SKY SPORTS FOOTBALL YEARBOOK 2008-2009

EDITORS: GLENDA ROLLIN AND JACK ROLLIN

headline

First published in 2008
by HEADLINE PUBLISHING GROUP

1

Front cover photographs: (left) Michael Ballack (Chelsea) – *Phil Cole/Getty Images Sport*; (centre and background) Fernando Torres (Liverpool) – *Stephen Pond/ EMPICS Sport/PA Photos*; (right) Cesc Fabregas (Arsenal) – *Adam Davy/ EMPICS Sport/PA Photos.*

Spine photograph: Manchester United celebrating victory in the 2008 Champions League – *Martin Rickett/PA Photos.*

Back cover photographs: (above) John Kennedy (Celtic) and Barry Ferguson (Rangers) – *Jeff J. Mitchell/Getty Images Sport*; (below) Joleon Lescott (Everton) – *John Walton/EMPICS Sport/PA Photos.*

Cataloguing in Publication Data is available from the British Library

ISBN 978 0 7553 1819 3 (Hardback)
ISBN 978 0 7553 1820 9 (Trade paperback)

Typeset by Wearset Ltd, Boldon, Tyne and Wear

Printed and bound in the UK by
CPI Mackays, Chatham ME5 8TD

Headline's policy is to use papers that are natural, renewable and recyclable products and made from wood grown in sustainable forests. The logging and manufacturing processes are expected to conform to the environmental regulations of the country of origin.

HEADLINE PUBLISHING GROUP
An Hachette Livre UK Company
338 Euston Road
London NW1 3BH

www.headline.co.uk
www.hachettelivre.co.uk

CONTENTS

INTERNATIONAL FOOTBALL

NON-LEAGUE FOOTBALL

INFORMATION AND RECORDS

FOREWORD

I work across a range of football programming for Sky Sports, and as it was as a player so it is in television – the weekends can be hectic! I'm usually at my desk by about 5 a.m. ready for Goals on Sunday after covering a game for Gillette Soccer Saturday. Two different roles but the same rules apply – you have to get your facts right.

You can be sure that the guys in the production teams have a Yearbook handy. In fact, it's a familiar sight in the office, while I know there's a few seasons' worth in the gallery of Soccer Saturday! But I often have to check the odd fact myself when I'm at games so I always have one with me. Internet sources can often vary wildly, so it's the big blue book for me. It's our 'bible'.

I've been a player, manager and now a broadcaster and the Yearbook has always been my favoured point of reference. It's not just football fans who own the book. I can assure you that it graces the shelves of any self-respecting manager in the game.

And you can also find it on the gantries and in the press boxes up and down the land. Trust me – Jeff will soon put me right in the studio if I get something wrong!! So in these days of information overload, it remains the only option. There's nothing unbelievable about that.

Chris Kamara, Sky Sports

Chris Kamara

INTRODUCTION

The 39th edition of the Yearbook, our sixth with sponsors Sky Sports, has maintained its expansion of recent years to 1,056 pages. Another new feature this time is Up for the Cup! highlighting an interesting feature from each of the 125 FA Cup finals since 1872. Statistical research in recent years has discovered discrepancies particularly from the early years of the competition. These changes have been noted.

In addition to the comprehensive coverage of the Euro 2008 tournament including all qualifying and final details, for the first time we have introduced complete line-ups of all UEFA Cup matches from 2007–08 to fall in line with our established treatment of the Champions League.

Attention is now focused on the World Cup 2010, finals of which will be held in South Africa. All qualifying results of matches played up to the time of going to press have been included as well as forthcoming fixtures for Europe and South America.

At international level for the first time there are national results for the previous year for all countries affiliated to FIFA. In order to accommodate such innovations it has been necessary to alter the presentation of international appearances for British and Irish clubs. Individual listing of matches for players has been omitted, though there are starting dates, clubs and total number of matches for each entry as well as the full teams as usual for each game played in 2007–08.

As last year and again in conjunction with the Sky Sports Football Yearbook Honours, the Editorial panel of the yearbook has produced a similar team of the season covering the Championship, to reflect its continually growing stature.

Once again, there is an A to Z index of names with a cross reference to the Players Directory, enabling readers to check on the whereabouts of any specific player during the 2007–08 season. The who's who style directory again provides a season-by-season account of individual player's appearances and goals. The fullest possible available details have been provided for players in this section, including all players who appeared in first-class matches.

Throughout the book players sent off are designated thus ■, substitutes in the club pages are 12, 13 and 14 with 15 for the substitute goalkeeper. Squad numbers are not used.

Because of the changes in designation of divisions in recent years for the Football League and references to levels, steps and pyramids, attempting to place in a historical sense just where to place any given club in any given season's finishing has become almost impossible. Therefore in any particular section of the Records Section, the top club in the Football League is mentioned regardless of its actual status at the time. Individual records of players on the other hand have been retained.

With the continual increase in interest in non-League football, all Blue Square Premier clubs have again been given the same style of recognition as the FA Premier League and Football League teams. For the coming season this competition continues with its recent sponsor for the Conference and its North and South sections.

As far as the club pages are concerned, the more uniform approach has been retained in respect of individual entries, without losing any of the essential information, including records over the previous ten seasons, latest sequences and runs of scoring and non-scoring.

The usual detailed and varied coverage in the Yearbook involves Scottish, Welsh and Irish football, amateur, schools, university, reserve team, extensive non-League information, awards, records and an international directory. Women's football, referees and the work of chaplains are also featured.

Transfer fees quoted in the Daily Round-Up are invariably those initially mentioned when a deal is imminent. They may not reflect the figures which appear elsewhere in the edition. Moves during the summer months, together with any specific changes affecting the book appear in the Stop Press section.

The Editors would like to express their appreciation of the response from FA Premier League and Football League clubs when requesting information. Thanks are also due to Alan Elliott for checking the Scottish section, Tony Brown for co-ordinating the changes to the FA Cup feature, sequences and instances of match results in the records section, Ian Nannestad for the obituaries and Andrew Howe on foreign players. Thanks are also due to John English, who provided invaluable and conscientious reading of the proofs.

ACKNOWLEDGEMENTS

The Editors would like to express appreciation of the following individuals and organisations for their co-operation: David Barber, Dawn Keleher and Jill Roberts (Football Association), David C. Thomson (Scottish League), Heather Elliott, Dr Malcolm Brodie, Rev. Nigel Sands, Ken Goldman, Grahame Lloyd, Marshall Gillespie, Sean Creedon, and Alan Platt. Special mention, too, of Rhea Halford (Headline Book Publishing). The highest praise is due to the indefatigable, ebullient and loquacious Lorraine Jerram, Headline's Managing Editor for her generosity, expertise, constant support, determined resilience, patience, sincerity, perspicacity and appreciation, not to mention her unfailing humour, stoicism, quick-wittedness, courtesy, quiet consideration and understated authority.

Finally sincere thanks to John Anderson, Simon Dunnington, Geoff Turner, Brian Tait and the staff at Wearset for their efforts in the production of this book, which were much appreciated throughout the year.

EDITORIAL

It was not so long ago that First Choice was merely either a travel agent or a bus company, even the Fourth Rock from the Sun could still get a mortgage from the Northern and before a Russian billionaire suddenly needed a Grant only to decide it was unnecessary after all. Then again, Alan Hansen had yet to become a supermarket sweeper, David Seaman's future career was still not on ice and Gary Lineker was not destroying old Routemasters under a bridge too low. You might also imagine FC in this context referred to the aforementioned First Choice. Not a bit of it – just the initials of Fabio Capello, an Italian who was hired to bring back the World Cup to England.

But where *is* the respect for those in authority? Poor Steve McClaren, the butt of the media stamped with the sobriquet of The Wally with the Brolly, sinking in the reign. Who would be a manager? Then there is the No. 10, dubbed Incapability Brown and the man who put the wraith in Raith Rovers. Who would want to be an unelected PM? Poor John Terry treated unmercifully for slipping up as he went to take a penalty in the Champions League final. Such is the life of the well-paid professional footballer, though many thousands would welcome the chance. Fortunately FC came to his rescue and gave him the England armband and he responded with a goal only a week later. Captain for the day is the new vogue; expect the first non-playing skipper ere long.

Our leader wants England to play fantasy football. One hopes this does not mean he will be ordering copies of the *Daily Telegraph* once the new season gets under way with another competition of this kind.

Fortunately our one-time "First Choice" has lined himself up with a job in Holland in charge of Twente. Say it twice and you could have a Dutch limited-overs cricket match perhaps. His predecessor Sven-Goran Eriksson seemed to have found his niche back in club football with Manchester City but he just about lasted a season before he was off again back in international waters and in charge of Mexico, finding time no doubt to strut his stuff on the beach at Acapulco. Like chairmen in business circles, they can always find someone to keep them in business, though in fairness they do stick to the same profession. Interesting, too, that Luiz Filipe Scolari – remember him when the FA unveiled its cunning plan to fool the media with a Jolly Boys outing to Portugal – has made it to England and Chelsea after all. But he has a different version of those earlier events.

As to the Premier League's 39th step, not the climb up to the Royal Box at the old Twin Towers, nothing remotely connected to John Buchan's novel filmed three times or even the faintest football connection with Charlie Buchan, distinguished international turned journalist and figurehead for a monthly magazine, a kind of *Soccer Star* for adolescents. No, it is just another money-making scheme to bring in even more revenue. It would have to be brought in during the season, not at the end if championships and relegation depend on it. Shudder at the thought of two teams fighting relegation and having to travel abroad to avoid the drop.

Referees continue to be clobbered. There will be no condemnation of them here. They are essential. But can we be allowed a few requests? The kind of unarmed combat which goes on in the penalty area at free-kicks and corners, a cross between the Military Two-Step and Hip Hop, will only be resolved with flashing cards. We know you are acting under instructions – but just try it. Also please punish the GBH when defenders are obstructing attackers as the ball runs towards the bye-line. Anywhere else on the pitch and it would be a hanging offence.

Players have many gripes about referees, one of which is when their momentum clatters them into an opponent. This is the classic of the official with little or no experience of the playing side. All referees should be made to play five-a-side football regularly – not to improve their ability but just to experience such contact. Conversely, players ought to have regular bouts of having to control games.

Penalty shoot-outs remain a curse, but why should a team that has had a player sent off during play be allowed the same number of penalty takers? Also, if for every two yellow cards you remove another spot kicker, one wonders if clubs would be as keen to favour shoot-outs. Discipline at least would improve. Why ditch the golden goal in the first place?

A watching brief was all we in the UK could console ourselves with in Euro 2008. Fifty years ago we were able to take more personal interest in what was then the World Cup in Sweden. England, Northern Ireland, Scotland and Wales were involved. For added measure the host nation even had an Englishman in charge, George Raynor!

Yes there was a bit of European cup football around in the shape of the European Cup of the Champions, reserved for what it purported to be – the champions of various countries. What a quaint, old fashioned notion that was, not a money-grabbing operation open to the rich and famous. Alas Real Madrid were making it their own, so not much British joy there. However, in the Inter-Cities Fairs Cup, London fielded a team from various clubs in the metropolis and were

England manager Steve McClaren weathers the storm but cannot help his team avoid a catastrophic Euro 2008 qualifying defeat to Croatia at Wembley in November. (EMPICS Sport/PA Photos/Mike Egerton)

soundly thrashed 6-0 in the second leg by Barcelona. Not enough foreigners in the team, obviously. The non-English were plentiful, though. Those days they just called them Scots, Welsh and Irish. That was then. This is now.

There was enough English interest in the events in Austria/Switzerland in early summer. Thirteen of the sixteen finalists had, to a greater or lesser extent, Premier League players in their squads. Only Italy, Romania and Russia lacked such talent. Irony or not, one might imagine. No Premiership players in Italy's squad – yet we have an Italian as our national team manager. Yet it was to Italy that the first international players left our shores in the early post-war period. John Charles (Yes, Welsh, of course), Jimmy Greaves, Denis Law (a Scot) and Joe Baker among them. But the exodus had gone on much earlier, with lower-profile additions and coaches, too. Jesse Carver is probably the best example of an Englishman making a name in Italian football as a coach. The old boot is now firmly on the other foot.

Good to see that even a high-profile tournament – albeit with memorably flowing and skilful attacking play – of the calibre of Euro 2008 can still produce delightfully archaic notions like expecting the whole of the ball to cross those white lines before it is out of play. More seriously, we mere mortals are unable to grasp the modern interpretation of the offside law. Heaven forfend someone receiving the last rites on the touchline can still play someone onside, but the door seems to be wide open to that awful situation. Then you have goalkeepers who invariably clear their lines by stepping over them – and assistant referees are too busy haring towards the centre to notice the indiscretions. Still you had to be impressed with the way Joachim Löw and Josef Hickersberger, the respective German and Austrian coaches, were banished to the stands for virtually nothing. Can we expect the same treatment in the coming season in England when the usual undignified hand-bagging goes on near our touchlines?

But you have to admire UEFA for the way they can organise such a competition in two countries and still find time to start the Intertoto Cup at the same time. That is masterly organisation. And who said there was too much football?

UEFA's head man Michel Platini does not like us. Make no mistake about that one. He was not around to remember Dunkirk, Agincourt was a bit before his time too, as was Trafalgar and Waterloo – though he might have taken offence if required to have his ticket punched on Eurostar. Taking a look at his international playing career when he was himself abroad with Juventus (Italian team, naturally), he was once on the winning side for France, another as a loser in the two games against England. That has to be ruled out as an excuse. He is also interested in opting out of any EU rules about freedom of labour movement.

Perhaps a history lesson is in order. In the early 1930s when the French were starting their professional competition, they attracted many players from English clubs. They included some of the calibre of Peter O'Dowd, the Chelsea and England international centre-half. Their arrival helped to enhance the French League, just as the Premier League has achieved similar recognition with foreign imports today.

Platini's mentor, dear old Sepp Blatter – who also imagines himself to be a kind of latter-day Abe Lincoln – wants to curb the foreign intake in the Premier League with his 6,5 special which he hopes will become top of the popular thinking in England. UEFA, mindful of EU laws, favours a much more watered down version. While we get the governments we deserve, there is precious little we can do about football administrators.

Moreover, both ideas are flawed. Surely the object is to improve the standard of the national team if that is the reason for the idea. One wonders if the record of two English teams appearing in the final has prompted the argument. But both Manchester United and Chelsea fielded a dozen or so international players qualified to play for their country and had done so in the quest to reach the final stages of Euro 2008. There were others with similar qualifications, not selected because of injury etc.

It is rather like setting an examination and deciding beforehand how many candidates are going to pass regardless of the marks obtained. This is of course the classic paper when the standard of those entering is known to be much lower than desired and quotas are necessary. One national Sunday newspaper conducted a poll of readers, of whom 80 per cent said they were more interested in their club team than the England national side. But the same survey did support the development of homegrown talent. The way to produce such is to improve the system of bringing on youth. No club is going to sign a player from abroad if there is a better one on the doorstep. No amount of culling and downsizing on foreigners will make the England team any better.

When Tom put on his glove he enquired: "Does my thumb look big in this?" Size as in all things is relative.

Michel Platini conducting on the pitch in his pomp. As President of UEFA, he now hopes to orchestrate some radical changes to the way football is governed in Europe.

SKY SPORTS FOOTBALL YEARBOOK HONOURS

The FWA members chose the following team for the season.

Sky Sports Football Yearbook Team of the Season 2007–08

David James
(Portsmouth)

Bakari Sagna *(Arsenal)*
Nemanja Vidic *(Manchester U)*
Rio Ferdinand *(Manchester U)*
Patrice Evra *(Manchester U)*

Steven Gerrard *(Liverpool)*
Frank Lampard *(Chelsea)*
Cesc Fabregas *(Arsenal)*
Cristiano Ronaldo *(Manchester U)*

Fernando Torres *(Liverpool)*
Emmanuel Adebayor *(Arsenal)*

Manager:
Sir Alex Ferguson CBE *(Manchester U)*

Substitutes:
Micah Richards (*Manchester C*), David Bentley (*Blackburn R*), Wayne Rooney (*Manchester U*)

FOOTBALL AWARDS 2008

FOOTBALLER OF THE YEAR

The Football Writers' Association Sir Stanley Matthews Trophy for the Footballer of the Year was awarded to Cristiano Ronaldo of Manchester United and Portugal. Fernando Torres of Liverpool was runner-up and David James of Portsmouth third.

Past Winners
1947–48 Stanley Matthews (Blackpool), 1948–49 Johnny Carey (Manchester U), 1949–50 Joe Mercer (Arsenal), 1950–51 Harry Johnston (Blackpool), 1951–52 Billy Wright (Wolverhampton W), 1952–53 Nat Lofthouse (Bolton W), 1953–54 Tom Finney (Preston NE), 1954–55 Don Revie (Manchester C), 1955–56 Bert Trautmann (Manchester C), 1956–57 Tom Finney (Preston NE), 1957–58 Danny Blanchflower (Tottenham H), 1958–59 Syd Owen (Luton T), 1959–60 Bill Slater (Wolverhampton W), 1960–61 Danny Blanchflower (Tottenham H), 1961–62 Jimmy Adamson (Burnley), 1962–63 Stanley Matthews (Stoke C), 1963–64 Bobby Moore (West Ham U), 1964–65 Bobby Collins (Leeds U), 1965–66 Bobby Charlton (Manchester U), 1966–67 Jackie Charlton (Leeds U), 1967–68 George Best (Manchester U), 1968–69 Dave Mackay (Derby Co) shared with Tony Book (Manchester C), 1969–70 Billy Bremner (Leeds U), 1970–71 Frank McLintock (Arsenal), 1971–72 Gordon Banks (Stoke C), 1972–73 Pat Jennings (Tottenham H), 1973–74 Ian Callaghan (Liverpool), 1974–75 Alan Mullery (Fulham), 1975–76 Kevin Keegan (Liverpool), 1976–77 Emlyn Hughes (Liverpool), 1977–78 Kenny Burns (Nottingham F), 1978–79 Kenny Dalglish (Liverpool), 1979–80 Terry McDermott (Liverpool), 1980–81 Frans Thijssen (Ipswich T), 1981–82 Steve Perryman (Tottenham H), 1982–83 Kenny Dalglish (Liverpool), 1983–84 Ian Rush (Liverpool), 1984–85 Neville Southall (Everton), 1985–86 Gary Lineker (Everton), 1986–87 Clive Allen (Tottenham H), 1987–88 John Barnes (Liverpool), 1988–89 Steve Nicol (Liverpool), 1989–90 John Barnes (Liverpool), 1990–91 Gordon Strachan (Leeds U), 1991–92 Gary Lineker (Tottenham H), 1992–93 Chris Waddle (Sheffield W), 1993–94 Alan Shearer (Blackburn R), 1994–95 Jurgen Klinsmann (Tottenham H), 1995–96 Eric Cantona (Manchester U), 1996–97 Gianfranco Zola (Chelsea), 1997–98 Dennis Bergkamp (Arsenal), 1998–99 David Ginola (Tottenham H), 1999–2000 Roy Keane (Manchester U), 2000–01 Teddy Sheringham (Manchester U), 2001–02 Robert Pires (Arsenal), 2002–03 Thierry Henry (Arsenal), 2003–04 Thierry Henry (Arsenal), 2004–05 Frank Lampard (Chelsea), 2005–06 Thierry Henry (Arsenal), 2006–07 Cristiano Ronaldo (Manchester U), 2007–08 Cristiano Ronaldo (Manchester U).

THE PFA AWARDS 2008

Player of the Year: Cristiano Ronaldo, Manchester U and Portugal.
Young Player of the Year: Cesc Fabregas, Arsenal and Spain.

Cristiano Ronaldo repeated his double of Football Writers' Association award and PFA Player of the Year. (Nick Potts/PA Archive/PA Photos)

The Football Yearbook Championship Team of the Season 2007–08

Wayne Hennessey
(Wolverhampton W)

Lloyd Doyley *(Watford)*	Jason De Vos *(Ipswich T)*	Mark Hudson *(Crystal Palace)*	Tony Capaldi *(Cardiff C)*
Liam Lawrence *(Stoke C)*	Ian Ashbee *(Hull C)*	Brian Howard *(Barnsley)*	Michael McIndoe *(Bristol C)*
	James Beattie *(Sheffield U)*	Kevin Phillips *(WBA)*	

Manager:
Phil Brown *(Hull C)*

Substitutes:
Krisztian Timar (*Plymouth Arg*), Zheng-Zhi (*Charlton Ath*), Kyle Lafferty (*Burnley*)

OTHER AWARDS

SCOTTISH FOOTBALL WRITERS' ASSOCIATION 2008

Player of the Year: Carlos Cuellar, Rangers and Spain
Manager of the Year: Billy Reid, Hamilton A

SCOTTISH PFA PLAYER OF THE YEAR AWARDS 2008

Player of the Year: Aiden McGeady, Celtic and Republic of Ireland
Young Player of the Year: Aiden McGeady, Celtic and Republic of Ireland

EUROPEAN FOOTBALLER OF THE YEAR 2007

Kaka, AC Milan and Brazil

WORLD PLAYER OF THE YEAR 2007

Kaka, AC Milan and Brazil

WOMEN'S PLAYER OF THE YEAR 2007

Marta, Umea and Brazil

UP FOR THE CUP

▪*Denotes player sent off.*

Kennington Oval, 16 March 1872 *2000*
The Wanderers (1) 1 *(Betts)*
Royal Engineers (0) 0
The Wanderers: Welch; Lubbock E., Thompson A.C., Alcock, Bowen, Bonsor, Betts, Crake, Hooman, Vidal, Wollaston.
Royal Engineers: Merriman; Marindin, Addison, Cresswell, Mitchell, Renny-Tailyour, Rich, Goodwyn, Muirhead, Cotter, Bogle.
Referee: A. Stair.
Lt Creswell broke collarbone 10 mins, soldiered on; A.H. Chequer was actually Betts.

Lillie Bridge, 29 March 1873 *3000*
The Wanderers (0) 2 *(Kinnaird, Wollaston)*
Oxford University (0) 0
The Wanderers: Welch; Howell, Bowen, Wollaston, Kingsford, Bonsor, Kenyon-Slaney, Thompson C.M., Sturgis, Kinnaird, Stewart.
Oxford University: Leach; Smith, Mackarness, Birley, Longman, Maddison, Dixon, Paton, Vidal, Sumner, Ottaway.
Referee: A. Stair.
Kick-off a.m. because of the boat-race. Oxford even moved goalie Leach up front!

Kennington Oval, 14 March 1874 *2000*
Oxford University (2) 2 *(Mackarness, Patton)*
Royal Engineers (0) 0
Oxford University: Neapean; Mackarness, Birley, Green, Vidal, Ottoway, Benson, Patton, Rawson, Maddison, Johnson.
Royal Engineers: Merriman; Marindin, Addison, Onslow, Olivier, Digby, Renny-Tailyour, Rawson, Blackburn, Wood, von Donop.
Referee: A. Stair.
Engineers had undergone special training for the game. Oxford had four caps.

Kennington Oval, 13 March 1875 *3000*
Royal Engineers (1) 1 *(Renny-Tailyour)*
Old Etonians (1) 1 *(Bonsor)*
Royal Engineers: Merriman; Sim, Onslow, Ruck, von Donop, Wood, Rawson, Stafford, Renny-Tailyour, Mein, Wingfield-Stratford.
Old Etonians: Farmer; Wilson, Merysey-Thompson A.C., Lubbock E., Benson, Kenyon-Slaney, Patton, Bonsor, Ottoway, Kinnaird, Stronge.
aet.
Referee: C.W. Alcock.
Ottaway injured after 37 mins and did not return. Stiff breeze hindered play, too.

***Replay:** Kennington Oval, 16 March 1875* *3000*
Royal Engineers (0) 2 *(Renny-Tailyour 2)*
Old Etonians (0) 0
Royal Engineers: Merriman; Sim, Onslow, Ruck, von Donop, Wood, Rawson, Stafford, Renny-Tailyour, Mein, Wingfield-Stratford.
Old Etonians: Drummond-Moray; Farrer, Lubbock E, Wilson, Kinnaird, Stronge, Patton, Farmer, Bonsor, Lubbock A, Hammond.
Referee: C.W. Alcock.
Engineers had goal disallowed for offside, 20th unbeaten game; Bonsor injured.

Kennington Oval, 11 March 1876 *3000*
The Wanderers (1) 1 *(Edwards)*
Old Etonians (0) 1 *(Bonsor)*
The Wanderers: Greig; Stratford, Lindsay, Maddison, Birley, Wollaston, Heron H, Heron F, Edwards, Kenrick, Hughes.
Old Etonians: Hogg; Welldon, Lyttelton E, Meysey-Thompson A.C., Kinnaird, Meysey-Thompson C.M., Kenyon-Slaney, Lyttelton A, Sturgis, Bonsor, Allene.
aet.
Referee: W.S. Rawson.
Bonsor's goal cannot be confirmed in contemporary accounts; Three pairs of brothers, Kinnaird and Meysey-Thompson carried on with injuries.

***Replay:** Kennington Oval, 18 March 1876* *3500*
The Wanderers (2) 3 *(Wollaston, Hughes 2)*
Old Etonians (0) 0
The Wanderers: Greig; Stratford, Lindsay, Maddison, Birley, Wollaston, Heron H, Heron F, Edwards, Kenrick, Hughes.
Old Etonians: Wilson; Lubbock E, Lyttelton E, Farrer, Kinnaird, Stronge, Kenyon-Slaney, Lyttelton A, Sturgis, Bonsor, Alleyne.
Referee: W.S. Rawson.
Wanderers benefited from being unchanged compared with their opponents.

Kennington Oval, 24 March 1877 *3000*
The Wanderers (0) 2 *(Lindsay, Kenrick)*
Oxford University (1) 1 *(Kinnaird (og))*
The Wanderers: Kinnaird; Lindsay, Stratford, Birley, Denton, Green, Heron H, Hughes, Kenrick, Wace, Wollaston.
Oxford University: Allington; Bain, Dunell, Savory, Todd, Waddington, Fernandez, Hills, Otter, Parry, Rawson.
aet.
Referee: S.H. Wright.
For years the score was given as 2-0 and Kinnaird's own goal was even annulled; the now accepted result is 2-1 after extra time, and Kinnaird's own goal is reinstated.

Kennington Oval, 23 March 1878 *4500*
The Wanderers (2) 3 *(Kenrick 2, Kinnaird)*
Royal Engineers (1) 1 *(unknown)*
The Wanderers: Kirkpatrick; Stratford, Lindsay, Kinnaird, Green, Wollaston, Heron H, Wylie, Wace, Denton, Kenrick.
Royal Engineers: Friend; Cowan, Morris, Mayne, Heath, Haynes, Lindsay, Hedley, Bond, Barnet, Ruck.
Referee: S.R. Bastard.
Kinnaird's goal cannot be confirmed in contemporary accounts; The Royal Engineers goal was scored "in a rush" and is therefore not credited to an individual player; Broken arm for Kirkpatrick 30 mins but carried on; Wanderers handed back cup.

Kennington Oval, 29 March 1879 *5000*
Old Etonians (0) 1 *(Clerke)*
Clapham Rovers (0) 0
Old Etonians: Hawtrey; Christian, Bury, Kinnaird, Lubbock E, Clerke, Pares, Goodhart, Whitfield, Chevalier, Beaufoy.
Clapham Rovers: Birkett; Ogilvie, Field, Bailey, Prinsep, Rawson, Stanley, Scott, Bevington, Growse, Keith-Falconer.
Referee: C.W. Alcock.
Prinsep at 17 years 245 days was the youngest finalist; Old Boys stamina told.

Kennington Oval, 10 April 1880 *6000*
Clapham Rovers (0) 1 *(Lloyd-Jones)*
Oxford University (0) 0
Clapham Rovers: Birkett; Ogilvie, Field, Weston, Bailey, Brougham, Stanley, Barry, Sparks, Lloyd-Jones, Ram.
Oxford University: Parr; Wilson, King, Phillips, Rogers, Heygate, Childs, Eyre, Crowdy, Hill, Lubbock J.
Referee: Major Marindin.
Wind buffeted Oxford in the first half, but it abated for the favourites Clapham.

Kennington Oval, 9 April 1881 *4500*
Old Carthusians (1) 3 *(Wynyard, Parry, Todd)*
Old Etonians (0) 0
Old Carthusians: Gillett; Norris, Colvin, Prinsep, Vintcent, Hansell, Richards, Page, Wynyard, Parry, Tod.
Old Etonians: Rawlinson; Foley, French, Kinnaird, Farrer, Chevalier, Anderson, Goodhart, Macaulay, Whitfield, Novelli.
Referee: W. Pierce Dix.
The far-fitter, organised Carthusians had Parry the first overseas born winning captain.

Kennington Oval, 25 March 1882 *6500*
Old Etonians (1) 1 *(Anderson)*
Blackburn Rovers (0) 0
Old Etonians: Rawlinson; French, de Paravicini, Kinnaird, Foley, Novelli, Dunn, Macaulay, Goodhart, Anderson, Chevalier.
Blackburn Rovers: Howarth; McIntyre, Suter, Sharples, Hargreaves F, Duckworth, Douglas, Strachan, Brown, Avery, Hargreaves J.
Referee: J.C. Clegg.
Avery injured near the break but the favourites were held up by goalie Rawlinson.

Kennington Oval, 31 March 1883 *8000*
Blackburn Olympic (0) 2 *(Costley, Matthews)*
Old Etonians (1) 1 *(Goodhart)*
Blackburn Olympic: Hacking; Ward, Warburton, Gibson, Astley, Hunter, Dewhurst, Matthews, Wilson, Costley, Yates.
Old Etonians: Rawlinson; French, de Paravicini, Kinnaird, Foley, Chevalier, Anderson, Macaulay, Goodhart, Dunn, Bainbridge.
aet.
Referee: C. Crump.
Old Etonians suffered several injuries and the well-trained cotton workers prevailed.

Kennington Oval, 29 March 1884 *12,000*
Blackburn Rovers (2) 2 *(Sowerbutts, Forrest)*
Queen's Park (0) 1 *(Christie)*
Blackburn Rovers: Arthur; Beverley, Suter, McIntyre, Hargreaves J, Forrest, Lofthouse, Douglas, Sowerbutts, Inglis, Brown.
Queen's Park: Gillespie; Arnott, McDonald, Campbell, Gow, Anderson, Watt, Smith, Harrower, Allan, Christie.
Referee: Major Marindin.
Scottish finalists bowed to "professional" Rovers, both had two goals disallowed.

Kennington Oval, 4 April 1885 *12,500*
Blackburn Rovers (1) 2 *(Forrest, Brown)*
Queen's Park (0) 0
Blackburn Rovers: Arthur; Turner, Suter, McIntyre, Haworth, Forrest, Lofthouse, Douglas, Brown, Fecitt, Sowerbutts.
Queen's Park: Gillespie; Arnott, MacLeod, Campbell, McDonald, Hamilton, Anderson, Sellar, Gray, McWhannel, Allan.
Referee: Major Marindin.
Professionalism had arrived, but it was the last entry for amateur Queen's Park.

Kennington Oval, 3 April 1886 *15,000*
Blackburn Rovers (0) 0
West Bromwich Albion (0) 0
Blackburn Rovers: Arthur; Turner, Suter, Douglas, Forrest, McIntyre, Heyes, Strachan, Brown, Fecitt, Sowerbutts.
West Bromwich Albion: Roberts; Green H, Bell H, Horton, Perry, Timmins, Woodhall, Green T, Bayliss, Loach, Bell G.
Referee: Major Marindin.
Boat race day kept crowd down yet fledgling Albion earned their replay chance.

***Replay:** County Ground, Derby, 10 April 1886* *12,000*
Blackburn Rovers (1) 2 *(Brown, Sowerbutts)*
West Bromwich Albion (0) 0
Blackburn Rovers: Arthur; Turner, Suter, Douglas, Forrest, McIntyre, Walton, Strachan, Brown, Fecitt, Sowerbutts.
West Bromwich Albion: Roberts; Green H, Bell H, Horton, Perry, Timmins, Woodhall, Green T, Bayliss, Loach, Bell G.
Referee: Major Marindin.
Rovers equalled the earlier feat of Wanderers and given a silver shield.

Kennington Oval, 2 April 1887 *15,500*
Aston Villa (0) 2 *(Hunter, Hodgetts)*
West Bromwich Albion (0) 0
Aston Villa: Warner; Coulton, Simmonds, Yates, Dawson, Burton, Davis, Brown, Hunter, Vaughton, Hodgetts.
West Bromwich Albion: Roberts; Green H, Aldridge, Horton, Perry, Timmins, Woodhall, Green T, Bayliss, Paddock, Pearson.
Referee: Major Marindin.
Aston Villa had gained the mastery over their midland rivals after the first 20 mins.

Kennington Oval, 24 March 1888 *19,000*
West Bromwich Albion (1) 2 *(Woodhall, Bayliss)*
Preston North End (0) 1 *(Dewhurst)*
West Bromwich Albion: Roberts; Aldridge, Green, Horton, Perry, Timmins, Bassett, Woodhall, Bayliss, Wilson, Pearson.
Preston North End: Mills-Roberts; Howarth, Ross N, Holmes, Russell, Graham, Gordon, Ross J, Goodall, Dewhurst, Drummond.
Referee: Major Marindin.
Triumph for the £5 total wage, all-English Albion against the Preston professionals.

Kennington Oval, 30 March 1889 *22,000*
Preston North End (2) 3 *(Dewhurst, Ross J, Thompson)*
Wolverhampton Wanderers (0) 0
Preston North End: Mills-Roberts; Howarth, Holmes, Drummond, Russell, Graham, Gordon, Ross J, Goodall, Dewhurst, Thompson.
Wolverhampton Wanderers: Baynton; Baugh, Mason, Fletcher, Allen, Lowder, Hunter, Wykes, Brodie, Wood, Knight.
Referee: Major Marindin.
Proud Preston completed the first League and Cup double, no goals conceded.

Kennington Oval, 29 March 1890 *20,000*
Blackburn Rovers (3) 6 *(Walton, John Southworth, Lofthouse, Townley 3)*
Sheffield Wednesday (0) 1 *(Mumford)*
Blackburn Rovers: Horne; James Southworth, Forbes, Barton, Dewar, Forrest, Lofthouse, Campbell, John Southworth, Walton, Townley.
Sheffield Wednesday: Smith; Brayshaw, Morley, Dungworth, Betts, Waller, Ingram, Woodhouse, Bennett, Mumford, Cawley.
Referee: Major Marindin.
Non-League Wednesday on the defensive and a goal down from the sixth minute.

Kennington Oval, 21 March 1891 *23,000*
Blackburn Rovers (3) 3 *(Dewar, John Southworth, Townley)*
Notts County (0) 1 *(Oswald)*
Blackburn Rovers: Pennington; Brandon, Forbes, Barton, Dewar, Forrest, Lofthouse, Walton, John Southworth, Hall, Townley.
Notts County: Thraves; Ferguson, Hendry, Osbourne, Calderhead, Shelton, McGregor, McInnes, Oswald, Locker, Daft.
Referee: C.J. Hughes.
Season of penalties. Rovers displayed the much better combination all-round.

Kennington Oval, 19 March 1892 *32,810*
West Bromwich Albion (2) 3 *(Geddes, Nicholls, Reynolds)*
Aston Villa (0) 0
West Bromwich Albion: Reader; Nicholson, McCulloch, Reynolds, Perry, Groves, Bassett, McLeod, Nicholls, Pearson, Geddes.
Aston Villa: Warner; Evans, Cox, Devey H, Cowan, Baird, Athersmith, Devey J, Dickson, Campbell, Hodgetts.
Referee: J.C. Clegg.
Fast moving, well-organised Albion, goal nets and crossbar featured.

Fallowfield, Manchester, 25 March 1893 *45,000*
Wolverhampton Wanderers (0) 1 *(Allen)*
Everton (0) 0
Wolverhampton Wanderers: Rose; Baugh, Swift, Malpass, Allen, Kinsey, Topham, Wykes, Butcher, Wood, Griffin.
Everton: Williams; Howarth, Kelso, Stewart, Holt, Boyle, Latta, Gordon, Maxwell, Chadwick, Milward.
Referee: C.J. Hughes.
Everton protested over the goal; good-natured crowd spilled near the touch-lines.

Goodison Park, Liverpool, 31 March 1894 *37,000*
Notts County (2) 4 *(Watson, Logan 3)*
Bolton Wanderers (0) 1 *(Cassidy)*
Notts County: Toone; Harper, Hendry, Bramley, Calderhead, Shelton, Watson, Donnelly, Logan, Bruce, Daft.
Bolton Wanderers: Sutcliffe; Somerville, Jones, Gardiner, Paton, Hughes, Dickenson, Wilson, Tannahill, Bentley, Cassidy.
Referee: C.J. Hughes.
Logan led his Second Division forwards in fine style and Bolton just had to be content.

Crystal Palace, 20 April 1895 *42,560*
Aston Villa (1) 1 *(Chatt)*
West Bromwich Albion (0) 0
Aston Villa: Wilkes; Spencer, Welford, Reynolds, James Cowan, Russell, Athersmith, Chatt, Devey J, Hodgetts, Smith.
West Bromwich Albion: Reader; Williams, Horton, Taggart, Higgins, Perry, Bassett, McLeod, Richards, Hutchinson, Banks.
Referee: J. Lewis.
A goal hit in 30 seconds, scorching heat and cup later stolen and never recovered.

Crystal Palace, 18 April 1896 *48,836*
Sheffield Wednesday (1) 2 *(Spiksley 2)*
Wolverhampton Wanderers (0) 1 *(Black)*
Sheffield Wednesday: Massey; Earp, Langley, Brandon, Crawshaw, Petrie, Brash, Brady, Bell, Davis, Spiksley.
Wolverhampton Wanderers: Tennant; Baugh, Dunn, Owen, Malpass, Griffiths, Tonks, Henderson, Beats, Wood, Black.
Referee: Captain W. Simpson.
Spiksley game, one goal in the first minute and the winning second in off the post.

Crystal Palace, 10 April 1897 *65,891*
Aston Villa (3) 3 *(Campbell, Wheldon, Crabtree)*
Everton (2) 2 *(Boyle, Bell)*
Aston Villa: Whitehouse; Spencer, Evans, Reynolds, James Cowan, Crabtree, Athersmith, Devey J, Campbell, Wheldon, John Cowan.
Everton: Menham; Meehan, Storrier, Boyle, Holt, Stewart, Taylor, Bell, Hartley, Chadwick, Milward.
Referee: J. Lewis.
Well-matched opponents, but Villa had the edge in midfield in their double season.

Crystal Palace, 16 April 1898 *62,017*
Nottingham Forest (2) 3 *(Capes 2, McPherson)*
Derby County (1) 1 *(Bloomer)*
Nottingham Forest: Allsop; Ritchie, Scott, Frank Forman, McPherson, Wragg, McInnes, Richards, Benbow, Capes, Spouncer.
Derby County: Fryer; Methven, Leiper, Cox, Goodall A, Turner, Goodall J, Bloomer, Boag, Stevenson, McQueen.
Referee: J. Lewis.
Forest found each other with more ease though their second goal was rather fortunate.

Crystal Palace, 15 April 1899 *73,833*
Sheffield United (0) 4 *(Bennett, Beers, Almond, Priest)*
Derby County (1) 1 *(Boag)*
Sheffield United: Foulke; Thickett, Boyle, Johnson, Morren, Needham, Bennett, Beers, Hedley, Almond, Priest.
Derby County: Fryer; Methvin, Staley, Cox, Paterson, May, Arkesden, Bloomer, Boag, McDonald, Allen.
Referee: A. Scragg.
United transformed in the second half and Thickett played on with broken ribs.

Crystal Palace, 21 April 1900 *68,945*
Bury (3) 4 *(McLuckie 2, Wood, Plant)*
Southampton (0) 0
Bury: Thompson; Darroch, Davidson, Pray, Leeming, Ross, Richards, Wood, McLuckie, Sagar, Plant.
Southampton: Robinson; Meehan, Durber, Meston, Chadwick, Petrie, Turner, Yates, Farrell, Wood, Milward.
Referee: A.G. Kingscott.
First southern professional team to reach the final beaten by Bury's superior fitness.

Crystal Palace, 20 April 1901 *110,820*
Tottenham Hotspur (1) 2 *(Brown 2)*
Sheffield United (1) 2 *(Bennett, Priest)*
Tottenham Hotspur: Clawley; Erentz, Tait, Morris, Hughes, Jones, Smith, Cameron, Brown, Copeland, Kirwan.
Sheffield United: Foulke; Thickett, Boyle, Johnson, Morren, Needham, Bennett, Field, Hedley, Priest, Lipsham.
Referee: A.G. Kingscott.
Spurs had to rally after going behind in a match which drew an unprecedented crowd.

***Replay:** Burnden Park, Bolton, 27 April 1901* *20,470*
Tottenham Hotspur (0) 3 *(Cameron, Smith, Brown)*
Sheffield United (1) 1 *(Priest)*
Tottenham Hotspur: Clawley; Erentz, Tait, Morris, Hughes, Jones, Smith, Cameron, Brown, Copeland, Kirwan.
Sheffield United: Foulke; Thickett, Boyle, Johnson, Morren, Needham, Bennett, Field, Hedley, Priest, Lipsham.
Referee: A.G. Kingscott.
Trailing a goal down, Spurs became the first southern professionals to win the cup.

Crystal Palace, 19 April 1902 *76,914*
Sheffield United (0) 1 *(Common)*
Southampton (0) 1 *(Wood)*
Sheffield United: Foulke; Thickett, Boyle, Needham, Wilkinson, Johnson, Bennett, Common, Hedley, Priest, Lipsham.
Southampton: Robinson; Fry, Molyneux, Meston, Bowman, Lee, Turner A, Wood, Brown, Chadwick, Turner J.
Referee: T. Kirkham.
Saints forced a replay with a goal three minutes from time in game of missed chances.

***Replay:** Crystal Palace, 26 April 1902* *33,068*
Sheffield United (1) 2 *(Hedley, Barnes)*
Southampton (0) 1 *(Brown)*
Sheffield United: Foulke; Thickett, Boyle, Needham, Wilkinson, Johnson, Barnes, Common, Hedley, Priest, Lipsham.
Southampton: Robinson; Fry, Molyneux, Meeston, Bowman, Lee, Turner A, Wood, Brown, Chadwick, Turner J.
Referee: T. Kirkham.
Both teams gave an improved display but United just had the advantage in the end.

Crystal Palace, 18 April 1903 *63,102*
Bury (1) 6 *(Ross, Sagar, Leeming 2, Wood, Plant)*
Derby County (0) 0
Bury: Monteith; Lindsey, McEwen, Johnstone, Thorpe, Ross, Richards, Wood, Sagar, Leeming, Plant.
Derby County: Fryer; Methven, Morris, Warren, Goodall A, May, Warrington, York, Boag, Richards, Davis.
Referee: J. Adams.
Bury, after a quiet start, equalled Preston's feat of not conceding a goal in the cup.

Crystal Palace, 23 April 1904 *61,374*
Manchester City (1) 1 *(Meredith)*
Bolton Wanderers (0) 0
Manchester City: Hillman; McMahon, Burgess, Frost, Hynds, Ashworth, Meredith, Livingstone, Gillespie, Turnbull A., Booth.
Bolton Wanderers: Davies; Brown, Struthers, Clifford, Greenhalgh, Freebairn, Stokes, Marsh, Yenson, White, Taylor.
Referee: A.J. Barker.
Disappointing match decided in 20 mins, the occasion proving too much for both.

Crystal Palace, 15 April 1905 *101,117*
Aston Villa (1) 2 *(Hampton 2)*
Newcastle United (0) 0
Aston Villa: George; Spencer, Miles, Pearson, Leake, Windmill, Brawn, Garraty, Hampton, Bache, Hall.

Newcastle United: Lawrence; McCombie, Carr, Gardner, Aitken, McWilliam, Rutherford, Howie, Appleyard, Veitch, Gosnell.
Referee: P.R. Harrower.
All out attacking play sparked by Hampton's goal in the third minute, first of two.

Crystal Palace, 21 April 1906 *75,609*
Everton (0) 1 *(Young)*
Newcastle United (0) 0
Everton: Scott; Balmer W, Crelley, Makepeace, Taylor, Abbott, Sharp, Bolton, Young, Settle, Hardman.
Newcastle United: Lawrence; McCombie, Carr, Gardner, Aitken, McWilliam, Rutherford, Howie, Veitch, Orr, Gosnell.
Referee: F. Kirkham.
Best move of the game produced the goal: Young finishing off a cross by Sharp.

Crystal Palace, 20 April 1907 *84,584*
Sheffield Wednesday (1) 2 *(Stewart, Simpson)*
Everton (1) 1 *(Sharp)*
Sheffield Wednesday: Lyall; Layton, Burton, Brittleton, Crawshaw, Bartlett, Chapman, Bradshaw, Wilson, Stewart, Simpson.
Everton: Scott; Balmer W, Balmer R, Makepeace, Taylor, Abbott, Sharp, Bolton, Young, Settle, Hardman.
Referee: N. Whittaker.
Defensive error gave Wednesday the first goal and a simple header for their second.

Crystal Palace, 25 April 1908 *74,967*
Wolverhampton Wanderers (2) 3 *(Hunt, Hedley, Harrison)*
Newcastle United (0) 1 *(Howie)*
Wolverhampton Wanderers: Lunn; Jones, Collins, Hunt, Wooldridge, Bishop, Harrison, Shelton, Hedley, Radford, Pedley.
Newcastle United: Lawrence; McCracken, Pudan, Gardner, Veitch, McWilliam, Rutherford, Howie, Appleyard, Speedie, Wilson.
Referee: T.P. Campbell.
Third defeat in four for Newcastle the "H" men of Second Division Wolves prevailed.

Crystal Palace, 24 April 1909 *71,401*
Manchester United (1) 1 *(Turnbull A)*
Bristol City (0) 0
Manchester United: Moger; Stacey, Hayes, Duckworth, Roberts, Bell, Meredith, Halse, Turnbull J, Turnbull A, Wall.
Bristol City: Clay; Annan, Cottle, Hanlin, Wedlock, Spear, Staniforth, Hardy, Gilligan, Burton, Hilton.
Referee: J. Mason.
Turnbull scored after Halse hit the crossbar, United's experience proving the answer.

Crystal Palace, 23 April 1910 *76,980*
Newcastle United (0) 1 *(Rutherford)*
Barnsley (1) 1 *(Tufnell)*
Newcastle United: Lawrence; McCracken, Whitson, Veitch, Low, McWilliam, Rutherford, Howie, Shepherd, Higgins, Wilson.
Barnsley: Mearns; Downs, Ness, Glendinning, Boyle, Utley, Bartrop, Gadsby, Lillycrop, Tufnell, Forman.
Referee: J.T. Ibbotson.
Late on Newcastle showed their true worth and outstanding Rutherford earned replay.

Replay: *Goodison Park, Liverpool, 28 April 1910* *55,364*
Newcastle United (0) 2 *(Shepherd 2 (1 pen))*
Barnsley (0) 0
Newcastle United: Lawrence; McCracken, Carr, Veitch, Low, McWilliam, Rutherford, Howie, Shepherd, Higgins, Wilson.
Barnsley: Mearns; Downs, Ness, Glendinning, Boyle, Utley, Bartrop, Gadsby, Lillycrop, Tufnell, Forman.
Referee: J.T. Ibbotson.
An improved United settled down quicker and Shepherd scored from a penalty.

Crystal Palace, 22 April 1911 *69,098*
Bradford City (0) 0
Newcastle United (0) 0
Bradford City: Mellors; Campbell, Taylor, Robinson, Gildea, McDonald, Logan, Speirs, O'Rourke, Devine, Thompson.
Newcastle United: Lawrence; McCracken, Whitson, Veitch, Low, Willis, Rutherford, Jobey, Stewart, Higgins, Wilson.
Referee: J.H. Pearson.
Evenly matched but neither able to raise their game sufficiently for a defining result.

Replay: *Old Trafford, Manchester, 26 April 1911* *58,000*
Bradford City (1) 1 *(Speirs)*
Newcastle United (0) 0
Bradford City: Mellors; Campbell, Taylor, Robinson, Torrance, McDonald, Logan, Speirs, O'Rourke, Devine, Thompson.
Newcastle United: Lawrence; McCracken, Whitson, Veitch, Low, Willis, Rutherford, Jobey, Stewart, Higgins, Wilson.
Referee: J.H. Pearson.
Bradford with the new cup made locally earned victory after a defensive error.

Crystal Palace, 20 April 1912 *54,556*
Barnsley (0) 0
West Bromwich Albion (0) 0
Barnsley: Cooper; Downs, Taylor, Glendinning, Bratley, Utley, Bartrop, Tufnell, Lillycrop, Travers, Moore.
West Bromwich Albion: Pearson; Cook, Pennington, Baddeley, Buck, McNeal, Jephcott, Wright, Pailor, Bowser, Shearman.
Referee: J.R. Schumacher.
Dour game finishing with West Bromwich slightly the more enterprising team.

Replay: *Bramall Lane, Sheffield, 24 April 1912* *38,555*
Barnsley (1) 1 *(Tufnell)*
West Bromwich Albion (0) 0
Barnsley: Cooper; Downs, Taylor, Glendinning, Bratley, Utley, Bartrop, Tufnell, Lillycrop, Travers, Moore.
West Bromwich Albion: Pearson; Cook, Pennington, Baddeley, Buck, McNeal, Jephcott, Wright, Pailor, Bowser, Shearman.
aet.
Referee: J.R. Schumacher.
Albion had the better of the first half but Barnsley's winner at the death.

Crystal Palace, 19 April 1913 *121,919*
Aston Villa (0) 1 *(Barber)*
Sunderland (0) 0
Aston Villa: Hardy; Lyons, Weston, Barber, Harrop, Leach, Wallace, Halse, Hampton, Stephenson, Bache.
Sunderland: Butler; Gladwin, Ness, Cuggy, Thomson, Low, Mordue, Buchan, Richardson, Holley, Martin.
Referee: A. Adams.
Attendance record for an erratic match with Villa having the edge in midfield.

Crystal Palace, 25 April 1914 *72,778*
Burnley (0) 1 *(Freeman)*
Liverpool (0) 0
Burnley: Sewell; Bamford, Taylor, Halley, Boyle, Watson, Nesbitt, Lindley, Freeman, Hodgson, Mosscrop.
Liverpool: Campbell; Longworth, Pursell, Fairfoul, Ferguson, McKinlay, Sheldon, Metcalf, Miller, Lacey, Nicholl.
Referee: H.S. Bamlett.
King George V present; even final decided by a ferocious shot in the 55th minute.

Old Trafford, Manchester, 24 April 1915 *49,557*
Sheffield United (1) 3 *(Simmons, Fazackerley, Kitchen)*
Chelsea (0) 0
Sheffield United: Gough; Cook, English, Sturgess, Brelsford, Utley, Simmons, Fazackerley, Kitchen, Masterman, Evans.
Chelsea: Molyneux; Bettridge, Harrow, Taylor, Logan, Walker, Ford, Halse, Thomson, Croal, McNeil.
Referee: H.H. Taylor.
The Khaki final; a low key occasion with United fairly comfortable winners.

Stamford Bridge, 24 April 1920 *50,018*
Aston Villa (0) 1 *(Kirton)*
Huddersfield Town (0) 0
Aston Villa: Hardy; Smart, Weston, Ducat, Barson, Moss, Wallace, Kirton, Walker, Stephenson, Dorrell.
Huddersfield Town: Mutch; Wood, Bullock, Slade, Wilson, Watson, Richardson, Mann, Taylor, Swann, Islip.
aet.
Referee: J.T. Howcroft.
Extra time before a decision, Kirton's header taken a deflection off Wilson's back.

Stamford Bridge, 23 April 1921 *72,805*
Tottenham Hotspur (0) 1 *(Dimmock)*
Wolverhampton Wanderers (0) 0
Tottenham Hotspur: Hunter; Clay, McDonald, Smith, Walters, Grimsdell, Banks, Seed, Cantrell, Bliss, Dimmock.
Wolverhampton Wanderers: George; Woodward, Marshall, Gregory, Hodnett, Riley, Lea, Burrill, Edmonds, Potts, Brooks.
Referee: J. Davies.
Spurs favourite crossfield pass executed by Seed and a slick solo by Dimmock.

Stamford Bridge, 29 April 1922 *53,000*
Huddersfield Town (0) 1 *(Smith (pen))*
Preston North End (0) 0
Huddersfield Town: Mutch; Wood, Wadsworth, Slade, Wilson, Watson, Richardson, Mann, Islip, Stephenson, Smith.
Preston North End: Mitchell; Hamilton, Doolan, Duxbury, McCall, Williamson, Rawlings, Jefferis, Roberts, Woodhouse, Quinn.
Referee: J.W.D. Fowler.
Sixty-five minutes, Smith tripped, got up and then scored from the penalty spot.

Wembley, 28 April 1923 *126,047*
Bolton Wanderers (1) 2 *(Jack, Smith JR)*
West Ham United (0) 0
Bolton Wanderers: Pym; Haworth, Finney, Nuttall, Seddon, Jennings, Butler, Jack, Smith JR, Smith J, Vizard.
West Ham United: Hufton; Henderson, Young, Bishop, Kay, Tresadern, Richards, Brown, Watson, Moore, Ruffell.
Referee: D.H. Asson.
Huge crowd ringed the touchline; PC Scorey and his white horse (grey) in charge.

Wembley, 26 April 1924 *91,695*
Newcastle United (0) 2 *(Harris, Seymour)*
Aston Villa (0) 0
Newcastle United: Bradley; Hampson, Hudspeth, Mooney, Spencer, Gibson, Low, Cowan, Harris, McDonald, Seymour.
Aston Villa: Jackson; Smart, Mort, Moss, Milne, Blackburn, York, Kirton, Capewell, Walker, Dorrell.
Referee: W.E. Russell.
First all-ticket game; Newcastle produced a devastating two goals in 90 seconds.

Wembley, 25 April 1925 *91,763*
Sheffield United (1) 1 *(Tunstall)*
Cardiff City (0) 0
Sheffield United: Sutcliffe; Cook, Milton, Pantling, King, Green, Mercer, Boyle, Johnson, Gillespie, Tunstall.
Cardiff City: Farquharson; Nelson, Blair, Wake, Keenor, Hardy, Davies, Gill, Nicholson, Beadles, Evans.
Referee: G.N. Watson.
One error Cardiff missed chances; skipper Gillespie was outstanding for United.

Wembley, 24 April 1926 *91,447*
Bolton Wanderers (0) 1 *(Jack)*
Manchester City (0) 0
Bolton Wanderers: Pym; Haworth, Greenhalgh, Nuttall, Seddon, Jennings, Butler, Jack, Smith JR, Smith J, Vizard.
Manchester City: Goodchild; Cookson, McCloy, Pringle, Cowan, McMullan, Austin, Browell, Roberts, Johnson, Hicks.
Referee: I. Baker.
Both defences in command, the winning goal arriving 12 minutes from time.

Wembley, 23 April 1927 *91,206*
Cardiff City (0) 1 *(Ferguson)*
Arsenal (0) 0
Cardiff City: Farquharson; Nelson, Watson, Keenor, Sloan, Hardy, Curtis, Irving, Ferguson, Davies, McLachlan.
Arsenal: Lewis; Parker, Kennedy, Baker, Butler, John, Hulme, Buchan, Brain, Blyth, Hoar.
Referee: W.F. Bunnell.
Slip-up by Welsh goalkeeper Lewis and the cup goes with Cardiff to Wales.

Wembley, 21 April 1928 *92,041*
Blackburn Rovers (2) 3 *(Roscamp 2, McLean)*
Huddersfield Town (0) 1 *(Jackson)*
Blackburn Rovers: Crawford; Hutton, Jones, Healless, Rankin, Campbell, Thornewell, Puddefoot, Roscamp, McLean, Rigby.
Huddersfield Town: Mercer; Goodall, Barkas, Redfern, Wilson, Steele, Jackson, Kelly, Brown, Stephenson, Smith.
Referee: T.G. Bryan.
BBC Radio coverage; Roscamp bundling keeper and ball after a minute.

Wembley, 27 April 1929 *92,576*
Bolton Wanderers (0) 2 *(Butler, Blackmore)*
Portsmouth (0) 0
Bolton Wanderers: Pym; Haworth, Finney, Kean, Seddon, Nuttall, Butler, McClelland, Blackmore, Gibson, Cook.
Portsmouth: Gilfillan; Mackie, Bell, Nichol, McIlwaine, Thackeray, Forward, Smith, Weddle, Watson, Cook.
Referee: A. Josephs.
Portsmouth had the better of the first half but Bolton gradually got on top.

Wembley, 26 April 1930 *92,488*
Arsenal (1) 2 *(James, Lambert)*
Huddersfield Town (0) 0
Arsenal: Preedy; Parker, Hapgood, Baker, Seddon, John, Hulme, Jack, Lambert, James, Bastin.
Huddersfield Town: Turner; Goodall, Spence, Naylor, Wilson, Campbell, Jackson, Kelly, Davies, Raw, Smith.
Referee: T. Crew.
Arsenal weathered a comeback by Huddersfield, thanks to their stout defence.

Wembley, 25 April 1931 *92,406*
West Bromwich Albion (1) 2 *(Richardson WG 2)*
Birmingham (0) 1 *(Bradford)*
West Bromwich Albion: Pearson; Shaw, Trentham, Magee, Richardson W, Edwards, Glidden, Carter, Richardson WG, Sandford, Wood.
Birmingham: Hibbs; Liddell, Barkas, Cringan, Morrall, Leslie, Briggs, Crosbie, Bradford, Gregg, Curtis.
Referee: A.H. Kingscott.
A unique double for Albion – the cup and promotion from Division Two.

Wembley, 23 April 1932 *92,298*
Newcastle United (1) 2 *(Allen 2)*
Arsenal (1) 1 *(John)*
Newcastle United: McInroy; Nelson, Fairhurst, McKenzie, Davidson, Weaver, Boyd, Richardson J.R., Allen, McMenemy, Lang.
Arsenal: Moss; Parker, Hapgood, Jones, Roberts, Male, Hulme, Jack, Lambert, Bastin, John.
Referee: W.P. Harper.
Controversy! Richardson's cross was already over the line for the Allen goal.

Wembley, 29 April 1933 *92,950*
Everton (1) 3 *(Stein, Dean, Dunn)*
Manchester City (0) 0
Everton: Sagar; Cook, Cresswell, Britton, White, Thomson, Geldard, Dunn, Dean, Johnson, Stein.
Manchester City: Langford; Cann, Dale, Busby, Cowan, Bray, Toseland, Marshall, Herd, McMullan, Brook.
Referee: E. Wood.
Players numbered for the first time but strangely from 1 to Langford's 22!

Wembley, 28 April 1934 *93,258*
Manchester City (0) 2 *(Tilson 2)*
Portsmouth (1) 1 *(Rutherford)*
Manchester City: Swift; Barnett, Dale, Busby, Cowan, Bray, Toseland, Marshall, Tilson, Herd, Brook.
Portsmouth: Gilfillan; Mackie, Smith W, Nichol, Allen, Thackeray, Worrall, Smith J, Weddle, Easson, Rutherford.
Referee: S.F. Rous.
Tilson who had been left out in 1933 predicted his duo and ensured City's win.

Wembley, 27 April 1935 *93,204*
Sheffield Wednesday (1) 4 *(Rimmer 2, Palethorpe, Hooper)*
West Bromwich Albion (1) 2 *(Boyes, Sandford)*
Sheffield Wednesday: Brown; Nibloe, Catlin, Sharp, Millership, Burrows, Hooper, Surtees, Palethorpe, Starling, Rimmer.
West Bromwich Albion: Pearson; Shaw, Trentham, Murphy, Richardson W, Edwards, Glidden, Carter, Richardson W G, Sandford, Boyes.
Referee: A.E. Fogg.
Rimmer double kept his record of scoring in every round with lucky horseshoe.

Wembley, 25 April 1936 *93,384*
Arsenal (0) 1 *(Drake)*
Sheffield United (0) 0
Arsenal: Wilson; Male, Hapgood, Crayston, Roberts, Copping, Hulme, Bowden, Drake, James, Bastin.
Sheffield United: Smith; Hooper, Wilkinson, Jackson, Johnson, McPherson, Barton, Barclay, Dodds, Pickering, Williams.
Referee: H. Nattrass.
Drake shrugs off discomfiture of his heavily bandaged knee; ban on cameras!

Wembley, 1 May 1937 *93,495*
Sunderland (0) 3 *(Gurney, Carter, Burbanks)*
Preston North End (1) 1 *(O'Donnell F)*
Sunderland: Mapson; Gorman, Hall, Thomson, Johnson, McNab, Duns, Carter, Gurney, Gallacher, Burbanks.
Preston North End: Burns; Gallimore, Beattie A, Shankly, Tremelling, Milne, Dougal, Beresford, O'Donnell F, Fagan, O'Donnell H.
Referee: R.G. Rudd.
First for TV cameras and Sunderland's recently-wed local boy Carter inspires.

Wembley, 30 April 1938 *93,497*
Preston North End (0) 1 *(Mutch (pen))*
Huddersfield Town (0) 0
Preston North End: Holdcroft; Gallimore, Beattie A, Shankly, Smith, Batey, Watmough, Mutch, Maxwell, Beattie R, O'Donnell H.
Huddersfield Town: Hesford; Craig, Mountford, Willingham, Young, Boot, Hulme, Isaac, McFadyen, Barclay, Beasley.
aet.
Referee: A.J. Jewell.
Controversial Mutch penalty in off the crossbar in the 119th minute.

Wembley, 29 April 1939 *99,370*
Portsmouth (2) 4 *(Parker 2, Barlow, Anderson)*
Wolverhampton Wanderers (0) 1 *(Dorsett)*
Portsmouth: Walker; Morgan, Rochford, Guthrie, Rowe, Wharton, Worrall, McAlinden, Anderson, Barlow, Parker.
Wolverhampton Wanderers: Scott; Morris, Taylor, Galley, Cullis, Gardiner, Burton, McIntosh, Westcott, Dorsett, Maguire.
Referee: T. Thompson.
Barlow scores against his old club; odds-on favourites are decisively beaten.

Wembley, 27 April 1946 *97,106*
Derby County (0) 4 *(Turner H (og), Doherty, Stamps 2)*
Charlton Athletic (0) 1 *(Turner H)*
Derby County: Woodley; Nicholas, Howe, Bullions, Leuty, Musson, Harrison, Carter, Stamps, Doherty, Duncan.
Charlton Athletic: Bartram; Phipps, Shreeve, Turner H, Oakes, Johnson, Fell, Brown, Turner A, Welsh, Duffy.
aet.
Referee: E.D. Smith.
Turner H scores for both teams and Derby really turn on the style.

Wembley, 26 April 1947 *98,215*
Charlton Athletic (0) 1 *(Duffy)*
Burnley (0) 0
Charlton Athletic: Bartram; Croker, Shreeve, Johnson, Phipps, Whittaker, Hurst, Dawson, Robinson, Welsh, Duffy.
Burnley: Strong; Woodruff, Mather, Attwell, Brown, Bray, Chew, Morris, Harrison, Potts, Kippax.
aet.
Referee: J.M. Wiltshire.
Winner six minutes from the end; ball bursts for second year running.

Wembley, 24 April 1948 *99,000*
Manchester United (1) 4 *(Rowley 2, Pearson, Anderson)*
Blackpool (2) 2 *(Shimwell (pen), Mortensen)*
Manchester United: Crompton; Carey, Aston, Anderson, Chilton, Cockburn, Delaney, Morris, Rowley, Pearson, Mitten.
Blackpool: Robinson; Shimwell, Crosland, Johnston, Hayward, Kelly, Matthews, Munro, Mortensen, Dick, Rickett.
Referee: C.J. Barrick.
Exceptional, enthralling contest Shimwell first full-back to score at Wembley.

Wembley, 30 April 1949 *98,920*
Wolverhampton Wanderers (2) 3 *(Pye 2, Smyth)*
Leicester City (0) 1 *(Griffiths)*
Wolverhampton Wanderers: Williams; Pritchard, Springthorpe, Crook, Shorthouse, Wright, Hancocks, Smyth, Pye, Dunn, Mullen.
Leicester City: Bradley; Jelly, Scott, Harrison W, Plummer, King, Griffiths, Lee, Harrison J, Chisholm, Adam.
Referee: R.A. Mortimer.
Leicester miss nosebleed victim Revie, Wolves four capped forwards supreme.

Wembley, 29 April 1950 *100,000*
Arsenal (1) 2 *(Lewis 2)*
Liverpool (0) 0
Arsenal: Swindin; Scott, Barnes, Forbes, Compton L, Mercer, Cox, Logie, Goring, Lewis, Compton D.
Liverpool: Sidlow; Lambert, Spicer, Taylor, Hughes, Jones, Payne, Baron, Stubbins, Fagan, Liddell.
Referee: H. Pearce.
Arsenal the oldest team to win the cup average age 30 years 2 months in control.

Wembley, 28 April 1951 *100,000*
Newcastle United (0) 2 *(Milburn 2)*
Blackpool (0) 0
Newcastle United: Fairbrother; Cowell, Corbett, Harvey, Brennan, Crowe, Walker, Taylor, Milburn, Robledo G, Mitchell.
Blackpool: Farm; Shimwell, Garrett, Johnston, Hayward, Kelly, Matthews, Mudie, Mortensen, Slater, Perry.
Referee: W. Ling.
Seymour (1924) first to play for and then manage a winning Cup Final team.

Wembley, 3 May 1952 *100,000*
Newcastle United (0) 1 *(Robledo G)*
Arsenal (0) 0
Newcastle United: Simpson; Cowell, McMichael, Harvey, Brennan, Robledo E, Walker, Foulkes, Milburn, Robledo G, Mitchell.
Arsenal: Swindin; Barnes, Smith, Forbes, Daniel, Mercer, Cox, Logie, Holton, Lishman, Roper.
Referee: A. Ellis.
Walley Barnes off with a split cartilage, Chilean Robledo scores in 84 minutes.

Wembley, 2 May 1953 *100,000*
Blackpool (1) 4 *(Mortensen 3, Perry)*
Bolton Wanderers (2) 3 *(Lofthouse, Moir, Bell)*
Blackpool: Farm; Shimwell, Garrett, Fenton, Johnston, Robinson, Matthews, Taylor, Mortensen, Mudie, Perry.
Bolton Wanderers: Hanson; Ball, Banks, Wheeler, Barrass, Bell, Holden, Moir, Lofthouse, Hassall, Langton.
Referee: M. Griffiths.
The Matthews Final; but injury-ridden Bolton suffer heavily in last 20 minutes.

Wembley, 1 May 1954 *100,000*
West Bromwich Albion (1) 3 *(Allen 2 (1 pen), Griffin)*
Preston North End (1) 2 *(Morrison, Wayman)*
West Bromwich Albion: Sanders; Kennedy, Millard, Dudley, Dugdale, Barlow, Griffin, Ryan, Allen, Nicholls, Lee.
Preston North End: Thompson; Cunningham, Walton, Docherty, Marston, Forbes, Finney, Foster, Wayman, Baxter, Morrison.
Referee: A. Luty.
Finney disappoints for Preston and Albion favourites win in the last minute.

Wembley, 7 May 1955 *100,000*
Newcastle United (1) 3 *(Milburn, Mitchell, Hannah)*
Manchester City (1) 1 *(Johnstone)*
Newcastle United: Simpson; Cowell, Batty, Scoular, Stokoe, Casey, White, Milburn, Keeble, Hannah, Mitchell.
Manchester City: Trautmann; Meadows, Little, Barnes, Ewing, Paul, Spurdle, Hayes, Revie, Johnstone, Fagan.
Referee: R. Leafe.
Meadows out with a twisted knee and City hit by Milburn's 45 second goal.

Wembley, 5 May 1956 *100,000*
Manchester City (1) 3 *(Hayes, Dyson, Johnstone)*
Birmingham City (1) 1 *(Kinsey)*
Manchester City: Trautmann; Leivers, Little, Barnes, Ewing, Paul, Johnstone, Hayes, Revie, Dyson, Clarke.
Birmingham City: Merrick; Hall, Green, Newman, Smith, Boyd, Astall, Kinsey, Brown, Murphy, Govan.
Referee: A. Bond.
The Revie plan works; Trautmann plays the last 20 minutes with a broken neck.

Wembley, 4 May 1957 *100,000*
Aston Villa (0) 2 *(McParland 2)*
Manchester United (0) 1 *(Taylor T)*
Aston Villa: Sims; Lynn, Aldis, Crowther, Dugdale, Saward, Smith, Sewell, Myerscough, Dixon, McParland.
Manchester United: Wood; Foulkes, Byrne, Colman, Blanchflower, Edwards, Berry, Whelan, Taylor T, Charlton, Pegg.
Referee: F. Coultas.
Wood broken collarbone after challenge by McParland, Blanchflower in goal.

Wembley, 3 May 1958 *100,000*
Bolton Wanderers (1) 2 *(Lofthouse 2)*
Manchester United (0) 0
Bolton Wanderers: Hopkinson; Hartle, Banks, Hennin, Higgins, Edwards, Birch, Stevens, Lofthouse, Parry, Holden.
Manchester United: Gregg; Foulkes, Greaves, Goodwin, Cope, Crowther, Dawson, Taylor E, Charlton, Viollet, Webster.
Referee: J. Sherlock.
Post-Munich Final, United given dispensation for Taylor and Crowther to play.

Wembley, 2 May 1959 *100,000*
Nottingham Forest (2) 2 *(Dwight, Wilson)*
Luton Town (0) 1 *(Pacey)*
Nottingham Forest: Thomson; Whare, McDonald, Whitefoot, McKinlay, Burkitt, Dwight, Quigley, Wilson, Gray, Imlach.
Luton Town: Baynham; McNally, Hawkes, Groves, Owen, Pacey, Bingham, Brown, Morton, Cummins, Gregory.
Referee: J. Clough.
Dwight scores, breaks his leg and watches the final on TV from hospital bed.

Wembley, 7 May 1960 *100,000*
Wolverhampton Wanderers (1) 3 *(McGrath (og), Deeley 2)*
Blackburn Rovers (0) 0
Wolverhampton Wanderers: Finlayson; Showell, Harris, Clamp, Slater, Flowers, Deeley, Stobart, Murray, Broadbent, Horne.
Blackburn Rovers: Leyland; Bray, Whelan, Clayton, Woods, McGrath, Bimpson, Dobing, Dougan, Douglas, MacLeod.
Referee: K. Howley.
Whelan breaks his leg and Wolves have an easy ride to winning their medals.

Wembley, 6 May 1961 *100,000*
Tottenham Hotspur (0) 2 *(Smith, Dyson)*
Leicester City (0) 0
Tottenham Hotspur: Brown; Baker, Henry, Blanchflower, Norman, Mackay, Jones, White, Smith, Allen, Dyson.
Leicester City: Banks; Chalmers, Norman, McLintock, King, Appleton, Riley, Walsh, McIlmoyle, Keyworth, Cheesebrough.
Referee: J. Kelly.
Blanchflower inspires the Spurs first League and Cup double of the century.

Wembley, 5 May 1962 *100,000*
Tottenham Hotspur (1) 3 *(Greaves, Smith, Blanchflower (pen))*
Burnley (0) 1 *(Robson)*
Tottenham Hotspur: Brown; Baker, Henry, Blanchflower, Norman, Mackay, Medwin, White, Smith, Greaves, Jones.
Burnley: Blacklaw; Angus, Elder, Adamson, Cummings, Miller, Connelly, McIlroy, Pointer, Robson, Harris.
Referee: J. Finney.
Robson scores the 100th Cup Final goal but Spurs prove the ultimate masters.

Wembley, 25 May 1963 *100,000*
Manchester United (1) 3 *(Herd 2, Law)*
Leicester City (0) 1 *(Keyworth)*
Manchester United: Gaskell; Dunne, Cantwell, Crerand, Foulkes, Setters, Giles, Quixall, Herd, Law, Charlton.
Leicester City: Banks; Sjoberg, Norman, McLintock, King, Appleton, Riley, Cross, Keyworth, Gibson, Stringfellow.
Referee: K. Aston.
Harsh winter decides late date and United are in control in all departments.

Wembley, 2 May 1964 *100,000*
West Ham United (1) 3 *(Sissons, Hurst, Boyce)*
Preston North End (2) 2 *(Holden, Dawson)*
West Ham United: Standen; Bond, Burkett, Bovington, Brown, Moore, Brabrook, Boyce, Byrne, Hurst, Sissons.
Preston North End: Kelly; Ross, Smith, Lawton, Singleton, Kendall, Wilson, Ashworth, Dawson, Spavin, Holden.
Referee: A. Holland.
Kendall 17 years 345 days Wembley's youngest, Sissons the youngest scorer.

Wembley, 1 May 1965 *100,000*
Liverpool (0) 2 *(Hunt, St John)*
Leeds United (0) 1 *(Bremner)*
Liverpool: Lawrence; Lawler, Byrne, Strong, Yeats, Stevenson, Callaghan, Hunt, St John, Smith, Thompson.
Leeds United: Sprake; Reaney, Bell, Bremner, Charlton, Hunter, Giles, Storrie, Peacock, Collins, Johanneson.
aet.
Referee: W. Clements.
Byrne breaks his collarbone, extra time and Liverpool cry of "ee-ay-addio".

Wembley, 14 May 1966 *100,000*
Everton (0) 3 *(Trebilcock 2, Temple)*
Sheffield Wednesday (1) 2 *(McCalliog, Ford)*
Everton: West; Wright, Wilson, Gabriel, Labone, Harris, Scott, Trebilcock, Young, Harvey, Temple.
Sheffield Wednesday: Springett; Smith, Megson, Eustace, Ellis, Young, Pugh, Fantham, McCalliog, Ford, Quinn.
Referee: J.K. Taylor.
Two down in 57 minutes Trebilcock (not mentioned in programme) wins it.

Wembley, 20 May 1967 *100,000*
Tottenham Hotspur (1) 2 *(Robertson, Saul)*
Chelsea (0) 1 *(Tambling)*
Tottenham Hotspur: Jennings; Kinnear, Knowles, Mullery, England, Mackay, Robertson, Greaves, Gilzean, Venables, Saul.
Chelsea: Bonetti; Harris A, McCreadie, Hollins, Hinton, Harris R, Cooke, Baldwin, Hateley, Tambling, Boyle.
Referee: K. Dagnall.
First all-London Final and all-action Spurs make it five wins in five finals.

Wembley, 18 May 1968 *100,000*
West Bromwich Albion (0) 1 *(Astle)*
Everton (0) 0
West Bromwich Albion: Osborne; Fraser, Williams, Brown, Talbut, Kaye (Clarke), Lovett, Collard, Astle, Hope, Clark.
Everton: West; Wright, Wilson, Kendall, Labone, Harvey, Husband, Ball, Royle, Hurst, Morrissey.
aet.
Referee: L. Callaghan.
Astle scores in every round the scuffed winner in the third minute of extra time.

Wembley, 26 April 1969 *100,000*
Manchester City (1) 1 *(Young)*
Leicester City (0) 0
Manchester City: Dowd; Book, Pardoe, Doyle, Booth, Oakes, Summerbee, Bell, Lee, Young, Coleman.
Leicester City: Shilton; Rodrigues, Nish, Roberts, Woollett, Cross, Fern, Gibson, Lochhead, Clarke, Glover (Manley).
Referee: G. McCabe.
The double for fourth finalists Leicester – defeat and relegation to Division Two.

Wembley, 11 April 1970 *100,000*
Chelsea (1) 2 *(Houseman, Hutchinson)*
Leeds United (1) 2 *(Charlton, Jones)*
Chelsea: Bonetti; Webb, McCreadie, Hollins, Dempsey, Harris R (Hinton), Baldwin, Houseman, Osgood, Hutchinson, Cooke.
Leeds United: Sprake; Madeley, Cooper, Bremner, Charlton, Hunter, Lorimer, Clarke, Jones, Giles, Gray E.
aet.
Referee: E. Jennings.
Chelsea twice behind force a replay – first since 1912 – against dominant Leeds.

Replay: *Old Trafford, Manchester, 29 April 1970* *62,078*
Chelsea (0) 2 *(Osgood, Webb)*
Leeds United (1) 1 *(Jones)*
Chelsea: Bonetti; Harris R, McCreadie, Hollins, Dempsey, Webb, Baldwin, Cooke, Osgood (Hinton), Hutchinson, Houseman.
Leeds United: Harvey; Madeley, Cooper, Bremner, Charlton, Hunter, Lorimer, Clarke, Jones, Giles, Gray E.
aet.
Referee: E. Jennings.
Chelsea out of town find a rarity – taking a late lead and winning the cup.

Wembley, 8 May 1971 *100,000*
Arsenal (0) 2 *(Kelly, George)*
Liverpool (0) 1 *(Heighway)*
Arsenal: Wilson; Rice, McNabb, Storey (Kelly), McLintock, Simpson, Armstrong, Graham, Radford, Kennedy, George.
Liverpool: Clemence; Lawler, Lindsay, Smith, Lloyd, Hughes, Callaghan, Evans (Thompson), Heighway, Toshack, Hall.
aet.
Referee: N. Burtenshaw.
Drawn away in every round, Arsenal double winners and Kelly first sub scorer.

Wembley, 6 May 1972 *100,000*
Leeds United (0) 1 *(Clarke)*
Arsenal (0) 0
Leeds United: Harvey; Reaney, Madeley, Bremner, Charlton, Hunter, Lorimer, Clarke, Jones, Giles, Gray E.
Arsenal: Barnett; Rice, McNab, Storey, McLintock, Simpson, Armstrong, Ball, George, Radford (Kennedy), Graham.
Referee: D.W. Smith.
Centenary Final, goal provider Jones dislocates his elbow in the last minute.

Wembley, 5 May 1973 *100,000*
Sunderland (1) 1 *(Porterfield)*
Leeds United (0) 0
Sunderland: Montgomery; Malone, Guthrie, Horswill, Watson, Pitt, Kerr, Hughes, Halom, Porterfield, Tueart.
Leeds United: Harvey; Reaney, Cherry, Bremner, Madeley, Hunter, Lorimer, Clarke, Jones, Giles, Gray E (Yorath).
Referee: K. Burns.
First Second Division winners in 42 years and the Montgomery double save.

Wembley, 4 May 1974 *100,000*
Liverpool (0) 3 *(Keegan 2, Heighway)*
Newcastle United (0) 0
Liverpool: Clemence; Smith, Lindsay, Thompson, Cormack, Hughes, Keegan, Hall, Heighway, Toshack, Callaghan.
Newcastle United: McFaul; Clark, Kennedy, McDermott, Howard, Moncur, Smith (Gibb), Cassidy, Macdonald, Tudor, Hibbitt.
Referee: G.C. Kew.
United's 11th final but suffer first Wembley defeat against skillful Liverpool.

Wembley, 3 May 1975 *100,000*
West Ham United (0) 2 *(Taylor A 2)*
Fulham (0) 0
West Ham United: Day; McDowell, Taylor T, Lock, Lampard, Bonds, Paddon, Brooking, Jennings, Taylor A, Holland.
Fulham: Mellor; Cutbush, Lacy, Moore, Fraser, Mullery, Conway, Slough, Mitchell, Busby, Barrett.
Referee: P. Partridge.
Hammers win is Taylor-made – striker signed in November from Rochdale.

Wembley, 1 May 1976 *100,000*
Southampton (0) 1 *(Stokes)*
Manchester United (0) 0
Southampton: Turner; Rodrigues, Peach, Holmes, Blyth, Steele, Gilchrist, Channon, Osgood, McCalliog, Stokes.
Manchester United: Stepney; Forsyth, Houston, Daly, Greenhoff B, Buchan, Coppell, McIlroy, Pearson, Macari, Hill (McCreery).
Referee: C. Thomas.
Third time lucky for the Second Division Saints, 83rd minute winner.

Wembley, 21 May 1977 *100,000*
Manchester United (0) 2 *(Pearson, Greenhoff J)*
Liverpool (0) 1 *(Case)*
Manchester United: Stepney; Nicholl, Albiston, McIlroy, Greenhoff B, Buchan, Coppell, Greenhoff J, Pearson, Macari, Hill (McCreery).
Liverpool: Clemence; Neal, Jones, Smith, Kennedy, Hughes, Keegan, Case, Heighway, Johnson (Callaghan), McDermott.
Referee: R. Matthewson.
All three goals in a five minute spell after half-time in well-fought display.

Wembley, 6 May 1978 *100,000*
Ipswich Town (0) 1 *(Osborne)*
Arsenal (0) 0
Ipswich Town: Cooper; Burley, Mills, Osborne (Lambert), Hunter, Beattie, Talbot, Wark, Mariner, Geddis, Woods.
Arsenal: Jennings; Rice, Nelson, Price, Young, O'Leary, Brady (Rix), Hudson, Macdonald, Stapleton, Sunderland.
Referee: D.R.G. Nippard.
Wembley's 50th Final, 40th different winners Osborne replaced – exhausted

Wembley, 12 May 1979 *100,000*
Arsenal (2) 3 *(Talbot, Stapleton, Sunderland)*
Manchester United (0) 2 *(McQueen, McIlroy)*
Arsenal: Jennings; Rice, Nelson, Talbot, O'Leary, Young, Brady, Sunderland, Stapleton, Price (Walford), Rix.
Manchester United: Bailey; Nicholl, Albiston, McIlroy, McQueen, Buchan, Coppell, Greenhoff J, Jordan, Macari, Thomas.
Referee: R. Challis.
Despite goals in 86 and 88 minutes to level, United are the ultimate losers.

Wembley, 10 May 1980 *100,000*
West Ham United (1) 1 *(Brooking)*
Arsenal (0) 0
West Ham United: Parkes; Stewart, Lampard, Bonds, Martin, Devonshire, Allen, Pearson, Cross, Brooking, Pike.
Arsenal: Jennings; Rice, Devine (Nelson), Talbot, O'Leary, Young, Brady, Sunderland, Stapleton, Price, Rix.
Referee: G. Courtney.
Allen at 17 years 256 days youngest Wembley finalist; Brooking header!

Wembley, 9 May 1981 *100,000*
Tottenham Hotspur (0) 1 *(Hutchison (og))*
Manchester City (1) 1 *(Hutchison)*
Tottenham Hotspur: Aleksic; Hughton, Miller, Roberts, Perryman, Villa (Brooke), Ardiles, Archibald, Galvin, Hoddle, Crooks.
Manchester City: Corrigan; Ranson, McDonald, Reid, Power, Caton, Bennett, Gow, MacKenzie, Hutchison (Henry), Reeves.
aet.
Referee: K. Hackett.
The 100th Final, well-matched teams given another chance after own goal.

Replay: *Wembley, 14 May 1981* *92,000*
Tottenham Hotspur (1) 3 *(Villa 2, Crooks)*
Manchester City (1) 2 *(MacKenzie, Reeves (pen))*
Tottenham Hotspur: Aleksic; Hughton, Miller, Roberts, Perryman, Villa, Ardiles, Archibald, Galvin, Hoddle, Crooks.
Manchester City: Corrigan; Ranson, McDonald (Tueart), Caton, Reid, Gow, Power, MacKenzie, Reeves, Bennett, Hutchison.
Referee: K. Hackett.
Villa caps an unfortgettable Final, beating three men in a 30 yard run.

Wembley, 22 May 1982 *100,000*
Tottenham Hotspur (0) 1 *(Hoddle)*
Queens Park Rangers (0) 1 *(Fenwick)*
Tottenham Hotspur: Clemence; Hughton, Miller, Price, Roberts, Perryman, Hazard (Brooke), Archibald, Galvin, Hoddle, Crooks.
Queens Park Rangers: Hucker; Fenwick, Gillard, Waddock, Hazell, Roeder, Currie, Flanagan, Allen (Micklewhite), Stainrod, Gregory.
aet.
Referee: C. White.
Spurs Centenary year but forced to try again against a plucky Rangers.

Replay: *Wembley, 27 May 1982* *90,000*
Tottenham Hotspur (1) 1 *(Hoddle (pen))*
Queens Park Rangers (0) 0
Tottenham Hotspur: Clemence; Hughton, Miller, Price, Roberts, Perryman, Hazard (Brooke), Archibald, Galvin, Hoddle, Crooks.
Queens Park Rangers: Hucker; Fenwick, Gillard, Waddock, Hazell, Neill, Currie, Flanagan, Micklewhite (Burke), Stainrod, Gregory.
Referee: C. White.
Hoddle's penalty makes it seven wins in seven for celebrating Spurs.

Wembley, 21 May 1983 *100,000*
Manchester United (0) 2 *(Stapleton, Wilkins)*
Brighton & Hove Albion (1) 2 *(Smith, Stevens)*
Manchester United: Bailey; Duxbury, Albiston, Wilkins, McQueen, Moran, Robson, Muhren, Stapleton, Whiteside, Davies.
Brighton & Hove Albion: Moseley; Ramsey (Ryan), Stevens, Gatting, Pearce, Smillie, Case, Grealish, Howlett, Robinson, Smith.
aet.
Referee: A.W. Grey.
Relegated Brighton and Smith misses easy chance in last minute.

Replay: *Wembley, 26 May 1983* *92,000*
Manchester United (3) 4 *(Robson 2, Whiteside, Muhren (pen))*
Brighton & Hove Albion (0) 0
Manchester United: Bailey; Duxbury, Albiston, Wilkins, McQueen, Moran, Robson, Muhren, Stapleton, Whiteside, Davies.
Brighton & Hove Albion: Moseley; Gatting, Pearce, Grealish, Foster, Stevens, Case, Howlett, Robinson, Smith, Smillie.
Referee: A.W. Grey.
Whiteside youngest final scorer at 18 years 18 days in one-sided game.

Wembley, 19 May 1984 *100,000*
Everton (1) 2 *(Sharp, Gray)*
Watford (0) 0
Everton: Southall; Stevens, Bailey, Ratcliffe, Mountfield, Reid, Steven, Heath, Sharp, Gray, Richardson.
Watford: Sherwood; Bardsley, Price (Atkinson), Taylor, Terry, Sinnott, Callaghan, Johnston, Reilly, Jackett, Barnes.
Referee: J. Hunting.
Sharp via post and Gray header out of goalkeeper's hands see off Watford.

Wembley, 18 May 1985 *100,000*
Manchester United (0) 1 *(Whiteside)*
Everton (0) 0
Manchester United: Bailey; Gidman, Albiston (Duxbury), Whiteside, McGrath, Moran■, Robson, Strachan, Hughes, Stapleton, Olsen.
Everton: Southall; Stevens, Van Den Hauwe, Ratcliffe, Mountfield, Reid, Steven, Gray, Sharp, Bracewell, Sheedy.
aet.
Referee: P. Willis.
Policeman Willis makes Moran first finalist to be sent off. £1m gate.

Wembley, 10 May 1986 *98,000*
Liverpool (0) 3 *(Rush 2, Johnston)*
Everton (1) 1 *(Lineker)*
Liverpool: Grobbelaar; Lawrenson, Beglin, Nicol, Whelan, Hansen, Dalglish, Johnston, Rush, Molby, MacDonald.
Everton: Mimms; Stevens (Heath), Van Den Hauwe, Ratcliffe, Mountfield, Reid, Steven, Lineker, Sharp, Bracewell, Sheedy.
Referee: A. Robinson.
All-Mersey Final and Liverpool with first non-English team.

Wembley, 16 May 1987 *98,000*
Coventry City (1) 3 *(Bennett, Houchen, Mabbutt (og))*
Tottenham Hotspur (2) 2 *(Allen C, Mabbutt)*
Coventry City: Ogrizovic; Phillips, Downs, McGrath, Kilcline (Rodger), Peake, Bennett, Gynn, Regis, Houchen, Pickering.
Tottenham Hotspur: Clemence; Hughton (Claeson), Thomas, Hodge, Gough, Mabbutt, Allen C, Allen P, Waddle, Hoddle, Ardiles (Stevens).
aet.
Referee: N. Midgley.
In their 104th year, twice in arrears Coventry achieve first major honour.

Wembley, 14 May 1988 *98,203*
Wimbledon (1) 1 *(Sanchez)*
Liverpool (0) 0
Wimbledon: Beasant; Goodyear, Phelan, Jones, Young, Thorn, Gibson (Scales), Cork (Cunningham), Fashanu, Sanchez, Wise.
Liverpool: Grobbelaar; Gillespie, Ablett, Nicol, Spackman (Molby), Hansen, Beardsley, Aldridge (Johnston), Houghton, Barnes, McMahon.
Referee: B. Hill.
Beasant saves an Aldridge penalty and the fledgling Dons cause a huge upset.

Wembley, 20 May 1989 *82,500*
Liverpool (1) 3 *(Aldridge, Rush 2)*
Everton (0) 2 *(McCall 2)*
Liverpool: Grobbelaar; Ablett, Staunton (Venison), Nicol, Whelan, Hansen, Beardsley, Aldridge (Rush), Houghton, Barnes, McMahon.
Everton: Southall; McDonald, Van Den Hauwe, Ratcliffe, Watson, Bracewell (McCall), Nevin, Steven, Sharp, Cottee, Sheedy (Wilson).
aet.
Referee: J. Worrall.
Poignant Merseyside final played in the aftermath of the Hillsborough disaster.

Wembley, 12 May 1990 *80,000*
Manchester United (1) 3 *(Robson, Hughes 2)*
Crystal Palace (1) 3 *(O'Reilly, Wright 2)*
Manchester United: Leighton; Ince, Martin (Blackmore), Bruce, Phelan, Pallister (Robins), Robson, Webb, McClair, Hughes, Wallace.
Crystal Palace: Martyn; Pemberton, Shaw, Gray (Madden), O'Reilly, Thorn, Barber (Wright), Thomas, Bright, Salako, Pardew.
aet.
Referee: A. Gunn.
Palace force a replay against much fancied United in a feast of goalscoring.

Replay: *Wembley, 17 May 1990* *80,000*
Manchester United (0) 1 *(Martin)*
Crystal Palace (0) 0
Manchester United: Sealey; Ince, Martin, Bruce, Phelan, Pallister, Robson, Webb, McClair, Hughes, Wallace.
Crystal Palace: Martyn; Pemberton, Shaw, Gray, O'Reilly, Thorn, Barber (Wright), Thomas, Bright, Salako (Madden), Pardew.
Referee: A. Gunn.
Match-winner Martin's goal was his only one in the entire season.

Wembley, 18 May 1991 *80,000*
Tottenham Hotspur (0) 2 *(Stewart, Walker (og))*
Nottingham Forest (1) 1 *(Pearce)*
Tottenham Hotspur: Thorstvedt; Edinburgh, Van Den Hauwe, Sedgley, Howells, Mabbutt, Stewart, Gascoigne (Nayim), Samways (Walsh), Lineker, Allen.
Nottingham Forest: Crossley; Charles, Pearce, Walker, Chettle, Keane, Crosby, Parker, Clough, Glover (Laws), Woan (Hodge).
aet.
Referee: R. Milford.
Gascoigne self-inflicted injury and Spurs need extra time own goal to win.

Wembley, 9 May 1992 *79,544*
Liverpool (0) 2 *(Thomas, Rush)*
Sunderland (0) 0
Liverpool: Grobbelaar; Jones, Burrows, Nicol, Molby, Wright, Saunders, Houghton, Rush, McManaman, Thomas.
Sunderland: Norman; Owers, Ball, Bennett, Rogan, Rush (Hardyman), Bracewell, Davenport, Armstrong, Byrne, Atkinson (Hawke).
Referee: P. Don.
Fourth trophy but winning medals given to wrong team! Rush goal record.

Wembley, 15 May 1993 *79,347*
Arsenal (1) 1 *(Wright)*
Sheffield Wednesday (0) 1 *(Hirst)*
Arsenal: Seaman; Dixon, Winterburn, Davis, Linighan, Adams, Jensen, Wright (O'Leary), Campbell, Merson, Parlour (Smith).
Sheffield Wednesday: Woods; Nilsson, Worthington, Palmer, Anderson (Hyde), Warhurst, Harkes, Waddle (Bart-Williams), Hirst, Bright, Sheridan.
aet.
Referee: K. Barratt.
Squad numbers and names but the League Cup finalists pushed to replay.

Replay: *Wembley, 20 May 1993* *62,267*
Arsenal (1) 2 *(Wright, Linighan)*
Sheffield Wednesday (0) 1 *(Waddle)*
Arsenal: Seaman; Dixon, Winterburn, Davis, Linighan, Adams, Jensen, Wright (O'Leary), Smith, Merson, Campbell.
Sheffield Wednesday: Woods; Nilsson (Bart-Williams), Worthington, Harkes, Palmer, Warhurst, Wilson (Hyde), Waddle, Hirst, Bright, Sheridan.
aet.
Referee: K. Barratt.
Penalty shoot-out avoided only by Linighan header 44 seconds from time.

Wembley, 14 May 1994 *79,634*
Manchester United (0) 4 *(Cantona 2 (2 pens), Hughes, McClair)*
Chelsea (0) 0
Manchester United: Schmeichel; Parker, Irwin (Sharpe), Bruce, Kanchelskis (McClair), Pallister, Cantona, Ince, Keane, Hughes, Giggs.
Chelsea: Kharine; Clarke, Sinclair, Kjeldbjerg, Johnsen, Burley (Hoddle), Spencer, Newton, Stein (Cascarino), Peacock, Wise.
Referee: D. Elleray.
United on the double again; Chelsea in contention for an hour.

Wembley, 20 May 1995 *79,592*
Everton (1) 1 *(Rideout)*
Manchester United (0) 0
Everton: Southall; Jackson, Ablett, Parkinson, Watson, Unsworth, Limpar (Amokachi), Horne, Stuart, Rideout (Ferguson), Hinchcliffe.
Manchester United: Schmeichel; Neville G, Irwin, Bruce (Giggs), Sharpe (Scholes), Pallister, Keane, Ince, McClair, Hughes, Butt.
Referee: G. Ashby.
It's the Littlewoods Pools Cup, Everton win after Stuart strikes the crossbar.

Wembley, 11 May 1996 *79,007*
Manchester United (0) 1 *(Cantona)*
Liverpool (0) 0
Manchester United: Schmeichel; Irwin, Neville P, May, Keane, Pallister, Cantona, Beckham (Neville G), Cole (Scholes), Butt, Giggs.
Liverpool: James; McAteer, Jones (Thomas), Scales, Wright, Babb, McManaman, Redknapp, Collymore (Rush), Barnes, Fowler.
Referee: D. Gallagher.
Liverpool lose a disappointing match to a classic from the edge of the area.

Wembley, 17 May 1997 *79,160*
Chelsea (1) 2 *(Di Matteo, Newton)*
Middlesbrough (0) 0
Chelsea: Grodas; Petrescu, Minto, Sinclair, Leboeuf, Clarke, Zola (Vialli), Di Matteo, Newton, Hughes M, Wise.
Middlesbrough: Roberts; Blackmore, Fleming, Stamp, Pearson, Festa, Emerson, Mustoe (Vickers), Ravanelli (Beck), Juninho, Hignett (Kinder).
Referee: S. Lodge.
Middlesbrough already relegated and on the back foot after 42 seconds goal.

Wembley, 16 May 1998 *79,183*
Arsenal (0) 2 *(Overmars, Anelka)*
Newcastle U (0) 0
Arsenal: Seaman; Dixon, Winterburn, Vieira, Keown, Adams, Parlour, Anelka, Petit, Wreh (Platt), Overmars.
Newcastle U: Given; Pistone, Pearce (Andersson), Batty, Dabizas, Howey, Lee, Barton (Watson), Shearer, Ketsbaia (Barnes), Speed.
Referee: P. Durkin.
Arsenal, League title secured, achieve their second League and Cup double.

Wembley, 22 May 1999 *79,101*
Manchester U (1) 2 *(Sheringham 11, Scholes 53)*
Newcastle U (0) 0
Manchester U: Schmeichel; Neville G, Neville P, May, Keane (Sheringham), Johnsen, Beckham, Scholes (Stam), Cole (Yorke), Solskjaer, Giggs.
Newcastle U: Harper; Griffin, Domi, Dabizas, Charvet, Solano (Maric), Lee, Hamann (Ferguson), Shearer, Ketsbaia (Glass), Speed.
Referee: P. Jones (Loughborough).
Manchester United on way to an historic treble home plus European, in a one-sided affair.

Wembley, 20 May 2000 *78,217*
Chelsea (0) 1 *(Di Matteo 72)*
Aston Villa (0) 0
Chelsea: De Goey; Melchiot, Babayaro, Deschamps, Leboeuf, Desailly, Poyet, Di Matteo, Weah (Flo), Zola (Morris), Wise.
Aston Villa: James; Delaney, Wright (Hendrie), Southgate, Ehiogu, Barry, Taylor (Stone), Boateng, Dublin, Carbone (Joachim), Merson.
Referee: G. Poll (Tring).
After a poor first half the game decided by a 73rd minute goalkeeping error.

Millennium Stadium, 12 May 2001 *74,200*
Liverpool (0) 2 *(Owen 83, 88)*
Arsenal (0) 1 *(Ljungberg 72)*
Liverpool: Westerveld; Babbel, Carragher, Hamann (McAllister), Henchoz, Hyypia, Murphy (Berger), Gerrard, Heskey, Owen, Smicer (Fowler).
Arsenal: Seaman; Dixon (Bergkamp), Cole, Vieira, Keown, Adams, Pires, Grimandi, Wiltord (Parlour), Henry, Ljungberg (Kanu).
Referee: S. Dunn (Bristol).
First final played outside of England, Liverpool gain second of three trophies.

Millennium Stadium, 4 May 2002 *73,963*
Arsenal (0) 2 *(Parlour 70, Ljungberg 80)*
Chelsea (0) 0
Arsenal: Seaman; Lauren, Cole, Vieira, Campbell, Adams, Wiltord (Keown), Parlour, Henry (Kanu), Bergkamp (Edu), Ljungberg.
Chelsea: Cudicini; Melchiot (Zenden), Babayaro (Terry), Petit, Gallas, Desailly, Gronkjaer, Lampard, Hasselbaink (Zola), Gudjohnsen, Le Saux.
Referee: M. Riley (Leeds).
For double Gunners, Ljungberg first to score in straight finals for 40 years.

Millennium Stadium, 17 May 2003 *73,726*
Arsenal (1) 1 *(Pires 38)*
Southampton (0) 0
Arsenal: Seaman; Lauren, Cole, Silva, Luzhny, Keown, Ljungberg, Parlour, Henry, Bergkamp (Wiltord), Pires.
Southampton: Niemi (Jones); Baird (Fernandez), Bridge, Marsden, Lundekvam, Svensson M, Telfer, Oakley, Beattie, Ormerod, Svensson A (Tessem).
Referee: G. Barber (Hertfordshire).
Goalkeeper substitute for the first time and Seaman even captains Arsenal.

Millennium Stadium, 22 May 2004 *72,350*
Manchester U (1) 3 *(Ronaldo 42, Van Nistelrooy 64 (pen), 80)*
Millwall (0) 0
Manchester U: Howard (Carroll); Neville G, O'Shea, Brown, Keane, Silvestre, Ronaldo (Solskjaer), Fletcher (Butt), Van Nistelrooy, Scholes, Giggs.
Millwall: Marshall; Elliott, Ryan (Cogan), Cahill, Lawrence, Ward, Ifill, Wise (Weston), Harris (McCammon), Livermore, Sweeney.
Referee: J. Winter (Stockton).
First non-Premier team and Weston 17 years 119 days is youngest ever.

Millennium Stadium, 21 May 2005 *71,896*
Arsenal (0) 0
Manchester U (0) 0
Arsenal: Lehmann; Lauren, Cole, Vieira, Toure, Senderos, Fabregas (Van Persie), Silva, Reyes■, Bergkamp (Ljungberg), Pires (Edu).
Manchester U: Carroll; Brown, O'Shea (Fortune), Ferdinand, Keane, Silvestre, Fletcher (Giggs), Scholes, Van Nistelrooy, Rooney, Ronaldo.
aet; Arsenal won 5-4 on penalties: Van Nistelrooy scored; Lauren scored; Scholes saved; Ljungberg scored; Ronaldo scored; Van Persie scored; Rooney scored; Cole scored; Keane scored; Vieira scored.
Referee: R. Styles (Waterlooville).
First Final unhappily decided on penalties Reyes sent off in extra time.

Millennium Stadium, 13 May 2006 *74,000*
Liverpool (1) 3 *(Cisse 32, Gerrard 54, 90)*
West Ham U (2) 3 *(Carragher 21 (og), Ashton 28, Konchesky 64)*
Liverpool: Reina; Finnan, Riise, Xabi Alonso (Kromkamp), Carragher, Hyypia, Sissoko, Gerrard, Crouch (Hamann), Cisse, Kewell (Morientes).
West Ham U: Hislop; Scaloni, Konchesky, Gabbidon, Ferdinand, Fletcher (Dailly), Benayoun, Reo-Coker, Harewood, Ashton (Zamora), Etherington (Sheringham).
aet; Liverpool won 3-1 on penalties: Hamann scored; Zamora saved; Hyypia saved; Sheringham scored; Gerrard scored; Konchesky saved; Riise scored; Ferdinand saved.
Referee: A. Wiley (Staffordshire).
Excellent contest Gerrard rescuing Liverpool with a lightning strike.

Wembley, 19 May 2007 *89,826*
Chelsea (0) 1 *(Drogba 116)*
Manchester U (0) 0
Chelsea: Cech; Paulo Ferreira, Bridge, Makelele, Terry, Essien, Wright-Phillips (Kalou), Lampard, Drogba, Mikel, Cole J (Robben) (Cole A).
Manchester U: Van der Sar; Brown, Heinze, Carrick (O'Shea), Ferdinand, Vidic, Ronaldo, Scholes, Rooney, Fletcher (Smith), Giggs (Solskjaer).
aet.
Referee: S. Bennett (Kent).
Eighth in-a-row Final with at least one London club; defence dominated.

Wembley, 17 May 2008 *89,874*
Portsmouth (1) 1 *(Kanu 37)*
Cardiff C (0) 0
Portsmouth: James; Johnson, Hreidarsson, Diarra, Campbell, Distin, Utaka (Nugent), Pedro Mendes (Diop), Kranjcar, Kanu (Baros), Muntari.
Cardiff C: Enckelman; McNaughton, Capaldi, Rae (Sinclair), Johnson, Loovens, Ledley, McPhail, Hasselbaink (Thompson), Whittingham (Ramsey), Parry.
Referee: M. Dean (Wirral).
Portsmouth gifted by goalkeeping error – shades of 1927 for Cardiff.

DAILY ROUND-UP 2007–08

JULY 2007

Sven back in Man City harness ... record man Torres ... Chelsea get a Grant ... Tevez tug to dock at Old Trafford? ... Henry the pot-hunter moves on ... Terry in the chips.

1 Lampard coy over Chelsea deal. Man City boss Thaksin to fight Thai government. Torres closer to Liverpool deal. Hargreaves lands at Man Utd £17m from Bayern. Hammers get Julien Faubert (Bordeaux) for £6.1m. Cliftonville win away at Dinaburg, Llanelli get five but still go out.
2 Leeds to offer Tax man more cash. Lamps wants to stay.
3 Sheff Utd get sympathy but no justice. Sven nearer to Man City job.
4 Torres costs Liverpool club record £22m from Atletico Madrid. Colchester get vintage Sheri from Hammers.
5 Now PL getting involved in Tevez affair. Spurs spending reaches £37m with Younes Kaboul from Auxerre at £8m. Steven Davis Villa to Fulham for half that.
6 Gerrard hails boss Benitez – with some reservations. Hammers get Bellamy, but holding on to Tevez. Sven officially appointed at Man City. Leeds up for sale.
7 Now Tevez may be loaned to Man Utd! Cliftonville beaten in Gent.
8 Hawk-Eye technology for goal-line arguments. Vetra, conquerors of Llanelli, have Intertoto game with Legia abandoned because of crowd trouble.
9 Florent Malouda joins Chelsea for £13.5m from Standard Liege. WBA have to sell the "K" men – Koumas and Kamara.
10 FIFA muscle in on Tevez saga. Becks hype in USA. Barton may face prosecution. Gerry Sutcliffe, new sports minister, concerned about foreign ownership. FA may start Under-21 League.
11 Bates i/c Leeds again. England to play Russia on artificial pitch. Chelsea appoint Avram Gant as Director of Football. Pompey spend £11m on Nugent (£6m) and John Utaka (£5m) from Rennes.
12 Liverpool take spending to well over £40m with arrival of Ryan Babel £11.5m from Ajax after Benayoun's £5m capture. Messi – chips with everything – wonder goal lifts Argies to Copa America final v Brazil, who qualified only on penalties against Uruguay. Sven gets Rolando Bianchi from Reggina for £8.8m. Morecambe record signing: £30,000 Baker from Southport.
13 Sheff Utd fail in High Court action. Now Interpol involved in Tevez. Fulham sign Healy, fourth close season Irishman. FA fury over £2000 fine over U-21 game with Serbia (their share £16,500).
14 Arsene Wenger hints at Henry departure over no-pot Gunners.
15 Copa: Underdogs Brazil beat Argentina 3-0! Celtic beat QPR 5-1, Rangers 4-2 over Lippstadt in Scottish warm-ups.
16 Police land morning raids on Newcastle, Portsmouth and Rangers! Now Birmingham braced for takeover. Everton contemplate ground switch. Richardson, Man Utd – Sunderland £5.5m.
17 West Ham stop Tevez medical at Old Trafford. Andrei Voronin new star of Liverpool. Even Owen scores for Newcastle. Ch Lge starts: TNS edge Ventspils, Linfield held by Elfsborg.
18 Chelsea's Terry has broken toe. FIFA still interested in Tevez move. Ch Lge: Derry held by Pyunik.
19 Hammers Faubert out for six months with injury! Pearce gets U-21 job for England. Leeds players unpaid. Eduardo duo on Arsenal debut. UEFA Cup: Carmarthen dumped 8-0 at home by Brann, Glentoran similarly ship five to AIK, St Patricks held by Odense, but Rhyl beat Haka 3-1 and Duncannon surprise Suduva; Drogheda draw away to Libertas.
20 Bernie Ecclestone interested in Arsenal. Man Utd have 75m fans worldwide – 40.7m in Asia!
21 Becks 12 min cameo sub role but toe-job Terry scores Chelsea winner, 27,000 present. PL hand FL £5.4m. Barton fractures foot. Fowler goes to Cardiff. David Preece, 44, ex-Luton dies. Former Lilleshall director John Cartwright savages FA over academy system.
22 WC 2018 might still come to England. Intertoto: Blackburn take crucial lead over Vetra.
23 Ljungberg becomes a Hammer and hits out at Arsenal. Scholes to miss kick-off with injury.
24 Tevez agent serves writ on West Ham. Heinze tug-of-war with Liverpool. Brighton get stadium green light.
25 Birmingham chase Spurs Mido and Ghaly. Sir Alex tells "Special One" to cool it. Ch Lge: TNS ousted on away goals, Linfield and Derry failing to score at all.
26 Sven signs Marin Petrov £6m Bulgarian. Death of Danny Bergara, ex-Stockport manager.
27 Terry now top earner on £130,000 a week.
28 Record Edinburgh crowd at Murrayfield 57,857 see Barca beat Hearts 3-1. Rangers beat Chelsea 2-0 at Ibrox. Blackburn ease to Intertoto win with Santa Cruz in the bag, too, at £3.4m.
29 Tevez: peace in sight? Beckenbauer backs England WC bid.
30 Real Madrid interested in Kaka.
31 Trouble in Toon? Sam Allardyce and Mike Ashley on collision course. Ch Lge: two joke goals enough for Rangers over Zeta.

AUGUST 2007

Leeds hit with 15 pt deduction ... England PL minority ... Rooney puts foot out ... PL refs – you're having a laugh ... England lose Wembley first to Germans ... Football fatalities.

1 Inter beat Man Utd 3-2 at Old Trafford, but Bolton cruise to 3-0 against Espanyol. SFA to clamp down on diving. Becks no play but the crowds roll in.
2 Tevez seems likely to go to Man Utd after all for £2m. Tax man after Leeds. Alan Smith interests Newcastle. Police charge Barton. Now it's seven up for Sven with Elano, Vedran Corluka and Javier Garrido. PSV's Alex nears Chelsea move. UEFA Cup: Curtains for Glentoran, Dungannon, St Patrick's and Carmarthen plus Rhyl on away goals, but Drogheda carry on regardless.
3 Becks and Owen may miss England start. Leeds have 15-pt deduction. Birmingham lose Ghaly interest. Ch Lge draw: Arsenal away to Sparta Prague; Celtic at Spartak Moscow, Liverpool in Toulouse. UEFA Cup: Blackburn away to MyPa; Drogheda home to Helsingborg, Dunfermline entertain Hacken.
4 SPL: Rangers off to a flier at Caley; fledgling Gretna dumped at home (Motherwell) by the Bairns and boss Rowan Alexander banned from ground!.

5 Community Shield settled by penalties – quite naturally – after 1-1 to give Man Utd first blood over Chelsea again. Terry latest England casualty. SPL: Celtic held by Killie.
6 Campbell recall for England? Heinze goes to arbitration. Newcastle sign Jose Enrique £6.3m from Villarreal.
7 Sunderland record £9m for Hearts goalie Gordon. Ch Lge: Rangers complete Zeta job. CIS Cup: Livi get five against Ayr.
8 Ch Lge: Rosenborg hit Astana for seven. Zeta in trouble over racist chants against Beasley.
9 Lennon new England doubt. FIFA man Warner hits at England WC bid. Lamps yet to sign contract. Leeds lose appeal.
10 Eve-of-PL season and Daily Telegraph survey lists only 233 English among 596 players.
11 Gerrard winner for Liverpool at Villa; big spending Sven dividend at West Ham; Black Cats Chopra swings late axe on Spurs; Santa Cruz delivers early gift for Rovers at Boro; Everton edge Wigan; Martins at the double for Toon; share issue for Derby and Pompey. Championship: Shot-shy Scowcroft sinks Saints with Palace treble; four-play winners, too, in Ipswich and Coventry; Watford snare Wolves late on. Lge 1: points-strapped Leeds win at Tranmere; Walsall over the Mooney with vets equaliser. Gills nine lose 1-0 to Cheltenham ten. Lge 2: new boys report: Daggers just out at Stockport, Morecambe draw with Barnet; Shrews get four at Lincoln. SPL: Gretna crash at Hibs after two up; Celtic hit four at Falkirk, Rangers take two off St Mirren. SL: Airdrie six at Alloa. BSP: Exeter 4-1 winners at Altrincham.
12 Uninspired Man Utd held by ten-man Reading and Rooney breaks metatarsal in foot; Chelsea have to battle to beat Brum; Arsenal even harder to clip Fulham at the death. SPL: Dons and Hearts draw.
13 Unlucky for Neil McDonald, first managerial casualty of the season at Carlisle. C Cup: Saints lose to Posh. SPL: Killie beat Dundee U.
14 Everton climb high with Spurs win. Ch Lge: Rangers narrow lead over Red Star. C Cup: hat-trick heroes: Ainsworth (Hereford), Bradbury (Southend); MK Dons knock-out Ipswich on penalties after six goal share; Morecambe stun Preston, but Daggers beaten by Luton; Norwich hit five. SC Cup: Montrose score five and even East Stirling win with four.
15 Man Utd (with Tevez) draw again but(t) Ronaldo red in ten-a-side at Pompey; Chelsea from behind win at Reading; Man City stroll on; Wigan one goal enough to ko Boro; Fulham edge Bolton and newcomers Birmingham and Sunderland draw. Ch Lge: Arsenal win in Prague, Liverpool in Toulouse while Celtic draw in Moscow. BSP: farce at Woking; drop ball "goal" and Grays gifted leveller! Millwall fined £30,000 for poor disciplinary record.
16 Gerrard (toe) latest England injury woe. Hammers unmoved by Sheff Utd £50m legal claim. UEFA Cup: Rovers owe it relatively to Santa again in win over MyPa; Drogheda held by Helsingborg, Dunfermline by Hacken. BSP: Cambridge beat Oxford.
17 Expectations of a Chinese takeaway at Birmingham. Leeds to appeal pts deduction.
18 Toffees toppled, Johnson can only hit post, Reading in the Hunt; Spurs off the bottom with four-play against poor Derby; Warner bothers and Healy denied obvious goal cost Fulham as Boro reap Mido touch; Utaka strike sparks Portsmouth over struggling Bolton; Bellamy goes to ground and Noble fires from the spot for Hammers to Brummie disgust; Toon goalless with Villa and not in scoring tune at home (560 mins and counting); woe for Sunderland at table-topping Wigan. Championship: Sheri goal for Colchester in ten-a-side with two-pens-Howard Barnsley. Lge 1 Leeds now only minus 9 after three in five mins against Southend. Lge 2: MK Dons in another six-goal shared affair v Paul Ince old boys Macc. BSP: Kedwell three for grafting Grays. SPL: Rangers seventh heaven over Falkirk; Gretna grab point at Hearts.
19 Anfield fury as ref Stokes gives joke penalty to Chelsea in 1-1; Manchester's sky blue as City edge out United; Lehmann gaffed Arsenal draw at ten-man Blackburn. Championship: Wolves win at Sheff Wed. SPL; Celtic keep up the pressure with late win at Dons.
20 Styles gets enforced weekend off for error as does Fulham game lino Gosling. Even Poll is critical! Under-fire still, Jol may be replaced by Ramos. QPR board jump ship as takeover looms.
21 U-21s: Wales win in Sweden, N Ireland beat Finns, Scots edge Czechs, while England draw with Romania and the Republic hold the Germans. U-17s: England whack New Zealand 5-0 in FIFA comp.
22 Euro 2008: another Healy double as N Ireland beat Liechtenstein. Friendlies see Wales (with Eastwood debut goal) winning in Bulgaria; the Republic four-play exhausting Denmark and Scotland just beating South Africa. Meanwhile at fortress Wembley, the Germans beat injury-depleted England 2-1 assisted by Robbo goalie error.
23 Platini plan FA Cup winners to get Ch Lge place. Chelsea home in on new capture after Robben flies off to Real for £25m.
24 Becks air miles burn out. Chelsea grab Juliano Belletti £3.75m. England U-17 beat Brazil 2-1. BSP: York lose again.
25 Schmeichel stops Van Persie pen but Fabregas ends City run; Sanchez rage again after hands deny Fulham draw at Villa; Lamps shines again but James slips for Pompey as Chelsea go top; Coppell hits out at Int friendlies as Reading slump 3-0 to Bolton; Jerome double enough for Brum at Derby – first in 33-secs; Liverpool hit 7000th League goal as Sunderland lose; Everton – Blackburn and West Ham – Wigan go for one apiece, goals and points. Championship: Charlton give Sheff Wed two goals start and beat them; Coventry clear top after 1-0 at Cardiff; Sheri again for rampant Colchester; Eastwood fires twice for Wolves; QPR call off Burnley game after Ray Jones, 18, dies in car crash. Lge 1: 100% Orient two points clear with win at Crewe; 100% Leeds knock off another three off deficit. Lge 2: Sub Luke Medley, 18, in tune with first touch winning goal debut for Bradford; Morecambe first victory. SPL: Rangers clip Killie as Celtic hit Hearts for five. SL: East Stirling second after 3-0 at Sten'muir! Real 2 Atletico 1 in Madrid derby but Sevilla's Puerta has heart attack. Juve get five – goals.
26 Nani 30 yarder gives Man Utd lucky first win but Jol argues for pen; Boro held by Toon whose owner Mike Ashley sports Smith's No. 17 replica. Championship: Ipswich level with Coventry after 1-0 against Palace. Barca held by ten man Santander, sub Henry hits post.
27 FA to target agents again. Injury forces Solskjaer to quit. BSP: first wins for York, Halifax; first point for Stafford.
28 Sevilla's Puerta, 22, dies; Leicester's on-loan Clive Clarke collapses at half-time and Forest game abandoned; Hammers Dyer breaks leg; Luton bag Black Cats in another C Cup tie; Blackpool oust Derby on pens; Hull win at Wigan; Morecambe trap Wolves at Molineux. Ch Lge: Sevilla game in Athens called off; Rangers hold Red Star and Liverpool crack Toulouse. CIS Cup: East Fife dump St Mirren at Paisley. Preston chairman Derek Shaw quits after car vandalised. Lee Hughes out of jail prepares for Oldham debut.

29 Ch Lge: Arsenal coast it over Sparta, Celtic need pens to beach Spartak. C Cup: Owen scores for Newcastle! Martin Allen axed at Leicester. Ecclestone buys into QPR. Yakubu, Boro to Everton £11.25m. Sunderland pay £9m for Saints Jones (£6M) Stoke's Higginbotham (£3m), while John moves to St Mary's as part of the deal.

30 David Dein behind Russian bid for Arsenal. Ch Lge draw: Liverpool in Porto group; Chelsea have Valencia in theirs; Celtic face AC Milan and Benfica; Rangers get Barca; Man Utd returning to Roma; Arsenal likely to meet Sevilla. UEFA Cup: D-Day but Dunfermline and Drogheda both ditched in Sweden. England U-17s dispose of Syria, now for Germany? Becks injured again.

31 Window closes with flurry of activity including: Hammers get Solano (Newcastle), Fulham and Reading swap Rosenior for Seol; Fulham and Pompey exchange Diop and Stefanovic. O'Neil, Portsmouth to Middlesbrough £5m. Derby pay £3m for Celtic's Miller. Hull pay club record fee for Wigan's Folan. Lamps out for England. AC Milan beat Sevilla in Super Cup.

SEPTEMBER 2007

Formula One at QPR ... England relieved over Israel – and Russia ... Scots frog march in Paris ... Mourinho bows out ... 11 goal PL record aggregate ... German Ladies are tops.

1 Merseyside joy: six-whacking Liverpool leave Rams reeling and go top; Yakubu debut goal for late-striking Everton at Bolton clinches second place on goal difference; super-sub Saha rescues Man Utd against Sunderland; Spurs twice throw two-goal lead at Fulham to draw amid Jol sub errors; three Hammer blows hit slumping Reading; Mido inspired Boro hit Brummies; Owen goal lifts Toon and England! Championship: Doyle thunderer keeps Coventry on track after slow start against Preston; Sheff Wed only FL team without a point; QPR all wear Jones name and board confirm Formula One takeover; fourth win for Leeds. Lge 1: Orient held but strike their 5000th League goal; Carlisle catch them after 1-0 over Cheltenham; Hughes bow for beaten Oldham but has to start ban from prison game!. Lge 2: Dagenham off the mark with sub Benyon beating Lincoln; Shrews edge ahead after 2-1 v Grimsby. SPL: Gretna hit by Rangers four-play; Caley still seek a point. SL: Bavidge (Peterhead), Weir (Raith) hat-tricksters, while Elgin also still chase a point. BSP: Hullo, hullo, Kiddy come to life with Constable trio over Exeter.

2 Knight leaves Chelsea in a daze for Villa; Sven boys lose again in ten-a-side with Blackburn; James lets in three at Arsenal. SPL: Celtic high five at St Mirren. End of the U-17 World Cup for England, beaten 4-1 by Germany in quarter-final.

3 Big Mac reviews mounting injury list. JM dismisses talk of more rift. Liverpool not to replace departing No.2 Pako Ayestaran. Ch Lge: Sevilla confirm place after rearranged victory in Athens. SPL: Hearts first win at Motherwell. Hull lose at Blackpool but fancy Okocha. Paint: Orient win at Notts Co.

4 Gerrard may need injection to play. Ballack not figuring in Ch Lge plans, may be away in January. Paint: Donny 5, Grimsby and Swindon 4 goals, and Daggers skewer the Shrimpers on penalties. BSP: Torquay hit Salisbury for four, Oxford and Exeter share them. SC Cup: five for Airdrie and East Stirling win, too.

5 Scots confident despite withdrawals; Republic keep McShane under wraps; Hennessey to face the Germans for Wales; Brunt now at WBA ready for N Ireland again. SC Cup: Fifers convincing win at Clyde.

6 Wenger signs £12m Arsenal deal. Derby's Fagan given four match ban for stamp. PFA get the needle over Gerrard.

7 Gerrard will play through pain barrier after all. England U-21s take three off Montenegro, Wales own goal ko in France, both Irish teams beaten, Republic by Portugal, Northern Ireland by Germany. Lge 1: Brighton convince with win over Millwall. Lge 2: Morecambe succeed again, MK Dons tie three on Notts.

8 Euro 2008: relief as England see off Israel 3-0, but ten Russians with sub goalie saving penalty do the same to Macedonia and Eduardo double for Croatia against Estonia; Scots inspired substitutions by McLeish help towards 3-1 v Lithuania, Klose brace for the Germans threaten Wales hopes; Baird own goal downs Irish in Latvia and Republic held up by late Slovakia equaliser. Lge 1: Leeds fifth win wipes out deficit in best start since Revie days 34 years ago; Orient still clear at top. Lge 2: Darlo overtake Friday leaders Chesterfield with 2-0 at Rotherham. BSP: Aldershot top after five over Northwich, Crawley nap hand, too, against nine-men Droylsden.

9 World U-17 final goes to penalties – of course – no goals then Nigeria beat Spain 3-0 on the spot. Standees aired their views on the terraces around FL games at the weekend.

10 Women's WC opens with non-PC Gerries beating Argies 11-0! BSP: Stevenage top after Torquay go for a Burton. Ronnie Jepson quits at Gillingham.

11 Draws in vogue in WWC: England with Japan; North Korea with USA and Sweden with Nigeria. England U-21s win in Bulgaria. Big Mac's big night awaits against the Guus men. Fit-again Healy to spark Northern Ireland, Republic must beat Czechs; Wales facing elimination; McLeish toys with forward thoughts. Death of Ian Porterfield, 61, Sunderland scoring hero of 1973 FA Cup final.

12 Euro 2008 – isle of joy as Owen double puts boot in Putin's lot, McFadden frogmarches the French in Paris and Wales harpoon Slovakia, but across the pond Irish reel to twin defeats in Iceland and Czech Republic. Plenty of PL scorers elsewhere including Shevchenko! U-21s: Scots held by Danes, but Northern Ireland win in Luxembourg. Gary Megson may be next Leicester boss.

13 Ballack may require third ankle op. WWC: the kissing has to stop says boss lady Hope Powell.

14 Lge 1: Leeds continue winning, so do Tranmere. BSP: Torquay see off Halifax with late rally. WWC: England tactics frustrate Germany.

15 Arsenal give Spurs goal start and win 3-1 in game of missed chances; JM rage over Kalou offside disallowed goal in Blackburn draw; 1-0 to the Man Utd again, courtesy Vidic at Everton; Reading edged out at Sunderland; Wigan and Fulham level it; rotating Rafa omits Torres, Gerrard – so it's goalless for Pool at Pompey thanks to Reina pen stop from Kanu; fit-again Ashton sparks Hammers against Boro; Bolton bow to Brummies Kapo. Championship: unbeaten Bristol City trample table-toppers Coventry at the Ricoh to take over; old U's pet Iwelumo upsets Colchester in Charlton draw; Baggies hit four against Ipswich; standing ovation at Hull for Okocha; Gary Megson has to settle for debut draw at Leicester unveiling. Lge 1: O's stay ahead with 1-0 at Yeovil; ten-man Southend keep Oldham bottom with L for loanee Clarke goal. Lge 2: goalie Harrison marks 300th Barnet game with point saving display v Rochdale; Darlo at home, Chesterfield away keep ahead with wins. SPL: Celtic hand Caley a five goal beating as Hearts trump Rangers. SL: first win for Elgin. BSP: Stevenage reclaim top spot at York.

16 Johnson special lifts Man City over Villa. Silvestre out for season with cruciate knee injury; Heskey six weeks with metatarsal problem. Championship: late Watford revival nips Saints.

17 After "eggs and omelette" speech has JM cracked at last? New boy Miller strikes right note for Derby over Toon. WWC: six of the best spanking for Argies at England hands who reach last eight with Germans. Redfearn resigns after nine Northwich games, another vet Warhurst takes over.

18 Ch Lge: Chelsea fail to beat Norwegians Rosenborg, Liverpool draw in Porto and Celtic lose two goals to Shakhtar. Platini hits out at PL money baggage. C Cup: Leicester stir Forest to earn O'Neill Villa renewal. Championship: last gasp Bristol C cling to top despite WBA draw. BSP: goal glut: Histon 4 Torquay 5, Crawley 5 Woking 3 and Stevenage hit four, too.

19 Chelsea's Jose Mourinho, the Special One, eggs-it. Ch Lge: Arsenal impress with three over Sevilla; the do-Ron run enough for Man Utd and Rangers comeback against Stuttgart. Championship: Watford regain top spot with win at Cardiff. Liverpool hit by injuries. Kerlon "seal dribble" with head tennis causes furore in Brazil. WWC: typhoon threat postpones two games!

20 UEFA Cup: Jo(l)y of six as Spurs clobber Anorthosis; Larissa stun Blackburn; Bolton get a Rabotnicki draw and Everton held by nine Metalists in Johnson double penalty woe – one retaken saved after scoring, the second fired over; Aberdeen also denied by Dnepr.

21 Official unveiling of Avram Grant at the Bridge, Sir Alex praises JM, Rafael refuses and Russians flex muscles over Arsenal bid – just another freaky PL Friday.

22 Adebayor treble-shooter as high-five Gunners destroy Derby; tinkering no aid for Liverpool in scoreless with Birmingham; Miller stays late for Black Cats to level at Boro, Harper even later hits Reading winner over Wigan; Fulham and Man City share six goals. Championship: Charlton cut Watford lead with win over Leicester; Sheff Wed end worst-ever start; Baggies finish Scunny nine-month home record; Nine Canaries devoured by Wolves; Coventry runover four times by Tractor Boys. Lge 1: Seven-in-a-row Leeds; Orient hit by Hartlepool four-play; Agogo hat-trick for blooming Forest, Paynter (Swindon), too, similarly wipes out Bournemouth. Lge 2: Grimsby break their duck; seven change Brentford surprise Chester; Rotherham 100 years at Millmoor tied in Notts; Darlo, Hereford, Chesterfield, Shrews level on 14 pts. SPL: Gretna first win, Caley first point after boss man Brewster winner. SL: Elgin's Shallicker trio shellacking for ten-man East Stirling. WWC: Brown goalie errors as USA beat England 3-0; Germans win similarly v N Korea. BSP: Stevenage clean sheets wiped out by Cambridge and Shots steal top.

23 Ref Mike Dean woe – sends Mikel off, misses a pen and gives one that was not as Chelsea bow to Man Utd; Viduka double for Mags over Hammers, but Owen limps off; Villa take out Everton; Kanu strikes for Pompey at Blackburn; Spurs get a point at Bolton. SPL: Boruc blunders give Hibees win over Celtic as Rangers take three off Dons. WWC: hosts China beaten 1-0 by Norway, Brazil just edge Aussies 3-2.

24 Owen may need another op. Arsenal top of PL rich list with £200m turnover. New National Football Centre undecided. Howard Wilkinson queries Avram Grant lack of licence.

25 C Cup: Torres hat-trick as Liverpool win 4-2 at Reading; Arsenal, Pompey, Luton, Man City, high-five Sheff Utd, Cardiff and extra timers Blackpool go through, too. Rumour academy agenda: Klinsmann, Hiddink, Van Basten for Chelsea, JM for Spurs, Arsenal: it's Russia v USA backers. BSP: Stevenage lost in the Forest Green. CIS Cup: Hamilton ko Killie – Dundee Utd, Hearts and Caley through.

26 C Cup: Man Utd stiffs sent to Coventry defeat as Mifsud the mosquito bites twice; O'Neill's Villa lose to his old Leicester; relief for Chelsea at Hull and Spurs over Boro; Rovers down Brummie; more Sheff Wed misery against Everton; Ashton late Hammers saviour over Pilgrims; Trotters even win at Fulham. CIS Cup: Rangers, Celtic, Aberdeen away day successes, Motherwell, too at Hibs. Martin Foyle quits Port Vale. WWC semi: Germans hit Norway 3-0.

27 FA to charge Chelsea over beaviour at Man Utd and reveal little known ban on U-16s playing senior football! WWC semi: Brazil shake USA with 4-0 drubbing.

28 Spurs speculation not all rubbish? Arsenal rumble among the roubles.

29 Pompey 7 (half-fit Mwaruwari 3) Reading 4 in PL aggregate record – and James on 600th outing saves pen! awesome Elano inspired "videodromers" Man City overcome Newcastle; Ronaldo it is as Man Utd win at Birmingham; Chelsea held by neighbours Fulham and Terry cheekbone injury; Liverpool need sub Benayoun for Wigan win; Rovers capitalize on Black Cats errors; Persie the main Van man for Arsenal at Upton Park; point apiece for Derby – Bolton. Championship: top trio all held, but Watford stay in front; ex-crock Pedersen two for Hull; now Sheff Wed win away! Lge 1: Leeds nine and boss Wise also banished held by the Gills; fourth trawl for in-form Southend Shrimpers. Lge 2: MK Dons grab top placing at Morecambe; Bury first home win for year!; fledgling loanee Fielding keeps Bradford at bay for Wycombe; Elding hat-trick for Stockport includes two pens. SPL: Aussie McDonald trio clinches Celtic win over Dundee Utd, but Rangers held at Motherwell; two pens in Donaldson trio for Hibs v Killie. SL: Hamilton first defeat at St J; McManus four in East Fife's second-half seven stun against nine-man Sten'-muir. BSP: Torquay leave it late again over Droylsden, Stevenage win at Grays. Ex-Gunner Henry breaks scoring duck for Barca with treble.

30 WBA snapping at Watford heels with 5-1 win over QPR. WWC final: Germany 2 Brazil 0 (Marta misses pen) triumph of efficiency over style; third place consolation for USA 4-1 against Norway.

OCTOBER 2007

Blatter seeks PL foreign cull ... England 2018 WC hopes and Euro 2008 improving? ... Hibs unbeaten record ends ... Ramos in at Spurs ... Ban on 15 year old doesn't work!

1 125th anniversary for Spurs, 4-1 down to Villa with 20 mins left, scrape a draw!

2 Ch Lge: Rooney, Van Persie with the minimum respectively for Man Utd against Roma, Arsenal v Steaua, but Rangers are three star Lyon kings in France. Championship: Watford, Charlton – ten a side at Hull – keep top two places, Preston shake Saints with five. unbeaten Bristol C lose at Barnsley. Lge 1: Orient go down to Gills and none of top five win – Leeds naturally succeed again. Lge 2: Top four all win including MK Dons at Mansfield. Ruskie Usmanov still taking steps towards Arsenal. BSP: Shots see off Exeter to cut Torquay lead by one point. SC Cup semis: Fifers edge Ayr, Saints win at Morton. Who was that masked man? It's Terry.

3 Ch Lge: under-fire Grant sees Chelsea win in Valencia, success for Celtic over AC Milan spoiled by fan intrusion and Liverpool's finest hit by the Mistral boys of Marseille. Championship: Rangers having axed manager John Gregory, still seeking first win after losing at Colchester; Baggies held by Stoke. Carlisle

Benjamin Mwaruwari leaves Michael Duberry in his wake as he completes his hat-trick during the 11-goal thriller at Fratton Park. Portsmouth ran out 7-4 winners against Reading. (Action Images/Henry Browne/Livepic)

likely to appoint John Ward as manager, Cheltenham filling gap with Keith Downing. Becks training again!

4 UEFA Cup: Everton do it away in the Ukraine, sub Anelka for Bolton at home, Aberdeen on away goals, even Spurs get a draw in Cyprus, but Blackburn's 2-1 not enough to oust Larissa.

5 Wenger warns on loss of PL status if Blatter insists on culling foreigners.

6 Football crazy! – just two PL games; Roo and Ron (2) roar Man Utd to top; Gardner free kick for Villa as Hammers lose Ashton injured again. Championship: Watford increase lead as Charlton are held by the Tykes; Saints Stern measures rule out Baggies; rare Cardiff home win. Lge 1: Tranmere catch the Shrimpers and peak it on goal difference as Swans upping the ante in five star at Oh! O's; De Vries proves loan sharp for Leeds; Gradel upgrades Bournemouth; Swindon 5 and four play for Walsall, Carlisle. Lge 2: MK Dons still the team to beat; Bullock repays loan twice over for Bury; Barnet fair enough four at Stockport. SPL: Rangers down to earth as Hibs win and snatch leader position. SL; Weatherson hat-trick for Morton. BSP: Stevenage call the Shots to close gap on Torquay beaten at Ebbsfleet.

7 Van Persie robs plucky Sunderland as Arsenal resume as No.1; exciting Elano duo keeps Man City ticking over Boro; Torres has to rescue unbeaten Liverpool as they labour to Spurs draw; Pompey finish better than Fulham at the Cottage; formation fancy Blackburn edge Brummies whose boss man Bruce fears the peril from the East; Chelsea PL 460 min goal famine ends – just – in win at Bolton; ex-op superman Owen hits crucial goal for Toon over Tofffes; Reading pile more misery on Derby. Lge 2: Chester climb to third against Shrews. SPL: so-close Gretna caught by Celtic at the death and the hoops hop back top.

8 Chelsea to bus in new coach Henk Ten Cate from Ajax. Hip-hop Hennessey to miss Wales game with injury. Dancing in the Loftus Road as QPR catch Canaries in first win. Managerial axing: Peter Taylor at Palace and Willie Donachie at Millwall.

9 Seb Coe to mastermind 2018 WC bid. Robinson still England No.1. Republic's Ireland to stay at home. Wigan fined £20,000 over loss of player control. FIFA to experiment with two goalmouth refs! UEFA groups: Everton fair one, Bolton and Aberdeen tough, Spurs in balance. Paint: Hartlepool hit five at Lincoln; Daggers upset the Orient. BSP: Stevenage held so Aldershot reclaim heading.

10 Terry doubtful for England, Bellamy ignores groin strain, Scots wary of Shevchenko (?). Becks still not fit. Barca get lawsuit victory over nursery development after losing players abroad. Ballack happy at Chelsea.

11 Neil Warnock becomes 11th Palace manager under chairman Simon Jordan. Speed resigns as Bolton player-coach. Dida two-match ban for threatrics in Celtic pitch "battle." 20 in for Indy-FA role. Gary Neville still not fit. U-21: Scots beat Lithuania 3-0. Victory Shield: England held 2-2 by Northern Ireland. BSP: Oxford chuck three goal lead to draw with Torquay.

12 Blatter U-turn on rotation fuels England WC hopes. U-21s top group after Montenegro win. Lge 1: Hartlepool edge Bristol R.

13 Euro 2008: Another trinity for Big Mac – now almost walking on water; Scots stay high and dry as two Macs pour it on Uk(rain)e; wilting Wales spring a leak in Cyprus; Republic hopes finally drain away in German draw. Elsewhere Germany sail on as first qualifiers. Lge 1: Boss Ling rages at ref as penalty missing Leeds survive disallowed goal and still get a point against ten-man O's; Commons rare hat-trick for Forest at Cheltenham; Southend shunt off Crewe; managerless Gills and Lions settle for a draw. Lge 2: Chesterfield go third as Shrews slump continues. BSP: Burton's undefeated 13th is unlucky for leaders Shots.

14 Lge 1: Swans preen themselves with table-topping 4-1 at Bournemouth. Lge 2: MK Dons surge on in front of record 13,037. BSP: Torquay reclaim top 4-2 over Stevenage.

15 Artificial ground zero in Moscow worries England; Scots to shrug off injury list. Luton score four. Lincoln axe managerial Johns – Schofield and Deehan. 2010 WC: (yes, already under way weeks ago) Brazil draw in Colombia.

16 Life's a pitch – Terry victim of Luzhniki; Lescott to get left-back nod. U-21s: England show bottle in Cork; Scots suffer Dutch hangover:. Toshack to fire the Dragons; Republic to put Cypriots in place; Irish still optimistic in Sweden. Steve Thompson axed at Notts County.

17 Euro 2008: turn of the tide – Rooney (offside?) scores, becomes silly tugger (outside area?) as England pay penalty before Robbo spills one and the Red sub sinks them; Scots no longer on the crest as Mchedlidze (!) at 17 surfaces for Georgia; Wales just manage to beach San Marino; the Irish lads draw – wishy washy in Dublin, more buoyant in Stockholm. Qualifiers confirmed: Czechs after easily beating the Germans and Greece following win in Turkey. U-21s: Northern Ireland lose at home to Israel, Wales beat Malta. Sammy Lee leaves Bolton 13th unlucky boss this season. Chelsea hold up their hands. England U-19s beat Belgium 3-1.

18 FA right behind McClaren as the rumours spread of his eventual replacement. Drogba wants to quit Chelsea. Ian McParland appointed Notts boss. Arsenal block takeover chances.

19 Scolari (second choice?) fined £24,000 for incident with Serbian player. Trevor Birch leaves Derby. Hartlepool to call off game as Michael Maidens, 20, dies in car crash.

20 Merseyside derby: Reds 2 (pens) Blues 1 (two reds); ref Clattenburg ends his 54 PL streak without a red card with double, but ignores Kuyt aerial assault and gets two penalty calls wrong, one in favour of Liverpool, one denying Everton – phew! Man Utd beat nine Villans 4-1; Arsenal leave late to tred on Trotters; ten man Fulham hold Derby scoreless; the Drog on song for Chelsea at Boro; oneup(front)manship again enough for Pompey at Wigan; Elano El-supremo for Man City; Blackburn 4-2 over Reading. Championship: Wolves go fourth after the Addicks 'ave had it; Watford maintain six point lead with minimum over Hull; Sheff Wed joy marred by Jeffers injury. Lge 1: Orient's three in seven second-half mins floor the Vale; Clarkes P and L pass test as Southend drive on to second spot at Walsall; unbeaten Leeds tenth win. Lge 2: MK Dons keep four point lead at Hereford; improving Barnet move to fifth. SPL: Rangers treble over Celtic clips hoops advantage to one goal difference; Hibs unbeaten record goes at Motherwell. SL: Stirling still off the goal standard despite draw; Clarke hat-trick for Cowden. BSP: Top Shots ride their luck to injury-time win over Halifax.

21 Subterfuge from the bench turns it for Hammers over Sunderland. Saints move up at expense of old boy Jones' Cardiff. Torquay reclaim leadership at York. Steve Staunton awaiting axe for the Republic.

22 More misery for Jol as Spurs lose to Mags. Man Utd loanee Campbell has two for Hull. Thais probe Thaksin. Ref Clattenburg to get weekend off. Becks USA contribution 360 mins – now Ipswich want him. WC: seven for Iraq and China, too, in qualifiers.

23 Ch Lge: Seven of one, a dozen of another – Arsenal goals and overall wins as Slavia wither away; Rangers hold firm against Barca; Man Utd do the motoring over Dynamo. Championship: Coventry recoil at the Ricoh against Watford; Pilgrims journey takes them fifth after 2-1 at Charlton. Gary Megson tipped for Bolton. Brown (our leader) and Blatter (FIFA's) to have 2018 talks.

24 Ch Lge: Bobo for Besiktas, boo-boo for Liverpool bottom of Group A; new-look Chelsea shoot to the top; Celtic concede late to Benfica. Republic seek Steve Staunton successor. Championship: Bristol C hold off Saints (with takeover looming) comeback to go second; Wolves clinch third with odd goal in five win at Cardiff; Sheri off in red menu for Colchester.

25 Levy imposed by Spurs on axed Martin Jol and they lose UEFA tie to Getafe at WHL with Juande Ramos the replacement; Clattenburg has a UEFA hat-trick: three goals each and three yellows in Loco – Atletico tie. Megson confirmed at Bolton and they are held by Braga; Everton beat Larissa 3-1 with Cahill scoring return; Dons slip up in Greece. Chelsea fined £30,000 for Man Utd furore. Kroenke still interested in Arsenal.

26 Ramos resigns as Sevilla coach heading for Spurs. Tranmere table-toppers in Lge 1.

27 Chelsea's six-pack embarrasses Sven with Grant becoming the special stylist; top aces Man Utd four-play four in a row habit best for 100 years; Green penalty save environmentally sound for Hammers holding Pompey; Kapo gives Brummies edge over Wigan; Long marker ends short-staying level Toon for Reading. Jones saves point for ten-man Sunderland against Fulham. Championship: Tractor Boys run over Wolves as Eastwood fluffs penalty; Plymouth Pilgrims progress stopped at Preston; Rangers Bolder rocks Charlton. Lge 1: Leeds (now 6th) 13 no loss watched by 30,319; Carlisle new leaders after win at Southend – watched by Jol; loanee Dickson again keeps Gills alive. Lge 2: MK Dons caught out by Stockport, but all six nearest rivals draw! SPL: Macs the man for Celtic three times over against old club Motherwell; Gretna beaten by Caley looking doomed already. SL; Stirling first win and climb two places! S Cup: Sten'muir stunned at Threave; Montrose held by the Pollok. FA Cup 4th qual: Staines leave their mark at Woking.

28 Arsenal reclaim leadership with draw at Liverpool; Spurs' Ramos reign starts losing late to Blackburn; Derby down again, Everton the winners; Villa draw at Bolton. Lge 1: Sun still setting on slipping Orient at Donny. SPL: Rangers falter at Dundee Utd.

29 Sunday's Gridiron expose ruins Wembley pitch. Scholes out till 2008. Watford sink Palace deeper in trouble, but John Bostock becomes Palace's and 17th youngest ever FL/PL player at 15 years 287 days. Ref Danny McDermid charged by FA with swearing at Wise (already fined £5000). QPR appoint Luigi de Canio as manager.

30 C Cup: Late Cole delivery fires Hammers at Coventry. Glenn Roeder appointed at Norwich, Peter Jackson at Lincoln. Platini hits out at Wenger youth policy.

31 C Cup: Lamps hat-trick but Shevy saves Chelsea against plucky Leicester; Eduardo double steers Arsenal at Sheff Utd; Spurs win! – but v Blackpool; Cahill on overtime for Everton at Luton; Blackburn ease it at Pompey; Man City need pen to oust Trotters. CIS Cup: Velicka lip-smacking double lifts Hearts at Celtic; Rangers comfort at the 'Well; Nicholson treble for Dons v Caley and Hunt trio enough for Dundee Utd against Hamilton. Riise's monthly wages on internet site – gross income £139,634. Dave Bassett is new Leeds assistant with Poyet now at Tottenham. Shepherd family lose executive pen at Newcastle. WC 2018 – here we come? Already concerns over Brazil 2014!

NOVEMBER 2007

Freeman is just a another boy ... Arsenal's 1000th PL goal ... Healy Euro record ... England out – McClaren sinking in the reign ... McLeish quits Scots for Birmingham.

1 Prince William to lead 2018 bid. G14 clubs flexing muscle against Platini. Richards injury not as bad as feared. Sports Minister Sutcliffe hits out at Terry wonga. Mark Stimson is new Gillingham manager, Peter Taylor taking the vacant Stevenage job. BSP: Oxford blues as Rushden whack five past them.

2 Grant aid for Terry at the Bridge. Gills break duck away to Swans! Shots top BSP – at least for the day.

3 Gallas: the Hyde and Jekyll episode – cancels og with Gunners last ditch leveller at 2-2, but Sir Alex hits at ref Webb sight while Arsene cheers lino Cann; Pompey three in four mins floors tumbling Toon; Liverpool blank with Blackburn; Toffees first four in a row for 17 years as shot-shy Carsley sticks one of two late two on Birmingham; Ramos settles for low key point at Boro; Belletti belter as Chelsea roar on at Wigan; Derby drift at Villa; sub Healy seals it for Fulham's late-finishing ten v Reading. Championship: Baggies pocket the points at shattered Watford; crucial point for Bristol City at Wolves; Rangers revival continues; ten-man Charlton stop rot at Soton. Lge 1: Leeds finally beaten by the Carlisle leading pack; vet Mooney hits 200th and 201st career goals for Walsall. Lge 2: Nine MK Dons rage over decisions in Wycombe stalemate; High fives: Mansfield (Brown 14-min trio), Hereford over Darlo; Barnet's 10-run Bur(y)ied. SPL: Rangers, Celtic both win but Gretna drifting away. SL: Hamilton lead then bow to Queens, Dundee trail to Saints then cut Accies advantage to three points. BSP: Torquay fail to recapture top spot as Cambridge win.

4 Third minute of injury enough for Bolton to draw at West Ham. Championship: East Anglian derby: ten Canaries swoop late to share with Ipswich. Shrews end poor spell at Wrexham. SPL: Edinburgh derby: Hibs claim pen but have to settle 1-1 with Hearts.

5 Ireland gets three points for Man City over Sunderland, but pants airing may get short shrift.PL now the biggest thing in worldwide TV. Lee Sinnott is new Port Vale boss. Ex-Welsh cap Ivor Powell, 91, world's oldest coach prepares his assistant role for FA Cup aspirants Team Bath. Sir Alex hits out at agents. Barnsley go fourth.

6 Ch Lge: Liverpool 8 – and not a zip code – with Benayoun treble over Besiktas; Chelsea draw at Schalke; Celtic edge ten-man Benfica (Binya bundle on Brown). Championship: Watford back to winning ways at Norwich and with Baggies held by the Owls, extend lead to eight points; Iwelumo again the matchwinner for Charlton at Bristol City. Lge 1: Leeds seventh after win at Bournemouth; Forest fire fries the ten Shrimpers to serve second place. Lge 2: Lester hat-trick for Chesterfield at rock bottom Lincoln. Chelsea not to join G14, Sir Alex against FIFA plan to cut foreigners. Kenny Jackett takes Millwall job.

7 Ch Lge: Man Utd and Arsenal in knock-out stages: after respectively beating Dynamo Kiev 4-0 and drawing with Slavia; Rangers bow to Barca. Cech has calf injury. Gullit for LA. Pele backs England WC bid. Jewell may return to Wigan.

8 UEFA Cup: Brits do well: Everton winning in Nuremberg, Spurs in Tel Aviv, Bolton drawing away to Bayern, though Aberdeen held by Loco Moscow. Burnley part with Steve Cotterill. Night of the short stabbing being prepared for Big Mac if Euro failure.

9 Rooney injured ankle ligaments in training – out for a month. Becks in squad after flying Mac visit to LA. FA Cup: Leeds get to replay with Hereford.

10 Liverpool leave it late against Fulham; one derby (Geordie) ends all square – but injury-hit Hammers rack up five at Derby itself. Championship: Ipswich – with Walters trio – switch to sixth gear to overrun ten-man Bristol City; nightmare Saints surrender five at Sheff Wed; King misses pen as Watford held by Colchester; Charlton on a roll now, go second; no-boss Burnley win at Leicester. FA Cup with everything: diamond studded giant-killing Rushden over Macclesfield; Ryman minnows Staines earning draw at Stockport; Barrow (19th in BSN) holding Bournemouth; Bailey (Southend) 22-sec early strike; youngest ever FA Cup player Luke Freeman sub for Gills at 15 years 233 days; ten-man Horsham in second round first time in 136 year history; Chasetown, too; hat-trick heroes: Mackail-Smith (Posh), Bishop with Bury's first trio for eight years; highest gate 7361 for Forest draw at Lincoln; Harrogate Railway (Unibond Div 1) take puff out of Droylsden; Havant administer ko to York; Billericay seven mins away from Swans replay. SPL: Caley nine taken out by 'Well. SL: Dorrans treble for Livi.

11 Ron at the double for Man Utd over Rovers as Sir Alex raves about his squad; improving Spurs four against Wigan; Villa win midland derby at Brum ex-Villan Ridgewell og, too; Bolton, home to Boro and Pompey – Redknapp's 200th i/c – hosting Man City finish goalless; Everton snatch late leveller (Cahill naturally) at Chelsea. FA Cup: Torquay turn giant-killers over Yeovil; Hartlepool six at Gainsborough; Millers have to earn replay at Forest Green. SPL: Hearts ease against Dons. More Italian violence – police shoot fan dead, trouble elsewhere. Benayoun out of crucial Israel Euro tie.

12 Peak hitting Arsenal's three at Reading includes Adebayor hitting the second, the Gunners 1000th in the PL. Baggies second-half four play brushes aside ten-man Coventry. Platini plan for Ch Lge rejected.

13 A Russian win in Israel will cancel all police leave at Wembley for Croatia game! Now Platini cool over England 2018. Scots may benefit from Italy's domestic woes. Death of ex-Busby Babe John Doherty at 72. Preston sack Paul Simpson. Paint: Leeds ten bow to Bury. Web-fans to buy Ebbsfleet.

14 Gerrard wants foreign cull. Brian Little likely to be Wrexham manager. Platini latest crusade – v American owners! SL: Jags hit Livi four times.

15 Austria friendly fails to mask Euro 2008 worries for Big Mac who recalls Becks. Paul Jewell turns down Wigan return for possible Republic role. Luton bowled over by 55 transfer charges. Little appointed, Carey to stay, too.

16 Crouch heads England win in Vienna, Owen injured, but Big Mac feels the strain. Wales and Republic to play for pride, Northern Ireland with hope, but Scots on brink of finest hour. Russian roulette is England's fear in Israel. U-21s: England beat Bulgaria, Republic lose to Montenegro. Binya binned for six games. Steve Bruce gets permission to talk to Wigan.

17 The two Macs in contrasting injury time sensations: Israel (McClaren my life-line) beat Russia – while for good measure Croatia bogged down in Macedonian mud – Scots suffer free-kick farce by ref Gonzalez and McLeish is crushed; Healy's record-breaking 13th Euro strike (33rd overall) gives Irish an outside chance of qualifying; Wales snatch late equaliser against Republic; Poland beating Belgium, Holland edging Luxembourg and Spaniards easy over Sweden add to finalists. Aussies beat Nigeria at Fulham – of course. U-21s: Scots four in Slovenia, Wales same at home to Bosnia, Irish even five over Luxembourg. Lge 1: Leeds go fourth after beating Wise's old Swindon outfit. Lge 2: Buoyant Bury end Posh nine game

run; injury-hit Owen watches MK Dons win at Chester; Ainsworth trio for Hereford at Stockport. BSP: status quo as top five win, but Peter Taylor's Stevenage hit by three goals in five mins by Burton.

18 England camp prepares for one last thrust for the Austro-Swiss finals. Lge 1: Yeovil late show beats Gills.

19 Rooney on mend, Carson may be No.1. Wigan say come on down to Steve Bruce, Ian Holloway could be Leicester boss. York sack Billy McEwan. Rain in Staines ko's replay. Graham Paddon, 1975 FA Cup winner, dies at 57.

20 Big Mac swings the axe ahead of chopping Croatia – Robbo, Becks out, Carson and W-Phillips in. Irish dream of Spain 25 years ago. Wales daunting prospect in Germany. U-21s: England snatch draw in Portugal, Wales shake French 4-2, Irish hit three against Moldova and even Republic put it over Bulgaria. B game: Scots and Republic level. FA Cup: Forest Green tre(e)mendous rout of Rotherham at Millmoor; Hereford topple Leeds, but Barrow just edged out at Bournemouth. Alan Irvine appointed Preston manager. WC: Tevez red card as Argies lose in Colombia.

21 Anger land not Eng-ger-land: two down in 14 mins level in 65, then ko with 13 to go; England out of Euro, as Russia survive scare with ten men in Andorra to qualify. Irish out, too, after 1-0 defeat in Spain; Wales get goalless draw in Germany. Other finalists: Portugal, Turkey edging Bosnia and Sweden from Northern Ireland's group. Bruce hits Wigan snag, Holloway awol at Plymouth heads for Leicester.

22 McClaren, Venables sacked by FA – O'Neill, Mourinho, Scolari, Shearer, Benitez, Redknapp etc. tipped. Roy Keane blames the "star" players. Luton deducted ten pts for administration. FA Cup: Staines indelible mark – in second round for first time in 115 year history as goalie Allaway earns and wins shoot-out against Stockport. Owen Coyle is new Burnley boss.

23 The Great Race starts: O'Neill a non-runner and England already in panic over WC 2010 draw. BSP: Cambridge win at Burton to go third.

24 Bolton muscle Man Utd (ten no loss) out and Sir Alex sees Clattenburg h-t red; late double for Arsenal against Wigan; Southgate under threat as Villa ease past Boro; Big Sam, too, as Liverpool turn screw at St James' Park, though Rafa has owners worry; Toffees stick seven past Sunderland; Ireland injury-time winner for Man City over Reading; Pompey chime in with a brace at Birmingham helped by gk Kingson gaffe; Essien red mars Chelsea win at Derby. Championship: Boothroyd unhappy over no-penalty award as Barnsley edge Watford; ref apologises to Blackpool boss after loss at Soton; Holloway celebrates first Leicester manager to start with win in 57 years; Warnock hails initial Palace victory; Plymouth first win at Sheff Utd for 69 years; Burnley's 125th anniversary and 0-0 with Stoke; vet Windass, Hull double; another rare Cardiff homer. Lge 1: ref Styles shares out four reds as Swindon clip Bristol R; golly it's two-goal Oli for Gills; admin boys Luton just account for Southend as Brill saves spot kick. Lge 2: Posh hit seven after Brentford gk sees 40-sec red; Lincoln end 15-game no win; MK Dons bow to Chesterfield. SPL: Celtic, Rangers win, Hibs held by Dundee Utd. SL: Dundee crucial win over Hamilton. S Cup: plucky Buckie seconds away from Morton replay; Stirling on goal standard with six at Stranraer; Raith five at Threave, East Stirling five, too, at Albion. BSP: Carey-Bertram's trio not enough for Forest Green at Droylsden; Torquay close on Aldershot after beating ten-man Woking; Northwich strike gold – beat Diamonds for first win. Last meaningless Euro 2008 game – Serbia beat Kazakhstan.

25 WC draw and England to face Croatia! Scots have Norway and Holland, Wales – Germans and Russia, Northern Ireland – Czechs and Poles, Republic face Italy. Fulham share it with Blackburn; Green pen save from Defoe and Spurs draw at West Ham. Black Country derby all square for Baggies and Wolves. Leeds not at the races at lowly Cheltenham. North-west derby even between Wrexham and Chester.

26 England may play Scotland at Wembley but Celtic Cup to go on without us. Platini wants PL reform. Bruce finally in at Wigan as Davies exits Derby and Sturrock prepares a Plymouth return after quitting Swindon.

27 Ch Lge: Ronaldo injury-time free-kick sees Man Utd home against Sporting; Stuttgart nip past Rangers; Arsenal well beaten in Seville. FA Cup: Nine-man Orient ousted in Bristol R – by a shoot-out. Championship: another Norwich success and for Palace, but more Watford woe; the Scunny nine get point at Coventry. Lge 1: Swans up to top downing Hartlepool. Alex McLeish lined up by Birmingham. Fans back Rafa.

28 Bung: Harry Redknapp, Peter Storrie, Milan Mandaric, Amdy Faye and Willie McKay arrested. Ch Lge: Liverpool power past Porto; Celtic clip Shakhtar. Villa hit four at Rovers. Wolves, WBA both win. McLeish quits Scots for Brummie, Paul Jewell gets Derby job.

29 Barwick casts net – for expert advice! Redknapp questioned by police over Faye transfer as chief executive, agent and Mandaric also involved. UEFA Cup: Spurs forced to overhaul two-goal Aalborg lead; Stelios steals Trotters draw with Aris. Sky Sports Victory Shield goes to England, 2-1 winners over the Scots.

30 Chelsea prepare to defend ref persecution complex. Barton hits out at Toon rail against Big Sam. Roy Hodgson quits Finns for Inter No.2 job. FA Cup: Horsham pen the Swans as replay is Taylor-made.

DECEMBER 2007

Giggs 100th League goal ... Capello is the new England first choice ... PL treble on both sides ... Arsenal have a point ... Hodgson – Fulham saviour? ... Death of Phil O'Donnell.

1 Determined Arsenal give Villa goal start but win; Geovanni 28-sec goal for Man City but Bruce's new ten-finishing boys get a draw; Stokes fires late to shoot Sunderland – who lose Edwards with leg-break – to 14th on Jewell bow for Rams; Everton frustrate Pompey at Fratton; Tuncay is Turkish delight in Boro draw with Reading; Drogba hit by lazer, Cole J just scores as Chelsea beat the Hammers in target-missing-day of 41 fouls; Rovers need a Bentley brace to power on over Newcastle. Championship: Watford still at a loss to Bristol C; 59th birthday boy Warnock gets a draw present; Sheri 349th career goal in 52-sec Colchester strike; tut-tut Charlton's second home defeat in a week – Wolves second 1-0 in the same time. FA Cup: It's Notts Waterloo as they haven't a clue against H & W; Bristol R gift Rushden lead then hit them five times; Burton snatch draw with Barnet; Mackail-Smith four for Posh wipes out Staines; Oxford earn Southend replay. SPL: Hearts hit back to pen back Celtic 1-1 as Rangers cut hoops lead to one point. SL: Raith edge into Ross advantage with 3-2 win there.

2 Liverpool foursome sees off Bolton; Spurs unhappy with Keane red card and Birmingham winner for new boss McLeish. FA Cup: Harrogate Railway shunted by the Stags, but Chasetown on track for replay with Port Vale.

3 Two-goal Ronaldo gets yellow from Styles for diving after foul by Niemi. Sir Alex alleged to have FA talks. Player revolt hints at Newcastle. UEFA in a fix over gambling games. Belgrade riot worries Bolton.

4 Ch Lge: Celtic lose to AC Milan but both qualify. Championship: Watford win at Colchester, Charlton away to Cardiff, so do Palace at QPR but Warnock red-carded; Coventry shake Baggies. Lge 1: Swans, Carlisle march on but Orient clipped by the Lions; Leeds back winning. Lge 2: MK Dons foil the Daggers; JM the front runner for England? Keane appeal turned down.

5 UEFA Cup: Cahill (who else?) pushes Everton through against ten-man Zenit. Big Sam relieved as Toon share points with Arsenal. Southend whack nine-man Huddersfield.

6 UEFA Cup: sub Berbatov pen is enough for Spurs draw but Anderlecht fan missiles hit them; Bolton win in Belgrade but supporters herded by nervous police. Platini and G14 settle differences.

7 FA may have short list of five. Anderlecht may be axed from UEFA Cup. Tyson double for Forest at Brighton.

8 Giggs 100th League goal – 11th such Man Utd centurian – in 4-1 romp over Rams (first away goal and Howard's first PL strike in 173 goals); 11th unbeaten Pompey (Muntari the long-ranger duo) at Villa, but Redknapp fury over crowd abuse; Shevy lives and scores in easy win against ten-finishing Sunderland; excellent Reading have first PL big-four victory 3-1 over tinkered Liverpool, who hit woodwork twice; Yakubu second half trio carpets Fulham for Everton; Beye heads 91st min winner for resurrected Toon over Brum. Championship: Burnley on a six-game unbeaten roll as Wolves fail at home; hat-trick Saint John teaches Hull a Soton lesson; eight no loss Palace draw at Barnsley; home wins return to ten-man Charlton against poor travelling Ipswich. Lge 1: Leeds derby day four against Huddersfield; Southend injury time winner over Swindon; Orient stop the slump; Tranmere first win in six. Lge 2: Proudlock three as Stockport six pulls rug from Wycombe Chairboys; MK Dons high five v Stanley; Rochdale hit high-flying Millers; Hereford's undefeated 10th finishes off ten-finishing Lincoln. Weather note: 2 off, 2 abandoned. SPL: St Mirren scare Celtic into late leveller – Rangers game off at Gretna. SL: Dundee win and Accies leaders loss puts them on same pts; Gemmell four of Albion's five in nine-goal thriller at East Stirling. BSP: Plucky Stafford three strikes – three goals, shake four-goal Shots.

9 Boro dig deep to prove travel-weary Arsenal are vulnerable; Ireland red then Defoe rare goal gives Spurs win over Man City; Green keeping and Ashton blooming raises Hammers at Blackburn; revitalised Bolton four-play finds Wigan wanting. Championship: Watford settle for goalless at Stoke. Lippi, Capello, JM alleged England pack leaders.

10 JM pulls out of race, Capello likely by a good length from Lippi. FA Cup: Horsham twice lead but six hitting Swans prevail.

11 Ch Lge: Liverpool deliver four times over in Marseille to qualify; Chelsea held by Valencia top Group B while Porto, Schalke, Real Madrid and Olympiakos also make it. FA Cup: Port Vale whose reserves beat Chasetown, lose to them and Rodgers misses two pens; Luton cut down Forest. SPL: Celtic's McGeady threesome puts Bairns to sleep. Championship: Burnley revival hit by resurging Rangers; home is best place for Ipswich over ten-man Leicester. Terry Butcher and Brentford part company. Coventry takeover in doubt.

12 Capello all but appointed. Ch Lge: Repercharge Rangers shuffled to UEFA Cup after Lyon's roar at Ibrox; six Man Utd fans stabbed in Rome – the game ends 1-1; Arsenal beat Steaua but finish second – though Barca, Lyon, Man Utd, Roma, Inter, Fenerbahce, Sevilla and the Gunners complete the knock-out stage teams. Gerrard dwelling burgled in absence – sixth Liverpool player so targeted overall. C Cup: Everton take advantage of Green errors to beat Hammers. BSP: Torquay close gap on Shots at Farsley. Ground approvals help Barnet, Oldham. Cardiff to escape administration. Boca reach CWC final beating Etoile Sahel.

13 Capello on board with Italian entourage; his salary £6.5m pa. Magnusson cuts ties with Hammers. AC Milan edge Urawa to meet Boca in CWC finale.

14 "Mamma" Capello doubts son's WC 2010 credentials! Cheltenham beat minus-ten pt Luton. Debt-ridden Coventry saved by Ranson "demand" as new chairman. Anderlecht fined £12,857 for hooli fans.

15 Eight goals, two trebles (first for opposing PL teams) nine yellow, one red, missed pen – that's Wigan 5 Blackburn 3 (Bent and Cruz trios); Everton in fine form at West Ham; Man City s/h revival batters Bolton; Brum and Reading in flowing 1-1 affair, Sunderland and Villa in more of a stutter, though Black Cats "winner" ruled out; Barton injury-time pen lifts Toon at Fulham; another Tuncay day for Boro at Derby; "Dim" Berbatov lights up Spurs at Pompey. Championship: Baggies head it after 4-2 over Charlton as Watford suffer fourth reverse in five home to Plymouth; Whaley almost subbed is Preston winner over nine-man Burnley; Ranson sees his Coventry held by his former fancy Soton; late Scunny loss at Ipswich, now ten no win; Super-sub Scannell, 17, Palace injury-time winner over Wednesday. Lge 1: Booming Bournemouth first home win in nine months over Gills; Hughes hat-trick for Oldham at Millwall; Leeds injury-time leveller at Walsall; Swans ease over ten-man Southend. Lge 2: Born-again Brentford after 520 goalless mins, succeed at Wrexham; MK Dons crucial win at Posh. SPL: Rangers late hit Hearts; point in six-goal share for Gretna at Killie. SL: East Fife eighth win on trot with no goals against Dumbarton; Hot-shot skipper Brand XXX for East Stirling. Trophy: holders Stevenage dumped at Dorchester.

16 Big four day leaves scrappy Liverpool and forward-weak Chelsea crying as one goal enough for Man Utd and Arsenal respectively, the Gunners now leading by a point. SPL: Caley clip Celtic and finish with ten men. CWC final: AC Milan 4 Boca 2 and Maldini, 39, announces retirement in June.

17 Capello unveiled in splendour. Liverpool revise new ground plan. No GB teams in Olympics.

18 C Cup: ten-man Spurs ruin Man City home record; Arsenal "stiffs" average age under-20 rigid in win at Blackburn. Brooking boost for Burton site.

19 C Cup: Liverpool lose to Chelsea and Crouch red-card for aerial attack on Mikel as Merseyside stadium cash is question-marked; s-f draw keeps Arsenal, Chelsea apart. UEFA Cup: Toni gets four of Bayern's six against Aris. Sol Campbell appeals for fan ban over racist abuse. QPR seek Mittal millions. Watford's Bangura may get work permit to stop extradiction. John Collins, ex-Fulham resigns as Hibs boss.

20 National Football Centre boost but is it Burton? Dave Sullivan to increase share in Birmingham. Abramovich clears Bates debt at Chelsea. Vodafone will not call UEFA again after 2008-09. UEFA Cup: Everton smash AZ's 32-home match unbeaten record; Aberdeen win at last as four-play floors FC Copenhagen.

21 Ch Lge: Arsenal v AC Milan, Liverpool v Inter; Lyon v Man Utd, Olympiakos v Chelsea, Celtic v Barca while UEFA draw pits Dons v Bayern, Bolton against Atletico Madrid, Everton at Brann, Rangers v

Panathinaikos and Spurs at Slavia Prague. Fulham sack Sanchez. Capello plans summer camp for stars, Sven wants winter break. Lge 2: MK Dons held by Brentford.

22 Torres duo helps Liverpool to four against Portsmouth; Arsenal edge it over Spurs; Anelka double welcome for Bolton against Brum; Parker late one aids Hammers at Boro; Villa and Man City level it as do managerless Fulham with Wigan; Sunderland anger at Reading winner. Championship: Fuller treble topples Albion as Watford win at Sheff Wed to reclaim leadership; ten-man Coventry blanked at Blackpool. Lge 1: goal famine oddity – only one match sees both teams scoring; Forest win to top Swans frozen off at Carlisle. Lge 2: Darlo four at Lincoln, Posh keep in touch with one goal in three win over Bradford. SPL: managerless Hibs hold slipping Celtic; Gretna win first away at Dundee Utd. SL: fog and frost kills off a third of games, East Fife beaten at Stennie.

23 Body-check by Pienaar on Giggs costly for previously 13-game unbeaten Everton and rampant Ron pen secures Man Utd win; Cole J does it for Chelsea at Blackburn, but Cech injured; Derby almost win at Newcastle. SPL: ten-man Rangers held at Aberdeen, leaving them two behind Celtic. Spain: Real win at Barca. Italy: Inter (with no Italians) beat AC Milan to lead by seven pts.

24 Speed could be loaned to Sheff Utd. Becks may train at Arsenal in New Year.

25 Tommy Harmer, Spurs midfield maestro, dies at 79.

26 Man Utd four-play at Sunderland, Arsenal held at Pompey gives Old Trafford pt lead and 8-13 on with the bookies; O'Neill cries "diver" as Ballack falls, complains of late free-kick as two-down Chelsea (two red) v Villa (one red) level in eight goal thriller; Liverpool need injury-time winner at Derby; Spurs high five over ten-man faltering Fulham; Reading ten hold Hammers at Upton Park; Big Sam booed by Toon fans in defeat at Wigan; own goal, penalty and one near the break give Birmingham relief over Boro; Everton return to winning ways against Bolton. Championship: Watford scrape draw with Cardiff but caught by Baggies who trounce Bristol C 4-1; two pens in Lawrence hat-trick for Stoke, 3-3 at ten-man Barnsley; ten-man sunny Scunny end misery with Preston victory. Lge 1: Eight-man Luton get a point at Bristol R!; Swans back on top after 4-1 over Cheltenham; Alexander treble for Millwall; late-again Leeds manage draw at Hartlepool. Lge 2: Morecambe 5 Chester 3, Puncheon hat-trick for ten-man Barnet; MK Dons still lead by six, after injury-time win at Notts. BSP: Exeter 4 Torquay 3 (7839), Cambridge 1-0 have 7125 for Histon game; Shots win at Woking, Burton easily at Stafford. SPL: Balde's return stiffens Celtic rearguard at Dundee Utd, Rangers leave it late to down 'Well. SL: Hamilton held by Clyde, but Dundee lose at QoS. East Fife beaten again.

27 Santa's late arrival gifts Rovers point at Man City – Sven (winter-break man) not amused. Barton arrested in Liverpool. Bookies say it's all over for chasing pack. Lamps out for weeks. Big Sam under more pressure says the media.

28 Roy Hodgson is new Fulham boss. Barton in jail, no bail. Toon in crisis, Shearer awaits? Gordon Taylor, 63, gets OBE in PFA's centenary year. Ivor Powell, 91, world's oldest coach at Team Bath and ex-Welsh cap is an MBE.

29 Arsenal – not ugly? – go top with 4-1, ten-a-side finish at Everton and David Moyes claims better team lost!; Man Utd with Roo bug victim, Ron firing pen wide, lose at rejuvenated West Ham; Spurs 4-3 down to Reading win 6-4, Berbatov netting four, but encroaching Defoe's rebound goal from Keane pen save was illegal; Big Sam rage at Kalou offside winner for Chelsea; Richardson back to fire Sunderland win over Bolton; Tuncay still Turkish delight for Boro at Pompey – nine hours at home minus a goal; Hodgson off to a Fulham point at Birmingham; Villa go seventh after win at Wigan. Championship: Albion bag five over ten-man Scunny as Watford collapse against QPR!; Warnock return to Sheff Utd sees his Palace 12 unbeaten; Saints recover from 16-second goal to draw at Barnsley. Lge 1: Scotland sparks ten-man Swansea against out-of-sorts Leeds; Gills cut down Forest; 11th away win for Walsall. Lge 2: Ten-man Morecambe two down v Posh, win 3-2; crucial win for MK Dons to end Darlo home run. SPL: tragedy as Phil O'Donnell, 35, dies after being subbed in Motherwell 5-3 over Dundee Utd. BSP: Shots miss pen have one sent off and lose to Grays while Torquay close the gap with Woking win; five each away for Stevenage, Crawley.

30 Rumour day: Shearer for Toon, Berbatov somewhere. Windass goal enough for Hull over Wednesday.

31 *The Daily Telegraph* extols PL virtue of goals – 549 at 2.76 a game. Auld Firm game put off in light of O'Donnell tragedy.

JANUARY 2008

Becks trains at Arsenal ... Rangers climb over Celtic ... Man Utd 333m fans ... Big Sam axed ... Havant in heaven ... Keegan in Toon again.

1 Arsenal hardly break sweat against Hammers, low key Man Utd leave it to Tevez v Brummie as Sir Alex gets twitchy; Fulham lose again after leading – naturally – as Chelsea need a Grant whip to lash them and born-again Ballack even scores a pen; dead ball deficiencies hit Spurs at Villa; Sonko early red hits Reading against Pompey; Everton take it in their stride at Boro. Championship: Watford bounce back convincingly at Soton and catch leaders Albion beaten at Ipswich; QPR keep up winning habit and Colchester off bottom with win at Charlton. Lge 1: Swansea draw at Swindon as Forest close gap beating Huddersfield; Brighton Revell in hat-trick; listing Leeds lose home record to Oldham. Lge 2: MK Dons stretch lead as Hereford tied by Notts; Lester is again Chesterfield key striker; Accrington lose eighth at home; beaten Wrexham, Mansfield drifting away. BSP: Shots, Torquay (6021 v Exeter), Stevenage, Burton all win, Cambridge lose at Histon. Transfer window opens: Gunter, Cardiff to Spurs £2m; Cooper, Ross Co to Liverpool; Cohen, Maccabi Netanya to Bolton among first moves.

2 Man City successful Toon raiders; Yorke red and Whitehead pen failure writes off Sunderland at Blackburn; Bramble thorn in Liverpool side as Wigan draw; Bolton leave it late against Derby. SPL: programme amended in respect for O'Donnell, but Hearts humiliated in sixth defeat in a row, finishing with eight men at Dundee Utd. SL: Hamilton edge away from drawing Dundee; goal glut sees 48 in 15 games. Moneybags QPR sign Buzsaky, Connolly, Ephraim.

3 Bailed Barton barred from playing. African Nations Cup has PL clubs in sweat. More Terry injury worry. Posh break club record with £400,000 Joe Lewis deal from Norwich.

4 Becks trains with Arsenal with 23 on track suit, of course. Accrington break club transfer record with £65,000 Craney after Swansea loan. Caretaker Andy Scott given keys at Brentford.

5 FA Cup: six PL clubs out, two more to go. Havant they done well – drawing ten-a-side at Swansea; Chasetown in 10th tie frighten Cardiff with og from only attempt and not disgraced in defeat; Capello

sees above sub-standard Rooney beat Villa for Man Utd; mossy Mifsud stings Rovers twice in Coventry raids; Addicks old boy Kiely earns Baggies replay; Brum glum at Huddersfield exit; Robbo fails again as eight-change Reading earn Spurs return; rich-list Chelsea need og to oust even more quids-in QPR; off street, pre-match fry up, then Oldham's McDonald batters six-change Everton; Carney carves Trotters for Blades; Wigan keep Black Cats in the bag; West Ham – Man City much adoo about 0-0; Cambridge scare Wolves; Pompey just beat ten-man Ipswich; Shittu rare double for Watford, ends Palace run; Mansfield in fourth round first time in two decades. Lge 1: loanee Kilkenny axe man for Oldham over Leeds changes sides to beat Cobblers. Scott at Brentford has win at Shrews. Lge 2: another crucial win for MK Dons at Rotherham. SPL: Hearts just stop rot with Killie draw after six game reverse; Rangers climb over Celtic by beating Dundee Utd. SL: Livi six-pack send Morton away. BSP: Shots win, Stevenage too.

6 FA Cup: four draw, only Arsenal win at Burnley as Bristol R surprise Fulham, Rams pecked back by Owls; Luton hold Liverpool and Toon survive at Stoke.

7 Capello bowled over by public response. Man Utd claim 333m fans! Havant get Liverpool in cup – if! Swindon takeover should see Maurice Malpas as new manager. BSP: Torquay go for a Burton to Clough's Albion.

8 C Cup s-f: Mikel off, but late og sees Chelsea take slender lead over Everton. Orient see off Tranmere, Wycombe win at Mansfield. Paint: Morecambe to play Grimsby (north), MK Dons – after pens – to face Swansea (south). Rams seek a Savage saviour, Robbie of that ilk.

9 C Cup s-f: Arsenal made to fight for draw with Spurs. Big Sam Allardyce bites the dust on Tyneside. Capello and Co visit Wembley. Mikel four game ban. Luton players get paid at last.

10 Harry Redknapp the front – and only ? – runner for Toon stakes. Becks and PM conflab towards 2018 WC role. Colchester record signing: Chris Coyne (Luton) £350,000.

11 Pompey give noon deadline to Harry boy. Anelka to Chelsea for £15m, now world's most expensive player at £87m over eight club moves. Bristol are top Rovers at Tranmere.

12 Ronaldo's first treble as Man Utd sink six past sad managerless Mags; below par Arsenal lose top spot as Brummies hold them; Torres rescues Liverpool in come back draw at Boro, so Everton are just goal difference away after beating Man City; Fulham lose lead again, this time at West Ham; Spurs usual reverse at Chelsea; Wigan pile more misery on Derby; Carew sails Villa to Reading win. Championship: Watford loss at Preston shoves them into third place, as Baggies win at Hull and Bristol C get a point; Palace 14 unbeaten, ravage the Wolves at Molineux; Rasiak 29th birthday boy on scoresheet for Soton. Lge 1: Swans first win at Luton in 54 years keeps them flying as Kevin Blackwell and Sam Ellis plan 9 Feb exit; Holt back on goal standard aids Forest to foursome. Lge 2: Barnet shock MK Dons at home; Wrexham's eighth straight defeat; Mansfield first away success in 13; Holmes has away day hat-trick for Millers; Thorne trio trips Notts for Bradford; Macc stun Posh; Walsall held in 18th overall unbeaten run; Vale off the foot. S Cup: Motherwell fight back to Hearts draw; Shiels treble for Hibs; Gretna chuck two-goal lead as Morton earn replay as weather ko's seven ties. Trophy: Sole outsiders AFC Wimbledon win at Tonbridge; Exeter, Forest Green lose to other BSP teams. Becks 100 likely to be his last.

13 Late arriving Roberts sneaks it for Rovers at Bolton; Richardson double lifts Sunderland against Pompey. Hereford go second in Lge 2 after derby win over Shrews. As Redknapp declines, Hughes, Shearer, Houllier, Keegan, the latest Toon tout.

14 Benitez ko could come as owners coax Jurgen Klinsmann. First win for Capello – the WC fixture list! PL hit out at Blatter cull plan. Beckford goal pushes Leeds third. Chris Casper and Bury part company.

15 FA Cup replays: Gerrard treble as Liverpool rout Luton, but saviour Nick Owen in attendance; Baggies beat Addicks on pens; Spurs win at Reading; Bury shake Canaries off perch; Lions end Saddlers run; three ties off. Lge 2: McLean threesome as Posh hit Stanley for eight. Chelsea to add Branislav Ivanovic at £10m from Loco Moscow. Bangura gets work permit. Bournemouth heading for administration. Swindon takeover completed, Maurice Malpas in hot seat. Didier Deschamps now a Newcastle possible.

16 FA Cup replays: Havant they done good again! – 4-2 Swans upping; Keegan in Toon again and Newcastle's ten floor Stoke; one goal enough for Man City, Hereford. Lge 2: Perkins rare treble for Rochdale at Chesterfield. Capello in Italian tax probe. Luton axe Blackwell, Ellis, Carver – Mick Harford takes over.

17 Transfer window bulging at £88m already. Shearer No.2 for Mags? FA Youth Cup shock – Man Utd out to Carlisle.

18 Man Utd David Gill's property vandalised. Wenger wants window shut. Cheltenham swap places with Millwall after win at Hartlepool.

19 Roo and Ron double act for Man Utd at Reading; "Nodding" Adebayor twosome as Arsenal hit three past drifting Fulham; Kamikaze Keegan forced into point blank landing with Bolton; Mwaruwari hat-trick ends Pompey 9 hrs 38 mins home goal famine after Rams lead; sub Robbie Keane's 100th Spurs goal – No.15 in club list – leaves Roy of that ilk an unhappy Black Cat; oddity: subs Pizarro for Chelsea at Birmingham, Derbyshire for Blackburn v Boro score, their only previous Lge goals also v same opposition. Championship: Home groan again for Watford, held by Charlton; Baggies share six with Cardiff in thriller; Palace 15 unbeaten ease past Bristol C; steel city derby goes Owls way; new look Rangers still winning; first win in nine for Wolves. Lge 1: Southend 4-1 at Bournemouth and miss pen; Bristol R pitch protection just pays off with draw; Swans shake off Havant hangover; Leeds stunned by bonny Donny; two ogs enough to Swindon over Forest. Lge 2: new look Wrexham take out MK Dons. SPL: Kalambay calamity gives Hearts lead over Hibs; Celtic need og to down Killie. SL: Hamilton lose, Dundee draw. Peterhead 9 ten-man Berwick 2 (just avoid worst defeat). BSP: huff and puff Shots lose to Forest in 49 secs; Stevenage get five, Torquay held, Burton win, Cambridge lose; Cook three for Crawley. Vase: Dunston shrivel Shrivenham eight times.

20 Man City in stall mode held by the Hammers; Everton overtake Liverpool after Wigan victory. Anfield owners to reject Dubai interest. SPL: Rangers win at Caley keeps them well clear. ANC: late Muntari strike gives Ghana edge over Guinea.

21 Sub Crouch salvages point for Liverpool against Villa. Chesterfield hit four off Hereford. ANC: Morocco high fivers. FIFA and UEFA to compensate clubs for international calls.

22 C Cup semi: Now it's "Cincode" Ramos as Spurs sink the Gunners 5-1, first win over them since 1999. FA Cup: Shoot-outs needed for Barnet, Derby and Bristol R to beat Swindon, Sheff Wed and falling Fulham. Lge 1: Bournemouth four lifts them off foot; Swans preening again; Hartlepool edge Southend 4-3. S Cup: Partick clip Dunfermline while Aberdeen and Motherwell win replays against Falkirk and Hearts. BSP: Cambridge hit five against Droylsden. ANC: Egypt impress against Cameroon. As Burley prepares for Scots job, Hoddle may return a Saint.

23 C Cup semi: Cole J confirms Chelsea as finalists over Everton. Lge 1: Tyson rescues point for Forest at Millwall. S Cup: Rangers six over East Stirling; Ross ease it at Cove. Chris Coleman joins Billy Davies, Alan Shearer in Soton job hunt. Havant thwarted in bid to get five-yellow Justin Gregory available for Liverpool tie, as Thurrock game is abandoned: floodlight failure. But FA had already pulled plug on that plan.

24 Geoff Thompson stands down at FA. Sir Alex wants Becks to get century. BSP: Stevenage held at Farsley. ANC: Agogo strike puts Ghana in frame.

25 FA Cup: Campbell-Ryce sinks old mates Southend for Tykes. Lge 1: Swans four soar at Donny, defeats for Carlisle, Orient. Yanks takeover Derby now! ANC: Toure injury as Ivory Coast it.

26 FA Cup: Havant scare pants off Liverpool at 2-1 before losing 5-2; Derby panned by Preston; Wolves find fangs at Watford – at last; no KK revolution for Newcastle yet as Arsenal get three second half goals; Chelsea through at Wigan after 2-1. PL: Carson saves Derbyshire pen as Villa held by Blackburn. Lge 1: Luton save point in late leveller against Leeds; Bournemouth win again! Lge 2: third 1-0 defeat on trot for MK Dons. BSP: York 13 unbeaten crack shaky Shots; Burton lose at Ebbsfleet. SPL: Rangers take four off St Mirren. SL: Dundee ahead lose 3-2 to QoS, Hamilton behind at Clyde win likewise. Five off waterlogged.

27 FA Cup: early goal but Dawson dismissal as Spurs hit by the Ronaldo factor at Man Utd and Man City balloons cause confusion as Sheff Utd cut a dash.

28 Dennis Wise joins the Toon club. Palace fall short of club record 16 unbeaten League games in Leicester defeat. Spurs tempt Woodgate. Yanks interested in Derby. BSP: Torquay close gap on Shots. S Cup: Morton oust Gretna in replay; wins for Killie, Brechin.

29 Toon in town again with same 3-0 to the Arsenal; Sunderland new boy Prica bursts Brummie bubble; Capello sees Boro beat Wigan; Barren hard-up for strikers Bolton held by Fulham. Championship: nine-man Preston hold off WBA; Watford get a point at Sheff Utd. Lge 1: Leeds without the Wise man beached at Southend as Gary McAllister takes charge; Donny go second after beating Hartlepool as Swansea draw at Forest. Lge 2: MK Dons stop losing but Macc get a point there; four play for Bradford, Rochdale, too. Becks shows off pecs on Rio beach. BSP: Shots edge Oxford, Cambridge lose, Burton beat Diamonds. ANC: Nigeria scorers: Mikel, Yakubu. As transfers hot up Sissoko goes to Juve for £8.2m. SFA order Brechin – Accies tie replayed through an ineligible City player, but then club admit another and are chucked out!

30 The do Ron-Ron double – including ace free kick – again as Man Utd top it over Pompey; Liverpool put on spot by Noble injury time pen; Spurs hold Everton at Goodison; it's Ballack for Chelsea against Reading; even Derby get a point off Man City. Transfers hit record with Hutton, Rangers to Spurs for £9m. CIS: Rangers beat Hearts in semi. ANC: Eto'o becomes record scorer with brace for Cameroon now 16. Capello gives Pearce gets "key position" – door man?

31 Window shuts with overall record broken at around £200m; Chelsea biggest spenders at £27.4m, Arsenal the misers even making £5.3m; Afonso Alves, Heerenveen to Boro for £14.9m and Liverpool hoping to secure agreement over Mascherano at £17.1m. Becks bombed out by Capello first squad, Villa's Agbonlahor and Davies the big surprises.

FEBRUARY 2008

Capello – a first time winner . . . The 39th steps . . . 5pt lead for Arsenal . . . Tykes take Anfield apart . . . Everton hit their Euro records . . . Spurs for the Carling.

1 Mwaruwari move to Man City in balance at £7.5m. Burley blocks England v Scots.

2 Spurs robbed of justified win over Man Utd by injury-time Dawson og as ref Clattenburg books 7 Utd, 3 Spurs; Adebayor becoming true Henry successor as he fires the Gunners at Man City; Pompey's debutant Defoe draws down on Chelsea to end their ten-in-a-row run; Derby get a point at Brum; Liverpool still unhappy despite three v Sunderland; Everton rage over Johnson ruled-out goal against Blackburn; Wigan hit off song Hammers; Bolton first away win, Reading's sixth reverse in succession. Championship: Borrowed Bednar bounces for Baggies; Watford snare Wolves; skint Saints draw at Palace; Norwich 11 unbeaten now; Ipswich rare away win; rampant Rangers rattle Bristol C; deb Dickov does it for Blackpool. Lge 1: Swans need Brandy to revive them; wheels off at Leeds; Walsall 17 run ends at Carlisle; Forest lack fire at Bournemouth. Lge 2: Brown, 18, Bradford Bantam bow buries Macc; Wrexham – 11 window signings – four no loss now; born again MK Dons five at Bury. S Cup: Celtic five at Killie. Trophy: Crawley eight over Droylsden, Vieira, Cook hat-tricks. BSP: Exeter hit Stevenage for four.

3 Owen scores but Toon held by Boro; Bullard blockbuster bolsters Fulham over Villa. S Cup: Rangers held at Hibs. ANC: Agogo for Ghana as Nigeria exit; Ivory Coast it five times against Guinea.

4 Tough man Capello will tax England players resolve as his Italian income is in focus. Billy Davies in Republic frame. Drogba rows with African Confederation over Awards. ANC: Egypt, Cameroon into semis now. Alan Knill takes over at Bury from caretaker Chris Brass.

5 Excitement as new era England await Swiss game, Gerrard skipper, lone striker, too, but well supported. U-21: Walcott shines in old Soton surroundings as England beat Republic 3-0; Wales four play in Malta; Pele beats Scots in Portugal. U-19: England 2 Croatia 0. Mwaruwari finally goes to Man City in staggered payment deal, as Defoe joins Pompey permanently; Hammers prepare for court battle over Tevez.

6 A win is a win as Capello starts with the odd goal in three; Nigel Worthington's full-time job with Northern Ireland starts with Bulgaria winning there; Koumas double helps Wales see off Norwegians; Robinho robs the Republic for Brazil. U-21: Scots hold Ukraine in Portugal; Northern Ireland lose in Israel. Heart scare Clive Clarke calls it a day. More backroom signings at Newcastle.

7 PL to have 39th League game around the world! Seven subs for Pl bench. ANC semis: Cameroon edge Ghana, Eygpt easily beat Ivorians.

8 Platini ridicules PL plan. Capello tax probe on back burner. Charlton with Varney double see off Palace.

9 Owen (another header) for Toon but they fail to repel Carew's Villa hat-trick; clean sheet James helps off-form Pompey to win at Bolton; Derby worn down by second-gear Spurs; Boro inflict more woe on Fulham; happier at home Sunderland take out Wigan; Hammers held by Brum in balloon game; Everton still looking secure in fourth place after grinding win over Reading. Championship: WBA taken to task by Barnsley Tykes as Watford inflict first home defeat on Ipswich to go top; Stoke devour Wolves at Molineux; Good Evans a brace for Norwich at his happy Ninian Park hunting-ground. Lge 1: Swans caught late in Crewe draw; bonny Donny still rattling them in; 43 sec goal for Jevons in Huddersfield win;

Leeds held at Northampton; Bournemouth easy win at Luton in admin-boys match. Lge 2: Rotherham's valuable point at MK Dons marred by Brogan broken leg; Daggers slip to 23rd after crash at Hereford. SPL: Rangers hit Falkirk to keep on track. SL; Ross Co get six; East Fife lose at home to Sten – again. BSP: Shots, Torquay, Cambridge win; Stevenage, Burton lose and Exeter draw.

10 Sven over the moon as Man City complete first double over Man Utd since 1970 on Munich commemoration day – late, late signing Mwaruwari the match-winner at 2-1; Chelsea and Liverpool bore away goalless but Grant laments no-pen award. SPL: Celtic take five off Killie. ANC: Egypt sixth title beating Cameroon to retain crown.

11 Arsenal go five pts ahead after win against Blackburn with 12 games left. FA to look at PL plans. Iain Dowie out at Coventry. S Cup: Dundee finish with nine but win at Motherwell.

12 Asian Confederation against PL global idea. Championship: old man Cole hits three for Burnley at QPR; Sheff Utd hold WBA at The Hawthorns as ten-man Watford edge Leicester and Stoke hold off Saints fight back; Colchester off the bottom after win over Preston. Lge 1: Crowd of 29,552 see Leeds held by Forest; Swans, Donny and Carlisle all win. Lge 2: Dagenham delight with six off Chester; MK Dons share six at Shrews; Darlo, Hereford (MacDonald three) both win but Rotherham shaken by Stockport (Rowe treble) four play. BSP: Shots held by Cambridge, as are Torquay at Weymouth. S Cup: Partick need pens against Livi; St Johnstone edge Ross Co.

13 UEFA Cup: record sixth win on trot for Everton in Europe; Rangers held by Panathinaikos. SPL: Fletcher hat-trick floors Gretna. S Cup: St Mirren surprise Dundee Utd. BSP: Forest Green hold Stevenage. Republic appoint ageing Giovanni Trapattoni, 69, as manager. Rich list puts four English clubs in top five for first time, but Real stay No.1.

14 Blatter batters PL's 39ers as "abuse of football." Bryan Robson declines upstairs move and leaves Sheff Utd as Kevin Blackwell takes over until end of season, 11th Championship departure this season. UEFA Cup: Diouf edge Bolton over ten-man Atletico Madrid; Spurs take 2-1 lead at Slavia Prague; Aberdeen held by Bayern. Women's international: England beat Norway 2-1.

15 FA and Man Utd to put knife into worldwide PL. Stoke, two down to Scunny, get three and go top!

16 FA Cup: loony Liverpool found out by Barnsley determination and loanee goalie Steele as the Tykes make it take out time at Anfield; talisman Rooney returns to set four play up for Man Utd as ten-man Arsenal (Eboue off) crumple and Sir Alex (100th cup tie) and Arsene have a disagreement; Bristol R return to last eight after 50 years to send Saints packing; Cardiff blunt and blank Wolves for quarter-final place 61 years after they won the cup!; Baggies high five at shambolic Coventry; Lampard 100th and 101st Chelsea goals in fight back against Huddersfield. Championship: Watford get a point at Charlton; born-again Leicester four goals hit ten-man Norwich. Lge 1: Scotland pen ends four spot failures for other Swans; rare away win for Orient; Walker debut goal for Southend. Lge 2: four goal Daggers can't stop winning or scoring; Stags clip ten-man Darlo; Hatch does in old Barnet mates for Posh; Logan gaffe lets in Bury against Stockport; it's a pitch for MK Dons frozen out. SPL: Celtic keep pressure on Rangers with 3-0 over Hearts. BSP: Torquay ease nearer inactive Shots.

17 FA Cup: og agony for Preston, James saves pen and Pompey's tie; Boro draw at steely Sheff Utd. SPL: Rangers keep four pt lead after win at Killie; Hibs climb back to fifth beating the Dons. BSP: Shots Sunday best sweeps Stevenage aside.

18 Gallas escapes FA wrath after altercation with Nani on Saturday. Palace valuable draw at Bristol C. FA Cup draw sends Chelsea to Barnsley and only one all-PL tie: Man Utd v Portsmouth, one non-Pl semi-finalist guaranteed with Bristol R v WBA and Sheff Utd or Boro meet Cardiff. Soton appoint Nigel Pearson as manager. Gretna crisis: owner in hospital, players not paid.

19 Ch Lge: Liverpool find ten-man Inter easier than the Tykes, but need two late goals; Chelsea scale no heights in dull draw at Olympiakos; Roma fight back floors Real; Schalke edge Porto. Chris Coleman gets Coventry post. No progress for Pearson at Soton, beaten by the Pilgrims. Paint: MK Dons take slender lead at Swansea. Frost kills off seven games. PL adamant over global games. Gretna boss and assistant join Morton.

20 Ch Lge: Tubby Tevez snatches Man Utd draw in Lyon on Giggs' 100th in it, but laser targets Ronaldo; Arsenal fail to break down AC Milan; Messi sweeps up Celtic for Barca; Fenerbahce edge Sevilla by odd goal in five. PL to woo FA over worldwide idea.

21 Troubled Gazza sectioned. UEFA Cup: Bolton hold out for draw with Atletico Madrid for best-ever place in Europe; Everton hit another Euro height with joy of six against Brann (Yakubu hat-trick); Spurs owe it to restored gk Robbo for "winning" draw against Slavia; Rangers level with Panathinaikos to go on, too, but Aberdeen ship five in Munich. UEFA concern over failure to identify laser launches. Redknapp pledges support for old club Bournemouth. Chelsea loss is £74.8m. Old Wolves legend Steve Bull is new Stafford Rangers boss.

22 Bolton complain to UEFA over Spanish police. PL and FA still at odds over 39th step. Swansea stroll on 1-0 over Luton.

23 Eduardo suffers compound fracture of left leg in red-card tackle from Martin Taylor as the Birmingham ten hold Arsenal and Gallas throws a wobbly; Keegan suffers from R & R as the dynamic duo hit a brace each in the high five at St James Park; Tor-Tor-Torres the Spaniard gets a treble for Liverpool to blunt plucky ten-man finishing Boro; Hammers put another nail in Fulham's relegation box with controversial effort on Bobby Moore remembrance day; dreaming Pompey need Defoe pen to see off the Black Cats; Paul Jewell riles over ragged Rams loss to old mates Wigan. Championship: Stoke prosper again as Watford are held by Preston, Albion beaten at home by Hull; Blackpool 5 Charlton 3 in Bloomfield bloomers; Wolves show fangs again at Palace. Lge 1: Forest gifted win at Orient by Nelson gaffe; three on travel for Walsall, Southend and at home for Millwall; Leeds can only draw again. Lge 2: MK Dons clip the Barnet ten; Keith Hill calls his Rochdale losers "a pub team"; Daggers still winning; first touch loanee scorer Dowson does it for Chesterfield; SPL: with no Auld Firm in action, Hibs, Hearts both win. BSP: Stevenage held, but Cambridge, Exeter win. Trophy: winners Torquay easily, Shots with difficulty, York at Rushden; Ebbsfleet and Burton draw.

24 C Cup final: Spurs rally sinks Grant-tinkered Chelsea. PL: Reading lose to Villa, their eighth defeat on the trot; McCarthy 2 pens as Rovers tread on Trotters. Taylor gets death threats. SPL: Rangers see off Gretna, Celtic leave it late at St Mirren.

25 The fourth is back for Everton at Man City. Eduardo fit in nine months? Yanks to ditch Liverpool? Paint: Scotland pen not enough at MK Dons as Swans upped in shoot-out Southern final.

Everton's Mikel Arteta scores his team's fifth goal in a 6-0 rout of Norwegian side SK Brann in the UEFA Cup Round of 32 second leg match at Goodison on 22 February. (EMPICS Sport/PA Photos/Tony Marshall)

26 PL scrap Blatter meeting. Man City boss flies back to Thailand. Abramovich unhappy over C Cup loss. Boro fury over Aliadiere extended ban. Championship: Stoke toppled at Preston but stay top. Lge 1: Carlisle second after win at Crewe. Lge 2: Posh second after 2-0 at Wrexham; Daggers dig for victory again against Hereford. Paint: Northern final first leg lifts Grimsby at Morecambe. BSP: Torquay held by Altrincham. Trophy: Ebbsfleet extra time winners over Burton. Setanta: Aldershot four in extra time hit Crawley for six; Woking threesome over Weymouth.

27 FA Cup: Joke own goal by Kenny is Boro extra time winner over Sheff Utd. SPL: Celtic edge Caley while Rangers hit a four at Hearts; Gretna fourth win over nearest sufferers Killie. SL: high five for Stranraer at Elgin. Ian Brightwell declines No.2 role at Macclesfield as Keith Alexander takes his place. Spurs seek new HQ.

28 Anfield rift as Hicks is stay-boy, Gillett jr the sale-away and Carragher in Police caution over neighbour spat. *France Football* reckon Chelsea have four players in richest-earning ten, but Kaka £6.60m, Ronaldinho ££6.31m are No.1 and No.2. Roy Keane lists Liam Miller for poor time-keeping. Ladies shock: Everton beat Arsenal (58 unbeaten domestically) in PL Cup final.

29 Mascherano finally signs for Liverpool at £18.6m – what about the window? – but Cousin move to Fulham from Rangers is ruled out.

MARCH 2008

Gretna facing extinction? ... Torres 20 League goal man ... East Fife already home and dry ... Rangers 50th game ... Super Sunday blow for Arsenal ... Becks 100th – England a duck.

1 The late, late (injury time) PL goal show: Arsenal grab point v Villa; father of twins Derbyshire has the Rovers winner at 14-corner Toon; similarly Harper for slump-addressed Reading at Boro; Jenas just a Spurs consolation as Forssell hits a Brummie hat-trick. Also only brief R & R sub outings as Man Utd ease past faltering Fulham; Chelsea suffer red Lamps departure but light up West Ham with four play; Derby, Man City goalless with Sunderland, Wigan respectively. Championship: Comic Purse og lets in Leicester at Cardiff; Bristol C top up over inactive Stoke; Palace reverse recent stalling; Barnsley goal drought since Liverpool win; Baggies hit three, Watford held at Burnley. Lge 1: Scotland gives Swansea club record 18 unbeaten run at Huddersfield; Moore debut goal for Walsall; Leeds win again at last. Lge 2: MK Dons one goal victors again but Gueret saves Chester pen; Dickinson spot on as Stockport equal club record seven away wins in a row; Daggers make it five anywhere on the trot; Lincoln send boss Peter Jackson for hospital treatment with another victory. SPL: Boyd's 18th goal leaves Rangers on track as Celtic win at Hibs, too. SL: Late goals give Dundee a win, Hamilton a draw. East Fife see off nearest rivals Stranraer and lead Div 3 by 25 pts! BSP: Torquay slip up at Grays managed by their chairman then Shots grind out another win.

2 Jaaskelainen joke og puts Liverpool on way to win at Bolton, but Everton keep the fourth with Yakubu double over Pompey. Championship: Stoke's ten not good enough at Rangers.

3 Villa's Davies out six months with Achilles injury. Carlisle second after win at Forest. Chester and Gary Peters part company. BSP: Shots clip the Torquay Gulls in fourth minute of injury time.

4 Ch Lge: Arsenal – and Fabregas' finest in Europe, victory in Milan; Celtic early loss and exit to Barca; Ronaldo, naturally, for Man Utd over Lyon. Dubai still have Anfield interest. Championship: Bristol C, Watford involved in drawn games; Albion late win at ten-man Sheff Wed while Plymouth hit Colchester four times; winners Hull and losers Burnley share four red cards in seven minutes! Lge 1: Donny win at Bristol R; Brighton hit nine-Gills for four, but Swindon's nine too good for Huddersfield. Lge 2; Posh go top after win at Barnet, Darlo put pressure on MK Dons with victory over Chester. Paint: Grimsby book Wembley place with Morecambe draw. BSP: Harriers hit six, so do Forest Green while Cambridge climb over Torquay in second place.

5 Ch Lge: Chelsea hit form over Olympiakos; Real's ten not enough to stop Roma. PL: Torres trio as Hammers concede four again to give Liverpool fourth spot. SL: Russell is a treble-shooter for Airdrie. Sheffield legend Derek Dooley, Wednesday player, manager then United director, dies at 78.

6 UEFA Cup: Everton disappoint in Florence; Bolton held by Sporting and Spurs find no way to stop PSV winning but Rangers at least take two-goal lead over Werder. JM finally closes love affair with Chelsea.

7 Blatter wants foul tacklers banned from the game. Trophy semi: Torquay take two goal lead over York.

8 FA Cup: Tyke that! Odejayi and Barnsley stun tinkerman Grant and Chelsea; Pompey chime in with pen after Kuszczak rare red at Old Trafford and ref Martin Aktinson riles Sir Alex with no pen in Portsmouth's first win there for 41 years. PL: cruel Liverpool fans put metaphorical boot into Keegan's tumbling Toon on Owen's 250th PL game; Gutsy Reading dent Man City Euro hopes; Bullard again the Fulham point saver at Blackburn. Championship: Bristol C, Stoke only manage drawn games at the top; Moses, one of four 17 year olds, is the right tablet to cure Palace ills; Coventry edge the Norwich nine. Lge 1: Donny, Carlisle – with club record 12th successive home win – make progress; Leeds near play-off range again. Lge 2: Posh end Daggers run; Knight's overhead strike for Wycombe sparks win over Darlo; Akinfenwa makes it six goals in six games for Northampton; Billy Dearden axed at Mansfield after four-goal home defeat. S Cup: Dundee shot out at QoS; Saints level – Johnstone and Mirren. BSP: Cambridge, Stevenage both lose. Trophy semi: Ebbsfleet sink the sad Shots. FIFA u-turn on Hawk-Eye – the last of the innovations!

9 FA Cup: Cardiff leave one PL in semis after taking out Middlesbrough; Albion bag five at Bristol Rovers with triple-Miller in the mood. PL: Arsenal bogged down in goalless at Wigan. Everton keeping pressure on Liverpool with win at Sunderland; Hammers concede four for third game as sub Gilberto hits 500th Spurs PL goal at WHL. S Cup: Vennegoor scrapes equaliser for Celtic at Aberdeen as Rangers win replay with Hibs.

10 West Ham board behind Alan Curbishley. MK Dons win at Chesterfield regains top spot. BSP: Exeter lose at York.

11 Ch Lge: Liverpool make it a PL quartet in quarter-finals after masterly display away to Inter. Championship: Howard hat-trick sparks Tykes over Ipswich; Stoke sandwich between drawing Bristol C and Watford (miss pen) after win at Norwich; Colchester looking adrift following loss to Sheff Wed; even Sharp gets a goal for Sheff Utd! Lge 1: Swans held by Rovers, but Donny, Carlisle both win. Lge 2: Posh leapfrog inactive MK Dons; Mansfield, Wrexham both toil but Macc win at Dagenham. Cardiff in legal battle over finance. Gretna heading out of business. SL: Dundee close gap on Hamilton held at Dunfermline. McLaughlin foursome in Cowden 5-4 at Berwick, while Ayr shake Ross 4-2.

12 UEFA Cup: Spurs, Everton fight-backs ruined by the curse of the shoot-out. PL: Lamps foursome as Chelsea crush Rams 6-1; Pompey hit Brummies with four of their own; Boro get a point at Villa. Championship: Baggies and Palace draw. Paul Simpson gets Shrewsbury post. SPL: Celtic held by Dundee Utd.

13 UEFA Cup; Bolton run ended at last in Lisbon; Rangers sole Brit qualifiers after surviving 19 Werder corners in 1-0 defeat. Gary Neville on comeback trail at Man Utd.

14 Ch Lge draw: Arsenal v Liverpool, Man Utd away to Roma first and Chelsea at the easier Fenerbahce. Foster awaits Man Utd debut after three year wait. Agger agony – out till next term.

15 Aliadiere shoots ahead for Boro against old Gunners mates and Toure has to strike late for a point, so with debutant Foster repelling boarders in Man Utd goal, a Ron effort over a better Derby gives Sir Alex back the PL lead; Liverpool grateful for Torres becoming first to hit 20 League goals since Fowler in 1996 against lead-taking Reading; one goal enough for Chelsea at Sunderland; Carson comic capers cost Villa dearly at Portsmouth; goal-a-game Freddie Sears, 19, is super-sub on senior bow for Hammers against Blackburn. Championship: ten-man Watford – their fifth draw – hold Stoke in sterility; Baggies ten hit by Howard treble for Leicester; Cardiff to appeal Hasselbaink red after draw at Colchester; Saints go to Hull and back five goals worse off; Scowcroft 100th career goal as Palace put it over Barnsley; Pilgrims make progress at Bristol C; Charlton, Norwich both slip up. Lge 1: Swansea seen off by the Cobblers; Donny dip out at Brighton; Carlisle, Forest v Walsall in drawn games with Southend taking advantage; Luton sparked by Charles, 18. Lge 2: Dons deliver against the Daggers; Macc – two in last eight mins – win again; Stags owe it to Boulding M with his 21st goal. SPL: Gretna living on handouts, minus ten pts, go down to the Dons; Fir Park pitch unfit again as Celtic game at Motherwell is off. SL: Hamilton take crucial advantage against ten-man Dundee. Flying East Fife take the Div 3 crown already! BSP: Cambridge cut a little into Shots lead with pen v Woking. Trophy: Shots held at the death by Ebbsfleet, who join Torquay in Wembley final despite defeat at York.

16 McBride leaves Everton at the faltering fifth in Fulham revival; Spurs undone by Man City comeback, too; Wigan put Bolton in bottom three. Lge 2: Rochdale Sunday best for three-goal Le Fondre. CIS Cup final: Rangers need a shoot-out to see off Dundee Utd.

17 Owen brings pointed relief to KK in Toon draw at Brum. Credit squeeze could hit big clubs. Sky to get more Ch Lge games. AFC Liverpool latest breakaway club for hard-up fans.

18 FA chairman Lord Triesman pleads for respect for the man in the middle. Rotherham back in administration. Hull on a roll, even Wolves win. Swans swim nine points clear. BSP: Cambridge, Forest Green lose ground. Setanta semi: Shots pen Woking out. S Cup replays: Aberdeen win at Celtic, Johnstone prevail in Saints battle with Mirren.

19 Chelsea ditch two goal lead and allow Spurs to settle for equal pieces of eight as Man Utd take the Ron route twice to overcome Bolton. S Cup: Jags put brake on Rangers to force replay. FA Youth Cup: Chelsea reach final after edging Villa. Police raid Birmingham on agent doings. Cardiff in financial relief but Hasselbaink red card enforced.

20 Capello, Coppell also on the whistlers side. Becks back for 100th chance.

21 WBA point at Charlton. Swans held by the Shrimpers, Donny lose but Forest win at Northampton. MK Dons draw with Posh. BSP: Stevenage go second.

22 Owen on song in Toons of glory rather than the last post for KK as Fulham go 32 without away win; Bikey pedal power pushes Reading ahead of Birmingham; Chopra hews out first away win for Sunderland at Villa; Bentley inspires Rovers against Wigan; bereft Bolton make a point with meandering Man City; Ashton rescues draw for Hammers at fourth-place dreamers Everton; Spurs leave it late to break down Pompey; Bargain buy Tuncay again the Boro scorer as Derby suffer more grief. Championship: Cardiff edge Bristol C in battle on and off the pitch; Palace 20 secs from defeat draw at Sheff Wed; Cureton with career 10th treble helps Norwich do in old Colchester mates; Watford held at ten-man Plymouth; Saints and Coventry scoreless; Barnsley eye-on-the-cup lose to Sheff Utd; Wolves share six with

QPR. Lge 1: Carlisle cut into Swans lead with win at Orient; Beckford double boosts Leeds. Lge 2: high five for Barnet; four for Chesterfield; Mansfield, Wrexham still drifting. BSP: Shots recover from Altrincham lead; Torquay, Burton and Exeter also win, Cambridge held. SPL: Rangers grind out another win in 50th overall game this season; Dundee U homing in on third place with Motherwell victory. SL: five for Brechin; Vase semis: Kirkham & W recover to edge Needham 3-2, but Lowestoft take four off Whitley Bay.

23 Super Sunday: Drogba double deals crucial blow to Arsenal for Chelsea as Mascherano red is no help to Liverpool in 3-0 defeat against champion-looking Man Utd. SPL: Celtic beat Gretna at Livingston! Real lose to Valencia; Barca wonder boy Krkic, 17, has brace v Valladolid.

24 Jairzinho (Brazil 1970) puts boot into English players skill factor. Lge 1: Swans call on Scotland to snatch point against Bristol R as Carlisle move to within five points; Donny, Forest both held but Southend gain ground at Swindon; welcome points for Vale over Gills. Lge 2: MK Dons, Posh win, Hereford lose, Darlo held. Dagnall three for Rochdale. BSP: Shots miss pen but win at Crawley; Cambridge ten go down at Ebbsfleet; Torquay beat ten-man Forest; Stevenage and Exeter also beaten.

25 Ferdinand to skipper England. U-21: England held by the Poles (local selection?!). £20m Kit sponsorship deal for QPR. Soton pair on alleged theft charge. Healy to receive award for Euro goals. U-17: England held by France.

26 Becks gets his century, England a duck as French pen is mightier on the sward; Scots held by Croatia; Wolves "reserve" Eastwood has a double for Wales in Luxembourg; Healy on the mark again as the Irish whack Georgia 4-1; Brazil beat Sweden at the Emirates (of course) 60,021 attend. U-21s: Scots edge Finns, Wales win in Bosnia, N Ireland lose to Romania. Mascherano charged with misconduct. Gretna axe nine seniors and entire youth team.

27 Becks to be new Ronaldo – says Fabio! Rupert Lowe may become a Saint again. BSP: Shots scrape a draw via og at ten-a-side with Droylsden.

28 Roy Keane hits out at hypocritical bosses. Wembley to miss 2010 Ch Lge final over UK government tax. Lge 1: Donny win over Forest.

29 Comeback Kings ten-man Arsenal give Bolton two goals and win – just – but Ron back-heeling cheek says it all for roaring Man Utd against Villa; Derby's Villa scores twice, so do Fulham and the Rams are earliest to leave PL; Brummies ten still too good for slipping Man City, though ref Styles errs over pen; definitive Defoe double and James pen save for Pompey subdues Wigan; Reid has Black Cats purring as 15 seconds past injury time edges Hammers; ten-man Reading goalless with Blackburn. Championship: Colchester 2-0 in 17 mins at WBA let in two in 1st and 3rd mins of injury-time to lose 4-3!; Bristol C in pole position after injury-time "hands" goal upsets Norwich; Hull (23,501) on a real roll overturn Watford, thanks to Dubai workout; Barnsley slump on; Cardiff add to Saints woe; Wolves late winner at Charlton. Lge 1: Swans in winning vein again; Carlisle's 13th unbeaten game; Southend go fourth with minimum over Walsall. Lge 2: Brisley, 17, Macc boot boy bags brace over ten-man Accrington; first-half treble for Newby gives Morecambe high five and their best League win; Posh top of the pops again. SPL: Rangers go six points clear with game in hand over Celtic in Auld Firm decider? Gretna relegated. SL: Berwick point not enough to stop demotion. BSP: Shots extend lead as Cambridge crash at home and Torquay only draw.

30 Born-again Newcastle hit four at Spurs!; Liverpool win Mersey derby with another Torres home goal; Chelsea early end Boro hopes. Paint final: Gueret pen save paves way for MK Dons to beat Grimsby – 56,615 at Wembley in weekend's second best. Juve v Parma called off on road death of fan.

31 More allegations: Capello linked to Juve corruption case; Mourinho in similar Portuguese incident. BSP: Burton lost in the Forest Green.

APRIL 2008

Arsenal's 100th but unlikely to celebrate? ... Cardiff in first final for 81 years ... Rangers 26th unbeaten ... Aldershot back in FL after 16 years ... Celtic close on Rangers ... Chelsea upset Man Utd.

1 Ch Lge: Ron and Roo rock and roll in Rome for two goal lead; Barca edge it over Schalke. Championship: Cardiff make a point with fellow finalists Albion, as do Sheff Wed late against Coventry. Lge 1: Forest end Carlisle run, Leeds win at Donny, Gills get lift against Luton. Lge 2: Mansfield win relegation affair with Wrexham. Huddersfield part with Andy Ritchie. BSP: Torquay, away – Stevenage home both win, Grays score five.

2 Ch Lge: Liverpool hold Gunners at the Emirates, but Arsenal claim Kuyt pen refused by his Dutch "neighbour" ref!; Deivid villan turns Fenerbahce hero against Chelsea. Ronaldo rated best in world, Kaka the richest.

3 UEFA Cup: Zenit crush at Leverkusen, Getafe hold Bayern as do PSV against Fiorentina and Sporting at Rangers. Liverpool livid over Mascherano ban and fine. FA Youth Cup: Man City draw first leg semi at Chelsea. Setanta Shd final: Rushden 3-1 down draw at Aldershot but lose in shoot-out.

4 Arsene Wenger calls for unknown bribe player to be banned. MK Dons catch Posh on points at least and have game in hand.

5 FA Cup semi: shot-shy Baggies bow to Harry's boys as Pompey reach first final since 1939, though suspicion of "hands" assist before goal? PL: despite 100th overall goal of season, Arsenal's draw with Liverpool spells end of title hopes?; Chelsea revive at sad Man City; terrier Toon now terrorise Reading!; Rovers rant over no-pen in Spurs draw – 101st clash since 1-1 in cup 101 spooky years ago; Sunderland in clear water but tide going out on Fulham; Wigan beat ten-man Brummies to give Steve Bruce satisfaction; bungling Bolton beaten by Villa. Championship: Watford end eight-game misery; Vernon pulls two for Colchester over Ipswich; Lita lifts ten-man Addicks at Plymouth; Beattie first half seven min treble as Sheff Utd beat Leicester, who rant at "diving" Sharp; Saints alive stitch-up Bristol C. Lge 1: three in a row for Port Vale now! Flahavan saves two pens, Barnard hits two goals against his loan boys Crewe for Southend; down and out Bournemouth win at Swansea!; Leeds win at Orient. Lge 2: controversial pen helps Wycombe draw with Posh; Rotherham (only 2979) lose again; super-sub Rene Howe second half hat-trick for Rochdale. SPL: now ten-man Motherwell sink Celtic – at Parkhead; Gretna's 431 gate at Motherwell, is poorest ever. SL: Ross are Div 2 champs after 4-0 v Berwick. BSP: nearly there Shots (3388) just edge Salisbury as Torquay, Burton and Stevenage all lose at home.

6 FA Cup semi: Cardiff reach first final for 81 years with Ledley volley to light up the valleys against Barnsley. PL: Rooney rescues point for Man Utd after Alves double for Boro; Everton one goal, Derby zero in their 27th record without-a-win run. Rangers make it 26 unbeaten in SPL in sharing six with Dundee Utd. AC Milan to bid for Ronaldinho.

7 Cech suffers 50-stitch facial injury – in training accident. Palace scrape into play-off position with win at Stoke. Cardiff "wild card" hope for UEFA place.

8 Ch Lge: Chelsea leave it late to oust Fenerbahce, so do Liverpool against Arsenal. PL: away day win for Portsmouth at West Ham. Championship: Baggies win at the seaside; Sheffield derby all square. Lge 1: win for Southend, Swans away, Forest at home gets a point each. Lge 2: winners MK Dons get four goals, so do Rochdale. BSP: Shots draw at Ebbsfleet but Torquay recover to beat Oxford. SL: Partick relegate Stirling.

9 Ch Lge: Minimum win for Barca, Man Utd – though De Rossi wastes a pen for Roma. Championship: Barnsley shake Watford at Vicarage Road. Lge 2: more Mansfield misery. SPL: Gretna crowd given as over 7000 is one naught too many! Birmingham's David Sullivan and Karren Brady questioned by police over alleged conspiracy to defraud.

10 UEFA Cup: Rangers finest hour in Lisbon on away day successes – Bayern on visiting goals, Fiorentina winning and Leverkusen just failing to overturn Zenit. Hicks calls for Parry axing at Liverpool.

11 Low-profile Benitez as Parry hits back. Calamity James may be PFA P of Y! Eighteen of 24 Championship clubs still have promotion chance! Donny keep up Lge 1 challenge.

12 Bolton (with Davies 100th career goal) home in on Hammers, Fulham rare away day joy at Reading, but barking Rams at Pride concede six to Villa – one Petrov 50 yarder and another laughingly offside; cup-eyed Pompey settle for Toon draw; Sunderland hit by Man City at S of L; Zarate the mark of a Brummie scorer as Everton get a point; Spurs need og to hold Boro. Championship: Stoke recover to win at Coventry; Wolves hold Bristol C; goalie gaffe gives Saints draw at Charlton; Palace relegate Scunthorpe; Hull leave it late for QPR leveller; Barnsley win again, Watford all square at Albion. Lge 1: Leeds edge Carlisle by odd goal in five; Forest in at Tranmere; Luton relegated by Brighton, Port Vale by Huddersfield draw but Swansea promoted at Gillingham. Lge 2: Stockport surprise Posh, MK Dons hit back so late to draw with Wycombe. S Cup s-f: Q of S stun Aberdeen in 4-3 win to turn clock back 58 years. SL: Hamilton almost there in Div 1. BSP: Shots (5791) still waiting as they – narrowly over Burton – and Torquay both win, United convincingly at Stevenage.

13 Man Utd close to title again as Arsenal lose lead to Ron pen and Hargreaves free-kick; Torres scores in seven consecutive home League games as Blackburn are beaten 3-1 and Rafa calls for crisis talks. Derby win for Ipswich over Norwich, Shrews against Wrexham. S Cup replay: Rangers see of Jags. SPL: Celtic ease in at Motherwell.

14 Cech returns but Chelsea caught at last gasp by Wigan equaliser as doubt cast over Grant future as title challenge hit. Ferdinand signs five year Man Utd deal. Klinsmann link looms again at Anfield. Mike Tyson to aid stricken Gazza! Tory boy Michael Ashcroft increases Spurs involvement. Sheff Wed get seventh successive draw v Argyle.

15 Chelsea fall out with Sky. Capello loves end of season friendlies, Rooney tipped as skipper. Championship: Hull – now second – stop the Barnsley bandwagon, Black Country derby sees Baggies pocket points at Wolves. Lge 1: Leeds lose at Huddersfield, Bristol R return with win at Walsall. Lge 2: MK Dons point nearer promotion, Wycombe consolidate at Grimsby, Rochdale home to Barnet. BSP: Aldershot return to FL after 16 years with draw at Exeter; Torquay and Burton both win.

16 Lord Triesman, one-time maverick politician, warns PL clubs to remember England team. Harry Redknapp to sue police. SPL: Celtic shake Rangers with last minute winner to close gap. FA Youth Cup final: Man City wrap up victory over ten-man Chelsea.

17 Tired Everton give Chelsea another title glimmer. 39th game still looks a step too far. Ref chief Hackett apologies to Sunderland for whistler error. Gillett calls for peace at Anfield.

18 Rafa happy at Liverpool, Eriksson confident at Man City. Bradford price cut lead to be followed by other FL clubs. BSP: bouncy Burton bury Stevenage.

19 Tevez saves Man Utd blushes at Blackburn with 88th minute leveller; Bolton win at Boro, Arsenal home to Reading, Spurs draw at Wigan, lacklustre Hammers just nail the Rams, Liverpool add to Keller erred Fulham woe. Championship: Watford's poor home form carries on as Palace win; slumping Saints bow to Burnley; Sidibe double lifts Stoke against Bristol C. Lge 1: Swans sunk at home but win the title!; Chris Martin, 18, lets in six on PV debut; Leeds attract best Millwall season gate (13,395). Lge 2: Lifeline for Wrexham against Notts and Boulding threesome aids Mansfield, too; MK Dons edge it at Edgeley Park; rare play-off place for Rochdale. SPL: ref saves Celtic with late whistle as Dons lose. SL: Hamilton 19 year out of top flight, return after beating Clyde. BSP: in-form Cambridge go fourth after beating Salisbury.

20 Villa's high five rattle Birmingham; Toon hero Owen at the double against Black Cats; Man City take out unfocused Pompey. S Cup semi: St Johnstone push Rangers all the way to penalties.

21 Carlos Alberto Parreira quits South Africa job over family illness.

22 Ch Lge semi: Chelsea gifted injury-time Riise og to level at Liverpool. Hereford win relegates Wrexham. Jimmy Mullen replaces Richard Money as Walsall manager.

23 Ch Lge: Ronaldo hits second minute pen high and wide as Man Utd draw in Barcelona on Scholes 100th competition appearance.

24 UEFA Cup semi: Rangers held at Ibrox by Fiorentina; Bayern by Zenit. Stan Ternent is new Huddersfield boss.

25 Leeds secure play-off berth after win at Yeovil.

26 It's all two-goal Ballack's as Chelsea edge a Sir Alex tinkered Man Utd to keep the title tilt in the balance, but scuffles off and on mar it; Fulham with a sub Kamara double and 94th minute winner, back from the dead, give Man City two goals and beat them; fourth time late again but now safe Sunderland clip Boro; Newcastle give Hammers two goal lead and hold them, as do Liverpool at Birmingham; Wigan and Reading (7 hours 41 mins goalless) draw, Spurs and Bolton one apiece. Championship: Speed duo first Sheff Utd into possible play-off berth after win over Bristol C; Sheri bows out – with Colchester from Layer Road, as Stoke nearer promotion; first reverse in 11 for Palace at Hull; Purse red for Cardiff threatens cup final outing in 3-3 at Burnley; now Watford lose at home to Scunny!; Leicester slump to Sheff Wed. Barnsley safe as beaten Charlton introduce Jonjo Shelvey, 16, their youngest debutant. Lge 1: Brighton provide disappointing farewell to Memorial Ground for Bristol R; Bauza 19 min

first half treble for Swansea; Southend first defeat in 14 at Tranmere. Lge 2: Mansfield, Wrexham – relegated after 87 years – both lose, but Notts out of danger, while Hereford get promotion at Brentford. SPL: Motherwell and Dundee Utd draw in UEFA place battle. SL: Clyde face play-off, Alloa, too, despite Peterhead's five elsewhere; wooden spoon for Forfar. BSP: Cash-straped Halifax safe, despite defeat, but Farsley, Altrincham join already demoted Stafford and Droylsden. Shots make it 18 without defeat.

27 Rovers Santa Cruz lets Pompey concentrate on cup! Everton and Villa share four goals and their UEFA ambitions. SPL: Celtic hit ten-man Rangers – again.

28 PFA warns players over abuse of refs. Adebayor treble as Arsenal savage the Rams in joy of six. WBA get point for promotion, Saints theirs towards salvation.

29 Ch Lge semi: searing Scholes shot against Barca propels Man Utd to final. Chester point against Stockport demotes Mansfield.

30 Ch Lge semi: Chelsea come good in overtime to beat Liverpool with Drogba double. SL play-offs: Alloa slender lead over Clyde, Airdrie surprise Raith; Cowden draw at Arbroath, Stranraer at Montrose.

MAY

Man Utd 10th PL title . . . Blatter's 6, 5 special . . . Ronaldo double awards . . . Pompey's cup overflows . . . Gretna – and Grant – axed . . . Celtic pip Rangers

1 UEFA semis: Rangers hold nerve at Fiorentina shoot-out for first final in 36 years; Zenit, zoom, too after routing Bayern. Capello was highest paid boss in Italy. Arsenal MD Keith Edelman quits. Liverpool – new ground concerns. Giovanni Trapattoni officially unveiled as Republic boss. Scunthorpe fined £15,000 over players accosting ref. BSP playoff: Torquay hit late at Exeter.

2 Barry to stay at Villa? Scolari in Man City frame? Harry Redknapp accuses police. Russia agrees speedy visas. BSP play-off: Cambridge claw back level at Burton.

3 Ron double – only 5th to reach 30 PL goal mark and 40 overall – as Man Utd cruise to win over West Ham; Fulham move out of bottom three beating Birmingham; Diouf leaves Bolton with goal towards survival against Sunderland; Spurs drop Reading into last three; Wigan safe after win at Villa; Blackburn give Derby worst ever PL record; Boro brace over Cup Final thinking Pompey. Lge 1: Swansea handed trophy at Brighton; Forest join the automatic duo, too; Cheltenham save themselves against Doncaster, but draw not enough for Bournemouth to stay and Leeds finish off Gills as well. Lge 2: schoolboy Curtis Main, 15, helps Darlo win at Posh; relegated Wrexham bow out with a 4-2 win at Lincoln; Gianluca Havern, 19, debut scorer for Stockport. SPL: Celtic eight points clear of four-in-hand Rangers after Motherwell beaten. SL play-offs: Airdrie draw enough to knock out Raiith; Clyde need extra time against Alloa; Arbroath stun Cowden, Stranraer ease over Montrose.

4 One goal enough for low key Arsenal against Everton and Liverpool over Man City – as Torres eight in-in-a-row at home equals Ian Rush record. Championship: WBA take title at QPR; Stoke point enough to accompany them, though insufficient for Leicester to survive the drop; Saints relief despite ten-men edging Sheff Utd; Sheff Wed ease worries against Norwich; play-off Watford point just enough to hold off Wolves late winners against Plymouth. SPL: tired Rangers draw at Hibs. Spain: ten-man Real (Cannavaro off) assured of title, Barca hit six (Henry 2). Germany: Bayern's 20th. Italy: AC Milan beat Inter to give Roma a chance.

5 Chelsea now level on points behind Man Utd after win at Newcastle. BSP play-off: Exeter make Torquay reel with a late foursome. Women's FA Cup final: Arsenal 4-1 over Leeds take ninth such trophjy with 24,582 at Forest.

6 The FA reveals a cunning plan: WC2010 qualifying, Euro 2012 semis and Capello happy with targets. Is PL boring? It's a devil – Man Utd debt £666m. KK wants more Toon cash to strengthen.. Sven will we see you again? Rangers row with SFA over fixtures. BSP play-off: Cambridge oust Burton.

7 Capello faces perjury charge in Italy. Danger for England fans in Russia. Arbitration costs Leeds £500,000. SPL: Rangers scrape win over Motherwell, two in hand and four points behind Celtic. SL play-offs: Clyde win at Airdrie, Arbroath go two up against Stranraer.

8 Luigi Di Canio sacked at QPR. Micky Adams is the new Brighton manager. Williams hat-trick as England Ladies beat Belarus 6-1 in Minsk.

9 Ahead of D-day Sunday, Grant wants play-off for title! Sacked Frank Rijkaard of Barca may be heading Chelsea way? Porto deducted six points and fined for match-fixing, but still win League! Lge 1 play-off: ten Donnys draw at Southend.

10 Championship play-off: injury-time winner for Bristol C at Palace; Lge 2 play-off: Darlo similarly late edging Rochdale. SPL: Dundee Utd rage over ref in defeat against Rangers. SL play-off finals: Clyde finish off Airdrie, one goal not enough for Stranraer over Arbroath. Trophy final: McPhee fluffs pen but hits only goal as Ebbsfleet sink Torquay.

11 Man Utd clinch 17th overall championship – 10th in PL – with 2-0 win at Wigan while Chelsea are even caught level at the death by Bolton; the dead men all win – four goal Birmingham and Reading, Fulham with one, but it's the Cottagers who escape on goal difference; ten-man Man City bow out with an 8-1 thrashing at Boro, who record their best PL result and an Alves hat-trick; Arsenal one goal winners at Sunderland; Everton secure fifth place beating Newcastle as Villa are held at West Ham; Liverpool win at Spurs on day of 34 goals. Championship play-off: Watford concede two at home to Hull. Lge 2: Stockport draw at Wycombe. SPL: Celtic win over Hibs gives them four point lead, two games more than Ramgers. Vase final: Kirkham and W late winners over Lowestoft. .

12 Sir Alex: Man Utd by life. Chelsea snap up Jose Bosingwa £16.2m from Porto. Blatter wants at least six home grown players in each team. Lge 1 play-off: Leeds shaken by Carlisle lead. Iain Dowie set to replace departed Luigi De Canio at QPR. Ian Holloway's job safe at Leicester. Arm wrestling out at Rochdale after Thorpe's broken limb last week!

13 Championship play-off: Trundle settles it for Bristol C in overtime after Palace fight-back. Veteran Larsson returns to Swedish international duty. Rupert Lowe is ready for Southampton role. SPL: Gretna win last game against Hearts, long-serving Skelton the scorer.

14 UEFA Cup final: Zenit just two goals better than Rangers, but rioting fans cause chaos in Manchester when giant screen fails in the city. Championship play-off: Hull recover from Watford strike to hit them four times. Grant turns his ranting on ref who "gave" title to Man Utd.

15 Ronaldo is FWA choice as Footballer of the Year and hints at Real move one day. More police for Moscow final. Lge 1 play-off: How's that son! Howson double turns tables on Carlisle. U-21s: Walcott impresses Capello as England beat Wales 2-0. FA worries over Manchester riots. Celtic legend Tommy Burns dies at 51.

16 127th FA Cup final looms, 500m viewers in 169 countries, winner takes all. Lge 1 play-off: It's a fair Coppinger, as Doncaster hat-trick boy in high five shreds the Shrimpers.

17 FA Cup final: Kanu is Pompey hero – and Cardiff are hit by Enckelman blip having won in 1927 through goalie slip. Lg 2 play-offs: Rochdale on penalties with scorer Perkins red carded, defeat Darlo and Dickinson wins it for Stockport against Wycombe.

18 Exeter back in FL after exiting Cambridge in the BSP play-off. Abroad: Lyon 7th record French title in a row; Ajax miss Ch Lge place; 1899 Hoffenheim (who?) win Bundesliga place; Inter win Serie A and relegate Parma.

19 Pitch patchy for Ch Lge finale as Chelsea reminded of "ghost goal" ref Michel from 2005 semi against Liverpool! SPL: Rangers win at St Mirren leaves them behind better goal difference Celtic with one to go. Gretna sack remaining 40 staff. "First choice" Steve McClaren will go Dutch with Twente.

20 Abramovich may quit Chelsea. Barton handed six months jail for assault. Paul Lambert resigns ast Wycombe boss, Steve Coppell takes pay cut at Reading.

21 Ch Lge final: another penned-in decider as Ronald flops, Terry slips and Van der Sar saves from Anelka after 1-1 from classic Ron header, battling Lampard equaliser and Drogba red card – plus Giggs breaks Sir Bobby's 758 game record.

22 SPL: it's Celtic the tortoise who hare in to thwart Rangers who lose Novo to a red and the game to the Dons. Blatter and Platini (of course) link to fight EU ruling over foreigners.

23 Harry back in police quizzing! Sir Alex says hands off Ron – Real-ly. Chelsea keen on Robinho. Leicester and Holloway part company.

24 Championship play-off: Icing on the cake for Hull as one-time frozen pea packer Windass drives his local team to the PL at Bristol City's expense. S Cup: weary Rangers given a bit of a scare by the Doonhamers before winning and boy Fleck is youngest ever finalist. Shevchenko not wanted by MLS! Republic scrape draw with Serbia.

25 Div 1 play-off: Bonny Donny end the Leeds dream. Republic held by Serbia. Mark Hughes rumoured for Chelsea?

26 Div 2 play-off: Stockport send Rochdale out to their 35th record season in lowest division. England U-19s beat Poland 2-0.

27 Terry appointed England skipper. Giovanni Dos Santos, 19, joins Spurs from Barca for £12.5m.

28 Tears to cheers for Terry header as England beat Yanks 2-0. U-19s win again 1-0 over Serbia. Ched Evans marks Wales debut with match-winning cheeky back-heel in Iceland. Sir Alex cleared of ref abuse!

29 Inter sack Roberto Mancini. Ten Cate follows Grant out of Chelsea. Peter Taylor is new Wycombe manager. Gretna demoted to Div Three, Airdrie and Stranraer move up accordingly. Republic beat Colombia 1-0 at Craven Cottage – of course. Rotherham to move to Don Valley Athletics Stadium.

30 Blatter's hit parade on the PL with his 6-5 special – quotas for foreigners in PL. Czechs beat Scots in Prague. Saints get a new boss: Jan Poortvliet as Nigel Pearson goes in return sweep of Rupert Lowe. Boy Bostock to leave Palace for Spurs.

31 Ballack goal wins friendly for Germany over Serbia. Mutu scores for Romania.

Celtic's Jan Vennegoor of Hesselink rises above the Dundee United defence to power home the only goal of the game during the final league game of the season at Tannadice Park. The win was enough to ensure Celtic had won the Scottish Premier League for the third successive season. (Action Images/Russell Cheyne)

Kris Boyd of Rangers (third from right) outjumps Queen of the South's Robert Harris (centre) to score the third and winning goal in the Scottish FA Cup Final at Hampden. (Action Images/John Clifton/Livepic)

JUNE

Seven English subs ... Sven for Mexico ... Scolari gets Chelsea job ... Russians flatter ... Croatia penned out ... Spain reign supreme

1 Trinidad 0 Becks capt England 3 with Defoe double; managerial rumours: Double-Dutch no treat for Wales. Rijkaard for Chelsea, Wenger for PSG. Pompey may sack three misbehaving players. Gazza recovering.

2 Jose Mourinho is Inter boss, Sven takes charge of Mexico. Gretna told to quit before axe falls.

3 Ancelotti "no" to Chelsea. FA give nod to Burton site for National Centre. Jack Warner now backs England WC bid! Pompey to sign £6m Marcelo (Panathinaikos). Henry's 100th French cap.

4 England might be sunk by seventh sub – but shoot to 10th in FIFA rankings. Mark Hughes installed as Man City boss. Porto banned from Ch Lge for match-fixing – four years ago. Ashton gets five years at West Ham. Luton deducted 10 points, more may follow. 39th step might just be friendlies.

5 England players can keep Trinidad caps ok. Spalletti is latest Chelsea speculation. Spurs pay £16.5m for Luka Modric. AC Milan want Adebayor for £23m. CSKA Sofia, Bulgarian champions banned from Ch Lge because of debts, Steaua Bucharest may join them. Sven's Mexicans beaten 4-1 by the Argies.

6 The Ronaldo – Real affair drifts on. Scolari free after Euro 2008 may be ok for Chelsea – and Mutu ordered to pay them £9.6m! Platini takes another swipe at PL.

7 Euro 2008 starts: Swiss on back foot against Czechs; Portugal find Turks tough but beatable.

8 Austrians go way of Swiss as Modric record 4 min pen for nervous Croatia. Podolski brace gives Germans Pole vaullting.

9 France in bore draw with Romania, but Dutch delight with five-star, three goal win over Italy. Capello wants England to play fantasy football – in a newspaper? 26 Portuguese refs suspended over corruption case.

10 Villa treble as Spain wreck the Russians, Swedes polish off Greeks. PL chairman Sir David Richards criticises "foreigners" in competition! UEFA dismiss that first Dutch "offside" goal furore. Cardiff's Ramsey to join Arsenal.

11 Scolari Oh! Oh! as Big Phil is new Chelsea boss as his Portugal bounce the Czechs; oop Swiss becomes oops as Turkey trot ends their hopes. Shearer not for Blackburn.

12 Whistler Webb points to the spot and gives Austria draw with Poland after Croatia see off Germany as Schweinsteiger sees red. Another Italian scandal is looming.

13 Mutu hero to villain as he scores then sees Buffon save his late pen in a draw, France succumb to Holland but unlucky not to have had a pen of their own.

14 Swedes caught late in Spanish net; Greek holders have a word for it – defeat and out to Russia.

15 Turkey give Czechs two goal start and gobble them up after Cech gaffe – then goalie Volkan blows his top! At least Big Phil has a job to go to as the Swiss win at last against a Ronaldo-less Portugal. WC qualifier sees Iraq in final Asian phase but 39 wounded in random gunfire!

16 Nervous Germans find target missing Austrians a problem until Ballack beauty of a free-kick, but respective coaches Low and Hickersberger banished to stands and shake hands! Croatia indebted to kidney transplant Klasnic for goal over Poles.

17 French lose Abidal to a red, Ribery to injury so it's au revoir as WC 2006 final revisited for Italy. Dutch rest a few but still two goals better than Romania.

18 Spain with reservists hit Greece late. Russia prove too strong for Sweden.
19 Germans fired by two early goals and hold off Portugal in an end-to-end classic. Riise moves to Roma and Kewell may join him.
20 Dramatic defeat on penalties for Croatia as the Turks come back from the dead yet again to deny one of the favourites in an absorbing contest. Nigel Pearson is new Leicester manager. Is Paul Ince heading for Blackburn?
21 Rampant Russians ravage the Dutch ranks in extra time and could have sown it up much earlier.
22 Spain and Italy cancel each other out goalless, but Spain manage it on penalties. Paul Ince becomes the first black manager in the Premier League with Blackburn Rovers. Real up the anti-Man Utd race for Ronaldo quoting £80m.
23 Roberto Donadoni falls on his Italian sword. Anton Ferdinand can leave West Ham – for £8m.
24 Platini fails in bid to have PL clubs regulated over finance. Liverpool's new ground takes step forward. Shrewsbury break record transfer fee paying £170,000 for Grant Holt from Nottingham Forest. Pearson appoints Craig Shakespeare as No.2.
25 See-sawing affair and Germans beat Turkey at their own late, late scoring game. Hiddink hailed as master tactician ahead of match with Spain
26 Spanish inquisition leaves Russia again with no answers. Platini platform pressurises Premiership again. Marcello Lippi gets Italian job. Ex-FIFA President Joao Havelange reopens WC 1966 wounds over use of English refs in crucial matches!
27 David Dein advises Arsenal to take Uzbekistani's dosh. Lampard reported on his way to Inter at £7.1m. Thuram has heart condition. Man City expect to sign Jo, CSKA Moscow's Brazilian at £18m.
28 Concern over Ballack fitness for final. UEFA tell Poland/Ukraine Euro 2012 hosts to shape up or ship out. McClaren starts with a friendly win in Holland.
29 Euro final: Spain massacre Germany 1-0, a delight of attacking football and classic individual goal from Torres. FIFA have plan B for WC 2010 finals! UEFA fine Croatia for fans' racism.
30 Scolari takes a Deco and it costs £7.9m. Sir Alex confident about Ronaldo. Barton pleads guilty to Dabo incident.

LANDMARKS

Emmanuel Adebayor scored Arsenal's 1000th Premier League goal v Reading on 12 November.

Derby County ended the season with the worst Premier League record – just one win, 20 goals, fewest points (11).

Luke Freeman (Gillingham) became the youngest FA Cup player at 15 years 233 days on 10 November.

Leyton Orient scored their 5000th League goal v Carlisle United on 1 September.

Liverpool scored their 7000th League goal v Sunderland 25 August and broke the Champions League scoring record in beating Besiktas 8-0 on 6 November.

Manchester United's Ryan Giggs caught up with Sir Bobby Charlton's 759 first-team appearances in the Champions League final.

First game of 11 Premier League goals: Portsmouth 7 Reading 4 and ten: Tottenham Hotspur 6 Reading 4.

Northern Ireland's David Healy broke the European Championship goalscoring record with his 13th goal on 17 November.

The Manchester United v Chelsea Champions League final is the first in the competition with two English teams.

ENGLISH LEAGUE TABLES 2007–08

FA BARCLAYCARD PREMIERSHIP

			Home					Away					Total						
		P	*W*	*D*	*L*	*F*	*A*	*W*	*D*	*L*	*F*	*A*	*W*	*D*	*L*	*F*	*A*	*GD*	*Pts*
1	Manchester U	38	17	1	1	47	7	10	5	4	33	15	27	6	5	80	22	58	87
2	Chelsea	38	12	7	0	36	13	13	3	3	29	13	25	10	3	65	26	39	85
3	Arsenal	38	14	5	0	37	11	10	6	3	37	20	24	11	3	74	31	43	83
4	Liverpool	38	12	6	1	43	13	9	7	3	24	15	21	13	4	67	28	39	76
5	Everton	38	11	4	4	34	17	8	4	7	21	16	19	8	11	55	33	22	65
6	Aston Villa	38	10	3	6	34	22	6	9	4	37	29	16	12	10	71	51	20	60
7	Blackburn R	38	8	7	4	26	19	7	6	6	24	29	15	13	10	50	48	2	58
8	Portsmouth	38	7	8	4	24	14	9	1	9	24	26	16	9	13	48	40	8	57
9	Manchester C	38	11	4	4	28	20	4	6	9	17	33	15	10	13	45	53	–8	55
10	West Ham U	38	7	7	5	24	24	6	3	10	18	26	13	10	15	42	50	–8	49
11	Tottenham H	38	8	5	6	46	34	3	8	8	20	27	11	13	14	66	61	5	46
12	Newcastle U	38	8	5	6	25	26	3	5	11	20	39	11	10	17	45	65	–20	43
13	Middlesbrough	38	7	5	7	27	23	3	7	9	16	30	10	12	16	43	53	–10	42
14	Wigan Ath	38	8	5	6	21	17	2	5	12	13	34	10	10	18	34	51	–17	40
15	Sunderland	38	9	3	7	23	21	2	3	14	13	38	11	6	21	36	59	–23	39
16	Bolton W	38	7	5	7	23	18	2	5	12	13	36	9	10	19	36	54	–18	37
17	Fulham	38	5	5	9	22	31	3	7	9	16	29	8	12	18	38	60	–22	36
18	Reading	38	8	2	9	19	25	2	4	13	22	41	10	6	22	41	66	–25	36
19	Birmingham C	38	6	8	5	30	23	2	3	14	16	39	8	11	19	46	62	–16	35
20	Derby Co	38	1	5	13	12	43	0	3	16	8	46	1	8	29	20	89	–69	11

COCA-COLA FOOTBALL LEAGUE CHAMPIONSHIP

			Home					Away					Total						
		P	*W*	*D*	*L*	*F*	*A*	*W*	*D*	*L*	*F*	*A*	*W*	*D*	*L*	*F*	*A*	*GD*	*Pts*
1	WBA	46	12	8	3	51	27	11	4	8	37	28	23	12	11	88	55	33	81
2	Stoke C	46	12	7	4	36	27	9	9	5	33	28	21	16	9	69	55	14	79
3	Hull C	46	13	7	3	43	19	8	5	10	22	28	21	12	13	65	47	18	75
4	Bristol C	46	13	7	3	33	20	7	7	9	21	33	20	14	12	54	53	1	74
5	Crystal Palace	46	9	9	5	31	23	9	8	6	27	19	18	17	11	58	42	16	71
6	Watford	46	8	7	8	26	29	10	9	4	36	27	18	16	12	62	56	6	70
7	Wolverhampton W	46	11	6	6	31	25	7	10	6	22	23	18	16	12	53	48	5	70
8	Ipswich T	46	15	7	1	44	14	3	8	12	21	42	18	15	13	65	56	9	69
9	Sheffield U	46	10	8	5	32	24	7	7	9	24	27	17	15	14	56	51	5	66
10	Plymouth Arg	46	9	9	5	37	22	8	4	11	23	28	17	13	16	60	50	10	64
11	Charlton Ath	46	9	7	7	38	29	8	6	9	25	29	17	13	16	63	58	5	64
12	Cardiff C	46	12	4	7	31	21	4	12	7	28	34	16	16	14	59	55	4	64
13	Burnley	46	7	9	7	31	31	9	5	9	29	36	16	14	16	60	67	–7	62
14	QPR	46	10	6	7	32	27	4	10	9	28	39	14	16	16	60	66	–6	58
15	Preston NE	46	11	5	7	29	20	4	6	13	21	36	15	11	20	50	56	–6	56
16	Sheffield W	46	9	5	9	29	25	5	8	10	25	30	14	13	19	54	55	–1	55
17	Norwich C	46	10	6	7	30	22	5	4	14	19	37	15	10	21	49	59	–10	55
18	Barnsley	46	11	7	5	35	26	3	6	14	17	39	14	13	19	52	65	–13	55
19	Blackpool	46	8	11	4	35	27	4	7	12	24	37	12	18	16	59	64	–5	54
20	Southampton	46	9	5	9	26	27	4	10	9	30	45	13	15	18	56	72	–16	54
21	Coventry C	46	8	8	7	25	26	6	3	14	27	38	14	11	21	52	64	–12	53
22	Leicester C	46	7	7	9	23	19	5	9	9	19	26	12	16	18	42	45	–3	52
23	Scunthorpe U	46	7	8	8	31	33	4	5	14	15	36	11	13	22	46	69	–23	46
24	Colchester U	46	4	8	11	31	41	3	9	11	31	45	7	17	22	62	86	–24	38

COCA–COLA FOOTBALL LEAGUE DIVISION 1

		Home						Away					Total						
		P	*W*	*D*	*L*	*F*	*A*	*W*	*D*	*L*	*F*	*A*	*W*	*D*	*L*	*F*	*A*	*GD*	*Pts*
1	Swansea C	46	13	5	5	38	21	14	6	3	44	21	27	11	8	82	42	40	92
2	Nottingham F	46	13	8	2	37	13	9	8	6	27	19	22	16	8	64	32	32	82
3	Doncaster R	46	14	4	5	34	18	9	7	7	31	23	23	11	12	65	41	24	80
4	Carlisle U	46	17	3	3	39	16	6	8	9	25	30	23	11	12	64	46	18	80
5	Leeds U*	46	15	4	4	41	18	12	6	5	31	20	27	10	9	72	38	34	76
6	Southend U	46	12	6	5	35	20	10	4	9	35	35	22	10	14	70	55	15	76
7	Brighton & HA	46	12	6	5	37	25	7	6	10	21	25	19	12	15	58	50	8	69
8	Oldham Ath	46	10	7	6	32	21	8	6	9	26	25	18	13	15	58	46	12	67
9	Northampton T	46	12	6	5	38	21	5	9	9	22	34	17	15	14	60	55	5	66
10	Huddersfield T	46	12	4	7	29	22	8	2	13	21	40	20	6	20	50	62	–12	66
11	Tranmere R	46	13	4	6	32	18	5	7	11	20	29	18	11	17	52	47	5	65
12	Walsall	46	7	9	7	27	26	9	7	7	25	20	16	16	14	52	46	6	64
13	Swindon T	46	12	5	6	41	24	4	8	11	22	32	16	13	17	63	56	7	61
14	Leyton Orient	46	9	6	8	27	29	7	6	10	22	34	16	12	18	49	63	–14	60
15	Hartlepool U	46	11	5	7	40	26	4	4	15	23	40	15	9	22	63	66	–3	54
16	Bristol R	46	5	10	8	25	30	7	7	9	20	23	12	17	17	45	53	–8	53
17	Millwall	46	9	4	10	30	26	5	6	12	15	34	14	10	22	45	60	–15	52
18	Yeovil T	46	9	4	10	19	27	5	6	12	19	32	14	10	22	38	59	–21	52
19	Cheltenham T	46	10	8	5	23	21	3	4	16	19	43	13	12	21	42	64	–22	51
20	Crewe Alex	46	8	6	9	27	33	4	8	11	20	32	12	14	20	47	65	–18	50
21	Bournemouth†	46	10	4	9	31	35	7	3	13	31	37	17	7	22	62	72	–10	48
22	Gillingham	46	9	9	5	26	22	2	4	17	18	51	11	13	22	44	73	–29	46
23	Port Vale	46	5	8	10	26	35	4	3	16	21	46	9	11	26	47	81	–34	38
24	Luton T†	46	10	5	8	29	25	1	5	17	14	38	11	10	25	43	63	–20	33

** Leeds U deducted 15 points; † Bournemouth and Luton Town deducted 10 points.*

COCA–COLA FOOTBALL LEAGUE DIVISION 2

		Home						Away					Total						
		P	*W*	*D*	*L*	*F*	*A*	*W*	*D*	*L*	*F*	*A*	*W*	*D*	*L*	*F*	*A*	*GD*	*Pts*
1	Milton Keynes D	46	11	7	5	39	17	18	3	2	43	20	29	10	7	82	37	45	97
2	Peterborough U	46	14	4	5	46	20	14	4	5	38	23	28	8	10	84	43	41	92
3	Hereford U	46	11	6	6	34	19	15	4	4	38	22	26	10	10	72	41	31	88
4	Stockport Co	46	11	5	7	40	30	13	5	5	32	24	24	10	12	72	54	18	82
5	Rochdale	46	11	4	8	37	28	12	7	4	40	26	23	11	12	77	54	23	80
6	Darlington	46	11	7	5	36	22	11	5	7	31	18	22	12	12	67	40	27	78
7	Wycombe W	46	13	6	4	29	15	9	6	8	27	27	22	12	12	56	42	14	78
8	Chesterfield	46	9	8	6	42	29	10	4	9	34	27	19	12	15	76	56	20	69
9	Rotherham U*	46	12	4	7	37	29	9	7	7	25	29	21	11	14	62	58	4	64
10	Bradford C	46	10	4	9	30	30	7	7	9	33	31	17	11	18	63	61	2	62
11	Morecambe	46	9	6	8	33	32	7	6	10	26	31–16	12	18	59	63		4	60
12	Barnet	46	10	6	7	37	30	6	6	11	19	33	16	12	18	56	63	–7	60
13	Bury	46	8	6	9	30	30	8	5	10	28	31	16	11	19	58	61	–3	59
14	Brentford	46	7	5	11	25	35	10	3	10	27	35	17	8	21	52	70	–18	59
15	Lincoln C	46	9	3	11	33	38	9	1	13	28	39	18	4	24	61	77	–16	58
16	Grimsby T	46	7	5	11	26	34	8	5	10	29	32	15	10	21	55	66	–11	55
17	Accrington S	46	7	1	15	20	39	9	2	12	29	44	16	3	27	49	83	–34	51
18	Shrewsbury T	46	9	6	8	31	22	3	8	12	25	43	12	14	20	56	65	–9	50
19	Macclesfield T	46	6	8	9	27	31	5	9	9	20	33	11	17	18	47	64	–17	50
20	Dagenham & R	46	6	7	10	27	32	7	3	13	22	38	13	10	23	49	70	–21.	49
21	Notts Co	46	8	5	10	19	23	2	13	8	18	30	10	18	18	37	53	–16	48
22	Chester C	46	5	5	13	21	30	7	6	10	30	38	12	11	23	51	68	–17	47
23	Mansfield T	46	6	3	14	30	39	5	6	12	18	29	11	9	26	48	68	–20	42
24	Wrexham	46	6	7	10	16	28	4	3	16	22	42	10	10	26	38	70	–32	40

** Rotherham U deducted 10 points.*

FOOTBALL LEAGUE PLAY-OFFS 2007–08

▪ *Denotes player sent off.*

CHAMPIONSHIP FIRST LEG

Saturday, 10 May 2008

Crystal Palace (0) 1 *(Watson 87 (pen))*

Bristol C (0) 2 *(Carey 53, Noble 90)* 22,869

Crystal Palace: Speroni; Butterfield, Hill, Watson, Hudson, Fonte, Soares, Derry (Lawrence), Moses (Scowcroft) (Ifill), Morrison, Sinclair.

Bristol C: Basso; Orr, McAllister, Noble (Johnson), Carey, McCombe, Carle, Elliott, Trundle (Fontaine), Adebola, McIndoe.

Sunday, 11 May 2008

Watford (0) 0

Hull C (2) 2 *(Barmby 8, Windass 23)* 14,713

Watford: Lee; Doyley (O'Toole), Sadler, Eustace▪, Shittu (DeMerit), Bromby, McAnuff, Williamson, Ellington, Ainsworth (Priskin), Smith.

Hull C: Myhill; Ricketts, Dawson, Ashbee, Turner, Brown, Barmby (Fagan), Hughes, Campbell, Windass (Folan), Garcia (Doyle).

CHAMPIONSHIP SECOND LEG

Tuesday, 13 May 2008

Bristol C (0) 2 *(Trundle 104, McIndoe 110)*

Crystal Palace (1) 1 *(Watson 24)* 18,842

Bristol C: Basso; Orr, McAllister, Carle (Fontaine), Carey, McCombe, Noble (Sproule), Elliott, Trundle (Johnson), Adebola, McIndoe.

Crystal Palace: Speroni; Butterfield, Hill, Watson, Hudson, Lawrence (Fonte), Soares, Derry (Moses), Sinclair (Ifill), Morrison, Scannell.

aet.

Wednesday, 14 May 2008

Hull C (1) 4 *(Barmby 43, Folan 70, Garcia 88, Doyle 90)*

Watford (1) 1 *(Henderson 12)* 23,155

Hull C: Myhill; Ricketts, Dawson, Ashbee, Turner, Brown, Garcia, Barmby (Fagan), Campbell (Doyle), Windass (Folan), Hughes.

Watford: Lee; Mariappa (Priskin), Sadler, Eustace, Bromby, DeMerit, McAnuff, Williamson, Henderson, Ellington (Ainsworth), Smith.

CHAMPIONSHIP FINAL (AT WEMBLEY)

Saturday, 24 May 2008

Bristol C (0) 0

Hull C (1) 1 *(Windass 38)* 86,703

Bristol C: Basso; Orr (Johnson), McAllister, Carle (Byfield), Carey, Fontaine, Noble (Sproule), Elliott, Trundle, Adebola, McIndoe.

Hull C: Myhill; Ricketts, Dawson, Ashbee, Turner, Brown, Garcia, Barmby (Fagan), Campbell (Marney), Windass (Folan), Hughes.

Referee: A. Wiley (Staffordshire).

LEAGUE 1 FIRST LEG

Friday, 9 May 2008

Southend U (0) 0

Doncaster R (0) 0 9109

Southend U: Flahavan; Francis, Mulgrew, Bailey, Clarke P, Barrett, Black (Revell), McCormack, Barnard, Walker, Gower.

Doncaster R: Sullivan; O'Connor, Roberts G, Hird, Mills, Stock, Green, Guy (Hayter), Heffernan▪, Price (McCammon), Coppinger (Taylor).

Monday, 12 May 2008

Leeds U (0) 1 *(Freedman 90)*

Carlisle U (1) 2 *(Graham 32, Bridge-Wilkinson 50)* 36,297

Leeds U: Ankergren; Richardson, Johnson, Kilkenny, Michalik, Huntington, Prutton (Carole), Howson (Hughes), Beckford (Kandol), Freedman, Douglas.

Carlisle U: Westwood; Arnison, Horwood, Smith G (Thirlwell), Livesey, Murphy, Dobie, Bridge-Wilkinson, Graham (Madine), Hackney (Taylor), Lumsdon.

Doncaster's James Hayter (right) scores the only goal against Leeds United in the League 1 play-off final at Wembley. (Action Images/Scott Heavey/Livepic)

Liam Dickinson (left) and Anthony Pilkington celebrate with the League 2 play-off trophy after their well-deserved 3-2 win over Rochdale at Wembley. (Empics Sport/PA Photos/Joe Giddens)

LEAGUE 1 SECOND LEG

Thursday, 15 May 2008

Carlisle U (0) 0

Leeds U (1) 2 *(Howson 10, 90)* 12,873

Carlisle U: Westwood; Raven, Horwood, Smith G, Livesey, Murphy, Dobie, Bridge-Wilkinson, Graham, Hackney, Lumsdon.
Leeds U: Ankergren; Richardson, Johnson, Kilkenny, Michalik, Huntington, Prutton, Howson, Beckford, Freedman, Douglas.

Friday, 16 May 2008

Doncaster R (3) 5 *(Stock 11 (pen), Coppinger 39, 52, 80, Barrett 21 (og))*

Southend U (0) 1 *(Bailey 88)* 13,081

Doncaster R: Sullivan; O'Connor, Roberts G (Guy), Hird, Mills, Stock, Green, Wellens (McCammon), Hayter, Price (Taylor), Coppinger.
Southend U: Flahavan; Francis, Mulgrew, Bailey, Clarke P, Barrett, Moussa, McCormack, Barnard (Revell), Walker (MacDonald), Gower.

LEAGUE 1 FINAL (AT WEMBLEY)

Sunday, 25 May 2008

Doncaster R (0) 1 *(Hayter 48)*

Leeds U (0) 0 75,132

Doncaster R: Sullivan; O'Connor, Roberts G, Hird, Mills, Stock, Green, Wellens (McCammon), Hayter, Price (Lockwood), Coppinger (Guy).
Leeds U: Ankergren; Richardson, Johnson, Kilkenny, Michalik, Huntington, Prutton (Kandol), Howson, Beckford, Freedman (Hughes), Douglas.
Referee: A. D'Urso (Essex).

LEAGUE 2 FIRST LEG

Saturday, 10 May 2008

Darlington (1) 2 *(Kennedy 28, Miller 90)*

Rochdale (0) 1 *(Dagnall 70)* 8057

Darlington: Stockdale; Wiseman, Purdie, Ravenhill, Foster, White (Miller), Joachim, Parker (Ndumbu-Nsungu), Kennedy, Wright (Wainwright), Cummins.
Rochdale: Lee; Ramsden, Kennedy, Jones, D'Laryea (Holness), McArdle, Higginbotham, Perkins, Howe, Dagnall (Le Fondre), Rundle (Muirhead).

Sunday, 11 May 2008

Wycombe W (1) 1 *(Facey 37)*

Stockport Co (0) 1 *(Gleeson 82)* 6371

Wycombe W: Fielding; Martin, Woodman, Oakes, Johnson, Williamson, Doherty (Phillips), Torres, Facey (Sutton), McGleish (Knight), Holt.
Stockport Co: Ruddy; James Smith, Rose, Turnbull, Raynes (McNulty), Owen, Pilkington, Dicker, Rowe (McSweeney), Dickinson, Blizzard (Gleeson).

LEAGUE 2 SECOND LEG

Saturday, 17 May 2008

Rochdale (1) 2 *(Dagnall 43, Perkins 78)*

Darlington (1) 1 *(Keltie 28 (pen))* 9870

Rochdale: Lee; Ramsden, Kennedy, Jones, Stanton, McArdle, Higginbotham (Muirhead), Perkins■, Howe (Le Fondre), Dagnall, Rundle (Doolan).
Darlington: Stockdale; Wiseman, Purdie, Ravenhill, Foster, White, Joachim, Keltie (Nelthorpe), Wainwright, Kennedy, Cummins (Ndumbu-Nsungu).
aet; Rochdale won 5-4 on penalties.

Stockport Co (1) 1 *(Dickinson 7)*

Wycombe W (0) 0 9245

Stockport Co: Logan C; James Smith, Rose, McSweeney (Pilkington), McNulty, Owen, Rowe, Dicker, Turnbull, Dickinson (Tunnicliffe), Gleeson (Taylor).
Wycombe W: Fielding; Martin, Woodman (Sutton), Oakes, Johnson, Williamson, Doherty, Torres (Knight), Facey, McGleish, Holt.

LEAGUE 2 FINAL (AT WEMBLEY)

Monday, 26 May 2008

Stockport Co (1) 3 *(Stanton 34 (og), Pilkington 49, Dickinson 67)*

Rochdale (1) 2 *(McArdle 23, Rundle 77)* 35,715

Stockport Co: Logan C; James Smith, Rose, Turnbull, McNulty, Owen, Pilkington, Dicker, Rowe, Dickinson (McNeil), Gleeson (McSweeney).
Rochdale: Lee; Ramsden, Kennedy, D'Laryea (Buckley), Stanton, McArdle, Higginbotham (Muirhead), Jones, Le Fondre (Howe), Dagnall, Rundle.
Referee: S. Attwell (Warwickshire).

LEADING GOALSCORERS 2007–08

BARCLAYS PREMIERSHIP	League	Carling Cup	FA Cup	Other	Total
Players in this competition scoring eleven or more League goals are listed. Other leading scorers classified by total number of goals in all competitions. Only goals scored in the same division are included.					
Cristiano Ronaldo *(Manchester U)*	31	0	3	8	42
Fernando Torres *(Liverpool)*	24	3	0	6	33
Emmanuel Adebayor *(Arsenal)*	24	1	2	3	30
Roque Santa Cruz *(Blackburn R)*	19	3	0	1	23
Dimitar Berbatov *(Tottenham H)*	15	1	2	5	23
Robbie Keane *(Tottenham H)*	15	2	2	4	23
Ayegbeni Yakubu *(Everton)*	15	3	0	3	21
Benjani Mwaruwari *(Manchester C)*	15	0	0	0	15
(Includes 12 League goals for Portsmouth.)					
Carlos Tevez *(Manchester U)*	14	0	1	4	19
John Carew *(Aston Villa)*	13	0	0	0	13
Wayne Rooney *(Manchester U)*	12	0	2	4	18
Jermain Defoe *(Portsmouth)*	12	1	0	3	16
(Includes 4 League goals, 1 Carling Cup and 3 other goals for Tottenham H.)					
Steven Gerrard *(Liverpool)*	11	1	3	6	21
Nicolas Anelka *(Chelsea)*	11	0	0	1	12
(Includes 10 League and 1 other goal for Bolton W.)					
Michael Owen *(Newcastle U)*	11	1	1	0	13
Frank Lampard *(Chelsea)*	10	4	2	4	20
In order of total goals:					
Didier Drogba *(Chelsea)*	8	1	0	6	15
Cese Fabregas *(Arsenal)*	7	0	0	6	13
COCA-COLA CHAMPIONSHIP					
Sylvain Ebanks-Blake*(Wolverhampton W)*	23	1	1	0	25
(Includes 11 League, 1 Carling Cup and 1 FA Cup goal for Plymouth Arg.)					
Kevin Phillips *(WBA)*	22	0	2	0	24
James Beattie *(Sheffield U)*	22	0	0	0	22
Stern John *(Southampton)*	19	0	0	0	19
Kevin Lisbie *(Colchester U)*	17	0	0	0	17
Clinton Morrison *(Crystal Palace)*	16	0	0	0	16
Fraizer Campbell *(Hull C)*	15	0	0	0	15
(on loan from Manchester U)					
Ricardo Fuller *(Stoke C)*	15	0	0	0	15
Liam Lawrence *(Stoke C)*	14	0	1	0	15
Roman Bednar *(WBA)*	13	0	4	0	17
Andy Gray *(Charlton Ath)*	13	2	0	0	15
(Includes 11 League and 2 Carling Cup goals for Burnley.)					
Jamie Cureton *(Norwich C)*	12	2	9	9	14
Brian Howard *(Barnsley)*	13	0	1	0	14
Martin Paterson *(Scunthorpe U)*	13	1	0	0	14
COCA-COLA LEAGUE 1					
Jason Scotland *(Swansea C)*	24	1	2	2	29
Jason Beckford *(Leeds U)*	20	0	0	0	20
Nicky Forster *(Brighton & HA)*	15	0	2	2	19
Simon Cox *(Swindon T)*	15	0	0	1	16
Danny Graham *(Carlisle U)*	14	1	0	2	17
Nicky Maynard *(Crewe Alex)*	14	0	0	0	14
Joe Garner *(Carlisle U)*	14	0	0	0	14
Rickie Lambert *(Bristol R)*	14	0	6	0	20
Adam Boyd *(Leyton Orient)*	14	1	2	0	17
Steven Gillespie *(Cheltenham T)*	14	0	2	0	16
Richard Barker *(Hartlepool U)*	13	0	2	1	16
Junior Agogo *(Nottingham F)*	13	0	0	0	13
Poul Hubertz *(Northampton T)*	13	0	0	0	13
Andy Kirk *(Yeovil T)*	12	1	2	0	15
(Includes 8 League, 1 Carling Cup and 2 FA Cup goals for Northampton T.)					
Jo Osei-Kuffour *(Bournemouth)*	12	0	0	1	13
COCA-COLA LEAGUE 2					
Aaron McLean *(Peterborough U)*	29	0	3	1	33
Scott McGleish *(Wycombe W)*	25	0	0	0	25
Jack Lester *(Chesterfield)*	23	1	1	0	25
Michael Boulding *(Mansfield T)*	20	0	3	0	23
Liam Dickinson *(Stockport Co)*	19	0	0	2	21
Andy Bishop *(Bury)*	19	0	5	1	25
Adam Le Fondre *(Rochdale)*	16	0	1	0	17
Ben Strevens *(Dagenham & R)*	15	1	3	1	20
Ben Wright *(Lincoln C)*	15	0	0	0	15
Peter Thorne *(Bradford C)*	14	0	1	0	15
Glenn Poole *(Brentford)*	14	0	0	0	14
Mark Wright *(Milton Keynes D)*	13	0	0	2	15
Theo Robinson *(Hereford U)*	13	1	2	0	16
(On loan from Watford.)					
Anthony Elding *(Stockport Co)*	13	1	0	1	15
(Transferred to Leeds U January 2008.)					

Other matches consist of European games, J Paint Trophy, Community Shield and Football League play-offs. Players listed in order of League goals total.

REVIEW OF THE SEASON

So after a couple of hiccups on the way, once the ingredients of the 2007–2008 Premier League season had been digested, Manchester United had retained their title after all. Even so it did not run smoothly all the way through the campaign.

Moreover, just for a moment it seemed that the Cristiano Ronaldo-led Old Trafford charge to another Premiership was to be thwarted in sight of the promised finishing line when Chelsea beat them 2-1 at Stamford Bridge on 26 April. The Portuguese swashbuckler did not even start the game as a confident Sir Alex Ferguson indulged in a spot of tinkering with the team. It could have proved fatal. But while United recovered their poise, Chelsea had to be content with runners-up again and it added to the debit side of manager Avram Grant who had replaced Jose Mourinho earlier in the season and was to be forced to walk the plank.

Naturally in the context of the squad system, ever-present players are a rare species. In 2007–2008, the Premier League produced just 12 and amazingly just one of them, Stephen Kelly the Birmingham City full-back, succeeded in playing every one of the 90 minutes throughout the 38 matches.

Not surprisingly perhaps, in view of the previous comments, Manchester United did not have one. Of the 25 different players called upon, Wes Brown came the nearest, missing just two games, though two of his appearances were as a substitute. Rio Ferdinand turned out in 35 full matches while Ronaldo and Carlos Tevez, spirited away from West Ham United, both had 34 outings, including three from the bench.

Ronaldo, with 31 League goals, once again a dual PFA and FWA player of the year as in 2006–2007 was top scorer, and only the fourth in the Premier League's short history to top the 30-goal mark. Tevez had 14 goals, Wayne Rooney, who missed a number of matches with injury, scored 12 goals himself from a total of 27 appearances.

Owen Hargreaves, prised out of Germany after many years, recovered from his broken leg and made an invaluable contribution in several midfield and defensive roles, the evergreen Ryan Giggs broke several personal records and in the Champions League final his substitute appearance caught up with Sir Bobby Charlton's 759 first team games for the Old Trafford club.

Chelsea, also second in the Carling Cup to Tottenham Hotspur and of course to Manchester United again in the Champions League final, produced a hat-trick of disappointment. Their home record remains outstanding and the 85 points obtained, despite being the highest attained by a team failing to win such a 20-team competition, is of little consolation. Early defeats at Villa Park and Old Trafford put them on the back foot, but the last 21 fixtures saw them unbeaten.

Arsenal's 1000th Premier League goal celebrated by scorer Emmanuel Adebayor (left) and Francesc Fabregas. The 3-1 victory over Reading at the Madejski Stadium saw Arsenal return to the top of the table on 12 November. (AP/PA Photos/Alastair Grant)

By Arsenal's standards, third place was just as disappointing. Still top but drawing games in a row into March, they had scant reward one might say for losing just three times, significantly perhaps at Manchester United, Chelsea and Middlesbrough. United, of course, had suffered five reverses.

Such are the expectations in the top echelon, fourth for Liverpool was equally frustrating for the Merseyside club, though they did pip Merseyside rivals Everton. United achieved the double over them and their other two losses were at West Ham United and, surprisingly, Reading. With the exciting arrival of Fernando Torres to lead the Anfield attack, and responding with a 20-goal return for the outlay of the same in £millions, they failed by drawing 13 times. Manager Rafael Benitez was accused on many occasions of tinkering with his selection.

There had been a curious start to their Champions League campaign, too, but subsequently included a competition record-breaking 8-0 win over Besiktas. Rivals Everton, who had to concede fourth place to them when only two wins came in the last nine, also had some impact in the UEFA Cup. At times Aston Villa looked capable of even better things but 12 drawn affairs were unhelpful. Blackburn Rovers, too, came through the Intertoto Cup to play their UEFA Cup part, but domestically a mid-season run of one win in nine proved a setback.

Though after reaching the FA Cup final Portsmouth seemed to lose concentration, they had been involved in the highest-scoring aggregate in the Premier League when they beat Reading 7-4. Oddly enough they managed only seven goals in their entire but successful cup journey! Manchester City, who promised much earlier on with a host of foreign imports, faded and even Sven-Goran Eriksson departed at the close of business.

West Ham United looked mid-table, only once winning two in a row. Tottenham Hotspur were erratic, capable of high-scoring including a 6-4 win over Reading and heavy defeats throughout. They were also heavily involved in Europe. Newcastle United improved enough with the return of Kevin Keegan, but only after a barren spell of 11 games which yielded only four goals! Middlesbrough also showed inconsistency, but finished with a flourish beating Manchester City 8-1, their best performance in the Premiership. Wigan Athletic rallied well after a disastrous eight consecutive defeats, while Sunderland kept out of serious trouble in the last third of the season.

Bolton Wanderers also made a decent effort in the UEFA Cup and just escaped with an unbeaten run of five in the run-in. Fulham's survival was more dramatic, only two wins into February but Roy Hodgson's arrival culminated in four victories from the last five outings.

Less fortunate were Reading, Birmingham City and Derby County, the latter breaking all the worst records, who all suffered relegation. Reading developed a distinct lack of scoring, with only 12 coming from their last 18 – and these included four at Derby in the last match. Birmingham managed only isolated wins throughout the season and the Rams' many woes included just one win over Newcastle, fewest goals and 777 minutes without one at one time.

Dimitar Berbatov confidently equalises from the penalty spot for Tottenham Hotspur after 70 minutes of the Carling Cup Final at Wembley. Tottenham went on to secure victory with an extra-time winner from Jonathan Woodgate. (EMPICS Sport/PA Photos/Mike Egerton)

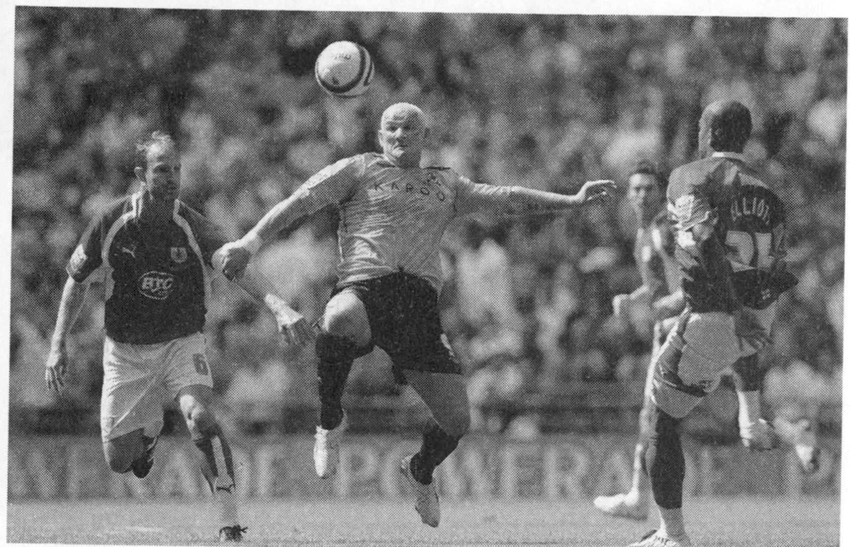

Dean Windass (centre) of Hull City challenged by Bristol City's Marvin Elliott (right) during the Championship play-off final at Wembley. The veteran striker scored the only goal of the game to send Hull to the top flight for the first time in their history. (Action Images/Eddie Keogh/Livepic)

Automatic promotion came for West Bromwich Albion and Stoke City. Albion had slipped a little after the turn of the year but regained top billing following an unbeaten sequence of nine matches at the end of season. Stoke's improvement was such that in late November they were as low as tenth but never out of the top two in the last quarter. Hull City emerged via the play-offs, disposing of Watford, then Bristol City in the final. Their turnaround was even more dramatic from the first half of the season when consistency was not a feature.

Fourth-placed Bristol City were top in mid-March but won just two of the last 11. Crystal Palace, beaten by City in the play-offs, had been second from the bottom in November and even recovered from another falter in February. However there was considerable disappointment for Watford, top in mid-December but then suffering a number of home reverses.

Not once did Ipswich Town win three in a row, Sheffield United staged a late rally, losing only two of the last 11, and Plymouth Argyle's best was four wins in a row from early February. Charlton Athletic, expected to do much better, managed wins spasmodically after the turn of the year.

For Cardiff City the consolation was reaching the FA Cup final. Eighth had been their highest position at one stage. Wolverhampton Wanderers flirted with the play-offfs and were third in December before an immediate disastrous run of eight matches without a win. Burnley were still eight in March but were unable to show further progress.

Queens Park Rangers, bottom in December, showed steady subsequent improvement, as did Preston North End from a similar position until a timely run of seven without defeat arrived. Sheffield Wednesday left it even later but in their last twelve there were seven successive draws and just one defeat.

A wretched start for Norwich City was forgotten for a time with 13 unbeaten, Barnsley recalled beating both Liverpool and Chelsea in the FA Cup but otherwise found goals hard to come by. Blackpool were able to step up a gear after the New Year while Southampton, in free-fall at one period, scraped enough points together when it mattered. Coventry City, in the top seven early in November, were restricted to a pattern of winning games here and there, but could count the scalp of Manchester United in the Carling Cup – at Old Trafford.

Sadly down went Leicester City, Scunthorpe United and Colchester United. Leicester had 19 games without scoring, Scunthorpe were never out of the bottom two from January and Colchester won only one of the last 15.

League One produced Swansea City and Nottingham Forest in first and second places. Swansea quickly shrugged off an indifferent opening, and a mid-season sequence of 18 without defeat set them up nicely. Forest slipped up after looking automatic candidates, but finished with a flourish losing only one of 13. Doncaster Rovers joined them through in the play-offs at the expense of points-penalised Leeds United after beating Southend United.

Doncaster solved their early season problems but Carlisle United, who became Leeds' victims, succeeded in gaining only one win in the last eight. Leeds had made light of their burden until ironically losing at Carlisle in November, but recovered after a blip from January. Southend were beaten only twice from mid-January, but Brighton & Hove Albion stayed just out of reach of the play-off zone.

Oldham Athletic's final position was their highest all season, as was that of Northampton Town, while one defeat out of nine was too little to help Huddersfield Town.

Tranmere Rovers, top in November, faltered at the end of the season, losing four of the last five. Walsall, fifth in early March, tailed off dramatically, and Swindon Town's next best was ten points from the last five games having gone nine undefeated earlier. Leyton Orient headed affairs in late November, but slowly fell back, while one success in the last nine was not enough to put Hartlepool into higher reckoning.

Bristol Rovers had to be satisfied with a useful FA Cup run, winning but one of the last 15. For Millwall, two wins in succession on three occasions was their best, three in a row Yeovil Town's marker and Cheltenham Town, not unused to last-ditch battles, did so again after only two wins in the first 16. Crewe Alexandra scored only 14 goals in a 21-game run, but survived as did others above them because of points deductions to other teams. Relegation came for Bournemouth, Gillingham, Port Vale and Luton Town. Bournemouth and Luton had points deducted for administration, too. Amazingly Bournemouth took 19 points from their last seven matches. Gillingham won a mere four games from the New Year, Port Vale scrambled two points from ten games to early March and Luton won two in the last half of the season.

Milton Keynes Dons, Peterborough United and Hereford United were the first-time teams promoted from League Two. The MK Dons might have clinched the title much earlier but for losing three on the trot in January, but reached the winning post unbeaten in the last 18. Additionally they took the Johnstone's Paint Trophy. Unusually, they won seven more away matches than at home, though this was a trait of the division as a whole. Free-scoring Peterborough managed an eight and a seven plus eight consecutive wins. Hereford showed consistency and were never out of the top four from early February. They were joined by Stockport County from the play-offs as, for the first time since they were introduced, the highest finishing team in all divisions were successful in this way. Stockport beat Rochdale in the final after taking out Wycombe Wanderers. Stockport set it up by dropping just two points from a possible 30. Unusually Rochdale had scored four goals on eight occasions, Darlington let down by winning two of the last 12, while Wycombe had never been out of the zone from Boxing Day.

Chesterfield's bid was nullified when they were left with too much to do from March, a points deduction for Rotherham United eroded what had been second place in December. Eight games without a win was Bradford City's worst run, while newcomers Morecambe had a satisfying first season with some cup successes, too. Failing to score in 18 games was Barnet's curse and what might have been for Bury was ruined by 12 without a win.

Brentford were yet another better away than at home, Lincoln City sufficiently put aside the trauma of an unlucky 13 without a victory, but previous good work was undone for Grimsby Town by losing the last seven. Accrington picked up enough wins to steer clear when it was required, but Shrewsbury fell like a stone from late January, winning only once. Macclesfield Town put on survival gear in March with four wins out of five, newcomers Dagenham & Redbridge had five wins in a row towards safety and goal-shy Notts County won two of the last four. Chester City, second in October and ninth in January, slumped to just two wins in the last 26. But it was Wrexham and Mansfield Town who were consigned to the Blue Square Premier. Mansfield were never out of the cellar positions from December, Wrexham rock bottom from February. They were replaced by two ex-League clubs, Aldershot Town (after 16 years' absence) and Exeter City.

Liverpool's Fernando Torres (centre) sees off the threat from West Ham United's Jonathan Spector to slide the ball past goalkeeper Robert Green to record his second hat-trick in successive games at Anfield. He became only the fourth player in the club's history to achieve the feat. (Action Images/Phil Noble/Livepic)

THE FA CHARITY SHIELD WINNERS 1908–2007

1908	Manchester U v QPR	4-0 after 1-1 draw
1909	Newcastle U v Northampton T	2-0
1910	Brighton v Aston Villa	1-0
1911	Manchester U v Swindon T	8-4
1912	Blackburn R v QPR	2-1
1913	Professionals v Amateurs	7-2
1920	WBA v Tottenham H	2-0
1921	Tottenham H v Burnley	2-0
1922	Huddersfield T v Liverpool	1-0
1923	Professionals v Amateurs	2-0
1924	Professionals v Amateurs	3-1
1925	Amateurs v Professionals	6-1
1926	Amateurs v Professionals	6-3
1927	Cardiff C v Corinthians	2-1
1928	Everton v Blackburn R	2-1
1929	Professionals v Amateurs	3-0
1930	Arsenal v Sheffield W	2-1
1931	Arsenal v WBA	1-0
1932	Everton v Newcastle U	5-3
1933	Arsenal v Everton	3-0
1934	Arsenal v Manchester C	4-0
1935	Sheffield W v Arsenal	1-0
1936	Sunderland v Arsenal	2-1
1937	Manchester C v Sunderland	2-0
1938	Arsenal v Preston NE	2-1
1948	Arsenal v Manchester U	4-3
1949	Portsmouth v Wolverhampton W	1-1*
1950	World Cup Team v Canadian Touring Team	4-2
1951	Tottenham H v Newcastle U	2-1
1952	Manchester U v Newcastle U	4-2
1953	Arsenal v Blackpool	3-1
1954	Wolverhampton W v WBA	4-4*
1955	Chelsea v Newcastle U	3-0
1956	Manchester U v Manchester C	1-0
1957	Manchester U v Aston Villa	4-0
1958	Bolton W v Wolverhampton W	4-1
1959	Wolverhampton W v Nottingham F	3-1
1960	Burnley v Wolverhampton W	2-2*
1961	Tottenham H v FA XI	3-2
1962	Tottenham H v Ipswich T	5-1
1963	Everton v Manchester U	4-0
1964	Liverpool v West Ham U	2-2*
1965	Manchester U v Liverpool	2-2*
1966	Liverpool v Everton	1-0
1967	Manchester U v Tottenham H	3-3*
1968	Manchester C v WBA	6-1
1969	Leeds U v Manchester C	2-1
1970	Everton v Chelsea	2-1
1971	Leicester C v Liverpool	1-0
1972	Manchester C v Aston Villa	1-0
1973	Burnley v Manchester C	1-0
1974	Liverpool† v Leeds U	1-1
1975	Derby Co v West Ham U	2-0
1976	Liverpool v Southampton	1-0
1977	Liverpool v Manchester U	0-0*
1978	Nottingham F v Ipswich T	5-0
1979	Liverpool v Arsenal	3-1
1980	Liverpool v West Ham U	1-0
1981	Aston Villa v Tottenham H	2-2*
1982	Liverpool v Tottenham H	1-0
1983	Manchester U v Liverpool	2-0
1984	Everton v Liverpool	1-0
1985	Everton v Manchester U	2-0
1986	Everton v Liverpool	1-1*
1987	Everton v Coventry C	1-0
1988	Liverpool v Wimbledon	2-1
1989	Liverpool v Arsenal	1-0
1990	Liverpool v Manchester U	1-1*
1991	Arsenal v Tottenham H	0-0*
1992	Leeds U v Liverpool	4-3
1993	Manchester U† v Arsenal	1-1
1994	Manchester U v Blackburn R	2-0
1995	Everton v Blackburn R	1-0
1996	Manchester U v Newcastle U	4-0
1997	Manchester U† v Chelsea	1-1
1998	Arsenal v Manchester U	3-0
1999	Arsenal v Manchester U	2-1
2000	Chelsea v Manchester U	2-0
2001	Liverpool v Manchester U	2-1
2002	Arsenal v Liverpool	1-0
2003	Manchester U† v Arsenal	1-1
2004	Arsenal v Manchester U	3-1
2005	Chelsea v Arsenal	2-1
2006	Liverpool v Chelsea	2-1
2007	Manchester U† v Chelsea	1-1

** Each club retained shield for six months. † Won on penalties.*

THE FA COMMUNITY SHIELD 2007

Chelsea (1) 1, Manchester United (1) 1

aet; Manchester U won 3-0 on penalties.

At Wembley Stadium, 5 August 2007, attendance 80,731

Chelsea: Cech; Johnson (Sidwell), Cole A (Diarra), Mikel, Ben Haim, Ricardo Carvalho, Wright-Phillips, Lampard, Cole J (Sinclair), Essien, Malouda (Pizarro).

Scorer: Malouda 45.

Manchester United: Van der Sar; Brown, Evra, Silvestre (Nani), Ferdinand, Vidic, Ronaldo, O'Shea, Rooney, Giggs (Fletcher), Carrick.

Scorer: Giggs 35.

Referee: M. Halsey (Lancashire).

ACCRINGTON STANLEY FL Championship 2

FOUNDATION

Accrington Football Club, founder members of the Football League in 1888, were not connected with Accrington Stanley. In fact both clubs ran concurrently between 1891 when Stanley were formed and 1895 when Accrington FC folded. Actually Stanley Villa was the original name, those responsible for forming the club living in Stanley Street and using the Stanley Arms as their meeting place. They became Accrington Stanley in 1893. In 1894–95 they joined the Accrington & District League, playing at Moorhead Park. Subsequently they played in the North-East Lancashire Combination and the Lancashire Combination before becoming founder members of the Third Division (North) in 1921, two years after moving to Peel Park. In 1962 they resigned from the Football League, were wound up, reformed 1963, disbanded in 1966 only to restart as Accrington Stanley (1968), returning to the Lancashire Combination in 1970.

The Fraser Eagle Stadium, Livingstone Road, Accrington, Lancashire BB5 5BX.

Telephone: (01254) 356 950.

Ticket Office: (01254) 356 950/(01254) 336 954.

Fax: (01254) 356 951.

Website: www.accringtonstanley.co.uk

Email: info@accringtonstanley.co.uk

Ground Capacity: 5,057.

Record Attendance: 4,368 v Colchester U, FA Cup 1st rd, 3 January 2004.

Pitch Measurements: 111yds × 72yds.

Chairman: Eric Whalley.

Vice-chairman: Peter Marsden.

Chief Executive: Robert Heys.

Secretary: Hannah Bailey.

Manager: John Coleman.

Assistant Manager: Jimmy Bell.

Physio: Ian Liversedge.

Club Nickname: 'Reds'.

Colours: Red shirts, white shorts, red stockings.

Change Colours: Blue shirts, blue shorts, blue stockings.

Year Formed: 1891, reformed 1968.

Turned Professional: 1919.

Grounds: 1891, Moorhead Park; 1897, Bell's Ground; 1919, Peel Park; 1970, Crown Inn.

HONOURS

Football League: Division 3 (N) – Runners-up 1954–55, 1957–58.

Conference: Champions 2005–06.

FA Cup: 4th rd 1927, 1937, 1959.

Football League Cup: never past 2nd rd.

Northern Premier League: Champions 2002–03.

Northern League: Division 1 – Champions 1999–2000.

North West Counties: Runners-up 1986–87.

Cheshire County League: Division 2 – Champions 1980–81; Runners-up 1979–80.

Lancashire Combination: Champions 1973–74, 1977–78; Runners-up 1971–72, 1975–76.

Lancashire Combination Cup: Winners 1971–72, 1972–73, 1973–74, 1976–77.

SKY SPORTS FACT FILE

John Jepson scored a hat-trick for Accrington Stanley at Wrexham on 24 October 1925 in a 6–5 win. A month later he hit three against them in a 4–0 success in the FA Cup and yet another trio on 2 March in a 4–2 home League win.

First Football League Game: 27 August 1921, Division 3 (N), v Rochdale (a) L 3-6 – Tattersall; Newton, Baines, Crawshaw, Popplewell, Burkinshaw, Oxley, Makin, Green (1), Hosker (2), Hartles.

Record League Victory: 8-0 v New Brighton, Division 3 (N), 17 March 1934 – Maidment; Armstrong (pen), Price, Dodds, Crawshaw, McCulloch, Wyper, Lennox (2), Cheetham (4), Leedham (1), Watson.

Record Cup Victory: 7-0 v Spennymoor U, FA Cup 2nd rd, 8 December 1938 – Tootill; Armstrong, Whittaker, Latham, Curran, Lee, Parry (2), Chadwick, Jepson (3), McLoughlin (2), Barclay.

Record Defeat: 9-1 v Lincoln C, Division 3 (N), 3 March 1951.

Most League Points (2 for a win): 61, Division 3 (N), 1954–55.

Most League Points (3 for a win): 50, FL 2, 2006–07.

Most League Goals: 96, Division 3 (N) 1954–55.

Highest League Scorer in Season: George Stewart, 35, 1955–56 Division 3 (N); George Hudson, 35, 1960–61, Division 4.

Most League Goals in Total Aggregate: George Stewart, 136, 1954–58.

Most League Goals in One Match: 5, Billy Harker v Gateshead, Division 3 (N), 16 November 1935; George Stewart v Gateshead, Division 3 (N), 27 November 1954.

Most Capped Player: Romuald Boco, (17), Benin.

Most League Appearances: Jim Armstrong, 260, 1927–34.

Record Transfer Fee Received: £180,000 from Ipswich T for Gary Roberts, January 2007.

Record Transfer Fee Paid: £85,000 to Swansea C for Ian Craney, January 2008

Football League Record: Original members of Division 3 (N) 1921–58; Division 3 1958–60; Division 4 1960–62; FL 2 2006–.

MANAGERS

William Cronshaw *c.*1894
John Haworth 1897–1910
Johnson Haworth c.1916
Sam Pilkingson 1919–24
(Tommy Booth p-m 1923–24)
Ernie Blackburn 1924–32
Amos Wade 1932–35
John Hacking 1935–49
Jimmy Porter 1949–51
Walter Crook 1951–53
Walter Galbraith 1953–58
George Eastham snr 1958–59
Harold Bodle 1959–60
James Harrower 1960–61
Harold Mather 1962–63
Jimmy Hinksman 1963–64
Terry Neville 1964–65
Ian Bryson 1965
Danny Parker 1965–66
John Coleman May 1999–

LATEST SEQUENCES

Longest Sequence of League Wins: 7, 27.12.1954 – 5.2.1955.

Longest Sequence of League Defeats: 9, 8.3.1030 – 21.4.1930.

Longest Sequence of League Draws: 4, 10.9.1927 – 27.9.1927.

Longest Sequence of Unbeaten League Matches: 11, 27.11.1954 – 5.2.1955.

Longest Sequence Without a League Win: 18, 17.9.1938 – 31.12.1938.

Successive Scoring Runs: 22 from 14.11.1936.

Successive Non-scoring Runs: 5 from 15.3.1930.

TEN YEAR LEAGUE RECORD

		P	*W*	*D*	*L*	*F*	*A*	*Pts*	*Pos*
1998-99	U Pr	42	9	9	24	47	77	36	22
1999-2000	U D I	42	25	9	8	96	43	84	1
2000-01	U Pr	44	18	10	16	72	67	64	9
2001-02	U Pr	44	21	9	14	89	64	72	6
2002-03	U Pr	44	30	10	4	97	44	100	1
2003-04	Conf	42	15	13	14	68	61	58	10
2004-05	Conf	42	18	11	13	72	58	65	10
2005-06	Conf	42	28	7	7	76	45	91	1
2006-07	FL 2	46	13	11	22	70	81	50	20
2007-08	FL 2	46	16	3	27	49	83	51	17

DID YOU KNOW ?

On 20 January 1923, Bradford Park Avenue were leading Accrington Stanley 3–0 before a recovery produced a turnaround in the losers' fortunes. They scored four times for a narrow win. Bradford were runners-up that season, Accrington finishing eighth.

ACCRINGTON STANLEY 2007–08 LEAGUE RECORD

Match No.	Date	Venue	Opponents	Result		H/T Score	Lg. Pos.	Goalscorers	Attendance
1	Aug 11	A	Wycombe W	W	1-0	0-0	—	Mullin 58	4408
2	18	H	Darlington	L	0-3	0-1	11		1805
3	25	A	Lincoln C	L	0-2	0-1	20		3189
4	Sept 1	H	Peterborough U	L	0-2	0-0	24		1484
5	8	H	Grimsby T	W	4-1	1-0	16	Proctor 2 (1 pen) 29 (p), 90, Mullin 2 48, 69	1350
6	15	A	Shrewsbury T	L	0-2	0-1	18		5789
7	22	H	Mansfield T	W	1-0	1-0	15	Mullin 26	1408
8	29	A	Bury	L	1-2	0-0	19	Mullin 46	2784
9	Oct 2	A	Bradford C	W	3-0	2-0	—	D'Sane 2 2, 32, Proctor 61	13,346
10	5	H	Wrexham	L	0-2	0-1	—		1822
11	14	A	Dagenham & R	W	3-1	2-1	12	McGivern 16, Proctor 27, Mullin 78	1596
12	19	H	Macclesfield T	W	3-2	0-0	—	D'Sane 2 51, 74, Mullin 54	1792
13	27	A	Barnet	D	2-2	0-0	10	Craney 51, D'Sane 83	2178
14	Nov 3	H	Notts Co	L	0-2	0-1	12		1722
15	6	A	Morecambe	W	1-0	1-0	—	Cresswell (og) 13	2814
16	17	H	Rotherham U	L	0-1	0-0	12		1918
17	24	A	Hereford U	D	0-0	0-0	12		2804
18	Dec 5	H	Rochdale	L	1-2	1-0	—	Craney 23	1621
19	8	A	Milton Keynes D	L	0-5	0-3	15		6917
20	15	H	Chesterfield	W	2-1	0-1	13	Proctor (pen) 74, D'Sane 89	1448
21	22	H	Shrewsbury T	L	1-2	1-0	13	Mullin 39	1410
22	26	A	Grimsby T	W	2-1	0-1	12	Mullin 48, Proctor 58	4240
23	29	A	Mansfield T	W	2-1	0-0	12	Mullin 75, Proctor (pen) 90	2494
24	Jan 1	H	Bradford C	L	0-2	0-0	13		2898
25	5	H	Chester C	D	3-3	1-1	13	Proctor 37, Craney 63, D'Sane 74	1311
26	12	A	Stockport Co	L	0-2	0-2	15		4714
27	15	A	Peterborough U	L	2-8	0-4	—	Mullin 46, Whalley 62	4257
28	29	A	Darlington	L	0-1	0-1	—		2808
29	Feb 2	H	Wycombe W	L	0-2	0-1	17		1200
30	9	A	Chester C	W	3-2	1-2	16	Thomas 2 14, 68, Craney 90	1957
31	12	H	Lincoln C	L	0-3	0-1	—		1281
32	16	A	Brentford	L	1-3	1-2	17	Craney 39	4635
33	23	H	Stockport Co	L	0-2	0-1	17		2576
34	26	H	Brentford	W	1-0	1-0	—	Richardson 31	1149
35	Mar 1	A	Rotherham U	W	1-0	0-0	15	Craney 64	3683
36	8	H	Hereford U	L	0-2	0-1	15		1262
37	12	H	Morecambe	W	3-2	1-1	—	Kempson 43, Mangan 72, Mullin 73	1448
38	16	A	Rochdale	L	1-4	1-1	15	Whalley 34	3247
39	22	A	Chesterfield	L	2-4	2-1	15	Proctor 2 (1 pen) 23, 31 (p)	3274
40	24	H	Milton Keynes D	L	0-1	0-0	17		1559
41	29	A	Macclesfield T	L	1-2	1-2	17	Craney 31	1853
42	Apr 4	H	Dagenham & R	W	1-0	0-0	—	Edwards 47	1262
43	12	A	Notts Co	L	0-1	0-1	17		5525
44	19	H	Barnet	L	0-2	0-0	18		1288
45	26	A	Wrexham	W	3-1	2-0	17	Pejic (og) 7, Cavanagh 28, Whalley 72	3657
46	May 3	H	Bury	L	0-2	0-2	17		2566

Final League Position: 17

GOALSCORERS

League (49): Mullin 12, Proctor 10 (4 pens), Craney 7, D'Sane 7, Whalley 3, Thomas 2, Cavanagh 1, Edwards 1, Kempson 1, Mangan 1, McGivern 1, Richardson 1, own goals 2.
Carling Cup (0).
FA Cup (2): Cavanagh 1, Mullin 1.
J Paint Trophy (2): D'Sane 1, Proctor 1 (pen).

Arthur K 24	Cavanagh P 19	Proctor A 40 + 3	Williams R 23 + 3	Roberts M 33 + 1	Harris J 38 + 3	Branch G 19 + 3	Boco R 6 + 5	McEvilly L 3 + 8	Mullin P 43	Miles J 12 + 4	Brown D 8 + 7	McGivern L 2 + 10	Whalley S 14 + 17	Edwards P 28 + 3	Richardson L 33 + 4	McGrail C — + 1	D'Sane R 18 + 4	Webb S 18	Carden P 4	Craney I 34	Dunbavin I 22 + 1	Dennehy B 2 + 5	Todd A 14 + 7	King M 4 + 2	Doughty P 3	Thomas A 13	Grant R 5 + 2	Turner C — + 1	Mannix D 9 + 3	Mangan A 3 + 4	Kempson D 8	Smith A — + 1	Bell J 2	Murphy P 2	*Match No.*
1	2	3	4	5	6	7	8	9	10	11^{1}	12																								1
1	2	3	4	5	6	7^{1}	8	9	10	11^{2}		12	13																						2
1		7	4	5	6^{1}		8^{2}	9	10^{3}	11	12		13	2	3	14																			3
1		7	4	5	6	$3^{\blacksquare}$	8	$12^{\blacksquare}$	10	9^{1}	13		11^{3}		2^{2}		14																		4
1	2	8	4	5	6	3^{1}			10	11^{2}	7		13	12	14		9^{3}																		5
1	2^{3}	8	5	6	$4^{\blacksquare}$	3	12		10	11^{2}	7		13		14		9^{1}																		6
1	2	4	5	6		8^{3}	12	13	10		7				14		9^{2}	3	11^{1}																7
1	2	4	5	6		11^{3}		12	10		9^{1}				13		14	3	7^{2}	8															8
1^{6}	2^{1}	4	5	6				12	10		13				7		9	3	11	8^{2}	15														9
	2	4	5	6				12	10	13	7^{2}		14		3^{3}		9^{1}	8	11		1														10
	2	4	5	6	8	3			10		9	11^{1}			7		12				1														11
	2	4	5	6	7	8	12		10	11^{1}					3		9				1														12
	2	4	5	6	8	3			10	12	13				7^{1}		9			11^{2}	1														13
	2	4	5	6	7	3			10	12			11^{1}				9			8	1														14
	2	4	3	6	7	11^{1}		12	10								9	5		8	1														15
	2	4	5	6	7		11^{2}	12	10^{1}			14	13	3			9^{3}			8	1														16
		4	2	5	7	11^{2}	13		10			12			3		9^{1}	6		8	1														17
		4^{1}	5	6	7	3^{3}	12		10		13	9^{2}			2			11		8	1	14													18
		4	5	6^{3}	7		9^{1}			12	10^{2}		13	2	3			11		8	1	14													19
		12	5	6	7	3^{2}			10	4^{1}			14	13	2		9			8	1	11^{3}													20
		4	5	6	7	3^{3}			10	11^{2}		12	13	14	2		9^{1}			8	1														21
		4	12	6	7				10	11^{1}				2	3		9	5		8	1														22
		4		6	7				10	11				2	3		9^{1}	5		8	1	12													23
		4		6	7				10	11^{2}	12	13		2	3^{1}		9	5			1	14	8^{3}												24
		4	12	6	7^{2}				10					3	2		9	5^{1}		8	1	13	11												25
		4	5	6	11			12	10^{1}			13	14	2			9^{2}			8	1		7^{3}	3											26
		4	12	6^{1}	7				10				13	2			14	5		8	1	11^{2}	9^{3}	3											27
		4	2^{1}		7	12			10			13	14	5	3					8	1		11^{3}	9^{2}	6										28
		4			7^{3}	6			10				13	3	2					8	1		11^{2}	9^{1}		5	12	14							29
		4		6^{1}	8^{2}	2			10				12	11	3					9	1		13	14		5			7^{3}						30
		4			7				10				11	2	3					9	1		8		6	5									31
1		4			7^{1}				10				11	2	3					9			8^{2}	12	6	5			13						32
1		4							10			12	11^{1}	3	2			6		9			8			5			7^{2}	13					33
1		12		5	11^{1}				10				13	4	3			6		8			14			2			7^{2}	9^{3}					34
1		12		5	11^{1}				10					2	3					8						4			7	9	6				35
1				5	11^{2}				10				13	4	3					8			12			2			7	9^{1}	6				36
1					8				10				11	2	3			5		9^{1}						4			7	12	6				37
1				5^{1}	8^{2}				10			12	11	2	3					9			13			4			7^{3}	14	6				38
1		7		5	8^{1}	13							11	2	3					9			12			4			10^{2}		6				39
1		4			8	12					10^{1}		11^{2}	2	3					9			7			5				13	6				40
1		4			8^{1}				10				11	2	3					9			7			$5^{\blacksquare}$	12				6				41
1	2	4			12				10				11^{1}	5	$3^{\blacksquare}$					9			7^{2}				8		13		6				42
1	2	4			12	3			10				13	5				6		9			8^{1}				11		7^{2}						43
1	2	4^{1}			7				10				11	5	3			6		8			12				9^{2}					13			44
1	2^{1}	7			13				10				11	5	3					9^{3}			12				8^{2}		14				4	6	45
1	2	4		12	8				10			13	11	5									7				9^{2}						3^{1}	6	46

FA Cup
First Round — Huddersfield T — (h) — 2-3

Carling Cup
First Round — Leicester C — (h) — 0-1

J Paint Trophy
First Round — Oldham Ath — (h) — 2-3

ALDERSHOT TOWN FL Championship 2

FOUNDATION

It was through the initiative of Councillor Jack White, a local newsagent, who immediately captured the interest of the Town Clerk D. Llewellyn Griffiths, that Aldershot Town was formed in 1926. Having established a limited liability company under the chairmanship of Norman Clinton, an Aldershot resident and chairman of the Hampshre County FA, they rented the Recreation Ground from the Aldershot Borough Council. Admitted to the Southern League for 1927–28, they were elected to the Football League in 1932 but were removed from the competition in March 1992 and their record expunged. Re-formed almost immediately as Aldershot Town Football Club.

The EBB Stadium at the Recreation Ground, High Street, Aldershot GU11 1TW.

Telephone: 01252 320211.

Fax: 01252 324347.

Ticket Office: 01252 320211.

Website: www.theshots.co.uk

Ground capacity: 7,500.

Record Attendance: 19,138 v Carlisle U, FA Cup 4th rd (replay), 28 January 1970.

Pitch Measurements: 117yd × 75yd.

Chairman: John McGinty.

Chief Executive: Doug Wilson.

Secretary: Graham Hortop.

Manager: Gary Waddock.

Assistant Manager: Martin Kuhl.

Physio: Jim Joyce.

Colours: All red with blue trim.

Change Colours: All dark blue with red trim.

Year Formed: 1926.

Turned Professional: 1927.

Ltd Co.: 1927.

Previous Names: 1926, Aldershot Town; c.1937 Aldershot; 1992, Aldershot Town.

Club nickname: 'The Shots'.

Ground: 1927, Recreation Ground.

First Football League Game: 27 August 1932, Division 3 (S), v Southend U (h) L 1–2 – Robb; Wade, McDougall, Lawson, Spence, Middleton, Proud, White, Gamble, Douglas, Fishlock (1).

HONOURS

Football League: Best season: 8th, Division 3, 1973–74.

FA Cup: Best season: 5th rd, 1932–33, 5th rd replay, 1978–79.

Football League Cup: Best season: 3rd rd replay, 1984–85.

Blue Square Premier League: Champions 2007–08.

Conference: Runners-up 2003–04.

Isthmian League Division 3: Champions 1992–93.

Isthmian First Division Champions: 1997–98.

Isthmian League Premier Division: Champions 2002–03.

Hampshire Senior Cup: Winners 1928, 1999, 2000, 2002, 2003, 2007.

Setanta Shield: Winners 2008.

SKY SPORTS FACT FILE

In March 1992 Aldershot became the first club to be kicked out of the Football League since Leeds City in 1919. Sixteen years later the Shots returned having won the Blue Square Premier League with record points (101) and wins (31), finishing with 18 games unbeaten.

Record League Victory: 8–1 v Gateshead, Division 4, 13 September 1958 – Marshall; Henry, Jackson, Mundy, Price, Gough, Walters, Stepney (3), Lacey (3), Matthews (2), Tyrer.

Record Cup Victory: 7–0 v Chelmsford, FA Cup, 1st rd, 28 November 1931 – Robb; Twine, McDougall (1), Norman Wilson, Gardiner, Middleton (1), Blackbourne, Stevenson (1), Thom (3), Hopkins (1), Edgar.

7–0 v Newport (IW), FA Cup, 2nd rd, 8 December 1945 – Reynolds; Horton, Sheppard, Ray, White, Summerbee, Sinclair, Hold (1), Brooks (5), Fitzgerald, Hobbs (1).

N.B. 11–1 v Kingstonian, FA Cup, 4th qual rd, 16 November 1929 – Mobbs; Thomas, McDougall, Norman Wilson, Gardiner, Middleton (2), Young (1), Common (1), Horton (2), Hopkins (3), Edgar (2).

Record Defeat: – 1–10 v Southend U, Leyland Daf Cup, Pr rd, 6 November 1990.

Most League Points: (2 for a win): 57, Division 4, 1978–79.

Most League Points (3 for a win): 75, Division 4, 1983–84.

Most League Goals: 83, Division 4, 1963–64.

Highest League Scorer in Season: John Dungworth, 26, Division 4, 1978–79.

Most League Goals in Total Aggregate: Jack Howarth, 171, 1965–71 and 1972–77.

Most Capped Player: Louie Soares, 3, Barbados.

Most League Appearances: Murray Brodie, 461, 1970–83.

Record Transfer Fee Received: £150,000 from Wolverhampton W for Tony Lange, July 1989.

Record Transfer Fee Paid: £54,000 to Portsmouth for Colin Garwood, February 1980.

Football League Record: 1932 elected to Division 3 (S); 1958–73 Division 4; 1973–76 Division 3; 1976–87 Division 4; 1987–89 Division 3; 1989–92 Division 4; 1992–93 Isthmian League Division 3; 1993–94 Isthmian League Division 2; 1994–98 Isthmian League Division 1; 1998–2003 Isthmian League Premier Division; 2003–08 Conference; 2008– FL 2.

MANAGERS

Angus Seed 1927–37
Bill McCracken 1937–49
Gordon Clark 1950–55
Harry Evans 1955–59
Dave Smith 1959–71
(GM from 1967)
Tommy McAnearney 1967–68
Jimmy Melia 1968–72
Tommy McAnearney 1972–81
Len Walker 1981–84
Ron Harris (GM) 1984–85
Len Walker 1985–91
Brian Talbot 1991–92
Ian McDonald 1992
Steve Wignall 1992–95
Steve Wigley 1995–97
George Borg 1997–2002
Terry Brown 2002–07
Gary Waddock May 2007–

LATEST SEQUENCES

Longest Sequence of League Wins: 5, 16.9.1961 – 2.10.61.

Longest Sequence of League Defeats: 9, 20.11.1965 – 5.2.1966.

Longest Sequence of League Draws: 6, 6.10.1962 – 27.10.1962.

Longest Sequence of Unbeaten League Matches: 13, 26.3.1966 – 3.9.1966.

Longest Sequence Without a League Win: 17, 10.10.1936 – 30.1.1937.

Successive Scoring Runs: 29 from 1.4.1961.

Successive Non-scoring Runs: 6 from 22.3.1988.

TEN YEAR LEAGUE RECORD

1997-98	Isth Div 1	42	28	8	6	89	36	92	1
1998-99	Isth PR	42	16	14	12	83	48	62	7
1999-2000	Isth PR	42	24	5	13	71	51	77	2
2000-01	Isth PR	41	21	11	9	73	39	74	4
2001-02	Isth PR	42	22	7	13	76	51	73	3
2002-03	Isth PR	46	33	6	7	81	36	105	1
2003-04	Conf	42	20	10	12	80	67	70	5
2004-05	Conf	42	21	10	11	68	52	73	4
2005-06	Conf	42	16	6	20	61	74	54	13
2006-07	Conf	46	18	11	17	64	62	65	9
2007-08	B Sq Pr	46	31	8	7	82	48	101	1

DID YOU KNOW ?

Though Derby County took the FA Cup honours in 1945–46 with Raich Carter (12 goals) and Peter Doherty (10) outstanding, Harry Brooks of Aldershot was the top scorer with 13 including a competition record five goals in successive matches.

ARSENAL

FA Premiership

FOUNDATION

Formed by workers at the Royal Arsenal, Woolwich in 1886, they began as Dial Square (name of one of the workshops), and included two former Nottingham Forest players, Fred Beardsley and Morris Bates. Beardsley wrote to his old club seeking help and they provided the new club with a full set of red jerseys and a ball. The club became known as the 'Woolwich Reds' although their official title soon after formation was Woolwich Arsenal.

Emirates Stadium, Drayton Park, Islington, London N5 1BU.

Telephone: (020) 7704 4000.

Fax: (020) 7704 4001.

Ticket Office: (020) 7704 4040.

Website: www.arsenal.com

Email: info@arsenal.co.uk

Ground Capacity: 60,361.

Record Attendance: 73,295 v Sunderland, Div 1, 9 March 1935.

At Wembley: 73,707 v RC Lens, UEFA Champions League, 25 November 1998.

Pitch Measurements: 105m × 68m.

Chairman: Peter Hill-Wood.

Managing Director: TBC.

Secretary: David Miles.

Manager: Arsène Wenger.

Assistant Manager: Pat Rice.

Physio: Gary Lewin.

Colours: Red shirts with white sleeves, white shorts, white stockings.

Change Colours: All yellow.

Year Formed: 1886.

Turned Professional: 1891.

Ltd Co: 1893.

Previous Names: 1886, Dial Square; 1886, Royal Arsenal; 1891, Woolwich Arsenal; 1914 Arsenal.

Club Nickname: 'Gunners'.

Grounds: 1886, Plumstead Common; 1887, Sportsman Ground; 1888, Manor Ground; 1890, Invicta Ground; 1893, Manor Ground; 1913, Highbury; 2006, Emirates Stadium.

HONOURS

FA Premier League: Champions 1997–98, 2001–02, 2003–04. Runners-up 1998–99, 1999–2000, 2000–01, 2002–03, 2004–05.

Football League: Division 1 – Champions 1930–31, 1932–33, 1933–34, 1934–35, 1937–38, 1947–48, 1952–53, 1970–71, 1988–89, 1990–91; Runners-up 1925–26, 1931–32, 1972–73; Division 2 – Runners-up 1903–04.

FA Cup: Winners 1930, 1936, 1950, 1971, 1979, 1993, 1998, 2002, 2003, 2005; Runners-up 1927, 1932, 1952, 1972, 1978, 1980, 2001.

Double performed: 1970–71, 1997–98, 2001–02.

Football League Cup: Winners 1987, 1993; Runners-up 1968, 1969, 1988, 2007.

European Competitions: *Fairs Cup:* 1963–64, 1969–70 (winners), 1970–71. *European Cup:* 1971–72, 1991–92. *UEFA Champions League:* 1998–99, 1999–2000, 2000–01, 2001–02, 2002–03, 2003–04, 2004–05, 2005–06 (runners-up), 2006–07, 2007–08 (q-f). *UEFA Cup:* 1978–79, 1981–82, 1982–83, 1996–97, 1997–98, 1999–2000 (runners-up). *European Cup-Winners' Cup:* 1979–80 (runners-up), 1993–94 (winners), 1994–95 (runners-up).

SKY SPORTS FACT FILE

Emmanuel Adebayor scored what was the 1000th Premier League goal for Arsenal in the match against Reading on 12 November. He was also particularly harsh on Derby County in the season scoring a hat-trick on both occasions, initially in the 5–0 win at the Emirates and then 6–3 away.

First Football League Game: 2 September 1893, Division 2, v Newcastle U (h) D 2–2 – Williams; Powell, Jeffrey; Devine, Buist, Howat; Gemmell, Henderson, Shaw (1), Elliott (1), Booth.

Record League Victory: 12–0 v Loughborough T, Division 2, 12 March 1900 – Orr; McNichol, Jackson; Moir, Dick (2), Anderson (1); Hunt, Cottrell (2), Main (2), Gaudie (3), Tennant (2).

Record Cup Victory: 11–1 v Darwen, FA Cup 3rd rd, 9 January 1932 – Moss; Parker, Hapgood; Jones, Roberts, John; Hulme (2), Jack (3), Lambert (2), James, Bastin (4).

Record Defeat: 0–8 v Loughborough T, Division 2, 12 December 1896.

Most League Points (2 for a win): 66, Division 1, 1930–31.

Most League Points (3 for a win): 90, Premier League 2003–04.

Most League Goals: 127, Division 1, 1930–31.

Highest League Scorer in Season: Ted Drake, 42, 1934–35.

Most League Goals in Total Aggregate: Thierry Henry, 174, 1999–2007.

Most League Goals in One Match: 7, Ted Drake v Aston Villa, Division 1, 14 December 1935.

Most Capped Player: Thierry Henry, 81 (102), France.

Most League Appearances: David O'Leary, 558, 1975–93.

Youngest League Player: Gerry Ward, 16 years 321 days v Huddersfield T, 22 August 1953 (Jermaine Pennant, 16 years 319 days v Middlesbrough, League Cup, 30 November 1999).

Record Transfer Fee Received: A reported £22,900,000 from Real Madrid for Nicolas Anelka, August 1999.

Record Transfer Fee Paid: A reported £11,000,000 to Bordeaux for Sylvain Wiltord, August 2000.

Football League Record: 1893 Elected to Division 2; 1904–13 Division 1; 1913–19 Division 2; 1919–92 Division 1; 1992– FA Premier League.

MANAGERS

Sam Hollis 1894–97
Tom Mitchell 1897–98
George Elcoat 1898–99
Harry Bradshaw 1899–1904
Phil Kelso 1904–08
George Morrell 1908–15
Leslie Knighton 1919–25
Herbert Chapman 1925–34
George Allison 1934–47
Tom Whittaker 1947–56
Jack Crayston 1956–58
George Swindin 1958–62
Billy Wright 1962–66
Bertie Mee 1966–76
Terry Neill 1976–83
Don Howe 1984–86
George Graham 1986–95
Bruce Rioch 1995–96
Arsène Wenger September 1996–

LATEST SEQUENCES

Longest Sequence of League Wins: 14, 10.2.2002 – 18.8.2002.

Longest Sequence of League Defeats: 7, 12.2.1977 – 12.3.1977.

Longest Sequence of League Draws: 6, 4.3.1961 – 1.4.1961.

Longest Sequence of Unbeaten League Matches: 49, 7.5.2003 – 24.10.2004.

Longest Sequence Without a League Win: 23, 28.9.1912 – 1.3.1913.

Successive Scoring Runs: 55 from 19.5.2001.

Successive Non-scoring Runs: 6 from 25.2.1987.

TEN YEAR LEAGUE RECORD

		P	W	D	L	F	A	Pts	Pos
1998-99	PR Lge	38	22	12	4	59	17	78	2
1999-2000	PR Lge	38	22	7	9	73	43	73	2
2000-01	PR Lge	38	20	10	8	63	38	70	2
2001-02	PR Lge	38	26	9	3	79	36	87	1
2002-03	PR Lge	38	23	9	6	85	42	78	2
2003-04	PR Lge	38	26	12	0	73	26	90	1
2004-05	PR Lge	38	25	8	5	87	36	83	2
2005-06	PR Lge	38	20	7	11	68	31	67	4
2006-07	PR Lge	38	19	11	8	63	35	68	4
2007-08	PR Lge	38	24	11	3	74	31	83	3

DID YOU KNOW ?

There is more to Arsène Wenger the successful Arsenal manager than his football prowess. He is fluent in four languages, speaks another three, has a degree in engineering and a Master's degree in economics from Strasbourg University.

ARSENAL 2007–08 LEAGUE RECORD

Match No.	Date	Venue	Opponents	Result		H/T Score	Lg. Pos.	Goalscorers	Attendance
1	Aug 12	H	Fulham	W	2-1	0-1	—	Van Persie (pen)[84], Hleb[90]	60,093
2	19	A	Blackburn R	D	1-1	1-0	7	Van Persie[18]	24,917
3	25	H	Manchester C	W	1-0	0-0	6	Fabregas[80]	60,114
4	Sept 2	H	Portsmouth	W	3-1	2-0	2	Adebayor (pen)[8], Fabregas[35], Rosicky[59]	60,114
5	15	A	Tottenham H	W	3-1	0-1	1	Adebayor 2[65, 90], Fabregas[80]	36,053
6	22	H	Derby Co	W	5-0	2-0	1	Diaby[10], Adebayor 3 (1 pen)[25, 50 (p), 79], Fabregas[70]	60,122
7	29	A	West Ham U	W	1-0	1-0	1	Van Persie[13]	34,966
8	Oct 7	H	Sunderland	W	3-2	2-1	1	Van Persie 2[7, 80], Senderos[14]	60,098
9	20	H	Bolton W	W	2-0	0-0	1	Toure[68], Rosicky[80]	59,442
10	28	A	Liverpool	D	1-1	0-1	1	Fabregas[80]	44,122
11	Nov 3	H	Manchester U	D	2-2	0-1	1	Fabregas[48], Gallas[90]	60,161
12	12	A	Reading	W	3-1	1-0	—	Flamini[44], Adebayor[52], Hleb[78]	24,024
13	24	H	Wigan Ath	W	2-0	0-0	1	Gallas[83], Rosicky[85]	60,126
14	Dec 1	A	Aston Villa	W	2-1	2-1	1	Flamini[23], Adebayor[36]	42,018
15	5	A	Newcastle U	D	1-1	1-0	—	Adebayor[4]	50,305
16	9	A	Middlesbrough	L	1-2	0-1	1	Rosicky[90]	26,428
17	16	H	Chelsea	W	1-0	1-0	1	Gallas[45]	60,139
18	22	H	Tottenham H	W	2-1	0-0	1	Adebayor[48], Bendtner[76]	60,087
19	26	A	Portsmouth	D	0-0	0-0	2		20,556
20	29	A	Everton	W	4-1	0-1	1	Eduardo 2[47, 58], Adebayor[78], Rosicky[90]	39,443
21	Jan 1	H	West Ham U	W	2-0	2-0	1	Eduardo[2], Adebayor[18]	60,102
22	12	H	Birmingham C	D	1-1	1-0	2	Adebayor (pen)[21]	60,037
23	19	A	Fulham	W	3-0	2-0	2	Adebayor 2[19, 38], Rosicky[81]	25,297
24	29	H	Newcastle U	W	3-0	1-0	—	Adebayor[40], Flamini[72], Fabregas[80]	60,127
25	Feb 2	A	Manchester C	W	3-1	2-1	1	Adebayor 2[9, 88], Eduardo[26]	46,426
26	11	H	Blackburn R	W	2-0	1-0	—	Senderos[4], Adebayor[90]	60,049
27	23	A	Birmingham C	D	2-2	0-1	1	Walcott 2[50, 55]	27,195
28	Mar 1	H	Aston Villa	D	1-1	0-1	1	Bendtner[90]	60,097
29	9	A	Wigan Ath	D	0-0	0-0	1		19,676
30	15	H	Middlesbrough	D	1-1	0-1	2	Toure[86]	60,084
31	23	A	Chelsea	L	1-2	0-0	3	Sagna[59]	41,824
32	29	A	Bolton W	W	3-2	0-2	3	Gallas[62], Van Persie (pen)[68], Samuel (og)[90]	22,431
33	Apr 5	H	Liverpool	D	1-1	0-1	3	Bendtner[54]	60,111
34	13	A	Manchester U	L	1-2	0-0	3	Adebayor[48]	75,985
35	19	H	Reading	W	2-0	2-0	3	Adebayor[30], Silva[38]	60,109
36	28	A	Derby Co	W	6-2	2-1	—	Bendtner[25], Van Persie[39], Adebayor 3[59, 81, 90], Walcott[78]	33,003
37	May 4	H	Everton	W	1-0	0-0	3	Bendtner[77]	60,123
38	11	A	Sunderland	W	1-0	1-0	3	Walcott[24]	47,802

Final League Position: 3

GOALSCORERS

League (74): Adebayor 24 (3 pens), Fabregas 7, Van Persie 7 (2 pens), Rosicky 6, Bendtner 5, Eduardo 4, Gallas 4, Walcott 4, Flamini 3, Hleb 2, Senderos 2, Toure 2, Diaby 1, Sagna 1, Silva 1, own goal 1.
Carling Cup (10): Eduardo 4, Denilson 2, Adebayor 1, Bendtner 1, Diaby 1, Walcott 1.
FA Cup (5): Adebayor 2, Bendtner 1, Eduardo 1, own goal 1.
Champions League (24): Fabregas 6, Adebayor 3, Eduardo 3, Bendtner 2, Diaby 2, Hleb 2, Van Persie 2, Walcott 2, Rosicky 1, own goal 1.

Lehmann J 6 + 1	Sagna B 29	Clichy G 37 + 1	Flamini M 30	Toure K 29 + 1	Gallas W 31	Eboue E 20 + 3	Fabregas F 32	Hleb A 29 + 2	Van Persie R 13 + 2	Rosicky T 15 + 3	Bendtner N 7 + 20	Song Billong A 5 + 4	Walcott T 11 + 14	Senderos P 14 + 3	Eduardo 13 + 4	Denilson 4 + 9	Almunia M 29	Silva G 12 + 11	Adebayor E 32 + 4	Diaby V 9 + 6	Diarra L 4 + 3	Hoyte J 2 + 3	Traore A 1 + 2	Fabianski L 3	Djourou J 1 + 1	Randall M — + 1	Match No.
1	2	3	4	5	6	7^3	8	9	10^2	11^1	12	13	14														1
1	2	3	4	5	6^2		8	11	10		12		7^1	13	9^3	14											2
	2^3	3	4	5			8	7	10^2	11		13			12	14	1	6	9^1								3
		3	4	2			8	7^3	10^2	11				5■	12	14	1	6	9^1	13							4
	2	3	4	5			8	7^2	10^3	12		13				14	1	6	9	11^1							5
	2	3	4^2	5			8^1					13	7^3	6	9	12	1		10	11	14						6
	2	3	4	5		12	8	7^1	10^2		13			6			1	14	9^3	11							7
	2^3	3	4	5		14	8	7	10^1				13	6			1	12	9	11^2							8
	2	3	4	5	6	7^1	8	11^2		12			14		10^3		1		9	13							9
	2	3^3	4	5	6	7^1	8	11		10^2	12		13				1	14	9								10
	2	3	4	5	6	7^1	8	10^2		11^3			12		14		1	13	9								11
	2	3	4	5	6	7	8	10^3		11^2	12		13				1		9^1		14						12
	2	3		5	6	7^2				11	12		10^1		13	8	1		9		4						13
	2	3	4	5	6	7		10^2		11^3	12		13				1	14	9^1		8						14
	2	3		5	6	7				11	12				10^1		1	4	9		8						15
	2	3		5	6	7^2				11	12		13		10^1	14	1	4	9		8^3						16
	2	3	4	5	6	7^1	8	10^3	12	11	13						1	14	9^2								17
	2	3	4	5	6	7^1	8	10^2		11	12						1	13	9								18
	2	3	4	5	6	7^2	8	10^1		11	12						1		9	13							19
	2	3	4	5	6		8^1	7^3		12	10■				9^2		1		13	11	14						20
		3	4	5	6	7^1	8	12		11^3			13		10^2		1		9	14		2					21
	2^2	3	4		6		8	11			12		7^1	5	10		1		9	13							22
	2	3	4		6		8	7		11				5	10		1		9								23
	2	3	4		6		8	7			12		13	5	10^1		1	14	9^2	11^3							24
1	2	3	4		6		8	7^1						5	10				9	11		12					25
1	2	3	4		6		8	11						5	10			7	9								26
	2	3	4		6		8	11^3			12		7^2	5	10^1	13	1	14	9								27
	2	3	4^3		6		8	7			12		10	5^2		13	1	14	9	11^1							28
	2	3	4	12	6		8	11	13		10^2			5			1	7^1	9								29
	2^1	3^2	4	5	6	7	8	11	10^3		12		14	13			1		9								30
	2^3	3	4^1	5	6	7	8	11	10^2		12		13				1		9	14							31
		3	4	2	6		8	7	10^2		9^3		12	5^1			1		14	11■		13					32
		12	4^2	5	6	7	8	13			10		9				1	11	14			2^3	3^1				33
1		3		2^3	6	7^2	8	11	10^1		12	5	13					4	9			14					34
1		3		2^2	6	13	8	11^3	10		12	5	7			14		4	9^1								35
		3		2^3	6	7	8		10^1		9	5	11			4^2		13	12					1	14		36
15		3		2^2	6	7					10	5	11	12		8		4	9^1				13	1^9			37
		3				7^2					10^1	2	11	5		8		4	9				12	1	6	13	38

Champions League

Third Qualifying Round	Sparta Prague	(a)	2-0
		(h)	3-0
Group H	Sevilla	(h)	3-0
	Steaua	(a)	1-0
	Slavia Prague	(h)	7-0
		(a)	0-0
	Sevilla	(a)	1-3
	Steaua	(h)	2-1
Knock-Out Round	AC Milan	(h)	0-0
		(a)	2-0
Quarter-Final	Liverpool	(h)	1-1
		(a)	2-4

FA Cup

Third Round	Burnley	(a)	2-0
Fourth Round	Newcastle U	(h)	3-0
Fifth Round	Manchester U	(a)	0-4

Carling Cup

Third Round	Newcastle U	(h)	2-0
Fourth Round	Sheffield U	(a)	3-0
Quarter-Final	Blackburn R	(a)	3-2
Semi-Final	Tottenham H	(h)	1-1
		(a)	1-5

ASTON VILLA

FA Premiership

FOUNDATION

Cricketing enthusiasts of Villa Cross Wesleyan Chapel, Aston, Birmingham decided to form a football club during the winter of 1874–75. Football clubs were few and far between in the Birmingham area and in their first game against Aston Brook St Mary's Rugby team they played one half rugby and the other soccer. In 1876 they were joined by a Scottish soccer enthusiast George Ramsay who was immediately appointed captain and went on to lead Aston Villa from obscurity to one of the country's top clubs in a period of less than 10 years.

Villa Park, Birmingham B6 6HE.

Telephone: (0121) 327 2299.

Fax: (0121) 322 2107.

Ticket Office/Consumer Sales: (0800) 612 0970.

Website: www.avfc.co.uk

Email: postmaster@avfc.co.uk

Ground Capacity: 42,640.

Record Attendance: 76,588 v Derby Co, FA Cup 6th rd, 2 March 1946.

Pitch Measurements: 115yd × 75yd.

Chairman: Randolph Lerner.

Secretary: Sharon Barnhurst.

Manager: Martin O'Neill.

Assistant Manager: John Robertson.

Physio: Alan Smith.

Sports Science Manager: Dr Stephen McGregor.

Colours: Claret body, blue sleeve shirts, white shorts, sky blue stockings with claret turnover.

Change Colours: Laser blue shirts with black sleeves, black shorts, black stockings with alternative laser blue.

Third Kit: White shirts with thin claret pinstripe, blue shorts, white stockings.

Year Formed: 1874.

Turned Professional: 1885.

Ltd Co.: 1896.

Public Ltd Company: 1969.

Club Nickname: 'The Villans'.

Grounds: 1874, Wilson Road and Aston Park (also used Aston Lower Grounds for some matches); 1876, Wellington Road, Perry Barr; 1897, Villa Park.

First Football League Game: 8 September 1888, Football League, v Wolverhampton W (a) D 1–1 – Warner; Cox, Coulton; Yates, H. Devey, Dawson; A. Brown, Green (1), Allen, Garvey, Hodgetts.

HONOURS

FA Premier League: Runners-up 1992–93.

Football League: Division 1 – Champions 1893–94, 1895–96, 1896–97, 1898–99, 1899–1900, 1909–10, 1980–81; Runners-up 1888–89, 1902–03, 1907–08, 1910–11, 1912–13, 1913–14, 1930–31, 1932–33, 1989–90; Division 2 – Champions 1937–38, 1959–60; Runners-up 1974–75, 1987–88; Division 3 – Champions 1971–72.

FA Cup: Winners 1887, 1895, 1897, 1905, 1913, 1920, 1957; Runners-up 1892, 1924, 2000.

Double Performed: 1896–97.

Football League Cup: Winners 1961, 1975, 1977, 1994, 1996; Runners-up 1963, 1971.

European Competitions: *European Cup:* 1981–82 (winners), 1982–83. *UEFA Cup:* 1975–76, 1977–78, 1983–84, 1990–91, 1993–94, 1994–95, 1996–97, 1997–98, 1998–99, 2001–02. *World Club Championship:* 1982. *European Super Cup:* 1982–83 (winners). *Intertoto Cup:* 2000, 2001 (winners), 2002.

SKY SPORTS FACT FILE

Aston Villa centre-forward Ralph Brown had the unusual distinction of playing just once for the first team but his League Cup outing against Rotherham United on 22 August 1961 made him the youngest player in the competition at the age of 17 years 177 days.

Record League Victory: 12–2 v Accrington S, Division 1, 12 March 1892 – Warner; Evans, Cox; Harry Devey, Jimmy Cowan, Baird; Athersmith (1), Dickson (2), John Devey (4), L. Campbell (4), Hodgetts (1).

Record Cup Victory: 13–0 v Wednesbury Old Ath, FA Cup 1st rd, 30 October 1886 – Warner; Coulton, Simmonds; Yates, Robertson, Burton (2); R. Davis (1), A. Brown (3), Hunter (3), Loach (2), Hodgetts (2).

Record Defeat: 1–8 v Blackburn R, FA Cup 3rd rd, 16 February 1889.

Most League Points (2 for a win): 70, Division 3, 1971–72.

Most League Points (3 for a win): 78, Division 2, 1987–88.

Most League Goals: 128, Division 1, 1930–31.

Highest League Scorer in Season: 'Pongo' Waring, 49, Division 1, 1930–31.

Most League Goals in Total Aggregate: Harry Hampton, 215, 1904–15.

Most League Goals in One Match: 5, Harry Hampton v Sheffield W, Division 1, 5 October 1912; 5, Harold Halse v Derby Co, Division 1, 19 October 1912; 5, Len Capewell v Burnley, Division 1, 29 August 1925; 5, George Brown v Leicester C, Division 1, 2 January 1932; 5, Gerry Hitchens v Charlton Ath, Division 2, 18 November 1959.

Most Capped Player: Steve Staunton 64 (102), Republic of Ireland.

Most League Appearances: Charlie Aitken, 561, 1961–76.

Youngest League Player: Jimmy Brown, 15 years 349 days v Bolton W, 17 September 1969.

MANAGERS

George Ramsay 1884–1926
(Secretary-Manager)
W. J. Smith 1926–34
(Secretary-Manager)
Jimmy McMullan 1934–35
Jimmy Hogan 1936–44
Alex Massie 1945–50
George Martin 1950–53
Eric Houghton 1953–58
Joe Mercer 1958–64
Dick Taylor 1964–67
Tommy Cummings 1967–68
Tommy Docherty 1968–70
Vic Crowe 1970–74
Ron Saunders 1974–82
Tony Barton 1982–84
Graham Turner 1984–86
Billy McNeill 1986–87
Graham Taylor 1987–90
Dr Jozef Venglos 1990–91
Ron Atkinson 1991–94
Brian Little 1994–98
John Gregory 1998–2002
Graham Taylor OBE 2002–03
David O'Leary 2003–2006
Martin O'Neill August 2006–

Record Transfer Fee Received: £12,600,000 from Manchester U for Dwight Yorke, August 1998.

Record Transfer Fee Paid: £9,600,000 to Watford for Ashley Young, January 2007.

Football League Record: 1888 Founder Member of the League; 1936–38 Division 2; 1938–59 Division 1; 1959–60 Division 2; 1960–67 Division 1; 1967–70 Division 2; 1970–72 Division 3; 1972–75 Division 2; 1975–87 Division 1; 1987–88 Division 2; 1988–92 Division 1; 1992– FA Premier League.

LATEST SEQUENCES

Longest Sequence of League Wins: 9, 15.10.1910 – 10.12.1910.

Longest Sequence of League Defeats: 11, 23.3.1963 – 4.5.1963.

Longest Sequence of League Draws: 6, 12.9.1981 – 10.10.1981.

Longest Sequence of Unbeaten League Matches: 15, 12.3.1949 – 27.8.1949.

Longest Sequence Without a League Win: 12, 27.12.1986 – 25.3.1987.

Successive Scoring Runs: 35 from 10.11.1895.

Successive Non-scoring Runs: 5 from 29.2.1992.

TEN YEAR LEAGUE RECORD

		P	*W*	*D*	*L*	*F*	*A*	*Pts*	*Pos*
1998-99	PR Lge	38	15	10	13	51	46	55	6
1999-2000	PR Lge	38	15	13	10	46	35	58	6
2000-01	PR Lge	38	13	15	10	46	43	54	8
2001-02	PR Lge	38	12	14	12	46	47	50	8
2002-03	PR Lge	38	12	9	17	42	47	45	16
2003-04	PR Lge	38	15	11	12	48	44	56	6
2004-05	PR Lge	38	12	11	15	45	52	47	10
2005-06	PR Lge	38	10	12	16	42	55	42	16
2006-07	PR Lge	38	11	17	10	43	41	50	11
2007-08	PR Lge	38	16	12	10	71	51	60	6

DID YOU KNOW ?

On 18 March 1922 it was a day of extreme goalscoring famine in the First Division. Of the eleven scheduled matches the total number of goals scored was just 13. Top scorers were Aston Villa with a 2–0 win over Arsenal.

ASTON VILLA 2007–08 LEAGUE RECORD

Match No.	*Date*	*Venue*	*Opponents*	*Result*		*H/T Score*	*Lg. Pos.*	*Goalscorers*	*Attendance*
1	Aug 11	H	Liverpool	L	1-2	0-1	—	Barry (pen) [85]	42,640
2	18	A	Newcastle U	D	0-0	0-0	17		51,049
3	25	H	Fulham	W	2-1	0-1	11	Young [51], Maloney [90]	36,638
4	Sept 2	H	Chelsea	W	2-0	0-0	10	Knight [47], Agbonlahor [88]	37,714
5	16	A	Manchester C	L	0-1	0-0	11		38,363
6	23	H	Everton	W	2-0	1-0	8	Carew [14], Agbonlahor [60]	38,235
7	Oct 1	A	Tottenham H	D	4-4	3-1	—	Laursen 2 [22, 33], Agbonlahor [40], Gardner [59]	36,094
8	6	H	West Ham U	W	1-0	1-0	8	Gardner [24]	40,842
9	20	H	Manchester U	L	1-4	1-3	9	Agbonlahor [13]	42,640
10	28	A	Bolton W	D	1-1	0-1	10	Moore [57]	18,413
11	Nov 3	H	Derby Co	W	2-0	0-0	9	Laursen [57], Young [61]	40,938
12	11	A	Birmingham C	W	2-1	1-0	8	Ridgewell (og) [11], Agbonlahor [87]	26,539
13	24	A	Middlesbrough	W	3-0	1-0	7	Carew [45], Mellberg [48], Agbonlahor [58]	23,900
14	28	A	Blackburn R	W	4-0	1-0	—	Carew [29], Barry (pen) [53], Young [81], Harewood [89]	20,776
15	Dec 1	H	Arsenal	L	1-2	1-2	7	Gardner [14]	42,018
16	8	H	Portsmouth	L	1-3	0-2	8	Barry (pen) [72]	35,790
17	15	A	Sunderland	D	1-1	0-1	8	Maloney [73]	43,248
18	22	H	Manchester C	D	1-1	1-1	8	Carew [14]	41,455
19	26	A	Chelsea	D	4-4	2-1	8	Maloney 2 [14, 44], Laursen [72], Barry (pen) [90]	41,686
20	29	A	Wigan Ath	W	2-1	0-1	7	Davies [55], Agbonlahor [70]	18,806
21	Jan 1	H	Tottenham H	W	2-1	1-0	6	Mellberg [41], Laursen [85]	41,609
22	12	H	Reading	W	3-1	1-0	6	Carew 2 [22, 88], Laursen [55]	32,288
23	21	A	Liverpool	D	2-2	0-1	—	Harewood [69], Fabio Aurelio (og) [72]	42,590
24	26	H	Blackburn R	D	1-1	0-0	—	Young [73]	39,602
25	Feb 3	A	Fulham	L	1-2	0-0	6	Hughes (og) [69]	24,760
26	9	H	Newcastle U	W	4-1	0-1	6	Bouma [48], Carew 3 (1 pen) [51, 72, 90 (p)]	42,640
27	24	A	Reading	W	2-1	1-0	6	Young [45], Harewood [83]	23,889
28	Mar 1	A	Arsenal	D	1-1	1-0	6	Senderos (og) [27]	60,097
29	12	H	Middlesbrough	D	1-1	0-1	—	Barry (pen) [74]	39,874
30	15	A	Portsmouth	L	0-2	0-2	7		20,388
31	22	H	Sunderland	L	0-1	0-0	7		42,640
32	29	A	Manchester U	L	0-4	0-2	8		75,932
33	Apr 5	H	Bolton W	W	4-0	1-0	7	Barry 2 [9, 60], Agbonlahor [56], Harewood [85]	37,773
34	12	A	Derby Co	W	6-0	3-0	7	Young [25], Carew [26], Petrov [36], Barry [58], Agbonlahor [76], Harewood [85]	33,036
35	20	H	Birmingham C	W	5-1	2-0	6	Young 2 [28, 63], Carew 2 [42, 53], Agbonlahor [78]	42,584
36	27	A	Everton	D	2-2	0-0	6	Agbonlahor [80], Carew [86]	37,936
37	May 3	H	Wigan Ath	L	0-2	0-0	6		42,640
38	11	A	West Ham U	D	2-2	1-1	6	Young [14], Barry [58]	34,969

Final League Position: 6

GOALSCORERS

League (71): Carew 13 (1 pen), Agbonlahor 11, Barry 9 (5 pens), Young 9, Laursen 6, Harewood 5, Maloney 4, Gardner 3, Mellberg 2, Bouma 1, Davies 1, Knight 1, Moore 1, Petrov 1, own goals 4.
Carling Cup (5): Maloney 2, Harewood 1, Moore 1, Reo-Coker 1.
FA Cup (0).

Taylor S 3 + 1	Gardner C 15 + 8	Bouma W 38	Reo-Coker N 36	Mellberg O 33 + 1	Laursen M 38	Petrov S 22 + 6	Young A 37	Agbonlahor G 37	Carew J 32	Barry G 37	Cahill G — + 1	Moore L 8 + 7	Carson S 35	Maloney S 11 + 11	Harewood M 1 + 22	Knight Z 25 + 2	Osbourne I 1 + 7	Berger P — + 8	Davies C 9 + 3	Salifou M — + 4	Routledge W — + 1	*Match No.*
1	2	3^{2}	4	5	6^{1}	7	8	9	10	11	12	13										1
	2	3	4	5	6	7	8	9	10^{1}	11		12	1									2
	2	3^{2}	4	5	6	7^{1}	8	9	10^{3}	11		12	1	13	14							3
		3	4	2	6	12	8	7	10^{1}	11		9	1			5						4
	12	3^{1}	4^{3}	2	6	14	8	7	10^{2}	11		9	1	13		5						5
	12	3	4	2	6		8	7	10^{1}	11		9^{2}	1		13	5						6
	7^{1}	3	4	2	6	12	8	9		11		10^{2}	1		13	5						7
	7^{1}	3	4	2	6	12	8	9		11		10^{2}	1	13		5						8
15	7^{1}	3	4■	2	6		8	9		11		10^{2}	1■	12		5^{6}	13					9
1		3		2	6	7	8	9		11		12		10^{1}		5	4^{2}	13				10
		3	4	2	6	7	8^{1}	9		11		10^{2}	1	12		5^{3}		13	14			11
		3	4	2	6	7	8	9	10^{1}	11		12	1			5						12
	12	3	4	2	6^{3}	7^{1}	8	9	10^{2}	11			1	13		5			14			13
	12	3	4	2	6	7^{1}	8	9^{2}	10	11			1		13	5						14
	4	3^{2}		2	6	7^{1}	8	9	10	11			1	12		5		13				15
	7^{1}	3^{2}	4	2	6		8	9	10	11			1		12	5		13				16
	7^{1}	3	4	2	6		8	9	10	11			1	12		5						17
		3	4	2	6	12	8	9	10	11			1	7^{1}		5						18
		3^{2}	4	2	6		8	9	10^{1}	11		12	1	7^{3}	13	5■			14			19
	12	3	4	2	6	13	8^{2}	9	10^{3}	11		14	1	7^{1}					5			20
	12	3^{2}	4	2	6	7	8	9		11		10^{1}	1	13					5			21
	2	3	4		6	7	8^{1}	9^{2}	10^{3}	11			1	12	13				5	14		22
1	11^{1}	3	4	2	6	7	8	9	10^{2}						12	13			5			23
		3	4	2	6	7^{1}	8	9	10	11			1		12				5			24
	12	3^{1}	4	2	6	7		9^{2}	10	11			1	8	13		14		5^{3}			25
	12	3	4	2^{1}	6	7^{2}	8^{3}		10	11			1	9	13		14		5			26
	2	3	4^{2}		6		8	9	10	11			1	7^{1}	12		13		5			27
	2	3	4^{3}		6		8	9	10	11			1	7^{2}	13	14	12		5^{1}			28
	2^{1}	3	4	12	6		8	9	10	11			1	7^{2}	13	5						29
		3^{2}	4	2■	6		8	9	10	11			1	7^{1}	12	5				13		30
	2	3	4^{1}		6		8	9	10	11			1	7^{2}	12	5	13					31
		3^{2}	2	5	6	7	8	9	10^{1}	11			1	12	4^{3}		13			14		32
		3	4	2	6	7^{3}	8^{2}	9	10^{1}	11			1		12	5		13			14	33
		3	4	2	6	7	8^{2}	9	10^{1}	11^{3}			1		12	5		13		14		34
		3	4	2^{1}	6	7	8	9	10	11			1		12	5						35
		3^{1}	4	2	6	7	8	9	10	11			1		12	5^{2}		13				36
		3^{1}	4	2	6	7	8	9	10	11			1		12	5^{2}		13				37
		3	4	2	6	7	8	9	10^{1}	11			1		12	5						38

FA Cup

Third Round	Manchester U	(h)	0-2

Carling Cup

Second Round	Wrexham	(a)	5-0
Third Round	Leicester C	(h)	0-1

BARNET FL Championship 2

FOUNDATION

Barnet Football Club was formed in 1888 as an amateur organisation and they played at a ground in Queen's Road until they disbanded in 1901. A club known as Alston Works FC was then formed and they played at Totteridge Lane until changing to Barnet Alston FC in 1906. They moved to their present ground a year later, combining with The Avenue to form Barnet and Alston in 1912. The club progressed to senior amateur football by way of the Athenian and Isthmian Leagues, turning professional in 1965. It was as a Southern League and Conference club that they made their name.

Underhill Stadium, Barnet Lane, Barnet, Herts EN5 2DN.

Telephone: (020) 8441 6932.

Fax: (020) 8447 0655.

Ticket Office: 0208 449 6325.

Website: www.barnetfc.com

Email: info@barnetfc.com

Ground Capacity: 5,568.

Record Attendance: 11,026 v Wycombe Wanderers, FA Amateur Cup 4th Round 1951–52.

Record Receipts: £31,202 v Portsmouth, FA Cup 3rd Round, 5 January 1991.

Pitch Measurements: 100m × 64m.

Chairman: Anthony Kleanthous.

Secretary: Andrew Adie.

Manager: Paul Fairclough.

Assistant Manager: Ian Hendon.

Physio: Mark Stein.

Colours: Amber and black.

Change Colours: White with red and black.

Year Formed: 1888.

Turned Professional: 1965.

Previous Names: 1906, Barnet Alston FC; 1919, Barnet.

Club Nickname: The Bees.

Grounds: 1888, Queens Road; 1901, Totteridge Lane; 1907, Barnet Lane.

First Football League Game: 17 August 1991, Division 4, v Crewe Alex (h) L 4–7 – Phillips; Blackford, Cooper (Murphy), Horton, Bodley (Stein), Johnson, Showler, Carter (2), Bull (2), Lowe, Evans.

HONOURS

Football League: Division 2 best season: 24th, 1993–94.

FA Amateur Cup: Winners 1946.

FA Trophy: Finalists 1972.

GM Vauxhall Conference: Winners 1990–91. *Conference:* Winners 2004–05

FA Cup: 4th rd, 2007, 2008.

League Cup: best season: 3rd rd, 2006.

SKY SPORTS FACT FILE

Ricky George, who left Barnet for Hereford United in 1971 to find FA Cup fame with the West Country club, returned to Underhill midway through 1972–73 from Stevenage Borough. He still contrived to finish top scorer for the then Southern League club.

Record League Victory: 7–0 v Blackpool, Division 3, 11 November 2000 – Naisbitt; Stockley, Sawyers, Niven (Brown), Heald, Arber (1), Currie (3), Doolan, Richards (2) (McGleish), Cottee (1) (Riza), Toms.

Record Cup Victory: 6–1 v Newport Co, FA Cup 1st rd, 21 November 1970 – McClelland; Lye, Jenkins, Ward, Embery, King, Powell (1), Ferry, Adams (1), Gray, George (3), (1 og).

Record Defeat: 1–9 v Peterborough U, Division 3, 5 September 1998.

Most League Points (3 for a win): 79, Division 3, 1992–93.

Most League Goals: 81, Division 4, 1991–92.

Highest League Scorer in Season: Dougie Freedman, 24, Division 3, 1994–95.

Most League Goals in Total Aggregate: Sean Devine, 47, 1995–99.

Most League Goals in One Match: 4, Dougie Freedman v Rochdale, Division 3, 13 September 1994; 4, Lee Hodges v Rochdale, Division 3, 8 April 1996.

Most Capped Player: Ken Charlery, 4, St Lucia.

Most League Appearances: Paul Wilson, 263, 1991–2000.

Youngest League Player: Kieran Adams, 17 years 71 days v Mansfield T, 31 December 1994.

Record Transfer Fee Received: £800,000 from Crystal Palace for Dougie Freedman, September 1995.

Record Transfer Fee Paid: £130,000 to Peterborough U for Greg Heald, August 1997.

Football League Record: Promoted to Division 4 from GMVC 1991; 1991–92 Division 4; 1992–93 Division 3; 1993–94 Division 2; 1994–2001 Division 3; 2001–05 Conference; 2005– FL 2.

MANAGERS

Lester Finch
George Wheeler
Dexter Adams
Tommy Coleman
Gerry Ward
Gordon Ferry
Brian Kelly
Bill Meadows 1976–79
Barry Fry 1979–85
Roger Thompson 1985
Don McAllister 1985–86
Barry Fry 1986–93
Edwin Stein 1993
Gary Phillips (Player–Manager) 1993–94
Ray Clemence 1994–96
Alan Mullery (Director of Football) 1996–97
Terry Bullivant 1997
John Still 1997–2000
Tony Cottee 2000–01
John Still 2001–02
Peter Shreeves 2002–03
Martin Allen 2003–04
Paul Fairclough March 2004–

LATEST SEQUENCES

Longest Sequence of League Wins: 6, 28.8.1993 – 25.9.1999.

Longest Sequence of League Defeats: 11, 8.5.1993 – 2.10.1993.

Longest Sequence of League Draws: 4, 22.1.1994 – 12.2.1994.

Longest Sequence of Unbeaten League Matches: 12, 5.12.1992 – 2.3.1993.

Longest Sequence Without a League Win: 14, 24.4.1993 – 10.10.1993.

Successive Scoring Runs: 12 from 19.3.1995.

Successive Non-scoring Runs: 5 from 12.2.2000.

TEN YEAR LEAGUE RECORD

		P	W	D	L	F	A	Pts	Pos
1998-99	Div 3	46	14	13	19	54	71	55	16
1999-2000	Div 3	46	21	12	13	59	53	75	6
2000–01	Div 3	46	12	9	25	67	81	45	24
2001–02	Conf	42	19	10	13	64	48	67	5
2002–03	Conf	42	13	14	15	65	68	53	11
2003–04	Conf	42	19	14	9	60	48	71	4
2004–05	Conf	42	26	8	8	90	44	86	1
2005-06	FL 2	46	12	18	16	44	57	54	18
2006-07	FL 2	46	16	11	19	55	70	59	14
2007-08	FL 2	46	16	12	18	56	63	60	12

DID YOU KNOW?

In eight years of Southern League football from 1965–66 to 1972–73 Les Eason amassed 477 appearances despite twice breaking his leg. He was also the leading marksman for the club, his marksmanship yielding 241 goals. He was capped at England amateur level.

BARNET 2007–08 LEAGUE RECORD

Match No.	Date	Venue	Opponents	Result	H/T Score	Lg. Pos.	Goalscorers	Attendance
1	Aug 11	A	Morecambe	D 0-0	0-0	—		3633
2	18	H	Hereford U	L 1-2	1-1	20	Puncheon 13	1790
3	25	A	Brentford	L 1-2	0-0	21	Puncheon 61	4744
4	Sept 1	H	Bradford C	W 2-1	1-0	15	Johnson (og) 43, Puncheon 90	2412
5	8	A	Dagenham & R	D 1-1	1-1	17	Thomas 45	2192
6	15	H	Rochdale	D 0-0	0-0	16		2040
7	22	A	Chesterfield	W 1-0	0-0	13	Norville 69	4088
8	29	H	Rotherham U	W 2-0	0-0	9	Birchall 52, Puncheon (pen) 83	2008
9	Oct 2	H	Wycombe W	W 2-1	0-1	—	Hatch 77, Puncheon 86	2023
10	6	A	Stockport Co	W 4-2	1-1	6	Birchall 2 14, 47, Wright 62, Carew 84	4751
11	13	H	Mansfield T	D 1-1	0-0	7	Hatch 71	2041
12	20	A	Wrexham	W 2-0	0-0	5	Hatch 2 59, 69	3591
13	27	H	Accrington S	D 2-2	0-0	5	Hatch 59, Burton 70	2178
14	Nov 3	A	Bury	L 0-3	0-1	8		2121
15	6	H	Notts Co	D 1-1	1-0	—	Puncheon 39	2089
16	17	A	Shrewsbury T	L 0-1	0-0	9		5197
17	24	H	Grimsby T	L 0-3	0-2	9		2059
18	Dec 4	A	Chester C	L 0-3	0-2	—		1858
19	8	H	Macclesfield T	D 2-2	1-2	12	Hatch 9, Bishop 90	1303
20	15	A	Lincoln C	L 1-4	0-2	14	Birchall 59	3549
21	26	H	Dagenham & R	W 3-1	1-0	13	Puncheon 3 (1 pen) 41 (p), 50, 78	2513
22	29	H	Chesterfield	L 0-2	0-1	14		2346
23	Jan 1	A	Wycombe W	D 0-0	0-0	14		4818
24	12	A	Milton Keynes D	W 1-0	1-0	16	Yakubu 22	9881
25	30	A	Hereford U	W 2-1	0-0	—	Adomah 52, Nicolau 85	2271
26	Feb 2	H	Morecambe	L 0-1	0-0	16		1619
27	9	A	Darlington	L 0-1	0-1	17		3145
28	12	H	Brentford	L 1-2	0-1	—	Birchall 90	2522
29	16	A	Peterborough U	L 0-1	0-0	18		5520
30	23	H	Milton Keynes D	L 0-2	0-2	18		2495
31	Mar 1	H	Shrewsbury T	W 4-1	3-1	19	Akurang 2 16, 54, Adomah 2 32, 45	1864
32	4	H	Peterborough U	L 0-2	0-1	—		2202
33	8	A	Notts Co	D 0-0	0-0	20		3687
34	11	A	Grimsby T	L 1-4	0-2	—	Akurang 80	3325
35	15	H	Chester C	W 3-1	0-0	18	Adomah 50, Akurang 2 (1 pen) 72 (p), 80	1663
36	22	H	Lincoln C	W 5-2	3-0	18	Birchall 2 28, 46, Adomah (pen) 38, Thomas 44, Porter 63	2115
37	24	A	Macclesfield T	L 0-3	0-2	16		1718
38	29	H	Wrexham	W 3-2	1-0	16	Yakubu 45, Thomas 51, Nicolau 62	2286
39	Apr 1	H	Darlington	D 0-0	0-0	—		1678
40	5	A	Mansfield T	D 2-2	0-1	15	Thomas 70, Birchall 77	2463
41	8	A	Bradford C	D 1-1	1-0	—	Birchall 23	13,072
42	12	H	Bury	W 3-0	0-0	14	Birchall 2 57, 70, Akurang 84	3054
43	15	A	Rochdale	L 0-3	0-1	—		2925
44	19	A	Accrington S	W 2-0	0-0	13	Bishop 54, Leary 82	1288
45	26	H	Stockport Co	W 2-1	0-0	11	Puncheon 47, Akurang 81	3074
46	May 3	A	Rotherham U	L 0-1	0-1	12		4834

Final League Position: 12

GOALSCORERS

League (56): Birchall 11, Puncheon 10 (2 pens), Akurang 7 (1 pen), Hatch 6, Adomah 5 (1 pen), Thomas 4, Bishop 2, Nicolau 2, Yakubu 2, Burton 1, Carew 1, Leary 1, Norville 1, Porter 1, Wright 1, own goal 1.
Carling Cup (2): Birchall 1, Puncheon 1.
FA Cup (6): Birchall 2, Hatch 2, Yakubu 1, own goal 1.
J Paint Trophy (1): Birchall 1.

Harrison L 37 + 1	Devera J 41	Nicolau N 31 + 7	Bishop N 39	Yakubu I 28	Burton S 29 + 1	Carew A 18 + 15	Leary M 19 + 3	Thomas A 14 + 12	Birchall A 36 + 6	Puncheon J 37 + 4	Porter M 26 + 4	Hatch L 10 + 11	Hendon I 2 + 2	Seanla C 1 + 2	Hart D — + 2	O'Cearuill J 9 + 5	Angus S 1	Gillet K 30 + 1	Wright J 31 + 1	Norville J 5 + 3	Grazioli G 2 + 9	Beckwith R 9	Akurang C 17 + 4	Adomah A 22	St Aimie K 5 + 5	Parkes J 7 + 3	*Match No.*
1	2	3	4	5	6	7^1	8	9^2	10	11	12	13															1
1	5■	3			6	4^2	8	9	10^1	11	7	12	2	13													2
1		3			6^1		8^2	9	10	11	7	14	2	4	13^3	12	5■										3
1	2	12		5	6	7		9	10^2	11	4	13						3	8^1								4
1	2		4	5	6	7^1		9^2	10	11	8	13						3	12								5
1	2	12	4	5	6			9^2	10^3	11	8^1	13						3	7	14							6
1	2	12	4	5^3	6			13	10	11	7					14		3^1	8	9^2							7
1	2	3	4	5	6	12		13	10^2	11	7^1	14							8	9^3							8
1	2^2	3	4	5	6	7			10	11		12				13			8	9^1							9
1	2	3	4	5^2	6	7			10	11		12				13			8	9^1							10
1	2^2	3	4		6	7		14	10	11	8^3	12	13			5				9^1							11
1	2	3	4		6	7			10^2	11		9^1		12		5			8		13						12
1	2	3	4		6	7			10^2	11		9^1				5			8	12	13						13
1	2	3^2	4		6	7^1	12		10	11^3		9				5		14	8	13							14
1	2	9^1	4		6	13	7^2		10	11		12				5		3	8								15
1	2	12	4	5	6		8^2		10	11	7^1	9	13					3									16
1	2^2	13	4	5^3	6	12	8^1		10	11		9				14		3	7								17
1	2^2		4^1	5		7^3	12		10	11	13	9				6		3	8		14						18
1	2	12	4	5		7^1	8		13	11		9				6		3			10^2						19
1	2		4	5		7^1	8	12	10	11		9				6■		3									20
1	2	3	4	5■		12	8^1		10	11	7	9^2						6			13						21
1	2	3	4			12	8^1	13	10	11	7	9^2				5		6									22
	2	3	4	5		7	8			11	9							6				1	10				23
	2	3	4	5		7				11	8							6	9			1	10				24
1	2	3	4	5		12			13	11	9							6	8				10^2	7^1			25
1	2	3	4	5				12	13	11^3	9							6	8				10^1	7^2	14		26
	2	3^2	4	5					12	11^1	9							6	8			1	10	7	13		27
	2		4	5		12		13	9		3^1							6	8			1	10	7	11^2		28
	2		4	5		12			13	11	6							3	8			1	10^2	7	9^1		29
	2			5	12	13	8■		9	11^3	6^2							3	4		14	1	10^1	7			30
	2		4	5	6			12	9^1	11	13							3	8^2		14	1	10^3	7			31
	2	12	4	5	6			13	9^2	11■								3^1	8			1	10	7			32
15	2	11	4	5	6				9^1									3	8		12	1G	10	7			33
1	2	3^2	4	5	6	12		13											8		9		10	7	11^1		34
1	2	11	4	5		12	13	9										3^1	8^2				10	7^3	14	6	35
1	2	11			6	12		9	10	13	4							3^2	8					7^1		5	36
1	2	11^2	4		6	12		9	10	13								3	8					7^1		5	37
1	2	11	4	5	6			9^2	10		12							3^1	8					7	13		38
1	2	3	4		6	12		9^3	10^1	13									8				14	7	11^2	5	39
1	2	3	4			7^1	8	12	13	14	6												10^3	9	11^2	5	40
1	2	3	4		6		5	9^1	10	11	8												12	7			41
1	2^3	3	4^1		6	12	5	9^2	10	11	8												13	7		14	42
1		3	4		6		5	9^1	10	11	8												12	7		2	43
1			4^1		6	3	5		10	11								2	8				9	7		12	44
1		3				4^2	5		10^1	11	2				14			6	8		12		9	7^3		13	45
1		3					5	12	10^1	11	4							6	8		13		9^2	7^3	14	2	46

FA Cup

First Round	Gillingham	(h)	2-1
Second Round	Burton Alb	(a)	1-1
		(h)	1-0
Third Round	Swindon T	(a)	1-1
		(h)	1-1
Fourth Round	Bristol R	(h)	0-1

Carling Cup

First Round	Norwich C	(a)	2-5

J Paint Trophy

Second Round	Brighton & HA	(a)	1-2

BARNSLEY FL Championship

FOUNDATION

Many clubs owe their inception to the church and Barnsley are among them, for they were formed in 1887 by the Rev. T. T. Preedy, curate of Barnsley St Peter's and went under that name until it was dropped in 1897 a year before being admitted to the Second Division of the Football League.

Oakwell Stadium, Grove Street, Barnsley, South Yorkshire S71 1ET.

Telephone: (01226) 211 211.

Fax: (01226) 211 444.

Ticket Office: (0871) 22 66 777.

Website: www.barnsleyfc.co.uk

Email: thereds@barnsleyfc.co.uk

Ground Capacity: 23,176.

Record Attendance: 40,255 v Stoke C, FA Cup 5th rd, 15 February 1936.

Pitch Measurements: 110yd × 73yd.

Chairman: James Gordon Shepherd.

General Manager/Secretary: Albert Donald Rowing.

Manager: Simon Davey.

Assistant Manager: Ryan Kidd.

Physio: Richard Kay.

Colours: Red shirts, white shorts, red stockings.

Change Colours: Black shirts with red trim, black shorts with red trim, black stockings with red trim.

Year Formed: 1887.

Turned Professional: 1888.

Ltd Co.: 1899.

Previous Name: 1887, Barnsley St Peter's; 1897, Barnsley.

Club Nickname: 'The Tykes', 'Reds' or 'Colliers'.

Ground: 1887, Oakwell.

First Football League Game: 1 September 1898, Division 2, v Lincoln C (a) L 0–1 – Fawcett; McArtney, Nixon; King, Burleigh, Porteous; Davis, Lees, Murray, McCullough, McGee.

Record League Victory: 9–0 v Loughborough T, Division 2, 28 January 1899 – Greaves; McArtney, Nixon; Porteous, Burleigh, Howard; Davis (4), Hepworth (1), Lees (1), McCullough (1), Jones (2). 9–0 v Accrington S, Division 3 (N), 3 February 1934 – Ellis; Cookson, Shotton; Harper, Henderson, Whitworth; Spence (2), Smith (1), Blight (4), Andrews (1), Ashton (1).

Record Cup Victory: 6–0 v Blackpool, FA Cup 1st rd replay, 20 January 1910 – Mearns; Downs, Ness; Glendinning, Boyle (1), Utley; Bartrop, Gadsby (1), Lillycrop (2), Tufnell (2), Forman. 6–0 v Peterborough U, League Cup 1st rd 2nd leg, 15 September 1981 – Horn; Joyce, Chambers, Glavin (2), Banks, McCarthy, Evans, Parker (2), Aylott (1), McHale, Barrowclough (1).

HONOURS

Football League: Division 1 – Runners-up 1996–97; Promoted from FL 1 (play-offs) 2005–06; Division 3 (N) – Champions 1933–34, 1938–39, 1954–55; Runners-up 1953–54; Division 3 – Runners-up 1980–81; Division 4 – Runners-up 1967–68; Promoted 1978–79.

FA Cup: Winners 1912; Runners-up 1910.

Football League Cup: best season: 5th rd, 1982.

SKY SPORTS FACT FILE

No other Football League club has managed to win successive FA Cup ties in disposing of two of the top four Premier League clubs as Barnsley did in 2007–08. After winning 2–1 against Liverpool at Anfield, they beat Chelsea 1–0 at Oakwell.

Record Defeat: 0–9 v Notts Co, Division 2, 19 November 1927.

Most League Points (2 for a win): 67, Division 3 (N), 1938–39.

Most League Points (3 for a win): 82, Division 1, 1999–2000.

Most League Goals: 118, Division 3 (N), 1933–34.

Highest League Scorer in Season: Cecil McCormack, 33, Division 2, 1950–51.

Most League Goals in Total Aggregate: Ernest Hine, 123, 1921–26 and 1934–38.

Most League Goals in One Match: 5, Frank Eaton v South Shields, Division 3N, 9 April 1927; 5, Peter Cunningham v Darlington, Division 3N, 4 February 1933; 5, Beau Asquith v Darlington, Division 3N, 12 November 1938; 5, Cecil McCormack v Luton T, Division 2, 9 September 1950.

Most Capped Player: Gerry Taggart, 35 (50), Northern Ireland.

Most League Appearances: Barry Murphy, 514, 1962–78.

Youngest League Player: Alan Ogley, 16 years 226 days v Bristol R, 18 September 1962.

Record Transfer Fee Received: £4,500,000 from Blackburn R for Ashley Ward, December 1998.

Record Transfer Fee Paid: £1,500,000 to Partizan Belgrade for Georgi Hristov, July 1997.

Football League Record: 1898 Elected to Division 2; 1932–34 Division 3 (N); 1934–38 Division 2; 1938–39 Division 3 (N); 1946–53 Division 2; 1953–55 Division 3 (N); 1955–59 Division 2; 1959–65 Division 3; 1965–68 Division 4; 1968–72 Division 3; 1972–79 Division 4; 1979–81 Division 3; 1981–92 Division 2; 1992–97 Division 1; 1997–98 FA Premier League; 1998–2002 Division 1; 2002–04 Division 2; 2004–06 FL 1; 2006– FL C.

MANAGERS

Arthur Fairclough 1898–1901 *(Secretary-Manager)*
John McCartney 1901–04 *(Secretary-Manager)*
Arthur Fairclough 1904–12
John Hastie 1912–14
Percy Lewis 1914–19
Peter Sant 1919–26
John Commins 1926–29
Arthur Fairclough 1929–30
Brough Fletcher 1930–37
Angus Seed 1937–53
Tim Ward 1953–60
Johnny Steele 1960–71 *(continued as General Manager)*
John McSeveney 1971–72
Johnny Steele *(General Manager)* 1972–73
Jim Iley 1973–78
Allan Clarke 1978–80
Norman Hunter 1980–84
Bobby Collins 1984–85
Allan Clarke 1985–89
Mel Machin 1989–93
Viv Anderson 1993–94
Danny Wilson 1994–98
John Hendrie 1998–99
Dave Bassett 1999–2000
Nigel Spackman 2001
Steve Parkin 2001–02
Glyn Hodges 2002–03
Gudjon Thordarson 2003–04
Paul Hart 2004–05
Andy Ritchie 2005–06
Simon Davey January 2007–

LATEST SEQUENCES

Longest Sequence of League Wins: 10, 5.3.1955 – 23.4.1955.

Longest Sequence of League Defeats: 9, 14.3.1953 – 25.4.1953.

Longest Sequence of League Draws: 7, 28.3.1911 – 22.4.1911.

Longest Sequence of Unbeaten League Matches: 21, 1.1.1934 – 5.5.1934.

Longest Sequence Without a League Win: 26, 13.12.1952 – 26.8.1953.

Successive Scoring Runs: 44 from 2.10.1926.

Successive Non-scoring Runs: 6 from 7.10.1899.

TEN YEAR LEAGUE RECORD

		P	*W*	*D*	*L*	*F*	*A*	*Pts*	*Pos*
1998-99	Div 1	46	14	17	15	59	56	59	13
1999-2000	Div 1	46	24	10	12	88	67	82	4
2000-01	Div 1	46	15	9	22	49	62	54	16
2001-02	Div 1	46	11	15	20	59	86	48	23
2002-03	Div 2	46	13	13	20	51	64	52	19
2003-04	Div 2	46	15	17	14	54	58	62	12
2004-05	FL 1	46	14	19	13	69	64	61	13
2005-06	FL 1	46	18	18	10	62	44	72	5
2006-07	FL C	46	15	5	26	53	85	50	20
2007-08	FL C	46	14	13	19	52	65	55	18

DID YOU KNOW ?

Barnsley, winners of the FA Cup in 1911–12 after a lengthy twelve matches, had a four game marathon en route with Bradford City in which no goals were scored until the third replay at Bramall Lane. Barnsley just edged it 3–2.

BARNSLEY 2007–08 LEAGUE RECORD

Match No.	Date	Venue	Opponents	Result	H/T Score	Lg. Pos.	Goalscorers	Atten-dance
1	Aug 11	H	Coventry C	L 1-4	1-1	—	Howard (pen) [9]	12,616
2	18	A	Colchester U	D 2-2	1-1	22	Howard 2 (2 pens) [28, 85]	4450
3	25	H	Plymouth Arg	W 3-2	2-0	17	Ferenczi [12], Werling [45], Howard [60]	9240
4	Sept 1	A	WBA	L 0-2	0-2	21		18,310
5	15	H	Scunthorpe U	W 2-0	1-0	14	Williams (og) [45], Odejayi [65]	11,230
6	18	A	Stoke C	D 0-0	0-0	—		13,071
7	22	A	Southampton	W 3-2	2-1	7	McCann 2 [27, 40], Devaney [90]	19,151
8	29	H	Cardiff C	D 1-1	0-0	8	Howard [84]	10,709
9	Oct 2	H	Bristol C	W 3-0	0-0	—	Howard [67], Souza [72], Devaney [88]	9679
10	6	A	Charlton Ath	D 1-1	0-0	6	Christensen [90]	21,801
11	20	H	Burnley	D 1-1	0-1	7	Mostto [71]	11,560
12	22	A	Hull C	L 0-3	0-2	—		15,761
13	27	A	Leicester C	L 0-2	0-2	13		24,133
14	Nov 3	H	Preston NE	W 1-0	1-0	11	Ferenczi [42]	10,223
15	5	H	Blackpool	W 2-1	1-0	—	Howard (pen) [21], Ferenczi [70]	8531
16	10	A	Wolverhampton W	L 0-1	0-1	10		22,231
17	24	H	Watford	W 3-2	2-2	7	Howard [31], Devaney [34], lee (og) [66]	10,117
18	27	A	Sheffield W	L 0-1	0-0	—		27,769
19	Dec 1	A	Ipswich T	D 0-0	0-0	12		19,540
20	4	H	Wolverhampton W	W 1-0	0-0	—	Ferenczi [47]	9956
21	8	H	Crystal Palace	D 0-0	0-0	9		10,298
22	15	A	Sheffield U	L 0-1	0-0	10		26,629
23	22	A	Bristol C	L 2-3	2-2	12	Macken [33], Souza [40]	16,588
24	26	H	Stoke C	D 3-3	1-1	12	Howard (pen) [23], Macken 2 [66, 85]	12,398
25	29	H	Southampton	D 2-2	2-0	13	Togwell [1], Campbell-Ryce [34]	10,425
26	Jan 1	A	Scunthorpe U	D 2-2	0-1	13	McCann [74], Howard (pen) [90]	6897
27	12	H	Norwich C	L 1-3	1-0	15	Devaney [18]	10,117
28	19	A	QPR	L 0-2	0-2	16		16,197
29	29	H	Colchester U	W 1-0	1-0	—	Nardiello [45]	9246
30	Feb 2	A	Coventry C	L 0-4	0-1	17		16,449
31	9	H	WBA	W 2-1	2-0	14	Nardiello [30], Macken [45]	13,083
32	12	A	Plymouth Arg	L 0-3	0-1	—		11,346
33	23	A	Norwich C	L 0-1	0-1	17		24,197
34	26	H	QPR	D 0-0	0-0	—		9019
35	Mar 1	H	Sheffield W	D 0-0	0-0	16		18,257
36	4	A	Blackpool	D 1-1	1-1	—	Campbell-Ryce [45]	8080
37	11	H	Ipswich T	W 4-1	1-1	—	Howard 2 (1 pen) [27, 83 (p)], Macken [50], Wright (og) [86]	11,333
38	15	A	Crystal Palace	L 0-2	0-0	17		17,459
39	22	H	Sheffield U	L 0-1	0-0	18		15,798
40	29	A	Burnley	L 1-2	1-2	20	Howard [43]	11,915
41	Apr 9	A	Watford	W 3-0	1-0	—	Odejayi 2 [36, 54], Foster [47]	16,129
42	12	A	Preston NE	W 2-1	1-0	17	Leon [33], Macken (pen) [55]	13,994
43	15	H	Hull C	L 1-3	0-1	—	Ferenczi [90]	13,061
44	19	H	Leicester C	L 0-1	0-0	19		14,644
45	26	H	Charlton Ath	W 3-0	2-0	17	Campbell-Ryce [11], Nyatanga [33], Macken [85]	11,228
46	May 4	A	Cardiff C	L 0-3	0-1	18		14,469

Final League Position: 18

GOALSCORERS

League (52): Howard 13 (7 pens), Macken 7 (1 pen), Ferenczi 5, Devaney 4, Campbell-Ryce 3, McCann 3, Odejayi 3, Nardiello 2, Souza 2, Christensen 1, Foster 1, Leon 1, Mostto 1, Nyatanga 1, Togwell 1, Werling 1, own goals 3.
Carling Cup (2): Ferenczi 1, Reid 1.
FA Cup (6): Foster 2, Campbell-Ryce 1, Coulson 1, Howard 1, Odejayi 1.

Colgan N 1	Souza D 45	Kozluk R 24	Reid P 2 + 1	Nyatanga L 40 + 1	Howard B 41	Devaney M 24 + 10	Johnson A 4	Ferenczi I 25 + 12	Mostto M 7 + 7	Ricketts R 2 + 8	Togwell S 10 + 12	Odejayi K 23 + 16	Werling D 16 + 1	Muller H 28	Christensen K — + 12	McCann G 11 + 8	Foster S 41	Anderson 20	Campbell-Ryce J 34 + 3	Macken J 28 + 1	Van Homoet M 17 + 2	Hassell B 17 + 3	Coulson M 1 + 11	Leon D 16 + 2	Tininho3	Nardiello D 8 + 3	Warner T 3	Steele L 14	Butterfield J 1 + 2	Mattis D — + 1	Adam J — + 1	*Match No.*
1	2^{3}	3	4	5	6	7	8^{1}	9	10^{2}	11	12	13	14																			1
	2	3	4■	5	6		8^{1}	9		11^{2}	12	10	7^{3}	1	13	14																2
	2	3		5	6		8	9		12		10^{2}	7^{1}	1	13		4	11														3
	2	3		5	6		8^{1}	9^{3}		14		10	7^{2}	1	13	12	4	11														4
	2	3			6	12		9^{3}			13	10	11	1	14	8	5	4^{2}	7^{1}													5
	2	3^{1}		12	6	13		9				10	8	1		11	5	4	7^{2}													6
	2		12	5	6	13		9^{3}			14	10	3■	1		11	4	8^{1}	7^{2}													7
	2	3		5	8	12		9^{2}	13			10		1		11	6	4	7^{1}													8
	2			5	6	12			10^{3}		13	9	3	1	14	11^{2}	4	8	7^{1}													9
	2^{2}			5	6	12			10			9	3	1	13	11	4	8	7^{1}													10
	2			5	6	11			10	12		9	3	1		8	4		7^{1}													11
	2			5	6	12			10	13		9	3	1	14	11^{1}	4^{3}	8	7^{2}													12
	2	3		5	6	7			10^{3}	12	8^{2}	9		1	14	13	4		11^{1}													13
	2	3		5	6	11^{3}		9^{1}	12		8	13		1		14	4		7	10^{2}												14
	2	3		5	6	11^{1}		9		12	8	13		1		14	4		7^{3}	10^{2}												15
	2			5	6	11		9		12	8^{3}	13	3^{2}	1		14	4		7^{1}	10												16
	2			5	6	11		9					3	1		12	4	8	7^{1}	10												17
	2			5	6	11		9^{1}				12	3^{2}	1	13		4	8	7	10												18
	2			5		7		9^{1}			6		3	1	12	11	4	8		10												19
	2			5	6	11^{2}		9^{3}	12		13		3	1	14		4	8	7	10^{1}												20
	2			5	6	11		9^{1}	12				3	1	13		4	8	7	10^{2}												21
	2			5	6	11^{2}		9^{1}	12			13		1			4	8	7	10	3											22
	2			5	6	11^{1}		9^{2}			12	13		1			4	8	7■	10	3											23
	2			5	6	7^{2}		9^{1}			8	12		1		11	4■			10	3	13										24
	2			5	6	11		9	12		8	10^{1}		1					7		3	4										25
	2			5^{1}	6	11^{2}		9^{3}	12		8	10		1		13	4		7		3		14									26
	2				6	11^{1}		12	10^{2}			9		1		8	4		7^{3}		3	5	13	14								27
	2				6	11^{3}		12		14		13		1			5		7		3	8	10^{2}	9^{1}	4							28
	2				6			12				13		1			4		7^{2}	10	3	5		8	11	9^{1}						29
	2			5	6	13		12				14					4	8	7^{2}	10				11^{3}	3	9^{1}	1					30
	2	3		5	6	11		12									4	8		10^{1}		13	14	7^{2}		9^{3}	1					31
	2	3		5■	6	11^{1}		12									4	8	13	10		14		7^{2}		9^{3}	1					32
	2	3			6	11		9				12					4	8^{2}		14	13	5		7^{1}		10^{3}		1				33
	2			5	6	11^{2}		9^{1}				12					4		7	10	3	8		13				1				34
		2■		5	6	13						12					4		7^{3}	10	3	8	14	11^{2}		9^{1}		1				35
	2			5	6	12					8	9					4		7	10^{2}	3^{1}	11	13					1				36
	2	3		5	6^{3}			12			13	9^{1}					4		7	10		8		11^{2}				1	14			37
	2	3		5	6			9^{2}			8	11					4		12	10^{3}	7^{1}		14			13		1				38
	2^{2}	3		5	6	11		12				9^{3}					4			10	13	8		7^{1}		14		1				39
	2	3		5	6							12					4		7^{2}	10		8	13	11^{1}		9		1				40
	2	3		5				12			13	9^{1}					4		7^{2}	10^{3}	6	8	14	11				1				41
	2	3		5				12			13	9^{3}					4		7^{2}	10^{1}	6	8	14	11				1				42
	2	3		5^{3}				12				9^{2}					4		7^{1}	10	6	8	14	11		13		1				43
	2	3		5	6	7^{1}						13					4		12	10		8^{3}	14	11		9^{2}		1				44
	2	3		5	6^{3}			12			13	9							7	10	4^{1}	8		11^{2}				1	14			45
	2	3^{2}		5				9^{3}			12								7	10	4	8^{1}		11				1	6	13	14	46

FA Cup

Third Round	Blackpool	(h)	2-1
Fourth Round	Southend U	(a)	1-0
Fifth Round	Liverpool	(a)	2-1
Sixth Round	Chelsea	(h)	1-0
Semi-Final *(at Wembley)*	Cardiff C		0-1

Carling Cup

First Round	Darlington	(h)	2-1
Second Round	Newcastle U	(a)	0-2

BIRMINGHAM CITY FL Championship

FOUNDATION

In 1875, cricketing enthusiasts who were largely members of Trinity Church, Bordesley, determined to continue their sporting relationships throughout the year by forming a football club which they called Small Heath Alliance. For their earliest games played on waste land in Arthur Street, the team included three Edden brothers and two James brothers.

St Andrews Stadium, Birmingham B9 4NH.

Telephone: 0844 557 1875.

Fax: 0844 557 1975.

Ticket Office: (0844) 557 1875 (then option 2).

Website: www.bcfc.com

Email: reception@bcfc.com

Ground Capacity: 30,079.

Record Attendance: 66,844 v Everton, FA Cup 5th rd, 11 February 1939.

Pitch Measurements: 101m × 68m.

Chairman: David Sullivan (PLC), David Gold (FC).

Vice-chairman: Jack Wiseman.

Managing Director: Karren Brady.

Secretary: Julia Shelton.

Manager: Alex McLeish.

First Team Coaches: Roy Aitken, Andy Watson.

Physio: Neil McDiarmid.

Colours: Blue shirts, blue shorts, white stockings.

Change Colours: White shirts with a broad red vertical panel, white shorts, red and white stockings.

Year Formed: 1875.

Turned Professional: 1885.

Ltd Co.: 1888.

Previous Names: 1875, Small Heath Alliance; 1888, dropped 'Alliance'; 1905, Birmingham; 1945, Birmingham City.

Club Nickname: 'Blues'.

Grounds: 1875, waste ground near Arthur St; 1877, Muntz St, Small Heath; 1906, St Andrews.

First Football League game: 3 September 1892, Division 2, v Burslem Port Vale (h) W 5–1 – Charsley; Bayley, Speller; Ollis, Jenkyns, Devey; Hallam (1), Edwards (1), Short (1), Wheldon (2), Hands.

Record League Victory: 12–0 v Walsall T Swifts, Division 2, 17 December 1892 – Charsley; Bayley, Jones; Ollis, Jenkyns, Devey; Hallam (2), Walton (3), Mobley (3), Wheldon (2), Hands (2). 12–0 v Doncaster R, Division 2, 11 April 1903 – Dorrington; Goldie, Wassell; Beer, Dougherty (1), Howard; Athersmith (1), Leonard (3), McRoberts (1), Wilcox (4), Field (1). Aston, (1 og).

HONOURS

Football League: Promoted from FL C – Runners-up 2006–07; Division 1 (play-offs) 2001–02; Division 2 – Champions 1892–93, 1920–21, 1947–48, 1954–55, 1994–95; Runners-up 1893–94, 1900–01, 1902–03, 1971–72, 1984–85; Division 3 Runners-up 1991–92.

FA Cup: Runners-up 1931, 1956.

Football League Cup: Winners 1963; Runners-up 2001.

Leyland Daf Cup: Winners 1991.

Auto Windscreens Shield: Winners 1995.

European Competitions: *European Fairs Cup:* 1955–58, 1958–60 (runners-up), 1960–61 (runners-up), 1961–62.

SKY SPORTS FACT FILE

Amateur goalkeeper Chris Charsley, signed by Small Heath Alliance in 1886, was capped for England in 1893. His status was such because of his role as a policeman. Eventually he graduated to become the Chief Constable of Coventry!

Record Cup Victory: 9–2 v Burton W, FA Cup 1st rd, 31 October 1885 – Hedges; Jones, Evetts (1); F. James, Felton, A. James (1); Davenport (2), Stanley (4), Simms, Figures, Morris (1).

Record Defeat: 1–9 v Sheffield W, Division 1, 13 December 1930. 1–9 v Blackburn R, Division 1, 5 January 1895.

Most League Points (2 for a win): 59, Division 2, 1947–48.

Most League Points (3 for a win): 89, Division 2, 1994–95.

Most League Goals: 103, Division 2, 1893–94 (only 28 games).

Highest League Scorer in Season: Joe Bradford, 29, Division 1, 1927–28.

Most League Goals in Total Aggregate: Joe Bradford, 249, 1920–35.

Most League Goals in One Match: 5, Walter Abbott v Darwen, Division 2, 26 November, 1898; 5, John McMillan v Blackpool, Division 2, 2 March 1901; 5, James Windridge v Glossop, Division 2, 23 January 1915.

Most Capped Player: Kenny Cunningham, 32 (72), Republic of Ireland.

Most League Appearances: Frank Womack, 491, 1908–28.

Youngest League Player: Trevor Francis, 16 years 7 months v Cardiff C, 5 September 1970.

Record Transfer Fee Received: £6,800,000 from Liverpool for Jermaine Pennant, July 2006.

Record Transfer Fee Paid: £5,875,000 to Liverpool for Emile Heskey, July 2004.

Football League Record: 1892 elected to Division 2; 1894–96 Division 1; 1896–1901 Division 2; 1901–02 Division 1; 1902–03 Division 2; 1903–08 Division 1; 1908–21 Division 2; 1921–39 Division 1; 1946–48 Division 2; 1948–50 Division 1; 1950–55 Division 2; 1955–65 Division 1; 1965–72 Division 2; 1972–79 Division 1; 1979–80 Division 2; 1980–84 Division 1; 1984–85 Division 2; 1985–86 Division 1; 1986–89 Division 2; 1989–92 Division 3; 1992–94 Division 1; 1994–95 Division 2; 1995–2002 Division 1; 2002–06 FA Premier League; 2006–07 FL C; 2007–08 FA Premier League; 2008– FL C.

MANAGERS

Alfred Jones 1892–1908
(Secretary-Manager)
Alec Watson 1908–10
Bob McRoberts 1910–15
Frank Richards 1915–23
Billy Beer 1923–27
William Harvey 1927–28
Leslie Knighton 1928–33
George Liddell 1933–39
Harry Storer 1945–48
Bob Brocklebank 1949–54
Arthur Turner 1954–58
Pat Beasley 1959–60
Gil Merrick 1960–64
Joe Mallett 1965
Stan Cullis 1965–70
Fred Goodwin 1970–75
Willie Bell 1975–77
Sir Alf Ramsay 1977–78
Jim Smith 1978–82
Ron Saunders 1982–86
John Bond 1986–87
Garry Pendrey 1987–89
Dave Mackay 1989–91
Lou Macari 1991
Terry Cooper 1991–93
Barry Fry 1993–96
Trevor Francis 1996–2001
Steve Bruce 2001–07
Alex McLeish November 2007–

LATEST SEQUENCES

Longest Sequence of League Wins: 13, 17.12.1892 – 16.9.1893.

Longest Sequence of League Defeats: 8, 28.9.1985 – 23.11.1985.

Longest Sequence of League Draws: 8, 18.9.1990 – 23.10.1990.

Longest Sequence of Unbeaten League Matches: 20, 3.9.1994 – 2.1.1995.

Longest Sequence Without a League Win: 17, 28.9.1985 – 18.1.1986.

Successive Scoring Runs: 24 from 24.9.1892.

Successive Non-scoring Runs: 6 from 1.10.1949.

TEN YEAR LEAGUE RECORD

		P	*W*	*D*	*L*	*F*	*A*	*Pts*	*Pos*
1998-99	Div 1	46	23	12	11	66	37	81	4
1999-2000	Div 1	46	22	11	13	65	44	77	5
2000-01	Div 1	46	23	9	14	59	48	78	5
2001-02	Div 1	46	21	13	12	70	49	76	5
2002-03	PR Lge	38	13	9	16	41	49	48	13
2003-04	PR Lge	38	12	14	12	43	48	50	10
2004-05	PR Lge	38	11	12	15	40	46	45	12
2005-06	PR Lge	38	8	10	20	28	50	34	18
2006-07	FL C	46	26	8	12	67	42	86	2
2007-08	PR Lge	38	8	11	19	46	62	35	19

DID YOU KNOW ?

Of the comparatively small number of players who appeared in every Premier League match in 2007–08, only right-back Stephen Kelly at Birmingham City managed to play the entire 90 minutes in every one of the club's 38 matches in the competition.

BIRMINGHAM CITY 2007–08 LEAGUE RECORD

Match No.	*Date*	*Venue*	*Opponents*	*Result*	*H/T Score*	*Lg. Pos.*	*Goalscorers*	*Attendance*
1	Aug 12	A	Chelsea	L 2-3	2-2	—	Forssell [15], Kapo [36]	41,590
2	15	H	Sunderland	D 2-2	1-0	—	McShane (og) [28], O'Connor [82]	24,898
3	18	H	West Ham U	L 0-1	0-0	18		24,961
4	25	A	Derby Co	W 2-1	1-0	12	Jerome 2 [1, 63]	31,117
5	Sept 1	A	Middlesbrough	L 0-2	0-2	16		22,920
6	15	H	Bolton W	W 1-0	1-0	12	Kapo [37]	28,124
7	22	A	Liverpool	D 0-0	0-0	14		44,215
8	29	H	Manchester U	L 0-1	0-0	13		26,526
9	Oct 7	A	Blackburn R	L 1-2	0-1	13	Jerome [68]	19,316
10	20	A	Manchester C	L 0-1	0-1	14		45,688
11	27	H	Wigan Ath	W 3-2	1-1	13	Kapo 2 (1 pen) [26 (p), 81], Ridgewell [67]	27,661
12	Nov 3	A	Everton	L 1-3	0-1	14	Kapo [80]	35,155
13	11	H	Aston Villa	L 1-2	0-1	15	Forssell [62]	26,539
14	24	H	Portsmouth	L 0-2	0-1	16		22,089
15	Dec 2	A	Tottenham H	W 3-2	1-0	12	McSheffrey (pen) [24], Jerome [62], Larsson [90]	35,635
16	8	A	Newcastle U	L 1-2	1-1	15	Jerome [9]	49,948
17	15	H	Reading	D 1-1	1-0	15	Forssell [4]	27,300
18	22	A	Bolton W	L 0-3	0-0	16		19,111
19	26	H	Middlesbrough	W 3-0	2-0	14	Downing (og) [22], Forssell [45], McSheffrey (pen) [90]	24,094
20	29	H	Fulham	D 1-1	0-1	15	Larsson [55]	28,923
21	Jan 1	A	Manchester U	L 0-1	0-1	15		75,459
22	12	A	Arsenal	D 1-1	0-1	16	O'Connor [48]	60,037
23	19	H	Chelsea	L 0-1	0-0	16		26,567
24	29	A	Sunderland	L 0-2	0-1	—		37,674
25	Feb 2	H	Derby Co	D 1-1	0-0	18	Larsson [68]	25,924
26	9	A	West Ham U	D 1-1	1-1	17	McFadden (pen) [16]	34,884
27	23	H	Arsenal	D 2-2	1-0	17	McFadden 2 (1 pen) [28, 90 (p)]	27,195
28	Mar 1	H	Tottenham H	W 4-1	1-0	16	Forssell 3 [7, 59, 81], Larsson [55]	26,055
29	12	A	Portsmouth	L 2-4	2-2	—	Muamba [10], Larsson [40]	20,138
30	17	H	Newcastle U	D 1-1	1-0	—	McFadden [33]	25,777
31	22	A	Reading	L 1-2	0-1	17	Zarate [64]	24,085
32	29	H	Manchester C	W 3-1	1-0	17	Zarate 2 [40, 54], McSheffrey (pen) [77]	22,962
33	Apr 5	A	Wigan Ath	L 0-2	0-1	17		17,926
34	12	H	Everton	D 1-1	0-0	17	Zarate [83]	25,923
35	20	A	Aston Villa	L 1-5	0-2	18	Forssell [67]	42,584
36	26	H	Liverpool	D 2-2	1-0	18	Forssell [34], Larsson [55]	29,252
37	May 3	A	Fulham	L 0-2	0-0	19		25,308
38	11	H	Blackburn R	W 4-1	1-0	19	Murphy [31], Jerome 2 [73, 89], Muamba [90]	26,668

Final League Position: 19

GOALSCORERS

League (46): Forssell 9, Jerome 7, Larsson 6, Kapo 5 (1 pen), McFadden 4 (2 pens), Zarate 4, McSheffrey 3 (3 pens), Muamba 2, O'Connor 2, Murphy 1, Ridgewell 1, own goals 2.
Carling Cup (2): O'Connor 1, McSheffrey 1.
FA Cup (1): O'Connor 1.

Doyle C 3	Kelly S 38	Queudrue F 14+2	Nafti M 19+7	Djourou J 13	Ridgewell L 35	Larsson S 32+3	Muamba F 37	Forssell M 21+9	Kapo O 22+4	McSheffrey G 24+8	Jerome C 21+12	De Ridder D 6+4	Parnaby S 4+9	O'Connor G 5+18	Jaidi R 18	Sadler M 3+2	Taylor Maik 34	Melendez B 1+1	Schmitz R 12+3	Palacios W 4+3	Danns N —+2	Kingson R 1	Johnson D 17	McFadden J 10+2	Zarate M 6+8	Murphy D 14	Taylor Martin 4	*Match No.*
1	2	3[3]	4[2]	5	6	7	8	9	10	11[1]	12	13	14															1
1	3		4	5	6	7	8	9[1]	10	11[2]	12		2	13														2
1	3		4[2]		6	7	8[3]	9[1]	11	12	13		2	10	5	14												3
	3		12	5	6	13	8[3]	9[2]	7	11[1]	10		2		4	14	1											4
	2		12	5	6	7[2]	8[1]	9[3]	11	13	10		3	14	4		1											5
	2	3	4	5	6	7	8[2]		10	11[3]	9[1]			12			1	13	14									6
	2	3	4	5	6	7			10	12	9[3]			13			1	11[1]	14	8[2]								7
	2	3	4[1]	5[3]	6	7	8[2]		10	11	9			12			1		14	13								8
	2	3	4[3]	5	6	7	8[2]		10	11[1]	9			12			1			13	14							9
	2	3	4[1]		6		8		10	11[2]	9	13		12			1		5[3]	7	14							10
	2	3	4		6	12	8[3]		10	13	9	7[2]		14			1		5	11[1]								11
	2		4[1]	5	3	11[3]	8	13	10	12	9	7[2]		14			1		6									12
	2		4[1]	5	6	12	8	13	10		9[3]	7		14			1		3	11[2]								13
	2		4	5	6		8	9	10	11[1]		7		12					3			1						14
	2		4	5	6	7	8	12	13	10[2]	9	11[1]	14				1		3[3]									15
	2		4		6	7	8	12	13	10[2]	9	11[1]				3	1		5									16
	2				6	7	8	9[1]		11	10			12		3	1		5				4					17
	2			10		7	8		12	11[2]	9			13	6	3[1]	1		5				4					18
	2	3	12		6	7[1]	8	9[2]		11	10			13	5		1						4					19
	2	3	12		6	7[3]	8	9[2]		11	10	14		13	5		1						4[1]					20
	2	3	4[2]		6	7	8	12		11[3]	9[1]	14		10	5		1			13								21
	2	3[3]			6	7	8	12	10	13	9[2]		14	11[1]			1		5				4					22
	2	3			6	7	8	12	10		9[2]			11[1]			1		5				4	13				23
	2	3			6	7[1]	8	12	10		9[2]						1		5				4	11	13			24
	2				6	7[1]	8		10					9			1						4	11	12	3	5	25
	2				6	7	8	9[1]		11[2]	12		13				1						4	10		3	5	26
	2		12		6	7[1]	8	9[2]	10[3]				13				1						4	11	14	3	5▮	27
	2				6	7	8	9[1]		11[2]	12		13		5		1						4	10[3]	14	3		28
	2				6	7	8	9[1]		11	12				5		1						4	13	10[2]	3		29
	2				6	7[2]	8	9[1]		11	12		13		5		1						4	10[3]	14	3		30
	2		4		6	7	8	9[1]		11[2]	12			13	5		1								10	3		31
	2	6▮				7	8	9[1]		11			12	13	5		1						4		10[2]	3		32
	2		12			7	8	9[2]		11[1]	13		14		6		1						4▮		10	3	5[3]	33
	2		4		6	7[1]	8	9[2]		11	12			13	5		1							10[3]	14	3		34
	2		4		6		8	13	12	11	7[1]				5		1							9	10[2]	3		35
	2	12	4		6[1]	7	8	9[3]	10[2]	13					5		1							11	14	3		36
	2	12			6[1]	7	8	9[2]	10[3]		13				5		1						4	11	14	3		37
	2		12		6	7	8	9[2]	11[3]	14	13				5		1						4[1]		10	3		38

FA Cup
Third Round Huddersfield T (a) 1-2

Carling Cup
Second Round Hereford U (h) 2-1
Third Round Blackburn R (a) 0-3

BLACKBURN ROVERS FA Premiership

FOUNDATION

It was in 1875 that some Public School old boys called a meeting at which the Blackburn Rovers club was formed and the colours blue and white adopted. The leading light was John Lewis, later to become a founder of the Lancashire FA, a famous referee who was in charge of two FA Cup Finals, and a vice-president of both the FA and the Football League.

Ewood Park, Blackburn BB2 4JF.

Telephone: 0871 702 1875.

Fax: (01254) 671 042.

Ticket Office: 0871 222 1444.

Website: www.rovers.co.uk

Email: enquiries@rovers.co.uk

Ground Capacity: 31,154.

Record Attendance: 62,522 v Bolton W, FA Cup 6th rd, 2 March 1929.

Pitch Measurements: 105m × 65.8m.

Chairman: John Williams.

Vice-chairman: David Brown.

Managing Director: Tom Finn.

Secretary: Andrew Pincher.

Manager: Paul Ince.

Assistant Manager: Ray Mathias.

Physio: Dave Fevre.

Colours: Blue and white halved shirts.

Change Colours: Red and black halved shirts.

Year Formed: 1875.

Turned Professional: 1880.

Ltd Co.: 1897.

Club Nickname: Rovers.

Grounds: 1875, all matches played away; 1876, Oozehead Ground; 1877, Pleasington Cricket Ground; 1878, Alexandra Meadows; 1881, Leamington Road; 1890, Ewood Park.

First Football League Game: 15 September 1888, Football League, v Accrington (h) D 5–5 – Arthur; Beverley, James Southworth; Douglas, Almond, Forrest; Beresford (1), Walton, John Southworth (1), Fecitt (1), Townley (2).

Record League Victory: 9–0 v Middlesbrough, Division 2, 6 November 1954 – Elvy; Suart, Eckersley; Clayton, Kelly, Bell; Mooney (3), Crossan (2), Briggs, Quigley (3), Langton (1).

HONOURS

FA Premier League: Champions 1994–95; Runners-up 1993–94.

Football League: Division 1 – Champions 1911–12, 1913–14; 1991–92 (play-offs); Runners-up 2000–01; Division 2 – Champions 1938–39; Runners-up 1957–58; Division 3 – Champions 1974–75; Runners-up 1979–80.

FA Cup: Winners 1884, 1885, 1886, 1890, 1891, 1928; Runners-up 1882, 1960.

Football League Cup: Winners 2002.

Full Members' Cup: Winners 1987.

European Competitions: *European Cup:* 1995–96. *UEFA Cup:* 1994–95, 1998–99, 2002–03, 2003–04, 2006–07, 2007–08. *Intertoto Cup:* 2007.

SKY SPORTS FACT FILE

The most sustained period of success in the Football League for Blackburn Rovers came in the years up to the First World War from 1908–09 to 1914–15. They recorded two First Division championships, two third places and only once were they out of the top five clubs.

Record Cup Victory: 11–0 v Rossendale, FA Cup 1st rd, 13 October 1884 – Arthur; Hopwood, McIntyre; Forrest, Blenkhorn, Lofthouse; Sowerbutts (2), J. Brown (1), Fecitt (4), Barton (3), Birtwistle (1).

Record Defeat: 0–8 v Arsenal, Division 1, 25 February 1933.

Most League Points (2 for a win): 60, Division 3, 1974–75.

Most League Points (3 for a win): 91, Division 1, 2000–01.

Most League Goals: 114, Division 2, 1954–55.

Highest League Scorer in Season: Ted Harper, 43, Division 1, 1925–26.

Most League Goals in Total Aggregate: Simon Garner, 168, 1978–92.

Most League Goals in One Match: 7, Tommy Briggs v Bristol R, Division 2, 5 February 1955.

Most Capped Player: Henning Berg, 58 (100), Norway.

Most League Appearances: Derek Fazackerley, 596, 1970–86.

Youngest League Player: Harry Dennison, 16 years 155 days v Bristol C, 8 April 1911.

Record Transfer Fee Received: £16,000,000 from Chelsea for Damian Duff, July 2003.

Record Transfer Fee Paid: £7,500,000 to Manchester U for Andy Cole, December 2001.

Football League Record: 1888 Founder Member of the League; 1936–39 Division 2; 1946–48 Division 1; 1948–58 Division 2; 1958–66 Division 1; 1966–71 Division 2; 1971–75 Division 3; 1975–79 Division 2; 1979–80 Division 3; 1980–92 Division 2; 1992–99 FA Premier League; 1999–2001 Division 1; 2001– FA Premier League.

LATEST SEQUENCES

Longest Sequence of League Wins: 8, 1.3.1980 – 7.4.1980.

Longest Sequence of League Defeats: 7, 12.3.1966 – 16.4.1966.

Longest Sequence of League Draws: 5, 11.10.1975 – 1.11.1975.

Longest Sequence of Unbeaten League Matches: 23, 30.9.1987 – 27.3.1988.

Longest Sequence Without a League Win: 16, 11.11.1978 – 24.3.1979.

Successive Scoring Runs: 32 from 24.4.1954.

Successive Non-scoring Runs: 4 from 12.12.1908.

MANAGERS

Thomas Mitchell 1884–96
(Secretary-Manager)
J. Walmsley 1896–1903
(Secretary-Manager)
R. B. Middleton 1903–25
Jack Carr 1922–26
(Team Manager under Middleton to 1925)
Bob Crompton 1926–30
(Hon. Team Manager)
Arthur Barritt 1931–36
(had been Secretary from 1927)
Reg Taylor 1936–38
Bob Crompton 1938–41
Eddie Hapgood 1944–47
Will Scott 1947
Jack Bruton 1947–49
Jackie Bestall 1949–53
Johnny Carey 1953–58
Dally Duncan 1958–60
Jack Marshall 1960–67
Eddie Quigley 1967–70
Johnny Carey 1970–71
Ken Furphy 1971–73
Gordon Lee 1974–75
Jim Smith 1975–78
Jim Iley 1978
John Pickering 1978–79
Howard Kendall 1979–81
Bobby Saxton 1981–86
Don Mackay 1987–91
Kenny Dalglish 1991–95
Ray Harford 1995–97
Roy Hodgson 1997–98
Brian Kidd 1998–99
Tony Parkes 1999–2000
Graeme Souness 2000–04
Mark Hughes 2004–08
Paul Ince June 2008–

TEN YEAR LEAGUE RECORD

		P	*W*	*D*	*L*	*F*	*A*	*Pts*	*Pos*
1998-99	PR Lge	38	7	14	17	38	52	35	19
1999-2000	Div 1	46	15	17	14	55	51	62	11
2000-01	Div 1	46	26	13	7	76	39	91	2
2001-02	PR Lge	38	12	10	16	55	51	46	10
2002-03	PR Lge	38	16	12	10	52	43	60	6
2003-04	PR Lge	38	12	8	18	51	59	44	15
2004-05	PR Lge	38	9	15	14	32	43	42	15
2005-06	PR Lge	38	19	6	13	51	42	63	6
2006-07	PR Lge	38	15	7	16	52	54	52	10
2007-08	PR Lge	38	15	13	10	50	48	58	7

DID YOU KNOW ?

The quaintly named Robert Haresnape came into his own during the FA Cup run for Blackburn Rovers in 1888–89. This outside-right was picked up from local football and produced six goals in his four outings in the competition.

BLACKBURN ROVERS 2007–08 LEAGUE RECORD

Match No.	*Date*	*Venue*	*Opponents*	*Result*		*H/T Score*	*Lg. Pos.*	*Goalscorers*	*Attendance*
1	Aug 11	A	Middlesbrough	W	2-1	0-1	—	Santa Cruz [63], Derbyshire [79]	25,058
2	19	H	Arsenal	D	1-1	0-1	8	Dunn [72]	24,917
3	25	A	Everton	D	1-1	1-0	9	Santa Cruz [15]	33,850
4	Sept 2	H	Manchester C	W	1-0	1-0	7	McCarthy [13]	26,881
5	15	A	Chelsea	D	0-0	0-0	8		41,062
6	23	H	Portsmouth	L	0-1	0-1	10		19,506
7	29	A	Sunderland	W	2-1	0-0	7	Bentley [53], Santa Cruz [55]	41,252
8	Oct 7	H	Birmingham C	W	2-1	1-0	6	Bentley [15], McCarthy (pen) [56]	19,316
9	20	H	Reading	W	4-2	3-0	6	McCarthy 2 (1 pen) [18, 82 (p)], Santa Cruz [22], Tugay [32]	19,425
10	28	A	Tottenham H	W	2-1	0-0	5	McCarthy [60], Samba [90]	36,086
11	Nov 3	H	Liverpool	D	0-0	0-0	5		30,033
12	11	A	Manchester U	L	0-2	0-2	7		75,710
13	25	A	Fulham	D	2-2	0-0	9	Emerton [57], Warnock [79]	22,826
14	28	H	Aston Villa	L	0-4	0-1	—		20,776
15	Dec 1	H	Newcastle U	W	3-1	0-0	8	Bentley 2 [54, 67], Tugay [90]	27,477
16	9	H	West Ham U	L	0-1	0-0	9		20,870
17	15	A	Wigan Ath	L	3-5	1-3	9	Santa Cruz 3 [45, 50, 61]	16,489
18	23	H	Chelsea	L	0-1	0-1	10		23,966
19	27	A	Manchester C	D	2-2	1-2	—	Santa Cruz 2 [28, 84]	42,112
20	30	A	Derby Co	W	2-1	2-1	9	Santa Cruz [39], Bentley [42]	30,048
21	Jan 2	H	Sunderland	W	1-0	0-0	—	McCarthy (pen) [57]	23,212
22	13	A	Bolton W	W	2-1	0-1	8	Samba [53], Roberts [90]	18,315
23	19	H	Middlesbrough	D	1-1	0-1	9	Derbyshire [75]	21,687
24	26	A	Aston Villa	D	1-1	0-0	—	Santa Cruz [68]	39,602
25	Feb 2	H	Everton	D	0-0	0-0	8		27,946
26	11	A	Arsenal	L	0-2	0-1	—		60,049
27	24	H	Bolton W	W	4-1	1-0	9	McCarthy 2 (2 pens) [25, 67], Bentley [71], Pedersen [90]	23,995
28	Mar 1	A	Newcastle U	W	1-0	0-0	7	Derbyshire [90]	50,796
29	8	H	Fulham	D	1-1	0-0	7	Pedersen [59]	20,362
30	15	A	West Ham U	L	1-2	1-1	9	Santa Cruz [19]	34,006
31	22	H	Wigan Ath	W	3-1	2-1	8	Santa Cruz 2 [12, 63], Roberts [45]	23,541
32	29	A	Reading	D	0-0	0-0	7		24,374
33	Apr 5	H	Tottenham H	D	1-1	1-1	8	Pedersen [30]	24,592
34	13	A	Liverpool	L	1-3	0-0	9	Santa Cruz [90]	43,283
35	19	H	Manchester U	D	1-1	1-0	9	Santa Cruz [21]	30,316
36	27	A	Portsmouth	W	1-0	0-0	8	Santa Cruz [74]	18,722
37	May 3	H	Derby Co	W	3-1	1-1	7	Santa Cruz 2 [45, 77], Roberts [47]	26,110
38	11	A	Birmingham C	L	1-4	0-1	7	Pedersen [49]	26,668

Final League Position: 7

GOALSCORERS

League (50): Santa Cruz 19, McCarthy 8 (5 pens), Bentley 6, Pedersen 4, Derbyshire 3, Roberts 3, Samba 2, Tugay 2, Dunn 1, Emerton 1, Warnock 1.
Carling Cup (7): Santa Cruz 3, Bentley 1, Derbyshire 1 (pen), McCarthy 1, Pedersen 1.
FA Cup (1): Bentley 1.
Inter-Toto Cup (6): McCarthy 2, Derbyshire 1, Pedersen 1, Roberts 1, Samba 1.
UEFA Cup (5): Bentley 1, Derbyshire 1 (pen), Roberts 1, Santa Cruz 1, Warnock 1.

Friedel B 38	Ooijer A 23 + 4	Warnock S 37	Dunn D 25 + 6	Nelsen R 22	Samba C 33	Bentley D 37	Savage R 10 + 2	Roberts J 11 + 15	McCarthy B 21 + 10	Pedersen M 32 + 5	Santa Cruz R 36 + 1	Derbyshire M 4 + 19	Mokoena A 8 + 10	Emerton B 31 + 2	Tugay K 12 + 8	Rigters M — + 2	Khizanishvili Z 10 + 3	Reid S 20 + 4	Berner B 2	Olsson M — + 2	Vogel J 6	*Match No.*
1	2	3	4^{3}	5	6	7	8	9^{2}	10^{1}	11	12	13	14									1
1	12	3	4	5■	6	7	8		13	11	10^{2}	9^{1}		2								2
1	5	3	4^{3}		6	7	8	12	10^{2}	11	9^{1}	13	14	2								3
1	12	3	4	5	6	7	8^{3}		10^{1}	11	9^{2}	13		2	14■							4
1	12	3	4^{3}	5	6^{1}	7	8	13	10^{2}	11	9		14	2								5
1	5	3	4^{3}		6	7	8	12	10^{2}	11^{1}	9	13		2	14							6
1	5	3	11^{3}		6	7	12			13	9	10^{2}	8	2	4^{1}	14						7
1	5	3	10^{1}		6	7	8^{3}		12	11	9	13	14	2	4^{2}							8
1	5	3^{3}	11^{1}		6	7	8		10	12	9^{2}	13		2	4		14					9
1	5	3	11^{2}		6	7	8^{3}		10	12	9	13	14	2	4^{1}							10
1	2	3	4^{2}	5	6	8			10^{1}	11	9	12		7	13							11
1		3	4■	5	6	7			10	11	9^{1}	12	8	2								12
1	2	3		5	6	7		12	10^{1}	11			8^{2}	9	4			13				13
1	2	3	8	5■	6	11^{2}		12	10^{1}	13	9		4^{3}	7				14				14
1	5	3	11^{2}		6	7		12	10^{1}	13	9		8^{3}	2	4			14				15
1	5	3	7^{3}		6		12	13	10	11^{2}	9		8^{1}	2	4			14				16
1		3	12	5	6	7	4		10^{2}	11	9^{1}	13		2■				8				17
1		3	7	5		10		12		11	9			2	4^{1}		6	8				18
1			4^{3}	5	6	10		12	13	11	9^{1}			7	14		2^{2}	8	3			19
1		3	12	5		7			10^{2}	11^{3}	9	13	8	2	4^{1}		6			14		20
1		3	13	5	6	7			10	11	9^{1}	12^{2}	8	2	4							21
1	2^{3}	3	4	5	6	7		12	10^{1}	11	9^{2}	13					14	8				22
1	2	3	4^{2}	5	6	7		10		11^{1}	9	13		12				8				23
1	5	3	4		6	7		12		11	9	10^{1}		2				8				24
1	5	3	4^{1}			7			12	11	9	10^{2}		2	13		6	8				25
1	5^{3}	3				7		12	10^{1}		9		13	2	4^{2}	14	6	8	11			26
1		3	4^{2}		6	7		12	10^{1}	11	9		13	2			5	8				27
1	2	3			6	8		12	10^{1}	11	9	13		7^{2}			5	4				28
1	2	3			6	7		12	10^{2}	11	9	13			4^{1}		5	8				29
1	5	3	4^{2}		6	7		10	12	11^{1}	9	13		2^{3}			14	8				30
1	2	3	4^{2}		6■	7		10^{3}	12	11	9^{1}		13		14		5	8				31
1	2^{1}	3	4^{2}	5		7		10	12	11	9	13					6	8				32
1	2^{2}	3		5	6	7		10	12	11^{1}	9		14	13				8^{3}			4	33
1		3	12	5	6	7		10	13	11^{2}	9			2				8			4^{1}	34
1		3		5	6	7		10		11	9		12	2				8			4^{1}	35
1	13	3	12	5	6^{2}	7		10^{1}		11	9			2				8			4	36
1		3		5	6	7		10^{1}		11^{3}	9	12		2	13			8		14	4^{2}	37
1		3^{1}	13	5	6	7		10	12	11^{3}	9			2	14			8			4^{2}	38

Intertoto Cup

Third Round	Vetra	(a)	2-0
		(h)	4-0

UEFA Cup

Second Qualifying Round			
	MyPa	(a)	1-0
		(h)	2-0
First Round	Larissa	(a)	0-2
		(h)	2-1

FA Cup

Third Round	Coventry C	(h)	1-4

Carling Cup

Third Round	Birmingham C	(h)	3-0
Fourth Round	Portsmouth	(a)	2-1
Quarter-Final	Arsenal	(h)	2-3

BLACKPOOL FL Championship

FOUNDATION

Old boys of St John's School who had formed themselves into a football club decided to establish a club bearing the name of their town and Blackpool FC came into being at a meeting at the Stanley Arms Hotel in the summer of 1887. In their first season playing at Raikes Hall Gardens, the club won both the Lancashire Junior Cup and the Fylde Cup.

Bloomfield Road, Seasiders Way, Blackpool FY1 6JJ.

Telephone: 0870 443 1953.

Fax: (01253) 405 011.

Ticket Office: 0870 443 1953 (option 1).

Website: www.blackpoolfc.co.uk

Email: info@blackpoolfc.co.uk

Ground Capacity: 9,731.

Record Attendance: 38,098 v Wolverhampton W, Division 1, 17 September 1955.

Pitch Measurements: 110yd × 74yd.

Chairman: Karl Oyston.

President: Valery Belokon.

Secretary: Matt Williams.

Manager: Simon Grayson.

Assistant Manager: Tony Parkes.

Physio: Phil Horner.

Colours: Tangerine shirts, white shorts, tangerine stockings.

Change Colours: White shirts, tangerine shorts, white stockings.

Year Formed: 1887.

Turned Professional: 1887.

Ltd Co.: 1896.

Previous Name: 'South Shore' combined with Blackpool in 1899, twelve years after the latter had been formed on the breaking up of the old 'Blackpool St John's' club.

Club Nickname: 'The Seasiders'.

Grounds: 1887, Raikes Hall Gardens; 1897, Athletic Grounds; 1899, Raikes Hall Gardens; 1899, Bloomfield Road.

First Football League game: 5 September 1896, Division 2, v Lincoln C (a) L 1–3 – Douglas; Parr, Bowman; Stuart, Stirzaker, Norris; Clarkin, Donnelly, R. Parkinson, Mount (1), J. Parkinson.

Record League Victory: 7–0 v Reading, Division 2, 10 November 1928 – Mercer; Gibson, Hamilton, Watson, Wilson, Grant, Ritchie, Oxberry (2), Hampson (5), Tufnell, Neal. 7–0 v Preston NE (away), Division 1, 1 May 1948 – Robinson; Shimwell, Crosland; Buchan, Hayward, Kelly; Hobson, Munro (1), McIntosh (5), McCall, Rickett (1). 7–0 v Sunderland, Division 1, 5 October 1957 – Farm; Armfield, Garrett, Kelly (J), Gratrix, Kelly (H), Matthews, Taylor (2), Charnley (2), Durie (2), Perry (1).

HONOURS

Football League: Division 1 – Runners-up 1955–56; Promoted from FL 1 – 2006–07 (play-offs); Division 2 – Champions 1929–30; Runners-up 1936–37, 1969–70; Promoted from Division 3 – 2000–01 (play-offs); Division 4 – Runners-up 1984–85.

FA Cup: Winners 1953; Runners-up 1948, 1951.

Football League Cup: Semi-final 1962.

Anglo-Italian Cup: Winners 1971; Runners-up 1972.

LDV Vans Trophy: Winners 2002, 2004.

SKY SPORTS FACT FILE

Goalkeeper Alex Roxburgh, previously on Manchester City's books, was rediscovered by Blackpool while saving penalties on Blackpool beach! Signed in 1932 he established himself and played in a wartime international for England v Wales at Wembley in 1943.

Record Cup Victory: 7–1 v Charlton Ath, League Cup 2nd rd, 25 September 1963 – Harvey; Armfield, Martin; Crawford, Gratrix, Cranston; Lea, Ball (1), Charnley (4), Durie (1), Oates (1).

Record Defeat: 1–10 v Small Heath, Division 2, 2 March 1901 and v Huddersfield T, Division 1, 13 December 1930.

Most League Points (2 for a win): 58, Division 2, 1929–30 and Division 2, 1967–68.

Most League Points (3 for a win): 86, Division 4, 1984–85.

Most League Goals: 98, Division 2, 1929–30.

Highest League Scorer in Season: Jimmy Hampson, 45, Division 2, 1929–30.

Most League Goals in Total Aggregate: Jimmy Hampson, 246, 1927–38.

Most League Goals in One Match: 5, Jimmy Hampson v Reading, Division 2, 10 November 1928; 5, Jimmy McIntosh v Preston NE, Division 1, 1 May 1948.

Most Capped Player: Jimmy Armfield, 43, England.

Most League Appearances: Jimmy Armfield, 568, 1952–71.

Youngest League Player: Matty Kay, 16 years 32 days v Scunthorpe U, 13 November 2005.

Record Transfer Fee Received: £1,750,000 from Southampton for Brett Ormerod, December 2001.

Record Transfer Fee Paid: £275,000 to Millwall for Chris Malkin, October 1996.

Football League Record: 1896 Elected to Division 2; 1899 Failed re-election; 1900 Re-elected; 1900–30 Division 2; 1930–33 Division 1; 1933–37 Division 2; 1937–67 Division 1; 1967–70 Division 2; 1970–71 Division 1; 1971–78 Division 2; 1978–81 Division 3; 1981–85 Division 4; 1985–90 Division 3; 1990–92 Division 4; 1992–2000 Division 2; 2000–01 Division 3; 2001–04 Division 2; 2004–07 FL 1; 2007– FL C.

MANAGERS

Tom Barcroft 1903–33
(Secretary-Manager)
John Cox 1909–11
Bill Norman 1919–23
Maj. Frank Buckley 1923–27
Sid Beaumont 1927–28
Harry Evans 1928–33
(Hon. Team Manager)
Alex 'Sandy' Macfarlane 1933–35
Joe Smith 1935–58
Ronnie Suart 1958–67
Stan Mortensen 1967–69
Les Shannon 1969–70
Bob Stokoe 1970–72
Harry Potts 1972–76
Allan Brown 1976–78
Bob Stokoe 1978–79
Stan Ternent 1979–80
Alan Ball 1980–81
Allan Brown 1981–82
Sam Ellis 1982–89
Jimmy Mullen 1989–90
Graham Carr 1990
Bill Ayre 1990–94
Sam Allardyce 1994–96
Gary Megson 1996–97
Nigel Worthington 1997–99
Steve McMahon 2000–04
Colin Hendry 2004–06
Simon Grayson June 2006–

LATEST SEQUENCES

Longest Sequence of League Wins: 9, 21.11.1936 – 1.1.1937.

Longest Sequence of League Defeats: 8, 26.11.1898 – 7.1.1899.

Longest Sequence of League Draws: 5, 4.12.1976 – 1.1.1977.

Longest Sequence of Unbeaten League Matches: 17, 6.4.1968 – 21.9.1968.

Longest Sequence Without a League Win: 19, 19.12.1970 – 24.4.1971.

Successive Scoring Runs: 33 from 23.2.1929.

Successive Non-scoring Runs: 5 from 12.4.1975.

TEN YEAR LEAGUE RECORD

		P	*W*	*D*	*L*	*F*	*A*	*Pts*	*Pos*
1998-99	Div 2	46	14	14	18	44	54	56	14
1999-2000	Div 2	46	8	17	21	49	77	41	22
2000-01	Div 2	46	22	6	18	74	58	72	7
2001-02	Div 2	46	14	14	18	66	69	56	16
2002-03	Div 2	46	15	13	18	56	64	58	13
2003-04	Div 2	46	16	11	19	58	65	59	14
2004-05	FL 1	46	15	12	19	54	59	57	16
2005-06	FL 1	46	12	17	17	56	64	53	19
2006-07	FL 1	46	24	11	11	76	49	83	3
2007-08	FL C	46	12	18	16	59	64	54	19

DID YOU KNOW ?

In 1934 Blackpool who had had a history of shirt colour changes, wore light and dark blue stripes before reverting to Tangerine in 1939 and leading the abortive pre-war season table after three matches. They also dominated wartime regional football thereafter.

BLACKPOOL 2007–08 LEAGUE RECORD

Match No.	Date	Venue	Opponents	Result	H/T Score	Lg. Pos.	Goalscorers	Atten-dance
1	Aug 11	A	Leicester C	W 1-0	0-0	—	Southern [63]	26,650
2	18	H	Bristol C	D 1-1	0-0	8	Morrell [52]	8983
3	25	A	Wolverhampton W	L 1-2	0-0	14	Taylor-Fletcher [51]	24,294
4	Sept 3	H	Hull C	W 2-1	0-0	—	Taylor-Fletcher [47], Burgess [90]	7902
5	15	A	Burnley	D 2-2	0-0	6	Hoolahan (pen) [73], Morrell [90]	16,843
6	18	H	Sheffield U	D 2-2	1-1	—	Crainey [45], Burgess [87]	9512
7	22	H	Colchester U	D 2-2	0-0	9	Morrell [54], Barker [84]	7959
8	29	A	Watford	D 1-1	0-1	10	Hoolahan (pen) [73]	16,580
9	Oct 2	A	Coventry C	L 1-3	1-1	—	Morrell [32]	15,803
10	6	H	Plymouth Arg	D 0-0	0-0	16		8784
11	20	H	Crystal Palace	D 1-1	0-0	16	Fox [69]	9037
12	23	A	WBA	L 1-2	1-1	—	Vernon [31]	22,030
13	27	A	Sheffield W	L 1-2	1-0	20	Hoolahan [37]	19,238
14	Nov 5	A	Barnsley	L 1-2	0-1	—	Southern [72]	8531
15	10	H	Scunthorpe U	W 1-0	0-0	19	Gorkss [73]	8051
16	24	A	Southampton	L 0-1	0-1	21		21,075
17	27	H	Norwich C	L 1-3	1-1	—	Slusarski [38]	7759
18	Dec 1	H	QPR	W 1-0	0-0	21	Burgess [90]	8527
19	3	A	Scunthorpe U	D 1-1	0-1	—	Michael Flynn [88]	4407
20	8	A	Preston NE	W 1-0	0-0	18	Hoolahan (pen) [68]	17,807
21	11	H	Cardiff C	L 0-1	0-1	—		7214
22	15	H	Stoke C	L 2-3	1-2	18	Michael Flynn [13], Barker [89]	9123
23	22	H	Coventry C	W 4-0	1-0	17	Hoolahan (pen) [28], Michael Flynn [65], Gorkss [72], Vernon [88]	8690
24	26	A	Sheffield U	D 1-1	0-1	17	Jorgensen [69]	26,409
25	29	A	Colchester U	W 2-0	2-0	17	Vernon 2 [26, 36]	5160
26	Jan 1	H	Burnley	W 3-0	1-0	14	Gorkss [23], Burgess [59], Jorgensen [63]	9599
27	12	A	Charlton Ath	L 1-4	1-3	16	Burgess [12]	21,412
28	19	H	Ipswich T	D 1-1	1-0	15	Jorgensen [39]	9154
29	26	A	Bristol C	L 0-1	0-1	—		15,465
30	Feb 2	H	Leicester C	W 2-1	1-0	15	Taylor-Fletcher [3], Dickov [90]	9298
31	9	A	Hull C	D 2-2	1-0	16	Dickov 2 [39, 50]	18,407
32	12	H	Wolverhampton W	D 0-0	0-0	—		9413
33	16	A	Ipswich T	L 1-2	0-0	—	Dickov [89]	21,059
34	23	H	Charlton Ath	W 5-3	2-2	14	McPhee [16], Gorkss [26], Taylor-Fletcher 2 [59, 69], Dickov [62]	9134
35	Mar 1	A	Norwich C	W 2-1	2-0	12	McPhee 2 [15, 39]	24,531
36	4	H	Barnsley	D 1-1	1-1	—	Taylor-Fletcher [20]	8080
37	8	H	Southampton	D 2-2	0-1	12	Southern [49], Gorkss [55]	9050
38	11	A	QPR	L 2-3	0-2	—	Burgess [60], McPhee [73]	11,538
39	15	H	Preston NE	D 0-0	0-0	15		9629
40	22	A	Stoke C	D 1-1	1-0	16	Burgess [37]	20,019
41	29	A	Crystal Palace	D 0-0	0-0	16		16,028
42	Apr 8	H	WBA	L 1-3	1-0	—	Burgess [35]	9628
43	12	A	Cardiff C	L 1-3	0-1	18	Morrell [73]	14,715
44	19	H	Sheffield W	W 2-1	2-1	16	Jorgensen [6], Dickov [30]	9633
45	26	A	Plymouth Arg	L 0-3	0-2	18		12,911
46	May 4	H	Watford	D 1-1	1-0	19	Burgess [2]	9640

Final League Position: 19

GOALSCORERS

League (59): Burgess 9, Dickov 6, Taylor-Fletcher 6, Gorkss 5, Hoolahan 5 (4 pens), Morrell 5, Jorgensen 4, McPhee 4, Vernon 4, Michael Flynn 3, Southern 3, Barker 2, Crainey 1, Fox 1, Slusarski 1.
Carling Cup (5): Gorkss 2, Burgess 1, Hoolahan 1, Michael Jackson 1.
FA Cup (1): Fox 1.

Rachubka P 46	Barker S 46	Crainey S 37 + 3	Fox D 16 + 12	Jackson Mike 23 + 2	Evatt I 27 + 2	Taylor-Fletcher G 40 + 2	Southern K 29 + 1	Morrell A 23 + 15	Parker K 10 + 11	Hoolahan W 43 + 2	Jorgensen C 30 + 7	Hills J 1 + 3	Gorkss K 39 + 1	Burgess B 25 + 10	Vernon S 6 + 9	Forbes A — + 2	Welsh A 3 + 18	Flynn Michael 20 + 8	Coid D 9 + 4	Jackson Matt 2 + 1	McMahon T 2	Slusarski B 4 + 2	McPhee S 16 + 3	Dickov P 7 + 4	Green S 1 + 5	Holt G — + 4	Martin J 1	*Match No.*
1	2	3	4	5	6	7^1	8	9	10	11^2	12	13																1
1	2	3	4	5		7^2	8	9^1	12	11	13		6	10^3	14													2
1	2	3	4	5		7^2	8	9^1	12	11	13		6	10^3	14													3
1	2	12	4	5	6	7^2	8	9^3	10	11			3^1	14		13												4
1	2	3	4	5	6	7^3	8^2	9	10^1	11				12			14	13										5
1	2	3	4	5	6	7^2	8	9^1	12	11				10			13											6
1	2	3	4	5	6^2	7^3	8	9^1	12	11			13	10			14											7
1	2		4	5		7	8	9^2	12	11^3	13	14	6					10^1	3									8
1	2		4	5		7^2	8^3	9^1	12	11			6■		13		14	10	3									9
1	2	3	4	5		7^3	8^1	9^2	10	11	12				13		14			6								10
1	2	3	4^2	5		7^1	8		10	11			6		9		12	13										11
1	2	3	4^2	5^3		12	8		10	11			6		9			13	7^1	14								12
1	2	3	4^1				8^3		10	11	12		6		9		13	14	7^2	5								13
1	2		4^2	5■		7^1	8	9^3	10	11	13	14	6		12				3									14
1	2	12				7^3	8	9^2	10	11^1	4		5		13		14		3		6							15
1	5	12	13			7	8	9		14	4^2		6				11^3		3		2^1	10						16
1	5	3				7^3	8	9	12	11	4		6		13		14		2^2			10^1						17
1	2	3	12	5		13	8^1	14		11	4		6	9			7^2					10^3						18
1	2	3	4^3	5^2		7		9^1	12	11	8		6	10			13	14										19
1	2	3		5^1	12	7^2		9	13	11^3	8		6	10			14	4										20
1	2	3		5	12	7^2		14	10^1		8		6	9		13	11^3	4										21
1	2	3	12		6	7^3		13		11	4^1		5	9			14	8				10^2						22
1	2	3	12		6	7^1		9^2		11	4		5	10	13		14	8^3										23
1	2	3	12	13	6■	7^3		9^2		11^1	4		5	10			14	8										24
1	2	3	12	5		7		9^2		11^1	4		6	13	10^3			8				14						25
1	2	3	12	5		7^1		13		11	4		6	10^3	9^2			8				14						26
1	2	3	12	5		7		13		11	4^1		6	10	9^3			8^2					14					27
1	2	3	12		6	7^3		13		11	4		5	9			14	8^1					10^2					28
1	2	3	4		6			9^2		12	7^3		5	10	13		14	8					11^1					29
1	2	3			6	7		12		11^2	4		5	10^1			13	8					9^3	14				30
1	2	3		12	6	7		13		11^1	4		5■	10				8^3						9^2	14			31
1	2	3		5	6	7	8^2			11	4			9									12	10^1	13			32
1	2			5^3	6^1	7	8			11	4	3		9^2					12				13	10	14			33
1	2	3			6	7^3	8	12		11^2	4		5	13									9	10^1	14			34
1	2	3			6	7^3	8	9^1		11	4		5	13				12	14				10^2					35
1	2	3			6	7^3	8	9^1		11	4^2		5	12			14	13					10					36
1	2	3			6	7^1	8	12		11	4^3		5	13				14					9	10^2				37
1	2	3	12		6	7^3	8^1	9^2	14	11			5	13				4					10					38
1	2	3			6	7^2		12	13	11	4		5	9				8					10^1					39
1	2	3			6	7^1				11	4		5	9				8					10			12		40
1	2	3			6	7^2				11	4		5	9^3				8	12				10^1	13		14		41
1	2	3			6	7	12			11	4		5	9^3				8^1					10^2	13		14		42
1	2	3	12		6	7	8	13		11			5	9^3				4^1					10^2	14				43
1	2	3			6	7^3	8	12		11	4		5	13									9^1	10^2	14			44
1	2			5^2	6		8	12		11	4		3	13					14				9	10^3	7^1			45
1	2		12		6		8	13		11	4		5	10^3					3				9^1			14	7^2	46

FA Cup

Third Round	Barnsley	(a)	1-2

Carling Cup

First Round	Huddersfield T	(h)	1-0
Second Round	Derby Co	(a)	2-2
Third Round	Southend U	(h)	2-1
Fourth Round	Tottenham H	(a)	0-2

BOLTON WANDERERS FA Premiership

FOUNDATION

In 1874 boys of Christ Church Sunday School, Blackburn Street, led by their master Thomas Ogden, established a football club which went under the name of the school and whose president was Vicar of Christ Church. Membership was 6d (two and a half pence). When their president began to lay down too many rules about the use of church premises, the club broke away and formed Bolton Wanderers in 1877, holding their earliest meetings at the Gladstone Hotel.

The Reebok Stadium, Burnden Way, Lostock, Bolton BL6 6JW.

Telephone: (01204) 673 673. ***Fax:*** (01204) 673 773.

Ticket Office: 0871 871 2932.

Website: www.bwfc.co.uk

Email: reception@bwfc.co.uk

Ground Capacity: 28,101.

Record Attendance: 69,912 v Manchester C, FA Cup 5th rd, 18 February 1933.

Pitch Measurements: 105m × 68m.

Chairman: Phil A. Gartside.

Chief Executive: Allan Duckworth.

Vice-chairman: Brett Warburton.

Secretary: Simon Marland.

Manager: Gary Megson.

Assistant Manager: Chris Evans.

Physio: Andy Barr.

Colours: White shirts, white shorts, white stockings.

Change Colours: Black shirts, black shorts, black stockings.

Year Formed: 1874. ***Turned Professional:*** 1880. ***Ltd Co.:*** 1895.

Previous Name: 1874, Christ Church FC; 1877, Bolton Wanderers.

Club Nickname: 'The Trotters'.

Grounds: Park Recreation Ground and Cockle's Field before moving to Pike's Lane ground 1881; 1895, Burnden Park; 1997, Reebok Stadium.

First Football League Game: 8 September 1888, Football League, v Derby Co (h) L 3–6 – Harrison; Robinson, Mitchell; Roberts, Weir, Bullough, Davenport (2), Milne, Coupar, Barbour, Brogan (1).

Record League Victory: 8–0 v Barnsley, Division 2, 6 October 1934 – Jones; Smith, Finney; Goslin, Atkinson, George Taylor; George T. Taylor (2), Eastham, Milsom (1), Westwood (4), Cook, (1 og).

HONOURS

Football League: Division 1 – Champions 1996–97; Promoted from Division 1 (play-offs) 2000–01. Division 2 – Champions 1908–09, 1977–78; Runners-up 1899–1900, 1904–05, 1910–11, 1934–35, 1992–93; Division 3 – Champions 1972–73; Promoted from Division 4 (3rd) 1987–88.

FA Cup: Winners 1923, 1926, 1929, 1958; Runners-up 1894, 1904, 1953.

Football League Cup: Runners-up 1995, 2004.

Freight Rover Trophy: Runners-up 1986.

Sherpa Van Trophy: Winners 1989.

European Competitions: *UEFA Cup:* 2005–06, 2007–08.

SKY SPORTS FACT FILE

In the 1926 FA Cup final when Bolton Wanderers defeated Manchester City 1–0, their opponents had scored 31 goals in six previous cup games including a replay with Corinthians. Bolton thus reversed the score of the 1904 final against City.

Record Cup Victory: 13–0 v Sheffield U, FA Cup 2nd rd, 1 February 1890 – Parkinson; Robinson (1), Jones; Bullough, Davenport, Roberts; Rushton, Brogan (3), Cassidy (5), McNee, Weir (4).

Record Defeat: 1–9 v Preston NE, FA Cup 2nd rd, 10 December 1887.

Most League Points (2 for a win): 61, Division 3, 1972–73.

Most League Points (3 for a win): 98, Division 1, 1996–97.

Most League Goals: 100, Division 1, 1996–97.

Highest League Scorer in Season: Joe Smith, 38, Division 1, 1920–21.

Most League Goals in Total Aggregate: Nat Lofthouse, 255, 1946–61.

Most League Goals in One Match: 5, Tony Caldwell v Walsall, Division 3, 10 September 1983.

Most Capped Player: Mark Fish, 34 (62), South Africa.

Most League Appearances: Eddie Hopkinson, 519, 1956–70.

Youngest League Player: Ray Parry, 15 years 267 days v Wolverhampton W, 13 October 1951.

Record Transfer Fee Received: £15,000,000 from Chelsea for Nicolas Anelka, January 2008.

Record Transfer Fee Paid: £8,000,000 to Fenerbahce for Nicolas Anelka, August 2006.

Football League Record: 1888 Founder Member of the League; 1899–1900 Division 2; 1900–03 Division 1; 1903–05 Division 2; 1905–08 Division 1; 1908–09 Division 2; 1909–10 Division 1; 1910–11 Division 2; 1911–33 Division 1; 1933–35 Division 2; 1935–64 Division 1; 1964–71 Division 2; 1971–73 Division 3; 1973–78 Division 2; 1978–80 Division 1; 1980–83 Division 2; 1983–87 Division 3; 1987–88 Division 4; 1988–92 Division 3; 1992–93 Division 2; 1993–95 Division 1; 1995–96 FA Premier League; 1996–97 Division 1; 1997–98 FA Premier League; 1998–2001 Division 1; 2001– FA Premier League.

MANAGERS

Tom Rawthorne 1874–85 *(Secretary)*
J. J. Bentley 1885–86 *(Secretary)*
W. G. Struthers 1886–87 *(Secretary)*
Fitzroy Norris 1887 *(Secretary)*
J. J. Bentley 1887–95 *(Secretary)*
Harry Downs 1895–96 *(Secretary)*
Frank Brettell 1896–98 *(Secretary)*
John Somerville 1898–1910
Will Settle 1910–15
Tom Mather 1915–19
Charles Foweraker 1919–44
Walter Rowley 1944–50
Bill Ridding 1951–68
Nat Lofthouse 1968–70
Jimmy McIlroy 1970
Jimmy Meadows 1971
Nat Lofthouse 1971 *(then Admin. Manager to 1972)*
Jimmy Armfield 1971–74
Ian Greaves 1974–80
Stan Anderson 1980–81
George Mulhall 1981–82
John McGovern 1982–85
Charlie Wright 1985
Phil Neal 1985–92
Bruce Rioch 1992–95
Roy McFarland 1995–96
Colin Todd 1996–99
Sam Allardyce 1999–2007
Sammy Lee 2007
Gary Megson October 2007–

LATEST SEQUENCES

Longest Sequence of League Wins: 11, 5.11.1904 – 2.1.1905.

Longest Sequence of League Defeats: 11, 7.4.1902 – 18.10.1902.

Longest Sequence of League Draws: 6, 25.1.1913 – 8.3.1913.

Longest Sequence of Unbeaten League Matches: 23, 13.10.1990 – 9.3.1991.

Longest Sequence Without a League Win: 26, 7.4.1902 – 10.1.1903.

Successive Scoring Runs: 24 from 22.11.1996.

Successive Non-scoring Runs: 5 from 3.1.1898.

TEN YEAR LEAGUE RECORD

		P	W	D	L	F	A	Pts	Pos
1998-99	Div 1	46	20	16	10	78	59	76	6
1999-2000	Div 1	46	21	13	12	69	50	76	6
2000-01	Div 1	46	24	15	7	76	45	87	3
2001-02	PR Lge	38	9	13	16	44	62	40	16
2002-03	PR Lge	38	10	14	14	41	51	44	17
2003-04	PR Lge	38	14	11	13	48	56	53	8
2004-05	PR Lge	38	16	10	12	49	44	58	6
2005-06	PR Lge	38	15	11	12	49	41	56	8
2006-07	PR Lge	38	16	8	14	47	52	56	7
2007-08	PR Lge	38	9	10	19	36	54	37	16

DID YOU KNOW ?

The first player to score a hat-trick for Bolton Wanderers was Davie Weir against Accrington on 22 December 1888. Signed from Halliwell he was brought up in Scotland but had been born in Aldershot and twice played for England. He later coached in Germany.

BOLTON WANDERERS 2007–08 LEAGUE RECORD

Match No.	*Date*	*Venue*	*Opponents*	*Result*		*H/T Score*	*Lg. Pos.*	*Goalscorers*	*Attendance*
1	Aug 11	H	Newcastle U	L	1-3	0-3	—	Anelka [50]	25,414
2	15	A	Fulham	L	1-2	1-2	—	Helguson [12]	21,102
3	18	A	Portsmouth	L	1-3	1-2	20	Anelka [12]	17,108
4	25	H	Reading	W	3-0	1-0	18	Speed [32], Anelka [55], Braaten [90]	20,023
5	Sept 1	H	Everton	L	1-2	0-1	19	Anelka [55]	22,064
6	15	A	Birmingham C	L	0-1	0-1	19		28,124
7	23	H	Tottenham H	D	1-1	1-1	19	Campo [39]	20,308
8	29	A	Derby Co	D	1-1	1-1	19	Anelka [32]	31,503
9	Oct 7	H	Chelsea	L	0-1	0-1	19		20,059
10	20	A	Arsenal	L	0-2	0-0	20		59,442
11	28	H	Aston Villa	D	1-1	1-0	19	Anelka [22]	18,413
12	Nov 4	A	West Ham U	D	1-1	0-1	19	Nolan [90]	33,867
13	11	H	Middlesbrough	D	0-0	0-0	18		17,624
14	24	H	Manchester U	W	1-0	1-0	15	Anelka [11]	25,028
15	Dec 2	A	Liverpool	L	0-4	0-2	17		43,270
16	9	H	Wigan Ath	W	4-1	2-1	14	Scharner (og) [3], Nolan [37], Davies [70], Anelka [89]	20,309
17	15	A	Manchester C	L	2-4	2-1	16	Diouf [31], Nolan [40]	40,506
18	22	H	Birmingham C	W	3-0	0-0	14	Diouf [72], Anelka 2 [78, 90]	19,111
19	26	A	Everton	L	0-2	0-0	15		38,918
20	29	A	Sunderland	L	1-3	1-2	16	Diouf [41]	42,058
21	Jan 2	H	Derby Co	W	1-0	0-0	—	Giannakopoulos [90]	17,014
22	13	H	Blackburn R	L	1-2	1-0	15	Nolan [43]	18,315
23	19	A	Newcastle U	D	0-0	0-0	15		52,250
24	29	H	Fulham	D	0-0	0-0	—		17,732
25	Feb 2	A	Reading	W	2-0	1-0	14	Nolan [33], Helguson [58]	21,893
26	9	H	Portsmouth	L	0-1	0-0	15		18,544
27	24	A	Blackburn R	L	1-4	0-1	16	Davies [50]	23,995
28	Mar 2	H	Liverpool	L	1-3	0-1	17	Cohen [79]	24,004
29	16	A	Wigan Ath	L	0-1	0-1	18		17,055
30	19	A	Manchester U	L	0-2	0-2	—		75,476
31	22	H	Manchester C	D	0-0	0-0	18		22,633
32	29	H	Arsenal	L	2-3	2-0	18	Taylor 2 [14, 43]	22,431
33	Apr 5	A	Aston Villa	L	0-4	0-1	18		37,773
34	12	H	West Ham U	W	1-0	0-0	18	Davies [47]	23,043
35	19	A	Middlesbrough	W	1-0	0-0	16	McCann [61]	25,037
36	26	A	Tottenham H	D	1-1	0-0	16	Giannakopoulos [46]	36,176
37	May 3	H	Sunderland	W	2-0	1-0	16	Diouf [42], Murphy (og) [83]	25,053
38	11	A	Chelsea	D	1-1	0-0	16	Taylor [90]	41,755

Final League Position: 16

GOALSCORERS

League (36): Anelka 10, Nolan 5, Diouf 4, Davies 3, Taylor 3, Giannakopoulos 2, Helguson 2, Braaten 1, Campo 1, Cohen 1, McCann 1, Speed 1, own goals 2.
Carling Cup (2): Giannakopoulos 1, Guthrie 1.
FA Cup (0).
UEFA Cup (9): Diouf 2, McCann 2, Anelka 1, Davies 1, Gardner 1, Giannakopoulos 1, Meite 1.

Jaaskelainen J 28	Hunt N 12 + 2	Samuel J 14 + 6	McCann G 21 + 10	Cid G 6 + 1	Diagne-Faye A 1	Nolan K 33	Speed G 11 + 3	Anelka N 18	Davies K 31 + 1	Vaz Te R 1	Diouf E 30 + 4	Alonso M 4 + 3	Helguson H 3 + 3	Meite A 21	Michalik L 5 + 2	Braaten D — + 6	Teimourian A 1 + 2	Wilhelmsson C — + 8	O'Brien A 31 + 1	Gardner R 25 + 1	Campo I 25 + 2	O'Brien J 15 + 4	Giannakopoulos S 1 + 14	Guthrie D 21 + 4	Cohen T 3 + 7	Steinsson G 16	Taylor M 16	Cahill G 13	Rasiak G 2 + 5	Al-Habsi A 10	*Match No.*
1	2	3	4	5	6	7	8^2	9	10^3	11^1	12	13	14																		1
1	2	3^2	4^1	5		7	8	9			11	12	10^3	6	13	14															2
1	2^1	3		5		10^2	8	9			11	4	12	6		13	7^3	14													3
1	2	3	4	5		7	8	9			10	11^1		6		12															4
1	2^1	3	4^3	5^2		7	8	9	12		10	11		6				14	13												5
1	2	3^3	4	12		7	8	9			10	11^2		6		13			5^1	14											6
1						7^1	8	9	10		11^2	12		6				13	5	3	4	2									7
1			12			7	8^1	9	10^3		11			6		13		14	5	3	4	2^2									8
1			8					9	10		11^1			6				12	5	3	4	2^2	13	7							9
1			8			7			10		9^1			6		12			5	3	4	2	13	11^2							10
1		12	8^3			7	13	9^1	10		11			6					5	3	4^2	2		14							11
1	2^1	14	12			7	8^3		10		9			6^2	13				5	3	4			11							12
1			2	3		7^1	8^2		10					6			13		5	9	4		12	11							13
1	2		12			7^1	13	9	10^2		11			6				14	5	3	4			8^3							14
1		2	7				8	9	10		11^1			6	5					3	4		12								15
1	2		12			7^3	13	9	10		11^1			6					5	3	4^2		14	8							16
1	2^1		12			7		9	10		11			6	5					3	4^2		13	8							17
1	2	12	13			7		9	10^1		11			6					5	3	4^2			8							18
1	2	12	13			7^3		9	10		11			6					5	3	4^1	14		8^2							19
1		2^3	4			7^1		9	10^2		11			6					5	3	12	8	13	14							20
1						7^1		9	10^2		11			6				13	5	3	4	2	12	8							21
1			12			7			10						6			13	5	3	4^1	2	11	8	9^2						22
1		12	4^3			7^2			10						6				5	3	13	11		8	14	2	9^1				23
1			4			11			10				12		6		13		5	3		7^3		8^2	14	2	9^1				24
1		12				7			10		13		9^2						5	3	4			8^3	14	2	11^1	6			25
1						7			10		11^3								5	3	4		12	8^2	13	2	9^1	6	14		26
1						7^2			10		9								5	3	4^1	12		8^3	13	2	11	6	14		27
1						8^1			10		9								5	3	4	7			12	2^2	11	6	13		28
			12			7			10		9^2								5	3	4	13			8^3	2	11	6^1	14	1	29
	12		4						10		9			6^1					5	3		7	13	8^2		2	11			1	30
			12			7			10		9								5	3^3	4^1	14	13	8		2	11^2	6		1	31
	12^2	3	7						10		9^3								5		4		14	8		2	11^1	6	13	1	32
			4						10		11		9						5			7^1		8	12	2	3	6		1	33
		3	8			7			10		9								5		4					2	11	6		1	34
		3	8			7					12								5		4			13	10^2	2	11	6	9^1	1	35
		3	8			7					12								5		4^2	11^3	13	14		2	10	6	9^1	1	36
		3	4			7			10		9								5					8		2	11	6		1	37
		3	4			8			10		9^1								5			7	12			2	11	6		1	38

UEFA Cup

First Round	Rabotnicki	(a)	1-1
		(h)	1-0
Group F	Braga	(h)	1-1
	Bayern Munich	(a)	2-2
	Aris Salonika	(h)	1-1
	Red Star Belgrade	(a)	1-0
Third Round	Atletico Madrid	(h)	1-0
		(a)	0-0
Fourth Round	Sporting Lisbon	(h)	1-1
		(a)	0-1

FA Cup

Third Round	Sheffield U	(h)	0-1

Carling Cup

Third Round	Fulham	(a)	2-1
Fourth Round	Manchester C	(h)	0-1

AFC BOURNEMOUTH FL Championship 2

FOUNDATION

There was a Bournemouth FC as early as 1875, but the present club arose out of the remnants of the Boscombe St John's club (formed 1890). The meeting at which Boscombe FC came into being was held at a house in Gladstone Road in 1899. They began by playing in the Boscombe and District Junior League.

The Fitness First Stadium at Dean Court, Bournemouth, Dorset BH7 7AF.

Telephone: (01202) 726 300.

Fax: (01202) 726 373.

Ticket Office: (01202) 726 338.

Website: www.afcb.co.uk

Email: tickets@afcb.co.uk / enquiries@afcb.co.uk

Ground Capacity: 10,375 (with temporary stand, 9,776 without).

Record Attendance: 28,799 v Manchester U, FA Cup 6th rd, 2 March 1957.

Pitch Measurements: 110yd × 70yd.

Chairman: Jeff Mostyn.

Vice-chairman: Steve Sly.

Secretary: Neil Vacher (Football Administrator).

Manager: Kevin Bond.

Assistant Manager: Rob Newman.

Physio: Steve Hard.

Colours: Red and black, design to be confirmed.

Change Colours: Gold shirts, black shorts and stockings.

Year Formed: 1899.

Turned Professional: 1912.

Ltd Co.: 1914.

Previous Names: 1890, Boscombe St Johns; 1899, Boscombe FC; 1923, Bournemouth & Boscombe Ath FC; 1971, AFC Bournemouth.

Club Nickname: 'Cherries'.

Grounds: 1899, Castlemain Road, Pokesdown; 1910, Dean Court.

First Football League Game: 25 August 1923, Division 3 (S), v Swindon T (a) L 1–3 – Heron; Wingham, Lamb; Butt, C. Smith, Voisey; Miller, Lister (1), Davey, Simpson, Robinson.

Record League Victory: 7–0 v Swindon T, Division 3 (S), 22 September 1956 – Godwin; Cunningham, Keetley; Clayton, Crosland, Rushworth; Siddall (1), Norris (2), Arnott (1), Newsham (2), Cutler (1). 10–0 win v Northampton T at start of 1939–40 expunged from the records on outbreak of war.

HONOURS

Football League: Division 3 – Champions 1986–87; Promoted from Division 3, 2002–03 (play-offs); Division 3 (S) – Runners-up 1947–48; Division 4 – Runners-up 1970–71; Promotion from Division 4 1981–82 (4th).

FA Cup: best season: 6th rd, 1957.

Football League Cup: best season: 4th rd, 1962, 1964.

Associate Members' Cup: Winners 1984.

Auto Windscreens Shield: Runners-up 1998.

SKY SPORTS FACT FILE

Longevity at Bournemouth: firstly trainer Harry Kinghorn aged 42, forced to play on the left-wing in 1929. He was a former Sheffield Wednesday goalkeeper c.1910! Then in 1976 Bobby McAlinden made a solitary outing, his only previous one having been 13 years before with Manchester City.

Record Cup Victory: 11–0 v Margate, FA Cup 1st rd, 20 November 1971 – Davies; Machin (1), Kitchener, Benson, Jones, Powell, Cave (1), Boyer, MacDougall (9 incl. 1p), Miller, Scott (De Garis).

Record Defeat: 0–9 v Lincoln C, Division 3, 18 December 1982.

Most League Points (2 for a win): 62, Division 3, 1971–72.

Most League Points (3 for a win): 97, Division 3, 1986–87.

Most League Goals: 88, Division 3 (S), 1956–57.

Highest League Scorer in Season: Ted MacDougall, 42, 1970–71.

Most League Goals in Total Aggregate: Ron Eyre, 202, 1924–33.

Most League Goals in One Match: 4, Jack Russell v Clapton Orient, Division 3S, 7 January 1933; 4, Jack Russell v Bristol C, Division 3S, 28 January 1933; 4, Harry Mardon v Southend U, Division 3S, 1 January 1938; 4, Jack McDonald v Torquay U, Division 3S, 8 November 1947; 4, Ted MacDougall v Colchester U, 18 September 1970; 4, Brian Clark v Rotherham U, 10 October 1972, 4, Luther Blissett v Hull C, 29 November 1988; 4, James Hayter v Bury, Division 2, 21 October 2000.

Most Capped Player: Gerry Peyton, 7 (33), Republic of Ireland.

Most League Appearances: Steve Fletcher, 466, 1992–2007.

Youngest League Player: Jimmy White, 15 years 321 days v Brentford, 30 April 1958.

Record Transfer Fee Received: £800,000 from Everton for Joe Parkinson, March 1994 and £800,000 from Ipswich T for Matt Holland, July 1997.

MANAGERS

Vincent Kitcher 1914–23
(Secretary-Manager)
Harry Kinghorn 1923–25
Leslie Knighton 1925–28
Frank Richards 1928–30
Billy Birrell 1930–35
Bob Crompton 1935–36
Charlie Bell 1936–39
Harry Kinghorn 1939–47
Harry Lowe 1947–50
Jack Bruton 1950–56
Fred Cox 1956–58
Don Welsh 1958–61
Bill McGarry 1961–63
Reg Flewin 1963–65
Fred Cox 1965–70
John Bond 1970–73
Trevor Hartley 1974–75
John Benson 1975–78
Alec Stock 1979–80
David Webb 1980–82
Don Megson 1983
Harry Redknapp 1983–92
Tony Pulis 1992–94
Mel Machin 1994–2000
Sean O'Driscoll 2000–2006
Kevin Bond October 2006–

Record Transfer Fee Paid: £210,000 to Gillingham for Gavin Peacock, August 1989.

Football League Record: 1923 Elected to Division 3 (S) and remained a Third Division club for record number of years until 1970; 1970–71 Division 4; 1971–75 Division 3; 1975–82 Division 4; 1982–87 Division 3; 1987–90 Division 2; 1990–92 Division 3; 1992–2002 Division 2; 2002–03 Division 3; 2003–04 Division 2; 2004–08 FL 1; 2008– FL 2.

LATEST SEQUENCES

Longest Sequence of League Wins: 7, 22.8.1970 – 23.9.1970.

Longest Sequence of League Defeats: 7, 13.8.1994 – 13.9.1994.

Longest Sequence of League Draws: 5, 25.4.2000 – 12.8.2000.

Longest Sequence of Unbeaten League Matches: 18, 6.3.1982 – 28.8.1982.

Longest Sequence Without a League Win: 14, 6.3.1974 – 27.4.1974.

Successive Scoring Runs: 31 from 28.10.2000.

Successive Non-scoring Runs: 6 from 1.2.1975.

TEN YEAR LEAGUE RECORD

		P	W	D	L	F	A	Pts	Pos
1998-99	Div 2	46	21	13	12	63	41	76	7
1999-2000	Div 2	46	16	9	21	59	62	57	16
2000-01	Div 2	46	20	13	13	79	55	73	7
2001-02	Div 2	46	10	14	22	56	71	44	21
2002-03	Div 3	46	20	14	12	60	48	74	4
2003-04	Div 2	46	17	15	14	56	51	66	9
2004-05	FL 1	46	20	10	16	77	64	70	8
2005-06	FL 1	46	12	19	15	49	53	55	17
2006-07	FL 1	46	13	13	20	50	64	52	19
2007-08	FL 1	46	17	7	22	62	72	48*	21

**10 pts deducted.*

DID YOU KNOW?

In 1925–26 Ron Eyre's 27 League goals were three times more than any other scorer with Bournemouth. The same season they forced a replay with Bolton Wanderers the eventual FA Cup winners. Eyre, the overall leading marksman in the club's history, hit many hat-tricks, but did not break into the four goal bracket in any of them.

AFC BOURNEMOUTH 2007–08 LEAGUE RECORD

Match No.	Date	Venue	Opponents	Result		H/T Score	Lg. Pos.	Goalscorers	Attendance
1	Aug 11	A	Nottingham F	D	0-0	0-0	—		18,791
2	18	H	Huddersfield T	L	0-1	0-1	21		5606
3	25	A	Doncaster R	W	2-1	1-1	11	Gradel [28], Osei-Kuffour [46]	6476
4	Sept 1	H	Port Vale	L	0-1	0-0	14		5444
5	8	A	Leyton Orient	L	0-1	0-0	17		4995
6	15	H	Northampton T	D	1-1	1-0	19	Anderton [34]	5009
7	22	A	Swindon T	L	1-4	1-1	21	Hollands [37]	6668
8	29	H	Carlisle U	L	1-3	0-2	24	Osei-Kuffour [54]	4940
9	Oct 2	H	Brighton & HA	L	0-2	0-0	—		4638
10	6	A	Crewe Alex	W	4-1	1-0	23	Bradbury [37], Gradel 2 [61, 77], Anderton [85]	4799
11	14	H	Swansea C	L	1-4	1-2	24	Bradbury (pen) [31]	5843
12	20	A	Millwall	L	1-2	0-1	24	Bradbury [90]	7805
13	27	H	Walsall	D	1-1	1-0	24	Osei-Kuffour [20]	5414
14	Nov 3	A	Bristol R	W	2-0	1-0	21	Henry 2 [41, 90]	6405
15	6	H	Leeds U	L	1-3	1-1	—	Karacan [37]	9632
16	18	A	Hartlepool U	D	1-1	1-1	21	Henry [16]	3496
17	24	H	Oldham Ath	L	0-3	0-0	22		5261
18	Dec 4	A	Yeovil T	L	1-2	0-2	—	Cummings (pen) [65]	5321
19	8	A	Tranmere R	L	1-3	0-2	24	Vokes [76]	5043
20	15	H	Gillingham	W	1-0	1-0	23	Pitman [34]	4746
21	21	A	Northampton T	L	1-4	1-2	24	Pitman [5]	4806
22	26	H	Leyton Orient	W	3-1	1-0	21	Gradel [19], Vokes [54], Henry [89]	5356
23	29	H	Swindon T	D	2-2	0-0	22	Osei-Kuffour [63], Vokes [78]	6540
24	Jan 1	A	Brighton & HA	L	2-3	1-1	22	Christophe [24], Pitman [79]	5963
25	12	A	Cheltenham T	L	0-1	0-0	24		3959
26	19	H	Southend U	L	1-4	0-3	24	Cummings [50]	5419
27	22	H	Luton T	W	4-3	2-1	—	Gradel [2], Osei-Kuffour [31], Vokes [89], Pitman [90]	3489
28	26	A	Port Vale	W	3-1	2-0	—	Vokes [10], Hollands [28], Cooper [84]	4047
29	29	A	Huddersfield T	L	0-1	0-1	—		7359
30	Feb 2	H	Nottingham F	W	2-0	2-0	22	Vokes 2 [20, 29]	7251
31	9	A	Luton T	W	4-1	3-0	23	Vokes [13], Osei-Kuffour 2 [14, 84], Gradel [45]	5897
32	12	H	Doncaster R	L	0-2	0-1	—		4947
33	16	A	Southend U	L	1-2	1-1	23	Pearce J [40]	7474
34	23	H	Cheltenham T	D	2-2	2-1	23	Gradel (pen) [17], Bartley [39]	4365
35	Mar 1	H	Hartlepool U	W	2-0	2-0	22	Vokes 2 [6, 45]	3984
36	8	A	Leeds U	L	0-2	0-1	22		21,199
37	11	A	Oldham Ath	L	0-2	0-1	—		3633
38	15	H	Yeovil T	W	2-0	2-0	22	Hollands [9], Vokes [32]	4145
39	22	A	Gillingham	L	1-2	1-2	23	Osei-Kuffour [28]	6540
40	24	H	Tranmere R	W	2-1	2-0	22	Goodison (og) [1], Osei-Kuffour [34]	4118
41	29	H	Millwall	W	2-0	0-0	22	Gradel 2 (1 pen) [75 (p), 89]	4962
42	Apr 5	A	Swansea C	W	2-1	0-0	22	Partington [89], Osei-Kuffour [90]	15,613
43	12	H	Bristol R	W	2-1	1-0	22	Anderton [18], Osei-Kuffour [55]	6867
44	19	A	Walsall	W	3-1	2-1	22	Hollands [10], Osei-Kuffour [35], Pitman (pen) [63]	4530
45	26	H	Crewe Alex	W	1-0	0-0	21	Vokes [55]	8621
46	May 3	A	Carlisle U	D	1-1	0-0	21	Pitman [68]	12,223

Final League Position: 21

GOALSCORERS

League (62): Osei-Kuffour 12, Vokes 12, Gradel 9 (2 pens), Pitman 6 (1 pen), Henry 4, Hollands 4, Anderton 3, Bradbury 3 (1 pen), Cummings 2 (1 pen), Bartley 1, Christophe 1, Cooper 1, Karacan 1, Partington 1, Pearce J 1, own goal 1.
Carling Cup (0).
FA Cup (5): Cooper 1, Golbourne 1, Gradel 1 (pen), Hollands 1, Karacan 1.
J Paint Trophy (3): Bradbury 2, Osei-Kuffour 1.

Begovic A 8	Pearce J 30 + 3	Garry R 6 + 2	Telfer P 17 + 1	Cummings W 31 + 1	Gowling J 36 + 1	O'Connor G 5 + 1	Anderton D 20	Pitman B 14 + 25	Osei-Kuffour J 37 + 5	Gradel M 31 + 3	Christophe J 5 + 5	Cooper S 33 + 5	Vokes S 30 + 11	Bradbury L 33 + 2	Young N 18 + 3	Perrett R 10	Hollands D 37	Wilson M 7	Moss N 7	Lallana A 2 + 1	McQuoid J 2 + 3	Karacan J 11 + 2	Pearce A 11	Henry J 8 + 3	Golbourne S 5	Stewart G 18	Shimmin D 1 + 1	Bartley M 14 + 6	Tessem J 5 + 6	Pryce R 2 + 2	Partington J — + 6	Forde D 11	Franks B 1	Finlay M — + 1	Hutchings S — + 1	Match No.
1	2	3	4	5	6	7[1]	8	9[3]	10	11[2]	12	13	14																							1
1	2	3	4	5	6	7[1]	8	9[3]	10	12	11[2]	13	14																							2
1	2	3		5	6	7[3]	8	12	10[2]	11[1]	4	14		9	13																					3
1	2	3	12	5	6	7[1]	8	13	10	11[2]	4[3]		14	9																						4
1		3	4	7[2]	6		8	12	10[1]	11	13			9	2	5																				5
1		3	4	12[2]	6		8		10[3]	11	13		14	9	2	5[1]	7																			6
1	2		4				8	7	10[2]		12	11[1]	13	9	5		6	3																		7
1	2		4[3]		6[2]	12	8	13	10	11		3	14	9			5	7[1]																		8
	3		2		6	7[2]	8		10	11		12	13	9			4[1]	5	1																	9
	3		2		6		8	12	10	11[2]		13	7[1]	9			4	5	1																	10
	3		2		12		8		10[1]			5	11	9			4	6	1	7																11
	3[1]		2		6		8		14			7	10[3]	9			4	5	1	12[2]	13	11														12
			2		6		8[1]	13	10			5	12	9			4	3	1	7[2]		11														13
	3		2		6		8	12	10[1]					9			4		1			11	5	7												14
			2		6		8[1]		10				12	9[■]			4		1			11	5	7	3											15
			2		6			9	10[1]			8					4				12	11	5	7	3	1										16
	12		2		6			13	14	11		4	10[3]	9[2]								8	5	7	3[1]	1										17
			2	3				10		11		6[2]	12	9[1]			4					8	5	7		1	13									18
	12		2[2]	3				10		13		6	9				4					8[3]	5	7		1	11[1]	14								19
	5			11				9				8	10[1]	12	2		4					13[3]	6	7[2]	3	1		14								20
	2			11				9	12			8[3]	10[1]	13	5		4					14	6	7	3[2]	1										21
	5			3				9	12	11[3]	13	8[2]	10[1]		2		4					7	6	14		1										22
	5			3				9[1]	12	11	8[2]		10		2		4					7	6	13		1										23
	5			3				12	10	11[1]	8[2]		9		2		4					7	6	13		1										24
				3	6			11[1]	10			8	12	9	2	5	4									1			7							25
				3	6			12	10	11		8[1]	9		2	5	4									1[G]		13	7[2]	15						26
				3	6			12	10[1]	11		7	8	9	2	5	4													1						27
				3	6			12	10			8	11[1]	9	2	5	4											7		1						28
				3	6			12	10	13		8[2]	11[3]	9[1]	2	5	4									1		7	14							29
				3	6			12	10	11		2	8[1]	9		5	4									1		7								30
	12			3[1]	6			13	10	11[2]		2	8	9		5	4									1		7[3]			14					31
	4			3	6			12	10[1]	11		2[■]	8	9[2]		5										1		7	13							32
	5			3[2]	6			12	10[1]	11			8	9	2		4									1		7	13							33
	5			3	6			12	10[2]	11		4	8[1]	9	2											1		7	13							34
				3	6			12	10[1]	11		5	8	9[2]	2		4									1[G]		7	13	15						35
	5			3	6			12	10	11		8	9		2		4											7[1]				1				36
	5			3	6			12	10	11		8	9		2[2]		4											7[1]			13	1				37
	5			3	6			8	10[1]	11		2	9				4				12							7				1				38
	5				6			3[1]	10	11		2	8	9			4											7[2]	12		13	1				39
	5								10	11		2		9			4				8[1]							7	6		12	1	3[2]	13		40
	3				6			12		11		2	10[3]	9			4				8[2]							7	5[1]		13	1			14	41
	5	13		3	6		8[3]	12	10	11		2	7[2]	9															4[1]		14	1				42
	5	13		3[2]	6		8[1]	12	10	11[3]		2	7	9	14		4															1				43
	5			2	6		8[2]	7	10			3	11[1]	9	12		4											13				1				44
	5			3	6		8		10	11[1]		2	7	9			4											12				1				45
	5			3[2]	6		8[1]	12	10	11		2	7	9			4											13				1				46

FA Cup

First Round	Barrow	(a)	1-1
		(h)	3-2
Second Round	Millwall	(a)	1-2

Carling Cup

First Round	WBA	(a)	0-1

J Paint Trophy

First Round	Walsall	(h)	2-0
Second Round	Bristol R	(a)	1-0
Quarter-Final	Milton Keynes D	(h)	0-2

BRADFORD CITY FL Championship 2

FOUNDATION

Bradford was a rugby stronghold around the turn of the century but after Manningham RFC held an archery contest to help them out of financial difficulties in 1903, they were persuaded to give up the handling code and turn to soccer. So they formed Bradford City and continued at Valley Parade. Recognising this as an opportunity of spreading the dribbling code in this part of Yorkshire, the Football League immediately accepted the new club's first application for membership of the Second Division.

Coral Window Stadium, Valley Parade, Bradford, West Yorkshire BD8 7DY.

Telephone: (01274) 773 355.

Fax: (01274) 773 356.

Ticket Office: (01274) 770 012.

Website: www.bradfordcityfc.co.uk

Email: bradfordcityfc@compuserve.com

Ground Capacity: 25,136.

Record Attendance: 39,146 v Burnley, FA Cup 4th rd, 11 March 1911.

Pitch Measurements: 113yd × 70yd.

Joint Chairmen: Julian Rhodes and Mark Lawn.

Head of Operations: David Baldwin.

Secretary: Jon Pollard.

Manager: Stuart McCall.

Assistant Manager: Wayne Jacobs.

Physio: Steve Redmond.

Colours: Claret and amber.

Change Colours: White.

Year Formed: 1903.

Turned Professional: 1903.

Ltd Co.: 1908.

Club Nickname: 'The Bantams'.

Ground: 1903, Valley Parade.

First Football League Game: 1 September 1903, Division 2, v Grimsby T (a) L 0–2 – Seymour; Wilson, Halliday; Robinson, Millar, Farnall; Guy, Beckram, Forrest, McMillan, Graham.

Record League Victory: 11–1 v Rotherham U, Division 3 (N), 25 August 1928 – Sherlaw; Russell, Watson; Burkinshaw (1), Summers, Bauld; Harvey (2), Edmunds (3), White (3), Cairns, Scriven (2).

Record Cup Victory: 11–3 v Walker Celtic, FA Cup 1st rd (replay), 1 December 1937 – Parker; Rookes, McDermott; Murphy, Mackie, Moore; Bagley (1), Whittingham (1), Deakin (4 incl. 1p), Cooke (1), Bartholomew (4).

HONOURS

Football League: Division 1 – Runners-up 1998–99; Division 2 – Champions 1907–08; Promoted from Division 2 1995–96 (play-offs); Division 3 – Champions 1984–85; Division 3 (N) – Champions 1928–29; Division 4 – Runners-up 1981–82.

FA Cup: Winners 1911.

Football League Cup: best season: 5th rd, 1965, 1989.

European Competitions: *Intertoto Cup:* 2000.

SKY SPORTS FACT FILE

Enterprising Bradford City were rewarded in 2007–08 when the club's sensible ticket pricing initiative resulted in a boost to the average attendance at home matches representing an increase of 50 per cent on the previous campaign.

Record Defeat: 1–9 v Colchester U, Division 4, 30 December 1961.

Most League Points (2 for a win): 63, Division 3 (N), 1928–29.

Most League Points (3 for a win): 94, Division 3, 1984–85.

Most League Goals: 128, Division 3 (N), 1928–29.

Highest League Scorer in Season: David Layne, 34, Division 4, 1961–62.

Most League Goals in Total Aggregate: Bobby Campbell, 121, 1981–84, 1984–86.

Most League Goals in One Match: 7, Albert Whitehurst v Tranmere R, Division 3N, 6 March 1929.

Most Capped Player: Jamie Lawrence (42), Jamaica.

Most League Appearances: Cec Podd, 502, 1970–84.

Youngest League Player: Robert Cullingford, 16 years 141 days v Mansfield T, 22 April 1970.

Record Transfer Fee Received: £2,000,000 from Newcastle U for Des Hamilton, March 1997 and £2,000,000 from Newcastle U for Andrew O'Brien, March 2001.

Record Transfer Fee Paid: £2,500,000 to Leeds U for David Hopkins, July 2000.

Football League Record: 1903 Elected to Division 2; 1908–22 Division 1; 1922–27 Division 2; 1927–29 Division 3 (N); 1929–37 Division 2; 1937–61 Division 3; 1961–69 Division 4; 1969–72 Division 3; 1972–77 Division 4; 1977–78 Division 3; 1978–82 Division 4; 1982–85 Division 3; 1985–90 Division 2; 1990–92 Division 3; 1992–96 Division 2; 1996–99 Division 1; 1999–2001 FA Premier League; 2001–04 Division 1; 2004–07 FL 1; 2007– FL 2.

MANAGERS

Robert Campbell 1903–05
Peter O'Rourke 1905–21
David Menzies 1921–26
Colin Veitch 1926–28
Peter O'Rourke 1928–30
Jack Peart 1930–35
Dick Ray 1935–37
Fred Westgarth 1938–43
Bob Sharp 1943–46
Jack Barker 1946–47
John Milburn 1947–48
David Steele 1948–52
Albert Harris 1952
Ivor Powell 1952–55
Peter Jackson 1955–61
Bob Brocklebank 1961–64
Bill Harris 1965–66
Willie Watson 1966–69
Grenville Hair 1967–68
Jimmy Wheeler 1968–71
Bryan Edwards 1971–75
Bobby Kennedy 1975–78
John Napier 1978
George Mulhall 1978–81
Roy McFarland 1981–82
Trevor Cherry 1982–87
Terry Dolan 1987–89
Terry Yorath 1989–90
John Docherty 1990–91
Frank Stapleton 1991–94
Lennie Lawrence 1994–95
Chris Kamara 1995–98
Paul Jewell 1998–2000
Chris Hutchings 2000
Jim Jefferies 2000–01
Nicky Law 2002–03
Bryan Robson 2003–04
Colin Todd 2004–07
Stuart McCall May 2007–

LATEST SEQUENCES

Longest Sequence of League Wins: 10, 26.11.1983 – 3.2.1984.

Longest Sequence of League Defeats: 8, 21.1.1933 – 11.3.1933.

Longest Sequence of League Draws: 6, 30.1.1976 – 13.3.1976.

Longest Sequence of Unbeaten League Matches: 21, 11.1.1969 – 2.5.1969.

Longest Sequence Without a League Win: 16, 28.8.1948 – 20.11.1948.

Successive Scoring Runs: 30 from 26.12.1961.

Successive Non-scoring Runs: 7 from 18.4.1925.

TEN YEAR LEAGUE RECORD

		P	W	D	L	F	A	Pts	Pos
1998-99	Div 1	46	26	9	11	82	47	87	2
1999-2000	PR Lge	38	9	9	20	38	68	36	17
2000-01	PR Lge	38	5	11	22	30	70	26	20
2001-02	Div 1	46	15	10	21	69	76	55	15
2002-03	Div 1	46	14	10	22	51	73	52	19
2003-04	Div 1	46	10	6	30	38	69	36	23
2004-05	FL 1	46	17	14	15	64	62	65	11
2005-06	FL 1	46	14	19	13	51	49	61	11
2006-07	FL 1	46	11	14	21	47	65	47	22
2007-08	FL 2	46	17	11	18	63	61	62	10

DID YOU KNOW ?

On 25 August 2007, Bradford City substitute Luke Medley aged 18 scored with his first for their winning goal. On 3 February 2008 it was another such teenager David Brown who achieved a similar feat against Macclesfield Town.

BRADFORD CITY 2007–08 LEAGUE RECORD

Match No.	Date	Venue	Opponents	Result		H/T Score	Lg. Pos.	Goalscorers	Attendance
1	Aug 11	H	Macclesfield T	D	1-1	1-1	—	N'Dumbu Nsungu [45]	13,401
2	18	A	Shrewsbury T	L	0-1	0-1	21		6413
3	25	H	Wrexham	W	2-1	0-0	12	Johnson [49], Medley [78]	13,546
4	Sept 1	A	Barnet	L	1-2	0-1	16	Johnson [52]	2412
5	7	A	Lincoln C	W	2-1	1-1	—	N'Dumbu Nsungu [35], Colbeck [79]	5286
6	15	H	Peterborough U	W	1-0	0-0	7	Bower [56]	13,019
7	22	A	Hereford U	L	2-4	1-2	12	N'Dumbu Nsungu 2 [30, 59]	3275
8	29	H	Wycombe W	L	0-1	0-1	15		13,530
9	Oct 2	H	Accrington S	L	0-3	0-2	—		13,346
10	6	A	Milton Keynes D	L	1-2	0-0	21	Conlon (pen) [90]	7903
11	12	A	Morecambe	L	1-2	1-0	—	Bower [43]	4761
12	20	H	Darlington	D	0-0	0-0	19		14,074
13	27	A	Grimsby T	D	1-1	0-0	20	N'Dumbu Nsungu (pen) [90]	4883
14	Nov 3	H	Brentford	L	1-2	0-1	21	Bower [88]	13,326
15	6	H	Chester C	W	2-1	1-0	—	Daley [36], Alex Rhodes [89]	13,211
16	17	A	Dagenham & R	W	4-1	1-0	18	Thorne [19], Wetherall [75], Law 2 [89, 90]	2247
17	24	H	Stockport Co	D	1-1	0-0	17	N'Dumbu Nsungu [71]	13,837
18	Dec 5	A	Mansfield T	D	0-0	0-0	—		2308
19	8	A	Chesterfield	D	1-1	0-1	17	Nix [77]	3727
20	22	A	Peterborough U	L	1-2	1-0	19	Nix [11]	5355
21	26	H	Lincoln C	W	2-1	1-0	15	Thorne [1], Conlon [90]	15,510
22	29	H	Hereford U	L	1-3	1-3	16	Wetherall [44]	13,640
23	Jan 1	A	Accrington S	W	2-0	0-0	16	Clarke [47], Colbeck [90]	2898
24	12	H	Notts Co	W	3-0	1-0	17	Thorne 3 [34, 58, 90]	13,494
25	22	A	Bury	D	2-2	1-0	—	Conlon (pen) [45], Nix [79]	2776
26	26	A	Wrexham	D	1-1	0-1	16	Nix [49]	4341
27	29	H	Shrewsbury T	W	4-2	2-0	—	Nix [7], Daley [40], Thorne [57], Conlon (pen) [85]	13,269
28	Feb 2	A	Macclesfield T	W	1-0	0-0	13	Brown D [75]	2778
29	9	H	Bury	L	1-2	1-0	14	Thorne [23]	13,844
30	16	H	Rochdale	L	1-2	1-1	15	Thorne [45]	14,017
31	23	A	Notts Co	W	3-1	0-0	13	Thorne [63], Colbeck [69], Alex Rhodes [76]	4717
32	26	H	Rotherham U	W	3-2	3-1	—	Daley [15], Alex Rhodes [17], Bullock [44]	13,436
33	Mar 1	H	Dagenham & R	L	0-2	0-1	13		13,537
34	8	A	Stockport Co	L	1-2	0-0	13	Thorne (pen) [53]	5763
35	12	A	Chester C	W	1-0	0-0	—	Conlon [66]	1566
36	15	H	Mansfield T	L	1-2	1-1	13	Conlon [45]	13,611
37	22	A	Rotherham U	D	1-1	0-0	13	Colbeck [48]	4157
38	24	H	Chesterfield	W	1-0	1-0	13	Thorne [16]	13,825
39	29	A	Darlington	W	3-1	0-1	12	Penford [50], Conlon [63], Colbeck [79]	4492
40	Apr 1	A	Rochdale	L	1-2	0-1	—	Thorne (pen) [60]	3811
41	5	H	Morecambe	W	1-0	0-0	10	Johnson [56]	13,562
42	8	H	Barnet	D	1-1	0-1	9	Johnson [76]	13,072
43	12	A	Brentford	D	2-2	2-2	9	Thorne [17], Nix [19]	4336
44	19	H	Grimsby T	W	2-1	0-1	9	Thorne [62], Colbeck [90]	13,448
45	26	H	Milton Keynes D	L	1-2	1-2	9	Daley [45]	14,609
46	May 3	A	Wycombe W	L	1-2	1-2	10	Medley (pen) [44]	5467

Final League Position: 10

GOALSCORERS

League (63): Thorne 14 (2 pens), Conlon 7 (3 pens), Colbeck 6, N'Dumbu Nsungu 6 (1 pen), Nix 6, Daley 4, Johnson 4, Bower 3, Alex Rhodes 3, Law 2, Medley 2 (1 pen), Wetherall 2, Brown D 1, Bullock 1, Clarke 1, Penford 1.
Carling Cup (1): Nix 1.
FA Cup (1): Thorne 1.
J Paint Trophy (1): Nix 1.

Ricketts D 22	Williams D 28	Heckingbottom P 44	Evans P 19 + 6	Wetherall D 46	Bower M 25 + 2	Daley O 37 + 4	Johnson E 30 + 2	Conlon B 21 + 21	N'Dumbu Nsungu G 17 + 1	Rhodes Alex 11 + 17	Colbeck J 27 + 6	Joynes N 1 + 1	Nix K 31 + 9	Ainge S — + 4	Medley L 1 + 8	Phelan S 8 + 5	Harban T 6	Thorne P 31 + 2	Bentham C — + 3	Evans R 4	Clarke M 15 + 2	Law N 10	Penford T 13 + 2	Topp W 6 + 5	Bullock L 12	Starosta B 12 + 3	Loach S 20	Brown D — + 5	Moncur T 6 + 1	O'Brien L 2	Taylforth S 1	Match No.
1	2	3	4	5	6	7	8	9	10^{1}	11^{2}	12	13																				1
1	2	3	4	5	6	7	8^{3}	12	10	11^{2}	13	9^{1}	14																			2
1	2^{1}	3	4	5	6	7	8	9^{2}	10^{3}				11	12	13	14																3
1		3	4^{3}	5	6	7	8	9^{2}	10^{1}		12		11		13	14	2															4
1		3		5	6	7^{3}	8	12	10^{2}		11		14			4	2	9^{1}	13													5
1		3	12	5	6	7^{3}	8	13	10^{1}		11		14			4	2	9^{2}														6
1		3	4	5	6	7^{1}	8	12	10		11^{2}		13				2	9														7
1		3	4^{2}	5	6	7	8	12	10	13			11^{3}			14	2	9^{1}														8
1		3		5	6	7	8	12	10^{1}	11^{2}			13			4	2	9														9
	2	3	4^{3}	5	6	7	8	12	10^{1}	11^{2}	13									1	14	9										10
	2	3^{1}		5	6	7	8	9	10	11^{2}			13	12						1		4										11
	2	3		5	6	7	8	9	10	12			11^{1}							1		4										12
	2	3		5	6	7	8	9^{2}	10	12			11^{1}		13					1^{G}	15	4										13
1	2	3	12	5	6	7	8	9^{3}	10^{1}	13			11^{2}		14							4										14
1	2	3	4^{3}	5	12	7	8		13	14			11^{1}					9^{2}			6	10										15
1	2	3	4	5		7				12			11^{1}			8		9			6	10										16
1	2	3■	4	5		12		13	10^{3}				11			8^{1}		9^{2}	14		6	7										17
1	2	3	12	5		7		9^{2}	10				11			8^{1}		13			6	4										18
1	2	3^{2}	4	5		7		12			10		11	13				9^{1}			6	8										19
1	2	3	4	5	6	7		12		13	10		8^{2}			14		9^{1}					11^{3}									20
1	2	3	4^{1}	5		7		13	10^{3}	14	11		8			12		9^{2}			6											21
1	2	3		5		7		12		13	11^{3}		8^{1}			4		9			6		10^{2}	14								22
1	2	3	4	5		7		9			11							10			6				8							23
1	2	3	4	5		11^{1}		9		12	7							10			6				8							24
1	2	3	4	5		7		9			11		12					10^{1}			6				8							25
1	2^{2}	3	12	5		7	8^{1}	9			11		10								6				4	13						26
		3	12	5		7^{2}		14			13		11					10			6		4^{1}	9^{3}	8	2	1					27
		3	12	5				13			7		11					10^{2}			6		4^{1}	9^{3}	8	2	1	14				28
		3		5		7	13	12					11					10^{1}			6		4^{2}	9^{3}	8	2	1	14				29
		3		5		7^{1}	8	13			12		11					10^{3}			6			9^{2}	4	2	1	14				30
		3		5		7^{1}	8			13	11		12					10						9^{2}	4	2	1		6			31
		3		5		7^{3}	8	12		9^{2}	11		13					10^{1}						14	4	2	1		6			32
		3		5		7^{1}		12		9	11		8^{2}					10					13	14	4	2^{3}	1		6			33
	2	3	4^{2}	5	12	14	8	13		9^{3}	11							10							7		1		6^{1}			34
	2	3	4	5			8	9		12	7		11^{1}					10									1		6			35
	2	3	4^{2}	5		12	8	9		11^{1}	7^{3}							10					13	14			1		6			36
	2^{2}	3		5	6	11■	8	9^{1}			7		10					12					4			13	1					37
		3		5	6		12	13		11^{1}	7		8					10^{2}					4	9^{3}		2	1	14				38
	2	3		5	6		8	9			7^{1}		11					10					4			12	1					39
		3		5	6		8^{3}	9		12	7		11^{1}		13			10^{2}					4			2	1		14			40
		3		5	6	11^{1}	10	9		12	7		8										4			2	1					41
		3		5	6	7^{1}	8	9			11		10		12								4^{2}	13		2	1					42
	3			5	6	12	9			11^{2}	7		8^{1}		13			10	14				4^{3}				1			2		43
	2			5	6	11^{3}	8	12		14	7		10		13			9^{2}					4^{1}				1			3		44
	2	3		5	6	11^{1}	8	9		12	7■		4					10									1					45
		3		5	6	7^{1}		9^{2}		12			8	14	10^{3}	4										2	1	13			11	46

FA Cup

First Round	Chester C	(h)	1-0
Second Round	Tranmere R	(h)	0-3

Carling Cup

First Round	Wolverhampton W	(a)	1-2

J Paint Trophy

First Round	Doncaster R	(a)	1-5

BRENTFORD FL Championship 2

FOUNDATION

Formed as a small amateur concern in 1889 they were very successful in local circles. They won the championship of the West London Alliance in 1893 and a year later the West Middlesex Junior Cup before carrying off the Senior Cup in 1895. After winning both the London Senior Amateur Cup and the Middlesex Senior Cup in 1898 they were admitted to the Second Division of the Southern League.

Griffin Park, Braemar Road, Brentford, Middlesex TW8 0NT.

Telephone: 0845 3456 442.

Fax: (0208) 568 9940.

Ticket Office: 0845 3456 442.

Website: www.brentfordfc.co.uk

E-mail: enquiries@brentfordfc.co.uk

Ground Capacity: 12,400.

Record Attendance: 38,678 v Leicester C, FA Cup 6th rd, 26 February 1949.

Pitch Measurements: 111yd × 74yd.

Chairman: Greg Dyke.

Chief Executive: David Heath.

Secretary: Lisa Hall.

Manager: Andy Scott.

Assistant Manager: Terry Bullivant.

Physio: Brett Hutchinson.

Colours: Red and white striped shirts, black shorts, red and black stockings.

Change Colours: Sky blue shirts, navy shorts, navy stockings with blue turnovers.

Year Formed: 1889.

Turned Professional: 1899.

Ltd Co.: 1901.

Club Nickname: 'The Bees'.

Grounds: 1889, Clifden Road; 1891, Benns Fields, Little Ealing; 1895, Shotters Field; 1898, Cross Road, S. Ealing; 1900, Boston Park; 1904, Griffin Park.

First Football League Game: 28 August 1920, Division 3, v Exeter C (a) L 0–3 – Young; Hodson, Rosier, Elliott J, Levitt, Amos, Smith, Thompson, Spreadbury, Morley, Henery.

Record League Victory: 9–0 v Wrexham, Division 3, 15 October 1963 – Cakebread; Coote, Jones; Slater, Scott, Higginson; Summers (1), Brooks (2), McAdams (2), Ward (2), Hales (1), (1 og).

Record Cup Victory: 7–0 v Windsor & Eton (away), FA Cup 1st rd, 20 November 1982 – Roche; Rowe, Harris (Booker), McNichol (1), Whitehead, Hurlock (2), Kamara, Joseph (1), Mahoney (3), Bowles, Roberts. *N.B.* 8–0 v Uxbridge, FA Cup, 3rd Qual rd, 31 October 1903.

HONOURS

Football League: Division 1 best season: 5th, 1935–36; Division 2 – Champions 1934–35; Division 3 – Champions 1991–92, 1998–99; Division 3 (S) – Champions 1932–33, Runners-up 1929–30, 1957–58; Division 4 – Champions 1962–63.

FA Cup: best season: 6th rd, 1938, 1946, 1949, 1989.

Football League Cup: best season: 4th rd, 1983.

Freight Rover Trophy: Runners-up 1985.

LDV Vans Trophy: Runners-up 2001.

SKY SPORTS FACT FILE

Two Brentford players scored in their only first team appearances for the Griffin Park club – and on successive days! Johnny Price did so on Good Friday 1928, John Cairns on Easter Saturday. Injuries had been responsible for the unusual situation.

Record Defeat: 0–7 v Swansea T, Division 3 (S), 8 November 1924 and v Walsall, Division 3 (S), 19 January 1957.

Most League Points (2 for a win): 62, Division 3 (S), 1932–33 and Division 4, 1962–63.

Most League Points (3 for a win): 85, Division 2, 1994–95 and Division 3, 1998–99.

Most League Goals: 98, Division 4, 1962–63.

Highest League Scorer in Season: Jack Holliday, 38, Division 3 (S), 1932–33.

Most League Goals in Total Aggregate: Jim Towers, 153, 1954–61.

Most League Goals in One Match: 5, Jack Holliday v Luton T, Division 3S, 28 January 1933; Billy Scott v Barnsley, Division 2, 15 December 1934; Peter McKennan v Bury, Division 2, 18 February 1949.

Most Capped Player: John Buttigieg, 22 (98), Malta.

Most League Appearances: Ken Coote, 514, 1949–64.

Youngest League Player: Danis Salman, 15 years 243 days v Watford, 15 November 1975.

Record Transfer Fee Received: £2,500,000 from Wimbledon for Hermann Hreidarsson, October 1999.

Record Transfer Fee Paid: £750,000 to Crystal Palace for Hermann Hreidarsson, September 1998.

Football League Record: 1920 Original Member of Division 3; 1921–33 Division 3 (S); 1933–35 Division 2; 1935–47 Division 1; 1947–54 Division 2; 1954–62 Division 3 (S); 1962–63 Division 4; 1963–66 Division 3; 1966–72 Division 4; 1972–73 Division 3; 1973–78 Division 4; 1978–92 Division 3; 1992–93 Division 1; 1993–98 Division 2; 1998–99 Division 3; 1999–04 Division 2; 2004–07 FL 1; 2007– FL 2.

MANAGERS

Will Lewis 1900–03
(Secretary-Manager)
Dick Molyneux 1902–06
W. G. Brown 1906–08
Fred Halliday 1908–12, 1915–21, 1924–26
(only Secretary to 1922)
Ephraim Rhodes 1912–15
Archie Mitchell 1921–24
Harry Curtis 1926–49
Jackie Gibbons 1949–52
Jimmy Bain 1952–53
Tommy Lawton 1953
Bill Dodgin Snr 1953–57
Malcolm Macdonald 1957–65
Tommy Cavanagh 1965–66
Billy Gray 1966–67
Jimmy Sirrel 1967–69
Frank Blunstone 1969–73
Mike Everitt 1973–75
John Docherty 1975–76
Bill Dodgin Jnr 1976–80
Fred Callaghan 1980–84
Frank McLintock 1984–87
Steve Perryman 1987–90
Phil Holder 1990–93
David Webb 1993–97
Eddie May 1997
Micky Adams 1997–98
Ron Noades 1998–2000
Ray Lewington 2001
Steve Coppell 2001–02
Wally Downes 2002–04
Martin Allen 2004–2006
Leroy Rosenior 2006
Scott Fitzgerald 2006–07
Terry Butcher 2007
Andy Scott December 2007–

LATEST SEQUENCES

Longest Sequence of League Wins: 9, 30.4.1932 – 24.9.1932.

Longest Sequence of League Defeats: 9, 20.10.1928 – 25.12.1928.

Longest Sequence of League Draws: 5, 16.3.1957 – 6.4.1957.

Longest Sequence of Unbeaten League Matches: 26, 20.2.1999 – 16.10.1999.

Longest Sequence Without a League Win: 18, 9.9.2006 – 26.12.2006.

Successive Scoring Runs: 26 from 4.3.1963.

Successive Non-scoring Runs: 7 from 7.3.2000.

TEN YEAR LEAGUE RECORD

		P	*W*	*D*	*L*	*F*	*A*	*Pts*	*Pos*
1998-99	Div 3	46	26	7	13	79	56	85	1
1999-2000	Div 2	46	13	13	20	47	61	52	17
2000-01	Div 2	46	14	17	15	56	70	59	14
2001-02	Div 2	46	24	11	11	77	43	83	3
2002-03	Div 2	46	14	12	20	47	56	54	16
2003-04	Div 2	46	14	11	21	52	69	53	17
2004-05	FL 1	46	22	9	15	57	60	75	4
2005-06	FL 1	46	20	16	10	72	52	76	3
2006-07	FL 1	46	8	13	25	40	79	37	24
2007-08	FL 2	46	17	8	21	52	70	59	14

DID YOU KNOW ?

In 1929–30 when Brentford won all 21 home League matches they scored in every game, hit two sixes, four fives and the Lanes, Jack and Billy, contributed 40 of the 60 goals registered.

BRENTFORD 2007–08 LEAGUE RECORD

Match No.	Date	Venue	Opponents	Result		H/T Score	Lg. Pos.	Goalscorers	Attendance
1	Aug 11	H	Mansfield T	D	1-1	1-1	—	Connell 14	4909
2	18	A	Notts Co	D	1-1	0-0	13	O'Connor 63	4670
3	25	H	Barnet	W	2-1	0-0	6	O'Connor (pen) 50, Mousinho 71	4744
4	Sept 1	A	Bury	W	2-1	1-0	6	Poole 21, Shakes 84	2301
5	9	A	Wycombe W	L	0-1	0-0	8		4711
6	15	H	Milton Keynes D	L	0-3	0-1	12		4476
7	22	A	Chester C	W	2-0	0-0	7	Thorpe 53, Moore S 90	2453
8	29	H	Stockport Co	L	1-3	0-2	12	Connell 80	4449
9	Oct 2	H	Dagenham & R	L	2-3	0-1	—	Mousinho 62, Thorpe 75	3662
10	6	A	Hereford U	L	0-2	0-2	17		2942
11	12	H	Rotherham U	D	1-1	0-0	—	Thorpe 55	3841
12	20	A	Rochdale	D	1-1	0-0	16	Poole 88	2424
13	27	H	Lincoln C	W	1-0	0-0	14	Moore S 80	4368
14	Nov 3	A	Bradford C	W	2-1	1-0	13	Poole 41, Thorpe 60	13,326
15	6	A	Macclesfield T	L	0-1	0-0	—		1378
16	17	H	Darlington	L	0-2	0-2	16		4657
17	24	A	Peterborough U	L	0-7	0-4	16		4865
18	Dec 4	H	Morecambe	L	0-1	0-0	—		3155
19	8	H	Grimsby T	L	0-1	0-0	19		3999
20	15	A	Wrexham	W	3-1	0-1	17	Connell 2 66, 77, Evans S (og) 72	3811
21	21	A	Milton Keynes D	D	1-1	1-0	—	Connell 16	8445
22	26	H	Wycombe W	L	1-3	1-0	17	Poole 23	5841
23	29	H	Chester C	W	3-0	1-0	15	Connell 4, Montague 76, Poole 79	4323
24	Jan 1	A	Dagenham & R	W	2-1	1-0	15	Poole 2 22, 68	2353
25	5	A	Shrewsbury T	W	1-0	0-0	14	Osborne 52	5083
26	12	H	Chesterfield	W	2-1	1-1	12	Smith G 25, Poole 61	4882
27	29	H	Notts Co	D	0-0	0-0	—		4332
28	Feb 2	A	Mansfield T	W	3-2	1-1	12	O'Connor 25, Connell 56, Elder 85	2511
29	9	H	Shrewsbury T	D	1-1	0-0	12	Connell 57	5353
30	12	A	Barnet	W	2-1	1-0	—	Poole 2 (1 pen) 36, 79 (p)	2522
31	16	H	Accrington S	W	3-1	2-1	11	Poole 34, Heywood 44, Connell 63	4635
32	23	A	Chesterfield	L	0-1	0-1	12		3728
33	26	A	Accrington S	L	0-1	0-1	—		1149
34	Mar 1	A	Darlington	L	1-3	0-0	12	Reid 82	3508
35	4	H	Bury	L	1-4	0-3	—	Poole (pen) 56	3333
36	8	H	Macclesfield T	W	1-0	0-0	12	Poole 90	3863
37	11	H	Peterborough U	L	1-2	0-1	—	Connell 62	4049
38	15	A	Morecambe	L	1-3	1-1	12	Elder 42	2180
39	22	H	Wrexham	W	2-0	1-0	12	Shakes 2 31, 81	4448
40	24	A	Grimsby T	W	2-1	0-1	10	Connell 51, Brown W 82	4620
41	29	H	Rochdale	L	0-2	0-0	11		4896
42	Apr 5	A	Rotherham U	W	2-1	1-0	9	Elder 39, Connell 90	2979
43	12	H	Bradford C	D	2-2	2-2	11	Poole 6, Bennett 26	4336
44	19	A	Lincoln C	L	1-3	1-1	11	Elder 45	3689
45	26	H	Hereford U	L	0-3	0-2	13		6246
46	May 3	A	Stockport Co	L	0-1	0-0	14		6284

Final League Position: 14

GOALSCORERS

League (52): Poole 14 (2 pens), Connell 12, Elder 4, Thorpe 4, O'Connor 3 (1 pen), Shakes 3, Moore S 2, Mousinho 2, Bennett 1, Brown W 1, Heywood 1, Montague 1, Osborne 1, Reid 1, Smith G 1, own goal 1.
Carling Cup (0).
FA Cup (1): Ide 1.
J Paint Trophy (1): Shakes 1.

Hamer B 20	Starosta B 20 + 1	Basey G 8	Moore S 13 + 7	Pettigrew A 9 + 2	Mackie J 14	O'Connor K 36 + 1	Mousinho J 13 + 10	Ide C 16 + 3	Connell A 35 + 7	Poole G 42 + 3	Smith G 26 + 3	Peters R — + 4	Brooker P — + 1	Osborne K 25 + 4	Tillen S — + 1	Thorpe L 17 + 2	Heywood M 30 + 2	Shakes R 25 + 14	Pead C 27 + 5	Brown S 26	Charles D 8 + 9	Emanuel L 3	Montague R 7 + 3	Dickson R 30 + 1	Masters C — + 1	Sinclair E 1 + 3	Sankofa O 10 + 1	Stone C 5 + 1	Parkes J — + 1	Elder N 16 + 1	Reid R 1 + 9	Milsom R 5 + 1	Brown W 7 + 4	Bennett A 11	*Match No.*
1	2	3	4	5	6	7	8^{1}	9	10^{2}	11^{3}	12	13	14																						1
1	2	3^{1}	4	5	6	7	8	9		11^{2}		12		10	13																				2
1	2	3	4	5	6	7^{2}	8	9^{1}		13		12		11		10■																			3
1	2	3	4	5		7	8^{1}	9^{2}		11				10			6	12	13																4
1	2	3	4■	5		7		9^{2}	12	11^{1}				8			6	10	13																5
1	2	3		5		7	8	9^{3}		12	11^{2}	14		4^{1}		10	6	13																	6
	2		4	5	6	7		12	10^{1}	11	13					9^{2}		8		1	3														7
	2		4	5	6^{1}	7		13	9	11				14		10		8^{2}	12	1	3^{3}														8
	2^{2}		4	5		8	13	9^{1}	10	11				12		6			7	1	3														9
	12	3^{1}	4^{2}		6	2	8		10^{3}	11						9	5	13	7	1	14														10
	2	3	12		6^{3}	7	8	9^{2}	13	11^{1}						10	5	4		1	14														11
	2			12	6^{1}	3		9	13	11	14					10	5	8^{2}	7^{3}	1	4														12
	7		13	12	6	2		4^{3}	10	11						9^{2}	5		8^{1}	1		3	14												13
	2		7		6	4			10^{2}	11^{1}						9^{3}	5	12	8	1	13	3	14												14
	2		7		6	4			10^{1}	11						9	5	12	8	1	13	3^{2}													15
	2		8		6	3		9	12	11						10	5^{2}	4^{1}	7^{3}	1	13			14											16
					6	2		7^{G}	12	11						9^{1}	5	13	8^{2}	1■	3			4	15	10									17
	2		4		6^{1}	7			13	11^{3}						9	5		12	1	3		10^{2}	8		14									18
	2		12			7		11^{2}	9		4^{1}			6		14	5	13		1	3		10^{3}	8											19
	2					4		7^{2}	10^{3}	12	8^{1}			6		9	5	13		1	3			11		14									20
	2		12			7		14	10^{1}	11	4^{2}			3		9	5	8^{3}	13	1				6											21
	2■					4		7	10^{1}	11^{2}	8			6		9	5			1	12			3		13									22
			12			2		9^{2}	10	11^{1}	4			6			5	13	7	1			8	3											23
1			12			4			9	11^{2}	8			6			5	7^{1}	2		13		10	3											24
1			12			4	13		9	11	8			6			5	7^{1}	2				10^{2}	3											25
1						2	12		9	11	4			6		13	5	8^{1}	7				10^{2}	3											26
1						4			9	11	8			6^{1}			5	7	2				10	3			12								27
1						4^{2}			9	11^{3}	8						5	7^{1}	2				12	3			6	13	14	10					28
1									9	11	8						5	7^{1}	2					3			6	4		10	12				29
1									9^{3}	11	8■			12			5	7	2^{1}					3			6	4		10^{2}	13	14			30
1									9	11				12			5	7	2^{1}					3			6	4		10^{2}	13	8			31
1							12		9	11	4			2			5^{2}	7			13			3			6^{1}			10^{3}	14	8			32
1							12		9	11	4			5				13	2					3			6			14	10^{3}	8^{1}	7^{2}		33
1							12		9	11	4			5				13	2					3			6			10^{3}	14	8^{1}	7^{2}		34
1							5		9	11	4			6				12						3			2^{1}			10	13	8	7^{2}		35
									9	11	4			5				7	2	1				3				8		10				6	36
							12		9	11	4			6				7	2	1				3				8^{1}		10				5	37
						12	8^{1}		9	11	4			6				7^{2}		1				3			2^{3}			10	14		13	5	38
						3	12		9	11	4^{1}			6				7	2	1				8						10				5	39
						4	8		9^{1}	11				6				7^{2}	2	1				3						10	12		13	5	40
						4	8		9	11							5	7^{1}	2	1				3						10			12	6	41
						6	12		13	11	4						5	9^{1}	2	1				3						10^{2}			8	7	42
						4			9	11	8						5	12	2	1				3						10			7^{1}	6	43
						8	2		9^{2}	11	4						5	12		1				3						10	13		7^{1}	6	44
1						6	13		9	11	8^{2}			5			12	10	2^{1}					3									7	4	45
1						2	8^{2}		9	11	7			4			12	10			14			3^{3}			6^{1}						13	5	46

FA Cup
First Round — Luton T — (a) 1-1; (h) 0-2

Carling Cup
First Round — Bristol C — (h) 0-3

J Paint Trophy
First Round — Swindon T — (a) 1-4

BRIGHTON & HOVE ALBION FL Championship 1

FOUNDATION

A professional club Brighton United was formed in November 1897 at the Imperial Hotel, Queen's Road, but folded in March 1900 after less than two seasons in the Southern League at the County Ground. An amateur team Brighton & Hove Rangers was then formed by some prominent United supporters and after one season at Withdean, decided to turn semi-professional and play at the County Ground. Rangers were accepted into the Southern League but then also folded June 1901. John Jackson the former United manager organised a meeting at the Seven Stars public house, Ship Street on 24 June 1901 at which a new third club Brighton & Hove United was formed. They took over Rangers' place in the Southern League and pitch at County Ground. The name was changed to Brighton & Hove Albion before a match was played because of objections by Hove FC.

Withdean Stadium, Tongdean Lane, Brighton, East Sussex BN1 5JD.

Telephone: (01273) 695 400 (admin office 44 North Road, Brighton).

Fax: (01273) 648 179 (admin office 44 North Road, Brighton).

Ticket Office: (01273) 776 992.

Website: www.seagulls.co.uk

Email: seagulls@bhafc.co.uk

Ground Capacity: 8,850.

Record Attendance: 36,747 v Fulham, Division 2, 27 December 1958 (at Goldstone Ground).

Pitch Measurements: 110yd × 70yd.

Chairman: Dick Knight.

Managing Director: Ken Brown.

Chief Executive: Martin Perry.

Secretary: Derek J. Allan.

Manager: Micky Adams.

Assistant to Manager: Dean White.

Physio: Malcolm Stuart.

Colours: Blue and white striped shirts, white shorts, white stockings.

Change Colours: Yellow and navy blue striped shirts, navy blue shorts, navy blue stockings.

Year Formed: 1901. ***Turned Professional:*** 1901.

Ltd Co.: 1904.

Grounds: 1901, County Ground; 1902, Goldstone Ground.

Club Nickname: 'The Seagulls'.

First Football League Game: 28 August 1920, Division 3, v Southend U (a) L 0–2 – Hayes; Woodhouse, Little; Hall, Comber, Bentley; Longstaff, Ritchie, Doran, Rodgerson, March.

HONOURS

Football League: Division 1 best season: 13th, 1981–82; Division 2 – Champions 2001–02; Runners-up 1978–79; Promoted from Division 2 2003–04 (play-offs); Division 3 (S) – Champions 1957–58; Runners-up 1953–54, 1955–56; Division 3 – Champions 2000–01; Runners-up 1971–72, 1976–77, 1987–88; Division 4 – Champions 1964–65.

FA Cup: Runners-up 1983.

Football League Cup: best season: 5th rd, 1979.

SKY SPORTS FACT FILE

Brighton & Hove Albion changed the official logo of the club to a Seagull in flight in 1977. On 19 May the board of directors acquired at a local auction, two stuffed seagulls housed in a glass display case which proved a commendable adjunct to it.

Record League Victory: 9–1 v Newport Co, Division 3 (S), 18 April 1951 – Ball; Tennant (1p), Mansell (1p); Willard, McCoy, Wilson; Reed, McNichol (4), Garbutt, Bennett (2), Keene (1). 9–1 v Southend U, Division 3, 27 November 1965 – Powney; Magill, Baxter; Leck, Gall, Turner; Gould (1), Collins (1), Livesey (2), Smith (3), Goodchild (2).

Record Cup Victory: 10–1 v Wisbech, FA Cup 1st rd, 13 November 1965 – Powney; Magill, Baxter; Collins (1), Gall, Turner; Gould, Smith (2), Livesey (3), Cassidy (2), Goodchild (1), (1 og).

Record Defeat: 0–9 v Middlesbrough, Division 2, 23 August 1958.

Most League Points (2 for a win): 65, Division 3 (S), 1955–56 and Division 3, 1971–72.

Most League Points (3 for a win): 92, Division 3, 2000–01.

Most League Goals: 112, Division 3 (S), 1955–56.

Highest League Scorer in Season: Peter Ward, 32, Division 3, 1976–77.

Most League Goals in Total Aggregate: Tommy Cook, 114, 1922–29.

Most League Goals in One Match: 5, Jack Doran v Northampton T, Division 3S, 5 November 1921; 5, Adrian Thorne v Watford, Division 3S, 30 April 1958.

Most Capped Player: Steve Penney, 17, Northern Ireland.

Most League Appearances: 'Tug' Wilson, 509, 1922–36.

Youngest League Player: Ian Chapman, 16 years 259 days v Birmingham C, 14 February 1987.

Record Transfer Fee Received: £1,500,000 from Tottenham H for Bobby Zamora, July 2003 and £1,500,000 from Celtic for Adam Virgo, July 2005.

Record Transfer Fee Paid: £500,000 to Manchester U for Andy Ritchie, October 1980.

Football League Record: 1920 Original Member of Division 3; 1921–58 Division 3 (S); 1958–62 Division 2; 1962–63 Division 3; 1963–65 Division 4; 1965–72 Division 3; 1972–73 Division 2; 1973–77 Division 3; 1977–79 Division 2; 1979–83 Division 1; 1983–87 Division 2; 1987–88 Division 3; 1988–96 Division 2; 1996–2001 Division 3; 2001–02 Division 2; 2002–03 Division 1; 2003–04 Division 2; 2004–06 FL C; 2006– FL 1.

MANAGERS

John Jackson 1901–05
Frank Scott-Walford 1905–08
John Robson 1908–14
Charles Webb 1919–47
Tommy Cook 1947
Don Welsh 1947–51
Billy Lane 1951–61
George Curtis 1961–63
Archie Macaulay 1963–68
Fred Goodwin 1968–70
Pat Saward 1970–73
Brian Clough 1973–74
Peter Taylor 1974–76
Alan Mullery 1976–81
Mike Bailey 1981–82
Jimmy Melia 1982–83
Chris Cattlin 1983–86
Alan Mullery 1986–87
Barry Lloyd 1987–93
Liam Brady 1993–95
Jimmy Case 1995–96
Steve Gritt 1996–98
Brian Horton 1998–99
Jeff Wood 1999
Micky Adams 1999–2001
Peter Taylor 2001–02
Martin Hinshelwood 2002
Steve Coppell 2002–03
Mark McGhee 2003–06
Dean Wilkins 2006–08
Micky Adams May 2008–

LATEST SEQUENCES

Longest Sequence of League Wins: 9, 2.10.1926 – 20.11.1926.

Longest Sequence of League Defeats: 12, 17.8.2002 – 26.10.2002.

Longest Sequence of League Draws: 6, 16.2.1980 – 15.3.1980.

Longest Sequence of Unbeaten League Matches: 16, 8.10.1930 – 28.1.1931.

Longest Sequence Without a League Win: 15, 21.10.1972 – 27.1.1973

Successive Scoring Runs: 31 from 4.2.1956.

Successive Non-scoring Runs: 6 from 8.11.1924.

TEN YEAR LEAGUE RECORD

		P	W	D	L	F	A	Pts	Pos
1998-99	Div 3	46	16	7	23	49	66	55	17
1999-2000	Div 3	46	17	16	13	64	46	67	11
2000-01	Div 3	46	28	8	10	73	35	92	1
2001-02	Div 2	46	25	15	6	66	42	90	1
2002-03	Div 1	46	11	12	23	49	67	45	23
2003-04	Div 2	46	22	11	13	64	43	77	4
2004-05	FL C	46	13	12	21	40	65	51	20
2005-06	FL C	46	7	17	22	39	71	38	24
2006-07	FL 1	46	14	11	21	49	58	53	18
2007-08	FL 1	46	19	12	15	58	50	69	7

DID YOU KNOW ?

The first season in which two Brighton & Hove Albion players succeeded in scoring 20 or more goals in the Football League was in 1926–27 when Sam Jennings hit 25 and Tommy Cook weighed in with 21.

BRIGHTON & HOVE ALBION 2007–08 LEAGUE RECORD

Match No.	*Date*	*Venue*	*Opponents*	*Result*		*H/T Score*	*Lg. Pos.*	*Goalscorers*	*Attendance*
1	Aug 11	A	Crewe Alex	L	1-2	1-1	—	Cox [14]	5394
2	18	H	Northampton T	W	2-1	1-1	8	Hammond (pen) [2], Revell [66]	5137
3	25	A	Tranmere R	L	0-2	0-0	16		5670
4	Sept 1	H	Southend U	W	3-2	0-1	10	Forster 2 [75, 85], Hammond [90]	5652
5	7	H	Millwall	W	3-0	2-0	—	Hammond (pen) [12], Cox [19], Martot [78]	6563
6	15	A	Gillingham	L	0-1	0-0	6		6118
7	22	H	Yeovil T	L	1-2	0-2	12	Hammond (pen) [61]	5231
8	29	A	Swansea C	D	0-0	0-0	12		11,058
9	Oct 2	A	Bournemouth	W	2-0	0-0	—	Cox [46], Savage [66]	4638
10	6	H	Bristol R	D	0-0	0-0	9		5820
11	13	A	Port Vale	W	1-0	0-0	8	Revell [64]	3490
12	20	H	Leeds U	L	0-1	0-0	11		8691
13	27	A	Hartlepool U	W	2-1	1-0	8	Nelson (og) [14], Savage [90]	5619
14	Nov 3	H	Luton T	W	3-1	1-0	7	Savage [40], Forster 2 [69, 85]	5317
15	6	H	Walsall	D	1-1	1-0	—	Robinson [36]	4717
16	17	A	Leyton Orient	D	2-2	0-1	7	Forster [68], Cox [75]	6496
17	24	H	Carlisle U	D	2-2	0-1	7	Forster 2 [47, 84]	5390
18	Dec 4	A	Doncaster R	D	0-0	0-0	—		6215
19	7	H	Nottingham F	L	0-2	0-1	—		6536
20	15	A	Swindon T	W	3-0	2-0	8	Forster [3], Robinson [45], Hammond [73]	6415
21	26	A	Millwall	L	0-3	0-1	11		9401
22	29	A	Yeovil T	L	1-2	1-1	12	Revell [19]	6881
23	Jan 1	H	Bournemouth	W	3-2	1-1	10	Revell 3 [15, 58, 90]	5963
24	12	A	Oldham Ath	D	1-1	0-1	9	Elder [90]	5168
25	19	H	Huddersfield T	D	1-1	0-0	12	Elphick [74]	5343
26	29	A	Northampton T	L	0-1	0-1	—		4657
27	Feb 2	H	Crewe Alex	W	3-0	3-0	12	Murray 2 [23, 45], Butters [41]	4802
28	9	A	Cheltenham T	L	1-2	0-0	14	Robinson [55]	3963
29	12	H	Tranmere R	D	0-0	0-0	—		4797
30	19	H	Cheltenham T	W	2-1	0-1	—	Murray [80], Lynch [88]	4395
31	23	H	Oldham Ath	W	1-0	0-0	11	Murray [61]	4815
32	Mar 1	H	Leyton Orient	D	1-1	0-0	12	Forster (pen) [90]	6242
33	4	H	Gillingham	W	4-2	3-1	—	Forster (pen) [23], El-Abd [43], Elphick [45], Robinson [68]	6836
34	8	A	Carlisle U	L	0-2	0-1	12		6793
35	11	A	Walsall	W	2-1	1-1	—	Forster [34], Murray [79]	4309
36	15	H	Doncaster R	W	1-0	0-0	9	Forster [57]	6252
37	18	A	Huddersfield T	L	1-2	0-1	—	Forster (pen) [47]	6004
38	22	H	Swindon T	W	2-1	1-1	7	Forster 2 [12, 66]	6849
39	24	A	Nottingham F	D	0-0	0-0	6-		18,165
40	29	A	Leeds U	D	0-0	0-0	7		22,575
41	Apr 5	H	Port Vale	L	2-3	1-2	9	Cox [26], Murray [90]	7741
42	8	A	Southend U	L	0-2	0-2	—		8428
43	12	A	Luton T	W	2-1	0-0	8	Westlake [51], Murray [59]	6652
44	19	H	Hartlepool U	W	2-1	1-0	7	Murray [38], Cox [89]	6178
45	26	A	Bristol R	W	2-0	0-0	7	Westlake [71], Murray [74]	7590
46	May 3	H	Swansea C	L	0-1	0-0	7		7283

Final League Position: 7

GOALSCORERS

League (58): Forster 15 (3 pens), Murray 9, Cox 6, Revell 6, Hammond 5 (3 pens), Robinson 4, Savage 3, Elphick 2, Westlake 2, Butters 1, El-Abd 1, Elder 1, Lynch 1, Martot 1, own goal 1.
Carling Cup (0).
FA Cup (6): Forster 2, El-Abd 1, Hammond 1 (pen), Loft 1, Revell 1.
J Paint Trophy (6): Forster 2, Cox 1, Martot 1, Robinson 1, Savage 1.

Kuipers M 46	Whing A 42	Mayo K 10 + 5	Butters G 19 + 2	Lynch J 18 + 4	El-Abd A 31 + 4	Cox D 40 + 2	Hammond D 24	Forster N 39 + 2	Revell A 14 + 7	Fraser T 15 + 9	Savage B 17 + 4	Elder N 1 + 8	Reid P 3 + 4	Elphick T 39	Rents S 4 + 1	Robinson J 16 + 18	O'Callaghan G 13 + 1	Martot D 17 + 9	Hinshelwood A — + 1	Richards M 28	Loft D 1 + 12	Gatting J — + 9	Fogden W 1 + 2	Hart G 2 + 5	Thomson S 20	Murray G 20 + 1	McFaul S — + 1	Bowditch D 5	Dixon J 2 + 2	Westlake I 11	Racon T 8	Gargan S — + 1	Match No.
1	2	3	4	5	6[1]	7	8	9	10[2]	11[3]	12	13	14																				1
1	2		4		6	7	8[1]	9	10	12	13			5	3	11[2]																	2
1	2■		4		6	7	8	9[1]	10		11	12		5	3																		3
1			4[1]	3	6	7[2]	8	9	10		14			5	12	13	2	11[3]															4
1	2		4	3[1]	12	7	8	9	14		10[3]			5		11[2]	6	13															5
1	2		4[3]		6	7	8	9	12		10[1]			5		13	3	11[2]	14														6
1	2		4[1]		12	7	8	9	13		10[2]			5		14	6	11[3]		3													7
1	2		4			7	8	9[1]	10		11			5			6			3	12												8
1	2		4		12	7[2]	8	9	10		11			5			6[1]			3	13												9
1	2		4[1]		12	7	8		10[2]		9	13		5		11	6			3													10
1	2				6	7[3]	8		10	12	11[2]	13		5		9	4[1]	14		3													11
1	2				6		8	12	10	4[3]	11[2]	13		5		9[1]		7		3	14												12
1	2				6	7[2]	8		10[1]	4	12			5		9		11		3	13												13
1	2				6	7[1]	8	12		4[2]	10			5		9	13	11		3													14
1	2				6	12	8	9[1]			10			5		7	4	11		3													15
1			4[1]	12	6	7	8	9			10			5		13	2	11[2]		3													16
1	2			5	6	7[1]	8	9		12	10					11[2]	4■	13		3													17
1	2			5	6	7	8	9[1]	12	4[3]	10		14					11[2]		3	13												18
1	2[3]			5	6	7	8[2]	9	12	4[1]	10		14			11				3	13												19
1	2			5	6		8	9	12	11[3]	10[1]		14			7[2]	4	13		3													20
1	2			5	6	12	8	9	13	7[1]	10[2]				3	11[3]	4	14															21
1	2			5	6	7	8	9	10	4[2]		12			3[1]	14		11[3]			13												22
1	2		5		6	7	8	9	10				4[1]	3		11[2]					12	13											23
1	2	12			6	7	8■	9	10[3]	4[2]		13		5				11					3[1]	14									24
1	2				6	7		9	10[2]			12	4	5				11[1]		3				13■	8								25
1	2				6	7		9		12		10[3]	8[1]	5		13		11[2]		3					4	14							26
1	2		4		6	7[1]		9						5		11[2]		13		3		14			8	10[3]	12						27
1	2		4[2]		6	7		9						5		11[1]				3		13	12		8	10							28
1	2	12	4[1]		6	7		9						5						3				13	8	10[2]		11					29
1	2	11[2]	4[1]	12		7		9		13				5		14				3					6	10		8[3]					30
1	2			12	6	7		9[1]		11[3]				5		13		14		3					4	10		8[2]					31
1	2				6	7[1]		9		11[3]				5		13		12		3					4	10		8[2]	14				32
1	2	12			6			9		7				5		13		11		3						10		8[2]		4[1]			33
1	2				6			9[3]		7[2]				5		13		11[1]		3	12			14	4	10				8			34
1	2			4	6	7[1]		9[2]		12				5		13				3					8	10				11			35
1	2	12		4	6	7		9[2]						5						3[1]				13	8	10				11			36
1	2	3[2]		4	6[1]	7[3]		9		12				5		13						14			8	10				11			37
1		3	12	4		7[1]		9[3]		13				5								14		2	8	10				11[2]	6		38
1		3	12	6		7[1]		9[2]						5		13		11			14			2	8[3]	10					4		39
1	2	3		6		7[1]		9						5		12		11[2]			13				8	10					4		40
1	2	3		6		7		9		12				5		13						14			8[3]	10				11[2]	4[1]		41
1	2	3	6[2]			7		9						5		12						13			8	10				11[1]	4		42
1	2	3	6			7[2]								5				13			12				8	10			9[1]	11	4		43
1	2	3	6[1]	12		7								5		13						14			8	10			9[2]	11[3]	4		44
1	2			6		7		9[1]						5						3		12			8	10[2]				11	4	13	45
1	2	12		6		7		9		4				5		11[3]				3[1]	8[2]		13			10			14				46

FA Cup

First Round	Cheltenham T	(a)	1-1
		(h)	2-1
Second Round	Torquay U	(a)	2-0
Third Round	Mansfield T	(h)	1-2

Carling Cup

First Round	Cardiff C	(a)	0-1

J Paint Trophy

Second Round	Barnet	(h)	2-1
Quarter-Final	Cheltenham T	(h)	4-1
Southern Semi-Final	Swansea C	(a)	0-1

BRISTOL CITY FL Championship

FOUNDATION

The name Bristol City came into being in 1897 when the Bristol South End club, formed three years earlier, decided to adopt professionalism and apply for admission to the Southern League after competing in the Western League. The historic meeting was held at The Albert Hall, Bedminster. Bristol City employed Sam Hollis from Woolwich Arsenal as manager and gave him £40 to buy players. In 1900 they merged with Bedminster, another leading Bristol club.

Ashton Gate Stadium, Bristol BS3 2EJ.

Telephone: (0871) 222 6666.

Fax: (0117) 9630 700.

Ticket Office: 0871 222 6666.

Website: www.bcfc.co.uk

Ground Capacity: 21,804.

Record Attendance: 43,335 v Preston NE, FA Cup 5th rd, 16 February 1935.

Pitch Measurements: 115yd × 75yd.

Chairman: Stephen Lansdown.

Vice-chairman: Keith Dawe.

Chief Executive: Colin Sexstone.

Secretary: Michelle McDonald.

Manager: Gary Johnson.

Assistant Manager: Keith Millen.

Physio: Nick Dawes.

Colours: Red shirts, white shorts, white stockings.

Change Colours: All black.

Year Formed: 1894.

Turned Professional: 1897.

Ltd Co.: 1897. Bristol City Football Club Ltd.

Previous Name: 1894, Bristol South End; 1897, Bristol City.

Club Nickname: 'Robins'.

Grounds: 1894, St John's Lane; 1904, Ashton Gate.

First Football League Game: 7 September 1901, Division 2, v Blackpool (a) W 2–0 – Moles; Tuft, Davies; Jones, McLean, Chambers; Bradbury, Connor, Boucher, O'Brien (2), Flynn.

Record League Victory: 9–0 v Aldershot, Division 3 (S), 28 December 1946 – Eddols; Morgan, Fox; Peacock, Roberts, Jones (1); Chilcott, Thomas, Clark (4 incl. 1p), Cyril Williams (1), Hargreaves (3).

HONOURS

Football League: Division 1 – Runners-up 1906–07; Division 2 – Champions 1905–06; Runners-up 1975–76, 1997–98; FL 1 – Runners-up 2006–07; Division 3 (S) – Champions 1922–23, 1926–27, 1954–55; Runners-up 1937–38; Division 3 – Runners-up 1964–65, 1989–90.

FA Cup: Runners-up 1909.

Football League Cup: Semi-final 1971, 1989.

Welsh Cup: Winners 1934.

Anglo-Scottish Cup: Winners 1978.

Freight Rover Trophy: Winners 1986; Runners-up 1987.

Auto Windscreens Shield: Runners-up 2000.

LDV Vans Trophy: Winners 2003.

SKY SPORTS FACT FILE

John Cowell made his name with Castleford Town scoring 72 goals in one season. Signed from Rotherham Town by Bristol City in 1909–10, he hit 20 goals including a hat-trick and four in a match against Nottingham Forest on 30 April.

Record Cup Victory: 11–0 v Chichester C, FA Cup 1st rd, 5 November 1960 – Cook; Collinson, Thresher; Connor, Alan Williams, Etheridge; Tait (1), Bobby Williams (1), Atyeo (5), Adrian Williams (3), Derrick, (1 og).

Record Defeat: 0–9 v Coventry C, Division 3 (S), 28 April 1934.

Most League Points (2 for a win): 70, Division 3 (S), 1954–55.

Most League Points (3 for a win): 91, Division 3, 1989–90.

Most League Goals: 104, Division 3 (S), 1926–27.

Highest League Scorer in Season: Don Clark, 36, Division 3 (S), 1946–47.

Most League Goals in Total Aggregate: John Atyeo, 314, 1951–66.

Most League Goals in One Match: 6, Tommy 'Tot' Walsh v Gillingham, Division 3S, 15 January 1927.

Most Capped Player: Billy Wedlock, 26, England.

Most League Appearances: John Atyeo, 597, 1951–66.

Youngest League Player: Marvin Brown, 16 years 105 days v Bristol R, 17 October 1999.

Record Transfer Fee Received: £3,000,000 from Wolverhampton W for Ade Akinbiyi, September 1999.

Record Transfer Fee Paid: £1,200,000 to Gillingham for Ade Akinbiyi, May 1998.

Football League Record: 1901 Elected to Division 2; 1906–11 Division 1; 1911–22 Division 2; 1922–23 Division 3 (S); 1923–24 Division 2; 1924–27 Division 3 (S); 1927–32 Division 2; 1932–55 Division 3 (S); 1955–60 Division 2; 1960–65 Division 3; 1965–76 Division 2; 1976–80 Division 1; 1980–81 Division 2; 1981–82 Division 3; 1982–84 Division 4; 1984–90 Division 3; 1990–92 Division 2; 1992–95 Division 1; 1995–98 Division 2; 1998–99 Division 1; 1999–04 Division 2; 2004–07 FL 1; 2007 – FL C.

MANAGERS

Sam Hollis 1897–99
Bob Campbell 1899–1901
Sam Hollis 1901–05
Harry Thickett 1905–10
Frank Bacon 1910–11
Sam Hollis 1911–13
George Hedley 1913–17
Jack Hamilton 1917–19
Joe Palmer 1919–21
Alex Raisbeck 1921–29
Joe Bradshaw 1929–32
Bob Hewison 1932–49
(under suspension 1938–39)
Bob Wright 1949–50
Pat Beasley 1950–58
Peter Doherty 1958–60
Fred Ford 1960–67
Alan Dicks 1967–80
Bobby Houghton 1980–82
Roy Hodgson 1982
Terry Cooper 1982–88
(Director from 1983)
Joe Jordan 1988–90
Jimmy Lumsden 1990–92
Denis Smith 1992–93
Russell Osman 1993–94
Joe Jordan 1994–97
John Ward 1997–98
Benny Lennartsson 1998–99
Tony Pulis 1999
Tony Fawthrop 2000
Danny Wilson 2000–04
Brian Tinnion 2004–05
Gary Johnson September 2005–

LATEST SEQUENCES

Longest Sequence of League Wins: 14, 9.9.1905 – 2.12.1905.

Longest Sequence of League Defeats: 7, 3.10.1970 – 7.11.1970.

Longest Sequence of League Draws: 4, 6.11.1999 – 27.11.1999.

Longest Sequence of Unbeaten League Matches: 24, 9.9.1905 – 10.2.1906.

Longest Sequence Without a League Win: 15, 29.4.1933 – 4.11.1933.

Successive Scoring Runs: 25 from 26.12.1905.

Successive Non-scoring Runs: 6 from 10.9.1910.

TEN YEAR LEAGUE RECORD

		P	W	D	L	F	A	Pts	Pos
1998-99	Div 1	46	9	15	22	57	80	42	24
1999-2000	Div 2	46	15	19	12	59	57	64	9
2000-01	Div 2	46	18	14	14	70	56	68	9
2001-02	Div 2	46	21	10	15	68	53	73	7
2002-03	Div 2	46	24	11	11	79	48	83	3
2003-04	Div 2	46	23	13	10	58	37	82	3
2004-05	FL 1	46	18	16	12	74	57	70	7
2005-06	FL 1	46	18	11	17	66	62	65	9
2006-07	FL 1	46	25	10	11	63	39	85	2
2007-08	FL C	46	20	14	12	54	53	74	4

DID YOU KNOW?

In both the 1905–06 season when they won the Second Division championship and again in 1954–55 when annexing the Third Division (South) title, Bristol City on each occasion won 30 League games out of 38 in the former term, 46 in the latter one.

BRISTOL CITY 2007–08 LEAGUE RECORD

Match No.	*Date*	*Venue*	*Opponents*	*Result*	*H/T Score*	*Lg. Pos.*	*Goalscorers*	*Attendance*
1	Aug 11	H	QPR	D 2-2	1-1	—	Johnson [33], Murray [89]	18,228
2	18	A	Blackpool	D 1-1	0-0	15	Murray [75]	8983
3	25	H	Scunthorpe U	W 2-1	2-1	7	Trundle 2 [36, 45]	12,474
4	Sept 1	A	Sheffield W	W 1-0	1-0	3	Wilson B [4]	17,559
5	15	A	Coventry C	W 3-0	1-0	2	McIndoe [15], Konstantopoulos (og) [74], Byfield [90]	21,538
6	18	H	WBA	D 1-1	0-0	—	Orr [89]	16,571
7	22	H	Burnley	D 2-2	0-0	4	Byfield 2 [80, 86]	14,079
8	29	A	Preston NE	D 0-0	0-0	4		12,098
9	Oct 2	A	Barnsley	L 0-3	0-0	—		9679
10	6	H	Sheffield U	W 2-0	1-0	4	Noble [44], McIndoe [72]	13,071
11	20	A	Norwich C	W 3-1	0-0	2	McIndoe [48], Murray [85], Trundle [90]	24,125
12	24	H	Southampton	W 2-1	2-0	—	Byfield [4], Sproule [17]	18,326
13	27	H	Stoke C	W 1-0	1-0	2	Elliott [35]	15,012
14	Nov 3	A	Wolverhampton W	D 1-1	1-1	2	Fontaine [27]	26,094
15	6	H	Charlton Ath	L 0-1	0-0	—		15,420
16	10	A	Ipswich T	L 0-6	0-2	4		22,020
17	24	H	Leicester C	L 0-2	0-1	6		15,040
18	27	A	Hull C	D 0-0	0-0	—		15,768
19	Dec 1	A	Watford	W 2-1	0-0	5	Showunmi [75], Byfield [90]	16,689
20	4	H	Ipswich T	W 2-0	2-0	—	Elliott [5], Orr (pen) [32]	14,062
21	8	A	Plymouth Arg	D 1-1	0-1	4	Timar (og) [74]	16,530
22	15	H	Cardiff C	W 1-0	0-0	3	Elliott [57]	15,753
23	22	H	Barnsley	W 3-2	2-2	3	Showunmi 2 [35, 45], Byfield [90]	16,588
24	26	A	WBA	L 1-4	0-0	4	Byfield [87]	27,314
25	29	A	Burnley	W 1-0	0-0	3	Vasko [67]	12,109
26	Jan 1	H	Coventry C	W 2-1	1-0	3	Byfield [5], Elliott [67]	15,899
27	12	H	Colchester U	D 1-1	1-1	2	Sproule [33]	16,484
28	19	A	Crystal Palace	L 0-2	0-1	3		19,010
29	26	H	Blackpool	W 1-0	1-0	—	Elliott [20]	15,465
30	Feb 2	A	QPR	L 0-3	0-2	3		16,502
31	9	H	Sheffield W	W 2-1	1-0	3	Adebola [7], Orr [56]	15,520
32	12	A	Scunthorpe U	W 1-0	0-0	—	Orr [83]	5423
33	18	H	Crystal Palace	D 1-1	0-0	—	McCombe [90]	16,446
34	23	A	Colchester U	W 2-1	0-0	2	Adebola [52], McIndoe [58]	5609
35	Mar 1	H	Hull C	W 2-1	1-1	1	Adebola [14], McCombe [46]	15,859
36	4	A	Charlton Ath	D 1-1	0-1	—	McCombe [62]	24,075
37	8	A	Leicester C	D 0-0	0-0	1		22,616
38	11	H	Watford	D 0-0	0-0	—		19,026
39	15	H	Plymouth Arg	L 1-2	0-1	2	Trundle (pen) [74]	19,011
40	22	A	Cardiff C	L 1-2	0-1	2	Adebola [73]	16,458
41	29	H	Norwich C	W 2-1	1-0	1	Adebola [41], Brooker [90]	17,511
42	Apr 5	A	Southampton	L 0-2	0-1	1		22,890
43	12	H	Wolverhampton W	D 0-0	0-0	3		19,332
44	19	A	Stoke C	L 1-2	0-2	4	Adebola [67]	24,475
45	26	A	Sheffield U	L 1-2	1-1	4	McIndoe (pen) [25]	29,787
46	May 4	H	Preston NE	W 3-0	2-0	4	Trundle [8], McIndoe [16], Noble [51]	19,169

Final League Position: 4

GOALSCORERS

League (54): Byfield 8, Adebola 6, McIndoe 6 (1 pen), Elliott 5, Trundle 5 (1 pen), Orr 4 (1 pen), McCombe 3, Murray 3, Showunmi 3, Noble 2, Sproule 2, Brooker 1, Fontaine 1, Johnson 1, Vasko 1, Wilson B 1, own goals 2.
Carling Cup (4): Jevons 2, Elliott 1, Orr 1.
FA Cup (1): Fontaine 1.
Play-Offs (4): Carey 1, McIndoe 1, Noble 1, Trundle 1.

Basso A 44	Orr B 42	McAllister J 40 + 1	Johnson L 39 + 1	Carey L 33	Vasko T 8 + 11	Wilson B 16 + 2	Elliott M 44 + 1	Trundle L 21 + 14	Showunmi E 10 + 7	McIndoe M 45	Fontaine L 32 + 6	Murray S 4 + 10	Henderson S — + 1	Weale C 2 + 1	Russell A 1	Skuse C 5 + 20	Jevons P — + 2	Betsy K — + 1	Sproule I 31 + 9	Byfield D 17 + 16	McCombe J 25 + 9	Noble D 16 + 10	Carle N 14 + 3	Adebola D 16 + 1	Brooker S 1 + 3	*Match No.*
1^{6}	2	3	4	5	6^{1}	7	8	9^{2}	10	11	12	13	15													1
	2	3		5		7^{1}	8	9	10^{3}	11	4	12		1	6^{2}	13	14									2
	2	3	4	5		7^{3}	8	9^{1}		11^{2}	6	10		1		13	12	14								3
1	2	3	4	5		7	8	9^{3}	12^{2}	11	6	14				13			10^{1}							4
1	2	3	4^{1}	5		7	8	9^{2}		11	6	13				12			10^{3}	14						5
1	2	3^{1}	4	5	12	7^{3}	8	9		11^{2}	6	13							10	14						6
1	2	3	4	5	12	7^{3}	8	9^{2}		11	6					13			10^{1}	14						7
1	2	3	4	5		7^{3}	8	9^{2}		11	6	12				13			10^{1}	14						8
1	2	3	4	5	12		8^{2}	9		11	6^{1}	7^{3}				13			14	10						9
1	2^{3}	3	4	5			8	12		11	6					13			7	10^{1}	14	9^{2}				10
1	2	3	7	5			8	12		11	4^{3}	13							9^{2}	10^{1}	14	6				11
1	2	3	4	5^{3}			8			11	6	12				13			7^{2}	10	14	9^{1}				12
1	2	3	4	5			8	9^{3}		11	6					12			7^{1}	13	14	10^{2}				13
1	2	3	4	5			8	9^{2}		11	6	12							7^{1}	10^{3}	13	14				14
1	2	3	4	5			8	9^{1}		11	6^{2}								7	10	13	12				15
1	2■	3	4	5^{3}		12	8		13	11	6								7^{1}	10	14	9^{2}				16
1			4	5		7^{1}	8	9^{2}	13	11	3					2^{3}			14	10	6	12				17
1	2	3■	4	5			8		9^{3}	11	6	12							7^{1}	14	13	10^{2}				18
1	2		4	5			8	12	9^{3}	11	6					13			7^{2}	14	3	10^{1}				19
1	2		4	5			8	12	10^{3}	11	6					13			7^{2}	14	3	9^{1}				20
1	2		4	5			8	12	10^{3}	11	6					13			7^{2}	14	3	9^{1}				21
1^{6}	2		4	5			8	9^{1}	10	11	3			15					7		6	12				22
1	2	12	4	5			8	9^{2}	10	11	3					13			7^{3}	14	6^{1}					23
1	2	3	4				8	9	10^{2}	11^{3}	6					12			7^{1}	14	5	13				24
1	2	3	4		6	12	8	13		11									7	10^{2}	5	9^{1}				25
1	2	3	4		6	7	8	12	13		14								11^{3}	10^{1}	5	9^{2}				26
1	2	3	4		6		8	9^{2}	12	11	5								7	10^{1}	13					27
1	2	3	4				8	12	10^{1}	11	6								7	13	5		9^{2}			28
1	2	3	4		6		8	9^{3}		11^{1}	12					13				10	5	14	7^{2}			29
1	2	3	4^{3}		6^{1}		8			11	12								13	10	5	14	7^{2}	9		30
1	2	3	4	5			8^{2}	12		11						13			7	14	6		10^{1}	9^{3}		31
1	2	3	4		12		8			11	6					13			7		5		10^{2}	9^{1}		32
1	2	3	4		12		8	13		11	6^{1}								7^{3}	14	5		10^{2}	9		33
1	2■	3	4		12		8			11	6					13			7^{2}	14	5		10^{3}	9^{1}		34
1		3	4^{1}		12	2	8			11	6								7^{2}		5	13	10	9		35
1		3^{1}	4		12	2	8			11	6								7^{2}	13	5	14	10^{3}	9		36
1		3	4^{1}		12	2	8	13		11	6								14	10^{2}	5		7^{3}	9		37
1	2	3	4^{3}	5	6	7^{2}	8	12		11									13			9^{1}	14	10		38
1	2	3		5	12	7^{3}	8	13		11	6^{1}								14	10^{2}			4	9		39
1	2	3		5	6^{1}		8	9		11	12					13			7^{3}				4^{2}	10	14	40
1	2	3	4^{2}	5						11		7				8			12		6	9^{1}	13	10^{3}	14	41
1	2	3	4	5			12			11		7^{2}				8^{1}			13		6	9^{3}		10	14	42
1	2	3^{1}		5			8			11	12					4			7^{2}	10^{3}	6		13	14	9	43
1	2	3		5	12	7^{3}	8^{1}	13		11						4				10^{2}	6	14		9		44
1	2	3		5			8^{1}	9	12	11											6	4	7	10		45
1	2	3	12	5			8	9^{2}	14	11									13		6	7	4^{1}	10^{3}		46

FA Cup

Third Round	Middlesbrough	(h)	1-2

Carling Cup

First Round	Brentford	(a)	3-0
Second Round	Manchester C	(h)	1-2

Play-Offs

Semi-Final	Crystal Palace	(a)	2-1
		(h)	2-1
Final *(at Wembley)*	Hull C		0-1

BRISTOL ROVERS FL Championship 1

FOUNDATION

Bristol Rovers were formed at a meeting in Stapleton Road, Eastville, in 1883. However, they first went under the name of the Black Arabs (wearing black shirts). Changing their name to Eastville Rovers in their second season, they won the Gloucestershire Senior Cup in 1888–89. Original members of the Bristol & District League in 1892, this eventually became the Western League and Eastville Rovers adopted professionalism in 1897.

The Memorial Stadium, Filton Avenue, Horfield, Bristol BS7 0BF.

Telephone: (0117) 909 6648.

Fax: (0117) 907 4312.

Ticket Office: (0117) 952 4001.

Website: www.bristolrovers.co.uk

Email: rodwesson@bristolrovers.co.uk; dave@bristolrovers.co.uk

Ground Capacity: 11,916.

Record Attendance: 11,530 v Bristol C, J Paint Trophy, Southern Final 2nd leg, 27 February 2007 (Memorial Stadium). 9,464 v Liverpool, FA Cup 4th rd, 8 February 1992 (Twerton Park). 38,472 v Preston NE, FA Cup 4th rd, 30 January 1960 (Eastville).

Pitch Measurements: 110yd × 73yd 6in.

Chairman: Ron Craig.

Vice-chairman: Nick Higgs.

Secretary: Rod Wesson.

Director of Football: Lennie Lawrence.

First Team Coach: Paul Trollope.

Physio: Phil Kite.

Colours: Blue and white quarters.

Change Colours: Green shirts, black shorts, green stockings.

Year Formed: 1883. ***Turned Professional:*** 1897. ***Ltd Co.:*** 1896.

Previous Names: 1883, Black Arabs; 1884, Eastville Rovers; 1897, Bristol Eastville Rovers; 1898, Bristol Rovers. ***Club Nickname:*** 'Pirates'.

Grounds: 1883, Purdown; Three Acres, Ashley Hill; Rudgeway, Fishponds; 1897, Eastville; 1986, Twerton Park; 1996, The Memorial Stadium.

First Football League Game: 28 August 1920, Division 3, v Millwall (a) L 0–2 – Stansfield; Bethune, Panes; Boxley, Kenny, Steele; Chance, Bird, Sims, Bell, Palmer.

Record League Victory: 7–0 v Brighton & HA, Division 3 (S), 29 November 1952 – Hoyle; Bamford, Fox; Pitt, Warren, Sampson; McIlvenny, Roost (2), Lambden (1), Bradford (1), Petherbridge (2), (1 og). 7–0 v Swansea T, Division 2, 2 October 1954 – Radford; Bamford, Watkins; Pitt, Muir, Anderson; Petherbridge, Bradford (2), Meyer, Roost (1), Hooper (2), (2 og). 7–0 v Shrewsbury T, Division 3, 21 March 1964 – Hall; Hillard, Gwyn Jones; Oldfield, Stone (1), Mabbutt; Jarman (2), Brown (1), Biggs (1p), Hamilton, Bobby Jones (2).

HONOURS

Football League: Division 2 best season: 4th, 1994–95; Promoted from FL 2 – 2006–07 (play-offs); Division 3 (S) – Champions 1952–53; Division 3 – Champions 1989–90; Runners-up 1973–74.

FA Cup: best season: 6th rd, 1951, 1958, 2008.

Football League Cup: best season: 5th rd, 1971, 1972.

J Paint Trophy: Runners-up 2007.

SKY SPORTS FACT FILE

In 1901–02 Bristol Rovers were leading Bristol City 2–0 in an FA Cup tie when the game was abandoned in fog after 80 minutes. A week later it was called off in bad light but on 27 November the tie was at last completed with Rovers winning 3–2.

Record Cup Victory: 6–0 v Merthyr Tydfil, FA Cup 1st rd, 14 November 1987 – Martyn; Alexander (Dryden), Tanner, Hibbitt, Twentyman, Jones, Holloway, Meacham (1), White (2), Penrice (3) (Reece), Purnell.

Most League Points (2 for a win): 64, Division 3 (S), 1952–53.

Most League Points (3 for a win): 93, Division 3, 1989–90.

Most League Goals: 92, Division 3 (S), 1952–53.

Highest League Scorer in Season: Geoff Bradford, 33, Division 3 (S), 1952–53.

Most League Goals in Total Aggregate: Geoff Bradford, 242, 1949–64.

Most League Goals in One Match: 4, Sidney Leigh v Exeter C, Division 3S, 2 May 1921; 4, Jonah Wilcox v Bournemouth, Division 3S, 12 December 1925; 4, Bill Culley v QPR, Division 3S, 5 March 1927; Frank Curran v Swindon T, Division 3S, 25 March 1939; Vic Lambden v Aldershot, Division 3S, 29 March 1947; George Petherbridge v Torquay U, Division 3S, 1 December 1951; Vic Lambden v Colchester U, Division 3S, 14 May 1952; Geoff Bradford v Rotherham U, Division 2, 14 March 1959; Robin Stubbs v Gillingham, Division 2, 10 October 1970; Alan Warboys v Brighton & HA, Division 3, 1 December 1973; Jamie Cureton v Reading, Division 2, 16 January 1999.

Most Capped Player: Vitalijs Astafjevs, 31 (142), Latvia.

Most League Appearances: Stuart Taylor, 546, 1966–80.

Youngest League Player: Ronnie Dix, 15 years 173 days v Charlton Ath, 25 February 1928.

Record Transfer Fee Received: £2,100,000 from Fulham for Barry Hayles, November 1998 and £2,100,000 from WBA for Jason Roberts, July 2000.

Record Transfer Fee Paid: £375,000 to QPR for Andy Tillson, November 1992.

Football League Record: 1920 Original Member of Division 3; 1921–53 Division 3 (S); 1953–62 Division 2; 1962–74 Division 3; 1974–81 Division 2; 1981–90 Division 3; 1990–92 Division 2. 1992–93 Division 1; 1993–2001 Division 2; 2001–04 Division 3; 2004–07 FL 2; 2007– FL 1.

MANAGERS

Alfred Homer 1899–1920 *(continued as Secretary to 1928)*
Ben Hall 1920–21
Andy Wilson 1921–26
Joe Palmer 1926–29
Dave McLean 1929–30
Albert Prince-Cox 1930–36
Percy Smith 1936–37
Brough Fletcher 1938–49
Bert Tann 1950–68 *(continued as General Manager to 1972)*
Fred Ford 1968–69
Bill Dodgin Snr 1969–72
Don Megson 1972–77
Bobby Campbell 1978–79
Harold Jarman 1979–80
Terry Cooper 1980–81
Bobby Gould 1981–83
David Williams 1983–85
Bobby Gould 1985–87
Gerry Francis 1987–91
Martin Dobson 1991
Dennis Rofe 1992
Malcolm Allison 1992–93
John Ward 1993–96
Ian Holloway 1996–2001
Garry Thompson 2001
Gerry Francis 2001
Garry Thompson 2001–02
Ray Graydon 2002–04
Ian Atkins 2004–05
Paul Trollope September 2005–

LATEST SEQUENCES

Longest Sequence of League Wins: 12, 18.10.1952 – 17.1.1953.

Longest Sequence of League Defeats: 8, 26.10.2002 – 21.12.2002.

Longest Sequence of League Draws: 5, 1.11.1975 – 22.11.1975.

Longest Sequence of Unbeaten League Matches: 32, 7.4.1973 – 27.1.1974.

Longest Sequence Without a League Win: 20, 5.4.1980 – 1.11.1980.

Successive Scoring Runs: 26 from 26.3.1927.

Successive Non-scoring Runs: 6 from 14.10.1922.

TEN YEAR LEAGUE RECORD

		P	*W*	*D*	*L*	*F*	*A*	*Pts*	*Pos*
1998-99	Div 2	46	13	17	16	65	56	56	13
1999-2000	Div 2	46	23	11	12	69	45	80	7
2000-01	Div 2	46	12	15	19	53	57	51	21
2001-02	Div 3	46	11	12	23	40	60	45	23
2002-03	Div 3	46	12	15	19	50	57	51	20
2003-04	Div 3	46	14	13	19	50	61	55	15
2004-05	FL 2	46	13	21	12	60	57	60	12
2005-06	FL 2	46	17	9	20	59	67	60	12
2006-07	FL 2	46	20	12	14	49	42	72	6
2007-08	FL 1	46	12	17	17	45	53	53	16

DID YOU KNOW ?

In 2007–08 Bristol Rovers reached the sixth round of the FA Cup for the first time in 50 years. Their list of victims included Premier League Fulham after a replay. The club had initially reached the same stage in 1950–51.

BRISTOL ROVERS 2007–08 LEAGUE RECORD

Match No.	Date	Venue	Opponents	Result		H/T Score	Lg. Pos.	Goalscorers	Attendance
1	Aug 11	A	Port Vale	D	1-1	0-0	—	Williams A [77]	6808
2	18	H	Crewe Alex	D	1-1	1-1	14	Disley [32]	7750
3	25	A	Oldham Ath	W	1-0	1-0	9	Jacobson [38]	5348
4	Sept 1	H	Nottingham F	D	2-2	2-2	8	Anthony [25], Walker (pen) [28]	9080
5	8	A	Luton T	W	2-1	1-1	7	Lambert 2 [2, 82]	6131
6	14	H	Leeds U	L	0-3	0-1	—		11,883
7	22	A	Carlisle U	D	1-1	1-0	9	Elliott [14]	6106
8	29	H	Leyton Orient	L	2-3	1-0	14	Walker 2 (2 pens) [41, 54]	7181
9	Oct 2	H	Southend U	D	1-1	1-0	—	Walker (pen) [11]	5762
10	6	A	Brighton & HA	D	0-0	0-0	—		5820
11	12	A	Hartlepool U	L	0-1	0-1	—		4963
12	20	H	Yeovil T	D	1-1	0-0	17	Elliott [90]	7726
13	27	A	Gillingham	L	2-3	1-1	19	Lambert [27], Pipe [46]	5333
14	Nov 3	H	Bournemouth	L	0-2	0-1	19		6405
15	6	A	Northampton T	W	1-0	0-0	—	Lambert [70]	5126
16	17	H	Millwall	W	2-1	0-1	18	Lambert (pen) [78], Haldane [90]	6991
17	24	A	Swindon T	L	0-1	0-0	18		9342
18	Dec 15	A	Huddersfield T	L	1-2	0-1	19	Pipe [51]	8118
19	22	A	Leeds U	L	0-1	0-0	19		27,863
20	26	H	Luton T	D	1-1	1-0	20	Lambert (pen) [17]	7556
21	29	H	Carlisle U	W	3-0	2-0	20	Lines [8], Hinton [15], Williams A [59]	6254
22	Jan 1	A	Southend U	W	1-0	0-0	19	Williams A [57]	7664
23	11	A	Tranmere R	W	2-0	1-0	—	Williams A [12], Lambert [58]	5887
24	19	H	Walsall	D	1-1	0-1	16	Disley [87]	6276
25	29	A	Crewe Alex	D	1-1	1-0	—	Williams (og) [45]	3942
26	Feb 2	H	Port Vale	W	3-2	1-1	17	Coles [13], Lines [81], Lambert (pen) [87]	6927
27	5	H	Cheltenham T	W	2-0	1-0	—	Hinton [40], Lambert [81]	6780
28	9	A	Doncaster R	L	0-2	0-0	16		8168
29	12	H	Oldham Ath	W	1-0	0-0	—	Disley [90]	5778
30	23	H	Tranmere R	D	1-1	0-0	15	Disley [81]	7777
31	Mar 1	A	Millwall	W	1-0	0-0	13	Disley [90]	9202
32	4	H	Doncaster R	L	0-1	0-1	—		3933
33	12	H	Northampton T	D	1-1	1-0	—	Rigg [45]	4657
34	15	A	Cheltenham T	L	0-1	0-0	16		5187
35	18	H	Swansea C	L	0-2	0-0	—		6410
36	22	H	Huddersfield T	L	2-3	1-1	17	Klein-Davies [20], Lines [49]	6585
37	24	A	Swansea C	D	2-2	2-0	18	Lambert [14], Disley [36]	15,048
38	29	A	Yeovil T	D	0-0	0-0	18		6654
39	Apr 5	H	Hartlepool U	D	0-0	0-0	17		5526
40	8	A	Nottingham F	D	1-1	0-1	—	Lambert [64]	15,860
41	12	A	Bournemouth	L	1-2	0-1	16	Lambert [56]	6867
42	15	A	Walsall	W	1-0	1-0	—	Lambert [34]	5200
43	19	H	Gillingham	D	1-1	0-1	16	Elliott [84]	6614
44	22	H	Swindon T	L	0-1	0-0	—		6102
45	26	H	Brighton & HA	L	0-2	0-0	16		7590
46	May 3	A	Leyton Orient	L	1-3	1-1	16	Lambert [29]	5132

Final League Position: 16

GOALSCORERS

League (45): Lambert 14 (3 pens), Disley 6, Walker 4 (4 pens), Williams A 4, Elliott 3, Lines 3, Hinton 2, Pipe 2, Anthony 1, Coles 1, Haldane 1, Jacobson 1, Klein-Davies 1, Rigg 1, own goal 1.
Carling Cup (2): Disley 1, Williams 1.
FA Cup (14): Lambert 6 (1 pen), Hinton 3, Coles 2, Disley 2, Williams 1.
J Paint Trophy (0).

Phillips S 46	Lescott A 34	Carruthers C 13 + 4	Campbell S 46	Anthony B 19 + 1	Elliott S 33	Pipe D 37 + 3	Disley C 41 + 3	Walker R 12 + 12	Lambert R 42 + 4	Jacobson J 34 + 6	Haldane L 22 + 10	Williams A 19 + 22	Rigg S 14 + 17	Igoe S 9 + 12	Green R 12	Hinton C 21 + 3	Coles D 24	Lines C 25 + 2	Groves M — + 1	Reece C — + 1	Klein-Davies J 2 + 8	Pulis A — + 1	Andrews W 1	Clough C — + 1	Match No.
1	2	3	4	5	6	7^1	8	9	10^2	11^3	12	13	14												1
1	2	3^3	4	5	6	7	8	9^2	10	11^1	12	13		14											2
1	2	3	4	5	6	7^1	8	9	10^2	11	12	13													3
1	2	3	4	5	6	7^3	8	9^1	12	13	11^2	10		14											4
1		3	4	5	6		8	12	10^2		11	9^1	13	7	2^3	14									5
1		3	4	5	6	12	8	13	10	14	11	9^2		7^1	2^3										6
1		3	4	5	6		8	9	10^2	11^1	12	13		7	2										7
1		3	4	5	6	12	8^1	9	10^3	13	11^2	14		7	2										8
1			4	5	6	7	8^2	9^1	12	3	11	10^3	14	13	2										9
1			4	5	6	7	8	9	12	3	11^2	10^1	13		2										10
1			4		6	7^1	8	9	10	3	11^2	12	13		2	5									11
1		3	4		6	7^3	8	9^1	10		11^2	12	13	14	2	5									12
1	2	3	4		6	7	8	9^1	10	12	11^2	13				5									13
1			4		6	7^1	8	12	10	3	11^3	13	9^2	14	2		5								14
1		12	4		6	7	8^2		10	3	11^1		9^3	13	2	14	5								15
1		3	4		6	12			10		11	13	9^2	7^1	2		5	8							16
1			4		6■	7^3	8	12■	10	3	11^1	13	9^2	14	2		5								17
1	2		4			7^1	8		10	3	11^2	9		12		6	5		13						18
1	2	12	4		6	7	8	13	10	3^1	11^2	14	9^3				5								19
1	2^2		4		6	7	8	12	10	3	11^1	9					5	13							20
1	2	12	4		6	7^1			10	3		9^3		11^2		5		8		13	14				21
1	2	12	4		6	7^2	13	14	10^3	3		9		11^1		5		8							22
1	2		4		6	7^1	12	13	10^2	3		9^3	14			5	8	11							23
1	2		4		6	7^2	12		10	3		9	14	13		5	8^1	11^3							24
1	2		4			7	8		10	3		9^1	12			5	6	11							25
1	2		4			7^2	8^1		10	3	12	9^3	14	13		5	6	11							26
1	2	3	4			7	8		10			9^1	12			5	6	11							27
1	2		4			7^3	8^1		10	3		9	12	13		5	6	11^2				14			28
1	2		4			7	8	12	10^1	3		9^2	13			5	6	11							29
1	2		4			7^2	8	12	10^3	3		9^1	13	14		5	6	11							30
1	2		4				8		10	3	12	9^2	13	7^1		5	6	11							31
1	2		4				8		10	3	11^2	9^1	12	7		5	6				13				32
1	2	3	4	5		7^3	8	9^1	12	13	11^2		10				6	14							33
1	2		4	5			8	12	10	3	11^1	13	9^2				6	7							34
1	2		4	5			8	12	10	3	7^1	13	9^2				6	11							35
1	2		4	5		7^1	8		10	3	12	13					6	11			9^2				36
1	2		4	12	6	7	8		10^1		13		9^2			3	5^3	11			14				37
1	2		4		6	7	8		10							3	5	11			12		9^1		38
1	2		4		6	7	8		10	12		13				5	3^1	11			9^2				39
1	2		4		6	7	8		10	3	9^1	12				5		11							40
1	2		4		6	7^1	8		10	3	9^3	12	13			5		11^2			14				41
1	2		4	5	6	7	8		10^1	3			9			12		11							42
1	2		4	5	6	7^1	8		10	3	12	13	9^3					11^2			14				43
1	2		4	5	6	7^1	8^3		10	3	12	13	9^2					11			14				44
1	2		4	5	6	7	8^1		10	3		12	9^2					11						13	45
1	2		4	5	6	7^1	8^2		10	3		12	9					11			13				46

FA Cup

First Round	Leyton Orient	(a)	1-1
		(h)	3-3
Second Round	Rushden & D	(h)	5-1
Third Round	Fulham	(a)	2-2
		(h)	0-0
Fourth Round	Barnet	(a)	1-0
Fifth Round	Southampton	(h)	1-0
Sixth Round	WBA	(h)	1-5

Carling Cup

First Round	Crystal Palace	(h)	1-1
Second Round	West Ham U	(h)	1-2

J Paint Trophy

Second Round	Bournemouth	(h)	0-1

BURNLEY

FL Championship

FOUNDATION

On 18 May 1882 Burnley (Association) Football Club was still known as Burnley Rovers as members of that Rugby Club had decided on that date to play Association Football in the future. It was only a matter of days later that the members met again and decided to drop Rovers from the club's name.

Turf Moor, Harry Potts Way, Burnley, Lancashire BB10 4BX.

Telephone: 0871 221 1882.

Fax: (01282) 700 014.

Ticket Office: 0871 221 1882.

Website: www.burnleyfc.com

Email: info@burnleyfc.com

Ground Capacity: 21,973.

Record Attendance: 54,775 v Huddersfield T, FA Cup 3rd rd, 23 February 1924.

Pitch Measurements: 112yd × 70yd.

Chairman: Barry Kilby.

Vice-chairman: Ray Ingleby.

Manager: Owen Coyle.

Assistant Manager: Sandy Stewart.

Physio: Andy Mitchell.

Colours: Claret and blue.

Change Colours: Sky blue and white.

Year Formed: 1882.

Turned Professional: 1883. ***Ltd Co.:*** 1897.

Previous Names: 1882, Burnley Rovers; 1882, Burnley.

Club Nickname: 'The Clarets'.

Grounds: 1882, Calder Vale; 1883, Turf Moor.

First Football League Game: 8 September 1888, Football League, v Preston NE (a) L 2–5 – Smith; Lang, Bury, Abrahams, Friel, Keenan, Brady, Tait, Poland (1), Gallocher (1), Yates.

Record League Victory: 9–0 v Darwen, Division 1, 9 January 1892 – Hillman; Walker, McFettridge, Lang, Matthews, Keenan, Nicol (3), Bowes, Espie (1), McLardie (3), Hill (2).

Record Cup Victory: 9–0 v Crystal Palace, FA Cup 2nd rd (replay), 10 February 1909 – Dawson; Barron, McLean; Cretney (2), Leake, Moffat; Morley, Ogden, Smith (3), Abbott (2), Smethams (1). 9–0 v New Brighton, FA Cup 4th rd, 26 January 1957 – Blacklaw; Angus, Winton; Seith, Adamson, Miller; Newlands (1), McIlroy (3), Lawson (3), Cheesebrough (1), Pilkington (1). 9–0 v Penrith, FA Cup 1st rd, 17 November 1984 – Hansbury; Miller, Hampton, Phelan, Overson (Kennedy), Hird (3 incl. 1p), Grewcock (1), Powell (2), Taylor (3), Biggins, Hutchison.

Record Defeat: 0–10 v Aston Villa, Division 1, 29 August 1925 and v Sheffield U, Division 1, 19 January 1929.

HONOURS

Football League: Division 1 – Champions 1920–21, 1959–60; Runners-up 1919–20, 1961–62; Division 2 – Champions 1897–98, 1972–73; Runners-up 1912–13, 1946–47, 1999–2000; Promoted from Division 2, 1993–94 (play-offs); Division 3 – Champions 1981–82; Division 4 – Champions 1991–92. Record 30 consecutive Division 1 games without defeat 1920–21.

FA Cup: Winners 1914; Runners-up 1947, 1962.

Football League Cup: Semi-final 1961, 1969, 1983.

Anglo–Scottish Cup: Winners 1979.

Sherpa Van Trophy: Runners-up 1988.

European Competitions: *European Cup:* 1960–61. *European Fairs Cup:* 1966–67.

SKY SPORTS FACT FILE

Burnley won the Anglo-Scottish Cup in 1978–79 with an impressive list of victims, Preston North End, Blackpool, Blackburn Rovers and Celtic (twice) plus Mansfield Town on penalties. They defeated Oldham Athletic in the final having played a total of nine matches.

Most League Points (2 for a win): 62, Division 2, 1972–73.

Most League Points (3 for a win): 88, Division 2, 1999–2000.

Most League Goals: 102, Division 1, 1960–61.

Highest League Scorer in Season: George Beel, 35, Division 1, 1927–28.

Most League Goals in Total Aggregate: George Beel, 179, 1923–32.

Most League Goals in One Match: 6, Louis Page v Birmingham C, Division 1, 10 April 1926.

Most Capped Player: Jimmy McIlroy, 51 (55), Northern Ireland.

Most League Appearances: Jerry Dawson, 522, 1907–28.

Youngest League Player: Tommy Lawton, 16 years 174 days v Doncaster R, 28 March 1936.

Record Transfer Fee Received: £3,250,000 from Glasgow Rangers for Kyle Lafferty, June 2008.

Record Transfer Fee Paid: £1,000,000 to Stockport Co for Ian Moore, November 2000 and £1,000,000 to Bradford C for Robbie Blake, January 2002.

Football League Record: 1888 Original Member of the Football League; 1897–98 Division 2; 1898–1900 Division 1; 1900–13 Division 2; 1913–30 Division 1; 1930–47 Division 2; 1947–71 Division 1; 1971–73 Division 2; 1973–76 Division 1; 1976–80 Division 2; 1980–82 Division 3; 1982–83 Division 2; 1983–85 Division 3; 1985–92 Division 4; 1992–94 Division 2; 1994–95 Division 1; 1995–2000 Division 2; 2000–04 Division 1; 2004– FL C.

MANAGERS

Harry Bradshaw 1894–99
(Secretary-Manager from 1897)
Club Directors 1899–1900
J. Ernest Mangnall 1900–03
(Secretary-Manager)
Spen Whittaker 1903–10
(Secretary-Manager)
John Haworth 1910–24
(Secretary-Manager)
Albert Pickles 1925–31
(Secretary-Manager)
Tom Bromilow 1932–35
Selection Committee 1935–45
Cliff Britton 1945–48
Frank Hill 1948–54
Alan Brown 1954–57
Billy Dougall 1957–58
Harry Potts 1958–70
(General Manager to 1972)
Jimmy Adamson 1970–76
Joe Brown 1976–77
Harry Potts 1977–79
Brian Miller 1979–83
John Bond 1983–84
John Benson 1984–85
Martin Buchan 1985
Tommy Cavanagh 1985–86
Brian Miller 1986–89
Frank Casper 1989–91
Jimmy Mullen 1991–96
Adrian Heath 1996–97
Chris Waddle 1997–98
Stan Ternent 1998–2004
Steve Cotterill 2004–07
Owen Coyle November 2007–

LATEST SEQUENCES

Longest Sequence of League Wins: 10, 16.11.1912 – 18.1.1913.

Longest Sequence of League Defeats: 8, 2.1.1995 – 25.2.1995.

Longest Sequence of League Draws: 6, 21.2.1931 – 28.3.1931.

Longest Sequence of Unbeaten League Matches: 30, 6.9.1920 – 25.3.1921.

Longest Sequence Without a League Win: 24, 16.4.1979 – 17.11.1979.

Successive Scoring Runs: 27 from 13.2.1926.

Successive Non-scoring Runs: 6 from 9.8.1997.

TEN YEAR LEAGUE RECORD

		P	*W*	*D*	*L*	*F*	*A*	*Pts*	*Pos*
1998-99	Div 2	46	13	16	17	54	73	55	15
1999-2000	Div 2	46	25	13	8	69	47	88	2
2000-01	Div 2	46	21	9	16	50	54	72	7
2001-02	Div 1	46	21	12	13	70	62	75	7
2002-03	Div 1	46	15	10	21	65	89	55	16
2003-04	Div 1	46	13	14	19	60	77	53	19
2004-05	FL C	46	15	15	16	38	39	60	13
2005-06	FL C	46	14	12	20	46	54	54	17
2006-07	FL C	46	15	12	19	52	49	57	15
2007-08	FL C	46	16	14	16	60	67	62	13

DID YOU KNOW ?

On 2 March 1889 John Yates, an outside-left, won his first international cap for England against Northern Ireland. England won 6–1 and scored a hat-trick but it was his only such honour. A cotton worker he served Burnley well as a weaving winger.

BURNLEY 2007–08 LEAGUE RECORD

Match No.	*Date*	*Venue*	*Opponents*	*Result*	*H/T Score*	*Lg. Pos.*	*Goalscorers*	*Attendance*
1	Aug 11	H	WBA	W 2-1	0-1	—	Blake [47], Gray (pen) [79]	15,337
2	18	A	Scunthorpe U	L 0-2	0-0	13		6975
3	Sept 1	A	Colchester U	W 3-2	2-1	12	Mahon [15], Gray 2 (1 pen) [29, 63 (p)]	4925
4	15	H	Blackpool	D 2-2	0-0	10	Jones [52], Akinbiyi [86]	16,843
5	18	A	Sheffield W	W 2-0	1-0	—	Blake [15], McCann [48]	18,359
6	22	A	Bristol C	D 2-2	0-0	7	Gray [52], Carlisle [90]	14,079
7	29	H	Crystal Palace	D 1-1	1-1	7	Duff [13]	10,711
8	Oct 2	H	Ipswich T	D 2-2	1-2	—	Lafferty [11], Gray [60]	9952
9	6	A	Cardiff C	L 1-2	0-1	13	Akinbiyi [50]	12,914
10	20	A	Barnsley	D 1-1	1-0	14	Gray [11]	11,560
11	23	H	Norwich C	W 2-1	2-0	—	Blake [1], Gray (pen) [4]	10,133
12	27	H	Southampton	L 2-3	1-2	12	McCann [31], Akinbiyi [83]	10,944
13	Nov 3	A	Sheffield U	D 0-0	0-0	13		25,306
14	6	H	Hull C	L 0-1	0-0	—		9978
15	10	A	Leicester C	W 1-0	1-0	13	Gray [23]	21,334
16	24	H	Stoke C	D 0-0	0-0	13		11,758
17	27	A	Watford	W 2-1	0-0	—	Gray [58], Gudjonsson [80]	15,021
18	Dec 1	A	Charlton Ath	W 3-1	2-1	9	Gray 2 (1 pen) [8, 70 (p)], McCann [13]	21,122
19	4	H	Leicester C	D 1-1	1-0	—	Unsworth [19]	10,688
20	8	A	Wolverhampton W	W 3-2	3-1	7	Blake [20], Lafferty [30], Ward D (og) [42]	20,763
21	11	H	QPR	L 0-2	0-0	—		10,522
22	15	H	Preston NE	L 2-3	1-1	9	Lafferty [31], McCann [62]	14,829
23	22	A	Ipswich T	D 0-0	0-0	9		20,077
24	26	H	Sheffield W	D 1-1	1-1	10	Akinbiyi [31]	15,326
25	29	H	Bristol C	L 0-1	0-0	11		12,109
26	Jan 1	A	Blackpool	L 0-3	0-1	12		9599
27	12	H	Plymouth Arg	W 1-0	0-0	11	Blake [66]	14,162
28	19	A	Coventry C	W 2-1	1-1	9	Akinbiyi [10], Blake [68]	17,347
29	26	H	Scunthorpe U	W 2-0	2-0	—	Blake [9], Akinbiyi [32]	14,516
30	Feb 2	A	WBA	L 1-2	1-1	10	O'Connor J [3]	22,206
31	9	H	Colchester U	D 1-1	1-1	9	Cole [23]	15,376
32	12	A	QPR	W 4-2	1-2	—	Cole 3 [41, 56, 86], Akinbiyi [77]	13,410
33	23	A	Plymouth Arg	L 1-3	1-2	9	O'Connor J [19]	13,557
34	26	H	Coventry C	W 2-0	1-0	—	McCann [20], Caldwell [85]	9779
35	Mar 1	H	Watford	D 2-2	0-1	8	Blake 2 [75, 88]	13,677
36	4	A	Hull C	L 0-2	0-2	—		15,838
37	8	A	Stoke C	D 1-1	1-0	10	Lafferty [3]	18,432
38	11	H	Charlton Ath	W 1-0	0-0	—	Elliott [59]	10,700
39	15	H	Wolverhampton W	L 1-3	0-2	10	Akinbiyi [76]	12,749
40	22	A	Preston NE	L 1-2	1-1	11	O'Connor J [38]	16,149
41	29	H	Barnsley	W 2-1	2-1	10	Elliott [30], Lafferty [36]	11,915
42	Apr 5	A	Norwich C	L 0-2	0-1	11		24,049
43	12	H	Sheffield U	L 1-2	0-1	13	Cole [80]	11,693
44	19	A	Southampton	W 1-0	1-0	12	Caldwell [45]	21,762
45	26	H	Cardiff C	D 3-3	1-0	11	Alexander [36], Cole [54], Carlisle [86]	10,694
46	May 4	A	Crystal Palace	L 0-5	0-3	13		23,950

Final League Position: 13

GOALSCORERS

League (60): Gray 11 (4 pens), Blake 9, Akinbiyi 8, Cole 6, Lafferty 5, McCann 5, O'Connor J 3, Caldwell 2, Carlisle 2, Elliott 2, Alexander 1, Duff 1, Gudjonsson 1, Jones 1, Mahon 1, Unsworth 1, own goal 1.
Carling Cup (4): Gray 2, Akinbiyi 1, Blake 1.
FA Cup (0).

Kiraly G 27	Duff M 8	Jordan S 20 + 1	McCann C 34 + 1	Thomas W 1	Caldwell S 26 + 3	Elliott W 45 + 1	Gudjonsson J 13 + 15	Blake R 41 + 4	Gray A 25	Harley J 31 + 2	Lafferty K 34 + 3	Akinbiyi A 14 + 25	Carlisle C 32 + 1	Unsworth D 26 + 3	Spicer J 9 + 15	Jensen B 19	Mahon A 13 + 13	Alexander G 43	Jones S 1 + 16	O'Connor J 24 + 5	Rodriguez J — + 1	Varga S 10	O'Connor G — + 1	Randall M 2 + 8	Cole A 8 + 5	MacDonald A — + 2	*Match No.*
1	2	3	4	5	6^{1}	7	8	9^{2}	10	11	12	13															1
1	2	3	4^{3}			7^{2}	8	9	10	11^{1}	12	13	5	6	14												2
	2	3	4		6	11		9^{1}	10	13		12	5		14	1	8^{2}	7^{3}									3
	2	3	4		6	7^{3}		9^{1}	10	11^{2}		12	5		14	1		8	13								4
1	2	3	4^{3}		6	11	14	9^{1}	10		8^{2}	12	5		13			7									5
1	2	3	4^{2}		6	11	13	9^{1}	10		8^{3}	12	5		14			7									6
1	2^{3}	3			6	7		11	10^{2}		9^{1}	12	5		14		8	4	13								7
1		3			6	7^{2}		9	10		8^{1}	12	5		11		4^{3}	2	13	14							8
1		3	12		6	13		9	10		11^{2}	14	5	4^{3}	7		8^{1}	2									9
1		3	4		6	11			10		12	9^{2}	5		7		8^{1}	2	13								10
1		3	4			11		8^{1}	10		9^{2}	13	5	6	7		12	2									11
1		3	4		6^{1}	11^{3}		8^{2}	10		9	14	5	12	7		13	2									12
1		3^{2}	4			11		8	10	13	9^{1}		5	6	7		12	2									13
1		3	4			11^{3}		8^{1}	10		9	14	5	6■	7^{2}		12	2	13								14
1		6^{2}	4			11		8	10	3	9^{3}	14	5		7^{1}		13	2		12							15
1			4			7	12	11^{3}	10	3	9^{2}	13	5	6			8^{1}	2	14								16
1			4			11	12	7^{3}	10^{2}	3	9^{1}	13	5	6			8	2	14								17
1			4			11^{3}	12	7^{2}	10	3	9	13	5	6			8^{1}	2	14								18
1			4			11	12	7^{2}	10	3	9		5	6			8^{1}	2	13								19
1			4			11	12	7^{3}	10^{2}	3	9	13	5	6			8^{1}	2		14							20
1			4			11	12	7^{2}	10	3	9		5^{1}	6			8^{3}	2	13	14							21
1		5	4■			11	12■	7^{3}	10	3	9^{2}			6			8^{1}	2	13	14							22
1					5	11		8^{2}	10^{1}	3	9	12		6	4■			2	13	7							23
1					4	11		8		3	9	10^{1}	5	6				2	12	7							24
1		2^{2}			4	11		8		3	9	10	5^{1}	6					12	7	13						25
1		12	4		5	11		8^{2}	10	3	9^{3}	13		6^{1}				2	14	7							26
					5	11	8^{2}	12	10	3				6	13	1		2	9^{1}	7		4					27
			4			11	8^{3}	10		3		9^{2}		6	14	1	12	2	13	7^{1}		5					28
			4		12	11	8^{2}	10^{3}		3		9^{1}		6	13	1		2		7		5	14				29
			4^{3}			11	8^{1}	10		3		9^{2}		6	12	1		2		7		5		14	13		30
					13	11	4^{2}	8^{1}		3	9	12		6		1		2		7^{3}		5		14	10		31
					5	11	4	8^{1}		3	9	12			13	1		2		7^{2}		6		14	10^{3}		32
			4^{3}		5	11	8	10		3^{1}	9		13	12		1		2		7		6^{2}		14			33
			4		6	11	8^{3}	12		3	9^{1}	10^{2}	5		13	1		2		7				14			34
			4		6	11		12		3	9	10^{1}	5			1		2		7					8		35
			4^{1}		6■	11	12■	13			9^{2}	10	5	3		1		2		7^{3}				14	8		36
1						11		8		3	9^{2}	10^{3}	5		13		12	2		7		6		4^{1}	14		37
1						11		8^{3}		3	9	12	5		13		4^{2}	2		7		6		14	10^{1}		38
1						11	4^{2}	8^{3}		3	9	10	5	12			13	2		7		6^{1}		14			39
			4		12	11	13	8		3	9^{3}	10	5■	6^{1}		1		2		7^{2}					14		40
			4		5	11^{2}	8	10^{3}		3	9^{1}	12		6		1	13	2		7					14		41
			4^{3}		5	11	8^{1}	10^{2}		3	9	13		6		1	12	2		7					14		42
		3	4		5	11	12	8^{2}			9	13		6		1		2		7^{1}					10		43
		3	4		6	11	12	8^{3}				9	5		14	1	13	2		7^{1}					10^{2}		44
		3	4^{1}		6	11^{3}	12	8^{2}				9	5			1	13	2		7					10	14	45
	8		4^{2}		6	11^{3}	12	9		3			5■			1	13	2		7				10^{1}		14	46

FA Cup

Third Round	Arsenal	(h)	0-2

Carling Cup

First Round	Grimsby T	(a)	1-1
Second Round	Oldham Ath	(h)	3-0
Third Round	Portsmouth	(h)	0-1

BURY FL Championship 2

FOUNDATION

A meeting at the Waggon & Horses Hotel, attended largely by members of Bury Wesleyans and Bury Unitarians football clubs, decided to form a new Bury club. This was officially formed at a subsequent gathering at the Old White Horse Hotel, Fleet Street, Bury on 24 April 1885.

Gigg Lane, Bury BL9 9HR.

Telephone: (0161) 764 4881.

Fax: (0161) 764 5521.

Ticket Office: (0161) 764 4881.

Website: www.buryfc.co.uk

Email: info@buryfc.co.uk

Ground Capacity: 11,669.

Record Attendance: 35,000 v Bolton W, FA Cup 3rd rd, 9 January 1960.

Pitch Measurements: 112yd × 72yd.

Secretary: Jill Neville.

Director of Football: Keith Alexander.

Manager: Alan Knill.

Physio: Alan Bent.

Colours: White shirts, royal blue shorts, royal blue stockings.

Change Colours: Red shirts, red shorts, red stockings ***Third Kit:*** Chocolate shirts, sky blue shorts, cholate stockings.

Year Formed: 1885.

Turned Professional: 1885.

Ltd Co.: 1897.

Club Nickname: 'Shakers'.

Ground: 1885, Gigg Lane.

First Football League Game: 1 September 1894, Division 2, v Manchester C (h) W 4–2 – Lowe; Gillespie, Davies; White, Clegg, Ross; Wylie, Barbour (2), Millar (1), Ostler (1), Plant.

Record League Victory: 8–0 v Tranmere R, Division 3, 10 January 1970 – Forrest; Tinney, Saile; Anderson, Turner, McDermott; Hince (1), Arrowsmith (1), Jones (4), Kerr (1), Grundy, (1 og).

Record Cup Victory: 12–1 v Stockton, FA Cup 1st rd (replay), 2 February 1897 – Montgomery; Darroch, Barbour; Hendry (1), Clegg, Ross (1); Wylie (3), Pangbourn, Millar (4), Henderson (2), Plant, (1 og).

Record Defeat: 0–10 v Blackburn R, FA Cup pr rd, 1 October 1887. 0–10 v West Ham U, Milk Cup 2nd rd 2nd leg, 25 October 1983.

HONOURS

Football League: Division 1 best season: 4th, 1925–26; Division 2 – Champions 1894–95, 1996–97; Runners-up 1923–24; Division 3 – Champions 1960–61; Runners-up 1967–68; Promoted from Division 3 (3rd) 1995–96.

FA Cup: Winners 1900, 1903.

Football League Cup: Semi-final 1963.

SKY SPORTS FACT FILE

Charlie Sagar had nearly seven years with Bury and in addition to his 71 League goals hit 17 in the FA Cup including a hat-trick against West Bromwich Albion in 1898–99. He moved on to Manchester United and grabbed another treble for them, too.

Most League Points (2 for a win): 68, Division 3, 1960–61.

Most League Points (3 for a win): 84, Division 4, 1984–85 and Division 2, 1996–97.

Most League Goals: 108, Division 3, 1960–61.

Highest League Scorer in Season: Craig Madden, 35, Division 4, 1981–82.

Most League Goals in Total Aggregate: Craig Madden, 129, 1978–86.

Most League Goals in One Match: 5, Eddie Quigley v Millwall, Division 2, 15 February 1947; 5, Ray Pointer v Rotherham U, Division 2, 2 October 1965.

Most Capped Player: Bill Gorman, 11 (13), Republic of Ireland and (4), Northern Ireland.

Most League Appearances: Norman Bullock, 506, 1920–35.

Youngest League Player: Brian Williams, 16 years 133 days v Stockport Co, 18 March 1972.

Record Transfer Fee Received: £1,100,000 from Ipswich T for David Johnson, November 1997.

Record Transfer Fee Paid: £200,000 to Ipswich T for Chris Swailes, November 1997 and £200,000 to Swindon T for Darren Bullock, February 1999.

Football League Record: 1894 Elected to Division 2; 1895–1912 Division 1; 1912–24 Division 2; 1924–29 Division 1; 1929–57 Division 2; 1957–61 Division 3; 1961–67 Division 2; 1967–68 Division 3; 1968–69 Division 2; 1969–71 Division 3; 1971–74 Division 4; 1974–80 Division 3; 1980–85 Division 4; 1985–96 Division 3; 1996–97 Division 2; 1997–99 Division 1; 1999–2002 Division 2; 2002–04 Division 3; 2004– FL 2.

MANAGERS

T. Hargreaves 1887
(Secretary-Manager)
H. S. Hamer 1887–1907
(Secretary-Manager)
Archie Montgomery 1907–15
William Cameron 1919–23
James Hunter Thompson 1923–27
Percy Smith 1927–30
Arthur Paine 1930–34
Norman Bullock 1934–38
Charlie Dean 1938–44
Jim Porter 1944–45
Norman Bullock 1945–49
John McNeil 1950–53
Dave Russell 1953–61
Bob Stokoe 1961–65
Bert Head 1965–66
Les Shannon 1966–69
Jack Marshall 1969
Colin McDonald 1970
Les Hart 1970
Tommy McAnearney 1970–72
Alan Brown 1972–73
Bobby Smith 1973–77
Bob Stokoe 1977–78
David Hatton 1978–79
Dave Connor 1979–80
Jim Iley 1980–84
Martin Dobson 1984–89
Sam Ellis 1989–90
Mike Walsh 1990–95
Stan Ternent 1995–98
Neil Warnock 1998–99
Andy Preece 2000–04
Graham Barrow 2004–05
Chris Casper 2005–08
Alan Knill February 2008–

LATEST SEQUENCES

Longest Sequence of League Wins: 9, 26.9.1960 – 19.11.1960.

Longest Sequence of League Defeats: 8, 18.8.2001 – 25.9.2001.

Longest Sequence of League Draws: 6, 6.3.1999 – 3.4.1999.

Longest Sequence of Unbeaten League Matches: 18, 4.2.1961 – 29.4.1961.

Longest Sequence Without a League Win: 19, 1.4.1911 – 2.12.1911.

Successive Scoring Runs: 24 from 1.9.1894.

Successive Non-scoring Runs: 6 from 11.1.1969.

TEN YEAR LEAGUE RECORD

		P	*W*	*D*	*L*	*F*	*A*	*Pts*	*Pos*
1998-99	Div 1	46	10	17	19	35	60	47	22
1999-2000	Div 2	46	13	18	15	61	64	57	15
2000-01	Div 2	46	16	10	20	45	59	58	16
2001-02	Div 2	46	11	11	24	43	75	44	22
2002-03	Div 3	46	18	16	12	57	56	70	7
2003-04	Div 3	46	15	11	20	54	64	56	12
2004-05	FL 2	46	14	16	16	54	54	58	17
2005-06	FL 2	46	12	17	17	45	57	52*	19
2006-07	FL 2	46	13	11	22	46	61	50	21
2007-08	FL 2	46	16	11	19	58	61	59	13

**1 pt deducted.*

DID YOU KNOW ?

In terms of his first team contribution to Bury, Jesse Carver was almost The Man Who Never Was. After a long centre-half career with Blackburn Rovers and Newcastle United in 1939, at only 28 he soon after took up coaching and was feted in Italian club circles.

BURY 2007–08 LEAGUE RECORD

Match No.	Date	Venue	Opponents	Result		H/T Score	Lg. Pos.	Goalscorers	Attendance
1	Aug 11	A	Milton Keynes D	W	2-1	0-1	—	Bishop 2 (1 pen) [51, 58 (p)]	7740
2	18	H	Grimsby T	D	1-1	0-1	4	Parrish [71]	2493
3	25	A	Wycombe W	L	0-1	0-0	13		4067
4	Sept 1	H	Brentford	L	1-2	0-1	17	Bishop [46]	2301
5	7	A	Chesterfield	L	1-3	0-1	—	Woodthorpe [75]	4161
6	15	H	Chester C	L	0-2	0-1	23		2539
7	22	A	Dagenham & R	D	1-1	1-1	22	Scott [21]	1597
8	29	H	Accrington S	W	2-1	0-0	21	Mangan [71], Adams [84]	2784
9	Oct 2	H	Lincoln C	D	1-1	1-1	—	Scott [24]	1690
10	6	A	Rochdale	W	2-1	2-0	13	Mangan [2], Adams [12]	4692
11	13	A	Notts Co	W	3-1	1-0	11	Haslam [35], Scott [67], Adams (pen) [90]	3710
12	20	H	Shrewsbury T	D	1-1	1-0	11	Scott [45]	2667
13	27	A	Macclesfield T	D	2-2	0-2	11	Mangan [49], Adams (pen) [64]	2672
14	Nov 3	H	Barnet	W	3-0	1-0	10	Hurst [31], Adams 2 [54, 86]	2121
15	6	A	Rotherham U	L	1-2	1-1	—	Adams (pen) [43]	3425
16	17	H	Peterborough U	W	2-0	1-0	10	Baker [32], Mangan [84]	2660
17	24	A	Morecambe	L	1-2	0-2	11	Bishop [76]	3124
18	Dec 4	H	Wrexham	L	0-1	0-1	—		2248
19	15	H	Hereford U	L	0-1	0-0	15		2099
20	22	A	Chester C	L	1-2	1-1	15	Bishop [16]	2260
21	26	H	Chesterfield	L	0-1	0-1	16		3158
22	29	H	Dagenham & R	L	0-2	0-1	18		1887
23	Jan 1	A	Lincoln C	D	1-1	0-0	18	Bishop [85]	3327
24	12	A	Darlington	L	0-3	0-2	19		3003
25	22	H	Bradford C	D	2-2	0-1	—	Bishop [57], Stephens [88]	2776
26	29	A	Grimsby T	L	0-1	0-1	—		3445
27	Feb 2	H	Milton Keynes D	L	1-5	0-3	21	Hurst [89]	2241
28	5	H	Stockport Co	L	2-3	1-1	—	Bishop [13], Hurst [48]	3142
29	9	A	Bradford C	W	2-1	0-1	21	Bishop 2 (1 pen) [56 (p), 87]	13,844
30	12	H	Wycombe W	D	2-2	0-2	—	Bishop (pen) [65], Barry-Murphy [88]	1895
31	16	A	Stockport Co	W	2-1	0-1	20	Scott [71], Adams [79]	5704
32	23	H	Darlington	L	1-2	0-1	21	Sodje [88]	2554
33	26	A	Mansfield T	D	1-1	0-0	—	Rooney [84]	1923
34	Mar 1	A	Peterborough U	L	0-1	0-0	21		6150
35	4	A	Brentford	W	4-1	3-0	—	Adams [13], Hurst [15], Bishop 2 [37, 83]	3333
36	8	H	Morecambe	W	2-1	1-0	19	Bishop 2 (1 pen) [45, 49 (p)]	2596
37	11	H	Rotherham U	W	3-0	1-0	—	Bishop 2 [16, 62], Adams [66]	1957
38	15	A	Wrexham	L	1-2	1-1	17	Hurst [45]	4431
39	22	A	Hereford U	D	0-0	0-0	17		3420
40	24	H	Mansfield T	W	2-0	2-0	15	Scott [10], Rooney [37]	2779
41	29	A	Shrewsbury T	W	1-0	0-0	14	Adams [71]	5213
42	Apr 5	H	Notts Co	W	2-1	1-0	14	Rooney [18], Hurst [87]	2463
43	12	A	Barnet	L	0-3	0-0	15		3054
44	19	H	Macclesfield T	W	1-0	1-0	14	Bennett [43]	2506
45	26	H	Rochdale	D	1-1	0-0	15	Adams [56]	6271
46	May 3	A	Accrington S	W	2-0	2-0	13	Bishop 2 (1 pen) [22 (p), 45]	2566

Final League Position: 13

GOALSCORERS

League (58): Bishop 19 (5 pens), Adams 12 (3 pens), Hurst 6, Scott 6, Mangan 4, Rooney 3, Baker 1, Barry-Murphy 1, Bennett 1, Haslam 1, Parrish 1, Sodje 1, Stephens 1, Woodthorpe 1.
Carling Cup (0).
FA Cup (8): Bishop 5, Adams 1, Futcher 1, Scott 1.
J Paint Trophy (5): Hurst 2, Bishop 1, Futcher 1, Rouse 1.

Provett J 32	Scott P 40	Parrish A 17 + 9	Futcher B 40	Challinor D 26	Morgan P 20	Baker R 21 + 11	Woodthorpe C 30 + 1	Hurst G 29 + 13	Richardson M 1	Adams N 41 + 2	Barry-Murphy B 27 + 4	Mangan A 7 + 13	Bishop A 37 + 7	Dean J 3 + 1	Dorney J 3 + 4	Buchanan D 24 + 11	Haslam S 37	Bullock L 8	Rouse D — + 6	Hughes L 1 + 3	Yeo S — + 8	Stephens D 4 + 2	Bennett E 18 + 1	Randolph D 14	Rooney A 10 + 6	Sodje E 16	Belford C — + 1	Match No.
1	2	3	4	5	6	7^{1}	8	9^{2}	10^{3}	11	12	13	14															1
1	2	3	4	5	6	7	8	9		11			12	10^{1}														2
1	2	3	4	5	6	7	8	9		11^{2}		13	12	10^{1}														3
1	2	3	4	5	6	7	8^{2}	9^{1}		11		12	10	13														4
1	2	3	4	5	6		8			11^{2}	7	12	10	9^{1}	13													5
1	2	3		5	6	12	8	9		11	7^{1}	13	10		4^{2}													6
1	2	3	4	5	6	7^{2}	8	9^{1}			11	12	10			13												7
1	2	3	4	5	6		8	9^{1}		13	11	12	10^{3}		7^{2}	14												8
1	2		4	5	6		8	12		11	7^{2}	9	10^{1}			13	3											9
1	2		4	5	6	12	8	13		7^{1}		9^{3}	10^{2}			14	3	11										10
1	2		4	5	6	12	8	9^{2}		11^{1}		10					3	7	13									11
1	2		4	5	6		8	9^{3}		11	12	10^{2}	13				3	7^{1}	14									12
1			4	5	6	7	8	9^{1}		3	11^{2}	10^{3}	12			13	2		14									13
1	2	3	4	5		12		9^{2}		8		10^{1}	13			11	6	7										14
1	2	3	4	5				9^{1}		8		10^{2}	12			11	6	7	13									15
1	2	12	4	5^{2}	6	13	8	9^{3}			11^{1}	14	10				3	7										16
1	2		4		6	7	5	9^{2}		12	11^{1}	13	10				3^{3}	8		14								17
1	2	3^{1}	4		6		8^{2}	12		7		13	10			11	5^{3}	9		14								18
1	2	3	4		6		8^{1}	9		7		12	10			11	5											19
1	2	3^{1}	4		6		8	9		7			10■			11	5			12								20
1	2■	3	4		6	12	8^{2}	9		7					13	11	5			10^{1}								21
1		12	4	5	6^{1}	7	8	9^{2}		3			10		14	11	2^{3}		13									22
1		3	4	5		7	8	9^{1}		11	6		10			12	2											23
1		3^{2}	4	5		7	8^{1}	9		6	11		10			12	2				13							24
1	2		6			7	3	12		9^{1}	4^{2}		10			11	5				13	8						25
1	2		4			7^{1}	3			9	8^{2}		10		13	11	5				12	6						26
1	2		4			7	3	12		9^{1}	8^{3}		10^{2}			11	5				13	6	14					27
1	2		4	5		7	3	9^{3}			13	14	10		11^{2}		6				12		8^{1}					28
	2	12	4	5		7	3			11^{2}			10			13	6						8^{1}	1	9			29
	2		4	5		7^{1}	3^{3}	13		11	12		10			14	6						8	1	9^{2}			30
	2			5			3^{2}	12		7^{3}	11	14	10			13	6						8	1	9^{1}	4		31
	2			5			3^{2}	12		9^{3}	11		10			13	7				14		4	1	8^{1}	6		32
	2			5				9^{1}		7	8		10			11	3						4	1	12	6		33
	2			5		12		13		7^{1}	8		10			11	3				14		4^{3}	1	9^{2}	6		34
	2	12	4			13		9^{2}		7	8		10			11	3						6^{1}	1		5		35
	2	12	4					9^{2}		7	8		10			11	3						6^{1}	1	13	5		36
	2	12	4					9^{2}		7	8		10			11	3						6^{1}	1	13	5		37
	2		4					9^{2}		7	8		10			11	3				12		6^{1}	1	13	5		38
	2		4			12		9^{2}		7	8		10			11	3						6^{1}	1	13	5		39
	2	12	4			13		14		7	8		10^{3}			11	3						6^{1}	1	9^{2}	5		40
	2	12	4			13				7	8		10			11	3						6^{1}	1	9^{2}	5		41
			4			7		12		2	8		10			11	3					13	6^{2}	1	9^{1}	5		42
1		3^{1}	4			7	12	13		2	8		10			11			14				6^{3}		9^{2}	5		43
1	2		6			7		12		8			10			11	3						4		9^{1}	5		44
1	2		6■			7		9^{1}		8			10			11	3					12	4			5		45
1^{6}	2	12				7		9		6	8		10^{2}			11^{1}	3					4			13	5	15	46

FA Cup

First Round	Workington	(h)	4-1
Second Round	Exeter C	(h)	1-0
Third Round	Norwich C	(a)	1-1
		(h)	2-1
Fourth Round	Southampton	(a)	0-2

Carling Cup

First Round	Carlisle U	(h)	0-1

J Paint Trophy

Second Round	Rochdale	(a)	3-1
Quarter-Final	Leeds U	(a)	2-1
Northern Semi-Final	Morecambe	(a)	0-2

CARDIFF CITY — FL Championship

FOUNDATION

Credit for the establishment of a first class professional football club in such a rugby stronghold as Cardiff, is due to members of the Riverside club formed in 1899 out of a cricket club of that name. Cardiff became a city in 1905 and in 1908 the South Wales and Monmouthshire FA granted Riverside permission to call themselves Cardiff City. The club turned professional under that name in 1910.

Ninian Park, Sloper Road, Cardiff CF11 8SX.

Telephone: (029) 2022 1001.

Fax: (029) 2034 1148.

Ticket Office: 0845 345 1400.

Website: www.cardiffcityfc.co.uk

Email: info@cardiffcityfc.co.uk

Ground Capacity: 20,500.

Record Attendance: 62,634, Wales v England, 17 October 1959.

Club Record Attendance: 57,893 v Arsenal, Division 1, 22 April 1953.

Pitch Measurements: 110yd × 75yd.

Chairman: Peter Ridsdale.

Secretary: Jason Turner.

Manager: Dave Jones.

Assistant Manager: Terry Burton.

Physio: Sean Connelly BHSc MCSP, SRP.

Colours: Blue shirts with yellow trim, white shorts with blue trim.

Change Colours: Red.

Year Formed: 1899.

Turned Professional: 1910.

Ltd Co.: 1910.

Previous Names: 1899, Riverside; 1902, Riverside Albion; 1908, Cardiff City.

Club Nickname: 'Bluebirds'.

Grounds: Riverside, Sophia Gardens, Old Park and Fir Gardens. Moved to Ninian Park, 1910.

First Football League Game: 28 August 1920, Division 2, v Stockport Co (a) W 5–2 – Kneeshaw; Brittan, Leyton; Keenor (1), Smith, Hardy; Grimshaw (1), Gill (2), Cashmore, West, Evans (1).

Record League Victory: 9–2 v Thames, Division 3 (S), 6 February 1932 – Farquharson; E. L. Morris, Roberts; Galbraith, Harris, Ronan; Emmerson (1), Keating (1), Jones (1), McCambridge (1), Robbins (5).

HONOURS

Football League: Division 1 – Runners-up 1923–24; Division 2 – Runners-up 1920–21, 1951–52, 1959–60; Division 2 – 2002–03 (play-offs); Division 3 (S) – Champions 1946–47; Division 3 – Champions 1992–93. Runners-up 1975–76, 1982–83, 2000–01; Division 4 – Runners-up 1987–88.

FA Cup: Winners 1927 (only occasion the Cup has been won by a club outside England); Runners-up 1925, 2008.

Football League Cup: Semi-final 1966.

Welsh Cup: Winners 22 times (joint record).

Charity Shield: Winners 1927.

European Competitions: *European Cup-Winners' Cup:* 1964–65, 1965–66, 1967–68 (semi-finalists), 1968–69, 1969–70, 1970–71, 1971–72, 1973–74, 1974–75, 1976–77, 1977–78, 1988–89, 1992–93, 1993–94.

SKY SPORTS FACT FILE

In January 1955 Cardiff City paid Kidderminster Harriers £1,500 for centre-forward Gerry Hitchens aged 17. He scored on his debut v Wolverhampton Wanderers to enable the club to avoid relegation. Two years later he was sold to Aston Villa for £22,500.

Record Cup Victory: 8–0 v Enfield, FA Cup 1st rd, 28 November 1931 – Farquharson; Smith, Roberts; Harris (1), Galbraith, Ronan; Emmerson (2), Keating (3); O'Neill (2), Robbins, McCambridge.

Record Defeat: 2–11 v Sheffield U, Division 1, 1 January 1926.

Most League Points (2 for a win): 66, Division 3 (S), 1946–47.

Most League Points (3 for a win): 86, Division 3, 1982–83.

Most League Goals: 95, Division 3, 2000–01.

Highest League Scorer in Season: Robert Earnshaw, 31, Division 2, 2002–03.

Most League Goals in Total Aggregate: Len Davies, 128, 1920–31.

Most League Goals in One Match: 5, Hugh Ferguson v Burnley, Division 1, 1 September 1928; 5, Walter Robbins v Thames, Division 3S, 6 February 1932; 5, William Henderson v Northampton T, Division 3S, 22 April 1933.

Most Capped Player: Alf Sherwood, 39 (41), Wales.

Most League Appearances: Phil Dwyer, 471, 1972–85.

Youngest League Player: Aaron Ramsey, 16 years 123 days v Hull C, 28 April 2007.

Record Transfer Fee Received: £5,000,000 from Sunderland for Michael Chopra, August 2006.

Record Transfer Fee Paid: £1,700,000 to Stoke C for Peter Thorne, September 2001.

Football League Record: 1920 Elected to Division 2; 1921–29 Division 1; 1929–31 Division 2; 1931–47 Division 3 (S); 1947–52 Division 2; 1952–57 Division 1; 1957–60 Division 2; 1960–62 Division 1; 1962–75 Division 2; 1975–76 Division 3; 1976–82 Division 2; 1982–83 Division 3; 1983–85 Division 2; 1985–86 Division 3; 1986–88 Division 4; 1988–90 Division 3; 1990–92 Division 4; 1992–93 Division 3; 1993–95 Division 2; 1995–99 Division 3; 1999–2000 Division 2; 2000–01 Division 3; 2001–03 Division 2; 2003–04 Division 1; 2004– FL C.

MANAGERS

Davy McDougall 1910–11
Fred Stewart 1911–33
Bartley Wilson 1933–34
B. Watts-Jones 1934–37
Bill Jennings 1937–39
Cyril Spiers 1939–46
Billy McCandless 1946–48
Cyril Spiers 1948–54
Trevor Morris 1954–58
Bill Jones 1958–62
George Swindin 1962–64
Jimmy Scoular 1964–73
Frank O'Farrell 1973–74
Jimmy Andrews 1974–78
Richie Morgan 1978–82
Len Ashurst 1982–84
Jimmy Goodfellow 1984
Alan Durban 1984–86
Frank Burrows 1986–89
Len Ashurst 1989–91
Eddie May 1991–94
Terry Yorath 1994–95
Eddie May 1995
Kenny Hibbitt *(Chief Coach)* 1995
Phil Neal 1996
Russell Osman 1996–97
Kenny Hibbitt 1996–98
Frank Burrows 1998–99
Billy Ayre 1999–2000
Bobby Gould 2000
Alan Cork 2000–02
Lennie Lawrence 2002–05
Dave Jones May 2005–

LATEST SEQUENCES

Longest Sequence of League Wins: 9, 26.10.1946 – 28.12.1946.

Longest Sequence of League Defeats: 7, 4.11.1933 – 25.12.1933.

Longest Sequence of League Draws: 6, 29.11.1980 – 17.1.1981.

Longest Sequence of Unbeaten League Matches: 21, 21.9.1946 – 1.3.1947.

Longest Sequence Without a League Win: 15, 21.11.1936 – 6.3.1937.

Successive Scoring Runs: 23 from 24.10.1992.

Successive Non-scoring Runs: 8 from 20.12.1952.

TEN YEAR LEAGUE RECORD

		P	*W*	*D*	*L*	*F*	*A*	*Pts*	*Pos*
1998-99	Div 3	46	22	14	10	60	39	80	3
1999-2000	Div 2	46	9	17	20	45	67	44	21
2000-01	Div 3	46	23	13	10	95	58	82	2
2001-02	Div 2	46	23	14	9	75	50	83	4
2002-03	Div 2	46	23	12	11	68	43	81	6
2003-04	Div 1	46	17	14	15	68	58	65	13
2004-05	FL C	46	13	15	18	48	51	54	16
2005-06	FL C	46	16	12	18	58	59	60	11
2006-07	FL C	46	17	13	16	57	53	64	13
2007-08	FL C	46	16	16	14	59	55	64	12

DID YOU KNOW ?

West Bromwich Albion wanted inside-left Walter Robbins from Ely United in 1928, but he signed for Cardiff City instead. Four years later they had to pay a transfer fee for the same player. His City debut was in a 1–0 win over Portsmouth on 8 December 1928.

CARDIFF CITY 2007–08 LEAGUE RECORD

Match No.	Date	Venue	Opponents	Result		H/T Score	Lg. Pos.	Goalscorers	Attendance
1	Aug 11	H	Stoke C	L	0-1	0-1	—		18,840
2	18	A	QPR	W	2-0	1-0	12	MacLean 29, Parry 59	12,596
3	25	H	Coventry C	L	0-1	0-1	19		16,407
4	Sept 1	A	Norwich C	W	2-1	0-1	10	Whittingham 64, Johnson 84	24,292
5	15	A	Plymouth Arg	D	2-2	0-1	9	Rae 71, Thompson 89	11,591
6	19	H	Watford	L	1-2	0-1	—	Hasselbaink 61	13,169
7	22	H	Preston NE	D	2-2	1-0	17	Fowler 2 28, 61	11,772
8	29	A	Barnsley	D	1-1	0-0	17	Hasselbaink 73	10,709
9	Oct 2	A	Sheffield U	D	3-3	2-1	—	Ledley 31, Fowler (pen) 45, Rae 59	26,186
10	6	H	Burnley	W	2-1	1-0	12	Ledley 36, Parry 55	12,914
11	21	A	Southampton	L	0-1	0-1	15		20,796
12	24	H	Wolverhampton W	L	2-3	2-1	—	Fowler (pen) 25, Hasselbaink 29	15,000
13	27	H	Scunthorpe U	D	1-1	1-0	17	McPhail 37	11,850
14	Nov 6	H	Crystal Palace	D	1-1	1-1	—	Purse 9	11,781
15	10	A	Charlton Ath	L	0-3	0-2	20		22,866
16	24	H	Ipswich T	W	1-0	1-0	18	Parry 33	15,173
17	26	A	Leicester C	D	0-0	0-0	—		27,246
18	Dec 1	A	Hull C	D	2-2	1-2	20	Thompson 6, Johnson 90	16,269
19	4	H	Charlton Ath	L	0-2	0-1	—		11,874
20	8	H	Colchester U	W	4-1	0-1	17	Thompson 52, Whittingham 57, Hasselbaink 66, Virgo (og) 70	11,006
21	11	A	Blackpool	W	1-0	1-0	—	Thompson 14	7214
22	15	A	Bristol C	L	0-1	0-0	16		15,753
23	22	H	Sheffield U	W	1-0	1-0	15	Parry 30	12,869
24	26	A	Watford	D	2-2	1-0	15	Johnson 34, Whittingham 56	17,014
25	29	A	Preston NE	W	2-1	0-1	12	Johnson 53, Ledley 67	12,046
26	Jan 1	H	Plymouth Arg	W	1-0	1-0	11	Ledley 30	14,965
27	12	H	Sheffield W	W	1-0	1-0	8	Hasselbaink 36	14,015
28	19	A	WBA	D	3-3	2-1	8	Parry 2 1, 33, Ledley 52	22,325
29	29	H	QPR	W	3-1	2-0	—	Ledley 2 12, 40, Parry 57	13,602
30	Feb 2	A	Stoke C	L	1-2	0-1	9	Hasselbaink 63	15,045
31	9	H	Norwich C	L	1-2	1-1	11	Rae 45	11,937
32	12	A	Coventry C	D	0-0	0-0	—		15,260
33	23	A	Sheffield W	L	0-1	0-1	13		18,539
34	Mar 1	H	Leicester C	L	0-1	0-1	14		13,355
35	4	A	Crystal Palace	D	0-0	0-0	—		13,446
36	12	H	Hull C	W	1-0	1-0	—	McPhail 2	17,555
37	15	A	Colchester U	D	1-1	1-0	14	Parry 11	4699
38	22	H	Bristol C	W	2-1	1-0	13	Johnson 44, Whittingham 81	16,458
39	29	H	Southampton	W	1-0	1-0	12	Parry 6	12,955
40	Apr 1	H	WBA	D	0-0	0-0	—		13,915
41	9	A	Ipswich T	D	1-1	1-0	—	Rae 37	20,311
42	12	H	Blackpool	W	3-1	1-0	10	McPhail 7, Sinclair 50, Whittingham 58	14,715
43	19	A	Scunthorpe U	L	2-3	1-0	13	Hasselbaink 45, Ledley 59	4727
44	22	A	Wolverhampton W	L	0-3	0-2	—		20,862
45	26	A	Burnley	D	3-3	0-1	13	Ledley (pen) 57, Ramsey 69, Thompson 89	10,694
46	May 4	H	Barnsley	W	3-0	1-0	12	Parry 44, McNaughton 49, Ledley 63	14,469

Final League Position: 12

GOALSCORERS

League (59): Ledley 10 (1 pen), Parry 10, Hasselbaink 7, Johnson 5, Thompson 5, Whittingham 5, Fowler 4 (2 pens), Rae 4, McPhail 3, MacLean 1, McNaughton 1, Purse 1, Ramsey 1, Sinclair 1, own goal 1.
Carling Cup (7): Fowler 2 (1 pen), Hasselbaink 1, Johnson 1, Purse 1, Sinclair 1, Whittingham 1.
FA Cup (10): Whittingham 3, Hasselbaink 1, Johnson 1, Ledley 1, McNaughton 1, Parry 1, Ramsey 1, Thompson 1 (pen).

Turnbull R 6	McNaughton K 35	Capaldi T 43 + 1	Rae G 40 + 5	Johnson R 41 + 1	Loovens G 36	Ledley J 38 + 3	McPhail S 42 + 1	MacLean S 6 + 9	Feeney W 1 + 4	Sinclair T 14 + 7	Whittingham P 25 + 16	Parry P 37 + 4	Gunter C 11 + 2	Purse D 12 + 6	Blake D 4 + 4	Hasselbaink J 33 + 3	Fowler R 10 + 3	Thompson S 17 + 19	Oakes M 11	Ramsey A 11 + 4	Schmeichel K 14	Enckelman P 15 + 1	Brown J — + 2	Scimeca R 4 + 5	Match No.
1	2	3	4	5	6	7	8^{1}	9	10^{2}	11	12	13													1
1	2^{3}	3^{2}	4	5	6	7	8	9^{1}	12	11	13	10	14												2
1		3	4	5	6	7^{2}	8	9^{1}	12	11	13	10	2^{3}	14											3
1		3	4	5	6	7^{1}	8			11	13	12	2^{3}		14	9	10^{2}								4
1	6	3	4	5		12	8			7	10^{3}	11	2^{2}			9^{1}	14	13							5
1	6	3	4	5			8			7	12	11	2^{2}			9	10^{1}	13							6
	6	3	4	5		2	8			7^{2}	13	11^{1}	12			9	10^{3}	14	1						7
	2	3	4	5	6	7	8			11^{1}		12				9	10		1						8
	2	3	4	5	6	7	8					11				9	10		1						9
	2	3	4	5	6^{1}	7					8	11		12		9^{3}	10^{2}	13	1	14					10
	2^{3}	3	4	5	6	7^{2}	8	14		13	12	11^{1}				9	10		1						11
	2	3	4		6	7^{2}	8	12		13		11		5		9^{1}	10^{3}	14	1						12
	2^{1}	3	4	6		7	8			11		12		5		9	10^{2}	13			1				13
	2	3	4	6		7	8			12		11^{1}		5		9	10^{2}	13			1				14
	2	3	4	5		7	8				12	11^{1}		6		9^{2}	13	10			1				15
		3	4	12	6	7^{2}	8				13	11	2	5		9		10^{1}			1				16
		3	4		6	7	8	12			13	11^{2}	2	5		9^{1}		10			1				17
		3^{2}	4^{1}	6		7	8	9			13	11	2	5		12		10			1				18
		3^{2}	4		6	7	8	9^{1}			13	11	2	5		12		10			1				19
	3^{1}	12	13	5	6	7	8^{2}	14			4	11	2			9^{3}		10			1				20
	3		12	5	6^{3}	7	8	13			4^{1}	11	2	14		9^{2}		10			1				21
	3^{3}		12	5	6	7	8	13			4^{1}	11	2			9^{2}	14	10■			1				22
	2	3	4	5	6	7	8	12			10^{2}	11		13		9^{1}					1				23
	2	3	4	5	6	7	8	9^{1}			10	11		12							1				24
	2	3	4	5	6	7	8	12			10	11				9^{1}					1				25
	2	3	4	5	6	7	8	12			10^{2}	11				9^{1}		13			1				26
	2	3	4	5	6	7	8				10	11				9^{1}		12	1						27
	2^{2}	3	4	5	6	7	8				10	11			13	9^{1}		12	1						28
	2	3	4	5	6	7					10^{2}	11			13	9^{1}		12	1^{G}	8		15			29
	2	3	4	5	6	7	8				10	11				9^{1}		12	1						30
	2	3	4	5	6	7	8				10	11				9^{1}		12	1						31
	2	3	4	5	6	7^{1}	12				10^{3}	11				9^{2}		13		8		1	14		32
	2	3	4	5			8^{1}				10	11		6		9		12		7		1			33
	2	3	4	5			8^{1}				10^{2}	11		6		9		12		7		1		13	34
	2	3	12	5	6		8			7^{2}	10	11						9		13		1		4^{1}	35
	2^{2}	3	12	5	6	13	8		14	7	10	11^{3}						9				1		4^{1}	36
		3	4	5	6	7^{1}				13	10^{2}	11			2	9■		12		8^{3}		1		14	37
		3	4	5	6	7	8				10^{1}	11			2			9		12		1			38
		3	4	5	6	7	8			12	10^{1}	11						9^{2}		2		1		13	39
	2	3	4	5	6	7	8		12^{2}	10	14	11^{3}						9^{1}				1		13	40
		3^{2}	4	5	6	7^{3}	8			12	13				2	14		9		11		1		10^{1}	41
	2	3	4	5			8			11^{1}	10			6				9		7		1	12		42
	2^{2}	3	4	5	6	7	8			13	12					9^{1}		10		11		1			43
	2	3	4	5	6	7	8				10^{1}				12	9^{3}		14		11^{2}		1		13	44
		3			6	12	8^{1}			11	13			5■	2	9^{2}		10		7		1		4	45
	2	3^{3}	4	5	6^{2}	7	8				10	11^{1}		13		9		12		14		1			46

FA Cup

Third Round	Chasetown	(a)	3-1
Fourth Round	Hereford U	(a)	2-1
Fifth Round	Wolverhampton W	(h)	2-0
Sixth Round	Middlesbrough	(a)	2-0
Semi-Final *(at Wembley)*	Barnsley		1-0
Final *(at Wembley)*	Portsmouth		0-1

Carling Cup

First Round	Brighton & HA	(h)	1-0
Second Round	Leyton Orient	(h)	1-0
Third Round	WBA	(a)	4-2
Fourth Round	Liverpool	(a)	1-2

CARLISLE UNITED FL Championship 1

FOUNDATION

Carlisle United came into being in 1903 through the amalgamation of Shaddongate United and Carlisle Red Rose. The new club was admitted to the Second Division of the Lancashire Combination in 1905–06, winning promotion the following season. Devonshire Park was officially opened on 2 September 1905, when St Helens Town were the visitors. Despite defeat in a disappointing 3-2 start, a respectable mid-table position was achieved.

Brunton Park, Warwick Road, Carlisle CA1 1LL.

Telephone: (01228) 526 237.

Fax: (01228) 554 141.

Ticket Office: (01228) 526 237 (option 1).

Website: www.carlisleunited.co.uk

Email: enquiries@carlisleunited.co.uk

Ground Capacity: 16,982.

Record Attendance: 27,500 v Birmingham C, FA Cup 3rd rd, 5 January 1957 and v Middlesbrough, FA Cup 5th rd, 7 February 1970.

Pitch Measurements: 114yd × 74yd.

Chairman: H. A. Jenkins.

Managing Director: John Nixon.

Secretary: Sarah McKnight.

Manager: John Ward.

Assistant Manager: Greg Abbott.

Physio: Neil Dalton.

Colours: Blue shirts, white shorts, blue stockings.

Change Colours: Red shirts, red shorts, red stockings.

Year Formed: 1903.

Ltd Co.: 1921.

Previous Name: 1903, Shaddongate United; 1904, Carlisle United.

Club Nicknames: 'Cumbrians' or 'The Blues'.

Grounds: 1903, Milholme Bank; 1905, Devonshire Park; 1909, Brunton Park.

First Football League Game: 25 August 1928, Division 3 (N), v Accrington S (a) W 3–2 – Prout; Coulthard, Cook; Harrison, Ross, Pigg; Agar (1), Hutchison, McConnell (1), Ward (1), Watson.

Record League Victory: 8–0 v Hartlepool U, Division 3 (N), 1 September 1928 – Prout; Smiles, Cook; Robinson (1) Ross, Pigg; Agar (1), Hutchison (1), McConnell (4), Ward (1), Watson. 8–0 v Scunthorpe U, Division 3 (N), 25 December 1952 – MacLaren; Hill, Scott; Stokoe, Twentyman, Waters; Harrison (1), Whitehouse (5), Ashman (2), Duffett, Bond.

Record Cup Victory: 6–0 v Shepshed Dynamo, FA Cup 1st rd, 16 November 1996 – Caig; Hopper, Archdeacon (pen), Walling, Robinson, Pounewatchy, Peacock (1), Conway (1) (Jansen), Smart (McAlindon (1)), Hayward, Aspinall (Thorpe), (2 og).

HONOURS

Football League: Division 1 best season: 22nd, 1974–75; Promoted from Division 2 (3rd) 1973–74; Division 3 – Champions 1964–65, 1994–95; Runners-up 1981–82; Promoted from Division 3 1996–97; Division 4 – Runners-up 1963–64; FL 2 – Champions 2005–06. Promoted from Conference (play-offs) 2004–05.

FA Cup: best season: 6th rd 1975.

Football League Cup: Semi-final 1970.

Auto Windscreens Shield: Winners 1997; Runners-up 1995.

LDV Vans Trophy: Runners-up 2003, 2006.

SKY SPORTS FACT FILE

On 1 June 1972 in the Anglo-Italian Cup, Carlisle United, tenth in Division Two, beat Roma 3–2 in the Olympic Stadium on their European debut. The Italian club at the time were still enjoying an unbeaten home record in Serie A.

Record Defeat: 1–11 v Hull C, Division 3 (N), 14 January 1939.

Most League Points (2 for a win): 62, Division 3 (N), 1950–51.

Most League Points (3 for a win): 91, Division 3, 1994–95.

Most League Goals: 113, Division 4, 1963–64.

Highest League Scorer in Season: Jimmy McConnell, 42, Division 3 (N), 1928–29.

Most League Goals in Total Aggregate: Jimmy McConnell, 126, 1928–32.

Most League Goals in One Match: 5, Hugh Mills v Halifax T, Division 3N, 11 September 1937; 5, Jim Whitehouse v Scunthorpe U, Division 3N, 25 December 1952.

Most Capped Player: Eric Welsh, 4, Northern Ireland.

Most League Appearances: Allan Ross, 466, 1963–79.

Youngest League Player: John Slaven, 16 years 162 days v Scunthorpe U, 16 March 2002.

Record Transfer Fee Received: £1,500,000 from Crystal Palace for Matt Jansen, February 1998.

Record Transfer Fee Paid: £121,000 to Notts Co for David Reeves, December 1993.

Football League Record: 1928 Elected to Division 3 (N); 1958–62 Division 4; 1962–63 Division 3; 1963–64 Division 4; 1964–65 Division 3; 1965–74 Division 2; 1974–75 Division 1; 1975–77 Division 2; 1977–82 Division 3; 1982–86 Division 2; 1986–87 Division 3; 1987–92 Division 4; 1992–95 Division 3; 1995–96 Division 2; 1996–97 Division 3; 1997–98 Division 2; 1998–04 Division 3; 2004–05 Conference; 2005–06 FL 2; 2006– FL 1.

LATEST SEQUENCES

Longest Sequence of League Wins: 7, 18.2.06 – 8.4.06.

Longest Sequence of League Defeats: 12, 27.9.2003 – 13.12.2003.

Longest Sequence of League Draws: 6, 11.2.1978 – 11.3.1978.

Longest Sequence of Unbeaten League Matches: 19, 1.10.1994 – 11.2.1995.

Longest Sequence Without a League Win: 14, 19.1.1935 – 19.4.1935.

Successive Scoring Runs: 26 from 23.8.1947.

Successive Non-scoring Runs: 5 from 24.8.1968.

MANAGERS

Harry Kirkbride 1904–05 *(Secretary-Manager)*
McCumiskey 1905–06 *(Secretary-Manager)*
Jack Houston 1906–08 *(Secretary-Manager)*
Bert Stansfield 1908–10
Jack Houston 1910–12
Davie Graham 1912–13
George Bristow 1913–30
Billy Hampson 1930–33
Bill Clarke 1933–35
Robert Kelly 1935–36
Fred Westgarth 1936–38
David Taylor 1938–40
Howard Harkness 1940–45
Bill Clark 1945–46 *(Secretary-Manager)*
Ivor Broadis 1946–49
Bill Shankly 1949–51
Fred Emery 1951–58
Andy Beattie 1958–60
Ivor Powell 1960–63
Alan Ashman 1963–67
Tim Ward 1967–68
Bob Stokoe 1968–70
Ian MacFarlane 1970–72
Alan Ashman 1972–75
Dick Young 1975–76
Bobby Moncur 1976–80
Martin Harvey 1980
Bob Stokoe 1980–85
Bryan 'Pop' Robson 1985
Bob Stokoe 1985–86
Harry Gregg 1986–87
Cliff Middlemass 1987–91
Aidan McCaffery 1991–92
David McCreery 1992–93
Mick Wadsworth *(Director of Coaching)* 1993–96
Mervyn Day 1996–97
David Wilkes and John Halpin (*Directors of Coaching*), and Michael Knighton 1997–99
Nigel Pearson 1998–99
Keith Mincher 1999
Martin Wilkinson 1999–2000
Ian Atkins 2000–01
Roddy Collins 2001–02; 2002–03
Paul Simpson 2003–06
Neil McDonald 2006–07
John Ward October 2007–

TEN YEAR LEAGUE RECORD

		P	W	D	L	F	A	Pts	Pos
1998-99	Div 3	46	11	16	19	43	53	49	23
1999-2000	Div 3	46	9	12	25	42	75	39	23
2000-01	Div 3	46	11	15	20	42	65	48	22
2001-02	Div 3	46	12	16	18	49	56	52	17
2002-03	Div 3	46	13	10	23	52	78	49	22
2003-04	Div 3	46	12	9	25	46	69	45	23
2004-05	Conf	42	20	13	9	74	37	73	3
2005-06	FL 2	46	25	11	10	84	42	86	1
2006-07	FL 1	46	19	11	16	54	55	68	8
2007-08	FL 1	46	23	11	12	64	46	80	4

DID YOU KNOW 

Jimmy Whitehouse scored his 100th and final League goal for Carlisle United against Oldham Athletic on 15 December 1956 in a 2–2 draw. It was his 196th League appearance. He retired from the first-class game at the end of the same season.

CARLISLE UNITED 2007–08 LEAGUE RECORD

Match No.	Date	Venue	Opponents	Result		H/T Score	Lg. Pos.	Goalscorers	Attendance
1	Aug 11	A	Walsall	D	1-1	1-0	—	Gall 19	6933
2	18	H	Oldham Ath	W	1-0	1-0	5	Graham (pen) 42	7777
3	25	A	Huddersfield T	W	2-0	2-0	2	Livesey 34, Garner 44	10,022
4	Sept 1	H	Cheltenham T	W	1-0	0-0	2	Livesey 90	6125
5	8	H	Tranmere R	L	0-1	0-1	3		6556
6	14	A	Swansea C	L	1-2	0-0	—	Graham (pen) 48	11,354
7	22	H	Bristol R	D	1-1	0-1	6	Graham 70	6106
8	29	A	Bournemouth	W	3-1	2-0	4	Garner 2 27, 39, Anyinsah 66	4940
9	Oct 2	A	Hartlepool U	D	2-2	2-1	—	Graham 2 19, 45	5359
10	6	H	Millwall	W	4-0	4-0	3	Garner 15, Graham 2 29, 34, Bridge-Wilkinson 45	7022
11	13	A	Yeovil T	L	1-2	0-0	6	Hackney 49	4757
12	20	H	Gillingham	W	2-0	1-0	3	Cox (og) 15, Hackney 54	6461
13	27	A	Southend U	W	1-0	0-0	1	Garner 59	9281
14	Nov 3	H	Leeds U	W	3-1	0-1	1	Hackney 61, Garner 70, Bridge-Wilkinson 90	16,668
15	6	A	Luton T	D	0-0	0-0	—		5462
16	24	A	Brighton & HA	D	2-2	1-0	3	Hackney 34, Garner 53	5390
17	Dec 4	H	Swindon T	W	3-0	1-0	—	Anyinsah 2 27, 54, Garner 75	5477
18	8	A	Northampton T	D	2-2	1-1	4	Bridge-Wilkinson 26, Garner 63	4908
19	15	H	Leyton Orient	W	1-0	0-0	2	Garner 50	6843
20	26	A	Tranmere R	L	0-2	0-2	4		8516
21	29	A	Bristol R	L	0-3	0-2	5		6254
22	Jan 1	H	Hartlepool U	W	4-2	1-1	3	Garner 2 42, 69, Smith J 66, Hackney 90	7496
23	5	H	Port Vale	W	3-2	0-2	—	Joyce 50, Hackney 2 65, 69	6313
24	12	A	Doncaster R	L	0-1	0-0	3		8197
25	19	H	Crewe Alex	W	1-0	0-0	2	Garner 52	6449
26	25	A	Cheltenham T	L	0-1	0-1	—		4221
27	29	A	Oldham Ath	L	0-2	0-2	—		4701
28	Feb 2	H	Walsall	W	2-1	1-1	3	Bridge-Wilkinson (pen) 33, Graham 75	6220
29	9	A	Port Vale	D	1-1	0-0	4	Garner 62	4221
30	12	H	Huddersfield T	W	2-1	1-0	—	Livesey 21, Graham 76	6196
31	23	H	Doncaster R	W	1-0	1-0	4	Graham 40	8390
32	26	A	Crewe Alex	W	1-0	0-0	—	Dobie 64	4786
33	Mar 3	A	Nottingham F	W	1-0	0-0	—	Graham 71	28,487
34	8	H	Brighton & HA	W	2-0	1-0	3	Graham 35, Livesey 59	6793
35	11	H	Luton T	W	2-1	2-0	—	Livesey 22, Murphy 29	5489
36	15	A	Swindon T	D	2-2	0-0	3	Bridge-Wilkinson 54, Murphy 86	6004
37	22	A	Leyton Orient	W	3-0	2-0	2	Graham 17, Raven 32, Smith G 49	6134
38	24	H	Northampton T	W	2-0	0-0	2-	Livesey 50, Bridge-Wilkinson 84	9038
39	29	A	Gillingham	D	0-0	0-0	2		6673
40	Apr 1	H	Nottingham F	L	0-2	0-0	—		9979
41	5	H	Yeovil T	W	2-1	0-1	2	Murphy 77, Dobie 90	6843
42	8	H	Swansea C	D	0-0	0-0	—		10,623
43	12	A	Leeds U	L	2-3	1-0	2	Dobie 17, Graham 60	28,530
44	19	H	Southend U	L	1-2	0-1	2	Hackney 52	9122
45	26	A	Millwall	L	0-3	0-1	4		10,075
46	May 3	H	Bournemouth	D	1-1	0-0	4	Dobie 57	12,223

Final League Position: 4

GOALSCORERS

League (64): Garner 14, Graham 14 (2 pens), Hackney 8, Bridge-Wilkinson 6 (1 pen), Livesey 6, Dobie 4, Anyinsah 3, Murphy 3, Gall 1, Joyce 1, Raven 1, Smith G 1, Smith J 1, own goal 1.
Carling Cup (1): Graham 1.
FA Cup (1): Aranalde 1 (pen).
J Paint Trophy (4): Gall 2, Bridge-Wilkinson 1, Graham 1.
Play-Offs (2): Bridge-Wilkinson 1, Graham 1.

Westwood K 46	Raven D 43	Aranalde Z 27	Thirlwell P 9 + 4	Livesey D 45	Murphy P 33 + 3	Hackney S 39 + 4	Bridge-Wilkinson M 44 + 1	Graham D 39 + 6	Gall K 10 + 11	Smith J 13 + 9	Arnison P 7 + 10	Garner J 30 + 1	Carlton D 5 + 26	Brittain M — + 1	Lumsdon C 38 + 2	Worley H 1	Anyinsah J 10 + 2	Keogh R 7	Joyce L 1 + 2	Dobie S 8 + 7	Horwood E 19	Taylor C 14 + 4	Smith G 15 + 1	Madine G 1 + 10	Reid P 1	Campion D 1 + 1	*Match No.*
1	2	3	4	5	6^{1}	7^{2}	8	9^{3}	10	11	12	13	14														1
1	6	3	4	5			8	9^{1}	7^{2}	11	2	10	12	13													2
1	6	3	4	5			8	10^{2}	7	11	2	9^{1}	12		13												3
1	2	3	4	5		12	8	10	7	11^{1}	13	9				6^{2}											4
1	6	3	4	5		12	8^{3}	10	7^{2}	11^{1}	2	9	13		14												5
1	6	3	4^{2}	5	12		8	13	10^{3}	11	2	9^{1}	14		7												6
1	2	3		5	6	12	4	10	7^{3}	11^{1}		9^{2}	13		8		14										7
1	2	3		5	6	7^{2}	8	10^{3}	12	13		9	14		11		4^{1}										8
1	2	3		5	6	7^{2}	8	10	13	12		9^{3}	14		11		4^{1}										9
1	2	3		5	6^{2}	7	8	10	12		13	9^{1}	14		11		4^{3}										10
1	2	3		5	6	7	8	9^{1}	10	11^{2}			12		4		13										11
1	2	3		5	6	7	8	10	12			9			11		4^{1}										12
1	2	3^{1}		5	6	7	8	10			12	9			11		4										13
1	2	3		5	6	7	8	10	12			9^{2}	13		11		4^{1}										14
1	2	3		5	6	7^{1}	4	10	8	12		9			11												15
1	2	3		5		7	8	12	13			9^{2}	10^{1}		11		4	6									16
1	2	3	12	5		7	8^{1}	13	14			9	10^{2}		11		4^{3}	6									17
1	2	3	12	5		7^{1}	8	13	14			9^{2}	10^{3}		11		4	6									18
1	2	3	12	5		7	8					9	10		11		4^{1}	6									19
1	2^{1}	3	4	5	12	7	8	10	13			9			11^{2}			6									20
1	2	3	4	5		7	8	10	11			9						6									21
1	2	3		5		7	4	10^{2}	12	13		9	8^{1}		11			6									22
1	2	3	4^{2}	5	6	7		10		11^{1}	12	9			8				13								23
1	2^{1}	3		5	6	7^{2}	4	10	12	11		9	13		8												24
1	2	3		5	6	7^{1}	4	10		11	12	9			8												25
1	2	3		5	6	7^{2}	4	10^{1}		11		9	12		8					13							26
1	2	3		5	6	12	4	13		11^{2}		9	14		8				7^{1}	10^{3}							27
1				5	6	7	8	12			2	9	13		11					10^{2}	3	4^{1}					28
1	2			5	6	7^{1}	8	10				9^{3}	13		11					4^{2}	3	14	12				29
1	2			5	6	7	8	10				9^{1}	12		11						3	4					30
1	2			5	6	7	8	10^{2}		13	12	9^{3}								14	3^{1}	4	11				31
1	2			5	6	7	8	10		12		9^{2}								13	3	11^{1}	4				32
1	2			5	6	10^{2}	8	9^{3}		12			13		11						3	7	4^{1}	14			33
1	2			5	6	10	8	9^{3}		12			13		11						3	7^{2}	4^{1}	14			34
1	2			5	6	10	8	9		12^{2}			14		11						3	7^{3}	4^{1}	13			35
1	2			5	6	10^{1}	8	9			12		13		11				14		3	7^{2}	4^{3}				36
1	2			5	6	10	8^{3}	9^{2}					12		11					13	3	7^{1}	4	14			37
1	2			5	6	10^{1}	8	9			13		12		11^{2}					14	3	7^{3}	4				38
1	2			5	6	10	8	9^{2}					12		11					13	3	7^{1}	4				39
1	2			5	6	10	8	9					12		11						3	7^{2}	4^{1}	13			40
1	2			5	6	10^{3}	8	9			12				11					13	3	7^{1}	4^{2}	14			41
1	2			5	6	10^{2}	8	9							11					7^{1}	3	12	4	13			42
1	2			5	6	10	8	9							11					7^{2}	3	12	4^{1}	13			43
1	2■		13	5	12	10	8	9^{2}							11					7	3		4^{3}	14	6^{1}		44
1				5■	6	10	8	9			2				11					4^{2}	3	7^{1}		12		13	45
1					6	10	12	9^{3}			2		14		11					7	3	13	4^{1}	8^{2}		5	46

FA Cup

First Round	Grimsby T	(h)	1-1
		(a)	0-1

Carling Cup

First Round	Bury	(a)	1-0
Second Round	Coventry C	(h)	0-2

J Paint Trophy

Second Round	Chester C	(h)	4-2
Quarter-Final	Stockport Co	(h)	0-3

Play-Offs

Semi-Final	Leeds U	(a)	2-2
		(h)	0-2

CHARLTON ATHLETIC FL Championship

FOUNDATION

The club was formed on 9 June 1905, by a group of 14- and 15-year-old youths living in streets by the Thames in the area which now borders the Thames Barrier. The club's progress through local leagues was so rapid that after the First World War they joined the Kent League where they spent a season before turning professional and joining the Southern League in 1920. A year later they were elected to the Football League's Division 3 (South).

The Valley, Floyd Road, Charlton, London SE7 8BL.

Telephone: (020) 8333 4000.

Fax: (020) 8333 4001.

Ticket Office: (0871) 226 1905.

Website: www.cafc.co.uk

Email: info@cafc.co.uk

Ground Capacity: 27,111.

Record Attendance: 75,031 v Aston Villa, FA Cup 5th rd, 12 February 1938 (at The Valley).

Pitch Measurements: 101.5m × 65.8m.

Chairman: Richard Murray.

Vice-chairman: Martin Simons.

Chief Executive: Peter Varney.

Secretary: Chris Parkes.

Manager: Alan Pardew.

Assistant Manager: Phil Parkinson.

Physio: Steve Allen.

Colours: Red shirts, white shorts, red stockings.

Change Colours: White shirts, black shorts, white stockings.

Year Formed: 1905.

Turned Professional: 1920.

Ltd Co.: 1919.

Club Nickname: 'Addicks'.

Grounds: 1906, Siemen's Meadow; 1907, Woolwich Common; 1909, Pound Park; 1913, Horn Lane; 1920, The Valley; 1923, Catford (The Mount); 1924, The Valley; 1985, Selhurst Park; 1991, Upton Park; 1992, The Valley.

First Football League Game: 27 August 1921, Division 3 (S), v Exeter C (h) W 1–0 – Hughes; J Mitchell, Goodman; Dowling (1), Hampson, Dunn; Castle, Bailey, Halse, Green, Wilson.

HONOURS

Football League: Division 1 – Champions 1999–2000; Runners-up 1936–37; Promoted from Division 1, 1997–98 (play-offs); Division 2 – Runners-up 1935–36, 1985–86; Division 3 (S) – Champions 1928–29, 1934–35; Promoted from Division 3 (3rd) 1974–75, 1980–81.

FA Cup: Winners 1947; Runners-up 1946.

Football League Cup: Quarter-final 2007.

Full Members' Cup: Runners-up 1987.

SKY SPORTS FACT FILE

George Moore, the left-wing understudy to Harold Hobbis, managed just one first team appearance for Charlton Athletic but had the satisfaction of scoring in the 4–3 win over Bournemouth on 26 August 1933. Signed from Tunbridge Wells Rangers he later played for Yeovil.

Record League Victory: 8–1 v Middlesbrough, Division 1, 12 September 1953 – Bartram; Campbell, Ellis; Fenton, Ufton, Hammond; Hurst (2), O'Linn (2), Leary (1), Firmani (3), Kiernan.

Record Cup Victory: 7–0 v Burton A, FA Cup 3rd rd, 7 January 1956 – Bartram; Campbell, Townsend; Hewie, Ufton, Hammond; Hurst (1), Gauld (1), Leary (3), White, Kiernan (2).

Record Defeat: 1–11 v Aston Villa, Division 2, 14 November 1959.

Most League Points (2 for a win): 61, Division 3 (S), 1934–35.

Most League Points (3 for a win): 91, Division 1, 1999–2000.

Most League Goals: 107, Division 2, 1957–58.

Highest League Scorer in Season: Ralph Allen, 32, Division 3 (S), 1934–35.

Most League Goals in Total Aggregate: Stuart Leary, 153, 1953–62.

Most League Goals in One Match: 5, Wilson Lennox v Exeter C, Division 3S, 2 February 1929; 5, Eddie Firmani v Aston Villa, Division 1, 5 February 1955; 5, John Summers v Huddersfield T, Division 2, 21 December 1957; 5, John Summers v Portsmouth, Division 2, 1 October 1960.

Most Capped Player: Jonatan Johansson, 42 (88), Finland.

Most League Appearances: Sam Bartram, 579, 1934–56.

Youngest League Player: Jonjo Shevley, 16 years 59 days v Burnley, 26 April 2008.

Record Transfer Fee Received: £16,500,000 from Tottenham H for Darren Bent, May 2007

Record Transfer Fee Paid: £5,380,000 to Ipswich T for Darren Bent, June 2005.

Football League Record: 1921 Elected to Division 3 (S); 1929–33 Division 2; 1933–35 Division 3 (S); 1935–36 Division 2; 1936–57 Division 1; 1957–72 Division 2; 1972–75 Division 3; 1975–80 Division 2; 1980–81 Division 3; 1981–86 Division 2; 1986–90 Division 1; 1990–92 Division 2; 1992–98 Division 1; 1998–99 FA Premier League; 1999–2000 Division 1; 2000–07 FA Premier League; 2007– FL C.

MANAGERS

Walter Rayner 1920–25
Alex Macfarlane 1925–27
Albert Lindon 1928
Alex Macfarlane 1928–32
Albert Lindon 1932–33
Jimmy Seed 1933–56
Jimmy Trotter 1956–61
Frank Hill 1961–65
Bob Stokoe 1965–67
Eddie Firmani 1967–70
Theo Foley 1970–74
Andy Nelson 1974–79
Mike Bailey 1979–81
Alan Mullery 1981–82
Ken Craggs 1982
Lennie Lawrence 1982–91
Steve Gritt/Alan Curbishley 1991–95
Alan Curbishley 1995–2006
Iain Dowie 2006
Les Reed 2006
Alan Pardew December 2006–

LATEST SEQUENCES

Longest Sequence of League Wins: 12, 26.12.1999 – 7.3.2000.

Longest Sequence of League Defeats: 10, 11.4.1990 – 15.9.1990.

Longest Sequence of League Draws: 6, 13.12.1992 – 16.1.1993.

Longest Sequence of Unbeaten League Matches: 15, 4.10.1980 – 20.12.1980.

Longest Sequence Without a League Win: 16, 26.2.1955 – 22.8.1955.

Successive Scoring Runs: 25 from 26.12.1935.

Successive Non-scoring Runs: 5 from 6.9.1922.

TEN YEAR LEAGUE RECORD

		P	*W*	*D*	*L*	*F*	*A*	*Pts*	*Pos*
1998-99	PR Lge	38	8	12	18	41	56	36	18
1999-2000	Div 1	46	27	10	9	79	45	91	1
2000-01	PR Lge	38	14	10	14	50	57	52	9
2001-02	PR Lge	38	10	14	14	38	49	44	14
2002-03	PR Lge	38	14	7	17	45	56	49	12
2003-04	PR Lge	38	14	11	13	51	51	53	7
2004-05	PR Lge	38	12	10	16	42	58	46	11
2005-06	PR Lge	38	13	8	17	41	55	47	13
2006-07	PR Lge	38	8	10	20	34	60	34	19
2007-08	FL C	46	17	13	16	63	58	64	11

DID YOU KNOW ?

On 26 April 2008 against Barnsley, Jonjo Shelvey, an England youth international, became the youngest debutant for Charlton Athletic in a League match. He was 16 years 59 days. A midfield player he formerly captained his country at Under-16 level.

CHARLTON ATHLETIC 2007–08 LEAGUE RECORD

Match No.	*Date*	*Venue*	*Opponents*	*Result*	*H/T Score*	*Lg. Pos.*	*Goalscorers*	*Attendance*
1	Aug 11	H	Scunthorpe U	D 1-1	0-0	—	Bent ^{62}	23,151
2	18	A	Stoke C	L 1-2	0-0	17	Fortune ^{55}	12,649
3	25	H	Sheffield W	W 3-2	0-2	12	Reid ^{51}, Iwelumo 2 $^{67, 87}$	22,033
4	Sept 1	A	Crystal Palace	W 1-0	0-0	7	Todorov ^{74}	18,556
5	15	A	Colchester U	D 2-2	1-2	5	Todorov ^{45}, Zheng-Zhi ^{73}	5860
6	18	H	Norwich C	W 2-0	0-0	—	Reid 2 (2 pens) $^{85, 88}$	21,543
7	22	H	Leicester C	W 2-0	2-0	2	Iwelumo ^{18}, Varney ^{23}	21,918
8	29	A	Coventry C	D 1-1	1-0	3	Sam ^{15}	19,021
9	Oct 2	A	Hull C	W 2-1	1-0	—	Varney ^{41}, Iwelumo ^{89}	15,001
10	6	H	Barnsley	D 1-1	0-0	2	Zheng-Zhi ^{82}	21,801
11	20	A	Wolverhampton W	L 0-2	0-0	3		24,058
12	23	H	Plymouth Arg	L 1-2	1-2	—	McCormick (og) ^{12}	22,123
13	27	H	QPR	L 0-1	0-0	8		23,671
14	Nov 3	A	Southampton	W 1-0	0-0	5	Iwelumo ^{90}	23,363
15	6	A	Bristol C	W 1-0	0-0	—	Iwelumo ^{90}	15,420
16	10	H	Cardiff C	W 3-0	2-0	2	Sodje ^{44}, Iwelumo ^{45}, Zheng-Zhi ^{80}	22,866
17	24	A	Preston NE	W 2-0	1-0	3	Zheng-Zhi ^{45}, Varney ^{90}	12,532
18	27	H	Sheffield U	L 0-3	0-1	—		20,737
19	Dec 1	H	Burnley	L 1-3	1-2	4	Reid ^{36}	21,122
20	4	A	Cardiff C	W 2-0	1-0	—	Holland ^{34}, Reid (pen) ^{79}	11,874
21	8	H	Ipswich T	W 3-1	3-0	3	Ambrose 2 $^{5, 39}$, Iwelumo ^{30}	24,680
22	15	A	WBA	L 2-4	1-1	5	Iwelumo ^{37}, McLeod ^{73}	20,346
23	22	H	Hull C	D 1-1	0-1	5	Bougherra ^{57}	22,040
24	26	A	Norwich C	D 1-1	1-0	8	Zheng-Zhi ^{21}	25,327
25	29	A	Leicester C	D 1-1	0-0	5	McCarthy ^{90}	23,667
26	Jan 1	H	Colchester U	L 1-2	1-2	5	Varney ^{45}	21,508
27	12	H	Blackpool	W 4-1	3-1	5	Bougherra ^{6}, Varney ^{10}, Zheng-Zhi 2 $^{24, 52}$	21,412
28	19	A	Watford	D 1-1	0-0	6	Ambrose ^{78}	17,214
29	29	H	Stoke C	W 1-0	0-0	—	Sam ^{83}	22,108
30	Feb 2	A	Scunthorpe U	L 0-1	0-0	5		6084
31	8	H	Crystal Palace	W 2-0	0-0	—	Varney 2 $^{60, 87}$	26,202
32	12	A	Sheffield W	D 0-0	0-0	—		17,211
33	16	H	Watford	D 2-2	2-0	—	Ambrose ^{15}, Shittu (og) ^{36}	26,337
34	23	A	Blackpool	L 3-5	2-2	6	Ambrose 2 $^{29, 30}$, Fortune ^{74}	9134
35	Mar 1	A	Sheffield U	W 2-0	1-0	5	Iwelumo ^{45}, Sodje ^{82}	23,180
36	4	H	Bristol C	D 1-1	1-0	—	Ambrose ^{8}	24,075
37	8	H	Preston NE	L 1-2	0-1	5	McCarthy ^{74}	25,124
38	11	A	Burnley	L 0-1	0-0	—		10,700
39	15	A	Ipswich T	L 0-2	0-1	9		23,539
40	21	H	WBA	D 1-1	1-1	—	Halford ^{30}	23,412
41	29	H	Wolverhampton W	L 2-3	1-1	11	Halford ^{31}, Lita ^{90}	23,187
42	Apr 5	A	Plymouth Arg	W 2-1	0-0	8	Lita 2 $^{65, 76}$	14,715
43	12	H	Southampton	D 1-1	0-1	9	Gray ^{69}	26,206
44	19	A	QPR	L 0-1	0-1	11		17,035
45	26	A	Barnsley	L 0-3	0-2	12		11,228
46	May 4	H	Coventry C	W 4-1	2-1	11	Varney ^{4}, Gray ^{19}, Basey ^{48}, Powell ^{86}	26,130

Final League Position: 11

GOALSCORERS

League (63): Iwelumo 10, Varney 8, Ambrose 7, Zheng-Zhi 7, Reid 5 (3 pens), Lita 3, Bougherra 2, Fortune 2, Gray 2, Halford 2, McCarthy 2, Sam 2, Sodje 2, Todorov 2, Basey 1, Bent 1, Holland 1, McLeod 1, Powell 1, own goals 2.
Carling Cup (7): Ambrose 1, McCarthy 1, Reid 1 (pen), Sam 1, Sinclair 1, Todorov 1, Zheng-Zhi 1 (pen).
FA Cup (3): Ambrose 1, Dickson 1, Zheng-Zhi 1.

Weaver N 45	Moutaouakil Y 7 + 3	Thatcher B 11	Semedo J 28 + 9	McCarthy P 27 + 2	Bougherra M 24 + 5	Sam L 24 + 4	Reid A 21 + 1	Todorov S 3 + 4	Bent M 3	Ambrose D 29 + 8	Iwelumo C 32 + 14	McLeod I 2 + 16	Fortune J 25 + 1	Thomas J 20 + 12	Zheng-Zhi 38 + 4	Faye A — + 1	Mills D 19	Powell C 16 + 1	Racon T 1 + 3	Varney L 23 + 16	Sodje S 20 + 7	Holland M 28 + 3	Basey G 8	Sankofa O — + 1	Youga K 11	Dickson C — + 2	Gray A 10 + 6	Halford G 16	Cook L 4 + 5	Sinclair S — + 3	Lita L 8	Elliot R — + 1	Randolph D 1	Shelvey J 2	Wagstaff S — + 2	Match No.
1	2	3	4	5	6	7	8	9[2]	10[1]	11	12	13																								1
1	2[1]	3	4	12	6	7[3]	8		9	11	13	10[2]	5	14																						2
1		2[2]	4	3	6[3]		8	12	9[1]	11	10		5	7	13	14																				3
1			4[3]	5			8	12		11	9[2]	13	6	7[1]	10		2	3	14																	4
1			4	5		12	13	10[1]		11	9[3]		6	7[2]	8		2	3		14																5
1			4		6	7[1]	8			12	9	13	5		10[3]		2	3		11[2]	14															6
1			4		6	7[1]	8[3]			12	9	13	5		10		2	3		11[2]	14															7
1			4		6	7[2]	8				9	12	5		10		2	3		11[1]		13														8
1			4[2]		6	7■	8				9	13	5	12	10[3]		2	3		11[1]	14															9
1			4		6		8	12		7[2]	9		5[3]	13	10		2	3		11[1]	14															10
1			4		6[1]		8	13		7[2]	9		5	12	10		2	3[3]		11	14															11
1	2		4[2]		6		8	10[1]			9	12	5[3]	13	11		3			7	14															12
1			4[2]			7[3]	8				9[1]	12	5	13	10		2		14	11	6		3													13
1	12		4■			7[1]	8[2]			13	9		5	11[3]	10		2			14	6		3													14
1					12	7[3]	8			13	9		5	11	10[2]		2		4[1]	14	6		3													15
1			4			7[2]	8			13	9[3]	12	5	11	10[1]		2			14	6		3													16
1			4[1]			7[2]	8[3]			13	9		5	11	10		2			14	6	12	3													17
1			4[3]		12	7[2]	8				9		5	11	10		2			13	6	14	3[1]													18
1					12	13	8			7	9	14	5		10[2]		2	3		11[3]	6[1]	4														19
1			12			7[3]	8			11[1]	9[2]	13	5		10		2	3		14	6	4														20
1			12		13	7[1]	8[3]			11	9		5■		10		2	3[2]		14	6	4														21
1			4		5		8[3]			7[2]	9[1]	12		11	10			3		13	2	6		14												22
1			12	13	6	7[3]				8	9	14		11	10		2■	3[1]			5[2]	4														23
1			4	5	2	13					9[1]	12[2]		11	10			3	14	7[3]	6■	8														24
1	12		4[2]	5	2	13					9		6[1]	11	10			3		7		8														25
1	12		4[1]	5[3]	2	7				13	9		6	11	10			3[2]		14		8														26
1	2			5	6	7[2]				11[3]	12	8[1]		13	10					9		4			3	14										27
1	2			5	6[1]	7[2]				8	9[3]		12		10					11		4			3	13	14									28
1	2		12	5	6	7[1]				11[2]	9[3]			13	10					14		4			3		8									29
1	2[1]			5	6	7[3]				11	13	12		14	10					9[2]		4			3		8									30
1			12	5	6	7				11[1]	13	14			10					9[3]		4			3		8[2]	2								31
1			12	5		7[3]				11	13		6		10					9		4			3[1]		8[2]	2	14							32
1				5		7[2]				11[3]	12		6	13	10					9		4			3		8[1]	2	14							33
1			12	5						7	13		6	14	10[1]					9		4	3				8[2]	2	11[3]							34
1			12	5						7[1]	9			11	10					8[2]	6	4			3			2		13						35
1				5						7[2]	9			11[3]	10					8[1]	6	4			3		12	2	13	14						36
1				5		7[3]				11	12				10					8[2]	6	4			3		13	2[1]		14	9					37
1		3	4[2]	5						7[3]	12			11	13					14	6	8					10[1]	2			9					38
1		3	4[1]	5						7	12			11	10[2]					13	6	8					14	2			9[3]					39
1		3	4[2]	5						7[3]	12			11	13						6	8					10	2	14		9[1]					40
1		3	4[2]	5						7[1]	9			11[3]	12					13	6	8						2	14		10					41
1■		3	4	5	12						9[2]				10					13	6[1]	7						2	11[G]		8	15				42
		3	4[1]	5	6					12	8[3]			13	10[2]							7					14	2	11		9		1			43
1		3	12	5	6					7	13				10[1]					14		4					8[2]	2	11[3]		9					44
1		3	4[3]	5	6[1]					7[2]	9									10	12	8					13	2						11	14	45
1				5	6						12			7[3]				13		9		4	3[1]		11		10	2						8[2]	14	46

FA Cup

Third Round	WBA	(h)	1-1	
		(a)	2-2	

Carling Cup

First Round	Swindon T	(a)	2-0
Second Round	Stockport Co	(h)	4-3
Third Round	Luton T	(a)	1-3

CHELSEA FA Premiership

FOUNDATION

Chelsea may never have existed but for the fact that Fulham rejected an offer to rent the Stamford Bridge ground from Mr H. A. Mears who had owned it since 1904. Fortunately he was determined to develop it as a football stadium rather than sell it to the Great Western Railway and got together with Frederick Parker, who persuaded Mears of the financial advantages of developing a major sporting venue. Chelsea FC was formed in 1905, and when admission to the Southern League was denied, they immediately gained admission to the Second Division of the Football League.

Stamford Bridge, Fulham Road, London SW6 1HS.

Telephone: 0871 984 1955.

Fax: (020) 7381 4831.

Ticket Office: 0871 984 1905.

Website: www.chelseafc.com

Ground Capacity: 41,841.

Record Attendance: 82,905 v Arsenal, Division 1, 12 October 1935.

Pitch Measurements: 103m × 67m.

Chairman: Bruce Buck.

Director: Eugene Tenenbaum.

Chief Executive: Peter Kenyon.

Secretary: David Barnard.

Manager: Luiz Felipe Scolari.

Assistant Manager: Steve Clarke.

Physio: Dave Hancock.

Colours: Reflex blue shirt, reflex blue shorts, white stockings.

Change Colours: All black with white trim.

Year Formed: 1905.

Turned Professional: 1905.

Ltd Co.: 1905.

Club Nickname: 'The Blues'.

Ground: 1905, Stamford Bridge.

First Football League Game: 2 September 1905, Division 2, v Stockport Co (a) L 0–1 – Foulke; Mackie, McEwan; Key, Harris, Miller; Moran, J. T. Robertson, Copeland, Windridge, Kirwan.

Record League Victory: 9–2 v Glossop N E, Division 2, 1 September 1906 – Byrne; Walton, Miller; Key (1), McRoberts, Henderson; Moran, McDermott (1), Hilsdon (5), Copeland (1), Kirwan (1).

HONOURS

FA Premier League: Champions 2004–05, 2005–06. Runners-up 2003–04, 2006–07, 2007–08.

Football League: Division 1 – Champions 1954–55; Division 2 – Champions 1983–84, 1988–89; Runners-up 1906–07, 1911–12, 1929–30, 1962–63, 1976–77.

FA Cup: Winners 1970, 1997, 2000, 2007. Runners-up 1915, 1967, 1994, 2002.

Football League Cup: Winners 1965, 1998, 2005, 2007; Runners-up 1972, 2008.

Full Members' Cup: Winners 1986.

Zenith Data Systems Cup: Winners 1990.

European Competitions: *Champions League:* 1999–2000, 2003–04 (semi-finals), 2004–05 (semi-finals), 2005–06, 2006–07 (semi-finals), 2007–08 (runners-up). *European Fairs Cup:* 1958–60, 1965–66, 1968–69. *European Cup-Winners' Cup:* 1970–71 (winners), 1971–72, 1994–95, 1997–98 (winners), 1998–99 (semi-finals). *UEFA Cup:* 2000–01, 2001–02, 2002–03. *Super Cup:* 1998–99 (winners).

SKY SPORTS FACT FILE

On 16 February 2008 Frank Lampard chose a suitable time to record his 100th and 101st goals for Chelsea in the FA Cup tie against Huddersfield Town to end the fightback by the Yorkshire club. His goals came in the 18th and 60th minutes during the 3–1 win.

Record Cup Victory: 13–0 v Jeunesse Hautcharage, ECWC, 1st rd 2nd leg, 29 September 1971 – Bonetti; Boyle, Harris (1), Hollins (1p), Webb (1), Hinton, Cooke, Baldwin (3), Osgood (5), Hudson (1), Houseman (1).

Record Defeat: 1–8 v Wolverhampton W, Division 1, 26 September 1953.

Most League Points (2 for a win): 57, Division 2, 1906–07.

Most League Points (3 for a win): 99, Division 2, 1988–89.

Most League Goals: 98, Division 1, 1960–61.

Highest League Scorer in Season: Jimmy Greaves, 41, 1960–61.

Most League Goals in Total Aggregate: Bobby Tambling, 164, 1958–70.

Most League Goals in One Match: 5, George Hilsdon v Glossop, Division 2, 1 September 1906; 5, Jimmy Greaves v Wolverhampton W, Division 1, 30 August 1958; 5, Jimmy Greaves v Preston NE, Division 1, 19 December 1959; 5, Jimmy Greaves v WBA, Division 1, 3 December 1960; 5, Bobby Tambling v Aston Villa, Division 1, 17 September 1966; 5, Gordon Durie v Walsall, Division 2, 4 February 1989.

Most Capped Player: Marcel Desailly, 67 (116), France.

Most League Appearances: Ron Harris, 655, 1962–80.

Youngest League Player: Ian Hamilton, 16 years 138 days v Tottenham H, 18 March 1967.

Record Transfer Fee Received: £12,000,000 from Rangers for Tore Andre Flo, November 2000.

Record Transfer Fee Paid: £29,500,000 to AC Milan for Andriy Shevchenko, June 2006.

Football League Record: 1905 Elected to Division 2; 1907–10 Division 1; 1910–12 Division 2; 1912–24 Division 1; 1924–30 Division 2; 1930–62 Division 1; 1962–63 Division 2; 1963–75 Division 1; 1975–77 Division 2; 1977–79 Division 1; 1979–84 Division 2; 1984–88 Division 1; 1988–89 Division 2; 1989–92 Division 1; 1992– FA Premier League.

MANAGERS

John Tait Robertson 1905–07
David Calderhead 1907–33
Leslie Knighton 1933–39
Billy Birrell 1939–52
Ted Drake 1952–61
Tommy Docherty 1961–67
Dave Sexton 1967–74
Ron Suart 1974–75
Eddie McCreadie 1975–77
Ken Shellito 1977–78
Danny Blanchflower 1978–79
Geoff Hurst 1979–81
John Neal 1981–85 *(Director to 1986)*
John Hollins 1985–88
Bobby Campbell 1988–91
Ian Porterfield 1991–93
David Webb 1993
Glenn Hoddle 1993–96
Ruud Gullit 1996–98
Gianluca Vialli 1998–2000
Claudio Ranieri 2000–04
Jose Mourinho 2004–07
Avram Grant 2007–08
Luiz Felipe Scolari June 2008–

LATEST SEQUENCES

Longest Sequence of League Wins: 10, 19.11.2005 – 15.1.2006.

Longest Sequence of League Defeats: 7, 1.11.1952 – 20.12.1952.

Longest Sequence of League Draws: 6, 20.8.1969 – 13.9.1969.

Longest Sequence of Unbeaten League Matches: 40, 23.10.2004 – 29.10.2005.

Longest Sequence Without a League Win: 21, 3.11.1987 – 2.4.1988.

Successive Scoring Runs: 27 from 29.10.1988.

Successive Non-scoring Runs: 9 from 14.3.1981.

TEN YEAR LEAGUE RECORD

		P	*W*	*D*	*L*	*F*	*A*	*Pts*	*Pos*
1998-99	PR Lge	38	20	15	3	57	30	75	3
1999-2000	PR Lge	38	18	11	9	53	34	65	5
2000-01	PR Lge	38	17	10	11	68	45	61	6
2001-02	PR Lge	38	17	13	8	66	38	64	6
2002-03	PR Lge	38	19	10	9	68	38	67	4
2003-04	PR Lge	38	24	7	7	67	30	79	2
2004-05	PR Lge	38	29	8	1	72	15	95	1
2005-06	PR Lge	38	29	4	5	72	22	91	1
2006-07	PR Lge	38	24	11	3	64	24	83	2
2007-08	PR Lge	38	25	10	3	65	26	85	2

DID YOU KNOW ?

When Chelsea paid £15 million for the signature of Nicolas Anelka from Bolton Wanderers, they had captured the most expensive player in the world at the time. His eight moves to various clubs since starting his career with Paris St Germain have aggregated transfer fees amounting to £87 million.

CHELSEA 2007–08 LEAGUE RECORD

Match No.	Date	Venue	Opponents	Result	H/T Score	Lg. Pos.	Goalscorers	Attendance
1	Aug 12	H	Birmingham C	W 3-2	2-2	—	Pizarro ^{17}, Malouda ^{31}, Essien ^{50}	41,590
2	15	A	Reading	W 2-1	0-1	—	Lampard ^{47}, Drogba ^{50}	24,031
3	19	A	Liverpool	D 1-1	0-1	2	Lampard (pen) ^{62}	43,924
4	25	H	Portsmouth	W 1-0	1-0	1	Lampard ^{31}	41,501
5	Sept 2	A	Aston Villa	L 0-2	0-0	4		37,714
6	15	H	Blackburn R	D 0-0	0-0	5		41,062
7	23	A	Manchester U	L 0-2	0-1	6		75,663
8	29	H	Fulham	D 0-0	0-0	8		41,837
9	Oct 7	A	Bolton W	W 1-0	1-0	7	Kalou ^{41}	20,059
10	20	A	Middlesbrough	W 2-0	1-0	7	Drogba ^{8}, Alex ^{57}	27,699
11	27	H	Manchester C	W 6-0	2-0	4	Essien ^{16}, Drogba 2 $^{31, 56}$, Cole J ^{60}, Kalou ^{75}, Shevchenko ^{90}	41,832
12	Nov 3	A	Wigan Ath	W 2-0	2-0	3	Lampard ^{11}, Belletti ^{18}	19,011
13	11	H	Everton	D 1-1	0-0	4	Drogba ^{70}	41,683
14	24	A	Derby Co	W 2-0	1-0	4	Kalou ^{17}, Wright-Phillips ^{73}	32,789
15	Dec 1	H	West Ham U	W 1-0	0-0	2	Cole J ^{76}	41,830
16	8	H	Sunderland	W 2-0	1-0	3	Shevchenko ^{23}, Lampard (pen) ^{75}	41,707
17	16	A	Arsenal	L 0-1	0-1	3		60,139
18	23	A	Blackburn R	W 1-0	1-0	3	Cole J ^{22}	23,966
19	26	H	Aston Villa	D 4-4	1-2	3	Shevchenko 2 (1 pen) $^{45 (p), 50}$, Alex ^{66}, Ballack ^{88}	41,686
20	29	H	Newcastle U	W 2-1	1-0	3	Essien ^{29}, Kalou ^{87}	41,751
21	Jan 1	A	Fulham	W 2-1	0-1	3	Kalou ^{54}, Ballack (pen) ^{62}	25,357
22	12	H	Tottenham H	W 2-0	1-0	3	Belletti ^{19}, Wright-Phillips ^{80}	41,777
23	19	A	Birmingham C	W 1-0	0-0	3	Pizarro ^{79}	26,567
24	30	H	Reading	W 1-0	1-0	—	Ballack ^{32}	41,171
25	Feb 2	A	Portsmouth	D 1-1	0-0	3	Anelka ^{55}	20,488
26	10	H	Liverpool	D 0-0	0-0	3		41,788
27	Mar 1	A	West Ham U	W 4-0	3-0	3	Lampard (pen) ^{17}, Cole J ^{20}, Ballack ^{22}, Cole A ^{64}	34,969
28	12	H	Derby Co	W 6-1	2-0	—	Lampard 4 (1 pen) $^{28 (p), 57, 66, 72}$, Kalou ^{42}, Cole J ^{64}	39,447
29	15	A	Sunderland	W 1-0	1-0	3	Terry ^{10}	44,679
30	19	A	Tottenham H	D 4-4	2-1	—	Drogba ^{3}, Essien ^{20}, Cole J 2 $^{52, 80}$	36,178
31	23	H	Arsenal	W 2-1	0-0	2	Drogba 2 $^{73, 82}$	41,824
32	30	H	Middlesbrough	W 1-0	1-0	2	Ricardo Carvalho ^{6}	39,993
33	Apr 5	A	Manchester C	W 2-0	1-0	2	Dunne (og) ^{6}, Kalou ^{53}	42,594
34	14	H	Wigan Ath	D 1-1	0-0	—	Essien ^{55}	40,487
35	17	A	Everton	W 1-0	1-0	—	Essien ^{41}	37,112
36	26	H	Manchester U	W 2-1	1-0	2	Ballack 2 (1 pen) $^{45, 86 (p)}$	41,828
37	May 5	A	Newcastle U	W 2-0	0-0	—	Ballack ^{61}, Malouda ^{82}	52,305
38	11	H	Bolton W	D 1-1	0-0	2	Shevchenko ^{62}	41,755

Final League Position: 2

GOALSCORERS

League (65): Lampard 10 (4 pens), Drogba 8, Ballack 7 (2 pens), Cole J 7, Kalou 7, Essien 6, Shevchenko 5 (1 pen), Alex 2, Belletti 2, Malouda 2, Pizarro 2, Wright-Phillips 2, Anelka 1, Cole A 1, Ricardo Carvalho 1, Terry 1, own goal 1.
Carling Cup (14): Lampard 4, Kalou 2, Shevchenko 2, Cole J 1, Drogba 1, Sidwell 1, Sinclair 1, Wright-Phillips 1, own goal 1.
FA Cup (6): Lampard 2, Anelka 1, Kalou 1, Wright-Phillips 1, own goal 1.
Champions League (20): Drogba 6, Lampard 4 (1 pen), Ballack 2, Cole J 2, Alex 1, Kalou 1, Malouda 1, Shevchenko 1, own goals 2.
Community Shield (1): Malouda 1.

Cech P 26	Johnson G 1 + 1	Cole A 27	Essien M 23 + 4	Ben Haim T 10 + 3	Ricardo Carvalho21	Wright-Phillips S 20 + 7	Lampard F 23 + 1	Pizarro C 4 + 17	Kalou S 24 + 6	Malouda F 16 + 5	Drogba D 17 + 2	Mikel J 21 + 8	Sidwell S 7 + 8	Paulo Ferreira15 + 3	Terry J 23	Cole J 28 + 5	Alex22 + 6	Belletti J 20 + 3	Makelele C 15 + 3	Shevchenko A 8 + 9	Bridge W 9 + 2	Cudicini C 10	Hilario2 + 1	Ballack M 16 + 2	Sinclair S — + 1	Anelka N 10 + 4	*Match No.*
1	2	3	4²	5	6	7	8	9¹	10	11³	12	13	14														1
1	12	3		5	6¹	7	8	13	10	11	9	14	4³	2²													2
1		3	2	6		7²	8	12	10¹	11³	9	4			5	13	14										3
1		3	2	6		7²	8	10¹	12	11	9	4³			5	13		14									4
1		3	8			7³		12	13	11	9	10¹			5	14	6	2	4²								5
1		3¹	4	12		7²			9	13		14	8³		5	11	6	2		10							6
1		3	7	6		12		13	14	11¹		8		2	5	9²			4	10³							7
1		3²		6				12	11	13	9■		8		5³	7	14	2	4	10¹							8
1		3			6		8	12	9¹	11²			7	14	5	10³		2	4	13							9
1			7²		6	12	8			11¹	9³	4	13	3		10	5	2		14							10
1			7		6		8	12	10		9¹	4		3		11²	5	2		13							11
1			10²		6	7	8		12	11	9¹	4	13				5	2			3						12
			7	12	6¹	11²	8		13		9	4				10	5	2			3	1					13
		3	12■	6		11	8²	13	9			4	7¹		5			2		10		1					14
						12	8		11		9	4	7¹		5	10²	6	2	13		3	1					15
		3				7	8	12	9¹			4	13		5	11²	6	2		10		1					16
1		3		12		7²	8	14	13			11		2	5¹	10	6		4³	9							17
1G		3	7		6	12	8	13	10			4		2		11²	5			9¹			15				18
1		3■	4		6■	12	8³	9²	7			13		2		11	5			10¹				14			19
			7	6		11²		12	9			4	13			10¹	5	2			3		1	8³	14		20
			4	5		7¹		12	9			13	8²	14		10³	6	2			3		1	11			21
1		3			6	7¹		9³		11²			12			10	5	2	4		13			8		14	22
1		3			6	7¹		12		11³			13			10²	5	2	4		14			8		9	23
1					6	7²		12		11¹			13	2		10	5		4		3			8		9	24
1		3		6		7		12		11¹						10	5	2	4					8		9	25
1		3			6	11²	8³	12		13		14				10¹	5	2	4					7		9	26
1		3	12		6		8■		11²	13				2	5	10¹	14		4³					7		9	27
		3	12		6		8		10		13			2	5	11³			4¹	14		1		7²		9	28
		3	12			13	8		10		9	4		2	5	11²	6					1		7¹			29
		3	7		6		8		10¹		9			2²	5	11³	12		4	13		1		14			30
		3	2		6		8		10		9	12			5	11¹		13	4³			1		7²		14	31
			8		6	12			10³		9²	4			5	11	13	2			3	1		7¹		14	32
		3	7			11¹	8		10			4		13	5	12	6	2²				1				9	33
1			8						10	11¹		4²			5	12	6	2		13	3			7		9	34
1		3	8		6	7²			10	12		4		2	5	11¹			13							9	35
1		3	8		6				10²		9	4		2³	5	11¹			12	13				7		14	36
1			7		6²		12			11	9³	4		2	5		13			14	3			8		10¹	37
1		3	2				8			11	9	12			5²	10¹	6	13	4³	14				7			38

Champions League

Group B	Rosenborg	(h)	1-1
	Valencia	(a)	2-1
	Schalke	(h)	2-0
		(a)	0-0
	Rosenborg	(a)	4-0
	Valencia	(h)	0-0
Knock-Out Round	Olympiakos	(a)	0-0
		(h)	3-0
Quarter-Final	Fenerbahce	(a)	1-2
		(h)	2-0
Semi-Final	Liverpool	(a)	1-1
		(h)	3-2
Final *(in Moscow)*	Manchester U		1-1

FA Cup

Third Round	QPR	(h)	1-0
Fourth Round	Wigan Ath	(a)	2-1
Fifth Round	Huddersfield T	(h)	3-1
Sixth Round	Barnsley	(a)	0-1

Carling Cup

Third Round	Hull C	(a)	4-0
Fourth Round	Leicester C	(h)	4-3
Quarter-Final	Liverpool	(h)	2-0
Semi-Final	Everton	(h)	2-1
		(a)	1-0
Final *(at Wembley)*	Tottenham H		1-2

Community Shield

	Manchester U		1-1

CHELTENHAM TOWN FL Championship 1

FOUNDATION

Although a scratch team representing Cheltenham played a match against Gloucester in 1884, the earliest recorded match for Cheltenham Town FC was a friendly against Dean Close School on 12 March 1892. The School won 4–3 and the match was played at Prestbury (half a mile from Whaddon Road). Cheltenham Town played Wednesday afternoon friendlies at a local cricket ground until entering the Mid Gloucester League. In those days the club played in deep red coloured shirts and were nicknamed 'the Rubies'. The club moved to Whaddon Lane for season 1901–02 and changed to red and white colours two years later.

Whaddon Road, Cheltenham, Gloucestershire GL52 5NA.

Telephone: (01242) 573 558.

Fax: (01242) 224 675.

Ticket Office: (01242) 573 558 (option 1).

Website: www.ctfc.com

Email: info@ctfc.com

Ground Capacity: 7,136.

Record Attendance: at Whaddon Road: 8,326 v Reading, FA Cup 1st rd, 17 November 1956; at Cheltenham Athletic Ground: 10,389 v Blackpool, FA Cup 3rd rd, 13 January 1934.

Pitch Measurements: 112yd × 72yd.

Chairman: Paul Baker.

Vice-chairman: Colin Farmer.

Chief Executive: Nick Hale.

Secretary: Paul Godfrey.

Manager: Keith Downing.

Assistant Manager: Bob Bloomer.

Physio: Ian Weston.

Colours: All red with white trim.

Change Colours: All yellow with red trim.

Year Formed: 1892.

Turned Professional: 1932.

Ltd Co.: 1937.

Club Nickname: 'The Robins'.

Grounds: Grafton Cricket Ground, Whaddon Lane, Carter's Field (pre 1932).

HONOURS

Football League: Promoted from Division 3 (play-offs) 2001–02; Promoted from FL 2 (play-offs) 2005–06.

FA Cup: best season: 5th rd 2002.

Football League Cup: never past 2nd rd.

Football Conference: Champions 1998–99, runners-up 1997–98.

Trophy: Winners 1997–98.

Southern League: Champions 1984–85; *Southern League Cup:* Winners 1957–58, runners-up 1968–69, 1984–85; *Southern League Merit Cup:* Winners 1984–85; *Southern League Championship Shield:* Winners 1985.

Gloucestershire Senior Cup: Winners 1998–99; *Gloucestershire Northern Senior Professional Cup:* Winners 30 times; *Midland Floodlit Cup:* Winners 1985–86, 1986–87, 1987–88; *Mid Gloucester League:* Champions 1896–97; *Gloucester and District League:* Champions 1902–03, 1905–06; *Cheltenham League:* Champions 1910–11, 1913–14; *North Gloucestershire League:* Champions 1913–14; *Gloucestershire Northern Senior League:* Champions 1928–29, 1932–33; *Gloucestershire Northern Senior Amateur Cup:* Winners 1929–30, 1930–31, 1932–33, 1933–34, 1934–35; *Leamington Hospital Cup:* Winners 1934–35.

SKY SPORTS FACT FILE

In 1933–34 Cheltenham Town fought their way to the third round of the FA Cup beating Carlisle United at Carlisle while members of the comparatively modest Birmingham Combination. Two years later they entered the Southern League.

Record League Victory: 11–0 v Bourneville Ath, Birmingham Combination, 29 April 1933 – Davis; Jones, Williams; Lang (1), Blackburn, Draper; Evans, Hazard (4), Haycox (4), Goodger (1), Hill (1).

Record Cup Victory: 12–0 v Chippenham R, FA Cup 3rd qual. rd, 2 November 1935 – Bowles; Whitehouse, Williams; Lang, Devonport (1), Partridge (2); Perkins, Hackett, Jones (4), Black (4), Griffiths (1).

Record Defeat: 0–7 v Crystal Palace, League Cup 2nd rd, 2 October 2002.
N.B. 1–10 v Merthyr T, Southern League, 8 March 1952.

Most League Points (2 for a win): 60, Southern League Division 1, 1963–64.

Most League Points (3 for a win): 78, Division 3, 2001–02.

Most League Goals: 66, Division 3, 2001–02.

Highest League Scorer in Season: Julian Alsop, 20, Division 3, 2001–02.

Most League Goals in Total Aggregate: Martin Devaney, 38, 1999–2005.

Most Capped Player: Grant McCann, 7 (16), Northern Ireland.

Most League Appearances: Jamie Victory, 258, 1999–.

Record Transfer Fee Received: £200,000 from Barnsley for Kayode Odejayi, June 2007.

Record Transfer Fee Paid: £50,000 to West Ham U for Grant McCann, January 2003 and £50,000 to Stoke C for Brian Wilson, March 2004.

Football League Record: 1999 Promoted to Division 3; 2002 Division 2; 2003–04 Division 3; 2004–06 FL 2; 2006– FL 1.

MANAGERS

George Blackburn 1932–34
George Carr 1934–37
Jimmy Brain 1937–48
Cyril Dean 1948–50
George Summerbee 1950–52
William Raeside 1952–53
Arch Anderson 1953–58
Ron Lewin 1958–60
Peter Donnelly 1960–61
Tommy Cavanagh 1961
Arch Anderson 1961–65
Harold Fletcher 1965–66
Bob Etheridge 1966–73
Willie Penman 1973–74
Dennis Allen 1974–79
Terry Paine 1979
Alan Grundy 1979–82
Alan Wood 1982–83
John Murphy 1983–88
Jim Barron 1988–90
John Murphy 1990
Dave Lewis 1990–91
Ally Robertson 1991–92
Lindsay Parsons 1992–95
Chris Robinson 1995–97
Steve Cotterill 1997–2002
Graham Allner 2002–03
Bobby Gould 2003
John Ward 2003–07
Keith Downing October 2007–

LATEST SEQUENCES

Longest Sequence of League Wins: 4, 29.4.2006 – 8.8.2006.

Longest Sequence of League Defeats: 5, 13.1.2001 – 13.2.2001.

Longest Sequence of League Draws: 5, 5.4.2003 – 21.4.2003.

Longest Sequence of Unbeaten League Matches: 16, 1.12.2001 – 12.3.2002.

Longest Sequence Without a League Win: 11, 18.9.2007 – 17.11.2007.

Successive Scoring Runs: 15 from 15.2.2003.

Successive Non-scoring Runs: 4 from 12.9.1999.

TEN YEAR LEAGUE RECORD

		P	*W*	*D*	*L*	*F*	*A*	*Pts*	*Pos*
1998-99	Conf.	42	22	14	6	71	36	80	1
1999-2000	Div 3	46	20	10	16	50	42	70	8
2000-01	Div 3	46	18	14	14	59	52	68	9
2001-02	Div 3	46	21	15	10	66	49	78	4
2002-03	Div 2	46	10	18	18	53	68	48	21
2003-04	Div 3	46	14	14	18	57	71	56	14
2004-05	FL 2	46	16	12	18	51	54	60	14
2005-06	FL 2	46	19	15	12	65	53	72	5
2006-07	FL 1	46	15	9	22	49	61	54	17
2007-08	FL 1	46	13	12	21	42	64	51	19

DID YOU KNOW ?

In 1950–51 Cheltenham Town had a successful season in the Southern League finishing sixth. But the nucleus of this team was broken up the following season when Frank Allcock and Johnny McIlvenny joined Bristol Rovers, Peter Rushworth, son of the club chairman, went to Leicester City and leading scorer Roy Shiner joined Huddersfield Town in December 1951.

CHELTENHAM TOWN 2007–08 LEAGUE RECORD

Match No.	Date	Venue	Opponents	Result	H/T Score	Lg. Pos.	Goalscorers	Attendance
1	Aug 11	H	Gillingham	W 1-0	1-0	—	Gillespie 24	4008
2	18	A	Millwall	L 0-1	0-1	12		8671
3	25	H	Swindon T	D 1-1	0-1	12	Vincent 72	5442
4	Sept 1	A	Carlisle U	L 0-1	0-0	15		6125
5	15	A	Huddersfield T	W 3-2	0-0	13	Spencer 2 62, 78, Finnigan 83	8756
6	18	H	Swansea C	L 1-2	1-0	—	Vincent 4	4323
7	22	H	Tranmere R	D 1-1	0-1	16	Caines 50	3742
8	29	A	Doncaster R	L 0-2	0-1	18		6150
9	Oct 2	A	Port Vale	L 0-3	0-1	—		3102
10	6	H	Oldham Ath	D 1-1	1-0	21	Townsend (pen) 45	3621
11	13	H	Nottingham F	L 0-3	0-2	22		5012
12	20	A	Northampton T	L 1-2	0-1	22	Spencer 50	5012
13	27	H	Crewe Alex	D 2-2	0-0	23	Wright 85, Bird 89	3605
14	Nov 3	A	Walsall	L 0-2	0-1	24		4810
15	6	H	Yeovil T	D 1-1	0-1	—	Caines 89	3169
16	17	A	Southend U	D 2-2	2-0	24	Gillespie 14, Sinclair 25	7158
17	25	H	Leeds U	W 1-0	0-0	21	Gillespie 86	7043
18	Dec 8	A	Leyton Orient	L 0-2	0-1	22		4156
19	14	H	Luton T	W 1-0	1-0	—	Lindegaard 2	3702
20	22	H	Huddersfield T	L 0-2	0-1	21		3998
21	26	A	Swansea C	L 1-4	0-2	22	Gillespie 82	14,049
22	29	A	Tranmere R	L 0-1	0-0	23		6111
23	Jan 2	H	Port Vale	W 1-0	1-0	—	Connor 22	3221
24	12	H	Bournemouth	W 1-0	0-0	21	Bird 90	3959
25	18	A	Hartlepool U	W 2-0	1-0	—	Gillespie 2 11, 84	4120
26	25	H	Carlisle U	W 1-0	1-0	—	Gillespie 20	4221
27	29	H	Millwall	L 0-1	0-0	—		3812
28	Feb 2	A	Gillingham	D 0-0	0-0	19		4993
29	5	A	Bristol R	L 0-2	0-1	—		6780
30	9	H	Brighton & HA	W 2-1	0-0	18	Russell 89, Gillespie 90	3963
31	12	A	Swindon T	L 0-3	0-2	—		6483
32	16	H	Hartlepool U	D 1-1	1-0	18	Lindegaard 40	3583
33	19	A	Brighton & HA	L 1-2	1-0	—	Brooker 3	4395
34	23	A	Bournemouth	D 2-2	1-2	19	Bird 45, Brooker 89	4365
35	29	H	Southend U	D 1-1	1-0	—	Brooker 25	3859
36	Mar 8	A	Yeovil T	L 1-2	0-1	20	Brooker 64	4588
37	11	A	Leeds U	W 2-1	1-0	—	Bird 38, Russell 63	20,257
38	15	H	Bristol R	W 1-0	0-0	19	Brooker 80	5187
39	22	A	Luton T	D 1-1	0-1	19	Gillespie 81	6087
40	24	H	Leyton Orient	W 1-0	0-0	17	Connor 47	3988
41	29	H	Northampton T	D 1-1	1-0	17	Gillespie 39	4024
42	Apr 5	A	Nottingham F	L 1-3	1-2	18	Gillespie 20	19,860
43	12	H	Walsall	L 1-2	0-2	19	Connor 74	4861
44	19	A	Crewe Alex	L 1-3	0-1	20	Gillespie 62	5279
45	26	A	Oldham Ath	L 1-2	0-1	20	Gillespie (pen) 50	6400
46	May 3	H	Doncaster R	W 2-1	1-0	19	Gillespie 24, Connor 85	6787

Final League Position: 19

GOALSCORERS

League (42): Gillespie 14 (1 pen), Brooker 5, Bird 4, Connor 4, Spencer 3, Caines 2, Lindegaard 2, Russell 2, Vincent 2, Finnigan 1, Sinclair 1, Townsend 1 (pen), Wright 1.
Carling Cup (1): Finnigan 1.
FA Cup (2): Gillespie 2.
J Paint Trophy (4): Connor 1, Myrie-Williams 1, Reid 1, own goal 1.

Higgs S 46	Gallinagh A 24 + 2	Ridley L 8	Bird D 46	Duff S 30	Gill J 43	Lindegaard A 31 + 10	Finnigan J 10	Gillespie S 35 + 2	Connor P 26 + 13	Vincent A 19 + 18	Yao S — + 5	Reid C 2 + 6	Myrie-Williams J 7 + 5	Townsend M 13	Gill B — + 2	Spencer D 22 + 8	Connolly A 3 + 12	Caines G 22 + 6	Sinclair D 12	Wright A 33	Madjo G 2 + 3	D'Agostino M 14 + 11	Brown S 9 + 11	Russell A 12 + 1	Brooker S 14	Armstrong C 13 + 1	Keogh R 10	Match No.
1	2	3	4	5	6	7^{1}	8	9■	10^{2}	11^{3}	12	13	14															1
1		3	4	5	2	7^{2}	8	9	10	11^{1}			12	6	13													2
1		3	4	5	2	7	8	9^{2}	10^{1}	12			11	6		13												3
1		3	4	5	2	7^{1}	8	12	9	10^{3}			11^{2}	6		14	13											4
1		3	4	5	2	7	8	9^{1}	10^{3}	12^{2}	13			6		11		14										5
1		3	4		2	7^{1}	8		10	11^{2}	12		13	6		9		5										6
1		3	4		2	7	8		10^{1}	11			12	6		9		5										7
1	12	3^{1}	4		2	7^{2}	8^{3}		13	10			11	6		9	14	5										8
1	3^{2}		4	5	2	7■			9^{1}	12	13		11^{3}	6		10	8	14										9
1	3		4	5	2■				10	7^{2}		13	11^{3}	6		9^{1}	12	14	8									10
1	2		4	5			8			12		10^{2}	11^{1}	6		9		13	7	3								11
1	2		4^{3}	5		12	8		10	13		14	11^{2}	6		9^{1}			7	3								12
1			4	5	2	7^{2}		9	10				12	6^{3}		11^{1}	13	14	8	3								13
1			4	5	2	7^{1}			9^{2}	14		10^{3}		6		11	12	13	8	3								14
1			4	5	2	7			9^{1}	11	12					10		6	8	3								15
1			4	5	2			9^{2}	10	11^{1}		13			12	8		6	7	3								16
1			4	5	2	12		9	10^{2}	7^{1}						11		6	8	3	13							17
1			4^{2}	5	2	7^{1}		9	10	12						11^{3}		6	8	3	13	14						18
1			4	5	2	7		9	12							11		6	8	3	10^{1}							19
1	12		4	5^{1}	2	7^{3}		9		13						11		6	8	3	10^{2}	14						20
1	5		4		2	7^{1}		12	9	10^{3}						11	13	6	8^{2}	3		14						21
1	5		4		2	7^{1}		9	10^{2}	12							11^{3}	6		3	13	8	14					22
1	5		4		2	7		9	10	12							8	6		3		11^{1}						23
1	5		4			2		9	12	11^{2}								6		3		7	13	8	10^{1}			24
1	5		4		2	11^{3}		9	12	13								6		3		7^{2}	14	8	10^{1}			25
1	5		4		2	11^{3}		9	12							13		6		3		7^{2}	14	8	10^{1}			26
1	5		4^{1}		2	7^{3}		9								13	12	6		3		11^{2}	14	8	10			27
1	5		4		2	7		9								12		6		3		11^{2}	13	8	10^{1}			28
1	5		4		2	7^{1}		9		12						10		6		3		13	11^{2}	8				29
1	5		4		2	7^{3}		9	12	13								6		3		11^{2}	14	8	10^{1}			30
1	5		4		2^{1}	7^{2}		9	12									6		3		11	13	8	10			31
1	5		4		2	7^{2}		9	12									6		3		11	13	8	10^{1}			32
1	5		4		2	7^{3}		9	12	13								6		3		11^{2}	14		10^{1}	8		33
1	5		4	6	2	7^{3}		9	12	13										3		11^{2}	14■		10	8^{1}		34
1	5		4	6	2			9		7^{1}						11				3		12			10	8		35
1	5		4	6	2	7^{1}		9	12	13										3^{3}		11^{2}		14	10	8		36
1			4	6	2			7	12	13						9^{2}				3				8	10^{1}	11	5	37
1			4	6	2	12		9^{1}	13							11				3		14	7^{3}		10^{2}	8	5	38
1			4	6	2	12		7		11^{1}		13				9^{3}				3		14	8^{2}			10	5	39
1	2		4	6	3	12		9	10^{3}	13						14						7^{2}	11^{1}			8	5	40
1			4	6	2	12		9	10^{2}	11^{3}						13				3		14	7^{1}			8	5	41
1			4	6	2	13		9	10	11^{3}						14	12			3^{1}			7^{2}			8	5	42
1	2^{1}		4	6	3	7		9	10			14					12					13	11^{3}			8^{2}	5	43
1			4	6	2	12		9	10	7^{1}							13			3		14	11^{3}			8^{2}	5	44
1	3^{1}		4	6	2	12		9^{3}	10	7^{2}							14					13		8		11	5	45
1			4	6	2	12		9^{2}	10	7							13			3			11^{1}	8^{3}		14	5	46

FA Cup

First Round	Brighton & HA	(h)	1-1
		(a)	1-2

Carling Cup

First Round	Southend U	(a)	1-4

J Paint Trophy

Second Round	Swindon T	(a)	3-1
Quarter-Final	Brighton & HA	(a)	1-4

CHESTER CITY FL Championship 2

FOUNDATION

All students of soccer history have read about the medieval games of football in Chester, but the present club was not formed until 1884 through the amalgamation of King's School Old Boys with Chester Rovers. For many years Chester were overshadowed in Cheshire by Northwich Victoria and Crewe Alexandra who had both won the Senior Cup several times before Chester's first success in 1894–95. The final against Macclesfield saw Chester face the team that had not only beaten them in the previous year's final, but also knocked them out of the FA Cup two seasons in succession. The final was held at the Drill Field, Northwich and Chester had the support of more than 1000 fans. Chester won 2-1.

Deva Stadium, Bumpers Lane, Chester CH1 4LT.

Telephone: (01244) 371 376.

Fax: (01244) 390 265.

Ticket Offfice: (01244) 371 376.

Website: www.chestercityfc.net

Email: info@chestercityfc.net

Ground Capacity: 5,556.

Record Attendance: 20,500 v Chelsea, FA Cup 3rd rd (replay), 16 January 1952 (at Sealand Road).

Pitch Measurements: 115yd × 75yd.

Chairman: TBC.

Managing Director: Rob Gray.

Secretary: Tony Allen.

Manager: Simon Davies.

Physio: Ben Holt.

Colours: Sky blue and white striped shirts, sky blue shorts, sky blue stockings.

Change Colours: Yellow shirts, yellow shorts, yellow stockings.

Year Formed: 1885.

Turned Professional: 1902.

Ltd Co.: 1909.

Previous Name: Chester until 1983.

Club Nickname: 'Blues' and 'City'.

Grounds: 1885, Faulkner Street; 1898, The Old Showground; 1901, Whipcord Lane; 1906, Sealand Road; 1990, Moss Rose Ground, Macclesfield; 1992, Deva Stadium, Bumpers Lane.

First Football League Game: 2 September 1931, Division 3 (N), v Wrexham (a) D 1–1 – Johnson; Herod, Jones; Keeley, Skitt, Reilly; Thompson, Ranson, Jennings (1), Cresswell, Hedley.

HONOURS

Football League: Division 3 – Runners-up 1993–94; Division 3 (N) – Runners-up 1935–36; Division 4 – Runners-up 1985–86.

Conference: Champions 2003–04.

FA Cup: best season: 5th rd, 1977, 1980.

Football League Cup: Semi-final 1975.

Welsh Cup: Winners 1908, 1933, 1947.

Debenhams Cup: Winners 1977.

SKY SPORTS FACT FILE

Chester manager Frank Brown obtained the signature of Ronnie Hughes in September 1950 in a telephone kiosk! The full-back had been playing for his local club Mold Alexandra and he went on to serve Chester on 399 League occasions alone.

Record League Victory: 12–0 v York C, Division 3 (N), 1 February 1936 – Middleton; Common, Hall; Wharton, Wilson, Howarth; Horsman (2), Hughes, Wrightson (4), Cresswell (2), Sargeant (4).

Record Cup Victory: 6–1 v Darlington, FA Cup 1st rd, 25 November 1933 – Burke; Bennett, Little; Pitcairn, Skitt, Duckworth; Armes (3), Whittam, Mantle (2), Cresswell (1), McLachlan.

Record Defeat: 2–11 v Oldham Ath, Division 3 (N), 19 January 1952.

Most League Points (2 for a win): 56, Division 3 (N), 1946–47 and Division 4, 1964–65.

Most League Points (3 for a win): 84, Division 4, 1985–86.

Most League Goals: 119, Division 4, 1964–65.

Highest League Scorer in Season: Dick Yates, 36, Division 3 (N), 1946–47.

Most League Goals in Total Aggregate: Stuart Rimmer, 135, 1985–88, 1991–98.

Most League Goals in One Match: 5, Tom Jennings v Walsall, Division 3N, 30 January 1932; 5, Barry Jepson v York C, Division 4, 8 February 1958.

Most Capped Player: Angus Eve, 35 (117), Trinidad & Tobago.

Most League Appearances: Ray Gill, 406, 1951–62.

Youngest League Player: Aidan Newhouse, 15 years 350 days v Bury, 7 May 1988.

Record Transfer Fee Received: £300,000 from Liverpool for Ian Rush, May 1980.

Record Transfer Fee Paid: £100,000 to Doncaster R for Gregg Blundell, July 2005.

Football League Record: 1931 Elected Division 3 (N); 1958–75 Division 4; 1975–82 Division 3; 1982–86 Division 4; 1986–92 Division 3; 1992–93 Division 2; 1993–94 Division 3; 1994–95 Division 2; 1995–2000 Division 3; 2000–04 Conference; 2004– FL 2.

MANAGERS

Charlie Hewitt 1930–36
Alex Raisbeck 1936–38
Frank Brown 1938–53
Louis Page 1953–56
John Harris 1956–59
Stan Pearson 1959–61
Bill Lambton 1962–63
Peter Hauser 1963–68
Ken Roberts 1968–76
Alan Oakes 1976–82
Cliff Sear 1982
John Sainty 1982–83
John McGrath 1984
Mick Speight 1985
Harry McNally 1985–92
Graham Barrow 1992–94
Mike Pejic 1994–95
Derek Mann 1995
Kevin Ratcliffe 1995–99
Terry Smith 1999
Ian Atkins 2000
Graham Barrow 2000–01
Gordon Hill 2001
Steve Mungall 2001
Mark Wright 2002–04
Ian Rush 2004–05
Keith Curle 2005–06.
Mark Wright 2006–07
Bobby Williamson 2007–08
Simon Davies March 2008–

LATEST SEQUENCES

Longest Sequence of League Wins: 8, 12.4.1978 – 26.8.1978.

Longest Sequence of League Defeats: 9, 30.4.1994 – 13.9.1994.

Longest Sequence of League Draws: 6, 11.10.1986 – 1.11.1986.

Longest Sequence of Unbeaten League Matches: 18, 27.10.1934 – 16.2.1935.

Longest Sequence Without a League Win: 25, 19.9.1961 – 3.3.1962.

Successive Scoring Runs: 24 from 31.8.1932.

Successive Non-scoring Runs: 5, 17.11.1951.

TEN YEAR LEAGUE RECORD

		P	W	D	L	F	A	Pts	Pos
1998-99	Div 3	46	13	18	15	57	66	57	14
1999-2000	Div 3	46	10	9	27	44	79	39	24
2000-01	Conf.	42	16	14	12	49	43	62	8
2001-02	Conf.	42	15	9	18	54	51	54	14
2002-03	Conf.	42	21	12	9	59	31	75	4
2003-04	Conf.	42	27	11	4	85	34	92	1
2004-05	FL 2	46	12	16	18	43	69	52	20
2005-06	FL 2	46	14	12	20	53	59	54	15
2006-07	FL 2	46	13	14	19	40	48	53	18
2007-08	FL 2	46	12	11	23	51	68	47	22

DID YOU KNOW ?

Robert Williams made his League debut for New Brighton as an amateur goalkeeper while only 16 years old, their youngest debutant. He next appeared in the League for Chester in 1951–52, but playing as a winger!

CHESTER CITY 2007–08 LEAGUE RECORD

Match No.	Date	Venue	Opponents	Result		H/T Score	Lg. Pos.	Goalscorers	Attendance
1	Aug 11	H	Chesterfield	D	0-0	0-0	—		3183
2	18	A	Rochdale	W	2-1	0-1	5	Grant [58], Ellison [90]	3243
3	25	H	Dagenham & R	W	4-0	0-0	2	Yeo 2 [50, 58], Murphy 2 [71, 81]	2098
4	Sept 1	A	Rotherham U	D	1-1	0-0	2	Roberts [72]	4036
5	7	H	Morecambe	L	0-1	0-0	—		3199
6	15	A	Bury	W	2-0	1-0	4	Butler [32], Hughes [52]	2539
7	22	H	Brentford	L	0-2	0-0	6		2453
8	29	A	Macclesfield T	W	2-1	2-0	5	Murphy [12], Wilson [41]	2647
9	Oct 2	A	Grimsby T	W	2-1	1-1	—	Murphy [10], Ellison [47]	3479
10	7	H	Shrewsbury T	W	3-1	0-0	3	Partridge [62], Murphy [72], Yeo [73]	3057
11	12	H	Hereford U	D	1-1	0-0	—	Yeo [58]	3430
12	20	A	Stockport Co	W	2-1	0-1	2	Partridge 2 [53, 81]	5566
13	27	H	Wycombe W	D	2-2	2-1	2	Holroyd [16], Murphy [40]	2598
14	Nov 2	A	Lincoln C	W	1-0	0-0	—	Dinning (pen) [57]	3960
15	6	A	Bradford C	L	1-2	0-1	—	Ellison [90]	13,211
16	17	H	Milton Keynes D	L	0-2	0-1	6		3102
17	25	A	Wrexham	D	2-2	2-1	7	Roberts [27], Linwood [45]	7687
18	Dec 4	H	Barnet	W	3-0	2-0	—	Partridge [6], Ellison 2 [40, 76]	1858
19	8	H	Peterborough U	L	1-2	1-0	6	Hughes [45]	2291
20	22	H	Bury	W	2-1	1-1	6	Hughes [45], Ellison [79]	2260
21	26	A	Morecambe	L	3-5	1-4	8	Ellison 2 [5, 73], Holroyd [76]	3419
22	29	A	Brentford	L	0-3	0-1	9		4323
23	Jan 1	H	Grimsby T	L	0-2	0-0	10		2255
24	5	A	Accrington S	D	3-3	1-1	9	Holroyd 2 [9, 78], Wilson [68]	1311
25	12	H	Mansfield T	L	0-1	0-0	11		2092
26	19	A	Notts Co	L	0-1	0-0	12		3774
27	26	H	Rotherham U	L	0-1	0-1	12		2536
28	29	H	Rochdale	L	0-4	0-2	—		2131
29	Feb 2	A	Chesterfield	D	1-1	0-0	15	Murphy [59]	3701
30	9	H	Accrington S	L	2-3	2-1	15	Butler [20], Murphy [34]	1957
31	12	A	Dagenham & R	L	2-6	0-3	—	Roberts [51], Murphy [89]	1328
32	16	H	Notts Co	L	0-1	0-0	16		1798
33	23	A	Mansfield T	W	3-1	0-1	15	Ellison 2 [56, 90], Dinning (pen) [72]	2362
34	Mar 1	A	Milton Keynes D	L	0-1	0-0	17		8172
35	4	A	Darlington	L	0-1	0-1	—		3294
36	9	H	Wrexham	L	0-2	0-1	17		3849
37	12	H	Bradford C	L	0-1	0-0	—		1566
38	15	A	Barnet	L	1-3	0-0	19	Hughes [90]	1663
39	22	H	Darlington	W	2-1	2-0	19	Rutherford [6], Partridge [36]	1759
40	24	A	Peterborough U	L	0-1	0-0	19		6457
41	Apr 5	A	Hereford U	D	2-2	0-2	20	Sandwith [68], Ellison (pen) [90]	3210
42	12	H	Lincoln C	L	1-2	1-2	20	McManus [20]	2089
43	19	A	Wycombe W	L	0-1	0-0	20		5497
44	26	A	Shrewsbury T	D	0-0	0-0	22		6417
45	29	H	Stockport Co	D	0-0	0-0	—		3060
46	May 3	H	Macclesfield T	D	0-0	0-0	22		2396

Final League Position: 22

GOALSCORERS

League (51): Ellison 11 (1 pen), Murphy 9, Partridge 5, Holroyd 4, Hughes 4, Yeo 4, Roberts 3, Butler 2, Dinning 2 (2 pens), Wilson 2, Grant 1, Linwood 1, McManus 1, Rutherford 1, Sandwith 1.
Carling Cup (0).
FA Cup (0).
J Paint Trophy (3): Partridge 2, Holroyd 1.

Danby J 46	Vaughan J 29 + 1	Wilson L 40	Grant T 15 + 4	Butler P 35	Linwood P 42	Partridge R 34 + 2	Hughes M 39 + 4	Murphy J 39	Lowndes N 8 + 4	Ellison K 36	Hand J — + 1	Holroyd C 14 + 11	Yeo S 7 + 14	Roberts K 30 + 7	Rutherford P 10 + 13	Sandwith K 12 + 10	Bolland P 2	Marples S 16	Carroll N 1	Dinning T 20	McManus P 9 + 10	Rule G 2 + 2	Newton S 2	Welsh J 6	Kelly S 7 + 3	Lindfield C 5 + 2	Mitchell A — + 4	Palethorpe P — + 1	*Match No.*
1	2	3	4^1	5	6	7	8	9^2	10^3	11	12	13	14																1
1	2	3	4	5	6		8^2		10^3	11		12	9^1	7	13	14													2
1	2	3	4	5	6	7	8	9		11			10																3
1	2	3	4^2	5	6	7	8	9^1		11		12	10	13															4
1	2	3	4^1	5	6■	7	8	9^2	13	11			10^3	12	14														5
1	2	3	4	5		7	8	9	12	11			10^1				6												6
1		3	4^2	5		7^3	8	9	12	11			10^1	13	14		6	2											7
1		3	4	5	6	7^1	8	9	12	11						13		2	10^2										8
1		3	4^2	5	6	7	8	9	10^1	11			12			13		2											9
1		3		5	6	7^2	8	9		11			12			10^1		2		4	13								10
1		3		5	6	7^3	8	9		11		13	12^2		14			2		4	10^1								11
1		3		5	6	7	8	9		11		10^1			12			2		4									12
1		3		5	6	7	8	9		11		10^1	12	13				2^2		4									13
1		3		5	6	7	8	9		11		10^1	12					2		4									14
1		3		5	6	7^2	8	9^3		11		10^1	12	14	13			2		4									15
1		3	12	5	6^1	7		9	10^2	11			13	8				2		4									16
1		3	12^2	5	6	7	10		9^3	11			13	8				2		4^1	14								17
1		3		5	6	7^3	8	9^1	10^2	11		12	13	4				2			14								18
1		3^2		5	6		8	9	10^1	11			12	4	7^3	13		2			14								19
1	2			5	6	7	8	9^1	10^2	11		12	13	4				3											20
1	2			5	6	7	8	9^1		11		13	12	4				3				10^2							21
1	2			5	6	7	8			11		9	10^1	4	12			3											22
1	2			5	6	7	13			11		9^1	12	8							10^2		3	4					23
1	2	3		5^2	6	7^1	8					9		4							12		10	11	13				24
1	2	3			6	7^2	8^1			11		9		4	12						13			10	5				25
1	2	3		5		7	8^1			11		9		4		6								10		12			26
1	2	3		5	6	7	12	9		11^2		10^3		4^1		13								8		14			27
1	2	3■	4^2	5	6^1	7^3	13	9		11■				12		14								8		10			28
1	2		4	5	6^1		8	9						11		3				7					12	10			29
1	2	3	4^1	5		12	8	9				13		6		11				7						10^2			30
1	2	3	4^1	5	6	12	8	9						11						7						10			31
1	2	3^2		5	6	7	8^3	9				12		11	14	13				4						10^1			32
1	2	3		5^1	6	7	8	9		11		12		10						4									33
1	2	3	4^1	5	6			9		11		10		7	12					8									34
1	2	3			6			9		11		10		5	8^1	7				4							12		35
1	2	3^1			6		8	9		11		10^2		5	12	7				4	13								36
1	2	3			6		8	9		11				5	7					4	10								37
1	2^1	3	13		6		8	9		11				5	7^2	12				4	10^3						14		38
1^G		3		5	6	7^1	8	9				10^2		2	11	12				4	13							15	39
1		3			6	7^3	8	9						2	10^2	12				4■	13	11^1			5		14		40
1		3		5^1	6	7^2	8	9		11				4	10	2					13				12				41
1	12	3			6		8	9		11				2	4^2	7					10	13			5^1				42
1	2	3			5		8	9				12		4	7	11					10^1				6				43
1	2	3			6	7	12	9		11^2				4	13	8					10^1				5				44
1	2	3	12		6	7^1	8	9						4	13	11					10^2				5				45
1	2		4		6^1	7^2	8	9						12	11^3	3					10	13			5		14		46

FA Cup
First Round — Bradford C — (a) — 0-1

Carling Cup
First Round — Nottingham F — (h) — 0-0

J Paint Trophy
First Round — Crewe Alex — (h) — 1-1
Second Round — Carlisle U — (a) — 2-4

CHESTERFIELD FL Championship 2

FOUNDATION

Chesterfield are fourth only to Stoke, Notts County and Nottingham Forest in age for they can trace their existence as far back as 1866, although it is fair to say that they were somewhat casual in the first few years of their history playing only a few friendlies a year. However, their rules of 1871 are still in existence showing an annual membership of 2s (10p), but it was not until 1891 that they won a trophy (the Barnes Cup) and followed this a year later by winning the Sheffield Cup, Barnes Cup and the Derbyshire Junior Cup.

The Recreation Ground, Saltergate, Chesterfield, Derbyshire S40 4SX.
Telephone: (01246) 209 765.
Fax: (01246) 556 799.
Ticket Office: (01246) 209 765.
Website: www.chesterfield-fc.co.uk
Email: reception@chesterfield-fc.co.uk
Ground Capacity: 8,502.
Record Attendance: 30,968 v Newcastle U, Division 2, 7 April 1939.
Pitch Measurements: 111yd × 71yd.
Chairman: Barrie Hubbard.
Vice-chairman: David Jones.
Chief Executive: Mike Warner.
Secretary: Alan Walters.
Manager: Lee Richardson.
Assistant Manager: Scott Sellars.
Physio: Jamie Hewitt.
Colours: Blue shirts, white shorts, white stockings.
Change Colours: Red shirts, red shorts, red stockings.
Year Formed: 1866.
Turned Professional: 1891.
Ltd Co: 1871.
Previous Name: Chesterfield Town.
Club Nicknames: 'Blues' or 'Spireites'.
Grounds: 1867, Drill Field; 1871, Recreation Ground.
First Football League Game: 2 September 1899, Division 2, v Sheffield W (a) L 1–5 – Hancock; Pilgrim, Fletcher; Ballantyne, Bell, Downie; Morley, Thacker, Gooing, Munday (1), Geary.
Record League Victory: 10–0 v Glossop NE, Division 2, 17 January 1903 – Clutterbuck; Thorpe, Lerper; Haig, Banner, Thacker; Tomlinson (2), Newton (1), Milward (3), Munday (2), Steel (2).
Record Cup Victory: 5–0 v Wath Ath (a), FA Cup 1st rd, 28 November 1925 – Birch; Saxby, Dennis; Wass, Abbott, Thompson; Fisher (1), Roseboom (1), Cookson (2), Whitfield (1), Hopkinson.

HONOURS

Football League: Division 2 best season: 4th, 1946–47; Division 3 (N) – Champions 1930–31, 1935–36; Runners-up 1933–34; Promoted to Division 2 (3rd) – 2000–01; Division 4 – Champions 1969–70, 1984–85.

FA Cup: Semi-final 1997.

Football League Cup: best season: 4th rd, 1965, 2007.

Anglo-Scottish Cup: Winners 1981.

SKY SPORTS FACT FILE

In the 1920–21 FA Cup campaign, Chesterfield were drawn against Dronfield Woodhouse in the preliminary round. They won easily 11–1. But there was a happier Woodhouse on the field that day – Chesterfield's similarly named goalkeeper!

Record Defeat: 0–10 v Gillingham, Division 3, 5 September 1987.

Most League Points (2 for a win): 64, Division 4, 1969–70.

Most League Points (3 for a win): 91, Division 4, 1984–85.

Most League Goals: 102, Division 3 (N), 1930–31.

Highest League Scorer in Season: Jimmy Cookson, 44, Division 3 (N), 1925–26.

Most League Goals in Total Aggregate: Ernie Moss, 161, 1969–76, 1979–81 and 1984–86.

Most League Goals in One Match: 4, Jimmy Cookson v Accrington S, Division 3N, 16 January 1926; 4, Jimmy Cookson v Ashington, Division 3N, 1 May 1926; 4, Jimmy Cookson v Wigan Borough, Division 3N, 4 September 1926; 4, Tommy Lyon v Southampton, Division 2, 3 December 1938.

Most Capped Player: Walter McMillen, 4 (7), Northern Ireland; Mark Williams, 4 (30), Northern Ireland.

Most League Appearances: Dave Blakey, 613, 1948–67.

Youngest League Player: Dennis Thompson, 16 years 160 days v Notts Co, 26 December 1950.

Record Transfer Fee Received: £750,000 from Southampton for Kevin Davies, May 1997.

Record Transfer Fee Paid: £250,000 to Watford for Jason Lee, August 1998.

Football League Record: 1899 Elected to Division 2; 1909 failed re-election; 1921–31 Division 3 (N); 1931–33 Division 2; 1933–36 Division 3 (N); 1936–51 Division 2; 1951–58 Division 3 (N); 1958–61 Division 3; 1961–70 Division 4; 1970–83 Division 3; 1983–85 Division 4; 1985–89 Division 3; 1989–92 Division 4; 1992–95 Division 3; 1995–2000 Division 2; 2000–01 Division 3; 2001–04 Division 2; 2004–07 FL 1; 2007– FL 2.

MANAGERS

E. Russell Timmeus 1891–95 *(Secretary-Manager)*
Gilbert Gillies 1895–1901
E. F. Hind 1901–02
Jack Hoskin 1902–06
W. Furness 1906–07
George Swift 1907–10
G. H. Jones 1911–13
R. L. Weston 1913–17
T. Callaghan 1919
J. J. Caffrey 1920–22
Harry Hadley 1922
Harry Parkes 1922–27
Alec Campbell 1927
Ted Davison 1927–32
Bill Harvey 1932–38
Norman Bullock 1938–45
Bob Brocklebank 1945–48
Bobby Marshall 1948–52
Ted Davison 1952–58
Duggie Livingstone 1958–62
Tony McShane 1962–67
Jimmy McGuigan 1967–73
Joe Shaw 1973–76
Arthur Cox 1976–80
Frank Barlow 1980–83
John Duncan 1983–87
Kevin Randall 1987–88
Paul Hart 1988–91
Chris McMenemy 1991–93
John Duncan 1993–2000
Nicky Law 2000–02
Dave Rushbury 2002–03
Roy McFarland 2003–07
Lee Richardson April 2007–

LATEST SEQUENCES

Longest Sequence of League Wins: 10, 6.9.1933 – 4.11.1933.

Longest Sequence of League Defeats: 9, 22.10.1960 – 27.12.1960.

Longest Sequence of League Draws: 8, 26.11.2005 – 2.1.2006.

Longest Sequence of Unbeaten League Matches: 21, 26.12.1994 – 29.4.1995.

Longest Sequence Without a League Win: 18, 11.9.1999 – 3.1.2000.

Successive Scoring Runs: 46 from 25.12.1929.

Successive Non-scoring Runs: 7 from 23.9.1977.

TEN YEAR LEAGUE RECORD

		P	W	D	L	F	A	Pts	Pos
1998-99	Div 2	46	17	13	16	46	44	64	9
1999-2000	Div 2	46	7	15	24	34	63	36	24
2000-01	Div 3	46	25	14	7	79	42	80*	3
2001-02	Div 2	46	13	13	20	53	65	52	18
2002-03	Div 2	46	14	8	24	43	73	50	20
2003-04	Div 2	46	12	15	19	49	71	51	20
2004-05	FL 1	46	14	15	17	55	62	57	17
2005-06	FL 1	46	14	14	18	63	73	56	16
2006-07	FL 1	46	12	11	23	45	53	47	21
2007-08	FL 2	46	19	12	15	76	56	69	8

**9 pts deducted.*

DID YOU KNOW?

The year 1890 was a milestone one for Chesterfield football. Walter Bannister was signed as its first semi-professional footballer, they won their first trophy, the Alfred Barnes Charity Cup, and a game was suspended by a pitch invasion from a bull!

CHESTERFIELD 2007–08 LEAGUE RECORD

Match No.	Date	Venue	Opponents	Result	H/T Score	Lg. Pos.	Goalscorers	Attendance
1	Aug 11	A	Chester C	D 0-0	0-0	—		3183
2	18	H	Stockport Co	D 1-1	0-0	16	Lester 79	4600
3	25	A	Peterborough U	W 3-2	1-2	7	Lester 19, Lowry 60, Niven 61	5005
4	Sept 1	H	Wycombe W	W 2-0	1-0	4	Niven 44, Lester 74	3757
5	7	H	Bury	W 3-1	1-0	—	Fletcher 2 33, 77, Lester 84	4161
6	15	A	Mansfield T	W 3-1	2-1	2	Robertson 3, Lowry 45, Lester 90	4514
7	22	H	Barnet	L 0-1	0-0	3		4088
8	29	A	Notts Co	L 0-1	0-1	4		5757
9	Oct 2	A	Wrexham	W 4-0	3-0	—	Lester 2 6, 15, Rooney 14, Leven 60	3058
10	6	H	Macclesfield T	D 2-2	1-1	5	Rooney 2 5, 46	4080
11	13	A	Shrewsbury T	W 3-2	1-1	3	Rooney 44, Lowry 49, Lester (pen) 65	5143
12	20	H	Dagenham & R	D 1-1	1-0	4	Downes 8	4101
13	27	A	Darlington	D 0-0	0-0	4		4205
14	Nov 3	H	Morecambe	D 2-2	0-1	6	Lester 2 56, 64	3721
15	6	A	Lincoln C	W 4-2	3-1	—	Lester 3 8, 18, 42, Kovacs 65	3893
16	24	A	Milton Keynes D	W 2-1	1-1	6	Bastians 33, Ward 52	9638
17	Dec 5	H	Rotherham U	L 0-2	0-1	—		5417
18	8	H	Bradford C	D 1-1	1-0	7	Rooney 13	3727
19	15	A	Accrington S	L 1-2	1-0	7	Ward 18	1448
20	22	H	Mansfield T	W 2-0	0-0	7	Lester 52, Ward 61	6300
21	26	A	Bury	W 1-0	1-0	6	Leven (pen) 45	3158
22	29	A	Barnet	W 2-0	1-0	5	Rooney 21, Kovacs 80	2346
23	Jan 1	H	Wrexham	W 2-1	2-0	4	Leven 7, Lester 41	4293
24	5	H	Grimsby T	L 1-2	0-1	4	Ward 83	4540
25	12	A	Brentford	L 1-2	1-1	5	Lester 41	4882
26	16	H	Rochdale	L 3-4	0-2	—	Downes 49, Lester 59, Rooney 90	3595
27	21	H	Hereford U	W 4-0	3-0	—	Lowry 2, Lester 2 21, 40, Moloney 90	3274
28	26	A	Wycombe W	L 0-1	0-1	7		5203
29	29	A	Stockport Co	D 2-2	1-1	—	Fletcher 16, Lester 51	5105
30	Feb 2	H	Chester C	D 1-1	0-0	7	Lester 54	3701
31	9	A	Grimsby T	L 2-4	0-2	7	Cooper 73, Ward 83	4601
32	13	H	Peterborough U	L 1-2	0-1	—	Leven 87	3973
33	16	A	Hereford U	L 0-2	0-2	10		3503
34	23	H	Brentford	W 1-0	1-0	8	Dowson 4	3728
35	Mar 1	A	Rochdale	W 1-0	0-0	8	Leven 89	3108
36	7	H	Lincoln C	W 4-1	1-0	—	Kerry 2 39, 81, Lester 52, Leven 59	4352
37	10	H	Milton Keynes D	L 1-2	0-1	—	Lowry 69	3834
38	15	A	Rotherham U	L 1-2	0-2	8	Ward 75	4550
39	22	H	Accrington S	W 4-2	1-2	7	Niven 31, Roberts (og) 58, Lowry 59, Ward 85	3274
40	24	A	Bradford C	L 0-1	0-1	7-		13,825
41	29	A	Dagenham & R	W 3-0	1-0	7	Ward 2 37, 46, Fletcher 79	2054
42	Apr 5	H	Shrewsbury T	W 4-1	0-0	8	Dowson 2 47, 90, Ward 2 50, 59	3570
43	12	A	Morecambe	D 1-1	1-0	8	Fletcher 35	2531
44	19	H	Darlington	D 1-1	0-0	8	Ward 50	3809
45	26	A	Macclesfield T	L 0-1	0-1	8		2573
46	May 3	H	Notts Co	D 1-1	0-1	8	Lester 59	4477

Final League Position: 8

GOALSCORERS

League (76): Lester 23 (1 pen), Ward 12, Rooney 7, Leven 6 (1 pen), Lowry 6, Fletcher 5, Dowson 3, Niven 3, Downes 2, Kerry 2, Kovacs 2, Bastians 1, Cooper 1, Moloney 1, Robertson 1, own goal 1.
Carling Cup (1): Lester 1.
FA Cup (1): Lester 1.
J Paint Trophy (1): Allison 1.

Roche B 45	Picken P 34 + 3	Robertson G 34 + 1	Downes A 38 + 2	Kovacs J 41	Niven D 38	Leven P 42	Winter J 20 + 5	Lester J 35 + 1	Fletcher S 23 + 15	Ward J 27 + 8	Smith A 2 + 6	Lowry J 41 + 1	Gray K 10 + 5	Jackson J — + 4	Allison W — + 9	Rooney A 11 + 11	O'Hare A 4 + 9	Algar B 1 + 1	Bastians F 12	Travis N — + 2	Davies G — + 1	Barnes M 1 + 2	Moloney B 8 + 1	Cooper K 2 + 5	Jordan M 1	Kerry L 8 + 5	Hartley P 12	Dowson D 9 + 3	Hawkins C 5	Owens G 2 + 2	Dyer B — + 3	Match No.
1	2	3	4	5	6	7¹	8	9²	10	11	12	13																				1
1	2	3	4¹	5	6	7	8	9	10³		11²		12	13	14																	2
1	2	3	4	5	6	7	8¹	9	10²		12	11	14		13³																	3
1	2³	3	4	5	6	7¹	8	9	10			11²	14			13	12															4
1	2	3		5	6	7		9	10			11	4				12	8¹														5
1	2	3	12	5	6	7²	8	9	10			11³	4¹			14	13															6
1	2	3	4	5	6	7	8¹	9	10			11²		12		13																7
1	2	3	4	5	6	7	8¹	9	10²			11³		12	14	13																8
1	2	3	4	5²	6	7		9¹				11	13		12	10			8³	14												9
1	2	3	4	5	6	7²		9				11				10	12		8¹	13												10
1	2	3	4	5	6		8¹	9		13		11				10	12		7²													11
1	2	3	4	5	6	7		9		12		11			13	10¹			8²													12
1	2	3	4	5	6	7		9¹		10		11				12			8													13
1	2	3	4	5	6	7		9²	13	10		11				12			8¹													14
1	2¹	3	4	5	6	7		9	13	10²			14			11	12		8³													15
1		3		5	6	7		9²	13	10		2	4			11	12		8¹													16
1	13	3		5	6	7			9	10	12	2	4			11¹			8²													17
1	2	3		5	6	7			12	10	13	11	4			9¹			8²													18
1	2	3	4		6	7			9¹	10	13	11³	5		12	14			8²													19
1	2	3	12	5		7	6	9¹	13	10		11	4■						8²													20
1	2	3	4	5	6	7	8	9²	12	10¹		11				13																21
1		3	4	5	6	7	8	9¹	10	12		2				11																22
1		3	4	5	6²	7	8	9		10		2				11¹	12				13											23
1		3	4¹	5	6	7	8²		9	10		2			12	11						13										24
1		2	4	5	6	7	8¹	9	12	10		11				13							3²									25
1	12	3	4	5	6	7		9	10	13		2²				14						8³	11¹									26
1		3	4	5	6	7		9	12	10¹		11					8						2									27
1		3	4	5	6²	7		9	12	10		11				13	8¹					14	2³									28
1	12	3	4	5	6	7		9	10	11			2										8¹									29
1		3	4	5	6		8	9	10¹	11			2²	13	12								7									30
1		3		5	6	7		9	12	13	10³	11	4				8¹						2²	14								31
1	2	3	4	5	6¹	7	13	9	12	10		11												8²								32
	2		4	5			8		9	10		11²			12		6						3	7¹	1	13						33
1	2		4	5		7²	8	9	12			11					13									6	3	10¹				34
1	2		4	5		7	8	9		12		11														6	3	10¹				35
1	2		4	5		7³	8	9¹	12	13		11												14		6	3	10²				36
1	2		4	5		7	8¹	9	12	13		11														6	3	10²				37
1	2		4	5		7¹	12	9	10	8		11²												13		6	3					38
1	2	3¹	4	5	6	7		9³	12	10		11														13	8²	14				39
1	2	3³	4	5	6¹	7	12		9		13	11²											14			8		10				40
1	2		4		6	7			9	11		8¹														12	3	10²	5	13		41
1	2		4		6	7			9³	11		8												12		13	3¹	10²	5		14	42
1	2		4		6	7			9³	10		11												12		13	3²	8¹	5		14	43
1	2		4¹		6	7²	13	12	9	10		11															3	8³	5	14		44
1	2	12		5¹	6²				9³	10		11														7	3	13	4	8	14	45
1	2		4	5²		7¹	12	9		10		11						14								6	3	13		8³		46

FA Cup
First Round — Tranmere R — (h) — 1-2

Carling Cup
First Round — Sheffield U — (a) — 1-3

J Paint Trophy
First Round — Hartlepool U — (h) — 1-3

COLCHESTER UNITED FL Championship 1

FOUNDATION

Colchester United was formed in 1937 when a number of enthusiasts of the much older Colchester Town club decided to establish a professional concern as a limited liability company. The new club continued at Layer Road which had been the amateur club's home since 1909.

Colchester Community Stadium, United Way, Colchester, Essex CO4 5HE.

Telephone: 0871 226 2161.

Fax: (01206) 715 327.

Ticket Office: 0871 226 2161.

Website: www.cu-fc.com

Email: caroline@colchesterunited.net

Ground Capacity: 10,000.

Record Attendance: 19,072 v Reading, FA Cup 1st rd, 27 November 1948.

Pitch Measurements: 106m × 68m.

Chairman: Mr Robbie Cowling.

Chief Executive: Mrs Marie Partner.

Secretary: Miss Caroline Pugh.

Manager: Geraint Williams.

Assistant Manager: Kit Symons.

Physio: Tony Flynn.

Colours: Royal blue and white striped shirts, royal blue shorts, royal blue stockings.

Change Colours: Yellow with royal blue piping shirts, yellow with royal blue panel shorts, yellow with royal blue trim stockings.

Year Formed: 1937.

Turned Professional: 1937.

Ltd Co.: 1937.

Club Nickname: 'The U's'.

Grounds: 1937, Layer Road.

First Football League Game: 19 August 1950, Division 3 (S), v Gillingham (a) D 0–0 – Wright; Kettle, Allen; Bearryman, Stewart, Elder; Jones, Curry, Turner, McKim, Church.

Record League Victory: 9–1 v Bradford C, Division 4, 30 December 1961 – Ames; Millar, Fowler; Harris, Abrey, Ron Hunt; Foster, Bobby Hunt (4), King (4), Hill (1), Wright.

HONOURS

Football League: Promoted from Division 3 – 1997–98 (play-offs); Division 4 – Runners-up 1961–62; FL 1 – Runners-up 2005–06.

FA Cup: best season: 6th rd, 1971.

Football League Cup: best season: 5th rd, 1975.

Auto Windscreens Shield: Runners-up 1997.

GM Vauxhall Conference: Winners 1991–92.

FA Trophy: Winners 1992.

SKY SPORTS FACT FILE

Personal milestones were achieved in successive games for Colchester United players in 1985–86: Roger Osborne's 300th League game v Cambridge United, Tony Adcock's 150th at Orient and Ian Phillips's 25th v Port Vale. There were also three victories as a result.

Record Cup Victory: 9-1 v Leamington, FA Cup 1st rd, 5 November 2005 – Davison; Stockley (Garcia), Duguid, Brown (1), Chilvers, Watson (1), Halford (1), Izzet (Danns) (2), Iwelumo (1) (Williams), Cureton (2), Yeates (1).

Record Defeat: 0–8 v Leyton Orient, Division 4, 15 October 1988.

Most League Points (2 for a win): 60, Division 4, 1973–74.

Most League Points (3 for a win): 81, Division 4, 1982–83.

Most League Goals: 104, Division 4, 1961–62.

Highest League Scorer in Season: Bobby Hunt, 38, Division 4, 1961–62.

Most League Goals in Total Aggregate: Martyn King, 130, 1956–64.

Most League Goals in One Match: 4, Bobby Hunt v Bradford C, Division 4, 30 December 1961; 4, Martyn King v Bradford C, Division 4, 30 December 1961; 4, Bobby Hunt v Doncaster R, Division 4, 30 April 1962.

Most Capped Player: Bela Balogh, 2 (9), Hungary.

Most League Appearances: Micky Cook, 613, 1969–84.

Youngest League Player: Lindsay Smith, 16 years 218 days v Grimsby T, 24 April 1971.

Record Transfer Fee Received: £2,500,000 from Reading for Greg Halford, January 2007.

Record Transfer Fee Paid: £350,000 to Luton T for Christopher Coyne, January 2008.

Football League Record: 1950 Elected to Division 3 (S); 1958–61 Division 3; 1961–62 Division 4; 1962–65 Division 3; 1965–66 Division 4; 1966–68 Division 3; 1968–74 Division 4; 1974–76 Division 3, 1976–77 Division 4; 1977–81 Division 3; 1981–90 Division 4; 1990–92 GM Vauxhall Conference; 1992–98 Division 3; 1998–04 Division 2; 2004–06 FL 1; 2006–08 FL C; 2008– FL 1.

MANAGERS

Ted Fenton 1946–48
Jimmy Allen 1948–53
Jack Butler 1953–55
Benny Fenton 1955–63
Neil Franklin 1963–68
Dick Graham 1968–72
Jim Smith 1972–75
Bobby Roberts 1975–82
Allan Hunter 1982–83
Cyril Lea 1983–86
Mike Walker 1986–87
Roger Brown 1987–88
Jock Wallace 1989
Mick Mills 1990
Ian Atkins 1990–91
Roy McDonough 1991–94
George Burley 1994
Steve Wignall 1995–99
Mick Wadsworth 1999
Steve Whitton 1999–2003
Phil Parkinson 2003–06
Geraint Williams July 2006–

LATEST SEQUENCES

Longest Sequence of League Wins: 7, 29.11.1968 – 1.2.1969.

Longest Sequence of League Defeats: 8, 9.10.1954 – 4.12.1954.

Longest Sequence of League Draws: 6, 21.3.1977 – 11.4.1977.

Longest Sequence of Unbeaten League Matches: 20, 22.12.1956 – 19.4.1957.

Longest Sequence Without a League Win: 20, 2.3.1968 – 31.8.1968.

Successive Scoring Runs: 24 from 15.9.1962.

Successive Non-scoring Runs: 5 from 7.4.1981.

TEN YEAR LEAGUE RECORD

		P	*W*	*D*	*L*	*F*	*A*	*Pts*	*Pos*
1998-99	Div 2	46	12	16	18	52	70	52	18
1999-2000	Div 2	46	14	10	22	59	82	52	18
2000-01	Div 2	46	15	12	19	55	59	57	17
2001-02	Div 2	46	15	12	19	65	76	57	15
2002-03	Div 2	46	14	16	16	52	56	58	12
2003-04	Div 2	46	17	13	16	52	56	64	11
2004-05	FL 1	46	14	17	15	60	50	59	15
2005-06	FL 1	46	22	13	11	58	40	79	2
2006-07	FL C	46	20	9	17	70	56	69	10
2007-08	FL C	46	7	17	22	62	86	38	24

DID YOU KNOW ?

On 1 December 2007 Teddy Sheringham hit a 52-second goal for Colchester United. It was the 349th of his distinguished career. Among his many honours including England international caps he was awarded the MBE in June 2007 and made over 700 League appearances.

COLCHESTER UNITED 2007–08 LEAGUE RECORD

Match No.	Date	Venue	Opponents	Result		H/T Score	Lg. Pos.	Goalscorers	Attendance
1	Aug 11	A	Sheffield U	D	2-2	0-0	—	McLeod K [68], Platt [89]	26,202
2	18	H	Barnsley	D	2-2	1-1	14	Sheringham [45], Connolly [48]	4450
3	25	A	Preston NE	W	3-0	1-0	6	Lisbie [41], Sheringham (pen) [61], Yeates [72]	11,582
4	Sept 1	H	Burnley	L	2-3	1-2	13	Lisbie [45], Virgo [88]	4925
5	15	H	Charlton Ath	D	2-2	2-1	16	Yeates [32], Lisbie [38]	5860
6	19	A	Southampton	D	1-1	0-0	—	Skacel (og) [58]	18,773
7	22	A	Blackpool	D	2-2	0-0	14	Yeates 2 [63, 86]	7959
8	29	H	Scunthorpe U	L	0-1	0-1	18		5218
9	Oct 3	H	QPR	W	4-2	3-1	—	Leigertwood (og) [19], Izzet [30], Yeates [38], Platt [63]	5361
10	6	A	Stoke C	L	1-2	0-1	17	Platt [58]	12,395
11	20	H	WBA	W	3-2	2-2	13	Yeates 2 (1 pen) [8, 68 (p)], Lisbie [19]	5798
12	23	A	Ipswich T	L	1-3	1-0	—	Platt [31]	25,727
13	27	A	Coventry C	L	0-1	0-0	16		23,431
14	Nov 3	H	Leicester C	D	1-1	1-1	16	Jackson [45]	5661
15	6	H	Plymouth Arg	D	1-1	0-0	—	Lisbie [56]	4833
16	10	A	Watford	D	2-2	1-1	18	Platt [20], Lisbie [46]	16,069
17	24	H	Crystal Palace	L	1-2	0-1	19	Jackson [69]	5856
18	28	A	Wolverhampton W	L	0-1	0-1	—		20,966
19	Dec 1	A	Sheffield W	W	2-1	2-1	19	Sheringham [1], Elokobi [26]	22,331
20	4	H	Watford	L	2-3	2-2	—	Connolly [28], Platt [77]	5760
21	8	A	Cardiff C	L	1-4	1-0	22	Jackson [45]	11,006
22	15	H	Norwich C	D	1-1	0-0	22	McLeod K [78]	5560
23	22	A	QPR	L	1-2	0-1	24	Yeates [62]	12,464
24	26	H	Southampton	D	1-1	0-1	24	Platt [47]	6157
25	29	H	Blackpool	L	0-2	0-2	24		5160
26	Jan 1	A	Charlton Ath	W	2-1	2-1	23	Lisbie 2 (1 pen) [16 (p), 29]	21,508
27	12	A	Bristol C	D	1-1	1-1	24	Lisbie [6]	16,484
28	29	A	Barnsley	L	0-1	0-1	—		9246
29	Feb 2	H	Sheffield U	D	2-2	0-1	24	Lisbie [46], Armstrong (og) [64]	5695
30	9	A	Burnley	D	1-1	1-1	24	Jackson [38]	15,376
31	12	H	Preston NE	W	2-1	0-0	—	Vernon (pen) [68], Jackson [88]	5122
32	16	A	Hull C	D	1-1	0-0	—	Jackson [47]	15,664
33	23	H	Bristol C	L	1-2	0-0	23	Platt [50]	5609
34	Mar 1	H	Wolverhampton W	L	0-1	0-1	24		5989
35	4	A	Plymouth Arg	L	1-4	0-1	—	Lisbie [64]	11,562
36	8	A	Crystal Palace	L	1-2	1-1	24	Lisbie [23]	13,895
37	11	H	Sheffield W	L	1-2	1-2	—	Lisbie [4]	5086
38	15	H	Cardiff C	D	1-1	0-1	24	Jackson [71]	4699
39	18	H	Hull C	L	1-3	1-2	—	Lisbie [37]	5497
40	22	A	Norwich C	L	1-5	1-2	24	Lisbie [41]	25,215
41	29	A	WBA	L	3-4	2-2	24	Coyne [14], Elito [17], Lisbie [76]	20,433
42	Apr 5	H	Ipswich T	W	2-0	1-0	24	Vernon 2 [29, 73]	6264
43	12	A	Leicester C	D	1-1	0-0	24	Lisbie [76]	22,719
44	19	H	Coventry C	L	1-5	1-0	24	Vernon [17]	5836
45	26	H	Stoke C	L	0-1	0-1	24		6300
46	May 4	A	Scunthorpe U	D	3-3	1-1	24	McLeod K 2 [11, 48], Vernon [47]	5554

Final League Position: 24

GOALSCORERS

League (62): Lisbie 17 (1 pen), Platt 8, Yeates 8 (1 pen), Jackson 7, Vernon 5 (1 pen), McLeod K 4, Sheringham 3 (1 pen), Connolly 2, Coyne 1, Elito 1, Elokobi 1, Izzet 1, Virgo 1, own goals 3.
Carling Cup (0).
FA Cup (1): Sheringham 1 (pen).

Gerken D 40	Duguid K 37	Connolly M 13 + 3	Izzet K 35 + 4	Baldwin P 23 + 3	Elokobi G 17	Jackson J 46	Yeates M 29	Platt C 34 + 7	Sheringham T 11 + 8	McLeod K 21 + 7	Guttridge L 5 + 9	Lisbie K 39 + 3	Virgo A 30 + 6	Cousins M — + 2	Davison A 6	White J 21	Granville D 14 + 5	Guy J — + 11	Balogh B 10 + 7	Watson K 7	Ifil P 20	Coyne C 16	Vernon S 8 + 9	Hammond D 11 + 2	McLeod I — + 2	Elito M 7 + 4	Wordsworth A 1 + 2	Heath M 5	*Match No.*
1	2	3	4^{1}	5	6	7	8	9	10	11	12																		1
1■	2	3	4	5	6	7	8^{2}		10	11^{1}	12	9^{6}	13	15															2
	11	3	4	5	6	7	8		10			9^{1}	12		1	2													3
1	2	3	4^{2}	5	6	7	11^{3}		10	12	13	9	14			8^{1}													4
1	2	3■	4	5	6	7	8^{2}	12	10^{1}	11		9	13																5
	2		4	5	6	7	8	9		11^{1}		10	3		1		12												6
	2		4^{1}	5	6	7	8^{2}	9		11	12	10^{3}	3		1		13	14											7
1	2		4^{1}	5	6	7	8	9		11^{2}	12	10	3					13											8
1	2		4	5	6	7	8	9				10	3				11												9
1	2^{2}		4	5	6	7	8	9				10	3				11^{1}	12	13										10
		12	4	5	6	7	8	9	13			10^{2}	3^{1}		1		11		2										11
		3	4	5	6	7	8^{1}	9	12	13		10			1		11^{2}		2										12
	2	3	4	5	6^{1}	7	8	9^{2}	13■	14		10	12		1		11^{3}												13
1	11	3	4	5		7	8	9		12		10					2			6^{1}									14
1	2	6	4	5		7	8	9				10					3			11									15
1	2		4	5		7	8	9		12		10					6		3	11^{1}									16
1	2	12	4^{1}	5■		7	8	9^{3}	13			10^{2}					6	14	3	11									17
1	2	12	4			7	8	9	13	14		10^{2}	5				3		6^{1}	11^{3}									18
1	2	3^{1}	4	12	6	7	8	13	10^{2}	11		9	5																19
1	2	3^{1}	4^{3}	12	6	7	8	9	13	11^{2}	14	10	5																20
1	2^{1}	3		12	6	7	8	13	10^{2}	11		9	5^{3}				14			4									21
1		6	4	5		7	8	9	10^{1}	11			2				3	12											22
1			4^{1}	5^{3}		7	8	9	10^{2}	11	12	13	6				3	14	2										23
1	2			5		7	8	9		11	4	10^{1}	6^{2}				3	12	13										24
1	2			5		7	8	9	10^{1}	11	4	12	6				3^{2}	13											25
1			12	5	3	7	8	9		11^{1}	4	10^{2}	6			2		13											26
1^{6}			4			7	8	9			11	10	6	15		3			12		2^{1}	5							27
1			4			7	8^{2}	9	12		11^{1}	10	6			3		13			2	5							28
1	11		4			7	8^{1}	9				10	6			3					2	5	12						29
1	11		4			7		9		8^{1}	12	10^{2}	6			3					2	5	13						30
1	8		4			7		9	10^{2}	11^{1}	12		6			3					2	5	13						31
1	7		4			8		9		11			6^{1}			3	12				2	5	10						32
1	7		4			8		9		11^{1}		12	6			3^{2}	13				2	5^{3}	10	14					33
1	7^{3}		4^{2}			8		9		11^{1}		10	6						12	3	2	5		13	14				34
1			4			7		12		11^{1}		10	6						3		2	5	9^{2}	8	13^{3}	14			35
1	11		4^{2}			7		9^{1}				10	6			3					2	5	12	8		13			36
1	7^{2}		4^{3}			11		9				10	6			3			12		2	5^{1}	13	8		14			37
1	7					11		9				10	6			3^{1}					2		12	4		8^{2}	13	5	38
1	7^{2}		12			8		9^{3}				10	6			3			13		2■		14	4			11^{1}	5	39
1			4			7		9				10^{2}	6			3			5		2		12	8		11^{1}	13		40
1	7		12	4^{2}		8		9^{3}				10	13			3					2	5	14	6		11^{1}			41
1	7					8						10				3					2	5	9	4		11		6	42
1	7		12			8		13				10^{3}				3		14			2	5	9^{2}	4		11^{1}		6	43
1	7					8				12		10				3^{1}			6		2	5	9	4		11			44
1	7^{1}					8		12	13			10	6^{3}			3			14		2	5	9^{2}	4		11			45
1	7		4			8		12		11		10				3			6		2^{2}		9^{1}			13		5	46

FA Cup
Third Round Peterborough U (h) 1-3

Carling Cup
First Round Shrewsbury T (a) 0-1

COVENTRY CITY FL Championship

FOUNDATION

Workers at Singers' cycle factory formed a club in 1883. The first success of Singers' FC was to win the Birmingham Junior Cup in 1891 and this led in 1894 to their election to the Birmingham and District League. Four years later they changed their name to Coventry City and joined the Southern League in 1908 at which time they were playing in blue and white quarters.

Ricoh Arena, Phoenix Way, Foleshill, Coventry CV6 6GE.

Telephone: 0870 421 1987.

Fax: 0870 421 1988.

Ticket Office: 0870 421 1987.

Website: www.ccfc.co.uk

Email: info@ccfc.co.uk

Ground Capacity: 32,609.

Record Attendance: 51,455 v Wolverhampton W, Division 2, 29 April 1967 (at Highfield Road). 27,212 v Birmingham C, FL Championship, 31 October 2006 (at Ricoh Arena).

Pitch Measurements: 110yd × 75yd.

Chairman: Ray Ranson.

Vice-chairman: Gary Hoffman.

Secretary: Paul Hindson.

Manager: Chris Coleman.

Assistant Manager: Steve Kean.

Physio: Michael McBride.

Colours: Sky blue and white striped shirts with navy sleeves and back, sky blue shorts with navy side trim, sky blue stockings with navy turn down and foot.

Change Colours: Black with gold trim shirts, black with gold side trim shorts, black stockings with gold turn down and foot.

Year Formed: 1883. ***Turned Professional:*** 1893. ***Ltd Co.:*** 1907.

Previous Names: 1883, Singers FC; 1898, Coventry City FC.

Club Nickname: 'Sky Blues'.

Grounds: 1883, Binley Road; 1887, Stoke Road; 1899, Highfield Road; 2005, Ricoh Arena.

First Football League Game: 30 August 1919, Division 2, v Tottenham H (h) L 0–5 – Lindon; Roberts, Chaplin, Allan, Hawley, Clarke, Sheldon, Mercer, Sambrooke, Lowes, Gibson.

Record League Victory: 9–0 v Bristol C, Division 3 (S), 28 April 1934 – Pearson; Brown, Bisby; Perry, Davidson, Frith; White (2), Lauderdale, Bourton (5), Jones (2), Lake.

Record Cup Victory: 8–0 v Rushden & D, League Cup 2nd rd, 2 October 2002 – Debec; Caldwell, Quinn, Betts (1p), Konjic (Shaw), Davenport, Pipe, Safri (Stanford), Mills (2) (Bothroyd (2)), McSheffery (3), Partridge.

HONOURS

Football League: Division 1 best season: 6th, 1969–70; Division 2 – Champions 1966–67; Division 3 – Champions 1963–64; Division 3 (S) – Champions 1935–36; Runners-up 1933–34; Division 4 – Runners-up 1958–59.

FA Cup: Winners 1987.

Football League Cup: Semi-final 1981, 1990.

European Competitions: *European Fairs Cup:* 1970–71.

SKY SPORTS FACT FILE

In 2007–08 Coventry City recorded three notable wins: 4–2 at West Bromwich Albion in the Championship, 4–1 in the FA Cup at Blackburn Rovers and 2–0 at Manchester United in the Carling Cup. Moreover Michael Mifsud scored twice in each game.

Record Defeat: 2–10 v Norwich C, Division 3 (S), 15 March 1930.

Most League Points (2 for a win): 60, Division 4, 1958–59 and Division 3, 1963–64.

Most League Points (3 for a win): 66, Division 1, 2001–02.

Most League Goals: 108, Division 3 (S), 1931–32.

Highest League Scorer in Season: Clarrie Bourton, 49, Division 3 (S), 1931–32.

Most League Goals in Total Aggregate: Clarrie Bourton, 171, 1931–37.

Most League Goals in One Match: 5, Clarrie Bourton v Bournemouth, Division 3S, 17 October 1931; 5, Arthur Bacon v Gillingham, Division 3S, 30 December 1933.

Most Capped Player: Magnus Hedman 44 (58), Sweden.

Most League Appearances: Steve Ogrizovic, 507, 1984–2000.

Youngest League Player: Ben Mackey, 16 years 167 days v Ipswich T, 12 April 2003.

Record Transfer Fee Received: £13,000,000 from Internazionale for Robbie Keane, July 2000.

Record Transfer Fee Paid: £6,500,000 to Wolverhampton W for Robbie Keane, August 1999.

Football League Record: 1919 Elected to Division 2; 1925–26 Division 3 (N); 1926–36 Division 3 (S); 1936–52 Division 2; 1952–58 Division 3 (S); 1958–59 Division 4; 1959–64 Division 3; 1964–67 Division 2; 1967–92 Division 1; 1992–2001 FA Premier League; 2001–04 Division 1; 2004– FL C.

LATEST SEQUENCES

Longest Sequence of League Wins: 6, 25.4.1964 – 5.9.1964.

Longest Sequence of League Defeats: 9, 30.8.1919 – 11.10.1919.

Longest Sequence of League Draws: 6, 1.11.2003 – 29.11.2003.

Longest Sequence of Unbeaten League Matches: 25, 26.11.1966 – 13.5.1967.

Longest Sequence Without a League Win: 19, 30.8.1919 – 20.12.1919.

Successive Scoring Runs: 25 from 10.9.1966.

Successive Non-scoring Runs: 11 from 11.10.1919.

MANAGERS

H. R. Buckle 1909–10
Robert Wallace 1910–13
(Secretary-Manager)
Frank Scott-Walford 1913–15
William Clayton 1917–19
H. Pollitt 1919–20
Albert Evans 1920–24
Jimmy Kerr 1924–28
James McIntyre 1928–31
Harry Storer 1931–45
Dick Bayliss 1945–47
Billy Frith 1947–48
Harry Storer 1948–53
Jack Fairbrother 1953–54
Charlie Elliott 1954–55
Jesse Carver 1955–56
George Raynor 1956
Harry Warren 1956–57
Billy Frith 1957–61
Jimmy Hill 1961–67
Noel Cantwell 1967–72
Bob Dennison 1972
Joe Mercer 1972–75
Gordon Milne 1972–81
Dave Sexton 1981–83
Bobby Gould 1983–84
Don Mackay 1985–86
George Curtis 1986–87
(became Managing Director)
John Sillett 1987–90
Terry Butcher 1990–92
Don Howe 1992
Bobby Gould 1992–93
Phil Neal 1993–95
Ron Atkinson 1995–96
(became Director of Football)
Gordon Strachan 1996–2001
Roland Nilsson 2001–02
Gary McAllister 2002–04
Eric Black 2004
Peter Reid 2004–05
Micky Adams 2005–07
Iain Dowie 2007
Chris Coleman February 2008–

TEN YEAR LEAGUE RECORD

		P	W	D	L	F	A	Pts	Pos
1998-99	PR Lge	38	11	9	18	39	51	42	15
1999-2000	PR Lge	38	12	8	18	47	54	44	14
2000-01	PR Lge	38	8	10	20	36	63	34	19
2001-02	Div 1	46	20	6	20	59	53	66	11
2002-03	Div 1	46	12	14	20	46	62	50	20
2003-04	Div 1	46	17	14	15	67	54	65	12
2004-05	FL C	46	13	13	20	61	73	52	19
2005-06	FL C	46	16	15	15	62	65	63	8
2006-07	FL C	46	16	8	22	47	62	56	17
2007-08	FL C	46	14	11	21	52	64	53	21

DID YOU KNOW

In 1920–21 Harry Nash played in a qualifying round FA Cup tie for Coventry City against Rochdale. Transferred to Cardiff City he played in their semi-final against Wolverhampton Wanderers watched by King George V and Queen Mary.

COVENTRY CITY 2007–08 LEAGUE RECORD

Match No.	Date	Venue	Opponents	Result	H/T Score	Lg. Pos.	Goalscorers	Attendance
1	Aug 11	A	Barnsley	W 4-1	1-1	—	McKenzie [6], Kyle [50], Gray [65], Mifsud [90]	12,616
2	18	H	Hull C	D 1-1	0-0	4	McKenzie [51]	21,059
3	25	A	Cardiff C	W 1-0	1-0	1	Tabb [34]	16,407
4	Sept 1	H	Preston NE	W 2-1	0-1	1	Adebola [80], Doyle [85]	17,551
5	15	H	Bristol C	L 0-3	0-1	3		21,538
6	18	A	Crystal Palace	D 1-1	0-1	—	Best [87]	14,455
7	22	A	Ipswich T	L 1-4	0-3	8	Hughes S [69]	18,840
8	29	H	Charlton Ath	D 1-1	0-1	9	Mifsud [84]	19,021
9	Oct 2	H	Blackpool	W 3-1	1-1	—	Doyle (pen) [44], Mifsud [69], Simpson [86]	15,803
10	6	A	Wolverhampton W	L 0-1	0-0	8		24,338
11	20	A	Plymouth Arg	L 0-1	0-1	11		11,576
12	23	H	Watford	L 0-3	0-2	—		17,032
13	27	H	Colchester U	W 1-0	0-0	11	Mifsud [81]	23,431
14	Nov 3	A	Stoke C	W 3-1	0-0	7	Mifsud 2 [58, 79], Adebola [63]	13,448
15	6	A	QPR	W 2-1	0-0	—	Mifsud [61], Kyle [90]	11,922
16	12	H	WBA	L 0-4	0-0	—		18,566
17	24	A	Norwich C	L 0-2	0-1	11		24,590
18	27	H	Scunthorpe U	D 1-1	0-0	—	Doyle (pen) [51]	14,036
19	Dec 1	H	Sheffield U	L 0-1	0-0	14		20,355
20	4	A	WBA	W 4-2	2-0	—	Best 2 [6, 83], Mifsud 2 [11, 86]	20,641
21	15	H	Southampton	D 1-1	1-0	14	Tabb [19]	19,143
22	22	A	Blackpool	L 0-4	0-1	16		8690
23	26	H	Crystal Palace	L 0-2	0-0	16		22,134
24	29	H	Ipswich T	W 2-1	1-1	15	Gray [11], Adebola [64]	18,346
25	Jan 1	A	Bristol C	L 1-2	0-1	17	Adebola [72]	15,899
26	12	A	Leicester C	L 0-2	0-1	17		23,905
27	19	H	Burnley	L 1-2	1-1	19	Doyle [26]	17,347
28	29	A	Hull C	L 0-1	0-0	—		14,822
29	Feb 2	H	Barnsley	W 4-0	1-0	19	Best 2 [37, 84], Gray [70], Tabb [75]	16,449
30	9	A	Preston NE	L 0-1	0-1	19		11,857
31	12	H	Cardiff C	D 0-0	0-0	—		15,260
32	23	H	Leicester C	W 2-0	1-0	18	Ward (pen) [32], Best [79]	23,129
33	26	A	Burnley	L 0-2	0-1	—		9779
34	Mar 1	A	Scunthorpe U	L 1-2	1-1	20	Thornton (pen) [21]	5866
35	5	H	QPR	D 0-0	0-0	—		15,225
36	8	H	Norwich C	W 1-0	1-0	18	Tabb [6]	18,108
37	11	A	Sheffield U	L 1-2	0-0	—	Ward (pen) [81]	23,864
38	15	H	Sheffield W	D 0-0	0-0	21		19,283
39	22	A	Southampton	D 0-0	0-0	20		22,014
40	29	H	Plymouth Arg	W 3-1	2-0	18	Doyle 2 [37, 43], Tabb [65]	18,775
41	Apr 1	A	Sheffield W	D 1-1	0-0	—	Hines [83]	21,110
42	5	A	Watford	L 1-2	0-1	18	Best [59]	17,188
43	12	H	Stoke C	L 1-2	1-0	20	Ward (pen) [31]	20,249
44	19	A	Colchester U	W 5-1	0-1	17	Best [48], Fox [51], Ward 2 (2 pens) [78, 90], Doyle [80]	5836
45	26	H	Wolverhampton W	D 1-1	1-0	19	Ward [18]	27,992
46	May 4	A	Charlton Ath	L 1-4	1-2	21	Mifsud [20]	26,130

Final League Position: 21

GOALSCORERS

League (52): Mifsud 10, Best 8, Doyle 7 (2 pens), Ward 6 (5 pens), Tabb 5, Adebola 4, Gray 3, Kyle 2, McKenzie 2, Fox 1, Hines 1, Hughes S 1, Simpson 1, Thornton 1 (pen).
Carling Cup (8): Mifsud 4, Adebola 1, Best 1, Simpson 1, Tabb 1.
FA Cup (6): Mifsud 3, Adebola 1, Hughes S 1, Ward 1 (pen).

Konstantopoulos D 21	Borrowdale G 20 + 1	Osbourne I 37 + 5	Doyle M 42	Hall M 17 + 1	Ward E 35 + 2	Gray J 20 + 6	Hughes M 16 + 2	Kyle K 7 + 6	McKenzie L 9 + 2	Tabb J 40 + 2	Mifsud M 34 + 7	Best L 29 + 5	Hughes S 32 + 5	Adebola D 15 + 11	Simpson R 10 + 18	Cairo E 4 + 3	Andrews W — + 7	De Zeeuw A 16 + 1	Thornton K 9 + 10	Marshall A 16	McNamee D 12 + 1	Turner B 19	Davis L 2 + 4	Birchall C 1	Fox D 18	Dann S 14 + 2	Schmeichel K 9	Hines Z — + 7	Duffy R 2	*Match No.*
1	2	3	4	5	6	7	8^{3}	9^{1}	10^{2}	11	12	13	14																	1
1	2	3	4	5	6	7	8^{2}	9^{3}	10	11^{1}	12		13	14																2
1	2	3	4	5	6	7^{2}			10^{1}	11	12		8	9	13															3
1	2	3	4	5	6	7			10^{1}	11^{2}	12		8	9		13														4
1	2		4	5^{2}	6				10	11^{1}			8	9	12	7	13	3												5
1	2		4	3	6				10^{2}	11		12	8	9^{1}	13	7^{3}		5	14											6
1	2	3	4	5						11^{3}	12	10	8	9^{1}	13	7^{2}		6	14											7
	3		4		6					11	9	10^{1}	8	12	7					1	2	5								8
	2^{2}	3	4		6					11^{3}	9	10^{1}	8	12	7				13	1	14	5								9
	2	3	4		6			12		11	9	13	8	10^{1}	7^{2}					1		5								10
	2^{2}	3	4		6	7	8	13			10		11	12	9^{1}					1		5								11
	2^{1}	3	4		6	7^{2}		9			10	13	8^{3}		14			12		1	11	5								12
		7	4	3		11^{1}		9^{2}		12	10	8^{3}		13	14			6		1	2	5								13
1		7	4	3				12		11	10	9^{1}		13	8^{2}			6			2	5								14
1		7	4	3				12		11	10	8^{1}	13	9				6			2^{2}	5								15
1		2	4	3				12	13	11	10■	8^{1}	7	9^{2}				6				5								16
1		2^{1}	4	3		12		10^{2}		11			8^{3}	9		13	14	6			7	5								17
1			4	3	6	7	12		10^{3}	11^{2}			8^{1}	9		13	14				2	5								18
1	3^{3}	12	4			7			13	11			8	9		10^{2}	14	6			2^{1}	5								19
1	3	12	4^{1}		6	14	7		8^{3}	11	10	9^{2}		13							2	5								20
1	3	12	4		6	13	7		8^{2}	11^{1}	10	9^{3}		14							2	5								21
1	3	12	4		6		7^{2}	9■		11	10^{1}	8^{3}	13	14							2	5								22
	3^{3}	8	4			12				11	10	9	7^{2}	13				6	14	1	2^{1}	5								23
	2	3	4		12	7^{3}				11^{2}	10		8^{1}	9				6	13	1		5	14							24
	2	3^{2}	4		13		7			12	10^{3}	8		9	11^{1}			6	14	1		5								25
1	2	3			6		4	12			10	8^{1}		9	13				11^{3}			5	14	7^{2}						26
1		2	4		6	7^{2}	8	9■		11^{3}	10		12	13	14			5					3^{1}							27
1	12	2	4		6					11	10^{2}	13	7	9	14			5					3^{3}		8^{1}					28
1		2	4		6	7^{2}				11	10^{1}	9	8		12			5^{3}					13		3	14				29
1		2	4	3^{3}	6	7	12			11	13	9	8^{1}		10^{2}			5								14				30
		2	4		6	7^{3}	8			11^{2}	10^{1}	9			12		13			1			14		3	5				31
		2		5	6	7^{2}	8			11	10	9^{3}	4^{1}		14		13		12	1					3					32
		2		5	6	7	4			11^{1}	10	9			12				8	1					3					33
		2		5		7	4^{1}			11	10	9^{2}			13		12		8	1					3	6				34
		2	4		6	12				11^{1}	10	9	7						8	1					3	5				35
		2	4		6					11	10	9^{1}	7		12				8	1					3	5				36
		2	4		6					11	10	9	7						8	1					3	5				37
		2	4^{1}		6					11	10	9	7		12				8						3	5	1			38
		2	4		6	12				11	10^{2}	9	7		13				8^{1}						3	5	1			39
		2	4		6	7^{1}				11	10^{2}		8		9				12						3	5	1	13		40
		12	4		6	7^{1}				11	10^{2}		8		9										3	5	1	13	2	41
		7	4		6	11^{2}					12	10	8		9^{3}				13						3	5	1	14	2^{1}	42
		2	4		6					11	10^{2}	9^{1}	7		12				8						3	5	1	13		43
		2^{1}	4	12	6		7			11	10	9^{2}	8												3	5	1	13		44
		2	4		6		7^{1}			11	10	9	8												3	5	1	12		45
		2^{2}	4		6		7^{1}			11	10	9	8						12						3	5	1	13		46

FA Cup

Third Round	Blackburn R	(a)	4-1
Fourth Round	Millwall	(h)	2-1
Fifth Round	WBA	(h)	0-5

Carling Cup

First Round	Notts Co	(h)	3-0
Second Round	Carlisle U	(a)	2-0
Third Round	Manchester U	(a)	2-0
Fourth Round	West Ham U	(h)	1-2

CREWE ALEXANDRA FL Championship 1

FOUNDATION

The first match played at Crewe was on 1 December 1877 against Basford, the leading North Staffordshire team of that time. During the club's history they have also played in a number of other leagues including the Football Alliance, Football Combination, Lancashire League, Manchester League, Central League and Lancashire Combination. Two former players, Aaron Scragg in 1899 and Jackie Pearson in 1911, had the distinction of refereeing FA Cup finals. Pearson was also capped for England against Ireland in 1892.

The Alexandra Stadium, Gresty Road, Crewe, Cheshire CW2 6EB.

Telephone: (01270) 213 014.

Fax: (01270) 216 320.

Ticket Office: (01270) 252 610.

Website: www.crewealex.net

Email: info@crewealex.net

Ground Capacity: 10,046.

Record Attendance: 20,000 v Tottenham H, FA Cup 4th rd, 30 January 1960.

Pitch Measurements: 112m × 74m.

Chairman: John Bowler.

Vice-chairman: Norman Hassall.

Business Operations Manager: Alison Bowler.

Secretary: Andry Blakemore.

Manager: Steve Holland.

Assistant Manager: Neil Baker.

Physios: Barry Holmes and Steve Walker.

Colours: Red and white.

Change Colours: All blue.

Year Formed: 1877.

Turned Professional: 1893.

Ltd Co.: 1892.

Club Nickname: 'Railwaymen'.

Ground: 1898, Gresty Road.

First Football League Game: 3 September 1892, Division 2, v Burton Swifts (a) L 1–7 – Hickton; Moore, Cope; Linnell, Johnson, Osborne; Bennett, Pearson (1), Bailey, Barnett, Roberts.

Record League Victory: 8–0 v Rotherham U, Division 3 (N), 1 October 1932 – Foster; Pringle, Dawson; Ward, Keenor (1), Turner (1); Gillespie, Swindells (1), McConnell (2), Deacon (2), Weale (1).

HONOURS

Football League: Division 2 – Runners-up 2002–03; Promoted from Division 2 1996–97 (play-offs).

FA Cup: Semi-final 1888.

Football League Cup: best season: 3rd rd, 1975, 1976, 1979, 1993, 1999, 2000, 2002, 2007.

Welsh Cup: Winners 1936, 1937.

SKY SPORTS FACT FILE

With only one win in the last 13 matches, Crewe Alexandra were facing relegation in 2007–08. But on 15 March Nick Maynard scored in a 3–0 win over Gillingham and also found the net in the next six outings for a total of 11 goals in the sequence.

Record Cup Victory: 8–0 v Hartlepool U, Auto Windscreens Shield 1st rd, 17 October 1995 – Gayle; Collins (1), Booty, Westwood (Unsworth), Macauley (1), Whalley (1), Garvey (1), Murphy (1), Savage (1) (Rivers (1p)), Lennon, Edwards, (1 og). 8–0 v Doncaster R, LDV Vans Trophy 3rd rd, 10 November 2002 – Bankole; Wright, Walker, Foster, Tierney; Lunt (1), Brammer, Sorvel, Vaughan (1) (Bell); Ashton (3) (Miles), Jack (2) (Jones (1)).

Record Defeat: 2–13 v Tottenham H, FA Cup 4th rd replay, 3 February 1960.

Most League Points (2 for a win): 59, Division 4, 1962–63.

Most League Points (3 for a win): 86, Division 2, 2002–03.

Most League Goals: 95, Division 3 (N), 1931–32.

Highest League Scorer in Season: Terry Harkin, 35, Division 4, 1964–65.

Most League Goals in Total Aggregate: Bert Swindells, 126, 1928–37.

Most League Goals in One Match: 5, Tony Naylor v Colchester U, Division 3, 24 April 1993.

Most Capped Player: Clayton Ince, 38 (66), Trinidad & Tobago.

Most League Appearances: Tommy Lowry, 436, 1966–78.

Youngest League Player: Steve Walters, 16 years 119 days v Peterborough U, 6 May 1988.

Record Transfer Fee Received: £3,400,000 from Norwich C for Dean Ashton, January 2005.

Record Transfer Fee Paid: £650,000 to Torquay U for Rodney Jack, June 1998.

Football League Record: 1892 Original Member of Division 2; 1896 Failed re-election; 1921 Re-entered Division (N); 1958–63 Division 4; 1963–64 Division 3; 1964–68 Division 4; 1968–69 Division 3; 1969–89 Division 4; 1989–91 Division 3; 1991–92 Division 4; 1992–94 Division 3; 1994–97 Division 2; 1997–2002 Division 1; 2002–03 Division 2; 2003–04 Division 1; 2004–06 FL C; 2006– FL 1.

MANAGERS

W. C. McNeill 1892–94 *(Secretary-Manager)*
J. G. Hall 1895–96 *(Secretary-Manager)*
R. Roberts *(1st team Secretary-Manager)* 1897
J. B. Blomerley 1898–1911 *(Secretary-Manager, continued as Hon. Secretary to 1925)*
Tom Bailey *(Secretary only)* 1925–38
George Lillycrop *(Trainer)* 1938–44
Frank Hill 1944–48
Arthur Turner 1948–51
Harry Catterick 1951–53
Ralph Ward 1953–55
Maurice Lindley 1956–57
Willie Cook 1957–58
Harry Ware 1958–60
Jimmy McGuigan 1960–64
Ernie Tagg 1964–71 *(continued as Secretary to 1972)*
Dennis Viollet 1971
Jimmy Melia 1972–74
Ernie Tagg 1974
Harry Gregg 1975–78
Warwick Rimmer 1978–79
Tony Waddington 1979–81
Arfon Griffiths 1981–82
Peter Morris 1982–83
Dario Gradi 1983–2007
Steve Holland May 2007–

LATEST SEQUENCES

Longest Sequence of League Wins: 7, 30.4.1994 – 3.9.1994.

Longest Sequence of League Defeats: 10, 16.4.1979 – 22.8.1979.

Longest Sequence of League Draws: 5, 31.8.1987 – 18.9.1987.

Longest Sequence of Unbeaten League Matches: 17, 25.3.1995 – 16.9.1995.

Longest Sequence Without a League Win: 30, 22.9.1956 – 6.4.1957.

Successive Scoring Runs: 26 from 7.4.1934.

Successive Non-scoring Runs: 9 from 6.11.1974.

TEN YEAR LEAGUE RECORD

		P	*W*	*D*	*L*	*F*	*A*	*Pts*	*Pos*
1998-99	Div 1	46	12	12	22	54	78	48	18
1999-2000	Div 1	46	14	9	23	46	67	51	19
2000-01	Div 1	46	15	10	21	47	62	55	14
2001-02	Div 1	46	12	13	21	47	76	49	22
2002-03	Div 2	46	25	11	10	76	40	86	2
2003-04	Div 1	46	14	11	21	57	66	53	18
2004-05	FL C	46	12	14	20	66	86	50	21
2005-06	FL C	46	9	15	22	57	86	42	22
2006-07	FL 1	46	17	9	20	66	72	60	13
2007-08	FL 1	46	12	14	20	47	65	50	20

DID YOU KNOW ?

On 15 April 1899 Crewe Alexandra met New Brighton Tower in the final of the Cheshire Senior Challenge Cup. Unfortunately the opposing team sent a telegram saying they were not fulfilling the tie. Crewe kicked off nonetheless, scored and won the cup!

CREWE ALEXANDRA 2007–08 LEAGUE RECORD

Match No.	Date	Venue	Opponents	Result		H/T Score	Lg. Pos.	Goalscorers	Attendance
1	Aug 11	H	Brighton & HA	W	2-1	1-1	—	Gary S Roberts 2 (1 pen) [22 (p), 79]	5394
2	18	A	Bristol R	D	1-1	1-1	3	Pope [34]	7750
3	25	H	Leyton Orient	L	0-2	0-1	14		4683
4	Sept 1	A	Swindon T	D	1-1	1-1	11	Schumacher [42]	6595
5	8	H	Huddersfield T	W	2-0	2-0	9	Barnard [16], Bopp [39]	5164
6	16	A	Doncaster R	L	0-2	0-1	10		6726
7	22	H	Millwall	D	0-0	0-0	14		4478
8	29	A	Oldham Ath	L	2-3	2-1	17	Barnard [17], Moore [26]	5082
9	Oct 2	A	Tranmere R	D	1-1	0-0	—	Gary S Roberts (pen) [56]	6155
10	6	H	Bournemouth	L	1-4	0-1	19	Miller [89]	4799
11	13	A	Southend U	L	0-3	0-1	20		6927
12	20	H	Luton T	W	2-0	2-0	18	Lowe 2 [14, 40]	4490
13	27	A	Cheltenham T	D	2-2	0-0	16	Church [74], Lowe [78]	3605
14	Nov 3	H	Yeovil T	W	2-0	2-0	16	McCready [28], Moore [40]	4363
15	6	A	Port Vale	W	1-0	0-0	—	Bennett [76]	5329
16	17	H	Northampton T	W	1-0	0-0	10	Lowe [59]	4531
17	24	A	Nottingham F	L	0-2	0-1	12		16,650
18	Dec 4	H	Gillingham	L	2-3	1-1	—	Moore [43], Gary S Roberts [49]	3929
19	8	H	Walsall	D	0-0	0-0	13		4639
20	15	A	Hartlepool U	L	0-3	0-0	15		3915
21	22	H	Doncaster R	L	0-4	0-1	17		4122
22	26	A	Huddersfield T	D	1-1	1-0	16	Barnard [19]	9759
23	29	A	Millwall	L	0-2	0-1	19		8068
24	Jan 1	H	Tranmere R	W	4-3	1-2	17	Gary S Roberts 2 (1 pen) [30 (p), 48], Maynard [67], O'Donnell [89]	5137
25	14	H	Leeds U	L	0-1	0-1	—		6771
26	19	A	Carlisle U	L	0-1	0-0	19		6449
27	22	A	Swansea C	L	1-2	0-1	—	Pope [90]	11,200
28	26	H	Swindon T	D	0-0	0-0	—		4344
29	29	H	Bristol R	D	1-1	0-1	—	Pope [47]	3942
30	Feb 2	A	Brighton & HA	L	0-3	0-3	21		4802
31	9	H	Swansea C	D	2-2	0-2	20	Baudet [82], Pope [90]	4955
32	12	A	Leyton Orient	W	1-0	1-0	—	Maynard [26]	3881
33	23	A	Leeds U	D	1-1	0-0	21	Maynard [47]	21,223
34	26	H	Carlisle U	L	0-1	0-0	—		4786
35	Mar 1	A	Northampton T	D	0-0	0-0	21		5507
36	8	H	Nottingham F	D	0-0	0-0	19		6314
37	11	H	Port Vale	L	0-2	0-0	—		5229
38	15	A	Gillingham	W	3-0	1-0	20	Pope [9], Maynard [50], Morgan [76]	4956
39	22	H	Hartlepool U	W	3-1	2-0	20	Maynard 2 [20, 30], Pope [85]	4412
40	24	A	Walsall	D	1-1	0-0	20	Maynard [61]	4741
41	29	A	Luton T	L	1-2	0-1	20	Maynard [58]	5465
42	Apr 5	H	Southend U	L	1-3	0-2	20	Maynard [74]	4895
43	12	A	Yeovil T	W	3-0	1-0	20	Maynard 2 [8, 58], Pope [90]	4785
44	19	H	Cheltenham T	W	3-1	1-0	18	Maynard 3 [14, 68, 76]	5279
45	26	A	Bournemouth	L	0-1	0-0	19		8621
46	May 3	H	Oldham Ath	L	1-4	0-2	20	Jones S [84]	6786

Final League Position: 20

GOALSCORERS

League (47): Maynard 14, Pope 7, Gary S Roberts 6 (3 pens), Lowe 4, Barnard 3, Moore 3, Baudet 1, Bennett 1, Bopp 1, Church 1, Jones S 1, McCready 1, Miller 1, Morgan 1, O'Donnell 1, Schumacher 1.
Carling Cup (0).
FA Cup (2): Cox 1, McCready 1.
J Paint Trophy (1): Lowe 1.

Williams B 46	Woodards D 36	Jones B 22	McCready C 32 + 2	Cox N 21 + 6	Baudet J 35	Schumacher S 24 + 2	Roberts Gary S 40 + 2	Maynard N 25 + 2	Miller S 5 + 10	Moore B 25 + 8	O'Donnell D 19 + 8	Pope T 15 + 11	Vaughan D — + 1	Rix B 21 + 4	Dickson C 2 + 1	Lynch R 1 + 1	Bopp E 5 + 5	Lowe R 16 + 11	Bailey M — + 2	Barnard L 9 + 1	Abbey G 20 + 3	O'Connor M 17 + 6	Church S 11 + 1	Bennett E 4 + 5	Baseya C 1 + 2	Gray D 1	Carrington M 3 + 6	Daniel C — + 1	Bailey J — + 1	Boyle P 17	Brown J — + 1	Roberts Gary M 4	Lunt K 14	Anyinsah J 6 + 2	Morgan D 7 + 2	Jones S 2 + 2	Match No.
1	2^{1}	3	4	5	6	7	8^{2}	9^{3}	10	11	12	13	14																								1
1	2	3	4^{2}	5	6	7^{3}	8		12		13	9		11	10^{1}	14																					2
1	2	3		5	6	7	8		12		4	9			10^{1}		11^{2}	13																			3
1	2	3		5	6	7	8		10^{1}		4	9^{3}		13	12			11^{2}	14																		4
1	2	3	13	5	6	7	8^{2}			12	4			14			11^{1}	10		9^{3}																	5
1	2	3	4	5^{1}	6^{3}	7	8			13				12			11^{2}	10		9	14																6
1	2	3	4			7	8			11				6			12	10^{1}		9	5																7
1	2	3^{1}	5			7	4			11	6	12		8				10^{2}		9		13															8
1	2	3	4	12		7	8		13	11^{2}	5			6^{1}				10		9^{3}		14															9
1	2	3	5			7	4^{1}		12	10	11	13		8^{3}			14	9				6^{2}															10
1	2	3	5	4	6^{2}		8^{1}			11	13	12		7				10		9																	11
1		3	5	4	6^{1}	7	13			10	12			11				14		9^{3}	2^{2}		8														12
1	2	3	5	6			8			11	4	12		7				10^{1}					9														13
1	2	4	5	6^{1}			8			11				7			12	10			3^{2}		9	13													14
1	2	3	5	4	6		8		12	11				7^{2}				10^{1}					9	13													15
1	2	3	5	4	6		8		12	11^{3}				7^{1}				10	13					14	9^{2}												16
1	6	3	5	4^{1}			8			11				7				10^{3}				12	9	13	14	2^{2}											17
1	2	3	5	4	6		8	10		11^{1}													9	7	12												18
1	2	3	5	4	6		8	10	12					13									9^{1}	7^{2}			11										19
1	2	3		4	6		8	9^{3}	10	12				7^{2}								11	13	5^{1}				14									20
1	2^{1}		5	4	6		8^{1}	9	10		11									13		7		3^{2}					12								21
1		3	5	12	6					11				7				13		10^{2}	2	4	9				8^{1}										22
1	2		5		6		8	12		11^{2}								13		10	3	4	9^{1}	14			7^{3}										23
1	2^{2}		5	4	6		8	11	12		13			7		3^{3}		10					9^{1}				14										24
1	2		5	4	6		8	9	12	13				7^{1}				10^{2}			3	11^{3}					14										25
1	2		5	4^{1}	6	7		9	13	11		12									3	8	10^{2}														26
1	2		5	12	6	13	8^{2}	9	11^{3}			10		7				14				4^{1}								3							27
1	2		5		6		8	9		11		10		7^{1}				12				4								3							28
1	2		5^{3}	12	6		8	9		11	14	10		7^{2}				13				4^{1}								3							29
1	2			4	6^{1}	7				11	5	10					9	8^{2}			12									3	13						30
1	2				6	8	10^{3}	9		11	5	12		7^{2}			13					4^{1}					14			3							31
1	2			12	6^{3}	4	8	9		10^{1}	5	13		7							14									3		11^{2}					32
1				12	6	4	8	9		10	5										2	13								3		11^{2}	7^{1}				33
1					6	4^{1}	8	9		10^{2}	5	13						12			2									3		11	7				34
1					6	4^{3}	8	9^{1}		10	5	12						13			2	14								3		11^{2}	7				35
1	2		5							10	6	9					8^{1}	12				4								3			7	11^{2}	13		36
1			5			11^{2}	13	12		14	6	9									2	4								3			7	8^{1}	10^{3}		37
1	5						8	10^{2}			6	9						12			2	4								3			7	13	11^{1}		38
1	2				6		8	9^{1}		12		10									3	4								5			7	13	11^{2}		39
1	5				6	12	4	9		13		10									2	8^{2}								3			7		11^{1}		40
1	5^{1}		12		6		4	9		13							14				2	8								3			7	11^{3}		10^{2}	41
1	3^{2}		5		6^{1}	7	8	9			12										2						13						11	4	10		42
1			5		6	7	4	9			12	10									2									3			8	11^{1}			43
1			5		6	7	4^{1}	9^{3}				10									2						12			3			8	11^{2}	13	14	44
1			5		6^{1}	7^{2}	4	9			3	10									2						12						8		11	13	45
1		3^{1}	5			7	4	9			6	13									2	12											8		11^{2}	10	46

FA Cup

First Round	Milton Keynes D	(h)	2-1
Second Round	Oldham Ath	(a)	0-1

Carling Cup

First Round	Hull C	(h)	0-3

J Paint Trophy

First Round	Chester C	(a)	1-1

CRYSTAL PALACE FL Championship

FOUNDATION

There was a Crystal Palace club as early as 1861 but the present organisation was born in 1905 after the formation of a club by the company that controlled the Crystal Palace (building), had been rejected by the FA who did not like the idea of the Cup Final hosts running their own club. A separate company had to be formed and they had their home on the old Cup Final ground until 1915.

Selhurst Park Stadium, Whitehorse Lane, London SE25 6PU.

Telephone: (020) 8768 6000.

Fax: (020) 8771 5311.

Ticket Office: 0871 200 0071.

Website: www.cpfc.co.uk

Email: info@cpfc.co.uk

Ground Capacity: 26,297.

Record Attendance: 51,482 v Burnley, Division 2, 11 May 1979.

Pitch Measurements: 110yd × 74yd.

Chairman: Simon Jordan.

Vice-chairman: Dominic Jordan.

Chief Executive: Phil Alexander.

Secretary: Christine Dowdeswell.

Manager: Neil Warnock.

Assistant Manager: Mick Jones.

Physio: Nigel Cox.

Colours: Red and blue striped shirts, red shorts.

Change Colours: White shirts, red shorts.

Year Formed: 1905.

Turned Professional: 1905.

Ltd Co.: 1905.

Club Nickname: 'The Eagles'.

Grounds: 1905, Crystal Palace; 1915, Herne Hill; 1918, The Nest; 1924, Selhurst Park.

First Football League Game: 28 August 1920, Division 3, v Merthyr T (a) L 1–2 – Alderson; Little, Rhodes; McCracken, Jones, Feebury; Bateman, Conner, Smith, Milligan (1), Whibley.

Record League Victory: 9–0 v Barrow, Division 4, 10 October 1959 – Rouse; Long, Noakes; Truett, Evans, McNichol; Gavin (1), Summersby (4 incl. 1p), Sexton, Byrne (2), Colfar (2).

Record Cup Victory: 8–0 v Southend U, Rumbelows League Cup 2nd rd (1st leg), 25 September 1989 – Martyn; Humphrey (Thompson (1)), Shaw, Pardew, Young, Thorn, McGoldrick, Thomas, Bright (3), Wright (3), Barber (Hodges (1)).

HONOURS

Football League: Division 1 – Champions 1993–94; Promoted from Division 1, 1996–97 (play-offs), 2003–04 (play-offs); Division 2 – Champions 1978–79; Runners-up 1968–69; Division 3 – Runners-up 1963–64; Division 3 (S) – Champions 1920–21; Runners-up 1928–29, 1930–31, 1938–39; Division 4 – Runners-up 1960–61.

FA Cup: Runners-up 1990.

Football League Cup: Semi-final 1993, 1995, 2001.

Zenith Data Systems Cup: Winners 1991.

European Competition: *Intertoto Cup:* 1998.

SKY SPORTS FACT FILE

To christen the opening of the Arthur Wait stand at Selhurst Park, Manchester United provided the opposition as the first visitors on 9 August 1969. A then record crowd of 48,610 was present for the 2–2 draw. The gate figure was beaten the same season.

Record Defeat: 0–9 v Burnley, FA Cup 2nd rd replay, 10 February 1909. 0–9 v Liverpool, Division 1, 12 September 1990.

Most League Points (2 for a win): 64, Division 4, 1960–61.

Most League Points (3 for a win): 90, Division 1, 1993–94.

Most League Goals: 110, Division 4, 1960–61.

Highest League Scorer in Season: Peter Simpson, 46, Division 3 (S), 1930–31.

Most League Goals in Total Aggregate: Peter Simpson, 153, 1930–36.

Most League Goals in One Match: 6, Peter Simpson v Exeter C, Division 3S, 4 October 1930.

Most Capped Player: Aleksandrs Kolinko 23 (76), Latvia.

Most League Appearances: Jim Cannon, 571, 1973–88.

Youngest League Player: John Bostock, 15 years 287 days v Watford, 29 October 2007.

Record Transfer Fee Received: £8,500,000 from Everton for Andy Johnson, May 2006.

Record Transfer Fee Paid: £2,750,000 to RC Strasbourg for Valerien Ismael, January 1998.

Football League Record: 1920 Original Members of Division 3; 1921–25 Division 2; 1925–58 Division 3 (S); 1958–61 Division 4; 1961–64 Division 3; 1964–69 Division 2; 1969–73 Division 1; 1973–74 Division 2; 1974–77 Division 3; 1977–79 Division 2; 1979–81 Division 1; 1981–89 Division 2; 1989–92 Division 1; 1992–93 FA Premier League; 1993–94 Division 1; 1994–95 FA Premier League; 1995–97 Division 1; 1997–98 FA Premier League; 1998–2004 Division 1; 2004–05 FA Premier League; 2005– FL C.

LATEST SEQUENCES

Longest Sequence of League Wins: 8, 9.2.1921 – 26.3.1921.

Longest Sequence of League Defeats: 8, 10.1.1998 – 14.3.1998.

Longest Sequence of League Draws: 5, 21.9.2002 – 19.10.2002.

Longest Sequence of Unbeaten League Matches: 18, 22.2.1969 – 13.8.1969.

Longest Sequence Without a League Win: 20, 3.3.1962 – 8.9.1962.

Successive Scoring Runs: 24 from 27.4.1929.

Successive Non-scoring Runs: 9 from 19.11.1994.

MANAGERS

John T. Robson 1905–07
Edmund Goodman 1907–25 *(had been Secretary since 1905 and afterwards continued in this position to 1933)*
Alex Maley 1925–27
Fred Mavin 1927–30
Jack Tresadern 1930–35
Tom Bromilow 1935–36
R. S. Moyes 1936
Tom Bromilow 1936–39
George Irwin 1939–47
Jack Butler 1947–49
Ronnie Rooke 1949–50
Charlie Slade and Fred Dawes *(Joint Managers)* 1950–51
Laurie Scott 1951–54
Cyril Spiers 1954–58
George Smith 1958–60
Arthur Rowe 1960–62
Dick Graham 1962–66
Bert Head 1966–72 *(continued as General Manager to 1973)*
Malcolm Allison 1973–76
Terry Venables 1976–80
Ernie Walley 1980
Malcolm Allison 1980–81
Dario Gradi 1981
Steve Kember 1981–82
Alan Mullery 1982–84
Steve Coppell 1984–93
Alan Smith 1993–95
Steve Coppell *(Technical Director)* 1995–96
Dave Bassett 1996–97
Steve Coppell 1997–98
Attilio Lombardo 1998
Terry Venables *(Head Coach)* 1998–99
Steve Coppell 1999–2000
Alan Smith 2000–01
Steve Bruce 2001
Trevor Francis 2001–03
Steve Kember 2003
Iain Dowie 2003–06
Peter Taylor 2006–07
Neil Warnock October 2007–

TEN YEAR LEAGUE RECORD

		P	W	D	L	F	A	Pts	Pos
1998-99	Div 1	46	14	16	16	58	71	58	14
1999-2000	Div 1	46	13	15	18	57	67	54	15
2000-01	Div 1	46	12	13	21	57	70	49	21
2001-02	Div 1	46	20	6	20	70	62	66	10
2002-03	Div 1	46	14	17	15	59	52	59	14
2003-04	Div 1	46	21	10	15	72	61	73	6
2004-05	PR Lge	38	7	12	19	41	62	33	18
2005-06	FL C	46	21	12	13	67	48	75	6
2006-07	FL C	46	18	11	17	59	51	65	12
2007-08	FL C	46	18	17	11	58	42	71	5

DID YOU KNOW ?

On 29 October 2007 Crystal Palace introduced John Bostock into their team against Watford. At the time he was 15 years 287 days old and the youngest to have made his League debut for the club and the 17th youngest in English League history.

CRYSTAL PALACE 2007–08 LEAGUE RECORD

Match No.	Date	Venue	Opponents	Result	H/T Score	Lg. Pos.	Goalscorers	Attendance
1	Aug 11	A	Southampton	W 4-1	2-1	—	Scowcroft 3 [30, 31, 55], Morrison [57]	25,054
2	18	H	Leicester C	D 2-2	1-0	3	Green [33], Morrison [90]	15,607
3	26	A	Ipswich T	L 0-1	0-0	8		19,382
4	Sept 1	H	Charlton Ath	L 0-1	0-0	16		18,556
5	15	A	Norwich C	L 0-1	0-0	21		24,228
6	18	H	Coventry C	D 1-1	1-0	—	Green [26]	14,455
7	22	H	Sheffield U	W 3-2	0-0	15	Soares [60], Fletcher [70], Watson (pen) [89]	14,131
8	29	A	Burnley	D 1-1	1-1	16	Hudson [5]	10,711
9	Oct 2	A	Plymouth Arg	L 0-1	0-0	—		10,451
10	6	H	Hull C	D 1-1	0-0	19	Scowcroft [81]	15,769
11	20	A	Blackpool	D 1-1	0-0	19	Soares [59]	9037
12	23	H	Stoke C	L 1-3	0-0	—	Freedman [51]	14,237
13	29	H	Watford	L 0-2	0-1	—		13,986
14	Nov 3	A	Scunthorpe U	D 0-0	0-0	23		6778
15	6	A	Cardiff C	D 1-1	1-1	—	Watson (pen) [44]	11,781
16	10	H	QPR	D 1-1	0-1	23	Morrison [88]	17,010
17	24	A	Colchester U	W 2-1	1-0	20	Morrison 2 [6, 74]	5856
18	27	H	Preston NE	W 2-1	2-1	—	Morrison [40], Hill [45]	13,048
19	Dec 1	H	WBA	D 1-1	1-1	17	Morrison [21]	15,247
20	4	A	QPR	W 2-1	0-1	—	Hill [65], Morrison [68]	13,300
21	8	A	Barnsley	D 0-0	0-0	15		10,298
22	15	H	Sheffield W	W 2-1	1-1	15	Morrison [37], Scannell [90]	14,865
23	22	H	Plymouth Arg	W 2-1	2-0	10	Hill [8], Scowcroft [44]	15,097
24	26	A	Coventry C	W 2-0	0-0	9	Morrison [47], Ifill [88]	22,134
25	29	A	Sheffield U	W 1-0	1-0	7	Scowcroft [38]	23,982
26	Jan 1	H	Norwich C	D 1-1	0-1	8	Morrison [50]	17,199
27	12	A	Wolverhampton W	W 3-0	1-0	6	Morrison [24], Scannell [49], Scowcroft [66]	22,650
28	19	H	Bristol C	W 2-0	1-0	5	Morrison [6], Hudson [85]	19,010
29	28	A	Leicester C	L 0-1	0-0	—		21,764
30	Feb 2	H	Southampton	D 1-1	0-0	7	Scowcroft [73]	17,967
31	8	A	Charlton Ath	L 0-2	0-0	—		26,202
32	12	H	Ipswich T	L 0-1	0-1	—		16,090
33	18	A	Bristol C	D 1-1	0-0	—	Hills [61]	16,446
34	23	H	Wolverhampton W	L 0-2	0-0	11		15,679
35	Mar 1	A	Preston NE	W 1-0	0-0	11	Morrison [76]	12,347
36	4	H	Cardiff C	D 0-0	0-0	—		13,446
37	8	H	Colchester U	W 2-1	1-1	9	Ifil (og) [21], Watson [74]	13,895
38	12	A	WBA	D 1-1	0-1	—	Moses [55]	20,378
39	15	H	Barnsley	W 2-0	0-0	7	Soares [46], Scowcroft [83]	17,459
40	22	A	Sheffield W	D 2-2	1-1	8	Watson [40], Lawrence [90]	19,875
41	29	H	Blackpool	D 0-0	0-0	9		16,028
42	Apr 7	A	Stoke C	W 2-1	2-0	—	Soares [23], Fonte [45]	15,756
43	12	H	Scunthorpe U	W 2-0	2-0	6	Soares [21], Morrison [39]	15,975
44	19	A	Watford	W 2-0	0-0	6	Ifill [72], Moses [75]	17,694
45	26	A	Hull C	L 1-2	1-1	6	Sinclair [38]	24,350
46	May 4	H	Burnley	W 5-0	3-0	5	Watson (pen) [8], Moses [10], Soares [37], Sinclair [61], Morrison [65]	23,950

Final League Position: 5

GOALSCORERS

League (58): Morrison 16, Scowcroft 9, Soares 6, Watson 5 (3 pens), Hill 3, Moses 3, Green 2, Hudson 2, Ifill 2, Scannell 2, Sinclair 2, Fletcher 1, Fonte 1, Freedman 1, Hills 1, Lawrence 1, own goal 1.
Carling Cup (1): Freedman 1.
FA Cup (0).
Play-Offs (2): Watson 2 (1 pen).

Speroni J 46	Lawrence M 36 + 1	Craig T 13	Watson B 41 + 1	Hudson M 45	Cort L 12	Green S 7 + 3	Soares T 38 + 1	Scowcroft J 35 + 3	Morrison C 33 + 10	Kennedy M 8	Freedman D 4 + 15	Kuqi S 2 + 6	Butterfield D 25 + 5	Fonte J 17 + 5	Fletcher C 17 + 11	Hughes J 4 + 6	Martin D 2 + 7	Hill P 5 + 8	Idrizaj B 3 + 4	Dickov P 6 + 3	Hills L 6 + 6	Bostock J 1 + 3	Songo'o F 9	Hill C 28	Moses V 9 + 4	Hall R — + 1	Derry S 30	Scannell S 10 + 13	Halls J 5	Grabban L — + 2	Danns N 2 + 2	Robinson A — + 6	Kudjodji B — + 1	Ashton N 1	Reid K — + 2	Sinclair S 6	Match No.
1	2	3	4	5	6	7	8	9^{1}	10^{2}	11^{3}	12	13	14																								1
1	2	3		5	6	7^{2}	8	9	10	11^{1}	12	13	14	4^{3}																							2
1	2	3		5	6	7^{2}	8	9	10^{3}	11	12	13			4^{1}	14																					3
1	2	3		5	6		8	9	10^{3}	11					4^{1}	7^{2}	12	13	14																		4
1		3		5	6	7^{3}	8	9	12		13		2		4	14			11^{2}	10^{1}																	5
1		3	4	5	6	7	8	9			10		2		11																						6
1		3	4	5	6	7^{1}	8	9^{3}			12		2		11	13			14	10^{2}																	7
1		3	4	5	6	7^{2}	8	9^{1}	12				2		11	13			14	10^{3}																	8
1	7	3	12	5	6	13	8^{1}		14				2^{2}		4	11			9^{3}	10																	9
1		3	4^{1}	5	6	12	8	9	13				2		7	11^{3}	14			10^{2}																	10
1	12	3	4^{2}	5	6		8	9	13		10^{1}		2		7		11^{3}			14																	11
1	2	3	4^{3}	5	6	13		9	10		12			14	7		11^{2}			8^{1}																	12
1	2		4^{3}	5				9	12		10^{2}			6	11	3^{1}			13		7	14	8														13
1	2	3	4	5				9	12	11	13			6	7^{2}				10^{1}			14	8^{3}														14
1	2		4	5			7	9^{1}	12	11				6				13				10^{3}	8^{2}	3	14												15
1	2		4^{3}	5			8^{1}		9	11	12			6				7				14	10^{2}	3		13											16
1	2		4	5			12	9	10^{3}	11^{1}			14	6			13	7^{2}						3			8										17
1	2		4	5			7^{1}	9	10^{2}		11^{3}		12	6			14			13				3			8										18
1	2		4	5			7	9	10^{1}					6			13			12			11^{2}	3			8										19
1			4	5			7^{1}	9	10				2	6^{2}	12						13		11^{3}	3			8	14									20
1	2		4	5			7^{1}	9^{2}	10				3		12						13		11^{3}	6			8	14									21
1	2		4^{2}	5			7	9	10^{1}				3		12		13						11^{3}	6			8	14									22
1	2		4	5			7^{2}	9	10^{1}		12		3				13						11^{3}	6			8	14									23
1	2		4	5			7^{1}	9	10^{3}				3		12			13			14			6			8	11^{2}									24
1	2		4	5			7^{2}	9	10^{1}				3		12			13			14			6			8	11^{3}									25
1	2		4^{2}	5			7	9	10		12		3^{3}	14	13									6			8	11^{1}									26
1	2		4	5			7	9	10												12			3^{1}	13		8^{2}	11^{3}	6	14							27
1	6		4	5			7	9	10^{1}												12			3			8	11^{2}	2	13							28
1	6		4	5			7	9	10			12												3	13		8^{2}	11^{1}	2								29
1	6		4	5			7^{3}	9	10^{1}		12													3	13		8	11^{2}	2		14						30
1	6		4	5				9	10^{2}		13	12	2					11^{3}									8	14	3		7^{1}						31
1	6		4^{2}	5				9^{3}	10		12	14	2		13						3						8^{1}	11			7						32
1	6		4	5			7^{3}	12				10^{1}	2	13	11						9			3			8^{2}	14									33
1	6		4	5			7^{3}	12	13			10^{1}	2		11			14			9^{2}			3			8										34
1	6		4	5					10		12		2		11			7^{1}			3				9^{2}		8					13					35
1	6		4	5				12	10		13		2		11^{2}			7^{1}						3	9^{3}		8	14									36
1	6		4				7	9	10				2	12							3^{1}			5	11^{2}		8^{3}	13				14					37
1	2		4^{3}	5			7^{1}	9	12					6	11	14								3	10^{2}		8	13									38
1	2		4	5			7	9	10^{2}					6										3			8	11^{1}				12	13				39
1	2		4	5			7^{1}	9	10					6		13								3			8^{3}	11^{2}			12	14					40
1	6		4	5			7^{2}	9^{1}	10				2	12													8					13		3^{1}	14	11	41
1	2		4	5			7^{2}		10					6	12									3	9^{3}		8	13							14	11^{1}	42
1			4	5			7		10^{3}				2	6	12									3	9^{2}		8^{1}	13				14				11	43
1	2^{1}		4	5			7		10^{2}				12	6	13			14						3	9		8									11^{3}	44
1			4	5			7		10				2	6				13						3	9		8^{1}	12								11^{2}	45
1			4	5			7		10^{2}				2	6	12			14						3	9^{3}		8^{1}	13								11	46

FA Cup
Third Round — Watford (a) 0-2

Carling Cup
First Round — Bristol R (a) 1-1

Play-Offs
Semi-Final — Bristol C (h) 1-2
(a) 1-2

DAGENHAM & REDBRIDGE FL Championship 2

FOUNDATION

The roots of Dagenham & Redbridge live firmly in the Essex side of the Greater London area. Though only formed in 1992 their complex origins date back to the 19th century involving Ilford (founded 1881) and Leytonstone (1886) who merged in 1979 to form Leytonstone-Ilford. They and Walthamstow Avenue (1900) joined together in 1988 to becom Redbridge Forest who in turn merged with Dagenham FC (1949) in 1992. Victoria Road has existed as a football ground since 1917. Initially used by Sterling Works, in the summer of 1955 Briggs Sports vacated the premises and Dagenham FC moved in and the pitch was enclosed.

The London Borough of Barking and Dagenham Stadium, Victoria Road, Dagenham, Essex RM10 7XL.

Telephone: (020) 8592 1549 or (020) 8592 7194.

Fax: (020) 8593 7227.

Ticket Office: (020) 8592 1549 (extension 21).

Website: www.daggers.co.uk

Email: info@daggers.co.uk

Ground Capacity: 6,087.

Record Attendance: 5,949 v Ipswich T, FA Cup 3rd rd, 5 January 2002.

Pitch Measurements: 100m × 64.5m.

Chairman: David J. Andrews.

Vice-chairman: David E. Ward.

Managing Director: Stephen R. Thompson.

Secretary: Terry Grover.

Manager: John L. Still.

Assistant Manager: Terry W. Harris.

Physio: John Gowens.

Colours: Red and blue striped shirts, white shorts, blue stockings.

Change Colours: All yellow or Dark blue shirts, light blue shorts, dark blue stockings.

Year Formed: 1992.

MANAGERS

John Still 1992–94
Dave Cusack 1994–95
Graham Carr 1995–96
Ted Hardy 1996–99
Garry Hill 1999–2004
John Still April 2004–

SKY SPORTS FACT FILE

Before 12 February 2008, Dagenham & Redbridge had managed to win just six League matches during the season. But a 6–2 win over Chester City was one of five successive victories which helped considerably to avoiding relegation.

Grounds: Victoria Road 1992.

Club Nickname: Daggers.

Record League Victory: 8-1 v Woking (a), Conference 19 April 1994.

Record Defeat: 0-9 v Hereford U, Conference 27 February 2004.

Most League Points (3 for a win): 101, 1999–2000 Ryman Premier.

Most League Goals: 97, Ryman Premier, 1999–2000.

Highest League Scorer in Season: Paul Benson, 28 Conference, 2006–07.

Most League Goals in Total Aggregate: 105, Danny Shipp, 1997–2004.

Most League Appearances: Jason Broom, 462, 1992–2003.

Record Transfer Fee Received: Reported figure of £250,000 from Peterborough U for Craig Mackail-Smith and Shane Blackett, January 2007.

Record Transfer Fee Paid: £16,000 to Purfleet for Paul Cobb, 1998.

Football League Record: Promoted from Conference 2006–07; FL 2 2007–.

HONOURS

FA Cup: best season: 3rd rd, 2008.

Conference: Champions – 2006–07. Runners-up – 2001–02.

Isthmian League (Premier): Champions 1999–2000.

Essex Senior Cup: Winners – 1997–98, 2000–01. Runners-up 2001–02.

AS DAGENHAM FC
FA Trophy: Winners 1979–80; Runners-up 1976–77. *Amateur Cup:* Runners-up 1969–70, 1970–71.

AS ILFORD
FA Amateur Cup: Winners 1929, 1930. *Isthmian League:* Champions 1906–07, 1920–21, 1921–22.

AS LEYTONSTONE
FA Amateur Cup: Winners 1947, 1948, 1968. *Isthmian League:* Champions 1918–19, 1937–38, 1938–39, 1946–47, 1947–48, 1949–50, 1950–51, 1951–52, 1965–66.

AS LEYTONSTONE/ILFORD
Isthmian League: Champions 1981–82, 1988–89.

AS WALTHAMSTOW AVENUE
FA Amateur Cup: Winners 1952, 1961. *Isthmian League:* Champions 1945–46, 1948–49, 1952–53, 1954–55. *Athenian League:* Champions 1929–30, 1932–33, 1933–34, 1937–38, 1938–39.

AS REDBRIDGE FOREST
Isthmian League: Winners 1990–91.

LATEST SEQUENCES

Longest Sequence of League Wins: 5, 12.2.2008 – 1.3.2008.

Longest Sequence of League Defeats: 4, 27.10.2007 – 17.11.2007.

Longest Sequence of League Draws: 2, 22.3.2008 – 24.3.2008.

Longest Sequence of Unbeaten League Matches: 5, 12.2.2008 – 1.3.2008.

Longest Sequence Without a League Win: 9, 6.10.2007 – 4.12.2007.

Successive Scoring Runs: 7 from 9.2.2008.

Successive Non-scoring Runs: 3 from 12.1.2008.

TEN YEAR LEAGUE RECORD

		P	W	D	L	F	A	Pts	Pos
1998-99	IPL	42	20	13	9	71	44	73	3
1999-00	IPL	42	32	5	5	97	35	101	1
2000-01	Conf	42	23	8	11	71	54	77	3
2001-02	Conf	42	24	12	8	70	47	84	3
2002-03	Conf	42	21	9	12	71	59	72	5
2003-04	Conf	42	15	9	18	59	64	54	13
2004-05	Conf	42	19	8	15	68	60	65	11
2005-06	Conf	42	16	19	16	63	59	58	10
2006-07	Conf	46	28	11	7	93	48	95	1
2007-08	FL 2	46	13	10	23	49	70	49	20

DID YOU KNOW 

That best Football League win for Dagenham & Redbridge in February 2008 coincided with another oddity. They were the only home winners from 11 midweek fixtures that week. Unusually, too, there were eight away winners from the same fixture list.

DAGENHAM & REDBRIDGE 2007–08 LEAGUE RECORD

Match No.	*Date*	*Venue*	*Opponents*	*Result*	*H/T Score*	*Lg. Pos.*	*Goalscorers*	*Attendance*
1	Aug 11	A	Stockport Co	L 0-1	0-0	—		5577
2	18	H	Wycombe W	D 2-2	1-0	18	Sloma [33], Moore [49]	2280
3	25	A	Chester C	L 0-4	0-0	24		2098
4	Sept 1	H	Lincoln C	W 1-0	0-0	21	Benson [88]	2060
5	8	H	Barnet	D 1-1	1-1	18	Strevens [20]	2192
6	15	A	Notts Co	L 0-1	0-0	20		3926
7	22	H	Bury	D 1-1	1-1	21	Rainford [39]	1597
8	29	A	Mansfield T	W 1-0	0-0	18	Huke [63]	2048
9	Oct 2	A	Brentford	W 3-2	1-0	—	Strevens [23], Rainford (pen) [47], Moore [60]	3662
10	6	H	Darlington	L 0-3	0-1	15		1888
11	14	H	Accrington S	L 1-3	1-2	18	Cavanagh (og) [26]	1596
12	20	A	Chesterfield	D 1-1	0-1	18	Benson [56]	4101
13	27	H	Rotherham U	L 0-2	0-1	19		2091
14	Nov 3	A	Rochdale	L 0-1	0-0	19		2278
15	6	A	Peterborough U	L 1-3	1-0	—	Benson [30]	4200
16	17	H	Bradford C	L 1-4	0-1	20	Benson [77]	2247
17	24	A	Macclesfield T	D 1-1	1-0	21	Southam (pen) [7]	1781
18	Dec 4	H	Milton Keynes D	L 0-1	0-1	—		1880
19	8	H	Wrexham	W 3-0	1-0	21	Evans S (og) [24], Strevens [86], Taylor [90]	1520
20	15	A	Shrewsbury T	L 0-4	0-0	22		4597
21	22	H	Notts Co	D 1-1	0-1	22	Southam (pen) [50]	1649
22	26	A	Barnet	L 1-3	0-1	22	Huke [88]	2513
23	29	A	Bury	W 2-0	1-0	21	Strevens 2 [21, 62]	1887
24	Jan 1	H	Brentford	L 1-2	0-1	21	Strevens [49]	2353
25	12	A	Morecambe	L 0-1	0-0	22		2754
26	19	H	Grimsby T	D 0-0	0-0	22		2216
27	26	A	Lincoln C	L 0-2	0-1	22		3779
28	29	A	Wycombe W	W 1-0	1-0	—	Rainford (pen) [45]	3974
29	Feb 2	H	Stockport Co	L 0-1	0-1	22		1834
30	9	A	Hereford U	L 1-4	1-3	23	Strevens [33]	2594
31	12	H	Chester C	W 6-2	3-0	—	Strevens 2 [13, 60], Uddin [15], Rainford [23], Nurse [83], Hall [90]	1328
32	16	A	Grimsby T	W 4-1	2-0	22	Smith [16], Rainford 2 (1 pen) [31 (p), 85], Strevens [82]	4060
33	23	H	Morecambe	W 2-0	1-0	19	Gain [20], Strevens [90]	1809
34	26	H	Hereford U	W 1-0	1-0	—	Foster [45]	1929
35	Mar 1	A	Bradford C	W 2-0	1-0	18	Arber [30], Strevens [79]	13,537
36	8	H	Peterborough U	L 2-3	0-0	18	Rainford (pen) [83], Hall [90]	3130
37	11	H	Macclesfield T	L 0-1	0-0	—		1350
38	15	A	Milton Keynes D	L 0-4	0-3	20		9417
39	22	H	Shrewsbury T	D 1-1	0-1	20	Benson [70]	1686
40	24	A	Wrexham	D 0-0	0-0	20		4692
41	29	H	Chesterfield	L 0-3	0-1	21		2054
42	Apr 4	A	Accrington S	L 0-1	0-0	—		1262
43	12	H	Rochdale	D 1-1	1-1	22	Strevens [33]	2032
44	19	A	Rotherham U	L 1-2	0-2	22	Strevens [52]	3203
45	26	A	Darlington	W 3-2	0-1	21	Sloma [63], Rainford (pen) [66], Keltie (og) [74]	3709
46	May 3	H	Mansfield T	W 2-0	0-0	20	Strevens [50], Benson (pen) [53]	3451

Final League Position: 20

GOALSCORERS

League (49): Strevens 15, Rainford 8 (5 pens), Benson 6 (1 pen), Hall 2, Huke 2, Moore 2, Sloma 2, Southam 2 (2 pens), Arber 1, Foster 1, Gain 1, Nurse 1, Smith 1, Taylor 1, Uddin 1, own goals 3.
Carling Cup (1): Strevens 1.
FA Cup (8): Benson 3, Strevens 3, Huke 1, Nurse 1.
J Paint Trophy (3): Moore 1, Saunders 1, Strevens 1.

Roberts T 43	Foster D 31 + 1	Griffiths S 41	Rainford D 28 + 1	Uddin A 40 + 1	Boardman J 22 + 5	Saunders S 21 + 1	Southam G 44 + 1	Benson P 19 + 3	Nurse J 23 + 7	Sloma S 22 + 7	Strevens B 39 + 7	Moore C 13 + 13	Huke S 31 + 5	Graham R 4 + 3	Taylor J 2 + 10	Patterson M 5 + 1	Okuonghae M 9 + 1	Smith R 23	Green D 2 + 10	Taiwo S 4 + 6	Cook A — + 1	Thompson E 3	Hall R 2 + 6	Gain P 18	Baidoo S 1 + 2	Arber M 16	Goodwin L — + 1	*Match No.*
1	2	3	4	5	6	7^{1}	8	9^{2}	10	11^{3}	12	13	14															1
1	2	3		5	6	7	8		10^{1}	11^{2}	12	9^{3}	4	13	14													2
1	2			5	6	7	8			11^{1}	10	9	4	12		3												3
1	2	3	4	5		7	8	12		11^{3}	10^{2}	9^{1}	14		13		6											4
1	2	3	4			7	8			11^{2}	10^{1}	9	13		12		5	6										5
1	2	3	4	5		7	8			11	10^{1}	9	12					6										6
1	2	3	4	5		7	8				10	9	11					6										7
1	2	3	4	5		7	8			12	10	9^{1}	11					6										8
1	2	3	4	5	12	7^{1}	8				10	9^{2}	11		13			6										9
1	2	3	4^{1}	5		7	8			12	10	9^{2}	11					6	13									10
1	2^{3}	3	4	5	12		8	13		11^{1}	10	9^{2}	7	14				6										11
1	2	3		5	12		8	9		11	10^{2}	13	7	4^{1}				6										12
1	2	3	4	5			8	9			10^{1}	12	7^{3}	11^{2}				6	13	14								13
1	2	3	4^{2}	12	5		8	9		11^{1}	10		13	7^{3}				6	14									14
1	2	3			6		8	9		11	12	10^{1}	7	4^{2}				5		13								15
1	2^{3}	3		5	6		8	9	12		11^{1}	10^{2}	7				13		14	4■								16
1	2	3		5	6		8	9^{1}	12	11	7	10	4															17
1		3		5	6		8	9^{1}	10	11^{2}	7	12	4				2		13									18
1				5	6		8	9	10^{2}	11	12		4		13	3	2		7^{1}									19
1				5			8	9	10^{2}	11	12		4^{3}		13	3	2		6^{1}	7■	14							20
1				5	6	7^{1}	8	9	10	11^{2}	12		4			3	2		13									21
1	12			5	6	7^{1}	8	9	10	11	13		4			3^{3}	2^{2}		14									22
1	2	3		5		7^{2}	8		9^{1}	11^{3}	10	12	4		13		6		14									23
1	2	3		5	12	7	8		9	11^{2}	10		4				6^{1}		13									24
	2	3^{3}		5	6	7^{2}	8		9	12	10		4		13	14						1	11^{1}					25
	2	3		5	6	7	8		9^{1}	11	10		4		12							1						26
	2	3		5	6	7	8		9^{3}	11^{1}	10		4^{2}		12					13		1	14					27
1	2	3	4	5	6		8				10	12			9^{1}			7		13				11^{2}				28
1	2	3	4^{1}	5	6^{2}		8		12		10				9^{3}			7					13	11	14			29
1	2	3		5	6	7^{1}	12		13		10									4			8	11	9^{2}			30
1	2	3	4	5		7^{1}	8		9^{2}	11	10												12		13	6		31
1	2	3	4	5			8		9		10							7						11		6		32
1	2	3	4	5			8		9	12	10							7						11^{1}		6		33
1	2	3	4	5			8		9		10							7						11		6		34
1		3	4	5	12		8		9^{2}		10		7^{1}					2					13	11		6		35
1		3	4	5	2		8^{2}		9		10	12	7^{1}										13	11		6		36
1	2^{2}	3	4	5	6		8^{1}		9		10	12											13	11		7		37
1	2	3	4	5			8^{2}		9	12	10	13						7^{1}						11		6		38
1		3	4^{1}	5			8	12	9		10		2					7						11		6		39
1		3	4	5			8	9			10^{1}	12	2					7						11		6		40
1		3	4^{1}	5			8^{3}	9	12	13	10	14	2					7^{2}						11		6		41
1		3	4	5			8^{1}	9	12		10		7					2^{2}		13				11		6		42
1		3	4	5			8	9	7		10		2											11		6		43
1		3^{2}	4		6	12	8	9^{1}	7		10	13						2^{3}		14				11		5		44
1		3	4		6	7	8^{2}	9^{1}	12	13	10^{3}	14	2											11		5		45
1		3	12		6	8^{3}		9		11^{2}	10		2^{1}						13	4				7		5	14	46

FA Cup

First Round	Hampton & R	(a)	3-0
Second Round	Kidderminster H	(h)	3-1
Third Round	Southend U	(a)	2-5

Carling Cup

First Round	Luton T	(h)	1-2

J Paint Trophy

First Round	Southend U	(a)	2-2
Second Round	Leyton Orient	(a)	1-0
Quarter-Final	Gillingham	(a)	0-4

DARLINGTON FL Championship 2

FOUNDATION

A football club was formed in Darlington as early as 1861 but the present club began in 1883 and reached the final of the Durham Senior Cup in their first season, losing to Sunderland in a replay after complaining that they had suffered from intimidation in the first. On 5 April 1884, Sunderland had defeated Darlington 4-3. Darlington's objection was upheld by the referee and the replay took place on 3 May. The new referee for the match was Major Marindin, appointed by the Football Association to ensure fair play. Sunderland won 2-0. The following season Darlington won this trophy and for many years were one of the leading amateur clubs in their area.

Darlington Arena, Neasham Road, Darlington DL2 1DL.

Telephone: (01325) 387 000.

Fax: (01325) 387 050.

Ticket Office: 0871 855 1883.

Website: www.darlington-fc.net

Email: commercial@darlington-fc.net

Ground Capacity: 27,000.

Record Attendance: 21,023 v Bolton W, League Cup 3rd rd, 14 November 1960.

Pitch Measurements: 112yd × 74yd.

Chairman: George Houghton.

Commercial Director: Graham McDonnell.

Secretary: Lisa Charlton.

Manager: Dave Penney.

Assistant Manager: Martin Gray.

Physio: Will Short.

Colours: Black and white hooped shirts, black shorts, white stockings.

Change Colours: All red.

Year Formed: 1883. ***Turned Professional:*** 1908. ***Ltd Co.:*** 1891.

Grounds: 1918, Feethams Ground; 2003, Reynolds Arena, Hurworth Moor.

Club Nickname: 'The Quakers'.

First Football League Game: 27 August 1921, Division 3 (N), v Halifax T (h) W 2–0 – Ward; Greaves, Barbour; Dickson (1), Sutcliffe, Malcolm; Dolphin, Hooper (1), Edmunds, Wolstenholme, Winship.

Record League Victory: 9–2 v Lincoln C, Division 3 (N), 7 January 1928 – Archibald; Brooks, Mellen; Kelly, Waugh, McKinnell; Cochrane (1), Gregg (1), Ruddy (3), Lees (3), McGiffen (1).

HONOURS

Football League: Division 2 best season: 15th, 1925–26; Division 3 (N) – Champions 1924–25; Runners-up 1921–22; Division 4 – Champions 1990–91; Runners-up 1965–66.

FA Cup: best season: 5th rd, 1958.

Football League Cup: best season: 5th rd, 1968.

GM Vauxhall Conference: Champions 1989–90.

SKY SPORTS FACT FILE

Geoff Barker managed to appear in 50 Football League matches in the 1974–75 season. He began with Darlington where he made 34 and finished the season at Reading where he added another 16. He is the only player to have reached half a century in one season.

Record Cup Victory: 7–2 v Evenwood T, FA Cup 1st rd, 17 November 1956 – Ward; Devlin, Henderson; Bell (1p), Greener, Furphy; Forster (1), Morton (3), Tulip (2), Davis, Moran.

Record Defeat: 0–10 v Doncaster R, Division 4, 25 January 1964.

Most League Points (2 for a win): 59, Division 4, 1965–66.

Most League Points (3 for a win): 85, Division 4, 1984–85.

Most League Goals: 108, Division 3 (N), 1929–30.

Highest League Scorer in Season: David Brown, 39, Division 3 (N), 1924–25.

Most League Goals in Total Aggregate: Alan Walsh, 90, 1978–84.

Most League Goals in One Match: 5, Tom Ruddy v South Shields, Division 2, 23 April 1927; 5, Maurice Wellock v Rotherham U, Division 3N, 15 February 1930.

Most Capped Player: Jason Devos, 3 (46), Canada; Adrian Webster, 3, New Zealand.

Most League Appearances: Ron Greener, 442, 1955–68.

Youngest League Player: Curtis Main, 15 years 318 days v Peterborough U, 3 May 2008.

Record Transfer Fee Received: £400,000 from Dundee U for Jason De Vos, October 1998.

Record Transfer Fee Paid: £100,000 to Boston U for Julian Joachim, September 2006 and £100,000 to Swansea C for Pawel Abbott, July 2007.

Football League Record: 1921 Original Member Division 3 (N); 1925–27 Division 2; 1927–58 Division 3 (N); 1958–66 Division 4; 1966–67 Division 3; 1967–85 Division 4; 1985–87 Division 3; 1987–89 Division 4; 1989–90 GM Vauxhall Conference; 1990–91 Division 4; 1991–2004 Division 3; 2004– FL 2.

LATEST SEQUENCES

Longest Sequence of League Wins: 6, 6.2.2000 – 7.3.2000.

Longest Sequence of League Defeats: 8, 31.8.1985 – 19.10.1985.

Longest Sequence of League Draws: 5, 31.12.1988 – 28.1.1989.

Longest Sequence of Unbeaten League Matches: 17, 27.4.1968 – 19.10.1968.

Longest Sequence Without a League Win: 19, 27.4.1988 – 8.11.1988.

Successive Scoring Runs: 22 from 3.12.1932.

Successive Non-scoring Runs: 7 from 5.9.1975.

MANAGERS

Tom McIntosh 1902–11
W. L. Lane 1911–12
(Secretary-Manager)
Dick Jackson 1912–19
Jack English 1919–28
Jack Fairless 1928–33
George Collins 1933–36
George Brown 1936–38
Jackie Carr 1938–42
Jack Surtees 1942
Jack English 1945–46
Bill Forrest 1946–50
George Irwin 1950–52
Bob Gurney 1952–57
Dick Duckworth 1957–60
Eddie Carr 1960–64
Lol Morgan 1964–66
Jimmy Greenhalgh 1966–68
Ray Yeoman 1968–70
Len Richley 1970–71
Frank Brennan 1971
Ken Hale 1971–72
Allan Jones 1972
Ralph Brand 1972–73
Dick Conner 1973–74
Billy Horner 1974–76
Peter Madden 1976–78
Len Walker 1978–79
Billy Elliott 1979–83
Cyril Knowles 1983–87
Dave Booth 1987–89
Brian Little 1989–91
Frank Gray 1991–92
Ray Hankin 1992
Billy McEwan 1992–93
Alan Murray 1993–95
Paul Futcher 1995
David Hodgson/Jim Platt
(Director of Coaching) 1995
Jim Platt 1995–96
David Hodgson 1996–2000
Gary Bennett 2000–01
Tommy Taylor 2001–02
Mick Tait 2003
David Hodgson 2003–06
Dave Penney October 2006–

TEN YEAR LEAGUE RECORD

		P	*W*	*D*	*L*	*F*	*A*	*Pts*	*Pos*
1998-99	Div 3	46	18	11	17	69	58	65	11
1999-2000	Div 3	46	21	16	9	66	36	79	4
2000-01	Div 3	46	12	13	21	44	56	49	20
2001-02	Div 3	46	15	11	20	60	71	56	15
2002-03	Div 3	46	12	18	16	58	59	54	14
2003-04	Div 3	46	14	11	21	53	61	53	18
2004-05	FL 2	46	20	12	14	57	49	72	8
2005-06	FL 2	46	16	15	15	58	52	63	8
2006-07	FL 2	46	17	14	15	52	56	65	11
2007-08	FL 2	46	22	12	12	67	40	78	6

DID YOU KNOW ?

Unusually for a cup competition, the pre-war Third Division version did not prevent players appearing for Southern and Northern clubs. Goalkeeper Jack Beby conceded 11 goals for Crystal Palace but transferred to Darlington he collected a winner's medal!

DARLINGTON 2007–08 LEAGUE RECORD

Match No.	Date	Venue	Opponents	Result		H/T Score	Lg. Pos.	Goalscorers	Attendance
1	Aug 11	H	Wrexham	W	2-0	1-0	—	McBride [42], Joachim [72]	4408
2	18	A	Accrington S	W	3-0	1-0	1	Wright [26], Abbott 2 (1 pen) [49, 90 (p)]	1805
3	25	H	Notts Co	D	2-2	1-0	1	Wright [40], Miller [86]	3763
4	Sept 1	A	Macclesfield T	D	0-0	0-0	3		2288
5	8	A	Rotherham U	W	2-0	1-0	1	Abbott [10], Blundell [76]	3988
6	15	H	Lincoln C	W	2-0	1-0	1	Abbott [34], Ravenhill [46]	4075
7	22	A	Milton Keynes D	L	0-1	0-0	1		7901
8	29	H	Peterborough U	D	1-1	0-0	2	Wright [63]	3974
9	Oct 2	H	Rochdale	D	1-1	0-0	—	Wright [59]	3031
10	6	A	Dagenham & R	W	3-0	1-0	4	Foster [45], Blundell [67], Wright [83]	1888
11	14	H	Stockport Co	W	4-0	2-0	2	Wright 2 [21, 85], Joachim [28], Blundell [81]	3841
12	20	A	Bradford C	D	0-0	0-0	3		14,074
13	27	H	Chesterfield	D	0-0	0-0	3		4205
14	Nov 3	A	Hereford U	L	1-5	1-2	5	Colbeck [16]	3516
15	6	H	Shrewsbury T	W	2-0	1-0	—	Joachim [27], Colbeck [63]	2628
16	17	A	Brentford	W	2-0	2-0	3	Keltie (pen) [17], Wright [37]	4657
17	24	H	Wycombe W	W	1-0	0-0	2	Abbott [77]	3002
18	Dec 4	A	Grimsby T	W	4-0	2-0	—	White [3], Blundell [25], Foran [50], Cummins [90]	3057
19	22	A	Lincoln C	W	4-0	3-0	3	Foran [11], Keltie (pen) [32], Cummins 2 [45, 51]	4025
20	26	H	Rotherham U	D	1-1	0-1	3	Cummins [68]	6965
21	29	H	Milton Keynes D	L	0-1	0-0	4		5304
22	Jan 1	A	Rochdale	L	1-3	0-3	6	Keltie (pen) [54]	3116
23	12	H	Bury	W	3-0	2-0	4-	Wright [12], Miller [22], Mayo [58]	3003
24	15	A	Morecambe	W	3-0	1-0	—	Austin [27], Joachim [63], Blundell [70]	2773
25	19	A	Mansfield T	W	1-0	1-0	3	Blundell (pen) [30]	3344
26	26	H	Macclesfield T	D	2-2	1-0	3	Wright [10], Cresswell (og) [72]	3585
27	29	H	Accrington S	W	1-0	1-0	—	Wright [1]	2808
28	Feb 2	A	Wrexham	L	0-2	0-1	2		4013
29	9	H	Barnet	W	1-0	1-0	2	Joachim [11]	3145
30	12	A	Notts Co	W	1-0	1-0	—	Ravenhill [45]	3421
31	16	H	Mansfield T	L	1-2	1-0	3	Austin [22]	3527
32	23	A	Bury	W	2-1	1-0	3	N'Dumbu Nsungu (pen) [6], Cummins [67]	2554
33	Mar 1	H	Brentford	W	3-1	0-0	3	N'Dumbu Nsungu [48], Joachim [59], Abbott [90]	3508
34	4	H	Chester C	W	1-0	1-0	—	Abbott [27]	3294
35	8	A	Wycombe W	L	0-2	0-1	3		5185
36	11	A	Shrewsbury T	D	0-0	0-0	—		4499
37	15	H	Grimsby T	W	3-2	2-2	4	Abbott 2 [33, 44], Wright [64]	3499
38	22	A	Chester C	L	1-2	0-2	4	Foster [84]	1759
39	24	H	Morecambe	D	2-2	0-2	4-	Kennedy [84], N'Dumbu Nsungu [89]	3719
40	29	H	Bradford C	L	1-3	1-0	4	Keltie (pen) [11]	4492
41	Apr 1	A	Barnet	D	0-0	0-0	—		1678
42	5	A	Stockport Co	L	0-1	0-1	4		6460
43	12	H	Hereford U	L	0-1	0-0	5		4331
44	19	A	Chesterfield	D	1-1	0-0	6	Wright [68]	3809
45	26	H	Dagenham & R	L	2-3	1-0	6	Ravenhill [20], Arber (og) [52]	3709
46	May 3	A	Peterborough U	W	2-0	1-0	6	Kennedy [3], Cummins [52]	10,400

Final League Position: 6

GOALSCORERS

League (67): Wright 13, Abbott 9 (1 pen), Blundell 6 (1 pen), Cummins 6, Joachim 6, Keltie 4 (4 pens), N'Dumbu Nsungu 3 (1 pen), Ravenhill 3, Austin 2, Colbeck 2, Foran 2, Foster 2, Kennedy 2, Miller 2, Mayo 1, McBride 1, White 1, own goals 2.
Carling Cup (1): Wright 1.
FA Cup (2): Blundell 1, Wright 1.
J Paint Trophy (0).
Play-Offs (3): Keltie 1 (pen), Kennedy 1, Miller 1.

Oakes A 6	Austin N 23 + 6	Ryan T 13	Ravenhill R 25 + 10	Foster S 42	Miller I 18 + 10	Joachim J 40	McBride K 3 + 3	Abbott P 16 + 8	Wright T 37 + 3	Palmer C 4	Stockdale D 40 + 1	Blundell G 17 + 19	Purdie R 30 + 9	White A 35	Cummins M 31 + 9	Nelthorpe C 4 + 3	Wainwright N 5 + 9	Harty I — + 1	Keltie C 21 + 6	Barrau X — + 1	Smith M — + 4	Green M 3 + 1 / Main C — + 1	Colbeck J 4 + 2	Brackstone J 3	Foran R 11 + 1	Ridley L 6	Wiseman S 2 + 5	Mayo P 7	Smith J 3	Valentine R 13 + 4	Gall K 7 + 1	Hodge B 7	N'Dumbu Nsungu G 4 + 4	Parker B 13	Kennedy J 13	Reay S — + 1	Kazimierczak P — + 1	*Match No.*
1■	2	3	4	5	6	7	8	9^{2}	10^{1}	11^{G}	15	12	13																									1
		3	4^{3}	5	12	7	8^{1}	9	10^{2}	2	1	13	11	6	14																							2
		3		5	12	7	8^{1}	9^{2}	10	6^{3}	1	13	2	4	11		14																					3
		3	4	5		7	12	9^{2}	10^{3}	8^{1}	1	13	2	6	11			14																				4
	2^{1}	3	4	5	12	7	14	9^{2}	10^{3}		1	13	8	6	11																							5
		3	4	5	2	7		9^{1}	10		1	12	8	6	11																							6
		3	4	5	2	7		9^{1}	10^{2}		1	12	8	6	11				13																			7
1		3	4^{2}	5	2^{3}	7			10^{1}			9	8	6	11		12		13	14■																		8
1		3	12	6		7			10			9	2	5	11		8		4^{1}																			9
1		3	12	6		7			10			9	2	5	11		8		4^{1}																			10
1		3^{1}	12	5	14	7			10^{3}			13	2	6	11				4			9^{2}							8									11
1	2		4	5	14				9			12	3	6	11^{2}		13		7			10^{1}							8^{3}									12
	2		4	5			12				1	9	3	0	13				0			10^{1}	7						11^{7}									13
	2	3^{2}	4	5		10			9^{3}		1	12	11	6	13				8^{1}			14	7															14
	2^{1}		13	5		8			10		1	9	12	6	11				4^{2}				7	3														15
	2			5	13	7		12	10^{1}		1	9^{2}		6	11				4				14	3	8^{3}													16
			12	5		7^{3}		9^{2}	14		1	13	2	6	11^{1}				8				4		10	3												17
	13		4^{2}	5		7		12	10		1	9^{1}	2	6	11								14		8^{3}	3												18
	12			5^{2}	13	7		14	10^{3}		1	9^{1}	2	6	11				4						8	3												19
	12		13	5		7		14	10^{3}		1	9	2	6	11				4						8^{2}	3^{1}												20
	2				6	7		9^{1}	10		1	12	8	5	11				4		13					3^{2}												21
	2		4		6	7^{1}		12	10		1	9^{3}	11	5■					8		13					3^{2}	14											22
	2		4	5	6	7		9	10^{1}		1	12	13						11^{2}		14				8^{3}			3										23
	2		4	5	6	7		9^{2}	10^{3}		1	13	12		11^{1}				14						8			3										24
	2		4^{3}	5	6	7			10^{2}		1	9	12		11^{1}				13						8			3		14								25
	2^{3}		4		6	7			10		1	9^{1}	12	5					11		13				8^{2}			3		14								26
		2	12	5	6	9			10^{2}		1	13	14		11^{3}				4									3^{1}		7	8							27
	2		4^{3}	5^{1}	12	10			9		1	13		6	11				14									3^{2}		7	8							28
			12	5		10			13		1	9	4	6	11^{1}													3		2	8^{2}	7						29
	2		4^{2}	5		7			10		1	9^{1}	11	6	12		13													3		8						30
	2		4	5	12	7			10		1	9^{2}	11^{1}	6■	13		14													3		8^{3}						31
	2		4	5	6	7^{2}		12			1				11		13							3^{3}			14				9	8	10^{1}					32
				5	6	7		12			1	13			11		14													2	9^{2}	8^{3}	10^{1}	3	4			33
	12			5	6	7		9	13		1				11^{1}		14													2	8^{3}		10^{2}	3	4			34
			4^{1}	5	6	7		10			1	9^{2}	12																	2	14	8^{3}	13	3	11			35
	2			5	6	9		14	10		1				11		12													7	8^{2}		13^{3}	3^{1}	4			36
	2			5	6	8		9^{1}	10^{3}		1	12	4		11^{2}															13			14	3	7			37
	2^{2}			5		7		9^{1}	10		1	12	8	6	11^{3}										14					13				3	4			38
	13			5		7			10^{2}		1	9^{3}	12	6											8					2		11^{1}	14	3	4			39
	13			5		7					1		3	6	12	11^{1}			10						8■					2^{2}				9	4			40
	2		12	5		10			9		1		7	6	13	11^{2}			4^{1}															3	8			41
	2		4^{1}	5		10^{2}			9		1		7	6	11	13^{3}			12								14							3	8			42
	2^{2}		12	5					9		1		7	6	11	14											13			3			10^{1}	8^{3}	4			43
			4	5					9		1		11^{3}	6	12	14	7^{2}		8								13			2				3	10^{1}			44
			4	5	13			9^{3}	10^{1}		1			6	12	11^{2}	7		8								2							3■		14		45
			4^{1}		6						1^{G}		3	5	11	10	7		8			12					2								9		15	46

FA Cup
First Round Northampton T (h) 1-1
(a) 1-2

Carling Cup
First Round Barnsley (a) 1-2

J Paint Trophy
Second Round Leeds U (h) 0-1

Play-Offs
Semi-Final Rochdale (h) 2-1
(a) 1-2

DERBY COUNTY — FL Championship

FOUNDATION

Derby County was formed by members of the Derbyshire County Cricket Club in 1884, when football was booming in the area and the cricketers thought that a football club would help boost finances for the summer game. To begin with, they sported the cricket club's colours of amber, chocolate and pale blue, and went into the game at the top immediately entering the FA Cup.

Pride Park Stadium, Pride Park, Derby DE24 8XL.

Telephone: 0871 472 1884.

Fax: (01332) 667 519.

Ticket Office: 0871 472 1884.

Website: www.dcfc.co.uk

Email: derby.county@dcfc.co.uk

Ground Capacity: 33,540.

Record Attendance: Baseball Ground: 41,826 v Tottenham H, Division 1, 20 September 1969. Pride Park: 33,475 Derby Co Legends v Rangers 9 in a Row Legends, 1 May 2006 (Ted McMinn Benefit).

Pitch Measurements: 100.58m × 67.66m.

Chairman of Football Operations: Adam Pearson.

Club Chairman: Andy Appleby.

President and Chief Executive: Tom Glick.

Secretary: Clare Morris.

Manager: Paul Jewell.

Assistant Manager: Chris Hutchings.

Physio: Alan Tomlinson.

Colours: White shirts, black shorts, white stockings.

Change Colours: Black shirts, white shorts, black stockings.

Year Formed: 1884.

Turned Professional: 1884.

Ltd Co.: 1896.

Club Nickname: 'The Rams'.

Grounds: 1884, Racecourse Ground; 1895, Baseball Ground; 1997, Pride Park.

First Football League Game: 8 September 1888, Football League, v Bolton W (a) W 6–3 – Marshall; Latham, Ferguson, Williamson; Monks, W. Roulstone; Bakewell (2), Cooper (2), Higgins, H. Plackett, L. Plackett (2).

Record League Victory: 9–0 v Wolverhampton W, Division 1, 10 January 1891 – Bunyan; Archie Goodall, Roberts; Walker, Chalmers, Roulstone (1); Bakewell, McLachlan, Johnny Goodall (1), Holmes (2), McMillan (5). 9–0 v Sheffield W, Division 1, 21 January 1899 – Fryer; Methven, Staley; Cox, Archie Goodall, May; Oakden (1), Bloomer (6), Boag, McDonald (1), Allen, (1 og).

HONOURS

Football League: Division 1 – Champions 1971–72, 1974–75; Runners-up 1895–96, 1929–30, 1935–36, 1995–96; Promoted from FL C – 2006–07 (play-offs); Division 2 – Champions 1911–12, 1914–15, 1968–69, 1986–87; Runners-up 1925–26; Division 3 (N) Champions 1956–57; Runners-up 1955–56.

FA Cup: Winners 1946; Runners-up 1898, 1899, 1903.

Football League Cup: Semi-final 1968.

Texaco Cup: Winners 1972.

European Competitions: *European Cup:* 1972–73, 1975–76. *UEFA Cup:* 1974–75, 1976–77. *Anglo-Italian Cup:* Runners-up 1993.

SKY SPORTS FACT FILE

On 7 December 1926 Mick O'Brien, a dual Irish international half-back on either side of the border, was transferred from Hull City to Derby County while he was residing in the United States of America and playing for Brooklyn Wanderers.

Record Cup Victory: 12–0 v Finn Harps, UEFA Cup 1st rd 1st leg, 15 September 1976 – Moseley; Thomas, Nish, Rioch (1), McFarland, Todd (King), Macken, Gemmill, Hector (5), George (3), James (3).

Record Defeat: 2–11 v Everton, FA Cup 1st rd, 1889–90.

Most League Points (2 for a win): 63, Division 2, 1968–69 and Division 3 (N), 1955–56 and 1956–57.

Most League Points (3 for a win): 84, Division 3, 1985–86, Division 3, 1986–87 and FL C, 2006–07.

Most League Goals: 111, Division 3 (N), 1956–57.

Highest League Scorer in Season: Jack Bowers, 37, Division 1, 1930–31; Ray Straw, 37 Division 3 (N), 1956–57.

Most League Goals in Total Aggregate: Steve Bloomer, 292, 1892–1906 and 1910–14.

Most League Goals in One Match: 6, Steve Bloomer v Sheffield W, Division 1, 2 January 1899.

Most Capped Players: Deon Burton, 41 (51), Jamaica and Mart Poom, 41 (118), Estonia.

Most League Appearances: Kevin Hector, 486, 1966–78 and 1980–82.

Youngest League Player: Lee Holmes, 15 years 268 days v Grimsby T, 26 December 2002.

Record Transfer Fee Received: £7,000,000 rising to £9,000,000 for Seth Johnson from Leeds U, October 2001.

Record Transfer Fee Paid: £3,500,000 to Norwich C for Robert Earnshaw, June 2007.

Football League Record: 1888 Founder Member of the Football League; 1907–12 Division 2; 1912–14 Division 1; 1914–15 Division 2; 1915–21 Division 1; 1921–26 Division 2; 1926–53 Division 1; 1953–55 Division 2; 1955–57 Division 3 (N); 1957–69 Division 2; 1969–80 Division 1; 1980–84 Division 2; 1984–86 Division 3; 1986–87 Division 2; 1987–91 Division 1; 1991–92 Division 2; 1992–96 Division 1; 1996–2002 FA Premier League; 2002–04 Division 1; 2004–07 FL C; 2007–08 FA Premier League; 2008– FL C.

MANAGERS

W. D. Clark 1896–1900
Harry Newbould 1900–06
Jimmy Methven 1906–22
Cecil Potter 1922–25
George Jobey 1925–41
Ted Magner 1944–46
Stuart McMillan 1946–53
Jack Barker 1953–55
Harry Storer 1955–62
Tim Ward 1962–67
Brian Clough 1967–73
Dave Mackay 1973–76
Colin Murphy 1977
Tommy Docherty 1977–79
Colin Addison 1979–82
Johnny Newman 1982
Peter Taylor 1982–84
Roy McFarland 1984
Arthur Cox 1984–93
Roy McFarland 1993–95
Jim Smith 1995–2001
Colin Todd 2001–02
John Gregory 2002–03
George Burley 2003–05
Phil Brown 2005–06
Billy Davies 2006–07
Paul Jewell November 2007–

LATEST SEQUENCES

Longest Sequence of League Wins: 9, 15.3.1969 – 19.4.1969.

Longest Sequence of League Defeats: 8, 12.12.1987 – 10.2.1988.

Longest Sequence of League Draws: 6, 26.3.1927 – 18.4.1927.

Longest Sequence of Unbeaten League Matches: 22, 8.3.1969 – 20.9.1969.

Longest Sequence Without a League Win: 32, 22.9.2007 – 11.5.2008.

Successive Scoring Runs: 29 from 3.12.1960.

Successive Non-scoring Runs: 8 from 30.10.1920.

TEN YEAR LEAGUE RECORD

		P	*W*	*D*	*L*	*F*	*A*	*Pts*	*Pos*
1998-99	PR Lge	38	13	13	12	40	45	52	8
1999-2000	PR Lge	38	9	11	18	44	57	38	16
2000-01	PR Lge	38	10	12	16	37	59	42	17
2001-02	PR Lge	38	8	6	24	33	63	30	19
2002-03	Div 1	46	15	7	24	55	74	52	18
2003-04	Div 1	46	13	13	20	53	67	52	20
2004-05	FL C	46	22	10	14	71	60	76	4
2005-06	FL C	46	10	20	16	53	67	50	20
2006-07	FL C	46	25	9	12	62	46	84	3
2007-08	PR Lge	38	1	8	29	20	89	11	20

DID YOU KNOW ?

Steve Bloomer at Derby County became the overall leading aggregate goalscorer in the Football League in 1901–02 with 182 goals. He retained the lead including four seasons at Middlesbrough until 1913–14 when his total had reached 352.

DERBY COUNTY 2007–08 LEAGUE RECORD

Match No.	Date	Venue	Opponents	Result		H/T Score	Lg. Pos.	Goalscorers	Attendance
1	Aug 11	H	Portsmouth	D	2-2	1-1	—	Oakley 5, Todd 84	32,176
2	15	A	Manchester C	L	0-1	0-1	—		43,620
3	18	A	Tottenham H	L	0-4	0-3	19		35,600
4	25	H	Birmingham C	L	1-2	0-1	20	Oakley 51	31,117
5	Sept 1	A	Liverpool	L	0-6	0-2	20		44,076
6	17	H	Newcastle U	W	1-0	1-0	—	Miller 39	33,016
7	22	A	Arsenal	L	0-5	0-2	20		60,122
8	29	H	Bolton W	D	1-1	1-1	20	Miller 19	31,503
9	Oct 7	A	Reading	L	0-1	0-0	20		23,091
10	20	A	Fulham	D	0-0	0-0	19		22,576
11	28	H	Everton	L	0-2	0-1	20		33,048
12	Nov 3	A	Aston Villa	L	0-2	0-0	20		40,938
13	10	H	West Ham U	L	0-5	0-1	20		32,440
14	24	H	Chelsea	L	0-2	0-1	20		32,789
15	Dec 1	A	Sunderland	L	0-1	0-0	20		42,380
16	8	A	Manchester U	L	1-4	0-2	20	Howard 76	75,725
17	15	H	Middlesbrough	L	0-1	0-1	20		32,676
18	23	A	Newcastle U	D	2-2	1-1	20	Barnes 6, Miller 52	51,386
19	26	H	Liverpool	L	1-2	0-1	20	McEveley 67	33,029
20	30	H	Blackburn R	L	1-2	1-2	20	Oakley 27	30,048
21	Jan 2	A	Bolton W	L	0-1	0-0	—		17,014
22	12	H	Wigan Ath	L	0-1	0-0	20		31,658
23	19	A	Portsmouth	L	1-3	1-2	20	Nyatanga 4	19,401
24	30	H	Manchester C	D	1-1	0-0	—	Jihai (og) 47	31,368
25	Feb 2	A	Birmingham C	D	1-1	0-0	20	Villa 89	25,924
26	9	H	Tottenham H	L	0-3	0-0	20		33,058
27	23	A	Wigan Ath	L	0-2	0-0	20		20,176
28	Mar 1	H	Sunderland	D	0-0	0-0	20		33,058
29	12	A	Chelsea	L	1-6	0-2	—	Jones 73	39,447
30	15	H	Manchester U	L	0-1	0-0	20		33,072
31	22	A	Middlesbrough	L	0-1	0-1	20		25,649
32	29	H	Fulham	D	2-2	1-1	20	Villa 2 10, 80	33,034
33	Apr 6	A	Everton	L	0-1	0-0	20		36,017
34	12	H	Aston Villa	L	0-6	0-3	20		33,036
35	19	A	West Ham U	L	1-2	0-1	20	Mears 65	34,612
36	28	H	Arsenal	L	2-6	1-2	—	McEveley 31, Earnshaw 77	33,003
37	May 3	A	Blackburn R	L	1-3	1-1	20	Miller 19	26,110
38	11	H	Reading	L	0-4	0-1	20		33,087

Final League Position: 20

GOALSCORERS

League (20): Miller 4, Oakley 3, Villa 3, McEveley 2, Barnes 1, Earnshaw 1, Howard 1, Jones 1, Mears 1, Nyatanga 1, Todd 1, own goal 1.
Carling Cup (2): Camara 1, Fagan 1.
FA Cup (4): Miller 2, Barnes 1, Earnshaw 1.

Bywater S 18	Mears T 22 + 3	Griffin A 13 + 2	Oakley M 19	Moore D 29 + 2	Davis C 19	Fagan C 17 + 5	Todd A 14 + 5	Howard S 14 + 6	Earnshaw R 7 + 15	Pearson S 23 + 1	Teale G 9 + 9	McEveley J 21 + 8	Jones D 11 + 3	Leacock D 22 + 4	Lewis E 22 + 2	Camara M 1	Malcolm B 1	Miller K 30	Feilhaber B 1 + 9	Barnes G 14 + 7	Edworthy M 7 + 2	Price L 6	Johnson M 1 + 2	Macken J — + 3	Mills D 2	Savage R 16	Robert L 3 + 1	Villa E 9 + 7	Ghaly H 13 + 2	Nyatanga L 2	Carroll R 14	Stubbs A 8	Sterjovski M 9 + 3	Addison M 1	Simmons P — + 1	*Match No.*
1	2	3^2	4	5	6	7	8	9	10^1	11	12	13																								1
1	2	3	4	5	6	7^1	8^3	9	12	10	13	14	11^2																							2
1	2^1	12	4	5		7	8^2	9	10	11	13	3		6																						3
1		2	4	12	6^1	10	5	9	14	8	7^2	3		13	11^3																					4
1	11	2^1	4	12	6	7	8	9		10	13	14				3^3	5^2																			5
1	2	3	4		6			9		8	7	12		5	11^1			10^2	13																	6
1	2	3	4^2		6			9^3		8	7	12		5	11			10^1	13	14																7
1	2		4		6			9		8	12	3	7^2	5	11^1			10		13																8
1	2	3^2	4		6			9^3	13	8		11		5	12			10	7^1	14																9
1	2	13	4	5	6^1	9		14		8		3^2		7^3	11			10		12																10
1	2		4	5	6	9^1		12	13	8		3	14		11^2			10^3		7																11
1		2	4	5	6^1	7^2		9	13	11	12	3		8						10																12
1	2	3	4	5		12		13	14	8	7^2				11^3			10^1		9	6															13
1		2	4^3	5	6	7^2		12	13			3	11	8				10	14	9^1																14
1		2	4	5	6	14		9	12	8	7^2	3		13				10^1		11^3																15
1	12	2	4	5	6	7^1		13		11	14	3^2		8				10		9^3																16
1	2	3^3	4	5	6			12	13	11	7^1	14		8				10^2		9																17
1	2			5		12		9		8	7^2	3		6	11^1			10	13	4																18
	2			5^2				9	12	8^3	7^1	3		6	11			10	13	4		1	14													19
	2		4		6	12		9				3		7^2	11			10^3	13	8		1	5^1	14												20
	2		4	5	6	9^3					7^2	3^1			11			10	14	8		1	12	13												21
	2				6	7	5				12									10	13	1		14	3	4	11^2	9^1	8^3							22
				5		7^1	6				12				13			10		14		1			2^2	4	11^3	9	8	3						23
				5	6^1	7	12		9^3	8^2				2				10		13	3	1				4		14	11							24
				5^1		7	12		9^3					2				10		13	3					4	11^2	14	8		1	6				25
				5^1		7	12			8			13	2				10		11	3^2					4^3		9			1	6	14			26
				5		7	12			11^3		3		2^1				10		9						4		14	8^2		1	6	13			27
				5		12			13	8		3	4^3		11			10^2			2							9	14		1	6	7^1			28
				5					12	9		3	13	14	11^2			10			2					4			8^1		1	6^3	7			29
				5			12		9^3			3	8	6	11			10			2^1					4	13	14			1		7^2			30
				5			2		9	12		3	8^1	6	11			10								4^2		14	13		1		7^3			31
	12			5			2^1		13				11	6	3			10^2								4		9	8		1		7			32
	12			5			2						11	6	3			10								4		9	8		1		7^1			33
	7			5^1			2^2		13			14	11^3	12	3			10								4		9	8		1	6				34
	7						2^1					12	11^2	5	3			10								4		13	8		1	6	9			35
	7			5			2		12			3			11				13							4		9	8^2		1	6	10^1			36
	7			5			2		9			3			11^1			10								4		12	8^2		1		13	6		37
	2			5									11		3			10	13		12					4^2		9^3	8	6	1		7^1		14	38

FA Cup

Third Round	Sheffield W	(h)	2-2
		(a)	1-1
Fourth Round	Preston NE	(h)	1-4

Carling Cup

Second Round	Blackpool	(h)	2-2

DONCASTER ROVERS FL Championship

FOUNDATION

In 1879, Mr Albert Jenkins assembled a team to play a match against the Yorkshire Institution for the Deaf. The players remained together as Doncaster Rovers, joining the Midland Alliance in 1889 and the Midland Counties League in 1891.

Keepmoat Stadium, Stadium Way, Lakeside, Doncaster, South Yorkshire DN4 5JW.

Telephone: (01302) 764 664.

Fax: (01302) 363 525.

Ticket Office: (01302) 762 576.

Website: www.doncasterroversfc.co.uk

Email: info@doncasterroversfc.co.uk

Ground Capacity: 15,269.

Record Attendance: 37,149 v Hull C, Division 3 (N), 2 October 1948.

Pitch Measurements: 100m × 70m.

Chairman: John Ryan.

Vice-chairman: Dick Watson.

Chief Executive/Secretary: David Morris.

Manager: Sean O'Driscoll.

Assistant Manager: Richard O'Kelly.

Physio: John Dickens.

Colours: Red and white hooped shirts, black shorts, black stockings.

Change Colours: Black shirts, red shorts, red stockings.

Year Formed: 1879.

Turned Professional: 1885.

Ltd Co.: 1905 & 1920.

Club Nickname: 'Rovers'.

Grounds: 1880–1916, Intake Ground; 1920, Benetthorpe Ground; 1922, Low Pasture, Belle Vue; 2007, Keepmoat Stadium.

Record League Victory: 10–0 v Darlington, Division 4, 25 January 1964: Potter; Raine, Meadows, Windross (1), White, Ripley (2), Robinson, Book (2), Hale (4), Jeffrey, Broadbent (1).

Record Cup Victory: 7–0 v Blyth Spartans, FA Cup 1st rd, 27 November 1937: Imrie; Shaw, Rodgers, McFarlane, Bycroft, Cyril Smith, Burton (1), Killourhy (4), Morgan (2), Malam, Dutton.

Record Defeat: 0–12 v Small Heath, Division 2, 11 April 1903.

HONOURS

Football League: Promoted from FL 1 2007–08 (play-offs); Division 3 Champions 2003–04; Division 3 (N) Champions – 1934–35, 1946–47, 1949–50; Runners-up: 1937–38, 1938–39; Division 4 Champions 1965–66, 1968–69; Runners-up: 1983–84. Promoted 1980–81 (3rd).

FA Cup: best season 5th rd, 1952, 1954, 1955, 1956.

Football League Cup: best season: 5th rd, 1976.

J Paint Trophy: Winners 2007.

Football Conference: Champions 2002–03

Sheffield County Cup: Winners 1891, 1912, 1936, 1938, 1956, 1968, 1976, 1986.

Midland Counties League: Champions 1897, 1899.

Conference Trophy: Winners 1999, 2000.

Sheffield & Hallamshire Senior Cup: Winners 2001, 2002.

SKY SPORTS FACT FILE

Striker James Hayter was the Doncaster Rovers matchwinner in the League One play-off final at Wembley on 24 May 2008. Bought from Bournemouth by Sean O'Driscoll the former Cherries manager, he cost a club record £200,000.

Most League Points (2 for a win): 72, Division 3 (N), 1946–47.

Most League Points (3 for a win): 92, Division 3, 2003–04.

Most League Goals: 123, Division 3 (N), 1946–47.

Highest League Scorer in Season: Clarrie Jordan, 42, Division 3 (N), 1946–47.

Most League Goals in Total Aggregate: Tom Keetley, 180, 1923–29.

Most League Goals in One Match: 6, Tom Keetley v Ashington, Division 3 (N), 16 February 1929.

Most Capped Player: Len Graham, 14, Northern Ireland.

Most League Appearances: Fred Emery, 417, 1925–36.

Youngest League Player: Alick Jeffrey, 15 years 229 days v Fulham, 15 September 1954.

Record Transfer Fee Received: £275,000 from QPR for Rufus Brevett, February 1991.

Record Transfer Fee Paid: £200,000 to AFC Bournemouth for James Hayter, May 2007.

Football League Record: 1901 Elected to Division 2; 1903 Failed re-election; 1904 Re-elected; 1905 Failed re-election; 1923 Re-elected to Division 3 (N); 1935–37 Division 2; 1937–47 Division 3 (N); 1947–48 Division 2; 1948–50 Division 3 (N); 1950–58 Division 2; 1958–59 Division 3; 1959–66 Division 4; 1966–67 Division 3; 1967–69 Division 4; 1969–71 Division 3; 1971–81 Division 4; 1981–83 Division 3; 1983–84 Division 4; 1984–88 Division 3; 1988–92 Division 4; 1992–98 Division 3; 1998–2003 Conference; 2003–04 Division 3; 2004–08 FL 1; 2008– FL C.

MANAGERS

Arthur Porter 1920–21
Harry Tufnell 1921–22
Arthur Porter 1922–23
Dick Ray 1923–27
David Menzies 1928–36
Fred Emery 1936–40
Bill Marsden 1944–46
Jackie Bestall 1946–49
Peter Doherty 1949–58
Jack Hodgson & Sid Bycroft (*Joint Managers*) 1958
Jack Crayston 1958–59 (*continued as Secretary-Manager to 1961*)
Jackie Bestall (TM) 1959–60
Norman Curtis 1960–61
Danny Malloy 1961–62
Oscar Hold 1962–64
Bill Leivers 1964–66
Keith Kettleborough 1966–67
George Raynor 1967–68
Lawrie McMenemy 1968–71
Morris Setters 1971–74
Stan Anderson 1975–78
Billy Bremner 1978–85
Dave Cusack 1985–87
Dave Mackay 1987–89
Billy Bremner 1989–91
Steve Beaglehole 1991–93
Ian Atkins 1994
Sammy Chung 1994–96
Kerry Dixon (*Player–Manager*) 1996–97
Dave Cowling 1997
Mark Weaver 1997–98
Ian Snodin 1998–99
Steve Wignall 1999–2001
Dave Penney 2002–06
Sean O'Driscoll September 2006–

LATEST SEQUENCES

Longest Sequence of League Wins: 10, 22.1.1947 – 4.4.1947.

Longest Sequence of League Defeats: 9, 14.1.1905 – 1.4.1905.

Longest Sequence of League Draws: 4, 29.10.1932 – 19.11.1932.

Longest Sequence of Unbeaten League Matches: 20, 26.12.1968 – 12.4.1969.

Longest Sequence Without a League Win: 20, 9.8.1997 – 29.11.1997.

Successive Scoring Runs: 27 from 10.11.1934.

Successive Non-scoring Runs: 7 from 27.9.1947.

TEN YEAR LEAGUE RECORD

		P	*W*	*D*	*L*	*F*	*A*	*Pts*	*Pos*
1998-99	Conf.	42	12	12	18	51	55	48	16
1999-2000	Conf.	42	15	9	18	46	48	54	12
2000-01	Conf.	42	15	13	14	47	43	58	9
2001-02	Conf.	42	18	13	11	68	46	67	4
2002-03	Conf.	42	22	12	8	73	47	78	3
2003-04	Div 3	46	27	11	8	79	37	92	1
2004-05	FL 1	46	16	18	12	65	60	66	10
2005-06	FL 1	46	20	9	17	55	51	69	8
2006-07	FL 1	46	16	15	15	52	47	63	11
2007-08	FL 1	46	23	11	12	65	41	80	3

DID YOU KNOW ?

In two post-war seasons Doncaster Rovers won championships by achieving more points away than at home. In 1946–47 they had 37 away, 35 at home while in the 1949–50 season their visiting form was just a shade better at 28 compared with 27 at Belle Vue.

DONCASTER ROVERS 2007–08 LEAGUE RECORD

Match No.	*Date*	*Venue*	*Opponents*	*Result*		*H/T Score*	*Lg. Pos.*	*Goalscorers*	*Attendance*
1	Aug 11	H	Millwall	D	0-0	0-0	—		7542
2	18	A	Hartlepool U	L	1-2	0-1	17	Hayter 71	5544
3	25	H	Bournemouth	L	1-2	1-1	20	Greer 24	6476
4	Sept 1	A	Swansea C	W	2-1	0-1	13	Wellens 2 68, 84	11,933
5	7	A	Northampton T	L	0-2	0-0	—		5274
6	16	H	Crewe Alex	W	2-0	1-0	14	Heffernan 31, Woodards (og) 48	6726
7	22	A	Southend U	L	2-3	2-1	17	Roberts G 28, Guy 36	8117
8	29	H	Cheltenham T	W	2-0	1-0	13	Guy 18, Mills 58	6150
9	Oct 2	H	Walsall	L	2-3	2-1	—	Mills 17, Guy 40	6038
10	6	A	Luton T	D	1-1	1-0	16	Hayter 26	6513
11	14	H	Huddersfield T	W	2-0	1-0	13	Stock 13, Wilson 65	6866
12	20	A	Nottingham F	D	0-0	0-0	13		23,108
13	28	H	Leyton Orient	W	4-2	0-0	11	Wellens 2 52, 88, Jason Price 69, Hayter 83	7184
14	Nov 3	A	Swindon T	W	2-1	1-0	8	Stock 31, Guy 73	6517
15	6	A	Gillingham	D	1-1	0-1	—	Hayter (pen) 65	5030
16	17	H	Tranmere R	D	0-0	0-0	9		7070
17	24	A	Port Vale	W	3-1	0-1	6	Guy 59, Hayter 68, Wellens 81	4581
18	Dec 4	H	Brighton & HA	D	0-0	0-0	—		6215
19	8	A	Oldham Ath	D	1-1	0-1	7	Hayter (pen) 90	4776
20	16	H	Yeovil T	L	1-2	0-1	10	Skiverton (og) 90	5967
21	22	A	Crewe Alex	W	4-0	1-0	9	Jason Price 2 38, 50, Green 89, Guy 90	4122
22	26	H	Northampton T	W	2-0	2-0	6	McCammon 11, Lockwood 29	7046
23	29	H	Southend U	W	3-1	3-1	4	Lockwood 6, Green 30, Roberts G 42	7163
24	Jan 1	A	Walsall	D	1-1	1-0	4	Jason Price 45	6266
25	12	H	Carlisle U	W	1-0	0-0	4	Hayter 84	8197
26	19	A	Leeds U	W	1-0	1-0	4	Stock 21	31,402
27	25	H	Swansea C	L	0-4	0-1	—		10,358
28	29	H	Hartlepool U	W	2-0	1-0	—	Wellens 34, Lockwood 54	6442
29	Feb 2	A	Millwall	W	3-0	1-0	2	Jason Price 43, Coppinger 77, Green 90	8230
30	9	H	Bristol R	W	2-0	0-0	2	Stock (pen) 65, Heffernan (pen) 90	8168
31	12	A	Bournemouth	W	2-0	1-0	—	Jason Price 2 1, 70	4947
32	23	A	Carlisle U	L	0-1	0-1	3		8390
33	Mar 1	A	Tranmere R	W	1-0	1-0	2	Coppinger 2	7551
34	4	A	Bristol R	W	1-0	1-0	—	Heffernan 3	3933
35	8	H	Port Vale	W	2-1	2-1	2	Heffernan 11, McCammon 19	8040
36	11	H	Gillingham	W	2-1	1-0	—	Coppinger 4, Heffernan (pen) 48	7867
37	15	A	Brighton & HA	L	0-1	0-0	2		6252
38	21	A	Yeovil T	L	1-2	0-2	—	Heffernan 73	6146
39	24	H	Oldham Ath	D	1-1	1-0	3-	Heffernan 37	8777
40	28	H	Nottingham F	W	1-0	0-0	—	Roberts G 74	12,508
41	Apr 1	H	Leeds U	L	0-1	0-1	—		15,001
42	5	A	Huddersfield T	D	2-2	0-1	3	Taylor 52, Green 84	10,279
43	11	H	Swindon T	W	2-0	1-0	—	McDaid 39, Stock (pen) 68	8371
44	19	A	Leyton Orient	D	1-1	0-1	3	McCammon 60	4582
45	26	H	Luton T	W	2-0	1-0	2	Mills 34, McCammon 82	9332
46	May 3	A	Cheltenham T	L	1-2	0-1	3	Green 76	6787

Final League Position: 3

GOALSCORERS

League (65): Hayter 7 (2 pens), Heffernan 7 (2 pens), Jason Price 7, Guy 6, Wellens 6, Green 5, Stock 5 (2 pens), McCammon 4, Coppinger 3, Lockwood 3, Mills 3, Roberts G 3, Greer 1, McDaid 1, Taylor 1, Wilson 1, own goals 2.
Carling Cup (4): Hayter 1, Heffernan 1, McCammon 1, Wellens 1.
FA Cup (3): Hayter 2, McCammon 1.
J Paint Trophy (10): Guy 2, McCammon 2, Woods 2, Green 1, Heffernan 1 (pen), Price 1, own goal 1.
Play-Offs (6): Coppinger 3, Hayter 1, Stock 1 (pen), own goal 1.

Sullivan N 46	O'Connor J 40	Roberts G 35 + 2	Woods M 7 + 8	Lockwood A 39	Greer G 10 + 1	Wilson M 23 + 8	Wellens R 45	Hayter J 21 + 13	Heffernan P 18 + 9	Coppinger J 31 + 8	McDaid S 14 + 10	Guy L 13 + 16	McCammon M 23 + 9	Mills M 29 + 5	Stock B 40	Green L 26 + 12	Price Jason 18 + 11	Roberts S 20 + 5	Hird S 3 + 1	Nelthorpe C — + 2	Elliott S 1 + 9	Taylor G 4 + 8	Lee G — + 1	Match No.
1	2	3	4[1]	5	6	7	8	9[2]	10	11[3]	12	13	14											1
1	2	3[2]	4	5	6	7[1]	8	9	10[3]	11	12	13	14											2
1	2	3[3]	4	5	6	7[2]	8	9	10	11[1]		12	13	14										3
1	2	3	13	5	6	7[3]	8	9[1]	12				10	4	11[2]	14								4
1	2	3	13	5	6[3]	7	8[1]	9[2]	12			14	10	4	11									5
1	2	3		5		7	8[2]	9	10[3]		12	11[1]		4	6	13	14							6
1	2	3		5	11[1]	7	8	13	10[2]	12	14	9		6	4[3]									7
1	2	3[1]		5		7	8	9	10		12	11[2]		6	4[3]	13		14						8
1	2			5		7	8	9[3]	10[1]	12	3	11■		4	6[2]	13	14							9
1	2			5		7	8[2]	9		10[1]	3			4	11	12	13	6[3]	14					10
1	2			5	3	7	8[2]	9[3]	12	10[1]	11			4	6	13				14				11
1	2	12		5	3[2]	7	8	9		10[3]	11[1]	13		4	6		14							12
1	2	3		5	12	7	8	9[1]			11[3]	10		4	6[2]	13	14							13
1	2	3	12	5		7	8[2]	9				10[1]		4	6	13	11[3]	14						14
1	2	3	12	5		7[2]	8	9		13		11[3]		4	6	14	10[1]							15
1	2		12	5		7[1]	8	9	10[3]	13	3	11[2]	14	4	6									16
1	2		12	5	4	7[1]	8	9	10[2]	13	3	11[3]			6			14						17
1	2		4	5	6	7	8	9[1]		12	3[2]	11[3]	10			13				14				18
1	2		4	5		7[1]	8[3]	9		12	3	10	13		11	14		6[2]						19
1	2		11	5		7[3]	8	9		12	3	10[1]			6	13	14	4[2]						20
1	2		12	5			8	9[2]		7	3	13	14		6[1]	11	10[3]	4						21
1	2	12		5		13	8	14		11	3[1]		10		6[2]	7	9[3]	4						22
1	2	3	12	5			8[1]	13		11[2]		14	10		6	7	9[3]	4						23
1	2	3		5		12	8	9[2]		11[1]		13	14		6	7	10[3]	4						24
1	2	3		5		12	8	13		11[2]		14	10[3]		6[1]	7	9	4						25
1	2	3		5		12	8[1]	13		11[2]			10	14	6	7	9[3]	4						26
1	2	3	4[2]	5[3]			8	12		11		13	10[1]	14		7	9	6■						27
1	2	3		5		7[2]	8		12	11[3]	13	14	10	6		4	9[1]							28
1	2	3		5		12	8		13	11			10[3]	14	6[1]	7	9[2]	4						29
1	2	3					8[2]		12	11[3]	13	14	10	5	6	7	9[1]	4						30
1	2	3				12	8		13	11		14	10[3]	5	6[1]	7	9[2]	4						31
1	2[2]	3		5			8		12	11			10[3]	13	6	7	9[1]	4			14			32
1		3		2		12	8[3]			11[1]			10	5	6	7	9[2]	4			13	14		33
1		3		5		12	8		9[3]	11			10[2]	2	6	7		4[1]			13	14		34
1		3		5		7	8		9[3]	11[1]	12		10[2]	4	6	2					13	14		35
1		3		5		7[2]	8	12	9	11[1]	13		10[3]	4	6	2					14			36
1		3		5			8	12	9[2]	7	11[3]		10[1]	4	6	2					13	14		37
1	2	3		5			8[3]	12	9	11			13	4[2]	6	7[1]					10	14		38
1		3		5			8	12	9[1]	11[3]			10[2]	2	6	7	13	4				14		39
1	2	3		5			8		9[3]	11[2]		12		4	6	7	10[1]	13				14		40
1	2	3		5[3]			8	12	9[1]	11[2]		13		4	6	7	10	14						41
1	2	3					8[3]		9[1]	11			12	5■	6	7	10[2]	4			14	13		42
1	2	3						12			11	9[2]	10[3]		6	7	13	4	5		14	8[1]		43
1	2	3					8[2]	13		9	12		10	5	6	7	14	4[1]				11[3]		44
1	2	3					8			11			10[2]	5	6[3]	7	12		4		14	9[1]	13	45
1	2	3					8		12	11[3]		14	10[1]	5	6	7	13		4			9[2]		46

FA Cup

First Round	Oldham Ath	(a)	2-2
		(h)	1-2

Carling Cup

First Round	Lincoln C	(h)	4-1
Second Round	Plymouth Arg	(a)	0-2

J Paint Trophy

First Round	Bradford C	(h)	5-1
Second Round	Oldham Ath	(h)	3-0
Quarter-Final	Grimsby T	(a)	2-2

Play-Offs

Semi-Final	Southend U	(a)	0-0
		(h)	5-1
Final *(at Wembley)*	Leeds U		1-0

EVERTON

FA Premiership

FOUNDATION

St Domingo Church Sunday School formed a football club in 1878 which played at Stanley Park. Enthusiasm was so great that in November 1879 they decided to expand membership and changed the name to Everton playing in black shirts with a scarlet sash and nicknamed the 'Black Watch'. After wearing several other colours, royal blue was adopted in 1901.

Goodison Park, Goodison Road, Liverpool L4 4EL.

Telephone: (0870) 442 1878.

Fax: (0151) 286 9112.

Ticket Office: 0870 442 1878.

Website: www.evertonfc.com

Email: everton@evertonfc.com

Ground Capacity: 40,157.

Record Attendance: 78,299 v Liverpool, Division 1, 18 September 1948.

Pitch Measurements: 100.48m × 68m.

Chairman: Bill Kenwright CBE.

Vice chairman: Jon Woods.

Chief Executive: Keith Wyness.

Secretary: David Harrison.

Manager: David Moyes.

Assistant Manager: Steve Round.

Head of Physiotherapy: Mick Rathbone Bsc (Hons), MCSP.

Colours: Blue shirts, white shorts, white stockings.

Change Colours: White shirts, dark navy shorts, dark navy stockings.

Year Formed: 1878.

Turned Professional: 1885.

Ltd Co.: 1892.

Previous Name: 1878, St Domingo FC; 1879, Everton.

Club Nickname: 'The Toffees'.

Grounds: 1878, Stanley Park; 1882, Priory Road; 1884, Anfield Road; 1892, Goodison Park.

First Football League Game: 8 September 1888, Football League, v Accrington (h) W 2–1 – Smalley; Dick, Ross; Holt, Jones, Dobson; Fleming (2), Waugh, Lewis, E. Chadwick, Farmer.

HONOURS

Football League: Division 1 – Champions 1890–91, 1914–15, 1927–28, 1931–32, 1938–39, 1962–63, 1969–70, 1984–85, 1986–87; Runners-up 1889–90, 1894–95, 1901–02, 1904–05, 1908–09, 1911–12, 1985–86; Division 2 – Champions 1930–31; Runners-up 1953–54.

FA Cup: Winners 1906, 1933, 1966, 1984, 1995; Runners-up 1893, 1897, 1907, 1968, 1985, 1986, 1989.

Football League Cup: Runners-up 1977, 1984.

League Super Cup: Runners-up 1986.

Simod Cup: Runners-up 1989.

Zenith Data Systems Cup: Runners-up 1991.

European Competitions: *European Cup:* 1963–64, 1970–71. *European Cup-Winners' Cup:* 1966–67, 1984–85 (winners), 1995–96. *European Fairs Cup:* 1962–63, 1964–65, 1965–66. *Champions League:* 2005–06. *UEFA Cup:* 1975–76, 1978–79, 1979–80, 2005–06, 2007–08.

SKY SPORTS FACT FILE

Landmarks for Everton in 2007–08 involved their exploits in the UEFA Cup campaign. On 20 December they beat AZ's 32-match unbeaten home record in Europe, then on 13 February they completed a club record sixth win in succession with a 2–0 win in Norway against Brann.

Record League Victory: 9–1 v Manchester C, Division 1, 3 September 1906 – Scott; Balmer, Crelley; Booth, Taylor (1), Abbott (1); Sharp, Bolton (1), Young (4), Settle (2), George Wilson. 9–1 v Plymouth Arg, Division 2, 27 December 1930 – Coggins; Williams, Cresswell; McPherson, Griffiths, Thomson; Critchley, Dunn, Dean (4), Johnson (1), Stein (4).

Record Cup Victory: 11–2 v Derby Co, FA Cup 1st rd, 18 January 1890 – Smalley; Hannah, Doyle (1); Kirkwood, Holt (1), Parry; Latta, Brady (3), Geary (3), Chadwick, Millward (3).

Record Defeat: 4–10 v Tottenham H, Division 1, 11 October 1958.

Most League Points (2 for a win): 66, Division 1, 1969–70.

Most League Points (3 for a win): 90, Division 1, 1984–85.

Most League Goals: 121, Division 2, 1930–31.

Highest League Scorer in Season: William Ralph 'Dixie' Dean, 60, Division 1, 1927–28 (All-time League record).

Most League Goals in Total Aggregate: William Ralph 'Dixie' Dean, 349, 1925–37.

Most League Goals in One Match: 6, Jack Southworth v WBA, Division 1, 30 December 1893.

Most Capped Player: Neville Southall, 92, Wales.

Most League Appearances: Neville Southall, 578, 1981–98.

Youngest League Player: James Vaughan, 16 years 271 days v Crystal Palace, 10 April 2005.

Record Transfer Fee Received: £23,000,000 rising to £27,000,000 from Manchester U for Wayne Rooney, August 2004.

Record Transfer Fee Paid: £11,250,000 to Middlesbrough for Yakubu, August 2007.

Football League Record: 1888 Founder Member of the Football League; 1930–31 Division 2; 1931–51 Division 1; 1951–54 Division 2; 1954–92 Division 1; 1992– FA Premier League.

MANAGERS

W. E. Barclay 1888–89
(Secretary-Manager)
Dick Molyneux 1889–1901
(Secretary-Manager)
William C. Cuff 1901–18
(Secretary-Manager)
W. J. Sawyer 1918–19
(Secretary-Manager)
Thomas H. McIntosh 1919–35
(Secretary-Manager)
Theo Kelly 1936–48
Cliff Britton 1948–56
Ian Buchan 1956–58
Johnny Carey 1958–61
Harry Catterick 1961–73
Billy Bingham 1973–77
Gordon Lee 1977–81
Howard Kendall 1981–87
Colin Harvey 1987–90
Howard Kendall 1990–93
Mike Walker 1994
Joe Royle 1994–97
Howard Kendall 1997–98
Walter Smith 1998–2002
David Moyes March 2002–

LATEST SEQUENCES

Longest Sequence of League Wins: 12, 24.3.1894 – 13.10.1894.

Longest Sequence of League Defeats: 6, 26.12.1996 – 29.1.1997.

Longest Sequence of League Draws: 5, 4.5.1977 – 16.5.1977.

Longest Sequence of Unbeaten League Matches: 20, 29.4.1978 – 16.12.1978.

Longest Sequence Without a League Win: 14, 6.3.1937 – 4.9.1937.

Successive Scoring Runs: 40 from 15.3.1930.

Successive Non-scoring Runs: 6 from 3.3.1951.

TEN YEAR LEAGUE RECORD

		P	*W*	*D*	*L*	*F*	*A*	*Pts*	*Pos*
1998-99	PR Lge	38	11	10	17	42	47	43	14
1999-2000	PR Lge	38	12	14	12	59	49	50	13
2000-01	PR Lge	38	11	9	18	45	59	42	16
2001-02	PR Lge	38	11	10	17	45	57	43	15
2002-03	PR Lge	38	17	8	13	48	49	59	7
2003-04	PR Lge	38	9	12	17	45	57	39	17
2004-05	PR Lge	38	18	7	13	45	46	61	4
2005-06	PR Lge	38	14	8	16	34	49	50	11
2006-07	PR Lge	38	15	13	10	52	36	58	6
2007-08	PR Lge	38	19	8	11	55	33	65	5

DID YOU KNOW?

Harry Makepeace and Jack Sharp, two members of the successful Everton team which captured the FA Cup for the first time in 1906, went on to play Test cricket for England as well as being capped for their country in the winter sport.

EVERTON 2007–08 LEAGUE RECORD

Match No.	*Date*	*Venue*	*Opponents*	*Result*		*H/T Score*	*Lg. Pos.*	*Goalscorers*	*Attendance*
1	Aug 11	H	Wigan Ath	W	2-1	1-0	—	Osman [26], Anichebe [75]	39,220
2	14	A	Tottenham H	W	3-1	3-1	—	Lescott [3], Osman [37], Stubbs [45]	35,716
3	18	A	Reading	L	0-1	0-1	4		22,813
4	25	H	Blackburn R	D	1-1	0-1	5	McFadden [78]	33,850
5	Sept 1	A	Bolton W	W	2-1	1-0	3	Yakubu [11], Lescott [90]	22,064
6	15	H	Manchester U	L	0-1	0-0	7		39,364
7	23	A	Aston Villa	L	0-2	0-1	9		38,235
8	30	H	Middlesbrough	W	2-0	1-0	5	Lescott [7], Pienaar [58]	31,885
9	Oct 7	A	Newcastle U	L	2-3	0-1	10	Johnson [53], Given (og) [90]	50,152
10	20	H	Liverpool	L	1-2	1-0	11	Hyypia (og) [38]	40,049
11	28	A	Derby Co	W	2-0	1-0	9	Arteta [26], Yakubu [63]	33,048
12	Nov 3	H	Birmingham C	W	3-1	1-0	8	Yakubu [10], Carsley [89], Vaughan [90]	35,155
13	11	A	Chelsea	D	1-1	0-0	9	Cahill [90]	41,683
14	24	H	Sunderland	W	7-1	3-1	8	Yakubu 2 [12, 73], Cahill 2 [17, 62], Pienaar [43], Johnson [80], Osman [85]	38,594
15	Dec 1	A	Portsmouth	D	0-0	0-0	9		20,102
16	8	H	Fulham	W	3-0	0-0	7	Yakubu 3 [51, 61, 79]	32,743
17	15	A	West Ham U	W	2-0	1-0	6	Yakubu [45], Johnson [90]	34,430
18	23	A	Manchester U	L	1-2	1-1	6	Cahill [27]	75,749
19	26	H	Bolton W	W	2-0	0-0	6	Neville [51], Cahill [70]	38,918
20	29	H	Arsenal	L	1-4	1-0	6	Cahill [19]	39,443
21	Jan 1	A	Middlesbrough	W	2-0	0-0	5	Johnson [67], McFadden [72]	27,028
22	12	H	Manchester C	W	1-0	1-0	5	Lescott [31]	38,474
23	20	A	Wigan Ath	W	2-1	2-0	4	Johnson [39], Lescott [42]	18,820
24	30	H	Tottenham H	D	0-0	0-0	—		35,840
25	Feb 2	A	Blackburn R	D	0-0	0-0	4		27,946
26	9	H	Reading	W	1-0	0-0	4	Jagielka [62]	36,582
27	25	A	Manchester C	W	2-0	2-0	—	Yakubu [30], Lescott [38]	41,728
28	Mar 2	H	Portsmouth	W	3-1	1-1	4	Yakubu 2 [1, 81], Cahill [73]	33,938
29	9	A	Sunderland	W	1-0	0-0	5	Johnson [55]	42,595
30	16	A	Fulham	L	0-1	0-0	5		25,262
31	22	H	West Ham U	D	1-1	1-0	5	Yakubu [8]	37,430
32	30	A	Liverpool	L	0-1	0-1	5		44,295
33	Apr 6	H	Derby Co	W	1-0	0-0	5	Osman [56]	36,017
34	12	A	Birmingham C	D	1-1	0-0	5	Lescott [78]	25,923
35	17	H	Chelsea	L	0-1	0-1	—		37,112
36	27	H	Aston Villa	D	2-2	0-0	5	Neville [56], Yobo [84]	37,936
37	May 4	A	Arsenal	L	0-1	0-0	5		60,123
38	11	H	Newcastle U	W	3-1	1-0	5	Yakubu 2 (1 pen) [28, 82 (p)], Lescott [70]	39,592

Final League Position: 5

GOALSCORERS

League (55): Yakubu 15 (1 pen), Lescott 8, Cahill 7, Johnson 6, Osman 4, McFadden 2, Neville 2, Pienaar 2, Anichebe 1, Arteta 1, Carsley 1, Jagielka 1, Stubbs 1, Vaughan 1, Yobo 1, own goals 2.
Carling Cup (7): Yakubu 3, McFadden 2, Cahill 1, Osman 1.
FA Cup (0).
UEFA Cup (23): Anichebe 4, Johnson 4, Arieta 3 (1 pen), Yakubu 3, Cahill 2, Lescott 2, Osman 2, Jagielka 1, McFadden 1, Vaughan 1.

Howard T 36	Hibbert T 22 + 2	Lescott J 37 + 1	Yobo J 29 + 1	Stubbs A 7 + 1	Carsley L 33 + 1	Osman L 26 + 2	Neville P 37	Johnson A 20 + 9	Anichebe V 10 + 17	Arteta M 27 + 1	Pienaar S 25 + 3	Jagielka P 27 + 7	Nuno Valente 8 + 1	McFadden J 5 + 7	Baines L 13 + 9	Gravesen T 1 + 7	Yakubu A 26 + 3	Wessels S 2	Cahill T 18	Vaughan J — + 8	Fernandes M 9 + 3	Rodwell J — + 2	*Match No.*
1	2	3	4	5	6	7^1	8	9	10	11	12												1
1	2	3	4	5	6	7	8	9	10^1	11		12											2
1	2^3	4		5	6	7^2	8	9	10^1	11	12	13	3	14									3
1	2^1	14	4	5^3	6^2	7	8	9	12	11		13		10	3								4
1		5	4		6^3	12	8	9	13	11	7^1	2			3	14	10^2						5
	2	5	4			7^2	8^3	9	12	11	13	6		14	3		10^1	1					6
	2	5	4			7	8	9^1	10^2		11	6		12	3		13	1					7
1	2	4	14	5	12		8		13	11^1	7	6		10^3	3		9^2						8
1	2	5	4		6	12	8^3	13	10	11	7^1			9^2	3		14						9
1	2■	3	4	5		7	8■		10^2	11		6		12	13		9^1						10
1		5	4	12	6	7			13	11	8	2		14	3^1		9^2		10^3				11
1		3	4	5^1	6	7^3	2			11	8^2	12				13	9		10	14			12
1	2	5	4		6^3	7	8^1		13		11		3	12		14	9^2		10				13
1		5	4^1		6	7	2	13	14	11	8	12	3				9^2		10^3				14
1		5	4		6	7	2	12	13	11	8^1		3				9^2		10				15
1		5	4		6	7	2	12		11	8	14		13	3^3		9^2		10^1				16
1		3	4		6	7	2	12		11	8	5					9^1		10				17
1	2	3	4		6		8	9	12		11	5				13	10^2		7^1				18
1	12	3	4		6		2^1	13		11	8	5				7^2	9^3		10	14			19
1	2^1	3	4		6		8	12		11■	7	5					9		10				20
1	2	5			6		8	9	12		7^1	4	3	11^2	13		10^3			14			21
1	2	5			6		8		9^1	11		4	3	7^2	12				10	13			22
1	2	5			6	7	8^1	9		11		4	3						10	12			23
1		5			6		2	9	10^1	7		4	3		11					12	8		24
1		5			6	7^1	2	9		11		4			3				10	12	8		25
1		3	5		6	7	2	9		11		4							10	12	8^1		26
1	2	3	4		6	7	8	13			11^1	5					9		10		12^2		27
1	2^1	3	4		6	7	8	12	13		11^3	5			14		9^2		10				28
1	2	3	4				8	9	12	11	7^2	5			13		10^1		6^3			14	29
1	12	3	4		6	7	2	9^1		11	8^2	5			13		10						30
1		5			6	7	2		10	11		4			3		9		8^1		12		31
1	2	3	4		6	7	8^1			11	10^2	5			12		9				13		32
1		5	4		6	7	2	9	12	11^3		13	14		3		10^1				8^2		33
1	2	5			6		8	9	12		11^1	4			3	13	10^2				7		34
1	2	3	4		6		8	9^2	12		11^1	5				13	10				7		35
1		3	4		6	7	2	9^2	13	12	11	5					10				8^1		36
1	2	3	4		6^2	11	8	9^1	12		10	5			14		13				7^3		37
1		3	4^1		6^3	7	2		10^2		11	5			12	13	9				8	14	38

UEFA Cup

First Round	Metalist Kharkiv	(h)	1-1
		(a)	3-2
Group A	Larissa	(h)	3-1
	Nuremberg	(a)	2-0
	Zenit	(h)	1-0
	AZ	(a)	3-2
Third Round	Brann	(a)	2-0
		(h)	6-1
Fourth Round	Fiorentina	(a)	0-2
		(h)	2-0

FA Cup

Third Round	Oldham Ath	(h)	0-1

Carling Cup

Third Round	Sheffield W	(a)	3-0
Fourth Round	Luton T	(a)	1-0
Quarter-Final	West Ham U	(a)	2-1
Semi-Final	Chelsea	(a)	1-2
		(h)	0-1

EXETER CITY FL Championship 2

FOUNDATION

Exeter City was formed in 1904 by the amalgamation of St Sidwell's United and Exeter United. The club first played in the East Devon League and then the Plymouth & District League. After an exhibition match between West Bromwich Albion and Woolwich Arsenal which was held to test interest as Exeter was then a rugby stronghold, it was decided to form Exeter City. At a meeting at the Red Lion Hotel in 1908, the club turned professional.

St James Park, Exeter EX4 6PX.

Telephone: (0871) 855 1904.

Fax: (01392) 413 959.

Website: www.exetercityfc.co.uk

Email: enquiries@exetercityfc.co.uk

Training Ground: (01395) 232784.

Ground Capacity: 9,036.

Record Attendance: 20,984 v Sunderland, FA Cup 6th rd (replay), 4 March 1931.

Record Receipts: £59,862.98 v Aston Villa, FA Cup 3rd rd, 8 January 1994.

Pitch Measurements: 114yd × 73yd.

Chairman: Dennis Watts.

Manager: Paul Tisdale.

Assistant Manager: John Yems.

Sports Therapist: Tamer James.

Secretary: Sally Cooke.

Colours: Red and white shirts, black shorts, black stockings.

Change Colours: All blue.

Year Formed: 1904.

Turned Professional: 1908.

Ltd Co.: 1908.

Club Nickname: 'The Grecians'.

First Football League Game: 28 August 1920, Division 3, v Brentford (h) W 3–0 – Pym; Coleburne, Feebury (1p); Crawshaw, Carrick, Mitton; Appleton, Makin, Wright (1), Vowles (1), Dockray.

Record League Victory: 8–1 v Coventry C, Division 3 (S), 4 December 1926 – Bailey; Pollard, Charlton; Pullen, Pool, Garrett; Purcell (2), McDevitt, Blackmore (2), Dent (2), Compton (2). 8–1 v Aldershot, Division 3 (S), 4 May 1935 – Chesters; Gray, Miller; Risdon, Webb, Angus; Jack Scott (1), Wrightson (1), Poulter (3), McArthur (1), Dryden (1), (1 og).

HONOURS

Football League: Division 3 best season: 8th, 1979–80; Division 3 (S) – Runners-up 1932–33; Division 4 – Champions 1989–90; Runners-up 1976–77.

FA Cup: best season: 6th rd replay, 1931, 6th rd 1981.

Football League Cup: never beyond 4th rd.

Division 3 (S) Cup: Winners 1934.

SKY SPORTS FACT FILE

In 1936–37 Exeter City signed centre-forward Rod Williams from Newport County. He achieved the remarkable feat of scoring almost half of the 59 League goals. He missed the first game so it could be argued that he had 50 per cent anyway with his 29.

Record Cup Victory: 14–0 v Weymouth, FA Cup 1st qual rd, 3 October 1908 – Fletcher; Craig, Bulcock; Ambler, Chadwick, Wake; Parnell (1), Watson (1), McGuigan (4), Bell (6), Copestake (2).

Record Defeat: 0–9 v Notts Co, Division 3 (S), 16 October 1948. 0–9 v Northampton T, Division 3 (S), 12 April 1958.

Most League Points (2 for a win): 62, Division 4, 1976–77.

Most League Points (3 for a win): 89, Division 4, 1989–90.

Most League Goals: 88, Division 3 (S), 1932–33.

Highest League Scorer in Season: Fred Whitlow, 33, Division 3 (S), 1932–33.

Most League Goals in Total Aggregate: Tony Kellow, 129, 1976–78, 1980–83, 1985–88.

Most League Goals in One Match: 4, Harold 'Jazzo' Kirk v Portsmouth, Division 3S, 3 March 1923; 4, Fred Dent v Bristol R, Division 3S, 5 November 1927; 4, Fred Whitlow v Watford, Division 3S, 29 October 1932.

Most Capped Player: Dermot Curtis, 1 (17), Eire.

Most League Appearances: Arnold Mitchell, 495, 1952–66.

Youngest League Player: Cliff Bastin, 16 years 31 days v Coventry C, 14 April 1928.

Record Transfer Fee Received: £500,000 from Manchester C for Martin Phillips, November 1995.

Record Transfer Fee Paid: £65,000 to Blackpool for Tony Kellow, March 1980.

Football League Record: 1920 Elected Division 3; 1921–58 Division 3 (S); 1958–64 Division 4; 1964–66 Division 3; 1966–77 Division 4; 1977–84 Division 3; 1984–90 Division 4; 1990–92 Division 3; 1992–94 Division 2; 1994–2003 Division 3; 2003–08 Conference; 2008– FL 2.

MANAGERS

Arthur Chadwick 1910–22
Fred Mavin 1923–27
Dave Wilson 1928–29
Billy McDevitt 1929–35
Jack English 1935–39
George Roughton 1945–52
Norman Kirkman 1952–53
Norman Dodgin 1953–57
Bill Thompson 1957–58
Frank Broome 1958–60
Glen Wilson 1960–62
Cyril Spiers 1962–63
Jack Edwards 1963–65
Ellis Stuttard 1965–66
Jock Basford 1966–67
Frank Broome 1967–69
Johnny Newman 1969–76
Bobby Saxton 1977–79
Brian Godfrey 1979–83
Gerry Francis 1983–84
Jim Iley 1984–85
Colin Appleton 1985–87
Terry Cooper 1988–91
Alan Ball 1991–94
Terry Cooper 1994–95
Peter Fox 1995–2000
Noel Blake 2000–01
John Cornforth 2001–02
Neil McNab 2002–03
Gary Peters 2003
Eamonn Dolan 2003–2004
Alex Inglethorpe 2004–06
Paul Tisdale June 2006–

LATEST SEQUENCES

Longest Sequence of League Wins: 7, 23.4.1977 – 20.8.1977.

Longest Sequence of League Defeats: 7, 14.1.1984 – 25.2.1984.

Longest Sequence of League Draws: 6, 13.9.1986 – 4.10.1986.

Longest Sequence of Unbeaten League Matches: 13, 23.8.1986 – 25.10.1986.

Longest Sequence Without a League Win: 18, 21.2.1995 – 19.8.1995.

Successive Scoring Runs: 22 from 15.9.1958.

Successive Non-scoring Runs: 6 from 24.11.1923.

TEN YEAR LEAGUE RECORD

		P	*W*	*D*	*L*	*F*	*A*	*Pts*	*Pos*
1998-99	Div 3	46	17	12	17	47	50	63	12
1999-2000	Div 3	46	11	11	24	46	72	44	21
2000-01	Div 3	46	12	14	20	40	58	50	19
2001-02	Div 3	46	14	13	19	48	73	55	16
2002-03	Div 3	46	11	15	20	50	64	48	23
2003-04	Conf	42	19	12	11	71	51	69	6
2004-05	Conf	42	20	11	11	71	50	71	6
2005-06	Conf	42	18	9	15	65	48	63	7
2006-07	Conf	46	22	12	12	67	48	78	5
2007-08	B Sq Pr	46	22	17	7	83	58	83	4

DID YOU KNOW ?

Exeter City revealed outstanding powers of recovery in 1923–24 as at the halfway stage they had scored in only five of 21 matches! Doubling their number of victories they finished a respectable 16th in the final table.

FULHAM — FA Premiership

FOUNDATION

Churchgoers were responsible for the foundation of Fulham, which first saw the light of day as Fulham St Andrew's Church Sunday School FC in 1879. They won the West London Amateur Cup in 1887 and the championship of the West London League in its initial season of 1892–93. The name Fulham had been adopted in 1888.

Craven Cottage, Stevenage Road, London SW6 6HH
Telephone: 0870 442 1222.
Fax: 0870 442 0236.
Ticket Office: 0870 442 1234.
Website: www.fulhamfc.co.uk
Email: enquiries@fulhamfc.com
Ground Capacity: 25,478.
Record Attendance: 49,335 v Millwall, Division 2, 8 October 1938.
Pitch Measurements: 100m × 65m.
Chairman: Mohamed Al Fayed.
Vice-chairman: Omar Al Fayed.
Managing Director: David McNally.
Secretary: Darren Preston.
Manager: Roy Hodgson.
Assistant Manager: Mike Kelly.
Head of Sports Medicine and Exercise Science: Mark Taylor.
Colours: White shirts, black shorts, white stockings.
Change Colours: Red and black striped shirts, white shorts, black stockings.
Year Formed: 1879.
Turned Professional: 1898.
Ltd Co.: 1903.
Reformed: 1987.
Previous Name: 1879, Fulham St Andrew's; 1888, Fulham.
Club Nickname: 'Cottagers'.
Grounds: 1879, Star Road, Fulham; c.1883, Eel Brook Common, 1884, Lillie Road; 1885, Putney Lower Common; 1886, Ranelagh House, Fulham; 1888, Barn Elms, Castelnau; 1889, Purser's Cross (Roskell's Field), Parsons Green Lane; 1891, Eel Brook Common; 1891, Half Moon, Putney; 1895, Captain James Field, West Brompton; 1896, Craven Cottage.
First Football League Game: 3 September 1907, Division 2, v Hull C (h) L 0–1 – Skene; Ross, Lindsay; Collins, Morrison, Goldie; Dalrymple, Freeman, Bevan, Hubbard, Threlfall.
Record League Victory: 10–1 v Ipswich T, Division 1, 26 December 1963 – Macedo; Cohen, Langley; Mullery (1), Keetch, Robson (1); Key, Cook (1), Leggat (4), Haynes, Howfield (3).
Record Cup Victory: 7–0 v Swansea C, FA Cup 1st rd, 11 November 1995 – Lange; Jupp (1), Herrera, Barkus (Brooker (1)), Moore, Angus, Thomas (1), Morgan, Brazil (Hamill), Conroy (3) (Bolt), Cusack (1).

HONOURS

Football League: Division 1 – Champions 2000–01; Division 2 – Champions 1948–49, 1998–99; Runners-up 1958–59; Division 3 (S) – Champions 1931–32; Division 3 – Runners-up 1970–71, 1996–97.

FA Cup: Runners-up 1975.

Football League Cup: best season: 5th rd, 1968, 1971, 2000.

European Competitions: *UEFA Cup:* 2002–03. *Intertoto Cup:* 2002 (winners)

SKY SPORTS FACT FILE

The appointment of Roy Hodgson and the return of Jimmy Bullard for his first game since 9 September 2006 for the last 17 matches of 2007–08 helped considerably towards avoiding relegation. Six wins – three times as many as hitherto – came in this period.

Record Defeat: 0–10 v Liverpool, League Cup 2nd rd 1st leg, 23 September 1986.

Most League Points (2 for a win): 60, Division 2, 1958–59 and Division 3, 1970–71.

Most League Points (3 for a win): 101, Division 2, 1998–99. 101, Division 1, 2000–01.

Most League Goals: 111, Division 3 (S), 1931–32.

Highest League Scorer in Season: Frank Newton, 43, Division 3 (S), 1931–32.

Most League Goals in Total Aggregate: Gordon Davies, 159, 1978–84, 1986–91.

Most League Goals in One Match: 5, Fred Harrison v Stockport Co, Division 2, 5 September 1908; 5, Bedford Jezzard v Hull C, Division 2, 8 October 1955; 5, Jimmy Hill v Doncaster R, Division 2, 15 March 1958; 5, Steve Earle v Halifax T, Division 3, 16 September 1969.

Most Capped Player: Johnny Haynes, 56, England.

Most League Appearances: Johnny Haynes, 594, 1952–70.

Youngest League Player: Matthew Briggs, 16 years 65 days v Middlesbrough, 13 May 2007.

Record Transfer Fee Received: £11,500,000 from Manchester U for Louis Saha, January 2004.

Record Transfer Fee Paid: £11,500,000 to Lyon for Steve Marlet, August 2001.

Football League Record: 1907 Elected to Division 2; 1928–32 Division 3 (S); 1932–49 Division 2; 1949–52 Division 1; 1952–59 Division 2; 1959–68 Division 1; 1968–69 Division 2; 1969–71 Division 3; 1971–80 Division 2; 1980–82 Division 3; 1982–86 Division 2; 1986–92 Division 3; 1992–94 Division 2; 1994–97 Division 3; 1997–99 Division 2; 1999–2001 Division 1; 2001– FA Premier League.

LATEST SEQUENCES

Longest Sequence of League Wins: 12, 7.5.2000 – 18.10.2000.

Longest Sequence of League Defeats: 11, 2.12.1961 – 24.2.1962.

Longest Sequence of League Draws: 6, 14.10.1995 – 18.11.1995.

Longest Sequence of Unbeaten League Matches: 15, 26.1.1999 – 13.4.1999.

Longest Sequence Without a League Win: 15, 25.2.1950 – 23.8.1950.

Successive Scoring Runs: 26 from 28.3.1931.

Successive Non-scoring Runs: 6 from 21.8.1971.

MANAGERS

Harry Bradshaw 1904–09
Phil Kelso 1909–24
Andy Ducat 1924–26
Joe Bradshaw 1926–29
Ned Liddell 1929–31
Jim McIntyre 1931–34
Jimmy Hogan 1934–35
Jack Peart 1935–48
Frank Osborne 1948–64
(was Secretary-Manager or General Manager for most of this period and Team Manager 1953–56)
Bill Dodgin Snr 1949–53
Duggie Livingstone 1956–58
Bedford Jezzard 1958–64
(General Manager for last two months)
Vic Buckingham 1965–68
Bobby Robson 1968
Bill Dodgin Jnr 1968–72
Alec Stock 1972–76
Bobby Campbell 1976–80
Malcolm Macdonald 1980–84
Ray Harford 1984–96
Ray Lewington 1986–90
Alan Dicks 1990–91
Don Mackay 1991–94
Ian Branfoot 1994–96
(continued as General Manager)
Micky Adams 1996–97
Ray Wilkins 1997–98
Kevin Keegan 1998–99
(Chief Operating Officer)
Paul Bracewell 1999–2000
Jean Tigana 2000–03
Chris Coleman 2003–07
Lawrie Sanchez 2007
Roy Hodgson December 2007–

TEN YEAR LEAGUE RECORD

		P	*W*	*D*	*L*	*F*	*A*	*Pts*	*Pos*
1998-99	Div 2	46	31	8	7	79	32	101	1
1999-2000	Div 1	46	17	16	13	49	41	67	9
2000-01	Div 1	46	30	11	5	90	32	101	1
2001-02	PR Lge	38	10	14	14	36	44	44	13
2002-03	PR Lge	38	13	9	16	41	50	48	14
2003-04	PR Lge	38	14	10	14	52	46	52	9
2004-05	PR Lge	38	12	8	18	52	60	44	13
2005-06	PR Lge	38	14	6	18	48	58	48	12
2006-07	PR Lge	38	8	15	15	38	60	39	16
2007-08	PR Lge	38	8	12	18	38	60	36	17

DID YOU KNOW ?

In 1925–26 Fulham battled their way to the sixth round of the FA Cup knocking out Everton – after a replay – Liverpool and Notts County with goalkeeper Ernest Cromwell Beecham outstanding in the run. He earned his second name as the first baby born in that new road!

FULHAM 2007–08 LEAGUE RECORD

Match No.	Date	Venue	Opponents	Result		H/T Score	Lg. Pos.	Goalscorers	Attendance
1	Aug 12	A	Arsenal	L	1-2	1-0	—	Healy 1	60,093
2	15	H	Bolton W	W	2-1	2-1	—	Healy 23, Cid (og) 26	21,102
3	18	H	Middlesbrough	L	1-2	1-0	13	McBride 16	20,948
4	25	A	Aston Villa	L	1-2	1-0	19	Dempsey 6	36,638
5	Sept 1	H	Tottenham H	D	3-3	1-2	15	Dempsey 42, Richardo Rocha (og) 77, Kamara 90	24,007
6	15	A	Wigan Ath	D	1-1	1-0	16	Dempsey 11	16,973
7	22	H	Manchester C	D	3-3	1-1	17	Davies 13, Bouazza 48, Murphy 75	24,674
8	29	A	Chelsea	D	0-0	0-0	16		41,837
9	Oct 7	H	Portsmouth	L	0-2	0-0	18		20,774
10	20	H	Derby Co	D	0-0	0-0	13		22,576
11	27	A	Sunderland	D	1-1	1-0	14	Davies 32	39,392
12	Nov 3	H	Reading	W	3-1	1-0	13	Davies 18, Dempsey 72, Healy 90	22,086
13	10	A	Liverpool	L	0-2	0-0	13		43,073
14	25	H	Blackburn R	D	2-2	0-0	12	Murphy (pen) 51, Kamara 63	22,826
15	Dec 3	A	Manchester U	L	0-2	0-1	—		75,055
16	8	A	Everton	L	0-3	0-0	17		32,743
17	15	H	Newcastle U	L	0-1	0-0	18		24,959
18	22	H	Wigan Ath	D	1-1	0-0	17	Dempsey 78	20,820
19	26	A	Tottenham H	L	1-5	0-2	18	Dempsey 60	36,077
20	29	A	Birmingham C	D	1-1	1-0	19	Bocanegra 8	28,923
21	Jan 1	H	Chelsea	L	1-2	1-0	19	Murphy (pen) 10	25,357
22	12	A	West Ham U	L	1-2	1-1	19	Davies 8	34,947
23	19	H	Arsenal	L	0-3	0-2	19		25,297
24	29	A	Bolton W	D	0-0	0-0	—		17,732
25	Feb 3	H	Aston Villa	W	2-1	0-0	19	Davies 73, Bullard 86	24,760
26	9	A	Middlesbrough	L	0-1	0-1	19		26,885
27	23	H	West Ham U	L	0-1	0-0	19		25,280
28	Mar 1	H	Manchester U	L	0-3	0-2	19		25,314
29	8	A	Blackburn R	D	1-1	0-0	19	Bullard 89	20,362
30	16	H	Everton	W	1-0	0-0	19	McBride 67	25,262
31	22	A	Newcastle U	L	0-2	0-1	19		52,293
32	29	A	Derby Co	D	2-2	1-1	19	Kamara 24, Leacock (og) 78	33,034
33	Apr 5	H	Sunderland	L	1-3	0-1	19	Healy 74	25,053
34	12	A	Reading	W	2-0	1-0	19	McBride 24, Nevland 90	24,112
35	19	H	Liverpool	L	0-2	0-1	19		25,311
36	26	A	Manchester C	W	3-2	0-2	19	Kamara 2 70, 90, Murphy 79	44,504
37	May 3	H	Birmingham C	W	2-0	0-0	17	McBride 52, Nevland 87	25,308
38	11	A	Portsmouth	W	1-0	0-0	17	Murphy 76	20,532

Final League Position: 17

GOALSCORERS

League (38): Dempsey 6, Davies 5, Kamara 5, Murphy 5 (2 pens), Healy 4, McBride 4, Bullard 2, Nevland 2, Bocanegra 1, Bouazza 1, own goals 3.
Carling Cup (2): Healy 1, Kamara 1.
FA Cup (2): Healy 1, Murphy 1.

Warner T 3	Baird C 17 + 1	Konchesky P 33	Davis S 22	Knight Z 4	Bocanegra C 18 + 4	Davies S 36 + 1	Smertin A 11 + 4	McBride B 14 + 3	Healy D 15 + 15	Bouazza H 15 + 5	Diop P — + 2	Dempsey C 29 + 7	Kamara D 17 + 11	Keller K 13	Pearce I — + 1	Volz M 5 + 4	John C — + 2	Niemi A 22	Stefanovic D 13	Hughes A 29 + 1	Murphy D 28 + 5	Seol K 4 + 8	Omozusi E 8	Kuqi S 3 + 7	Ashton N 1	Bullard J 15 + 2	Andreasen L 9 + 4	Hangeland B 15	Christanval P — + 1	Nevland E 2 + 6	Stalteri P 13	Johnson E 4 + 2	*Match No.*
1	2	3	4	5	6	7	8^1	9	10^3	11^2	12	13	14																				1
1	2	3	4	5	6	7	8	9	10^2	11^1		12	13																				2
1	2	3	4^1	5	6	7	8	9^3	10	11^2	12	13	14																				3
	2▪	3	4	5^1	6	7	8		10^3			11	9^2	1	12	13	14																4
	2	3	4		5	7	8^2		12	10^1		11	9				13	1	6														5
	2	3	4		6	7^2	8		12	11^3		10	9^1					1		5	13	14											6
	2	3	4		5	7^1	8		10^2	11^3		9	12					1		6	13	14											7
	2	3	4		6	7	8^3		10^1	13		9	12	1						5	14	11^2											8
	2^2	3	4		6	7	8^3		10^1	11		9	12	1						5	13	14											9
	2	3▪	4^1		13	12			14	7		10	9^3					1	6	5	8	11^2											10
			4		3	7			10^2			11	9^1					1	6	5	8	12	2	13									11
			4			7			12	11^2		10	9^1					1	2	5	8		3▪	13	6								12
	2		4		3	7			10^1	12		11^2	13					1	6	5	8			9									13
	2	3	4			8			12	11^3		10	9^2					1	6	5	7^1	13		14									14
		3	4			8			12	11^2		9^1						1	6	5	7	13	2	10									15
		3	4			8			12			9^1	11					1	6	5	7^2	13	2	10									16
			4^1		3	8			10	11		9						1	6	5	7		2	12									17
	12	3	4^2		6	8			13	11^3		10	9					1		5	7		2^1	14									18
	2^3	3			6	7	8		12	13		10	9			14▪		1		5^1	4	11^2											19
		3	4		5	7	12		10^2	11▪		9						1	6		8^1		2	13									20
		3	4^1		5	7	12		13			10	9^2			2^3		1	6		8	14	11										21
	2	3	4		5^2	11	12		10^1			9				7^3		1	6	13	8					14							22
			4^3		3	11	8^2		12			9				2		1	6	5	10	7^1		13		14							23
	2	3			12	11				13		9				7^3		1		5	10					8^2	4^1	6	14				24
	2	3				7		12				9^2	13					1		5	11					8	4	6		10^1			25
	5	3				7		12				13	9^2					1			11					8	4	6		10^1	2		26
		3						9				11^1	10					1		5	7					8	4▪	6			2	12	27
		3				4	12	9					13			7^2		1		5	11^1					8		6		14	2	10^3	28
		3				11		13	12			10^2		1						5	7^1					8	4	6			2	9	29
		3			12	11		9^2				13		1		14				5	7^1					8^3	4	6			2	10	30
		3				11		9^3	12			14		1		13				5	7^2					8	4	6			2^1	10	31
		3				7		9		11^2			10	1						5	12					8^1	4	6			2	13	32
		3				7		9	12	13		14	10^2	1						5	11					8	4^1	6			2^3		33
		3			12	4		9	10^3			11^1		1						5	7^2					8	13	6		14	2		34
		3				4		9^1	10^3			11	12	1						5	7^2					8	13	6		14	2		35
		3				4		9^2	10^1			11	12	1						5	7					8		6		13	2		36
		3				4		9	12			11^1	10^3	1						5	7					8^2	13	6		14	2		37
		3				4		9				11^2	10^1	1						5	7					8	12	6		13	2		38

FA Cup
Third Round — Bristol R (h) 2-2
(a) 0-0

Carling Cup
Second Round — Shrewsbury T (a) 1-0
Third Round — Bolton W (h) 1-2

GILLINGHAM — FL Championship 2

FOUNDATION

The success of the pioneering Royal Engineers of Chatham excited the interest of the residents of the Medway Towns and led to the formation of many clubs including Excelsior. After winning the Kent Junior Cup and the Chatham District League in 1893, Excelsior decided to go for bigger things and it was at a meeting in the Napier Arms, Brompton, in 1893 that New Brompton FC came into being, buying and developing the ground which is now Priestfield Stadium. Changed name to Gillingham in 1913, when they also changed their strip from black and white stripes to predominantly blue.

Priestfield Stadium, Redfern Avenue, Gillingham, Kent ME7 4DD.

Telephone: (01634) 300 000.

Fax: (01634) 850 986.

Ticket Office: (01634) 300 000 (option 3).

Website: www.gillinghamfootballclub.com

Email: info@gillinghamfootballclub.com

Ground Capacity: 11,440.

Record Attendance: 23,002 v QPR, FA Cup 3rd rd, 10 January 1948.

Pitch Measurements: 110yd × 70yd.

Chairman: Paul D. P. Scally.

Chief Executive: Mark Jones.

Secretary: Gwendoline Poynter.

Manager: Mark Stimson.

Assistant Manager: Scott Barrett.

Physio: Paul Smith.

Colours: Blue with white insert.

Change Colours: Yellow with blue insert.

Year Formed: 1893.

Turned Professional: 1894.

Ltd Co.: 1893.

Previous Name: 1893, New Brompton; 1913, Gillingham.

Club Nickname: 'The Gills'.

Ground: 1893, Priestfield Stadium.

First Football League Game: 28 August 1920, Division 3, v Southampton (h) D 1–1 – Branfield; Robertson, Sissons; Battiste, Baxter, Wigmore; Holt, Hall, Gilbey (1), Roe, Gore.

HONOURS

Football League: Promoted from Division 2 1999–2000 (play-offs); Division 3 – Runners-up 1995-96; Division 4 – Champions 1963–64; Runners-up 1973–74.

FA Cup: best season: 6th rd, 2000.

Football League Cup: best season: 4th rd, 1964, 1997.

SKY SPORTS FACT FILE

Chris Dickson, on loan from Charlton Athletic, scored 11 goals in 14 League and Cup matches while on loan at Gillingham in 2007–08. His tally included a hat-trick against Luton Town in the Johnstone's Paint Trophy match on 9 October.

Record League Victory: 10–0 v Chesterfield, Division 3, 5 September 1987 – Kite; Haylock, Pearce, Shipley (2) (Lillis), West, Greenall (1), Pritchard (2), Shearer (2), Lovell, Elsey (2), David Smith (1).

Record Cup Victory: 10–1 v Gorleston, FA Cup 1st rd, 16 November 1957 – Brodie; Parry, Hannaway; Riggs, Boswell, Laing; Payne, Fletcher (2), Saunders (5), Morgan (1), Clark (2).

Record Defeat: 2–9 v Nottingham F, Division 3 (S), 18 November 1950.

Most League Points (2 for a win): 62, Division 4, 1973–74.

Most League Points (3 for a win): 85, Division 2, 1999–2000.

Most League Goals: 90, Division 4, 1973–74.

Highest League Scorer in Season: Ernie Morgan, 31, Division 3 (S), 1954–55; Brian Yeo, 31, Division 4, 1973–74.

Most League Goals in Total Aggregate: Brian Yeo, 135, 1963–75.

Most League Goals in One Match: 6, Fred Cheesmur v Merthyr T, Division 3S, 26 April 1930.

Most Capped Player: Mamady Sidibe, 7, Mali.

Most League Appearances: John Simpson, 571, 1957–72.

Youngest League Player: Luke Freeman, 15 years 247 days v Hartlepool U, 24 November 2007.

Record Transfer Fee Received: £1,500,000 from Manchester C for Robert Taylor, November 1999.

Record Transfer Fee Paid: £600,000 to Reading for Carl Asaba, August 1998.

Football League Record: 1920 Original Member of Division 3; 1921 Division 3 (S); 1938 Failed re-election; Southern League 1938–44; Kent League 1944–46; Southern League 1946–50; 1950 Re-elected to Division 3 (S); 1958–64 Division 4; 1964–71 Division 3; 1971–74 Division 4; 1974–89 Division 3; 1989–92 Division 4; 1992–96; Division 3; 1996–2000 Division 2; 2000–04 Division 1; 2004–05 FL C; 2005–08 FL 1; 2008– FL 2.

MANAGERS

W. Ironside Groombridge 1896–1906 *(Secretary-Manager) (previously Financial Secretary)*
Steve Smith 1906–08
W. I. Groombridge 1908–19 *(Secretary-Manager)*
George Collins 1919–20
John McMillan 1920–23
Harry Curtis 1923–26
Albert Hoskins 1926–29
Dick Hendrie 1929–31
Fred Mavin 1932–37
Alan Ure 1937–38
Bill Harvey 1938–39
Archie Clark 1939–58
Harry Barratt 1958–62
Freddie Cox 1962–65
Basil Hayward 1966–71
Andy Nelson 1971–74
Len Ashurst 1974–75
Gerry Summers 1975–81
Keith Peacock 1981–87
Paul Taylor 1988
Keith Burkinshaw 1988–89
Damien Richardson 1989–92
Glenn Roeder 1992–93
Mike Flanagan 1993–95
Neil Smillie 1995
Tony Pulis 1995–99
Peter Taylor 1999–2000
Andy Hessenthaler 2000–04
Stan Ternent 2004–05
Neale Cooper 2005
Ronnie Jepson 2005–07
Mark Stimson November 2007

LATEST SEQUENCES

Longest Sequence of League Wins: 7, 18.12.1954 – 29.1.1955.

Longest Sequence of League Defeats: 10, 20.9.1988 – 5.11.1988.

Longest Sequence of League Draws: 5, 28.8.1993 – 18.9.1993.

Longest Sequence of Unbeaten League Matches: 20, 13.10.1973 – 10.2.1974.

Longest Sequence Without a League Win: 15, 1.4.1972 – 2.9.1972.

Successive Scoring Runs: 20 from 31.10.1959.

Successive Non-scoring Runs: 6 from 11.2.1961.

TEN YEAR LEAGUE RECORD

		P	*W*	*D*	*L*	*F*	*A*	*Pts*	*Pos*
1998-99	Div 2	46	22	14	10	75	44	80	4
1999-2000	Div 2	46	25	10	11	79	48	85	3
2000-01	Div 1	46	13	16	17	61	66	55	13
2001-02	Div 1	46	18	10	18	64	67	64	12
2002-03	Div 1	46	16	14	16	56	65	62	11
2003-04	Div 1	46	14	9	23	48	67	51	21
2004-05	FL C	46	12	14	20	45	66	50	22
2005-06	FL 1	46	16	12	18	50	64	60	14
2006-07	FL 1	46	17	8	21	56	77	59	16
2007-08	FL 1	46	11	13	22	44	73	46	22

DID YOU KNOW ?

Luke Freeman, the youngest debutant for Gillingham, had already become the youngest player in the FA Cup proper at 15 years 273 days when he appeared against Barnet on 10 November 2007. The previous most youthful player had been just four days older!

GILLINGHAM 2007–08 LEAGUE RECORD

Match No.	*Date*	*Venue*	*Opponents*	*Result*		*H/T Score*	*Lg. Pos.*	*Goalscorers*	*Attendance*
1	Aug 11	A	Cheltenham T	L	0-1	0-1	—		4008
2	18	H	Tranmere R	L	0-2	0-1	22		5302
3	25	A	Luton T	L	1-3	1-2	23	Bentley ^{22}	6178
4	Sept 1	H	Walsall	W	2-1	2-1	20	Mulligan 2 $^{15, 34}$	4806
5	8	A	Southend U	L	0-3	0-2	22		7348
6	15	H	Brighton & HA	W	1-0	0-0	18	Facey ^{82}	6118
7	22	A	Nottingham F	L	0-4	0-1	20		16,330
8	29	H	Leeds U	D	1-1	0-1	21	Cox ^{90}	8719
9	Oct 2	H	Leyton Orient	W	3-1	1-0	—	Graham 2 $^{25, 50}$, Cogan ^{67}	5632
10	6	A	Swindon T	L	0-5	0-2	20		6345
11	13	H	Millwall	D	1-1	1-0	18	Dickson ^{16}	6120
12	20	A	Carlisle U	L	0-2	0-1	21		6461
13	27	H	Bristol R	W	3-2	1-1	18	Brown ^{19}, Graham ^{85}, Dickson ^{89}	5333
14	Nov 2	A	Swansea C	D	1-1	1-0	—	Facey ^{10}	13,452
15	6	H	Doncaster R	D	1-1	1-0	—	Dickson ^{18}	5030
16	18	A	Yeovil T	L	1-2	0-0	20	Dickson ^{76}	4408
17	24	H	Hartlepool U	W	2-1	0-1	19	Oli 2 $^{46, 59}$	5488
18	Dec 4	A	Crewe Alex	W	3-2	1-1	—	Bentley ^{8}, Dickson 2 (1 pen) $^{56 (p), 73}$	3929
19	8	H	Port Vale	L	1-2	1-2	16	Dickson ^{32}	7001
20	15	A	Bournemouth	L	0-1	0-1	17		4746
21	26	H	Southend U	D	1-1	0-0	18	Miller ^{89}	8268
22	29	H	Nottingham F	W	3-0	0-0	17	Mulligan ^{49}, Miller ^{61}, Griffiths ^{81}	7712
23	Jan 1	A	Leyton Orient	D	0-0	0-0	18		5369
24	12	A	Huddersfield T	W	3-1	1-1	15	Mulligan 2 (1 pen) $^{45, 75 (p)}$, Facey ^{82}	11,212
25	19	H	Northampton T	L	0-1	0-1	18		5579
26	22	H	Oldham Ath	D	0-0	0-0	—		4402
27	26	A	Walsall	L	1-2	0-1	—	Crofts ^{90}	4914
28	29	A	Tranmere R	L	0-2	0-2	—		5006
29	Feb 2	H	Cheltenham T	D	0-0	0-0	18		4993
30	9	A	Oldham Ath	L	1-2	1-1	19	Oli ^{25}	4866
31	16	A	Northampton T	L	0-4	0-2	21		4978
32	23	H	Huddersfield T	W	1-0	0-0	20	Miller (pen) ^{88}	5022
33	Mar 1	H	Yeovil T	D	0-0	0-0	20		5083
34	4	A	Brighton & HA	L	2-4	1-3	—	Crofts 2 $^{4, 76}$	6836
35	8	A	Hartlepool U	L	0-4	0-2	21		4055
36	11	A	Doncaster R	L	1-2	0-1	—	Crofts ^{56}	7867
37	15	H	Crewe Alex	L	0-3	0-1	21		4956
38	22	H	Bournemouth	W	2-1	2-1	21	Crofts ^{9}, Jackson ^{26}	6540
39	24	A	Port Vale	L	1-2	0-1	21	Griffiths ^{78}	3157
40	29	H	Carlisle U	D	0-0	0-0	21		6673
41	Apr 1	H	Luton T	W	2-1	0-1	—	Jackson 2 $^{75, 87}$	6142
42	5	A	Millwall	D	1-1	1-0	21	Southall ^{26}	10,006
43	12	H	Swansea C	L	1-2	1-2	21	Oli ^{22}	8520
44	19	A	Bristol R	D	1-1	1-0	21	Nutter ^{38}	6614
45	26	H	Swindon T	D	1-1	1-0	22	Richards ^{2}	6334
46	May 3	A	Leeds U	L	1-2	1-0	22	Jackson ^{20}	38,256

Final League Position: 22

GOALSCORERS

League (44): Dickson 7 (1 pen), Crofts 5, Mulligan 5 (1 pen), Jackson 4, Oli 4, Facey 3, Graham 3, Miller 3 (1 pen), Bentley 2, Griffiths 2, Brown 1, Cogan 1, Cox 1, Nutter 1, Richards 1, Southall 1.
Carling Cup (0).
FA Cup (1): Graham 1.
J Paint Trophy (9): Dickson 4 (1 pen), Armstrong 1, Bentley 1, Brown 1, Oli 1, Stone 1.

Royce S 33	Southall N 31 + 2	Armstrong C 12 + 1	Lomas S 8	Simmonds D — + 3	Cox I 20	Sodje E 12 + 1	Bentley M 32 + 1	Crofts A 41	Ba G 1 + 3	Graham D 7 + 9	Facey D 27 + 5	Brown A 10 + 1	King S 39 + 3	Stone C 4 + 5	Mulligan G 15 + 15	Pugh A — + 2	Cogan B 9 + 7	Cumbers L 2 + 4	Hamilton M 3 + 2	Clohessy S 16 + 1	Stillie D 13 + 1	Nowland A 4 + 1	Dickson C 9 + 3	Jupp D 2	Griffiths L 4 + 20	Oli D 17 + 5	Thurgood S 11 + 1	Bygrave A 13 + 2	Freeman L — + 1	Miller A 26 + 2	Nutter J 23 + 1	Rocastle C 2	Richards G 12 + 2	Fuller B 9 + 1	Lewis S 6 + 4	Jackson S 14 + 4	Cullip D 11	Maher K 7	Howard C 1	*Match No.*
1	2	3	4■		5■	6	7	8		9^2	10^3	11^1	12	13	14																									1
1	2	3^1	4		5		7	8		9	10	11	6			12																								2
1	2	3	4		5		7	8		9^2	10	11^1					6	13	12																					3
1	2	3	4^1		5		7	8		13	10		6^3	12	9^2				14	11																				4
1	2	3^2	4^3		5	6	7			13	10	12	8	14	9					11^1																				5
1	2	12	4		5	6	7	8		13	10	11^3	3^1		9^2		14																							6
	2	9^1	4		5	6	7^3	8		12	10	11^2	3								1	14	13																	7
1			4^1		5	6		8		9	10				12		11		3^2	2		7	13																	8
1	7				5	6		8		9^1	10		13	14	12		11		3^2	2		4^3																		9
1	7				5^3	6	12	8		9^2	10		14		13		11		3	2		4^1																		10
1	7				5	6	8			12	9		3^3		13		11^1			14		4^2	10	2																11
1	7				5	6	8	4^3		12	9	11	3	14	13					2^1			10^2																	12
1	7				5	6	8	4^1		13	9	11	3^3		12		14						10	2^2																13
1	2				5	6	7	8		9^1	10	11	3		4^2		12						13																	14
1	2				5	6	7	8		12	9	11	3				4^1						10																	15
1	13	3			5^1	12^2	7					11	6	4			8^3			2			10		14	9														16
1	12	3					7						5	8^1						2			10		9^2	11^3	4	6	14	13										17
1		3					7	8			12		5							2			10			9	4	6		11^1										18
1		3					7	8			12		5				13			2^1			10			9	4	6^2		11										19
1	7^1	3					5	8			12		6							2			10^2		13	9	4			11										20
1	2	3^3					4	8			10		5	7^2	12		13									9^1	6■			11	14									21
1	2						7	8			10		5		9^2		12								13	11^1		6		4	3									22
1	2						7	8		12	10^1		5		9^2		4								13			6		11	3									23
1	2						7	8			10^2		5		9^1			12							13			6		11■	3	4								24
1	2				5		7	8			10^1		6^2		9										12		14	13		11	3	4^3								25
1■	2				5		7	8^G							9			10^1			15				12		4	6		11	3									26
	2				5^3		7^1	8			10^2				9		12				1				13		4	6		11	3		14							27
1								8					5		9		7^1	10^2							13		4^3	12		11	3		6	2	14					28
1							7^1	8			10		5													12	4^2	6		11	3			2	13	9				29
1	7^3							8			12		5		13											10^2	4^1	6		11	3			2	14	9				30
1	7							8					5		12											9^3	4	6^1		11^2	3		14	2	13	10				31
1								8			12		5		9^1					2					13					11	3		4		7	10^2	6			32
1								8			10^2		5^3		12					2					9^1	14				11	3		6		7	13	4			33
								8			10		5		12					2■	1				9^3					11	3		6■	13	7^1	14	4^2			34
					4			8			10		5		12						1				13	9^2				11	3			2		7^1		6		35
1								8			10		5		12										9^1	7^2		6		11	3			2		13		4		36
1							7^2	8			10^3		5		9^1										14	13		6		11	3			2		12		4■		37
							7	8					5					12		2	1				13	9^1				11^2	3		6			10	4			38
							7						5	8^2				12		2	1				13	9				11	3		6			10			4^1	39
	2						7	8					5								1				12	9				11^1	3		6			10	4			40
	2			13			7	8	14				5								1				12	9^2				11^3	3^1		6			10	4			41
	2						7	8	13				5								1				12	9^2				11^1			3	6		10	4			42
	2^1			14				8					5			12					1				13	9^3				11^2			3	7		10	6	4		43
	2			14				8	9^1				5		12						1				13						3		6		11^2	10^3	4	7		44
	2							8	13				5		9^1						1					12					3		6		11^2	10	4	7		45
	2						7	8					5		9^1						1				13	14				12	3				11^3	10	4^2	6		46

FA Cup

First Round	Barnet	(a)	1-2

Carling Cup

First Round	Watford	(a)	0-3

J Paint Trophy

Second Round	Luton T	(h)	4-3
Quarter-Final	Dagenham & R	(h)	4-0
Southern Semi-Final	Milton Keynes D	(h)	1-1

GRIMSBY TOWN FL Championship 2

FOUNDATION

Grimsby Pelham FC, as they were first known, came into being at a meeting held at the Wellington Arms in September 1878. Pelham is the family name of big landowners in the area, the Earls of Yarborough. The receipts for their first game amounted to 6s. 9d. (approx. 39p). After a year, the club name was changed to Grimsby Town.

Blundell Park, Cleethorpes, North East Lincolnshire DN35 8DB.

Telephone: (01472) 605 050.

Fax: (01472) 693 665.

Ticket Office: (01472) 608 025.

Website: www.gtfc.co.uk.

Email: enquiries@gtfc.co.uk.

Ground Capacity: 10,033.

Record Attendance: 31,657 v Wolverhampton W, FA Cup 5th rd, 20 February 1937.

Pitch Measurements: 111yd × 75yd.

Chairman: John Fenty.

Chief Executive/Secretary: Ian Fleming.

Manager: Alan Buckley.

Assistant Manager: Stuart Watkiss.

Physio: David Moore.

Colours: Black and white shirts, black shorts, black stockings.

Change Colours: Red shirts, white shorts, red stockings.

Year Formed. 1878.

Turned Professional: 1890. ***Ltd Co.:*** 1890.

Previous Name: 1878, Grimsby Pelham; 1879, Grimsby Town.

Club Nickname: 'The Mariners'.

Grounds: 1880, Clee Park; 1889, Abbey Park; 1899, Blundell Park.

First Football League Game: 3 September 1892, Division 2, v Northwich Victoria (h) W 2–1 – Whitehouse; Lundie, T. Frith; C. Frith, Walker, Murrell; Higgins, Henderson, Brayshaw, Riddoch (2), Ackroyd.

Record League Victory: 9–2 v Darwen, Division 2, 15 April 1899 – Bagshaw; Lockie, Nidd; Griffiths, Bell (1), Nelmes; Jenkinson (3), Richards (1), Cockshutt (3), Robinson, Chadburn (1).

Record Cup Victory: 8–0 v Darlington, FA Cup 2nd rd, 21 November 1885 – G. Atkinson; J. H. Taylor, H. Taylor; Hall, Kimpson, Hopewell; H. Atkinson (1), Garnham, Seal (3), Sharman, Monument (4).

HONOURS

Football League: Division 1 best season: 5th, 1934–35; Division 2 – Champions 1900–01, 1933–34; Runners-up 1928–29; Promoted from Division 2 1997–98 (play-offs); Division 3 (N) – Champions 1925–26, 1955–56; Runners-up 1951–52; Division 3 – Champions 1979–80; Runners-up 1961–62; Division 4 – Champions 1971–72; Runners-up 1978–79; 1989–90.

FA Cup: Semi-finals, 1936, 1939.

Football League Cup: best season: 5th rd, 1980, 1985.

League Group Cup: Winners 1982.

Auto Windscreen Shield: Winners 1998.

Johnstone's Paint Trophy: Runners-up 2008.

SKY SPORTS FACT FILE

Legendary Football League manager Herbert Chapman, associated with Huddersfield Town and Arsenal, is not often recalled as making a double goal debut for Grimsby Town. He achieved this feat in September 1898 against Manchester City.

Record Defeat: 1–9 v Arsenal, Division 1, 28 January 1931.

Most League Points (2 for a win): 68, Division 3 (N), 1955–56.

Most League Points (3 for a win): 83, Division 3, 1990–91.

Most League Goals: 103, Division 2, 1933–34.

Highest League Scorer in Season: Pat Glover, 42, Division 2, 1933–34.

Most League Goals in Total Aggregate: Pat Glover, 180, 1930–39.

Most League Goals in One Match: 6, Tommy McCairns v Leicester Fosse, Division 2, 11 April 1896.

Most Capped Player: Pat Glover, 7, Wales.

Most League Appearances: John McDermott, 647, 1987– 2007.

Youngest League Player: Tony Ford, 16 years 143 days v Walsall, 4 October 1975.

Record Transfer Fee Received: £1,500,000 from Everton for John Oster, July 1997.

Record Transfer Fee Paid: £500,000 to Preston NE for Lee Ashcroft, August 1998.

Football League Record: 1892 Original Member Division 2; 1901–03 Division 1; 1903 Division 2; 1910 Failed re-election; 1911 re-elected Division 2; 1920–21 Division 3; 1921–26 Division 3 (N); 1926–29 Division 2; 1929–32 Division 1; 1932–34 Division 2; 1934–48 Division 1; 1948–51 Division 2; 1951–56 Division 3 (N); 1956–59 Division 2; 1959–62 Division 3; 1962–64 Division 2; 1964–68 Division 3; 1968–72 Division 4; 1972–77 Division 3; 1977–79 Division 4; 1979–80 Division 3; 1980–87 Division 2; 1987–88 Division 3; 1988–90 Division 4; 1990–91 Division 3; 1991–92 Division 2; 1992–97 Division 1; 1997–98 Division 2; 1998–2003 Division 1; 2003–04 Division 2; 2004– FL 2.

MANAGERS

H. N. Hickson 1902–20
(Secretary-Manager)
Haydn Price 1920
George Fraser 1921–24
Wilf Gillow 1924–32
Frank Womack 1932–36
Charles Spencer 1937–51
Bill Shankly 1951–53
Billy Walsh 1954–55
Allenby Chilton 1955–59
Tim Ward 1960–62
Tom Johnston 1962–64
Jimmy McGuigan 1964–67
Don McEvoy 1967–68
Bill Harvey 1968–69
Bobby Kennedy 1969–71
Lawrie McMenemy 1971–73
Ron Ashman 1973–75
Tom Casey 1975–76
Johnny Newman 1976–79
George Kerr 1979–82
David Booth 1982–85
Mike Lyons 1985–87
Bobby Roberts 1987–88
Alan Buckley 1988–94
Brian Laws 1994–96
Kenny Swain 1997
Alan Buckley 1997–2000
Lennie Lawrence 2000–01
Paul Groves 2001–04
Nicky Law 2004
Russell Slade 2004–06
Graham Rodger 2006
Alan Buckley November 2006–

LATEST SEQUENCES

Longest Sequence of League Wins: 11, 19.1.1952 – 29.3.1952.

Longest Sequence of League Defeats: 9, 30.11.1907 – 18.1.1908.

Longest Sequence of League Draws: 5, 6.2.1965 – 6.3.1965.

Longest Sequence of Unbeaten League Matches: 19, 16.2.1980 – 30.8.1980.

Longest Sequence Without a League Win: 18, 10.10.1981 – 16.3.1982.

Successive Scoring Runs: 33 from 6.10.1928.

Successive Non-scoring Runs: 6 from 11.3.2000.

TEN YEAR LEAGUE RECORD

		P	*W*	*D*	*L*	*F*	*A*	*Pts*	*Pos*
1998-99	Div 1	46	17	10	19	40	52	61	11
1999-2000	Div 1	46	13	12	21	41	67	51	20
2000-01	Div 1	46	14	10	22	43	62	52	18
2001-02	Div 1	46	12	14	20	50	72	50	19
2002-03	Div 1	46	9	12	25	48	85	39	24
2003-04	Div 2	46	13	11	22	55	81	50	21
2004-05	FL 2	46	14	16	16	51	52	58	18
2005-06	FL 2	46	22	12	12	64	44	78	4
2006-07	FL 2	46	17	8	21	57	73	59	15
2007-08	FL 2	46	15	10	21	55	66	55	16

DID YOU KNOW?

To be given the nickname of Rocket, one might expect it to refer to a goalscorer. But Tommy Read was a goalkeeper famous for dashing out to deal with dangerous situations. Signed in 1927 he made over 250 senior appearances for Grimsby Town.

GRIMSBY TOWN 2007–08 LEAGUE RECORD

Match No.	*Date*	*Venue*	*Opponents*	*Result*		*H/T Score*	*Lg. Pos.*	*Goalscorers*	*Atten-dance*
1	Aug 11	H	Notts Co	D	1-1	1-1	—	Bennett [12]	5483
2	18	A	Bury	D	1-1	1-0	14	Bolland [10]	2493
3	25	H	Macclesfield T	D	1-1	0-0	18	Taylor [74]	3701
4	Sept 1	A	Shrewsbury T	L	1-2	0-0	22	Toner (pen) [68]	5490
5	8	A	Accrington S	L	1-4	0-1	23	Bolland [57]	1350
6	15	H	Stockport Co	D	1-1	0-1	21	Bolland [51]	3726
7	22	A	Lincoln C	W	2-1	1-1	18	Whittle [19], Toner (pen) [52]	4428
8	29	H	Hereford U	W	2-1	1-0	14	Boshell [20], Newey [52]	3699
9	Oct 2	H	Chester C	L	1-2	1-1	—	Boshell [25]	3479
10	6	A	Peterborough U	L	1-2	0-0	20	Toner (pen) [59]	4786
11	12	H	Rochdale	L	1-2	1-1	—	Logan [18]	5829
12	20	A	Wycombe W	L	0-3	0-1	21		4052
13	27	H	Bradford C	D	1-1	0-0	21	Logan [49]	4883
14	Nov 3	A	Rotherham U	L	1-2	0-1	22	Fenton [53]	4162
15	6	A	Milton Keynes D	L	0-2	0-2	—		6797
16	17	H	Morecambe	L	1-2	0-1	22	Taylor [53]	4897
17	24	A	Barnet	W	3-0	2-0	20	North 2 [11, 44], Taylor [89]	2059
18	Dec 4	H	Darlington	L	0-4	0-2	—		3057
19	8	A	Brentford	W	1-0	0-0	20	Jones [57]	3999
20	15	H	Mansfield T	W	1-0	0-0	20	Jones [62]	3836
21	22	A	Stockport Co	D	1-1	1-0	20	Butler [25]	4711
22	26	H	Accrington S	L	1-2	1-0	20	Hegarty [8]	4240
23	29	H	Lincoln C	W	1-0	0-0	17	Jones [85]	5533
24	Jan 1	A	Chester C	W	2-0	0-0	17	Boshell (pen) [65], Atkinson [84]	2255
25	5	A	Chesterfield	W	2-1	1-0	15	North 2 (1 pen) [45, 78 (p)]	4540
26	12	H	Wrexham	W	1-0	0-0	14	North [68]	4084
27	19	A	Dagenham & R	D	0-0	0-0	14		2216
28	26	H	Shrewsbury T	D	1-1	0-0	13	North [90]	3785
29	29	H	Bury	W	1-0	1-0	—	Clarke [40]	3445
30	Feb 2	A	Notts Co	D	1-1	0-0	11	Fenton [61]	4902
31	9	H	Chesterfield	W	4-2	2-0	11	Boshell 2 (2 pens) [19, 86], North [31], Hegarty [53]	4601
32	12	A	Macclesfield T	W	2-1	1-0	—	North [5], Clarke [82]	2194
33	16	H	Dagenham & R	L	1-4	0-2	12	Jones [90]	4060
34	23	A	Wrexham	D	0-0	0-0	11		4217
35	Mar 1	A	Morecambe	W	4-0	2-0	11	Bore 2 [22, 25], Hegarty [59], Butler [81]	2303
36	7	H	Milton Keynes D	L	0-1	0-1	—		4106
37	11	H	Barnet	W	4-1	2-0	—	Hegarty [29], Butler [43], Bolland [55], Taylor [85]	3325
38	15	A	Darlington	L	2-3	2-2	11	Butler 2 [29, 30]	3499
39	22	A	Mansfield T	W	2-1	1-0	10	Till [32], Boshell [74]	2616
40	24	H	Brentford	L	1-2	1-0	9	North [19]	4620
41	Apr 5	A	Rochdale	L	1-3	0-0	12	Taylor [85]	2974
42	12	H	Rotherham U	L	0-1	0-1	13		3583
43	15	H	Wycombe W	L	0-1	0-1	—		2537
44	19	A	Bradford C	L	1-2	1-0	15	Till [9]	13,448
45	26	H	Peterborough U	L	1-4	0-1	16	Butler [63]	4125
46	May 3	A	Hereford U	L	0-2	0-2	16		6020

Final League Position: 16

GOALSCORERS

League (55): North 9 (1 pen), Boshell 6 (3 pens), Butler 6, Taylor 5, Bolland 4, Hegarty 4, Jones 4, Toner 3 (3 pens), Bore 2, Clarke 2, Fenton 2, Logan 2, Till 2, Atkinson 1, Bennett 1, Newey 1, Whittle 1.
Carling Cup (1): North 1.
FA Cup (2): Bolland 1, Jones 1.
J Paint Trophy (10): Till 2, Bolland 1, Boshell 1, Clarke 1, Fenton 1, Rankin 1, Toner 1, own goals 2.

Barnes P 42	Fenton N 40 + 2	Newey T 42	Hunt J 32 + 5	Bennett R 28 + 12	Whittle J 14 + 4	Till P 31 + 3	Bolland P 33 + 2	Rankin I 12 + 5	Toner C 25 + 5	Boshell D 38 + 2	Jones G 15 + 21	Bore P 4 + 13	North D 21 + 6	Taylor A 1 + 25	Mulligan D 4 + 2	Clarke J 27 + 2	Logan S 5	Butler M 15 + 6	Montgomery G 4 + 1	Hegarty N 27 + 3	Jarman N 5 + 2	Atkinson R 24	Hird S 17	Bird M — + 2	Match No.
1	2	3	4[1]	5	6	7[2]	8	9[3]	10	11	12	13	14												1
1	2	3	4	5	6	7	8	12	10	11[1]	13		9[2]												2
1	2	3	12	5	6	7[2]	8	9[3]	11	4	13		10[1]	14											3
1	2	3	4	5■	6	7	8[1]	9[3]	10	11	13		14		12[2]										4
1	5	3	4		6	7[1]	8	9[3]	10	11[2]	14	12		13	2										5
1	5	3	12	2[3]	6	7[2]	8	9	10	11		13		4[1]	14										6
1	5	3	4[2]		6	7	8	9[1]	10	11	12				2	13									7
1	5	3		12	6	7	8[3]	9[2]	10	11[1]	13			14	2	4									8
1	5	3		6	12	7	8	9[2]	10	11	14			13	2[1]	4[3]									9
1	5	3		2	6	7[3]	8	9[2]	10	11	14		13	12		4[1]									10
1	5	3	12	6		7	8	9[3]	11[2]		10	13		14		4[1]	2								11
1	5	3	4	12	6	7[1]		9[2]	11	8[3]				13		14	2	10							12
1■	5	3[G]	4	12	6	7[1]		9[2]	11	8				13			2	10	15						13
	5■	3	4	12	6	7[1]			11	10	9	13		14			2[2]		1	8[3]					14
1		3	4	8	6	7[1]			11[2]	10				12		5[3]	2	9		13	14				15
1	5	3	4[1]			7	8		12	11■	13		9[3]	14		2		10[2]		6					16
	5	3	4	6		7[1]		14	11		10	12	9[2]	13[3]					1			2	8		17
	5	3	4[2]	12		7[3]	8	14	10	11			9	13					1			6	2[1]		18
1	5		7[2]	2	13		8	12	11		10		9[1]							6		4	3		19
1		3		2			8		11	7	10[2]		9[1]	12				13		4		5	6		20
1	5	3	13	2			8	12	11[1]	4	10[2]							9		7			6		21
1	5	3	7	2			8			4[1]	10[2]	12	13					9		11			6		22
1		3	4	2			8			11	12		9[1]	13				10[2]		7		5	6		23
1	12	3	4	2			8			11	10		13					9[2]		7[1]		5	6		24
1	12	3	4	2[1]			8				10		9			11				7		5	6		25
1	5[1]	3	4		12	13	8		14		10		9			11[3]				7		2	6[2]		26
1	5[1]	3	4	12			8			13	10		9[3]	14		11[2]				7		2	6		27
1	5	3	4			12	8[2]			13	10		9	14		11[3]				7		2	6[1]		28
1	5	3	8	13						4	10		9[1]	12		11				7		2	6[2]		29
1	5		8	3		10				4	12		9[1]			11				7		2	6		30
1	5	3	4	12		10[2]				8	13	14	9[3]			11				7		2	6[1]		31
1	5	3	4	14		10[2]	12			8[1]	13		9			11				7[3]		2	6		32
1	5	3[3]	4	14		10	8[2]				12	13	9			11				7		2	6[1]		33
1	5		4	2		10[1]	13		11[2]	8	12	14	9[3]			3				7		6			34
	5		4	2	6		8			11	10[2]	9[3]		12		3		13	1	7[1]	14				35
1	5	3	4[3]	14		10[1]	8			6	12	9[2]				11		13		7		2			36
1	5	3		6		12	8			11[1]	10[3]	13		14		7		9[2]		4		2			37
1	5	3	4	6[2]	13	10	8		12	11[3]		14				7		9				2[1]			38
1	5	3	13	14		7	8[1]			4	12		9[2]			6		10		11		2[3]			39
1	5	3	4[1]	2		7			13	6	12		9[2]	14		11		10[3]		8					40
1	5	3	4[2]	2					11	8	12			13		6[1]		9		7	10■				41
1	5	3		2		10			11[2]	8	12	7[1]		13		6[3]		9		4				14	42
1	5[1]	3				11	4		12	8		13		14		6		9[2]		7	10[3]	2			43
1	5	3	4[2]	2		7[1]	8		9	11								13		12	10	6			44
1	5	3		2			4		9[3]	11[1]		7[2]	12			8		14		13	10	6			45
1		3		2		7[2]	8			4			9[3]	13		6		12		11	10[1]	5		14	46

FA Cup

First Round	Carlisle U	(a)	1-1
		(h)	1-0
Second Round	Huddersfield T	(a)	0-3

Carling Cup

First Round	Burnley	(h)	1-1

J Paint Trophy

First Round	Huddersfield T	(h)	4-1
Second Round	Rotherham U	(a)	1-1
Quarter-Final	Doncaster R	(h)	2-2
Northern Semi-Final	Stockport Co	(a)	2-1
Northern Final	Morecambe	(a)	1-0
		(h)	0-0
Final *(at Wembley)*	Milton Keynes D		0-2

HARTLEPOOL UNITED FL Championship 1

FOUNDATION

The inspiration for the launching of Hartlepool United was the West Hartlepool club which won the FA Amateur Cup in 1904–05. They had been in existence since 1881 and their Cup success led in 1908 to the formation of the new professional concern which first joined the North-Eastern League. In those days they were Hartlepools United and won the Durham Senior Cup in their first two seasons.

Victoria Park, Clarence Road, Hartlepool TS24 8BZ.

Telephone: (01429) 272 584.

Fax: (01429) 863 007.

Ticket Office: (01429) 272 584 (option 2).

Website: www.hartlepoolunited.co.uk

Email: enquires@hartlepoolunited.co.uk

Ground Capacity: 7,787.

Record Attendance: 17,426 v Manchester U, FA Cup 3rd rd, 5 January 1957.

Pitch Measurements: 110yd × 74yd.

Chairman: Ken Hodcroft.

Chief Executive: Russ Green.

Secretary: Maureen Smith.

Manager: Danny Wilson.

Reserve Team Manager: Ian Butterworth.

Physio: James Haycock.

Colours: White shirts with blue trim, blue shorts, white stockings.

Change Colours: Red and black striped shirts, black shorts, black stockings.

Year Formed: 1908.

Turned Professional: 1908.

Ltd Co.: 1908.

Previous Names: 1908, Hartlepools United; 1968, Hartlepool; 1977, Hartlepool United.

Club Nickname: 'The Pool'.

Ground: 1908, Victoria Park.

First Football League Game: 27 August 1921, Division 3 (N), v Wrexham (a) W 2–0 – Gill; Thomas, Crilly; Dougherty, Hopkins, Short; Kessler, Mulholland (1), Lister (1), Robertson, Donald.

Record League Victory: 10–1 v Barrow, Division 4, 4 April 1959 – Oakley; Cameron, Waugh; Johnson, Moore, Anderson; Scott (1), Langland (1), Smith (3), Clark (2), Luke (2), (1 og).

Record Cup Victory: 6–0 v North Shields, FA Cup 1st rd, 30 November 1946 – Heywood; Brown, Gregory; Spelman, Lambert, Jones; Price, Scott (2), Sloan (4), Moses, McMahon.

HONOURS

Football League: FL 2 – Runners-up 2006–07; Division 3 – Runners-up 2002–03; Division 3 (N) – Runners-up 1956–57.

FA Cup: best season: 4th rd, 1955, 1978, 1989, 1993, 2005.

Football League Cup, best season: 4th rd, 1975.

SKY SPORTS FACT FILE

Winger Billy Linacre joined Hartlepools United in 1953–54 after making his name with Manchester City. His two sons John and Phil followed him at United from the late 1970s and the family between them logged over 400 League and Cup appearances there.

Record Defeat: 1–10 v Wrexham, Division 4, 3 March 1962.

Most League Points (2 for a win): 60, Division 4, 1967–68.

Most League Points (3 for a win): 88, FL 2, 2006–07.

Most League Goals: 90, Division 3 (N), 1956–57.

Highest League Scorer in Season: William Robinson, 28, Division 3 (N), 1927–28; Joe Allon, 28, Division 4, 1990–91.

Most League Goals in Total Aggregate: Ken Johnson, 98, 1949–64.

Most League Goals in One Match: 5, Harry Simmons v Wigan Borough, Division 3N, 1 January 1931; 5, Bobby Folland v Oldham Ath, Division 3N, 15 April 1961.

Most Capped Player: Ambrose Fogarty, 1 (11), Republic of Ireland.

Most League Appearances: Wattie Moore, 447, 1948–64.

Youngest League Player: David Foley, 16 years 105 days v Port Vale, 25 August 2003.

Record Transfer Fee Received: £750,000 from Ipswich T for Tommy Miller, July 2001.

Record Transfer Fee Paid: £75,000 to Northampton for Chris Freestone, March 1993; £75,000 to Notts Co for Gary Jones, March 1999; £75,000 to Mansfield T for Darrell Clarke, July 2001.

Football League Record: 1921 Original Member of Division 3 (N); 1958–68 Division 4; 1968–69 Division 3; 1969–91 Division 4; 1991–92 Division 3; 1992–94 Division 2; 1994–2003 Division 3; 2003–04 Division 2; 2004–06 FL 1; 2006–07 FL 2; 2007– FL 1.

LATEST SEQUENCES

Longest Sequence of League Wins: 9, 18.11.2006 – 1.1.2007.

Longest Sequence of League Defeats: 8, 27.1.1993 – 27.2.1993.

Longest Sequence of League Draws: 5, 24.2.2001 – 17.3.2001.

Longest Sequence of Unbeaten League Matches: 23, 18.11.2006 – 30.3.2007.

Longest Sequence Without a League Win: 18, 9.1.1993 – 3.4.1993.

Successive Scoring Runs: 27 from 18.11.2006.

Successive Non-scoring Runs: 11 from 9.1.1993.

MANAGERS

Alfred Priest 1908–12
Percy Humphreys 1912–13
Jack Manners 1913–20
Cecil Potter 1920–22
David Gordon 1922–24
Jack Manners 1924–27
Bill Norman 1927–31
Jack Carr 1932–35
(had been Player-Coach since 1931)
Jimmy Hamilton 1935–43
Fred Westgarth 1943–57
Ray Middleton 1957–59
Bill Robinson 1959–62
Allenby Chilton 1962–63
Bob Gurney 1963–64
Alvan Williams 1964–65
Geoff Twentyman 1965
Brian Clough 1965–67
Angus McLean 1967–70
John Simpson 1970–71
Len Ashurst 1971–74
Ken Hale 1974–76
Billy Horner 1976–83
Johnny Duncan 1983
Mike Docherty 1983
Billy Horner 1984–86
John Bird 1986–88
Bobby Moncur 1988–89
Cyril Knowles 1989–91
Alan Murray 1991–93
Viv Busby 1993
John MacPhail 1993–94
David McCreery 1994–95
Keith Houchen 1995–96
Mick Tait 1996–99
Chris Turner 1999–2002
Mike Newell 2002–03
Neale Cooper 2003–05
Martin Scott 2005–06
Danny Wilson June 2006–

TEN YEAR LEAGUE RECORD

		P	W	D	L	F	A	Pts	Pos
1998-99	Div 3	46	13	12	21	52	65	51	22
1999-2000	Div 3	46	21	9	16	60	49	72	7
2000-01	Div 3	46	21	14	11	71	54	77	4
2001-02	Div 3	46	20	11	15	74	48	71	7
2002-03	Div 3	46	24	13	9	71	51	85	2
2003-04	Div 2	46	20	13	13	76	61	73	6
2004-05	FL 1	46	21	8	17	76	66	71	6
2005-06	FL 1	46	11	17	18	44	59	50	21
2006-07	FL 2	46	26	10	10	65	40	88	2
2007-08	FL 1	46	15	9	22	63	66	54	15

DID YOU KNOW 

Billy Smith scored seven of the ten goals by which Hartlepools United beat St Peters Albion 10–1 in a fourth qualifying round FA Cup tie in 1923. Five of the goals came in the first half of the match and included one from the penalty spot.

HARTLEPOOL UNITED 2007–08 LEAGUE RECORD

Match No.	Date	Venue	Opponents	Result		H/T Score	Lg. Pos.	Goalscorers	Attendance
1	Aug 11	A	Luton T	L	1-2	0-1	—	Barker (pen) 90	8013
2	18	H	Doncaster R	W	2-1	1-0	9	Antwi-Birago 43, Barker (pen) 81	5544
3	25	A	Port Vale	W	2-0	1-0	5	Robson 6, Brown 88	3978
4	Sept 1	H	Oldham Ath	W	4-1	3-1	3	Moore 15, Brown 26, Barker (pen) 44, Porter 83	5015
5	8	A	Leeds U	L	0-2	0-1	5		26,877
6	15	H	Swindon T	D	1-1	0-1	3	Porter 68	4943
7	22	A	Leyton Orient	W	4-2	1-0	3	Moore 2 10, 90, Brown 51, Monkhouse 84	5325
8	29	H	Walsall	L	0-1	0-0	5		4948
9	Oct 2	H	Carlisle U	D	2-2	1-2	—	Barker 39, MacKay 86	5359
10	6	A	Nottingham F	L	1-2	1-1	8	Barker 38	17,520
11	12	H	Bristol R	W	1-0	1-0	—	Brown 39	4963
12	27	H	Brighton & HA	L	1-2	0-1	13	Barker 86	5619
13	Nov 3	A	Millwall	W	1-0	0-0	10	Sweeney 51	7731
14	6	A	Huddersfield T	L	0-2	0-1	—		8154
15	18	H	Bournemouth	D	1-1	1-1	13	Moore 41	3496
16	24	A	Gillingham	L	1-2	1-0	15	Brown 25	5488
17	27	A	Swansea C	L	0-1	0-0	—		11,421
18	Dec 4	H	Tranmere R	W	3-1	2-0	—	Liddle 3, Brown 11, Porter 58	3583
19	8	A	Yeovil T	L	1-3	1-2	12	MacKay 10	4694
20	15	H	Crewe Alex	W	3-0	0-0	12	Nelson 67, Barker 2 (1 pen) 85, 88 (p)	3915
21	22	A	Swindon T	L	1-2	1-0	13	Moore 45	5875
22	26	H	Leeds U	D	1-1	1-0	14	Nelson 21	7784
23	29	H	Leyton Orient	D	1-1	0-1	14	Moore 55	4379
24	Jan 1	A	Carlisle U	L	2-4	1-1	15	Humphreys 2 39, 48	7496
25	12	A	Northampton T	D	1-1	1-1	14	Clark 45	4639
26	18	H	Cheltenham T	L	0-2	0-1	—		4120
27	22	H	Southend U	W	4-3	1-1	—	Barker (pen) 17, Brown 2 47, 53, Sweeney 90	3217
28	29	A	Doncaster R	L	0-2	0-1	—		6442
29	Feb 2	H	Luton T	W	4-0	1-0	16	Barker 2 (1 pen) 30 (p), 73, Thompson 61, Porter 64	3913
30	9	A	Southend U	L	1-2	1-0	17	Sweeney 9	7436
31	12	H	Port Vale	W	3-2	0-2	—	Barker 2 68, 90, Sweeney 87	3630
32	16	A	Cheltenham T	D	1-1	0-1	14	Porter 53	3583
33	22	H	Northampton T	L	0-1	0-0	—		3945
34	Mar 1	A	Bournemouth	L	0-2	0-2	17		3984
35	4	A	Oldham Ath	W	1-0	0-0	—	MacKay 74	3765
36	8	H	Gillingham	W	4-0	2-0	14	Monkhouse 21, Porter 26, Collins 74, McCunnie 90	4055
37	11	H	Huddersfield T	W	2-1	1-0	—	Collins 30, MacKay 50	3650
38	15	A	Tranmere R	L	1-3	0-1	13	Humphreys 71	5608
39	22	A	Crewe Alex	L	1-3	0-2	14	Porter 81	4412
40	24	H	Yeovil T	W	2-0	1-0	13	Brown 28, Porter 67	3808
41	29	H	Swansea C	L	1-3	1-2	13	Liddle 1	4484
42	Apr 5	A	Bristol R	D	0-0	0-0	13		5526
43	12	H	Millwall	L	0-1	0-1	14		4077
44	19	A	Brighton & HA	L	1-2	0-1	15	Porter 75	6178
45	26	H	Nottingham F	L	0-1	0-0	15		5206
46	May 3	A	Walsall	D	2-2	1-2	15	MacKay 19, Brown 90	5021

Final League Position: 15

GOALSCORERS

League (63): Barker 13 (6 pens), Brown 10, Porter 9, Moore 6, MacKay 5, Sweeney 4, Humphreys 3, Collins 2, Liddle 2, Monkhouse 2, Nelson 2, Antwi-Birago 1, Clark 1, McCunnie 1, Robson 1, Thompson 1.
Carling Cup (3): Foley 2, Moore 1.
FA Cup (6): Barker 2, Brown 1, Liddle 1, Moore 1, Porter 1.
J Paint Trophy (9): Porter 3, Brown 2, Barker 1, Foley 1, Mackay 1, Moore 1.

Lee-Barrett A 18	McCunnie J 23 + 6	Antwi-Birago G 27	Elliott R 14 + 1	Nelson M 44 + 1	Liddle G 41	Boland W 32 + 2	Brown J 31 + 4	Barker R 31 + 5	Moore I 22 + 2	Humphreys R 43 + 2	Sweeney A 27 + 9	Porter J 24 + 15	Budtz J 28	Robson M 6 + 11	Clark B 14 + 5	Foley D 11 + 23	Monkhouse A 21 + 4	Gibb A 4 + 2	MacKay M 10 + 14	Coles D 3	Nolan E 11	Bullock L — + 1	Thompson A 7	Turnbull S — + 1	Collins S 10	Lee G 3	Craddock T 1 + 3	*Match No.*
1	2	3	4	5	6	7^{1}	8	9	10	11^{2}	12	13																1
	2	3^{2}	4■	5	6	7	8	9	10^{1}			12	1	11	13													2
	2	6		5	4	7^{1}	8	9^{2}	10^{3}	3	12	13	1	11		14												3
	2	6	3	5	4		7^{1}	9	10	13	8^{2}	12	1			14	11^{3}											4
	2	6	3^{2}	5	4		8	9	10^{1}	11		12	1				7	13										5
	2	6	3^{3}	5^{2}	4		8	9	10^{1}	11		12	1		13		7	14										6
	2	6		5	4	7^{2}	8^{1}	9^{3}	10	3		12	1		13		11		14									7
	2	6		5	4	7^{2}	8	9		3	13	10^{3}	1		12		11^{1}		14									8
	2	6		5	4	7	8^{3}	9	10^{1}	3		13	1	12		11^{2}			14									9
	12	6		5	4	7	8^{3}	9	10	3		13	1			14	11^{2}			2^{1}								10
	12			5	4	7	8^{2}	9	10	3		11^{1}	1		6	13				2								11
	3^{2}			5	4	7■	8	9		11	13	10^{3}	1		6^{1}		12		14	2								12
				5	6		8	9	12	3	7	10^{1}	1		4		11	2										13
				5	6		7^{2}	9	12	3	8	10^{3}	1		4	13	11^{1}	2	14									14
	2			5		8^{1}	11	9	10	3	12	7^{2}	1		6	13		4										15
	7	6		5		8	11	9	10^{1}	3		12	1			13		4^{2}			2							16
	7	6		5		4^{2}	11	9^{1}	10	3	8	12	1			13					2							17
		6		5	4		7^{3}	12	10	3	8	9^{1}	1	13		14	11^{2}				2							18
		6	3	5	4		7	12	10^{1}	11^{2}	8		1			13			9		2							19
		6	3	5	4^{2}	8	7^{3}	12	10	11	13		1			14			9^{1}		2							20
		3	4	5	6	8^{2}	7^{3}	12	10	11	13		1			14			9^{1}		2							21
		6	3	5	4	7	8^{1}	9	10	11	12		1								2							22
		6	3	5	4			9	10	11	8		1			7^{2}			13		2^{1}	12						23
		6	3	5	4		12	9	10	11^{2}	8		1	13		7^{1}					2							24
1			3^{1}	5	4	8	13	9^{3}	10	11		14		12	6	7^{2}					2							25
1			3^{1}	5	4	8^{2}	7	9	10	11		13		12	6						2							26
1	2	6		5	4		7	9		3	12	10		11									8^{1}					27
1	7^{3}	6		5	4		8	12		3	2	10^{2}				9			13				11^{1}	14				28
	12			5	4	8^{1}	7^{2}	9		3	2	10	1			13	14						11^{3}		6			29
		2		5	4	8^{1}		9		3	7	10^{3}	1			13	12		14				11^{2}		6■			30
	12	6^{1}		5	4	8^{3}		9		3^{2}	2	10	1	13		7			14				11					31
	12	6			4	8^{1}		9		3	2	10	1			7							11^{2}			5	13	32
	12	2^{1}		5	6	8^{2}		9		3	7	10	1			13							11^{3}			4	14	33
1		2		5	6	8^{2}		9		3	7	12				11^{1}	13		14							4	10^{3}	34
1	2			5	6	8		10^{1}		3	7	12				13	11		9^{2}						4			35
1	2		12	5	6	8^{2}				3^{1}	7	10		14		13	11^{3}		9						4			36
1	2			5	6	8				3	7	10					11		9						4			37
1	2■			5	6	8				3	7	10^{1}			13	12	11		9^{3}						4^{2}		14	38
1		6		5	4	8^{2}	12			3^{3}	7	10		14		13	11		9^{1}						2			39
1	2			12	6	8^{3}	13	9^{2}		3	7	10			4	14	11								5^{1}			40
1	2			5	6^{1}	12	9^{3}			3^{2}	7	10		8	4	13	11		14									41
1	2			5		8				3	7	9		6	4	10^{1}	11		12									42
1	2		3^{1}	5		4	10^{3}			12	7	9		8^{2}	6	13	11		14									43
1				5	4	8^{2}	7			3	2	10		13	6	12	11		9^{1}									44
1				5	6		9			3	7	10^{2}		12	4	8^{1}	11		13						2			45
1				5	6^{1}	12	10			3^{2}	2			13	8	7	11		9						4			46

FA Cup

First Round	Gainsborough T	(a)	6-0
Second Round	Hereford U	(a)	0-2

Carling Cup

First Round	Scunthorpe U	(a)	2-1
Second Round	Sheffield W	(a)	1-2

J Paint Trophy

First Round	Chesterfield	(a)	3-1
Second Round	Lincoln C	(a)	5-2
Quarter-Final	Morecambe	(h)	1-1

HEREFORD UNITED FL Championship 1

FOUNDATION

Two local teams RAOC and St Martins amalgamated in 1924 under the chairmanship of Dr. E.W. Maples to form Hereford United and joined the Birmingham Combination. The first game at Edgar Street was against Atherstone Town on 24 August 1924, the visitors winnning 3-2. The players used the Wellington Hotel as a changing room. They graduated to the Birmingham League four years later and the Southern League in 1939.

Edgar Street, Hereford HR4 9JU.

Telephone: (01432) 276 666.

Fax: (01432) 341 359.

Ticket Office: (01432) 276 666.

Website: www.herefordunited.co.uk

Email: hufc1939@hotmail.com

Ground capacity: 7,149.

Record Attendance: 18,114 v Sheffield W, FA Cup 3rd rd, 4 January 1958.

Pitch measurements: 100m × 72m.

Chairman: Graham Turner.

Secretary: Joan Fennessy.

Manager: Graham Turner.

Physio: Wayne Jones.

Colours: White shirts, black shorts, white stockings.

Change colours: Yellow shirts, blue shorts, blue stockings.

Year Formed: 1924.

Turned Professional: 1924.

Ltd Co.: 1939.

Club Nickname: 'United'.

Ground: 1924, Edgar Street.

First Football League game: 12 August 1972, Division 4, v Colchester U (a) L 0-1 – Potter; Mallender, Naylor; Jones, McLaughlin, Tucker; Slattery, Hollett, Owen, Radford, Wallace.

HONOURS

Football League: Division 2 best season: 22nd, 1976–77; Division 3 – Champions 1975–76; Division 4 – Runners-up 1972–73.

FA Cup: best season: 4th rd, 1972, 1974, 1977, 1982, 1990, 1992, 2008.

Football League Cup: best season: 3rd rd, 1975.

Welsh Cup: Winners 1990.

Conference (runners-up): 2003–04, 2004–05. Promoted from Conference 2005–06 (Play-offs).

SKY SPORTS FACT FILE

The 1945–46 transitional season saw the return of the Southern League to almost a full programme. Sadly Hereford United finished second, deprived of the title when cancelled matches gave extra points to Chelmsford City the declared winners.

Record League Victory: 6–0 v Burnley (away), Division 4, 24 January 1987 – Rose; Rodgerson, Devine, Halliday, Pejic, Dalziel, Harvey (1p), Wells, Phillips (3), Kearns (2), Spooner.

Record Cup Victory: 6–1 v QPR, FA Cup 2nd rd, 7 December 1957 – Sewell; Tomkins, Wade; Masters, Niblett, Horton (2p); Reg Bowen (1), Clayton (1), Fidler, Williams (1), Cyril Beech (1).

Record Defeat: 0–7 v Middlesbrough, Coca-Cola Cup 2nd rd, 1st leg, 18 September 1996.

Most League Points (2 for a win): 63, Division 3, 1975–76.

Most League Points (3 for a win): 77, Division 4, 1984–85.

Most League Goals: 86, Division 3, 1975–76.

Highest League Scorer in Season: Dixie McNeil, 35, 1975–76.

Most League Goals in Total Aggregate: Stewart Phillips, 93, 1980–88, 1990–91.

Most Capped Player: Trevor Benjamin, 2, Jamaica.

Most League Appearances: Mel Pejic, 412, 1980–92.

Record Transfer Fee Received: £440,000 from QPR for Darren Peacock, December 1990.

Record Transfer Fee Paid: £80,000 to Walsall for Dean Smith, June 1994.

Football League Record: 1972 Elected to Division 4; 1973–76 Division 3; 1976–77 Division 2; 1977–78 Division 3; 1978–92 Division 4; 1992–97 Division 3; 1997–2006 Vauxhall Conference; 2006–08 FL 2; 2008– FL 1.

MANAGERS

Eric Keen 1939
George Tranter 1948–49
Alex Massie 1952
George Tranter 1953–55
Joe Wade 1956–62
Ray Daniels 1962–63
Bob Dennison 1963–67
John Charles 1967–71
Colin Addison 1971–74
John Sillett 1974–78
Mike Bailey 1978–79
Frank Lord 1979–82
Tommy Hughes 1982–83
Johnny Newman 1983–87
Ian Bowyer 1987–90
Colin Addison 1990–91
John Sillett 1991–92
Greg Downs 1992–94
John Layton 1994–95
Graham Turner August 1995–

LATEST SEQUENCES

Longest Sequence of League Wins: 6, 2.4.1996 – 20.4.1996.

Longest Sequence of League Defeats: 8, 7.2.1987 – 18.3.1987.

Longest Sequence of League Draws: 6, 12.4.1975 – 23.8.1975.

Longest Sequence of Unbeaten League Matches: 14, 21.10.1972 – 17.1.1973.

Longest Sequence Without a League Win: 13, 19.11.1977 – 25.2.1978.

Successive Scoring Runs: 23 from 20.9.1975.

Successive Non-scoring Runs: 6 from 10.3.2007.

TEN YEAR LEAGUE RECORD

		P	*W*	*D*	*L*	*F*	*A*	*Pts*	*Pos*
1998-99	Conf	42	15	10	17	49	46	55	13
1999-2000	Conf	42	15	14	13	61	52	59	8
2000-01	Conf	42	14	15	13	60	46	57	11
2001-02	Conf	42	14	10	18	50	53	52	17
2002-03	Conf	42	19	7	16	64	51	64	6
2003-04	Conf	42	28	7	7	103	44	91	2
2004-05	Conf	42	21	11	10	68	41	74	2
2005-06	Conf	42	22	14	6	59	33	80	2
2006-07	FL 2	46	14	13	19	45	53	55	16
2007-08	FL 2	46	26	10	10	72	41	88	3

DID YOU KNOW ?

In 1949–50 Charlie Thompson was granted a benefit match which attracted over 8,000 to Edgar Street. Apart from his eight FA Cup goal achievement, he also scored a hat-trick on his home debut and hit five of six goals v Guildford City in 1948–49.

HEREFORD UNITED 2007–08 LEAGUE RECORD

Match No.	Date	Venue	Opponents	Result		H/T Score	Lg. Pos.	Goalscorers	Attendance
1	Aug 11	H	Rotherham U	D	0-0	0-0	—		3566
2	18	A	Barnet	W	2-1	1-1	6	Benjamin (pen) ^{44}, Robinson ^{67}	1790
3	25	H	Rochdale	D	1-1	1-1	9	Robinson ^{27}	2732
4	Sept 1	A	Wrexham	W	2-0	0-0	5	Taylor ^{53}, Benjamin ^{74}	4004
5	8	H	Macclesfield T	L	0-1	0-0	7		2725
6	15	A	Morecambe	W	3-0	0-0	5	Benjamin ^{80}, Ainsworth ^{84}, Webb ^{90}	2949
7	22	H	Bradford C	W	4-2	2-1	2	Diagouraga ^{15}, Guinan ^{18}, Benjamin (pen) ^{52}, Robinson ^{84}	3275
8	29	A	Grimsby T	L	1-2	0-1	3	Benjamin ^{56}	3699
9	Oct 2	A	Notts Co	W	3-2	2-0	—	Smith ^{13}, Guinan 2 $^{26, 70}$	3576
10	6	H	Brentford	W	2-0	2-0	2	Webb 2 $^{31, 34}$	2942
11	12	A	Chester C	D	1-1	0-0	—	Diagouraga ^{77}	3430
12	20	H	Milton Keynes D	L	0-1	0-0	6		3936
13	27	A	Peterborough U	D	1-1	0-1	6	Easton ^{72}	5008
14	Nov 3	H	Darlington	W	5-1	2-1	3	Rose ^{4}, Robinson ^{22}, Smith ^{47}, Benjamin ^{58}, Easton ^{90}	3516
15	6	H	Mansfield T	W	2-1	1-0	—	Robinson ^{25}, Benjamin ^{48}	2272
16	17	A	Stockport Co	W	3-2	1-0	2	Ainsworth 3 $^{37, 54, 70}$	5103
17	24	H	Accrington S	D	0-0	0-0	4		2804
18	Dec 4	A	Wycombe W	D	2-2	0-2	—	Robinson ^{86}, Johnson ^{89}	4081
19	8	H	Lincoln C	W	3-1	2-1	4	Robinson (pen) ^{10}, McClenahan ^{44}, Smith ^{84}	2528
20	15	A	Bury	W	1-0	0-0	2	Robinson ^{90}	2099
21	22	H	Morecambe	L	0-3	0-2	4		3058
22	26	A	Macclesfield T	W	1-0	0-0	2	Robinson ^{57}	2393
23	29	A	Bradford C	W	3-1	3-1	2	Robinson ^{17}, Beckwith ^{39}, Benjamin ^{45}	13,640
24	Jan 1	H	Notts Co	D	0-0	0-0	2		3945
25	13	H	Shrewsbury T	W	3-1	1-1	2	Benjamin (pen) ^{41}, Beckwith ^{73}, Johnson ^{79}	4707
26	21	A	Chesterfield	L	0-4	0-3	—		3274
27	30	H	Barnet	L	1-2	0-0	—	Benjamin ^{64}	2271
28	Feb 2	A	Rotherham U	W	1-0	1-0	5	Hooper ^{40}	4748
29	9	H	Dagenham & R	W	4-1	3-1	3	MacDonald 2 $^{9, 67}$, Hooper ^{21}, Johnson (pen) ^{45}	2594
30	12	A	Rochdale	W	4-2	3-1	—	MacDonald 3 $^{14, 21, 31}$, Hooper ^{73}	2884
31	16	H	Chesterfield	W	2-0	2-0	2	MacDonald ^{8}, Hooper ^{45}	3503
32	23	A	Shrewsbury T	W	2-1	1-1	2	Johnson ^{27}, Hooper ^{67}	7402
33	26	A	Dagenham & R	L	0-1	0-1	—		1929
34	Mar 1	H	Stockport Co	L	0-1	0-0	4		3526
35	8	A	Accrington S	W	2-0	1-0	4	Hooper ^{43}, Roberts (og) ^{52}	1262
36	11	A	Mansfield T	W	1-0	1-0	—	Easton ^{8}	1606
37	15	H	Wycombe W	W	1-0	0-0	3	Martin (og) ^{72}	3126
38	22	H	Bury	D	0-0	0-0	3		3420
39	24	A	Lincoln C	L	1-2	0-1	3-	Hooper ^{62}	3614
40	Apr 5	H	Chester C	D	2-2	2-0	3	Smith ^{25}, Hooper ^{35}	3210
41	12	A	Darlington	W	1-0	0-0	3	Hooper ^{69}	4331
42	15	A	Milton Keynes D	D	0-0	0-0	—		11,428
43	19	H	Peterborough U	L	0-1	0-1	3		5279
44	22	H	Wrexham	W	2-0	1-0	—	Hooper ^{42}, Robinson ^{60}	3739
45	26	A	Brentford	W	3-0	2-0	3	Hooper ^{18}, Robinson ^{36}, Johnson ^{90}	6246
46	May 3	H	Grimsby T	W	2-0	2-0	3	Smith ^{36}, Robinson ^{42}	6020

Final League Position: 3

GOALSCORERS

League (72): Robinson 13 (1 pen), Hooper 11, Benjamin 10 (3 pens), MacDonald 6, Johnson 5 (1 pen), Smith 5, Ainsworth 4, Easton 3, Guinan 3, Webb 3, Beckwith 2, Diagouraga 2, McClenahan 1, Rose 1, Taylor 1, own goals 2.
Carling Cup (5): Ainsworth 3, Easton 1, Robinson 1.
FA Cup (7): Robinson 2, Ainsworth 1, Benjamin 1, Johnson 1, McCombe 1, Smith 1.
J Paint Trophy (0).

Weale C 1	McClenahan T 38	Rose R 31	Diagouraga T 41	Beckwith D 38	Broadhurst K 22+1	Ainsworth L 13+2	Taylor K 22+9	Guinan S 20+8	Benjamin T 15+19	Easton C 36+3	Smith B 42+2	Robinson T 32+11	Brown W 44	Gwynne S 9+6	McCombe J 23+4	Webb L 3+11	Johnson S 22+11	Threlfall R 6+3	Collins L 14+2	Hooper G 19	MacDonald S 7	Palmer M —+1	Gleeson S 3+1	Igoe S 4	Esson R 1	*Match No.*
1	2	3	4	5	6	7	8^1	9	10^2	11	12	13														1
	2	3	4	5	6	7	12	13	10^2	11	8^1	9^3	1	14												2
	2	3	4	5	6^3	7	12	13	10^2	11	8^1	9	1		14											3
	2	3	4	5	6	7^3	8^2	9^1	12	11	13	10	1	14												4
		2	4	5	6	7	8	9	12	3	11^2	10^1	1			13										5
		3	4	5	6	7^2	2	9	10^1	11	8		1			13	12									6
		2	4	5	6	7^2	3	9	10^1	11	8	12	1			13										7
		2	4^2	5	6	7	3	9^1	10	11	8	12	1			13										8
	2		4	5	6	7^1	3	9		11	8	10	1			12										9
	2		4	5	6		3	9^1	12	11	8	10	1			7										10
	2		4	5^3	6	12	3	9^2	13	11	8	10	1		14	7^1										11
	2		4		6	7^2	3^3	9^4	12	11	8^1	10	1		5	13	14									12
	2		4		6	12	3		10	11	8	9	1		5	7^1										13
	2	3	4			7^2	12		10^1	11	8	9^3	1		5	13	14	6								14
		2	4		6	7^2	12		10^3	11	8^1	9	1		5	13	14	3								15
		3	4			7		12	10^1	11	8	9^2	1		5	13		2	6							16
		2^2	4	5			11^3	12	10^1		8	9	1	7	6		14	3	13							17
	2		4	5			8^1	9			7	10	1	6	3		12		11							18
	2		4	5				9^1	12		8	10	1	7	6		11		3							19
	2		4	5				9^1	12	13	8	10	1	7^3	6	14	11^2		3							20
	2		4		6^1		12	9		11	8	10	1	7^2	5		13		3							21
	2		4	5			3	12	10^1	11	8	9	1	14		13^3	7^2		6							22
	2		4	5			3	12	10	11^1	8	9	1	13			7^2		6							23
	2		4	5			3	9	12		8	10	1	7^1			11		6							24
	2	3		5			4		10		8	9	1	7			11		6							25
	2	3^1	4	5			7		10^2	12	8	9	1	13	14		11		6^3							26
	2		4	5	6		12		13		8	9	1	7^2			11^1		3	10						27
		2	4	5					12	11	8	9	1		6		7		3	10^1						28
	2	3	4	5^3					12	11	8		1		6		7		14	9^1	10^2	13				29
	2	3	4^2				7			11		12	1	13	5		8		6	9	10^1					30
	2	3		5			8		12	11		13	1	7^3	6		4	14		9^1	10^2					31
	2	3		5					12	11^3	8	13	1		4		6	14		9^1	10^2		7			32
	2	3		5			12		13	11^3	4^1	14	1		6		8^2			9	10		7			33
	2				6		11^3		12	13	4	8	1		5		14	3		9	10^1		7^2			34
	2	3	4	5					12	11	8	13	1		6		7			9^1	10^2					35
	2	3	4	5			12		13	11	8	10^1	1		6		7^2			9						36
	2	3	4	5						11	8	10	1		6		7^1	12		9						37
	2	3	4	5						11	8	10	1		6		7^1			9			12			38
	2	3	4	5				12		11	8	10	1		6		7^1			9						39
	2	3	4	5				10		11	8		1		6		12			9				7^1		40
	2	3	4	5	6			10		11	8	12	1				7			9^1						41
	2	3	4	5	6		13	10^2		11	8	12	1				7			9^1						42
	2	3	4	5	6			10^2	13	11^3	8	12	1				14			9				7^1		43
	2	3	4	5	6					11	8	10	1							9				7		44
	2	3	4	5	6			12		11	8	10^2	1				13			9^1				7		45
	2^1		4	5^2	12		11	9^3	14		8	10			13		7	3	6						1	46

FA Cup

First Round	Leeds U	(h)	0-0
		(a)	1-0
Second Round	Hartlepool U	(h)	2-0
Third Round	Tranmere R	(a)	2-2
		(h)	1-0
Fourth Round	Cardiff C	(h)	1-2

Carling Cup

First Round	Yeovil T	(h)	4-1
Second Round	Birmingham C	(a)	1-2

J Paint Trophy

Second Round	Yeovil T	(h)	0-0

HUDDERSFIELD TOWN FL Championship 1

FOUNDATION

A meeting, attended largely by members of the Huddersfield & District FA, was held at the Imperial Hotel in 1906 to discuss the feasibility of establishing a football club in this rugby stronghold. However, it was not until a man with both the enthusiasm and the money to back the scheme came on the scene, that real progress was made. This benefactor was Mr Hilton Crowther and it was at a meeting at the Albert Hotel in 1908, that the club formally came into existence with a capital of £2,000 and joined the North-Eastern League.

The Galpharm Stadium, Stadium Way, Leeds Road, Huddersfield HD1 6PX.

Telephone: 0870 4444 677.

Fax: (01484) 484 101.

Ticket Office: 0870 4444 552.

Website: www.htafc.com

Email: info@htafc.com

Ground Capacity: 24,500.

Record Attendance: 67,037 v Arsenal, FA Cup 6th rd, 27 February 1932 (at Leeds Road); 23,678 v Liverpool, FA Cup 3rd rd, 12 December 1999 (at Alfred McAlpine Stadium).

Pitch Measurements: 115yd × 76yd.

Chairman: Ken Davy.

Vice-chairman: Andrew Watson.

Secretary: J. Ann Hough.

Manager: Stan Ternent.

Assistant Manager: Ronnie Jepson.

Physio: Lee Martin MCSP SRP.

Colours: Blue and white striped shirts, white shorts, white and blue hooped stockings.

Change Colours: All black kit with gold and red trim.

Year Formed: 1908. ***Turned Professional:*** 1908. ***Ltd Co.:*** 1908. ***Club Nickname:*** 'The Terriers'.

Grounds: 1908, Leeds Road; 1994, The Alfred McAlpine Stadium (renamed the Galpharm Stadium 2004).

First Football League Game: 3 September 1910, Division 2, v Bradford PA (a) W 1–0 – Mutch; Taylor, Morris; Beaton, Hall, Bartlett; Blackburn, Wood, Hamilton (1), McCubbin, Jee.

Record League Victory: 10–1 v Blackpool, Division 1, 13 December 1930 – Turner; Goodall, Spencer; Redfern, Wilson, Campbell; Bob Kelly (1), McLean (4), Robson (3), Davies (1), Smailes (1).

Record Cup Victory: 7–0 v Lincoln U, FA Cup 1st rd, 16 November 1991 – Clarke; Trevitt, Charlton, Donovan (2), Mitchell, Doherty, O'Regan (1), Stapleton (1) (Wright), Roberts (2), Onuora (1), Barnett (Ireland). *N.B.* 11-0 v Heckmondwike (a), FA Cup pr rd, 18 September 1909 – Doggart; Roberts, Ewing; Hooton, Stevenson, Randall; Kenworthy (2), McCreadie (1), Foster (4), Stacey (4), Jee.

HONOURS

Football League: Division 1 – Champions 1923–24, 1924–25, 1925–26; Runners-up 1926–27, 1927–28, 1933–34; Division 2 – Champions 1969–70; Runners-up 1919–20, 1952–53; Promoted from Division 2 1994–95 (play-offs); Promoted from Division 3 2003–04 (play-offs); Division 4 – Champions 1979–80.

FA Cup: Winners 1922; Runners-up 1920, 1928, 1930, 1938.

Football League Cup: Semi-final 1968.

Autoglass Trophy: Runners-up 1994.

SKY SPORTS FACT FILE

On 10 November 1934 Huddersfield Town beat Liverpool 8–0 in a First Division match. Albert Malam scored a hat-trick including a twice-taken penalty. The win equalled Liverpool's heaviest goal margin reverse and was Town's highspot of the season.

Record Defeat: 1–10 v Manchester C, Division 2, 7 November 1987.

Most League Points (2 for a win): 66, Division 4, 1979–80.

Most League Points (3 for a win): 82, Division 3, 1982–83.

Most League Goals: 101, Division 4, 1979–80.

Highest League Scorer in Season: Sam Taylor, 35, Division 2, 1919–20; George Brown, 35, Division 1, 1925–26.

Most League Goals in Total Aggregate: George Brown, 142, 1921–29; Jimmy Glazzard, 142, 1946–56.

Most League Goals in One Match: 5, Dave Mangnall v Derby Co, Division 1, 21 November 1931; 5, Alf Lythgoe v Blackburn R, Division 1, 13 April 1935.

Most Capped Player: Jimmy Nicholson, 31 (41), Northern Ireland.

Most League Appearances: Billy Smith, 520, 1914–34.

Youngest League Player: Denis Law, 16 years 303 days v Notts Co, 24 December 1956.

Record Transfer Fee Received: £2,750,000 from Ipswich T for Marcus Stewart, February 2000.

Record Transfer Fee Paid: £1,200,000 to Bristol R for Marcus Stewart, July 1996.

Football League Record: 1910 Elected to Division 2; 1920–52 Division 1; 1952–53 Division 2; 1953–56 Division 1; 1956–70 Division 2; 1970–72 Division 1; 1972–73 Division 2; 1973–75 Division 3; 1975–80 Division 4; 1980–83 Division 3; 1983–88 Division 2; 1988–92 Division 3; 1992–95 Division 2; 1995–2001 Division 1; 2001–03 Division 2; 2003–04 Division 3; 2004– FL 1.

MANAGERS

Fred Walker 1908–10
Richard Pudan 1910–12
Arthur Fairclough 1912–19
Ambrose Langley 1919–21
Herbert Chapman 1921–25
Cecil Potter 1925–26
Jack Chaplin 1926–29
Clem Stephenson 1929–42
David Steele 1943–47
George Stephenson 1947–52
Andy Beattie 1952–56
Bill Shankly 1956–59
Eddie Boot 1960–64
Tom Johnston 1964–68
Ian Greaves 1968–74
Bobby Collins 1974
Tom Johnston 1975–78
(had been General Manager since 1975)
Mike Buxton 1978–86
Steve Smith 1986–87
Malcolm Macdonald 1987–88
Eoin Hand 1988–92
Ian Ross 1992–93
Neil Warnock 1993–95
Brian Horton 1995–97
Peter Jackson 1997–99
Steve Bruce 1999–2000
Lou Macari 2000–02
Mick Wadsworth 2002–03
Peter Jackson 2003–07
Andy Ritchie 2007
Stan Ternent April 2008–

LATEST SEQUENCES

Longest Sequence of League Wins: 11, 5.4.1920 – 4.9.1920.

Longest Sequence of League Defeats: 7, 8.10.1955 – 19.11.1955.

Longest Sequence of League Draws: 6, 3.3.1987 – 3.4.1987.

Longest Sequence of Unbeaten League Matches: 27, 24.1.1925 – 17.10.1925.

Longest Sequence Without a League Win: 22, 4.12.1971 – 29.4.1972.

Successive Scoring Runs: 27 from 12.3.2005.

Successive Non-scoring Runs: 7 from 22.1.1972.

TEN YEAR LEAGUE RECORD

		P	W	D	L	F	A	Pts	Pos
1998-99	Div 1	46	15	16	15	62	71	61	10
1999-2000	Div 1	46	21	11	14	62	49	74	8
2000-01	Div 1	46	11	15	20	48	57	48	22
2001-02	Div 2	46	21	15	10	65	47	78	6
2002-03	Div 2	46	11	12	23	39	61	45	22
2003-04	Div 3	46	23	12	11	68	52	81	4
2004-05	FL 1	46	20	10	16	74	65	70	9
2005-06	FL 1	46	19	16	11	72	59	73	4
2006-07	FL 1	46	14	17	15	60	69	59	15
2007-08	FL 1	46	20	6	20	50	62	66	10

DID YOU KNOW?

In May 1951 Festival of Britain matches, Huddersfield Town pulled off two notable victories which in another era of European football would have been hailed as outstanding. They beat PSV Eindhoven 4–1 and then Stade Rennais 5–1.

HUDDERSFIELD TOWN 2007–08 LEAGUE RECORD

Match No.	*Date*	*Venue*	*Opponents*	*Result*		*H/T Score*	*Lg. Pos.*	*Goalscorers*	*Attendance*
1	Aug 11	H	Yeovil T	W	1-0	1-0	—	Beckett [17]	9876
2	18	A	Bournemouth	W	1-0	1-0	2	Beckett [43]	5606
3	25	H	Carlisle U	L	0-2	0-2	7		10,022
4	Sept 1	A	Millwall	W	2-1	1-1	4	Booth [44], Kamara [52]	9004
5	8	A	Crewe Alex	L	0-2	0-2	8		5164
6	15	H	Cheltenham T	L	2-3	0-0	9	Kamara [48], Keogh [90]	8756
7	22	A	Northampton T	L	0-3	0-1	15		5014
8	29	H	Luton T	W	2-0	1-0	9	Beckett [36], Cadamarteri [60]	9028
9	Oct 2	H	Nottingham F	D	1-1	0-0	—	Cadamarteri [67]	10,994
10	6	A	Walsall	L	0-4	0-2	14		5112
11	14	A	Doncaster R	L	0-2	0-1	15		6866
12	20	H	Oldham Ath	D	1-1	0-1	16	Wallwork [80]	10,909
13	26	A	Tranmere R	L	0-3	0-1	—		6008
14	Nov 3	H	Port Vale	W	3-1	3-1	17	Booth [3], Wallwork [9], Clarke N [21]	8555
15	6	H	Hartlepool U	W	2-0	1-0	—	Cadamarteri [12], Beckett [87]	8154
16	16	A	Swansea C	W	1-0	0-0	—	Kamara [54]	12,184
17	24	H	Leyton Orient	L	0-1	0-1	13		9697
18	Dec 5	A	Southend U	L	1-4	0-1	—	Schofield [67]	6844
19	8	A	Leeds U	L	0-4	0-1	15		32,501
20	15	H	Bristol R	W	2-1	1-0	13	Wallwork [16], Jevons [55]	8118
21	22	A	Cheltenham T	W	2-0	1-0	11	Booth 2 [14, 66]	3998
22	26	H	Crewe Alex	D	1-1	0-1	12	Booth [85]	9759
23	29	H	Northampton T	L	1-2	1-0	13	Booth [45]	8566
24	Jan 1	A	Nottingham F	L	1-2	1-0	14	Jevons (pen) [37]	18,762
25	12	H	Gillingham	L	1-3	1-1	16	Brandon [32]	11,212
26	19	A	Brighton & HA	D	1-1	0-0	15	Williams [77]	5343
27	29	H	Bournemouth	W	1-0	1-0	—	Jevons [35]	7359
28	Feb 2	A	Yeovil T	W	2-0	1-0	15	Beckett (pen) [25], Collins [51]	4823
29	9	H	Swindon T	W	1-0	1-0	13	Jevons [1]	9388
30	12	A	Carlisle U	L	1-2	0-1	—	Page [87]	6196
31	19	H	Millwall	W	1-0	1-0	—	Beckett (pen) [29]	6326
32	23	A	Gillingham	L	0-1	0-0	14		5022
33	Mar 1	H	Swansea C	L	0-1	0-1	15		10,471
34	4	A	Swindon T	L	2-3	1-3	—	Jevons 2 (2 pens) [39, 77]	4840
35	8	A	Leyton Orient	W	1-0	0-0	15	Beckett [75]	4660
36	11	A	Hartlepool U	L	1-2	0-1	—	Clarke N [64]	3650
37	15	H	Southend U	L	1-2	0-1	15	Booth [73]	7823
38	18	H	Brighton & HA	W	2-1	1-0	—	Holdsworth [4], Beckett (pen) [79]	6004
39	22	A	Bristol R	W	3-2	1-1	13	Berrett [39], Brandon [70], Collins [88]	6585
40	29	A	Oldham Ath	L	1-4	0-3	14	Mirfin [90]	5637
41	Apr 5	H	Doncaster R	D	2-2	1-0	14	Williams [7], Holdsworth [61]	10,279
42	12	A	Port Vale	D	0-0	0-0	13		4150
43	15	H	Leeds U	W	1-0	0-0	—	Holdsworth [76]	16,413
44	19	H	Tranmere R	W	1-0	0-0	12	Booth [61]	8315
45	26	H	Walsall	W	2-0	1-0	12	Schofield [41], Booth [56]	9969
46	May 3	A	Luton T	W	1-0	0-0	10	Jevons [77]	6539

Final League Position: 10

GOALSCORERS

League (50): Booth 9, Beckett 8 (3 pens), Jevons 7 (3 pens), Cadamarteri 3, Holdsworth 3, Kamara 3, Wallwork 3, Brandon 2, Clarke N 2, Collins 2, Schofield 2, Williams 2, Berrett 1, Keogh 1, Mirfin 1, Page 1.
Carling Cup (0).
FA Cup (10): Beckett 4, Jevons 2, Kamara 2, Brandon 1, Collins 1.
J Paint Trophy (1): Collins 1.

Glennon M 45	Skarz J 22 + 5	Sinclair F 28 + 1	Holdsworth A 43 + 1	Mirfin D 23 + 6	Clarke N 44	Brandon C 25 + 3	Collins M 35 + 6	Kamara M 33 + 10	Beckett L 25 + 11	Schofield D 19 + 6	Worthington J 19 + 6	Akins L — + 3	Booth A 28 + 10	Hardy A 5 + 1	Young M 4 + 4	Keogh R 9	Killock S 1	Racchi D — + 3	Cadamarteri D 10 + 2	Wallwork R 16	Broadbent D — + 5	Jevons P 17 + 4	Smithies A 1 + 1	Williams R 24 + 1	Berrett J 10 + 5	Page R 18	Clarke T 2 + 1	Match No.
1	2	3	4	5	6	7[1]	8	9[2]	10[3]	11	12	13	14															1
1	3		2		6	7	8	9	10[1]		11		12	5	4													2
1	3		2		6	8	4	9	10		7	12	13	5[1]	11[2]													3
1	3	2[1]	4		6	7	8	11	10[2]				9	12	13	5												4
1	3		4	5		7		11	10[1]	12			9	2	8[2]		6	13										5
1	3		4	5		7	8	11	10	12			9	2[1]		6												6
1	3	12	4		6	7	8	11[3]	10				9	2[2]		5[1]		13	14									7
1	3	2	4		6	7[3]	12	11	10[2]				13		14	5			9[1]	8								8
1	3	2	4	12	6	13	7[2]	11	10[1]						14	5			9■	8[3]								9
1	3	2■	4[1]	12	6		7	9	10[3]			14	13		11[2]	5				8								10
1	3		4	5[2]	6	11[1]	7	13	10	12						2			9	8								11
1	3	2	4		6			7	10	11						5			9	8								12
1	3[1]	2	4		6			7	10	11						5			9	8	12							13
1	3	2	4	5	6		12	7[1]	13	11[3]			10[2]		14				9	8								14
1	3	2	4	5	6		12	7[1]	13	11			10[2]						9	8								15
1	3	2	4	5	6			7	12	11			10[1]						9	8								16
1	3[1]	2	4	5	6		12	7	10	11[2]									9	8		13						17
1■	3	2■	4	5	6		12	7[2]		11			10[G]						9	8[1]		13	15					18
			2	5	6		4	7	12	11			10[1]						13	8		9[2]	1	3				19
1	12		2	5	6		4	7		11[1]	13		10							8[2]		9		3				20
1			2	5	6		4	7[1]		11	12		10							8		9		3				21
1	12		2	5	6		4	7	13	11[2]	14		10							8[3]		9		3[1]				22
1		5	2		6		4	7		11[1]	12		10							8		9		3				23
1	12	2	4	5	6	13	8	7[2]		14	11[3]		10									9[1]		3				24
1		2[1]		5	6	9		7	10	11[2]	8							12				13		3	4			25
1	3[1]		2[2]	5	6	7■	4	12	10		8											9		11	13			26
1			4		6		2	7	10[1]	11[2]	8		12									9		3	13	5		27
1		3	4		6		7	12	10[2]	11	8		13									9[1]		2		5		28
1		2	4	12	6	13	7[1]	14	10	11[2]	8[3]											9		3		5		29
1		2	4	12	6[1]	8	7	13					10									9		3	11[2]	5		30
1		2	4		6	7	8	12	10				13									9[2]		3	11[1]	5		31
1		2	4		6	7	8	12	10[2]		11		13									9		3		5[1]		32
1		2	4	12	6	7	8[1]	11[2]	10	13			14									9[3]		3		5■		33
1		2	4	5	6	7	8	11	12				10									9		3[1]				34
1		2	4		6	7	8[3]	11[2]	12		14		10									9[1]		3	13	5		35
1		2[2]	4		6	7	13	11	12		8		10									9[1]		3		5		36
1		2	4		6	7	11[3]	9	12		8[2]		10[1]								14			3	13	5		37
1		3	4[1]		6	7	2	11	10[2]		8		9								13				12	5		38
1		3			6	7	2	11[1]	10[2]		8		9								13			12	4	5		39
1		2	12	13	6	7	4	14	10[2]		8[1]		9											3	11[3]	5		40
1	12		4	2	6	7	8				11		9											3[1]	10	5		41
1			2	4	6	7	8	12			11[1]		9											3	10	5		42
1	12		2	4	6	7[3]	8	14	13		11■		9[2]											3[1]	10	5		43
1	3		2	4	6		8	10[2]	12	13			9[1]											11		5	7	44
1	3		2	4	6		8			11[1]	7[2]		9								12				10	5	13	45
1	3		2	4	6		8			11	7		9									12			10[1]		5	46

FA Cup

First Round	Accrington S	(a)	3-2
Second Round	Grimsby T	(h)	3-0
Third Round	Birmingham C	(h)	2-1
Fourth Round	Oldham Ath	(a)	1-0
Fifth Round	Chelsea	(a)	1-3

Carling Cup

First Round	Blackpool	(a)	0-1

J Paint Trophy

First Round	Grimsby T	(a)	1-4

HULL CITY

FA Premiership

FOUNDATION

The enthusiasts who formed Hull City in 1904 were brave men indeed. More than that they were audacious for they immediately put the club on the map in this Rugby League fortress by obtaining a three-year agreement with the Hull Rugby League club to rent their ground! They had obtained quite a number of conversions to the dribbling code, before the Rugby League forbade the use of any of their club grounds by Association Football clubs. By that time, Hull City were well away having entered the FA Cup in their initial season and the Football League, Second Division after only a year.

Kingston Communications Stadium, Walton Street, Hull, East Yorkshire HU3 6HU.

Telephone: 0870 837 0003.

Fax: (01482) 304 882.

Ticket Office: 0870 837 0004.

Website: www.hullcityafc.net

Email: info@hulltigers.com

Ground Capacity: 25,417.

Record Attendance: KC Stadium: 25,512 v Sunderland, FL C, 28 October 2007. Boothferry Park: 55,019 v Manchester U, FA Cup 6th rd, 26 February 1949.

Pitch Measurements: 100.5m × 67.5m.

Chairman/Chief Executive: Paul Duffen.

Secretary: Phil Hough.

Manager: Phil Brown.

Assistant Manager: Brian Horton.

Physio: Simon Maltby.

Colours: Black and amber striped shirts, black shorts.

Change Colours: Grey shirt, grey shorts, grey stockings.

Year Formed: 1904. ***Turned Professional:*** 1905.

Ltd Co.: 1905.

Club Nickname: 'The Tigers'.

Grounds: 1904, Boulevard Ground (Hull RFC); 1905, Anlaby Road (Hull CC); 1944, Boulevard Ground; 1946, Boothferry Park; 2002, Kingston Communications Stadium.

First Football League Game: 2 September 1905, Division 2, v Barnsley (h) W 4–1 – Spendiff; Langley, Jones; Martin, Robinson, Gordon (2); Rushton, Spence (1), Wilson (1), Howe, Raisbeck.

Record League Victory: 11–1 v Carlisle U, Division 3 (N), 14 January 1939 – Ellis; Woodhead, Dowen; Robinson (1), Blyth, Hardy; Hubbard (2), Richardson (2), Dickinson (2), Davies (2), Cunliffe (2).

HONOURS

Football League: Promoted from FL C – 2008 (play-offs); Championship 1 runners-up 2004–05; Division 2 best season: 3rd, 1909–10; Division 3 (N) – Champions 1932–33, 1948–49; Division 3 – Champions 1965–66; Runners-up 1958–59, 2003–04; Division 4 – Runners-up 1982–83.

FA Cup: Semi-final 1930.

Football League Cup: best season: 4th, 1974, 1976, 1978.

Associate Members' Cup: Runners-up 1984.

SKY SPORTS FACT FILE

On 23 May 2008, locally born Dean Windass, 39, scored the only goal of the play-off final against Bristol City. It was the icing on the promotion cake for the one-time frozen food packer and one of the oldest goalscorers at Wembley Stadium.

Record Cup Victory: 8–2 v Stalybridge Celtic (a), FA Cup 1st rd, 26 November 1932 – Maddison; Goldsmith, Woodhead; Gardner, Hill (1), Denby; Forward (1), Duncan, McNaughton (1), Wainscoat (4), Sargeant (1).

Record Defeat: 0–8 v Wolverhampton W, Division 2, 4 November 1911.

Most League Points (2 for a win): 69, Division 3, 1965–66.

Most League Points (3 for a win): 90, Division 4, 1982–83.

Most League Goals: 109, Division 3, 1965–66.

Highest League Scorer in Season: Bill McNaughton, 39, Division 3 (N), 1932–33.

Most League Goals in Total Aggregate: Chris Chilton, 195, 1960–71.

Most League Goals in One Match: 5, Ken McDonald v Bristol C, Division 2, 17 November 1928; 5, Simon 'Slim' Raleigh v Halifax T, Division 3N, 26 December 1930.

Most Capped Player: Theo Whitmore, Jamaica.

Most League Appearances: Andy Davidson, 520, 1952–67.

Youngest League Player: Matthew Edeson, 16 years 63 days v Fulham, 10 October 1992.

Record Transfer Fee Received: £1,000,000 from Crystal Palace for Leon Cort, June 2006.

Record Transfer Fee Paid: £1,000,000 to Wigan Ath for Caleb Folan, August 2007.

Football League Record: 1905 Elected to Division 2; 1930–33 Division 3 (N); 1933–36 Division 2; 1936–49 Division 3 (N); 1949–56 Division 2; 1956–58 Division 3 (N); 1958–59 Division 3; 1959–60 Division 2; 1960–66 Division 3; 1966–78 Division 2; 1978–81 Division 3; 1981–83 Division 4; 1983–85 Division 3; 1985–91 Division 2; 1991–92 Division 3; 1992–96 Division 2; 1996–2004 Division 3; 2004–05 FL 1; 2005–08 FL C; 2008– FA Premier League.

MANAGERS

James Ramster 1904–05
(Secretary-Manager)
Ambrose Langley 1905–13
Harry Chapman 1913–14
Fred Stringer 1914–16
David Menzies 1916–21
Percy Lewis 1921–23
Bill McCracken 1923–31
Haydn Green 1931–34
John Hill 1934–36
David Menzies 1936
Ernest Blackburn 1936–46
Major Frank Buckley 1946–48
Raich Carter 1948–51
Bob Jackson 1952–55
Bob Brocklebank 1955–61
Cliff Britton 1961–70
(continued as General Manager to 1971)
Terry Neill 1970–74
John Kaye 1974–77
Bobby Collins 1977–78
Ken Houghton 1978–79
Mike Smith 1979–82
Bobby Brown 1982
Colin Appleton 1982–84
Brian Horton 1984–88
Eddie Gray 1988–89
Colin Appleton 1989
Stan Ternent 1989–91
Terry Dolan 1991–97
Mark Hateley 1997–98
Warren Joyce 1998–2000
Brian Little 2000–02
Jan Molby 2002
Peter Taylor 2002–06
Phil Parkinson 2006
Phil Brown January 2007–

LATEST SEQUENCES

Longest Sequence of League Wins: 10, 23.2.1966 – 20.4.1966.

Longest Sequence of League Defeats: 8, 7.4.1934 – 8.9.1934.

Longest Sequence of League Draws: 5, 30.3.1929 – 15.4.1929.

Longest Sequence of Unbeaten League Matches: 19, 13.3.2001 – 22.9.2001.

Longest Sequence Without a League Win: 27, 27.3.1989 – 4.11.1989.

Successive Scoring Runs: 26 from 10.4.1990.

Successive Non-scoring Runs: 6 from 13.11.1920.

TEN YEAR LEAGUE RECORD

		P	W	D	L	F	A	Pts	Pos
1998-99	Div 3	46	14	11	21	44	62	53	21
1999-2000	Div 3	46	15	14	17	43	43	59	14
2000-01	Div 3	46	19	17	10	47	39	74	6
2001-02	Div 3	46	16	13	17	57	51	61	11
2002-03	Div 3	46	14	17	15	58	53	59	13
2003-04	Div 3	46	25	13	8	82	44	88	2
2004-05	FL 1	46	26	8	12	80	53	86	2
2005-06	FL C	46	12	16	18	49	55	52	18
2006-07	FL C	46	13	10	23	51	67	49	21
2007-08	FL C	46	21	12	13	65	47	75	3

DID YOU KNOW?

For five seasons from 1905–06 Hull City had two forwards named Smith – Jackie and Joe (known as Stanley, signed from West Stanley). By 1910–11 they were joined by two more, Ted and Wally by name. Later there were three Browells, three Gordons and two Wrights!

HULL CITY 2007–08 LEAGUE RECORD

Match No.	*Date*	*Venue*	*Opponents*	*Result*		*H/T Score*	*Lg. Pos.*	*Goalscorers*	*Attendance*
1	Aug 11	H	Plymouth Arg	L	2-3	1-2	—	Windass [3], Marney [49]	16,633
2	18	A	Coventry C	D	1-1	0-0	16	Barmby [62]	21,059
3	25	H	Norwich C	W	2-1	0-0	13	Windass [49], Garcia [77]	15,939
4	Sept 3	A	Blackpool	L	1-2	0-0	—	Ashbee [50]	7902
5	15	H	Stoke C	D	1-1	0-1	20	Livermore [87]	19,642
6	18	A	Wolverhampton W	W	1-0	0-0	—	Windass (pen) [49]	21,352
7	22	A	Sheffield W	L	0-1	0-1	18		21,518
8	29	H	Ipswich T	W	3-1	3-1	11	Pedersen 2 [11, 40], Brown [45]	15,456
9	Oct 2	H	Charlton Ath	L	1-2	0-1	—	McPhee [90]	15,001
10	6	A	Crystal Palace	D	1-1	0-0	15	Marney (pen) [90]	15,769
11	20	A	Watford	L	0-1	0-1	18		15,803
12	22	H	Barnsley	W	3-0	2-0	—	Campbell 2 [7, 18], Marney [90]	15,761
13	27	H	Sheffield U	D	1-1	0-1	14	Windass (pen) [54]	20,185
14	Nov 3	A	QPR	L	0-2	0-1	15		12,375
15	6	A	Burnley	W	1-0	0-0	—	Turner [90]	9978
16	10	H	Preston NE	W	3-0	2-0	11	Windass [11], Campbell [21], Dawson [63]	16,358
17	24	A	Scunthorpe U	W	2-1	2-1	9	Windass 2 [4, 16]	8633
18	27	H	Bristol C	D	0-0	0-0	—		15,768
19	Dec 1	H	Cardiff C	D	2-2	2-1	10	McPhee [3], Garcia [43]	16,269
20	4	A	Preston NE	L	0-3	0-0	—		11,311
21	8	A	Southampton	L	0-4	0-1	14		18,125
22	15	H	Leicester C	W	2-0	1-0	13	Folan [17], Campbell [78]	16,006
23	22	A	Charlton Ath	D	1-1	1-0	11	Campbell [37]	22,040
24	26	H	Wolverhampton W	W	2-0	0-0	11	Garcia [47], Campbell [61]	19,127
25	30	H	Sheffield W	W	1-0	1-0	8	Windass [33]	21,252
26	Jan 1	A	Stoke C	D	1-1	0-1	9	Folan [61]	15,788
27	12	H	WBA	L	1-3	0-2	10	Garcia [71]	18,391
28	29	H	Coventry C	W	1-0	0-0	—	Folan [90]	14,822
29	Feb 2	A	Plymouth Arg	W	1-0	1-0	8	Windass [45]	11,011
30	9	H	Blackpool	D	2-2	0-1	8	Folan [60], Windass [71]	18,407
31	12	A	Norwich C	D	1-1	0-1	—	Campbell [53]	25,259
32	16	H	Colchester U	D	1-1	0-0	—	Campbell [64]	15,664
33	23	A	WBA	W	2-1	1-1	8	Campbell [29], Folan [82]	22,716
34	Mar 1	A	Bristol C	L	1-2	1-1	9	Fontaine (og) [45]	15,859
35	4	H	Burnley	W	2-0	2-0	—	Campbell [14], Garcia [28]	15,838
36	8	H	Scunthorpe U	W	2-0	2-0	6	Pedersen [27], Turner [37]	20,906
37	12	A	Cardiff C	L	0-1	0-1	—		17,555
38	15	H	Southampton	W	5-0	1-0	5	Campbell [7], Pedersen [55], Turner [57], Marney [68], Hughes [90]	16,829
39	18	A	Colchester U	W	3-1	2-1	—	Campbell 2 [20, 33], Folan [87]	5497
40	22	A	Leicester C	W	2-0	1-0	3	Marney [45], Folan [76]	30,374
41	29	H	Watford	W	3-0	2-0	3	Turner [1], Campbell [13], Folan [73]	23,501
42	Apr 12	H	QPR	D	1-1	0-1	4	Turner [90]	22,468
43	15	A	Barnsley	W	3-1	1-0	—	Marney (pen) [24], Ashbee [52], Windass [83]	13,061
44	19	A	Sheffield U	L	0-2	0-0	3		28,188
45	26	H	Crystal Palace	W	2-1	1-1	3	Campbell [18], Ashbee [85]	24,350
46	May 4	A	Ipswich T	L	0-1	0-0	3		28,233

Final League Position: 3

GOALSCORERS

League (65): Campbell 15, Windass 11 (2 pens), Folan 8, Marney 6 (2 pens), Garcia 5, Turner 5, Pedersen 4, Ashbee 3, McPhee 2, Barmby 1, Brown 1, Dawson 1, Hughes 1, Livermore 1, own goal 1.
Carling Cup (4): Bridges 1, Elliott 1, Garcia 1, McPhee 1.
FA Cup (2): Windass 2.
Play-Offs (7): Barmby 2, Windass 2, Doyle 1, Folan 1, Garcia 1.

Myhill B 43	Ricketts S 44	Dawson A 24 + 5	Ashbee I 42	Coles D 1	Delaney D 20 + 2	Marney D 35 + 6	Hughes B 26 + 9	Barmby N 5 + 10	Windass D 29 + 8	Garcia R 35 + 3	Livermore D 9 + 11	McPhee S 7 + 12	Bridges M 1 + 6	Duke M 3	Turner M 44	Brown W 41	Elliott S 3 + 4	Folan C 18 + 11	Okocha J 10 + 8	Pedersen H 18 + 3	Featherstone N — + 6	Campbell F 32 + 2	France R 3 + 10	Walton S 5 + 5	Clement N 4 + 1	Fagan C 4 + 4	Doyle N — + 1	Match No.
1	2	3	4	5	6	7	8^{1}	9^{2}	10^{3}	11	12	13	14															1
	2■	12	4		3	7		9^{2}	10^{3}	11	13	14		1	6	5	8^{1}											2
		2	4		3	7	12	9^{3}	10^{2}	11	13		14	1	6	5	8^{1}											3
		3	4		2	7	13		10^{3}	11^{2}		14	12	1	6	5	8	9^{1}										4
1	2		4		3	7^{3}	8^{1}		10	11^{2}	13		12		6	5		9	14									5
1	2		4		3	7	8		12^{2}	11	14		13		6	5		9^{1}	10^{3}									6
1	2		4		3	7^{1}	8^{2}			11	13	12	9^{3}		6	5			10	14								7
1	2	3	4			7	12		9^{3}	8	13	14			6	5			10^{2}	11^{1}								8
1	2	3	4■			7^{2}	8		10^{1}	9^{3}	13	14			6	5	12			11								9
1	2				3	7	12^{2}		10^{3}	8	4	14			6	5			9^{1}	11	13							10
1	2^{1}				3	7	8		13	10^{2}	11^{3}	4			5	6	12				14	9						11
1	2				3	4	8		10^{1}	7	11	12			5	6					13	9^{2}						12
1	2		4		3		8		10	7^{2}	11^{3}	12			5	6			14		13	9^{1}						13
1	2		4		3	7^{1}			10	8		12			5	6			11^{2}		13	9						14
1	2		4		3	7	8^{1}		12	11		10			5	6			13			9^{2}						15
1	2	12	4		3	7	8		10^{3}			11			5	6^{1}	13		14			9^{2}						16
1	2	12	4		3	7	8		10^{3}	14		11^{1}			5	6		13				9^{2}						17
1	2		4		3	7	8^{2}		10	13		11^{3}			5	6		12	14			9^{1}						18
1	2	12	4		3	7			10^{3}	8	13	11^{2}			5	6		14				9^{1}						19
1	2		4		3	7			12	8	13	11^{3}			5	6		10^{1}	14			9^{2}						20
1	2	12	4		3	7^{2}	8		10	13		14			5^{1}	6		9	11^{3}									21
1	2	3	4			7	8		10^{1}	11	12				5	6		9^{2}				13						22
1	2	3	4		14		8^{1}	12		11^{2}	7	13			5	6		10				9^{3}						23
1	2	3	4^{1}			12	8	13	14	11	7				5	6		10^{3}				9^{2}						24
1	2	3	4		14		8	12	13^{3}	11	7				5	6		10^{1}				9^{2}						25
1	2	3	4				8^{1}	13	10^{2}	11	7				5	6	12	9										26
1	2		4		3^{3}	7^{2}	8	12	10^{1}	11					5	6		9				13	14					27
1	2	3				7^{1}	8	12	10^{2}	11^{3}					5	6		13		14		9		4				28
1	2		4				8	12	10^{2}	11^{3}					5	6		13		3		9^{1}	14	7				29
1	2		4			12	8^{2}	13	10^{1}						5	6		14		3		9	7	11^{3}				30
1	2		4			12		10^{1}							5	6			11^{2}	3	13	9	7	8				31
1	2		4			12		10^{1}							5	6		13	11	3		9	7	8^{2}				32
1	2	3	4			12				7^{2}					5	6		10	8^{1}	11		9^{3}	13	14				33
1	2	3	4			8^{1}				7^{2}						6		10	13	11		9	12		5			34
1	2	3	4			12				7^{1}					5	6		10■	8■	11^{3}		9^{2}	13	14				35
1	2	3	4			8				7^{1}					5	6				11^{2}		9	12	13		10		36
1	2	3	4			8	12			7					5	6^{2}				11		9^{1}			13	10		37
1	2	3	4			8	12		10^{1}	7^{2}			13		5					11^{3}		9	14		6			38
1	2	3	4			8	12		10^{3}	7					5			14	13	11^{1}		9^{2}			6			39
1	2	3	4^{3}			8			10	7^{1}					5			13		11		9^{2}	12	14	6			40
1	2	3	4^{1}			8	12		10^{2}	7					5	6		13		11		9^{3}				14		41
1	2	3	4			8	12		10^{3}	7^{1}					5	6		13		11^{2}		9				14		42
1	2	3	4			7	8		12						5	6		10^{1}				9^{3}	13	14		11^{2}		43
1	2	3^{1}	4			7	8		12		6^{2}				5			10		14		9	13			11^{3}		44
1	2		4			8	11^{1}	12	10^{2}						5	6		7		3^{3}		9				13	14	45
1	2	3	4			8	11^{2}	12	10						5	6		7^{1}				9				13		46

FA Cup
Third Round — Plymouth Arg — (a) 2-3

Carling Cup
First Round — Crewe Alex — (a) 3-0
Second Round — Wigan Ath — (a) 1-0
Third Round — Chelsea — (h) 0-4

Play-Offs
Semi-Final — Watford — (a) 2-0; (h) 4-1
Final *(at Wembley)* — Bristol C — 1-0

IPSWICH TOWN FL Championship

FOUNDATION

Considering that Ipswich Town only reached the Football League in 1938, many people outside of East Anglia may be surprised to learn that this club was formed at a meeting held in the Town Hall as far back as 1878 when Mr T. C. Cobbold, MP, was voted president. Originally it was the Ipswich Association FC to distinguish it from the older Ipswich Football Club which played rugby. These two amalgamated in 1888 and the handling game was dropped in 1893.

Portman Road, Ipswich, Suffolk IP1 2DA.

Telephone: (01473) 400 500.

Fax: (01473) 400 042.

Ticket Office: 0870 1110 555.

Website: www.itfc.co.uk

Email: enquiries@itfc.co.uk

Ground Capacity: 30,311.

Record Attendance: 38,010 v Leeds U, FA Cup 6th rd, 8 March 1975.

Pitch Measurements: 102.46m × 66m.

Chairman: David Sheepshanks.

Chief Executive: Derek Bowden.

Secretary: Sally Webb.

Manager: Jim Magilton.

Assistant Manager: Bryan Klug.

Physio: Matt Byard.

Colours: Blue shirts, white shorts, blue stockings.

Change Colours: TBC.

Year Formed: 1878.

Turned Professional: 1936.

Ltd Co.: 1936.

Club Nicknames: 'Blues' or 'Town' or 'Tractor Boys'.

Grounds: 1878, Broom Hill and Brook's Hall; 1884, Portman Road.

Record League Victory: 7–0 v Portsmouth, Division 2, 7 November 1964 – Thorburn; Smith, McNeil; Baxter, Bolton, Thompson; Broadfoot (1), Hegan (2), Baker (1), Leadbetter, Brogan (3). 7–0 v Southampton, Division 1, 2 February 1974 – Sivell; Burley, Mills (1), Morris, Hunter, Beattie (1), Hamilton (2), Viljoen, Johnson, Whymark (2), Lambert (1) (Woods). 7–0 v WBA, Division 1, 6 November 1976 – Sivell; Burley, Mills, Talbot, Hunter, Beattie (1), Osborne, Wark (1), Mariner (1) (Bertschin), Whymark (4), Woods.

HONOURS

Football League: Division 1 – Champions 1961–62; Runners-up 1980–81, 1981–82; Promoted from Division 1 1999–2000 (play-offs); Division 2 – Champions 1960–61, 1967–68, 1991–92; Division 3 (S) – Champions 1953–54, 1956–57.

FA Cup: Winners 1978.

Football League Cup: Semi-final 1982, 1985.

Texaco Cup: Winners 1973.

European Competitions: *European Cup:* 1962–63. *European Cup-Winners' Cup:* 1978–79. *UEFA Cup:* 1973–74, 1974–75, 1975–76, 1977–78, 1979–80, 1980–81 (winners), 1981–82, 1982–83, 2001–02, 2002–03.

SKY SPORTS FACT FILE

In addition to the players capped for the four home countries and the Republic of Ireland, Ipswich Town have had international players from Bulgaria, Canada, Denmark, Finland, Holland, Iceland, Jamaica, Nigeria and Slovenia in the last 25 years.

First Football League Game: 27 August 1938, Division 3 (S), v Southend U (h) W 4–2 – Burns; Dale, Parry; Perrett, Fillingham, McLuckie; Williams, Davies (1), Jones (2), Alsop (1), Little.

Record Cup Victory: 10–0 v Floriana, European Cup prel. rd, 25 September 1962 – Bailey; Malcolm, Compton; Baxter, Laurel, Elsworthy (1); Stephenson, Moran (2), Crawford (5), Phillips (2), Blackwood.

Record Defeat: 1–10 v Fulham, Division 1, 26 December 1963.

Most League Points (2 for a win): 64, Division 3 (S), 1953–54 and 1955–56.

Most League Points (3 for a win): 87, Division 1, 1999–2000.

Most League Goals: 106, Division 3 (S), 1955–56.

Highest League Scorer in Season: Ted Phillips, 41, Division 3 (S), 1956–57.

Most League Goals in Total Aggregate: Ray Crawford, 204, 1958–63 and 1966–69.

Most League Goals in One Match: 5, Alan Brazil v Southampton, Division 1, 16 February 1981.

Most Capped Player: Allan Hunter, 47 (53), Northern Ireland.

Most League Appearances: Mick Mills, 591, 1966–82.

Youngest League Player: Jason Dozzell, 16 years 56 days v Coventry C, 4 February 1984.

Record Transfer Fee Received: £6,000,000 from Newcastle U for Kieron Dyer, July 1999 and £6,000,000 from Arsenal for Richard Wright, July 2001.

Record Transfer Fee Paid: £5,000,000 to Sampdoria for Matteo Sereni, August 2001.

Football League Record: 1938 Elected to Division 3 (S); 1954–55 Division 2; 1955–57 Division 3 (S); 1957–61 Division 2; 1961–64 Division 1; 1964–68 Division 2; 1968–86 Division 1; 1986–92 Division 2; 1992–95 FA Premier League; 1995–2000 Division 1; 2000–02 FA Premier League; 2002–04 Division 1; 2004– FL C.

MANAGERS

Mick O'Brien 1936–37
Scott Duncan 1937–55
(continued as Secretary)
Alf Ramsey 1955–63
Jackie Milburn 1963–64
Bill McGarry 1964–68
Bobby Robson 1969–82
Bobby Ferguson 1982–87
Johnny Duncan 1987–90
John Lyall 1990–94
George Burley 1994–2002
Joe Royle 2002–06
Jim Magilton June 2006–

LATEST SEQUENCES

Longest Sequence of League Wins: 8, 23.9.1953 – 31.10.1953.

Longest Sequence of League Defeats: 10, 4.9.1954 – 16.10.1954.

Longest Sequence of League Draws: 7, 10.11.1990 – 21.12.1990.

Longest Sequence of Unbeaten League Matches: 23, 8.12.1979 – 26.4.1980.

Longest Sequence Without a League Win: 21, 28.8.1963 – 14.12.1963.

Successive Scoring Runs: 31 from 7.3.2004.

Successive Non-scoring Runs: 7 from 28.2.1995.

TEN YEAR LEAGUE RECORD

		P	*W*	*D*	*L*	*F*	*A*	*Pts*	*Pos*
1998-99	Div 1	46	26	8	12	69	32	86	3
1999-2000	Div 1	46	25	12	9	71	42	87	3
2000-01	PR Lge	38	20	6	12	57	42	66	5
2001-02	PR Lge	38	9	9	20	41	64	36	18
2002-03	Div 1	46	19	13	14	80	64	70	7
2003-04	Div 1	46	21	10	15	84	72	73	5
2004-05	FL C	46	24	13	9	85	56	85	3
2005-06	FL C	46	14	14	18	53	66	56	15
2006-07	FL C	46	18	8	20	64	59	62	14
2007-08	FL C	46	18	15	13	65	56	69	8

DID YOU KNOW ?

Half a dozen Ipswich Town players were involved in the 1981 film *Escape to Victory*. In addition to Kevin Beattie playing as Michael Caine and Paul Cooper as Sylvester Stallone, Kevin O'Callaghan, Russell Osman, Laurie Sivell and John Wark played in the match.

IPSWICH TOWN 2007–08 LEAGUE RECORD

Match No.	Date	Venue	Opponents	Result		H/T Score	Lg. Pos.	Goalscorers	Attendance
1	Aug 11	H	Sheffield W	W	4-1	3-0	—	Lee 2 (1 pen) [2 (p), 25], Roberts [11], Counago [60]	23,099
2	18	A	Plymouth Arg	D	1-1	1-0	5	Lee [2]	13,260
3	26	H	Crystal Palace	W	1-0	0-0	2	Walters [72]	19,382
4	Sept 1	A	Watford	L	0-2	0-1	5		17,295
5	15	A	WBA	L	0-4	0-1	15		19,460
6	22	H	Coventry C	W	4-1	3-0	10	De Vos [10], Counago 2 [24, 57], Walters [40]	18,840
7	29	A	Hull C	L	1-3	1-3	15	Harding [45]	15,456
8	Oct 2	A	Burnley	D	2-2	2-1	—	Legwinski [7], Lee [9]	9952
9	6	H	Preston NE	W	2-1	1-0	10	Lee [34], Miller T [74]	19,243
10	20	A	QPR	D	1-1	0-0	10	Legwinski [53]	13,946
11	23	H	Colchester U	W	3-1	0-1	—	Walters [71], Trotter [81], Haynes [84]	25,727
12	27	H	Wolverhampton W	W	3-0	1-0	4	Lee [42], Counago [52], Haynes [90]	23,308
13	Nov 4	A	Norwich C	D	2-2	2-0	4	Lee [27], Counago [41]	25,461
14	6	A	Sheffield U	L	1-3	0-1	—	Walters [54]	25,033
15	10	H	Bristol C	W	6-0	2-0	6	Walters 3 [5, 55, 72], Wright [15], Miller T (pen) [48], Counago [65]	22,020
16	24	A	Cardiff C	L	0-1	0-1	8		15,173
17	27	H	Southampton	W	2-0	1-0	—	Walters [34], Counago [69]	19,791
18	Dec 1	H	Barnsley	D	0-0	0-0	8		19,540
19	4	A	Bristol C	L	0-2	0-2	—		14,062
20	8	A	Charlton Ath	L	1-3	0-3	11	Counago [70]	24,680
21	11	H	Leicester C	W	3-1	2-1	—	Counago [19], Lee (pen) [41], Walters [65]	17,938
22	15	H	Scunthorpe U	W	3-2	2-2	6	Counago [18], Garvan [21], Miller T [83]	19,306
23	22	H	Burnley	D	0-0	0-0	6		20,077
24	26	A	Leicester C	L	0-2	0-2	7		24,049
25	29	A	Coventry C	L	1-2	1-1	9	Haynes [42]	18,346
26	Jan 1	H	WBA	W	2-0	0-0	6	Wright [75], De Vos [84]	24,000
27	12	H	Stoke C	D	1-1	1-1	7	Haynes [19]	20,346
28	19	A	Blackpool	D	1-1	0-1	7	Walters [65]	9154
29	29	H	Plymouth Arg	D	0-0	0-0	—		20,095
30	Feb 2	A	Sheffield W	W	2-1	1-1	6	Quinn [4], Lee [71]	19,092
31	9	H	Watford	L	1-2	0-1	6	Walters [71]	24,227
32	12	A	Crystal Palace	W	1-0	1-0	—	Haynes [45]	16,090
33	16	H	Blackpool	W	2-1	0-0	—	Sumulikoski [50], Walters [58]	21,059
34	23	A	Stoke C	L	0-1	0-1	7		23,563
35	Mar 1	A	Southampton	D	1-1	0-0	6	Norris [56]	23,299
36	4	H	Sheffield U	D	1-1	0-1	—	Lee [54]	20,190
37	11	A	Barnsley	L	1-4	1-1	—	Counago [20]	11,333
38	15	H	Charlton Ath	W	2-0	1-0	8	Garvan [20], Haynes [53]	23,539
39	22	A	Scunthorpe U	W	2-1	1-0	7	Counago [19], Sito [71]	6636
40	29	H	QPR	D	0-0	0-0	7		24,570
41	Apr 5	A	Colchester U	L	0-2	0-1	7		6264
42	9	H	Cardiff C	D	1-1	0-1	—	Rhodes [73]	20,311
43	13	H	Norwich C	W	2-1	2-1	7	Pearce (og) [13], Haynes [40]	29,656
44	19	A	Wolverhampton W	D	1-1	0-0	7	Miller T [90]	26,072
45	26	A	Preston NE	D	2-2	1-1	8	Miller T [11], Walters [87]	14,187
46	May 4	H	Hull C	W	1-0	0-0	8	Lee [70]	28,233

Final League Position: 8

GOALSCORERS

League (65): Walters 13, Counago 12, Lee 11 (2 pens), Haynes 7, Miller T 5 (1 pen), De Vos 2, Garvan 2, Legwinski 2, Wright 2, Harding 1, Norris 1, Quinn 1, Rhodes 1, Roberts 1, Sito 1, Sumulikoski 1, Trotter 1, own goal 1.
Carling Cup (3): Garvan 1, Lee 1 (pen), own goal 1.
FA Cup (0).

Alexander N 29	Wright D 39 + 2	Harding D 29 + 1	Garvan O 39 + 4	De Vos J 46	Bruce A 35 + 1	Walters J 39 + 1	Miller T 32 + 5	Lee A 37 + 8	Counago P 35 + 8	Roberts G 10 + 11	Legwinski S 9 + 6	Clarke B 9 + 11	Haynes D 18 + 23	O'Callaghan G 1	Wilnis F 9 + 4	Peters J — + 5	Casement C 2 + 1	Trotter L 2 + 4	Williams G 10 + 3	Sito11 + 2	Rhodes J — + 8	Naylor R 6 + 1	Quinn A 14 + 2	Bywater S 17	Sumulikoski V 10 + 6	Norris D 9	Kuqi S 2 + 2	Simpson D 7 + 1	Match No.
1	2	3	4	5	6	7	8^{1}	9^{3}	10^{2}	11	12	13	14																1
1	2	3	4	5	6^{3}	7	8	9^{2}	10^{1}	12			13	11	14■														2
1	2	3	4	5	6	7	8	9^{2}	10^{3}	11^{1}	13	14	12																3
1	2	3	4	5	6	7	8	9^{1}	10	11^{2}		12				13													4
1	2	3	4	5	6	7	8	9	10^{1}		11^{2}	12				13													5
1	2	3	4	5	6^{3}	7	8	9	10^{2}	11^{1}		13				12	14												6
1		3	4	5	6	7	8^{1}	9^{2}	10	11^{3}	12		14			13	2												7
1	2	3	4	5	6	7	8	9	12		11	10^{1}																	8
1	2	3	4	5		7	8	9	10^{2}	12		11^{1}	13		6														9
1	2	3	4	5		7	8^{1}	9^{2}	13	12	11	10^{3}	14		6														10
1	2	3	4	5		7		9	10^{1}	12	8^{3}	11^{2}	13		6			14											11
1	2	3	4	5	12	7		9^{3}	10^{1}	13	8	11^{2}	14		6														12
1	2	3	4	5		7		9	10^{3}	12	8^{2}	11^{1}	13		6			14											13
1	2	3	12	5	6	10	8	9	13	11^{3}	4^{1}					14		7^{2}											14
1	2	3	4^{1}	5	6	7^{2}	8	9^{3}	10	13	12	11	14																15
1	2	3	4^{2}	5	6	7	8	9	10^{1}			13	12						11										16
1	2	3	4^{3}	5	6	7	8^{1}	9	10		12	11^{2}	13						14										17
1	2	3		5	6	7	8	9^{2}	10	12		11^{1}	13						4										18
1	2	3	4	5	6^{3}	7		9	12	11^{2}	8^{1}		13		14				10										19
1	2	3^{3}	4	5		7	8	9	12	11^{2}			13		6				10^{1}	14									20
1	2		4	5		7^{2}		9^{1}	10			12	11		6			13	8	3									21
1	2		4	5		7	12	9	10			13	11^{2}		6				8^{1}	3									22
1	2		4	5	6	7	8	9^{3}	10				11^{2}		12				13	3^{1}	14								23
1	2	3	4	5	6^{3}	7	8	9	10^{1}			13	12		14				11^{2}										24
1	2		4	5		7	8■	9^{3}	10^{2}				11		6		3^{1}	12	13		14								25
1	2		4	5	6	9		12	10^{2}			13	11					8^{1}	7	3									26
1	2		4	5	6	7	8^{1}	9	10^{2}		12	13	11							3									27
1	2		4	5	6	9	12	13	10^{2}	11^{1}	8		7^{3}							3■		14							28
1	2	3	4	5	6	9	8	12	10	13			7^{1}										11^{2}						29
	2	3	4^{3}	5	6	9	8	12	10^{1}				13										11^{2}	1	14	7			30
	2	3	4^{3}	5	6	9	8^{1}	12	10^{2}				13										11	1	14	7			31
	12	3		5	2^{1}	9	8	10^{2}	13				11									6		1	4	7			32
		3		5	2	9	8	10^{1}	12				11^{2}									6	13	1	4	7			33
		3	12	5	2	9	8	10^{2}	13				14									6	11^{3}	1	4	7^{1}			34
	2	3	12	5		11	8^{1}	9	10^{2}				13									6		1	4	7			35
	2	3	12	5		11		9	10				8^{2}									6	13	1	4^{1}	7			36
	2	12	4	5	3^{1}			9	10				13								14	6	11^{2}	1	8^{3}	7			37
	3		4	5	6		12	9^{1}	10^{3}				13							2			11	1	8	7^{2}	14		38
	2		4	5	6		12	9^{2}	10■				7^{3}							3	13		11	1	8^{1}			14	39
			4	5	6			9		12			10						7^{1}	3	13		11^{2}	1	8			2	40
			4	5	6		12	9		13			10						7^{1}	3	14		11^{2}	1	8^{3}			2	41
	12		4	5	6		8	9		7^{2}			10							3^{1}	13		11^{3}	1	14			2	42
	3		4	5	6^{2}	12	8		10^{3}				7							13			11	1	14		9^{1}	2	43
	3		4	5	6	9	8	12	10^{2}				7^{1}								13		11	1				2	44
	3		4	5	6	9	8	12	10^{2}				7^{1}										11^{3}	1	14		13	2	45
	3		4	5	6	7	8	12	10^{3}				13										11^{1}	1	14		9^{2}	2	46

FA Cup
Third Round Portsmouth (h) 0-1

Carling Cup
First Round Milton Keynes D (a) 3-3

LEEDS UNITED FL Championship 1

FOUNDATION

Immediately the Leeds City club (founded in 1904) was wound up by the FA in October 1919, following allegations of illegal payments to players, a meeting was called by a Leeds solicitor, Mr Alf Masser, at which Leeds United was formed. They joined the Midland League playing their first game in that competition in November 1919. It was in this same month that the new club had discussions with the directors of a virtually bankrupt Huddersfield Town who wanted to move to Leeds in an amalgamation. But Huddersfield survived even that crisis.

Elland Road, Leeds, West Yorkshire LS11 0ES.

Telephone: (0113) 367 6000.

Fax: (0113) 367 6050.

Ticket Office: 0871 334 1992.

Website: www.leedsunited.com

Email: reception@leedsunited.com

Ground Capacity: 39,450.

Record Attendance: 57,892 v Sunderland, FA Cup 5th rd (replay), 15 March 1967.

Pitch Measurements: 115yd × 76yd.

Chairman: Ken Bates.

Chief Executive: Shaun Harvey.

Manager: Gary McAllister.

Assistant Manager: Steve Staunton.

Physio: Harvey Sharman.

Colours: White shirts, white shorts, white stockings.

Change Colours: Yellow shirts, yellow shorts, yellow stockings.

Year Formed: 1919, as Leeds United after disbandment (by FA order) of Leeds City (formed in 1904).

Turned Professional: 1920.

Ltd Co.: 1920.

Club Nickname: 'The Whites'.

Ground: 1919, Elland Road.

First Football League Game: 28 August 1920, Division 2, v Port Vale (a) L 0–2 – Down; Duffield, Tillotson; Musgrove, Baker, Walton; Mason, Goldthorpe, Thompson, Lyon, Best.

Record League Victory: 8–0 v Leicester C, Division 1, 7 April 1934 – Moore; George Milburn, Jack Milburn; Edwards, Hart, Copping; Mahon (2), Firth (2), Duggan (2), Furness (2), Cochrane.

HONOURS

Football League: Division 1 – Champions 1968–69, 1973–74, 1991–92; Runners-up 1964–65, 1965–66, 1969–70, 1970–71, 1971–72; Division 2 – Champions 1923–24, 1963–64, 1989–90; Runners-up 1927–28, 1931–32, 1955–56.

FA Cup: Winners 1972; Runners-up 1965, 1970, 1973.

Football League Cup: Winners 1968; Runners-up 1996.

European Competitions: *European Cup:* 1969–70, 1974–75 (runners-up). *Champions League:* 1992–93, 2000–01 (semi-finalists). *European Cup-Winners' Cup:* 1972–73 (runners-up). *European Fairs Cup:* 1965–66, 1966–67 (runners-up), 1967–68 (winners), 1968–69, 1970–71 (winners). *UEFA Cup:* 1971–72, 1973–74, 1979–80, 1995–96, 1998–99, 1999–2000 (semi-finalists), 2001–02, 2002–03.

SKY SPORTS FACT FILE

Jim Baker made 167 consecutive League and Cup appearances for Leeds United from 1920–21. Centre-half and captain he went on to complete 200 League appearances alone for Leeds.

Record Cup Victory: 10–0 v Lyn (Oslo), European Cup 1st rd 1st leg, 17 September 1969 – Sprake; Reaney, Cooper, Bremner (2), Charlton, Hunter, Madeley, Clarke (2), Jones (3), Giles (2) (Bates), O'Grady (1).

Record Defeat: 1–8 v Stoke C, Division 1, 27 August 1934.

Most League Points (2 for a win): 67, Division 1, 1968–69.

Most League Points (3 for a win): 85, Division 2, 1989–90.

Most League Goals: 98, Division 2, 1927–28.

Highest League Scorer in Season: John Charles, 42, Division 2, 1953–54.

Most League Goals in Total Aggregate: Peter Lorimer, 168, 1965–79 and 1983–86.

Most League Goals in One Match: 5, Gordon Hodgson v Leicester C, Division 1, 1 October 1938.

Most Capped Player: Lucas Radebe, 58 (70), South Africa.

Most League Appearances: Jack Charlton, 629, 1953–73.

Youngest League Player: Peter Lorimer, 15 years 289 days v Southampton, 29 September 1962.

Record Transfer Fee Received: £30,000,000 from Manchester U for Rio Ferdinand, July 2002.

Record Transfer Fee Paid: £18,000,000 to West Ham United for Rio Ferdinand, November 2000.

Football League Record: 1920 Elected to Division 2; 1924–27 Division 1; 1927–28 Division 2; 1928–31 Division 1; 1931–32 Division 2; 1932–47 Division 1; 1947–56 Division 2; 1956–60 Division 1; 1960–64 Division 2; 1964–82 Division 1; 1982–90 Division 2; 1990–92 Division 1; 1992–2004 FA Premier League; 2004–07 FL C; 2007– FL 1.

MANAGERS

Dick Ray 1919–20
Arthur Fairclough 1920–27
Dick Ray 1927–35
Bill Hampson 1935–47
Willis Edwards 1947–48
Major Frank Buckley 1948–53
Raich Carter 1953–58
Bill Lambton 1958–59
Jack Taylor 1959–61
Don Revie OBE 1961–74
Brian Clough 1974
Jimmy Armfield 1974–78
Jock Stein CBE 1978
Jimmy Adamson 1978–80
Allan Clarke 1980–82
Eddie Gray MBE 1982–85
Billy Bremner 1985–88
Howard Wilkinson 1988–96
George Graham 1996–98
David O'Leary 1998–2002
Terry Venables 2002–03
Peter Reid 2003
Eddie Gray *(Caretaker)* 2003–04
Kevin Blackwell 2004–06
Dennis Wise 2006–08
Gary McAllister January 2008–

LATEST SEQUENCES

Longest Sequence of League Wins: 9, 26.9.1931 – 21.11.1931.

Longest Sequence of League Defeats: 6, 28.12.2003 – 7.2.2004.

Longest Sequence of League Draws: 5, 19.4.1997 – 9.8.1997.

Longest Sequence of Unbeaten League Matches: 34, 26.10.1968 – 26.8.1969.

Longest Sequence Without a League Win: 17, 1.2.1947 – 26.5.1947.

Successive Scoring Runs: 30 from 27.8.1927.

Successive Non-scoring Runs: 6 from 30.1.1982.

TEN YEAR LEAGUE RECORD

		P	*W*	*D*	*L*	*F*	*A*	*Pts*	*Pos*
1998-99	PR Lge	38	18	13	7	62	34	67	4
1999-2000	PR Lge	38	21	6	11	58	43	69	3
2000-01	PR Lge	38	20	8	10	64	43	68	4
2001-02	PR Lge	38	18	12	8	53	37	66	5
2002-03	PR Lge	38	14	5	19	58	57	47	15
2003-04	PR Lge	38	8	9	21	40	79	33	19
2004-05	FL C	46	14	18	14	49	52	60	14
2005-06	FL C	46	21	15	10	57	38	78	5
2006-07	FL C	46	13	7	26	46	72	36*	24
2007-08	FL 1	46	27	10	9	72	38	76†	5

**10 pts deducted; †15 pts deducted.*

DID YOU KNOW 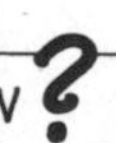

On 1 January 2008 Leeds United were beaten 3–1 at home by Oldham Athletic, the architect of their defeat being midfield player Neil Kilkenny on loan from Birmingham City. Four days later he was signed by Leeds and helped in a 3–0 win over Northampton Town.

LEEDS UNITED 2007–08 LEAGUE RECORD

Match No.	Date	Venue	Opponents	Result	H/T Score	Lg. Pos.	Goalscorers	Attendance
1	Aug 11	A	Tranmere R	W 2-1	0-1	—	Heath [55], Kandol [89]	11,008
2	18	H	Southend U	W 4-1	1-0	24	Thompson [3], Flo [85], Rui Marques [88], Beckford [90]	24,036
3	25	A	Nottingham F	W 2-1	1-0	24	Kandol [17], Beckford [89]	25,237
4	Sept 1	H	Luton T	W 1-0	1-0	24	Kandol [44]	26,856
5	8	H	Hartlepool U	W 2-0	1-0	24	Kandol [20], Beckford [50]	26,877
6	14	A	Bristol R	W 3-0	1-0	—	Beckford 2 [9, 90], Kandol [77]	11,883
7	22	H	Swansea C	W 2-0	0-0	18	Beckford [62], Prutton [67]	29,467
8	29	A	Gillingham	D 1-1	1-0	20	Carole [28]	8719
9	Oct 2	A	Oldham Ath	W 1-0	0-0	—	Westlake [90]	10,054
10	6	H	Yeovil T	W 1-0	0-0	12	De Vries [89]	27,808
11	13	H	Leyton Orient	D 1-1	0-1	12	Carole [55]	29,177
12	20	A	Brighton & HA	W 1-0	0-0	9	Kandol [79]	8691
13	27	H	Millwall	W 4-2	1-0	6	Prutton [37], Beckford [53], Douglas 2 [57, 60]	30,319
14	Nov 3	A	Carlisle U	L 1-3	1-0	9	Beckford [28]	16,668
15	6	A	Bournemouth	W 3-1	1-1	—	Kandol 2 [4, 86], Carole [54]	9632
16	17	H	Swindon T	W 2-1	1-0	4	Beckford 2 (1 pen) [32 (p), 56]	27,900
17	25	A	Cheltenham T	L 0-1	0-0	5		7043
18	Dec 4	H	Port Vale	W 3-0	1-0	—	Prutton [18], Beckford [55], Flo [83]	20,301
19	8	H	Huddersfield T	W 4-0	1-0	5	Douglas [24], Beckford 2 [49, 69], Flo [87]	32,501
20	15	A	Walsall	D 1-1	0-0	5	Thompson [90]	10,102
21	22	H	Bristol R	W 1-0	0-0	3	Howson [84]	27,863
22	26	A	Hartlepool U	D 1-1	0-1	3	Beckford [90]	7784
23	29	A	Swansea C	L 2-3	1-3	3	Beckford [12], Thompson [46]	19,010
24	Jan 1	H	Oldham Ath	L 1-3	0-3	5	Constantine [46]	25,906
25	5	H	Northampton T	W 3-0	1-0	—	Richardson [43], Rui Marques [52], Weston [90]	24,472
26	14	A	Crewe Alex	W 1-0	1-0	—	Beckford [36]	6771
27	19	H	Doncaster R	L 0-1	0-1	5		31,402
28	26	A	Luton T	D 1-1	1-0	—	Huntington [27]	9297
29	29	A	Southend U	L 0-1	0-1	—		9819
30	Feb 2	H	Tranmere R	L 0-2	0-0	8		24,907
31	9	A	Northampton T	D 1-1	1-0	8	Howson [38]	7260
32	12	H	Nottingham F	D 1-1	0-0	—	Beckford (pen) [83]	29,552
33	23	H	Crewe Alex	D 1-1	0-0	9	Kandol [86]	21,223
34	Mar 1	A	Swindon T	W 1-0	1-0	8	Kandol [25]	13,270
35	8	H	Bournemouth	W 2-0	1-0	7	Johnson [11], Kilkenny [63]	21,199
36	11	H	Cheltenham T	L 1-2	0-1	—	Elding [85]	20,257
37	15	A	Port Vale	D 3-3	2-0	10	Rui Marques [39], Freedman 2 [41, 86]	7908
38	22	H	Walsall	W 2-0	1-0	8	Beckford 2 [29, 80]	19,095
39	29	H	Brighton & HA	D 0-0	0-0	8		22,575
40	Apr 1	A	Doncaster R	W 1-0	1-0	—	Sheehan [20]	15,001
41	5	A	Leyton Orient	W 2-0	1-0	6	Johnson [16], Beckford [50]	7602
42	12	H	Carlisle U	W 3-2	0-1	6	Freedman 2 [50, 69], Howson [59]	28,530
43	15	A	Huddersfield T	L 0-1	0-0	—		16,413
44	19	A	Millwall	W 2-0	0-0	6	Prutton [70], Hughes [79]	13,895
45	25	A	Yeovil T	W 1-0	1-0	—	Freedman [4]	9527
46	May 3	H	Gillingham	W 2-1	0-1	5	Johnson [69], Kandol [88]	38,256

Final League Position: 5

GOALSCORERS

League (72): Beckford 20 (2 pens), Kandol 11, Freedman 5, Prutton 4, Carole 3, Douglas 3, Flo 3, Howson 3, Johnson 3, Rui Marques 3, Thompson 3, Constantine 1, De Vries 1, Elding 1, Heath 1, Hughes 1, Huntington 1, Kilkenny 1, Richardson 1, Sheehan 1, Westlake 1, Weston 1.
Carling Cup (1): Westlake 1.
FA Cup (0).
J Paint Trophy (2): Constantine 1, Huntington 1.
Play-Offs (3): Howson 2, Freedman 1.

Ankergren C 43	Richardson F 39	Lewis E 1	Westlake I 10 + 10	Heath M 25 + 1	Rui Marques M 34 + 2	Weston C 1 + 6	Thompson A 9 + 4	Beckford J 40	Kandol T 32 + 9	Hughes A 32 + 8	Flo T 4 + 18	Howson J 21 + 5	Prutton D 38 + 5	Douglas J 22 + 2	Parker B 6 + 3	Carole S 17 + 11	Clapham J 12 + 1	Huntington P 12 + 5	De Vries M 1 + 5	Andrews W 1	Da Costa F — + 4	Constantine L 1 + 3	Kishishev R 5 + 2	Lucas D 3	Kilkenny N 16	Kenton D 16	Johnson B 18 + 3	Sweeney P 6 + 3	Sheehan A 10	Michalik L 17	Elding A 4 + 5	Freedman D 9 + 2	Gardner S 1	Delph F — + 1	Match No.
1	2	3	4	5	6	7^1	8	9^2	10	11	12	13																							1
1	2		11^3	5	6		8	9	10	3^2	12		7^1	4	13	14																			2
1	2			5	6		8^1	9^3	10		13	12	7^2	4	14	11	3																		3
1	2			5	6		8^1	9	10	3			7	4		11	12																		4
1	2		12	5	6			9	10	8		4^2	7			11^1	3	13																	5
1	2^2		12	5	6			9	10	8			7	4		11^1	3	13																	6
1	2		12	5	6			9^2	10	8	13		7	4		11^1	3																		7
1	2		12	5	6	13		9■	10■	8^1			7	4		11^2	3^3	14																	8
1	2		12	5	6		8^1			3			7	4		11			9	10															9
1	2		12	5	6			9	10	8^1	13		7^2	4		11^3	3		14																10
1	2		12	5	6		8^1	9	10	4			7^3			11	3^2		13		14														11
1	2		12	5	6			9^2	10	8^1			7	4		11	3		13																12
1	2		8	5	6	12		9^2	10				7	4		11^1	3				13														13
1	2			5	6			9	10	8			7^3	4		11^2	3^1	12			13	14													14
1	2			5	6	12		9	10	8^2			7	4		11^1	3				13														15
1	2			5	6			9^2	10^1	8		4	7			11^3	3		12			13	14												16
	2		12	5	6			9	10	8	13		7^2	4	3^3	11^1			14					1											17
1	2		11^1	5	6		12	9^2	10	3	13	14	7	4									8^3												18
1	2		11	5	6			9^2	10^1	3	13	14	7	4		12							8^3												19
1	2		11	5	6		12	9		3	13	14	7^3	4								10^2	8^1												20
1	2		11^1	5	6		8	9^3	10	3	12	4	7^2			13							14												21
1	2		11^2	5	6		12	9	10	3	13	4	7^3			14							8^1												22
1	2		11^2	5	6	14	3	9	10	8	13	4^1	12			7^3																			23
1	2			5	6		8^2	9	10	3	12		7		13	11^1						14	4^3												24
1	2		11^3		6	12		9	13	8	10^2		7^1		3	14		5							4										25
1	2							9	12	8	10^1		7^2		3			5							4	6	13	11							26
1	2			12		13		9	14	8	10^3				3			5							4^2	6^1	7	11							27
1	2		12					9^2	10	8	13		7		3			5								6	4	11^1							28
	2							9	10	11	12		7^1		3	13		5						1	4^3	6	14	8^2							29
				5				9		8	12	4	7			13		14						1		3^2	11		2^3	6	10^1				30
1					6			9	10	8	12	4	7^1													3	11^2	13	2	5					31
1					6			9	10^3	8	12	4	7^1													3	11^2	13	2	5	14				32
1	2				6				10		9^3	4	7			12										3^1	13	8^2	11	5	14				33
1	2				6		12	9	10			8	7												4^1	3	11			5					34
1	3				6			9	10^2	12		8^1	7												4^3	2	11			5	13	14			35
1	3^1				6			9	10^2	12		8^3	7												4	2	11			5	13	14			36
1					6			9	12	3		8	7			13									4^2	2	11^1			5		10			37
1					6			9	12			8	7	13											4	2	11^2		3	5		10^1			38
1					6			9	12			8	7	13											4^1	2	11^2		3	5	14	10^3			39
1	2							9		12		8		7				6							4		11^1		3	5		10			40
1	2							9^2	13	12		8	14	7				6							4^1		11^3		3	5		10			41
1	2							9^2	13	12		8	14	7				6							4^3	3	11^1			5		10			42
1	2								9	12		8^1	13	7■		14		6							4^3	3	11^2			5		10			43
1	2								13	12		8	7					6							4		11^3	14	3	5	9^1	10^2			44
1	2				12					14		8	13	7				6							4^1		11^2		3■	5	9^3	10			45
1					12				10	8			7	4^3		13		6									11	3^2		5	9^1		2	14	46

FA Cup
First Round — Hereford U (a) 0-0; (h) 0-1

Carling Cup
First Round — Macclesfield T (a) 1-0
Second Round — Portsmouth (a) 0-3

J Paint Trophy
Second Round — Darlington (a) 1-0
Quarter-Final — Bury (h) 1-2

Play-Offs
Semi-Final — Carlisle U (h) 1-2; (a) 2-0
Final (*at Wembley*) — Doncaster R 0-1

LEICESTER CITY FL Championship 1

FOUNDATION

In 1884 a number of young footballers who were mostly old boys of Wyggeston School, held a meeting at a house on the Roman Fosse Way and formed Leicester Fosse FC. They collected 9d (less than 4p) towards the cost of a ball, plus the same amount for membership. Their first professional, Harry Webb from Stafford Rangers, was signed in 1888 for 2s 6d (12p) per week, plus travelling expenses.

Walkers Stadium, Filbert Way, Leicester LE2 7FL.

Telephone: 0844 815 6000.

Fax: (0116) 229 4549.

Ticket Office: 0844 815 5000.

Website: www.lcfc.co.uk

Email: customer.relations@lcfc.co.uk

Ground Capacity: 32,312.

Record Attendance: 47,298 v Tottenham H, FA Cup 5th rd, 18 February 1928.

Pitch Measurements: 110yd × 74yd.

Chairman: Milan Mandaric.

Chief Executive: Paul Aldridge.

Secretary: Andrew Neville.

Manager: Nigel Pearson.

Assistant Managers: Craig Shakespeare, Steve Walsh.

Physio: David Rennie.

Colours: All blue.

Change Colours: All black. ***Third Kit:*** Amber and navy.

Year Formed: 1884.

Turned Professional: 1888. ***Ltd Co:*** 1897.

Previous Name: 1884, Leicester Fosse; 1919, Leicester City.

Club Nickname: 'Foxes'.

Grounds: 1884, Victoria Park; 1887, Belgrave Road; 1888, Victoria Park; 1891, Filbert Street; 2002, Walkers Stadium.

First Football League Game: 1 September 1894, Division 2, v Grimsby T (a) L 3–4 – Thraves; Smith, Bailey; Seymour, Brown, Henrys; Hill, Hughes, McArthur (1), Skea (2), Priestman.

Record League Victory: 10–0 v Portsmouth, Division 1, 20 October 1928 – McLaren; Black, Brown; Findlay, Carr, Watson; Adcock, Hine (3), Chandler (6), Lochhead, Barry (1).

Record Cup Victory: 8–1 v Coventry C (a), League Cup 5th rd, 1 December 1964 – Banks; Sjoberg, Norman (2); Roberts, King, McDerment; Hodgson (2), Cross, Goodfellow, Gibson (1), Stringfellow (2), (1 og).

HONOURS

Football League: Division 1 – Runners-up 1928–29; Promoted from Division 1 1993–94 (play-offs) and 1995–96 (play-offs); Division 2 – Champions 1924–25, 1936–37, 1953–54, 1956–57, 1970–71, 1979–80; Runners-up 1907–08.

FA Cup: Runners-up 1949, 1961, 1963, 1969.

Football League Cup: Winners 1964, 1997, 2000; Runners-up 1965, 1999.

European Competitions: *European Cup-Winners' Cup:* 1961–62. *UEFA Cup:* 1997–98, 2000–01.

SKY SPORTS FACT FILE

Leicester City were involved in the only Football League match played on the High Road, Leyton ground of Essex County Cricket Club, when they visited the then Woolwich Arsenal whose ground was under suspension. The game on 9 March 1895 ended in a 3–3 draw.

Record Defeat: 0–12 (as Leicester Fosse) v Nottingham F, Division 1, 21 April 1909.

Most League Points (2 for a win): 61, Division 2, 1956–57.

Most League Points (3 for a win): 92, Division 1, 2002–03.

Most League Goals: 109, Division 2, 1956–57.

Highest League Scorer in Season: Arthur Rowley, 44, Division 2, 1956–57.

Most League Goals in Total Aggregate: Arthur Chandler, 259, 1923–35.

Most League Goals in One Match: 6, John Duncan v Port Vale, Division 2, 25 December 1924; 6, Arthur Chandler v Portsmouth, Division 1, 20 October 1928.

Most Capped Player: John O'Neill, 39, Northern Ireland.

Most League Appearances: Adam Black, 528, 1920–35.

Youngest League Player: Dave Buchanan, 16 years 192 days v Oldham Ath, 1 January 1979.

Record Transfer Fee Received: £11,000,000 from Liverpool for Emile Heskey, March 2000.

Record Transfer Fee Paid: £5,000,000 to Wolverhampton W for Ade Akinbiyi, July 2000.

Football League Record: 1894 Elected to Division 2; 1908–09 Division 1; 1909–25 Division 2; 1925–35 Division 1; 1935–37 Division 2; 1937–39 Division 1; 1946–54 Division 2; 1954–55 Division 1; 1955–57 Division 2; 1957–69 Division 1; 1969–71 Division 2; 1971–78 Division 1; 1978–80 Division 2; 1980–81 Division 1; 1981–83 Division 2; 1983–87 Division 1; 1987–92 Division 2; 1992–94 Division 1; 1994–95 FA Premier League; 1995–96 Division 1; 1996–2002 FA Premier League; 2002–03 Division 1; 2003–04 FA Premier League; 2004–08 FL C; 2008– FL 1.

LATEST SEQUENCES

Longest Sequence of League Wins: 7, 28.2.1993 – 27.3.1993.

Longest Sequence of League Defeats: 8, 17.3.2001 – 28.4.2001.

Longest Sequence of League Draws: 6, 21.8.1976 – 18.9.1976.

Longest Sequence of Unbeaten League Matches: 19, 6.2.1971 – 18.8.1971.

Longest Sequence Without a League Win: 18, 12.4.1975 – 1.11.1975.

Successive Scoring Runs: 31 from 12.11.1932.

Successive Non-scoring Runs: 7 from 21.11.1987.

MANAGERS

Frank Gardner 1884–92
Ernest Marson 1892–94
J. Lee 1894–95
Henry Jackson 1895–97
William Clark 1897–98
George Johnson 1898–1912
Jack Bartlett 1912–14
Louis Ford 1914–15
Harry Linney 1915–19
Peter Hodge 1919–26
Willie Orr 1926–32
Peter Hodge 1932–34
Arthur Lochhead 1934–36
Frank Womack 1936–39
Tom Bromilow 1939–45
Tom Mather 1945–46
John Duncan 1946–49
Norman Bullock 1949–55
David Halliday 1955–58
Matt Gillies 1958–68
Frank O'Farrell 1968–71
Jimmy Bloomfield 1971–77
Frank McLintock 1977–78
Jock Wallace 1978–82
Gordon Milne 1982–86
Bryan Hamilton 1986–87
David Pleat 1987–91
Gordon Lee 1991
Brian Little 1991–94
Mark McGhee 1994–95
Martin O'Neill 1995–2000
Peter Taylor 2000–01
Dave Bassett 2001–02
Micky Adams 2002–04
Craig Levein 2004–06
Robert Kelly 2006–07
Martin Allen 2007
Gary Megson 2007
Ian Holloway 2007–08
Nigel Pearson June 2008–

TEN YEAR LEAGUE RECORD

		P	*W*	*D*	*L*	*F*	*A*	*Pts*	*Pos*
1998-99	PR Lge	38	12	13	13	40	46	49	10
1999-2000	PR Lge	38	16	7	15	55	55	55	8
2000-01	PR Lge	38	14	6	18	39	51	48	13
2001-02	PR Lge	38	5	13	20	30	64	28	20
2002-03	Div 1	46	26	14	6	73	40	92	2
2003-04	PR Lge	38	6	15	17	48	65	33	18
2004-05	FL C	46	12	21	13	49	46	57	15
2005-06	FL C	46	13	15	18	51	59	54	16
2006-07	FL C	46	13	14	19	49	64	53	19
2007-08	FL C	46	12	16	18	42	45	52	22

DID YOU KNOW?

Goalkeeper Ben Davies was 35 years 182 days old when he made his debut for Leicester City on 8 December 1923 in a Second Division match against South Shields. A former Middlesbrough player he appeared three times for City and was not on the losing side.

LEICESTER CITY 2007–08 LEAGUE RECORD

Match No.	*Date*	*Venue*	*Opponents*	*Result*		*H/T Score*	*Lg. Pos.*	*Goalscorers*	*Attendance*
1	Aug 11	H	Blackpool	L	0-1	0-0	—		26,650
2	18	A	Crystal Palace	D	2-2	0-1	18	Campbell [63], Kisnorbo [87]	15,607
3	25	H	Watford	W	4-1	1-0	9	Hume [15], Campbell [51], Sheehan [54], De Vries [85]	21,642
4	Sept 1	A	Plymouth Arg	D	0-0	0-0	14		11,850
5	15	H	QPR	D	1-1	0-0	17	Hume (pen) [63]	21,893
6	22	A	Charlton Ath	L	0-2	0-2	21		21,918
7	29	H	Stoke C	D	1-1	0-1	20	Fryatt [47]	23,654
8	Oct 2	H	Wolverhampton W	D	0-0	0-0	—		21,311
9	6	A	Sheffield W	W	2-0	2-0	18	McAuley [7], Sodje (og) [14]	20,010
10	20	A	Scunthorpe U	D	0-0	0-0	17		6006
11	23	H	Sheffield U	L	0-1	0-0	—		21,146
12	27	H	Barnsley	W	2-0	2-0	15	John [22], Kisnorbo [30]	24,133
13	Nov 3	A	Colchester U	D	1-1	1-1	14	John [7]	5661
14	6	A	Preston NE	D	1-1	0-1	—	Campbell [59]	10,930
15	10	H	Burnley	L	0-1	0-1	17		21,334
16	24	A	Bristol C	W	2-0	1-0	15	Stearman [23], Fryatt [78]	15,040
17	26	H	Cardiff C	D	0-0	0-0	—		27,246
18	Dec 1	H	Southampton	L	1-2	1-1	16	King [45]	20,070
19	4	A	Burnley	D	1-1	0-1	—	Hume [78]	10,688
20	8	H	WBA	L	1-2	0-1	20	Hume [75]	22,088
21	11	A	Ipswich T	L	1-3	1-2	—	Hume [27]	17,938
22	15	A	Hull C	L	0-2	0-1	20		16,006
23	22	A	Wolverhampton W	D	1-1	1-0	22	Hume [4]	23,477
24	26	H	Ipswich T	W	2-0	2-0	18	Stearman [12], Kisnorbo [33]	24,049
25	29	H	Charlton Ath	D	1-1	0-0	18	Clemence [78]	23,667
26	Jan 1	A	QPR	L	1-3	0-2	21	Hume [59]	13,326
27	12	H	Coventry C	W	2-0	1-0	19	Howard [11], Hayles [85]	23,905
28	19	A	Norwich C	D	0-0	0-0	20		25,462
29	28	H	Crystal Palace	W	1-0	0-0	—	Hayles [89]	21,764
30	Feb 2	A	Blackpool	L	1-2	0-1	20	Howard [62]	9298
31	9	H	Plymouth Arg	L	0-1	0-1	20		21,264
32	12	A	Watford	L	0-1	0-1	—		15,944
33	16	H	Norwich C	W	4-0	1-0	—	Hume [22], Howard [57], Campbell [77], Clemence [82]	25,854
34	23	A	Coventry C	L	0-2	0-1	20		23,129
35	Mar 1	A	Cardiff C	W	1-0	1-0	17	Purse (og) [27]	13,355
36	4	H	Preston NE	L	0-1	0-0	—		19,264
37	8	H	Bristol C	D	0-0	0-0	21		22,616
38	11	A	Southampton	L	0-1	0-0	—		17,741
39	15	A	WBA	W	4-1	1-1	20	McAuley [38], Howard 3 (1 pen) [59 (p), 79, 86]	22,038
40	22	H	Hull C	L	0-2	0-1	21		30,374
41	29	H	Scunthorpe U	W	1-0	1-0	19	Hendrie [41]	22,165
42	Apr 5	A	Sheffield U	L	0-3	0-3	20		24,818
43	12	H	Colchester U	D	1-1	0-0	21	Hume [89]	22,719
44	19	A	Barnsley	W	1-0	0-0	20	Hume [72]	14,644
45	26	H	Sheffield W	L	1-3	1-1	21	Hume [9]	31,892
46	May 4	A	Stoke C	D	0-0	0-0	22		26,609

Final League Position: 22

GOALSCORERS

League (42): Hume 11 (1 pen), Howard 6 (1 pen), Campbell 4, Kisnorbo 3, Clemence 2, Fryatt 2, Hayles 2, John 2, McAuley 2, Stearman 2, De Vries 1, Hendrie 1, King 1, Sheehan 1, own goals 2.
Carling Cup (8): Campbell 1, Clemence 1, Cort 1, Fryatt 1, McAuley 1, Sheehan 1, Stearman 1, Wesolowski 1.
FA Cup (0).

Henderson P 14	Chambers J 15 + 9	Mattock J 26 + 5	Clemence S 30 + 1	McAuley G 43 + 1	N'Gotty B 30 + 8	Newton S 7 + 3	Kishishev R 2 + 5	Hume I 34 + 6	De Vries M 5 + 1	Wesolowski J 15 + 7	Stearman R 37 + 2	Hayes J 1 + 6	Campbell D 17 + 11	Fulop M 24	Clarke C 2	Kisnorbo P 41	Sheehan A 17 + 3	Porter L 1 + 3 / Worley H 1 + 1	Kaebi H 2 + 1	Cort C 7 + 7	Fryatt M 21 + 9	King A 5 + 6	Kenton D 6 + 4	John C 7 + 4	Sappleton R — + 1	Maybury A 1	Chambers A 1 + 4	Howard S 20 + 1	Hayles B 9 + 9	Alnwick B 8	Bori G 4 + 2	Oakley M 20	Laczko Z 5 + 4	Clapham J 11	Hendrie L 9	Etuhu K 2 + 2	Bell D 6	*Match No.*
1	2^1	3^2	4	5	6	7	8^3	9	10	11	12	13	14																									1
	12		4	5	2	7^1		13	10^2	11			9	1	3	6	8^3	14																				2
	12		4	5	2		13	9^3	10	11			8^1	1	3	6	7^2		14																			3
		3^2	4	5	2		12	9	10^3	11			8^1	1		6	7	13		14																		4
	12		4	5	2		13	9	14	11			8^1	1		6	3	7^2		10^3																		5
	8	3	4	5	12		13	9^2			2		14	1		6	11^1			7	10^3																	6
	2	11	4	5	3		12	13	10^1		7		8^3	1		6				9^2	14																	7
	2	11		5	4		8^2	9			3		12	1		6				13	10^1	7																8
	2			5	4	7		9^1			3		12	1		6	11			13	10^2	8^3	14															9
	2		4	5	6	7^2		9■		13	8		12	1		3	11				10^1																	10
	3		4^1	5	2^2	12				7	8		9^3	1		6	11	13			10			14														11
	12			5	2	7		9		4^1	3			1		6	11			13	10			8^2														12
	2			5	3	12					7		8^1	1		6	11			13	10		4	9^2														13
	4			5^2	2	12					3		8^1	1		6	11			14	10	13	7	9^3														14
		3	4	5	7^1			12		13	2		8	1		6				9^3	10		11^2	14														15
		11	4	5	12			7^1		8	2			1		6	3				10■		13	9^2														16
		3^3	4	5		7^1		9		8^2	2	14		1		6	11				10	13					12											17
			4	5	14	7^1		9			2	8^2		1		6	11			10^3		3			13		12											18
		11	4	5				9			2			1		6	3^2			10		13	8			7^1	12											19
		3	4	5				9		11^2	2	12		1		6				10		13	8				7^1											20
	12	3	4	5	2			9^3				13		1		6■	11^1		7		10	8^2		14														21
		3	4	5	2			9^1			12			1		6	11^3		7^2	13	10	8		14														22
	11^2	3	4	5	7			9			2	12		1		6					10^1		13	8														23
	7	3^1	4	5	2			9			11			1		6	12				10		13	8^2														24
		3^2	4	5	2			9		14	7	12		1		6	13^3				10		11	8^1														25
1	8^2	3^3	4	5	7^1			9		13	2					6	12				10							14	11									26
		3	4	5				9^1		12	2					6												10	13	1	7	8	11^2					27
	12	3^1		5	6			9		8	2											13						10	14	1	7^2	4	11^3					28
		3	4	5	12			9^2			2^1		13			6												10	11	1	14	8	7^3					29
	12	3^1	7	5				8^2			2		14			6												9	10	1	13	4	11^3					30
	2		4	5				9					12			6					13							10	11^3	1	7^1	8	14	3^2				31
	2^3		4	5^2				12			3		9			6												10	13	1	7^1	8	14	11				32
	12	3^3	4	5				9			2^1		11^2			6					13							10		1		8	14	7				33
	2	12	4	5^2	13			9					8			6												10	14	1		7	11^1	3^3				34
1		12	4		5			9^2		13	2		11^3			6												10	14			8		3	7^1			35
1		12	4^1		5			7			2		10^2			6					13							9^3	14			8		3	11			36
1		12		5	6			11^1			2		10^3								13							9	14			4		3	7	8^2		37
1		3		5	6			9^2			2		11^1								12							10	13			4			7	8		38
1		3		5	4			12		13	2					6					10							9^1	11			8^2			7^3	14		39
1		12		5	3^3						2		13			6					10^2							9	11			4		8^1	7	14		40
1		3	12^2	5	13					11^1	2					6					10							9				4	14		7^3		8	41
1	12	3		5^3	4					11	2^1					6■		14			10	13						9				8^2					7	42
1				12	5^1			13			2		10			6					14							9^3	11^2			4		3	7		8	43
1				5	14			9^3		11	2		13			6												10	12			4		3	7^1		8^2	44
1				5	12			9^3		11	2		14			6^1					13							10	8^2			4		3			7	45
1		3		5	6			9			2							4^1			12						13	10	11			8					7^2	46

FA Cup

Third Round	Southampton	(a)	0-2

Carling Cup

First Round	Accrington S	(a)	1-0
Second Round	Nottingham F	(a)	3-2
Third Round	Aston Villa	(a)	1-0
Fourth Round	Chelsea	(a)	3-4

LEYTON ORIENT FL Championship 1

FOUNDATION

There is some doubt about the foundation of Leyton Orient, and, indeed, some confusion with clubs like Leyton and Clapton over their early history. As regards the foundation, the most favoured version is that Leyton Orient was formed originally by members of Homerton Theological College who established Glyn Cricket Club in 1881 and then carried on through the following winter playing football. Eventually many employees of the Orient Shipping Line became involved and so the name Orient was chosen in 1888.

Matchroom Stadium, Brisbane Road, Leyton, London E10 5NF.

Telephone: 0871 310 1881.

Fax: 0871 310 1882.

Ticket Office: 0871 310 1883.

Website: www.leytonorient.com

Email: info@leytonorient.net

Ground Capacity: 9,271

Record Attendance: 34,345 v West Ham U, FA Cup 4th rd, 25 January 1964.

Pitch Measurements: 110yd × 76yd.

Chairman: Barry Hearn.

Vice-chairman: Nick Levene.

Chief Executive: Matthew Porter.

Secretary: Lindsey Martin.

Manager: Martin Ling.

Assistant Manager: Dean Smith.

Physio: Lewis Manning.

Colours: Red and white. ***Change Colours:*** Blue and white.

Year Formed: 1881. ***Turned Professional:*** 1903.

Ltd Co.: 1906.

HONOURS

Football League: Division 1 best season: 22nd, 1962–63; Division 2 – Runners-up 1961–62; Division 3 – Champions 1969–70; Division 3 (S) – Champions 1955–56; Runners-up 1954–55; Promoted from Division 4 1988–89 (play-offs); Promoted from FL 2 (3rd) 2005–06.

FA Cup: Semi-final 1978.

Football League Cup: best season: 5th rd, 1963.

Previous Names: 1881, Glyn Cricket and Football Club; 1886, Eagle Football Club; 1888, Orient Football Club; 1898, Clapton Orient; 1946, Leyton Orient; 1966, Orient; 1987, Leyton Orient.

Club Nickname: 'The O's'.

Grounds: 1884, Glyn Road; 1896, Whittles Athletic Ground; 1900, Millfields Road; 1930, Lea Bridge Road; 1937, Brisbane Road.

First Football League Game: 2 September 1905, Division 2, v Leicester Fosse (a) L 1–2 – Butler; Holmes, Codling; Lamberton, Boden, Boyle; Kingaby (1), Wootten, Leigh, Evenson, Bourne.

Record League Victory: 8–0 v Crystal Palace, Division 3 (S), 12 November 1955 – Welton; Lee, Earl; Blizzard, Aldous, McKnight; White (1), Facey (3), Burgess (2), Heckman, Hartburn (2). 8–0 v Rochdale, Division 4, 20 October 1987 – Wells; Howard, Dickenson (1), Smalley (1), Day, Hull, Hales (2), Castle (Sussex), Shinners (2), Godfrey (Harvey), Comfort (2). 8–0 v Colchester U,

SKY SPORTS FACT FILE

On 22 January 1955 left-winger Johnny Hartburn scored three goals in three minutes for Leyton Orient against Shrewsbury Town in a 5–0 win. He was one of four different Orient players to hit hat-tricks during the season, Stan Morgan even netting a foursome.

Division 4, 15 October 1988 – Wells; Howard, Dickenson, Hales (1p), Day (1), Sitton (1), Baker (1), Ward, Hull (3), Juryeff, Comfort (1). 8–0 v Doncaster R, Division 3, 28 December 1997 – Hyde; Channing, Naylor, Smith (1p), Hicks, Clark, Ling, Joseph R, Griffiths (3) (Harris), Richards (2) (Baker (1)), Inglethorpe (1) (Simpson).

Record Cup Victory: 9–2 v Chester, League Cup 3rd rd, 15 October 1962 – Robertson; Charlton, Taylor; Gibbs, Bishop, Lea; Deeley (1), Waites (3), Dunmore (2), Graham (3), Wedge.

Record Defeat: 0–8 v Aston Villa, FA Cup 4th rd, 30 January 1929.

Most League Points (2 for a win): 66, Division 3 (S), 1955–56.

Most League Points (3 for a win): 81, FL 2, 2005–06.

Most League Goals: 106, Division 3 (S), 1955–56.

Highest League Scorer in Season: Tom Johnston, 35, Division 2, 1957–58.

Most League Goals in Total Aggregate: Tom Johnston, 121, 1956–58, 1959–61.

Most League Goals in One Match: 4, Wally Leigh v Bradford C, Division 2, 13 April 1906; 4, Albert Pape v Oldham Ath, Division 2, 1 September 1924; 4, Peter Kitchen v Millwall, Division 3, 21 April 1984.

Most Capped Players: Tunji Banjo, 7 (7), Nigeria; John Chiedozie, 7 (9), Nigeria; Tony Grealish, 7 (45), Republic of Ireland.

Most League Appearances: Peter Allen, 432, 1965–78.

Youngest League Player: Paul Went, 15 years 327 days v Preston NE, 4 September 1965.

Record Transfer Fee Received: £1,000,000 from Fulham for Gabriel Zakuani, July 2006.

Record Transfer Fee Paid: £175,000 to Wigan Ath for Paul Beesley, October 1989.

Football League Record: 1905 Elected to Division 2; 1929–56 Division 3 (S); 1956–62 Division 2; 1962–63 Division 1; 1963–66 Division 2; 1966–70 Division 3; 1970–82 Division 2; 1982–85 Division 3; 1985–89 Division 4; 1989–92 Division 3; 1992–95 Division 2; 1995–2004 Division 3; 2004–06 FL 2; 2006– FL 1.

MANAGERS

Sam Omerod 1905–06
Ike Ivenson 1906
Billy Holmes 1907–22
Peter Proudfoot 1922–29
Arthur Grimsdell 1929–30
Peter Proudfoot 1930–31
Jimmy Seed 1931–33
David Pratt 1933–34
Peter Proudfoot 1935–39
Tom Halsey 1939
Bill Wright 1939–45
Willie Hall 1945
Bill Wright 1945–46
Charlie Hewitt 1946–48
Neil McBain 1948–49
Alec Stock 1949–59
Les Gore 1959–61
Johnny Carey 1961–63
Benny Fenton 1963–64
Dave Sexton 1965
Dick Graham 1966–68
Jimmy Bloomfield 1968–71
George Petchey 1971–77
Jimmy Bloomfield 1977–81
Paul Went 1981
Ken Knighton 1981–83
Frank Clark 1983–91
(Managing Director)
Peter Eustace 1991–94
Chris Turner/John Sitton 1994–95
Pat Holland 1995–96
Tommy Taylor 1996–2001
Paul Brush 2001–03
Martin Ling January 2004–

LATEST SEQUENCES

Longest Sequence of League Wins: 10, 21.1.1956 – 30.3.1956.

Longest Sequence of League Defeats: 9, 1.4.1995 – 6.5.1995.

Longest Sequence of League Draws: 6, 30.11.1974 – 28.12.1974.

Longest Sequence of Unbeaten League Matches: 13, 30.10.1954 – 19.2.1955.

Longest Sequence Without a League Win: 23, 6.10.1962 – 13.4.1963.

Successive Scoring Runs: 24 from 3.5.2003.

Successive Non-scoring Runs: 8 from 19.11.1994.

TEN YEAR LEAGUE RECORD

		P	*W*	*D*	*L*	*F*	*A*	*Pts*	*Pos*
1998-99	Div 3	46	19	15	12	68	59	72	6
1999-2000	Div 3	46	13	13	20	47	52	52	19
2000-01	Div 3	46	20	15	11	59	51	75	5
2001-02	Div 3	46	13	13	20	55	71	52	18
2002-03	Div 3	46	14	11	21	51	61	53	18
2003-04	Div 3	46	13	14	19	48	65	53	19
2004-05	FL 2	46	16	15	15	65	67	63	11
2005-06	FL 2	46	22	15	9	67	51	81	3
2006-07	FL 1	46	12	15	19	61	77	51	20
2007-08	FL 1	46	16	12	18	49	63	60	14

DID YOU KNOW?

In May 1905 the then Clapton Orient manager Sam Ormerod hired a Manchester hotel room to sign prospective players. Six were signed at £4 a week including Billy Holmes from Manchester City who was eventually to succeed him in the managerial role.

LEYTON ORIENT 2007–08 LEAGUE RECORD

Match No.	Date	Venue	Opponents	Result		H/T Score	Lg. Pos.	Goalscorers	Attendance
1	Aug 11	A	Southend U	W	2-1	1-1	—	Thornton 38, Boyd 86	9828
2	18	H	Walsall	W	1-0	0-0	1	Gray 52	4524
3	25	A	Crewe Alex	W	2-0	1-0	1	Melligan 35, Boyd (pen) 85	4683
4	Sept 1	H	Northampton T	D	2-2	0-2	1	Chambers 52, Mkandawire 57	5170
5	8	H	Bournemouth	W	1-0	0-0	1	Boyd 71	4995
6	15	A	Yeovil T	W	1-0	0-0	1	Boyd 57	5217
7	22	H	Hartlepool U	L	2-4	0-1	1	Melligan 57, Daniels 87	5325
8	29	A	Bristol R	W	3-2	0-1	1	Gray 59, Mkandawire 77, Demetriou 81	7181
9	Oct 2	A	Gillingham	L	1-3	0-1	—	Ibehre 72	5632
10	6	H	Swansea C	L	0-5	0-1	2		5586
11	13	A	Leeds U	D	1-1	1-0	3	Thornton 9	29,177
12	20	H	Port Vale	W	3-1	0-1	1	Mkandawire 53, Ibehre 55, Boyd (pen) 60	4555
13	28	A	Doncaster R	L	2-4	0-0	4	Ibehre 56, Purches 68	7184
14	Nov 3	H	Oldham Ath	W	1-0	1-0	2	Daniels 8	4690
15	6	A	Swindon T	D	1-1	0-0	—	Boyd 87	5874
16	17	H	Brighton & HA	D	2-2	1-0	2	Gray 27, Demetriou 70	6496
17	24	A	Huddersfield T	W	1-0	1-0	1	Boyd 4	9697
18	Dec 4	H	Millwall	L	0-1	0-1	—		6220
19	8	H	Cheltenham T	W	2-0	1-0	2	Boyd 41, Melligan 76	4156
20	15	A	Carlisle U	L	0-1	0-0	4		6843
21	22	H	Yeovil T	D	0-0	0-0	5		4687
22	26	A	Bournemouth	L	1-3	0-1	5	Saah 72	5356
23	29	A	Hartlepool U	D	1-1	1-0	7	Chambers 33	4379
24	Jan 1	H	Gillingham	D	0-0	0-0	7		5369
25	8	H	Tranmere R	W	3-0	1-0	—	Gray 11, Thornton 84, Demetriou 90	3447
26	12	A	Nottingham F	L	0-4	0-1	7		17,805
27	19	H	Luton T	W	2-1	1-0	6	Boyd 39, Barcham 55	5516
28	25	A	Northampton T	L	0-2	0-1	—		5405
29	29	A	Walsall	D	0-0	0-0	—		4643
30	Feb 2	H	Southend U	D	2-2	0-1	7	Boyd (pen) 51, Ibehre 90	6886
31	9	A	Tranmere R	D	1-1	0-1	7	Chambers 87	6530
32	12	H	Crewe Alex	L	0-1	0-1	—		3881
33	16	A	Luton T	W	1-0	1-0	7	Ibehre 26	6412
34	23	H	Nottingham F	L	0-1	0-0	8		7136
35	Mar 1	A	Brighton & HA	D	1-1	0-0	9	Ibehre 80	6242
36	8	H	Huddersfield T	L	0-1	0-0	11		4660
37	11	H	Swindon T	W	2-1	0-1	—	Boyd 2 (1 pen) 51 (p), 55	3082
38	15	A	Millwall	W	1-0	0-0	8	Gray 50	10,986
39	22	H	Carlisle U	L	0-3	0-2	10		6134
40	24	A	Cheltenham T	L	0-1	0-0	10		3988
41	29	A	Port Vale	L	1-2	1-0	11	Boyd (pen) 26	3252
42	Apr 5	H	Leeds U	L	0-2	0-1	12		7602
43	12	A	Oldham Ath	L	0-2	0-2	12		4325
44	19	H	Doncaster R	D	1-1	1-0	13	Gray 44	4582
45	26	A	Swansea C	L	1-4	0-4	14	Gray 63	16,856
46	May 3	H	Bristol R	W	3-1	1-1	14	Gray (pen) 12, Boyd 81, Ibehre 90	5132

Final League Position: 14

GOALSCORERS

League (49): Boyd 14 (5 pens), Gray 8 (1 pen), Ibehre 7, Chambers 3, Demetriou 3, Melligan 3, Mkandawire 3, Thornton 3, Daniels 2, Barcham 1, Purches 1, Saah 1.
Carling Cup (2): Boyd 1 (pen), Demetriou 1.
FA Cup (4): Boyd 2 (1 pen), Gray 2.
J Paint Trophy (1): Echanomi 1.

Nelson S 30	Purches S 35 + 2	Palmer A 23	Chambers A 45	Mkandawire T 35	Saah B 23 + 2	Melligan J 25 + 7	Thornton S 22 + 9	Boyd A 40 + 4	Gray W 30 + 8	Corden W 17 + 9	Demetriou J 31 + 12	Echanomi E — + 14	Daniels C 24 + 7	Thelwell A 27 + 1	Terry P 41 + 2	Oji S 9 + 4	Ibehre J 18 + 13	Morris G 16	Barcham A 15 + 10	Fortune C — + 1	Pires L — + 1	Match No.
1	2	3	4	5	6	7^1	8	9	10^2	11^3	12	13	14									1
1	2	3	4	5		7^1	8	9^2	10	11^3	12	13	14	6								2
1		3	4	5		7	8	9	10	11				6	2							3
1	2^1	3	4	5		7		9	10	11^2	12	13		6	8							4
1		3	4	5		7^1	8	9	10	11^2	12			6	2	13						5
1		3	4	5		7^2	8	9	10^1	11		12		6	2	13						6
1		3	4	5		7	8	9	10^2	11^3	12	13	14	6	2^1							7
1		3	4	5		7	8	9^3	10	11^2	12		13	6	2^1		14					8
1		3	4	5		7^2	8^1	9	10^3	11	2		13	6	12		14					9
1	2	3^2	4	5		7^1	8	9	10^3	13	12		11	6			14					10
1	2		4	5			8■	9	10^1		11		3	6	7		12					11
1	2		4	5	6	7		9	12	13	11^2		3		8		10^1					12
1	2		4	5	6	7		9^1	12	13	11^2		3		8		10					13
1	2		4	5	12	7^2		9	14	13	11^1		3	6	8		10^3					14
1	2		4	5	12	7^1		9	10		11		3	6	8							15
1	2		4	5		12	8^1	9^2	10		11		3	6	7		13					16
	2		4	5				9	10^1	11	7		3	6	8		12	1				17
	2		4	5				9	10		11^1	12	3	6	8			1	7			18
	2		4	5		12		9	10^1		11		3	6	8		7	1				19
	2		4	5		7^3		9		12	11^1	13	3	6	8		10^2	1	14			20
1	2		4	5		7^1	12	9		13	11^2	14	3	6	8		10^3					21
1	2		4	5	6		8^1	9		12	11^3	13	3		7		10^2		14			22
1	2	3	4	5		7		9		11				6	8		10^1		12			23
1	2	3	4	5		7^1	12	9		11^2	13	14		6	8				10^3			24
1	2	3	4	5	6		8		10^2	11^1	12	13			7				9			25
1	2	3	4	5	6	12	8		10^3	11^2	13	14			7^1				9			26
1			4	5	6		8	9			11	12	3		2	7			10^1			27
1	12		4	5	6	13	8^2	9		14	11^3		3		7	2^1			10			28
1	2		4	5	6	7^1		9		11	12	13	3		8				10^2			29
1	2			5	6	7^1		9	12	11^2	8		3		4		13		10			30
1	2		4	5	6	12		9^2	13	14	11^3		3		8		10		7^1			31
1	2		4	5^3	6			9	12	11^1	13		3		8	14	10		7^2			32
1	2	3	4		6		12	9^1	10		11				7	5	8					33
1	2	3	4		6		12	9^3	10^1		11^2		13		7	5	8		14			34
	2	3	4		6		8^3	12	10^1		11			13	7	5^2	9	1	14			35
	2^1	3	4		6	12	8^3	13	10^2		11			5	7		9	1	14			36
		3	2		6	7	8	9^2	10^1		11			5	4		12	1	13			37
		3	2		6	7^2	8	9^1	10		11			5	4		12	1	13			38
	12	3	2		6	7■	8^1	9^3	10		11		13	5^2	4		14	1				39
	2		4		6^3		12	9	10		11^2		3	5	8^1		13	1	7	14		40
	2		4	5			12	9	13		11		3	6	8		10^2	1	7^1			41
	2		4	5			12	9	13		11		3	6^3	7^1	14	10	1	8^2			42
	2	3	4	5		7^1	8^3	9	10^2		11				12	6	13	1	14			43
	2		4		6			12	10^2		11		3		7	5	9	1	8^1		13	44
	2		4		6	12	14	13	10		11^3		3		7	5	9^2	1	8^1			45
	2	3	4		6	7^3	12	9	10^2		11				8	5^1	13	1	14			46

FA Cup

First Round	Bristol R	(h)	1-1
		(a)	3-3

Carling Cup

First Round	QPR	(a)	2-1
Second Round	Cardiff C	(a)	0-1

J Paint Trophy

First Round	Notts Co	(a)	1-0
Second Round	Dagenham & R	(h)	0-1

LINCOLN CITY — FL Championship 2

FOUNDATION

The original Lincoln Football Club was established in the early 1860s and was one of the first provisional clubs to affiliate to the Football Association. In their early years, they regularly played matches against the famous Sheffield Club and later became known as Lincoln Lindum. The present organisation was formed at a public meeting held in the Monson Arms Hotel in June 1884 and won the Lincolnshire Cup in only their third season. They were founder members of the Midland League in 1889 and that competition's first champions.

Sincil Bank Stadium, Sincil Bank, Lincoln LN5 8LD.
Telephone: 0870 899 2005.
Fax: (01522) 880 020.
Ticket Office: 0870 899 1976.
Website: www.redimps.com
Email: lcfc@redimps.com
Ground Capacity: 10,120.
Record Attendance: 23,196 v Derby Co, League Cup 4th rd, 15 November 1967.
Pitch Measurements: 100m × 65m.
Chairman: Steff Wright.
Vice-chairman: David Beck.
Chief Executive: Dave Roberts.
Secretary (football): Fran Martin.
Manager: Peter Jackson.
Assistant Manager: Iffy Onuora.
Physio: Michael Wait.
Colours: Red and white.
Change Colours: White and red.
Year Formed: 1884.
Turned Professional: 1892.
Ltd Co.: 1895.
Club Nickname: 'The Red Imps'.
Grounds: 1883, John O'Gaunt's; 1894, Sincil Bank.
First Football League Game: 3 September 1892, Division 2, v Sheffield U (a) L 2–4 – W. Gresham; Coulton, Neill; Shaw, Mettam, Moore; Smallman, Irving (1), Cameron (1), Kelly, J. Gresham.
Record League Victory: 11–1 v Crewe Alex, Division 3 (N), 29 September 1951 – Jones; Green (1p), Varney; Wright, Emery, Grummett (1); Troops (1), Garvey, Graver (6), Whittle (1), Johnson (1).
Record Cup Victory: 8–1 v Bromley, FA Cup 2nd rd, 10 December 1938 – McPhail; Hartshorne, Corbett; Bean, Leach, Whyte (1); Hancock, Wilson (1), Ponting (3), Deacon (1), Clare (2).

HONOURS

Football League: Division 2 best season: 5th, 1901–02; Promotion from Division 3, 1997–98; Division 3 (N) – Champions 1931–32, 1947–48, 1951–52; Runners-up 1927–28, 1930–31, 1936–37; Division 4 – Champions 1975–76; Runners-up 1980–81.
FA Cup: best season: 1st rd of Second Series (5th rd equivalent), 1887, 2nd rd (5th rd equivalent), 1890, 1902.
Football League Cup: best season: 4th rd, 1968.
GM Vauxhall Conference: Champions 1987–88.

SKY SPORTS FACT FILE

Allan Hall's goalscoring at Lincoln City over two seasons rated one successful strike every 100 minutes as he scored 65 in 72 matches. Apart from his record-breaking 1930–31 season he had a run of 12 successive League and Cup scoring games in 1931–32.

Record Defeat: 3–11 v Manchester C, Division 2, 23 March 1895.

Most League Points (2 for a win): 74, Division 4, 1975–76.

Most League Points (3 for a win): 77, Division 3, 1981–82.

Most League Goals: 121, Division 3 (N), 1951–52.

Highest League Scorer in Season: Allan Hall, 41, Division 3 (N), 1931–32.

Most League Goals in Total Aggregate: Andy Graver, 143, 1950–55 and 1958–61.

Most League Goals in One Match: 6, Frank Keetley v Halifax T, Division 3N, 16 January 1932; 6, Andy Graver v Crewe Alex, Division 3N, 29 September 1951.

Most Capped Player: Gareth McAuley, 5 (10), Northern Ireland.

Most League Appearances: Grant Brown, 407, 1989–2002.

Youngest League Player: Shane Nicholson, 16 years 172 days v Burnley, 22 November 1986.

Record Transfer Fee Received: £750,000 from Liverpool for Jack Hobbs, August 2005.

Record Transfer Fee Paid: £75,000 to Carlisle U for Dean Walling, October 1997 and £75,000 to Bury for Tony Battersby, August 1998.

Football League Record: 1892 Founder member of Division 2. Remained in Division 2 until 1920 when they failed re-election but also missed seasons 1908–09 and 1911–12 when not re-elected. 1921–32 Division 3 (N); 1932–34 Division 2; 1934–48 Division 3 (N); 1948–49 Division 2; 1949–52 Division 3 (N); 1952–61 Division 2; 1961–62 Division 3; 1962–76 Division 4; 1976–79 Division 3; 1979–81 Division 4; 1981–86 Division 3; 1986–87 Division 4; 1987–88 GM Vauxhall Conference; 1988–92 Division 4; 1992–98 Division 3; 1998–99 Division 2; 1999–2004 Division 3; 2004– FL 2.

MANAGERS

David Calderhead 1900–07
John Henry Strawson 1907–14
(had been Secretary)
George Fraser 1919–21
David Calderhead Jnr. 1921–24
Horace Henshall 1924–27
Harry Parkes 1927–36
Joe McClelland 1936–46
Bill Anderson 1946–65
(General Manager to 1966)
Roy Chapman 1965–66
Ron Gray 1966–70
Bert Loxley 1970–71
David Herd 1971–72
Graham Taylor 1972–77
George Kerr 1977–78
Willie Bell 1977–78
Colin Murphy 1978–85
John Pickering 1985
George Kerr 1985–87
Peter Daniel 1987
Colin Murphy 1987–90
Allan Clarke 1990
Steve Thompson 1990–93
Keith Alexander 1993–94
Sam Ellis 1994–95
Steve Wicks *(Head Coach)* 1995
John Beck 1995–98
Shane Westley 1998
John Reames 1998–99
Phil Stant 2000–01
Alan Buckley 2001–02
Keith Alexander 2002–06
John Schofield 2006–07
Peter Jackson October 2007–

LATEST SEQUENCES

Longest Sequence of League Wins: 10, 1.9.1930 – 18.10.1930.

Longest Sequence of League Defeats: 12, 21.9.1896 – 9.1.1897.

Longest Sequence of League Draws: 5, 21.2.1981 – 7.3.1981.

Longest Sequence of Unbeaten League Matches: 18, 11.3.1980 – 13.9.1980.

Longest Sequence Without a League Win: 19, 22.8.1978 – 23.12.1978.

Successive Scoring Runs: 37 from 1.3.1930.

Successive Non-scoring Runs: 5 from 15.11.1913.

TEN YEAR LEAGUE RECORD

		P	*W*	*D*	*L*	*F*	*A*	*Pts*	*Pos*
1998-99	Div 2	46	13	7	26	42	74	46	23
1999-2000	Div 3	46	15	14	17	67	69	59	15
2000-01	Div 3	46	12	15	19	58	66	51	18
2001-02	Div 3	46	10	16	20	44	62	46	22
2002-03	Div 3	46	18	16	12	46	37	70	6
2003-04	Div 3	46	19	17	10	68	47	74	7
2004-05	FL 2	46	20	12	14	64	47	72	6
2005-06	FL 2	46	15	21	10	65	53	66	7
2006-07	FL 2	46	21	11	14	70	59	74	5
2007-08	FL 2	46	18	4	24	61	77	58	15

DID YOU KNOW ?

In preparation for their last home game in 1931–32, Lincoln City trained at Skegness. They achieved the promotion point against Wrexham before a then record 14,981 attendance. The game was filmed and shown subsequently in a local cinema.

LINCOLN CITY 2007–08 LEAGUE RECORD

Match No.	Date	Venue	Opponents	Result		H/T Score	Lg. Pos.	Goalscorers	Attendance
1	Aug 11	H	Shrewsbury T	L	0-4	0-0	—		3893
2	18	A	Mansfield T	W	3-1	2-1	10	Dodds [2], McIntosh (og) [36], Stallard [54]	3357
3	25	H	Accrington S	W	2-0	1-0	4	N'Guessan [31], Dodds [66]	3189
4	Sept 1	A	Dagenham & R	L	0-1	0-0	9		2060
5	7	H	Bradford C	L	1-2	1-1	—	Dodds [26]	5286
6	15	A	Darlington	L	0-2	0-1	17		4075
7	22	H	Grimsby T	L	1-2	1-1	20	Forrester [38]	4428
8	29	A	Wrexham	L	0-1	0-0	23		3614
9	Oct 2	A	Bury	D	1-1	1-1	—	Kerr [19]	1690
10	6	H	Morecambe	D	1-1	1-1	23	Amoo [22]	3281
11	14	A	Milton Keynes D	L	0-4	0-1	23		13,037
12	20	H	Peterborough U	D	1-1	1-0	22	Wright [45]	5036
13	27	A	Brentford	L	0-1	0-0	23		4368
14	Nov 2	H	Chester C	L	0-1	0-0	—		3960
15	6	H	Chesterfield	L	2-4	1-3	—	N'Guessan [44], Bencherif [67]	3893
16	17	A	Wycombe W	L	0-1	0-1	24		4297
17	24	H	Notts Co	W	2-1	1-0	23	Wright [44], Frecklington [75]	4503
18	Dec 4	A	Stockport Co	W	3-1	0-0	—	Wright 2 [50, 53], John-Lewis [86]	5260
19	8	A	Hereford U	L	1-3	1-2	22	Frecklington [21]	2528
20	15	H	Barnet	W	4-1	2-0	21	Wright 2 [9, 90], Forrester (pen) [32], Dodds [50]	3549
21	22	H	Darlington	L	0-4	0-3	21		4025
22	26	A	Bradford C	L	1-2	0-1	21	John-Lewis [51]	15,510
23	29	A	Grimsby T	L	0-1	0-0	22		5533
24	Jan 1	H	Bury	D	1-1	0-0	22	Dodds [79]	3327
25	5	A	Rochdale	W	2-0	0-0	21	Forrester [82], Frecklington [83]	2721
26	12	H	Rotherham U	L	1-3	0-1	21	Forrester [55]	5016
27	26	H	Dagenham & R	W	2-0	1-0	21	Wright [15], N'Guessan [90]	3779
28	29	H	Mansfield T	L	1-2	0-0	—	Forrester (pen) [60]	4280
29	Feb 2	A	Shrewsbury T	W	2-1	1-0	20	Dodds 2 [12, 85]	4892
30	5	A	Macclesfield T	W	2-1	0-0	—	N'Guessan [81], Forrester [89]	1576
31	9	H	Rochdale	W	2-1	1-0	18	Forrester [45], Hone [81]	3955
32	12	A	Accrington S	W	3-0	1-0	—	Stallard [6], Wright [70], Beevers [75]	1281
33	16	H	Macclesfield T	W	3-1	0-1	14	John-Lewis [72], Forrester [81], N'Guessan [90]	3682
34	23	A	Rotherham U	L	2-3	1-1	16	Dodds [25], Wright [87]	4321
35	Mar 1	H	Wycombe W	W	1-0	0-0	14	Dodds [66]	4002
36	7	A	Chesterfield	L	1-4	0-1	—	Wright [58]	4352
37	11	A	Notts Co	W	1-0	1-0	—	Forrester [16]	3858
38	15	H	Stockport Co	L	0-1	0-0	14		4544
39	22	A	Barnet	L	2-5	0-3	14	Wright 2 [76, 81]	2115
40	24	H	Hereford U	W	2-1	1-0	16	N'Guessan 2 (1 pen) [31, 85 (p)]	3614
41	29	A	Peterborough U	L	0-4	0-1	15		8035
42	Apr 4	H	Milton Keynes D	L	1-2	0-1	—	Wright [59]	3896
43	12	A	Chester C	W	2-1	2-1	16	Forrester 2 [21, 23]	2089
44	19	H	Brentford	W	3-1	1-1	16	King [39], Forrester [67], Frecklington [83]	3689
45	26	A	Morecambe	W	2-1	1-0	14	Wright [42], Green [70]	2762
46	May 3	H	Wrexham	L	2-4	1-2	15	Evans S (og) [39], Wright [90]	4958

Final League Position: 15

GOALSCORERS

League (61): Wright 15, Forrester 12 (2 pens), Dodds 9, N'Guessan 7 (1 pen), Frecklington 4, John-Lewis 3, Stallard 2, Amoo 1, Beevers 1, Bencherif 1, Green 1, Hone 1, Kerr 1, King 1, own goals 2.
Carling Cup (1): Forrester 1.
FA Cup (2): Forrester 1, own goal 1.
J Paint Trophy (2): Stallard 2 (1 pen).

Marriott A 34	Green P 36	Croft G 20	Brown N 23+4	Watt P 1	Kerr S 33+3	Dodds L 38+3	Frecklington L 31+3	Forrester J 37+3	Torpey S 7+6	Amoo R 10+3	Ryan O 4+11	Stallard M 14+11	N'Guessan D 23+14	Moses A 16+2	Hand J 19+6	Warlow O 6+11	Beevers L 37	Bencherif H 11+1	Wright B 26+8	Hone D 20+3	Smith B 9	John-Lewis L 15+6	Clarke S 11+5	Smith Adam —+4	Ridley L 15	King G 3+3	Pembleton M 4+2	Duffy A 3+1	Match No.
1	2	3	4	5	6[1]	7[2]	8	9	10	11[3]	12	13	14																1
1	2		4		12	7[2]	8[1]	9		11	14	10[3]	3	5	6	13													2
1			4			7[3]	8	9[2]	12	2	13	10[1]	11	5	6	14	3												3
1			4			7[2]	8	9[1]	12	2	13	10	11[3]	5	6	14	3												4
1		3[2]	4		12	7[1]	8	9	13	2		10	11[3]		6	14	5												5
1		3[2]	4		12	7	8	9[3]	10	2		13	11		6[1]	14	5												6
1		3[2]	4			7	8[3]	9	10[1]	13	14	12	11	5	6		2												7
1	2	3■	4		6	7[1]	12	9[2]			13	10	14	5[3]	8		11												8
1	2		4		6	9[2]	13		10[1]	3	11	12		14	8		7	5[3]											9
1	2				6	9[1]	7		10	3	11		12		8		4	5											10
1			4		6		8	12	13	2	11[3]	10[2]	9		7[1]	14	3	5											11
1	3[2]	7	4		6	9[1]	8		12	13	14			5	11		2		10[3]										12
1	2	3[2]			6	9	8		12	7			13		11		5	4	10[1]										13
1	2	3			6	9	8[2]		10[1]				11		7	13	5[3]	4	12	14									14
1	2	3			6	9	8	12	10[1]				11	5	7[2]			4	13										15
	2	3			6	7[3]	8				10■			5	12	11[1]		13	9	4[2]	1	14							16
	2	3			6	7	8	9					12	5		11[1]			10	4	1								17
	2	3			6[1]		8	9					7[2]		12	11		5	10	4	1	13							18
	2[2]	3■			6[1]	12	8	9[3]					7		13	11		5	10	4	1	14							19
	2				6	7	8	9[2]				12	11[1]			3		5	10	4	1	13							20
	2				6[1]	7[2]	8	9				10[3]	11		12	13	3	5		4	1	14							21
	2	3[2]	13		6		8[3]	9				12	11[1]	4	14		5		10		1	7							22
			4		6■	7[1]	8[2]	9			12			2	13		3	5	10		1	11							23
	2[1]		4			13	8	9		12				5	6	7[2]	3		10		1	11							24
1	2		4			7	8	9									5		10[1]			11	6	12	3				25
1	2		4		6	7[1]	8[2]	9[3]			12						5		10			11	13■	14	3				26
1	2		4		6	7		9[3]				12	13		8		5		10[1]			11[2]		14	3				27
1	2		4		6	7[1]		9[3]				13	12		8		5		10[2]			11		14	3				28
1	2				6	7		9				13	12		8		5		10[1]	4		11[2]			3				29
1	2				6	7		9				10	12		8		5		11[1]	4					3				30
1			2		6	7	8	9			12	10[2]	11[1]				5		13	4					3				31
1	2		12		6	7	8[3]	9[2]				10[1]					5		13	4		11	14		3				32
1	2[3]		12		6			9			14	10[1]	13				5		8[2]	4		11	7		3				33
1	2				6	7		9[2]				10■	12				5		13	4		11	8[1]		3				34
1	2				6	7		9					12				5		10[1]	4		11	8		3				35
1	2		5		6	7		9[2]					11			13	3		12	4		8[1]	10						36
1	2		3		6	7		9					11				5		10	4			8						37
1	3		2		6	7[2]		9				10[1]	11				5		12	4			8			13			38
1	2[1]		12		6	7[3]		9				10[2]	11				5		13	4		14	8		3				39
1	2		4		6■			9[2]					7	12					10	5		11	8		3[1]		13		40
1	2[2]	3	4			12	13	14					7				5		10	6		11[1]	8				9[3]		41
1		2				7[1]	8	9[2]				12	11	4			5		10				6[3]		3	13	14		42
1[6]		2				7	8	9[2]					11■	4			5		10	12					3	13	6[1]	15	43
	2	3				7[2]	8	9[3]				14		5		13	6		10				12			11	4[1]	1	44
	2	3				7	8	9					14	5[2]			6		10	13			12			11[3]	4[1]	1	45
	2	3[2]			6	7[1]	8[3]	9					12			13	5		10	4			14			11		1	46

FA Cup

First Round	Nottingham F	(h)	1-1
		(a)	1-3

Carling Cup

First Round	Doncaster R	(a)	1-4

J Paint Trophy

Second Round	Hartlepool U	(h)	2-5

LIVERPOOL FA Premiership

FOUNDATION

But for a dispute between Everton FC and their landlord at Anfield in 1892, there may never have been a Liverpool club. This dispute persuaded the majority of Evertonians to quit Anfield for Goodison Park, leaving the landlord, Mr John Houlding, to form a new club. He originally tried to retain the name 'Everton' but when this failed, he founded Liverpool Association FC on 15 March 1892.

Anfield Stadium, Anfield Road, Liverpool L4 0TH.

Telephone: (0151) 263 2361.

Fax: (0151) 260 8813.

Ticket Office: 0844 844 0844.

Website: www.liverpoolfc.tv

Email: customercontact@liverpoolfc.tv or customerservices@liverpoolfc.tv

Ground Capacity: 45,362.

Record Attendance: 61,905 v Wolverhampton W, FA Cup 4th rd, 2 February 1952.

Pitch Measurements: 101m × 68m.

Chairmen: George Gillett and Tom Hicks.

Chief Executive: Rick Parry BSC, FCA.

Secretary: William Bryce Morrison.

Manager: Rafael Benitez.

Assistant Manager: Sammy Lee.

Physio: Robert Price.

Colours: Red shirts, red shorts, red stockings.

Change Colours: Grey with red trim.

Year Formed: 1892.

Turned Professional: 1892.

Ltd Co.: 1892.

Club Nicknames: 'Reds' or 'Pool'.

Ground: 1892, Anfield.

First Football League Game: 2 September 1893, Division 2, v Middlesbrough Ironopolis (a) W 2–0 – McOwen; Hannah, McLean; Henderson, McQue (1), McBride; Gordon, McVean (1), M. McQueen, Stott, H. McQueen.

HONOURS

Football League: Division 1 – Champions 1900–01, 1905–06, 1921–22, 1922–23, 1946–47, 1963–64, 1965–66, 1972–73, 1975–76, 1976–77, 1978–79, 1979–80, 1981–82, 1982–83, 1983–84, 1985–86, 1987–88, 1989–90 (Liverpool have a record number of 18 League Championship wins); Runners-up 1898–99, 1909–10, 1968–69, 1973–74, 1974–75, 1977–78, 1984–85, 1986–87, 1988–89, 1990–91, 2001–02; Division 2 – Champions 1893–94, 1895–96, 1904–05, 1961–62.

FA Cup: Winners 1965, 1974, 1986, 1989, 1992, 2001, 2006; Runners-up 1914, 1950, 1971, 1977, 1988, 1996.

Football League Cup: Winners 1981, 1982, 1983, 1984, 1995, 2001, 2003; Runners-up 1978, 1987, 2005.

League Super Cup: Winners 1986.

European Competitions: *European Cup:* 1964–65, 1966–67, 1973–74, 1976–77 (winners), 1977–78 (winners), 1978–79, 1979–80, 1980–81 (winners), 1981–82, 1982–83, 1983–84 (winners), 1984–85 (runners-up). *Champions League:* 2001–02, 2002–03, 2004–05 (winners), 2005–06, 2006–07 (runners-up), 2007–08 (s-f). *European Cup-Winners' Cup:* 1965–66 (runners-up), 1971–72, 1974–75, 1992–93, 1996–97 (s-f). *European Fairs Cup:* 1967–68, 1968–69, 1969–70, 1970–71. *UEFA Cup:* 1972–73 (winners), 1975–76 (winners), 1991–92, 1995–96, 1997–98, 1998–99, 2000–01 (winners), 2002–03, 2003–04. *Super Cup:* 1977 (winners), 1978, 1984, 2001 (winners), 2005 (winners). *World Club Championship:* 1981 (runners-up), 1984 (runners-up). *FIFA Club World Championship:* 2005 (runners-up).

SKY SPORTS FACT FILE

On 25 August 2007 Liverpool scored their 7,000th League goal in the 2–0 win at Sunderland. Then on 6 November they defeated Besiktas 8–0 to establish a Champions League record. Of all English clubs in the European season only goalkeeper Jose Reina played unchanged.

Record League Victory: 10–1 v Rotherham T, Division 2, 18 February 1896 – Storer; Goldie, Wilkie; McCartney, McQue, Holmes; McVean (3), Ross (2), Allan (4), Becton (1), Bradshaw.

Record Cup Victory: 11–0 v Stromsgodset Drammen, ECWC 1st rd 1st leg, 17 September 1974 – Clemence; Smith (1), Lindsay (1p), Thompson (2), Cormack (1), Hughes (1), Boersma (2), Hall, Heighway (1), Kennedy (1), Callaghan (1).

Record Defeat: 1–9 v Birmingham C, Division 2, 11 December 1954.

Most League Points (2 for a win): 68, Division 1, 1978–79.

Most League Points (3 for a win): 90, Division 1, 1987–88.

Most League Goals: 106, Division 2, 1895–96.

Highest League Scorer in Season: Roger Hunt, 41, Division 2, 1961–62.

Most League Goals in Total Aggregate: Roger Hunt, 245, 1959–69.

Most League Goals in One Match: 5, Andy McGuigan v Stoke C, Division 1, 4 January 1902; 5, John Evans v Bristol R, Division 2, 15 September 1954; 5, Ian Rush v Luton T, Division 1, 29 October 1983.

Most Capped Player: Ian Rush, 67 (73), Wales.

Most League Appearances: Ian Callaghan, 640, 1960–78.

Youngest League Player: Max Thompson, 17 years 128 days v Tottenham H, 8 May 1974.

Record Transfer Fee Received: £12,500,000 from Leeds U for Robbie Fowler, November 2001.

Record Transfer Fee Paid: £22,000,000 to Atletico Madrid for Fernando Torres, July 2007.

Football League Record: 1893 Elected to Division 2; 1894–95 Division 1; 1895–96 Division 2; 1896–1904 Division 1; 1904–05 Division 2; 1905–54 Division 1; 1954–62 Division 2; 1962–92 Division 1; 1992– FA Premier League.

MANAGERS

W. E. Barclay 1892–96
Tom Watson 1896–1915
David Ashworth 1920–23
Matt McQueen 1923–28
George Patterson 1928–36
(continued as Secretary)
George Kay 1936–51
Don Welsh 1951–56
Phil Taylor 1956–59
Bill Shankly 1959–74
Bob Paisley 1974–83
Joe Fagan 1983–85
Kenny Dalglish 1985–91
Graeme Souness 1991–94
Roy Evans 1994–98
(then Joint Manager)
Gerard Houllier 1998–2004
Rafael Benitez June 2004–

LATEST SEQUENCES

Longest Sequence of League Wins: 12, 21.4.1990 – 6.10.1990.

Longest Sequence of League Defeats: 9, 29.4.1899 – 14.10.1899.

Longest Sequence of League Draws: 6, 19.2.1975 – 19.3.1975.

Longest Sequence of Unbeaten League Matches: 31, 4.5.1987 – 16.3.1988.

Longest Sequence Without a League Win: 14, 12.12.1953 – 20.3.1954.

Successive Scoring Runs: 29 from 27.4.1957.

Successive Non-scoring Runs: 5 from 22.12.1906.

TEN YEAR LEAGUE RECORD

		P	W	D	L	F	A	Pts	Pos
1998-99	PR Lge	38	15	9	14	68	49	54	7
1999-2000	PR Lge	38	19	10	9	51	30	67	4
2000-01	PR Lge	38	20	9	9	71	39	69	3
2001-02	PR Lge	38	24	8	6	67	30	80	2
2002-03	PR Lge	38	18	10	10	61	41	64	5
2003-04	PR Lge	38	16	12	10	55	37	60	4
2004-05	PR Lge	38	17	7	14	52	41	58	5
2005-06	PR Lge	38	25	7	6	57	25	82	3
2006-07	PR Lge	38	20	8	10	57	27	68	3
2007-08	PR Lge	38	21	13	4	67	28	76	4

DID YOU KNOW ?

Fernando Torres in his initial season with Liverpool became the first player since Robbie Fowler in 1996 to hit 20 League goals. He also equalled Roger Hunt's 1961–62 record of scoring in eight successive home games. Torres finished with 23 League goals.

LIVERPOOL 2007–08 LEAGUE RECORD

Match No.	Date	Venue	Opponents	Result	H/T Score	Lg. Pos.	Goalscorers	Attendance
1	Aug 11	A	Aston Villa	W 2-1	1-0	—	Laursen (og) [31], Gerrard [87]	42,640
2	19	H	Chelsea	D 1-1	1-0	9	Torres [16]	43,924
3	25	A	Sunderland	W 2-0	1-0	4	Sissoko [37], Voronin [87]	45,645
4	Sept 1	H	Derby Co	W 6-0	2-0	1	Alonso 2 [27, 69], Babel [45], Torres 2 [56, 78], Voronin [76]	44,076
5	15	A	Portsmouth	D 0-0	0-0	3		20,388
6	22	H	Birmingham C	D 0-0	0-0	4		44,215
7	29	A	Wigan Ath	W 1-0	0-0	4	Benayoun [75]	24,311
8	Oct 7	H	Tottenham H	D 2-2	1-1	4	Voronin [12], Torres [90]	43,986
9	20	A	Everton	W 2-1	0-1	4	Kuyt 2 (2 pens) [54, 90]	40,049
10	28	H	Arsenal	D 1-1	1-0	6	Gerrard [7]	44,122
11	Nov 3	A	Blackburn R	D 0-0	0-0	7		30,033
12	10	H	Fulham	W 2-0	0-0	5	Torres [81], Gerrard (pen) [85]	43,073
13	24	A	Newcastle U	W 3-0	1-0	5	Gerrard [28], Kuyt [46], Babel [66]	52,307
14	Dec 2	H	Bolton W	W 4-0	2-0	3	Hyypia [17], Torres [45], Gerrard (pen) [56], Babel [86]	43,270
15	8	A	Reading	L 1-3	1-1	4	Gerrard [28]	24,022
16	16	H	Manchester U	L 0-1	0-1	5		44,459
17	22	H	Portsmouth	W 4-1	2-0	5	Benayoun [13], Distin (og) [16], Torres 2 [67, 85]	43,071
18	26	A	Derby Co	W 2-1	1-0	4	Torres [12], Gerrard [90]	33,029
19	30	A	Manchester C	D 0-0	0-0	4		47,321
20	Jan 2	H	Wigan Ath	D 1-1	0-0	—	Torres [49]	42,308
21	12	A	Middlesbrough	D 1-1	0-1	4	Torres [71]	33,035
22	21	H	Aston Villa	D 2-2	1-0	—	Benayoun [19], Crouch [88]	42,590
23	30	A	West Ham U	L 0-1	0-0	—		34,977
24	Feb 2	H	Sunderland	W 3-0	0-0	5	Crouch [57], Torres [69], Gerrard (pen) [89]	43,244
25	10	A	Chelsea	D 0-0	0-0	5		41,788
26	23	H	Middlesbrough	W 3-2	2-1	4	Torres 3 [28, 29, 61]	43,612
27	Mar 2	A	Bolton W	W 3-1	1-0	5	Jaaskelainen (og) [12], Babel [60], Fabio Aurelio [75]	24,004
28	5	H	West Ham U	W 4-0	1-0	—	Torres 3 [8, 61, 81], Gerrard [83]	42,954
29	8	H	Newcastle U	W 3-0	2-0	4	Pennant [43], Torres [45], Gerrard [51]	44,031
30	15	H	Reading	W 2-1	1-1	4	Mascherano [19], Torres [48]	43,524
31	23	A	Manchester U	L 0-3	0-1	4		76,000
32	30	H	Everton	W 1-0	1-0	4	Torres [7]	44,295
33	Apr 5	A	Arsenal	D 1-1	1-0	4	Crouch [42]	60,111
34	13	H	Blackburn R	W 3-1	0-0	4	Gerrard [60], Torres [82], Voronin [90]	43,283
35	19	A	Fulham	W 2-0	1-0	4	Pennant [17], Crouch [70]	25,311
36	26	A	Birmingham C	D 2-2	0-1	4	Crouch [63], Benayoun [76]	29,252
37	May 4	H	Manchester C	W 1-0	0-0	4	Torres [58]	43,074
38	11	A	Tottenham H	W 2-0	0-0	4	Voronin [69], Torres [74]	36,063

Final League Position: 4

GOALSCORERS

League (67): Torres 24, Gerrard 11 (3 pens), Crouch 5, Voronin 5, Babel 4, Benayoun 4, Kuyt 3 (2 pens), Alonso 2, Pennant 2, Fabio Aurelio 1, Hyypia 1, Mascherano 1, Sissoko 1, own goals 3.
Carling Cup (6): Torres 3, Benayoun 1, El-Zhar 1, Gerrard 1.
FA Cup (12): Benayoun 3, Gerrard 3, Crouch 2, Babel 1, Hyypia 1, Kuyt 1, Lucas 1.
Champions League (34): Kuyt 7, Gerrard 6 (2 pens), Torres 6, Babel 5, Crouch 4, Benayoun 3, Hyypia 2, Voronin 1.

Reina J 38	Finnan S 21 + 3	Arbeloa A 26 + 2	Alonso X 16 + 3	Carragher J 34 + 1	Agger D 4 + 1	Pennant J 14 + 4	Gerrard S 32 + 2	Torres F 29 + 4	Kuyt D 24 + 8	Riise J 22 + 7	Sissoko M 6 + 3	Voronin A 13 + 6	Babel R 15 + 15	Crouch P 9 + 12	Hyypia S 24 + 3	Mascherano J 25	Benayoun Y 15 + 15	Fabio Aurelio13 + 3	Lucas 12 + 6	Kewell H 8 + 2	Hobbs J 1 + 1	Skrtel M 13 + 1	Plessis D 2	Insua E 2 + 1	*Match No.*
1	2	3	4	5	6	7³	8	9²	10¹	11	12	13	14												1
1	2	3	4	5	6	7¹	8	9	10	11²			12	13											2
1	2	3	4	5³	12	7		9	13	14	8	10	11²		6¹										3
1	2	3	4		6	7³		9	10		12	13	11²		5	8¹	14								4
1	2	3	4³	5	6	7¹	12	13			8	10	14	9²			11								5
1	12	2		5		7¹	8	13	10	3		9³	11²	14	6	4									6
1		2		5		7²	8	9¹	10	11	12	13			6	4	14	3³							7
1	2	3²		5		7¹	8	9	12	11		10³	13		6	4	14								8
1	2			5		12	7³		10	3	8¹	9	13		6	4	11²		14						9
1	2	12	4¹	5			8	9²	10	3		11³		13	6	7	14								10
1	2			5			9		10	3	8		11²	12	6	4	7¹			13					11
1		2		5			8	12		11²		10¹	13	9	6	4³	7	3	14						12
1	2	3		5			8²	9	10¹	12	7		14	13	6				4	11³					13
1		2		5³			8	9¹	12	3			13	10	6		7		4	11²	14				14
1		2		5¹			7²	9³		3	8	11	13	10	12	4				14	6				15
1		2		5			8	9	10²	3³			12	13	6	4	7	14		11¹					16
1		2		5			8	9³	10	3			12		6	4	7¹	13	14	11²					17
1	2		4	5			8	9	12	3		10³	7¹		6²		13	11	14						18
1	2	6		5			8	9	10				12			4	7	3		11¹					19
1	2	6	4	5		7¹	10	9	12					13		8²	14	3		11³					20
1	2	7³	12	5			8	9	13	3		10²	14		6	4	11¹								21
1		2³		5			8	9	10				12	13	6	4	7²	3		11¹		14			22
1	2		4	5			8	9	10				12		6		7¹	3	13	11²					23
1	12			2		7	8	9	13					10²	6	4	14	3¹	11³			5			24
1	2			5		12	8		10	3			11¹	9		4			7			6			25
1	2	5					8	9²	10¹	12			11³	13	6	4	14	3	7						26
1		12	8	2			7	9²	10¹	13			11		6	4		3				5			27
1		2	8	5		12	7	9²	10³	3			11¹	13		4	14					6			28
1		2	4	5		7²	8¹	9³	12	3				14	13		10		11			6			29
1		2	7	5			8²	9	10³	12			11¹		13	4	14	3				6			30
1		2	7	5			8	9¹	10	12			11²			4[illegible]	13	3				6			31
1			4	2		12	8³	9¹	10	3			11²	14	6		13		7			5			32
1	2	3		5		7¹	12	13		11		14		9²			10³		8			6	4		33
1		2	4²	5			8	9¹	10	13		12	11³				14	3	7			6			34
1	2		12	13		7				3		10³		9	6²	4¹	11	14	8			5			35
1	2					7				3¹		10		9	6		11		8			5	4	12	36
1	2		12	5			8²	9	10			13	11³		6	4	14		7¹					3	37
1	12	2		5			7	9	10³			8¹	11²			4	13		14			6		3	38

Champions League

Third Qualifying Round	Toulouse	(a)	1-0
		(h)	4-0
Group A	Porto	(a)	1-1
	Marseille	(h)	0-1
	Besiktas	(a)	1-2
		(h)	8-0
	Porto	(h)	4-1
	Marseille	(a)	4-0
Knock-Out Round	Internazionale	(h)	2-0
		(a)	1-0
Quarter-Final	Arsenal	(a)	1-1
		(h)	4-2
Semi-Final	Chelsea	(h)	1-1
		(a)	2-3

FA Cup

Third Round	Luton T	(a)	1-1
		(h)	5-0
Fourth Round	Havant & W	(h)	5-2
Fifth Round	Barnsley	(h)	1-2

Carling Cup

Third Round	Reading	(a)	4-2
Fourth Round	Cardiff C	(h)	2-1
Quarter-Final	Chelsea	(a)	0-2

LUTON TOWN FL Championship 2

FOUNDATION

Formed by an amalgamation of two leading local clubs, Wanderers and Excelsior a works team, at a meeting in Luton Town Hall in April 1885. The Wanderers had three months earlier changed their name to Luton Town Wanderers and did not take too kindly to the formation of another Town club but were talked around at this meeting. Wanderers had already appeared in the FA Cup and the new club entered in its inaugural season.

Kenilworth Stadium, 1 Maple Road, Luton, Beds LU4 8AW.

Telephone: (01582) 411 622.

Fax: (01582) 405 070.

Ticket Office: 0870 017 0656.

Website: www.lutontown.co.uk

Email: clubsec@lutontown.co.uk

Ground Capacity: 10,260.

Record Attendance: 30,069 v Blackpool, FA Cup 6th rd replay, 4 March 1959.

Pitch Measurements: 110yd × 72yd.

Chairman: TBC.

Chief Executive: TBC.

Secretary: Cherry Newbery.

Manager: Mick Harford.

Assistant Manager: TBC.

Physio: TBC.

Colours: TBC.

Change Colours: TBC.

Year Formed: 1885.

Turned Professional: 1890.

Ltd Co.: 1897.

Club Nickname: 'The Hatters'.

Grounds: 1885, Excelsior, Dallow Lane; 1897, Dunstable Road; 1905, Kenilworth Road.

First Football League Game: 4 September 1897, Division 2, v Leicester Fosse (a) D 1–1 – Williams; McCartney, McEwen; Davies, Stewart, Docherty; Gallacher, Coupar, Birch, McInnes, Ekins (1).

Record League Victory: 12–0 v Bristol R, Division 3 (S), 13 April 1936 – Dolman; Mackey, Smith; Finlayson, Nelson, Godfrey; Rich, Martin (1), Payne (10), Roberts (1), Stephenson.

Record Cup Victory: 9–0 v Clapton, FA Cup 1st rd (replay after abandoned game), 30 November 1927 – Abbott; Kingham, Graham; Black, Rennie, Fraser; Pointon, Yardley (4), Reid (2), Woods (1), Dennis (2).

HONOURS

Football League: Championship 1 – Winners 2004–05; Division 1 best season: 7th, 1986–87; Division 2 – Champions 1981–82; Runners-up 1954–55, 1973–74; Division 3 – Runners-up 1969–70, 2001–02; Division 4 – Champions 1967–68; Division 3 (S) – Champions 1936–37; Runners-up 1935–36.

FA Cup: Runners-up 1959.

Football League Cup: Winners 1988; Runners-up 1989.

Simod Cup: Runners-up 1988.

SKY SPORTS FACT FILE

Three pre-First World War stalwarts of Luton Town: Ernie Simms wounded in Italy, Sydney Hoar a wartime gas victim and Arthur Roe who received severe wounds in France all played regularly for the club in 1919–20 having each made full recoveries.

Record Defeat: 0–9 v Small Heath, Division 2, 12 November 1898.

Most League Points (2 for a win): 66, Division 4, 1967–68.

Most League Points (3 for a win): 98, Championship 1 2004–05.

Most League Goals: 103, Division 3 (S), 1936–37.

Highest League Scorer in Season: Joe Payne, 55, Division 3 (S), 1936–37.

Most League Goals in Total Aggregate: Gordon Turner, 243, 1949–64.

Most League Goals in One Match: 10, Joe Payne v Bristol R, Division 3S, 13 April 1936.

Most Capped Player: Mal Donaghy, 58 (91), Northern Ireland.

Most League Appearances: Bob Morton, 495, 1948–64.

Youngest League Player: Mike O'Hara, 16 years 32 days v Stoke C, 1 October 1960.

Record Transfer Fee Received: £3,000,000 from WBA for Curtis Davies, August 2005.

Record Transfer Fee Paid: £850,000 to Odense for Lars Elstrup, August 1989.

Football League Record: 1897 Elected to Division 2; 1900 Failed re-election; 1920 Division 3; 1921–37 Division 3 (S); 1937–55 Division 2; 1955–60 Division 1; 1960–63 Division 2; 1963–65 Division 3; 1965–68 Division 4; 1968–70 Division 3; 1970–74 Division 2; 1974–75 Division 1; 1975–82 Division 2; 1982–96 Division 1; 1996–2001 Division 2; 2001–02 Division 3; 2002–04 Division 2; 2004–05 FL 1; 2005–07 FL C; 2007–08 FL 1; 2008– FL 2.

MANAGERS

Charlie Green 1901–28
(Secretary-Manager)
George Thomson 1925
John McCartney 1927–29
George Kay 1929–31
Harold Wightman 1931–35
Ted Liddell 1936–38
Neil McBain 1938–39
George Martin 1939–47
Dally Duncan 1947–58
Syd Owen 1959–60
Sam Bartram 1960–62
Bill Harvey 1962–64
George Martin 1965–66
Allan Brown 1966–68
Alec Stock 1968–72
Harry Haslam 1972–78
David Pleat 1978–86
John Moore 1986–87
Ray Harford 1987–89
Jim Ryan 1990–91
David Pleat 1991–95
Terry Westley 1995
Lennie Lawrence 1995–2000
Ricky Hill 2000
Lil Fuccillo 2000
Joe Kinnear 2001–03
Mike Newell 2003–07
Kevin Blackwell 2007–08
Mick Harford January 2008–

LATEST SEQUENCES

Longest Sequence of League Wins: 12, 19.2.2002 – 6.4.2002.

Longest Sequence of League Defeats: 8, 11.11.1899 – 6.1.1900.

Longest Sequence of League Draws: 5, 28.8.1971 – 18.9.1971.

Longest Sequence of Unbeaten League Matches: 19, 8.4.1969 – 7.10.1969.

Longest Sequence Without a League Win: 16, 9.9.1964 – 6.11.1964.

Successive Scoring Runs: 25 from 24.10.1931.

Successive Non-scoring Runs: 5 from 10.4.1973.

TEN YEAR LEAGUE RECORD

		P	W	D	L	F	A	Pts	Pos
1998-99	Div 2	46	16	10	20	51	60	58	12
1999-2000	Div 2	46	17	10	19	61	65	61	13
2000-01	Div 2	46	9	13	24	52	80	40	22
2001-02	Div 3	46	30	7	9	96	48	97	2
2002-03	Div 2	46	17	14	15	67	62	65	9
2003-04	Div 2	46	17	15	14	69	66	66	10
2004-05	FL 1	46	29	11	6	87	48	98	1
2005-06	FL C	46	17	10	19	66	67	61	10
2006-07	FL C	46	10	10	26	53	81	40	23
2007-08	FL 1	46	11	10	25	43	63	33*	24

**10 pts deducted.*

DID YOU KNOW ?

Luton Town produced several outstanding performances in what proved to be an overall disappointing 2007–08 season for the club. In the FA Cup they forced Liverpool to a replay and defeated Sunderland 3–0 in the second round of the Carling Cup.

LUTON TOWN 2007–08 LEAGUE RECORD

Match No.	Date	Venue	Opponents	Result		H/T Score	Lg. Pos.	Goalscorers	Atten-dance
1	Aug 11	H	Hartlepool U	W	2-1	1-0	—	Currie[36], Goodall[84]	8013
2	18	A	Swindon T	L	1-2	0-0	10	Edwards[66]	7520
3	25	H	Gillingham	W	3-1	2-1	4	Bell[17], Furlong[27], Spring (pen)[80]	6178
4	Sept 1	A	Leeds U	L	0-1	0-1	7		26,856
5	8	H	Bristol R	L	1-2	1-1	10	Spring (pen)[19]	6131
6	14	A	Tranmere R	L	1-2	1-0	—	Furlong[5]	6525
7	22	H	Port Vale	W	2-1	1-0	13	Furlong[30], Bell[86]	6084
8	29	A	Huddersfield T	L	0-2	0-1	16		9028
9	Oct 2	A	Yeovil T	D	0-0	0-0	—		4848
10	6	H	Doncaster R	D	1-1	0-1	17	Furlong[57]	6513
11	15	H	Northampton T	W	4-1	1-1	—	Currie[4], Spring 2 (2 pens)[49, 90], Furlong[62]	5881
12	20	A	Crewe Alex	L	0-2	0-2	15		4490
13	27	H	Nottingham F	W	2-1	0-0	14	Perry[52], Bell[88]	8524
14	Nov 3	A	Brighton & HA	L	1-3	0-1	15	Edwards[79]	5317
15	6	H	Carlisle U	D	0-0	0-0	—		5462
16	17	A	Walsall	D	0-0	0-0	17		5056
17	24	H	Southend U	W	1-0	0-0	23	Andrew[74]	6820
18	Dec 4	A	Oldham Ath	D	1-1	1-1	—	Fojut[34]	4251
19	14	A	Cheltenham T	L	0-1	0-1	—		3702
20	22	H	Tranmere R	W	1-0	0-0	22	Edwards[70]	6070
21	26	A	Bristol R	D	1-1	0-1	23	Edwards[49]	7556
22	29	A	Port Vale	W	2-1	1-1	21	Fojut[3], Spring[90]	4224
23	Jan 1	H	Yeovil T	W	1-0	0-0	21	Andrew[48]	6811
24	12	H	Swansea C	L	1-3	0-1	22	Furlong[74]	6756
25	19	A	Leyton Orient	L	1-2	0-1	22	Keane[67]	5516
26	22	A	Bournemouth	L	3-4	1-2	—	Spring (pen)[45], Morgan[60], Furlong[78]	3489
27	26	H	Leeds U	D	1-1	0-1	—	Parkin[90]	9297
28	29	H	Swindon T	L	0-1	0-0	—		5738
29	Feb 2	A	Hartlepool U	L	0-4	0-1	23		3913
30	9	H	Bournemouth	L	1-4	0-3	22	Emanuel[50]	5897
31	16	H	Leyton Orient	L	0-1	0-1	22		6412
32	22	A	Swansea C	L	0-1	0-0	—		14,122
33	26	H	Millwall	D	1-1	1-1	—	Furlong[19]	6417
34	Mar 1	H	Walsall	L	0-1	0-1	23		6157
35	8	A	Southend U	L	0-2	0-1	23		8241
36	11	A	Carlisle U	L	1-2	0-2	—	Bell[51]	5489
37	15	H	Oldham Ath	W	3-0	3-0	23	Charles[20], Spring (pen)[33], Emanuel[35]	5417
38	22	H	Cheltenham T	D	1-1	1-0	22	Parkin[24]	6087
39	24	A	Millwall	D	0-0	0-0	23		8375
40	29	H	Crewe Alex	W	2-1	1-0	23	Spring 2 (1 pen)[4, 78 (p)]	5465
41	Apr 1	A	Gillingham	L	1-2	1-0	—	Parkin[19]	6142
42	5	A	Northampton T	L	1-2	0-2	24	Parkin[90]	5132
43	12	H	Brighton & HA	L	1-2	0-0	24	Parkin[49]	6652
44	19	A	Nottingham F	L	0-1	0-0	24		17,531
45	26	A	Doncaster R	L	0-2	0-1	24		9332
46	May 3	H	Huddersfield T	L	0-1	0-0	24		6539

Final League Position: 24

GOALSCORERS

League (43): Spring 9 (7 pens), Furlong 8, Parkin 5, Bell 4, Edwards 4, Andrew 2, Currie 2, Emanuel 2, Fojut 2, Charles 1, Goodall 1, Keane 1, Morgan 1, Perry 1.
Carling Cup (8): Furlong 2, Spring 2 (1 pen), Talbot 2, Bell 1, Robinson 1.
FA Cup (5): Andrew 2, Coyne 1, Fojut 1, own goal 1.
J Paint Trophy (5): Furlong 2, Hutchison 1, Peschisolido 1, Spring 1 (pen).

Brill D 37	Goodall A 25 + 4	Jackson R 27 + 2	Robinson S 24 + 3	Coyne C 18	Perry C 35	Currie D 25 + 6	Edwards D 18 + 1	Furlong P 24 + 8	Peschisolido P 2 + 2	Spring M 44	Hutchison D 15 + 6	McVeigh P 15 + 10	Parkin S 12 + 7	Talbot D 16 + 11	Morgan D 8 + 8	Forde D 5	Bell D 32	Andrew C 19 + 20	Keane K 27 + 1	Fojut J 15 + 1	Brkovic A — + 1	Alnwick B 4	Wilson M 4	Grant A 1 + 3	Emanuel L 15 + 2	O'Leary S 10 + 6	Davis S 15	Beavan G 1 + 1	Charles R 6 + 1	Asafu-Adjaye E 7	Howells J — + 1	Langley R — + 1	Match No.
1	2	3	4	5	6	7^1	8	9^3	10^2	11	12	13	14																				1
1	2	3	4	5	6	7^2	8	9^3	10^1	11		12		13	14																		2
	3	2		5	6	7	8^2	9^3		11	13	12		10^1		1	4	14															3
	3			5	6	7^1	8	9^3		11		13		10^2	12	1	4	14	2														4
	2^1	3	4	5	6	7^2		9	14	11	12			10^3	13	1	8																5
	3	2	4^3	5	6		8	9	12	11					10^1	1	7^2			14	13												6
	2	3	4	5	6	12	8^2	9^3		11		13			10^1	1	7	14															7
	2	3^3	4		6	12		9■		11		10^2		13	7^1		8	14		5		1											8
	3		4	5	2	7	8			11				12			10^1	9		6		1											9
	2	12	4	5^1	3	7^2	8	9		11		13						10		6		1											10
1	2	3			6	7		9		11	8			10^1			4	12		5													11
	2	3^1	12		6	7	13	9		11	8^2				14		4	10^3		5		1											12
1	3		4	5	6	7	8	9		11							10			2													13
1	2■	12	4	5	6	7	10^2			11	13	14					8^3	9^1		3													14
1		2	4	5	6	7^2	10^1			11				13	12		8	9		3													15
1		3		5	6					11	4	10^1		12			8	9		2			7										16
1		3		5		12	8			11		7^1					4	9	6	2^2			10	13									17
1		2	4	5	6	12	8^3	9						13			7^1	10^2		3			11	14									18
1		3^2	4^1	5	6	7	8^3	9		11				12				13	2				10	14									19
1	2		4	5	6	7^1	10	9^2		11				12			8	13		3													20
1	2^2		4■	5■	6		8	12		11							7	9^1	13	3				10■									21
1	2				6	7^3	8	12		11	13	14		9^1			4^2	10	5	3													22
1	2				6	7^2	8	12		11		13		9^1			4	10	5	3													23
1	2	3^1	4		6^2	7		12			8			9			11	10	5						13								24
1	2^3		4^1		5	7		12		11	6			9	13		8	10^2	3						14								25
1	2		4		5	7		9		11	6			10^1	8^2			12	3							13							26
1	2	3	4		6	7^2		9		11			12	8^3	13			10^1	5							14							27
1	2	3			6	7^1		9		11			12	8^3	13		4	10^2	5							14							28
1	12	2	4^2		6^1			9		11	7^3			10			8	13	5							14	3						29
1	2		4^1			7^2				11			10	12	9		8	13	5^3						3		6	14					30
1			4					12		11			10		8		7^1	9	5						2		6	3					31
1	12	2	4^3		6			13		11			10^2	9^1			8	14	5						7		3■						32
1	12	3			6			9		11		13		10^3	7^2		8	14	5						2^1	4							33
1	12	2			6			9		11		8^2	13	10	7^3			14	5							4	3^1						34
1	2	3	4^3		6			9^1		11		7	12	10^2			8	13	5										14				35
1		2			6			9^2		11		7	13	12			4		5						8		3		10^1				36
1		2			6^2			9^1		11	13	7	12				4		5						8	14	3^3		10				37
1		2			6					11		7^3	10	12			4	13	5						8	14	3^2		9^1				38
1		2								11	6	7	10				8	12	5						3	4			9^1				39
1										11	6	7^1	10					12	5						2	8	3		9	4			40
1										11	6	7	10					12	5						3	8	4		9^1	2			41
1						12				11	6	7	10					9	5						8	4	3^1			2			42
1			12			13				11	6	7^2	10					9	5						8	4	3^1			2			43
1						7				11	6	9^1	10					12	5						8	4	3			2			44
1			12			7				11	6	9^1	10					13	5						8	4	3^2			2			45
1		3				7^3		12		11	6		10					9^1							8	4	5^2			2	13	14	46

FA Cup

First Round	Brentford	(h)	1-1
		(a)	2-0
Second Round	Nottingham F	(h)	1-0
Third Round	Liverpool	(h)	1-1
		(a)	0-5

Carling Cup

First Round	Dagenham & R	(a)	2-1
Second Round	Sunderland	(h)	3-0
Third Round	Charlton Ath	(h)	3-1
Fourth Round	Everton	(h)	0-1

J Paint Trophy

First Round	Northampton T	(h)	2-0
Second Round	Gillingham	(a)	3-4

MACCLESFIELD TOWN FL Championship 2

FOUNDATION

From the mid-19th Century until 1874, Macclesfield Town FC played under rugby rules. In 1891 they moved to the Moss Rose and finished champions of the Manchester & District League in 1906 and 1908. By 1911, they had carried off the Cheshire Senior Cup five times. Macclesfield were founder members of the Cheshire County League in 1919.

Moss Rose Ground, London Road, Macclesfield, Cheshire SK11 7SP.

Telephone: (01625) 264 686.

Fax: (01625) 264 692.

Ticket Office: (01625) 264 686.

Website: www.mtfc.co.uk

Email: admin@mtfc.co.uk

Ground Capacity: 6,335.

Record Attendance: 9,008 v Winsford U, Cheshire Senior Cup 2nd rd, 4 February 1948.

Pitch Measurements: 100m × 60m.

Chairman: Mike Rance.

Vice-chairman: Andy Scott.

Chief Executive: Patrick Nelson.

Manager: Keith Alexander.

Assistant Manager: Gary Simpson.

Physio: Nick Reid.

Colours: Blue shirts, white shorts and blue stockings.

Change Colours: Black shirts, black shorts, black stockings.

Year formed: 1874.

Club Nickname: 'The Silkmen'.

Grounds: 1874, Rostron Field; 1891, Moss Rose.

First Football League Game: 9 August 1997, Division 3, v Torquay U (h) W 2–1 – Price; Tinson, Rose, Payne (Edey), Howarth, Sodje (1), Askey, Wood, Landon (1) (Power), Mason, Sorvel.

HONOURS

Football League: Division 3 – Runners-up 1997–98.

FA Cup: best season: 3rd rd, 1968, 1988, 2002, 2003, 2004, 2007.

Football League Cup: never past 2nd rd.

Vauxhall Conference: Champions 1994–95, 1996–97.

FA Trophy: Winners 1969–70, 1995–96; Runners-up 1988–89.

Bob Lord Trophy: Winners 1993–94; Runners-up 1995–96, 1996–97.

Vauxhall Conference Championship Shield: Winners 1996, 1997, 1998.

Northern Premier League: Winners 1968–69, 1969–70, 1986–87; Runners-up 1984–85.

Northern Premier League Challenge Cup: Winners 1986–87; Runners-up 1969–70, 1970–71, 1982–83.

Northern Premier League Presidents Cup: Winners 1986–87; Runners-up 1984–85.

Cheshire Senior Cup: Winners 20 times; Runners-up 11.

SKY SPORTS FACT FILE

On 29 March 2008 Shaun Brisley, 17, scholar at Macclesfield Town and boot boy at the club, made an indelible impression against Accrington Stanley when he scored twice for his club, before returning to more down-to-earth dressing-room duties the following Monday.

Record League Victory: 6–0 v Stockport Co, FL 1, 26 December 2005 – Fettis; Harsley, Sandwith, Morley, Swailes (Teague), Navarro, Whitaker (Miles (1)), Bullock (1), Parkin (2), Wijnhard (2) (Townson), McIntyre.

Record Win: 15–0 v Chester St Marys, Cheshire Senior Cup, 2nd rd, 16 February 1886.

Record Defeat: 1–13 v Tranmere R reserves, 3 May 1929.

Most League Points (3 for a win): 82, Division 3, 1997–98.

Most League Goals: 66, Division 3, 1999–2000.

Highest League Scorer in Season: Jon Parkin, 22, League 2, 2004–05.

Most League Goals in Total Aggregate: Matt Tipton, 45, 2002–05; 2006–07.

Most Capped Player: George Abbey, 10, Nigeria.

Most League Appearances: Darren Tinson, 263, 1997–2003.

Youngest League Player: Peter Griffiths, 18 years 44 days v Reading, 26 September 1998.

Record Transfer Fee Received: £300,000 from Stockport Co for Rickie Lambert, April 2002.

Record Transfer Fee Paid: £40,000 to Bury for Danny Swailes, January 2005.

Football League Record: 1997 Promoted to Division 3; 1998–99 Division 2; 1999–2004 Division 3; 2004– FL 2.

MANAGERS

Since 1967
Keith Goalen 1967–68
Frank Beaumont 1968–72
Billy Haydock 1972–74
Eddie Brown 1974
John Collins 1974
Willie Stevenson 1974
John Collins 1975–76
Tony Coleman 1976
John Barnes 1976
Brian Taylor 1976
Dave Connor 1976–78
Derek Partridge 1978
Phil Staley 1978–80
Jimmy Williams 1980–81
Brian Booth 1981–85
Neil Griffiths 1985–86
Roy Campbell 1986
Peter Wragg 1986–93
Sammy McIlroy 1993–2000
Peter Davenport 2000
Gil Prescott 2001
David Moss 2001–03
John Askey 2003–04
Brian Horton 2004–06
Paul Ince 2006–07
Ian Brightwell 2007–08
Keith Alexander February 2008–

LATEST SEQUENCES

Longest Sequence of League Wins: 6, 25.1.2005 – 26.2.2005.

Longest Sequence of League Defeats: 6, 26.12.1998 – 6.2.1999.

Longest Sequence of League Draws: 5, 5.5.2007 – 1.9.2007.

Longest Sequence of Unbeaten League Matches: 8, 16.10.1999 – 27.11.1999.

Longest Sequence Without a League Win: 19, 5.8.2006 – 25.11.2006.

Successive Scoring Runs: 14 from 11.10.2003.

Successive Non-scoring Runs: 5 from 18.12.1998.

TEN YEAR LEAGUE RECORD

		P	*W*	*D*	*L*	*F*	*A*	*Pts*	*Pos*
1998-99	Div 2	46	11	10	25	43	63	43	24
1999-2000	Div 3	46	18	11	17	66	61	65	13
2000-01	Div 3	46	14	14	18	51	62	56	14
2001-02	Div 3	46	15	13	18	41	52	58	13
2002-03	Div 3	46	14	12	20	57	63	54	16
2003-04	Div 3	46	13	13	20	54	69	52	20
2004-05	FL 2	46	22	9	15	60	49	75	5
2005-06	FL 2	46	12	18	16	60	71	54	17
2006-07	FL 2	46	12	12	22	55	77	48	22
2007-08	FL 2	46	11	17	18	47	64	50	19

DID YOU KNOW ?

In 1968 Macclesfield Town reached the third round of the FA Cup for the first time and despite losing 4–2 to Fulham, Keith Goalen became the first non-league player to be awarded the Footballer of the Month by the London based *Evening Standard* newspaper.

MACCLESFIELD TOWN 2007–08 LEAGUE RECORD

Match No.	Date	Venue	Opponents	Result		H/T Score	Lg. Pos.	Goalscorers	Attendance
1	Aug 11	A	Bradford C	D	1-1	1-1	—	Green [9]	13,401
2	18	H	Milton Keynes D	D	3-3	1-1	12	Green 2 [33, 63], Gritton [57]	2257
3	25	A	Grimsby T	D	1-1	0-0	16	Gritton [63]	3701
4	Sept 1	H	Darlington	D	0-0	0-0	13		2288
5	8	A	Hereford U	W	1-0	0-0	10	Green [82]	2725
6	15	H	Wycombe W	L	1-2	0-0	13	Evans [90]	2173
7	22	A	Rochdale	D	1-1	1-1	16	McIntyre (pen) [22]	3066
8	29	H	Chester C	L	1-2	0-2	20	Dunfield [53]	2647
9	Oct 2	H	Rotherham U	D	1-1	0-1	—	Gritton [61]	1715
10	6	A	Chesterfield	D	2-2	1-1	18	Gritton [29], Green [73]	4080
11	13	H	Wrexham	W	3-2	1-2	14	Gritton [36], Morley [89], Thomas [90]	2256
12	19	A	Accrington S	L	2-3	0-0	—	McIntyre (pen) [71], Evans [73]	1792
13	27	H	Bury	D	2-2	2-0	17	Thomas [21], Gritton [45]	2672
14	Nov 3	A	Mansfield T	L	0-5	0-4	18		2853
15	6	H	Brentford	W	1-0	0-0	—	Thomas [76]	1378
16	17	A	Notts Co	W	1-0	0-0	14	Green [63]	4390
17	24	H	Dagenham & R	D	1-1	0-1	15	Blackman [90]	1781
18	Dec 1	A	Shrewsbury T	L	0-2	0-1	—		4763
19	8	A	Barnet	D	2-2	2-1	16	McNulty [3], Reid L [7]	1303
20	15	H	Stockport Co	L	0-2	0-0	16		3585
21	22	A	Wycombe W	L	1-2	1-1	18	Green [17]	3887
22	26	H	Hereford U	L	0-1	0-0	19		2393
23	29	H	Rochdale	D	2-2	2-0	19	Reid L [20], Evans [30]	2742
24	Jan 1	A	Rotherham U	L	0-3	0-0	20		4464
25	5	H	Morecambe	L	1-2	1-1	20	Gritton [25]	2254
26	12	A	Peterborough U	W	1-0	1-0	18	Reid I [37]	5238
27	26	A	Darlington	D	2-2	0-1	19	Gritton [60], Cresswell [64]	3585
28	29	A	Milton Keynes D	D	1-1	1-0	—	Symes [3]	6483
29	Feb 2	H	Bradford C	L	0-1	0-0	19		2778
30	5	H	Lincoln C	L	1-2	0-0	—	Evans [90]	1576
31	9	A	Morecambe	W	1-0	0-0	19	Green [87]	2626
32	12	H	Grimsby T	L	1-2	0-1	—	Evans [79]	2194
33	16	A	Lincoln C	L	1-3	1-0	21	Evans [8]	3682
34	23	H	Peterborough U	L	0-3	0-0	22		2094
35	Mar 1	H	Notts Co	D	1-1	1-0	22	Reid I [22]	2193
36	8	A	Brentford	L	0-1	0-0	22		3863
37	11	A	Dagenham & R	W	1-0	0-0	—	Green [72]	1350
38	15	H	Shrewsbury T	W	2-1	0-0	21	Tolley [82], Green [85]	2473
39	21	A	Stockport Co	L	0-2	0-1	—		7824
40	24	H	Barnet	W	3-0	2-0	21	Thomas [31], Ashton [41], Green [48]	1718
41	29	H	Accrington S	W	2-1	2-1	19	Brisley 2 [15, 38]	1853
42	Apr 5	A	Wrexham	D	1-1	0-0	18	Tolley [52]	3993
43	12	H	Mansfield T	D	0-0	0-0	19		3250
44	19	A	Bury	L	0-1	0-1	19		2506
45	26	H	Chesterfield	W	1-0	1-0	19	Evans [42]	2573
46	May 3	A	Chester C	D	0-0	0-0	19		2396

Final League Position: 19

GOALSCORERS

League (47): Green 11, Gritton 8, Evans 7, Thomas 4, Brisley 2, McIntyre 2 (2 pens), Reid I 2, Reid L 2, Tolley 2, Ashton 1, Blackman 1, Cresswell 1, Dunfield 1, McNulty 1, Morley 1, Symes 1.
Carling Cup (0).
FA Cup (1): Gritton 1.
J Paint Trophy (0).

Lee T 17+1	Edghill R 13+2	Regan C 18+2	Thomas D 43	Dimech L 23+3	Dunfield T 40+1	Murray A 22+1	Reid I 17+8	Green F 35+6	Husbands M 2	McIntyre K 22+1	Jennings J 5+6	Evans G 20+22	McNulty J 13+6	Hadfield J —+2	Gritton M 27+4	Wiles S 1+16	Reid L 29+2	Morley D 2+2	Tolley J 20+4	Hessey S 26	Blackman N 1+10	Brain J 29	Doughty P 5+1	Dennis K —+1	Millar C —+2	Ashton N 19	Cresswell R 19	Ashmore J 7+1	Symes M 10+4	Brisley S 9+1	Onibuje F —+1	Spencer S —+3	Walker R 10	Rooney J 1+1	Teague A 1	*Match No.*
1	2	3	4^{1}	5	6	7		9	10^{3}	11	12	13	14				8^{2}																			1
1	2	3	4^{2}	5	6	7		9	10^{3}	11			12	13	14		8^{1}																			2
1	4	2	11^{1}	5	6^{3}	7		9		3		13	12		10^{2}	14	8																			3
1	2		4	5	6	7		10		3		12	11		9^{1}		8																			4
1	2	3^{1}	4		6	7		10		11		14	5^{2}	13	9^{3}		8	12																		5
1	2		4	5	11	7		10		3		12	6		9^{1}	13	8^{2}																			6
1	2		4	5	6	7		10^{1}		11		12	3		9	13	8^{2}																			7
1			11	5	6	7	2^{3}	10		3		12	4		9^{1}	13	8^{2}	14																		8
1			11	5	6	7	2	10		3		12	4		9^{1}	13	8^{2}																			9
1			11	5	6	7	2	10		3		12	4		9^{1}	13	8^{2}																			10
1	2		11		6	7		10^{2}		3		13	4		9	12	8^{1}	5																		11
1	2	12	11		6	7		10		3		13	5		9		8^{2}	4^{1}																		12
1	4	2	11	5	6	7		10^{2}		3		13			9	12	8^{1}																			13
1	4	2	11^{2}	5^{3}		7		10		3		13	14		9	12	8^{1}		6																	14
1	2^{2}	12	11	5	6	7^{3}				3		10	4^{1}		9	13	8		14																	15
1		2	11	5	6^{1}	12		10		3		13	14		9^{2}		8		7	4^{3}																16
1	2		11^{3}	5		7		9		3		10	13			12	8^{1}		4	6^{2}	14															17
		2	11		12	7		10		3		9^{2}	4		13	14	8^{3}		6^{1}			1	5													18
		2	11	5	6	7		10				12	3		9^{1}		8					1	4													19
		2	11^{2}	5	6	7		10^{1}		13		12	3		9	14	8^{3}					1	4													20
		2	11	5	6	7		10		3		12			9		8^{1}			4		1														21
		2	11	5	6	7		10^{1}		3		12			9	13	8^{2}			4		1														22
		2	11	5^{2}	6	7				3		10			9^{3}	12	8^{1}			4	14	1	13													23
		2	11^{2}		6					3		10				12	8		7	4	9^{1}	1	5	13												24
		2	11^{2}	5	6		12					10			9	8^{1}			7^{3}	4	13	1	3		14											25
		2^{2}	11	12	6		8					10▪								4	13	1			14	3	5^{1}	7	9^{3}							26
		2	11^{1}		6		8	13							9^{2}		12			4		1				3	5	7	10							27
		2	11		6		8^{2}	12							9^{1}		13			4	14	1				3	5	7	10^{3}							28
			11^{3}		6		2	12							9		8^{1}		13	4	14	1				3	5	7^{2}	10							29
			11		6		2	14				12			9^{3}		8^{1}		13	4		1				3	5	7^{2}	10							30
			11		6		2	9				12					8^{1}		13	4		1				3	5	7^{2}	10							31
			11^{2}	12	6		2	9				7							8	4^{1}	13	1				3	5		10							32
15			11^{1}		6^{2}		2	9				7							8	4	12	1^{6}				3	5	13	10							33
			11	12			2	10^{3}				9					8		6	4^{1}	13	1				3	5	7^{2}	14							34
				5			11	7			4	9^{1}							8			1				3	6		10	2	12					35
					6		8	7^{1}				9							11	2		1				3	5		10	4		12				36
			11^{2}		6		2^{1}	12			8	9							10	4		1				7	5			13			3			37
			11		6		12	10			4^{2}	9^{3}			13				8	2		1					5^{1}			3		14	7			38
			11		6		12	10^{1}			4^{3}	13			9^{2}				8	2		1					5			7		14	3			39
			11^{3}		6		12	10^{1}			13	9							7	2		1				8^{2}	5			3			4	14		40
			11^{1}		6		12	10^{2}			13	9							7	2		1				8	5			3			4			41
			11^{2}		6		13	10^{3}			14	9^{1}							7	4		1				8	5		12	3			2			42
	12		11		6		13	10			14	9^{2}							8^{3}	2		1				4	5			3^{1}			7			43
			11		6		12	10			3	9^{3}			14					4		1				7	5^{2}		13	2^{1}			8			44
			11^{3}	5	6		2	12			14	10^{2}			9^{1}				8	4		1				3			13				7			45
	12			5			3	11^{2}				13			9^{3}		7^{1}		8		14	1				6							4	10	2	46

FA Cup
First Round — Rushden & D — (a) — 1-3

Carling Cup
First Round — Leeds U — (h) — 0-1

J Paint Trophy
Second Round — Stockport Co — (h) — 0-1

MANCHESTER CITY FA Premiership

FOUNDATION

Manchester City was formed as a Limited Company in 1894 after their predecessors Ardwick had been forced into bankruptcy. However, many historians like to trace the club's lineage as far back as 1880 when St Mark's Church, West Gorton added a football section to their cricket club. They amalgamated with Gorton Athletic in 1884 as Gorton FC. Because of a change of ground they became Ardwick in 1887.

The City of Manchester Stadium, SportCity, Manchester M11 3FF.

Telephone: 0870 062 1894.

Fax: (0161) 438 7999.

Ticket Office: 0870 062 1894 (option 2).

Club Museum and Ground Tours: 0870 062 1894.

Website: www.mcfc.co.uk

Email: mcfc@mcfc.co.uk

Ground Capacity: 47,715.

Record Attendance: (at Maine Road) 85,569 v Stoke C, FA Cup 6th rd, 3 March 1934 (British record for any game outside London or Glasgow). (At City of Manchester Stadium) 47,304 v Chelsea, FA Premier League, 28 February 2004.

Pitch Measurements: 105m × 68m.

Chairman: Dr Thaksin Shinawatra.

Vice-chairman: John Wardle.

Chief Executive: Alistair Mackintosh.

Secretary: J. B. Halford.

Manager: Mark Hughes.

Assistant Manager: Mark Bowen.

Physio: Ally Beattie.

Colours: Sky blue shirts, white shorts, sky blue stockings.

Change Colours: Red and black striped shirts, black shorts, black stockings.

Year Formed: 1887 as Ardwick FC; 1894 as Manchester City.

Turned Professional: 1887 as Ardwick FC. ***Ltd Co.:*** 1894.

Previous Names: 1887, Ardwick FC (formed through the amalgamation of West Gorton and Gorton Athletic, the latter having been formed in 1880); 1894, Manchester City.

Club Nicknames: 'Blues' or 'The Citizens'.

Grounds: 1880, Clowes Street; 1881, Kirkmanshulme Cricket Ground; 1882, Queens Road; 1884, Pink Bank Lane; 1887, Hyde Road (1894–1923 as City); 1923, Maine Road; 2003, City of Manchester Stadium.

First Football League Game: 3 September 1892, Division 2, v Bootle (h) W 7–0 – Douglas; McVickers, Robson; Middleton, Russell, Hopkins; Davies (3), Morris (2), Angus (1), Weir (1), Milarvie.

Record League Victory: 10–1 v Huddersfield T, Division 2, 7 November 1987 – Nixon; Gidman, Hinchcliffe, Clements, Lake, Redmond, White (3), Stewart (3), Adcock (3), McNab (1), Simpson.

HONOURS

Football League: Division 1 – Champions 1936–37, 1967–68, 2001–02; Runners-up 1903–04, 1920–21, 1976–77, 1999–2000; Division 2 – Champions 1898–99, 1902–03, 1909–10, 1927–28, 1946–47, 1965–66; Runners-up 1895–96, 1950–51, 1987–88; Promoted from Division 2 (play-offs) 1998–99.

FA Cup: Winners 1904, 1934, 1956, 1969; Runners-up 1926, 1933, 1955, 1981.

Football League Cup: Winners 1970, 1976; Runners-up 1974.

European Competitions: *European Cup:* 1968–69. *European Cup-Winners' Cup:* 1969–70 (winners), 1970–71. *UEFA Cup:* 1972–73, 1976–77, 1977–78, 1978–79, 2003–04.

SKY SPORTS FACT FILE

In 2007–08 Manchester City had international players from 15 different countries: Belgium, Brazil and Bulgaria (two each), China, Croatia, Denmark, Ecuador, Germany, Greece, Italy, Mexico, Spain, Sweden, Switzerland and Zimbabwe.

Record Cup Victory: 10–1 v Swindon T, FA Cup 4th rd, 29 January 1930 – Barber; Felton, McCloy; Barrass, Cowan, Heinemann; Toseland, Marshall (5), Tait (3), Johnson (1), Brook (1).

Record Defeat: 1–9 v Everton, Division 1, 3 September 1906.

Most League Points (2 for a win): 62, Division 2, 1946–47.

Most League Points (3 for a win): 99, Division 1, 2001–02.

Most League Goals: 108, Division 2, 1926–27, 108, Division 1, 2001–02.

Highest League Scorer in Season: Tommy Johnson, 38, Division 1, 1928–29.

Most League Goals in Total Aggregate: Tommy Johnson, 158, 1919–30.

Most League Goals in One Match: 5, Fred Williams v Darwen, Division 2, 18 February 1899; 5, Tom Browell v Burnley, Division 2, 24 October 1925; 5, Tom Johnson v Everton, Division 1, 15 September 1928; 5, George Smith v Newport Co, Division 2, 14 June 1947.

Most Capped Player: Colin Bell, 48, England.

Most League Appearances: Alan Oakes, 565, 1959–76.

Youngest League Player: Glyn Pardoe, 15 years 314 days v Birmingham C, 11 April 1962.

Record Transfer Fee Received: £21,000,000 from Chelsea for Shaun Wright-Phillips, July 2005.

Record Transfer Fee Paid: Reported £18,000,000 to CSKA Moscow for Jo, July 2008.

Football League Record: 1892 Ardwick elected founder member of Division 2; 1894 Newly-formed Manchester C elected to Division 2; Division 1 1899–1902, 1903–09, 1910–26, 1928–38, 1947–50, 1951–63, 1966–83, 1985–87, 1989–92; Division 2 1902–03, 1909–10, 1926–28, 1938–47, 1950–51, 1963–66, 1983–85, 1987–89; 1992–96 FA Premier League; 1996–98 Division 1; 1998–99 Division 2; 1999–2000 Division 1; 2000–01 FA Premier League; 2001–02 Division 1; 2002– FA Premier League.

MANAGERS

Joshua Parlby 1893–95
(Secretary-Manager)
Sam Omerod 1895–1902
Tom Maley 1902–06
Harry Newbould 1906–12
Ernest Magnall 1912–24
David Ashworth 1924–25
Peter Hodge 1926–32
Wilf Wild 1932–46
(continued as Secretary to 1950)
Sam Cowan 1946–47
John 'Jock' Thomson 1947–50
Leslie McDowall 1950–63
George Poyser 1963–65
Joe Mercer 1965–71
(continued as General Manager to 1972)
Malcolm Allison 1972–73
Johnny Hart 1973
Ron Saunders 1973–74
Tony Book 1974–79
Malcolm Allison 1979–80
John Bond 1980–83
John Benson 1983
Billy McNeill 1983–86
Jimmy Frizzell 1986–87
(continued as General Manager)
Mel Machin 1987–89
Howard Kendall 1990
Peter Reid 1990–93
Brian Horton 1993–95
Alan Ball 1995–96
Steve Coppell 1996
Frank Clark 1996–98
Joe Royle 1998–2001
Kevin Keegan 2001–05
Stuart Pearce 2005–07
Sven-Göran Eriksson 2007–08
Mark Hughes June 2008–

LATEST SEQUENCES

Longest Sequence of League Wins: 9, 8.4.1912 – 28.9.1912.

Longest Sequence of League Defeats: 8, 23.8.1995 – 14.10.1995.

Longest Sequence of League Draws: 6, 5.4.1913 – 6.9.1913.

Longest Sequence of Unbeaten League Matches: 22, 16.11.1946 – 19.4.1947.

Longest Sequence Without a League Win: 17, 26.12.1979 – 7.4.1980.

Successive Scoring Runs: 44 from 3.10.1936.

Successive Non-scoring Runs: 6 from 30.1.1971.

TEN YEAR LEAGUE RECORD

		P	W	D	L	F	A	Pts	Pos
1998-99	Div 2	46	22	16	8	69	33	82	3
1999-2000	Div 1	46	26	11	9	78	40	89	2
2000-01	PR Lge	38	8	10	20	41	65	34	18
2001-02	Div 1	46	31	6	9	108	52	99	1
2002-03	PR Lge	38	15	6	17	47	54	51	9
2003-04	PR Lge	38	9	14	15	55	54	41	16
2004-05	PR Lge	38	13	13	12	47	39	52	8
2005-06	PR Lge	38	13	4	21	43	48	43	15
2006-07	PR Lge	38	11	9	18	29	44	42	14
2007-08	PR Lge	38	15	10	13	45	53	55	9

DID YOU KNOW 

In 1895–96 Manchester City remained undefeated at home and overall failed to score in just two League games. They finished second but lost out in the subsequent Test matches. Unusually for a winger, the legendary Billy Meredith ended the season as the club's leading scorer hitting twelve goals in the Second Division.

MANCHESTER CITY 2007–08 LEAGUE RECORD

Match No.	*Date*	*Venue*	*Opponents*	*Result*		*H/T Score*	*Lg. Pos.*	*Goalscorers*	*Attendance*
1	Aug 11	A	West Ham U	W	2-0	1-0	—	Bianchi [18], Geovanni [87]	34,921
2	15	H	Derby Co	W	1-0	1-0	—	Johnson [43]	43,620
3	19	H	Manchester U	W	1-0	1-0	1	Geovanni [31]	44,955
4	25	A	Arsenal	L	0-1	0-0	2		60,114
5	Sept 2	A	Blackburn R	L	0-1	0-1	5		26,881
6	16	H	Aston Villa	W	1-0	0-0	2	Johnson [48]	38,363
7	22	A	Fulham	D	3-3	1-1	3	Petrov 2 [36, 60], Mpenza [50]	24,674
8	29	H	Newcastle U	W	3-1	1-1	3	Petrov [38], Mpenza [47], Elano [87]	40,606
9	Oct 7	H	Middlesbrough	W	3-1	2-0	3	Riggott (og) [10], Elano 2 [33, 63]	40,438
10	20	H	Birmingham C	W	1-0	1-0	3	Elano [37]	45,688
11	27	A	Chelsea	L	0-6	0-2	3		41,832
12	Nov 5	H	Sunderland	W	1-0	0-0	—	Ireland [67]	40,038
13	11	A	Portsmouth	D	0-0	0-0	3		19,529
14	24	H	Reading	W	2-1	1-1	3	Petrov [11], Ireland [90]	43,813
15	Dec 1	A	Wigan Ath	D	1-1	1-1	5	Geovanni [1]	18,614
16	9	A	Tottenham H	L	1-2	0-1	6	Bianchi [61]	35,646
17	15	H	Bolton W	W	4-2	1-2	4	Bianchi [7], Michalik (og) [48], Vassell [77], Etuhu [90]	40,506
18	22	A	Aston Villa	D	1-1	1-1	4	Bianchi [11]	41,455
19	27	H	Blackburn R	D	2-2	2-1	—	Vassell [27], Nelsen (og) [30]	42,112
20	30	H	Liverpool	D	0-0	0-0	5		47,321
21	Jan 2	A	Newcastle U	W	2-0	1-0	—	Elano [38], Gelson [76]	50,956
22	12	A	Everton	L	0-1	0-1	7		38,474
23	20	H	West Ham U	D	1-1	1-1	5	Vassell [16]	39,042
24	30	A	Derby Co	D	1-1	0-0	—	Sturridge [63]	31,368
25	Feb 2	H	Arsenal	L	1-3	1-2	7	Gelson [28]	46,426
26	10	A	Manchester U	W	2-1	2-0	7	Vassell [25], Mwaruwari [45]	75,970
27	25	H	Everton	L	0-2	0-2	—		41,728
28	Mar 1	H	Wigan Ath	D	0-0	0-0	8		38,261
29	8	A	Reading	L	0-2	0-0	8		24,062
30	16	H	Tottenham H	W	2-1	0-1	8	Ireland [59], Onuoha [72]	40,180
31	22	A	Bolton W	D	0-0	0-0	9		22,633
32	29	A	Birmingham C	L	1-3	0-1	9	Elano (pen) [59]	22,962
33	Apr 5	H	Chelsea	L	0-2	0-1	9		42,594
34	12	A	Sunderland	W	2-1	0-0	8	Elano (pen) [79], Vassell [87]	46,797
35	20	H	Portsmouth	W	3-1	2-1	8	Vassell [11], Petrov [13], Mwaruwari [74]	40,205
36	26	H	Fulham	L	2-3	2-0	9	Ireland [10], Mwaruwari [21]	44,504
37	May 4	A	Liverpool	L	0-1	0-0	9		43,074
38	11	A	Middlesbrough	L	1-8	0-2	9	Elano [87]	27,613

Final League Position: 9

GOALSCORERS

League (45): Elano 8 (2 pens), Vassell 6, Petrov 5, Bianchi 4, Ireland 4, Geovanni 3, Mwaruwari 3, Gelson 2, Johnson 2, Mpenza 2, Etuhu 1, Onuoha 1, Sturridge 1, own goals 3.
Carling Cup (4): Bianchi 1, Elano 1 (pen), Mpenza 1, Sammaras 1.
FA Cup (2): Elano 1, Sturridge 1.

Schmeichel K 7	Corluka V 34 + 1	Garrido J 21 + 6	Dunne R 36	Richards M 25	Johnson M 23	Ireland S 32 + 1	Hamann D 26 + 3	Elano 29 + 5	Bianchi R 7 + 12	Petrov M 34	Onuoha N 13 + 3	Geovanni 2 + 17	Bojinov V 1 + 2	Mpenza E 8 + 7	Ball M 19 + 9	Vassell D 21 + 6	Jihai S 7 + 7	Hart J 26	Samaras G 2 + 3	Gelson 21 + 5	Isaksson A 5	Etuhu K 2 + 4	Castillo N 2 + 5	Sturridge D 2 + 1	Mwaruwari B 13	Caicedo F — + 10	Williamson S — + 1	*Match No.*
1	2^{1}	3	4	5	6	7	8	9^{2}	10^{3}	11	12	13	14															1
1	2	3	4	5	6	7	8	9^{1}	10^{3}	11^{2}		13	14	12														2
1	2	3	4	5	6		8	9^{3}	14	11		7^{2}	10^{1}	12	13													3
1	2	3	4	5	6	7^{3}	8	9^{2}	12	11		13		10^{1}	14													4
1	2	3	4■	5	6^{1}	7^{3}	8	9	10	11^{2}	14	13		12														5
1	4	3		5	6		8	9^{2}	12	11	2			10^{1}	13	7^{3}	14											6
1	2	3	4	5	6	7^{3}	8	9^{2}	12	11		13		10^{1}			14											7
	2^{2}	3	4	5	6^{3}	7	8	9^{1}		11	13	12		10	14			1										8
	2	3	4	5	6^{2}	7	8	9^{1}		11		12		10^{3}	13			1	14									9
	2	3	4	5	6	7^{1}	8	9^{3}		11				10^{2}	12			1	13	14								10
	2	3	4	5	6	7^{3}	8^{2}	9^{1}	12	11					13	14		1	10									11
	5	3	4		6^{2}	7	8	9^{3}	12	11				10^{1}	14	13	2	1										12
	2	3	4	5		7	8	9^{2}	12	11		13				10^{1}		1		6								13
	2^{2}	3	4	5		7	8	9^{1}		11		12		10^{3}			13		14	6	1							14
	2	3^{2}	4	5		7	8		12	11		10^{3}			13				9^{1}	6	1	14						15
	2	3	4	5	6	7■			12	11		13				9^{2}				8	1	10^{1}						16
	2	12	4	5	6		8		10^{2}	11^{1}				13	3	9				7^{3}	1	14						17
	12	13	4	5			8^{1}	9^{2}	10^{3}	11	2				3	7		1		6		14						18
	8	12	4	5		7^{1}		13	10^{2}	11	2				3	9		1		6								19
	6		4	5		7^{3}	8	9^{1}	12	11	2	13			3	10^{2}		1		14								20
	6		4	5		7^{2}	8	9^{3}	12	11	2				3	10^{1}		1		13		14						21
	7		4	5		12	8^{3}	9	13	11	2				3	10^{1}		1		14			6^{2}					22
	2	12	4	5		7^{2}	6	9^{1}	10	11		13			3	8^{3}		1		14								23
	5		4			7		12		11		13		14	3	10^{3}	2	1		6		8^{1}		9^{2}				24
	2		4	5		7^{3}	8^{1}	9		11		12		14	3	13		1		6				10^{2}				25
		12	4	5		7	8^{2}			11^{1}	2				3	10	13	1		6					9^{3}	14		26
			4	5		7^{3}	8^{1}	12		11■	2				3	10^{2}		1		6			13		9	14		27
	2		4		6	7^{1}		11^{2}			5				3	10		1		8			12		9	13		28
	5	2	4^{1}		6		8^{2}	10							3	7^{3}	12	1		11			13		9	14		29
	2	3	4		6	7		10^{3}			5					12	13	1		8			11^{1}		9^{2}	14		30
	2	3	4		6	7^{1}		12		11	5					10^{2}		1		8					9	13		31
		3	4			7	8^{1}	10			5	12		13		11^{3}	2	1		6					9^{2}	14		32
	2		4		6	7^{3}		10^{1}		11	5^{2}				3	12	13	1		8					9	14		33
	5		4		6	7^{2}	12	10^{1}		11					3	14	2	1		8				13^{3}	9			34
	5		4^{3}		6	7^{1}		2^{2}		11		12			3	10		1		8					9	13	14	35
	5				6	7^{1}		2		11		12			4	10^{2}	3	1		8					9	13		36
	2	13	4		6	7	12	10^{1}		11^{3}					5	8^{2}	3	1					14		9			37
	5	8	4■			7	12	13		11^{2}					3	10^{1}	2			6	1		14		9^{3}			38

FA Cup

Third Round	West Ham U	(a)	0-0
		(h)	1-0
Fourth Round	Sheffield U	(a)	1-2

Carling Cup

Second Round	Bristol C	(a)	2-1
Third Round	Norwich C	(h)	1-0
Fourth Round	Bolton W	(a)	1-0
Quarter-Final	Tottenham H	(h)	0-2

MANCHESTER UNITED FA Premiership

FOUNDATION

Manchester United was formed as comparatively recently as 1902 after their predecessors, Newton Heath, went bankrupt. However, it is usual to give the date of the club's foundation as 1878 when the dining room committee of the carriage and waggon works of the Lancashire and Yorkshire Railway Company formed Newton Heath L and YR Cricket and Football Club. They won the Manchester Cup in 1886 and as Newton Heath FC were admitted to the Second Division in 1892.

Old Trafford, Sir Matt Busby Way, Manchester M16 0RA.

Telephone: (0161) 868 8000.

Fax: (0161) 868 8804.

Ticket Office: 0870 442 1968.

Website: www.manutd.com

Email: enquiries@manutd.co.uk

Ground Capacity: 76,212.

Record Attendance: 76,962 Wolverhampton W v Grimsby T, FA Cup semi-final, 25 March 1939.
Club Record Attendance: 76,098 v Blackburn R, FA Premier League, 31 March 2007.

Pitch Measurements: 105m × 68m.

Chief Executive: David Gill.

Secretary: Ken Ramsden.

Manager: Sir Alex Ferguson CBE.

Assistant Manager: TBC.

Physio: Robert Swire.

Colours: Red shirts, white shorts, black stockings.

Change Colours: All black.

Year Formed: 1878 as Newton Heath LYR; 1902, Manchester United.

Turned Professional: 1885. ***Ltd Co.:*** 1907.

Previous Name: 1880, Newton Heath; 1902, Manchester United.

Club Nickname: 'Red Devils'.

Grounds: 1880, North Road, Monsall Road; 1893, Bank Street; 1910, Old Trafford (played at Maine Road 1941–49).

First Football League Game: 3 September 1892, Division 1, v Blackburn R (a) L 3–4 – Warner; Clements, Brown; Perrins, Stewart, Erentz; Farman (1), Coupar (1), Donaldson (1), Carson, Mathieson.

HONOURS

FA Premier League – Champions 1992–93, 1993–94, 1995–96, 1996–97, 1998–99, 1999–2000, 2000–01, 2002–03, 2006–07, 2007–08; Runners-up 1994–95, 1997–98, 2005–06.

Football League: Division 1 – Champions 1907–08, 1910–11, 1951–52, 1955–56, 1956–57, 1964–65, 1966–67; Runners-up 1946–47, 1947–48, 1948–49, 1950–51, 1958–59, 1963–64, 1967–68, 1979–80, 1987–88, 1991–92. Division 2 – Champions 1935–36, 1974–75; Runners-up 1896–97, 1905–06, 1924–25, 1937–38.

FA Cup: Winners 1909, 1948, 1963, 1977, 1983, 1985, 1990, 1994, 1996, 1999, 2004; Runners-up 1957, 1958, 1976, 1979, 1995, 2005, 2007.

Football League Cup: Winners 1992, 2006; Runners-up 1983, 1991, 1994, 2003.

European Competitions: *European Cup:* 1956–57 (s-f), 1957–58 (s-f), 1965–66 (s-f), 1967–68 (winners), 1968–69 (s-f). *Champions League:* 1993–94, 1994–95, 1996–97 (s-f), 1997–98, 1998–99 (winners), 1999–2000, 2000–01, 2001–02 (s-f), 2002–03, 2003–04, 2004–05, 2005–06, 2006–07 (s-f), 2007–08 (winners). *European Cup-Winners' Cup:* 1963–64, 1977–78, 1983–84, 1990–91 (winners). 1991–92. *Inter Cities Fairs Cup:* 1964–65. *UEFA Cup:* 1976–77, 1980–81, 1982–83, 1984–85, 1992–93, 1995–96. *Super Cup:* 1991 (winners), 1999 (runners-up). *Inter-Continental Cup:* 1999 (winners), 1968 (runners-up).

SKY SPORTS FACT FILE

Ryan Giggs had a memorable 2007–08. On 8 December he scored his 100th League goal, on 20 February played in his 100th European cup game and in the Champions League final he caught up with Sir Bobby Charlton's record of 759 first class matches for Manchester United.

Record League Victory (as Newton Heath): 10–1 v Wolverhampton W, Division 1, 15 October 1892 – Warner; Mitchell, Clements; Perrins, Stewart (3), Erentz; Farman (1), Hood (1), Donaldson (3), Carson (1), Hendry (1).

Record League Victory (as Manchester U): 9–0 v Ipswich T, FA Premier League, 4 March 1995 – Schmeichel; Keane (1) (Sharpe), Irwin, Bruce (Butt), Kanchelskis, Pallister, Cole (5), Ince (1), McClair, Hughes (2), Giggs.

Record Cup Victory: 10–0 v RSC Anderlecht, European Cup prel. rd 2nd leg, 26 September 1956 – Wood; Foulkes, Byrne; Colman, Jones, Edwards; Berry (1), Whelan (2), Taylor (3), Viollet (4), Pegg.

Record Defeat: 0–7 v Blackburn R, Division 1, 10 April 1926. 0–7 v Aston Villa, Division 1, 27 December 1930. 0–7 v Wolverhampton W, Division 2, 26 December 1931.

Most League Points (2 for a win): 64, Division 1, 1956–57.

Most League Points (3 for a win): 92, FA Premier League, 1993–94.

Most League Goals: 103, Division 1, 1956–57 and 1958–59.

Highest League Scorer in Season: Dennis Viollet, 32, 1959–60.

Most League Goals in Total Aggregate: Bobby Charlton, 199, 1956–73.

Most Capped Player: Bobby Charlton, 106, England.

Most League Appearances: Bobby Charlton, 606, 1956–73.

Youngest League Player: Jeff Whitefoot, 16 years 105 days v Portsmouth, 15 April 1950.

Record Transfer Fee Received: £25,000,000 from Real Madrid for David Beckham, July 2003.

Record Transfer Fee Paid: £30,000,000 to Leeds U for Rio Ferdinand, July 2002.

Football League Record: 1892 Newton Heath elected to Division 1; 1894–1906 Division 2; 1906–22 Division 1; 1922–25 Division 2; 1925–31 Division 1; 1931–36 Division 2; 1936–37 Division 1; 1937–38 Division 2; 1938–74 Division 1; 1974–75 Division 2; 1975–92 Division 1; 1992– FA Premier League.

MANAGERS

J. Ernest Mangnall 1903–12
John Bentley 1912–14
John Robson 1914–21
(Secretary-Manager from 1916)
John Chapman 1921–26
Clarence Hilditch 1926–27
Herbert Bamlett 1927–31
Walter Crickmer 1931–32
Scott Duncan 1932–37
Walter Crickmer 1937–45
(Secretary-Manager)
Matt Busby 1945–69
(continued as General Manager then Director)
Wilf McGuinness 1969–70
Sir Matt Busby 1970–71
Frank O'Farrell 1971–72
Tommy Docherty 1972–77
Dave Sexton 1977–81
Ron Atkinson 1981–86
Sir Alex Ferguson November 1986–

LATEST SEQUENCES

Longest Sequence of League Wins: 14, 15.10.1904 – 3.1.1905.

Longest Sequence of League Defeats: 14, 26.4.1930 – 25.10.1930.

Longest Sequence of League Draws: 6, 30.10.1988 – 27.11.1988.

Longest Sequence of Unbeaten League Matches: 29, 26.12.1998 – 25.9.1999.

Longest Sequence Without a League Win: 16, 19.4.1930 – 25.10.1930.

Successive Scoring Runs: 27 from 11.10.1958.

Successive Non-scoring Runs: 5 from 22.2.1902.

TEN YEAR LEAGUE RECORD

		P	*W*	*D*	*L*	*F*	*A*	*Pts*	*Pos*
1998-99	PR Lge	38	22	13	3	80	37	79	1
1999-2000	PR Lge	38	28	7	3	97	45	91	1
2000-01	PR Lge	38	24	8	6	79	31	80	1
2001-02	PR Lge	38	24	5	9	87	45	77	3
2002-03	PR Lge	38	25	8	5	74	34	83	1
2003-04	PR Lge	38	23	6	9	64	35	75	3
2004-05	PR Lge	38	22	11	5	58	26	77	3
2005-06	PR Lge	38	25	8	5	72	34	83	2
2006-07	PR Lge	38	28	5	5	83	27	89	1
2007-08	PR Lge	38	27	6	5	80	22	87	1

DID YOU KNOW ?

Cristiano Ronaldo, with a double and back-to-back FWA and PFA player awards to his credit, scored 42 League and Cup goals in 2007–08 for Manchester United including three in the FA Cup and eight in the Champions League.

MANCHESTER UNITED 2007–08 LEAGUE RECORD

Match No.	*Date*	*Venue*	*Opponents*	*Result*	*H/T Score*	*Lg. Pos.*	*Goalscorers*	*Attendance*
1	Aug 12	H	Reading	D 0-0	0-0	—		75,655
2	15	A	Portsmouth	D 1-1	1-0	—	Scholes ^{15}	20,510
3	19	A	Manchester C	L 0-1	0-1	16		44,955
4	26	H	Tottenham H	W 1-0	0-0	10	Nani ^{68}	75,696
5	Sept 1	H	Sunderland	W 1-0	0-0	8	Saha ^{72}	75,648
6	15	A	Everton	W 1-0	0-0	4	Vidic ^{83}	39,364
7	23	H	Chelsea	W 2-0	1-0	2	Tevez ^{45}, Saha (pen) ^{90}	75,663
8	29	A	Birmingham C	W 1-0	0-0	2	Ronaldo ^{51}	26,526
9	Oct 6	H	Wigan Ath	W 4-0	0-0	2	Tevez ^{54}, Ronaldo 2 $^{59, 76}$, Rooney ^{82}	75,300
10	20	A	Aston Villa	W 4-1	3-1	2	Rooney 2 $^{36, 44}$, Ferdinand ^{45}, Giggs ^{75}	42,640
11	27	H	Middlesbrough	W 4-1	2-1	2	Nani ^{3}, Rooney ^{33}, Tevez 2 $^{55, 85}$	75,720
12	Nov 3	A	Arsenal	D 2-2	1-0	2	Gallas (og) ^{45}, Ronaldo ^{82}	60,161
13	11	H	Blackburn R	W 2-0	2-0	1	Ronaldo 2 $^{34, 35}$	75,710
14	24	A	Bolton W	L 0-1	0-1	2		25,028
15	Dec 3	H	Fulham	W 2-0	1-0	—	Ronaldo 2 $^{10, 58}$	75,055
16	8	H	Derby Co	W 4-1	2-0	2	Giggs ^{40}, Tevez 2 $^{45, 60}$, Ronaldo (pen) ^{90}	75,725
17	16	A	Liverpool	W 1-0	1-0	2	Tevez ^{43}	44,459
18	23	H	Everton	W 2-1	1-1	2	Ronaldo 2 (1 pen) $^{22, 88 (p)}$	75,749
19	26	A	Sunderland	W 4-0	3-0	1	Rooney ^{20}, Saha 2 (1 pen) $^{30, 86 (p)}$, Ronaldo ^{45}	47,360
20	29	A	West Ham U	L 1-2	1-0	2	Ronaldo ^{14}	34,956
21	Jan 1	H	Birmingham C	W 1-0	1-0	2	Tevez ^{25}	75,459
22	12	H	Newcastle U	W 6-0	0-0	1	Ronaldo 3 $^{49, 70, 88}$, Tevez 2 $^{55, 90}$, Ferdinand ^{85}	75,965
23	19	A	Reading	W 2-0	0-0	1	Rooney ^{77}, Ronaldo ^{90}	24,135
24	30	H	Portsmouth	W 2-0	2-0	—	Ronaldo 2 $^{10, 13}$	75,415
25	Feb 2	A	Tottenham H	D 1-1	0-1	2	Tevez ^{90}	36,075
26	10	H	Manchester C	L 1-2	0-2	2	Carrick ^{90}	75,970
27	23	A	Newcastle U	W 5-1	2-0	2	Rooney 2 $^{25, 80}$, Ronaldo 2 $^{45, 56}$, Saha ^{90}	52,291
28	Mar 1	A	Fulham	W 3-0	2-0	2	Hargreaves ^{15}, Park ^{44}, Davies (og) ^{72}	25,314
29	15	A	Derby Co	W 1-0	0-0	1	Ronaldo ^{76}	33,072
30	19	H	Bolton W	W 2-0	2-0	—	Ronaldo 2 $^{9, 19}$	75,476
31	23	H	Liverpool	W 3-0	1-0	1	Brown ^{34}, Ronaldo ^{79}, Nani ^{81}	76,000
32	29	H	Aston Villa	W 4-0	2-0	1	Ronaldo ^{17}, Tevez ^{33}, Rooney 2 $^{53, 70}$	75,932
33	Apr 6	A	Middlesbrough	D 2-2	1-1	1	Ronaldo ^{10}, Rooney ^{74}	33,952
34	13	H	Arsenal	W 2-1	0-0	1	Ronaldo (pen) ^{54}, Hargreaves ^{72}	75,985
35	19	A	Blackburn R	D 1-1	0-1	1	Tevez ^{88}	30,316
36	26	A	Chelsea	L 1-2	0-1	1	Rooney ^{57}	41,828
37	May 3	H	West Ham U	W 4-1	3-1	1	Ronaldo 2 $^{3, 24}$, Tevez ^{26}, Carrick ^{59}	76,013
38	11	A	Wigan Ath	W 2-0	1-0	1	Ronaldo (pen) ^{33}, Giggs ^{80}	25,133

Final League Position: 1

GOALSCORERS

League (80): Ronaldo 31 (4 pens), Tevez 14, Rooney 12, Saha 5 (2 pens), Giggs 3, Nani 3, Carrick 2, Ferdinand 2, Hargreaves 2, Brown 1, Park 1, Scholes 1, Vidic 1, own goals 2.
Carling Cup (0).
FA Cup (9): Ronaldo 3 (1 pen), Fletcher 2, Rooney 2, Nani 1, Tevez 1.
Champions League (20): Ronaldo 8 (1 pen), Rooney 4, Tevez 4, Pique 2, Ferdinand 1, Scholes 1.
Community Shield (1): Giggs 1.

Van der Sar E 29	Brown W 34 + 2	Silvestre M 3	Carrick M 24 + 7	Ferdinand R 35	Vidic N 32	Ronaldo C 31 + 3	Scholes P 22 + 2	Giggs R 26 + 5	Rooney W 25 + 2	Evra P 33	Nani 16 + 10	O'Shea J 10 + 18	Fletcher D 5 + 11	Tevez C 31 + 3	Eagles C 1 + 3	Hargreaves O 16 + 7	Campbell F — + 1	Anderson 16 + 8	Saha L 6 + 11	Pique G 5 + 4	Kuszczak T 8 + 1	Simpson D 1 + 2	Park J 8 + 4	Foster B 1	*Match No.*
1	2^{3}	3^{2}	4	5	6	7	8	9	10^{1}	11	12	13	14												1
1	2^{2}		4	5	6	7■	8	11^{1}		3	9	12		10	13										2
1	2^{1}		4^{3}	5	6		8	11		3	9^{2}	12		10	13	7	14								3
1	2		4^{2}	5	6		8	9		3	7		12	10^{1}	13	11									4
1	2			5	6		8			3	11^{1}	12	13	10	7^{2}	4		9^{3}	14						5
1	2	3^{1}	4	5	6	7	8	9^{3}		11	12^{2}			10					14	13					6
1	2		4	5	6	7	8	11	9	3				10^{1}					12						7
1^{G}	2		4	5	6	7	8	11^{2}	9	3		12		10^{1}					13		15				8
				5	6^{2}	7	8	11	9	3	12	4^{3}		10^{1}				13		2	1	14			9
1	4			5		12	8^{2}	11^{1}	9	3	7	13	14	10^{3}				6		2					10
1	2			5^{3}	6	7		12	9		11	3	13	10		4^{2}		8^{1}		14					11
1	2^{1}		13	5	6	7		11	9	3		12		10^{3}		4		8^{2}	14						12
1	2		12	5	6	7		11		3	13			10		4^{1}		8	9^{2}						13
1	2^{1}		4	5				11		3	7	12		10		8		13	9	6^{2}					14
1	2		12	5^{1}	6	7		11	9^{3}	3^{2}		13		10		4		8	14						15
1	2		4	5^{1}	6	7		11^{3}	9	3		12	13	10				8^{2}	14						16
1	2		12	5	6	7		11	9	3		13		10^{1}		4		8^{2}							17
	5		4^{3}		6	7		11	9	3		12	13	10				8^{2}	14		1	2^{1}			18
	3		4	5	6^{1}	7^{2}			9		11	2	8						10	12	1		13		19
	2^{1}			5	6	7		11		3	13	12	8	10^{3}		4^{2}		14	9		1				20
	12		4	5	6	7				3^{1}	11	2		10^{3}		13		8	14		1		9^{2}		21
1			4	5	6	7		11^{2}	9	3^{3}	13	2	12	10				8^{1}				14			22
1	2		4	5	6	7		12	9	3	13		14	10^{3}		8^{2}							11^{1}		23
1	2		4	5	6	7^{2}	8^{3}		9^{1}	3	11			12		13		14					10		24
1	2		12	5	6	7	8^{3}	11^{2}	9	3	13			10		4^{1}		14							25
1	2		12	5	6	9	8	11			7^{3}	3^{1}		10		13		4^{2}					14		26
1	2		4	5	6^{1}	7^{3}	12		9	3^{2}	11	13	8	10					14						27
1	2			5		12	8		13	3	7^{3}	6		10^{1}		4		14	9^{2}				11		28
	5		12		6	10	8^{1}	11	9	3		2	13					4^{2}	14				7^{3}	1	29
	12				6^{1}	7	13		14		11	3	8	10		2		4^{2}	9^{3}	5	1				30
1	2		4	5	6	7	8	11^{2}	9	3	13			12				10^{1}							31
	2		4^{3}	5^{2}	6	7	8	11	9	3^{1}		12		10		13		14			1				32
1	6		4	5^{3}		7	8	11	9	3		2^{1}		10^{2}		12				14			13		33
1	2		4	5		7	8^{3}	12	9	3				13		10^{1}		14		6			11^{2}		34
	2^{1}		4	5	6	7	8	11^{2}	9^{3}	3	13	12		10							1		14		35
1	2	3	4	5	6^{3}	12		10	9^{1}		11	13	7			14		8^{2}							36
1	6		4	5		9^{1}	8^{2}	14		3	7■	13	12	10		2							11^{3}		37
1	2		4	5	6	7	8^{2}	12	9	3				10		13							11^{1}		38

Champions League

Group F	Sporting Lisbon	(a)	1-0
	Roma	(h)	1-0
	Dynamo Kiev	(a)	4-2
		(h)	4-0
	Sporting Lisbon	(h)	2-1
	Roma	(a)	1-1
Knock-Out Round	Lyon	(a)	1-1
		(h)	1-0
Quarter-Final	Roma	(a)	2-0
		(h)	1-0
Semi-Final	Barcelona	(a)	0-0
		(h)	1-0
Final *(in Moscow)*	Chelsea		1-1

FA Cup

Third Round	Aston Villa	(a)	2-0
Fourth Round	Tottenham H	(h)	3-1
Fifth Round	Arsenal	(h)	4-0
Sixth Round	Portsmouth	(h)	0-1

Carling Cup

Third Round	Coventry C	(h)	0-2

Community Shield

	Chelsea		1-1

MANSFIELD TOWN Blue Square Premier

FOUNDATION

The club was formed as Mansfield Wesleyans in 1897, and changed their name to Mansfield Wesley in 1906 and Mansfield Town in 1910. This was after the Mansfield Wesleyan Chapel trustees had requested that the club change its name as 'it has no longer had any connection with either the chapel or school'. The new club participated in the Notts and Derby District League, but in the following season 1911–12 joined the Central Alliance.

Field Mill Ground, Quarry Lane, Mansfield, Notts NG18 5DA.

Telephone: 0870 756 3160.

Fax: (01623) 482 495.

Ticket Office: 0870 756 3160.

Website: www.mansfieldtown.net

Email: info@mansfieldtown.net

Ground Capacity: 7,225.

Record Attendance: 24,467 v Nottingham F, FA Cup 3rd rd, 10 January 1953.

Pitch Measurements: 113yd × 70yd.

Chairman: Tony Egginton.

Chief Executive: Stephen Booth.

Secretary: Sharon Roberts.

Manager: Billy McEwan.

Assistant Manager: Ivan Hollett.

Physio: Paul Madin IIST, SPORTS THERAPY DIP.

Colours: Amber shirts, blue shorts, amber stockings.

Change Colours: Light blue shirts, navy shorts, light blue stockings.

Year Formed: 1897.

Turned Professional: 1906.

Ltd Co.: 1922.

Previous Name: 1897, Mansfield Wesleyans; 1906, Mansfield Wesley; 1910, Mansfield Town.

Grounds: 1897–99, Westfield Lane; 1899–1901, Ratcliffe Gate; 1901–12, Newgate Lane; 1912–16, Ratcliffe Gate; 1916, Field Mill.

Club Nickname: 'The Stags'.

First Football League Game: 29 August 1931, Division 3 (S), v Swindon T (h) W 3–2 – Wilson; Clifford, England; Wake, Davis, Blackburn; Gilhespy, Readman (1), Johnson, Broom (2), Baxter.

Record League Victory: 9–2 v Rotherham U, Division 3 (N), 27 December 1932 – Wilson; Anthony, England; Davies, S. Robinson, Slack; Prior, Broom, Readman (3), Hoyland (3), Bowater (3).

HONOURS

Football League: Division 2 best season: 21st, 1977–78; Division 3 – Champions 1976–77; Promoted to Division 2 (3rd) 2001–02; Division 4 – Champions 1974–75; Division 3 (N) – Runners-up 1950–51.

FA Cup: best season: 6th rd, 1969.

Football League Cup: best season: 5th rd, 1976.

Freight Rover Trophy: Winners 1987.

SKY SPORTS FACT FILE

Despite the disappointment of the 2007–08 season for Mansfield Town striker, Michael Boulding, the former professional tennis player, served the club well in the scoring department with 24 League and cup goals to his credit.

Record Cup Victory: 8–0 v Scarborough (a), FA Cup 1st rd, 22 November 1952 – Bramley; Chessell, Bradley; Field, Plummer, Lewis; Scott, Fox (3), Marron (2), Sid Watson (1), Adam (2).

Record Defeat: 1–8 v Walsall, Division 3 (N), 19 January 1933.

Most League Points (2 for a win): 68, Division 4, 1974–75.

Most League Points (3 for a win): 81, Division 4, 1985–86.

Most League Goals: 108, Division 4, 1962–63.

Highest League Scorer in Season: Ted Harston, 55, Division 3 (N), 1936–37.

Most League Goals in Total Aggregate: Harry Johnson, 104, 1931–36.

Most League Goals in One Match: 7, Ted Harston v Hartlepools U, Division 3N, 23 January 1937.

Most Capped Player: John McClelland, 6 (53), Northern Ireland.

Most League Appearances: Rod Arnold, 440, 1970–83.

Youngest League Player: Cyril Poole, 15 years 351 days v New Brighton, 27 February 1937.

Record Transfer Fee Received: £655,000 from Tottenham H for Colin Calderwood, July 1993.

Record Transfer Fee Paid: £150,000 to Carlisle U for Lee Peacock, October 1997.

Football League Record: 1931 Elected to Division 3 (S); 1932–37 Division 3 (N); 1937–47 Division 3 (S); 1947–58 Division 3 (N); 1958–60 Division 3; 1960–63 Division 4; 1963–72 Division 3; 1972–75 Division 4; 1975–77 Division 3; 1977–78 Division 2; 1978–80 Division 3; 1980–86 Division 4; 1986–91 Division 3; 1991–92 Division 4; 1992–93 Division 2; 1993–2002 Division 3; 2002–03 Division 2; 2003–04 Division 3; 2004–08 FL 2; 2008– Blue Square Premier.

MANAGERS

John Baynes 1922–25
Ted Davison 1926–28
Jack Hickling 1928–33
Henry Martin 1933–35
Charlie Bell 1935
Harold Wightman 1936
Harold Parkes 1936–38
Jack Poole 1938–44
Lloyd Barke 1944–45
Roy Goodall 1945–49
Freddie Steele 1949–51
George Jobey 1952–53
Stan Mercer 1953–55
Charlie Mitten 1956–58
Sam Weaver 1958–60
Raich Carter 1960–63
Tommy Cummings 1963–67
Tommy Eggleston 1967–70
Jock Basford 1970–71
Danny Williams 1971–74
Dave Smith 1974–76
Peter Morris 1976–78
Billy Bingham 1978–79
Mick Jones 1979–81
Stuart Boam 1981–83
Ian Greaves 1983–89
George Foster 1989–93
Andy King 1993–96
Steve Parkin 1996–99
Billy Dearden 1999–2002
Stuart Watkiss 2002
Keith Curle 2002–05
Carlton Palmer 2005
Peter Shirtliff 2005–06
Billy Dearden 2006–08
Paul Holland 2008
Billy McEwan June 2008–

LATEST SEQUENCES

Longest Sequence of League Wins: 7, 13.9.1991 – 26.10.1991.

Longest Sequence of League Defeats: 7, 18.1.1947 – 15.3.1947.

Longest Sequence of League Draws: 5, 18.10.1986 – 22.11.1986.

Longest Sequence of Unbeaten League Matches: 20, 14.2.1976 – 21.8.1976.

Longest Sequence Without a League Win: 14, 25.3.2000 – 2.9.2000.

Successive Scoring Runs: 27 from 1.10.1962.

Successive Non-scoring Runs: 8 from 25.3.2000.

TEN YEAR LEAGUE RECORD

		P	*W*	*D*	*L*	*F*	*A*	*Pts*	*Pos*
1998-99	Div 3	46	19	10	17	60	58	67	8
1999-2000	Div 3	46	16	8	22	50	65	56	17
2000-01	Div 3	46	15	13	18	64	72	68	13
2001-02	Div 3	46	24	7	15	72	60	79	3
2002-03	Div 2	46	12	8	26	66	97	44	23
2003-04	Div 3	46	22	9	15	76	62	75	5
2004-05	FL 2	46	15	15	16	56	56	60	13
2005-06	FL 2	46	13	15	18	59	66	54	16
2006-07	FL 2	46	14	12	20	58	63	54	17
2007-08	FL 2	46	11	9	26	48	68	42	23

DID YOU KNOW?

Full-back Ernest England – known as Mac – joined Mansfield Town in 1931 after a long career with Sunderland including their 1922–23 runners-up season. At Roker Park he received FA representative recognition and came to Field Mill from West Ham United.

MANSFIELD TOWN 2007–08 LEAGUE RECORD

Match No.	Date	Venue	Opponents	Result		H/T Score	Lg. Pos.	Goalscorers	Attendance
1	Aug 11	A	Brentford	D	1-1	1-1	—	Boulding M [23]	4909
2	18	H	Lincoln C	L	1-3	1-2	23	Boulding M (pen) [36]	3357
3	25	A	Morecambe	L	1-3	1-2	22	Boulding M [40]	2980
4	Sept 1	H	Stockport Co	W	4-2	4-2	18	McAliskey [3], McIntosh [9], Buxton [25], Boulding M (pen) [32]	2747
5	9	A	Peterborough U	L	1-2	0-1	19	McAliskey [53]	4721
6	15	H	Chesterfield	L	1-3	1-2	22	Dawson [9]	4514
7	22	A	Accrington S	L	0-1	0-1	23		1408
8	29	H	Dagenham & R	L	0-1	0-0	24		2048
9	Oct 2	H	Milton Keynes D	L	1-2	1-0	—	Boulding M [29]	1984
10	6	A	Rotherham U	L	2-3	0-2	24	Boulding M [76], Arnold [83]	3881
11	13	A	Barnet	D	1-1	0-0	24	Brown [47]	2041
12	20	H	Notts Co	W	2-0	0-0	24	Boulding M 2 (1 pen) [57 (p), 61]	4002
13	27	A	Shrewsbury T	D	0-0	0-0	22		5347
14	Nov 3	H	Macclesfield T	W	5-0	4-0	20	Brown 3 [8, 19, 22], Arnold [21], Boulding M [54]	2853
15	6	A	Hereford U	L	1-2	0-1	—	Boulding M [66]	2272
16	24	A	Rochdale	L	0-1	0-0	22		2431
17	Dec 5	H	Bradford C	D	0-0	0-0	—		2308
18	15	A	Grimsby T	L	0-1	0-0	24		3836
19	22	A	Chesterfield	L	0-2	0-0	24		6300
20	26	H	Peterborough U	W	2-0	1-0	23	Boulding M 2 [35, 61]	3107
21	29	H	Accrington S	L	1-2	0-0	23	Holmes [90]	2494
22	Jan 1	A	Milton Keynes D	L	0-1	0-0	23		9583
23	8	H	Wycombe W	L	0-4	0-1	—		1959
24	12	A	Chester C	W	1-0	0-0	23	Hamshaw [49]	2092
25	19	H	Darlington	L	0-1	0-1	23		3344
26	29	A	Lincoln C	W	2-1	0-0	—	Boulding M 2 [49, 90]	4280
27	Feb 2	H	Brentford	L	2-3	1-1	24	Elder (og) [15], Louis [64]	2511
28	9	A	Wycombe W	W	2-1	1-1	22	Boulding M (pen) [9], Louis [90]	5963
29	12	H	Morecambe	L	1-2	0-2	—	Bell [48]	2287
30	16	A	Darlington	W	2-1	0-1	23	Louis [56], Dawson [64]	3527
31	23	H	Chester C	L	1-3	1-0	23	Mullins [45]	2362
32	26	H	Bury	D	1-1	0-0	—	Buxton [56]	1923
33	Mar 1	A	Wrexham	D	1-1	0-0	23	Boulding M [53]	4865
34	8	H	Rochdale	L	0-4	0-1	23		2351
35	11	H	Hereford U	L	0-1	0-1	—		1606
36	15	A	Bradford C	W	2-1	1-1	23	Arnold [14], Boulding M [51]	13,611
37	22	H	Grimsby T	L	1-2	0-1	23	Arnold [49]	2616
38	24	A	Bury	L	0-2	0-2	23		2779
39	29	A	Notts Co	D	0-0	0-0	23		10,027
40	Apr 1	H	Wrexham	W	2-1	0-0	—	Louis (pen) [51], Mullins [54]	3435
41	5	H	Barnet	D	2-2	1-0	23	Boulding M [14], Hamshaw [55]	2463
42	9	A	Stockport Co	L	1-2	1-1	—	Dicker (og) [39]	4982
43	12	A	Macclesfield T	D	0-0	0-0	23		3250
44	19	H	Shrewsbury T	W	3-1	2-1	23	Boulding M 3 [22, 37, 87]	3334
45	26	H	Rotherham U	L	0-1	0-0	23		5271
46	May 3	A	Dagenham & R	L	0-2	0-0	23		3451

Final League Position: 23

GOALSCORERS

League (48): Boulding M 21 (4 pens), Arnold 4, Brown 4, Louis 4 (1 pen), Buxton 2, Dawson 2, Hamshaw 2, McAliskey 2, Mullins 2, Bell 1, Holmes 1, McIntosh 1, own goals 2.
Carling Cup (1): Mullins 1.
FA Cup (8): Boulding M 3, Holmes 2, Boulding R 1, Hamshaw 1, Jelleyman 1.
J Paint Trophy (0).

White J 10 + 3	John-Baptiste A 25	Jelleyman G 37 + 2	Dawson S 43	Buxton J 40	McIntosh M 9 + 2	Hamshaw M 45	Bell L 23	McAliskey J 9 + 7	Boulding M 43	Martin D 21 + 5	Arnold N 21 + 11	Reet D — + 2	Mullins J 42 + 1	Sleath D 2 + 5	Boulding R 4 + 7	Muggleton C 36	Holmes I 4 + 12	Bullock L 5	McAllister S 5 + 2	Wood C 8 + 5	Burrell W — + 1	Brown S 15 + 14	Kitchen A 1	Goward R — + 2	D'Laryea J 23 + 6	Trimmer L — + 2	Atkinson W 10 + 2	Louis J 14 + 4	Briggs K 10 + 3	Horlock K — + 5	Wainwright N 1 + 4	*Match No.*
1	2	3	4	5	6	7^1	8	9^2	10	11^3	12	13	14																			1
1	2	3	4	5	6	7	8^2	9	10	11^1	12			13																		2
1		3^2	4	5	6	7	8	9^3	10		13	12	2	11^1	14																	3
		3	4	5	6^2	7	8■	9^1	10	13			2			1	12	11														4
		3^1	4	5	6	7		9	10		13		2			1	12	11	8^2													5
		3	4	5■	6	7		9^1	10				2	13		1	12	11	8^2													6
		3	4		6^2	7			10	13	12		2			1	9^3	8	11^1	5		14										7
	6		4	5		7	8^3	9^1	10	14	13		2			1		11		3^2		12										8
15	6		4	5		7	8	12	10	3	13		2			1^6			11^1			9^2										9
15	6		4			7^1	8	12	10	11	13		2			1^6			3			9	5^2									10
	6		4	5		7	8		10	3^2	11^1		2	12		1						9		13								11
	6	12	4	5		7	8		10	3	11^1		2			1						9										12
	6	12	4	5		7^1	8		10	3^2	11^3		2■	13		1			14			9										13
	6	3^3	4	5		7	8	12	10^1	2	11					1	13					9^2			14							14
	6		4	5		7	8^1		10	3	11^3		2			1	13		12			9^2			14							15
	6	11^2	4	5		7^3	8	12	10	3			2		9^1	1	13								14							16
	6	11	4	5		7	8^1		10	3			2		9	1						12										17
	6	3	4	5	12	7		13	10				2^1		9^2	1						11			8							18
	6	3^2	4^1	5	12	7			10		11		2		13	1	14					9			8^3							19
		3	4		5	7		9^1	10^2	6	11		2		13	1						12			8							20
		3^1		5^2	6■	7		9^3	10	4	11		2		14	1	13					12			8							21
		3	11	5		7		13^3	10^2	4	12		2	6^1		1	14					9			8							22
		3	4	5			7^1			2^2	11		6	12		1	10					9			8	13						23
		3	4			7	11			6			5		12	1	10^1			2		9			8							24
		3	4	5		7	11	12	10	6^2			2			1	13					9			8^1							25
		3	4	5		7	11^3		10	6^1			2			1	13			12		9^2			8		14					26
		3	4	5		7	11		10				2			1	9^2			6					8^1		12	13				27
		3	4	5		7^1	8		10	11			2			1									12		6	9				28
		3	4	5^2		7	8		10	2^3			6			1	13			14		12					11^1	9				29
		3	4	5		7	8^1		10				6			1				14		13			12^2		11	9	2^3			30
		3^1	4	5		7			10				6			1						12			8		11	9	2			31
		3		5		7			10				4			1				6					8		11	9	2			32
		3		5		7^1			10		12		4			1				6					8		11	9	2			33
	6^2	3^3	4	5		7			10		13		8			1				12					14		11	9	2^1			34
15	6	3^2	4	5		7			10		9		2		12	1^6									8^1		11	13				35
1	6	3	4	5		7^2			10	12	9		2												8^1		11^3	14	13			36
1	6	3	4	5		7^1			10		9		2												8^2		11^3	12		13	14	37
1	6	3	4	5		7			10		9		2									12							8^2	13	11^1	38
	6	3	4	5		7			10		11		2			1						12			8			9^1				39
	6	3	4	5		7^2			10^3		11		2		12	1									8			9^1	13	14		40
	6	3	4	5		7			10		11^2		2			1						12			8			9^1			13	41
	6	3^1	4^3	5■		7			10		11		2			1									8			9^2	12	13	14	42
1	6	3^2	4			7			10^3		11^1		5							13		12			8			9	2		14	43
1	6		4^3			7			10	12	11^2		5							3^1		13			8			9	2	14		44
1		3	6	5		7			10		11		2									12			8			9^1	4			45
1			4	5■		7	8			3^1	11^3				9^2					6	14	10		12		13			2			46

FA Cup

First Round	Lewes	(h)	3-0
Second Round	Harrogate R	(a)	3-2
Third Round	Brighton & HA	(a)	2-1
Fourth Round	Middlesbrough	(h)	0-2

Carling Cup

First Round	Oldham Ath	(a)	1-4

J Paint Trophy

First Round	Rotherham U	(h)	0-1

MIDDLESBROUGH — FA Premiership

FOUNDATION

A previous belief that Middlesbrough Football Club was founded at a tripe supper at the Corporation Hotel has proved to be erroneous. In fact, members of Middlesbrough Cricket Club were responsible for forming it at a meeting in the gymnasium of the Albert Park Hotel in 1875.

Riverside Stadium, Middlesbrough TS3 6RS.

Telephone: 0844 499 6789.

Fax: (01642) 757 690.

Ticket Office: 0844 499 2676.

Website: www.mfc.co.uk

Email: enquiries@mfc.co.uk

Ground Capacity: 35,041.

Record Attendance: Ayresome Park: 53,536 v Newcastle U, Division 1, 27 December 1949. Riverside Stadium: 34,814 v Newcastle U, FA Premier League, 5 March 2003.

Pitch Measurements: 105m × 68m.

Chairman: Steve Gibson.

Chief Executive: Keith Lamb.

Secretary: Karen Nelson.

Manager: Gareth Southgate.

Assistant Manager: Malcolm Crosby.

Physio: Grant Downie.

Colours: Red shirts with white chestband, red shorts, red stockings.

Change Colours: TBC.

Year Formed: 1876; reformed 1986.

Turned Professional: 1889; became amateur 1892, and professional again, 1899.

Ltd Co: 1892.

Club Nickname: 'Boro'.

Grounds: 1877, Old Archery Ground, Albert Park; 1879, Breckon Hill; 1882, Linthorpe Road Ground; 1903, Ayresome Park; 1995, Riverside Stadium.

First Football League Game: 2 September 1899, Division 2, v Lincoln C (a) L 0–3 – Smith; Shaw, Ramsey; Allport, McNally, McCracken; Wanless, Longstaffe, Gettins, Page, Pugh.

Record League Victory: 9–0 v Brighton & HA, Division 2, 23 August 1958 – Taylor; Bilcliff, Robinson; Harris (2p), Phillips, Walley; Day, McLean, Clough (5), Peacock (2), Holliday.

Record Cup Victory: 7–0 v Hereford U, Coca-Cola Cup 2nd rd, 1st leg, 18 September 1996 – Miller; Fleming (1), Branco (1), Whyte, Vickers, Whelan, Emerson (1), Mustoe, Stamp, Juninho, Ravanelli (4).

HONOURS

Football League: Division 1 – Champions 1994–95; Runners-up 1997–98; Division 2 – Champions 1926–27, 1928–29, 1973–74; Runners-up 1901–02, 1991–92; Division 3 – Runners-up 1966–67, 1986–87.

FA Cup: Runners-up 1997.

Football League Cup: Winners 2004; Runners-up 1997, 1998.

Amateur Cup: Winners 1895, 1898.

Anglo-Scottish Cup: Winners 1976.

Zenith Data Systems Cup: Runners-up 1990.

European Competitions: *UEFA Cup:* 2004–05, 2005–06 (runners-up).

SKY SPORTS FACT FILE

One of George Camsell's finest solo performances for Middlesbrough was achieved on the last day of the 1930–31 season when he scored all four goals at Old Trafford against Manchester United to earn a point for his team in the eight-goal thriller.

Record Defeat: 0–9 v Blackburn R, Division 2, 6 November 1954.

Most League Points (2 for a win): 65, Division 2, 1973–74.

Most League Points (3 for a win): 94, Division 3, 1986–87.

Most League Goals: 122, Division 2, 1926–27.

Highest League Scorer in Season: George Camsell, 59, Division 2, 1926–27 (Second Division record).

Most League Goals in Total Aggregate: George Camsell, 325, 1925–39.

Most League Goals in One Match: 5, John Wilkie v Gainsborough T, Division 2, 2 March 1901; 5, Andy Wilson v Nottingham F, Division 1, 6 October 1923; 5, George Camsell v Manchester C, Division 2, 25 December 1926; 5, George Camsell v Aston Villa, Division 1, 9 September 1935; 5, Brian Clough v Brighton & HA, Division 2, 22 August 1958.

Most Capped Player: Wilf Mannion, 26, England.

Most League Appearances: Tim Williamson, 563, 1902–23.

Youngest League Player: Stephen Bell, 16 years 323 days v Southampton, 30 January 1982; Sam Lawrie, 16 years 323 days v Arsenal, 3 November 1951.

Record Transfer Fee Received: £12,000,000 from Atletico Madrid for Juninho, July 1997.

Record Transfer Fee Paid: £8,150,000 to Empoli for Massimo Maccarone, August 2002.

Football League Record: 1899 Elected to Division 2; 1902–24 Division 1; 1924–27 Division 2; 1927–28 Division 1; 1928–29 Division 2; 1929–54 Division 1; 1954–66 Division 2; 1966–67 Division 3; 1967–74 Division 2; 1974–82 Division 1; 1982–86 Division 2; 1986–87 Division 3; 1987–88 Division 2; 1988–89 Division 1; 1989–92 Division 2; 1992–93 FA Premier League; 1993–95 Division 1; 1995–97 FA Premier League; 1997–98 Division 1; 1998– FA Premier League.

MANAGERS

John Robson 1899–1905
Alex Mackie 1905–06
Andy Aitken 1906–09
J. Gunter 1908–10
(Secretary-Manager)
Andy Walker 1910–11
Tom McIntosh 1911–19
Jimmy Howie 1920–23
Herbert Bamlett 1923–26
Peter McWilliam 1927–34
Wilf Gillow 1934–44
David Jack 1944–52
Walter Rowley 1952–54
Bob Dennison 1954–63
Raich Carter 1963–66
Stan Anderson 1966–73
Jack Charlton 1973–77
John Neal 1977–81
Bobby Murdoch 1981–82
Malcolm Allison 1982–84
Willie Maddren 1984–86
Bruce Rioch 1986–90
Colin Todd 1990–91
Lennie Lawrence 1991–94
Bryan Robson 1994–2001
Steve McClaren 2001–06
Gareth Southgate June 2006–

LATEST SEQUENCES

Longest Sequence of League Wins: 9, 16.2.1974 – 6.4.1974.

Longest Sequence of League Defeats: 8, 26.12.1995 – 17.2.1996.

Longest Sequence of League Draws: 8, 3.4.1971 – 1.5.1971.

Longest Sequence of Unbeaten League Matches: 24, 8.9.1973 – 19.1.1974.

Longest Sequence Without a League Win: 19, 3.10.1981 – 6.3.1982.

Successive Scoring Runs: 26 from 21.9.1946.

Successive Non-scoring Runs: 4 from 24.11.1923.

TEN YEAR LEAGUE RECORD

		P	*W*	*D*	*L*	*F*	*A*	*Pts*	*Pos*
1998-99	PR Lge	38	12	15	11	48	54	51	9
1999-2000	PR Lge	38	14	10	14	46	52	52	12
2000-01	PR Lge	38	9	15	14	44	44	42	14
2001-02	PR Lge	38	12	9	17	35	47	45	12
2002-03	PR Lge	38	13	10	15	48	44	49	11
2003-04	PR Lge	38	13	9	16	44	52	48	11
2004-05	PR Lge	38	14	13	11	53	46	55	7
2005-06	PR Lge	38	12	9	17	48	58	45	14
2006-07	PR Lge	38	12	10	16	44	49	46	12
2007-08	PR Lge	38	10	12	16	43	53	42	13

DID YOU KNOW ?

When Afonso Alves scored a hat-trick in Middlesbrough's 8–1 win over Manchester City on 11 May 2008, it was the second game in which he figured where nine goals had been scored that season. On 7 October 2007 he had hit seven of the Heerenveen goals in their 9–0 win over Heracles for an individual Dutch scoring record.

MIDDLESBROUGH 2007–08 LEAGUE RECORD

Match No.	Date	Venue	Opponents	Result	H/T Score	Lg. Pos.	Goalscorers	Attendance
1	Aug 11	H	Blackburn R	L 1-2	1-0	—	Downing [31]	25,058
2	15	A	Wigan Ath	L 0-1	0-0	—		14,007
3	18	A	Fulham	W 2-1	0-1	14	Mido [55], Cattermole [88]	20,948
4	26	H	Newcastle U	D 2-2	1-1	13	Mido [28], Arca [80]	28,875
5	Sept 1	H	Birmingham C	W 2-0	2-0	12	Wheater [12], Downing [37]	22,920
6	15	A	West Ham U	L 0-3	0-0	13		34,351
7	22	H	Sunderland	D 2-2	1-1	13	Arca [15], Downing [67]	30,675
8	30	A	Everton	L 0-2	0-1	14		31,885
9	Oct 7	A	Manchester C	L 1-3	0-2	15	Hutchinson [89]	40,438
10	20	H	Chelsea	L 0-2	0-1	17		27,699
11	27	A	Manchester U	L 1-4	1-2	17	Aliadiere [6]	75,720
12	Nov 3	H	Tottenham H	D 1-1	0-1	16	Young [52]	25,625
13	11	A	Bolton W	D 0-0	0-0	17		17,624
14	24	H	Aston Villa	L 0-3	0-1	17		23,900
15	Dec 1	A	Reading	D 1-1	0-0	18	Tuncay [83]	22,262
16	9	H	Arsenal	W 2-1	1-0	16	Downing (pen) [4], Tuncay [74]	26,428
17	15	A	Derby Co	W 1-0	1-0	14	Tuncay [38]	32,676
18	22	H	West Ham U	L 1-2	1-1	15	Wheater [40]	26,007
19	26	A	Birmingham C	L 0-3	0-2	16		24,094
20	29	A	Portsmouth	W 1-0	1-0	14	Tuncay [20]	20,089
21	Jan 1	H	Everton	L 0-2	0-0	14		27,028
22	12	H	Liverpool	D 1-1	1-0	14	Boateng [26]	33,035
23	19	A	Blackburn R	D 1-1	1-0	13	Wheater [13]	21,687
24	29	H	Wigan Ath	W 1-0	1-0	—	Aliadiere [19]	22,963
25	Feb 3	A	Newcastle U	D 1-1	0-0	13	Huth [87]	51,105
26	9	H	Fulham	W 1-0	1-0	12	Aliadiere [11]	26,885
27	23	A	Liverpool	L 2-3	1-2	12	Tuncay [9], Downing [83]	43,612
28	Mar 1	H	Reading	L 0-1	0-0	12		23,273
29	12	A	Aston Villa	D 1-1	1-0	—	Downing [23]	39,874
30	15	A	Arsenal	D 1-1	1-0	13	Aliadiere [25]	60,084
31	22	H	Derby Co	W 1-0	1-0	12	Tuncay [32]	25,649
32	30	A	Chelsea	L 0-1	0-1	13		39,993
33	Apr 6	H	Manchester U	D 2-2	1-1	14	Alves 2 [35, 56]	33,952
34	12	A	Tottenham H	D 1-1	0-1	13	Downing [69]	36,092
35	19	H	Bolton W	L 0-1	0-0	14		25,037
36	26	A	Sunderland	L 2-3	1-2	15	Tuncay [4], Alves [73]	45,059
37	May 3	H	Portsmouth	W 2-0	1-0	14	Riggott [40], Tuncay [53]	24,828
38	11	H	Manchester C	W 8-1	2-0	13	Downing 2 (1 pen) [16 (p), 58], Alves 3 [37, 60, 90], Johnson [70], Rochemback [80], Aliadiere [85]	27,613

Final League Position: 13

GOALSCORERS

League (43): Downing 9 (2 pens), Tuncay 8, Alves 6, Aliadiere 5, Wheater 3, Arca 2, Mido 2, Boateng 1, Cattermole 1, Hutchinson 1, Huth 1, Johnson 1, Riggott 1, Rochemback 1, Young 1.
Carling Cup (2): Lee 1, Rochemback 1.
FA Cup (5): Downing 1, Lee 1, Wheater 1, own goals 2.

Schwarzer M 34	Davies A 3+1	Taylor A 18+1	Riggott C 9+1	Wheater D 34	Boateng G 29+4	Tuncay S 27+7	Arca J 23+1	Yakubu A 2	Aliadiere J 26+3	Downing S 38	Johnson A 3+16	Cattermole L 10+14	Lee D 5+9	Mido8+4	Hines S —+1	Young L 35	Woodgate J 16	Rochemback F 21+5	O'Neil G 25+1	Craddock T 1+2	Hutchinson B —+8	Pogatetz E 23+1	Turnbull R 3	Huth R 9+4	Shawki M 3+2	Grounds J 5	Alves A 7+4	Jones B 1	McMahon T —+1	Match No.
1	2	3	4	5	6	7^{1}	8^{2}	9	10^{3}	11	12	13	14																	1
1	2	3	4	5	6	7^{1}	8	9^{3}	10^{2}	11	12	13	14																	2
1	2	3	4	5	6	7^{1}	8		12	11		10	13^{3}	9^{2}	14															3
1		3		5	6^{2}	12	8		10^{1}	11		13		9		2	4	7												4
1		3		5	6	12	8		10^{1}	11		13	14	9^{3}		2	4	7^{2}												5
1	12	3^{1}		5	6	13	8		10^{2}	11				9		2	4	7^{3}	14											6
1		3		5	12	10^{2}	8^{1}			11		14	13	9^{3}		2	4	7	6											7
1		3	12	5	6					11			10^{1}	9^{2}		2	4	7	8	13										8
1		3	5		6^{1}	12				11		8				2	4	7	10	9^{2}	13									9
1		3	5		6^{1}	10^{2}				11		12		9		2	4	7	8	13										10
1		3		5	12	10^{2}			9^{3}	11		8^{1}	13			2	4	7	6		14									11
1		3	6	5	12	10^{3}			9^{2}	11		8	13			2		7^{1}	4		14									12
1		3^{1}	4	5	6	10^{2}			9	11		8				2			7		13	12								13
1				5	6				9^{2}	11	10	8^{1}				2	4	12	7		13	3								14
				5	6	12			9	11	7^{2}	13	10^{1}			2	4^{3}	8				3	1	14						15
				5	6	10^{2}	12		9^{1}	11	13					2	4^{3}	7	8			3	1	14						16
1				5	6	10			9	11^{1}	12					2	4	7	8			3								17
1				5	6	10	8		9	11	7^{1}	12				2	4^{2}					3		13						18
1				5^{3}	6	10	8^{2}		9^{1}	11	13		12			2	4	7				3		14						19
1						10	8			11	12		9^{2}			2	4		7^{1}		13	3		5	6					20
1						10	8			11	12	13	9^{3}			2	4	7^{2}	6^{1}		14	3		5						21
1				4	6	10			9^{1}	11						2		8	7		12			5		3				22
1				4	6	10	8^{1}		9	11						2		12	7			3		5						23
1				4		10^{3}	8		9^{1}	11^{2}	12	13		14		2		7	6					5		3				24
1				4			8		9	11	12	10^{2}	13			2		7^{1}	6			3		5						25
1				4	12		8		9^{1}	11			10^{2}			2		7	6			3		5			13			26
1				4		10^{2}	8		9■	11				12		2		7	6^{1}			5				3	13			27
1				4	6^{2}	10	8^{1}			11	13	12		14		2			7			5				3	9^{3}			28
1				4	6	10				11		12		9^{1}		2			8			3		5	7					29
1		14		4	6	10^{3}			9^{2}	11		12		13■		2			8			3		5	7^{1}					30
1		3		4	6	10^{1}			9^{3}	11	12	8				2^{2}			7			5			13		14			31
1		3		4	6	10^{3}			9	11	12	8^{2}				2			7^{1}			5			13		14			32
1		3		4	6	12	8		9^{2}	11	13					2			7			5					10^{1}			33
1				4	6	12	8^{2}		9	11	14					2		13	7^{1}			5				3^{3}	10			34
		3^{1}		4	6	10^{2}	8		7	11	13					2		12				5	1				9			35
		3		4	6	10	8			11		7^{1}				2		12				5					9	1		36
1			5	4	6^{1}	10	8		13	11		12				2		7				3					9^{2}			37
1			5	4	6	10^{1}	8^{2}		12	11	13					2^{3}		7				3					9		14	38

FA Cup

Third Round	Bristol C	(a)	2-1
Fourth Round	Mansfield T	(a)	2-0
Fifth Round	Sheffield U	(a)	0-0
		(h)	1-0
Sixth Round	Cardiff C	(h)	0-2

Carling Cup

Second Round	Northampton T	(h)	2-0
Third Round	Tottenham H	(a)	0-2

MILLWALL — FL Championship 1

FOUNDATION

Formed in 1885 as Millwall Rovers by employees of Morton & Co, a jam and marmalade factory in West Ferry Road. The founders were predominantly Scotsmen. Their first headquarters was The Islanders pub in Tooke Street, Millwall. Their first trophy was the East End Cup in 1887.

The Den, Zampa Road, London SE16 3LN.

Telephone: (020) 7232 1222.

Fax: (020) 7231 3663.

Ticket Office: (020) 7231 9999.

Website: www.millwallfc.co.uk

Email: questions@millwallplc.com

Ground Capacity: 20,146.

Record Attendance: 20,093 v Arsenal, FA Cup 3rd rd, 10 January 1994.

Pitch Measurements: 105m × 68m.

Chairman: John G Berylson.

Executive Deputy Chairman: Heather Rabbatts.

Chief Operating Officer: Andy Ambler.

Secretary: Yvonne Haines.

Manager: Kenny Jackett.

Assistant Manager: Joe Gallen.

Physio: Bobby Bacic.

Colours: Royal blue shirts, white shorts, royal blue stockings.

Change Colours: White shirts, navy blue shorts, navy blue stockings.

Year Formed: 1885. ***Turned Professional:*** 1893. ***Ltd Co.:*** 1894.

Previous Names: 1885, Millwall Rovers; 1889, Millwall Athletic; 1899, Millwall; 1985, Millwall Football & Athletic Company.

Club Nickname: 'The Lions'.

Grounds: 1885, Glengall Road, Millwall; 1886, Back of 'Lord Nelson'; 1890, East Ferry Road; 1901, North Greenwich; 1910, The Den, Cold Blow Lane; 1993, The Den, Bermondsey.

First Football League Game: 28 August 1920, Division 3, v Bristol R (h) W 2–0 – Lansdale; Fort, Hodge; Voisey (1), Riddell, McAlpine; Waterall, Travers, Broad (1), Sutherland, Dempsey.

Record League Victory: 9–1 v Torquay U, Division 3 (S), 29 August 1927 – Lansdale, Tilling, Hill, Amos, Bryant (3), Graham, Chance, Hawkins (3), Landells (1), Phillips (2), Black. 9–1 v Coventry C, Division 3 (S), 19 November 1927 – Lansdale, Fort, Hill, Amos, Collins (1), Graham, Chance, Landells (4), Cock (2), Phillips (2), Black.

HONOURS

Football League: Division 1 best season: 3rd, 1993–94; Division 2 – Champions 1987–88, 2000–01; Division 3 (S) – Champions 1927–28, 1937–38; Runners-up 1952–53; Division 3 – Runners–up 1965–66, 1984–85; Division 4 – Champions 1961–62; Runners-up 1964–65.

FA Cup: Runners-up 2004; Semi-final 1900, 1903, 1937 (first Division 3 side to reach semi-final).

Football League Cup: best season: 5th rd, 1974, 1977, 1995.

Football League Trophy: Winners 1983.

Auto Windscreens Shield: Runners-up 1999.

European Competitions: *UEFA Cup:* 2004–05.

SKY SPORTS FACT FILE

Left-winger Billy Hunter who graduated from Millwall to Bolton Wanderers before the First World War went on to a successful career as a coach. In 1924 after leaving the Hakoah club in Vienna, he was in charge of the Turkish Olympic team.

Record Cup Victory: 7–0 v Gateshead, FA Cup 2nd rd, 12 December 1936 – Yuill; Ted Smith, Inns; Brolly, Hancock, Forsyth; Thomas (1), Mangnall (1), Ken Burditt (2), McCartney (2), Thorogood (1).

Record Defeat: 1–9 v Aston Villa, FA Cup 4th rd, 28 January 1946.

Most League Points (2 for a win): 65, Division 3 (S), 1927–28 and Division 3, 1965–66.

Most League Points (3 for a win): 93, Division 2, 2000–01.

Most League Goals: 127, Division 3 (S), 1927–28.

Highest League Scorer in Season: Richard Parker, 37, Division 3 (S), 1926–27.

Most League Goals in Total Aggregate: Neil Harris 101, 1995–2004; 2006–07.

Most League Goals in One Match: 5, Richard Parker v Norwich C, Division 3S, 28 August 1926.

Most Capped Player: Eamonn Dunphy, 22 (23), Republic of Ireland.

Most League Appearances: Barry Kitchener, 523, 1967–82.

Youngest League Player: Moses Ashikodi, 15 years 240 days v Brighton & HA, 22 February 2003.

Record Transfer Fee Received: £2,300,000 from Liverpool for Mark Kennedy, March 1995.

Record Transfer Fee Paid: £800,000 to Derby Co for Paul Goddard, December 1989.

Football League Record: 1920 Original Members of Division 3; 1921 Division 3 (S); 1928–34 Division 2; 1934–38 Division 3 (S); 1938–48 Division 2; 1948–58 Division 3 (S); 1958–62 Division 4; 1962–64 Division 3; 1964–65 Division 4; 1965–66 Division 3; 1966–75 Division 2; 1975–76 Division 3; 1976–79 Division 2; 1979–85 Division 3; 1985–88 Division 2; 1988–90 Division 1; 1990–92 Division 2; 1992–96 Division 1; 1996–2001 Division 2; 2001–04 Division 1; 2004–06 FL C; 2006– FL 1.

LATEST SEQUENCES

Longest Sequence of League Wins: 10, 10.3.1928 – 25.4.1928.

Longest Sequence of League Defeats: 11, 10.4.1929 – 16.9.1929.

Longest Sequence of League Draws: 5, 22.12.1973 – 12.1.1974.

Longest Sequence of Unbeaten League Matches: 19, 22.8.1959 – 31.10.1959.

Longest Sequence Without a League Win: 20, 26.12.1989 – 5.5.1990.

Successive Scoring Runs: 22 from 8.12.1923.

Successive Non-scoring Runs: 6 from 20.12.1947.

MANAGERS

F. B. Kidd 1894–99
(Hon. Treasurer/Manager)
E. R. Stopher 1899–1900
(Hon. Treasurer/Manager)
George Saunders 1900–11
(Hon. Treasurer/Manager)
Herbert Lipsham 1911–19
Robert Hunter 1919–33
Bill McCracken 1933–36
Charlie Hewitt 1936–40
Bill Voisey 1940–44
Jack Cock 1944–48
Charlie Hewitt 1948–56
Ron Gray 1956–57
Jimmy Seed 1958–59
Reg Smith 1959–61
Ron Gray 1961–63
Billy Gray 1963–66
Benny Fenton 1966–74
Gordon Jago 1974–77
George Petchey 1978–80
Peter Anderson 1980–82
George Graham 1982–86
John Docherty 1986–90
Bob Pearson 1990
Bruce Rioch 1990–92
Mick McCarthy 1992–96
Jimmy Nicholl 1996–97
John Docherty 1997
Billy Bonds 1997–98
Keith Stevens May 1998–2000
(then Joint Manager)
(*plus* Alan McLeary 1999–2000)
Mark McGhee 2000–03
Dennis Wise 2003–05
Steve Claridge 2005
Colin Lee 2005–06
Nigel Spackman 2006
Willie Donachie 2006–07
Kenny Jackett November 2007–

TEN YEAR LEAGUE RECORD

		P	W	D	L	F	A	Pts	Pos
1998-99	Div 2	46	17	11	18	52	59	62	10
1999-2000	Div 2	46	23	13	10	76	50	82	5
2000-01	Div 2	46	28	9	9	89	38	93	1
2001-02	Div 1	46	22	11	13	69	48	77	4
2002-03	Div 1	46	19	9	18	59	69	66	9
2003-04	Div 1	46	18	15	13	55	48	69	10
2004-05	FL C	46	18	12	16	51	45	66	10
2005-06	FL C	46	8	17	21	35	61	40	23
2006-07	FL 1	46	19	9	18	59	62	66	10
2007-08	FL 1	46	14	10	22	45	60	52	17

DID YOU KNOW ?

In 1902–03 Millwall beat West Ham United 7–1 away in the Southern Professional Challenge Cup semi-final. The victory was achieved with six second-half goals in the space of 35 minutes and included the 100th of the season for them.

MILLWALL 2007–08 LEAGUE RECORD

Match No.	Date	Venue	Opponents	Result	H/T Score	Lg. Pos.	Goalscorers	Attendance
1	Aug 11	A	Doncaster R	D 0-0	0-0	—		7542
2	18	H	Cheltenham T	W 1-0	1-0	6	Spiller 45	8671
3	25	A	Southend U	L 0-1	0-0	13		8758
4	Sept 1	H	Huddersfield T	L 1-2	1-1	16	Robinson P 41	9004
5	7	A	Brighton & HA	L 0-3	0-2	—		6563
6	15	H	Walsall	L 1-2	0-1	22	Frampton 83	7720
7	22	A	Crewe Alex	D 0-0	0-0	22		4478
8	29	H	Swindon T	L 1-2	0-1	22	Simpson 56	8744
9	Oct 2	H	Northampton T	W 2-0	2-0	—	Dunne 12, Robinson P 31	6520
10	6	A	Carlisle U	L 0-4	0-4	24		7022
11	13	A	Gillingham	D 1-1	0-1	21	Dunne 61	6120
12	20	H	Bournemouth	W 2-1	1-0	19	O'Hara 33, Hoskins 55	7805
13	27	A	Leeds U	L 2-4	0-1	20	Hoskins 65, Brkovic 76	30,319
14	Nov 3	H	Hartlepool U	L 0-1	0-0	22		7731
15	6	H	Swansea C	D 2-2	0-1	—	Whitbread 58, Dunne (pen) 70	6750
16	17	A	Bristol R	L 1-2	1-0	22	Fuseini 8	6991
17	24	H	Yeovil T	W 2-1	0-0	20	O'Hara 71, Fuseini 82	8105
18	Dec 4	A	Leyton Orient	W 1-0	1-0	—	Whitbread 9	6220
19	15	H	Oldham Ath	L 2-3	2-1	20	Simpson 38, Whitbread 45	8033
20	22	A	Walsall	L 0-3	0-3	20		5433
21	26	H	Brighton & HA	W 3-0	1-0	19	Alexander 3 (1 pen) 7, 54, 71 (p)	9401
22	29	H	Crewe Alex	W 2-0	1-0	18	Harris (pen) 45, Brkovic 53	8068
23	Jan 1	A	Northampton T	D 1-1	0-1	20	Alexander 90	5329
24	12	A	Port Vale	L 1-3	1-1	20	Alexander 14	3724
25	19	H	Tranmere R	L 0-1	0-0	21		8925
26	23	H	Nottingham F	D 2-2	1-0	—	Harris 27, Simpson 53	8436
27	29	A	Cheltenham T	W 1-0	0-0	—	Alexander 55	3812
28	Feb 2	H	Doncaster R	L 0-3	0-1	20		8230
29	9	A	Nottingham F	L 0-2	0-0	21		17,046
30	12	H	Southend U	W 2-1	1-1	—	Alexander 41, Martin 54	7425
31	16	A	Tranmere R	L 0-2	0-2	20		6108
32	19	A	Huddersfield T	L 0-1	0-1	—		6326
33	23	H	Port Vale	W 3-0	2-0	18	Grabban 18, Laird 44, Martin 68	7775
34	26	A	Luton T	D 1-1	1-1	—	Grabban 39	6417
35	Mar 1	H	Bristol R	L 0-1	0-0	18		9202
36	7	A	Swansea C	W 2-1	1-0	—	Grabban 1, Simpson 70	15,561
37	11	A	Yeovil T	W 1-0	0-0	—	Savage 70	4439
38	15	H	Leyton Orient	L 0-1	0-0	18		10,986
39	22	A	Oldham Ath	D 1-1	0-0	18	Savage 76	4391
40	24	H	Luton T	D 0-0	0-0	19		8375
41	29	A	Bournemouth	L 0-2	0-0	19		4962
42	Apr 5	H	Gillingham	D 1-1	0-1	19	Robinson P 75	10,006
43	12	A	Hartlepool U	W 1-0	1-0	17	Simpson 11	4077
44	19	H	Leeds U	L 0-2	0-0	19		13,895
45	26	H	Carlisle U	W 3-0	1-0	17	Simpson 43, Harris (pen) 56, Craig 64	10,075
46	May 3	A	Swindon T	L 1-2	1-1	17	Senda 6	7781

Final League Position: 17

GOALSCORERS

League (45): Alexander 7 (1 pen), Simpson 6, Dunne 3 (1 pen), Grabban 3, Harris 3 (2 pens), Robinson P 3, Whitbread 3, Brkovic 2, Fuseini 2, Hoskins 2, Martin 2, O'Hara 2, Savage 2, Craig 1, Frampton 1, Laird 1, Senda 1, Spiller 1.
Carling Cup (0).
FA Cup (7): Hoskins 2, Alexander 1, Brkovic 1, Dunne 1 (pen), May 1, Simpson 1.
J Paint Trophy (2): May 1, Simpson 1.

Day C 5	Senda D 39 + 1	Frampton A 28 + 2	Dunne A 17 + 2	Robinson P 45	Shaw R 16 + 2	Spiller D 6	Brammer D 23	Harris N 19 + 8	Alexander G 32 + 4	May B 4 + 4 Craig T 5	Barron S 7 + 5	Smith R 9 + 7	Ardley N — + 1	O'Hara J 10 + 4	Simpson J 34 + 7	Whitbread Z 21 + 2	Hackett C 1 + 5	Douglas R 7	Fuseini A 31 + 6	Hoskins W 9 + 1	Bakayogo Z 5 + 5	Pidgeley L 13	Brkovic A 15 + 10	Hodge B 10	Bignot M 17 + 5	Akinfenwa A 1 + 6	Gaynor R 1 + 2	Forbes A 6 + 5	Laird M 16 + 1	Bowes G — + 1	Evans R 21	Grabban L 10 + 3	Edwards P — + 1	Martin D 7 + 4	Savage B 9 + 2	Karacan J 7	Cochrane J — + 1	*Match No.*
1	2	3	4	5	6	7^1	8	9	10^2	11	12	13																										1
1	2	3^2	4	5	6	7^3	8	9	12	10	13	11^1	14																									2
1	2	3^1	4	5	6	7^2	8	9	12	10		11		13																								3
1	2	3	4^2	5	6	7^1	8	9	10			11		13	12																							4
1	2	3	4	5		7	8	9^1	10^3	11		12^2			14	6■	13																					5
	2	3		5	6	7	8	9^3	10	12		11^2		4^1	14		13	1																				6
		3	4	5	6		8		10	12		13		7	2^2			1	11	9^1																		7
	2	3		5	6		8					11^1		4^2	9		12	1	7	10	13																	8
	2	3	4	5	6		8^2	9	10^3					13	7^1		12	1	11	14																		9
	2	3	4	5	6^3		8	9^1	10					11^2	7		12	1	13		14																	10
	2	3	4	5	6		8	12	9					13	14		7^3	1	11^2	10^1																		11
	2	3	4	5	6		8^2	12	9		14			11^3	7^1			1	13	10																		12
	2	3	4	5	6				9					7	12				11^1	10		1	8															13
	2	3	4	5	6^3			12	9	13				11	10^1	14						1	8	7^2														14
		3	2	5	6^1				9					11	10	12			7			1	8	4														15
			4^1	5					9					11		6			12	10	3	1	8^2	7	2	13												16
				5				12	9					4	8^1	6			11	10^2	3	1		7	2	13												17
	2^1			5				8^2	9		14				13	6			11	10	12	1	4^3	7	3													18
	2			5			8		9						4■	6			11^1	10		1		7	3	12												19
	2^1			5	12		8^2	11	9		4					6			13			1		7	3	10^3	14											20
	2			5			8	10^1	9						4	6			11			1		7	3	12												21
	2			5			8	10^2	9^1						4	6			11			1	12	7	3	13												22
	2^2			5			8	9■	12		13				10	6			11			1	4^1	7^3	3	14												23
	2	12			6■		8		9	13	3				10^1	5			11			1						4^2	7^3	14								24
	2^3	6		5			8	13	9		3				10				11		12^2	1			14		7^1	4										25
	2	6	12	5			8	9	13		3				7				11^1									4			1	10^2						26
	2	6	12	5			8^2		9		3				7				11				14		13			4^1			1	10^3						27
	2	6	7^1	5					9		3				8				11				12					4	13		1^G	10^2	15					28
		3		5				10^2	9						7	6			11				8^1		2				4		1	13		12				29
		3		5					9						8	6			11				12		2			13	4		1	10^1		7^2				30
	12	6		5			8	13	9		3^1				10^3								11		2			4^2	7		1	14						31
	2			5			8^1		9						11^2	6			12				7		3			13	4		1	10						32
	2	12		5					9^3						8^2	6			11				13		3^1			14	4		1	10		7				33
	2			5					9^3						8	6			11^1				12		3			13	4		1	10		7^2	14			34
	2			5					9			12			8	6			11				10^2		3			13	4		1			7^1				35
	2	3	7^1	5					9						8	6			11		12								4		1	10						36
	2	3	4^1	5					9^2			12			8	6			11										7		1	10			13			37
	2	3		5				12				10			8^1	6			11				13						4■		1			7^2	9			38
	2			5				12				10			8	6			11		3^2		7^1		13						1				9	4^3	14	39
	2			5								8^2			7	6			11		3		12								1	10^1		13	9	4		40
	2			5	6^2			10		3					8				11				12				13				1			7	9^1	4		41
	2	3		5				10		6		8^1			12				11				7^2						4		1			13	9			42
	2			5						6		12			10				11				13		3				8^2		1			7^1	9	4		43
	2^1	3		5						6					8				11^2				7^3		12				4		1	14		13	9	10		44
	2	3^1		5				10		6					7								8		12				4		1				9	11		45
	2^1			5	12			10				13			11				14		6		8		3				4		1				9^2	7^3		46

FA Cup

First Round	Altrincham	(a)	2-1
Second Round	Bournemouth	(h)	2-1
Third Round	Walsall	(a)	0-0
		(h)	2-1
Fourth Round	Coventry C	(a)	1-2

Carling Cup

First Round	Northampton T	(a)	0-2

J Paint Trophy

First Round	Swansea C	(a)	2-3

MILTON KEYNES DONS FL Championship 1

FOUNDATION

Old boys from Central School formed this club as Wimbledon Old Centrals in 1889. Their earliest successes were in the Clapham League before switching to the Southern Suburban League in 1902. In July 2004 Wimbledon became MK Dons and relocated to Milton Keynes.

Stadiummk, *Stadium Way, Milton Keynes MK1 1ST.*

Telephone: (01908) 622 922.

Fax: (01908) 622 933.

Ticket Office: (01908) 622 900.

Website: www.mkdons.com

Email: info@mkdons.com

Ground Capacity: 22,000 (rising to 31,000).

Record Attendance: 30,115 v Manchester U, FA Premier League, 9 May 1993 (at Selhurst Park).

Pitch Measurements: 105m × 68m.

Chairman: Pete Winkelman.

Vice-chairman: Berni Winkelman.

General manager: Keith Dickens.

Head of Football Operations: Kirstine Nicholson.

Manager: Roberto Di Matteo.

Assistant Manager: Eddie Newton.

Physio: Simon Crampton.

Colours: White shirts, white shorts, white stockings.

Change Colours: Red shirts, black shorts, black stockings.

Year Formed: 1889.

Turned Professional: 1964.

Ltd Co.: 1964.

Previous Names: 1899, Wimbledon Old Centrals; 1905, Wimbledon; 2004, Milton Keynes Dons.

Grounds: 1899, Plough Lane; 1991, Selhurst Park; 2003, The National Hockey Stadium; 2007, Stadium:mk.

Club Nicknames: 'The Dons', 'The Crazy Gang'.

First Football League Game: 20 August 1977, Division 4, v Halifax T (h) D 3–3 – Guy; Bryant (1), Galvin, Donaldson, Aitken, Davies, Galliers, Smith, Connell (1), Holmes, Leslie (1).

HONOURS

As Wimbledon

FA Premier League: best season: 6th, 1993–94.

Football League: Division 3 – Runners-up 1983–84; Division 4 – Champions 1982–83.

FA Cup: Winners 1988.

Football League Cup: Semi-final 1996–97, 1998–99.

League Group Cup: Runners-up 1982.

Amateur Cup: Winners 1963; Runners-up 1935, 1947.

European Competitions: *Intertoto Cup:* 1995.

As Milton Keynes Dons

Football League: FL 2 – Champions 2007–08.

Johnstone's Paint Trophy: Winners 2008.

SKY SPORTS FACT FILE

On 26 April 2008, Milton Keynes Dons' 2–1 victory at Bradford City was their 18th away win which equalled the Football League record established by Doncaster Rovers in the 1946–47 season and ensured themselves of the championship in League Two.

Record League Victory: 6–0 v Newport Co, Division 3, 3 September 1983 – Beasant; Peters, Winterburn, Galliers, Morris, Hatter, Evans (2), Ketteridge (1), Cork (3 incl. 1p), Downes, Hodges (Driver).

Record Cup Victory: 7–2 v Windsor & Eton, FA Cup 1st rd, 22 November 1980 – Beasant; Jones, Armstrong, Galliers, Mick Smith (2), Cunningham (1), Ketteridge, Hodges, Leslie, Cork (1), Hubbick (3).

Record Defeat: 0–8 v Everton, League Cup 2nd rd, 29 August 1978.

Most League Points (2 for a win): 61, Division 4, 1978–79.

Most League Points (3 for a win): 98, Division 4, 1982–83.

Most League Goals: 97, Division 3, 1983–84.

Highest League Scorer in Season: Alan Cork, 29, 1983–84.

Most League Goals in Total Aggregate: Alan Cork, 145, 1977–92.

Most League Goals in One Match: 4, Alan Cork v Torquay U, Division 4, 28 February 1979.

MANAGERS

Les Henley 1955–71
Mike Everitt 1971–73
Dick Graham 1973–74
Allen Batsford 1974–78
Dario Gradi 1978–81
Dave Bassett 1981–87
Bobby Gould 1987–90
Ray Harford 1990–91
Peter Withe 1991
Joe Kinnear 1992–99
Egil Olsen 1999–2000
Terry Burton 2000–02
Stuart Murdock 2002–04
Danny Wilson 2004–06
Martin Allen 2006–07
Paul Ince 2007–08
Roberto Di Matteo July 2008–

Most Capped Player: Kenny Cunningham, 40 (72), Republic of Ireland.

Most League Appearances: Alan Cork, 430, 1977–92.

Youngest League Player: Kevin Gage, 17 years 15 days v Bury, 2 May 1981.

Record Transfer Fee Received: £7,000,000 from Newcastle U for Carl Cort, July 2000.

Record Transfer Fee Paid: £7,500,000 to West Ham U for John Hartson, January 1999.

Football League Record: 1977 Elected to Division 4; 1979–80 Division 3; 1980–81 Division 4; 1981–82 Division 3; 1982–83 Division 4; 1983–84 Division 3; 1984–86 Division 2; 1986–92 Division 1; 1992–2000 FA Premier League; 2000–04 Division 1; 2004–06 FL 1; 2006–08 FL 2; 2008– FL 1.

LATEST SEQUENCES (as Milton Keynes Dons)

Longest Sequence of League Wins: 8, 7.9.2007 – 20.10.2007.

Longest Sequence of League Defeats: 4, 10.8.2004 – 28.8.2004.

Longest Sequence of League Draws: 3, 19.2.2005 – 26.2.2005.

Longest Sequence of Unbeaten League Matches: 18, 29.1.2008 (continuing).

Longest Sequence Without a League Win: 10, 2.10.2004 – 7.12.2004.

Successive Scoring Runs: 18 from 7.4.2007.

Successive Non-scoring Runs: 4, 17.12.2005–2.1.2006.

TEN YEAR LEAGUE RECORD

		P	W	D	L	F	A	Pts	Pos
1998-99	PR Lge	38	10	12	16	40	63	42	16
1999-2000	PR Lge	38	7	12	19	46	74	33	18
2000-01	Div 1	46	17	18	11	71	50	69	8
2001-02	Div 1	46	18	13	15	63	57	67	9
2002-03	Div 1	46	18	11	17	76	73	65	10
2003-04	Div 1	46	8	5	33	41	89	29	24
2004-05	FL 1	46	12	15	19	54	68	51	20
2005-06	FL 1	46	12	14	20	45	66	50	22
2006-07	FL 2	46	25	9	12	76	58	84	4
2007-08	FL 2	46	29	10	7	82	37	97	1

DID YOU KNOW ?

Silverware for the fledging MK Dons came via the Johnstone's Paint Trophy in 2007–08. Victims included promotion rivals Peterborough United, Gillingham, Swansea City and Grimsby Town in the final at Wembley 20 years after a Wimbledon triumph there.

MILTON KEYNES DONS 2007–08 LEAGUE RECORD

Match No.	*Date*	*Venue*	*Opponents*	*Result*		*H/T Score*	*Lg. Pos.*	*Goalscorers*	*Attendance*
1	Aug 11	H	Bury	L	1-2	1-0	—	Andrews [21]	7740
2	18	A	Macclesfield T	D	3-3	1-1	17	Andrews [20], Knight [73], Cameron [90]	2257
3	25	H	Shrewsbury T	W	3-0	0-0	10	Knight [47], Dyer [78], Andrews [84]	7380
4	Sept 1	A	Rochdale	L	2-3	2-1	12	Gallen 2 [16, 28]	2743
5	7	H	Notts Co	W	3-0	1-0	—	Andrews [41], Swailes [67], Wilbraham [85]	7977
6	15	A	Brentford	W	3-0	1-0	6	Andrews 2 [24, 79], Johnson [90]	4476
7	22	H	Darlington	W	1-0	0-0	5	Diallo [89]	7901
8	29	A	Morecambe	W	1-0	1-0	1	Dyer [21]	2688
9	Oct 2	A	Mansfield T	W	2-1	0-1	—	Dyer [72], Stirling [83]	1984
10	6	H	Bradford C	W	2-1	0-0	1	Andrews [73], Swailes [81]	7903
11	14	H	Lincoln C	W	4-0	1-0	1	Knight 2 [45, 82], Dyer [70], Wilbraham [78]	13,037
12	20	A	Hereford U	W	1-0	0-0	1	Wright [87]	3936
13	27	H	Stockport Co	L	0-2	0-0	1		8290
14	Nov 3	A	Wycombe W	D	1-1	1-1	1	Cameron [45]	5929
15	6	H	Grimsby T	W	2-0	2-0	—	Wilbraham [1], Wright [41]	6797
16	17	A	Chester C	W	2-0	1-0	1	Wright [38], Johnson [64]	3102
17	24	H	Chesterfield	L	1-2	1-1	1	Wright [10]	9638
18	Dec 4	A	Dagenham & R	W	1-0	1-0	—	Diallo [24]	1880
19	8	H	Accrington S	W	5-0	3-0	1	Andrews [9], Navarro [25], Cameron [33], Dyer 2 [49, 77]	6917
20	15	A	Peterborough U	W	2-1	0-0	1	Gallen [47], Andrews [57]	10,351
21	21	H	Brentford	D	1-1	0-1	—	Gallen [68]	8445
22	26	A	Notts Co	W	2-1	1-1	1	Wright [15], Johnson [90]	5106
23	29	A	Darlington	W	1-0	0-0	1	Johnson [84]	5304
24	Jan 1	H	Mansfield T	W	1-0	0-0	1	Andrews [58]	9583
25	5	A	Rotherham U	W	1-0	0-0	1	Wright [82]	5421
26	12	H	Barnet	L	0-1	0-1	1		9881
27	19	A	Wrexham	L	0-1	0-0	1		4319
28	26	H	Rochdale	L	0-1	0-1	1		7882
29	29	H	Macclesfield T	D	1-1	0-1	—	O'Hanlon [50]	6483
30	Feb 2	A	Bury	W	5-1	3-0	1	Wright 3 [10, 36, 68], Dyer [23], Gallen [81]	2241
31	9	H	Rotherham U	D	1-1	1-0	1	Gallen [16]	9455
32	12	A	Shrewsbury T	D	3-3	3-1	—	Wright 2 [32, 40], Gallen [35]	5474
33	23	A	Barnet	W	2-0	2-0	1	Navarro [13], Dyer [17]	2495
34	Mar 1	H	Chester C	W	1-0	0-0	1	Swailes [57]	8172
35	7	A	Grimsby T	W	1-0	1-0	—	O'Hanlon [10]	4106
36	10	A	Chesterfield	W	2-1	1-0	—	Andrews [42], Dyer [70]	3834
37	15	H	Dagenham & R	W	4-0	3-0	1	Wilbraham 2 [3, 37], Dyer [10], Gallen [82]	9417
38	21	H	Peterborough U	D	1-1	1-1	—	Wilbraham [12]	14,521
39	24	A	Accrington S	W	1-0	0-0	1-	Wright [83]	1559
40	Apr 4	A	Lincoln C	W	2-1	1-0	—	Regan [3], Johnson [55]	3896
41	8	H	Wrexham	W	4-1	2-0	—	Swailes [2], Wilbraham 2 [10, 90], O'Hanlon [75]	8646
42	12	H	Wycombe W	D	2-2	0-1	2	Wilbraham [72], O'Hanlon [90]	12,747
43	15	H	Hereford U	D	0-0	0-0	—		11,428
44	19	A	Stockport Co	W	3-2	1-1	1	Wright [31], Navarro [59], Andrews [74]	8838
45	26	A	Bradford C	W	2-1	2-1	1	Stirling [13], Dyer [18]	14,609
46	May 3	H	Morecambe	D	1-1	1-0	1	Wilbraham [41]	17,250

Final League Position: 1

GOALSCORERS

League (82): Wright 13, Andrews 12, Dyer 11, Wilbraham 10, Gallen 8, Johnson 5, Knight 4, O'Hanlon 4, Swailes 4, Cameron 3, Navarro 3, Diallo 2, Stirling 2, Regan 1.
Carling Cup (5): Broughton 1, Gallen 1 (pen), Knight 1, McGovern 1, own goal 1.
FA Cup (1): Johnson 1 (pen).
J Paint Trophy (9): Andrews 2 (2 pens), Johnson 2, Wright 2, Cameron 1, O'Hanlon 1, Swailes 1.

Gueret W 46	Edds G 2 + 5	Lewington D 45	Andrews K 40 + 1	O'Hanlon S 41 + 2	Diallo D 30	McGovern J 2 + 1	Cameron C 21 + 8	Knight L 15 + 2	Gallen K 15 + 9	Dyer L 43 + 2	Wilbraham A 28 + 7	Wright M 29 + 5	Murphy K 1 + 2	Stirling J 21 + 13	Broughton D 2 + 11	Swailes D 40	Navarro A 38 + 1	Johnson J 17 + 22	Smart B — + 8	Howell L 8	Hadfield J 6 + 7	Baldock S — + 5	Carbon M — + 3	Miles J 7 + 5	Regan C 8 + 1	Livermore J — + 5	Dobson C 1	*Match No.*
1	2	3	4	5	6■	7^{1}	8^{2}	9^{3}	10	11	12	13	14															1
1	2	3	4	5		7^{2}	8	9	10^{1}	11^{3}	12		6	13	14													2
1		3	4	5		12	8	9		11	10^{2}	7^{1}		2	13	6												3
1		3	4	5			8^{1}	9^{2}	10	11		7		2		6	12	13										4
1		3	4	5^{1}	6			9^{3}	10^{2}	11	13		14	7		2	8	12										5
1	12	3	4	5	2			9^{2}		11^{1}	10^{3}			7		6	8	13	14									6
1	12	3	4^{1}	5	2			9^{2}		11^{3}	10			7		6	8	13	14									7
1		3	4	5	2			9^{2}		11^{3}	10^{1}			7	12	6	8	13	14									8
1	12	3	4	5	2			9^{3}		11^{1}	10^{2}			7	13	6		14		8								9
1		3	4	5	2			9^{2}		11^{1}	10			7^{3}	12	6	8	13	14									10
1		3^{2}	4	5	2			9		11	10^{1}	14		7^{3}		6	8	12	13									11
1		3	4	5	2		12	9^{3}		11^{2}	10	7				6	8^{1}	14	13									12
1		3	4	5	2		12	9^{2}		11^{3}	10	7^{1}				6	8	13	14									13
1	12	3	4■	5	2		7	9^{1}		11■	10	8				6												14
1		2		5	6		7	9^{1}	12		10^{2}	3			13	4	8	11^{3}	14									15
1		3	4	5	2		12	13		11^{2}	10	7^{1}				6	8	9										16
1		3	4	5	2^{1}		12		13	11	10^{2}	7			14	6	8	9^{3}										17
1		3		5	6		4	12		11	10^{2}	7^{4}		2	13		8	9^{1}			14							18
1		3	4	5	2^{1}		7^{2}		10	11		9		12		6	8^{3}	13				14						19
1		3	4	5	2■		10^{2}		9^{1}	11^{3}	12	7		14		6	8	13										20
1		3	4	5			7		9	11^{1}		10		2^{2}	12	6	8	13										21
1		3	4	5^{3}			7^{2}		9^{1}	11		10			12	6	8	13		2			14					22
1		3	4		5		7^{1}			11^{3}		10		13	9^{2}	6	8	12		2	14							23
1		3	4		5		7			11		10		12	9^{1}	6	8^{2}			2	13							24
1		3		12	5		7^{2}			11		10		4^{3}		6	8	13		2^{1}	9	14						25
1		3	4	5	6		12			11^{1}	13	10		7^{2}	14		8	9		2^{3}								26
1		3	4	5	6		11^{2}		12	13	10	7					8	9^{3}		2^{1}			14					27
1		3	4^{3}	5	2				12	11	10^{1}	7				6	8	9^{2}					13	14				28
1		3	4	5	2^{3}		12		9	11	10	7^{2}		14		6	8^{1}	13										29
1		3^{1}	4	5^{3}	2		12		13	11	10	9		14		6	8				7^{2}							30
1		3	4		5				9	11		10				6	8	12			7^{1}				2			31
1		3	4	5	2				9^{2}	11^{1}		7		12		6	8	10^{3}			14	13						32
1		3	4	5	2		12		9	11				7^{3}		6	8^{1}	10^{2}			13			14				33
1				5			7^{1}			11				3		6	8	9			4^{2}	12		10	2	13		34
1		3		5			4			11^{3}	12			13		6	8	9			10^{1}			7^{2}	2	14		35
1		3	4	5			7^{3}			11	12			13		6	8	9						10^{1}	2^{2}	14		36
1		3	4	5	6		7^{3}		12	11	10			2				9^{2}				13		8^{1}		14		37
1		3	4	5	2^{2}		7^{3}		12	11	10	8^{1}		13		6		9								14		38
1		3	4	5					9^{2}	11	10	12		2		6	8	13						7^{1}				39
1	12	3	4'	5^{1}			7^{2}			11^{3}	10	9				6	8	13			14				2			40
1		3	4	5					12	11^{1}	10	7		13		6	8	9^{3}						14	2^{2}			41
1		3	4	5					9^{3}	11	10	7^{2}		12		6	8	13						14	2^{1}			42
1		3	4	5					12	11	10	13		2		6	8	9^{2}						7^{1}				43
1		3	4	5					9^{3}	11^{1}	10	7^{2}		2		6	8	12			14				13			44
1		3	4	12						11	10	7		2^{1}		6	8				9^{2}			13	5			45
1		3	12	5						14	10	13		2		6^{1}	8	9^{2}		11				7			4^{3}	46

FA Cup

First Round	Crewe Alex	(a)	1-2

Carling Cup

First Round	Ipswich T	(h)	3-3
Second Round	Sheffield U	(h)	2-3

J Paint Trophy

Second Round	Peterborough U	(h)	3-1
Quarter-Final	Bournemouth	(a)	2-0
Southern Semi-Final	Gillingham	(a)	1-1
Southern Final	Swansea C	(a)	1-0
		(h)	0-1
Final *(at Wembley)*	Grimsby T		2-0

MORECAMBE FL Championship 2

FOUNDATION

Several attempts to start a senior football club in a rugby stronghold finally succeeded on 7 May 1920 at the West View Hotel, Morecambe and a team competed in the Lancashire Combination for 1920–21. The club shared with a local cricket club at Woodhill Lane for the first season and a crowd of 3,000 watched the first game. The club moved to Roseberry Park the name of which was changed to Christie Park after J.B. Christie who as President had purchased the ground.

Christie Park, Lancaster Road, Morecambe LA4 5TJ.

Telephone: (01524) 411797.

Fax: (01524) 832 230.

Ticket Office: (01524) 411797.

Website: www.morecambefc.com.

Email: office@morecambefc.com

Ground Capacity: 6,030.

Pitch Measurements: 103m × 70m.

Record Attendance: 9,383 v Weymouth, FA Cup 3rd rd, 6 January 1962.

Chairman: Peter McGuigan.

Vice-chairman: Graham Hodgson.

Chief Executive: Rod Taylor.

Secretary: Neil Marsdin.

Manager: Sammy McIlroy.

Assistant Manager: Mark Lillis.

Physio: David Edge.

Colours: Red shirts, white shorts, white stockings.

Change Colours: All sky blue.

HONOURS

FA Cup: best season: 3rd rd, 1962, 2001, 2003.

League Cup: best season: 3rd rd, 2008.

Conference: Promoted to Football League (play-offs) 2006–07. Semi-finalists – 2002–03, 2005–06.

Northern Premier League: Runners-up – 1994–95.

Presidents Cup: Winners – 1991–92.

FA Trophy: Winners 1973–74.

Lancs Senior Cup: Winners 1967–68.

Lancs Combination: Champions – 1924–25, 1961–62, 1962–63, 1967–68. Runners-up – 1925–26.

Lancs Combination Cup: Winners – 1926–27, 1945–46, 1964–65, 1966–67, 1967–68. Runners-up – 1923–24, 1924–25, 1962–63.

Lancs Junior Cup: Winners – 1927, 1928, 1962, 1963, 1969, 1986, 1987, 1994, 1996, 1999, 2004.

SKY SPORTS FACT FILE

Few newcomers to the Football League have won their first two away cup ties in the League Cup against higher opposition and also reached the final of another competition. They were Northern finalists in the Johnstone's Paint Trophy.

Year Formed: 1920.

Club Nickname: The Shrimps.

Grounds: 1920, Woodhill Lane; 1921, Christie Park.

Record League Victory: 16-0 v Rossendale U, Lancashire Combination, September 1967.

Most League Points (3 for a win): 78, Conference, 2002–03.

Most League Goals: 86, Conference 2002–03.

Highest League Scorer in Season: Justin Jackson, 29, 1999–2000.

Most League Goals in Total Aggregate: 100, John Norman, 1994–99; 2000–02.

Most League Goals in One Match: 8, Jim Ashworth v Gt Harwood T, 1946–47; 8, Arnold Timmons v Rossendale, 1967–68.

Most League Appearances: 299, Dave McKearney, 1995–2004.

Record Transfer Fee Received: undisclosed from Rushden & D for Justin Jackson, June 2000.

Record Transfer Fee Paid: undisclosed to Southport for Carl Baker, July 2007.

Football League Record: 2006–07 Promoted from Conference; 2007– FL2.

MANAGERS

Jimmy Milne 1947–48
Albert Dainty 1955–56
Ken Horton 1956–61
Joe Dunn 1961–64
Geoff Twentyman 1964–65
Ken Waterhouse 1965–69
Ronnie Clayton 1969–70
Gerry Irving/Ronnie Mitchell 1970
Ken Waterhouse 1970–72
Dave Roberts 1972–75
Alan Spavin 1975–76
Johnny Johnson 1976–77
Tommy Ferber 1977–78
Mick Hogarth 1978–79
Don Curbage 1979–81
Jim Thompson 1981
Les Rigby 1981–84
Sean Gallagher 1984–85
Joe Wojciechowicz 1985–88
Eric Whalley 1988
Billy Wright 1988–89
Lawrie Milligan 1989
Bryan Griffiths 1989–93
Leighton James 1994
Jim Harvey 1994–2006
Sammy McIlroy May 2006–

LATEST SEQUENCES

Longest Sequence of League Wins: 3, 17.11.2007 – 4.12.2007.

Longest Sequence of League Defeats: 4, 23.2.2008 – 12.3.2008.

Longest Sequence of League Draws: 2, 27.10.2007 – 3.11.2007.

Longest Sequence of Unbeaten League Matches: 3, 25.8.2007 – 7.9.2007.

Longest Sequence Without a League Win: 6, 5.4.2008 (continuing).

Successive Scoring Runs: 6 from 2.10.2007.

Successive Non-scoring Runs: 2 from 15.1.2008.

TEN YEAR LEAGUE RECORD

		P	*W*	*D*	*L*	*F*	*A*	*Pts*	*Pos*
1998-99	Conf	42	15	8	19	60	76	53	14
1999-2000	Conf	42	18	16	8	70	48	70	3
2000-01	Conf	42	11	12	19	64	66	45	19
2001-02	Conf	42	17	11	14	63	67	62	6
2002-03	Conf	42	23	9	10	86	42	78	2
2003-04	Conf	42	20	7	15	66	66	67	7
2004-05	Conf	42	19	14	9	69	50	71	7
2005-06	Conf	42	22	8	12	68	41	74	5
2006-07	Conf	46	23	12	11	64	46	81	3
2007-08	FL 2	46	16	12	18	59	63	60	11

DID YOU KNOW?

On 29 December 2007 Morecambe found themselves losing 2–0 at home to promotion chasing Peterborough United. They pulled a goal back, but were reduced to ten men before a concerted recovery led to them eventually winning 3–2.

MORECAMBE 2007–08 LEAGUE RECORD

Match No.	*Date*	*Venue*	*Opponents*	*Result*		*H/T Score*	*Lg. Pos.*	*Goalscorers*	*Attendance*
1	Aug 11	H	Barnet	D	0-0	0-0	—		3633
2	18	A	Wrexham	L	1-2	0-2	22	Newby [56]	5504
3	25	H	Mansfield T	W	3-1	2-1	11	White (og) [5], Stanley [44], Baker (pen) [51]	2980
4	Sept 1	A	Notts Co	D	1-1	1-0	10	Twiss [34]	4434
5	7	A	Chester C	W	1-0	0-0	—	Baker (pen) [90]	3199
6	15	H	Hereford U	L	0-3	0-0	11		2949
7	22	A	Peterborough U	D	1-1	0-0	14	Thompson [83]	4473
8	29	H	Milton Keynes D	L	0-1	0-1	17		2688
9	Oct 2	H	Stockport Co	W	2-0	1-0	—	Baker 2 [45, 66]	2871
10	6	A	Lincoln C	D	1-1	1-1	11	Beevers (og) [36]	3281
11	12	H	Bradford C	W	2-1	0-1	—	Thompson [64], Baker [90]	4761
12	20	A	Rotherham U	L	1-3	0-0	12	Bentley [46]	4181
13	27	H	Rochdale	D	1-1	1-0	12	Artell [17]	3651
14	Nov 3	A	Chesterfield	D	2-2	1-0	15	Curtis [1], Grand [90]	3721
15	6	H	Accrington S	L	0-1	0-1	—		2814
16	17	A	Grimsby T	W	2-1	1-0	13	Newby [28], Twiss [50]	4897
17	24	H	Bury	W	2-1	2-0	10	Bentley [11], Twiss [27]	3124
18	Dec 4	A	Brentford	W	1-0	0-0	—	Twiss [56]	3155
19	14	A	Wycombe W	L	0-2	0-1	—		3821
20	22	A	Hereford U	W	3-0	2-0	10	Bentley [27], Blinkhorn [38], Artell [64]	3058
21	26	H	Chester C	W	5-3	4-1	10	Bentley 2 [18, 70], Thompson [20], Blinkhorn [25], Baker [45]	3419
22	29	H	Peterborough U	W	3-2	1-2	8	Artell [27], Baker 2 (1 pen) [52, 71 (p)]	2371
23	Jan 1	A	Stockport Co	L	1-2	0-2	8	Blinkhorn [80]	5489
24	5	A	Macclesfield T	W	2-1	1-1	8	Blinkhorn [30], Thompson [86]	2254
25	12	H	Dagenham & R	W	1-0	0-0	8	Blinkhorn [90]	2754
26	15	H	Darlington	L	0-3	0-1	—		2773
27	19	A	Shrewsbury T	L	0-2	0-2	8		5036
28	26	H	Notts Co	D	1-1	0-1	9	Baker [72]	2727
29	29	H	Wrexham	D	2-2	1-1	—	Curtis [8], Roberts (og) [52]	2421
30	Feb 2	A	Barnet	W	1-0	0-0	9	Thompson [62]	1619
31	9	H	Macclesfield T	L	0-1	0-0	10		2626
32	12	A	Mansfield T	W	2-1	2-0	—	Bentley [6], Blinkhorn [24]	2287
33	23	A	Dagenham & R	L	0-2	0-1	10		1809
34	Mar 1	H	Grimsby T	L	0-4	0-2	10		2303
35	8	A	Bury	L	1-2	0-1	10	Drummond [53]	2596
36	12	A	Accrington S	L	2-3	1-1	—	Blinkhorn [14], Twiss [50]	1448
37	15	H	Brentford	W	3-1	1-1	10	Drummond [31], Thompson [53], Hunter [88]	2180
38	22	H	Wycombe W	L	0-1	0-1	9		2524
39	24	A	Darlington	D	2-2	2-0	11	Thompson (pen) [38], Newby [41]	3719
40	29	H	Rotherham U	W	5-1	4-1	9	Blinkhorn [8], Newby 3 [9, 18, 42], Stanley [73]	2171
41	Apr 5	A	Bradford C	L	0-1	0-0	11		13,562
42	8	H	Shrewsbury T	D	1-1	1-0	—	Baker [32]	1634
43	12	H	Chesterfield	D	1-1	0-1	11	Blinkhorn [74]	2531
44	19	A	Rochdale	L	0-1	0-0	10		3706
45	26	H	Lincoln C	L	1-2	0-1	12	Blinkhorn [90]	2762
46	May 3	A	Milton Keynes D	D	1-1	0-1	11	Twiss [78]	17,250

Final League Position: 11

GOALSCORERS

League (59): Baker 10 (3 pens), Blinkhorn 10, Thompson 7 (1 pen), Bentley 6, Newby 6, Twiss 6, Artell 3, Curtis 2, Drummond 2, Stanley 2, Grand 1, Hunter 1, own goals 3.
Carling Cup (5): Artell 1, Baker 1 (pen), Bentley 1, Newby 1, Thompson 1.
J Paint Trophy (6): Newby 3 (1 pen), Blinkhorn 1, Burns 1, Hunter 1.

Lewis J 19	Yates A 42 + 2	Adams D 42	Artell D 34 + 2	Bentley J 43	Stanley C 41	Baker C 40 + 2	Sorvel N 14 + 8	Twiss M 27 + 9	Curtis W 16 + 20	Hunter G 19 + 19	Burns J 4 + 3	Newby J 11 + 21	Thompson G 36 + 4	Allen D 16 + 4	Blinkhorn M 36 + 5	Howard M 2 + 2	Drench S 3 + 1	Grand S 4 + 2	Cresswell R 2	Loach S 2	Drummond S 17 + 1	Jalal S 12	McStay H 12 + 1	Lloyd P 1 + 6	Davies S 10	McLachlan F 1	Match No.
1	2	3	4	5	6	7^{1}	8	9^{2}	10	11^{3}	12	13	14														1
1	2	3	4	5	6	7	8	9^{2}	12	13	11^{3}	14	10^{1}														2
1	2	3	4	5	6^{1}	7^{2}	8	9^{3}	10	12		13	11	14													3
1	2	3	4	5	6	7^{2}	8	9		12		13	11^{1}	10^{3}	14												4
1	2	3	4	5	6	7	8^{1}	12		13			11	10^{2}	9												5
1	2	3	4	5	6^{1}	7	8^{3}	12		13		14	11	10	9^{2}												6
1	2	3^{3}	4	5	6	7^{1}	8	9				12	13	11^{2}	10	14											7
1	2	3	4	5	6	7^{2}		9		12		13	11	8^{1}	10												8
1	2	3	4	5	6	7^{1}	12	9		13		14	11	8^{2}	10^{3}												9
1	2	3	4	5	6	7^{1}	12	9^{3}		13		14	11	8^{2}	10												10
1	2	3	4	5	6	7^{1}	12	9^{2}		14		13	11	8^{3}	10												11
1^{6}	2	3	4	5	6	7		9		12		13	11	8^{1}	10^{2}		15										12
	2		4	5	6^{2}		8	11■	12	14	13	10^{1}	7		9^{3}	3	1										13
		3		5	6	7^{2}	8^{1}		10	9		13	11		12		1	2	4								14
	2	3	12	5	6	7^{1}	8^{2}		10	13		14	11		9^{3}		1		4								15
1	2	3	4	5	6	7		9	12	11		10^{1}		8													16
1	2	3	4	5	6	7	12	9	13	11^{1}		10		8^{2}													17
1	2	3	4	5	6	7^{3}	12	9^{1}	13	11		10^{2}		8	14												18
1	2	3	4	5	6	7		9^{1}	12	11^{2}		10^{3}	13	8	14												19
1	2	3	4	5	6	7^{2}	12	9	13	11^{1}			8		10												20
1	2	3^{3}	4	5	6	7	12	9^{2}	13	11^{1}			8		10	14											21
1	2	3	4■	5	6	7	12	9^{2}	13	11			8		10^{1}												22
	2	3	4	5	6	7		9^{1}	12	11			8		10					1							23
	2	3		5		7^{2}		12	13	11			9	4^{1}	10	6				1	8						24
	2	3		5	6	7^{1}		9^{2}	12			13	11		10			4			8	1					25
	2	3		5	6	7		9	12	13			11^{1}		10			4			8^{2}	1					26
	2	3		5	6	7^{1}		9	12	11			8^{2}	13	10			4				1					27
	2	3	4	5	6	7		9^{1}	12	13			14	11^{3}	10						8^{2}	1					28
	2	3	4	5	6	7		12	10^{1}				11		9						8	1					29
	2	3	4	5	6	7^{1}			10^{2}	12	13		11		9						8	1					30
	2	3	4	5	6	7		12	10^{1}				11		9						8	1					31
	2	3	4	5	6	7^{2}			10			12	11		9^{1}						8^{3}	1	14	13			32
	2	3	4		6	7^{2}		12	10^{1}			13	11		9						8	1	5				33
	12	3	4^{1}	5	6^{3}	7		13		11		10	8^{2}		9						14		2		1		34
	2	3	4	5		7^{3}	8		10^{1}	11^{2}		12	9		13						6	1		14			35
	2	3	4	5		12	8	9	13				7		10^{2}						6	1		11^{1}			36
	2	3		5		7^{1}	8	9^{2}	13	12		14	11		10^{3}						6		4		1		37
	2	3		5		12	8^{1}	9^{3}	13	11		14	7		10^{2}						4		6		1		38
	2		12	5^{1}	6			13	3		11	9^{2}	7		10						8		4		1		39
	2		4		6				10	12	3	8^{1}	7	13	9			14			11^{2}		5^{3}		1		40
	2		4		6				11	12	3	10^{1}	7^{2}		9						8		5	13	1		41
	2	3		5	6	7			11^{2}	12		10^{3}			9			14			8^{1}		4	13	1		42
	2	3		5	6	7^{2}			10	11		8^{1}		12	9								4	13	1		43
	2	3		5	6^{1}	7			10	11		12		8	9^{2}								4	13	1		44
		3	4	5	6	7		9^{1}	12	11		13	8^{2}		10								2		1		45
	12	3	4	5	6	7		13	14	11			8		9^{3}							1	2^{1}			10^{2}	46

FA Cup

First Round	Port Vale	(h)	0-2

Carling Cup

First Round	Preston NE	(a)	2-1
Second Round	Wolverhampton W	(a)	3-1
Third Round	Sheffield U	(a)	0-5

J Paint Trophy

First Round	Tranmere R	(a)	1-0
Second Round	Port Vale	(h)	2-2
Quarter-Final	Hartlepool U	(a)	1-1
Northern Semi-Final	Bury	(h)	2-0
Northern Final	Grimsby T	(h)	0-1
		(a)	0-0

NEWCASTLE UNITED FA Premiership

FOUNDATION

It stemmed from a newly formed club called Stanley in 1881. In October 1882 they changed their name to Newcastle East End to avoid confusion with two other local clubs, Stanley Nops and Stanley Albion. Shortly afterwards another club Rosewood merged with them. Newcastle West End had been formed in August 1882 and they played on a pitch which was part of the Town Moor. Moved to Brandling Park 1885 and St James' Park 1886 (home of Newcastle Rangers). West End went out of existence after a bad run and the remaining committee men invited East End to move to St James' Park. They accepted and, at a meeting in Bath Lane Hall in 1892, changed their name to Newcastle United.

St James' Park, Newcastle-upon-Tyne NE1 4ST.

Telephone: (0191) 201 8400.

Fax: (0191) 201 8600.

Ticket Office: (0191) 261 1571.

Website: www.nufc.co.uk

Email: admin@nufc.co.uk

Ground Capacity: 52,387.

Record Attendance: 68,386 v Chelsea, Division 1, 3 September 1930.

Pitch Measurements: 105m × 68m.

Managing Director: Derek Llambias.

Exex Director Operations: David Williamson.

Manager: Kevin Keegan.

First Team Coaches: Terry McDermott, Chris Hughton.

Physio: Derek Wright.

Colours: Black and white striped shirts, black shorts, black stockings.

Change Colours: All purple with white trim.

Year Formed: 1881.

Turned Professional: 1889.

Ltd Co.: 1890.

Previous Names: 1881, Stanley; 1882, Newcastle East End; 1892, Newcastle United.

Club Nickname: 'The Magpies'.

Grounds: 1881, South Byker; 1886, Chillingham Road, Heaton; 1892, St James' Park.

First Football League Game: 2 September 1893, Division 2, v Royal Arsenal (a) D 2–2 – Ramsay; Jeffery, Miller; Crielly, Graham, McKane; Bowman, Crate (1), Thompson, Sorley (1), Wallace. Graham and not Crate scored according to some reports.

HONOURS

FA Premier League: Runners-up 1995–96, 1996–97; *Football League:* Division 1 – Champions 1904–05, 1906–07, 1908–09, 1926–27, 1992–93; Division 2 – Champions 1964–65; Runners-up 1897–98, 1947–48.

FA Cup: Winners 1910, 1924, 1932, 1951, 1952, 1955; Runners-up 1905, 1906, 1908, 1911, 1974, 1998, 1999.

Football League Cup: Runners-up 1976.

Texaco Cup: Winners 1974, 1975.

European Competitions: *Champions League:* 1997–98, 2002–03, 2003–04. *European Fairs Cup:* 1968–69 (winners), 1969–70, 1970–71. *UEFA Cup:* 1977–78, 1994–95, 1996–97, 1999–2000, 2003–04 (semi-final), 2004–05, 2006–07. *European Cup Winners' Cup:* 1998–99. *Anglo-Italian Cup:* Winners 1972–73. *Intertoto Cup:* 2001 (runners-up), 2005, 2006 (winners).

SKY SPORTS FACT FILE

In 1924 Newcastle United were involved in a marathon FA Cup tie with Derby County which produced 20 goals in seven hours of play. There were three 2–2 draws, the third of them at Bolton. Attempt number four was at Newcastle with United at last 5–3 winners.

Record League Victory: 13–0 v Newport Co, Division 2, 5 October 1946 – Garbutt; Cowell, Graham; Harvey, Brennan, Wright; Milburn (2), Bentley (1), Wayman (4), Shackleton (6), Pearson.

Record Cup Victory: 9–0 v Southport (at Hillsborough), FA Cup 4th rd, 1 February 1932 – McInroy; Nelson, Fairhurst; McKenzie, Davidson, Weaver (1); Boyd (1), Jimmy Richardson (3), Cape (2), McMenemy (1), Lang (1).

Record Defeat: 0–9 v Burton Wanderers, Division 2, 15 April 1895.

Most League Points (2 for a win): 57, Division 2, 1964–65.

Most League Points (3 for a win): 96, Division 1, 1992–93.

Most League Goals: 98, Division 1, 1951–52.

Highest League Scorer in Season: Hughie Gallacher, 36, Division 1, 1926–27.

Most League Goals in Total Aggregate: Jackie Milburn, 177, 1946–57.

Most League Goals in One Match: 6, Len Shackleton v Newport Co, Division 2, 5 October 1946.

Most Capped Player: Shay Given, 77 (86), Republic of Ireland.

Most League Appearances: Jim Lawrence, 432, 1904–22.

Youngest League Player: Steve Watson, 16 years 223 days v Wolverhampton W, 10 November 1990.

Record Transfer Fee Received: £13,650,000 from Real Madrid for Jonathan Woodgate, August 2004.

Record Transfer Fee Paid: £16,000,000 to Real Madrid for Michael Owen, September 2005.

Football League Record: 1893 Elected to Division 2; 1898–1934 Division 1; 1934–48 Division 2; 1948–61 Division 1; 1961–65 Division 2; 1965–78 Division 1; 1978–84 Division 2; 1984–89 Division 1; 1989–92 Division 2; 1992–93 Division 1; 1993– FA Premier League.

MANAGERS

Frank Watt 1895–32
(Secretary-Manager)
Andy Cunningham 1930–35
Tom Mather 1935–39
Stan Seymour 1939–47
(Hon. Manager)
George Martin 1947–50
Stan Seymour 1950–54
(Hon. Manager)
Duggie Livingstone 1954–56
Stan Seymour 1956–58
(Hon. Manager)
Charlie Mitten 1958–61
Norman Smith 1961–62
Joe Harvey 1962–75
Gordon Lee 1975–77
Richard Dinnis 1977
Bill McGarry 1977–80
Arthur Cox 1980–84
Jack Charlton 1984
Willie McFaul 1985–88
Jim Smith 1988–91
Ossie Ardiles 1991–92
Kevin Keegan 1992–97
Kenny Dalglish 1997–98
Ruud Gullit 1998–99
Sir Bobby Robson 1999–2004
Graeme Souness 2004–06
Glenn Roeder 2006–07
Sam Allardyce 2007–08
Kevin Keegan January 2008–

LATEST SEQUENCES

Longest Sequence of League Wins: 13, 25.4.1992 – 18.10.1992.

Longest Sequence of League Defeats: 10, 23.8.1977 – 15.10.1977.

Longest Sequence of League Draws: 4, 20.1.1990 – 24.2.1990.

Longest Sequence of Unbeaten League Matches: 14, 22.4.1950 – 30.9.1950.

Longest Sequence Without a League Win: 21, 14.1.1978 – 23.8.1978.

Successive Scoring Runs: 25 from 15.4.1939.

Successive Non-scoring Runs: 6 from 31.12.1938.

TEN YEAR LEAGUE RECORD

		P	*W*	*D*	*L*	*F*	*A*	*Pts*	*Pos*
1998-99	PR Lge	38	11	13	14	48	54	46	13
1999-2000	PR Lge	38	14	10	14	63	54	52	11
2000-01	PR Lge	38	14	9	15	44	50	51	11
2001-02	PR Lge	38	21	8	9	74	52	71	4
2002-03	PR Lge	38	21	6	11	63	48	69	3
2003-04	PR Lge	38	13	17	8	52	40	56	5
2004-05	PR Lge	38	10	14	14	47	57	44	14
2005-06	PR Lge	38	17	7	14	47	42	58	7
2006-07	PR Lge	38	11	10	17	38	47	43	13
2007-08	PR Lge	38	11	10	17	45	65	43	12

DID YOU KNOW ?

Outside-right Joe Rogers was the first Newcastle United player to receive any kind of international recognition when he was included in the FA's 1899 tour of Germany in what was virtually an England XI. He had been signed from Grimsby Town the previous season.

NEWCASTLE UNITED 2007–08 LEAGUE RECORD

Match No.	Date	Venue	Opponents	Result	H/T Score	Lg. Pos.	Goalscorers	Attendance
1	Aug 11	A	Bolton W	W 3-1	3-0	—	N'Zogbia [11], Martins 2 [21, 27]	25,414
2	18	H	Aston Villa	D 0-0	0-0	6		51,049
3	26	A	Middlesbrough	D 2-2	1-1	7	N'Zogbia [22], Viduka [77]	28,875
4	Sept 1	H	Wigan Ath	W 1-0	0-0	6	Owen [87]	50,461
5	17	A	Derby Co	L 0-1	0-1	—		33,016
6	23	H	West Ham U	W 3-1	2-1	5	Viduka 2 [2, 41], N'Zogbia [76]	50,104
7	29	A	Manchester C	L 1-3	1-1	9	Martins [29]	40,606
8	Oct 7	H	Everton	W 3-2	1-0	9	Butt [42], Emre [86], Owen [89]	50,152
9	22	H	Tottenham H	W 3-1	1-0	—	Martins [45], Cacapa [51], Milner [73]	51,411
10	27	A	Reading	L 1-2	0-0	8	Duberry (og) [76]	24,119
11	Nov 3	H	Portsmouth	L 1-4	1-3	10	Campbell (og) [16]	51,490
12	10	A	Sunderland	D 1-1	0-0	11	Milner [65]	47,701
13	24	H	Liverpool	L 0-3	0-1	11		52,307
14	Dec 1	A	Blackburn R	L 1-3	0-0	11	Martins [47]	27,477
15	5	H	Arsenal	D 1-1	0-1	—	Taylor [60]	50,305
16	8	H	Birmingham C	W 2-1	1-1	11	Martins (pen) [37], Beye [90]	49,948
17	15	A	Fulham	W 1-0	0-0	10	Barton (pen) [90]	24,959
18	23	H	Derby Co	D 2-2	1-1	9	Viduka 2 [27, 87]	51,386
19	26	A	Wigan Ath	L 0-1	0-0	11		20,304
20	29	A	Chelsea	L 1-2	0-1	11	Butt [56]	41,751
21	Jan 2	H	Manchester C	L 0-2	0-1	—		50,956
22	12	A	Manchester U	L 0-6	0-0	11		75,965
23	19	H	Bolton W	D 0-0	0-0	12		52,250
24	29	A	Arsenal	L 0-3	0-1	—		60,127
25	Feb 3	H	Middlesbrough	D 1-1	0-0	12	Owen [60]	51,105
26	9	A	Aston Villa	L 1-4	1-0	13	Owen [4]	42,640
27	23	H	Manchester U	L 1-5	0-2	13	Diagne-Faye [79]	52,291
28	Mar 1	H	Blackburn R	L 0-1	0-0	13		50,796
29	8	A	Liverpool	L 0-3	0-2	15		44,031
30	17	A	Birmingham C	D 1-1	0-1	—	Owen [56]	25,777
31	22	H	Fulham	W 2-0	1-0	13	Viduka [6], Owen [83]	52,293
32	30	A	Tottenham H	W 4-1	1-1	12	Butt [45], Geremi [52], Owen [65], Martins [83]	36,067
33	Apr 5	H	Reading	W 3-0	2-0	12	Martins [18], Owen [43], Viduka [58]	52,179
34	12	A	Portsmouth	D 0-0	0-0	12		20,507
35	20	H	Sunderland	W 2-0	2-0	12	Owen 2 (1 pen) [4, 45 (p)]	52,305
36	26	A	West Ham U	D 2-2	2-2	12	Martins [42], McCartney (og) [45]	34,980
37	May 5	H	Chelsea	L 0-2	0-0	—		52,305
38	11	A	Everton	L 1-3	0-1	12	Owen (pen) [47]	39,592

Final League Position: 12

GOALSCORERS

League (45): Owen 11 (2 pens), Martins 9 (1 pen), Viduka 7, Butt 3, N'Zogbia 3, Milner 2, Barton 1 (pen), Beye 1, Cacapa 1, Diagne-Faye 1, Emre 1, Geremi 1, Taylor 1, own goals 3.
Carling Cup (2): Martins 1, Owen 1.
FA Cup (4): Cacapa 1, Duff 1, Milner 1, Owen 1.

Harper S 19 + 2	Carr S 8 + 2	N'Zogbia C 27 + 4	Butt N 35	Taylor S 29 + 2	Rozehnal D 16 + 5	Geremi 24 + 3	Smith A 26 + 7	Martins O 23 + 8	Viduka M 19 + 7	Milner J 25 + 4	Solano N — + 1	Ameobi S 2 + 4	Ramage P — + 3	Cacapa C 16 + 3	Owen M 24 + 5	Beye H 27 + 2	Jose Enrique 18 + 5	Diagne-Faye A 20 + 2	Given S 19	Emre B 6 + 8	Barton J 20 + 3	Duff D 12 + 4	LuaLua K — + 2	Carroll A 1 + 3	Edgar D 2 + 3	Diatta L — + 2	*Match No.*
1	2	3	4	5	6	7	8	9^{1}	10^{2}	11^{3}	12	13	14														1
1	2	3	4	5	6	7^{2}	8	9^{3}	10^{1}	11		12		13	14												2
1	2^{2}	3	4	5	6	7	8	9^{1}	10	11			13^{3}	14	12												3
1		3	4	2	6	7	8^{1}	12	10^{2}	11		13		5	9												4
1		3	4	2^{2}	6	7^{3}	8	12		11		10		5	9^{1}	13		14									5
1		3	4	12	6	7	8	13	10^{3}	11				5^{1}	9^{2}	2	14										6
		3	4	5^{1}	6	7^{4}	8	9	10^{3}	11						2	13	12	1	14							7
		11	4		12	7^{1}	8	9^{2}		10^{3}				5	13	2	3	6	1	14							8
		11^{1}	4		13	7		9		12				5	10^{2}	2	3	6	1	8^{3}	14						9
		12	4^{1}			7	13	9^{2}		14				5	10	2	3	6^{3}	1	11	8						10
1		11	4	2	12		9	13		7^{3}				5^{1}	10		3^{2}	6		14	8						11
1		3		2	6	12	7	13	10	11					9^{2}	14		5^{3}		8^{1}	4						12
	12	11^{2}	4		6	2	7	9	10	13						5	3^{1}		1	8^{3}	14						13
	12^{2}	3	4		6	7	10	9	13	11						2		5^{1}	1		8						14
		3	4	5	6	7^{1}	10	9	12	11						2			1		8						15
		3	4^{1}	5	6	7^{2}	10	9^{3}	12	11						2	14		1	13	8						16
		3	4		6	7^{2}	10	9^{1}	12	11				5		2			1	13	8						17
		3	4^{3}	12	6^{1}		7	9	10	11				5		2			1	13	8^{2}	14					18
		3		5		7^{1}	4	12	10	11						2	13	6	1	8		9^{2}					19
		3	4	6	12		8^{1}	9^{3}	13	11				5	14	2		7	1			10^{2}					20
		3	4	6				9^{1}	10	7				5	12	2	13	8^{3}	1	14		11^{2}					21
	2	11	4	6	12		8		13	7^{2}				5	9^{1}		3		1			10					22
	2	11		4	6					7		10		5	9		3		1			8^{1}	12				23
	2	3	4	6	8^{2}		10			7^{1}		12		5	9				1		13	11					24
	2	3	4	6			10^{2}		13	12				5	9				1	7^{1}	8	11					25
15	2		4	6			10			7				5	9	3			1^{G}	12	8^{1}	11					26
15		3	4	5		12	10			7^{1}					9	2		6	1^{G}		8^{2}	11		13			27
1		12	4^{2}	5			10	13		7					9	2	3	6			8	11^{1}					28
1		11	4	5		12	10	13		7^{1}					9	2	3	6				8^{2}					29
1		12	4	5		7		11^{1}	10						9	2	3	6			8						30
1		12	4	5		7	13	11^{1}	10^{2}						9	2^{3}	3	6			8				14		31
1			4	5		7^{3}	12	11	10^{1}						9^{2}	2	3	6			8			13	14		32
1			4^{1}			7	12	11	10^{2}						9	2	3	6^{3}			8	13			5	14	33
1			4	5		7	12	11	10^{1}						9	2	3	6			8						34
1			4	5		7		11^{1}	10^{2}						9	2	3^{3}	6			8	12		13	14		35
1			4	5		7	12	11	10^{1}						9	2	3				8				6^{2}	13	36
1			4	5		7^{2}	12	11	10^{1}						9	2	3	6			8	13					37
1		11	4	5^{2}			8						13	14	9	2	3^{1}	6^{3}				7	12	10			38

FA Cup

Third Round	Stoke C	(a)	0-0
		(h)	4-1
Fourth Round	Arsenal	(a)	0-3

Carling Cup

Second Round	Barnsley	(h)	2-0
Third Round	Arsenal	(a)	0-2

NORTHAMPTON TOWN FL Championship 1

FOUNDATION

Formed in 1897 by school teachers connected with the Northampton and District Elementary Schools' Association, they survived a financial crisis at the end of their first year when they were £675 in the red and became members of the Midland League – a fast move indeed for a new club. They achieved Southern League membership in 1901.

Sixfields Stadium, Upton Way, Northampton NN5 5QA.

Telephone: (01604) 683 700.

Fax: (01604) 751 613.

Ticket Office: (01604) 683 777.

Website: www.ntfc.co.uk

Email: secretary@ntfc.co.uk

Ground Capacity: 7,653.

Record Attendance: (at County Ground): 24,523 v Fulham, Division 1, 23 April 1966; (at Sixfields Stadium): 7,557 v Manchester C, Division 2, 26 September 1998.

Pitch Measurements: 116yd × 72yd.

Chairman: David Cardoza.

Secretary: Norman Howells.

Manager: Stuart Gray.

Assistant Manager: Ian Sampson.

Physio: Stuart Barker.

Colours: Claret shirts, white shorts, claret stockings.

Change Colours: Black shirts, black shorts, black stockings.

Year Formed: 1897.

Turned Professional: 1901.

Ltd Co.: 1901.

Grounds: 1897, County Ground; 1994, Sixfields Stadium.

Club Nickname: 'The Cobblers'.

First Football League Game: 28 August 1920, Division 3, v Grimsby T (a) L 0–2 – Thorpe; Sproston, Hewison; Jobey, Tomkins, Pease; Whitworth, Lockett, Thomas, Freeman, MacKechnie.

Record League Victory: 10–0 v Walsall, Division 3 (S), 5 November 1927 – Hammond; Watson, Jeffs; Allen, Brett, Odell; Daley, Smith (3), Loasby (3), Hoten (1), Wells (3).

Record Cup Victory: 10–0 v Sutton T, FA Cup prel rd, 7 December 1907 – Cooch; Drennan, Lloyd Davies, Tirrell (1), McCartney, Hickleton, Badenock (3), Platt (3), Lowe (1), Chapman (2), McDiarmid.

HONOURS

Football League: Division 1 best season: 21st, 1965–66; Division 2 – Runners-up 1964–65; Division 3 – Champions 1962–63; Promoted from Division 3 1996–97 (play-offs); Division 3 (S) – Runners-up 1927–28, 1949–50; Division 4 – Champions 1986–87; Runners-up 1975–76; FL 2 – Runners-up 2005–06.

FA Cup: best season: 5th rd, 1934, 1950, 1970.

Football League Cup: best season: 5th rd, 1965, 1967.

SKY SPORTS FACT FILE

Signed on transfer deadline day by Northampton Town, Colin Russell made a brief but decisive contribution to the club's goalscoring in the last seven matches of the 1931–32 season. Including a hat-trick against Swindon Town he scored eight times – his only games for them.

Record Defeat: 0–11 v Southampton, Southern League, 28 December 1901.

Most League Points (2 for a win): 68, Division 4, 1975–76.

Most League Points (3 for a win): 99, Division 4, 1986–87.

Most League Goals: 109, Division 3, 1962–63 and Division 3 (S), 1952–53.

Highest League Scorer in Season: Cliff Holton, 36, Division 3, 1961–62.

Most League Goals in Total Aggregate: Jack English, 135, 1947–60.

Most League Goals in One Match: 5, Ralph Hoten v Crystal Palace, Division 3S, 27 October 1928.

Most Capped Player: Edwin Lloyd Davies, 12 (16), Wales.

Most League Appearances: Tommy Fowler, 521, 1946–61.

Youngest League Player: Adrian Mann, 16 years 297 days v Bury, 5 May 1984.

Record Transfer Fee Received: £265,000 from Watford for Richard Hill, July 1987.

Record Transfer Fee Paid: £165,000 to Oldham Ath for Josh Low, July 2003.

Football League Record: 1920 Original Member of Division 3; 1921 Division 3 (S); 1958–61 Division 4; 1961–63 Division 3; 1963–65 Division 2; 1965–66 Division 1; 1966–67 Division 2; 1967–69 Division 3; 1969–76 Division 4; 1976–77 Division 3; 1977–87 Division 4; 1987–90 Division 3; 1990–92 Division 4; 1992–97 Division 3; 1997–99 Division 2; 1999–2000 Division 3; 2000–03 Division 2; 2003–04 Division 3; 2004–06 FL 2; 2006– FL 1.

LATEST SEQUENCES

Longest Sequence of League Wins: 8, 27.8.1960 – 19.9.1960.

Longest Sequence of League Defeats: 8, 26.10.1935 – 21.12.1935.

Longest Sequence of League Draws: 6, 18.9.1983 – 15.10.1983.

Longest Sequence of Unbeaten League Matches: 21, 27.9.1986 – 6.2.1987.

Longest Sequence Without a League Win: 18, 26.3.1969 – 20.9.1969.

Successive Scoring Runs: 27 from 23.8.1986.

Successive Non-scoring Runs: 7 from 7.4.1939.

MANAGERS

Arthur Jones 1897–1907
(Secretary-Manager)
Herbert Chapman 1907–12
Walter Bull 1912–13
Fred Lessons 1913–19
Bob Hewison 1920–25
Jack Tresadern 1925–30
Jack English 1931–35
Syd Puddefoot 1935–37
Warney Cresswell 1937–39
Tom Smith 1939–49
Bob Dennison 1949–54
Dave Smith 1954–59
David Bowen 1959–67
Tony Marchi 1967–68
Ron Flowers 1968–69
Dave Bowen 1969–72
(continued as General Manager and Secretary to 1985 when joined the board)
Billy Baxter 1972–73
Bill Dodgin Jnr 1973–76
Pat Crerand 1976–77
Bill Dodgin Jnr 1977
John Petts 1977–78
Mike Keen 1978–79
Clive Walker 1979–80
Bill Dodgin Jnr 1980–82
Clive Walker 1982–84
Tony Barton 1984–85
Graham Carr 1985–90
Theo Foley 1990–92
Phil Chard 1992–93
John Barnwell 1993–95
Ian Atkins 1995–99
Kevin Wilson 1999–2001
Kevan Broadhurst 2001–03
Terry Fenwick 2003
Martin Wilkinson 2003
Colin Calderwood 2003–06
John Gorman 2006
Stuart Gray January 2007–

TEN YEAR LEAGUE RECORD

		P	W	D	L	F	A	Pts	Pos
1998-99	Div 2	46	10	18	18	43	57	48	22
1999-2000	Div 3	46	25	7	14	63	45	82	3
2000-01	Div 2	46	15	12	19	46	59	57	18
2001-02	Div 2	46	14	7	25	54	79	49	20
2002-03	Div 2	46	10	9	27	40	79	39	24
2003-04	Div 3	46	22	9	15	58	51	75	6
2004-05	FL 2	46	20	12	14	62	51	72	7
2005-06	FL 2	46	22	17	7	63	37	83	2
2006-07	FL 1	46	15	14	17	48	51	59	14
2007-08	FL 1	46	17	15	14	60	55	66	9

DID YOU KNOW

In the same 1931–32 season Northampton Town scored only 18 League goals in the first half of the season but still beat Metropolitan Police 9–0 in the FA Cup! Transformation thereafter with two 6s, a five and two matches where they hit four goals.

NORTHAMPTON TOWN 2007–08 LEAGUE RECORD

Match No.	Date	Venue	Opponents	Result		H/T Score	Lg. Pos.	Goalscorers	Attendance
1	Aug 11	H	Swindon T	D	1-1	1-1	—	Kirk[9]	6210
2	18	A	Brighton & HA	L	1-2	1-1	16	Kirk[23]	5137
3	25	H	Yeovil T	L	1-2	1-1	19	Hubertz[32]	4555
4	Sept 1	A	Leyton Orient	D	2-2	2-0	22	Hubertz[15], Doig[19]	5170
5	7	H	Doncaster R	W	2-0	0-0	—	Gilligan[50], Kirk[71]	5274
6	15	A	Bournemouth	D	1-1	0-1	16	Larkin[78]	5009
7	22	H	Huddersfield T	W	3-0	1-0	11	Hubertz[44], Holt[62], Kirk[66]	5014
8	29	A	Tranmere R	D	2-2	2-0	11	Kirk[12], Hubertz[39]	6338
9	Oct 2	A	Millwall	L	0-2	0-2	—		6520
10	6	H	Port Vale	W	2-1	2-0	13	Kirk 2[19, 33]	4755
11	15	A	Luton T	L	1-4	1-1	—	Bradley Johnson[23]	5881
12	20	H	Cheltenham T	W	2-1	1-0	12	Kirk[22], Gilligan[80]	5012
13	27	A	Oldham Ath	W	1-0	0-0	10	Russell[66]	4870
14	Nov 3	H	Southend U	L	0-1	0-0	12		6646
15	6	H	Bristol R	L	0-1	0-0	—		5126
16	17	A	Crewe Alex	L	0-1	0-0	16		4531
17	24	H	Walsall	L	0-2	0-1	17		5767
18	Dec 4	A	Swansea C	L	0-3	0-2	—		10,957
19	8	H	Carlisle U	D	2-2	1-1	18	Crowe[28], Bradley Johnson[90]	4908
20	15	A	Nottingham F	D	2-2	0-1	18	Hubertz[59], Jones[65]	17,081
21	21	H	Bournemouth	W	4-1	2-1	—	Bowditch[4], Crowe[33], Jones[50], Bradley Johnson[67]	4806
22	26	A	Doncaster R	L	0-2	0-2	17		7046
23	29	A	Huddersfield T	W	2-1	0-1	16	Hubertz[71], Crowe[85]	8566
24	Jan 1	H	Millwall	D	1-1	1-0	16	Bowditch[37]	5329
25	5	A	Leeds U	L	0-3	0-1	—		24,472
26	12	H	Hartlepool U	D	1-1	1-1	18	Dolman[16]	4639
27	19	A	Gillingham	W	1-0	1-0	14	Jones[3]	5579
28	25	H	Leyton Orient	W	2-0	1-0	—	Coke[14], Hubertz (pen)[78]	5405
29	29	H	Brighton & HA	W	1-0	1-0	—	Hughes[44]	4657
30	Feb 2	A	Swindon T	D	1-1	0-0	11	Akinfenwa[87]	7375
31	9	H	Leeds U	D	1-1	0-1	12	Akinfenwa[75]	7260
32	12	A	Yeovil T	L	0-1	0-0	—		5001
33	16	H	Gillingham	W	4-0	2-0	12	Crowe[44], Akinfenwa 2[45, 53], Coke[64]	4978
34	22	A	Hartlepool U	W	1-0	0-0	—	Coke[82]	3945
35	Mar 1	H	Crewe Alex	D	0-0	0-0	11		5507
36	8	A	Walsall	W	2-0	1-0	10	Akinfenwa 2[8, 71]	6844
37	12	A	Bristol R	D	1-1	0-1	—	Hubertz[55]	4657
38	15	H	Swansea C	W	4-2	3-1	11	Hubertz 2 (1 pen)[14, 23 (p)], Tate (og)[20], Jackman[52]	5926
39	21	H	Nottingham F	L	1-2	1-1	—	Hubertz[32]	7244
40	24	A	Carlisle U	L	0-2	0-0	12		9038
41	29	A	Cheltenham T	D	1-1	0-1	12	Coke[76]	4024
42	Apr 5	H	Luton T	W	2-1	2-0	11	Hubertz (pen)[34], Dyer[41]	5132
43	12	A	Southend U	D	1-1	1-0	11	Larkin[24]	9286
44	19	H	Oldham Ath	W	2-0	0-0	9	Coke[51], Gilligan[64]	5171
45	26	A	Port Vale	D	2-2	2-1	11	Gilligan[24], Holt[27]	4556
46	May 3	H	Tranmere R	W	2-1	1-1	9	Akinfenwa[3], Hubertz[68]	5088

Final League Position: 9

GOALSCORERS

League (60): Hubertz 13 (3 pens), Kirk 8, Akinfenwa 7, Coke 5, Crowe 4, Gilligan 4, Bradley Johnson 3, Jones 3, Bowditch 2, Holt 2, Larkin 2, Doig 1, Dolman 1, Dyer 1, Hughes 1, Jackman 1, Russell 1, own goal 1.
Carling Cup (2): Bradley Johnson 1, Kirk 1.
FA Cup (4): Kirk 2, Bradley Johnson 1, Larkin 1.
J Paint Trophy (0).

Bunn M 45	Crowe J 44	Jackman D 34 + 5	Hughes M 34 + 1	Doig C 15	Gilligan R 28 + 10	Johnson Bradley 22 + 1	Henderson I 9 + 14	Larkin C 14 + 19	Kirk A 25	Holt A 29 + 7	Jones D 27 + 6	Hubertz P 33 + 7	Burnell J 26 + 7	Johnson Brett 10 + 6	Dolman L 27 + 3	Russell A 11 + 2	Dyer A 3 + 3	Branston G 3	Aiston S — + 1	Bowditch D 7 + 3	May D — + 2	Coke G 11 + 9	Little M 17	Hayes J 5 + 6	Akinfenwa A 13 + 2	Gyepes G 13	Dunn C 1	Match No.
1	2	3	4	5	6	7	8^1	9^2	10^3	11	12	13	14															1
1	2	3^2	4	5	6	7	8^1	14	10	11^3	12	9		13														2
1	2		4	5	6	7		12	10^1	3	11	9	8^2		13													3
1	2		4	5	12	7	8^2	13	10	11^3	3	9	6^1		14													4
1	2		4		12	7			10	11	3^2	9	8^1	13	5	6												5
1	2		4	5	6^1	7		12	10	11		9		13	3	8^2												6
1	3		4	5	12	7	13	8^1	10^2	11		9			2	6^3	14											7
1	2		4	5	12	7	13	8	10^2	11^3		9^1		14	3	6												8
1	2^1	3	4	5^3		7	13	8	10^2		14	9	12		6	11												9
1		3	4		12	7	8^2	11	10		2	9^1	14	13	5	6^3												10
1	2	3^1	4		12	7	13	9^2	10	11	6				5	8												11
1	2	12	4		13	7		8	10	11	3^1	9^2	14		5	6^3												12
1	2	3^3	4	5	11	7		9^1	10		14	12	8^2		6	13												13
1	2		4	5	11^2	7		12	10	13	3	9			6^1	8												14
1	2	12	4^2	5	11	7^3		14	10	13	3^1	9			6	8												15
1	2	3			7	12		9	10	11^2	13		8^1		4	6^3		5	14									16
1	2	3	4			7		8	10^3	11^2	13	9	6^1			12		5		14								17
1	2	3	4		11	7	8	9^1	10						6			5		12								18
1	2	3^1	4		12	7	8^2		10^3	11	6	13	14		5					9								19
1	2	3	4		11^3	7^2	8	12			6	9^1	10	13	5					14								20
1	2	3	4		12	7		13	10		6^3	9^2	8^1		5					11	14							21
1	2	3	4			7		12	10		6	9	8^2		5		13			11^1								22
1	2	12	4		11^2	7		13	10		3	9^1	8	6	5													23
1	2^1	3^2	4					12	10	13	7	9	8	6	5					11								24
1	2	3^1	4				12	9^2	10^3	11			8	6	5					7	13	14						25
1	2	3	12		13		14		10^3		11			6	5^1					9		8	4	7^2				26
1	2	3	4		6		13	12			11		8	5						9^2		7^1	10					27
1	2	3	4		6^2		13			12	10	9	8	5								7^1	11					28
1	2	3	4		11		12			13		9	8^1	6								7^2	5	10				29
1	2	3	4		7^1		12			11^2		9	8	6									5	10	13			30
1	2	3	4		7		12			11^3		9	8^2	6								13	5	10^1	14			31
1	2	3	4		10					11		9	12	6^3	13							8^1	7^2	14		5		32
1	2	3	4		7^2					11		9	8									12	6	13	10^1	5		33
1	2	3	4		7					11		9	8									12	6		10^1	5		34
1	2	3	4		7^1					11^2		9	8									12	6	13	10	5		35
1	2^3	3	4		7		9^1	12		11		13	8									14	6		10^2	5		36
1		3			7^2		10^1	12		11	2	9	8		4							13	6			5		37
1	2	3			7					11	4	9	8									12	6		10^1	5		38
1	2	3			7^3			12		11^1	4	9	8^2									13	6	14	10	5		39
1	2	3^1						12		13	11	9^3	8		4							7	6	14	10	5^2		40
1	2	3					14	12		11^3	5	13	8^1		4							7	6	9^2	10			41
1	2	3					12			11	4	9	13		5		7^3					8^2	6	14	10^1			42
1	2	12		6	7		13	9^3		11	3	14			4		8^1								10^2	5		43
1	2	3		6	7^1			12		11	4	9										8			10	5		44
1	2	3^1		6	7			12		11	4	9^2					13					8			10	5		45
	2	12		6	7			9^1		14	4	13			3		11^3					8^2			10	5	1	46

FA Cup

First Round	Darlington	(a)	1-1
		(h)	2-1
Second Round	Walsall	(h)	1-1
		(a)	0-1

Carling Cup

First Round	Millwall	(h)	2-0
Second Round	Middlesbrough	(a)	0-2

J Paint Trophy

First Round	Luton T	(a)	0-2

NORWICH CITY FL Championship

FOUNDATION

Formed in 1902, largely through the initiative of two local schoolmasters who called a meeting at the Criterion Cafe, they were shocked by an FA Commission which in 1904 declared the club professional and ejected them from the FA Amateur Cup. However, this only served to strengthen their determination. New officials were appointed and a professional club established at a meeting in the Agricultural Hall in March 1905.

Carrow Road, Norwich NR1 1JE.

Telephone: (01603) 760 760.

Fax: (01603) 613 886.

Ticket Office: 0870 444 1902.

Website: www.canaries.co.uk

Email: reception@ncfc-canaries.co.uk

Ground Capacity: 26,034.

Record Attendance: 43,984 v Leicester C, FA Cup 6th rd, 30 March 1963.

Pitch Measurements: 105m × 67m.

Chairman: Roger Munby.

Chief Executive: Neil Doncaster.

Secretary: Kevan Platt.

Manager: Glenn Roeder.

Assistant Manager: Lee Clark.

Physio: Neil Reynolds MCSP, SRP.

Colours: Yellow shirts, green shorts, yellow stockings.

Change Colours: Black shirts, black shorts, black stockings.

Year Formed: 1902.

Turned Professional: 1905.

Ltd Co.: 1905.

Club Nickname: 'The Canaries'.

Grounds: 1902, Newmarket Road; 1908, The Nest, Rosary Road; 1935, Carrow Road.

First Football League Game: 28 August 1920, Division 3, v Plymouth Arg (a) D 1–1 – Skermer; Gray, Gadsden; Wilkinson, Addy, Martin; Laxton, Kidger, Parker, Whitham (1), Dobson.

Record League Victory: 10–2 v Coventry C, Division 3 (S), 15 March 1930 – Jarvie; Hannah, Graham; Brown, O'Brien, Lochhead (1); Porter (1), Anderson, Hunt (5), Scott (2), Slicer (1).

HONOURS

FA Premier League: best season: 3rd 1992–93.

Football League: Division 1 – Champions 2003–04; Division 2 – Champions 1971–72, 1985–86; Division 3 (S) – Champions 1933–34; Division 3 – Runners-up 1959–60.

FA Cup: Semi-finals 1959, 1989, 1992.

Football League Cup: Winners 1962, 1985; Runners-up 1973, 1975.

European Competitions: *UEFA Cup:* 1993–94.

SKY SPORTS FACT FILE

On 24 December 1921 James Silverthorne became the youngest goalscorer for Norwich City against Brighton & Hove Albion at the age of 17 years 131 days. He also returned to the club for a second spell at Carrow Road two seasons later.

Record Cup Victory: 8–0 v Sutton U, FA Cup 4th rd, 28 January 1989 – Gunn; Culverhouse, Bowen, Butterworth, Linighan, Townsend (Crook), Gordon, Fleck (3), Allen (4), Phelan, Putney (1).

Record Defeat: 2–10 v Swindon T, Southern League, 5 September 1908.

Most League Points (2 for a win): 64, Division 3 (S), 1950–51.

Most League Points (3 for a win): 94, Division 1, 2003–04.

Most League Goals: 99, Division 3 (S), 1952–53.

Highest League Scorer in Season: Ralph Hunt, 31, Division 3 (S), 1955–56.

Most League Goals in Total Aggregate: Johnny Gavin, 122, 1945–54, 1955–58.

Most League Goals in One Match: 5, Tommy Hunt v Coventry C, Division 3S, 15 March 1930; 5, Roy Hollis v Walsall, Division 3S, 29 December 1951.

Most Capped Player: Mark Bowen, 35 (41), Wales.

Most League Appearances: Ron Ashman, 592, 1947–64.

Youngest League Player: Ryan Jarvis, 16 years 282 days v Walsall, 19 April 2003.

Record Transfer Fee Received: £7,250,000 from West Ham U for Dean Ashton, January 2006.

Record Transfer Fee Paid: £3,400,000 to Crewe Alex for Dean Ashton, January 2005.

Football League Record: 1920 Original Member of Division 3; 1921 Division 3 (S): 1934–39 Division 2; 1946–58 Division 3 (S); 1958–60 Division 3; 1960–72 Division 2; 1972–74 Division 1; 1974–75 Division 2; 1975–81 Division 1; 1981–82 Division 2; 1982–85 Division 1; 1985–86 Division 2; 1986–92 Division 1; 1992–95 FA Premier League; 1995–2004 Division 1; 2004–05 FA Premier League; 2005– FL C.

MANAGERS

John Bowman 1905–07
James McEwen 1907–08
Arthur Turner 1909–10
Bert Stansfield 1910–15
Major Frank Buckley 1919–20
Charles O'Hagan 1920–21
Albert Gosnell 1921–26
Bert Stansfield 1926
Cecil Potter 1926–29
James Kerr 1929–33
Tom Parker 1933–37
Bob Young 1937–39
Jimmy Jewell 1939
Bob Young 1939–45
Cyril Spiers 1946–47
Duggie Lochhead 1947–50
Norman Low 1950–55
Tom Parker 1955–57
Archie Macaulay 1957–61
Willie Reid 1961–62
George Swindin 1962
Ron Ashman 1962–66
Lol Morgan 1966–69
Ron Saunders 1969–73
John Bond 1973–80
Ken Brown 1980–87
Dave Stringer 1987–92
Mike Walker 1992–94
John Deehan 1994–95
Martin O'Neill 1995
Gary Megson 1995–96
Mike Walker 1996–98
Bruce Rioch 1998–2000
Bryan Hamilton 2000
Nigel Worthington 2001–06
Peter Grant 2006–07
Glenn Roeder October 2007–

LATEST SEQUENCES

Longest Sequence of League Wins: 10, 23.11.1985 – 25.1.1986.

Longest Sequence of League Defeats: 7, 1.4.1995 – 6.5.1995.

Longest Sequence of League Draws: 7, 15.1.1994 – 26.2.1994.

Longest Sequence of Unbeaten League Matches: 20, 31.8.1950 – 30.12.1950.

Longest Sequence Without a League Win: 25, 22.9.1956 – 23.2.1957.

Successive Scoring Runs: 25 from 31.8.1963.

Successive Non-scoring Runs: 5 from 21.2.1925.

TEN YEAR LEAGUE RECORD

		P	*W*	*D*	*L*	*F*	*A*	*Pts*	*Pos*
1998-99	Div 1	46	15	17	14	62	61	62	9
1999-2000	Div 1	46	14	15	17	45	50	57	12
2000-01	Div 1	46	14	12	20	46	58	54	15
2001-02	Div 1	46	22	9	15	60	51	75	6
2002-03	Div 1	46	19	12	15	60	49	69	8
2003-04	Div 1	46	28	10	8	79	39	94	1
2004-05	PR Lge	38	7	12	19	42	77	33	19
2005-06	FL C	46	18	8	20	56	65	62	9
2006-07	FL C	46	16	9	21	56	71	57	16
2007-08	FL C	46	15	10	21	49	59	55	17

DID YOU KNOW ?

On 22 March 2008 Jamie Cureton hit his tenth career hat-trick while playing for Norwich City against his former club Colchester United. He had also started his career at Carrow Road before returning at the beginning of the season.

NORWICH CITY 2007–08 LEAGUE RECORD

Match No.	Date	Venue	Opponents	Result		H/T Score	Lg. Pos.	Goalscorers	Attendance
1	Aug 11	A	Preston NE	D	0-0	0-0	—		13,408
2	18	H	Southampton	W	2-1	0-1	9	Cureton 2 61, 71	24,004
3	25	A	Hull C	L	1-2	0-0	15	Dublin 71	15,939
4	Sept 1	H	Cardiff C	L	1-2	1-0	20	Lappin 12	24,292
5	15	H	Crystal Palace	W	1-0	0-0	13	Strihavka 75	24,228
6	18	A	Charlton Ath	L	0-2	0-0	—		21,543
7	22	A	Wolverhampton W	L	0-2	0-2	20		22,564
8	29	H	Sheffield W	L	0-1	0-0	21		23,293
9	Oct 2	H	Scunthorpe U	D	0-0	0-0	—		23,176
10	8	A	QPR	L	0-1	0-0	—		10,514
11	20	H	Bristol C	L	1-3	0-0	23	Huckerby 82	24,125
12	23	A	Burnley	L	1-2	0-2	—	Brown 68	10,133
13	27	A	WBA	L	0-2	0-1	24		20,247
14	Nov 4	H	Ipswich T	D	2-2	0-2	24	Garvan (og) 56, Cureton 67	25,461
15	6	H	Watford	L	1-3	0-2	—	Croft 65	24,192
16	10	A	Plymouth Arg	L	0-3	0-1	24		11,222
17	24	H	Coventry C	W	2-0	1-0	24	Chadwick 34, Cureton 77	24,590
18	27	A	Blackpool	W	3-1	1-1	—	Dublin 2 30, 90, Taylor 74	7759
19	Dec 1	A	Stoke C	L	1-2	1-0	24	Huckerby 5	19,285
20	4	H	Plymouth Arg	W	2-1	1-0	—	Evans 2, Huckerby (pen) 87	25,434
21	8	H	Sheffield U	W	1-0	1-0	21	Evans 10	24,493
22	15	A	Colchester U	D	1-1	0-0	21	Granville (og) 90	5560
23	22	A	Scunthorpe U	W	1-0	0-0	18	Cureton 78	6648
24	26	H	Charlton Ath	D	1-1	0-1	20	Russell 73	25,327
25	29	H	Wolverhampton W	D	1-1	0-0	20	Cureton 75	24,300
26	Jan 1	A	Crystal Palace	D	1-1	1-0	20	Russell 9	17,199
27	12	A	Barnsley	W	3-1	0-1	18	Evans 48, Fotheringham 70, Dublin 74	10,117
28	19	H	Leicester C	D	0-0	0-0	18		25,462
29	29	A	Southampton	W	1-0	1-0	—	Evans 45	18,004
30	Feb 2	H	Preston NE	W	1-0	0-0	13	Russell 90	24,092
31	9	A	Cardiff C	W	2-1	1-1	13	Evans 2 15, 88	11,937
32	12	H	Hull C	D	1-1	1-0	—	Dublin 19	25,259
33	16	A	Leicester C	L	0-4	0-1	—		25,854
34	23	H	Barnsley	W	1-0	1-0	12	Cureton 26	24,197
35	Mar 1	H	Blackpool	L	1-2	0-2	13	Cureton (pen) 65	24,531
36	4	A	Watford	D	1-1	0-1	—	Cureton 81	16,537
37	8	A	Coventry C	L	0-1	0-1	13		18,108
38	11	H	Stoke C	L	0-1	0-0	—		23,471
39	15	A	Sheffield U	L	0-2	0-0	18		25,536
40	22	H	Colchester U	W	5-1	2-1	17	Otsemobor 6, Cureton 3 (1 pen) 36, 53 (p), 87, Dublin 90	25,215
41	29	A	Bristol C	L	1-2	0-1	17	Huckerby 70	17,511
42	Apr 5	H	Burnley	W	2-0	1-0	16	Dublin 2, Evans 90	24,049
43	13	A	Ipswich T	L	1-2	1-2	16	Evans 4	29,656
44	19	H	WBA	L	1-2	0-1	18	Evans (pen) 73	25,442
45	26	H	QPR	W	3-0	1-0	16	Evans 7, Fotheringham 56, Russell 83	25,497
46	May 4	A	Sheffield W	L	1-4	1-1	17	Huckerby 9	36,208

Final League Position: 17

GOALSCORERS

League (49): Cureton 12 (2 pens), Evans 10 (1 pen), Dublin 7, Huckerby 5 (1 pen), Russell 4, Fotheringham 2, Brown 1, Chadwick 1, Croft 1, Lappin 1, Otsemobor 1, Strihavka 1, Taylor 1, own goals 2.
Carling Cup (6): Cureton 2, Dublin 1, Fotheringham 1, Lappin 1, Russell 1.
FA Cup (2): Doherty 1, Dublin 1.

Marshall D 46	Otsemobor J 41 + 2	Drury A 9	Shackell J 36 + 3	Doherty G 32 + 2	Russell D 37 + 2	Chadwick L 9 + 4	Brellier J 8 + 2	Dublin D 28 + 9	Brown C 8 + 6	Lappin S 15	Croft L 19 + 22	Fotheringham M 26 + 2	Strihavka D 3 + 7	Cureton J 29 + 12	Murray I 8 + 1	Huckerby D 26 + 8	Spillane M 4 + 2	Martin C 3 + 4	Jarvis Rossi 4	Hartson J 2 + 2	Smith J 6 + 3	Taylor M 8	Camara M 20 + 1	Pattison M 22 + 5	Evans C 20 + 8	Bertrand R 18	Bates M 2 + 1	Henry J 1 + 2	Gibbs K 6 + 1	Pearce A 8 + 3	Velasco J 2 + 1	Rigters M — + 2	Jarvis Ryan — + 1	*Match No.*
1	2	3	4	5	6	7^{1}	8^{2}	9^{3}	10	11	12	13	14																					1
1	2	3	4	5	6	13	8^{1}		10	11	7	12^{2}	14	9^{3}																				2
1	2		4	5	6		8^{1}	12	10	11	7^{2}		13	9	3																			3
1	2	3		5	6	7^{2}	8^{1}	4	10	11	12			9		13																		4
1	2	3		5	6	7^{1}	13	4	10^{3}	11	12		14	9		8^{2}																		5
1	2	3	12	5	6	7^{2}	8^{3}	4■	10^{1}	11	13			14		9																		6
1	2		4■	5	6		8■		12	11			7^{3}	10^{1}	3	9^{2}	13	14																7
1	2	3		5					10^{2}	11	12		13	9	4	7	6^{1}		8															8
1	2	3		5	6			9			7			10^{1}	4	11		12	8															9
1	2	3	4		6			5^{3}	12	11^{2}	7		13		14	9		10^{1}	8															10
1	2	3^{3}	4		6					11	12		7		5^{1}	9	14	13	8	10^{2}														11
1	2		4		6^{3}	7^{1}			10	3			8^{2}	12	5	9	11			13	14													12
1	2		4		6	12				11	13			10^{2}	3	9	5	8			7^{1}													13
1	2		4		6	7^{1}	8	9^{2}		3	12			10^{3}		11■				13	14	5												14
1	2		4		6	7^{2}	8		13	3	12			9				14		10^{3}	11^{1}	5												15
1	2		4		6		12		13	3	7^{3}		14	10	11		8	9^{2}				5^{1}												16
1	2		4		6	7^{1}		9^{2}	13		12	8		10								5	3	11										17
1	2		4		6	7^{1}		9			13	8		10^{3}		12						5	3	11^{2}	14									18
1			4	2	6			9			7^{1}	8		12		10						5	3	11^{2}	13									19
1	2		12	4	6			13			14	8		10^{2}		7						5^{1}	3	11^{3}	9									20
1	2		4					12			13	8		10		7					6^{2}	5	3	11	9^{1}									21
1	2		4	5	6			12			13	8		10		14					7^{2}		3	11^{3}	9^{1}									22
1	2		4	5	6			9^{2}			12	8		13		7^{1}					14		3	11^{3}	10									23
1	2		4	5	6			12			13			10^{1}		7					8^{2}		3	11	9									24
1	2		4	5	6			12	13		14			10		7^{2}					8^{3}		3	11	9^{1}									25
1	2		4	5	6			9			7^{1}	8		10^{2}		12							3	11	13									26
1	2		4	5	6			10^{3}			7^{2}	8		12		13							11		9^{1}	3							14	27
1	2		4	5	6			9			7	8		12									3		10^{1}	11								28
1	2		4	5	6			9			7	8^{3}		12		13							3^{2}	14	10^{1}	11								29
1	2^{2}		4	5	6			9			7^{3}	8		12									3		10^{1}	11	13	14						30
1			4	5	6			9			7^{1}	8				12							3	13	10	11^{2}	2							31
1	12		4	5	6			9			7^{2}	8				13								14	10	11	2^{1}		3^{3}					32
1	2		4	5	6■			9			7	8		12									3^{1}	13	10			11^{2}						33
1	2			5							7			9		8								11^{2}	10^{1}	3		12	4	6	13			34
1	2			5				9			7^{2}	8^{1}		10		11								12	13	3			4	6				35
1	12		13	5				9			7^{1}	8		14									6^{3}	11	10	3				4	2^{2}			36
1			4	5■	6■			9			7^{2}	8		12									10^{1}	11	13	3				14	2^{3}			37
1	2		4					9			7	8		10									3^{1}	6	12	11				5				38
1	2		4^{1}	12				13			14	8		10		7								11	9^{2}	3			6^{3}	5				39
1	2		4	5^{2}	6			9			12	8		10		7^{3}								11^{1}		3				13		14		40
1	2		4		6^{1}			9^{2}			12	8		10		7								11	14	3				5		13^{3}		41
1	2		4	12	6			9^{1}				8		10^{2}		7								11	13	3				5				42
1	2			5	6			9^{1}			12^{2}			8		7							14	11	10	3^{3}			13	4				43
1	2		4	5	12	14		13				8		9^{2}		7							3^{1}	11	10				6^{3}					44
1	2		4	5	12	14		13				8		9^{2}		7								11^{3}	10	3			6^{1}					45
1	2^{3}		4	5	6			9^{2}			12	8		13		7								11^{1}	10	3				14				46

FA Cup

Third Round	Bury	(h)	1-1
		(a)	1-2

Carling Cup

First Round	Barnet	(h)	5-2
Second Round	Rochdale	(a)	1-1
Third Round	Manchester C	(a)	0-1

NOTTINGHAM FOREST FL Championship

FOUNDATION

One of the oldest football clubs in the world, Nottingham Forest was formed at a meeting in the Clinton Arms in 1865. Known originally as the Forest Football Club, the game which first drew the founders together was 'shinney', a form of hockey. When they determined to change to football in 1865, one of their first moves was to buy a set of red caps to wear on the field.

The City Ground, Nottingham NG2 5FJ.

Telephone: (0115) 982 4444.

Fax: (0115) 982 4455.

Ticket Office: 0871 226 1980.

Website: www.nottinghamforest.co.uk

Email: info@nottinghamforest.co.uk

Ground Capacity: 30,576.

Record Attendance: 49,946 v Manchester U, Division 1, 28 October 1967.

Pitch Measurements: 112yd × 76yd.

Chairman: Nigel Doughty.

Chief Executive: Mark Arthur.

Finance Director: John Pelling.

Football Administrator: Jane Carnelly.

Manager: Colin Calderwood.

First Team Coaches: David Kerslake, John Pemberton, Barry Richardson.

Physios: Steve Devine, Andy Hunt.

Colours: Red shirts, white shorts, red stockings.

Change Colours: White shirts, red shorts, white stockings.

Year Formed: 1865. ***Turned Professional:*** 1889.

Ltd Co.: 1982.

Club Nickname: 'Reds'.

Grounds: 1865, Forest Racecourse; 1879, The Meadows; 1880, Trent Bridge Cricket Ground; 1882, Parkside, Lenton; 1885, Gregory, Lenton; 1890, Town Ground; 1898, City Ground.

First Football League Game: 3 September 1892, Division 1, v Everton (a) D 2–2 – Brown; Earp, Scott; Hamilton, A. Smith, McCracken; McCallum, W. Smith, Higgins (2), Pike, McInnes.

Record League Victory: 12–0 v Leicester Fosse, Division 1, 12 April 1909 – Iremonger; Dudley, Maltby; Hughes (1), Needham, Armstrong; Hooper (3), Marrison, West (3), Morris (2), Spouncer (3 incl. 1p).

Record Cup Victory: 14–0 v Clapton (away), FA Cup 1st rd, 17 January 1891 – Brown; Earp, Scott; A. Smith, Russell, Jeacock; McCallum (2), 'Tich' Smith (1), Higgins (5), Lindley (4), Shaw (2).

HONOURS

Football League: Division 1 – Champions 1977–78, 1997–98; Runners-up 1966–67, 1978–79; FL 1 – Runners-up 2007–08. Division 2 – Champions 1906–07, 1921–22; Runners-up 1956–57; Division 3 (S) – Champions 1950–51.

FA Cup: Winners 1898, 1959; Runners-up 1991.

Football League Cup: Winners 1978, 1979, 1989, 1990; Runners-up 1980, 1992.

Anglo-Scottish Cup: Winners 1977;

Simod Cup: Winners 1989.

Zenith Data Systems Cup: Winners: 1992.

European Competitions: *European Cup:* 1978–79 (winners), 1979–80 (winners), 1980–81. *European Fairs Cup:* 1961–62, 1967–68. *UEFA Cup:* 1983–84, 1984–85, 1995–96. *Super Cup:* 1979–80 (winners), 1980–81 (runners-up). *World Club Championship:* 1980.

SKY SPORTS FACT FILE

After Arron Davies scored twice for Yeovil Town against Nottingham Forest in the 2006–07 play-offs, the midland club signed him. Injury kept him out for several weeks in 2007–08 until the last match of the season when he came on as a substitute against Yeovil!

Record Defeat: 1–9 v Blackburn R, Division 2, 10 April 1937.

Most League Points (2 for a win): 70, Division 3 (S), 1950–51.

Most League Points (3 for a win): 94, Division 1, 1997–98.

Most League Goals: 110, Division 3 (S), 1950–51.

Highest League Scorer in Season: Wally Ardron, 36, Division 3 (S), 1950–51.

Most League Goals in Total Aggregate: Grenville Morris, 199, 1898–1913.

Most League Goals in One Match: 4, Enoch West v Sunderland, Division 1, 9 November 1907; 4, Tommy Gibson v Burnley, Division 2, 25 January 1913; 4, Tom Peacock v Port Vale, Division 2, 23 December 1933; 4, Tom Peacock v Barnsley, Division 2, 9 November 1935; 4, Tom Peacock v Port Vale, Division 2, 23 November 1935; 4, Tom Peacock v Doncaster R, Division 2, 26 December 1935; 4, Tommy Capel v Gillingham, Division 3S, 18 November 1950; 4, Wally Ardron v Hull C, Division 2, 26 December 1952; 4, Tommy Wilson v Barnsley, Division 2, 9 February 1957; 4, Peter Withe v Ipswich T, Division 1, 4 October 1977.

Most Capped Player: Stuart Pearce, 76 (78), England.

Most League Appearances: Bob McKinlay, 614, 1951–70.

Youngest League Player: Craig Westcarr, 16 years 257 days v Burnley, 13 October 2001.

Record Transfer Fee Received: £8,500,000 from Liverpool for Stan Collymore, June 1995.

Record Transfer Fee Paid: £3,500,000 to Celtic for Pierre van Hooijdonk, March 1997.

Football League Record: 1892 Elected to Division 1; 1906–07 Division 2; 1907–11 Division 1; 1911–22 Division 2; 1922–25 Division 1; 1925–49 Division 2; 1949–51 Division 3 (S); 1951–57 Division 2; 1957–72 Division 1; 1972–77 Division 2; 1977–92 Division 1; 1992–93 FA Premier League; 1993–94 Division 1; 1994–97 FA Premier League; 1997–98 Division 1; 1998–99 FA Premier League; 1999–2004 Division 1; 2004–05 FL C; 2005–08 FL 1; 2008– FL C.

MANAGERS

Harry Radford 1889–97 *(Secretary-Manager)*
Harry Haslam 1897–1909 *(Secretary-Manager)*
Fred Earp 1909–12
Bob Masters 1912–25
John Baynes 1925–29
Stan Hardy 1930–31
Noel Watson 1931–36
Harold Wightman 1936–39
Billy Walker 1939–60
Andy Beattie 1960–63
Johnny Carey 1963–68
Matt Gillies 1969–72
Dave Mackay 1972
Allan Brown 1973–75
Brian Clough 1975–93
Frank Clark 1993–96
Stuart Pearce 1996–97
Dave Bassett 1997–98 *(previously General Manager from February)*
Ron Atkinson 1998–99
David Platt 1999–2001
Paul Hart 2001–04
Joe Kinnear 2004
Gary Megson 2005
Colin Calderwood May 2006–

LATEST SEQUENCES

Longest Sequence of League Wins: 7, 9.5.1979 – 1.9.1979.

Longest Sequence of League Defeats: 14, 21.3.1913 – 27.9.1913.

Longest Sequence of League Draws: 7, 29.4.1978 – 2.9.1978.

Longest Sequence of Unbeaten League Matches: 42, 26.11.1977 – 25.11.1978.

Longest Sequence Without a League Win: 19, 8.9.1998 – 16.1.1999.

Successive Scoring Runs: 22 from 28.3.1931.

Successive Non-scoring Runs: 7 from 13.12.2003.

TEN YEAR LEAGUE RECORD

		P	*W*	*D*	*L*	*F*	*A*	*Pts*	*Pos*
1998-99	PR Lge	38	7	9	22	35	69	30	20
1999-2000	Div 1	46	14	14	18	53	55	56	14
2000-01	Div 1	46	20	8	18	55	53	68	11
2001-02	Div 1	46	12	18	16	50	51	54	16
2002-03	Div 1	46	20	14	12	82	50	74	6
2003-04	Div 1	46	15	15	16	61	58	60	14
2004-05	FL C	46	9	17	20	42	66	44	23
2005-06	FL 1	46	19	12	15	67	52	69	7
2006-07	FL 1	46	23	13	10	65	41	82	4
2007-08	FL 1	46	22	16	8	64	32	82	2

DID YOU KNOW ?

Had substitutions been permitted in the FA Cup during the 1958–59 season, it is obvious that Nottingham Forest would not have been unchanged throughout their nine matches in the tournament, solely because Roy Dwight broke his leg after scoring in the final.

NOTTINGHAM FOREST 2007–08 LEAGUE RECORD

Match No.	*Date*	*Venue*	*Opponents*	*Result*	*H/T Score*	*Lg. Pos.*	*Goalscorers*	*Attendance*
1	Aug 11	H	Bournemouth	D 0-0	0-0	—		18,791
2	18	A	Swansea C	D 0-0	0-0	15		17,220
3	25	H	Leeds U	L 1-2	0-1	18	Commons [50]	25,237
4	Sept 1	A	Bristol R	D 2-2	2-2	18	Anthony (og) [29], Grant Holt [45]	9080
5	15	A	Port Vale	W 2-0	1-0	15	Edwards (og) [3], Chambers [86]	6521
6	22	H	Gillingham	W 4-0	1-0	10	Agogo 3 [43, 61, 73], Sinclair [84]	16,330
7	29	A	Yeovil T	W 3-0	0-0	8	Chambers [57], Agogo [79], Commons [84]	6818
8	Oct 2	A	Huddersfield T	D 1-1	0-0	—	Commons [75]	10,994
9	6	H	Hartlepool U	W 2-1	1-1	5	Commons [11], Agogo [83]	17,520
10	13	A	Cheltenham T	W 3-0	2-0	4	Commons 3 [11, 45, 66]	5012
11	20	H	Doncaster R	D 0-0	0-0	4		23,108
12	27	A	Luton T	L 1-2	0-0	7	Bennett [90]	8524
13	30	H	Oldham Ath	D 0-0	0-0	—		16,423
14	Nov 3	H	Tranmere R	W 2-0	0-0	4	Agogo (pen) [50], Tyson [78]	16,825
15	6	H	Southend U	W 4-1	1-1	—	Breckin [41], Tyson [65], Agogo 2 [73, 88]	26,094
16	24	H	Crewe Alex	W 2-0	1-0	2	Davies [45], Clingan [52]	16,650
17	Dec 4	A	Walsall	L 0-1	0-0	—		6605
18	7	A	Brighton & HA	W 2-0	1-0	—	Tyson 2 [30, 49]	6536
19	15	H	Northampton T	D 2-2	1-0	3	McGugan [15], Agogo [90]	17,081
20	22	H	Port Vale	W 2-0	1-0	1	Agogo [24], McGugan [67]	21,407
21	26	A	Oldham Ath	D 0-0	0-0	2		8140
22	29	A	Gillingham	L 0-3	0-0	2		7712
23	Jan 1	H	Huddersfield T	W 2-1	0-1	2	Cohen [68], McGugan [90]	18,762
24	12	H	Leyton Orient	W 4-0	1-0	2	Grant Holt 2 (1 pen) [31, 54 (p)], Commons [72], Thornhill [89]	17,805
25	19	A	Swindon T	L 1-2	0-1	3	Chambers [63]	9815
26	23	A	Millwall	D 2-2	0-1	—	Cohen [85], Tyson [88]	8436
27	29	H	Swansea C	D 0-0	0-0	4		21,065
28	Feb 2	A	Bournemouth	L 0-2	0-2	4		7251
29	9	H	Millwall	W 2-0	0-0	3	Bennett [48], Chambers [58]	17,046
30	12	A	Leeds U	D 1-1	0-0	—	Bennett [69]	29,552
31	16	H	Swindon T	W 1-0	0-0	3	Tyson [50]	23,439
32	23	A	Leyton Orient	W 1-0	0-0	2	Agogo [61]	7136
33	Mar 3	H	Carlisle U	L 0-1	0-0	—		28,487
34	8	A	Crewe Alex	D 0-0	0-0	4		6314
35	11	A	Southend U	D 1-1	0-1	—	Thornhill [65]	8376
36	15	H	Walsall	D 1-1	0-0	4	Ormerod [49]	17,177
37	21	A	Northampton T	W 2-1	1-1	—	Ormerod [9], Tyson (pen) [63]	7244
38	24	H	Brighton & HA	D 0-0	0-0	4-		18,165
39	28	A	Doncaster R	L 0-1	0-0	—		12,508
40	Apr 1	A	Carlisle U	W 2-0	0-0	—	Chambers [76], McCleary [90]	9979
41	5	H	Cheltenham T	W 3-1	2-1	4	Agogo 2 [26, 47], Chambers [45]	19,860
42	8	H	Bristol R	D 1-1	1-0	—	McGugan [33]	15,860
43	12	A	Tranmere R	W 2-0	1-0	4	Tyson [34], Morgan [51]	8689
44	19	H	Luton T	W 1-0	0-0	4	Tyson [67]	17,531
45	26	A	Hartlepool U	W 1-0	0-0	3	McGugan [84]	5206
46	May 3	H	Yeovil T	W 3-2	3-1	2	Bennett [12], Commons [18], McGugan [28]	28,520

Final League Position: 2

GOALSCORERS

League (64): Agogo 13 (1 pen), Commons 9, Tyson 9 (1 pen), Chambers 6, McGugan 6, Bennett 4, Grant Holt 3 (1 pen), Cohen 2, Ormerod 2, Thornhill 2, Breckin 1, Clingan 1, Davies 1, McCleary 1, Morgan 1, Sinclair 1, own goals 2.
Carling Cup (2): Smith 1, Tyson 1.
FA Cup (4): Tyson 2, Commons 1, McGugan 1.
J Paint Trophy (2): Chambers 2.

Smith P 46	Wilson K 40 + 2	Lockwood M 11	Chambers L 40 + 2	Morgan W 37 + 5	Clingan S 40 + 2	Perch J 19 + 11	Lennon N 15 + 3	Moloney B 2	Dobie S 1 + 1	Commons K 29 + 10	Holt Grant 22 + 10	Agogo J 27 + 8	Bennett J 33 + 1	Thornhill M 5 + 9	Sinclair E — + 12	Tyson N 26 + 8	Bastians F — + 1	Breckin I 22 + 6	Cohen C 40 + 1	McGugan L 24 + 9	Davies A 9 + 10	Hoskins W 2	McCleary G 3 + 5	Ormerod B 13	Byrne M — + 1	*Match No.*
1	2	3^{3}	4	5	6	7	8	9^{1}	10^{2}	11	12	13	14													1
1	2		4	5	6	12	8	9^{1}		11^{2}	10	7^{3}	3	13	14											2
1	2		4	5	6	7	8			11^{1}	10	9^{2}	3			13	12									3
1	2		4	5	6	7^{1}	8			11^{2}	10■	9^{3}	3	12		13		14								4
1	2		4	5	12	7^{1}	8		13	14	10	9^{2}	3			11^{3}			6							5
1	2		4^{1}	5	6	12	8^{2}			13	10	9^{3}	3		14	11			7							6
1	2		4	5	6		8			12	10	9^{2}	3		13	11^{1}			7							7
1	2		4	5	6	12	8			13	10	9	3^{1}			11^{2}			7							8
1	2		4	5	6		8			11	12	9	3			10^{1}			7							9
1	2		4	5^{2}	6		8			11^{1}	10	9	3			12		13	7							10
1	2		4		6		8			11	12	9	3			10^{1}		5	7							11
1	2		4	12	6^{1}		8^{2}			11	10	9	3					5	7	13						12
1	2		4		6					11	10^{2}	9	3	12				5	7	8^{1}	13					13
1	2		4	12	6					11^{2}		9	3			13		5	7	8	10^{1}					14
1	2		4	12	6					11^{1}		9^{3}	3		14	13		5	7	8	10^{2}					15
1	2		4	12	6					11	13		3			9		5	7	8^{1}	10^{2}					16
1	2	3^{1}	4		6					11^{2}	12	13				9		5	7	8	10					17
1	2	3	4	12	6■	14	13				10	11^{3}				9^{2}		5	7	8^{1}						18
1	2	3^{3}	4^{1}			7	14			11^{2}	12	13				9		5	6	8	10					19
1		3^{1}	2	5		12	4			11	13	9				10^{2}		6	7	8^{3}	14					20
1	12		2	4	6	7	3^{1}			13	10	9						5	11^{2}	8						21
1	3		2	4	6					11	10	9		12				5	7	8^{1}						22
1	2■	3		4	6	12	7^{1}			11^{3}	10^{2}	9						5	13	8	14					23
1		3	12	4	6	2^{1}				11	10			13	14			5	7^{2}	8	9^{3}					24
1	12	3^{1}	2	4		7				11^{2}	10					13		5	6	8	9					25
1	2		4^{2}	5	6	7^{3}				12	10		3			9		13	11	8^{1}	14					26
1	2		4	5	6		12			11	10		3	7^{2}	13	9				8^{1}						27
1	2		4^{1}	5	6	7					10^{2}		3		13	9		12	11		8					28
1	2		4	5	6	12				11^{1}	13		3			9			7	8^{3}	14	10^{2}				29
1	2		4	6	12	13				11^{2}	14		3			9		5	7	8^{1}		10^{3}				30
1	2	3	4	5	6	12				11		9^{2}			13	10^{3}			7	8^{1}	14					31
1	2		4^{1}	5	6	12				11^{3}	10	9^{2}	8					3	7	13	14					32
1	2			5	6	7^{2}				11	10	9	3						4	8^{1}	12		13			33
1	2			5	6	7						9	3	12		13		4^{1}	11	14	8^{3}			10^{2}		34
1	2			5	6	7					10^{1}	9^{3}	3	14		12		4	11	13				8^{2}		35
1	2		12	5	6	7^{1}					13	14	3	11^{2}		10			4^{3}	8				9		36
1	2		4	5	6	7■				12		13	3	8^{3}		9^{2}			11	14				10^{1}		37
1	2		4^{3}	5	6					11		12	3	7^{2}		9			8^{1}	13			14	10		38
1	2		4	5	6							12	3	8^{1}	14	9		7	11^{2}	13				10^{3}		39
1	2		4	5^{1}	6							9^{2}	3		13	10^{3}		12	7	8			14	11		40
1	2		4	5	6					12		9	3^{1}		13				7	8			10^{3}	11^{2}	14	41
1	2	3	4	5	6	12				11		9^{3}			13				7^{2}	8^{1}			14	10		42
1			2	5	6	7				12			3	13		9		4	8				11^{1}	10^{2}		43
1			2	5	6	7				11^{2}			3	12		9^{1}		4	8	13			14	10^{3}		44
1	2	3^{3}	4	5	6	7^{2}				12						9			8	13	14		11	10^{1}		45
1	4		2^{2}	5		7^{1}				11		12	3			9		13	6	8	14			10^{3}		46

FA Cup

First Round	Lincoln C	(a)	1-1
		(h)	3-1
Second Round	Luton T	(a)	0-1

Carling Cup

First Round	Chester C	(a)	0-0
Second Round	Leicester C	(h)	2-3

J Paint Trophy

First Round	Peterborough U	(h)	2-3

NOTTS COUNTY FL Championship 2

FOUNDATION

According to the official history of Notts County 'the true date of Notts' foundation has to be the meeting at the George Hotel on 7 December 1864'. However, there is documented evidence of continuous play from 1862, when club members played organised matches amongst themselves in The Park in Nottingham.

Meadow Lane Stadium, Meadow Lane, Nottingham NG2 3HJ.

Telephone: (0115) 952 9000.

Fax: (0115) 955 3994.

Ticket Office: (0115) 955 7204 (weekdays), (0115) 955 7210 (match days).

Website: www.nottscountyfc.co.uk

Email: info@nottscountyfc.co.uk

Ground Capacity: 20,300.

Record Attendance: 47,310 v York C, FA Cup 6th rd, 12 March 1955.

Pitch Measurements: 113yd × 72yd.

Chairman: John Armstrong-Holmes.

Vice-chairman: Roy Parker.

Chief Executive: Geoff Davey.

Secretary: Tony Cuthbert.

Manager: Ian McParland.

Assistant Manager: Dave Kevan.

Physio: Paul Smith.

Colours: Black and white striped shirts, black shorts, black stockings.

Change Colours: Claret and blue halved shirts, claret shorts with sky blue trim, sky blue stockings.

Year Formed: 1862* (*see Foundation*). ***Turned Professional:*** 1885. ***Ltd Co.:*** 1890.

Club Nickname: 'Magpies'.

Grounds: 1862, The Park; 1864, The Meadows; 1877, Beeston Cricket Ground; 1880, Castle Ground; 1883, Trent Bridge; 1910, Meadow Lane.

First Football League Game: 15 September 1888, Football League, v Everton (a) L 1–2 – Holland; Guttridge, McLean; Brown, Warburton, Shelton; Hodder, Harker, Jardine, Moore (1), Wardle.

Record League Victory: 11–1 v Newport Co, Division 3 (S), 15 January 1949 – Smith; Southwell, Purvis; Gannon, Baxter, Adamson; Houghton (1), Sewell (4), Lawton (4), Pimbley, Johnston (2).

Record Cup Victory: 15–0 v Rotherham T (at Trent Bridge), FA Cup 1st rd, 24 October 1885 – Sherwin; Snook, H. T. Moore; Dobson (1), Emmett (1), Chapman; Gunn (1), Albert Moore (2),

HONOURS

Football League: Division 1 best season: 3rd, 1890–91, 1900–01; Division 2 – Champions 1896–97, 1913–14, 1922–23; Runners-up 1894–95, 1980–81; Promoted from Division 2 1990–91 (play-offs); Division 3 (S) – Champions 1930–31, 1949–50; Runners-up 1936–37; Division 3 – Champions 1997–98; Runners-up 1972–73; Promoted from Division 3 1989–90 (play-offs); Division 4 – Champions 1970–71; Runners-up 1959–60.

FA Cup: Winners 1894; Runners-up 1891.

Football League Cup: best season: 5th rd, 1964, 1973, 1976.

Anglo-Italian Cup: Winners 1995; Runners-up 1994.

SKY SPORTS FACT FILE

Notts County might claim to have had the shortest five forwards on record, but not in terms of the players' height. In 1963–64 on the books were Fry (Keith), Astle (Jeff), Bly (Terry), Tait (Bob) and Jones (Barrie) – just 20 characters in their surnames.

Jackson (3), Daft (2), Cursham (4), (1 og).

Record Defeat: 1–9 v Blackburn R, Division 1, 16 November 1889. 1–9 v Aston Villa, Division 1, 29 September 1888. 1–9 v Portsmouth, Division 2, 9 April 1927.

Most League Points (2 for a win): 69, Division 4, 1970–71.

Most League Points (3 for a win): 99, Division 3, 1997–98.

Most League Goals: 107, Division 4, 1959–60.

Highest League Scorer in Season: Tom Keetley, 39, Division 3 (S), 1930–31.

Most League Goals in Total Aggregate: Les Bradd, 125, 1967–78.

Most League Goals in One Match: 5, Robert Jardine v Burnley, Division 1, 27 October 1888; 5, Daniel Bruce v Port Vale, Division 2, 26 February 1895; 5, Bertie Mills v Barnsley, Division 2, 19 November 1927.

Most Capped Player: Kevin Wilson, 15 (42), Northern Ireland.

Most League Appearances: Albert Iremonger, 564, 1904–26.

Youngest League Player: Tony Bircumshaw, 16 years 54 days v Brentford, 3 April 1961.

Record Transfer Fee Received: £2,500,000 from Derby Co for Craig Short, September 1992.

Record Transfer Fee Paid: £685,000 to Sheffield U for Tony Agana, November 1991.

Football League Record: 1888 Founder Member of the Football League; 1893–97 Division 2; 1897–1913 Division 1; 1913–14 Division 2; 1914–20 Division 1; 1920–23 Division 2; 1923–26 Division 1; 1926–30 Division 2; 1930–31 Division 3 (S); 1931–35 Division 2; 1935–50 Division 3 (S); 1950–58 Division 2; 1958–59 Division 3; 1959–60 Division 4; 1960–64 Division 3; 1964–71 Division 4; 1971–73 Division 3; 1973–81 Division 2; 1981–84 Division 1; 1984–85 Division 2; 1985–90 Division 3; 1990–91 Division 2; 1991–95 Division 1; 1995–97 Division 2; 1997–98 Division 3; 1998–2004 Division 2; 2004– FL 2.

LATEST SEQUENCES

Longest Sequence of League Wins: 10, 3.12.1997 – 31.1.1998.

Longest Sequence of League Defeats: 7, 3.9.1983 – 16.10.1983.

Longest Sequence of League Draws: 5, 2.12.1978 – 26.12.1978.

Longest Sequence of Unbeaten League Matches: 19, 26.4.1930 – 6.12.1930.

Longest Sequence Without a League Win: 20, 3.12.1996 – 31.3.1997.

Successive Scoring Runs: 35 from 26.4.1930.

Successive Non-scoring Runs: 5 from 30.11.1912.

MANAGERS

Albert Fisher 1913–27
Horace Henshall 1927–34
Charlie Jones 1934
David Pratt 1935
Percy Smith 1935–36
Jimmy McMullan 1936–37
Harry Parkes 1938–39
Tony Towers 1939–42
Frank Womack 1942–43
Major Frank Buckley 1944–46
Arthur Stollery 1946–49
Eric Houghton 1949–53
George Poyser 1953–57
Tommy Lawton 1957–58
Frank Hill 1958–61
Tim Coleman 1961–63
Eddie Lowe 1963–65
Tim Coleman 1965–66
Jack Burkitt 1966–67
Andy Beattie *(General Manager)* 1967
Billy Gray 1967–68
Jack Wheeler (*Caretaker Manager*) 1968–69
Jimmy Sirrel 1969–75
Ron Fenton 1975–77
Jimmy Sirrel 1978–82 *(continued as General Manager to 1984)*
Howard Wilkinson 1982–83
Larry Lloyd 1983–84
Richie Barker 1984–85
Jimmy Sirrel 1985–87
John Barnwell 1987–88
Neil Warnock 1989–93
Mick Walker 1993–94
Russell Slade 1994–95
Howard Kendall 1995
Colin Murphy 1995 *(continued as General Manager to 1996)*
Steve Thompson 1996
Sam Allardyce 1997–99
Gary Brazil 1999–2000
Jocky Scott 2000–01
Gary Brazil 2001
Billy Dearden 2002–04
Gary Mills 2004
Ian Richardson 2004–05
Gudjon Thordarson 2005–06
Steve Thompson 2006–07
Ian McParland October 2007–

TEN YEAR LEAGUE RECORD

		P	W	D	L	F	A	Pts	Pos
1998-99	Div 2	46	14	12	20	52	61	54	16
1999-2000	Div 2	46	18	11	17	61	55	65	8
2000-01	Div 2	46	19	12	15	62	66	69	8
2001-02	Div 2	46	13	11	22	59	71	50	19
2002-03	Div 2	46	13	16	17	62	70	55	15
2003-04	Div 2	46	10	12	24	50	78	42	23
2004-05	FL 2	46	13	13	20	46	62	52	19
2005-06	FL 2	46	12	16	18	48	63	52	21
2006-07	FL 2	46	16	14	16	55	53	62	13
2007-08	FL 2	46	10	18	18	37	53	48	21

DID YOU KNOW 

In 2008–09 Notts County will become the first club to have played 4,500 League games when they complete their 20th fixture. They will have beaten Preston North End the first Football League champions, who will reach the same milestone in their last game.

NOTTS COUNTY 2007–08 LEAGUE RECORD

Match No.	Date	Venue	Opponents	Result		H/T Score	Lg. Pos.	Goalscorers	Attendance
1	Aug 11	A	Grimsby T	D	1-1	1-1	—	MacKenzie [29]	5483
2	18	H	Brentford	D	1-1	0-0	15	Butcher [82]	4670
3	25	A	Darlington	D	2-2	0-1	17	Butcher 2 [72, 90]	3763
4	Sept 1	H	Morecambe	D	1-1	0-1	14	Butcher [87]	4434
5	7	A	Milton Keynes D	L	0-3	0-1	—		7977
6	15	H	Dagenham & R	W	1-0	0-0	15	MacKenzie [83]	3926
7	22	A	Rotherham U	D	1-1	1-1	17	Weir-Daley [36]	4181
8	29	H	Chesterfield	W	1-0	1-0	11	Hunt [21]	5757
9	Oct 2	H	Hereford U	L	2-3	0-2	—	Silk [64], Sam [74]	3576
10	6	A	Wycombe W	L	1-3	0-0	16	Butcher [68]	4199
11	13	H	Bury	L	1-3	0-1	19	MacKenzie (pen) [64]	3710
12	20	A	Mansfield T	L	0-2	0-0	20		4002
13	27	H	Wrexham	W	2-1	1-0	18	Weir-Daley [17], MacKenzie [90]	4359
14	Nov 3	A	Accrington S	W	2-0	1-0	16	Lindfield [23], Dudfield [87]	1722
15	6	A	Barnet	D	1-1	0-1	—	Butcher [49]	2089
16	17	H	Macclesfield T	L	0-1	0-0	19		4390
17	24	A	Lincoln C	L	1-2	0-1	19	Silk [50]	4503
18	Dec 4	H	Peterborough U	L	0-1	0-0	—		4412
19	8	H	Shrewsbury T	W	2-1	0-1	18	Pearce [69], MacKenzie [75]	3819
20	22	A	Dagenham & R	D	1-1	1-0	17	Butcher [6]	1649
21	26	H	Milton Keynes D	L	1-2	1-1	18	Butcher [9]	5106
22	29	H	Rotherham U	L	0-1	0-1	20		5290
23	Jan 1	A	Hereford U	D	0-0	0-0	19		3945
24	5	H	Stockport Co	L	1-2	1-2	19	Hunt [7]	4120
25	12	A	Bradford C	L	0-3	0-1	20		13,494
26	19	H	Chester C	W	1-0	0-0	18	Tann [58]	3774
27	26	A	Morecambe	D	1-1	1-0	18	Butcher [28]	2727
28	29	A	Brentford	D	0-0	0-0	—		4332
29	Feb 2	H	Grimsby T	D	1-1	0-0	18	Butcher [59]	4902
30	9	A	Stockport Co	D	1-1	1-1	20	Edwards [9]	5849
31	12	H	Darlington	L	0-1	0-1	—		3421
32	16	A	Chester C	W	1-0	0-0	19	Crow [69]	1798
33	23	H	Bradford C	L	1-3	0-0	20	Jarvis [59]	4717
34	Mar 1	A	Macclesfield T	D	1-1	0-1	20	Butcher [72]	2193
35	8	H	Barnet	D	0-0	0-0	21		3687
36	11	H	Lincoln C	L	0-1	0-1	—		3858
37	15	A	Peterborough U	D	0-0	0-0	22		7173
38	22	H	Rochdale	W	1-0	1-0	22	Johnson [28]	4030
39	24	A	Shrewsbury T	D	0-0	0-0	22		5673
40	29	H	Mansfield T	D	0-0	0-0	22		10,027
41	Apr 5	A	Bury	L	1-2	0-1	22	Crow [71]	2463
42	8	A	Rochdale	L	2-4	0-0	—	Lee [72], MacKenzie (pen) [90]	2536
43	12	H	Accrington S	W	1-0	1-0	22	Jarvis [37]	5525
44	19	A	Wrexham	L	0-1	0-0	21		4076
45	26	H	Wycombe W	W	1-0	0-0	20	Butcher [66]	7327
46	May 3	A	Chesterfield	D	1-1	1-0	21	Weir-Daley [45]	4477

Final League Position: 21

GOALSCORERS

League (37): Butcher 12, MacKenzie 6 (2 pens), Weir-Daley 3, Crow 2, Hunt 2, Jarvis 2, Silk 2, Dudfield 1, Edwards 1, Johnson 1, Lee 1, Lindfield 1, Pearce 1, Sam 1, Tann 1.
Carling Cup (0).
FA Cup (3): Dudfield 2, Sam 1.
J Paint Trophy (0).

Pilkington K 32	Silk G 22 + 11	Mayo P 27 + 2	Hunt S 36 + 1	Canoville L 32 + 3	Somner M 12 + 4	Butcher R 46	MacKenzie N 24 + 5	Lee J 22 + 9	Dudfield L 26 + 7	Parkinson A 11 + 12	Smith J 16 + 4	Sam H 7 + 13	Weir-Daley S 12 + 18	Tann A 40 + 1	Weston M 14 + 11	McCann A 13 + 9	Frost S — + 2	Crow D 13 + 1	Lindfield C 3	Pearce K 8	Branston G 1	Bastians F 5	Gibb A 9	Strachan G 7	Edwards M 19	Jarvis R 17	Hoult R 14	Johnson M 11 + 1	Corden W 7 + 2	*Match No.*
1	2	3	4	5	6	7[1]	8	9	10[2]	11[3]	12	13	14																	1
1		3	4	5	6[1]	7	8	9	10[3]	11[2]	12	13		2	14															2
1	12	11	4	2[1]	13	7	8[2]		10	14	6		9[3]	5		3														3
1		11	6	2	12	7	8			9	4[3]	10[2]	13	5		3[1]	14													4
1		3	4	2	12	7		9	10[3]	11[2]	8	14	13	5		6[1]														5
1	12	3	4	2	6	7[2]	13	9	10[3]		8[1]	14	11	5																6
1	12	3	4	2	6	7[1]	8[3]	9	10[2]	13			11	5		14														7
1	12	3	4	2	6	7	8[1]	9	13	14		11[2]	10[3]	5																8
1	12	3	4	2[1]	6	7	8	9[2]	10	11[3]		14	13	5																9
1		3■	4	2[2]	6	7	8	9[1]	10	12		11[3]	14	5		13														10
1	2		4		6	7	8[1]		10	12		13	11[2]	5	14	3		9[3]												11
1	2	3	4			7	8		10	11[2]		12	9	5	13	6[1]														12
1		3	4	2	6	7	8		10	12		13	9[2]	5	11[1]															13
1	7	3	4	2		11	8		10			12		5	6[2]	13			9[1]											14
1	7	3	4[1]	2	12	11	8		10			13		5	6[2]	14			9[3]											15
1	7	3		2	6[1]	8			10	11[3]		13	12	5	14				9[2]	4										16
1	7	3	4	2		6	8		10			9[1]	12	5	11															17
1	2		3		4[1]	7	12	9	10[3]			13	11[2]	5		8	14			6										18
1	2		3	12	4[2]	7	13	9[3]	10	14			11	5[1]		8				6										19
1	12		4	5		7	8[1]	9	10[2]	13				2	3	11				6■										20
1	7		4	2		6	8	12	10	11[1]				5	9	3														21
1	7		4	2		8		12	10[3]	11		14	9[1]	5	3[2]	13				6										22
1	12	13	4	2		7	8		10	11		9[1]		5		3[2]				6										23
1	12		4			7[1]	8		10	11		9[2]	13	2		14				6	5[3]	3								24
1			3	2		7			10			9[1]	12	5						6		11	4	8						25
1	7		4	2		8		9	10[2]		12		13	5	14	3						11[3]		6[1]						26
1	7		4			8		9	10					2	12	3						11[1]		6	5					27
1	7[3]		3	2		10		9[1]	12		14			5		13						11[2]	8	4	6					28
1	7		3	2		8		9[2]	12				13	5	14								11[3]	4	6	10[1]				29
1	12		3	2		11			10[2]		8[1]			5	13								7	4	6	9				30
1			3[1]	2		11		9			8		13	5	14	12							7[2]	4[3]	6	10				31
1	12	3		2		11		13			8[1]		14	5	4			9[2]					7		6	10[3]				32
	12	3		2[1]		8	13				4		14	5	11[3]			9					7[2]		6	10	1			33
		3	4[2]			8	12	13			6			2	11[3]			9					7[1]		5	10	1	14		34
	7	3				11	8	12			4[2]		13	5				9[1]							2	10	1	6		35
		11				8		12		13	4		10	2		3[1]							7[2]		5	9	1	6		36
	7	3	12			8		9		13	4			2											6	10[2]	1	5	11[1]	37
	7	3		12		8		13		14	4			2				9[2]							5[1]	10	1	6[3]	11	38
	7	3	6	2		8		12			4		13	5		14		9[2]								10[1]	1		11[3]	39
	7	3				8					4		12	2				9							5	10[1]	1	6	11	40
	7	3		12		8[3]		13			4			2[1]	14			9							5	10[2]	1	6	11	41
			3	2		4	8	9					12		13			10[1]							5	7	1	6	11[2]	42
			3	2		4	8	9	12						11[2]			10[1]							5	7	1	6	13	43
		12	3	2		11	0	9	14						4			10[3]							5	7[2]	1	6[1]	13	44
			3	2[1]		11	8	9	13					12	4			10[2]							5	7	1	6		45
	2	3				8	4	9[2]	13	12			10[3]		11			14							5		1	6	7[1]	46

FA Cup

First Round	Histon	(h)	3-0
Second Round	Havant & W	(h)	0-1

Carling Cup

First Round	Coventry C	(a)	0-3

J Paint Trophy

First Round	Leyton Orient	(h)	0-1

OLDHAM ATHLETIC FL Championship 1

FOUNDATION

It was in 1895 that John Garland, the landlord of the Featherstall and Junction Hotel, decided to form a football club. As Pine Villa they played in the Oldham Junior League. In 1899 the local professional club, Oldham County, went out of existence and one of the liquidators persuaded Pine Villa to take over their ground at Sheepfoot Lane and change their name to Oldham Athletic.

Boundary Park, Furtherwood Road, Oldham OL1 2PA.

Telephone: 0871 226 2235.

Fax: 0871 226 1715.

Ticket Office: 0871 226 1653.

Website: www.oldhamathletic.co.uk

Email: enquiries@oldhamathletic.co.uk

Ground Capacity: 10,850.

Record Attendance: 46,471 v Sheffield W, FA Cup 4th rd, 25 January 1930.

Pitch Measurements: 106yd × 72yd.

Chairman: Simon Blitz.

Vice-chairman: Simon Corney.

Chief Executive/Secretary: Alan Hardy.

Manager: John Sheridan.

Assistant Manager: Tommy Wright.

Physio: Marc Czuczman.

Colours: Blue shirts, blue shorts, white stockings.

Change Colours: Fluo yellow shirts, black shorts, black stockings.

Year Formed: 1895.

Turned Professional: 1899.

Ltd Co.: 1906.

Previous Name: 1895, Pine Villa; 1899, Oldham Athletic.

Club Nickname: 'The Latics'.

Grounds: 1895, Sheepfoot Lane; 1900, Hudson Field; 1906, Sheepfoot Lane; 1907, Boundary Park.

First Football League Game: 9 September 1907, Division 2, v Stoke (a) W 3–1 – Hewitson; Hodson, Hamilton; Fay, Walders, Wilson; Ward, W. Dodds (1), Newton (1), Hancock, Swarbrick (1).

Record League Victory: 11–0 v Southport, Division 4, 26 December 1962 – Bollands; Branagan, Marshall; McCall, Williams, Scott; Ledger (1), Johnstone, Lister (6), Colquhoun (1), Whitaker (3).

HONOURS

Football League: Division 1 – Runners-up 1914–15; Division 2 – Champions 1990–91; Runners-up 1909–10; Division 3 (N) – Champions 1952–53; Division 3 – Champions 1973–74; Division 4 – Runners-up 1962–63.

FA Cup: Semi-final 1913, 1990, 1994.

Football League Cup: Runners-up 1990.

SKY SPORTS FACT FILE

At the age of 42 years 63 days the much-travelled former Scottish international Bobby Collins played for Oldham Athletic against Rochdale on 20 April 1973. He had just returned from a spell playing in Australia.

Record Cup Victory: 10–1 v Lytham, FA Cup 1st rd, 28 November 1925 – Gray; Wynne, Grundy; Adlam, Heaton, Naylor (1), Douglas, Pynegar (2), Ormston (2), Barnes (3), Watson (2).

Record Defeat: 4–13 v Tranmere R, Division 3 (N), 26 December 1935.

Most League Points (2 for a win): 62, Division 3, 1973–74.

Most League Points (3 for a win): 88, Division 2, 1990–91.

Most League Goals: 95, Division 4, 1962–63.

Highest League Scorer in Season: Tom Davis, 33, Division 3 (N), 1936–37.

Most League Goals in Total Aggregate: Roger Palmer, 141, 1980–94.

Most League Goals in One Match: 7, Eric Gemmell v Chester, Division 3N, 19 January 1952.

Most Capped Player: Gunnar Halle, 24 (64), Norway.

Most League Appearances: Ian Wood, 525, 1966–80.

Youngest League Player: Wayne Harrison, 15 years 11 months v Notts Co, 27 October 1984.

Record Transfer Fee Received: £1,700,000 from Aston Villa for Earl Barrett, February 1992.

Record Transfer Fee Paid: £750,000 to Aston Villa for Ian Olney, June 1992.

Football League Record: 1907 Elected to Division 2; 1910–23 Division 1; 1923–35 Division 2; 1935–53 Division 3 (N); 1953–54 Division 2; 1954–58 Division 3 (N); 1958–63 Division 4; 1963–69 Division 3; 1969–71 Division 4; 1971–74 Division 3; 1974–91 Division 2; 1991–92 Division 1; 1992–94 FA Premier League; 1994–97 Division 1; 1997–2004 Division 2; 2004– FL 1.

MANAGERS

David Ashworth 1906–14
Herbert Bamlett 1914–21
Charlie Roberts 1921–22
David Ashworth 1923–24
Bob Mellor 1924–27
Andy Wilson 1927–32
Jimmy McMullan 1933–34
Bob Mellor 1934–45
(continued as Secretary to 1953)
Frank Womack 1945–47
Billy Wootton 1947–50
George Hardwick 1950–56
Ted Goodier 1956–58
Norman Dodgin 1958–60
Jack Rowley 1960–63
Les McDowall 1963–65
Gordon Hurst 1965–66
Jimmy McIlroy 1966–68
Jack Rowley 1968–69
Jimmy Frizzell 1970–82
Joe Royle 1982–94
Graeme Sharp 1994–97
Neil Warnock 1997–98
Andy Ritchie 1998–2001
Mick Wadsworth 2001–02
Iain Dowie 2002–03
Brian Talbot 2004–05
Ronnie Moore 2005–06
John Sheridan June 2006–

LATEST SEQUENCES

Longest Sequence of League Wins: 10, 12.1.1974 – 12.3.1974.

Longest Sequence of League Defeats: 8, 15.12.1934 – 2.2.1935.

Longest Sequence of League Draws: 5, 26.12.1982 – 15.1.1983.

Longest Sequence of Unbeaten League Matches: 20, 1.5.1990 – 10.11.1990.

Longest Sequence Without a League Win: 17, 4.9.1920 – 18.12.1920.

Successive Scoring Runs: 25 from 15.1.1927.

Successive Non-scoring Runs: 6 from 4.2.1922.

TEN YEAR LEAGUE RECORD

		P	*W*	*D*	*L*	*F*	*A*	*Pts*	*Pos*
1998-99	Div 2	46	14	9	23	48	66	51	20
1999-2000	Div 2	46	16	12	18	50	55	60	14
2000-01	Div 2	46	15	13	18	53	65	58	15
2001-02	Div 2	46	18	16	12	77	65	70	9
2002-03	Div 2	46	22	16	8	68	38	82	5
2003-04	Div 2	46	12	21	13	66	60	57	15
2004-05	FL 1	46	14	10	22	60	73	52	19
2005-06	FL 1	46	18	11	17	58	60	65	10
2006-07	FL 1	46	21	12	13	69	47	75	6
2007-08	FL 1	46	18	13	15	58	46	67	8

DID YOU KNOW ?

On 9 May 1987 substitute Mike Cecere, aged 19, the club's former apprentice, scored a hat-trick for Oldham Athletic against Blackburn Rovers in a Second Division match.

OLDHAM ATHLETIC 2007–08 LEAGUE RECORD

Match No.	Date	Venue	Opponents	Result		H/T Score	Lg. Pos.	Goalscorers	Attendance
1	Aug 11	H	Swansea C	W	2-1	1-0	—	Ricketts (pen) [3], Davies [90]	7397
2	18	A	Carlisle U	L	0-1	0-1	11		7777
3	25	H	Bristol R	L	0-1	0-1	15		5348
4	Sept 1	A	Hartlepool U	L	1-4	1-3	21	Davies [14]	5015
5	15	H	Southend U	L	0-1	0-1	24		5151
6	22	A	Walsall	W	3-0	1-0	19	Ricketts [33], Liddell (pen) [65], Davies [90]	6202
7	29	H	Crewe Alex	W	3-2	1-2	15	Allott [36], Wolfenden [83], Kilkenny [90]	5082
8	Oct 2	H	Leeds U	L	0-1	0-0	—		10,054
9	6	A	Cheltenham T	D	1-1	0-1	18	Liddell [46]	3621
10	20	A	Huddersfield T	D	1-1	1-0	20	Davies [27]	10,909
11	27	H	Northampton T	L	0-1	0-0	21		4870
12	30	A	Nottingham F	D	0-0	0-0	—		16,423
13	Nov 3	A	Leyton Orient	L	0-1	0-1	20		4690
14	6	A	Tranmere R	W	1-0	0-0	—	Davies [90]	5473
15	17	H	Port Vale	D	1-1	1-1	19	Davies [23]	5097
16	24	A	Bournemouth	W	3-0	0-0	16	Hughes 2 (1 pen) [56, 87 (p)], Taylor [70]	5261
17	Dec 4	H	Luton T	D	1-1	1-1	—	Davies [32]	4251
18	8	H	Doncaster R	D	1-1	1-0	17	Allott [44]	4776
19	15	A	Millwall	W	3-2	1-2	14	Hughes 3 (1 pen) [32, 74 (p), 80]	8033
20	22	A	Southend U	W	1-0	1-0	14	Hughes [4]	7388
21	26	H	Nottingham F	D	0-0	0-0	15		8140
22	29	H	Walsall	L	0-2	0-1	15		5292
23	Jan 1	A	Leeds U	W	3-1	3-0	13	Hazell [28], Trotman [36], Hughes (og) [41]	25,906
24	12	H	Brighton & HA	D	1-1	1-0	13	Hughes [40]	5168
25	19	A	Yeovil T	D	0-0	0-0	13		4905
26	22	A	Gillingham	D	0-0	0-0	—		4402
27	29	H	Carlisle U	W	2-0	2-0	—	McDonald 2 [21, 44]	4701
28	Feb 2	A	Swansea C	L	1-2	0-0	14	Davies (pen) [76]	12,458
29	9	H	Gillingham	W	2-1	1-1	10	Taylor [42], Davies [67]	4866
30	12	A	Bristol R	L	0-1	0-0	—		5778
31	16	H	Yeovil T	W	3-0	1-0	10	McDonald [15], Peltier (og) [77], Davies [87]	4781
32	23	A	Brighton & HA	L	0-1	0-0	12		4815
33	26	H	Swindon T	D	2-2	0-1	—	Livermore [50], Allott [55]	3923
34	Mar 1	A	Port Vale	W	3-0	1-0	10	Robertson [23], Eardley [78], Wolfenden [90]	3715
35	4	H	Hartlepool U	L	0-1	0-0	—		3765
36	8	H	Tranmere R	W	3-1	2-0	9	Eardley (pen) [41], Taylor [45], Alessandra [76]	5442
37	11	H	Bournemouth	W	2-0	1-0	—	Eardley 2 (2 pens) [24, 80]	3633
38	15	A	Luton T	L	0-3	0-3	12		5417
39	22	H	Millwall	D	1-1	0-0	11	Constantine [79]	4391
40	24	A	Doncaster R	D	1-1	0-1	11	Jarrett [52]	8777
41	29	H	Huddersfield T	W	4-1	3-0	9	Jarrett 2 [8, 45], Constantine [40], Taylor [61]	5637
42	Apr 5	A	Swindon T	L	0-3	0-0	10		5384
43	12	H	Leyton Orient	W	2-0	2-0	10	Taylor [22], Allott [42]	4325
44	19	A	Northampton T	L	0-2	0-0	10		5171
45	26	H	Cheltenham T	W	2-1	1-0	20	Smalley [16], Alessandra [87]	6400
46	May 3	A	Crewe Alex	W	4-1	2-0	8	Smalley [5], Eardley 2 [32, 59], McDonald [69]	6786

Final League Position: 8

GOALSCORERS

League (58): Davies 10 (1 pen), Hughes 7 (2 pens), Eardley 6 (3 pens), Taylor 5, Allott 4, McDonald 4, Jarrett 3, Alessandra 2, Constantine 2, Liddell 2 (1 pen), Ricketts 2 (1 pen), Smalley 2, Wolfenden 2, Hazell 1, Kilkenny 1, Livermore 1, Robertson 1, Trotman 1, own goals 2.
Carling Cup (4): Davies 1, Kamudimba Kalala 1, Kilkenny 1, Smalley 1.
FA Cup (6): McDonald 2, Davies 1, Hughes 1, Kilkenny 1, Trotman 1.
J Paint Trophy (3): Davies 1, Liddell 1, Wolfenden 1.

Crossley M 38	Eardley N 40+2	Giddings S 2	Kilkenny N 19+1	Thompson J 6+1	Gregan S 15	Allott M 34+8	Kamudimba Kalala J 14+6	Ricketts M 8+1	Davies C 31+1	Taylor C 40+2	McDonald G 31+4	Smalley D 19+18	Liddell A 16+2	Bertrand R 21	Wolfenden M 7+18	Trotman N 16+1	Pearson M —+1	Hughes L 15+3	Hazell R 32+2	Beresford M 5	Alessandra L 12+3	Stam S 34+2	Lomax K 17+4	Jarrett J 12+3	Livermore D 10	Robertson J 2+1	Constantine L 7+1	O'Donnell R 3+1	Black P —+2	Kelly A —+1	Chalmers A —+2	Match No.
1	2^1	3	4	5	6	7	8	9^3	10	11^2	12	13	14																			1
1	2	3	4	5	6	7	8^1	9	10	12		13	11^2																			2
1	2		4	5	6		8^1	9^3	10	11	12	13	7^2	3	14																	3
1	2			5^2	6	12	8^1		10	11	4		7^3	3		13	14	9														4
1	12			5^1	6	7		13	10	11	4^3		8	3	14			9^2	2													5
1	2				6	7	8	9^1	10	11^2			4	3	13			12	5													6
1	2		12		6	7^1	8	9^2	10	11			4	3	13				5													7
1	2		4		6		8	9^1	10	11			7	3	12				5													8
1	2		4		6	7^1		9	10^2	11	12		8	3	13				5													9
	2		4^1		6	12	8		10	11		13	7^3	3	9^2				5	1	14											10
	2		4			12	8^1	9	10	11^2		13	7	3		6			5^3	1		14										11
	2		4^1			12			10	11	8	13	7	3	9^2	5				1		6										12
	2		4			12			10	11	8^1	9^2	7^3	3	13	5		14		1		6										13
	2^1		4			12			10	11	8	9^2	7	3		5		13		1		6										14
1			4			12	13		10	11	8^1	7^2		3	14	5		9^3	2			6										15
1	2		4			12			10	11	8^1	7^3		3	13	5		9^2	14			6										16
1	2		4			7			10	11	8^1	12		3		5		9				6										17
1	2		4			7			10	11	8			3		5		9				6										18
1	2■		4			7			10	11	8^2	13		3		5		9^1	12			6										19
1			4			7	12		10	11	8^1			3		5		9	2			6										20
1	2		4			7	12		10	11	8^1			3		5		9				6										21
1	2		4			7			10^1	11	8^2	13		3	12	5		9				6										22
1			4			7	12		10	11^2	8	13		3		5		9^1	2			6										23
1						7	8		10^1		4	11			12	5		9	2			6	3									24
1	12					7	8		10	13	4^2	11				5		9	2			6	3^1									25
1	2					7	8		10	11	4^1	12				5^2		9	3			6	13									26
1	2					7	12			11	8	10						9^2	5		13	6	3	4^1								27
1	2					7	12		10		8^3	14			13				5		9^2	6	3	4^1	11							28
1	2					7			10	11	8	12							5		9^1	6		4	3							29
1	2					7			10	11	8	12							5		9^1	6		4	3							30
1	2					7			10^1	11	8^2	13			12				5		9	6	14	4^3	3							31
1	2					7			10^1	11	8	12							5		9	6	13	4^2	3							32
1	2					7				11	8	10							5		9	6^1	12	4^2	3	13						33
1	2					7				11	8^1	12			13				5		9	6	3		4	10^2						34
1	2					7				11	8	12							5		9	6	3	4^1		10^2	13					35
1	2					7				11	8	4			12				5		9^1	6	3				10					36
1	2						7			11	8	4			12				5		9^1	6	3				10					37
	2			13			7^1			11	8	9			12				5■			6	3	4^2			10	1				38
	2			5^1		7				11	8	4			13							6	3	12^2	9		10	1				39
	2					7				11		9			4^1				5			6	3	12	8		10	1				40
1	2					7				11		9							5			6	3^1	4	8		10		12			41
1	2				4	7				11		9	12						5			6	3	8^1			10					42
1	2				4^1	7				11		9	8		10^2				5			6	3							12	13	43
1	11				5	7						10	8^1		9				2		12	6	3	4^2							13	44
1	11				5	7					12	4^2	8		10^3				2		9	6^1	3	13					14			45
1^6	2				5	7			13	11	4	8			10^2				6^1		9	12	3					15				46

FA Cup

First Round	Doncaster R	(h)	2-2
		(a)	2-1
Second Round	Crewe Alex	(h)	1-0
Third Round	Everton	(a)	1-0
Fourth Round	Huddersfield T	(h)	0-1

Carling Cup

First Round	Mansfield T	(h)	4-1
Second Round	Burnley	(a)	0-3

J Paint Trophy

First Round	Accrington S	(a)	3-2
Second Round	Doncaster R	(a)	0-3

PETERBOROUGH UNITED FL Championship 1

FOUNDATION

The old Peterborough & Fletton club, founded in 1923, was suspended by the FA during season 1932–33 and disbanded. Local enthusiasts determined to carry on and in 1934 a new professional club, Peterborough United, was formed and entered the Midland League the following year. Peterborough's first success came in 1939–40, but from 1955–56 to 1959–60 they won five successive titles. During the 1958–59 season they were undefeated in the Midland League. They reached the third round of the FA Cup, won the Northamptonshire Senior Cup, the Maunsell Cup and were runners-up in the East Anglian Cup.

London Road, Peterborough PE2 8AL.

Telephone: (01733) 563 947.

Fax: (01733) 344 140.

Ticket Office: (01733) 563 947.

Website: www.theposh.com

Email: phil@theposh.com

Ground Capacity: 15,000.

Record Attendance: 30,096 v Swansea T, FA Cup 5th rd, 20 February 1965.

Pitch Measurements: 112yd × 71yd.

Chairman: Darragh MacAnthony.

Chief Executive: Bob Symns.

Secretary: Karen Turner.

Manager: Darren Ferguson.

Assistant Manager: Kevin Russell.

Physio: Keith Oakes.

Colours: Blue shirts, white shorts, blue stockings.

Change Colours: All black.

Year Formed: 1934.

Turned Professional: 1934.

Ltd Co.: 1934.

Club Nickname: 'The Posh'.

Ground: 1934, London Road Stadium.

First Football League Game: 20 August 1960, Division 4, v Wrexham (h) W 3–0 – Walls; Stafford, Walker; Rayner, Rigby, Norris; Hails, Emery (1), Bly (1), Smith, McNamee (1).

Record League Victory: 9–1 v Barnet (a) Division 3, 5 September 1998 – Griemink; Hooper (1), Drury (Farell), Gill, Bodley, Edwards, Davies, Payne, Grazioli (5), Quinn (2) (Rowe), Houghton (Etherington) (1).

HONOURS

Football League: Division 1 best season: 10th, 1992–93; Division 2 1991–92 (play-offs). Promoted from Division 3 1999–2000 (play-offs); FL 2 – Runners-up 2007–08. Division 4 – Champions 1960–61, 1973–74.

FA Cup: best season: 6th rd, 1965.

Football League Cup: Semi-final 1966.

SKY SPORTS FACT FILE

Analysing Terry Bly's record-breaking 52 goals in 1960–61 it is interesting to note he failed to score in only 17 games with just Gillingham and Oldham Athletic prevented him from scoring. His tally included a five, two fours and four hat-tricks.

Record Cup Victory: 7–0 v Harlow T, FA Cup 1st rd, 16 November 1991 – Barber; Luke, Johnson, Halsall (1), Robinson D, Welsh, Sterling (1) (Butterworth), Cooper G (2 incl. 1p), Riley (1) (Culpin (1)), Charlery (1), Kimble.

Record Defeat: 1–8 v Northampton T, FA Cup 2nd rd (2nd replay), 18 December 1946.

Most League Points (2 for a win): 66, Division 4, 1960–61.

Most League Points (3 for a win): 82, Division 4, 1981–82.

Most League Goals: 134, Division 4, 1960–61.

Highest League Scorer in Season: Terry Bly, 52, Division 4, 1960–61.

Most League Goals in Total Aggregate: Jim Hall, 122, 1967–75.

Most League Goals in One Match: 5, Guiliano Grazioli v Barnet, Division 3, 5 September 1998.

Most Capped Player: James Quinn, 9 (50), Northern Ireland.

Most League Appearances: Tommy Robson, 482, 1968–81.

Youngest League Player: Matthew Etherington, 15 years 262 days v Brentford, 3 May 1997.

Record Transfer Fee Received: £700,000 from Tottenham H for Simon Davies, December 1999.

Record Transfer Fee Paid: £400,000 to Norwich C for Joe Lewis, January 2008.

Football League Record: 1960 Elected to Division 4; 1961–68 Division 3, when they were demoted for financial irregularities; 1968–74 Division 4; 1974–79 Division 3; 1979–91 Division 4; 1991–92 Division 3; 1992–94 Division 1; 1994–97 Division 2; 1997–2000 Division 3; 2000–04 Division 2; 2004–05 FL 1; 2005–08 FL 2; 2008– FL 1.

MANAGERS

Jock Porter 1934–36
Fred Taylor 1936–37
Vic Poulter 1937–38
Sam Madden 1938–48
Jack Blood 1948–50
Bob Gurney 1950–52
Jack Fairbrother 1952–54
George Swindin 1954–58
Jimmy Hagan 1958–62
Jack Fairbrother 1962–64
Gordon Clark 1964–67
Norman Rigby 1967–69
Jim Iley 1969–72
Noel Cantwell 1972–77
John Barnwell 1977–78
Billy Hails 1978–79
Peter Morris 1979–82
Martin Wilkinson 1982–83
John Wile 1983–86
Noel Cantwell 1986–88 *(continued as General Manager)*
Mick Jones 1988–89
Mark Lawrenson 1989–90
Dave Booth 1990–91
Chris Turner 1991–92
Lil Fuccillo 1992–93
John Still 1994–95
Mick Halsall 1995–96
Barry Fry 1996–2005
Mark Wright 2005–06
Keith Alexander 2006–07
Darren Ferguson January 2007–

LATEST SEQUENCES

Longest Sequence of League Wins: 9, 1.2.1992 – 14.3.1992.

Longest Sequence of League Defeats: 6, 16.12.2006 – 21.1.2007.

Longest Sequence of League Draws: 8, 18.12.1971 – 12.2.1972.

Longest Sequence of Unbeaten League Matches: 17, 17.12.1960 – 8.4.1961.

Longest Sequence Without a League Win: 17, 23.9.1978 – 30.12.1978.

Successive Scoring Runs: 33 from 20.9.1960.

Successive Non-scoring Runs: 6 from 13.8.2002.

TEN YEAR LEAGUE RECORD

		P	W	D	L	F	A	Pts	Pos
1998-99	Div 3	46	18	12	16	72	56	66	9
1999-2000	Div 3	46	22	12	12	63	54	78	5
2000-01	Div 2	46	15	14	17	61	66	59	12
2001-02	Div 2	46	15	10	21	64	59	55	17
2002-03	Div 2	46	14	16	16	51	54	58	11
2003-04	Div 2	46	12	16	18	58	58	52	18
2004-05	FL 1	46	9	12	25	49	73	39	23
2005-06	FL 2	46	17	11	18	57	49	62	9
2006-07	FL 2	46	18	11	17	70	61	65	10
2007-08	FL 2	46	28	8	10	84	43	92	2

DID YOU KNOW 

Despite scoring in just two FA Cup ties during 2007–08, Craig Mackail-Smith succeeded in becoming the tournament's leading marksman with a four and a treble. His total of seven goals was as many as cup winners Portsmouth managed in the entire campaign!

PETERBOROUGH UNITED 2007–08 LEAGUE RECORD

Match No.	Date	Venue	Opponents	Result		H/T Score	Lg. Pos.	Goalscorers	Attendance
1	Aug 11	H	Rochdale	W	3-0	2-0	—	Low 10, McLean 44, Crow 90	5575
2	19	A	Rotherham U	L	1-3	0-3	8	McLean 88	4291
3	25	H	Chesterfield	L	2-3	2-1	15	McLean 9, Lee 45	5005
4	Sept 1	A	Accrington S	W	2-0	0-0	7	Lee 55, McLean 90	1484
5	9	H	Mansfield T	W	2-1	1-0	4	Low 29, Crow 75	4721
6	15	A	Bradford C	L	0-1	0-0	9		13,019
7	22	H	Morecambe	D	1-1	0-0	9	McLean (pen) 63	4473
8	29	A	Darlington	D	1-1	0-0	10	Mackail-Smith 90	3974
9	Oct 2	A	Shrewsbury T	W	2-0	1-0	—	Lee 33, Boyd 81	5220
10	6	H	Grimsby T	W	2-1	0-0	7	Boyd 65, McLean (pen) 80	4786
11	14	H	Wycombe W	W	2-1	0-0	6	Boyd 48, McLean 87	4584
12	20	A	Lincoln C	D	1-1	0-1	7	Croft (og) 89	5036
13	27	H	Hereford U	D	1-1	1-0	7	Mackail-Smith 43	5008
14	Nov 3	A	Stockport Co	W	2-1	2-1	4	Mackail-Smith 15, McLean 45	5042
15	6	H	Dagenham & R	W	3-1	0-1	—	Keates 69, McLean 2 79, 82	4200
16	17	A	Bury	L	0-2	0-1	5		2660
17	24	H	Brentford	W	7-0	4-0	5	McLean 3 (1 pen) 3 (p), 14, 41, Whelpdale 45, Boyd 49, Mackail-Smith 56, Howe 76	4865
18	Dec 4	A	Notts Co	W	1-0	0-0	—	Mackail-Smith 52	4412
19	8	A	Chester C	W	2-1	0-1	2	McLean 80, Mackail-Smith (pen) 85	2291
20	15	H	Milton Keynes D	L	1-2	0-0	3	McLean 75	10,351
21	22	H	Bradford C	W	2-1	0-1	2	McLean 58, Hughes 88	5355
22	26	A	Mansfield T	L	0-2	0-1	4		3107
23	29	A	Morecambe	L	2-3	2-1	6	Morgan 5, Lee 12	2371
24	Jan 1	H	Shrewsbury T	W	2-1	0-1	5	Lee 55, Morgan 57	5062
25	12	H	Macclesfield T	L	0-1	0-1	6		5238
26	15	H	Accrington S	W	8-2	4-0	—	Mackail-Smith 2 12, 89, Boyd 3 27, 33, 76, McLean 3 39, 78, 82	4257
27	29	H	Rotherham U	W	3-1	1-0	—	Lee 22, McLean 81, Mackail-Smith 90	5152
28	Feb 2	A	Rochdale	W	2-0	0-0	4	Boyd 57, McLean 76	3076
29	9	H	Wrexham	D	0-0	0-0	5		5505
30	13	A	Chesterfield	W	2-1	1-0	—	McLean 45, Boyd 47	3973
31	16	H	Barnet	W	1-0	0-0	4	Hatch 73	5520
32	23	A	Macclesfield T	W	3-0	0-0	4	Boyd 46, Whelpdale 65, McLean 72	2094
33	26	A	Wrexham	W	2-0	0-0	—	Day 2 65, 81	4103
34	Mar 1	H	Bury	W	1-0	0-0	2	Keates 59	6150
35	4	A	Barnet	W	2-0	1-0	—	Keates 32, Day 90	2202
36	8	A	Dagenham & R	W	3-2	0-0	1	Boyd 57, Mackail-Smith 73, McLean 86	3130
37	11	A	Brentford	W	2-1	1-0	—	McLean 10, Mackail-Smith 58	4049
38	15	H	Notts Co	D	0-0	0-0	2		7173
39	21	A	Milton Keynes D	D	1-1	1-1	—	Whelpdale 27	14,521
40	24	H	Chester C	W	1-0	0-0	2-	Keates 71	6457
41	29	H	Lincoln C	W	4-0	1-0	1	McLean 2 18, 49, Rendell 2 56, 67	8035
42	Apr 5	A	Wycombe W	D	2-2	0-1	1	Boyd 66, Hatch 83	6202
43	12	H	Stockport Co	L	0-1	0-0	1		10,023
44	19	A	Hereford U	W	1-0	1-0	2	Keates 29	5279
45	26	A	Grimsby T	W	4-1	1-0	2	McLean 2 33, 49, Mackail-Smith 73, Rendell 82	4125
46	May 3	H	Darlington	L	0-2	0-1	2		10,400

Final League Position: 2

GOALSCORERS

League (84): McLean 29 (3 pens), Boyd 12, Mackail-Smith 12 (1 pen), Lee 6, Keates 5, Day 3, Rendell 3, Whelpdale 3, Crow 2, Hatch 2, Low 2, Morgan 2, Howe 1, Hughes 1, own goal 1.
Carling Cup (2): Boyd 1, own goal 1.
FA Cup (12): Mackail-Smith 7, McLean 3, Boyd 1, Lee 1.
J Paint Trophy (4): Boyd 1, Lee 1, McLean 1, own goal 1.

Jalal S 7	Newton A 26 + 6	Day J 42	Hyde M 33 + 4	Morgan C 41	Blackett S 9 + 2	Whelpdale C 29 + 6	Keates D 33 + 7	Boyd G 41 + 5	McLean A 45	Low J 9 + 6	Westwood C 35 + 2	Crow D 2 + 2	Howe R 2 + 13	Lee C 32 + 10	Strachan G — + 3	Tyler M 17	Gnapka C 25 + 3	Charnock K 10	Mackail-Smith C 34 + 2	Branston G 1 + 1	Hughes J 2 + 5	Hatch L 1 + 10	Lewis J 22	Williams T 3 + 4	Mitchell S 1 + 4	McKeown J — + 1	Blanchett D 1	Rendell S 3 + 7	Potter A — + 2	*Match No.*
1	2	3	4	5	6	7^{1}	8	9^{2}	10^{3}	11	12	13	14																	1
1	2	3	4^{3}	5	6^{1}	7	8	9^{2}	10	11	12		13	14																2
1	2	3	4	5^{1}	12		8^{2}	9	10	13	6		11	7^{3}	14															3
	12	3	4	5	6			9	10	11	2			8		1	7^{1}													4
	12	3^{2}	8		6		14	9^{3}	10	11	5^{1}	13		7		1	2	4												5
	12	3	8	5	6^{2}	14		13	10	11^{3}		9		7		1	2^{1}	4												6
	12	3	4	5		7^{1}		13	10	11^{2}		9^{3}		8		1	2	6	14											7
1	2	3	4	5			8^{1}	12	10		7^{2}		13	11				6	9											8
1	2	3	7	5			8	12	10		4			11^{2}	13			6	9^{1}											9
1	2^{1}	3	7	5		13	8^{2}	12	10		4		14	11				6	9^{3}											10
1	2^{1}	3	4			12	8	9	10		6		13	7			5^{3}		11^{2}	14										11
	2^{1}	3	8^{3}	6		12	7	9	10		4		13	11		1			14	5^{2}										12
	2^{1}	3		5		12	8^{2}	9	10		6		14	7	13	1	4		11^{3}											13
		3		5		7	8	9	10		6		12	2		1	4		11^{1}											14
		3	12	5		7	8	9	10		6			2		1	4^{1}		11											15
	12	3	6			7^{2}	8	9	10	13	5		14	2		1	4^{1}		11^{3}											16
		3^{3}	8	5		7	12	9	10^{2}		6		13	2^{1}		1	4		11		14									17
		3^{3}	8	5		7^{1}		9	10^{2}	12	6		13	2		1	4		11		14									18
		3	8	5		7^{1}	13	9	10	12	6^{3}			2^{2}		1	4		11		14									19
		3	8	5	6			9	10	7^{2}			12	2^{1}		1	4		11		13									20
	2	3	4^{2}	5	6	12	8^{1}	9	10					13		1			7		11									21
	2	3	4	5	6		8	9	10^{1}				12	13		1			7		11^{2}									22
	2	3	4	5	6^{1}	7	12	9					10^{2}	8		1			11		13									23
	2	3	4	5		7		9	10					8		1	12	6^{1}	11^{2}			13								24
	2^{1}	3^{2}	4			7	12	9	10					8			6	5	11^{3}			13	1	14						25
	2	3^{2}	4^{1}	5		7	12	9	10					8^{3}				6	11			14	1	13						26
	2	3	4^{1}			7^{2}	12	9	10		5			8			13	6^{3}	11				1	14						27
	2	3		5		7^{1}	8	9	10		6						12		11				1		4					28
	2^{1}	3		5			8	9	10		6			7			4		11				1^{G}		12	15				29
	2	3		5			8	9^{1}	10		6			7^{2}			4		11^{3}			14	1	12■	13					30
	2	3		5		7^{1}	8	9	10		6			4					11^{2}			12	1		13					31
				5		7	8	9	10^{1}		6			2^{2}			4		11^{3}			12	1		13		3	14		32
		3	12	5		7	8	9	10		6			2^{1}			4		11^{2}			13	1							33
		3	12	5		7^{1}	8	9	10		6			2			4		11				1							34
		3	2	5	12	7^{1}	8	9	10		6						4		11^{2}			13	1							35
		3	2	5		7^{1}	8	9	10		6			12			4		11				1							36
	12	3	7^{2}	5			8	9	10	2^{1}	6			13			4		11				1							37
		3	7	5			8	9^{3}	10	2^{1}	6			12			4		11^{2}			13	1					14		38
		3	2^{1}	5		7	8	9	10		6			12			4		11^{2}				1					13		39
		3		5		7	8	9	10		6			2			4						1					11		40
	2	3		5		7	8	9^{1}	10	12	6			4									1					11		41
	2	3	12	5		7^{1}	8	9	10	13	6			4^{2}								14	1					11^{3}		42
	2	3	4	5		7^{1}	8	9	10		6			12								11^{2}	1					13		43
	2		4	5		7	8	9	10		6								11^{1}				1	3				12		44
	2		4	5		7^{3}	8^{1}	9	10^{2}		6			12					11				1	3				13	14	45
	2^{3}		4	5		7^{1}	8	9	10^{2}		6			12					11				1	3				13	14	46

FA Cup

First Round	Wrexham	(h)	4-1
Second Round	Staines T	(a)	5-0
Third Round	Colchester U	(a)	3-1
Fourth Round	WBA	(h)	0-3

Carling Cup

First Round	Southampton	(h)	2-1
Second Round	WBA	(h)	0-2

J Paint Trophy

First Round	Nottingham F	(a)	3-2
Second Round	Milton Keynes D	(a)	1-3

PLYMOUTH ARGYLE FL Championship

FOUNDATION

The club was formed in September 1886 as the Argyle Football Club by former public and private school pupils who wanted to continue playing the game. The meeting was held in a room above the Borough Arms (a Coffee House), Bedford Street, Plymouth. It was common then to choose a local street/terrace as a club name and Argyle or Argyll was a fashionable name throughout the land due to Queen Victoria's great interest in Scotland.

Home Park, Plymouth, Devon PL2 3DQ.

Telephone: (01752) 562 561.

Fax: (01752) 606 167.

Ticket Office: 0845 338 7232.

Website: www.pafc.co.uk

Email: argyle@pafc.co.uk

Ground Capacity: 20,000.

Record Attendance: 43,596 v Aston Villa, Division 2, 10 October 1936.

Pitch Measurements: 112yd × 73yd.

Chairman: Paul Stapleton.

Vice-chairman: Robert Dennerly.

Chief Executive: Michael Dunford.

Secretary: Mrs Carole Rowntree.

Manager: Paul Sturrock.

Assistant Manager: Kevin Summerfield.

Physio: Paul Maxwell.

Colours: Green shirts, white shorts, black stockings.

Change Colours: Tangerine shirts, green shorts.

Year Formed: 1886.

Turned Professional: 1903.

Ltd Co.: 1903.

Previous Name: 1886, Argyle Athletic Club; 1903, Plymouth Argyle.

Club Nickname: 'The Pilgrims'.

Ground: 1886, Home Park.

First Football League Game: 28 August 1920, Division 3, v Norwich C (h) D 1–1 – Craig; Russell, Atterbury; Logan, Dickinson, Forbes; Kirkpatrick, Jack, Bowler, Heeps (1), Dixon.

Record League Victory: 8–1 v Millwall, Division 2, 16 January 1932 – Harper; Roberts, Titmuss; Mackay, Pullan, Reed; Grozier, Bowden (2), Vidler (3), Leslie (1), Black (1), (1 og). 8–1 v Hartlepool U (a), Division 2, 7 May 1994 – Nicholls; Patterson (Naylor), Hill, Burrows, Comyn, McCall (1), Barlow, Castle (1), Landon (3), Marshall (1), Dalton (2).

HONOURS

Football League: Division 2 – Champions 2003–04; Division 3 (S) – Champions 1929–30, 1951–52; Runners-up 1921–22, 1922–23, 1923–24, 1924–25, 1925–26, 1926–27 (record of six consecutive years); Division 3 – Champions 1958–59, 2001–02; Runners-up 1974–75, 1985–86, Promoted 1995–96 (play-offs).

FA Cup: Semi-final 1984.

Football League Cup: Semi-final 1965, 1974.

SKY SPORTS FACT FILE

During the early months of the 2006–07 season Plymouth Argyle midfield player and captain Bob Wotton had his ferocious free-kicks monitored by a speed camera which reported them to be timed as fast as 83 mph.

Record Cup Victory: 6–0 v Corby T, FA Cup 3rd rd, 22 January 1966 – Leiper; Book, Baird; Williams, Nelson, Newman; Jones (1), Jackson (1), Bickle (3), Piper (1), Jennings.

Record Defeat: 0–9 v Stoke C, Division 2, 17 December 1960.

Most League Points (2 for a win): 68, Division 3 (S), 1929–30.

Most League Points (3 for a win): 102, Division 3, 2001–02.

Most League Goals: 107, Division 3 (S), 1925–26 and 1951–52.

Highest League Scorer in Season: Jack Cock, 32, Division 3 (S), 1926–27.

Most League Goals in Total Aggregate: Sammy Black, 180, 1924–38.

Most League Goals in One Match: 5, Wilf Carter v Charlton Ath, Division 2, 27 December 1960.

Most Capped Player: Moses Russell, 20 (23), Wales.

Most League Appearances: Kevin Hodges, 530, 1978–92.

Youngest League Player: Lee Phillips, 16 years 43 days v Gillingham, 29 October 1996.

Record Transfer Fee Received: £2,250,000 from Ipswich T for David Norris, January 2008.

Record Transfer Fee Paid: £500,000 to Cardiff C for Steve MacLean, January 2008.

Football League Record: 1920 Original Member of Division 3; 1921–30 Division 3 (S); 1930–50 Division 2; 1950–52 Division 3 (S); 1952–56 Division 2; 1956–58 Division 3 (S); 1958–59 Division 3; 1959–68 Division 2; 1968–75 Division 3; 1975–77 Division 2; 1977–86 Division 3; 1986–95 Division 2; 1995–96 Division 3; 1996–98 Division 2; 1998–2002 Division 3; 2002–04 Division 2; 2004– FL C.

MANAGERS

Frank Brettell 1903–05
Bob Jack 1905–06
Bill Fullerton 1906–07
Bob Jack 1910–38
Jack Tresadern 1938–47
Jimmy Rae 1948–55
Jack Rowley 1955–60
Neil Dougall 1961
Ellis Stuttard 1961–63
Andy Beattie 1963–64
Malcolm Allison 1964–65
Derek Ufton 1965–68
Billy Bingham 1968–70
Ellis Stuttard 1970–72
Tony Waiters 1972–77
Mike Kelly 1977–78
Malcolm Allison 1978–79
Bobby Saxton 1979–81
Bobby Moncur 1981–83
Johnny Hore 1983–84
Dave Smith 1984–88
Ken Brown 1988–90
David Kemp 1990–92
Peter Shilton 1992–95
Steve McCall 1995
Neil Warnock 1995–97
Mick Jones 1997–98
Kevin Hodges 1998–2000
Paul Sturrock 2000–04
Bobby Williamson 2004–05
Tony Pulis 2005–06
Ian Holloway 2006–07
Paul Sturrock November 2007–

LATEST SEQUENCES

Longest Sequence of League Wins: 9, 8.3.1986 – 12.4.1986.

Longest Sequence of League Defeats: 9, 12.10.1963 – 7.12.1963.

Longest Sequence of League Draws: 5, 26.2.2000 – 14.3.2000.

Longest Sequence of Unbeaten League Matches: 22, 20.4.1929 – 21.12.1929.

Longest Sequence Without a League Win: 13, 27.4.1963 – 2.10.1963.

Successive Scoring Runs: 39 from 15.4.1939.

Successive Non-scoring Runs: 5 from 20.9.1947.

TEN YEAR LEAGUE RECORD

		P	W	D	L	F	A	Pts	Pos
1998-99	Div 3	46	17	10	19	58	54	61	13
1999-2000	Div 3	46	16	18	12	55	51	66	12
2000-01	Div 3	46	15	13	18	54	61	58	12
2001-02	Div 3	46	31	9	6	71	28	102	1
2002-03	Div 2	46	17	14	15	63	52	65	8
2003-04	Div 2	46	26	12	8	85	41	90	1
2004-05	FL C	46	14	11	21	52	64	53	17
2005-06	FL C	46	13	17	16	39	46	56	14
2006-07	FL C	46	17	16	13	63	62	67	11
2007-08	FL C	46	17	13	16	60	50	64	10

DID YOU KNOW 

Dave Thomas scored in ten successive League matches during 1946–47. He finished as top goalscorer with 19, while his brother Bob had 17. Largely as a result of their marksmanship Plymouth Argyle survived to finish in seventeenth place.

PLYMOUTH ARGYLE 2007–08 LEAGUE RECORD

Match No.	Date	Venue	Opponents	Result		H/T Score	Lg. Pos.	Goalscorers	Attendance
1	Aug 11	A	Hull C	W	3-2	2-1	—	Norris 15, Fallon 45, Ebanks-Blake 81	16,633
2	18	H	Ipswich T	D	1-1	0-1	7	Ebanks-Blake (pen) 85	13,260
3	25	A	Barnsley	L	2-3	0-2	11	Hayles 63, Chadwick 68	9240
4	Sept 1	H	Leicester C	D	0-0	0-0	15		11,850
5	15	H	Cardiff C	D	2-2	1-0	18	Ebanks-Blake 2 30, 58	11,591
6	18	A	QPR	W	2-0	0-0	—	Halmosi 50, Norris 62	10,850
7	22	A	Stoke C	L	2-3	0-1	13	Seip 52, Fallon 59	12,533
8	29	H	Wolverhampton W	D	1-1	0-1	13	Chadwick 61	13,638
9	Oct 2	H	Crystal Palace	W	1-0	0-0	—	Halmosi 50	10,451
10	6	A	Blackpool	D	0-0	0-0	9		8784
11	20	H	Coventry C	W	1-0	1-0	6	Martin 16	11,576
12	23	A	Charlton Ath	W	2-1	2-1	—	Ebanks-Blake 5, Hayles 38	22,123
13	27	A	Preston NE	L	0-2	0-1	7		11,055
14	Nov 3	H	Sheffield W	L	1-2	0-0	8	Ebanks-Blake (pen) 47	12,145
15	6	A	Colchester U	D	1-1	0-0	—	Norris 88	4833
16	10	H	Norwich C	W	3-0	1-0	7	Martin 26, Connolly 47, Norris 49	11,222
17	24	A	Sheffield U	W	1-0	1-0	4	Halmosi 24	23,811
18	28	H	WBA	L	1-2	0-2	—	Easter 84	14,348
19	Dec 1	H	Scunthorpe U	W	3-0	0-0	6	Ebanks-Blake 51, Timar 64, Abdou 77	10,520
20	4	A	Norwich C	L	1-2	0-1	—	Timar 89	25,434
21	8	H	Bristol C	D	1-1	1-0	8	Ebanks-Blake (pen) 23	16,530
22	15	A	Watford	W	1-0	0-0	7	Norris 89	18,532
23	22	A	Crystal Palace	L	1-2	0-2	8	Easter 49	15,097
24	26	H	QPR	W	2-1	0-1	6	Ebanks-Blake 2 (1 pen) 50 (p), 90	16,502
25	29	H	Stoke C	D	2-2	1-1	6	Ebanks-Blake 44, Timar 67	13,692
26	Jan 1	A	Cardiff C	L	0-1	0-1	7		14,965
27	12	A	Burnley	L	0-1	0-0	9		14,162
28	19	H	Southampton	D	1-1	0-1	11	Fallon 49	14,676
29	29	A	Ipswich T	D	0-0	0-0	—		20,095
30	Feb 2	H	Hull C	L	0-1	0-1	12		11,011
31	9	A	Leicester C	W	1-0	1-0	10	Halmosi 34	21,264
32	12	H	Barnsley	W	3-0	1-0	—	MacLean 6, Mackie 2 76, 85	11,346
33	19	A	Southampton	W	2-0	2-0	—	Halmosi 31, Paterson 33	17,806
34	23	H	Burnley	W	3-1	2-1	5	Nalis 12, Halmosi 2 35, 76	13,557
35	Mar 1	A	WBA	L	0-3	0-1	7		22,503
36	4	H	Colchester U	W	4-1	1-0	—	Ifil (og) 11, Easter 57, MacLean 60, Sawyer 68	11,562
37	8	H	Sheffield U	L	0-1	0-0	7		13,669
38	11	A	Scunthorpe U	L	0-1	0-0	—		4920
39	15	A	Bristol C	W	2-1	1-0	6	Fallon 2 45, 59	19,011
40	22	H	Watford	D	1-1	1-1	6	Easter 34	17,511
41	29	A	Coventry C	L	1-3	0-2	8	MacLean 81	18,775
42	Apr 5	H	Charlton Ath	L	1-2	0-0	9	Easter 60	14,715
43	14	A	Sheffield W	D	1-1	1-0	—	Halmosi 2	20,635
44	19	H	Preston NE	D	2-2	1-0	10	Mackie 12, Wotton (pen) 75	10,727
45	26	H	Blackpool	W	3-0	2-0	10	Easter 4, Fallon 2 25, 55	12,911
46	May 4	A	Wolverhampton W	L	0-1	0-0	10		26,293

Final League Position: 10

GOALSCORERS

League (60): Ebanks-Blake 11 (4 pens), Halmosi 8, Fallon 7, Easter 6, Norris 5, MacLean 3, Mackie 3, Timar 3, Chadwick 2, Hayles 2, Martin 2, Abdou 1, Connolly 1, Nalis 1, Paterson 1, Sawyer 1, Seip 1, Wotton 1 (pen), own goal 1.
Carling Cup (4): Ebanks-Blake 1, Hodges 1, Summerfield 1, own goal 1.
FA Cup (4): Abdou 1, Clark 1, Ebanks-Blake 1, Halmosi 1.

Larrieu R 15	Connolly P 42	Sawyer G 28 + 3	Buzsaky A 8 + 3	Doumbe S 10 + 2	Seip M 32 + 2	Norris D 27	Nalis L 35 + 5	Fallon R 13 + 16	Hayles B 21 + 2	Halmosi P 41 + 2	Hodges L 20 + 7	Ebanks-Blake S 19 + 6	Chadwick N 3 + 6	Abdou N 22 + 9	McCormick L 30	Timar K 36 + 2	Gosling D 5 + 5	Djordjic B 1	Martin L 10 + 2	Easter J 20 + 12	Summerfield L 5 + 2	Jutkiewicz L 1 + 2	Smith D — + 2	Folly Y 1 + 3	MacLean S 14 + 3	Clark C 8 + 4	Paterson J 7 + 1	Wotton P 5 + 3	Mackie J 4 + 9	Anderson R 14	Teale G 8 + 4	Douglas R 1	*Match No.*
1	2	3	4	5	6	7	8	9^{3}	10^{2}	11^{1}	12	13	14																				1
1	2	3	4	5	6	7	8	9^{1}	10	11		12																					2
1	2	3	4^{3}	5^{1}	6	7	8	9^{2}	10	11		12	13	14																			3
	2	3^{2}	4		6	7	8^{3}	12	10^{1}	11	13	9		14	1	5																	4
	2	3	12		6	7			10	13		9^{3}	14	8	1	5	4^{1}	11^{2}															5
	2	3	4		6	7	8		10^{1}	11	12	9			1	5																	6
	2	3^{3}	4		6	7	8	9^{1}	12	11	14	13	10^{2}		1	5																	7
	2	3	4^{2}		6	7	8	12	10	11^{3}		9^{1}	13		1	5	14																8
	2		12	14	6	7	8		10^{2}	11	3	13	9^{3}		1	5	4^{1}																9
	2		4^{3}		6	7	8	12	13	11	3	10^{1}	9^{2}		1	5			14														10
	2	12			6	7	8		10	11^{1}	3	9			1	5			4														11
	2	12	13		6	7	8		10^{3}	11	3^{2}	9^{1}	14		1	5			4														12
	2				6	7	8	12	10	11	3^{2}	9^{3}			1	5	13		4^{1}	14													13
	2^{2}				6	7	8	12	10^{1}	11	3	9^{3}			1	5	13		4	14													14
1	2				6	7	8	12	10^{3}	13	3	9		4^{2}		5			11^{1}	14													15
1	2				6	7	8^{1}		10^{2}	11	3^{3}	9		12		5	14		4	13													16
1	2	12		5	6	7	8		10	11^{1}	3	9^{2}							4	13													17
1	2			5	6	7	8	12	10^{2}	11	3^{1}	9		14			4^{3}			13													18
1	2				6	7	8	12	10^{3}	11	3	9^{1}		13		5			4^{2}	14													19
1	2				6	7	8		10	11	3^{2}	9		4^{1}		5	12			13													20
1	2				6	7	8	12		11	3	9^{2}	13	4		5				10^{1}													21
1		2			6	7			10	11	3			8		5	4			9													22
1		3			6	7			10^{1}	11	2^{2}	12		8		5	4			9	13												23
1	2				6	7	8		10^{2}	11	3	9		4^{1}		5			12	13													24
1	2				6	7	8			11	3	9		12		5			4^{1}	10													25
1	2			12	6	7	13			11	3	9		8^{3}		5^{1}			4^{2}	10		14											26
	2	5			6		8^{2}	12		11	3			4^{3}	1					10	7	9^{1}	14	13									27
	2	3			6	7	8	10		11					1	5					4^{1}			12	9								28
	2	3		6			8	10^{1}		11^{2}	12				1	5				13	14			4^{3}	9	7							29
	2	3		6			8	10^{2}		11				12	1	5				13	4^{1}	14			9	7^{3}							30
	2	3		6			8	12		11^{2}	13			4	1	5				10					9^{1}		7						31
	2	3		6			8			11				4^{2}	1	5				10^{1}					9		7	13	12				32
	2	3					8			11				4	1	5				10^{1}					9		7^{2}		12	6	13		33
	2	3					8	12		11				4	1	5				10^{2}					9^{1}			14	13	6	7^{3}		34
	2	3			12		8			11^{3}				4	1	5^{1}				10					9	14			13	6	7^{2}		35
	2	3			12		8	13		11				4	1	5^{1}				10					9^{2}	14				6	7^{3}		36
	2	3					8^{1}	12		11				4	1	5				10^{2}					9	14			13	6	7^{3}		37
	2				6		8^{3}	12		11	3			4	1■										9	7^{2}		14	10^{1}	5	13		38
	2	3			6		12	9		11^{1}				13						10^{3}						8		4	14	5	7^{2}	1	39
	2	3			6		12	9^{2}		11■					1	13				10						8^{1}	14	4		5	7^{3}		40
	2	3^{3}			6									12	1	13				10					9	8^{1}	11	4	14	5^{2}	7		41
	2	3^{3}					12	9						4	1	6				10					13		11	8^{1}	14	5	7^{2}		42
	2	3					8	12		7^{3}				4	1	5				10					9^{2}	14	11^{1}		13	6			43
	2						13	10		11^{2}				4	1	5				14					9^{3}		3	8	7^{1}	6	12		44
		3						9		11^{3}	12			4^{1}	1	5				10^{2}	8		14		13	2			7	6			45
		3		2				9						4	1	5^{2}				10^{1}	8			13	12	7^{3}			11	6	14		46

FA Cup

Third Round	Hull C	(h)	3-2
Fourth Round	Portsmouth	(a)	1-2

Carling Cup

First Round	Wycombe W	(h)	2-1
Second Round	Doncaster R	(h)	2-0
Third Round	West Ham U	(a)	0-1

PORTSMOUTH FA Premiership

FOUNDATION

At a meeting held in his High Street, Portsmouth offices in 1898, solicitor Alderman J. E. Pink and five other business and professional men agreed to buy some ground close to Goldsmith Avenue for £4,950 which they developed into Fratton Park in record breaking time. A team of professionals was signed up by manager Frank Brettell and entry to the Southern League obtained for the new club's September 1899 kick-off.

Fratton Park, Frogmore Road, Portsmouth, Hampshire PO4 8RA.

Telephone: (02392) 731 204.

Fax: (02392) 734 129.

Ticket Office: 0871 230 1898.

Website: www.pompeyfc.co.uk

Email: info@pompeyfc.co.uk

Ground Capacity: 20,338.

Record Attendance: 51,385 v Derby Co, FA Cup 6th rd, 26 February 1949.

Pitch Measurements: 100m × 65m.

Owner: Alexander Gaydamak.

Chief Executive: Peter Storrie.

Secretary: Paul Weld.

Manager: Harry Redknapp.

Assistant Manager: Tony Adams.

Physio: Gary Sadler MCSP, SROP.

Colours: Blue shirts, white shorts, red stockings.

Change Colours: White shirts, blue shorts, blue stockings.

Year Formed: 1898.

Turned Professional: 1898.

Ltd Co.: 1898.

Club Nickname: 'Pompey'.

Ground: 1898, Fratton Park.

First Football League Game: 28 August 1920, Division 3, v Swansea T (h) W 3–0 – Robson; Probert, Potts; Abbott, Harwood, Turner; Thompson, Stringfellow (1), Reid (1), James (1), Beedie.

Record League Victory: 9–1 v Notts Co, Division 2, 9 April 1927 – McPhail; Clifford, Ted Smith; Reg Davies (1), Foxall, Moffat; Forward (1), Mackie (2), Haines (3), Watson, Cook (2).

Record Cup Victory: 7–0 v Stockport Co, FA Cup 3rd rd, 8 January 1949 – Butler; Rookes, Ferrier; Scoular, Flewin, Dickinson; Harris (3), Barlow, Clarke (2), Phillips (2), Froggatt.

HONOURS

Football League: Division 1 – Champions 1948–49, 1949–50, 2002–03; Division 2 – Runners-up 1926–27, 1986–87; Division 3 (S) – Champions 1923–24; Division 3 – Champions 1961–62, 1982–83.

FA Cup: Winners 1939, 2008; Runners-up 1929, 1934.

Football League Cup: best season: 5th rd, 1961, 1986.

SKY SPORTS FACT FILE

On 8 March 2008 Portsmouth defeated Manchester United 1–0 in the quarter-final of the FA Cup. It was their first win at Old Trafford since 1957 and the first against them in the competition since a 1934 replay the year they reached the final at Wembley.

Record Defeat: 0–10 v Leicester C, Division 1, 20 October 1928.

Most League Points (2 for a win): 65, Division 3, 1961–62.

Most League Points (3 for a win): 98, Division 1, 2002–03.

Most League Goals: 97, Division 1, 2002–03.

Highest League Scorer in Season: Guy Whittingham, 42, Division 1, 1992–93.

Most League Goals in Total Aggregate: Peter Harris, 194, 1946–60.

Most League Goals in One Match: 5, Alf Strange v Gillingham, Division 3, 27 January 1923; 5, Peter Harris v Aston Villa, Division 1, 3 September 1958.

Most Capped Player: Jimmy Dickinson, 48, England.

Most League Appearances: Jimmy Dickinson, 764, 1946–65.

Youngest League Player: Clive Green, 16 years 259 days v Wrexham, 21 August 1976.

Record Transfer Fee Received: £7,500,000 from Middlesbrough for Ayegbeni Yakubu, July 2005.

Record Transfer Fee Paid: Reported fee of £11,000,000 to Liverpool for Peter Crouch, July 2008.

Football League Record: 1920 Original Member of Division 3; 1921 Division 3 (S); 1924–27 Division 2; 1927–59 Division 1; 1959–61 Division 2; 1961–62 Division 3; 1962–76 Division 2; 1976–78 Division 3; 1978–80 Division 4; 1980–83 Division 3; 1983–87 Division 2; 1987–88 Division 1; 1988–92 Division 2; 1992–2003 Division 1; 2003– FA Premier League.

MANAGERS

Frank Brettell 1898–1901
Bob Blyth 1901–04
Richard Bonney 1905–08
Bob Brown 1911–20
John McCartney 1920–27
Jack Tinn 1927–47
Bob Jackson 1947–52
Eddie Lever 1952–58
Freddie Cox 1958–61
George Smith 1961–70
Ron Tindall 1970–73
(General Manager to 1974)
John Mortimore 1973–74
Ian St John 1974–77
Jimmy Dickinson 1977–79
Frank Burrows 1979–82
Bobby Campbell 1982–84
Alan Ball 1984–89
John Gregory 1989–90
Frank Burrows 1990–91
Jim Smith 1991–95
Terry Fenwick 1995–98
Alan Ball 1998–99
Tony Pulis 2000
Steve Claridge 2000–01
Graham Rix 2001–02
Harry Redknapp 2002–04
Velimir Zajec 2004–05
Alain Perrin 2005
Harry Redknapp December 2005–

LATEST SEQUENCES

Longest Sequence of League Wins: 7, 17.8.2002 – 17.9.2002.

Longest Sequence of League Defeats: 9, 21.10.1975 – 6.12.1975.

Longest Sequence of League Draws: 5, 16.12.2000 – 13.1.2001.

Longest Sequence of Unbeaten League Matches: 15, 18.4.1924 – 18.10.1924.

Longest Sequence Without a League Win: 25, 29.11.1958 – 22.8.1959.

Successive Scoring Runs: 23 from 30.8.1930.

Successive Non-scoring Runs: 6 from 14.1.1939.

TEN YEAR LEAGUE RECORD

		P	*W*	*D*	*L*	*F*	*A*	*Pts*	*Pos*
1998-99	Div 1	46	11	14	21	57	73	47	19
1999-2000	Div 1	46	13	12	21	55	66	51	18
2000-01	Div 1	46	10	19	17	47	59	49	20
2001-02	Div 1	46	13	14	19	60	72	53	17
2002-03	Div 1	46	29	11	6	97	45	98	1
2003-04	PR Lge	38	12	9	17	47	54	45	13
2004-05	PR Lge	38	10	9	19	43	59	39	16
2005-06	PR Lge	38	10	8	20	37	62	38	17
2006-07	PR Lge	38	14	12	12	45	42	54	9
2007-08	PR Lge	38	16	9	13	48	40	57	8

DID YOU KNOW ?

The record aggregate of goals in the Premier League was achieved when Portsmouth beat Reading 7–4 at Fratton Park on 29 September 2007. It could have been a higher scoreline as David James on his 600th overall match saved a penalty for Pompey.

PORTSMOUTH 2007–08 LEAGUE RECORD

Match No.	*Date*	*Venue*	*Opponents*	*Result*		*H/T Score*	*Lg. Pos.*	*Goalscorers*	*Attendance*
1	Aug 11	A	Derby Co	D	2-2	1-1	—	Mwaruwari [27], Utaka [83]	32,176
2	15	H	Manchester U	D	1-1	0-1	—	Mwaruwari [53]	20,510
3	18	H	Bolton W	W	3-1	2-1	5	Kanu [16], Utaka [30], Taylor (pen) [88]	17,108
4	25	A	Chelsea	L	0-1	0-1	8		41,501
5	Sept 2	A	Arsenal	L	1-3	0-2	13	Kanu [60]	60,114
6	15	H	Liverpool	D	0-0	0-0	15		20,388
7	23	A	Blackburn R	W	1-0	1-0	11	Kanu [25]	19,506
8	29	H	Reading	W	7-4	2-1	6	Mwaruwari 3 [7, 37, 70], Hreidarsson [55], Kranjcar [75], Ingimarsson (og) [81], Muntari (pen) [90]	20,102
9	Oct 7	A	Fulham	W	2-0	0-0	5	Mwaruwari [50], Hreidarsson [52]	20,774
10	20	A	Wigan Ath	W	2-0	0-0	5	Mwaruwari [81], Johnson [86]	17,695
11	27	H	West Ham U	D	0-0	0-0	7		20,525
12	Nov 3	A	Newcastle U	W	4-1	3-1	4	Pamarot [8], Mwaruwari [9], Utaka [11], Kranjcar [71]	51,490
13	11	H	Manchester C	D	0-0	0-0	6		19,529
14	24	A	Birmingham C	W	2-0	1-0	6	Muntari [34], Kranjcar [82]	22,089
15	Dec 1	H	Everton	D	0-0	0-0	6		20,102
16	8	A	Aston Villa	W	3-1	2-0	5	Gardner (og) [10], Muntari 2 [40, 61]	35,790
17	15	H	Tottenham H	L	0-1	0-0	7		20,520
18	22	A	Liverpool	L	1-4	0-2	7	Mwaruwari [57]	43,071
19	26	H	Arsenal	D	0-0	0-0	7		20,556
20	29	H	Middlesbrough	L	0-1	0-1	8		20,089
21	Jan 1	A	Reading	W	2-0	1-0	8	Campbell [9], Utaka [66]	24,084
22	13	A	Sunderland	L	0-2	0-2	9		37,369
23	19	H	Derby Co	W	3-1	2-1	8	Mwaruwari 3 [38, 42, 55]	19,401
24	30	A	Manchester U	L	0-2	0-2	—		75,415
25	Feb 2	H	Chelsea	D	1-1	0-0	9	Defoe [64]	20,488
26	9	A	Bolton W	W	1-0	0-0	8	Diarra [81]	18,544
27	23	H	Sunderland	W	1-0	0-0	7	Defoe (pen) [69]	20,139
28	Mar 2	A	Everton	L	1-3	1-1	9	Defoe [38]	33,938
29	12	H	Birmingham C	W	4-2	2-2	—	Defoe 2 (1 pen) [6 (p), 9], Hreidarsson [49], Kanu [90]	20,138
30	15	H	Aston Villa	W	2-0	2-0	6	Defoe [11], Reo-Coker (og) [38]	20,388
31	22	A	Tottenham H	L	0-2	0-0	6		35,998
32	29	H	Wigan Ath	W	2-0	1-0	6	Defoe 2 [32, 90]	18,623
33	Apr 8	A	West Ham U	W	1-0	0-0	—	Kranjcar [61]	33,629
34	12	H	Newcastle U	D	0-0	0-0	6		20,507
35	20	A	Manchester C	L	1-3	1-2	7	Utaka [24]	40,205
36	27	H	Blackburn R	L	0-1	0-0	7		18,722
37	May 3	A	Middlesbrough	L	0-2	0-1	8		24,828
38	11	H	Fulham	L	0-1	0-0	8		20,532

Final League Position: 8

GOALSCORERS

League (48): Mwaruwari 12, Defoe 8 (2 pens), Utaka 5, Kanu 4, Kranjcar 4, Muntari 4 (1 pen), Hreidarsson 3, Campbell 1, Diarra 1, Johnson 1, Pamarot 1, Taylor 1 (pen), own goals 3.
Carling Cup (5): Nugent 2, Pamarot 2, Kanu 1.
FA Cup (7): Kanu 2, Diarra 1, Kranjcar 1, Muntari 1 (pen), Nugent 1, own goal 1.

James D 35	Lauren E 11 + 4	Hreidarsson H 30 + 2	Davis S 18 + 4	Campbell S 31	Distin S 36	Utaka J 25 + 4	Pedro Mendes 14 + 4	Mwaruwari B 21 + 2	Nugent D 5 + 10	Muntari S 27 + 2	Taylor M 3 + 10	Kanu N 13 + 12	Pamarot N 14 + 4	Cranie M 1 + 1	Hughes R 8 + 5	Traore D 1 + 2	O'Neil G 2	Mvuemba A 3 + 5	Johnson G 29	Kranjcar N 31 + 3	Diop P 25	Songo'o F — + 1	Diarra L 11 + 1	Baros M 8 + 4	Defoe J 12	Aubey L 1 + 2	Ashdown J 3	Match No.
1	2	3	4	5	6	7	8	9^{3}	10^{2}	11^{1}	12	13	14															1
1		3	4		6	7	8^{1}	9	10	11■	12		5^{2}	2^{3}	13	14												2
1		5	4		6	11		9^{1}	12		3	10^{3}		13	8	2	7^{2}	14										3
1	2^{3}	3	4	5	6	9		12	13	8	11^{2}	10	14				7^{1}											4
1	7^{1}	3^{3}	4^{2}		6	9	12		13	8	11	10	5						2	14								5
1		3	4	5	6	7		9^{1}		11		10							2	12	8							6
1		3	4	5	6	9^{3}		12		11	13	10^{1}	14						2	7^{2}	8							7
1		3	4	5	6	10		9^{1}	12	11									2	7	8							8
1		3^{2}	4	5	6	10	12	9		11			13						2	7	8^{1}							9
1		3	4^{1}	5	6	10	12	9		11									2	7	8							10
1		3		5	6	10^{1}	8	9		11		12							2	7	4							11
1			4	5	6	10	12	9^{2}		11^{1}		13	3						2	7	8							12
1			4	5	6	8^{2}		9	12	11	13	10^{1}	3						2	7								13
1			4	5	6	10^{1}		9		11	12		3						2	7	8							14
1				5	6	10^{1}	8	9		11		12	3						2	7	4							15
1				5	6	10^{1}	8	9		11	13	12	3						2	7^{2}	4							16
1		12	13	5	6	10	8^{2}	9	14	11^{3}			3^{1}						2	7	4							17
1	12	3		5	6	10^{3}	8	9		11^{2}	13	14							2^{1}	7	4							18
1	2	3		5	6	12		9^{1}		11	13	10			4					7^{2}	8							19
1	2	3^{3}		5	6	7^{1}		9	12	13	14	10			4^{2}					11	8							20
1	12	3		5	6	10		9^{2}		11	14	13			4^{1}				2	7^{3}	8							21
1		3		5	6^{1}		8	9	10				2		11	12		4^{2}		7		13						22
1	7	3			6		8	9^{2}	10				5		12			13	2	11			4^{1}					23
1	7^{3}	12	4	5	6^{1}			9					3		13			14	2	11			8	10^{2}				24
1		3	4^{1}	5									6		7			12	2	11			8	9	10			25
1	2	6		5		12						13	3^{3}		7					11^{1}	8		4	9^{2}	10	14		26
1		3		5	6					11		12							2	7	8		4	9^{1}	10			27
1		3		5	6	12				11		9							2	7	8^{1}		4		10			28
1	13	3		5	6		8			11		12							2	7	4^{3}		14	9^{1}	10^{2}			29
1	3	5			6	12				11■		13							2	7	8		4	9^{2}	10^{1}			30
1		5	4		6	10	8					9^{2}			11^{1}			12	2	7				13		3		31
1	12	3^{1}	4	5	6	7^{3}	8		13						14				2	11				9^{2}	10			32
1		3		5	6		8^{2}		10^{1}	11		12			13			7	2	9	4							33
1		3	4	5	6				12	11		10^{1}							2	7	8				9			34
1	2	3■	12	5	6	10^{2}				11										7^{1}	8^{3}		4	13	9	14		35
	3			5	6	7^{1}				11^{2}		10							2	12	8		4	13	9		1	36
		3	13	5	6				12									7	2	11	8^{2}		4	9^{1}	10		1	37
		3	12		6	7	8^{1}			13		10^{3}	5						2	11			4^{2}	14	9		1	38

FA Cup

Third Round	Ipswich T	(a)	1-0
Fourth Round	Plymouth Arg	(h)	2-1
Fifth Round	Preston NE	(a)	1-0
Sixth Round	Manchester U	(a)	1-0
Semi-Final *(at Wembley)*	WBA		1-0
Final *(at Wembley)*	Cardiff C		1-0

Carling Cup

Second Round	Leeds U	(h)	3-0
Third Round	Burnley	(a)	1-0
Fourth Round	Blackburn R	(h)	1-2

PORT VALE

FL Championship 2

FOUNDATION

Formed in 1876 as Port Vale, adopting the prefix 'Burslem' in 1884 upon moving to that part of the city. It was dropped in 1909.

Vale Park, Hamil Road, Burslem, Stoke-on-Trent ST6 1AW.

Telephone: (01782) 655 800.

Fax: (01782) 834 981.

Ticket Office: (01782) 655 832.

Website: www.port-vale.co.uk

Email: lodey@port-vale.co.uk

Ground Capacity: 18,982.

Record Attendance: 49,768 v Aston Villa, FA Cup 5th rd, 20 February 1960.

Pitch Measurements: 114yd × 75yd.

Chairman/Chief Executive: William A. Bratt.

Vice-chairmen: David Smith, Peter L. Jackson.

Secretary: Bill Lodey.

Manager: Lee Sinnott.

Assistant Manager: Dean Glover.

Physio: John Bowers.

Colours: White shirts, white shorts, white stockings.

Change Colours: Black shirts, black shorts, black stockings.

Year Formed: 1876.

Turned Professional: 1885.

Ltd Co.: 1911.

Previous Names: 1876, Port Vale; 1884, Burslem Port Vale; 1909, Port Vale.

Club Nickname: 'Valiants'.

Grounds: 1876, Limekin Lane, Longport; 1881, Westport; 1884, Moorland Road, Burslem; 1886, Athletic Ground, Cobridge; 1913, Recreation Ground, Hanley; 1950, Vale Park.

First Football League Game: 3 September 1892, Division 2, v Small Heath (a) L 1–5 – Frail; Clutton, Elson; Farrington, McCrindle, Delves; Walker, Scarratt, Bliss (1), Jones. (Only 10 men).

Record League Victory: 9–1 v Chesterfield, Division 2, 24 September 1932 – Leckie; Shenton, Poyser; Sherlock, Round, Jones; McGrath, Mills, Littlewood (6), Kirkham (2), Morton (1).

Record Cup Victory: 7–1 v Irthlingborough, FA Cup 1st rd, 12 January 1907 – Matthews; Dunn, Hamilton; Eardley, Baddeley, Holyhead; Carter, Dodds (2), Beats, Mountford (2), Coxon (3).

Record Defeat: 0–10 v Sheffield U, Division 2, 10 December 1892. 0–10 v Notts Co, Division 2, 26 February 1895.

HONOURS

Football League: Division 2 – Runners-up 1993–94; Division 3 (N) – Champions 1929–30, 1953–54; Runners-up 1952–53; Division 4 – Champions 1958–59; Promoted 1969–70 (4th).

FA Cup: Semi-final 1954, when in Division 3.

Football League Cup: best season: 4th rd 2007.

Autoglass Trophy: Winners 1993.

Anglo-Italian Cup: Runners-up 1996.

LDV Vans Trophy: Winners 2001.

SKY SPORTS FACT FILE

Lucien Boullemier made 186 first team appearances for Port Vale. His tally included making the most club outings in 1898–99 with 44 in all games. Signed as a right-half the previous season he was a ceramic artist of French extraction!

Most League Points (2 for a win): 69, Division 3 (N), 1953–54.

Most League Points (3 for a win): 89, Division 2, 1992–93.

Most League Goals: 110, Division 4, 1958–59.

Highest League Scorer in Season: Wilf Kirkham 38, Division 2, 1926–27.

Most League Goals in Total Aggregate: Wilf Kirkham, 154, 1923–29, 1931–33.

Most League Goals in One Match: 6, Stewart Littlewood v Chesterfield, Division 2, 24 September 1922.

Most Capped Player: Chris Birchall, 22 (26), Trinidad & Tobago.

Most League Appearances: Roy Sproson, 761, 1950–72.

Youngest League Player: Malcolm McKenzie, 15 years 347 days v Newport Co, 12 April 1966.

Record Transfer Fee Received: £2,000,000 from Wimbledon for Gareth Ainsworth, October 1998.

Record Transfer Fee Paid: £500,000 to York C for Jon McCarthy, August 1995 and £500,000 to Lincoln C for Gareth Ainsworth, September 1997.

Football League Record: 1892 Original Member of Division 2. Failed re-election in 1896; Re-elected 1898; Resigned 1907; Returned in Oct, 1919, when they took over the fixtures of Leeds City; 1929–30 Division 3 (N); 1930–36 Division 2; 1936–38 Division 3 (N); 1938–52 Division 3 (S); 1952–54 Division 3 (N); 1954–57 Division 2; 1957–58 Division 3 (S); 1958–59 Division 4; 1959–65 Division 3; 1965–70 Division 4; 1970–78 Division 3; 1978–83 Division 4; 1983–84 Division 3; 1984–86 Division 4; 1986–89 Division 3; 1989–94 Division 2; 1994–2000 Division 1; 2000–04 Division 2; 2004–08 FL 1; 2008– FL 2.

MANAGERS

Sam Gleaves 1896–1905 *(Secretary-Manager)*
Tom Clare 1905–11
A. S. Walker 1911–12
H. Myatt 1912–14
Tom Holford 1919–24 *(continued as Trainer)*
Joe Schofield 1924–30
Tom Morgan 1930–32
Tom Holford 1932–35
Warney Cresswell 1936–37
Tom Morgan 1937–38
Billy Frith 1945–46
Gordon Hodgson 1946–51
Ivor Powell 1951
Freddie Steele 1951–57
Norman Low 1957–62
Freddie Steele 1962–65
Jackie Mudie 1965–67
Sir Stanley Matthews *(General Manager)* 1965–68
Gordon Lee 1968–74
Roy Sproson 1974–77
Colin Harper 1977
Bobby Smith 1977–78
Dennis Butler 1978–79
Alan Bloor 1979
John McGrath 1980–83
John Rudge 1984–99
Brian Horton 1999–2004
Martin Foyle 2004–07
Lee Sinnott November 2007–

LATEST SEQUENCES

Longest Sequence of League Wins: 8, 8.4.1893 – 30.9.1893.

Longest Sequence of League Defeats: 9, 9.3.1957 – 20.4.1957.

Longest Sequence of League Draws: 6, 26.4.1981 – 12.9.1981.

Longest Sequence of Unbeaten League Matches: 19, 5.5.1969 – 8.11.1969.

Longest Sequence Without a League Win: 17, 7.12.1991 – 21.3.1992.

Successive Scoring Runs: 22 from 12.9.1992.

Successive Non-scoring Runs: 4 from 10.2.1896.

TEN YEAR LEAGUE RECORD

		P	*W*	*D*	*L*	*F*	*A*	*Pts*	*Pos*
1998-99	Div 1	46	13	8	25	45	75	47	21
1999-2000	Div 1	46	7	15	24	48	69	36	23
2000-01	Div 2	46	16	14	16	55	49	62	11
2001-02	Div 2	46	16	10	20	51	62	58	14
2002-03	Div 2	46	14	11	21	54	70	53	17
2003-04	Div 2	46	21	10	15	73	63	73	7
2004-05	FL 1	46	17	5	24	49	59	56	18
2005-06	FL 1	46	16	12	18	49	54	60	13
2006-07	FL 1	46	18	6	22	64	65	60	12
2007-08	FL 1	46	9	11	26	47	81	38	23

DID YOU KNOW ?

The circumstances of Port Vale making their League bow with only ten men in 1892 came about because Billy Beats missed his train to Birmingham, while another player had put pen to paper for two clubs and played for Darlington his original signing!

PORT VALE 2007–08 LEAGUE RECORD

Match No.	*Date*	*Venue*	*Opponents*	*Result*		*H/T Score*	*Lg. Pos.*	*Goalscorers*	*Attendance*
1	Aug 11	H	Bristol R	D	1-1	0-0	—	Rodgers (pen) [66]	6808
2	18	A	Yeovil T	L	0-1	0-1	18		5071
3	25	H	Hartlepool U	L	0-2	0-1	22		3978
4	Sept 1	A	Bournemouth	W	1-0	0-0	17	Rodgers [82]	5444
5	8	A	Walsall	D	0-0	0-0	14		4967
6	15	H	Nottingham F	L	0-2	0-1	21		6521
7	22	A	Luton T	L	1-2	0-1	23	Rodgers [90]	6084
8	29	H	Southend U	L	1-2	0-2	23	Rodgers (pen) [59]	3969
9	Oct 2	H	Cheltenham T	W	3-0	1-0	—	McGoldrick [21], Edwards [73], Rocastle [88]	3102
10	6	A	Northampton T	L	1-2	0-2	22	McGoldrick [55]	4755
11	13	H	Brighton & HA	L	0-1	0-0	23		3490
12	20	A	Leyton Orient	L	1-3	1-0	23	Rodgers [40]	4555
13	27	H	Swindon T	W	2-1	2-1	22	Rodgers (pen) [18], Whitaker [26]	4013
14	Nov 3	A	Huddersfield T	L	1-3	1-3	23	Rodgers [43]	8555
15	6	H	Crewe Alex	L	0-1	0-0	—		5329
16	17	A	Oldham Ath	D	1-1	1-1	23	Willock [32]	5097
17	24	H	Doncaster R	L	1-3	1-0	24	Pilkington [10]	4581
18	Dec 4	A	Leeds U	L	0-3	0-1	—		20,301
19	8	A	Gillingham	W	2-1	2-1	21	Willock [34], King (og) [45]	7001
20	15	H	Tranmere R	D	0-0	0-0	22		3604
21	22	A	Nottingham F	L	0-2	0-1	23		21,407
22	26	H	Walsall	D	1-1	1-0	24	Laird [12]	6029
23	29	H	Luton T	L	1-2	1-1	24	Willock [45]	4224
24	Jan 2	A	Cheltenham T	L	0-1	0-1	—		3221
25	5	A	Carlisle U	L	2-3	2-0	—	Harsley [27], Whitaker [38]	6313
26	12	H	Millwall	W	3-1	1-1	23	Whitaker [24], Lowe 2 [75, 90]	3724
27	19	A	Swansea C	L	0-2	0-1	23		12,310
28	26	H	Bournemouth	L	1-3	0-2	—	Pilkington [49]	4047
29	29	H	Yeovil T	D	2-2	1-1	—	Eckersley [38], Edwards [58]	2869
30	Feb 2	A	Bristol R	L	2-3	1-1	24	Harsley (pen) [12], Lowe [64]	6927
31	9	H	Carlisle U	D	1-1	0-0	24	Harsley (pen) [84]	4221
32	12	A	Hartlepool U	L	2-3	2-0	—	Herd 2 [3, 15]	3630
33	16	H	Swansea C	L	0-2	0-0	24		4347
34	23	A	Millwall	L	0-3	0-2	24		7775
35	Mar 1	H	Oldham Ath	L	0-3	0-1	24		3715
36	8	A	Doncaster R	L	1-2	1-2	24	Whitaker [34]	8040
37	11	A	Crewe Alex	W	2-0	0-0	—	Harsley (pen) [57], Rodgers [81]	5229
38	15	H	Leeds U	D	3-3	0-2	24	Harsley (pen) [65], Whitaker [67], Rodgers [90]	7908
39	20	A	Tranmere R	L	0-2	0-0	—		6484
40	24	H	Gillingham	W	2-1	1-0	24	Richards [19], Whitaker [53]	3157
41	29	H	Leyton Orient	W	2-1	0-1	24	Richards [75], Howland [90]	3252
42	Apr 5	A	Brighton & HA	W	3-2	2-1	23	Richards 2 [12, 19], Whitaker [87]	7741
43	12	H	Huddersfield T	D	0-0	0-0	23		4150
44	19	A	Swindon T	L	0-6	0-5	23		7361
45	26	H	Northampton T	D	2-2	1-2	23	Richards [30], Glover [49]	4556
46	May 3	A	Southend U	D	1-1	1-0	23	Mulligan [23]	9292

Final League Position: 23

GOALSCORERS

League (47): Rodgers 9 (3 pens), Whitaker 7, Harsley 5 (4 pens), Richards 5, Lowe 3, Willock 3, Edwards 2, Herd 2, McGoldrick 2, Pilkington 2, Eckersley 1, Glover 1, Howland 1, Laird 1, Mulligan 1, Rocastle 1, own goal 1.
Carling Cup (1): Rodgers 1 (pen).
FA Cup (3): Pilkington 1, Rodgers 1, Willock 1.
J Paint Trophy (2): Miller 1, Rodgers 1.

Anyon J 44	McGregor M 18 + 2	Talbot J 21 + 4	Hulbert R 15 + 7	Pilkington G 45	Lowe K 24 + 4	Tudor S 8 + 6	Rocastle C 17 + 6	Sodje A 3	Rodgers L 29 + 7	Whitaker D 36 + 5	Willock C 8 + 7	Edwards P 17 + 8	Harsley P 39 + 2	Richards M 19 + 10	Miller J 12 + 2	Miles C 1 + 2	Chapman L — + 1	Westwood A 11 + 1	McGoldrick D 15 + 2	Eckersley A 18	Atkinson W 3 + 1	Laird M 7	Salmon M 8 + 1	Lawrie J — + 6	Glover D 9 + 6	O'Loughlin C — + 3	Cardle J 4 + 5	Mulligan D 10 + 3	Herd C 11	Perry K 9 + 7	Slater C 1 + 4	Mikaelsson T 5 + 1	Howland D 17	Pearce K 11 + 1	Richman S 6	Prosser L 3 + 2	Martin C 2	Davidson R — + 3	*Match No.*
1	2	3	4	5	6	7	8	9^{1}	10	11	12																												1
1	2	3^{1}	4	5	6	7^{3}	8^{2}	9	10	11		12	13	14																									2
1		3	4	5		7		9	12	13	14	11^{3}	8^{2}	10^{1}	2	6																							3
1				5	12	7^{1}	8		13	11	14	3	4	9^{2}	2			6	10^{3}																				4
1		12	14	5		7^{2}	8		13	11^{3}		3	4	9	2^{1}			6	10																				5
1	12			5	6^{1}	7	8		13	11^{3}	14	3	4	9^{2}				2	10																				6
1	2			5		12	8		9	11	7^{3}	3	4^{2}	14	13			6▮	10^{1}																				7
1	2	3		5	6	12	8		9	11^{1}	13	7^{2}	4	14					10^{3}																				8
1	2	3▮	12	5		13	8		9^{2}	7^{1}		11	4	14	6				10^{3}																				9
1	2^{1}		13	5		12	8		9	7		11	4^{2}	14	3			6	10^{3}																				10
1			4^{1}	5		7	8		9	12		11^{3}		13	2			6	10^{2}	3▮	14																		11
1	6	13	4	5		7^{1}	8		9	11^{2}	12	3		10	2^{3}			14																					12
1				5			8		9	11	12		4^{1}	10^{2}	2			6	13	3	7																		13
1	2		12			13	8		9	11		3	4		6^{1}			5	10		7^{2}																		14
1	2	3^{1}	4	5	13	12	8		9	7			14					6^{2}	10		11^{3}																		15
1	2	3		5	12		8		9^{1}	7	10^{3}	11^{2}		14				6	13			4																	16
1	2	3		5			8		9	11	10^{2}	13	7^{1}	12				6				4^{3}	14																17
1	3^{2}	7		5	6				9				8		2^{1}				11			10	4	12	13														18
1	2	3		5	6				9^{2}	12	10		8			13			11			7	4^{1}																19
1	2	3		5	6		12		9		10^{2}		8	13					11			7	4^{1}																20
1	2	3^{3}	12	5	6		13		9^{1}		10	14	8						11			7	4^{2}																21
1	2	3^{1}	14	5	6				9	13	10		8			12^{2}			11			7^{3}	4																22
1	2	3	4	5	6		8^{2}		12	11	10	13											7^{1}		9														23
1			4	5	6		12			11^{1}			8	9^{3}	2^{2}					3			7		10	13	14												24
1	2	3^{2}	4	5	6		12			11			8^{1}							9			7^{3}		10	13	14												25
1			4^{1}	5	6				9	11		12	8							3				14	10^{3}		13	2	7^{2}										26
1				5	6				9	11		2^{1}	8							3					10^{3}			4^{2}	7	12	13	14							27
1				5	6^{3}				9	11^{1}		12	8							3					13			2	7		14	10^{2}	4						28
1				5	6				9			11	8							3								2	7	12		10^{1}	4						29
1				5	6				9	12		11^{2}	8							3								2	7▮	14		10^{3}	4^{1}	13					30
1				5	2					11			8							3					7^{1}		12			9		10	4	6					31
1				5	2				12	11^{2}			8							3									7	9	13	10^{1}	4	6▮					32
1		3^{1}		5	6		13		9^{3}	11			8		12										14			2	7	10			4^{2}						33
1				5	6		12			11^{3}			8	14	2										9^{2}		13		7	10	3		4^{1}						34
1		3	12	5	2^{2}					11		13	8	9^{3}										14					7	10			4^{1}	6					35
1		3^{2}	7	5					12	11		13	8	9															2	10			4^{1}	6					36
1		3	2	5					9	11			8	10^{1}															7	12			4	6					37
1		3	2^{1}	5					9	11		7^{3}	8	10^{2}											13			12		14			4	6					38
1		3	2	5					9^{1}	11		7^{2}	8	10											12					13			4	6					39
1		12	2^{2}	5					9	11			8	10						3^{1}								13		7			4	6					40
1		12		5					9^{2}	11			8	10						3^{1}				14				13		7			4	6	2^{3}				41
1	12			5						11			8	10						3							7^{2}	9					4	6	2^{1}	13			42
1				5						11			8	10						3				14	12		7^{3}	9					4	6^{2}	2^{1}	13			43
				5^{1}	12					11^{3}			8	9						3							10	2^{2}			13		4		7	6	1	14	44
				5	2					11			8	10						3				12	9^{1}		7^{2}			13					4^{3}	6	1	14	45
1				5	2^{1}								8	10			14			3					9^{3}	13		7^{2}		11					4	6		12	46

FA Cup

First Round	Morecambe	(a)	2-0
Second Round	Chasetown	(h)	1-1
		(a)	0-1

Carling Cup

First Round	Wrexham	(h)	1-1

J Paint Trophy

Second Round	Morecambe	(a)	2-2

PRESTON NORTH END FL Championship

FOUNDATION

North End Cricket and Rugby Club which was formed in 1863, indulged in most sports before taking up soccer in about 1879. In 1881 they decided to stick to football to the exclusion of other sports and even a 16–0 drubbing by Blackburn Rovers in an invitation game at Deepdale, a few weeks after taking this decision, did not deter them for they immediately became affiliated to the Lancashire FA.

Deepdale Stadium, Sir Tom Finney Way, Deepdale, Preston PR1 6RU.

Telephone: 0870 442 1964.

Fax: (01772) 693 366.

Ticket Office: 0870 442 1965.

Website: www.pne.com

Email: enquiries@pne.com

Ground Capacity: 24,000 (with completion of new stand).

Record Attendance: 42,684 v Arsenal, Division 1, 23 April 1938.

Pitch Measurements: 110yd × 77yd.

Chairman: Derek Shaw.

Vice-chairman: David Taylor.

Secretary: Janet Parr.

Manager: Alan Irvine.

First Team Coach: Robert Kelly.

Physio: Matt Radcliffe.

Colours: White shirts, blue shorts, white and blue hooped stockings.

Change Colours: Yellow shirts, yellow shorts, yellow stockings.

Year Formed: 1881.

Turned Professional: 1885. ***Ltd Co.:*** 1893.

Club Nicknames: 'The Lilywhites' or 'North End'.

Ground: 1881, Deepdale.

First Football League Game: 8 September 1888, Football League, v Burnley (h) W 5–2 – Trainer; Howarth, Holmes; Robertson, W. Graham, J. Graham; Gordon (1), Ross (2), Goodall, Dewhurst (2), Drummond.

Record League Victory: 10–0 v Stoke, Division 1, 14 September 1889 – Trainer; Howarth, Holmes; Kelso, Russell (1), Graham; Gordon, Jimmy Ross (2), Nick Ross (3), Thomson (2), Drummond (2).

Record Cup Victory: 26–0 v Hyde, FA Cup 1st rd, 15 October 1887 – Addision; Howarth, Nick Ross; Russell (1), Thomson (5), Graham (1); Gordon (5), Jimmy Ross (8), John Goodall (1), Dewhurst (3), Drummond (2).

Record Defeat: 0–7 v Blackpool, Division 1, 1 May 1948.

Most League Points (2 for a win): 61, Division 3, 1970–71.

HONOURS

Football League: Division 1 – Champions 1888–89 (first champions) 1889–90; Runners-up 1890–91, 1891–92, 1892–93, 1905–06, 1952–53, 1957–58; Division 2 – Champions 1903–04, 1912–13, 1950–51, 1999–2000; Runners-up 1914–15, 1933–34; Division 3 – Champions 1970–71, 1995–96; Division 4 – Runners-up 1986–87.

FA Cup: Winners 1889, 1938; Runners-up 1888, 1922, 1937, 1954, 1964.

Football League Cup: best season: 4th rd, 2003.

Double Performed: 1888–89.

Football League Cup: best season: 4th rd, 1963, 1966, 1972, 1981.

SKY SPORTS FACT FILE

When centre-forward Tommy Roberts re-signed for Preston North End from Burnley in 1926, the news was flashed onto the cinema screen at the Empire theatre, owned by one of the club's directors. He missed the last eleven games but still hit 30 goals in League and Cup.

Most League Points (3 for a win): 95, Division 2, 1999–2000.

Most League Goals: 100, Division 2, 1927–28 and Division 1, 1957–58.

Highest League Scorer in Season: Ted Harper, 37, Division 2, 1932–33.

Most League Goals in Total Aggregate: Tom Finney, 187, 1946–60.

Most League Goals in One Match: 4, Jimmy Ross v Stoke, Division 1, 6 October 1888; 4, Nick Ross v Derby Co, Division 1, 11 January 1890; 4, George Drummond v Notts Co, Division 1, 12 December 1891; 4, Frank Becton v Notts Co, Division 1, 31 March 1893; 4, George Harrison v Grimsby T, Division 2, 3 November 1928; 4, Alex Reid v Port Vale, Division 2, 23 February 1929; 4, James McClelland v Reading, Division 2, 6 September 1930; 4, Dick Rowley v Notts Co, Division 2, 16 April 1932; 4, Ted Harper v Burnley, Division 2, 29 August 1932; 4, Ted Harper v Lincoln C, Division 2, 11 March 1933; 4, Charlie Wayman v QPR, Division 2, 25 December 1950; 4, Alex Bruce v Colchester U, Division 3, 28 February 1978.

Most Capped Player: Tom Finney, 76, England.

Most League Appearances: Alan Kelly, 447, 1961–75.

Youngest League Player: Steve Doyle, 16 years 166 days v Tranmere R, 15 November 1974.

Record Transfer Fee Received: £6,000,000 from Portsmouth for David Nugent, August 2007.

Record Transfer Fee Paid: £1,500,000 to Manchester U for David Healy, December 2000.

Football League Record: 1888 Founder Member of League; 1901–04 Division 2; 1904–12 Division 1; 1912–13 Division 2; 1913–14 Division 1; 1914–15 Division 2; 1919–25 Division 1; 1925–34 Division 2; 1934–49 Division 1; 1949–51 Division 2; 1951–61 Division 1; 1961–70 Division 2; 1970–71 Division 3; 1971–74 Division 2; 1974–78 Division 3; 1978–81 Division 2; 1981–85 Division 3; 1985–87 Division 4; 1987–92 Division 3; 1992–93 Division 2; 1993–96 Division 3; 1996–2000 Division 2; 2000–04 Division 1; 2004– FL C.

MANAGERS

Charlie Parker 1906–15
Vincent Hayes 1919–23
Jim Lawrence 1923–25
Frank Richards 1925–27
Alex Gibson 1927–31
Lincoln Hayes 1931–32
Run by committee 1932–36
Tommy Muirhead 1936–37
Run by committee 1937–49
Will Scott 1949–53
Scot Symon 1953–54
Frank Hill 1954–56
Cliff Britton 1956–61
Jimmy Milne 1961–68
Bobby Seith 1968–70
Alan Ball Sr 1970–73
Bobby Charlton 1973–75
Harry Catterick 1975–77
Nobby Stiles 1977–81
Tommy Docherty 1981
Gordon Lee 1981–83
Alan Kelly 1983–85
Tommy Booth 1985–86
Brian Kidd 1986
John McGrath 1986–90
Les Chapman 1990–92
Sam Allardyce 1992 (*Caretaker*)
John Beck 1992–94
Gary Peters 1994–98
David Moyes 1998–2002
Kelham O'Hanlon 2002 (*Caretaker*)
Craig Brown 2002–04
Billy Davies 2004–06
Paul Simpson 2006–07
Alan Irvine November 2007–

LATEST SEQUENCES

Longest Sequence of League Wins: 14, 25.12.1950 – 27.3.1951.

Longest Sequence of League Defeats: 8, 22.9.1984 – 27.10.1984.

Longest Sequence of League Draws: 6, 24.2.1979 – 20.3.1979.

Longest Sequence of Unbeaten League Matches: 23, 8.9.1888 – 14.9.1889.

Longest Sequence Without a League Win: 15, 14.4.1923 – 20.10.1923.

Successive Scoring Runs: 30 from 15.11.1952.

Successive Non-scoring Runs: 6 from 8.4.1897.

TEN YEAR LEAGUE RECORD

		P	W	D	L	F	A	Pts	Pos
1998-99	Div 2	46	22	13	11	78	50	79	5
1999-2000	Div 2	46	28	11	7	74	37	95	1
2000-01	Div 1	46	23	9	14	64	52	78	4
2001-02	Div 1	46	20	12	14	71	59	72	8
2002-03	Div 1	46	16	13	17	68	70	61	12
2003-04	Div 1	46	15	14	17	69	71	59	15
2004-05	FL C	46	21	12	13	67	58	75	5
2005-06	FL C	46	20	20	6	59	30	80	4
2006-07	FL C	46	22	8	16	64	53	74	7
2007-08	FL C	46	15	11	20	50	56	56	15

DID YOU KNOW

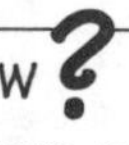

A record-breaking 1950–51 season for Preston North End in several respects, notably 14 successive victories, it also included the 3,000th League goal achieved by the club on 17 October, registered by Ken Horton at Luton Town in a 2–1 win.

PRESTON NORTH END 2007–08 LEAGUE RECORD

Match No.	Date	Venue	Opponents	Result		H/T Score	Lg. Pos.	Goalscorers	Attendance
1	Aug 11	H	Norwich C	D	0-0	0-0	—		13,408
2	18	A	WBA	L	0-2	0-0	21		19,556
3	25	H	Colchester U	L	0-3	0-1	23		11,582
4	Sept 1	A	Coventry C	L	1-2	1-0	23	Agyemang[16]	17,551
5	15	H	Sheffield W	W	1-0	1-0	22	Gallagher[28]	13,062
6	18	A	Scunthorpe U	L	1-2	1-1	—	Mawene[44]	5754
7	22	A	Cardiff C	D	2-2	0-1	22	Davidson 2[51, 90]	11,772
8	29	H	Bristol C	D	0-0	0-0	22		12,098
9	Oct 2	H	Southampton	W	5-1	1-1	—	Hawley[12], Carter[58], Sedgwick[75], Agyemang 2[83, 90]	10,279
10	6	A	Ipswich T	L	1-2	0-1	21	Mellor (pen)[88]	19,243
11	20	A	Sheffield U	D	1-1	1-0	21	Carter[35]	23,661
12	23	H	QPR	D	0-0	0-0	—		11,407
13	27	H	Plymouth Arg	W	2-0	1-0	18	Ormerod[11], Carter[67]	11,055
14	Nov 3	A	Barnsley	L	0-1	0-1	20		10,223
15	6	H	Leicester C	D	1-1	1-0	—	Carroll[14]	10,930
16	10	A	Hull C	L	0-3	0-2	21		16,358
17	24	H	Charlton Ath	L	0-2	0-1	23		12,532
18	27	A	Crystal Palace	L	1-2	1-2	—	Mawene[36]	13,048
19	Dec 1	A	Wolverhampton W	L	0-1	0-0	23		22,836
20	4	H	Hull C	W	3-0	0-0	—	Agyemang[60], Whaley[68], Neal L[89]	11,311
21	8	H	Blackpool	L	0-1	0-0	23		17,807
22	15	A	Burnley	W	3-2	1-1	23	Sedgwick[45], Mellor[54], Whaley[82]	14,829
23	22	A	Southampton	W	1-0	0-0	20	Neal L[90]	23,267
24	26	H	Scunthorpe U	L	0-1	0-1	22		12,920
25	29	H	Cardiff C	L	1-2	1-0	23	Whaley[5]	12,046
26	Jan 1	A	Sheffield W	L	1-2	1-0	24	Hawley[35]	20,690
27	12	H	Watford	W	1-0	0-0	22	Mellor[75]	12,347
28	19	A	Stoke C	L	1-3	0-2	22	Brown C[68]	15,011
29	29	H	WBA	W	2-1	1-0	—	Mawene[6], Hawley[72]	12,473
30	Feb 2	A	Norwich C	L	0-1	0-0	22		24,092
31	9	H	Coventry C	W	1-0	1-0	21	St Ledger-Hall[21]	11,857
32	12	A	Colchester U	L	1-2	0-0	—	Mellor[81]	5122
33	23	A	Watford	D	0-0	0-0	22		16,798
34	26	H	Stoke C	W	2-0	2-0	—	Chaplow 2[22, 33]	10,347
35	Mar 1	H	Crystal Palace	L	0-1	0-0	21		12,347
36	4	A	Leicester C	W	1-0	0-0	—	Carter[90]	19,264
37	8	A	Charlton Ath	W	2-1	1-0	17	Brown C 2[15, 77]	25,124
38	11	H	Wolverhampton W	W	2-1	0-0	—	Davidson (pen)[60], Whaley[81]	12,090
39	15	A	Blackpool	D	0-0	0-0	16		9629
40	22	H	Burnley	W	2-1	1-1	15	Priskin[5], Brown C[54]	16,149
41	29	H	Sheffield U	W	3-1	1-0	15	Davidson (pen)[28], Mellor 2[63, 90]	14,647
42	Apr 5	A	QPR	D	2-2	1-0	15	Mellor[37], Priskin[64]	14,966
43	12	H	Barnsley	L	1-2	0-1	15	Foster (og)[67]	13,994
44	19	A	Plymouth Arg	D	2-2	0-1	15	Mellor[77], Chaplow[90]	10,727
45	26	H	Ipswich T	D	2-2	1-1	15	Brown C[34], Mellor[79]	14,187
46	May 4	A	Bristol C	L	0-3	0-2	15		19,169

Final League Position: 15

GOALSCORERS

League (50): Mellor 9 (1 pen), Brown C 5, Agyemang 4, Carter 4, Davidson 4 (2 pens), Whaley 4, Chaplow 3, Hawley 3, Mawene 3, Neal L 2, Priskin 2, Sedgwick 2, Carroll 1, Gallagher 1, Ormerod 1, St Ledger-Hall 1, own goal 1.
Carling Cup (1): Pugh 1.
FA Cup (5): Hawley 2, Whaley 2, Mellor 1 (pen).

Henderson W 3	Alexander G 3	Davidson C 39 + 1	Nicholls K 17 + 1	St Ledger-Hall S 34 + 3	Mawene Y 36 + 2	Whaley S 29 + 14	Carter D 30 + 9	Ormerod B 8 + 10	Mellor N 12 + 24	Pugh D 5 + 2	Sedgwick C 40 + 2	Hawley K 20 + 5	Carroll A 7 + 4	Agyemang P 11 + 11	Lonergan A 43	Jones B 28 + 1	Chilvers L 27 + 1	Gallagher P 15 + 4	Hill M 21 + 5	Neal L 8 + 9	McKenna P 33	Halls J 4	Brown C 17	Chaplow R 7 + 5	Beattie C 1 + 1	Priskin T 4 + 1	Trotman N 2 + 1	Hart M 2	*Match No.*
1	2	3	4	5	6	7	8	9[2]	10[1]	11	12	13																	1
1	2	3	4[1]	5	6	12	8	9[2]	10[3]	11	7	13	14																2
1	2	3	4	5	6	12	8	13		11[1]	7		10	9[2]															3
		3	4		6	12	8	13		11[1]	7		10[3]	9[2]	1	2	5	14											4
		3	4		6	12	8	13		14	7[3]		10	9[2]	1	2	5	11[1]											5
		3	4		6	12	8	13		14	7[1]		10■	9[2]	1	2	5	11[3]											6
		3	4		6		8		12		7	13		9[2]	1	11	5	10[1]	2[3]	14									7
		11	4	12	6[1]		8		13		7	10[3]		14	1	2	5	9[2]	3										8
		11	4		6		8		12		7	10[1]		13	1	2	5	9[2]	3[3]	14									9
		11	4		6	12	8[1]		13	3	7	10[2]		14	1	2	5	9[3]											10
		11	4	12	6	13	8[2]				7	10		14	1	2	5[1]	9[3]	3										11
		11	4	5	6	12		13	14		7[3]	10[2]		9	1	2		8[1]	3										12
			4	5	6	12	8	9[3]	13		7	10[2]		14	1	2[1]			3		11								13
			4[1]	5		12	8	9[2]	13		7	10[3]		14	1		6		3		11	2							14
		12	4	5	6	11		9[2]			7		10	13	1	2[1]			3		8								15
		11		5	6	4	12	13			7[1]	9[2]	10[3]	14	1				3		8	2							16
		3	4[1]	5	6	13	12	9[3]			7		10	14	1			11[2]			8	2							17
		3	4[3]	5	6	11	10[1]				7		14	9	1		13	12			8	2[2]							18
		11		2	6	4		9[1]	12		7[2]		14	10[3]	1		5	13	3		8								19
		11		2	6	4[3]		9[2]	12		7			10[1]	1		5	13	3	14	8								20
		11[1]		2	6[2]	4			12		7[3]			10	1	13	5	9	3	14	8								21
		11		5	12	4	14		10		7	13			1	2[1]	6	9[2]	3		8[3]								22
		11	12	5		4	8		10[2]		7[3]			13	1	2	6	9[1]	3	14									23
		11		5		4	12		10		7[2]			13	1	2[1]	6	9	3[3]	14	8								24
		2		5[3]		4[1]	11		13		12	14		10	1		6	9	3	7[2]	8								25
		2		5		4	8	12	13			10[2]	14		1		6	9[3]	3	7[1]	11								26
		3		2	6	4	12		13			10			1		5			11	8		9[2]	7[1]					27
		3		2	6	4	12		13			10[2]			1		5			11	8		9	7[1]					28
		2		5	6■	4	8				7[2]	10[1]			1		3		12		11		9■	13					29
		3[2]		5		4	8	12	9[1]			10			1	2	6		13	7[3]	11			14					30
				5		4	8	12	13		7	10[1]			1	2	6		3		11		9[2]						31
		3		5■	12	4[3]	8		13		7[1]	10[2]			1	2	6				11		9	14					32
		3		12	6	4[1]			13		7	10[2]			1	2	5		14		11		9	8[3]					33
		3			6	4	12		13		7	10[2]			1	2	5				11		9	8[1]					34
					6	4[3]	8	12	13		7[1]	10[2]			1	2	5		3	14	11		9						35
				2	6	4[2]	8		12		7				1		5		3	13	11		9		10[1]				36
		3		2	6	4[2]	8		12		7				1	5			13		11		9			10[1]			37
		3		5	6	4	8		12		7				1	2					11		9			10[1]			38
		3		5	6	4	8		12		7				1	2					11		9			10[1]			39
		3		5	6	4	8		12		7				1	2					11		9			10[1]			40
		3[1]		5	6	4[2]	8		10		7				1	2			12		11		9	13					41
		3		5	6	4	8		10[1]		7				1	2					11		9			12			42
		3		5	6	4[1]	8[2]		10		7	9			1	2				12	11			13					43
		3		5[3]	6	12	13		10		7[2]	9			1	2				11[1]	8			4			14		44
		3			6	12			10		7				1					11[1]	8		9	4			5	2	45
				5		12	13		10		7[2]				1				3	11[1]	8		9[3]	4	14		6	2	46

FA Cup

Third Round	Scunthorpe U	(h)	1-0
Fourth Round	Derby Co	(a)	4-1
Fifth Round	Portsmouth	(h)	0-1

Carling Cup

First Round	Morecambe	(h)	1-2

QUEENS PARK RANGERS FL Championship

FOUNDATION

There is an element of doubt about the date of the foundation of this club, but it is believed that in either 1885 or 1886 it was formed through the amalgamation of Christchurch Rangers and St Jude's Institute FC. The leading light was George Wodehouse, whose family maintained a connection with the club until comparatively recent times. Most of the players came from the Queen's Park district so this name was adopted after a year as St Jude's Institute.

Loftus Road Stadium, South Africa Road, Shepherds Bush, London W12 7PA.

Telephone: (020) 8743 0262

Fax: (020) 8749 0994

Ticket Office: 08444 777077

Website: www.qpr.co.uk

Ground Capacity: 18,682.

Record Attendance: 35,353 v Leeds U, Division 1, 27 April 1974.

Pitch Measurements: 110yd × 73yd.

Chairman: Gianni Paladini.

Secretary: Mrs Sheila Marson.

Manager: Iain Dowie.

Assistant Manager: Tim Flowers.

Physio: Paul Hunter.

Colours: Blue and white hooped shirts.

Change Colours: All red and blue.

Year Formed: 1885* (*see Foundation*).

Turned Professional: 1898. ***Ltd Co.:*** 1899.

Previous Names: 1885, St Jude's; 1887, Queens Park Rangers. ***Club Nicknames:*** 'Rangers' or 'Rs'.

Grounds: 1885* (*see Foundation*), Welford's Fields; 1888–99; London Scottish Ground, Brondesbury, Home Farm, Kensal Rise Green, Gun Club Wormwood Scrubs, Kilburn Cricket Ground; 1899, Kensal Rise Athletic Ground; 1901, Latimer Road, Notting Hill; 1904, Agricultural Society, Park Royal; 1907, Park Royal Ground; 1917, Loftus Road; 1931, White City; 1933, Loftus Road; 1962, White City; 1963, Loftus Road.

First Football League Game: 28 August 1920, Division 3, v Watford (h) L 1–2 – Price; Blackman, Wingrove; McGovern, Grant, O'Brien; Faulkner, Birch (1), Smith, Gregory, Middlemiss.

Record League Victory: 9–2 v Tranmere R, Division 3, 3 December 1960 – Drinkwater; Woods, Ingham; Keen, Rutter, Angell; Lazarus (2), Bedford (2), Evans (2), Andrews (1), Clark (2).

Record Cup Victory: 8–1 v Bristol R (away), FA Cup 1st rd, 27 November 1937 – Gilfillan; Smith, Jefferson; Lowe, James, March; Cape, Mallett, Cheetham (3), Fitzgerald (3) Bott (2). 8–1 v Crewe Alex, Milk Cup 1st rd, 3 October 1983 – Hucker; Neill, Dawes, Waddock (1), McDonald (1), Fenwick, Micklewhite (1), Stewart (1), Allen (1), Stainrod (3), Gregory.

Record Defeat: 1–8 v Mansfield T, Division 3, 15 March 1965. 1–8 v Manchester U, Division 1, 19 March 1969.

HONOURS

Football League: Division 1 – Runners-up 1975–76; Division 2 – Champions 1982–83; Runners-up 1967–68, 1972–73, 2003–04; Division 3 (S) – Champions 1947–48; Runners-up 1946–47; Division 3 – Champions 1966–67.

FA Cup: Runners-up 1982.

Football League Cup: Winners 1967; Runners-up 1986. (In 1966–67 won Division 3 and Football League Cup).

European Competitions: *UEFA Cup:* 1976–77, 1984–85.

SKY SPORTS FACT FILE

George Gofton had been briefly on the books of Newcastle United when he signed for Queens Park Rangers midway through the 1932–33 season. He played in seven League matches and four FA Cup ties during consecutive appearances and hit eight League goals!

Most League Points (2 for a win): 67, Division 3, 1966–67.

Most League Points (3 for a win): 85, Division 2, 1982–83.

Most League Goals: 111, Division 3, 1961–62.

Highest League Scorer in Season: George Goddard, 37, Division 3 (S), 1929–30.

Most League Goals in Total Aggregate: George Goddard, 172, 1926–34.

Most League Goals in One Match: 4, George Goddard v Merthyr T, Division 3S, 9 March 1929; 4, George Goddard v Swindon T, Division 3S, 12 April 1930; 4, George Goddard v Exeter C, Division 3S, 20 December 1930; 4, George Goddard v Watford, Division 3S, 19 September 1931; 4, Tom Cheetham v Aldershot, Division 3S, 14 September 1935; 4, Tom Cheetham v Aldershot, Division 3S, 12 November 1938.

Most Capped Player: Alan McDonald, 52, Northern Ireland.

Most League Appearances: Tony Ingham, 519, 1950–63.

Youngest League Player: Frank Sibley, 16 years 97 days v Bristol C, 10 March 1964.

Record Transfer Fee Received: £6,000,000 from Newcastle U for Les Ferdinand, June 1995.

Record Transfer Fee Paid: £2,350,000 to Stoke C for Mike Sheron, July 1997.

Football League Record: 1920 Original Members of Division 3; 1921–48 Division 3 (S); 1948–52 Division 2; 1952–58 Division 3 (S); 1958–67 Division 3; 1967–68 Division 2; 1968–69 Division 1; 1969–73 Division 2; 1973–79 Division 1; 1979–83 Division 2; 1983–92 Division 1; 1992–96 FA Premier League; 1996–2001 Division 1; 2001–04 Division 2; 2004– FL C.

LATEST SEQUENCES

Longest Sequence of League Wins: 8, 7.11.1931 – 28.12.1931.

Longest Sequence of League Defeats: 9, 25.2.1969 – 5.4.1969.

Longest Sequence of League Draws: 6, 29.1.2000 – 5.3.2000.

Longest Sequence of Unbeaten League Matches: 20, 11.3.1972 – 23.9.1972.

Longest Sequence Without a League Win: 20, 7.12.1968 – 7.4.1969.

Successive Scoring Runs: 33 from 9.12.1961.

Successive Non-scoring Runs: 6 from 18.3.1939.

MANAGERS

James Cowan 1906–13
Jimmy Howie 1913–20
Ned Liddell 1920–24
Will Wood 1924–25
(had been Secretary since 1903)
Bob Hewison 1925–31
John Bowman 1931
Archie Mitchell 1931–33
Mick O'Brien 1933–35
Billy Birrell 1935–39
Ted Vizard 1939–44
Dave Mangnall 1944–52
Jack Taylor 1952–59
Alec Stock 1959–65
(General Manager to 1968)
Bill Dodgin Jnr 1968
Tommy Docherty 1968
Les Allen 1968–71
Gordon Jago 1971–74
Dave Sexton 1974–77
Frank Sibley 1977–78
Steve Burtenshaw 1978–79
Tommy Docherty 1979–80
Terry Venables 1980–84
Gordon Jago 1984
Alan Mullery 1984
Frank Sibley 1984–85
Jim Smith 1985–88
Trevor Francis 1988–90
Don Howe 1990–91
Gerry Francis 1991–94
Ray Wilkins 1994–96
Stewart Houston 1996–97
Ray Harford 1997–98
Gerry Francis 1998–2001
Ian Holloway 2001–06
Gary Waddock 2006
John Gregory 2006–07
Luigi Di Canio 2007–08
Iain Dowie May 2008–

TEN YEAR LEAGUE RECORD

		P	W	D	L	F	A	Pts	Pos
1998-99	Div 1	46	12	11	23	52	61	47	20
1999-2000	Div 1	46	16	18	12	62	53	66	10
2000-01	Div 1	46	7	19	20	45	75	40	23
2001-02	Div 2	46	19	14	13	60	49	71	8
2002-03	Div 2	46	24	11	11	69	45	83	4
2003-04	Div 2	46	22	17	7	80	45	83	2
2004-05	FL C	46	17	11	18	54	58	62	11
2005-06	FL C	46	12	14	20	50	65	50	21
2006-07	FL C	46	14	11	21	54	68	53	18
2007-08	FL C	46	14	16	16	60	66	58	14

DID YOU KNOW

The first Queens Park Rangers player to score as many as four goals in an FA Cup tie was centre-forward Harry Millar, formerly with Preston North End, Bury, Reading and Sheffield Wednesday. On 20 November 1901 he did so in a qualifying match against West Norwood.

QUEENS PARK RANGERS 2007–08 LEAGUE RECORD

Match No.	*Date*	*Venue*	*Opponents*	*Result*		*H/T Score*	*Lg. Pos.*	*Goalscorers*	*Attendance*
1	Aug 11	A	Bristol C	D	2-2	1-1	—	Blackstock [34], Stewart [90]	18,228
2	18	H	Cardiff C	L	0-2	0-1	20		12,596
3	Sept 1	H	Southampton	L	0-3	0-2	22		15,560
4	15	A	Leicester C	D	1-1	0-0	23	Leigertwood [82]	21,893
5	18	H	Plymouth Arg	L	0-2	0-0	—		10,850
6	22	H	Watford	D	1-1	0-0	23	Moore [59]	14,240
7	30	A	WBA	L	1-5	1-3	24	Ainsworth [24]	24,757
8	Oct 3	A	Colchester U	L	2-4	1-3	—	Ephraim [29], Vine [58]	5361
9	8	H	Norwich C	W	1-0	0-0	—	Rowlands (pen) [67]	10,514
10	20	H	Ipswich T	D	1-1	0-0	24	Nygaard [73]	13,946
11	23	A	Preston NE	D	0-0	0-0	—		11,407
12	27	A	Charlton Ath	W	1-0	0-0	23	Bolder [72]	23,671
13	Nov 3	H	Hull C	W	2-0	1-0	21	Ephraim [26], Leigertwood [56]	12,375
14	6	H	Coventry C	L	1-2	0-0	—	Buzsaky [50]	11,922
15	10	A	Crystal Palace	D	1-1	1-0	22	Sinclair [45]	17,010
16	24	H	Sheffield W	D	0-0	0-0	22		15,241
17	27	A	Stoke C	L	1-3	0-2	—	Vine [63]	11,147
18	Dec 1	A	Blackpool	L	0-1	0-0	22		8527
19	4	H	Crystal Palace	L	1-2	1-0	—	Stewart [10]	13,300
20	8	A	Scunthorpe U	D	2-2	2-1	24	Buzsaky 2 [12, 42]	5612
21	11	A	Burnley	W	2-0	0-0	—	Stewart [60], Vine [90]	10,522
22	15	H	Wolverhampton W	D	0-0	0-0	24		13,482
23	22	H	Colchester U	W	2-1	1-0	21	Buzsaky 2 [27, 52]	12,464
24	26	A	Plymouth Arg	L	1-2	1-0	23	Ainsworth [20]	16,502
25	29	A	Watford	W	4-2	3-0	19	Rowlands 2 (1 pen) [13 (p), 40], Stewart [29], Buzsaky [80]	18,698
26	Jan 1	H	Leicester C	W	3-1	2-0	18	Stewart [15], Bolder [26], Blackstock [56]	13,326
27	12	A	Sheffield U	L	1-2	1-0	20	Agyemang [45]	28,894
28	19	H	Barnsley	W	2-0	2-0	17	Agyemang [5], Vine [45]	16,197
29	29	A	Cardiff C	L	1-3	0-2	—	Ephraim [76]	13,602
30	Feb 2	H	Bristol C	W	3-0	2-0	18	Agyemang 2 [18, 33], Buzsaky [63]	16,502
31	9	A	Southampton	W	3-2	2-1	15	Rowlands [38], Agyemang 2 [45, 60]	22,505
32	12	H	Burnley	L	2-4	2-1	—	Mahon [14], Agyemang [30]	13,410
33	23	H	Sheffield U	D	1-1	1-0	16	Balanta [19]	15,383
34	26	A	Barnsley	D	0-0	0-0	—		9019
35	Mar 2	H	Stoke C	W	3-0	2-0	15	Leigertwood 2 [12, 21], Buzsaky [56]	13,398
36	5	A	Coventry C	D	0-0	0-0	—		15,225
37	8	A	Sheffield W	L	1-2	1-1	15	Delaney [15]	18,555
38	11	H	Blackpool	W	3-2	2-0	—	Buzsaky [11], Vine [40], Rowlands [47]	11,538
39	15	H	Scunthorpe U	W	3-1	1-1	12	Rowlands (pen) [43], Agyemang [79], Vine [90]	14,499
40	22	A	Wolverhampton W	D	3-3	1-1	14	Buzsaky [28], Blackstock (pen) [49], Leigertwood [79]	24,290
41	29	A	Ipswich T	D	0-0	0-0	14		24,570
42	Apr 5	H	Preston NE	D	2-2	0-1	14	Ainsworth [89], Blackstock [90]	14,966
43	12	A	Hull C	D	1-1	1-0	14	Blackstock [14]	22,468
44	19	H	Charlton Ath	W	1-0	1-0	14	Blackstock [15]	17,035
45	26	A	Norwich C	L	0-3	0-1	14		25,497
46	May 4	H	WBA	L	0-2	0-0	14		18,309

Final League Position: 14

GOALSCORERS

League (60): Buzsaky 10, Agyemang 8, Blackstock 6 (1 pen), Rowlands 6 (3 pens), Vine 6, Leigertwood 5, Stewart 5, Ainsworth 3, Ephraim 3, Bolder 2, Balanta 1, Delaney 1, Mahon 1, Moore 1, Nygaard 1, Sinclair 1.
Carling Cup (1): Rowlands 1.
FA Cup (0).

Camp L 46	Rehman Z 17 + 4	Curtis J 3 + 1	Bolder A 20 + 4	Mancienne M 26 + 4	Stewart D 35 + 4	Rowlands M 43 + 1	Bailey S 1	Nardiello D 4 + 4	Blackstock D 26 + 9	Moore S 5 + 6	Ephraim H 20 + 9	Nygaard M 6 + 13	Ward N — + 1	Barker C 25	Cullip D 5 + 1	Leigertwood M 33 + 7	Sahar B 6 + 3	Timoska S 3 + 4	Bignot M — + 2	Ainsworth G 16 + 8	Jarrett J 1 + 1	Vine R 31 + 2	Cranie M 6	Buzsaky A 24 + 3	Sinclair S 8 + 1	Malcolm B 10 + 1	Balanta A 6 + 5	Walton S 1 + 4	Mahon G 11 + 5	Connolly M 18 + 2	Hall F 14	Agyemang P 17	Lee K 2 + 5	Delaney D 17	Rose R — + 1	Match No.
1	2	3	4	5	6	7	8	9^{1}	10^{2}	11	12	13																								1
1	2	3	4	5	6	7		9^{1}	10	11^{2}	8	12	13																							2
1		2	4	5^{3}	6	7		12	10^{2}		11	13		3	14	8	9^{1}																			3
1	2		4^{2}		6	7		12	10	11	13			3	5	8	9^{1}																			4
1	2^{1}		4		6	7		9^{3}	10	11^{2}	13			3	5	8	14		12																	5
1			4		6	11		9^{2}	10	12	13			3	5	8■		2		7^{1}																6
1	2^{1}	12	4		6	7			10	11	13			3^{3}	5		9^{2}		14	8																7
1			4			2			10	12	11			3	6	5	13			7^{1}	8^{2}	9														8
1			4		6	2				12	11^{2}			3		8	10^{1}	13		7^{3}	14	9	5													9
1			4	2^{2}	6	11				12	10	13		3		8				7^{1}		9	5													10
1			4	2	6	11					10	12		3		8				7^{1}		9	5													11
1			4	2	6	7					11	10		3		8						9	5													12
1			12	2	6	7		13			11	10^{1}		3		8				14		9^{2}	5	4^{3}												13
1			12	2	6	7		13				10^{2}		3		8^{1}		14				9	5^{3}	4	11											14
1	12		10^{1}	5	6	7^{2}								3		8	14	2		13		9^{3}		4	11											15
1				5	6	7			10^{1}			12		3		8		13				9		4	11	2^{2}										16
1			12	2^{3}	6	7^{1}			10■			13		3		8		5				9^{2}		4	11	14										17
1			8		6	7				12		13		3		5	10^{2}			14		9^{3}		4^{1}	11	2										18
1	2		12		6	7^{2}						13		3		8	10^{3}					9		4^{1}	11	5	14									19
1	2^{3}		10		6	7						12		3		8		14		13		9		4^{2}	11^{1}	5										20
1	2		4		6				12	13		10		3		8^{3}				7^{2}		9			11^{1}	5		14								21
1	5				6	11			10^{1}			9		3		8				7				4	12	2										22
1	5		11		6■				10^{1}			12		3		8^{2}				7		9		4		2		13								23
1	5		11			7^{2}			12			13		3		8■				10		9		4^{1}		2		6								24
1	5		4		6	7			10			9^{3}		3						8^{2}		13		12		2	11^{1}	14								25
1	5		8^{1}		6	11			10^{2}			12		3						7^{3}		9		4		2		13	14							26
1					6	7			12					3^{1}								9		4					8	2	5	10	11			27
1				12	6^{3}	7			10^{2}		13					8						9		4						5	3^{1}	11	14	2		28
1				12	6	7			13		14					8						9		4^{3}					11	5^{2}	3^{1}	10		2		29
1	5^{3}			2	6	7					11^{2}					12						9^{1}		4					8	14		10	13	3		30
1	6			2		7			12		11^{2}					13						9		14					4	5		10^{1}	8^{3}	3		31
1	5			12	6	7^{3}			13		11^{2}					14						9		4					8	2^{1}		10		3		32
1				2	13	7			12		11					8						9					4^{1}			5^{2}	6	10		3		33
1				2	12	7			9^{2}		14					8						13		4^{1}			11^{3}			5	6	10		3		34
1				2	12	7^{3}			13		11					8				14		9^{2}		4						5	6^{1}	10		3		35
1				2		7^{2}			12		11					8				13		9		4						5	6	10^{1}		3		36
1				2	6	7			11		12■					8^{3}						9^{1}		4^{2}			13		14	5		10		3		37
1	12			2		7^{1}			8							6						9		4^{3}					13	5	11	10^{2}	14	3		38
1				2	12	7^{1}			8							6						9		4^{2}					13	5	11	10^{3}	14	3		39
1	12			2		7^{3}			11							8				13		9		4^{2}					14	5^{1}	6	10		3		40
1				2	3	12			11		7^{2}					8^{1}						9^{3}					13		4	5	6	10	14			41
1				2	3	7			9		11^{2}					8				12							13		4^{1}	5	6	10				42
1				2	5	8			9^{1}		11					12				7^{3}							13		4	14	6	10^{2}		3		43
1				12	5	8			9		11^{2}					13				7^{3}				14			10		4	2	6^{1}			3		44
1	13			2	6■	8			9		11^{2}					12				7^{1}							10		4	5				3		45
1	6			2		8■			9		11^{2}					12				7							10^{1}		4	5				3	13	46

FA Cup
Third Round Chelsea (a) 0-1

Carling Cup
First Round Leyton Orient (h) 1-2

READING FL Championship

FOUNDATION

Reading was formed as far back as 1871 at a public meeting held at the Bridge Street Rooms. They first entered the FA Cup as early as 1877 when they amalgamated with the Reading Hornets. The club was further strengthened in 1889 when Earley FC joined them. They were the first winners of the Berks and Bucks Cup in 1878–79.

Madejski Stadium, Junction 11, M4, Reading, Berkshire RG2 0FL.

Telephone: (0118) 968 1100.

Fax: (0118) 968 1101.

Ticket Office: 0870 999 1871.

Website: www.readingfc.co.uk

Email: customerservice@readingfc.co.uk

Ground Capacity: 24,161.

Record Attendance: Madejski Stadium: 24,122 v Aston Villa, Premiershp, 10 February 2007. Elm Park: 33,042 v Brentford, FA Cup 5th rd, 19 February 1927.

Pitch Measurements: 105m × 68m.

Chairman: John Madejski OBE, DL.

Vice-chairman: Ian Wood-Smith.

Chief Executive: Nigel Howe.

Secretary: Sue Hewett.

Manager: Steve Coppell.

Assistant Manager: Kevin Dillon, Wally Downes.

Physio: Jon Fearn MMACP, MCSP.

Colours: Blue and white.

Change Colours: Grey and black.

Year Formed: 1871.

Turned Professional: 1895. ***Ltd Co.:*** 1895.

Club Nickname: 'The Royals'.

Grounds: 1871, Reading Recreation; Reading Cricket Ground; 1882, Coley Park; 1889, Caversham Cricket Ground; 1896, Elm Park; 1998, Madejski Stadium.

First Football League Game: 28 August 1920, Division 3, v Newport Co (a) W 1–0 – Crawford; Smith, Horler; Christie, Mavin, Getgood; Spence, Weston, Yarnell, Bailey (1), Andrews.

Record League Victory: 10–2 v Crystal Palace, Division 3 (S), 4 September 1946 – Groves; Glidden, Gulliver; McKenna, Ratcliffe, Young; Chitty, Maurice Edelston (3), McPhee (4), Barney (1), Deverell (2).

HONOURS

FA Premier League: Best season – 8th 2006–07.
Football League: FL C – Champions 2005–06; Division 1 – Runners-up 1994–95; Division 2 – Champions 1993–94; Runners-up 2001–02; Division 3 – Champions 1985–86; Division 3 (S) – Champions 1925–26; Runners-up 1931–32, 1934–35, 1948–49, 1951–52; Division 4 – Champions 1978–79.
FA Cup: Semi-final 1927.
Football League Cup: best season: 5th rd, 1996.
Simod Cup: Winners 1988.

SKY SPORTS FACT FILE

Dick Pegg scored six of the goals by which Reading beat Chesham Generals 11–0 in a fourth qualifying round FA Cup tie on 17 November 1900. Subsequently associated with Manchester United he also managed an early hat-trick for them, too.

Record Cup Victory: 6–0 v Leyton, FA Cup 2nd rd, 12 December 1925 – Duckworth; Eggo, McConnell; Wilson, Messer, Evans; Smith (2), Braithwaite (1), Davey (1), Tinsley, Robson (2).

Record Defeat: 0–18 v Preston NE, FA Cup 1st rd, 1893–94.

Most League Points (2 for a win): 65, Division 4, 1978–79.

Most League Points (3 for a win): 106, Championship, 2005–06.

Most League Goals: 112, Division 3 (S), 1951–52.

Highest League Scorer in Season: Ronnie Blackman, 39, Division 3 (S), 1951–52.

Most League Goals in Total Aggregate: Ronnie Blackman, 158, 1947–54.

Most League Goals in One Match: 6, Arthur Bacon v Stoke C, Division 2, 3 April 1931.

Most Capped Player: Jimmy Quinn, 17 (46), Northern Ireland.

Most League Appearances: Martin Hicks, 500, 1978–91.

Youngest League Player: Peter Castle, 16 years 49 days v Watford, 30 April 2003.

Record Transfer Fee Received: Undisclosed from Sunderland for Greg Halford, June 2007.

Record Transfer Fee Paid: Undisclosed to Nantes for Emerse Fae, August 2007.

Football League Record: 1920 Original Member of Division 3; 1921–26 Division 3 (S); 1926–31 Division 2; 1931–58 Division 3 (S); 1958–71 Division 3; 1971–76 Division 4; 1976–77 Division 3; 1977–79 Division 4; 1979–83 Division 3; 1983–84 Division 4; 1984–86 Division 3; 1986–88 Division 2; 1988–92 Division 3; 1992–94 Division 2; 1994–98 Division 1; 1998–2002 Division 2; 2002–04 Division 1; 2004–06 FL C; 2006–08 FA Premier League; 2008– FL C.

MANAGERS

Thomas Sefton 1897–1901 *(Secretary-Manager)*
James Sharp 1901–02
Harry Matthews 1902–20
Harry Marshall 1920–22
Arthur Chadwick 1923–25
H. S. Bray 1925–26 *(Secretary only since 1922 and 1926–35)*
Andrew Wylie 1926–31
Joe Smith 1931–35
Billy Butler 1935–39
John Cochrane 1939
Joe Edelston 1939–47
Ted Drake 1947–52
Jack Smith 1952–55
Harry Johnston 1955–63
Roy Bentley 1963–69
Jack Mansell 1969–71
Charlie Hurley 1972–77
Maurice Evans 1977–84
Ian Branfoot 1984–89
Ian Porterfield 1989–91
Mark McGhee 1991–94
Jimmy Quinn/Mick Gooding 1994–97
Terry Bullivant 1997–98
Tommy Burns 1998–99
Alan Pardew 1999–2003
Steve Coppell October 2003–

LATEST SEQUENCES

Longest Sequence of League Wins: 13, 17.8.1985 – 19.10.1985.

Longest Sequence of League Defeats: 8, 29.12.2007 – 24.2.2008.

Longest Sequence of League Draws: 6, 23.3.2002 – 20.4.2002.

Longest Sequence of Unbeaten League Matches: 33, 9.8.2005 – 14.2.2006.

Longest Sequence Without a League Win: 14, 30.4.1927 – 29.10.1927.

Successive Scoring Runs: 32 from 1.10.1932.

Successive Non-scoring Runs: 6 from 13.4.1925.

TEN YEAR LEAGUE RECORD

		P	W	D	L	F	A	Pts	Pos
1998-99	Div 2	46	16	13	17	54	63	61	11
1999-2000	Div 2	46	16	14	16	57	63	62	10
2000-01	Div 2	46	25	11	10	86	52	86	3
2001-02	Div 2	46	23	15	8	70	43	84	2
2002-03	Div 1	46	25	4	17	61	46	79	4
2003-04	Div 1	46	20	10	16	55	57	70	9
2004-05	FL C	46	19	13	14	51	44	70	7
2005-06	FL C	46	31	13	2	99	32	106	1
2006-07	PR Lge	38	16	7	15	52	47	55	8
2007-08	PR Lge	38	10	6	22	41	66	36	18

DID YOU KNOW ?

On a purely goals per game ratio Irish international Hugh Davey produced a healthy average during his time with Reading from 1925 to 1927. His 61 League matches produced 46 goals. Capped five times for Northern Ireland he subsequently played for Portsmouth.

READING 2007–08 LEAGUE RECORD

Match No.	Date	Venue	Opponents	Result		H/T Score	Lg. Pos.	Goalscorers	Attendance
1	Aug 12	A	Manchester U	D	0-0	0-0	—		75,655
2	15	H	Chelsea	L	1-2	1-0	—	Bikey [30]	24,031
3	18	H	Everton	W	1-0	1-0	10	Hunt [44]	22,813
4	25	A	Bolton W	L	0-3	0-1	15		20,023
5	Sept 1	H	West Ham U	L	0-3	0-1	18		23,533
6	15	A	Sunderland	L	1-2	0-1	18	Kitson [85]	39,272
7	22	H	Wigan Ath	W	2-1	1-0	16	Kitson [29], Harper [90]	21,379
8	29	A	Portsmouth	L	4-7	1-2	17	Hunt [45], Kitson [48], Long [79], Campbell (og) [90]	20,102
9	Oct 7	H	Derby Co	W	1-0	0-0	12	Doyle [63]	23,091
10	20	A	Blackburn R	L	2-4	0-3	12	Doyle 2 [80, 90]	19,425
11	27	H	Newcastle U	W	2-1	0-0	12	Kitson [53], Long [84]	24,119
12	Nov 3	A	Fulham	L	1-3	0-1	12	Doyle [54]	22,086
13	12	H	Arsenal	L	1-3	0-1	—	Shorey [87]	24,024
14	24	A	Manchester C	L	1-2	1-1	13	Harper [43]	43,813
15	Dec 1	H	Middlesbrough	D	1-1	0-0	13	Kitson [54]	22,262
16	8	H	Liverpool	W	3-1	1-1	12	Hunt (pen) [17], Doyle [60], Harper [67]	24,022
17	15	A	Birmingham C	D	1-1	0-1	13	Hunt (pen) [51]	27,300
18	22	H	Sunderland	W	2-1	0-0	12	Ingimarsson [69], Hunt [90]	24,082
19	26	A	West Ham U	D	1-1	0-1	12	Kitson [60]	34,277
20	29	A	Tottenham H	L	4-6	1-1	13	Cisse [16], Ingimarsson [53], Kitson 2 [69, 74]	36,178
21	Jan 1	H	Portsmouth	L	0-2	0-1	13		24,084
22	12	A	Aston Villa	L	1-3	0-1	13	Harper [90]	32,288
23	19	H	Manchester U	L	0-2	0-0	14		24,135
24	30	A	Chelsea	L	0-1	0-1	—		41,171
25	Feb 2	H	Bolton W	L	0-2	0-1	17		21,893
26	9	A	Everton	L	0-1	0-0	18		36,582
27	24	H	Aston Villa	L	1-2	0-1	18	Shorey [90]	23,889
28	Mar 1	A	Middlesbrough	W	1-0	0-0	18	Harper [90]	23,273
29	8	H	Manchester C	W	2-0	0-0	14	Long [62], Kitson [88]	24,062
30	15	A	Liverpool	L	1-2	1-1	14	Matejovsky [5]	43,524
31	22	H	Birmingham C	W	2-1	1-0	15	Bikey 2 [31, 79]	24,085
32	29	H	Blackburn R	D	0-0	0-0	15		24,374
33	Apr 5	A	Newcastle U	L	0-3	0-2	16		52,179
34	12	H	Fulham	L	0-2	0-1	16		24,112
35	19	A	Arsenal	L	0-2	0-2	17		60,109
36	26	A	Wigan Ath	D	0-0	0-0	17		19,043
37	May 3	H	Tottenham H	L	0-1	0-1	18		24,125
38	11	A	Derby Co	W	4-0	1-0	18	Harper [15], Kitson [61], Doyle [69], Lita [90]	33,087

Final League Position: 18

GOALSCORERS

League (41): Kitson 10, Doyle 6, Harper 6, Hunt 5 (2 pens), Bikey 3, Long 3, Ingimarsson 2, Shorey 2, Cisse 1, Lita 1, Matejovsky 1, own goal 1.
Carling Cup (3): Convey 1, Halls 1, Lita 1.
FA Cup (2): Hunt 2.

Hahnemann M 38	De la Cruz U 3 + 3	Shorey N 36	Ingimarsson I 33 + 1	Duberry M 12 + 1	Harper J 38	Murty G 28	Gunnarsson B 18 + 2	Hunt S 37	Doyle K 34 + 2	Seol K 2 + 1	Kitson D 28 + 6	Bikey A 14 + 8	Oster J 12 + 6	Cisse K 11 + 11	Long S 7 + 22	Convey B 12 + 8	Halls J — + 1	Golbourne S 1	Fae E 3 + 5	Lita L 10 + 4	Rosenior L 15 + 2	Sonko I 15 + 1	Matejovsky M 10 + 4	Kebe J 1 + 4	Little G — + 2	*Match No.*
1	2	3	4	5	6	7	8	9^{2}	10^{1}	11^{3}	12■	13	14													1
1		3	4	5^{3}	6	2	12	11	10	13		14	7^{2}	8■	9^{1}											2
1	12	3	4		6	2^{1}	8	11^{3}	10	7^{2}		5	13		9	14										3
1	2^{2}		4		6		8	11	10			5			9	12	13	3^{1}	7^{3}	14						4
1		3	4	5	6	2	8^{3}	11	10		12			14		13			7^{1}	9^{2}						5
1		3	4		6	2	8^{3}	11			10	5			12	13			14	9^{1}	7^{2}					6
1		3	4	5	6	2	8	11	10^{1}		9	12				13					7^{2}					7
1		3	4	5	6	2^{1}	8^{2}	11	10		9				12				13		7					8
1		3	4	5	6	2	8	11	10		9		12								7^{1}					9
1		3		5	6	2	12	10	13		9	8^{3}							7^{2}	14	11^{1}	4				10
1		3		5	6	2^{2}	8	11	10		9				12					7^{1}	13	4				11
1		3		5	6	2^{1}	8	11	10		9				12	13				7^{2}		4				12
1		3	4		6^{3}	2	8	11	10^{2}		9		12		13	7^{1}			14			5				13
1		3	4		6	2	8	11	10^{1}		9				12	7						5				14
1		3	4		6	2	8^{1}	11	10		9	13			12	7^{2}						5				15
1		3	4		6	2^{3}	8	11	10		9	13		14		7^{1}				12		5^{2}				16
1		3	4		6	2	8^{2}	11	10		9			13	12	7^{1}						5				17
1		3	4		6	2	8	11	10		9				12	7^{1}						5				18
1		3	4		6	2	8■	11	10^{1}		9^{2}	12		14	13	7^{3}						5				19
1	12	3	4		6	2^{1}		11	10		9			8	13	7^{2}						5				20
1	12	3^{1}	4		6	2		11	10^{3}		9	13		8	14	7^{2}						5■				21
1	7^{1}	3	4		6	2	5	11	10^{2}		9^{3}			8	13	12				14						22
1		3	4		6	2		11	10		9			5	12	7^{2}				8^{1}			13			23
1		3	4		6	2		8	10				7^{2}	5		11^{1}				9	12		13			24
1		3	4		6^{3}	2		11	10		9^{2}		13	5	12					8^{1}		14	7			25
1		3			6	2		11	10		9^{1}		7^{2}	5	12							4	8	13		26
1		3	12		6	2		11	10^{2}		9		7^{3}	4^{1}	13							5	8	14		27
1		3	4		6			11	10^{2}		12	5	7^{1}	13	9						2		8^{3}	14		28
1		3	4		6			11	10		12	5	7	13	9^{1}						2		8^{2}			29
1		3	4		6			11	10		12	5	7^{3}	13	9^{1}						2		8^{2}	14		30
1		3	4		6			11	10		9	5	7^{1}	13	12						2		8^{2}			31
1		3	4		6			11	10		9^{2}	5	7^{1}	13	12						2		8■			32
1		3	4		6			11	10		9^{1}	5	7^{2}	8^{3}	12	13			14		2					33
1		3	4		6			11	10		12	5	7^{3}	13	9^{1}						2		8^{2}		14	34
1			4	12	6^{2}	2					9	3		8		10			13		7	5^{1}	14	11^{3}		35
1		3	4	5	6			11	10^{2}		9	7			12					8^{1}	2				13	36
1		3	4	5	6			11	10^{1}		9	7^{3}	13		12					8	2^{2}		14			37
1		3	4	5	6^{2}	2		11	12		9^{1}	13	7	14						10			8^{3}			38

FA Cup

Third Round	Tottenham H	(a)	2-2
		(h)	0-1

Carling Cup

Second Round	Swansea C	(a)	1-0
Third Round	Liverpool	(h)	2-4

ROCHDALE FL Championship 2

FOUNDATION

Considering the love of rugby in their area, it is not surprising that Rochdale had difficulty in establishing an Association Football club. The earlier Rochdale Town club formed in 1900 went out of existence in 1907 when the present club was immediately established and joined the Manchester League, before graduating to the Lancashire Combination in 1908.

Spotland Stadium, Sandy Lane, Rochdale OL11 5DS.

Telephone: (01706) 644 648.

Fax: (01706) 648 466.

Ticket Office: (01706) 648 466.

Website: www.rochdaleafc.co.uk

Email: office@rochdaleafc.co.uk

Ground Capacity: 10,208.

Record Attendance: 24,231 v Notts Co, FA Cup 2nd rd, 10 December 1949.

Pitch Measurements: 114yd × 76yd.

Chairman: Chris Dunphy.

Vice-chairman: Graham Morris.

Chief Executive/Secretary: Colin Garlick.

Manager: Keith Hill.

Assistant Manager: David Flitcroft.

Physio: Andy Thorpe.

Colours: Black and blue striped shirts, white shorts, blue stockings.

Change Colours: White shirts, blue shorts, white stockings.

Year Formed: 1907.

Turned Professional: 1907.

Ltd Co.: 1910.

Club Nickname: 'The Dale'.

Ground: 1907, St Clements Playing Fields (original name Spotland).

First Football League Game: 27 August 1921, Division 3 (N), v Accrington Stanley (h) W 6–3 – Crabtree; Nuttall, Sheehan; Hill, Farrer, Yarwood; Hoad, Sandiford, Dennison (2), Owens (3), Carney (1).

Record League Victory: 8–1 v Chesterfield, Division 3 (N), 18 December 1926 – Hill; Brown, Ward; Hillhouse, Parkes, Braidwood; Hughes, Bertram, Whitehurst (5), Schofield (2), Martin (1).

HONOURS

Football League: Division 3 best season: 9th, 1969–70; Division 3 (N) – Runners-up 1923–24, 1926–27.

FA Cup: best season: 5th rd, 1990, 2003.

Football League Cup: Runners-up 1962 (record for 4th Division club).

SKY SPORTS FACT FILE

For a variety of reasons, Rochdale were forced to field five different goalkeepers in a run of six games over 19 days from January 1928. They were Harry Moody (injured), Eddie Plane (two games), Napper Heywood, William Wood and Jackie Mittell.

Record Cup Victory: 8–2 v Crook T, FA Cup 1st rd, 26 November 1927 – Moody; Hopkins, Ward; Braidwood, Parkes, Barker; Tompkinson, Clennell (3) Whitehurst (4), Hall, Martin (1).

Record Defeat: 1–9 v Tranmere R, Division 3 (N), 25 December 1931.

Most League Points (2 for a win): 62, Division 3 (N), 1923–24.

Most League Points (3 for a win): 78, Division 3, 2001–02.

Most League Goals: 105, Division 3 (N), 1926–27.

Highest League Scorer in Season: Albert Whitehurst, 44, Division 3 (N), 1926–27.

Most League Goals in Total Aggregate: Reg Jenkins, 119, 1964–73.

Most League Goals in One Match: 6, Tommy Tippett v Hartlepools U, Division 3N, 21 April 1930.

Most Capped Player: Leo Bertos, 6 (7), New Zealand.

Most League Appearances: Graham Smith, 317, 1966–74.

Youngest League Player: Zac Hughes, 16 years 105 days v Exeter C, 19 September 1987.

Record Transfer Fee Received: £400,000 from West Ham U for Stephen Bywater, August 1998.

Record Transfer Fee Paid: £150,000 to Stoke C for Paul Connor, March 2001.

Football League Record: 1921 Elected to Division 3 (N); 1958–59 Division 3; 1959–69 Division 4; 1969–74 Division 3; 1974–92 Division 4; 1992–2004 Division 3; 2004– FL 2.

MANAGERS

Billy Bradshaw 1920
Run by committee 1920–22
Tom Wilson 1922–23
Jack Peart 1923–30
Will Cameron 1930–31
Herbert Hopkinson 1932–34
Billy Smith 1934–35
Ernest Nixon 1935–37
Sam Jennings 1937–38
Ted Goodier 1938–52
Jack Warner 1952–53
Harry Catterick 1953–58
Jack Marshall 1958–60
Tony Collins 1960–68
Bob Stokoe 1967–68
Len Richley 1968–70
Dick Conner 1970–73
Walter Joyce 1973–76
Brian Green 1976–77
Mike Ferguson 1977–78
Doug Collins 1979
Bob Stokoe 1979–80
Peter Madden 1980–83
Jimmy Greenhoff 1983–84
Vic Halom 1984–86
Eddie Gray 1986–88
Danny Bergara 1988–89
Terry Dolan 1989–91
Dave Sutton 1991–94
Mick Docherty 1995–96
Graham Barrow 1996–99
Steve Parkin 1999–2001
John Hollins 2001–02
Paul Simpson 2002–03
Alan Buckley 2003–04
Steve Parkin 2004–06
Keith Hill January 2007–

LATEST SEQUENCES

Longest Sequence of League Wins: 8, 29.9.1969 – 3.11.1969.

Longest Sequence of League Defeats: 17, 14.11.1931 – 12.3.1932.

Longest Sequence of League Draws: 6, 17.8.1968 – 14.9.1968.

Longest Sequence of Unbeaten League Matches: 20, 15.9.1923 – 19.1.1924.

Longest Sequence Without a League Win: 28, 14.11.1931 – 29.8.1932.

Successive Scoring Runs: 29 from 8.1.1927.

Successive Non-scoring Runs: 9 from 14.3.1980.

TEN YEAR LEAGUE RECORD

		P	*W*	*D*	*L*	*F*	*A*	*Pts*	*Pos*
1998-99	Div 3	46	13	15	18	42	55	54	19
1999-2000	Div 3	46	18	14	14	57	54	68	10
2000-01	Div 3	46	18	17	11	59	48	71	8
2001-02	Div 3	46	21	15	10	65	52	78	5
2002-03	Div 3	46	12	16	18	63	70	52	19
2003-04	Div 3	46	12	14	20	49	58	50	21
2004-05	FL 2	46	16	18	12	54	48	66	9
2005-06	FL 2	46	14	14	18	66	69	56	14
2006-07	FL 2	46	18	12	16	70	50	66	9
2007-08	FL 2	46	23	11	12	77	54	80	5

DID YOU KNOW

In 2007–08 Rochdale eight times scored four goals. In three of these there were different hat-trick scorers: David Perkins, Adam Le Fondre and Chris Dagnall. Then in a 3–1 win over Grimsby Town on 5 April 2008, Rene Howe scored all three goals!

ROCHDALE 2007–08 LEAGUE RECORD

Match No.	Date	Venue	Opponents	Result		H/T Score	Lg. Pos.	Goalscorers	Atten-dance
1	Aug 11	A	Peterborough U	L	0-3	0-2	—		5575
2	18	H	Chester C	L	1-2	1-0	24	Ramsden ^{21}	3243
3	25	A	Hereford U	D	1-1	1-1	23	Dagnall (pen) ^{22}	2732
4	Sept 1	H	Milton Keynes D	W	3-2	1-2	20	Dagnall 2 $^{27, 90}$, Le Fondre ^{89}	2743
5	15	A	Barnet	D	0-0	0-0	19		2040
6	22	H	Macclesfield T	D	1-1	1-1	19	McNulty (og) ^{17}	3066
7	29	A	Shrewsbury T	W	4-3	0-1	16	Rundle ^{46}, Murray ^{80}, Jones ^{85}, Le Fondre ^{90}	6262
8	Oct 2	A	Darlington	D	1-1	0-0	—	Prendergast ^{88}	3031
9	6	H	Bury	L	1-2	0-2	19	McArdle ^{61}	4692
10	12	A	Grimsby T	W	2-1	1-1	—	Le Fondre ^{12}, Murray ^{59}	5829
11	20	H	Brentford	D	1-1	0-0	14	Murray ^{63}	2424
12	27	A	Morecambe	D	1-1	0-1	16	McArdle ^{55}	3651
13	Nov 3	H	Dagenham & R	W	1-0	0-0	14	Foster (og) ^{59}	2278
14	6	H	Stockport Co	L	1-2	0-1	—	Le Fondre (pen) ^{69}	2915
15	24	H	Mansfield T	W	1-0	0-0	14	McEvilly ^{67}	2431
16	Dec 1	H	Wrexham	D	0-0	0-0	—		2808
17	5	A	Accrington S	W	2-1	0-1	—	Higginbotham ^{56}, Murray ^{75}	1621
18	8	A	Rotherham U	W	4-2	2-2	8	Jones ^{4}, Le Fondre ^{7}, Murray ^{48}, McEvilly ^{90}	3808
19	26	A	Wrexham	W	2-0	1-0	11	Murray ^{7}, McEvilly ^{60}	4302
20	29	A	Macclesfield T	D	2-2	0-2	11	Rundle ^{63}, Murray ^{90}	2742
21	Jan 1	H	Darlington	W	3-1	3-0	9	Thompson ^{22}, Murray ^{37}, Le Fondre (pen) ^{45}	3116
22	5	H	Lincoln C	L	0-2	0-0	11		2721
23	12	A	Wycombe W	W	1-0	0-0	10	Kennedy (pen) ^{90}	4493
24	16	A	Chesterfield	W	4-3	2-0	—	Perkins 3 $^{18, 39, 86}$, Murray ^{88}	3595
25	26	A	Milton Keynes D	W	1-0	1-0	8	Jones ^{32}	7882
26	29	A	Chester C	W	4-0	2-0	—	Le Fondre ^{29}, Butler (og) ^{44}, Kennedy ^{60}, Rundle ^{88}	2131
27	Feb 2	H	Peterborough U	L	0-2	0-0	8		3076
28	9	A	Lincoln C	L	1-2	0-1	8	Howe ^{56}	3955
29	12	H	Hereford U	L	2-4	1-3	—	Ramsden ^{7}, Howe ^{90}	2884
30	16	A	Bradford C	W	2-1	1-1	8	Clarke (og) ^{12}, Le Fondre ^{90}	14,017
31	23	H	Wycombe W	L	0-1	0-1	9		2616
32	Mar 1	H	Chesterfield	L	0-1	0-0	9		3108
33	8	A	Mansfield T	W	4-0	1-0	9	Jones 2 $^{27, 55}$, Le Fondre ^{47}, Howe ^{67}	2351
34	11	A	Stockport Co	L	0-2	0-1	—		5530
35	16	H	Accrington S	W	4-1	1-1	9	Le Fondre 3 (1 pen) $^{45 (p), 65, 83}$, Jones ^{48}	3247
36	22	A	Notts Co	L	0-1	0-1	8		4030
37	24	H	Rotherham U	W	4-1	1-1	8-	Jones ^{30}, Dagnall 3 $^{81, 86, 90}$	2985
38	29	A	Brentford	W	2-0	0-0	8	Thorpe ^{76}, Rundle ^{90}	4896
39	Apr 1	H	Bradford C	W	2-1	1-0	—	Perkins ^{1}, Le Fondre ^{87}	3811
40	5	H	Grimsby T	W	3-1	0-0	6	Howe 3 $^{47, 55, 90}$	2974
41	8	H	Notts Co	W	4-2	0-0	—	Howe ^{58}, Rundle ^{70}, Le Fondre ^{78}, Johnson (og) ^{85}	2536
42	12	A	Dagenham & R	D	1-1	1-1	6	Higginbotham ^{28}	2032
43	15	H	Barnet	W	3-0	1-0	—	Le Fondre ^{34}, Howe ^{50}, Higginbotham ^{72}	2925
44	19	H	Morecambe	W	1-0	0-0	4	Howe ^{66}	3706
45	26	A	Bury	D	1-1	0-0	4	Le Fondre (pen) ^{90}	6271
46	May 3	H	Shrewsbury T	D	1-1	0-1	5	Dagnall ^{54}	4000

Final League Position: 5

GOALSCORERS

League (77): Le Fondre 16 (4 pens), Howe 9, Murray 9, Dagnall 7 (1 pen), Jones 7, Rundle 5, Perkins 4, Higginbotham 3, McEvilly 3, Kennedy 2 (1 pen), McArdle 2, Ramsden 2, Prendergast 1, Thompson 1, Thorpe 1, own goals 5.
Carling Cup (3): Murray 1, Perkins 1, Prendergast 1.
FA Cup (1): Le Fondre 1.
J Paint Trophy (1): Prendergast 1.
Play-Offs (5): Dagnall 2, McArdle 1, Perkins 1, Rundle 1.

Spencer J 20	Ramsden S 35	Kennedy T 43	Jones G 43	Crooks L 5 + 4	McArdle R 42 + 1	Muirhead B 18 + 13	Perkins D 40	Dagnall C 7 + 7	Le Fondre A 30 + 16	Rundle A 37 + 5	D'Laryea N 2 + 4	Murray G 21 + 2	Thompson J 4 + 7	Prendergast R 2 + 12	Doolan J 19 + 6	Branston G 4	Higginbotham K 22 + 11	Lomax K 10	Holness M 13 + 6	Atkinson R — + 2	Taylor S 2 + 2	Russell S 15	Stanton N 27	McEvilly L 3 + 4	Wharton B — + 1	Howe R 19 + 1	Thorpe L 5 + 3	Buckley W 1 + 6	Basham C 5 + 8	Lee T 11	Evans R 1	Bowyer G — + 1	Match No.
1	2	3	4	5	6	7^{1}	8	9	10	11^{2}	12	13																					1
1	2	3	4	5	6	7^{1}	8	14	10	11^{2}		9^{3}	12	13																			2
1	2	3	4^{1}	12	6		8■	9^{3}	13	14		10		11^{2}	7	5																	3
1	2	3			6	7^{3}	8	9	12	11^{2}		10^{1}		13	4	5	14																4
1		3	4		6	12	8	9	10^{1}			11		13	7^{2}	5		2															5
1		3		12	6	7	8	9^{2}	13	11^{3}		10		14	4	5^{1}		2															6
1		3	4	5^{1}	6	7^{3}	8		12	10^{2}		9		13	11		14	2															7
1		5	8		6	7^{2}	3		10	11^{1}		9		12	4		13	2															8
1		5	8		6	7^{2}	3		10	11^{1}		9		12	4		13	2															9
1		5	8		6	7	3		10	11		9			4^{1}			2	12														10
1		3	4		6	7^{1}	8		10^{3}	11		9		12				2	5^{2}	13	14												11
1		3	4		6	7^{3}	8		12	11^{2}		9		13			14	2	5		10^{1}												12
1		3	4		6	7^{2}	8		12	11		9					13	2	5^{3}	14	10^{1}												13
1		3	4	12	6	13	8		10			9		11^{3}			7^{2}	2^{1}	5		14												14
	2	3	4				8		12	11^{3}		9^{1}		14	13		7		6			1	5	10^{2}									15
	2	3	4				8^{3}		10	11^{1}		12		13	14		7		5			1	6	9^{2}									16
	2	3	4		6		8■		10^{1}	11		9			12		7^{2}					1	5		13								17
	2	3	8	12	6				10^{3}	11		9			4^{1}		7		13			1	5^{2}	14									18
	2	3	4	8	6				10^{3}	11^{1}		9	13	12			7^{2}					1	5	14									19
	2		8	4^{2}	6				12	11		9	14		13		7^{3}		3			1	5	10^{1}									20
	2	3	8		6				10^{1}	11		9	7^{2}		4		13					1	5	12									21
	2	3	8		6				10^{2}	11		9^{1}	7		4		13					1	5	12									22
	2	3	7		6	12	8		10^{2}				13		4		11^{1}					1	5			9							23
	2	3	11		6	12	8		10^{1}	13		9			4^{2}		7					1	5										24
	2	3	7		6		8		10^{3}	12			13		4		11^{1}		14			1	5■			9^{2}							25
	2	3	11		6^{3}	12	8		10	13	14				4^{2}		7^{1}		5			1				9							26
	2	3	11		6	12	8		10	13					4^{1}		7^{2}					1	5				9						27
	2	3	7		6^{2}		8		10^{1}	11^{3}					4		12		13			1	5			9	14						28
	2	3	7^{3}		6^{1}		8		10	11					4^{2}		12					1	5			9		13	14				29
1	2	3	4		6	7^{2}	8		12	11									5							9	10^{1}	13					30
1	2	3	4		6	7^{3}	8		12	11^{2}					13		14		5							9		10^{1}					31
1	2		4		6	12	3		13	11							7^{1}						5			9^{2}	10^{3}	14	8				32
1	2	3	4^{3}		6	12	8		10	11							7^{1}		13				5^{2}			9			14				33
1	2	3^{3}	4		6	12	8		10	11^{2}							7^{1}						5			9		13	14				34
1	2	3	4^{2}		6	12	8		10^{3}	11			14		13								5			9			7^{1}				35
	2	3	4		6	12	8		10	11^{1}			13										5			9			7^{2}	1			36
	2	3	4		6	7^{3}	8	12	10^{1}	11													5			9^{2}	13		14	1			37
	2	3	4		6	12	8	13	10^{3}	11													5			9^{2}	14		7^{1}	1			38
	2	3	4		6	7^{2}	8	13	12	11							9^{1}						5				10			1			39
	2	3	4		6	7^{1}	8^{2}		12	11							9						5			14	10^{3}		13	1			40
	2	3^{1}	4		12		8^{3}		13	11	6		7^{2}				9		5							10			14	1			41
	2	3	4		6	7^{3}	8	12	13	11^{2}							9						5			10^{1}			14	1			42
	2^{2}	3	4		6		8^{3}	12	10^{1}	11							7		13				5			9			14	1			43
		3	4		6	12	8	13	10^{2}	11^{1}	14						7		2^{3}				5			9				1			44
	2	3	4		6		8	10^{1}	12	11^{2}	14						7^{3}						5■			9		13		1			45
	2					11		8	10^{1}		3		7		4				5^{2}									12	9	1	6	13	46

FA Cup
First Round — Southend U — (a) — 1-2

Carling Cup
First Round — Stoke C — (h) — 2-2
Second Round — Norwich C — (h) — 1-1

J Paint Trophy
Second Round — Bury — (h) — 1-3

Play-Offs
Semi-Final — Darlington — (a) — 1-2
(h) — 2-1
Final *(at Wembley)* — Stockport Co — 2-3

ROTHERHAM UNITED FL Championship 2

FOUNDATION

Rotherham were formed in 1870 before becoming Town in the late 1880s. Thornhill United were founded in 1877 and changed their name to Rotherham County in 1905. The Town amalgamated with Rotherham County to form Rotherham United in 1925.

Don Valley Stadium, Worksop Road, Sheffield, South Yorkshire S9 3TL.

Telephone: (08444) 140737.

Ticket Office: (01709) 512 760.

Website: www.themillers.co.uk

Email: office@rotherhamunited.net

Ground Capacity: 25,000.

Record Attendance: 25,170 v Sheffield U, Division 2, 13 December 1952.

Pitch Measurements. 108yd × 72yd.

Chairman: Tony Stewart.

Chief Executive: Paul Douglas.

Secretary: J. Pilmner.

Media Officer: Mark Hitchens.

Manager: Mark Robins.

Assistant Manager: John Breckin.

Physios: Denis Circuit, Ian Baily.

Colours: Red and white.

Change Colours: TBC.

Year Formed: 1870.

Turned Professional: 1905.

Ltd Co.: 1920.

Club Nickname: 'The Merry Millers'.

Previous Names: 1877, Thornhill United; 1905, Rotherham County; 1925, amalgamated with Rotherham Town under Rotherham United.

Grounds: 1870, Red House Ground; 1907, Millmoor; 2008, Don Valley Stadium.

First Football League Game: 2 September 1893, Division 2, Rotherham T v Lincoln C (a) D 1–1 – McKay; Thickett, Watson; Barr, Brown, Broadhead; Longden, Cutts, Leatherbarrow, McCormick, Pickering, (1 og). 30 August 1919, Division 2, Rotherham Co v Nottingham F (h) W 2–0 – Branston; Alton, Baines; Bailey, Coe, Stanton; Lee (1), Cawley (1), Glennon, Lees, Lamb.

Record League Victory: 8–0 v Oldham Ath, Division 3 (N), 26 May 1947 – Warnes; Selkirk, Ibbotson; Edwards, Horace Williams, Danny Williams; Wilson (2), Shaw (1), Ardron (3), Guest (1), Hainsworth (1).

Record Cup Victory: 6–0 v Spennymoor U, FA Cup 2nd rd, 17 December 1977 – McAlister; Forrest, Breckin, Womble, Stancliffe, Green, Finney, Phillips (3), Gwyther (2) (Smith), Goodfellow, Crawford (1). 6–0 v Wolverhampton W, FA Cup 1st rd, 16 November 1985 – O'Hanlon; Forrest, Dungworth, Gooding (1), Smith (1), Pickering, Birch (2), Emerson, Tynan (1), Simmons (1), Pugh. 6–0 v Kings Lynn, FA Cup 2nd rd, 6 December 1997 – Mimms; Clark, Hurst (Goodwin), Garner (1) (Hudson) (1), Warner (Bass), Richardson (1), Berry (1), Thompson, Druce (1), Glover (1), Roscoe.

HONOURS

Football League: Division 2 – runners-up 2000–01; Division 3 – Champions 1980–81; Runners-up 1999–2000; Division 3 (N) – Champions 1950–51; Runners-up 1946–47, 1947–48, 1948–49; Division 4 – Champions 1988–89; Runners-up 1991–92.

FA Cup: best season: 5th rd, 1953, 1968.

Football League Cup: Runners-up 1961.

Auto Windscreens Shield: Winners 1996.

SKY SPORTS FACT FILE

When known as Rotherham County in 1921–22 the club struggled to score goals. Only 32 came in 42 matches including 21 without scoring at all. But they still finished 16th in the table and at home conceded just seven goals.

Record Defeat: 1–11 v Bradford C, Division 3 (N), 25 August 1928.

Most League Points (2 for a win): 71, Division 3 (N), 1950–51.

Most League Points (3 for a win): 91, Division 2, 2000–01.

Most League Goals: 114, Division 3 (N), 1946–47.

Highest League Scorer in Season: Wally Ardron, 38, Division 3 (N), 1946–47.

Most League Goals in Total Aggregate: Gladstone Guest, 130, 1946–56.

Most League Goals in One Match: 4, Roland Bastow v York C, Division 3N, 9 November 1935; 4, Roland Bastow v Rochdale, Division 3N, 7 March 1936; 4, Wally Ardron v Crewe Alex, Division 3N, 5 October 1946; 4, Wally Ardron v Carlisle U, Division 3N, 13 September 1947; 4, Wally Ardron v Hartlepools U, Division 3N, 13 October 1948; 4, Ian Wilson v Liverpool, Division 2, 2 May 1955; 4, Carl Gilbert v Swansea C, Division 3, 28 September 1971; 4, Carl Airey v Chester, Division 3, 31 August 1987; 4, Shaun Goater v Hartlepool U, Division 3, 9 April 1994; 4, Lee Glover v Hull C, Division 3, 28 December 1997; 4, Darren Byfield v Millwall, Division 1, 10 August 2002.

Most Capped Player: Shaun Goater 14 (19), Bermuda.

Most League Appearances: Danny Williams, 459, 1946–62.

Youngest League Player: Kevin Eley, 16 years 72 days v Scunthorpe U, 15 May 1984.

Record Transfer Fee Received: £850,000 from Cardiff C for Alan Lee, August 2003.

Record Transfer Fee Paid: £150,000 to Millwall for Tony Towner, August 1980; £150,000 to Port Vale for Lee Glover, August 1996; £150,000 to Burnley for Alan Lee, September 2000; £150,000 to Reading for Martin Butler, September 2003.

Football League Record: 1893 Rotherham Town elected to Division 2; 1896 Failed re-election; 1919 Rotherham County elected to Division 2; 1923–51 Division 3 (N); 1951–68 Division 2; 1968–73 Division 3; 1973–75 Division 4; 1975–81 Division 3; 1981–83 Division 2; 1983–88 Division 3; 1988–89 Division 4; 1989–91 Division 3; 1991–92 Division 4; 1992–97 Division 2; 1997–2000 Division 3; 2000–01 Division 2; 2001–04 Division 1; 2004–05 FL C; 2005–07 FL 1; 2007– FL 2.

MANAGERS

Billy Heald 1925–29 *(Secretary only for long spell)*
Stanley Davies 1929–30
Billy Heald 1930–33
Reg Freeman 1934–52
Andy Smailes 1952–58
Tom Johnston 1958–62
Danny Williams 1962–65
Jack Mansell 1965–67
Tommy Docherty 1967–68
Jimmy McAnearney 1968–73
Jimmy McGuigan 1973–79
Ian Porterfield 1979–81
Emlyn Hughes 1981–83
George Kerr 1983–85
Norman Hunter 1985–87
Dave Cusack 1987–88
Billy McEwan 1988–91
Phil Henson 1991–94
Archie Gemmill/John McGovern 1994–96
Danny Bergara 1996–97
Ronnie Moore 1997–2005
Mick Harford 2005
Alan Knill 2005–07
Mark Robins April 2007–

LATEST SEQUENCES

Longest Sequence of League Wins: 9, 2.2.1982 – 6.3.1982.

Longest Sequence of League Defeats: 8, 7.4.1956 – 18.8.1956.

Longest Sequence of League Draws: 6, 13.10.1969 – 22.11.1969.

Longest Sequence of Unbeaten League Matches: 18, 13.10.1969 – 7.2.1970.

Longest Sequence Without a League Win: 21, 9.5.2004 – 20.11.2004.

Successive Scoring Runs: 30 from 3.4.1954.

Successive Non-scoring Runs: 6 from 21.8.2004.

TEN YEAR LEAGUE RECORD

		P	*W*	*D*	*L*	*F*	*A*	*Pts*	*Pos*
1998-99	Div 3	46	20	13	13	79	61	73	5
1999-2000	Div 3	46	24	12	10	72	36	84	2
2000-01	Div 2	46	27	10	9	79	55	91	2
2001-02	Div 1	46	10	19	17	52	66	49	21
2002-03	Div 1	46	15	14	17	62	62	59	15
2003-04	Div 1	46	13	15	18	53	61	54	17
2004-05	FL C	46	5	14	27	35	69	29	24
2005-06	FL 1	46	12	16	18	52	62	52	20
2006-07	FL 1	46	13	9	24	58	75	38	23
2007-08	FL 2	46	21	11	14	62	58	64*	9

**10 pts deducted.*

DID YOU KNOW ?

In 11 spasmodic League appearances over three seasons local boy Redvers Boulton did not score for Rotherham United, but on 28 November 1925 he hit two in the FA Cup win over Halifax Town. It was the club's first game under their new name, too.

ROTHERHAM UNITED 2007–08 LEAGUE RECORD

Match No.	Date	Venue	Opponents	Result	H/T Score	Lg. Pos.	Goalscorers	Attendance
1	Aug 11	A	Hereford U	D 0-0	0-0	—		3566
2	19	H	Peterborough U	W 3-1	3-0	3	Holmes D 2 [8, 35], O'Grady [33]	4291
3	25	A	Stockport Co	D 2-2	0-1	5	Sharps [55], McNeil (og) [72]	5764
4	Sept 1	H	Chester C	D 1-1	0-0	8	O'Grady [57]	4036
5	8	H	Darlington	L 0-2	0-1	13		3988
6	15	A	Wrexham	W 1-0	0-0	10	O'Grady [78]	3711
7	22	H	Notts Co	D 1-1	1-1	10	Holmes P [7]	4181
8	29	A	Barnet	L 0-2	0-0	13		2008
9	Oct 2	A	Macclesfield T	D 1-1	1-0	—	Holmes D [13]	1715
10	6	H	Mansfield T	W 3-2	2-0	10	Bean [4], Newsham [20], Brogan [67]	3881
11	12	A	Brentford	D 1-1	0-0	—	Coughlan [62]	3841
12	20	H	Morecambe	W 3-1	0-0	9	Brogan (pen) [71], Yates 2 [81, 87]	4181
13	27	A	Dagenham & R	W 2-0	1-0	8	Harrison 2 [45, 52]	2091
14	Nov 3	H	Grimsby T	W 2-1	1-0	7	Hudson [39], O'Grady [77]	4162
15	6	H	Bury	W 2-1	1-1	—	Newsham [22], O'Grady [55]	3425
16	17	A	Accrington S	W 1-0	0-0	4	Hudson [52]	1918
17	24	H	Shrewsbury T	W 2-0	1-0	3	Taylor [38], Holmes D [81]	3832
18	Dec 5	A	Chesterfield	W 2-0	1-0	—	Holmes D [8], Hudson [55]	5417
19	8	H	Rochdale	L 2-4	2-2	5	Sharps [14], Holmes D [16]	3808
20	22	H	Wrexham	W 3-0	1-0	5	Holmes D 2 [40, 72], Newsham [82]	3773
21	26	A	Darlington	D 1-1	1-0	5	O'Grady [36]	6965
22	29	A	Notts Co	W 1-0	1-0	3	Joseph [34]	5290
23	Jan 1	H	Macclesfield T	W 3-0	0-0	3	Hudson [70], Taylor 2 [80, 87]	4464
24	5	H	Milton Keynes D	L 0-1	0-0	3		5421
25	12	A	Lincoln C	W 3-1	1-0	3	Holmes D 3 [24, 57, 84]	5016
26	19	H	Wycombe W	D 1-1	1-0	2	Brogan [14]	6709
27	26	A	Chester C	W 1-0	1-0	2	O'Grady [7]	2536
28	29	A	Peterborough U	L 1-3	0-1	—	Taylor [89]	5152
29	Feb 2	H	Hereford U	L 0-1	0-1	3		4748
30	9	A	Milton Keynes D	D 1-1	0-1	4	Harrison [82]	9455
31	12	H	Stockport Co	L 1-4	1-1	—	Hudson [37]	4004
32	16	A	Wycombe W	L 0-1	0-0	5		4610
33	23	H	Lincoln C	W 3-2	1-1	5	Joseph [35], Hudson [65], Newsham [74]	4321
34	26	A	Bradford C	L 2-3	1-3	—	Taylor [29], O'Grady [84]	13,436
35	Mar 1	H	Accrington S	L 0-1	0-0	5		3683
36	8	A	Shrewsbury T	D 1-1	1-1	7	Mills [37]	5265
37	11	A	Bury	L 0-3	0-1	—		1957
38	15	H	Chesterfield	W 2-1	2-0	7	Holmes P [30], Joseph [45]	4550
39	22	H	Bradford C	D 1-1	0-0	11	O'Grady [65]	4157
40	24	A	Rochdale	L 1-4	1-1	12	Joseph [7]	2985
41	29	A	Morecambe	L 1-5	1-4	13	Hudson [35]	2171
42	Apr 5	H	Brentford	L 1-2	0-1	13	Hudson [87]	2979
43	12	A	Grimsby T	W 1-0	1-0	12	Taylor [40]	3583
44	19	H	Dagenham & R	W 2-1	2-0	12	Hudson (pen) [8], Harrison D [41]	3203
45	26	A	Mansfield T	W 1-0	0-0	10	Yates [71]	5271
46	May 3	H	Barnet	W 1-0	1-0	9	Green [8]	4834

Final League Position: 9

GOALSCORERS

League (62): Holmes D 11, Hudson 9 (1 pen), O'Grady 9, Taylor 6, Harrison D 4, Joseph 4, Newsham 4, Brogan 3 (1 pen), Yates 3, Holmes P 2, Sharps 2, Bean 1, Coughlan 1, Green 1, Mills 1, own goal 1.
Carling Cup (1): Harrison D 1.
FA Cup (2): Brogan 1 (pen), O'Grady 1.
J Paint Trophy (2): O'Grady 1, Sharps 1.

Warrington A 46	Tonge D 31 + 6	Hurst P 8 + 3	Harrison D 44	Sharps I 33	Coughlan G 45	Brogan S 28 + 1	Holmes P 19 + 5	Holmes D 33 + 4	O'Grady C 35 + 3	Todd A 11 + 2	Bean M 11 + 1	Newsham M 11 + 14	Joseph M 34 + 2	Taylor R 22 + 13	Duncum S — + 2	Dyer B 3	Yates J 3 + 17	Cresswell R 1 + 2	King L — + 1	Cahill T 5 + 2	Hudson M 30 + 1	Mills P 32 + 1	Ross I 9 + 8	Pettigrew A 3 + 1	Green J 6 + 3	Widdowson J 3	Haggarty D — + 1	Match No.
1	2	3	4	5	6	7^1	8	9^2	10	11	12	13																1
1	2		4	5	6		8	9	10	11	7		3															2
1	2			5	6	7	8	9	10	11	4		3															3
1	2		7	5	6	12	8^3	9	10	11^2	4	13	3^1	14														4
1	2	3	8		6	7		9^1	10^2	11^3	4	13	5	12	14													5
1	2		4		6	7	8	9^1	12	11	5	13	3			10^3												6
1	2		4		6	3	8	9	12	7^2	11		5			10^1	13											7
1	2			5	6	3	8^3		10	11^2	4	12				9^1	14	7	13									8
1	2	3	4	5	6	11^1		9	10	7	8				12													9
1	2	3	4	5	6	11		9^2		7	8^1	10						12		13								10
1	2	3^1	4	5	6	11	12	9^2	13	7^3	8	10					14											11
1	2	3^3	4	5	6	7	8^2		9^1		11	10					12	13			14							12
1	2	12	4	5	6	3			9^2	13		11		10							8	7^1						13
1	2		4	5	6	3			9			10^2	13	11^1			12				8	7						14
1	2	13	4	5	6	3			10			11		9^2			12				8^1	7						15
1	2^1	3	4	5	6	11			9			10^2	12	13							8	7						16
1		12	4	5	6	3^1		8	9				2	10							11	7						17
1	12		4	5	6	3	13	8^1	10				2	9^2							11	7						18
1	12		4	5	6	3	8	9^3	10	13		14	2^1								11	7^2						19
1	12		4^1	5	6	3		9^3	10			13	2	7^2			14					8	11					20
1	12		4	5	6	3		9^2	10			11	2^1	13								7	8					21
1			4	5	6	11		9^1	10				2	12							8	3	7					22
1			4	5	6	3		9				11^1	2	12							8	10	7					23
1			4	5	6	3		9^2	10				2	12			13				8	11	7^1					24
1			4	5	6	3		9	10				2	11^1							8	7	12					25
1			4	5	6	3		9	10				2	11							8	7						26
1	2		4	5		3		9^1	10				6	11^2			12				8	7	13					27
1			4	5	6	3		9^1	10				2	11			12				8	7^2	13					28
1	2		4	5	6	3		12	10			9^2		11^1			13				8	7^3	14					29
1	2^3		4	5	6	3^1	12	9^2	10				11	13			14					7		8				30
1	2	3	4	5	6		8	9^1	10					12							11	7						31
1	2		4		6			9^1	10				3	11			12				8	7^2	13	5^3	14			32
1	12		4	5	6			9^3	10			14	2	11							8^2	13	7	3^1				33
1	3		4	5	6				10			9^1	2	11			12				8		7					34
1			4	5	6			9^1	10			12	2	11								8^2	7		13	3		35
1			4	5	6		12	9^1	10				2	11							8	7				3		36
1	12		4	5^1	6		11	13	10				2	9^2							8	7^3	14			3		37
1	2		4		6		8	9^2	10				3	12			11^1				7	5	13					38
1	2^2		4		6		8	9^1	10			12	3	13			11^3				7	5			14			39
1	2		4		6		8^3	9^1	10			12	3	13			7^2				11	5	14					40
1	2		4		6		8	9^1				12	3	10^2						13	11	5		14	7^3			41
1	2		4		6		12	9				13	5	14						10^2	8	3	11^1		7^3			42
1	3		4		6		8					12	2	10						9^1	11	5			7			43
1	3		4		6		8						2	9			12			10^1	7	5			11			44
1	3		4		6		9	12					2	11^1			13			10^2	8	5			7			45
1	2		4		6^3		9	12					3	11^2			13			10^1	8	5			7		14	46

FA Cup
First Round — Forest Green R — (a) 2-2
(h) 0-3

Carling Cup
First Round — Sheffield W — (h) 1-3

J Paint Trophy
First Round — Mansfield T — (a) 1-0
Second Round — Grimsby T — (h) 1-1

SCUNTHORPE UNITED FL Championship 1

FOUNDATION

The year of foundation for Scunthorpe United has often been quoted as 1910, but the club can trace its history back to 1899 when Brumby Hall FC, who played on the Old Showground, consolidated their position by amalgamating with some other clubs and changing their name to Scunthorpe United. The year 1910 was when that club amalgamated with North Lindsey United as Scunthorpe and Lindsey United. The link is Mr W. T. Lockwood whose chairmanship covers both years.

Glanford Park, Doncaster Road, Scunthorpe DN15 8TD.

Telephone: (0871) 2211 899.

Fax: (01724) 857 986.

Ticket Office: (0871) 2211 899.

Website: www.scunthorpe-united.co.uk

Email: admin@scunthorpe-united.co.uk

Ground Capacity: 9,203.

Record Attendance: Old Showground: 23,935 v Portsmouth, FA Cup 4th rd, 30 January 1954. Glanford Park: 8,906 v Nottingham F, FL 1, 10 March 2007.

Pitch Measurements: 112yd × 72yd.

Chairman: J. S. Wharton.

Vice-chairman: R. Garton.

Chief Executive/Secretary: Jamie Hammond.

Manager: Nigel Adkins.

Assistant Managers: Ian Baraclough, Andy Crosby.

Physio: Alex Dalton.

Colours: Claret and blue.

Change Colours: White and blue.

Year Formed: 1899.

Turned Professional: 1912.

Ltd Co.: 1912.

Club Nickname: 'The Iron'.

Previous Names: Amalgamated first with Brumby Hall then North Lindsey United to become Scunthorpe & Lindsey United, 1910; dropped '& Lindsey' in 1958.

Grounds: 1899, Old Showground; 1988, Glanford Park.

First Football League Game: 19 August 1950, Division 3 (N), v Shrewsbury T (h) D 0–0 – Thompson; Barker, Brownsword; Allen, Taylor, McCormick; Mosby, Payne, Gorin, Rees, Boyes.

HONOURS

Football League: FL 1 – Champions 2006–07; FL 2 – Runners-up 2004–05; Division 3 (N) – Champions 1957–58. Promoted from Division 3 1998–99 (play-offs).

FA Cup: best season: 5th rd, 1958, 1970.

Football League Cup: never past 3rd rd.

SKY SPORTS FACT FILE

The much-travelled inside-forward Syd Ottewell played for Scunthorpe United in their last 14 matches of the 1951–52 season, scoring eight goals. In fact these were the only games in which the club registered any League goals at all in that period.

Record League Victory: 8–1 v Luton T, Division 3, 24 April 1965 – Sidebottom; Horstead, Hemstead; Smith, Neale, Lindsey; Bramley (1), Scott, Thomas (5), Mahy (1), Wilson (1). 8–1 v Torquay U (a), Division 3, 28 October 1995 – Samways; Housham, Wilson, Ford (1), Knill (1), Hope (Nicholson), Thornber, Bullimore (Walsh), McFarlane (4) (Young), Eyre (2), Paterson.

Record Cup Victory: 9–0 v Boston U, FA Cup 1st rd, 21 November 1953 – Malan; Hubbard, Brownsword; Sharpe, White, Bushby; Mosby (1), Haigh (3), Whitfield (2), Gregory (1), Mervyn Jones (2).

Record Defeat: 0–8 v Carlisle U, Division 3 (N), 25 December 1952.

Most League Points (2 for a win): 66, Division 3 (N), 1956–57, 1957–58.

Most League Points (3 for a win): 91, FL 1, 2006–07.

Most League Goals: 88, Division 3 (N), 1957–58.

Highest League Scorer in Season: Barrie Thomas, 31, Division 2, 1961–62.

Most League Goals in Total Aggregate: Steve Cammack, 110, 1979–81, 1981–86.

Most League Goals in One Match: 5, Barrie Thomas v Luton T, Division 3, 24 April 1965.

Most Capped Player: Dave Mulligan 1(12), New Zealand.

Most League Appearances: Jack Brownsword, 595, 1950–65.

Youngest League Player: Mike Farrell, 16 years 240 days v Workington, 8 November 1975.

Record Transfer Fee Received: £2,000,000 from Sheffield U for Billy Sharp, July 2007.

Record Transfer Fee Paid: £425,000 to Stoke C for Martin Paterson, July 2007.

Football League Record: 1950 Elected to Division 3 (N); 1958–64 Division 2; 1964–68 Division 3; 1968–72 Division 4; 1972–73 Division 3; 1973–83 Division 4; 1983–84 Division 3; 1984–92 Division 4; 1992–99 Division 3; 1999–2000 Division 2; 2000–04 Division 3; 2004–05 FL 2; 2005–07 FL 1; 2007–08 FL C; 2008– FL 1.

MANAGERS

Harry Allcock 1915–53
(Secretary-Manager)
Tom Crilly 1936–37
Bernard Harper 1946–48
Leslie Jones 1950–51
Bill Corkhill 1952–56
Ron Suart 1956–58
Tony McShane 1959
Bill Lambton 1959
Frank Soo 1959–60
Dick Duckworth 1960–64
Fred Goodwin 1964–66
Ron Ashman 1967–73
Ron Bradley 1973–74
Dick Rooks 1974–76
Ron Ashman 1976–81
John Duncan 1981–83
Allan Clarke 1983–84
Frank Barlow 1984–87
Mick Buxton 1987–91
Bill Green 1991–93
Richard Money 1993–94
David Moore 1994–96
Mick Buxton 1996–97
Brian Laws 1997–2004; 2004–06
Nigel Adkins December 2006–

LATEST SEQUENCES

Longest Sequence of League Wins: 7, 27.1.2007 – 3.3.2007.

Longest Sequence of League Defeats: 8, 29.11.1997 – 20.1.1998.

Longest Sequence of League Draws: 6, 2.1.1984 – 25.2.1984.

Longest Sequence of Unbeaten League Matches: 19, 22.12.2006 – 6.4.2007.

Longest Sequence Without a League Win: 14, 22.3.1975 – 6.9.1975.

Successive Scoring Runs: 24 from 13.1.2007.

Successive Non-scoring Runs: 7 from 19.4.1975.

TEN YEAR LEAGUE RECORD

		P	W	D	L	F	A	Pts	Pos
1998-99	Div 3	46	22	8	16	69	58	74	4
1999-2000	Div 2	46	9	12	25	40	74	39	23
2000-01	Div 3	46	18	11	17	62	52	65	10
2001-02	Div 3	46	19	14	13	74	56	71	8
2002-03	Div 3	46	19	15	12	68	49	72	5
2003-04	Div 3	46	11	16	19	69	72	49	22
2004-05	FL 2	46	22	14	10	69	42	80	2
2005-06	FL 1	46	15	15	16	68	73	60	12
2006-07	FL 1	46	26	13	7	73	35	91	1
2007-08	FL C	46	11	13	22	46	69	46	23

DID YOU KNOW ?

In 1954–55 Scunthorpe United called upon the services of 20 players. However, two were ever present, two more missed just one game, another two were absent twice, one made 43 appearances and goalkeeper Norman Malan turned out in 40 League games.

SCUNTHORPE UNITED 2007–08 LEAGUE RECORD

Match No.	Date	Venue	Opponents	Result	H/T Score	Lg. Pos.	Goalscorers	Attendance
1	Aug 11	A	Charlton Ath	D 1-1	0-0	—	Iriekpen 69	23,151
2	18	H	Burnley	W 2-0	0-0	6	Paterson 47, Goodwin 64	6975
3	25	A	Bristol C	L 1-2	1-2	10	Paterson 44	12,474
4	Sept 1	H	Sheffield U	W 3-2	1-0	4	Crosby 37, Paterson 61, Sparrow 90	8801
5	15	A	Barnsley	L 0-2	0-1	11		11,230
6	18	H	Preston NE	W 2-1	1-1	—	Crosby 24, Hayes 49	5754
7	22	H	WBA	L 2-3	1-0	12	Crosby (pen) 16, Paterson 90	8307
8	29	A	Colchester U	W 1-0	1-0	6	Hayes 41	5218
9	Oct 2	A	Norwich C	D 0-0	0-0	—		23,176
10	6	H	Watford	L 1-3	1-1	11	Forte 20	7515
11	20	H	Leicester C	D 0-0	0-0	12		6006
12	23	A	Sheffield W	W 2-1	2-1	—	Paterson 2 24, 40	21,557
13	27	A	Cardiff C	D 1-1	0-1	9	Goodwin 55	11,850
14	Nov 3	H	Crystal Palace	D 0-0	0-0	10		6778
15	6	H	Stoke C	L 2-3	1-1	—	Hayes 31, Goodwin 85	5521
16	10	A	Blackpool	L 0-1	0-0	14		8051
17	24	H	Hull C	L 1-2	1-2	17	Forte 45	8633
18	27	A	Coventry C	D 1-1	0-0	—	Cork 68	14,036
19	Dec 1	A	Plymouth Arg	L 0-3	0-0	18		10,520
20	3	H	Blackpool	D 1-1	1-0	—	Butler 19	4407
21	8	H	QPR	D 2-2	1-2	19	Paterson 24, Forte 55	5612
22	15	A	Ipswich T	L 2-3	2-2	19	Paterson 2 16, 33	19,306
23	22	H	Norwich C	L 0-1	0-0	23		6648
24	26	A	Preston NE	W 1-0	1-0	19	Paterson 43	12,920
25	29	A	WBA	L 0-5	0-2	21		25,238
26	Jan 1	H	Barnsley	D 2-2	1-0	22	Morris 45, Youga 47	6897
27	12	A	Southampton	L 0-1	0-1	23		18,146
28	19	H	Wolverhampton W	L 0-2	0-1	23		7465
29	26	A	Burnley	L 0-2	0-2	—		14,516
30	Feb 2	H	Charlton Ath	W 1-0	0-0	23	Paterson 63	6084
31	9	A	Sheffield U	D 0-0	0-0	23		25,668
32	12	H	Bristol C	L 0-1	0-0	—		5423
33	15	A	Stoke C	L 2-3	2-0	—	Paterson 7, Hobbs 23	20,979
34	23	H	Southampton	D 1-1	1-0	24	Crosby 41	6035
35	Mar 1	H	Coventry C	W 2-1	1-1	23	Paterson 15, Cork 66	5866
36	8	A	Hull C	L 0-2	0-2	23		20,906
37	11	H	Plymouth Arg	W 1-0	0-0	—	Morris 55	4920
38	15	A	QPR	L 1-3	1-1	23	McCann 8	14,499
39	18	A	Wolverhampton W	L 1-2	1-0	—	Butler 5	21,628
40	22	H	Ipswich T	L 1-2	0-1	23	May 90	6636
41	29	A	Leicester C	L 0-1	0-1	23		22,165
42	Apr 5	H	Sheffield W	D 1-1	1-0	23	Morris 18	7425
43	12	A	Crystal Palace	L 0-2	0-2	23		15,975
44	19	H	Cardiff C	W 3-2	0-1	23	Hayes 2 (1 pen) 53, 90 (p), Hurst 56	4727
45	26	A	Watford	W 1-0	0-0	23	Hayes 69	16,454
46	May 4	H	Colchester U	D 3-3	1-1	23	Forte 15, Hayes 2 67, 82	5554

Final League Position: 23

GOALSCORERS

League (46): Paterson 13, Hayes 8 (1 pen), Crosby 4 (1 pen), Forte 4, Goodwin 3, Morris 3, Butler 2, Cork 2, Hobbs 1, Hurst 1, Iriekpen 1, May 1, McCann 1, Sparrow 1, Youga 1.
Carling Cup (1): Paterson 1.
FA Cup (0).

Murphy J 45	Byrne C 25	Williams M 29 + 5	Iriekpen E 12 + 5	Crosby A 38	Baraclough I 17	Taylor C 12 + 8	Goodwin J 39 + 1	Hayes P 32 + 8	Forte J 18 + 20	Hurst K 31 + 2	Sparrow M 24 + 8	Paterson M 34 + 6	Butler A 34 + 2	Cork J 32 + 2	Youga K 18 + 1	May B 6 + 15	Lillis J 1 + 2	Morris I 20 + 5	Logan S 4	Ameobi T — + 9	Winn P — + 4	Seck M — + 1	Martis S 3	McCann G 12 + 2	Hobbs J 7 + 2	Horsfield G 11 + 1	Weston C 2 + 5	Wright A — + 2	*Match No.*
1	2	3	4	5	6	7	8	9^{1}	10^{2}	11	12	13																	1
1	2	3	4^{3}	5	6	12	8	9	10^{2}	11	13	7^{1}	14																2
1	2	3		5		7^{1}	8	9^{3}	12	11^{2}	4	10	6	13	14														3
1	2■			5	6	12	8	9^{2}	13	11	7	10^{1}	4		3														4
1		3	12	5	6^{1}		8	9	13	11	7	10^{2}	4		2														5
1	2		12	5	6^{2}	13	8	9^{3}	14	11	7	10^{1}	4		3														6
1	2		12	5^{1}	6^{2}	13	8	9^{3}	14	11	7	10	4		3														7
1	5	12				7^{1}	8	9	10^{2}	11	6		4	2	3	13													8
1	2^{1}		12	5		7	8	9^{3}	10^{2}	11	6	13	4		3	14													9
1	2^{2}			5		7^{1}	8	12	10^{3}	11	6	9	4	13	3	14													10
1	2			5			8	9	7^{1}	11	6	10	4		3	12													11
1	2	12		5		7	8	9^{2}	13	11	6^{1}	10^{3}	4		3	14													12
1^{G}	2			5		7	8	9	12	11		10^{1}	4	6	3		15												13
1		13		5		7^{2}	8	9^{1}	12	11	6	10	4	2	3														14
1	2^{1}	12		5		7	8	9		11		10	4	6	3														15
1		12		5		7^{3}	8	9^{2}	13	11		10^{1}	4	6	3			14	2										16
1		6^{1}		5				9^{2}	10	11	7	12	4	2	3				8	13									17
1■		2		5		12	8^{2}	9	10	11^{G}		13	4	6	3■		15		7^{1}										18
		3		5	6^{1}	7^{3}		12	10^{2}	13	9	11	4	8			1		2	14									19
1		3		5			8	9	12	11	7	10^{1}	4	6	2■														20
1		3		5			8	9^{2}	6^{1}	11	7	10	4	2				12		13									21
1		3		5	6	12	8	9^{3}	13	11		10^{2}	4^{1}	2				7		14									22
1		3		5	6^{3}	12	8	7^{1}	9	11^{2}	13	10		2				4		14									23
1	2■	3		5	6		8	9^{1}	13	11	12	10^{2}		4				7^{3}		14									24
1		3■		5	6	11	8^{1}	12	9^{3}			10^{2}		4	2			7		13	14								25
1		3		5	6	12	8	9^{1}	13	11^{2}		10^{3}		4	2			7		14									26
1	2^{3}	3		5				9	12	11^{1}	7^{2}	10		4				8		13		14	6						27
1	2^{3}	3		5				9^{2}	12	11^{1}	7	10		4		13		8					6	14					28
1		3					12	13	14		7	10^{3}	5	4		9^{2}		8^{1}					6	11	2				29
1	2	3		5			8	9^{3}		11^{1}		12	6■	4				13						7	14	10^{2}			30
1	2^{1}	3		5			8	9	10^{2}		12			4		13		11						7■	6				31
1	2^{1}	3		5			8	7^{2}	14	11^{3}	13	10	12	4											6	9			32
1		3		5			8	12	13		7^{3}	10	2	4		14		11^{2}							6	9^{1}			33
1		3	12	5			8		13		7■	10^{3}	4	6		14		11							2^{1}	9^{2}			34
1		3	4	5			8					10		6		9		11						7	2				35
1		3	4	5			8^{2}		12			10		6		9		11^{1}						7^{3}	2	13	14		36
1			2	5^{2}	6		8					10^{3}	4	3		12		11						7	13	9^{1}	14		37
1			2	5	6		8	9^{1}		12	7		3	4		13								11^{2}		10			38
1				5	6		8				7	10^{1}	4	2		12		11^{2}						3		9	13		39
1				5	6^{1}		8^{2}				7^{3}	10	4	2■		12		11						3		9	14	13	40
1	2		5		6^{1}		8	12		11^{3}	13		4			9		14						3		10	7^{2}		41
1	2	3	4				8	12	9			13	5			14		11						6^{1}		10^{3}	7^{2}		42
1	2	3	4				8	12	7			10	5					11						6^{1}		9^{2}	13		43
1	2	3	4				8^{2}	9	7^{1}	11		10^{3}	5	6		12		13			14								44
1	2	3	4					9^{2}	8^{3}	11^{1}	12		5	6		10		7			14							13	45
1	2	3	4					9	7		8		5	6^{1}		10		11^{2}			13			12					46

FA Cup
Third Round Preston NE (a) 0-1

Carling Cup
First Round Hartlepool U (h) 1-2

SHEFFIELD UNITED FL Championship

FOUNDATION

In March 1889, Yorkshire County Cricket Club formed Sheffield United six days after an FA Cup semi-final between Preston North End and West Bromwich Albion had finally convinced Charles Stokes, a member of the cricket club, that the formation of a professional football club would prove successful at Bramall Lane. The United's first secretary, Mr J. B. Wostinholm was also secretary of the cricket club.

Bramall Lane Ground, Cherry Street, Bramall Lane, Sheffield S2 4SU.
Telephone: 0871 222 1899.
Fax: 0871 663 2430.
Ticket Office: 0871 222 1889.
Website: www.sufc.co.uk
Email: info@sufc.co.uk
Ground Capacity: 32,500.
Record Attendance: 68,287 v Leeds U, FA Cup 5th rd, 15 February 1936.
Pitch Measurements: 101.1m × 62.2m.
Chairman: Kevin McCabe.
Vice-chairman: Chris Steer.
Football Executive: Terry Robinson, Simon McCabe, Jason Rockett, Kevin Blackwell, Scott McCabe.
Secretary: Donna Fletcher.
Manager: Kevin Blackwell.
Assistant Manager: Sam Ellis.
Physio: Dennis Pettitt.
Colours: Red and white striped shirts, black shorts, black stockings.
Change Colours: Black shirts, black shorts, black stockings.
Year Formed: 1889. ***Turned Professional:*** 1889. ***Ltd Co.:*** 1899.
Club Nickname: 'The Blades'.
Ground: 1889, Bramall Lane.
First Football League Game: 3 September 1892, Division 2, v Lincoln C (h) W 4–2 – Lilley; Witham, Cain; Howell, Hendry, Needham (1); Wallace, Dobson, Hammond (3), Davies, Drummond.
Record League Victory: 10–0 v Burslem Port Vale (a), Division 2, 10 December 1892 – Howlett; Witham, Lilley; Howell, Hendry, Needham; Drummond (1), Wallace (1), Hammond (4), Davies (2), Watson (2).
Record Cup Victory: 6–1 v Lincoln C, League Cup, 22 August 2000 – Tracey; Uhlenbeek, Weber, Woodhouse (Ford), Murphy, Sandford, Devlin (pen), Ribeiro (Santos), Bent (3), Kelly (1) (Thompson), Jagielka, og (1). 6–1 v Loughborough, FA Cup 4th qualifying rd, 6 December 1890; 6–1 v Scarborough (a), FA Cup 1st qualifying rd, 5 October 1889.
Record Defeat: 0–13 v Bolton W, FA Cup 2nd rd, 1 February 1890.

HONOURS

Football League: FL C – Runners-up 2005–06; Division 1 – Champions 1897–98; Runners-up 1896–97, 1899–1900; Division 2 – Champions 1952–53; Runners-up 1892–93, 1938–39, 1960–61, 1970–71, 1989–90; Division 4 – Champions 1981–82.

FA Cup: Winners 1899, 1902, 1915, 1925; Runners-up 1901, 1936.

Football League Cup: semi-final 2003.

SKY SPORTS FACT FILE

Jimmy Hagan scored his 100th League goal for Sheffield United against Blackburn Rovers on 21 February 1953. The Blades were Second Division champions that season and celebrated with a tour of West Germany and Holland winning three games and drawing the other two.

Most League Points (2 for a win): 60, Division 2, 1952–53.

Most League Points (3 for a win): 96, Division 4, 1981–82.

Most League Goals: 102, Division 1, 1925–26.

Highest League Scorer in Season: Jimmy Dunne, 41, Division 1, 1930–31.

Most League Goals in Total Aggregate: Harry Johnson, 205, 1919–30.

Most League Goals in One Match: 5, Harry Hammond v Bootle, Division 2, 26 November 1892; 5, Harry Johnson v West Ham U, Division 1, 26 December 1927.

Most Capped Player: Billy Gillespie, 25, Northern Ireland.

Most League Appearances: Joe Shaw, 629, 1948–66.

Youngest League Player: Steve Hawes, 17 years 47 days v WBA, 2 September 1995.

Record Transfer Fee Received: £4,000,000 from Everton for Phil Jagielka, July 2007.

Record Transfer Fee Paid: £4,000,000 to Everton for James Beattie, August 2007.

Football League Record: 1892 Elected to Division 2; 1893–1934 Division 1; 1934–39 Division 2; 1946–49 Division 1; 1949–53 Division 2; 1953–56 Division 1; 1956–61 Division 2; 1961–68 Division 1; 1968–71 Division 2; 1971–76 Division 1; 1976–79 Division 2; 1979–81 Division 3; 1981–82 Division 4; 1982–84 Division 3; 1984–88 Division 2; 1988–89 Division 3; 1989–90 Division 2; 1990–92 Division 1; 1992–94 FA Premier League; 1994–2004 Division 1; 2004–06 FL C; 2006–07 FA Premier League; 2007– FL C.

MANAGERS

J. B. Wostinholm 1889–99 *(Secretary-Manager)*
John Nicholson 1899–1932
Ted Davison 1932–52
Reg Freeman 1952–55
Joe Mercer 1955–58
Johnny Harris 1959–68 *(continued as General Manager to 1970)*
Arthur Rowley 1968–69
Johnny Harris *(General Manager resumed Team Manager duties)* 1969 73
Ken Furphy 1973–75
Jimmy Sirrel 1975–77
Harry Haslam 1978–81
Martin Peters 1981
Ian Porterfield 1981–86
Billy McEwan 1986–88
Dave Bassett 1988–95
Howard Kendall 1995–97
Nigel Spackman 1997–98
Steve Bruce 1998–99
Adrian Heath 1999
Neil Warnock 1999–2007
Bryan Robson 2007–08
Kevin Blackwell February 2008–

LATEST SEQUENCES

Longest Sequence of League Wins: 8, 14.9.1960 – 22.10.1960.

Longest Sequence of League Defeats: 7, 19.8.1975 – 20.9.1975.

Longest Sequence of League Draws: 6, 6.5.2001 – 8.9.2001.

Longest Sequence of Unbeaten League Matches: 22, 2.9.1899 – 13.1.1900.

Longest Sequence Without a League Win: 19, 27.9.1975 – 7.2.1976.

Successive Scoring Runs: 34 from 30.3.1956.

Successive Non-scoring Runs: 6 from 4.12.1993.

TEN YEAR LEAGUE RECORD

		P	W	D	L	F	A	Pts	Pos
1998-99	Div 1	46	18	13	15	71	66	67	8
1999-2000	Div 1	46	13	15	18	59	71	54	16
2000-01	Div 1	46	19	11	16	52	49	68	10
2001-02	Div 1	46	15	15	16	53	54	60	13
2002-03	Div 1	46	23	11	12	72	52	80	3
2003-04	Div 1	46	20	11	15	65	56	71	8
2004-05	FL C	46	18	13	15	57	56	67	8
2005-06	FL C	46	26	12	8	76	46	90	2
2006-07	PR Lge	38	10	8	20	32	55	38	18
2007-08	FL C	46	17	15	14	56	51	66	9

DID YOU KNOW ?

It took a marathon semi-final against Liverpool before Sheffield United went on to win the FA Cup in 1898–99. A 2–2 draw at Forest, 4–4 at Bolton, losing 1–0 at Fallowfield until a pitch invasion and darkness called a halt, before winning 1–0 on Derby's ground, coincidentally their final opponents!

SHEFFIELD UNITED 2007–08 LEAGUE RECORD

Match No.	Date	Venue	Opponents	Result		H/T Score	Lg. Pos.	Goalscorers	Attendance
1	Aug 11	H	Colchester U	D	2-2	0-0	—	Beattie 68, Tonge 82	26,202
2	18	A	Watford	L	0-1	0-0	19		16,414
3	25	H	WBA	W	1-0	1-0	16	Beattie 37	23,491
4	Sept 1	A	Scunthorpe U	L	2-3	0-1	19	Webber 2 79, 83	8801
5	15	H	Wolverhampton W	W	3-1	0-1	8	Beattie 2 (1 pen) 57, 83 (p), Stead 90	26,003
6	18	A	Blackpool	D	2-2	1-1	—	Beattie 2 13, 88	9512
7	22	A	Crystal Palace	L	2-3	0-0	16	Hudson (og) 48, Beattie 76	14,131
8	29	H	Southampton	L	1-2	1-2	19	Gillespie 12	24,561
9	Oct 2	H	Cardiff C	D	3-3	1-2	—	Beattie 18, Armstrong 85, Morgan 90	26,186
10	6	A	Bristol C	L	0-2	0-1	20		13,071
11	20	H	Preston NE	D	1-1	0-1	20	Beattie (pen) 80	23,661
12	23	A	Leicester C	W	1-0	0-0	—	Webber 56	21,146
13	27	A	Hull C	D	1-1	1-0	19	Stead 35	20,185
14	Nov 3	H	Burnley	D	0-0	0-0	17		25,306
15	6	H	Ipswich T	W	3-1	1-0	—	Beattie 2 (1 pen) 33, 72 (p), Gillespie 86	25,033
16	10	A	Stoke C	W	1-0	1-0	12	Cahill 43	12,158
17	24	H	Plymouth Arg	L	0-1	0-1	14		23,811
18	27	A	Charlton Ath	W	3-0	1-0	—	Beattie (pen) 34, Cahill 75, Armstrong 89	20,737
19	Dec 1	A	Coventry C	W	1-0	0-0	11	Armstrong 62	20,355
20	4	H	Stoke C	L	0-3	0-3	—		23,378
21	8	A	Norwich C	L	0-1	0-1	13		24,493
22	15	H	Barnsley	W	1-0	0-0	12	Kilgallon 64	26,629
23	22	A	Cardiff C	L	0-1	0-1	14		12,869
24	26	H	Blackpool	D	1-1	1-0	14	Beattie 23	26,409
25	29	H	Crystal Palace	L	0-1	0-1	16		23,982
26	Jan 1	A	Wolverhampton W	D	0-0	0-0	16		24,791
27	12	H	QPR	W	2-1	0-1	14	Stewart (og) 64, Hendrie 69	28,894
28	19	A	Sheffield W	L	0-2	0-1	14		30,486
29	29	H	Watford	D	1-1	0-1	—	Carney 67	23,161
30	Feb 2	A	Colchester U	D	2-2	1-0	16	Shelton 45, Carney 66	5695
31	9	H	Scunthorpe U	D	0-0	0-0	17		25,668
32	12	A	WBA	D	0-0	0-0	—		22,643
33	23	A	QPR	D	1-1	0-1	15	Morgan 78	15,383
34	Mar 1	H	Charlton Ath	L	0-2	0-1	18		23,180
35	4	A	Ipswich T	D	1-1	1-0	—	Beattie 32	20,190
36	8	A	Plymouth Arg	W	1-0	0-0	16	Beattie 63	13,669
37	11	H	Coventry C	W	2-1	0-0	—	Sharp 69, Speed 78	23,864
38	15	H	Norwich C	W	2-0	0-0	13	Sharp 52, Kilgallon 56	25,536
39	22	A	Barnsley	W	1-0	0-0	12	Sharp 77	15,798
40	29	A	Preston NE	L	1-3	0-1	13	Beattie (pen) 87	14,647
41	Apr 5	H	Leicester C	W	3-0	3-0	13	Beattie 3 12, 14, 19	24,818
42	8	H	Sheffield W	D	2-2	0-1	—	Wood (og) 62, Beattie 85	31,760
43	12	A	Burnley	W	2-1	1-0	11	Beattie 33, Sharp 53	11,693
44	19	H	Hull C	W	2-0	0-0	8	Quinn S 51, Beattie (pen) 72	28,188
45	26	H	Bristol C	W	2-1	1-1	9	Speed 2 (1 pen) 29, 55 (p)	29,787
46	May 4	A	Southampton	L	2-3	1-1	9	Quinn S 23, Stead 65	31,957

Final League Position: 9

GOALSCORERS

League (56): Beattie 22 (6 pens), Sharp 4, Armstrong 3, Speed 3 (1 pen), Stead 3, Webber 3, Cahill 2, Carney 2, Gillespie 2, Kilgallon 2, Morgan 2, Quinn S 2, Hendrie 1, Shelton 1, Tonge 1, own goals 3.
Carling Cup (11): Sharp 2, Shelton 2, Stead 2, Hendrie 1, Horsfield 1, Law 1, Lucketti 1, Webber 1.
FA Cup (3): Carney 1, Shelton 1, Stead 1.

Kenny P 40	Geary D 19 + 2	Naysmith G 38	Montgomery N 18 + 2	Luckett C 4 + 2	Kilgallon M 39 + 1	Gillespie K 23 + 12	Leigertwood M 1 + 1	Beattie J 36 + 3	Sharp B 21 + 8	Hendrie L 7 + 5	Tonge M 37 + 8	Armstrong C 27 + 5	Webber D 8 + 6	Morgan C 25	Bromby L 11	Stead J 12 + 12	Shelton L 5 + 10	Quinn A 4 + 4	Quinn S 15 + 4	Carney D 18 + 3	Cahill G 16	Bardsley P 16	Bennett I 6 + 1	Hulse R 10 + 11	Speed G 20	Martin L 5 + 1	Ehiogu U 5 + 5	Cotterill D 15 + 1	Halls J 5 + 1	Law N — + 1	Match No.
1	2	3	4	5	6	7	8^{2}	9	10^{3}	11^{1}	12	13	14																		1
1	12		4		6	7		9			11	3	10^{2}	2	5	8^{1}	13														2
1	2		4		6	7^{2}	13	9	10^{1}		8	11		5	3	12															3
1	2■		4		6	7^{1}		9	10^{2}		8	11^{3}	12	5	3	13		14													4
1		3			6	7		9			8	11	10^{1}	5	2	12		13	4^{2}												5
1		4			6	7^{2}		9			8^{1}	3	12	5	2	10		13	11^{3}	14											6
1		3	4			7^{2}		9			8	11	12	5	2^{1}	10			13		6										7
1	2	3^{1}	4			7^{3}		9		8^{2}	13	12		5		10	14		11		6										8
1						7^{3}		9	12	4^{1}	8	3		5	2	10^{2}	13	11		14	6										9
1				2^{1}				9	12	4^{3}	8	3		5		10^{2}	13	11	14	7	6										10
1		3			6	7		9			12	11	13			10^{3}	14	4^{1}	8^{2}		5	2									11
1^{6}		3			6	7^{1}		9			4	11	10			12	8				5	2	15								12
		3			6			9			4	11	10			8		7			5	2	1								13
		3	12		6	7^{1}		9			4^{2}	11	10				8	13			5	2	1								14
		3	4		6	7		9			12	11	10							8^{1}	5	2	1								15
		3	4	12	6	7		9			13	11	10^{1}							8^{2}	5	2	1								16
		3	4		6	7^{1}		9	13		12	11	10							8^{2}	5	2	1								17
1		3	4		6	7		9			8	11								10	5	2									18
1		3	4		6	7		9			8	11	12							10^{1}	5	2									19
1		3^{3}	4^{2}		6	7		9	12		8	11				13			14	10	5	2^{1}									20
1		3	4		6	7		9	12	13	8	11^{1}								10^{2}	5	2									21
1		3	4		6	7		9^{2}	10	12	8						13			11^{1}	5	2									22
1		3	4	12	6	7		9	10^{3}	13	8			5^{1}						11^{2}		2		14							23
1		3	4	5	6	7^{2}		9^{3}	10^{1}	13	8	11				12						2		14							24
1		3	4	5	6	7^{1}			12	13	8	11^{2}				10						2		9							25
1		3	12		6	13				7^{1}	8	11			5	10^{2}						2		9	4						26
1	2^{1}				6	12			10^{3}	7^{2}	11	3			5	13	14			8				9	4						27
1	2		4^{1}		6	12			13		11	3			5					7^{2}				9	8	10					28
1		3								7^{3}	12	13		5	2		10^{2}		11^{1}	14				9	4	8	6				29
1	2	3						12			13	14		5		9	10		11	7^{1}					4^{3}	8^{2}	6				30
1	2	3			12			10^{2}	13		8			5			14							9	4	11^{3}	6^{1}	7			31
1	2	3			6	12		9^{3}				13		5			10^{1}		11					14	4^{2}	8		7			32
1	2	3			6			9^{2}	10^{3}		8	11		5		7^{1}	12		4					13				14			33
1	2				6	12		9^{3}	10^{2}		8	3		5		13			11■					14	4			7^{1}			34
1	2	3			6			9	10^{1}		8	11		5										12	4			7			35
1	2	3			6	12		9^{2}	10^{3}		8			5						11^{1}				13	4		14	7			36
1	2	3			6	12		9^{2}	10		8			5						11^{1}				13	4		14	7^{3}			37
1	2	3			6				10^{2}		8			5		12				11				9^{1}	4		13	7			38
1	2^{3}	3			6	12		13	10		8			5						11^{1}				9^{2}	4			7	14		39
1		3^{2}			6	12		13	10		8			5■					14	11^{3}				9	4			7^{1}	2		40
		3			6	12		9^{2}	10		8^{3}					13			11				1		4		5	7^{1}	2	14	41
1	2	3			6			9	10		8			5		12			11^{1}						4			7			42
1	2	3			6	12		9^{1}	10^{2}		8			5					11					13	4		14	7^{3}			43
1		3			6			9	10^{1}		8			5■					11					12	4		13	7^{2}	2		44
1	14	3			6			9^{1}	10		8								11					12	4	13^{3}	5^{2}	7	2		45
1	2	5			6	12			10^{3}		8					13	14		11					9^{2}	4			7^{1}	3		46

FA Cup

Third Round	Bolton W	(a)	1-0
Fourth Round	Manchester C	(h)	2-1
Fifth Round	Middlesbrough	(h)	0-0
		(a)	0-1

Carling Cup

First Round	Chesterfield	(h)	3-1
Second Round	Milton Keynes D	(a)	3-2
Third Round	Morecambe	(h)	5-0
Fourth Round	Arsenal	(h)	0-3

SHEFFIELD WEDNESDAY FL Championship

FOUNDATION

Sheffield being one of the principal centres of early Association Football, this club was formed as long ago as 1867 by the Sheffield Wednesday Cricket Club (formed 1825) and their colours from the start were blue and white. The inaugural meeting was held at the Adelphi Hotel and the original committee included Charles Stokes who was subsequently a founder member of Sheffield United.

Hillsborough, Sheffield S6 1SW.

Telephone: 0870 999 1867.

Fax: (0114) 221 2122.

Ticket Office: 0870 999 1867 (option 2).

Website: www.swfc.co.uk

Email: enquiries@swfc.co.uk

Ground Capacity: 39,812.

Record Attendance: 72,841 v Manchester C, FA Cup 5th rd, 17 February 1934.

Pitch Measurements: 110yd × 71yd.

Chief Executive: Kaven Walker

Secretary: Kaven Walker (football secretary).

Manager: Brian Laws.

Assistant Manager: Russ Wilcox.

Physio: Mark Palmer.

Colours: Blue and white striped shirts, black shorts, black stockings.

Change Colours: White shirts, blue shorts, white stockings.

Year Formed: 1867 (fifth oldest League club).

Turned Professional: 1887.

Ltd Co.: 1899.

Former Names: The Wednesday until 1929.

Club Nickname: 'The Owls'.

Grounds: 1867, Highfield; 1869, Myrtle Road; 1877, Sheaf House; 1887, Olive Grove; 1899, Owlerton (since 1912 known as Hillsborough). Some games were played at Endcliffe in the 1880s. Until 1895 Bramall Lane was used for some games.

First Football League Game: 3 September 1892, Division 1, v Notts Co (a) W 1–0 – Allan; Tom Brandon (1), Mumford; Hall, Betts, Harry Brandon; Spiksley, Brady, Davis, R. N. Brown, Dunlop.

Record League Victory: 9–1 v Birmingham, Division 1, 13 December 1930 – Brown; Walker, Blenkinsop; Strange, Leach, Wilson; Hooper (3), Seed (2), Ball (2), Burgess (1), Rimmer (1).

HONOURS

Football League: Division 1 – Champions 1902–03, 1903–04, 1928–29, 1929–30; Runners-up 1960–61; Promotion from Championship 1 2004–05 (play-offs); Division 2 – Champions 1899–1900, 1925–26, 1951–52, 1955–56, 1958–59; Runners-up 1949–50, 1983–84.

FA Cup: Winners 1896, 1907, 1935; Runners-up 1890, 1966, 1993.

Football League Cup: Winners 1991; Runners-up 1993.

European Competitions: *European Fairs Cup:* 1961–62, 1963–64. *UEFA Cup:* 1992–93. *Intertoto Cup:* 1995.

SKY SPORTS FACT FILE

Sheffield Wednesday while still a non-league club accounted for several Football League team scalps in the FA Cup between 1888 and 1892. Their victims were Notts County and Bolton Wanderers twice each plus Accrington and Derby County.

Record Cup Victory: 12–0 v Halliwell, FA Cup 1st rd, 17 January 1891 – Smith; Thompson, Brayshaw; Harry Brandon (1), Betts, Cawley (2); Winterbottom, Mumford (2), Bob Brandon (1), Woolhouse (5), Ingram (1).

Record Defeat: 0–10 v Aston Villa, Division 1, 5 October 1912.

Most League Points (2 for a win): 62, Division 2, 1958–59.

Most League Points (3 for a win): 88, Division 2, 1983–84.

Most League Goals: 106, Division 2, 1958–59.

Highest League Scorer in Season: Derek Dooley, 46, Division 2, 1951–52.

Most League Goals in Total Aggregate: Andrew Wilson, 199, 1900–20.

Most League Goals in One Match: 6, Doug Hunt v Norwich C, Division 2, 19 November 1938.

Most Capped Player: Nigel Worthington, 50 (66), Northern Ireland.

Most League Appearances: Andrew Wilson, 501, 1900–20.

Youngest League Player: Peter Fox, 15 years 269 days v Orient, 31 March 1973.

Record Transfer Fee Received: £2,750,000 from Blackburn R for Paul Warhurst, September 1993.

Record Transfer Fee Paid: £4,500,000 to Celtic for Paolo Di Canio, August 1997.

Football League Record: 1892 Elected to Division 1; 1899–1900 Division 2; 1900–20 Division 1; 1920–26 Division 2; 1926–37 Division 1; 1937–50 Division 2; 1950–51 Division 1; 1951–52 Division 2; 1952–55 Division 1; 1955–56 Division 2; 1956–58 Division 1; 1958–59 Division 2; 1959–70 Division 1; 1970–75 Division 2; 1975–80 Division 3; 1980–84 Division 2; 1984–90 Division 1; 1990–91 Division 2; 1991–92 Division 1; 1992–2000 FA Premier League; 2000–03 Division 1; 2003–04 Division 2; 2004–05 FL 1; 2005– FL C.

MANAGERS

Arthur Dickinson 1891–1920
(Secretary-Manager)
Robert Brown 1920–33
Billy Walker 1933–37
Jimmy McMullan 1937–42
Eric Taylor 1942–58
(continued as General Manager to 1974)
Harry Catterick 1958–61
Vic Buckingham 1961–64
Alan Brown 1964–68
Jack Marshall 1968–69
Danny Williams 1969–71
Derek Dooley 1971–73
Steve Burtenshaw 1974–75
Len Ashurst 1975–77
Jackie Charlton 1977–83
Howard Wilkinson 1983–88
Peter Eustace 1988–89
Ron Atkinson 1989–91
Trevor Francis 1991–95
David Pleat 1995–97
Ron Atkinson 1997–98
Danny Wilson 1998–2000
Peter Shreeves (Acting) 2000
Paul Jewell 2000–01
Peter Shreeves 2001
Terry Yorath 2001–02
Chris Turner 2002–04
Paul Sturrock 2004–06
Brian Laws November 2006–

LATEST SEQUENCES

Longest Sequence of League Wins: 9, 23.4.1904 – 15.10.1904.

Longest Sequence of League Defeats: 8, 9.9.2000 – 17.10.2000.

Longest Sequence of League Draws: 7, 15.3.2008 – 14.4.2008.

Longest Sequence of Unbeaten League Matches: 19, 10.12.1960 – 8.4.1961.

Longest Sequence Without a League Win: 20, 11.1.1975 – 30.8.1975.

Successive Scoring Runs: 40 from 14.11.1959.

Successive Non-scoring Runs: 8 from 8.3.1975.

TEN YEAR LEAGUE RECORD

		P	W	D	L	F	A	Pts	Pos
1998-99	PR Lge	38	13	7	18	41	42	46	12
1999-2000	PR Lge	38	8	7	23	38	70	31	19
2000-01	Div 1	46	15	8	23	52	71	53	17
2001-02	Div 1	46	12	14	20	49	71	50	20
2002-03	Div 1	46	10	16	20	56	73	46	22
2003-04	Div 2	46	13	14	19	48	64	53	16
2004-05	FL 1	46	19	15	12	77	59	72	5
2005-06	FL C	46	13	13	20	39	52	52	19
2006-07	FL C	46	20	11	15	70	66	71	9
2007-08	FL C	46	14	13	19	54	55	55	16

DID YOU KNOW

The first and highly successful continental tour undertaken by Sheffield Wednesday took place in 1911 to Scandinavia. Victories were achieved as follows: Orgryte 5–0, Swedish XI 2–1, Denmark 3–2, Copenhagen Select 3–2, Denmark XI 3–2.

SHEFFIELD WEDNESDAY 2007–08 LEAGUE RECORD

Match No.	Date	Venue	Opponents	Result		H/T Score	Lg. Pos.	Goalscorers	Attendance
1	Aug 11	A	Ipswich T	L	1-4	0-3	—	Clarke [89]	23,099
2	19	H	Wolverhampton W	L	1-3	1-1	24	Small [45]	22,131
3	25	A	Charlton Ath	L	2-3	2-0	24	O'Brien [6], Spurr [15]	22,033
4	Sept 1	H	Bristol C	L	0-1	0-1	24		17,559
5	15	A	Preston NE	L	0-1	0-1	24		13,062
6	18	H	Burnley	L	0-2	0-1	—		18,359
7	22	H	Hull C	W	1-0	1-0	24	Jeffers [40]	21,518
8	29	A	Norwich C	W	1-0	0-0	23	Small [76]	23,293
9	Oct 2	A	Watford	L	1-2	1-2	—	Kavanagh [36]	15,473
10	6	H	Leicester C	L	0-2	0-2	23		20,010
11	20	A	Stoke C	W	4-2	2-2	22	Johnson J [16], Tudgay 2 [23, 85], Burton [87]	14,019
12	23	H	Scunthorpe U	L	1-2	1-2	—	Burton (pen) [23]	21,557
13	27	H	Blackpool	W	2-1	0-1	21	Tudgay [66], Hinds [71]	19,238
14	Nov 3	A	Plymouth Arg	W	2-1	0-0	18	Sodje [52], O'Brien [56]	12,145
15	6	A	WBA	D	1-1	0-0	—	Watson [90]	19,807
16	10	H	Southampton	W	5-0	1-0	16	Whelan 2 (1 pen) [41 (p), 56], Sodje 2 [51, 62], O'Brien [65]	19,442
17	24	A	QPR	D	0-0	0-0	16		15,241
18	27	H	Barnsley	W	1-0	0-0	—	Sodje [60]	27,769
19	Dec 1	H	Colchester U	L	1-2	1-2	15	Sodje [36]	22,331
20	4	A	Southampton	D	0-0	0-0	—		17,981
21	15	A	Crystal Palace	L	1-2	1-1	17	Hinds [11]	14,865
22	22	H	Watford	L	0-1	0-1	19		19,641
23	26	A	Burnley	D	1-1	1-1	21	Burton (pen) [30]	15,326
24	30	A	Hull C	L	0-1	0-1	22		21,252
25	Jan 1	H	Preston NE	W	2-1	0-1	19	Sodje [51], Jeffers (pen) [82]	20,690
26	12	A	Cardiff C	L	0-1	0-1	21		14,015
27	19	H	Sheffield U	W	2-0	1-0	21	Sodje [25], Tudgay [76]	30,486
28	29	A	Wolverhampton W	L	1-2	1-1	—	Tudgay [19]	22,746
29	Feb 2	H	Ipswich T	L	1-2	1-1	21	Tudgay [13]	19,092
30	9	A	Bristol C	L	1-2	0-1	22	Bullen [90]	15,520
31	12	H	Charlton Ath	D	0-0	0-0	—		17,211
32	23	H	Cardiff C	W	1-0	1-0	21	Tudgay [41]	18,539
33	Mar 1	A	Barnsley	D	0-0	0-0	22		18,257
34	4	H	WBA	L	0-1	0-0	—		18,805
35	8	H	QPR	W	2-1	1-1	22	Kavanagh [45], Burton (pen) [52]	18,555
36	11	A	Colchester U	W	2-1	2-1	—	Burton [18], Small [44]	5086
37	15	A	Coventry C	D	0-0	0-0	22		19,283
38	22	H	Crystal Palace	D	2-2	1-1	22	Sahar [18], Small [68]	19,875
39	29	H	Stoke C	D	1-1	0-1	22	Songo'o [82]	21,857
40	Apr 1	H	Coventry C	D	1-1	0-0	—	Wood [90]	21,110
41	5	A	Scunthorpe U	D	1-1	0-1	21	Sahar [49]	7425
42	8	A	Sheffield U	D	2-2	1-0	—	Bolder 2 [39, 56]	31,760
43	14	H	Plymouth Arg	D	1-1	0-1	—	Spurr [81]	20,635
44	19	A	Blackpool	L	1-2	1-2	22	Wood [12]	9633
45	26	A	Leicester C	W	3-1	1-1	20	Slusarski [45], Watson [53], Clarke [89]	31,892
46	May 4	H	Norwich C	W	4-1	1-1	16	Burton 2 (1 pen) [23 (p), 76], Sahar [53], Clarke [87]	36,208

Final League Position: 16

GOALSCORERS

League (54): Burton 7 (4 pens), Sodje 7, Tudgay 7, Small 4, Clarke 3, O'Brien 3, Sahar 3, Bolder 2, Hinds 2, Jeffers 2 (1 pen), Kavanagh 2, Spurr 2, Watson 2, Whelan 2 (1 pen), Wood 2, Bullen 1, Johnson J 1, Slusarski 1, Songo'o 1.
Carling Cup (5): Burton 2, Folly 1, Small 1, Whelan 1.
FA Cup (3): Beevers 1, Tudgay 1, Watson 1.

Grant L 44	Simek F 17	Gilbert P 9 + 1	Whelan G 25	Bullen L 17 + 5	Wood R 26 + 1	Watson S 20 + 3	Johnson J 30 + 5	Jeffers F 7 + 3	Tudgay M 29 + 6	Brunt C 1	Lunt K 3 + 1	Small W 18 + 11	Clarke L 2 + 6	Burton D 23 + 17	Hinds R 30 + 8	O'Brien B 26 + 7	Spurr T 40 + 1	Folly Y 7 + 3	Burch R 2	Esajas E 5 + 13	Sodje A 16 + 3	Kavanagh G 21 + 2	Johnson M 13	Beevers M 26 + 2	Boden L — + 2	Wallwork R 4 + 3	Showunmi E 6 + 4	Bolder A 11 + 2	McAllister S 5 + 3	Sahar B 8 + 4	Songo'o F 12	Slusarski B 3 + 4	*Match No.*
1	2	3	4	5^{1}	6	7	8^{2}	9^{3}	10	11	12	13	14																				1
1	2		4^{3}	5	6		8	9^{1}			7^{2}	11	12	10	13	14	3																2
1	2	12	4		6		8^{3}		13		11		9^{2}	10	5	7	3^{1}	14															3
	2		4	12	6	11	8^{3}		9					10	5^{1}	7^{2}	3		1	13	14												4
1	2		4		6	5	12	9^{2}				8^{1}		13	14		3	7		11^{3}	10												5
1	2		4		6	5^{3}		9^{1}	12		7	11		13	14		3			8	10^{2}												6
1	2		4		6	7^{2}		9^{1}	12			13		10	14		3^{3}			8		11	5										7
1	2		4		6	7^{2}	13	9^{1}	12			8		10	14		3^{3}					11	5										8
	2^{2}	3	4	12			8■		9					10	6^{1}				1	13	7	11	5										9
1		3	4	2				12	9					10^{1}	6	13				7	8^{2}	11	5^{3}	14									10
1			4	2^{2}	6		8^{3}	9^{1}	10					12	13	7	3				14	11	5										11
1			4	12	6^{1}		8		9					10^{3}	2	7^{2}	3			13	14	11	5										12
1	2		4^{1}			12	8^{3}		9					13	6	7	3			14	10^{2}	11	5										13
1	2					4	8^{2}		9					12	5	11	3	7		13	10^{1}		6										14
1	2		4			7	8^{2}		9			13		12	5	11^{1}	3			14	10^{3}			6									15
1	2		4			7	8^{2}		9			13		12	6	11	3				10^{1}		5^{3}	14									16
1	2					7	8^{2}		9			13		12	6	11	3	4			10^{1}		5										17
1	2					7	8^{2}		9^{1}			13		12	6	11	3	4			10		5										18
1	2		4			7	8		9^{1}			12			6	11^{2}	3			13	10			5									19
1			4	2			8		12			9^{2}			6	11	3	7		13	10^{1}			5									20
1	2^{1}		4	12		7	8		9			10^{2}			6	11	3			13			5										21
1			4	2		7^{2}	8^{1}		9			10		12	6	11^{3}	3	13		14			5										22
1			4	2		7^{2}			9			8^{1}		10^{3}	6	11	3	12		13				5	14								23
1			4	2				12	9					10^{1}	6	11	3	7^{2}		13	8			5									24
1			4	2			8^{3}	12	13					10^{1}	6	11	3	7^{2}		14	9			5									25
1			4	2		7^{3}	12		9				10^{2}	13	6	11	3			8^{1}				5		14							26
1			4	2			8^{1}		9			12	13		6	11	3				10^{2}			5		7							27
1			4	2			8^{2}		9			11		12	6	13	3				10^{1}			5		7							28
1				2			8^{1}		9			13	14	12	6	11	3					4		5		7^{2}	10^{3}						29
1		3		2	12				9^{2}			7		10	6^{1}	11^{3}						4		5	13			8	14				30
1				2	6		8^{1}		9			11		12			3					4^{2}		5		13	10	7					31
1		3		2^{2}	6		8^{3}		9			11		12	13							4		5			10^{1}	7		14			32
1		3^{2}			6				9			11^{3}		12	2	7	13					4		5			10^{1}	8		14			33
1					6		8■		9						2	11^{1}	3					4		5			10	7		12			34
1					6				9			7^{2}		12	2	13	3					4		5		8^{3}	10^{1}		14		11		35
1					6				9			11^{1}		10	2	12	3					4		5			13		8		7^{2}		36
1					6				9^{3}			11		10^{2}	2	12	3					4		5			14	13	8		7^{1}		37
1					6							11^{1}		10	2		3					4		5			12		8	9	7		38
1					6	12	13					11^{2}		10	2^{1}		3					4		5			14		8	9^{3}	7		39
1					5	12	8							10		11^{3}	3					4^{1}		2				13	6^{2}	9	7	14	40
1		2			5	11	8					12		10			3					4						6		9^{2}	7^{1}	13	41
1					6	2	8							10	12	13	3					4^{2}		5				11		9^{3}	7^{1}	14	42
1		2			6		8^{1}					12		10		7	3							5				4		9^{2}	11	13	43
1		2■		12	6		8^{1}							10		7^{2}	3					13		5				4		14	11	9^{3}	44
1				2^{1}	6	7	12						13	10			3							5		14		4		9^{2}	11^{3}	8	45
1					6	2^{1}	8						13	10			3					12		5				4	14	9^{2}	7^{3}	11	46

FA Cup
Third Round Derby Co (a) 2-2
(h) 1-1

Carling Cup
First Round Rotherham U (a) 3-1
Second Round Hartlepool U (h) 2-1
Third Round Everton (h) 0-3

SHREWSBURY TOWN FL Championship 2

FOUNDATION

Shrewsbury School having provided a number of the early England and Wales international players it is not surprising that there was a Town club as early as 1876 which won the Birmingham Senior Cup in 1879. However, the present Shrewsbury Town club was formed in 1886 and won the Welsh FA Cup as early as 1891.

The New Stadium, Oteley Road, Shrewsbury, Shropshire SY2 6ST.

Telephone: (0871) 811 8800.

Fax: (0871) 811 8801.

Ticket Office: (01743) 273 943.

Website: www.shrewsburytown.com

Email: ian@shrewsburytown.co.uk

Ground Capacity: 9,875.

Record Attendance: 18,917 v Walsall, Division 3, 26 April 1961.

Pitch Measurements: 114yd × 73yd.

Chairman: Roland Wycherley.

Vice-chairman: Keith Sayfritz.

Managing Director: Robert Bickerton.

Secretary/General Manager: Jonathan Harris.

Manager: Paul Simpson.

Assistant Manager: John McMahon.

Physio: Nathan Ring.

Colours: Blue and amber.

Change Colours: Red and dark blue.

Year Formed: 1886.

Turned Professional: 1896.

Ltd Co.: 1936.

Club Nickname: 'Town', 'Blues' or 'Salop'. The name 'Salop' is a colloquialism for the county of Shropshire. Since Shrewsbury is the only club in Shropshire, cries of 'Come on Salop' are frequently used!

Grounds: 1886, Old Shrewsbury Racecourse; 1910, Gay Meadow; 2007, The New Stadium.

First Football League Game: 19 August 1950, Division 3 (N), v Scunthorpe U (a) D 0–0 – Egglestone; Fisher, Lewis; Wheatley, Depear, Robinson; Griffin, Hope, Jackson, Brown, Barker.

Record League Victory: 7–0 v Swindon T, Division 3 (S), 6 May 1955 – McBride; Bannister, Skeech; Wallace, Maloney, Candlin; Price, O'Donnell (1), Weigh (4), Russell, McCue (2).

HONOURS

Football League: Division 2 best season: 8th, 1983–84, 1984–85; Division 3 – Champions 1978–79, 1993–94; Division 4 – Runners-up 1974–75.

Conference: Promotion 2003–04 (play-offs)

FA Cup: best season: 6th rd, 1979, 1982.

Football League Cup: Semi-final 1961.

Welsh Cup: Winners 1891, 1938, 1977, 1979, 1984, 1985; Runners-up 1931, 1948, 1980.

Auto Windscreens Shield: Runners-up 1996.

SKY SPORTS FACT FILE

On 13 October 1962 Shrewsbury Town playing against Bristol Rovers scored seven goals for the first time in the Football League. Both Jimmy McLaughlin and Frank Clarke hit hat-tricks leaving leading marksman Arthur Rowley with just one to his credit.

Record Cup Victory: 11–2 v Marine, FA Cup 1st rd, 11 November 1995 – Edwards, Seabury (Dempsey (1)), Withe (1), Evans (1), Whiston (2), Scott (1), Woods, Stevens (1), Spink (3) (Anthrobus), Walton, Berkley, (1 og).

Record Defeat: 1–8 v Norwich C, Division 3 (S), 13 September 1952. 1–8 v Coventry C, Division 3, 22 October 1963.

Most League Points (2 for a win): 62, Division 4, 1974–75.

Most League Points (3 for a win): 79, Division 3, 1993–94.

Most League Goals: 101, Division 4, 1958–59.

Highest League Scorer in Season: Arthur Rowley, 38, Division 4, 1958–59.

Most League Goals in Total Aggregate: Arthur Rowley, 152, 1958–65 (thus completing his League record of 434 goals).

Most League Goals in One Match: 5, Alf Wood v Blackburn R, Division 3, 2 October 1971.

Most Capped Player: Jimmy McLaughlin, 5 (12), Northern Ireland; Bernard McNally, 5, Northern Ireland.

Most League Appearances: Mickey Brown, 418, 1986–91; 1992–94; 1996–2001.

Youngest League Player: Graham French, 16 years 177 days v Reading, 30 September 1961.

Record Transfer Fee Received: £600,000 from Manchester C for Joe Hart, May 2006.

Record Transfer Fee Paid: £100,000 to Aldershot for John Dungworth, November 1979 and £100,000 to Southampton for Mark Blake, August 1990.

Football League Record: 1950 Elected to Division 3 (N); 1951–58 Division 3 (S); 1958–59 Division 4; 1959–74 Division 3; 1974–75 Division 4; 1975–79 Division 3; 1979–89 Division 2; 1989–94 Division 3; 1994–97 Division 2; 1997–2003 Division 3; 2003–04 Conference; 2004– FL 2.

MANAGERS

W. Adams 1905–12
(Secretary-Manager)
A. Weston 1912–34
(Secretary-Manager)
Jack Roscamp 1934–35
Sam Ramsey 1935–36
Ted Bousted 1936–40
Leslie Knighton 1945–49
Harry Chapman 1949–50
Sammy Crooks 1950–54
Walter Rowley 1955–57
Harry Potts 1957–58
Johnny Spuhler 1958
Arthur Rowley 1958–68
Harry Gregg 1968–72
Maurice Evans 1972–73
Alan Durban 1974–78
Richie Barker 1978
Graham Turner 1978–84
Chic Bates 1984–87
Ian McNeill 1987–90
Asa Hartford 1990–91
John Bond 1991–93
Fred Davies 1994–97
(previously Caretaker-Manager 1993–94)
Jake King 1997–99
Kevin Ratcliffe 1999–2003
Jimmy Quinn 2003–04
Gary Peters 2004–08
Paul Simpson March 2008–

LATEST SEQUENCES

Longest Sequence of League Wins: 7, 28.10.1995 – 16.12.1995.

Longest Sequence of League Defeats: 11, 9.4.2003 – 14.8.2004.

Longest Sequence of League Draws: 6, 30.10.1963 – 14.12.1963.

Longest Sequence of Unbeaten League Matches: 16, 30.10.1993 – 26.2.1994.

Longest Sequence Without a League Win: 18, 8.3.2003 – 14.8.2004.

Successive Scoring Runs: 28 from 7.9.1960.

Successive Non-scoring Runs: 6 from 1.1.1991.

TEN YEAR LEAGUE RECORD

		P	*W*	*D*	*L*	*F*	*A*	*Pts*	*Pos*
1998-99	Div 3	46	14	14	18	52	63	56	15
1999-2000	Div 3	46	9	13	24	40	67	40	22
2000-01	Div 3	46	15	10	21	49	65	55	15
2001-02	Div 3	46	20	10	16	64	53	70	9
2002-03	Div 3	46	9	14	23	62	92	41	24
2003-04	Conf.	42	20	14	8	67	42	74	3
2004-05	FL 2	46	11	16	19	48	53	49	21
2005-06	FL 2	46	16	13	17	55	55	61	10
2006-07	FL 2	46	18	17	11	68	46	71	7
2007-08	FL 2	46	12	14	20	56	65	50	18

DID YOU KNOW ?

On 16 January 1937 Shrewsbury Town beat Bangor 11–1 with Ernie Breeze scoring six times including once from the penalty spot. It was a season of goal gluts in the Birmingham League and in all games the club achieved a total of 197.

SHREWSBURY TOWN 2007–08 LEAGUE RECORD

Match No.	Date	Venue	Opponents	Result	H/T Score	Lg. Pos.	Goalscorers	Attendance
1	Aug 11	A	Lincoln C	W 4-0	0-0	—	Cooke 2 [52, 81], Hibbert [57], Leslie [82]	3893
2	18	H	Bradford C	W 1-0	1-0	2	Hibbert (pen) [9]	6413
3	25	A	Milton Keynes D	L 0-3	0-0	3		7380
4	Sept 1	H	Grimsby T	W 2-1	0-0	1	Hibbert [50], Symes [59]	5490
5	8	A	Stockport Co	D 1-1	1-1	3	Hibbert [25]	5473
6	15	H	Accrington S	W 2-0	1-0	3	Nicholson [3], Hibbert (pen) [52]	5789
7	22	A	Wycombe W	D 1-1	1-1	4	Murdock [27]	4936
8	29	H	Rochdale	L 3-4	1-0	6	Hibbert [38], Drummond [62], Hunt [88]	6262
9	Oct 2	H	Peterborough U	L 0-2	0-1	—		5220
10	7	A	Chester C	L 1-3	0-0	9	Moss [69]	3057
11	13	H	Chesterfield	L 2-3	1-1	13	Hibbert [5], Murdock [68]	5143
12	20	A	Bury	D 1-1	0-1	13	Drummond [82]	2667
13	27	H	Mansfield T	D 0-0	0-0	13		5347
14	Nov 4	A	Wrexham	W 1-0	0-0	11	Symes [59]	4305
15	6	A	Darlington	L 0-2	0-1	—		2628
16	17	H	Barnet	W 1-0	0-0	11	Symes [90]	5197
17	24	A	Rotherham U	L 0-2	0-1	13		3832
18	Dec 1	H	Macclesfield T	W 2-0	1-0	—	Drummond [33], Hunt [65]	4763
19	8	A	Notts Co	L 1-2	1-0	11	Hibbert (pen) [41]	3819
20	15	H	Dagenham & R	W 4-0	0-0	9	Davies 2 [54, 69], Pugh [78], Tierney [81]	4597
21	22	A	Accrington S	W 2-1	0-1	9	Davies [64], Hibbert [68]	1410
22	26	H	Stockport Co	W 3-1	1-0	9	Cooke [22], Davies [76], Hibbert (pen) [86]	7707
23	29	H	Wycombe W	L 0-1	0-1	10		6208
24	Jan 1	A	Peterborough U	L 1-2	1-0	11	Cooke [27]	5062
25	5	H	Brentford	L 0-1	0-0	12		5083
26	13	A	Hereford U	L 1-3	1-1	13	Briggs K [31]	4707
27	19	H	Morecambe	W 2-0	2-0	11	Hall A [4], Madjo [31]	5036
28	26	A	Grimsby T	D 1-1	0-0	11	Madjo [75]	3785
29	29	A	Bradford C	L 2-4	0-2	—	Hibbert [48], Pugh [65]	13,269
30	Feb 2	H	Lincoln C	L 1-2	0-1	14	Davies [76]	4892
31	9	A	Brentford	D 1-1	0-0	13	Constable [79]	5353
32	12	H	Milton Keynes D	D 3-3	1-3	—	Langmead [44], Constable 2 [70, 90]	5474
33	23	H	Hereford U	L 1-2	1-1	14	Hall A [6]	7402
34	Mar 1	A	Barnet	L 1-4	1-3	16	Madjo [10]	1864
35	8	H	Rotherham U	D 1-1	1-1	16	Davies [43]	5265
36	11	H	Darlington	D 0-0	0-0	—		4499
37	15	A	Macclesfield T	L 1-2	0-0	16	Hibbert [65]	2473
38	22	A	Dagenham & R	D 1-1	1-0	16	Cooke [34]	1686
39	24	H	Notts Co	D 0-0	0-0	18		5673
40	29	H	Bury	L 0-1	0-0	18		5213
41	Apr 5	A	Chesterfield	L 1-4	0-0	19	McIntyre [81]	3570
42	8	A	Morecambe	D 1-1	0-1	—	Pugh [70]	1634
43	13	H	Wrexham	W 3-0	1-0	19	McIntyre [7], Moss [58], Constable [68]	7065
44	19	A	Mansfield T	L 1-3	1-2	17	Pugh [2]	3334
45	26	H	Chester C	D 0-0	0-0	18		6417
46	May 3	A	Rochdale	D 1-1	1-0	18	Hall A [34]	4000

Final League Position: 18

GOALSCORERS

League (56): Hibbert 12 (4 pens), Davies 6, Cooke 5, Constable 4, Pugh 4, Drummond 3, Hall A 3, Madjo 3, Symes 3, Hunt 2, McIntyre 2, Moss 2, Murdock 2, Briggs K 1, Langmead 1, Leslie 1, Nicholson 1, Tierney 1.
Carling Cup (1): Kempson 1.
FA Cup (0).
J Paint Trophy (0).

Garner G 41	Moss D 28 + 3	Herd B 42 + 3	Drummond S 22 + 1	Kempson D 18 + 5	Murdock C 29	Hall D 7 + 8	Hibbert D 36 + 8	Cooke A 10 + 4	Langmead K 39	Pugh M 27 + 10	Leslie S 10 + 7	Symes M 12 + 9	Humphrey C 7 + 18	Tierney M 42 + 1	Nicholson S 6 + 8	Hunt D 22 + 5	Ashton N 6 + 9	Ryan J 1 + 3	Wainwright N 2 + 1	Jones L 6 + 1	Davies B 26 + 1	McIntyre K 22	Briggs K 1 + 1	Madjo G 10 + 5	Hall A 13 + 2	Constable J 7 + 7	Meredith J 3	Lee G 4 + 1	Barnes M 2	Bevan S 5	*Match No.*
1	2	3	4	5	6	7	8¹	9²	10	11³	12	13	14																		1
1	2	11	4		6	7	10¹		5	8	12			3	9																2
1	2	5	4	12	6¹	7³	8²		10	11		13		3	9	14															3
1	2	7	4	12	6	13	10¹		5	11		9³		3	14	8²															4
1	2¹	7	4	5	6	13	10		3	11²		9³			14	8	12														5
1	2	7²	4	12	5¹	13	10³		6	11		14		3	9	8															6
1	12	7	4	2¹	5		9		6	11²		14		3	10³	8	13														7
1		2	4		5		9		6	11		12	7²	3	10¹	8	13														8
1	2	7	12	5		4¹	9		6	11		10		3²		8	13														9
1	2	7	8	5	4¹		9		6	12²		10³			14	11	3	13													10
1		2	8	4	5		9		6			10¹	11²	13	12	7	3														11
1		2	8	4²	5	12	9		6	10¹	14			3	13	7³	11														12
1		2	4	6¹	5		9		10	7		12		3		8²	11		13												13
1	2¹	12	4		5	13	9³		6	11²		10		3		8	14		7												14
1	2²	7	4		5	12	9		6		11	10		3	13	8¹															15
1	2	12	4				9		6	13	11²	14		3	10³	8			7¹	5											16
1	2		4			7	9		6		12	10		3		8¹	11²			5	13										17
1	2	7	4		5	12	9		6			10²		3	13	11					8¹										18
1	2	3	4		5²		9		6			10¹		11	12	8	13				7										19
1	2	3	4		5³		9²		6	13		10		11		8	12			14	7¹										20
1	2	7	4	12		13	9²		6	14		10³		3		8				5¹	11										21
1	2³	3	4		5		9	10²	6	13			14	11		8¹	12				7										22
1	2	3³	4		5		9	10²	6	13			14	11		8¹	12				7										23
1	2³	7		5		4	9²	10¹	6	13	8	12	14	3			11														24
1	2²	3		5		4³	9	10¹	6	13		12	14	7							8	11									25
1	2¹	12		5			13	9²	6	14				3				8			4	11	7³	10							26
1		2			5			12	6	9¹			7²	3							4	11	13	10	8						27
1	12	2		13	5¹		14		6	9³			4²	3							8	11		10¹	7						28
1	12	2¹		5			13		6	9			4²	3		14					8	11³		10	7						29
1		2¹		5			9²		6	4			12	3							8	11		10	7	13					30
1		2			5		9²		6	4¹			12	3							8	11		10	7	13					31
1		2			5		9³		6	8¹			13	3		12					4²	11		14	7	10					32
1	8³	2						12	6	4²	14		13	3								11		10	7	9	5¹				33
1	2	4²					12		6				13	3		14					8	11³		10¹	7	9	5				34
1		2			5		8³	13	6	14				3		12					4	11		10²	7¹	9					35
1		2			5		12	10¹	6	8²			13	3		7³					4	11			14	9					36
1		2					12	9³	6	5			13	3¹		10				4	8	11			7²	14					37
1		2					12	9¹	6	8	4			3							10	11			7			5			38
1		2					9¹	12	6	8³	4		13	3							10	11			7²	14		5			39
1		2					9	10²			4¹		12	3						6	7	11		13				5	8		40
1	7	2					9				10³		12	3				13		5	8	11		14				6²	4¹		41
	7	2		6	5		9			10	8¹		12	3							4²	11				13				1	42
	7	2		6	5		9			10³	8		12	3				13			4¹	11²				14				1	43
	4	2		6	5		9¹			8	7³		12	3								11		13		10²		14		1	44
	4²	2		6	5¹		9³				12		7	3							8	11		10	13	14				1	45
		2		6			12			5¹	13		4	3							8	11		14	7	10³	9²			1	46

FA Cup
First Round — Walsall — (a) — 0-2

Carling Cup
First Round — Colchester U — (h) — 1-0
Second Round — Fulham — (h) — 0-1

J Paint Trophy
First Round — Yeovil T — (a) — 0-1

SOUTHAMPTON FL Championship

FOUNDATION

The club was formed by members of the St Mary's Church of England Young Men's Association at a meeting of the Y.M.A. in November 1885 and it was named as such. For the sake of brevity this was usually shortened to St Mary's Y.M.A. The rector Canon Albert Basil Orme Wilberforce was elected president. The name was changed to plain St Mary's during 1887–88 and did not become Southampton St Mary's until 1894, the inaugural season in the Southern League.

St Mary's Stadium, Britannia Road, Southampton SO14 5FP.

Telephone: 0845 688 9448.

Fax: 0238 072 7727

Ticket Office: 0845 688 9288.

Website: www.saintsfc.co.uk

Email: sfc@saintsfc.co.uk

Ground Capacity: 32,689.

Record Attendance: 32,104 v Liverpool, FA Premier League, 18 January 2003.

Pitch Measurements: 112yd × 72yd.

Chairman: Rupert Lowe.

Football Secretary: Ros Wheeler.

Head Coach: Jan Poortvliet.

Coach: Mark Wotte.

Physio: Mo Gimpel.

Colours: Red and white striped shirts, black shorts, white and red hooped stockings.

Change Colours: Flint shirts, flint shorts, flint stockings.

Year Formed: 1885.

Turned Professional: 1894. ***Ltd Co.:*** 1897.

Previous Name: 1885, St Mary's Young Men's Association; 1887–88, St Mary's; 1894–95 Southampton St Mary's; 1897, Southampton.

Club Nickname: 'The Saints'.

Grounds: 1885, 'The Common' (from 1887 also used the County Cricket Ground and Antelope Cricket Ground); 1889, Antelope Cricket Ground; 1896 The County Cricket Ground; 1898, The Dell; 2001, St Mary's.

First Football League Game: 28 August 1920, Division 3, v Gillingham (a) D 1–1 – Allen; Parker, Titmuss; Shelley, Campbell, Turner; Barratt, Dominy (1), Rawlings, Moore, Foxall.

Record League Victory: 9–3 v Wolverhampton W, Division 2, 18 September 1965 – Godfrey; Jones, Williams; Walker, Knapp, Huxford; Paine (2), O'Brien (1), Melia, Chivers (4), Sydenham (2).

HONOURS

Football League: Division 1 – Runners-up 1983–84; Division 2 – Runners-up 1965–66, 1977–78; Division 3 (S) – Champions 1921–22; Division 3 – Champions 1959–60: Runners-up 1920–21.

FA Cup: Winners 1976; Runners-up 1900, 1902, 2003.

Football League Cup: Runners-up 1979.

Zenith Data Systems Cup: Runners-up 1992.

European Competitions: *European Fairs Cup:* 1969–70. *UEFA Cup:* 1971–72, 1981–82, 1982–83, 1984–85, 2003–04. *European Cup-Winners' Cup:* 1976–77.

SKY SPORTS FACT FILE

Terry Paine was ever present for Southampton in more seasons than any other player involved with the club – seven terms in total and consecutively from 1958–59 to 1960–61, then alternate seasons from 1962–63 until 1968–69.

Record Cup Victory: 7–1 v Ipswich T, FA Cup 3rd rd, 7 January 1961 – Reynolds; Davies, Traynor, Conner, Page, Huxford, Paine (1), O'Brien (3 incl. 1p), Reeves, Mulgrew (2), Penk (1).

Record Defeat: 0–8 v Tottenham H, Division 2, 28 March 1936. 0–8 v Everton, Division 1, 20 November 1971.

Most League Points (2 for a win): 61, Division 3 (S), 1921–22 and Division 3, 1959–60.

Most League Points (3 for a win): 77, Division 1, 1983–84.

Most League Goals: 112, Division 3 (S), 1957–58.

Highest League Scorer in Season: Derek Reeves, 39, Division 3, 1959–60.

Most League Goals in Total Aggregate: Mike Channon, 185, 1966–77, 1979–82.

Most League Goals in One Match: 5, Charlie Wayman v Leicester C, Division 2, 23 October 1948.

Most Capped Player: Peter Shilton, 49 (125), England.

Most League Appearances: Terry Paine, 713, 1956–74.

Youngest League Player: Theo Walcott, 16 years 143 days v Wolverhampton W, 6 August 2005.

Record Transfer Fee Received: Up to £10,000,000 from Arsenal for Theo Walcott, January 2006.

Record Transfer Fee Paid: £4,000,000 to Derby Co for Rory Delap, July 2001.

Football League Record: 1920 Original Member of Division 3; 1921–22 Division 3 (S); 1922–53 Division 2; 1953–58 Division 3 (S); 1958–60 Division 3; 1960–66 Division 2; 1966–74 Division 1; 1974–78 Division 2; 1978–92 Division 1; 1992–2005 FA Premier League; 2005– FL C.

LATEST SEQUENCES

Longest Sequence of League Wins: 6, 3.3.1992 – 4.4.1992.

Longest Sequence of League Defeats: 5, 16.8.1998 – 12.9.1998.

Longest Sequence of League Draws: 8, 29.8.2005 – 15.10.2005.

Longest Sequence of Unbeaten League Matches: 19, 5.9.1921 – 31.12.1921.

Longest Sequence Without a League Win: 20, 30.8.1969 – 27.12.1969.

Successive Scoring Runs: 28 from 10.2.2008.

Successive Non-scoring Runs: 5 from 1.9.1937.

MANAGERS

Cecil Knight 1894–95
(Secretary-Manager)
Charles Robson 1895–97
Er Arnfield 1897–1911
(Secretary-Manager)
(continued as Secretary)
George Swift 1911–12
Er Arnfield 1912–19
Jimmy McIntyre 1919–24
Arthur Chadwick 1925–31
George Kay 1931–36
George Gross 1936–37
Tom Parker 1937–43
J. R. Sarjantson stepped down from the board to act as Secretary-Manager 1943–47 with the next two listed being team Managers during this period
Arthur Dominy 1943–46
Bill Dodgin Snr 1946–49
Sid Cann 1949–51
George Roughton 1952–55
Ted Bates 1955–73
Lawrie McMenemy 1973–85
Chris Nicholl 1985–91
Ian Branfoot 1991–94
Alan Ball 1994–95
Dave Merrington 1995–96
Graeme Souness 1996–97
Dave Jones 1997–2000
Glenn Hoddle 2000–01
Stuart Gray 2001
Gordon Strachan 2001–04
Paul Sturrock 2004
Steve Wigley 2004
Harry Redknapp 2004–05
George Burley 2005–08
Nigel Pearson 2008
Jan Poortvliet June 2008–

TEN YEAR LEAGUE RECORD

		P	W	D	L	F	A	Pts	Pos
1998-99	PR Lge	38	11	8	19	37	64	41	17
1999-2000	PR Lge	38	12	8	18	45	62	44	15
2000-01	PR Lge	38	14	10	14	40	48	52	10
2001-02	PR Lge	38	12	9	17	46	54	45	11
2002-03	PR Lge	38	13	13	12	43	46	52	8
2003-04	PR Lge	38	12	11	15	44	45	47	12
2004-05	PR Lge	38	6	14	18	45	66	32	20
2005-06	FL C	46	13	19	14	49	50	58	12
2006-07	FL C	46	21	12	13	77	53	75	6
2007-08	FL C	46	13	15	18	56	72	54	20

DID YOU KNOW ?

Previously with the uniquely named club Nil Desperandum (never despair), full-back George Carter was also an Ordnance Survey Officer and posted to the Southampton area played and skippered the Saints, becoming the first to lead them in an FA Cup tie in October 1891.

SOUTHAMPTON 2007–08 LEAGUE RECORD

Match No.	Date	Venue	Opponents	Result	H/T Score	Lg. Pos.	Goalscorers	Attendance
1	Aug 11	H	Crystal Palace	L 1-4	1-2	—	Saganowski [45]	25,054
2	18	A	Norwich C	L 1-2	1-0	23	Jones [37]	24,004
3	25	H	Stoke C	W 3-2	1-1	21	Surman [36], Rasiak [71], Viafara [75]	20,300
4	Sept 1	A	QPR	W 3-0	2-0	11	Rasiak 2 [18, 45], Wright-Phillips [49]	15,560
5	16	A	Watford	L 2-3	1-1	19	Rasiak [45], Dyer [69]	15,915
6	19	H	Colchester U	D 1-1	0-0	—	Wright-Phillips [52]	18,773
7	22	H	Barnsley	L 2-3	1-2	19	Saganowski [45], Idiakez [89]	19,151
8	29	A	Sheffield U	W 2-1	2-1	14	Rasiak [19], Viafara [31]	24,561
9	Oct 2	A	Preston NE	L 1-5	1-1	—	Jones (og) [45]	10,279
10	6	H	WBA	W 3-2	2-1	14	John 2 [17, 64], Skacel [23]	21,967
11	21	H	Cardiff C	W 1-0	1-0	9	John [15]	20,796
12	24	A	Bristol C	L 1-2	0-2	—	McAllister (og) [54]	18,326
13	27	A	Burnley	W 3-2	2-1	10	Wright-Phillips [3], Euell [15], John [51]	10,944
14	Nov 3	H	Charlton Ath	L 0-1	0-0	12		23,363
15	6	H	Wolverhampton W	D 0-0	0-0	—		19,856
16	10	A	Sheffield W	L 0-5	0-1	15		19,442
17	24	H	Blackpool	W 1-0	1-0	12	John [35]	21,075
18	27	A	Ipswich T	L 0-2	0-1	—		19,791
19	Dec 1	A	Leicester C	W 2-1	1-1	13	John [32], Surman (pen) [56]	20,070
20	4	H	Sheffield W	D 0-0	0-0	—		17,981
21	8	H	Hull C	W 4-0	1-0	10	Wright-Phillips [43], John 3 [58, 76, 78]	18,125
22	15	A	Coventry C	D 1-1	0-1	11	Wright-Phillips [59]	19,143
23	22	H	Preston NE	L 0-1	0-0	13		23,267
24	26	A	Colchester U	D 1-1	1-0	13	Viafara [19]	6157
25	29	A	Barnsley	D 2-2	0-2	14	Wright-Phillips 2 [61, 70]	10,425
26	Jan 1	H	Watford	L 0-3	0-1	15		23,008
27	12	H	Scunthorpe U	W 1-0	1-0	13	Rasiak [25]	18,146
28	19	A	Plymouth Arg	D 1-1	1-0	13	Wright-Phillips [12]	14,676
29	29	H	Norwich C	L 0-1	0-1	—		18,004
30	Feb 2	A	Crystal Palace	D 1-1	0-0	14	John [84]	17,967
31	9	H	QPR	L 2-3	1-2	18	Powell [1], John [90]	22,505
32	12	A	Stoke C	L 2-3	0-3	—	John 2 [46, 54]	19,481
33	19	H	Plymouth Arg	L 0-2	0-2	—		17,806
34	23	A	Scunthorpe U	D 1-1	0-1	19	Vignal (pen) [88]	6035
35	Mar 1	H	Ipswich T	D 1-1	0-0	19	John [51]	23,299
36	4	A	Wolverhampton W	D 2-2	0-0	—	Vignal (pen) [75], Euell [90]	21,795
37	8	A	Blackpool	D 2-2	1-0	20	Vignal (pen) [31], John [63]	9050
38	11	H	Leicester C	W 1-0	0-0	—	John [76]	17,741
39	15	A	Hull C	L 0-5	0-1	19		16,829
40	22	H	Coventry C	D 0-0	0-0	19		22,014
41	29	A	Cardiff C	L 0-1	0-1	21		12,955
42	Apr 5	H	Bristol C	W 2-0	1-0	19	John [35], Euell [84]	22,890
43	12	A	Charlton Ath	D 1-1	1-0	19	McCarthy (og) [11]	26,206
44	19	H	Burnley	L 0-1	0-1	21		21,762
45	28	A	WBA	D 1-1	0-0	—	Lallana [77]	26,167
46	May 4	H	Sheffield U	W 3-2	1-1	20	Saganowski [42], John 2 [53, 69]	31,957

Final League Position: 20

GOALSCORERS

League (56): John 19, Wright-Phillips 8, Rasiak 6, Euell 3, Saganowski 3, Viafara 3, Vignal 3 (3 pens), Surman 2 (1 pen), Dyer 1, Idiakez 1, Jones 1, Lallana 1, Powell 1, Skacel 1, own goals 3.
Carling Cup (1): Rasiak 1.
FA Cup (4): Surman 2, Rasiak 1, Vignal 1.

Bialkowski B 1	Ostlund A 8 + 4	Vignal G 20	Bennett A 10	Makin C 5	Safri Y 37	Viafara J 30 + 10	Wright J 33 + 3	Rasiak G 13 + 10	Saganowski M 14 + 16	Surman A 35 + 5	Skacel R 13 + 3	Hammill A 12 + 13	Wright-Phillips B 27 + 12	Davis K 35	Thomas W 29 + 1	Dyer N 15 + 2	Jones K 1	Powell D 10	John S 35 + 5	Euell J 31 + 7	Idiakez I 14 + 7	Dailly C 11	Ifil P 11 + 1	Davies A 22 + 1	Lallana A — + 5	McGoldrick D 2 + 6	O'Halloran S — + 1	Licka M 10 + 2	Pearce I 1	Baseya C — + 1	Poke M 3 + 1	Gillett S — + 2	Pericard V 1 + 4	Wright R 7	Perry C 6	Lucketti C 4	Match No.
1	2	3^1	4	5	6	7^2	8	9	10^3	11	12	13	14																								1
				4	6	8	2	9^1	12	11^3	3	13	14	1	5	7^2	10																				2
	12				6	8	2	9	13	11	3^1		10^2	1	5	7		4																			3
		3		5	6	8	2	9^3	12	11^2			10^1	1	4	7			14	13																	4
	12	3		5	6	8	2	9^2		11^1			13	1	4	7			10^3	14																	5
	12			5	6	8	2	9	13	11^3	3^1	14	10^2	1	4	7																					6
		3			6	8	2^3	12	9^1	11		7	10^2	1	4				13		14	5															7
	2				6	8		9	12	11^2			10^1	1	4	7				13		5	3														8
	2^1				6	8^3	12	9	10^2	11				1	4	7			13	14		5	3														9
					6	8			10^2	12	3			1	4	7			9	13	11^1	5	2														10
	2^2		4		6	8			10^1		13		12	1		7			9	14	11^3	5	3														11
		3			6■	4		12		11^3	13		10	1		7			9^1	8^2	14	5	2														12
		3				4		12		13			10	1	6	7			9^1	8	11^2	5	2														13
		3^3				4		12		11^2		13	10^1	1	5	7			9		8	6	2	14													14
						4		9^2	13	12	11	14	10^3	1	6	7^1				8		5	2	3													15
					6	4^1			10^2	7	11		12	1	2				9	8	13	5		3													16
					6	12		13		11	3	14	10	1		7^3			9^2	8^1		5	2	4													17
					6	4	12	13	14	11^1	3	7	10	1					9^2	8^3			2	5													18
			3		6		4			11		12	10	1		7^1			9	8			2	5													19
			4		6	12	2		13	11	3	7^3	10^2	1					9	8				5^1	14												20
			4		6	12	2	13	14	11	3	7^1	10^3	1					9^2	8				5													21
			4		6	12	2		13	11	3	7^1	10^2	1					9	8				5													22
			4		6		2	12	13	11	3	7	10^2	1					9^1	8				5													23
			4		6	7^2	2	12		11		13	10^1	1	3				9	8				5													24
			3		6		2	10		11		7^3	12	1	5			4^2	9^1	8			13		14												25
			4		6	7	2	12		11^2		13	10	1	3				9^1	8				5													26
		3				12	2	9^2		11		7	10^3	1	4				13	8	6^1			5		14											27
	2^2	3					4	9^3		11		7^1	10	1	13			6	14	8	12			5													28
		3^3					2	9		7^2	11	12	6^1	1	4				10	8	13			5			14										29
					6^2		3		12	11		7^3	10^1	1	2			4	9	8	13			5		14											30
					6■	12	3		13	11		7^2	10^3	1	2^1			4	9	8				5	14												31
	2					7	11		10	3			12	1				6	9	8	4^2			5^1		13											32
		3				12	4		7	11		13	10^2	1	2			6^1	9	8^3	14			5													33
		3				7^3	8		10	11^2		13	12	1	2^1				9		4			5				14	6								34
		3			6	7	2		10^1					1	4				9^2		8			5		12		11		13							35
		3■			6	7	2		10^2					1^6	4				9	12	8^1			5		13		11			15						36
	12	3			6	7	2		10^2				13		4				9^3	8				5^1		14		11			1						37
	2	3			6	4			12	11^2		13			5				9^3	8						10^1		7			1	14					38
	2	11			6	4	12								3			5	9^1	8						10^3		7^2			1	13	14				39
		3			6	7	2						12		5			4	9	8								11					10^1	1			40
		3			6	7^1	2			13		11	12		5				9	8^2								10^3					14	1	4		41
		3^1			6	13	2			12			10						9^3	8	11^2							7					14	1	4	5	42
					6	13	2		12	3			10^1						9^3	8	11^2							7					14	1	4	5	43
					6	14	2		12	3			10^1			13			9	8	11^3							7^2						1	4	5	44
					6^2	7	2		10^3	3			12			13			9^1	8	11				14									1	4	5	45
					6	7	2		10^2	3								5	9■	8	11^1				13			12						1	4		46

FA Cup

Third Round	Leicester C	(h)	2-0
Fourth Round	Bury	(h)	2-0
Fifth Round	Bristol R	(a)	0-1

Carling Cup

First Round	Peterborough U	(a)	1-2

SOUTHEND UNITED FL Championship 1

FOUNDATION

The leading club in Southend around the turn of the century was Southend Athletic, but they were an amateur concern. Southend United was a more ambitious professional club when they were founded in 1906, employing Bob Jack as secretary-manager and immediately joining the Second Division of the Southern League.

Roots Hall Stadium, Victoria Avenue, Southend-on-Sea, Essex SS2 6NQ.

Telephone: (01702) 304 050.

Fax: (01702) 304 124.

Ticket Office: (08444) 770 077.

Website: www.southendunited.co.uk

Email: info@southend-united.co.uk

Ground Capacity: 12,168.

Record Attendance: 31,090 v Liverpool, FA Cup 3rd rd, 10 January 1979.

Pitch Measurements: 110yd × 76yd.

Chairman: Ronald Martin.

Chief Executive: Geoffrey King.

Secretary: Mrs Helen Norbury.

Manager: Stephen Tilson.

Assistant Manager: Paul Brush.

Physio: John Stannard.

Club Nickname: 'The Blues' or 'The Shrimpers'.

Colours: Navy blue.

Change Colours: Sky blue.

Year Formed: 1906.

Turned Professional: 1906. ***Ltd Co.:*** 1919.

Grounds: 1906, Roots Hall, Prittlewell; 1920, Kursaal; 1934, Southend Stadium; 1955, Roots Hall Football Ground.

First Football League Game: 28 August 1920, Division 3, v Brighton & HA (a) W 2–0 – Capper; Reid, Newton; Wileman, Henderson, Martin; Nicholls, Nuttall, Fairclough (2), Myers, Dorsett.

Record League Victory: 9–2 v Newport Co, Division 3 (S), 5 September 1936 – McKenzie; Nelson, Everest (1); Deacon, Turner, Carr; Bolan, Lane (1), Goddard (4), Dickinson (2), Oswald (1).

Record Cup Victory: 10–1 v Golders Green, FA Cup 1st rd, 24 November 1934 – Moore; Morfitt, Kelly; Mackay, Joe Wilson, Carr (1); Lane (1), Johnson (5), Cheesmuir (2), Deacon (1), Oswald. 10–1 v Brentwood, FA Cup 2nd rd, 7 December 1968 – Roberts; Bentley, Birks; McMillan (1) Beesley, Kurila; Clayton, Chisnall, Moore (4), Best (5), Hamilton. 10–1 v Aldershot, Leyland Daf Cup Prel rd, 6 November 1990 – Sansome; Austin, Powell, Cornwell, Prior (1), Tilson (3), Cawley, Butler, Ansah (1), Benjamin (1), Angell (4).

HONOURS

Football League: FL 1 – Champions 2005–06; Division 1 best season: 13th, 1994–95; Promoted from FL 2 2004–05 (play-offs); Division 3 – Runners-up 1990–91; Division 4 – Champions 1980–81; Runners-up 1971–72, 1977–78.

FA Cup: best season: old 3rd rd, 1921; 5th rd, 1926, 1952, 1976, 1993.

Football League Cup: Quarter final 2007.

LDV Vans Trophy: Runners-up 2004, 2005.

SKY SPORTS FACT FILE

Harry Johnson, the first Southend United player to score as many as five goals in an FA Cup tie during the record win over Golders Green, was the same player who later registered in the competition for Scunthorpe United before and after the Second World War.

Record Defeat: 1–9 v Brighton & HA, Division 3, 27 November 1965.

Most League Points (2 for a win): 67, Division 4, 1980–81.

Most League Points (3 for a win): 85, Division 3, 1990–91.

Most League Goals: 92, Division 3 (S), 1950–51.

Highest League Scorer in Season: Jim Shankly, 31, 1928–29; Sammy McCrory, 1957–58, both in Division 3 (S).

Most League Goals in Total Aggregate: Roy Hollis, 122, 1953–60.

Most League Goals in One Match: 5, Jim Shankly v Merthyr T, Division 3S, 1 March 1930.

Most Capped Player: George Mackenzie, 9, Eire.

Most League Appearances: Sandy Anderson, 452, 1950–63.

Youngest League Player: Phil O'Connor, 16 years 76 days v Lincoln C, 26 December 1969.

Record Transfer Fee Received: £4,200,000 from Nottingham F for Stan Collymore, June 1993.

Record Transfer Fee Paid: £750,000 to Crystal Palace for Stan Collymore, November 1992.

Football League Record: 1920 Original Member of Division 3; 1921–58 Division 3 (S); 1958–66 Division 3; 1966–72 Division 4; 1972–76 Division 3; 1976–78 Division 4; 1978–80 Division 3; 1980–81 Division 4; 1981–84 Division 3; 1984–87 Division 4; 1987–89 Division 3; 1989–90 Division 4; 1990–91 Division 3; 1991–92 Division 2; 1992–97 Division 1; 1997–98 Division 2; 1998–2004 Division 3; 2004–05 FL 2; 2005–06 FL 1; 2006–07 FL C; 2007– FL 1.

MANAGERS

Bob Jack 1906–10
George Molyneux 1910–11
O. M. Howard 1911–12
Joe Bradshaw 1912–19
Ned Liddell 1919–20
Tom Mather 1920–21
Ted Birnie 1921–34
David Jack 1934–40
Harry Warren 1946–56
Eddie Perry 1956–60
Frank Broome 1960
Ted Fenton 1961–65
Alvan Williams 1965–67
Ernie Shepherd 1967–69
Geoff Hudson 1969–70
Arthur Rowley 1970–76
Dave Smith 1976–83
Peter Morris 1983–84
Bobby Moore 1984–86
Dave Webb 1986–87
Dick Bate 1987
Paul Clark 1987–88
Dave Webb *(General Manager)* 1988–92
Colin Murphy 1992–93
Barry Fry 1993
Peter Taylor 1993–95
Steve Thompson 1995
Ronnie Whelan 1995–97
Alvin Martin 1997–99
Alan Little 1999–2000
David Webb 2000–01
Rob Newman 2001–03
Steve Wignall 2003–04
Steve Tilson May 2004–

LATEST SEQUENCES

Longest Sequence of League Wins: 8, 29.8.2005 – 9.10.2005.

Longest Sequence of League Defeats: 6, 29.8.1987 – 19.9.1987.

Longest Sequence of League Draws: 6, 30.1.1982 – 19.2.1982.

Longest Sequence of Unbeaten League Matches: 16, 20.2.1932 – 29.8.1932.

Longest Sequence Without a League Win: 17, 31.12.1983 – 14.4.1984.

Successive Scoring Runs: 24 from 23.3.1929.

Successive Non-scoring Runs: 6 from 28.10.1933.

TEN YEAR LEAGUE RECORD

		P	W	D	L	F	A	Pts	Pos
1998-99	Div 3	46	14	12	20	52	58	54	18
1999-2000	Div 3	46	15	11	20	53	61	56	16
2000-01	Div 3	46	15	18	13	55	53	63	11
2001-02	Div 3	46	15	13	18	51	54	58	12
2002-03	Div 3	46	17	3	26	47	59	54	17
2003-04	Div 3	46	14	12	20	51	63	54	17
2004-05	FL 2	46	22	12	12	65	46	78	4
2005-06	FL 1	46	23	13	10	72	43	82	1
2006-07	FL C	46	10	12	24	47	80	42	22
2007-08	FL 1	46	22	10	14	70	55	76	6

DID YOU KNOW ?

Legendary David Jack, scorer of the first FA Cup final goal at Wembley in 1923 for Bolton Wanderers, became the oldest debutant for Southend United when as the manager he played in the Cup against Crystal Palace on 28 November 1936 aged 37 years 235 days.

SOUTHEND UNITED 2007–08 LEAGUE RECORD

Match No.	Date	Venue	Opponents	Result	H/T Score	Lg. Pos.	Goalscorers	Attendance
1	Aug 11	H	Leyton Orient	L 1-2	1-1	—	Gower [24]	9828
2	18	A	Leeds U	L 1-4	0-1	23	Barrett [69]	24,036
3	25	H	Millwall	W 1-0	0-0	17	Bailey [55]	8758
4	Sept 1	A	Brighton & HA	L 2-3	1-0	19	McCormack [40], Bailey [78]	5652
5	8	H	Gillingham	W 3-0	2-0	12	Bailey [8], McCormack [44], Clarke L [59]	7348
6	15	A	Oldham Ath	W 1-0	1-0	7	Clarke L [28]	5151
7	22	H	Doncaster R	W 3-2	1-2	5	Barrett [25], McCormack [49], Clarke L (pen) [59]	8117
8	29	A	Port Vale	W 2-1	2-0	3	Clarke L [32], McCormack [45]	3969
9	Oct 2	A	Bristol R	D 1-1	0-1	—	Clarke L [90]	5762
10	6	H	Tranmere R	L 1-2	1-1	7	Barrett [43]	7619
11	13	H	Crewe Alex	W 3-0	1-0	5	Bailey [17], Hooper [63], Clarke L (pen) [82]	6927
12	20	A	Walsall	W 2-0	1-0	2	Clarke P [38], Clarke L [51]	5661
13	27	H	Carlisle U	L 0-1	0-0	5		9281
14	Nov 3	A	Northampton T	W 1-0	0-0	3	Barrett [65]	6646
15	6	A	Nottingham F	L 1-4	1-1	—	Gower [3]	26,094
16	17	H	Cheltenham T	D 2-2	0-2	5	Gower [50], Hammell [56]	7158
17	24	A	Luton T	L 0-1	0-0	8		6820
18	Dec 5	H	Huddersfield T	W 4-1	1-0	—	Clarke L [3], McCormack 2 [57, 90], Gower [84]	6844
19	8	H	Swindon T	W 2-1	1-1	6	Barrett [32], Gower [90]	7403
20	15	A	Swansea C	L 0-3	0-1	6		12,629
21	22	H	Oldham Ath	L 0-1	0-1	7		7388
22	26	A	Gillingham	D 1-1	0-0	8	Clarke P [54]	8268
23	29	A	Doncaster R	L 1-3	1-3	10	MacDonald [18]	7163
24	Jan 1	H	Bristol R	L 0-1	0-0	11		7664
25	12	H	Yeovil T	D 1-1	1-0	11	Bailey [20]	7352
26	19	A	Bournemouth	W 4-1	3-0	8	Gower [18], Francis [23], Black [44], Hooper [65]	5419
27	22	A	Hartlepool U	L 3-4	1-1	—	Hammell (pen) [30], Gower [83], Black [90]	3217
28	29	H	Leeds U	W 1-0	1-0	—	Barnard [41]	9819
29	Feb 2	A	Leyton Orient	D 2-2	1-0	9	Barnard [27], Clarke P [56]	6886
30	9	H	Hartlepool U	W 2-1	0-1	9	McCormack [61], Bailey [66]	7436
31	12	A	Millwall	L 1-2	1-1	—	Bailey [9]	7425
32	16	H	Bournemouth	W 2-1	1-1	8	Barnard [10], Walker [79]	7474
33	23	A	Yeovil T	W 3-0	2-0	7	Barnard [20], Clarke P [34], Gower [64]	4820
34	29	A	Cheltenham T	D 1-1	0-1	—	Bailey [74]	3859
35	Mar 8	H	Luton T	W 2-0	1-0	6	Bailey [37], Walker [90]	8241
36	11	H	Nottingham F	D 1-1	1-0	—	Robson-Kanu [20]	8376
37	15	A	Huddersfield T	W 2-1	1-0	5	Robson-Kanu [40], McCormack [90]	7823
38	21	H	Swansea C	D 1-1	1-1	—	Robson-Kanu [45]	9797
39	24	A	Swindon T	W 1-0	1-0	5	Francis [18]	6378
40	29	H	Walsall	W 1-0	0-0	4	Barnard [47]	8145
41	Apr 5	A	Crewe Alex	W 3-1	2-0	5	Barnard 2 [2, 80], Walker [19]	4895
42	8	H	Brighton & HA	W 2-0	2-0	—	Gower [24], Barrett [30]	8428
43	12	H	Northampton T	D 1-1	0-1	5	Barnard [51]	9286
44	19	A	Carlisle U	W 2-1	1-0	5	Mulgrew [7], Barnard [90]	9122
45	26	A	Tranmere R	L 0-1	0-0	5		5842
46	May 3	H	Port Vale	D 1-1	0-1	6	Walker [84]	9292

Final League Position: 6

GOALSCORERS

League (70): Bailey 9, Barnard 9, Gower 9, Clarke L 8 (2 pens), McCormack 8, Barrett 6, Clarke P 4, Walker 4, Robson-Kanu 3, Black 2, Francis 2, Hammell 2 (1 pen), Hooper 2, MacDonald 1, Mulgrew 1.
Carling Cup (7): Bradbury 3 (1 pen), Harrold 2 (1 pen), Barrett 1, MacDonald 1.
FA Cup (10): MacDonald 3, Morgan 3 (1 pen), Bailey 2, Francis 1, Harrold 1 (pen).
J Paint Trophy (2): Foran 1, McCormack 1.
Play-Offs (1): Bailey 1.

Flahavan D 26	Gilbert K 5	Wilson C 4 + 2	Maher K 18 + 1	Clarke P 45	Barrett A 45	Campbell-Ryce J 2	McCormack A 42	Harrold M 12 + 4	Hooper G 9 + 4	Gower M 40 + 2	MacDonald C 11 + 14	Black T 29 + 9	Bailey N 42 + 2	Bradbury L 1	Richards G 8 + 2	Odhiambo E 2 + 3	Collis S 20	Foran R — + 6	Clarke L 16	Hunt L 23 + 1	Hammell S 16	Moussa F 6 + 10	Francis S 24 + 3	Morgan D 6 + 2	Scannell D — + 9	Barnard L 11 + 4	Mulgrew C 18	Robson-Kanu 6 + 2	Revell A 5 + 3	Grant A — + 10	Walker J 14 + 1	*Match No.*
1	2	3	4	5	6	7	8■	9^{1}	10^{3}	11^{2}	12	13	14																			1
1	2^{3}	3		5	6	7	8	9		11^{2}	12	13	4	10^{1}	14																	2
1	2	3	4	5	6		8	9	12	11^{2}	10^{1}	13	7																			3
1	2	3	4	5	6		8	9		11^{1}	10^{2}	12	7			13																4
	2		4	5	3		8	9^{3}		12		11^{1}	7		6	14	1	13	10^{2}													5
		12	4	5	3		8	9				11^{1}	7		6■		1	13	10^{2}	2												6
			4	5	3		8^{2}	9^{1}			12	11	7		6		1	13	10	2												7
			4	5	3		8^{2}			11^{1}		12	7		6	10	1	13	9	2												8
			4	5	3		8^{1}	9^{2}		11		12	7		6	13	1		10	2												9
			4	5	3		8^{3}	12		11^{2}		13	7		6	9^{1}	1	14	10	2												10
		12		5	6		8		9	11^{2}		7^{3}	4				1	13	10	2	3^{1}	14										11
			12	5	6		8		9^{2}	11	13	7^{1}	4				1		10	2	3											12
				5	6		8	12	9^{2}	11^{1}	13	7	4				1		10	2	3											13
				5	6		8	12	9^{1}	11			4				1		10	2	3	7										14
				5	6		8^{2}	9^{1}	12	11			4				1		10■	2	3	7	13									15
			4	5	6		8	9		11	12						1			2	3	7^{1}		10								16
			4	5	3		8	9	10^{1}				7		6		1			2	11		12									17
			4	5	6		8			11	12		7				1		10	2	3			9^{1}								18
			4	5	6^{2}		8			11	12		7		13		1		10	2	3			9^{1}								19
			4	5			8^{1}			11	10		7■		6		1			2	3	12	13	9^{2}								20
			4	5	6		8■				9	11					1		10	2^{1}	3	12		7								21
			4	5	6					11	9^{1}	7	8				1		10	2	3			12								22
			4	5	6				12	11^{2}	9	7	8				1		10^{1}	3			2	13								23
			4	5	6		8		12	11^{1}	10	13	7				1			3			2	9^{2}								24
1				5	6		8	9■		11^{2}	10^{1}	12	4							2	3		7		13							25
1				5	6		8		10^{1}	11		9	4							2	3		7		12							26
1				5	6		8		10^{1}	11		9	4							7	3		2		12							27
1				5	6		8			11	10^{2}	7^{1}	4								3	12	2		13	9						28
1				5	6		8			11	12	7^{2}	4										2			9^{1}	3	13	10			29
1				5	6		8			11^{2}	12	7	4										2		14	9^{1}	3	13^{3}	10			30
1				5	6		8			11^{1}	10^{2}	7	4									12	2		13■		3		9			31
1					6		8			11^{1}	10^{2}	7	4							5			2			9	3			12	13	32
1				5	6		8^{2}			11	12	7^{3}	4									13	2			9^{1}	3			14	10	33
1				5	6		8	12		11		7^{1}	4										2			9	3				10	34
1				5	6					11		9	4							14		8^{2}	2		12		3	7^{1}		13^{3}	10	35
1				5	6					11		7	4									8	2				3	9^{1}		12	10	36
1				5	6		8			11		7^{1}	4									12	2			14	3^{2}	9^{3}		13	10	37
1				5	6		8			11		7^{2}	4										2			12	3	9		13	10^{1}	38
1				5	6		8			11		7^{2}	4										2			12	3	9^{1}		13	10	39
1				5	6		8			11^{1}		7^{3}	4									12	2		13	9^{2}	3			14	10	40
1				5	6		8			11^{2}	12	7^{3}	4									14	2			9	3			13	10^{1}	41
1				5	6		8			11	12	7^{2}	4										2			9^{3}	3		14	13	10^{1}	42
1				5	6		8			11		7^{1}	4										2			9	3		12		10	43
1				5	6		8			11		7^{1}	4										2			9	3		12		10	44
1				5	6		8			11^{2}	12	7^{3}	4									13	2		14		3		9^{1}		10	45
1				5	6		8^{2}		9^{3}	12			13									4	2			14	3	11^{1}	10		7	46

FA Cup

First Round	Rochdale	(h)	2-1
Second Round	Oxford U	(a)	0-0
		(h)	3-0
Third Round	Dagenham & R	(h)	5-2
Fourth Round	Barnsley	(h)	0-1

J Paint Trophy

First Round	Dagenham & R	(h)	2-2

Carling Cup

First Round	Cheltenham T	(h)	4-1
Second Round	Watford	(h)	2-0
Third Round	Blackpool	(a)	1-2

Play-Offs

Semi-Final	Doncaster R	(h)	0-0
		(a)	1-5

STOCKPORT COUNTY FL Championship 1

FOUNDATION

Formed at a meeting held at Wellington Road South by members of Wycliffe Congregational Chapel in 1883, they called themselves Heaton Norris Rovers until changing to Stockport County in 1890, a year before joining the Football Combination.

Edgeley Park, Hardcastle Road, Edgeley, Stockport, Cheshire SK3 9DD.

Telephone: (0161) 286 8888 (ext 257).

Fax: (0161) 286 8927.

Ticket Office: 0845 688 5799.

Website: www.stockportcounty.com

Email: rachael.moss@stockportcounty.com

Ground Capacity: 10,812.

Record Attendance: 27,833 v Liverpool, FA Cup 5th rd, 11 February 1950.

Pitch Measurements: 104m × 66m.

Chairman: Martin Reid.

Managing Director: Mark Maguire.

Acting Secretary: Rachael Moss.

Manager: Jim Gannon.

Assistant Manager: Peter Ward.

Physio: Rodger Wylde.

Colours: Reflex blue shirts, reflex blue shorts, white stockings.

Change Colours: White shirts, white shorts, white stockings.

Year Formed: 1883.

Turned Professional: 1891.

Ltd Co.: 1908.

Previous Names: 1883, Heaton Norris Rovers; 1888, Heaton Norris; 1890, Stockport County.

Club Nicknames: 'County' or 'Hatters'.

Grounds: 1883 Heaton Norris Recreation Ground; 1884 Heaton Norris Wanderers Cricket Ground; 1885 Chorlton's Farm, Chorlton's Lane; 1886 Heaton Norris Cricket Ground; 1887 Wilkes' Field, Belmont Street; 1889 Nursery Inn, Green Lane; 1902 Edgeley Park.

First Football League Game: 1 September 1900, Division 2, v Leicester Fosse (a) D 2–2 – Moores; Earp, Wainwright; Pickford, Limond, Harvey; Stansfield, Smith (1), Patterson, Foster, Betteley (1).

Record League Victory: 13–0 v Halifax T, Division 3 (N), 6 January 1934 – McGann; Vincent (1p), Jenkinson; Robinson, Stevens, Len Jones; Foulkes (1), Hill (3), Lythgoe (2), Stevenson (2), Downes (4).

Record Cup Victory: 5–0 v Lincoln C, FA Cup 1st rd, 11 November 1995 – Edwards; Connelly, Todd, Bennett, Flynn, Gannon (Dinning), Beaumont, Oliver, Ware, Eckhardt (3), Armstrong (1) (Mike), Chalk, (1 og).

Record Defeat: 1–8 v Chesterfield, Division 2, 19 April 1902.

HONOURS

Football League: Division 1 best season: 8th, 1997–98; Division 2 – Runners-up 1996–97; Division 3 (N) – Champions 1921–22, 1936–37; Runners-up 1928–29, 1929-30, 1996–97; Promoted from FL 2 – 2007–08 (play-offs); Division 4 – Champions 1966–67; Runners-up 1990–91.

FA Cup: best season: 5th rd, 1935, 1950, 2001.

Football League Cup: Semi-final 1997.

Autoglass Trophy: Runners-up 1992, 1993.

SKY SPORTS FACT FILE

Jimmy Molyneux had two spells with Stockport County either side of the First World War, the second signing in 1925. In between he was wounded at Ypres but managed a full recovery. He also kept goal in the annual event against blind players of St Dunstans.

Most League Points (2 for a win): 64, Division 4, 1966–67.

Most League Points (3 for a win): 85, Division 2, 1993–94.

Most League Goals: 115, Division 3 (N), 1933–34.

Highest League Scorer in Season: Alf Lythgoe, 46, Division 3 (N), 1933–34.

Most League Goals in Total Aggregate: Jack Connor, 132, 1951–56.

Most League Goals in One Match: 5, Joe Smith v Southport, Division 3N, 7 January 1928; 5, Joe Smith v Lincoln C, Division 3N, 15 September 1928; 5, Frank Newton v Nelson, Division 3N, 21 September 1929; 5, Alf Lythgoe v Southport, Division 3N, 25 August 1934; 5, Billy McNaughton v Mansfield T, Division 3N, 14 December 1935; 5, Jack Connor v Workington, Division 3N, 8 November 1952; 5, Jack Connor v Carlisle U, Division 3N, 7 April 1956.

Most Capped Player: Jarkko Wiss, 9 (43), Finland.

Most League Appearances: Andy Thorpe, 489, 1978–86, 1988–92.

Youngest League Player: Paul Turnbull, 16 years 97 days v Wrexham, 30 April 2005.

Record Transfer Fee Received: £1,600,000 from Middlesbrough for Alun Armstrong, February 1998.

Record Transfer Fee Paid: £800,000 to Nottingham F for Ian Moore, July 1998.

Football League Record: 1900 Elected to Division 2; 1904 Failed re-election; 1905–21 Division 2; 1921–22 Division 3 (N); 1922–26 Division 2; 1926–37 Division 3 (N); 1937–38 Division 2; 1938–58 Division 3 (N); 1958–59 Division 3; 1959–67 Division 4; 1967–70 Division 3; 1970–91 Division 4; 1991–92 Division 3; 1992–97 Division 2; 1997–2002 Division 1; 2002–04 Division 2; 2004–05 FL 1; 2005–08 FL 2; 2008– FL 1.

LATEST SEQUENCES

Longest Sequence of League Wins: 9, 13.1.2007 – 3.3.2007.

Longest Sequence of League Defeats: 10, 24.11.2001 – 13.01.2002.

Longest Sequence of League Draws: 7, 17.3.1989 – 14.4.1989.

Longest Sequence of Unbeaten League Matches: 18, 28.1.1933 – 28.8.1933.

Longest Sequence Without a League Win: 19, 28.12.1999 – 22.4.2000.

Successive Scoring Runs: 27 from 20.10.2007.

Successive Non-scoring Runs: 7 from 10.3.1923.

MANAGERS

Fred Stewart 1894–1911
Harry Lewis 1911–14
David Ashworth 1914–19
Albert Williams 1919–24
Fred Scotchbrook 1924–26
Lincoln Hyde 1926–31
Andrew Wilson 1932–33
Fred Westgarth 1934–36
Bob Kelly 1936–38
George Hunt 1938–39
Bob Marshall 1939–49
Andy Beattie 1949–52
Dick Duckworth 1952–56
Billy Moir 1956–60
Reg Flewin 1960–63
Trevor Porteous 1963–65
Bert Trautmann *(General Manager)* 1965–66
Eddie Quigley *(Team Manager)* 1965–66
Jimmy Meadows 1966–69
Wally Galbraith 1969–70
Matt Woods 1970–71
Brian Doyle 1972–74
Jimmy Meadows 1974–75
Roy Chapman 1975–76
Eddie Quigley 1976–77
Alan Thompson 1977–78
Mike Summerbee 1978–79
Jimmy McGuigan 1979–82
Eric Webster 1982–85
Colin Murphy 1985
Les Chapman 1985–86
Jimmy Melia 1986
Colin Murphy 1986–87
Asa Hartford 1987–89
Danny Bergara 1989–95
Dave Jones 1995–97
Gary Megson 1997–99
Andy Kilner 1999–2001
Carlton Palmer 2001–03
Sammy McIlroy 2003–04
Chris Turner 2004–05
Jim Gannon January 2006–

TEN YEAR LEAGUE RECORD

		P	W	D	L	F	A	Pts	Pos
1998-99	Div 1	46	12	17	17	49	60	53	16
1999-2000	Div 1	46	13	15	18	55	67	54	17
2000-01	Div 1	46	11	18	17	58	65	51	19
2001-02	Div 1	46	6	8	32	42	102	26	24
2002-03	Div 2	46	15	10	21	65	70	55	14
2003-04	Div 2	46	11	19	16	62	70	52	19
2004-05	FL 1	46	6	8	32	49	98	26	24
2005-06	FL 2	46	11	19	16	57	78	52	22
2006-07	FL 2	46	21	8	17	65	54	71	8
2007-08	FL 2	46	24	10	12	72	54	82	4

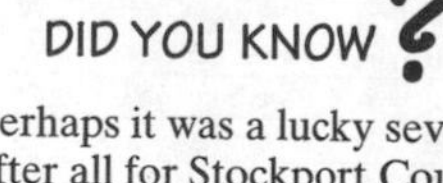

Perhaps it was a lucky seven after all for Stockport County when they equalled a club record of seven away wins in succession on 1 March 2008. Promotion followed via the play-off final, the first year all three best-placed divisional winners had achieved it.

STOCKPORT COUNTY 2007–08 LEAGUE RECORD

Match No.	Date	Venue	Opponents	Result		H/T Score	Lg. Pos.	Goalscorers	Attendance
1	Aug 11	H	Dagenham & R	W	1-0	0-0	—	Dickinson 85	5577
2	18	A	Chesterfield	D	1-1	0-0	7	Dickinson 64	4600
3	25	H	Rotherham U	D	2-2	1-0	8	Elding 13, Griffin 67	5764
4	Sept 1	A	Mansfield T	L	2-4	2-4	11	Proudlock 2 35, 42	2747
5	8	H	Shrewsbury T	D	1-1	1-1	14	Proudlock 32	5473
6	15	A	Grimsby T	D	1-1	1-0	14	McNeil 45	3726
7	22	H	Wrexham	W	2-1	1-1	11	Elding 29, Blizzard 65	5513
8	29	A	Brentford	W	3-1	2-0	8	Elding 3 (2 pens) 7 (p), 44 (p), 61	4449
9	Oct 2	A	Morecambe	L	0-2	0-1	—		2871
10	6	H	Barnet	L	2-4	1-1	12	Elding (pen) 25, Dickinson 90	4751
11	14	A	Darlington	L	0-4	0-2	16		3841
12	20	H	Chester C	L	1-2	1-0	17	Taylor 45	5566
13	27	A	Milton Keynes D	W	2-0	0-0	15	Elding 74, Pilkington 90	8290
14	Nov 3	H	Peterborough U	L	1-2	1-2	17	McNeil 22	5042
15	6	A	Rochdale	W	2-1	1-0	—	Dickinson 2 28, 53	2915
16	17	H	Hereford U	L	2-3	0-1	15	Elding (pen) 61, Brown (og) 83	5103
17	24	A	Bradford C	D	1-1	0-0	16	Poole 90	13,837
18	Dec 4	H	Lincoln C	L	1-3	0-0	—	Dickinson 84	5260
19	8	H	Wycombe W	W	6-0	2-0	14	Proudlock 3 34, 60, 74, Dickinson 37, Christon (og) 64, Martin (og) 78	4477
20	15	A	Macclesfield T	W	2-0	0-0	12	Dickinson 63, Proudlock 90	3585
21	22	H	Grimsby T	D	1-1	0-1	12	Rose 83	4711
22	26	A	Shrewsbury T	L	1-3	0-1	14	Pilkington 72	7707
23	29	A	Wrexham	W	1-0	0-0	13	Elding 59	4287
24	Jan 1	H	Morecambe	W	2-1	2-0	12	Elding 9, Dickinson 41	5489
25	5	A	Notts Co	W	2-1	2-1	10	Elding 13, Dickinson 35	4120
26	12	H	Accrington S	W	2-0	2-0	9	Rose 3, Elding 45	4714
27	29	H	Chesterfield	D	2-2	1-1	—	Dickinson 34, Elding 63	5105
28	Feb 2	A	Dagenham & R	W	1-0	1-0	10	McSweeney 6	1834
29	5	A	Bury	W	3-2	1-1	—	Pilkington 2 7, 58, Taylor 52	3142
30	9	H	Notts Co	D	1-1	1-1	9	Rowe 22	5849
31	12	A	Rotherham U	W	4-1	1-1	—	Rowe 3 8, 49, 63, Pilkington 56	4004
32	16	H	Bury	L	1-2	1-0	7	Randolph (og) 21	5704
33	23	A	Accrington S	W	2-0	1-0	7	Dickinson 2 33, 63	2576
34	Mar 1	A	Hereford U	W	1-0	0-0	7	Dickinson (pen) 54	3526
35	8	H	Bradford C	W	2-1	0-0	6	Pilkington 69, Rose 79	5763
36	11	H	Rochdale	W	2-0	1-0	—	Dickinson 2 10, 56	5530
37	15	A	Lincoln C	W	1-0	0-0	5	Poole 68	4544
38	21	H	Macclesfield T	W	2-0	1-0	—	Taylor 2 10, 46	7824
39	24	A	Wycombe W	D	0-0	0-0	5-		5380
40	Apr 5	H	Darlington	W	1-0	1-0	5	Dickinson 37	6460
41	9	H	Mansfield T	W	2-1	1-1	—	Muggleton (og) 44, Dickinson (pen) 74	4982
42	12	A	Peterborough U	W	1-0	0-0	5	Rowe 59	10,023
43	19	H	Milton Keynes D	L	2-3	1-1	5	Dickinson 30, Proudlock 58	8838
44	26	A	Barnet	L	1-2	0-0	5	Rowe 51	3074
45	29	A	Chester C	D	0-0	0-0	—		3060
46	May 3	H	Brentford	W	1-0	0-0	4	Havern 49	6284

Final League Position: 4

GOALSCORERS

League (72): Dickinson 19 (2 pens), Elding 13 (4 pens), Proudlock 8, Pilkington 6, Rowe 6, Taylor 4, Rose 3, McNeil 2, Poole 2, Blizzard 1, Griffin 1, Havern 1, McSweeney 1, own goals 5.
Carling Cup (4): Blizzard 1, Elding 1, McNeil 1, Proudlock 1.
FA Cup (2): McNeil 2.
J Paint Trophy (5): Elding 1, McNeil 1, Pilkington 1, Proudlock 1, Tierney 1.
Play-Offs (5): Dickinson 2, Gleeson 1, Pilkington 1, own goal 1.

Logan C 34	Tierney P 15 + 1	Smith James 24 + 2	Taylor J 40 + 2	Williams A 26	Owen G 35 + 1	Griffin A 19 + 9	Dicker G 29 + 1	Elding A 18 + 7	McNeil M 17	Poole D 13 + 9	Dickinson L 34 + 6	Blizzard D 22 + 5	Proudlock A 18 + 15	Briggs K 5 + 8	Tansey G 5 + 8	Pilkington A 23 + 6	Rowe T 17 + 7	Thompson L 3	Bowler M 4 + 1	Raynes M 20 + 7	Turnbull P 12 + 7	Rose M 25 + 3	Nowland A 4	Tunnicliffe J 1 + 4	McSweeney L 5 + 6	McNulty J 11	Ruddy J 12	Logan S 6 + 1	Smith Johann — + 2	Gleeson S 4 + 2	Lowe R 4	Havern G 1	Vincent J — + 1	Morgan-Smith A — + 1	Match No.
1	2	3	4	5	6	7^{1}	8^{2}	9	10	11^{3}	12	13	14																						1
1	2	3	4	5	6	7^{1}	8^{3}	9	10	11^{2}	12	13	14																						2
1	3	2	4	5	6	12	8^{2}	9	10	7^{1}	11^{3}	13	14																						3
1	2		4^{1}	5	6	12	13	9	10^{2}			8	7	3^{3}	14	11																			4
1	2	3	12	5	6	7^{3}	8	14	10			4^{2}	9	13		11^{1}																			5
1	2	3	4	5	6		8^{2}	12	10	11^{3}			9^{1}	13	14	7																			6
1	3	2	4	5	6	7^{2}		9	10	12		8	11^{1}				13																		7
1	2	3	4	5	6	7^{2}		9	10			8	11^{1}	12			13																		8
1	2	3^{2}	4	5	6	7		9	10		12	8^{3}	11^{1}	13	14																				9
1	3		4	5	6	7^{1}		9^{2}	10		13	8	12	2^{3}	14			11																	10
1	3		4	5		12			10		9	8	13			11^{3}		7^{2}	2	6^{1}	14														11
1	3		4	5		11	8^{1}	13	10		9^{2}		14		12	7			2	6^{3}															12
1	11	2	4	5		3		9	10		12				7^{3}	13		8^{2}		6^{1}	14														13
1	3	2	4	5^{1}	6	7		9	10		12	8^{3}	11^{2}		13						14														14
1	3	2	4		5	7		9^{1}	10		8^{2}			12		11^{3}			13		6	14													15
1			4			7^{3}		9	10	12	8		11^{1}		13		14		2^{2}	5		3	6												16
1			4^{3}		6	12		9	10	7	8			11		13	5		2^{2}		14	3^{1}													17
1			4		6	11		9^{1}		7	10		12■	13	8^{2}		14			5	2	3^{3}													18
1			4		6	11^{3}		12		7^{2}	10		9^{1}	13			14			5	2	3	8												19
1			2^{1}		6	11				7	9		10	12						5	8	3	4												20
1					6	11^{2}		12		7	9		10	2^{1}		13				5	8	3	4												21
1	13				6	3	4	12		7^{3}	9^{1}		10^{2}	2		11				5■	8			14											22
1			2		6	12	4	13		11^{1}	9		10^{2}			7				5	8	3													23
1			2		6	3	4	9^{2}		13	10		12		11	7^{1}				5	8														24
1		2	4		6^{2}		8	9		7^{1}	10					11^{3}				5	12	3		13	14										25
1			4			11^{2}	7	9		12	10	13								2^{3}	8	6		14	3^{1}	5									26
1			4	2	6^{3}			9		12	8		10^{1}				13			5	7	14			11^{2}	3									27
1			2	5		14	4			13	9		10^{2}		7^{1}	8				12		3			11^{3}	6									28
1		2	4	5		12	8				9^{2}		14			7^{1}	10			13		3			11^{3}	6									29
1		2	4	5			8				9		12		11^{2}	7^{1}	10			6		3			13										30
1		2^{2}	8	5			11				9	13			12	7^{1}	10			6^{3}		3			14	4									31
1■		12^{2}	2	5	14		8				9	4^{1}	11				10				7	3			13	6^{3}									32
			4	5	6	12	8				9^{2}	7	10^{3}			13	11^{1}				14	3					1	2							33
		12	4	5	6	13	8				10	11				7^{3}	9^{2}					3			14		1	2^{1}							34
			4^{1}	5	6		8				10	11				7	9			12		3					1	2							35
			4	5	6		8^{1}			13	10	7				11^{2}	9			12		3					1	2							36
		2	4	5	6		8^{1}			14	9^{2}	7	12			11^{3}	10			13		3					1								37
		2	4^{1}	5	6		8				10	11				7^{3}	9^{2}			12		3					1	13	14						38
		2	4^{2}		6		8			12	10	11				7^{1}	9			5		3					1		13						39
		2	12		6		8				10	4				11^{1}	13			5		3					1			7	9^{2}				40
		2	4^{1}		6		8				10	11	12			13	9			5		3					1			7^{2}					41
		2	4		6		8				10	11				12	9			5^{1}		13				3^{2}	1	7							42
		3	4		6		8				10	11	13			7^{2}	9									5	1	2^{1}		12					43
		2			6		8				10	11	12				4					3^{2}		13	14	5	1			7^{3}	9^{1}				44
1		3	2^{2}		6		8				10^{1}	4	12			7	11				13					5				14	9^{3}				45
1										7			10							12	4^{1}	3		5	11^{3}	6				8	9	2^{2}	13	14	46

FA Cup

First Round	Staines T	(h)	1-1
		(a)	1-1

Play-Offs

Semi-Final	Wycombe W	(a)	1-1
		(h)	1-0
Final *(at Wembley)*	Rochdale		3-2

Carling Cup

First Round	Tranmere R	(h)	1-0
Second Round	Charlton Ath	(a)	3-4

J Paint Trophy

Second Round	Macclesfield T	(a)	1-0
Quarter-Final	Carlisle U	(a)	3-0
Northern Semi-Final	Grimsby T	(h)	1-2

STOKE CITY

FA Premiership

FOUNDATION

The date of the formation of this club has long been in doubt. The year 1863 was claimed, but more recent research by Wade Martin has uncovered nothing earlier than 1868, when a couple of Old Carthusians, who were apprentices at the local works of the old North Staffordshire Railway Company, met with some others from that works, to form Stoke Ramblers. It should also be noted that the old Stoke club went bankrupt in 1908 when a new club was formed.

Britannia Stadium, Stanley Matthews Way, Stoke-on-Trent, Staffs ST4 4EG.

Telephone: (0871) 663 2008.

Fax: (01782) 592 299.

Ticket Office: (0871) 663 2007.

Website: www.stokecityfc.com

Email: info@stokecityfc.com

Ground Capacity: 28,218.

Record Attendance: 51,380 v Arsenal, Division 1, 29 March 1937 (at Victoria Ground).

Pitch Measurements: 100m × 64m.

Chairman: Peter Coates.

Chief Executive: Tony Scholes.

Football Administrator: Eddie Harrison.

Manager: Tony Pulis.

Assistant Manager: Dave Kemp.

Physio: Dave Watson.

Colours: Red and white striped shirts, white shorts, white stockings.

Change Colours: Yellow shirts, royal blue shorts, yellow stockings.

Year Formed: 1863* (*see Foundation*). ***Turned Professional:*** 1885. ***Ltd Co.:*** 1908.

Previous Names: 1868, Stoke Ramblers; 1870, Stoke; 1925, Stoke City.

Club Nickname: 'The Potters'.

Grounds: 1875, Sweeting's Field; 1878, Victoria Ground (previously known as the Athletic Club Ground); 1997, Britannia Stadium.

First Football League Game: 8 September 1888, Football League, v WBA (h) L 0–2 – Rowley; Clare, Underwood; Ramsey, Shutt, Smith; Sayer, McSkimming, Staton, Edge, Tunnicliffe.

Record League Victory: 10–3 v WBA, Division 1, 4 February 1937 – Doug Westland; Brigham, Harbot; Tutin, Turner (1p), Kirton; Matthews, Antonio (2), Freddie Steele (5), Jimmy Westland, Johnson (2).

Record Cup Victory: 7–1 v Burnley, FA Cup 2nd rd (replay), 20 February 1896 – Clawley; Clare, Eccles; Turner, Grewe, Robertson; Willie Maxwell, Dickson, A. Maxwell (3), Hyslop (4), Schofield.

HONOURS

Football League: Division 1 best season: 4th, 1935–36, 1946–47; Promoted from FL C – 2007–08 (runners-up); Division 2 – Champions 1932–33, 1962–63, 1992–93; Runners-up 1921–22; Promoted 1978–79 (3rd), Promoted from Division 2 (play-offs) 2001–02; Division 3 (N) – Champions 1926–27.

FA Cup: Semi-finals 1899, 1971, 1972.

Football League Cup: Winners 1972.

Autoglass Trophy: Winners: 1992.

Auto Windscreens Shield: Winners: 2000.

European Competitions: *UEFA Cup:* 1972–73, 1974–75.

SKY SPORTS FACT FILE

Between 4 March 1911 and 29 April Stoke played 19 matches winning twelve in the Southern League Division Two and Birmingham League. Twenty-four players were called upon during the period in question but only Sam Baddeley and Billy Smith were ever present.

Record Defeat: 0–10 v Preston NE, Division 1, 14 September 1889.

Most League Points (2 for a win): 63, Division 3 (N), 1926–27.

Most League Points (3 for a win): 93, Division 2, 1992–93.

Most League Goals: 92, Division 3 (N), 1926–27.

Highest League Scorer in Season: Freddie Steele, 33, Division 1, 1936–37.

Most League Goals in Total Aggregate: Freddie Steele, 142, 1934–49.

Most League Goals in One Match: 7, Neville Coleman v Lincoln C, Division 2, 23 February 1957.

Most Capped Player: Gordon Banks, 36 (73), England.

Most League Appearances: Eric Skeels, 506, 1958–76.

Youngest League Player: Peter Bullock, 16 years 163 days v Swansea C, 19 April 1958.

Record Transfer Fee Received: £2,750,000 from QPR for Mike Sheron, July 1997.

Record Transfer Fee Paid: £1,500,000 to Crystal Palace for Leon Cort, January 2008 and £1,500,000 to Manchester U for Ryan Shawcross, January 2008.

Football League Record: 1888 Founder Member of Football League; 1890 Not re-elected; 1891 Re-elected; relegated in 1907, and after one year in Division 2, resigned for financial reasons; 1919 re-elected to Division 2; 1922–23 Division 1; 1923–26 Division 2; 1926–27 Division 3 (N); 1927–33 Division 2; 1933–53 Division 1; 1953–63 Division 2; 1963–77 Division 1; 1977–79 Division 2; 1979–85 Division 1; 1985–90 Division 2; 1990–92 Division 3; 1992–93 Division 2; 1993–98 Division 1; 1998–2002 Division 2; 2002–04 Division 1; 2004–08 FL C; 2008– FA Premier League.

MANAGERS

Tom Slaney 1874–83
(Secretary-Manager)
Walter Cox 1883–84
(Secretary-Manager)
Harry Lockett 1884–90
Joseph Bradshaw 1890–92
Arthur Reeves 1892–95
William Rowley 1895–97
H. D. Austerberry 1897–1908
A. J. Barker 1908–14
Peter Hodge 1914–15
Joe Schofield 1915–19
Arthur Shallcross 1919–23
John 'Jock' Rutherford 1923
Tom Mather 1923–35
Bob McGrory 1935–52
Frank Taylor 1952–60
Tony Waddington 1960–77
George Eastham 1977–78
Alan A'Court 1978
Alan Durban 1978–81
Richie Barker 1981–83
Bill Asprey 1984–85
Mick Mills 1985–89
Alan Ball 1989–91
Lou Macari 1991–93
Joe Jordan 1993–94
Lou Macari 1994–97
Chic Bates 1997–98
Chris Kamara 1998
Brian Little 1998–99
Gary Megson 1999
Gudjon Thordarson 1999–2002
Steve Cotterill 2002
Tony Pulis 2002–05
Johan Boskamp 2005–06
Tony Pulis June 2006–

LATEST SEQUENCES

Longest Sequence of League Wins: 8, 30.3.1895 – 21.9.1895.

Longest Sequence of League Defeats: 11, 6.4.1985 – 17.8.1985.

Longest Sequence of League Draws: 5, 21.3.1987 – 11.4.1987.

Longest Sequence of Unbeaten League Matches: 25, 5.9.1992 – 20.2.1993.

Longest Sequence Without a League Win: 17, 22.4.1989 – 14.10.1989.

Successive Scoring Runs: 21 from 24.12.1921.

Successive Non-scoring Runs: 8 from 29.12.1984.

TEN YEAR LEAGUE RECORD

		P	W	D	L	F	A	Pts	Pos
1998-99	Div 2	46	21	6	19	59	63	69	8
1999-2000	Div 2	46	23	13	10	68	42	82	6
2000-01	Div 2	46	21	14	11	74	49	77	5
2001-02	Div 2	46	23	11	12	67	40	80	5
2002-03	Div 1	46	12	14	20	45	69	50	21
2003-04	Div 1	46	18	12	16	58	55	66	11
2004-05	FL C	46	17	10	19	36	38	61	12
2005-06	FL C	46	17	7	22	54	63	58	13
2006-07	FL C	46	19	16	11	62	41	73	8
2007-08	FL C	46	21	16	9	69	55	79	2

DID YOU KNOW ?

In 1954–55 Stoke City were concerned in a long drawn out third round FA Cup tie against Bury which began at Gigg Lane 1–1, abandoned in a snowstorm after 112 minutes at 1–1, followed by 3–3 and 2–2 drawn affairs before Stoke won 3–2 at Old Trafford.

STOKE CITY 2007–08 LEAGUE RECORD

Match No.	Date	Venue	Opponents	Result		H/T Score	Lg. Pos.	Goalscorers	Attendance
1	Aug 11	A	Cardiff C	W	1-0	1-0	—	Shawcross 27	18,840
2	18	H	Charlton Ath	W	2-1	0-0	1	Fuller 57, Parkin 78	12,649
3	25	A	Southampton	L	2-3	1-1	4	Fuller 10, Parkin 82	20,300
4	Sept 1	H	Wolverhampton W	D	0-0	0-0	8		17,135
5	15	A	Hull C	D	1-1	1-0	7	Delap 44	19,642
6	18	H	Barnsley	D	0-0	0-0	—		13,071
7	22	H	Plymouth Arg	W	3-2	1-0	5	Seip (og) 10, Lawrence 66, Fuller 73	12,533
8	29	A	Leicester C	D	1-1	1-0	5	Fuller 15	23,654
9	Oct 3	A	WBA	D	1-1	1-0	—	Shawcross 27	20,048
10	6	H	Colchester U	W	2-1	1-0	5	Shawcross 8, Lawrence 73	12,395
11	20	H	Sheffield W	L	2-4	2-2	8	Fuller 2 12, 41	14,019
12	23	A	Crystal Palace	W	3-1	0-0	—	Cresswell 2 49, 59, Shawcross 74	14,237
13	27	A	Bristol C	L	0-1	0-1	6		15,012
14	Nov 3	H	Coventry C	L	1-3	0-0	9	Lawrence (pen) 72	13,448
15	6	A	Scunthorpe U	W	3-2	1-1	—	Cresswell 26, Hayes (og) 88, Lawrence 90	5521
16	10	H	Sheffield U	L	0-1	0-1	9		12,158
17	24	A	Burnley	D	0-0	0-0	10		11,758
18	27	H	QPR	W	3-1	2-0	—	Cresswell 5, Lawrence 19, Cort 77	11,147
19	Dec 1	H	Norwich C	W	2-1	0-1	7	Cort 46, Cresswell 89	19,285
20	4	A	Sheffield U	W	3-0	3-0	—	Cresswell 2, Beattie (og) 7, Shawcross 19	23,378
21	9	H	Watford	D	0-0	0-0	5		15,516
22	15	A	Blackpool	W	3-2	2-1	4	Fuller 2 37, 61, Cort 41	9123
23	22	H	WBA	W	3-1	2-0	4	Fuller 3 5, 38, 66	18,420
24	26	A	Barnsley	D	3-3	1-1	3	Lawrence 3 (2 pens) 31 (p), 84, 90 (p)	12,398
25	29	A	Plymouth Arg	D	2-2	1-1	4	Cresswell 8, Shawcross 57	13,692
26	Jan 1	H	Hull C	D	1-1	1-0	4	Cort 33	15,788
27	12	A	Ipswich T	D	1-1	1-1	4	Fuller 33	20,346
28	19	H	Preston NE	W	3-1	2-0	4	Cort 2 16, 72, Cresswell 28	15,011
29	29	A	Charlton Ath	L	0-1	0-0	—		22,108
30	Feb 2	H	Cardiff C	W	2-1	1-0	4	Johnson (og) 39, Fuller (pen) 57	15,045
31	9	A	Wolverhampton W	W	4-2	1-1	4	Delap 4, Lawrence 49, Cort 74, Fuller 90	25,373
32	12	H	Southampton	W	3-2	3-0	—	Powell (og) 27, Shawcross 35, Sidibe 44	19,481
33	15	H	Scunthorpe U	W	3-2	0-2	—	Lawrence 2 53, 67, Cresswell 63	20,979
34	23	H	Ipswich T	W	1-0	1-0	1	Lawrence 42	23,563
35	26	A	Preston NE	L	0-2	0-2	—		10,347
36	Mar 2	A	QPR	L	0-3	0-2	2		13,398
37	8	H	Burnley	D	1-1	0-1	2	Lawrence (pen) 90	18,432
38	11	A	Norwich C	W	1-0	0-0	—	Sidibe 58	23,471
39	15	A	Watford	D	0-0	0-0	1		18,338
40	22	H	Blackpool	D	1-1	0-1	1	Cort 47	20,019
41	29	A	Sheffield W	D	1-1	1-0	2	Cresswell 21	21,857
42	Apr 7	H	Crystal Palace	L	1-2	0-2	—	Whelan 85	15,756
43	12	A	Coventry C	W	2-1	0-1	1	Fuller (pen) 55, Lawrence 79	20,249
44	19	H	Bristol C	W	2-1	2-0	2	Sidibe 2 14, 36	24,475
45	26	A	Colchester U	W	1-0	1-0	1	Cresswell 45	6300
46	May 4	H	Leicester C	D	0-0	0-0	2		26,609

Final League Position: 2

GOALSCORERS

League (69): Fuller 15 (2 pens), Lawrence 14 (4 pens), Cresswell 11, Cort 8, Shawcross 7, Sidibe 4, Delap 2, Parkin 2, Whelan 1, own goals 5.
Carling Cup (2): Cresswell 1, Shawcross 1.
FA Cup (1): Lawrence 1.

Simonsen S 35 + 1	Wright S 14 + 2	Dickinson C 19 + 8	Delap R 44	Shawcross R 39 + 2	Higginbotham D 1	Lawrence L 40 + 1	Matteo D 14	Sidibe M 33 + 2	Fuller R 39 + 3	Cresswell R 42 + 1	Eustace J 20 + 6	Craddock J 4	Buxton L — + 4	Parkin J 4 + 25	Wilkinson A 16 + 7	Hill C 4 + 1	Pulis A — + 1	Zakuani G 11 + 8	Sweeney P — + 5	Pericard V 2 + 3	Cort L 33	Pugh D 27 + 3	Phillips D — + 2	Hoult R 1	Griffin A 15	Diao S 8 + 3	Whelan G 13 + 1	Gallagher P 2 + 5	Nash C 10	Riggott C 9	Bothroyd J 1 + 3	Ameobi S 3 + 3	Pearson S 3 + 1	Match No.
1	2	3	4	5	6	7	8	9	10^1	11	12																							1
1	2^2	3	4	5		7^1	8	9	10^3	11	12	6	13	14																				2
1			4	5		7^3	8^2	9^1	10	11	13	6		12	2	3	14																	3
1		3	4	6		7^1	8	9^2	10	11	13			12		5		2																4
1			4	5		7^2	8	9	10^1	11	13	3		12		6		2																5
1	2	3^2	4	5		7^3	8	12	10	11		6		9^1				13	14															6
1	2		4	5		7	8	9^1	10	11^3				12	13	6^2		3	14															7
1	2		4^1	5		7	8		10	11	12			9	3			6																8
1	2	12		5		7	8	9^2	10	11	4			13	3			6^1																9
1	2	12	4	5		7^3	8	9^2	10	11	6			13	3^1				14															10
1			4	5		7	8		10	11	6			9^1	3			2	12															11
1		3	4	5		7	8		10^1	9^2	11			12	2	13		6																12
1	12	3	4	5		7^3	8		10		11			13	2^1			6	14	9^2														13
1	2^2	12	4	5		7			10	9	8			13	3						6	11^1												14
1	12	3	4	5		7			10	9	8							2^1			6	11												15
1	2^3		4	6				9^1	10	11	8			12	3^2					13	5	7	14											16
1	2		4	5			6	9		11	8			12						10^1	3	7												17
1	2^2		4	6		7		9^1	10^3	11	8			12	13						5	3	14											18
1	2^2		4	6		7		9^1	10	11	8			12	13						5	3												19
1		12	4^1	6		7		9^2	10	11	8			13	3^3			14			5	2												20
1	2^2	3	4			7		9^1	10	11			13	12				5			6	8												21
1		12	4	6		7		9^2	10^1	11	8			13	2						5	3												22
1		12	4	6		7		9^1	10^2	11	8			13	2						5	3												23
1			4	6		7		9^1	10	11	8			12	2						5	3												24
15			4	6		7		9^1	10	11	8			12^6	2^2			13			5	3		1■										25
1	2^3	12	4	6		7		9^1		11	8			10^2				14		13	5	3												26
1		3^1	4	6		7			10	9	8			12	2^2			13			5	11												27
1		3	4^1	6		7^3			10^2	9	8			12						13	5	11			2	14								28
1		3^1	4	6		7			10	9	8			12							5	11			2									29
1			4	6		7		9^1	10	11											5	3			2	8	12							30
1		12	4	6		7^1		9	13									2			5	3				8	11	10^2						31
1			4	6		7^1		9	10									12			5	3			2	8	11							32
1			4	6		7		9	10^2	12								13			5	3			2	8^1	11							33
1		3	4	6		7		9^1	10	11											5				2	12	8							34
1			4	6		7		9^1	10	11				12	13						5^2	3			2		8^3	14						35
1				6		7^2		9^1	10	11			13		12						5	3			2■	8^3	4	14						36
			4			7		9^2	10	11				12							5	3			2	8^1		13	1	6				37
		3	4	12		7		9^3	13	10											5^1	11			2	8^2		14	1	6				38
		11^2	4	6					10	3											5^3	13			2	12	7	14	1	8	9^1			39
			4					9		10					13^3			12			5^1	3			2	8^2	7	11	1	6	14			40
		3	4			7				10											5	12			2		8		1	6	13	9^1	11^2	41
			4					9^1	12	11											5	3			2		7		1	6	13	10	8^2	42
		3	4	12		13		14	10	7											5	11			2^1				1	6		9^3	8^2	43
		3	4	6		7^1		9^3	10	11^2					12						5						8		1	2		14	13	44
		3	4	6		7		9^1	10	11											5						8		1	2		12		45
		3	4	6		7^2		9^3	10	11			12		2^1						5	13					8		1			14		46

FA Cup
Third Round Newcastle U (h) 0-0
(a) 1-4

Carling Cup
First Round Rochdale (a) 2-2

SUNDERLAND FA Premiership

FOUNDATION

A Scottish schoolmaster named James Allan, working at Hendon Board School, took the initiative in the foundation of Sunderland in 1879 when they were formed as The Sunderland and District Teachers' Association FC at a meeting in the Adults School, Norfolk Street. Due to financial difficulties, they quickly allowed members from outside the teaching profession and so became Sunderland AFC in October 1880.

Stadium of Light, Sunderland, Tyne and Wear SR5 1SU.

Telephone: (0191) 551 5000.

Fax: (0191) 551 5123.

Ticket Office: 0845 671 1973.

Website: www.safc.com

Email: enquiries@safc.com

Ground Capacity: 49,000.

Record Attendance: Stadium of Light: 48,353 v Liverpool, FA Premier League, 13 April 2002. FA Premier League figure (46,062). Roker Park: 75,118 v Derby Co, FA Cup 6th rd replay, 8 March 1933.

Pitch Measurements: 105m × 68m.

Chairman: Niall Quinn.

Vice-chairman: John Hays.

Chief Executive: Peter Walker.

Club Secretary: Margaret Byrne.

Manager: Roy Keane.

Head Coach: Tony Loughlan.

First Team Coach: Ricky Sbragia.

Head of Sports Therapy: Pete Friar.

Colours: Red and white striped shirts, black shorts, black and red stockings.

Change Colours: Dark navy and deep royal blue striped shirts, dark navy shorts, dark navy and deep royal blue stockings.

Year Formed: 1879. ***Turned Professional:*** 1886. ***Ltd Co.:*** 1906.

Club Nickname: Black Cats.

Previous Name: 1879, Sunderland and District Teacher's AFC; 1880, Sunderland.

Grounds: 1879, Blue House Field, Hendon; 1882, Groves Field, Ashbrooke; 1883, Horatio Street; 1884, Abbs Field, Fulwell; 1886, Newcastle Road; 1898, Roker Park; 1997, Stadium of Light.

First Football League Game: 13 September 1890, Football League, v Burnley (h) L 2–3 – Kirtley; Porteous, Oliver; Wilson, Auld, Gibson; Spence (1), Miller, Campbell (1), Scott, D. Hannah.

Record League Victory: 9–1 v Newcastle U (a), Division 1, 5 December 1908 – Roose; Forster, Melton; Daykin, Thomson, Low; Mordue (1), Hogg (3), Brown, Holley (3), Bridgett (2).

HONOURS

Football League: FL C – Champions 2004–05, 2006–07; Division 1 – Champions 1891–92, 1892–93, 1894–95, 1901–02, 1912–13, 1935–36, 1995–96, 1998–99; Runners-up 1893–94, 1897–98, 1900–01, 1922–23, 1934–35; Division 2 – Champions 1975–76; Runners-up 1963–64, 1979–80; 1989–90 (play-offs). Division 3 – Champions 1987–88.

FA Cup: Winners 1937, 1973; Runners-up 1913, 1992.

Football League Cup: Runners-up 1985.

European Competitions: *European Cup-Winners' Cup:* 1973–74.

SKY SPORTS FACT FILE

Amateur centre-forward Harry Poulter picked up from Shiney Row Swifts by Sunderland played just three first team games for the Roker Park club, all FA Cup ties, and scored twice in a replay at Southampton to earn them a 4–2 win. Ex-Royal Navy he later went to Exeter City.

Record Cup Victory: 11–1 v Fairfield, FA Cup 1st rd, 2 February 1895 – Doig; McNeill, Johnston; Dunlop, McCreadie (1), Wilson; Gillespie (1), Millar (5), Campbell, Hannah (3), Scott (1).

Record Defeat: 0–8 v Sheff Wed, Division 1, 26 December 1911. 0–8 v West Ham U, Division 1, 19 October 1968. 0–8 v Watford, Division 1, 25 September 1982.

Most League Points (2 for a win): 61, Division 2, 1963–64.

Most League Points (3 for a win): 105, Division 1, 1998–99 (Football League Record).

Most League Goals: 109, Division 1, 1935–36.

Highest League Scorer in Season: Dave Halliday, 43, Division 1, 1928–29.

Most League Goals in Total Aggregate: Charlie Buchan, 209, 1911–25.

Most League Goals in One Match: 5, Charlie Buchan v Liverpool, Division 1, 7 December 1919; 5, Bobby Gurney v Bolton W, Division 1, 7 December 1935; 5, Dominic Sharkey v Norwich C, Division 2, 20 February 1962.

Most Capped Player: Charlie Hurley, 38 (40), Republic of Ireland.

Most League Appearances: Jim Montgomery, 537, 1962–77.

Youngest League Player: Derek Forster, 15 years 184 days v Leicester C, 22 August 1964.

Record Transfer Fee Received: £5,500,000 from Leeds U for Michael Bridges, July 1999.

MANAGERS

Tom Watson 1888–96
Bob Campbell 1896–99
Alex Mackie 1899–1905
Bob Kyle 1905–28
Johnny Cochrane 1928–39
Bill Murray 1939–57
Alan Brown 1957–64
George Hardwick 1964–65
Ian McColl 1965–68
Alan Brown 1968–72
Bob Stokoe 1972–76
Jimmy Adamson 1976–78
Ken Knighton 1979–81
Alan Durban 1981–84
Len Ashurst 1984–85
Lawrie McMenemy 1985–87
Denis Smith 1987–91
Malcolm Crosby 1992–93
Terry Butcher 1993
Mick Buxton 1993–95
Peter Reid 1995–2002
Howard Wilkinson 2002–03
Mick McCarthy 2003–06
Niall Quinn 2006
Roy Keane August 2006–

Record Transfer Fee Paid: £9,000,000 to Hearts for Craig Gordon, August 2007.

Football League Record: 1890 Elected to Division 1; 1958–64 Division 2; 1964–70 Division 1; 1970–76 Division 2; 1976–77 Division 1; 1977–80 Division 2; 1980–85 Division 1; 1985–87 Division 2; 1987–88 Division 3; 1988–90 Division 2; 1990–91 Division 1; 1991–92 Division 2; 1992–96 Division 1; 1996–97 FA Premier League; 1997–99 Division 1; 1999–2003 FA Premier League; 2003–04 Division 1; 2004–05 FL C; 2005–06 FA Premier League; 2006–07 FL C; 2007– FA Premier League.

LATEST SEQUENCES

Longest Sequence of League Wins: 13, 14.11.1891 – 2.4.1892.

Longest Sequence of League Defeats: 17, 18.1.2003 – 16.8.2003.

Longest Sequence of League Draws: 6, 26.3.1949 – 19.4.1949.

Longest Sequence of Unbeaten League Matches: 19, 3.5.1998 – 14.11.1998.

Longest Sequence Without a League Win: 22, 21.12.2002 – 16.8.2003.

Successive Scoring Runs: 29 from 8.11.1997.

Successive Non-scoring Runs: 10 from 27.11.1976.

TEN YEAR LEAGUE RECORD

		P	W	D	L	F	A	Pts	Pos
1998-99	Div 1	46	31	12	3	91	28	105	1
1999-2000	PR Lge	38	16	10	12	57	56	58	7
2000-01	PR Lge	38	15	12	11	46	41	57	7
2001-02	PR Lge	38	10	10	18	29	51	40	17
2002-03	PR Lge	38	4	7	27	21	65	19	20
2003-04	Div 1	46	22	13	11	62	45	79	3
2004-05	FL C	46	29	7	10	76	41	94	1
2005-06	PR Lge	38	3	6	29	26	69	15	20
2006-07	FL C	46	27	7	12	76	47	88	1
2007-08	PR Lge	38	11	6	21	36	59	39	15

DID YOU KNOW ?

Sunderland and Aston Villa became the first clubs to play against each other 100 times in the Football League. They met at Roker Park on 1 January 1953 in a 2–2 draw. That same season also saw the installation of floodlights at the ground.

SUNDERLAND 2007–08 LEAGUE RECORD

Match No.	Date	Venue	Opponents	Result		H/T Score	Lg. Pos.	Goalscorers	Attendance
1	Aug 11	H	Tottenham H	W	1-0	0-0	—	Chopra [90]	43,967
2	15	A	Birmingham C	D	2-2	0-1	—	Chopra [75], John [90]	24,898
3	18	A	Wigan Ath	L	0-3	0-1	11		18,639
4	25	H	Liverpool	L	0-2	0-1	16		45,645
5	Sept 1	A	Manchester U	L	0-1	0-0	17		75,648
6	15	H	Reading	W	2-1	1-0	14	Jones [29], Wallace [47]	39,272
7	22	A	Middlesbrough	D	2-2	1-1	15	Leadbitter [2], Miller [89]	30,675
8	29	H	Blackburn R	L	1-2	0-0	15	Leadbitter [90]	41,252
9	Oct 7	A	Arsenal	L	2-3	1-2	16	Wallace [25], Jones [48]	60,098
10	21	A	West Ham U	L	1-3	0-1	16	Jones [52]	34,913
11	27	H	Fulham	D	1-1	0-1	15	Jones [86]	39,392
12	Nov 5	A	Manchester C	L	0-1	0-0	—		40,038
13	10	H	Newcastle U	D	1-1	0-0	16	Higginbotham [52]	47,701
14	24	A	Everton	L	1-7	1-3	18	Yorke [45]	38,594
15	Dec 1	H	Derby Co	W	1-0	0-0	15	Stokes [90]	42,380
16	8	A	Chelsea	L	0-2	0-1	18		41,707
17	15	H	Aston Villa	D	1-1	1-0	17	Higginbotham [10]	43,248
18	22	A	Reading	L	1-2	0-0	18	Chopra (pen) [82]	24,082
19	26	H	Manchester U	L	0-4	0-3	19		47,360
20	29	H	Bolton W	W	3-1	2-1	17	Richardson K [13], Jones [32], Murphy [90]	42,058
21	Jan 2	A	Blackburn R	L	0-1	0-0	—		23,212
22	13	H	Portsmouth	W	2-0	2-0	22	Richardson K 2 [33, 44]	37,369
23	19	A	Tottenham H	L	0-2	0-1	18		36,070
24	29	H	Birmingham C	W	2-0	1-0	—	Murphy [15], Prica [65]	37,674
25	Feb 2	A	Liverpool	L	0-3	0-0	16		43,244
26	9	H	Wigan Ath	W	2-0	1-0	14	Etuhu [42], Murphy [75]	43,600
27	23	A	Portsmouth	L	0-1	0-0	15		20,139
28	Mar 1	A	Derby Co	D	0-0	0-0	15		33,058
29	9	H	Everton	L	0-1	0-0	16		42,595
30	15	H	Chelsea	L	0-1	0-1	16		44,679
31	22	A	Aston Villa	W	1-0	0-0	16	Chopra [83]	42,640
32	29	H	West Ham U	W	2-1	1-1	14	Jones [29], Reid [90]	45,690
33	Apr 5	A	Fulham	W	3-1	1-0	13	Collins [45], Chopra [54], Jones [76]	25,053
34	12	H	Manchester C	L	1-2	0-0	14	Whitehead [82]	46,797
35	20	A	Newcastle U	L	0-2	0-2	15		52,305
36	26	H	Middlesbrough	W	3-2	2-1	13	Higginbotham [6], Chopra [45], Pogatetz (og) [90]	45,059
37	May 3	A	Bolton W	L	0-2	0-1	15		25,053
38	11	H	Arsenal	L	0-1	0-1	15		47,802

Final League Position: 15

GOALSCORERS

League (36): Jones 7, Chopra 6 (1 pen), Higginbotham 3, Murphy 3, Richardson K 3, Leadbitter 2, Wallace 2, Collins 1, Etuhu 1, John 1, Miller 1, Prica 1, Reid 1, Stokes 1, Whitehead 1, Yorke 1, own goal 1.
Carling Cup (0).
FA Cup (0).

Gordon C 34	Whitehead D 27	Wallace R 18 + 3	Yorke D 17 + 3	Nosworthy N 29	McShane P 20 + 1	Edwards C 11 + 2	Etuhu D 18 + 2	Murphy D 20 + 8	Stokes A 8 + 12	Richardson K 15 + 2	Collins D 32 + 4	Miller L 16 + 8	Chopra M 21 + 12	Halford G 8	O'Donovan R 4 + 13	John S — + 1	Anderson R — + 1	Connolly D 1 + 2	Leadbitter G 17 + 14	Higginbotham D 21	Jones K 33	Harte I 3 + 5	Cole A 3 + 4	Ward D 3	Waghorn M 1 + 2	Evans J 15	Bardsley P 11	Prica R — + 6	Reid A 11 + 2	Fulop M 1	*Match No.*
1	2	3	4[2]	5	6	7	8	9	10[3]	11[1]	12	13	14																		1
1	4[3]	11		5	6	7	8				2	14	9	3[1]	12	13		10[2]													2
1		3	4[1]	5	6[3]		8	7	10[2]	11	12	13	9	2			14														3
1		3	4[3]	5	6		8	9[2]	12	11[1]		7	10	2				13	14												4
1		11[3]	4	2	5		8[1]	13	14		3	12	10						7	6	9[2]										5
1		11[2]	4	5	2		8	12	13		3	14	10[3]						7	6	9[1]										6
1		11[3]	4[2]		5		8[1]		13		3	12	10	2	14				7	6	9										7
1		11[2]	4[1]	5	2			12			3	8	10[3]		14			13	7	6	9										8
1		11[1]	4[3]	5	2■		12		13		3	8	10[2]						7	6	9	14									9
1		11[1]		5			8		12		3[3]	4	13	2	10[2]				7	6	9	14									10
1		11[3]		5			8[2]	12	13		3	4	10[1]	2■					7	6	9	14									11
1		12		2			8	9[1]	7[2]		6	4	13						11	5	10	3									12
1		11[2]		5[1]	2	7	8		13		12		10						4	6	9	3									13
1	2	12	4[2]		5	7	8[1]				13		10[3]						11	6	9	3	14								14
	4	11			5	7[3]			14		3	12	13	2					8[1]	6	9		10[2]	1							15
	4	11			5		8	12	13		3	10■		2					7[2]	6	9[1]			1							16
	2	11[3]	4		5		8[2]	7	10[1]		3		12						13	6	9		14	1							17
1	2	12	4		5		13	11[1]	14		3		10[3]						7	6	9		8[2]								18
1	2	11[1]	4[2]		5		8			13	3		10[3]		14				12	6	9				7						19
1	2				5		8	12		7[3]	3	4	10[2]		14				13	6	9		11[1]								20
1	2	11[2]	4■		5			9		7[3]	3	8							12	6	10[1]		13		14						21
1	2		4	5	12			9	7[2]	11	3	8			14				13		10[3]					6[1]					22
1	2		8	5	4[2]			11	10[1]		3	7	12								9		13			6					23
1	7		4[2]	5				9	11[1]		3	8			12						10					6	2	13			24
1	7			5				9		11[1]	3	4	8[3]		13						10				14	6	2	12[2]			25
1	7			5			8[1]	9			3		11[3]		4[2]				12		10					6	2	13	14		26
1	7		12	5			8	9[2]			3		14						4[1]		10					6	2	13	11[3]		27
1	4			5				9[2]	13	11			7						12	3	10					6	2		8[1]		28
1	8			5				9[3]	11[2]	7	3		14						4[1]		10					6	2	12	13		29
1	8		12	5		7[2]					3				4[1]				11[3]		9	14				6	2	13	10		30
1	4		12	5		7[2]		9[1]		11	3		14		10[3]				13							6	2		8		31
1	4			5		12		7[3]		11[1]	3		10[2]		14				13		9					6	2		8		32
1	4			5		7[3]		10[1]		11[2]	3		14		12				13		9					6	2		8		33
1	4			5		12		10[1]		11[2]	3		7[3]		14				13		9					6	2		8		34
1	4			5	2[2]	7[1]		10[3]		12	3	11	14							6	9	13							8		35
1	2			5		7[2]		12		11	3	4	10[1]						13	6	9								8		36
1	7			2[1]				12		11	3	4[2]	10[3]		14				13	5	9					6			8		37
	2	11	4[2]	5		7[1]					3	12	13		14				8		9[3]					6			10	1	38

FA Cup				**Carling Cup**			
Third Round	Wigan Ath	(h)	0-3	Second Round	Luton T	(a)	0-3

SWANSEA CITY FL Championship

FOUNDATION

The earliest Association Football in Wales was played in the Northern part of the country and no international took place in the South until 1894, when a local paper still thought it necessary to publish an outline of the rules and an illustration of the pitch markings. There had been an earlier Swansea club, but this has no connection with Swansea Town (now City) formed at a public meeting in June 1912.

Liberty Stadium, Landore, Swansea SA1 2FA.

Telephone: (01792) 616 600.

Fax: (01792) 616 606.

Ticket Office: (0870) 040 0004.

Website: www.swanseacity.net

Email: info@swanseacityfc.co.uk

Ground Capacity: 20,520.

Record Attendance: 32,796 v Arsenal, FA Cup 4th rd, 17 February 1968 (at Vetch Field).

Pitch Measurements: 115yd × 74yd.

Chairman: Huw Jenkins.

Vice-chairman: Leigh Dineen.

General Manager: Alun Cowie.

Secretary: Jackie Rockey.

Manager: Roberto Martinez.

Assistant Manager: Graeme Jones.

Physio: Richard Evans.

Colours: All white.

Change Colours: Flint grey and navy.

Year Formed: 1912. ***Turned Professional:*** 1912.

Ltd Co.: 1912.

Previous Name: 1912, Swansea Town; 1970, Swansea City.

Club Nicknames: 'The Swans', 'The Jacks'.

Grounds: 1912, Vetch Field; 2005, Liberty Stadium.

First Football League Game: 28 August 1920, Division 3, v Portsmouth (a) L 0–3 – Crumley; Robson, Evans; Smith, Holdsworth, Williams; Hole, I. Jones, Edmundson, Rigsby, Spottiswood.

Record League Victory: 8–0 v Hartlepool U, Division 4, 1 April 1978 – Barber; Evans, Bartley, Lally (1) (Morris), May, Bruton, Kevin Moore, Robbie James (3 incl. 1p), Curtis (3), Toshack (1), Chappell.

Record Cup Victory: 12–0 v Sliema W (Malta), ECWC 1st rd 1st leg, 15 September 1982 – Davies; Marustik, Hadziabdic (1), Irwin (1), Kennedy, Rajkovic (1), Loveridge (2) (Leighton James), Robbie James, Charles (2), Stevenson (1), Latchford (1) (Walsh (3)).

HONOURS

Football League: Championship 2 – promoted 2004–05 (3rd); Division 1 best season: 6th, 1981–82; FL 1 – Champions 2007–08; Division 2 – Promoted 1980–81 (3rd); Division 3 (S) – Champions 1924–25, 1948–49; Division 3 – Champions 1999–2000; Promoted 1978–79 (3rd); Division 4 – Promoted 1969–70 (3rd), 1977–78 (3rd), 1987–88 (play-offs).

FA Cup: Semi-finals 1926, 1964.

Football League Cup: best season: 4th rd, 1965, 1977.

Welsh Cup: Winners 11 times; Runners-up 8 times.

Autoglass Trophy: Winners 1994, 2006.

Football League Trophy: Winners 2006.

European Competitions: *European Cup-Winners' Cup:* 1961–62, 1966–67, 1981–82, 1982–83, 1983–84, 1989–90, 1991–92.

SKY SPORTS FACT FILE

Not obvious from bare statistics alone, Frank Lampard actually made his League debut on loan to Swansea City secured by caretaker manager Bobby Smith on 6 October 1995. He made his first appearance the following day against Bradford City.

Record Defeat: 0–8 v Liverpool, FA Cup 3rd rd, 9 January 1990. 0–8 v Monaco, ECWC, 1st rd 2nd leg, 1 October 1991.

Most League Points (2 for a win): 62, Division 3 (S), 1948–49.

Most League Points (3 for a win): 85, Division 3, 1999–2000.

Most League Goals: 90, Division 2, 1956–57.

Highest League Scorer in Season: Cyril Pearce, 35, Division 2, 1931–32.

Most League Goals in Total Aggregate: Ivor Allchurch, 166, 1949–58, 1965–68.

Most League Goals in One Match: 5, Jack Fowler v Charlton Ath, Division 3S, 27 December 1924.

Most Capped Player: Ivor Allchurch, 42 (68), Wales.

Most League Appearances: Wilfred Milne, 585, 1919–37.

Youngest League Player: Nigel Dalling, 15 years 289 days v Southport, 6 December 1974.

Record Transfer Fee Received: £1,000,000 from Bristol C for Lee Trundle, July 2007.

Record Transfer Fee Paid: £340,000 to Liverpool for Colin Irwin, August 1981.

Football League Record: 1920 Original Member of Division 3; 1921–25 Division 3 (S); 1925–47 Division 2; 1947–49 Division 3 (S); 1949–65 Division 2; 1965–67 Division 3; 1967–70 Division 4; 1970–73 Division 3; 1973–78 Division 4; 1978–79 Division 3; 1979–81 Division 2; 1981–83 Division 1; 1983–84 Division 2; 1984–86 Division 3; 1986–88 Division 4; 1988–92 Division 3; 1992–96 Division 2; 1996–2000 Division 3; 2000–01 Division 2; 2001–04 Division 3; 2004–05 FL 2; 2005–08 FL 1; 2008– FL C.

MANAGERS

Walter Whittaker 1912–14
William Bartlett 1914–15
Joe Bradshaw 1919–26
Jimmy Thomson 1927–31
Neil Harris 1934–39
Haydn Green 1939–47
Bill McCandless 1947–55
Ron Burgess 1955–58
Trevor Morris 1958–65
Glyn Davies 1965–66
Billy Lucas 1967–69
Roy Bentley 1969–72
Harry Gregg 1972–75
Harry Griffiths 1975–77
John Toshack 1978–83 *(resigned October re-appointed in December) 1983–84*
Colin Appleton 1984
John Bond 1984–85
Tommy Hutchison 1985–86
Terry Yorath 1986–89
Ian Evans 1989–90
Terry Yorath 1990–91
Frank Burrows 1991–95
Bobby Smith 1995
Kevin Cullis 1996
Jan Molby 1996–97
Micky Adams 1997
Alan Cork 1997–98
John Hollins 1998–2001
Colin Addison 2001–02
Nick Cusack 2002
Brian Flynn 2002–04
Kenny Jackett 2004–07
Roberto Martinez February 2007–

LATEST SEQUENCES

Longest Sequence of League Wins: 9, 27.11.1999 – 22.01.2000.

Longest Sequence of League Defeats: 9, 26.1.1991 – 19.3.1991.

Longest Sequence of League Draws: 5, 5.1.1993 – 5.2.1993.

Longest Sequence of Unbeaten League Matches: 19, 19.10.1970 – 9.3.1971.

Longest Sequence Without a League Win: 15, 25.3.1989 – 2.9.1989.

Successive Scoring Runs: 27 from 28.8.1947.

Successive Non-scoring Runs: 6 from 6.2.1996.

TEN YEAR LEAGUE RECORD

		P	W	D	L	F	A	Pts	Pos
1998-99	Div 3	46	19	14	13	56	48	71	7
1999-2000	Div 3	46	24	13	9	51	30	85	1
2000-01	Div 2	46	8	13	25	47	73	37	23
2001-02	Div 3	46	13	12	21	53	77	51	20
2002-03	Div 3	46	12	13	21	48	65	49	21
2003-04	Div 3	46	15	14	17	58	61	59	10
2004-05	FL 2	46	24	8	14	62	43	80	3
2005-06	FL 1	46	18	17	11	78	55	71	6
2006-07	FL 1	46	20	12	14	69	53	72	7
2007-08	FL 1	46	27	11	8	82	42	92	1

DID YOU KNOW ?

Jason Scotland was born in Trinidad but was signed by the Welsh club Swansea City from the Scottish club St Johnstone at the start of 2007–08. Moreover his first competitive goal for the club was scored on an English ground at Oldham on 11 August.

SWANSEA CITY 2007–08 LEAGUE RECORD

Match No.	*Date*	*Venue*	*Opponents*	*Result*		*H/T Score*	*Lg. Pos.*	*Goalscorers*	*Attendance*
1	Aug 11	A	Oldham Ath	L	1-2	0-1	—	Scotland [55]	7397
2	18	H	Nottingham F	D	0-0	0-0	19		17,220
3	25	A	Walsall	W	3-1	2-1	10	Robinson 2 (1 pen) [12, 66 (p)], Scotland [26]	5673
4	Sept 1	H	Doncaster R	L	1-2	1-0	12	Scotland [41]	11,933
5	14	H	Carlisle U	W	2-1	0-0	—	Duffy [81], Anderson [83]	11,354
6	18	A	Cheltenham T	W	2-1	0-1	—	Scotland [50], Robinson [69]	4323
7	22	A	Leeds U	L	0-2	0-0	8		29,467
8	29	H	Brighton & HA	D	0-0	0-0	10		11,058
9	Oct 2	H	Swindon T	W	2-1	1-0	—	Anderson [21], Feeney [74]	10,135
10	6	A	Leyton Orient	W	5-0	1-0	4	Butler 2 [4, 51], Pratley [46], Anderson [57], Feeney [90]	5586
11	14	A	Bournemouth	W	4-1	2-1	1	Bodde [15], Lawrence [28], Feeney 2 (1 pen) [83 (p), 88]	5843
12	27	A	Yeovil T	W	2-1	1-0	2	Scotland [40], Bodde [79]	6207
13	Nov 2	H	Gillingham	D	1-1	0-1	—	Anderson [79]	13,452
14	6	A	Millwall	D	2-2	1-0	—	Scotland [18], Anderson [78]	6750
15	16	H	Huddersfield T	L	0-1	0-0	—		12,184
16	24	A	Tranmere R	W	1-0	0-0	4	Jennings (og) [81]	6149
17	27	H	Hartlepool U	W	1-0	0-0	—	Rangel [82]	11,421
18	Dec 4	H	Northampton T	W	3-0	2-0	—	Scotland 2 (1 pen) [16, 66 (p)], Pratley [19]	10,957
19	15	H	Southend U	W	3-0	1-0	1	Feeney [18], Rangel [58], Butler [83]	12,629
20	26	H	Cheltenham T	W	4-1	2-0	1	Robinson 2 [18, 20], Bodde [47], Scotland [78]	14,049
21	29	H	Leeds U	W	3-2	3-1	1	Robinson [9], Monk [23], Scotland [45]	19,010
22	Jan 1	A	Swindon T	D	1-1	0-0	1-	Butler [87]	9426
23	12	A	Luton T	W	3-1	1-0	1	Keane (og) [5], Bauza [64], Scotland [82]	6756
24	19	H	Port Vale	W	2-0	1-0	1	Bodde [28], Pratley [47]	12,310
25	22	H	Crewe Alex	W	2-1	1-0	—	Butler [14], Anderson [77]	11,200
26	25	A	Doncaster R	W	4-0	1-0	—	Bodde [28], Bauza [52], Scotland (pen) [86], Brandy [90]	10,358
27	29	A	Nottingham F	D	0-0	0-0	—		21,065
28	Feb 2	H	Oldham Ath	W	2-1	0-0	1	McDonald (og) [67], Brandy [85]	12,458
29	9	A	Crewe Alex	D	2-2	2-0	1	Scotland (pen) [9], Roberts (og) [40]	4955
30	12	H	Walsall	W	1-0	0-0	—	Bodde [53]	13,020
31	16	A	Port Vale	W	2-0	0-0	1	Scotland 2 (1 pen) [63 (p), 76]	4347
32	22	H	Luton T	W	1-0	0-0	—	Butler [79]	14,122
33	Mar 1	A	Huddersfield T	W	1-0	1-0	1	Scotland [45]	10,471
34	7	H	Millwall	L	1-2	0-1	—	Scotland (pen) [73]	15,561
35	11	H	Tranmere R	D	1-1	1-0	—	Tate [43]	11,039
36	15	A	Northampton T	L	2-4	1-3	1	Scotland 2 [29, 83]	5926
37	18	A	Bristol R	W	2-0	0-0	—	Lawrence [72], Scotland (pen) [79]	6410
38	21	A	Southend U	D	1-1	1-1	—	Scotland (pen) [24]	9797
39	24	H	Bristol R	D	2-2	0-2	1-	Scotland 2 [50, 84]	15,048
40	29	A	Hartlepool U	W	3-1	2-1	1	Pratley 2 [23, 73], Scotland (pen) [45]	4484
41	Apr 5	H	Bournemouth	L	1-2	0-0	1	Robinson [50]	15,613
42	8	A	Carlisle U	D	0-0	0-0	—		10,623
43	12	A	Gillingham	W	2-1	2-1	1	Bauza 2 [44, 45]	8520
44	19	H	Yeovil T	L	1-2	0-1	1	Robinson [79]	18,321
45	26	H	Leyton Orient	W	4-1	4-0	1	Anderson [18], Bauza 3 [25, 35, 44]	16,856
46	May 3	A	Brighton & HA	W	1-0	0-0	1	Brandy [78]	7283

Final League Position: 1

GOALSCORERS

League (82): Scotland 24 (8 pens), Robinson 8 (1 pen), Anderson 7, Bauza 7, Bodde 6, Butler 6, Feeney 5 (1 pen), Pratley 5, Brandy 3, Lawrence 2, Rangel 2, Duffy 1, Monk 1, Tate 1, own goals 4.
Carling Cup (2): Anderson 1, Scotland 1.
FA Cup (12): Bauza 4, Robinson 2, Scotland 2, Bodde 1, Britton 1, Feeney 1, Pratley 1.
J Paint Trophy (8): Anderson 2, Bauza 2, Scotland 2 (1 pen), Duffy 1, own goal 1.

De Vries D 46	Rangel A 43	Painter M 29+1	Bodde F 33	Tate A 18+3	Lawrence D 40	Britton L 35+5	Pratley D 39+3	Scotland J 43+2	Duffy D 12+8	Robinson A 34+6	O'Leary K 5+6	Anderson P 22+9	Monk G 32	Bauza G 12+16	Austin K 17+2	Craney I —+1	Butler T 29+13	Allen J 2+4	Feeney W 7+3	Orlandi A 1+7	Brandy F 2+17	Tudur Jones O 2+6	Way D —+2	Williams A 3	Macdonald S —+1	*Match No.*
1	2	3	4	5	6	7	8^{1}	9	10	11^{2}	12	13														1
1	2	3	4		6	7	8	9	10^{1}	11			5	12												2
1	2		4^{1}		6	7^{2}	8^{3}	9	10	11	12	13	5		3	14										3
1	2		4■		6	7^{1}	8	9	10^{2}	11^{3}	13	12	5		3		14									4
1	2				6	7	8	9^{3}	10	11		12	5		3^{1}		13	4^{2}	14							5
1	2	12			6	7^{2}	8^{3}	9	10	11	4	13	5		3^{1}		14									6
1	2	3	4		6		12	9	10^{2}		8^{1}	11^{3}	5				7		13	14						7
1	2	3	4		6		8	9				12	5	13			11		10^{1}	7^{2}						8
1	2	3	4		6		8	9^{2}	10^{1}			7^{3}	5				11	13	12	14						9
1	2	3	4		6		8^{1}	9^{3}			12	7	5				11^{2}	13	10	14						10
1	2	3	4		6		8	9^{1}				7^{2}	5				11	12	10	13						11
1	2	3	4		6	12	8	9	13	14		11^{1}	5				7^{3}		10^{2}							12
1	2	3^{1}			6^{3}	7	8	9	13	14		4	5		12		11^{2}		10■							13
1	2				6	4^{1}	8	9	12	10^{2}	13	7	5		3		11^{3}			14						14
1	2		4		6	12	8	9	10^{3}	13		7	5	14	3^{1}		11^{2}									15
1	2	3	4		6	12	8^{1}	9^{2}		11		7	5	14					10^{3}	13						16
1	2	3	4		6	7	8^{1}	9^{2}	12	11		10^{3}	5	13			14									17
1	2	3^{2}	4	5	6	7	8	9^{3}		11^{1}		10		14	13		12									18
1	2	3	4		6	7	8			11^{3}		9^{2}	5	12			13		10^{1}	14						19
1	2	3	4	12	6	7^{2}	8	14		11		9	5^{1}	10^{3}			13									20
1	2	3	4■	12	6	7	8	9^{2}		11^{3}		10^{1}	5	13			14									21
1	2	3			6	12	8	9^{2}		13	4	11^{1}	5	10			7									22
1	2	3			6	4	8	9	12	7^{2}		11	5	10^{1}			13									23
1	2	3	4	5		7	8^{2}	9^{1}		12		10^{3}	6	13			11				14					24
1	2	3	4		6	7	8	12		11^{3}		13	5	10^{1}			9^{2}				14					25
1	2	3	4		6	7^{2}		9		12		8	5	10^{3}			11^{1}	13			14					26
1	2	3	4		6	7		9^{2}		11		8^{1}	5	10			12				13					27
1	2	3	4		6	7		9^{2}		11			5	12			8	10^{1}			13					28
1	2		4	12	6^{1}	7	13	9^{3}		8			5	10	3		11^{2}				14					29
1	2	3	4	5		7	8	9^{1}		11			6	12			10									30
1	2	3	4	5		7	8	9		11^{2}			6	10^{1}			12				13					31
1	2	3	4^{1}	5		7^{2}	8	9		11	12		6				10				13					32
1	2		4	5		7	8	9^{1}	12	10^{2}	6				3		11				13					33
1	2		4	5		7	8^{1}	9		11	6^{2}			12	3		10				13					34
1	2		4	5	6	7	8	9^{1}		11^{2}				12	3		10				13					35
1	2	3^{1}	4	5	6	7	12	9		11				10^{2}			8				13					36
1	2		4	5	6	12	8^{1}	9	10^{2}	11^{3}					3		7				13■	14				37
1	2		4	5	6	7	8^{2}	9	12	10^{1}					3		11					13				38
1	2		4^{2}	5	6	7	8^{1}	9	12	10					3		11					13				39
1	2			5	6	7^{1}	8	9	10	11					3		4^{2}					13	12			40
1	2			5	6	7	8	9^{1}	10^{2}	11				12	3		4^{3}				13	14				41
1				2	6	7	8	9		11		12		13	3		4^{1}				10^{2}			5		42
1		3		2	6	7	8	9^{2}		11^{1}		4		10^{3}			12				13	14		5		43
1				5	6	7	8■	9		4		12		13	2^{2}		11^{1}				10			3		44
1	2	3			6	7^{2}		9		8		11^{1}	5	10^{3}			12				14	4	13			45
1	2	3			6		8	9				7^{2}	5	10^{1}			11				12	4			13	46

FA Cup

First Round	Billericay T	(a)	2-1
Second Round	Horsham	(a)	1-1
		(h)	6-2
Third Round	Havant & W	(h)	1-1
		(a)	2-4

Carling Cup

First Round	Walsall	(h)	2-0
Second Round	Reading	(h)	0-1

J Paint Trophy

First Round	Millwall	(h)	3-2
Second Round	Wycombe W	(h)	2-0
Quarter-Final	Yeovil T	(h)	1-0
Southern Semi-Final	Brighton & HA	(h)	1-0
Southern Final	Milton Keynes D	(h)	0-1
		(a)	1-0

SWINDON TOWN FL Championship 1

FOUNDATION

It is generally accepted that Swindon Town came into being in 1881, although there is no firm evidence that the club's founder, Rev. William Pitt, captain of the Spartans (an offshoot of a cricket club) changed his club's name to Swindon Town before 1883, when the Spartans amalgamated with St Mark's Young Men's Friendly Society.

The County Ground, County Road, Swindon, Wiltshire SN1 2ED.

Telephone: 0871 423 6433.

Fax: (0844) 880 1112.

Ticket Office: 0871 223 2300.

Website: www.swindontownfc.co.uk

Email: enquiries@swindontownfc.co.uk

Ground Capacity: 14,800.

Record Attendance: 32,000 v Arsenal, FA Cup 3rd rd, 15 January 1972.

Pitch Measurements: 110yd × 70yd.

Chairman: Andrew Fitton.

Chief Executive: Nicholas Watkins.

Secretary: Louise Fletcher.

Manager: Maurice Malpas.

Assistant Manager: David Byrne.

Physio: Dick Mackey.

Colours: All red.

Change Colours: Blue shirts with white trim, white shorts, blue stockings.

Year Formed: 1881* (*see Foundation*).

Turned Professional: 1894.

Ltd Co.: 1894.

Club Nickname: 'Robins'.

Grounds: 1881, The Croft; 1896, County Ground.

First Football League Game: 28 August 1920, Division 3, v Luton T (h) W 9–1 – Nash; Kay, Macconachie; Langford, Hawley, Wareing; Jefferson (1), Fleming (4), Rogers, Batty (2), Davies (1), (1 og).

Record League Victory: 9–1 v Luton T, Division 3 (S), 28 August 1920 – Nash; Kay, Macconachie; Langford, Hawley, Wareing; Jefferson (1), Fleming (4), Rogers, Batty (2), Davies (1), (1 og).

HONOURS

Football League: Promoted to FA Premier League from Division 1 – 1992–93 (play-offs); Promoted from FL 2 (3rd) 2006–07.

Division 2 – Champions 1995–96; Division 3 – Runners-up 1962–63, 1968–69; Division 4 – Champions 1985–86 (with record 102 points).

FA Cup: Semi-finals 1910, 1912.

Football League Cup: Winners 1969.

Anglo-Italian Cup: Winners 1970.

SKY SPORTS FACT FILE

Frank Richardson scored ten FA Cup goals for Swindon Town unusually in three successive ties in the 1925–26 season, comprising two fours and a two out of 20 for the team. He had two spells with the club sandwiching a stint at Reading.

Record Cup Victory: 10–1 v Farnham U Breweries (away), FA Cup 1st rd (replay), 28 November 1925 – Nash; Dickenson, Weston, Archer, Bew, Adey; Denyer (2), Wall (1), Richardson (4), Johnson (3), Davies.

Record Defeat: 1–10 v Manchester C, FA Cup 4th rd (replay), 25 January 1930.

Most League Points (2 for a win): 64, Division 3, 1968–69.

Most League Points (3 for a win): 102, Division 4, 1985–86.

Most League Goals: 100, Division 3 (S), 1926–27.

Highest League Scorer in Season: Harry Morris, 47, Division 3 (S), 1926–27.

Most League Goals in Total Aggregate: Harry Morris, 216, 1926–33.

Most League Goals in One Match: 5, Harry Morris v QPR, Division 3S, 18 December 1926; 5, Harry Morris v Norwich C, Division 3S, 26 April 1930; 5, Keith East v Mansfield T, Division 3, 20 November 1965.

Most Capped Player: Rod Thomas, 30 (50), Wales.

Most League Appearances: John Trollope, 770, 1960–80.

Youngest League Player: Paul Rideout, 16 years 107 days v Hull C, 29 November 1980.

Record Transfer Fee Received: £1,500,000 from Manchester C for Kevin Horlock, January 1997.

Record Transfer Fee Paid: £800,000 to West Ham U for Joey Beauchamp, August 1994.

Football League Record: 1920 Original Member of Division 3; 1921–58 Division 3 (S); 1958–63 Division 3; 1963–65 Division 2; 1965–69 Division 3; 1969–74 Division 2; 1974–82 Division 3; 1982–86 Division 4; 1986–87 Division 3; 1987–92 Division 2; 1992–93 Division 1; 1993–94 FA Premier League; 1994–95 Division 1; 1995–96 Division 2; 1996–2000 Division 1; 2000–04 Division 2; 2004–06 FL 1; 2006–07 FL 2; 2007– FL 1.

MANAGERS

Sam Allen 1902–33
Ted Vizard 1933–39
Neil Harris 1939–41
Louis Page 1945–53
Maurice Lindley 1953–55
Bert Head 1956–65
Danny Williams 1965–69
Fred Ford 1969–71
Dave Mackay 1971–72
Les Allen 1972–74
Danny Williams 1974–78
Bobby Smith 1978–80
John Trollope 1980–83
Ken Beamish 1983–84
Lou Macari 1984–89
Ossie Ardiles 1989–91
Glenn Hoddle 1991–93
John Gorman 1993–94
Steve McMahon 1994–99
Jimmy Quinn 1999–2000
Colin Todd 2000
Andy King 2000–01
Roy Evans 2001
Andy King 2002–06
Iffy Onuora 2006
Dennis Wise 2006
Paul Sturrock 2006–07
Maurice Malpas January 2008–

LATEST SEQUENCES

Longest Sequence of League Wins: 8, 12.1.1986 – 15.3.1986.

Longest Sequence of League Defeats: 8, 29.8.2005 – 8.10.2005.

Longest Sequence of League Draws: 6, 22.11.1991 – 28.12.1991.

Longest Sequence of Unbeaten League Matches: 22, 12.1.1986 – 23.8.86.

Longest Sequence Without a League Win: 19, 30.10.1999 – 4.3.2000.

Successive Scoring Runs: 31 from 17.4.1926.

Successive Non-scoring Runs: 5 from 16.11.1963.

TEN YEAR LEAGUE RECORD

		P	W	D	L	F	A	Pts	Pos
1998-99	Div 1	46	13	11	22	59	81	50	17
1999-2000	Div 1	46	8	12	26	38	77	36	24
2000-01	Div 2	46	13	13	20	47	65	52	20
2001-02	Div 2	46	15	14	17	46	56	59	13
2002-03	Div 2	46	16	12	18	59	63	60	10
2003-04	Div 2	46	20	13	13	76	58	73	5
2004-05	FL 1	46	17	12	17	66	68	63	12
2005-06	FL 1	46	11	15	20	46	65	48	23
2006-07	FL 2	46	25	10	11	58	38	85	3
2007-08	FL 1	46	16	13	17	63	56	61	13

DID YOU KNOW ?

When Swindon Town achieved their second Southern League championship title in 1913–14, they also produced the club's first significant attendance figure. The visit of Bristol Rovers drew a crowd of 9,712.

SWINDON TOWN 2007–08 LEAGUE RECORD

Match No.	*Date*	*Venue*	*Opponents*	*Result*		*H/T Score*	*Lg. Pos.*	*Goalscorers*	*Attendance*
1	Aug 11	A	Northampton T	D	1-1	1-1	—	Roberts (pen) [44]	6210
2	18	H	Luton T	W	2-1	0-0	4	Peacock [56], Easton [88]	7520
3	25	A	Cheltenham T	D	1-1	1-0	8	Sturrock [35]	5442
4	Sept 1	H	Crewe Alex	D	1-1	1-1	9	Pook [24]	6595
5	9	H	Yeovil T	L	0-1	0-0	11		6944
6	15	A	Hartlepool U	D	1-1	1-0	12	McGovern [31]	4943
7	22	H	Bournemouth	W	4-1	1-1	7	Cox [7], Paynter 3 [48, 64, 85]	6668
8	29	A	Millwall	W	2-1	1-0	6	Cox [8], Ifil [79]	8744
9	Oct 2	A	Swansea C	L	1-2	0-1	—	Roberts [70]	10,135
10	6	H	Gillingham	W	5-0	2-0	6	McGovern [4], Cox 2 [6, 62], Paynter 2 [52, 84]	6345
11	20	H	Tranmere R	W	1-0	0-0	7	Corr [88]	6430
12	27	A	Port Vale	L	1-2	1-2	9	Peacock [19]	4013
13	Nov 3	H	Doncaster R	L	1-2	0-1	11	Cox [47]	6517
14	6	H	Leyton Orient	D	1-1	0-0	—	Aljofree [90]	5874
15	17	A	Leeds U	L	1-2	0-1	15	Peacock [47]	27,900
16	24	H	Bristol R	W	1-0	0-0	11	Roberts (pen) [67]	9342
17	Dec 4	A	Carlisle U	L	0-3	0-1	—		5477
18	8	A	Southend U	L	1-2	1-1	14	Cox [2]	7403
19	15	H	Brighton & HA	L	0-3	0-2	16		6415
20	22	H	Hartlepool U	W	2-1	0-1	15	Cox [49], Corr (pen) [73]	5875
21	26	A	Yeovil T	W	1-0	0-0	13	Corr [66]	6539
22	29	A	Bournemouth	D	2-2	0-0	11	Corr 2 [49, 83]	6540
23	Jan 1	H	Swansea C	D	1-1	0-0	12	Cox (pen) [90]	9426
24	12	A	Walsall	D	2-2	0-1	12	Nicholas [65], Easton [67]	5449
25	19	H	Nottingham F	W	2-1	1-0	11	Perch (og) [35], Breckin (og) [82]	9815
26	26	A	Crewe Alex	D	0-0	0-0	—		4344
27	29	A	Luton T	W	1-0	0-0	—	Roberts [52]	5738
28	Feb 2	H	Northampton T	D	1-1	0-0	10	Sturrock [56]	7375
29	9	A	Huddersfield T	L	0-1	0-1	11		9388
30	12	H	Cheltenham T	W	3-0	2-0	—	Cox [20], Paynter [41], Roberts [80]	6483
31	16	A	Nottingham F	L	0-1	0-0	11		23,439
32	23	H	Walsall	L	0-3	0-1	13		6265
33	26	A	Oldham Ath	D	2-2	1-0	—	Peacock [29], Cox [58]	3923
34	Mar 1	H	Leeds U	L	0-1	0-1	14		13,270
35	4	H	Huddersfield T	W	3-2	3-1	—	Paynter [4], Easton 2 [23, 31]	4840
36	11	A	Leyton Orient	L	1-2	1-0	—	Thelwell (og) [20]	3082
37	15	H	Carlisle U	D	2-2	0-0	14	Cox [61], Sturrock [80]	6004
38	22	A	Brighton & HA	L	1-2	1-1	15	Easton [8]	6849
39	24	H	Southend U	l	0-1	0-1	15		6378
40	28	A	Tranmere R	L	1-2	0-2	—	Paynter [68]	5815
41	Apr 5	H	Oldham Ath	W	3-0	0-0	15	Peacock [49], Cox 2 [53, 70]	5384
42	11	A	Doncaster R	L	0-2	0-1	—		8371
43	19	H	Port Vale	W	6-0	5-0	14	Peacock [16], Easton [21], Smith J [33], McNamee [44], Timlin [45], Joyce [90]	7361
44	22	A	Bristol R	W	1-0	0-0	—	Cox [74]	6102
45	26	A	Gillingham	D	1-1	0-1	13	Aljofree [88]	6334
46	May 3	H	Millwall	W	2-1	1-1	13	Cox (pen) [31], McNamee [51]	7781

Final League Position: 13

GOALSCORERS

League (63): Cox 15 (2 pens), Paynter 8, Easton 6, Peacock 6, Corr 5 (1 pen), Roberts 5 (2 pens), Sturrock 3, Aljofree 2, McGovern 2, McNamee 2, Ifil 1, Joyce 1, Nicholas 1, Pook 1, Smith J 1, Timlin 1, own goals 3.
Carling Cup (0).
FA Cup (7): Paynter 2, Sturrock 2, Aljofree 1, McGovern 1, Roberts 1.
J Paint Trophy (5): Blackburn 2, Arrieta 1, Cox 1, Sturrock 1.

Smith P 15	Smith J 21	Vincent J 32	Adams S 2	Ifil J 39 + 1	Aljofree H 38 + 1	Roberts C 16 + 11	Pook M 13 + 9	Sturrock B 13 + 8	Peacock L 36 + 1	Zaaboub S 18 + 11	Mohammed K 3 + 8	Arrieta I — + 4	Comminges M 32 + 8	Easton C 40	McGovern J 34 + 7	Paynter B 23 + 13	Cox S 35 + 1	Blackburn C 4 + 3	Collins S 3 + 1	Nicholas A 8 + 3	Corr B 7 + 10	Brezovan P 31	Tozer B 1 + 1	Allen C 7 + 1	Williams A — + 1	Ashikodi M 4 + 6	McNamee A 18 + 1	Kanyuka P 3 + 1	Timlin M 9 + 1	Joyce B — + 3	Morrison S 1 + 1	*Match No.*
1	2	3	4	5	6	7^{1}	8	9^{2}	10	11^{3}	12	13	14																			1
1	2	3		5	6	7	8	9^{1}	10	11^{2}		12	13	4																		2
1	2	3		5	6	7^{1}	8	9^{2}	10	11		13	12	4																		3
1	2	3		5	6	7^{3}	8	9^{2}	10	11^{1}	14	13	12	4																		4
1	2	3		5	6	7^{1}	8^{7}	9^{3}	10	11				4	12	13	14															5
1		3		5	6^{3}	12	13		10	11			2	4	7^{2}	9	8^{1}	14														6
1		3		5		12			10	11^{1}			2	4	7	9	8	6														7
1	2	3		5		7^{3}	12		10	13			14	4	8^{2}	9^{1}	11		6													8
1	2^{2}	3		5		7	12		10	11^{3}			13	4	14	9	8		6^{1}													9
1		3^{1}		5		7^{2}	12		10		13		2	4	11	9	8	14	6^{3}													10
1				5	6	7^{2}	12		10^{1}	13			2	4	11	9^{3}	8			3	14											11
				5^{2}	6	12			10	11			2	4	7	9^{3}	8		13	3^{1}	14	1										12
				5	6	12		13	10	11^{1}			2	4	7	9^{3}	8			3^{2}	14	1										13
			3^{2}	5	6	12	13		10	11			2	4^{1}	7	9^{3}	8				14	1										14
				5	6	7^{1}	11		10	3			2	4^{2}	12	9	8				13	1										15
	3			5■	6	11^{3}	8			12■			2	4	7^{1}	9^{2}	10				13	1	14									16
	2				6		8	12					7^{2}	4	11	9^{3}	10^{1}	13		3	14	1	5■									17
	2				6		8	9^{3}			11^{2}		12	4	13	14	10^{1}	5		3		1		7								18
	2^{2}				6		8	9^{3}			10^{1}		13	4	12	14	11	5		3		1		7								19
		3		5	6^{1}		13		10	11			2	4	7	14	8				9^{3}	1			12^{2}							20
		3		5	6^{1}				10		11^{3}		2	4	7	13	8			12	9^{2}	1		14								21
		3		5				12	10	11^{2}	13			4	7^{1}		8	2		6	9	1										22
		3		5	6		12		10^{2}	11^{3}	13		2	4^{1}	7	14	8				9■	1										23
		3		5		12		8^{1}	10	11	13		2	4	7^{2}	9				6		1										24
		3		5	6			8^{1}	10	11			2	4	7	9						1				12						25
		3		5	6	12	4		10				2		7	9■					13	1				8^{2}	11^{1}					26
		3			6^{2}	4		14	10	12			2		7					13	8	1				9^{3}	11^{1}	5				27
		3		5	6	4		13	10	12			2		7						8^{2}	1				9	11^{1}					28
		3		5	6	4^{3}	12	13	10	11^{2}			2		7		8					1				9^{1}	14					29
		3		5	6	12	4	13	10				2		7	9^{3}	8^{2}				14	1					11^{1}					30
		3		5	6	12	8	10^{3}		13			2	4	7^{2}	9						1				14	11^{1}					31
1		3		5	6	12			10				2^{2}	4	7^{1}	9	8									13	11					32
1		3			6	11		12	10^{2}	13			2	4		9	8^{1}							7				5				33
1		3		12	6	11			10				2	4	13	9	8							7^{2}				5^{1}				34
1	3			5	6	14			10■				2	4	12	9■	8^{1}							7		13^{3}	11^{2}					35
	2			5	6			9		12			3	4	7		10					1		8^{1}		13	11^{2}					36
	2			5	6			9^{1}					3	4	7		10					1				12	11		8			37
	2			5	6			9^{2}		12			3	4^{1}	7	13	10^{3}				14	1					11		8			38
	2			5	6				12	13			3	4	7^{2}	14	10				9^{3}	1					11		8^{1}			39
		3		5	6				10		12		2	4^{2}	7^{1}	9	8					1					11		13			40
	2	3		5	6				10	12				4	7	13	9^{2}					1					11^{1}		8			41
	2	3		5	6■				10					4	7	12	9^{2}			13		1					11^{1}		8			42
	3	6		5					10^{1}		13		2	4	7	12	9^{3}					1					11^{2}		8	14		43
	2	6		5	12				10				3^{1}	4	7	13	9^{2}					1					11		8			44
	2^{2}	3		5^{3}	6				10					4	7	12	9					1					11^{1}		8	13	14	45
		3			6									4	2	10^{1}	9					1		7^{2}			11	13	8	12	5	46

FA Cup

First Round	Wycombe W	(a)	2-1
Second Round	Forest Green R	(h)	3-2
Third Round	Barnet	(h)	1-1
		(a)	1-1

Carling Cup

First Round	Charlton Ath	(h)	0-2

J Paint Trophy

First Round	Brentford	(h)	4-1
Second Round	Cheltenham T	(h)	1-3

TOTTENHAM HOTSPUR FA Premiership

FOUNDATION

The Hotspur Football Club was formed from an older cricket club in 1882. Most of the founders were old boys of St John's Presbyterian School and Tottenham Grammar School. The Casey brothers were well to the fore as the family provided the club's first goalposts (painted blue and white) and their first ball. They soon adopted the local YMCA as their meeting place, but after a couple of moves settled at the Red House, which is still their headquarters, although now known simply as 748 High Road.

White Hart Lane, Bill Nicholson Way, 748 High Road, Tottenham, London N17 0AP.

Telephone: 0870 420 5000.

Fax: (020) 8365 5175.

Ticket Office: 0844 844 0102.

Website: www.tottenhamhotspur.co.uk

Email: email@tottenhamhotspur.co.uk

Ground Capacity: 36,310.

Record Attendance: 75,038 v Sunderland, FA Cup 6th rd. 5 March 1938.

Pitch Measurements: 100m × 67m.

Chairman: Daniel Levy.

Secretary: John Alexander.

Manager: Juande Ramos.

First Team Coaches: Marcos Alvarez, Gus Poyet.

Head of Medical Services: Wayne Diesel.

Colours: White shirts, white shorts, white and blue hooped stockings.

Change Colours: Light blue shirts, light blue shorts, light blue stockings.

Year Formed: 1882.

Turned Professional: 1895.

Ltd Co.: 1898.

Previous Name: 1882, Hotspur Football Club; 1884, Tottenham Hotspur.

Club Nickname: 'Spurs'.

Grounds: 1882, Tottenham Marshes; 1888, Northumberland Park; 1899, White Hart Lane.

First Football League Game: 1 September 1908, Division 2, v Wolverhampton W (h) W 3–0 – Hewitson; Coquet, Burton; Morris (1), D. Steel, Darnell; Walton, Woodward (2), Macfarlane, R. Steel, Middlemiss.

HONOURS

Football League: Division 1 – Champions 1950–51, 1960–61; Runners-up 1921–22, 1951–52, 1956–57, 1962–63; Division 2 – Champions 1919–20, 1949–50; Runners-up 1908–09, 1932–33; Promoted 1977–78 (3rd).

FA Cup: Winners 1901 (as non-League club), 1921, 1961, 1962, 1967, 1981, 1982, 1991; Runners-up 1987.

Football League Cup: Winners 1971, 1973, 1999, 2008; Runners-up 1982, 2002.

European Competitions: *European Cup:* 1961–62. *European Cup-Winners' Cup:* 1962–63 (winners), 1963–64, 1967–68, 1981–82, 1982–83, 1991–92. *UEFA Cup:* 1971–72 (winners), 1972–73, 1973–74 (runners-up), 1983–84 (winners), 1984–85, 1999–2000, 2006–07, 2007–08. *Intertoto Cup:* 1995.

SKY SPORTS FACT FILE

Tottenham Hotspur celebrated their 125th anniversary on 1 October 2007 against Aston Villa. With twenty minutes remaining, Spurs were trailing 4–1, but fought back to a dramatic draw in the dying seconds. On 29 December they beat Reading 6–4 in another goal feast.

TRANMERE ROVERS FL Championship 1

FOUNDATION

Formed in 1884 as Belmont they adopted their present title the following year and eventually joined their first league, the West Lancashire League in 1889–90, the same year as their first success in the Wirral Challenge Cup. The club almost folded in 1899–1900 when all the players left en bloc to join a rival club, but they survived the crisis and went from strength to strength winning the 'Combination' title in 1907–08 and the Lancashire Combination in 1913–14. They joined the Football League in 1921 from the Central League.

Prenton Park, Prenton Road West, Birkenhead, Merseyside CH42 9PY.

Telephone: 0870 460 3333.

Fax: (0151) 608 6144.

Ticket Office: 0870 460 3332.

Website: www.tranmererovers.co.uk

Email: info@tranmererovers.co.uk

Ground Capacity: 16,567.

Record Attendance: 24,424 v Stoke C, FA Cup 4th rd, 5 February 1972.

Pitch Measurements: 100yd × 70yd.

Chairperson: Lorraine Rogers.

Chief Executive/Secretary: Mick Horton.

Manager: Ronnie Moore.

Assistant Manager: Peter Shirtliff.

Physio: Les Parry.

Colours: White.

Change Colours: Gold.

Year Formed: 1884.

Turned Professional: 1912.

Ltd Co.: 1920.

Previous Name: 1884, Belmont AFC; 1885, Tranmere Rovers.

Club Nickname: 'The Rovers'.

Grounds: 1884, Steeles Field; 1887, Ravenshaws Field/Old Prenton Park; 1912, Prenton Park.

First Football League Game: 27 August 1921, Division 3 (N), v Crewe Alex (h) W 4–1 – Bradshaw; Grainger, Stuart (1); Campbell, Milnes (1), Heslop; Moreton, Groves (1), Hyam, Ford (1), Hughes.

Record League Victory: 13–4 v Oldham Ath, Division 3 (N), 26 December 1935 – Gray; Platt, Fairhurst; McLaren, Newton, Spencer; Eden, MacDonald (1), Bell (9), Woodward (2), Urmson (1).

HONOURS

Football League Division 1 best season: 4th, 1992–93; Promoted from Division 3 1990–91 (play-offs); Division 3 (N) – Champions 1937–38; Promotion to 3rd Division: 1966–67, 1975–76; Division 4 – Runners-up 1988–89.

FA Cup: best season: 6th rd, 2000, 2001, 2004.

Football League Cup: Runners-up, 2000.

Welsh Cup: Winners 1935; Runners-up 1934.

Leyland Daf Cup: Winners 1990; Runners-up 1991.

SKY SPORTS FACT FILE

On two occasions Tranmere Rovers have recorded the feat of providing six different goalscorers in a match. On 15 January 1927 they did so in the 8–3 win over Durham City and repeated the feat on 5 September 1960 when they defeated Port Vale 6–0.

Record League Victory: 9–0 v Bristol R, Division 2, 22 October 1977 – Daines; Naylor, Holmes, Hoddle (1), McAllister, Perryman, Pratt, McNab, Moores (3), Lee (4), Taylor (1).

Record Cup Victory: 13–2 v Crewe Alex, FA Cup 4th rd (replay), 3 February 1960 – Brown; Hills, Henry; Blanchflower, Norman, Mackay; White, Harmer (1), Smith (4), Allen (5), Jones (3 incl. 1p).

Record Defeat: 0–8 v Cologne, UEFA Intertoto Cup, 22 July 1995.

Most League Points (2 for a win): 70, Division 2, 1919–20.

Most League Points (3 for a win): 77, Division 1, 1984–85.

Most League Goals: 115, Division 1, 1960–61.

Highest League Scorer in Season: Jimmy Greaves, 37, Division 1, 1962–63.

Most League Goals in Total Aggregate: Jimmy Greaves, 220, 1961–70.

Most League Goals in One Match: 5, Ted Harper v Reading, Division 2, 30 August 1930; 5, Alf Stokes v Birmingham C, Division 1, 18 September 1957; 5, Bobby Smith v Aston Villa, Division 1, 29 March 1958.

Most Capped Player: Pat Jennings, 74 (119), Northern Ireland.

Most League Appearances: Steve Perryman, 655, 1969–86.

Youngest League Player: Ally Dick, 16 years 301 days v Manchester C, 20 February 1982.

Record Transfer Fee Received: £18,600,000 from Manchester U for Michael Carrick, July 2006.

Record Transfer Fee Paid: £16,500,000 to Charlton Ath for Darren Bent, May 2007.

Football League Record: 1908 Elected to Division 2; 1909–15 Division 1; 1919–20 Division 2; 1920–28 Division 1; 1928–33 Division 2; 1933–35 Division 1; 1935–50 Division 2; 1950–77 Division 1; 1977–78 Division 2; 1978–92 Division 1; 1992– FA Premier League.

MANAGERS

Frank Brettell 1898–99
John Cameron 1899–1906
Fred Kirkham 1907–08
Peter McWilliam 1912–27
Billy Minter 1927–29
Percy Smith 1930–35
Jack Tresadern 1935–38
Peter McWilliam 1938–42
Arthur Turner 1942–46
Joe Hulme 1946–49
Arthur Rowe 1949–55
Jimmy Anderson 1955–58
Bill Nicholson 1958–74
Terry Neill 1974–76
Keith Burkinshaw 1976–84
Peter Shreeves 1984–86
David Pleat 1986–87
Terry Venables 1987–91
Peter Shreeves 1991–92
Doug Livermore 1992–93
Ossie Ardiles 1993–94
Gerry Francis 1994–97
Christian Gross *(Head Coach)* 1997–98
George Graham 1998–2001
Glenn Hoddle 2001–03
David Pleat (*Caretaker*) 2003–04
Jacques Santini 2004
Martin Jol 2004–07
Juande Ramos October 2007–

LATEST SEQUENCES

Longest Sequence of League Wins: 13, 23.4.1960 – 1.10.1960.

Longest Sequence of League Defeats: 7, 1.1.1994 – 27.2.1994.

Longest Sequence of League Draws: 6, 9.1.1999 – 27.2.1999.

Longest Sequence of Unbeaten League Matches: 22, 31.8.1949 – 31.12.1949.

Longest Sequence Without a League Win: 16, 29.12.1934 – 13.4.1935.

Successive Scoring Runs: 32 from 24.2.1962.

Successive Non-scoring Runs: 6 from 28.12.1985.

TEN YEAR LEAGUE RECORD

		P	*W*	*D*	*L*	*F*	*A*	*Pts*	*Pos*
1998-99	PR Lge	38	11	14	13	47	50	47	11
1999-2000	PR Lge	38	15	8	15	57	49	53	10
2000-01	PR Lge	38	13	10	15	47	54	49	12
2001-02	PR Lge	38	14	8	16	49	53	50	9
2002-03	PR Lge	38	14	8	16	51	62	50	10
2003-04	PR Lge	38	13	6	19	47	57	45	14
2004-05	PR Lge	38	14	10	14	47	41	52	9
2005-06	PR Lge	38	18	11	9	53	38	65	5
2006-07	PR Lge	38	17	9	12	57	54	60	5
2007-08	PR Lge	38	11	13	14	66	61	46	11

DID YOU KNOW ?

On 19 January 2008 Robbie Keane came on as a substitute for Tottenham Hotspur and scored his 100th goal for the club putting him 15th in the club's pecking order. Then on 9 March sub Gilberto hit Spurs 500th home Premier League goal against West Ham United.

TOTTENHAM HOTSPUR 2007–08 LEAGUE RECORD

Match No.	Date	Venue	Opponents	Result		H/T Score	Lg. Pos.	Goalscorers	Attendance
1	Aug 11	A	Sunderland	L	0-1	0-0	—		43,967
2	14	H	Everton	L	1-3	1-3	—	Gardner ^{26}	35,716
3	18	H	Derby Co	W	4-0	3-0	12	Malbranque 2 $^{2, 6}$, Jenas ^{14}, Bent ^{80}	35,600
4	26	A	Manchester U	L	0-1	0-0	17		75,696
5	Sept 1	A	Fulham	D	3-3	2-1	14	Kaboul ^{10}, Berbatov ^{28}, Bale ^{61}	24,007
6	15	H	Arsenal	L	1-3	1-0	17	Bale ^{15}	36,053
7	23	A	Bolton W	D	1-1	1-1	18	Keane ^{34}	20,308
8	Oct 1	H	Aston Villa	D	4-4	1-3	—	Berbatov ^{20}, Chimbonda ^{69}, Keane (pen) ^{82}, Kaboul ^{90}	36,094
9	7	A	Liverpool	D	2-2	1-1	17	Keane 2 $^{45, 47}$	43,986
10	22	A	Newcastle U	L	1-3	0-1	—	Keane ^{57}	51,411
11	28	H	Blackburn R	L	1-2	0-0	18	Keane (pen) ^{49}	36,086
12	Nov 3	A	Middlesbrough	D	1-1	1-0	17	Bent ^{35}	25,625
13	11	H	Wigan Ath	W	4-0	3-0	14	Jenas 2 $^{13, 26}$, Lennon ^{34}, Bent ^{72}	35,504
14	25	A	West Ham U	D	1-1	0-1	14	Dawson ^{67}	34,966
15	Dec 2	H	Birmingham C	L	2-3	0-1	16	Keane 2 (1 pen) $^{50 (p), 53}$	35,635
16	9	H	Manchester C	W	2-1	1-0	13	Chimbonda ^{45}, Defoe ^{83}	35,646
17	15	A	Portsmouth	W	1-0	0-0	12	Berbatov ^{81}	20,520
18	22	A	Arsenal	L	1-2	0-0	13	Berbatov ^{66}	60,087
19	26	H	Fulham	W	5-1	2-0	13	Keane 2 $^{27, 62}$, Huddlestone 2 $^{45, 71}$, Defoe ^{90}	36,077
20	29	H	Reading	W	6-4	1-1	12	Berbatov 4 $^{7, 63, 73, 83}$, Malbranque ^{76}, Defoe ^{79}	36,178
21	Jan 1	A	Aston Villa	L	1-2	0-1	12	Defoe ^{79}	41,609
22	12	A	Chelsea	L	0-2	0-1	12		41,777
23	19	H	Sunderland	W	2-0	1-0	11	Lennon ^{2}, Keane ^{90}	36,070
24	30	A	Everton	D	0-0	0-0	—		35,840
25	Feb 2	H	Manchester U	D	1-1	1-0	11	Berbatov ^{21}	36,075
26	9	A	Derby Co	W	3-0	0-0	11	Keane ^{68}, Kaboul ^{81}, Berbatov (pen) ^{90}	33,058
27	Mar 1	A	Birmingham C	L	1-4	0-1	11	Jenas ^{90}	26,055
28	9	H	West Ham U	W	4-0	2-0	11	Berbatov 2 $^{8, 11}$, Gilberto ^{85}, Bent ^{90}	36,062
29	16	A	Manchester C	L	1-2	1-0	11	Keane ^{32}	40,180
30	19	H	Chelsea	D	4-4	1-2	—	Woodgate ^{12}, Berbatov ^{61}, Huddlestone ^{75}, Keane ^{88}	36,178
31	22	H	Portsmouth	W	2-0	0-0	11	Bent ^{80}, O'Hara ^{82}	35,998
32	30	H	Newcastle U	L	1-4	1-1	11	Bent ^{26}	36,067
33	Apr 5	A	Blackburn R	D	1-1	1-1	11	Berbatov ^{7}	24,592
34	12	H	Middlesbrough	D	1-1	1-0	11	Grounds (og) ^{27}	36,092
35	19	A	Wigan Ath	D	1-1	1-1	11	Berbatov ^{6}	18,673
36	26	H	Bolton W	D	1-1	0-0	11	Malbranque ^{52}	36,176
37	May 3	A	Reading	W	1-0	1-0	11	Keane ^{16}	24,125
38	11	H	Liverpool	L	0-2	0-0	11		36,063

Final League Position: 11

GOALSCORERS

League (66): Berbatov 15 (1 pen), Keane 15 (3 pens), Bent 6, Defoe 4, Jenas 4, Malbranque 4, Huddlestone 3, Kaboul 3, Bale 2, Chimbonda 2, Lennon 2, Dawson 1, Gardner 1, Gilberto 1, O'Hara 1, Woodgate 1, own goal 1.
Carling Cup (14): Jenas 2, Keane 2, Malbranque 2, Bale 1, Berbatov 1 (pen), Chimbonda 1, Defoe 1, Huddlestone 1, Lennon 1, Woodgate 1, own goal 1.
FA Cup (4): Berbatov 2 (1 pen), Keane 2.
UEFA Cup (18): Berbatov 5 (1 pen), Keane 4, Defoe 3, Bent 2, Dawson 1, Kaboul 1, Malbranque 1, O'Hara 1.

Robinson P 25	Chimbonda P 31 + 1	Stalteri P 3	Zokora D 25 + 3	Kaboul Y 19 + 2	Gardner A 4	Tainio T 6 + 10	Jenas J 28 + 1	Berbatov D 33 + 3	Keane R 32 + 4	Malbranque S 35 + 2	Bent D 11 + 16	Huddlestone T 18 + 10	Defoe J 3 + 16	Ricardo Rocha 4 + 1	Routledge W 1 + 1	Lee Y 17 + 1	Taarabt A — + 6	Bale G 8	Dawson M 26 + 1	Lennon A 25 + 4	Assou-Ekotto B 1	Cerny R 13	Boateng K 7 + 6	O'Hara J 9 + 8	King L 4	Gunter C 1 + 1	Woodgate J 12	Hutton A 14	Gilberto 3 + 3	Match No.
1	2	3	4^{2}	5	6	7^{1}	8	9^{3}	10	11	12	13	14																	1
1	2	3^{3}	4	5^{2}	6		8	9	7	11	10^{1}		12	13	14															2
1	2^{2}		13		6		8		10^{1}	11	9	4	12	5	7^{3}	3	14													3
1	2		12		6		8	9	10^{2}	7		4	13	5^{1}		3^{3}	14	11												4
1	2			5			8	9	10^{1}	7^{2}		4	12	6		3		11	13											5
1	2			5			8	9	10	7^{1}	12	4				3		11^{2}	6	13										6
1	2		4			11^{2}	8	9^{1}	10	7	12			6					5	13	3									7
1	2		4	5		11^{2}		9^{3}	10	12	14	8	13					3	6	7^{1}										8
1	2		4	5		7^{1}	8	9	10	12						3		11	6											9
	2		4	5		12	8	13	10	7^{2}	9^{3}					3		11^{1}	6	14		1								10
	2		4	5				9^{1}	10	11^{2}	13	8	12			3			6	7		1								11
1	2		12	5			8	13	14	11	9^{2}		10^{3}			3			6	7			4^{1}							12
1	2		4	5		12	8	9	10^{3}	11^{1}	14		13			3			6	7^{2}										13
1	2		4	5^{2}			8	9	10^{1}	11	13		12					3	6	7										14
1	2		4	5^{2}				9	10[illegible]	11	8^{1}	13	12			14		3^{3}	6	7										15
1	2		4	5		12	8	9^{1}		11	10^{2}		13			3			6	7^{3}			14							16
1	2		4	5		12	8	9		11	10^{2}		13			3				7^{1}			6^{3}	14						17
1	4			5		2		9	10^{2}	11		12	13			3^{3}	14			7			6^{1}	8						18
1	2			5				9^{3}	10^{1}	11		8	12			3	13			7			14	4	6^{2}					19
1	2			5		12	8	9	10^{1}	11		4	13			3				7^{3}			14		6^{2}					20
1			2	5^{3}			8	9	12	11		13	10			3			4	7^{1}			6^{2}	14						21
	2			12				9	10	11^{3}			13			3	14		5	7		1	8^{1}	4^{2}	6					22
	12	2^{1}				13	8	9	14			4	10^{3}			3			5	7		1	6	11^{2}						23
	2						8	9	10	11		4								7		1	12	6		3^{1}	5			24
	2						8	9	10^{2}	11		4							6	7^{1}		1	12	13			5	3		25
	2			12			8	13	10	11	9^{2}	4							5^{1}	7		1	6^{3}	14				3		26
1	3		4^{3}	5		7^{1}	12	9	13	11^{2}	10	8												6		14		2		27
1	3		4			12		9	10^{2}	11^{3}	13	8							6	7							5^{1}	2	14	28
1	3		4				8	9	10^{2}	11^{3}	13	12							6	7^{1}				14			5	2		29
1	3		4				8^{2}	9	10	11	12	13								7					6^{1}		5	2		30
1	3		4			12		9	10^{1}	11	13	8							6^{2}	7^{3}				14			5	2		31
1			4^{1}			12		9	10^{2}	11^{3}	7	8					13		6	14				3			5	2		32
	3^{3}		4				8	9	10^{2}	11^{1}	13	12							6	7		1					5	2	14	33
	3^{3}		4				8	9	10	11^{2}	12	13							6	7^{1}		1					5	2	14	34
			4				8	9	10^{1}	11	12	6							5	7		1		3				2		35
			4				8	9	10	11^{3}	13	12							6^{2}	7		1		14			5	2^{1}	3	36
			4				8		9^{2}	11	10	7^{1}							6			1	13	12			5	2	3	37
			4			14	8^{1}	9	10	11	13	12							6^{2}			1		7^{3}			5	2	3	38

UEFA Cup

First Round	Anorthosis	(h)	6-1
		(a)	1-1
Group G	Getafe	(h)	1-2
	Hapoel Tel Aviv	(a)	2-0
	Aalborg	(h)	3-2
	Anderlecht	(a)	1-1
Third Round	Slavia Prague	(a)	2-1
		(h)	1-1
Fourth Round	PSV Eindhoven	(h)	0-1
		(a)	1-0

FA Cup

Third Round	Reading	(h)	2-2
		(a)	1-0
Fourth Round	Manchester U	(a)	1-3

Carling Cup

Third Round	Middlesbrough	(h)	2-0
Fourth Round	Blackpool	(h)	2-0
Quarter-Final	Manchester C	(a)	2-0
Semi-Final	Arsenal	(a)	1-1
		(h)	5-1
Final *(at Wembley)*	Chelsea		2-1

Record Cup Victory: 13–0 v Oswestry U, FA Cup 2nd prel rd, 10 October 1914 – Ashcroft; Stevenson, Bullough, Hancock, Taylor, Holden (1), Moreton (1), Cunningham (2), Smith (5), Leck (3), Gould (1).

Record Defeat: 1–9 v Tottenham H, FA Cup 3rd rd (replay), 14 January 1953.

Most League Points (2 for a win): 60, Division 4, 1964–65.

Most League Points (3 for a win): 80, Division 4, 1988–89; Division 3, 1989–90; Division 2, 2002–03.

Most League Goals: 111, Division 3 (N), 1930–31.

Highest League Scorer in Season: Bunny Bell, 35, Division 3 (N), 1933–34.

Most League Goals in Total Aggregate: Ian Muir, 142, 1985–95.

Most League Goals in One Match: 9, Bunny Bell v Oldham Ath, Division 3N, 26 December 1935.

Most Capped Player: John Aldridge, 30 (69), Republic of Ireland.

Most League Appearances: Harold Bell, 595, 1946–64 (incl. League record 401 consecutive appearances).

Youngest League Player: Iain Hume, 16 years 167 days v Swindon T, 15 April 2000.

Record Transfer Fee Received: £2,500,000 from WBA for Jason Koumas, August 2002.

Record Transfer Fee Paid: £450,000 to Aston Villa for Shaun Teale, August 1995.

Football League Record: 1921 Original Member of Division 3 (N): 1938–39 Division 2; 1946–58 Division 3 (N); 1958–61 Division 3; 1961–67 Division 4; 1967–75 Division 3; 1975–76 Division 4; 1976–79 Division 3; 1979–89 Division 4; 1989–91 Division 3; 1991–92 Division 2; 1992–2001 Division 1; 2001–04 Division 2; 2004– FL 1.

MANAGERS

Bert Cooke 1912–35
Jackie Carr 1935–36
Jim Knowles 1936–39
Bill Ridding 1939–45
Ernie Blackburn 1946–55
Noel Kelly 1955–57
Peter Farrell 1957–60
Walter Galbraith 1961
Dave Russell 1961–69
Jackie Wright 1969–72
Ron Yeats 1972–75
John King 1975–80
Bryan Hamilton 1980–85
Frank Worthington 1985–87
Ronnie Moore 1987
John King 1987–96
John Aldridge 1996–2001
Dave Watson 2001–02
Ray Mathias 2002–03
Brian Little 2003–06
Ronnie Moore June 2006–

LATEST SEQUENCES

Longest Sequence of League Wins: 9, 9.2.1990 – 19.3.1990.

Longest Sequence of League Defeats: 8, 29.10.1938 – 17.12.1938.

Longest Sequence of League Draws: 5, 26.12.1997 – 31.1.1998.

Longest Sequence of Unbeaten League Matches: 18, 16.3.1970 – 4.9.1970.

Longest Sequence Without a League Win: 16, 8.11.1969 – 14.3.1970.

Successive Scoring Runs: 32 from 24.2.1934.

Successive Non-scoring Runs: 7 from 20.12.1997.

TEN YEAR LEAGUE RECORD

		P	W	D	L	F	A	Pts	Pos
1998-99	Div 1	46	12	20	14	63	61	56	15
1999-2000	Div 1	46	15	12	19	57	68	57	13
2000-01	Div 1	46	9	11	26	46	77	38	24
2001-02	Div 2	46	16	15	15	63	60	63	12
2002-03	Div 2	46	23	11	12	66	57	80	7
2003-04	Div 2	46	17	16	13	59	56	67	8
2004-05	FL 1	46	22	13	11	73	55	79	3
2005-06	FL 1	46	13	15	18	50	52	54	18
2006-07	FL 1	46	18	13	15	58	53	67	9
2007-08	FL 1	46	18	11	17	52	47	65	11

DID YOU KNOW ?

Even though they finished fourth in 1930–31, Tranmere Rovers total of 111 goals was the highest in the division. Jack Kennedy signed as an inside-forward from Sheffield United was their leading marksman with a total of 34 goals from 36 matches.

TRANMERE ROVERS 2007–08 LEAGUE RECORD

Match No.	Date	Venue	Opponents	Result		H/T Score	Lg. Pos.	Goalscorers	Attendance
1	Aug 11	H	Leeds U	L	1-2	1-0	—	Greenacre 22	11,008
2	18	A	Gillingham	W	2-0	1-0	7	Greenacre 19, Davies 50	5302
3	25	H	Brighton & HA	W	2-0	0-0	3	Greenacre 78, Shuker 90	5670
4	Sept 1	A	Yeovil T	D	1-1	0-0	5	Davies 90	4985
5	8	A	Carlisle U	W	1-0	1-0	2	Curran 42	6556
6	14	H	Luton T	W	2-1	0-1	—	Curran 83, Kay 86	6525
7	22	A	Cheltenham T	D	1-1	1-0	2	Greenacre 34	3742
8	29	H	Northampton T	D	2-2	0-2	2	Shuker 69, Taylor G 88	6338
9	Oct 2	H	Crewe Alex	D	1-1	0-0	—	Shuker 65	6155
10	6	A	Southend U	W	2-1	1-1	1	Chorley 30, Taylor G 55	7619
11	12	H	Walsall	D	0-0	0-0	—		7697
12	20	A	Swindon T	L	0-1	0-0	6		6430
13	26	H	Huddersfield T	W	3-0	1-0	—	McLaren 29, Cansdell-Sheriff 53, Taylor G 83	6008
14	Nov 3	A	Nottingham F	L	0-2	0-0	6		16,825
15	6	H	Oldham Ath	L	0-1	0-0	—		5473
16	17	A	Doncaster R	D	0-0	0-0	8		7070
17	24	H	Swansea C	L	0-1	0-0	9		6149
18	Dec 4	A	Hartlepool U	L	1-3	0-2	—	Cansdell-Sherriff 54	3583
19	8	H	Bournemouth	W	3-1	2-0	10	Zola 23, Greenacre (pen) 28, Jennings 63	5043
20	15	A	Port Vale	D	0-0	0-0	11		3604
21	22	A	Luton T	L	0-1	0-0	12		6070
22	26	H	Carlisle U	W	2-0	2-0	10	McLaren 16, Kay 45	8516
23	29	H	Cheltenham T	W	1-0	0-0	9	Zola 59	6111
24	Jan 1	A	Crewe Alex	L	3-4	2-1	9	Taylor A 8, Greenacre 31, McLaren 74	5137
25	8	A	Leyton Orient	L	0-3	0-1	—		3447
26	11	H	Bristol R	L	0-2	0-1	—		5887
27	19	A	Millwall	W	1-0	0-0	9	Kay 87	8925
28	26	H	Yeovil T	W	2-1	1-0	—	Zola 4, Myrie-Williams (pen) 62	5386
29	29	H	Gillingham	W	2-0	2-0	—	McLaren 7, Zola 14	5006
30	Feb 2	A	Leeds U	W	2-0	0-0	6	Myrie-Williams 61, Moore 69	24,907
31	9	H	Leyton Orient	D	1-1	1-0	6	Zola 2	6530
32	12	A	Brighton & HA	D	0-0	0-0	—		4797
33	16	H	Millwall	W	2-0	2-0	5	Taylor A 10, Moore 45	6108
34	23	A	Bristol R	D	1-1	0-0	6	Kay 74	7777
35	Mar 1	H	Doncaster R	L	0-1	0-1	6		7551
36	8	A	Oldham Ath	L	1-3	0-2	8	Jones 70	5442
37	11	A	Swansea C	D	1-1	0-1	—	Greenacre 90	11,039
38	15	H	Hartlepool U	W	3-1	1-0	7	Greenacre 36, Nelson (og) 64, Cansdell-Sherriff 90	5608
39	20	H	Port Vale	W	2-0	0-0	—	Greenacre (pen) 68, Moore 88	6484
40	24	A	Bournemouth	L	1-2	0-2	7-	Kay 87	4118
41	28	H	Swindon T	W	2-1	2-0	—	Jennings 12, Greenacre 40	5815
42	Apr 5	A	Walsall	L	1-2	1-1	7	Myrie-Williams 3	5745
43	12	H	Nottingham F	L	0-2	0-1	9		8689
44	19	A	Huddersfield T	L	0-1	0-0	9		8315
45	26	H	Southend U	W	1-0	0-0	8	Kay 53	5842
46	May 3	A	Northampton T	L	1-2	1-1	11	Greenacre 43	5088

Final League Position: 11

GOALSCORERS

League (52): Greenacre 11 (2 pens), Kay 6, Zola 5, McLaren 4, Cansdell-Sherriff 3, Moore 3, Myrie-Williams 3 (1 pen), Shuker 3, Taylor G 3, Curran 2, Davies 2, Jennings 2, Taylor A 2, Chorley 1, Jones 1, own goal 1.
Carling Cup (0).
FA Cup (7): Greenacre 3 (1 pen), Jennings 2, Kay 1, Taylor G 1.
J Paint Trophy (0).

Coyne D 41	Stockdale R 43 + 1	Cansdell-Sherriff S 43 + 1	Jennings S 39 + 2	Chorley B 30 + 1	Goodison I 42	McLaren P 43	Shuker C 22 + 1	Davies S 8 + 2	Greenacre C 36 + 4	Zola C 18 + 12	Curran C 1 + 34	Taylor G 19 + 4	Ahmed A 3 + 3	Tremarco C 4 + 4	Kay A 30 + 8	Achterberg J 5	Jones M 4 + 5	Cooper K 3 + 1	Taylor A 29 + 1	Henry P 1 + 1	Myrie-Williams J 21 + 4	Mullin J 4 + 6	Moore I 17	Match No.
1	2	3	4	5	6	7	8^{1}	9	10^{2}	11	12	13												1
1	2	3	4	5	6	7	8	9	10	11^{1}		12												2
1	2	3	4	5	6	7	8	9	10		12	11^{1}												3
1	2	3	4	5	6	7^{1}	8	9	10		11^{2}		12	13										4
1	2^{3}	3	4	5	6	7	8	9	10	11^{1}	12^{2}			13	14									5
1	2	3	4^{2}	5	6	7	8	9	10		12	11^{1}			13									6
	2	3	4^{2}	5	6	7	8	9	10		12	11^{1}			13	1								7
	2^{2}	3	4^{1}	5	6	7	8	9^{3}	10		12	11			13	1	14							8
	2	3	4	5	6	7^{2}	8		10		12	9			13	1	11^{1}							9
	2	3	4	5	6	7	8^{2}			12	13	9^{1}		10	11	1								10
	2	3	4^{2}	5	6	7	8^{3}			9^{1}	12	10		11	13	1	14							11
1	2	3	4^{2}	5	6	7			10	12	13	9^{1}		8	11									12
1	2	3		5	6	7			10^{1}		12	9		13	8		4	11^{2}						13
1	2	3	4^{2}	5	6	7			10		12	9	13		8			11^{1}						14
1	2	3	13	5	6	7	8^{1}		10		12	9			4^{2}		14	11^{3}						15
1	2		4		6	7	8^{3}		10^{1}			9	11^{2}	3▪	5			12	14	13				16
1	2	12	4		6	7	8^{3}		10	13	14	9^{2}			5				3		11^{1}			17
1		11	4	5	6	7			10	9					2		8^{1}		3		12			18
1	12	11	4	5	6^{1}	7			10	9					2				3		8			19
1		11		5	6	7			10	9^{2}	12	13			2				3		8^{1}	4		20
1	2	5	4		6		8		10^{1}		12	9	11^{2}						3	7	13			21
1	2	11	4		6	7	8^{2}		10	9^{1}	12				5				3		13			22
1	2	11	4		6	7			10^{1}	9	12				5				3		8			23
1	2	11^{2}	4	12	6▪	7			10	9^{3}	13	14			5				3		8^{1}			24
1	2	3▪	4	5		7			10^{2}	11	12	9^{1}		13	6						8			25
1	2		4	5		7			10	12	13	9^{2}			6		11^{1}		3		8			26
1	2	11^{3}	4^{2}		6	7				10^{1}	12	9			5		14		3		8	13		27
1	2	11	4		6	7^{2}				10	12	9^{1}			5				3		8	13		28
1	2	11	4^{2}		6	7				10	12	9			5				3		8^{1}	13		29
1	2	11	4		6	7			12	10	13				5				3		8^{2}		9^{1}	30
1	2	11	4		6	7				10	12				5				3		8^{1}		9	31
1	2	11	4		6	7			12	10^{1}					5				3		8		9	32
1	2	11	4		6	7			10^{1}		12				5				3		8		9	33
1	2	11	4▪		6	7			10	12					5				3		8^{2}	13	9^{1}	34
1	2	11			6	7			10^{2}	12	13				5				3		8^{1}	4	9	35
1	2	11		5	6^{2}	7			12	10^{3}			14				13		3		8	4^{1}	9	36
1	2	11		5		7			12	13			4		6				3		8^{1}	10^{2}	9	37
1	2	11	4^{2}	5		7	8^{1}		10	12					6				3			13	9	38
1	2	11	4	5	6	7	8^{2}		10^{1}	12									3		13		9	39
1	2	11	4^{3}	5	6	7			10	12	13				14				3		8^{1}		9^{2}	40
1	2	11	4	5	6	7			10^{2}	12	13								3		8^{1}		9	41
1	2	11	4^{1}	5▪	6	7	12		10^{2}	13					14				3		8^{3}		9	42
1	2	11^{2}	4		6	7	8^{1}	13	10		12				5				3				9	43
1	2	11^{2}	4	7	6		8		10		12				5				3			13	9^{1}	44
1	2	11	4	5	6		7^{1}		10		12				8				3				9	45
1	2^{3}	11^{2}	14	5	6▪	8	7^{1}	12	10		13				4				3				9	46

FA Cup

First Round	Chesterfield	(a)	2-1
Second Round	Bradford C	(a)	3-0
Third Round	Hereford U	(h)	2-2
		(a)	0-1

Carling Cup

First Round	Stockport Co	(a)	0-1

J Paint Trophy

First Round	Morecambe	(h)	0-1

WALSALL FL Championship 1

FOUNDATION

Two of the leading clubs around Walsall in the 1880s were Walsall Swifts (formed 1877) and Walsall Town (formed 1879). The Swifts were winners of the Birmingham Senior Cup in 1881, while the Town reached the 4th round (5th round modern equivalent) of the FA Cup in 1883. These clubs amalgamated as Walsall Town Swifts in 1888, becoming simply Walsall in 1895.

Banks's Stadium, Bescot Crescent, Walsall WS1 4SA.

Telephone: 0871 221 0442.

Fax: (01922) 613 202.

Ticket Office: 0871 663 0111 or 0871 663 0222.

Website: www.saddlers.co.uk

Email: info@walsallfc.co.uk

Ground Capacity: 11,230.

Record Attendance: 11,037 v Wolverhampton W, Division 1, 11 January 2003.

Pitch Measurements: 110yd × 73yd.

Chairman: Jeff Bonser.

Chief Executive/Secretary: K. R. Whalley.

Manager: Jimmy Mullen.

First Team Coach: John Schofield.

Physio: Jon Whitney.

Colours: White shirts with red trim, red shorts with white stripe, white stockings with red stripe.

Change Colours: Black shirts with red trim, black shorts, black stockings with red stripe.

Year Formed: 1888.

Turned Professional: 1888.

Ltd Co.: 1921.

Previous Names: Walsall Swifts (founded 1877) and Walsall Town (founded 1879) amalgamated in 1888 and were known as Walsall Town Swifts until 1895.

Club Nickname: 'The Saddlers'.

Grounds: 1888, Fellows Park; 1990, Bescot Stadium.

First Football League Game: 3 September 1892, Division 2, v Darwen (h) L 1–2 – Hawkins; Withington, Pinches; Robinson, Whitrick, Forsyth; Marshall, Holmes, Turner, Gray (1), Pangbourn.

Record League Victory: 10–0 v Darwen, Division 2, 4 March 1899 – Tennent; E. Peers (1), Davies; Hickinbotham, Jenkyns, Taggart; Dean (3), Vail (2), Aston (4), Martin, Griffin.

Record Cup Victory: 7–0 v Macclesfield T (a), FA Cup 2nd rd, 6 December 1997 – Walker; Evans, Marsh, Viveash (1), Ryder, Peron, Boli (2 incl. 1p) (Ricketts), Porter (2), Keates, Watson (Platt), Hodge (2 incl. 1p).

Record Defeat: 0–12 v Small Heath, 17 December 1892. 0–12 v Darwen, 26 December 1896, both Division 2.

HONOURS

Football League: Division 2: Runners-up, 1998–99, Promoted to Division 1 – 2000–01 (play-offs); FL 2 – Champions 2006–07; Division 3 – Runners-up 1960–61, 1994–95; Division 4 – Champions 1959–60; Runners-up 1979–80.

FA Cup: best season: 5th rd, 1939, 1975, 1978, 1987, 2002, 2003 and last 16 1889.

Football League Cup: Semi-final 1984.

SKY SPORTS FACT FILE

In successive seasons 1897–98 and 1898–99, Walsall were particularly harsh against visitors Blackpool. On both occasions they won 6–0. Jack Aston scored twice in each match and in the first encounter there was a hat-trick for Sammy Holmes, too.

Most League Points (2 for a win): 65, Division 4, 1959–60.

Most League Points (3 for a win): 89, FL 2, 2006–07.

Most League Goals: 102, Division 4, 1959–60.

Highest League Scorer in Season: Gilbert Alsop, 40, Division 3 (N), 1933–34 and 1934–35.

Most League Goals in Total Aggregate: Tony Richards, 184, 1954–63; Colin Taylor, 184, 1958–63, 1964–68, 1969–73.

Most League Goals in One Match: 5, Gilbert Alsop v Carlisle U, Division 3N, 2 February 1935; 5, Bill Evans v Mansfield T, Division 3N, 5 October 1935; 5, Johnny Devlin v Torquay U, Division 3S, 1 September 1949.

Most Capped Player: Mick Kearns, 15 (18), Republic of Ireland.

Most League Appearances: Colin Harrison, 467, 1964–82.

Youngest League Player: Geoff Morris, 16 years 218 days v Scunthorpe U, 14 September 1965.

Record Transfer Fee Received: £750,000 from Coventry C for Scott Dann, January 2008.

Record Transfer Fee Paid: £175,000 to Birmingham C for Alan Buckley, June 1979.

Football League Record: 1892 Elected to Division 2; 1895 Failed re-election; 1896–1901 Division 2; 1901 Failed re-election; 1921 Original Member of Division 3 (N); 1927–31 Division 3 (S); 1931–36 Division 3 (N); 1936–58 Division 3 (S); 1958–60 Division 4; 1960–61 Division 3; 1961–63 Division 2; 1963–79 Division 3; 1979–80 Division 4; 1980–88 Division 3; 1988–89 Division 2; 1989–90 Division 3; 1990–92 Division 4; 1992–95 Division 3; 1995–99 Division 2; 1999–2000 Division 1; 2000–01 Division 2; 2001–04 Division 1; 2004–06 FL 1; 2006–07 FL 2; 2007– FL 1.

LATEST SEQUENCES

Longest Sequence of League Wins: 7, 10.10.1959 – 21.11.1959.

Longest Sequence of League Defeats: 15, 29.10.1988 – 4.2.1989.

Longest Sequence of League Draws: 5, 7.5.1988 – 17.9.1988.

Longest Sequence of Unbeaten League Matches: 21, 6.11.1979 – 22.3.1980.

Longest Sequence Without a League Win: 18, 15.10.1988 – 4.2.1989.

Successive Scoring Runs: 27 from 9.2.1928.

Successive Non-scoring Runs: 5 from 8.10.1927.

MANAGERS

H. Smallwood 1888–91
(Secretary-Manager)
A. G. Burton 1891–93
J. H. Robinson 1893–95
C. H. Ailso 1895–96
(Secretary-Manager)
A. E. Parsloe 1896–97
(Secretary-Manager)
L. Ford 1897–98 *(Secretary-Manager)*
G. Hughes 1898–99
(Secretary-Manager)
L. Ford 1899–1901
(Secretary-Manager)
J. E. Shutt 1908–13
(Secretary-Manager)
Haydn Price 1914–20
Joe Burchell 1920–26
David Ashworth 1926–27
Jack Torrance 1927–28
James Kerr 1928–29
Sid Scholey 1929–30
Peter O'Rourke 1930–32
Bill Slade 1932–34
Andy Wilson 1934–37
Tommy Lowes 1937–44
Harry Hibbs 1944–51
Tony McPhee 1951
Brough Fletcher 1952–53
Major Frank Buckley 1953–55
John Love 1955–57
Billy Moore 1957–64
Alf Wood 1964
Reg Shaw 1964–68
Dick Graham 1968
Ron Lewin 1968–69
Billy Moore 1969–72
John Smith 1972–73
Doug Fraser 1973–77
Dave Mackay 1977–78
Alan Ashman 1978
Frank Sibley 1979
Alan Buckley 1979–86
Neil Martin *(Joint Manager with Buckley)* 1981–82
Tommy Coakley 1986–88
John Barnwell 1989–90
Kenny Hibbitt 1990–94
Chris Nicholl 1994–97
Jan Sorensen 1997–98
Ray Graydon 1998–2002
Colin Lee 2002–04
Paul Merson 2004–06
Kevin Broadhurst 2006
Richard Money 2006–08
Jimmy Mullen April 2008–

TEN YEAR LEAGUE RECORD

		P	W	D	L	F	A	Pts	Pos
1998-99	Div 2	46	26	9	11	63	47	87	2
1999-2000	Div 1	46	11	13	22	52	77	46	22
2000-01	Div 2	46	23	12	11	79	50	81	4
2001-02	Div 1	46	13	12	21	51	71	51	18
2002-03	Div 1	46	15	9	22	57	69	54	17
2003-04	Div 1	46	13	12	21	45	65	51	22
2004-05	FL 1	46	16	12	18	65	69	60	14
2005-06	FL 1	46	11	14	21	47	70	47	24
2006-07	FL 2	46	25	14	7	66	34	89	1
2007-08	FL 1	46	16	16	14	52	46	64	12

DID YOU KNOW 

On 3 November 2007 the much travelled striker Tommy Mooney, discovered by Aston Villa, in his first season with Walsall hit his 200th and 201st career goals against Cheltenham Town including a penalty in the 2–0 win.

WALSALL 2007–08 LEAGUE RECORD

Match No.	Date	Venue	Opponents	Result		H/T Score	Lg. Pos.	Goalscorers	Attendance
1	Aug 11	H	Carlisle U	D	1-1	0-1	—	Mooney 47	6933
2	18	A	Leyton Orient	L	0-1	0-0	20		4524
3	25	H	Swansea C	L	1-3	1-2	21	Butler 7	5673
4	Sept 1	A	Gillingham	L	1-2	1-2	23	Fox 20	4806
5	8	H	Port Vale	D	0-0	0-0	23		4967
6	15	A	Millwall	W	2-1	1-0	20	Fox 42, Deeney 86	7720
7	22	H	Oldham Ath	L	0-3	0-1	24		6202
8	29	A	Hartlepool U	W	1-0	0-0	19	Hall 90	4948
9	Oct 2	A	Doncaster R	W	3-2	1-2	—	Fox 28, Bradley 66, Mooney (pen) 71	6038
10	6	H	Huddersfield T	W	4-0	2-0	10	Gerrard 31, Sonko 43, Bradley 50, Mooney 67	5112
11	12	A	Tranmere R	D	0-0	0-0	—		7697
12	20	H	Southend U	L	0-2	0-1	14		5661
13	27	A	Bournemouth	D	1-1	0-1	15	Wrack 81	5414
14	Nov 3	H	Cheltenham T	W	2-0	1-0	13	Mooney 2 (1 pen) 10 (p), 56	4810
15	6	A	Brighton & HA	D	1-1	0-1	—	Demontagnac 78	4717
16	17	H	Luton T	D	0-0	0-0	14		5056
17	24	A	Northampton T	W	2-0	1-0	10	Bradley 45, Demontagnac 86	5767
18	Dec 4	H	Nottingham F	W	1-0	0-0	—	Ricketts 48	6605
19	8	A	Crewe Alex	D	0-0	0-0	8		4639
20	15	H	Leeds U	D	1-1	0-0	9	Mooney 76	10,102
21	22	H	Millwall	W	3-0	3-0	6	Mooney 2 29, 38, Harris (og) 45	5433
22	26	A	Port Vale	D	1-1	0-1	7	Ricketts 90	6029
23	29	A	Oldham Ath	W	2-0	1-0	6	Dann 2, Ricketts 65	5292
24	Jan 1	H	Doncaster R	D	1-1	0-1	6	Dann 75	6266
25	8	A	Yeovil T	W	2-0	0-0	—	Dann 59, Nicholls 64	4319
26	12	H	Swindon T	D	2-2	1-0	5	Sonko 2 22, 68	5449
27	19	A	Bristol R	D	1-1	1-0	7	Sonko 37	6276
28	26	H	Gillingham	W	2-1	1-0	—	Mooney 28, Sonko 72	4914
29	29	H	Leyton Orient	D	0-0	0-0	—		4643
30	Feb 2	A	Carlisle U	L	1-2	1-1	5	Holmes 23	6220
31	9	H	Yeovil T	W	2-0	0-0	5	Holmes 67, Betsy 90	5034
32	12	A	Swansea C	L	0-1	0-0	—		13,020
33	23	A	Swindon T	W	3-0	1-0	5	Holmes 2 11, 57, Nicholls 90	6265
34	Mar 1	A	Luton T	W	1-0	1-0	5	Moore 4	6157
35	8	H	Northampton T	L	0-2	0-1	5		6844
36	11	H	Brighton & HA	L	1-2	1-1	—	Gerrard 29	4309
37	15	A	Nottingham F	D	1-1	0-0	6	Wilson (og) 54	17,177
38	22	A	Leeds U	L	0-2	0-1	9		19,095
39	24	H	Crewe Alex	D	1-1	0-0	9-	Roper 90	4741
40	29	A	Southend U	L	0-1	0-0	10		8145
41	Apr 5	H	Tranmere R	W	2-1	1-1	8	N'Dour 45, Demontagnac 59	5745
42	12	A	Cheltenham T	W	2-1	2-0	7	Mooney (pen) 27, Gerrard 28	4861
43	15	H	Bristol R	L	0-1	0-1	—		5200
44	19	H	Bournemouth	L	1-3	1-2	8	Betsy 33	4530
45	26	A	Huddersfield T	L	0-2	0-1	10		9969
46	May 3	H	Hartlepool U	D	2-2	2-1	12	Dobson 9, Mooney 15	5021

Final League Position: 12

GOALSCORERS

League (52): Mooney 11 (3 pens), Sonko 5, Holmes 4, Bradley 3, Dann 3, Demontagnac 3, Fox 3, Gerrard 3, Ricketts 3, Betsy 2, Nicholls 2, Butler 1, Deeney 1, Dobson 1, Hall 1, Moore 1, N'Dour 1, Roper 1, Wrack 1, own goals 2.
Carling Cup (0).
FA Cup (5): Ricketts 2 (1 pen), Demontagnac 1, Mooney 1, Nicholls 1.
J Paint Trophy (0).

Ince C 46	Wrack D 35 + 2	Boertien P 20	Sonner D 6	Gerrard A 44	Dann S 28	Hall P 7 + 12	Dobson M 21 + 3	Carneiro C 2 + 1	Mooney T 36	Fox D 21 + 1	Nicholls A 7 + 12	Deeney T 16 + 19	Weston R 43 + 1	Roper I 19	Bradley M 29 + 6	Demontagnac I 10 + 20	Sonko E 30 + 7	Butler M 5	McDermott D 1 + 12	Mattis D 4	Ricketts M 12	Taundry R 12 + 9	Sweeney P 7	Brittain M — + 1	Holmes L 19	Betsy K 16	N'Dour A 3 + 6	Moore S 3 + 2	Smith E 4	Craddock J — + 1	*Match No.*
1	2	3	4	5	6	7^1	8	9^2	10	11	12	13																			1
1	11	3	4		6	7	8^2	9	10				2^1	5	12	13															2
1	7	3	4		6	11^2	8^3	13		12			2	5■		10^1	14	9													3
1	7	3		5	6	12	8^3			11		10^2	2		4^1	13	14	9													4
1	7	3	8^3	4^1	6	10				11^2	12		2	5		13		9	14												5
1	7	3	8	4	6	10^1				11		13	2	5^3		12^2	14	9													6
1	7		8^2	4^3	6	12			9	3		14	2	5		13	11^1	10													7
1	2			5	6	12	8		9	3		7^1			13	10^3	11		14	4^2											8
1	2^1			5	6		8		9	3			12		4	10^2	11		13	7											9
1				5	6	12	8		9^2	3		13	2		7	10^1	11^3		14	4											10
1				5	6		8		9	3		12	2		4	10	7^2		13	11^1											11
1	12			5	6	13	8		9	3	14	10^3	2		11^2		7		4^1												12
1	11			5	6	12	4^2		9	3		13	2		8	10^3	7^1		14												13
1	7			5	6	12	4^1		9^2	3		14	2		8	13	11				10^3										14
1	11			5	6	7			9	3			2		4	12	8^1				10										15
1	11			5	6	7^1			9	3			2			8^2	4		12		10	13									16
1	11			5	6	12			10	3			2		4	13	7^1				9^2		8								17
1	11			5	6	12			9	3			2		4		7^1				10		8								18
1	11			5	6				9	3		13	2		4	12	7				10^2		8^1								19
1	7			5	6				9	3		11^1	2		4		12				10		8								20
1	7			5	6				9		12	11^2	2		4^3	13	14				10^1	3	8								21
1	11			5	6				9^3	3■	12	7^2	2		4	13	14				10		8^1								22
1	11			5	6	12						7^2	2		4	9^1	13				10	3	8								23
1	7			5	6	12				11	13	14	2		4	9^1	8^3				10	3^2									24
1	7			5	6	12				3	10^3	11	2		4		8^1				9^2	13		14							25
1	7			5	6						9	11	2		4	12	10					3			8^1						26
1	7	3		5	6		9^1				12	10^3	2		4	13	11					14			8^2						27
1	7	3		5			12		9^2		13	10	2	6	4^1		11								8						28
1	7	3		5	6				9		10^3	11^1	2		13	12	8^2					14			4						29
1	7^1	3		5					9			12	2	6	4^3		11		13			14			8	10^2					30
1	7^1	3		5					9		13^3	10^2	2	6			11					12			4	8	14				31
1		3		5							9^2	10	2	6		12	8					4^1			7	11	13				32
1	7	3		5					9^1		12	13	2	6	4^3		11^2								8	10	14				33
1	7	3		5			13		9			12	2	6			11^2					14			4	10^3		8^1			34
1	7	3^2		5			12		9			13	2^1	6	4							14			8	11		10^3			35
1	7	3^2		5					9			12	2	6	4^3				13			14■			8	11		10^1			36
1		3		5			7		9			13	2	6	4	12	11^2		14						8^1	10^3					37
1	7^1	3		5			4		9^2				2	6	12		11								8	10		13			38
1	7^2	3		5			4		9		12	13	2	6			11^3								8	10^1	14				39
1		3		5					9		7^3	10^2	2	6	4				12			11			8^1		14	13			40
1				5			8		9			13	2	6	14	12	7^1					3			11^2	10	4^3				41
1				5			4		9			14	2	6^1	12	13^3	7					3			11^2	10	8				42
1				5			4^2		9			14	2			12	7^3		13			3			11^1	10	8		6		43
1				5			4		9		12	7^2	2		8^1							3			11	10	13		6		44
1	7			5			8		9		10		2^1		4	12						3				11			6		45
1	12			5			11		9		7^2		2		4^1	8						3				10			6	13	46

FA Cup			
First Round	Shrewsbury T	(h)	2-0
Second Round	Northampton T	(a)	1-1
		(h)	1-0
Third Round	Millwall	(h)	0-0
		(a)	1-2

Carling Cup			
First Round	Swansea C	(a)	0-2

J Paint Trophy			
First Round	Bournemouth	(a)	0-2

WATFORD FL Championship

FOUNDATION

The club was formed as Watford Rovers in 1881. The name was changed to West Herts in 1893 and then the name Watford was adopted after rival club Watford St Mary's was absorbed in 1898.

Vicarage Road Stadium, Vicarage Road, Watford, Hertsfordshire, WD18 0ER.

Telephone: 0845 442 1881.

Fax: (01923) 496 001.

Ticket Office: 0845 442 1881.

Website: www.watfordfc.com

Email: yourvoice@watfordfc.com

Ground Capacity: 18,400.

Record Attendance: 34,099 v Manchester U, FA Cup 4th rd (replay), 3 February 1969.

Pitch Measurements: 114 yd × 73yd.

Chairman: Graham Simpson.

Chief Executive: Mark Ashton.

Secretary: Michelle Ives.

Manager: Adrian Boothroyd.

Physio: Andy Rolls.

Colours: Yellow shirts, black shorts, yellow stockings.

Change Colours: Red shirts, red shorts, red stockings.

Year Formed: 1881.

Turned Professional: 1897.

Ltd Co.: 1909.

Club Nickname: 'The Hornets'.

Previous Names: 1881, Watford Rovers; 1893, West Herts; 1898, Watford.

Grounds: 1883, Vicarage Meadow, Rose and Crown Meadow; 1889, Colney Butts; 1890, Cassio Road; 1922, Vicarage Road.

First Football League Game: 28 August 1920, Division 3, v QPR (a) W 2–1 – Williams; Horseman, F. Gregory; Bacon, Toone, Wilkinson; Bassett, Ronald (1), Hoddinott, White (1), Waterall.

Record League Victory: 8–0 v Sunderland, Division 1, 25 September 1982 – Sherwood; Rice, Rostron, Taylor, Terry, Bolton, Callaghan (2), Blissett (4), Jenkins (2), Jackett, Barnes.

Record Cup Victory: 10–1 v Lowestoft T, FA Cup 1st rd, 27 November 1926 – Yates; Prior, Fletcher (1); F. Smith, 'Bert' Smith, Strain; Stephenson, Warner (3), Edmonds (3), Swan (1), Daniels (1), (1 og).

Record Defeat: 0–10 v Wolverhampton W, FA Cup 1st rd (replay), 24 January 1912.

Most League Points (2 for a win): 71, Division 4, 1977–78.

HONOURS

Football League: Division 1 – Runners-up 1982–83, promoted from Division 1 1998–99 (play-offs); promoted from FL C (play-offs) 2005–06; Division 2 – Champions 1997–98; Runners-up 1981–82; Division 3 – Champions 1968–69; Runners-up 1978–79; Division 4 – Champions 1977–78; Promoted 1959–60 (4th).

FA Cup: Runners-up 1984, semi-finals 1970, 1984, 1987, 2003, 2007.

Football League Cup: Semi-final 1979.

European Competitions: *UEFA Cup:* 1983–84.

SKY SPORTS FACT FILE

Signed in 1913–14 by Watford, goalkeeper Skilly Williams served the club for twelve seasons and had the satisfaction of saving a penalty in the club's first League game. He was employed as an attendant at Leavesden Mental Hospital Asylum.

Most League Points (3 for a win): 88, Division 2, 1997–98.

Most League Goals: 92, Division 4, 1959–60.

Highest League Scorer in Season: Cliff Holton, 42, Division 4, 1959–60.

Most League Goals in Total Aggregate: Luther Blissett, 148, 1976–83, 1984–88, 1991–92.

Most League Goals in One Match: 5, Eddie Mummery v Newport Co, Division 3S, 5 January 1924.

Most Capped Player: John Barnes, 31 (79), England and Kenny Jackett, 31, Wales.

Most League Appearances: Luther Blissett, 415, 1976–83, 1984–88, 1991–92.

Youngest League Player: Keith Mercer, 16 years 125 days v Tranmere R, 16 February 1973.

Record Transfer Fee Received: £9,600,000 from Aston V for Ashley Young, January 2007.

Record Transfer Fee Paid: £3,250,000 to WBA for Nathan Ellington, August 2007.

Football League Record: 1920 Original Member of Division 3; 1921–58 Division 3 (S); 1958–60 Division 4; 1960–69 Division 3; 1969–72 Division 2; 1972–75 Division 3; 1975–78 Division 4; 1978–79 Division 3; 1979–82 Division 2; 1982–88 Division 1; 1988–92 Division 2; 1992–96 Division 1; 1996–98 Division 2; 1998–99 Division 1; 1999–2000 FA Premier League; 2000–04 Division 1; 2004–06 FL C; 2006–07 FA Premier League; 2007– FL C.

MANAGERS

John Goodall 1903–10
Harry Kent 1910–26
Fred Pagnam 1926–29
Neil McBain 1929–37
Bill Findlay 1938–47
Jack Bray 1947–48
Eddie Hapgood 1948–50
Ron Gray 1950–51
Haydn Green 1951–52
Len Goulden 1952–55
(General Manager to 1956)
Johnny Paton 1955–56
Neil McBain 1956–59
Ron Burgess 1959–63
Bill McGarry 1963–64
Ken Furphy 1964–71
George Kirby 1971–73
Mike Keen 1973–77
Graham Taylor 1977–87
Dave Bassett 1987–88
Steve Harrison 1988–90
Colin Lee 1990
Steve Perryman 1990–93
Glenn Roeder 1993–96
Kenny Jackett 1996–97
Graham Taylor 1997–2001
Gianluca Vialli 2001–02
Ray Lewington 2002–05
Adrian Boothroyd March 2005–

LATEST SEQUENCES

Longest Sequence of League Wins: 7, 28.8.2000 – 14.10.2000.

Longest Sequence of League Defeats: 9, 26.12.1972 – 27.2.1973.

Longest Sequence of League Draws: 7, 30.11.1996 – 27.1.1997.

Longest Sequence of Unbeaten League Matches: 22, 1.10.1996 – 1.3.1997.

Longest Sequence Without a League Win: 19, 27.11.1971 – 8.4.1972.

Successive Scoring Runs: 22 from 20.8.1985.

Successive Non-scoring Runs: 7 from 18.12.1971.

TEN YEAR LEAGUE RECORD

		P	*W*	*D*	*L*	*F*	*A*	*Pts*	*Pos*
1998-99	Div 1	46	21	14	11	65	56	77	5
1999-2000	PR Lge	38	6	6	26	35	77	24	20
2000-01	Div 1	46	20	9	17	76	67	69	9
2001-02	Div 1	46	16	11	19	62	56	59	14
2002-03	Div 1	46	17	9	20	54	70	60	13
2003-04	Div 1	46	15	12	19	54	68	57	16
2004-05	FL C	46	12	16	18	52	59	52	18
2005-06	FL C	46	22	15	9	77	53	81	3
2006-07	PR Lge	38	5	13	20	29	59	28	20
2007-08	FL C	46	18	16	12	62	56	70	6

DID YOU KNOW ?

In the 1980–81 League Cup, Watford were drawn against the reigning European Cup holders Nottingham Forest. They produced an outstanding performance to win 4–1. Luther Blissett put them ahead from the penalty spot and Ross Jenkins completed the win with a hat-trick.

WATFORD 2007–08 LEAGUE RECORD

Match No.	Date	Venue	Opponents	Result		H/T Score	Lg. Pos.	Goalscorers	Attendance
1	Aug 11	A	Wolverhampton W	W	2-1	0-1	—	Stewart 87, King (pen) 90	23,115
2	18	H	Sheffield U	W	1-0	0-0	2	Williamson 56	16,414
3	25	A	Leicester C	L	1-4	0-1	5	King (pen) 90	21,642
4	Sept 1	H	Ipswich T	W	2-0	1-0	2	Henderson 6, Smith 75	17,295
5	16	H	Southampton	W	3-2	1-1	1	Shittu 42, Henderson 2 81, 90	15,915
6	19	A	Cardiff C	W	2-1	1-0	—	Henderson 2 17, 78	13,169
7	22	A	QPR	D	1-1	0-0	1	Johnson 49	14,240
8	29	H	Blackpool	D	1-1	1-0	1	Johnson 41	16,580
9	Oct 2	H	Sheffield W	W	2-1	2-1	—	Henderson 6, King (pen) 16	15,473
10	6	A	Scunthorpe U	W	3-1	1-1	1	Johnson 10, Henderson 61, King 63	7515
11	20	H	Hull C	W	1-0	1-0	1	King 20	15,803
12	23	A	Coventry C	W	3-0	2-0	—	Johnson 30, King 42, Henderson 46	17,032
13	29	A	Crystal Palace	W	2-0	1-0	—	Smith 32, King 67	13,986
14	Nov 3	H	WBA	L	0-3	0-2	1		18,273
15	6	A	Norwich C	W	3-1	2-0	—	Henderson 36, Marshall (og) 43, King 88	24,192
16	10	H	Colchester U	D	2-2	1-1	1	Johnson 4, King 64	16,069
17	24	A	Barnsley	L	2-3	2-2	1	Shittu 2 36, 45	10,117
18	27	H	Burnley	L	1-2	0-0	—	Shittu 86	15,021
19	Dec 1	H	Bristol C	L	1-2	0-0	1	O'Toole 87	16,689
20	4	A	Colchester U	W	3-2	2-2	—	King 40, O'Toole 42, Priskin 64	5760
21	9	A	Stoke C	D	0-0	0-0	1		15,516
22	15	H	Plymouth Arg	L	0-1	0-0	2		18,532
23	22	A	Sheffield W	W	1-0	1-0	1	McAnuff 6	19,641
24	26	H	Cardiff C	D	2-2	0-1	2	DeMerit 49, McAnuff 90	17,014
25	29	H	QPR	L	2-4	0-3	2	Francis 52, Shittu 84	18,698
26	Jan 1	A	Southampton	W	3-0	1-0	2	Francis 45, King 55, Henderson 62	23,008
27	12	A	Preston NE	L	0-1	0-0	3		12,347
28	19	H	Charlton Ath	D	1-1	0-0	2	Ellington 59	17,214
29	29	A	Sheffield U	D	1-1	1-0	—	Ellington 21	23,161
30	Feb 2	H	Wolverhampton W	W	3-0	1-0	2	Kabba 1, Smith 2 76, 78	18,082
31	9	A	Ipswich T	W	2-1	1-0	1	Smith 33, Ellington 56	24,227
32	12	H	Leicester C	W	1-0	1-0	—	Henderson 45	15,944
33	16	A	Charlton Ath	D	2-2	0-2	—	O'Toole 54, Shittu 55	26,337
34	23	H	Preston NE	D	0-0	0-0	3		16,798
35	Mar 1	A	Burnley	D	2-2	1-0	3	Henderson 23, Stewart 85	13,677
36	4	H	Norwich C	D	1-1	1-0	—	Shittu 11	16,537
37	11	A	Bristol C	D	0-0	0-0	—		19,026
38	15	H	Stoke C	D	0-0	0-0	3		18,338
39	22	A	Plymouth Arg	D	1-1	1-1	4	Williamson 37	17,511
40	29	A	Hull C	L	0-3	0-2	5		23,501
41	Apr 5	H	Coventry C	W	2-1	1-0	4	Ellington 7, Smith 79	17,188
42	9	H	Barnsley	L	0-3	0-1	—		16,129
43	12	A	WBA	D	1-1	1-0	5	Bromby 6	26,508
44	19	H	Crystal Palace	L	0-2	0-0	5		17,694
45	26	H	Scunthorpe U	L	0-1	0-0	5		16,454
46	May 4	A	Blackpool	D	1-1	0-1	6	Smith 62	9640

Final League Position: 6

GOALSCORERS

League (62): Henderson 12, King 11 (3 pens), Shittu 7, Smith 7, Johnson 5, Ellington 4, O'Toole 3, Francis 2, McAnuff 2, Stewart 2, Williamson 2, Bromby 1, DeMerit 1, Kabba 1, Priskin 1, own goal 1.
Carling Cup (3): Campana 1, Priskin 1, Rinaldi 1.
FA Cup (3): Shittu 2, O'Toole 1.
Play-Offs (1): Henderson 1.

Poom M 12	Doyley L 36	Stewart J 33 + 6	Mahon G 19	Shittu D 37 + 2	DeMerit J 30 + 5	McAnuff J 31 + 8	Williamson L 27 + 5	Priskin T 7 + 7	King M 25 + 2	Smith T 44	Henderson D 34 + 6	Kabba S 7 + 7	Hoskins W — + 1	Mariappa A 13 + 12	Ellington N 18 + 16	O'Toole J 23 + 12	Johnson A 11 + 1	Lee R 34 + 1	Francis D 6 + 5	Ainsworth L 3 + 5	Jackson M 6	Davenport C 1	Bangura A 3 + 4	Sadler M 14 + 1	Eustace J 13	Bromby L 16	John C 3 + 2	*Match No.*
1	2	3	4	5	6	7	8	9^1	10	11^2	12	13																1
1	2	3	4	5	6	7	8		10	11^1	9	12																2
1	2	3	4	5	6^3	7^2	8	12	10	11		9^1	14	13														3
1	2	3	4	5	6	7	8		10	11^2	9^1				12	13												4
1	2	3	4	5	6	7^3	8^2		10	11	12			13	9^1		14											5
1	2	3	4	5	6	12			13	11	9			7^3	10^2	14	8^1											6
1	2	3	4	5	6^2	12	8		10	11^1	9^3			13	14		7											7
1	2	3	4	5	6	12	8		10	11	9^2				13		7^1											8
1	2	3	4	5	6	12	8		10^2	11	9					13	7^1											9
	2	3	4	5	6	12	8■	13	10^2	11	9^3					14	7^1	1										10
	2	3	4	5	6	12			10	11^1	9^2				13	7	8	1										11
	2	3	4	5	6	12		13	10^3	11^1	9^2				14	7	8	1										12
	2	3	4	5	6	12		13	10^3	7^1	9^2				14	11	8	1										13
	2	3	4^1	5	6^2		12		10	11	9^3			13	14	7	8	1										14
	2	3	4	5			8	12	10^1	11	9			6		13	7^2	1										15
	2	3^1	4	5			8		10	11	9			6	12		7	1										16
	2	3	4^1	5			8		10	11	9	7		6^2				1	12	13								17
1	2	3^3	4^2	5	6		8	12	10	11	9^1	7			13				14									18
1	2	3	4^2	5	6	7	8		10	11	9^1				12	13												19
1^6	2	3		5	6	7^2	8	9^1	10	11	12					4		15	13									20
	2	3			6	7	8	9^2	10	11^1					12	4		1	13		5							21
	2	3^2			6		8	9^1	10	11				13	12	4		1	14	7^3	5							22
	2	3			6	7^1	12		10	11	13				9^2	8		1	4		5							23
	2	3		12	6	7	13		10^3	11	14				9	4^2		1	8		5^1							24
	2^3	3		12	6	7	8		13	11	9				10^2	14		1	4		5^1							25
	2	3		5	6	7	8^1		10	11^2	9			12		13		1	4									26
	2	3			6	7	8		10	11	9			12		13		1	4^2		5^1							27
	2	3			6	7	8			11	9			12^2	10^3	13		1	4			5^1	14					28
	3	12			6	7^1	8			11		9		2	10^2	4		1					13	5				29
	2					7^2				11	12	9^1		6	10^3	4		1		13			14	3	8	5		30
		12		5						11^2	9	13		2	10^3	14		1		7^1			4	3	8	6		31
		12		5		7^2					9	13		2	10^1	11■		1		8^3			14	3	4	6		32
				5		7				11	9			2	10	12		1					4^1	3	8	6		33
				5	12	7				11^2	9			2^1	10	8		1		13				3	4	6		34
		12		5	13	7				11^1	9	14		2^2	10^3	8		1						3	4	6		35
		12		5		7				11	9			2	10^2	8		1						3^1	4	6	13	36
		3		5	12	7	13			11	9			2^1		8		1							4	6	10^2	37
				5	6	7	12			11	9					8		1						3	4■	2	10^1	38
				5	6	7	8			11	9				12	4		1						3		2	10^1	39
				5	6^3	7	8			11		9■		12	10^2			1		13			4^1	3		2	14	40
	2^1	13		5	12	7^2	8			11		9		14	10^3	4		1						3		6		41
	2	11		5	12	7	8	13			9^1	14			10^2	4		1						3^3		6		42
	2	3		5		7^3		10^1		11	9	14		12	13	4^2		1							8	6		43
	2	3^1		5		7^2		10		11	9				12	4		1						13	8	6		44
	2	3		5	6	7^1		10		11	9^2				12	4		1		13					8			45
	2			5		7	8^1			11	9■			12	10			1						3	4	6		46

FA Cup

Third Round	Crystal Palace	(h)	2-0
Fourth Round	Wolverhampton W	(h)	1-4

Carling Cup

First Round	Gillingham	(h)	3-0
Second Round	Southend U	(a)	0-2

Play-Offs

Semi-Final	Hull C	(h)	0-2
		(a)	1-4

WEST BROMWICH ALBION FA Premiership

FOUNDATION

There is a well known story that when employees of Salter's Spring Works in West Bromwich decided to form a football club, they had to send someone to the nearby Association Football stronghold of Wednesbury to purchase a football. A weekly subscription of 2d (less than 1p) was imposed and the name of the new club was West Bromwich Strollers.

The Hawthorns, West Bromwich, West Midlands B71 4LF.

Telephone: 0871 271 1100.

Fax: 0871 271 9861.

Ticket Office: 0871 271 9780.

Website: www.wbafc.co.uk

Email: enquiries@wbafc.co.uk

Ground Capacity: 27,877.

Record Attendance: 64,815 v Arsenal, FA Cup 6th rd, 6 March 1937.

Pitch Measurements: 115yd × 74yd.

Chairman: Jeremy Peace.

Legal Director/Secretary: Darren Eales.

Manager: Tony Mowbray.

Assistant Manager: Mark Venus.

Physio: Richard Rawlins.

Colours: Navy blue and white striped shirts, white shorts, navy blue stockings.

Change Colours: White shirts, navy blue shorts, white stockings. ***Third Kit:*** Black shirts, black shorts, black stockings.

Year Formed: 1878.

Turned Professional: 1885.

Ltd Co.: 1892.

Plc: 1996.

Previous Name: 1878, West Bromwich Strollers; 1881, West Bromwich Albion.

Club Nicknames: 'Throstles', 'Baggies', 'Albion'.

Grounds: 1878, Coopers Hill; 1879, Dartmouth Park; 1881, Bunns Field, Walsall Street; 1882, Four Acres (Dartmouth Cricket Club); 1885, Stoney Lane; 1900, The Hawthorns.

First Football League Game: 8 September 1888, Football League, v Stoke (a) W 2–0 – Roberts; J. Horton, Green; E. Horton, Perry, Bayliss; Bassett, Woodhall (1), Hendry, Pearson, Wilson (1).

Record League Victory: 12–0 v Darwen, Division 1, 4 April 1892 – Reader; J. Horton, McCulloch; Reynolds (2), Perry, Groves; Bassett (3), McLeod, Nicholls (1), Pearson (4), Geddes (1), (1 og).

HONOURS

Football League: Division 1 – Champions 1919–20; Runners-up 1924–25, 1953–54, 2001–02, 2003–04; FLC – Champions 2007–08; Division 2 – Champions 1901–02, 1910–11; Runners-up 1930–31, 1948–49; Promoted to Division 1 1975–76 (3rd); 1992–93 (play-offs); Promoted to FA Premier League 2001–02.

FA Cup: Winners 1888, 1892, 1931, 1954, 1968; Runners-up 1886, 1887, 1895, 1912, 1935.

Football League Cup: Winners 1966; Runners-up 1967, 1970.

European Competitions: *European Cup-Winners' Cup:* 1968–69. *European Fairs Cup:* 1966–67. *UEFA Cup:* 1978–79, 1979–80, 1981–82.

SKY SPORTS FACT FILE

William G. Richardson, the West Bromwich Albion centre-forward, hit four goals in five minutes against West Ham United on 7 November 1931, and three in six minutes v Derby County on 30 September 1933.

Record Cup Victory: 10–1 v Chatham (away), FA Cup 3rd rd, 2 March 1889 – Roberts; J. Horton, Green; Timmins (1), Charles Perry, E. Horton; Bassett (2), Perry (1), Bayliss (2), Pearson, Wilson (3), (1 og).

Record Defeat: 3–10 v Stoke C, Division 1, 4 February 1937.

Most League Points (2 for a win): 60, Division 1, 1919–20.

Most League Points (3 for a win): 89, Division 1, 2001–02.

Most League Goals: 105, Division 2, 1929–30.

Highest League Scorer in Season: William 'Ginger' Richardson, 39, Division 1, 1935–36.

Most League Goals in Total Aggregate: Tony Brown, 218, 1963–79.

Most League Goals in One Match: 6, Jimmy Cookson v Blackpool, Division 2, 17 September 1927.

Most Capped Player: Stuart Williams, 33 (43), Wales.

Most League Appearances: Tony Brown, 574, 1963–80.

Youngest League Player: Charlie Wilson, 16 years 73 days v Oldham Ath, 1 October 1921.

Record Transfer Fee Received: £6,000,000 from Fulham for Diomansy Kamara, July 2007.

Record Transfer Fee Paid: £3,500,000 to Cardiff C for Robert Earnshaw, August 2004.

Football League Record: 1888 Founder Member of Football League; 1901–02 Division 2; 1902–04 Division 1; 1904–11 Division 2; 1911–27 Division 1; 1927–31 Division 2; 1931–38 Division 1; 1938–49 Division 2; 1949–73 Division 1; 1973–76 Division 2; 1976–86 Division 1; 1986–91 Division 2; 1991–92 Division 3; 1992–93 Division 2; 1993–2002 Division 1; 2002–03 FA Premier League; 2003–04 Division 1; 2004–06 FA Premier League; 2006–08 FL C; 2008– FA Premier League.

MANAGERS

Louis Ford 1890–92
(Secretary-Manager)
Henry Jackson 1892–94
(Secretary-Manager)
Edward Stephenson 1894–95
(Secretary-Manager)
Clement Keys 1895–96
(Secretary-Manager)
Frank Heaven 1896–1902
(Secretary-Manager)
Fred Everiss 1902–48
Jack Smith 1948–52
Jesse Carver 1952
Vic Buckingham 1953–59
Gordon Clark 1959–61
Archie Macaulay 1961–63
Jimmy Hagan 1963–67
Alan Ashman 1967–71
Don Howe 1971–75
Johnny Giles 1975–77
Ronnie Allen 1977
Ron Atkinson 1978–81
Ronnie Allen 1981–82
Ron Wylie 1982–84
Johnny Giles 1984–85
Ron Saunders 1986–87
Ron Atkinson 1987–88
Brian Talbot 1988–91
Bobby Gould 1991–92
Ossie Ardiles 1992–93
Keith Burkinshaw 1993–94
Alan Buckley 1994–97
Ray Harford 1997
Denis Smith 1997–2000
Brian Little 2000
Gary Megson 2000–04
Bryan Robson 2004–06
Tony Mowbray October 2006–

LATEST SEQUENCES

Longest Sequence of League Wins: 11, 5.4.1930 – 8.9.1930.

Longest Sequence of League Defeats: 11, 28.10.1995 – 26.12.1995.

Longest Sequence of League Draws: 5, 30.8.1999 – 3.10.1999.

Longest Sequence of Unbeaten League Matches: 17, 7.9.1957 – 7.12.1957.

Longest Sequence Without a League Win: 15, 16.10.2004 – 25.9.2004.

Successive Scoring Runs: 36 from 26.4.1958.

Successive Non-scoring Runs: 4 from 15.2.1913.

TEN YEAR LEAGUE RECORD

		P	W	D	L	F	A	Pts	Pos
1998-99	Div 1	46	16	11	19	69	76	59	12
1999-2000	Div 1	46	10	19	17	43	60	49	21
2000-01	Div 1	46	21	11	14	60	52	74	6
2001-02	Div 1	46	27	8	11	61	29	89	2
2002-03	PR Lge	38	6	8	24	29	65	26	19
2003-04	Div 1	46	25	11	10	64	42	86	2
2004-05	PR Lge	38	6	16	16	36	61	34	17
2005-06	PR Lge	38	7	9	22	31	58	30	19
2006-07	FL C	46	22	10	14	81	55	76	4
2007-08	FL C	46	23	12	11	88	55	81	1

DID YOU KNOW ?

On 10 April 1920 West Bromwich Albion clinched the First Division championship with four games to spare beating Bradford 3–1 watched by a crowd of 29,414. Fred Morris was top scorer with 37 of the 104 goals and 13 players made all but 14 appearances.

WEST BROMWICH ALBION 2007–08 LEAGUE RECORD

Match No.	Date	Venue	Opponents	Result	H/T Score	Lg. Pos.	Goalscorers	Attendance
1	Aug 11	A	Burnley	L 1-2	1-0	—	Phillips [18]	15,337
2	18	H	Preston NE	W 2-0	0-0	11	Phillips [65], Miller [71]	19,556
3	25	A	Sheffield U	L 0-1	0-1	18		23,491
4	Sept 1	H	Barnsley	W 2-0	2-0	9	Teixeira [30], Beattie [38]	18,310
5	15	H	Ipswich T	W 4-0	1-0	4	Miller [23], Teixeira [87], Phillips 2 [89, 90]	19,460
6	18	A	Bristol C	D 1-1	0-0	—	Koren [74]	16,571
7	22	A	Scunthorpe U	W 3-2	0-1	3	Barnett [49], Brunt [60], Teixeira [78]	8307
8	30	H	QPR	W 5-1	3-1	2	Phillips 2 [17, 39], Miller [18], Koren [57], Greening [66]	24,757
9	Oct 3	H	Stoke C	D 1-1	0-1	—	Barnett [73]	20,048
10	6	A	Southampton	L 2-3	1-2	3	Koren 2 [32, 62]	21,967
11	20	A	Colchester U	L 2-3	2-2	5	Phillips [6], Miller [39]	5798
12	23	H	Blackpool	W 2-1	1-1	—	Miller [22], Morrison [79]	22,030
13	27	H	Norwich C	W 2-0	1-0	3	Miller [16], Phillips [51]	20,247
14	Nov 3	A	Watford	W 3-0	2-0	3	Miller [33], Phillips [35], Albrechtsen [49]	18,273
15	6	H	Sheffield W	D 1-1	0-0	—	Phillips [77]	19,807
16	12	A	Coventry C	W 4-0	0-0	—	Robinson [56], Teixeira 2 [58, 73], Koren [90]	18,566
17	25	H	Wolverhampton W	D 0-0	0-0	2		27,493
18	28	A	Plymouth Arg	W 2-1	2-0	—	Bednar 2 [9, 43]	14,348
19	Dec 1	A	Crystal Palace	D 1-1	1-1	2	Hudson (og) [8]	15,247
20	4	H	Coventry C	L 2-4	0-2	—	Bednar 2 [52, 65]	20,641
21	8	A	Leicester C	W 2-1	1-0	2	Gera [31], Beattie [88]	22,088
22	15	H	Charlton Ath	W 4-2	1-1	1	Bednar [43], Gera 2 [50, 80], Phillips [84]	20,346
23	22	A	Stoke C	L 1-3	0-2	2	Bednar [72]	18,420
24	26	H	Bristol C	W 4-1	0-0	1	Bednar [48], Koren [67], Phillips 2 [72, 75]	27,314
25	29	H	Scunthorpe U	W 5-0	2-0	1	Phillips 2 [35, 52], Koren [45], Gera [77], Beattie [81]	25,238
26	Jan 1	A	Ipswich T	L 0-2	0-0	1		24,000
27	12	A	Hull C	W 3-1	2-0	2	Phillips [2], Morrison [32], Bednar [90]	18,391
28	19	H	Cardiff C	D 3-3	1-2	1	Bednar [35], Albrechtsen [72], Johnson (og) [88]	22,325
29	29	A	Preston NE	L 1-2	0-1	—	Gera [50]	12,473
30	Feb 2	H	Burnley	W 2-1	1-1	1	Cesar [26], Bednar [60]	22,206
31	9	A	Barnsley	L 1-2	0-2	2	Morrison [58]	13,083
32	12	H	Sheffield U	D 0-0	0-0	—		22,643
33	23	H	Hull C	L 1-2	1-1	4	Bednar [42]	22,716
34	Mar 1	H	Plymouth Arg	W 3-0	1-0	4	Gera [45], Miller [59], Bednar [67]	22,503
35	4	A	Sheffield W	W 1-0	0-0	—	Phillips [90]	18,805
36	12	H	Crystal Palace	D 1-1	1-0	—	Phillips [30]	20,378
37	15	H	Leicester C	L 1-4	1-1	4	Koren [22]	22,038
38	21	A	Charlton Ath	D 1-1	1-1	—	Phillips [42]	23,412
39	29	H	Colchester U	W 4-3	2-2	4	Phillips [36], Brunt [39], Morrison [89], Bednar [90]	20,433
40	Apr 1	A	Cardiff C	D 0-0	0-0	—		13,915
41	8	A	Blackpool	W 3-1	0-1	—	Phillips 2 (1 pen) [81 (p), 84], Miller [87]	9628
42	12	H	Watford	D 1-1	0-1	2	Barnett [49]	26,508
43	15	A	Wolverhampton W	W 1-0	0-0	—	Gera [59]	27,883
44	19	A	Norwich C	W 2-1	1-0	1	Koren [2], Gera [71]	25,442
45	28	H	Southampton	D 1-1	0-0	—	Brunt [84]	26,167
46	May 4	A	QPR	W 2-0	0-0	1	Kim [53], Brunt [77]	18,309

Final League Position: 1

GOALSCORERS

League (88): Phillips 22 (1 pen), Bednar 13, Koren 9, Miller 9, Gera 8, Teixeira 5, Brunt 4, Morrison 4, Barnett 3, Beattie 3, Albrechtsen 2, Cesar 1, Greening 1, Kim 1, Robinson 1, own goals 2.
Carling Cup (5): Miller 2 (1 pen), Beattie 1, Ellington 1, Gera 1.
FA Cup (16): Miller 5, Bednar 4 (1 pen), Morrison 2, Phillips 2 (1 pen), Brunt 1, Gera 1, Koren 1.

Kiely D 44	Hoefkens C 42	Tininho 1	Chaplow R 2 + 3	Barnett L 30 + 2	Clement N 8 + 1	Gera Z 33 + 10	Teixeira F 24 + 6	Phillips K 29 + 6	Beattie C 6 + 15	Greening J 46	Morrison J 25 + 10	Ellington N — + 3	Pele 13 + 8	Albrechtsen M 28 + 4	Robinson P 43	Miller I 24 + 10	Brunt C 22 + 12	Koren R 38 + 2	MacDonald S — + 10	Slusarski B — + 1	Cesar B 19 + 1	Bednar R 18 + 11	Hodgkiss J 3 + 1	Steele L 2	Martis S 2	Moore L 3 + 7	Kim D 1 + 3	*Match No.*
1	2	3	4^{1}	5	6	7	8^{3}	9	10^{2}	11	12	13	14															1
1	2			5		7	12	9^{3}	10^{2}	11	8	13	6^{1}	4	3	14												2
1	2			5		12	8	9	10^{2}	11	7	13	6^{1}	4	3													3
1	2		12	5		7	8^{1}	9	10^{2}	11	6^{3}			4	3	13	14											4
1	2		12	5			8	9		11	4^{3}		13	6	3	10^{2}	7^{1}	14										5
1	2		4	5		7		9^{3}	10^{2}	11	14		12	6	3	13		8^{1}										6
1	2			5		7	8		12	11	14		13	6	3^{2}	10^{1}	9^{3}	4										7
1	2			5		12	8^{3}	9	13	11^{1}	7			6	3	10^{2}	14	4										8
1	2^{1}			5		12	8^{3}		9^{2}	11	4			6	3	10	13	7	14									9
1	2			5		7^{1}	8^{3}		12	11	13			6	3	9	10^{2}	4	14									10
1	2^{3}			5		12	8^{2}	9		11	7			6	3	10	13	4^{1}		14								11
1	2					12	8^{1}	9		11^{2}	4			6	3	10	7^{3}	13	14		5							12
1	2					12	13	9	14	11	4^{1}			6	3	10^{3}	7^{2}	8			5							13
1	2					7	12	9^{1}		11	4^{2}			6	3	10^{3}	13	8			5	14						14
1	2					7^{3}	8^{2}	9		11	13		12	6^{1}	3	10	14	4			5							15
1	2			6		7	9			11	8^{1}				3	10^{2}	12	4			5	13						16
1	2			6		7	9^{2}		12	11					3	10^{3}	8^{1}	4	13		5	14						17
1	2			6		7	8^{2}		12	11					3		10	4	13		5	9^{1}						18
1	2			6		7	8		12	11					3		10^{1}	4^{2}	13		5	9						19
1	2			6		7^{1}	8^{2}			11			13		3■		10	4	12		5^{3}	9	14					20
			12	5		7	8		13	11			6				10	4^{1}				9^{2}	3	1	2			21
						7	8^{1}	12		11			6		3		10	4	13		5	9^{2}	2	1				22
1	2					7	8^{1}	12		11			6	13	3	14	10^{3}	4			5^{2}	9						23
1	2					7		10^{3}	12	11	8^{1}		6	14	3	13		4			5	9^{2}						24
1	2					7		9^{1}	12	11	8		6		3	13	14	4^{3}			5	10^{2}						25
1	2					7	12	9^{2}	13	11	8^{1}		6		3	10^{3}		4			5	14						26
1	2			5		12		9^{2}		11	8		6		3■	10^{3}	7^{1}	4			13	14						27
1	2			5		12	8	9		11	13		6^{2}	3		10^{3}	7	4^{1}				14						28
1	2^{1}					7^{2}	8^{3}		12	11	10			6	3		14	4	13		5	9						29
1	2					7	12	9^{2}	13	11	8			6	3			4			5	10^{1}						30
1	2			12		13	8	9	14	11	4			6	3		7^{2}				5^{1}	10^{3}						31
1	2			5			8	9	12	11	4			6	3	10^{1}	7											32
1	2			5		7	12	9^{3}		11^{1}	8			6	3	13		4				10^{2}				14		33
1	2			5		12	8^{1}			11				6	3	10^{2}	7	4				9^{3}				13	14	34
1	2			5		7		12		11	13			6	3	14	8^{2}	4				9^{3}				10^{1}		35
1				5		7^{1}		9		11	13^{3}			6	3	10	8^{2}	4					2			12	14	36
1				5		7^{2}		12		11			13	6	3			4	14			10^{1}			2	9■	8^{3}	37
1	2					7		9		11			4	6	3	10^{1}		8			5	12						38
1	2^{3}				12	7		9		11	13			6	3	14	8	4^{2}			5^{1}	10						39
1	2				6	7^{2}		12		11	9		4	5	3	10^{3}	13	8^{1}				14						40
1	2			12	6			13		11	14		4^{3}	5^{1}	3	10	7^{2}	8								9		41
1	2			5	6	7		9		11	8^{1}				3	10^{2}	12	4				13						42
1	2			5	6	7		9^{1}		11	8^{2}		12		3	10^{3}		4				14				13		43
1	2			5	6	7		9^{2}		11	8			12	3^{1}	14		4				10^{3}				13		44
1	2			5	6	7		9		11^{1}	8^{2}				3	10^{3}	13	4				14				12		45
1	2			5	6^{1}	7		9		11				12	3^{2}		8	4				10^{3}				13	14	46

FA Cup

Third Round	Charlton Ath	(a)	1-1
		(h)	2-2
Fourth Round	Peterborough U	(a)	3-0
Fifth Round	Coventry C	(a)	5-0
Sixth Round	Bristol R	(a)	5-1
Semi-Final *(at Wembley)*	Portsmouth		0-1

Carling Cup

First Round	Bournemouth	(h)	1-0
Second Round	Peterborough U	(a)	2-0
Third Round	Cardiff C	(h)	2-4

WEST HAM UNITED FA Premiership

FOUNDATION

Thames Iron Works FC was formed by employees of this famous shipbuilding company in 1895 and entered the FA Cup in their initial season at Chatham and the London League in their second. The committee wanted to introduce professional players, so Thames Iron Works was wound up in June 1900 and relaunched a month later as West Ham United.

The Boleyn Ground, Upton Park, Green Street, London E13 9AZ.

Telephone: (020) 8548 2748.

Fax: (020) 8548 2758.

Ticket Office: 0870 112 2700.

Website: www.whufc.co.uk

Email: yourcomments@westhamunited.co.uk

Ground Capacity: 35,303.

Record Attendance: 42,322 v Tottenham H, Division 1, 17 October 1970.

Pitch Measurements: 100.58m × 66.84m.

Chairman: Bjorgolfur Gudmundsson.

Vice-chairman: Asgeir Fridgeirsson.

Chief Executive: Scott Duxbury.

Secretary: Peter Barnes.

Manager: Alan Curbishley.

Assistant Manager: Mervyn Day.

Physio: George Cooper.

Colours: Claret and sky blue shirts, white shorts, white stockings.

Change Colours: Sky blue shirts, sky blue shorts, sky blue stockings.

Year Formed: 1895.

Turned Professional: 1900.

Ltd Co.: 1900.

Previous Name: 1895, Thames Iron Works FC; 1900, West Ham United.

Club Nicknames: 'The Hammers', 'The Irons'.

Grounds: 1895, Memorial Recreation Ground, Canning Town; 1904, Boleyn Ground.

First Football League Game: 30 August 1919, Division 2, v Lincoln C (h) D 1–1 – Hufton; Cope, Lee; Lane, Fenwick, McCrae; D. Smith, Moyes (1), Puddefoot, Morris, Bradshaw.

HONOURS

Football League: Promotion from Championship 2004–05 (play-offs); Division 2 – Champions 1957–58, 1980–81; Runners-up 1922–23, 1990–91.

FA Cup: Winners 1964, 1975, 1980; Runners-up 1923, 2006.

Football League Cup: Runners-up 1966, 1981.

European Competitions: *European Cup-Winners' Cup:* 1964–65 (winners), 1965–66, 1975–76 (runners-up), 1980–81. *UEFA Cup:* 1999–2000; 2006–07. *Intertoto Cup:* 1999 (winners).

SKY SPORTS FACT FILE

Few goalkeepers score on their debut, but George Kitchen did so for West Ham United against Swindon Town from a penalty and was also on the spot against Woolwich Arsenal in an FA Cup tie on 13 January 1906 at Plumstead Common which forced a replay.

Record League Victory: 8–0 v Rotherham U, Division 2, 8 March 1958 – Gregory; Bond, Wright; Malcolm, Brown, Lansdowne; Grice, Smith (2), Keeble (2), Dick (4), Musgrove. 8–0 v Sunderland, Division 1, 19 October 1968 – Ferguson; Bonds, Charles; Peters, Stephenson, Moore (1); Redknapp, Boyce, Brooking (1), Hurst (6), Sissons.

Record Cup Victory: 10–0 v Bury, League Cup 2nd rd (2nd leg), 25 October 1983 – Parkes; Stewart (1), Walford, Bonds (Orr), Martin (1), Devonshire (2), Allen, Cottee (4), Swindlehurst, Brooking (2), Pike.

Record Defeat: 2–8 v Blackburn R, Division 1, 26 December 1963.

Most League Points (2 for a win): 66, Division 2, 1980–81.

Most League Points (3 for a win): 88, Division 1, 1992–93.

Most League Goals: 101, Division 2, 1957–58.

Highest League Scorer in Season: Vic Watson, 42, Division 1, 1929–30.

Most League Goals in Total Aggregate: Vic Watson, 298, 1920–35.

Most League Goals in One Match: 6, Vic Watson v Leeds U, Division 1, 9 February 1929; 6, Geoff Hurst v Sunderland, Division 1, 19 October 1968.

Most Capped Player: Bobby Moore, 108, England.

Most League Appearances: Billy Bonds, 663, 1967–88.

Youngest League Player: Billy Williams, 16 years 221 days v Blackpool, 6 May 1922.

Record Transfer Fee Received: £18,000,000 from Leeds U for Rio Ferdinand, November 2000.

Record Transfer Fee Paid: £7,500,000 to Liverpool for Craig Bellamy, July 2007.

Football League Record: 1919 Elected to Division 2; 1923–32 Division 1; 1932–58 Division 2; 1958–78 Division 1; 1978–81 Division 2; 1981–89 Division 1; 1989–91 Division 2; 1991–93 Division 1; 1993–2003 FA Premier League; 2003–04 Division 1; 2004–05 FL C; 2005– FA Premier League.

MANAGERS

Syd King 1902–32
Charlie Paynter 1932–50
Ted Fenton 1950–61
Ron Greenwood 1961–74
(continued as General Manager to 1977)
John Lyall 1974–89
Lou Macari 1989–90
Billy Bonds 1990–94
Harry Redknapp 1994–2001
Glenn Roeder 2001–03
Alan Pardew 2003–06
Alan Curbishley December 2006–

LATEST SEQUENCES

Longest Sequence of League Wins: 9, 19.10.1985 – 14.12.1985.

Longest Sequence of League Defeats: 9, 28.3.1932 – 29.8.1932.

Longest Sequence of League Draws: 5, 15.10.2003 – 1.11.2003.

Longest Sequence of Unbeaten League Matches: 27, 27.12.80 – 10.10.81.

Longest Sequence Without a League Win: 17, 31.1.1976 – 21.8.1976.

Successive Scoring Runs: 27 from 5.10.1957.

Successive Non-scoring Runs: 5 from 1.5.1971.

TEN YEAR LEAGUE RECORD

		P	*W*	*D*	*L*	*F*	*A*	*Pts*	*Pos*
1998-99	PR Lge	38	16	9	13	46	53	57	5
1999-2000	PR Lge	38	15	10	13	52	53	55	9
2000-01	PR Lge	38	10	12	16	45	50	42	15
2001-02	PR Lge	38	15	8	15	48	57	53	7
2002-03	PR Lge	38	10	12	16	42	59	42	18
2003-04	Div 1	46	19	17	10	67	45	74	4
2004-05	FL C	46	21	10	15	66	56	73	6
2005-06	PR Lge	38	16	7	15	52	55	55	9
2006-07	PR Lge	38	12	5	21	35	59	41	15
2007-08	PR Lge	38	13	10	15	42	50	49	10

DID YOU KNOW?

When West Ham United beat Arsenal 1–0 in the 1980 FA Cup final they had an all-English team and were the last to win it while outside of the top division. They were also the last team to win at Highbury and the first to win at the Gunners' Emirates Stadium in 2007.

WEST HAM UNITED 2007–08 LEAGUE RECORD

Match No.	Date	Venue	Opponents	Result		H/T Score	Lg. Pos.	Goalscorers	Attendance
1	Aug 11	H	Manchester C	L	0-2	0-1	—		34,921
2	18	A	Birmingham C	W	1-0	0-0	15	Noble (pen) 70	24,961
3	25	H	Wigan Ath	D	1-1	0-0	14	Bowyer 81	33,793
4	Sept 1	A	Reading	W	3-0	1-0	11	Bellamy 6, Etherington 2 49, 90	23,533
5	15	H	Middlesbrough	W	3-0	0-0	6	Bowyer 46, Young (og) 51, Ashton 62	34,351
6	23	A	Newcastle U	L	1-3	1-2	7	Ashton 32	50,104
7	29	H	Arsenal	L	0-1	0-1	11		34,966
8	Oct 6	A	Aston Villa	L	0-1	0-1	11		40,842
9	21	H	Sunderland	W	3-1	1-0	10	Cole 9, Gordon (og) 78, Bellamy 90	34,913
10	27	A	Portsmouth	D	0-0	0-0	11		20,525
11	Nov 4	H	Bolton W	D	1-1	1-0	11	McCartney 20	33,867
12	10	A	Derby Co	W	5-0	1-0	10	Bowyer 2 42, 59, Etherington 51, Lewis (og) 55, Solano 69	32,440
13	25	H	Tottenham H	D	1-1	1-0	10	Cole 20	34,966
14	Dec 1	A	Chelsea	L	0-1	0-0	10		41,830
15	9	A	Blackburn R	W	1-0	0-0	10	Ashton 52	20,870
16	15	H	Everton	L	0-2	0-1	11		34,430
17	22	A	Middlesbrough	W	2-1	1-1	11	Ashton 44, Parker 90	26,007
18	26	H	Reading	D	1-1	1-0	9	Solano 42	34,277
19	29	H	Manchester U	W	2-1	0-1	10	Ferdinand 77, Upson 82	34,956
20	Jan 1	A	Arsenal	L	0-2	0-2	10		60,102
21	12	H	Fulham	W	2-1	1-1	10	Ashton 28, Ferdinand 69	34,947
22	20	A	Manchester C	D	1-1	1-1	10	Cole 8	39,042
23	30	H	Liverpool	W	1-0	0-0	—	Noble (pen) 90	34,977
24	Feb 2	A	Wigan Ath	L	0-1	0-1	10		20,525
25	9	H	Birmingham C	D	1-1	1-1	10	Ljungberg 7	34,884
26	23	A	Fulham	W	1-0	0-0	10	Solano 87	25,280
27	Mar 1	H	Chelsea	L	0-4	0-3	10		34,969
28	5	A	Liverpool	L	0-4	0-1	—		42,954
29	9	A	Tottenham H	L	0-4	0-2	10		36,062
30	15	H	Blackburn R	W	2-1	1-1	10	Ashton 39, Sears 81	34,006
31	22	A	Everton	D	1-1	0-1	10	Ashton 68	37,430
32	29	A	Sunderland	L	1-2	1-1	10	Ljungberg 18	45,690
33	Apr 8	H	Portsmouth	L	0-1	0-0	—		33,629
34	12	A	Bolton W	L	0-1	0-0	10		23,043
35	19	H	Derby Co	W	2-1	1-0	10	Zamora 20, Cole 77	34,612
36	26	H	Newcastle U	D	2-2	2-2	10	Noble 10, Ashton 23	34,980
37	May 3	A	Manchester U	L	1-4	1-3	10	Ashton 28	76,013
38	11	H	Aston Villa	D	2-2	1-1	10	Solano 8, Ashton 88	34,969

Final League Position: 10

GOALSCORERS

League (42): Ashton 10, Bowyer 4, Cole 4, Solano 4, Etherington 3, Noble 3 (2 pens), Bellamy 2, Ferdinand 2, Ljungberg 2, McCartney 1, Parker 1, Sears 1, Upson 1, Zamora 1, own goals 3.
Carling Cup (6): Bellamy 2, Cole 2, Ashton 1, own goal 1.
FA Cup (0).

Green R 38	Spector J 13 + 13	McCartney G 38	Noble M 25 + 6	Ferdinand A 22 + 3	Upson M 29	Ljungberg F 22 + 3	Bowyer L 12 + 3	Zamora B 11 + 2	Bellamy C 7 + 1	Boa Morte L 18 + 9	Ashton D 20 + 11	Mullins H 32 + 2	Etherington M 15 + 3	Dyer K 2	Gabbidon D 8 + 2	Neill L 34	Cole C 21 + 10	Collins J 2 + 1	Camara H 3 + 7	Parker S 17 + 1	Solano N 14 + 9	Pantsil J 4 + 10	Reid K — + 1	Collison J 1 + 1	Faubert J 4 + 3	Sears F 1 + 6	Tomkins J 5 + 1	*Match No.*
1	2	3^{1}	4	5	6	7	8^{2}	9	10	11^{3}	12	13	14															1
1	2^{1}	3	8	5	6			9	10			4	11	7	12													2
1		3	8	5	6		12	9^{3}	10^{2}	13	14	4^{1}	11	7		2												3
1	12	3	8	5	6		7^{1}		10^{2}	13	9^{3}	4	11			2	14											4
1		3	8		6	12	7		10^{3}	13	9^{1}	4	11^{2}			2	14	5										5
1	12	3	8	5	6	13	7				9	4^{2}	11^{1}			2	10^{3}		14									6
1		3	4	5^{3}	6	10	7^{1}			12	9	13			14	2			11	8^{2}								7
1		3	12		6	7	8			13	9	4^{1}	11^{2}		5	2	14		10^{3}									8
1		3	8^{3}	12	5		7		10	13		6	11^{2}		4	2	9^{1}				14							9
1	12	3	8	13	5				10^{3}	11		6	14		4	2	9^{2}				7^{1}							10
1	12	3			5		8^{3}			10		6^{1}	11		4	2	9^{2}		13		7	14						11
1	4	3^{1}			6		8^{2}			10			11		5	2	9	13			7	12						12
1	12	3	8^{2}		6					10^{3}	14	4	11		5	2	9			13	7^{1}							13
1	12	3			5	13				10	14	6	11^{3}		4	2	9			8^{1}	7^{2}							14
1	12	3			6					10	13	4	11^{2}		5	2	9^{3}		14	8	7^{1}							15
1		3	12		6	11					10	4^{3}				2	9^{2}	5	13	8	7^{1}		14					16
1	3	5	12		6	11					10	4				2			9^{2}	8	7^{1}	13						17
1	6	3	12		5	11					10	4				2	9^{2}		13	8	7^{1}							18
1	6	3	11	12	5	10^{3}					14	4				2	9			8^{1}	7^{2}	13						19
1	8	3	11	5	6	10^{3}					12	4^{2}				2	9^{1}		13			7		14				20
1	2	3	4	5	6	7^{3}	12			13	10	8	11^{1}				9^{2}								14			21
1	12	3	8	5	6	7	11^{1}			10^{2}		4				2	9								13			22
1	12	3	4	5	6	7	11^{3}			10^{2}	14	8	13			2	9^{1}											23
1		3	4^{1}	5	6	7	12		13		10	8	11^{3}			2	9^{2}				14							24
1	12	3		5	6	7	8■				10^{1}	4	11^{2}			2	9^{3}		13						14			25
1	12	3	4	5	6	7^{1}				10	13	8				2	9^{2}				14				11^{3}			26
1		3	4	5	6	7		12		10^{2}	13	8				2	9^{1}				14				11^{3}			27
1	12	3	4	5	6^{1}	11		13		10	14	8				2	9^{2}				7^{3}							28
1	6	3	12	5		7^{3}		9		11■	10^{2}	4				2	13			8^{1}		14						29
1	6	3	12	5		11^{2}		9			10	4				2				8^{1}	7^{3}	13				14		30
1	12	3	4	5		7^{2}				9^{3}	10	11				2				8^{1}	13					14	6	31
1	6	3^{1}	4	5		7					10	11				2	9^{3}			8	14	12^{2}					13	32
1	6	3		5				9^{3}		11	10	4^{1}				2	12			8	7^{2}	13				14		33
1	2	3		5^{2}	6			9^{3}		11	10	4					12			8		13		7^{1}		14		34
1		3	4			11^{1}		9		12						5	13			8	14	2			7^{3}	10^{2}	6	35
1		3	4			11^{1}		9^{2}		12	10					5	13			8	14	2			7^{3}		6	36
1		3	7					9		11^{2}	10^{1}	4^{3}				5	12			8	13	2				14	6	37
1		3^{2}	4	5				9^{1}		11	10					2	12			8	7^{3}	13				14	6	38

FA Cup

Third Round	Manchester C	(h)	0-0
		(a)	0-1

Carling Cup

Second Round	Bristol R	(a)	2-1
Third Round	Plymouth Arg	(h)	1-0
Fourth Round	Coventry C	(a)	2-1
Quarter-Final	Everton	(h)	1-2

WIGAN ATHLETIC

FA Premiership

FOUNDATION

Following the demise of Wigan Borough and their resignation from the Football League in 1931, a public meeting was called in Wigan at the Queen's Hall in May 1932 at which a new club, Wigan Athletic, was founded in the hope of carrying on in the Football League. With this in mind, they bought Springfield Park for £2,250, but failed to gain admission to the Football League until 46 years later.

JJB Stadium, Robin Park, Newtown, Wigan, Lancashire WN5 0UZ.

Telephone: (01942) 774 000.

Fax: (01942) 770 477.

Ticket Office: 0871 6633 252.

Website: www.wiganathletic.tv

Email: latics@jjbstadium.co.uk

Ground Capacity: 25,138.

Record Attendance: 27,526 v Hereford U, 12 December 1953 (at Springfield Park).

Pitch Measurements: 105m × 68m.

Chairman: David Whelan.

Vice-chairman: Phillip Williams.

Chief Executive: Brenda Spencer.

Secretary: Stuart Hayton.

Manager: Steve Bruce.

Assistant Manager: Eric Black.

Physio: David Galley.

Colours: Blue and white striped shirts, blue shorts, white stockings.

Change Colours: Fluo yellow shirts, black shorts, black stockings.

Year Formed: 1932.

Grounds: 1932, Springfield Park; 1999, JJB Stadium.

Club Nickname: 'The Latics'.

First Football League Game: 19 August 1978, Division 4, v Hereford U (a) D 0–0 – Brown; Hinnigan, Gore, Gillibrand, Ward, Davids, Corrigan, Purdie, Houghton, Wilkie, Wright.

Record League Victory: 7–1 v Scarborough, Division 3, 11 March 1997 – Butler L, Butler J, Sharp (Morgan), Greenall, McGibbon (Biggins (1)), Martinez (1), Diaz (2), Jones (Lancashire (1)), Lowe (2), Rogers, Kilford.

Record Cup Victory: 6–0 v Carlisle U (away), FA Cup 1st rd, 24 November 1934 – Caunce; Robinson,

HONOURS

Football League: Championship – Runners-up 2004–05; Division 2 Champions, 2002–03; Division 3 Champions, 1996–97; Division 4 – Promoted (3rd) 1981–82.

FA Cup: best season: 6th rd, 1987.

Football League Cup: Runners up: 2006.

Freight Rover Trophy: Winners 1985.

Auto Windscreens Shield: Winners 1999.

SKY SPORTS FACT FILE

Hotshot hat-trick hero Harry Lyon scored three second half goals in an FA Cup tie for Wigan Athletic against Doncaster Rovers on 17 November 1965 despite being carried off with a suspected broken ankle in the first half. Wigan won 3–1.

Talbot; Paterson, Watson, Tufnell; Armes (2), Robson (1), Roberts (2), Felton, Scott (1).

Record Defeat: 1–6 v Bristol R, Division 3, 3 March 1990.

Most League Points (2 for a win): 55, Division 4, 1978–79 and 1979–80.

Most League Points (3 for a win): 100, Division 2, 2002–03.

Most League Goals: 84, Division 3, 1996–97.

Highest League Scorer in Season: Graeme Jones, 31, Division 3, 1996–97.

Most League Goals in Total Aggregate: Andy Liddell, 70, 1998–2004.

Most League Goals in One Match: Not more than three goals by one player.

Most Capped Player: Lee McCulloch, 11 (15), Scotland.

Most League Appearances: Kevin Langley, 317, 1981–86, 1990–94.

Youngest League Player: Steve Nugent, 16 years 132 days v Leyton Orient, 16 September 1989.

Record Transfer Fee Received: £5,000,000 from Everton for Leighton Baines, August 2007.

Record Transfer Fee Paid: £5,500,000 to Birmingham C for Emile Heskey, July 2006.

Football League Record: 1978 Elected to Division 4; 1982–92 Division 3; 1992–93 Division 2; 1993–97 Division 3; 1997–2003 Division 2; 2003–04 Division 1; 2004–05 FL C; 2005– FA Premier League.

MANAGERS

Charlie Spencer 1932–37
Jimmy Milne 1946–47
Bob Pryde 1949–52
Ted Goodier 1952–54
Walter Crook 1954–55
Ron Suart 1955–56
Billy Cooke 1956
Sam Barkas 1957
Trevor Hitchen 1957–58
Malcolm Barrass 1958–59
Jimmy Shirley 1959
Pat Murphy 1959–60
Allenby Chilton 1960
Johnny Ball 1961–63
Allan Brown 1963–66
Alf Craig 1966–67
Harry Leyland 1967–68
Alan Saunders 1968
Ian McNeill 1968–70
Gordon Milne 1970–72
Les Rigby 1972–74
Brian Tiler 1974–76
Ian McNeill 1976–81
Larry Lloyd 1981–83
Harry McNally 1983–85
Bryan Hamilton 1985–86
Ray Mathias 1986–89
Bryan Hamilton 1989–93
Dave Philpotts 1993
Kenny Swain 1993–94
Graham Barrow 1994–95
John Deehan 1995–98
Ray Mathias 1998–99
John Benson 1999–2000
Bruce Rioch 2000–01
Steve Bruce 2001
Paul Jewell 2001–07
Chris Hutchings 2007
Steve Bruce November 2007–

LATEST SEQUENCES

Longest Sequence of League Wins: 11, 2.11.2002 – 18.1.2003.

Longest Sequence of League Defeats: 8, 13.12.2006 – 30.1.2007.

Longest Sequence of League Draws: 6, 11.12.2001 – 5.1.2002.

Longest Sequence of Unbeaten League Matches: 25, 8.5.1999 – 3.1.2000.

Longest Sequence Without a League Win: 14, 9.5.1989 – 17.10.1989.

Successive Scoring Runs: 24 from 27.4.1996.

Successive Non-scoring Runs: 4 from 15.4.1995.

TEN YEAR LEAGUE RECORD

		P	*W*	*D*	*L*	*F*	*A*	*Pts*	*Pos*
1998-99	Div 2	46	22	10	14	75	48	76	6
1999-2000	Div 2	46	22	17	7	72	38	83	4
2000-01	Div 2	46	19	18	9	53	42	75	6
2001-02	Div 2	46	16	16	14	66	51	64	10
2002-03	Div 2	46	29	13	4	68	25	100	1
2003-04	Div 1	46	18	17	11	60	45	71	7
2004-05	FL C	46	25	12	9	79	35	87	2
2005-06	PR Lge	38	15	6	17	45	52	51	10
2006-07	PR Lge	38	10	8	20	37	59	38	17
2007-08	PR Lge	38	10	10	18	34	51	40	14

DID YOU KNOW?

On 15 December 2007 Wigan Athletic were involved in the first Premier League match in which both teams produced a hat-trick marksman. Wigan won 5–3 against Blackburn Rovers with Marcus Bent scoring his treble for the Latics and Roque Santa Cruz replying for Rovers.

WIGAN ATHLETIC 2007–08 LEAGUE RECORD

Match No.	Date	Venue	Opponents	Result		H/T Score	Lg. Pos.	Goalscorers	Attendance
1	Aug 11	A	Everton	L	1-2	0-1	—	Sibierski [80]	39,220
2	15	H	Middlesbrough	W	1-0	0-0	—	Sibierski [55]	14,007
3	18	H	Sunderland	W	3-0	1-0	3	Heskey [19], Landzaat (pen) [62], Sibierski (pen) [69]	18,639
4	25	A	West Ham U	D	1-1	0-0	3	Scharner [78]	33,793
5	Sept 1	A	Newcastle U	L	0-1	0-0	9		50,461
6	15	H	Fulham	D	1-1	0-1	10	Koumas (pen) [80]	16,973
7	22	A	Reading	L	1-2	0-1	12	Bent [50]	21,379
8	29	H	Liverpool	L	0-1	0-0	12		24,311
9	Oct 6	A	Manchester U	L	0-4	0-0	14		75,300
10	20	H	Portsmouth	L	0-2	0-0	15		17,695
11	27	A	Birmingham C	L	2-3	1-1	16	Bent 2 [23, 59]	27,661
12	Nov 3	H	Chelsea	L	0-2	0-2	18		19,011
13	11	A	Tottenham H	L	0-4	0-3	19		35,504
14	24	A	Arsenal	L	0-2	0-0	19		60,126
15	Dec 1	H	Manchester C	D	1-1	1-1	19	Scharner [25]	18,614
16	9	A	Bolton W	L	1-4	1-2	19	Landzaat [14]	20,309
17	15	H	Blackburn R	W	5-3	3-1	19	Landzaat [10], Bent 3 [12, 66, 81], Scharner [37]	16,489
18	22	A	Fulham	D	1-1	0-0	19	Bent [70]	20,820
19	26	H	Newcastle U	W	1-0	0-0	17	Taylor [65]	20,304
20	29	H	Aston Villa	L	1-2	1-0	18	Bramble [28]	18,806
21	Jan 2	A	Liverpool	D	1-1	0-0	—	Bramble [80]	42,308
22	12	A	Derby Co	W	1-0	0-0	17	Sibierski [82]	31,658
23	20	H	Everton	L	1-2	0-2	17	Jagielka (og) [53]	18,820
24	29	A	Middlesbrough	L	0-1	0-1	—		22,963
25	Feb 2	H	West Ham U	W	1-0	1-0	15	Kilbane [45]	20,525
26	9	A	Sunderland	L	0-2	0-1	16		43,600
27	23	H	Derby Co	W	2-0	0-0	14	Scharner [60], Valencia [84]	20,176
28	Mar 1	A	Manchester C	D	0-0	0-0	14		38,261
29	9	H	Arsenal	D	0-0	0-0	13		19,676
30	16	H	Bolton W	W	1-0	1-0	12	Heskey [34]	17,055
31	22	A	Blackburn R	L	1-3	1-2	14	King (pen) [17]	23,541
32	29	A	Portsmouth	L	0-2	0-1	16		18,623
33	Apr 5	H	Birmingham C	W	2-0	1-0	15	Taylor 2 [15, 55]	17,926
34	14	A	Chelsea	D	1-1	0-0	—	Heskey [90]	40,487
35	19	H	Tottenham H	D	1-1	1-1	13	Heskey [12]	18,673
36	26	H	Reading	D	0-0	0-0	14		19,043
37	May 3	A	Aston Villa	W	2-0	0-0	13	Valencia 2 [52, 63]	42,640
38	11	H	Manchester U	L	0-2	0-1	14		25,133

Final League Position: 14

GOALSCORERS

League (34): Bent 7, Heskey 4, Scharner 4, Sibierski 4 (1 pen), Landzaat 3 (1 pen), Taylor 3, Valencia 3, Bramble 2, Kilbane 1, King 1 (pen), Koumas 1 (pen), own goal 1.
Carling Cup (0).
FA Cup (4): Cotterill 1, Scharner 1, Sibierski 1, own goal 1.

Kirkland C 37	Melchiot M 31	Kilbane K 33 + 2	Landzaat D 19	Bramble T 26	Granqvist A 13 + 1	Valencia L 30 + 1	Scharner P 37	Folan C 1 + 1	Heskey E 27 + 1	Koumas J 21 + 9	Sibierski A 10 + 20	Aghahowa J 2 + 12	Brown M 27 + 4	Skoko J 7 + 5	Boyce E 24 + 1	Bent M 25 + 6	Cotterill D 2	Taylor R 12 + 5	Hall F — + 1	Olembe S 2 + 6	Pollitt M 1	Palacios W 16	King M 8 + 7	Edman E 5	Hagen E 1	Figueroa M 1 + 1	*Match No.*
1	2	3	4	5	6	7	8	9^{1}	10	11	12																1
1	2	3	4	5	6	7	8		10	11	9^{1}	12															2
1	2	3	4	5	6	7	8^{3}	12	10^{1}	11	9^{2}	13	14														3
1	2	3	4	5	6	7^{2}	8		10	11	9^{1}	12	13														4
1	2	3■	4^{1}	5	6		8		10	11^{2}	9^{3}		7	12	14	13											5
1	2			5	6		8		10^{3}	11	9^{1}	12	4	13	3	14	7^{2}										6
1	2	3		5	6		8			11	9^{1}	12	4	7		10											7
1	2	3		5			8^{1}			11		9	4	7	6	10		12									8
1	2^{2}	3		5		12	8			11			4	7	6	10			13	9^{1}							9
1		3	4	5	6		8			11	9^{1}	12	7		2	10											10
1	2	3	4	5	6	7	8			11	9^{1}	12				10											11
1	2	3	4^{1}	5	6	7	8			10	12		11^{2}	13		9											12
1	2	3	4	5	6		8				12		13	7^{2}		10	9^{1}	11									13
		3	4	5	6		8^{2}		12	11	14		7	13	2	10^{3}				9^{1}	1						14
1	2■	3	4	5		7	8		9^{1}	11					6	10		12									15
1		3	4	5	6	7	8		9^{1}	11			12		2	10											16
1		3	4	5	13	7	8		9^{1}			12^{2}	11		6	10		2^{3}		14							17
1		3	4	5		7	6				12	9^{1}	8		2	10		11^{2}		13							18
1	2	3	4	5		7	6				9^{1}	12	8			10		11^{2}		13							19
1	2	3	4^{2}	5		7	6				9^{1}	12	8			10		11		13							20
1	2	3	4	5		7	6		9^{2}	12	13		8			10		11^{1}									21
1	2	3	4^{1}	5		7			9	13	12		8		6	10^{3}				14		11^{2}					22
1	2	3	4^{2}	5		7	6		9^{1}	13	12	14	8^{3}			10						11					23
1	2	3		5		7	6		9	12	13		11			10^{2}						4	8^{1}				24
1	2	3				7	6		9^{3}	12	13		8		5	14		11^{1}				4	10^{2}				25
1	2^{1}	3				7	6		9^{2}	12			8		5	13		11^{3}		14		4	10				26
1	2	11				7	6		9^{3}	12	13		8		5	14						4	10^{2}	3^{1}			27
1	2					7	6		9	11	12		8		5							4	10^{1}	3			28
1	2	12				7	6		9^{2}	11	13		8		5							4	10^{1}	3			29
1	2	12				7	6		9	11■			8		5			13				4^{2}	10^{1}	3			30
1	2	11				7	6		9				8		5	12		13				4■	10^{1}	3^{2}			31
1	2^{2}	3				7	8		9		12	13		4	5	10		11^{1}					14		6^{3}		32
1	2	3				7	6		9^{2}		12			8^{3}	5	10		11^{1}				4	13			14	33
1	2	3				7	6		9	12	13			8^{1}	5	10^{2}		11^{3}				4	14				34
1	2	3				7	6		9^{2}	12	13		8		5	10^{3}		11^{1}				4	14				35
1	2^{2}	3				7	6		9^{3}	11	12		8		5	10^{1}		13				4	14				36
1		3		5		7	6		9^{1}	11	12		8	13	2	10^{3}						4^{2}	14				37
1				5		7	6		9	11	12		8^{2}		2	10^{1}						4	13			3	38

FA Cup

Third Round	Sunderland	(a)	3-0
Fourth Round	Chelsea	(h)	1-2

Carling Cup

Second Round	Hull C	(h)	0-1

WOLVERHAMPTON WANDERERS FL Championship

FOUNDATION

Enthusiasts of the game at St Luke's School, Blakenhall formed a club in 1877. In the same neighbourhood a cricket club called Blakenhall Wanderers had a football section. Several St Luke's footballers played cricket for them and shortly before the start of the 1879–80 season the two amalgamated and Wolverhampton Wanderers FC was brought into being.

Molineux, Waterloo Road, Wolverhampton WV1 4QR.

Telephone: 0871 880 8442.

Fax: (01902) 687 006.

Ticket Office: 0871 880 8433

Website: wolves.co.uk

Email: info@wolves.co.uk

Ground Capacity: 28,576.

Record Attendance: 61,315 v Liverpool, FA Cup 5th rd, 11 February 1939.

Pitch Measurements: 110yd × 75yd.

Chairman: Steve Morgan OBE.

Chief Executive: Jez Moxey.

Secretary: Richard Skirrow.

Manager: Mick McCarthy.

Assistant Manager: Ian Evans.

Physio: Steve Kemp.

Colours: Old gold and black.

Change Colours: Black.

Year Formed: 1877* (*see Foundation*).

Turned Professional: 1888.

Ltd Co.: 1923 (but current club is WWFC (1986) Ltd).

Previous Names: 1879, St Luke's combined with Wanderers Cricket Club to become Wolverhampton Wanderers (1923) Ltd. New limited companies followed in 1982 and 1986 (current).

Club Nickname: 'Wolves'.

Grounds: 1877, Windmill Field; 1879, John Harper's Field; 1881, Dudley Road; 1889, Molineux.

First Football League Game: 8 September 1888, Football League, v Aston Villa (h) D 1–1 – Baynton; Baugh, Mason; Fletcher, Allen, Lowder; Hunter, Cooper, Anderson, White, Cannon, (1 og).

Record League Victory: 10–1 v Leicester C, Division 1, 15 April 1938 – Sidlow; Morris, Dowen; Galley, Cullis, Gardiner; Maguire (1), Horace Wright, Westcott (4), Jones (1), Dorsett (4).

HONOURS

Football League: Division 1 – Champions 1953–54, 1957–58, 1958–59; Runners-up 1937–38, 1938–39, 1949–50, 1954–55, 1959–60; 2002–03 (play-offs). Division 2 – Champions 1931–32, 1976–77; Runners-up 1966–67, 1982–83; Division 3 (N) – Champions 1923–24; Division 3 – Champions 1988–89; Division 4 – Champions 1987–88.

FA Cup: Winners 1893, 1908, 1949, 1960; Runners-up 1889, 1896, 1921, 1939.

Football League Cup: Winners 1974, 1980.

Texaco Cup: Winners 1971.

Sherpa Van Trophy: Winners 1988.

European Competitions: *European Cup:* 1958–59, 1959–60. *European Cup-Winners' Cup:* 1960–61. *UEFA Cup:* 1971–72 (runners-up), 1973–74, 1974–75, 1980–81.

SKY SPORTS FACT FILE

Major Frank Buckley was never frightened of transferring players to the financial benefit of the club. In March 1929 he sold popular centre-forward Reg Weaver to Chelsea for £5,000. His 29 goals in 50 League games included ten in six in a row.

Record Cup Victory: 14–0 v Crosswell's Brewery, FA Cup 2nd rd, 13 November 1886 – I. Griffiths; Baugh, Mason; Pearson, Allen (1), Lowder; Hunter (4), Knight (2), Brodie (4), B. Griffiths (2), Wood. Plus one goal 'scrambled through'.

Record Defeat: 1–10 v Newton Heath, Division 1, 15 October 1892.

Most League Points (2 for a win): 64, Division 1, 1957–58.

Most League Points (3 for a win): 92, Division 3, 1988–89.

Most League Goals: 115, Division 2, 1931–32.

Highest League Scorer in Season: Dennis Westcott, 38, Division 1, 1946–47.

Most League Goals in Total Aggregate: Steve Bull, 250, 1986–99.

Most League Goals in One Match: 5, Joe Butcher v Accrington, Division 1, 19 November 1892; 5, Tom Phillipson v Barnsley, Division 2, 26 April 1926; 5, Tom Phillipson v Bradford C, Division 2, 25 December 1926; 5, Billy Hartill v Notts Co, Division 2, 12 October 1929; 5, Billy Hartill v Aston Villa, Division 1, 3 September 1934.

Most Capped Player: Billy Wright, 105, England (70 consecutive).

Most League Appearances: Derek Parkin, 501, 1967–82.

Youngest League Player: Jimmy Mullen, 16 years 43 days v Leeds U, 18 February 1939.

Record Transfer Fee Received: £6,000,000 from Coventry C for Robbie Keane, August 1999.

Record Transfer Fee Paid: £3,500,000 to Bristol C for Ade Akinbiyi, September 1999.

Football League Record: 1888 Founder Member of Football League: 1906–23 Division 2; 1923–24 Division 3 (N); 1924–32 Division 2; 1932–65 Division 1; 1965–67 Division 2; 1967–76 Division 1; 1976–77 Division 2; 1977–82 Division 1; 1982–83 Division 2; 1983–84 Division 1; 1984–85 Division 2; 1985–86 Division 3; 1986–88 Division 4; 1988–89 Division 3; 1989–92 Division 2; 1992–2003 Division 1; 2003–04 FA Premier League; 2004– FL C.

MANAGERS

George Worrall 1877–85
(Secretary-Manager)
John Addenbrooke 1885–1922
George Jobey 1922–24
Albert Hoskins 1924–26
(had been Secretary since 1922)
Fred Scotchbrook 1926–27
Major Frank Buckley 1927–44
Ted Vizard 1944–48
Stan Cullis 1948–64
Andy Beattie 1964–65
Ronnie Allen 1966–68
Bill McGarry 1968–76
Sammy Chung 1976–78
John Barnwell 1978–81
Ian Greaves 1982
Graham Hawkins 1982–84
Tommy Docherty 1984–85
Bill McGarry 1985
Sammy Chapman 1985–86
Brian Little 1986
Graham Turner 1986–94
Graham Taylor 1994–95
Mark McGhee 1995–98
Colin Lee 1998–2000
Dave Jones 2001–04
Glenn Hoddle 2004–2006
Mick McCarthy July 2006–

LATEST SEQUENCES

Longest Sequence of League Wins: 8, 15.10.1988 – 26.11.1988.

Longest Sequence of League Defeats: 8, 5.12.1981 – 13.2.1982.

Longest Sequence of League Draws: 6, 22.4.1995 – 20.8.1995.

Longest Sequence of Unbeaten League Matches: 21, 15.1.2005 – 13.8.2005.

Longest Sequence Without a League Win: 19, 1.12.1984 – 6.4.1985.

Successive Scoring Runs: 41 from 20.12.1958.

Successive Non-scoring Runs: 7 from 2.2.1985.

TEN YEAR LEAGUE RECORD

		P	*W*	*D*	*L*	*F*	*A*	*Pts*	*Pos*
1998-99	Div 1	46	19	16	11	64	43	73	7
1999-2000	Div 1	46	21	11	14	64	48	74	7
2000-01	Div 1	46	14	13	19	45	48	55	12
2001-02	Div 1	46	25	11	10	76	43	86	3
2002-03	Div 1	46	20	16	10	81	44	76	5
2003-04	PR Lge	38	7	12	19	38	77	33	20
2004-05	FL C	46	15	21	10	72	59	66	9
2005-06	FL C	46	16	19	11	50	42	67	7
2006-07	FL C	46	22	10	14	59	56	76	5
2007-08	FL C	46	18	16	12	53	48	70	7

DID YOU KNOW?

On 25 September 1920 with no apparent offside decision awarded, Wolverhampton Wanderers centre-forward George Edmonds hit the ball straight through the Bristol City goal but the referee refused to signal a goal! The match ended in a goalless draw.

WOLVERHAMPTON WANDERERS 2007–08 LEAGUE RECORD

Match No.	*Date*	*Venue*	*Opponents*	*Result*		*H/T Score*	*Lg. Pos.*	*Goalscorers*	*Attendance*
1	Aug 11	H	Watford	L	1-2	1-0	—	Olofinjana [45]	23,115
2	19	A	Sheffield W	W	3-1	1-1	10	Eastwood [14], Kightly [48], Bothroyd [90]	22,131
3	25	H	Blackpool	W	2-1	0-0	3	Eastwood 2 [69, 78]	24,294
4	Sept 1	A	Stoke C	D	0-0	0-0	6		17,135
5	15	A	Sheffield U	L	1-3	1-0	12	Elliott [24]	26,003
6	18	H	Hull C	L	0-1	0-0	—		21,352
7	22	H	Norwich C	W	2-0	2-0	11	Foley [23], Keogh [35]	22,564
8	29	A	Plymouth Arg	D	1-1	1-0	12	Elliott [41]	13,638
9	Oct 2	A	Leicester C	D	0-0	0-0	—		21,311
10	6	H	Coventry C	W	1-0	0-0	7	Collins N [90]	24,338
11	20	H	Charlton Ath	W	2-0	0-0	4	Bothroyd [46], Henry [85]	24,058
12	24	A	Cardiff C	W	3-2	1-2	—	Kightly 2 [13, 66], Craddock [74]	15,000
13	27	A	Ipswich T	L	0-3	0-1	5		23,308
14	Nov 3	H	Bristol C	D	1-1	1-1	6	Bothroyd [22]	26,094
15	6	A	Southampton	D	0-0	0-0	—		19,856
16	10	H	Barnsley	W	1-0	1-0	5	Collins N [13]	22,231
17	25	A	WBA	D	0-0	0-0	5		27,493
18	28	H	Colchester U	W	1-0	1-0	—	Elliott [32]	20,966
19	Dec 1	H	Preston NE	W	1-0	0-0	3	Henry [55]	22,836
20	4	A	Barnsley	L	0-1	0-0	—		9956
21	8	H	Burnley	L	2-3	1-3	6	Gibson [24], Elliott (pen) [60]	20,763
22	15	A	QPR	D	0-0	0-0	8		13,482
23	22	H	Leicester C	D	1-1	0-1	7	Jarvis [73]	23,477
24	26	A	Hull C	L	0-2	0-0	8		19,127
25	29	A	Norwich C	D	1-1	0-0	10	Keogh [52]	24,300
26	Jan 1	H	Sheffield U	D	0-0	0-0	10		24,791
27	12	H	Crystal Palace	L	0-3	0-1	12		22,650
28	19	A	Scunthorpe U	W	2-0	1-0	10	Edwards D [8], Ebanks-Blake [46]	7465
29	29	H	Sheffield W	W	2-1	1-1	—	Keogh [11], Ebanks-Blake [90]	22,746
30	Feb 2	A	Watford	L	0-3	0-1	11		18,082
31	9	H	Stoke C	L	2-4	1-1	12	Edwards R [45], Keogh [47]	25,373
32	12	A	Blackpool	D	0-0	0-0	—		9413
33	23	A	Crystal Palace	W	2-0	0-0	10	Gray [76], Kyle [89]	15,679
34	Mar 1	A	Colchester U	W	1-0	1-0	10	Ebanks-Blake [30]	5989
35	4	H	Southampton	D	2-2	0-0	—	Ebanks-Blake 2 [61, 88]	21,795
36	11	A	Preston NE	L	1-2	0-0	—	Keogh [52]	12,090
37	15	A	Burnley	W	3-1	2-0	11	Olofinjana [14], Gray [16], Ebanks-Blake [56]	12,749
38	18	H	Scunthorpe U	W	2-1	0-1	—	Gray [57], Collins N [83]	21,628
39	22	H	QPR	D	3-3	1-1	9	Keogh 2 [45, 90], Ebanks-Blake (pen) [67]	24,290
40	29	A	Charlton Ath	W	3-2	1-1	6	Ebanks-Blake 2 [15, 81], Henry [90]	23,187
41	Apr 12	A	Bristol C	D	0-0	0-0	8		19,332
42	15	H	WBA	L	0-1	0-0	—		27,883
43	19	H	Ipswich T	D	1-1	0-0	9	Ebanks-Blake [73]	26,072
44	22	H	Cardiff C	W	3-0	2-0	—	Keogh [8], Ebanks-Blake [44], Kightly [56]	20,862
45	26	A	Coventry C	D	1-1	0-1	7	Ebanks-Blake (pen) [53]	27,992
46	May 4	H	Plymouth Arg	W	1-0	0-0	7	Olofinjana [87]	26,293

Final League Position: 7

GOALSCORERS

League (53): Ebanks-Blake 12 (2 pens), Keogh 8, Elliott 4 (1 pen), Kightly 4, Bothroyd 3, Collins N 3, Eastwood 3, Gray 3, Henry 3, Olofinjana 3, Craddock 1, Edwards D 1, Edwards R 1, Foley 1, Gibson 1, Jarvis 1, Kyle 1.
Carling Cup (3): Craddock 1, Eastwood 1, Keogh 1 (pen).
FA Cup (6): Keogh 2, Bothroyd 1, Collins N 1, Elliott 1, Kightly 1.

Hennessey W 46	Collins N 34 + 5	Gray M 29 + 4	Olofinjana S 35 + 1	Breen G 18 + 1	Ward D 30	Kightly M 20 + 1	Potter D 11 + 7	Keogh A 33 + 10	Elliott S 18 + 11	Ward S 23 + 6	Edwards R 4 + 4	Bothroyd J 13 + 9	Foley K 42 + 2	Eastwood F 10 + 21	Henry K 38 + 2	Craddock J 22 + 1	Stack G — + 2	Jarvis M 17 + 9	Gibson D 15 + 6	Little M — + 1	Ebanks-Blake S 20	Edwards D 10	Jones D — + 1	Kyle K 3 + 9	Elokobi G 15	*Match No.*
1	2	3	4	5^1	6	7	8	9	10^2	11	12	13														1
1	12	3	4	5^1	6	7	8^3	9		11		13	2	10^2	14											2
1	12	3^1	4	5	6	7	8^3	9		11^2		13	2	10	14											3
1	3		4	5	6	7		9	12	11			2	10^1	8											4
1	3		4	5	6	7		9	10^2	11		13	2^1	12	8											5
1	3	12	4	5	6^1	7		9^2	14	11^3		13	2	10	8											6
1		3	4	5		7		9	10	11			2		8	6										7
1		3	4	5		7	12	9	10^2	11^1		13	2		8	6										8
1	12	3	4	5		7		9	10^2	11^1			2	13	8	6										9
1^G	12	3^1	4	5		7		9	10	11^2			2	13	8	6	15									10
1	3		4		6	7		9				10^1	2		8	5		12	11							11
1	3		4		6	7	12	9^2		14		10^1	2	13	8	5			11^3							12
1	3		4		6	7^1		12		11		10	2	9^2	8	5^3		13		14						13
1	3		4		6	7^1	12	9		11^2		10^3	2	13	8	5		14								14
1	3		4		6	7^3	12	9^2		11^1		13	2	10	8	5		14								15
1	3		4		6	7^1	12	13		11		9^2	2	10	8	5										16
1	3		4		6	7^1			13	11		10^2	2	12	8	5			9							17
1	3	13			6		7	12	9^1	11			2	10	8	5^2			4							18
1	5	3	4		6		12	13	9^2	11			2	10^1	7			14	8^3							19
1	5	3	4		6		8^3	9	12	11^2			2	13	10			7^1	14							20
1	5	3	4		6			12	9	11^3		10^1	2	13	8			14	7^2							21
1	5	3	4		6			12	10	11		9^1	2		8				7							22
1	5	3^2	4		6			12	10^3	13		9	2	14	8			11	7^1							23
1	3		4^3		6			9	12	13	5	10	2	11^2	8			7^1	14							24
1	5	3^2	4		6			9^1	12	11	13	10	2		8				7							25
1	5	3	4		6			9^1	12	11^2		10	2	13	8				7							26
1	5	3			6		4	12		11^2		10	2	13	8			14	7^3		9^1					27
1	5	3^1			6			9	10	13	12		2		8			7			11^2	4				28
1	5^1	3			6			9^2	7^3		12	13	2		8			11			10	4	14			29
1		3			6			9^1	10^2		5	12	2		8			11			7	4		13		30
1		3			6			9^2	12		5		2	13	8			11			10	4^1		7		31
1			12	5	6			11^1					2	13	8			7			10^2	4		9	3	32
1^6	2	11		5			7		10^1				12		8	6	15				9^2	4		13	3	33
1	2	11^2		5			7		10				12		8	6^1			13		9^3	4		14	3	34
1	6			5			12	13	10^3				2	14	7^1			11			9	4		8^2	3	35
1	2	11^3		5			8	12	10^2						7	6		14	13		9	4^1			3	36
1	5	11^2	4^1		6		8	9					2	12	7				13		10^3			14	3	37
1	5	11^1	4		6		8^2	9					2	12	7			13			10^3			14	3	38
1	5	11^1	4					9			6^2		2^3	12	7	13		8			10			14	3	39
1	5	11^2	4					9					2	12	8	6		7^1	13		10^3			14	3	40
1	6	11^1	4					9					2	12		5		7	8		10				3	41
1	5	11^1	4					9					2^2	12		6		7	8		10			13	3	42
1	5	11^2	4	12		13		9					2			6		7			10^3	8^1		14	3	43
1	12		4	5		7^2		9	14	13			2^1			6		11^3	8		10				3	44
1		12	4	5		7^1		9	13	14			2			6		11^3	8^2		10				3	45
1		13	4	5		7^2		9^3	12				2^1	14	8	6		11			10				3	46

FA Cup

Third Round	Cambridge U	(h)	2-1
Fourth Round	Watford	(a)	4-1
Fifth Round	Cardiff C	(a)	0-2

Carling Cup

First Round	Bradford C	(h)	2-1
Second Round	Morecambe	(h)	1-3

WREXHAM

Blue Square Premier

FOUNDATION

The club was formed on 28 September 1872 by members of Wrexham Cricket Club, so they could continue playing a sport during the winter months. This meeting was held at the Turf Hotel, which although rebuilt since, still stands at one corner of the present ground. Their first game was a few weeks later and matches often included 17 players on either side! By 1875 team formations were reduced to 11 men and a year later the club was among the founder members of the Cambrian Football Association, which quickly changed its title to the Football Association of Wales.

Racecourse Ground, Mold Road, Wrexham LL11 2AH.

Telephone: (01978) 262 129.

Fax: (01978) 357 821.

Ticket Office: (01978) 262 129 (ext 1).

Website: www.wrexhamafc.co.uk

Email: info@wrexhamafc.co.uk

Ground Capacity: 15,500.

Record Attendance: 34,445 v Manchester U, FA Cup 4th rd, 26 January 1957.

Pitch Measurements: 111yd × 71 yd.

Chairman: Neville Dickens.

Vice-chairman: Geoff Moss.

Chief Executive: Anthony Fairclough.

Secretary: Geraint Parry.

Manager: Brian Little.

Assistant Manager: Brian Carey.

Physio: Mel Pejic BSc (Hons).

Colours: Red shirts, white shorts, red stockings.

Change Colours: Light blue shirts, dark blue shorts, dark blue stockings.

Year Formed: 1872 (oldest club in Wales).

Turned Professional: 1912.

Ltd Co.: 1912.

Club Nickname: 'Red Dragons'.

Grounds: 1872, Racecourse Ground; 1883, Rhosddu Recreation Ground; 1887, Racecourse Ground.

First Football League Game: 27 August 1921, Division 3 (N), v Hartlepools U (h) L 0–2 – Godding; Ellis, Simpson; Matthias, Foster, Griffiths; Burton, Goode, Cotton, Edwards, Lloyd.

Record League Victory: 10–1 v Hartlepool U, Division 4, 3 March 1962 – Keelan; Peter Jones, McGavan; Tecwyn Jones, Fox, Ken Barnes; Ron Barnes (3), Bennion (1), Davies (3), Ambler (3), Ron Roberts.

HONOURS

Football League: Division 3 – Champions 1977–78; Runners-up 1992–93; Promoted (3rd) 2002–03; Division 3 (N) – Runners-up 1932–33; Division 4 – Runners-up 1969–70.

FA Cup: best season: 6th rd, 1974, 1978, 1997.

Football League Cup: best season: 5th rd, 1961, 1978.

Welsh Cup: Winners 22 times (joint record); Runners-up 22 times (record).

FAW Premier Cup: Winners 1998, 2000, 2001, 2003.

LDV Vans Trophy: Winners 2005

European Competition: *European Cup-Winners' Cup:* 1972–73, 1975–76, 1978–79, 1979–80, 1984–85, 1986–87, 1990–91, 1995–96.

SKY SPORTS FACT FILE

On 14 December 1960 Wrexham beat Blackburn Rovers 3–1 in a League Cup replay after extra time. Rovers had been FA Cup finalists earlier in the year and were a middle of the table First Division team at the time. A crowd of 8,870 saw a Mickey Metcalf hat-trick.

Record Cup Victory: 11–1 v New Brighton, Football League Northern Section Cup 1st rd, 3 January 1934 – Foster; Alfred Jones, Hamilton, Bulling, McMahon, Lawrence, Bryant (3), Findlay (1), Bamford (5), Snow, Waller (1), (o.g. 1).

Record Defeat: 0–9 v Brentford, Division 3, 15 October 1963.

Most League Points (2 for a win): 61, Division 4, 1969–70 and Division 3, 1977–78.

Most League Points (3 for a win): 84, Division 3, 2002–03.

Most League Goals: 106, Division 3 (N), 1932–33.

Highest League Scorer in Season: Tom Bamford, 44, Division 3 (N), 1933–34.

Most League Goals in Total Aggregate: Tom Bamford, 175, 1928–34.

Most League Goals in One Match: 5, Tom Bamford v Carlisle U, Division 3N, 17 March 1934; 5, Lee Jones v Cambridge U, Division 2, 6 April 2002; 5 Juan Ugarte v Hartlepool U, League Championship 1, 5 March 2005.

Most Capped Player: Joey Jones, 29 (72), Wales.

Most League Appearances: Arfon Griffiths, 592, 1959–61, 1962–79.

Youngest League Player: Ken Roberts, 15 years 158 days v Bradford PA, 1 September 1951.

Record Transfer Fee Received: £800,000 from Birmingham C for Bryan Hughes, March 1997.

Record Transfer Fee Paid: £210,000 to Liverpool for Joey Jones, October 1978.

Football League Record: 1921 Original Member of Division 3 (N); 1958–60 Division 3; 1960–62 Division 4; 1962–64 Division 3; 1964–70 Division 4; 1970–78 Division 3; 1978–82 Division 2; 1982–83 Division 3; 1983–92 Division 4; 1992–93 Division 3; 1993–2002 Division 2; 2002–03 Division 3; 2003–04 Division 2; 2004–05 FL 1; 2005–08 FL 2; 2008– Blue Square Premier.

MANAGERS

Selection Committee 1872–1924
Charlie Hewitt 1924–25
Selection Committee 1925–29
Jack Baynes 1929–31
Ernest Blackburn 1932–37
James Logan 1937–38
Arthur Cowell 1938
Tom Morgan 1938–42
Tom Williams 1942–49
Les McDowell 1949–50
Peter Jackson 1950–55
Cliff Lloyd 1955–57
John Love 1957–59
Cliff Lloyd 1959–60
Billy Morris 1960–61
Ken Barnes 1961–65
Billy Morris 1965
Jack Rowley 1966–67
Alvan Williams 1967–68
John Neal 1968–77
Arfon Griffiths 1977–81
Mel Sutton 1981–82
Bobby Roberts 1982–85
Dixie McNeil 1985–89
Brian Flynn 1989–2001
Denis Smith 2001–07
Brian Carey 2007
Brian Little November 2007–

LATEST SEQUENCES

Longest Sequence of League Wins: 8, 5.4.2003 – 3.5.2003.

Longest Sequence of League Defeats: 9, 2.10.1963 – 30.10.1963.

Longest Sequence of League Draws: 6, 12.11.1999 – 26.12.1999.

Longest Sequence of Unbeaten League Matches: 18, 8.3.2003 – 25.8.2003.

Longest Sequence Without a League Win: 16, 25.9.1999 – 3.1.2000.

Successive Scoring Runs: 25 from 5.5.1928.

Successive Non-scoring Runs: 6 from 12.9.1973.

TEN YEAR LEAGUE RECORD

		P	W	D	L	F	A	Pts	Pos
1998-99	Div 2	46	13	14	19	43	62	53	17
1999-2000	Div 2	46	17	11	18	52	61	62	11
2000-01	Div 2	46	17	12	17	65	71	63	10
2001-02	Div 2	46	11	10	25	56	89	43	23
2002-03	Div 3	46	23	15	8	84	50	84	3
2003-04	Div 2	46	17	9	20	50	60	60	13
2004-05	FL 1	46	13	14	19	62	80	43*	22
2005-06	FL 2	46	15	14	17	61	54	59	13
2006-07	FL 2	46	13	12	21	43	65	51	19
2007-08	FL 2	46	10	10	26	38	70	40	24

**10 points deducted.*

DID YOU KNOW ?

In the 1932–33 season, Wrexham produced an impressive goalscoring record in home games. Included in their 75 notched at the Racecourse Ground, they had one spell of producing 39 in seven such successive matches with this impressive sequence: 7 5 3 8 6 5 5. The five most regularly used forwards all reached double figures in scoring.

WREXHAM 2007–08 LEAGUE RECORD

Match No.	Date	Venue	Opponents	Result	H/T Score	Lg. Pos.	Goalscorers	Attendance
1	Aug 11	A	Darlington	L 0-2	0-1	—		4408
2	18	H	Morecambe	W 2-1	2-0	9	Proctor 2 [6, 22]	5504
3	25	A	Bradford C	L 1-2	0-0	19	Roberts [54]	13,546
4	Sept 1	H	Hereford U	L 0-2	0-0	23		4004
5	15	H	Rotherham U	L 0-1	0-0	24		3711
6	22	A	Stockport Co	L 1-2	1-1	24	Marc Williams [26]	5513
7	29	H	Lincoln C	W 1-0	0-0	22	Marc Williams [51]	3614
8	Oct 2	H	Chesterfield	L 0-4	0-3	—		3058
9	5	A	Accrington S	W 2-0	1-0	—	Roberts 2 [37, 66]	1822
10	13	A	Macclesfield T	L 2-3	2-1	22	Proctor (pen) [6], Llewellyn [22]	2256
11	20	H	Barnet	L 0-2	0-0	23		3591
12	27	A	Notts Co	L 1-2	0-1	24	Spann [70]	4359
13	Nov 4	H	Shrewsbury T	L 0-1	0-0	23		4305
14	7	H	Wycombe W	D 0-0	0-0	—		2805
15	25	H	Chester C	D 2-2	1-2	24	Proctor 2 [37, 75]	7687
16	Dec 1	A	Rochdale	D 0-0	0-0	—		2808
17	4	A	Bury	W 1-0	1-0	—	Williams E [31]	2248
18	8	A	Dagenham & R	L 0-3	0-1	23		1520
19	15	H	Brentford	L 1-3	1-0	23	Llewellyn [41]	3811
20	22	A	Rotherham U	L 0-3	0-1	23		3773
21	26	H	Rochdale	L 0-2	0-1	24		4302
22	29	H	Stockport Co	L 0-1	0-0	24		4287
23	Jan 1	A	Chesterfield	L 1-2	0-2	24	Evans S [68]	4293
24	12	A	Grimsby T	L 0-1	0-0	24		4084
25	19	H	Milton Keynes D	W 1-0	0-0	24	Roberts [71]	4319
26	26	H	Bradford C	D 1-1	1-0	24	Roberts [38]	4341
27	29	A	Morecambe	D 2-2	1-1	—	Sonner (pen) [30], Proctor (pen) [79]	2421
28	Feb 2	H	Darlington	W 2-0	1-0	23	Evans S [21], Proctor [86]	4013
29	9	A	Peterborough U	D 0-0	0-0	24		5505
30	23	H	Grimsby T	D 0-0	0-0	24		4217
31	26	H	Peterborough U	L 0-2	0-0	—		4103
32	Mar 1	H	Mansfield T	D 1-1	0-0	24	Proctor [70]	4865
33	9	A	Chester C	W 2-0	1-0	24	Hall [22], Proctor [65]	3849
34	11	A	Wycombe W	L 1-2	0-2	—	Proctor [53]	4002
35	15	H	Bury	W 2-1	1-1	24	Broughton [25], Proctor [77]	4431
36	22	A	Brentford	L 0-2	0-1	24		4448
37	24	H	Dagenham & R	D 0-0	0-0	24		4692
38	29	A	Barnet	L 2-3	0-1	24	Broughton [55], Spender [66]	2286
39	Apr 1	A	Mansfield T	L 1-2	0-0	—	Marc Williams [78]	3435
40	5	H	Macclesfield T	D 1-1	0-0	24	Evans S [79]	3993
41	8	A	Milton Keynes D	L 1-4	0-2	—	Roberts (pen) [59]	8646
42	13	A	Shrewsbury T	L 0-3	0-1	24		7065
43	19	H	Notts Co	W 1-0	0-0	24	Roberts [77]	4076
44	22	A	Hereford U	L 0-2	0-1	—		3739
45	26	H	Accrington S	L 1-3	0-2	24	Roberts (pen) [90]	3657
46	May 3	A	Lincoln C	W 4-2	2-1	24	Mackin [11], Baynes 2 [33, 88], Llewellyn [90]	4958

Final League Position: 24

GOALSCORERS

League (38): Proctor 11 (2 pens), Roberts 8 (2 pens), Evans S 3, Llewellyn 3, Marc Williams 3, Baynes 2, Broughton 2, Hall 1, Mackin 1, Sonner 1 (pen), Spann 1, Spender 1, Williams E 1.
Carling Cup (1): Proctor 1.
FA Cup (1): Roberts 1.

Williams T 22	Spender S 32 + 2	Valentine R 14	Williams D 11 + 4	Pejic S 17 + 2	Hope R 33	Jones Mark 14 + 2	Duffy R — + 6	Williams E 7 + 6	Roberts N 35 + 1	Proctor M 23 + 17	Llewellyn C 38 + 2	Mackin L 8 + 1	Done M 13 + 13	Williams Marc 11 + 8	Johnson J — + 7	Evans S 30 + 1	Carvill M 5 + 3	Spann S 7 + 2	Crowell M 3 + 3	Taylor N 21 + 5	Ugarte J — + 1	Garrett R 9 + 3	Williams Mike 15 + 3	Evans G 10 + 3	Jones M 2	Collins Michael 2	Baynes W 10 + 2	Aiston S 13 + 6	Murtagh C 3 + 1	Ward G 22	Bolland P 18	Sonner D 9	Fleming A 2 + 2	Hall P 7 + 4	Tremarco C 10	Nicholson S 9 + 4	Whitley Jeff 5 + 6	Broughton D 16	*Match No.*
1	2	3	4	5	6	7^{1}		8^{2}	9^{3}	10	11	12	13	14																									1
1	2	3	4	5	6	12		13	9	10	7^{3}	8^{1}	11^{2}		14																								2
1	2	3	4^{2}	5	6	12		14	9^{3}	10	7	8	11^{1}		13																								3
1	2	3	4	12	6	7		13	9	10^{2}	8^{3}		11			5^{1}	14																						4
1	2	3			6	7^{2}		8	9	10	12	4^{3}	11^{1}			5		14	13																				5
1	2		4	12	6	7							11^{3}	9		5	8	10^{2}	13	3^{1}	14																		6
1			2		6	7			9^{2}				12	10	13	5	3		8	4^{1}		11																	7
1	12		2		6	7			9		13		14	10^{2}		5	3^{1}		4^{3}	8		11																	8
1	2		4^{3}	5	6	7^{2}		12	9^{1}	10	8					14			13	3		11																	9
1	2		4^{2}	5	6	7		12	9	10^{1}	11									8		3■	13																10
	2				6	7		12	9^{2}	10^{1}	11		14	13				4		8			5^{3}	3	1														11
1	2^{1}				6	7^{3}		9	10	12	11		13			5^{2}		14■		4		8		3															12
1	2	3			6			9	10^{3}	12	11^{1}		13	14		5	7^{2}					8				4													13
1	2	3			6			9^{2}		12	10		11^{3}	13				4^{1}		14		7		5		8													14
1	12			6^{2}	4			9	10^{3}	7	8		13			5				2		14					3	11^{1}											15
1				6	2				10	9^{1}	8		7^{2}	12	13	5				4							3	11											16
1		3		4	6			9^{2}	8	10^{1}	11			13	12	5						7					2												17
1		3		4	6				8^{1}	9	11		12	10^{2}	13	5						7					2^{3}	14											18
1				2^{1}	6	7^{2}			9	12	10		13			5		4^{3}		8		14					3	11											19
1		3			6	7^{1}			9	10	8				12	5			4■								2	11											20
1		3			6	7			9	10	8					5		4^{1}		2				12				11											21
1		3		6					9^{1}	10^{2}	11			12		5	13			8			4				2	7											22
1	2	3		6					9	12	10	7				5				13			4					11^{1}	8^{2}										23
	2	3			6	7^{2}			9^{3}	12			14	10^{1}		5														1	4	8	13	11					24
	2				6				8	12	11					5														1	4	7		9^{1}	3	10^{2}	13		25
	2				6				7	12	11					5														1	4^{1}	8			3	10^{2}	13	9	26
	2^{1}			4	6■				7	12	11					5				13										1		8^{3}			3^{2}	10	14	9	27
	2						14		7	12	11					5				3			6							1	4	8^{2}				10^{1}	13	9^{3}	28
	2						14		7	12	11					5				3			6							1	4	8^{2}				10^{1}	13	9^{3}	29
	2						14			12	11					5							6					13		1	4	8			3	10^{3}	7^{2}	9^{1}	30
	2						14			12	11					5		8					6^{2}							1	4			13	3	10^{1}	7	9^{3}	31
	2				5		14			10	11^{2}							8					6^{1}					12		1	4			13	3		7	9^{3}	32
	2				5		14			10^{1}	11												6					12		1	4			8^{2}	3	13	7	9^{3}	33
	2				5^{1}					10	11									14			6	12				13		1	4^{3}			8	3		7^{2}	9	34
	2									10	11		12							6^{1}			13	5				7		1	4			8^{3}	3^{2}	14		9	35
	2								8^{1}	7	11		12										6	5				3		1	4	10^{2}		13				9	36
	2^{3}				6				13	10^{1}	3		11											5			14	7		1	4	8^{2}				12		9	37
	2				6^{1}					10	3		11										12	5				7^{2}		1	4			8			13	9	38
	2		12						8^{2}	13	11			14									6	5				3		1	4			7^{1}		10		9^{3}	39
	2^{2}		7^{1}		6^{3}				8	12	11			10		5				3								13		1	4					14		9	40
			7^{1}		6				8	12	11		13	9		4				2				5						1	3					10^{2}			41
	2		12		6				4	8			11	10^{1}						3								7^{2}		1	5			13				9	42
			12	2					9			8^{1}	11^{2}	10		5				3			6	13			7		14	1			4^{3}						43
			12	4					9	13		8	11	10^{2}		5				3		14	6				2^{3}		7^{1}	1									44
				4					9		10	8	11			5^{1}	7^{2}			12			6	3	1		13						2						45
	2			6							10	7		9		5	12			11							8		4^{2}	1			13		3^{1}				46

FA Cup
First Round Peterborough U (a) 1-4

Carling Cup
First Round Port Vale (a) 1-1
Second Round Aston Villa (h) 0-5

WYCOMBE WANDERERS FL Championship 2

FOUNDATION

In 1887 a group of young furniture trade workers called a meeting at the Steam Engine public house with the aim of forming a football club and entering junior football. It is thought that they were named after the famous FA Cup winners, The Wanderers who had visited the town in 1877 for a tie with the original High Wycombe club. It is also possible that they played informally before their formation, although there is no proof of this.

Adams Park, Hillbottom Road, Sands, High Wycombe HP12 4HJ.

Telephone: (01494) 472 100.

Fax: (01494) 527 633.

Ticket Office: (01494) 441 118.

Website: www.wwfc.com

Email: wwfc@wwfc.com

Ground Capacity: 10,000.

Record Attendance: 9,921 v Fulham, FA Cup 3rd rd, 9 January 2002.

Pitch Measurements: 115yd × 75yd.

Chairman: Ivor L. Beeks.

Managing Director: Steve Hayes.

Secretary: Keith Allen.

Manager: Peter Taylor.

Assistant Manager: Ian Culverhouse.

Physio: Shay Connolly.

Colours: Light blue and dark blue.

Change Colours: Red and white.

Year Formed: 1887.

Turned Professional: 1974.

Club Nicknames: 'Chairboys' (after High Wycombe's tradition of furniture making), 'The Blues'.

Grounds: 1887, The Rye; 1893, Spring Meadow; 1895, Loakes Park; 1899, Daws Hill Park; 1901, Loakes Park; 1990, Adams Park.

First Football League Game: 14 August 1993, Division 3 v Carlisle U (a) D 2–2: Hyde; Cousins, Horton (Langford), Kerr, Crossley, Ryan, Carroll, Stapleton, Thompson, Scott, Guppy (1) (Hutchinson), (1 og).

Record League Victory: 5–0 v Burnley, Division 2, 15 April 1997 – Parkin; Cousins, Bell, Kavanagh, McCarthy, Forsyth, Carroll (2p) (Simpson), Scott (Farrell), Stallard (1), McGavin (1) (Read (1)), Brown.

Record Cup Victory: 5–0 v Hitchin T (a), FA Cup 2nd rd, 3 December 1994 – Hyde; Cousins, Brown,

HONOURS

Football League: Division 2 best season: 6th, 1994–95. Division 3 1993–94 (play-offs).

FA Amateur Cup: Winners 1931.

FA Trophy: Winners 1991, 1993.

GM Vauxhall Conference: Winners 1992–93.

FA Cup: semi-final 2001.

Football League Cup: semi-final 2007.

SKY SPORTS FACT FILE

Wycombe Wanderers played in the Spartan League for just two seasons 1919–20 and 1920–21 winning the championship both times and losing just once in each season. They scored an impressive 222 goals in the 42 matches involved.

Crossley, Evans, Ryan (1), Carroll, Bell (1), Thompson, Garner (3) (Hemmings), Stapleton (Langford).

Record Defeat: 0–5 v Walsall, Auto Windscreens Shield 1st rd, 7 November 1995.

Most League Points (3 for a win): 78, Division 2, 1994–95.

Most League Goals: 72, FL 2, 2005–06.

Highest League Goalscorer in Season: Sean Devine, 23, 1999–2000.

Most League Goals in Total Aggregate: Nathan Tyson, 42, 2004–06.

Most League Goals in One Match: 3, Miquel Desouza v Bradford C, Division 2, 2 September 1995; 3, John Williams v Stockport Co, Division 2, 24 February 1996; 3, Mark Stallard v Walsall, Division 2, 21 October 1997; 3, Sean Devine v Reading, Division 2, 2 October 1999; 3, Sean Divine v Bury, Division 2, 26 February 2000; 3, Nathan Tyson v Lincoln C, FL 2, 5 March 2005; 3 Nathan Tyson v Kidderminster H, FL 2, 2 April 2005; 3 Nathan Tyson v Stockport Co, FL 2, 10 September 2005; 3 Kevin Betsy v Mansfield T 24 September 2005.

Most Capped Player: Mark Rogers, 7, Canada.

Most League Appearances: Steve Brown, 371, 1994–2004.

Youngest League Player: Ikechi Anya, 16 years 279 days v Scunthorpe U, 8 October 2004.

Record Transfer Fee Received: £600,000 from Nottingham F for Nathan Tyson, January 2006.

Record Transfer Fee Paid: £200,000 to Barnet for Sean Devine, 15 April 1999.

Football League Record: Promoted to Division 3 from GM Vauxhall Conference in 1993; 1993–94 Division 3; 1994–2004 Division 2; 2004– FL 2.

MANAGERS

First coach appointed 1951.
Prior to Brian Lee's appointment in 1969 the team was selected by a Match Committee which met every Monday evening.

James McCormack 1951–52
Sid Cann 1952–61
Graham Adams 1961–62
Don Welsh 1962–64
Barry Darvill 1964–68
Brian Lee 1969–76
Ted Powell 1976–77
John Reardon 1977–78
Andy Williams 1978–80
Mike Keen 1980–84
Paul Bence 1984–86
Alan Gane 1986–87
Peter Suddaby 1987–88
Jim Kelman 1988–90
Martin O'Neill 1990–95
Alan Smith 1995–96
John Gregory 1996–98
Neil Smillie 1998–99
Lawrie Sanchez 1999–2003
Tony Adams 2003–04
John Gorman 2004–06
Paul Lambert 2006–08
Peter Taylor May 2008–

LATEST SEQUENCES

Longest Sequence of League Wins: 6, 19.8.2006 – 16.9.2006.

Longest Sequence of League Defeats: 6, 18.3.2006 – 17.4.2006.

Longest Sequence of League Draws: 5, 24.1.2004 – 21.2.2004.

Longest Sequence of Unbeaten League Matches: 21, 6.8.2005 – 10.12.2005.

Longest Sequence Without a League Win: 13, 16.8.2003 – 18.10.2003 and 10.1.2004 – 20.3.2004.

Successive Scoring Runs: 15 from 28.12.2004.

Successive Non-scoring Runs: 5 from 15.10.1996.

TEN YEAR LEAGUE RECORD

		P	W	D	L	F	A	Pts	Pos
1998-99	Div 2	46	13	12	21	52	58	51	19
1999-2000	Div 2	46	16	13	17	56	53	61	12
2000-01	Div 2	46	15	14	17	46	53	59	13
2001-02	Div 2	46	17	13	16	58	64	64	11
2002-03	Div 2	46	13	13	20	59	66	52	18
2003-04	Div 2	46	6	19	21	50	75	37	24
2004-05	FL 2	46	17	14	15	58	52	65	10
2005-06	FL 2	46	18	17	11	72	56	71	6
2006-07	FL 2	46	16	14	16	52	47	62	12
2007-08	FL 2	46	22	12	12	56	42	78	7

DID YOU KNOW ?

On 23 September 2000 Wycombe Wanderers emphasised that two of the most appropriate times in which to score goals are just before and immediately after the interval. Against Peterborough United Jamie Bates scored with the last kick of the first half and on the resumption, Jermaine McSporran made it 2–0 within nine seconds without the opposition touching the ball!

WYCOMBE WANDERERS 2007–08 LEAGUE RECORD

Match No.	*Date*	*Venue*	*Opponents*	*Result*		*H/T Score*	*Lg. Pos.*	*Goalscorers*	*Attendance*
1	Aug 11	H	Accrington S	L	0-1	0-0	—		4408
2	18	A	Dagenham & R	D	2-2	0-1	19	Bloomfield [69], Easter (pen) [90]	2280
3	25	H	Bury	W	1-0	0-0	14	Torres [70]	4067
4	Sept 1	A	Chesterfield	L	0-2	0-1	19		3757
5	9	H	Brentford	W	1-0	0-0	12	Easter (pen) [82]	4711
6	15	A	Macclesfield T	W	2-1	0-0	8	McGleish [65], Reid [89]	2173
7	22	H	Shrewsbury T	D	1-1	1-1	8	McGleish [37]	4936
8	29	A	Bradford C	W	1-0	1-0	7	McGleish [7]	13,530
9	Oct 2	A	Barnet	L	1-2	1-0	—	Sutton [22]	2023
10	6	H	Notts Co	W	3-1	0-0	8	Sutton (pen) [48], McGleish [71], Bloomfield [82]	4199
11	14	A	Peterborough U	L	1-2	0-0	8	Bloomfield [53]	4584
12	20	H	Grimsby T	W	3-0	1-0	8	Holt [24], McGleish 2 (1 pen) [77, 90 (p)]	4052
13	27	A	Chester C	D	2-2	1-2	9	Torres [13], Sutton [64]	2598
14	Nov 3	H	Milton Keynes D	D	1-1	1-1	9	Bloomfield [37]	5929
15	7	A	Wrexham	D	0-0	0-0	—		2805
16	17	H	Lincoln C	W	1-0	1-0	8	McGleish [39]	4297
17	24	A	Darlington	L	0-1	0-0	8		3002
18	Dec 4	H	Hereford U	D	2-2	2-0	—	Oakes [6], Holt [45]	4081
19	8	A	Stockport Co	L	0-6	0-2	—		4477
20	14	H	Morecambe	W	2-0	1-0	—	McGleish [19], Sutton [69]	3821
21	22	H	Macclesfield T	W	2-1	1-1	8	McGleish 2 (1 pen) [32 (p), 73]	3887
22	26	A	Brentford	W	3-1	0-1	7	Torres [55], McGleish [61], Sutton [65]	5841
23	29	A	Shrewsbury T	W	1-0	1-0	7	Sutton [8]	6208
24	Jan 1	H	Barnet	D	0-0	0-0	7		4818
25	8	A	Mansfield T	W	4-0	1-0	—	McGleish 3 [5, 69, 73], Jelleyman (og) [58]	1959
26	12	H	Rochdale	L	0-1	0-0	7		4493
27	19	A	Rotherham U	D	1-1	0-1	6	McGleish [56]	6709
28	26	H	Chesterfield	W	1-0	1-0	5	McGleish [26]	5203
29	29	H	Dagenham & R	L	0-1	0-1	—		3974
30	Feb 2	A	Accrington S	W	2-0	1-0	6	McGleish [13], Knight [75]	1200
31	9	H	Mansfield T	L	1-2	1-1	6	McGleish [42]	5963
32	12	A	Bury	D	2-2	2-0	—	Torres [14], McGleish (pen) [39]	1895
33	16	H	Rotherham U	W	1-0	0-0	6	McCracken [50]	4610
34	23	A	Rochdale	W	1-0	1-0	6	Knight [13]	2616
35	Mar 1	A	Lincoln C	L	0-1	0-0	6		4002
36	8	H	Darlington	W	2-0	1-0	5	Knight [24], McGleish [84]	5185
37	11	H	Wrexham	W	2-1	2-0	—	Knight [14], McGleish [21]	4002
38	15	A	Hereford U	L	0-1	0-0	6		3126
39	22	A	Morecambe	W	1-0	1-0	6	Oakes [36]	2524
40	24	H	Stockport Co	D	0-0	0-0	6-		5380
41	Apr 5	H	Peterborough U	D	2-2	1-0	7	Oakes [5], McGleish (pen) [90]	6202
42	12	A	Milton Keynes D	D	2-2	1-0	7	McGleish 2 [37, 73]	12,747
43	15	A	Grimsby T	W	1-0	1-0	—	Torres [19]	2537
44	19	H	Chester C	W	1-0	0-0	7	McGleish [78]	5497
45	26	A	Notts Co	L	0-1	0-0	7		7327
46	May 3	H	Bradford C	W	2-1	2-1	7	Facey [6], Knight [25]	5467

Final League Position: 7

GOALSCORERS

League (56): McGleish 25 (4 pens), Sutton 6 (1 pen), Knight 5, Torres 5, Bloomfield 4, Oakes 3, Easter 2 (2 pens), Holt 2, Facey 1, McCracken 1, Reid 1, own goal 1.
Carling Cup (1): Oakes 1.
FA Cup (1): Bloomfield 1.
J Paint Trophy (0).
Play-Offs (1): Facey 1.

Shearer S 4 + 1	Stockley S 18 + 4	Woodman C 27 + 2	Bloomfield M 26 + 9	Johnson L 44 + 1	McCracken D 35 + 2	Bullock M 17 + 8	Torres S 36 + 6	Sutton J 23 + 20	McGleish S 45 + 1	Holt G 42 + 1	Boucaud A 2 + 8	Williams T 6 + 4	Oakes S 23 + 11	Martin R 44	Christon L 2	Easter J 6	Young J 3 + 1	Reid R 1 + 10	Fielding F 36	Antwi W 6	Douglas R 3	Doherty T 21 + 3	Daly G — + 2	Knight L 12 + 8	Lennon N 8 + 1	Williamson M 7 + 5	Herd C 3 + 1	Facey D 4 + 2	Rice R — + 1	Phillips M 1 + 1	Palmer C 1	Match No.
1	2	3^{1}	4	5	6	7^{2}	8	9	10	11^{3}	12	13	14																			1
1			4	3	5	12	13	14	10^{3}	11	7^{1}		8^{2}	2	6	9																2
1	12		4^{2}	5	6	7	8^{1}	14	10^{3}	11		3	13	2		9																3
1	2		4^{2}	5	6	7	8	12	10	11^{1}			13	3		9																4
	2		4	5	6	7	12	14	10^{3}	11^{2}		8^{1}	13	3		9	1															5
	2		4^{1}	5	6	7	12	13	10^{2}	11			8	3		9^{3}	1	14														6
15	2^{2}		12	5	6	7	8		10	11^{1}		13	4	3		9	1^{G}															7
	2		12	5	6	7	8	9^{3}	10	11		13	4^{1}	3^{2}				14	1													8
	2		12	5	6	7	8	9	10^{3}	11		13	4^{1}	3^{2}				14	1													9
	2		12	5	6	7	8^{2}	9^{3}	10	11	13		4^{1}	3				14	1													10
	2		12	5	6	7^{2}	8	9^{3}	10^{1}	11	13		4	3				14	1													11
			4	5	6	7^{1}	8^{2}	9^{3}	10	11	13	3	12	2				14	1													12
			4	5	6	7	8	9	10^{1}	11		3		2				12	1													13
			4	5^{2}		7	8	9	10	11^{1}		3	12	2				13	1	6												14
	12		4	13	6	7	8	14	10^{3}			3	11	2^{1}				9	1	5^{2}												15
	2		4	5		7	8	12	10^{1}	11	13		9^{2}	3					1	6												16
	2^{1}	13	4	5		7^{3}	8	12	10	11			9^{2}	3				14	1	6												17
	2	12	4	5			8^{3}	9	10	11	13		7^{2}	3						6^{1}	1	14										18
	2^{2}		4	5		12	8	9	10	11			7^{1}	3	6			13	1													19
	2	3^{2}	4^{1}	5	6	12	8	9	10	11			13	7					1													20
	2^{1}	3	4^{2}	5	6	12	8	9	10	11				7					1			13										21
	2^{1}	3	4	5	6	13	8^{2}	9	10^{3}	11				7					1			12	14									22
		3	4	5	6		8	9	10^{3}	12	13		7^{1}	2					1			11^{2}	14									23
		3	4	5	6		8	9	10	11			12	2							1	7^{1}										24
		3	4	5	6		8	9	10^{3}	11^{2}	13		12	2							1	7^{1}		14								25
		3	4	5	6	12	8^{1}	9^{3}	10	11			13	2					1			7^{2}		14								26
		3	4	5	6		8	9	10	11				2					1			7^{1}		12								27
	12	3^{1}	4	5	6		8	9^{2}	10	11				2					1			7		13								28
		3		5	6	7^{1}	8	9	10	11				2					1			4		12								29
		3	12	5	6		8^{1}	9	10^{2}	11				2					1			4		13	7							30
		3	12	5^{3}	6		8^{1}	9^{2}	10	11				2					1			4		13	7	14						31
		3	12	5	6		8	13	10	11				2					1			4^{1}		9^{2}	7							32
		3	12	5	6		8	13	10^{2}	11				2					1			4		9^{1}	7							33
		3	4	5	6		8^{2}	12	10					2					1			11		9^{1}	7	13						34
		3^{1}	4	5	6	13		12	10	11				2					1			7		9	8^{2}							35
		3	4^{3}	5	6	12		13	10	11			8^{2}	2					1			7		9^{1}		14						36
	2	3		5	6			12	10^{1}	11			8^{3}	4					1			7■		9^{2}	13	14						37
	12	3		5	6^{3}			13	10	11			8	2					1					9^{2}	4^{1}	14	7					38
		3		5			12	13	10^{2}	11			4	2					1					9	8	6	7^{1}					39
		3		5			12	13	10	11			4	2					1			8		9^{2}		6	7^{1}					40
		3^{1}		5			8	12	10	11			4	2					1			7		9^{2}		6		13				41
		3		5			8		10	11			4^{2}	2					1			7		9^{1}		6	13	12				42
		3		5	12		8^{1}	13	10^{3}	11			4	2					1			7		14		6		9^{2}				43
		3		5	12		8^{1}	13	10^{2}	11			4	2					1			7				6		9				44
	2■				6		12	9^{3}	10		8		4	3^{2}					1	5								11	13	14	7^{1}	45
		3		5	6		8		13	11			12				15		1^{G}			7		9		4		10^{2}		2^{1}		46

FA Cup
First Round | Swindon T | (h) | 1-2

Carling Cup
First Round | Plymouth Arg | (a) | 1-2

J Paint Trophy
Second Round | Swansea C | (a) | 0-2

Play-Offs
Semi-Final | Stockport Co | (h) | 1-1
| | (a) | 0-1

YEOVIL TOWN — FL Championship 1

FOUNDATION

One of the prime movers of Yeovil football was Ernest J. Sercombe. His association with the club began in 1895 as a playing member of Yeovil Casuals, of which team he became vice-captain and in his last season 1899–1900, he was chosen to play for Somerset against Devon. Upon the reorganisation of the club, he became secretary of the old Yeovil Town FC and with the amalgamation with Petters United in 1914, he continued to serve until his resignation in 1930.

Huish Park, Lufton Way, Yeovil, Somerset BA22 8YF.

Telephone: (01935) 423 662.

Fax: (01935) 473 956.

Ticket Office: (01935) 847 888.

Website: www.ytfc.net

Email: jcotton@ytfc.co.uk

Ground Capacity: 9,665.

Record Attendance: 9,527 v Leeds U, FL 1, 25 April 2008 (16,318 v Sunderland at Huish).

Pitch Measurements: 110m × 69m.

Chairman: John R. Fry.

Chief Executive: Martyne Starnes.

Secretary: Jean Cotton.

Manager: Russell Slade.

Assistant Manager: Steve Thompson.

Colours: Green and white shirts, green shorts, white stockings.

Change Colours: Black and green shirts, black shorts, black stockings.

Year Formed: 1895.

Turned Professional: 1921.

Ltd Co.: 1923.

Club Nickname: 'Glovers'.

Previous Names: 1895, Yeovil Casuals; 1907, Yeovil Town; 1915, Yeovil & Petters United; 1946, Yeovil Town.

Grounds: 1895, Pen Mill Ground; 1921, Huish; 1990, Huish Park.

HONOURS

FL Championship 2 winners 2004–05.

Conference: Champions 2002–03.

FA Cup: 5th rd 1949.

League Cup: 2nd rd 2006.

Southern League: Champions 1954–55, 1963–64, 1970–71; Runners-up: 1923–24, 1931–32, 1934–35, 1969–70, 1972–73.

Southern League Cup: Winners 1948–49, 1954–55, 1960–61, 1965–66; Runners-up: 1946–47, 1955–56.

Isthmian League: Winners 1987–88; Runners-up: 1985–86, 1986–87, 1996–97.

AC Delco Cup: Winners 1987–88.

Bob Lord Trophy: Winners 1989–90.

FA Trophy: Winners 2002.

London Combination: Runners-up 1930–31, 1932–33.

SKY SPORTS FACT FILE

Welsh international forward Wilf Lewis playing for Yeovil Town scored the club's first hat-trick in the competition proper in an FA Cup replay against Dartford on 1 December 1932. He was transferred to Bath City because of a financial crisis before a return to Cardiff City.

First Football League Game: 9 August 2003, Division 3 v Rochdale (a) W 3-1: Weale; Williams (Lindegaard), Crittenden, Lockwood, O'Brien, Pluck (Rodrigues), Gosling (El Kholti), Way, Jackson, Gall (2), Johnson (1).

Record League Victory: 10–0 v Kidderminster H, Southern League, 27 December 1955. 10–0 v Bedford T, Southern League, 4 March 1961.

Record Cup Victory: 12–1 v Westbury United, FA Cup 1st qual rd, 1923–24.

Record Defeat: 0–8 v Manchester United, FA Cup 5th rd, 12 February 1949.

Most League Points (3 for a win): – 83, FL 2, 2004–05.

Most League Goals: 90, FL 2, 2004–05.

Highest League Goalscorer in Season: Phil Jevons, 27, 2004–05

Most League Goals in Total Aggregate: Phil Jevons, 42, 2004–06

Most Capped Player: Andrejs Stolcers, 1 (81) Latvia and Arron Davies, 1, Wales.

Most League Appearances: Terry Skiverton, 170, 2003–.

Record Transfer Fee Received: Undisclosed from Nottingham F for Arron Davies, July 2007.

Record Transfer Fee Paid: Undisclosed to Atletico Penarol de Rafaela (Argentina) for Pablo Bastianini, August 2005.

Football League Record: 2003 Promoted to Division 3 from Conference; 2003–04 Division 3; 2004–05 FL 2; 2005– FL 1.

LATEST SEQUENCES

Longest Sequence of League Wins: 7, 7.12.2004 – 15.1.2005.

Longest Sequence of League Defeats: 5, 29.10.05 – 6.12.05.

Longest Sequence of Unbeaten League Matches: 7, 7.12.2004 – 15.1.2005.

Longest Sequence Without a League Win: 6, 6.8.05 – 29.8.05.

Successive Scoring Runs: 22 from 30.10.2004.

Successive Non-scoring Runs: 3 from 21.1.2006.

MANAGERS

Jack Gregory 1922–28
Tommy Lawes 1928–29
Dave Pratt 1929–33
Louis Page 1933–35
Dave Halliday 1935–38
Billy Kingdon 1938–46
Alec Stock 1946–49
George Patterson 1949–51
Harry Lowe 1951–53
Ike Clarke 1953–57
Norman Dodgin 1957
Jimmy Baldwin 1957–60
Basil Hayward 1960–64
Glyn Davies 1964–65
Joe McDonald 1965–67
Ron Saunders 1967–69
Mike Hughes 1969–72
Cecil Irwin 1972–75
Stan Harland 1975–81
Barry Lloyd 1978–81
Malcolm Allison 1981
Jimmy Giles 1981–83
Trevor Finnigan/Mike Hughes 1983
Steve Coles 1983–84
Ian McFarlane 1984
Gerry Gow 1984–87
Brian Hall 1987–90
Clive Whitehead 1990–91
Steve Rutter 1991–93
Brian Hall 1994–95
Graham Roberts 1995–98
Colin Lippiatt 1998–99
Steve Thompson 1999–2000
Dave Webb 2000
Gary Johnson 2001–05
Steve Thompson 2005–06
Russell Slade June 2006–

TEN YEAR LEAGUE RECORD

		P	W	D	L	F	A	Pts	Pos
1998-99	Conf.	42	20	11	11	68	54	71	5
1999-2000	Conf.	42	18	10	14	60	63	64	7
2000-01	Conf.	42	24	8	10	73	50	80	2
2001-02	Conf.	42	19	13	10	66	53	70	3
2002-03	Conf.	42	28	11	3	100	37	95	1
2003-04	Div 3	46	23	5	18	70	57	74	8
2004-05	FL 2	46	25	8	13	90	65	83	1
2005-06	FL 1	46	15	11	20	54	62	56	15
2006-07	FL 1	46	23	10	13	55	39	79	5
2007-08	FL 1	46	14	10	22	38	59	52	18

DID YOU KNOW ?

David Halliday was a prolific goalscoring centre-forward in the years between the wars north and south of the border hitting some 347 League goals in the process. After leaving Clapton Orient he joined Yeovil & Petters United as player-manager and despite his 39 years of age was still a menacing marksman getting a hat-trick on his first appearance.

YEOVIL TOWN 2007–08 LEAGUE RECORD

Match No.	Date	Venue	Opponents	Result		H/T Score	Lg. Pos.	Goalscorers	Attendance
1	Aug 11	A	Huddersfield T	L	0-1	0-1	—		9876
2	18	H	Port Vale	W	1-0	1-0	13	Cochrane 17	5071
3	25	A	Northampton T	W	2-1	1-1	6	Cochrane 26, Owusu 90	4555
4	Sept 1	H	Tranmere R	D	1-1	0-0	6	Stewart 57	4985
5	9	A	Swindon T	W	1-0	0-0	4	Owusu 77	6944
6	15	H	Leyton Orient	L	0-1	0-0	5		5217
7	22	A	Brighton & HA	W	2-1	2-0	4	Owusu 15, Warne 43	5231
8	29	H	Nottingham F	L	0-3	0-0	7		6818
9	Oct 2	H	Luton T	D	0-0	0-0	—		4848
10	6	A	Leeds U	L	0-1	0-0	11		27,808
11	13	H	Carlisle U	W	2-1	0-0	9	Owusu 54, Jones N 65	4757
12	20	A	Bristol R	D	1-1	0-0	8	Rose 62	7726
13	27	H	Swansea C	L	1-2	0-1	12	Betsy 48	6207
14	Nov 3	A	Crewe Alex	L	0-2	0-2	14		4363
15	6	A	Cheltenham T	D	1-1	1-0	—	Owusu 31	3169
16	18	H	Gillingham	W	2-1	0-0	12	Owusu 66, Walker 88	4408
17	24	A	Millwall	L	1-2	0-0	14	Walker 49	8105
18	Dec 4	H	Bournemouth	W	2-1	2-0	—	Skiverton 3, Walker 38	5321
19	8	H	Hartlepool U	W	3-1	2-1	9	Skiverton 27, Stewart 31, Owusu 77	4694
20	16	A	Doncaster R	W	2-1	1-0	7	Way 37, Stewart 78	5967
21	22	A	Leyton Orient	D	0-0	0-0	8		4687
22	26	H	Swindon T	L	0-1	0-0	9		6539
23	29	H	Brighton & HA	W	2-1	1-1	8	Dempsey 42, Stieber 50	6881
24	Jan 1	A	Luton T	L	0-1	0-0	8		6811
25	8	H	Walsall	L	0-2	0-0	—		4319
26	12	A	Southend U	D	1-1	0-1	8	Owusu 71	7352
27	19	H	Oldham Ath	D	0-0	0-0	10		4905
28	26	A	Tranmere R	L	1-2	0-1	—	Kirk 51	5386
29	29	A	Port Vale	D	2-2	1-1	—	Dempsey 6, Kirk 52	2869
30	Feb 2	H	Huddersfield T	L	0-2	0-1	13		4823
31	9	A	Walsall	L	0-2	0-0	15		5034
32	12	H	Northampton T	W	1-0	0-0	—	Skiverton 90	5001
33	16	A	Oldham Ath	L	0-3	0-1	13		4781
34	23	H	Southend U	L	0-3	0-2	16		4820
35	Mar 1	A	Gillingham	D	0-0	0-0	16		5083
36	8	H	Cheltenham T	W	2-1	1-0	16	Wright (og) 9, Kirk 73	4588
37	11	H	Millwall	L	0-1	0-0	—		4439
38	15	A	Bournemouth	L	0-2	0-2	17		4145
39	21	H	Doncaster R	W	2-1	2-0	—	Skiverton 22, Owusu 31	6146
40	24	A	Hartlepool U	L	0-2	0-1	16		3808
41	29	H	Bristol R	D	0-0	0-0	15		6654
42	Apr 5	A	Carlisle U	L	1-2	1-0	16	Stewart 38	6843
43	12	H	Crewe Alex	L	0-3	0-1	18		4785
44	19	A	Swansea C	W	2-1	1-0	17	Skiverton 23, Downes 60	18,321
45	25	H	Leeds U	L	0-1	0-1	—		9527
46	May 3	A	Nottingham F	L	2-3	1-3	18	Peters 20, Kirk 75	28,520

Final League Position: 18

GOALSCORERS

League (38): Owusu 9, Skiverton 5, Kirk 4, Stewart 4, Walker 3, Cochrane 2, Dempsey 2, Betsy 1, Downes 1, Jones N 1, Peters 1, Rose 1, Stieber 1, Warne 1, Way 1, own goal 1.
Carling Cup (1): Owusu 1.
FA Cup (1): Stewart 1.
J Paint Trophy (1): Owusu 1.

Mildenhall S 29	Lynch M 12 + 2	Jones N 29 + 2	Peltier L 34	Guyett S 34	Forbes T 41	Barry A 25 + 11	Warne P 26 + 7	Owusu L 31 + 12	Stewart M 35 + 1	Williams M 8 + 15	Cochrane J 6 + 6	Rose M 27 + 3	Morris L — + 1	Alcock C 5 + 3	Knights D — + 3	Jones R 6 + 3	Skiverton T 27 + 4	Hughes J — + 1	Domoraud W — + 5	Begovic A 2	Larrieu R 6	Gillett S 3 + 1	Downes A 3 + 2	Betsy K 5	Dempsey G 10 + 6	Walker J 11 + 2	Stieber Z 14 + 1	Way D 7	Bircham M 9 + 4	Welsh I — + 3	Kirk A 15 + 4	Peters J 12 + 2	Bridcutt L 6 + 3	Church S 2 + 4	Woods M 3	Flinders S 9	Maher S 4 + 2	Christophe J 4 + 1	Smith N 6 + 1	Match No.
1	2^1	3	4	5^2	6	7	8	9	10	11^3	12	13	14																											1
1			4	5	6		12	9	10^2	7^1	8	3		2	13	11																								2
1			4	5	6	13	8^1	9	10	12^2	11	3		2		7																								3
1		3	4	5	6	12	8	9^2	10	14	7^1	2			13^3	11																								4
1	12	3	4	5	6	7	8	9	10^2			2^1				11	13																							5
1^6		3	4	5	6	7	8	9	10			2^1				11^2	15	12	13																					6
		3	4	5	6	7	8	9	10							12	2				1	11^1																		7
		3	4	5	6	7	8	9	10^2			11			13	12	2^1				1																			8
		3	4	5	6	7	8	9	10			2									1	11																		9
	2	3		5	6	7	8^1	9	10			4							12		1			11																10
	2	3	4^1	5	6	7	8^2	9			12	10									1	13		11																11
	12	3	4^1	5	6	7	8	9			10^2	2									1			11	13															12
1	2	3		5	6	7	12	9^2	10^1		8^3	4							13					11		14														13
1	2^3	3		5	6	7	8	9^1			10^2	4							12					11	14	13														14
1		3		5	2		8	9			12	7^1				4	6		13						11	10^2														15
1		3	4		6	7	8	9			12						5					2			11^1	10														16
1		3	4		6	7^1	8^2	9			13	2^3					5								12	10	14	11												17
1		3■	4^3	6	2		8	12	10^1					13			5								14	9	7^2	11												18
1			4	6	2	13	8	12	10							14	5								3	9^1	7^3	11^2												19
1		3	2	5	6	12	8		10■								13								11^2	9	7^1	4												20
1		3	4	5	2	12	8	13									6								10^2	9	7^1	11												21
1		3^3	2		4	12	8^2	13	10			14					5■								11^1	9	7	6												22
1		3	2	5	6		8^2	12	10^1	13		4													11	9	7^3		14											23
1		3		5	6	12	8■	13	10	14		2													11^1	9	7^3	4^2												24
1	2	3^1		5	6	7		9	10	13															4^2	8	11^3		12	14										25
1		3		5	6	7^2	12	9	10	13		2					4										11^3		8^1	14										26
1		3		5			8^2	9	10	13		2					6								12		7		4^1		11									27
1		3^2		5	2		8	9	10	13							6								12		7^1		4■		11									28
1		3			6	12	8	9			13	4^1		2			5								11^2		7^3			14	10									29
1	2		3		6	12		9^2	13	14		4					5										7		8^1		10	11^3								30
1^6		3	2	6			12	13	10			4		15			5														9	7^2	11	8^1						31
		3	2	5		7		9^2		12		4					6														10	11^1	8	13		1				32
		3^2	2	5		7	12	9^1				4					6														10	13	8	14	11^3	1				33
	3		2		6	12	13	9	10	11^2		4^1					5														8^3	14	7			1				34
	2		3		6	7		12	9	11^3							5														10^2	4	8^1	14		1	13■			35
	3				6	7	8^3		9	12		4^2		2			5												13		10	11^1	14			1				36
	3			6		7^1	13	12	10	14				2			5														9	8^3			11^2	1		4		37
	3		2	5	6	13		12	10^2	14		7^3																			9			8^1	11	1		4		38
			2	6	3	7		9	10					12			5^1												13		8^3			14		1	11^2	4		39
			3	6	2	7^2		9	10	12							5														11		13			1	8^1	4^3	14	40
			2		6			9	10			4^2					5			1							11				14	7^1	12				8^3	13	3	41
			3	5	2			9	10	6										1			14						4^2		12	7^3	8^1				13		11	42
1			2	5	6			9	10	12							13						14						4		11^2	7^1					8^3		3	43
1		13	2		6	7		12	10	8							5						9^2						4^1			11							3	44
1			2		6	7^1		12	10	8^2							5						11						4		13	9							3	45
1		12	2		6	7^3			10	9^2		14					5						8^1						4		13	11							3	46

FA Cup
First Round Torquay U (a) 1-4

Carling Cup
First Round Hereford U (a) 1-4

J Paint Trophy
First Round Shrewsbury T (h) 1-0
Second Round Hereford U (a) 0-0
Quarter-Final Swansea C (a) 0-1

ENGLISH LEAGUE PLAYERS DIRECTORY

Players listed represent those with their clubs during the 2007–08 season.

Players are listed alphabetically on pages 561–567.

The number alongside each player corresponds to the team number heading. (Abbey, George 27 = team 27 (Crewe Alex))

ACCRINGTON S (1)

ARTHUR, Kenny (G) **267 0**
H: 6 3 W: 13 08 b.Bellshill 7-12-78
1997–98 Partick T 19 0
1998–99 Partick T 26 0
1999–2000 Partick T 4 0
2000–01 Partick T 34 0
2001–02 Partick T 23 0
2002–03 Partick T 35 0
2003–04 Partick T 22 0
2004–05 Partick T 35 0
2005–06 Partick T 24 0
2006–07 Partick T 21 0 **243 0**
2007–08 Accrington S 24 0 **24 0**

BELL, James (M) **2 0**
H: 6 0 W: 12 00 b.Liverpool 24-11-89
Source: Scholar.
2007–08 Accrington S 2 0 **2 0**

BOCO, Romuald (F) **43 3**
H: 5 10 W: 10 12 b.Bernay 8-7-85
Source: Niort. *Honours:* Benin 17 full caps.
2006–07 Accrington S 32 3
2007–08 Accrington S 11 0 **43 3**

BRANCH, Graham (F) **409 31**
H: 6 2 W: 12 02 b.Liverpool 12-2-72
Source: Heswall.
1991–92 Tranmere R 4 0
1992–93 Tranmere R 3 0
1992–93 *Bury* 4 1 **4 1**
1993–94 Tranmere R 13 0
1994–95 Tranmere R 1 0
1995–96 Tranmere R 21 2
1996–97 Tranmere R 35 5
1997–98 Tranmere R 25 3 **102 10**
1997–98 *Wigan Ath* 3 0 **3 0**
1998–99 Stockport Co 14 3 **14 3**
1998–99 Burnley 20 1
1999–2000 Burnley 44 3
2000–01 Burnley 35 5
2001–02 Burnley 10 0
2002–03 Burnley 32 0
2003–04 Burnley 38 3
2004–05 Burnley 43 3
2005–06 Burnley 37 2
2006–07 Burnley 5 0 **264 17**
2007–08 Accrington S 22 0 **22 0**

BROWN, David (F) **165 28**
H: 5 10 W: 11 02 b.Bolton 2-10-78
Source: Trainee.
1995–96 Manchester U 0 0
1996–97 Manchester U 0 0
1997–98 Manchester U 0 0
1997–98 *Hull C* 7 2
1998–99 Hull C 42 11
1999–2000 Hull C 45 6
2000–01 Hull C 37 4 **131 23**
2001–02 Torquay U 2 0 **2 0**
From Chester C, Telford U, Hereford U.
2006–07 Accrington S 17 5
2007–08 Accrington S 15 0 **32 5**

CARDEN, Paul (M) **145 0**
H: 5 9 W: 11 10 b.Liverpool 29-3-79
Source: Trainee.
1996–97 Blackpool 1 0
1997–98 Blackpool 0 0 **1 0**
1997–98 Rochdale 7 0
1998–99 Rochdale 25 0
1999–2000 Rochdale 13 0 **45 0**
1999–2000 Chester C 11 0
From Doncaster R.
2004–05 Chester C 40 0 **51 0**
2005–06 Peterborough U 42 0
2006–07 Peterborough U 2 0 **44 0**
2007–08 Accrington S 4 0 **4 0**

CAVANAGH, Paul (D) **45 5**
H: 5 11 W: 11 09 b.Liverpool 14-10-81
Source: Liverpool Scholar.
2006–07 Accrington S 26 4
2007–08 Accrington S 19 1 **45 5**

CRANEY, Ian (M) **80 12**
H: 5 10 W: 12 00 b.Liverpool 21-7-82
Source: Runcorn, Altrincham.
2006–07 Accrington S 18 5
2006–07 Swansea C 27 0
2007–08 Swansea C 1 0 **28 0**
2007–08 Accrington S 34 7 **52 12**

D'SANE, Roscoe (M) **24 7**
H: 5 4 W: 11 00 b.Epsom 16-10-80
Source: Trainee.
1999–2000 Crystal Palace 0 0
2000–01 Crystal Palace 0 0
2001–02 Southend U 2 0 **2 0**
From Woking, Aldershot T, AFC Wimbledon
2007–08 Accrington S 22 7 **22 7**

DUNBAVIN, Ian (G) **142 0**
H: 6 1 W: 12 10 b.Knowsley 27-5-80
Source: Trainee.
1998–99 Liverpool 0 0
1999–2000 Liverpool 0 0
1999–2000 Shrewsbury T 7 0
2000–01 Shrewsbury T 22 0
2001–02 Shrewsbury T 34 0
2002–03 Shrewsbury T 33 0
2003–04 Shrewsbury T 0 0 **96 0**
From Halifax T.
2006–07 Accrington S 23 0
2007–08 Accrington S 23 0 **46 0**

EDWARDS, Phil (D) **64 2**
H: 5 8 W: 11 03 b.Bootle 8-11-85
Source: Scholar.
2005–06 Wigan Ath 0 0
2006–07 Accrington S 33 1
2007–08 Accrington S 31 1 **64 2**

FEARON, Martin (G) **0 0**
H: 6 2 W: 12 02 b.Liverpool 30-10-88
2007–08 Accrington S 0 0

GRANT, Robert (M) **8 0**
H: 5 11 W: 12 00 b.Blackpool 27-3-87
Source: Scholar.
2006–07 Accrington S 1 0
2007–08 Accrington S 7 0 **8 0**

HARRIS, James (M) **73 2**
H: 5 7 W: 11 06 b.Liverpool 15-4-87
2005–06 Everton 0 0
2005–06 Everton 0 0
2006–07 Accrington S 32 2
2007–08 Accrington S 41 0 **73 2**

KING, Mark (M) **6 0**
H: 5 11 W: 12 04 b.Blackburn 6-6-88
Source: Scholar.
2007–08 Blackburn R 0 0
2007–08 Accrington S 6 0 **6 0**

MANGAN, Andrew (M) **63 9**
H: 5 9 W: 10 03 b.Liverpool 30-8-86
Source: Scholar.
2003–04 Blackpool 2 0
2004–05 Blackpool 0 0 **2 0**
2006–07 Accrington S 34 4
2007–08 Bury 20 4 **20 4**
2007–08 Accrington S 7 1 **41 5**

MANNIX, David (M) **13 0**
H: 5 8 W: 11 06 b.Winsford 24-9-85
Source: Trainee. *Honours:* England Under-20.
2003–04 Liverpool 0 0
2004–05 Liverpool 0 0
2005–06 Liverpool 0 0
2006–07 Liverpool 0 0
2006–07 *Accrington S* 1 0
2007–08 Liverpool 0 0
2007–08 Accrington S 12 0 **13 0**

McEVILLY, Lee (F) **154 42**
H: 6 0 W: 13 00 b.Liverpool 15-4-82
Source: Burscough. *Honours:* Northern Ireland Under-21, 1 full cap.
2001–02 Rochdale 18 4
2002–03 Rochdale 37 15
2003–04 Rochdale 30 6
From Accrington S
2005–06 Wrexham 23 7
2006–07 Wrexham 28 7 **51 14**
2007–08 Accrington S 11 0 **11 0**
2007–08 *Rochdale* 7 3 **92 28**

McGIVERN, Leighton (M) **44 3**
H: 5 8 W: 11 01 b.Liverpool 2-6-84
Honours: from Vauxhall Motors.
2004–05 Rochdale 25 1
2005–06 Rochdale 0 0 **25 1**
2006–07 Accrington S 7 1
2007–08 Accrington S 12 1 **19 2**

MILES, John (F) **156 22**
H: 5 10 W: 10 08 b.Fazackerley 28-9-81
Source: Trainee.
1998–99 Liverpool 0 0
1999–2000 Liverpool 0 0
2000–01 Liverpool 0 0
2001–02 Liverpool 0 0
2001–02 Stoke C 1 0 **1 0**
2002–03 Crewe Alex 5 1 **5 1**
2002–03 Macclesfield T 8 4
2003–04 Macclesfield T 29 6
2004–05 Macclesfield T 30 3
2005–06 Macclesfield T 25 4
2006–07 Macclesfield T 30 4 **122 21**
2007–08 Accrington S 16 0 **16 0**
2007–08 *Milton Keynes D* 12 0 **12 0**

MULLIN, Paul (F) **89 26**
H: 6 0 W: 12 01 b.Bury 16-3-74
Source: Clitheroe, Darwen, Radcliffe Borough.
2006–07 Accrington S 46 14
2007–08 Accrington S 43 12 **89 26**

MURPHY, Peter (M) **2 0**
H: 6 0 W: 11 10 b.Liverpool 13-2-90
Source: Scholar.
2007–08 Accrington S 2 0 **2 0**

PROCTOR, Andy (M) **86 13**
H: 6 0 W: 12 04 b.Blackburn 13-3-83
Source: Great Harwood T.
2006–07 Accrington S 43 3
2007–08 Accrington S 43 10 **86 13**

RICHARDSON, Leam (D) **180 1**
H: 5 7 W: 11 04 b.Leeds 19-11-79
Source: Trainee.
1997–98 Blackburn R 0 0
1998–99 Blackburn R 0 0
1999–2000 Blackburn R 0 0
2000–01 Bolton W 12 0
2001–02 Bolton W 1 0
2001–02 *Notts Co* 21 0 **21 0**
2002–03 Bolton W 0 0 **13 0**
2002–03 *Blackpool* 20 0
2003–04 Blackpool 28 0
2004–05 Blackpool 23 0 **71 0**
2006–07 Accrington S 38 0
2007–08 Accrington S 37 1 **75 1**

ROBERTS, Mark (D) **41 0**
H: 6 1 W: 12 00 b.Northwich 16-10-83
Source: Scholar.
2002–03 Crewe Alex 0 0
2003–04 Crewe Alex 0 0
2004–05 Crewe Alex 6 0
2005–06 Crewe Alex 0 0

2005–06 *Chester C* 1 0 **1 0**
2006–07 Crewe Alex 0 0 **6 0**
From Northwich Vic.
2007–08 Accrington S 34 0 **34 0**

SMITH, Andrew (F) 1 0
H: 5 10 W: 11 02 b.Burnley 22-12-89
Source: Scholar.
2007–08 Accrington S 1 0 **1 0**

TURNER, Chris (M) 1 0
H: 5 10 W: 11 10 b.Manchester 12-8-87
Source: Scholar.
2007–08 Accrington S 1 0 **1 0**

WEBB, Sean (D) 18 0
H: 6 2 W: 12 04 b.Dungannon 4-1-83
2007–08 Accrington S 18 0 **18 0**

WHALLEY, Shaun (F) 54 5
H: 5 9 W: 10 07 b.Prescot 7-8-87
Source: Southport.
2004–05 Chester C 3 0 **3 0**
From Witton Alb.
2006–07 Accrington S 20 2
2007–08 Accrington S 31 3 **51 5**

WILLIAMS, Robbie (D) 69 3
H: 5 10 W: 12 00 b.Liverpool 12-4-79
Source: St Dominics.
2006–07 Accrington S 43 3
2007–08 Accrington S 26 0 **69 3**

ARSENAL (2)

ADEBAYOR, Emmanuel (F) 200 69
H: 6 4 W: 11 08 b.Lome 26-2-84
Source: Lome. *Honours:* Togo 37 full caps, 16 goals.
2001–02 Metz 10 2
2002–03 Metz 34 13 **44 15**
2003–04 Monaco 31 8
2004–05 Monaco 34 9
2005–06 Monaco 13 1 **78 18**
2005–06 Arsenal 13 4
2006–07 Arsenal 29 8
2007–08 Arsenal 36 24 **78 36**

ALMUNIA, Manuel (G) 173 0
H: 6 3 W: 13 00 b.Pamplona 19-5-77
1997–98 Osasuna B 31 0
1998–99 Osasuna B 13 0 **44 0**
1999–2000 Cartagonova 3 0 **3 0**
2000–01 Sabadell 25 0 **25 0**
2001–02 Celta Vigo 0 0
2001–02 *Eibar* 35 0 **35 0**
2002–03 *Recreativo* 2 0 **2 0**
2003–04 Albacete 24 0 **24 0**
2004–05 Arsenal 10 0
2005–06 Arsenal 0 0
2006–07 Arsenal 1 0
2007–08 Arsenal 29 0 **40 0**

BARAZITE, Nacer (M) 0 0
H: 6 2 W: 13 01 b.Arnhem 27-5-90
Source: Scholar. *Honours:* Holland Youth.
2007–08 Arsenal 0 0

BENDTNER, Nicklas (F) 69 16
H: 6 2 W: 13 00 b.Copenhagen 16-1-88
Source: Scholar. *Honours:* Denmark Youth, Under-21, 18 full caps, 7 goals.
2005–06 Arsenal 0 0
2006–07 Arsenal 0 0
2006–07 *Birmingham C* 42 11 **42 11**
2007–08 Arsenal 27 5 **27 5**

BOTHELO, Pedro (D) 0 0
H: 6 2 W: 13 00 b.Salvador 14-12-89
Source: Salamanca.
2007–08 Arsenal 0 0

CLICHY, Gael (D) 99 0
H: 5 9 W: 10 04 b.Toulouse 26-7-85
Source: Cannes. *Honours:* France Under-21, B.
2003–04 Arsenal 12 0
2004–05 Arsenal 15 0
2005–06 Arsenal 7 0
2006–07 Arsenal 27 0
2007–08 Arsenal 38 0 **99 0**

DENILSON (M) 35 0
H: 5 10 W: 10 10 b.Sao Paulo 16-2-88
Honours: Brazil Youth, Under-20.
2005 Sao Paulo 10 0
2006 Sao Paulo 2 0 **12 0**
2006–07 Arsenal 10 0
2007–08 Arsenal 13 0 **23 0**

DIABY, Vassiriki (M) 49 4
H: 6 2 W: 12 04 b.Paris 11-5-86
Honours: France Youth, Under-21, 3 full caps.
2004–05 Auxerre 5 0
2005–06 Auxerre 5 1 **10 1**
2005–06 Arsenal 12 1
2006–07 Arsenal 12 1
2007–08 Arsenal 15 1 **39 3**

DJOUROU, Johan (D) 43 0
H: 6 2 W: 12 05 b.Ivory Coast 18-1-87
Source: Scholar. *Honours:* Switzerland Youth, Under-20, Under-21, 17 full caps, 1 goal.
2004–05 Arsenal 0 0
2005–06 Arsenal 7 0
2006–07 Arsenal 21 0
2007–08 Arsenal 2 0 **30 0**
2007–08 *Birmingham C* 13 0 **13 0**

DUNNE, James (M) 0 0
b.Farnborough 18-9-89
Source: Scholar.
2007–08 Arsenal 0 0

EBOUE, Emmanuel (D) 136 4
H: 5 10 W: 11 08 b.Abidjan 4-6-83
Honours: Ivory Coast 23 full caps.
2002–03 Beveren 23 0
2003–04 Beveren 30 2
2004–05 Beveren 17 2 **70 4**
2004–05 Arsenal 1 0
2005–06 Arsenal 18 0
2006–07 Arsenal 24 0
2007–08 Arsenal 23 0 **66 0**

EDUARDO (F) 143 87
H: 5 10 W: 10 03 b.Rio 25-2-83
Source: Bangu. *Honours:* Croatia Under-21, 22 full caps, 13 goals.
2001–02 Dinamo Zagreb 4 0
2002–03 *Inter Zapresic* 15 10 **15 10**
2003–04 Dinamo Zagreb 24 9
2004–05 Dinamo Zagreb 22 10
2005–06 Dinamo Zagreb 29 20
2006–07 Dinamo Zagreb 32 34 **111 73**
2007–08 Arsenal 17 4 **17 4**

FABIANSKI, Lukasz (G) 56 0
H: 6 3 W: 13 01 b.Costrzyn nad Odra 18-4-85
Honours: Poland Under-21, 8 full caps.
2005–06 Legia 30 0
2006–07 Legia 23 0 **53 0**
2007–08 Arsenal 3 0 **3 0**

FABREGAS, Francesc (M) 138 14
H: 5 11 W: 11 01 b.Vilessoc de Mar 4-5-87
Source: Barcelona. *Honours:* Spain Youth, Under-21, 32 full caps, 1 goal.
2003–04 Arsenal 0 0
2004–05 Arsenal 33 2
2005–06 Arsenal 35 3
2006–07 Arsenal 38 2
2007–08 Arsenal 32 7 **138 14**

FLAMINI, Mathieu (M) 116 7
H: 5 11 W: 11 10 b.Marseille 7-3-84
Source: Marseille. *Honours:* France Under-21, 2 full caps.
2003–04 Marseille 14 0 **14 0**
2004–05 Arsenal 21 1
2005–06 Arsenal 31 0
2006–07 Arsenal 20 3
2007–08 Arsenal 30 3 **102 7**

FONTE, Rui (F) 0 0
b.Lisbon 23-9-90
Source: Scholar.
2007–08 Arsenal 0 0

GALLAS, William (D) 314 21
H: 6 0 W: 12 12 b.Asnieres 17-8-77
Honours: France Under-21, 65 full caps, 2 goals.
1996–97 Caen 18 0 **18 0**
1997–98 Marseille 3 0
1998–99 Marseille 30 0
1999–2000 Marseille 22 0
2000–01 Marseille 30 2 **85 2**
2001–02 Chelsea 30 1
2002–03 Chelsea 38 4
2003–04 Chelsea 29 0
2004–05 Chelsea 28 2
2005–06 Chelsea 34 5
2006–07 Chelsea 0 0 **159 12**
2006–07 Arsenal 21 3
2007–08 Arsenal 31 4 **52 7**

GIBBS, Kieran (M) 7 0
H: 5 10 W: 10 02 b.Lambeth 26-9-89
Source: Scholar. *Honours:* England Youth.
2007–08 Arsenal 0 0
2007–08 *Norwich C* 7 0 **7 0**

GILBERT, Kerrea (D) 31 0
H: 5 6 W: 11 03 b.Hammersmith 28-2-87
Source: Scholar. *Honours:* England Youth.
2005–06 Arsenal 2 0
2006–07 Arsenal 0 0
2006–07 *Cardiff C* 24 0 **24 0**
2007–08 Arsenal 0 0 **2 0**
2007–08 *Southend U* 5 0 **5 0**

HLEB, Aleksandr (M) 268 28
H: 5 10 W: 11 07 b.Minsk 1-5-81
Honours: Belarus 41 full caps, 4 goals.
1999 BATE 13 1
2000 BATE 12 3 **25 4**
2000–01 Stuttgart B 17 4 **17 4**
2000–01 Stuttgart 6 0
2001–02 Stuttgart 32 2
2002–03 Stuttgart 34 4
2003–04 Stuttgart 31 5
2004–05 Stuttgart 34 2 **137 13**
2005–06 Arsenal 25 3
2006–07 Arsenal 33 2
2007–08 Arsenal 31 2 **89 7**

HOYTE, Gavin (D) 0 0
H: 5 11 W: 11 00 b.Waltham Forest 6-6-90
Source: Scholar. *Honours:* England Youth.
2007–08 Arsenal 0 0

HOYTE, Justin (D) 61 2
H: 5 11 W: 11 00 b.Waltham Forest 20-11-84
Source: Scholar. *Honours:* England Youth, Under-20, Under-21.
2002–03 Arsenal 1 0
2003–04 Arsenal 1 0
2004–05 Arsenal 5 0
2005–06 Arsenal 0 0
2005–06 *Sunderland* 27 1 **27 1**
2006–07 Arsenal 22 1
2007–08 Arsenal 5 0 **34 1**

LANSBURY, Henri (M) 0 0
H: 6 0 W: 13 06 b.Enfield 12-10-90
Source: Scholar. *Honours:* England Youth.
2007–08 Arsenal 0 0

LEHMANN, Jens (G) 481 2
H: 6 4 W: 13 05 b.Essen 10-11-69
Honours: Germany Youth, Under-21, 61 full caps.
1991–92 Schalke 37 0
1992–93 Schalke 8 0
1993–94 Schalke 21 0
1994–95 Schalke 34 1
1995–96 Schalke 32 0
1996–97 Schalke 34 0
1997–98 Schalke 34 1 **200 2**
1998–99 AC Milan 5 0 **5 0**
1998–99 Borussia Dortmd 13 0
1999–2000 Borussia Dortmd 31 0
2000–01 Borussia Dortmd 31 0
2001–02 Borussia Dortmd 30 0
2002–03 Borussia Dortmd 24 0 **129 0**
2003–04 Arsenal 38 0
2004–05 Arsenal 28 0
2005–06 Arsenal 38 0
2006–07 Arsenal 36 0
2007–08 Arsenal 7 0 **147 0**

MANNONE, Vito (G) 2 0
H: 6 0 W: 11 08 b.Desio 2-3-88
Source: Atalanta.
2005–06 Arsenal 0 0
2006–07 Arsenal 0 0
2006–07 *Barnsley* 2 0 **2 0**
2007–08 Arsenal 0 0

MERIDA PEREZ, Fran (M) **0 0**
H: 5 11 W: 13 00 b.Barcelona 4-3-90
Source: Scholar.

2006–07	Arsenal	0	0		
2007–08	Arsenal	0	0		

MURPHY, Rhys (F) **0 0**
H: 6 1 W: 11 13 b.Shoreham 6-11-90

2007–08	Arsenal	0	0		

NORDTVEIT, Havard (D) **9 0**
H: 6 2 W: 11 09 b.Vats 21-6-90
Honours: Norway Youth.

2007	Haugesund	9	0	**9**	**0**
2007–08	Arsenal	0	0		

OGOGO, Abu (D) **0 0**
b.Epsom 3-11-89
Source: Scholar.

2007–08	Arsenal	0	0		

PARISIO, Carl (D) **0 0**
b.Cannes 7-8-89
Source: Scholar.

2006–07	Arsenal	0	0		
2007–08	Arsenal	0	0		

RANDALL, Mark (M) **11 0**
H: 6 0 W: 12 12 b.Milton Keynes 28-9-89
Source: Scholar.

2006–07	Arsenal	0	0		
2007–08	Arsenal	1	0	**1**	**0**
2007–08	*Burnley*	10	0	**10**	**0**

RODGERS, Paul (D) **0 0**
b.Edmonton 6-10-89
Source: Scholar.

2007–08	Arsenal	0	0		

ROSICKY, Tomas (M) **234 36**
H: 5 10 W: 10 10 b.Prague 4-10-80
Honours: Czech Republic Under-21, 67 full caps, 18 goals.

1998–99	Sparta Prague	3	0		
1999–2000	Sparta Prague	24	5		
2000–01	Sparta Prague	14	3	**41**	**8**
2000–01	Borussia Dotmund	15	0		
2001–02	Borussia Dotmund	30	5		
2002–03	Borussia Dotmund	30	3		
2003–04	Borussia Dotmund	19	2		
2004–05	Borussia Dotmund	27	4		
2005–06	Borussia Dotmund	28	5	**149**	**19**
2006–07	Arsenal	26	3		
2007–08	Arsenal	18	6	**44**	**9**

SAGNA, Bakari (D) **116 1**
H: 5 10 W: 11 05 b.Sens 14-2-83
Source: Auxerre B. *Honours:* France Under-21, 2 full caps.

2004–05	Auxerre	26	0		
2005–06	Auxerre	23	0		
2006–07	Auxerre	38	0	**87**	**0**
2007–08	Arsenal	29	1	**29**	**1**

SENDEROS, Philippe (D) **90 7**
H: 6 1 W: 13 10 b.Geneva 14-2-85
Honours: Switzerland Youth, Under-20, Under-21, 31 full caps, 3 goals.

2001–02	Servette	3	0		
2002–03	Servette	23	3	**26**	**3**
2003–04	Arsenal	0	0		
2004–05	Arsenal	13	0		
2005–06	Arsenal	20	2		
2006–07	Arsenal	14	0		
2007–08	Arsenal	17	2	**64**	**4**

SILVA, Gilberto (M) **197 20**
H: 6 3 W: 12 04 b.Lagoa da Prata 7-10-76
Honours: Brazil 63 full caps, 3 goals.

2000	Atletico Mineiro	1	0		
2001	Atletico Mineiro	26	3	**27**	**3**
2002–03	Arsenal	35	0		
2003–04	Arsenal	32	4		
2004–05	Arsenal	13	0		
2005–06	Arsenal	33	2		
2006–07	Arsenal	34	10		
2007–08	Arsenal	23	1	**170**	**17**

SIMPSON, Jay (M) **41 6**
H: 5 11 W: 13 04 b.Enfield 1-12-88
Source: Scholar.

2007–08	Arsenal	0	0		
2007–08	*Millwall*	41	6	**41**	**6**

SONG BILLONG, Alexandre (M) **28 0**
H: 5 11 W: 12 04 b.Douala 9-9-87
Source: Bastia. *Honours:* France Youth, Cameroon Youth. Cameroon 8 full caps.

2005–06	Arsenal	5	0		
2006–07	Arsenal	2	0		
2006–07	*Charlton Ath*	12	0	**12**	**0**
2007–08	Arsenal	9	0	**16**	**0**

STEER, Rene (D) **0 0**
b.Luton 31-1-90
Source: Scholar.

2007–08	Arsenal	0	0		

SUNU, Gilles (F) **0 0**
b.Chateauroux 30-3-91
Source: Scholar.

2007–08	Arsenal	0	0		

SZCZESNY, Wojciech (G) **0 0**
b.Warsaw 18-4-90
Source: Scholar.

2007–08	Arsenal	0	0		

TOURE, Kolo (D) **196 8**
H: 5 10 W: 13 08 b.Sokuora Bouake 19-3-81
Source: ASEC Mimosas. *Honours:* Ivory Coast 45 full caps, 2 goals.

2001–02	Arsenal	0	0		
2002–03	Arsenal	26	2		
2003–04	Arsenal	37	1		
2004–05	Arsenal	35	0		
2005–06	Arsenal	33	0		
2006–07	Arsenal	35	3		
2007–08	Arsenal	30	2	**196**	**8**

TRAORE, Armand (D) **3 0**
H: 6 1 W: 12 12 b.Paris 8-10-89
Source: Monaco. *Honours:* France Youth.

2006–07	Arsenal	0	0		
2007–08	Arsenal	3	0	**3**	**0**

VAN DEN BERG, Vincent (M) **5 0**
b.Holland 19-1-89
Source: Heerenveen.

2006–07	Arsenal	0	0		
2007–08	*Go Ahead*	5	0	**5**	**0**
2007–08	Arsenal	0	0		

VAN PERSIE, Robin (F) **148 42**
H: 6 0 W: 11 00 b.Rotterdam 6-8-83
Honours: Holland Under-21, 28 full caps, 8 goals.

2001–02	Feyenoord	10	0		
2002–03	Feyenoord	23	8		
2003–04	Feyenoord	28	6	**61**	**14**
2004–05	Arsenal	26	5		
2005–06	Arsenal	24	5		
2006–07	Arsenal	22	11		
2007–08	Arsenal	15	7	**87**	**28**

VELA, Carlos (F) **0 0**
b.Mexico 1-3-89
Source: Celta Vigo.

2007–08	Arsenal	0	0		

WALCOTT, Theo (F) **62 8**
H: 5 9 W: 11 01 b.Compton 16-3-89
Source: Scholar. *Honours:* England Youth, Under-21, B, 2 full caps.

2005–06	Southampton	21	4	**21**	**4**
2005–06	Arsenal	0	0		
2006–07	Arsenal	16	0		
2007–08	Arsenal	25	4	**41**	**4**

Scholars
Ayling, Luke David; Bartley, Kyle; Blackwood, Anton; Cruise, Thomas Daniel; Eastmond, Craig Leon; Emmanuel-Thomas, Jay-Aston; Lansbury, Henri George; Murphy, Rhys Philip Elliot; Rasmussen, Jonas Hebo; Shea, James; Watt, Herschel Oulio Sanchez

ASTON VILLA (3)

AGBONLAHOR, Gabriel (F) **94 21**
H: 5 11 W: 12 05 b.Birmingham 13-10-86
Source: Scholar. *Honours:* England Under-20, Under-21.

2005–06	Aston Villa	9	1		
2005–06	*Watford*	2	0	**2**	**0**
2005–06	*Sheffield W*	8	0	**8**	**0**
2006–07	Aston Villa	38	9		
2007–08	Aston Villa	37	11	**84**	**21**

BARRY, Gareth (D) **327 36**
H: 5 11 W: 12 06 b.Hastings 23-2-81
Source: Trainee. *Honours:* England Youth, B, Under-21, 20 full caps, 1 goal.

1997–98	Aston Villa	2	0		
1998–99	Aston Villa	32	2		
1999–2000	Aston Villa	30	1		
2000–01	Aston Villa	30	0		
2001–02	Aston Villa	20	0		
2002–03	Aston Villa	35	3		
2003–04	Aston Villa	36	3		
2004–05	Aston Villa	34	7		
2005–06	Aston Villa	36	3		
2006–07	Aston Villa	35	8		
2007–08	Aston Villa	37	9	**327**	**36**

BELLON, Damien (M) **0 0**
H: 5 8 W: 11 05 b.St Gallen 28-8-89
Source: Scholar.

2006–07	Aston Villa	0	0		
2007–08	Aston Villa	0	0		

BELLON, Yago (M) **0 0**
H: 5 8 W: 10 11 b.St Gallen 28-8-89
Source: Scholar.

2006–07	Aston Villa	0	0		
2007–08	Aston Villa	0	0		

BERGER, Patrik (M) **350 66**
H: 6 1 W: 12 06 b.Prague 10-11-73
Honours: Czechoslovakia 2 full caps.Czech Republic Under-21, 44 full caps, 18 goals.

1991–92	Slavia Prague	20	3		
1992–93	Slavia Prague	29	10		
1993–94	Slavia Prague	12	4		
1994–95	Slavia Prague	28	7	**89**	**24**
1995–96	Borussia Dotmund	25	4	**25**	**4**
1996–97	Liverpool	23	6		
1997–98	Liverpool	22	3		
1998–99	Liverpool	32	7		
1999–2000	Liverpool	34	9		
2000–01	Liverpool	14	2		
2001–02	Liverpool	21	1		
2002–03	Liverpool	2	0	**148**	**28**
2003–04	Portsmouth	20	5		
2004–05	Portsmouth	32	3	**52**	**8**
2005–06	Aston Villa	8	0		
2006–07	Aston Villa	13	2		
2006–07	*Stoke C*	7	0	**7**	**0**
2007–08	Aston Villa	8	0	**29**	**2**

BEVAN, David (G) **0 0**
H: 6 2 W: 13 00 b.Cork 24-6-89
Source: Scholar.

2007–08	Aston Villa	0	0		

BOUMA, Wilfred (D) **334 38**
H: 5 10 W: 13 01 b.Helmond 15-6-78
Honours: Holland 34 full caps, 2 goals.

1994–95	PSV Eindhoven	1	0		
1995–96	PSV Eindhoven	4	0		
1996–97	PSV Eindhoven	1	0		
1996–97	MVV	18	7		
1997–98	MVV	33	6	**51**	**13**
1998–99	Fortuna Sittard	33	5	**33**	**5**
1999–2000	PSV Eindhoven	27	9		
2000–01	PSV Eindhoven	20	0		
2001–02	PSV Eindhoven	27	3		
2002–03	PSV Eindhoven	27	1		
2003–04	PSV Eindhoven	32	5		
2004–05	PSV Eindhoven	28	1	**167**	**19**
2005–06	Aston Villa	20	0		
2006–07	Aston Villa	25	0		
2007–08	Aston Villa	38	1	**83**	**1**

BOYLE, Lee (G) **0 0**
H: 5 11 W: 10 08 b.Donegal 22-1-88
Source: Scholar.

2005–06	Aston Villa	0	0		
2006–07	Aston Villa	0	0		
2007–08	Aston Villa	0	0		

BRIDGES, Scott (D) **0 0**
H: 5 7 W: 13 08 b.Oxford 3-5-88
Source: Scholar.

2005–06	Aston Villa	0	0		
2006–07	Aston Villa	0	0		
2007–08	Aston Villa	0	0		

CAREW, John (F) 257 99
H: 6 5 W: 14 11 b.Lorenskog 5-9-79
Source: Lorenskog. *Honours:* Norway Youth, Under-21, 71 full caps, 21 goals.

1998	Valerenga	18	7		
1999	Valerenga	15	7	**33**	**14**
1999	Rosenborg	8	10		
2000	Rosenborg	10	8	**18**	**18**
2000–01	Valencia	37	11		
2001–02	Valencia	15	1		
2002–03	Valencia	32	8	**84**	**20**
2003–04	Roma	20	8	**20**	**8**
2004–05	Besiktas	24	13	**24**	**13**
2005–06	Lyon	26	9		
2006–07	Lyon	9	1	**35**	**10**
2006–07	Aston Villa	11	3		
2007–08	Aston Villa	32	13	**43**	**16**

COLLINS, Jordan (F) 0 0
H: 5 7 W: 11 08 b.Birmingham 11-3-89
Source: Scholar.

2007–08	Aston Villa	0	0		

DELFOUNESCO, Nathan (F) 0 0
b. *Honours:* 2-2-91
Source: Scholar. *Honours:* England Youth.

2007–08	Aston Villa	0	0		

FORRESTER, Harry (M) 0 0
b. 2-1-91

2007–08	Aston Villa	0	0		

GARDNER, Craig (M) 44 5
H: 5 10 W: 11 13 b.Solihull 25-11-86
Source: Scholar. *Honours:* England Under-21.

2004–05	Aston Villa	0	0		
2005–06	Aston Villa	8	0		
2006–07	Aston Villa	13	2		
2007–08	Aston Villa	23	3	**44**	**5**

HAREWOOD, Marlon (F) 353 104
H: 6 1 W: 13 07 b.Hampstead 25-8-79
Source: Trainee.

1996–97	Nottingham F	0	0		
1997–98	Nottingham F	1	0		
1998–99	Nottingham F	23	1		
1998–99	*Ipswich T*	6	1	**6**	**1**
1999–2000	Nottingham F	34	4		
2000–01	Nottingham F	33	3		
2001–02	Nottingham F	28	11		
2002–03	Nottingham F	44	20		
2003–04	Nottingham F	19	12	**182**	**51**
2003–04	West Ham U	28	13		
2004–05	West Ham U	45	17		
2005–06	West Ham U	37	14		
2006–07	West Ham U	32	3	**142**	**47**
2007–08	Aston Villa	23	5	**23**	**5**

HERD, Chris (M) 15 2
H: 5 9 W: 11 04 b.Melbourne 4-4-89
Source: Scholar.

2007–08	Aston Villa	0	0		
2007–08	*Port Vale*	11	2	**11**	**2**
2007–08	*Wycombe W*	4	0	**4**	**0**

HOFBAUER, Dominik (M) 0 0
b.Eggenberg 19-9-90
Source: Scholar.

2007–08	Aston Villa	0	0		

HOGG, Jonathan (M) 0 0
H: 5 7 W: 10 05 b.Middlesbrough 6-12-88
Source: Scholar.

2007–08	Aston Villa	0	0		

KNIGHT, Zat (D) 185 4
H: 6 6 W: 15 02 b.Solihull 2-5-80
Source: Rushall Olympic. *Honours:* England Under-21, 2 full caps.

1998–99	Fulham	0	0		
1999–2000	Fulham	0	0		
1999–2000	*Peterborough U*	8	0	**8**	**0**
2000–01	Fulham	0	0		
2001–02	Fulham	10	0		
2002–03	Fulham	17	0		
2003–04	Fulham	31	0		
2004–05	Fulham	35	1		
2005–06	Fulham	30	0		
2006–07	Fulham	23	2		
2007–08	Fulham	4	0	**150**	**3**
2007–08	Aston Villa	27	1	**27**	**1**

LAURSEN, Martin (D) 198 12
H: 6 2 W: 12 05 b.Farvoug 26-7-77
Honours: Denmark Youth, Under-21, 49 full caps, 2 goals.

1995–96	Silkeborg	1	0		
1996–97	Silkeborg	12	0		
1997–98	Silkeborg	22	1	**35**	**1**
1998–99	Verona	6	0		
1999–2000	Verona	19	2		
2000–01	Verona	31	0	**56**	**2**
2001–02	AC Milan	22	2		
2002–03	AC Milan	10	0		
2003–04	AC Milan	10	0	**42**	**2**
2004–05	Aston Villa	12	1		
2005–06	Aston Villa	1	0		
2006–07	Aston Villa	14	0		
2007–08	Aston Villa	38	6	**65**	**7**

LICHAJ, Eric (M) 0 0
b.Denwers Grove 17-11-88
Source: Univ of North Carolina, Chicago Magic.

2007–08	Aston Villa	0	0		

LOWRY, Shane (D) 0 0
H: 6 1 W: 13 01 b.Perth 12-6-89
Source: Scholar.

2007–08	Aston Villa	0	0		

LUND, Eric (D) 0 0
H: 6 1 W: 12 00 b.Gothenburg 6-11-88
Source: Scholar.

2006–07	Aston Villa	0	0		
2007–08	Aston Villa	0	0		

MALONEY, Shaun (M) 134 31
H: 5 7 W: 10 01 b.Miri 24-1-83
Honours: Scotland Under-20, Under-21, B, 11 full caps, 2 goals.

1999–2000	Celtic	0	0		
2000–01	Celtic	4	0		
2001–02	Celtic	16	5		
2002–03	Celtic	20	3		
2003–04	Celtic	17	5		
2004–05	Celtic	2	0		
2005–06	Celtic	36	13		
2006–07	Celtic	9	0	**104**	**26**
2006–07	Aston Villa	8	1		
2007–08	Aston Villa	22	4	**30**	**5**

McGURK, Adam (F) 0 0
H: 5 9 W: 12 13 b.St Helier 24-1-89
Source: Scholar.

2005–06	Aston Villa	0	0		
2006–07	Aston Villa	0	0		
2007–08	Aston Villa	0	0		

MELLBERG, Olof (D) 394 8
H: 6 1 W: 12 10 b.Amncharad 3-9-77
Honours: Sweden Under-21, 85 full caps, 4 goals.

1996	Degerfors	22	0		
1997	Degerfors	25	0	**47**	**0**
1998	AIK Stockholm	17	0	**17**	**0**
1998–99	Santander	25	0		
1999–2000	Santander	37	0		
2000–01	Santander	36	0	**98**	**0**
2001–02	Aston Villa	32	0		
2002–03	Aston Villa	38	1		
2003–04	Aston Villa	33	1		
2004–05	Aston Villa	30	3		
2005–06	Aston Villa	27	0		
2006–07	Aston Villa	38	1		
2007–08	Aston Villa	34	2	**232**	**8**

MIKAELSSON, Tobias (F) 6 0
H: 6 3 W: 11 04 b.Jorlanda 17-11-88
Source: Scholar.

2005–06	Aston Villa	0	0		
2006–07	Aston Villa	0	0		
2007–08	Aston Villa	0	0		
2007–08	*Port Vale*	6	0	**6**	**0**

MOORE, Luke (F) 103 18
H: 5 11 W: 11 13 b.Birmingham 13-2-86
Source: Trainee. *Honours:* FA Schools, England Youth, Under-21.

2002–03	Aston Villa	0	0		
2003–04	Aston Villa	7	0		
2003–04	*Wycombe W*	6	4	**6**	**4**
2004–05	Aston Villa	25	1		
2005–06	Aston Villa	27	8		
2006–07	Aston Villa	13	4		
2007–08	Aston Villa	15	1	**87**	**14**
2007–08	*WBA*	10	0	**10**	**0**

O'HALLORAN, Stephen (D) 12 0
H: 6 0 W: 11 07 b.Cork 29-11-87
Source: Scholar. *Honours:* Eire Under-21, 2 full caps.

2005–06	Aston Villa	0	0		
2006–07	Aston Villa	0	0		
2006–07	*Wycombe W*	11	0	**11**	**0**
2007–08	Aston Villa	0	0		
2007–08	*Southampton*	1	0	**1**	**0**

OSBOURNE, Isaiah (M) 19 0
H: 6 2 W: 12 07 b.Birmingham 5-11-87
Source: Scholar.

2005–06	Aston Villa	0	0		
2006–07	Aston Villa	11	0		
2007–08	Aston Villa	8	0	**19**	**0**

PETROV, Stilian (M) 324 59
H: 5 11 W: 11 09 b.Sofia 5-7-79
Source: FC Montana. *Honours:* Bulgaria 78 full caps, 7 goals.

1997–98	CSKA Sofia	10	0		
1998–99	CSKA Sofia	29	3	**39**	**3**
1999–2000	Celtic	29	1		
2000–01	Celtic	28	7		
2001–02	Celtic	27	6		
2002–03	Celtic	34	12		
2003–04	Celtic	35	6		
2004–05	Celtic	37	11		
2005–06	Celtic	37	10	**227**	**53**
2006–07	Aston Villa	30	2		
2007–08	Aston Villa	28	1	**58**	**3**

REO-COKER, Nigel (M) 214 17
H: 5 8 W: 12 03 b.Southwark 14-5-84
Source: Scholar. *Honours:* England Youth, Under-20, Under-21.

2001–02	Wimbledon	1	0		
2002–03	Wimbledon	32	2		
2003–04	Wimbledon	25	4	**58**	**6**
2003–04	West Ham U	15	2		
2004–05	West Ham U	39	3		
2005–06	West Ham U	31	5		
2006–07	West Ham U	35	1	**120**	**11**
2007–08	Aston Villa	36	0	**36**	**0**

ROUTLEDGE, Wayne (M) 153 10
H: 5 6 W: 11 02 b.Sidcup 7-1-85
Source: Scholar. *Honours:* England Youth, Under-20, Under-21.

2001–02	Crystal Palace	2	0		
2002–03	Crystal Palace	26	4		
2003–04	Crystal Palace	44	6		
2004–05	Crystal Palace	38	0	**110**	**10**
2005–06	Tottenham H	3	0		
2005–06	*Portsmouth*	13	0	**13**	**0**
2006–07	Tottenham H	0	0		
2006–07	*Fulham*	24	0	**24**	**0**
2007–08	Tottenham H	2	0	**5**	**0**
2007–08	Aston Villa	1	0	**1**	**0**

SALIFOU, Moustapha (M) 67 3
H: 5 11 W: 10 12 b.Lome 1-6-83
Source: Modele de Lome. *Honours:* Togo 37 full caps, 4 goals.

2002–03	Oberhausen	11	1		
2003–04	Oberhausen	6	0		
2004–05	Oberhausen	16	0	**33**	**1**
2005–06	Stade Brest	7	0	**7**	**0**
2006–07	FC Wil	19	2		
2007–08	FC Wil	4	0	**23**	**2**
2007–08	Aston Villa	4	0	**4**	**0**

SORENSEN, Thomas (G) 310 0
H: 6 4 W: 13 10 b.Fredericia 12-6-76
Source: Odense. *Honours:* Denmark Youth, Under-21, B, 73 full caps.

1998–99	Sunderland	45	0		
1999–2000	Sunderland	37	0		
2000–01	Sunderland	34	0		
2001–02	Sunderland	34	0		
2002–03	Sunderland	21	0	**171**	**0**
2003–04	Aston Villa	38	0		
2004–05	Aston Villa	36	0		
2005–06	Aston Villa	36	0		
2006–07	Aston Villa	29	0		
2007–08	Aston Villa	0	0	**139**	**0**

STIEBER, Zoltan (M) 15 1
H: 5 8 W: 9 10 b.Savar 16-10-88
Source: Scholar. *Honours:* Hungary Youth.

2006–07	Aston Villa	0	0		
2007–08	Aston Villa	0	0		
2007–08	*Yeovil T*	15	1	**15**	**1**

TAYLOR, Stuart (G) **60 0**
H: 6 5 W: 13 07 b.Romford 28-11-80
Source: Trainee. *Honours:* FA Schools, England Youth, Under-21.
1998–99 Arsenal 0 0
1999–2000 Arsenal 0 0
1999–2000 *Bristol R* 4 0 **4 0**
2000–01 Arsenal 0 0
2000–01 *Crystal Palace* 10 0 **10 0**
2000–01 *Peterborough U* 6 0 **6 0**
2001–02 Arsenal 10 0
2002–03 Arsenal 8 0
2003–04 Arsenal 0 0
2004–05 Arsenal 0 0 **18 0**
2004–05 *Leicester C* 10 0 **10 0**
2005–06 Aston Villa 2 0
2006–07 Aston Villa 6 0
2007–08 Aston Villa 4 0 **12 0**

WILLIAMS, Sam (M) **18 3**
H: 5 11 W: 10 08 b.London 9-6-87
Source: Scholar.
2004–05 Aston Villa 0 0
2005–06 Aston Villa 0 0
2005–06 *Wrexham* 15 2 **15 2**
2006–07 Aston Villa 0 0
2006–07 *Brighton & HA* 3 1 **3 1**
2007–08 Aston Villa 0 0

YOUNG, Ashley (M) **148 30**
H: 5 10 W: 10 03 b.Stevenage 9-7-85
Source: Juniors. *Honours:* England Under-21, 3 full caps.
2002–03 Watford 0 0
2003–04 Watford 5 3
2004–05 Watford 34 0
2005–06 Watford 39 13
2006–07 Watford 20 3 **98 19**
2006–07 Aston Villa 13 2
2007–08 Aston Villa 37 9 **50 11**

Scholars
Albrighton, Marc Kevin; Baker, Nathan; Bannan, Barry; Bradley, Daniel David; Clark, Ciaran; Collins, James Steven; Dau, Thomas Roland Leonard; Parish, Elliott Charles; Roome, Matthew John; Simmonds, Sam; Weimann, Andreas

BARNET (4)

ADOMAH, Albert (F) **22 5**
H: 6 1 W: 11 08 b.Harrow 13-12-87
Source: Harrow Borough.
2007–08 Barnet 22 5 **22 5**

AKURANG, Cliff (F) **21 7**
H: 6 2 W: 12 03 b.Histon 27-2-81
Source: Histon.
2007–08 Barnet 21 7 **21 7**

ANGUS, Stevland (D) **192 2**
H: 6 0 W: 12 00 b.Westminster 16-9-80
Source: Trainee.
1999–2000 West Ham U 0 0
2000–01 West Ham U 0 0
2000–01 *Bournemouth* 9 0 **9 0**
2001–02 Cambridge U 41 0
2002–03 Cambridge U 40 0
2003–04 Cambridge U 40 1
2004–05 Cambridge U 14 0 **135 1**
2004–05 *Hull C* 2 0 **2 0**
2004–05 *Scunthorpe U* 9 0 **9 0**
From Grays Ath
2005–06 Barnet 0 0
2006–07 Torquay U 36 1 **36 1**
2007–08 Barnet 1 0 **1 0**

BECKWITH, Rob (G) **28 0**
H: 6 1 W: 13 12 b.Hackney 12-9-84
Source: Scholar.
2002–03 Luton T 4 0
2003–04 Luton T 13 0
2004–05 Luton T 0 0
2005–06 Luton T 0 0
2005–06 *Chesterfield* 2 0 **2 0**
2006–07 Luton T 0 0 **17 0**
2007–08 Barnet 9 0 **9 0**

BIRCHALL, Adam (F) **113 23**
H: 5 7 W: 10 09 b.Maidstone 2-12-84
Source: Trainee. *Honours:* Wales Under-21.
2002–03 Arsenal 0 0
2003–04 Arsenal 0 0
2004–05 Arsenal 0 0
2004–05 *Wycombe W* 12 4 **12 4**
2005–06 Mansfield T 31 2
2006–07 Mansfield T 5 0 **36 2**
2006–07 Barnet 23 6
2007–08 Barnet 42 11 **65 17**

BISHOP, Neil (M) **39 2**
H: 6 1 W: 12 10 b.Stockton 7-8-81
Source: Billingham T, Gateshead, Spennymoor U, Whitby T, Scarborough, York C.
2007–08 Barnet 39 2 **39 2**

BURTON, Sagi (D) **291 13**
H: 6 2 W: 14 02 b.Birmingham 25-11-77
Source: Trainee. *Honours:* St Kitts & Nevis 3 full caps.
1995–96 Crystal Palace 0 0
1996–97 Crystal Palace 0 0
1997–98 Crystal Palace 2 0
1998–99 Crystal Palace 23 1 **25 1**
1999–2000 Colchester U 9 0 **9 0**
1999–2000 Sheffield U 0 0
1999–2000 Port Vale 20 2
2000–01 Port Vale 29 0
2001–02 Port Vale 37 0 **86 2**
2002–03 Crewe Alex 1 0 **1 0**
2002–03 Peterborough U 31 0
2003–04 Peterborough U 30 1
2004–05 Peterborough U 16 1
2005–06 Peterborough U 19 2 **96 4**
2005–06 Shrewsbury T 16 4
2006–07 Shrewsbury T 28 1 **44 5**
2007–08 Barnet 30 1 **30 1**

CAREW, Ashley (M) **33 1**
H: 6 0 W: 11 00 b.Lambeth 17-12-85
2006–07 Barnet 0 0
2007–08 Barnet 33 1 **33 1**

DEVERA, Joe (D) **67 0**
H: 6 2 W: 12 00 b.Southgate 6-2-87
2005–06 Barnet 0 0
2006–07 Barnet 26 0
2007–08 Barnet 41 0 **67 0**

GILLET, Kenny (M) **31 0**
H: 5 10 W: 12 04 b.Bordeaux 3-1-86
Source: Caen.
2007–08 Barnet 31 0 **31 0**

GRAZIOLI, Giuliano (F) **210 54**
H: 5 10 W: 12 00 b.Marylebone 23-3-75
Source: Wembley.
1995–96 Peterborough U 3 1
1996–97 Peterborough U 4 0
1997–98 Peterborough U 0 0
1998–99 Peterborough U 34 15 **41 16**
1999–2000 Swindon T 19 8
2000–01 Swindon T 28 2
2001–02 Swindon T 31 8 **78 18**
2002–03 Bristol R 34 11 **34 11**
2003–04 Barnet 0 0
2004–05 Barnet 0 0
2005–06 Barnet 29 7
2006–07 Barnet 17 2
2007–08 Barnet 11 0 **57 9**

GROSS, Adam (D) **47 1**
H: 5 10 W: 10 09 b.Greenwich 16-2-86
Source: Charlton Ath Scholar.
2005–06 Barnet 20 0
2006–07 Barnet 27 1
2007–08 Barnet 0 0 **47 1**

HARRISON, Lee (G) **341 0**
H: 6 2 W: 11 13 b.Billericay 12-9-71
Source: Trainee.
1990–91 Charlton Ath 0 0
1991–92 Charlton Ath 0 0
1991–92 *Fulham* 0 0
1991–92 *Gillingham* 2 0 **2 0**
1992–93 Charlton Ath 0 0
1992–93 *Fulham* 0 0
1993–94 Fulham 0 0
1994–95 Fulham 7 0
1995–96 Fulham 5 0 **12 0**
1996–97 Barnet 21 0
1997–98 Barnet 46 0
1998–99 Barnet 43 0
1999–2000 Barnet 43 0
2000–01 Barnet 30 0
2001–02 Barnet 0 0
2002–03 Peterborough U 12 0
2002–03 Leyton Orient 6 0
2003–04 Leyton Orient 20 0
2004–05 Leyton Orient 34 0 **60 0**
2005–06 Peterborough U 6 0 **18 0**
2006–07 Barnet 28 0
2007–08 Barnet 38 0 **249 0**

HART, Danny (M) **2 0**
H: 5 10 W: 11 09 b.London 26-4-89
Source: Boreham Wood.
2007–08 Barnet 2 0 **2 0**

HENDON, Ian (D) **418 25**
H: 6 1 W: 13 02 b.Ilford 5-12-71
Source: Trainee. *Honours:* England Youth, Under-21.
1989–90 Tottenham H 0 0
1990–91 Tottenham H 2 0
1991–92 Tottenham H 2 0
1991–92 *Portsmouth* 4 0 **4 0**
1991–92 *Leyton Orient* 6 0
1992–93 Tottenham H 0 0 **4 0**
1992–93 *Barnsley* 6 0 **6 0**
1993–94 Leyton Orient 36 2
1994–95 Leyton Orient 29 0
1994–95 *Birmingham C* 4 0 **4 0**
1995–96 Leyton Orient 38 2
1996–97 Leyton Orient 28 1 **137 5**
1996–97 Notts Co 12 0
1997–98 Notts Co 38 0
1998–99 Notts Co 32 6 **82 6**
1998–99 Northampton T 7 0
1999–2000 Northampton T 44 2
2000–01 Northampton T 9 1 **60 3**
2000–01 Sheffield W 31 2
2001–02 Sheffield W 9 0
2002–03 Sheffield W 9 0 **49 2**
2002–03 Peterborough U 7 1 **7 1**
2004–05 Barnet 0 0
2005–06 Barnet 35 4
2006–07 Barnet 26 4
2007–08 Barnet 4 0 **65 8**

LEARY, Michael (M) **91 4**
H: 6 0 W: 11 11 b.Ealing 17-4-83
Source: Scholar.
2001–02 Luton T 0 0
2002–03 Luton T 0 0
2003–04 Luton T 14 2
2004–05 Luton T 8 0
2005–06 Luton T 0 0
2005–06 *Bristol R* 13 0 **13 0**
2005–06 *Walsall* 15 1 **15 1**
2006–07 Luton T 0 0 **22 2**
2006–07 *Torquay U* 2 0 **2 0**
2006–07 *Brentford* 17 0 **17 0**
2007–08 Barnet 22 1 **22 1**

NICOLAU, Nicky (D) **96 4**
H: 5 8 W: 10 03 b.Camden 12-10-83
Source: Trainee.
2002–03 Arsenal 0 0
2003–04 Arsenal 0 0
2003–04 *Southend U* 9 0
2004–05 Southend U 22 1 **31 1**
2005–06 Swindon T 5 0 **5 0**
2006–07 Barnet 22 1
2007–08 Barnet 38 2 **60 3**

NORVILLE, Jason (F) **47 4**
H: 6 0 W: 11 03 b.Trinidad 9-9-83
Source: Scholar.
2001–02 Watford 2 0
2002–03 Watford 12 1
2003–04 Watford 0 0
2004–05 Watford 0 0 **14 1**
2005–06 Barnet 22 2
2006–07 Barnet 3 0
2007–08 Barnet 8 1 **33 3**

O'CEARUILL, Joe (D) **22 0**
H: 5 11 W: 12 11 b.Edmonton 9-2-87
Source: Watford Youth. *Honours:* Eire B, Under-21, 2 full caps.
2006–07 Arsenal 0 0
2006–07 *Brighton & HA* 8 0 **8 0**
2007–08 Arsenal 0 0
2007–08 Barnet 14 0 **14 0**

PORTER, Max (M) **30 1**
H: 5 10 W: 12 04 b.Hornchurch 29-6-87
Source: Bishop's Stortford.
2007–08 Barnet 30 1 **30 1**

PUNCHEON, Jason (M) 112 16
H: 5 9 W: 12 05 b.Croydon 26-6-86
Source: Scholar.

2003–04	Wimbledon	8	0	**8**	**0**
2004–05	Milton Keynes D	25	1		
2005–06	Milton Keynes D	1	0	**26**	**1**
2006–07	Barnet	37	5		
2007–08	Barnet	41	10	**78**	**15**

SEANLA, Claude (F) 3 0
H: 6 0 W: 13 00 b.Abidjan 2-6-88
Source: Scholar.

2006–07	Watford	0	0		
2007–08	Barnet	3	0	**3**	**0**

ST AIMIE, Kieron (M) 10 0
H: 6 1 W: 13 00 b.Brent 4-5-89

2006–07	QPR	0	0		
2007–08	QPR	0	0		
2007–08	Barnet	10	0	**10**	**0**

THOMAS, Anthony (F) 26 4
H: 5 11 W: 12 08 b.Hemel Hempstead 30-8-82
Source: Hemel Hempstead T.

2007–08	Barnet	26	4	**26**	**4**

YAKUBU, Ismail (D) 83 4
H: 6 1 W: 13 09 b.Kano 8-4-85
Source: Trainee.

2005–06	Barnet	26	1		
2006–07	Barnet	29	1		
2007–08	Barnet	28	2	**83**	**4**

BARNSLEY (5)

ADAM, Jamil (M) 1 0
H: 5 10 W: 10 00 b.Bolton 5-6-91
Source: Scholar.

2007–08	Barnsley	1	0	**1**	**0**

ANDERSON (M) 92 4
H: 6 2 W: 12 11 b.Sao Paulo 29-8-82
Honours: Brazil 4 full caps.

2003	Santiago Wanderers	18	2	**18**	**2**
2003–04	Santander	8	0		
2004–05	Santander	30	2	**38**	**2**
2005–06	Malaga	15	0	**15**	**0**
2006–07	Everton	1	0		
2007–08	Everton	0	0	**1**	**0**
2007–08	Barnsley	20	0	**20**	**0**

ATKINSON, Rob (D) 34 1
H: 6 1 W: 12 00 b.Beverley 29-4-87
Source: Scholar.

2003–04	Barnsley	1	0		
2004–05	Barnsley	1	0		
2005–06	Barnsley	0	0		
2006–07	Barnsley	6	0		
2007–08	Barnsley	0	0	**8**	**0**
2007–08	*Rochdale*	2	0	**2**	**0**
2007–08	*Grimsby T*	24	1	**24**	**1**

BUTTERFIELD, Jacob (D) 3 0
H: 5 10 W: 11 00 b.Manchester 10-6-90
Source: Scholar.

2007–08	Barnsley	3	0	**3**	**0**

CAMPBELL-RYCE, Jamal (M) 168 7
H: 5 7 W: 12 03 b.Lambeth 6-4-83
Source: Scholar. *Honours:* Jamaica 7 full caps.

2002–03	Charlton Ath	1	0		
2002–03	*Leyton Orient*	17	2	**17**	**2**
2003–04	Charlton Ath	2	0		
2003–04	*Wimbledon*	4	0	**4**	**0**
2004–05	Charlton Ath	0	0	**3**	**0**
2004–05	*Chesterfield*	14	0	**14**	**0**
2004–05	Rotherham U	24	0		
2005–06	Rotherham U	7	0	**31**	**0**
2005–06	*Southend U*	13	0		
2005–06	*Colchester U*	4	0	**4**	**0**
2006–07	Southend U	43	2		
2007–08	Southend U	2	0	**58**	**2**
2007–08	Barnsley	37	3	**37**	**3**

CHRISTENSEN, Kim (F) 205 39
H: 6 2 W: 12 08 b.Frederiksvaerk 8-5-80
Honours: Denmark Under-21.

1998–99	Lyngby	6	1		
1999–2000	Lyngby	18	5		
2000–01	Lyngby	33	10		
2001–02	Lyngby	13	2	**70**	**18**
2001–02	Hamburg	4	0		
2002–03	Hamburg II	13	1		
2002–03	Hamburg	8	1	**12**	**1**
2003–04	Twente	30	7		
2004–05	Twente	23	3	**53**	**10**
2004–05	Brondby	0	0		
2005–06	Brondby	16	2		
2006–07	Brondby	3	1	**19**	**3**
2006–07	Odense	23	4		
2007–08	Odense	3	1	**26**	**5**
2007–08	Barnsley	12	1	**12**	**1**

COULSON, Michael (F) 14 0
H: 5 10 W: 10 00 b.Scarborough 4-4-88
Source: Scarborough.

2006–07	Barnsley	2	0		
2007–08	Barnsley	12	0	**14**	**0**

DEVANEY, Martin (M) 316 53
H: 5 11 W: 12 00 b.Cheltenham 1-6-80
Source: Trainee.

1997–98	Coventry C	0	0		
1998–99	Coventry C	0	0		
1999–2000	Cheltenham T	26	6		
2000–01	Cheltenham T	34	10		
2001–02	Cheltenham T	25	1		
2002–03	Cheltenham T	40	6		
2003–04	Cheltenham T	40	5		
2004–05	Cheltenham T	38	10	**203**	**38**
2005–06	Watford	0	0		
2005–06	Barnsley	38	6		
2006–07	Barnsley	41	5		
2007–08	Barnsley	34	4	**113**	**15**

FERENCZI, Istvan (F) 261 89
H: 6 3 W: 13 10 b.Gyor 14-9-77
Honours: Hungary 9 full caps, 2 goals.

1995–96	Gyor	8	0		
1996–97	Gyor	8	0		
1997–98	Gyor	18	5		
1998–99	Zalaegerszeg	24	8		
1999–2000	Zalaegerszeg	12	7	**36**	**15**
1999–2000	Gyor	14	3	**48**	**8**
2000–01	MTK	31	14		
2001–02	MTK	28	14		
2001–02	Levski	4	3	**4**	**3**
2002–03	MTK	19	7	**78**	**35**
2003–04	Osnabruck	0	0		
2004–05	Vasas	15	8	**15**	**8**
2005–06	Debrecen	11	5	**11**	**5**
2006–07	Zalaegerszeg	16	5	**16**	**5**
2006–07	Barnsley	16	5		
2007–08	Barnsley	37	5	**53**	**10**

FOSTER, Stephen (D) 276 16
H: 6 0 W: 11 05 b.Warrington 10-9-80
Source: Trainee. *Honours:* England Schools.

1998–99	Crewe Alex	1	0		
1999–2000	Crewe Alex	0	0		
2000–01	Crewe Alex	30	0		
2001–02	Crewe Alex	34	5		
2002–03	Crewe Alex	35	4		
2003–04	Crewe Alex	45	2		
2004–05	Crewe Alex	34	1		
2005–06	Crewe Alex	39	3	**218**	**15**
2006–07	Burnley	17	0		
2007–08	Burnley	0	0	**17**	**0**
2007–08	Barnsley	41	1	**41**	**1**

HARBAN, Thomas (D) 6 0
H: 6 0 W: 11 09 b.Barnsley 12-11-85
Source: Scholar.

2005–06	Barnsley	0	0		
2006–07	Barnsley	0	0		
2007–08	Barnsley	0	0		
2007–08	*Bradford C*	6	0	**6**	**0**

HASSELL, Bobby (D) 286 7
H: 5 10 W: 12 00 b.Derby 4-6-80
Source: Trainee.

1997–98	Mansfield T	9	0		
1998–99	Mansfield T	3	0		
1999–2000	Mansfield T	11	1		
2000–01	Mansfield T	40	1		
2001–02	Mansfield T	43	1		
2002–03	Mansfield T	20	0		
2003–04	Mansfield T	34	0	**160**	**3**
2004–05	Barnsley	39	0		
2005–06	Barnsley	28	2		
2006–07	Barnsley	39	2		
2007–08	Barnsley	20	0	**126**	**4**

HESLOP, Simon (M) 1 0
H: 5 11 W: 11 00 b.York 1-5-87
Source: Scholar.

2005–06	Barnsley	0	0		
2006–07	Barnsley	1	0		
2007–08	Barnsley	0	0	**1**	**0**

HOWARD, Brian (M) 184 35
H: 5 8 W: 11 00 b.Winchester 23-1-83
Source: Trainee. *Honours:* England Schools, Youth, Under-20.

1999–2000	Southampton	0	0		
2000–01	Southampton	0	0		
2001–02	Southampton	0	0		
2002–03	Southampton	0	0		
2003–04	Swindon T	35	4		
2004–05	Swindon T	35	5	**70**	**9**
2005–06	Barnsley	31	5		
2006–07	Barnsley	42	8		
2007–08	Barnsley	41	13	**114**	**26**

JOHNSON, Andy (M) 343 30
H: 6 0 W: 13 00 b.Bristol 2-5-74
Source: Trainee. *Honours:* England Youth, Wales 15 full caps.

1991–92	Norwich C	2	0		
1992–93	Norwich C	2	1		
1993–94	Norwich C	2	0		
1994–95	Norwich C	7	0		
1995–96	Norwich C	26	7		
1996–97	Norwich C	27	5	**66**	**13**
1997–98	Nottingham F	34	4		
1998–99	Nottingham F	28	0		
1999–2000	Nottingham F	25	2		
2000–01	Nottingham F	31	3		
2001–02	Nottingham F	1	0	**119**	**9**
2001–02	WBA	32	4		
2002–03	WBA	32	1		
2003–04	WBA	38	2		
2004–05	WBA	22	0		
2005–06	WBA	8	0	**132**	**7**
2006–07	Leicester C	22	1	**22**	**1**
2007–08	Barnsley	4	0	**4**	**0**

JOYNES, Nathan (F) 13 1
H: 6 1 W: 12 02 b.Hoyland 7-8-85
Source: Scholar.

2004–05	Barnsley	1	0		
2005–06	Barnsley	0	0		
2006–07	Barnsley	0	0		
2006–07	*Boston U*	10	1	**10**	**1**
2007–08	Barnsley	0	0	**1**	**0**
2007–08	*Bradford C*	2	0	**2**	**0**

KOZLUK, Rob (D) 268 2
H: 5 8 W: 10 02 b.Mansfield 5-8-77
Source: Trainee. *Honours:* England Under-21.

1995–96	Derby Co	0	0		
1996–97	Derby Co	0	0		
1997–98	Derby Co	9	0		
1998–99	Derby Co	7	0	**16**	**0**
1998–99	Sheffield U	10	0		
1999–2000	Sheffield U	39	0		
2000–01	Sheffield U	27	0		
2000–01	*Huddersfield T*	14	0	**14**	**0**
2001–02	Sheffield U	8	0		
2002–03	Sheffield U	32	1		
2003–04	Sheffield U	42	1		
2004–05	Sheffield U	9	0		
2004–05	*Preston NE*	1	0	**1**	**0**
2005–06	Sheffield U	27	0		
2006–07	Sheffield U	19	0	**213**	**2**
2007–08	Barnsley	24	0	**24**	**0**

LAIGHT, Ryan (D) 1 0
H: 6 2 W: 11 09 b.Barnsley 16-11-85
Source: Scholar.

2002–03	Barnsley	0	0		
2003–04	Barnsley	0	0		
2004–05	Barnsley	0	0		
2005–06	Barnsley	1	0		
2006–07	Barnsley	0	0		
2007–08	Barnsley	0	0	**1**	**0**

LEON, Diego (M) 62 5
H: 5 7 W: 10 10 b.Palencia 16-1-84

2005–06	Real Madrid	0	0		
2005–06	*Arm Bielefeld*	14	1	**14**	**1**
2006–07	Grasshoppers	30	3	**30**	**3**
2007–08	Barnsley	18	1	**18**	**1**

LETHEREN, Kyle (G) **0 0**
H: 6 2 W: 12 02 b.Llanelli 26-12-87
Source: Swansea C Scholar. *Honours:* Wales Under-21.

2006–07	Barnsley	0	0		
2007–08	Barnsley	0	0		

MACKEN, Jon (F) **314 83**
H: 5 11 W: 12 04 b.Manchester 7-9-77
Source: Trainee. *Honours:* England Youth. Eire 1 full cap.

1996–97	Manchester U	0	0		
1997–98	Preston NE	29	6		
1998–99	Preston NE	42	8		
1999–2000	Preston NE	44	22		
2000–01	Preston NE	38	19		
2001–02	Preston NE	31	8	**184**	**63**
2001–02	Manchester C	8	5		
2002–03	Manchester C	5	0		
2003–04	Manchester C	15	1		
2004–05	Manchester C	23	1	**51**	**7**
2005–06	Crystal Palace	24	2		
2006–07	Crystal Palace	1	0	**25**	**2**
2006–07	*Ipswich T*	14	4	**14**	**4**
2006–07	Derby Co	8	0		
2007–08	Derby Co	3	0	**11**	**0**
2007–08	Barnsley	29	7	**29**	**7**

MATTIS, Dwayne (M) **174 13**
H: 6 1 W: 11 12 b.Huddersfield 31-7-81
Source: Trainee. *Honours:* Eire Youth, Under-21.

1998–99	Huddersfield T	2	0		
1999–2000	Huddersfield T	0	0		
2000–01	Huddersfield T	0	0		
2001–02	Huddersfield T	29	1		
2002–03	Huddersfield T	33	1		
2003–04	Huddersfield T	5	0	**69**	**2**
2004–05	Bury	39	5		
2005–06	Bury	36	5		
2006–07	Bury	22	1	**97**	**11**
2006–07	Barnsley	3	0		
2007–08	Barnsley	1	0	**4**	**0**
2007–08	*Walsall*	4	0	**4**	**0**

McGRORY, Scott (F) **0 0**
H: 5 11 W: 10 11 b.Aberdeen 5-4-87
Source: Scholar.

2006–07	Barnsley	0	0		
2007–08	Barnsley	0	0		

MEYNELL, Rhys (D) **0 0**
H: 5 11 W: 12 03 b.Barnsley 17-8-88
Source: Scholar.

2006–07	Barnsley	0	0		
2007–08	Barnsley	0	0		

MOSTTO, Miguel (F) **14 1**
H: 5 10 W: 11 11 b.Ica 11-1-79
Source: Universitario, Coronel Bolognesi, Cienciano. *Honours:* Peru 10 full caps, 1 goal.

2007–08	Barnsley	14	1	**14**	**1**

MULLER, Heinz (G) **102 0**
H: 6 4 W: 15 04 b.Frankfurt-on-Main 30-5-78
Source: FSV Frankfurt.

1999–2000	Hanover	4	0	**4**	**0**
2000–01	Arm Bielefeld	0	0		
2001–02	Arm Bielefeld	1	0	**1**	**0**
2002–03	St Pauli	16	0	**16**	**0**
2003–04	Regensberg	4	0	**4**	**0**
2004	Odd Grenland	7	0	**7**	**0**
2005	Lillestrom	5	0		
2006	Lillestrom	24	0		
2007	Lillestrom	13	0	**42**	**0**
2007–08	Barnsley	28	0	**28**	**0**

ODEJAYI, Kayode (F) **193 33**
H: 6 2 W: 12 02 b.Ibadon 21-2-82
Source: Scholar. *Honours:* Nigeria 1 full cap.

1999–2000	Bristol C	3	0		
2000–01	Bristol C	3	0		
2001–02	Bristol C	0	0		
2002–03	Bristol C	0	0	**6**	**0**
2003–04	Cheltenham T	30	5		
2004–05	Cheltenham T	32	1		
2005–06	Cheltenham T	41	11		
2006–07	Cheltenham T	45	13	**148**	**30**
2007–08	Barnsley	39	3	**39**	**3**

POTTER, Luke (D) **1 0**
H: 6 2 W: 12 07 b.Barnsley 13-7-89
Source: Scholar.

2006–07	Barnsley	1	0		
2007–08	Barnsley	0	0	**1**	**0**

REID, Paul (D) **187 6**
H: 6 2 W: 11 08 b.Carlisle 18-2-82
Source: Trainee. *Honours:* England Youth, Under-20.

1998–99	Carlisle U	0	0		
1999–2000	Carlisle U	19	0		
2000–01	Rangers	0	0		
2001–02	Rangers	0	0		
2001–02	*Preston NE*	1	1	**1**	**1**
2002–03	Rangers	0	0		
2002–03	*Northampton T*	19	0		
2003–04	Northampton T	33	2	**52**	**2**
2004–05	Barnsley	41	3		
2005–06	Barnsley	33	0		
2006–07	Barnsley	37	0		
2007–08	Barnsley	3	0	**114**	**3**
2007–08	*Carlisle U*	1	0	**20**	**0**

RICKETTS, Rohan (M) **99 2**
H: 5 10 W: 11 07 b.Clapham 22-12-82
Source: Scholar. *Honours:* England Youth, Under-20.

2001–02	Arsenal	0	0		
2002–03	Tottenham H	0	0		
2003–04	Tottenham H	24	1		
2004–05	Tottenham H	6	0	**30**	**1**
2004–05	*Coventry C*	6	0	**6**	**0**
2004–05	*Wolverhampton W*	7	1		
2005–06	Wolverhampton W	25	0		
2006–07	Wolverhampton W	19	0	**51**	**1**
2006–07	*QPR*	2	0	**2**	**0**
2007–08	Barnsley	10	0	**10**	**0**

SOUZA, Dennis (M) **141 6**
H: 6 3 W: 13 05 b.Sao Paulo 1-9-80
Source: Matsubara, Roda JC.

2000–01	*Harelbeke*	0	0		
2002–03	*RAEC Mons*	25	1		
2003–04	*KBHZ*	31	0	**31**	**0**
2004–05	Standard	0	0		
2004–05	RAEC Mons	8	0		
2005–06	RAEC Mons	16	1	**49**	**2**
2006–07	Charleroi	16	2	**16**	**2**
2007–08	Barnsley	45	2	**45**	**2**

TOGWELL, Sam (D) **106 4**
H: 5 11 W: 12 04 b.Beaconsfield 14-10-84
Source: Scholar.

2002–03	Crystal Palace	1	0		
2003–04	Crystal Palace	0	0		
2004–05	Crystal Palace	0	0		
2004–05	*Oxford U*	4	0	**4**	**0**
2004–05	*Northampton T*	8	0	**8**	**0**
2005–06	Crystal Palace	0	0	**1**	**0**
2005–06	*Port Vale*	27	2	**27**	**2**
2006–07	Barnsley	44	1		
2007–08	Barnsley	22	1	**66**	**2**

VAN HOMOET, Marciano (D) **47 1**
H: 5 9 W: 11 11 b.Rotterdam 7-3-84

2004–05	Sparta Rotterdam	23	1		
2005–06	Sparta Rotterdam	5	0		
2006–07	Sparta Rotterdam	0	0	**28**	**1**
2007–08	Barnsley	19	0	**19**	**0**

WERLING, Dominik (M) **72 4**
H: 5 8 W: 12 08 b.Ludwigshafen 13-12-82

2003–04	Bielefeld II	20	0	**20**	**0**
2004–05	Union Berlin	9	0	**9**	**0**
2005–06	Crailsheim	26	3	**26**	**3**
2006–07	Sakarya	0	0		
2007–08	Barnsley	17	1	**17**	**1**

BIRMINGHAM C (6)

ALUKO, Sone (F) **20 3**
H: 5 8 W: 9 11 b.Birmingham 19-2-89
Source: Scholar. *Honours:* England Schools, Youth.

2005–06	Birmingham C	0	0		
2006–07	Birmingham C	0	0		
2007–08	*Aberdeen*	20	3	**20**	**3**
2007–08	Birmingham C	0	0		

AYDILEK, Semih (F) **0 0**
H: 6 1 W: 11 13 b.Frankfurt 16-1-89
Source: Eintracht Frankfurt.

2007–08	Birmingham C	0	0		

BURGE, Ryan (M) **0 0**
H: 5 10 W: 10 03 b.Cheltenham 12-10-88
Source: Scholar.

2005–06	Birmingham C	0	0		
2006–07	Birmingham C	0	0		
2007–08	Birmingham C	0	0		

DE RIDDER, Daniel (M) **60 4**
H: 5 11 W: 10 12 b.Amsterdam 6-3-84
Honours: Holland Under-21.

2003–04	Ajax	15	1		
2004–05	Ajax	15	2	**30**	**3**
2005–06	Celta Vigo	17	1		
2006–07	Celta Vigo	3	0	**20**	**1**
2007–08	Birmingham C	10	0	**10**	**0**

DOYLE, Colin (G) **39 0**
H: 6 5 W: 14 05 b.Cork 12-8-85
Honours: Eire Youth, Under-21, 1 full cap.

2004–05	Birmingham C	0	0		
2004–05	*Chester C*	0	0		
2004–05	*Nottingham F*	3	0	**3**	**0**
2005–06	Birmingham C	0	0		
2005–06	*Millwall*	14	0	**14**	**0**
2006–07	Birmingham C	19	0		
2007–08	Birmingham C	3	0	**22**	**0**

FORSSELL, Mikael (F) **219 59**
H: 5 10 W: 10 10 b.Steinfurt 15-3-81
Honours: Finland Youth, Under-20, Under-21, 55 full caps, 17 goals.

1997	HJK Helsinki	1	0		
1998	HJK Helsinki	16	1	**17**	**1**
1998–99	Chelsea	10	1		
1999–2000	Chelsea	0	0		
1999–2000	*Crystal Palace*	13	3		
2000–01	Chelsea	0	0		
2000–01	*Crystal Palace*	39	13	**52**	**16**
2001–02	Chelsea	22	4		
2002–03	*M'gladbach*	16	7	**16**	**7**
2002–03	Chelsea	0	0		
2003–04	Chelsea	0	0		
2003–04	*Birmingham C*	32	17		
2004–05	Chelsea	1	0	**33**	**5**
2004–05	*Birmingham C*	4	0		
2005–06	Birmingham C	27	3		
2006–07	Birmingham C	8	1		
2007–08	Birmingham C	30	9	**101**	**30**

HALL, Asa (M) **27 3**
H: 6 2 W: 11 09 b.Sandwell 29-11-86
Source: Scholar. *Honours:* England Youth, Under-20.

2004–05	Birmingham C	0	0		
2005–06	Birmingham C	0	0		
2005–06	*Boston U*	12	0	**12**	**0**
2006–07	Birmingham C	0	0		
2007–08	Birmingham C	0	0		
2007–08	*Shrewsbury T*	15	3	**15**	**3**

HOWLAND, David (M) **17 1**
H: 5 11 W: 10 08 b.Ballynahinch 17-9-86
Source: Scholar. *Honours:* Northern Ireland Under-21.

2004–05	Birmingham C	0	0		
2005–06	Birmingham C	0	0		
2006–07	Birmingham C	0	0		
2007–08	Birmingham C	0	0		
2007–08	*Port Vale*	17	1	**17**	**1**

JAIDI, Radhi (D) **99 14**
H: 6 2 W: 14 00 b.Tunis 30-8-75
Source: Esperance. *Honours:* Tunisia 99 full caps, 6 goals.

2004–05	Bolton W	27	5		
2005–06	Bolton W	16	3	**43**	**8**
2006–07	Birmingham C	38	6		
2007–08	Birmingham C	18	0	**56**	**6**

JEROME, Cameron (F) **144 38**
H: 6 1 W: 13 06 b.Huddersfield 14-8-86
Honours: England Under-21.

2004–05	Cardiff C	29	6		
2005–06	Cardiff C	44	18	**73**	**24**
2005–06	Birmingham C	0	0		
2006–07	Birmingham C	38	7		
2007–08	Birmingham C	33	7	**71**	**14**

JOHNSON, Damien (M) **249 7**
H: 5 9 W: 11 09 b.Lisburn 18-11-78
Source: Trainee. *Honours:* Northern Ireland Youth, Under-21, 48 full caps.

1995–96	Blackburn R	0	0		
1996–97	Blackburn R	0	0		
1997–98	Blackburn R	0	0		
1997–98	*Nottingham F*	6	0	**6**	**0**
1998–99	Blackburn R	21	1		
1999–2000	Blackburn R	16	1		
2000–01	Blackburn R	16	0		

Season	Club	App	Gls	Total App	Total Gls
2001–02	Blackburn R	7	1	60	3
2001–02	Birmingham C	8	1		
2002–03	Birmingham C	30	1		
2003–04	Birmingham C	35	1		
2004–05	Birmingham C	36	0		
2005–06	Birmingham C	31	0		
2006–07	Birmingham C	26	1		
2007–08	Birmingham C	17	0	183	4

JOYCE, David (D) **0 0**
H: 5 10 W: 12 13 b.County Mayo 8-8-90
Source: Scholar.

Season	Club	App	Gls	Total App	Total Gls
2007–08	Birmingham C	0	0		

KAPO, Olivier (M) **214 34**
H: 6 1 W: 12 06 b.Abidjan 27-9-80
Honours: France 9 full caps, 3 goals.

Season	Club	App	Gls	Total App	Total Gls
1999–2000	Auxerre	15	3		
2000–01	Auxerre	29	4		
2001–02	Auxerre	25	4		
2002–03	Auxerre	21	6		
2003–04	Auxerre	29	2	119	19
2004–05	Juventus	14	0	14	0
2005–06	Monaco	25	5	25	5
2006–07	Levante	30	5	30	5
2007–08	Birmingham C	26	5	26	5

KELLY, Stephen (D) **141 2**
H: 6 0 W: 12 04 b.Dublin 6-9-83
Source: Juniors. *Honours:* Eire Youth, Under-21, 11 full caps.

Season	Club	App	Gls	Total App	Total Gls
2000–01	Tottenham H	0	0		
2001–02	Tottenham H	0	0		
2002–03	Tottenham H	0	0		
2002–03	*Southend U*	10	0	10	0
2002–03	*QPR*	7	0	7	0
2003–04	Tottenham H	11	0		
2003–04	*Watford*	13	0	13	0
2004–05	Tottenham H	17	2		
2005–06	Tottenham H	9	0	37	2
2006–07	Birmingham C	36	0		
2007–08	Birmingham C	38	0	74	0

KINGSON, Richard (G) **102 0**
H: 6 3 W: 13 10 b.Accra 13-6-78
Honours: Ghana 55 full caps.

Season	Club	App	Gls	Total App	Total Gls
1998–99	Sakarya	21	0	21	0
1999–2000	Goztepe	19	0		
2000–01	Goztepe	10	0	29	0
2001–02	Antalya	15	0	15	0
2002–03	Elazig	20	0	20	0
2003–04	Ankara	0	0		
2004–05	Galatasaray	1	0	1	0
2005–06	Ankara	1	0		
2006–07	Ankara	3	0	4	0
2007	Hammarby	11	0	11	0
2007–08	Birmingham C	1	0	1	0

KRYSIAK, Artur (G) **4 0**
H: 6 1 W: 12.00 b.Lodz 11-8-89
Source: LKS Lodz.

Season	Club	App	Gls	Total App	Total Gls
2006–07	Birmingham C	0	0		
2007–08	*Gretna*	4	0	4	0
2007–08	Birmingham C	0	0		

LARSSON, Sebastian (M) **81 10**
H: 5 11 W: 11 02 b.Eskilstuna 6-6-85
Source: Trainee. *Honours:* Sweden Under-21, 5 full caps.

Season	Club	App	Gls	Total App	Total Gls
2002–03	Arsenal	0	0		
2003–04	Arsenal	0	0		
2004–05	Arsenal	0	0		
2005–06	Arsenal	3	0		
2006–07	Arsenal	0	0	3	0
2006–07	Birmingham C	43	4		
2007–08	Birmingham C	35	6	78	10

LEGZDINS, Adam (G) **0 0**
H: 6 1 W: 14 02 b.Stafford 28-11-86
Source: Scholar.

Season	Club	App	Gls	Total App	Total Gls
2006–07	Birmingham C	0	0		
2007–08	Birmingham C	0	0		

McFADDEN, James (M) **184 41**
H: 6 0 W: 12 11 b.Glasgow 14-4-83
Honours: Scotland Under-21, B, 37 full caps, 13 goals.

Season	Club	App	Gls	Total App	Total Gls
2000–01	Motherwell	6	0		
2001–02	Motherwell	24	10		
2002–03	Motherwell	30	13		
2003–04	Motherwell	3	3	63	26
2003–04	Everton	23	0		
2004–05	Everton	23	1		
2005–06	Everton	32	6		
2006–07	Everton	19	2		
2007–08	Everton	12	2	109	11
2007–08	Birmingham C	12	4	12	4

McKERR, Michael (D) **16 0**
b. 23-2-84
Source: Scholar.

Season	Club	App	Gls	Total App	Total Gls
2006–07	Glenavon	6	0		
2007–08	*Glenavon*	10	0	16	0
2007–08	Birmingham C	0	0		

McPIKE, James (F) **0 0**
H: 5 10 W: 11 02 b.Birmingham 4-10-88
Source: Scholar.

Season	Club	App	Gls	Total App	Total Gls
2005–06	Birmingham C	0	0		
2006–07	Birmingham C	0	0		
2007–08	Birmingham C	0	0		

McSHEFFREY, Gary (F) **243 71**
H: 5 8 W: 10 06 b.Coventry 13-8-82
Source: Trainee. *Honours:* England Youth, Under-20.

Season	Club	App	Gls	Total App	Total Gls
1998–99	Coventry C	1	0		
1999–2000	Coventry C	3	0		
2000–01	Coventry C	0	0		
2001–02	*Stockport Co*	5	1	5	1
2001–02	Coventry C	8	1		
2002–03	Coventry C	29	4		
2003–04	Coventry C	19	11		
2003–04	*Luton T*	18	9		
2004–05	Coventry C	37	12		
2004–05	*Luton T*	5	1	23	10
2005–06	Coventry C	43	15		
2006–07	Coventry C	3	1	143	44
2006–07	Birmingham C	40	13		
2007–08	Birmingham C	32	3	72	16

MILOJEVIC, Stefan (M) **0 0**
H: 5 9 W: 11 03 b.Paris 6-2-89

Season	Club	App	Gls	Total App	Total Gls
2007–08	Birmingham C	0	0		

MOSES-GARVEY, Aaron (F) **0 0**
H: 5 8 W: 11 13 b.Birmingham 6-9-89
Source: Scholar.

Season	Club	App	Gls	Total App	Total Gls
2007–08	Birmingham C	0	0		

MUAMBA, Fabrice (M) **71 2**
H: 6 1 W: 11 10 b.DR Congo 6-4-88
Source: Scholar. *Honours:* England Youth, Under-21.

Season	Club	App	Gls	Total App	Total Gls
2005–06	Arsenal	0	0		
2006–07	Arsenal	0	0		
2006–07	Birmingham C	34	0		
2007–08	Birmingham C	37	2	71	2

MURPHY, David (D) **144 7**
H: 6 1 W: 12 03 b.Hartlepool 1-3-84
Source: Scholar. *Honours:* England Youth.

Season	Club	App	Gls	Total App	Total Gls
2001–02	Middlesbrough	5	0		
2002–03	Middlesbrough	8	0		
2003–04	Middlesbrough	0	0	13	0
2003–04	*Barnsley*	10	2	10	2
2004–05	Hibernian	27	1		
2005–06	Hibernian	30	1		
2006–07	Hibernian	33	0		
2007–08	Hibernian	17	2	107	4
2007–08	Birmingham C	14	1	14	1

MUTCH, Jordon (M) **0 0**
H: 5 9 W: 10 03 b.Birmingham 2-12-91
Source: Derby Co. *Honours:* England Youth.

Season	Club	App	Gls	Total App	Total Gls
2007–08	Birmingham C	0	0		

NAFTI, Mehdi (M) **225 4**
H: 5 10 W: 12 02 b.Toulouse 28-11-78
Honours: Tunisia 41 full caps, 1 goal.

Season	Club	App	Gls	Total App	Total Gls
1998–99	Toulouse	11	0		
1999–2000	Toulouse	13	1	24	1
2000–01	Santander B	21	0	21	0
2000–01	Santander	3	0		
2001–02	Santander	30	0		
2002–03	Santander	31	2		
2003–04	Santander	31	1		
2004–05	Santander	16	0	111	3
2004–05	Birmingham C	10	0		
2005–06	Birmingham C	1	0		
2006–07	Birmingham C	32	0		
2007–08	Birmingham C	26	0	69	0

O'BRIEN, James (M) **0 0**
b.Dublin 8-6-90
Source: Scholar. *Honours:* Eire Youth.

Season	Club	App	Gls	Total App	Total Gls
2007–08	Birmingham C	0	0		

O'CONNOR, Garry (F) **163 50**
H: 6 1 W: 12 02 b.Edinburgh 7-5-83
Honours: Scotland Under-21, 15 full caps, 5 goals.

Season	Club	App	Gls	Total App	Total Gls
2000–01	Hibernian	1	0		
2001–02	Hibernian	4	1		
2002–03	Hibernian	19	10		
2003–04	Hibernian	24	6		
2004–05	Hibernian	35	13		
2005–06	Hibernian	24	11	107	41
2006	Lokomotiv Moscow	24	7		
2007	Lokomotiv Moscow	9	0	33	7
2007–08	Birmingham C	23	2	23	2

OUBINA, Borja (M) **80 2**
H: 6 0 W: 11 11 b.Vigo 17-5-82
Honours: Spain 2 full caps.

Season	Club	App	Gls	Total App	Total Gls
2003–04	Celta Vigo	12	0		
2004–05	Celta Vigo	0	0		
2005–06	Celta Vigo	36	1		
2006–07	Celta Vigo	30	1	78	2
2007–08	Birmingham C	2	0	2	0

PARNABY, Stuart (M) **110 2**
H: 5 11 W: 11 00 b.Durham 19-7-82
Source: Trainee. *Honours:* England Youth, Under-20, Under-21.

Season	Club	App	Gls	Total App	Total Gls
1999–2000	Middlesbrough	0	0		
2000–01	Middlesbrough	0	0		
2000–01	*Halifax T*	6	0	6	0
2001–02	Middlesbrough	0	0		
2002–03	Middlesbrough	21	0		
2003–04	Middlesbrough	13	0		
2004–05	Middlesbrough	19	0		
2005–06	Middlesbrough	20	2		
2006–07	Middlesbrough	18	0	91	2
2007–08	Birmingham C	13	0	13	0

PEARCE, Krystian (D) **20 1**
H: 6 1 W: 12 00 b.Birmingham 5-1-90
Honours: England Youth.

Season	Club	App	Gls	Total App	Total Gls
2007–08	Birmingham C	0	0		
2007–08	*Port Vale*	12	0	12	0
2007–08	*Notts Co*	8	1	8	1

QUEUDRUE, Franck (D) **237 14**
H: 6 1 W: 12 01 b.Paris 27-8-78
Source: Meaux. *Honours:* France B.

Season	Club	App	Gls	Total App	Total Gls
1999–2000	Lens	16	1		
2000–01	Lens	24	1		
2001–02	Lens	2	0	42	2
2001–02	Middlesbrough	28	2		
2002–03	Middlesbrough	31	1		
2003–04	Middlesbrough	31	0		
2004–05	Middlesbrough	31	5		
2005–06	Middlesbrough	29	3	150	11
2006–07	Fulham	29	1	29	1
2007–08	Birmingham C	16	0	16	0

RIDGEWELL, Liam (D) **119 7**
H: 5 10 W: 10 03 b.Bexley 21-7-84
Source: Scholar. *Honours:* England Youth, Under-20, Under-21.

Season	Club	App	Gls	Total App	Total Gls
2001–02	Aston Villa	0	0		
2002–03	Aston Villa	0	0		
2002–03	*Bournemouth*	5	0	5	0
2003–04	Aston Villa	11	0		
2004–05	Aston Villa	15	0		
2005–06	Aston Villa	32	5		
2006–07	Aston Villa	21	1	79	6
2007–08	Birmingham C	35	1	35	1

SCHMITZ, Rafael (D) **123 2**
H: 5 9 W: 11 07 b.Blumerau 17-12-80
Source: Malutrum.

Season	Club	App	Gls	Total App	Total Gls
2001–02	Lille	15	0		
2002–03	Lille	2	0		
2003–04	Lille	5	0		
2003–04	Krylia	9	0	9	0
2004–05	Lille	27	1		
2005–06	Lille	26	1		
2006–07	Lille	24	0	99	2
2007–08	Birmingham C	15	0	15	0

TAYLOR, Maik (G) **439 0**
H: 6 4 W: 14 02 b.Hildeshein 4-9-71
Source: Farnborough T. *Honours:* Northern Ireland Under-21, B, 68 full caps.

Season	Club	App	Gls	Total App	Total Gls
1995–96	Barnet	45	0		
1996–97	Barnet	25	0	70	0
1996–97	Southampton	18	0		
1997–98	Southampton	0	0	18	0
1997–98	Fulham	28	0		
1998–99	Fulham	46	0		

1999–2000	Fulham	46	0		
2000–01	Fulham	44	0		
2001–02	Fulham	1	0		
2002–03	Fulham	19	0		
2003–04	Fulham	0	0	**184**	**0**
2003–04	Birmingham C	34	0		
2004–05	Birmingham C	38	0		
2005–06	Birmingham C	34	0		
2006–07	Birmingham C	27	0		
2007–08	Birmingham C	34	0	**167**	**0**

TAYLOR, Martin (D) **182 7**
H: 6 4 W: 15 00 b.Ashington 9-11-79
Source: Trainee. *Honours:* England Youth, Under-21.

1997–98	Blackburn R	0	0		
1998–99	Blackburn R	3	0		
1999–2000	Blackburn R	6	0		
1999–2000	*Darlington*	4	0	**4**	**0**
1999–2000	*Stockport Co*	7	0	**7**	**0**
2000–01	Blackburn R	16	3		
2001–02	Blackburn R	19	0		
2002–03	Blackburn R	33	2		
2003–04	Blackburn R	11	0	**88**	**5**
2003–04	Birmingham C	12	1		
2004–05	Birmingham C	7	0		
2005–06	Birmingham C	21	0		
2006–07	Birmingham C	31	0		
2007–08	Birmingham C	4	0	**75**	**1**
2007–08	*Norwich C*	8	1	**8**	**1**

WILSON, Jared (D) **0 0**
b.Cheltenham 24-11-89
Source: Scholar.

2007–08	Birmingham C	0	0

WRIGHT, Nick (M) **8 0**
H: 6 2 W: 12 00 b.Birmingham 25-11-87
Source: Scholar.

2006–07	Birmingham C	0	0		
2006–07	*Bristol C*	4	0	**4**	**0**
2006–07	*Northampton T*	4	0	**4**	**0**
2007–08	Birmingham C	0	0		

ZARATE, Mauro (F) **87 26**
H: 5 9 W: 11 13 b.Haedo 18-3-87
Honours: Argentina Under-20.

2003–04	Velez Sarsfield	4	1		
2004–05	Velez Sarsfield	14	2		
2005–06	Velez Sarsfield	23	3		
2006–07	Velez Sarsfield	32	16	**73**	**22**
From Al Saad.					
2007–08	Birmingham C	14	4	**14**	**4**

Scholars
Gradwell, Robert; Lyness, Dean James; Osman, Toby James; Rowe, Jacob; Rutter, Jack; Sheldon, Jamie; Timmins, Shaun

BLACKBURN R (7)

ARESTIDOU, Andreas (G) **0 0**
b. 6-12-89
Source: Scholar.

2007–08	Blackburn R	0	0

BENTLEY, David (F) **129 15**
H: 5 10 W: 11 03 b.Peterborough 27-8-84
Source: Scholar. *Honours:* England Youth, Under-20, Under-21, B, 6 full caps.

2001–02	Arsenal	0	0		
2002–03	Arsenal	0	0		
2003–04	Arsenal	1	0		
2004–05	Arsenal	0	0		
2004–05	*Norwich C*	26	2	**26**	**2**
2005–06	Arsenal	0	0	**1**	**0**
2005–06	Blackburn R	29	3		
2006–07	Blackburn R	36	4		
2007–08	Blackburn R	37	6	**102**	**13**

BERNER, Bruno (M) **184 6**
H: 6 1 W: 12 13 b.Zurich 21-11-77
Honours: Switzerland Youth, Under-20, Under-21, 16 full caps.

1997–98	Grasshoppers	2	0		
1998–99	Grasshoppers	21	0		
1999–2000	Grasshoppers	6	1		
1999–2000	*Oviedo*	1	1	**1**	**1**
2000–01	Grasshoppers	27	1		
2001–02	Grasshoppers	16	0	**72**	**2**
2002–03	Freiburg	31	2		
2003–04	Freiburg	33	1		
2004–05	Freiburg	12	0	**76**	**3**
2005–06	Basle	17	0		
2006–07	Basle	15	0	**32**	**0**
2006–07	Blackburn R	1	0		
2007–08	Blackburn R	2	0	**3**	**0**

BROWN, Jason (G) **127 0**
H: 6 0 W: 15 07 b.Southwark 18-5-82
Source: Charlton Ath Scholar. *Honours:* Wales Youth, Under-21, 2 full caps.

2000–01	Gillingham	0	0		
2001–02	Gillingham	10	0		
2002–03	Gillingham	39	0		
2003–04	Gillingham	22	0		
2004–05	Gillingham	16	0		
2005–06	Gillingham	39	0	**126**	**0**
2006–07	Blackburn R	1	0		
2007–08	Blackburn R	0	0	**1**	**0**

BUSSMANN, Bjorn (G) **0 0**
H: 6 0 W: 12 00 b.Germany 18-3-91
Source: Scholar.

2007–08	Blackburn R	0	0

CLARKE, Jamie (F) **0 0**
H: 5 10 W: 11 11 b.Sunderland 11-9-88
Source: Scholar.

2007–08	Blackburn R	0	0

DE VITA, Raffaele (F) **0 0**
H: 6 0 W: 11 09 b.Rome 23-9-87
Source: Scholar.

2005–06	Blackburn R	0	0
2006–07	Blackburn R	0	0
2007–08	Blackburn R	0	0

DERBYSHIRE, Matt (F) **74 18**
H: 5 10 W: 11 01 b.Gt Harwood 14-4-86
Source: Gt Harwood T. *Honours:* England Under-21.

2003–04	Blackburn R	0	0		
2004–05	Blackburn R	1	0		
2005–06	Blackburn R	0	0		
2005–06	*Plymouth Arg*	12	0	**12**	**0**
2005–06	*Wrexham*	16	10	**16**	**10**
2006–07	Blackburn R	22	5		
2007–08	Blackburn R	23	3	**46**	**8**

DORAN, Aaron (M) **0 0**
b.Ireland 13-5-91
Source: Scholar.

2007–08	Blackburn R	0	0

DUNN, David (M) **236 38**
H: 5 9 W: 12 03 b.Gt Harwood 27-12-79
Source: Trainee. *Honours:* England Youth, Under-21, 1 full cap.

1997–98	Blackburn R	0	0		
1998–99	Blackburn R	15	1		
1999–2000	Blackburn R	22	2		
2000–01	Blackburn R	42	12		
2001–02	Blackburn R	29	7		
2002–03	Blackburn R	28	8		
2003–04	Birmingham C	21	2		
2004–05	Birmingham C	11	2		
2005–06	Birmingham C	15	2		
2006–07	Birmingham C	11	1	**58**	**7**
2006–07	Blackburn R	11	0		
2007–08	Blackburn R	31	1	**178**	**31**

EMERTON, Brett (M) **357 35**
H: 6 1 W: 13 05 b.Bankstown 22-2-79
Honours: Australia Youth, Under-20, Under-23, 64 full caps, 12 goals.

1996–97	Sydney Olympic	18	2		
1997–98	Sydney Olympic	24	3		
1998–99	Sydney Olympic	21	2		
1999–2000	Sydney Olympic	31	9	**94**	**16**
2000–01	Feyenoord	28	2		
2001–02	Feyenoord	31	6		
2002–03	Feyenoord	33	3	**92**	**11**
2003–04	Blackburn R	37	2		
2004–05	Blackburn R	37	4		
2005–06	Blackburn R	30	1		
2006–07	Blackburn R	34	0		
2007–08	Blackburn R	33	1	**171**	**8**

ENCKELMAN, Peter (G) **149 0**
H: 6 2 W: 12 05 b.Turku 10-3-77
Source: TPS Turku. *Honours:* Finland Under-21, 11 full caps.

1995	TPS Turku	6	0		
1996	TPS Turku	24	0		
1997	TPS Turku	25	0		
1998	TPS Turku	24	0	**79**	**0**
1998–99	Aston Villa	0	0		
1999–2000	Aston Villa	10	0		
2000–01	Aston Villa	0	0		
2001–02	Aston Villa	9	0		
2002–03	Aston Villa	33	0		
2003–04	Aston Villa	0	0	**52**	**0**
2003–04	Blackburn R	2	0		
2004–05	Blackburn R	0	0		
2005–06	Blackburn R	0	0		
2006–07	Blackburn R	0	0		
2007–08	Blackburn R	0	0	**2**	**0**
2007–08	*Cardiff C*	16	0	**16**	**0**

FIELDING, Frank (G) **36 0**
H: 5 11 W: 12 00 b.Blackburn 4-4-88
Source: Scholar. *Honours:* England Youth.

2006–07	Blackburn R	0	0		
2007–08	Blackburn R	0	0		
2007–08	*Wycombe W*	36	0	**36**	**0**

FLYNN, Jonathan (D) **0 0**
H: 5 10 W: 11 00 b.Ballymena 18-11-89
Source: Ballymena U.

2007–08	Blackburn R	0	0

FRIEDEL, Brad (G) **351 1**
H: 6 3 W: 14 00 b.Lakewood 18-5-71
Honours: USA 82 full caps.

1996	Columbus Crew	9	0		
1997	Columbus Crew	29	0	**38**	**0**
1997–98	Liverpool	11	0		
1998–99	Liverpool	12	0		
1999–2000	Liverpool	2	0		
2000–01	Liverpool	0	0	**25**	**0**
2000–01	Blackburn R	27	0		
2001–02	Blackburn R	36	0		
2002–03	Blackburn R	37	0		
2003–04	Blackburn R	36	1		
2004–05	Blackburn R	38	0		
2005–06	Blackburn R	38	0		
2006–07	Blackburn R	38	0		
2007–08	Blackburn R	38	0	**288**	**1**

GALLAGHER, Paul (F) **123 18**
H: 6 1 W: 11 00 b.Glasgow 9-8-84
Source: Trainee. *Honours:* Scotland Under-21, B, 1 full cap.

2002–03	Blackburn R	1	0		
2003–04	Blackburn R	26	3		
2004–05	Blackburn R	16	2		
2005–06	Blackburn R	1	0		
2005–06	*Stoke C*	37	11		
2006–07	Blackburn R	16	1		
2007–08	Blackburn R	0	0	**60**	**6**
2007–08	*Preston NE*	19	1	**19**	**1**
2007–08	*Stoke C*	7	0	**44**	**11**

GRIFFITHS, Rostyn (M) **0 0**
H: 6 2 W: 12 08 b.Stoke 10-3-88
Source: Scholar.

2005–06	Blackburn R	0	0
2006–07	Blackburn R	0	0
2007–08	Blackburn R	0	0

GUNNING, Gavin (D) **0 0**
b.Dublin 26-1-91

2007–08	Blackburn R	0	0

HAWORTH, Andrew (M) **0 0**
b.Lancaster 28-11-88
Source: Scholar.

2007–08	Blackburn R	0	0

HENCHOZ, Stephane (D) **389 3**
H: 6 1 W: 12 08 b.Billens 7-9-74
Source: Bulle. *Honours:* Switzerland Youth, Under-21, 72 full caps.

1992–93	Neuchatel Xamax	35	0		
1993–94	Neuchatel Xamax	21	1		
1994–95	Neuchatel Xamax	35	0	**91**	**1**
1995–96	Hamburg	31	2		
1996–97	Hamburg	18	0	**49**	**2**
1997–98	Blackburn R	36	0		
1998–99	Blackburn R	34	0		
1999–2000	Liverpool	29	0		
2000–01	Liverpool	32	0		
2001–02	Liverpool	37	0		
2002–03	Liverpool	19	0		
2003–04	Liverpool	18	0	**135**	**0**
2004–05	*Celtic*	6	0	**6**	**0**
2005–06	Wigan Ath	26	0		
2006–07	Wigan Ath	0	0	**26**	**0**

2006–07 Blackburn R 12 0
2007–08 Blackburn R 0 0 **82 0**

HODGE, Bryan (M) 26 0
H: 5 11 W: 11 07 b.Hamilton 23-9-87
Source: Scholar.
2004–05 Blackburn R 0 0
2005–06 Blackburn R 0 0
2006–07 Blackburn R 0 0
2006–07 *Mansfield T* 9 0 **9 0**
2007–08 Blackburn R 0 0
2007–08 *Millwall* 10 0 **10 0**
2007–08 *Darlington* 7 0 **7 0**

JONES, Zak (G) 0 0
H: 5 11 W: 12 08 b.Darwen 24-11-88
Source: Scholar. *Honours:* England Youth.
2005–06 Blackburn R 0 0
2006–07 Blackburn R 0 0
2007–08 Blackburn R 0 0
2007–08 *Stockport Co* 0 0

JUDGE, Alan (F) 0 0
b.Dublin 11-11-88
2006–07 Blackburn R 0 0
2007–08 Blackburn R 0 0

KANE, Tony (D) 4 0
H: 5 11 W: 11 00 b.Belfast 29-8-87
Source: Scholar. *Honours:* Eire Under-21, Northern Ireland Youth, Under-21.
2004–05 Blackburn R 0 0
2005–06 Blackburn R 0 0
2006–07 Blackburn R 0 0
2006–07 *Stockport Co* 4 0 **4 0**
2007–08 Blackburn R 0 0

KAVANAGH, Conor (D) 0 0
b.Limerick 8-1-90
2007–08 Blackburn R 0 0

KEITA, Mamadi (M) 0 0
b. 14-11-89
2006–07 Blackburn R 0 0
2007–08 Blackburn R 0 0

KHIZANISHVILI, Zurab (D) 186 6
H: 6 1 W: 12 08 b.Tbilisi 6-10-81
Honours: Georgia 51 full caps.
1998–99 Dynamo Tbilisi B 17 3 **17 3**
1998–99 Dynamo Tbilisi 2 1 **2 1**
1999–2000 Tbilisi 9 0 **9 0**
1999–2000 Lokomotivi 5 1
2000–01 Lokomotivi 11 0 **16 1**
2000–01 Dundee 6 0
2001–02 Dundee 18 0
2002–03 Dundee 19 0 **43 0**
2003–04 Rangers 26 0
2004–05 Rangers 16 0
2005–06 Rangers 0 0 **42 0**
2005–06 *Blackburn R* 26 1
2006–07 Blackburn R 18 0
2007–08 Blackburn R 13 0 **57 1**

MARROW, Alex (M) 0 0
b. 21-1-90
2007–08 Blackburn R 0 0

MARSHALL, Marcus (F) 0 0
b.Hammersmith 7-10-89
2007–08 Blackburn R 0 0

McCARTHY, Benni (F) 311 145
H: 6 0 W: 12 08 b.Ciudad de Cabo 11-12-77
Honours: South Africa 70 caps, 30 goals.
1995–96 Seven Stars 29 27
1996–97 Seven Stars 20 12 **49 39**
1997–98 Cape Town Spurs 7 4 **7 4**
1997–98 Ajax 17 9
1998–99 Ajax 19 11 **36 20**
1999–2000 Celta Vigo 31 8
2000–01 Celta Vigo 19 0
2001–02 Celta Vigo 2 0
2001–02 Porto 11 12
2002–03 Celta Vigo 14 2 **66 10**
2003–04 Porto 29 20
2004–05 Porto 23 11
2005–06 Porto 23 3 **86 46**
2006–07 Blackburn R 36 18
2007–08 Blackburn R 31 8 **67 26**

MOKOENA, Aaron (D) 149 2
H: 6 2 W: 14 00 b.Johannesburg 25-11-80
Honours: South Africa 57 full caps, 1 goal.
2000–01 Ajax 0 0
2000–01 Antwerp 6 0
2001–02 Antwerp 13 1
2002–03 Antwerp 29 1 **48 2**
2003–04 Genk 18 0 **18 0**
2004–05 Blackburn R 16 0
2005–06 Blackburn R 22 0
2006–07 Blackburn R 27 0
2007–08 Blackburn R 18 0 **83 0**

NELSEN, Ryan (D) 161 7
H: 5 11 W: 14 02 b.Christchurch, NZ 18-10-77
Honours: New Zealand Under-23, 34 full caps, 7 goals.
2001 DC United 19 0
2002 DC United 20 4
2003 DC United 25 1
2004 DC United 17 2 **81 7**
2004–05 Blackburn R 15 0
2005–06 Blackburn R 31 0
2006–07 Blackburn R 12 0
2007–08 Blackburn R 22 0 **80 0**

NIELSEN, Gunnar (G) 0 0
H: 6 3 W: 14 00 b.Faeroes 7-10-86
Source: Frem. *Honours:* Faeroes Under-21.
2007–08 Blackburn R 0 0

NOLAN, Eddie (D) 15 0
H: 6 0 W: 13 05 b.Waterford 5-8-88
Source: Scholar. *Honours:* Eire Under-21.
2005–06 Blackburn R 0 0
2006–07 Blackburn R 0 0
2006–07 *Stockport Co* 4 0 **4 0**
2007–08 Blackburn R 0 0
2007–08 *Hartlepool U* 11 0 **11 0**

O'KEEFE, Josh (M) 0 0
H: 6 1 W: 11 05 b.Whalley 22-12-88
Source: Scholar.
2005–06 Blackburn R 0 0
2006–07 Blackburn R 0 0
2007–08 Blackburn R 0 0

OLSSON, Martin (D) 2 0
H: 5 7 W: 12 12 b.Sweden 17-5-88
Source: Hogaborg. *Honours:* Sweden Under-21.
2005–06 Blackburn R 0 0
2006–07 Blackburn R 0 0
2007–08 Blackburn R 2 0 **2 0**

OOIJER, Andre (D) 346 32
H: 6 0 W: 11 13 b.Amsterdam 11-7-74
Source: SDW, SDZ, Ajax.Holland 40 full caps, 2 goals.
1994–95 Volendam 32 4 **32 4**
1995–96 Roda JC 23 1
1996–97 Roda JC 33 2
1997–98 Roda JC 19 6 **75 9**
1997–98 PSV Eindhoven 12 2
1998–99 PSV Eindhoven 21 2
1999–2000 PSV Eindhoven 18 1
2000–01 PSV Eindhoven 20 2
2001–02 PSV Eindhoven 26 5
2002–03 PSV Eindhoven 32 3
2003–04 PSV Eindhoven 15 2
2004–05 PSV Eindhoven 24 2
2005–06 PSV Eindhoven 24 0 **192 19**
2006–07 Blackburn R 20 0
2007–08 Blackburn R 27 0 **47 0**

PEDERSEN, Morten (F) 289 68
H: 5 11 W: 11 00 b.Vadso 8-9-81
Honours: Norway Youth, Under-21, 40 full caps, 8 goals.
2004 Tromso 18 7
1997 Norlid 21 0
1998 Pola 20 4 **20 4**
1999 Norlid 19 0 **40 0**
2000 Tromso 10 3
2001 Tromso 26 5
2002 Tromso 23 18
2003 Tromso 26 8 **103 41**
2004–05 Blackburn R 19 4
2005–06 Blackburn R 34 9
2006–07 Blackburn R 36 6
2007–08 Blackburn R 37 4 **126 23**

PETER, Sergio (M) 17 0
H: 5 8 W: 11 00 b.Ludwigshafen 12-10-86
Source: Scholar. *Honours:* Germany Youth, Under-21.
2004–05 Blackburn R 0 0
2005–06 Blackburn R 8 0
2006–07 Blackburn R 9 0
2007–08 Blackburn R 0 0 **17 0**

PEZZONI, Kevin (D) 0 0
b. 22-3-89
2006–07 Blackburn R 0 0
2007–08 Blackburn R 0 0

REID, Steven (M) 244 24
H: 6 0 W: 12 07 b.Kingston 10-3-81
Source: Trainee. *Honours:* England Youth. Eire Under-21, 22 full caps, 2 goals.
1997–98 Millwall 1 0
1998–99 Millwall 25 0
1999–2000 Millwall 21 0
2000–01 Millwall 37 7
2001–02 Millwall 35 5
2002–03 Millwall 20 6 **139 18**
2003–04 Blackburn R 16 0
2004–05 Blackburn R 28 2
2005–06 Blackburn R 34 4
2006–07 Blackburn R 3 0
2007–08 Blackburn R 24 0 **105 6**

RIGTERS, Maceo (F) 60 5
H: 5 10 W: 14 07 b.Amsterdam 22-1-84
Honours: Holland Under-21.
2005–06 NAC Breda 24 2
2006–07 NAC Breda 32 3 **56 5**
2007–08 Blackburn R 2 0 **2 0**
2007–08 *Norwich C* 2 0 **2 0**

ROBERTS, Jason (F) 331 114
H: 6 0 W: 14 01 b.Park Royal 25-1-78
Source: Hayes. *Honours:* Grenada 22 full caps, 12 goals.
1997–98 Wolverhampton W 0 0
1997–98 *Torquay U* 14 6 **14 6**
1997–98 *Bristol C* 3 1 **3 1**
1998–99 Bristol R 37 16
1999–2000 Bristol R 41 22 **78 38**
2000–01 WBA 43 14
2001–02 WBA 14 7
2002–03 WBA 32 3
2003–04 WBA 0 0 **89 24**
2003–04 *Portsmouth* 10 1 **10 1**
2003–04 Wigan Ath 14 8
2004–05 Wigan Ath 45 21
2005–06 Wigan Ath 34 8 **93 37**
2006–07 Blackburn R 18 4
2007–08 Blackburn R 26 3 **44 7**

SAMBA, Christopher (D) 71 4
H: 6 5 W: 13 03 b.Creteil 28-3-84
Source: Issy-les-Moulineaux, Rouen.Congo 20 full caps.
2001–02 Sedan 1 0
2002–03 Sedan 0 0
2003–04 Sedan 3 0 **4 0**
2004–05 Hertha Berlin 0 0
2005–06 Hertha Berlin 12 0
2006–07 Hertha Berlin 8 0 **20 0**
2006–07 Blackburn R 14 2
2007–08 Blackburn R 33 2 **47 4**

SANTA CRUZ, Roque (F) 200 53
H: 6 2 W: 13 12 b.Asuncion 16-8-81
Honours: Paraguay Under-20, 59 full caps, 18 goals.
1998–99 Olimpia 9 3 **9 3**
1999–2000 Bayern Munich 28 5
2000–01 Bayern Munich 19 5
2001–02 Bayern Munich 22 5
2002–03 Bayern Munich 14 5
2003–04 Bayern Munich 28 5
2004–05 Bayern Munich 4 0
2005–06 Bayern Munich 13 4
2006–07 Bayern Munich 26 2 **154 31**
2007–08 Blackburn R 37 19 **37 19**

TREACY, Keith (M) 4 0
H: 6 0 W: 13 02 b.Dublin 13-9-88
Source: Scholar. *Honours:* Eire Under-21.
2005–06 Blackburn R 0 0
2006–07 Blackburn R 0 0
2006–07 *Stockport Co* 4 0 **4 0**
2007–08 Blackburn R 0 0

TUFFY, Darragh (D) 0 0
b. 28-2-90
2007–08 Blackburn R 0 0

TUGAY, Kerimoglu (M) **521 47**
H: 5 9 W: 11 07 b.Istanbul 24-8-70
Honours: Turkey Youth, Under-21, Under-23, 93 full caps, 2 goals.

1988–89	Galatasaray	16	0		
1989–90	Galatasaray	23	0		
1990–91	Galatasaray	12	0		
1991–92	Galatasaray	26	3		
1992–93	Galatasaray	25	6		
1993–94	Galatasaray	25	12		
1994–95	Galatasaray	23	1		
1995–96	Galatasaray	30	3		
1996–97	Galatasaray	33	4		
1997–98	Galatasaray	30	2		
1998–99	Galatasaray	22	2		
1999–2000	Galatasaray	10	1	**275**	**34**
1999–2000	Rangers	16	1		
2000–01	Rangers	26	3	**42**	**4**
2001–02	Blackburn R	33	3		
2002–03	Blackburn R	37	1		
2003–04	Blackburn R	36	1		
2004–05	Blackburn R	21	0		
2005–06	Blackburn R	27	1		
2006–07	Blackburn R	30	1		
2007–08	Blackburn R	20	2	**204**	**9**

VOGEL, Johann (M) **338 20**
H: 5 10 W: 11 03 b.Geneva 8-3-77
Honours: Switzerland Under-21, 94 full caps, 2 goals.

1992–93	Grasshoppers	3	0		
1993–94	Grasshoppers	4	0		
1994–95	Grasshoppers	23	0		
1995–96	Grasshoppers	24	0		
1996–97	Grasshoppers	28	3		
1997–98	Grasshoppers	24	5		
1998–99	Grasshoppers	27	5	**133**	**13**
1999–2000	PSV Eindhoven	31	2		
2000–01	PSV Eindhoven	30	1		
2001–02	PSV Eindhoven	25	1		
2002–03	PSV Eindhoven	32	1		
2003–04	PSV Eindhoven	24	1		
2004–05	PSV Eindhoven	27	1	**169**	**7**
2005–06	AC Milan	13	0	**13**	**0**
2006–07	Betis	17	0		
2007–08	Betis	0	0	**17**	**0**
2007–08	Blackburn R	6	0	**6**	**0**

WARNOCK, Stephen (D) **146 7**
H: 5 7 W: 11 09 b.Ormskirk 12-12-81
Source: Trainee. *Honours:* England Schools, Youth, 1 full cap.

1998–99	Liverpool	0	0		
1999–2000	Liverpool	0	0		
2000–01	Liverpool	0	0		
2001–02	Liverpool	0	0		
2002–03	Liverpool	0	0		
2002–03	*Bradford C*	12	1	**12**	**1**
2003–04	Liverpool	0	0		
2003–04	*Coventry C*	44	3	**44**	**3**
2004–05	Liverpool	19	0		
2005–06	Liverpool	20	1		
2006–07	Liverpool	1	0	**40**	**1**
2006–07	Blackburn R	13	1		
2007–08	Blackburn R	37	1	**50**	**2**

WINNARD, Dean (D) **0 0**
H: 5 9 W: 10 04 b.Wigan 20-8-89

2006–07	Blackburn R	0	0
2007–08	Blackburn R	0	0

ZENABA, Francis (M) **0 0**
b.DR Congo 3-9-89

2007–08	Blackburn R	0	0

Scholars
Bateson, Jonathan; Brierley, Jack Oliver; Hall, Michael James Angelo; Kennedy, John Nicholas; McCubbin, Martin Kenneth; O'Connor, Callum Anthony; Paterson, Kris Andrew; Ryan, David Patrick; Simpson, Jacob David

BLACKPOOL (8)

BARKER, Shaun (D) **214 12**
H: 6 2 W: 12 08 b.Nottingham 19-9-82
Source: Scholar.

2002–03	Rotherham U	11	0		
2003–04	Rotherham U	36	2		
2004–05	Rotherham U	33	2		
2005–06	Rotherham U	43	3	**123**	**7**
2006–07	Blackpool	45	3		
2007–08	Blackpool	46	2	**91**	**5**

BAYLISS, Ashton (M) **0 0**
Source: Scholar.

2007–08	Blackpool	0	0

BEAN, Marcus (M) **119 5**
H: 5 11 W: 11 06 b.Hammersmith 2-11-84
Source: Scholar.

2002–03	QPR	7	0		
2003–04	QPR	31	1		
2004–05	QPR	20	1		
2004–05	*Swansea C*	8	0		
2005–06	QPR	9	0	**67**	**2**
2005–06	*Swansea C*	9	1	**17**	**1**
2005–06	Blackpool	17	1		
2006–07	Blackpool	6	0		
2007–08	Blackpool	0	0	**23**	**1**
2007–08	*Rotherham U*	12	1	**12**	**1**

BURGESS, Ben (F) **230 72**
H: 6 3 W: 14 04 b.Buxton 9-11-81
Source: Trainee. *Honours:* Eire Youth, Under-21.

1998–99	Blackburn R	0	0		
1999–2000	Blackburn R	2	0		
2000–01	Blackburn R	0	0		
2000–01	Northern Spirit	27	16	**27**	**16**
2001–02	Blackburn R	0	0	**2**	**0**
2001–02	*Brentford*	43	17	**43**	**17**
2002–03	Stockport Co	19	4	**19**	**4**
2002–03	*Oldham Ath*	7	0	**7**	**0**
2002–03	Hull C	7	4		
2003–04	Hull C	44	18		
2004–05	Hull C	2	0		
2005–06	Hull C	14	2		
2006–07	Hull C	3	0	**70**	**24**
2006–07	Blackpool	27	2		
2007–08	Blackpool	35	9	**62**	**11**

COID, Danny (D) **245 9**
H: 5 11 W: 11 07 b.Liverpool 3-10-81
Source: Trainee.

1998–99	Blackpool	1	0		
1999–2000	Blackpool	21	1		
2000–01	Blackpool	46	1		
2001–02	Blackpool	27	3		
2002–03	Blackpool	36	1		
2003–04	Blackpool	35	3		
2004–05	Blackpool	35	0		
2005–06	Blackpool	13	0		
2006–07	Blackpool	18	0		
2007–08	Blackpool	13	0	**245**	**9**

CRAINEY, Stephen (D) **138 1**
H: 5 9 W: 9 11 b.Glasgow 22-6-81
Honours: Scotland B, Under-21, 6 full caps.

1999–2000	Celtic	9	0		
2000–01	Celtic	2	0		
2001–02	Celtic	15	0		
2002–03	Celtic	13	0		
2003–04	Celtic	2	0	**41**	**0**
2003–04	Southampton	5	0	**5**	**0**
2004–05	Leeds U	9	0		
2005–06	Leeds U	24	0		
2006–07	Leeds U	19	0	**52**	**0**
2007–08	Blackpool	40	1	**40**	**1**

D'AGOSTINO, Michael (M) **25 0**
H: 5 9 W: 11 08 b.Vancouver 7-1-87
Source: Kentucky Wildcats, Whitecaps. *Honours:* Canada Youth.

2007–08	Blackpool	0	0		
2007–08	*Cheltenham T*	25	0	**25**	**0**

DOUGHTY, Phil (D) **9 0**
H: 6 2 W: 13 02 b.Kirkham 6-9-86
Source: Scholar.

2003–04	Blackpool	0	0		
2004–05	Blackpool	0	0		
2005–06	Blackpool	0	0		
2006–07	Blackpool	0	0		
2007–08	Blackpool	0	0		
2007–08	*Macclesfield T*	6	0	**6**	**0**
2007–08	*Accrington S*	3	0	**3**	**0**

EDGE, Lewis (G) **4 0**
H: 6 1 W: 12 10 b.Lancaster 12-1-87
Source: Scholar.

2003–04	Blackpool	1	0		
2004–05	Blackpool	0	0		
2005–06	Blackpool	1	0		
2006–07	Blackpool	1	0		
2006–07	*Bury*	1	0	**1**	**0**
2007–08	Blackpool	0	0	**3**	**0**

EVATT, Ian (D) **229 9**
H: 6 3 W: 13 12 b.Coventry 19-11-81
Source: Trainee.

1998–99	Derby Co	0	0		
1999–2000	Derby Co	0	0		
2000–01	Derby Co	1	0		
2001–02	*Northampton T*	11	0	**11**	**0**
2001–02	Derby Co	3	0		
2002–03	Derby Co	30	0	**34**	**0**
2003–04	Chesterfield	43	5		
2004–05	Chesterfield	41	4	**84**	**9**
2005–06	QPR	27	0		
2006–07	QPR	0	0	**27**	**0**
2006–07	Blackpool	44	0		
2007–08	Blackpool	29	0	**73**	**0**

FLYNN, Michael (M) **169 24**
H: 5 10 W: 13 04 b.Newport 17-10-80
Source: Barry T.

2002–03	Wigan Ath	17	1		
2003–04	Wigan Ath	8	0		
2004–05	Wigan Ath	13	1	**38**	**2**
2004–05	*Blackpool*	6	0		
2004–05	Gillingham	16	3		
2005–06	Gillingham	36	6		
2006–07	Gillingham	45	10	**97**	**19**
2007–08	Blackpool	28	3	**34**	**3**

FOX, David (M) **76 7**
H: 5 9 W: 11 08 b.Leek 13-12-83
Source: Scholar. *Honours:* England Youth, Under-20.

2000–01	Manchester U	0	0		
2001–02	Manchester U	0	0		
2002–03	Manchester U	0	0		
2003–04	Manchester U	0	0		
2004–05	Manchester U	0	0		
2004–05	*Shrewsbury T*	4	1	**4**	**1**
2005–06	Manchester U	0	0		
2005–06	Blackpool	7	1		
2006–07	Blackpool	37	4		
2007–08	Blackpool	28	1	**72**	**6**

GORKSS, Kaspars (D) **161 11**
H: 6 3 W: 13 05 b.Riga 6-11-81
Honours: Latvia 15 full caps, 1 goal.

2002	Auda Riga	28	0	**28**	**0**
2003	Oster	8	0		
2004	Oster	24	1	**32**	**1**
2005	Assyriska	23	0	**23**	**0**
2006	Ventspils	28	5	**28**	**5**
2006–07	Blackpool	10	0		
2007–08	Blackpool	40	5	**50**	**5**

GREEN, Stuart (M) **193 33**
H: 5 10 W: 11 01 b.Whitehaven 15-6-81
Source: Trainee.

1999–2000	Newcastle U	0	0		
2000–01	Newcastle U	0	0		
2001–02	Newcastle U	0	0		
2001–02	*Carlisle U*	16	3		
2002–03	Newcastle U	0	0		
2002–03	Hull C	28	6		
2002–03	*Carlisle U*	10	2	**26**	**5**
2003–04	Hull C	42	6		
2004–05	Hull C	29	8		
2005–06	Hull C	38	4		
2006–07	Hull C	0	0	**137**	**24**
2006–07	Crystal Palace	14	2		
2007–08	Crystal Palace	10	2	**24**	**4**
2007–08	Blackpool	6	0	**6**	**0**

HILLS, John (D) **282 19**
H: 5 9 W: 12 08 b.St Annes-on-Sea 21-4-78
Source: Trainee.

1995–96	Blackpool	0	0		
1995–96	Everton	0	0		
1996–97	Everton	3	0		
1996–97	*Swansea C*	11	0		
1997–98	Everton	0	0	**3**	**0**
1997–98	*Swansea C*	7	1	**18**	**1**
1997–98	Blackpool	19	1		
1998–99	Blackpool	28	1		
1999–2000	Blackpool	33	2		
2000–01	Blackpool	18	2		
2001–02	Blackpool	37	5		
2002–03	Blackpool	27	5		
2003–04	Gillingham	29	2		
2004–05	Gillingham	23	0	**52**	**2**
2005–06	Sheffield W	27	0		

2006–07 Sheffield W 16 0 **43 0**
2007–08 Blackpool 4 0 **166 16**

HOOLAHAN, Wes (M) 206 22
H: 5 6 W: 10 03 b.Dublin 10-8-83
Honours: Eire Under-21, 1 full cap.
2001–02 Shelbourne 20 3
2002–03 Shelbourne 23 0
2004 Shelbourne 31 2
2005 Shelbourne 29 4 **103 9**
2005–06 Livingston 16 0 **16 0**
2006–07 Blackpool 42 8
2007–08 Blackpool 45 5 **87 13**

JACKSON, Mike (D) 533 35
H: 6 0 W: 13 08 b.Runcorn 4-12-73
Source: Trainee.
1991–92 Crewe Alex 1 0
1992–93 Crewe Alex 4 0 **5 0**
1993–94 Bury 39 0
1994–95 Bury 24 2
1995–96 Bury 31 4
1996–97 Bury 31 3 **125 9**
1996–97 Preston NE 7 0
1997–98 Preston NE 40 2
1998–99 Preston NE 44 8
1999–2000 Preston NE 46 5
2000–01 Preston NE 30 1
2001–02 Preston NE 13 0
2002–03 Preston NE 22 1
2002–03 *Tranmere R* 6 0
2003–04 Preston NE 43 0 **245 17**
2004–05 Tranmere R 43 5
2005–06 Tranmere R 41 3 **90 8**
2006–07 Blackpool 43 1
2007–08 Blackpool 25 0 **68 1**

JORGENSEN, Claus (M) 274 38
H: 5 10 W: 10 06 b.Holstebro 27-4-76
Source: Resen-Humlum, Struer BK, Holstebro, Aarhus, AC Horsens. *Honours:* Faeroes 10 full caps, 1 goal.
1999–2000 Bournemouth 44 6
2000–01 Bournemouth 43 8
2001–02 Bradford C 18 1
2002–03 Bradford C 32 11 **50 12**
2003–04 Coventry C 8 0
2003–04 *Bournemouth* 17 0 **104 14**
2004–05 Coventry C 17 3
2005–06 Coventry C 27 3 **52 6**
2006–07 Blackpool 31 2
2007–08 Blackpool 37 4 **68 6**

KAY, Matty (M) 1 0
H: 5 9 W: 11 00 b.Blackpool 12-10-89
2005–06 Blackpool 1 0
2006–07 Blackpool 0 0
2007–08 Blackpool 0 0 **1 0**

LAWLOR, Matthew (M) 0 0
H: 5 11 W: 12 00 b.Kirkham 20-8-88
2006–07 Blackpool 0 0
2007–08 Blackpool 0 0

MARSH, Phil (F) 0 0
H: 5 10 W: 11 13 b.St Helens 15-11-86
Source: Scholar.
2006–07 Manchester U 0 0
2007–08 Blackpool 0 0

McPHEE, Stephen (F) 215 50
H: 5 7 W: 10 08 b.Glasgow 5-6-81
Honours: Scotland Under-21.
1998–99 Coventry C 0 0
1999–2000 Coventry C 0 0
2000–01 Coventry C 0 0
2001–02 Port Vale 44 11
2002–03 Port Vale 40 3
2003–04 Port Vale 46 25 **130 39**
2004–05 Beira Mar 31 5 **31 5**
2005–06 Hull C 4 0
2006–07 Hull C 12 0
2007–08 Hull C 19 2 **35 2**
2007–08 Blackpool 19 4 **19 4**

MITCHLEY, Daniel (M) 0 0
Source: Scholar.
2007–08 Blackpool 0 0

MORRELL, Andy (F) 286 78
H: 5 11 W: 12 00 b.Doncaster 28-9-74
Source: Newcastle Blue Star.
1998–99 Wrexham 7 0
1999–2000 Wrexham 13 1
2000–01 Wrexham 20 3
2001–02 Wrexham 25 2
2002–03 Wrexham 45 34 **110 40**
2003–04 Coventry C 30 9
2004–05 Coventry C 34 6
2005–06 Coventry C 34 2
2006–07 Coventry C 0 0 **98 17**
2006–07 Blackpool 40 16
2007–08 Blackpool 38 5 **78 21**

PARKER, Keigan (F) 273 55
H: 5 7 W: 10 05 b.Livingston 8-6-82
Source: St Johnstone BC. *Honours:* Scotland Youth, Under-21.
1998–99 St Johnstone 2 0
1999–2000 St Johnstone 10 2
2000–01 St Johnstone 37 9
2001–02 St Johnstone 21 1
2002–03 St Johnstone 31 1
2003–04 St Johnstone 31 8 **132 21**
2004–05 Blackpool 35 9
2005–06 Blackpool 40 12
2006–07 Blackpool 45 13
2007–08 Blackpool 21 0 **141 34**

RACHUBKA, Paul (G) 165 0
H: 6 1 W: 13 05 b.San Luis Opispo 21-5-81
Source: Trainee. *Honours:* England Youth, Under-20.
1999–2000 Manchester U 0 0
2000–01 Manchester U 1 0
2001–02 Manchester U 0 0 **1 0**
2001–02 *Oldham Ath* 16 0 **16 0**
2001–02 Charlton Ath 0 0
2002–03 Charlton Ath 0 0
2003–04 Charlton Ath 0 0
2003–04 *Huddersfield T* 13 0
2004–05 Charlton Ath 0 0
2004–05 *Milton Keynes D* 4 0 **4 0**
2004–05 *Northampton T* 10 0 **10 0**
2004–05 Huddersfield T 29 0
2005–06 Huddersfield T 34 0
2006–07 Huddersfield T 0 0 **76 0**
2006–07 *Peterborough U* 4 0 **4 0**
2006–07 *Blackpool* 8 0
2007–08 Blackpool 46 0 **54 0**

SOUTHERN, Keith (M) 204 19
H: 5 10 W: 12 06 b.Gateshead 24-4-81
Source: Trainee.
1998–99 Everton 0 0
1999–2000 Everton 0 0
2000–01 Everton 0 0
2001–02 Everton 0 0
2002–03 Everton 0 0
2002–03 Blackpool 38 1
2003–04 Blackpool 28 2
2004–05 Blackpool 27 6
2005–06 Blackpool 42 2
2006–07 Blackpool 39 5
2007–08 Blackpool 30 3 **204 19**

STEINBORS, Pavels (G) 0 0
H: 6 2 W: 13 00 b.Latvia 21-9-85
Source: FK Jurmala.
2007–08 Blackpool 0 0

TAYLOR-FLETCHER, Gary (F) 230 55
H: 6 0 W: 11 00 b.Liverpool 4-6-81
Source: Northwich Vic. *Honours:* England Schools.
2000–01 Hull C 5 0 **5 0**
2001–02 Leyton Orient 9 0
2002–03 Leyton Orient 12 1 **21 1**
2003–04 Lincoln C 42 16
2004–05 Lincoln C 38 11 **80 27**
2005–06 Huddersfield T 43 10
2006–07 Huddersfield T 39 11 **82 21**
2007–08 Blackpool 42 6 **42 6**

TIERNEY, Paul (D) 92 1
H: 5 10 W: 12 05 b.Salford 15-9-82
Source: Scholar. *Honours:* Eire Under-21.
2000–01 Manchester U 0 0
2000–01 Manchester U 0 0
2001–02 Manchester U 0 0
2002–03 Manchester U 0 0
2002–03 *Crewe Alex* 17 1 **17 1**
2003–04 Manchester U 0 0
2003–04 *Colchester U* 2 0 **2 0**
2004–05 Manchester U 0 0
2004–05 *Bradford C* 16 0 **16 0**
2005–06 Livingston 31 0 **31 0**
2006–07 Blackpool 10 0
2007–08 Blackpool 0 0 **10 0**
2007–08 *Stockport Co* 16 0 **16 0**

WELSH, Andy (M) 160 8
H: 5 8 W: 10 03 b.Manchester 24-11-83
Source: Scholar. *Honours:* Scotland Youth.
2001–02 Stockport Co 15 0
2002–03 Stockport Co 13 2
2002–03 *Macclesfield T* 6 2 **6 2**
2003–04 Stockport Co 34 1
2004–05 Stockport Co 13 0 **75 3**
2004–05 Sunderland 7 1
2005–06 Sunderland 14 0
2005–06 *Leicester C* 10 1
2006–07 Sunderland 0 0 **21 1**
2006–07 *Leicester C* 7 0 **17 1**
2007 Toronto Lynx 20 1 **20 1**
2007–08 Blackpool 21 0 **21 0**

WILES, Simon (F) 55 3
H: 5 11 W: 11 04 b.Preston 22-4-85
Source: Scholar.
2003–04 Blackpool 4 0
2004–05 Blackpool 0 0
2005–06 Blackpool 27 3
2006–07 Blackpool 0 0
2006–07 *Macclesfield T* 7 0
2007–08 Blackpool 0 0 **31 3**
2007–08 *Macclesfield T* 17 0 **24 0**

BOLTON W (9)

AL-HABSI, Ali (G) 72 0
H: 6 4 W: 12 06 b.Oman 30-12-81
Source: Al-Nasser, Al-Mudhaibi. *Honours:* Oman 66 full caps.
2003 Lyn 13 0
2004 Lyn 24 0
2005 Lyn 25 0 **62 0**
2005–06 Bolton W 0 0
2006–07 Bolton W 0 0
2007–08 Bolton W 10 0 **10 0**

ALONSO, Mikel (M) 154 4
H: 5 10 W: 11 12 b.Tolosa 16-5-80
2000–01 Real Sociedad 1 0
2001–02 Real Sociedad B 34 2
2001–02 Real Sociedad 1 0
2002–03 Real Sociedad 9 1
2003–04 Real Sociedad 2 0
2003–04 *Numancia* 10 1 **10 1**
2004–05 Real Sociedad 35 0
2005–06 Real Sociedad 37 0
2006–07 Real Sociedad 18 0 **103 1**
2007–08 Bolton W 7 0 **7 0**

AUGUSTYN, Blazej (M) 0 0
H: 6 3 W: 13 00 b.Strzelin 26-1-88
Source: Scholar. *Honours:* Poland Youth.
2006–07 Bolton W 0 0
2007–08 Bolton W 0 0

BASHAM, Chris (M) 13 0
H: 5 11 W: 12 08 b.Stafford 20-7-88
Source: Scholar.
2007–08 Bolton W 0 0
2007–08 *Rochdale* 13 0 **13 0**

BOGDAN, Adam (G) 0 0
H: 6 4 W: 14 02 b.Budapest 27-9-87
Source: Vasas.
2007–08 Bolton W 0 0

BRAATEN, Daniel Omoya (F) 169 35
H: 6 0 W: 13 05 b.Oslo 25-2-82
Honours: Norway 16 full caps, 2 goals.
2000 Skeid 12 0
2001 Skeid 28 3
2002 Skeid 25 4
2003 Skeid 21 6
2004 Skeid 14 9 **100 22**
2004 Rosenborg 10 5
2005 Rosenborg 19 2
2006 Rosenborg 19 3
2007 Rosenborg 15 2 **63 12**
2007–08 Bolton W 6 1 **6 1**

BURNS, Michael (D) 0 0
b.Huyton 4-10-88
Source: Liverpool Scholar.
2007–08 Bolton W 0 0

CAHILL, Gary (D) **84 4**
H: 6 2 W: 12 06 b.Dronfield 19-12-85
Source: Trainee. *Honours:* England Youth, Under-20, Under-21.

2003–04	Aston Villa	0	0		
2004–05	Aston Villa	0	0		
2004–05	*Burnley*	27	1	**27**	**1**
2005–06	Aston Villa	7	1		
2006–07	Aston Villa	20	0		
2007–08	Aston Villa	1	0	**28**	**1**
2007–08	*Sheffield U*	16	2	**16**	**2**
2007–08	Bolton W	13	0	**13**	**0**

CAMPO, Ivan (M) **341 20**
H: 6 1 W: 12 10 b.San Sebastian 21-2-74
Honours: Spain 4 full caps.

1993–94	Alaves	11	1		
1994–95	Alaves	23	1		
1995–96	Alaves	11	0	**45**	**2**
1995–96	Valladolid	24	2	**24**	**2**
1996–97	Valencia	7	1	**7**	**1**
1997–98	Mallorca	33	1	**33**	**1**
1998–99	Real Madrid	27	1		
1999–2000	Real Madrid	20	0		
2000–01	Real Madrid	10	0		
2001–02	Real Madrid	3	0	**60**	**1**
2002–03	Bolton W	31	2		
2003–04	Bolton W	38	4		
2004–05	Bolton W	27	0		
2005–06	Bolton W	15	2		
2006–07	Bolton W	34	4		
2007–08	Bolton W	27	1	**172**	**13**

CASSIDY, Matthew (M) **0 0**
H: 6 0 W: 12 00 b.Blackburn 12-7-87

2007–08	Bolton W	0	0

CID, Gerald (D) **50 2**
H: 6 2 W: 11 07 b.Talence 17-2-83

2003–04	Bordeaux	1	0		
2004–05	Bordeaux	8	1		
2005–06	Istres	24	0	**24**	**0**
2006–07	Bordeaux	10	1	**19**	**2**
2007–08	Bolton W	7	0	**7**	**0**

To Nice January 2008.

COHEN, Tamir (M) **109 6**
H: 5 11 W: 11 09 b.Israel 4-3-84
Honours: Israel 6 full caps.

2002–03	Maccabi Tel Aviv	13	0		
2003–04	Maccabi Tel Aviv	30	2		
2004–05	Maccabi Tel Aviv	22	2		
2005–06	Maccabi Tel Aviv	16	0		
2006–07	Maccabi Tel Aviv	3	0	**84**	**4**
2006–07	Maccabi Netanya	15	1	**15**	**1**
2007–08	Bolton W	10	1	**10**	**1**

DAVIES, Kevin (F) **440 80**
H: 6 0 W: 12 10 b.Sheffield 26-3-77
Source: Trainee. *Honours:* England Youth, Under-21.

1993–94	Chesterfield	24	4		
1994–95	Chesterfield	41	11		
1995–96	Chesterfield	30	4		
1996–97	Chesterfield	34	3	**129**	**22**
1996–97	Southampton	0	0		
1997–98	Southampton	25	9		
1998–99	Blackburn R	21	1		
1999–2000	Blackburn R	2	0	**23**	**1**
1999–2000	Southampton	23	6		
2000–01	Southampton	27	1		
2001–02	Southampton	23	2		
2002–03	Southampton	9	1	**107**	**19**
2002–03	*Millwall*	9	3	**9**	**3**
2003–04	Bolton W	38	9		
2004–05	Bolton W	35	8		
2005–06	Bolton W	37	7		
2006–07	Bolton W	30	8		
2007–08	Bolton W	32	3	**172**	**35**

DIOUF, El Hadji (F) **266 43**
H: 5 11 W: 11 11 b.Dakar 15-1-81
Honours: Senegal 41 full caps, 16 goals.

1998–99	Sochaux	15	0	**15**	**0**
1999–2000	Rennes	28	1	**28**	**1**
2000–01	Lens	28	8		
2001–02	Lens	26	10	**54**	**18**
2002–03	Liverpool	29	3		
2003–04	Liverpool	26	0		
2004–05	Liverpool	0	0	**55**	**3**
2004–05	*Bolton W*	27	9		
2005–06	Bolton W	20	3		
2006–07	Bolton W	33	5		
2007–08	Bolton W	34	4	**114**	**21**

DZEMAILI, Blerim (M) **108 9**
H: 5 10 W: 11 07 b.Tetovo 12-4-86
Honours: Switzerland 7 full caps.

2003–04	Zurich	30	2		
2004–05	Zurich	23	1		
2005–06	Zurich	34	3		
2006–07	Zurich	21	3	**108**	**9**
2007–08	Bolton W	0	0		

ELLIS, Mark (D) **0 0**
b.Plymouth 30-9-88

2007–08	Bolton W	0	0

FOJUT, Jaroslaw (D) **17 2**
H: 6 2 W: 13 00 b.Legionowo 17-10-87
Source: Scholar. *Honours:* Poland Youth.

2005–06	Bolton W	1	0		
2006–07	Bolton W	0	0		
2007–08	Bolton W	0	0	**1**	**0**
2007–08	*Luton T*	16	2	**16**	**2**

GARDNER, Ricardo (D) **283 15**
H: 5 9 W: 11 00 b.St Andrews 25-9-78
Source: Harbour View. *Honours:* Jamaica 58 full caps, 4 goals.

1998–99	Bolton W	30	2		
1999–2000	Bolton W	29	5		
2000–01	Bolton W	32	3		
2001–02	Bolton W	31	3		
2002–03	Bolton W	32	2		
2003–04	Bolton W	22	0		
2004–05	Bolton W	33	0		
2005–06	Bolton W	30	0		
2006–07	Bolton W	18	0		
2007–08	Bolton W	26	0	**283**	**15**

GIANNAKOPOULOS, Stelios (M) **443 116**
H: 5 8 W: 11 00 b.Athens 12-7-74
Honours: Greece 76 full caps, 12 goals.

1992–93	Ethnikos	32	6	**32**	**6**
1993–94	Paniliakos	26	9		
1994–95	Paniliakos	31	10		
1995–96	Paniliakos	27	7	**84**	**26**
1996–97	Olympiakos	31	7		
1997–98	Olympiakos	31	3		
1998–99	Olympiakos	23	7		
1999–2000	Olympiakos	29	10		
2000–01	Olympiakos	26	11		
2001–02	Olympiakos	21	11		
2002–03	Olympiakos	29	15	**190**	**64**
2003–04	Bolton W	31	2		
2004–05	Bolton W	34	7		
2005–06	Bolton W	34	9		
2006–07	Bolton W	23	0		
2007–08	Bolton W	15	2	**137**	**20**

HARSANYI, Zoltan (D) **11 1**
H: 6 1 W: 12 00 b.Bratislava 1-6-87
Honours: Slovakia Youth, Under-20.

2006–07	Senec	11	1	**11**	**1**
2006–07	Bolton W	0	0		
2007–08	Bolton W	0	0		

HELGUSON, Heidar (F) **281 87**
H: 5 10 W: 12 09 b.Akureyri 22-8-77
Source: Throttur. *Honours:* Iceland Youth, Under-21, 44 full caps, 6 goals.

1998	Lillestrom	19	2		
1999	Lillestrom	25	16	**44**	**18**
1999–2000	Watford	16	6		
2000–01	Watford	33	8		
2001–02	Watford	34	6		
2002–03	Watford	30	11		
2003–04	Watford	22	8		
2004–05	Watford	39	16	**174**	**55**
2005–06	Fulham	27	8		
2006–07	Fulham	30	4	**57**	**12**
2007–08	Bolton W	6	2	**6**	**2**

HUNT, Nicky (D) **128 1**
H: 6 1 W: 13 07 b.Westhoughton 3-9-83
Source: Scholar. *Honours:* England Under-21.

2000–01	Bolton W	1	0		
2001–02	Bolton W	0	0		
2002–03	Bolton W	0	0		
2003–04	Bolton W	31	1		
2004–05	Bolton W	29	0		
2005–06	Bolton W	20	0		
2006–07	Bolton W	33	0		
2007–08	Bolton W	14	0	**128**	**1**

JAASKELAINEN, Jussi (G) **463 0**
H: 6 3 W: 12 10 b.Vaasa 19-4-75
Honours: Finland Youth, Under-21, 42 full caps.

1992	MP	6	0		
1993	MP	6	0		
1994	MP	26	0		
1995	MP	26	0	**64**	**0**
1996	VPS	27	0		
1997	VPS	27	0	**54**	**0**
1997–98	Bolton W	0	0		
1998–99	Bolton W	34	0		
1999–2000	Bolton W	34	0		
2000–01	Bolton W	27	0		
2001–02	Bolton W	34	0		
2002–03	Bolton W	38	0		
2003–04	Bolton W	38	0		
2004–05	Bolton W	36	0		
2005–06	Bolton W	38	0		
2006–07	Bolton W	38	0		
2007–08	Bolton W	28	0	**345**	**0**

JAMIESON, Scott (D) **0 0**
H: 5 10 W: 12 00 b.Auburn 13-10-88
Source: Scholar.

2007–08	Bolton W	0	0

McCANN, Gavin (M) **268 12**
H: 5 11 W: 11 00 b.Blackpool 10-1-78
Source: Trainee. *Honours:* England 1 full cap.

1995–96	Everton	0	0		
1996–97	Everton	0	0		
1997–98	Everton	11	0		
1998–99	Everton	0	0	**11**	**0**
1998–99	Sunderland	11	0		
1999–2000	Sunderland	24	4		
2000–01	Sunderland	22	3		
2001–02	Sunderland	29	0		
2002–03	Sunderland	30	1	**116**	**8**
2003–04	Aston Villa	28	0		
2004–05	Aston Villa	20	1		
2005–06	Aston Villa	32	1		
2006–07	Aston Villa	30	1	**110**	**3**
2007–08	Bolton W	31	1	**31**	**1**

MEITE, Abdoulaye (D) **176 2**
H: 6 1 W: 12 13 b.Paris 6-10-80
Honours: Ivory Coast 20 full caps.

1998–99	Red Star 93	4	1		
1999–2000	Red Star 93	0	0	**4**	**1**
2000–01	Marseille	1	0		
2001–02	Marseille	10	0		
2002–03	Marseille	28	0		
2003–04	Marseille	30	0		
2004–05	Marseille	34	1		
2005–06	Marseille	13	0	**116**	**1**
2006–07	Bolton W	35	0		
2007–08	Bolton W	21	0	**56**	**0**

NOLAN, Kevin (M) **276 40**
H: 6 0 W: 14 00 b.Liverpool 24-6-82
Source: Scholar. *Honours:* England Youth, Under-20, Under-21.

1999–2000	Bolton W	4	0		
2000–01	Bolton W	31	1		
2001–02	Bolton W	35	8		
2002–03	Bolton W	33	1		
2003–04	Bolton W	37	9		
2004–05	Bolton W	36	4		
2005–06	Bolton W	36	9		
2006–07	Bolton W	31	3		
2007–08	Bolton W	33	5	**276**	**40**

O'BRIEN, Andy (D) **317 9**
H: 6 2 W: 11 13 b.Harrogate 29-6-79
Source: Trainee. *Honours:* England Youth, Under-21, Eire Under-21, 26 full caps, 1 goal.

1996–97	Bradford C	22	2		
1997–98	Bradford C	26	0		
1998–99	Bradford C	31	0		
1999–2000	Bradford C	36	1		
2000–01	Bradford C	18	0	**133**	**3**
2000–01	Newcastle U	9	1		
2001–02	Newcastle U	34	2		
2002–03	Newcastle U	26	0		
2003–04	Newcastle U	28	1		
2004–05	Newcastle U	23	2	**120**	**6**
2005–06	Portsmouth	29	0		
2006–07	Portsmouth	3	0		
2007–08	Portsmouth	0	0	**32**	**0**
2007–08	Bolton W	32	0	**32**	**0**

O'BRIEN, Joey (M) **58 2**
H: 5 11 W: 10 13 b.Dublin 17-2-86
Source: Scholar. *Honours:* Eire Youth, Under-21, 3 full caps.

2004–05	Bolton W	1	0		
2004–05	*Sheffield W*	15	2	**15**	**2**
2005–06	Bolton W	23	0		
2006–07	Bolton W	0	0		
2007–08	Bolton W	19	0	**43**	**0**

OBADEYI, Temitope (F) **0 0**
b.Birmingham
Source: Coventry C. *Honours:* England Youth.

2006–07	Bolton W	0	0		
2007–08	Bolton W	0	0		

SAMUEL, JLloyd (D) **197 2**
H: 5 11 W: 11 04 b.Trinidad 29-3-81
Source: Charlton Ath Trainee. *Honours:* England Youth, Under-20, Under-21.

1998–99	Aston Villa	0	0		
1999–2000	Aston Villa	9	0		
2000–01	Aston Villa	3	0		
2001–02	*Gillingham*	8	0	**8**	**0**
2001–02	Aston Villa	23	0		
2002–03	Aston Villa	38	0		
2003–04	Aston Villa	38	2		
2004–05	Aston Villa	35	0		
2005–06	Aston Villa	19	0		
2006–07	Aston Villa	4	0	**169**	**2**
2007–08	Bolton W	20	0	**20**	**0**

SINCLAIR, James (F) **2 0**
H: 5 6 W: 10 05 b.Newcastle 22-10-87
Source: Scholar.

2005–06	Bolton W	0	0		
2006–07	Bolton W	2	0		
2007–08	Bolton W	0	0	**2**	**0**

SISSONS, Robert (M) **0 0**
H: 5 8 W: 11 02 b.Stockport 29-9-88
Source: Scholar. *Honours:* England Youth.

2005–06	Bolton W	0	0		
2006–07	Bolton W	0	0		
2007–08	Bolton W	0	0		

SMITH, Johann (M) **20 1**
H: 5 11 W: 12 06 b.Hartford 25-4-87
Source: Scholar. *Honours:* USA Youth.

2005–06	Bolton W	0	0		
2006–07	Bolton W	1	0		
2006–07	*Carlisle U*	14	1	**14**	**1**
2007–08	Bolton W	0	0	**1**	**0**
2007–08	*Darlington*	3	0	**3**	**0**
2007–08	*Stockport Co*	2	0	**2**	**0**

STEINSSON, Gretar Rafn (D) **158 20**
H: 6 2 W: 12 04 b.Siglufjordur 9-1-82
Honours: Iceland 24 full caps, 3 goals.

1999	IA Akranes	0	0		
2000	IA Akranes	13	0		
2001	IA Akranes	18	6		
2002	IA Akranes	17	2		
2003	IA Akranes	11	2		
2004	IA Akranes	17	2	**76**	**12**
2004–05	Young Boys	14	3		
2005–06	Young Boys	7	0	**21**	**3**
2005–06	AZ	20	4		
2006–07	AZ	25	1	**45**	**5**
2007–08	Bolton W	16	0	**16**	**0**

TAYLOR, Matthew (D) **324 42**
H: 5 11 W: 12 03 b.Oxford 27-11-81
Source: Trainee. *Honours:* England Youth, Under-21.

1998–99	Luton T	0	0		
1999–2000	Luton T	41	4		
2000–01	Luton T	45	1		
2001–02	Luton T	43	11	**129**	**16**
2002–03	Portsmouth	35	7		
2003–04	Portsmouth	30	0		
2004–05	Portsmouth	32	1		
2005–06	Portsmouth	34	6		
2006–07	Portsmouth	35	8		
2007–08	Portsmouth	13	1	**179**	**23**
2007–08	Bolton W	16	3	**16**	**3**

TEIMOURIAN, Andranik (M) **20 2**
H: 5 11 W: 11 07 b.Tehran 6-3-83
Source: Ararat, Keshavirz, Esteghal, Oghab, ABV Moslem. *Honours:* Iran 28 full caps, 2 goals.

2006–07	Bolton W	17	2		
2007–08	Bolton W	3	0	**20**	**2**

THOMPSON, Leslie (M) **3 0**
H: 5 10 W: 11 02 b.Newham 3-10-88
Source: Scholar.

2007–08	Bolton W	0	0		
2007–08	*Stockport Co*	3	0	**3**	**0**

VAZ TE, Ricardo (F) **62 3**
H: 6 2 W: 12 07 b.Lisbon 1-10-86
Source: Trainee. *Honours:* Portugal Youth, Under-20, Under-21.

2003–04	Bolton W	1	0		
2004–05	Bolton W	7	0		
2005–06	Bolton W	22	3		
2006–07	Bolton W	25	0		
2006–07	*Hull C*	6	0	**6**	**0**
2007–08	Bolton W	1	0	**56**	**3**

WALKER, Ian (G) **401 0**
H: 6 2 W: 13 01 b.Watford 31-10-71
Source: Trainee. *Honours:* England Youth, Under-21, B, 4 full caps.

1989–90	Tottenham H	0	0		
1990–91	Tottenham H	1	0		
1990–91	*Oxford U*	2	0	**2**	**0**
1990–91	*Ipswich T*	0	0		
1991–92	Tottenham H	18	0		
1992–93	Tottenham H	17	0		
1993–94	Tottenham H	11	0		
1994–95	Tottenham H	41	0		
1995–96	Tottenham H	38	0		
1996–97	Tottenham H	37	0		
1997–98	Tottenham H	29	0		
1998–99	Tottenham H	25	0		
1999–2000	Tottenham H	38	0		
2000–01	Tottenham H	4	0	**259**	**0**
2001–02	Leicester C	35	0		
2002–03	Leicester C	46	0		
2003–04	Leicester C	37	0		
2004–05	Leicester C	22	0	**140**	**0**
2005–06	Bolton W	0	0		
2006–07	Bolton W	0	0		
2007–08	Bolton W	0	0		

WILHELMSSON, Christian (M) **281 52**
H: 5 10 W: 10 10 b.Malmo 8-2-79
Honours: Sweden 51 full caps, 4 goals.

1997	Mjallby	6	0		
1998	Mjallby	21	4		
1999	Mjallby	25	7	**52**	**11**
2000	Stabaek	24	9		
2001	Stabaek	25	6		
2002	Stabaek	26	6		
2003	Stabaek	9	4	**84**	**25**
2003–04	Anderlecht	27	5		
2004–05	Anderlecht	32	4		
2005–06	Anderlecht	31	5	**90**	**14**
2006–07	Nantes	13	0	**13**	**0**
2006–07	Roma	19	1	**19**	**1**
2007–08	*La Coruna*	15	1	**15**	**1**
2007–08	Bolton W	8	0	**8**	**0**

WOOLFE, Nathan (M) **0 0**
H: 5 11 W: 12 05 b.Florida 6-10-88
Source: Scholar.

2007–08	Bolton W	0	0		

Scholars
Brocklehurst, Tom Matthew; Carlisle, Matthew James; Gbemie, David; Lainton, Robert; McDonald, Stuart Robert; Michail, Marcos; Mooy, Aaron Frank; O'Halloran, Michael Francis; Sheridan, Samuel; Stokes, Christopher Martin Thomas; Ward, Daniel Carl; Wolze, Kevin; Woolfe, Nathan Bret

BOURNEMOUTH (10)

ANDERTON, Darren (M) **453 54**
H: 6 1 W: 12 05 b.Southampton 3-3-72
Source: Trainee. *Honours:* England Youth, Under-21, B, 30 full caps, 7 goals.

1989–90	Portsmouth	0	0		
1990–91	Portsmouth	20	0		
1991–92	Portsmouth	42	7	**62**	**7**
1992–93	Tottenham H	34	6		
1993–94	Tottenham H	37	6		
1994–95	Tottenham H	37	5		
1995–96	Tottenham H	8	2		
1996–97	Tottenham H	16	3		
1997–98	Tottenham H	15	0		
1998–99	Tottenham H	32	3		
1999–2000	Tottenham H	22	3		
2000–01	Tottenham H	23	2		
2001–02	Tottenham H	35	3		
2002–03	Tottenham H	20	0		
2003–04	Tottenham H	20	1	**299**	**34**
2004–05	Birmingham C	20	3		
2005–06	Birmingham C	0	0	**20**	**3**
2005–06	Wolverhampton W	24	1	**24**	**1**
2006–07	Bournemouth	28	6		
2007–08	Bournemouth	20	3	**48**	**9**

BARTLEY, Marvyn (M) **20 1**
H: 6 1 W: 12 04 b.Reading 4-7-86
Source: Hampton & Richmond B.

2007–08	Bournemouth	20	1	**20**	**1**

BRADBURY, Lee (F) **417 85**
H: 6 0 W: 12 07 b.Isle of Wight 3-7-75
Source: Cowes. *Honours:* England Under-21.

1995–96	Portsmouth	12	0		
1995–96	*Exeter C*	14	5	**14**	**5**
1996–97	Portsmouth	42	15		
1997–98	Manchester C	27	7		
1998–99	Manchester C	13	3	**40**	**10**
1998–99	Crystal Palace	22	4		
1998–99	*Birmingham C*	7	0	**7**	**0**
1999–2000	Crystal Palace	10	2	**32**	**6**
1999–2000	Portsmouth	35	10		
2000–01	Portsmouth	39	10		
2001–02	Portsmouth	22	7		
2002–03	Portsmouth	3	1		
2002–03	*Sheffield W*	11	3	**11**	**3**
2003–04	Portsmouth	0	0	**153**	**43**
2003–04	*Derby Co*	7	0	**7**	**0**
2003–04	Walsall	8	1	**8**	**1**
2004–05	Oxford U	41	4		
2005–06	Oxford U	22	5	**63**	**9**
2005–06	Southend U	15	1		
2006–07	Southend U	31	4		
2007–08	Southend U	1	0	**47**	**5**
2007–08	Bournemouth	35	3	**35**	**3**

COOPER, Shaun (D) **132 1**
H: 5 10 W: 10 05 b.Newport (IW) 5-10-83
Source: School.

2000–01	Portsmouth	0	0		
2001–02	Portsmouth	7	0		
2002–03	Portsmouth	0	0		
2003–04	Portsmouth	0	0		
2003–04	*Leyton Orient*	9	0	**9**	**0**
2004–05	Portsmouth	0	0		
2004–05	*Kidderminster H*	10	0	**10**	**0**
2005–06	Portsmouth	0	0	**7**	**0**
2005–06	Bournemouth	35	0		
2006–07	Bournemouth	33	0		
2007–08	Bournemouth	38	1	**106**	**1**

CUMMINGS, Warren (D) **182 7**
H: 5 9 W: 11 05 b.Aberdeen 15-10-80
Source: Trainee. *Honours:* Scotland Under-21, 1 full cap.

1999–2000	Chelsea	0	0		
2000–01	Chelsea	0	0		
2000–01	*Bournemouth*	10	1		
2000–01	*WBA*	3	0		
2001–02	Chelsea	0	0		
2001–02	*WBA*	14	0	**17**	**0**
2002–03	Chelsea	0	0		
2002–03	Bournemouth	20	0		
2003–04	Bournemouth	42	2		
2004–05	Bournemouth	30	2		
2005–06	Bournemouth	0	0		
2006–07	Bournemouth	31	0		
2007–08	Bournemouth	32	2	**165**	**7**

FINLAY, Matt (M) **1 0**
H: 6 2 W: 12 00 b.Salisbury 25-1-90

2007–08	Bournemouth	1	0	**1**	**0**

FOLEY-SHERIDAN, Steven (M) **53 6**
H: 5 4 W: 9 00 b.Dublin 10-2-86
Source: Trainee. *Honours:* Eire Youth.

2002–03	Aston Villa	0	0		
2003–04	Aston Villa	0	0		
2004–05	Aston Villa	0	0		
2005–06	Aston Villa	0	0		
2005–06	Bournemouth	35	5		
2006–07	Bournemouth	18	1		
2007–08	Bournemouth	0	0	**53**	**6**

FRANKS, Billy (D) **1 0**
H: 6 2 W: 12 07 b.Shoreham 26-11-89

2007–08	Bournemouth	1	0	**1**	**0**

GARRY, Ryan (D) **9 0**

H: 6 0 W: 11 05 b.Hornchurch 29-9-83

Source: Scholar. *Honours:* England Youth, Under-20.

2001–02	Arsenal	0	0		
2002–03	Arsenal	1	0		
2003–04	Arsenal	0	0		
2004–05	Arsenal	0	0		
2005–06	Arsenal	0	0		
2006–07	Arsenal	0	0	**1**	**0**
2007–08	Bournemouth	8	0	**8**	**0**

GOWLING, Josh (D) **96 1**

H: 6 3 W: 12 08 b.Coventry 29-11-83

Source: WBA Scholar.

2004–05	Herfolge	13	0	**13**	**0**
2005–06	Bournemouth	13	0		
2006–07	Bournemouth	33	1		
2007–08	Bournemouth	37	0	**83**	**1**

HOLLANDS, Danny (M) **80 6**

H: 6 0 W: 11 11 b.Ashford 6-11-85

Source: Trainee.

2003–04	Chelsea	0	0		
2004–05	Chelsea	0	0		
2005–06	Chelsea	0	0		
2005–06	*Torquay U*	10	1	**10**	**1**
2006–07	Bournemouth	33	1		
2007–08	Bournemouth	37	4	**70**	**5**

HUTCHINGS, Steve (M) **1 0**

H: 6 0 W: 12 00 b.Portsmouth 13-12-90

2007–08	Bournemouth	1	0	**1**	**0**

McQUOID, Josh (M) **7 0**

H: 5 9 W: 10 10 b.Southampton 15-12-89

Source: Scholar.

2006–07	Bournemouth	2	0		
2007–08	Bournemouth	5	0	**7**	**0**

MOSS, Neil (G) **218 0**

H: 6 0 W: 13 10 b.New Milton 10-5-75

Source: Trainee.

1992–93	Bournemouth	1	0		
1993–94	Bournemouth	6	0		
1994–95	Bournemouth	8	0		
1995–96	Bournemouth	7	0		
1995–96	Southampton	0	0		
1996–97	Southampton	3	0		
1997–98	Southampton	0	0		
1997–98	*Gillingham*	10	0	**10**	**0**
1998–99	Southampton	7	0		
1999–2000	Southampton	9	0		
2000–01	Southampton	3	0		
2001–02	Southampton	2	0		
2002–03	Southampton	0	0	**24**	**0**
2002–03	Bournemouth	33	0		
2003–04	Bournemouth	46	0		
2004–05	Bournemouth	46	0		
2005–06	Bournemouth	4	0		
2006–07	Bournemouth	26	0		
2007–08	Bournemouth	7	0	**184**	**0**

OSEI-KUFFOUR, Jo (F) **240 55**

H: 5 8 W: 11 11 b.Edmonton 17-11-81

Source: Scholar.

2000–01	Arsenal	0	0		
2001–02	Arsenal	0	0		
2001–02	*Swindon T*	11	2	**11**	**2**
2002–03	Torquay U	30	5		
2003–04	Torquay U	41	10		
2004–05	Torquay U	34	6		
2005–06	Torquay U	43	8	**148**	**29**
2006–07	Brentford	39	12	**39**	**12**
2007–08	Bournemouth	42	12	**42**	**12**

PARTINGTON, Joe (M) **6 1**

H: 5 11 W: 11 13 b.Portsmouth 1-4-90

Honours: Wales Youth.

2007–08	Bournemouth	6	1	**6**	**1**

PEARCE, Jason (D) **33 1**

H: 5 11 W: 12 00 b.Hillingdon 6-12-87

Source: Scholar.

2006–07	Portsmouth	0	0		
2007–08	Bournemouth	33	1	**33**	**1**

PERRETT, Russell (D) **210 12**

H: 6 1 W: 12 08 b.Barton-on-Sea 18-6-73

Source: AFC Lymington.

1995–96	Portsmouth	9	0		
1996–97	Portsmouth	32	1		
1997–98	Portsmouth	16	1		
1998–99	Portsmouth	15	0	**72**	**2**
1999–2000	Cardiff C	27	1		
2000–01	Cardiff C	2	0	**29**	**1**
2001–02	Luton T	40	3		
2002–03	Luton T	20	2		
2003–04	Luton T	6	2		
2004–05	Luton T	12	1		
2005–06	Luton T	11	0		
2006–07	Luton T	10	1	**99**	**9**
2007–08	Bournemouth	10	0	**10**	**0**

PITMAN, Brett (M) **87 12**

H: 6 0 W: 11 00 b.Jersey 31-1-88

2005–06	Bournemouth	19	1		
2006–07	Bournemouth	29	5		
2007–08	Bournemouth	39	6	**87**	**12**

PRYCE, Ryan (G) **4 0**

H: 6 0 W: 11 09 b.Bournemouth 20-9-86

2007–08	Bournemouth	4	0	**4**	**0**

STEWART, Gareth (G) **164 0**

H: 6 0 W: 12 08 b.Preston 3-2-80

Source: Trainee. *Honours:* England Schools, Youth.

1996–97	Blackburn R	0	0		
1997–98	Blackburn R	0	0		
1998–99	Blackburn R	0	0		
1999–2000	Bournemouth	3	0		
2000–01	Bournemouth	35	0		
2001–02	Bournemouth	45	0		
2002–03	Bournemouth	1	0		
2003–04	Bournemouth	0	0		
2004–05	Bournemouth	0	0		
2005–06	Bournemouth	42	0		
2006–07	Bournemouth	20	0		
2007–08	Bournemouth	18	0	**164**	**0**

TELFER, Paul (D) **481 26**

H: 5 10 W: 11 13 b.Edinburgh 21-10-71

Source: Trainee. *Honours:* Scotland Under-21, B, 1 full cap.

1988–89	Luton T	0	0		
1989–90	Luton T	0	0		
1990–91	Luton T	1	0		
1991–92	Luton T	20	1		
1992–93	Luton T	32	2		
1993–94	Luton T	45	7		
1994–95	Luton T	46	9	**144**	**19**
1995–96	Coventry C	31	1		
1996–97	Coventry C	34	0		
1997–98	Coventry C	33	3		
1998–99	Coventry C	32	2		
1999–2000	Coventry C	30	0		
2000–01	Coventry C	31	0		
2001–02	Coventry C	0	0	**191**	**6**
2001–02	Southampton	28	1		
2002–03	Southampton	33	0		
2003–04	Southampton	37	0		
2004–05	Southampton	30	0		
2005–06	Southampton	0	0		
2006–07	Southampton	0	0	**128**	**1**
2007–08	Bournemouth	18	0	**18**	**0**

TESSEM, Jo (M) **320 64**

H: 6 2 W: 13 01 b.Orlandet 28-2-72

Honours: Norway 9 full caps.

1996	Lyn	22	15		
1997	Lyn	26	8		
1998	Molde	26	8		
1999	Molde	26	6	**52**	**14**
1999–2000	Southampton	25	4		
2000–01	Southampton	33	4		
2001–02	Southampton	22	2		
2002–03	Southampton	27	2		
2003–04	Southampton	3	0		
2004	Lyn	12	2		
2004–05	Southampton	0	0	**110**	**12**
2004–05	*Millwall*	12	1	**12**	**1**
2005	Lyn	26	8		
2006	Lyn	25	2		
2007	Lyn	24	2	**135**	**37**
2007–08	Bournemouth	11	0	**11**	**0**

VOKES, Sam (F) **54 16**

H: 6 1 W: 13 10 b.Southampton 21-10-89

Source: Scholar. *Honours:* Wales Under-21, 2 full caps.

2006–07	Bournemouth	13	4		
2007–08	Bournemouth	41	12	**54**	**16**

YOUNG, Neil (D) **429 4**

H: 5 9 W: 12 04 b.Harlow 31-8-73

Source: Trainee.

1991–92	Tottenham H	0	0		
1992–93	Tottenham H	0	0		
1993–94	Tottenham H	0	0		
1994–95	Bournemouth	32	0		
1995–96	Bournemouth	41	0		
1996–97	Bournemouth	44	0		
1997–98	Bournemouth	44	2		
1998–99	Bournemouth	44	1		
1999–2000	Bournemouth	37	0		
2000–01	Bournemouth	7	0		
2001–02	Bournemouth	11	0		
2002–03	Bournemouth	32	1		
2003–04	Bournemouth	10	0		
2004–05	Bournemouth	30	0		
2005–06	Bournemouth	42	0		
2006–07	Bournemouth	34	0		
2007–08	Bournemouth	21	0	**429**	**4**

BRADFORD C (11)

AINGE, Simon (D) **13 0**

H: 6 1 W: 12 02 b.Shipley 18-2-88

Source: Scholar.

2005–06	Bradford C	0	0		
2006–07	Bradford C	9	0		
2007–08	Bradford C	4	0	**13**	**0**

BENTHAM, Craig (D) **30 0**

H: 5 9 W: 11 06 b.Bingley 7-3-85

Source: Scholar.

2004–05	Bradford C	2	0		
2005–06	Bradford C	7	0		
2006–07	Bradford C	18	0		
2007–08	Bradford C	3	0	**30**	**0**

BOWER, Mark (D) **264 14**

H: 5 10 W: 11 00 b.Bradford 23-1-80

Source: Trainee.

1997–98	Bradford C	3	0		
1998–99	Bradford C	0	0		
1999–2000	Bradford C	0	0		
1999–2000	*York C*	15	1		
2000–01	Bradford C	0	0		
2000–01	*York C*	21	1	**36**	**2**
2001–02	Bradford C	10	2		
2002–03	Bradford C	37	0		
2003–04	Bradford C	14	0		
2004–05	Bradford C	46	2		
2005–06	Bradford C	45	2		
2006–07	Bradford C	46	3		
2007–08	Bradford C	27	3	**228**	**12**

BROWN, David (F) **5 1**

H: 5 11 W: 11 09 b.Tadcaster 29-5-89

2007–08	Nottingham F	0	0		
2007–08	Bradford C	5	1	**5**	**1**

BULLOCK, Lee (M) **285 36**

H: 6 0 W: 11 04 b.Stockton 22-5-81

Source: Trainee.

1999–2000	York C	24	0		
2000–01	York C	33	3		
2001–02	York C	40	8		
2002–03	York C	39	6		
2003–04	York C	35	7	**171**	**24**
2003–04	*Cardiff C*	11	3		
2004–05	Cardiff C	21	3	**32**	**6**
2005–06	Hartlepool U	31	4		
2006–07	Hartlepool U	25	1		
2007–08	Hartlepool U	1	0	**57**	**5**
2007–08	*Mansfield T*	5	0	**5**	**0**
2007–08	*Bury*	8	0	**8**	**0**
2007–08	Bradford C	12	1	**12**	**1**

CLARKE, Matthew (D) **265 16**

H: 6 3 W: 13 00 b.Leeds 18-12-80

Source: Wolverhampton W Trainee.

1999–2000	Halifax T	19	0		
2000–01	Halifax T	19	1		
2001–02	Halifax T	31	1	**69**	**2**
2002–03	Darlington	38	3		
2003–04	Darlington	45	4		
2004–05	Darlington	43	3		
2005–06	Darlington	43	3		
2006–07	Bradford C	8	0		
2006–07	*Darlington*	2	0	**171**	**13**
2007–08	Bradford C	17	1	**25**	**1**

COLBECK, Joe (M) **82 8**

H: 5 10 W: 10 12 b.Bradford 29-11-86

Source: Scholar.

2004–05	Bradford C	0	0		
2005–06	Bradford C	11	0		
2006–07	Bradford C	32	0		

2007–08 Bradford C 33 6 **76 6**
2007–08 *Darlington* 6 2 **6 2**

CONLON, Barry (F) 359 94
H: 6 3 W: 14 00 b.Drogheda 1-10-78
Source: QPR Trainee. *Honours:* Eire Under-21.
1997–98 Manchester C 7 0
1997–98 *Plymouth Arg* 13 2 **13 2**
1998–99 Manchester C 0 0 **7 0**
1998–99 Southend U 34 7 **34 7**
1999–2000 York C 40 11
2000–01 York C 8 0 **48 11**
2000–01 *Colchester U* 26 8 **26 8**
2001–02 Darlington 35 10
2002–03 Darlington 41 15
2003–04 Darlington 39 14
2004–05 Barnsley 24 6
2005–06 Barnsley 11 1 **35 7**
2005–06 *Rotherham U* 3 1 **3 1**
2006–07 Darlington 19 6 **134 45**
2006–07 Mansfield T 17 6 **17 6**
2007–08 Bradford C 42 7 **42 7**

DALEY, Omar (M) 75 6
H: 5 10 W: 11 03 b.Kingston, Jamaica 25-4-81
Source: Portmore U. *Honours:* Jamaica Under-20, 52 full caps, 4 goals.
2003–04 Reading 6 0 **6 0**
2004–05 Preston NE 14 0 **14 0**
From Charleston B, Portmore U.
2006–07 Bradford C 14 2
2007–08 Bradford C 41 4 **55 6**

EVANS, Paul (M) 471 70
H: 5 8 W: 12 06 b.Oswestry 1-9-74
Source: Trainee. *Honours:* Wales Youth, Under-21, 2 full caps.
1991–92 Shrewsbury T 2 0
1992–93 Shrewsbury T 4 0
1993–94 Shrewsbury T 13 0
1994–95 Shrewsbury T 32 5
1995–96 Shrewsbury T 34 3
1996–97 Shrewsbury T 42 6
1997–98 Shrewsbury T 39 6
1998–99 Shrewsbury T 32 6 **198 26**
1998–99 Brentford 14 3
1999–2000 Brentford 33 7
2000–01 Brentford 43 7
2001–02 Brentford 40 14 **130 31**
2002–03 Bradford C 19 2
2002–03 *Blackpool* 10 1 **10 1**
2003–04 Bradford C 23 3
2003–04 Nottingham F 8 0
2004–05 Nottingham F 39 4
2005–06 Nottingham F 0 0 **47 4**
2005–06 *Rotherham U* 4 0 **4 0**
2006–07 Swindon T 15 3 **15 3**
2007–08 Bradford C 25 0 **67 5**

HECKINGBOTTOM, Paul (D) 342 11
H: 6 0 W: 13 01 b.Barnsley 17-7-77
Source: Manchester U Trainee.
1995–96 Sunderland 0 0
1996–97 Sunderland 0 0
1997–98 Sunderland 0 0
1997–98 *Scarborough* 29 0 **29 0**
1998–99 Sunderland 0 0
1998–99 *Hartlepool U* 5 1 **5 1**
1998–99 *Darlington* 10 0
1999–2000 Darlington 45 1
2000–01 Darlington 18 1
2001–02 Darlington 42 3 **115 5**
2002–03 Norwich C 15 0 **15 0**
2003–04 Bradford C 43 0
2004–05 Sheffield W 38 4
2005–06 Sheffield W 4 0 **42 4**
2005–06 Barnsley 18 1
2006–07 Barnsley 31 0
2007–08 Barnsley 0 0 **49 1**
2007–08 Bradford C 44 0 **87 0**

HOPKINS, Damian (D) 0 0
H: 5 11 W: 10 06 b.Bradford 1-3-89
Source: Scholar.
2007–08 Bradford C 0 0

JOHNSON, Eddie (F) 112 17
H: 5 10 W: 13 05 b.Chester 20-9-84
Source: Scholar. *Honours:* England Youth, Under-20.
2001–02 Manchester U 0 0
2002–03 Manchester U 0 0
2003–04 Manchester U 0 0
2004–05 Manchester U 0 0
2004–05 *Coventry C* 26 5 **26 5**
2005–06 Manchester U 0 0
2005–06 *Crewe Alex* 22 5 **22 5**
2006–07 Bradford C 32 3
2007–08 Bradford C 32 4 **64 7**

MEDLEY, Luke (F) 9 2
H: 6 1 W: 13 03 b.Greenwich 21-6-89
Source: Tottenham H Scholar.
2007–08 Bradford C 9 2 **9 2**

MORGAN, Luke (M) 0 0
H: 5 8 W: 10 02 b.Leeds 26-10-88
Source: Scholar.
2007–08 Bradford C 0 0

NIX, Kyle (F) 40 6
H: 5 6 W: 9 10 b.Sydney 21-1-86
Source: Manchester U Trainee. *Honours:* FA Schools, England Youth, Under-20.
2002–03 Aston Villa 0 0
2003–04 Aston Villa 0 0
2004–05 Aston Villa 0 0
2005–06 Sheffield U 0 0
2005–06 *Barnsley* 0 0
2006–07 Sheffield U 0 0
2007–08 Bradford C 40 6 **40 6**

O'BRIEN, Luke (D) 2 0
H: 5 9 W: 12 01 b.Halifax 11-9-88
Source: Scholar.
2007–08 Bradford C 2 0 **2 0**

OSBORNE, Leon (F) 1 0
H: 5 10 W: 10 10 b.Doncaster 28-10-89
Source: Scholar.
2006–07 Bradford C 1 0
2007–08 Bradford C 0 0 **1 0**

PENFORD, Tom (M) 38 1
H: 5 10 W: 11 03 b.Leeds 5-1-85
Source: Scholar.
2002–03 Bradford C 3 0
2003–04 Bradford C 4 0
2004–05 Bradford C 3 0
2005–06 Bradford C 10 0
2006–07 Bradford C 3 0
2007–08 Bradford C 15 1 **38 1**

PHELAN, Scott (M) 13 0
H: 5 7 W: 10 07 b.Liverpool 13-3-88
Source: Scholar. *Honours:* England Youth.
2005–06 Everton 0 0
2006–07 Everton 0 0
2007–08 Bradford C 13 0 **13 0**

RHODES, Alex (F) 89 8
H: 5 9 W: 10 04 b.Cambridge 23-1-82
Source: Newmarket T.
2003–04 Brentford 3 1
2004–05 Brentford 22 3
2005–06 Brentford 17 1
2006–07 Brentford 15 0 **57 5**
2006–07 *Swindon T* 4 0 **4 0**
2007–08 Bradford C 28 3 **28 3**

RICKETTS, Donovan (G) 108 0
H: 6 1 W: 11 05 b.Kingston 7-6-77
Source: Village U. *Honours:* Jamaica Under-23, 46 full caps.
2003–04 Bolton W 0 0
2004–05 Bolton W 0 0
2004–05 Bradford C 4 0
2005–06 Bradford C 36 0
2006–07 Bradford C 46 0
2007–08 Bradford C 22 0 **108 0**

SAYNOR, Ben (G) 0 0
H: 6 3 W: 12 04 b.Leeds 6-3-89
Source: Scholar.
2007–08 Bradford C 0 0

TAYLFORTH, Sean (F) 1 0
H: 5 11 W: 10 03 b.Middlewich 10-3-89
Source: Scholar.
2007–08 Bradford C 1 0 **1 0**

THORNE, Peter (F) 441 153
H: 6 1 W: 13 13 b.Manchester 21-6-73
Source: Trainee.
1991–92 Blackburn R 0 0
1992–93 Blackburn R 0 0
1993–94 Blackburn R 0 0
1993–94 *Wigan Ath* 11 0 **11 0**
1994–95 Blackburn R 0 0
1994–95 Swindon T 20 9
1995–96 Swindon T 26 10
1996–97 Swindon T 31 8 **77 27**
1997–98 Stoke C 36 12
1998–99 Stoke C 34 9
1999–2000 Stoke C 45 24
2000–01 Stoke C 38 16
2001–02 Stoke C 5 4 **158 65**
2001–02 Cardiff C 26 8
2002–03 Cardiff C 46 13
2003–04 Cardiff C 23 13
2004–05 Cardiff C 31 12 **126 46**
2005–06 Norwich C 21 1
2006–07 Norwich C 15 0 **36 1**
2007–08 Bradford C 33 14 **33 14**

TOPP, Willy (F) 11 0
H: 5 9 W: 11 04 b.Temuco 4-3-86
Source: Univ Catolica. *Honours:* Chile Youth.
2007–08 Bradford C 11 0 **11 0**

WAITE, Jamie (G) 0 0
H: 6 2 W: 13 02 b.Plymouth 20-2-86
Source: Rotherham U, Milton Keynes D, St Albans.
2006–07 Milton Keynes D 0 0
2007–08 Bradford C 0 0

WETHERALL, David (D) 506 30
H: 6 3 W: 13 12 b.Sheffield 14-3-71
Source: School. *Honours:* England Schools.
1989–90 Sheffield W 0 0
1990–91 Sheffield W 0 0
1991–92 Leeds U 1 0
1992–93 Leeds U 13 1
1993–94 Leeds U 32 1
1994–95 Leeds U 38 3
1995–96 Leeds U 34 4
1996–97 Leeds U 29 0
1997–98 Leeds U 34 3
1998–99 Leeds U 21 0 **202 12**
1999–2000 Bradford C 38 2
2000–01 Bradford C 18 1
2001–02 Bradford C 19 2
2002–03 Bradford C 17 0
2003–04 Bradford C 34 1
2004–05 Bradford C 45 4
2005–06 Bradford C 46 5
2006–07 Bradford C 41 1
2007–08 Bradford C 46 2 **304 18**

WILLIAMS, Darren (D) 332 4
H: 5 11 W: 11 00 b.Middlesbrough 28-4-77
Source: Trainee. *Honours:* England Under-21, B.
1994–95 York C 1 0
1995–96 York C 18 0
1996–97 York C 1 0 **20 0**
1996–97 Sunderland 11 2
1997–98 Sunderland 36 2
1998–99 Sunderland 25 0
1999–2000 Sunderland 25 0
2000–01 Sunderland 28 0
2001–02 Sunderland 28 0
2002–03 Sunderland 16 0
2003–04 Sunderland 29 0
2004–05 Sunderland 1 0 **199 4**
2004–05 Cardiff C 20 0 **20 0**
2005–06 Hartlepool U 39 0
2006–07 Hartlepool U 26 0 **65 0**
2007–08 Bradford C 28 0 **28 0**

BRENTFORD (12)

BROOKER, Paul (M) 306 23
H: 5 8 W: 10 00 b.Hammersmith 25-11-76
Source: Trainee.
1995–96 Fulham 20 2
1996–97 Fulham 26 2
1997–98 Fulham 9 0
1998–99 Fulham 1 0
1999–2000 Fulham 0 0 **56 4**
1999–2000 *Brighton & HA* 15 2
2000–01 Brighton & HA 41 3
2001–02 Brighton & HA 41 4
2002–03 Brighton & HA 37 6 **134 15**
2003–04 Leicester C 3 0 **3 0**
2003–04 *Reading* 11 0
2004–05 Reading 31 0 **42 0**
2005–06 Brentford 36 4
2006–07 Brentford 34 0
2007–08 Brentford 1 0 **71 4**

BROWN, Simon (G) **217 0**
H: 6 2 W: 15 00 b.Chelmsford 3-12-76
Source: Trainee.

1995–96	Tottenham H	0	0		
1996–97	Tottenham H	0	0		
1997–98	Tottenham H	0	0		
1997–98	*Lincoln C*	1	0	**1**	**0**
1998–99	Tottenham H	0	0		
1998–99	*Fulham*	0	0		
1999–2000	Colchester U	38	0		
2000–01	Colchester U	18	0		
2001–02	Colchester U	19	0		
2002–03	Colchester U	27	0		
2003–04	Colchester U	40	0	**142**	**0**
2004–05	Hibernian	36	0		
2005–06	Hibernian	8	0		
2006–07	Hibernian	4	0	**48**	**0**
2007–08	Brentford	26	0	**26**	**0**

CARDER-ANDREWS, Karle (M) **5 0**
H: 5 11 W: 10 08 b.Feltham 13-3-89
Source: Scholar.

2006–07	Brentford	5	0		
2007–08	Brentford	0	0	**5**	**0**

CHARLES, Darius (M) **37 1**
H: 6 1 W: 13 05 b.Ealing 10-12-87
Source: Scholar.

2004–05	Brentford	1	0		
2005–06	Brentford	2	0		
2006–07	Brentford	17	1		
2007–08	Brentford	17	0	**37**	**1**

CONNELL, Alan (F) **162 36**
H: 6 0 W: 12 00 b.Enfield 5-2-83
Source: Ipswich T Trainee.

2002–03	Bournemouth	13	6		
2003–04	Bournemouth	7	0		
2004–05	Bournemouth	34	2	**54**	**8**
2005–06	Torquay U	22	7	**22**	**7**
2006–07	Hereford U	44	9	**44**	**9**
2007–08	Brentford	42	12	**42**	**12**

DARK, Lewis (M) **3 0**
H: 5 8 W: 11 06 b.Harlow 10-4-89
Source: Scholar.

2006–07	Brentford	3	0		
2007–08	Brentford	0	0	**3**	**0**

DICKSON, Ryan (M) **45 1**
H: 5 10 W: 11 05 b.Saltash 14-12-86
Source: Scholar.

2004–05	Plymouth Arg	3	0		
2005–06	Plymouth Arg	0	0		
2006–07	Plymouth Arg	2	0		
2006–07	*Torquay U*	9	1	**9**	**1**
2007–08	Plymouth Arg	0	0	**5**	**0**
2007–08	Brentford	31	0	**31**	**0**

ELDER, Nathan (F) **39 6**
H: 6 1 W: 13 12 b.Hornchurch 5-4-85
Source: Billericay T.

2006–07	Brighton & HA	13	1		
2007–08	Brighton & HA	9	1	**22**	**2**
2007–08	Brentford	17	4	**17**	**4**

HEYWOOD, Matthew (D) **280 12**
H: 6 3 W: 14 00 b.Chatham 26-8-79
Source: Trainee.

1998–99	Burnley	13	0		
1999–2000	Burnley	0	0		
2000–01	Burnley	0	0	**13**	**0**
2000–01	Swindon T	21	2		
2001–02	Swindon T	44	3		
2002–03	Swindon T	46	1		
2003–04	Swindon T	40	1		
2004–05	Swindon T	32	1	**183**	**8**
2005–06	Bristol C	24	2	**24**	**2**
2006–07	Brentford	28	1		
2007–08	Brentford	32	1	**60**	**2**

IDE, Charlie (M) **46 7**
H: 5 9 W: 11 00 b.Sunbury 10-5-88

2004–05	Brentford	1	0		
2005–06	Brentford	0	0		
2006–07	Brentford	26	7		
2007–08	Brentford	19	0	**46**	**7**

MACKIE, John (D) **207 14**
H: 6 1 W: 12 08 b.Enfield 5-7-76
Source: Sutton U.

1999–2000	Reading	0	0		
2000–01	Reading	10	0		
2001–02	Reading	27	2		
2002–03	Reading	25	0		
2003–04	Reading	9	1	**71**	**3**
2003–04	Leyton Orient	20	1		
2004–05	Leyton Orient	27	4		
2005–06	Leyton Orient	40	6		
2006–07	Leyton Orient	35	0	**122**	**11**
2007–08	Brentford	14	0	**14**	**0**

MONTAGUE, Ross (F) **14 1**
H: 6 0 W: 12 11 b.Twickenham 1-11-88
Source: Scholar.

2006–07	Brentford	4	0		
2007–08	Brentford	10	1	**14**	**1**

MOUSINHO, John (D) **64 2**
H: 6 1 W: 12 07 b.Buckingham 30-4-86
Source: Univ of Notre Dame.

2005–06	Brentford	7	0		
2006–07	Brentford	34	0		
2007–08	Brentford	23	2	**64**	**2**

O'CONNOR, Kevin (F) **273 25**
H: 5 11 W: 12 00 b.Blackburn 24-2-82
Source: Trainee. *Honours:* Eire Youth, Under-21.

1999–2000	Brentford	6	0		
2000–01	Brentford	11	1		
2001–02	Brentford	25	0		
2002–03	Brentford	45	5		
2003–04	Brentford	43	1		
2004–05	Brentford	37	2		
2005–06	Brentford	30	7		
2006–07	Brentford	39	6		
2007–08	Brentford	37	3	**273**	**25**

OSBORNE, Karleigh (D) **52 1**
H: 6 2 W: 12 04 b.Southall 19-3-88
Source: Scholar.

2004–05	Brentford	1	0		
2005–06	Brentford	1	0		
2006–07	Brentford	21	0		
2007–08	Brentford	29	1	**52**	**1**

PEAD, Craig (M) **167 3**
H: 5 9 W: 11 06 b.Bromsgrove 15-9-81
Source: Trainee. *Honours:* England Youth, Under-20.

1998–99	Coventry C	0	0		
1999–2000	Coventry C	0	0		
2000–01	Coventry C	0	0		
2001–02	Coventry C	1	0		
2002–03	Coventry C	24	2		
2003–04	Coventry C	17	1		
2004–05	Coventry C	0	0	**42**	**3**
2004–05	*Notts Co*	5	0	**5**	**0**
2004–05	*Walsall*	8	0		
2005–06	Walsall	39	0		
2006–07	Walsall	41	0	**88**	**0**
2007–08	Brentford	32	0	**32**	**0**

PETERS, Ryan (F) **47 2**
H: 5 8 W: 10 05 b.Wandsworth 21-8-87
Source: Scholar.

2000–01	Southampton	0	0		
2001–02	Southampton	0	0		
2001–02	Brentford	0	0		
2002–03	Brentford	11	1		
2003–04	Brentford	9	0		
2004–05	Brentford	0	0		
2005–06	Brentford	10	1		
2006–07	Brentford	13	0		
2007–08	Brentford	4	0	**47**	**2**

POOLE, Glenn (M) **51 14**
H: 5 7 W: 11 04 b.Essex 3-2-81
Source: Thurrock, Grays Ath.

2006–07	Rochdale	6	0	**6**	**0**
2007–08	Brentford	45	14	**45**	**14**

REID, Reuben (F) **37 4**
H: 6 0 W: 12 02 b.Bristol 26-7-88

2005–06	Plymouth Arg	1	0		
2006–07	Plymouth Arg	6	0		
2006–07	*Rochdale*	2	0	**2**	**0**
2006–07	*Torquay U*	7	2	**7**	**2**
2007–08	Plymouth Arg	0	0	**7**	**0**
2007–08	*Wycombe W*	11	1	**11**	**1**
2007–08	Brentford	10	1	**10**	**1**

SHAKES, Ricky (M) **116 10**
H: 5 10 W: 12 00 b.Brixton 26-1-85
Source: Scholar. *Honours:* Trinidad & Tobago 1 full cap.

2003–04	Bolton W	0	0		
2004–05	Bolton W	0	0		
2004–05	*Bristol R*	1	0	**1**	**0**
2004–05	*Bury*	7	2	**7**	**2**
2005–06	Swindon T	37	3		
2006–07	Swindon T	32	2	**69**	**5**
2007–08	Brentford	39	3	**39**	**3**

SMITH, Gary (M) **111 9**
H: 5 8 W: 10 09 b.Middlesbrough 30-1-84
Source: Trainee.

2002–03	Middlesbrough	0	0		
2003–04	Middlesbrough	0	0		
2003–04	*Wimbledon*	11	3	**11**	**3**
2004–05	Milton Keynes D	23	1		
2005–06	Milton Keynes D	25	3		
2006–07	Milton Keynes D	23	1	**71**	**5**
2007–08	Brentford	29	1	**29**	**1**

TILLEN, Sam (D) **68 1**
H: 5 10 W: 11 09 b.Reading 16-4-85
Source: Trainee. *Honours:* England Youth.

2002–03	Chelsea	0	0		
2003–04	Chelsea	0	0		
2004–05	Chelsea	0	0		
2005–06	Brentford	33	0		
2006–07	Brentford	34	1		
2007–08	Brentford	1	0	**68**	**1**

BRIGHTON & HA (13)

BUTTERS, Guy (D) **554 35**
H: 6 3 W: 13 00 b.Hillingdon 30-10-69
Source: Trainee. *Honours:* England Under-21.

1988–89	Tottenham H	28	1		
1989–90	Tottenham H	7	0	**35**	**1**
1989–90	*Southend U*	16	3	**16**	**3**
1990–91	Portsmouth	23	0		
1991–92	Portsmouth	33	2		
1992–93	Portsmouth	15	1		
1993–94	Portsmouth	15	1		
1994–95	Portsmouth	24	0		
1994–95	*Oxford U*	3	1	**3**	**1**
1995–96	Portsmouth	37	2		
1996–97	Portsmouth	7	0	**154**	**6**
1996–97	Gillingham	30	0		
1997–98	Gillingham	31	7		
1998–99	Gillingham	23	3		
1999–2000	Gillingham	40	2		
2000–01	Gillingham	12	3		
2001–02	Gillingham	23	1	**159**	**16**
2002–03	Brighton & HA	6	0		
2003–04	Brighton & HA	43	3		
2004–05	Brighton & HA	41	2		
2005–06	Brighton & HA	45	2		
2006–07	Brighton & HA	31	0		
2007–08	Brighton & HA	21	1	**187**	**8**

CHAMBERLAIN, Scott (M) **0 0**
H: 5 9 W: 10 08 b.Eastbourne 15-1-88
Source: Scholar.

2006–07	Brighton & HA	0	0		
2007–08	Brighton & HA	0	0		

COBBS, Sonny (D) **0 0**
Source: Scholar.

2007–08	Brighton & HA	0	0		

COX, Dean (M) **85 12**
H: 5 4 W: 9 08 b.Cuckfield 12-8-87
Source: Scholar.

2005–06	Brighton & HA	1	0		
2006–07	Brighton & HA	42	6		
2007–08	Brighton & HA	42	6	**85**	**12**

DIXON, Jonny (F) **77 7**
H: 5 9 W: 11 01 b.Murcia 16-1-84
Source: Scholar.

2002–03	Wycombe W	22	5		
2003–04	Wycombe W	8	0		
2004–05	Wycombe W	16	1		
2005–06	Wycombe W	17	0		
2006–07	Wycombe W	10	1	**73**	**7**
From Aldershot T.					
2007–08	Brighton & HA	4	0	**4**	**0**

EL-ABD, Adam (D) **133 2**
H: 5 10 W: 13 05 b.Brighton 11-9-84
Source: Scholar.

2003–04	Brighton & HA	11	0		
2004–05	Brighton & HA	16	0		
2005–06	Brighton & HA	29	0		
2006–07	Brighton & HA	42	1		
2007–08	Brighton & HA	35	1	**133**	**2**

ELPHICK, Tommy (M) 43 2
H: 5 11 W: 11 07 b.Brighton 7-9-87
Source: Scholar.
2005–06 Brighton & HA 1 0
2006–07 Brighton & HA 3 0
2007–08 Brighton & HA 39 2 **43 2**

FOGDEN, Wes (F) 3 0
H: 5 8 W: 10 04 b.Brighton 12-4-88
Source: Scholar.
2006–07 Brighton & HA 0 0
2007–08 Brighton & HA 3 0 **3 0**

FORSTER, Nicky (F) 531 162
H: 5 9 W: 11 05 b.Caterham 8-9-73
Source: Horley T. *Honours:* England Under-21.
1992–93 Gillingham 26 6
1993–94 Gillingham 41 18 **67 24**
1994–95 Brentford 46 24
1995–96 Brentford 38 5
1996–97 Brentford 25 10 **109 39**
1996–97 Birmingham C 7 3
1997–98 Birmingham C 28 3
1998–99 Birmingham C 33 5 **68 11**
1999–2000 Reading 36 10
2000–01 Reading 9 1
2001–02 Reading 42 19
2002–03 Reading 40 16
2003–04 Reading 30 7
2004–05 Reading 30 7 **187 60**
2005–06 Ipswich T 20 7
2006–07 Ipswich T 4 1 **24 8**
2006–07 Hull C 35 5 **35 5**
2007–08 Brighton & HA 41 15 **41 15**

FRASER, Tom (M) 52 1
H: 5 10 W: 11 00 b.Brighton 5-12-87
Source: Bognor Regis T.
2006–07 Brighton & HA 28 1
2007–08 Brighton & HA 24 0 **52 1**

GARGAN, Sam (F) 1 0
H: 6 3 W: 11 12 b.Hurstpierpoint 24-6-88
Source: Scholar.
2007–08 Brighton & HA 1 0 **1 0**

GATTING, Joe (D) 44 4
H: 5 11 W: 12 04 b.Brighton 25-11-87
Source: Scholar.
2005–06 Brighton & HA 12 0
2006–07 Brighton & HA 23 4
2007–08 Brighton & HA 9 0 **44 4**

HART, Gary (F) 342 44
H: 5 9 W: 12 03 b.Harlow 21-9-76
Source: Stansted.
1998–99 Brighton & HA 44 12
1999–2000 Brighton & HA 43 9
2000–01 Brighton & HA 45 7
2001–02 Brighton & HA 39 4
2002–03 Brighton & HA 36 4
2003–04 Brighton & HA 42 3
2004–05 Brighton & HA 26 2
2005–06 Brighton & HA 35 1
2006–07 Brighton & HA 25 2
2007–08 Brighton & HA 7 0 **342 44**

HINSHELWOOD, Adam (D) 85 1
H: 5 10 W: 12 10 b.Oxford 8-1-84
Source: Scholar.
2002–03 Brighton & HA 7 0
2003–04 Brighton & HA 17 0
2004–05 Brighton & HA 38 1
2005–06 Brighton & HA 11 0
2006–07 Brighton & HA 11 0
2007–08 Brighton & HA 1 0 **85 1**

KUIPERS, Michels (G) 218 0
H: 6 2 W: 14 03 b.Amsterdam 26-6-74
Source: SDW Amsterdam.
1998–99 Bristol R 1 0
1999–2000 Bristol R 0 0 **1 0**
2000–01 Brighton & HA 34 0
2001–02 Brighton & HA 39 0
2002–03 Brighton & HA 21 0
2003–04 Brighton & HA 10 0
2003–04 *Hull C* 3 0 **3 0**
2004–05 Brighton & HA 30 0
2005–06 Brighton & HA 5 0
2005–06 *Boston U* 15 0 **15 0**
2006–07 Brighton & HA 14 0
2007–08 Brighton & HA 46 0 **199 0**

LOFT, Doug (M) 27 2
H: 6 0 W: 12 01 b.Maidstone 25-12-86
Source: Hastings U.
2005–06 Brighton & HA 3 1
2006–07 Brighton & HA 11 1
2007–08 Brighton & HA 13 0 **27 2**

LYNCH, Joel (G) 77 2
H: 6 1 W: 12 10 b.Eastbourne 3-10-87
Source: Scholar. *Honours:* England Youth.
2005–06 Brighton & HA 16 1
2006–07 Brighton & HA 39 0
2007–08 Brighton & HA 22 1 **77 2**

MARTOT, David (M) 137 12
H: 5 8 W: 11 00 b.Fecamp 1-2-81
2001–02 Le Havre B 0 0
2002–03 Le Havre 25 2
2003–04 Le Havre 25 1
2004–05 Le Havre 6 1
2005–06 Le Havre 32 5
2006–07 Le Havre 23 2 **111 11**
2007–08 Brighton & HA 26 1 **26 1**

MAYO, Kerry (D) 366 12
H: 5 10 W: 12 08 b.Haywards Heath 21-9-77
Source: Trainee.
1996–97 Brighton & HA 24 0
1997–98 Brighton & HA 44 6
1998–99 Brighton & HA 25 1
1999–2000 Brighton & HA 31 1
2000–01 Brighton & HA 45 1
2001–02 Brighton & HA 33 0
2002–03 Brighton & HA 41 1
2003–04 Brighton & HA 33 0
2004–05 Brighton & HA 27 1
2005–06 Brighton & HA 18 1
2006–07 Brighton & HA 30 0
2007–08 Brighton & HA 15 0 **366 12**

McFAUL, Shane (M) 31 0
H: 6 1 W: 11 11 b.Dublin 23-5-86
Source: Scholar. *Honours:* Eire Youth, Under-21.
2003–04 Notts Co 6 0
2004–05 Notts Co 24 0
2005–06 Notts Co 0 0
2006–07 Notts Co 0 0
2007–08 Notts Co 0 0 **30 0**
2007–08 Brighton & HA 1 0 **1 0**

MURRAY, Glenn (F) 113 40
H: 6 1 W: 12 12 b.Maryport 25-9-83
Source: Wilmington Hammerheads, Workington.
2005–06 Carlisle U 26 3
2006–07 Carlisle U 1 0 **27 3**
2006–07 *Stockport Co* 11 3 **11 3**
2006–07 Rochdale 31 16
2007–08 Rochdale 23 9 **54 25**
2007–08 Brighton & HA 21 9 **21 9**

OATWAY, Charlie (M) 383 10
H: 5 7 W: 10 10 b.Hammersmith 28-11-73
Source: Yeading.
1994–95 Cardiff C 30 0
1995–96 Cardiff C 2 0 **32 0**
1995–96 Torquay U 24 0
1996–97 Torquay U 41 1
1997–98 Torquay U 2 0 **67 1**
1997–98 Brentford 33 0
1998–99 Brentford 24 0 **57 0**
1998–99 *Lincoln C* 3 0 **3 0**
1999–2000 Brighton & HA 42 4
2000–01 Brighton & HA 38 0
2001–02 Brighton & HA 32 1
2002–03 Brighton & HA 29 1
2003–04 Brighton & HA 31 1
2004–05 Brighton & HA 34 1
2005–06 Brighton & HA 18 1
2006–07 Brighton & HA 0 0
2007–08 Brighton & HA 0 0 **224 9**

REID, Paul (M) 200 22
H: 5 10 W: 10 10 b.Sydney 6-7-79
Honours: Australia Under-20.
1998–99 Wollongong Wolves 22 2
1999–2000 Wollongong Wolves 31 3
2000–01 Wollongong Wolves 30 7
2001–02 Wollongong Wolves 15 3 **98 15**
2002–03 Bradford C 8 2
2003–04 Bradford C 0 0 **8 2**
2003–04 Brighton & HA 5 0

2004–05 Brighton & HA 34 2
2005–06 Brighton & HA 38 2
2006–07 Brighton & HA 10 1
2007–08 Brighton & HA 7 0 **94 5**

RENTS, Sam (D) 30 0
H: 5 9 W: 11 03 b.Brighton 22-6-87
Source: Scholar.
2006–07 Brighton & HA 25 0
2007–08 Brighton & HA 5 0 **30 0**

ROBINSON, Jake (F) 118 12
H: 5 7 W: 10 10 b.Brighton 23-10-86
Source: Scholar.
2003–04 Brighton & HA 9 0
2004–05 Brighton & HA 10 1
2005–06 Brighton & HA 27 1
2006–07 Brighton & HA 38 6
2007–08 Brighton & HA 34 4 **118 12**

SKINNER, Lloyd (D) 0 0
Source: Scholar.
2007–08 Brighton & HA 0 0

SULLIVAN, John (M) 0 0
H: 5 10 W: 11 04 b.Brighton 8-3-88
Source: Scholar. *Honours:* England Youth.
2005–06 Brighton & HA 0 0
2006–07 Brighton & HA 0 0
2007–08 Brighton & HA 0 0

THOMSON, Steve (M) 191 4
H: 5 8 W: 10 04 b.Glasgow 23-1-78
Source: Trainee. *Honours:* Scotland Youth.
1995–96 Crystal Palace 0 0
1996–97 Crystal Palace 0 0
1997–98 Crystal Palace 0 0
1998–99 Crystal Palace 16 0
1999–2000 Crystal Palace 21 0
2000–01 Crystal Palace 18 0
2001–02 Crystal Palace 23 0
2002–03 Crystal Palace 27 1 **105 1**
2003–04 Peterborough U 35 1
2004–05 Peterborough U 31 2
2005–06 Peterborough U 0 0
2006–07 Peterborough U 0 0 **66 3**
2007–08 Brighton & HA 20 0 **20 0**

WHING, Andrew (D) 160 2
H: 6 0 W: 12 00 b.Birmingham 20-9-84
Source: Scholar.
2002–03 Coventry C 14 0
2003–04 Coventry C 28 1
2004–05 Coventry C 16 1
2005–06 Coventry C 32 0
2006–07 Coventry C 16 0 **106 2**
2006–07 *Brighton & HA* 12 0
2007–08 Brighton & HA 42 0 **54 0**

BRISTOL C (14)

ADEBOLA, Dele (F) 495 116
H: 6 3 W: 12 08 b.Lagos 23-6-75
Source: Trainee.
1992–93 Crewe Alex 6 0
1993–94 Crewe Alex 0 0
1994–95 Crewe Alex 30 8
1995–96 Crewe Alex 29 8
1996–97 Crewe Alex 32 16
1997–98 Crewe Alex 27 7 **124 39**
1997–98 Birmingham C 17 7
1998–99 Birmingham C 39 13
1999–2000 Birmingham C 42 5
2000–01 Birmingham C 31 6
2001–02 Birmingham C 0 0 **129 31**
2001–02 *Oldham Ath* 5 0 **5 0**
2002–03 Crystal Palace 39 5 **39 5**
2003–04 Coventry C 28 2
2003–04 *Burnley* 3 1 **3 1**
2004–05 Coventry C 25 5
2004–05 *Bradford C* 15 3 **15 3**
2005–06 Coventry C 44 12
2006–07 Coventry C 40 8
2007–08 Coventry C 26 4 **163 31**
2007–08 Bristol C 17 6 **17 6**

ARTUS, Frankie (M) 0 0
H: 6 0 W: 11 02 b.Bristol 27-9-88
Source: Scholar.
2005–06 Bristol C 0 0
2006–07 Bristol C 0 0
2007–08 Bristol C 0 0

BASSO, Adriano (G) **118 0**
H: 6 1 W: 11 07 b.Jundiai 18-4-75
Source: Woking.

2005–06	Bristol C	29	0		
2006–07	Bristol C	45	0		
2007–08	Bristol C	44	0	**118**	**0**

BETSY, Kevin (M) **268 39**
H: 6 1 W: 12 00 b.Seychelles 20-3-78
Source: Woking.

1998–99	Fulham	7	1		
1999–2000	Fulham	2	0		
1999–2000	*Bournemouth*	5	0	**5**	**0**
1999–2000	*Hull C*	2	0	**2**	**0**
2000–01	Fulham	5	0		
2001–02	Fulham	1	0	**15**	**1**
2001–02	Barnsley	10	0		
2002–03	Barnsley	39	5		
2003–04	Barnsley	45	10		
2004–05	Barnsley	0	0	**94**	**15**
2004–05	*Hartlepool U*	6	1	**6**	**1**
2004–05	Oldham Ath	36	5	**36**	**5**
2005–06	Wycombe W	42	8		
2006–07	Wycombe W	29	5	**71**	**13**
2006–07	Bristol C	17	1		
2007–08	Bristol C	1	0	**18**	**1**
2007–08	*Yeovil T*	5	1	**5**	**1**
2007–08	*Walsall*	16	2	**16**	**2**

BROOKER, Stephen (F) **243 75**
H: 6 0 W: 14 00 b.Newport Pagnell 21-5-81
Source: Trainee.

1999–2000	Watford	1	0		
2000–01	Watford	0	0	**1**	**0**
2000–01	Port Vale	23	8		
2001–02	Port Vale	41	9		
2002–03	Port Vale	26	5		
2003–04	Port Vale	32	8		
2004–05	Port Vale	9	5	**131**	**35**
2004–05	Bristol C	33	16		
2005–06	Bristol C	37	16		
2006–07	Bristol C	23	2		
2007–08	Bristol C	4	1	**97**	**35**
2007–08	*Cheltenham T*	14	5	**14**	**5**

BYFIELD, Darren (F) **318 85**
H: 5 11 W: 12 07 b.Sutton Coldfield 29-9-76
Source: Trainee. *Honours:* Jamaica 7 full caps.

1993–94	Aston Villa	0	0		
1994–95	Aston Villa	0	0		
1995–96	Aston Villa	0	0		
1996–97	Aston Villa	0	0		
1997–98	Aston Villa	7	0		
1998–99	Aston Villa	0	0		
1998–99	*Preston NE*	5	1	**5**	**1**
1999–2000	Aston Villa	0	0	**7**	**0**
1999–2000	*Northampton T*	6	1	**6**	**1**
1999–2000	*Cambridge U*	4	0	**4**	**0**
1999–2000	*Blackpool*	3	0	**3**	**0**
2000–01	Walsall	40	9		
2001–02	Walsall	37	4	**77**	**13**
2001–02	Rotherham U	3	2		
2002–03	Rotherham U	37	13		
2003–04	Rotherham U	28	7	**68**	**22**
2003–04	Sunderland	17	5	**17**	**5**
2004–05	Gillingham	38	6		
2005–06	Gillingham	29	13	**67**	**19**
2006–07	Millwall	31	16		
2007–08	Millwall	0	0	**31**	**16**
2007–08	Bristol C	33	8	**33**	**8**

CAREY, Louis (D) **458 10**
H: 5 10 W: 11 00 b.Bristol 20-1-77
Source: Trainee. *Honours:* Scotland Under-21.

1995–96	Bristol C	23	0		
1996–97	Bristol C	42	0		
1997–98	Bristol C	38	0		
1998–99	Bristol C	41	0		
1999–2000	Bristol C	22	0		
2000–01	Bristol C	46	3		
2001–02	Bristol C	35	0		
2002–03	Bristol C	24	1		
2003–04	Bristol C	41	1		
2004–05	Coventry C	23	0	**23**	**0**
2004–05	Bristol C	14	0		
2005–06	Bristol C	38	3		
2006–07	Bristol C	38	2		
2007–08	Bristol C	33	0	**435**	**10**

CARLE, Nick (F) **198 27**
H: 5 9 W: 12 04 b.Sydney 23-11-81
Honours: Australia Youth, Under-20, Under-23, 7 full caps.

1997–98	Sydney Olympic	16	3		
1998–99	Sydney Olympic	11	3		
1999–2000	Sydney Olympic	24	1		
2000–01	Sydney Olympic	23	2		
2001–02	Sydney Olympic	12	3	**86**	**12**
2001–02	Troyes	5	0		
2002–03	Troyes	0	0	**5**	**0**
2003–04	Marconi Stallions	24	6		
2004	Ryde City	7	1	**7**	**1**
2004–05	Marconi Stallions	0	0	**24**	**6**
2005–06	Newcastle U Jets	22	3		
2006–07	Newcastle U Jets	23	4	**45**	**7**
2007–08	Genclerbirligi	14	1	**14**	**1**
2007–08	Bristol C	17	0	**17**	**0**

ELLIOTT, Marvin (M) **189 8**
H: 6 0 W: 12 02 b.Wandsworth 15-9-84
Source: Scholar.

2001–02	Millwall	0	0		
2002–03	Millwall	1	0		
2003–04	Millwall	21	0		
2004–05	Millwall	41	1		
2005–06	Millwall	39	2		
2006–07	Millwall	42	0	**144**	**3**
2007–08	Bristol C	45	5	**45**	**5**

FONTAINE, Liam (D) **109 1**
H: 5 11 W: 11 09 b.Beckenham 7-1-86
Source: Trainee. *Honours:* England Youth, Under-20.

2003–04	Fulham	0	0		
2004–05	Fulham	1	0		
2004–05	*Yeovil T*	15	0		
2005–06	Fulham	0	0	**1**	**0**
2005–06	*Yeovil T*	10	0	**25**	**0**
2005–06	*Bristol C*	15	0		
2006–07	Bristol C	30	0		
2007–08	Bristol C	38	1	**83**	**1**

HENDERSON, Stephen (G) **1 0**
H: 6 3 W: 11 00 b.Dublin 2-5-88
Source: Scholar. *Honours:* Eire Under-21.

2005–06	Aston Villa	0	0		
2006–07	Aston Villa	0	0		
2007–08	Bristol C	1	0	**1**	**0**

JOHNSON, Lee (M) **201 20**
H: 5 6 W: 10 07 b.Newmarket 7-6-81
Source: Trainee.

1998–99	Watford	0	0		
1999–2000	Watford	0	0		
2000–01	Brighton & HA	0	0		
2000–01	Brentford	0	0		
2001–02	Brentford	0	0		
2003–04	Yeovil T	45	5		
2004–05	Yeovil T	44	7		
2005–06	Yeovil T	26	2	**115**	**14**
2005–06	Hearts	4	0	**4**	**0**
2006–07	Bristol C	42	5		
2007–08	Bristol C	40	1	**82**	**6**

KEOGH, Richard (M) **69 4**
H: 6 0 W: 11 02 b.Harlow 11-8-86
Source: Scholar. *Honours:* Eire Under-21.

2004–05	Stoke C	0	0		
2005–06	Bristol C	9	1		
2005–06	*Wycombe W*	3	0	**3**	**0**
2006–07	Bristol C	31	2		
2007–08	Bristol C	0	0	**40**	**3**
2007–08	*Huddersfield T*	9	1	**9**	**1**
2007–08	*Carlisle U*	7	0	**7**	**0**
2007–08	*Cheltenham T*	10	0	**10**	**0**

McALLISTER, Jamie (D) **320 2**
H: 5 10 W: 11 00 b.Glasgow 26-4-78
Honours: Scotland1 full cap.

1995–96	Q of S	2	0		
1996–97	Q of S	6	0		
1997–98	Q of S	15	0		
1998–99	Q of S	27	0	**50**	**0**
1999–2000	Aberdeen	34	0		
2000–01	Aberdeen	25	0		
2001–02	Aberdeen	29	0		
2002–03	Aberdeen	29	0	**117**	**0**
2003–04	Livingston	34	1	**34**	**1**
2004–05	Hearts	30	0		
2005–06	Hearts	17	0	**47**	**0**
2006–07	Bristol C	31	1		
2007–08	Bristol C	41	0	**72**	**1**

McCOMBE, Jamie (D) **225 15**
H: 6 5 W: 12 05 b.Scunthorpe 1-1-83
Source: Scholar.

2001–02	Scunthorpe U	17	0		
2002–03	Scunthorpe U	31	1		
2003–04	Scunthorpe U	15	0	**63**	**1**
2003–04	Lincoln C	8	0		
2004–05	Lincoln C	41	3		
2005–06	Lincoln C	38	4	**87**	**7**
2006–07	Bristol C	41	4		
2007–08	Bristol C	34	3	**75**	**7**

McINDOE, Michael (M) **259 41**
H: 5 8 W: 11 00 b.Edinburgh 2-12-79
Source: Trainee. *Honours:* Scotland B.

1997–98	Luton T	0	0		
1998–99	Luton T	22	0		
1999–2000	Luton T	17	0	**39**	**0**
Fr Hereford, Yeovil					
2003–04	Doncaster R	45	10		
2004–05	Doncaster R	44	10		
2005–06	Doncaster R	33	8	**122**	**28**
2005–06	*Derby Co*	8	0	**8**	**0**
2006–07	Barnsley	18	4	**18**	**4**
2006–07	Wolverhampton W	27	3	**27**	**3**
2007–08	Bristol C	45	6	**45**	**6**

MEGYERI, Balazs (G) **0 0**
b.Hungary

2007–08	Bristol C	0	0		

MURRAY, Scott (M) **389 79**
H: 5 9 W: 11 00 b.Aberdeen 26-5-74
Source: Fraserburgh. *Honours:* Scotland B.

1993–94	Aston Villa	0	0		
1994–95	Aston Villa	0	0		
1995–96	Aston Villa	3	0		
1996–97	Aston Villa	1	0		
1997–98	Aston Villa	0	0	**4**	**0**
1997–98	Bristol C	23	0		
1998–99	Bristol C	32	3		
1999–2000	Bristol C	41	6		
2000–01	Bristol C	46	10		
2001–02	Bristol C	37	8		
2002–03	Bristol C	45	19		
2003–04	Reading	34	5	**34**	**5**
2003–04	Bristol C	6	0		
2004–05	Bristol C	42	8		
2005–06	Bristol C	37	10		
2006–07	Bristol C	28	7		
2007–08	Bristol C	14	3	**351**	**74**

MYRIE-WILLIAMS, Jennison (F) **63 5**
H: 5 11 W: 12 08 b.London 17-5-88
Source: Scholar.

2005–06	Bristol C	1	0		
2006–07	Bristol C	25	2		
2007–08	Bristol C	0	0	**26**	**2**
2007–08	*Cheltenham T*	12	0	**12**	**0**
2007–08	*Tranmere R*	25	3	**25**	**3**

NOBLE, David (M) **151 12**
H: 6 0 W: 12 04 b.Hitchin 2-2-82
Source: Scholar. *Honours:* England Youth, Under-20. Scotland Under-21, B.

2000–01	Arsenal	0	0		
2001–02	Arsenal	0	0		
2001–02	*Watford*	15	1	**15**	**1**
2002–03	Arsenal	0	0		
2002–03	West Ham U	0	0		
2003–04	West Ham U	3	0	**3**	**0**
2003–04	Boston U	14	2		
2004–05	Boston U	32	3		
2005–06	Boston U	11	0	**57**	**5**
2005–06	Bristol C	24	1		
2006–07	Bristol C	26	3		
2007–08	Bristol C	26	2	**76**	**6**

ORR, Bradley (M) **156 9**
H: 6 0 W: 11 11 b.Liverpool 1-11-82
Source: Scholar.

2001–02	Newcastle U	0	0		
2002–03	Newcastle U	0	0		
2003–04	Newcastle U	0	0		
2003–04	*Burnley*	4	0	**4**	**0**
2004–05	Bristol C	37	0		
2005–06	Bristol C	38	1		
2006–07	Bristol C	35	4		
2007–08	Bristol C	42	4	**152**	**9**

PLUMMER, Tristan (F) **0 0**
H: 5 6 W: 10 07 b.Bristol 30-1-90
Source: Scholar. *Honours:* England Youth.

2007–08	Bristol C	0	0		

RIBEIRO, Christian (D) 0 0
H: 5 11 W: 12 02 b.Neath 14-12-89
Source: Scholar. *Honours:* Wales Youth, Under-21.
2006–07 Bristol C 0 0
2007–08 Bristol C 0 0

RUSSELL, Alex (M) 418 52
H: 5 10 W: 11 07 b.Crosby 17-3-73
Source: Burscough.
1994–95 Rochdale 7 1
1995–96 Rochdale 25 0
1996–97 Rochdale 39 9
1997–98 Rochdale 31 4 **102 14**
1998–99 Cambridge U 37 6
1999–2000 Cambridge U 15 0
2000–01 Cambridge U 29 2 **81 8**
2001–02 Torquay U 33 7
2002–03 Torquay U 39 9
2003–04 Torquay U 43 2
2004–05 Torquay U 38 3 **153 21**
2005–06 Bristol C 27 4
2006–07 Bristol C 28 2
2007–08 Bristol C 1 0 **56 6**
2007–08 *Northampton T* 13 1 **13 1**
2007–08 *Cheltenham T* 13 2 **13 2**

SHOWUNMI, Enoch (F) 162 27
H: 6 3 W: 14 11 b.Kilburn 21-4-82
Source: Willesden Constantine. *Honours:* Nigeria 2 full caps.
2003–04 Luton T 26 7
2004–05 Luton T 35 6
2005–06 Luton T 41 1 **102 14**
2006–07 Bristol C 33 10
2007–08 Bristol C 17 3 **50 13**
2007–08 *Sheffield W* 10 0 **10 0**

SKUSE, Cole (M) 112 2
H: 6 1 W: 11 05 b.Bristol 29-3-86
Source: Scholar.
2004–05 Bristol C 7 0
2005–06 Bristol C 38 2
2006–07 Bristol C 42 0
2007–08 Bristol C 25 0 **112 2**

SLOCOMBE, Martin (M) 0 0
b.Weston-Super-Mare
2006–07 Bristol C 0 0
2007–08 Bristol C 0 0

SPROULE, Ivan (M) 104 13
H: 5 8 W: 11 09 b.Castlederg 18-2-81
Source: Omagh Town, Institute. *Honours:* Northern Ireland 11 full caps, 1 goal.
2005–06 Hibernian 32 4
2006–07 Hibernian 32 7 **64 11**
2007–08 Bristol C 40 2 **40 2**

TRUNDLE, Lee (F) 272 109
H: 6 0 W: 11 06 b.Liverpool 10-10-76
Source: Rhyl.
2000–01 Wrexham 14 8
2001–02 Wrexham 36 8
2002–03 Wrexham 44 11 **94 27**
2003–04 Swansea C 31 16
2004–05 Swansea C 42 22
2005–06 Swansea C 36 20
2006–07 Swansea C 34 19 **143 77**
2007–08 Bristol C 35 5 **35 5**

VASKO, Tamas (D) 64 6
H: 6 4 W: 14 13 b.Budapest 20-2-84
Honours: Hungary 10 full caps.
2003–04 Ujpest 3 0
2004–05 *Tatabanya* 0 0
2004–05 Ujpest 0 0
2005–06 Ujpest 15 2
2006–07 Ujpest 27 3 **45 5**
2007–08 Bristol C 19 1 **19 1**

WALKER, Jordan (D) 0 0
b.Bristol 1-8-89
2006–07 Bristol C 0 0
2007–08 Bristol C 0 0

WEALE, Chris (G) 103 0
H: 6 2 W: 13 03 b.Yeovil 9-2-82
Source: Juniors.
2003–04 Yeovil T 35 0
2004–05 Yeovil T 38 0
2005–06 Yeovil T 25 0 **98 0**
2006–07 Bristol C 1 0
2007–08 Hereford U 1 0 **1 0**
2007–08 Bristol C 3 0 **4 0**

WILSON, Brian (D) 168 15
H: 5 10 W: 11 00 b.Manchester 9-5-83
Source: Scholar.
2001–02 Stoke C 1 0
2002–03 Stoke C 3 0
2003–04 Stoke C 2 0 **6 0**
2003–04 Cheltenham T 14 0
2004–05 Cheltenham T 43 3
2005–06 Cheltenham T 43 9
2006–07 Cheltenham T 25 2 **125 14**
2006–07 Bristol C 19 0
2007–08 Bristol C 18 1 **37 1**

WILSON, James (D) 0 0
H: 6 2 W: 11 05 b.Chepstow 26-2-89
Source: Scholar. *Honours:* Wales Youth.
2005–06 Bristol C 0 0
2006–07 Bristol C 0 0
2007–08 Bristol C 0 0

BRISTOL R (15)

ANTHONY, Byron (D) 43 1
H: 6 1 W: 11 02 b.Newport 20-9-84
Source: Scholar. *Honours:* Wales Youth, Under-21.
2003–04 Cardiff C 0 0
2004–05 Cardiff C 0 0
2005–06 Cardiff C 0 0
2006–07 Bristol R 23 0
2007–08 Bristol R 20 1 **43 1**

CAMPBELL, Stuart (M) 344 14
H: 5 10 W: 10 08 b.Corby 9-12-77
Source: Trainee. *Honours:* Scotland Under-21.
1996–97 Leicester C 10 0
1997–98 Leicester C 11 0
1998–99 Leicester C 12 0
1999–2000 Leicester C 4 0
1999–2000 *Birmingham C* 2 0 **2 0**
2000–01 Leicester C 0 0 **37 0**
2000–01 *Grimsby T* 38 2
2001–02 Grimsby T 33 3
2002–03 Grimsby T 45 6
2003–04 Grimsby T 39 1 **155 12**
2004–05 Bristol R 25 0
2005–06 Bristol R 38 1
2006–07 Bristol R 41 1
2007–08 Bristol R 46 0 **150 2**

CARRUTHERS, Chris (M) 174 2
H: 5 10 W: 12 00 b.Kettering 19-8-83
Source: Scholar. *Honours:* England Under-20.
2000–01 Northampton T 3 0
2001–02 Northampton T 13 1
2002–03 Northampton T 33 0
2003–04 Northampton T 24 0
2004–05 Northampton T 1 0 **74 1**
2004–05 *Bristol R* 5 0
2005–06 Bristol R 40 1
2006–07 Bristol R 38 0
2007–08 Bristol R 17 0 **100 1**

CLOUGH, Charlie (M) 1 0
H: 6 2 W: 12 07 b.Taunton 4-9-90
Source: Scholar.
2007–08 Bristol R 1 0 **1 0**

COLES, Danny (D) 206 6
H: 6 1 W: 11 05 b.Bristol 31-10-81
Source: Scholarship.
1999–2000 Bristol C 1 0
2000–01 Bristol C 2 0
2001–02 Bristol C 23 0
2002–03 Bristol C 39 2
2003–04 Bristol C 45 2
2004–05 Bristol C 38 1 **148 5**
2005–06 Hull C 9 0
2006–07 Hull C 21 0
2007–08 Hull C 1 0 **31 0**
2007–08 *Hartlepool U* 3 0 **3 0**
2007–08 Bristol R 24 1 **24 1**

DISLEY, Craig (M) 300 38
H: 5 10 W: 10 13 b.Worksop 24-8-81
Source: Trainee.
1999–2000 Mansfield T 5 0
2000–01 Mansfield T 24 0
2001–02 Mansfield T 36 7
2002–03 Mansfield T 42 4
2003–04 Mansfield T 34 5 **141 16**
2004–05 Bristol R 28 4
2005–06 Bristol R 42 8
2006–07 Bristol R 45 4
2007–08 Bristol R 44 6 **159 22**

ELLIOTT, Steve (D) 259 13
H: 6 1 W: 14 00 b.Derby 29-10-78
Source: Trainee. *Honours:* England Under-21.
1996–97 Derby Co 0 0
1997–98 Derby Co 3 0
1998–99 Derby Co 11 0
1999–2000 Derby Co 20 0
2000–01 Derby Co 6 0
2001–02 Derby Co 6 0
2002–03 Derby Co 23 1
2003–04 Derby Co 4 0 **73 1**
2003–04 Blackpool 28 0 **28 0**
2004–05 Bristol R 41 2
2005–06 Bristol R 45 2
2006–07 Bristol R 39 5
2007–08 Bristol R 33 3 **158 12**

FRASER, James (M) 0 0
H: 5 9 W: 12 07 b.Brighton 26-4-89
Source: Scholar.
2007–08 Bristol R 0 0

GODSELL, Tom (D) 0 0
H: 5 11 W: 11 08 b.Bristol 26-11-88
Source: Scholar.
2007–08 Bristol R 0 0

GREEN, Mike (G) 0 0
H: 6 1 W: 13 01 b.Bristol 23-7-89
Source: Scholar.
2006–07 Bristol R 0 0
2007–08 Bristol R 0 0

GREEN, Ryan (M) 80 0
H: 5 7 W: 10 10 b.Cardiff 20-10-80
Source: Danes Court. *Honours:* Wales Youth, Under-21, 2 full caps.
1997–98 Wolverhampton W 0 0
1998–99 Wolverhampton W 1 0
1999–2000 Wolverhampton W 0 0
2000–01 Wolverhampton W 7 0
2000–01 *Torquay U* 10 0 **10 0**
2001–02 Wolverhampton W 0 0 **8 0**
2001–02 Millwall 13 0 **13 0**
2002–03 Cardiff C 0 0
2002–03 Sheffield W 4 0 **4 0**
From Hereford U.
2006–07 Bristol R 33 0
2007–08 Bristol R 12 0 **45 0**

GROVES, Matt (F) 1 0
H: 5 8 W: 11 07 b.Bristol 11-12-88
Source: Scholar.
2007–08 Bristol R 1 0 **1 0**

HALDANE, Lewis (F) 147 15
H: 6 0 W: 11 03 b.Trowbridge 13-3-85
Source: Scholar. *Honours:* Wales Under-21.
2003–04 Bristol R 27 5
2004–05 Bristol R 13 0
2005–06 Bristol R 30 3
2006–07 Bristol R 45 6
2007–08 Bristol R 32 1 **147 15**

HINTON, Craig (D) 301 5
H: 6 0 W: 12 00 b.Wolverhampton 26-11-77
Source: Trainee.
1996–97 Birmingham C 0 0
1997–98 Birmingham C 0 0
2000–01 Kidderminster H 46 2
2001–02 Kidderminster H 41 0
2002–03 Kidderminster H 44 0
2003–04 Kidderminster H 42 1 **173 3**
2004–05 Bristol R 38 0
2005–06 Bristol R 36 0
2006–07 Bristol R 30 0
2007–08 Bristol R 24 2 **128 2**

IGOE, Sammy (M) 409 29
H: 5 6 W: 10 00 b.Staines 30-9-75
Source: Trainee.
1993–94 Portsmouth 0 0
1994–95 Portsmouth 1 0
1995–96 Portsmouth 22 0
1996–97 Portsmouth 40 2
1997–98 Portsmouth 31 3
1998–99 Portsmouth 40 5
1999–2000 Portsmouth 26 1 **160 11**

1999–2000 Reading 6 0
2000–01 Reading 31 6
2001–02 Reading 35 1
2002–03 Reading 15 0 **87 7**
2002–03 *Luton T* 2 0 **2 0**
2003–04 Swindon T 36 5
2004–05 Swindon T 43 4 **79 9**
2005–06 Millwall 5 0 **5 0**
2005–06 *Bristol R* 11 1
2006–07 Bristol R 40 1
2007–08 Bristol R 21 0 **72 2**
2007–08 *Hereford U* 4 0 **4 0**

JACOBSON, Joe (D) 58 2
H: 5 11 W: 12 06 b.Cardiff 17-11-86
Source: Scholar. *Honours:* Wales Under-21.
2005–06 Cardiff C 1 0
2006–07 Cardiff C 0 0 **1 0**
2006–07 *Accrington S* 6 1 **6 1**
2006–07 *Bristol R* 11 0
2007–08 Bristol R 40 1 **51 1**

KITE, Alex (D) 0 0
H: 6 0 W: 12 05 b.Kent 7-3-89
Source: Scholar.
2007–08 Bristol R 0 0

KLEIN-DAVIES, Josh (F) 10 1
H: 5 11 W: 13 09 b.Bristol 6-7-89
Source: Bristol C Scholar. *Honours:* Wales Youth.
2007–08 Bristol R 10 1 **10 1**

LAMBERT, Ricky (F) 291 76
H: 6 2 W: 14 08 b.Liverpool 16-2-82
Source: Trainee.
1999–2000 Blackpool 3 0
2000–01 Blackpool 0 0 **3 0**
2000–01 Macclesfield T 9 0
2001–02 Macclesfield T 35 8 **44 8**
2001–02 Stockport Co 0 0
2002–03 Stockport Co 29 2
2003–04 Stockport Co 40 12
2004–05 Stockport Co 29 4 **98 18**
2004–05 Rochdale 15 6
2005–06 Rochdale 46 22
2006–07 Rochdale 3 0 **64 28**
2006–07 Bristol R 36 8
2007–08 Bristol R 46 14 **82 22**

LESCOTT, Aaron (M) 253 1
H: 5 8 W: 10 09 b.Birmingham 2-12-78
Source: Trainee. *Honours:* England Schools.
1996–97 Aston Villa 0 0
1997–98 Aston Villa 0 0
1998–99 Aston Villa 0 0
1999–2000 Aston Villa 0 0
1999–2000 *Lincoln C* 5 0 **5 0**
2000–01 Aston Villa 0 0
2000–01 Sheffield W 30 0
2001–02 Sheffield W 7 0 **37 0**
2001–02 Stockport Co 17 0
2002–03 Stockport Co 41 1
2003–04 Stockport Co 14 0 **72 1**
2003–04 *Bristol R* 8 0
2004–05 Bristol R 26 0
2005–06 Bristol R 37 0
2006–07 Bristol R 34 0
2007–08 Bristol R 34 0 **139 0**

LINES, Chris (M) 38 3
H: 6 2 W: 12 00 b.Bristol 30-11-85
Source: Youth.
2005–06 Bristol R 4 0
2006–07 Bristol R 7 0
2007–08 Bristol R 27 3 **38 3**

MAHDI, Adam (M) 0 0
H: 5 8 W: 11 00 b.London 2-12-89
Source: Scholar.
2007–08 Bristol R 0 0

PADDOCK, Ryan (D) 0 0
H: 6 3 W: 12 06 b.Newport 8-10-88
Source: Scholar.
2007–08 Bristol R 0 0

PALMER, James (M) 0 0
H: 5 7 W: 11 04 b.Bristol 30-3-88
Source: Scholar.
2006–07 Bristol R 0 0
2007–08 Bristol R 0 0

PARRINELLO, Tom (D) 0 0
H: 5 6 W: 10 07 b.Parkway 11-11-89
Source: Scholar.
2006–07 Bristol R 0 0
2007–08 Bristol R 0 0

PHILLIPS, Steve (G) 347 0
H: 6 1 W: 11 10 b.Bath 6-5-78
Source: Paulton R.
1996–97 Bristol C 0 0
1997–98 Bristol C 0 0
1998–99 Bristol C 15 0
1999–2000 Bristol C 21 0
2000–01 Bristol C 42 0
2001–02 Bristol C 22 0
2002–03 Bristol C 46 0
2003–04 Bristol C 46 0
2004–05 Bristol C 46 0
2005–06 Bristol C 19 0 **257 0**
2006–07 Bristol R 44 0
2007–08 Bristol R 46 0 **90 0**

PIPE, David (M) 202 7
H: 5 9 W: 12 01 b.Caerphilly 5-11-83
Source: Scholar. *Honours:* Wales Youth, Under-21, 1 full cap.
2000–01 Coventry C 0 0
2001–02 Coventry C 0 0
2002–03 Coventry C 21 1
2003–04 Coventry C 0 0 **21 1**
2003–04 Notts Co 18 0
2004–05 Notts Co 41 2
2005–06 Notts Co 43 2
2006–07 Notts Co 39 0 **141 4**
2007–08 Bristol R 40 2 **40 2**

REECE, Charlie (M) 1 0
H: 5 11 W: 11 03 b.Birmingham 8-9-88
Source: Scholar.
2007–08 Bristol R 1 0 **1 0**

RIGG, Sean (F) 49 2
H: 5 9 W: 12 01 b.Bristol 1-10-88
Source: Forest Green R.
2006–07 Bristol R 18 1
2007–08 Bristol R 31 1 **49 2**

WALKER, Richard (F) 278 73
H: 6 0 W: 12 04 b.Sutton Coldfield 8-11-77
Source: Trainee.
1995–96 Aston Villa 0 0
1996–97 Aston Villa 0 0
1997–98 Aston Villa 1 0
1998–99 Aston Villa 0 0
1998–99 *Cambridge U* 21 3 **21 3**
1999–2000 Aston Villa 5 2
2000–01 Aston Villa 0 0
2000–01 *Blackpool* 18 3
2001–02 Aston Villa 0 0 **6 2**
2001–02 *Wycombe W* 12 3 **12 3**
2001–02 Blackpool 21 8
2002–03 Blackpool 32 4
2003–04 Blackpool 9 0 **80 15**
2003–04 *Northampton T* 12 4 **12 4**
2003–04 Oxford U 4 0 **4 0**
2004–05 Bristol R 27 10
2005–06 Bristol R 46 20
2006–07 Bristol R 46 12
2007–08 Bristol R 24 4 **143 46**

WILLIAMS, Andy (F) 82 12
H: 5 11 W: 11 09 b.Hereford 14-8-86
Source: Pershore College.
2006–07 Hereford U 41 8 **41 8**
2007–08 Bristol R 41 4 **41 4**

BURNLEY (16)

AKINBIYI, Ade (F) 468 136
H: 6 1 W: 13 08 b.Hackney 10-10-74
Source: Trainee. *Honours:* Nigeria 1 full cap.
1992–93 Norwich C 0 0
1993–94 Norwich C 2 0
1993–94 *Hereford U* 4 2 **4 2**
1994–95 Norwich C 13 0
1994–95 *Brighton & HA* 7 4 **7 4**
1995–96 Norwich C 22 3
1996–97 Norwich C 12 0 **49 3**
1996–97 Gillingham 19 7
1997–98 Gillingham 44 21 **63 28**
1998–99 Bristol C 44 19
1999–2000 Bristol C 3 2 **47 21**
1999–2000 Wolverhampton W 37 16 **37 16**
2000–01 Leicester C 37 9
2001–02 Leicester C 21 2 **58 11**
2001–02 Crystal Palace 14 2
2002–03 Crystal Palace 10 1
2002–03 *Stoke C* 4 2
2003–04 Crystal Palace 0 0 **24 3**
2003–04 Stoke C 30 10
2004–05 Stoke C 29 7 **63 19**
2004–05 Burnley 10 4
2005–06 Burnley 29 12
2005–06 Sheffield U 15 3
2006–07 Sheffield U 3 0 **18 3**
2006–07 Burnley 20 2
2007–08 Burnley 39 8 **98 26**

ALEXANDER, Graham (D) 704 86
H: 5 10 W: 12 07 b.Coventry 10-10-71
Source: Trainee. *Honours:* Scotland B, 33 full caps.
1989–90 Scunthorpe U 0 0
1990–91 Scunthorpe U 1 0
1991–92 Scunthorpe U 36 5
1992–93 Scunthorpe U 41 5
1993–94 Scunthorpe U 41 4
1994–95 Scunthorpe U 40 4 **159 18**
1995–96 Luton T 37 1
1996–97 Luton T 45 2
1997–98 Luton T 39 8
1998–99 Luton T 29 4 **150 15**
1998–99 Preston NE 10 0
1999–2000 Preston NE 46 6
2000–01 Preston NE 34 5
2001–02 Preston NE 45 6
2002–03 Preston NE 45 10
2003–04 Preston NE 45 9
2004–05 Preston NE 42 7
2005–06 Preston NE 40 3
2006–07 Preston NE 42 6
2007–08 Preston NE 3 0 **352 52**
2007–08 Burnley 43 1 **43 1**

BERISHA, Besart (M) 46 12
H: 5 11 W: 11 12 b.Pristina 29-7-85
Honours: Albania 9 full caps, 3 goals.
2004–05 Hamburg 0 0
2004–05 *Aalborg* 2 0 **2 0**
2005–06 Hamburg 0 0
2005–06 *Horsens* 33 11 **33 11**
2006–07 Hamburg 11 1 **11 1**
2007–08 Burnley 0 0

BLAKE, Robbie (F) 485 134
H: 5 9 W: 12 00 b.Middlesbrough 4-3-76
Source: Trainee.
1994–95 Darlington 9 0
1995–96 Darlington 29 11
1996–97 Darlington 30 10 **68 21**
1996–97 Bradford C 5 0
1997–98 Bradford C 34 8
1998–99 Bradford C 39 16
1999–2000 Bradford C 28 2
2000–01 Bradford C 21 4
2000–01 *Nottingham F* 11 1 **11 1**
2001–02 Bradford C 26 10 **153 40**
2001–02 Burnley 10 0
2002–03 Burnley 41 13
2003–04 Burnley 45 19
2004–05 Burnley 24 10
2004–05 Birmingham C 11 2 **11 2**
2005–06 Leeds U 41 11
2006–07 Leeds U 36 8 **77 19**
2007–08 Burnley 45 9 **165 51**

CALDWELL, Steven (D) 178 8
H: 6 2 W: 13 12 b.Stirling 12-9-80
Source: Trainee. *Honours:* Scotland Youth, Under-21, B, 9 full caps.
1997–98 Newcastle U 0 0
1998–99 Newcastle U 0 0
1999–2000 Newcastle U 0 0
2000–01 Newcastle U 9 0
2001–02 Newcastle U 0 0
2001–02 *Blackpool* 6 0 **6 0**
2001–02 *Bradford C* 9 0 **9 0**
2002–03 Newcastle U 14 1
2003–04 Newcastle U 5 0 **28 1**
2003–04 *Leeds U* 13 1 **13 1**
2004–05 Sunderland 41 4
2005–06 Sunderland 24 0
2006–07 Sunderland 11 0 **76 4**
2006–07 Burnley 17 0
2007–08 Burnley 29 2 **46 2**

CARLISLE, Clarke (D) **298 22**

H: 6 2 W: 14 11 b.Preston 14-10-79
Source: Trainee. *Honours:* England Under-21.

1997–98	Blackpool	11	2		
1998–99	Blackpool	39	1		
1999–2000	Blackpool	43	4	**93**	**7**
2000–01	QPR	27	3		
2001–02	QPR	0	0		
2002–03	QPR	36	2		
2003–04	QPR	33	1	**96**	**6**
2004–05	Leeds U	35	4	**35**	**4**
2005–06	Watford	32	3		
2006–07	Watford	4	0		
2006–07	*Luton T*	5	0	**5**	**0**
2007–08	Watford	0	0	**36**	**3**
2007–08	Burnley	33	2	**33**	**2**

DUFF, Michael (D) **336 15**

H: 6 1 W: 11 08 b.Belfast 11-1-78
Source: Trainee. *Honours:* Northern Ireland 20 full caps.

1999–2000	Cheltenham T	31	2		
2000–01	Cheltenham T	39	5		
2001–02	Cheltenham T	45	3		
2002–03	Cheltenham T	44	2		
2003–04	Cheltenham T	42	0	**201**	**12**
2004–05	Burnley	42	0		
2005–06	Burnley	41	0		
2006–07	Burnley	44	2		
2007–08	Burnley	8	1	**135**	**3**

ELLIOTT, Wade (M) **344 40**

H: 5 10 W: 10 03 b.Southampton 14-12-78
Source: Bashley.

1999–2000	Bournemouth	12	3		
2000–01	Bournemouth	36	9		
2001–02	Bournemouth	46	8		
2002–03	Bournemouth	44	4		
2003–04	Bournemouth	39	3		
2004–05	Bournemouth	43	4	**220**	**31**
2005–06	Burnley	36	3		
2006–07	Burnley	42	4		
2007–08	Burnley	46	2	**124**	**9**

GUDJONSSON, Joey (M) **209 22**

H: 5 9 W: 12 04 b.Akranes 25-5-80
Honours: Iceland Youth, Under-21, 34 full caps, 1 goal.

1998–99	Genk	5	0	**5**	**0**
1999–2000	MVV	19	5	**19**	**5**
2000–01	RKC	31	4	**31**	**4**
2001–02	Betis	11	0	**11**	**0**
2002–03	Aston Villa	11	2	**11**	**2**
2003–04	Wolverhampton W	11	0	**11**	**0**
2004–05	Leicester C	35	2		
2005–06	Leicester C	42	8	**77**	**10**
2006–07	AZ	5	0	**5**	**0**
2006–07	Burnley	11	0		
2007–08	Burnley	28	1	**39**	**1**

HARLEY, Jon (D) **257 12**

H: 5 8 W: 10 03 b.Maidstone 26-9-79
Source: Trainee. *Honours:* England Under-21.

1996–97	Chelsea	0	0		
1997–98	Chelsea	3	0		
1998–99	Chelsea	0	0		
1999–2000	Chelsea	17	2		
2000–01	Chelsea	10	0	**30**	**2**
2000–01	*Wimbledon*	6	2	**6**	**2**
2001–02	Fulham	10	0		
2002–03	Fulham	11	1		
2002–03	*Sheffield U*	9	1		
2003–04	Fulham	4	0	**25**	**1**
2003–04	*Sheffield U*	5	0		
2003–04	*West Ham U*	15	1	**15**	**1**
2004–05	Sheffield U	44	2		
2005–06	Sheffield U	4	0	**62**	**3**
2005–06	Burnley	41	2		
2006–07	Burnley	45	1		
2007–08	Burnley	33	0	**119**	**3**

JENSEN, Brian (G) **209 0**

H: 6 1 W: 12 04 b.Copenhagen 8-6-75
Source: Hvidovre, B93.

1997–98	AZ	0	0		
1998–99	AZ	1	0	**1**	**0**
1999–2000	WBA	12	0		
2000–01	WBA	33	0		
2001–02	WBA	1	0		
2002–03	WBA	0	0	**46**	**0**
2003–04	Burnley	46	0		
2004–05	Burnley	27	0		
2005–06	Burnley	39	0		
2006–07	Burnley	31	0		
2007–08	Burnley	19	0	**162**	**0**

JONES, Steve (F) **230 47**

H: 5 10 W: 10 05 b.Derry 25-10-76
Source: Leigh RMI. *Honours:* Northern Ireland B, 29 full caps, 1 goal.

2001–02	*Rochdale*	9	1	**9**	**1**
2001–02	Crewe Alex	6	0		
2002–03	Crewe Alex	31	9		
2003–04	Crewe Alex	45	15		
2004–05	Crewe Alex	36	10		
2005–06	Crewe Alex	41	5		
2006–07	Burnley	41	5		
2007–08	Burnley	17	1	**58**	**6**
2007–08	*Crewe Alex*	4	1	**163**	**40**

JORDAN, Stephen (D) **85 0**

H: 6 1 W: 13 00 b.Warrington 6-3-82
Source: Scholarship.

1998–99	Manchester C	0	0		
1999–2000	Manchester C	0	0		
2000–01	Manchester C	0	0		
2001–02	Manchester C	0	0		
2002–03	Manchester C	1	0		
2002–03	*Cambridge U*	11	0	**11**	**0**
2003–04	Manchester C	2	0		
2004–05	Manchester C	19	0		
2005–06	Manchester C	18	0		
2006–07	Manchester C	13	0	**53**	**0**
2007–08	Burnley	21	0	**21**	**0**

KIRALY, Gabor (G) **401 0**

H: 6 3 W: 13 06 b.Szombathely 1-4-76
Honours: Hungary Youth, Under-21, 70 full caps.

1993–94	Haladas	15	0		
1994–95	Haladas	0	0		
1995–96	Haladas	19	0		
1996–97	Haladas	33	0	**67**	**0**
1997–98	Hertha Berlin	27	0		
1998–99	Hertha Berlin	34	0		
1999–2000	Hertha Berlin	27	0		
2000–01	Hertha Berlin	34	0		
2001–02	Hertha Berlin	25	0		
2002–03	Hertha Berlin	33	0		
2003–04	Hertha Berlin	18	0	**198**	**0**
2004–05	Crystal Palace	32	0		
2005–06	Crystal Palace	43	0		
2006–07	Crystal Palace	29	0	**104**	**0**
2006–07	*Aston Villa*	5	0	**5**	**0**
2007–08	Burnley	27	0	**27**	**0**

LAFFERTY, Kyle (F) **92 13**

H: 6 4 W: 11 02 b.Belfast 21-7-87
Source: Scholar. *Honours:* Northern Ireland Youth, Under-21, 16 full caps, 5 goals.

2005–06	Burnley	11	1		
2005–06	*Darlington*	9	3	**9**	**3**
2006–07	Burnley	35	4		
2007–08	Burnley	37	5	**83**	**10**

MACDONALD, Alex (F) **2 0**

H: 5 7 W: 11 04 b.Warrington 14-4-90
Source: Scholar.

2007–08	Burnley	2	0	**2**	**0**

MAHON, Alan (M) **289 29**

H: 5 8 W: 12 03 b.Dublin 4-4-78
Source: Crumplin U. *Honours:* Eire School, Youth, Under-21, 2 full caps.

1994–95	Tranmere R	0	0		
1995–96	Tranmere R	2	0		
1996–97	Tranmere R	25	2		
1997–98	Tranmere R	18	1		
1998–99	Tranmere R	39	6		
1999–2000	Tranmere R	36	4	**120**	**13**
2000–01	Sporting Lisbon	1	0	**1**	**0**
2000–01	Blackburn R	18	0		
2001–02	Blackburn R	13	1		
2002–03	Blackburn R	2	0		
2002–03	*Cardiff C*	15	2	**15**	**2**
2003–04	Blackburn R	3	0	**36**	**1**
2003–04	*Ipswich T*	11	1	**11**	**1**
2003–04	Wigan Ath	14	1		
2004–05	Wigan Ath	27	7		
2005–06	Wigan Ath	6	1	**47**	**9**
2005–06	Burnley	8	0		
2006–07	Burnley	25	2		
2007–08	Burnley	26	1	**59**	**3**

McCANN, Chris (M) **96 12**

H: 6 1 W: 11 11 b.Dublin 21-7-87
Source: Scholar. *Honours:* Eire Youth.

2005–06	Burnley	23	2		
2006–07	Burnley	38	5		
2007–08	Burnley	35	5	**96**	**12**

O'CONNOR, Gareth (M) **242 35**

H: 5 10 W: 11 00 b.Dublin 10-11-78
Source: Bohemians.

1998–99	Shamrock R	8	0	**8**	**0**
1999–2000	Bohemians	22	4	**22**	**4**
2000–01	Bournemouth	22	1		
2001–02	Bournemouth	28	0		
2002–03	Bournemouth	41	8		
2003–04	Bournemouth	37	2		
2004–05	Bournemouth	40	13		
2005–06	Burnley	29	7		
2006–07	Burnley	8	0		
2007–08	Burnley	1	0	**38**	**7**
2007–08	*Bournemouth*	6	0	**174**	**24**

O'CONNOR, James (M) **345 27**

H: 5 8 W: 11 00 b.Dublin 1-9-79
Source: Trainee. *Honours:* Eire Youth, Under-21.

1996–97	Stoke C	0	0		
1997–98	Stoke C	0	0		
1998–99	Stoke C	4	0		
1999–2000	Stoke C	42	6		
2000–01	Stoke C	44	8		
2001–02	Stoke C	43	2		
2002–03	Stoke C	43	0	**176**	**16**
2003–04	WBA	30	0		
2004–05	WBA	0	0	**30**	**0**
2004–05	Burnley	21	2		
2005–06	Burnley	46	3		
2006–07	Burnley	43	3		
2007–08	Burnley	29	3	**139**	**11**

RODRIGUEZ, Jay (F) **12 3**

H: 6 0 W: 12 00 b.Burnley 27-7-89
Source: Scholar.

2007–08	Burnley	1	0	**1**	**0**
2007–08	Stirling Alb	11	3	**11**	**3**

SPICER, John (M) **112 10**

H: 5 11 W: 11 07 b.Romford 13-9-83
Source: Scholar. *Honours:* England Schools, Youth, Under-20.

2001–02	Arsenal	0	0		
2002–03	Arsenal	0	0		
2003–04	Arsenal	0	0		
2004–05	Arsenal	0	0		
2004–05	Bournemouth	39	6		
2005–06	Bournemouth	4	0	**43**	**6**
2005–06	Burnley	34	3		
2006–07	Burnley	11	1		
2007–08	Burnley	24	0	**69**	**4**

UNSWORTH, Dave (D) **445 45**

H: 6 1 W: 13 07 b.Chorley 16-10-73
Source: Trainee. *Honours:* England Youth, Under-21, 1 full cap.

1991–92	Everton	2	1		
1992–93	Everton	3	0		
1993–94	Everton	8	0		
1994–95	Everton	38	3		
1995–96	Everton	31	2		
1996–97	Everton	34	5		
1997–98	West Ham U	32	2	**32**	**2**
1998–99	Aston Villa	0	0		
1998–99	Everton	34	1		
1999–2000	Everton	33	6		
2000–01	Everton	29	5		
2001–02	Everton	33	3		
2002–03	Everton	33	5		
2003–04	Everton	26	3	**304**	**34**
2004–05	Portsmouth	15	2		
2004–05	*Ipswich T*	16	1	**16**	**1**
2005–06	Portsmouth	0	0	**15**	**2**
2005–06	Sheffield U	34	4		
2006–07	Sheffield U	5	0	**39**	**4**
2006–07	Wigan Ath	10	1	**10**	**1**
2007–08	Burnley	29	1	**29**	**1**

BURY (17)

ADAMS, Nicky (F) **77 14**

H: 5 10 W: 11 00 b.Bolton 16-10-86
Source: Scholar. *Honours:* Wales Under-21.

2005–06	Bury	15	1		

2006–07 Bury 19 1
2007–08 Bury 43 12 **77 14**

BAKER, Richie (M) **71 6**
H: 5 10 W: 11 05 b.Burnley 29-12-87
Source: Preston NE Scholar.
2006–07 Bury 39 5
2007–08 Bury 32 1 **71 6**

BARRY-MURPHY, Brian (M) **304 13**
H: 5 10 W: 13 01 b.Cork 27-7-78
Honours: Eire Youth, Under-21.
1995–96 Cork City 13 0
1996–97 Cork City 25 0
1997–98 Cork City 15 1
1998–99 Cork City 27 1 **80 2**
1999–2000 Preston NE 1 0
2000–01 Preston NE 14 0
2001–02 Preston NE 4 0
2001–02 *Southend U* 8 1 **8 1**
2002–03 Preston NE 2 0 **21 0**
2002–03 *Hartlepool U* 7 0 **7 0**
2002–03 Sheffield W 17 0
2003–04 Sheffield W 41 0 **58 0**
2004–05 Bury 45 6
2005–06 Bury 40 3
2006–07 Bury 14 0
2007–08 Bury 31 1 **130 10**

BELFORD, Cameron (G) **1 0**
H: 6 1 W: 11 10 b.Nuneaton 16-10-88
2006–07 Coventry C 0 0
2007–08 Bury 1 0 **1 0**

BISHOP, Andy (F) **142 44**
H: 6 0 W: 10 10 b.Stone 19-10-82
Source: Scholar.
2002–03 Walsall 0 0
2002–03 *Kidderminster H* 29 5
2003–04 *Kidderminster H* 11 2 **40 7**
2003–04 *Rochdale* 10 1 **10 1**
2003–04 *Yeovil T* 5 2 **5 2**
From York C.
2006–07 Bury 43 15
2007–08 Bury 44 19 **87 34**

BUCHANAN, David (M) **102 0**
H: 5 7 W: 11 03 b.Rochdale 6-5-86
Source: Scholar. *Honours:* Northern Ireland Youth, Under-21.
2004–05 Bury 3 0
2005–06 Bury 23 0
2006–07 Bury 41 0
2007–08 Bury 35 0 **102 0**

CHALLINOR, Dave (D) **394 9**
H: 6 1 W: 12 06 b.Chester 2-10-75
Source: Brombrough Pool. *Honours:* England Schools, Youth.
1994–95 Tranmere R 0 0
1995–96 Tranmere R 0 0
1996–97 Tranmere R 5 0
1997–98 Tranmere R 32 1
1998–99 Tranmere R 34 2
1999–2000 Tranmere R 41 3
2000–01 Tranmere R 22 0
2001–02 Tranmere R 6 0 **140 6**
2001–02 Stockport Co 18 0
2002–03 Stockport Co 46 1
2003–04 Stockport Co 17 0 **81 1**
2003–04 *Bury* 15 0
2004–05 Bury 43 1
2005–06 Bury 46 1
2006–07 Bury 43 0
2007–08 Bury 26 0 **173 2**

DEAN, James (F) **4 0**
H: 5 10 W: 12 00 b.Cardiff 16-3-89
2007–08 Bury 4 0 **4 0**

DORNEY, Jack (M) **7 0**
H: 5 9 W: 10 00 b.Ashton-under-Lyne 9-1-90
Source: Scholar.
2007–08 Bury 7 0 **7 0**

FUTCHER, Ben (D) **229 18**
H: 6 7 W: 12 05 b.Manchester 20-2-81
Source: Trainee.
1999–2000 Oldham Ath 5 0
2000–01 Oldham Ath 5 0
2001–02 Oldham Ath 0 0 **10 0**
From Stalybridge C, Doncaster R
2002–03 Lincoln C 43 8
2003–04 Lincoln C 43 2
2004–05 Lincoln C 35 3 **121 13**
2005–06 Boston U 14 0 **14 0**
2005–06 Grimsby T 15 2
2006–07 Grimsby T 4 0 **19 2**
2006–07 Peterborough U 25 3 **25 3**
2007–08 Bury 40 0 **40 0**

GRUNDY, Aaron (G) **2 0**
H: 6 1 W: 12 07 b.Bolton 21-1-88
Source: Scholar.
2005–06 Bury 1 0
2006–07 Bury 1 0
2007–08 Bury 0 0 **2 0**

HASLAM, Steven (M) **184 3**
H: 5 11 W: 10 10 b.Sheffield 6-9-79
Source: Trainee. *Honours:* England Schools, Youth.
1996–97 Sheffield W 0 0
1997–98 Sheffield W 0 0
1998–99 Sheffield W 2 0
1999–2000 Sheffield W 23 0
2000–01 Sheffield W 27 1
2001–02 Sheffield W 41 0
2002–03 Sheffield W 26 1
2003–04 Sheffield W 25 0 **144 2**
2004–05 Northampton T 3 0
2005–06 Northampton T 0 0
2006–07 Northampton T 0 0 **3 0**
From Halifax T.
2007–08 Bury 37 1 **37 1**

HURST, Glynn (F) **337 109**
H: 5 10 W: 11 06 b.Barnsley 17-1-76
Source: Tottenham H Trainee.
1994–95 Barnsley 2 0
1995–96 Barnsley 5 0
1995–96 *Swansea C* 2 1 **2 1**
1996–97 Barnsley 1 0 **8 0**
1996–97 *Mansfield T* 6 0 **6 0**
1998–99 Ayr U 34 18
1999–2000 Ayr U 25 14 **59 32**
2000–01 Stockport Co 11 0
2001–02 Stockport Co 15 4 **26 4**
2001–02 Chesterfield 23 9
2002–03 Chesterfield 32 7
2003–04 Chesterfield 29 13 **84 29**
2004–05 Notts Co 41 14
2005–06 Notts Co 18 9 **59 23**
2005–06 Shrewsbury T 16 3
2006–07 Shrewsbury T 0 0 **16 3**
2006–07 Bury 35 11
2007–08 Bury 42 6 **77 17**

LEONARD, Benjamin (M) **0 0**
H: 6 3 W: 12 01
Source: Dinnington T.
2007–08 Bury 0 0

MORGAN, Paul (D) **232 2**
H: 6 0 W: 11 05 b.Belfast 23-10-78
Source: Trainee. *Honours:* Northern Ireland Under-21.
1997–98 Preston NE 0 0
1998–99 Preston NE 0 0
1999–2000 Preston NE 0 0
2000–01 Preston NE 0 0
2001–02 Lincoln C 34 1
2002–03 Lincoln C 45 0
2003–04 Lincoln C 41 0
2004–05 Lincoln C 39 0
2005–06 Lincoln C 20 0
2006–07 Lincoln C 33 1 **212 2**
2007–08 Bury 20 0 **20 0**

PARRISH, Andy (D) **43 1**
H: 6 0 W: 11 00 b.Bolton 22-6-88
Source: Scholar.
2005–06 Bury 8 0
2006–07 Bury 9 0
2007–08 Bury 26 1 **43 1**

PROVETT, Jim (G) **98 0**
H: 6 0 W: 13 04 b.Stockton 22-12-82
Source: Trainee.
1999–2000 Hartlepool U 0 0
2000–01 Hartlepool U 0 0
2001–02 Hartlepool U 0 0
2002–03 Hartlepool U 0 0
2003–04 Hartlepool U 45 0
2004–05 Hartlepool U 21 0
2005–06 Hartlepool U 0 0
2006–07 Hartlepool U 0 0 **66 0**
2007–08 Bury 32 0 **32 0**

RICHARDSON, Marcus (F) **183 36**
H: 6 1 W: 14 10 b.Reading 31-8-77
Source: Harrow B.
2000–01 Cambridge U 10 2
2001–02 Cambridge U 6 0 **16 2**
2001–02 Torquay U 30 6
2002–03 Torquay U 9 2 **39 8**
2002–03 Hartlepool U 24 5
2003–04 Hartlepool U 3 0 **27 5**
2003–04 Lincoln C 38 10
2004–05 Lincoln C 14 4 **52 14**
2004–05 *Rochdale* 2 0 **2 0**
2004–05 Yeovil T 4 0 **4 0**
2005–06 Chester C 34 4
2005–06 *Macclesfield T* 8 3 **8 3**
2006–07 Chester C 0 0 **34 4**
From Crawley T.
2007–08 Bury 1 0 **1 0**

ROUSE, Domaine (F) **8 0**
H: 5 6 W: 10 10 b.Stretford 4-7-89
Source: Scholar.
2006–07 Bury 2 0
2007–08 Bury 6 0 **8 0**

SCOTT, Paul (D) **182 12**
H: 5 11 W: 12 00 b.Wakefield 5-11-79
Source: Trainee.
1998–99 Huddersfield T 0 0
1999–2000 Huddersfield T 0 0
2000–01 Huddersfield T 0 0
2001–02 Huddersfield T 0 0
2002–03 Huddersfield T 13 0
2003–04 Huddersfield T 19 2
2004–05 Huddersfield T 0 0 **32 2**
2004–05 Bury 23 0
2005–06 Bury 41 2
2006–07 Bury 46 2
2007–08 Bury 40 6 **150 10**

STEPHENS, Dale (M) **9 1**
H: 5 7 W: 11 04 b.Bolton 12-12-87
Source: Scholar.
2006–07 Bury 3 0
2007–08 Bury 6 1 **9 1**

STEPIEN, Jordan (F) **0 0**
b.Manchester 13-9-88
Source: Scholar.
2007–08 Bury 0 0

WOODTHORPE, Colin (D) **580 13**
H: 6 0 W: 11 08 b.Ellesmere Pt 13-1-69
Source: Apprentice.
1986–87 Chester C 30 2
1987–88 Chester C 35 0
1988–89 Chester C 44 3
1989–90 Chester C 46 1 **155 6**
1990–91 Norwich C 1 0
1991–92 Norwich C 15 1
1992–93 Norwich C 7 0
1993–94 Norwich C 20 0 **43 1**
1994–95 Aberdeen 14 0
1995–96 Aberdeen 15 1
1996–97 Aberdeen 19 0 **48 1**
1997–98 Stockport Co 32 1
1998–99 Stockport Co 37 2
1999–2000 Stockport Co 26 0
2000–01 Stockport Co 24 1
2001–02 Stockport Co 34 0
2002–03 Stockport Co 0 0 **153 4**
2002–03 Bury 32 0
2003–04 Bury 39 0
2004–05 Bury 30 0
2005–06 Bury 33 0
2006–07 Bury 16 0
2007–08 Bury 31 1 **181 1**

CARDIFF C (18)

BLAKE, Darcy (M) **19 0**
H: 5 10 W: 12 05 b.Caerphilly 13-12-88
Source: Scholar. *Honours:* Wales Youth, Under-21.
2005–06 Cardiff C 1 0
2006–07 Cardiff C 10 0
2007–08 Cardiff C 8 0 **19 0**

BROWN, Jon (M) **2 0**
H: 5 10 W: 11 04 b.Llanelli 20-7-88
Source: Scholar. *Honours:* Wales Youth, Under-21.

2007–08	Cardiff C	2	0	**2**	**0**

BYRNE, Jason (F) **260 133**
H: 5 11 W: 11 11 b.Dublin 23-2-78
Honours: Eire 2 full caps.

1998–99	Bray W	17	5		
1999–2000	Bray W	31	7		
2000–01	Bray W	30	11		
2001–02	Bray W	30	14		
2002–03	Bray W	20	12	**128**	**49**
2003	Shelbourne	32	21		
2004	Shelbourne	33	25		
2005	Shelbourne	31	22		
2006	Shelbourne	26	15	**122**	**83**
2006–07	Cardiff C	10	1		
2007–08	Cardiff C	0	0	**10**	**1**

To Bohemians January 2008.

CAPALDI, Tony (D) **185 12**
H: 6 0 W: 11 08 b.Porsgrunn 12-8-81
Source: Trainee. *Honours:* Northern Ireland Youth, Under-21, 22 full caps.

1999–2000	Birmingham C	0	0		
2000–01	Birmingham C	0	0		
2001–02	Birmingham C	0	0		
2002–03	Birmingham C	0	0		
2002–03	Plymouth Arg	1	0		
2003–04	Plymouth Arg	33	7		
2004–05	Plymouth Arg	35	2		
2005–06	Plymouth Arg	41	3		
2006–07	Plymouth Arg	31	0	**141**	**12**
2007–08	Cardiff C	44	0	**44**	**0**

FEENEY, Warren (F) **237 64**
H: 5 8 W: 12 04 b.Belfast 17-1-81
Source: Trainee. *Honours:* Northern Ireland Schools, Youth, Under-21, 24 full caps, 3 goals.

1997–98	Leeds U	0	0		
1998–99	Leeds U	0	0		
1999–2000	Leeds U	0	0		
2000–01	Leeds U	0	0		
2000–01	*Bournemouth*	10	4		
2001–02	Bournemouth	37	13		
2002–03	Bournemouth	21	7		
2003–04	Bournemouth	40	12	**108**	**36**
2004–05	Stockport Co	31	15	**31**	**15**
2004–05	Luton T	6	0		
2005–06	Luton T	42	6		
2006–07	Luton T	29	2	**77**	**8**
2006–07	*Cardiff C*	6	0		
2007–08	Cardiff C	5	0	**11**	**0**
2007–08	*Swansea C*	10	5	**10**	**5**

FLOOD, Willo (M) **53 3**
H: 5 7 W: 10 05 b.Dublin 10-4-85
Source: Trainee. *Honours:* Eire Youth, Under-21.

2001–02	Manchester C	0	0		
2002–03	Manchester C	0	0		
2003–04	Manchester C	0	0		
2003–04	*Rochdale*	6	0	**6**	**0**
2004–05	Manchester C	9	1		
2005–06	Manchester C	5	0	**14**	**1**
2005–06	*Coventry C*	8	1	**8**	**1**
2006–07	Cardiff C	25	1		
2007–08	Cardiff C	0	0	**25**	**1**

FORDE, David (G) **23 0**
H: 6 3 W: 13 06 b.Galway 20-12-79
Source: Barry T.

2001–02	West Ham U	0	0		
2002–03	West Ham U	0	0		
2003–04	West Ham U	0	0		
2004–05	West Ham U	0	0		
2005–06	West Ham U	0	0		
2006–07	Cardiff C	7	0		
2007–08	Cardiff C	0	0	**7**	**0**
2007–08	*Luton T*	5	0	**5**	**0**
2007–08	*Bournemouth*	11	0	**11**	**0**

FOWLER, Robbie (F) **389 167**
H: 5 10 W: 12 05 b.Liverpool 9-4-75
Source: Trainee. *Honours:* England Youth, B, Under-21, 26 full caps, 7 goals.

1991–92	Liverpool	0	0		
1992–93	Liverpool	0	0		
1993–94	Liverpool	28	12		
1994–95	Liverpool	42	25		
1995–96	Liverpool	38	28		
1996–97	Liverpool	32	18		
1997–98	Liverpool	20	9		
1998–99	Liverpool	25	14		
1999–2000	Liverpool	14	3		
2000–01	Liverpool	27	8		
2001–02	Liverpool	10	3		
2001–02	Leeds U	22	12		
2002–03	Leeds U	8	2	**30**	**14**
2002–03	Manchester C	13	2		
2003–04	Manchester C	31	7		
2004–05	Manchester C	32	11		
2005–06	Manchester C	4	1	**80**	**21**
2005–06	Liverpool	14	5		
2006–07	Liverpool	16	3	**266**	**128**
2007–08	Cardiff C	13	4	**13**	**4**

GREEN, Matt (F) **10 0**
H: 5 5 W: 10 06 b.Bath 2-1-87
Source: Newport Co.

2006–07	Cardiff C	6	0		
2007–08	Cardiff C	0	0	**6**	**0**
2007–08	*Darlington*	4	0	**4**	**0**

HASSELBAINK, Jimmy Floyd (F) **418 190**
H: 5 10 W: 13 10 b.Paramaribo 27-3-72
Honours: Holland 23 full caps, 9 goals.

1995–96	Campomairorense	31	12	**31**	**12**
1996–97	Boavista	29	20	**29**	**20**
1997–98	Leeds U	33	16		
1998–99	Leeds U	36	18	**69**	**34**
1999–2000	Atletico Madrid	34	24	**34**	**24**
2000–01	Chelsea	35	23		
2001–02	Chelsea	35	23		
2002–03	Chelsea	36	11		
2003–04	Chelsea	30	12	**136**	**69**
2004–05	Middlesbrough	36	13		
2005–06	Middlesbrough	22	9	**58**	**22**
2006–07	Charlton Ath	25	2		
2007–08	Charlton Ath	0	0	**25**	**2**
2007–08	Cardiff C	36	7	**36**	**7**

JOHNSON, Roger (D) **231 26**
H: 6 3 W: 11 00 b.Ashford 28-4-83
Source: Trainee.

1999–2000	Wycombe W	1	0		
2000–01	Wycombe W	1	0		
2001–02	Wycombe W	7	1		
2002–03	Wycombe W	33	3		
2003–04	Wycombe W	28	2		
2004–05	Wycombe W	42	6		
2005–06	Wycombe W	45	7	**157**	**19**
2006–07	Cardiff C	32	2		
2007–08	Cardiff C	42	5	**74**	**7**

LEDLEY, Joe (M) **157 18**
H: 6 0 W: 11 07 b.Cardiff 23-1-87
Source: Scholar. *Honours:* Wales Youth, Under-21, 22 full caps, 1 goal.

2004–05	Cardiff C	28	3		
2005–06	Cardiff C	42	3		
2006–07	Cardiff C	46	2		
2007–08	Cardiff C	41	10	**157**	**18**

LOOVENS, Glenn (D) **161 5**
H: 6 1 W: 12 11 b.Doetinchem 22-9-83
Honours: Holland Youth, Under-21.

2001–02	Feyenoord	8	0		
2002–03	Feyenoord	12	0		
2003–04	Feyenoord	1	0		
2003–04	Excelsior	24	2	**24**	**2**
2004–05	Feyenoord	6	0	**27**	**0**
2004–05	De Graafschap	11	0	**11**	**0**
2005–06	Cardiff C	33	2		
2006–07	Cardiff C	30	1		
2007–08	Cardiff C	36	0	**99**	**3**

McNAUGHTON, Kevin (D) **252 4**
H: 5 10 W: 10 06 b.Dundee 28-8-82
Honours: Scotland Under-21, 4 full caps.

1999–2000	Aberdeen	0	0		
2000–01	Aberdeen	33	0		
2001–02	Aberdeen	34	0		
2002–03	Aberdeen	22	1		
2003–04	Aberdeen	17	0		
2004–05	Aberdeen	35	2		
2005–06	Aberdeen	34	0	**175**	**3**
2006–07	Cardiff C	42	0		
2007–08	Cardiff C	35	1	**77**	**1**

McPHAIL, Stephen (M) **251 10**
H: 5 8 W: 11 04 b.Westminster 9-12-79
Source: Trainee. *Honours:* Eire Youth, B, Under-21, 10 full caps, 1 goal.

1996–97	Leeds U	0	0		
1997–98	Leeds U	4	0		
1998–99	Leeds U	17	0		
1999–2000	Leeds U	24	2		
2000–01	Leeds U	7	0		
2001–02	Leeds U	1	0		
2001–02	*Millwall*	3	0	**3**	**0**
2002–03	Leeds U	13	0		
2003–04	Leeds U	12	1	**78**	**3**
2003–04	*Nottingham F*	14	0	**14**	**0**
2004–05	Barnsley	36	2		
2005–06	Barnsley	34	2	**70**	**4**
2006–07	Cardiff C	43	0		
2007–08	Cardiff C	43	3	**86**	**3**

OAKES, Michael (G) **262 0**
H: 6 2 W: 14 06 b.Northwich 30-10-73
Source: Trainee. *Honours:* England Under-21.

1991–92	Aston Villa	0	0		
1992–93	Aston Villa	0	0		
1993–94	Aston Villa	0	0		
1993–94	*Scarborough*	1	0	**1**	**0**
1993–94	*Tranmere R*	0	0		
1994–95	Aston Villa	0	0		
1995–96	Aston Villa	0	0		
1996–97	Aston Villa	20	0		
1997–98	Aston Villa	8	0		
1998–99	Aston Villa	23	0		
1999–2000	Aston Villa	0	0	**51**	**0**
1999–2000	Wolverhampton W	28	0		
2000–01	Wolverhampton W	46	0		
2001–02	Wolverhampton W	46	0		
2002–03	Wolverhampton W	6	0		
2003–04	Wolverhampton W	21	0		
2004–05	Wolverhampton W	35	0		
2005–06	Wolverhampton W	17	0		
2006–07	Wolverhampton W	0	0	**199**	**0**
2007–08	Cardiff C	11	0	**11**	**0**

PARRY, Paul (M) **151 22**
H: 5 11 W: 12 12 b.Chepstow 19-8-80
Source: Hereford U. *Honours:* Wales 11 full caps, 1 goal.

2003–04	Cardiff C	17	1		
2004–05	Cardiff C	24	4		
2005–06	Cardiff C	27	1		
2006–07	Cardiff C	42	6		
2007–08	Cardiff C	41	10	**151**	**22**

PURSE, Darren (D) **392 27**
H: 6 2 W: 12 08 b.Stepney 14-2-77
Source: Trainee. *Honours:* England Under-21.

1993–94	Leyton Orient	5	0		
1994–95	Leyton Orient	38	3		
1995–96	Leyton Orient	12	0	**55**	**3**
1996–97	Oxford U	31	1		
1997–98	Oxford U	28	4	**59**	**5**
1997–98	Birmingham C	8	0		
1998–99	Birmingham C	20	0		
1999–2000	Birmingham C	38	2		
2000–01	Birmingham C	37	3		
2001–02	Birmingham C	36	3		
2002–03	Birmingham C	20	1		
2003–04	Birmingham C	9	0	**168**	**9**
2004–05	WBA	22	0	**22**	**0**
2005–06	Cardiff C	39	5		
2006–07	Cardiff C	31	4		
2007–08	Cardiff C	18	1	**88**	**10**

RAE, Gavin (D) **285 30**
H: 5 11 W: 10 04 b.Aberdeen 28-11-77
Source: Hermes J. *Honours:* Scotland Under-21, 13 full caps.

1995–96	Dundee	6	0		
1996–97	Dundee	17	2		
1997–98	Dundee	6	0		
1998–99	Dundee	30	1		
1999–2000	Dundee	35	4		
2000–01	Dundee	32	4		
2001–02	Dundee	36	6		
2002–03	Dundee	37	4		
2003–04	Dundee	13	2	**212**	**23**
2003–04	Rangers	10	2		
2004–05	Rangers	0	0		
2005–06	Rangers	8	0		
2006–07	Rangers	10	1	**28**	**3**
2007–08	Cardiff C	45	4	**45**	**4**

RAMSEY, Aaron (M) **16 1**
H: 5 9 W: 10 07 b.Caerphilly 26-12-90
Source: School. *Honours:* Wales Youth, Under-21.

2006–07	Cardiff C	1	0		
2007–08	Cardiff C	15	1	**16**	**1**

SAK, Erwin (G) **0 0**
Source: Sokol Pniewi.
2007–08 Cardiff C 0 0

SCIMECA, Riccardo (D) **350 16**
H: 6 1 W: 12 09 b.Leamington Spa 13-6-75
Source: Trainee. *Honours:* England Under-21, B.

Season	Club	Apps	Gls	Tot Apps	Tot Gls
1993–94	Aston Villa	0	0		
1994–95	Aston Villa	0	0		
1995–96	Aston Villa	17	0		
1996–97	Aston Villa	17	0		
1997–98	Aston Villa	21	0		
1998–99	Aston Villa	18	2	**73**	**2**
1999–2000	Nottingham F	38	0		
2000–01	Nottingham F	36	4		
2001–02	Nottingham F	37	0		
2002–03	Nottingham F	40	3	**151**	**7**
2003–04	Leicester C	29	1	**29**	**1**
2004–05	WBA	33	0		
2005–06	WBA	2	0	**35**	**0**
2005–06	Cardiff C	18	1		
2006–07	Cardiff C	35	5		
2007–08	Cardiff C	9	0	**62**	**6**

SINCLAIR, Trevor (M) **559 74**
H: 5 9 W: 13 05 b.Dulwich 2-3-73
Source: Trainee. *Honours:* England Youth, Under-21, B, 12 full caps.

Season	Club	Apps	Gls	Tot Apps	Tot Gls
1989–90	Blackpool	9	0		
1990–91	Blackpool	31	1		
1991–92	Blackpool	27	3		
1992–93	Blackpool	45	11	**112**	**15**
1993–94	QPR	32	4		
1994–95	QPR	33	4		
1995–96	QPR	37	2		
1996–97	QPR	39	3		
1997–98	QPR	26	3	**167**	**16**
1997–98	West Ham U	14	7		
1998–99	West Ham U	36	7		
1999–2000	West Ham U	36	7		
2000–01	West Ham U	19	3		
2001–02	West Ham U	34	5		
2002–03	West Ham U	38	8	**177**	**37**
2003–04	Manchester C	29	1		
2004–05	Manchester C	4	1		
2005–06	Manchester C	31	3		
2006–07	Manchester C	18	0	**82**	**5**
2007–08	Cardiff C	21	1	**21**	**1**

SMITH, Matthew (D) **0 0**
H: 5 10 W: 12 00 b.Newport 5-10-88
Source: Scholar.
2007–08 Cardiff C 0 0

THOMPSON, Steven (F) **284 50**
H: 6 2 W: 12 05 b.Paisley 14-10-78
Source: Dundee U BC. *Honours:* Scotland Under-21, 16 full caps, 3 goals.

Season	Club	Apps	Gls	Tot Apps	Tot Gls
1996–97	Dundee U	1	0		
1997–98	Dundee U	8	0		
1998–99	Dundee U	15	1		
1999–2000	Dundee U	27	1		
2000–01	Dundee U	31	4		
2001–02	Dundee U	32	6		
2002–03	Dundee U	20	6	**134**	**18**
2002–03	Rangers	8	2		
2003–04	Rangers	16	8		
2004–05	Rangers	19	5		
2005–06	Rangers	14	2	**57**	**17**
2005–06	Cardiff C	14	4		
2006–07	Cardiff C	43	6		
2007–08	Cardiff C	36	5	**93**	**15**

WHITTINGHAM, Peter (D) **134 10**
H: 5 10 W: 9 13 b.Nuneaton 8-9-84
Source: Trainee. *Honours:* England Youth, Under-20, Under-21.

Season	Club	Apps	Gls	Tot Apps	Tot Gls
2002–03	Aston Villa	4	0		
2003–04	Aston Villa	32	0		
2004–05	Aston Villa	13	1		
2004–05	*Burnley*	7	0	**7**	**0**
2005–06	Aston Villa	4	0		
2005–06	*Derby Co*	11	0	**11**	**0**
2006–07	Aston Villa	3	0	**56**	**1**
2006–07	Cardiff C	19	4		
2007–08	Cardiff C	41	5	**60**	**9**

CARLISLE U (19)

ARANALDE, Zigor (D) **306 11**
H: 6 1 W: 13 03 b.Ibarra 28-2-73
Source: Logrones.

Season	Club	Apps	Gls	Tot Apps	Tot Gls
2000–01	Walsall	45	0		
2001–02	Walsall	45	2		
2002–03	Walsall	39	3		
2003–04	Walsall	36	0		
2004–05	Walsall	30	0	**195**	**5**
2004–05	Sheffield W	2	0	**2**	**0**
2005–06	Carlisle U	39	5		
2006–07	Carlisle U	43	1		
2007–08	Carlisle U	27	0	**109**	**6**

ARNISON, Paul (D) **172 4**
H: 5 10 W: 10 12 b.Hartlepool 18-9-77
Source: Trainee.

Season	Club	Apps	Gls	Tot Apps	Tot Gls
1995–96	Newcastle U	0	0		
1996–97	Newcastle U	0	0		
1997–98	Newcastle U	0	0		
1998–99	Newcastle U	0	0		
1999–2000	Newcastle U	0	0		
1999–2000	Hartlepool U	8	1		
2000–01	Hartlepool U	27	1		
2001–02	Hartlepool U	19	0		
2002–03	Hartlepool U	19	1		
2003–04	Hartlepool U	4	0	**77**	**3**
2003–04	Carlisle U	26	1		
2004–05	Carlisle U	0	0		
2005–06	Carlisle U	41	0		
2006–07	Carlisle U	11	0		
2007–08	Carlisle U	17	0	**95**	**1**

BILLY, Chris (M) **500 25**
H: 5 11 W: 11 08 b.Huddersfield 2-1-73
Source: Trainee.

Season	Club	Apps	Gls	Tot Apps	Tot Gls
1991–92	Huddersfield T	10	2		
1992–93	Huddersfield T	13	0		
1993–94	Huddersfield T	34	0		
1994–95	Huddersfield T	37	2	**94**	**4**
1995–96	Plymouth Arg	32	4		
1996–97	Plymouth Arg	45	3		
1997–98	Plymouth Arg	41	2	**118**	**9**
1998–99	Notts Co	6	0	**6**	**0**
1998–99	Bury	37	0		
1999–2000	Bury	36	4		
2000–01	Bury	46	0		
2001–02	Bury	21	3		
2002–03	Bury	38	4	**178**	**11**
2003–04	Carlisle U	39	1		
2004–05	Carlisle U	0	0		
2005–06	Carlisle U	45	0		
2006–07	Carlisle U	20	0		
2007–08	Carlisle U	0	0	**104**	**1**

BRADLEY, Adam (G) **0 0**
H: 6 0 W: 12 06 b.Carlisle 25-8-88

Season	Club	Apps	Gls
2005–06	Carlisle U	0	0
2006–07	Carlisle U	0	0
2007–08	Carlisle U	0	0

BRIDGE-WILKINSON, Marc (M) **286 51**
H: 5 6 W: 11 00 b.Coventry 16-3-79
Source: Trainee.

Season	Club	Apps	Gls	Tot Apps	Tot Gls
1996–97	Derby Co	0	0		
1997–98	Derby Co	0	0		
1998–99	Derby Co	1	0		
1998–99	*Carlisle U*	7	0		
1999–2000	Derby Co	0	0	**1**	**0**
2000–01	Port Vale	42	9		
2001–02	Port Vale	19	6		
2002–03	Port Vale	31	9		
2003–04	Port Vale	32	7	**124**	**31**
2004–05	Stockport Co	22	2	**22**	**2**
2004–05	*Bradford C*	12	3		
2005–06	Bradford C	36	5		
2006–07	Bradford C	39	4	**87**	**12**
2007–08	Carlisle U	45	6	**52**	**6**

CAMPION, Darren (D) **2 0**
H: 5 11 W: 12 00 b.Birmingham 17-10-88
Source: Scholar.
2007–08 Carlisle U 2 0 **2 0**

CARLTON, Danny (F) **31 0**
H: 5 11 W: 12 04 b.Leeds 22-12-83
Source: Morecambe.
2007–08 Carlisle U 31 0 **31 0**

DALTON, Ged (M) **0 0**
H: 5 8 W: 10 04 b.Beverley 30-3-90
2007–08 Carlisle U 0 0

DOBIE, Scott (F) **324 55**
H: 6 1 W: 12 05 b.Workington 10-10-78
Source: Trainee. *Honours:* Scotland 6 full caps, 1 goal.

Season	Club	Apps	Gls	Tot Apps	Tot Gls
1996–97	Carlisle U	2	1		
1997–98	Carlisle U	23	0		
1998–99	Carlisle U	33	6		
1998–99	*Clydebank*	6	0	**6**	**0**
1999–2000	Carlisle U	34	7		
2000–01	Carlisle U	44	10		
2001–02	WBA	43	10		
2002–03	WBA	31	5		
2003–04	WBA	31	5		
2004–05	WBA	5	1	**110**	**21**
2004–05	Millwall	16	3	**16**	**3**
2004–05	Nottingham F	12	1		
2005–06	Nottingham F	8	2		
2006–07	Nottingham F	19	0		
2007–08	Nottingham F	2	0	**41**	**3**
2007–08	Carlisle U	15	4	**151**	**28**

GALL, Kevin (F) **247 27**
H: 5 9 W: 10 08 b.Merthyr 4-2-82
Source: Trainee. *Honours:* Wales Schools, Youth, Under-21.

Season	Club	Apps	Gls	Tot Apps	Tot Gls
1998–99	Newcastle U	0	0		
1999–2000	Newcastle U	0	0		
2000–01	Newcastle U	0	0		
2000–01	Bristol R	10	2		
2001–02	Bristol R	31	3		
2002–03	Bristol R	9	0	**50**	**5**
2003–04	Yeovil T	43	8		
2004–05	Yeovil T	43	3		
2005–06	Yeovil T	37	2	**123**	**13**
2006–07	Carlisle U	45	8		
2007–08	Carlisle U	21	1	**66**	**9**
2007–08	*Darlington*	8	0	**8**	**0**

GARNER, Joe (F) **49 19**
H: 5 10 W: 11 02 b.Blackburn 12-4-88
Source: Scholar. *Honours:* England Schools, Youth.

Season	Club	Apps	Gls	Tot Apps	Tot Gls
2004–05	Blackburn R	0	0		
2005–06	Blackburn R	0	0		
2006–07	Blackburn R	0	0		
2006–07	*Carlisle U*	18	5		
2007–08	Carlisle U	31	14	**49**	**19**

GRAHAM, Danny (F) **101 25**
H: 5 11 W: 12 05 b.Gateshead 12-8-85
Source: Trainee. *Honours:* England Youth, Under-20.

Season	Club	Apps	Gls	Tot Apps	Tot Gls
2003–04	Middlesbrough	0	0		
2003–04	*Darlington*	9	2	**9**	**2**
2004–05	Middlesbrough	11	1		
2005–06	Middlesbrough	3	0		
2005–06	*Derby Co*	14	0	**14**	**0**
2005–06	*Leeds U*	3	0	**3**	**0**
2006–07	Middlesbrough	1	0	**15**	**1**
2006–07	*Blackpool*	4	1	**4**	**1**
2006–07	*Carlisle U*	11	7		
2007–08	Carlisle U	45	14	**56**	**21**

HACKNEY, Simon (M) **91 16**
H: 5 8 W: 9 13 b.Manchester 5-2-84
Source: Woodley Sports.

Season	Club	Apps	Gls	Tot Apps	Tot Gls
2005–06	Carlisle U	30	6		
2006–07	Carlisle U	18	2		
2007–08	Carlisle U	43	8	**91**	**16**

HINDMARCH, Stephen (F) **7 0**
H: 5 10 W: 11 11 b.Keswick 16-11-89
Source: Scholar.

Season	Club	Apps	Gls	Tot Apps	Tot Gls
2006–07	Carlisle U	7	0		
2007–08	Carlisle U	0	0	**7**	**0**

HORWOOD, Evan (D) **65 1**
H: 6 0 W: 10 06 b.Billingham 10-3-86
Source: Scholar.

Season	Club	Apps	Gls	Tot Apps	Tot Gls
2004–05	Sheffield U	0	0		
2004–05	*Stockport Co*	10	0	**10**	**0**
2005–06	Sheffield U	0	0		
2005–06	*Scunthorpe U*	0	0		
2005–06	*Chester C*	1	0	**1**	**0**
2006–07	Sheffield U	0	0		
2006–07	*Darlington*	20	0	**20**	**0**
2007–08	Sheffield U	0	0		
2007–08	Gretna	15	1	**15**	**1**
2007–08	Carlisle U	19	0	**19**	**0**

HOWARTH, Chris (G) **3 0**
H: 6 2 W: 12 10 b.Bolton 23-5-86
Source: Scholar. *Honours:* England Schools, Youth.
2005–06 Bolton W 0 0
2005–06 *Stockport Co* 0 0
2006–07 Bolton W 0 0
2006–07 *Oldham Ath* 3 0 **3 0**
2007–08 Carlisle U 0 0

JOYCE, Luke (M) **19 2**
H: 5 11 W: 12 03 b.Bolton 9-7-87
Source: Scholar.
2005–06 Wigan Ath 0 0
2005–06 Carlisle U 0 0
2006–07 Carlisle U 16 1
2007–08 Carlisle U 3 1 **19 2**

KIRKUP, Dan (D) **0 0**
H: 6 3 W: 12 07 b.Hexham 19-5-88
Source: Scholar.
2006–07 Carlisle U 0 0
2007–08 Carlisle U 0 0

LIVESEY, Danny (D) **139 11**
H: 6 3 W: 13 01 b.Salford 31-12-84
Source: Trainee.
2002–03 Bolton W 2 0
2003–04 Bolton W 0 0
2003–04 *Notts Co* 11 0 **11 0**
2003–04 *Rochdale* 13 0 **13 0**
2004–05 Bolton W 0 0 **2 0**
2004–05 *Blackpool* 1 0 **1 0**
2005–06 Carlisle U 36 4
2006–07 Carlisle U 31 1
2007–08 Carlisle U 45 6 **112 11**

LUMSDON, Chris (M) **226 23**
H: 5 11 W: 10 06 b.Newcastle 15-12-79
Source: Trainee.
1997–98 Sunderland 1 0
1998–99 Sunderland 0 0
1999–2000 Sunderland 1 0
1999–2000 *Blackpool* 6 1 **6 1**
2000–01 Sunderland 0 0
2000–01 *Crewe Alex* 16 0 **16 0**
2001–02 Sunderland 0 0 **2 0**
2001–02 Barnsley 32 7
2002–03 Barnsley 25 3
2003–04 Barnsley 28 3
2004–05 Barnsley 0 0 **85 13**
2005–06 Carlisle U 38 7
2006–07 Carlisle U 39 2
2007–08 Carlisle U 40 0 **117 9**

MADINE, Gary (F) **11 0**
H: 6 1 W: 12 00 b.Gateshead 24-8-90
2007–08 Carlisle U 11 0 **11 0**

McDERMOTT, Neale (M) **31 5**
H: 5 9 W: 10 11 b.Newcastle 8-3-85
Source: Scholar. *Honours:* England Schools, Youth.
2001–02 Newcastle U 0 0
2002–03 Newcastle U 0 0
2002–03 Fulham 0 0
2003–04 Fulham 0 0
2004–05 Fulham 0 0
2005–06 Fulham 0 0
2005–06 *Swindon T* 13 2 **13 2**
2005–06 *Darlington* 3 0 **3 0**
2006–07 Carlisle U 15 3
2007–08 Carlisle U 0 0 **15 3**

MURPHY, Peter (M) **256 11**
H: 5 10 W: 12 10 b.Dublin 27-10-80
Source: Trainee. *Honours:* Eire Youth, Under-21, 1 full cap.
1998–99 Blackburn R 0 0
1999–2000 Blackburn R 0 0
2000–01 Blackburn R 0 0
2000–01 *Halifax T* 21 1 **21 1**
2001–02 Blackburn R 0 0
2001–02 Carlisle U 40 0
2002–03 Carlisle U 40 2
2003–04 Carlisle U 35 1
2004–05 Carlisle U 0 0
2005–06 Carlisle U 44 2
2006–07 Carlisle U 40 2
2007–08 Carlisle U 36 3 **235 10**

RAVEN, David (D) **91 1**
H: 6 0 W: 11 04 b.Birkenhead 10-3-85
Source: Scholar. *Honours:* England Youth, Under-20.
2001–02 Liverpool 0 0
2002–03 Liverpool 0 0
2003–04 Liverpool 0 0
2004–05 Liverpool 1 0
2005–06 Liverpool 0 0 **1 0**
2005–06 *Tranmere R* 11 0 **11 0**
2006–07 Carlisle U 36 0
2007–08 Carlisle U 43 1 **79 1**

SMITH, Grant (M) **109 15**
H: 6 1 W: 12 07 b.Irvine 5-5-80
1998–99 Reading 0 0
1999–2000 Reading 0 0
2000–01 Reading 0 0
2001–02 *Halifax T* 11 0 **11 0**
2001–02 Sheffield U 7 0
2002–03 Sheffield U 3 0 **10 0**
2002–03 *Plymouth Arg* 5 1 **5 1**
2003–04 Swindon T 7 0
2004–05 Swindon T 30 10 **37 10**
2005–06 Bristol C 11 0
2005–06 *Walsall* 13 3 **13 3**
2006–07 Bristol C 0 0 **11 0**
2006–07 Dundee U 6 0
2007–08 Dundee U 0 0 **6 0**
2007–08 Carlisle U 16 1 **16 1**

SMITH, Jeff (M) **147 9**
H: 5 11 W: 11 10 b.Middlesbrough 28-6-80
Source: Trainee.
1998–99 Hartlepool U 3 0
1999–2000 Hartlepool U 0 0 **3 0**
From Bishop Auckland
2000–01 Bolton W 1 0
2001–02 *Macclesfield T* 8 2 **8 2**
2001–02 Bolton W 1 0
2002–03 Bolton W 0 0
2003–04 Bolton W 0 0 **2 0**
2003–04 *Scunthorpe U* 1 0 **1 0**
2003–04 *Rochdale* 1 0 **1 0**
2003–04 Preston NE 5 0 **5 0**
2004–05 Port Vale 34 1
2005–06 Port Vale 27 1
2006–07 Port Vale 27 3 **88 5**
2006–07 Carlisle U 17 1
2007–08 Carlisle U 22 1 **39 2**

TAYLOR, Cleveland (M) **195 15**
H: 5 8 W: 10 07 b.Leicester 9-9-83
Source: Scholar. *Honours:* Jamaica Youth.
2001–02 Bolton W 0 0
2002–03 Bolton W 0 0
2002–03 *Exeter C* 3 0 **3 0**
2003–04 Bolton W 0 0
2003–04 Scunthorpe U 20 3
2004–05 Scunthorpe U 44 6
2005–06 Scunthorpe U 45 3
2006–07 Scunthorpe U 45 3
2007–08 Scunthorpe U 20 0 **174 15**
2007–08 Carlisle U 18 0 **18 0**

THIRLWELL, Paul (M) **183 1**
H: 5 11 W: 12 08 b.Springwell 13-2-79
Source: Trainee. *Honours:* England Under-21.
1996–97 Sunderland 0 0
1997–98 Sunderland 0 0
1998–99 Sunderland 2 0
1999–2000 Sunderland 8 0
1999–2000 *Swindon T* 12 0 **12 0**
2000–01 Sunderland 5 0
2001–02 Sunderland 14 0
2002–03 Sunderland 19 0
2003–04 Sunderland 29 0 **77 0**
2004–05 Sheffield U 30 1 **30 1**
2005–06 Derby Co 21 0
2006–07 Derby Co 0 0 **21 0**
2006–07 Carlisle U 30 0
2007–08 Carlisle U 13 0 **43 0**

VIPOND, Shaun (M) **4 0**
H: 5 11 W: 11 04 b.Hexham 25-12-88
Source: Scholar.
2006–07 Carlisle U 4 0
2007–08 Carlisle U 0 0 **4 0**

WESTWOOD, Keiren (G) **127 0**
H: 6 1 W: 13 10 b.Manchester 23-10-84
Source: Scholar.
2001–02 Manchester C 0 0
2002–03 Manchester C 0 0
2003–04 Manchester C 0 0
2003–04 *Oldham Ath* 0 0
2004–05 Manchester C 0 0
2005–06 Manchester C 0 0
2005–06 Carlisle U 35 0
2006–07 Carlisle U 46 0
2007–08 Carlisle U 46 0 **127 0**

CHARLTON ATH (20)

AMBROSE, Darren (M) **158 26**
H: 6 0 W: 11 00 b.Harlow 29-2-84
Source: Scholar. *Honours:* England Youth, Under-20, Under-21.
2001–02 Ipswich T 1 0
2002–03 Ipswich T 29 8 **30 8**
2002–03 Newcastle U 1 0
2003–04 Newcastle U 24 2
2004–05 Newcastle U 12 3 **37 5**
2005–06 Charlton Ath 28 3
2006–07 Charlton Ath 26 3
2007–08 Charlton Ath 37 7 **91 13**

ARTER, Harry (M) **0 0**
H: 5 9 W: 11 07 b.Sidcup 23-12-89
Source: Scholar. *Honours:* Eire Youth.
2007–08 Charlton Ath 0 0

BASEY, Grant (D) **16 1**
H: 6 2 W: 13 12 b.Farnborough 30-11-88
Source: Scholar.
2007–08 Charlton Ath 8 1 **8 1**
2007–08 *Brentford* 8 0 **8 0**

BENT, Marcus (F) **432 90**
H: 6 2 W: 13 03 b.Hammersmith 19-5-78
Source: Trainee. *Honours:* England Under-21.
1995–96 Brentford 12 1
1996–97 Brentford 34 3
1997–98 Brentford 24 4 **70 8**
1997–98 Crystal Palace 16 5
1998–99 Crystal Palace 12 0 **28 5**
1998–99 Port Vale 15 0
1999–2000 Port Vale 8 1 **23 1**
1999–2000 Sheffield U 32 15
2000–01 Sheffield U 16 5 **48 20**
2000–01 Blackburn R 28 8
2001–02 Blackburn R 9 0 **37 8**
2001–02 Ipswich T 25 9
2002–03 Ipswich T 32 11
2003–04 Ipswich T 4 1 **61 21**
2003–04 *Leicester C* 33 9 **33 9**
2004–05 Everton 37 6
2005–06 Everton 18 1 **55 7**
2005–06 Charlton Ath 13 2
2006–07 Charlton Ath 30 1
2007–08 Charlton Ath 3 1 **46 4**
2007–08 *Wigan Ath* 31 7 **31 7**

BOUGHERRA, Madjid (D) **122 6**
H: 6 2 W: 14 00 b.Dijon 7-10-82
Source: Longvic. *Honours:* Algeria 21 full caps, 1 goal.
2002–03 Gueugnon 1 0
2003–04 Gueugnon 8 1
2004–05 Gueugnon 30 0
2005–06 Gueugnon 10 0 **49 1**
2005–06 Crewe Alex 11 1 **11 1**
2006–07 Sheffield W 28 2 **28 2**
2006–07 Charlton Ath 5 0
2007–08 Charlton Ath 29 2 **34 2**

CHRISTENSEN, Martin (D) **0 0**
H: 5 11 W: 12 10 b.Ishoj 23-12-87
Source: Herfolge. *Honours:* Denmark Youth, Under-21.
2007–08 Charlton Ath 0 0

DA SILVA MONTEIRO, Paulo (D) **0 0**
H: 6 3 W: 13 00 b.Guimaraes 21-1-85
Source: Farul Constanta, Sporting Braga, Istres. *Honours:* Portugal Youth.
2007–08 Charlton Ath 0 0

DICKSON, Chris (F) **17 7**
H: 5 11 W: 11 09 b.East Dulwich 28-12-84
Source: Dulwich H.
2006–07 Charlton Ath 0 0
2007–08 Charlton Ath 2 0 **2 0**
2007–08 *Crewe Alex* 3 0 **3 0**
2007–08 *Gillingham* 12 7 **12 7**

ELLIOT, Rob (G) **12 0**
H: 6 3 W: 14 10 b.Chatham 30-4-86
Source: Scholar.
2004–05 Charlton Ath 0 0
2004–05 *Notts Co* 4 0 **4 0**
2005–06 Charlton Ath 0 0
2006–07 Charlton Ath 0 0
2006–07 *Accrington S* 7 0 **7 0**
2007–08 Charlton Ath 1 0 **1 0**

FAYE, Amdy (M) **187 3**
H: 6 1 W: 12 06 b.Dakar 12-3-77
Source: Frejus. *Honours:* Senegal 18 full caps.
1998–99 Auxerre 0 0
1999–2000 Auxerre 3 0
2000–01 Auxerre 23 0
2001–02 Auxerre 20 0
2002–03 Auxerre 34 2 **80 2**
2003–04 Portsmouth 27 0
2004–05 Portsmouth 20 0 **47 0**
2004–05 Newcastle U 9 0
2005–06 Newcastle U 22 0 **31 0**
2006–07 Charlton Ath 28 1
2007–08 Charlton Ath 1 0 **29 1**

FOFANA, Beko (F) **0 0**
b.Abidjan 8-9-89
Source: ASEC Mimosas.
2007–08 Charlton Ath 0 0

FORTUNE, Jon (D) **181 8**
H: 6 2 W: 12 12 b.Islington 23-8-80
Source: Trainee.
1998–99 Charlton Ath 0 0
1999–2000 Charlton Ath 0 0
1999–2000 *Mansfield T* 4 0
2000–01 Charlton Ath 0 0
2000–01 *Mansfield T* 14 0 **18 0**
2001–02 Charlton Ath 19 0
2002–03 Charlton Ath 26 1
2003–04 Charlton Ath 28 2
2004–05 Charlton Ath 31 2
2005–06 Charlton Ath 11 0
2006–07 Charlton Ath 8 0
2006–07 *Stoke C* 14 1 **14 1**
2007–08 Charlton Ath 26 2 **149 7**

GIBBS, Cory (D) **106 6**
H: 6 3 W: 12 12 b.Fort Lauderdale 14-1-80
Source: Brown Univ. *Honours:* USA Under-21, Under-23, 19 full caps.
2001–02 St Pauli II 5 1 **5 1**
2001–02 St Pauli 25 1
2002–03 St Pauli 21 0
2003–04 St Pauli 14 3 **60 4**
2004 Dallas Burn 21 0 **21 0**
2004–05 Feyenoord 15 1 **15 1**
2005–06 *Den Haag* 5 0 **5 0**
2006–07 Charlton Ath 0 0
2007–08 Charlton Ath 0 0

GRAY, Andy (F) **342 78**
H: 6 1 W: 13 00 b.Harrogate 15-11-77
Source: Trainee. *Honours:* Scotland Youth, B, 2 full caps.
1995–96 Leeds U 15 0
1996–97 Leeds U 7 0
1997–98 Leeds U 0 0
1997–98 *Bury* 6 1 **6 1**
1998–99 Leeds U 0 0 **22 0**
1998–99 Nottingham F 8 0
1998–99 *Preston NE* 5 0 **5 0**
1998–99 *Oldham Ath* 4 0 **4 0**
1999–2000 Nottingham F 22 0
2000–01 Nottingham F 18 0
2001–02 Nottingham F 16 1 **64 1**
2002–03 Bradford C 44 15
2003–04 Bradford C 33 5 **77 20**
2003–04 Sheffield U 14 9
2004–05 Sheffield U 43 15
2005–06 Sheffield U 1 1 **58 25**
2005–06 Sunderland 21 1 **21 1**
2005–06 Burnley 9 3
2006–07 Burnley 35 14
2007–08 Burnley 25 11 **69 28**
2007–08 Charlton Ath 16 2 **16 2**

HARKIN, Ruairi (M) **0 0**
H: 5 10 W: 11 04 b.Derry 11-10-89
Source: Don Boscos, Charlton Ath Scholar.
2007–08 Charlton Ath 0 0

HOLLAND, Matt (M) **520 68**
H: 5 10 W: 12 03 b.Bury 11-4-74
Source: Trainee. *Honours:* Eire B, 49 full caps, 5 goals.
1992–93 West Ham U 0 0
1993–94 West Ham U 0 0
1994–95 West Ham U 0 0
1994–95 Bournemouth 16 1
1995–96 Bournemouth 43 10
1996–97 Bournemouth 45 7 **104 18**
1997–98 Ipswich T 46 10
1998–99 Ipswich T 46 5
1999–2000 Ipswich T 46 10
2000–01 Ipswich T 38 3
2001–02 Ipswich T 38 3
2002–03 Ipswich T 45 7 **259 38**
2003–04 Charlton Ath 38 6
2004–05 Charlton Ath 32 3
2005–06 Charlton Ath 23 1
2006–07 Charlton Ath 33 1
2007–08 Charlton Ath 31 1 **157 12**

IWELUMO, Chris (F) **310 72**
H: 6 3 W: 15 03 b.Coatbridge 1-8-78
Source: Juniors. *Honours:* Scotland B.
1996–97 St Mirren 14 0
1997–98 St Mirren 12 0 **26 0**
1998–99 Aarhus Fremad 27 4 **27 4**
1999–2000 Stoke C 3 0
2000–01 Stoke C 2 1
2000–01 *York C* 12 2 **12 2**
2000–01 *Cheltenham T* 4 1 **4 1**
2001–02 Stoke C 38 10
2002–03 Stoke C 32 5
2003–04 Stoke C 9 0 **84 16**
2003–04 Brighton & HA 10 4 **10 4**
2004–05 Aachen 9 0 **9 0**
2005–06 Colchester U 46 17
2006–07 Colchester U 46 18 **92 35**
2007–08 Charlton Ath 46 10 **46 10**

KOUADIO, Konan (M) **0 0**
b.Abidjan 31-12-88
Source: ASEC Mimosas.
2007–08 Charlton Ath 0 0

McCARTHY, Patrick (D) **119 5**
H: 6 2 W: 13 07 b.Dublin 31-5-83
Source: Scholar. *Honours:* Eire Youth, B, Under-21.
2000–01 Manchester C 0 0
2001–02 Manchester C 0 0
2002–03 Manchester C 0 0
2002–03 *Boston U* 12 0 **12 0**
2002–03 *Notts Co* 6 0 **6 0**
2003–04 Manchester C 0 0
2004–05 Manchester C 0 0
2004–05 Leicester C 12 0
2005–06 Leicester C 38 2
2006–07 Leicester C 22 1 **72 3**
2007–08 Charlton Ath 29 2 **29 2**

McLEOD, Izale (F) **182 59**
H: 6 1 W: 11 02 b.Birmingham 15-10-84
Source: Scholar. *Honours:* England Under-21.
2002–03 Derby Co 29 3
2003–04 Derby Co 10 1 **39 4**
2003–04 *Sheffield U* 7 0 **7 0**
2004–05 Milton Keynes D 43 16
2005–06 Milton Keynes D 39 17
2006–07 Milton Keynes D 34 21 **116 54**
2007–08 Charlton Ath 18 1 **18 1**
2007–08 *Colchester U* 2 0 **2 0**

MOUTAOUAKIL, Yassin (D) **10 0**
H: 5 10 W: 11 05 b.Nice 18-7-86
Honours: France Youth, Under-21.
2006–07 Chateauroux 0 0
2007–08 Charlton Ath 10 0 **10 0**

POWELL, Chris (D) **648 6**
H: 5 11 W: 11 12 b.Lambeth 8-9-69
Source: Trainee. *Honours:* England 5 full caps.
1987–88 Crystal Palace 0 0
1988–89 Crystal Palace 3 0
1989–90 Crystal Palace 0 0 **3 0**
1989–90 *Aldershot* 11 0 **11 0**
1990–91 Southend U 45 1
1991–92 Southend U 44 0
1992–93 Southend U 42 2
1993–94 Southend U 46 0
1994–95 Southend U 44 0
1995–96 Southend U 27 0 **248 3**
1995–96 Derby Co 19 0
1996–97 Derby Co 35 0
1997–98 Derby Co 37 1 **91 1**
1998–99 Charlton Ath 38 0
1999–2000 Charlton Ath 40 0
2000–01 Charlton Ath 33 0
2001–02 Charlton Ath 36 1
2002–03 Charlton Ath 37 0
2003–04 Charlton Ath 16 0
2004–05 Charlton Ath 0 0
2004–05 West Ham U 36 0 **36 0**
2005–06 Charlton Ath 27 0
2006–07 Watford 15 0 **15 0**
2007–08 Charlton Ath 17 1 **244 2**

RACON, Therry (M) **40 3**
H: 5 10 W: 10 02 b.Villeneuve-St-Georges 1-5-84
2004–05 Lorient 28 3 **28 3**
2005–06 Guingamp 0 0
2006–07 Guingamp 0 0
2007–08 Charlton Ath 4 0 **4 0**
2007–08 *Brighton & HA* 8 0 **8 0**

RANDOLPH, Darren (G) **19 0**
H: 6 2 W: 14 00 b.Dublin 12-5-87
Source: Ardmore R Scholar, Eire B, Under-21.
2004–05 Charlton Ath 0 0
2005–06 Charlton Ath 0 0
2006–07 Charlton Ath 1 0
2006–07 *Gillingham* 3 0 **3 0**
2007–08 Charlton Ath 1 0 **2 0**
2007–08 *Bury* 14 0 **14 0**

SAM, Lloyd (F) **54 2**
H: 5 10 W: 11 00 b.Leeds 27-9-84
Honours: England Youth, Under-20.
2002–03 Charlton Ath 0 0
2003–04 Charlton Ath 0 0
2003–04 *Leyton Orient* 10 0 **10 0**
2004–05 Charlton Ath 1 0
2005–06 Charlton Ath 2 0
2006–07 Charlton Ath 7 0
2006–07 *Sheffield W* 4 0 **4 0**
2006–07 *Southend U* 2 0 **2 0**
2007–08 Charlton Ath 28 2 **38 2**

SANKOFA, Osei (D) **34 0**
H: 6 0 W: 12 04 b.London 19-3-85
Source: Scholar. *Honours:* England Youth, Under-20.
2002–03 Charlton Ath 1 0
2003–04 Charlton Ath 0 0
2004–05 Charlton Ath 0 0
2005–06 Charlton Ath 4 0
2005–06 *Bristol C* 8 0 **8 0**
2006–07 Charlton Ath 9 0
2007–08 Charlton Ath 1 0 **15 0**
2007–08 *Brentford* 11 0 **11 0**

SEMEDO, Jose (D) **92 2**
H: 6 0 W: 12 08 b.Setubal 11-1-85
Honours: Portugal Under-21.
2004–05 Sporting Lisbon 0 0
2004–05 *Casa Pia* 34 2 **34 2**
2005–06 *Feirense* 18 0 **18 0**
2006–07 *Cagliari* 3 0 **3 0**
2007–08 Charlton Ath 37 0 **37 0**

SHELVEY, Jonjo (M) **2 0**
H: 6 1 W: 11 02 b.Romford 27-2-92
Honours: England Youth.
2007–08 Charlton Ath 2 0 **2 0**

SINCLAIR, Dean (M) **100 9**
H: 5 10 W: 11 03 b.St Albans 17-12-84
Source: Scholar.
2002–03 Norwich C 2 0
2003–04 Norwich C 0 0 **2 0**
2004–05 Barnet 0 0
2005–06 Barnet 44 2
2006–07 Barnet 42 6 **86 8**
2007–08 Charlton Ath 0 0
2007–08 *Cheltenham T* 12 1 **12 1**

SMITH, Dorian (M) **0 0**
Source: Tooting & Mitcham U.
2007–08 Charlton Ath 0 0

THATCHER, Ben (D) **310 2**
H: 5 10 W: 12 07 b.Swindon 30-11-75
Source: Trainee. *Honours:* England Youth, Under-21, Wales 7 full caps.
1992–93 Millwall 0 0

1993–94	Millwall	8	0		
1994–95	Millwall	40	1		
1995–96	Millwall	42	0	**90**	**1**
1996–97	Wimbledon	9	0		
1997–98	Wimbledon	26	0		
1998–99	Wimbledon	31	0		
1999–2000	Wimbledon	20	0	**86**	**0**
2000–01	Tottenham H	12	0		
2001–02	Tottenham H	12	0		
2002–03	Tottenham H	12	0	**36**	**0**
2003–04	Leicester C	29	1	**29**	**1**
2004–05	Manchester C	18	0		
2005–06	Manchester C	18	0		
2006–07	Manchester C	11	0	**47**	**0**
2006–07	Charlton Ath	11	0		
2007–08	Charlton Ath	11	0	**22**	**0**

THOMAS, Aswad (D) **13 2**
H: 5 11 W: 12 08 b.Westminster 9-8-89
Source: Scholar.

2007–08	Charlton Ath	0	0		
2007–08	*Accrington S*	13	2	**13**	**2**

THOMAS, Jerome (M) **112 10**
H: 5 9 W: 11 09 b.Wembley 23-3-83
Source: Scholar. *Honours:* England Youth, Under-20, Under-21.

2001–02	Arsenal	0	0		
2001–02	*QPR*	4	1		
2002–03	Arsenal	0	0		
2002–03	*QPR*	6	2	**10**	**3**
2003–04	Arsenal	0	0		
2003–04	Charlton Ath	1	0		
2004–05	Charlton Ath	24	3		
2005–06	Charlton Ath	25	1		
2006–07	Charlton Ath	20	3		
2007–08	Charlton Ath	32	0	**102**	**7**

TODOROV, Svetoslav (F) **186 75**
H: 5 8 W: 11 11 b.Dobrich 30-8-78
Honours: Bulgaria Youth, 42 full caps, 6 goals.

1996–97	Dobrudzha	12	2	**12**	**2**
1997–98	Litets Lovech	19	9		
1998–99	Litets Lovech	11	2		
1999–2000	Litets Lovech	26	19		
2000–01	Litets Lovech	15	7	**71**	**37**
2000–01	West Ham U	8	1		
2001–02	West Ham U	6	0	**14**	**1**
2001–02	Portsmouth	3	1		
2002–03	Portsmouth	45	26		
2003–04	Portsmouth	1	0		
2004–05	Portsmouth	0	0		
2005–06	Portsmouth	24	4		
2006–07	Portsmouth	4	2	**77**	**33**
2006–07	*Wigan Ath*	5	0	**5**	**0**
2007–08	Charlton Ath	7	2	**7**	**2**

VARNEY, Alex (F) **1 0**
H: 5 11 W: 11 13 b.Bromley 27-12-84
Source: Trainee.

2003–04	Charlton Ath	0	0		
2004–05	Charlton Ath	0	0		
2005–06	Charlton Ath	0	0		
2005–06	*Barnet*	1	0	**1**	**0**
2006–07	Charlton Ath	0	0		
2007–08	Charlton Ath	0	0		

VARNEY, Luke (F) **134 35**
H: 5 11 W: 11 00 b.Leicester 28-9-82
Source: Quorn.

2002–03	Crewe Alex	0	0		
2003–04	Crewe Alex	8	1		
2004–05	Crewe Alex	26	4		
2005–06	Crewe Alex	27	5		
2006–07	Crewe Alex	34	17	**95**	**27**
2007–08	Charlton Ath	39	8	**39**	**8**

WAGSTAFF, Scott (F) **2 0**
H: 5 10 W: 10 03 b.Maidstone 31-3-90
Source: Scholar.

2007–08	Charlton Ath	2	0	**2**	**0**

WALKER, James (F) **58 10**
H: 5 10 W: 11 10 b.Hackney 25-11-87
Source: Scholar. *Honours:* England Youth.

2004–05	Charlton Ath	0	0		
2005–06	Charlton Ath	0	0		
2005–06	*Hartlepool U*	4	0	**4**	**0**
2006–07	Charlton Ath	0	0		
2006–07	*Bristol R*	4	1	**4**	**1**
2006–07	*Leyton Orient*	14	2	**14**	**2**
2006–07	*Notts Co*	8	0	**8**	**0**
2007–08	Charlton Ath	0	0		

2007–08	*Yeovil T*	13	3	**13**	**3**
2007–08	*Southend U*	15	4	**15**	**4**

WEAVER, Nick (G) **232 0**
H: 6 4 W: 14 07 b.Sheffield 2-3-79
Source: Trainee. *Honours:* England Under-21.

1995–96	Mansfield T	1	0		
1996–97	Mansfield T	0	0	**1**	**0**
1996–97	Manchester C	0	0		
1997–98	Manchester C	0	0		
1998–99	Manchester C	45	0		
1999–2000	Manchester C	45	0		
2000–01	Manchester C	31	0		
2001–02	Manchester C	25	0		
2002–03	Manchester C	0	0		
2003–04	Manchester C	0	0		
2004–05	Manchester C	1	0		
2005–06	Manchester C	0	0		
2005–06	*Sheffield W*	14	0	**14**	**0**
2006–07	Manchester C	25	0	**172**	**0**
2007–08	Charlton Ath	45	0	**45**	**0**

WRIGHT, Josh (M) **32 1**
H: 6 1 W: 11 07 b.Tower Hamlets 6-11-89
Source: Scholar. *Honours:* England Youth.

2007–08	Charlton Ath	0	0		
2007–08	*Barnet*	32	1	**32**	**1**

YOUGA, Kelly (D) **45 1**
H: 6 1 W: 12 00 b.Bangui 22-9-85
Source: Lyon.

2005–06	Charlton Ath	0	0		
2005–06	*Bristol C*	4	0	**4**	**0**
2006–07	Charlton Ath	0	0		
2006–07	*Bradford C*	11	0	**11**	**0**
2007–08	Charlton Ath	11	0	**11**	**0**
2007–08	*Scunthorpe U*	19	1	**19**	**1**

YUSSUF, Rashid (M) **0 0**
b.Poplar 23-9-89

2007–08	Charlton Ath	0	0		

ZHENG-ZHI (M) **174 51**
H: 5 11 W: 11 11 b.Shenyang 20-8-80
Honours: China 41 full caps, 12 goals.

2001	Shenzhen	23	3		
2002	Shenzhen	22	6		
2003	Shenzhen	16	3		
2004	Shenzhen	16	2	**77**	**14**
2005	Shandong Luneng	17	8		
2006	Shandong Luneng	26	21	**43**	**29**
2006–07	Charlton Ath	12	1		
2007–08	Charlton Ath	42	7	**54**	**8**

CHELSEA (21)

ALEX (D) **175 25**
H: 6 2 W: 14 00 b.Niteroi 17-6-82
Honours: Brazil 12 full caps.

2002	Santos	25	3		
2003	Santos	34	9		
2004	Santos	4	0	**63**	**12**
2004–05	PSV Eindhoven	27	3		
2005–06	PSV Eindhoven	28	2		
2006–07	PSV Eindhoven	29	6	**84**	**11**
2007–08	Chelsea	28	2	**28**	**2**

ANELKA, Nicolas (F) **348 113**
H: 6 1 W: 13 03 b.Versailles 14-3-79
Honours: France Youth, Under-21, 51 full caps, 11 goals.

1995–96	Paris St Germain	2	0		
1996–97	Paris St Germain	8	1		
1996–97	Arsenal	4	0		
1997–98	Arsenal	26	6		
1998–99	Arsenal	35	17	**65**	**23**
1999–2000	Real Madrid	19	2	**19**	**2**
2000–01	Paris St Germain	27	8		
2001–02	Paris St Germain	12	2	**49**	**11**
2001–02	Liverpool	20	4	**20**	**4**
2002–03	Manchester C	38	14		
2003–04	Manchester C	32	16		
2004–05	Manchester C	19	7	**89**	**37**
2004–05	Fenerbahce	14	4		
2005–06	Fenerbahce	25	10	**39**	**14**
2006–07	Bolton W	35	11		
2007–08	Bolton W	18	10	**53**	**21**
2007–08	Chelsea	14	1	**14**	**1**

BALLACK, Michael (M) **342 104**
H: 6 2 W: 12 08 b.Gorlitz 26-9-76
Source: Motor Karl-Marx-Stadt.Germany Under-21, 87 full caps, 38 goals.

1995–96	Chemnitzer	15	0		
1996–97	Chemnitzer	34	10	**49**	**10**
1997–98	Kaiserslautern A	17	8	**17**	**8**
1997–98	Kaiserslautern	16	0		
1998–99	Kaiserslautern	30	4	**46**	**4**
1999–2000	Leverkusen	23	3		
2000–01	Leverkusen	27	7		
2001–02	Leverkusen	29	17	**79**	**27**
2002–03	Bayern Munich	26	10		
2003–04	Bayern Munich	28	7		
2004–05	Bayern Munich	27	13		
2005–06	Bayern Munich	26	13	**107**	**43**
2006–07	Chelsea	26	5		
2007–08	Chelsea	18	7	**44**	**12**

BELLETTI, Juliano (D) **245 17**
H: 5 9 W: 10 12 b.Casacvel 20-6-76
Honours: Brazil 23 full caps, 2 goals.

1994	Cruzeiro	5	0		
1995	Cruzeiro	17	0	**22**	**0**
1996	Sao Paulo	13	1		
1997	Sao Paulo	12	1		
1998	Sao Paulo	4	1		
1999	Atletico Mineiro	17	5	**17**	**5**
2000	Sao Paulo	11	0		
2001	Sao Paulo	14	1		
2002	Sao Paulo	0	0	**54**	**4**
2002–03	Villarreal	31	3		
2003–04	Villarreal	28	3	**59**	**6**
2004–05	Barcelona	31	0		
2005–06	Barcelona	26	0		
2006–07	Barcelona	13	0	**70**	**0**
2007–08	Chelsea	23	2	**23**	**2**

BEN HAIM, Tal (D) **187 3**
H: 5 11 W: 11 09 b.Rishon Le Zion 31-3-82
Source: Maccabi Tel Aviv. *Honours:* Israel Under-21, 40 full caps.

2000–01	Maccabi Tel Aviv	1	0		
2001–02	Maccabi Tel Aviv	29	1		
2002–03	Maccabi Tel Aviv	30	0		
2003–04	Maccabi Tel Aviv	26	1	**86**	**2**
2004–05	Bolton W	21	1		
2005–06	Bolton W	35	0		
2006–07	Bolton W	32	0	**88**	**1**
2007–08	Chelsea	13	0	**13**	**0**

BERTRAND, Ryan (D) **44 0**
H: 5 10 W: 11 00 b.Southwark 5-8-89
Source: Scholar. *Honours:* England Youth.

2006–07	Chelsea	0	0		
2006–07	*Bournemouth*	5	0	**5**	**0**
2007–08	Chelsea	0	0		
2007–08	*Oldham Ath*	21	0	**21**	**0**
2007–08	*Norwich C*	18	0	**18**	**0**

BOULAHROUZ, Khalid (D) **135 5**
H: 6 0 W: 12 10 b.Maassluis 28-12-81
Source: Excelsior Maassluis, Ajax, Haarlem. *Honours:* Holland 23 full caps.

2001–02	RKC Waalwijk	1	0		
2002–03	RKC Waalwijk	31	0		
2003–04	RKC Waalwijk	29	4		
2004–05	RKC Waalwijk	3	0	**64**	**4**
2004–05	Hamburg	24	1		
2005–06	Hamburg	28	0	**52**	**1**
2006–07	Chelsea	13	0		
2007–08	*Sevilla*	6	0	**6**	**0**
2007–08	Chelsea	0	0	**13**	**0**

BRIDCUTT, Liam (M) **9 0**
H: 5 9 W: 11 07 b.Reading 8-5-89
Source: Scholar.

2007–08	Chelsea	0	0		
2007–08	*Yeovil T*	9	0	**9**	**0**

BRIDGE, Wayne (D) **245 3**
H: 5 10 W: 12 13 b.Southampton 5-8-80
Source: Trainee. *Honours:* England Youth, Under-21, 30 full caps, 1 goal.

1997–98	Southampton	0	0		
1998–99	Southampton	23	0		
1999–2000	Southampton	19	1		
2000–01	Southampton	38	0		
2001–02	Southampton	38	0		
2002–03	Southampton	34	1	**152**	**2**
2003–04	Chelsea	33	1		
2004–05	Chelsea	15	0		
2005–06	Chelsea	0	0		
2005–06	*Fulham*	12	0	**12**	**0**

2006–07	Chelsea	22	0		
2007–08	Chelsea	11	0	**81**	**1**

CECH, Petr (G) **243 0**
H: 6 5 W: 14 07 b.Plzen 20-5-82
Honours: Czech Republic Youth, Under-20, Under-21, 62 full caps.

1998–99	Viktoria Plzen	0	0		
1999–2000	Chmel	1	0		
2000–01	Chmel	26	0	**27**	**0**
2001–02	Sparta Prague	26	0	**26**	**0**
2002–03	Rennes	37	0		
2003–04	Rennes	38	0	**75**	**0**
2004–05	Chelsea	35	0		
2005–06	Chelsea	34	0		
2006–07	Chelsea	20	0		
2007–08	Chelsea	26	0	**115**	**0**

COLE, Ashley (D) **220 10**
H: 5 8 W: 10 05 b.Stepney 20-12-80
Source: Trainee. *Honours:* England Schools, Youth, Under-21, B, 64 full caps.

1998–99	Arsenal	0	0		
1999–2000	Arsenal	1	0		
1999–2000	*Crystal Palace*	14	1	**14**	**1**
2000–01	Arsenal	17	3		
2001–02	Arsenal	29	2		
2002–03	Arsenal	31	1		
2003–04	Arsenal	32	0		
2004–05	Arsenal	35	2		
2005–06	Arsenal	11	0		
2006–07	Arsenal	0	0	**156**	**8**
2006–07	Chelsea	23	0		
2007–08	Chelsea	27	1	**50**	**1**

COLE, Joe (M) **269 33**
H: 5 9 W: 11 09 b.Romford 8-11-81
Source: Trainee. *Honours:* England Schools, Youth, Under-21, B, 50 full caps, 7 goals.

1998–99	West Ham U	8	0		
1999–2000	West Ham U	22	1		
2000–01	West Ham U	30	5		
2001–02	West Ham U	30	0		
2002–03	West Ham U	36	4	**126**	**10**
2003–04	Chelsea	35	1		
2004–05	Chelsea	28	8		
2005–06	Chelsea	34	7		
2006–07	Chelsea	13	0		
2007–08	Chelsea	33	7	**143**	**23**

CORK, Jack (D) **41 2**
H: 6 0 W: 10 12 b.Carshalton 25-6-89
Source: Scholar. *Honours:* England Youth.

2006–07	Chelsea	0	0		
2006–07	*Bournemouth*	7	0	**7**	**0**
2007–08	Chelsea	0	0		
2007–08	*Scunthorpe U*	34	2	**34**	**2**

CRESPO, Hernan (F) **377 178**
H: 6 0 W: 12 11 b.Florida, Arg 5-7-75
Honours: Argentina 65 full caps, 36 goals.

1993–94	River Plate	25	13		
1994–95	River Plate	18	5		
1995–96	River Plate	21	5	**64**	**23**
1996–97	Parma	27	12		
1997–98	Parma	25	12		
1998–99	Parma	30	16		
1999–2000	Parma	34	22	**116**	**62**
2000–01	Lazio	32	26		
2001–02	Lazio	22	13	**54**	**39**
2002–03	Internazionale	18	7		
2003–04	Chelsea	19	10		
2004–05	*AC Milan*	28	10	**28**	**10**
2005–06	Chelsea	30	10		
2006–07	Chelsea	0	0		
2006–07	*Internazionale*	29	13		
2007–08	Chelsea	0	0	**49**	**20**
2007–08	*Internazionale*	19	4	**66**	**24**

CUDICINI, Carlo (G) **223 0**
H: 6 1 W: 12 08 b.Milan 6-9-73
Honours: Italy Youth, Under-21.

1991–92	AC Milan	0	0		
1992–93	AC Milan	0	0		
1993–94	Como	6	0	**6**	**0**
1994–95	AC Milan	0	0		
1995–96	AC Milan	0	0		
1995–96	Prato	30	0	**30**	**0**
1996–97	Lazio	1	0	**1**	**0**
1997–98	Castel di Sangro	14	0		
1998–99	Castel di Sangro	32	0	**46**	**0**
1999–2000	Chelsea	1	0		
2000–01	Chelsea	24	0		
2001–02	Chelsea	28	0		
2002–03	Chelsea	36	0		
2003–04	Chelsea	26	0		
2004–05	Chelsea	3	0		
2005–06	Chelsea	4	0		
2006–07	Chelsea	8	0		
2007–08	Chelsea	10	0	**140**	**0**

CUMMINGS, Shaun (F) **0 0**
b.Hammersmith 25-2-89

2007–08	Chelsea	0	0		

DI SANTO, Franko (F) **0 0**
b.Mendoza 7-4-89
Source: Audax Italiano.

2007–08	Chelsea	0	0		

DROGBA, Didier (F) **254 99**
H: 6 2 W: 14 05 b.Abidjan 11-3-78
Honours: Ivory Coast 41 full caps, 33 goals.

1998–99	Le Mans	2	0		
1999–2000	Le Mans	30	6		
2000–01	Le Mans	11	0		
2001–02	Le Mans	21	5	**64**	**11**
2001–02	Guingamp	11	3		
2002–03	Guingamp	34	17	**45**	**20**
2003–04	Marseille	35	18	**35**	**18**
2004–05	Chelsea	26	10		
2005–06	Chelsea	29	12		
2006–07	Chelsea	36	20		
2007–08	Chelsea	19	8	**110**	**50**

ESSIEN, Michael (M) **228 28**
H: 5 10 W: 13 06 b.Accra 3-12-82
Honours: Ghana 39 full caps, 8 goals.

2000–01	Bastia	13	1		
2001–02	Bastia	24	4		
2002–03	Bastia	29	6	**66**	**11**
2003–04	Lyon	34	3		
2004–05	Lyon	37	4	**71**	**7**
2005–06	Chelsea	31	2		
2006–07	Chelsea	33	2		
2007–08	Chelsea	27	6	**91**	**10**

FERNANDES, Ricardo (M) **0 0**
b.Portugal 20-4-78
Source: Scholar.

2006–07	Chelsea	0	0		
2007–08	Chelsea	0	0		

FERREIRA, Fabio (M) **0 0**
b.Barreiro 3-5-89
Source: Scholar.

2006–07	Chelsea	0	0		
2007–08	Chelsea	0	0		

GRANT, Anthony (M) **57 0**
H: 5 10 W: 11 01 b.Lambeth 4-6-87
Source: Scholar. *Honours:* England Youth.

2004–05	Chelsea	1	0		
2005–06	Chelsea	0	0		
2005–06	*Oldham Ath*	2	0	**2**	**0**
2006–07	Chelsea	0	0		
2006–07	*Wycombe W*	40	0	**40**	**0**
2007–08	Chelsea	0	0	**1**	**0**
2007–08	*Luton T*	4	0	**4**	**0**
2007–08	*Southend U*	10	0	**10**	**0**

HIBBERT, Jordan (M) **0 0**
H: 5 10 W: 11 05 b.Hampstead 25-10-90
Source: Scholar.

2007–08	Chelsea	0	0		

HILARIO (G) **169 0**
H: 6 2 W: 13 05 b.San Pedro da Cova 21-10-75
Honours: Portugal Under-21, B.

1997–98	Porto	3	0		
1998–99	Amadora	27	0	**27**	**0**
1999–2000	Porto	19	0		
2000–01	Porto	0	0		
2001–02	Varzim	24	0	**24**	**0**
2002–03	Porto	0	0	**22**	**0**
2002–03	Academica	10	0	**10**	**0**
2003–04	Nacional	29	0		
2004–05	Nacional	32	0		
2005–06	Nacional	11	0	**72**	**0**
2006–07	Chelsea	11	0		
2007–08	Chelsea	3	0	**14**	**0**

HUTCHINSON, Sam (M) **1 0**
H: 6 0 W: 11 07 b.Windsor 3-8-89
Source: Scholar. *Honours:* England Youth.

2006–07	Chelsea	1	0		
2007–08	Chelsea	0	0	**1**	**0**

IVANOVIC, Branislav (M) **128 12**
H: 6 0 W: 12 04 b.Sremska Mitreovica 22-2-84
Honours: Serbia Under-21, 13 full caps, 1 goal.

2002–03	Sremska	19	2	**19**	**2**
2003–04	OFK Belgrade	13	0		
2004–05	OFK Belgrade	27	2		
2005–06	OFK Belgrade	15	3	**55**	**5**
2006	Lokomotiv Moscow	28	2		
2007	Lokomotiv Moscow	26	3	**54**	**5**
2007–08	Chelsea	0	0		

KALOU, Salomon (F) **141 53**
H: 6 0 W: 12 02 b.Oume 5-8-85
Source: Oume, ASEC Abidjan. *Honours:* Ivory Coast 6 full caps, 2 goals.

2003–04	Excelsior	11	4	**11**	**4**
2003–04	Feyenoord	2	0		
2004–05	Feyenoord	31	20		
2005–06	Feyenoord	34	15	**67**	**35**
2006–07	Chelsea	33	7		
2007–08	Chelsea	30	7	**63**	**14**

LAMPARD, Frank (M) **404 95**
H: 6 0 W: 14 02 b.Romford 20-6-78
Source: Trainee. *Honours:* England Youth, Under-21, B, 61 full caps, 14 goals.

1994–95	West Ham U	0	0		
1995–96	West Ham U	2	0		
1995–96	*Swansea C*	9	1	**9**	**1**
1996–97	West Ham U	13	0		
1997–98	West Ham U	31	4		
1998–99	West Ham U	38	5		
1999–2000	West Ham U	34	7		
2000–01	West Ham U	30	7	**148**	**23**
2001–02	Chelsea	37	5		
2002–03	Chelsea	38	6		
2003–04	Chelsea	38	10		
2004–05	Chelsea	38	13		
2005–06	Chelsea	35	16		
2006–07	Chelsea	37	11		
2007–08	Chelsea	24	10	**247**	**71**

MAGNAY, Carl (D) **0 0**
b.Durham 27-1-89

2006–07	Chelsea	0	0		
2007–08	Chelsea	0	0		

MAKELELE, Claude (M) **510 18**
H: 5 7 W: 10 05 b.Kinshasa 18-2-73
Source: Brest. *Honours:* France Under-20, Under-21, Under-23, B, 71 full caps.

1992–93	Nantes	34	1		
1993–94	Nantes	30	0		
1994–95	Nantes	36	3		
1995–96	Nantes	33	0		
1996–97	Nantes	36	5	**169**	**9**
1997–98	Marseille	33	4	**33**	**4**
1998–99	Celta Vigo	36	2		
1999–2000	Celta Vigo	34	1	**70**	**3**
2000–01	Real Madrid	33	0		
2001–02	Real Madrid	32	0		
2002–03	Real Madrid	29	0	**94**	**0**
2003–04	Chelsea	30	0		
2004–05	Chelsea	36	1		
2005–06	Chelsea	31	0		
2006–07	Chelsea	29	1		
2007–08	Chelsea	18	0	**144**	**2**

MALOUDA, Florent (M) **310 47**
H: 6 0 W: 11 06 b.Cayenne 13-6-80
Honours: France 41 full caps, 3 goals.

1996–97	Chateauroux	2	0		
1997–98	Chateauroux	1	0		
1998–99	Chateauroux	28	3		
1999–2000	Chateauroux	28	2	**59**	**5**
2000–01	Guingamp	23	1		
2001–02	Guingamp	32	4		
2002–03	Guingamp	37	10	**92**	**15**
2003–04	Lyon	35	4		
2004–05	Lyon	37	5		
2005–06	Lyon	31	6		
2006–07	Lyon	35	10	**138**	**25**
2007–08	Chelsea	21	2	**21**	**2**

MANCIENNE, Michael (D) **58 0**
H: 6 0 W: 11 09 b.Isleworth 8-1-88
Source: Scholar. *Honours:* England Youth, Under-21.

2005–06	Chelsea	0	0		
2006–07	Chelsea	0	0		
2006–07	*QPR*	28	0		

2007–08 Chelsea 0 0
2007–08 *QPR* 30 0 **58 0**

MIKEL, John Obi (M) 57 1
H: 6 0 W: 13 05 b.Plateau State 22-4-87
Source: Plateau U. *Honours:* Nigeria Youth, 16 full caps, 1 goal.
2005 Lyn 6 1 **6 1**
2006–07 Chelsea 22 0
2007–08 Chelsea 29 0 **51 0**

MODUBI, Michael (M) 0 0
b.Polokwane 22-4-85
2007–08 Chelsea 0 0

NIELSEN, Morten (F) 0 0
H: 6 3 W: 13 12 b.Copenhagen 24-2-90
Source: Scholar.
2007–08 Chelsea 0 0

NTUKA, Pule (M) 0 0
b.South Africa 10-5-85
Source: Westerlo.
2007–08 Chelsea 0 0

OFORI-TWUMASI, Nana (D) 0 0
H: 5 8 W: 11 09 b.Accra 15-5-90
Source: Scholar.
2007–08 Chelsea 0 0

PAULO FERREIRA (D) 257 4
H: 6 0 W: 11 13 b.Cascais 18-1-79
Honours: Portugal Under-21, 51 full caps.
1997–98 Estoril 1 0
1998–99 Estoril 16 0
1999–2000 Estoril 18 2 **35 2**
2000–01 Vitoria Setubal 34 2
2001–02 Vitoria Setubal 34 0 **68 2**
2002–03 Porto 30 0
2003–04 Porto 32 0 **62 0**
2004–05 Chelsea 29 0
2005–06 Chelsea 21 0
2006–07 Chelsea 24 0
2007–08 Chelsea 18 0 **92 0**

PETTIGREW, Adrian (D) 16 0
H: 6 0 W: 13 01 b.Hackney 12-11-86
Source: Scholar.
2004–05 Chelsea 0 0
2005–06 Chelsea 0 0
2006–07 Chelsea 0 0
2006–07 *Wycombe W* 1 0 **1 0**
2007–08 Chelsea 0 0
2007–08 *Brentford* 11 0 **11 0**
2007–08 *Rotherham U* 4 0 **4 0**

PIZARRO, Claudio (F) 336 138
H: 6 06 W: 12 06 b.Lima 3-10-78
Honours: Peru 53 full caps, 13 goals.
1995–96 Dep Pesquero 25 8
1996–97 Dep Pesquero 16 3 **41 11**
1997–98 Alianza 22 7
1998–99 Alianza 22 18 **44 25**
1999–2000 Werder Bremen 25 10
2000–01 Werder Bremen 31 19 **56 29**
2001–02 Bayern Munich 30 15
2002–03 Bayern Munich 31 15
2003–04 Bayern Munich 31 11
2004–05 Bayern Munich 23 11
2005–06 Bayern Munich 26 11
2006–07 Bayern Munich 33 8 **174 71**
2007–08 Chelsea 21 2 **21 2**

RAJKOVIC, Slobodan (D) 75 1
H: 6 5 W: 14 00 b.Belgrade 3-3-89
Honours: Serbia Under-21, 2 full caps.
2004–05 OFK Belgrade 26 1
2005–06 Chelsea 0 0
2005–06 *OFK Belgrade* 25 0
2006–07 Chelsea 0 0
2006–07 *OFK Belgrade* 11 0 **62 1**
2007–08 Chelsea 0 0
2007–08 *PSV Eindhoven* 13 0 **13 0**

RICARDO CARVALHO (D) 249 13
H: 6 0 W: 12 04 b.Amarante 18-5-78
Honours: Portugal Under-21, 46 full caps, 4 goals.
1996–97 Leca 0 0
1997–98 Leca 22 1 **22 1**
1998–99 Porto 1 0
1999–2000 Vitoria Setubal 25 2 **25 2**
2000–01 Alverca 29 1 **29 1**
2001–02 Porto 25 0
2002–03 Porto 17 1
2003–04 Porto 29 2 **72 3**
2004–05 Chelsea 25 1
2005–06 Chelsea 24 1
2006–07 Chelsea 31 3
2007–08 Chelsea 21 1 **101 6**

SAHAR, Ben (F) 24 3
H: 5 10 W: 12 05 b.Holon 10-8-89
Honours: Israel Under-21, 7 full caps, 2 goals.
2006–07 Chelsea 3 0
2007–08 Chelsea 0 0 **3 0**
2007–08 *QPR* 9 0 **9 0**
2007–08 *Sheffield W* 12 3 **12 3**

SARKI, Emmanuel (M) 7 0
b.Nigeria 26-12-87
2005–06 Chelsea 0 0
2005–06 *Westerlo* 7 0 **7 0**
2006–07 Chelsea 0 0
2007–08 Chelsea 0 0

SAWYER, Lee (M) 0 0
H: 5 10 W: 10 03 b.Leytonstone 10-9-89
Source: Scholar. *Honours:* England Youth.
2007–08 Chelsea 0 0

SHEVCHENKO, Andriy (F) 373 196
H: 6 0 W: 11 05 b.Dvirkivshchyna 29-9-76
Honours: Ukraine Youth, Under-21, 81 full caps, 37 goals.
1994–95 Dynamo Kiev 16 1
1995–96 Dynamo Kiev 31 16
1996–97 Dynamo Kiev 20 6
1997–98 Dynamo Kiev 23 19
1998–99 Dynamo Kiev 28 18 **118 60**
1999–2000 AC Milan 32 24
2000–01 AC Milan 34 24
2001–02 AC Milan 29 14
2002–03 AC Milan 24 5
2003–04 AC Milan 32 24
2004–05 AC Milan 29 17
2005–06 AC Milan 28 19 **208 127**
2006–07 Chelsea 30 4
2007–08 Chelsea 17 5 **47 9**

SIDWELL, Steve (M) 225 38
H: 5 10 W: 11 00 b.Wandsworth 14-12-82
Source: Scholar. *Honours:* England Under-20, Under-21.
2001–02 Arsenal 0 0
2001–02 *Brentford* 30 4 **30 4**
2002–03 Arsenal 0 0
2002–03 *Brighton & HA* 12 5 **12 5**
2002–03 Reading 13 2
2003–04 Reading 43 8
2004–05 Reading 44 5
2005–06 Reading 33 10
2006–07 Reading 35 4 **168 29**
2007–08 Chelsea 15 0 **15 0**

SIMMONDS, James (M) 0 0
b.Hammersmith 3-12-87
Source: Scholar. *Honours:* Eire Under-21.
2005–06 Chelsea 0 0
2006–07 Chelsea 0 0
2007–08 Chelsea 0 0

SINCLAIR, Scott (F) 38 5
H: 5 10 W: 10 00 b.Bath 26-3-89
Source: Bristol R Schoolboy, England Youth.
2004–05 Bristol R 2 0 **2 0**
2005–06 Chelsea 0 0
2006–07 Chelsea 2 0
2006–07 *Plymouth Arg* 15 2 **15 2**
2007–08 Chelsea 1 0 **3 0**
2007–08 *QPR* 9 1 **9 1**
2007–08 *Charlton Ath* 3 0 **3 0**
2007–08 *Crystal Palace* 6 2 **6 2**

SMITH, Jimmy (M) 39 6
H: 6 0 W: 10 03 b.Newham 7-1-87
Source: Scholar. *Honours:* England Youth.
2004–05 Chelsea 0 0
2005–06 Chelsea 1 0
2006–07 Chelsea 0 0
2006–07 *QPR* 29 6 **29 6**
2007–08 Chelsea 0 0 **1 0**
2007–08 *Norwich C* 9 0 **9 0**

STOCH, Miroslav (F) 0 0
H: 5 6 W: 10 01 b.Nitra 19-10-89
Source: Scholar.
2007–08 Chelsea 0 0

TAIWO, Tom (M) 0 0
H: 5 8 W: 10 07 b.Leeds 27-2-90
Source: Scholar.
2007–08 Chelsea 0 0

TAYLOR, Rhys (G) 0 0
H: 6 2 W: 12 08 b.Neath 7-4-90
Honours: Wales Under-21.
2007–08 Chelsea 0 0

TEJERA RODRIQUEZ, Sergio (M) 0 0
H: 5 11 W: 10 10 b.Barcelona 28-5-90
Source: Scholar.
2007–08 Chelsea 0 0

TERRY, John (D) 243 16
H: 6 1 W: 14 02 b.Barking 7-12-80
Source: Trainee. *Honours:* England Under-21, 44 full caps, 4 goals.
1997–98 Chelsea 0 0
1998–99 Chelsea 2 0
1999–2000 Chelsea 4 0
1999–2000 *Nottingham F* 6 0 **6 0**
2000–01 Chelsea 22 1
2001–02 Chelsea 33 1
2002–03 Chelsea 20 3
2003–04 Chelsea 33 2
2004–05 Chelsea 36 3
2005–06 Chelsea 36 4
2006–07 Chelsea 28 1
2007–08 Chelsea 23 1 **237 16**

VAN AANHOLT, Patrick (D) 0 0
H: 5 9 W: 10 08 b.S'Hertogenbosch 3-7-88
2007–08 Chelsea 0 0

WEIHRAUCH, Per (F) 0 0
b.Copenhagen 3-7-88
Source: Ajax.
2006–07 Chelsea 0 0
2007–08 Chelsea 0 0

WOODS, Michael (M) 0 0
H: 6 0 W: 12 07 b.York 6-4-90
Source: Scholar. *Honours:* England Youth. Scotland B.
2006–07 Chelsea 0 0
2007–08 Chelsea 0 0

WRIGHT-PHILLIPS, Shaun (F) 234 30
H: 5 5 W: 10 01 b.Lewisham 25-10-81
Source: Scholar. *Honours:* England Under-21, 19 full caps, 4 goals.
1998–99 Manchester C 0 0
1999–2000 Manchester C 4 0
2000–01 Manchester C 15 0
2001–02 Manchester C 35 8
2002–03 Manchester C 31 1
2003–04 Manchester C 34 7
2004–05 Manchester C 34 10 **153 26**
2005–06 Chelsea 27 0
2006–07 Chelsea 27 2
2007–08 Chelsea 27 2 **81 4**

YOUNGHUSBAND, Phil (F) 0 0
H: 5 10 W: 10 08 b.Ashford 4-8-87
Source: Scholar.
2004–05 Chelsea 0 0
2005–06 Chelsea 0 0
2006–07 Chelsea 0 0
2007–08 Chelsea 0 0

Scholars
Ahamed, Nikki; Borini, Fabio; Gordon, Benjamin Lawrence; Heimann, Niclas; Kakuta, Gael; King, Billy Joe; Mellis, Jacob Alexzander; Phillip, Adam; Philliskirk, Daniel; Saville, Jack William; Sebek, Jan; Tabor, Jordan Benjamin

CHELTENHAM T (22)

ARMSTRONG, Craig (M) 344 9
H: 5 11 W: 12 09 b.South Shields 23-5-75
Source: Trainee.
1992–93 Nottingham F 0 0
1993–94 Nottingham F 0 0
1994–95 Nottingham F 0 0
1994–95 *Burnley* 4 0 **4 0**
1995–96 Nottingham F 0 0
1995–96 *Bristol R* 14 0 **14 0**
1996–97 Nottingham F 0 0
1996–97 *Gillingham* 10 0
1996–97 *Watford* 15 0 **15 0**

1997–98 Nottingham F 18 0
1998–99 Nottingham F 22 0 **40 0**
1998–99 Huddersfield T 13 1
1999–2000 Huddersfield T 39 0
2000–01 Huddersfield T 44 3
2001–02 Huddersfield T 11 1 **107 5**
2001–02 Sheffield W 8 0
2002–03 Sheffield W 17 1
2003–04 Sheffield W 10 0
2003–04 *Grimsby T* 9 1 **9 1**
2004–05 Sheffield W 0 0 **35 1**
2004–05 Bradford C 7 0 **7 0**
2005–06 Cheltenham T 34 2
2006–07 Cheltenham T 42 0
2007–08 Gillingham 13 0 **23 0**
2007–08 Cheltenham T 14 0 **90 2**

BIRD, David (M) 185 7
H: 5 9 W: 12 00 b.Gloucester 26-12-84
Source: Cinderford T.
2001–02 Cheltenham T 0 0
2002–03 Cheltenham T 14 0
2003–04 Cheltenham T 24 0
2004–05 Cheltenham T 34 0
2005–06 Cheltenham T 36 1
2006–07 Cheltenham T 31 2
2007–08 Cheltenham T 46 4 **185 7**

BROWN, Scott (M) 87 5
H: 5 9 W: 10 03 b.Runcorn 8-5-85
Source: Scholar. *Honours:* England Youth.
2001–02 Everton 0 0
2002–03 Everton 0 0
2003–04 Everton 0 0
2004–05 Bristol C 19 0
2005–06 Bristol C 29 1
2006–07 Bristol C 15 4 **63 5**
2006–07 Cheltenham T 4 0
2007–08 Cheltenham T 20 0 **24 0**

BROWN, Scott P (G) 12 0
H: 6 2 W: 13 01 b.Wolverhampton 26-4-85
Source: Wolverhampton W Trainee.
From Welshpool T
2003–04 Bristol C 0 0
2004–05 Cheltenham T 0 0
2005–06 Cheltenham T 1 0
2006–07 Cheltenham T 11 0
2007–08 Cheltenham T 0 0 **12 0**

CAINES, Gavin (D) 135 6
H: 6 1 W: 12 00 b.Birmingham 20-9-83
Source: Scholar.
2003–04 Walsall 0 0
2004–05 Cheltenham T 29 2
2005–06 Cheltenham T 39 2
2006–07 Cheltenham T 39 0
2007–08 Cheltenham T 28 2 **135 6**

CONNOLLY, Adam (M) 32 1
H: 5 9 W: 12 04 b.Manchester 10-4-86
Source: Scholar.
2004–05 Cheltenham T 4 0
2005–06 Cheltenham T 5 1
2006–07 Cheltenham T 8 0
2007–08 Cheltenham T 15 0 **32 1**

CONNOR, Paul (F) 301 68
H: 6 2 W: 11 08 b.Bishop Auckland 12-1-79
Source: Trainee.
1996–97 Middlesbrough 0 0
1997–98 Middlesbrough 0 0
1997–98 *Hartlepool U* 5 0 **5 0**
1998–99 Middlesbrough 0 0
1998–99 *Stoke C* 3 2
1999–2000 Stoke C 26 5
2000–01 Stoke C 7 0 **36 7**
2000–01 *Cambridge U* 13 5 **13 5**
2000–01 Rochdale 14 10
2001–02 Rochdale 17 1
2002–03 Rochdale 39 12
2003–04 Rochdale 24 5 **94 28**
2003–04 Swansea C 12 5
2004–05 Swansea C 40 10
2005–06 Swansea C 13 1 **65 16**
2005–06 Leyton Orient 16 5
2006–07 Leyton Orient 18 2 **34 7**
2006–07 Cheltenham T 15 1
2007–08 Cheltenham T 39 4 **54 5**

DUFF, Shane (D) 162 2
H: 6 1 W: 12 10 b.Wroughton 2-4-82
Source: Juniors. *Honours:* Northern Ireland Under-21.
2000–01 Cheltenham T 0 0
2001–02 Cheltenham T 0 0
2002–03 Cheltenham T 18 0
2003–04 Cheltenham T 15 1
2004–05 Cheltenham T 45 1
2005–06 Cheltenham T 20 0
2006–07 Cheltenham T 34 0
2007–08 Cheltenham T 30 0 **162 2**

FINNIGAN, John (M) 346 22
H: 5 8 W: 10 09 b.Wakefield 29-3-76
Source: Trainee.
1992–93 Nottingham F 0 0
1993–94 Nottingham F 0 0
1994–95 Nottingham F 0 0
1995–96 Nottingham F 0 0
1996–97 Nottingham F 0 0
1997–98 Nottingham F 0 0
1997–98 *Lincoln C* 6 0
1998–99 Lincoln C 37 1
1999–2000 Lincoln C 37 2
2000–01 Lincoln C 40 0
2001–02 Lincoln C 23 0 **143 3**
2001–02 Cheltenham T 12 2
2002–03 Cheltenham T 37 1
2003–04 Cheltenham T 33 1
2004–05 Cheltenham T 32 3
2005–06 Cheltenham T 39 4
2006–07 Cheltenham T 40 7
2007–08 Cheltenham T 10 1 **203 19**

FOLEY, Sam (M) 0 0
H: 6 0 W: 10 08 b.Upton-on-Severn 17-10-86
Source: Scholar.
2005–06 Cheltenham T 0 0
2006–07 Cheltenham T 0 0
2007–08 Cheltenham T 0 0

GALLINAGH, Andy (D) 28 0
H: 5 8 W: 11 08 b.Sutton Coldfield 16-3-85
Source: Stratford T.
2004–05 Cheltenham T 0 0
2005–06 Cheltenham T 1 0
2006–07 Cheltenham T 1 0
2007–08 Cheltenham T 26 0 **28 0**

GILL, Ben (M) 2 0
H: 5 9 W: 10 11 b.Harrow 9-10-87
Source: Scholar.
2005–06 Watford 0 0
2006–07 Watford 0 0
2007–08 Cheltenham T 2 0 **2 0**

GILL, Jerry (D) 276 0
H: 5 11 W: 12 00 b.Clevedon 8-9-70
Source: Yeovil T.
1997–98 Birmingham C 3 0
1998–99 Birmingham C 3 0
1999–2000 Birmingham C 11 0
2000–01 Birmingham C 29 0
2001–02 Birmingham C 14 0
2002–03 Birmingham C 0 0 **60 0**
2002–03 Northampton T 41 0
2003–04 Northampton T 0 0 **41 0**
2003–04 Cheltenham T 7 0
2004–05 Cheltenham T 44 0
2005–06 Cheltenham T 42 0
2006–07 Cheltenham T 39 0
2007–08 Cheltenham T 43 0 **175 0**

GILLESPIE, Steven (F) 98 30
H: 5 9 W: 11 02 b.Liverpool 4-6-84
Source: Liverpool Scholar.
2004–05 Bristol C 8 0
2004–05 *Cheltenham T* 12 5
2005–06 Bristol C 4 1 **12 1**
2005–06 Cheltenham T 14 5
2006–07 Cheltenham T 23 5
2007–08 Cheltenham T 37 14 **86 29**

HIGGS, Shane (G) 237 0
H: 6 3 W: 14 06 b.Oxford 13-5-77
Source: Trainee.
1994–95 Bristol R 0 0
1995–96 Bristol R 0 0
1996–97 Bristol R 2 0
1997–98 Bristol R 8 0 **10 0**
From Worcester C.
1999–2000 Cheltenham T 0 0
2000–01 Cheltenham T 1 0
2001–02 Cheltenham T 1 0
2002–03 Cheltenham T 10 0
2003–04 Cheltenham T 42 0
2004–05 Cheltenham T 46 0
2005–06 Cheltenham T 45 0
2006–07 Cheltenham T 36 0
2007–08 Cheltenham T 46 0 **227 0**

LEDGISTER, Aaron (M) 0 0
H: 5 10 W: 11 07 b.Hong Kong 15-11-88
Source: Bristol C.
2007–08 Cheltenham T 0 0

LINDEGAARD, Andy (M) 130 5
H: 5 8 W: 11 04 b.Taunton 10-9-80
Source: Westland Sp.
2003–04 Yeovil T 23 2
2004–05 Yeovil T 29 1
2005–06 Yeovil T 23 0
2006–07 Yeovil T 14 0 **89 3**
2007–08 Cheltenham T 41 2 **41 2**

MANSHIP, Tommy (M) 0 0
H: 5 11 W: 11 08 b.Melton Mowbray 27-3-87
Source: Hinckley U.
2007–08 Cheltenham T 0 0

PAUL, Shane (F) 0 0
H: 5 6 W: 10 07 b.Walsall 25-1-87
Source: Scholar. *Honours:* England Youth.
2004–05 Aston Villa 0 0
2005–06 Aston Villa 0 0
2006–07 Cheltenham T 0 0
2007–08 Cheltenham T 0 0

PUDDY, Will (G) 0 0
H: 5 10 W: 11 07 b.Salisbury 4-10-87
Source: Scholar.
2005–06 Cheltenham T 0 0
2006–07 Cheltenham T 0 0
2007–08 Cheltenham T 0 0

REID, Craig (F) 14 0
H: 5 10 W: 11 10 b.Coventry 17-12-85
Honours: Ipswich T Scholar.
2004–05 Coventry C 0 0
2005–06 Coventry C 0 0
2006–07 Coventry C 0 0
2006–07 Cheltenham T 6 0
2007–08 Cheltenham T 8 0 **14 0**

RIDLEY, Lee (D) 129 2
H: 5 9 W: 11 11 b.Scunthorpe 5-12-81
Source: Scholar.
2000–01 Scunthorpe U 2 0
2001–02 Scunthorpe U 4 0
2002–03 Scunthorpe U 11 0
2003–04 Scunthorpe U 18 1
2004–05 Scunthorpe U 44 0
2005–06 Scunthorpe U 3 1
2006–07 Scunthorpe U 18 0 **100 2**
2007–08 Cheltenham T 8 0 **8 0**
2007–08 *Darlington* 6 0 **6 0**
2007–08 *Lincoln C* 15 0 **15 0**

SPENCER, Damien (F) 229 33
H: 6 1 W: 14 00 b.Ascot 19-9-81
Source: Scholarship.
1999–2000 Bristol C 9 1
2000–01 Bristol C 4 0
2000–01 *Exeter C* 6 0 **6 0**
2001–02 Bristol C 0 0 **13 1**
2002–03 Cheltenham T 30 6
2003–04 Cheltenham T 36 9
2004–05 Cheltenham T 41 8
2005–06 Cheltenham T 46 3
2006–07 Cheltenham T 27 3
2007–08 Cheltenham T 30 3 **210 32**

TOWNSEND, Michael (D) 74 2
H: 6 1 W: 13 12 b.Walsall 17-5-86
Source: Wolverhampton W scholar.
2004–05 Cheltenham T 0 0
2005–06 Cheltenham T 31 0
2006–07 Cheltenham T 30 1
2007–08 Cheltenham T 13 1 **74 2**

VINCENT, Ashley (F) 81 5
H: 5 10 W: 11 08 b.Oldbury 26-5-85
Source: Wolverhampton W Scholar.
2004–05 Cheltenham T 26 1
2005–06 Cheltenham T 13 2
2006–07 Cheltenham T 5 0
2007–08 Cheltenham T 37 2 **81 5**

WRIGHT, Alan (D) **536 8**
H: 5 4 W: 9 09 b.Ashton-under-Lyme 28-9-71
Source: Trainee. *Honours:* England Schools, Youth, Under-21.
1987–88 Blackpool 1 0
1988–89 Blackpool 16 0
1989–90 Blackpool 24 0
1990–91 Blackpool 45 0
1991–92 Blackpool 12 0 **98 0**
1991–92 Blackburn R 33 1
1992–93 Blackburn R 24 0
1993–94 Blackburn R 12 0
1994–95 Blackburn R 5 0 **74 1**
1994–95 Aston Villa 8 0
1995–96 Aston Villa 38 2
1996–97 Aston Villa 38 1
1997–98 Aston Villa 37 0
1998–99 Aston Villa 38 0
1999–2000 Aston Villa 32 1
2000–01 Aston Villa 36 1
2001–02 Aston Villa 23 0
2002–03 Aston Villa 10 0 **260 5**
2003–04 Middlesbrough 2 0 **2 0**
2003–04 Sheffield U 21 1
2004–05 Sheffield U 14 0
2005–06 Sheffield U 6 0
2005–06 *Derby Co* 7 0 **7 0**
2006–07 Sheffield U 1 0
2006–07 *Leeds U* 1 0 **1 0**
2006–07 *Cardiff C* 7 0 **7 0**
2006–07 *Doncaster R* 3 0 **3 0**
2006–07 *Nottingham F* 9 0 **9 0**
2007–08 Sheffield U 0 0 **42 1**
2007–08 Cheltenham T 33 1 **33 1**

WYLDE, Michael (M) **8 0**
H: 6 2 W: 13 02 b.Birmingham 6-1-87
Source: Scholar.
2005–06 Cheltenham T 1 0
2006–07 Cheltenham T 7 0
2007–08 Cheltenham T 0 0 **8 0**

YAO, Sosthene (M) **23 0**
H: 5 4 W: 11 09 b.Ivory Coast 7-8-87
Source: West Ham U Scholar.
2005–06 Cheltenham T 3 0
2006–07 Cheltenham T 15 0
2007–08 Cheltenham T 5 0 **23 0**

CHESTER C (23)

BENNETT, Dean (M) **252 19**
H: 5 11 W: 11 00 b.Wolverhampton 13-12-77
Source: Aston Villa Juniors.
1996–97 WBA 1 0
1997–98 WBA 0 0 **1 0**
2000–01 Kidderminster H 42 4
2001–02 Kidderminster H 42 8
2002–03 Kidderminster H 32 1
2003–04 Kidderminster H 38 3 **154 16**
2002–03 Wrexham 18 0
2003–04 Wrexham 0 0
2004–05 Wrexham 14 0
2005–06 Wrexham 33 2 **65 2**
2006–07 Chester C 32 1
2007–08 Chester C 0 0 **32 1**

BUTLER, Paul (D) **596 26**
H: 6 2 W: 13 00 b.Manchester 2-11-72
Source: Trainee. *Honours:* Eire B, 1 full cap.
1990–91 Rochdale 2 0
1991–92 Rochdale 25 0
1992–93 Rochdale 16 2
1993–94 Rochdale 38 2
1994–95 Rochdale 39 3
1995–96 Rochdale 38 3 **158 10**
1996–97 Bury 41 2
1997–98 Bury 43 2 **84 4**
1998–99 Sunderland 44 2
1999–2000 Sunderland 32 1
2000–01 Sunderland 3 0 **79 3**
2000–01 Wolverhampton W 12 0
2001–02 Wolverhampton W 43 1
2002–03 Wolverhampton W 32 1
2003–04 Wolverhampton W 37 1 **124 3**
2004–05 Leeds U 39 0
2005–06 Leeds U 44 3
2006–07 Leeds U 16 1 **99 4**
2006–07 *Milton Keynes D* 17 0 **17 0**
2007–08 Chester C 35 2 **35 2**

CARROLL, Neil (M) **1 0**
H: 6 0 W: 12 00 b.Liverpool 21-9-88
2006–07 Chester C 0 0
2007–08 Chester C 1 0 **1 0**

CRONIN, Glenn (M) **73 0**
H: 5 8 W: 10 08 b.Dublin 14-9-81
Source: Trainee.
2000–01 Exeter C 0 0
2001–02 Exeter C 30 0
2002–03 Exeter C 39 0
2003–04 Exeter C 0 0
2004–05 Exeter C 0 0
2005–06 Exeter C 0 0 **69 0**
2006–07 Chester C 4 0
2007–08 Chester C 0 0 **4 0**

DANBY, John (G) **140 0**
H: 6 2 W: 14 06 b.Stoke 20-9-83
Source: Juniors.
2001–02 Kidderminster H 2 0
2002–03 Kidderminster H 0 0
2003–04 Kidderminster H 9 0
2004–05 Kidderminster H 37 0
2005–06 Kidderminster H 0 0 **48 0**
2006–07 Chester C 46 0
2007–08 Chester C 46 0 **92 0**

DINNING, Tony (M) **450 55**
H: 6 0 W: 13 05 b.Wallsend 12-4-75
Source: Trainee.
1993–94 Newcastle U 0 0
1994–95 Stockport Co 40 1
1995–96 Stockport Co 10 1
1996–97 Stockport Co 20 2
1997–98 Stockport Co 30 4
1998–99 Stockport Co 41 5
1999–2000 Stockport Co 44 12
2000–01 Stockport Co 6 0
2000–01 Wolverhampton W 31 6
2001–02 Wolverhampton W 4 0 **35 6**
2001–02 Wigan Ath 33 5
2001–02 *Stoke C* 5 0 **5 0**
2002–03 Wigan Ath 38 7
2003–04 Wigan Ath 13 0
2003–04 *Walsall* 5 0 **5 0**
2003–04 *Blackpool* 10 3 **10 3**
2004–05 Wigan Ath 0 0 **84 12**
2004–05 *Ipswich T* 7 0 **7 0**
2004–05 *Bristol C* 19 0 **19 0**
2004–05 *Port Vale* 7 3
2005–06 Port Vale 35 2 **42 5**
2006–07 Stockport Co 32 2
2007–08 Stockport Co 0 0 **223 27**
2007–08 Chester C 20 2 **20 2**

ELLISON, Kevin (M) **193 28**
H: 6 0 W: 12 00 b.Liverpool 23-2-79
Source: Altrincham.
2000–01 Leicester C 1 0
2001–02 Leicester C 0 0 **1 0**
2001–02 Stockport Co 11 0
2002–03 Stockport Co 23 1
2003–04 Stockport Co 14 1 **48 2**
2003–04 *Lincoln C* 11 0 **11 0**
2004–05 Chester C 24 9
2004–05 Hull C 16 1
2005–06 Hull C 23 1 **39 2**
2006–07 Tranmere R 34 4 **34 4**
2007–08 Chester C 36 11 **60 20**

GRANT, Tony (M) **279 7**
H: 5 9 W: 11 00 b.Liverpool 14-11-74
Source: Trainee. *Honours:* England Under-21.
1993–94 Everton 0 0
1994–95 Everton 5 0
1995–96 Everton 13 1
1995–96 *Swindon T* 3 1 **3 1**
1996–97 Everton 18 0
1997–98 Everton 7 1
1998–99 Everton 16 0
1999–2000 Everton 2 0 **61 2**
1999–2000 *Tranmere R* 9 0 **9 0**
1999–2000 Manchester C 8 0
2000–01 Manchester C 10 0
2000–01 *WBA* 5 0 **5 0**
2001–02 Manchester C 3 0 **21 0**
2001–02 Burnley 28 0
2002–03 Burnley 34 1
2003–04 Burnley 37 0
2004–05 Burnley 42 2 **141 3**
2005–06 Bristol C 0 0
2005–06 Crewe Alex 10 0
2006–07 Crewe Alex 4 0 **14 0**
2006–07 Accrington S 6 0 **6 0**
2007–08 Chester C 19 1 **19 1**

HESSEY, Sean (D) **166 2**
H: 5 11 W: 12 08 b.Whiston 19-9-78
Source: Liverpool Trainee.
1997–98 Wigan Ath 0 0
1997–98 Leeds U 0 0
1997–98 Huddersfield T 1 0
1998–99 Huddersfield T 10 0 **11 0**
1999–2000 Kilmarnock 11 0
2000–01 Kilmarnock 6 0
2001–02 Kilmarnock 15 0
2002–03 Kilmarnock 5 0
2003–04 Kilmarnock 7 1 **44 1**
2003–04 Blackpool 6 0 **6 0**
2004–05 Chester C 34 1
2005–06 Chester C 19 0
2006–07 Chester C 26 0
2007–08 Chester C 0 0 **79 1**
2007–08 *Macclesfield T* 26 0 **26 0**

HOLROYD, Chris (M) **47 4**
H: 5 11 W: 12 03 b.Macclesfield 24-10-86
Source: Crewe Alex Scholar.
2005–06 Chester C 0 0
2006–07 Chester C 22 0
2007–08 Chester C 25 4 **47 4**

HUGHES, Mark (M) **108 6**
H: 5 10 W: 12 05 b.Dungannon 16-9-83
Source: Scholar. *Honours:* Northern Ireland Schools, Youth, Under-21, Under-23, 2 full caps.
2001–02 Tottenham H 0 0
2002–03 Tottenham H 0 0
2003–04 Tottenham H 0 0
2004–05 Tottenham H 0 0
2004–05 *Northampton T* 3 0 **3 0**
2004–05 *Oldham Ath* 27 0
2005–06 Oldham Ath 33 1
2006–07 Oldham Ath 0 0 **60 1**
From Thurrock.
2006–07 Chesterfield 2 1 **2 1**
From Stevenage B.
2007–08 Chester C 43 4 **43 4**

KELLY, Shaun (D) **12 0**
H: 6 1 W: 11 04 b.Southampton 4-7-86
Source: Scholar.
2006–07 Chester C 2 0
2007–08 Chester C 10 0 **12 0**

LINWOOD, Paul (D) **132 2**
H: 6 2 W: 13 03 b.Birkenhead 24-10-83
Source: Scholar.
2001–02 Tranmere R 0 0
2002–03 Tranmere R 0 0
2003–04 Tranmere R 20 0
2004–05 Tranmere R 10 0
2005–06 Tranmere R 14 0 **44 0**
2005–06 *Wrexham* 9 0 **9 0**
2006–07 Chester C 37 1
2007–08 Chester C 42 1 **79 2**

LOWNDES, Nathan (F) **218 33**
H: 6 0 W: 11 10 b.Salford 2-6-77
Source: Trainee.
1994–95 Leeds U 0 0
1995–96 Leeds U 0 0
1995–96 Watford 0 0
1996–97 Watford 3 0
1997–98 Watford 4 0 **7 0**
1998–99 St Johnstone 29 2
1999–2000 St Johnstone 25 10
2000–01 St Johnstone 10 2 **64 14**
2001–02 Livingston 21 3 **21 3**
2001–02 *Rotherham U* 2 0 **2 0**
2002–03 Plymouth Arg 16 2
2003–04 Plymouth Arg 33 8
2004–05 Plymouth Arg 4 0 **53 10**
2004–05 Port Vale 12 1
2005–06 Port Vale 35 5
2006–07 Port Vale 12 0 **59 6**
2007–08 Chester C 12 0 **12 0**

MARPLES, Simon (D) **89 0**
H: 5 10 W: 11 00 b.Sheffield 30-7-75
Source: Stocksbridge Park Steels.
2003–04 Doncaster R 16 0

2004–05 Doncaster R 12 0
2005–06 Doncaster R 15 0 **43 0**
2006–07 Chester C 30 0
2007–08 Chester C 16 0 **46 0**

MARSH-EVANS, Robert (D) 0 0
H: 6 3 W: 12 08 b.Abergele 13-10-86
Source: Ruthin T.
2006–07 Chester C 0 0
2007–08 Chester C 0 0

McMANUS, Paul (F) 19 1
H: 5 6 W: 10 00 b.Liverpool 22-4-90
Source: Scholar.
2007–08 Chester C 19 1 **19 1**

McSPORRAN, Jermaine (M) 195 31
H: 5 10 W: 10 12 b.Manchester 1-1-77
Source: Oxford C.
1998–99 Wycombe W 26 4
1999–2000 Wycombe W 38 9
2000–01 Wycombe W 20 2
2001–02 Wycombe W 32 7
2002–03 Wycombe W 9 1
2003–04 Wycombe W 33 7 **158 30**
2003–04 Walsall 6 0 **6 0**
2004–05 Doncaster R 26 1
2005–06 Doncaster R 2 0 **28 1**
2005–06 *Boston U* 2 0 **2 0**
2006–07 Chester C 1 0
2007–08 Chester C 0 0 **1 0**

MITCHELL, Andy (F) 4 0
H: 6 0 W: 12 03 b.Liverpool 18-4-90
Source: Scholar.
2007–08 Chester C 4 0 **4 0**

MURPHY, John (F) 423 119
H: 6 2 W: 14 00 b.Whiston 18-10-76
Source: Trainee.
1994–95 Chester C 5 0
1995–96 Chester C 18 3
1996–97 Chester C 11 1
1997–98 Chester C 27 4
1998–99 Chester C 42 12
1999–2000 Blackpool 39 10
2000–01 Blackpool 46 18
2001–02 Blackpool 37 13
2002–03 Blackpool 35 16
2003–04 Blackpool 30 9
2004–05 Blackpool 31 9
2005–06 Blackpool 34 8
2006–07 Blackpool 0 0 **252 83**
2006–07 Macclesfield T 29 7 **29 7**
2007–08 Chester C 39 9 **142 29**

NEWTON, Sean (D) 2 0
H: 6 2 W: 13 00 b.Liverpool 23-9-88
2006–07 Chester C 0 0
2007–08 Chester C 2 0 **2 0**

PALETHORPE, Philip (G) 1 0
H: 6 2 W: 11 08 b.Wallasey 17-9-86
Source: Scholar.
2003–04 Tranmere R 0 0
2004–05 Tranmere R 0 0
2005–06 Tranmere R 0 0
2006–07 Chester C 0 0
2007–08 Chester C 1 0 **1 0**

PARTRIDGE, Richie (M) 120 13
H: 5 8 W: 11 00 b.Dublin 12-9-80
Source: Trainee. *Honours:* Eire Youth, Under-21.
1998–99 Liverpool 0 0
1999–2000 Liverpool 0 0
2000–01 Liverpool 0 0
2000–01 *Bristol R* 6 1 **6 1**
2001–02 Liverpool 0 0
2002–03 Liverpool 0 0
2002–03 *Coventry C* 27 4 **27 4**
2003–04 Liverpool 0 0
2004–05 Liverpool 0 0
2005–06 Sheffield W 18 0 **18 0**
2006–07 Rotherham U 33 3 **33 3**
2007–08 Chester C 36 5 **36 5**

ROBERTS, Kevin (D) 37 3
H: 6 2 W: 14 00 b.Liverpool 17-8-89
Source: Scholar.
2006–07 Chester C 0 0
2007–08 Chester C 37 3 **37 3**

RULE, Glenn (M) 4 0
H: 5 11 W: 11 07 b.Birkenhead 30-11-89
Source: Scholar.
2007–08 Chester C 4 0 **4 0**

RUTHERFORD, Paul (M) 38 1
H: 5 9 W: 11 07 b.Moreton 10-7-87
Source: Greenleas.
2005–06 Chester C 6 0
2006–07 Chester C 9 0
2007–08 Chester C 23 1 **38 1**

SANDWITH, Kevin (D) 132 8
H: 5 11 W: 12 05 b.Workington 30-4-78
Source: Trainee.
1996–97 Carlisle U 0 0
1997–98 Carlisle U 3 0
1998–99 Carlisle U 0 0 **3 0**
From Halifax T
2003–04 Lincoln C 3 0
2004–05 Lincoln C 37 2 **40 2**
2005–06 Macclesfield T 35 3 **35 3**
2006–07 Chester C 32 2
2007–08 Chester C 22 1 **54 3**

VAUGHAN, James (D) 36 0
H: 5 10 W: 12 09 b.Liverpool 6-12-86
Source: Scholar.
2004–05 Tranmere R 0 0
2005–06 Chester C 0 0
2006–07 Chester C 6 0
2007–08 Chester C 30 0 **36 0**

VAUGHAN, Stephen (D) 65 0
H: 5 6 W: 11 11 b.Liverpool 22-1-85
Source: Scholar.
2001–02 Liverpool 0 0
2002–03 Liverpool 0 0
2003–04 Liverpool 0 0
2004–05 Chester C 21 0
2005–06 Chester C 17 0
2006–07 Chester C 20 0
2006–07 *Boston U* 7 0 **7 0**
2007–08 Chester C 0 0 **58 0**

WALKER, Adam (M) 0 0
H: 5 6 W: 9 00 b.Chester 23-3-87
2007–08 Chester C 0 0

WILSON, Laurence (M) 96 4
H: 5 10 W: 10 09 b.Huyton 10-10-86
Source: Scholar. *Honours:* England Youth.
2004–05 Everton 0 0
2005–06 Everton 0 0
2005–06 *Mansfield T* 15 1 **15 1**
2006–07 Chester C 41 1
2007–08 Chester C 40 2 **81 3**

YEO, Simon (F) 191 52
H: 5 10 W: 11 08 b.Stockport 20-10-73
Source: Hyde U.
2002–03 Lincoln C 37 5
2003–04 Lincoln C 41 11
2004–05 Lincoln C 44 21
From New Zealand Knights
2005–06 Lincoln C 12 5 **134 42**
2006–07 Peterborough U 13 2 **13 2**
2006–07 Chester C 15 4
2007–08 Chester C 21 4 **36 8**
2007–08 *Bury* 8 0 **8 0**

CHESTERFIELD (24)

ALGAR, Ben (M) 2 0
H: 6 1 W: 12 00 b.Dronfield 3-12-89
2007–08 Chesterfield 2 0 **2 0**

ALLISON, Wayne (F) 752 171
H: 6 0 W: 14 13 b.Huddersfield 16-10-68
Source: Trainee.
1986–87 Halifax T 8 4
1987–88 Halifax T 35 4
1988–89 Halifax T 41 15 **84 23**
1989–90 Watford 7 0 **7 0**
1990–91 Bristol C 37 6
1991–92 Bristol C 43 10
1992–93 Bristol C 39 4
1993–94 Bristol C 39 15
1994–95 Bristol C 37 13 **195 48**
1995–96 Swindon T 44 17
1996–97 Swindon T 41 11
1997–98 Swindon T 16 3 **101 31**
1997–98 Huddersfield T 27 6
1998–99 Huddersfield T 44 9
1999–2000 Huddersfield T 3 0 **74 15**
1999–2000 Tranmere R 40 16
2000–01 Tranmere R 36 6
2001–02 Tranmere R 27 4 **103 26**
2002–03 Sheffield U 34 6
2003–04 Sheffield U 39 1 **73 7**
2004–05 Chesterfield 38 6
2005–06 Chesterfield 32 11
2006–07 Chesterfield 36 4
2007–08 Chesterfield 9 0 **115 21**

COOPER, Kevin (M) 357 46
H: 5 8 W: 10 04 b.Derby 8-2-75
Source: Trainee.
1993–94 Derby Co 0 0
1994–95 Derby Co 1 0
1995–96 Derby Co 1 0
1996–97 Derby Co 0 0 **2 0**
1996–97 *Stockport Co* 12 3
1997–98 Stockport Co 38 8
1998–99 Stockport Co 38 1
1999–2000 Stockport Co 46 4
2000–01 Stockport Co 34 5 **168 21**
2000–01 Wimbledon 11 3
2001–02 Wimbledon 40 10 **51 13**
2001–02 Wolverhampton W 5 0
2002–03 Wolverhampton W 26 3
2003–04 Wolverhampton W 1 0
2003–04 *Sunderland* 1 0 **1 0**
2003–04 *Norwich C* 10 0 **10 0**
2004–05 Wolverhampton W 30 6 **62 9**
2005–06 Cardiff C 36 2
2006–07 Cardiff C 4 0
2006–07 *Yeovil T* 4 0 **4 0**
2006–07 *Walsall* 8 0 **8 0**
2007–08 Cardiff C 0 0 **40 2**
2007–08 *Tranmere R* 4 0 **4 0**
2007–08 Chesterfield 7 1 **7 1**

DAVIES, Gareth (M) 116 2
H: 6 1 W: 12 10 b.Chesterfield 4-2-83
Source: Trainee.
2001–02 Chesterfield 0 0
2002–03 Chesterfield 34 1
2003–04 Chesterfield 28 0
2004–05 Chesterfield 19 1
2005–06 Chesterfield 20 0
2006–07 Chesterfield 14 0
2007–08 Chesterfield 1 0 **116 2**

DOWNES, Aaron (D) 116 7
H: 6 2 W: 13 02 b.Mudgee 15-5-85
Honours: Australia Youth, Under-20, Under-21, Under-23.
2004–05 Chesterfield 9 2
2005–06 Chesterfield 22 0
2006–07 Chesterfield 45 3
2007–08 Chesterfield 40 2 **116 7**

DYER, Bruce (F) 468 119
H: 6 0 W: 11 03 b.Ilford 13-4-75
Source: Trainee. *Honours:* England Under-21.
1992–93 Watford 2 0
1993–94 Watford 29 6
1993–94 Crystal Palace 11 0
1994–95 Crystal Palace 16 1
1995–96 Crystal Palace 35 13
1996–97 Crystal Palace 43 17
1997–98 Crystal Palace 24 4
1998–99 Crystal Palace 6 2 **135 37**
1998–99 Barnsley 28 7
1999–2000 Barnsley 32 6
2000–01 Barnsley 38 15
2001–02 Barnsley 44 14
2002–03 Barnsley 40 17 **182 59**
2003–04 Watford 32 3
2004–05 Watford 36 9 **99 18**
2005–06 Stoke C 11 0 **11 0**
2005–06 *Millwall* 10 2 **10 2**
2005–06 Sheffield U 5 1 **5 1**
2006–07 Doncaster R 15 1
2006–07 *Bradford C* 5 1 **5 1**
2007–08 Doncaster R 0 0 **15 1**
2007–08 *Rotherham U* 3 0 **3 0**
2007–08 Chesterfield 3 0 **3 0**

FLETCHER, Steve (F) 563 97
H: 6 2 W: 14 09 b.Hartlepool 26-7-72
Source: Trainee.
1990–91 Hartlepool U 14 2
1991–92 Hartlepool U 18 2 **32 4**
1992–93 Bournemouth 31 4

1993–94 Bournemouth 36 6
1994–95 Bournemouth 40 6
1995–96 Bournemouth 7 1
1996–97 Bournemouth 35 7
1997–98 Bournemouth 42 12
1998–99 Bournemouth 39 8
1999–2000 Bournemouth 36 7
2000–01 Bournemouth 45 9
2001–02 Bournemouth 2 0
2002–03 Bournemouth 35 5
2003–04 Bournemouth 41 9
2004–05 Bournemouth 36 9
2005–06 Bournemouth 27 4
2006–07 Bournemouth 41 1 **493 88**
2007–08 Chesterfield 38 5 **38 5**

GRAY, Kevin (D) 499 19
H: 6 0 W: 14 00 b.Sheffield 7-1-72
Source: Trainee.
1988–89 Mansfield T 1 0
1989–90 Mansfield T 16 0
1990–91 Mansfield T 31 1
1991–92 Mansfield T 18 0
1992–93 Mansfield T 33 0
1993–94 Mansfield T 42 2 **141 3**
1994–95 Huddersfield T 5 0
1995–96 Huddersfield T 38 0
1996–97 Huddersfield T 39 1
1997–98 Huddersfield T 35 1
1998–99 Huddersfield T 34 1
1999–2000 Huddersfield T 18 2
2000–01 *Stockport Co* 1 0 **1 0**
2000–01 Huddersfield T 17 0
2001–02 Huddersfield T 44 1 **230 6**
2002–03 Tranmere R 10 1
2003–04 Tranmere R 2 0 **12 1**
2003–04 Carlisle U 25 3
2004–05 Carlisle U 0 0
2005–06 Carlisle U 44 3
2006–07 Carlisle U 31 3 **100 9**
2007–08 Chesterfield 15 0 **15 0**

JACKSON, Jamie (F) 20 0
H: 5 6 W: 10 04 b.Sheffield 1-11-86
Source: Scholar.
2005–06 Chesterfield 2 0
2006–07 Chesterfield 14 0
2007–08 Chesterfield 4 0 **20 0**

JORDAN, Michael (G) 7 0
H: 6 2 W: 13 02 b.Cheshunt 7-4-86
Source: Scholar.
2003–04 Arsenal 0 0
2004–05 Arsenal 0 0
2005–06 Arsenal 0 0
2005–06 *Yeovil T* 0 0
2006–07 Chesterfield 6 0
2007–08 Chesterfield 1 0 **7 0**

KOVACS, Janos (D) 57 2
H: 6 4 W: 14 10 b.Budapest 11-9-85
Source: MTK. *Honours:* Hungary Under-20.
2005–06 Chesterfield 9 0
2006–07 Chesterfield 7 0
2007–08 Chesterfield 41 2 **57 2**

LESTER, Jack (F) 399 86
H: 5 9 W: 12 08 b.Sheffield 8-10-75
Source: Trainee. *Honours:* England Schools.
1994–95 Grimsby T 7 0
1995–96 Grimsby T 5 0
1996–97 Grimsby T 22 5
1996–97 *Doncaster R* 11 1 **11 1**
1997–98 Grimsby T 40 4
1998–99 Grimsby T 33 4
1999–2000 Grimsby T 26 4 **133 17**
1999–2000 Nottingham F 15 2
2000–01 Nottingham F 19 7
2001–02 Nottingham F 32 5
2002–03 Nottingham F 33 7
2003–04 Sheffield U 32 12
2004–05 Sheffield U 12 0 **44 12**
2004–05 Nottingham F 3 1
2005–06 Nottingham F 38 5
2006–07 Nottingham F 35 6 **175 33**
2007–08 Chesterfield 36 23 **36 23**

LEVEN, Peter (M) 107 11
H: 5 11 W: 12 13 b.Glasgow 27-9-83
Source: Rangers.
2004–05 Kilmarnock 32 4
2005–06 Kilmarnock 6 0
2006–07 Kilmarnock 27 1 **65 5**
2007–08 Chesterfield 42 6 **42 6**

LOWRY, Jamie (D) 50 6
H: 6 0 W: 12 00 b.Newquay 18-3-87
Source: Scholar.
2006–07 Chesterfield 8 0
2007–08 Chesterfield 42 6 **50 6**

NIVEN, Derek (M) 186 13
H: 5 11 W: 12 05 b.Falkirk 12-12-83
Source: Stenhousemuir.
2000–01 Raith R 1 0 **1 0**
2001–02 Bolton W 0 0
2002–03 Bolton W 0 0
2003–04 Bolton W 0 0
2003–04 Chesterfield 22 1
2004–05 Chesterfield 38 1
2005–06 Chesterfield 42 5
2006–07 Chesterfield 45 3
2007–08 Chesterfield 38 3 **185 13**

O'HARE, Alan (D) 154 3
H: 6 1 W: 12 09 b.Drogheda 31-7-82
Source: Scholar. *Honours:* Eire Youth.
2001–02 Bolton W 0 0
2001–02 *Chesterfield* 19 0
2002–03 Bolton W 0 0
2002–03 Chesterfield 22 0
2003–04 Chesterfield 40 1
2004–05 Chesterfield 21 0
2005–06 Chesterfield 22 0
2006–07 Chesterfield 17 2
2007–08 Chesterfield 13 0 **154 3**

PICKEN, Phil (D) 108 2
H: 5 9 W: 10 07 b.Droylsden 12-11-85
Source: Scholar.
2004–05 Manchester U 0 0
2005–06 Manchester U 0 0
2005–06 *Chesterfield* 32 1
2006–07 Chesterfield 39 1
2007–08 Chesterfield 37 0 **108 2**

ROBERTSON, Gregor (D) 124 2
H: 6 0 W: 12 04 b.Edinburgh 19-1-84
Honours: Scotland Under-21.
2000–01 Nottingham F 0 0
2001–02 Nottingham F 0 0
2002–03 Nottingham F 0 0
2003–04 Nottingham F 16 0
2004–05 Nottingham F 20 0 **36 0**
2005–06 Rotherham U 35 1
2006–07 Rotherham U 18 0 **53 1**
2007–08 Chesterfield 35 1 **35 1**

ROCHE, Barry (G) 139 0
H: 6 5 W: 14 08 b.Dublin 6-4-82
Source: Trainee.
1999–2000 Nottingham F 0 0
2000–01 Nottingham F 2 0
2001–02 Nottingham F 0 0
2002–03 Nottingham F 1 0
2003–04 Nottingham F 8 0
2004–05 Nottingham F 2 0 **13 0**
2005–06 Chesterfield 41 0
2006–07 Chesterfield 40 0
2007–08 Chesterfield 45 0 **126 0**

SMITH, Adam (M) 70 3
H: 5 11 W: 12 00 b.Huddersfield 20-2-85
Source: Scholar.
2003–04 Chesterfield 3 0
2004–05 Chesterfield 16 0
2005–06 Chesterfield 26 3
2006–07 Chesterfield 13 0
2007–08 Chesterfield 8 0 **66 3**
2007–08 *Lincoln C* 4 0 **4 0**

WARD, Jamie (M) 78 25
H: 5 5 W: 9 04 b.Birmingham 12-5-86
Source: Scholar. *Honours:* Northern Ireland Youth, Under-21.
2003–04 Aston Villa 0 0
2004–05 Aston Villa 0 0
2005–06 Aston Villa 0 0
2005–06 *Stockport Co* 9 1 **9 1**
2006–07 Torquay U 25 9 **25 9**
2006–07 Chesterfield 9 3
2007–08 Chesterfield 35 12 **44 15**

WINTER, Jamie (M) 25 0
H: 5 10 W: 13 10 b.Dundee 4-8-85
Source: Scholar.
2002–03 Leeds U 0 0
2003–04 Leeds U 0 0
2004–05 Leeds U 0 0
2005–06 Leeds U 0 0
2006–07 Leeds U 0 0
2007–08 Chesterfield 25 0 **25 0**

COLCHESTER U (25)

BALDWIN, Pat (D) 150 1
H: 6 3 W: 12 07 b.City of London 12-11-82
Source: Chelsea Academy.
2002–03 Colchester U 19 0
2003–04 Colchester U 4 0
2004–05 Colchester U 38 0
2005–06 Colchester U 25 0
2006–07 Colchester U 38 1
2007–08 Colchester U 26 0 **150 1**

BALOGH, Bela (M) 96 9
H: 6 2 W: 12 08 b.Budapest 30-12-84
Honours: Hungary 9 full caps.
2003–04 MTK 3 0
2004–05 MTK 30 4
2005–06 MTK 25 4
2006–07 MTK 21 1 **79 9**
2007–08 Colchester U 17 0 **17 0**

COUSINS, Mark (G) 2 0
H: 6 2 W: 12 02 b.Chelmsford 9-1-87
Source: Scholar.
2005–06 Colchester U 0 0
2006–07 Colchester U 0 0
2007–08 Colchester U 2 0 **2 0**

COYNE, Chris (D) 266 15
H: 6 2 W: 13 10 b.Brisbane 20-12-78
Source: Perth SC. *Honours:* Australia Youth, Under-23, 1 full cap.
1995–96 West Ham U 0 0
1996–97 West Ham U 0 0
1997–98 West Ham U 0 0
1998–99 West Ham U 1 0 **1 0**
1998–99 *Brentford* 7 0 **7 0**
1998–99 *Southend U* 1 0 **1 0**
1999–2000 Dundee 2 0
2000–01 Dundee 18 0 **20 0**
2001–02 Luton T 31 3
2002–03 Luton T 40 1
2003–04 Luton T 44 2
2004–05 Luton T 40 5
2005–06 Luton T 30 2
2006–07 Luton T 18 1
2007–08 Luton T 18 0 **221 14**
2007–08 Colchester U 16 1 **16 1**

DAVISON, Aidan (G) 352 0
H: 6 2 W: 13 12 b.Sedgefield 11-5-68
Source: Billingham Synthonia. *Honours:* Northern Ireland B, 3 full caps.
1987–88 Notts Co 0 0
1988–89 Notts Co 1 0
1989–90 Notts Co 0 0 **1 0**
1989–90 *Leyton Orient* 0 0
1989–90 Bury 0 0
1989–90 *Chester C* 0 0
1990–91 Bury 0 0
1990–91 *Blackpool* 0 0
1991–92 Millwall 33 0
1992–93 Millwall 1 0 **34 0**
1993–94 Bolton W 31 0
1994–95 Bolton W 4 0
1995–96 Bolton W 2 0
1996–97 Bolton W 0 0 **37 0**
1996–97 *Ipswich T* 0 0
1996–97 *Hull C* 9 0 **9 0**
1996–97 Bradford C 10 0
1997–98 Grimsby T 42 0
1998–99 Grimsby T 35 0
1999–2000 Grimsby T 0 0
1999–2000 Sheffield U 2 0 **2 0**
1999–2000 Bradford C 6 0
2000–01 Bradford C 2 0
2001–02 Bradford C 9 0
2002–03 Bradford C 34 0 **61 0**
2003–04 Grimsby T 32 0 **109 0**
2004–05 Colchester U 33 0
2005–06 Colchester U 41 0
2006–07 Colchester U 19 0
2007–08 Colchester U 6 0 **99 0**

DEVAUX, Thomas (D) 0 0
H: 6 2 W: 12 04 b.Clacton 12-1-89
Source: Scholar.
2007–08 Colchester U 0 0

DUGUID, Karl (M) **385 42**
H: 5 11 W: 11 06 b.Hitchin 21-3-78
Source: Trainee.

1995–96	Colchester U	16	1		
1996–97	Colchester U	20	3		
1997–98	Colchester U	21	3		
1998–99	Colchester U	33	4		
1999–2000	Colchester U	41	12		
2000–01	Colchester U	41	5		
2001–02	Colchester U	41	4		
2002–03	Colchester U	27	3		
2003–04	Colchester U	30	2		
2004–05	Colchester U	0	0		
2005–06	Colchester U	35	0		
2006–07	Colchester U	43	5		
2007–08	Colchester U	37	0	**385**	**42**

ELITO, Medy (M) **11 1**
H: 6 2 W: 13 00 b.Kinshasa 20-3-90
Source: Scholar. *Honours:* England Youth.

2007–08	Colchester U	11	1	**11**	**1**

GERKEN, Dean (G) **88 0**
H: 6 3 W: 12 08 b.Rochford 22-5-85
Source: Scholar.

2003–04	Colchester U	1	0		
2004–05	Colchester U	13	0		
2005–06	Colchester U	7	0		
2006–07	Colchester U	27	0		
2007–08	Colchester U	40	0	**88**	**0**

GRANVILLE, Danny (D) **343 19**
H: 6 0 W: 12 00 b.Islington 19-1-75
Source: Trainee. *Honours:* England Under-21.

1993–94	Cambridge U	11	5		
1994–95	Cambridge U	16	2		
1995–96	Cambridge U	35	0		
1996–97	Cambridge U	37	0	**99**	**7**
1996–97	Chelsea	5	0		
1997–98	Chelsea	13	0	**18**	**0**
1998–99	Leeds U	9	0		
1999–2000	Leeds U	0	0	**9**	**0**
1999–2000	Manchester C	35	2		
2000–01	Manchester C	19	0		
2000–01	*Norwich C*	6	0	**6**	**0**
2001–02	Manchester C	16	1	**70**	**3**
2001–02	Crystal Palace	16	0		
2002–03	Crystal Palace	35	3		
2003–04	Crystal Palace	21	3		
2004–05	Crystal Palace	35	3		
2005–06	Crystal Palace	0	0		
2006–07	Crystal Palace	15	0	**122**	**9**
2007–08	Colchester U	19	0	**19**	**0**

GUTTRIDGE, Luke (M) **231 23**
H: 5 6 W: 8 07 b.Barnstaple 27-3-82
Source: Trainee.

1999–2000	Torquay U	1	0		
2000–01	Torquay U	0	0	**1**	**0**
2000–01	Cambridge U	1	1		
2001–02	Cambridge U	29	2		
2002–03	Cambridge U	43	3		
2003–04	Cambridge U	46	11		
2004–05	Cambridge U	17	0	**136**	**17**
2004–05	Southend U	5	0		
2005–06	Southend U	41	5		
2006–07	Southend U	17	0	**63**	**5**
2006–07	Leyton Orient	17	1	**17**	**1**
2007–08	Colchester U	14	0	**14**	**0**

GUY, Jamie (M) **47 3**
H: 6 1 W: 13 00 b.Barking 1-8-87
Source: Scholar.

2004–05	Colchester U	2	0		
2005–06	Colchester U	2	0		
2006–07	Colchester U	32	3		
2007–08	Colchester U	11	0	**47**	**3**

HAMMOND, Dean (M) **157 21**
H: 6 0 W: 11 09 b.Hastings 7-3-83
Source: Scholar.

2002–03	Brighton & HA	4	0		
2003–04	Brighton & HA	0	0		
2003–04	*Leyton Orient*	8	0	**8**	**0**
2004–05	Brighton & HA	30	4		
2005–06	Brighton & HA	41	4		
2006–07	Brighton & HA	37	8		
2007–08	Brighton & HA	24	5	**136**	**21**
2007–08	Colchester U	13	0	**13**	**0**

IFIL, Phil (D) **51 0**
H: 5 10 W: 12 02 b.Willesden 18-11-86
Honours: England Youth, Under-20.

2004–05	Tottenham H	2	0		
2005–06	Tottenham H	0	0		
2005–06	*Millwall*	16	0	**16**	**0**
2006–07	Tottenham H	1	0		
2007–08	Tottenham H	0	0	**3**	**0**
2007–08	*Southampton*	12	0	**12**	**0**
2007–08	Colchester U	20	0	**20**	**0**

IZZET, Kem (M) **256 17**
H: 5 7 W: 10 05 b.Mile End 29-9-80
Source: Trainee.

1998–99	Charlton Ath	0	0		
1999–2000	Charlton Ath	0	0		
2000–01	Charlton Ath	0	0		
2000–01	Colchester U	6	1		
2001–02	Colchester U	40	3		
2002–03	Colchester U	45	8		
2003–04	Colchester U	44	3		
2004–05	Colchester U	4	0		
2005–06	Colchester U	33	0		
2006–07	Colchester U	45	1		
2007–08	Colchester U	39	1	**256**	**17**

JACKSON, Johnnie (M) **145 13**
H: 6 1 W: 12 00 b.Camden 15-8-82
Source: Trainee. *Honours:* England Youth, Under-20.

1999–2000	Tottenham H	0	0		
2000–01	Tottenham H	0	0		
2001–02	Tottenham H	0	0		
2002–03	Tottenham H	0	0		
2002–03	*Swindon T*	13	1	**13**	**1**
2002–03	*Colchester U*	8	0		
2003–04	Tottenham H	11	1		
2003–04	*Coventry C*	5	2	**5**	**2**
2004–05	Tottenham H	8	0		
2004–05	*Watford*	15	0	**15**	**0**
2005–06	Tottenham H	1	0	**20**	**1**
2005–06	*Derby Co*	6	0	**6**	**0**
2006–07	Colchester U	32	2		
2007–08	Colchester U	46	7	**86**	**9**

LISBIE, Kevin (F) **221 39**
H: 5 10 W: 11 06 b.Hackney 17-10-78
Source: Trainee. *Honours:* England Youth. Jamaica 10 full caps, 2 goals.

1996–97	Charlton Ath	25	1		
1997–98	Charlton Ath	17	1		
1998–99	Charlton Ath	1	0		
1998–99	*Gillingham*	7	4	**7**	**4**
1999–2000	Charlton Ath	0	0		
1999–2000	*Reading*	2	0	**2**	**0**
2000–01	Charlton Ath	18	0		
2000–01	*QPR*	2	0	**2**	**0**
2001–02	Charlton Ath	22	5		
2002–03	Charlton Ath	32	4		
2003–04	Charlton Ath	9	4		
2004–05	Charlton Ath	17	1		
2005–06	Charlton Ath	6	0		
2005–06	*Norwich C*	6	1	**6**	**1**
2005–06	*Derby Co*	7	1	**7**	**1**
2006–07	Charlton Ath	8	0	**155**	**16**
2007–08	Colchester U	42	17	**42**	**17**

McLEOD, Kevin (M) **168 20**
H: 5 11 W: 11 00 b.Liverpool 12-9-80
Source: Trainee.

1998–99	Everton	0	0		
1999–2000	Everton	0	0		
2000–01	Everton	5	0		
2001–02	Everton	0	0		
2002–03	Everton	0	0		
2002–03	*QPR*	8	2		
2003–04	Everton	0	0	**5**	**0**
2003–04	QPR	35	3		
2004–05	QPR	24	1	**67**	**6**
2004–05	Swansea C	11	0		
2005–06	Swansea C	29	7		
2006–07	Swansea C	4	0	**44**	**7**
2006–07	Colchester U	24	3		
2007–08	Colchester U	28	4	**52**	**7**

PLATT, Clive (F) **400 78**
H: 6 4 W: 12 07 b.Wolverhampton 27-10-77
Source: Trainee.

1995–96	Walsall	4	2		
1996–97	Walsall	1	0		
1997–98	Walsall	20	1		
1998–99	Walsall	7	1		
1999–2000	Walsall	0	0	**32**	**4**
1999–2000	Rochdale	41	9		
2000–01	Rochdale	43	8		
2001–02	Rochdale	43	7		
2002–03	Rochdale	42	6	**169**	**30**
2003–04	Notts Co	19	3	**19**	**3**
2003–04	Peterborough U	18	2		
2004–05	Peterborough U	19	4	**37**	**6**
2004–05	Milton Keynes D	20	3		
2005–06	Milton Keynes D	40	6		
2006–07	Milton Keynes D	42	18	**102**	**27**
2007–08	Colchester U	41	8	**41**	**8**

SHERINGHAM, Teddy (F) **734 275**
H: 6 0 W: 12 05 b.Highams Park 2-4-66
Source: Apprentice. *Honours:* England Youth, Under-21, 51 full caps, 11 goals.

1983–84	Millwall	7	1		
1984–85	Millwall	0	0		
1984–85	*Aldershot*	5	0	**5**	**0**
1985–86	Millwall	18	4		
1986–87	Millwall	42	13		
1987–88	Millwall	43	22		
1988–89	Millwall	33	11		
1989–90	Millwall	31	9		
1990–91	Millwall	46	33	**220**	**93**
1991–92	Nottingham F	39	13		
1992–93	Nottingham F	3	1	**42**	**14**
1992–93	Tottenham H	38	21		
1993–94	Tottenham H	19	13		
1994–95	Tottenham H	42	18		
1995–96	Tottenham H	38	16		
1996–97	Tottenham H	29	7		
1997–98	Manchester U	31	9		
1998–99	Manchester U	17	2		
1999–2000	Manchester U	27	5		
2000–01	Manchester U	29	15	**104**	**31**
2001–02	Tottenham H	34	10		
2002–03	Tottenham H	36	12	**236**	**97**
2003–04	Portsmouth	32	9	**32**	**9**
2004–05	West Ham U	33	20		
2005–06	West Ham U	26	6		
2006–07	West Ham U	17	2	**76**	**28**
2007–08	Colchester U	19	3	**19**	**3**

VERNON, Scott (F) **173 45**
H: 6 1 W: 11 06 b.Manchester 13-12-83
Source: Scholar.

2002–03	Oldham Ath	8	1		
2003–04	Oldham Ath	45	12		
2004–05	Oldham Ath	22	7	**75**	**20**
2004–05	*Blackpool*	4	3		
2005–06	Blackpool	17	1		
2005–06	*Colchester U*	7	1		
2006–07	Blackpool	38	11		
2007–08	Blackpool	15	4	**74**	**19**
2007–08	Colchester U	17	5	**24**	**6**

VIRGO, Adam (D) **143 11**
H: 6 2 W: 13 12 b.Brighton 25-1-83
Source: Juniors. *Honours:* Scotland B.

2000–01	Brighton & HA	6	0		
2001–02	Brighton & HA	6	0		
2002–03	Brighton & HA	3	0		
2002–03	*Exeter C*	9	0	**9**	**0**
2003–04	Brighton & HA	22	1		
2004–05	Brighton & HA	36	8	**73**	**9**
2005–06	Celtic	10	0		
2006–07	Celtic	0	0	**10**	**0**
2006–07	Coventry C	15	1		
2007–08	Coventry C	0	0	**15**	**1**
2007–08	Colchester U	36	1	**36**	**1**

WATSON, Kevin (M) **396 13**
H: 6 0 W: 12 06 b.Hackney 3-1-74
Source: Trainee.

1991–92	Tottenham H	0	0		
1992–93	Tottenham H	5	0		
1993–94	Tottenham H	0	0		
1993–94	*Brentford*	3	0	**3**	**0**
1994–95	Tottenham H	0	0		
1994–95	*Bristol C*	2	0	**2**	**0**
1994–95	*Barnet*	13	0	**13**	**0**
1995–96	Tottenham H	0	0	**5**	**0**
1996–97	Swindon T	27	1		
1997–98	Swindon T	18	0		
1998–99	Swindon T	18	0	**63**	**1**
1999–2000	Rotherham U	44	1		
2000–01	Rotherham U	46	5		
2001–02	Rotherham U	19	1	**109**	**7**
2001–02	Reading	12	1		
2002–03	Reading	32	1		
2003–04	Reading	22	0	**66**	**2**

2004–05	Colchester U	44	2		
2005–06	Colchester U	44	0		
2006–07	Colchester U	40	1		
2007–08	Colchester U	7	0	**135**	**3**

WEBB, Thomas (F) **0 0**
H: 5 11 W: 10 05 b.Chelmsford 14-4-89
Source: Scholar.

2007–08	Colchester U	0	0		

WHITE, John (D) **92 0**
H: 6 0 W: 12 01 b.Maldon 26-7-86
Source: Scholar.

2004–05	Colchester U	20	0		
2005–06	Colchester U	35	0		
2006–07	Colchester U	16	0		
2007–08	Colchester U	21	0	**92**	**0**

WORDSWORTH, Anthony (M) **3 0**
H: 6 1 W: 12 00 b.Camden 3-1-89
Source: Scholar.

2007–08	Colchester U	3	0	**3**	**0**

YEATES, Mark (F) **103 14**
H: 5 8 W: 13 03 b.Dublin 11-1-85
Source: Trainee. *Honours:* Eire Youth, Under-21.

2002–03	Tottenham H	0	0		
2003–04	Tottenham H	1	0		
2003–04	*Brighton & HA*	9	0	**9**	**0**
2004–05	Tottenham H	2	0		
2004–05	*Swindon T*	4	0	**4**	**0**
2005–06	Tottenham H	0	0		
2005–06	*Colchester U*	44	5		
2006–07	Tottenham H	0	0	**3**	**0**
2006–07	*Hull C*	5	0	**5**	**0**
2006–07	*Leicester C*	9	1	**9**	**1**
2007–08	Colchester U	29	8	**73**	**13**

COVENTRY C (26)

ANDREWS, Wayne (F) **184 39**
H: 5 10 W: 11 06 b.Paddington 25-11-77
Source: Trainee.

1995–96	Watford	1	0		
1996–97	Watford	25	4		
1997–98	Watford	2	0		
1998–99	Watford	0	0	**28**	**4**
1998–99	*Cambridge U*	2	0	**2**	**0**
1998–99	*Peterborough U*	10	5	**10**	**5**
From Aldershot T, Chesham U					
2001–02	Oldham Ath	0	0		
2002–03	Oldham Ath	37	11	**37**	**11**
2003–04	Colchester U	41	12		
2004–05	Colchester U	5	2	**46**	**14**
2004–05	Crystal Palace	9	0		
2005–06	Crystal Palace	24	1	**33**	**1**
2006–07	Coventry C	3	1		
2006–07	*Sheffield W*	9	1	**9**	**1**
2006–07	*Bristol C*	7	2	**7**	**2**
2007–08	Coventry C	7	0	**10**	**1**
2007–08	*Leeds U*	1	0	**1**	**0**
2007–08	*Bristol R*	1	0	**1**	**0**

BEST, Leon (F) **97 27**
H: 6 1 W: 13 03 b.Nottingham 19-9-86
Source: Scholar. *Honours:* Eire Youth, Under-21.

2004–05	Southampton	3	0		
2004–05	*QPR*	5	0	**5**	**0**
2005–06	Southampton	3	0		
2005–06	*Sheffield W*	13	2	**13**	**2**
2006–07	Southampton	9	4	**15**	**4**
2006–07	*Bournemouth*	15	3	**15**	**3**
2006–07	*Yeovil T*	15	10	**15**	**10**
2007–08	Coventry C	34	8	**34**	**8**

BIRCHALL, Chris (M) **107 9**
H: 5 7 W: 13 05 b.Stafford 5-5-84
Source: Scholar. *Honours:* Trinidad & Tobago 26 full caps, 4 goals.

2001–02	Port Vale	1	0		
2002–03	Port Vale	2	0		
2003–04	Port Vale	10	0		
2004–05	Port Vale	34	6		
2005–06	Port Vale	31	1	**78**	**7**
2006–07	Coventry C	28	2		
2007–08	Coventry C	1	0	**29**	**2**

BORROWDALE, Gary (D) **119 0**
H: 6 0 W: 12 01 b.Sutton 16-7-85
Source: Scholar. *Honours:* England Youth, Under-20.

2002–03	Crystal Palace	13	0		
2003–04	Crystal Palace	23	0		
2004–05	Crystal Palace	7	0		
2005–06	Crystal Palace	30	0		
2006–07	Crystal Palace	25	0	**98**	**0**
2007–08	Coventry C	21	0	**21**	**0**

CAIRO, Ellery (M) **262 35**
H: 5 7 W: 11 00 b.Rotterdam 3-8-78

1994–95	Feyenoord	1	0		
1995–96	Feyenoord	0	0		
1996–97	Feyenoord	0	0		
1997–98	Excelsior	34	4		
1998–99	Excelsior	19	9	**53**	**13**
1998–99	Feyenoord	9	2		
1999–2000	Feyenoord	19	3	**29**	**5**
2000–01	Twente	27	3		
2001–02	Twente	29	2		
2002–03	Twente	30	7	**86**	**12**
2003–04	Freiburg	30	1		
2004–05	Freiburg	28	3	**58**	**4**
2005–06	Hertha Berlin	11	0		
2006–07	Hertha Berlin	18	1	**29**	**1**
2007–08	Coventry C	7	0	**7**	**0**

DANN, Scott (D) **75 7**
H: 6 2 W: 12 00 b.Liverpool 14-2-87
Source: Scholar. *Honours:* England Under-21.

2004–05	Walsall	1	0		
2005–06	Walsall	0	0		
2006–07	Walsall	30	4		
2007–08	Walsall	28	3	**59**	**7**
2007–08	Coventry C	16	0	**16**	**0**

DAVIS, Liam (M) **18 0**
H: 5 9 W: 11 07 b.Wandsworth 23-11-86
Source: Scholar.

2005–06	Coventry C	2	0		
2006–07	Coventry C	3	0		
2006–07	*Peterborough U*	7	0	**7**	**0**
2007–08	Coventry C	6	0	**11**	**0**

DE ZEEUW, Arjan (D) **541 23**
H: 6 0 W: 13 06 b.Castricum 16-4-70
Source: Vitesse 22.

1992–93	Telstar	30	1		
1993–94	Telstar	31	2		
1994–95	Telstar	29	1		
1995–96	Telstar	12	1	**102**	**5**
1995–96	Barnsley	31	1		
1996–97	Barnsley	43	2		
1997–98	Barnsley	26	0		
1998–99	Barnsley	38	4	**138**	**7**
1999–2000	Wigan Ath	39	3		
2000–01	Wigan Ath	45	1		
2001–02	Wigan Ath	42	2		
2002–03	Portsmouth	38	1		
2003–04	Portsmouth	36	1		
2004–05	Portsmouth	32	3	**106**	**5**
2005–06	Wigan Ath	31	0		
2006–07	Wigan Ath	21	0	**178**	**6**
2007–08	Coventry C	17	0	**17**	**0**

DOYLE, Micky (M) **210 17**
H: 5 10 W: 11 00 b.Dublin 8-7-81
Source: Celtic. *Honours:* Eire Under-21, 1 full cap.

2003–04	Coventry C	40	5		
2004–05	Coventry C	44	2		
2005–06	Coventry C	44	0		
2006–07	Coventry C	40	3		
2007–08	Coventry C	42	7	**210**	**17**

FOX, Daniel (D) **128 8**
H: 5 11 W: 12 06 b.Crewe 29-5-86
Source: Scholar. *Honours:* England Under-21.

2004–05	Everton	0	0		
2004–05	*Stranraer*	11	1	**11**	**1**
2005–06	Walsall	33	0		
2006–07	Walsall	44	3		
2007–08	Walsall	22	3	**99**	**6**
2007–08	Coventry C	18	1	**18**	**1**

GIDDINGS, Stuart (M) **18 0**
H: 6 0 W: 11 08 b.Coventry 27-3-86
Source: Scholar. *Honours:* England Youth.

2003–04	Coventry C	1	0		
2004–05	Coventry C	12	0		
2005–06	Coventry C	2	0		
2006–07	Coventry C	1	0		
2007–08	Coventry C	0	0	**16**	**0**
2007–08	*Oldham Ath*	2	0	**2**	**0**

GOODING, Andy (M) **0 0**
H: 5 7 W: 10 05 b.Coventry 30-4-88
Source: Scholar.

2006–07	Coventry C	0	0		
2007–08	Coventry C	0	0		

GRAY, Julian (M) **221 16**
H: 6 1 W: 11 00 b.Lewisham 21-9-79
Source: Trainee.

1998–99	Arsenal	0	0		
1999–2000	Arsenal	1	0	**1**	**0**
2000–01	Crystal Palace	23	1		
2001–02	Crystal Palace	43	2		
2002–03	Crystal Palace	35	5		
2003–04	Crystal Palace	24	2	**125**	**10**
2003–04	*Cardiff C*	9	0	**9**	**0**
2004–05	Birmingham C	32	2		
2005–06	Birmingham C	21	1		
2006–07	Birmingham C	7	0	**60**	**3**
2007–08	Coventry C	26	3	**26**	**3**

HALL, Marcus (D) **319 3**
H: 6 1 W: 12 02 b.Coventry 24-3-76
Source: Trainee. *Honours:* England Under-21, B.

1994–95	Coventry C	5	0		
1995–96	Coventry C	25	0		
1996–97	Coventry C	13	0		
1997–98	Coventry C	25	1		
1998–99	Coventry C	5	0		
1999–2000	Coventry C	9	0		
2000–01	Coventry C	21	0		
2001–02	Coventry C	29	1		
2002–03	Nottingham F	1	0	**1**	**0**
2002–03	Stoke C	24	0		
2003–04	Stoke C	35	0		
2004–05	Stoke C	20	1	**79**	**1**
2004–05	Coventry C	10	0		
2005–06	Coventry C	39	0		
2006–07	Coventry C	40	0		
2007–08	Coventry C	18	0	**239**	**2**

HAWKINS, Colin (D) **243 20**
H: 6 1 W: 12 06 b.Galway 17-8-77
Honours: Eire Youth, Under-20, Under-21.

1995–96	Coventry C	0	0		
1996–97	Coventry C	0	0		
1997–98	St Patrick's Ath	32	4		
1998–99	St Patrick's Ath	26	7		
1999–2000	St Patrick's Ath	27	2	**85**	**13**
From Doncaster R					
2001–02	Bohemians	9	1		
2002–03	Bohemians	21	2		
2003	Bohemians	30	1		
2004	Bohemians	29	1	**89**	**5**
2005	Shelbourne	26	0		
2006	Shelbourne	25	2	**51**	**2**
2006–07	Coventry C	13	0		
2007–08	Coventry C	0	0	**13**	**0**
2007–08	*Chesterfield*	5	0	**5**	**0**

HILDRETH, Lee (M) **1 0**
H: 6 0 W: 11 02 b.Nuneaton 22-11-88
Source: Scholar.

2006–07	Coventry C	1	0		
2007–08	Coventry C	0	0	**1**	**0**

HUGHES, Michael (M) **454 35**
H: 5 6 W: 10 08 b.Larne 2-8-71
Source: Carrick R. *Honours:* Northern Ireland Schools, Youth, Under-21, Under-23, 71 full caps, 5 goals.

1988–89	Manchester C	1	0		
1989–90	Manchester C	0	0		
1990–91	Manchester C	1	0		
1991–92	Manchester C	24	1	**26**	**1**
1992–93	Strasbourg	36	2		
1993–94	Strasbourg	34	7		
1994–95	Strasbourg	13	0	**83**	**9**
1994–95	*West Ham U*	17	2		
1995–96	*West Ham U*	28	0		
1996–97	West Ham U	33	3		
1997–98	West Ham U	5	0	**83**	**5**
1997–98	Wimbledon	29	4		
1998–99	Wimbledon	30	2		
1999–2000	Wimbledon	20	2		
2000–01	Wimbledon	10	1		
2001–02	Wimbledon	26	4		
2001–02	*Birmingham C*	3	0	**3**	**0**
2002–03	Wimbledon	0	0	**115**	**13**
2003–04	Crystal Palace	34	3		

2004–05 Crystal Palace 36 2
2005–06 Crystal Palace 40 2
2006–07 Crystal Palace 16 0 **126 7**
2007–08 Coventry C 18 0 **18 0**

HUGHES, Stephen (M) 229 11
H: 6 0 W: 12 12 b.Wokingham 18-9-76
Source: Trainee. *Honours:* England Schools, Youth, Under-21.
1994–95 Arsenal 1 0
1995–96 Arsenal 1 0
1996–97 Arsenal 14 1
1997–98 Arsenal 17 2
1998–99 Arsenal 14 1
1999–2000 Fulham 3 0 **3 0**
1999–2000 Arsenal 2 0 **49 4**
1999–2000 Everton 11 1
2000–01 Everton 18 0 **29 1**
2001–02 Watford 15 0
2002–03 Watford 0 0 **15 0**
2003–04 Charlton Ath 0 0
2004–05 Coventry C 40 4
2005–06 Coventry C 19 0
2006–07 Coventry C 37 1
2007–08 Coventry C 37 1 **133 6**

IRELAND, Daniel (G) 0 0
H: 6 2 W: 13 00 b.Sydney 20-1-89
2007–08 Coventry C 0 0

KONSTANTOPOULOS, Dimitrios (G) 138 0
H: 6 4 W: 14 02 b.Kalamata 29-11-78
Source: Farense. *Honours:* Greece Under-21.
2003–04 Hartlepool U 0 0
2004–05 Hartlepool U 25 0
2005–06 Hartlepool U 46 0
2006–07 Hartlepool U 46 0 **117 0**
2007–08 Coventry C 21 0 **21 0**

KYLE, Kevin (F) 162 18
H: 6 4 W: 14 07 b.Stranraer 7-6-81
Source: Ayr Boswell. *Honours:* Scotland Under-21, B, 9 full caps, 1 goal.
1998–99 Sunderland 0 0
1999–2000 Sunderland 0 0
2000–01 Sunderland 3 0
2000–01 *Huddersfield T* 4 0 **4 0**
2000–01 *Darlington* 5 1 **5 1**
2000–01 *Rochdale* 6 0 **6 0**
2001–02 Sunderland 6 0
2002–03 Sunderland 17 0
2003–04 Sunderland 44 10
2004–05 Sunderland 6 0
2005–06 Sunderland 13 1
2006–07 Sunderland 2 0 **91 11**
2006–07 Coventry C 31 3
2007–08 Coventry C 13 2 **44 5**
2007–08 *Wolverhampton W* 12 1 **12 1**

MARSHALL, Andy (G) 388 0
H: 6 3 W: 14 08 b.Bury St Edmunds 14-4-75
Source: Trainee. *Honours:* England Youth, Under-21.
1993–94 Norwich C 0 0
1994–95 Norwich C 21 0
1995–96 Norwich C 3 0
1996–97 Norwich C 7 0
1996–97 *Bournemouth* 11 0 **11 0**
1996–97 *Gillingham* 5 0 **5 0**
1997–98 Norwich C 42 0
1998–99 Norwich C 37 0
1999–2000 Norwich C 44 0
2000–01 Norwich C 41 0 **195 0**
2001–02 Ipswich T 13 0
2002–03 Ipswich T 40 0
2003–04 Ipswich T 0 0 **53 0**
2003–04 Millwall 16 0
2004–05 Millwall 22 0
2005–06 Millwall 29 0 **67 0**
2006–07 Coventry C 41 0
2007–08 Coventry C 16 0 **57 0**

McKENZIE, Leon (F) 313 89
H: 5 11 W: 12 11 b.Croydon 17-5-78
Source: Trainee.
1995–96 Crystal Palace 12 0
1996–97 Crystal Palace 21 2
1997–98 Crystal Palace 3 0
1997–98 *Fulham* 3 0 **3 0**
1998–99 Crystal Palace 16 1
1998–99 *Peterborough U* 14 8
1999–2000 Crystal Palace 25 4
2000–01 Crystal Palace 8 0 **85 7**
2000–01 Peterborough U 30 13
2001–02 Peterborough U 30 18
2002–03 Peterborough U 11 5
2003–04 Peterborough U 19 9 **104 53**
2003–04 Norwich C 18 9
2004–05 Norwich C 37 7
2005–06 Norwich C 20 4
2006–07 Norwich C 4 0 **79 20**
2006–07 Coventry C 31 7
2007–08 Coventry C 11 2 **42 9**

McNAMEE, David (D) 146 4
H: 5 11 W: 11 02 b.Glasgow 10-10-80
Source: St Mirren BC. *Honours:* Scotland B, 4 full caps.
1997–98 St Mirren 1 0
1998–99 St Mirren 31 0 **32 0**
1998–99 Blackburn R 0 0
1999–2000 Blackburn R 0 0
2000–01 Blackburn R 0 0
2001–02 Blackburn R 0 0
2002–03 Livingston 12 0
2003–04 Livingston 30 3
2004–05 Livingston 29 1
2005–06 Livingston 14 0 **85 4**
2006–07 Coventry C 16 0
2007–08 Coventry C 13 0 **29 0**

MIFSUD, Michael (F) 191 87
H: 5 6 W: 10 00 b.Pieta 17-4-81
Honours: Malta 56 full caps, 19 goals.
1997–98 Sliema Wanderers 7 1
1998–99 Sliema Wanderers 22 8
1999–2000 Sliema Wanderers 26 21
2000–01 Sliema Wanderers 25 30 **80 60**
2001–02 Kaiserslautern 5 0
2002–03 Kaiserslautern 16 2
2003–04 Kaiserslautern 0 0 **21 2**
2004 Lillestrom 9 0
2005 Lillestrom 2 0
2006 Lillestrom 19 11 **30 11**
2006–07 Coventry C 19 4
2007–08 Coventry C 41 10 **60 14**

OSBOURNE, Isaac (M) 84 0
H: 5 10 W: 11 11 b.Birmingham 22-6-86
Source: Scholar.
2002–03 Coventry C 2 0
2003–04 Coventry C 0 0
2004–05 Coventry C 9 0
2005–06 Coventry C 10 0
2006–07 Coventry C 19 0
2006–07 *Crewe Alex* 2 0 **2 0**
2007–08 Coventry C 42 0 **82 0**

SIMMONDS, Donovan (F) 3 0
H: 5 11 W: 11 00 b.Walthamstow 12-10-88
Source: Charlton Ath.
2007–08 Coventry C 0 0
2007–08 *Gillingham* 3 0 **3 0**

SIMPSON, Robbie (F) 28 1
H: 6 1 W: 11 11 b.Poole 15-3-85
Source: Cambridge U.
2007–08 Coventry C 28 1 **28 1**

TABB, Jay (M) 201 28
H: 5 7 W: 10 00 b.Tooting 21-2-84
Source: Trainee. *Honours:* Eire Under-21.
2000–01 Brentford 2 0
2001–02 Brentford 3 0
2002–03 Brentford 5 0
2003–04 Brentford 36 9
2004–05 Brentford 40 5
2005–06 Brentford 42 6 **128 20**
2006–07 Coventry C 31 3
2007–08 Coventry C 42 5 **73 8**

THORNTON, Kevin (M) 46 2
H: 5 7 W: 11 00 b.Drogheda 9-7-86
Source: Scholar. *Honours:* Eire Youth.
2003–04 Coventry C 0 0
2004–05 Coventry C 0 0
2005–06 Coventry C 16 0
2006–07 Coventry C 11 1
2007–08 Coventry C 19 1 **46 2**

TURNER, Ben (D) 30 0
H: 6 4 W: 14 04 b.Birmingham 21-1-88
Source: Scholar. *Honours:* England Youth.
2005–06 Coventry C 1 0
2006–07 Coventry C 1 0
2006–07 *Peterborough U* 8 0 **8 0**
2006–07 *Oldham Ath* 1 0 **1 0**
2007–08 Coventry C 19 0 **21 0**

WARD, Elliot (D) 110 10
H: 6 2 W: 13 00 b.Harrow 19-1-85
Source: Scholar.
2001–02 West Ham U 0 0
2002–03 West Ham U 0 0
2003–04 West Ham U 0 0
2004–05 West Ham U 11 0
2004–05 *Bristol R* 3 0 **3 0**
2005–06 West Ham U 4 0 **15 0**
2005–06 *Plymouth Arg* 16 1 **16 1**
2006–07 Coventry C 39 3
2007–08 Coventry C 37 6 **76 9**

CREWE ALEX (27)

ABBEY, George (D) 185 2
H: 5 10 W: 12 04 b.Port Harcourt 20-10-78
Source: Sharks. *Honours:* Nigeria 16 full caps.
1999–2000 Macclesfield T 18 0
2000–01 Macclesfield T 18 0
2001–02 Macclesfield T 17 0
2002–03 Macclesfield T 22 1
2003–04 Macclesfield T 25 0
2004–05 Macclesfield T 0 0 **100 1**
2004–05 Port Vale 18 0
2005–06 Port Vale 20 0
2006–07 Port Vale 24 1 **62 1**
2007–08 Crewe Alex 23 0 **23 0**

BAILEY, James (M) 1 0
H: 6 0 W: 12 05 b.Bollington 18-9-88
Source: Scholar.
2006–07 Crewe Alex 0 0
2007–08 Crewe Alex 1 0 **1 0**

BAILEY, Matt (F) 7 0
H: 6 4 W: 11 06 b.Crewe 12-3-86
Source: Nantwich T.
2003–04 Stockport Co 0 0
2004–05 Stockport Co 1 0 **1 0**
2004–05 *Scunthorpe U* 4 0 **4 0**
From Northwich Vic.
2005–06 Crewe Alex 0 0
2006–07 Crewe Alex 0 0
2007–08 Crewe Alex 2 0 **2 0**

BAUDET, Julien (D) 213 16
H: 6 2 W: 13 07 b.Grenoble 13-1-79
Source: Toulouse.
2001–02 Oldham Ath 20 1
2002–03 Oldham Ath 24 2 **44 3**
2003–04 Rotherham U 11 0 **11 0**
2004–05 Notts Co 39 5
2005–06 Notts Co 42 6 **81 11**
2006–07 Crewe Alex 42 1
2007–08 Crewe Alex 35 1 **77 2**

BOPP, Eugene (M) 116 14
H: 5 11 W: 12 03 b.Kiev 5-9-83
Source: Bayern Munich.
2000–01 Nottingham F 0 0
2001–02 Nottingham F 19 1
2002–03 Nottingham F 13 2
2003–04 Nottingham F 15 1
2004–05 Nottingham F 18 3
2005–06 Nottingham F 12 1 **77 8**
2006–07 Rotherham U 29 5 **29 5**
2007–08 Crewe Alex 10 1 **10 1**

BROWN, Junior (M) 1 0
H: 5 9 W: 10 09 b.Crewe 7-5-89
2006–07 Crewe Alex 0 0
2007–08 Crewe Alex 1 0 **1 0**

CARRINGTON, Mark (M) 12 0
H: 6 0 W: 11 00 b.Warrington 4-5-87
Source: Scholar.
2006–07 Crewe Alex 3 0
2007–08 Crewe Alex 9 0 **12 0**

COX, Neil (D) 549 37
H: 5 11 W: 13 08 b.Scunthorpe 8-10-71
Source: Trainee. *Honours:* England Under-21.
1989–90 Scunthorpe U 0 0
1990–91 Scunthorpe U 17 1 **17 1**
1990–91 Aston Villa 0 0
1991–92 Aston Villa 7 0
1992–93 Aston Villa 15 1
1993–94 Aston Villa 20 2 **42 3**
1994–95 Middlesbrough 40 1
1995–96 Middlesbrough 35 2
1996–97 Middlesbrough 31 0 **106 3**

1997–98	Bolton W	21	1		
1998–99	Bolton W	44	4		
1999–2000	Bolton W	15	2	**80**	**7**
1999–2000	Watford	21	0		
2000–01	Watford	44	5		
2001–02	Watford	40	2		
2002–03	Watford	40	9		
2003–04	Watford	35	4		
2004–05	Watford	39	0	**219**	**20**
2005–06	Cardiff C	27	2	**27**	**2**
2006–07	Crewe Alex	31	1		
2007–08	Crewe Alex	27	0	**58**	**1**

DANIEL, Colin (M) **1** **0**
H: 5 11 W: 11 06 b.Crewe 15-2-88
Source: Eastwood T.

2006–07	Crewe Alex	0	0		
2007–08	Crewe Alex	1	0	**1**	**0**

FARQUHARSON, Nick (M) **0** **0**
b.Coventry 7-9-88

2006–07	Crewe Alex	0	0
2007–08	Crewe Alex	0	0

HIGDON, Michael (F) **81** **10**
H: 6 2 W: 11 05 b.Liverpool 2-9-83
Source: School.

2000–01	Crewe Alex	0	0		
2001–02	Crewe Alex	0	0		
2002–03	Crewe Alex	0	0		
2003–04	Crewe Alex	10	1		
2004–05	Crewe Alex	20	3		
2005–06	Crewe Alex	26	3		
2006–07	Crewe Alex	25	3		
2007–08	Crewe Alex	0	0	**81**	**10**

JONES, Billy (D) **106** **0**
H: 6 1 W: 11 05 b.Chatham 26-3-83
Source: Trainee.

2000–01	Leyton Orient	1	0		
2001–02	Leyton Orient	16	0		
2002–03	Leyton Orient	24	0		
2003–04	Leyton Orient	31	0		
2004–05	Leyton Orient	0	0	**72**	**0**
2004–05	Kidderminster H	12	0		
2005–06	Kidderminster H	0	0		
2006–07	Kidderminster H	0	0	**12**	**0**
2007–08	Crewe Alex	22	0	**22**	**0**

LOWE, Ryan (F) **245** **49**
H: 5 10 W: 12 08 b.Liverpool 18-9-78
Source: Burscough.

2000–01	Shrewsbury T	30	4		
2001–02	Shrewsbury T	38	7		
2002–03	Shrewsbury T	39	9		
2003–04	Shrewsbury T	0	0		
2004–05	Shrewsbury T	30	3	**137**	**23**
2004–05	Chester C	8	4		
2005–06	Chester C	32	10	**40**	**14**
2005–06	Crewe Alex	0	0		
2006–07	Crewe Alex	37	8		
2007–08	Crewe Alex	27	4	**64**	**12**
2007–08	*Stockport Co*	4	0	**4**	**0**

LYNCH, Ryan (M) **2** **0**
H: 5 11 W: 11 09 b.Solihull 13-3-87
Source: Scholar.

2005–06	Coventry C	0	0		
2006–07	Coventry C	0	0		
2007–08	Crewe Alex	2	0	**2**	**0**

MAYNARD, Nicky (F) **59** **31**
H: 5 11 W: 11 00 b.Winsford 11-12-86
Source: Scholar.

2005–06	Crewe Alex	1	1		
2006–07	Crewe Alex	31	16		
2007–08	Crewe Alex	27	14	**59**	**31**

McCREADY, Chris (D) **152** **2**
H: 6 1 W: 12 05 b.Ellesmere Port 5-9-81
Source: Scholar.

2000–01	Crewe Alex	0	0		
2001–02	Crewe Alex	1	0		
2002–03	Crewe Alex	8	0		
2003–04	Crewe Alex	22	0		
2004–05	Crewe Alex	20	0		
2005–06	Crewe Alex	25	0		
2006–07	Tranmere R	42	1	**42**	**1**
2007–08	Crewe Alex	34	1	**110**	**1**

MELLOR, Kelvin (D) **0** **0**
Source: Nantwich T.

2007–08	Crewe Alex	0	0

MILLER, Shaun (F) **22** **4**
H: 5 10 W: 11 08 b.Alsager 25-9-87
Source: Scholar.

2006–07	Crewe Alex	7	3		
2007–08	Crewe Alex	15	1	**22**	**4**

MOORE, Byron (M) **33** **3**
H: 6 0 W: 10 06 b.Stoke 24-8-88
Source: Scholar.

2006–07	Crewe Alex	0	0		
2007–08	Crewe Alex	33	3	**33**	**3**

O'CONNOR, Michael (M) **54** **0**
H: 6 1 W: 11 08 b.Belfast 6-10-87
Source: Scholar. *Honours:* Northern Ireland Youth, Under-21, 1 full cap.

2005–06	Crewe Alex	2	0		
2006–07	Crewe Alex	29	0		
2007–08	Crewe Alex	23	0	**54**	**0**

O'DONNELL, Daniel (D) **52** **2**
H: 6 2 W: 11 11 b.Livepool 10-3-86
Source: Scholar.

2004–05	Liverpool	0	0		
2005–06	Liverpool	0	0		
2006–07	Liverpool	0	0		
2006–07	*Crewe Alex*	25	1		
2007–08	Crewe Alex	27	1	**52**	**2**

POPE, Tom (M) **30** **7**
H: 6 3 W: 11 03 b.Stoke 27-8-85
Source: Lancaster C.

2005–06	Crewe Alex	0	0		
2006–07	Crewe Alex	4	0		
2007–08	Crewe Alex	26	7	**30**	**7**

RIX, Ben (M) **139** **4**
H: 5 9 W: 11 13 b.Wolverhampton 11-12-82
Source: Scholar.

2000–01	Crewe Alex	0	0		
2001–02	Crewe Alex	21	0		
2002–03	Crewe Alex	23	0		
2003–04	Crewe Alex	26	2		
2004–05	Crewe Alex	0	0		
2005–06	Crewe Alex	2	0		
2005–06	*Bournemouth*	11	0	**11**	**0**
2006–07	Crewe Alex	31	2		
2007–08	Crewe Alex	25	0	**128**	**4**

ROBERTS, Gary S (M) **122** **11**
H: 5 8 W: 10 05 b.Chester 4-2-87
Source: Scholar. *Honours:* England Youth.

2003–04	Crewe Alex	2	0		
2004–05	Crewe Alex	2	0		
2005–06	Crewe Alex	33	2		
2006–07	Crewe Alex	43	3		
2007–08	Crewe Alex	42	6	**122**	**11**

SCHUMACHER, Steven (M) **147** **14**
H: 5 10 W: 11 00 b.Liverpool 30-4-84
Source: Scholar. *Honours:* England Youth.

2000–01	Everton	0	0		
2001–02	Everton	0	0		
2002–03	Everton	0	0		
2003–04	Everton	0	0		
2003–04	*Carlisle U*	4	0	**4**	**0**
2004–05	Bradford C	43	6		
2005–06	Bradford C	30	1		
2006–07	Bradford C	44	6	**117**	**13**
2007–08	Crewe Alex	26	1	**26**	**1**

TOMLINSON, Stuart (G) **11** **0**
H: 6 1 W: 11 02 b.Chester 10-5-85
Source: Scholar.

2002–03	Crewe Alex	1	0		
2003–04	Crewe Alex	1	0		
2004–05	Crewe Alex	0	0		
2005–06	Crewe Alex	2	0		
2006–07	Crewe Alex	7	0		
2007–08	Crewe Alex	0	0	**11**	**0**

VAUGHAN, David (M) **185** **18**
H: 5 7 W: 11 00 b.Rhuddlan 18-2-83
Source: Scholar. *Honours:* Wales Youth, Under-21, 13 full caps.

2000–01	Crewe Alex	1	0		
2001–02	Crewe Alex	13	0		
2002–03	Crewe Alex	32	3		
2003–04	Crewe Alex	31	0		
2004–05	Crewe Alex	44	6		
2005–06	Crewe Alex	34	5		
2006–07	Crewe Alex	29	4		
2007–08	Crewe Alex	1	0	**185**	**18**

WILLIAMS, Ben (G) **149** **0**
H: 6 0 W: 13 01 b.Manchester 27-8-82
Source: Scholar. *Honours:* England Schools.

2001–02	Manchester U	0	0		
2002–03	Manchester U	0	0		
2002–03	*Coventry C*	0	0		
2002–03	*Chesterfield*	14	0	**14**	**0**
2003–04	Manchester U	0	0		
2003–04	*Crewe Alex*	10	0		
2004–05	Crewe Alex	23	0		
2005–06	Crewe Alex	17	0		
2006–07	Crewe Alex	39	0		
2007–08	Crewe Alex	46	0	**135**	**0**

WILLIAMS, Owain Fon (G) **0** **0**
H: 6 1 W: 12 09 b.Gwynedd 17-3-87
Source: Scholar. *Honours:* Wales Youth, Under-21.

2005–06	Crewe Alex	0	0
2006–07	Crewe Alex	0	0
2007–08	Crewe Alex	0	0

WOODARDS, Danny (M) **47** **0**
H: 5 11 W: 11 01 b.Forest Gate 7-10-83
Source: Trainee.

2003–04	Chelsea	0	0		
2004–05	Chelsea	0	0		
2005–06	Chelsea	0	0		
From Exeter C.					
2006–07	Crewe Alex	11	0		
2007–08	Crewe Alex	36	0	**47**	**0**

CRYSTAL PALACE (28)

BOSTOCK, John (M) **4** **0**
H: 5 10 W: 11 11 b.Romford 13-10-91
Honours: England Youth.

2007–08	Crystal Palace	4	0	**4**	**0**

BUTTERFIELD, Danny (D) **293** **8**
H: 5 10 W: 11 06 b.Boston 21-11-79
Source: Trainee. *Honours:* England Youth.

1997–98	Grimsby T	7	0		
1998–99	Grimsby T	12	0		
1999–2000	Grimsby T	29	0		
2000–01	Grimsby T	30	1		
2001–02	Grimsby T	46	2	**124**	**3**
2002–03	Crystal Palace	46	1		
2003–04	Crystal Palace	45	4		
2004–05	Crystal Palace	7	0		
2005–06	Crystal Palace	13	0		
2006–07	Crystal Palace	28	0		
2007–08	Crystal Palace	30	0	**169**	**5**

CADOGAN, Kieron (M) **0** **0**
b.Wandsworth
Source: Scholar.

2007–08	Crystal Palace	0	0

CRAIG, Tony (D) **111** **3**
H: 6 0 W: 10 03 b.Greenwich 20-4-85
Source: Scholar.

2002–03	Millwall	2	1		
2003–04	Millwall	9	0		
2004–05	Millwall	10	0		
2004–05	*Wycombe W*	14	0	**14**	**0**
2005–06	Millwall	28	0		
2006–07	Millwall	30	1		
2007–08	Crystal Palace	13	0	**13**	**0**
2007–08	*Millwall*	5	1	**84**	**3**

DANNS, Neil (M) **132** **25**
H: 5 10 W: 10 12 b.Liverpool 23-11-82
Source: Scholar.

2000–01	Blackburn R	0	0		
2001–02	Blackburn R	0	0		
2002–03	Blackburn R	2	0		
2003–04	Blackpool	12	2	**12**	**2**
2003–04	Blackburn R	1	0		
2003–04	*Hartlepool U*	9	1	**9**	**1**
2004–05	Blackburn R	0	0	**3**	**0**
2004–05	Colchester U	32	11		
2005–06	Colchester U	41	8	**73**	**19**
2006–07	Birmingham C	29	3		
2007–08	Birmingham C	2	0	**31**	**3**
2007–08	Crystal Palace	4	0	**4**	**0**

DAYTON, James (M) **0** **0**
H: 5 8 W: 10 01 b.Enfield 12-12-88
Source: Scholar.

2007–08	Crystal Palace	0	0

DERRY, Shaun (M) 391 11
H: 5 10 W: 10 13 b.Nottingham 6-12-77
Source: Trainee.
1995–96 Notts Co 12 0
1996–97 Notts Co 39 2
1997–98 Notts Co 28 2 **79 4**
1997–98 Sheffield U 12 0
1998–99 Sheffield U 26 0
1999–2000 Sheffield U 34 0 **72 0**
1999–2000 Portsmouth 9 1
2000–01 Portsmouth 28 0
2001–02 Portsmouth 12 0 **49 1**
2002–03 Crystal Palace 39 1
2003–04 Crystal Palace 37 2
2004–05 Crystal Palace 7 0
2004–05 *Nottingham F* 7 0 **7 0**
2004–05 Leeds U 7 2
2005–06 Leeds U 41 0
2006–07 Leeds U 23 1
2007–08 Leeds U 0 0 **71 3**
2007–08 Crystal Palace 30 0 **113 3**

FLETCHER, Carl (M) 305 26
H: 5 10 W: 11 07 b.Camberley 7-4-80
Source: Trainee. *Honours:* Wales 29 full caps, 1 goal.
1997–98 Bournemouth 1 0
1998–99 Bournemouth 1 0
1999–2000 Bournemouth 25 3
2000–01 Bournemouth 43 6
2001–02 Bournemouth 35 5
2002–03 Bournemouth 42 1
2003–04 Bournemouth 40 2
2004–05 Bournemouth 6 2 **193 19**
2004–05 West Ham U 32 2
2005–06 West Ham U 12 1 **44 3**
2005–06 *Watford* 3 0 **3 0**
2006–07 Crystal Palace 37 3
2007–08 Crystal Palace 28 1 **65 4**

FLINDERS, Scott (G) 52 0
H: 6 4 W: 13 00 b.Rotherham 12-6-86
Source: Scholar. *Honours:* England Youth, Under-20.
2004–05 Barnsley 11 0
2005–06 Barnsley 3 0 **14 0**
2006–07 Crystal Palace 8 0
2006–07 *Gillingham* 9 0 **9 0**
2006–07 *Brighton & HA* 12 0 **12 0**
2007–08 Crystal Palace 0 0 **8 0**
2007–08 *Yeovil T* 9 0 **9 0**

FONTE, Jose (D) 102 4
H: 6 2 W: 12 08 b.Penafiel 22-12-83
Source: Sporting Lisbon, Salgueiros.
Honours: Portugal Under-21.
2004–05 Felgueiros 28 1 **28 1**
2005–06 Setubal 15 0 **15 0**
2005–06 Benfica 1 0 **1 0**
2005–06 *Pacos* 11 1 **11 1**
2006–07 *Amadora* 25 1 **25 1**
2007–08 Crystal Palace 22 1 **22 1**

FRAY, Arron (D) 0 0
H: 5 11 W: 11 02 b.Bromley 1-5-87
Source: Scholar.
2005–06 Crystal Palace 0 0
2006–07 Crystal Palace 0 0
2007–08 Crystal Palace 0 0

FREEDMAN, Dougie (F) 484 154
H: 5 9 W: 12 05 b.Glasgow 21-1-74
Source: Trainee. *Honours:* Scotland Schools, Under-21, B, 2 full caps, 1 goal.
1991–92 QPR 0 0
1992–93 QPR 0 0
1993–94 QPR 0 0
1994–95 Barnet 42 24
1995–96 Barnet 5 3 **47 27**
1995–96 Crystal Palace 39 20
1996–97 Crystal Palace 44 11
1997–98 Crystal Palace 7 0
1997–98 Wolverhampton W 29 10 **29 10**
1998–99 Nottingham F 31 9
1999–2000 Nottingham F 34 9
2000–01 Nottingham F 5 0 **70 18**
2000–01 Crystal Palace 26 11
2001–02 Crystal Palace 40 20
2002–03 Crystal Palace 29 9
2003–04 Crystal Palace 35 13
2004–05 Crystal Palace 20 1
2005–06 Crystal Palace 34 5
2006–07 Crystal Palace 34 3
2007–08 Crystal Palace 19 1 **327 94**
2007–08 *Leeds U* 11 5 **11 5**

HALL, Ryan (M) 9 2
H: 5 10 W: 10 04 b.Dulwich 4-1-88
Source: Scholar.
2005–06 Crystal Palace 0 0
2006–07 Crystal Palace 0 0
2007–08 Crystal Palace 1 0 **1 0**
2007–08 *Dagenham & R* 8 2 **8 2**

HILL, Clint (D) 265 23
H: 6 0 W: 11 06 b.Liverpool 19-10-78
Source: Trainee.
1997–98 Tranmere R 14 0
1998–99 Tranmere R 33 4
1999–2000 Tranmere R 29 5
2000–01 Tranmere R 34 5
2001–02 Tranmere R 30 2 **140 16**
2002–03 Oldham Ath 17 1 **17 1**
2003–04 Stoke C 12 0
2004–05 Stoke C 32 1
2005–06 Stoke C 13 0
2006–07 Stoke C 18 2
2007–08 Stoke C 5 0 **80 3**
2007–08 Crystal Palace 28 3 **28 3**

HILLS, Lee (D) 12 1
H: 5 10 W: 11 11 b.Croydon 3-4-90
Source: Scholar. *Honours:* England Youth.
2007–08 Crystal Palace 12 1 **12 1**

HUDSON, Mark (D) 135 7
H: 6 1 W: 12 01 b.Guildford 30-3-82
Source: Trainee.
1998–99 Fulham 0 0
1999–2000 Fulham 0 0
2000–01 Fulham 0 0
2001–02 Fulham 0 0
2002–03 Fulham 0 0
2003–04 Fulham 0 0
2003–04 *Oldham Ath* 15 0 **15 0**
2003–04 *Crystal Palace* 14 0
2004–05 Crystal Palace 7 1
2005–06 Crystal Palace 15 0
2006–07 Crystal Palace 39 4
2007–08 Crystal Palace 45 2 **120 7**

HUGHES, Jeff (D) 130 10
H: 6 1 W: 11 00 b.Larne 29-5-85
Source: Larne Tech Old Boys. *Honours:* Northern Ireland Under-21, 2 full caps.
2003–04 Larne 21 1
2004–05 Larne 29 0 **50 1**
2005–06 Lincoln C 22 2
2006–07 Lincoln C 41 6 **63 8**
2007–08 Crystal Palace 10 0 **10 0**
2007–08 *Peterborough U* 7 1 **7 1**

IFILL, Paul (M) 298 53
H: 6 0 W: 12 09 b.Brighton 20-10-79
Source: Trainee. *Honours:* England Youth, Barbados 8 full caps, 6 goals.
1998–99 Millwall 15 1
1999–2000 Millwall 44 11
2000–01 Millwall 35 6
2001–02 Millwall 40 4
2002–03 Millwall 45 6
2003–04 Millwall 33 8
2004–05 Millwall 18 4 **230 40**
2005–06 Sheffield U 39 9
2006–07 Sheffield U 3 0 **42 9**
2006–07 Crystal Palace 13 2
2007–08 Crystal Palace 13 2 **26 4**

KENNEDY, Mark (M) 367 32
H: 5 11 W: 11 09 b.Dublin 15-5-76
Source: Belvedere, Trainee. *Honours:* Eire Schools, Youth, Under-21, 34 full caps, 3 goals.
1992–93 Millwall 1 0
1993–94 Millwall 12 4
1994–95 Millwall 30 5 **43 9**
1994–95 Liverpool 6 0
1995–96 Liverpool 4 0
1996–97 Liverpool 5 0
1997–98 Liverpool 1 0 **16 0**
1997–98 *QPR* 8 2 **8 2**
1997–98 Wimbledon 4 0
1998–99 Wimbledon 17 0 **21 0**
1999–2000 Manchester C 41 8
2000–01 Manchester C 25 0 **66 8**
2001–02 Wolverhampton W 35 5
2002–03 Wolverhampton W 31 3
2003–04 Wolverhampton W 31 2
2004–05 Wolverhampton W 30 0
2005–06 Wolverhampton W 40 2 **167 12**
2006–07 Crystal Palace 38 1
2007–08 Crystal Palace 8 0 **46 1**

KUDJODJI, Ben (F) 1 0
H: 6 0 W: 11 11 b.Luton 23-4-89
Source: Scholar.
2007–08 Crystal Palace 1 0 **1 0**

KUQI, Shefki (F) 391 102
H: 6 2 W: 13 13 b.Albania 10-11-76
Source: Trepka, Miki. *Honours:* Albania 8 full caps, 1 goal, Finland 52 full caps, 6 goals.
1995 MP 24 3
1996 MP 26 7 **50 10**
1997 HJK Helsinki 25 6
1998 HJK Helsinki 22 1
1999 HJK Helsinki 25 11 **72 18**
From Jokerit
2000–01 Stockport Co 17 6
2001–02 Stockport Co 18 5 **35 11**
2001–02 Sheffield W 17 6
2002–03 Sheffield W 40 8
2003–04 Sheffield W 7 5 **64 19**
2003–04 Ipswich T 36 11
2004–05 Ipswich T 43 19
2005–06 Blackburn R 33 7
2006–07 Blackburn R 1 0 **34 7**
2006–07 Crystal Palace 35 7
2007–08 Crystal Palace 8 0 **43 7**
2007–08 *Fulham* 10 0 **10 0**
2007–08 *Ipswich T* 4 0 **83 30**

LAWRENCE, Matt (D) 433 6
H: 6 1 W: 12 12 b.Northampton 19-6-74
Source: Grays Ath. *Honours:* England Schools.
1995–96 Wycombe W 3 0
1996–97 Wycombe W 13 1
1996–97 Fulham 15 0
1997–98 Fulham 43 0
1998–99 Fulham 1 0 **59 0**
1998–99 Wycombe W 34 2
1999–2000 Wycombe W 29 2 **79 5**
1999–2000 Millwall 9 0
2000–01 Millwall 45 0
2001–02 Millwall 26 0
2002–03 Millwall 33 0
2003–04 Millwall 36 0
2004–05 Millwall 44 0
2005–06 Millwall 31 0 **224 0**
2006–07 Crystal Palace 34 0
2007–08 Crystal Palace 37 1 **71 1**

MORRISON, Clinton (F) 368 117
H: 6 0 W: 12 00 b.Tooting 14-5-79
Source: Trainee. *Honours:* Eire Under-21, 36 full caps, 9 goals.
1996–97 Crystal Palace 0 0
1997–98 Crystal Palace 1 1
1998–99 Crystal Palace 37 12
1999–2000 Crystal Palace 29 13
2000–01 Crystal Palace 45 14
2001–02 Crystal Palace 45 22
2002–03 Birmingham C 28 6
2003–04 Birmingham C 32 4
2004–05 Birmingham C 26 4
2005–06 Birmingham C 1 0 **87 14**
2005–06 Crystal Palace 40 13
2006–07 Crystal Palace 41 12
2007–08 Crystal Palace 43 16 **281 103**

MOSES, Victor (F) 13 3
H: 5 10 W: 11 07 b.Lagos 12-12-90
Source: Scholar. *Honours:* England Youth.
2007–08 Crystal Palace 13 3 **13 3**

ROBINSON, Ashley (F) 6 0
H: 5 9 W: 14 01 b. 5-12-89
Source: Scholar.
2007–08 Crystal Palace 6 0 **6 0**

SCANNELL, Sean (F) 23 2
H: 5 9 W: 11 07 b.Cork 21-3-89
Source: Scholar. *Honours:* Eire Youth, Under-21.
2007–08 Crystal Palace 23 2 **23 2**

SCOWCROFT, James (F) **458** **88**
H: 6 1 W: 14 07 b.Bury St Edmunds 15-11-75
Source: Trainee. *Honours:* England Under-21.

1994–95	Ipswich T	0	0		
1995–96	Ipswich T	23	2		
1996–97	Ipswich T	41	9		
1997–98	Ipswich T	31	6		
1998–99	Ipswich T	32	13		
1999–2000	Ipswich T	41	13		
2000–01	Ipswich T	34	4		
2001–02	Leicester C	24	5		
2002–03	Leicester C	43	10		
2003–04	Leicester C	35	5		
2004–05	Leicester C	31	4	**133**	**24**
2004–05	*Ipswich T*	9	0	**211**	**47**
2005–06	Coventry C	41	3	**41**	**3**
2006–07	Crystal Palace	35	5		
2007–08	Crystal Palace	38	9	**73**	**14**

SHERINGHAM, Charlie (F) **0** **0**
H: 6 1 W: 11 06 b.London 17-4-88

2006–07	Crystal Palace	0	0
2007–08	Crystal Palace	0	0

SOARES, Tom (M) **145** **10**
H: 6 0 W: 11 04 b.Reading 10-7-86
Source: Scholar. *Honours:* England Youth, Under-20, Under-21.

2003–04	Crystal Palace	3	0		
2004–05	Crystal Palace	22	0		
2005–06	Crystal Palace	44	1		
2006–07	Crystal Palace	37	3		
2007–08	Crystal Palace	39	6	**145**	**10**

SPENCE, Lewis (M) **2** **0**
H: 5 9 W: 11 02 b.Lambeth 29-10-87
Source: Scholar.

2006–07	Crystal Palace	2	0		
2007–08	Crystal Palace	0	0	**2**	**0**

SPERONI, Julian (G) **155** **0**
H: 6 0 W: 11 00 b.Buenos Aires 18-5-79
Honours: Argentina Under-20, Under-21.

1999–2000	Platense	2	0		
2000–01	Platense	0	0	**2**	**0**
2001–02	Dundee	17	0		
2002–03	Dundee	38	0		
2003–04	Dundee	37	0	**92**	**0**
2004–05	Crystal Palace	6	0		
2005–06	Crystal Palace	4	0		
2006–07	Crystal Palace	5	0		
2007–08	Crystal Palace	46	0	**61**	**0**

SWAIBU, Moses (D) **0** **0**
H: 6 2 W: 11 11 b.Croydon 9-5-89
Source: Scholar.

2007–08	Crystal Palace	0	0

WATSON, Ben (M) **151** **13**
H: 5 10 W: 10 11 b.Camberwell 9-7-85
Source: Scholar. *Honours:* England Under-21.

2002–03	Crystal Palace	5	0		
2003–04	Crystal Palace	16	1		
2004–05	Crystal Palace	21	0		
2005–06	Crystal Palace	42	4		
2006–07	Crystal Palace	25	3		
2007–08	Crystal Palace	42	5	**151**	**13**

WIGGINS, Rhoys (D) **0** **0**
H: 5 8 W: 11 05 b.Hillingdon 4-11-87
Source: Scholar. *Honours:* Wales Youth, Under-21.

2006–07	Crystal Palace	0	0
2007–08	Crystal Palace	0	0

WILKINSON, David (G) **0** **0**
H: 5 11 W: 12 00 b.Croydon 17-4-88
Source: Scholar.

2006–07	Crystal Palace	0	0
2007–08	Crystal Palace	0	0

DAGENHAM & R (29)

BAIDOO, Shabazz (M) **31** **3**
H: 5 8 W: 10 07 b.Hackney 13-4-88
Source: Scholar.

2004–05	QPR	4	0		
2005–06	QPR	15	2		
2006–07	QPR	9	1		
2007–08	QPR	0	0	**28**	**3**
2007–08	Dagenham & R	3	0	**3**	**0**

BENSON, Paul (F) **22** **6**
H: 6 1 W: 11 01 b.Rochford 12-10-79
Source: White Notley.

2007–08	Dagenham & R	22	6	**22**	**6**

BOARDMAN, Jon (D) **52** **1**
H: 6 2 W: 12 09 b.Reading 27-1-81
Source: Trainee.

1999–2000	Crystal Palace	0	0		
2000–01	Crystal Palace	0	0		
2001–02	Crystal Palace	0	0		
From Woking.					
2005–06	Rochdale	21	1		
2006–07	Rochdale	4	0	**25**	**1**
2007–08	Dagenham & R	27	0	**27**	**0**

CHARGE, Daniel (M) **0** **0**
Source: Scholar.

2007–08	Dagenham & R	0	0

COOK, Anthony (D) **1** **0**
H: 5 7 W: 11 02 b.London 10-8-89
Source: Croydon Ath.

2007–08	Dagenham & R	1	0	**1**	**0**

ERSKINE, Emmanuel (F) **0** **0**
H: 6 1 W: 13 06 b.London 13-1-89
Source: Wingate & Finchley.

2007–08	Dagenham & R	0	0

FOSTER, Danny (D) **32** **1**
H: 5 10 W: 12 10 b.Enfield 23-9-84
Source: Trainee.

2002–03	Tottenham H	0	0		
2003–04	Tottenham H	0	0		
2004–05	Tottenham H	0	0		
2005–06	Tottenham H	0	0		
2006–07	Tottenham H	0	0		
2007–08	Dagenham & R	32	1	**32**	**1**

GAIN, Peter (M) **316** **31**
H: 5 9 W: 11 07 b.Hammersmith 11-11-76
Source: Trainee.

1995–96	Tottenham H	0	0		
1996–97	Tottenham H	0	0		
1997–98	Tottenham H	0	0		
1998–99	Tottenham H	0	0		
1998–99	Lincoln C	4	0		
1999–2000	Lincoln C	32	2		
2000–01	Lincoln C	24	5		
2001–02	Lincoln C	42	2		
2002–03	Lincoln C	43	5		
2003–04	Lincoln C	42	7		
2004–05	Lincoln C	40	0	**227**	**21**
2005–06	Peterborough U	37	3		
2006–07	Peterborough U	34	6		
2007–08	Peterborough U	0	0	**71**	**9**
2007–08	Dagenham & R	18	1	**18**	**1**

GOODWIN, Lee (D) **1** **0**
H: 6 1 W: 13 12 b.Stepney 5-9-78
Source: Trainee.

1997–98	West Ham U	0	0		
1998–99	West Ham U	0	0		
2007–08	Dagenham & R	1	0	**1**	**0**

GRAHAM, Richard (M) **58** **3**
H: 5 10 W: 11 10 b.Newry 5-8-79
Source: Trainee. *Honours:* Northern Ireland Youth, Under-21.

1996–97	QPR	0	0		
1997–98	QPR	0	0		
1998–99	QPR	2	0		
1999–2000	QPR	0	0		
2000–01	QPR	0	0	**2**	**0**
From Chesham, Billericay, Kettering					
2004–05	Barnet	0	0		
2005–06	Barnet	15	1		
2006–07	Barnet	34	2	**49**	**3**
2007–08	Dagenham & R	7	0	**7**	**0**

GREEN, Dominic (F) **12** **0**
H: 5 6 W: 11 02 b.London 5-7-89
Source: Scholar.

2007–08	Dagenham & R	12	0	**12**	**0**

GRIFFITHS, Scott (D) **41** **0**
H: 5 9 W: 11 08 b.London 27-11-85
Source: Aveley.

2007–08	Dagenham & R	41	0	**41**	**0**

HUKE, Shane (M) **65** **3**
H: 5 11 W: 12 07 b.Reading 2-10-85
Source: Scholar.

2003–04	Peterborough U	0	0		
2004–05	Peterborough U	8	0		
2005–06	Peterborough U	3	0		
2006–07	Peterborough U	18	1	**29**	**1**
2007–08	Dagenham & R	36	2	**36**	**2**

KALIPHA, Kayan (F) **0** **0**
Source: MK Dons, Harrow B.

2007–08	Dagenham & R	0	0

MOORE, Chris (F) **42** **4**
H: 5 9 W: 11 05 b.Middlesex 13-1-80
Source: Northwood, Dagenham & R.

2006–07	Brentford	16	2	**16**	**2**
2007–08	Dagenham & R	26	2	**26**	**2**

NURSE, Jon (F) **30** **1**
H: 5 9 W: 12 04 b.Barbados 28-3-81
Source: Stevenage B. *Honours:* Barbados 2 full caps.

2007–08	Dagenham & R	30	1	**30**	**1**

OKUONGHAE, Magnus (D) **32** **1**
H: 6 3 W: 13 04 b.Nigeria 16-2-86
Source: Scholar.

2003–04	Rushden & D	1	0		
2004–05	Rushden & D	0	0		
2005–06	Rushden & D	21	1		
2006–07	Rushden & D	0	0	**22**	**1**
2007–08	Dagenham & R	10	0	**10**	**0**

PATTERSON, Marlon (D) **6** **0**
H: 5 9 W: 11 10 b.London 24-6-83
Source: Yeading.

2007–08	Dagenham & R	6	0	**6**	**0**

RAINFORD, David (M) **32** **8**
H: 6 1 W: 12 08 b.Stepney 21-4-79

1997–98	Colchester U	1	0	**1**	**0**
1998–99	*Scarborough*	2	0	**2**	**0**
From Slough, Grays, B Stortford.					
2007–08	Dagenham & R	29	8	**29**	**8**

ROBERTS, Tony (G) **173** **0**
H: 6 0 W: 13 11 b.Holyhead 4-8-69
Source: Trainee. *Honours:* Wales Under-21, 2 full caps.

1987 88	QPR	1	0		
1988–89	QPR	0	0		
1989–90	QPR	5	0		
1990–91	QPR	12	0		
1991–92	QPR	1	0		
1992–93	QPR	28	0		
1993–94	QPR	16	0		
1994–95	QPR	31	0		
1995–96	QPR	5	0		
1996–97	QPR	13	0		
1997–98	QPR	10	0	**122**	**0**
1998–99	Millwall	8	0	**8**	**0**
From St Albans C.					
2007–08	Dagenham & R	43	0	**43**	**0**

ROCHESTER, Kraig (M) **0** **0**
H: 6 1 W: 13 01 b.London 3-11-88
Source: Leicester C.

2007–08	Dagenham & R	0	0

SAUNDERS, Sam (M) **22** **0**
H: 5 6 W: 11 04 b.London 29-10-82
Source: Welling U, Hastings T, Ashford T, Carshalton Ath.

2007–08	Dagenham & R	22	0	**22**	**0**

SLOMA, Sam (M) **29** **2**
H: 5 8 W: 11 06 b.London 29-10-82
Source: Thurrock.

2007–08	Dagenham & R	29	2	**29**	**2**

SMITH, Ross (D) **23** **1**
H: 6 0 W: 12 07 b.Ontario 4-11-80
Source: Margate, Ebbsfleet U.

2007–08	Dagenham & R	23	1	**23**	**1**

SOUTHAM, Glen (M) **45** **2**
H: 5 7 W: 11 10 b.Enfield 27-8-80
Source: Bishop's Stortford.

2007–08	Dagenham & R	45	2	**45**	**2**

STREVENS, Ben (M) **115** **24**
H: 6 1 W: 12 00 b.Edgware 24-5-80
Source: Wingate & Finchley.

1998–99	Barnet	0	0
1999–2000	Barnet	6	0
2000–01	Barnet	28	4
2001–02	Barnet	0	0
2002–03	Barnet	0	0
2003–04	Barnet	0	0
2004–05	Barnet	0	0
2005–06	Barnet	35	5

2006–07 Barnet 0 0 **69 9**
From Crawley T.
2007–08 Dagenham & R 46 15 **46 15**

TAIWO, Soloman (M) 10 0
H: 6 1 W: 13 02 b.Lagos 29-4-85
Source: Sutton U.
2007–08 Dagenham & R 10 0 **10 0**

TAYLOR, Jamie (F) 12 1
H: 5 9 W: 12 06 b.Crawley 16-12-82
Source: Broadbridge Heath, Horsham, Aldershot T, Woking.
2007–08 Dagenham & R 12 1 **12 1**

TEJAN-SIE, Thomas (F) 0 0
H: 5 6 W: 11 08 b.London 23-11-88
Source: Wingate & Finchley.
2007–08 Dagenham & R 0 0

THOMPSON, Ed (G) 3 0
H: 5 10 W: 12 12 b.Enfield 8-1-83
Source: Wingate & Finchley.
2007–08 Dagenham & R 3 0 **3 0**

UDDIN, Anwar (D) 60 2
H: 5 11 W: 11 10 b.Whitechapel 1-11-81
Source: West Ham U Scholar.
2001–02 West Ham U 0 0
2001–02 Sheffield W 0 0
2002–03 Bristol R 18 1
2003–04 Bristol R 1 0
2004–05 Bristol R 0 0
2005–06 Bristol R 0 0
2006–07 Bristol R 0 0 **19 1**
2007–08 Dagenham & R 41 1 **41 1**

DARLINGTON (30)

ABBOTT, Pawel (F) 195 70
H: 6 2 W: 13 10 b.York 5-5-82
Source: LKS Lodz. *Honours:* Poland Under-21.
2000–01 Preston NE 0 0
2001–02 Preston NE 0 0
2002–03 Preston NE 16 4
2002–03 *Bury* 17 6 **17 6**
2003–04 Preston NE 9 2 **25 6**
2003–04 Huddersfield T 13 5
2004–05 Huddersfield T 44 26
2005–06 Huddersfield T 36 12
2006–07 Huddersfield T 18 5 **111 48**
2006–07 Swansea C 18 1 **18 1**
2007–08 Darlington 24 9 **24 9**

AUSTIN, Neil (D) 177 2
H: 5 10 W: 11 09 b.Barnsley 26-4-83
Source: Trainee. *Honours:* England Youth, Under-20.
1999–2000 Barnsley 0 0
2000–01 Barnsley 0 0
2001–02 Barnsley 0 0
2002–03 Barnsley 34 0
2003–04 Barnsley 37 0
2004–05 Barnsley 15 0
2005–06 Barnsley 38 0
2006–07 Barnsley 24 0 **148 0**
2007–08 Darlington 29 2 **29 2**

BARRAU, Xavi (M) 17 4
H: 5 10 W: 11 00 b.Lyon 26-8-82
Source: Vitry-Chatillon, Meyrin, Lyon.
2006–07 Airdrie U 13 2 **13 2**
2006–07 Bradford C 3 2
2007–08 Bradford C 0 0 **3 2**
2007–08 Darlington 1 0 **1 0**

BLUNDELL, Greg (F) 193 49
H: 5 10 W: 11 06 b.Liverpool 3-10-77
Source: Tranmere R Trainee, Vauxhall M, Northwich Vic.
2003–04 Doncaster R 44 18
2004–05 Doncaster R 41 9 **85 27**
2005–06 Chester C 30 7
2006–07 Chester C 27 6 **57 13**
2006–07 Darlington 15 3
2007–08 Darlington 36 6 **51 9**

BRACKSTONE, John (D) 28 0
H: 6 0 W: 11 06 b.Hartlepool 9-2-85
Source: Scholar.
2003–04 Hartlepool U 6 0
2004–05 Hartlepool U 9 0
2005–06 Hartlepool U 2 0
2006–07 Hartlepool U 8 0 **25 0**
2007–08 Darlington 3 0 **3 0**

BURGESS, Kevin (D) 1 0
H: 6 0 W: 12 00 b.Eston 8-1-88
Source: Scholar.
2006–07 Middlesbrough 0 0
2006–07 Darlington 1 0
2007–08 Darlington 0 0 **1 0**

CLARKE, Wayne (M) 0 0
b.Crook 30-9-88
2006–07 Darlington 0 0
2007–08 Darlington 0 0

COLLINS, Patrick (D) 75 1
H: 6 2 W: 12 08 b.Oman 4-2-85
Source: Scholar. *Honours:* England Youth, Under-20.
2001–02 Sunderland 0 0
2002–03 Sunderland 0 0
2003–04 Sunderland 0 0
2004–05 Sheffield W 28 1
2005–06 Sheffield W 3 0 **31 1**
2005–06 *Swindon T* 13 0 **13 0**
2006–07 Darlington 31 0
2007–08 Darlington 0 0 **31 0**

CUMMINS, Michael (M) 334 41
H: 6 0 W: 13 06 b.Dublin 1-6-78
Source: Trainee. *Honours:* Eire Youth, Under-21.
1995–96 Middlesbrough 0 0
1996–97 Middlesbrough 0 0
1997–98 Middlesbrough 0 0
1998–99 Middlesbrough 1 0
1999–2000 Middlesbrough 1 0 **2 0**
1999–2000 Port Vale 12 1
2000–01 Port Vale 45 2
2001–02 Port Vale 46 8
2002–03 Port Vale 30 4
2003–04 Port Vale 42 4
2004–05 Port Vale 39 2
2005–06 Port Vale 39 10 **253 31**
2006–07 Darlington 39 4
2007–08 Darlington 40 6 **79 10**

FOSTER, Steve (D) 401 11
H: 6 1 W: 13 00 b.Mansfield 3-12-74
Source: Trainee.
1993–94 Mansfield T 5 0 **5 0**
From Telford U, Woking
1997–98 Bristol R 34 0
1998–99 Bristol R 43 1
1999–2000 Bristol R 43 1
2000–01 Bristol R 44 4
2001–02 Bristol R 33 1 **197 7**
2002–03 Doncaster R 0 0
2003–04 Doncaster R 44 1
2004–05 Doncaster R 34 1
2005–06 Doncaster R 17 0 **95 2**
2005–06 Scunthorpe U 18 0
2006–07 Scunthorpe U 44 0 **62 0**
2007–08 Darlington 42 2 **42 2**

HARDMAN, Lewis (D) 1 0
H: 5 10 W: 11 00 b.Sunderland 12-4-85
Source: Scholar.
2006–07 Darlington 1 0
2007–08 Darlington 0 0 **1 0**

HARTY, Ian (M) 284 91
H: 5 8 W: 10 07 b.Airdrie 8-4-78
Source: Hearts.
1996–97 Albion R 9 0
1997–98 Albion R 26 2 **35 2**
1998–99 Stranraer 21 2
1999–2000 Stranraer 32 8
2000–01 Stranraer 35 13
2001–02 Stranraer 30 16
2002–03 Stranraer 32 12
2003–04 Clyde 34 15
2004–05 Clyde 33 15 **67 30**
2005–06 Hamilton A 3 1 **3 1**
2005–06 Stranraer 5 0 **155 51**
2006–07 Raith R 12 4 **12 4**
2006–07 Airdrie U 11 3 **11 3**
2007–08 Darlington 1 0 **1 0**

JOACHIM, Julian (F) 453 113
H: 5 6 W: 12 02 b.Boston 20-9-74
Source: Trainee. *Honours:* England Youth, Under-21.
1992–93 Leicester C 26 10
1993–94 Leicester C 36 11
1994–95 Leicester C 15 3
1995–96 Leicester C 22 1 **99 25**
1995–96 Aston Villa 11 1
1996–97 Aston Villa 15 3
1997–98 Aston Villa 26 8
1998–99 Aston Villa 36 14
1999–2000 Aston Villa 33 6
2000–01 Aston Villa 20 7 **141 39**
2001–02 Coventry C 16 1
2002–03 Coventry C 11 2
2003–04 Coventry C 29 8 **56 11**
2004–05 Leeds U 27 2 **27 2**
2004–05 *Walsall* 8 6 **8 6**
2005–06 Boston U 43 14
2006–07 Boston U 3 3 **46 17**
2006–07 Darlington 36 7
2007–08 Darlington 40 6 **76 13**

KAZIMIERCZAK, Prezemek (G) 9 0
H: 6 0 W: 12 02 b.Lodz 22-2-88
Source: Scholar.
2006–07 Bolton W 0 0
2006–07 *Accrington S* 8 0 **8 0**
2007–08 Bolton W 0 0
2007–08 Darlington 1 0 **1 0**

KELTIE, Clark (M) 161 9
H: 5 11 W: 11 08 b.Newcastle 31-8-83
Source: Shildon.
2001–02 Darlington 1 0
2002–03 Darlington 30 3
2003–04 Darlington 31 1
2004–05 Darlington 21 0
2005–06 Darlington 24 0
2006–07 Darlington 27 1
2007–08 Darlington 27 4 **161 9**

LIVERSEDGE, Nick (G) 0 0
H: 6 1 W: 11 07 b.Huddersfield 18-7-88
Source: Scholar.
2007–08 Darlington 0 0

MAIN, Curtis (F) 1 0
H: 5 9 W: 12 02 b.South Shields 20-6-92
2007–08 Darlington 1 0 **1 0**

McBRIDE, Kevin (M) 69 7
H: 5 10 W: 10 05 b.Airdrie 14-6-81
Source: Celtic BC.
2004–05 Celtic 0 0
2004–05 *Motherwell* 25 5
2005–06 Motherwell 21 1
2006–07 Motherwell 17 0 **63 6**
2007–08 Darlington 6 1 **6 1**
To Falkirk January 2008.

MILLER, Ian (M) 48 3
H: 6 2 W: 12 02 b.Colchester 23-11-83
2006–07 Ipswich T 1 0
2006–07 *Boston U* 12 0 **12 0**
2006–07 *Darlington* 7 1
2007–08 Ipswich T 0 0 **1 0**
2007–08 Darlington 28 2 **35 3**

N'DUMBU NSUNGU, Guylain (F) 139 33
H: 6 1 W: 12 08 b.Kinshasa 26-12-82
Source: Amiens. *Honours:* DR Congo Under-21.
2003–04 Sheffield W 24 9
2004–05 Sheffield W 11 1 **35 10**
2004–05 *Preston NE* 6 0 **6 0**
2004–05 Colchester U 8 1 **8 1**
2005–06 Darlington 21 10
2005–06 Cardiff C 11 0 **11 0**
2006–07 Gillingham 32 3 **32 3**
2007–08 Bradford C 18 6 **18 6**
2007–08 Darlington 8 3 **29 13**

OAKES, Andy (G) 107 0
H: 6 3 W: 12 04 b.Northwich 11-1-77
Source: Burnley Trainee.
1995–96 Bury 0 0
1996–97 Bury 0 0
1997–98 Bury 0 0
From Winsford U.
1998–99 Hull C 19 0 **19 0**
1999–2000 Derby Co 0 0
1999–2000 *Port Vale* 0 0
2000–01 Derby Co 6 0
2001–02 Derby Co 20 0
2002–03 Derby Co 7 0
2003–04 Derby Co 10 0
2004–05 Derby Co 0 0 **43 0**
2004–05 *Bolton W* 1 0 **1 0**
2004–05 Walsall 9 0

2005–06 Walsall 25 0 **34 0**
2006–07 Swansea C 4 0 **4 0**
2007–08 Darlington 6 0 **6 0**

PURDIE, Rob (M) 83 6
H: 5 9 W: 11 06 b.Leicester 28-9-82
Source: Leicester C.
2006–07 Hereford U 44 6 **44 6**
2007–08 Darlington 39 0 **39 0**

RAVENHILL, Ricky (M) 168 15
H: 5 10 W: 11 02 b.Doncaster 16-1-81
Source: Barnsley Trainee.
2003–04 Doncaster R 36 3
2004–05 Doncaster R 35 3
2005–06 Doncaster R 27 3 **98 9**
2006–07 Chester C 3 0 **3 0**
2006–07 Grimsby T 17 2 **17 2**
2006–07 Darlington 15 1
2007–08 Darlington 35 3 **50 4**

REAY, Sean (F) 4 0
H: 6 1 W: 12 00 b.Jarrow 20-5-89
Source: Scholar.
2005–06 Darlington 0 0
2006–07 Darlington 3 0
2007–08 Darlington 1 0 **4 0**

RYAN, Tim (D) 166 11
H: 5 10 W: 11 00 b.Stockport 10-12-74
Source: Trainee.
1992–93 Scunthorpe U 1 0
1993–94 Scunthorpe U 1 0
1994–95 Scunthorpe U 0 0 **2 0**
From Buxton.
1996–97 Doncaster R 28 0
From Southport
2003–04 Doncaster R 42 2
2004–05 Doncaster R 39 4
2005–06 Doncaster R 7 0 **116 6**
2005–06 Peterborough U 7 0 **7 0**
2006–07 Boston U 23 4 **23 4**
2006–07 Darlington 5 1
2007–08 Darlington 13 0 **18 1**

SMITH, Martin (F) 367 93
H: 5 11 W: 12 07 b.Sunderland 13-11-74
Source: Trainee. *Honours:* England Schools, Under-21.
1992–93 Sunderland 0 0
1993–94 Sunderland 29 8
1994–95 Sunderland 35 10
1995–96 Sunderland 20 2
1996–97 Sunderland 11 0
1997–98 Sunderland 16 2
1998–99 Sunderland 8 3 **119 25**
1999–2000 Sheffield U 26 10 **26 10**
1999–2000 Huddersfield T 12 4
2000–01 Huddersfield T 30 8
2001–02 Huddersfield T 0 0
2002–03 Huddersfield T 38 17 **80 29**
2003–04 Northampton T 44 11
2004–05 Northampton T 34 10
2005–06 Northampton T 26 3 **104 24**
2006–07 Darlington 34 5
2007–08 Darlington 4 0 **38 5**

STOCKDALE, David (G) 48 0
H: 6 3 W: 13 04 b.Leeds 20-9-85
Source: Scholar.
2002–03 York C 1 0
2003–04 York C 0 0
2004–05 York C 0 0
2005–06 York C 0 0 **1 0**
2006–07 Darlington 6 0
2007–08 Darlington 41 0 **47 0**

VALENTINE, Ryan (D) 227 6
H: 5 10 W: 11 05 b.Wrexham 19-8-82
Source: Trainee. *Honours:* Wales Youth, Under-21.
1999–2000 Everton 0 0
2000–01 Everton 0 0
2001–02 Everton 0 0
2002–03 Darlington 43 1
2003–04 Darlington 40 2
2004–05 Darlington 36 1
2005–06 Darlington 43 0
2006–07 Wrexham 34 2
2007–08 Wrexham 14 0 **48 2**
2007–08 Darlington 17 0 **179 4**

WAINWRIGHT, Neil (M) 286 31
H: 6 0 W: 12 00 b.Warrington 4-11-77
Source: Trainee.
1996–97 Wrexham 0 0
1997–98 Wrexham 11 3 **11 3**
1998–99 Sunderland 2 0
1999–2000 Sunderland 0 0
1999–2000 *Darlington* 17 4
2000–01 Sunderland 0 0
2000–01 *Halifax T* 13 0 **13 0**
2001–02 Sunderland 0 0 **2 0**
2001–02 Darlington 35 4
2002–03 Darlington 33 1
2003–04 Darlington 35 7
2004–05 Darlington 38 4
2005–06 Darlington 39 3
2006–07 Darlington 41 5
2007–08 Darlington 14 0 **252 28**
2007–08 *Shrewsbury T* 3 0 **3 0**
2007–08 *Mansfield T* 5 0 **5 0**

WHITE, Alan (D) 374 20
H: 6 0 W: 13 04 b.Darlington 22-3-76
Source: Derby Co Schoolboy.
1994–95 Middlesbrough 0 0
1995–96 Middlesbrough 0 0
1996–97 Middlesbrough 0 0
1997–98 Middlesbrough 0 0
1997–98 Luton T 28 1
1998–99 Luton T 33 1
1999–2000 Luton T 19 1 **80 3**
1999–2000 *Colchester U* 4 0
2000–01 Colchester U 32 0
2001–02 Colchester U 33 3
2002–03 Colchester U 41 0
2003–04 Colchester U 33 1 **143 4**
2004–05 Leyton Orient 26 0 **26 0**
2004–05 Boston U 11 0
2005–06 Boston U 37 4 **48 4**
2006–07 Notts Co 35 5 **35 5**
2006–07 *Peterborough U* 7 3 **7 3**
2007–08 Darlington 35 1 **35 1**

WISEMAN, Scott (D) 53 1
H: 6 0 W: 11 06 b.Hull 9-10-85
Source: Scholar. *Honours:* England Youth, Under-20.
2003–04 Hull C 2 0
2004–05 Hull C 3 0
2004–05 *Boston U* 2 0 **2 0**
2005–06 Hull C 11 0
2006–07 Hull C 0 0 **16 0**
2006–07 *Rotherham U* 18 1 **18 1**
2006–07 *Darlington* 10 0
2007–08 Darlington 7 0 **17 0**

WRIGHT, Tommy (F) 152 32
H: 6 0 W: 12 02 b.Leicester 28-9-84
Source: Scholar. *Honours:* England Youth, Under-20.
2001–02 Leicester C 1 0
2002–03 Leicester C 13 2
2003–04 Leicester C 0 0
2003–04 *Brentford* 25 3 **25 3**
2004–05 Leicester C 7 0
2005–06 Leicester C 0 0 **21 2**
2005–06 *Blackpool* 13 6 **13 6**
2005–06 Barnsley 17 1
2006–07 Barnsley 17 1 **34 2**
2006–07 *Walsall* 6 2 **6 2**
2006–07 Darlington 13 4
2007–08 Darlington 40 13 **53 17**

DERBY CO (31)

ADDISON, Miles (D) 3 0
H: 6 2 W: 13 03 b.London 7-1-89
Source: Scholar.
2005–06 Derby Co 2 0
2006–07 Derby Co 0 0
2007–08 Derby Co 1 0 **3 0**

BARNES, Giles (M) 79 10
H: 6 0 W: 12 10 b.Barking 5-8-88
Source: Scholar. *Honours:* England Youth.
2005–06 Derby Co 19 1
2006–07 Derby Co 39 8
2007–08 Derby Co 21 1 **79 10**

BEARDSLEY, Jason (D) 0 0
H: 6 0 W: 11 00 b.Burton 12-7-89
Source: Scholar.
2007–08 Derby Co 0 0

BYWATER, Steve (G) 151 0
H: 6 2 W: 12 10 b.Manchester 7-6-81
Source: Trainee. *Honours:* England Youth, Under-20, Under-21.
1997–98 Rochdale 0 0
1998–99 West Ham U 0 0
1999–2000 West Ham U 4 0
1999–2000 *Wycombe W* 2 0 **2 0**
1999–2000 *Hull C* 4 0 **4 0**
2000–01 West Ham U 1 0
2001–02 West Ham U 0 0
2001–02 *Wolverhampton W* 0 0
2001–02 *Cardiff C* 0 0
2002–03 West Ham U 0 0
2003–04 West Ham U 17 0
2004–05 West Ham U 36 0
2005–06 West Ham U 1 0
2005–06 *Coventry C* 14 0 **14 0**
2006–07 West Ham U 0 0 **59 0**
2006–07 Derby Co 37 0
2007–08 Derby Co 18 0 **55 0**
2007–08 *Ipswich T* 17 0 **17 0**

CAMARA, Mo (D) 312 2
H: 5 11 W: 11 03 b.Conakry 25-6-75
Honours: Guinea 79 full caps.
1993–94 Beauvais 19 0
1994–95 Beauvais 0 0
1995–96 Troyes 13 0 **13 0**
1996–97 Beauvais 35 0 **54 0**
1997–98 Le Havre 14 0
1998–99 Lille 34 2 **34 2**
1999–2000 Le Havre 2 0 **16 0**
2000–01 Wolverhampton W 18 0
2001–02 Wolverhampton W 27 0
2002–03 Wolverhampton W 0 0 **45 0**
2003–04 Burnley 45 0
2004–05 Burnley 45 0 **90 0**
2005–06 Celtic 18 0
2006–07 Celtic 1 0 **19 0**
2006–07 Derby Co 19 0
2007–08 Derby Co 1 0 **20 0**
2007–08 *Norwich C* 21 0 **21 0**

CARROLL, Roy (G) 275 0
H: 6 2 W: 13 12 b.Enniskillen 30-9-77
Source: Trainee. *Honours:* Northern Ireland Youth, Under-21, 19 full caps.
1995–96 Hull C 23 0
1996–97 Hull C 23 0 **46 0**
1996–97 Wigan Ath 0 0
1997–98 Wigan Ath 29 0
1998–99 Wigan Ath 43 0
1999–2000 Wigan Ath 34 0
2000–01 Wigan Ath 29 0 **135 0**
2001–02 Manchester U 7 0
2002–03 Manchester U 10 0
2003–04 Manchester U 6 0
2004–05 Manchester U 26 0 **49 0**
2005–06 West Ham U 19 0
2006–07 West Ham U 12 0 **31 0**
2007–08 Rangers 0 0
2007–08 Derby Co 14 0 **14 0**

DAVIS, Claude (D) 134 4
H: 6 3 W: 14 04 b.Kingston, Jam 6-3-79
Source: Portmore U. *Honours:* Jamaica 47 full caps, 2 goals.
2003–04 Preston NE 22 1
2004–05 Preston NE 32 0
2005–06 Preston NE 40 3 **94 4**
2006–07 Sheffield U 21 0 **21 0**
2007–08 Derby Co 19 0 **19 0**

EARNSHAW, Robert (F) 291 127
H: 5 6 W: 9 09 b.Mulfulira 6-4-81
Source: Trainee. *Honours:* Wales Youth, Under-21, 38 full caps, 13 goals.
1997–98 Cardiff C 5 0
1998–99 Cardiff C 5 1
1998–99 *Middlesbrough* 0 0
1999–2000 Cardiff C 6 1
1999–2000 *Morton* 3 2 **3 2**
2000–01 Cardiff C 36 19
2001–02 Cardiff C 30 11
2002–03 Cardiff C 46 31
2003–04 Cardiff C 46 21
2004–05 Cardiff C 4 1 **178 85**

Season	Club				
2004–05	WBA	31	11		
2005–06	WBA	12	1	**43**	**12**
2005–06	Norwich C	15	8		
2006–07	Norwich C	30	19	**45**	**27**
2007–08	Derby Co	22	1	**22**	**1**

EDWORTHY, Marc (D) **441 2**

H: 5 10 W: 11 11 b.Barnstaple 24-12-72

Source: Trainee.

Season	Club				
1990–91	Plymouth Arg	0	0		
1991–92	Plymouth Arg	15	0		
1992–93	Plymouth Arg	15	0		
1993–94	Plymouth Arg	12	0		
1994–95	Plymouth Arg	27	1	**69**	**1**
1995–96	Crystal Palace	44	0		
1996–97	Crystal Palace	45	0		
1997–98	Crystal Palace	34	0		
1998–99	Crystal Palace	3	0	**126**	**0**
1998–99	Coventry C	22	0		
1999–2000	Coventry C	10	0		
2000–01	Coventry C	24	1		
2001–02	Coventry C	20	0	**76**	**1**
2002–03	Wolverhampton W	22	0	**22**	**0**
2003–04	Norwich C	43	0		
2004–05	Norwich C	28	0	**71**	**0**
2005–06	Derby Co	30	0		
2006–07	Derby Co	38	0		
2007–08	Derby Co	9	0	**77**	**0**

FAGAN, Craig (F) **197 34**

H: 5 11 W: 11 11 b.Birmingham 11-12-82

Source: Scholar.

Season	Club				
2001–02	Birmingham C	0	0		
2002–03	Birmingham C	1	0		
2002–03	*Bristol C*	6	1	**6**	**1**
2003–04	Birmingham C	0	0	**1**	**0**
2003–04	Colchester U	37	9		
2004–05	Colchester U	26	8	**63**	**17**
2004–05	Hull C	12	4		
2005–06	Hull C	41	5		
2006–07	Hull C	27	6		
2006–07	Derby Co	17	1		
2007–08	Derby Co	22	0	**39**	**1**
2007–08	*Hull C*	8	0	**88**	**15**

FEILHABER, Benny (M) **68 3**

H: 5 9 W: 10 10 b.Rio 19-1-85

Honours: USA 16 full caps, 2 goals.

Season	Club				
2005–06	Hamburg II	30	2		
2006–07	Hamburg II	19	1	**49**	**3**
2006–07	Hamburg	9	0	**9**	**0**
2007–08	Derby Co	10	0	**10**	**0**

HANSON, Mitchell (D) **0 0**

H: 6 1 W: 13 07 b.Derby 2-9-88

Source: Scholar.

Season	Club				
2007–08	Derby Co	0	0		

HOLMES, Lee (M) **96 7**

H: 5 8 W: 10 06 b.Mansfield 2-4-87

Source: Scholar. *Honours:* FA Schools, England Youth.

Season	Club				
2002–03	Derby Co	2	0		
2003–04	Derby Co	23	2		
2004–05	Derby Co	3	0		
2004–05	*Swindon T*	15	1	**15**	**1**
2005–06	Derby Co	18	0		
2006–07	Derby Co	0	0		
2006–07	*Bradford C*	16	0	**16**	**0**
2007–08	Derby Co	0	0	**46**	**2**
2007–08	*Walsall*	19	4	**19**	**4**

JOHNSON, Michael (D) **532 18**

H: 5 11 W: 11 12 b.Nottingham 4-7-73

Source: Trainee. *Honours:* Jamaica 14 full caps.

Season	Club				
1991–92	Notts Co	5	0		
1992–93	Notts Co	37	0		
1993–94	Notts Co	34	0		
1994–95	Notts Co	31	0		
1995–96	Notts Co	0	0		
1995–96	Birmingham C	33	0		
1996–97	Birmingham C	35	0		
1997–98	Birmingham C	38	3		
1998–99	Birmingham C	45	5		
1999–2000	Birmingham C	34	2		
2000–01	Birmingham C	39	2		
2001–02	Birmingham C	32	1		
2002–03	Birmingham C	6	0		
2003–04	Birmingham C	0	0	**262**	**13**
2003–04	Derby Co	39	1		
2004–05	Derby Co	36	1		
2005–06	Derby Co	31	1		
2006–07	Derby Co	29	1		
2007–08	Derby Co	3	0	**138**	**4**
2007–08	*Sheffield W*	13	0	**13**	**0**
2007–08	*Notts Co*	12	1	**119**	**1**

JONES, David (M) **83 16**

H: 5 11 W: 10 10 b.Southport 4-11-84

Source: Trainee. *Honours:* England Youth, Under-21.

Season	Club				
2003–04	Manchester U	0	0		
2004–05	Manchester U	0	0		
2005–06	Manchester U	0	0		
2005–06	*Preston NE*	24	3	**24**	**3**
2005–06	NEC Nijmegen	17	6	**17**	**6**
2006–07	Manchester U	0	0		
2006–07	Derby Co	28	6		
2007–08	Derby Co	14	1	**42**	**7**

LEACOCK, Dean (D) **86 0**

H: 6 2 W: 12 04 b.Croydon 10-6-84

Source: Trainee. *Honours:* England Youth, Under-20.

Season	Club				
2002–03	Fulham	0	0		
2003–04	Fulham	4	0		
2004–05	Fulham	0	0		
2004–05	*Coventry C*	13	0	**13**	**0**
2005–06	Fulham	5	0		
2006–07	Fulham	0	0	**9**	**0**
2006–07	Derby Co	38	0		
2007–08	Derby Co	26	0	**64**	**0**

LEWIS, Eddie (M) **351 32**

H: 5 10 W: 11 02 b.Cerritos 17-5-74

Honours: USA 76 full caps, 9 goals.

Season	Club				
1996	San Jose Clash	25	0		
1997	San Jose Clash	29	2		
1998	San Jose Clash	32	3		
1999	San Jose Clash	29	4	**115**	**9**
1999–2000	Fulham	8	0		
2000–01	Fulham	7	0		
2001–02	Fulham	1	0	**16**	**0**
2002–03	Preston NE	38	5		
2003–04	Preston NE	33	6		
2004–05	Preston NE	40	4	**111**	**15**
2005–06	Leeds U	43	5		
2006–07	Leeds U	41	3		
2007–08	Leeds U	1	0	**85**	**8**
2007–08	Derby Co	24	0	**24**	**0**

MALCOLM, Bob (D) **111 3**

H: 5 11 W: 11 02 b.Glasgow 12-11-80

Honours: Scotland Under-21, B.

Season	Club				
1997–98	Rangers	0	0		
1998–99	Rangers	0	0		
1999–2000	Rangers	3	0		
2000–01	Rangers	6	1		
2001–02	Rangers	7	0		
2002–03	Rangers	24	1		
2003–04	Rangers	14	0		
2004–05	Rangers	22	1		
2005–06	Rangers	14	0	**90**	**3**
2006–07	Derby Co	9	0		
2007–08	Derby Co	1	0	**10**	**0**
2007–08	*QPR*	11	0	**11**	**0**

McEVELEY, James (D) **95 4**

H: 6 1 W: 13 03 b.Liverpool 11-2-85

Source: Trainee. *Honours:* England Under-20, Under-21. Scotland B, 3 full caps.

Season	Club				
2002–03	Blackburn R	9	0		
2003–04	Blackburn R	0	0		
2003–04	*Burnley*	4	0	**4**	**0**
2004–05	Blackburn R	5	0		
2004–05	*Gillingham*	10	1	**10**	**1**
2005–06	Blackburn R	0	0		
2005–06	*Ipswich T*	19	1	**19**	**1**
2006–07	Blackburn R	4	0	**18**	**0**
2006–07	Derby Co	15	0		
2007–08	Derby Co	29	2	**44**	**2**

MEARS, Tyrone (D) **114 6**

H: 5 11 W: 11 10 b.Stockport 18-2-83

Source: Manchester C Juniors.

Season	Club				
2000–01	Manchester C	0	0		
2001–02	Manchester C	1	0	**1**	**0**
2002–03	Preston NE	22	1		
2003–04	Preston NE	12	1		
2004–05	Preston NE	4	0		
2005–06	Preston NE	32	2	**70**	**4**
2006–07	West Ham U	5	0	**5**	**0**
2006–07	*Derby Co*	13	1		
2007–08	Derby Co	25	1	**38**	**2**

MILLER, Kenny (F) **305 80**

H: 5 10 W: 10 09 b.Edinburgh 23-12-79

Source: Hutchison Vale. *Honours:* Scotland Under-21, B, 37 full caps, 11 goals.

Season	Club				
1996–97	Hibernian	0	0		
1997–98	Hibernian	7	0		
1998–99	Hibernian	7	1		
1999–2000	Hibernian	31	11	**45**	**12**
2000–01	Rangers	27	8		
2001–02	Rangers	3	0	**30**	**8**
2001–02	Wolverhampton W	20	2		
2002–03	Wolverhampton W	43	19		
2003–04	Wolverhampton W	25	2		
2004–05	Wolverhampton W	44	19		
2005–06	Wolverhampton W	35	10	**167**	**52**
2006–07	Celtic	31	4		
2007–08	Celtic	2	0	**33**	**4**
2007–08	Derby Co	30	4	**30**	**4**

MOORE, Darren (D) **484 29**

H: 6 2 W: 15 07 b.Birmingham 22-4-74

Source: Trainee. *Honours:* Jamaica 3 full caps.

Season	Club				
1991–92	Torquay U	5	1		
1992–93	Torquay U	31	2		
1993–94	Torquay U	37	2		
1994–95	Torquay U	30	3	**103**	**8**
1995–96	Doncaster R	35	2		
1996–97	Doncaster R	41	5	**76**	**7**
1997–98	Bradford C	18	0		
1998–99	Bradford C	44	3		
1999–2000	Bradford C	0	0	**62**	**3**
1999–2000	Portsmouth	25	1		
2000–01	Portsmouth	32	1		
2001–02	Portsmouth	2	0	**59**	**2**
2001–02	WBA	32	2		
2002–03	WBA	29	2		
2003–04	WBA	22	2		
2004–05	WBA	16	0		
2005–06	WBA	5	0	**104**	**6**
2005–06	Derby Co	14	1		
2006–07	Derby Co	35	2		
2007–08	Derby Co	31	0	**80**	**3**

NYATANGA, Lewin (D) **95 5**

H: 6 2 W: 12 08 b.Burton 18-8-88

Source: Scholar. *Honours:* Wales Under-21, 21 full caps.

Season	Club				
2005–06	Derby Co	24	1		
2006–07	Derby Co	7	1		
2006–07	*Sunderland*	11	0	**11**	**0**
2006–07	*Barnsley*	10	1		
2007–08	Derby Co	2	1	**33**	**3**
2007–08	*Barnsley*	41	1	**51**	**2**

PEARSON, Stephen (M) **173 18**

H: 6 0 W: 11 01 b.Lanark 2-10-82

Honours: Scotland Under-21, B, 10 full caps.

Season	Club				
2000–01	Motherwell	6	0		
2001–02	Motherwell	27	2		
2002–03	Motherwell	29	6		
2003–04	Motherwell	18	4	**80**	**12**
2003–04	Celtic	17	3		
2004–05	Celtic	8	0		
2005–06	Celtic	18	2		
2006–07	Celtic	13	1	**56**	**6**
2006–07	Derby Co	9	0		
2007–08	Derby Co	24	0	**33**	**0**
2007–08	*Stoke C*	4	0	**4**	**0**

PRICE, Lewis (G) **80 0**

H: 6 3 W: 13 05 b.Bournemouth 19-7-84

Source: Southampton Academy. *Honours:* Wales Youth, Under-21, 6 full caps.

Season	Club				
2002–03	Ipswich T	0	0		
2003–04	Ipswich T	1	0		
2004–05	Ipswich T	8	0		
2004–05	*Cambridge U*	6	0	**6**	**0**
2005–06	Ipswich T	25	0		
2006–07	Ipswich T	34	0	**68**	**0**
2007–08	Derby Co	6	0	**6**	**0**

RICHARDS, Matthew (M) **0 0**

H: 5 9 W: 11 07 b.Derby 1-12-89

Source: Scholar.

Season	Club				
2006–07	Derby Co	0	0		
2007–08	Derby Co	0	0		

ROBERT, Laurent (M) **361 67**

H: 5 9 W: 11 02 b.Saint-Benoit 21-5-75

Honours: France 9 full caps, 1 goal.

Season	Club				
1994–95	Montpellier	7	0		
1995–96	Montpellier	21	5		
1996–97	Montpellier	38	1		
1997–98	Montpellier	26	2		

1998–99 Montpellier 32 11 **124 19**
1999–2000 Paris St Germain 28 9
2000–01 Paris St Germain 32 14
2001–02 Paris St Germain 1 0 **61 23**
2001–02 Newcastle U 36 8
2002–03 Newcastle U 27 5
2003–04 Newcastle U 35 6
2004–05 Newcastle U 31 3 **129 22**
2005–06 *Portsmouth* 17 1 **17 1**
2005–06 Benfica 13 2 **13 2**
2006–07 Levante 13 0 **13 0**
2007–08 Derby Co 4 0 **4 0**

SAVAGE, Robbie (M) 423 30
H: 5 11 W: 11 00 b.Wrexham 18-10-74
Source: Trainee. *Honours:* Wales Schools, Youth, Under-21, 39 full caps, 2 goals.
1993–94 Manchester U 0 0
1994–95 Crewe Alex 6 2
1995–96 Crewe Alex 30 7
1996–97 Crewe Alex 41 1 **77 10**
1997–98 Leicester C 35 2
1998–99 Leicester C 34 1
1999–2000 Leicester C 35 1
2000–01 Leicester C 33 4
2001–02 Leicester C 35 0 **172 8**
2002–03 Birmingham C 33 4
2003–04 Birmingham C 31 3
2004–05 Birmingham C 18 4 **82 11**
2004–05 Blackburn R 9 0
2005–06 Blackburn R 34 1
2006–07 Blackburn R 21 0
2007–08 Blackburn R 12 0 **76 1**
2007–08 Derby Co 16 0 **16 0**

SIMMONS, Paris (F) 1 0
H: 5 10 W: 11 12 b.London 2-1-90
2007–08 Derby Co 1 0 **1 0**

STERJOVSKI, Mile (M) 280 64
H: 6 1 W: 12 08 b.Wollongong 27-5-79
Honours: Australia Under-20, Under-23, 34 full caps, 6 goals.
1995–96 Wollongong Wolves 2 0
1996–97 Wollongong Wolves 0 0 **2 0**
1997–98 Sydney United 11 2
1998–99 Sydney United 26 18 **37 20**
1999–2000 Parramatta Power 31 11 **31 11**
2000–01 Lille 22 4
2001–02 Lille 25 6
2002–03 Lille 22 5
2003–04 Lille 21 0 **90 15**
2004–05 Basle 28 1
2005–06 Basle 32 7
2006–07 Basle 34 7 **94 15**
2007–08 Genclerbirligi 14 3 **14 3**
2007–08 Derby Co 12 0 **12 0**

STUBBS, Alan (D) 495 19
H: 6 2 W: 14 02 b.Kirkby 6-10-71
Source: Trainee. *Honours:* England B.
1990–91 Bolton W 23 0
1991–92 Bolton W 32 1
1992–93 Bolton W 42 2
1993–94 Bolton W 41 1
1994–95 Bolton W 39 1
1995–96 Bolton W 25 4 **202 9**
1996–97 Celtic 20 0
1997–98 Celtic 29 1
1998–99 Celtic 23 1
1999–2000 Celtic 23 0
2000–01 Celtic 11 1 **106 3**
2001–02 Everton 31 2
2002–03 Everton 35 0
2003–04 Everton 27 0
2004–05 Everton 31 1
2005–06 Sunderland 10 1 **10 1**
2005–06 Everton 14 0
2006–07 Everton 23 2
2007–08 Everton 8 1 **169 6**
2007–08 Derby Co 8 0 **8 0**

TEALE, Gary (F) 378 36
H: 5 11 W: 12 02 b.Glasgow 21-7-78
Honours: Scotland Under-21, B, 11 full caps.
1996–97 Clydebank 33 6
1997–98 Clydebank 27 6
1998–99 Clydebank 8 2 **68 14**
1998–99 Ayr U 23 4
1999–2000 Ayr U 32 0
2000–01 Ayr U 29 5
2001–02 Ayr U 18 4 **102 13**
2001–02 Wigan Ath 23 1
2002–03 Wigan Ath 38 2
2003–04 Wigan Ath 28 2
2004–05 Wigan Ath 37 3
2005–06 Wigan Ath 24 0
2006–07 Wigan Ath 12 0 **162 8**
2006–07 Derby Co 16 1
2007–08 Derby Co 18 0 **34 1**
2007–08 *Plymouth Arg* 12 0 **12 0**

TODD, Andy (D) 271 11
H: 5 11 W: 13 04 b.Derby 21-9-74
Source: Trainee.
1991–92 Middlesbrough 0 0
1992–93 Middlesbrough 0 0
1993–94 Middlesbrough 3 0
1994–95 Middlesbrough 5 0 **8 0**
1994–95 *Swindon T* 13 0 **13 0**
1995–96 Bolton W 12 2
1996–97 Bolton W 15 0
1997–98 Bolton W 25 0
1998–99 Bolton W 20 0
1999–2000 Bolton W 12 0 **84 2**
1999–2000 Charlton Ath 12 0
2000–01 Charlton Ath 23 1
2001–02 Charlton Ath 5 0 **40 1**
2001–02 *Grimsby T* 12 3 **12 3**
2002–03 Blackburn R 12 1
2003–04 Blackburn R 19 0
2003–04 *Burnley* 7 0 **7 0**
2004–05 Blackburn R 26 1
2005–06 Blackburn R 22 2
2006–07 Blackburn R 9 0 **88 4**
2007–08 Derby Co 19 1 **19 1**

VILLA, Emanuel (F) 177 63
H: 6 0 W: 12 00 b.Capital Federal 24-2-82
2001–02 Huracan 18 8
2002–03 Huracan 28 3 **46 11**
2003–04 Atletico Rafaela 25 9 **25 9**
2004–05 Rosario Central 32 14
2005–06 Atlas 16 10
2005–06 Rosario Central 10 4 **42 18**
2006–07 Tecos UAG 17 7 **17 7**
2006–07 Atlas 15 5 **31 15**
2007–08 Derby Co 16 3 **16 3**

Scholars
Atkins, Ross Michael; Booth, Jack; Dudley, Mark; Forde, Alexander Michael; Johnson, Jermaine; Kean, Jacob; Mills, Gregory Adam; Ojamaa, Henrik; Simmons, Paris Michael

DONCASTER R (32)

COPPINGER, James (F) 213 22
H: 5 7 W: 10 03 b.Middlesbrough 10-1-81
Source: Darlington Trainee. *Honours:* England Youth.
1997–98 Newcastle U 0 0
1998–99 Newcastle U 0 0
1999–2000 Newcastle U 0 0
1999–2000 *Hartlepool U* 10 3
2000–01 Newcastle U 1 0
2001–02 Newcastle U 0 0 **1 0**
2001–02 *Hartlepool U* 14 2 **24 5**
2002–03 Exeter C 43 5
2003–04 Exeter C 0 0 **43 5**
2004–05 Doncaster R 31 0
2005–06 Doncaster R 36 5
2006–07 Doncaster R 39 4
2007–08 Doncaster R 39 3 **145 12**

GREEN, Liam (M) 2 0
H: 5 9 W: 10 00 b.Grimsby 17-3-88
Source: Scholar.
2006–07 Doncaster R 2 0
2007–08 Doncaster R 0 0 **2 0**

GREEN, Paul (M) 198 25
H: 5 9 W: 10 02 b.Pontefract 10-4-83
Source: Scholar.
2003–04 Doncaster R 43 8
2004–05 Doncaster R 42 7
2005–06 Doncaster R 34 3
2006–07 Doncaster R 41 2
2007–08 Doncaster R 38 5 **198 25**

GREER, Gordon (D) 46 2
H: 6 2 W: 12 05 b.Glasgow 14-12-80
Source: Port Glasgow. *Honours:* Scotland B.
2000–01 Clyde 30 0 **30 0**
2000–01 Blackburn R 0 0
2001–02 Blackburn R 0 0
2002–03 Blackburn R 0 0
2002–03 *Stockport Co* 5 1 **5 1**
2003–04 Blackburn R 0 0
2004–05 Blackburn R 0 0
2005–06 Blackburn R 0 0
2006–07 Blackburn R 0 0
2007–08 Doncaster R 11 1 **11 1**

GUY, Lewis (F) 105 16
H: 5 10 W: 10 07 b.Penrith 27-8-85
Source: Trainee. *Honours:* England Youth, Under-20.
2002–03 Newcastle U 0 0
2003–04 Newcastle U 0 0
2004–05 Newcastle U 0 0
2004–05 Doncaster R 9 3
2005–06 Doncaster R 31 3
2006–07 Doncaster R 36 4
2007–08 Doncaster R 29 6 **105 16**

HAYTER, James (F) 392 101
H: 5 9 W: 10 13 b.Newport (IW) 9-4-79
Source: Trainee.
1996–97 Bournemouth 2 0
1997–98 Bournemouth 5 0
1998–99 Bournemouth 20 2
1999–2000 Bournemouth 31 2
2000–01 Bournemouth 40 11
2001–02 Bournemouth 44 7
2002–03 Bournemouth 45 9
2003–04 Bournemouth 44 14
2004–05 Bournemouth 39 19
2005–06 Bournemouth 46 20
2006–07 Bournemouth 42 10 **358 94**
2007–08 Doncaster R 34 7 **34 7**

HEFFERNAN, Paul (F) 209 67
H: 5 10 W: 11 00 b.Dublin 29-12-81
Source: Newton.
1999–2000 Notts Co 2 0
2000–01 Notts Co 1 0
2001–02 Notts Co 23 6
2002–03 Notts Co 36 10
2003–04 Notts Co 38 20 **100 36**
2004–05 Bristol C 27 5 **27 5**
2005–06 Doncaster R 26 8
2006–07 Doncaster R 29 11
2007–08 Doncaster R 27 7 **82 26**

HIRD, Samuel (D) 26 0
H: 5 7 W: 10 12 b.Askern 7-9-87
Source: Scholar.
2005–06 Leeds U 0 0
2006–07 Leeds U 0 0
2006–07 *Doncaster R* 5 0
2007–08 Doncaster R 4 0 **9 0**
2007–08 *Grimsby T* 17 0 **17 0**

LEE, Graeme (D) 354 29
H: 6 2 W: 13 07 b.Middlesbrough 31-5-78
Source: Trainee.
1995–96 Hartlepool U 6 0
1996–97 Hartlepool U 24 0
1997–98 Hartlepool U 37 3
1998–99 Hartlepool U 24 3
1999–2000 Hartlepool U 38 7
2000–01 Hartlepool U 6 0
2001–02 Hartlepool U 39 4
2002–03 Hartlepool U 45 2
2003–04 Sheffield W 30 3
2004–05 Sheffield W 22 1
2005–06 Sheffield W 15 1 **67 5**
2005–06 Doncaster R 20 1
2006–07 Doncaster R 39 4
2007–08 Doncaster R 1 0 **60 5**
2007–08 *Hartlepool U* 3 0 **222 19**
2007–08 *Shrewsbury T* 5 0 **5 0**

LOCKWOOD, Adam (D) 165 12
H: 6 0 W: 12 07 b.Wakefield 26-10-81
Source: Reading Trainee.
2003–04 Yeovil T 43 4
2004–05 Yeovil T 10 0
2005–06 Yeovil T 20 0 **73 4**
2005–06 *Torquay U* 9 3 **9 3**
2006–07 Doncaster R 44 2
2007–08 Doncaster R 39 3 **83 5**

McCAMMON, Mark (F) 199 25
H: 6 2 W: 14 05 b.Barnet 7-8-78
Source: Cambridge C. *Honours:* Barbados 2 full caps, 4 goals.
1997–98 Cambridge U 2 0
1998–99 Cambridge U 2 0 **4 0**
1998–99 Charlton Ath 0 0

1999–2000 Charlton Ath 4 0 **4 0**
1999–2000 *Swindon T* 4 0 **4 0**
2000–01 Brentford 24 3
2001–02 Brentford 14 0
2002–03 Brentford 37 7 **75 10**
2002–03 Millwall 7 2
2003–04 Millwall 7 0
2004–05 Millwall 8 0 **22 2**
2004–05 Brighton & HA 18 3
2005–06 Brighton & HA 7 0 **25 3**
2005–06 *Bristol C* 11 4 **11 4**
2006–07 Doncaster R 22 2
2007–08 Doncaster R 32 4 **54 6**

McDAID, Sean (D) **79 1**
H: 5 6 W: 9 08 b.Harrogate 6-3-86
Source: Trainee.
2002–03 Leeds U 0 0
2003–04 Leeds U 0 0
2004–05 Leeds U 0 0
2005–06 Doncaster R 35 0
2006–07 Doncaster R 20 0
2007–08 Doncaster R 24 1 **79 1**

NELTHORPE, Craig (M) **17 1**
H: 5 10 W: 11 00 b.Doncaster 10-6-87
Source: Scholar.
2004–05 Doncaster R 1 0
2005–06 Doncaster R 1 0
2006–07 Doncaster R 6 1
2007–08 Doncaster R 2 0 **10 1**
2007–08 *Darlington* 7 0 **7 0**

NOBLE, Matthew (D) **0 0**
H: 5 10 W: 11 00 b.Newcastle 23-11-88
Source: Scholar.
2007–08 Doncaster R 0 0

O'CONNOR, James (D) **138 2**
H: 5 10 W: 12 05 b.Birmingham 20-11-84
Source: Scholar.
2003–04 Aston Villa 0 0
2004–05 Aston Villa 0 0
2004–05 *Port Vale* 13 0 **13 0**
2004–05 Bournemouth 6 0
2005–06 Bournemouth 39 1 **45 1**
2006–07 Doncaster R 40 1
2007–08 Doncaster R 40 0 **80 1**

PRICE, Jason (M) **354 59**
H: 6 2 W: 11 05 b.Pontypridd 12-4-77
Source: Aberaman Ath. *Honours:* Wales Under-21.
1995–96 Swansea C 0 0
1996–97 Swansea C 2 0
1997–98 Swansea C 34 3
1998–99 Swansea C 28 4
1999–2000 Swansea C 39 6
2000–01 Swansea C 41 4 **144 17**
2001–02 Brentford 15 1 **15 1**
2001–02 Tranmere R 24 7
2002–03 Tranmere R 25 4 **49 11**
2003–04 Hull C 33 9
2004–05 Hull C 27 2
2005–06 Hull C 15 2 **75 13**
2005–06 Doncaster R 11 4
2006–07 Doncaster R 31 6
2007–08 Doncaster R 29 7 **71 17**

ROBERTS, Gareth (D) **348 17**
H: 5 8 W: 11 12 b.Wrexham 6-2-78
Source: Trainee. *Honours:* Wales Under-21, B, 9 full caps.
1995–96 Liverpool 0 0
1996–97 Liverpool 0 0
1997–98 Liverpool 0 0
1998–99 Liverpool 0 0
1999–2000 Tranmere R 37 1
2000–01 Tranmere R 34 0
2001–02 Tranmere R 45 2
2002–03 Tranmere R 37 4
2003–04 Tranmere R 44 1
2004–05 Tranmere R 40 3
2005–06 Tranmere R 44 2 **281 13**
2006–07 Doncaster R 30 1
2007–08 Doncaster R 37 3 **67 4**

ROBERTS, Steve (D) **223 7**
H: 6 1 W: 11 02 b.Wrexham 24-2-80
Source: Trainee. *Honours:* Wales Youth, Under-21, 1 full cap.
1997–98 Wrexham 0 0
1998–99 Wrexham 0 0
1999–2000 Wrexham 19 0
2000–01 Wrexham 7 0
2001–02 Wrexham 24 1
2002–03 Wrexham 39 2
2003–04 Wrexham 27 0
2004–05 Wrexham 34 3 **150 6**
2005–06 Doncaster R 27 1
2006–07 Doncaster R 21 0
2007–08 Doncaster R 25 0 **73 1**

SHIELIS, Valentino (M) **0 0**
H: 6 2 W: 12 00 b.Cyprus 1-3-90
Source: Arsenal Youth.
2007–08 Doncaster R 0 0

SMITH, Benjamin (G) **22 0**
H: 6 1 W: 12 11 b.Newcastle 5-9-86
Source: Newcastle U Scholar.
2006–07 Stockport Co 0 0
2006–07 Doncaster R 13 0
2007–08 Doncaster R 0 0 **13 0**
2007–08 *Lincoln C* 9 0 **9 0**

STOCK, Brian (M) **229 25**
H: 5 11 W: 11 02 b.Winchester 24-12-81
Source: Trainee. *Honours:* Wales Under-21.
1999–2000 Bournemouth 5 0
2000–01 Bournemouth 1 0
2001–02 Bournemouth 26 2
2002–03 Bournemouth 27 2
2003–04 Bournemouth 19 3
2004–05 Bournemouth 41 6
2005–06 Bournemouth 26 3 **145 16**
2005–06 Preston NE 6 1
2006–07 Preston NE 2 0 **8 1**
2006–07 Doncaster R 36 3
2007–08 Doncaster R 40 5 **76 8**

SULLIVAN, Neil (G) **407 0**
H: 6 2 W: 12 00 b.Sutton 24-2-70
Source: Trainee. *Honours:* Scotland 28 full caps.
1988–89 Wimbledon 0 0
1989–90 Wimbledon 0 0
1990–91 Wimbledon 1 0
1991–92 Wimbledon 1 0
1991–92 *Crystal Palace* 1 0 **1 0**
1992–93 Wimbledon 1 0
1993–94 Wimbledon 2 0
1994–95 Wimbledon 11 0
1995–96 Wimbledon 16 0
1996–97 Wimbledon 36 0
1997–98 Wimbledon 38 0
1998–99 Wimbledon 38 0
1999–2000 Wimbledon 37 0 **181 0**
2000–01 Tottenham H 35 0
2001–02 Tottenham H 29 0
2002–03 Tottenham H 0 0 **64 0**
2003–04 Chelsea 4 0 **4 0**
2004–05 Leeds U 46 0
2005–06 Leeds U 42 0
2006–07 Leeds U 7 0 **95 0**
2006–07 *Doncaster R* 16 0
2007–08 Doncaster R 46 0 **62 0**

TAYLOR, Gareth (F) **476 122**
H: 6 2 W: 13 07 b.Weston-Super-Mare 25-2-73
Source: Southampton Trainee. *Honours:* Wales Under-21, 15 full caps, 1 goal.
1991–92 Bristol R 1 0
1992–93 Bristol R 0 0
1993–94 Bristol R 0 0
1994–95 Bristol R 39 12
1995–96 Bristol R 7 4 **47 16**
1995–96 Crystal Palace 20 1 **20 1**
1995–96 Sheffield U 10 2
1996–97 Sheffield U 34 12
1997–98 Sheffield U 28 10
1998–99 Sheffield U 12 1 **84 25**
1998–99 Manchester C 26 4
1999–2000 Manchester C 17 5
1999–2000 *Port Vale* 4 0 **4 0**
1999–2000 *QPR* 6 1 **6 1**
2000–01 Manchester C 0 0 **43 9**
2000–01 *Burnley* 15 4
2001–02 Burnley 40 16
2002–03 Burnley 40 16
2003–04 Burnley 0 0 **95 36**
2003–04 Nottingham F 34 8
2004–05 Nottingham F 36 7
2005–06 Nottingham F 20 4 **90 19**
2005–06 *Crewe Alex* 15 4 **15 4**
2006–07 Tranmere R 37 7
2007–08 Tranmere R 23 3 **60 10**
2007–08 Doncaster R 12 1 **12 1**

WELLENS, Richard (M) **320 30**
H: 5 9 W: 11 06 b.Manchester 26-3-80
Source: Trainee. *Honours:* England Youth.
1996–97 Manchester U 0 0
1997–98 Manchester U 0 0
1998–99 Manchester U 0 0
1999–2000 Manchester U 0 0
1999–2000 Blackpool 8 0
2000–01 Blackpool 36 8
2001–02 Blackpool 36 1
2002–03 Blackpool 39 1
2003–04 Blackpool 41 3
2004–05 Blackpool 28 3 **188 16**
2005–06 Oldham Ath 45 4
2006–07 Oldham Ath 42 4 **87 8**
2007–08 Doncaster R 45 6 **45 6**

WILSON, Mark (M) **124 9**
H: 5 10 W: 12 07 b.Scunthorpe 9-2-79
Source: Trainee. *Honours:* England Schools, Youth, Under-21.
1995–96 Manchester U 0 0
1996–97 Manchester U 0 0
1997–98 Manchester U 0 0
1997–98 *Wrexham* 13 4 **13 4**
1998–99 Manchester U 0 0
1999–2000 Manchester U 3 0
2000–01 Manchester U 0 0 **3 0**
2001–02 Middlesbrough 10 0
2002–03 Middlesbrough 6 0
2002–03 *Stoke C* 4 0 **4 0**
2003–04 Middlesbrough 0 0
2003–04 *Swansea C* 12 2 **12 2**
2003–04 *Sheffield W* 3 0 **3 0**
2004–05 Middlesbrough 0 0 **16 0**
2004–05 *Doncaster R* 3 0
2004–05 *Livingston* 5 0 **5 0**
2006 Dallas 12 1 **12 1**
2006–07 Doncaster R 22 1
2007–08 Doncaster R 31 1 **56 2**

WOODS, Martin (M) **68 4**
H: 5 11 W: 11 13 b.Airdrie 1-1-86
Source: Trainee. *Honours:* Scotland Youth, Under-21.
2002–03 Leeds U 0 0
2003–04 Leeds U 0 0
2004–05 Leeds U 1 0 **1 0**
2004–05 *Hartlepool U* 6 0 **6 0**
2005–06 Sunderland 7 0 **7 0**
2006–07 Rotherham U 36 4 **36 4**
2007–08 Doncaster R 15 0 **15 0**
2007–08 *Yeovil T* 3 0 **3 0**

EVERTON (33)

AGARD, Kieran (F) **0 0**
b.Newham 10-10-89
Source: Scholar.
2006–07 Everton 0 0
2007–08 Everton 0 0

AKPAN, Hope (M) **0 0**
b.Liverpool 14-8-91
Source: Scholar.
2007–08 Everton 0 0

ANICHEBE, Victor (F) **48 5**
H: 6 1 W: 13 00 b.Nigeria 23-4-88
Source: Scholar. *Honours:* Nigeria Under-23, 4 full caps, 1 goal.
2005–06 Everton 2 1
2006–07 Everton 19 3
2007–08 Everton 27 1 **48 5**

ARTETA, Mikel (M) **199 27**
H: 5 9 W: 10 08 b.San Sebastian 26-3-82
Honours: Spain Youth, Under-21.
2000–01 Barcelona B 0 0
2000–01 Paris St Germain 6 1
2001–02 Paris St Germain 25 1 **31 2**
2002–03 Rangers 27 4
2003–04 Rangers 23 8 **50 12**
2004–05 Real Sociedad 14 1 **14 1**
2004–05 Everton 12 1
2005–06 Everton 29 1
2006–07 Everton 35 9
2007–08 Everton 28 1 **104 12**

BAINES, Leighton (D) 167 4
H: 5 8 W: 11 00 b.Liverpool 11-12-84
Source: Trainee. *Honours:* England Under-21.

2002–03	Wigan Ath	6	0		
2003–04	Wigan Ath	26	0		
2004–05	Wigan Ath	41	1		
2005–06	Wigan Ath	37	0		
2006–07	Wigan Ath	35	3		
2007–08	Wigan Ath	0	0	**145**	**4**
2007–08	Everton	22	0	**22**	**0**

BARNETT, Moses (D) 0 0
b.London 3-12-90
Source: Arsenal.

2007–08	Everton	0	0		

BOYLE, Patrick (D) 20 0
H: 6 0 W: 12 09 b.Glasgow 20-3-87
Source: Scholar.

2005–06	Everton	0	0		
2006–07	Everton	0	0		
2006–07	*Norwich C*	3	0	**3**	**0**
2007–08	Everton	0	0		
2007–08	*Crewe Alex*	17	0	**17**	**0**

CAHILL, Tim (M) 318 81
H: 5 10 W: 10 12 b.Sydney 6-12-79
Source: Sydney U. *Honours:* Western Samoa Youth, Australia Under-23, 28 full caps, 13 goals.

1997–98	Millwall	1	0		
1998–99	Millwall	36	6		
1999–2000	Millwall	45	12		
2000–01	Millwall	41	9		
2001–02	Millwall	43	13		
2002–03	Millwall	11	3		
2003–04	Millwall	40	9	**217**	**52**
2004–05	Everton	33	11		
2005–06	Everton	32	6		
2006–07	Everton	18	5		
2007–08	Everton	18	7	**101**	**29**

CARSLEY, Lee (M) 397 31
H: 5 10 W: 12 04 b.Birmingham 28-2-74
Source: Trainee. *Honours:* Eire 39 full caps.

1992–93	Derby Co	0	0		
1993–94	Derby Co	0	0		
1994–95	Derby Co	23	2		
1995–96	Derby Co	35	1		
1996–97	Derby Co	24	0		
1997–98	Derby Co	34	1		
1998–99	Derby Co	22	1	**138**	**5**
1998–99	Blackburn R	8	0		
1999–2000	Blackburn R	30	10		
2000–01	Blackburn R	8	0	**46**	**10**
2000–01	Coventry C	21	2		
2001–02	Coventry C	26	2	**47**	**4**
2001–02	Everton	8	1		
2002–03	Everton	24	3		
2003–04	Everton	21	2		
2004–05	Everton	36	4		
2005–06	Everton	5	0		
2006–07	Everton	38	1		
2007–08	Everton	34	1	**166**	**12**

CONNOR, Stephen (F) 1 0
b.Wirral 27-1-89
Source: Scholar.

2007–08	*Partick T*	1	0	**1**	**0**
2007–08	Everton	0	0		

DENNEHY, Darren (D) 0 0
H: 6 3 W: 11 11 b.Republic of Ireland 21-9-88
Source: Scholar.

2005–06	Everton	0	0		
2006–07	Everton	0	0		
2007–08	Everton	0	0		

DENSMORE, Shaun (M) 0 0
b.Liverpool 11-11-88 *Source:* Scholar.

2007–08	Everton	0	0		

DOWNES, Aiden (F) 5 1
H: 5 8 W: 11 07 b.Dublin 24-7-88
Source: Scholar. *Honours:* Eire Youth, Under-21.

2005–06	Everton	0	0		
2006–07	Everton	0	0		
2007–08	Everton	0	0		
2007–08	*Yeovil T*	5	1	**5**	**1**

FERNANDES, Manuel (M) 105 5
H: 5 9 W: 10 12 b.Lisbon 5-2-86
Honours: Portugal Youth, Under-20, Under-21, 3 full caps, 1 goal.

2003–04	Benfica	10	1		
2004–05	Benfica	29	1		
2005–06	Benfica	28	1	**67**	**3**
2006–07	Portsmouth	10	0	**10**	**0**
2006–07	*Everton*	9	2		
2007–08	Valencia	7	0	**7**	**0**
2007–08	*Everton*	12	0	**21**	**2**

GOSLING, Dan (M) 22 2
H: 6 0 W: 11 00 b.Brixham 2-2-90
Source: Scholar. *Honours:* England Youth.

2006–07	Plymouth Arg	12	2		
2007–08	Plymouth Arg	10	0	**22**	**2**
2007–08	Everton	0	0		

GRAVESEN, Thomas (M) 315 28
H: 5 9 W: 13 06 b.Vejle 11-3-76
Honours: Denmark Under-21, 56 full caps, 5 goals.

1995–96	Vejle	28	2		
1996–97	Vejle	30	8	**58**	**10**
1997–98	Hamburg	26	2		
1998–99	Hamburg	22	3		
1999–2000	Hamburg	26	1	**74**	**6**
2000–01	Everton	32	2		
2001–02	Everton	25	2		
2002–03	Everton	33	1		
2003–04	Everton	30	2		
2004–05	Everton	21	4		
2005–06	Real Madrid	17	1		
2006–07	Real Madrid	17	0	**34**	**1**
2007–08	Everton	8	0	**149**	**11**

HALL, James (M) 0 0
b.Glasgow 16-7-89
Source: Scholar.

2007–08	Everton	0	0		

HARPUR, Ryan (M) 0 0
H: 5 9 W: 11 11 b.Craigavon 1-12-88
Source: Scholar.

2005–06	Everton	0	0		
2006–07	Everton	0	0		
2007–08	Everton	0	0		

HIBBERT, Tony (D) 164 0
H: 5 9 W: 11 05 b.Liverpool 20-2-81
Source: Trainee.

1998–99	Everton	0	0		
1999–2000	Everton	0	0		
2000–01	Everton	3	0		
2001–02	Everton	10	0		
2002–03	Everton	24	0		
2003–04	Everton	25	0		
2004–05	Everton	36	0		
2005–06	Everton	29	0		
2006–07	Everton	13	0		
2007–08	Everton	24	0	**164**	**0**

HOWARD, Tim (G) 202 0
H: 6 3 W: 14 12 b.North Brunswick 6-3-79
Honours: USA Under-21, Under-23, 29 full caps.

1998	NY/NJ MetroStars	1	0		
1999	NY/NJ MetroStars	9	0		
2000	NY/NJ MetroStars	9	0		
2001	NY/NJ MetroStars	26	0		
2002	NY/NJ MetroStars	27	0		
2003	NY/NJ MetroStars	13	0	**85**	**0**
2003–04	Manchester U	32	0		
2004–05	Manchester U	12	0		
2005–06	Manchester U	1	0		
2006–07	Manchester U	0	0	**45**	**0**
2006–07	Everton	36	0		
2007–08	Everton	36	0	**72**	**0**

IRVING, John (M) 0 0
H: 5 10 W: 11 00 b.Liverpool 17-9-88
Source: Scholar.

2005–06	Everton	0	0		
2006–07	Everton	0	0		
2007–08	Everton	0	0		

JAGIELKA, Phil (D) 288 19
H: 6 0 W: 13 01 b.Manchester 17-8-82
Source: Scholar. *Honours:* England Youth, Under-20, Under-21, B, 1 full cap.

1999–2000	Sheffield U	1	0		
2000–01	Sheffield U	15	0		
2001–02	Sheffield U	23	3		
2002–03	Sheffield U	42	0		
2003–04	Sheffield U	43	3		
2004–05	Sheffield U	46	0		
2005–06	Sheffield U	46	8		
2006–07	Sheffield U	38	4	**254**	**18**
2007–08	Everton	34	1	**34**	**1**

JOHNSON, Andy (F) 284 99
H: 5 7 W: 10 09 b.Bedford 10-2-81
Source: Trainee. *Honours:* England Youth, Under-20, 8 full caps.

1997–98	Birmingham C	0	0		
1998–99	Birmingham C	4	0		
1999–2000	Birmingham C	22	1		
2000–01	Birmingham C	34	4		
2001–02	Birmingham C	23	3	**83**	**8**
2002–03	Crystal Palace	28	11		
2003–04	Crystal Palace	42	27		
2004–05	Crystal Palace	37	21		
2005–06	Crystal Palace	33	15	**140**	**74**
2006–07	Everton	32	11		
2007–08	Everton	29	6	**61**	**17**

JONES, Jamie (G) 0 0
b.Kirkby 18-2-89
Source: Scholar.

2007–08	Everton	0	0		

JUTKIEWICZ, Lucas (F) 41 5
H: 6 1 W: 12 11 b.Southampton 20-3-89
Source: Scholar.

2005–06	Swindon T	5	0		
2006–07	Swindon T	33	5	**38**	**5**
2006–07	Everton	0	0		
2007–08	Everton	0	0		
2007–08	*Plymouth Arg*	3	0	**3**	**0**

KISSOCK, John (M) 11 0
b.Fazackerley 1-12-89
Source: Scholar.

2006–07	Everton	0	0		
2007–08	*Gretna*	11	0	**11**	**0**
2007–08	Everton	0	0		

KRENN, George (M) 0 0
b.Austria 4-10-90
Source: Scholar.

2007–08	Everton	0	0		

LESCOTT, Jolean (D) 288 23
H: 6 2 W: 13 00 b.Birmingham 16-8-82
Source: Trainee. *Honours:* England Youth, Under-20, Under-21, B, 5 full caps.

1999–2000	Wolverhampton W	0	0		
2000–01	Wolverhampton W	37	2		
2001–02	Wolverhampton W	44	5		
2002–03	Wolverhampton W	44	1		
2003–04	Wolverhampton W	0	0		
2004–05	Wolverhampton W	41	4		
2005–06	Wolverhampton W	46	1	**212**	**13**
2006–07	Everton	38	2		
2007–08	Everton	38	8	**76**	**10**

MOLYNEUX, Lee (D) 0 0
H: 5 10 W: 11 07 b.Liverpool 24-2-89
Source: Scholar. *Honours:* England Schools, Youth.

2005–06	Everton	0	0		
2006–07	Everton	0	0		
2007–08	Everton	0	0		

MORRISON, Steven (M) 0 0
H: 6 0 W: 10 13 b.Southport 10-9-88
Source: Scholar.

2005–06	Everton	0	0		
2006–07	Everton	0	0		
2007–08	Everton	0	0		

NEVILLE, Phil (M) 369 8
H: 5 11 W: 12 00 b.Bury 21-1-77
Source: Trainee. *Honours:* England Schools, Youth, B, Under-21, 59 full caps.

1994–95	Manchester U	2	0		
1995–96	Manchester U	24	0		
1996–97	Manchester U	18	0		
1997–98	Manchester U	30	1		
1998–99	Manchester U	28	0		
1999–2000	Manchester U	29	0		
2000–01	Manchester U	29	1		
2001–02	Manchester U	28	2		
2002–03	Manchester U	25	1		
2003–04	Manchester U	31	0		
2004–05	Manchester U	19	0	**263**	**5**
2005–06	Everton	34	0		
2006–07	Everton	35	1		
2007–08	Everton	37	2	**106**	**3**

NUNO VALENTE (D) 278 4
H: 6 0 W: 12 03 b.Lisbon 12-9-74
Honours: Portugal Under-21, 33 full caps, 1 goal.

1993–94	Portimonense	26	1	**26**	**1**
1994–95	Sporting Lisbon	9	0		
1995–96	Sporting Lisbon	9	0		
1996–97	Maritimo	30	0	**30**	**0**
1997–98	Sporting Lisbon	6	0		
1998–99	Sporting Lisbon	12	1	**36**	**1**
1999–2000	Uniao Leiria	28	0		
2000–01	Uniao Leiria	31	2		
2001–02	Uniao Leiria	28	0	**87**	**2**
2002–03	Porto	21	0		
2003–04	Porto	27	0		
2004–05	Porto	8	0	**56**	**0**
2005–06	Everton	20	0		
2006–07	Everton	14	0		
2007–08	Everton	9	0	**43**	**0**

O'KANE, Eunan (M) 0 0
b.County Derry 10-7-90

2007–08	Everton	0	0		

OSMAN, Leon (F) 161 21
H: 5 8 W: 10 09 b.Billinge 17-5-81
Source: Trainee. *Honours:* England Schools, Youth.

1998–99	Everton	0	0		
1999–2000	Everton	0	0		
2000–01	Everton	0	0		
2001–02	Everton	0	0		
2002–03	Everton	2	0		
2002–03	*Carlisle U*	12	1	**12**	**1**
2003–04	Everton	4	1		
2003–04	*Derby Co*	17	3	**17**	**3**
2004–05	Everton	29	6		
2005–06	Everton	35	3		
2006–07	Everton	34	3		
2007–08	Everton	28	4	**132**	**17**

PIENAAR, Steven (M) 147 17
H: 5 10 W: 10 06 b.Westbury 17-3-82
Honours: South Africa 21 full caps.

2001–02	Ajax	8	1		
2002–03	Ajax	31	5		
2003–04	Ajax	16	3		
2004–05	Ajax	24	4		
2005–06	Ajax	15	2	**94**	**15**
2006–07	Bor Dortmund	25	0	**25**	**0**
2007–08	Everton	28	2	**28**	**2**

PISTONE, Alessandro (D) 249 8
H: 5 11 W: 11 08 b.Milan 27-7-75
Honours: Italy Under-21.

1992–93	Vicenza	0	0		
1993–94	Solbiatese	20	1	**20**	**1**
1994–95	Crevalcore	29	4	**29**	**4**
1995–96	Vicenza	6	0	**6**	**0**
1995–96	Internazionale	19	1		
1996–97	Internazionale	26	0	**45**	**1**
1997–98	Newcastle U	28	0		
1998–99	Newcastle U	3	0		
1999–2000	Newcastle U	15	1	**46**	**1**
2000–01	Everton	7	0		
2001–02	Everton	25	1		
2002–03	Everton	15	0		
2003–04	Everton	21	0		
2004–05	Everton	33	0		
2005–06	Everton	2	0		
2006–07	Everton	0	0		
2007–08	Everton	0	0	**103**	**1**

RODWELL, Jack (D) 2 0
H: 6 2 W: 12 08 b.Birkdale 11-3-91
Source: Scholar. *Honours:* England Youth.

2007–08	Everton	2	0	**2**	**0**

RUDDY, John (G) 81 0
H: 6 3 W: 12 07 b.St Ives 24-10-86
Source: Scholar. *Honours:* England Youth.

2003–04	Cambridge U	1	0		
2004–05	Cambridge U	38	0	**39**	**0**
2005–06	Everton	1	0		
2005–06	*Walsall*	5	0	**5**	**0**
2005–06	*Rushden & D*	3	0	**3**	**0**
2005–06	*Chester C*	4	0	**4**	**0**
2006–07	Everton	0	0		
2006–07	*Stockport Co*	11	0		
2006–07	*Wrexham*	5	0	**5**	**0**
2006–07	*Bristol C*	1	0	**1**	**0**
2007–08	Everton	0	0	**1**	**0**
2007–08	*Stockport Co*	12	0	**23**	**0**

SHEPPARD, Karl (F) 0 0
b.Shelbourne 14-2-91
Source: Scholar.

2007–08	Everton	0	0		

SINNOTT, Cory (D) 0 0
b.Liverpool 21-8-90
Source: Scholar.

2007–08	Everton	0	0		

SPENCER, Scott (F) 3 0
H: 5 11 W: 12 08 b.Manchester 1-1-89
Source: Oldham Ath Scholar.

2006–07	Everton	0	0		
2007–08	Everton	0	0		
2007–08	*Yeovil T*	0	0		
2007–08	*Macclesfield T*	3	0	**3**	**0**

STEWART, Michael (M) 0 0
b.Warrington 3-1-91
Source: Scholar.

2007–08	Everton	0	0		

STUBHAUG, Lars (G) 0 0
b.Haugesund 18-4-90
Source: Vard-Haugesund.

2006–07	Everton	0	0		
2007–08	Everton	0	0		

TURNER, Iain (G) 45 0
H: 6 3 W: 12 10 b.Stirling 26-1-84
Source: Riverside BC. *Honours:* Scotland Youth, Under-21, B.

2002–03	Stirling A	14	0	**14**	**0**
2002–03	Everton	0	0		
2003–04	Everton	0	0		
2004–05	Everton	0	0		
2004–05	*Doncaster R*	8	0	**8**	**0**
2005–06	Everton	3	0		
2005–06	*Wycombe W*	3	0	**3**	**0**
2006–07	Everton	1	0		
2006–07	*Crystal Palace*	5	0	**5**	**0**
2006–07	*Sheffield W*	11	0	**11**	**0**
2007–08	Everton	0	0	**4**	**0**

VAN DER MEYDE, Andy (M) 173 22
H: 5 10 W: 12 04 b.Arnhem 30-9-79
Honours: Holland 18 full caps, 1 goal.

1997–98	Ajax	4	0		
1998–99	Ajax	1	0		
1999–2000	Twente	32	2	**32**	**2**
2000–01	Ajax	27	3		
2001–02	Ajax	30	5		
2002–03	Ajax	29	11	**91**	**19**
2003–04	Internazionale	14	1		
2004–05	Internazionale	18	0	**32**	**1**
2005–06	Everton	10	0		
2006–07	Everton	8	0		
2007–08	Everton	0	0	**18**	**0**

VAUGHAN, James (F) 25 6
H: 5 11 W: 13 00 b.Birmingham 14-7-88
Source: Scholar. *Honours:* England Youth, Under-21.

2004–05	Everton	2	1		
2005–06	Everton	1	0		
2006–07	Everton	14	4		
2007–08	Everton	8	1	**25**	**6**

VIDARSSON, Bjarni (M) 6 1
H: 6 1 W: 11 08 b.Iceland 5-3-88
Source: Scholar. *Honours:* Iceland Youth, Under-21.

2005–06	Everton	0	0		
2006–07	Everton	0	0		
2006–07	*Bournemouth*	6	1	**6**	**1**
2007–08	*Twente*	0	0		
2007–08	Everton	0	0		

WESSELS, Stefan (G) 130 0
H: 6 2 W: 13 03 b.Rahden 28-2-79
Honours: Germany Under-21.

1999–2000	Bayern Munich	2	0		
2000–01	Bayern Munich II	18	0		
2000–01	Bayern Munich	1	0		
2001–02	Bayern Munich II	9	0		
2001–02	Bayern Munich	2	0		
2002–03	Bayern Munich	1	0	**6**	**0**
2003–04	Cologne	32	0		
2004–05	Cologne II	2	0		
2004–05	Cologne	7	0		
2005–06	Cologne	22	0		
2006–07	Cologne	32	0	**93**	**0**
2007–08	Everton	2	0	**2**	**0**

YAKUBU, Ayegbeni (F) 242 97
H: 6 0 W: 14 07 b.Benin City 22-11-82
Source: Julius Berger. *Honours:* Nigeria Under-21, Under-23, 41 full caps, 17 goals.

1999–2000	Gil Vicente	0	0		
1999–2000	Hapoel Kfar-Sava	23	6	**23**	**6**
2000–01	Maccabi Haifa	14	3		
2001–02	Maccabi Haifa	22	13	**36**	**16**
2002–03	Portsmouth	14	7		
2003–04	Portsmouth	37	16		
2004–05	Portsmouth	30	12	**81**	**35**
2005–06	Middlesbrough	34	13		
2006–07	Middlesbrough	37	12		
2007–08	Middlesbrough	2	0	**73**	**25**
2007–08	Everton	29	15	**29**	**15**

YOBO, Joseph (D) 247 8
H: 6 1 W: 13 00 b.Kano 6-9-80
Source: Mechelen. *Honours:* Nigeria B, 59 full caps, 4 goals.

1998–99	Standard Liege	0	0		
1999–2000	Standard Liege	18	0		
2000–01	Standard Liege	30	2	**48**	**2**
2001–02	Marseille	23	0	**23**	**0**
2002–03	Everton	24	0		
2003–04	Everton	28	2		
2004–05	Everton	27	0		
2005–06	Everton	29	1		
2006–07	Everton	38	2		
2007–08	Everton	30	1	**176**	**6**

Scholars
Akpan, Hope; Codling, Lewis; Jensen, Michael; McCarten, James; McCready, Thomas Richard; Powell, Luke; Redmond, Daniel Stephen

FULHAM (34)

ANDREASEN, Leon (D) 165 23
H: 6 1 W: 13 03 b.Aarhus 23-4-83
Honours: Denmark Youth, Under-20, Under-21, 10 full caps, 1 goal.

2001–02	Aarhus	17	3		
2002–03	Aarhus	32	8		
2003–04	Aarhus	25	3		
2004–05	Aarhus	31	3	**105**	**17**
2005–06	Werder Bremen	18	0		
2006–07	Werder Bremen	4	0		
2006–07	Mainz	15	4	**15**	**4**
2007–08	Werder Bremen	10	2	**32**	**2**
2007–08	Fulham	13	0	**13**	**0**

ASHTON, Nathan (D) 2 0
H: 5 8 W: 9 07 b.Plaistow 30-1-87
Source: Scholar. *Honours:* England Youth, Under-20.

2004–05	Charlton Ath	0	0		
2005–06	Charlton Ath	0	0		
2006–07	Charlton Ath	0	0		
2006–07	*Millwall*	0	0		
2007–08	Fulham	1	0	**1**	**0**
2007–08	*Crystal Palace*	1	0	**1**	**0**

BAIRD, Chris (D) 104 3
H: 5 10 W: 11 11 b.Ballymoney 25-2-82
Source: Scholar. *Honours:* Northern Ireland Youth, Under-21, 32 full caps.

2000–01	Southampton	0	0		
2001–02	Southampton	0	0		
2002–03	Southampton	3	0		
2003–04	Southampton	4	0		
2003–04	*Walsall*	10	0	**10**	**0**
2003–04	*Watford*	8	0	**8**	**0**
2004–05	Southampton	0	0		
2005–06	Southampton	17	0		
2006–07	Southampton	44	3	**68**	**3**
2007–08	Fulham	18	0	**18**	**0**

BATISTA, Ricardo (G) 38 0
H: 6 2 W: 12 06 b.Portugal 19-11-86
Source: Vitoria Setubal. *Honours:* Portugal Youth, Under-21.

2004–05	Fulham	0	0		
2005–06	Fulham	0	0		
2005–06	*Milton Keynes D*	9	0	**9**	**0**
2006–07	Fulham	0	0		
2006–07	*Wycombe W*	29	0	**29**	**0**
2007–08	Fulham	0	0		

BOCANEGRA, Carlos (D) 203 13
H: 5 11 W: 12 07 b.Alta Loma 25-5-79
Honours: USA Under-21, Under-23, 56 full caps, 8 goals.

2000	Chicago Fire	27	1		
2001	Chicago Fire	15	1		
2002	Chicago Fire	26	2		
2003	Chicago Fire	19	1	**87**	**5**
2003–04	Fulham	15	0		
2004–05	Fulham	28	1		
2005–06	Fulham	21	1		
2006–07	Fulham	30	5		
2007–08	Fulham	22	1	**116**	**8**

BOUAZZA, Hameur (F) 116 12
H: 5 10 W: 12 01 b.Evry 22-2-85
Source: Scholar. *Honours:* Algeria 5 full caps, 1 goal.

2003–04	Watford	9	1		
2004–05	Watford	28	1		
2005–06	Watford	14	1		
2005–06	*Swindon T*	13	2	**13**	**2**
2006–07	Watford	32	6	**83**	**9**
2007–08	Fulham	20	1	**20**	**1**

BRIGGS, Matthew (D) 1 0
H: 6 1 W: 11 12 b.Wandsworth 6-3-91
Source: School.

2006–07	Fulham	1	0		
2007–08	Fulham	0	0	**1**	**0**

BROOKS-MEADE, Corrin (G) 0 0
H: 6 1 W: 14 00 b.London 19-3-88
Source: Scholar.

2006–07	Fulham	0	0		
2007–08	*Darlington*	0	0		
2007–08	Fulham	0	0		

BROWN, Wayne (M) 11 1
b.Surrey 6-8-88
Source: Scholar.

2006–07	Fulham	0	0		
2007–08	Fulham	0	0		
2007–08	*Brentford*	11	1	**11**	**1**

BULLARD, Jimmy (M) 232 25
H: 5 10 W: 11 05 b.Newham 23-10-78
Source: Corinthian, Dartford, Gravesend & N.

1998–99	West Ham U	0	0		
1999–2000	West Ham U	0	0		
2000–01	West Ham U	0	0		
2001–02	Peterborough U	40	8		
2002–03	Peterborough U	26	3	**66**	**11**
2002–03	Wigan Ath	17	1		
2003–04	Wigan Ath	46	2		
2004–05	Wigan Ath	46	3		
2005–06	Wigan Ath	36	4	**145**	**10**
2005–06	Fulham	0	0		
2006–07	Fulham	4	2		
2007–08	Fulham	17	2	**21**	**4**

CHRISTANVAL, Philippe (D) 161 2
H: 6 2 W: 12 10 b.Paris 31-8-78
Honours: France Under-21, 6 full caps.

1997–98	Monaco	10	0		
1998–99	Monaco	23	1		
1999–2000	Monaco	25	0		
2000–01	Monaco	23	0	**81**	**1**
2001–02	Barcelona	26	0		
2002–03	Barcelona	5	0	**31**	**0**
2003–04	Marseille	13	0		
2004–05	Marseille	0	0	**13**	**0**
2005–06	Fulham	15	0		
2006–07	Fulham	20	1		
2007–08	Fulham	1	0	**36**	**1**

COOK, Lee (M) 207 18
H: 5 8 W: 11 10 b.Hammersmith 3-8-82
Source: Aylesbury U.

1999–2000	Watford	0	0		
2000–01	Watford	4	0		
2001–02	Watford	10	0		
2002–03	Watford	4	0		
2002–03	*York C*	7	1	**7**	**1**
2002–03	*QPR*	13	1		
2003–04	Watford	41	7	**59**	**7**
2004–05	QPR	42	2		
2005–06	QPR	40	4		
2006–07	QPR	37	3	**132**	**10**
2007–08	Fulham	0	0		
2007–08	Charlton Ath	9	0	**9**	**0**

DAVIES, Simon (M) 282 27
H: 5 10 W: 11 07 b.Haverfordwest 23-10-79
Source: Trainee. *Honours:* Wales Youth, Under-21, B, 50 full caps, 6 goals.

1997–98	Peterborough U	6	0		
1998–99	Peterborough U	43	4		
1999–2000	Peterborough U	16	2	**65**	**6**
1999–2000	Tottenham H	3	0		
2000–01	Tottenham H	13	2		
2001–02	Tottenham H	31	4		
2002–03	Tottenham H	36	5		
2003–04	Tottenham H	17	2		
2004–05	Tottenham H	21	0	**121**	**13**
2005–06	Everton	30	1		
2006–07	Everton	15	0	**45**	**1**
2006–07	Fulham	14	2		
2007–08	Fulham	37	5	**51**	**7**

DAVIS, Steve (M) 125 5
H: 5 7 W: 9 07 b.Ballymena 1-1-85
Source: Scholar. *Honours:* Northern Ireland Schools, Youth, Under-21, Under-23, 28 full caps, 1 goal.

2001–02	Aston Villa	0	0		
2002–03	Aston Villa	0	0		
2003–04	Aston Villa	0	0		
2004–05	Aston Villa	28	1		
2005–06	Aston Villa	35	4		
2006–07	Aston Villa	28	0	**91**	**5**
2007–08	*Rangers*	12	0	**12**	**0**
2007–08	Fulham	22	0	**22**	**0**

DEMPSEY, Clint (M) 123 33
H: 6 1 W: 12 02 b.Nacogdoches 9-3-83
Source: Furman Univ. *Honours:* USA Under-21, 41 full caps, 11 goals.

2004	New England Rev	24	7		
2005	New England Rev	30	11		
2006	New England Rev	23	8	**77**	**26**
2006–07	Fulham	10	1		
2007–08	Fulham	36	6	**46**	**7**

EHUI, Ismael (F) 3 0
H: 5 5 W: 10 02 b.Lille 10-12-86
Source: Scholar.

2004–05	Fulham	0	0		
2005–06	Fulham	0	0		
2005–06	*Scunthorpe U*	3	0	**3**	**0**
2006–07	Fulham	0	0		
2007–08	Fulham	0	0		

ELLIOTT, Simon (M) 193 11
H: 6 0 W: 13 02 b.Wellington 10-6-74
Source: Waterside Karori, Wellington Coll, Wellington U, Wellington Olympic AFC, Miramar R, Western Suburbs, Stanford Univ, Boston Bulldogs. *Honours:* New Zealand Under-20, Under-23, 48 full caps, 6 goals.

1999	Los Angeles G	23	2		
2000	Los Angeles G	27	5		
2001	Los Angeles G	23	1		
2002	Los Angeles G	25	1		
2003	Los Angeles G	24	1	**122**	**10**
2004	Columbus Crew	27	0		
2005	Columbus Crew	32	1	**59**	**1**
2005–06	Fulham	12	0		
2006–07	Fulham	0	0		
2007–08	Fulham	0	0	**12**	**0**

HANGELAND, Brede (D) 192 9
H: 6 4 W: 13 05 b.Houston 20-6-81
Honours: Norway Under-21, 44 full caps.

2000	Vidar	0	0		
2001	Viking	22	0		
2002	Viking	26	2		
2003	Viking	26	1		
2004	Viking	14	3		
2005	Viking	26	0	**114**	**6**
2005–06	FC Copenhagen	13	1		
2006–07	FC Copenhagen	32	0		
2007–08	FC Copenhagen	18	2	**63**	**3**
2007–08	Fulham	15	0	**15**	**0**

HEALY, David (F) 310 82
H: 5 8 W: 10 09 b.Downpatrick 5-8-79
Source: Trainee. *Honours:* Northern Ireland Schools, Youth, Under-21, B, 64 full caps, 34 goals.

1997–98	Manchester U	0	0		
1998–99	Manchester U	0	0		
1999–2000	Manchester U	0	0		
1999–2000	*Port Vale*	16	3	**16**	**3**
2000–01	Manchester U	1	0	**1**	**0**
2000–01	Preston NE	22	9		
2001–02	Preston NE	44	10		
2002–03	Preston NE	24	5		
2002–03	*Norwich C*	13	2	**13**	**2**
2003–04	Preston NE	38	15		
2004–05	Preston NE	11	5	**139**	**44**
2004–05	Leeds U	28	7		
2005–06	Leeds U	42	12		
2006–07	Leeds U	41	10	**111**	**29**
2007–08	Fulham	30	4	**30**	**4**

HUGHES, Aaron (D) 289 4
H: 6 0 W: 11 02 b.Cookstown 8-11-79
Source: Trainee. *Honours:* Northern Ireland Youth, B, 59 full caps.

1996–97	Newcastle U	0	0		
1997–98	Newcastle U	4	0		
1998–99	Newcastle U	14	0		
1999–2000	Newcastle U	27	2		
2000–01	Newcastle U	35	0		
2001–02	Newcastle U	34	0		
2002–03	Newcastle U	35	1		
2003–04	Newcastle U	34	0		
2004–05	Newcastle U	22	1	**205**	**4**
2005–06	Aston Villa	35	0		
2006–07	Aston Villa	19	0	**54**	**0**
2007–08	Fulham	30	0	**30**	**0**

JAMES, Chris (M) 0 0
H: 5 8 W: 10 12 b.New Zealand 4-7-87
Source: Scholar. *Honours:* England Youth.

2005–06	Fulham	0	0		
2006–07	Fulham	0	0		
2007–08	Fulham	0	0		

JOHN, Collins (F) 146 33
H: 5 11 W: 12 13 b.Zwandru 17-10-85
Honours: Holland Youth, Under-21, 2 full caps.

2002–03	Twente	17	2		
2003–04	Twente	18	9	**35**	**11**
2003–04	Fulham	8	4		
2004–05	Fulham	27	4		
2005–06	Fulham	35	11		
2006–07	Fulham	23	1		
2007–08	Fulham	2	0	**95**	**20**
2007–08	*Leicester C*	11	2	**11**	**2**
2007–08	*Watford*	5	0	**5**	**0**

JOHNSON, Eddie (F) 136 41
H: 6 0 W: 12 02 b.Bunnell 31-3-84
Honours: USA 34 full caps, 11 goals.

2001	Dallas Burn	10	2		
2002	Dallas Burn	14	2		
2003	Dallas Burn	22	3		
2004	Dallas Burn	26	12		
2005	Dallas Burn	15	5	**87**	**24**
2006	Kansas City Wizards19 2				
2007	Kansas City Wizards2415			**43**	**17**
2007–08	Fulham	6	0	**6**	**0**

KALLIO, Tony (D) 199 24
H: 6 4 W: 13 05 b.Tampere 9-8-78
Source: HJK Helsinki. *Honours:* Finland 38 full caps, 2 goals.

1997	Jazz	1	0	**1**	**0**
1997	Tampere U	19	1		
1998	Tampere U	19	2	**38**	**3**
1998	HJK Helsinki	9	0		
2000	HJK Helsinki	19	1		
2001	HJK Helsinki	32	5		
2002	HJK Helsinki	26	7		
2003	HJK Helsinki	0	0	**86**	**13**
2004	Molde	7	2		
2005	Molde	22	3		
2006	Molde	24	1	**53**	**6**
2006–07	Young Boys	15	0		
2007–08	Young Boys	6	2	**21**	**2**
2007–08	Fulham	0	0		

KAMARA, Diomansy (F) 200 48
H: 6 0 W: 11 05 b.Paris 8-11-80
Honours: Senegal 35 full caps, 7 goals.

1999–2000	Catanzaro	11	4		
2000–01	Catanzaro	23	5	**34**	**9**
2001–02	Chievo	0	0		
2001–02	Modena	24	4		
2002–03	Modena	29	5	**53**	**9**
2004–05	Portsmouth	25	4	**25**	**4**
2005–06	WBA	26	1		
2006–07	WBA	34	20	**60**	**21**
2007–08	Fulham	28	5	**28**	**5**

KELLER, Kasey (G) **506 0**
H: 6 1 W: 13 08 b.Washington 27-11-69
Source: Portland Univ. *Honours:* USA 102 full caps.
1991–92 Millwall 1 0
1992–93 Millwall 45 0
1993–94 Millwall 44 0
1994–95 Millwall 44 0
1995–96 Millwall 42 0 **176 0**
1996–97 Leicester C 31 0
1997–98 Leicester C 32 0
1998–99 Leicester C 36 0 **99 0**
1999–2000 Rayo Vallecano 28 0
2000–01 Rayo Vallecano 23 0 **51 0**
2001–02 Tottenham H 9 0
2002–03 Tottenham H 38 0
2003–04 Tottenham H 38 0
2004–05 Tottenham H 0 0 **85 0**
2004–05 *Southampton* 4 0 **4 0**
2004–05 Moenchengladbach 17 0
2005–06 Moenchengladbach 33 0
2006–07 Moenchengladbach 28 0 **78 0**
2007–08 Fulham 13 0 **13 0**

KONCHESKY, Paul (D) **253 6**
H: 5 10 W: 11 07 b.Barking 15-5-81
Source: Trainee. *Honours:* England Youth, Under-20, Under-21, 2 full caps.
1997–98 Charlton Ath 3 0
1998–99 Charlton Ath 2 0
1999–2000 Charlton Ath 8 0
2000–01 Charlton Ath 23 0
2001–02 Charlton Ath 34 1
2002–03 Charlton Ath 30 3
2003–04 Charlton Ath 21 0
2003–04 *Tottenham H* 12 0 **12 0**
2004–05 Charlton Ath 28 1 **149 5**
2005–06 West Ham U 37 1
2006–07 West Ham U 22 0 **59 1**
2007–08 Fulham 33 0 **33 0**

LARIBI, Karim (D) **0 0**
b.Tunisia
Source: Internazionale Academy.
2007–08 Fulham 0 0

LEIJER, Adrian (D) **61 1**
H: 6 1 W: 12 08 b.Dubbo 25-3-86
Honours: Australia Youth, Under-20, Under-23, 1 full cap.
2003–04 Melbourne Knights 20 0
2004–05 Melbourne Knights 0 0 **20 0**
2005–06 Melbourne Victory 20 1
2006–07 Melbourne Victory 21 0 **41 1**
2007–08 Fulham 0 0

LITMANEN, Jari (F) **391 161**
H: 6 0 W: 12 10 b.Lahti 20-2-71
Honours: Finland 114 full caps, 30 goals.
1987 Reipas Lahti 9 0
1988 Reipas Lahti 26 8
1989 Reipas Lahti 25 6
1990 Reipas Lahti 26 14 **86 28**
1991 HJK Helsinki 27 16 **27 16**
1992 MyPa 18 7 **18 7**
1992–93 Ajax 12 1
1993–94 Ajax 30 26
1994–95 Ajax 27 17
1995–96 Ajax 26 13
1996–97 Ajax 16 6
1997–98 Ajax 25 16
1998–99 Ajax 23 11
1999–2000 Barcelona 21 3
2000–01 Barcelona 0 0 **21 3**
2000–01 Liverpool 5 1
2001–02 Liverpool 21 4 **26 5**
2002–03 Ajax 14 5
2003–04 Ajax 6 0 **179 95**
2004 Lahti 11 3 **11 3**
2004–05 Hansa Rostock 13 1 **13 1**
2005 Malmo 2 1
2006 Malmo 8 2 **10 3**
2007–08 Fulham 0 0

McBRIDE, Brian (F) **330 100**
H: 6 0 W: 12 08 b.Chicago 19-6-72
Source: St Louis Univ. *Honours:* USA 95 full caps, 30 goals.
1994–95 Wolfsburg 12 1 **12 1**
1996 Columbus Crew 28 17
1997 Columbus Crew 13 6
1998 Columbus Crew 24 10
1999 Columbus Crew 25 5
2000 Columbus Crew 18 6
2000–01 Preston NE 9 1 **9 1**
2001 Columbus Crew 15 1
2002 Columbus Crew 14 5
2002–03 Everton 8 4 **8 4**
2003 Columbus Crew 24 12 **161 62**
2003–04 Fulham 16 4
2004–05 Fulham 31 6
2005–06 Fulham 38 9
2006–07 Fulham 38 9
2007–08 Fulham 17 4 **140 32**

MILSOM, Robert (D) **6 0**
H: 5 10 W: 11 05 b.Redhill 2-1-87
Source: Scholar.
2005–06 Fulham 0 0
2006–07 Fulham 0 0
2007–08 Fulham 0 0
2007–08 *Brentford* 6 0 **6 0**

MONCUR, T J (D) **7 0**
H: 5 10 W: 12 08 b.Hackney 23-9-87
Source: Scholar.
2005–06 Fulham 0 0
2006–07 Fulham 0 0
2007–08 Fulham 0 0
2007–08 *Bradford C* 7 0 **7 0**

MURPHY, Danny (M) **431 66**
H: 5 10 W: 11 09 b.Chester 18-3-77
Source: Trainee. *Honours:* England Schools, Youth, Under-21, 9 full caps, 1 goal.
1993–94 Crewe Alex 12 2
1994–95 Crewe Alex 35 5
1995–96 Crewe Alex 42 10
1996–97 Crewe Alex 45 10
1997–98 Liverpool 16 0
1998–99 Liverpool 1 0
1998–99 *Crewe Alex* 16 1 **150 28**
1999–2000 Liverpool 23 3
2000–01 Liverpool 27 4
2001–02 Liverpool 36 6
2002–03 Liverpool 36 7
2003–04 Liverpool 31 5 **170 25**
2004–05 Charlton Ath 38 3
2005–06 Charlton Ath 18 4 **56 7**
2005–06 Tottenham H 10 0
2006–07 Tottenham H 12 1
2007–08 Tottenham H 0 0 **22 1**
2007–08 Fulham 33 5 **33 5**

NEVLAND, Erik (F) **262 125**
H: 5 10 W: 11 12 b.Stavanger 10-11-77
Honours: Norway 6 full caps.
1996 Viking 1 0
1997 Viking 13 5
1997–98 Manchester U 1 0 **1 0**
1998 Viking 8 3
1999 IFK Gothenburg 4 0 **4 0**
2000 Viking 20 14
2001 Viking 37 18
2002 Viking 27 23
2003 Viking 25 11
2004 Viking 23 6 **154 80**
2004–05 Groningen 20 16
2005–06 Groningen 29 8
2006–07 Groningen 31 13
2007–08 Groningen 15 6 **95 43**
2007–08 Fulham 8 2 **8 2**

NIEMI, Antti (G) **419 0**
H: 6 1 W: 12 04 b.Oulu 31-5-72
Honours: Finland Youth, Under-21, 66 full caps.
1991 HJK Helsinki 2 0
1992 HJK Helsinki 28 0
1993 HJK Helsinki 24 0
1994 HJK Helsinki 24 0
1995 HJK Helsinki 24 0 **102 0**
1995–96 FC Copenhagen 17 0
1996–97 FC Copenhagen 30 0 **47 0**
1997–98 Rangers 5 0
1998–99 Rangers 7 0
1999–2000 Rangers 1 0 **13 0**
1999–2000 Hearts 17 0
2000–01 Hearts 37 0
2001–02 Hearts 32 0
2002–03 Hearts 3 0 **89 0**
2002–03 Southampton 25 0
2003–04 Southampton 28 0
2004–05 Southampton 28 0
2005–06 Southampton 25 0 **106 0**
2005–06 Fulham 9 0
2006–07 Fulham 31 0
2007–08 Fulham 22 0 **62 0**

OMOZUSI, Elliot (D) **8 0**
H: 5 11 W: 12 09 b.Hackney 15-12-88
Source: Scholar. *Honours:* England Youth.
2005–06 Fulham 0 0
2006–07 Fulham 0 0
2007–08 Fulham 8 0 **8 0**

OSEI-GYAN, King (M) **0 0**
b.Ghana 22-12-88
2006–07 Fulham 0 0
2007–08 Fulham 0 0

OWUSU, Daniel (M) **0 0**
H: 5 8 W: 10 03 b.Ghana 13-6-89
Source: Scholar.
2007–08 Fulham 0 0

PEARCE, Ian (D) **266 12**
H: 6 3 W: 15 06 b.Bury St Edmunds 7-5-74
Source: School. *Honours:* England Youth, Under-21.
1990–91 Chelsea 1 0
1991–92 Chelsea 2 0
1992–93 Chelsea 1 0
1993–94 Chelsea 0 0 **4 0**
1993–94 Blackburn R 5 1
1994–95 Blackburn R 28 0
1995–96 Blackburn R 12 1
1996–97 Blackburn R 12 0
1997–98 Blackburn R 5 0 **62 2**
1997–98 West Ham U 30 1
1998–99 West Ham U 33 2
1999–2000 West Ham U 1 0
2000–01 West Ham U 15 1
2001–02 West Ham U 9 2
2002–03 West Ham U 30 2
2003–04 West Ham U 24 1 **142 9**
2003–04 Fulham 13 0
2004–05 Fulham 11 0
2005–06 Fulham 10 0
2006–07 Fulham 22 1
2007–08 Fulham 1 0 **57 1**
2007–08 *Southampton* 1 0 **1 0**

RUNSTROM, Bjorn (F) **94 24**
H: 6 1 W: 12 08 b.Stockholm 1-3-84
Source: Bologna, Chievo, Fiorentina.
Honours: Sweden Youth, Under-21.
2004 Hammarby 25 5
2005 Hammarby 23 9
2006 Hammarby 9 4 **57 18**
2006–07 Fulham 1 0
2006–07 *Luton T* 8 2 **8 2**
2007–08 *Kaiserslautern* 28 4 **28 4**
2007–08 Fulham 0 0 **1 0**

SEOL, Ki-Hyun (F) **207 40**
H: 6 0 W: 11 07 b.South Korea 8-1-79
Honours: South Korea 77 full caps, 18 goals.
2000–01 Antwerp 25 10 **25 10**
2001–02 Anderlecht 20 3
2002–03 Anderlecht 32 12
2003–04 Anderlecht 19 3 **71 18**
2004–05 Wolverhampton W 37 4
2005–06 Wolverhampton W 32 4 **69 8**
2006–07 Reading 27 4
2007–08 Reading 3 0 **30 4**
2007–08 Fulham 12 0 **12 0**

SMERTIN, Alexei (M) **451 27**
H: 5 9 W: 10 10 b.Barnaul 1-5-75
Honours: Russia 55 full caps.
1992 Dynamo Barnaul 18 2
1993 Dynamo Barnaul 24 0 **42 2**
1994 Zarya 49 2
1995 Zarya 37 7
1996 Zarya 34 4
1997 Zarya 13 0 **133 13**
1997 Uralan 23 0
1998 Uralan 26 3 **49 3**
1999 Lokomotiv Moscow 29 6
2000 Lokomotiv Moscow 10 1 **39 7**
2000–01 Bordeaux 23 0
2001–02 Bordeaux 28 0
2002–03 Bordeaux 33 2 **84 2**
2003–04 Chelsea 0 0
2003–04 *Portsmouth* 26 0 **26 0**
2004–05 Chelsea 16 0
2005–06 Chelsea 0 0 **16 0**
2005–06 *Charlton Ath* 18 0 **18 0**
2006 Dynamo Moscow 22 0 **22 0**
2006–07 Fulham 7 0
2007–08 Fulham 15 0 **22 0**

STEFANOVIC, Dejan (D) **331 20**
H: 6 2 W: 13 01 b.Belgrade 28-10-74
Honours: Serbia-Montenegro 23 full caps.

1992–93	Red Star Belgrade	14	0		
1993–94	Red Star Belgrade	2	0		
1994–95	Red Star Belgrade	30	9	**46**	**9**
1995–96	Sheffield W	6	0		
1996–97	Sheffield W	29	2		
1997–98	Sheffield W	20	2		
1998–99	Sheffield W	11	0	**66**	**4**
1999–2000	Perugia	0	0		
1999–2000	OFK Belgrade	0	0		
1999–2000	Vitesse	14	0		
2000–01	Vitesse	27	1		
2001–02	Vitesse	25	3		
2002–03	Vitesse	28	0	**94**	**4**
2003–04	Portsmouth	32	3		
2004–05	Portsmouth	32	0		
2005–06	Portsmouth	28	0		
2006–07	Portsmouth	20	0		
2007–08	Portsmouth	0	0	**112**	**3**
2007–08	Fulham	13	0	**13**	**0**

TIMLIN, Michael (M) **38 2**
H: 5 8 W: 11 08 b.Lambeth 19-3-85
Source: Trainee. *Honours:* Eire Youth, Under-21.

2002–03	Fulham	0	0		
2003–04	Fulham	0	0		
2004–05	Fulham	0	0		
2005–06	Fulham	0	0		
2005–06	*Scunthorpe U*	1	0	**1**	**0**
2005–06	*Doncaster R*	3	0	**3**	**0**
2006–07	Fulham	0	0		
2006–07	*Swindon T*	24	1		
2007–08	Fulham	0	0		
2007–08	*Swindon T*	10	1	**34**	**2**

VOLZ, Moritz (D) **135 3**
H: 5 10 W: 11 07 b.Siegen 21-1-83
Source: Schalke. *Honours:* Germany Youth, Under-21.

1999–2000	Arsenal	0	0		
2000–01	Arsenal	0	0		
2001–02	Arsenal	0	0		
2002–03	Arsenal	0	0		
2002–03	*Wimbledon*	10	1	**10**	**1**
2003–04	Arsenal	0	0		
2003–04	Fulham	33	0		
2004–05	Fulham	31	0		
2005–06	Fulham	23	0		
2006–07	Fulham	29	2		
2007–08	Fulham	9	0	**125**	**2**

WARNER, Tony (G) **287 0**
H: 6 4 W: 15 06 b.Liverpool 11-5-74
Source: School. *Honours:* Trinidad & Tobago 1 full cap.

1993–94	Liverpool	0	0		
1994–95	Liverpool	0	0		
1995–96	Liverpool	0	0		
1996–97	Liverpool	0	0		
1997–98	Liverpool	0	0		
1997–98	*Swindon T*	2	0	**2**	**0**
1998–99	Liverpool	0	0		
1998–99	*Celtic*	3	0	**3**	**0**
1998–99	*Aberdeen*	6	0	**6**	**0**
1999–2000	Millwall	45	0		
2000–01	Millwall	35	0		
2001–02	Millwall	46	0		
2002–03	Millwall	46	0		
2003–04	Millwall	28	0	**200**	**0**
2004–05	Cardiff C	26	0		
2005–06	Cardiff C	0	0	**26**	**0**
2005–06	Fulham	18	0		
2006–07	Fulham	0	0		
2006–07	*Leeds U*	13	0	**13**	**0**
2006–07	*Norwich C*	13	0	**13**	**0**
2007–08	Fulham	3	0	**21**	**0**
2007–08	*Barnsley*	3	0	**3**	**0**

WATTS, Adam (D) **2 0**
H: 6 1 W: 11 09 b.London 4-3-88
Source: Scholar.

2006–07	Fulham	0	0		
2006–07	*Milton Keynes D*	2	0	**2**	**0**
2007–08	Fulham	0	0		

ZAKUANI, Gaby (D) **115 3**
H: 6 1 W: 12 13 b.DR Congo 31-5-86
Source: Scholar. *Honours:* DR Congo 1 full cap.

2002–03	Leyton Orient	1	0		
2003–04	Leyton Orient	10	2		
2004–05	Leyton Orient	33	0		
2005–06	Leyton Orient	43	1	**87**	**3**
2006–07	Fulham	0	0		
2006–07	*Stoke C*	9	0		
2007–08	Fulham	0	0		
2007–08	*Stoke C*	19	0	**28**	**0**

Scholars
Anderson, Joe; Bichard, Kai Courtney; Briggs, Matthew; Brown, Troy; Cumber, Lewis Perry; Etheridge, Neil; Foderingham, Wesley Andrew; Hall, Pierre; Jackson, Wayne Darren; Moscatiello, Luca; Pemberton, Donald Jeffrey; Saunders, Matthew; Smith, Lewis George; Thompson, Ashley; Wilson, Jordan Garfield

GILLINGHAM (35)

BA, George (F) **4 0**
H: 6 1 W: 13 05 b.Abidjan 24-1-79
Source: Maccabi Nethanya.

2007–08	Gillingham	4	0	**4**	**0**

BENTLEY, Mark (M) **167 18**
H: 6 2 W: 13 04 b.Hertford 7-1-78
Source: Enfield, Aldershot T, Gravesend & N, Dagenham & R.

2003–04	Southend U	21	2		
2004–05	Southend U	39	5		
2005–06	Southend U	33	5	**93**	**12**
2006–07	Gillingham	41	4		
2007–08	Gillingham	33	2	**74**	**6**

BROWN, Aaron (M) **244 18**
H: 5 10 W: 11 11 b.Bristol 14-3-80
Source: Trainee. *Honours:* England Schools.

1997–98	Bristol C	0	0		
1998–99	Bristol C	14	0		
1999–2000	Bristol C	13	2		
1999–2000	*Exeter C*	5	1	**5**	**1**
2000–01	Bristol C	35	2		
2001–02	Bristol C	36	1		
2002–03	Bristol C	32	2		
2003–04	Bristol C	30	5	**160**	**12**
2004–05	QPR	1	0		
2004–05	*Torquay U*	5	0	**5**	**0**
2005–06	QPR	2	0	**3**	**0**
2005–06	*Cheltenham T*	3	0	**3**	**0**
2005–06	Swindon T	27	2		
2006–07	Swindon T	30	2	**57**	**4**
2007–08	Gillingham	11	1	**11**	**1**

BRYANT, Tom (D) **0 0**
H: 6 2 W: 12 05 b.Chatham 7-10-88
Source: Scholar.

2007–08	Gillingham	0	0		

CLOHESSY, Sean (D) **43 1**
H: 5 11 W: 12 07 b.Croydon 12-12-86
Source: Arsenal Scholar.

2005–06	Gillingham	20	1		
2006–07	Gillingham	6	0		
2007–08	Gillingham	17	0	**43**	**1**

COGAN, Barry (F) **79 4**
H: 5 9 W: 9 0 b.Sligo 4-11-84
Source: Scholar. *Honours:* Eire Under-21.

2001–02	Millwall	0	0		
2002–03	Millwall	0	0		
2003–04	Millwall	3	0		
2004–05	Millwall	7	0		
2005–06	Millwall	14	0	**24**	**0**
2006–07	Barnet	39	3	**39**	**3**
2007–08	Gillingham	16	1	**16**	**1**

COX, Ian (D) **455 27**
H: 6 1 W: 12 08 b.Croydon 25-3-71
Source: Carshalton Ath. *Honours:* Trinidad & Tobago 16 full caps.

1993–94	Crystal Palace	0	0		
1994–95	Crystal Palace	11	0		
1995–96	Crystal Palace	4	0	**15**	**0**
1995–96	Bournemouth	8	0		
1996–97	Bournemouth	44	8		
1997–98	Bournemouth	46	3		
1998–99	Bournemouth	46	5		
1999–2000	Bournemouth	28	0	**172**	**16**
1999–2000	Burnley	17	1		
2000–01	Burnley	38	1		
2001–02	Burnley	34	2		
2002–03	Burnley	26	1	**115**	**5**
2003–04	Gillingham	33	0		
2004–05	Gillingham	31	2		
2005–06	Gillingham	36	0		
2006–07	Gillingham	33	3		
2007–08	Gillingham	20	1	**153**	**6**

CROFTS, Andrew (D) **165 17**
H: 5 10 W: 12 09 b.Chatham 29-5-84
Source: Trainee. *Honours:* Wales Youth, Under-21, 12 full caps.

2000–01	Gillingham	1	0		
2001–02	Gillingham	0	0		
2002–03	Gillingham	0	0		
2003–04	Gillingham	8	0		
2004–05	Gillingham	27	2		
2005–06	Gillingham	45	2		
2006–07	Gillingham	43	8		
2007–08	Gillingham	41	5	**165**	**17**

CULLIP, Danny (D) **358 9**
H: 6 0 W: 12 12 b.Bracknell 17-9-76
Source: Trainee.

1995–96	Oxford U	0	0		
1996–97	Fulham	29	1		
1997–98	Fulham	21	1	**50**	**2**
1997–98	Brentford	13	0		
1998–99	Brentford	2	0		
1999–2000	Brentford	0	0	**15**	**0**
1999–2000	Brighton & HA	33	2		
2000–01	Brighton & HA	38	2		
2001–02	Brighton & HA	44	0		
2002–03	Brighton & HA	44	2		
2003–04	Brighton & HA	40	1		
2004–05	Brighton & HA	18	0	**217**	**7**
2004–05	Sheffield U	11	0	**11**	**0**
2004–05	*Watford*	4	0	**4**	**0**
2005–06	Nottingham F	11	0		
2006–07	Nottingham F	20	0	**31**	**0**
2006–07	QPR	13	0		
2007–08	QPR	6	0	**19**	**0**
2007–08	Gillingham	11	0	**11**	**0**

CUMBERS, Luis (M) **7 0**
H: 6 0 W: 11 10 b.Chelmsford 6-9-88
Source: Scholar.

2006–07	Gillingham	1	0		
2007–08	Gillingham	6	0	**7**	**0**

FACEY, Delroy (F) **263 48**
H: 6 0 W: 15 02 b.Huddersfield 22-4-80
Source: Trainee.

1996–97	Huddersfield T	3	0		
1997–98	Huddersfield T	3	0		
1998–99	Huddersfield T	20	3		
1999–2000	Huddersfield T	2	0		
2000–01	Huddersfield T	34	10		
2001–02	Huddersfield T	13	2		
2002–03	Huddersfield T	0	0		
2002–03	*Bradford C*	6	1	**6**	**1**
2002–03	Bolton W	9	1		
2003–04	Bolton W	1	0	**10**	**1**
2003–04	*Burnley*	14	5	**14**	**5**
2003–04	WBA	9	0	**9**	**0**
2004–05	Hull C	21	4	**21**	**4**
2004–05	*Huddersfield T*	4	0	**79**	**15**
2004–05	Oldham Ath	6	0		
2005–06	Oldham Ath	3	0	**9**	**0**
2005–06	Tranmere R	37	8	**37**	**8**
2006–07	Rotherham U	40	10	**40**	**10**
2007–08	Gillingham	32	3	**32**	**3**
2007–08	*Wycombe W*	6	1	**6**	**1**

FREEMAN, Luke (F) **1 0**
H: 6 0 W: 10 00 b.London 22-3-92
Source: Scholar.

2007–08	Gillingham	1	0	**1**	**0**

FULLER, Barry (M) **25 1**
H: 5 10 W: 11 10 b.Ashford 25-9-84
Source: Scholar.

2004–05	Charlton Ath	0	0		
2005–06	Charlton Ath	0	0		
2005–06	*Barnet*	15	1	**15**	**1**
From Stevenage B.					
2007–08	Gillingham	10	0	**10**	**0**

GRAHAM, David (F) **282 69**
H: 5 10 W: 11 02 b.Edinburgh 6-10-78
Source: Rangers SABC. *Honours:* Scotland Under-21.

1995–96	Rangers	0	0		
1996–97	Rangers	0	0		
1997–98	Rangers	0	0		
1998–99	Rangers	3	0	**3**	**0**

1998–99 Dunfermline Ath 21 2
1999–2000 Dunfermline Ath 15 2
2000–01 Dunfermline Ath 4 0 **40 4**
2000–01 Torquay U 5 2
2001–02 Torquay U 36 8
2002–03 Torquay U 34 15
2003–04 Torquay U 45 22
2004–05 Wigan Ath 30 1
2005–06 Wigan Ath 0 0 **30 1**
2005–06 Sheffield W 24 2
2005–06 *Huddersfield T* 16 9 **16 9**
2006–07 Sheffield W 4 0 **28 2**
2006–07 *Bradford C* 22 3 **22 3**
2006–07 *Torquay U* 7 0 **127 47**
2007–08 Gillingham 16 3 **16 3**

GRIFFITHS, Leroy (F) 60 5
H: 5 11 W: 13 05 b.London 30-12-76
Source: Hampton & Richmond B.
2000–01 QPR 0 0
2001–02 QPR 30 3
2002–03 QPR 6 0
2003–04 QPR 0 0
2004–05 QPR 0 0
2005–06 QPR 0 0
2006–07 QPR 0 0 **36 3**
From Farnborough, Fisher Ath.
2007–08 Gillingham 24 2 **24 2**

HAMILTON, Marvin (D) 5 0
H: 6 0 W: 11 05 b.Leytonstone 8-10-88
Source: Scholar.
2007–08 Gillingham 5 0 **5 0**

HOWARD, Charlie (M) 1 0
H: 6 0 W: 15 00 b.London 26-11-89
Source: Scholar.
2007–08 Gillingham 1 0 **1 0**

JACK, Kelvin (G) 25 0
H: 6 3 W: 16 00 b.Trinidad 29-4-76
Honours: Holy Cross Coll, Yavapai Coll, Doc's Khelwalaas, W Connection. From San Juan. Trinidad & Tobago Under-23, 33 full caps.
2003–04 Reading 0 0
2004–05 Dundee 2 0
2005–06 Dundee 14 0 **16 0**
2006–07 Gillingham 9 0
2007–08 Gillingham 0 0 **9 0**

JACKSON, Simeon (M) 35 9
H: 5 10 W: 10 12 b.Kingston, Jamaica 28-3-87
Source: Scholar. *Honours:* Canada Youth.
2004–05 Rushden & D 3 0
2005–06 Rushden & D 14 5
2006–07 Rushden & D 0 0
2007–08 Rushden & D 0 0 **17 5**
2007–08 Gillingham 18 4 **18 4**

JUPP, Duncan (D) 277 2
H: 6 0 W: 12 12 b.Haslemere 25-1-75
Source: Trainee. *Honours:* Scotland Under-21.
1992–93 Fulham 3 0
1993–94 Fulham 30 0
1994–95 Fulham 36 2
1995–96 Fulham 36 0 **105 2**
1996–97 Wimbledon 6 0
1997–98 Wimbledon 3 0
1998–99 Wimbledon 6 0
1999–2000 Wimbledon 9 0
2000–01 Wimbledon 4 0
2001–02 Wimbledon 2 0
2002–03 Wimbledon 0 0 **30 0**
2002–03 *Notts Co* 8 0 **8 0**
2002–03 Luton T 5 0 **5 0**
2003–04 Southend U 40 0
2004–05 Southend U 31 0
2005–06 Southend U 29 0 **100 0**
2006–07 Gillingham 27 0
2007–08 Gillingham 2 0 **29 0**

KING, Simon (D) 121 2
H: 6 0 W: 13 00 b.Oxford 11-4-83
Source: Scholar.
2000–01 Oxford U 2 0
2001–02 Oxford U 2 0
2002–03 Oxford U 0 0
2003–04 Oxford U 0 0
2004–05 Oxford U 0 0 **4 0**
2005–06 Barnet 32 0
2006–07 Barnet 43 2 **75 2**
2007–08 Gillingham 42 0 **42 0**

LEWIS, Stuart (M) 14 0
H: 5 10 W: 11 06 b.Welwyn 15-10-87
Source: Scholar. *Honours:* England Youth.
2005–06 Tottenham H 0 0
2006–07 Tottenham H 0 0
2006–07 Barnet 4 0 **4 0**
From Stevenage B.
2007–08 Gillingham 10 0 **10 0**

LOMAS, Steve (M) 361 20
H: 6 0 W: 12 08 b.Hanover 18-1-74
Source: Trainee. *Honours:* Northern Ireland Schools, Youth, B, 45 full caps, 3 goals.
1991–92 Manchester C 0 0
1992–93 Manchester C 0 0
1993–94 Manchester C 23 0
1994–95 Manchester C 20 2
1995–96 Manchester C 33 3
1996–97 Manchester C 35 3 **111 8**
1996–97 West Ham U 7 0
1997–98 West Ham U 33 2
1998–99 West Ham U 30 1
1999–2000 West Ham U 25 1
2000–01 West Ham U 20 1
2001–02 West Ham U 15 4
2002–03 West Ham U 29 0
2003–04 West Ham U 5 0
2004–05 West Ham U 23 1
2005–06 West Ham U 0 0 **187 10**
2005–06 QPR 21 0
2006–07 QPR 34 2 **55 2**
2007–08 Gillingham 8 0 **8 0**

MILLER, Adam (M) 45 3
H: 5 11 W: 11 06 b.Hemel Hempstead 19-2-82
Source: Aldershot T.
2004–05 QPR 14 0
2005–06 QPR 1 0 **15 0**
2005–06 *Peterborough U* 2 0 **2 0**
From Stevenage B
2007–08 Gillingham 28 3 **28 3**

MULLIGAN, Gary (M) 105 17
H: 6 1 W: 12 03 b.Dublin 23-4-85
Source: Scholar.
2002–03 Wolverhampton W 0 0
2003–04 Wolverhampton W 0 0
2004–05 Wolverhampton W 1 0 **1 0**
2004–05 *Rushden & D* 13 3 **13 3**
2005–06 Sheffield U 0 0
2005–06 *Port Vale* 10 1 **10 1**
2005–06 *Gillingham* 13 1
2006–07 Gillingham 38 7
2007–08 Gillingham 30 5 **81 13**

NUTTER, John (D) 25 1
H: 6 2 W: 12 10 b.Taplow 13-6-82
Source: Blackburn R Scholar.
2000–01 Wycombe W 1 0
2001–02 Wycombe W 0 0
2007–08 Wycombe W 0 0 **1 0**
From Ald'shot T, Grays Ath, Stevenage B
2007–08 Gillingham 24 1 **24 1**

OLI, Dennis (F) 50 5
H: 6 0 W: 12 00 b.Newham 28-1-84
2001–02 QPR 2 0
2002–03 QPR 18 0
2003–04 QPR 3 0 **23 0**
2004–05 Swansea C 1 0 **1 0**
2004–05 Cambridge U 4 1
2005–06 Cambridge U 0 0
2006–07 Cambridge U 0 0 **4 1**
From Grays Ath.
2007–08 Gillingham 22 4 **22 4**

PUGH, Andy (F) 5 0
H: 5 9 W: 12 02 b.Gravesend 28-1-89
Source: Scholar.
2006–07 Gillingham 3 0
2007–08 Gillingham 2 0 **5 0**

RICHARDS, Garry (D) 54 3
H: 6 3 W: 13 00 b.Romford 11-6-86
Source: Scholar.
2005–06 Colchester U 15 0
2006–07 Colchester U 5 1 **20 1**
2006–07 *Brentford* 10 1 **10 1**
2007–08 Southend U 10 0 **10 0**
2007–08 Gillingham 14 1 **14 1**

ROYCE, Simon (G) 300 0
H: 6 2 W: 12 10 b.Forest Gate 9-9-71
Source: Heybridge Swifts.
1991–92 Southend U 1 0
1992–93 Southend U 3 0
1993–94 Southend U 6 0
1994–95 Southend U 13 0
1995–96 Southend U 46 0
1996–97 Southend U 43 0
1997–98 Southend U 37 0 **149 0**
1998–99 Charlton Ath 8 0
1999–2000 Charlton Ath 0 0
2000–01 Leicester C 19 0
2001–02 Leicester C 0 0
2001–02 *Brighton & HA* 6 0 **6 0**
2001–02 *Manchester C* 0 0
2002–03 Leicester C 0 0 **19 0**
2002–03 *QPR* 16 0
2003–04 Charlton Ath 1 0
2004–05 Charlton Ath 0 0 **9 0**
2004–05 *Luton T* 2 0 **2 0**
2004–05 *QPR* 13 0
2005–06 QPR 30 0
2006–07 QPR 20 0 **79 0**
2006–07 *Gillingham* 3 0
2007–08 Gillingham 33 0 **36 0**

SODJE, Efe (D) 351 20
H: 6 1 W: 12 00 b.Greenwich 5-10-72
Source: Delta Steel Pioneer, Stevenage Bor. *Honours:* Nigeria 9 full caps, 1 goal.
1997–98 Macclesfield T 41 3
1998–99 Macclesfield T 42 3 **83 6**
1999–2000 Luton T 9 0 **9 0**
1999–2000 Colchester U 3 0 **3 0**
2000–01 Crewe Alex 32 0
2001–02 Crewe Alex 36 2
2002–03 Crewe Alex 30 1 **98 3**
2003–04 Huddersfield T 39 4
2004–05 Huddersfield T 28 1 **67 5**
2004–05 Yeovil T 6 2
2005–06 Yeovil T 19 1 **25 3**
2005–06 Southend U 13 1
2006–07 Southend U 24 1 **37 2**
2007–08 Gillingham 13 0 **13 0**
2007–08 *Bury* 16 1 **16 1**

SOUTHALL, Nicky (M) 598 63
H: 5 11 W: 12 04 b.Stockton 28-1-72
Source: Trainee.
1990–91 Hartlepool U 0 0
1991–92 Hartlepool U 22 3
1992–93 Hartlepool U 39 6
1993–94 Hartlepool U 40 9
1994–95 Hartlepool U 37 6 **138 24**
1995–96 Grimsby T 33 2
1996–97 Grimsby T 34 3
1997–98 Grimsby T 5 0 **72 5**
1997–98 Gillingham 23 2
1998–99 Gillingham 42 4
1999–2000 Gillingham 45 9
2000–01 Gillingham 44 2
2001–02 Bolton W 18 1
2002–03 Bolton W 0 0 **18 1**
2002–03 *Norwich C* 9 0 **9 0**
2002–03 Gillingham 24 1
2003–04 Gillingham 35 0
2004–05 Gillingham 33 1
2005–06 Nottingham F 40 8
2006–07 Nottingham F 27 5 **67 13**
2006–07 Gillingham 15 0
2007–08 Gillingham 33 1 **294 20**

STILLIE, Derek (G) 244 0
H: 6 0 W: 12 07 b.Cumnock 3-12-73
Source: Notts Co. *Honours:* Scotland Under-21.
1991–92 Aberdeen 0 0
1992–93 Aberdeen 0 0
1993–94 Aberdeen 5 0
1994–95 Aberdeen 0 0
1995–96 Aberdeen 0 0
1996–97 Aberdeen 8 0
1997–98 Aberdeen 2 0
1998–99 Aberdeen 8 0 **23 0**
1999–2000 Wigan Ath 13 0
2000–01 Wigan Ath 18 0
2001–02 Wigan Ath 13 0 **44 0**
2002–03 Dunfermline Ath 21 0
2003–04 Dunfermline Ath 37 0
2004–05 Dunfermline Ath 38 0 **96 0**
2005–06 Dundee U 30 0

2006–07 Dundee U 37 0 **67 0**
2007–08 Gillingham 14 0 **14 0**

STONE, Craig (M) 21 0
H: 6 1 W: 12 05 b.Rochester 29-12-88
Source: Scholar.
2005–06 Gillingham 3 0
2006–07 Gillingham 3 0
2007–08 Gillingham 9 0 **15 0**
2007–08 *Brentford* 6 0 **6 0**

THURGOOD, Stuart (M) 91 1
H: 5 8 W: 12 03 b.Enfield 4-11-81
From Shimizu S-Pulse
2000–01 Southend U 13 1
2001–02 Southend U 39 0
2002–03 Southend U 27 0
2003–04 Southend U 0 0 **79 1**
From Grays Ath
2007–08 Gillingham 12 0 **12 0**

GRIMSBY T (36)

BARNES, Phil (G) 238 0
H: 6 1 W: 11 01 b.Sheffield 2-3-79
Source: Trainee.
1996–97 Rotherham U 2 0 **2 0**
1997–98 Blackpool 1 0
1998–99 Blackpool 1 0
1999–2000 Blackpool 12 0
2000–01 Blackpool 34 0
2001–02 Blackpool 30 0
2002–03 Blackpool 44 0
2003–04 Blackpool 19 0 **141 0**
2004–05 Sheffield U 1 0
2004–05 *Torquay U* 5 0 **5 0**
2005–06 Sheffield U 0 0 **1 0**
2005–06 *QPR* 1 0 **1 0**
2006–07 Grimsby T 46 0
2007–08 Grimsby T 42 0 **88 0**

BENNETT, Ryan (M) 45 1
H: 6 2 W: 11 00 b.Orsett 6-3-90
Source: Scholar. *Honours:* England Youth.
2006–07 Grimsby T 5 0
2007–08 Grimsby T 40 1 **45 1**

BIRD, Matthew (D) 2 0
H: 6 0 W: 11 07 b.Grimsby 31-10-90
Source: Scholar.
2007–08 Grimsby T 2 0 **2 0**

BOLLAND, Paul (M) 302 19
H: 5 10 W: 10 12 b.Bradford 23-12-79
Source: Trainee.
1997–98 Bradford C 10 0
1998–99 Bradford C 2 0 **12 0**
1998–99 Notts Co 13 0
1999–2000 Notts Co 25 1
2000–01 Notts Co 7 0
2001–02 Notts Co 19 0
2002–03 Notts Co 29 3
2003–04 Notts Co 39 1
2004–05 Notts Co 40 1 **172 6**
2005–06 Grimsby T 44 4
2006–07 Grimsby T 39 5
2007–08 Grimsby T 35 4 **118 13**

BORE, Peter (M) 49 10
H: 5 11 W: 11 04 b.Grimsby 4-11-87
Source: Scholar.
2006–07 Grimsby T 32 8
2007–08 Grimsby T 17 2 **49 10**

BOSHELL, Danny (M) 178 11
H: 5 11 W: 11 09 b.Bradford 30-5-81
Source: Trainee.
1998–99 Oldham Ath 0 0
1999–2000 Oldham Ath 8 0
2000–01 Oldham Ath 18 1
2001–02 Oldham Ath 4 0
2002–03 Oldham Ath 2 0
2003–04 Oldham Ath 22 0
2004–05 Oldham Ath 16 1 **70 2**
2004–05 *Bury* 6 0 **6 0**
2005–06 Stockport Co 33 1 **33 1**
2006–07 Grimsby T 29 2
2007–08 Grimsby T 40 6 **69 8**

BUTLER, Martin (F) 447 127
H: 5 11 W: 11 09 b.Wordsley 15-9-74
Source: Trainee.
1993–94 Walsall 15 3
1994–95 Walsall 8 0
1995–96 Walsall 28 4
1996–97 Walsall 23 1
1997–98 Cambridge U 31 10
1998–99 Cambridge U 46 17
1999–2000 Cambridge U 26 14 **103 41**
1999–2000 Reading 17 4
2000–01 Reading 45 24
2001–02 Reading 17 2
2002–03 Reading 21 2
2003–04 Reading 3 0 **103 32**
2003–04 Rotherham U 37 15
2004–05 Rotherham U 21 6
2005–06 Rotherham U 39 7 **97 28**
2006–07 Walsall 44 11
2007–08 Walsall 5 1 **123 20**
2007–08 Grimsby T 21 6 **21 6**

CLARKE, Jamie (D) 178 7
H: 6 2 W: 12 03 b.Sunderland 18-9-82
Source: Scholar.
2001–02 Mansfield T 1 0
2002–03 Mansfield T 21 1
2003–04 Mansfield T 12 0 **34 1**
2004–05 Rochdale 41 1
2005–06 Rochdale 22 0 **63 1**
2005–06 Boston U 15 1
2006–07 Boston U 37 2 **52 3**
2007–08 Grimsby T 29 2 **29 2**

FENTON, Nick (D) 339 19
H: 6 0 W: 10 02 b.Preston 23-11-79
Source: Trainee. *Honours:* England Youth.
1996–97 Manchester C 0 0
1997–98 Manchester C 0 0
1998–99 Manchester C 15 0
1999–2000 Manchester C 0 0
1999–2000 *Notts Co* 13 1
1999–2000 *Bournemouth* 8 0
2000–01 Manchester C 0 0 **15 0**
2000–01 *Bournemouth* 5 0 **13 0**
2000–01 Notts Co 30 2
2001–02 Notts Co 42 3
2002–03 Notts Co 40 3
2003–04 Notts Co 43 1 **168 10**
2004–05 Doncaster R 38 1
2005–06 Doncaster R 25 2
2006–07 Doncaster R 0 0 **63 3**
2006–07 Grimsby T 38 4
2007–08 Grimsby T 42 2 **80 6**

HEGARTY, Nick (M) 48 4
H: 5 10 W: 11 00 b.Hemsworth 25-6-86
Source: Scholar.
2004–05 Grimsby T 1 0
2005–06 Grimsby T 2 0
2006–07 Grimsby T 15 0
2007–08 Grimsby T 30 4 **48 4**

HUNT, James (M) 418 20
H: 5 8 W: 10 03 b.Derby 17-12-76
Source: Trainee.
1994–95 Notts Co 0 0
1995–96 Notts Co 10 1
1996–97 Notts Co 9 0 **19 1**
1997–98 Northampton T 21 0
1998–99 Northampton T 35 2
1999–2000 Northampton T 37 1
2000–01 Northampton T 41 1
2001–02 Northampton T 38 4 **172 8**
2002–03 Oxford U 39 1
2003–04 Oxford U 41 2 **80 3**
2004–05 Bristol R 41 4
2005–06 Bristol R 40 1
2006–07 Bristol R 14 1 **95 6**
2006–07 *Grimsby T* 15 2
2007–08 Grimsby T 37 0 **52 2**

JARMAN, Nathan (F) 24 0
H: 5 11 W: 11 03 b.Scunthorpe 19-9-86
Source: Scholar.
2004–05 Barnsley 6 0
2005–06 Barnsley 9 0
2005–06 *Bury* 2 0 **2 0**
2006–07 Barnsley 0 0
2007–08 Barnsley 0 0 **15 0**
2007–08 Grimsby T 7 0 **7 0**

JONES, Gary (M) 421 71
H: 6 3 W: 15 02 b.Chester 10-5-75
Source: Trainee.
1993–94 Tranmere R 6 2
1994–95 Tranmere R 19 3
1995–96 Tranmere R 23 1
1996–97 Tranmere R 30 6
1997–98 Tranmere R 43 8
1998–99 Tranmere R 26 5
1999–2000 Tranmere R 31 3
2000–01 Nottingham F 31 1
2001–02 Nottingham F 5 1
2002–03 Nottingham F 0 0 **36 2**
2002–03 Tranmere R 40 6
2003–04 Tranmere R 42 9
2004–05 Tranmere R 10 1 **270 44**
2005–06 Grimsby T 40 13
2006–07 Grimsby T 39 8
2007–08 Grimsby T 36 4 **115 25**

MONTGOMERY, Gary (G) 50 0
H: 5 11 W: 13 08 b.Leamington Spa 8-10-82
Source: Scholar.
2000–01 Coventry C 0 0
2001–02 Coventry C 0 0
2001–02 *Crewe Alex* 0 0
2001–02 *Kidderminster H* 2 0 **2 0**
2002–03 Coventry C 8 0 **8 0**
2003–04 Rotherham U 4 0
2004–05 Rotherham U 1 0
2005–06 Rotherham U 24 0
2006–07 Rotherham U 6 0 **35 0**
2007–08 Grimsby T 5 0 **5 0**

MURRAY, Robert (M) 0 0
H: 5 8 W: 9 00 b.Leamington Spa 11-7-88
Source: Scholar.
2004–05 Grimsby T 0 0
2005–06 Grimsby T 0 0
2006–07 Grimsby T 0 0
2007–08 Grimsby T 0 0

NEWEY, Tom (D) 206 7
H: 5 10 W: 10 02 b.Sheffield 31-10-82
Source: Scholar.
2000–01 Leeds U 0 0
2001–02 Leeds U 0 0
2002–03 Leeds U 0 0
2002–03 *Cambridge U* 6 0
2002–03 *Darlington* 7 1 **7 1**
2003–04 Leyton Orient 34 2
2004–05 Leyton Orient 20 1 **54 3**
2004–05 *Cambridge U* 16 0 **22 0**
2005–06 Grimsby T 38 1
2006–07 Grimsby T 43 1
2007–08 Grimsby T 42 1 **123 3**

NORTH, Danny (F) 49 15
H: 5 9 W: 12 08 b.Grimsby 7-9-87
Source: Scholar.
2004–05 Grimsby T 1 0
2005–06 Grimsby T 1 0
2006–07 Grimsby T 20 6
2007–08 Grimsby T 27 9 **49 15**

RANKIN, Isiah (F) 256 44
H: 5 10 W: 11 00 b.London 22-5-78
Source: Trainee.
1995–96 Arsenal 0 0
1996–97 Arsenal 0 0
1997–98 Arsenal 1 0 **1 0**
1997–98 *Colchester U* 11 5 **11 5**
1998–99 Bradford C 27 4
1999–2000 Bradford C 9 0
1999–2000 *Birmingham C* 13 4 **13 4**
2000–01 Bradford C 1 0 **37 4**
2000–01 *Bolton W* 16 2 **16 2**
2000–01 Barnsley 9 1
2001–02 Barnsley 9 1
2002–03 Barnsley 9 1
2003–04 Barnsley 20 5 **47 8**
2003–04 Grimsby T 12 4
2004–05 Brentford 41 8
2005–06 Brentford 37 7 **78 15**
2006–07 Grimsby T 20 2
2006–07 *Macclesfield T* 4 0 **4 0**
2007–08 Grimsby T 17 0 **49 6**

TAYLOR, Andy (F) 37 7
H: 6 2 W: 13 00 b.Caistor 30-10-88
Source: Scholar.
2005–06 Grimsby T 0 0
2006–07 Grimsby T 11 2
2007–08 Grimsby T 26 5 **37 7**

TILL, Peter (M) 84 3
H: 5 11 W: 11 04 b.Walsall 7-9-85
Source: Scholar.
2005–06 Birmingham C 0 0
2005–06 *Scunthorpe U* 8 0 **8 0**

2005–06 *Boston U* 16 1 **16 1**
2006–07 Birmingham C 0 0
2006–07 *Leyton Orient* 4 0 **4 0**
2006–07 Grimsby T 22 0
2007–08 Grimsby T 34 2 **56 2**

TONER, Ciaran (M) 181 18
H: 6 1 W: 12 02 b.Craigavon 30-6-81
Source: Trainee. *Honours:* Northern Ireland Schools, Youth, Under-21, 2 full caps.
1999–2000 Tottenham H 0 0
2000–01 Tottenham H 0 0
2001–02 Tottenham H 0 0
2001–02 *Peterborough U* 6 0 **6 0**
2001–02 Bristol R 6 0 **6 0**
2001–02 Leyton Orient 0 0
2002–03 Leyton Orient 25 1
2003–04 Leyton Orient 27 1 **52 2**
2004–05 Lincoln C 15 2 **15 2**
2004–05 *Cambridge U* 8 0 **8 0**
2005–06 Grimsby T 31 3
2006–07 Grimsby T 33 8
2007–08 Grimsby T 30 3 **94 14**

WHITTLE, Justin (D) 399 6
H: 6 1 W: 12 12 b.Derby 18-3-71
Source: Celtic.
1994–95 Stoke C 0 0
1995–96 Stoke C 8 0
1996–97 Stoke C 37 0
1997–98 Stoke C 20 0
1998–99 Stoke C 14 1 **79 1**
1998–99 Hull C 24 1
1999–2000 Hull C 38 0
2000–01 Hull C 38 0
2001–02 Hull C 36 0
2002–03 Hull C 39 1
2003–04 Hull C 18 0 **193 2**
2004–05 Grimsby T 40 1
2005–06 Grimsby T 32 0
2006–07 Grimsby T 37 1
2007–08 Grimsby T 18 1 **127 3**

HARTLEPOOL U (37)

ALLISON, Scott (G) 0 0
H: 6 1 W: 13 05 b.Guisborough 3-11-87
2007–08 Hartlepool U 0 0

BARKER, Richard (F) 413 109
H: 6 0 W: 14 03 b.Sheffield 30-5-75
Source: Trainee. *Honours:* England Schools.
1993–94 Sheffield W 0 0
1994–95 Sheffield W 0 0
1995–96 Sheffield W 0 0
1995–96 *Doncaster R* 6 0 **6 0**
1996–97 Sheffield W 0 0
From Linfield
1997–98 Brighton & HA 17 2
1998–99 Brighton & HA 43 10 **60 12**
1999–2000 Macclesfield T 35 16
2000–01 Macclesfield T 23 7 **58 23**
2000–01 Rotherham U 19 1
2001–02 Rotherham U 35 3
2002–03 Rotherham U 37 7
2003–04 Rotherham U 32 1
2004–05 Rotherham U 17 0 **140 12**
2004–05 Mansfield T 28 10
2005–06 Mansfield T 43 18
2006–07 Mansfield T 24 12 **95 40**
2006–07 Hartlepool U 18 9
2007–08 Hartlepool U 36 13 **54 22**

BARRON, Micky (D) 328 3
H: 5 11 W: 11 10 b.Chester-le-Street 22-12-74
Source: Trainee.
1992–93 Middlesbrough 0 0
1993–94 Middlesbrough 2 0
1994–95 Middlesbrough 0 0
1995–96 Middlesbrough 1 0
1996–97 Middlesbrough 0 0 **3 0**
1996–97 *Hartlepool U* 16 0
1997–98 Hartlepool U 33 0
1998–99 Hartlepool U 38 1
1999–2000 Hartlepool U 40 0
2000–01 Hartlepool U 28 0
2001–02 Hartlepool U 39 1
2002–03 Hartlepool U 42 0
2003–04 Hartlepool U 32 1
2004–05 Hartlepool U 13 0
2005–06 Hartlepool U 15 0
2006–07 Hartlepool U 29 0
2007–08 Hartlepool U 0 0 **325 3**

BOLAND, Willie (M) 333 3
H: 5 9 W: 12 04 b.Ennis 6-8-75
Source: Trainee. *Honours:* Eire Youth, B, Under-21.
1992–93 Coventry C 1 0
1993–94 Coventry C 27 0
1994–95 Coventry C 12 0
1995–96 Coventry C 3 0
1996–97 Coventry C 1 0
1997–98 Coventry C 19 0
1998–99 Coventry C 0 0 **63 0**
1999–2000 Cardiff C 28 1
2000–01 Cardiff C 25 1
2001–02 Cardiff C 42 1
2002–03 Cardiff C 41 0
2003–04 Cardiff C 37 0
2004–05 Cardiff C 21 0
2005–06 Cardiff C 15 0 **209 3**
2006–07 Hartlepool U 27 0
2007–08 Hartlepool U 34 0 **61 0**

BROWN, James (F) 75 17
H: 5 11 W: 11 00 b.Newcastle 3-1-87
Source: Cramlington Jun.
2004–05 Hartlepool U 0 0
2005–06 Hartlepool U 4 1
2006–07 Hartlepool U 36 6
2007–08 Hartlepool U 35 10 **75 17**

BUDTZ, Jan (G) 59 0
H: 6 0 W: 13 05 b.Denmark 20-4-79
Source: B1909 Odense.
2004–05 Nordsjaelland 0 0
2005–06 Doncaster R 20 0
2006–07 Doncaster R 7 0 **27 0**
2006–07 *Wolverhampton W* 4 0 **4 0**
2007–08 Hartlepool U 28 0 **28 0**

CLARK, Ben (D) 124 4
H: 6 1 W: 13 11 b.Shotley Bridge 24-1-83
Source: Manchester U Trainee. *Honours:* England Youth, Under-20.
2000–01 Sunderland 0 0
2001–02 Sunderland 0 0
2002–03 Sunderland 1 0
2003–04 Sunderland 5 0
2004–05 Sunderland 2 0 **8 0**
2004–05 Hartlepool U 25 0
2005–06 Hartlepool U 32 0
2006–07 Hartlepool U 40 3
2007–08 Hartlepool U 19 1 **116 4**

COLLINS, Sam (D) 291 15
H: 6 2 W: 14 03 b.Pontefract 5-6-77
Source: Trainee.
1994–95 Huddersfield T 0 0
1995–96 Huddersfield T 0 0
1996–97 Huddersfield T 4 0
1997–98 Huddersfield T 10 0
1998–99 Huddersfield T 23 0 **37 0**
1999–2000 Bury 19 0
2000–01 Bury 34 2
2001–02 Bury 29 0 **82 2**
2002–03 Port Vale 44 5
2003–04 Port Vale 43 4
2004–05 Port Vale 33 2
2005–06 Port Vale 15 0 **135 11**
2005–06 Hull C 17 0
2006–07 Hull C 6 0
2007–08 Hull C 0 0 **23 0**
2007–08 *Swindon T* 4 0 **4 0**
2007–08 Hartlepool U 10 2 **10 2**

ELLIOTT, Robbie (D) 257 16
H: 5 10 W: 10 12 b.Gosforth 25-12-73
Source: Trainee. *Honours:* England Youth, Under-21.
1990–91 Newcastle U 6 0
1991–92 Newcastle U 9 0
1992–93 Newcastle U 0 0
1993–94 Newcastle U 15 0
1994–95 Newcastle U 14 2
1995–96 Newcastle U 6 0
1996–97 Newcastle U 29 7
1997–98 Bolton W 4 0
1998–99 Bolton W 22 0
1999–2000 Bolton W 27 3
2000–01 Bolton W 33 2 **86 5**
2001–02 Newcastle U 27 1
2002–03 Newcastle U 2 0
2003–04 Newcastle U 0 0
2004–05 Newcastle U 17 1
2005–06 Newcastle U 17 0 **142 11**
2006–07 Sunderland 7 0 **7 0**
2006–07 Leeds U 7 0 **7 0**
2007–08 Hartlepool U 15 0 **15 0**

FOLEY, David (F) 73 0
H: 5 4 W: 8 09 b.South Shields 12-5-87
Source: Scholar.
2003–04 Hartlepool U 1 0
2004–05 Hartlepool U 2 0
2005–06 Hartlepool U 11 0
2006–07 Hartlepool U 25 0
2007–08 Hartlepool U 34 0 **73 0**

GIBB, Ali (M) 400 6
H: 5 9 W: 11 07 b.Salisbury 17-2-76
Source: Trainee.
1994–95 Norwich C 0 0
1995–96 Norwich C 0 0
1995–96 Northampton T 23 2
1996–97 Northampton T 18 1
1997–98 Northampton T 35 1
1998–99 Northampton T 41 0
1999–2000 Northampton T 14 0 **131 4**
1999–2000 Stockport Co 14 0
2000–01 Stockport Co 39 0
2001–02 Stockport Co 41 0
2002–03 Stockport Co 45 1
2003–04 Stockport Co 26 0 **165 1**
2003–04 Bristol R 8 1
2004–05 Bristol R 23 0
2005–06 Bristol R 33 0 **64 1**
2006–07 Hartlepool U 25 0
2007–08 Hartlepool U 6 0 **31 0**
2007–08 *Notts Co* 9 0 **9 0**

HAIGH, Tom (M) 0 0
H: 6 0 W: 11 01 b.Sunderland 15-10-88
Source: Scholar.
2007–08 Hartlepool U 0 0

HUMPHREYS, Richie (M) 409 41
H: 5 11 W: 12 07 b.Sheffield 30-11-77
Source: Trainee. *Honours:* England Youth, Under-21.
1995–96 Sheffield W 5 0
1996–97 Sheffield W 29 3
1997–98 Sheffield W 7 0
1998–99 Sheffield W 19 1
1999–2000 Sheffield W 0 0
1999–2000 *Scunthorpe U* 6 2 **6 2**
1999–2000 *Cardiff C* 9 2 **9 2**
2000–01 Sheffield W 7 0 **67 4**
2000–01 Cambridge U 7 3 **7 3**
2001–02 Hartlepool U 46 5
2002–03 Hartlepool U 46 11
2003–04 Hartlepool U 46 3
2004–05 Hartlepool U 46 3
2005–06 Hartlepool U 46 2
2006–07 Hartlepool U 38 3
2006–07 *Port Vale* 7 0 **7 0**
2007–08 Hartlepool U 45 3 **313 30**

LEE-BARRETT, Arran (G) 18 0
H: 6 2 W: 14 01 b.Ipswich 28-2-84
Source: Norwich C Scholar.
2002–03 Cardiff C 0 0
2003–04 Cardiff C 0 0
2004–05 Cardiff C 0 0
2005–06 Cardiff C 0 0
From Weymouth
2006–07 Coventry C 0 0
2007–08 Hartlepool U 18 0 **18 0**

LIDDLE, Gary (D) 83 5
H: 6 1 W: 12 06 b.Middlesbrough 15-6-86
Source: Trainee. *Honours:* England Youth.
2003–04 Middlesbrough 0 0
2004–05 Middlesbrough 0 0
2005–06 Middlesbrough 0 0
2006–07 Hartlepool U 42 3
2007–08 Hartlepool U 41 2 **83 5**

MACKAY, Michael (F) 25 5
H: 6 0 W: 11 06 b.Durham 11-10-82
Source: Consett.
2006–07 Hartlepool U 1 0
2007–08 Hartlepool U 24 5 **25 5**

MAIDENS (DECEASED), Michael (M)25 1
H: 5 11 W: 11 04 b.Middlesbrough 7-5-87
Source: Scholar.
2004–05 Hartlepool U 1 0
2005–06 Hartlepool U 20 1

2006–07 Hartlepool U 4 0
2007–08 Hartlepool U 0 0 **25 1**

McCUNNIE, Jamie (D) 188 1
H: 5 10 W: 10 11 b.Airdrie 15-4-83
Source: Dundee U BC. *Honours:* Scotland Under-21.
2000–01 Dundee U 15 0
2001–02 Dundee U 28 0
2002–03 Dundee U 18 0 **61 0**
2003–04 Ross Co 35 0
2004–05 Ross Co 27 0 **62 0**
2005–06 Dunfermline Ath 22 0
2006–07 Dunfermline Ath 14 0 **36 0**
2007–08 Hartlepool U 29 1 **29 1**

MONKHOUSE, Andy (M) 189 20
H: 6 1 W: 11 06 b.Leeds 23-10-80
Source: Trainee.
1998–99 Rotherham U 5 1
1999–2000 Rotherham U 0 0
2000–01 Rotherham U 12 0
2001–02 Rotherham U 38 2
2002–03 Rotherham U 20 0
2003–04 Rotherham U 27 3
2004–05 Rotherham U 14 2
2005–06 Rotherham U 12 1 **128 9**
2006–07 Swindon T 10 2 **10 2**
2006–07 Hartlepool U 26 7
2007–08 Hartlepool U 25 2 **51 9**

NELSON, Michael (D) 285 17
H: 6 2 W: 13 03 b.Gateshead 15-3-82
Source: Bishop Auckland.
2000–01 Bury 2 1
2001–02 Bury 31 2
2002–03 Bury 39 5 **72 8**
2003–04 Hartlepool U 40 3
2004–05 Hartlepool U 43 1
2005–06 Hartlepool U 43 2
2006–07 Hartlepool U 42 1
2007–08 Hartlepool U 45 2 **213 9**

PORTER, Joel (F) 243 69
H: 5 9 W: 11 13 b.Adelaide 25-12-78
Honours: Australia 4 full caps, 5 goals.
1998–99 West Adelaide 20 3 **20 3**
2000–01 Melbrne Knights 30 12
2001–02 Melbrne Knights 26 12 **56 24**
2002–03 Sydney Olympic 32 8 **32 8**
2003–04 Hartlepool U 27 3
2004–05 Hartlepool U 39 14
2005–06 Hartlepool U 8 3
2006–07 Hartlepool U 22 5
2007–08 Hartlepool U 39 9 **135 34**

RAE, Michael (F) 0 0
H: 5 10 W: 12 04 b.North Cleveland 23-10-87
Source: Scholar.
2006–07 Hartlepool U 0 0
2007–08 Hartlepool U 0 0

ROBSON, Matty (D) 106 7
H: 5 10 W: 11 02 b.Durham 23-1-85
Source: Scholar.
2002–03 Hartlepool U 0 0
2003–04 Hartlepool U 23 1
2004–05 Hartlepool U 27 2
2005–06 Hartlepool U 19 1
2006–07 Hartlepool U 20 2
2007–08 Hartlepool U 17 1 **106 7**

ROWELL, Jonathan (M) 0 0
b.Newcastle 10-9-89
2007–08 Hartlepool U 0 0

SWEENEY, Anthony (M) 167 27
H: 6 0 W: 11 07 b.Stockton 5-9-83
Source: Scholar.
2001–02 Hartlepool U 2 0
2002–03 Hartlepool U 4 0
2003–04 Hartlepool U 11 1
2004–05 Hartlepool U 44 13
2005–06 Hartlepool U 35 5
2006–07 Hartlepool U 35 4
2007–08 Hartlepool U 36 4 **167 27**

TURNBULL, Stephen (M) 33 0
H: 5 10 W: 11 00 b.South Shields 7-1-87
Source: Scholar.
2004–05 Hartlepool U 2 0
2005–06 Hartlepool U 21 0
2006–07 Hartlepool U 0 0
2006–07 *Bury* 5 0 **5 0**

2006–07 *Rochdale* 4 0 **4 0**
2007–08 Hartlepool U 1 0 **24 0**

YOUNG, Martin (M) 0 0
H: 5 11 W: 11 07 b.Hartlepool 8-9-88
Source: Scholar.
2007–08 Hartlepool U 0 0

HEREFORD U (38)

BECKWITH, Dean (D) 71 2
H: 6 3 W: 13 04 b.Southwark 18-9-83
Source: Scholar.
2003–04 Gillingham 0 0
2004–05 Gillingham 1 0 **1 0**
2006–07 Hereford U 32 0
2007–08 Hereford U 38 2 **70 2**

BENJAMIN, Trevor (F) 358 80
H: 6 2 W: 13 07 b.Kettering 8-2-79
Source: Trainee. *Honours:* England Under-21, Jamaica 2 full caps.
1995–96 Cambridge U 5 0
1996–97 Cambridge U 7 1
1997–98 Cambridge U 25 4
1998–99 Cambridge U 42 10
1999–2000 Cambridge U 44 20 **123 35**
2000–01 Leicester C 21 1
2001–02 Leicester C 11 0
2001–02 *Crystal Palace* 6 1 **6 1**
2001–02 *Norwich C* 6 0 **6 0**
2001–02 *WBA* 3 1 **3 1**
2002–03 Leicester C 35 8
2003–04 Leicester C 4 0
2003–04 *Gillingham* 4 1 **4 1**
2003–04 *Rushden & D* 6 1 **6 1**
2003–04 *Brighton & HA* 10 5 **10 5**
2004–05 Leicester C 10 2 **81 11**
2004–05 *Northampton T* 5 2 **5 2**
2004–05 Coventry C 12 1 **12 1**
2005–06 Peterborough U 20 1
2005–06 *Watford* 2 0 **2 0**
2005–06 *Swindon T* 8 2 **8 2**
2006–07 Peterborough U 27 7 **47 8**
2006–07 *Boston U* 3 0 **3 0**
2006–07 *Walsall* 8 2 **8 2**
2007–08 Hereford U 34 10 **34 10**

BROADHURST, Karl (D) 215 3
H: 6 1 W: 11 07 b.Portsmouth 18-3-80
Source: Trainee.
1998–99 Bournemouth 0 0
1999–2000 Bournemouth 16 0
2000–01 Bournemouth 30 0
2001–02 Bournemouth 23 0
2002–03 Bournemouth 21 1
2003–04 Bournemouth 39 1
2004–05 Bournemouth 29 1
2005–06 Bournemouth 7 0
2006–07 Bournemouth 27 0 **192 3**
2007–08 Hereford U 23 0 **23 0**

BROWN, Wayne (G) 191 0
H: 6 0 W: 13 11 b.Southampton 14-1-77
Source: Trainee.
1993–94 Bristol C 1 0
1994–95 Bristol C 0 0
1995–96 Bristol C 0 0 **1 0**
From Weston-S-Mare
1996–97 Chester C 2 0
1997–98 Chester C 13 0
1998–99 Chester C 23 0
1999–2000 Chester C 46 0
2000–01 Chester C 0 0
2001–02 Chester C 0 0
2004–05 Chester C 23 0
2005–06 Chester C 0 0 **107 0**
2006–07 Hereford U 39 0
2007–08 Hereford U 44 0 **83 0**

EASTON, Clint (M) 262 12
H: 5 11 W: 11 00 b.Barking 1-10-77
Source: Trainee. *Honours:* England Youth.
1996–97 Watford 17 1
1997–98 Watford 12 0
1998–99 Watford 7 0
1999–2000 Watford 17 0
2000–01 Watford 11 0 **64 1**
2001–02 Norwich C 14 1
2002–03 Norwich C 26 2
2003–04 Norwich C 10 2 **50 5**
2004–05 Wycombe W 33 1
2005–06 Wycombe W 44 1 **77 2**
2006–07 Gillingham 32 1 **32 1**
2007–08 Hereford U 39 3 **39 3**

ESSON, Ryan (G) 105 0
H: 6 1 W: 12 06 b.Aberdeen 19-3-80
Honours: Scotland Youth, Under-21.
1999–2000 Aberdeen 1 0
2000–01 Aberdeen 36 0
2001–02 Aberdeen 9 0
2001–02 Aberdeen 9 0
2001–02 *Rotherham U* 0 0
2002–03 Aberdeen 0 0
2003–04 Aberdeen 2 0
2004–05 Aberdeen 23 0
2005–06 Aberdeen 18 0 **98 0**
2006–07 Shrewsbury T 6 0
2007–08 Shrewsbury T 0 0 **6 0**
2007–08 Hereford U 1 0 **1 0**

FITZPATRICK, Jordan (M) 1 0
H: 6 0 W: 12 00 b.Stourbridge 15-6-88
Source: Wolverhampton W Scholar.
2006–07 Hereford U 1 0
2007–08 Hereford U 0 0 **1 0**

GUINAN, Stephen (F) 222 37
H: 6 1 W: 13 02 b.Birmingham 24-12-75
Source: Trainee.
1992–93 Nottingham F 0 0
1993–94 Nottingham F 0 0
1994–95 Nottingham F 0 0
1995–96 Nottingham F 2 0
1995–96 *Darlington* 3 1 **3 1**
1996–97 Nottingham F 2 0
1996–97 *Burnley* 6 0 **6 0**
1997–98 Nottingham F 2 0
1997–98 *Crewe Alex* 3 0 **3 0**
1998–99 Nottingham F 0 0
1998–99 *Halifax T* 12 2 **12 2**
1998–99 *Plymouth Arg* 11 7
1999–2000 Nottingham F 1 0 **7 0**
1999–2000 *Scunthorpe U* 3 1 **3 1**
1999–2000 Cambridge U 6 0 **6 0**
1999–2000 Plymouth Arg 8 2
2000–01 Plymouth Arg 22 1
2001–02 Plymouth Arg 0 0 **41 10**
2001–02 Shrewsbury T 5 0
2002–03 Shrewsbury T 0 0
2003–04 Shrewsbury T 0 0 **5 0**
2004–05 Cheltenham T 43 6
2005–06 Cheltenham T 30 7
2006–07 Cheltenham T 19 0 **92 13**
2006–07 *Hereford U* 16 7
2007–08 Hereford U 28 3 **44 10**

GWYNNE, Sam (M) 15 0
H: 5 9 W: 11 11 b.Hereford 17-12-87
Source: Scholar.
2006–07 Hereford U 0 0
2007–08 Hereford U 15 0 **15 0**

INGHAM, Michael (G) 130 0
H: 6 4 W: 13 10 b.Preston 9-7-80
Source: Malachians. *Honours:* Northern Ireland Youth, Under-21, 3 full caps.
1998–99 Cliftonville 18 0 **18 0**
1999–2000 Sunderland 0 0
1999–2000 *Carlisle U* 7 0 **7 0**
2000–01 Sunderland 0 0
2001–02 Sunderland 0 0
2001–02 *Stoke C* 0 0
2002–03 Sunderland 0 0
2002–03 *Darlington* 3 0 **3 0**
2002–03 *York C* 17 0 **17 0**
2003–04 Sunderland 0 0
2003–04 *Wrexham* 11 0
2004–05 Sunderland 2 0 **2 0**
2004–05 *Doncaster R* 1 0 **1 0**
2005–06 Wrexham 40 0
2006–07 Wrexham 31 0 **82 0**
2007–08 Hereford U 0 0

JOHNSON, Simon (F) 153 22
H: 5 9 W: 11 09 b.West Bromwich 9-3-83
Source: Scholar. *Honours:* England Youth, Under-20.
2000–01 Leeds U 0 0
2001–02 Leeds U 0 0
2002–03 Leeds U 4 0
2002–03 *Hull C* 12 2 **12 2**
2003–04 Leeds U 5 0
2003–04 *Blackpool* 4 1 **4 1**
2004–05 Leeds U 2 0 **11 0**

2004–05	*Sunderland*	5	0	**5**	**0**
2004–05	*Doncaster R*	11	3	**11**	**3**
2004–05	*Barnsley*	11	2	**11**	**2**
2005–06	Darlington	42	7		
2006–07	Darlington	24	2	**66**	**9**
2007–08	Hereford U	33	5	**33**	**5**

JONES, Craig (M) 0 0
b.Hereford 12-12-89
Source: Cardiff C.

2007–08	Hereford U	0	0

MACLEOD, Jack (M) 0 0
b.Epsom 3-7-88
Source: Millwall Scholar, Carshalton Ath.

2007–08	Hereford U	0	0

McCLENAHAN, Trent (D) 103 2
H: 5 11 W: 12 00 b.Sydney 4-2-85
Source: Scholar. *Honours:* Australia Under-20, Under-23.

2004–05	West Ham U	2	0		
2004–05	*Milton Keynes D*	8	0		
2005–06	West Ham U	0	0	**2**	**0**
2005–06	*Milton Keynes D*	29	0	**37**	**0**
2006–07	Hereford U	26	1		
2007–08	Hereford U	38	1	**64**	**2**

McCOMBE, John (D) 41 0
H: 6 2 W: 13 00 b.Pontefract 7-5-85
Source: Scholar.

2002–03	Huddersfield T	1	0		
2003–04	Huddersfield T	0	0		
2004–05	Huddersfield T	5	0		
2005–06	Huddersfield T	1	0		
2005–06	*Torquay U*	0	0		
2006–07	Huddersfield T	7	0	**14**	**0**
2007–08	Hereford U	27	0	**27**	**0**

PALMER, Marcus (F) 4 0
H: 6 0 W: 11 07 b.Gloucester 22-12-88
Source: Cheltenham T Scholar.

2006–07	Hereford U	3	0		
2007–08	Hereford U	1	0	**4**	**0**

ROSE, Richard (D) 131 2
H: 6 0 W: 12 04 b.Pembury 8-9-82
Source: Trainee.

2000–01	Gillingham	4	0		
2001–02	Gillingham	3	0		
2002–03	Gillingham	2	0		
2002–03	*Bristol R*	9	0	**9**	**0**
2003–04	Gillingham	17	0		
2004–05	Gillingham	18	0		
2005–06	Gillingham	14	0	**58**	**0**
2006–07	Hereford U	33	1		
2007–08	Hereford U	31	1	**64**	**2**

SMITH, Ben (M) 87 10
H: 5 9 W: 11 09 b.Chelmsford 23-11-78
Source: Yeovil T.

2001–02	Southend U	1	0	**1**	**0**
From Hereford U					
2004–05	Shrewsbury T	12	3		
2005–06	Shrewsbury T	12	1	**24**	**4**
From Weymouth.					
2006–07	Hereford U	18	1		
2007–08	Hereford U	44	5	**62**	**6**

TAYLOR, Kris (M) 111 7
H: 5 9 W: 11 05 b.Stafford 12-1-84
Source: Scholar. *Honours:* England Schools, Youth.

2000–01	Manchester U	0	0		
2001–02	Manchester U	0	0		
2002–03	Manchester U	0	0		
2002–03	Walsall	0	0		
2003–04	Walsall	11	1		
2004–05	Walsall	12	2		
2005–06	Walsall	22	2		
2006–07	Walsall	35	1	**80**	**6**
2007–08	Hereford U	31	1	**31**	**1**

WEBB, Luke (M) 35 3
H: 6 0 W: 12 01 b.Nottingham 12-9-86
Source: Arsenal Scholar.

2005–06	Coventry C	0	0		
2006–07	Hereford U	21	0		
2007–08	Hereford U	14	3	**35**	**3**

HUDDERSFIELD T (39)

AKINS, Lucas (F) 5 0
H: 5 10 W: 11 07 b.Huddersfield 25-2-89
Source: Scholar.

2006–07	Huddersfield T	2	0		
2007–08	Huddersfield T	3	0	**5**	**0**

BAILEY, Mitchell (M) 0 0
H: 5 9 W: 12 04 b.Manchester 31-12-88
Source: Scholar.

2007–08	Huddersfield T	0	0

BECKETT, Luke (F) 352 145
H: 5 11 W: 11 02 b.Sheffield 25-11-76
Source: Trainee.

1995–96	Barnsley	0	0		
1996–97	Barnsley	0	0		
1997–98	Barnsley	0	0		
1998–99	Chester C	28	11		
1999–2000	Chester C	46	14	**74**	**25**
2000–01	Chesterfield	41	16		
2001–02	Chesterfield	21	6	**62**	**22**
2001–02	Stockport Co	19	7		
2002–03	Stockport Co	42	27		
2003–04	Stockport Co	8	4		
2004–05	Stockport Co	15	7	**84**	**45**
2004–05	Sheffield U	5	0		
2004–05	*Huddersfield T*	7	6		
2004–05	*Oldham Ath*	9	6		
2005–06	Sheffield U	0	0	**5**	**0**
2005–06	*Oldham Ath*	34	18	**43**	**24**
2006–07	Huddersfield T	41	15		
2007–08	Huddersfield T	36	8	**84**	**29**

BERRETT, James (M) 17 1
H: 5 10 W: 10 13 b.Halifax 13-1-89
Source: Scholar. *Honours:* Eire Youth.

2006–07	Huddersfield T	2	0		
2007–08	Huddersfield T	15	1	**17**	**1**

BOOTH, Andy (F) 511 154
H: 6 0 W: 12 06 b.Huddersfield 6-12-73
Source: Trainee. *Honours:* England Under-21.

1991–92	Huddersfield T	3	0		
1992–93	Huddersfield T	5	2		
1993–94	Huddersfield T	26	10		
1994–95	Huddersfield T	46	26		
1995–96	Huddersfield T	43	16		
1996–97	Sheffield W	35	10		
1997–98	Sheffield W	23	7		
1998–99	Sheffield W	34	6		
1999–2000	Sheffield W	23	2		
2000–01	Sheffield W	18	3	**133**	**28**
2000–01	*Tottenham H*	4	0	**4**	**0**
2000–01	Huddersfield T	8	3		
2001–02	Huddersfield T	36	11		
2002–03	Huddersfield T	33	6		
2003–04	Huddersfield T	37	13		
2004–05	Huddersfield T	29	10		
2005–06	Huddersfield T	36	13		
2006–07	Huddersfield T	34	7		
2007–08	Huddersfield T	38	9	**374**	**126**

BRANDON, Chris (M) 290 33
H: 5 8 W: 10 00 b.Bradford 7-4-76
Source: Bradford PA.

1999–2000	Torquay U	42	5		
2000–01	Torquay U	2	0		
2001–02	Torquay U	27	3	**71**	**8**
2002–03	Chesterfield	36	7		
2003–04	Chesterfield	43	4	**79**	**11**
2004–05	Huddersfield T	44	6		
2005–06	Huddersfield T	40	3		
2006–07	Huddersfield T	23	1		
2006–07	*Blackpool*	5	2	**5**	**2**
2007–08	Huddersfield T	28	2	**135**	**12**

BROADBENT, Daniel (M) 5 0
H: 5 10 W: 12 00 b.Leeds 2-3-90
Source: Scholar. *Honours:* England Youth.

2006–07	Huddersfield T	0	0		
2007–08	Huddersfield T	5	0	**5**	**0**

CADAMARTERI, Danny (F) 237 26
H: 5 7 W: 13 05 b.Bradford 12-10-79
Source: Trainee. *Honours:* England Youth, Under-21.

1996–97	Everton	1	0		
1997–98	Everton	26	4		
1998–99	Everton	30	4		
1999–2000	Everton	17	1		
1999–2000	*Fulham*	5	1	**5**	**1**
2000–01	Everton	16	4		
2001–02	Everton	3	0	**93**	**13**
2001–02	Bradford C	14	2		
2002–03	Bradford C	20	0		
2003–04	Bradford C	18	3		
2004–05	Leeds U	0	0		
2004–05	Sheffield U	21	1	**21**	**1**
2005–06	Bradford C	39	2		
2006–07	Bradford C	0	0	**91**	**7**
2006–07	*Doncaster R*	6	1	**6**	**1**
2006–07	Leicester C	9	0	**9**	**0**
2007–08	Huddersfield T	12	3	**12**	**3**

CLARKE, Nathan (D) 208 4
H: 6 2 W: 12 00 b.Halifax 30-11-83
Source: Scholar.

2001–02	Huddersfield T	36	1		
2002–03	Huddersfield T	3	0		
2003–04	Huddersfield T	26	1		
2004–05	Huddersfield T	37	0		
2005–06	Huddersfield T	46	0		
2006–07	Huddersfield T	16	0		
2007–08	Huddersfield T	44	2	**208**	**4**

CLARKE, Tom (D) 41 1
H: 6 0 W: 11 02 b.Halifax 21-12-87
Source: Scholar. *Honours:* England Youth.

2004–05	Huddersfield T	12	0		
2005–06	Huddersfield T	17	1		
2006–07	Huddersfield T	9	0		
2007–08	Huddersfield T	3	0	**41**	**1**

COLLINS, Michael (M) 109 7
H: 6 0 W: 11 00 b.Halifax 30-4-86
Source: Scholar. *Honours:* Eire Youth, Under-21.

2004–05	Huddersfield T	8	0		
2005–06	Huddersfield T	17	1		
2006–07	Huddersfield T	43	4		
2007–08	Huddersfield T	41	2	**109**	**7**

EASTWOOD, Simon (G) 0 0
H: 6 2 W: 13 00 b.Luton 26-6-89
Source: Scholar. *Honours:* England Youth.

2005–06	Huddersfield T	0	0
2006–07	Huddersfield T	0	0
2007–08	Huddersfield T	0	0

GLENNON, Matty (G) 244 0
H: 6 2 W: 14 08 b.Stockport 8-10-78
Source: Trainee.

1997–98	Bolton W	0	0		
1998–99	Bolton W	0	0		
1999–2000	Bolton W	0	0		
1999–2000	*Port Vale*	0	0		
1999–2000	*Stockport Co*	0	0		
2000–01	Bolton W	0	0		
2000–01	*Bristol R*	1	0	**1**	**0**
2000–01	*Carlisle U*	29	0		
2001–02	Hull C	26	0		
2002–03	Hull C	9	0	**35**	**0**
2002–03	Carlisle U	32	0		
2003–04	Carlisle U	44	0		
2004–05	Carlisle U	0	0	**105**	**0**
2005–06	St Johnstone	12	0	**12**	**0**
2006–07	Huddersfield T	46	0		
2007–08	Huddersfield T	45	0	**91**	**0**

HARDY, Aaron (M) 15 0
H: 5 8 W: 11 04 b.Pontefract 26-5-86
Source: Scholar.

2005–06	Huddersfield T	0	0		
2006–07	Huddersfield T	9	0		
2007–08	Huddersfield T	6	0	**15**	**0**

HOLDSWORTH, Andy (D) 197 6
H: 5 9 W: 11 02 b.Pontefract 29-1-84
Source: Scholar.

2003–04	Huddersfield T	36	0		
2004–05	Huddersfield T	40	0		
2005–06	Huddersfield T	42	1		
2006–07	Huddersfield T	35	2		
2007–08	Huddersfield T	44	3	**197**	**6**

JEVONS, Phil (F) 243 81
H: 5 11 W: 12 00 b.Liverpool 1-8-79
Source: Trainee.

1996–97	Everton	0	0		
1997–98	Everton	0	0		
1998–99	Everton	1	0		
1999–2000	Everton	3	0		
2000–01	Everton	4	0	**8**	**0**
2001–02	Grimsby T	31	6		
2002–03	Grimsby T	3	0		

2002–03 *Hull C* 24 3 **24 3**
2003–04 Grimsby T 29 12 **63 18**
2004–05 Yeovil T 46 27
2005–06 Yeovil T 38 15 **84 42**
2006–07 Bristol C 41 11
2007–08 Bristol C 2 0 **43 11**
2007–08 Huddersfield T 21 7 **21 7**

KAMARA, Malvin (M) 153 10
H: 5 11 W: 13 00 b.Southwark 17-11-83
Source: Scholar. *Honours:* Sierra Leone 1 full cap.
2002–03 Wimbledon 2 0
2003–04 Wimbledon 27 2 **29 2**
2004–05 Milton Keynes D 25 1
2005–06 Milton Keynes D 23 2 **48 3**
2006–07 Cardiff C 15 1 **15 1**
2006–07 Port Vale 18 1 **18 1**
2007–08 Huddersfield T 43 3 **43 3**

KILLOCK, Shane (D) 1 0
H: 6 0 W: 12 04 b.Huddersfield 12-3-89
Source: Ossett Albion.
2007–08 Huddersfield T 1 0 **1 0**

MALCHER, Luke (F) 0 0
H: 5 8 W: 10 05 b.Huddersfield 8-11-88
Source: Scholar.
2007–08 Huddersfield T 0 0

MIRFIN, David (M) 161 9
H: 6 3 W: 13 00 b.Sheffield 18-4-85
Source: Scholar.
2002–03 Huddersfield T 1 0
2003–04 Huddersfield T 21 2
2004–05 Huddersfield T 41 4
2005–06 Huddersfield T 31 1
2006–07 Huddersfield T 38 1
2007–08 Huddersfield T 29 1 **161 9**

PAGE, Robert (D) 420 5
H: 6 0 W: 12 05 b.Llwynpia 3-9-74
Source: Trainee. *Honours:* Wales Schools, Youth, Under-21, B, 41 full caps.
1992–93 Watford 0 0
1993–94 Watford 4 0
1994–95 Watford 5 0
1995–96 Watford 19 0
1996–97 Watford 36 0
1997–98 Watford 41 0
1998–99 Watford 39 0
1999–2000 Watford 36 1
2000–01 Watford 36 1
2001–02 Watford 0 0 **216 2**
2001–02 Sheffield U 43 0
2002–03 Sheffield U 34 0
2003–04 Sheffield U 30 1 **107 1**
2004–05 Cardiff C 9 0 **9 0**
2004–05 Coventry C 9 0
2005–06 Coventry C 32 1
2006–07 Coventry C 29 0
2007–08 Coventry C 0 0 **70 1**
2007–08 Huddersfield T 18 1 **18 1**

RACCHI, Danny (D) 6 0
H: 5 8 W: 10 04 b.Halifax 22-11-87
Source: Scholar.
2006–07 Huddersfield T 3 0
2007–08 Huddersfield T 3 0 **6 0**

SCHOFIELD, Danny (F) 248 39
H: 5 10 W: 11 02 b.Doncaster 10-4-80
Source: Brodsworth.
1998–99 Huddersfield T 1 0
1999–2000 Huddersfield T 2 0
2000–01 Huddersfield T 1 0
2001–02 Huddersfield T 40 8
2002–03 Huddersfield T 30 2
2003–04 Huddersfield T 40 8
2004–05 Huddersfield T 33 5
2005–06 Huddersfield T 41 9
2006–07 Huddersfield T 35 5
2007–08 Huddersfield T 25 2 **248 39**

SINCLAIR, Frank (D) 473 12
H: 5 8 W: 12 09 b.Lambeth 3-12-71
Source: Trainee. *Honours:* Jamaica 28 full caps, 1 goal.
1989–90 Chelsea 0 0
1990–91 Chelsea 4 0
1991–92 Chelsea 8 1
1991–92 *WBA* 6 1 **6 1**
1992–93 Chelsea 32 0
1993–94 Chelsea 35 0
1994–95 Chelsea 35 3
1995–96 Chelsea 13 1
1996–97 Chelsea 20 1
1997–98 Chelsea 22 1 **169 7**
1998–99 Leicester C 31 1
1999–2000 Leicester C 34 0
2000–01 Leicester C 17 0
2001–02 Leicester C 35 0
2002–03 Leicester C 33 1
2003–04 Leicester C 14 1 **164 3**
2004–05 Burnley 36 1
2005–06 Burnley 37 0
2006–07 Burnley 19 0 **92 1**
2006–07 *Huddersfield T* 13 0
2007–08 Huddersfield T 29 0 **42 0**

SKARZ, Joe (D) 44 0
H: 5 10 W: 11 04 b.Huddersfield 13-7-89
Source: Scholar.
2006–07 Huddersfield T 17 0
2007–08 Huddersfield T 27 0 **44 0**

SMITHIES, Alex (G) 2 0
H: 6 1 W: 10 01 b.Huddersfield 25-3-90
Source: Scholar. *Honours:* England Youth.
2006–07 Huddersfield T 0 0
2007–08 Huddersfield T 2 0 **2 0**

WILLIAMS, Robbie (D) 100 10
H: 5 10 W: 11 13 b.Pontefract 2-10-84
Source: Scholar.
2002–03 Barnsley 8 0
2003–04 Barnsley 4 1
2004–05 Barnsley 17 1
2005–06 Barnsley 22 2
2006–07 Barnsley 15 0
2006–07 *Blackpool* 9 4 **9 4**
2007–08 Barnsley 0 0 **66 4**
2007–08 Huddersfield T 25 2 **25 2**

WORTHINGTON, Jon (M) 194 12
H: 5 9 W: 11 05 b.Dewsbury 16-4-83
Source: Scholar.
2001–02 Huddersfield T 0 0
2002–03 Huddersfield T 22 0
2003–04 Huddersfield T 39 3
2004–05 Huddersfield T 39 3
2005–06 Huddersfield T 41 4
2006–07 Huddersfield T 28 2
2007–08 Huddersfield T 25 0 **194 12**

YOUNG, Matthew (M) 39 2
H: 5 8 W: 11 03 b.Woodlesford 25-10-85
Source: Scholar.
2005–06 Huddersfield T 2 0
2006–07 Huddersfield T 29 2
2007–08 Huddersfield T 8 0 **39 2**

HULL C (40)

ASHBEE, Ian (M) 397 19
H: 6 1 W: 13 07 b.Birmingham 6-9-76
Source: Trainee. *Honours:* England Youth.
1994–95 Derby Co 1 0
1995–96 Derby Co 0 0
1996–97 Derby Co 0 0 **1 0**
1996–97 Cambridge U 18 0
1997–98 Cambridge U 27 1
1998–99 Cambridge U 31 4
1999–2000 Cambridge U 45 1
2000–01 Cambridge U 44 3
2001–02 Cambridge U 38 2 **203 11**
2002–03 Hull C 31 1
2003–04 Hull C 39 2
2004–05 Hull C 40 1
2005–06 Hull C 6 0
2006–07 Hull C 35 1
2007–08 Hull C 42 3 **193 8**

ASPDEN, Curtis (G) 0 0
H: 6 1 W: 11 12 b.Darwen 16-11-87
Source: Scholar.
2005–06 Hull C 0 0
2006–07 Hull C 0 0
2007–08 Hull C 0 0

ATKINSON, Will (M) 16 0
H: 5 10 W: 10 07 b.Driffield 14-10-88
Source: Scholar.
2006–07 Hull C 0 0
2007–08 Hull C 0 0
2007–08 *Port Vale* 4 0 **4 0**
2007–08 *Mansfield T* 12 0 **12 0**

BARMBY, Nick (F) 408 72
H: 5 7 W: 11 03 b.Hull 11-2-74
Source: Trainee. *Honours:* England Schools, Youth, Under-21, B, 23 full caps, 4 goals.
1991–92 Tottenham H 0 0
1992–93 Tottenham H 22 6
1993–94 Tottenham H 27 5
1994–95 Tottenham H 38 9 **87 20**
1995–96 Middlesbrough 32 7
1996–97 Middlesbrough 10 1 **42 8**
1996–97 Everton 25 4
1997–98 Everton 30 2
1998–99 Everton 24 3
1999–2000 Everton 37 9 **116 18**
2000–01 Liverpool 26 2
2001–02 Liverpool 6 0 **32 2**
2002–03 Leeds U 19 4
2003–04 *Nottingham F* 6 1 **6 1**
2003–04 Leeds U 6 0 **25 4**
2004–05 Hull C 39 9
2005–06 Hull C 26 5
2006–07 Hull C 20 4
2007–08 Hull C 15 1 **100 19**

BELT, Frank (D) 0 0
b.Bridlington 16-10-88
Source: Scholar.
2007–08 Hull C 0 0

BENNETT, James (M) 0 0
H: 5 10 W: 12 03 b.Beverley 4-9-88
Source: Scholar.
2006–07 Hull C 0 0
2007–08 Hull C 0 0

BRIDGES, Michael (F) 223 53
H: 6 1 W: 10 11 b.North Shields 5-8-78
Source: Trainee. *Honours:* England Schools, Youth, Under-21.
1995–96 Sunderland 15 4
1996–97 Sunderland 25 3
1997–98 Sunderland 9 1
1998–99 Sunderland 30 8
1999–2000 Leeds U 34 19
2000–01 Leeds U 7 0
2001–02 Leeds U 0 0
2002–03 Leeds U 5 0
2003–04 Leeds U 10 0 **56 19**
2003–04 *Newcastle U* 6 0 **6 0**
2004–05 Bolton W 0 0
2004–05 Sunderland 19 1 **98 17**
2005–06 Bristol C 11 0 **11 0**
2005–06 Carlisle U 25 15
2006–07 Carlisle U 5 0 **30 15**
2006–07 Hull C 15 2
2007–08 Hull C 7 0 **22 2**

BROWN, Wayne (D) 282 11
H: 6 0 W: 12 06 b.Barking 20-8-77
Source: Trainee.
1995–96 Ipswich T 0 0
1996–97 Ipswich T 0 0
1997–98 Ipswich T 1 0
1997–98 *Colchester U* 2 0
1998–99 Ipswich T 1 0
1999–2000 Ipswich T 25 0
2000–01 Ipswich T 4 0
2000–01 *QPR* 2 0 **2 0**
2001–02 Ipswich T 0 0
2001–02 *Wimbledon* 17 1 **17 1**
2001–02 *Watford* 11 3
2002–03 Ipswich T 9 0 **40 0**
2002–03 Watford 13 1
2003–04 Watford 12 0 **36 4**
2003–04 *Gillingham* 4 1 **4 1**
2003–04 *Colchester U* 16 0
2004–05 Colchester U 40 1
2005–06 Colchester U 38 2
2006–07 Colchester U 46 1 **142 4**
2007–08 Hull C 41 1 **41 1**

DAWSON, Andy (D) 347 14
H: 5 9 W: 11 02 b.Northallerton 20-10-78
Source: Trainee.
1995–96 Nottingham F 0 0
1996–97 Nottingham F 0 0
1997–98 Nottingham F 0 0
1998–99 Nottingham F 0 0
1998–99 Scunthorpe U 24 0
1999–2000 Scunthorpe U 43 2
2000–01 Scunthorpe U 41 4
2001–02 Scunthorpe U 44 0
2002–03 Scunthorpe U 43 2 **195 8**

2003–04 Hull C 33 3
2004–05 Hull C 34 0
2005–06 Hull C 18 0
2006–07 Hull C 38 2
2007–08 Hull C 29 1 **152 6**

DEVITT, Jamie (F) 0 0
b.Dublin
Source: Cherry Orchard BC, Hull C Scholar.
2007–08 Hull C 0 0

DOYLE, Nathan (M) 51 0
H: 5 11 W: 12 06 b.Derby 12-1-87
Source: Scholar. *Honours:* England Youth, Under-20.
2003–04 Derby Co 2 0
2004–05 Derby Co 3 0
2005–06 Derby Co 4 0
2005–06 *Notts Co* 12 0 **12 0**
2006–07 Derby Co 0 0 **9 0**
2006–07 *Bradford C* 28 0 **28 0**
2006–07 Hull C 1 0
2007–08 Hull C 1 0 **2 0**

DUKE, Matt (G) 16 0
H: 6 5 W: 13 04 b.Sheffield 16-7-77
Source: Alfreton T.
1999–2000 Sheffield U 0 0
2000–01 Sheffield U 0 0
2001–02 Sheffield U 0 0
2004–05 Hull C 2 0
2005–06 Hull C 2 0
2005–06 *Stockport Co* 3 0 **3 0**
2005–06 *Wycombe W* 5 0 **5 0**
2006–07 Hull C 1 0
2007–08 Hull C 3 0 **8 0**

ELLIOTT, Stuart (M) 369 114
H: 5 10 W: 11 09 b.Belfast 23-7-78
Honours: Northern Ireland Under-21, B, 39 full caps, 4 goals.
1994–95 Glentoran 0 0
1995–96 Glentoran 1 0
1996–97 Glentoran 8 1
1997–98 Glentoran 22 5
1998–99 Glentoran 31 7
1999–2000 Glentoran 34 16 **96 29**
2000–01 Motherwell 33 10
2001–02 Motherwell 37 10 **70 20**
2002–03 Hull C 36 12
2003–04 Hull C 42 14
2004–05 Hull C 36 27
2005–06 Hull C 40 7
2006–07 Hull C 32 5
2007–08 Hull C 7 0 **193 65**
2007–08 *Doncaster R* 10 0 **10 0**

FEATHERSTONE, Nicky (F) 8 0
H: 5 6 W: 11 02 b.North Ferriby 22-9-88
Source: Scholar.
2006–07 Hull C 2 0
2007–08 Hull C 6 0 **8 0**

FOLAN, Caleb (F) 153 25
H: 6 2 W: 14 07 b.Leeds 26-10-82
Source: Trainee.
1999–2000 Leeds U 0 0
2000–01 Leeds U 0 0
2001–02 Leeds U 0 0
2001–02 *Rushden & D* 6 0 **6 0**
2001–02 *Hull C* 1 0
2002–03 Leeds U 0 0
2002–03 Chesterfield 13 1
2003–04 Chesterfield 7 0
2004–05 Chesterfield 32 6
2005–06 Chesterfield 27 0
2006–07 Chesterfield 23 8 **102 15**
2006–07 Wigan Ath 13 2
2007–08 Wigan Ath 2 0 **15 2**
2007–08 Hull C 29 8 **30 8**

FRANCE, Ryan (M) 131 6
H: 5 11 W: 11 11 b.Sheffield 13-12-80
Source: Alfreton T.
2003–04 Hull C 28 2
2004–05 Hull C 31 2
2005–06 Hull C 35 2
2006–07 Hull C 24 0
2007–08 Hull C 13 0 **131 6**

FRIZZELL, Brewster (D) 0 0
b.Manchester 15-2-89
Source: Scholar.
2007–08 Hull C 0 0

GARCIA, Richard (F) 154 25
H: 5 11 W: 12 01 b.Perth 4-9-81
Source: Trainee. *Honours:* Australia Under-23.
1998–99 West Ham U 0 0
1999–2000 West Ham U 0 0
2000–01 West Ham U 0 0
2000–01 *Leyton Orient* 18 4 **18 4**
2001–02 West Ham U 8 0
2002–03 West Ham U 0 0
2003–04 West Ham U 7 0
2004–05 West Ham U 1 0 **16 0**
2004–05 Colchester U 24 4
2005–06 Colchester U 22 5
2006–07 Colchester U 36 7 **82 16**
2007–08 Hull C 38 5 **38 5**

HUGHES, Bryan (M) 451 52
H: 5 10 W: 11 08 b.Liverpool 19-6-76
Source: Trainee.
1993–94 Wrexham 11 0
1994–95 Wrexham 38 9
1995–96 Wrexham 22 0
1996–97 Wrexham 23 3 **94 12**
1996–97 Birmingham C 11 0
1997–98 Birmingham C 40 5
1998–99 Birmingham C 28 3
1999–2000 Birmingham C 45 10
2000–01 Birmingham C 45 4
2001–02 Birmingham C 31 7
2002–03 Birmingham C 22 2
2003–04 Birmingham C 26 3 **248 34**
2004–05 Charlton Ath 17 1
2005–06 Charlton Ath 33 3
2006–07 Charlton Ath 24 1 **74 5**
2007–08 Hull C 35 1 **35 1**

LIVERMORE, David (M) 328 18
H: 5 11 W: 12 02 b.Edmonton 20-5-80
Source: Trainee.
1998–99 Arsenal 0 0
1999–2000 Millwall 32 2
2000–01 Millwall 39 3
2001–02 Millwall 43 0
2002–03 Millwall 41 2
2003–04 Millwall 36 1
2004–05 Millwall 41 2
2005–06 Millwall 41 2 **273 12**
2006–07 Hull C 25 4
2007–08 Hull C 20 1 **45 5**
2007–08 *Oldham Ath* 10 1 **10 1**

MARNEY, Dean (M) 113 10
H: 5 10 W: 11 09 b.Barking 31-1-84
Source: Scholar. *Honours:* England Under-21.
2002–03 Tottenham H 0 0
2002–03 *Swindon T* 9 0 **9 0**
2003–04 Tottenham H 3 0
2003–04 *QPR* 2 0 **2 0**
2004–05 Tottenham H 5 2
2004–05 *Gillingham* 3 0 **3 0**
2005–06 Tottenham H 0 0 **8 2**
2005–06 *Norwich C* 13 0 **13 0**
2006–07 Hull C 37 2
2007–08 Hull C 41 6 **78 8**

MYHILL, Boaz (G) 221 0
H: 6 3 W: 14 06 b.Modesto 9-11-82
Source: Scholar. *Honours:* England Youth, Under-20. Wales 1 full cap.
2000–01 Aston Villa 0 0
2001–02 Aston Villa 0 0
2001–02 *Stoke C* 0 0
2002–03 Aston Villa 0 0
2002–03 *Bristol C* 0 0
2002–03 *Bradford C* 2 0 **2 0**
2003–04 Aston Villa 0 0
2003–04 *Macclesfield T* 15 0 **15 0**
2003–04 *Stockport Co* 2 0 **2 0**
2003–04 Hull C 23 0
2004–05 Hull C 45 0
2005–06 Hull C 45 0
2006–07 Hull C 46 0
2007–08 Hull C 43 0 **202 0**

OKOCHA, Jay-Jay (M) 378 73
H: 5 8 W: 11 00 b.Enugu 14-8-73
Source: Enugu Rangers, Neunkirchen.
Honours: Nigeria 65 full caps, 12 goals.
1992–93 Eintracht Frankfurt20 2
1993–94 Eintracht Frankfurt19 2
1994–95 Eintracht Frankfurt27 6
1995–96 Eintracht Frankfurt24 7 **90 17**
1996–97 Fenerbahce 33 16
1997–98 Fenerbahce 30 14 **63 30**
1998–99 Paris St Germain 25 4
1999–2000 Paris St Germain 23 2
2000–01 Paris St Germain 15 2
2001–02 Paris St Germain 20 4 **83 12**
2002–03 Bolton W 31 7
2003–04 Bolton W 35 0
2004–05 Bolton W 31 6
2005–06 Bolton W 27 1 **124 14**
From Qatar Sports Club
2007–08 Hull C 18 0 **18 0**

PEDERSEN, Henrik (F) 286 88
H: 6 1 W: 13 03 b.Copenhagen 10-6-75
Honours: Denmark 3 full caps.
1995–96 Silkeborg 12 4
1996–97 Silkeborg 2 0
1997–98 Silkeborg 15 9
1998–99 Silkeborg 33 16
1999–2000 Silkeborg 28 13
2000–01 Silkeborg 32 20 **122 62**
2001–02 Bolton W 11 0
2002–03 Bolton W 33 7
2003–04 Bolton W 33 7
2004–05 Bolton W 27 6
2005–06 Bolton W 21 1
2006–07 Bolton W 18 1
2007–08 Bolton W 0 0 **143 22**
2007–08 Hull C 21 4 **21 4**

PLUMMER, Matthew (D) 0 0
H: 6 1 W: 12 01 b.Hull 18-1-89
Source: Scholar.
2006–07 Hull C 0 0
2007–08 Hull C 0 0

RICKETTS, Sam (D) 215 3
H: 6 1 W: 12 01 b.Aylesbury 11-10-81
Source: Trainee. *Honours:* Wales 28 full caps.
1999–2000 Oxford U 0 0
2000–01 Oxford U 14 0
2001–02 Oxford U 29 1
2002–03 Oxford U 2 0 **45 1**
From Telford U
2004–05 Swansea C 42 0
2005–06 Swansea C 44 1 **86 1**
2006–07 Hull C 40 1
2007–08 Hull C 44 0 **84 1**

TURNER, Michael (D) 185 12
H: 6 4 W: 13 05 b.Lewisham 9-11-83
Source: Scholar.
2001–02 Charlton Ath 0 0
2002–03 Charlton Ath 0 0
2002–03 *Leyton Orient* 7 1 **7 1**
2003–04 Charlton Ath 0 0
2004–05 Charlton Ath 0 0
2004–05 Brentford 45 1
2005–06 Brentford 46 2 **91 3**
2006–07 Hull C 43 3
2007–08 Hull C 44 5 **87 8**

WELSH, John (M) 60 3
H: 5 7 W: 12 02 b.Liverpool 10-1-84
Source: Scholar. *Honours:* England Youth, Under-20, Under-21.
2000–01 Liverpool 0 0
2001–02 Liverpool 0 0
2002–03 Liverpool 0 0
2003–04 Liverpool 1 0
2004–05 Liverpool 3 0
2005–06 Liverpool 0 0 **4 0**
2005–06 Hull C 32 2
2006–07 Hull C 18 1
2007–08 Hull C 0 0 **50 3**
2007–08 *Chester C* 6 0 **6 0**

WILKINSON, Ben (M) 13 0
H: 5 11 W: 12 01 b.Sheffield 25-4-87
Source: Derby Co Scholar.
2005–06 Hull C 0 0
2006–07 Hull C 0 0
2007–08 *Gretna* 13 0 **13 0**
2007–08 Hull C 0 0

WINDASS, Dean (F) 612 197
H: 5 10 W: 12 03 b.North Ferriby 1-4-69
Source: N Ferriby U.
1991–92 Hull C 32 6
1992–93 Hull C 41 7
1993–94 Hull C 43 23
1994–95 Hull C 44 17
1995–96 Hull C 16 4

1995–96	Aberdeen	20	6		
1996–97	Aberdeen	29	10		
1997–98	Aberdeen	24	5	**73**	**21**
1998–99	Oxford U	33	15	**33**	**15**
1998–99	Bradford C	12	3		
1999–2000	Bradford C	38	10		
2000–01	Bradford C	24	3		
2000–01	Middlesbrough	8	2		
2001–02	Middlesbrough	27	1		
2001–02	*Sheffield W*	2	0	**2**	**0**
2002–03	Middlesbrough	2	0	**37**	**3**
2002–03	Sheffield U	20	6	**20**	**6**
2003–04	Bradford C	36	6		
2004–05	Bradford C	41	27		
2005–06	Bradford C	40	16		
2006–07	Bradford C	25	11	**216**	**76**
2006–07	*Hull C*	18	8		
2007–08	Hull C	37	11	**231**	**76**

WOODHEAD, Tom (G) **0 0**
H: 5 10 W: 12 00 b.Beverley 1-5-88
Source: Scholar.

2007–08	Hull C	0	0		

IPSWICH T (41)

ALEXANDER, Neil (G) **350 0**
H: 6 1 W: 12 08 b.Edinburgh 10-3-78
Source: Edina Hibs. *Honours:* Scotland Under-21, B, 3 full caps.

1996–97	Stenhousemuir	12	0		
1997–98	Stenhousemuir	36	0	**48**	**0**
1998–99	Livingston	21	0		
1999–2000	Livingston	13	0		
2000–01	Livingston	26	0	**60**	**0**
2001–02	Cardiff C	46	0		
2002–03	Cardiff C	40	0		
2003–04	Cardiff C	25	0		
2004–05	Cardiff C	17	0		
2005–06	Cardiff C	46	0		
2006–07	Cardiff C	39	0	**213**	**0**
2007–08	Ipswich T	29	0	**29**	**0**

To Rangers January 2008.

BOWDITCH, Dean (F) **111 13**
H: 5 11 W: 11 05 b.Bishops Stortford 15-6-86
Source: Trainee. *Honours:* FA Schools, England Youth.

2002–03	Ipswich T	5	0		
2003–04	Ipswich T	16	4		
2004–05	Ipswich T	21	3		
2004–05	*Burnley*	10	1	**10**	**1**
2005–06	Ipswich T	21	0		
2005–06	*Wycombe W*	11	1	**11**	**1**
2006–07	Ipswich T	9	1		
2006–07	*Brighton & HA*	3	1		
2007–08	Ipswich T	0	0	**72**	**8**
2007–08	*Northampton T*	10	2	**10**	**2**
2007–08	*Brighton & HA*	5	0	**8**	**1**

BRUCE, Alex (D) **112 0**
H: 6 0 W: 11 06 b.Norwich 28-9-84
Source: Trainee. *Honours:* Eire B, Under-21, 1 full cap.

2002–03	Blackburn R	0	0		
2003–04	Blackburn R	0	0		
2004–05	Blackburn R	0	0		
2004–05	*Oldham Ath*	12	0	**12**	**0**
2004–05	Birmingham C	0	0		
2004–05	*Sheffield W*	6	0	**6**	**0**
2005–06	Birmingham C	6	0	**6**	**0**
2005–06	*Tranmere R*	11	0	**11**	**0**
2006–07	Ipswich T	41	0		
2007–08	Ipswich T	36	0	**77**	**0**

CASEMENT, Chris (M) **8 0**
H: 6 0 W: 12 02 b.Belfast 12-1-88
Source: Scholar. *Honours:* Northern Ireland Youth, Under-21.

2005–06	Ipswich T	5	0		
2006–07	Ipswich T	0	0		
2007–08	Ipswich T	3	0	**8**	**0**

CLARKE, Billy (F) **63 4**
H: 5 7 W: 10 01 b.Cork 13-12-87
Source: Scholar. *Honours:* Eire Youth, Under-21.

2004–05	Ipswich T	0	0		
2005–06	Ipswich T	2	0		
2005–06	*Colchester U*	6	0	**6**	**0**
2006–07	Ipswich T	27	3		
2007–08	*Falkirk*	8	1	**8**	**1**
2007–08	Ipswich T	20	0	**49**	**3**

COLGAN, Nick (G) **248 0**
H: 6 1 W: 12 00 b.Drogheda 19-9-73
Source: Drogheda. *Honours:* Eire Schools, Youth, Under-21, B, 9 full caps.

1992–93	Chelsea	0	0		
1993–94	Chelsea	0	0		
1993–94	*Crewe Alex*	0	0		
1994–95	Chelsea	0	0		
1994–95	*Grimsby T*	0	0		
1995–96	Chelsea	0	0		
1995–96	*Millwall*	0	0		
1996–97	Chelsea	1	0		
1997–98	Chelsea	0	0	**1**	**0**
1997–98	*Brentford*	5	0	**5**	**0**
1997–98	*Reading*	5	0	**5**	**0**
1998–99	Bournemouth	0	0		
1999–2000	Hibernian	24	0		
2000–01	Hibernian	37	0		
2001–02	Hibernian	30	0		
2002–03	Hibernian	30	0		
2003–04	Hibernian	0	0	**121**	**0**
2003–04	*Stockport Co*	15	0	**15**	**0**
2004–05	Barnsley	13	0		
2005–06	Barnsley	43	0		
2006–07	Barnsley	44	0		
2007–08	Barnsley	1	0	**101**	**0**
2007–08	Ipswich T	0	0		

COUNAGO, Pablo (F) **239 58**
H: 5 11 W: 11 06 b.Pontevedra 9-8-79

1998–99	Numancia	13	1	**13**	**1**
1998–99	Celta Vigo	1	0		
1999–2000	Huelva	26	4	**26**	**4**
2000–01	Celta Vigo	8	0	**9**	**0**
2001–02	Ipswich T	13	0		
2002–03	Ipswich T	39	17		
2003–04	Ipswich T	29	11		
2004–05	Ipswich T	19	3		
2005–06	Malaga	27	3		
2006–07	Malaga	21	7	**48**	**10**
2007–08	Ipswich T	43	12	**143**	**43**

DE VOS, Jason (D) **398 32**
H: 6 4 W: 13 07 b.London, Can 2-1-74
Source: Montreal Impact. *Honours:* Canada Youth, Under-20, Under-23, 49 full caps, 4 goals.

1996–97	Darlington	8	0		
1997–98	Darlington	24	3		
1998–99	Darlington	12	2	**44**	**5**
1998–99	Dundee U	25	0		
1999–2000	Dundee U	35	2		
2000–01	Dundee U	33	0	**93**	**2**
2001–02	Wigan Ath	20	5		
2002–03	Wigan Ath	43	8		
2003–04	Wigan Ath	27	2	**90**	**15**
2004–05	Ipswich T	45	3		
2005–06	Ipswich T	41	3		
2006–07	Ipswich T	39	2		
2007–08	Ipswich T	46	2	**171**	**10**

GARVAN, Owen (M) **102 6**
H: 6 0 W: 10 07 b.Dublin 29-1-88
Source: Scholar. *Honours:* Eire Youth, Under-21.

2005–06	Ipswich T	32	3		
2006–07	Ipswich T	27	1		
2007–08	Ipswich T	43	2	**102**	**6**

HARDING, Dan (D) **159 2**
H: 6 0 W: 11 11 b.Gloucester 23-12-83
Source: Scholar. *Honours:* England Under-21.

2002–03	Brighton & HA	1	0		
2003–04	Brighton & HA	23	0		
2004–05	Brighton & HA	43	1	**67**	**1**
2005–06	Leeds U	20	0	**20**	**0**
2006–07	Ipswich T	42	0		
2007–08	Ipswich T	30	1	**72**	**1**

HAYNES, Danny (F) **96 19**
H: 5 11 W: 12 04 b.London 19-1-88
Source: Scholar. *Honours:* England Youth.

2005–06	Ipswich T	19	3		
2006–07	Ipswich T	31	7		
2006–07	*Millwall*	5	2	**5**	**2**
2007–08	Ipswich T	41	7	**91**	**17**

LEE, Alan (F) **330 82**
H: 6 2 W: 13 09 b.Galway 21-8-78
Source: Trainee. *Honours:* Eire Under-21, 10 full caps.

1995–96	Aston Villa	0	0		
1996–97	Aston Villa	0	0		
1997–98	Aston Villa	0	0		
1998–99	Aston Villa	0	0		
1998–99	*Torquay U*	7	2	**7**	**2**
1998–99	*Port Vale*	11	2	**11**	**2**
1999–2000	Burnley	15	0		
2000–01	Burnley	0	0	**15**	**0**
2000–01	Rotherham U	31	13		
2001–02	Rotherham U	38	9		
2002–03	Rotherham U	41	15		
2003–04	Rotherham U	1	0	**111**	**37**
2003–04	Cardiff C	23	3		
2004–05	Cardiff C	38	5		
2005–06	Cardiff C	25	2	**86**	**10**
2005–06	Ipswich T	14	4		
2006–07	Ipswich T	41	16		
2007–08	Ipswich T	45	11	**100**	**31**

LEGWINSKI, Sylvain (M) **349 30**
H: 6 1 W: 11 07 b.Clermont-Ferrand 6-10-73
Honours: France Under-21, B.

1992–93	Monaco	2	0		
1993–94	Monaco	0	0		
1994–95	Monaco	21	1		
1995–96	Monaco	29	2		
1996–97	Monaco	37	9		
1997–98	Monaco	22	0		
1998–99	Monaco	14	1	**125**	**13**
1999–2000	Bordeaux	13	1		
2000–01	Bordeaux	32	1		
2001–02	Bordeaux	4	0	**49**	**2**
2001–02	Fulham	33	3		
2002–03	Fulham	35	4		
2003–04	Fulham	32	0		
2004–05	Fulham	15	1		
2005–06	Fulham	13	0		
2006–07	Fulham	0	0	**128**	**8**
2006–07	Ipswich T	32	5		
2007–08	Ipswich T	15	2	**47**	**7**

MILLER, Tommy (M) **331 73**
H: 6 0 W: 11 07 b.Easington 8-1-79
Source: Trainee.

1997–98	Hartlepool U	13	1		
1998–99	Hartlepool U	34	4		
1999–2000	Hartlepool U	44	14		
2000–01	Hartlepool U	46	16		
2001–02	Hartlepool U	0	0	**137**	**35**
2001–02	Ipswich T	8	0		
2002–03	Ipswich T	30	6		
2003–04	Ipswich T	34	11		
2004–05	Ipswich T	45	13		
2005–06	Sunderland	29	3		
2006–07	Sunderland	4	0	**33**	**3**
2006–07	*Preston NE*	7	0	**7**	**0**
2007–08	Ipswich T	37	5	**154**	**35**

MOORE, Sammy (M) **21 2**
H: 5 8 W: 9 00 b.Dover 7-9-87
Source: Scholar.

2006–07	Ipswich T	1	0		
2007–08	Ipswich T	0	0	**1**	**0**
2007–08	*Brentford*	20	2	**20**	**2**

NAYLOR, Richard (D) **312 37**
H: 6 1 W: 13 07 b.Leeds 28-2-77
Source: Trainee.

1995–96	Ipswich T	0	0		
1996–97	Ipswich T	27	4		
1997–98	Ipswich T	5	2		
1998–99	Ipswich T	30	5		
1999–2000	Ipswich T	36	8		
2000–01	Ipswich T	13	1		
2001–02	Ipswich T	14	1		
2001–02	*Millwall*	3	0	**3**	**0**
2001–02	*Barnsley*	8	0	**8**	**0**
2002–03	Ipswich T	17	2		
2003–04	Ipswich T	39	5		
2004–05	Ipswich T	46	6		
2005–06	Ipswich T	42	3		
2006–07	Ipswich T	25	0		
2007–08	Ipswich T	7	0	**301**	**37**

NORRIS, David (M) **241 29**
H: 5 7 W: 11 06 b.Stamford 22-2-81
Source: Boston U.

1999–2000	Bolton W	0	0		

2000–01 Bolton W 0 0
2001–02 Bolton W 0 0
2001–02 *Hull C* 6 1 **6 1**
2002–03 Bolton W 0 0
2002–03 Plymouth Arg 33 6
2003–04 Plymouth Arg 45 5
2004–05 Plymouth Arg 35 3
2005–06 Plymouth Arg 45 2
2006–07 Plymouth Arg 41 6
2007–08 Plymouth Arg 27 5 **226 27**
2007–08 Ipswich T 9 1 **9 1**

O'CALLAGHAN, George (M) 153 20
H: 6 1 W: 10 11 b.Cork 5-9-79
Source: Trainee. *Honours:* Eire Youth.
1998–99 Port Vale 4 0
1999–2000 Port Vale 11 0
2000–01 Port Vale 8 1
2001–02 Port Vale 11 3 **34 4**
2002–03 Cork C 26 6
2003–04 Cork C 0 0
2004–05 Cork C 35 3
2005–06 Cork C 32 6 **93 15**
2006–07 Ipswich T 11 1
2007–08 Ipswich T 1 0 **12 1**
2007–08 *Brighton & HA* 14 0 **14 0**

PETERS, Jaime (M) 55 3
H: 5 7 W: 10 12 b.Pickering 4-5-87
Source: Moor Green. *Honours:* Canada Youth, Under-20, Under-23, 15 full caps, 1 goal.
2005–06 Ipswich T 13 0
2006–07 Ipswich T 23 2
2007–08 Ipswich T 5 0 **41 2**
2007–08 *Yeovil T* 14 1 **14 1**

PLUMMER, Andrew (G) 0 0
H: 6 0 W: 12 13 b.Ipswich 3-10-89
Source: Scholar.
2006–07 Ipswich T 0 0
2007–08 Ipswich T 0 0

QUINN, Alan (M) 276 28
H: 5 9 W: 10 06 b.Dublin 13-6-79
Source: Cherry Orchard. *Honours:* Eire Youth, Under-21, 8 full caps.
1997–98 Sheffield W 1 0
1998–99 Sheffield W 1 0
1999–2000 Sheffield W 19 3
2000–01 Sheffield W 37 2
2001–02 Sheffield W 38 2
2002–03 Sheffield W 37 5
2003–04 Sheffield W 24 4 **157 16**
2003–04 *Sunderland* 6 0 **6 0**
2004–05 Sheffield U 43 7
2005–06 Sheffield U 27 4
2006–07 Sheffield U 19 0
2007–08 Sheffield U 8 0 **97 11**
2007–08 Ipswich T 16 1 **16 1**

RHODES, Jordan (F) 8 1
H: 6 1 W: 11 03 b.Oldham 5-2-90
2007–08 Ipswich T 8 1 **8 1**

RICHARDS, Matt (D) 175 8
H: 5 8 W: 11 00 b.Harlow 26-12-84
Source: Scholar. *Honours:* England Under-21.
2001–02 Ipswich T 0 0
2002–03 Ipswich T 13 0
2003–04 Ipswich T 44 1
2004–05 Ipswich T 24 1
2005–06 Ipswich T 38 4
2006–07 Ipswich T 28 2
2007–08 Ipswich T 0 0 **147 8**
2007–08 *Brighton & HA* 28 0 **28 0**

ROBERTS, Gary M (F) 72 11
H: 5 10 W: 11 09 b.Wales 18-3-84
Source: Denbigh T, Bangor C.
2006–07 Accrington S 14 8 **14 8**
2006–07 Ipswich T 33 2
2007–08 Ipswich T 21 1 **54 3**
2007–08 *Crewe Alex* 4 0 **4 0**

ROBINSON, Kurt (D) 0 0
H: 5 8 W: 11 00 b.Basildon 21-10-89
Source: Southend U.
2007–08 Ipswich T 0 0

SITO (D) 120 1
H: 5 8 W: 11 07 b.Coruna 21-5-80
2001–02 Lugo 10 0 **10 0**
2001–02 Calahorra 18 0 **18 0**
2002–03 Racing Ferrol 12 0
2003–04 Racing Ferrol 21 0
2004–05 Racing Ferrol 0 0 **33 0**
2005–06 Ipswich T 38 0
2006–07 Ipswich T 8 0
2007–08 Ipswich T 13 1 **59 1**

SMITH, Tommy (D) 0 0
H: 6 2 W: 12 02 b.Macclesfield 31-3-90
Source: Scholar.
2007–08 Ipswich T 0 0

SUMULIKOSKI, Velice (M) 173 7
H: 6 0 W: 12 02 b.Macedonia 24-1-81
Honours: Macedonia 50 full caps, 1 goal.
1999–2000 Publikum 21 2
2000–01 Publikum 28 1
2001–02 Publikum 7 0 **56 3**
2001–02 Slovacko 13 0
2002–03 Slovacko 29 2
2003–04 Slovacko 13 0 **55 2**
2004 Zenit 25 0
2005 Zenit 16 1
2006 Zenit 5 0 **46 1**
2007–08 Ipswich T 16 1 **16 1**

SUPPLE, Shane (G) 38 0
H: 6 0 W: 11 13 b.Dublin 4-5-87
Source: Scholar. *Honours:* Eire Youth, Under-21.
2004–05 Ipswich T 0 0
2005–06 Ipswich T 22 0
2006–07 Ipswich T 12 0
2007–08 *Falkirk* 4 0 **4 0**
2007–08 Ipswich T 0 0 **34 0**

TROTTER, Liam (M) 9 1
H: 6 2 W: 12 02 b.Ipswich 24-8-88
Source: Scholar.
2005–06 Ipswich T 1 0
2006–07 Ipswich T 0 0
2006–07 *Millwall* 2 0 **2 0**
2007–08 Ipswich T 6 1 **7 1**

UPSON, Edward (M) 0 0
H: 5 10 W: 11 07 b.Bury St Edmunds 21-11-89
Source: Scholar. *Honours:* England Youth.
2006–07 Ipswich T 0 0
2007–08 Ipswich T 0 0

WALTERS, Jon (F) 183 38
H: 6 0 W: 12 06 b.Birkenhead 20-9-83
Source: Blackburn R Scholar. *Honours:* Eire Youth, Under-21, B.
2001–02 Bolton W 0 0
2002–03 Bolton W 4 0
2002–03 *Hull C* 11 5
2003–04 Bolton W 0 0 **4 0**
2003–04 Crewe Alex 0 0
2003–04 *Barnsley* 8 0 **8 0**
2003–04 Hull C 16 1
2004–05 Hull C 21 1 **48 7**
2004–05 *Scunthorpe U* 3 0 **3 0**
2005–06 Wrexham 38 5 **38 5**
2006–07 Chester C 26 9 **26 9**
2006–07 Ipswich T 16 4
2007–08 Ipswich T 40 13 **56 17**

WILLIAMS, Gavin (M) 119 15
H: 5 10 W: 11 05 b.Pontypridd 20-6-80
Source: Hereford U. *Honours:* Wales 2 full caps.
2003–04 Yeovil T 42 9
2004–05 Yeovil T 13 2 **55 11**
2004–05 West Ham U 10 1
2005–06 West Ham U 0 0 **10 1**
2005–06 Ipswich T 12 1
2006–07 Ipswich T 29 2
2007–08 Ipswich T 13 0 **54 3**

WILNIS, Fabian (D) 523 10
H: 5 8 W: 12 06 b.Paramaribo 23-8-70
Source: Het Noorden, NOC, De Zwervers, Sparta.
1990–91 NAC 7 3
1991–92 NAC 30 0
1992–93 NAC 32 0
1993–94 NAC 34 0
1994–95 NAC 31 0 **134 3**
1995–96 De Graafschap 32 0
1996–97 De Graafschap 23 0
1997–98 De Graafschap 33 1
1998–99 De Graafschap 19 0 **107 1**
1998–99 Ipswich T 18 1
1999–2000 Ipswich T 35 0
2000–01 Ipswich T 29 2
2001–02 Ipswich T 14 0
2002–03 Ipswich T 35 2
2003–04 Ipswich T 41 0
2004–05 Ipswich T 41 0
2005–06 Ipswich T 35 1
2006–07 Ipswich T 21 0
2007–08 Ipswich T 13 0 **282 6**

WRIGHT, David (D) 321 6
H: 5 11 W: 11 01 b.Warrington 1-5-80
Source: Trainee. *Honours:* England Youth.
1997–98 Crewe Alex 3 0
1998–99 Crewe Alex 20 1
1999–2000 Crewe Alex 45 0
2000–01 Crewe Alex 42 0
2001–02 Crewe Alex 30 0
2002–03 Crewe Alex 31 1
2003–04 Crewe Alex 40 1 **211 3**
2004–05 Wigan Ath 31 0
2005–06 Wigan Ath 2 0
2005–06 *Norwich C* 5 0 **5 0**
2006–07 Wigan Ath 12 0 **45 0**
2006–07 Ipswich T 19 1
2007–08 Ipswich T 41 2 **60 3**

LEEDS U (42)

AMEOBI, Tomi (F) 9 0
H: 6 3 W: 12 10 b.Newcastle 16-8-88
Source: Scholar.
2007–08 Leeds U 0 0
2007–08 *Scunthorpe U* 9 0 **9 0**

ANKERGREN, Casper (G) 143 0
H: 6 3 W: 14 07 b.Koge 9-11-79
Source: Koge. *Honours:* Denmark Youth, Under-21.
2001–02 Brondby 1 0
2002–03 Brondby 16 0
2003–04 Brondby 1 0
2004–05 Brondby 32 0
2005–06 Brondby 18 0
2006–07 Brondby 18 0 **86 0**
2006–07 Leeds U 14 0
2007–08 Leeds U 43 0 **57 0**

BAYLY, Robert (M) 1 0
H: 5 9 W: 11 09 b.Dublin 22-2-88
Source: Scholar.
2005–06 Leeds U 0 0
2006–07 Leeds U 1 0
2007–08 Leeds U 0 0 **1 0**

BECKFORD, Jermaine (F) 72 29
H: 6 2 W: 13 02 b.London 9-12-83
Source: Wealdstone.
2005–06 Leeds U 5 0
2006–07 Leeds U 5 0
2006–07 *Carlisle U* 4 1 **4 1**
2006–07 *Scunthorpe U* 18 8 **18 8**
2007–08 Leeds U 40 20 **50 20**

CAROLE, Sebastien (M) 97 6
H: 5 7 W: 11 05 b.Pontoise 8-9-82
Source: Monaco.
2003–04 West Ham U 1 0 **1 0**
2004–05 Chateauroux 11 1 **11 1**
2005–06 Brighton & HA 40 2 **40 2**
2006–07 Leeds U 17 0
2007–08 Leeds U 28 3 **45 3**

CONSTANTINE, Leon (F) 210 70
H: 6 2 W: 12 00 b.Hackney 24-2-78
Source: Edgware T.
2000–01 Millwall 1 0
2001–02 Millwall 0 0 **1 0**
2001–02 *Leyton Orient* 10 3 **10 3**
2001–02 *Partick T* 2 0 **2 0**
2002–03 Brentford 17 0 **17 0**
2003–04 Southend U 43 21 **43 21**
2004–05 Peterborough U 11 1 **11 1**
2004–05 Torquay U 27 9
2005–06 Torquay U 15 1 **42 10**
2005–06 Port Vale 30 10
2006–07 Port Vale 42 22
2007–08 Port Vale 0 0 **72 32**
2007–08 Leeds U 4 1 **4 1**
2007–08 *Oldham Ath* 8 2 **8 2**

DA COSTA, Filipe (M) **57 6**
H: 5 11 W: 11 05 b.San Sebastian 30-8-84
Source: Amora.

2002–03	Braga	3	0	**3**	**0**
2003–04	Reggiana	0	0		
2004–05	Ionikos	9	0		
2005–06	Ionikos	24	4		
2006–07	Ionikos	17	2	**50**	**6**
2007–08	Leeds U	4	0	**4**	**0**

DELPH, Fabian (D) **2 0**
H: 5 8 W: 11 00 b.Bradford 5-5-91
Source: Scholar. *Honours:* England Youth.

2006–07	Leeds U	1	0		
2007–08	Leeds U	1	0	**2**	**0**

DOUGLAS, Jonathan (M) **148 14**
H: 5 11 W: 11 11 b.Monaghan 22-11-81
Source: Trainee. *Honours:* Eire Under-21, 8 full caps.

1999–2000	Blackburn R	0	0		
2000–01	Blackburn R	0	0		
2001–02	Blackburn R	0	0		
2002–03	Blackburn R	1	0		
2002–03	*Chesterfield*	7	1	**7**	**1**
2003–04	Blackpool	16	3	**16**	**3**
2003–04	Blackburn R	14	1		
2004–05	Blackburn R	1	0		
2004–05	*Gillingham*	10	0	**10**	**0**
2005–06	Blackburn R	0	0		
2005–06	*Leeds U*	40	5		
2006–07	Blackburn R	0	0	**16**	**1**
2006–07	Leeds U	35	1		
2007–08	Leeds U	24	3	**99**	**9**

ELDING, Anthony (F) **81 30**
H: 6 1 W: 12 02 b.Boston 16-4-82
Source: Trainee.

2002–03	Boston U	8	0		
From Stevenage B, Kettering T.					
2006–07	Boston U	19	5	**27**	**5**
2006–07	Stockport Co	20	11		
2007–08	Stockport Co	25	13	**45**	**24**
2007–08	Leeds U	9	1	**9**	**1**

FLO, Tore Andre (F) **394 140**
H: 6 4 W: 13 08 b.Strin 15-6-73
Honours: Norway Under-21, 76 full caps, 23 goals.

1994	Sogndal	22	5	**22**	**5**
1995	Tromso	26	18	**26**	**18**
1996	Brann	24	19		
1997	Brann	16	9	**40**	**28**
1997–98	Chelsea	34	11		
1998–99	Chelsea	30	10		
1999–2000	Chelsea	34	10		
2000–01	Chelsea	14	3	**112**	**34**
2000–01	Rangers	19	11		
2001–02	Rangers	30	17		
2002–03	Rangers	4	0	**53**	**28**
2002–03	Sunderland	29	4	**29**	**4**
2003–04	Siena	33	8		
2004–05	Siena	32	7	**65**	**15**
2005	Valerenga	8	0		
2006	Valerenga	16	4	**24**	**4**
2006–07	Leeds U	1	1		
2007–08	Leeds U	22	3	**23**	**4**

GARDNER, Scott (M) **1 0**
H: 5 9 W: 11 04 b.Luxembourg 1-4-88
Source: Scholar. *Honours:* England Youth.

2005–06	Leeds U	0	0		
2006–07	Leeds U	0	0		
2007–08	Leeds U	1	0	**1**	**0**

HEATH, Matt (D) **148 11**
H: 6 4 W: 13 13 b.Leicester 1-11-81
Source: Scholar.

2000–01	Leicester C	0	0		
2001–02	Leicester C	5	0		
2002–03	Leicester C	11	3		
2003–04	Leicester C	13	0		
2003–04	*Stockport Co*	8	0	**8**	**0**
2004–05	Leicester C	22	3	**51**	**6**
2005–06	Coventry C	25	1		
2006–07	Coventry C	7	0	**32**	**1**
2006–07	Leeds U	26	3		
2007–08	Leeds U	26	1	**52**	**4**
2007–08	*Colchester U*	5	0	**5**	**0**

HOTCHKISS, Oliver (M) **0 0**
b.Houghton-le-Spring 27-9-89
Source: Scholar.

2007–08	Leeds U	0	0		

HOWSON, Jonathan (M) **35 4**
H: 5 11 W: 12 01 b.Morley 21-5-88
Source: Scholar.

2006–07	Leeds U	9	1		
2007–08	Leeds U	26	3	**35**	**4**

HUGHES, Andy (M) **421 39**
H: 5 11 W: 12 01 b.Stockport 2-1-78
Source: Trainee.

1995–96	Oldham Ath	15	1		
1996–97	Oldham Ath	8	0		
1997–98	Oldham Ath	10	0	**33**	**1**
1997–98	Notts Co	15	2		
1998–99	Notts Co	30	3		
1999–2000	Notts Co	35	7		
2000–01	Notts Co	30	5	**110**	**17**
2001–02	Reading	39	6		
2002–03	Reading	43	9		
2003–04	Reading	43	3		
2004–05	Reading	41	0	**166**	**18**
2005–06	Norwich C	36	2		
2006–07	Norwich C	36	0	**72**	**2**
2007–08	Leeds U	40	1	**40**	**1**

HUNTINGTON, Paul (D) **28 2**
H: 6 3 W: 12 08 b.Carlisle 17-9-87
Source: Scholar. *Honours:* England Youth.

2005–06	Newcastle U	0	0		
2006–07	Newcastle U	11	1		
2007–08	Newcastle U	0	0	**11**	**1**
2007–08	Leeds U	17	1	**17**	**1**

JOHNSON, Brad (M) **75 11**
H: 6 0 W: 12 10 b.Hackney 28-4-87
Source: Cambridge U Juniors.

2004–05	Cambridge U	1	0	**1**	**0**
2005–06	Northampton T	3	0		
2006–07	Northampton T	27	5		
2007–08	Northampton T	23	3	**53**	**8**
2007–08	Leeds U	21	3	**21**	**3**

KANDOL, Tresor (F) **128 27**
H: 6 0 W: 13 07 b.Banga 30-8-81
Source: Trainee. *Honours:* DR Congo 1 full cap.

1998–99	Luton T	4	0		
1999–2000	Luton T	4	0		
2000–01	Luton T	13	3	**21**	**3**
2001–02	Bournemouth	12	0	**12**	**0**
From Thurrock, Dagenham					
2005–06	*Darlington*	7	2	**7**	**2**
From Dagenham & R.					
2005–06	Barnet	13	4		
2006–07	Barnet	16	6	**29**	**10**
2006–07	Leeds U	18	1		
2007–08	Leeds U	41	11	**59**	**12**

KENTON, Darren (D) **246 11**
H: 5 10 W: 12 06 b.Wandsworth 13-9-78
Source: Trainee.

1997–98	Norwich C	11	0		
1998–99	Norwich C	22	1		
1999–2000	Norwich C	26	1		
2000–01	Norwich C	29	2		
2001–02	Norwich C	33	4		
2002–03	Norwich C	37	1	**158**	**9**
2002–03	Southampton	0	0		
2003–04	Southampton	7	0		
2004–05	Southampton	9	0		
2004–05	*Leicester C*	10	0		
2005–06	Southampton	13	0	**29**	**0**
2006–07	Leicester C	23	2		
2007–08	Leicester C	10	0	**43**	**2**
2007–08	Leeds U	16	0	**16**	**0**

KILKENNY, Neil (M) **89 6**
H: 5 8 W: 10 08 b.Enfield 19-12-85
Source: Arsenal Trainee. *Honours:* England Youth, Under-20, Australia Under-23, 2 full caps.

2003–04	Birmingham C	0	0		
2004–05	Birmingham C	0	0		
2004–05	*Oldham Ath*	27	4		
2005–06	Birmingham C	18	0		
2006–07	Birmingham C	8	0		
2007–08	Birmingham C	0	0	**26**	**0**
2007–08	*Oldham Ath*	20	1	**47**	**5**
2007–08	Leeds U	16	1	**16**	**1**

LUCAS, David (G) **215 0**
H: 6 1 W: 13 07 b.Preston 23-11-77
Source: Trainee. *Honours:* England Youth.

1995–96	Preston NE	1	0		
1995–96	*Darlington*	6	0		
1996–97	Preston NE	2	0		
1996–97	*Darlington*	7	0	**13**	**0**
1996–97	*Scunthorpe U*	6	0	**6**	**0**
1997–98	Preston NE	6	0		
1998–99	Preston NE	30	0		
1999–2000	Preston NE	6	0		
2000–01	Preston NE	29	0		
2001–02	Preston NE	24	0		
2002–03	Preston NE	21	0		
2003–04	Preston NE	2	0	**121**	**0**
2003–04	*Sheffield W*	17	0		
2004–05	Sheffield W	34	0		
2005–06	Sheffield W	18	0		
2006–07	Sheffield W	0	0	**69**	**0**
2006–07	Barnsley	3	0		
2007–08	Barnsley	0	0	**3**	**0**
2007–08	Leeds U	3	0	**3**	**0**

LUND, Jonny (G) **0 0**
H: 5 10 W: 11 10 b.Leeds 1-11-88
Source: Scholar.

2006–07	Leeds U	0	0		
2007–08	Leeds U	0	0		

MADDEN, Simon (D) **0 0**
H: 5 9 W: 11 10 b.Dublin 1-5-88
Source: Shelbourne.

2005–06	Leeds U	0	0		
2006–07	Leeds U	0	0		
2007–08	Leeds U	0	0		

MARTIN, Alan (G) **0 0**
H: 6 0 W: 11 11 b.Glasgow 1-1-89
Source: Motherwell. *Honours:* Scotland Youth.

2007–08	Leeds U	0	0		

MICHALIK, Lubomir (D) **55 4**
H: 6 4 W: 13 00 b.Cadca 13-8-83
Source: Cadca, Martin. *Honours:* Slovakia 4 full caps, 1 goal.

2005–06	Senec	8	1		
2006–07	Senec	12	1	**20**	**2**
2006–07	*Leeds U*	7	1		
2006–07	Bolton W	4	1		
2007–08	Bolton W	7	0	**11**	**1**
2007–08	Leeds U	17	0	**24**	**1**

PARKER, Ben (D) **61 0**
H: 5 11 W: 11 06 b.Pontefract 8-11-87
Source: Scholar. *Honours:* England Youth.

2004–05	Leeds U	0	0		
2005–06	Leeds U	0	0		
2006–07	Leeds U	0	0		
2006–07	*Bradford C*	39	0	**39**	**0**
2007–08	Leeds U	9	0	**9**	**0**
2007–08	*Darlington*	13	0	**13**	**0**

PRUTTON, David (M) **280 16**
H: 5 10 W: 13 00 b.Hull 12-9-81
Source: Trainee. *Honours:* England Youth, Under-21.

1998–99	Nottingham F	0	0		
1999–2000	Nottingham F	34	2		
2000–01	Nottingham F	42	1		
2001–02	Nottingham F	43	3		
2002–03	Nottingham F	24	1		
2002–03	Southampton	12	0		
2003–04	Southampton	27	1		
2004–05	Southampton	23	1		
2005–06	Southampton	17	0		
2006–07	Southampton	3	1	**82**	**3**
2006–07	*Nottingham F*	12	2	**155**	**9**
2007–08	Leeds U	43	4	**43**	**4**

RICHARDSON, Frazer (D) **139 4**
H: 5 11 W: 11 12 b.Rotherham 29-10-82
Source: Trainee. *Honours:* England Youth, Under-20.

1999–2000	Leeds U	0	0		
2000–01	Leeds U	0	0		
2001–02	Leeds U	0	0		
2002–03	Leeds U	0	0		
2002–03	*Stoke C*	7	0		
2003–04	Leeds U	4	0		
2003–04	*Stoke C*	6	1	**13**	**1**
2004–05	Leeds U	38	1		
2005–06	Leeds U	23	1		
2006–07	Leeds U	22	0		
2007–08	Leeds U	39	1	**126**	**3**

ROSS, Damian (G) **0 0**
b.Bishop Auckland

2007–08	Leeds U	0	0		

ROTHERY, Gavin (F) **0 0**
b.Morley 22-9-87
Source: Scholar. *Honours:* England Youth.
2005–06 Leeds U 0 0
2006–07 Leeds U 0 0
2007–08 Leeds U 0 0

RUI MARQUES, Manuel (D) **169 3**
H: 5 11 W: 11 13 b.Luanda 3-9-77
Source: Benfica. *Honours:* Angola 7 full caps.
1998–99 Baden 27 0 **27 0**
1999–2000 SSV Ulm 32 0 **32 0**
2000–01 Hertha 1 0 **1 0**
2000–01 Stuttgart 12 0
2001–02 Stuttgart 23 0
2002–03 Stuttgart 12 0
2003–04 Stuttgart 0 0 **47 0**
2004–05 Maritimo 8 0 **8 0**
2005–06 Leeds U 0 0
2005–06 *Hull C* 1 0 **1 0**
2006–07 Leeds U 17 0
2007–08 Leeds U 36 3 **53 3**

SORSA, Sebastian (M) **0 0**
H: 5 9 W: 11 00 b.Helsinki 25-1-84
Source: HJK Helsinki.
2007–08 Leeds U 0 0

SWEENEY, Peter (M) **118 7**
H: 6 0 W: 12 11 b.Glasgow 25-9-84
Source: Scholar. *Honours:* Scotland Youth, Under-21, B.
2001–02 Millwall 1 0
2002–03 Millwall 5 1
2003–04 Millwall 29 2
2004–05 Millwall 24 2 **59 5**
2005–06 Stoke C 17 1
2006–07 Stoke C 13 1
2006–07 *Yeovil T* 8 0 **8 0**
2007–08 Stoke C 5 0 **35 2**
2007–08 *Walsall* 7 0 **7 0**
2007–08 Leeds U 9 0 **9 0**

THOMPSON, Alan (M) **409 81**
H: 6 0 W: 12 08 b.Newcastle 22-12-73
Source: Trainee. *Honours:* England Youth, Under-21, B, 1 full cap.
1990–91 Newcastle U 0 0
1991–92 Newcastle U 14 0
1992–93 Newcastle U 2 0 **16 0**
1993–94 Bolton W 27 6
1994–95 Bolton W 37 7
1995–96 Bolton W 26 1
1996–97 Bolton W 34 10
1997–98 Bolton W 33 9 **157 33**
1998–99 Aston Villa 25 2
1999–2000 Aston Villa 21 2
2000–01 Aston Villa 30 4 **76 8**
2001–02 Celtic 25 6
2002–03 Celtic 29 8
2003–04 Celtic 26 11
2004–05 Celtic 32 7
2005–06 Celtic 17 2
2006–07 Celtic 0 0 **129 34**
2006–07 Leeds U 11 2
2007–08 Leeds U 13 3 **24 5**
2007–08 *Hartlepool U* 7 1 **7 1**

WESTLAKE, Ian (M) **172 18**
H: 5 10 W: 11 06 b.Clacton 10-7-83
Source: Scholar.
2002–03 Ipswich T 4 0
2003–04 Ipswich T 39 6
2004–05 Ipswich T 45 7
2005–06 Ipswich T 26 2 **114 15**
2006–07 Leeds U 27 0
2007–08 Leeds U 20 1 **47 1**
2007–08 *Brighton & HA* 11 2 **11 2**

WESTON, Curtis (M) **45 2**
H: 5 11 W: 11 09 b.Greenwich 24-1-87
Source: Scholar.
2003–04 Millwall 1 0
2004–05 Millwall 3 0
2005–06 Millwall 0 0 **4 0**
2006–07 Swindon T 27 1 **27 1**
2007–08 Leeds U 7 1 **7 1**
2007–08 *Scunthorpe U* 7 0 **7 0**

LEICESTER C (43)

BESWICK, Ryan (M) **0 0**
b.Walton-on-Thames 12-1-88
2007–08 Leicester C 0 0

BORI, Gabor (M) **97 14**
H: 5 10 W: 11 00 b.Hungary 16-1-84
Honours: Hungary 1 full cap.
2004–05 MTK 24 3
2005–06 MTK 29 3
2006–07 MTK 24 3
2007–08 MTK 14 5 **91 14**
2007–08 Leicester C 6 0 **6 0**

CAMPBELL, Dudley (F) **94 22**
H: 5 10 W: 11 00 b.London 12-11-81
Source: Aston Villa Trainee, QPR, Chesham U, Stevenage B, Yeading.
2005–06 Brentford 23 9 **23 9**
2005–06 Birmingham C 11 0
2006–07 Birmingham C 32 9 **43 9**
2007–08 Leicester C 28 4 **28 4**

CHAMBERS, Ashley (F) **5 0**
H: 5 10 W: 11 06 b.Leicester 1-3-90
Source: Scholar. *Honours:* England Schools, Youth.
2005–06 Leicester C 0 0
2006–07 Leicester C 0 0
2007–08 Leicester C 5 0 **5 0**

CHAMBERS, James (D) **194 0**
H: 5 10 W: 11 11 b.West Bromwich 20-11-80
Source: Trainee. *Honours:* England Youth.
1998–99 WBA 0 0
1999–2000 WBA 12 0
2000–01 WBA 31 0
2001–02 WBA 5 0
2002–03 WBA 8 0
2003–04 WBA 17 0
2004–05 WBA 0 0 **73 0**
2004–05 Watford 40 0
2005–06 Watford 38 0
2006–07 Watford 12 0 **90 0**
2006–07 *Cardiff C* 7 0 **7 0**
2007–08 Leicester C 24 0 **24 0**

CISAK, Aleksander (G) **0 0**
H: 6 3 W: 14 11 b.Krakow 19-5-89
Source: Scholar.
2006–07 Leicester C 0 0
2007–08 Leicester C 0 0

CLAPHAM, Jamie (M) **353 11**
H: 5 9 W: 11 09 b.Lincoln 7-12-75
Source: Trainee.
1994–95 Tottenham H 0 0
1995–96 Tottenham H 0 0
1996–97 Tottenham H 1 0
1996–97 *Leyton Orient* 6 0 **6 0**
1996–97 *Bristol R* 5 0 **5 0**
1997–98 Tottenham H 0 0 **1 0**
1997–98 Ipswich T 22 0
1998–99 Ipswich T 46 3
1999–2000 Ipswich T 46 2
2000–01 Ipswich T 35 2
2001–02 Ipswich T 32 2
2002–03 Ipswich T 26 1 **207 10**
2002–03 Birmingham C 16 0
2003–04 Birmingham C 25 0
2004–05 Birmingham C 27 0
2005–06 Birmingham C 16 1 **84 1**
2006–07 Wolverhampton W 26 0
2007–08 Wolverhampton W 0 0 **26 0**
2007–08 *Leeds U* 13 0 **13 0**
2007–08 Leicester C 11 0 **11 0**

CLEMENCE, Stephen (M) **242 12**
H: 6 0 W: 12 09 b.Liverpool 31-3-78
Source: Trainee. *Honours:* England Schools, Youth, Under-21.
1994–95 Tottenham H 0 0
1995–96 Tottenham H 0 0
1996–97 Tottenham H 0 0
1997–98 Tottenham H 17 0
1998–99 Tottenham H 18 0
1999–2000 Tottenham H 20 1
2000–01 Tottenham H 29 1
2001–02 Tottenham H 6 0
2002–03 Tottenham H 0 0 **90 2**
2002–03 Birmingham C 15 2
2003–04 Birmingham C 35 2
2004–05 Birmingham C 22 0
2005–06 Birmingham C 15 0
2006–07 Birmingham C 34 4 **121 8**
2007–08 Leicester C 31 2 **31 2**

CORT, Carl (F) **209 55**
H: 6 4 W: 12 04 b.Southwark 1-11-77
Source: Trainee. *Honours:* England Under-21.
1996–97 Wimbledon 1 0
1996–97 *Lincoln C* 6 1 **6 1**
1997–98 Wimbledon 22 4
1998–99 Wimbledon 16 3
1999–2000 Wimbledon 34 9 **73 16**
2000–01 Newcastle U 13 6
2001–02 Newcastle U 8 1
2002–03 Newcastle U 1 0
2003–04 Newcastle U 0 0 **22 7**
2003–04 Wolverhampton W 16 5
2004–05 Wolverhampton W 37 15
2005–06 Wolverhampton W 31 11
2006–07 Wolverhampton W 10 0 **94 31**
2007–08 Leicester C 14 0 **14 0**

COX, Lee (D) **0 0**
Source: Scholar.
2007–08 Leicester C 0 0

DE VRIES, Mark (F) **209 51**
H: 6 3 W: 13 05 b.Surinam 24-8-75
1995–96 Volendam 4 0
1996–97 Volendam 10 0
1997–98 Volendam 14 1 **28 1**
1998–99 Niort 0 0
1999–2000 Dordrecht 8 0
2000–01 Dordrecht 30 11
2001–02 Dordrecht 0 0 **38 11**
2002–03 Hearts 32 15
2003–04 Hearts 31 12
2004–05 Hearts 9 1 **72 28**
2004–05 Leicester C 16 1
2005–06 Leicester C 29 6
2006–07 Leicester C 0 0
2007–08 Leicester C 6 1 **51 8**
2007–08 *Dundee U* 14 2 **14 2**
2007–08 *Leeds U* 6 1 **6 1**

DODDS, Louis (F) **53 11**
H: 5 10 W: 12 04 b.Leicester 8-10-86
Source: Scholar.
2005–06 Leicester C 0 0
2006–07 Leicester C 0 0
2006–07 *Rochdale* 12 2 **12 2**
2007–08 Leicester C 0 0
2007–08 *Lincoln C* 41 9 **41 9**

DOUGLAS, Rab (G) **340 0**
H: 6 3 W: 14 12 b.Lanark 24-4-72
Source: Forth Wanderers. *Honours:* Scotland B, 19 full caps.
1992–93 Meadowbank T 0 0
1993–94 Meadowbank T 4 0
1994–95 Meadowbank T 8 0 **12 0**
1995–96 Livingston 24 0
1996–97 Livingston 36 0 **60 0**
1997–98 Dundee 36 0
1998–99 Dundee 35 0
1999–2000 Dundee 35 0
2000–01 Dundee 11 0 **117 0**
2000–01 Celtic 22 0
2001–02 Celtic 35 0
2002–03 Celtic 21 0
2003–04 Celtic 16 0
2004–05 Celtic 14 0 **108 0**
2005–06 Leicester C 32 0
2006–07 Leicester C 0 0
2007–08 Leicester C 0 0 **32 0**
2007–08 *Millwall* 7 0 **7 0**
2007–08 *Wycombe W* 3 0 **3 0**
2007–08 *Plymouth Arg* 1 0 **1 0**

FRYATT, Matty (F) **161 39**
H: 5 10 W: 11 00 b.Nuneaton 5-3-86
Source: Scholar. *Honours:* England Youth.
2002–03 Walsall 0 0
2003–04 Walsall 11 1
2003–04 *Carlisle U* 10 1 **10 1**
2004–05 Walsall 36 15
2005–06 Walsall 23 11 **70 27**
2005–06 Leicester C 19 6
2006–07 Leicester C 32 3
2007–08 Leicester C 30 2 **81 11**

GERRBRAND, Patrik (D) **82** **2**
H: 6 2 W: 12 06 b.Stockholm 27-4-81
Source: Alvsjo. *Honours:* Sweden Under-21.

2000	Hammarby	6	0		
2001	Hammarby	5	0		
2002	Hammarby	0	0		
2003	Hammarby	16	1		
2004	Hammarby	25	1		
2005	Hammarby	13	0	**65**	**2**
2005–06	Leicester C	17	0		
2006–07	Leicester C	0	0		
2007–08	Leicester C	0	0	**17**	**0**

GRADEL, Max (M) **34** **9**
H: 5 8 W: 12 03 b.Ivory Coast 30-9-87

2005–06	Leicester C	0	0		
2006–07	Leicester C	0	0		
2007–08	Leicester C	0	0		
2007–08	*Bournemouth*	34	9	**34**	**9**

HAMMOND, Elvis (F) **100** **10**
H: 5 10 W: 11 02 b.Accra 6-10-80
Source: Trainee. *Honours:* Ghana 1 full cap.

1999–2000	Fulham	0	0		
2000–01	Fulham	0	0		
2001–02	Fulham	0	0		
2001–02	*Bristol R*	7	0	**7**	**0**
2002–03	Fulham	10	0		
2003–04	Fulham	0	0		
2003–04	*Norwich C*	4	0	**4**	**0**
2004–05	Fulham	1	0		
2004–05	RBC Roosendaal	14	2	**14**	**2**
2005–06	Fulham	0	0	**11**	**0**
2005–06	Leicester C	33	3		
2006–07	Leicester C	31	5		
2007–08	Leicester C	0	0	**64**	**8**

HAYES, Jonathan (M) **29** **0**
H: 5 7 W: 11 00 b.Dublin 9-7-87
Source: Scholar. *Honours:* Eire Under-21.

2004–05	Reading	0	0		
2005–06	Reading	0	0		
2006–07	Reading	0	0		
2006–07	*Milton Keynes D*	11	0	**11**	**0**
2007–08	Leicester C	7	0	**7**	**0**
2007–08	*Northampton T*	11	0	**11**	**0**

HAYLES, Barry (F) **376** **109**
H: 5 10 W: 12 11 b.Lambeth 17-5-72
Source: Stevenage Bor. *Honours:* Jamaica 10 full caps.

1997–98	Bristol R	45	23		
1998–99	Bristol R	17	9	**62**	**32**
1998–99	Fulham	30	8		
1999–2000	Fulham	35	5		
2000–01	Fulham	35	18		
2001–02	Fulham	35	8		
2002–03	Fulham	14	1		
2003–04	Fulham	26	4	**175**	**44**
2004–05	Sheffield U	4	0	**4**	**0**
2004–05	Millwall	32	12		
2005–06	Millwall	23	4	**55**	**16**
2006–07	Plymouth Arg	39	13		
2007–08	Plymouth Arg	23	2	**62**	**15**
2007–08	Leicester C	18	2	**18**	**2**

HELLINGS, Sergio (M) **68** **3**
H: 6 0 W: 12 00 b.Amsterdam 11-10-84
Source: Anderlecht. *Honours:* Holland Under-21.

2004–05	Anderlecht	0	0		
2004–05	Heracles	23	2		
2005–06	Heracles	20	1	**43**	**3**
2006–07	AGOVV Apeldoorn	25	0	**25**	**0**
2007–08	Leicester C	0	0		

HENDERSON, Paul (G) **231** **0**
H: 6 1 W: 12 06 b.Sydney 22-4-76

1998–99	Northern Spirit	30	0		
1999–2000	Northern Spirit	14	0		
2000–01	Northern Spirit	21	0		
2001–02	Northern Spirit	13	0		
2002–03	Northern Spirit	33	0		
2003–04	Northern Spirit	23	0	**134**	**0**
2004–05	Bradford C	40	0	**40**	**0**
2005–06	Leicester C	15	0		
2006–07	Leicester C	28	0		
2007–08	Leicester C	14	0	**57**	**0**

HOWARD, Steve (F) **524** **163**
H: 6 3 W: 15 00 b.Durham 10-5-76
Source: Tow Law T. *Honours:* Scotland B.

1995–96	Hartlepool U	39	7		
1996–97	Hartlepool U	32	8		
1997–98	Hartlepool U	43	7		
1998–99	Hartlepool U	28	5	**142**	**27**
1998–99	Northampton T	12	0		
1999–2000	Northampton T	41	10		
2000–01	Northampton T	33	8	**86**	**18**
2000–01	Luton T	12	3		
2001–02	Luton T	42	24		
2002–03	Luton T	41	22		
2003–04	Luton T	34	14		
2004–05	Luton T	40	18		
2005–06	Luton T	43	14	**212**	**95**
2006–07	Derby Co	43	16		
2007–08	Derby Co	20	1	**63**	**17**
2007–08	Leicester C	21	6	**21**	**6**

HUME, Iain (F) **272** **65**
H: 5 7 W: 11 02 b.Brampton 31-10-83
Source: Juniors. *Honours:* Canada Youth, Under-20, 21 full caps, 2 goals.

1999–2000	Tranmere R	3	0		
2000–01	Tranmere R	10	0		
2001–02	Tranmere R	14	0		
2002–03	Tranmere R	35	6		
2003–04	Tranmere R	40	10		
2004–05	Tranmere R	42	15		
2005–06	Tranmere R	6	1	**150**	**32**
2005–06	Leicester C	37	9		
2006–07	Leicester C	45	13		
2007–08	Leicester C	40	11	**122**	**33**

KAEBI, Hossein (D) **42** **6**
H: 5 9 W: 10 03 b.Ahvaz 23-9-85
Source: Foolad, Al-Sadd. *Honours:* Iran 57 full caps, 1 goal.

2005–06	Foolad	26	2	**26**	**2**
2006–07	Emirates	7	1	**7**	**1**
2007	Persepolis	6	3	**6**	**3**
2007–08	Leicester C	3	0	**3**	**0**

KING, Andy (M) **11** **1**
H: 6 0 W: 11 10 b.Luton 29-10-88
Source: Scholar. *Honours:* Wales Youth, Under-21.

2007–08	Leicester C	11	1	**11**	**1**

KISHISHEV, Radostin (D) **396** **19**
H: 5 11 W: 12 03 b.Bourgas 30-7-74
Honours: Bulgaria 78 full caps.

1991–92	Chernomorets	6	1		
1992–93	Chernomorets	23	2		
1993–94	Chernomorets	23	1	**52**	**4**
1994–95	Neftochimik	14	0		
1995–96	Neftochimik	30	0		
1996–97	Neftochimik	30	6		
1997–98	Neftochimik	1	0	**75**	**6**
1997–98	Bursaspor	20	3	**20**	**3**
1997–98	Litets Lovech	5	0		
1998–99	Litets Lovech	26	2		
1999–2000	Litets Lovech	15	2	**46**	**4**
2000–01	Charlton Ath	27	0		
2001–02	Charlton Ath	3	0		
2002–03	Charlton Ath	34	2		
2003–04	Charlton Ath	33	0		
2004–05	Charlton Ath	31	0		
2005–06	Charlton Ath	37	0		
2006–07	Charlton Ath	14	0	**179**	**2**
2006–07	*Leeds U*	10	0		
2007–08	Leicester C	7	0	**7**	**0**
2007–08	*Leeds U*	7	0	**17**	**0**

KISNORBO, Patrick (D) **233** **13**
H: 6 1 W: 11 11 b.Melbourne 24-3-81
Honours: Australia Schools, Under-20, Under-23, 14 full caps.

2000–01	South Melbourne	25	0		
2001–02	South Melbourne	23	2		
2002–03	South Melbourne	19	1	**67**	**3**
2003–04	Hearts	31	0		
2004–05	Hearts	17	1	**48**	**1**
2005–06	Leicester C	37	1		
2006–07	Leicester C	40	5		
2007–08	Leicester C	41	3	**118**	**9**

LACZKO, Zsolt (F) **9** **0**
H: 6 0 W: 12 11 b.Szeged 18-12-86
Source: Ferencvaros, Olympiakos. *Honours:* Hungary Under-21.

2007–08	Leicester C	9	0	**9**	**0**

LOGAN, Conrad (G) **65** **0**
H: 6 2 W: 14 00 b.Letterkenny 18-4-86
Source: Scholar. *Honours:* Eire Youth.

2003–04	Leicester C	0	0		
2004–05	Leicester C	0	0		
2005–06	Leicester C	0	0		
2005–06	*Boston U*	13	0	**13**	**0**
2006–07	Leicester C	18	0		
2007–08	Leicester C	0	0	**18**	**0**
2007–08	*Stockport Co*	34	0	**34**	**0**

MAGUNDA, Joseph (D) **0** **0**
b.Leamington 16-4-89

2007–08	Leicester C	0	0		

MATTOCK, Joe (D) **35** **0**
H: 5 11 W: 12 05 b.Leicester 15-5-90
Source: Scholar. *Honours:* England Youth, Under-21.

2006–07	Leicester C	4	0		
2007–08	Leicester C	31	0	**35**	**0**

MAYBURY, Alan (D) **223** **7**
H: 5 8 W: 11 08 b.Dublin 8-8-78
Source: Trainee. *Honours:* Eire Youth, Under-21, B, 10 full caps.

1995–96	Leeds U	1	0		
1996–97	Leeds U	0	0		
1997–98	Leeds U	12	0		
1998–99	Leeds U	0	0		
1998–99	*Reading*	8	0	**8**	**0**
1999–2000	Leeds U	0	0		
2000–01	Leeds U	0	0		
2000–01	*Crewe Alex*	6	0	**6**	**0**
2001–02	Leeds U	1	0	**14**	**0**
2001–02	Hearts	27	0		
2002–03	Hearts	35	2		
2003–04	Hearts	33	2		
2004–05	Hearts	15	0	**110**	**4**
2004–05	Leicester C	17	2		
2005–06	Leicester C	40	1		
2006–07	Leicester C	27	0		
2007–08	Leicester C	1	0	**85**	**3**

McAULEY, Gareth (D) **146** **13**
H: 6 3 W: 13 00 b.Larne 5-12-79
Source: Coleraine. *Honours:* Northern Ireland Schools, B, 10 full caps.

2004–05	Lincoln C	37	3		
2005–06	Lincoln C	35	5	**72**	**8**
2006–07	Leicester C	30	3		
2007–08	Leicester C	44	2	**74**	**5**

McKAY, William (F) **0** **0**
b.Corby 22-10-88

2007–08	Leicester C	0	0		

N'GOTTY, Bruno (D) **578** **25**
H: 6 1 W: 13 07 b.Lyon 10-6-71
Honours: France Youth, Under-21, Under-23, B, 6 full caps.

1989–90	Lyon	27	0		
1990–91	Lyon	37	2		
1991–92	Lyon	36	1		
1992–93	Lyon	36	3		
1993–94	Lyon	36	3		
1994–95	Lyon	35	3	**207**	**12**
1995–96	Paris St Germain	24	1		
1996–97	Paris St Germain	30	4		
1997–98	Paris St Germain	26	2	**80**	**7**
1998–99	AC Milan	25	1		
1999–2000	AC Milan	9	0	**34**	**1**
1999–2000	Venezia	16	0	**16**	**0**
2000–01	Marseille	30	0	**30**	**0**
2001–02	Bolton W	26	1		
2002–03	Bolton W	23	1		
2003–04	Bolton W	33	2		
2004–05	Bolton W	37	0		
2005–06	Bolton W	29	0	**148**	**4**
2006–07	Birmingham C	25	1	**25**	**1**
2007–08	Leicester C	38	0	**38**	**0**

NEWTON, Shaun (M) **429** **34**
H: 5 8 W: 11 00 b.Camberwell 20-8-75
Source: Trainee. *Honours:* England Under-21.

1992–93	Charlton Ath	2	0		
1993–94	Charlton Ath	19	2		
1994–95	Charlton Ath	26	0		
1995–96	Charlton Ath	41	5		
1996–97	Charlton Ath	43	3		
1997–98	Charlton Ath	41	5		
1998–99	Charlton Ath	16	0		
1999–2000	Charlton Ath	42	5		
2000–01	Charlton Ath	10	0	**240**	**20**
2001–02	Wolverhampton W	45	8		
2002–03	Wolverhampton W	33	3		
2003–04	Wolverhampton W	28	0		
2004–05	Wolverhampton W	24	1	**130**	**12**

2004–05	West Ham U	11	0		
2005–06	West Ham U	26	1		
2006–07	West Ham U	3	0	**40**	**1**
2006–07	*Leicester C*	9	1		
2007–08	Leicester C	10	0	**19**	**1**

OAKLEY, Matthew (M) **337 23**
H: 5 10 W: 12 06 b.Peterborough 17-8-77
Source: Trainee. *Honours:* England Under-21.

1994–95	Southampton	1	0		
1995–96	Southampton	10	0		
1996–97	Southampton	28	3		
1997–98	Southampton	33	1		
1998–99	Southampton	22	2		
1999–2000	Southampton	31	3		
2000–01	Southampton	35	1		
2001–02	Southampton	27	1		
2002–03	Southampton	31	0		
2003–04	Southampton	7	0		
2004–05	Southampton	7	1		
2005–06	Southampton	29	2	**261**	**14**
2006–07	Derby Co	37	6		
2007–08	Derby Co	19	3	**56**	**9**
2007–08	Leicester C	20	0	**20**	**0**

ODHIAMBO, Eric (F) **9 0**
H: 5 9 W: 11 02 b.Oxford 12-5-89
Source: Scholar.

2006–07	Leicester C	0	0		
2007–08	Leicester C	0	0		
2007–08	*Dundee U*	4	0	**4**	**0**
2007–08	*Southend U*	5	0	**5**	**0**

PENTNEY, Carl (G) **0 0**
b.Leicester 3-2-89

2007–08	Leicester C	0	0		

PORTER, Levi (F) **38 3**
H: 5 4 W: 10 05 b.Leicester 6-4-87
Source: Scholar. *Honours:* England Youth.

2005–06	Leicester C	0	0		
2006–07	Leicester C	34	3		
2007–08	Leicester C	4	0	**38**	**3**

ROWE-TURNER, Lathanial (D) **0 0**
b.Leicester 12-11-89
Source: Scholar.

2007–08	Leicester C	0	0		

SAPPLETON, Reneil (M) **1 0**
H: 5 10 W: 11 13 b.Kingston 8-12-89

2007–08	Leicester C	1	0	**1**	**0**

SHEEHAN, Alan (D) **43 2**
H: 5 11 W: 11 02 b.Athlone 14-9-86
Source: Scholar. *Honours:* Eire Youth, Under-21.

2004–05	Leicester C	1	0		
2005–06	Leicester C	2	0		
2006–07	Leicester C	0	0		
2006–07	*Mansfield T*	10	0	**10**	**0**
2007–08	Leicester C	20	1	**23**	**1**
2007–08	*Leeds U*	10	1	**10**	**1**

STEARMAN, Richard (D) **116 7**
H: 6 2 W: 10 08 b.Wolverhampton 19-8-87
Source: Scholar. *Honours:* England Youth.

2004–05	Leicester C	8	1		
2005–06	Leicester C	34	3		
2006–07	Leicester C	35	1		
2007–08	Leicester C	39	2	**116**	**7**

WATSON, Marcus (M) **0 0**
b.Leicester 16-9-89
Source: Scholar.

2007–08	Leicester C	0	0		

WESOLOWSKI, James (D) **46 0**
H: 5 8 W: 11 11 b.Sydney 25-8-87
Source: Scholar. *Honours:* Australia Youth, Under-20.

2004–05	Leicester C	0	0		
2005–06	Leicester C	5	0		
2006–07	Leicester C	19	0		
2007–08	Leicester C	22	0	**46**	**0**

WORLEY, Harry (D) **13 0**
H: 6 3 W: 13 00 b.Warrington 25-11-88
Source: Scholar.

2005–06	Chelsea	0	0		
2006–07	Chelsea	0	0		
2006–07	*Doncaster R*	10	0	**10**	**0**
2007–08	Chelsea	0	0		
2007–08	*Carlisle U*	1	0	**1**	**0**
2007–08	Leicester C	2	0	**2**	**0**

LEYTON ORIENT (44)

BOYD, Adam (F) **221 72**
H: 5 9 W: 10 12 b.Hartlepool 25-5-82
Source: Scholarship.

1999–2000	Hartlepool U	4	1		
2000–01	Hartlepool U	5	0		
2001–02	Hartlepool U	29	9		
2002–03	Hartlepool U	22	5		
2003–04	Hartlepool U	18	12		
2003–04	*Boston U*	14	4	**14**	**4**
2004–05	Hartlepool U	45	22		
2005–06	Hartlepool U	21	4	**144**	**53**
2006–07	Luton T	19	1	**19**	**1**
2007–08	Leyton Orient	44	14	**44**	**14**

CHAMBERS, Adam (D) **152 8**
H: 5 10 W: 11 12 b.Sandwell 20-11-80
Source: Trainee. *Honours:* England Youth.

1998–99	WBA	0	0		
1999–2000	WBA	0	0		
2000–01	WBA	11	1		
2001–02	WBA	32	0		
2002–03	WBA	13	0		
2003–04	WBA	0	0		
2003–04	*Sheffield W*	11	0	**11**	**0**
2004–05	WBA	0	0	**56**	**1**
2004–05	Kidderminster H	2	0	**2**	**0**
2006–07	Leyton Orient	38	4		
2007–08	Leyton Orient	45	3	**83**	**7**

CORDEN, Wayne (M) **362 41**
H: 5 10 W: 11 05 b.Leek 1-11-75
Source: Trainee.

1994–95	Port Vale	1	0		
1995–96	Port Vale	2	0		
1996–97	Port Vale	12	0		
1997–98	Port Vale	33	1		
1998–99	Port Vale	16	0		
1999–2000	Port Vale	2	0	**66**	**1**
2000–01	Mansfield T	34	3		
2001–02	Mansfield T	46	8		
2002–03	Mansfield T	44	13		
2003–04	Mansfield T	44	8		
2004–05	Mansfield T	24	3	**192**	**35**
2004–05	Scunthorpe U	8	0		
2005–06	Scunthorpe U	9	0	**17**	**0**
2005–06	*Chester C*	2	0	**2**	**0**
2005–06	*Leyton Orient*	8	2		
2006–07	Leyton Orient	42	3		
2007–08	Leyton Orient	26	0	**76**	**5**
2007–08	*Notts Co*	9	0	**9**	**0**

DEMETRIOU, Jason (M) **61 5**
H: 5 11 W: 10 08 b.Newham 18-11-87
Source: Scholar.

2005–06	Leyton Orient	3	0		
2006–07	Leyton Orient	15	2		
2007–08	Leyton Orient	43	3	**61**	**5**

ECHANOMI, Efe (F) **51 8**
H: 5 7 W: 11 13 b.Nigeria 27-9-86

2004–05	Leyton Orient	18	5		
2005–06	Leyton Orient	16	3		
2006–07	Leyton Orient	3	0		
2007–08	Leyton Orient	14	0	**51**	**8**

FORTUNE, Clayton (D) **101 2**
H: 6 3 W: 13 10 b.Forest Gate 10-11-82
Source: Tottenham H Scholar.

2000–01	Bristol C	0	0		
2001–02	Bristol C	1	0		
2002–03	Bristol C	10	0		
2003–04	Bristol C	6	0		
2004–05	Bristol C	30	0		
2005–06	Bristol C	6	0	**53**	**0**
2005–06	*Port Vale*	25	2		
2006–07	Leyton Orient	9	0		
2006–07	*Port Vale*	13	0	**38**	**2**
2007–08	Leyton Orient	1	0	**10**	**0**

GRAY, Wayne (F) **276 53**
H: 5 10 W: 11 05 b.Dulwich 7-11-80
Source: Trainee.

1998–99	Wimbledon	0	0		
1999–2000	Wimbledon	1	0		
1999–2000	*Swindon T*	12	2	**12**	**2**
2000–01	Wimbledon	11	0		
2000–01	*Port Vale*	3	0	**3**	**0**
2001–02	Wimbledon	0	0		
2001–02	*Leyton Orient*	15	5		
2001–02	*Brighton & HA*	4	1	**4**	**1**
2002–03	Wimbledon	30	2		
2003–04	Wimbledon	33	4	**75**	**6**
2004–05	Southend U	44	11		
2005–06	Southend U	39	9	**83**	**20**
2006–07	Yeovil T	46	11	**46**	**11**
2007–08	Leyton Orient	38	8	**53**	**13**

IBEHRE, Jabo (F) **209 36**
H: 6 2 W: 13 13 b.Islington 28-1-83
Source: Trainee.

1999–2000	Leyton Orient	3	0		
2000–01	Leyton Orient	5	2		
2001–02	Leyton Orient	28	4		
2002–03	Leyton Orient	25	5		
2003–04	Leyton Orient	35	4		
2004–05	Leyton Orient	19	2		
2005–06	Leyton Orient	33	8		
2006–07	Leyton Orient	30	4		
2007–08	Leyton Orient	31	7	**209**	**36**

MELLIGAN, John (M) **211 31**
H: 5 9 W: 11 02 b.Dublin 11-2-82
Source: Trainee. *Honours:* Eire Youth, Under-21.

2000–01	Wolverhampton W	0	0		
2001–02	Wolverhampton W	0	0		
2001–02	*Bournemouth*	8	0	**8**	**0**
2002–03	Wolverhampton W	2	0		
2002–03	*Kidderminster H*	29	10		
2003–04	Wolverhampton W	0	0	**2**	**0**
2003–04	*Kidderminster H*	5	1	**34**	**11**
2003–04	*Doncaster R*	21	2	**21**	**2**
2004–05	Cheltenham T	29	2		
2005–06	Cheltenham T	42	6		
2006–07	Cheltenham T	43	7	**114**	**15**
2007–08	Leyton Orient	32	3	**32**	**3**

MKANDAWIRE, Tamika (D) **74 5**
H: 6 1 W: 12 03 b.Malawi 28-5-83
Source: Scholar.

2002–03	WBA	0	0		
2003–04	WBA	0	0		
2006–07	Hereford U	39	2	**39**	**2**
2007–08	Leyton Orient	35	3	**35**	**3**

MORRIS, Glenn (G) **87 0**
H: 6 0 W: 12 03 b.Woolwich 20-12-83
Source: Scholar.

2001–02	Leyton Orient	2	0		
2002–03	Leyton Orient	23	0		
2003–04	Leyton Orient	27	0		
2004–05	Leyton Orient	12	0		
2005–06	Leyton Orient	4	0		
2006–07	Leyton Orient	3	0		
2007–08	Leyton Orient	16	0	**87**	**0**

NELSON, Stuart (G) **146 0**
H: 6 1 W: 12 12 b.Stroud 17-9-81
Source: Doncaster R, Hucknall T.

2003–04	Brentford	9	0		
2004–05	Brentford	43	0		
2005–06	Brentford	45	0		
2006–07	Brentford	19	0	**116**	**0**
2007–08	Leyton Orient	30	0	**30**	**0**

OJI, Sam (D) **22 0**
H: 6 0 W: 14 05 b.Westminster 9-10-85
Source: Arsenal Scholar.

2003–04	Birmingham C	0	0		
2004–05	Birmingham C	0	0		
2005–06	Birmingham C	0	0		
2005–06	*Doncaster R*	4	0	**4**	**0**
2006–07	Birmingham C	0	0		
2006–07	*Bristol R*	5	0	**5**	**0**
2007–08	Birmingham C	0	0		
2007–08	Leyton Orient	13	0	**13**	**0**

PAGE, Jack (M) **1 0**
H: 6 0 W: 11 07 b.Purley 16-12-89
Source: Scholar.

2006–07	Leyton Orient	1	0		
2007–08	Leyton Orient	0	0	**1**	**0**

PALMER, Aiden (D) **37 0**
H: 5 8 W: 10 10 b.Enfield 2-1-87
Source: Scholar.

2004–05	Leyton Orient	5	0		
2005–06	Leyton Orient	3	0		
2006–07	Leyton Orient	6	0		
2007–08	Leyton Orient	23	0	**37**	**0**

PIRES, Loick (F) **1 0**
H: 6 3 W 13 02 b.Lisbon 20-11-89
Source: Scholar.

2007–08	Leyton Orient	1	0	**1**	**0**

PURCHES, Stephen (D) **281 11**
H: 5 11 W: 11 13 b.Ilford 14-1-80
1998–99 West Ham U 0 0
1999–2000 West Ham U 0 0
2000–01 Bournemouth 34 0
2001–02 Bournemouth 41 2
2002–03 Bournemouth 44 3
2003–04 Bournemouth 42 3
2004–05 Bournemouth 14 1
2005–06 Bournemouth 26 0
2006–07 Bournemouth 43 1 **244 10**
2007–08 Leyton Orient 37 1 **37 1**

SAAH, Brian (M) **78 1**
H: 6 3 W: 12 03 b.Rush Green 16-12-86
Source: Scholar.
2003–04 Leyton Orient 6 0
2004–05 Leyton Orient 12 0
2005–06 Leyton Orient 3 0
2006–07 Leyton Orient 32 0
2007–08 Leyton Orient 25 1 **78 1**

SHIELDS, Solomon (M) **1 0**
H: 5 10 W: 12 00 b.Leyton 14-10-89
Source: Scholar.
2006–07 Leyton Orient 1 0
2007–08 Leyton Orient 0 0 **1 0**

SYLVESTER, Raphael (F) **0 0**
H: 5 10 W: 11 00 b.Upper Holloway 23-9-88
Source: Scholar.
2007–08 Leyton Orient 0 0

TERRY, Paul (M) **178 10**
H: 5 10 W: 12 06 b.Barking 3-4-79
Source: Dagenham & R.
2003–04 Yeovil T 34 1
2004–05 Yeovil T 39 6
2005–06 Yeovil T 42 1
2006–07 Yeovil T 20 2 **135 10**
2007–08 Leyton Orient 43 0 **43 0**

THELWELL, Alton (D) **108 2**
H: 6 0 W: 12 05 b.Islington 5-9-80
Source: Trainee. *Honours:* England Under-21.
1998–99 Tottenham H 0 0
1999–2000 Tottenham H 0 0
2000–01 Tottenham H 16 0
2001–02 Tottenham H 2 0
2002–03 Tottenham H 0 0 **18 0**
2003–04 Hull C 26 1
2004–05 Hull C 3 0
2005–06 Hull C 9 0
2006–07 Hull C 2 0 **40 1**
2006–07 Leyton Orient 22 1
2007–08 Leyton Orient 28 0 **50 1**

THORNTON, Sean (M) **153 15**
H: 5 10 W: 11 00 b.Drogheda 18-5-83
Source: Scholar. *Honours:* Eire Youth, Under-21.
2001–02 Tranmere R 11 1 **11 1**
2002–03 Sunderland 11 1
2002–03 *Blackpool* 3 0 **3 0**
2003–04 Sunderland 22 4
2004–05 Sunderland 16 4 **49 9**
2005–06 Doncaster R 29 2
2006–07 Doncaster R 30 0 **59 2**
2007–08 Leyton Orient 31 3 **31 3**

LINCOLN C (45)

AMOO, Ryan (M) **62 3**
H: 5 10 W: 9 12 b.Leicester 11-10-83
Source: Scholar.
2001–02 Aston Villa 0 0
2002–03 Aston Villa 0 0
2003–04 Aston Villa 0 0
2003–04 Northampton T 1 0
2004–05 Northampton T 5 0
2005–06 Northampton T 0 0 **6 0**
2006–07 Lincoln C 43 2
2007–08 Lincoln C 13 1 **56 3**

BEEVERS, Lee (D) **194 10**
H: 6 2 W: 11 07 b.Doncaster 4-12-83
Source: Scholar. *Honours:* Wales Youth, Under-21.
2000–01 Ipswich T 0 0
2001–02 Ipswich T 0 0
2002–03 Ipswich T 0 0
2002–03 *Boston U* 1 0
2003–04 Boston U 40 2
2004–05 Boston U 31 1 **72 3**
2004–05 Lincoln C 8 0
2005–06 Lincoln C 33 1
2006–07 Lincoln C 44 5
2007–08 Lincoln C 37 1 **122 7**

BROWN, Nat (F) **170 8**
H: 6 2 W: 12 05 b.Sheffield 15-6-81
Source: Trainee.
1999–2000 Huddersfield T 0 0
2000–01 Huddersfield T 0 0
2001–02 Huddersfield T 0 0
2002–03 Huddersfield T 38 0
2003–04 Huddersfield T 21 0
2004–05 Huddersfield T 17 0 **76 0**
2005–06 Lincoln C 39 7
2006–07 Lincoln C 28 1
2007–08 Lincoln C 27 0 **94 8**

CLARKE, Shane (D) **16 0**
H: 6 1 W: 13 03 b.Lincoln 7-11-87
Source: Scholar.
2006–07 Lincoln C 0 0
2007–08 Lincoln C 16 0 **16 0**

CROFT, Gary (D) **383 8**
H: 5 9 W: 11 08 b.Burton-on-Trent 17-2-74
Source: Trainee. *Honours:* England Under-21.
1990–91 Grimsby T 1 0
1991–92 Grimsby T 0 0
1992–93 Grimsby T 32 0
1993–94 Grimsby T 36 1
1994–95 Grimsby T 44 1
1995–96 Grimsby T 36 1
1995–96 Blackburn R 0 0
1996–97 Blackburn R 5 0
1997–98 Blackburn R 23 1
1998–99 Blackburn R 12 0
1999–2000 Blackburn R 0 0 **40 1**
1999–2000 Ipswich T 21 1
2000–01 Ipswich T 8 0
2001–02 Ipswich T 0 0 **29 1**
2001–02 *Wigan Ath* 7 0 **7 0**
2001–02 *Cardiff C* 6 1
2002–03 Cardiff C 43 1
2003–04 Cardiff C 27 1
2004–05 Cardiff C 1 0 **77 3**
2005–06 Grimsby T 33 0
2006–07 Grimsby T 28 0 **210 3**
2007–08 Lincoln C 20 0 **20 0**

DUFFY, Ayden (M) **4 0**
H: 5 8 W: 10 12 b.Kettering 16-11-86
Source: Scholar.
2006–07 Lincoln C 0 0
2007–08 Lincoln C 4 0 **4 0**

FORRESTER, Jamie (F) **466 140**
H: 5 7 W: 11 00 b.Bradford 1-11-74
Source: Auxerre. *Honours:* England Schools, Youth.
1992–93 Leeds U 6 0
1993–94 Leeds U 3 0
1994–95 Leeds U 0 0
1994–95 *Southend U* 5 0 **5 0**
1994–95 *Grimsby T* 9 1
1995–96 Leeds U 0 0 **9 0**
1995–96 Grimsby T 28 5
1996–97 Grimsby T 13 1 **50 7**
1996–97 Scunthorpe U 10 6
1997–98 Scunthorpe U 45 11
1998–99 Scunthorpe U 46 20 **101 37**
1999–2000 Utrecht 1 0 **1 0**
1999–2000 Walsall 5 0 **5 0**
1999–2000 *Northampton T* 10 6
2000–01 Northampton T 43 17
2001–02 Northampton T 43 17
2002–03 Northampton T 25 5 **121 45**
2002–03 Hull C 11 3
2003–04 Hull C 21 4 **32 7**
2004–05 Bristol R 35 7
2005–06 Bristol R 17 2 **52 9**
2005–06 *Lincoln C* 9 5
2006–07 Lincoln C 41 18
2007–08 Lincoln C 40 12 **90 35**

FRECKLINGTON, Lee (M) **97 14**
H: 5 8 W: 11 00 b.Lincoln 8-9-85
Source: Scholar. *Honours:* Eire B.
2003–04 Lincoln C 0 0
2004–05 Lincoln C 3 0
2005–06 Lincoln C 18 2
2006–07 Lincoln C 42 8
2007–08 Lincoln C 34 4 **97 14**

GREEN, Paul (D) **52 2**
H: 5 8 W: 10 04 b.Birmingham 15-4-87
Source: Scholar.
2005–06 Aston Villa 0 0
2006–07 Aston Villa 0 0
2006–07 Lincoln C 16 1
2007–08 Lincoln C 36 1 **52 2**

HAND, Jamie (M) **155 2**
H: 6 0 W: 11 08 b.Uxbridge 7-2-84
Source: Scholar. *Honours:* England Youth.
2001–02 Watford 10 0
2002–03 Watford 23 0
2003–04 Watford 22 0
2004–05 Watford 0 0
2004–05 *Oxford U* 11 0 **11 0**
2005–06 Watford 0 0 **55 0**
2005–06 *Peterborough U* 9 0 **9 0**
From Fisher Ath.
2005–06 *Northampton T* 11 0 **11 0**
2006–07 Chester C 43 2
2007–08 Chester C 1 0 **44 2**
2007–08 Lincoln C 25 0 **25 0**

HONE, Daniel (D) **23 1**
H: 6 2 W: 12 00 b.Croydon 15-9-89
Source: Scholar.
2007–08 Lincoln C 23 1 **23 1**

JOHN-LEWIS, Leneli (M) **21 3**
H: 5 10 W: 11 10 b.Hammersmith 17-5-89
Source: Scholar.
2006–07 Lincoln C 0 0
2007–08 Lincoln C 21 3 **21 3**

KERR, Scott (M) **122 6**
H: 5 9 W: 10 07 b.Leeds 11-12-81
Source: Scholar.
2000–01 Bradford C 1 0 **1 0**
2001–02 Hull C 0 0
2002–03 Hull C 0 0
2003–04 Hull C 0 0
2004–05 Hull C 0 0
From Scarborough.
2005–06 Lincoln C 41 2
2006–07 Lincoln C 44 3
2007–08 Lincoln C 36 1 **121 6**

KING, Gary (M) **6 1**
H: 5 10 W: 11 04 b.Grimsby 27-1-90
Source: Scholar.
2007–08 Lincoln C 6 1 **6 1**

MARRIOTT, Alan (G) **351 0**
H: 5 11 W: 12 05 b.Bedford 3-9-78
Source: Trainee.
1997–98 Tottenham H 0 0
1998–99 Tottenham H 0 0
1999–2000 Lincoln C 18 0
2000–01 Lincoln C 30 0
2001–02 Lincoln C 43 0
2002–03 Lincoln C 46 0
2003–04 Lincoln C 46 0
2004–05 Lincoln C 45 0
2005–06 Lincoln C 43 0
2006–07 Lincoln C 46 0
2007–08 Lincoln C 34 0 **351 0**

MOSES, Adi (D) **327 5**
H: 5 11 W: 13 01 b.Doncaster 4-5-75
Source: School. *Honours:* England Under-21.
1993–94 Barnsley 0 0
1994–95 Barnsley 4 0
1995–96 Barnsley 24 1
1996–97 Barnsley 28 2
1997–98 Barnsley 35 0
1998–99 Barnsley 34 0
1999–2000 Barnsley 12 0
2000–01 Barnsley 14 0 **151 3**
2000–01 Huddersfield T 12 0
2001–02 Huddersfield T 17 0
2002–03 Huddersfield T 40 1 **69 1**
2003–04 Crewe Alex 21 0
2004–05 Crewe Alex 21 0
2005–06 Crewe Alex 15 0 **57 0**
2006–07 Lincoln C 32 1
2007–08 Lincoln C 18 0 **50 1**

N'GUESSAN, Dany (M) 69 12
H: 6 0 W: 12 13 b.Ivry-sur-Seine 11-8-87
Source: Auxerre, Rangers.
2006–07 Boston U 23 5 **23 5**
2006–07 Lincoln C 9 0
2007–08 Lincoln C 37 7 **46 7**

PEMBLETON, Martin (M) 6 0
H: 5 7 W: 10 09 b.Scunthorpe 1-6-90
Source: Scholar.
2007–08 Lincoln C 6 0 **6 0**

RYAN, Oliver (M) 38 0
H: 5 9 W: 11 00 b.Boston 26-9-85
Source: Scholar.
2004–05 Lincoln C 6 0
2005–06 Lincoln C 10 0
2006–07 Lincoln C 7 0
2007–08 Lincoln C 15 0 **38 0**

SEMPLE, Ryan (M) 48 3
H: 5 11 W: 10 11 b.Belfast 4-7-85
Source: Scholar.
2002–03 Peterborough U 3 0
2003–04 Peterborough U 2 0
2004–05 Peterborough U 8 0
2005–06 Peterborough U 28 3 **41 3**
2006–07 Lincoln C 4 0
2006–07 *Chester C* 3 0 **3 0**
2007–08 Lincoln C 0 0 **4 0**

STALLARD, Mark (F) 476 135
H: 6 0 W: 13 09 b.Derby 24-10-74
Source: Trainee.
1991–92 Derby Co 3 0
1992–93 Derby Co 5 0
1993–94 Derby Co 0 0
1994–95 Derby Co 16 2
1994–95 *Fulham* 4 3 **4 3**
1995–96 Derby Co 3 0 **27 2**
1995–96 Bradford C 21 9
1996–97 Bradford C 22 1 **43 10**
1996–97 *Preston NE* 4 1 **4 1**
1996–97 Wycombe W 12 4
1997–98 Wycombe W 43 17
1998–99 Wycombe W 15 2 **70 23**
1998–99 Notts Co 14 4
1999–2000 Notts Co 36 14
2000–01 Notts Co 42 17
2001–02 Notts Co 26 4
2002–03 Notts Co 45 24
2003–04 Notts Co 22 4
2003–04 Barnsley 10 1
2004–05 Barnsley 5 0 **15 1**
2004–05 *Chesterfield* 9 2 **9 2**
2004–05 *Notts Co* 16 3 **201 70**
2005–06 Shrewsbury T 37 6 **37 6**
2006–07 Lincoln C 41 15
2007–08 Lincoln C 25 2 **66 17**

TORPEY, Steve (F) 593 139
H: 6 3 W: 13 06 b.Islington 8-12-70
Source: Trainee.
1988–89 Millwall 0 0
1989–90 Millwall 7 0
1990–91 Millwall 0 0 **7 0**
1990–91 Bradford C 29 7
1991–92 Bradford C 43 10
1992–93 Bradford C 24 5 **96 22**
1993–94 Swansea C 40 9
1994–95 Swansea C 41 11
1995–96 Swansea C 42 15
1996–97 Swansea C 39 9 **162 44**
1997–98 Bristol C 29 8
1998–99 Bristol C 21 4
1998–99 *Notts Co* 6 1 **6 1**
1999–2000 Bristol C 20 1 **70 13**
1999–2000 Scunthorpe U 15 1
2000–01 Scunthorpe U 40 10
2001–02 Scunthorpe U 39 13
2002–03 Scunthorpe U 28 10
2003–04 Scunthorpe U 43 11
2004–05 Scunthorpe U 34 12
2005–06 Scunthorpe U 26 1
2006–07 Scunthorpe U 14 1 **239 59**
2007–08 Lincoln C 13 0 **13 0**

WARLOW, Owain (M) 22 0
H: 6 0 W: 12 00 b.Treforest 3-7-88
Source: Scholar. *Honours:* Wales Under-21.
2006–07 Lincoln C 5 0
2007–08 Lincoln C 17 0 **22 0**

WATT, Phil (F) 1 0
H: 5 11 W: 11 04 b.Rotherham 10-1-88
Source: Scholar.
2006–07 Lincoln C 0 0
2007–08 Lincoln C 1 0 **1 0**

WRIGHT, Ben (F) 157 47
H: 6 1 W: 13 07 b.Munster 1-7-80
1998–99 Bristol C 0 0
1999–2000 Bristol C 2 0
2000–01 Bristol C 0 0 **2 0**
2001 Viking 22 0
2002 Viking 18 1 **40 1**
2003 Start 30 13
2004 Start 29 15
2005 Start *9 1*
2006 Moss 11 2 **11 2**
2007 Start 2 0 **70 29**
2007–08 Lincoln C 34 15 **34 15**

LIVERPOOL (46)

AGGER, Daniel (D) 70 7
H: 6 2 W: 12 06 b.Hvidovre 12-12-84
Honours: Denmark Youth, Under-20, Under-21, 18 full caps, 2 goals.
2004–05 Brondby 26 5
2005–06 Brondby 8 0 **34 5**
2005–06 Liverpool 4 0
2006–07 Liverpool 27 2
2007–08 Liverpool 5 0 **36 2**

AJDAREVIC, Astrit (M) 0 0
b.Kosovo 20-9-90
Source: Falkenberg.
2006–07 Liverpool 0 0
2007–08 Liverpool 0 0

ALONSO, Xabi (M) 239 20
H: 6 0 W: 12 02 b.Tolosa 25-11-81
Honours: Spain Under-21, 47 full caps, 1 goal.
1999–2000 Real Sociedad 0 0
2000–01 Eibar 14 0 **14 0**
2000–01 Real Sociedad 18 0
2001–02 Real Sociedad 29 3
2002–03 Real Sociedad 33 3
2003–04 Real Sociedad 35 3 **115 9**
2004–05 Liverpool 24 2
2005–06 Liverpool 35 3
2006–07 Liverpool 32 4
2007–08 Liverpool 19 2 **110 11**

AMOO, David (M) 0 0
b. 23-4-91
2007–08 Liverpool 0 0

ANDERSON, Paul (M) 31 7
H: 5 9 W: 10 04 b.Leicester 23-7-88
Source: Scholar. *Honours:* England Youth.
2005–06 Hull C 0 0
2005–06 Liverpool 0 0
2006–07 Liverpool 0 0
2007–08 Liverpool 0 0
2007–08 *Swansea C* 31 7 **31 7**

ANTWI-BIRAGO, Godwin (D) 36 1
H: 6 1 W: 13 09 b.Tafu 7-6-88
Source: San Gregorio.
2005–06 Liverpool 0 0
2006–07 Liverpool 0 0
2006–07 *Accrington S* 9 0 **9 0**
2007–08 Liverpool 0 0
2007–08 *Hartlepool U* 27 1 **27 1**

ARBELOA, Alvaro (D) 144 2
H: 6 0 W: 12 06 b.Salamanca 17-1-83
Honours: Spain Under-21, 2 full caps.
2003–04 Real Madrid B 22 0
2004–05 Real Madrid B 28 1 **50 1**
2004–05 Real Madrid 2 0
2005–06 Real Madrid Castilla 34 0 **2 0**
2006–07 La Coruna 21 0 **21 0**
2006–07 Liverpool 9 1
2007–08 Liverpool 28 0 **37 1**

AYALA, Daniel (M) 0 0
H: 6 3 W: 13 03 b.Sevilla 7-11-90
2007–08 Liverpool 0 0

BABEL, Ryan (F) 103 18
H: 6 1 W: 12 04 b.Amsterdam 19-12-86
Honours: Holland Under-21, 25 full caps, 5 goals.
2003–04 Ajax 1 0
2004–05 Ajax 20 7
2005–06 Ajax 25 2
2006–07 Ajax 27 5 **73 14**
2007–08 Liverpool 30 4 **30 4**

BARNETT, Charlie (M) 0 0
b.Liverpool 19-9-88
Source: Scholar.
2006–07 Liverpool 0 0
2007–08 Liverpool 0 0

BENAYOUN, Yossi (M) 314 93
H: 5 10 W: 11 00 b.Beer Sheva 6-6-80
Honours: Israel 64 full caps, 16 goals.
1997–98 Hapoel Beer Sheva25 15 **25 15**
1998–99 Maccabi Haifa 29 16
1999–2000 Maccabi Haifa 38 19
2000–01 Maccabi Haifa 37 13
2001–02 Maccabi Haifa 26 7 **130 55**
2002–03 Santander 31 4
2003–04 Santander 35 7
2004–05 Santander 0 0 **66 11**
2005–06 West Ham U 34 5
2006–07 West Ham U 29 3 **63 8**
2007–08 Liverpool 30 4 **30 4**

BOUZANIS, Dean (G) 0 0
H: 6 1 W: 13 06 b.Sydney 2-10-90
Source: St George Saints, Sydney.
2007–08 Liverpool 0 0

BROUWER, Jordy (F) 0 0
H: 6 2 W: 12 05 b.Den Haag 26-2-88
Source: Ajax.
2006–07 Liverpool 0 0
2007–08 Liverpool 0 0

BRUNA, Gerardo (M) 0 0
b.Mendoza 21-1-91
2007–08 Liverpool 0 0

CARRAGHER, Jamie (D) 360 3
H: 5 9 W: 12 01 b.Liverpool 28-1-78
Source: Trainee. *Honours:* England Youth, Under-21, B, 34 full caps.
1995–96 Liverpool 0 0
1996–97 Liverpool 2 1
1997–98 Liverpool 20 0
1998–99 Liverpool 34 1
1999–2000 Liverpool 36 0
2000–01 Liverpool 34 0
2001–02 Liverpool 33 0
2002–03 Liverpool 35 0
2003–04 Liverpool 22 0
2004–05 Liverpool 38 0
2005–06 Liverpool 36 0
2006–07 Liverpool 35 1
2007–08 Liverpool 35 0 **360 3**

CARSON, Scott (G) 87 0
H: 6 3 W: 14 00 b.Whitehaven 3-9-85
Source: Scholar. *Honours:* England Youth, Under-21, B, 2 full caps.
2002–03 Leeds U 0 0
2003–04 Leeds U 3 0
2004–05 Leeds U 0 0 **3 0**
2004–05 Liverpool 4 0
2005–06 Liverpool 0 0
2005–06 *Sheffield W* 9 0 **9 0**
2006–07 Liverpool 0 0
2006–07 *Charlton Ath* 36 0 **36 0**
2007–08 Liverpool 0 0 **4 0**
2007–08 *Aston Villa* 35 0 **35 0**

COLLINS, Michael (F) 0 0
Source: Scholar.
2007–08 Liverpool 0 0

CROUCH, Peter (F) 243 72
H: 6 7 W: 13 03 b.Macclesfield 30-1-81
Source: Trainee. *Honours:* England Youth, Under-20, Under-21, B, 28 full caps, 14 goals.
1998–99 Tottenham H 0 0
1999–2000 Tottenham H 0 0
2000–01 QPR 42 10 **42 10**
2001–02 Portsmouth 37 18 **37 18**
2001–02 Aston Villa 7 2
2002–03 Aston Villa 14 0
2003–04 Aston Villa 16 4 **37 6**
2003–04 *Norwich C* 15 4 **15 4**

2004–05 Southampton 27 12 27 12
2005–06 Liverpool 32 8
2006–07 Liverpool 32 9
2007–08 Liverpool 21 5 85 22

CROWTHER, Ryan (M) 2 0
H: 5 11 W: 11 00 b.Stockport 17-9-88
Source: Scholar.
2005–06 Stockport Co 1 0
2006–07 Stockport Co 1 0 2 0
2007–08 Liverpool 0 0

DARBY, Stephen (D) 0 0
H: 5 9 W: 10 00 b.Liverpool 6-10-88
Source: Scholar. *Honours:* England Youth.
2006–07 Liverpool 0 0
2007–08 Liverpool 0 0

DURAN VAZQUEZ, Francisco (M) 0 0
H: 5 10 W: 12 04 b.Malaga 28-4-88
Source: Malaga.
2006–07 Liverpool 0 0
2007–08 Liverpool 0 0

ECCLESTON, Nathan (F) 0 0
b.Manchester 30-12-90
Source: Scholar.
2007–08 Liverpool 0 0

EL ZHAR, Nabil (F) 3 0
H: 5 9 W: 11 05 b.Ales 27-8-86
Source: St Etienne. *Honours:* France Youth, Morocco Under-20, 5 full caps, 2 goals.
2006–07 Liverpool 3 0
2007–08 Liverpool 0 0 3 0

FABIO AURELIO (M) 181 15
H: 5 10 W: 11 11 b.Sao Carlos 24-9-79
Honours: Brazil Youth, Under-20, Under-21.
1997 Sao Paulo 15 1
1998 Sao Paulo 11 1
1998 Santos 0 0
1999 Sao Paulo 23 1
2000 Sao Paulo 4 0 53 3
2000–01 Valencia 7 0
2001–02 Valencia 15 1
2002–03 Valencia 26 8
2003–04 Valencia 2 0
2004–05 Valencia 21 0
2005–06 Valencia 24 2 95 11
2006–07 Liverpool 17 0
2007–08 Liverpool 16 1 33 1

FINNAN, Steve (D) 429 15
H: 6 0 W: 12 03 b.Limerick 24-4-76
Source: Welling U. *Honours:* Eire Under-21, B, 50 full caps, 2 goals.
1995–96 Birmingham C 12 1
1995–96 *Notts Co* 17 2
1996–97 Birmingham C 3 0 15 1
1996–97 Notts Co 23 0
1997–98 Notts Co 44 5
1998–99 Notts Co 13 0 97 7
1998–99 Fulham 22 2
1999–2000 Fulham 35 2
2000–01 Fulham 45 2
2001–02 Fulham 38 0
2002–03 Fulham 32 0 172 6
2003–04 Liverpool 22 0
2004–05 Liverpool 33 1
2005–06 Liverpool 33 0
2006–07 Liverpool 33 0
2007–08 Liverpool 24 0 145 1

FLYNN, Ryan (M) 0 0
H: 5 8 W: 10 00 b.Scotland 4-9-88
Source: Scholar.
2006–07 Liverpool 0 0
2007–08 *Hereford U* 0 0
2007–08 Liverpool 0 0

GERRARD, Steven (M) 302 55
H: 6 0 W: 12 05 b.Whiston 30-5-80
Source: Trainee. *Honours:* England Youth, Under-21, 67 full caps, 13 goals.
1997–98 Liverpool 0 0
1998–99 Liverpool 12 0
1999–2000 Liverpool 29 1
2000–01 Liverpool 33 7
2001–02 Liverpool 28 3
2002–03 Liverpool 34 5
2003–04 Liverpool 34 4
2004–05 Liverpool 30 7
2005–06 Liverpool 32 10
2006–07 Liverpool 36 7
2007–08 Liverpool 34 11 302 55

GULACSI, Peter (G) 0 0
b.Budapest 6-5-90
Source: MTK.
2007–08 Liverpool 0 0

GUTHRIE, Danny (M) 38 0
H: 5 9 W: 11 06 b.Shrewsbury 18-4-87
Source: Scholar. *Honours:* England Schools, Youth.
2004–05 Liverpool 0 0
2005–06 Liverpool 0 0
2006–07 Liverpool 3 0
2006–07 *Southampton* 10 0 10 0
2007–08 Liverpool 0 0 3 0
2007–08 *Bolton W* 25 0 25 0

HAMMILL, Adam (M) 25 0
H: 5 11 W: 11 07 b.Liverpool 25-1-88
Source: Scholar. *Honours:* England Youth.
2005–06 Liverpool 0 0
2006–07 Liverpool 0 0
2007–08 Liverpool 0 0
2007–08 *Southampton* 25 0 25 0

HANSEN, Martin (G) 0 0
H: 6 2 W: 12 07 b.Glostrup 15-6-90
Source: Brondby.
2007–08 Liverpool 0 0

HIGHDALE, Sean (M) 0 0
b.Liverpool 4-3-91
2007–08 Liverpool 0 0

HOBBS, Jack (D) 12 1
H: 6 3 W: 13 05 b.Portsmouth 18-8-88
Source: Scholar. *Honours:* England Youth.
2004–05 Lincoln C 1 0 1 0
2005–06 Liverpool 0 0
2006–07 Liverpool 0 0
2007–08 Liverpool 2 0 2 0
2007–08 *Scunthorpe U* 9 1 9 1

HUTH, Ronald (D) 0 0
H: 6 2 W: 14 01 b.Asuncion 30-10-89
Source: Tacuary.
2006–07 Liverpool 0 0
2007–08 Liverpool 0 0

HYYPIA, Sami (D) 465 27
H: 6 3 W: 13 09 b.Porvoo 7-10-73
Source: KuMu. *Honours:* Finland Youth, Under-21, 90 full caps, 5 goals.
1993 MyPa 47 12 0
1994 MyPa 47 25 0
1995 MyPa 47 26 3 63 3
1995–96 Willem II 14 0
1996–97 Willem II 30 1
1997–98 Willem II 30 0
1998–99 Willem II 26 2 100 3
1999–2000 Liverpool 38 2
2000–01 Liverpool 35 3
2001–02 Liverpool 37 3
2002–03 Liverpool 36 3
2003–04 Liverpool 38 4
2004–05 Liverpool 32 2
2005–06 Liverpool 36 1
2006–07 Liverpool 23 2
2007–08 Liverpool 27 1 302 21

IDRIZAJ, Bezian (F) 14 1
H: 6 2 W: 12 02 b.Austria 12-10-87
Source: LASK Linz.
2005–06 Liverpool 0 0
2006–07 Liverpool 0 0
2006–07 *Luton T* 7 1 7 1
2007–08 Liverpool 0 0
2007–08 *Crystal Palace* 7 0 7 0

INSUA, Emiliano (D) 5 0
H: 5 10 W: 12 08 b.Buenos Aires 7-1-89
Source: Boca Juniors. *Honours:* Argentina Youth, Under-20, Under-23.
2006–07 Liverpool 2 0
2007–08 Liverpool 3 0 5 0

IRWIN, Steven (M) 0 0
b.Liverpool 29-9-90
Source: Scholar.
2007–08 Liverpool 0 0

ITANDJE, Charles (G) 179 0
H: 6 3 W: 13 01 b.Paris 2-11-82
Honours: France Under-21.
2000–01 Red Star 93 9 0 9 0
2001–02 Lens 0 0
2002–03 Lens 22 0
2003–04 Lens 35 0
2004–05 Lens 38 0
2005–06 Lens 37 0
2006–07 Lens 38 0 170 0
2007–08 Liverpool 0 0

KELLY, Martin (D) 0 0
H: 6 3 W: 12 02 b.Bolton 27-4-90
Source: Scholar.
2007–08 Liverpool 0 0

KEWELL, Harry (M) 274 57
H: 5 9 W: 12 06 b.Sydney 22-9-78
Source: NSW Soccer Academy. *Honours:* Australia Youth, Under-20, 35 full caps, 11 goals.
1995–96 Leeds U 2 0
1996–97 Leeds U 1 0
1997–98 Leeds U 29 5
1998–99 Leeds U 38 6
1999–2000 Leeds U 36 10
2000–01 Leeds U 17 2
2001–02 Leeds U 27 8
2002–03 Leeds U 31 14 181 45
2003–04 Liverpool 36 7
2004–05 Liverpool 18 1
2005–06 Liverpool 27 3
2006–07 Liverpool 2 1
2007–08 Liverpool 10 0 93 12

KUYT, Dirk (F) 327 137
H: 6 0 W: 12 02 b.Katwijk 22-7-80
Source: Quick Boys.Holland 42 full caps, 8 goals.
1998–99 Utrecht 28 5
1999–2000 Utrecht 32 6
2000–01 Utrecht 32 13
2001–02 Utrecht 34 7
2002–03 Utrecht 34 20 160 51
2003–04 Feyenoord 34 20
2004–05 Feyenoord 34 29
2005–06 Feyenoord 33 22 101 71
2006–07 Liverpool 34 12
2007–08 Liverpool 32 3 66 15

LE TALLEC, Anthony (M) 127 16
H: 6 0 W: 12 00 b.Hennebont 3-10-84
Honours: France Under-21.
2001–02 Le Havre 24 5
2002–03 Le Havre 30 2 54 7
2003–04 Liverpool 13 0
2004–05 Liverpool 4 0
2004–05 *St Etienne* 7 1 7 1
2005–06 Liverpool 0 0
2005–06 *Sunderland* 27 3 27 3
2006–07 Liverpool 0 0
2007–08 *Le Mans* 22 5 22 5
2007–08 Liverpool 0 0 17 0

LETO, Sebastian (M) 45 7
H: 6 2 W: 12 04 b.San Vicente 30-8-86
2006 Lanus 27 5
2007 Lanus 18 2 45 7
2007–08 Liverpool 0 0

LINDFIELD, Craig (F) 10 1
H: 6 0 W: 10 05 b.Wirral 7-9-88
Source: Scholar. *Honours:* England Youth.
2006–07 Liverpool 0 0
2007–08 Liverpool 0 0
2007–08 *Notts Co* 3 1 3 1
2007–08 *Chester C* 7 0 7 0

LUCAS (M) 51 4
H: 5 10 W: 11 09 b.Dourados 9-1-87
Honours: Brazil Under-20, 2 full caps.
2005 Gremio 3 0
2006 Gremio 30 4 33 4
2007–08 Liverpool 18 0 18 0

MACKAY-STEVEN, Gary (F) 0 0
b.Thurso 31-8-90
Source: Ross Co.
2007–08 Liverpool 0 0

MARTIN, David (G) 27 0
H: 6 1 W: 13 04 b.Romford 22-1-86
Source: Scholar. *Honours:* England Youth, Under-20.
2003–04 Wimbledon 2 0 2 0
2004–05 Milton Keynes D 15 0
2005–06 Milton Keynes D 0 0 15 0
2005–06 Liverpool 0 0

2006–07 Liverpool 0 0
2006–07 *Accrington S* 10 0 **10 0**
2007–08 Liverpool 0 0

MASCHERANO, Javier (M) 90 1
H: 5 7 W: 10 05 b.San Lorenzo 8-6-84
Honours: Argentina Youth, Under-20, Under-23, 36 full caps, 2 goals.
2003–04 River Plate 21 0
2004–05 River Plate 25 0 **46 0**
2005 Corinthians 7 0 **7 0**
2006–07 West Ham U 5 0 **5 0**
2006–07 Liverpool 7 0
2007–08 Liverpool 25 1 **32 1**

MIHAYLOV, Nikolay (G) 44 0
H: 6 3 W: 14 00 b.Bulgaria 28-6-88
2004–05 Levski 10 0
2005–06 Levski 21 0
2006–07 Levski 13 0 **44 0**
2007–08 Liverpool 0 0

NEMETH, Kristian (F) 37 14
H: 5 10 W: 11 07 b.Gyor 5-1-89
2005–06 MTK 13 2
2006–07 MTK 24 12 **37 14**
2007–08 Liverpool 0 0

PACHECO, Daniel (F) 0 0
H: 5 6 W: 10 03
2007–08 Liverpool 0 0

PALETTA, Gabriel (D) 45 5
H: 6 3 W: 12 08 b.Longchamps 15-2-86
Honours: Argentina Under-20.
2004–05 Banfield 9 2
2005–06 Banfield 33 3 **42 5**
2006–07 Liverpool 3 0
2007–08 Liverpool 0 0 **3 0**

PENNANT, Jermaine (M) 171 12
H: 5 9 W: 10 06 b.Nottingham 15-1-83
Honours: England Schools, Youth, Under-21.
1998–99 Notts Co 0 0
1998–99 Arsenal 0 0
1999–2000 Arsenal 0 0
2000–01 Arsenal 0 0
2001–02 Arsenal 0 0
2001–02 *Watford* 9 2
2002–03 Arsenal 5 3
2002–03 *Watford* 12 0 **21 2**
2003–04 Arsenal 0 0
2003–04 *Leeds U* 36 2 **36 2**
2004–05 Arsenal 7 0 **12 3**
2004–05 Birmingham C 12 0
2005–06 Birmingham C 38 2 **50 2**
2006–07 Liverpool 34 1
2007–08 Liverpool 18 2 **52 3**

PLESSIS, Damien (M) 18 0
H: 6 3 W: 12 02 b.Neuvy-sous-Bois 5-3-88
Honours: France Youth.
2005–06 Lyon B 7 0
2006–07 Lyon B 9 0 **16 0**
2007–08 Liverpool 2 0 **2 0**

POURIE, Marvin (F) 0 0
b.Germany 8-1-91
2007–08 Liverpool 0 0

PUTTERILL, Ray (M) 0 0
H: 5 8 W: 12 03 b.Liverpool 2-3-89
Source: Scholar.
2007–08 Liverpool 0 0

REINA, Jose (G) 237 0
H: 6 2 W: 14 06 b.Madrid 31-8-82
Honours: Spain Youth, Under-21, 10 full caps.
1999–2000 Barcelona B 30 0 **30 0**
2000–01 Barcelona 19 0
2001–02 Barcelona 11 0 **30 0**
2002–03 Villarreal 33 0
2003–04 Villarreal 38 0
2004–05 Villarreal 0 0 **71 0**
2005–06 Liverpool 33 0
2006–07 Liverpool 35 0
2007–08 Liverpool 38 0 **106 0**

RIISE, John Arne (M) 278 25
H: 6 1 W: 14 00 b.Molde 24-9-80
Honours: Norway Youth, Under-21, 71 full caps, 8 goals.
1998–99 Monaco 7 0
1999–2000 Monaco 21 1
2000–01 Monaco 16 3 **44 4**
2001–02 Liverpool 38 7
2002–03 Liverpool 37 6
2003–04 Liverpool 28 0
2004–05 Liverpool 37 6
2005–06 Liverpool 32 1
2006–07 Liverpool 33 1
2007–08 Liverpool 29 0 **234 21**

ROQUE, Miguel (D) 4 0
H: 6 2 W: 12 03 b.Lleida 8-7-88
Source: EU Lleida.
2005–06 Liverpool 0 0
2006–07 Liverpool 0 0
2006–07 *Oldham Ath* 4 0 **4 0**
2007–08 Liverpool 0 0

RYAN, Jimmy (M) 4 0
H: 5 11 W: 10 06 b.Maghull 6-9-88
Source: Scholar.
2007–08 Liverpool 0 0
2007–08 *Shrewsbury T* 4 0 **4 0**

SAN JOSE DOMINGUEZ, Mikel (D) 0 0
H: 6 0 W: 12 04 b.Pamplona 30-5-89
Source: Athletic Bilbao.
2007–08 Liverpool 0 0

SIMON, Andras (F) 1 0
H: 6 0 W: 11 05 b.Salgotarjan 30-3-90
2006–07 MTK 1 0 **1 0**
2007–08 Liverpool 0 0

SISSOKO, Mohamed (M) 96 1
H: 6 2 W: 12 08 b.Mont Saint Aigan 22-1-85
Source: Auxerre. *Honours:* Mali 14 full caps, 2 goals.
2003–04 Valencia 21 0
2004–05 Valencia 24 0 **45 0**
2005–06 Liverpool 26 0
2006–07 Liverpool 16 0
2007–08 Liverpool 9 1 **51 1**
To Juventus January 2008.

SKRTEL, Martin (D) 123 3
H: 6 3 W: 12 10 b.Handlova 15-12-84
Honours: Slovakia 25 full caps, 4 goals.
2002–03 Trencin 1 0
2003–04 Trencin 34 0 **35 0**
2004 Zenit 7 0
2005 Zenit 18 1
2006 Zenit 26 1
2007 Zenit 23 1 **74 3**
2007–08 Liverpool 14 0 **14 0**

SPEARING, Jay (D) 0 0
H: 5 6 W: 11 01 b.Wirral 25-11-88
Source: Scholar.
2006–07 Liverpool 0 0
2007–08 Liverpool 0 0

THRELFALL, Robert (D) 9 0
H: 5 11 W: 11 00 b.Liverpool 25-11-88
Source: Scholar. *Honours:* England Youth.
2006–07 Liverpool 0 0
2007–08 Liverpool 0 0
2007–08 *Hereford U* 9 0 **9 0**

TORRES, Fernando (F) 207 99
H: 5 9 W: 12 03 b.Madrid 20-3-84
Honours: Spain 54 full caps, 17 goals.
2002–03 Atletico Madrid 29 13
2003–04 Atletico Madrid 35 19
2004–05 Atletico Madrid 38 16
2005–06 Atletico Madrid 36 13
2006–07 Atletico Madrid 36 14 **174 75**
2007–08 Liverpool 33 24 **33 24**

VORONIN, Andrei (F) 213 70
H: 5 11 W: 11 08 b.Odessa 21-7-79
Honours: Ukraine 53 full caps, 6 goals.
1997–98 M Gladbach 7 1
1998–99 M Gladbach 0 0
1999–2000 M Gladbach 2 0 **9 1**
2000–01 Mainz 10 1
2001–02 Mainz 34 8
2002–03 Mainz 31 20 **75 29**
2003–04 Cologne 19 4 **19 4**
2004–05 Leverkusen 31 14
2005–06 Leverkusen 29 7
2006–07 Leverkusen 31 10 **91 31**
2007–08 Liverpool 19 5 **19 5**

Scholars
Kacaniklic, Alexander; Kennedy, Charles Joseph; O'Connor, Shane; Oldfield, Christopher; Scott, Michael David

LUTON T (47)

ANDREW, Calvin (F) 66 5
H: 6 0 W: 12 11 b.Luton 19-12-86
Source: Scholar.
2004–05 Luton T 8 0
2005–06 Luton T 1 1
2005–06 *Grimsby T* 8 1 **8 1**
2005–06 *Bristol C* 3 0 **3 0**
2006–07 Luton T 7 1
2007–08 Luton T 39 2 **55 4**

ASAFU-ADJAYE, Ed (D) 7 0
H: 5 11 W: 12 04 b.Southwark 22-12-88
Source: Scholar.
2007–08 Luton T 7 0 **7 0**

BARRETT, Zach (G) 0 0
H: 6 2 W: 11 07 b.Stevenage 26-5-88
Source: Scholar.
2006–07 Luton T 0 0
2007–08 Luton T 0 0

BEAVAN, George (D) 2 0
H: 5 9 W: 12 02 b.Luton 12-1-90
Source: Scholar.
2007–08 Luton T 2 0 **2 0**

BELL, David (M) 202 17
H: 5 10 W: 11 05 b.Kettering 21-1-84
Source: Trainee. *Honours:* Eire Youth, Under-21.
2001–02 Rushden & D 0 0
2002–03 Rushden & D 30 3
2003–04 Rushden & D 37 1
2004–05 Rushden & D 40 3
2005–06 Rushden & D 14 3 **121 10**
2005–06 Luton T 9 0
2006–07 Luton T 34 3
2007–08 Luton T 32 4 **75 7**
2007–08 *Leicester C* 6 0 **6 0**

BERESFORD, Marlon (G) 479 0
H: 6 1 W: 13 10 b.Lincoln 2-9-69
Source: Trainee.
1987–88 Sheffield W 0 0
1988–89 Sheffield W 0 0
1989–90 Sheffield W 0 0
1989–90 *Bury* 1 0 **1 0**
1989–90 *Ipswich T* 0 0
1990–91 Sheffield W 0 0
1990–91 *Northampton T* 13 0
1990–91 *Crewe Alex* 3 0 **3 0**
1991–92 Sheffield W 0 0
1991–92 *Northampton T* 15 0 **28 0**
1992–93 Burnley 44 0
1993–94 Burnley 46 0
1994–95 Burnley 40 0
1995–96 Burnley 36 0
1996–97 Burnley 40 0
1997–98 Burnley 34 0
1997–98 Middlesbrough 3 0
1998–99 Middlesbrough 4 0
1999–2000 Middlesbrough 1 0
2000–01 Middlesbrough 1 0
2000–01 *Sheffield W* 4 0 **4 0**
2001–02 Middlesbrough 1 0 **10 0**
2001–02 *Wolverhampton W* 0 0
2001–02 *Burnley* 13 0
2002–03 York C 6 0 **6 0**
2002–03 Burnley 34 0
2003–04 Burnley 0 0 **287 0**
2003–04 Bradford C 5 0 **5 0**
2003–04 Luton T 11 0
2003–04 Barnsley 14 0 **14 0**
2004–05 Luton T 38 0
2005–06 Luton T 41 0
2006–07 Luton T 26 0
2007–08 Luton T 0 0 **116 0**
2007–08 *Oldham Ath* 5 0 **5 0**

BRILL, Dean (G) 66 0
H: 6 2 W: 14 05 b.Luton 2-12-85
Source: Scholar.
2003–04 Luton T 5 0
2004–05 Luton T 0 0
2005–06 Luton T 5 0
2006–07 Luton T 11 0
2006–07 *Gillingham* 8 0 **8 0**
2007–08 Luton T 37 0 **58 0**

CHARLES, Ryan (F) **7 1**
H: 6 0 W: 12 00 b.Enfield 30-9-89
Source: Scholar.
2007–08 Luton T 7 1 **7 1**

CURRIE, Darren (M) **504 57**
H: 5 11 W: 12 07 b.Hampstead 29-11-74
Source: Trainee.
1993–94 West Ham U 0 0
1994–95 West Ham U 0 0
1994–95 *Shrewsbury T* 17 2
1995–96 West Ham U 0 0
1995–96 *Leyton Orient* 10 0 **10 0**
1995–96 Shrewsbury T 13 2
1996–97 Shrewsbury T 37 2
1997–98 Shrewsbury T 16 4 **83 10**
1997–98 Plymouth Arg 7 0 **7 0**
1998–99 Barnet 38 4
1999–2000 Barnet 44 5
2000–01 Barnet 45 10 **127 19**
2001–02 Wycombe W 46 3
2002–03 Wycombe W 38 4
2003–04 Wycombe W 42 7 **126 14**
2004–05 Brighton & HA 22 2 **22 2**
2004–05 Ipswich T 24 3
2005–06 Ipswich T 46 5
2006–07 Ipswich T 13 1 **83 9**
2006–07 *Coventry C* 8 0 **8 0**
2006–07 *Derby Co* 7 1 **7 1**
2007–08 Luton T 31 2 **31 2**

DAVIS, Sol (D) **292 2**
H: 5 7 W: 12 04 b.Cheltenham 4-9-79
Source: Trainee.
1997–98 Swindon T 6 0
1998–99 Swindon T 25 0
1999–2000 Swindon T 29 0
2000–01 Swindon T 36 0
2001–02 Swindon T 21 0
2002–03 Swindon T 0 0 **117 0**
2002–03 Luton T 34 0
2003–04 Luton T 36 0
2004 05 Luton T 45 2
2005–06 Luton T 21 0
2006–07 Luton T 24 0
2007–08 Luton T 15 0 **175 2**

EMANUEL, Lewis (D) **199 8**
H: 5 8 W: 12 01 b.Bradford 14-10-83
Source: Scholar. *Honours:* England Schools, Youth. Eire B.
2001–02 Bradford C 9 0
2002–03 Bradford C 29 0
2003–04 Bradford C 28 2
2004–05 Bradford C 36 0
2005–06 Bradford C 37 2 **139 4**
2006–07 Luton T 40 2
2007–08 Luton T 17 2 **57 4**
2007–08 *Brentford* 3 0 **3 0**

FURLONG, Paul (F) **518 171**
H: 6 0 W: 13 11 b.Wood Green 1-10-68
Source: Enfield.
1991–92 Coventry C 37 4 **37 4**
1992–93 Watford 41 19
1993–94 Watford 38 18 **79 37**
1994–95 Chelsea 36 10
1995–96 Chelsea 28 3 **64 13**
1996–97 Birmingham C 43 10
1997–98 Birmingham C 25 15
1998–99 Birmingham C 29 13
1999–2000 Birmingham C 19 11
2000–01 Birmingham C 4 0
2000–01 *QPR* 3 1
2001–02 Birmingham C 11 1
2001–02 *Sheffield U* 4 2 **4 2**
2002–03 Birmingham C 0 0 **131 50**
2002–03 QPR 33 13
2003–04 QPR 36 16
2004–05 QPR 40 18
2005–06 QPR 37 7
2006–07 QPR 22 2 **171 57**
2007–08 Luton T 32 8 **32 8**

GOODALL, Alan (D) **149 9**
H: 5 7 W: 11 08 b.Birkenhead 2-12-81
Source: Bangor C.
2004–05 Rochdale 34 2
2005–06 Rochdale 40 3
2006–07 Rochdale 46 3 **120 8**
2007–08 Luton T 29 1 **29 1**

HOWELLS, Jake (M) **1 0**
H: 5 9 W: 11 08 b.St Albans 18-4-91
Source: Scholar.
2007–08 Luton T 1 0 **1 0**

HUTCHISON, Don (M) **424 54**
H: 6 1 W: 11 08 b.Gateshead 9-5-71
Source: Trainee. *Honours:* Scotland B, 26 full caps, 6 goals.
1989–90 Hartlepool U 13 2
1990–91 Hartlepool U 11 0 **24 2**
1990–91 Liverpool 0 0
1991–92 Liverpool 3 0
1992–93 Liverpool 31 7
1993–94 Liverpool 11 0 **45 7**
1994–95 West Ham U 23 9
1995–96 West Ham U 12 2
1995–96 Sheffield U 19 2
1996–97 Sheffield U 41 3
1997–98 Sheffield U 18 0 **78 5**
1997–98 Everton 11 1
1998–99 Everton 33 3
1999–2000 Everton 31 6 **75 10**
2000–01 Sunderland 32 8
2001–02 Sunderland 2 0 **34 8**
2001–02 West Ham U 24 1
2002–03 West Ham U 10 0
2003–04 West Ham U 24 4
2004–05 West Ham U 5 0 **98 16**
2005–06 Millwall 11 2 **11 2**
2005–06 Coventry C 24 4
2006–07 Coventry C 14 0 **38 4**
2007–08 Luton T 21 0 **21 0**

JACKSON, Richard (D) **169 0**
H: 5 8 W: 12 10 b.Whitby 18-4-80
Source: Trainee.
1997–98 Scarborough 2 0
1998–99 Scarborough 20 0 **22 0**
1998–99 Derby Co 0 0
1999–2000 Derby Co 2 0
2000–01 Derby Co 2 0
2001–02 Derby Co 7 0
2002–03 Derby Co 21 0
2003–04 Derby Co 36 0
2004–05 Derby Co 19 0
2005–06 Derby Co 26 0
2006–07 Derby Co 5 0 **118 0**
2007–08 Luton T 29 0 **29 0**

KEANE, Keith (M) **89 4**
H: 5 9 W: 12 02 b.Luton 20-11-86
Source: Scholar. *Honours:* Eire Youth, Under-21.
2003–04 Luton T 15 1
2004–05 Luton T 17 0
2005–06 Luton T 10 1
2006–07 Luton T 19 1
2007–08 Luton T 28 1 **89 4**

LANGLEY, Richard (M) **265 30**
H: 6 0 W: 11 04 b.Harlesden 27-12-79
Source: Trainee. *Honours:* England Youth, Jamaica 12 full caps, 2 goals.
1996–97 QPR 0 0
1997–98 QPR 0 0
1998–99 QPR 8 1
1999–2000 QPR 41 3
2000–01 QPR 26 1
2001–02 QPR 18 3
2002–03 QPR 39 9
2003–04 QPR 1 1
2003–04 Cardiff C 44 6
2004–05 Cardiff C 25 2
2005–06 Cardiff C 0 0 **69 8**
2005–06 QPR 33 3 **166 21**
2006–07 Luton T 29 1
2007–08 Luton T 1 0 **30 1**

McVEIGH, Paul (F) **252 40**
H: 5 7 W: 11 00 b.Belfast 6-12-77
Source: Trainee. *Honours:* Northern Ireland Schools, Youth, Under-21, 20 full caps.
1995–96 Tottenham H 0 0
1996–97 Tottenham H 3 1
1997–98 Tottenham H 0 0
1998–99 Tottenham H 0 0
1999–2000 Tottenham H 0 0 **3 1**
1999–2000 Norwich C 1 0
2000–01 Norwich C 11 1
2001–02 Norwich C 42 8
2002–03 Norwich C 44 14
2003–04 Norwich C 44 5
2004–05 Norwich C 17 1
2005–06 Norwich C 36 7
2006–07 Norwich C 21 0 **216 36**
2006–07 *Burnley* 8 3 **8 3**
2007–08 Luton T 25 0 **25 0**

MORGAN, Dean (M) **207 21**
H: 5 11 W: 13 00 b.Enfield 3-10-83
Source: Scholar.
2000–01 Colchester U 4 0
2001–02 Colchester U 30 0
2002–03 Colchester U 37 6
2003–04 Colchester U 0 0 **71 6**
2003–04 Reading 13 1
2004–05 Reading 18 2 **31 3**
2005–06 Luton T 36 6
2006–07 Luton T 36 4
2007–08 Luton T 16 1 **88 11**
2007–08 *Southend U* 8 0 **8 0**
2007–08 *Crewe Alex* 9 1 **9 1**

O'LEARY, Stephen (M) **66 6**
H: 6 0 W: 11 09 b.Barnet 12-2-85
Source: Scholar. *Honours:* Eire Youth.
2003–04 Luton T 5 1
2004–05 Luton T 17 1
2005–06 Luton T 0 0
2005–06 *Tranmere R* 21 3 **21 3**
2006–07 Luton T 7 1
2007–08 Luton T 16 0 **45 3**

PARKIN, Sam (F) **235 90**
H: 6 2 W: 13 00 b.Roehampton 14-3-81
Honours: England Schools. Scotland B.
1998–99 Chelsea 0 0
1999–2000 Chelsea 0 0
2000–01 Chelsea 0 0
2000–01 *Millwall* 7 4 **7 4**
2000–01 *Wycombe W* 8 1 **8 1**
2000–01 *Oldham Ath* 7 3 **7 3**
2001–02 Chelsea 0 0
2001–02 *Northampton T* 40 4 **40 4**
2002–03 Swindon T 43 25
2003–04 Swindon T 40 19
2004–05 Swindon T 41 23 **124 67**
2005–06 Ipswich T 20 5
2006–07 Ipswich T 2 0 **22 5**
2006–07 Luton T 8 1
2007–08 Luton T 19 5 **27 6**

PERRY, Chris (D) **427 9**
H: 5 8 W: 11 03 b.Carshalton 26-4-73
Source: Trainee.
1991–92 Wimbledon 0 0
1992–93 Wimbledon 0 0
1993–94 Wimbledon 2 0
1994–95 Wimbledon 22 0
1995–96 Wimbledon 37 0
1996–97 Wimbledon 37 1
1997–98 Wimbledon 35 1
1998–99 Wimbledon 34 0 **167 2**
1999–2000 Tottenham H 37 1
2000–01 Tottenham H 32 1
2001–02 Tottenham H 33 0
2002–03 Tottenham H 18 1
2003–04 Tottenham H 0 0 **120 3**
2003–04 Charlton Ath 29 1
2004–05 Charlton Ath 19 1
2005–06 Charlton Ath 28 1 **76 3**
2006–07 WBA 23 0 **23 0**
2007–08 Luton T 35 1 **35 1**
2007–08 *Southampton* 6 0 **6 0**

PESCHISOLIDO, Paul (F) **447 118**
H: 5 7 W: 10 12 b.Scarborough, Can 25-5-71
Source: Toronto Blizzard. *Honours:* Canada Youth, Under-21, 53 full caps, 11 goals.
1992–93 Birmingham C 19 7
1993–94 Birmingham C 24 9
1994–95 Stoke C 40 13
1995–96 Stoke C 26 6 **66 19**
1995–96 Birmingham C 9 1 **52 17**
1996–97 WBA 37 15
1997–98 WBA 8 3 **45 18**
1997–98 Fulham 32 13
1998–99 Fulham 33 7
1999–2000 Fulham 30 4
2000–01 Fulham 0 0 **95 24**
2000–01 *QPR* 5 1 **5 1**
2000–01 *Sheffield U* 5 2
2000–01 *Norwich C* 5 0 **5 0**
2001–02 Sheffield U 29 6
2002–03 Sheffield U 23 3

2003–04	Sheffield U	27	8	**84**	**19**
2003–04	Derby Co	11	4		
2004–05	Derby Co	32	8		
2005–06	Derby Co	34	5		
2006–07	Derby Co	14	3	**91**	**20**
2007–08	Luton T	4	0	**4**	**0**

ROBINSON, Steve (M) 457 62
H: 5 7 W: 11 09 b.Lisburn 10-12-74
Source: Trainee. *Honours:* Northern Ireland Schools, Youth, Under-21, B, 7 full caps.

1992–93	Tottenham H	0	0		
1993–94	Tottenham H	2	0		
1994–95	Tottenham H	0	0	**2**	**0**
1994–95	*Leyton Orient*	0	0		
1994–95	Bournemouth	32	5		
1995–96	Bournemouth	41	7		
1996–97	Bournemouth	40	7		
1997–98	Bournemouth	45	10		
1998–99	Bournemouth	42	13		
1999–2000	Bournemouth	40	9	**240**	**51**
2000–01	Preston NE	22	1		
2001–02	Preston NE	2	0	**24**	**1**
2001–02	*Bristol C*	6	1	**6**	**1**
2002–03	Luton T	29	1		
2003–04	Luton T	34	2		
2004–05	Luton T	31	4		
2005–06	Luton T	26	2		
2006–07	Luton T	38	0		
2007–08	Luton T	27	0	**185**	**9**

SINCLAIR, Robert (D) 0 0
Source: Scholar.

2007–08	Luton T	0	0

SPRING, Matthew (M) 366 44
H: 5 11 W: 12 05 b.Harlow 17-11-79
Source: Trainee.

1997–98	Luton T	12	0		
1998–99	Luton T	45	3		
1999–2000	Luton T	45	6		
2000–01	Luton T	41	4		
2001–02	Luton T	42	6		
2002–03	Luton T	41	5		
2003–04	Luton T	24	1		
2004–05	Leeds U	13	1		
2005–06	Leeds U	0	0	**13**	**1**
2005–06	Watford	39	8		
2006–07	Watford	6	0	**45**	**8**
2006–07	Luton T	14	1		
2007–08	Luton T	44	9	**308**	**35**

STEVENS, Danny (F) 1 0
H: 5 5 W: 9 09 b.Enfield 26-11-86
Source: Tottenham H Scholar.

2004–05	Luton T	0	0		
2005–06	Luton T	1	0		
2006–07	Luton T	0	0		
2007–08	Luton T	0	0	**1**	**0**

TALBOT, Drew (F) 74 8
H: 5 10 W: 11 00 b.Barnsley 19-7-86
Source: Trainee.

2003–04	Sheffield W	0	0		
2004–05	Sheffield W	21	4		
2005–06	Sheffield W	0	0		
2006–07	Sheffield W	8	0	**29**	**4**
2006–07	*Scunthorpe U*	3	1	**3**	**1**
2006–07	Luton T	15	3		
2007–08	Luton T	27	0	**42**	**3**

UNDERWOOD, Paul (M) 177 6
H: 5 9 W: 12 13 b.Wimbledon 16-8-73
Source: Enfield.

2001–02	Rushden & D	40	0		
2002–03	Rushden & D	40	1		
2003–04	Rushden & D	30	0	**110**	**1**
2003–04	Luton T	1	0		
2004–05	Luton T	37	5		
2005–06	Luton T	29	0		
2006–07	Luton T	0	0		
2007–08	Luton T	0	0	**67**	**5**

MACCLESFIELD T (48)

BLACKMAN, Nick (F) 12 1
H: 6 2 W: 11 08 b.Whitefield 11-11-89
Source: Scholar.

2006–07	Macclesfield T	1	0		
2007–08	Macclesfield T	11	1	**12**	**1**

BRAIN, Jonny (G) 97 0
H: 6 3 W: 13 05 b.Carlisle 11-2-83
Source: Newcastle U Trainee.

2003–04	Port Vale	32	0		
2004–05	Port Vale	27	0		
2005–06	Port Vale	0	0	**59**	**0**
2006–07	Macclesfield T	9	0		
2007–08	Macclesfield T	29	0	**38**	**0**

BRISLEY, Shaun (M) 10 2
H: 6 2 W: 12 02
Source: Scholar.

2007–08	Macclesfield T	10	2	**10**	**2**

DENNIS, Kristian (F) 1 0
H: 5 11 W: 11 00 b.Macclesfield 12-3-90

2007–08	Macclesfield T	1	0	**1**	**0**

DIMECH, Luke (D) 101 1
H: 5 11 W: 14 10 b.Malta 11-1-77
Source: Shamrock R. *Honours:* Malta 56 full caps, 1 goal.

2003–04	Mansfield T	20	1		
2004–05	Mansfield T	25	0	**45**	**1**
2005–06	Chester C	30	0		
2006–07	Chester C	0	0	**30**	**0**
2007–08	Macclesfield T	26	0	**26**	**0**

DUNFIELD, Terry (M) 116 6
H: 5 11 W: 12 04 b.Vancouver 20-2-82
Source: Trainee. *Honours:* Canada Under-23, England Youth.

1998–99	Manchester C	0	0		
1999–2000	Manchester C	0	0		
2000–01	Manchester C	1	0		
2001–02	Manchester C	0	0		
2002–03	Manchester C	0	0	**1**	**0**
2002–03	Bury	29	2		
2003–04	Bury	30	2		
2004–05	Bury	15	1		
2005–06	Bury	0	0		
2006–07	Bury	0	0	**74**	**5**
2007–08	Macclesfield T	41	1	**41**	**1**

EDGHILL, Richard (D) 283 2
H: 5 9 W: 12 01 b.Oldham 23-9-74
Source: Trainee. *Honours:* England Under-21, B.

1992–93	Manchester C	0	0		
1993–94	Manchester C	22	0		
1994–95	Manchester C	14	0		
1995–96	Manchester C	13	0		
1996–97	Manchester C	0	0		
1997–98	Manchester C	36	0		
1998–99	Manchester C	38	0		
1999–2000	Manchester C	41	1		
2000–01	Manchester C	6	0		
2000–01	*Birmingham C*	3	0	**3**	**0**
2001–02	Manchester C	11	0	**181**	**1**
2002–03	Wigan Ath	0	0		
2002–03	Sheffield U	1	0	**1**	**0**
2003–04	QPR	20	0		
2004–05	QPR	20	0	**40**	**0**
2005–06	Bradford C	19	1		
2006–07	Bradford C	24	0	**43**	**1**
2007–08	Macclesfield T	15	0	**15**	**0**

EVANS, Gary (F) 42 7
H: 6 0 W: 12 08 b.Macclesfield 26-4-88
Source: Crewe Alex.

2007–08	Macclesfield T	42	7	**42**	**7**

FLYNN, Matthew (D) 0 0
H: 6 0 W: 11 08 b.Warrington 10-5-89
Source: Warrington T.

2007–08	Macclesfield T	0	0

GREEN, Francis (F) 294 48
H: 5 9 W: 11 04 b.Nottingham 25-4-80
Source: Ilkeston T.

1997–98	Peterborough U	4	1		
1998–99	Peterborough U	7	1		
1999–2000	Peterborough U	20	1		
2000–01	Peterborough U	32	6		
2001–02	Peterborough U	23	3		
2002–03	Peterborough U	19	2		
2003–04	Peterborough U	3	0	**108**	**14**
2003–04	Lincoln C	35	7		
2004–05	Lincoln C	37	8		
2005–06	Lincoln C	28	3	**100**	**18**
2005–06	*Boston U*	6	1		
2006–07	Boston U	39	4	**45**	**5**
2007–08	Macclesfield T	41	11	**41**	**11**

GRITTON, Martin (F) 263 53
H: 6 1 W: 12 02 b.Glasgow 1-6-78
Source: Porthleven.

1998–99	Plymouth Arg	2	0		
1999–2000	Plymouth Arg	30	6		
2000–01	Plymouth Arg	10	1		
2001–02	Plymouth Arg	2	0		
2002–03	Plymouth Arg	0	0	**44**	**7**
2002–03	Torquay U	43	13		
2003–04	Torquay U	31	4		
2004–05	Torquay U	19	6	**93**	**23**
2004–05	Grimsby T	23	4		
2005–06	Grimsby T	26	2	**49**	**6**
2005–06	Lincoln C	10	1		
2006–07	Lincoln C	17	2	**27**	**3**
2006–07	*Mansfield T*	19	6	**19**	**6**
2007–08	Macclesfield T	31	8	**31**	**8**

HADFIELD, Jordan (M) 53 1
H: 5 10 W: 11 04 b.Swinton 12-8-87
Source: Trainee.

2004–05	Stockport Co	1	0		
2005–06	Stockport Co	0	0	**1**	**0**
2006–07	Macclesfield T	37	1		
2007–08	Macclesfield T	2	0	**39**	**1**
2007–08	*Milton Keynes D*	13	0	**13**	**0**

HUSBANDS, Michael (F) 64 5
H: 5 8 W: 10 10 b.Birmingham 13-11-83
Source: Scholar.

2001–02	Aston Villa	0	0		
2002–03	Aston Villa	0	0		
2003–04	Southend U	9	0		
2004–05	Southend U	2	0	**11**	**0**
2005–06	Bristol R	0	0		
2005–06	Walsall	4	0	**4**	**0**
From Rushall Olympic.					
2005–06	Port Vale	24	4		
2006–07	Port Vale	23	1	**47**	**5**
2007–08	Macclesfield T	2	0	**2**	**0**

JENNINGS, James (D) 20 0
H: 5 10 W: 11 02 b.Manchester 2-9-87
Source: Scholar.

2006–07	Macclesfield T	9	0		
2007–08	Macclesfield T	11	0	**20**	**0**

LEE, Tommy (G) 74 0
H: 6 2 W: 12 00 b.Keighley 3-1-86
Source: Scholar.

2005–06	Manchester U	0	0		
2005–06	*Macclesfield T*	11	0		
2006–07	Macclesfield T	34	0		
2007–08	Macclesfield T	18	0	**63**	**0**
2007–08	*Rochdale*	11	0	**11**	**0**

McDONALD, Marvin (F) 0 0
H: 5 7 W: 10 00 b.Wythenshawe 24-8-86
Source: Scholar.

2005–06	Macclesfield T	0	0
2006–07	Macclesfield T	0	0
2007–08	Macclesfield T	0	0

MILLAR, Christian (M) 2 0
H: 5 11 W: 11 00 b.Stoke 23-11-89

2007–08	Macclesfield T	2	0	**2**	**0**

MORLEY, Dave (D) 275 13
H: 6 1 W: 13 02 b.St Helens 25-9-77
Source: Trainee.

1995–96	Manchester C	0	0		
1996–97	Manchester C	0	0		
1997–98	Manchester C	3	1		
1997–98	*Ayr U*	4	0	**4**	**0**
1998–99	Manchester C	0	0	**3**	**1**
1998–99	Southend U	27	0		
1999–2000	Southend U	32	0		
2000–01	Southend U	17	0	**76**	**0**
2000–01	Carlisle U	23	1		
2001–02	Carlisle U	18	0	**41**	**1**
2001–02	Oxford U	18	3	**18**	**3**
2003–04	Doncaster R	21	1		
2004–05	Doncaster R	9	0	**30**	**1**
2004–05	Macclesfield T	19	2		
2005–06	Macclesfield T	45	1		
2006–07	Macclesfield T	35	3		
2007–08	Macclesfield T	4	1	**103**	**7**

MURRAY, Adam (M) 218 16
H: 5 8 W: 10 12 b.Birmingham 30-9-81
Source: Trainee. *Honours:* England Youth, Under-20.

1998–99	Derby Co	4	0
1999–2000	Derby Co	8	0
2000–01	Derby Co	14	0

2001–02 Derby Co 6 0
2001–02 *Mansfield T* 13 7
2002–03 Derby Co 24 0
2003–04 Derby Co 0 0 **56 0**
2003–04 Kidderminster H 22 3 **22 3**
From Burton Alb.
2003–04 Notts Co 3 0 **3 0**
2004–05 Mansfield T 32 5 **45 12**
2004–05 Carlisle U 0 0
2005–06 Carlisle U 37 1
2006–07 Carlisle U 0 0 **37 1**
2006–07 Torquay U 21 0 **21 0**
2006–07 Macclesfield T 11 0
2007–08 Macclesfield T 23 0 **34 0**

ONIBUJE, Fola (F) 29 2
H: 6 7 W: 12 00 b.Lagos 25-9-84
Source: Charlton Ath Juniors.
2002–03 Preston NE 0 0
2003–04 Preston NE 0 0
2003–04 *Huddersfield T* 2 0 **2 0**
2004–05 Barnsley 3 0 **3 0**
2004–05 Peterborough U 2 0 **2 0**
From Cambridge U.
2006–07 Swindon T 14 2 **14 2**
2006–07 *Brentford* 2 0 **2 0**
2006–07 Wycombe W 5 0 **5 0**
2007–08 Shrewsbury T 0 0
2007–08 Macclesfield T 1 0 **1 0**

REID, Izak (M) 33 2
H: 5 5 W: 10 05 b.Sheffield 8-7-87
Source: Scholar.
2006–07 Macclesfield T 8 0
2007–08 Macclesfield T 25 2 **33 2**

REID, Levi (M) 73 2
H: 5 7 W: 11 12 b.Stafford 19-12-83
Source: Scholar.
2002–03 Port Vale 1 0
2003–04 Port Vale 11 0
2004–05 Port Vale 30 0
2005–06 Port Vale 0 0
2006–07 Port Vale 0 0 **42 0**
2007–08 Macclesfield T 31 2 **31 2**

ROONEY, John (F) 2 0
H: 5 10 W: 12 00 b.Liverpool 17-12-90
Source: Scholar.
2007–08 Macclesfield T 2 0 **2 0**

TEAGUE, Andrew (D) 44 2
H: 6 2 W: 12 00 b.Preston 5-2-86
Source: Scholar.
2004–05 Macclesfield T 5 0
2005–06 Macclesfield T 25 1
2006–07 Macclesfield T 13 1
2007–08 Macclesfield T 1 0 **44 2**

THOMAS, Danny (M) 208 16
H: 5 7 W: 10 10 b.Leamington Spa 1-5-81
Source: Trainee.
1997–98 Nottingham F 0 0
1997–98 Leicester C 0 0
1998–99 Leicester C 0 0
1999–2000 Leicester C 3 0
2000–01 Leicester C 0 0
2001–02 Leicester C 0 0 **3 0**
2001–02 Bournemouth 12 0
2002–03 Bournemouth 37 2
2003–04 Bournemouth 10 0 **59 2**
2003–04 Boston U 8 3
2004–05 Boston U 39 3
2005–06 Boston U 35 2
2006–07 Boston U 0 0 **82 8**
2006–07 Shrewsbury T 6 0 **6 0**
2006–07 Hereford U 15 2 **15 2**
2007–08 Macclesfield T 43 4 **43 4**

TOLLEY, Jamie (M) 207 17
H: 6 1 W: 11 03 b.Ludlow 12-5-83
Source: Scholarship. *Honours:* Wales Under-21.
1999–2000 Shrewsbury T 2 0
2000–01 Shrewsbury T 24 2
2001–02 Shrewsbury T 23 1
2002–03 Shrewsbury T 39 3
2003–04 Shrewsbury T 0 0
2004–05 Shrewsbury T 36 4
2005–06 Shrewsbury T 36 4 **160 14**
2006–07 Macclesfield T 23 1
2007–08 Macclesfield T 24 2 **47 3**

WALKER, Richard (D) 129 6
H: 6 2 W: 12 08 b.Stafford 17-9-80
Source: Brook House.
1999–2000 Crewe Alex 0 0
2000–01 Crewe Alex 3 0
2001–02 Crewe Alex 1 0
2002–03 Crewe Alex 35 2
2003–04 Crewe Alex 20 1
2004–05 Crewe Alex 23 2
2005–06 Crewe Alex 18 1 **100 6**
2006–07 Port Vale 16 0
2006–07 *Wrexham* 3 0 **3 0**
2007–08 Port Vale 0 0 **16 0**
2007–08 Macclesfield T 10 0 **10 0**

MANCHESTER C (49)

BALL, David (F) 0 0
b.Whitefield
Source: Scholar.
2007–08 Manchester C 0 0

BALL, Michael (D) 230 9
H: 5 11 W: 11 12 b.Liverpool 2-10-79
Source: Trainee. *Honours:* England Schools, Youth, Under-21, 1 full cap.
1996–97 Everton 5 0
1997–98 Everton 25 1
1998–99 Everton 37 3
1999–2000 Everton 25 1
2000–01 Everton 29 3 **121 8**
2001–02 Rangers 8 0
2002–03 Rangers 0 0
2003–04 Rangers 32 1
2004–05 Rangers 15 0
2005–06 Rangers 2 0 **57 1**
2005–06 PSV Eindhoven 12 0
2006–07 PSV Eindhoven 0 0 **12 0**
2006–07 Manchester C 12 0
2007–08 Manchester C 28 0 **40 0**

BIANCHI, Rolando (F) 182 41
H: 5 10 W: 10 11 b.Lovere 15-2-83
2000–01 Atalanta 1 0
2000–01 Atalanta Youth 23 4
2001–02 Atalanta 3 0
2001–02 Atalanta Youth 19 6
2002–03 Atalanta 16 0
2003–04 Atalanta 1 0 **21 0**
2003–04 Cagliari 14 2
2004–05 Cagliari 25 2 **39 4**
2005–06 Reggina 9 1
2006–07 Reggina 37 18 **46 19**
2007–08 *Lazio* 15 4 **15 4**
2007–08 Manchester C 19 4 **19 4**

BOJINOV, Valeri (F) 122 29
H: 5 10 W: 12 04 b.Oriahovizca 15-2-86
Honours: Bulgaria 21 full caps, 5 goals.
2001–02 Lecce 2 0
2002–03 Lecce 15 2
2003–04 Lecce 28 3
2004–05 Lecce 20 11 **65 16**
2004–05 Fiorentina 9 2
2005–06 Fiorentina 27 6 **36 8**
2006–07 Juventus 18 5 **18 5**
2007–08 Manchester C 3 0 **3 0**

BREEN, Garry (D) 0 0
b.Kilkenny
Source: Scholar.
2006–07 Manchester C 0 0
2007–08 Manchester C 0 0

BROWN, Matthew (D) 0 0
Source: Scholar.
2007–08 Manchester C 0 0

CAICEDO, Felipe (F) 55 11
H: 6 1 W: 12 08 b.Guayaquil 5-9-88
Source: Rocafuerte. *Honours:* Ecuador 15 full caps, 2 goals.
2006–07 Basle 27 7
2007–08 Basle 18 4 **45 11**
2007–08 Manchester C 10 0 **10 0**

CASTILLO, Nery Alberto (M) 118 30
H: 5 5 W: 9 00 b.San Luis Potosi 13-6-84
Honours: Mexico 13 full caps, 5 goals.
2000 Danubio 0 0
2000–01 Olympiakos 1 0
2001–02 Olympiakos 1 0
2002–03 Olympiakos 9 3
2003–04 Olympiakos 26 7
2004–05 Olympiakos 26 6
2005–06 Olympiakos 17 2
2006–07 Olympiakos 25 12 **105 30**
2007–08 Shakhtar Donetsk 6 0 **6 0**
2007–08 Manchester C 7 0 **7 0**

CLAYTON, Adam (M) 0 0
H: 5 9 W: 11 11 b.Manchester 14-1-89
Source: Scholar.
2007–08 Manchester C 0 0

CORLUKA, Vedran (D) 123 11
H: 6 3 W: 13 03 b.Zagreb 9-2-86
Honours: Croatia 23 full caps.
2003–04 Dynamo Zagreb 0 0
2004–05 Inter Zapresic 27 4 **27 4**
2005–06 Dynamo Zagreb 32 3
2006–07 Dynamo Zagreb 29 4 **61 7**
2007–08 Manchester C 35 0 **35 0**

CORRADI, Bernardo (F) 371 85
H: 6 2 W: 13 08 b.Siena 30-3-76
Source: Siena. *Honours:* Italy 13 full caps, 2 goals.
1994–95 Poggibonsi 16 1
1995–96 Poggibonsi 31 8 **47 9**
1996–97 Mobilieri 31 6 **31 6**
1997–98 Cagliari 2 0
1997–98 *Montevarchi* 26 5 **26 5**
1998–99 Fidelis Andria 31 7 **31 7**
1999–2000 Cagliari 20 0 **22 0**
2000–01 Chievo 36 12
2001–02 Chievo 32 10 **68 22**
2002–03 Internazionale 0 0
2002–03 *Lazio* 32 10
2003–04 Lazio 32 10 **64 20**
2004–05 Valencia 21 3
2005–06 Valencia 0 0 **21 3**
2005–06 *Parma* 36 10 **36 10**
2006–07 Manchester C 25 3
2007–08 Manchester C 0 0 **25 3**

DABO, Ousmane (M) 260 11
H: 6 1 W: 13 04 b.Laval 8-2-77
Honours: France Under-21, 3 full caps.
1995–96 Rennes 5 1
1996–97 Rennes 24 1
1997–98 Rennes 12 1 **41 3**
1998–99 Internazionale 5 0
1998–99 *Vicenza* 13 0
1999–2000 Internazionale 8 0 **13 0**
1999–2000 Parma 16 0 **16 0**
2000–01 Monaco 16 0 **16 0**
2000–01 Vicenza 17 1 **30 1**
2001–02 Atalanta 21 0
2002–03 Atalanta 31 4 **52 4**
2003–04 Lazio 19 0
2004–05 Lazio 29 1
2005–06 Lazio 31 2 **79 3**
2006–07 Manchester C 13 0
2007–08 Manchester C 0 0 **13 0**
To Lazio January 2008.

DALY, Ian (F) 0 0
b.Dublin 20-3-90
Source: Scholar. *Honours:* Eire Youth.
2007–08 Manchester C 0 0

DALY, Michael (M) 0 0
2006–07 Manchester C 0 0
2007–08 Manchester C 0 0

DICKOV, Paul (F) 375 94
H: 5 6 W: 10 06 b.Livingston 1-11-72
Source: Trainee. *Honours:* Scotland Schools, Youth, Under-21, 10 full caps, 1 goal.
1992–93 Arsenal 3 2
1993–94 Arsenal 1 0
1993–94 *Luton T* 15 1 **15 1**
1993–94 *Brighton & HA* 8 5 **8 5**
1994–95 Arsenal 9 0
1995–96 Arsenal 7 1
1996–97 Arsenal 1 0 **21 3**
1996–97 Manchester C 29 5
1997–98 Manchester C 30 9
1998–99 Manchester C 35 10
1999–2000 Manchester C 34 5
2000–01 Manchester C 21 4
2001–02 Manchester C 7 0
2001–02 Leicester C 12 4
2002–03 Leicester C 42 17
2003–04 Leicester C 35 11 **89 32**
2004–05 Blackburn R 29 9

2005–06	Blackburn R	21	5	**50**	**14**
2006–07	Manchester C	16	0		
2007–08	Manchester C	0	0	**172**	**33**
2007–08	*Crystal Palace*	9	0	**9**	**0**
2007–08	*Blackpool*	11	6	**11**	**6**

DUNNE, Richard (D) 323 7
H: 6 2 W: 15 10 b.Dublin 21-9-79
Source: Trainee. *Honours:* Eire Schools, Youth, Under-21, B, 42 full caps, 5 goals.

1996–97	Everton	7	0		
1997–98	Everton	3	0		
1998–99	Everton	16	0		
1999–2000	Everton	31	0		
2000–01	Everton	3	0	**60**	**0**
2000–01	Manchester C	25	0		
2001–02	Manchester C	43	1		
2002–03	Manchester C	25	0		
2003–04	Manchester C	29	0		
2004–05	Manchester C	35	2		
2005–06	Manchester C	32	3		
2006–07	Manchester C	38	1		
2007–08	Manchester C	36	0	**263**	**7**

ELANO (M) 214 55
H: 5 9 W: 10 03 b.Iracemapolis 14-6-81
Source: Guarani, Internacional. *Honours:* Brazil 28 full caps, 4 goals.

2001	Santos	24	2		
2002	Santos	28	8		
2003	Santos	39	8		
2004	Santos	40	15	**131**	**33**
2004–05	Shakhter Donetsk	13	4		
2005–06	Shakhter Donetsk	25	5		
2006–07	Shakhter Donetsk	11	5	**49**	**14**
2007–08	Manchester C	34	8	**34**	**8**

ETUHU, Kelvin (F) 14 3
H: 5 11 W: 11 02 b.Kano 30-5-88
Source: Scholar.

2005–06	Manchester C	0	0		
2006–07	Manchester C	0	0		
2006–07	*Rochdale*	4	2	**4**	**2**
2007–08	Manchester C	6	1	**6**	**1**
2007–08	*Leicester C*	4	0	**4**	**0**

EVANS, Ched (F) 28 10
H: 6 0 W: 12 00 b.Rhyl 28-12-88
Source: Scholar. *Honours:* Wales Under-21, 2 full caps, 1 goal.

2006–07	Manchester C	0	0		
2007–08	Manchester C	0	0		
2007–08	*Norwich C*	28	10	**28**	**10**

GARRIDO, Javier (M) 113 1
H: 5 10 W: 11 11 b.Irun 15-3-85
Honours: Spain Under-21.

2004–05	Real Sociedad	28	0		
2005–06	Real Sociedad	33	0		
2006–07	Real Sociedad	25	1	**86**	**1**
2007–08	Manchester C	27	0	**27**	**0**

GELSON (M) 125 3
H: 6 0 W: 11 03 b.Cape Verde Isl 2-9-86
Honours: Switzerland Under-21, 11 full caps.

2002–03	Sion	6	0		
2003–04	Sion	28	0		
2004–05	Sion	9	0		
2005–06	Sion	22	0		
2006–07	Sion	34	1	**99**	**1**
2007–08	Manchester C	26	2	**26**	**2**

GEOVANNI (F) 206 31
H: 5 8 W: 10 08 b.Acaiaca 11-1-80
Honours: Brazil 4 full caps, 1 goal.

1997	Cruzeiro	7	0		
1998	America	15	1	**15**	**1**
1999	Cruzeiro	21	2		
2000	Cruzeiro	12	6		
2001–02	Barcelona	21	1		
2002–03	Barcelona	5	0	**26**	**1**
2002–03	Benfica	17	2		
2003–04	Benfica	21	5		
2004–05	Benfica	31	6		
2005–06	Benfica	25	3	**94**	**16**
2006	Cruzeiro	10	2		
2007	Cruzeiro	2	0	**52**	**10**
2007–08	Manchester C	19	3	**19**	**3**

GIOMBETTI, Andrea (G) 0 0

2007–08	Manchester C	0	0		

GRIMES, Ashley (M) 4 0
H: 6 0 W: 11 02 b.Swinton 9-12-86
Source: Scholar.

2006–07	Manchester C	0	0		
2006–07	*Swindon T*	4	0	**4**	**0**
2007–08	Manchester C	0	0		

HAMANN, Dietmar (M) 364 18
H: 6 2 W: 13 00 b.Waldasson 27-8-73
Source: Wacker Munich. *Honours:* Germany Youth, Under-21, 59 full caps, 5 goals.

1993–94	Bayern Munich	5	1		
1994–95	Bayern Munich	30	0		
1995–96	Bayern Munich	20	2		
1996–97	Bayern Munich	22	1		
1997–98	Bayern Munich	28	2	**105**	**6**
1998–99	Newcastle U	23	4	**23**	**4**
1999–2000	Liverpool	28	1		
2000–01	Liverpool	30	2		
2001–02	Liverpool	31	1		
2002–03	Liverpool	30	2		
2003–04	Liverpool	25	2		
2004–05	Liverpool	30	0		
2005–06	Liverpool	17	0	**191**	**8**
2006–07	Manchester C	16	0		
2007–08	Manchester C	29	0	**45**	**0**

HART, Joe (G) 90 0
H: 6 3 W: 13 03 b.Shrewsbury 19-4-87
Source: Scholar, England Youth, Under-21, 1 full cap.

2004–05	Shrewsbury T	6	0		
2005–06	Shrewsbury T	46	0	**52**	**0**
2006–07	Manchester C	1	0		
2006–07	*Tranmere R*	6	0	**6**	**0**
2006–07	*Blackpool*	5	0	**5**	**0**
2007–08	Manchester C	26	0	**27**	**0**

IRELAND, Stephen (F) 81 5
H: 5 8 W: 10 07 b.Cork 22-8-86
Source: Scholar. *Honours:* Eire Youth, Under-21, 6 full caps, 4 goals.

2005–06	Manchester C	24	0		
2006–07	Manchester C	24	1		
2007–08	Manchester C	33	4	**81**	**5**

ISAKSSON, Andreas (G) 160 0
H: 6 6 W: 13 12 b.Trelleborg 3-10-81
Honours: Sweden Under-21, 59 full caps.

1999	Trelleborg	11	0	**11**	**0**
1999–2000	Juventus	0	0		
2000–01	Juventus	0	0		
2001	Djurgaarden	22	0		
2002	Djurgaarden	20	0		
2003	Djurgaarden	26	0	**68**	**0**
2004–05	Rennes	38	0		
2005–06	Rennes	24	0	**62**	**0**
2006–07	Manchester C	14	0		
2007–08	Manchester C	5	0	**19**	**0**

JIHAI, Sun (D) 153 3
H: 5 9 W: 12 02 b.Dalian 30-9-77
Source: Dalian Wanda. *Honours:* China 71 full caps, 1 goal.

1998–99	Crystal Palace	23	0	**23**	**0**
From Dalian Wanda.					
2001–02	Manchester C	7	0		
2002–03	Manchester C	28	2		
2003–04	Manchester C	33	1		
2004–05	Manchester C	6	0		
2005–06	Manchester C	29	0		
2006–07	Manchester C	13	0		
2007–08	Manchester C	14	0	**130**	**3**

JOHANSEN, Tobias (G) 0 0
b.Denmark

2007–08	Manchester C	0	0		

JOHNSON, Michael (M) 33 2
H: 6 1 W: 12 07 b.Urmston 3-3-88
Source: Scholar. *Honours:* England Youth, Under-21.

2005–06	Manchester C	0	0		
2006–07	Manchester C	10	0		
2007–08	Manchester C	23	2	**33**	**2**

KAY, Scott (D) 0 0
b.Denton
Source: Scholar.

2007–08	Manchester C	0	0		

LOGAN, Shaleum (M) 16 2
H: 6 1 W: 12 07 b.Manchester 6-11-88
Source: Scholar.

2006–07	Manchester C	0	0		
2007–08	Manchester C	0	0		
2007–08	*Grimsby T*	5	2	**5**	**2**
2007–08	*Scunthorpe U*	4	0	**4**	**0**
2007–08	*Stockport Co*	7	0	**7**	**0**

MANCINI, Filippo (F) 0 0
b.Genoa 13-10-90
Source: Internazionale.

2007–08	Manchester C	0	0		

MARSHALL, Paul (M) 0 0
H: 6 1 W: 12 03 b.Manchester 9-7-89
Source: Scholar.

2007–08	Manchester C	0	0		

MARTIN, Richard (G) 0 0
H: 6 2 W: 12 13 b.Chelmsford 1-9-87
Source: Scholar.

2005–06	Brighton & HA	0	0		
2006–07	Brighton & HA	0	0		
2007–08	Manchester C	0	0		

McDERMOTT, Donal (M) 0 0
b.Dublin
Source: Scholar. *Honours:* Eire Youth.

2007–08	Manchester C	0	0		

McDONALD, Clayton (D) 0 0
H: 6 6 W: 16 05 b.Liverpool 26-12-88
Source: Scholar.

2007–08	Manchester C	0	0		

McGIVERN, Ryan (D) 0 0
b.Newry 8-1-90
Source: Scholar. *Honours:* Northern Ireland Youth.

2007–08	Manchester C	0	0		

MEE, Benjamin (D) 0 0
b.Sale
Source: Scholar.

2007–08	Manchester C	0	0		

MENTEL, Filip (G) 0 0
b.Slovakia
Source: Scholar.

2007–08	Manchester C	0	0		

MILLS, Danny (D) 321 7
H: 5 11 W: 12 13 b.Norwich 18-5-77
Source: Trainee. *Honours:* England Youth, Under-21, 19 full caps.

1994–95	Norwich C	0	0		
1995–96	Norwich C	14	0		
1996–97	Norwich C	32	0		
1997–98	Norwich C	20	0	**66**	**0**
1997–98	Charlton Ath	9	1		
1998–99	Charlton Ath	36	2		
1999–2000	Leeds U	17	1		
2000–01	Leeds U	23	0		
2001–02	Leeds U	28	1		
2002–03	Leeds U	33	1		
2003–04	Leeds U	0	0	**101**	**3**
2003–04	*Middlesbrough*	28	0	**28**	**0**
2004–05	Manchester C	32	0		
2005–06	Manchester C	18	1		
2006–07	Manchester C	1	0		
2006–07	*Hull C*	9	0	**9**	**0**
2007–08	Manchester C	0	0	**51**	**1**
2007–08	*Charlton Ath*	19	0	**64**	**3**
2007–08	*Derby Co*	2	0	**2**	**0**

MILLS, Matthew (D) 65 6
H: 6 3 W: 12 12 b.Swindon 14-7-86
Source: Scholar. *Honours:* England Youth.

2004–05	Southampton	0	0		
2004–05	*Coventry C*	4	0	**4**	**0**
2004–05	*Bournemouth*	12	3	**12**	**3**
2005–06	Southampton	4	0	**4**	**0**
2005–06	Manchester C	1	0		
2006–07	Manchester C	1	0		
2006–07	*Colchester U*	9	0	**9**	**0**
2007–08	Manchester C	0	0	**2**	**0**
2007–08	*Doncaster R*	34	3	**34**	**3**

MOORE, Karl (M) 0 0
b.Dublin 9-11-88
Source: Scholar.

2006–07	Manchester C	0	0		
2007–08	Manchester C	0	0		

MOURITSEN, Christian (M) 0 0
b.Faroe Islands
Source: Scholar.

2006–07	Manchester C	0	0		
2007–08	Manchester C	0	0		

MPENZA, Emile (F) 247 92
H: 5 9 W: 10 12 b.Zellik 4-7-78
Honours: Belgium 54 full caps, 17 goals.

1995–96	Kortrijk	0	0		
1996–97	Mouscron	31	12	**31**	**12**
1997–98	Standard Liege	20	6		
1998–99	Standard Liege	17	10		
1999–2000	Standard Liege	11	4		
1999–2000	Schalke	15	6		
2000–01	Schalke	27	13		
2001–02	Schalke	16	4		
2002–03	Schalke	21	5	**79**	**28**
2003–04	Standard Liege	28	21	**76**	**41**
2004–05	Hamburg	26	5		
2005–06	Hamburg	10	1	**36**	**6**
From Al Rayyan.					
2006–07	Manchester C	10	3		
2007–08	Manchester C	15	2	**25**	**5**

MWARUWARI, Benjamin (F) 225 62
H: 6 2 W: 12 03 b.Harare 13-8-78
Honours: Zimbabwe 33 full caps, 9 goals.

1999–2000	Jomo Cosmos	15	7		
2000–01	Jomo Cosmos	30	13	**45**	**20**
2001–02	Grasshoppers	25	1	**25**	**1**
2002–03	Auxerre	27	7		
2003–04	Auxerre	3	0		
2004–05	Auxerre	31	11		
2005–06	Auxerre	11	1	**72**	**19**
2005–06	Portsmouth	16	1		
2006–07	Portsmouth	31	6		
2007–08	Portsmouth	23	12	**70**	**19**
2007–08	Manchester C	13	3	**13**	**3**

OBENG, Curtis (D) 0 0
H: 5 8 W: 10 08 b.Manchester 14-2-89
Source: Scholar. *Honours:* England Youth.

2007–08	Manchester C	0	0		

ONUOHA, Nedum (D) 61 1
H: 6 2 W: 12 04 b.Warri 12-11-86
Source: Scholar. *Honours:* England Youth, Under-20, Under-21.

2004–05	Manchester C	17	0		
2005–06	Manchester C	10	0		
2006–07	Manchester C	18	0		
2007–08	Manchester C	16	1	**61**	**1**

PETROV, Martin (F) 281 58
H: 6 0 W: 12 02 b.Vzatza 15-1-79
Honours: Bulgaria 74 full caps, 17 goals.

1996–97	CSKA Sofia	3	0		
1997–98	CSKA Sofia	4	0	**7**	**0**
1998–99	Servette	12	2		
1999–2000	Servette	31	9		
2000–01	Servette	32	11	**75**	**22**
2001–02	Wolfsburg	32	6		
2002–03	Wolfsburg	26	2		
2003–04	Wolfsburg	28	8		
2004–05	Wolfsburg	30	12	**116**	**28**
2005–06	Atletico Madrid	36	1		
2006–07	Atletico Madrid	13	2	**49**	**3**
2007–08	Manchester C	34	5	**34**	**5**

RICHARDS, Micah (D) 66 1
H: 5 11 W: 13 00 b.Birmingham 24-6-88
Source: Scholar. *Honours:* England Youth, Under-21, 11 full caps, 1 goal.

2005–06	Manchester C	13	0		
2006–07	Manchester C	28	1		
2007–08	Manchester C	25	0	**66**	**1**

SAMARAS, Georgios (F) 156 38
H: 6 3 W: 13 07 b.Heraklion 21-2-85
Source: OFI Crete. *Honours:* Greece Under-21, 11 full caps, 3 goals.

2002–03	Heerenveen	15	4		
2003–04	Heerenveen	27	4		
2004–05	Heerenveen	31	11		
2005–06	Heerenveen	13	6	**86**	**25**
2005–06	Manchester C	14	4		
2006–07	Manchester C	36	4		
2007–08	*Celtic*	15	5	**15**	**5**
2007–08	Manchester C	5	0	**55**	**8**

SCHMEICHEL, Kasper (G) 78 0
H: 6 1 W: 13 00 b.Denmark 5-11-86
Source: Scholar. *Honours:* Denmark Youth, Under-20, Under-21.

2003–04	Manchester C	0	0		
2004–05	Manchester C	0	0		
2005–06	Manchester C	0	0		
2005–06	*Darlington*	4	0	**4**	**0**
2005–06	*Bury*	15	0		
2006–07	Manchester C	0	0		
2006–07	*Falkirk*	15	0	**15**	**0**
2006–07	*Bury*	14	0	**29**	**0**
2007–08	Manchester C	7	0	**7**	**0**
2007–08	*Cardiff C*	14	0	**14**	**0**
2007–08	*Coventry C*	9	0	**9**	**0**

STURRIDGE, Daniel (F) 5 1
H: 6 2 W: 12 00 b.Manchester 1-9-89
Source: Scholar. *Honours:* England Youth.

2006–07	Manchester C	2	0		
2007–08	Manchester C	3	1	**5**	**1**

TRABELSI, Hatem (D) 119 3
H: 5 10 W: 11 02 b.Ariana 25-1-77
Source: Sfaxien. *Honours:* Tunisia 61 full caps, 1 goal.

2001–02	Ajax	21	0		
2002–03	Ajax	26	1		
2003–04	Ajax	8	1		
2004–05	Ajax	24	0		
2005–06	Ajax	20	0	**99**	**2**
2006–07	Manchester C	20	1		
2007–08	Manchester C	0	0	**20**	**1**

TRIPPIER, Keiran (D) 0 0
b.Bury
Source: Scholar.

2007–08	Manchester C	0	0		

TUTTLE, Andrew (M) 0 0
Source: Scholar.

2007–08	Manchester C	0	0		

VASSELL, Darius (F) 257 52
H: 5 9 W: 13 00 b.Birmingham 13-6-80
Source: Trainee. *Honours:* England Youth, Under-21, 22 full caps, 6 goals.

1998–99	Aston Villa	6	0		
1999–2000	Aston Villa	11	0		
2000–01	Aston Villa	23	4		
2001–02	Aston Villa	36	12		
2002–03	Aston Villa	33	8		
2003–04	Aston Villa	32	9		
2004–05	Aston Villa	21	2	**162**	**35**
2005–06	Manchester C	36	8		
2006–07	Manchester C	32	3		
2007–08	Manchester C	27	6	**95**	**17**

VIDAL, Javan (D) 0 0
H: 5 10 W: 10 10 b.Manchester 10-5-89
Source: Scholar.

2007–08	Manchester C	0	0		

WEISS, Vladimir (M) 0 0
b.Slovakia
Source: Scholar.

2007–08	Manchester C	0	0		

WILLIAMSON, Samuel (D) 1 0
H: 5 8 W: 11 09 b.Macclesfield 15-10-87
Source: Scholar.

2006–07	Manchester C	0	0		
2007–08	Manchester C	1	0	**1**	**0**

Scholars
Boyata, Anga Dedryck; Carter, Aaron Luke; Chantler, Christopher Steven; Cieslewicz, Adrian; Clegg, Joe; Cunningham, Gregory Richard; Frater, Craig; Hartley, Gregory, Hulme, Lee; Ibrahim, Abdisalam; Mak, Robert; Morris, Benjamin Thomas; Nimely-Tchuimeni, Alex; Nolan, Gary Thomas; Paldan, Igor; Poole, James Alexander; Ramsey, Christopher; Redshaw, Jack; Robinson, Dylan; Tsiaklis, Angelos; Varga, Peter

MANCHESTER U (50)

AMOS, Ben (G) 0 0
b.Macclesfield 10-4-90
Source: Scholar.

2007–08	Manchester U	0	0		

ANDERSON (M) 47 3
H: 5 8 W: 10 07 b.Porto Alegre 13-4-88

2004–05	Gremio	5	1	**5**	**1**
2005–06	Porto	3	0		
2006–07	Porto	15	2	**18**	**2**
2007–08	Manchester U	24	0	**24**	**0**

BARNES, Michael (M) 5 0
H: 5 10 W: 11 05 b.Chorley 24-6-88
Source: Lancaster C.

2006–07	Manchester U	0	0		
2007–08	Manchester U	0	0		
2007–08	*Chesterfield*	3	0	**3**	**0**
2007–08	*Shrewsbury T*	2	0	**2**	**0**

BRANDY, Febian (F) 19 3
H: 5 5 W: 10 00 b.Manchester 4-2-89
Source: Scholar. *Honours:* England Youth.

2006–07	Manchester U	0	0		
2007–08	Manchester U	0	0		
2007–08	*Swansea C*	19	3	**19**	**3**

BROWN, Wes (D) 198 2
H: 6 1 W: 13 08 b.Manchester 13-10-79
Source: Trainee. *Honours:* England Schools, Youth, Under-21, 17 full caps.

1996–97	Manchester U	0	0		
1997–98	Manchester U	2	0		
1998–99	Manchester U	14	0		
1999–2000	Manchester U	0	0		
2000–01	Manchester U	28	0		
2001–02	Manchester U	17	0		
2002–03	Manchester U	22	0		
2003–04	Manchester U	17	0		
2004–05	Manchester U	21	1		
2005–06	Manchester U	19	0		
2006–07	Manchester U	22	0		
2007–08	Manchester U	36	1	**198**	**2**

CAMPBELL, Frazier (F) 35 15
H: 5 11 W: 12 04 b.Huddersfield 13-9-87
Source: Scholar. *Honours:* England Youth, Under-21.

2005–06	Manchester U	0	0		
2006–07	Manchester U	0	0		
2007–08	Manchester U	1	0	**1**	**0**
2007–08	*Hull C*	34	15	**34**	**15**

CARRICK, Michael (M) 272 15
H: 6 1 W: 11 10 b.Wallsend 28-7-81
Source: Trainee. *Honours:* England Youth, Under-21, B, 14 full caps.

1998–99	West Ham U	0	0		
1999–2000	West Ham U	8	1		
1999–2000	*Swindon T*	6	2	**6**	**2**
1999–2000	*Birmingham C*	2	0	**2**	**0**
2000–01	West Ham U	33	1		
2001–02	West Ham U	30	2		
2002–03	West Ham U	30	1		
2003–04	West Ham U	35	1		
2004–05	West Ham U	0	0	**136**	**6**
2004–05	Tottenham H	29	0		
2005–06	Tottenham H	35	2	**64**	**2**
2006–07	Manchester U	33	3		
2007–08	Manchester U	31	2	**64**	**5**

CATHCART, Craig (D) 0 0
H: 6 2 W: 11 06 b.Belfast 6-2-89
Source: Scholar. *Honours:* Northern Ireland Under-21.

2005–06	Manchester U	0	0		
2006–07	Manchester U	0	0		
2007–08	Manchester U	0	0		

CHESTER, James (D) 0 0
b.Warrington 23-1-89
Source: Scholar.

2007–08	Manchester U	0	0		

CLEVERLEY, Tom (M) 0 0
b.Basingstoke 12-8-89
Source: Scholar.

2007–08	Manchester U	0	0		

DONG FANGZHOU (M) 93 54
H: 6 1 W: 11 09 b.Liaoning 23-1-85
Honours: China Under-23, 13 full caps, 1 goal.

2002	Dalian Saidelong	14	20	**14**	**20**
2003	Dalian Shide	8	0	**8**	**0**
2003–04	Manchester U	0	0		
2003–04	*Antwerp*	9	1		
2004–05	*Antwerp*	19	6		
2005–06	*Antwerp*	28	18		
2006–07	*Antwerp*	14	9	**70**	**34**
2006–07	Manchester U	1	0		
2007–08	Manchester U	0	0	**1**	**0**

EAGLES, Chris (M) 61 8
H: 5 10 W: 11 07 b.Hemel Hempstead 19-11-85
Source: Trainee. *Honours:* England Youth.
2003–04 Manchester U 0 0
2004–05 Manchester U 0 0
2004–05 *Watford* 13 1
2005–06 Manchester U 0 0
2005–06 *Sheffield W* 25 3 **25 3**
2005–06 *Watford* 17 3 **30 4**
2006–07 Manchester U 2 1
2007–08 Manchester U 4 0 **6 1**

ECKERSLEY, Richard (D) 0 0
b.Salford 12-3-89
Source: Scholar.
2007–08 Manchester U 0 0

EVANS, Corry (M) 0 0
Source: Scholar.
2007–08 Manchester U 0 0

EVANS, Jonny (D) 33 1
H: 6 2 W: 12 02 b.Belfast 3-1-88
Source: Scholar. *Honours:* Northern Ireland Schools, Youth, Under-21, 10 full caps.
2004–05 Manchester U 0 0
2005–06 Manchester U 0 0
2006–07 Manchester U 0 0
2006–07 *Sunderland* 18 1
2007–08 Manchester U 0 0
2007–08 *Sunderland* 15 0 **33 1**

EVANS, Sean (F) 0 0
H: 5 9 W: 11 00 b.Ludlow 25-9-87
Source: Scholar.
2006–07 Manchester U 0 0
2007–08 Manchester U 0 0

EVRA, Patrice (D) 254 6
H: 5 8 W: 11 10 b.Dakar 15-5-81
Honours: France 13 full caps.
1998–99 Marsala 24 3 **24 3**
1999–2000 Monza 3 0 **3 0**
2000–01 Nice 5 0
2001–02 Nice 34 1 **39 1**
2002–03 Monaco 36 1
2003–04 Monaco 33 0
2004–05 Monaco 36 0
2005–06 Monaco 15 0 **120 1**
2005–06 Manchester U 11 0
2006–07 Manchester U 24 1
2007–08 Manchester U 33 0 **68 1**

FAGAN, Chris (F) 0 0
H: 5 8 W: 10 05 b.Dublin 11-5-89
Source: Scholar.
2006–07 Manchester U 0 0
2007–08 Manchester U 0 0

FERDINAND, Rio (D) 375 10
H: 6 2 W: 13 12 b.Peckham 7-11-78
Source: Trainee. *Honours:* England Youth, Under-21, B, 68 full caps, 2 goals.
1995–96 West Ham U 1 0
1996–97 West Ham U 15 2
1996–97 *Bournemouth* 10 0 **10 0**
1997–98 West Ham U 35 0
1998–99 West Ham U 31 0
1999–2000 West Ham U 33 0
2000–01 West Ham U 12 0 **127 2**
2000–01 Leeds U 23 2
2001–02 Leeds U 31 0 **54 2**
2002–03 Manchester U 28 0
2003–04 Manchester U 20 0
2004–05 Manchester U 31 0
2005–06 Manchester U 37 3
2006–07 Manchester U 33 1
2007–08 Manchester U 35 2 **184 6**

FLETCHER, Darren (M) 107 7
H: 6 0 W: 11 09 b.Edinburgh 1-2-84
Source: Scholar. *Honours:* Scotland Under-21, B, 36 full caps, 4 goals.
2000–01 Manchester U 0 0
2001–02 Manchester U 0 0
2002–03 Manchester U 0 0
2003–04 Manchester U 22 0
2004–05 Manchester U 18 3
2005–06 Manchester U 27 1
2006–07 Manchester U 24 3
2007–08 Manchester U 16 0 **107 7**

FOSTER, Ben (G) 93 0
H: 6 2 W: 12 08 b.Leamington Spa 3-4-83
Source: Racing Club Warwick. *Honours:* England 1 full cap.
2000–01 Stoke C 0 0
2001–02 Stoke C 0 0
2002–03 Stoke C 0 0
2003–04 Stoke C 0 0
2004–05 Stoke C 0 0
2004–05 *Kidderminster H* 2 0 **2 0**
2004–05 *Wrexham* 17 0 **17 0**
2005–06 Manchester U 0 0
2005–06 *Watford* 44 0
2006–07 Manchester U 0 0
2006–07 *Watford* 29 0 **73 0**
2007–08 Manchester U 1 0 **1 0**

GALBRAITH, Daniel (F) 0 0
H: 5 9 W: 10 03 b.Manchester 5-3-90
Source: Scholar.
2007–08 Manchester U 0 0

GIBSON, Darron (M) 21 1
H: 6 0 W: 12 04 b.Londonderry 25-10-87
Source: Scholar. *Honours:* Eire Youth, Under-21, 2 full caps.
2005–06 Manchester U 0 0
2006–07 Manchester U 0 0
2007–08 Manchester U 0 0
2007–08 *Wolverhampton W* 21 1 **21 1**

GIGGS, Ryan (F) 535 101
H: 5 11 W: 11 02 b.Cardiff 29-11-73
Source: School. *Honours:* England Schools, Wales Youth, Under-21, 64 full caps, 12 goals.
1990–91 Manchester U 2 1
1991–92 Manchester U 38 4
1992–93 Manchester U 41 9
1993–94 Manchester U 38 13
1994–95 Manchester U 29 1
1995–96 Manchester U 33 11
1996–97 Manchester U 26 3
1997–98 Manchester U 29 8
1998–99 Manchester U 24 3
1999–2000 Manchester U 30 6
2000–01 Manchester U 31 5
2001–02 Manchester U 25 7
2002–03 Manchester U 36 8
2003–04 Manchester U 33 7
2004–05 Manchester U 32 5
2005–06 Manchester U 27 3
2006–07 Manchester U 30 4
2007–08 Manchester U 31 3 **535 101**

GRAY, David (F) 1 0
H: 5 11 W: 11 02 b.Edinburgh 4-5-88
Source: Scholar.
2005–06 Manchester U 0 0
2006–07 Manchester U 0 0
2007–08 Manchester U 0 0
2007–08 *Crewe Alex* 1 0 **1 0**

HARGREAVES, Owen (M) 168 7
H: 5 11 W: 11 07 b.Calgary 20-1-81
Source: Calgary Foothills. *Honours:* England Under-21, B, 42 full caps.
2000–01 Bayern Munich 14 0
2001–02 Bayern Munich 29 0
2002–03 Bayern Munich 25 1
2003–04 Bayern Munich 25 2
2004–05 Bayern Munich 27 1
2005–06 Bayern Munich 16 0
2006–07 Bayern Munich 9 0 **145 5**
2007–08 Manchester U 23 2 **23 2**

HEATON, Tom (G) 14 0
H: 6 1 W: 13 12 b.Chester 15-4-86
Source: Trainee. *Honours:* England Youth, Under-21.
2003–04 Manchester U 0 0
2004–05 Manchester U 0 0
2005–06 Manchester U 0 0
2005–06 *Swindon T* 14 0 **14 0**
2006–07 Manchester U 0 0
2007–08 Manchester U 0 0

HEWSON, Sam (M) 0 0
H: 5 8 W: 11 00 b.Bolton 28-11-88
Source: Scholar.
2007–08 Manchester U 0 0

JAMES, Matthew (M) 0 0
b.Rochdale 22-7-91
Source: Scholar.
2007–08 Manchester U 0 0

JONES, Richie (M) 19 0
H: 6 0 W: 11 00 b.Manchester 26-9-86
Source: Scholar. *Honours:* England Youth.
2004–05 Manchester U 0 0
2005–06 Manchester U 0 0
2006–07 Manchester U 0 0
2006–07 *Colchester U* 6 0 **6 0**
2006–07 *Barnsley* 4 0 **4 0**
2007–08 Manchester U 0 0
2007–08 *Yeovil T* 9 0 **9 0**

KUSZCZAK, Tomasz (G) 46 0
H: 6 3 W: 13 03 b.Krosno Odrzansia 20-3-82
Source: Uerdingen. *Honours:* Poland Youth, Under-21, 6 full caps.
2001–02 Hertha Berlin 0 0
2002–03 Hertha Berlin 0 0
2003–04 Hertha Berlin 0 0
2004–05 WBA 3 0
2005–06 WBA 28 0
2006–07 WBA 0 0 **31 0**
2006–07 *Manchester U* 6 0
2007–08 Manchester U 9 0 **15 0**

LEA, Michael (D) 0 0
b.Salford 4-11-87
Source: Scholar.
2007–08 Manchester U 0 0

LEE, Kieran (D) 8 0
H: 6 1 W: 12 00 b.Tameside 22-6-88
Source: Scholar.
2006–07 Manchester U 1 0
2007–08 Manchester U 0 0 **1 0**
2007–08 *QPR* 7 0 **7 0**

MANUCHO (F) 7 4
H: 6 2 W: 13 00 b.Luanda 7-3-83
Source: Benfica de Luanda, Petro Atletico.
Honours: Angola 14 full caps, 6 goals.
2007–08 *Panathinaikos* 7 4 **7 4**
2007–08 Manchester U 0 0

MARTIN, Lee (M) 38 3
H: 5 10 W: 10 03 b.Taunton 9-2-87
Source: Scholar. *Honours:* England Youth.
2004–05 Manchester U 0 0
2005–06 Manchester U 0 0
2006–07 Manchester U 0 0
2006–07 *Rangers* 7 0 **7 0**
2006–07 *Stoke C* 13 1 **13 1**
2007–08 Manchester U 0 0
2007–08 *Plymouth Arg* 12 2 **12 2**
2007–08 *Sheffield U* 6 0 **6 0**

NANI (M) 84 12
H: 5 9 W: 10 04 b.Amadora 17-11-86
Honours: Portugal Under-21, 16 full caps, 2 goals.
2005–06 Sporting Lisbon 29 4
2006–07 Sporting Lisbon 29 5 **58 9**
2007–08 Manchester U 26 3 **26 3**

NEVILLE, Gary (D) 364 5
H: 5 11 W: 12 10 b.Bury 18-2-75
Source: Trainee. *Honours:* England Youth, 85 full caps.
1992–93 Manchester U 0 0
1993–94 Manchester U 1 0
1994–95 Manchester U 18 0
1995–96 Manchester U 31 0
1996–97 Manchester U 31 1
1997–98 Manchester U 34 0
1998–99 Manchester U 34 1
1999–2000 Manchester U 22 0
2000–01 Manchester U 32 1
2001–02 Manchester U 34 0
2002–03 Manchester U 26 0
2003–04 Manchester U 30 2
2004–05 Manchester U 22 0
2005–06 Manchester U 25 0
2006–07 Manchester U 24 0
2007–08 Manchester U 0 0 **364 5**

O'SHEA, John (D) 201 10
H: 6 3 W: 13 07 b.Waterford 30-4-81
Source: Waterford. *Honours:* Eire Youth, Under-21, 45 full caps, 1 goal.
1998–99 Manchester U 0 0
1999–2000 Manchester U 0 0
1999–2000 *Bournemouth* 10 1 **10 1**
2000–01 Manchester U 0 0
2001–02 Manchester U 9 0
2002–03 Manchester U 32 0

2003–04 Manchester U 33 2
2004–05 Manchester U 23 2
2005–06 Manchester U 34 1
2006–07 Manchester U 32 4
2007–08 Manchester U 28 0 **191 9**

PARK, Ji-Sung (M) 199 31
H: 5 9 W: 11 06 b.Seoul 25-2-81
Honours: South Korea 70 full caps, 8 goals.
2000 Kyoto Purple S 13 1
2001 Kyoto Purple S 38 3
2002 Kyoto Purple S 25 7 **76 11**
2002–03 PSV Eindhoven 8 0
2003–04 PSV Eindhoven 28 6
2004–05 PSV Eindhoven 28 7 **64 13**
2005–06 Manchester U 33 1
2006–07 Manchester U 14 5
2007–08 Manchester U 12 1 **59 7**

PIQUE, Gerard (D) 12 0
H: 6 3 W: 13 03 b.Barcelona 2-2-87
Source: Scholar. *Honours:* Spain Youth.
2004–05 Manchester U 0 0
2005–06 Manchester U 3 0
2006–07 Manchester U 0 0
2007–08 Manchester U 9 0 **12 0**

POSSEBON, Rodrigo (M) 0 0
Source: Internacional.
2007–08 Manchester U 0 0

RONALDO, Cristiano (M) 188 69
H: 6 1 W: 13 02 b.Funchal 5-2-85
Honours: Portugal Youth, Under-21, 58 full caps, 21 goals.
2002–03 Sporting Lisbon 25 3 **25 3**
2003–04 Manchester U 29 4
2004–05 Manchester U 33 5
2005–06 Manchester U 33 9
2006–07 Manchester U 34 17
2007–08 Manchester U 34 31 **163 66**

ROONEY, Wayne (F) 194 68
H: 5 10 W: 12 13 b.Liverpool 24-10-85
Source: Scholar. *Honours:* FA Schools, England Youth, 43 full caps, 14 goals.
2002–03 Everton 33 6
2003–04 Everton 34 9 **67 15**
2004–05 Manchester U 29 11
2005–06 Manchester U 36 16
2006–07 Manchester U 35 14
2007–08 Manchester U 27 12 **127 53**

ROSE, Danny (M) 0 0
H: 5 7 W: 10 01 b.Bristol 21-2-88
Source: Scholar. *Honours:* England Youth.
2006–07 Manchester U 0 0
2007–08 Manchester U 0 0

SAHA, Louis (F) 261 87
H: 6 1 W: 12 08 b.Paris 8-8-78
Honours: France Youth, Under-21, 18 full caps, 4 goals.
1997–98 Metz 21 1
1998–99 Metz 3 0
1998–99 Newcastle U 11 1 **11 1**
1999–2000 Metz 23 4 **47 5**
2000–01 Fulham 43 27
2001–02 Fulham 36 8
2002–03 Fulham 17 5
2003–04 Fulham 21 13 **117 53**
2003–04 Manchester U 12 7
2004–05 Manchester U 14 1
2005–06 Manchester U 19 7
2006–07 Manchester U 24 8
2007–08 Manchester U 17 5 **86 28**

SCHOLES, Paul (M) 395 96
H: 5 7 W: 11 00 b.Salford 16-11-74
Source: Trainee. *Honours:* England Youth, 66 full caps, 14 goals.
1992–93 Manchester U 0 0
1993–94 Manchester U 0 0
1994–95 Manchester U 17 5
1995–96 Manchester U 26 10
1996–97 Manchester U 24 3
1997–98 Manchester U 31 8
1998–99 Manchester U 31 6
1999–2000 Manchester U 31 9
2000–01 Manchester U 32 6
2001–02 Manchester U 35 8
2002–03 Manchester U 33 14
2003–04 Manchester U 28 9
2004–05 Manchester U 33 9
2005–06 Manchester U 20 2
2006–07 Manchester U 30 6
2007–08 Manchester U 24 1 **395 96**

SILVESTRE, Mikael (D) 316 7
H: 6 0 W: 13 12 b.Chambray les Tours 9-8-77
Honours: France Youth, Under-21, 40 full caps, 2 goals.
1995–96 Rennes 1 0
1996–97 Rennes 16 0
1997–98 Rennes 32 0 **49 0**
1998–99 Internazionale 18 1 **18 1**
1999–2000 Manchester U 31 0
2000–01 Manchester U 30 1
2001–02 Manchester U 35 0
2002–03 Manchester U 34 1
2003–04 Manchester U 34 0
2004–05 Manchester U 35 2
2005–06 Manchester U 33 1
2006–07 Manchester U 14 1
2007–08 Manchester U 3 0 **249 6**

SIMPSON, Danny (D) 25 0
H: 5 9 W: 11 05 b.Eccles 4-1-87
Source: Scholar.
2005–06 Manchester U 0 0
2006–07 Manchester U 0 0
2006–07 *Sunderland* 14 0 **14 0**
2007–08 Manchester U 3 0 **3 0**
2007–08 *Ipswich T* 8 0 **8 0**

SOLSKJAER, Ole Gunnar (F) 277 122
H: 5 10 W: 11 07 b.Kristiansund 26-2-73
Honours: Norway Under-21, 67 full caps, 23 goals.
1995 Molde 26 20
1996 Molde 16 11 **42 31**
1996–97 Manchester U 33 18
1997–98 Manchester U 22 6
1998–99 Manchester U 19 12
1999–2000 Manchester U 28 12
2000–01 Manchester U 31 10
2001–02 Manchester U 30 17
2002–03 Manchester U 37 9
2003–04 Manchester U 13 0
2004–05 Manchester U 0 0
2005–06 Manchester U 3 0
2006–07 Manchester U 19 7
2007–08 Manchester U 0 0 **235 91**

TEVEZ, Carlos (F) 164 67
H: 5 8 W: 11 11 b.Cuidadela 5-2-84
Source: All Boys. *Honours:* Argentina Youth, Under-20, Under-23, 38 full caps, 7 goals.
2001–02 Boca Juniors 11 1
2002–03 Boca Juniors 32 11
2003–04 Boca Juniors 23 12
2004–05 Boca Juniors 9 2 **75 26**
2005 Corinthians 29 20 **29 20**
2006–07 West Ham U 26 7 **26 7**
2007–08 Manchester U 34 14 **34 14**

VAN DER SAR, Edwin (G) 518 1
H: 6 5 W: 14 11 b.Voorhout 29-10-70
Honours: Holland 128 full caps.
1990–91 Ajax 9 0
1991–92 Ajax 0 0
1992–93 Ajax 19 0
1993–94 Ajax 32 0
1994–95 Ajax 33 0
1995–96 Ajax 33 0
1996–97 Ajax 33 0
1997–98 Ajax 33 1 **192 1**
1998–99 Juventus 34 0
1999–2000 Juventus 32 0
2000–01 Juventus 34 0 **100 0**
2001–02 Fulham 37 0
2002–03 Fulham 19 0
2003–04 Fulham 37 0
2004–05 Fulham 34 0 **127 0**
2005–06 Manchester U 38 0
2006–07 Manchester U 32 0
2007–08 Manchester U 29 0 **99 0**

VIDIC, Nemanja (D) 202 26
H: 6 1 W: 13 02 b.Uzice 21-10-81
Honours: Serbia & Montenegro 31 full caps, 2 goals.
2000–01 Subotica 27 6 **27 6**
2001–02 Red Star Belgrade 22 2
2002–03 Red Star Belgrade 26 5
2003–04 Red Star Belgrade 20 5 **68 12**
2004 Spartak Moscow 12 2
2005 Spartak Moscow 27 2 **39 4**
2005–06 Manchester U 11 0
2006–07 Manchester U 25 3
2007–08 Manchester U 32 1 **68 4**

WELBECK, Danny (F) 0 0
H: 6 1 W: 11 07 b.Manchester 26-11-90
Source: Scholar. *Honours:* England Youth.
2007–08 Manchester U 0 0

ZIELER, Ron-Robert (G) 0 0
H: 6 1 W: 11 07 b.Cologne 12-2-89
Source: Scholar.
2006–07 Manchester U 0 0
2007–08 Manchester U 0 0

Scholars
Bryan, Antonio Stefan; Curran, Christopher; De Carvalho Brandao, Evandro Elmer; Derbyshire, James Jeffrey; Drinkwater, Daniel Noel; Dudgeon, Joseph Patrick; Eikrem, Magnus Wolff; James, Matthew; Macheda, Federico; Moffatt, Scott Lee; Norwood, Oliver James; Stewart, Cameron Reece; Strickland, Kenneth Andrew; Welbeck, Daniel; Woods, Gary

MANSFIELD T (51)

ARNOLD, Nathan (F) 62 8
H: 5 8 W: 10 07 b.Mansfield 26-7-87
2005–06 Mansfield T 8 1
2006–07 Mansfield T 22 3
2007–08 Mansfield T 32 4 **62 8**

BELL, Lee (M) 77 4
H: 5 11 W: 12 04 b.Crewe 26-1-83
Source: Scholar.
2000–01 Crewe Alex 0 0
2001–02 Crewe Alex 0 0
2002–03 Crewe Alex 17 1
2003–04 Crewe Alex 3 0
2004–05 Crewe Alex 17 0
2005–06 Crewe Alex 17 2
2006–07 Crewe Alex 0 0 **54 3**
2007–08 Mansfield T 23 1 **23 1**

BOULDING, Mick (F) 267 75
H: 5 10 W: 11 05 b.Sheffield 8-2-76
Source: Hallam.
1999–2000 Mansfield T 33 6
2000–01 Mansfield T 33 6
2001–02 Mansfield T 0 0
2001–02 Grimsby T 35 11
2002–03 Aston Villa 0 0
2002–03 *Sheffield U* 6 0 **6 0**
2002–03 Grimsby T 12 4
2003–04 Grimsby T 27 12 **74 27**
2003–04 Barnsley 6 0
2004–05 Barnsley 29 10 **35 10**
2004–05 *Cardiff C* 4 0 **4 0**
2005–06 Rotherham U 0 0
2006–07 Mansfield T 39 5
2007–08 Mansfield T 43 21 **148 38**

BOULDING, Rory (F) 20 0
H: 6 0 W: 12 02 b.Sheffield 21-7-88
Source: Ilkeston T.
2006–07 Mansfield T 9 0
2007–08 Mansfield T 11 0 **20 0**

BROWN, Simon (F) 134 23
H: 5 10 W: 11 00 b.West Bromwich 18-9-83
Source: Scholar.
2003–04 WBA 0 0
2003–04 *Kidderminster H* 8 2
2004–05 WBA 0 0
2004–05 *Kidderminster H* 13 0 **21 2**
2004–05 Mansfield T 21 2
2005–06 Mansfield T 29 10
2006–07 Mansfield T 34 5
2007–08 Mansfield T 29 4 **113 21**

BURRELL, Warren (M) 1 0
H: 5 10 W: 10 06 b.Mansfield 3-6-90
2007–08 Mansfield T 1 0 **1 0**

BUXTON, Jake (D) 151 5
H: 6 1 W: 13 05 b.Sutton-in-Ashfield 4-3-85
Source: Scholar.
2002–03 Mansfield T 3 0
2003–04 Mansfield T 9 1
2004–05 Mansfield T 30 1

2005–06 Mansfield T 39 0
2006–07 Mansfield T 30 1
2007–08 Mansfield T 40 2 **151 5**

D'LARYEA, Jonathan (M) 95 1
H: 5 10 W: 12 02 b.Manchester 3-9-85
Source: Trainee.
2003–04 Manchester C 0 0
2004–05 Manchester C 0 0
2005–06 Manchester C 0 0
2005–06 Mansfield T 29 0
2006–07 Mansfield T 37 1
2007–08 Mansfield T 29 0 **95 1**

DAWSON, Stephen (M) 117 4
H: 5 9 W: 11 09 b.Dublin 4-12-85
Source: Scholar. *Honours:* Eire Under-21.
2003–04 Leicester C 0 0
2004–05 Leicester C 0 0
2005–06 Mansfield T 40 1
2006–07 Mansfield T 34 1
2007–08 Mansfield T 43 2 **117 4**

GOWARD, Ryan (M) 2 0
H: 6 0 W: 12 00 b.Mansfield 1-11-89
2007–08 Mansfield T 2 0 **2 0**

HAMSHAW, Matt (M) 198 13
H: 5 10 W: 11 08 b.Rotherham 1-1-82
Source: Trainee. *Honours:* England Youth, Under-20.
1998–99 Sheffield W 0 0
1999–2000 Sheffield W 0 0
2000–01 Sheffield W 18 0
2001–02 Sheffield W 21 0
2002–03 Sheffield W 15 1
2003–04 Sheffield W 0 0
2004–05 Sheffield W 20 1 **74 2**
2005–06 Stockport Co 39 5 **39 5**
2006–07 Mansfield T 40 4
2007–08 Mansfield T 45 2 **85 6**

HOLMES, Ian (F) 16 1
H: 6 0 W: 12 05 b.Ellesmere Port 29-6-85
2007–08 Mansfield T 16 1 **16 1**

JELLEYMAN, Gareth (D) 231 1
H: 5 10 W: 10 02 b.Holywell 14-11-80
Source: Trainee. *Honours:* Wales Youth, Under-21.
1998–99 Peterborough U 0 0
1999–2000 Peterborough U 20 0
2000–01 Peterborough U 8 0
2001–02 Peterborough U 10 0
2002–03 Peterborough U 32 0
2003–04 Peterborough U 17 0
2004–05 Peterborough U 14 0 **101 0**
2004–05 *Boston U* 3 0 **3 0**
2004–05 Mansfield T 14 0
2005–06 Mansfield T 34 1
2006–07 Mansfield T 40 0
2007–08 Mansfield T 39 0 **127 1**

JOHN-BAPTISTE, Alex (D) 174 5
H: 6 0 W: 11 11 b.Sutton-in-Ashfield 31-1-86
Source: Scholar.
2002–03 Mansfield T 4 0
2003–04 Mansfield T 17 0
2004–05 Mansfield T 41 1
2005–06 Mansfield T 41 1
2006–07 Mansfield T 46 3
2007–08 Mansfield T 25 0 **174 5**

KITCHEN, Ashley (M) 5 0
H: 5 11 W: 11 06 b.Edwinstowe 10-10-88
Source: Scholar.
2006–07 Mansfield T 4 0
2007–08 Mansfield T 1 0 **5 0**

LLOYD, Callum (M) 41 4
H: 5 9 W: 11 07 b.Nottingham 1-1-86
Source: Scholar.
2004–05 Mansfield T 10 4
2005–06 Mansfield T 12 0
2006–07 Mansfield T 19 0
2007–08 Mansfield T 0 0 **41 4**

LOUIS, Jefferson (F) 83 12
H: 6 2 W: 15 00 b.Harrow 22-2-79
Source: Thame U. *Honours:* Dominica 1 full cap.
2001–02 Oxford U 1 0
2002–03 Oxford U 34 6
2003–04 Oxford U 20 2
2004–05 Oxford U 1 0 **56 8**
From For GR, Woking
2004–05 Bristol R 1 0
2005–06 Bristol R 8 0 **9 0**
From Weymouth.
2007–08 Mansfield T 18 4 **18 4**

MARTIN, Dan (D) 77 8
H: 6 1 W: 12 13 b.Derby 27-9-86
Source: Scholar. *Honours:* Wales Under-21.
2004–05 Derby Co 0 0
2005–06 Notts Co 22 4
2006–07 Notts Co 29 4 **51 8**
2007–08 Mansfield T 26 0 **26 0**

McALISKEY, John (F) 65 9
H: 6 4 W: 12 01 b.Huddersfield 2-9-84
Source: Scholar. *Honours:* Eire Under-21.
2003–04 Huddersfield T 8 4
2004–05 Huddersfield T 18 2
2005–06 Huddersfield T 9 0
2005–06 *Torquay U* 3 0 **3 0**
2006–07 Huddersfield T 8 1 **43 7**
2006–07 *Wrexham* 3 0 **3 0**
2007–08 Mansfield T 16 2 **16 2**

McGHEE, Jamie (M) 2 0
H: 5 8 W: 10 07 b.Grantham 28-9-89
Source: Scholar.
2006–07 Mansfield T 2 0
2007–08 Mansfield T 0 0 **2 0**

McINTOSH, Martin (D) 465 48
H: 6 3 W: 13 07 b.East Kilbride 19-3-71
Honours: Scotland B.
1988–89 St Mirren 2 0
1989–90 St Mirren 2 0
1990–91 St Mirren 0 0 **4 0**
1991–92 Clydebank 28 5
1992–93 Clydebank 33 4
1993–94 Clydebank 4 1 **65 10**
1993–94 Hamilton A 13 2
1994–95 Hamilton A 30 2
1995–96 Hamilton A 23 1
1996–97 Hamilton A 33 7 **99 12**
1997–98 Stockport Co 38 2
1998–99 Stockport Co 41 3
1999–2000 Stockport Co 20 0 **99 5**
1999–2000 Hibernian 9 0
2000–01 Hibernian 4 0 **13 0**
2001–02 Rotherham U 39 4
2002–03 Rotherham U 42 5
2003–04 Rotherham U 18 2
2004–05 Rotherham U 23 5 **122 16**
2005–06 Huddersfield T 22 4
2006–07 Huddersfield T 26 0 **48 4**
2006–07 *Grimsby T* 4 0 **4 0**
2007–08 Mansfield T 11 1 **11 1**

MUGGLETON, Carl (G) 446 0
H: 6 2 W: 14 12 b.Leicester 13-9-68
Source: Apprentice. *Honours:* England Under-21.
1986–87 Leicester C 0 0
1987–88 Leicester C 0 0
1987–88 *Chesterfield* 17 0
1987–88 *Blackpool* 2 0 **2 0**
1988–89 Leicester C 3 0
1988–89 *Hartlepool U* 8 0 **8 0**
1989–90 Leicester C 0 0
1989–90 *Stockport Co* 4 0 **4 0**
1990–91 Leicester C 22 0
1990–91 *Liverpool* 0 0
1991–92 Leicester C 4 0
1992–93 Leicester C 17 0
1993–94 Leicester C 0 0 **46 0**
1993–94 *Stoke C* 6 0
1993–94 *Sheffield U* 0 0
1993–94 Celtic 12 0 **12 0**
1994–95 Stoke C 24 0
1995–96 Stoke C 6 0
1995–96 *Rotherham U* 6 0 **6 0**
1995–96 *Sheffield U* 1 0 **1 0**
1996–97 Stoke C 33 0
1997–98 Stoke C 34 0
1998–99 Stoke C 40 0
1999–2000 Stoke C 0 0
1999–2000 *Mansfield T* 9 0
1999–2000 *Chesterfield* 5 0
2000–01 Stoke C 12 0 **155 0**
2000–01 *Cardiff C* 6 0 **6 0**
2001–02 Cheltenham T 7 0 **7 0**
2001–02 *Bradford C* 4 0 **4 0**
2002–03 Chesterfield 26 0
2003–04 Chesterfield 46 0
2004–05 Chesterfield 37 0
2005–06 Chesterfield 3 0 **134 0**
2006–07 Mansfield T 16 0
2007–08 Mansfield T 36 0 **61 0**

MULLINS, John (D) 107 6
H: 5 11 W: 12 07 b.Hampstead 6-11-85
Source: Scholar.
2004–05 Reading 0 0
2004–05 *Kidderminster H* 21 2 **21 2**
2005–06 Reading 0 0
2006–07 Mansfield T 43 2
2007–08 Mansfield T 43 2 **86 4**

REET, Danny (F) 53 15
H: 6 1 W: 14 02 b.Sheffield 31-1-87
Source: Juniors.
2005–06 Sheffield W 0 0
2005–06 *Bury* 6 4 **6 4**
2005–06 Mansfield T 18 5
2006–07 Mansfield T 21 6
2006–07 *Rochdale* 6 0 **6 0**
2007–08 Mansfield T 2 0 **41 11**

SLEATH, Danny (M) 14 0
H: 5 8 W: 9 07 b.Matlock 14-12-86
Source: Juniors.
2005–06 Mansfield T 0 0
2006–07 Mansfield T 7 0
2007–08 Mansfield T 7 0 **14 0**

TRIMMER, Lewis (M) 3 0
H: 5 7 W: 10 00 b.Norwich 30-10-89
Source: Juniors.
2006–07 Mansfield T 1 0
2007–08 Mansfield T 2 0 **3 0**

WHITE, Jason (G) 53 0
H: 6 2 W: 12 01 b.Sutton-in-Ashfield 28-1-84
Source: Trainee.
2002–03 Mansfield T 1 0
2003–04 Mansfield T 0 0
2004–05 Mansfield T 4 0
2005–06 Mansfield T 5 0
2006–07 Mansfield T 30 0
2007–08 Mansfield T 13 0 **53 0**

WOOD, Chris (M) 15 0
H: 6 0 W: 10 11 b.Worksop 24-1-87
Source: Scholar.
2004–05 Mansfield T 1 0
2005–06 Mansfield T 0 0
2006–07 Mansfield T 1 0
2007–08 Mansfield T 13 0 **15 0**

MIDDLESBROUGH (52)

ALIADIERE, Jeremie (F) 79 8
H: 6 0 W: 11 00 b.Rambouillet 30-3-83
Source: Scholar. *Honours:* France Youth, Under-21.
1999–2000 Arsenal 0 0
2000–01 Arsenal 0 0
2001–02 Arsenal 1 0
2002–03 Arsenal 3 1
2003–04 Arsenal 10 0
2004–05 Arsenal 4 0
2005–06 Arsenal 0 0
2005–06 *West Ham U* 7 0 **7 0**
2005–06 *Wolverhampton W* 14 2 **14 2**
2006–07 Arsenal 11 0 **29 1**
2007–08 Middlesbrough 29 5 **29 5**

ALVES, Afonso (F) 144 103
H: 6 1 W: 11 09 b.Belo Horizonte 30-1-81
Honours: Brazil 8 full caps, 1 goal.
2002 Orgryte 18 13
2003 Orgryte 21 10 **39 23**
2004 Malmo 24 12
2005 Malmo 24 14
2006 Malmo 7 3 **55 29**
2006–07 Heerenveen 31 34
2007–08 Heerenveen 8 11 **39 45**
2007–08 Middlesbrough 11 6 **11 6**

ARCA, Julio (M) 238 22
H: 5 9 W: 11 13 b.Quilmes 31-1-81
Honours: Argentina Youth, Under-21.
1999–2000 Argentinos Jun 19 0
2000–01 Argentinos Jun 17 1 **36 1**
2000–01 Sunderland 27 2
2001–02 Sunderland 22 1

2002–03	Sunderland	13	0		
2003–04	Sunderland	31	4		
2004–05	Sunderland	40	9		
2005–06	Sunderland	24	1	**157**	**17**
2006–07	Middlesbrough	21	2		
2007–08	Middlesbrough	24	2	**45**	**4**

BATES, Matthew (D) **28** **0**

H: 5 10 W: 12 03 b.Stockton 10-12-86

Source: Scholar. *Honours:* England Youth, Under-20.

2003–04	Middlesbrough	0	0		
2004–05	Middlesbrough	2	0		
2004–05	*Darlington*	4	0	**4**	**0**
2005–06	Middlesbrough	16	0		
2006–07	Middlesbrough	1	0		
2006–07	*Ipswich T*	2	0	**2**	**0**
2007–08	Middlesbrough	0	0	**19**	**0**
2007–08	*Norwich C*	3	0	**3**	**0**

BOATENG, George (M) **409** **17**

H: 5 9 W: 12 06 b.Nkawkaw 5-9-75

Honours: Holland Under-21, 4 full caps.

1994–95	Excelsior	9	0	**9**	**0**
1995–96	Feyenoord	24	1		
1996–97	Feyenoord	26	0		
1997–98	Feyenoord	18	0	**68**	**1**
1997–98	Coventry C	14	1		
1998–99	Coventry C	33	4	**47**	**5**
1999–2000	Aston Villa	33	2		
2000–01	Aston Villa	33	1		
2001–02	Aston Villa	37	1	**103**	**4**
2002–03	Middlesbrough	28	0		
2003–04	Middlesbrough	35	0		
2004–05	Middlesbrough	25	3		
2005–06	Middlesbrough	26	2		
2006–07	Middlesbrough	35	1		
2007–08	Middlesbrough	33	1	**182**	**7**

CATTERMOLE, Lee (M) **69** **3**

H: 5 10 W: 11 13 b.Stockton 21-3-88

Source: Scholar. *Honours:* England Youth, Under-21.

2005–06	Middlesbrough	14	1		
2006–07	Middlesbrough	31	1		
2007–08	Middlesbrough	24	1	**69**	**3**

CRADDOCK, Tom (F) **9** **1**

H: 5 11 W: 11 10 b.Durham 14-10-86

Source: Scholar.

2005–06	Middlesbrough	1	0		
2006–07	Middlesbrough	0	0		
2006–07	*Wrexham*	1	1	**1**	**1**
2007–08	Middlesbrough	3	0	**4**	**0**
2007–08	*Hartlepool U*	4	0	**4**	**0**

DOWNING, Stewart (M) **151** **20**

H: 5 11 W: 10 04 b.Middlesbrough 22-7-84

Source: Scholar. *Honours:* England Youth, Under-21, B, 18 full caps.

2001–02	Middlesbrough	3	0		
2002–03	Middlesbrough	2	0		
2003–04	Middlesbrough	20	0		
2003–04	*Sunderland*	7	3	**7**	**3**
2004–05	Middlesbrough	35	5		
2005–06	Middlesbrough	12	1		
2006–07	Middlesbrough	34	2		
2007–08	Middlesbrough	38	9	**144**	**17**

FRANKS, Jonathan (M) **0** **0**

Source: Scholar.

2007–08	Middlesbrough	0	0		

GOULON, Herold (M) **0** **0**

H: 6 4 W: 14 07 b.Paris 12-6-88

2005–06	Lyon	0	0		
2006–07	Middlesbrough	0	0		
2007–08	Middlesbrough	0	0		

GROUNDS, Jonathan (D) **5** **0**

H: 6 1 W: 13 10 b.Thornaby 2-2-88

Source: Scholar.

2007–08	Middlesbrough	5	0	**5**	**0**

HINES, Seb (D) **1** **0**

H: 6 1 W: 12 02 b.Wetherby 29-5-88

Source: Scholar. *Honours:* England Youth.

2005–06	Middlesbrough	0	0		
2006–07	Middlesbrough	0	0		
2007–08	Middlesbrough	1	0	**1**	**0**

HUTCHINSON, Ben (F) **8** **1**

H: 5 11 W: 12 07 b.Nottingham 27-11-87

Source: Arnold T.

2005–06	Middlesbrough	0	0		
2006–07	Middlesbrough	0	0		
2007–08	Middlesbrough	8	1	**8**	**1**

To Celtic January 2008.

HUTH, Robert (D) **67** **2**

H: 6 3 W: 14 07 b.Berlin 18-8-84

Source: Scholar. *Honours:* Germany Youth, Under-21, 17 full caps, 2 goals.

2001–02	Chelsea	1	0		
2002–03	Chelsea	2	0		
2003–04	Chelsea	16	0		
2004–05	Chelsea	10	0		
2005–06	Chelsea	13	0	**42**	**0**
2006–07	Middlesbrough	12	1		
2007–08	Middlesbrough	13	1	**25**	**2**

JOHNSON, Adam (M) **61** **7**

H: 5 8 W: 10 00 b.Sunderland 14-7-87

Source: Scholar. *Honours:* England Youth, Under-21.

2004–05	Middlesbrough	0	0		
2005–06	Middlesbrough	13	1		
2006–07	Middlesbrough	12	0		
2006–07	*Leeds U*	5	0	**5**	**0**
2007–08	Middlesbrough	19	1	**44**	**2**
2007–08	*Watford*	12	5	**12**	**5**

JOHNSON, John (D) **0** **0**

b.Middlesbrough 16-9-88

Source: Scholar.

2007–08	Middlesbrough	0	0		

JONES, Brad (G) **53** **0**

H: 6 3 W: 12 01 b.Armadale 19-3-82

Source: Trainee. *Honours:* Australia Under-20, Under-23, 1 full cap.

1998–99	Middlesbrough	0	0		
1999–2000	Middlesbrough	0	0		
2000–01	Middlesbrough	0	0		
2001–02	Middlesbrough	0	0		
2002	Shelbourne	2	0	**2**	**0**
2002–03	Middlesbrough	0	0		
2002–03	*Stockport Co*	1	0	**1**	**0**
2003–04	Middlesbrough	1	0		
2003–04	*Blackpool*	5	0		
2003–04	*Rotherham U*	0	0		
2004–05	Middlesbrough	5	0		
2004–05	*Blackpool*	12	0	**17**	**0**
2005–06	Middlesbrough	9	0		
2006–07	Middlesbrough	2	0		
2006–07	*Sheffield W*	15	0	**15**	**0**
2007–08	Middlesbrough	1	0	**18**	**0**

KENNEDY, Jason (M) **60** **5**

H: 6 1 W: 13 02 b.Stockton 11-9-86

Source: Scholar.

2004–05	Middlesbrough	1	0		
2005–06	Middlesbrough	3	0		
2006–07	Middlesbrough	0	0		
2006–07	*Boston U*	13	1	**13**	**1**
2006–07	*Bury*	12	0	**12**	**0**
2007–08	Middlesbrough	0	0	**4**	**0**
2007–08	*Livingston*	18	2	**18**	**2**
2007–08	*Darlington*	13	2	**13**	**2**

LEE, Dong-Gook (F) **116** **22**

H: 6 2 W: 12 13 b.Pohang 29-4-79

Source: Pohang Steelers. *Honours:* South Korea 71 full caps, 22 goals.

2000–01	Werder Bremen	7	0	**7**	**0**
From Pohang					
2003	Gwangiu	41	11		
2004	Gwangiu	19	1	**60**	**12**
2005	Pohang	17	3		
2006	Pohang	9	7	**26**	**10**
2006–07	Middlesbrough	9	0		
2007–08	Middlesbrough	14	0	**23**	**0**

McMAHON, Tony (D) **19** **0**

H: 5 10 W: 11 04 b.Bishop Auckland 24-3-86

Source: Scholar. *Honours:* England Youth.

2003–04	Middlesbrough	0	0		
2004–05	Middlesbrough	13	0		
2005–06	Middlesbrough	3	0		
2006–07	Middlesbrough	0	0		
2007–08	Middlesbrough	1	0	**17**	**0**
2007–08	*Blackpool*	2	0	**2**	**0**

MENDIETA, Gaizka (M) **409** **52**

H: 5 9 W: 11 02 b.Bilbao 27-3-74

Honours: Spain 40 full caps, 8 goals.

1991–92	Castellon	16	0	**16**	**0**
1992–93	Valencia B	31	2		
1992–93	Valencia	2	0		
1993–94	Valencia B	17	0	**48**	**2**
1993–94	Valencia	20	0		
1994–95	Valencia	13	1		
1995–96	Valencia	34	0		
1996–97	Valencia	29	1		
1997–98	Valencia	30	10		
1998–99	Valencia	38	7		
1999–2000	Valencia	33	13		
2000–01	Valencia	31	10	**230**	**42**
2001–02	Lazio	20	0	**20**	**0**
2002–03	Barcelona	33	4	**33**	**4**
2003–04	Middlesbrough	31	2		
2004–05	Middlesbrough	7	0		
2005–06	Middlesbrough	17	2		
2006–07	Middlesbrough	7	0		
2007–08	Middlesbrough	0	0	**62**	**4**

MIDO (F) **163** **62**

H: 6 2 W: 14 09 b.Cairo 23-2-83

Honours: Egypt 44 full caps, 18 goals.

1999–2000	Zamalek	4	3	**4**	**3**
2000–01	Gent	21	11	**21**	**11**
2001–02	Ajax	24	12		
2002–03	Ajax	16	9	**40**	**21**
2002–03	Celta Vigo	8	4	**8**	**4**
2003–04	Marseille	22	7	**22**	**7**
2004–05	Roma	8	0	**8**	**0**
2004–05	Tottenham H	9	2		
2005–06	Tottenham H	27	11		
2006–07	Tottenham H	12	1		
2007–08	Tottenham H	0	0	**48**	**14**
2007–08	Middlesbrough	12	2	**12**	**2**

O'NEIL, Gary (M) **217** **17**

H: 5 10 W: 11 00 b.Bromley 18-5-83

Source: Scholar. *Honours:* England Youth, Under-20, Under-21.

1999–2000	Portsmouth	1	0		
2000–01	Portsmouth	10	1		
2001–02	Portsmouth	33	1		
2002–03	Portsmouth	31	3		
2003–04	Portsmouth	3	2		
2003–04	*Walsall*	7	0	**7**	**0**
2004–05	Portsmouth	24	2		
2004–05	*Cardiff C*	9	1	**9**	**1**
2005–06	Portsmouth	36	6		
2006–07	Portsmouth	35	1		
2007–08	Portsmouth	2	0	**175**	**16**
2007–08	Middlesbrough	26	0	**26**	**0**

OWENS, Graeme (M) **4** **0**

H: 5 10 W: 11 06 b.Cramlington 1-6-88

2007–08	Middlesbrough	0	0		
2007–08	*Chesterfield*	4	0	**4**	**0**

POGATETZ, Emanuel (D) **206** **5**

H: 6 2 W: 13 05 b.Steinbock 16-1-83

Honours: Austria 30 full caps, 1 goal.

1999–2000	Sturm Graz	0	0		
2000–01	Karntern	33	0	**33**	**0**
2001–02	Leverkusen B	23	0		
2001–02	Leverkusen	0	0		
2002–03	Leverkusen B	3	0	**26**	**0**
2002–03	Leverkusen	0	0		
2002–03	Aarau	11	0	**11**	**0**
2003–04	Graz	31	1		
2004–05	Graz	22	1	**53**	**2**
2005–06	Middlesbrough	24	1		
2006–07	Middlesbrough	35	2		
2007–08	Middlesbrough	24	0	**83**	**3**

RIGGOTT, Chris (D) **181** **10**

H: 6 2 W: 13 09 b.Derby 1-9-80

Source: Trainee. *Honours:* England Youth, Under-21.

1998–99	Derby Co	0	0		
1999–2000	Derby Co	1	0		
2000–01	Derby Co	31	3		
2001–02	Derby Co	37	0		
2002–03	Derby Co	22	2	**91**	**5**
2002–03	Middlesbrough	5	2		
2003–04	Middlesbrough	17	0		
2004–05	Middlesbrough	21	2		
2005–06	Middlesbrough	22	0		
2006–07	Middlesbrough	6	0		
2007–08	Middlesbrough	10	1	**81**	**5**
2007–08	*Stoke C*	9	0	**9**	**0**

ROCHEMBACK, Fabio (M) **179** **20**

H: 6 0 W: 13 01 b.Soledade 10-12-81

Honours: Brazil 7 full caps.

2000	Internacional	20	4		
2001	Internacional	0	0	**20**	**4**
2001–02	Barcelona	24	1		
2002–03	Barcelona	21	1	**45**	**2**

2003–04 Sporting Lisbon 21 8
2004–05 Sporting Lisbon 23 1
2005–06 Sporting Lisbon 2 0 **46 9**
2005–06 Middlesbrough 22 2
2006–07 Middlesbrough 20 2
2007–08 Middlesbrough 26 1 **68 5**

SCHWARZER, Mark (G) 444 0
H: 6 4 W: 14 07 b.Sydney 6-10-72
Honours: Australia Youth, Under-20, Under-23, 58 full caps.
1990–91 Marconi Stallions 1 0
1991–92 Marconi Stallions 9 0
1992–93 Marconi Stallions 23 0
1993–94 Marconi Stallions 25 0 **58 0**
1994–95 Dynamo Dresden 2 0 **2 0**
1995–96 Kaiserslautern 4 0
1996–97 Kaiserslautern 0 0 **4 0**
1996–97 Bradford C 13 0 **13 0**
1996–97 Middlesbrough 7 0
1997–98 Middlesbrough 35 0
1998–99 Middlesbrough 34 0
1999–2000 Middlesbrough 37 0
2000–01 Middlesbrough 31 0
2001–02 Middlesbrough 21 0
2002–03 Middlesbrough 38 0
2003–04 Middlesbrough 36 0
2004–05 Middlesbrough 31 0
2005–06 Middlesbrough 27 0
2006–07 Middlesbrough 36 0
2007–08 Middlesbrough 34 0 **367 0**

SHAWKY, Mohamed (M) 5 0
H: 5 11 W: 11 11 b.Port Said 5-10-81
Source: Al Ahly. *Honours:* Egypt Under-21, 48 full caps, 3 goals.
2007–08 Middlesbrough 5 0 **5 0**

STEELE, Jason (G) 0 0
H: 6 2 W: 12 07 b.Stockton 18-8-90
Source: Scholar. *Honours:* England Youth.
2007–08 Middlesbrough 0 0

TAYLOR, Andrew (D) 90 0
H: 5 10 W: 11 04 b.Hartlepool 1-8-86
Source: Trainee. *Honours:* England Youth, Under-20, Under-21.
2003–04 Middlesbrough 0 0
2004–05 Middlesbrough 0 0
2005–06 Middlesbrough 13 0
2005–06 *Bradford C* 24 0 **24 0**
2006–07 Middlesbrough 34 0
2007–08 Middlesbrough 19 0 **66 0**

TUNCAY, Sanli (F) 251 97
H: 5 10 W: 11 00 b.Sakarya 16-1-82
Honours: Turkey 58 full caps, 16 goals.
2000–01 Sakarya 31 16
2001–02 Sakarya 35 16 **66 32**
2002–03 Fenerbahce 29 9
2003–04 Fenerbahce 31 19
2004–05 Fenerbahce 31 7
2005–06 Fenerbahce 27 13
2006–07 Fenerbahce 33 9 **151 57**
2007–08 Middlesbrough 34 8 **34 8**

TURNBULL, Ross (G) 69 0
H: 6 4 W: 15 00 b.Bishop Auckland 4-1-85
Source: Trainee. *Honours:* England Youth, Under-20.
2002–03 Middlesbrough 0 0
2003–04 Middlesbrough 0 0
2003–04 *Darlington* 1 0 **1 0**
2003–04 *Barnsley* 3 0
2004–05 Middlesbrough 0 0
2004–05 *Bradford C* 2 0 **2 0**
2004–05 *Barnsley* 23 0 **26 0**
2005–06 Middlesbrough 2 0
2005–06 *Crewe Alex* 29 0 **29 0**
2006–07 Middlesbrough 0 0
2007–08 Middlesbrough 3 0 **5 0**
2007–08 *Cardiff C* 6 0 **6 0**

WALKER, Josh (M) 15 0
H: 5 11 W: 11 13 b.Newcastle 21-2-89
Source: Scholar. *Honours:* England Schools, Youth.
2005–06 Middlesbrough 1 0
2006–07 Middlesbrough 0 0
2006–07 *Bournemouth* 6 0 **6 0**
2007–08 *Aberdeen* 8 0 **8 0**
2007–08 Middlesbrough 0 0 **1 0**

WHEATER, David (D) 65 7
H: 6 5 W: 12 12 b.Redcar 14-2-87
Source: Scholar. *Honours:* England Youth, Under-21.
2004–05 Middlesbrough 0 0
2005–06 Middlesbrough 6 0
2005–06 *Doncaster R* 7 1 **7 1**
2006–07 Middlesbrough 2 1
2006–07 *Wolverhampton W* 1 0 **1 0**
2006–07 *Darlington* 15 2 **15 2**
2007–08 Middlesbrough 34 3 **42 4**

WILLIAMS, Rhys (D) 0 0
b.Perth 14-7-88
Source: Scholar. *Honours:* Wales Under-21.
2006–07 Middlesbrough 0 0
2007–08 Middlesbrough 0 0

YOUNG, Luke (D) 280 5
H: 6 0 W: 12 04 b.Harlow 19-7-79
Source: Trainee. *Honours:* England Youth, Under-21, 7 full caps.
1997–98 Tottenham H 0 0
1998–99 Tottenham H 15 0
1999–2000 Tottenham H 20 0
2000–01 Tottenham H 23 0 **58 0**
2001–02 Charlton Ath 34 0
2002–03 Charlton Ath 32 0
2003–04 Charlton Ath 24 0
2004–05 Charlton Ath 36 2
2005–06 Charlton Ath 32 1
2006–07 Charlton Ath 29 1 **187 4**
2007–08 Middlesbrough 35 1 **35 1**

Scholars
Bennett, Joseph; Bonar, Nathan Robert; Burton, Ryan; Corker, Ashley; Cronesberry, James Liam; Filler, Samuel Edward; Furness, Theodore Eugene; Harris, Jonathan; Martin, Gary; Porritt, Nathan John; Robinson, Jordan; Saiko, Shaun; Smallwood, Richard; White, Jason Doni

MILLWALL (53)

ALEXANDER, Gary (F) 357 105
H: 6 0 W: 13 04 b.Lambeth 15-8-79
Source: Trainee.
1998–99 West Ham U 0 0
1999–2000 West Ham U 0 0
1999–2000 *Exeter C* 37 16 **37 16**
2000–01 Swindon T 37 7 **37 7**
2001–02 Hull C 43 17
2002–03 Hull C 25 6 **68 23**
2002–03 Leyton Orient 17 2
2003–04 Leyton Orient 44 15
2004–05 Leyton Orient 28 9
2005–06 Leyton Orient 46 14
2006–07 Leyton Orient 44 12 **179 52**
2007–08 Millwall 36 7 **36 7**

ARDLEY, Neal (M) 415 26
H: 5 10 W: 12 12 b.Epsom 1-9-72
Source: Trainee. *Honours:* England Under-21.
1990–91 Wimbledon 1 0
1991–92 Wimbledon 8 0
1992–93 Wimbledon 26 4
1993–94 Wimbledon 16 1
1994–95 Wimbledon 14 1
1995–96 Wimbledon 6 0
1996–97 Wimbledon 34 2
1997–98 Wimbledon 34 2
1998–99 Wimbledon 23 0
1999–2000 Wimbledon 17 2
2000–01 Wimbledon 37 3
2001–02 Wimbledon 29 3 **245 18**
2002–03 Watford 43 2
2003–04 Watford 38 1
2004–05 Watford 30 4 **111 7**
2004–05 Cardiff C 8 1
2005–06 Cardiff C 30 0 **38 1**
2006–07 Millwall 20 0
2007–08 Millwall 1 0 **21 0**

BAKAYOGO, Zaoumana (D) 15 0
H: 5 9 W: 10 08 b.Paris 11-8-86
Source: Paris St Germain. *Honours:* Ivory Coast Under-23.
2006–07 Millwall 5 0
2007–08 Millwall 10 0 **15 0**

BARRON, Scott (D) 30 0
H: 5 9 W: 9 08 b.Preston 2-9-85
Source: Scholar.
2003–04 Ipswich T 0 0
2004–05 Ipswich T 0 0
2005–06 Ipswich T 15 0
2006–07 Ipswich T 0 0 **15 0**
2006–07 *Wrexham* 3 0 **3 0**
2007–08 Millwall 12 0 **12 0**

BIGNOT, Marcus (D) 393 4
H: 5 7 W: 11 04 b.Birmingham 22-8-74
Source: Kidderminster H.
1997–98 Crewe Alex 42 0
1998–99 Crewe Alex 26 0
1999–2000 Crewe Alex 27 0 **95 0**
2000–01 Bristol R 26 1 **26 1**
2000–01 QPR 9 1
2001–02 QPR 45 0
2002–03 Rushden & D 33 0
2003–04 Rushden & D 35 2 **68 2**
2003–04 QPR 6 0
2004–05 QPR 43 0
2005–06 QPR 44 0
2006–07 QPR 33 0
2007–08 QPR 2 0 **182 1**
2007–08 Millwall 22 0 **22 0**

BOWES, Gary (F) 1 0
H: 5 11 W: 12 00 b.Ilford 14-2-80
Source: Scholar.
2007–08 Millwall 1 0 **1 0**

BRAMMER, Dave (M) 442 22
H: 5 8 W: 12 00 b.Bromborough 28-2-75
Source: Trainee.
1992–93 Wrexham 2 0
1993–94 Wrexham 22 2
1994–95 Wrexham 14 1
1995–96 Wrexham 11 2
1996–97 Wrexham 21 1
1997–98 Wrexham 33 4
1998–99 Wrexham 34 2 **137 12**
1998–99 Port Vale 9 0
1999–2000 Port Vale 29 0
2000–01 Port Vale 35 3 **73 3**
2001–02 Crewe Alex 30 2
2002–03 Crewe Alex 41 1
2003–04 Crewe Alex 16 1 **87 4**
2004–05 Stoke C 43 1
2005–06 Stoke C 40 1
2006–07 Stoke C 22 0 **105 2**
2006–07 Millwall 17 1
2007–08 Millwall 23 0 **40 1**

BRIGHTON, Tom (M) 58 9
H: 5 10 W: 11 11 b.Irvine 28-3-84
Honours: Scotland Youth, Under-21.
2001–02 Rangers 1 0
2002–03 Rangers 0 0
2003–04 Rangers 0 0 **1 0**
2004–05 Scunthorpe U 5 0 **5 0**
2005–06 Clyde 36 8 **36 8**
2006–07 Millwall 16 1
2007–08 Millwall 0 0 **16 1**

BRKOVIC, Ahmet (M) 288 41
H: 5 8 W: 11 11 b.Dubrovnik 23-9-74
Source: Dubrovnik.
1999–2000 Leyton Orient 29 5
2000–01 Leyton Orient 40 3
2001–02 Leyton Orient 0 0 **69 8**
2001–02 Luton T 21 1
2002–03 Luton T 36 3
2003–04 Luton T 32 1
2004–05 Luton T 42 15
2005–06 Luton T 42 8
2006–07 Luton T 20 3
2007–08 Luton T 1 0 **194 31**
2007–08 Millwall 25 2 **25 2**

CALLAGHAN, Andrew (F) 0 0
H: 5 11 W: 13 00 b.London 29-12-89
Source: Scholar.
2007–08 Millwall 0 0

COCHRANE, Justin (M) 122 4
H: 5 11 W: 11 07 b.Hackney 26-1-82
Source: Scholarship.
1999–2000 QPR 0 0
2000–01 QPR 1 0
2001–02 QPR 0 0
2002–03 QPR 0 0 **1 0**
From Hayes.

2003–04	Crewe Alex	39	0		
2004–05	Crewe Alex	29	0		
2005–06	Crewe Alex	4	0	**72**	**0**
2005–06	*Gillingham*	5	1	**5**	**1**
2006–07	Rotherham U	31	1	**31**	**1**
2007–08	Yeovil T	12	2	**12**	**2**
2007–08	Millwall	1	0	**1**	**0**

DAY, Chris (G) **182 0**
H: 6 2 W: 13 07 b.Whipps Cross 28-7-75
Source: Trainee. *Honours:* England Youth, Under-21.

1992–93	Tottenham H	0	0		
1993–94	Tottenham H	0	0		
1994–95	Tottenham H	0	0		
1995–96	Tottenham H	0	0		
1996–97	Crystal Palace	24	0	**24**	**0**
1997–98	Watford	0	0		
1998–99	Watford	0	0		
1999–2000	Watford	11	0		
2000–01	Watford	0	0	**11**	**0**
2000–01	*Lincoln C*	14	0	**14**	**0**
2001–02	QPR	16	0		
2002–03	QPR	12	0		
2003–04	QPR	29	0		
2004–05	QPR	30	0	**87**	**0**
2004–05	*Preston NE*	6	0	**6**	**0**
2005–06	Oldham Ath	30	0	**30**	**0**
2006–07	Millwall	5	0		
2007–08	Millwall	5	0	**10**	**0**

DUNNE, Alan (D) **123 12**
H: 5 10 W: 10 13 b.Dublin 23-8-82
Source: Trainee.

1999–2000	Millwall	0	0		
2000–01	Millwall	0	0		
2001–02	Millwall	1	0		
2002–03	Millwall	4	0		
2003–04	Millwall	8	0		
2004–05	Millwall	19	3		
2005–06	Millwall	40	0		
2006–07	Millwall	32	6		
2007–08	Millwall	19	3	**123**	**12**

EBBSWORTH, Darren (D) **0 0**
H: 5 10 W: 10 02 b.London 23-8-90
Source: Scholar.

2007–08	Millwall	0	0		

EDWARDS, Preston (G) **1 0**
H: 6 0 W: 12 07 b.Cheshunt 5-9-89
Source: Scholar.

2006–07	Millwall	0	0		
2007–08	Millwall	1	0	**1**	**0**

EVANS, Rhys (G) **197 0**
H: 6 1 W: 13 12 b.Swindon 27-1-82
Source: Trainee. *Honours:* England Schools, Youth, Under-20, Under-21.

1998–99	Chelsea	0	0		
1999–2000	Chelsea	0	0		
1999–2000	*Bristol R*	4	0	**4**	**0**
2000–01	Chelsea	0	0		
2001–02	Chelsea	0	0		
2001–02	*QPR*	11	0	**11**	**0**
2002–03	Chelsea	0	0		
2002–03	*Leyton Orient*	7	0	**7**	**0**
2003–04	Swindon T	41	0		
2004–05	Swindon T	45	0		
2005–06	Swindon T	32	0	**118**	**0**
2006–07	Blackpool	32	0		
2007–08	Blackpool	0	0	**32**	**0**
2007–08	*Bradford C*	4	0	**4**	**0**
2007–08	Millwall	21	0	**21**	**0**

FORBES, Adrian (F) **300 34**
H: 5 8 W: 11 10 b.Greenford 23-1-79
Source: Trainee. *Honours:* England Youth.

1996–97	Norwich C	10	0		
1997–98	Norwich C	33	4		
1998–99	Norwich C	15	0		
1999–2000	Norwich C	25	1		
2000–01	Norwich C	29	3	**112**	**8**
2001–02	Luton T	40	4		
2002–03	Luton T	5	1		
2003–04	Luton T	27	9	**72**	**14**
2004–05	Swansea C	40	7		
2005–06	Swansea C	29	4	**69**	**11**
2006–07	Blackpool	34	1		
2007–08	Blackpool	2	0	**36**	**1**
2007–08	Millwall	11	0	**11**	**0**

FRAMPTON, Andrew (D) **192 5**
H: 5 11 W: 10 10 b.Wimbledon 3-9-79
Source: Trainee.

1998–99	Crystal Palace	6	0		
1999–2000	Crystal Palace	9	0		
2000–01	Crystal Palace	10	0		
2001–02	Crystal Palace	2	0		
2002–03	Crystal Palace	1	0	**28**	**0**
2002–03	Brentford	15	0		
2003–04	Brentford	16	0		
2004–05	Brentford	35	0		
2005–06	Brentford	36	3		
2006–07	Brentford	32	1	**134**	**4**
2007–08	Millwall	30	1	**30**	**1**

FUSEINI, Ali (M) **44 2**
H: 5 6 W: 9 10 b.Ghana 7-12-88
Source: Scholar.

2006–07	Millwall	7	0		
2007–08	Millwall	37	2	**44**	**2**

GAYNOR, Ross (F) **3 0**
H: 5 10 W: 11 12 b.Drogheda 9-9-87
Source: Scholar. *Honours:* Eire Youth, Under-21.

2005–06	Millwall	0	0		
2006–07	Millwall	0	0		
2007–08	Millwall	3	0	**3**	**0**

GRABBAN, Lewis (F) **32 4**
H: 6 0 W: 11 03 b.Croydon 12-1-88
Source: Scholar.

2005–06	Crystal Palace	0	0		
2006–07	Crystal Palace	8	1		
2006–07	*Oldham Ath*	9	0	**9**	**0**
2007–08	Crystal Palace	2	0	**10**	**1**
2007–08	Millwall	13	3	**13**	**3**

GRANT, Gavin (F) **14 1**
H: 5 11 W: 11 00 b.Middlesex 27-3-84
Source: Tooting & Mitcham U.

2005–06	Gillingham	10	1	**10**	**1**
2005–06	Millwall	0	0		
2006–07	Millwall	4	0		
2007–08	Millwall	0	0	**4**	**0**

HACKETT, Chris (M) **166 12**
H: 6 0 W: 12 08 b.Oxford 1-3-83
Source: Scholarship.

1999–2000	Oxford U	2	0		
2000–01	Oxford U	16	2		
2001–02	Oxford U	15	0		
2002–03	Oxford U	12	0		
2003–04	Oxford U	22	1		
2004–05	Oxford U	37	4		
2005–06	Oxford U	21	2	**125**	**9**
2005–06	Hearts	2	0	**2**	**0**
2006–07	Millwall	33	3		
2007–08	Millwall	6	0	**39**	**3**

HARRIS, Neil (F) **353 109**
H: 5 10 W: 12 08 b.Orsett 12-7-77
Source: Cambridge C.

1997–98	Millwall	3	0		
1998–99	Millwall	39	15		
1999–2000	Millwall	38	25		
2000–01	Millwall	42	27		
2001–02	Millwall	21	4		
2002–03	Millwall	40	12		
2003–04	Millwall	38	9		
2004–05	Millwall	12	1		
2004–05	*Cardiff C*	3	1	**3**	**1**
2004–05	Nottingham F	13	0		
2005–06	Nottingham F	1	0		
2005–06	*Gillingham*	36	6	**36**	**6**
2006–07	Nottingham F	19	1	**33**	**1**
2006–07	Millwall	21	5		
2007–08	Millwall	27	3	**281**	**101**

JAMES, Ryan (F) **0 0**
Source: Scholar.

2007–08	Millwall	0	0		

LAIRD, Marc (M) **30 2**
H: 6 1 W: 10 07 b.Edinburgh 23-1-86
Source: Trainee.

2003–04	Manchester C	0	0		
2004–05	Manchester C	0	0		
2005–06	Manchester C	0	0		
2006–07	Manchester C	0	0		
2006–07	*Northampton T*	6	0	**6**	**0**
2007–08	Manchester C	0	0		
2007–08	*Port Vale*	7	1	**7**	**1**
2007–08	Millwall	17	1	**17**	**1**

MARTIN, David (M) **25 2**
H: 5 9 W: 10 10 b.Erith 3-6-85
Source: Dartford.

2006–07	Crystal Palace	5	0		
2007–08	Crystal Palace	9	0	**14**	**0**
2007–08	Millwall	11	2	**11**	**2**

PHILLIPS, Mark (D) **75 1**
H: 6 2 W: 11 00 b.Lambeth 27-1-82
Source: Scholarship.

1999–2000	Millwall	0	0		
2000–01	Millwall	0	0		
2001–02	Millwall	1	0		
2002–03	Millwall	7	0		
2003–04	Millwall	0	0		
2004–05	Millwall	25	1		
2005–06	Millwall	22	0		
2006–07	Millwall	12	0		
2006–07	*Darlington*	8	0	**8**	**0**
2007–08	Millwall	0	0	**67**	**1**

PIDGELEY, Lenny (G) **84 0**
H: 6 4 W: 14 09 b.Isleworth 7-2-84
Source: Scholar. *Honours:* England Under-20.

2003–04	Chelsea	0	0		
2003–04	*Watford*	27	0	**27**	**0**
2004–05	Chelsea	1	0		
2005–06	Chelsea	1	0	**2**	**0**
2005–06	*Millwall*	0	0		
2006–07	Millwall	42	0		
2007–08	Millwall	13	0	**55**	**0**

ROBINSON, Paul (D) **150 6**
H: 6 1 W: 11 09 b.Barnet 7-1-82
Source: Scholar.

2000–01	Millwall	0	0		
2001–02	Millwall	0	0		
2002–03	Millwall	14	0		
2003–04	Millwall	9	0		
2004–05	Millwall	0	0		
2004–05	*Torquay U*	12	0	**12**	**0**
2005–06	Millwall	32	0		
2006–07	Millwall	38	3		
2007–08	Millwall	45	3	**138**	**6**

SAVAGE, Bas (F) **109 13**
H: 6 3 W: 13 08 b.London 7-1-82
Source: Walton & Hersham.

2001–02	Reading	1	0		
2002–03	Reading	0	0		
2003–04	Reading	15	0		
2004–05	Reading	0	0	**16**	**0**
2004–05	*Wycombe W*	4	0	**4**	**0**
2004–05	*Bury*	5	0	**5**	**0**
2005–06	Bristol C	23	1		
2006–07	Bristol C	0	0	**23**	**1**
2006–07	Gillingham	14	1	**14**	**1**
2006–07	Brighton & HA	15	6		
2007–08	Brighton & HA	21	3	**36**	**9**
2007–08	Millwall	11	2	**11**	**2**

SENDA, Danny (M) **352 10**
H: 5 10 W: 10 02 b.Harrow 17-4-81
Source: Southampton Trainee. *Honours:* England Youth.

1998–99	Wycombe W	6	0		
1999–2000	Wycombe W	27	1		
2000–01	Wycombe W	31	2		
2001–02	Wycombe W	43	0		
2002–03	Wycombe W	41	2		
2003–04	Wycombe W	40	0		
2004–05	Wycombe W	44	4		
2005–06	Wycombe W	44	0	**276**	**9**
2006–07	Millwall	36	0		
2007–08	Millwall	40	1	**76**	**1**

SHAW, Richard (D) **587 4**
H: 5 9 W: 12 08 b.Brentford 11-9-68
Source: Apprentice.

1986–87	Crystal Palace	0	0		
1987–88	Crystal Palace	3	0		
1988–89	Crystal Palace	14	0		
1989–90	Crystal Palace	21	0		
1989–90	*Hull C*	4	0	**4**	**0**
1990–91	Crystal Palace	36	1		
1991–92	Crystal Palace	10	0		
1992–93	Crystal Palace	33	0		
1993–94	Crystal Palace	34	2		
1994–95	Crystal Palace	41	0		
1995–96	Crystal Palace	15	0	**207**	**3**
1995–96	Coventry C	21	0		
1996–97	Coventry C	35	0		
1997–98	Coventry C	33	0		
1998–99	Coventry C	37	0		

1999–2000	Coventry C	29	0		
2000–01	Coventry C	24	0		
2001–02	Coventry C	32	0		
2002–03	Coventry C	29	0		
2003–04	Coventry C	19	1		
2004–05	Coventry C	33	0		
2005–06	Coventry C	25	0	**317**	**1**
2006–07	Millwall	41	0		
2007–08	Millwall	18	0	**59**	**0**

SMITH, Ryan (M) **54** **1**

H: 5 10 W: 11 00 b.Islington 10-11-86

Source: Scholar. *Honours:* England Youth, Under-20.

2004–05	Arsenal	0	0		
2005–06	Arsenal	0	0		
2005–06	*Leicester C*	17	1	**17**	**1**
2006–07	Derby Co	15	0	**15**	**0**
2006–07	*Millwall*	6	0		
2007–08	Millwall	16	0	**22**	**0**

SPILLER, Danny (M) **135** **7**

H: 5 8 W: 11 00 b.Maidstone 10-10-81

Source: Trainee.

2000–01	Gillingham	0	0		
2001–02	Gillingham	1	0		
2002–03	Gillingham	10	0		
2003–04	Gillingham	39	6		
2004–05	Gillingham	22	0		
2005–06	Gillingham	32	0		
2006–07	Gillingham	25	0	**129**	**6**
2007–08	Millwall	6	1	**6**	**1**

TAYLOR, Lyle (F) **0** **0**

b.Greenwich

2007–08	Millwall	0	0		

WHITBREAD, Zak (D) **62** **3**

H: 6 2 W: 12 07 b.Houston 4-3-84

Honours: USA Under-23.

2002–03	Liverpool	0	0		
2003–04	Liverpool	0	0		
2004–05	Liverpool	0	0		
2005–06	Liverpool	0	0		
2005–06	*Millwall*	25	0		
2006–07	Millwall	14	0		
2007–08	Millwall	23	3	**62**	**3**

ZEBROSKI, Chris (F) **29** **3**

H: 6 1 W: 11 08 b.Swindon 29-10-86

Source: Cirencester T, Scholar.

2005–06	Plymouth Arg	4	0		
2006–07	Plymouth Arg	0	0	**4**	**0**
2006–07	Millwall	25	3		
2007–08	Millwall	0	0	**25**	**3**

MILTON KEYNES D (54)

ABBEY, Nathan (G) **208** **0**

H: 6 1 W: 11 13 b.Islington 11-7-78

Source: Trainee.

1995–96	Luton T	0	0		
1996–97	Luton T	0	0		
1997–98	Luton T	0	0		
1998–99	Luton T	2	0		
1999–2000	Luton T	33	0		
2000–01	Luton T	20	0		
2001–02	Chesterfield	46	0	**46**	**0**
2002–03	Northampton T	5	0	**5**	**0**
2003–04	Luton T	0	0	**55**	**0**
2003–04	Macclesfield T	0	0		
2003–04	Ipswich T	0	0		
2003–04	Burnley	0	0		
2004–05	Boston U	44	0		
2005–06	Boston U	17	0	**61**	**0**
2005–06	*Leyton Orient*	0	0		
2005–06	Bristol C	1	0	**1**	**0**
2006–07	Torquay U	24	0	**24**	**0**
2006–07	Brentford	16	0	**16**	**0**
2007–08	Milton Keynes D	0	0		

ANDREWS, Keith (M) **199** **21**

H: 6 0 W: 12 04 b.Dublin 13-9-80

Source: Trainee. *Honours:* Eire Youth.

1997–98	Wolverhampton W	0	0		
1998–99	Wolverhampton W	0	0		
1999–2000	Wolverhampton W	2	0		
2000–01	Wolverhampton W	22	0		
2000–01	*Oxford U*	4	1	**4**	**1**
2001–02	Wolverhampton W	11	0		
2002–03	Wolverhampton W	9	0		
2003–04	Wolverhampton W	1	0		
2003–04	*Stoke C*	16	0	**16**	**0**
2003–04	*Walsall*	10	2	**10**	**2**
2004–05	Wolverhampton W	20	0	**65**	**0**
2005–06	Hull C	26	0		
2006–07	Hull C	3	0	**29**	**0**
2006–07	Milton Keynes D	34	6		
2007–08	Milton Keynes D	41	12	**75**	**18**

BALDOCK, Sam (F) **6** **0**

H: 5 7 W: 10 07 b.Bedford 15-3-89

Source: Scholar.

2005–06	Milton Keynes D	0	0		
2006–07	Milton Keynes D	1	0		
2007–08	Milton Keynes D	5	0	**6**	**0**

BANKOLE, Ademola (G) **70** **0**

H: 6 3 W: 13 00 b.Lagos 9-9-69

Source: Leyton Orient.

1996–97	Crewe Alex	3	0		
1997–98	Crewe Alex	3	0		
1998–99	QPR	0	0		
1998–99	*Grimsby T*	0	0		
1999–2000	QPR	1	0	**1**	**0**
1999–2000	*Bradford C*	0	0		
2000–01	Crewe Alex	21	0		
2001–02	Crewe Alex	28	0		
2002–03	Crewe Alex	3	0		
2003–04	Crewe Alex	0	0	**58**	**0**
2004–05	Brentford	3	0		
2005–06	Brentford	2	0	**5**	**0**
2006–07	Milton Keynes D	6	0		
2007–08	Milton Keynes D	0	0	**6**	**0**

BROUGHTON, Drewe (F) **316** **58**

H: 6 3 W: 12 01 b.Hitchin 25-10-78

Source: Trainee.

1996–97	Norwich C	8	1		
1997–98	Norwich C	1	0		
1997–98	*Wigan Ath*	4	0	**4**	**0**
1998–99	Norwich C	0	0	**9**	**1**
1998–99	Brentford	1	0	**1**	**0**
1998–99	Peterborough U	25	7		
1999–2000	Peterborough U	10	1		
2000–01	Peterborough U	0	0	**35**	**8**
2000–01	Kidderminster H	19	7		
2001–02	Kidderminster H	38	8		
2002–03	Kidderminster H	37	4	**94**	**19**
2003–04	Southend U	35	2		
2004–05	Southend U	9	0	**44**	**2**
2004–05	Rushden & D	21	6		
2004–05	*Wycombe W*	3	0	**3**	**0**
2005–06	Rushden & D	37	10	**58**	**16**
2006–07	Chester C	14	2	**14**	**2**
2006–07	*Boston U*	25	8	**25**	**8**
2007–08	Milton Keynes D	13	0	**13**	**0**
2007–08	*Wrexham*	16	2	**16**	**2**

CAMERON, Colin (M) **503** **96**

H: 5 8 W: 11 00 b.Kirkcaldy 23-10-72

Source: Lochore Welfare. *Honours:* Scotland B, 28 full caps, 2 goals.

1990–91	Raith R	0	0		
1991–92	*Sligo R*	0	0		
1992–93	Raith R	16	1		
1993–94	Raith R	41	6		
1994–95	Raith R	35	7		
1995–96	Raith R	30	9	**122**	**23**
1995–96	Hearts	4	2		
1996–97	Hearts	36	7		
1997–98	Hearts	31	8		
1998–99	Hearts	11	6		
1999–2000	Hearts	32	8		
2000–01	Hearts	37	12		
2001–02	Hearts	4	3	**155**	**46**
2001–02	Wolverhampton W	41	4		
2002–03	Wolverhampton W	33	7		
2003–04	Wolverhampton W	30	4		
2004–05	Wolverhampton W	37	3		
2005–06	Wolverhampton W	27	4	**168**	**22**
2005–06	*Millwall*	5	0	**5**	**0**
2006–07	Coventry C	24	2	**24**	**2**
2007–08	Milton Keynes D	29	3	**29**	**3**

CARAYOL, Mustapha (M) **0** **0**

H: 5 10 W: 11 11 b.Gambia 10-4-90

2007–08	Milton Keynes D	0	0		

CARBON, Matt (D) **311** **18**

H: 6 2 W: 11 13 b.Nottingham 8-6-75

Source: Trainee. *Honours:* England Under-21.

1992–93	Lincoln C	1	0		
1993–94	Lincoln C	9	0		
1994–95	Lincoln C	33	7		
1995–96	Lincoln C	26	3		
1995–96	Derby Co	6	0		
1996–97	Derby Co	10	0		
1997–98	Derby Co	4	0	**20**	**0**
1997–98	WBA	16	1		
1998–99	WBA	39	2		
1999–2000	WBA	34	2		
2000–01	WBA	24	0	**113**	**5**
2001–02	Walsall	22	1		
2002–03	Walsall	25	1		
2003–04	Walsall	8	0	**55**	**2**
2003–04	*Lincoln C*	1	0	**70**	**10**
2004–05	Barnsley	26	0		
2005–06	Barnsley	24	1		
2006–07	Barnsley	0	0		
2007–08	Barnsley	0	0	**50**	**1**
2007–08	Milton Keynes D	3	0	**3**	**0**

COLLINS, Sam (M) **0** **0**

H: 6 0 W: 12 06 b.London 25-6-89

Source: Scholar.

2006–07	Milton Keynes D	0	0		
2007–08	Milton Keynes D	0	0		

DIALLO, Drissa (D) **140** **3**

H: 6 1 W: 11 13 b.Nouadhibou 4-1-73

Honours: Guinea full caps.

2002–03	Burnley	14	1	**14**	**1**
2003–04	Ipswich T	19	0		
2004–05	Ipswich T	26	0	**45**	**0**
2005–06	Sheffield W	11	0	**11**	**0**
2006–07	Milton Keynes D	40	0		
2007–08	Milton Keynes D	30	2	**70**	**2**

DOBSON, Craig (M) **3** **0**

H: 5 7 W: 10 06 b.Chingford 23-1-84

Source: Crystal Palace scholar. *Honours:* Jamaica 1 full cap.

2003–04	Cheltenham T	2	0	**2**	**0**
From Barnet, Camb C, Stevenage.					
2007–08	Milton Keynes D	1	0	**1**	**0**

DYER, Lloyd (M) **141** **19**

H: 5 8 W: 10 03 b.Birmingham 13-9-82

Source: Aston Villa Juniors.

2001–02	WBA	0	0		
2002–03	WBA	0	0		
2003–04	WBA	17	2		
2003–04	*Kidderminster H*	7	1	**7**	**1**
2004–05	WBA	4	0		
2004–05	*Coventry C*	6	0	**6**	**0**
2005–06	WBA	0	0	**21**	**2**
2005–06	*QPR*	15	0	**15**	**0**
2005–06	Millwall	6	0	**6**	**0**
2006–07	Milton Keynes D	41	5		
2007–08	Milton Keynes D	45	11	**86**	**16**

EDDS, Gareth (D) **175** **11**

H: 5 11 W: 11 01 b.Sydney 3-2-81

Source: Trainee. *Honours:* Australia Under-20, Under-23.

1997–98	Nottingham F	0	0		
1998–99	Nottingham F	0	0		
1999–2000	Nottingham F	2	0		
2000–01	Nottingham F	13	1		
2001–02	Nottingham F	1	0	**16**	**1**
2002–03	Swindon T	14	0	**14**	**0**
2003–04	Bradford C	23	0	**23**	**0**
2004–05	Milton Keynes D	39	5		
2005–06	Milton Keynes D	41	3		
2006–07	Milton Keynes D	35	2		
2007–08	Milton Keynes D	7	0	**122**	**10**

GALLEN, Kevin (F) **449** **111**

H: 5 11 W: 13 05 b.Hammersmith 21-9-75

Source: Trainee. *Honours:* England Schools, Youth, Under-21.

1992–93	QPR	0	0		
1993–94	QPR	0	0		
1994–95	QPR	37	10		
1995–96	QPR	30	8		
1996–97	QPR	2	3		
1997–98	QPR	27	3		
1998–99	QPR	44	8		
1999–2000	QPR	31	4		
2000–01	Huddersfield T	38	10	**38**	**10**
2001–02	Barnsley	9	2	**9**	**2**
2001–02	QPR	25	7		
2002–03	QPR	42	13		
2003–04	QPR	45	17		
2004–05	QPR	46	10		
2005–06	QPR	18	4		
2006–07	QPR	18	3	**365**	**90**

2006–07	*Plymouth Arg*	13	1	13	1
2007–08	Milton Keynes D	24	8	24	8

GUERET, Willy (G) **192 0**
H: 6 1 W: 13 02 b.Saint Claude 3-8-73
Source: Le Mans.

2000–01	Millwall	11	0		
2001–02	Millwall	1	0		
2002–03	Millwall	0	0		
2003–04	Millwall	2	0	**14**	**0**
2004–05	Swansea C	44	0		
2005–06	Swansea C	46	0		
2006–07	Swansea C	42	0	**132**	**0**
2007–08	Milton Keynes D	46	0	**46**	**0**

HASTINGS, John (F) **7 0**
H: 6 1 W: 11 11 b.London 9-5-98
Source: Hayes, Tooting & Mitcham U.

2006–07	Milton Keynes D	7	0		
2007–08	Milton Keynes D	0	0	**7**	**0**

HOWELL, Luke (D) **9 0**
H: 5 10 W: 10 05 b.Cuckfield 5-1-87
Source: Scholar.

2006–07	Gillingham	1	0	**1**	**0**
2007–08	Milton Keynes D	8	0	**8**	**0**

JOHNSON, Jemal (F) **82 12**
H: 5 8 W: 11 09 b.New Jersey 3-5-84
Source: Scholar.

2001–02	Blackburn R	0	0		
2002–03	Blackburn R	0	0		
2003–04	Blackburn R	0	0		
2004–05	Blackburn R	3	0		
2005–06	Blackburn R	3	0		
2005–06	*Preston NE*	3	1	**3**	**1**
2005–06	*Darlington*	9	3	**9**	**3**
2006–07	Blackburn R	0	0	**6**	**0**
2006–07	Wolverhampton W	20	3		
2006–07	*Leeds U*	5	0	**5**	**0**
2007–08	Wolverhampton W	0	0	**20**	**3**
2007–08	Milton Keynes D	39	5	**39**	**5**

LEWINGTON, Dean (D) **206 5**
H: 5 11 W: 11 07 b.Kingston 18-5-84
Source: Scholar.

2002–03	Wimbledon	1	0		
2003–04	Wimbledon	28	1	**29**	**1**
2004–05	Milton Keynes D	43	2		
2005–06	Milton Keynes D	44	1		
2006–07	Milton Keynes D	45	1		
2007–08	Milton Keynes D	45	0	**177**	**4**

MURPHY, Kieron (D) **3 0**
H: 5 11 W: 10 12 b.Kingston 21-12-87
Honours: Eire Under-21.

2006–07	Milton Keynes D	0	0		
2007–08	Milton Keynes D	3	0	**3**	**0**

NAVARRO, Alan (M) **172 8**
H: 5 10 W: 11 07 b.Liverpool 31-5-81
Source: Trainee.

1998–99	Liverpool	0	0		
1999–2000	Liverpool	0	0		
2000–01	Liverpool	0	0		
2000–01	*Crewe Alex*	8	1		
2001–02	Liverpool	0	0		
2001–02	*Crewe Alex*	7	0	**15**	**1**
2001–02	Tranmere R	21	1		
2002–03	Tranmere R	5	0		
2003–04	Tranmere R	19	0		
2004–05	Tranmere R	0	0		
2004–05	*Chester C*	3	0	**3**	**0**
2004–05	*Macclesfield T*	11	1		
2005–06	Tranmere R	0	0	**45**	**1**
From Accrington S.					
2005–06	Macclesfield T	27	0		
2006–07	Macclesfield T	32	2	**70**	**3**
2007–08	Milton Keynes D	39	3	**39**	**3**

O'HANLON, Sean (D) **178 17**
H: 6 1 W: 12 05 b.Southport 2-1-83
Honours: England Schools, Youth, Under-20.

1999–2000	Everton	0	0		
2000–01	Everton	0	0		
2001–02	Everton	0	0		
2002–03	Everton	0	0		
2003–04	Everton	0	0		
2003–04	Swindon T	19	2		
2004–05	Swindon T	40	3		
2005–06	Swindon T	40	4	**99**	**9**
2006–07	Milton Keynes D	36	4		
2007–08	Milton Keynes D	43	4	**79**	**8**

PAGE, Sam (D) **1 0**
H: 6 4 W: 13 02 b.Croydon 30-10-87
Source: Scholar.

2006–07	Milton Keynes D	1	0		
2007–08	Milton Keynes D	0	0	**1**	**0**

REGAN, Carl (D) **189 3**
H: 5 11 W: 11 12 b.Liverpool 14-1-80
Source: Trainee. *Honours:* England Youth.

1997–98	Everton	0	0		
1998–99	Everton	0	0		
1999–2000	Everton	0	0		
2000–01	Barnsley	27	0		
2001–02	Barnsley	10	0		
2002–03	Barnsley	0	0	**37**	**0**
2002–03	Hull C	38	0		
2003–04	Hull C	0	0		
2004–05	Hull C	0	0	**38**	**0**
2004–05	Chester C	6	0		
2005–06	Chester C	41	0	**47**	**0**
2006–07	Macclesfield T	38	2		
2007–08	Macclesfield T	20	0	**58**	**2**
2007–08	Milton Keynes D	9	1	**9**	**1**

STIRLING, Jude (D) **98 3**
H: 6 2 W: 11 12 b.Enfield 29-6-82
Source: Trainee.

1999–2000	Luton T	0	0		
2000–01	Luton T	9	0		
2001–02	Luton T	1	0	**10**	**0**
From Tamworth.					
2005–06	Oxford U	10	0	**10**	**0**
From Stevenage B, Hornchurch, Tamworth					
2005–06	Lincoln C	6	0	**6**	**0**
2006–07	Peterborough U	22	0	**22**	**0**
2006–07	Milton Keynes D	16	1		
2007–08	Milton Keynes D	34	2	**50**	**3**

SWAILES, Danny (D) **298 22**
H: 6 3 W: 12 06 b.Bolton 1-4-79
Source: Trainee.

1997–98	Bury	0	0		
1998–99	Bury	0	0		
1999–2000	Bury	24	3		
2000–01	Bury	11	0		
2001–02	Bury	28	1		
2002–03	Bury	39	3		
2003–04	Bury	42	5		
2004–05	Bury	20	1	**164**	**13**
2004–05	Macclesfield T	17	0		
2005–06	Macclesfield T	39	2		
2006–07	Macclesfield T	38	3		
2007–08	Macclesfield T	0	0	**94**	**5**
2007–08	Milton Keynes D	40	4	**40**	**4**

TAYLOR, Scott (F) **396 78**
H: 5 10 W: 11 04 b.Chertsey 5-5-76
Source: Staines T.

1994–95	Millwall	6	0		
1995–96	Millwall	22	0	**28**	**0**
1995–96	Bolton W	1	0		
1996–97	Bolton W	11	1		
1997–98	Bolton W	0	0		
1997–98	*Rotherham U*	10	3	**10**	**3**
1997–98	*Blackpool*	5	1		
1998–99	Bolton W	0	0	**12**	**1**
1998–99	Tranmere R	36	9		
1999–2000	Tranmere R	35	3		
2000–01	Tranmere R	37	5	**108**	**17**
2001–02	Stockport Co	28	4	**28**	**4**
2001–02	Blackpool	17	2		
2002–03	Blackpool	44	13		
2003–04	Blackpool	31	16		
2004–05	Blackpool	24	12	**121**	**44**
2004–05	Plymouth Arg	16	3		
2005–06	Plymouth Arg	18	1	**34**	**4**
2005–06	Milton Keynes D	17	3		
2006–07	Milton Keynes D	28	2		
2006–07	*Brentford*	6	0	**6**	**0**
2007–08	Milton Keynes D	0	0	**45**	**5**
2007–08	*Rochdale*	4	0	**4**	**0**

WILBRAHAM, Aaron (F) **298 61**
H: 6 3 W: 12 04 b.Knutsford 21-10-79
Source: Trainee.

1997–98	Stockport Co	7	1		
1998–99	Stockport Co	26	0		
1999–2000	Stockport Co	26	4		
2000–01	Stockport Co	36	12		
2001–02	Stockport Co	21	3		
2002–03	Stockport Co	15	7		
2003–04	Stockport Co	41	8	**172**	**35**
2004–05	Hull C	19	2	**19**	**2**
2004–05	*Oldham Ath*	4	2	**4**	**2**
2005–06	Milton Keynes D	31	4		
2005–06	*Bradford C*	5	1	**5**	**1**
2006–07	Milton Keynes D	32	7		
2007–08	Milton Keynes D	35	10	**98**	**21**

WRIGHT, Mark (M) **158 22**
H: 5 11 W: 11 00 b.Wolverhampton 24-2-82
Source: Scholar.

2000–01	Walsall	4	0		
2001–02	Walsall	0	0		
2002–03	Walsall	5	0		
2003–04	Walsall	11	2		
2004–05	Walsall	37	2		
2005–06	Walsall	30	2		
2006–07	Walsall	37	3	**124**	**9**
2007–08	Milton Keynes D	34	13	**34**	**13**

MORECAMBE (55)

ADAMS, Danny (D) **297 2**
H: 5 8 W: 13 08 b.Manchester 3-1-76
Source: Altrincham.

2000–01	Macclesfield T	37	0		
2001–02	Macclesfield T	39	0		
2002–03	Macclesfield T	45	1		
2003–04	Macclesfield T	27	0	**148**	**1**
2003–04	Stockport Co	12	0		
2004–05	Stockport Co	27	1	**39**	**1**
2004–05	Huddersfield T	5	0		
2005–06	Huddersfield T	40	0		
2006–07	Huddersfield T	23	0	**68**	**0**
2007–08	Morecambe	42	0	**42**	**0**

ALLEN, Damien (M) **70 1**
H: 5 11 W: 11 04 b.Cheadle 1-8-86
Source: Trainee.

2004–05	Stockport Co	21	1		
2005–06	Stockport Co	22	0		
2006–07	Stockport Co	7	0	**50**	**1**
2006–07	*Antwerp*	0	0		
2007–08	Morecambe	20	0	**20**	**0**

ARTELL, Dave (D) **226 16**
H: 6 3 W: 14 01 b.Rotherham 22-11-80
Source: Trainee.

1999–2000	Rotherham U	1	0		
2000–01	Rotherham U	36	4		
2001–02	Rotherham U	0	0		
2002–03	Rotherham U	0	0	**37**	**4**
2002–03	*Shrewsbury T*	28	1	**28**	**1**
2003–04	Mansfield T	26	3		
2004–05	Mansfield T	19	2	**45**	**5**
2005–06	Chester C	37	2		
2006–07	Chester C	43	1	**80**	**3**
2007–08	Morecambe	36	3	**36**	**3**

BAKER, Carl (M) **42 10**
H: 6 2 W: 12 06 b.Prescot 26-12-82
Source: Southport.

2007–08	Morecambe	42	10	**42**	**10**

BENTLEY, Jim (D) **43 6**
H: 6 1 W: 13 00 b.Liverpool 11-6-76
Source: Trainee.

1993–94	Manchester C	0	0		
1994–95	Manchester C	0	0		
1995–96	Manchester C	0	0		
1996–97	Manchester C	0	0		
1997–98	Manchester C	0	0		
1998–99	Manchester C	0	0		
2007–08	Morecambe	43	6	**43**	**6**

BLINKHORN, Matthew (F) **97 15**
H: 5 11 W: 10 10 b.Blackpool 2-3-85
Source: Scholar.

2001–02	Blackpool	3	0		
2002–03	Blackpool	7	2		
2003–04	Blackpool	12	1		
2004–05	Blackpool	4	0		
2004–05	*Luton T*	2	0	**2**	**0**
2005–06	Blackpool	16	2		
2006–07	Blackpool	2	0	**44**	**5**
2006–07	*Bury*	10	0	**10**	**0**
2007–08	Morecambe	41	10	**41**	**10**

BURNS, Jamie (F) **55 1**
H: 5 9 W: 10 11 b.Blackpool 6-3-84
Source: Scholar.

2002–03	Blackpool	7	0		
2003–04	Blackpool	11	0		
2004–05	Blackpool	23	0		

2005–06	Blackpool	6	1		
2005–06	*Bury*	1	0	**1**	**0**
2006–07	Blackpool	0	0	**47**	**1**
2007–08	Morecambe	7	0	**7**	**0**

CURTIS, Wayne (M) **36 2**
H: 6 0 W: 12 00 b.Barrow 6-3-80
Source: Holker Old Boys.

2007–08	Morecambe	36	2	**36**	**2**

DAVIES, Jamie (D) **0 0**
H: 6 0 W: 11 10 b.Lancaster 1-6-89

2007–08	Morecambe	0	0

DAVIES, Scott (G) **10 0**
H: 6 0 W: 11 00 b.Blackpool 27-2-87

2007–08	Morecambe	10	0	**10**	**0**

DRENCH, Steven (G) **4 0**
H: 5 11 W: 12 08 b.Salford 11-9-85
Source: Trainee.

2002–03	Blackburn R	0	0		
2003–04	Blackburn R	0	0		
2004–05	Blackburn R	0	0		
2005–06	Blackburn R	0	0		
2006–07	Blackburn R	0	0		
2007–08	Morecambe	4	0	**4**	**0**

DRUMMOND, Stuart (M) **172 21**
H: 6 2 W: 13 08 b.Preston 11-12-75
Source: Morecambe.

2004–05	Chester C	45	6		
2005–06	Chester C	42	6	**87**	**12**
2006–07	Shrewsbury T	44	4		
2007–08	Shrewsbury T	23	3	**67**	**7**
2007–08	Morecambe	18	2	**18**	**2**

GRAND, Simon (D) **65 5**
H: 6 0 W: 10 03 b.Chorley 23-2-84
Source: Scholar.

2002–03	Rochdale	23	2		
2003–04	Rochdale	17	0	**40**	**2**
2004–05	Carlisle U	0	0		
2005–06	Carlisle U	8	2		
2006–07	Carlisle U	4	0	**12**	**2**
2006–07	Grimsby T	7	0	**7**	**0**
2007–08	Morecambe	6	1	**6**	**1**

HOWARD, Mike (D) **232 2**
H: 5 6 W: 10 07 b.Birkenhead 2-12-78
Source: Tranmere R Trainee.

1997–98	Swansea C	3	0		
1998–99	Swansea C	39	1		
1999–2000	Swansea C	40	0		
2000–01	Swansea C	41	0		
2001–02	Swansea C	42	1		
2002–03	Swansea C	38	0		
2003–04	Swansea C	25	0		
2004–05	Swansea C	0	0		
2005–06	Swansea C	0	0		
2006–07	Swansea C	0	0	**228**	**2**
2007–08	Morecambe	4	0	**4**	**0**

HUNTER, Garry (M) **38 1**
H: 5 7 W: 10 03 b.Morecambe 1-1-85
Source: Scholar.

2007–08	Morecambe	38	1	**38**	**1**

JARVIS, Paul (M) **0 0**
H: 5 11 W: 11 00 b.Devon 21-8-88

2007–08	Morecambe	0	0

LANGFORD, Andy (M) **0 0**
H: 5 11 W: 12 05 b.Manchester 3-7-88

2007–08	Morecambe	0	0

LLOYD, Paul (M) **7 0**
H: 5 9 W: 10 11 b.Preston 26-3-87

2007–08	Morecambe	7	0	**7**	**0**

McLACHLAN, Fraser (M) **83 4**
H: 5 11 W: 12 07 b.Manchester 9-11-82
Source: Scholar.

2001–02	Stockport Co	11	1		
2002–03	Stockport Co	22	0		
2003–04	Stockport Co	20	3		
2004–05	Stockport Co	0	0	**53**	**4**
2004–05	Mansfield T	21	0		
2005–06	Mansfield T	8	0	**29**	**0**
2007–08	Morecambe	1	0	**1**	**0**

McSTAY, Henry (D) **26 0**
H: 6 0 W: 11 11 b.Co Armagh 6-3-85
Source: Scholar. *Honours:* Eire Under-21.

2001–02	Leeds U	0	0		
2002–03	Leeds U	0	0		
2003–04	Leeds U	0	0		
2004–05	Leeds U	0	0		
2005–06	Leeds U	0	0		
2006–07	Leeds U	0	0		
2007–08	Antwerp	13	0	**13**	**0**
2007–08	Morecambe	13	0	**13**	**0**

NEWBY, Jon (F) **239 32**
H: 5 11 W: 11 00 b.Warrington 28-11-78
Source: Trainee.

1998–99	Liverpool	0	0		
1999–2000	Liverpool	1	0		
1999–2000	*Crewe Alex*	6	0	**6**	**0**
2000–01	Liverpool	0	0	**1**	**0**
2000–01	*Sheffield U*	13	0	**13**	**0**
2000–01	Bury	17	5		
2001–02	Bury	46	6		
2002–03	Bury	46	10		
2003–04	Huddersfield T	14	0	**14**	**0**
2003–04	*York C*	7	0	**7**	**0**
2004–05	Bury	36	4		
2005–06	Bury	10	1	**155**	**26**
2006–07	Wrexham	11	0	**11**	**0**
2007–08	Morecambe	32	6	**32**	**6**

SORVEL, Neil (M) **430 25**
H: 5 10 W: 11 04 b.Whiston 2-3-73
Source: Trainee.

1991–92	Crewe Alex	9	0		
1992–93	Crewe Alex	0	0		
1997–98	Macclesfield T	45	3		
1998–99	Macclesfield T	41	4	**86**	**7**
1999–2000	Crewe Alex	46	6		
2000–01	Crewe Alex	46	1		
2001–02	Crewe Alex	38	0		
2002–03	Crewe Alex	43	3		
2003–04	Crewe Alex	31	0		
2004–05	Crewe Alex	46	3	**259**	**13**
2005–06	Shrewsbury T	45	4		
2006–07	Shrewsbury T	18	1	**63**	**5**
2007–08	Morecambe	22	0	**22**	**0**

STANLEY, Craig (M) **41 2**
H: 5 8 W: 10 08 b.Bedworth 3-3-83
Source: Scholar.

2002–03	Walsall	0	0		
2003–04	Walsall	0	0		
2004–05	Walsall	0	0		
2005–06	Walsall	0	0		
2006–07	Walsall	0	0		
2007–08	Morecambe	41	2	**41**	**2**

THOMPSON, Gary (M) **40 7**
H: 6 0 W: 14 02 b.Kendal 24-11-80
Source: Scholar.

2007–08	Morecambe	40	7	**40**	**7**

TWISS, Michael (M) **66 9**
H: 5 11 W: 13 03 b.Salford 28-12-77
Source: Trainee.

1996–97	Manchester U	0	0		
1997–98	Manchester U	0	0		
1998–99	*Sheffield U*	12	1	**12**	**1**
1999–2000	Manchester U	0	0		
2000–01	Port Vale	18	2		
2001–02	Port Vale	0	0	**18**	**2**
2007–08	Morecambe	36	6	**36**	**6**

YATES, Adam (D) **44 0**
H: 5 10 W: 10 07 b.Stoke 28-5-83
Source: Scholar.

2000–01	Crewe Alex	0	0		
2001–02	Crewe Alex	0	0		
2002–03	Crewe Alex	0	0		
2003–04	Crewe Alex	0	0		
2004–05	Crewe Alex	0	0		
2005–06	Crewe Alex	0	0		
2006–07	Crewe Alex	0	0		
2007–08	Morecambe	44	0	**44**	**0**

NEWCASTLE U (56)

AMEOBI, Shola (F) **174 28**
H: 6 3 W: 11 13 b.Zaria 12-10-81
Source: Trainee. *Honours:* England Under-21.

1998–99	Newcastle U	0	0		
1999–2000	Newcastle U	0	0		
2000–01	Newcastle U	20	2		
2001–02	Newcastle U	15	0		
2002–03	Newcastle U	28	5		
2003–04	Newcastle U	26	7		
2004–05	Newcastle U	31	2		
2005–06	Newcastle U	30	9		
2006–07	Newcastle U	12	3		
2007–08	Newcastle U	6	0	**168**	**28**
2007–08	*Stoke C*	6	0	**6**	**0**

BABAYARO, Celestine (D) **254 13**
H: 5 10 W: 11 11 b.Kaduna 29-8-78
Source: Plateau U. *Honours:* Nigeria 26 full caps.

1994–95	Anderlecht	22	0		
1995–96	Anderlecht	28	5		
1996–97	Anderlecht	25	3	**75**	**8**
1997–98	Chelsea	8	0		
1998–99	Chelsea	28	3		
1999–2000	Chelsea	25	0		
2000–01	Chelsea	24	0		
2001–02	Chelsea	18	0		
2002–03	Chelsea	19	1		
2003–04	Chelsea	6	1		
2004–05	Chelsea	4	0	**132**	**5**
2004–05	Newcastle U	7	0		
2005–06	Newcastle U	28	0		
2006–07	Newcastle U	12	0		
2007–08	Newcastle U	0	0	**47**	**0**

BARTON, Joey (M) **153 16**
H: 5 11 W: 12 05 b.Huyton 2-9-82
Source: Scholar. *Honours:* England Under-21, 1 full cap.

2001–02	Manchester C	0	0		
2002–03	Manchester C	7	1		
2003–04	Manchester C	28	1		
2004–05	Manchester C	31	1		
2005–06	Manchester C	31	6		
2006–07	Manchester C	33	6	**130**	**15**
2007–08	Newcastle U	23	1	**23**	**1**

BEYE, Habib (D) **291 11**
H: 6 0 W: 12 06 b.Paris 19-10-77
Honours: Senegal 35 full caps, 1 goal.

1997–98	Paris St Germain	0	0		
1998–99	Strasbourg	23	0		
1999–2000	Strasbourg	33	1		
2000–01	Strasbourg	31	3		
2001–02	Strasbourg	20	3		
2002–03	Strasbourg	26	1		
2003–04	Strasbourg	1	0	**134**	**8**
2003–04	Marseille	22	0		
2004–05	Marseille	37	1		
2005–06	Marseille	29	1		
2006–07	Marseille	36	0		
2007–08	Marseille	4	0	**128**	**2**
2007–08	Newcastle U	29	1	**29**	**1**

BUTT, Nicky (M) **378 29**
H: 5 10 W: 11 05 b.Manchester 21-1-75
Source: Trainee. *Honours:* England Schools, Youth, Under-21, 39 full caps.

1992–93	Manchester U	1	0		
1993–94	Manchester U	1	0		
1994–95	Manchester U	22	1		
1995–96	Manchester U	32	2		
1996–97	Manchester U	26	5		
1997–98	Manchester U	33	3		
1998–99	Manchester U	31	2		
1999–2000	Manchester U	32	3		
2000–01	Manchester U	28	3		
2001–02	Manchester U	25	1		
2002–03	Manchester U	18	0		
2003–04	Manchester U	21	1	**270**	**21**
2004–05	Newcastle U	18	1		
2005–06	*Birmingham C*	24	3	**24**	**3**
2006–07	Newcastle U	31	1		
2007–08	Newcastle U	35	3	**84**	**5**

CACAPA, Claudio (D) **212 10**
H: 6 0 W: 12 01 b.Lavras 29-5-76
Honours: Brazil 4 full caps.

1997	Atletico Mineiro	6	0		
1998	Atletico Mineiro	15	0		
1999	Atletico Mineiro	29	1		
2000	Atletico Mineiro	18	1	**68**	**2**
2000–01	Lyon	6	1		
2001–02	Lyon	15	0		
2002–03	Lyon	36	2		
2003–04	Lyon	15	1		
2004–05	Lyon	21	1		
2005–06	Lyon	26	2		
2006–07	Lyon	6	0	**125**	**7**
2007–08	Newcastle U	19	1	**19**	**1**

CARR, Stephen (D) **304 8**
H: 5 9 W: 11 13 b.Dublin 29-8-76
Source: Trainee. *Honours:* Eire Schools, Youth, Under-21, 44 full caps.

1993–94	Tottenham H	1	0		
1994–95	Tottenham H	0	0		
1995–96	Tottenham H	0	0		
1996–97	Tottenham H	26	0		
1997–98	Tottenham H	38	0		
1998–99	Tottenham H	37	0		
1999–2000	Tottenham H	34	3		
2000–01	Tottenham H	28	3		
2001–02	Tottenham H	0	0		
2002–03	Tottenham H	30	0		
2003–04	Tottenham H	32	1	**226**	**7**
2004–05	Newcastle U	26	1		
2005–06	Newcastle U	19	0		
2006–07	Newcastle U	23	0		
2007–08	Newcastle U	10	0	**78**	**1**

CARROLL, Andy (F) **19 1**
H: 6 4 W: 11 00 b.Gateshead 6-1-89
Source: Scholar. *Honours:* England Youth.

2006–07	Newcastle U	4	0		
2007–08	Newcastle U	4	0	**8**	**0**
2007–08	*Preston NE*	11	1	**11**	**1**

DIAGNE-FAYE, Aboulaye (M) **176 8**
H: 6 2 W: 13 10 b.Dakar 26-2-78
Source: Ndiambour Louga. *Honours:* Senegal 14 full caps, 3 goals.

2001–02	Jeanne D'Arc	32	4	**32**	**4**
2002–03	Lens	15	0		
2003–04	Lens	19	0	**34**	**0**
2004–05	Istres	28	0	**28**	**0**
2005–06	Bolton W	27	1		
2006–07	Bolton W	32	2		
2007–08	Bolton W	1	0	**60**	**3**
2007–08	Newcastle U	22	1	**22**	**1**

DIATTA, Lamine (D) **219 10**
H: 6 0 W: 11 13 b.Dakar 2-7-75

1998–99	Toulouse	25	0	**25**	**0**
1999–2000	Marseille	0	0		
1999–2000	Rennes	33	3		
2000–01	Rennes	23	2		
2001–02	Rennes	21	1		
2002–03	Rennes	20	0		
2003–04	Rennes	32	3	**129**	**9**
2004–05	Lyon	19	0		
2005–06	Lyon	13	0	**32**	**0**
2006–07	St Etienne	25	1	**25**	**1**
2007–08	Besiktas	6	0	**6**	**0**
2007–08	Newcastle U	2	0	**2**	**0**

DONINGER, Mark (M) **0 0**
b.Newcastle 19-10-89

2007–08	Newcastle U	0	0

DUFF, Damien (F) **303 42**
H: 5 9 W: 12 06 b.Ballyboden 2-3-79
Source: Lourdes Celtic. *Honours:* Eire Schools, Youth, Under-20, B, 68 full caps, 7 goals.

1995–96	Blackburn R	0	0		
1996–97	Blackburn R	1	0		
1997–98	Blackburn R	26	4		
1998–99	Blackburn R	28	1		
1999–2000	Blackburn R	39	5		
2000–01	Blackburn R	32	1		
2001–02	Blackburn R	32	7		
2002–03	Blackburn R	26	9	**184**	**27**
2003–04	Chelsea	23	5		
2004–05	Chelsea	30	6		
2005–06	Chelsea	28	3	**81**	**14**
2006–07	Newcastle U	22	1		
2007–08	Newcastle U	16	0	**38**	**1**

EDGAR, David (D) **8 1**
H: 6 2 W: 12 13 b.Ontario 19-5-87
Source: Scholar. *Honours:* Canada Youth, Under-20.

2005–06	Newcastle U	0	0		
2006–07	Newcastle U	3	1		
2007–08	Newcastle U	5	0	**8**	**1**

EMRE, Belezoglu (M) **219 21**
H: 5 8 W: 10 10 b.Istanbul 7-9-80
Honours: Turkey Youth, Under-21, 58 full caps, 4 goals.

1997–98	Galatasaray	24	2		
1998–99	Galatasaray	27	2		
1999–2000	Galatasaray	24	5		
2000–01	Galatasaray	26	4	**101**	**13**
2001–02	Internazionale	14	0		
2002–03	Internazionale	25	3		
2003–04	Internazionale	21	0		
2004–05	Internazionale	0	0	**60**	**3**
2005–06	Newcastle U	20	2		
2006–07	Newcastle U	24	2		
2007–08	Newcastle U	14	1	**58**	**5**

FORSTER, Fraser (G) **0 0**
H: 6 0 W: 12 00 b.Hexham 17-3-88
Source: Scholar.

2007–08	Newcastle U	0	0

GEREMI (M) **240 21**
H: 5 9 W: 13 01 b.Bafoussam 20-12-78
Source: Racing Bafousam. *Honours:* Cameroon 68 full caps, 9 goals.

1997	Cerro Porteno	6	0	**6**	**0**
1997–98	Genclerbirligi	28	4		
1998–99	Genclerbirligi	29	5	**57**	**9**
1999–2000	Real Madrid	20	0		
2000–01	Real Madrid	16	0		
2001–02	Real Madrid	9	0	**45**	**0**
2002–03	Middlesbrough	33	7	**33**	**7**
2003–04	Chelsea	25	1		
2004–05	Chelsea	13	0		
2005–06	Chelsea	15	2		
2006–07	Chelsea	19	1	**72**	**4**
2007–08	Newcastle U	27	1	**27**	**1**

GIVEN, Shay (G) **356 0**
H: 6 0 W: 13 03 b.Lifford 20-4-76
Source: Celtic. *Honours:* Eire Youth, Under-21, 86 full caps.

1994–95	Blackburn R	0	0		
1994–95	*Swindon T*	0	0		
1995–96	Blackburn R	0	0		
1995–96	*Swindon T*	5	0	**5**	**0**
1995–96	*Sunderland*	17	0	**17**	**0**
1996–97	Blackburn R	2	0	**2**	**0**
1997–98	Newcastle U	24	0		
1998–99	Newcastle U	31	0		
1999–2000	Newcastle U	14	0		
2000–01	Newcastle U	34	0		
2001–02	Newcastle U	38	0		
2002 03	Newcastle U	38	0		
2003–04	Newcastle U	38	0		
2004–05	Newcastle U	36	0		
2005–06	Newcastle U	38	0		
2006–07	Newcastle U	22	0		
2007–08	Newcastle U	19	0	**332**	**0**

HARPER, Steve (G) **112 0**
H: 6 2 W: 13 10 b.Easington 14-3-75
Source: Seaham Red Star.

1993–94	Newcastle U	0	0		
1994–95	Newcastle U	0	0		
1995–96	Newcastle U	0	0		
1995–96	*Bradford C*	1	0	**1**	**0**
1996–97	Newcastle U	0	0		
1996–97	*Stockport Co*	0	0		
1997–98	Newcastle U	0	0		
1997–98	*Hartlepool U*	15	0	**15**	**0**
1997–98	*Huddersfield T*	24	0	**24**	**0**
1998–99	Newcastle U	8	0		
1999–2000	Newcastle U	18	0		
2000–01	Newcastle U	5	0		
2001–02	Newcastle U	0	0		
2002–03	Newcastle U	0	0		
2003–04	Newcastle U	0	0		
2004–05	Newcastle U	2	0		
2005–06	Newcastle U	0	0		
2006–07	Newcastle U	18	0		
2007–08	Newcastle U	21	0	**72**	**0**

JOSE ENRIQUE (D) **79 1**
H: 6 0 W: 12 00 b.Valencia 23-1-86
Honours: Spain Under-21.

2004–05	Levante	19	1	**19**	**1**
2005–06	Valencia	0	0		
2005–06	*Celta Vigo*	14	0	**14**	**0**
2006–07	Villarreal	23	0	**23**	**0**
2007–08	Newcastle U	23	0	**23**	**0**

KADAR, Tamas (D) **0 0**
H: 6 0 W: 12 10 b.Veszprem 14-3-90

2007–08	Newcastle U	0	0

KRUL, Tim (G) **22 0**
H: 6 2 W: 11 08 b.Den Haag 3-4-88
Source: Academy. *Honours:* Holland Youth.

2005–06	Newcastle U	0	0		
2006–07	Newcastle U	0	0		
2007–08	*Falkirk*	22	0	**22**	**0**
2007–08	Newcastle U	0	0		

LUALUA, Kazenga (F) **2 0**
H: 5 11 W: 12 00 b.Kinshasa 10-12-90
Source: Scholar.

2007–08	Newcastle U	2	0	**2**	**0**

MARTINS, Obafemi (F) **154 47**
H: 5 9 W: 10 07 b.Lagos 28-10-84
Honours: Nigeria 21 full caps, 13 goals.

2000–01	Reggiana	2	0	**2**	**0**
2001–02	Internazionale	0	0		
2002–03	Internazionale	4	1		
2003–04	Internazionale	25	7		
2004–05	Internazionale	31	11		
2005–06	Internazionale	28	8	**88**	**27**
2006–07	Newcastle U	33	11		
2007–08	Newcastle U	31	9	**64**	**20**

McLAUGHLIN, Patrick (M) **0 0**
b.Larne 14-1-91

2007–08	Newcastle U	0	0

MILNER, James (M) **173 14**
H: 5 9 W: 11 00 b.Leeds 4-1-86
Source: Trainee. *Honours:* FA Schools, Youth, England Under-20, Under-21.

2002–03	Leeds U	18	2		
2003–04	Leeds U	30	3	**48**	**5**
2003–04	*Swindon T*	6	2	**6**	**2**
2004–05	Newcastle U	25	1		
2005–06	Newcastle U	3	0		
2005–06	*Aston Villa*	27	1	**27**	**1**
2006–07	Newcastle U	35	3		
2007–08	Newcastle U	29	2	**92**	**6**

N'ZOGBIA, Charles (M) **99 8**
H: 5 9 W: 11 00 b.Le Havre 28-5-86
Honours: France Youth, Under-21.

2004–05	Newcastle U	14	0		
2005–06	Newcastle U	32	5		
2006–07	Newcastle U	22	0		
2007–08	Newcastle U	31	3	**99**	**8**

NGO BAHENG, Wesley (F) **0 0**
H: 5 11 W: 11 06 b.Blanc Mesnil 23-9-89

2007–08	Newcastle U	0	0

OWEN, Michael (F) **295 149**
H: 5 8 W: 10 12 b.Chester 14-12-79
Source: Trainee. *Honours:* England Schools, Youth, Under-21, B, 89 full caps, 40 goals.

1996–97	Liverpool	2	1		
1997–98	Liverpool	36	18		
1998–99	Liverpool	30	18		
1999–2000	Liverpool	27	11		
2000–01	Liverpool	28	16		
2001–02	Liverpool	29	19		
2002–03	Liverpool	35	19		
2003–04	Liverpool	29	16	**216**	**118**
2004–05	Real Madrid	36	13	**36**	**13**
2005–06	Newcastle U	11	7		
2006–07	Newcastle U	3	0		
2007–08	Newcastle U	29	11	**43**	**18**

RAMAGE, Peter (D) **51 0**
H: 6 3 W: 11 02 b.Whitley Bay 22-11-83
Source: Trainee.

2003–04	Newcastle U	0	0		
2004–05	Newcastle U	4	0		
2005–06	Newcastle U	23	0		
2006–07	Newcastle U	21	0		
2007–08	Newcastle U	3	0	**51**	**0**

ROZEHNAL, David (D) **223 5**
H: 6 3 W: 12 04 b.Stembeck 5-7-80
Honours: Czech Republic Under-21, 42 full caps.

1999–2000	Olomouc	4	0		
2000–01	Olomouc	12	1		
2001–02	Olomouc	28	1		
2002–03	Olomouc	26	0	**70**	**2**
2003–04	FC Brugge	26	0		
2004–05	FC Brugge	24	1	**50**	**1**
2005–06	Paris St Germain	38	0		
2006–07	Paris St Germain	37	2	**75**	**2**
2007–08	*Lazio*	7	0	**7**	**0**
2007–08	Newcastle U	21	0	**21**	**0**

SHANKS, Chris (D) **0 0**
H: 6 0 W: 11 00 b.Ashington 16-10-86
Source: Scholar.

2004–05	Newcastle U	0	0
2005–06	Newcastle U	0	0
2006–07	Newcastle U	0	0
2007–08	Newcastle U	0	0

SMITH, Alan (F) 266 45
H: 5 10 W: 12 04 b.Rothwell 28-10-80
Source: Trainee. *Honours:* England Youth, Under-21, B, 19 full caps, 1 goal.
1997–98 Leeds U 0 0
1998–99 Leeds U 22 7
1999–2000 Leeds U 26 4
2000–01 Leeds U 33 11
2001–02 Leeds U 23 4
2002–03 Leeds U 33 3
2003–04 Leeds U 35 9 **172 38**
2004–05 Manchester U 31 6
2005–06 Manchester U 21 1
2006–07 Manchester U 9 0 **61 7**
2007–08 Newcastle U 33 0 **33 0**

SODERBERG, Ole (D) 0 0
b.Norrkoping 20-7-90
Source: BK Hacken.
2007–08 Newcastle U 0 0

TAYLOR, Steven (D) 90 3
H: 6 2 W: 13 01 b.Greenwich 23-1-86
Source: Trainee. *Honours:* FA Schools, Youth, England Under-20, Under-21, B.
2002–03 Newcastle U 0 0
2003–04 Newcastle U 1 0
2003–04 *Wycombe W* 6 0 **6 0**
2004–05 Newcastle U 13 0
2005–06 Newcastle U 12 0
2006–07 Newcastle U 27 2
2007–08 Newcastle U 31 1 **84 3**

TOZER, Ben (D) 2 0
H: 6 1 W: 12 11 b.Plymouth 1-3-90
Source: Scholar.
2007–08 Swindon T 2 0 **2 0**
2007–08 Newcastle U 0 0

TROISI, James (F) 0 0
H: 5 10 W: 11 03 b.Adelaide 3-7-88
Source: Scholar. *Honours:* Australia Under-23, 3 full caps.
2006–07 Newcastle U 0 0
2007–08 Newcastle U 0 0

VIDUKA, Mark (F) 397 202
H: 6 2 W: 15 01 b.Melbourne 9-10-75
Honours: Australia Youth, Under-20, Under-23, 43 full caps, 11 goals.
1992–93 Melbourne Knights 4 2
1993–94 Melbourne Knights 20 17
1994–95 Melbourne Knights 24 21 **48 40**
1995–96 Croatia Zagreb 27 12
1996–97 Croatia Zagreb 25 18
1997–98 Croatia Zagreb 25 8
1998–99 Croatia Zagreb 7 2 **84 40**
1998–99 Celtic 9 5
1999–2000 Celtic 28 25 **37 30**
2000–01 Leeds U 34 17
2001–02 Leeds U 33 11
2002–03 Leeds U 33 20
2003–04 Leeds U 30 11 **130 59**
2004–05 Middlesbrough 16 5
2005–06 Middlesbrough 27 7
2006–07 Middlesbrough 29 14 **72 26**
2007–08 Newcastle U 26 7 **26 7**

ZAMBLERA, Fabio (F) 0 0
b.Bergamo
Source: Atalanta. *Honours:* Italy Youth.
2007–08 Newcastle U 0 0

Scholars
Bath, Stewart; Bell, Adam Campbell; Danquah, Frank Wiafe; Donaldson, Ryan Mark; Ferguson, Shane; Godsmark, Jonathan; Grieve, Matthew Andrias; Johnson, Max Declan Ross John; Leadbetter, Daniel William; Lough, Darren; Marwood, James William; McCrudden, Michael; Morris, Callum Edward; Neary, Daniel; Taylor, James Edward; Wrightson, Kieran

NORTHAMPTON T (57)

AKINFENWA, Adebayo (F) 154 44
H: 5 11 W: 13 07 b.Nigeria 10-5-82
2001 Atlantas 19 4
2002 Atlantas 4 1 **23 5**
From Barry T
2003–04 Boston U 3 0 **3 0**
2003–04 Leyton Orient 1 0 **1 0**
2003–04 Rushden & D 0 0
2003–04 Doncaster R 9 4 **9 4**
2004–05 Torquay U 37 14 **37 14**
2005–06 Swansea C 34 9
2006–07 Swansea C 25 5
2007–08 Swansea C 0 0 **59 14**
2007–08 Millwall 7 0 **7 0**
2007–08 Northampton T 15 7 **15 7**

BUNN, Mark (G) 87 0
H: 6 0 W: 12 02 b.Camden 16-11-84
Source: Scholar.
2004–05 Northampton T 0 0
2005–06 Northampton T 0 0
2006–07 Northampton T 42 0
2007–08 Northampton T 45 0 **87 0**

BURNELL, Joe (M) 245 2
H: 5 8 W: 12 00 b.Bristol 10-10-80
Source: Trainee.
1999–2000 Bristol C 17 0
2000–01 Bristol C 23 0
2001–02 Bristol C 30 0
2002–03 Bristol C 44 0
2003–04 Bristol C 17 1 **131 1**
2004–05 Wycombe W 24 0
2005–06 Wycombe W 33 0 **57 0**
2006–07 Northampton T 24 1
2007–08 Northampton T 33 0 **57 1**

COKE, Gilles (M) 90 10
H: 6 0 W: 11 11 b.London 3-6-86
Source: Kingstonian.
2004–05 Mansfield T 9 0
2005–06 Mansfield T 40 4
2006–07 Mansfield T 21 1 **70 5**
2007–08 Northampton T 20 5 **20 5**

CROWE, Jason (D) 300 18
H: 5 9 W: 10 09 b.Sidcup 30-9-78
Source: Trainee. *Honours:* England Schools, Youth.
1995–96 Arsenal 0 0
1996–97 Arsenal 0 0
1997–98 Arsenal 0 0
1998–99 Arsenal 0 0
1998–99 *Crystal Palace* 8 0 **8 0**
1999–2000 Portsmouth 25 0
2000–01 Portsmouth 23 0
2000–01 *Brentford* 9 0 **9 0**
2001–02 Portsmouth 22 1
2002–03 Portsmouth 16 4 **86 5**
2003–04 Grimsby T 32 0
2004–05 Grimsby T 37 4 **69 4**
2005–06 Northampton T 41 2
2006–07 Northampton T 43 3
2007–08 Northampton T 44 4 **128 9**

DOIG, Chris (D) 178 4
H: 6 2 W: 12 06 b.Dumfries 13-2-81
Source: Trainee. *Honours:* Scotland Schools, Youth, Under-21.
1997–98 Nottingham F 0 0
1998–99 Nottingham F 2 0
1999–2000 Nottingham F 11 0
2000–01 Nottingham F 15 0
2001–02 Nottingham F 8 1
2002–03 Nottingham F 10 0
2003–04 Nottingham F 10 0
2003–04 *Northampton T* 9 0
2004–05 Nottingham F 21 0 **77 1**
2005–06 Northampton T 38 2
2006–07 Northampton T 39 0
2007–08 Northampton T 15 1 **101 3**

DOLMAN, Liam (D) 31 1
H: 6 0 W: 14 05 b.Brixworth 26-9-87
Source: Scholar.
2005–06 Northampton T 0 0
2006–07 Northampton T 1 0
2007–08 Northampton T 30 1 **31 1**

DUNN, Chris (G) 1 0
H: 6 5 W: 13 11 b.Essex 23-10-87
Source: Scholar.
2006–07 Northampton T 0 0
2007–08 Northampton T 1 0 **1 0**

DYER, Alex (M) 6 1
H: 5 8 W: 11 07 b.Sweden 1-6-90
Source: Scholar.
2007–08 Northampton T 6 1 **6 1**

GILLIGAN, Ryan (M) 85 8
H: 5 10 W: 11 07 b.Swindon 18-1-87
Source: Watford Scholar.
2005–06 Northampton T 23 4
2006–07 Northampton T 24 0
2007–08 Northampton T 38 4 **85 8**

GYEPES, Gabor (D) 147 12
H: 6 3 W: 13 01 b.Hungary 26-6-81
Honours: Hungary 22 full caps, 1 goal.
1999–2000 Ferencvaros 2 0
2000–01 Ferencvaros 29 2
2001–02 Ferencvaros 33 3
2002–03 Ferencvaros 17 2
2003–04 Ferencvaros 7 0
2004–05 Ferencvaros 26 5 **114 12**
2005–06 Wolverhampton W 20 0
2006–07 Wolverhampton W 0 0 **20 0**
2007–08 Northampton T 13 0 **13 0**

HENDERSON, Ian (F) 109 7
H: 5 10 W: 11 06 b.Thetford 24-1-85
Source: Scholar. *Honours:* England Youth, Under-20.
2002–03 Norwich C 20 1
2003–04 Norwich C 19 4
2004–05 Norwich C 3 0
2005–06 Norwich C 24 1
2006–07 Norwich C 2 0 **68 6**
2006–07 *Rotherham U* 18 1 **18 1**
2007–08 Northampton T 23 0 **23 0**

HOLT, Andy (M) 363 26
H: 6 1 W: 12 07 b.Stockport 21-5-78
Source: Trainee.
1996–97 Oldham Ath 1 0
1997–98 Oldham Ath 14 1
1998–99 Oldham Ath 43 5
1999–2000 Oldham Ath 46 3
2000–01 Oldham Ath 20 1 **124 10**
2000–01 *Hull C* 10 2
2001–02 Hull C 30 0
2002–03 Hull C 6 0
2002–03 *Barnsley* 7 0 **7 0**
2002–03 *Shrewsbury T* 9 0 **9 0**
2003–04 Hull C 25 1 **71 3**
2004–05 Wrexham 45 6
2005–06 Wrexham 36 3 **81 9**
2006–07 Northampton T 35 2
2007–08 Northampton T 36 2 **71 4**

HUBERTZ, Poul (F) 198 58
H: 6 5 W: 14 09 b.Viborg 21-9-76
2000 Frem 25 7
From Farum
2003 *Frem* 15 8 **40 15**
2003–04 Herfolge 30 7
2004–05 Herfolge 28 11 **58 18**
2005–06 Aalborg 26 3 **26 3**
2006–07 Millwall 34 9 **34 9**
2007–08 Northampton T 40 13 **40 13**

HUGHES, Mark (D) 56 4
H: 6 1 W: 13 03 b.Liverpool 9-12-86
Source: Scholar.
2004–05 Everton 0 0
2005–06 Everton 0 0
2005–06 *Stockport Co* 3 1 **3 1**
2006–07 Everton 1 0 **1 0**
2006–07 Northampton T 17 2
2007–08 Northampton T 35 1 **52 3**

JACKMAN, Danny (D) 179 7
H: 5 4 W: 10 00 b.Worcester 3-1-83
Source: Scholar.
2000–01 Aston Villa 0 0
2001–02 Aston Villa 0 0
2001–02 *Cambridge U* 7 1 **7 1**
2002–03 Aston Villa 0 0
2003–04 Aston Villa 0 0
2003–04 Stockport Co 27 2
2004–05 Stockport Co 33 2 **60 4**
2005–06 Gillingham 42 0
2006–07 Gillingham 31 1 **73 1**
2007–08 Northampton T 39 1 **39 1**

JOHNSON, Brett (D) 26 0
H: 6 1 W: 13 00 b.Hammersmith 15-8-85
Source: Ashford T, Aldershot T.
2005–06 Northampton T 6 0
2006–07 Northampton T 4 0
2007–08 Northampton T 16 0 **26 0**

LARKIN, Colin (F) **241 44**
H: 5 9 W: 11 07 b.Dundalk 27-4-82
Source: Trainee.

1998–99	Wolverhampton W	0	0		
1999–2000	Wolverhampton W	1	0		
2000–01	Wolverhampton W	2	0		
2001–02	Wolverhampton W	0	0	**3**	**0**
2001–02	*Kidderminster H*	33	6	**33**	**6**
2002–03	Mansfield T	22	7		
2003–04	Mansfield T	37	7		
2004–05	Mansfield T	33	11	**92**	**25**
2005–06	Chesterfield	41	7		
2006–07	Chesterfield	39	4	**80**	**11**
2007–08	Northampton T	33	2	**33**	**2**

MAY, Danny (D) **5 0**
H: 5 8 W: 10 09 b.Northampton 19-11-88
Source: Scholar.

2006–07	Northampton T	3	0		
2007–08	Northampton T	2	0	**5**	**0**

QUINN, James (M) **342 61**
H: 6 1 W: 12 10 b.Coventry 15-12-74
Source: Trainee. *Honours:* Northern Ireland Youth, Under-21, B, 50 full caps, 4 goals.

1992–93	Birmingham C	4	0	**4**	**0**
1993–94	Blackpool	14	2		
1993–94	*Stockport Co*	1	0	**1**	**0**
1994–95	Blackpool	41	9		
1995–96	Blackpool	44	9		
1996–97	Blackpool	38	13		
1997–98	Blackpool	14	4	**151**	**37**
1997–98	WBA	13	2		
1998–99	WBA	43	6		
1999–2000	WBA	37	0		
2000–01	WBA	14	1		
2001–02	WBA	7	0		
2001–02	*Notts Co*	6	3	**6**	**3**
2001–02	*Bristol R*	6	1	**6**	**1**
2002–03	WBA	0	0		
2003–04	WBA	0	0	**114**	**9**
2004–05	Sheffield W	15	2	**15**	**2**
2005–06	Peterborough U	24	7	**24**	**7**
2005–06	*Bristol C*	3	1	**3**	**1**
2006–07	Northampton T	18	1		
2007–08	Northampton T	0	0	**18**	**1**

NORWICH C (58)

ARNOLD, Steven (G) **0 0**
H: 6 1 W: 13 02 b.Welham Green 22-8-89
Source: Scholar.

2007–08	Norwich C	0	0		

BEXFIELD, Patrick (D) **0 0**
H: 6 0 W: 13 03 b.Cambridge 9-11-88
Source: Scholar.

2007–08	Norwich C	0	0		

BRELLIER, Julien (M) **62 0**
H: 5 9 W: 12 08 b.Grenoble 10-1-82
Source: Montpellier, Internazionale, Venezia.

2005–06	Hearts	30	0		
2006–07	Hearts	22	0	**52**	**0**
2007–08	Norwich C	10	0	**10**	**0**

CAVE-BROWN, Andrew (D) **0 0**
H: 5 10 W: 12 02 b.Gravesend 5-8-88
Source: Scholar. *Honours:* Scotland Youth.

2005–06	Norwich C	0	0		
2006–07	Norwich C	0	0		
2007–08	Norwich C	0	0		

CHADWICK, Luke (M) **176 16**
H: 5 11 W: 11 08 b.Cambridge 18-11-80
Source: Trainee. *Honours:* England Youth, Under-21.

1998–99	Manchester U	0	0		
1999–2000	Manchester U	0	0		
2000–01	Manchester U	16	2		
2001–02	Manchester U	8	0		
2002–03	Manchester U	1	0		
2002–03	*Reading*	15	1	**15**	**1**
2003–04	Manchester U	0	0	**25**	**2**
2003–04	*Burnley*	36	5	**36**	**5**
2004–05	West Ham U	32	1		
2005–06	West Ham U	0	0	**32**	**1**
2005–06	Stoke C	36	2		
2006–07	Stoke C	15	3	**51**	**5**
2006–07	Norwich C	4	1		
2007–08	Norwich C	13	1	**17**	**2**

CROFT, Lee (F) **117 5**
H: 5 11 W: 13 00 b.Wigan 21-6-85
Source: Scholar. *Honours:* England Youth, Under-20.

2002–03	Manchester C	0	0		
2003–04	Manchester C	0	0		
2004–05	Manchester C	7	0		
2004–05	*Oldham Ath*	12	0	**12**	**0**
2005–06	Manchester C	21	1	**28**	**1**
2006–07	Norwich C	36	3		
2007–08	Norwich C	41	1	**77**	**4**

CURETON, Jamie (F) **482 180**
H: 5 8 W: 10 07 b.Bristol 28-8-75
Source: Trainee. *Honours:* England Youth.

1992–93	Norwich C	0	0		
1993–94	Norwich C	0	0		
1994–95	Norwich C	17	4		
1995–96	Norwich C	12	2		
1995–96	*Bournemouth*	5	0	**5**	**0**
1996–97	Norwich C	0	0		
1996–97	Bristol R	38	11		
1997–98	Bristol R	43	13		
1998–99	Bristol R	46	25		
1999–2000	Bristol R	46	22		
2000–01	Bristol R	1	1	**174**	**72**
2000–01	Reading	43	26		
2001–02	Reading	38	15		
2002–03	Reading	27	9	**108**	**50**
From Busan Icons.					
2003–04	QPR	13	2		
2004–05	QPR	30	4	**43**	**6**
2005–06	Swindon T	30	7	**30**	**7**
2005–06	*Colchester U*	8	4		
2006–07	Colchester U	44	23	**52**	**27**
2007–08	Norwich C	41	12	**70**	**18**

DALEY, Luke (F) **0 0**
b.Northampton 10-11-89
Source: Scholar.

2007–08	Norwich C	0	0		

DOHERTY, Gary (D) **264 19**
H: 6 3 W: 13 13 b.Carndonagh 31-1-80
Source: Trainee. *Honours:* Eire Youth, Under-20, Under-21, 34 full caps, 4 goals.

1997–98	Luton T	10	0		
1998–99	Luton T	20	6		
1999–2000	Luton T	40	6	**70**	**12**
1999–2000	Tottenham H	2	0		
2000–01	Tottenham H	22	3		
2001–02	Tottenham H	7	0		
2002–03	Tottenham H	15	1		
2003–04	Tottenham H	17	0		
2004–05	Tottenham H	1	0	**64**	**4**
2004–05	Norwich C	20	2		
2005–06	Norwich C	42	1		
2006–07	Norwich C	34	0		
2007–08	Norwich C	34	0	**130**	**3**

DRURY, Adam (D) **396 5**
H: 5 10 W: 11 09 b.Cambridge 29-8-78
Source: Trainee.

1995–96	Peterborough U	1	0		
1996–97	Peterborough U	5	1		
1997–98	Peterborough U	31	0		
1998–99	Peterborough U	40	0		
1999–2000	Peterborough U	42	1		
2000–01	Peterborough U	29	0	**148**	**2**
2000–01	Norwich C	6	0		
2001–02	Norwich C	35	0		
2002–03	Norwich C	45	2		
2003–04	Norwich C	42	0		
2004–05	Norwich C	33	1		
2005–06	Norwich C	39	0		
2006–07	Norwich C	39	0		
2007–08	Norwich C	9	0	**248**	**3**

DUBLIN, Dion (F) **612 183**
H: 6 2 W: 15 00 b.Leicester 22-4-69
Source: Oakham U. *Honours:* England 4 full caps.

1987–88	Norwich C	0	0		
1988–89	Cambridge U	21	6		
1989–90	Cambridge U	46	15		
1990–91	Cambridge U	46	16		
1991–92	Cambridge U	43	15	**156**	**52**
1992–93	Manchester U	7	1		
1993–94	Manchester U	5	1	**12**	**2**
1994–95	Coventry C	31	13		
1995–96	Coventry C	34	14		
1996–97	Coventry C	34	13		
1997–98	Coventry C	36	18		
1998–99	Coventry C	10	3	**145**	**61**
1998–99	Aston Villa	24	11		
1999–2000	Aston Villa	26	12		
2000–01	Aston Villa	33	8		
2001–02	Aston Villa	21	4		
2001–02	*Millwall*	5	2	**5**	**2**
2002–03	Aston Villa	28	10		
2003–04	Aston Villa	23	3	**155**	**48**
2004–05	Leicester C	37	5		
2005–06	Leicester C	21	0	**58**	**5**
2005–06	Celtic	11	1		
2006–07	Celtic	0	0	**11**	**1**
2006–07	Norwich C	33	5		
2007–08	Norwich C	37	7	**70**	**12**

EAGLE, Robert (M) **10 0**
H: 5 7 W: 10 08 b.Leiston 23-2-87
Source: Scholar.

2006–07	Norwich C	10	0		
2007–08	Norwich C	0	0	**10**	**0**

FOTHERINGHAM, Mark (M) **118 6**
H: 5 7 W: 12 00 b.Dundee 22-10-83
Honours: Scotland Youth, Under-20, Under-21, B.

1999–2000	Celtic	2	0		
2000–01	Celtic	1	0		
2001–02	Celtic	0	0		
2002–03	Celtic	0	0	**3**	**0**
2003–04	Dundee	24	4		
2004–05	Dundee	27	0	**51**	**4**
2005–06	Freiburg	9	0	**9**	**0**
2006–07	Aarau	13	0	**13**	**0**
2006–07	Norwich C	14	0		
2007–08	Norwich C	28	2	**42**	**2**

GILKS, Matthew (G) **176 0**
H: 6 3 W: 13 12 b.Rochdale 4-6-82
Source: Scholar.

2000–01	Rochdale	3	0		
2001–02	Rochdale	19	0		
2002–03	Rochdale	20	0		
2003–04	Rochdale	12	0		
2004–05	Rochdale	30	0		
2005–06	Rochdale	46	0		
2006–07	Rochdale	46	0	**176**	**0**
2007–08	Norwich C	0	0		

HALLIDAY, Matthew (D) **3 0**
H: 6 2 W: 12 05 b.Norwich 21-1-87
Source: Scholar.

2006–07	Norwich C	0	0		
2006–07	*Torquay U*	3	0	**3**	**0**
2007–08	Norwich C	0	0		

HUCKERBY, Darren (F) **437 106**
H: 5 10 W: 12 09 b.Nottingham 23-4-76
Source: Trainee. *Honours:* England Under-21, B.

1993–94	Lincoln C	6	1		
1994–95	Lincoln C	6	2		
1995–96	Lincoln C	16	2	**28**	**5**
1995–96	Newcastle U	1	0		
1996–97	Newcastle U	0	0	**1**	**0**
1996–97	*Millwall*	6	3	**6**	**3**
1996–97	Coventry C	25	5		
1997–98	Coventry C	34	14		
1998–99	Coventry C	34	9		
1999–2000	Coventry C	1	0	**94**	**28**
1999–2000	Leeds U	33	2		
2000–01	Leeds U	7	0	**40**	**2**
2000–01	Manchester C	13	1		
2001–02	Manchester C	40	20		
2002–03	Manchester C	16	1		
2002–03	*Nottingham F*	9	5	**9**	**5**
2003–04	Manchester C	0	0	**69**	**22**
2003–04	Norwich C	36	14		
2004–05	Norwich C	37	6		
2005–06	Norwich C	43	8		
2006–07	Norwich C	40	8		
2007–08	Norwich C	34	5	**190**	**41**

JARVIS, Rossi (D) **21 0**
H: 5 11 W: 11 12 b.Fakenham 11-3-88
Source: Scholar. *Honours:* England Youth.

2005–06	Norwich C	3	0		
2006–07	Norwich C	0	0		
2006–07	*Torquay U*	4	0	**4**	**0**
2006–07	*Rotherham U*	10	0	**10**	**0**
2007–08	Norwich C	4	0	**7**	**0**

JARVIS, Ryan (F) **75** **12**
H: 6 1 W: 11 11 b.Fakenham 11-7-86
Source: Scholar. *Honours:* FA Schools, England Youth.

2002–03	Norwich C	3	0		
2003–04	Norwich C	12	1		
2004–05	Norwich C	4	1		
2004–05	*Colchester U*	6	0	**6**	**0**
2005–06	Norwich C	4	1		
2006–07	Norwich C	5	0		
2006–07	*Leyton Orient*	14	6	**14**	**6**
2007–08	Norwich C	1	0	**29**	**3**
2007–08	*Kilmarnock*	9	1	**9**	**1**
2007–08	*Notts Co*	17	2	**17**	**2**

LAPPIN, Simon (M) **43** **4**
H: 5 11 W: 9 06 b.Glasgow 25-1-83
Honours: Scotland Under-21.

2006–07	Norwich C	14	1		
2007–08	*Motherwell*	14	2	**14**	**2**
2007–08	Norwich C	15	1	**29**	**2**

LATHROPE, Damon (M) **0** **0**
b. 28-10-89
Source: Scholar.

2007–08	Norwich C	0	0		

MARSHALL, David (G) **83** **0**
H: 6 3 W: 13 04 b.Glasgow 5-3-85
Source: Celtic Youth. *Honours:* Scotland Youth, Under-21, B, 2 full caps.

2003–04	Celtic	11	0		
2004–05	Celtic	18	0		
2005–06	Celtic	4	0		
2006–07	Celtic	2	0	**35**	**0**
2006–07	Norwich C	2	0		
2007–08	Norwich C	46	0	**48**	**0**

MARTIN, Chris (F) **25** **4**
H: 6 2 W: 12 06 b.Beccles 4-11-88
Source: Scholar. *Honours:* England Youth.

2006–07	Norwich C	18	4		
2007–08	Norwich C	7	0	**25**	**4**

MURRAY, Ian (M) **9** **0**
H: 5 10 W: 11 05 b.Edinburgh 20-3-81
Honours: Scotland Under-21, 6 full caps.

2007–08	Norwich C	9	0	**9**	**0**

To Hibernian January 2008.

OTSEMOBOR, John (D) **124** **5**
H: 5 10 W: 12 07 b.Liverpool 23-3-83
Source: Trainee. *Honours:* England Youth, Under-20.

1999–2000	Liverpool	0	0		
2000–01	Liverpool	0	0		
2001–02	Liverpool	0	0		
2002–03	Liverpool	0	0		
2002–03	*Hull C*	9	3	**9**	**3**
2003–04	Liverpool	4	0		
2003–04	*Bolton W*	1	0	**1**	**0**
2004–05	Liverpool	0	0	**4**	**0**
2004–05	*Crewe Alex*	14	1		
2005–06	Rotherham U	10	0	**10**	**0**
2005–06	Crewe Alex	16	0		
2006–07	Crewe Alex	27	0	**57**	**1**
2007–08	Norwich C	43	1	**43**	**1**

PATTISON, Matt (M) **37** **0**
H: 5 9 W: 11 00 b.Johannesburg 27-10-86
Source: Scholar.

2005–06	Newcastle U	3	0		
2006–07	Newcastle U	7	0		
2007–08	Newcastle U	0	0	**10**	**0**
2007–08	Norwich C	27	0	**27**	**0**

RENTON, Kris (F) **3** **0**
H: 6 3 W: 12 06 b.Musselburgh 12-7-90
Source: Scholar.

2006–07	Norwich C	3	0		
2007–08	Norwich C	0	0	**3**	**0**

RUSSELL, Darel (M) **342** **27**
H: 5 10 W: 11 09 b.Mile End 22-10-80
Source: Trainee. *Honours:* England Youth.

1997–98	Norwich C	1	0		
1998–99	Norwich C	13	1		
1999–2000	Norwich C	33	4		
2000–01	Norwich C	41	2		
2001–02	Norwich C	23	0		
2002–03	Norwich C	21	0		
2003–04	Stoke C	46	4		
2004–05	Stoke C	45	2		
2005–06	Stoke C	37	3		
2006–07	Stoke C	43	7	**171**	**16**
2007–08	Norwich C	39	4	**171**	**11**

SHACKELL, Jason (D) **118** **3**
H: 6 4 W: 13 06 b.Stevenage 27-9-83
Source: Scholar.

2002–03	Norwich C	2	0		
2003–04	Norwich C	6	0		
2004–05	Norwich C	11	0		
2005–06	Norwich C	17	0		
2006–07	Norwich C	43	3		
2007–08	Norwich C	39	0	**118**	**3**

SMART, Bally (M) **9** **0**
H: 5 10 W: 10 00 b.Polokwane 27-4-89
Source: Scholar.

2006–07	Norwich C	1	0		
2007–08	Norwich C	0	0	**1**	**0**
2007–08	*Milton Keynes D*	8	0	**8**	**0**

SPILLANE, Michael (M) **13** **0**
H: 5 9 W: 11 10 b.Cambridge 23-3-89
Source: Scholar. *Honours:* Eire Youth, Under-21.

2005–06	Norwich C	2	0		
2006–07	Norwich C	5	0		
2007–08	Norwich C	6	0	**13**	**0**

STRIHAVKA, David (F) **62** **18**
H: 6 2 W: 12 11 b.Prague 4-3-83
Source: Bohemians, Sparta Prague, Jablonec, Bohemians. *Honours:* Czech Republic Youth.

2004–05	Sparta Prague	2	0	**2**	**0**
2004–05	Chmel Blsany	11	2	**11**	**2**
2005–06	Banik Ostrava	11	2		
2006–07	Banik Ostrava	28	13	**39**	**15**
2007–08	Norwich C	10	1	**10**	**1**

VELASCO, Juan (M) **284** **5**
H: 5 10 W: 11 11 b.Seville 17-5-77
Honours: Spain 4 full caps.

1996–97	Sevilla	13	0		
1997–98	Sevilla	34	2		
1998–99	Sevilla	34	2	**81**	**4**
1999–2000	Celta Vigo	29	1		
2000–01	Celta Vigo	33	0		
2001–02	Celta Vigo	16	0		
2002–03	Celta Vigo	31	0		
2003–04	Celta Vigo	25	0	**134**	**1**
2004–05	Atletico Madrid	21	0		
2005–06	Atletico Madrid	25	0	**46**	**0**
2006–07	Espanyol	20	0	**20**	**0**
2007–08	Norwich C	3	0	**3**	**0**

NOTTINGHAM F (59)

AGOGO, Junior (F) **213** **68**
H: 5 10 W: 11 07 b.Accra 1-8-79
Source: Willesden. *Honours:* Ghana 19 full caps, 10 goals.

1996–97	Sheffield W	0	0		
1997–98	Sheffield W	1	0		
1998–99	Sheffield W	1	0		
1999–2000	Sheffield W	0	0	**2**	**0**
1999–2000	*Oldham Ath*	2	0	**2**	**0**
1999–2000	*Chester C*	10	6	**10**	**6**
1999–2000	*Chesterfield*	4	0	**4**	**0**
1999–2000	*Lincoln C*	3	1	**3**	**1**

From Colorado R, San Jose E.

2001–02	QPR	2	0	**2**	**0**
2002–03	Barnet	0	0		
2003–04	Bristol R	38	6		
2004–05	Bristol R	43	19		
2005–06	Bristol R	42	16		
2006–07	Bristol R	3	0	**126**	**41**
2006–07	Nottingham F	29	7		
2007–08	Nottingham F	35	13	**64**	**20**

BASTIANS, Felix (M) **36** **2**
H: 6 2 W: 12 00 b.Bochum 9-5-88
Source: Scholar. *Honours:* Germany Youth.

2005–06	Nottingham F	11	0		
2006–07	Nottingham F	2	0		
2006–07	*Gillingham*	5	1	**5**	**1**
2007–08	Nottingham F	1	0	**14**	**0**
2007–08	*Chesterfield*	12	1	**12**	**1**
2007–08	*Milton Keynes D*	0	0		
2007–08	*Notts Co*	5	0	**5**	**0**

BENCHERIF, Hamza (D) **12** **1**
H: 5 9 W: 12 03 b.France 9-2-88
Source: Scholar.

2006–07	Nottingham F	0	0		
2007–08	*Lincoln C*	12	1	**12**	**1**

BENNETT, Julian (D) **133** **11**
H: 6 1 W: 13 00 b.Nottingham 17-12-84
Source: Scholar.

2003–04	Walsall	1	0		
2004–05	Walsall	31	2		
2005–06	Walsall	19	1	**51**	**3**
2005–06	Nottingham F	18	2		
2006–07	Nottingham F	30	2		
2007–08	Nottingham F	34	4	**82**	**8**

BRECKIN, Ian (D) **560** **26**
H: 6 2 W: 13 05 b.Rotherham 24-2-75
Source: Trainee.

1993–94	Rotherham U	10	0		
1994–95	Rotherham U	41	2		
1995–96	Rotherham U	39	1		
1996–97	Rotherham U	42	3	**132**	**6**
1997–98	Chesterfield	43	1		
1998–99	Chesterfield	44	2		
1999–2000	Chesterfield	38	1		
2000–01	Chesterfield	45	3		
2001–02	Chesterfield	42	1	**212**	**8**
2002–03	Wigan Ath	9	0		
2003–04	Wigan Ath	45	0		
2004–05	Wigan Ath	42	0	**96**	**0**
2005–06	Nottingham F	46	8		
2006–07	Nottingham F	46	3		
2007–08	Nottingham F	28	1	**120**	**12**

BYRNE, Mark (M) **1** **0**
b.Dublin 9-11-88

2006–07	Nottingham F	0	0		
2007–08	Nottingham F	1	0	**1**	**0**

CHAMBERS, Luke (D) **180** **7**
H: 6 1 W: 11 13 b.Kettering 29-8-85
Source: Scholar.

2002–03	Northampton T	1	0		
2003–04	Northampton T	24	0		
2004–05	Northampton T	27	0		
2005–06	Northampton T	43	0		
2006–07	Northampton T	29	1	**124**	**1**
2006–07	Nottingham F	14	0		
2007–08	Nottingham F	42	6	**56**	**6**

CLINGAN, Sammy (M) **121** **4**
H: 5 11 W: 11 06 b.Belfast 13-1-84
Source: Scholar. *Honours:* Northern Ireland Schools, Youth, Under-21, Under-23, 15 full caps.

2001–02	Wolverhampton W	0	0		
2002–03	Wolverhampton W	0	0		
2003–04	Wolverhampton W	0	0		
2004–05	Wolverhampton W	0	0		
2004–05	*Chesterfield*	15	2		
2005–06	Wolverhampton W	0	0		
2005–06	*Chesterfield*	21	1	**36**	**3**
2005–06	Nottingham F	15	0		
2006–07	Nottingham F	28	0		
2007–08	Nottingham F	42	1	**85**	**1**

COHEN, Chris (M) **133** **9**
H: 5 11 W: 10 11 b.Norwich 5-3-87
Source: Scholar. *Honours:* England Youth.

2003–04	West Ham U	7	0		
2004–05	West Ham U	11	0		
2005–06	West Ham U	0	0	**18**	**0**
2005–06	*Yeovil T*	30	1		
2006–07	Yeovil T	44	6	**74**	**7**
2007–08	Nottingham F	41	2	**41**	**2**

COMMONS, Kris (M) **179** **37**
H: 5 6 W: 9 08 b.Mansfield 30-8-83
Source: Scholar.

2000–01	Stoke C	0	0		
2001–02	Stoke C	0	0		
2002–03	Stoke C	8	1		
2003–04	Stoke C	33	4	**41**	**5**
2004–05	Nottingham F	30	6		
2005–06	Nottingham F	37	8		
2006–07	Nottingham F	32	9		
2007–08	Nottingham F	39	9	**138**	**32**

DAVIES, Arron (M) **124** **23**
H: 5 9 W: 11 00 b.Cardiff 22-6-84
Source: Trainee. *Honours:* Wales Under-21, 1 full cap.

2002–03	Southampton	0	0		
2003–04	Southampton	0	0		
2003–04	*Barnsley*	4	0	**4**	**0**
2004–05	Southampton	0	0		
2004–05	Yeovil T	23	8		
2005–06	Yeovil T	39	8		

2006–07 Yeovil T 39 6 **101 22**
2007–08 Nottingham F 19 1 **19 1**

GAMBLE, Paddy (G) 0 0
b.Nottingham 1-9-88
Source: Scholar. *Honours:* England Youth.
2005–06 Nottingham F 0 0
2006–07 Nottingham F 0 0
2007–08 Nottingham F 0 0

HEATH, Joe (D) 0 0
b.Birkenhead 4-10-88
2005–06 Nottingham F 0 0
2006–07 Nottingham F 0 0
2007–08 Nottingham F 0 0

HOLT, Grant (F) 205 59
H: 6 1 W: 14 02 b.Carlisle 12-4-81
Source: Workington.
1999–2000 Halifax T 4 0
2000–01 Halifax T 2 0 **6 0**
From Sengkang,Barrow
2002–03 Sheffield W 7 1
2003–04 Sheffield W 17 2 **24 3**
2003–04 Rochdale 14 4
2004–05 Rochdale 40 17
2005–06 Rochdale 21 14 **75 35**
2005–06 Nottingham F 19 4
2006–07 Nottingham F 45 14
2007–08 Nottingham F 32 3 **96 21**
2007–08 *Blackpool* 4 0 **4 0**

KAVANAGH, Gavin (D) 0 0
b.Dublin
Source: Crumlin U.
2007–08 Nottingham F 0 0

LOCKWOOD, Matt (D) 402 51
H: 5 11 W: 11 10 b.Southend 17-10-76
Source: Trainee.
1994–95 QPR 0 0
1995–96 QPR 0 0
1996–97 Bristol R 39 1
1997–98 Bristol R 24 0 **63 1**
1998–99 Leyton Orient 37 3
1999–2000 Leyton Orient 41 6
2000–01 Leyton Orient 32 7
2001–02 Leyton Orient 24 2
2002–03 Leyton Orient 43 5
2003–04 Leyton Orient 25 2
2004–05 Leyton Orient 43 6
2005–06 Leyton Orient 42 8
2006–07 Leyton Orient 41 11 **328 50**
2007–08 Nottingham F 11 0 **11 0**

McCLEARY, Garath (F) 8 1
H: 5 10 W: 12 06 b.Oxford 15-5-87
Source: Bromley.
2007–08 Nottingham F 8 1 **8 1**

McGUGAN, Lewis (M) 46 8
H: 5 9 W: 11 06 b.Long Eaton 25-10-88
Source: Scholar.
2006–07 Nottingham F 13 2
2007–08 Nottingham F 33 6 **46 8**

MITCHELL, Aaron (D) 0 0
b. *Honours:* 5-2-90
Source: Scholar.
2007–08 Nottingham F 0 0

MOLONEY, Brendan (M) 12 1
H: 6 1 W: 11 12 b.Enfield 18-1-89
Source: Scholar.
2005–06 Nottingham F 0 0
2006–07 Nottingham F 1 0
2007–08 Nottingham F 2 0 **3 0**
2007–08 *Chesterfield* 9 1 **9 1**

MORGAN, Wes (D) 203 7
H: 6 2 W: 14 00 b.Nottingham 21-1-84
Source: Scholar.
2002–03 Nottingham F 0 0
2002–03 *Kidderminster H* 5 1 **5 1**
2003–04 Nottingham F 32 2
2004–05 Nottingham F 43 1
2005–06 Nottingham F 43 2
2006–07 Nottingham F 38 0
2007–08 Nottingham F 42 1 **198 6**

NEWBOLD, Adam (F) 0 0
b.Nottingham 16-11-89
Source: Scholar.
2006–07 Nottingham F 0 0
2007–08 Nottingham F 0 0

PERCH, James (D) 136 8
H: 5 11 W: 11 05 b.Mansfield 29-9-85
Source: Scholar.
2002–03 Nottingham F 0 0
2003–04 Nottingham F 0 0
2004–05 Nottingham F 22 0
2005–06 Nottingham F 38 3
2006–07 Nottingham F 46 5
2007–08 Nottingham F 30 0 **136 8**

REDMOND, Shane (G) 0 0
b.Dublin 23-3-89
Source: Scholar.
2006–07 Nottingham F 0 0
2007–08 Nottingham F 0 0

REID, James (D) 0 0
b.Ashbourne 28-2-90
Source: Scholar. *Honours:* England Youth.
2007–08 Nottingham F 0 0

ROBERTS, Dale (M) 0 0
H: 6 3 W: 11 06 b.Horden 22-10-86
Source: Scholar.
2005–06 Nottingham F 0 0
2006–07 Nottingham F 0 0
2007–08 Nottingham F 0 0

SHARPE, Thomas (D) 0 0
b.Nottingham 12-10-88
Source: Scholar.
2007–08 Nottingham F 0 0

SINCLAIR, Emile (F) 16 1
H: 6 0 W: 11 04 b.Leeds 20-12-87
Source: Scholar.
2007–08 Nottingham F 12 1 **12 1**
2007–08 *Brentford* 4 0 **4 0**

SMITH, Paul (G) 193 0
H: 6 3 W: 14 00 b.Epsom 17-12-79
Source: Walton & Hersham.
1998–99 Charlton Ath 0 0
1998–99 *Brentford* 0 0
1999–2000 Charlton Ath 0 0
From Carshalton Ath.
2000–01 Brentford 2 0
2001–02 Brentford 18 0
2002–03 Brentford 43 0
2003–04 Brentford 24 0 **87 0**
2003–04 Southampton 0 0
2004–05 Southampton 6 0
2005–06 Southampton 9 0 **15 0**
2006–07 Nottingham F 45 0
2007–08 Nottingham F 46 0 **91 0**

STAPLES, Reece (M) 0 0
b.Nottingham 10-9-89
Source: Scholar.
2006–07 Nottingham F 0 0
2007–08 Nottingham F 0 0

TAIT, Richard (D) 0 0
b.Gallashields 2-12-89
Source: Curzon Ashton.
2007–08 Nottingham F 0 0

THORNHILL, Matt (M) 14 2
H: 6 1 W: 13 10 b.Nottingham 11-10-88
Source: Scholar.
2007–08 Nottingham F 14 2 **14 2**

TYSON, Nathan (F) 216 71
H: 5 10 W: 10 02 b.Reading 4-5-82
Source: Trainee. *Honours:* England Under-20.
1999–2000 Reading 1 0
2000–01 Reading 0 0
2001–02 Reading 1 0
2001–02 *Swansea C* 11 1 **11 1**
2001–02 *Cheltenham T* 8 1 **8 1**
2002–03 Reading 23 1
2003–04 Reading 8 0 **33 1**
2003–04 Wycombe W 21 9
2004–05 Wycombe W 42 22
2005–06 Wycombe W 15 11 **78 42**
2005–06 Nottingham F 28 10
2006–07 Nottingham F 24 7
2007–08 Nottingham F 34 9 **86 26**

WILSON, Kelvin (D) 147 4
H: 6 2 W: 12 12 b.Nottingham 3-9-85
Source: Scholar.
2003–04 Notts Co 3 0
2004–05 Notts Co 41 2
2005–06 Notts Co 34 1 **78 3**
2005–06 *Preston NE* 6 0
2006–07 Preston NE 21 1 **27 1**
2007–08 Nottingham F 42 0 **42 0**

NOTTS CO (60)

AKERS, Steven (M) 0 0
H: 5 7 W: 10 07 b.Worksop 26-9-89
Source: Scholar.
2006–07 Notts Co 0 0
2007–08 Notts Co 0 0

AUSTIN, Rob (D) 0 0
b. *Honours:* 15-2-89
Source: Scholar.
2007–08 Notts Co 0 0

BRANSTON, Guy (D) 245 18
H: 6 1 W: 15 01 b.Leicester 9-1-79
Source: Trainee.
1997–98 Leicester C 0 0
1997–98 *Colchester U* 12 1
1998–99 Leicester C 0 0
1998–99 *Colchester U* 1 0 **13 1**
1998–99 *Plymouth Arg* 7 1 **7 1**
1999–2000 Leicester C 0 0
1999–2000 *Lincoln C* 4 0 **4 0**
1999–2000 Rotherham U 30 4
2000–01 Rotherham U 41 6
2001–02 Rotherham U 10 1
2002–03 Rotherham U 15 2
2003–04 Rotherham U 8 0 **104 13**
2003–04 *Wycombe W* 9 0 **9 0**
2003–04 *Peterborough U* 14 0
2004–05 Sheffield W 11 0 **11 0**
2004–05 *Peterborough U* 4 1
2004–05 Oldham Ath 7 1
2005–06 Oldham Ath 38 1 **45 2**
2006–07 Peterborough U 24 0
2007–08 Peterborough U 2 0 **44 1**
2007–08 *Rochdale* 4 0 **4 0**
2007–08 *Northampton T* 3 0 **3 0**
2007–08 Notts Co 1 0 **1 0**

BUTCHER, Richard (M) 233 32
H: 6 0 W: 13 01 b.Peterborough 22-1-81
Source: Kettering T.
2002–03 Lincoln C 26 3
2003–04 Lincoln C 32 6
2004–05 Lincoln C 46 2
2005–06 Oldham Ath 36 4 **36 4**
2005–06 *Lincoln C* 4 1 **108 12**
2006–07 Peterborough U 43 4 **43 4**
2007–08 Notts Co 46 12 **46 12**

CANOVILLE, Lee (D) 215 3
H: 6 1 W: 12 00 b.Ealing 14-3-81
Source: Trainee. *Honours:* FA Schools, England Youth.
1998–99 Arsenal 0 0
1999–2000 Arsenal 0 0
2000–01 Arsenal 0 0
2000–01 *Northampton T* 2 0 **2 0**
2001–02 Torquay U 12 1
2002–03 Torquay U 36 0
2003–04 Torquay U 33 1
2004–05 Torquay U 31 0 **112 2**
2005–06 Boston U 43 1
2006–07 Boston U 16 0 **59 1**
2006–07 *Shrewsbury T* 7 0 **7 0**
2007–08 Notts Co 35 0 **35 0**

DUDFIELD, Lawrie (F) 272 43
H: 6 1 W: 13 05 b.Southwark 7-5-80
Source: Kettering T.
1997–98 Leicester C 0 0
1998–99 Leicester C 0 0
1999–2000 Leicester C 2 0
2000–01 Leicester C 0 0 **2 0**
2000–01 *Lincoln C* 3 0 **3 0**
2000–01 *Chesterfield* 14 3 **14 3**
2001–02 Hull C 38 12
2002–03 Hull C 21 1 **59 13**
2002–03 Northampton T 10 1
2003–04 Northampton T 19 3
2003–04 Southend U 13 5
2004–05 Southend U 36 4 **49 9**
2005–06 Northampton T 6 1 **35 5**
2005–06 Boston U 36 5 **36 5**
2006–07 Notts Co 41 7
2007–08 Notts Co 33 1 **74 8**

EDWARDS, Mike (D) **335 18**
H: 6 0 W: 12 10 b.Hessle 25-4-80
Source: Trainee.
1997–98 Hull C 21 0
1998–99 Hull C 30 0
1999–2000 Hull C 40 1
2000–01 Hull C 42 4
2001–02 Hull C 39 1
2002–03 Hull C 6 0 **178 6**
2002–03 Colchester U 5 0 **5 0**
2003–04 Grimsby T 33 1 **33 1**
2004–05 Notts Co 9 0
2005–06 Notts Co 46 7
2006–07 Notts Co 45 3
2007–08 Notts Co 19 1 **119 11**

FROST, Stef (M) **6 0**
H: 6 2 W: 11 05 b.Nottingham 3-7-89
Source: Scholar.
2005–06 Notts Co 4 0
2006–07 Notts Co 0 0
2007–08 Notts Co 2 0 **6 0**

HUNT, Stephen (D) **91 4**
H: 6 2 W: 13 00 b.Southampton 11-11-84
Source: Southampton Scholar.
2004–05 Colchester U 20 1
2005–06 Colchester U 2 0 **22 1**
2006–07 Notts Co 32 1
2007–08 Notts Co 37 2 **69 3**

LEE, Jason (F) **519 107**
H: 6 3 W: 13 08 b.Forest Gate 9-5-71
Source: Trainee.
1989–90 Charlton Ath 1 0
1990–91 Charlton Ath 0 0
1990–91 *Stockport Co* 2 0 **2 0**
1990–91 Lincoln C 17 3
1991–92 Lincoln C 35 6
1992–93 Lincoln C 41 12 **93 21**
1993–94 Southend U 24 3 **24 3**
1993–94 Nottingham F 13 2
1994–95 Nottingham F 22 3
1995–96 Nottingham F 28 8
1996–97 Nottingham F 13 1 **76 14**
1996–97 *Charlton Ath* 8 3 **9 3**
1996–97 *Grimsby T* 7 1 **7 1**
1997–98 Watford 36 10
1998–99 Watford 1 1 **37 11**
1998–99 Chesterfield 22 1
1999–2000 Chesterfield 6 0 **28 1**
1999–2000 Peterborough U 23 6
2000–01 Peterborough U 30 8
2001–02 Peterborough U 0 0
2002–03 Peterborough U 25 3 **78 17**
2003–04 Falkirk 29 8 **29 8**
2004–05 Boston U 39 9
2005–06 Boston U 17 2 **56 11**
2005–06 Northampton T 11 1 **11 1**
2006–07 Notts Co 38 15
2007–08 Notts Co 31 1 **69 16**

MACKENZIE, Neil (M) **280 21**
H: 6 2 W: 12 05 b.Birmingham 15-4-76
Source: WBA schoolboy.
1996–97 Stoke C 22 1
1997–98 Stoke C 12 0
1998–99 Stoke C 6 0
1998–99 *Cambridge U* 4 1
1999–2000 Stoke C 2 0 **42 1**
1999–2000 Cambridge U 22 0
2000–01 Cambridge U 6 0 **32 1**
2000–01 Kidderminster H 23 3 **23 3**
2001–02 Blackpool 14 1 **14 1**
2002–03 Mansfield T 24 1
2003–04 Mansfield T 32 2
2004–05 Mansfield T 15 1 **71 4**
2004–05 Macclesfield T 18 0
2005–06 Macclesfield T 6 1 **24 1**
2005–06 Scunthorpe U 14 2
2006–07 Scunthorpe U 24 2 **38 4**
2006–07 *Hereford U* 7 0 **7 0**
2007–08 Notts Co 29 6 **29 6**

MAYO, Paul (D) **229 11**
H: 5 11 W: 11 09 b.Lincoln 13-10-81
Source: Scholarship.
1999–2000 Lincoln C 19 0
2000–01 Lincoln C 27 0
2001–02 Lincoln C 14 0
2002–03 Lincoln C 15 0
2003–04 Lincoln C 31 6
2003–04 Watford 12 0
2004–05 Watford 13 0 **25 0**
2005–06 Lincoln C 28 3
2006–07 Lincoln C 34 1 **168 10**
2007–08 Notts Co 29 0 **29 0**
2007–08 *Darlington* 7 1 **7 1**

McCANN, Austin (D) **284 9**
H: 5 9 W: 11 13 b.Alexandria 21-1-80
Source: Wolverhampton W Trainee.
1997–98 Airdrieonians 14 0
1998–99 Airdrieonians 31 4
1999–2000 Airdrieonians 29 2
2000–01 Airdrieonians 20 1 **94 7**
2000–01 Hearts 10 0
2001–02 Hearts 6 0
2002–03 Hearts 17 1
2003–04 Hearts 6 0 **39 1**
2003–04 Clyde 6 0 **6 0**
2004–05 Boston U 45 1
2005–06 Boston U 35 0 **80 1**
2006–07 Notts Co 43 0
2007–08 Notts Co 22 0 **65 0**

PARKINSON, Andy (F) **338 38**
H: 5 8 W: 10 12 b.Liverpool 27-5-79
Source: Liverpool Trainee.
1996–97 Tranmere R 0 0
1997–98 Tranmere R 18 1
1998–99 Tranmere R 29 2
1999–2000 Tranmere R 37 7
2000–01 Tranmere R 39 6
2001–02 Tranmere R 31 2
2002–03 Tranmere R 10 0 **164 18**
2003–04 Sheffield U 7 0 **7 0**
2003–04 *Notts Co* 14 3
2004–05 Grimsby T 45 8
2005–06 Grimsby T 40 4 **85 12**
2006–07 Notts Co 45 5
2007–08 Notts Co 23 0 **82 8**

PILKINGTON, Kevin (G) **335 0**
H: 6 1 W: 13 00 b.Hitchin 8-3-74
Source: Trainee. *Honours:* England Schools.
1992–93 Manchester U 0 0
1993–94 Manchester U 0 0
1994–95 Manchester U 1 0
1995–96 Manchester U 3 0
1995–96 *Rochdale* 6 0 **6 0**
1996–97 Manchester U 0 0
1996–97 *Rotherham U* 17 0 **17 0**
1997–98 Manchester U 2 0
1998–99 Manchester U 0 0 **6 0**
1998–99 Port Vale 8 0
1999–2000 Port Vale 15 0 **23 0**
2000–01 Macclesfield T 0 0
2000–01 Wigan Ath 0 0
2000–01 Mansfield T 2 0
2001–02 Mansfield T 45 0
2002–03 Mansfield T 32 0
2003–04 Mansfield T 46 0
2004–05 Mansfield T 42 0 **167 0**
2005–06 Notts Co 45 0
2006–07 Notts Co 39 0
2007–08 Notts Co 32 0 **116 0**

SAM, Hector (F) **216 43**
H: 5 10 W: 12 07 b.Mount Hope 25-2-78
Source: San Juan Jabloteh. *Honours:* Trinidad & Tobago Under-21, 20 full caps, 2 goals.
2000–01 Wrexham 20 6
2001–02 Wrexham 29 5
2002–03 Wrexham 26 5
2003–04 Wrexham 37 10
2004–05 Wrexham 38 9 **150 35**
2005–06 Port Vale 4 0 **4 0**
2006–07 Walsall 42 7 **42 7**
2007–08 Notts Co 20 1 **20 1**

SANDERCOMBE, Timothy (G) **0 0**
H: 6 4 W: 13 12 b.Plymouth 15-6-89
Source: Plymouth Arg.
2007–08 Notts Co 0 0

SILK, Gary (M) **99 2**
H: 5 9 W: 13 07 b.Newport (IW) 13-9-84
Source: Scholar.
2003–04 Portsmouth 0 0
2004–05 Portsmouth 0 0
2004–05 *Wycombe W* 22 0 **22 0**
2005–06 Portsmouth 0 0
2005–06 *Boston U* 14 0 **14 0**
2006–07 Notts Co 30 0
2007–08 Notts Co 33 2 **63 2**

SMITH, Jay (M) **115 11**
H: 5 7 W: 12 00 b.Lambeth 24-9-81
Source: Scholar.
2000–01 Aston Villa 0 0
2001–02 Aston Villa 0 0
2002–03 Aston Villa 0 0
2002–03 Southend U 31 5
2003–04 Southend U 18 1
2004–05 Southend U 0 0
2005–06 Southend U 13 1
2005–06 *Oxford U* 6 0 **6 0**
2006–07 Southend U 0 0 **62 7**
2006–07 Notts Co 27 4
2007–08 Notts Co 20 0 **47 4**

SOMNER, Matt (D) **163 2**
H: 6 0 W: 13 00 b.Isleworth 8-12-82
Source: Trainee. *Honours:* Wales Under-21.
2000–01 Brentford 3 0
2001–02 Brentford 0 0
2002–03 Brentford 40 1
2003–04 Brentford 39 0
2004–05 Brentford 2 0 **84 1**
2004–05 Cambridge U 24 0 **24 0**
2005–06 Bristol R 1 0 **1 0**
From Aldershot T.
2006–07 Notts Co 38 1
2007–08 Notts Co 16 0 **54 1**

STRACHAN, Gavin (M) **139 10**
H: 5 10 W: 11 07 b.Aberdeen 23-12-78
Source: Trainee. *Honours:* Scotland Youth, Under-21.
1996–97 Coventry C 0 0
1997–98 Coventry C 9 0
1998–99 Coventry C 0 0
1998–99 *Dundee* 6 0 **6 0**
1999–2000 Coventry C 3 0
2000–01 Coventry C 2 0
2001–02 Coventry C 1 0
2002–03 Coventry C 1 0 **16 0**
2002–03 *Peterborough U* 2 0
2002–03 Southend U 7 0 **7 0**
2003–04 Hartlepool U 36 5
2004–05 Hartlepool U 29 1
2005–06 Hartlepool U 9 1
2005–06 *Stockport Co* 4 0 **4 0**
2006–07 Hartlepool U 4 0 **78 7**
2006–07 Peterborough U 16 3
2007–08 Peterborough U 3 0 **21 3**
2007–08 Notts Co 7 0 **7 0**

TANN, Adam (D) **198 7**
H: 6 0 W: 11 05 b.Fakenham 12-5-82
Source: Scholar. *Honours:* England Youth.
1999–2000 Cambridge U 0 0
2000–01 Cambridge U 1 0
2001–02 Cambridge U 25 0
2002–03 Cambridge U 25 1
2003–04 Cambridge U 34 2
2004–05 Cambridge U 36 1 **121 4**
From Gravesend & N.
2005–06 Notts Co 5 0
2005–06 Leyton Orient 10 1
2006–07 Leyton Orient 21 1 **31 2**
2007–08 Notts Co 41 1 **46 1**

WEIR-DALEY, Spencer (F) **60 12**
H: 5 9 W: 10 11 b.Leicester 5-9-85
Source: Scholar.
2003–04 Nottingham F 0 0
2004–05 Nottingham F 0 0
2005–06 Nottingham F 6 1
2006–07 Nottingham F 1 0 **7 1**
2006–07 *Macclesfield T* 7 2 **7 2**
2006–07 *Lincoln C* 11 5 **11 5**
2006–07 *Bradford C* 5 1 **5 1**
2007–08 Notts Co 30 3 **30 3**

WESTON, Myles (F) **29 0**
H: 5 11 W: 12 05 b.Lewisham 12-3-88
Source: Scholar.
2006–07 Charlton Ath 0 0
2006–07 *Notts Co* 4 0
2007–08 Notts Co 25 0 **29 0**

OLDHAM ATH (61)

ALESSANDRA, Lewis (F) **15 2**
H: 5 9 W: 11 07 b.Oldham 8-2-89
Source: Scholar.
2007–08 Oldham Ath 15 2 **15 2**

ALLOTT, Mark (M) 417 46
H: 5 11 W: 11 07 b.Manchester 3-10-77
Source: Trainee.

1995–96	Oldham Ath	0	0		
1996–97	Oldham Ath	5	1		
1997–98	Oldham Ath	22	2		
1998–99	Oldham Ath	41	7		
1999–2000	Oldham Ath	32	10		
2000–01	Oldham Ath	39	7		
2001–02	Oldham Ath	15	4		
2001–02	Chesterfield	21	4		
2002–03	Chesterfield	33	0		
2003–04	Chesterfield	40	2		
2004–05	Chesterfield	45	2		
2005–06	Chesterfield	43	3		
2006–07	Chesterfield	39	0	**221**	**11**
2007–08	Oldham Ath	42	4	**196**	**35**

BLACK, Paul (D) 2 0
H: 6 0 W: 12 10 b.Middleton 18-1-90
Source: Scholar.

2007–08	Oldham Ath	2	0	**2**	**0**

CHALMERS, Aaron (M) 2 0
H: 5 10 W: 12 08 b.Manchester 2-2-91
Source: Scholar.

2007–08	Oldham Ath	2	0	**2**	**0**

CROSSLEY, Mark (G) 426 1
H: 6 3 W: 15 09 b.Barnsley 16-6-69
Source: Trainee. *Honours:* England Under-21, B, Wales B, 8 full caps.

1987–88	Nottingham F	0	0		
1988–89	Nottingham F	2	0		
1989–90	Nottingham F	8	0		
1989–90	*Manchester U*	0	0		
1990–91	Nottingham F	38	0		
1991–92	Nottingham F	36	0		
1992–93	Nottingham F	37	0		
1993–94	Nottingham F	37	0		
1994–95	Nottingham F	42	0		
1995–96	Nottingham F	38	0		
1996–97	Nottingham F	33	0		
1997–98	Nottingham F	0	0		
1997–98	*Millwall*	13	0	**13**	**0**
1998–99	Nottingham F	12	0		
1999–2000	Nottingham F	20	0	**303**	**0**
2000–01	Middlesbrough	5	0		
2001–02	Middlesbrough	18	0		
2002–03	Middlesbrough	0	0	**23**	**0**
2002–03	*Stoke C*	12	0	**12**	**0**
2003–04	Fulham	1	0		
2004–05	Fulham	6	0		
2005–06	Fulham	13	0		
2006–07	Fulham	0	0	**20**	**0**
2006–07	*Sheffield W*	17	1	**17**	**1**
2007–08	Oldham Ath	38	0	**38**	**0**

DAVIES, Craig (F) 103 18
H: 6 2 W: 13 05 b.Burton-on-Trent 9-1-86
Source: Manchester C.Wales Youth, Under-21, 5 full caps.

2004–05	Oxford U	28	6		
2005–06	Oxford U	20	2	**48**	**8**
2005–06	Verona	0	0		
2006–07	Wolverhampton W	23	0	**23**	**0**
2007–08	Oldham Ath	32	10	**32**	**10**

EARDLEY, Neal (M) 79 8
H: 5 11 W: 11 10 b.Llandudno 6-11-88
Source: Scholar. *Honours:* Wales Under-21, 7 full caps.

2005–06	Oldham Ath	1	0		
2006–07	Oldham Ath	36	2		
2007–08	Oldham Ath	42	6	**79**	**8**

GREGAN, Sean (M) 533 18
H: 6 2 W: 14 00 b.Guisborough 29-3-74
Source: Trainee.

1991–92	Darlington	17	0		
1992–93	Darlington	17	1		
1993–94	Darlington	23	1		
1994–95	Darlington	25	2		
1995–96	Darlington	38	0		
1996–97	Darlington	16	0	**136**	**4**
1996–97	Preston NE	21	1		
1997–98	Preston NE	35	2		
1998–99	Preston NE	41	3		
1999–2000	Preston NE	33	3		
2000–01	Preston NE	41	2		
2001–02	Preston NE	41	1	**212**	**12**
2002–03	WBA	36	1		
2003–04	WBA	43	1		
2004–05	WBA	0	0	**79**	**2**
2004–05	Leeds U	35	0		
2005–06	Leeds U	28	0		
2006–07	Leeds U	1	0	**64**	**0**
2006–07	Oldham Ath	27	0		
2007–08	Oldham Ath	15	0	**42**	**0**

HAZELL, Reuben (D) 232 6
H: 5 11 W: 12 05 b.Birmingham 24-4-79
Source: Trainee.

1996–97	Aston Villa	0	0		
1997–98	Aston Villa	0	0		
1998–99	Aston Villa	0	0		
1999–2000	Tranmere R	23	1		
2000–01	Tranmere R	13	0		
2001–02	Tranmere R	6	0	**42**	**1**
2001–02	Torquay U	19	0		
2002–03	Torquay U	46	1		
2003–04	Torquay U	19	1		
2004–05	Torquay U	0	0	**84**	**2**
2005–06	Chesterfield	33	0		
2006–07	Chesterfield	39	2		
2007–08	Chesterfield	0	0	**72**	**2**
2007–08	Oldham Ath	34	1	**34**	**1**

HUGHES, Lee (F) 271 111
H: 5 10 W: 12 00 b.Smethwick 22-5-76
Source: Kidderminster H.

1997–98	WBA	37	14		
1998–99	WBA	42	31		
1999–2000	WBA	36	12		
2000–01	WBA	41	21		
2001–02	Coventry C	38	14		
2002–03	Coventry C	4	1	**42**	**15**
2002–03	WBA	23	0		
2003–04	WBA	32	11		
2004–05	WBA	0	0		
2005–06	WBA	0	0		
2006–07	WBA	0	0	**211**	**89**
2007–08	Oldham Ath	18	7	**18**	**7**

KAMUD'A KALALA, Jean-Paul (M)81 6
H: 5 10 W: 12 02 b.Lubumbashi 16-2-82
Honours: DR Congo 6 full caps.

2003–04	Nice	2	0		
2004–05	Nice	0	0	**2**	**0**
2005–06	Grimsby T	21	5	**21**	**5**
2006–07	Yeovil T	38	1	**38**	**1**
2007–08	Oldham Ath	20	0	**20**	**0**

KELLY, Ashley (M) 1 0
H: 5 8 W: 11 05 b.Aston-under-Lyne 22-12-88

2007–08	Oldham Ath	1	0	**1**	**0**

LEVER, Chris (D) 0 0
H: 5 11 W: 11 02 b.Oldham 13-2-87
Source: Scholar.

2006–07	Oldham Ath	0	0		
2007–08	Oldham Ath	0	0		

LIDDELL, Andy (F) 541 128
H: 5 7 W: 11 11 b.Leeds 28-6-73
Source: Trainee. *Honours:* Scotland Under-21.

1990–91	Barnsley	0	0		
1991–92	Barnsley	1	0		
1992–93	Barnsley	21	2		
1993–94	Barnsley	22	1		
1994–95	Barnsley	39	13		
1995–96	Barnsley	43	9		
1996–97	Barnsley	38	8		
1997–98	Barnsley	26	1		
1998–99	Barnsley	8	0	**198**	**34**
1998–99	Wigan Ath	28	10		
1999–2000	Wigan Ath	41	8		
2000–01	Wigan Ath	37	9		
2001–02	Wigan Ath	34	18		
2002–03	Wigan Ath	37	16		
2003–04	Wigan Ath	40	9	**217**	**70**
2004–05	Sheffield U	33	3	**33**	**3**
2005–06	Oldham Ath	29	9		
2006–07	Oldham Ath	46	10		
2007–08	Oldham Ath	18	2	**93**	**21**

LOMAX, Kelvin (D) 50 0
H: 5 11 W: 12 03 b.Bury 12-11-86
Source: Scholar.

2003–04	Oldham Ath	1	0		
2004–05	Oldham Ath	9	0		
2005–06	Oldham Ath	0	0		
2006–07	Oldham Ath	9	0		
2007–08	Oldham Ath	21	0	**40**	**0**
2007–08	*Rochdale*	10	0	**10**	**0**

McDONALD, Gary (F) 184 22
H: 6 0 W: 11 06 b.Irvine 10-4-82
Honours: Scotland B.

1999–2000	Kilmarnock	0	0		
2000–01	Kilmarnock	0	0		
2001–02	Kilmarnock	6	0		
2002–03	Kilmarnock	12	2		
2003–04	Kilmarnock	23	3		
2004–05	Kilmarnock	38	3		
2005–06	Kilmarnock	27	3	**106**	**11**
2006–07	Oldham Ath	43	7		
2007–08	Oldham Ath	35	4	**78**	**11**

PEARSON, Michael (M) 2 0
H: 5 11 W: 11 01 b.Bangor 19-1-88
Source: Scholar.

2006–07	Oldham Ath	1	0		
2007–08	Oldham Ath	1	0	**2**	**0**

POGLIACOMI, Les (G) 280 0
H: 6 4 W: 13 02 b.Sydney 3-5-76
Honours: Australia Schools, Under-20.

1994–95	Marconi Stallions	11	0		
1995–96	Marconi Stallions	1	0		
1996–97	Marconi Stallions	10	0	**22**	**0**
1997–98	Adelaide City	0	0		
1998–99	Wollongong W	22	0		
1999–2000	Wollongong W	34	0	**56**	**0**
2000–01	Parramatta Power	8	0		
2001–02	Parramatta Power	19	0	**27**	**0**
2002–03	Oldham Ath	37	0		
2003–04	Oldham Ath	46	0		
2004–05	Oldham Ath	37	0		
2005–06	Oldham Ath	0	0		
2005–06	Blackpool	15	0	**15**	**0**
2006–07	Oldham Ath	40	0		
2007–08	Oldham Ath	0	0	**160**	**0**

PORTER, Chris (F) 137 46
H: 6 1 W: 12 09 b.Wigan 12-12-83
Source: School.

2002–03	Bury	2	0		
2003–04	Bury	37	9		
2004–05	Bury	32	9	**71**	**18**
2005–06	Oldham Ath	31	7		
2006–07	Oldham Ath	35	21		
2007–08	Oldham Ath	0	0	**66**	**28**

RICKETTS, Michael (F) 309 67
H: 6 2 W: 11 12 b.Birmingham 4-12-78
Source: Trainee. *Honours:* England 1 full cap.

1995–96	Walsall	1	1		
1996–97	Walsall	11	1		
1997–98	Walsall	24	1		
1998–99	Walsall	8	0		
1999–2000	Walsall	32	11		
2000–01	Bolton W	39	19		
2001–02	Bolton W	37	12		
2002–03	Bolton W	22	6	**98**	**37**
2002–03	Middlesbrough	9	1		
2003–04	Middlesbrough	23	2	**32**	**3**
2004–05	Leeds U	21	0		
2004–05	*Stoke C*	11	0	**11**	**0**
2005–06	Leeds U	4	0	**25**	**0**
2005–06	*Cardiff C*	17	5	**17**	**5**
2005–06	*Burnley*	13	2	**13**	**2**
2006–07	Southend U	2	0	**2**	**0**
2006–07	Preston NE	14	1	**14**	**1**
2007–08	Oldham Ath	9	2	**9**	**2**
2007–08	*Walsall*	12	3	**88**	**17**

SMALLEY, Deane (M) 39 2
H: 6 0 W: 11 10 b.Chadderton 5-9-88
Source: Scholar.

2006–07	Oldham Ath	2	0		
2007–08	Oldham Ath	37	2	**39**	**2**

STAM, Stefan (D) 84 1
H: 6 2 W: 13 02 b.Amersfoort 14-9-79
Honours: Holland Under-21.

2004–05	Oldham Ath	13	0		
2005–06	Oldham Ath	13	0		
2006–07	Oldham Ath	22	1		
2007–08	Oldham Ath	36	0	**84**	**1**

TAYLOR, Chris (M) 100 9
H: 5 11 W: 11 00 b.Oldham 20-12-86
Source: Scholar.

2005–06	Oldham Ath	14	0		
2006–07	Oldham Ath	44	4		
2007–08	Oldham Ath	42	5	**100**	**9**

THOMPSON, John (D) 148 7
H: 6 0 W: 12 01 b.Dublin 12-10-81
Source: Home Farm. *Honours:* Eire Youth, Under-21, 1 full cap.
1999–2000 Nottingham F 0 0
2000–01 Nottingham F 0 0
2001–02 Nottingham F 8 0
2002–03 Nottingham F 20 3
2003–04 Nottingham F 32 1
2004–05 Nottingham F 20 0
2005–06 Nottingham F 35 3
2006–07 Nottingham F 14 0 **129 7**
2006–07 *Tranmere R* 12 0 **12 0**
2007–08 Oldham Ath 7 0 **7 0**

WOLFENDEN, Matthew (F) 34 2
H: 5 9 W: 11 02 b.Oldham 23-7-87
Source: Scholar.
2003–04 Oldham Ath 1 0
2004–05 Oldham Ath 1 0
2005–06 Oldham Ath 1 0
2006–07 Oldham Ath 6 0
2007–08 Oldham Ath 25 2 **34 2**

PETERBOROUGH U (62)

ARBER, Mark (D) 325 25
H: 6 1 W: 11 09 b.Johannesburg 9-10-77
Source: Trainee.
1995–96 Tottenham H 0 0
1996–97 Tottenham H 0 0
1997–98 Tottenham H 0 0
1998–99 Tottenham H 0 0
1998–99 Barnet 35 2
1999–2000 Barnet 45 6
2000–01 Barnet 45 7
2001–02 Barnet 0 0 **125 15**
2002–03 Peterborough U 25 2
2003–04 Peterborough U 44 3
2004–05 Oldham Ath 14 1 **14 1**
2004–05 Peterborough U 21 0
2005–06 Peterborough U 46 2
2006–07 Peterborough U 34 1
2007–08 Peterborough U 0 0 **170 8**
2007–08 *Dagenham & R* 16 1 **16 1**

BLACKETT, Shane (D) 24 0
H: 6 0 W: 12 11 b.Luton 26-6-81
Source: Arlesey, Dagenham & R.
2006–07 Peterborough U 13 0
2007–08 Peterborough U 11 0 **24 0**

BLANCHETT, Danny (D) 4 1
H: 5 11 W: 11 12 b.Wembley 12-3-88
Source: Northwood, Hendon, Harrow Borough, Cambridge C.
2006–07 Peterborough U 3 1
2007–08 Peterborough U 1 0 **4 1**

BOYD, George (M) 66 18
H: 5 10 W: 11 07 b.Chatham 2-10-85
Source: Stevenage B.
2006–07 Peterborough U 20 6
2007–08 Peterborough U 46 12 **66 18**

CHARNOCK, Kieran (D) 10 0
H: 6 1 W: 13 07 b.Preston 3-8-84
Source: Scholar.
2002–03 Wigan Ath 0 0
2003–04 Wigan Ath 0 0
2004–05 Wigan Ath 0 0
2005–06 Wigan Ath 0 0
2006–07 Wigan Ath 0 0
From Southport, Northwich Vic.
2007–08 Peterborough U 10 0 **10 0**

CROW, Danny (F) 104 27
H: 5 10 W: 11 00 b.Great Yarmouth 26-1-86
Source: Scholar.
2004–05 Norwich C 3 0 **3 0**
2004–05 *Northampton T* 10 2 **10 2**
2005–06 Peterborough U 38 15
2006–07 Peterborough U 35 6
2007–08 Peterborough U 4 2 **77 23**
2007–08 *Notts Co* 14 2 **14 2**

DAY, Jamie (M) 92 5
H: 5 9 W: 10 07 b.Wycombe 7-5-86
Source: Scholar.
2003–04 Peterborough U 0 0
2004–05 Peterborough U 1 0
2005–06 Peterborough U 25 1
2006–07 Peterborough U 24 1
2007–08 Peterborough U 42 3 **92 5**

GNAPKA, Claude (D) 28 0
H: 6 0 W: 13 05 b.Marseille 9-6-83
Source: Montpellier, Santander, Alaves, Vaduz.
2006–07 Swindon T 0 0
2007–08 Peterborough U 28 0 **28 0**

HATCH, Liam (F) 98 13
H: 6 4 W: 13 09 b.Hitchin 3-4-84
Source: Herne Bay, Gravesend & N.
2005–06 Barnet 35 2
2006–07 Barnet 31 3
2007–08 Barnet 21 6 **87 11**
2007–08 Peterborough U 11 2 **11 2**

HOWE, Rene (F) 35 10
H: 6 0 W: 14 03 b.Bedford 22-10-86
Source: Kettering T.
2007–08 Peterborough U 15 1 **15 1**
2007–08 *Rochdale* 20 9 **20 9**

HYDE, Micah (M) 517 38
H: 5 10 W: 11 02 b.Newham 10-11-74
Source: Trainee. *Honours:* Jamaica 16 full caps, 1 goal.
1993–94 Cambridge U 18 2
1994–95 Cambridge U 27 0
1995–96 Cambridge U 24 4
1996–97 Cambridge U 38 7 **107 13**
1997–98 Watford 40 4
1998–99 Watford 44 2
1999–2000 Watford 34 3
2000–01 Watford 26 6
2001–02 Watford 39 4
2002–03 Watford 37 4
2003–04 Watford 33 1 **253 24**
2004–05 Burnley 38 1
2005–06 Burnley 41 0
2006–07 Burnley 23 0 **102 1**
2006–07 Peterborough U 18 0
2007–08 Peterborough U 37 0 **55 0**

JALAL, Shwan (G) 20 0
H: 6 2 W: 14 02 b.Baghdad 14-8-83
Source: Hastings T.
2001–02 Tottenham H 0 0
2002–03 Tottenham H 0 0
2003–04 Tottenham H 0 0
From Woking.
2006–07 *Sheffield W* 0 0
2006–07 Peterborough U 1 0
2007–08 Peterborough U 7 0 **8 0**
2007–08 *Morecambe* 12 0 **12 0**

KEATES, Dean (M) 372 44
H: 5 6 W: 10 06 b.Walsall 30-6-78
Source: Trainee.
1996–97 Walsall 2 0
1997–98 Walsall 33 1
1998–99 Walsall 43 2
1999–2000 Walsall 35 1
2000–01 Walsall 33 4
2001–02 Walsall 13 1
2002–03 Hull C 36 4
2003–04 Hull C 14 0 **50 4**
2003–04 Kidderminster H 8 2
2004–05 Kidderminster H 41 5 **49 7**
2005–06 Lincoln C 21 4 **21 4**
2005–06 Walsall 14 2
2006–07 Walsall 39 13 **212 24**
2007–08 Peterborough U 40 5 **40 5**

LEE, Charlie (M) 47 6
H: 5 11 W: 11 07 b.Whitechapel 5-1-87
Source: Scholar.
2005–06 Tottenham H 0 0
2006–07 Tottenham H 0 0
2006–07 *Millwall* 5 0 **5 0**
2007–08 Peterborough U 42 6 **42 6**

LEWIS, Joe (G) 46 0
H: 6 5 W: 12 10 b.Bury St Edmunds 6-10-87
Source: Scholar. *Honours:* England Youth, Under-21.
2004–05 Norwich C 0 0
2005–06 Norwich C 0 0
2006–07 Norwich C 0 0
2006–07 *Stockport Co* 5 0 **5 0**
2007–08 Norwich C 0 0
2007–08 *Morecambe* 19 0 **19 0**
2007–08 Peterborough U 22 0 **22 0**

LOW, Josh (M) 275 28
H: 6 2 W: 14 03 b.Bristol 15-2-79
Source: Trainee. *Honours:* Wales Youth, Under-21.
1995–96 Bristol R 1 0
1996–97 Bristol R 3 0
1997–98 Bristol R 10 0
1998–99 Bristol R 8 0 **22 0**
1999–2000 Leyton Orient 5 1 **5 1**
1999–2000 Cardiff C 17 2
2000–01 Cardiff C 36 4
2001–02 Cardiff C 22 0
2002–03 Cardiff C 0 0 **75 6**
2002–03 Oldham Ath 21 3 **21 3**
2003–04 Northampton T 33 3
2004–05 Northampton T 34 7
2005–06 Northampton T 35 5 **102 15**
2006–07 Leicester C 16 0 **16 0**
2006–07 Peterborough U 19 1
2007–08 Peterborough U 15 2 **34 3**

MACKAIL-SMITH, Craig (F) 51 20
H: 6 3 W: 12 04 b.Hertford 25-2-84
Source: Dagenham & R.
2006–07 Peterborough U 15 8
2007–08 Peterborough U 36 12 **51 20**

McKEOWN, James (G) 1 0
H: 6 1 W: 13 07 b.Sutton Coldfield 24-7-89
Source: Scholar.
2005–06 Walsall 0 0
2006–07 Walsall 0 0
2007–08 Peterborough U 1 0 **1 0**

McLEAN, Aaron (F) 101 38
H: 5 9 W: 10 10 b.Hammersmith 25-5-83
Source: Trainee.
1999–2000 Leyton Orient 3 0
2000–01 Leyton Orient 2 1
2001–02 Leyton Orient 27 1
2002–03 Leyton Orient 8 0 **40 2**
From Aldershot T, Grays Ath.
2006–07 Peterborough U 16 7
2007–08 Peterborough U 45 29 **61 36**

MITCHELL, Scott (M) 48 4
H: 5 11 W: 12 00 b.Ely 2-9-85
Source: Scholar.
2003–04 Ipswich T 2 0
2004–05 Ipswich T 0 0
2005–06 Ipswich T 0 0 **2 0**
2006–07 Livingston 32 4
2007–08 Livingston 9 0 **41 4**
2007–08 Peterborough U 5 0 **5 0**

MORGAN, Craig (D) 160 4
H: 6 0 W: 11 04 b.St Asaph 18-6-85
Source: Scholar. *Honours:* Wales Youth, Under-21, 8 full caps.
2001–02 Wrexham 2 0
2002–03 Wrexham 6 1
2003–04 Wrexham 18 0
2004–05 Wrexham 26 0
2005–06 Milton Keynes D 40 0
2006–07 Milton Keynes D 3 0 **43 0**
2006–07 *Wrexham* 1 0 **53 1**
2006–07 Peterborough U 23 1
2007–08 Peterborough U 41 2 **64 3**

NEWTON, Adam (M) 253 10
H: 5 10 W: 11 00 b.Ascot 4-12-80
Source: West Ham U Trainee. *Honours:* England Under-21. St Kitts & Nevis 2 full caps, 1 goal.
1999–2000 West Ham U 2 0
1999–2000 *Portsmouth* 3 0 **3 0**
2000–01 West Ham U 0 0
2000–01 *Notts Co* 20 1 **20 1**
2001–02 West Ham U 0 0 **2 0**
2001–02 *Leyton Orient* 10 1 **10 1**
2002–03 Peterborough U 36 2
2003–04 Peterborough U 37 2
2004–05 Peterborough U 30 0
2005–06 Peterborough U 40 3
2006–07 Peterborough U 43 1
2007–08 Peterborough U 32 0 **218 8**

POTTER, Alfie (M) 2 0
H: 5 7 W: 9 06 b. 9-1-89
Source: Millwall.
2007–08 Peterborough U 2 0 **2 0**

RENDELL, Scott (F) **10 3**
H: 6 1 W: 13 00 b.Ashford 21-10-86
Source: Aldershot T, Forest Green R, Crawley T.
On loan from Cambridge U.
2007–08 Peterborough U 10 3 **10 3**

SMITH, Adam (D) **9 1**
H: 5 7 W: 10 05 b.Lingwood 11-9-85
Source: Norwich C Scholar.
From Kings Lynn.
2006–07 Peterborough U 9 1
2007–08 Peterborough U 0 0 **9 1**

TYLER, Mark (G) **413 0**
H: 6 0 W: 12 09 b.Norwich 2-4-77
Source: Trainee. *Honours:* England Youth, Under-20.
1994–95 Peterborough U 5 0
1995–96 Peterborough U 0 0
1996–97 Peterborough U 3 0
1997–98 Peterborough U 46 0
1998–99 Peterborough U 27 0
1999–2000 Peterborough U 32 0
2000–01 Peterborough U 40 0
2001–02 Peterborough U 44 0
2002–03 Peterborough U 29 0
2003–04 Peterborough U 43 0
2004–05 Peterborough U 46 0
2005–06 Peterborough U 40 0
2006–07 Peterborough U 41 0
2007–08 Peterborough U 17 0 **413 0**

WESTWOOD, Chris (D) **360 13**
H: 5 11 W: 12 10 b.Dudley 13-2-77
Source: Trainee.
1995–96 Wolverhampton W 0 0
1996–97 Wolverhampton W 0 0
1997–98 Wolverhampton W 4 1
1998–99 Wolverhampton W 0 0 **4 1**
1998–99 Hartlepool U 4 0
1999–2000 Hartlepool U 37 0
2000–01 Hartlepool U 46 1
2001–02 Hartlepool U 35 1
2002–03 Hartlepool U 46 1
2003–04 Hartlepool U 45 0
2004–05 Hartlepool U 37 4 **250 7**
2005–06 Walsall 29 3
2006–07 Walsall 40 2 **69 5**
2007–08 Peterborough U 37 0 **37 0**

WHELPDALE, Chris (M) **35 3**
H: 6 0 W: 12 08 b.Harold Wood 27-1-87
Source: Billericay T.
2006–07 Peterborough U 0 0
2007–08 Peterborough U 35 3 **35 3**

WILLIAMS, Tom (M) **207 4**
H: 5 11 W: 12 06 b.Carshalton 8-7-80
Source: Walton & Hersham. *Honours:* Cyprus 1 full cap.
1999–2000 West Ham U 0 0
2000–01 West Ham U 0 0
2000–01 *Peterborough U* 2 0
2001–02 Peterborough U 34 2
2001–02 Birmingham C 4 0
2002–03 Birmingham C 0 0
2002–03 *QPR* 26 1
2003–04 Birmingham C 0 0 **4 0**
2003–04 *QPR* 5 0 **31 1**
2003–04 *Peterborough U* 21 1
2004–05 Barnsley 39 0 **39 0**
2005–06 Gillingham 13 0 **13 0**
2005–06 Swansea C 17 0
2006–07 Swansea C 29 0 **46 0**
2007–08 Wycombe W 10 0 **10 0**
2007–08 Peterborough U 7 0 **64 3**

PLYMOUTH ARG (63)

ABDOU, Nadjim (M) **137 4**
H: 5 10 W: 11 02 b.Martigues 13-7-84
2002–03 Martigues 26 1 **26 1**
2003–04 Sedan 17 0
2004–05 Sedan 32 2
2005–06 Sedan 14 0
2006–07 Sedan 17 0 **80 2**
2007–08 Plymouth Arg 31 1 **31 1**

BARNES, Ashley (F) **0 0**
H: 6 0 W: 12 00 b.Bath 30-10-89
Source: Paulton R.
2006–07 Plymouth Arg 0 0
2007–08 Plymouth Arg 0 0

CHADWICK, Nick (F) **112 17**
H: 6 0 W: 12 08 b.Market Drayton 26-10-82
Source: Scholar.
1999–2000 Everton 0 0
2000–01 Everton 0 0
2001–02 Everton 9 3
2002–03 Everton 1 0
2002–03 *Derby Co* 6 0 **6 0**
2003–04 Everton 3 0
2003–04 *Millwall* 15 4 **15 4**
2004–05 Everton 1 0 **14 3**
2004–05 Plymouth Arg 15 1
2005–06 Plymouth Arg 37 5
2006–07 Plymouth Arg 16 2
2007–08 Plymouth Arg 9 2 **77 10**

CLARK, Chris (F) **193 8**
H: 5 7 W: 10 05 b.Aberdeen 15-9-80
1999–2000 Aberdeen 2 0
2000–01 Aberdeen 24 0
2001–02 Aberdeen 8 0
2002–03 Aberdeen 25 1
2003–04 Aberdeen 23 1
2004–05 Aberdeen 31 2
2005–06 Aberdeen 31 3
2006–07 Aberdeen 37 1 **181 8**
2007–08 Plymouth Arg 12 0 **12 0**

CONNOLLY, Paul (D) **162 1**
H: 6 0 W: 11 09 b.Liverpool 29-9-83
Source: Scholar.
2000–01 Plymouth Arg 1 0
2001–02 Plymouth Arg 0 0
2002–03 Plymouth Arg 2 0
2003–04 Plymouth Arg 29 0
2004–05 Plymouth Arg 19 0
2005–06 Plymouth Arg 31 0
2006–07 Plymouth Arg 38 0
2007–08 Plymouth Arg 42 1 **162 1**

DJORDJIC, Bojan (M) **69 4**
H: 5 10 W: 11 01 b.Belgrade 6-2-82
Honours: Sweden Under-21.
1998–99 Manchester U 0 0
1999–2000 Manchester U 0 0
2000–01 Manchester U 1 0
2001–02 Manchester U 0 0
2001–02 *Sheffield W* 5 0 **5 0**
2002–03 Manchester U 0 0
2003–04 *Red St Belgrade* 19 0 **19 0**
2004–05 Manchester U 0 0 **1 0**
2004–05 Rangers 4 0 **4 0**
2005–06 Plymouth Arg 22 1
2006–07 Plymouth Arg 17 3
2007–08 Plymouth Arg 1 0 **40 4**

DOUMBE, Stephen (D) **155 5**
H: 6 1 W: 12 05 b.Paris 28-10-79
Source: Paris St Germain. *Honours:* France Youth.
2001–02 Hibernian 0 0
2002–03 Hibernian 12 0
2003–04 Hibernian 33 2 **45 2**
2004–05 Plymouth Arg 26 2
2005–06 Plymouth Arg 43 1
2006–07 Plymouth Arg 29 0
2007–08 Plymouth Arg 12 0 **110 3**

EASTER, Jermaine (F) **185 48**
H: 5 9 W: 12 02 b.Cardiff 15-1-82
Source: Trainee. *Honours:* Wales Youth, 7 full caps.
2000–01 Wolverhampton W 0 0
2000–01 Hartlepool U 4 0
2001–02 Hartlepool U 12 2
2002–03 Hartlepool U 8 0
2003–04 Hartlepool U 3 0 **27 2**
2003–04 *Cambridge U* 15 2
2004–05 Cambridge U 24 6 **39 8**
2004–05 Boston U 9 3 **9 3**
2005–06 Stockport Co 19 8 **19 8**
2005–06 Wycombe W 15 2
2006–07 Wycombe W 38 17
2007–08 Wycombe W 6 2 **59 21**
2007–08 Plymouth Arg 32 6 **32 6**

FALLON, Rory (F) **229 53**
H: 6 2 W: 11 09 b.Gisbourne 20-3-82
Source: North Shore U. *Honours:* England Youth.
1998–99 Barnsley 0 0
1999–2000 Barnsley 0 0
2000–01 Barnsley 1 0
2001–02 Barnsley 9 0
2001–02 *Shrewsbury T* 11 0 **11 0**
2002–03 Barnsley 26 7
2003–04 Barnsley 16 4 **52 11**
2003–04 Swindon T 19 6
2004–05 Swindon T 31 3
2004–05 *Yeovil T* 6 1 **6 1**
2005–06 Swindon T 25 12 **75 21**
2005–06 Swansea C 17 4
2006–07 Swansea C 24 8 **41 12**
2006–07 Plymouth Arg 15 1
2007–08 Plymouth Arg 29 7 **44 8**

FOLLY, Yoann (M) **74 0**
H: 5 9 W: 11 04 b.Togo 6-6-85
Source: St Etienne. *Honours:* France Youth, Under-21.
2003–04 Southampton 9 0
2004–05 Southampton 3 0
2004–05 *Nottingham F* 1 0 **1 0**
2004–05 *Preston NE* 2 0 **2 0**
2005–06 Southampton 2 0 **14 0**
2005–06 *Sheffield W* 14 0
2006–07 Sheffield W 29 0
2007–08 Sheffield W 10 0 **53 0**
2007–08 Plymouth Arg 4 0 **4 0**

HALMOSI, Peter (M) **253 39**
H: 5 10 W: 10 12 b.Szombathely 25-9-79
Honours: Hungary 18 full caps.
1998–99 Haladas 2 0
1999–2000 Haladas 26 2
2000–01 Haladas 14 2
2001–02 Haladas 38 2 **80 6**
2002–03 Graz 17 3 **17 3**
2003–04 Debrecen 29 5
2004–05 Debrecen 28 5
2005–06 Debrecen 26 7
2006–07 Debrecen 14 1 **97 18**
2006–07 Plymouth Arg 16 4
2007–08 Plymouth Arg 43 8 **59 12**

HODGES, Lee (M) **394 49**
H: 6 0 W: 12 01 b.Epping 4-9-73
Source: Trainee.
1991–92 Tottenham H 0 0
1992–93 Tottenham H 4 0
1992–93 *Plymouth Arg* 7 2
1993–94 Tottenham H 0 0 **4 0**
1993–94 *Wycombe W* 4 0 **4 0**
1994–95 Barnet 34 4
1995–96 Barnet 40 17
1996–97 Barnet 31 5 **105 26**
1997–98 Reading 24 6
1998–99 Reading 1 0
1999–2000 Reading 25 2
2000–01 Reading 29 2
2001–02 Reading 0 0 **79 10**
2001–02 Plymouth Arg 45 6
2002–03 Plymouth Arg 39 2
2003–04 Plymouth Arg 37 3
2004–05 Plymouth Arg 19 0
2005–06 Plymouth Arg 13 0
2006–07 Plymouth Arg 15 0
2007–08 Plymouth Arg 27 0 **202 13**

KENDALL, Paul (D) **0 0**
Source: Scholar.
2007–08 Plymouth Arg 0 0

LAIRD, Scott (D) **0 0**
H: 5 11 W: 11 05 b.Taunton 15-5-88
Source: Scholar.
2006–07 Plymouth Arg 0 0
2007–08 Plymouth Arg 0 0

LARRIEU, Romain (G) **218 0**
H: 6 4 W: 13 01 b.Mont-de-Marsan 31-8-76
Source: Montpellier, ASOA Valence.
Honours: France Youth.
2000–01 Plymouth Arg 15 0
2001–02 Plymouth Arg 45 0
2002–03 Plymouth Arg 43 0
2003–04 Plymouth Arg 6 0
2004–05 Plymouth Arg 23 0
2005–06 Plymouth Arg 45 0
2006–07 Plymouth Arg 6 0

Season	Club	App	Gls	Tot App	Tot Gls
2006–07	*Gillingham*	14	0	**14**	**0**
2007–08	Plymouth Arg	15	0	**198**	**0**
2007–08	*Yeovil T*	6	0	**6**	**0**

MACLEAN, Steve (F) **160 59**
H: 5 11 W: 12 06 b.Edinburgh 23-8-82
Honours: Scotland Under-21.

Season	Club	App	Gls	Tot App	Tot Gls
2002–03	Rangers	3	0	**3**	**0**
2003–04	Scunthorpe U	42	23	**42**	**23**
2004–05	Sheffield W	36	18		
2005–06	Sheffield W	6	2		
2006–07	Sheffield W	41	12	**83**	**32**
2007–08	Cardiff C	15	1	**15**	**1**
2007–08	Plymouth Arg	17	3	**17**	**3**

MACKIE, Jamie (F) **29 3**
H: 5 8 W: 11 00 b.Dorking 22-9-85
Source: Leatherhead.

Season	Club	App	Gls	Tot App	Tot Gls
2003–04	Wimbledon	13	0	**13**	**0**
2004–05	Milton Keynes D	3	0	**3**	**0**
From Exeter C					
2007–08	Plymouth Arg	13	3	**13**	**3**

MASON, Anthony (F) **0 0**
H: 5 11 W: 12 01 b.Plymouth 10-10-88

Season	Club	App	Gls	Tot App	Tot Gls
2007–08	Plymouth Arg	0	0		

McCORMICK, Luke (G) **140 0**
H: 6 0 W: 13 12 b.Coventry 15-8-83
Source: Scholar.

Season	Club	App	Gls	Tot App	Tot Gls
2000–01	Plymouth Arg	1	0		
2001–02	Plymouth Arg	0	0		
2002–03	Plymouth Arg	3	0		
2003–04	Plymouth Arg	40	0		
2004–05	Plymouth Arg	23	0		
2004–05	*Boston U*	2	0	**2**	**0**
2005–06	Plymouth Arg	1	0		
2006–07	Plymouth Arg	40	0		
2007–08	Plymouth Arg	30	0	**138**	**0**

MOULT, Jake (M) **0 0**
H: 5 11 W: 10 08 b.Stoke 10-2-89
Source: Port Vale.

Season	Club	App	Gls	Tot App	Tot Gls
2007–08	Plymouth Arg	0	0		

NALIS, Lilian (M) **419 33**
H: 6 1 W: 11 00 b.Nogent sur Marne 29-9-71

Season	Club	App	Gls	Tot App	Tot Gls
1992–93	Auxerre	0	0		
1993–94	Caen	16	0		
1994–95	Caen	4	0	**20**	**0**
1995–96	Laval	42	4		
1996–97	Laval	39	8	**81**	**12**
1997–98	Guingamp	30	0	**30**	**0**
1998–99	Le Havre	27	3	**27**	**3**
1999–2000	Bastia	28	1		
2000–01	Bastia	28	1		
2001–02	Bastia	26	2	**82**	**4**
2002–03	Chievo	8	0	**8**	**0**
2003–04	Leicester C	20	1		
2004–05	Leicester C	39	5	**59**	**6**
2005–06	Sheffield U	4	0	**4**	**0**
2005–06	*Coventry C*	6	2	**6**	**2**
2005–06	Plymouth Arg	20	1		
2006–07	Plymouth Arg	42	4		
2007–08	Plymouth Arg	40	1	**102**	**6**

PATERSON, Jim (M) **201 11**
H: 5 11 W: 12 13 b.Airdrie 25-9-79
Source: Dundee U BC. *Honours:* Scotland Under-21.

Season	Club	App	Gls	Tot App	Tot Gls
1998–99	Dundee U	15	0		
1999–2000	Dundee U	8	1		
2000–01	Dundee U	6	1		
2001–02	Dundee U	27	2		
2002–03	Dundee U	33	1		
2003–04	Dundee U	16	0	**105**	**5**
2004–05	Motherwell	35	3		
2005–06	Motherwell	19	1		
2006–07	Motherwell	34	1	**88**	**5**
2007–08	Plymouth Arg	8	1	**8**	**1**

To Motherwell January 2008.

SAMBA, Cherno (M) **21 1**
H: 5 10 W: 10 01 b.Gambia 10-1-85
Source: Scholar. *Honours:* England Youth, Under-20.

Season	Club	App	Gls	Tot App	Tot Gls
2001–02	Millwall	0	0		
2002–03	Millwall	0	0		
2003–04	Millwall	0	0		
2004–05	Cadiz	1	0	**1**	**0**
2005–06	Malaga B	4	0	**4**	**0**
2006–07	Plymouth Arg	13	1		
2006–07	*Wrexham*	3	0	**3**	**0**
2007–08	Plymouth Arg	0	0	**13**	**1**

SAWYER, Gary (D) **53 1**
H: 6 0 W: 11 08 b.Bideford 5-7-85
Source: Scholar.

Season	Club	App	Gls	Tot App	Tot Gls
2004–05	Plymouth Arg	0	0		
2005–06	Plymouth Arg	0	0		
2006–07	Plymouth Arg	22	0		
2007–08	Plymouth Arg	31	1	**53**	**1**

SEIP, Marcel (D) **193 5**
H: 6 0 W: 11 03 b.Winschoten 5-4-82

Season	Club	App	Gls	Tot App	Tot Gls
1999–2000	Veendam	9	0		
2000–01	Veendam	18	0	**27**	**0**
2001–02	Heerenveen	0	0		
2002–03	Heerenveen	6	0		
2003–04	Heerenveen	31	1		
2004–05	Heerenveen	30	1		
2005–06	Heerenveen	28	0	**95**	**2**
2006–07	Plymouth Arg	37	2		
2007–08	Plymouth Arg	34	1	**71**	**3**

SMITH, Dan (M) **2 0**
H: 5 10 W: 10 07 b.Saltash 5-10-86
Source: Scholar.

Season	Club	App	Gls	Tot App	Tot Gls
2007–08	Plymouth Arg	2	0	**2**	**0**

SUMMERFIELD, Luke (M) **39 2**
H: 6 0 W: 11 00 b.Ivybridge 6-12-87
Source: Scholar.

Season	Club	App	Gls	Tot App	Tot Gls
2004–05	Plymouth Arg	1	0		
2005–06	Plymouth Arg	0	0		
2006–07	Plymouth Arg	23	1		
2006–07	*Bournemouth*	8	1	**8**	**1**
2007–08	Plymouth Arg	7	0	**31**	**1**

TIMAR, Krisztian (D) **128 11**
H: 6 3 W: 13 08 b.Budapest 4-10-79
Source: Ferencvaros, MTK, Elore. *Honours:* Hungary Youth, Under-21, Under-23, 1 full cap.

Season	Club	App	Gls	Tot App	Tot Gls
2001–02	Videoton	31	4		
2002–03	Videoton	15	0	**46**	**4**
2003	Jokerit	0	0		
2003–04	Tatabanya	0	0		
2004–05	Nyiregyhaza	12	0	**12**	**0**
2005–06	Ferencvaros	23	3	**23**	**3**
2006–07	Plymouth Arg	9	1		
2007–08	Plymouth Arg	38	3	**47**	**4**

WATTS, Martin (D) **0 0**
H: 5 11 W: 10 08 b.Truro 20-11-88
Source: Scholar.

Season	Club	App	Gls	Tot App	Tot Gls
2007–08	Plymouth Arg	0	0		

WOTTON, Paul (D) **394 54**
H: 5 11 W: 12 00 b.Plymouth 17-8-77
Source: Trainee.

Season	Club	App	Gls	Tot App	Tot Gls
1994–95	Plymouth Arg	7	0		
1995–96	Plymouth Arg	1	0		
1996–97	Plymouth Arg	9	1		
1997–98	Plymouth Arg	34	1		
1998–99	Plymouth Arg	36	1		
1999–2000	Plymouth Arg	23	0		
2000–01	Plymouth Arg	42	4		
2001–02	Plymouth Arg	46	5		
2002–03	Plymouth Arg	43	8		
2003–04	Plymouth Arg	38	9		
2004–05	Plymouth Arg	40	12		
2005–06	Plymouth Arg	45	8		
2006–07	Plymouth Arg	22	4		
2007–08	Plymouth Arg	8	1	**394**	**54**

PORT VALE (64)

ANYON, Joe (G) **66 0**
H: 6 1 W: 12 11 b.Poulton-le-Fylde 29-12-86
Source: Scholar.

Season	Club	App	Gls	Tot App	Tot Gls
2005–06	Port Vale	0	0		
2006–07	Port Vale	22	0		
2007–08	Port Vale	44	0	**66**	**0**

BRISCOE, Louie (F) **0 0**
H: 6 0 W: 13 07 b.Burton-on-Trent 2-4-88
Source: Scholar.

Season	Club	App	Gls	Tot App	Tot Gls
2006–07	Port Vale	0	0		
2007–08	Port Vale	0	0		

CARDLE, Joe (M) **22 0**
H: 5 8 W: 9 05 b.Blackpool 27-2-87
Source: Scholar.

Season	Club	App	Gls	Tot App	Tot Gls
2005–06	Port Vale	6	0		
2006–07	Port Vale	7	0		
2007–08	Port Vale	9	0	**22**	**0**

CHAPMAN, Luke (M) **1 0**
H: 6 1 W: 11 10
Source: Scholar.

Season	Club	App	Gls	Tot App	Tot Gls
2007–08	Port Vale	1	0	**1**	**0**

DAVIDSON, Ross (M) **3 0**
H: 6 2 W: 11 05 b.Burton 6-9-89
Source: Scholar.

Season	Club	App	Gls	Tot App	Tot Gls
2007–08	Port Vale	3	0	**3**	**0**

ECKERSLEY, Adam (D) **24 1**
H: 5 9 W: 11 13 b.Manchester 7-9-85
Source: Scholar. *Honours:* England Youth.

Season	Club	App	Gls	Tot App	Tot Gls
2004–05	Manchester U	0	0		
2005–06	Manchester U	0	0		
2006–07	Manchester U	0	0		
2006–07	*Barnsley*	6	0	**6**	**0**
2007–08	Manchester U	0	0		
2007–08	Port Vale	18	1	**18**	**1**

EDWARDS, Paul (M) **212 9**
H: 5 11 W: 10 12 b.Manchester 1-1-80
Source: Altrincham.

Season	Club	App	Gls	Tot App	Tot Gls
2001–02	Swindon T	20	0	**20**	**0**
2002–03	Wrexham	38	4		
2003–04	Wrexham	41	0	**79**	**4**
2004–05	Blackpool	28	3	**28**	**3**
2005–06	Oldham Ath	34	0		
2006–07	Oldham Ath	26	0	**60**	**0**
2007–08	Port Vale	25	2	**25**	**2**

GARDNER, Ross (M) **44 1**
H: 5 8 W: 10 06 b.South Shields 15-12-85
Source: Scholar. *Honours:* England Youth, Under-20.

Season	Club	App	Gls	Tot App	Tot Gls
2001–02	Newcastle U	0	0		
2002–03	Newcastle U	0	0		
2003–04	Nottingham F	2	0		
2004–05	Nottingham F	14	0		
2005–06	Nottingham F	12	0		
2006–07	Nottingham F	0	0	**28**	**0**
2006–07	Port Vale	16	1		
2007–08	Port Vale	0	0	**16**	**1**

GLOVER, Danny (M) **15 1**
H: 6 0 W: 11 02 b.Crewe 24-10-89
Source: Scholar.

Season	Club	App	Gls	Tot App	Tot Gls
2007–08	Port Vale	15	1	**15**	**1**

GOODLAD, Mark (G) **215 0**
H: 6 1 W: 14 05 b.Barnsley 9-9-79
Source: Trainee.

Season	Club	App	Gls	Tot App	Tot Gls
1996–97	Nottingham F	0	0		
1997–98	Nottingham F	0	0		
1998–99	Nottingham F	0	0		
1998–99	*Scarborough*	3	0	**3**	**0**
1999–2000	Nottingham F	0	0		
1999–2000	Port Vale	1	0		
2000–01	Port Vale	40	0		
2001–02	Port Vale	43	0		
2002–03	Port Vale	37	0		
2003–04	Port Vale	0	0		
2004–05	Port Vale	20	0		
2005–06	Port Vale	46	0		
2006–07	Port Vale	25	0		
2007–08	Port Vale	0	0	**212**	**0**

GRIFFITH, Anthony (M) **10 0**
H: 6 0 W: 12 00 b.Huddersfield 28-10-86
Source: Glasshoughton W.

Season	Club	App	Gls	Tot App	Tot Gls
2005–06	Doncaster R	4	0		
2005–06	*Oxford U*	0	0		
2006–07	Doncaster R	2	0		
2006–07	*Darlington*	4	0	**4**	**0**
2007–08	Doncaster R	0	0	**6**	**0**
2007–08	Port Vale	0	0		

HARSLEY, Paul (M) **412 35**
H: 5 8 W: 11 05 b.Scunthorpe 29-5-78
Source: Trainee.

Season	Club	App	Gls	Tot App	Tot Gls
1996–97	Grimsby T	0	0		
1997–98	Scunthorpe U	15	1		
1998–99	Scunthorpe U	34	0		
1999–2000	Scunthorpe U	46	3		
2000–01	Scunthorpe U	33	1	**128**	**5**
2001–02	Halifax T	45	11	**45**	**11**
2002–03	Northampton T	45	2		
2003–04	Northampton T	14	0	**59**	**2**
2003–04	Macclesfield T	16	2		
2004–05	Macclesfield T	46	3		
2005–06	Macclesfield T	45	6	**107**	**11**
2006–07	Port Vale	32	1		
2007–08	Port Vale	41	5	**73**	**6**

HULBERT, Robin (M) **142** **1**
H: 5 9 W: 12 02 b.Plymouth 14-3-80
Source: Trainee. *Honours:* England Schools, Youth.

1997–98	Swindon T	1	0		
1997–98	*Newcastle U*	0	0		
1998–99	Swindon T	16	0		
1999–2000	Swindon T	12	0	**29**	**0**
1999–2000	Bristol C	2	0		
2000–01	Bristol C	19	0		
2001–02	Bristol C	11	0		
2002–03	Bristol C	7	0		
2002–03	*Shrewsbury T*	7	0	**7**	**0**
2003–04	Bristol C	0	0	**39**	**0**
2004–05	Port Vale	24	0		
2005–06	Port Vale	1	0		
2006–07	Port Vale	20	1		
2007–08	Port Vale	22	0	**67**	**1**

LAWRIE, James (F) **6** **0**
H: 6 0 W: 12 05 b.Belfast 18-12-90
Source: Scholar.

2007–08	Port Vale	6	0	**6**	**0**

MARTIN, Chris (G) **2** **0**
H: 6 0 W: 13 05 b.Mansfield 21-7-90
Source: Scholar.

2007–08	Port Vale	2	0	**2**	**0**

McGREGOR, Mark (D) **423** **13**
H: 5 11 W: 11 05 b.Chester 16-2-77
Source: Trainee.

1994–95	Wrexham	1	0		
1995–96	Wrexham	32	1		
1996–97	Wrexham	38	1		
1997–98	Wrexham	42	2		
1998–99	Wrexham	43	1		
1999–2000	Wrexham	45	1		
2000–01	Wrexham	43	5		
2001–02	Wrexham	0	0	**244**	**11**
2001–02	Burnley	1	0		
2002–03	Burnley	30	1		
2003–04	Burnley	23	1	**54**	**2**
2004–05	Blackpool	38	0		
2005–06	Blackpool	21	0	**59**	**0**
2005–06	Port Vale	14	0		
2006–07	Port Vale	32	0		
2007–08	Port Vale	20	0	**66**	**0**

MILES, Colin (D) **124** **4**
H: 6 0 W: 13 10 b.Edmonton 6-9-78
Source: Trainee.

1996–97	Watford	0	0		
1997–98	Watford	1	0		
1998–99	Watford	0	0	**1**	**0**
1999–2000	Morton	4	0	**4**	**0**
From Dover Ath					
2003–04	Yeovil T	36	4		
2004–05	Yeovil T	21	0		
2005–06	Yeovil T	30	0	**87**	**4**
2006–07	Port Vale	29	0		
2007–08	Port Vale	3	0	**32**	**0**

MILLER, Justin (D) **177** **5**
H: 6 1 W: 12 12 b.Johannesburg 16-12-80
Source: Academy.

1999–2000	Ipswich T	0	0		
2000–01	Ipswich T	0	0		
2001–02	Ipswich T	0	0		
2002–03	Ipswich T	0	0		
2002–03	Leyton Orient	19	0		
2003–04	Leyton Orient	34	2		
2004–05	Leyton Orient	43	0		
2005–06	Leyton Orient	36	1		
2006–07	Leyton Orient	31	2	**163**	**5**
2007–08	Port Vale	14	0	**14**	**0**

MULLIGAN, Dave (D) **185** **7**
H: 5 8 W: 9 13 b.Bootle 24-3-82
Source: Scholar. *Honours:* New Zealand Youth, Under-20, Under-23, 16 full caps.

2000–01	Barnsley	0	0		
2001–02	Barnsley	28	0		
2002–03	Barnsley	33	1		
2003–04	Barnsley	4	0	**65**	**1**
2003–04	Doncaster R	14	1		
2004–05	Doncaster R	31	1		
2005–06	Doncaster R	32	2	**77**	**4**
2006–07	Scunthorpe U	24	1		
2007–08	Scunthorpe U	0	0	**24**	**1**
2007–08	*Grimsby T*	6	0	**6**	**0**
2007–08	Port Vale	13	1	**13**	**1**

O'LOUGHLIN, Charlie (D) **3** **0**
H: 6 1 W: 13 02 b.Birmingham 17-3-89
Source: Scholar.

2007–08	Port Vale	3	0	**3**	**0**

PERRY, Kyle (F) **16** **0**
H: 6 4 W: 14 05 b.Birmingham 5-3-86
Source: Chasetown.

2007–08	Port Vale	16	0	**16**	**0**

PILKINGTON, George (D) **231** **11**
H: 5 11 W: 12 05 b.Rugeley 7-11-81
Source: Trainee. *Honours:* England Youth.

1998–99	Everton	0	0		
1999–2000	Everton	0	0		
2000–01	Everton	0	0		
2001–02	Everton	0	0		
2002–03	Everton	0	0		
2002–03	*Exeter C*	7	0	**7**	**0**
2003–04	Port Vale	44	1		
2004–05	Port Vale	43	0		
2005–06	Port Vale	46	2		
2006–07	Port Vale	46	6		
2007–08	Port Vale	45	2	**224**	**11**

PROSSER, Luke (M) **5** **0**
H: 6 2 W: 12 04 b.Enfield 28-5-88
Source: Scholar.

2005–06	Port Vale	0	0		
2006–07	Port Vale	0	0		
2007–08	Port Vale	5	0	**5**	**0**

RICHARDS, Marc (F) **187** **42**
H: 6 2 W: 12 06 b.Wolverhampton 8-7-82
Source: Trainee. *Honours:* England Youth, Under-20.

1999–2000	Blackburn R	0	0		
2000–01	Blackburn R	0	0		
2001–02	Blackburn R	0	0		
2001–02	*Crewe Alex*	4	0	**4**	**0**
2001–02	*Oldham Ath*	5	0	**5**	**0**
2001–02	*Halifax T*	5	0	**5**	**0**
2002–03	Blackburn R	0	0		
2002–03	*Swansea C*	17	7	**17**	**7**
2003–04	Northampton T	41	8		
2004–05	Northampton T	12	2		
2004–05	*Rochdale*	5	2	**5**	**2**
2005–06	Northampton T	0	0	**53**	**10**
2005–06	Barnsley	38	12		
2006–07	Barnsley	31	6	**69**	**18**
2007–08	Port Vale	29	5	**29**	**5**

RICHMAN, Simon (M) **6** **0**
H: 5 11 W: 11 12 b.Ormskirk 2-6-90
Source: Scholar.

2007–08	Port Vale	6	0	**6**	**0**

ROCASTLE, Craig (M) **103** **4**
H: 6 1 W: 13 09 b.Lewisham 17-8-81
Source: Kingstonian.

2003–04	Chelsea	0	0		
2003–04	*Barnsley*	5	0	**5**	**0**
2003–04	*Lincoln C*	2	0	**2**	**0**
2004–05	Chelsea	0	0		
2004–05	Sheffield W	11	1		
2005–06	Sheffield W	17	0	**28**	**1**
2005–06	*Yeovil T*	8	0	**8**	**0**
2006–07	Oldham Ath	35	2	**35**	**2**
2007–08	Port Vale	23	1	**23**	**1**
2007–08	*Gillingham*	2	0	**2**	**0**

RODGERS, Luke (F) **224** **73**
H: 5 8 W: 11 00 b.Birmingham 1-1-82
Source: Trainee.

1999–2000	Shrewsbury T	6	1		
2000–01	Shrewsbury T	26	7		
2001–02	Shrewsbury T	38	22		
2002–03	Shrewsbury T	36	16		
2003–04	Shrewsbury T	0	0		
2004–05	Shrewsbury T	36	6	**142**	**52**
2005–06	Crewe Alex	26	6		
2006–07	Crewe Alex	12	3	**38**	**9**
2006–07	Port Vale	8	3		
2007–08	Port Vale	36	9	**44**	**12**

SLATER, Chris (D) **5** **0**
H: 6 0 W: 13 03 b.Dudley 14-1-84
Source: Chasetown.

2007–08	Port Vale	5	0	**5**	**0**

TALBOT, Jason (D) **62** **0**
H: 5 8 W: 10 01 b.Irlam 30-9-85
Source: Scholar.

2004–05	Bolton W	0	0		
2004–05	*Derby Co*	2	0	**2**	**0**
2004–05	*Mansfield T*	2	0		
2005–06	Mansfield T	6	0	**8**	**0**
2005–06	*Port Vale*	5	0		
2006–07	Port Vale	22	0		
2007–08	Port Vale	25	0	**52**	**0**

TUDOR, Shane (M) **202** **27**
H: 5 7 W: 11 12 b.Wolverhampton 10-2-82
Source: Trainee.

1999–2000	Wolverhampton W	0	0		
2000–01	Wolverhampton W	1	0		
2001–02	Wolverhampton W	0	0	**1**	**0**
2001–02	Cambridge U	32	3		
2002–03	Cambridge U	27	9		
2003–04	Cambridge U	36	3		
2004–05	Cambridge U	26	6	**121**	**21**
2005–06	Leyton Orient	33	4		
2006–07	Leyton Orient	33	2	**66**	**6**
2007–08	*Shrewsbury T*	0	0		
2007–08	Port Vale	14	0	**14**	**0**

WESTWOOD, Ashley (D) **277** **21**
H: 6 0 W: 12 09 b.Bridgnorth 31-8-76
Source: Trainee. *Honours:* England Youth.

1994–95	Manchester U	0	0		
1995–96	Crewe Alex	33	4		
1996–97	Crewe Alex	44	2		
1997–98	Crewe Alex	21	3	**98**	**9**
1998–99	Bradford C	19	2		
1999–2000	Bradford C	5	0		
2000–01	Bradford C	0	0	**24**	**2**
2000–01	Sheffield W	33	2		
2001–02	Sheffield W	26	1		
2002–03	Sheffield W	23	2	**82**	**5**
2003–04	Northampton T	9	0		
2004–05	Northampton T	19	2		
2005–06	Northampton T	3	0	**31**	**2**
2006–07	Chester C	21	3		
2006–07	*Swindon T*	9	0	**9**	**0**
2007–08	Chester C	0	0	**21**	**3**
2007–08	Port Vale	12	0	**12**	**0**

WHITAKER, Danny (M) **257** **37**
H: 5 10 W: 11 00 b.Manchester 14-11-80
Source: Wilmslow Sports.

2000–01	Macclesfield T	0	0		
2001–02	Macclesfield T	16	2		
2002–03	Macclesfield T	41	10		
2003–04	Macclesfield T	36	5		
2004–05	Macclesfield T	36	2		
2005–06	Macclesfield T	42	4	**171**	**23**
2006–07	Port Vale	45	7		
2007–08	Port Vale	41	7	**86**	**14**

WILLOCK, Calum (F) **148** **30**
H: 6 1 W: 12 08 b.Lambeth 29-10-81
Source: Scholar. *Honours:* England Schools. St Kitts & Nevis 2 full caps, 2 goals.

2000–01	Fulham	1	0		
2001–02	Fulham	2	0		
2002–03	Fulham	2	0		
2002–03	*QPR*	3	0	**3**	**0**
2003–04	Fulham	0	0	**5**	**0**
2003–04	*Bristol R*	5	0	**5**	**0**
2003–04	Peterborough U	29	8		
2004–05	Peterborough U	35	12		
2005–06	Peterborough U	15	3	**79**	**23**
2005–06	Brentford	13	1		
2006–07	Brentford	28	3	**41**	**4**
2007–08	Port Vale	15	3	**15**	**3**

PORTSMOUTH (65)

ASHDOWN, Jamie (G) **72** **0**
H: 6 1 W: 13 05 b.Reading 30-11-80
Source: Scholar.

1999–2000	Reading	0	0		
2000–01	Reading	1	0		
2001–02	Reading	1	0		
2001–02	*Arsenal*	0	0		
2002–03	Reading	1	0		
2002–03	*Bournemouth*	2	0	**2**	**0**
2003–04	Reading	10	0	**13**	**0**
2003–04	*Rushden & D*	19	0	**19**	**0**
2004–05	Portsmouth	16	0		
2005–06	Portsmouth	17	0		
2006–07	Portsmouth	0	0		
2006–07	*Norwich C*	2	0	**2**	**0**
2007–08	Portsmouth	3	0	**36**	**0**

AUBEY, Lucien (D) **167** **0**
H: 5 11 W: 11 11 b.Brazzaville 24-5-84
Honours: France Under-21.

2001–02	Toulouse	4	0		
2002–03	Toulouse	30	0		
2003–04	Toulouse	36	0		
2004–05	Toulouse	33	0		
2005–06	Toulouse	33	0		
2006–07	Toulouse	16	0	**152**	**0**
2007–08	Lens	12	0	**12**	**0**
2007–08	Portsmouth	3	0	**3**	**0**

BAROS, Milan (F) **207** **46**
H: 6 0 W: 12 00 b.Valasske Mezirici 28-10-81
Honours: Czech Republic Youth, Under-21, 60 full caps, 31 goals.

1998–99	Banik Ostrava	6	0		
1999–2000	Banik Ostrava	29	6		
2000–01	Banik Ostrava	26	5	**61**	**11**
2001–02	Liverpool	0	0		
2002–03	Liverpool	27	9		
2003–04	Liverpool	13	1		
2004–05	Liverpool	26	9		
2005–06	Liverpool	2	0	**68**	**19**
2005–06	Aston Villa	25	8		
2006–07	Aston Villa	17	1	**42**	**9**
2006–07	Lyon	12	4		
2007–08	Lyon	12	3	**24**	**7**
2007–08	Portsmouth	12	0	**12**	**0**

BEGOVIC, Asmir (G) **13** **0**
H: 6 5 W: 13 01 b.Trebinje 20-6-87
Source: La Louviere. *Honours:* Canada Under-20.

2006–07	Portsmouth	0	0		
2006–07	*Macclesfield T*	3	0	**3**	**0**
2007–08	Portsmouth	0	0		
2007–08	*Bournemouth*	8	0	**8**	**0**
2007–08	*Yeovil T*	2	0	**2**	**0**

CAMPBELL, Sol (D) **453** **20**
H: 6 2 W: 15 07 b.Plaistow 18-9-74
Source: Trainee. *Honours:* England Youth, Under-21, B, 73 full caps, 1 goal.

1992–93	Tottenham H	1	1		
1993–94	Tottenham H	34	0		
1994–95	Tottenham H	30	0		
1995–96	Tottenham H	31	1		
1996–97	Tottenham H	38	0		
1997–98	Tottenham H	34	0		
1998–99	Tottenham H	37	6		
1999–2000	Tottenham H	29	0		
2000–01	Tottenham H	21	2	**255**	**10**
2001–02	Arsenal	31	2		
2002–03	Arsenal	33	2		
2003–04	Arsenal	35	1		
2004–05	Arsenal	16	1		
2005–06	Arsenal	20	2	**135**	**8**
2006–07	Portsmouth	32	1		
2007–08	Portsmouth	31	1	**63**	**2**

CHRISTOPHE, Jean-Francois (M) **15** **1**
H: 6 1 W: 13 01 b.Creil 13-6-82
Source: Lens.

2007–08	Portsmouth	0	0		
2007–08	*Bournemouth*	10	1	**10**	**1**
2007–08	*Yeovil T*	5	0	**5**	**0**

CRANIE, Martin (D) **39** **0**
H: 6 1 W: 12 09 b.Yeovil 23-9-86
Source: Scholar. *Honours:* England Youth, Under-20, Under-21.

2003–04	Southampton	1	0		
2004–05	Southampton	3	0		
2004–05	*Bournemouth*	3	0	**3**	**0**
2005–06	Southampton	11	0		
2006–07	Southampton	1	0	**16**	**0**
2006–07	*Yeovil T*	12	0	**12**	**0**
2007–08	Portsmouth	2	0	**2**	**0**
2007–08	*QPR*	6	0	**6**	**0**

DAVIS, Sean (M) **240** **15**
H: 5 10 W: 12 00 b.Clapham 20-9-79
Source: Trainee. *Honours:* England Under-21.

1996–97	Fulham	1	0		
1997–98	Fulham	0	0		
1998–99	Fulham	6	0		
1999–2000	Fulham	26	0		
2000–01	Fulham	40	6		
2001–02	Fulham	30	0		
2002–03	Fulham	28	3		
2003–04	Fulham	24	5	**155**	**14**
2004–05	Tottenham H	15	0		
2005–06	Tottenham H	0	0	**15**	**0**
2005–06	Portsmouth	17	1		
2006–07	Portsmouth	31	0		
2007–08	Portsmouth	22	0	**70**	**1**

DEFOE, Jermain (F) **273** **98**
H: 5 7 W: 10 04 b.Beckton 7-10-82
Source: Charlton Ath. *Honours:* England Youth, Under-21, B, 28full caps, 5 goals.

1999–2000	West Ham U	0	0		
2000–01	West Ham U	1	0		
2000–01	*Bournemouth*	29	18	**29**	**18**
2001–02	West Ham U	35	10		
2002–03	West Ham U	38	8		
2003–04	West Ham U	19	11	**93**	**29**
2003–04	Tottenham H	15	7		
2004–05	Tottenham H	35	13		
2005–06	Tottenham H	36	9		
2006–07	Tottenham H	34	10		
2007–08	Tottenham H	19	4	**139**	**43**
2007–08	Portsmouth	12	8	**12**	**8**

DIARRA, Lassana (M) **32** **1**
H: 5 8 W: 11 02 b.Paris 10-3-85
Source: Le Havre. *Honours:* France Youth, Under-21, Under-23, 13 full caps.

2005–06	Chelsea	3	0		
2006–07	Chelsea	10	0		
2007–08	Chelsea	0	0	**13**	**0**
2007–08	Arsenal	7	0	**7**	**0**
2007–08	Portsmouth	12	1	**12**	**1**

DIOP, Papa Bouba (M) **195** **23**
H: 6 4 W: 14 12 b.Dakar 28-1-78
Source: Espoir, Jaraaf, Vevey Sports. *Honours:* Senegal 38 full caps, 9 goals.

1999–2000	Neuchatel Xamax	0	0		
2000–01	Neuchatel Xamax	18	4	**18**	**4**
2000–01	Grasshoppers	11	1		
2001–02	Grasshoppers	18	4	**29**	**5**
2001–02	Lens	5	0		
2002–03	Lens	16	3		
2003–04	Lens	26	3	**47**	**6**
2004–05	Fulham	29	6		
2005–06	Fulham	22	2		
2006–07	Fulham	23	0		
2007–08	Fulham	2	0	**76**	**8**
2007–08	Portsmouth	25	0	**25**	**0**

DISTIN, Sylvain (D) **329** **9**
H: 6 3 W: 14 06 b.Bagnolet 16-12-77

1998–99	Tours	26	3	**26**	**3**
1999–2000	Gueugnon	33	1	**33**	**1**
2000–01	Paris St Germain	28	0	**28**	**0**
2001–02	Newcastle U	28	0	**28**	**0**
2002–03	Manchester C	34	0		
2003–04	Manchester C	38	2		
2004–05	Manchester C	38	1		
2005–06	Manchester C	31	0		
2006–07	Manchester C	37	2	**178**	**5**
2007–08	Portsmouth	36	0	**36**	**0**

DUFFY, Richard (D) **98** **2**
H: 5 9 W: 10 03 b.Swansea 30-8-85
Source: Scholar. *Honours:* Wales Youth, Under-21, 13 full caps.

2002–03	Swansea C	0	0		
2003–04	Swansea C	18	1		
2003–04	Portsmouth	1	0		
2004–05	Portsmouth	0	0		
2004–05	*Burnley*	7	1	**7**	**1**
2004–05	*Coventry C*	14	0		
2005–06	Portsmouth	0	0		
2005–06	*Coventry C*	32	0		
2006–07	Portsmouth	0	0		
2006–07	*Coventry C*	13	0		
2006–07	*Swansea C*	11	0	**29**	**1**
2007–08	Portsmouth	0	0	**1**	**0**
2007–08	*Coventry C*	2	0	**61**	**0**

GAZET DUCHATTELIER, Ryan (M) **0** **0**
Source: Scholar.

2007–08	Portsmouth	0	0		

HREIDARSSON, Hermann (D) **434** **22**
H: 6 3 W: 12 12 b.Reykjavik 11-7-74
Honours: Iceland Under-21, 75 full caps, 5 goals.

1993	IBV	2	0		
1994	IBV	18	2		
1995	IBV	18	1		
1996	IBV	17	2		
1997	IBV	11	0	**66**	**5**
1997–98	Crystal Palace	30	2		
1998–99	Crystal Palace	7	0	**37**	**2**
1998–99	Brentford	33	4		
1999–2000	Brentford	8	2	**41**	**6**
1999–2000	Wimbledon	24	1	**24**	**1**
2000–01	Ipswich T	36	1		
2001–02	Ipswich T	38	1		
2002–03	Ipswich T	28	0	**102**	**2**
2002–03	Charlton Ath	0	0		
2003–04	Charlton Ath	33	2		
2004–05	Charlton Ath	34	1		
2005–06	Charlton Ath	34	0		
2006–07	Charlton Ath	31	0	**132**	**3**
2007–08	Portsmouth	32	3	**32**	**3**

HUGHES, Richard (M) **233** **15**
H: 6 0 W: 13 03 b.Glasgow 25-6-79
Source: Atalanta. *Honours:* Scotland Youth, Under-21, 5 full caps.

1997–98	Arsenal	0	0		
1998–99	Bournemouth	44	2		
1999–2000	Bournemouth	21	2		
2000–01	Bournemouth	44	8		
2001–02	Bournemouth	22	2	**131**	**14**
2002–03	Portsmouth	6	0		
2002–03	*Grimsby T*	12	1	**12**	**1**
2003–04	Portsmouth	11	0		
2004–05	Portsmouth	16	0		
2005–06	Portsmouth	26	0		
2006–07	Portsmouth	18	0		
2007–08	Portsmouth	13	0	**90**	**0**

JAMES, David (G) **627** **0**
H: 6 5 W: 15 07 b.Welwyn 1-8-70
Source: Trainee. *Honours:* England Youth, Under-21, B, 39 full caps.

1988–89	Watford	0	0		
1989–90	Watford	0	0		
1990–91	Watford	46	0		
1991–92	Watford	43	0	**89**	**0**
1992–93	Liverpool	29	0		
1993–94	Liverpool	14	0		
1994–95	Liverpool	42	0		
1995–96	Liverpool	38	0		
1996–97	Liverpool	38	0		
1997–98	Liverpool	27	0		
1998–99	Liverpool	26	0	**214**	**0**
1999–2000	Aston Villa	29	0		
2000–01	Aston Villa	38	0	**67**	**0**
2001–02	West Ham U	26	0		
2002–03	West Ham U	38	0		
2003–04	West Ham U	27	0	**91**	**0**
2003–04	Manchester C	17	0		
2004–05	Manchester C	38	0		
2005–06	Manchester C	38	0	**93**	**0**
2006–07	Portsmouth	38	0		
2007–08	Portsmouth	35	0	**73**	**0**

JOHNSON, Glen (D) **120** **4**
H: 6 0 W: 13 04 b.Greenwich 23-8-84
Source: Scholar. *Honours:* England Youth, Under-20, Under-21, 8 full caps.

2001–02	West Ham U	0	0		
2002–03	West Ham U	15	0	**15**	**0**
2002–03	*Millwall*	8	0	**8**	**0**
2003–04	Chelsea	19	3		
2004–05	Chelsea	17	0		
2005–06	Chelsea	4	0		
2006–07	Chelsea	0	0		
2006–07	*Portsmouth*	26	0		
2007–08	Chelsea	2	0	**42**	**3**
2007–08	Portsmouth	29	1	**55**	**1**

KANU, Nwankwo (F) **359** **92**
H: 6 5 W: 12 08 b.Owerri 1-8-76
Honours: Nigeria 73 full caps, 13 goals.

1991–92	Federation Works	30	9	**30**	**9**
1992–93	Iwanyanwu	30	6	**30**	**6**
1993–94	Ajax	6	2		
1994–95	Ajax	18	10		
1995–96	Ajax	30	13	**54**	**25**
1996–97	Internazionale	0	0		
1997–98	Internazionale	11	1		
1998–99	Internazionale	1	0	**12**	**1**
1998–99	Arsenal	12	6		
1999–2000	Arsenal	31	12		
2000–01	Arsenal	27	3		
2001–02	Arsenal	23	3		
2002–03	Arsenal	16	5		
2003–04	Arsenal	10	1	**119**	**30**
2004–05	WBA	28	2		
2005–06	WBA	25	5	**53**	**7**

2006–07	Portsmouth	36	10		
2007–08	Portsmouth	25	4	**61**	**14**

KILBEY, Tom (M) 0 0
H: 6 3 W: 13 08 b.Waltham Forest 19-10-90
Source: Millwall.

2007–08	Portsmouth	0	0		

KRANJCAR, Niko (M) 193 39
H: 6 1 W: 12 13 b.Zagreb 13-8-84
Honours: Croatia Youth, Under-21, 44 full caps, 3 goals.

2001–02	Dynamo Zagreb	24	3		
2002–03	Dynamo Zagreb	21	4		
2003–04	Dynamo Zagreb	24	10		
2004–05	Dynamo Zagreb	16	2	**85**	**19**
2004–05	Hajduk Split	13	1		
2005–06	Hajduk Split	32	10		
2006–07	Hajduk Split	5	3	**50**	**14**
2006–07	Portsmouth	24	2		
2007–08	Portsmouth	34	4	**58**	**6**

LAUREN, Etame-Mayer (D) 327 24
H: 5 11 W: 11 07 b.Londi Kribi 19-1-77
Honours: Cameroon 25 full caps, 8 goals.

1995–96	Utrera	30	5	**30**	**5**
1996–97	Sevilla B	17	3	**17**	**3**
1997–98	Levante	34	6	**34**	**6**
1998–99	Mallorca	32	1		
1999–2000	Mallorca	30	3	**62**	**4**
2000–01	Arsenal	18	2		
2001–02	Arsenal	27	2		
2002–03	Arsenal	27	1		
2003–04	Arsenal	32	0		
2004–05	Arsenal	33	1		
2005–06	Arsenal	22	0		
2006–07	Arsenal	0	0	**159**	**6**
2006–07	Portsmouth	10	0		
2007–08	Portsmouth	15	0	**25**	**0**

LUA-LUA, Lomano (F) 207 39
H: 5 8 W: 12 02 b.Kinshasa 28-12-80
Honours: DR Congo 6 full caps, 1 goal.

1998–99	Colchester U	13	1		
1999–2000	Colchester U	41	12		
2000–01	Colchester U	7	2	**61**	**15**
2000–01	Newcastle U	21	0		
2001–02	Newcastle U	20	3		
2002–03	Newcastle U	11	2		
2003–04	Newcastle U	7	0	**59**	**5**
2003–04	*Portsmouth*	15	4		
2004–05	Portsmouth	25	6		
2005–06	Portsmouth	25	7		
2006–07	Portsmouth	22	2		
2007–08	Portsmouth	0	0	**87**	**19**

MANTYLA, Tero (D) 0 0
b.Finland

2007–08	Portsmouth	0	0		

MUNTARI, Sulley Ali (M) 154 12
H: 5 10 W: 12 00 b.Konongo 27-8-84
Honours: Ghana 39 full caps, 11 goals.

2002–03	Udinese	12	0		
2003–04	Udinese	23	0		
2004–05	Udinese	33	2		
2005–06	Udinese	29	3		
2006–07	Udinese	28	3	**125**	**8**
2007–08	Portsmouth	29	4	**29**	**4**

MVUEMBA, Arnold (M) 48 2
H: 5 8 W: 10 07 b.Alencon 28-1-85
Honours: France Under-21.

2003–04	Rennes	8	0		
2004–05	Rennes	8	0		
2005–06	Rennes	16	1		
2006–07	Rennes	1	0	**33**	**1**
2006–07	Portsmouth	7	1		
2007–08	Portsmouth	8	0	**15**	**1**

NUGENT, Dave (F) 197 51
H: 5 11 W: 12 13 b.Liverpool 2-5-85
Source: Scholar. *Honours:* England Youth, Under-20, Under-21, 1 full cap, 1 goal.

2001–02	Bury	5	0		
2002–03	Bury	31	4		
2003–04	Bury	26	3		
2004–05	Bury	26	11	**88**	**18**
2004–05	Preston NE	18	8		
2005–06	Preston NE	32	10		
2006–07	Preston NE	44	15	**94**	**33**
2007–08	Portsmouth	15	0	**15**	**0**

PAMAROT, Noe (D) 223 12
H: 5 11 W: 13 07 b.Fontenay-sous-Bois 14-4-79
Source: Martigues, Nice.

1997–98	Martigues	25	2		
1998–99	Martigues	0	0	**25**	**2**
1999–2000	Nice	0	0		
1999–2000	Portsmouth	2	0		
2000–01	Nice	23	0		
2001–02	Nice	33	3		
2002–03	Nice	33	1		
2003–04	Nice	33	2	**122**	**6**
2004–05	Tottenham H	23	1		
2005–06	Tottenham H	2	0	**25**	**1**
2005–06	Portsmouth	8	0		
2006–07	Portsmouth	23	2		
2007–08	Portsmouth	18	1	**51**	**3**

PEDRO MENDES (M) 228 15
H: 5 9 W: 12 04 b.Guimaraes 26-2-79
Honours: Portugal Under-21, 2 full caps.

1998–99	Felgueiras	31	2	**31**	**2**
1999–2000	Guimaraes	13	1		
2000–01	Guimaraes	12	0		
2001–02	Guimaraes	26	0		
2002–03	Guimaraes	32	6	**83**	**7**
2003–04	Porto	26	0	**26**	**0**
2004–05	Tottenham H	24	1		
2005–06	Tottenham H	6	0	**30**	**1**
2005–06	Portsmouth	14	3		
2006–07	Portsmouth	26	2		
2007–08	Portsmouth	18	0	**58**	**5**

PRIMUS, Linvoy (D) 423 13
H: 5 10 W: 12 04 b.Forest Gate 14-9-73
Source: Trainee.

1992–93	Charlton Ath	4	0		
1993–94	Charlton Ath	0	0	**4**	**0**
1994–95	Barnet	39	0		
1995–96	Barnet	42	4		
1996–97	Barnet	46	3	**127**	**7**
1997–98	Reading	36	1		
1998–99	Reading	31	0		
1999–2000	Reading	28	0	**95**	**1**
2000–01	Portsmouth	23	0		
2001–02	Portsmouth	22	2		
2002–03	Portsmouth	40	0		
2003–04	Portsmouth	21	0		
2004 05	Portsmouth	35	1		
2005–06	Portsmouth	20	0		
2006–07	Portsmouth	36	2		
2007–08	Portsmouth	0	0	**197**	**5**

REYNOLDS, Callum (D) 0 0
b.Luton 10-11-89
Source: Rushden & D Scholar.

2007–08	Portsmouth	0	0		

SONGO'O, Frank (M) 34 1
H: 6 2 W: 12 06 b.Yaounde 14-5-87
Source: Barcelona. *Honours:* France Youth.

2005–06	Portsmouth	2	0		
2006–07	Portsmouth	0	0		
2006–07	*Bournemouth*	4	0	**4**	**0**
2006–07	*Preston NE*	6	0	**6**	**0**
2007–08	Portsmouth	1	0	**3**	**0**
2007–08	*Crystal Palace*	9	0	**9**	**0**
2007–08	*Sheffield W*	12	1	**12**	**1**

SUBOTIC, Danijel (F) 0 0
H: 6 2 W: 12 00 b.Doboj 31-1-89
Source: Basle.

2007–08	Portsmouth	0	0		

TRAORE, Djimi (D) 146 0
H: 6 2 W: 12 07 b.Saint-Ouen 1-3-80
Source: Laval. *Honours:* France Youth, Under-21, Mali 5 full caps, 1 goal.

1998–99	Liverpool	0	0		
1999–2000	Liverpool	0	0		
2000–01	Liverpool	8	0		
2001–02	Liverpool	0	0		
2001–02	Lens	19	0	**19**	**0**
2002–03	Liverpool	32	0		
2003–04	Liverpool	7	0		
2004–05	Liverpool	26	0		
2005–06	Liverpool	15	0	**88**	**0**
2006–07	Charlton Ath	11	0	**11**	**0**
2006–07	Portsmouth	10	0		
2007–08	*Rennes*	15	0	**15**	**0**
2007–08	Portsmouth	3	0	**13**	**0**

UTAKA, John (F) 194 51
H: 5 9 W: 11 02 b.Enugu 8-1-82
Source: Ismaily, Al Saad. *Honours:* Nigeria 30 full caps, 5 goals.

2002–03	Lens	36	8		
2003–04	Lens	32	4		
2004–05	Lens	34	12	**102**	**24**
2005–06	Rennes	28	11		
2006–07	Rennes	35	11	**63**	**22**
2007–08	Portsmouth	29	5	**29**	**5**

WILSON, Marc (M) 32 3
H: 6 2 W: 12 07 b.Belfast 17-8-87
Source: Scholar. *Honours:* Eire Under-21.

2005–06	Portsmouth	0	0		
2005–06	*Yeovil T*	2	0	**2**	**0**
2006–07	Portsmouth	0	0		
2006–07	*Bournemouth*	19	3		
2007–08	Portsmouth	0	0		
2007–08	*Bournemouth*	7	0	**26**	**3**
2007–08	*Luton T*	4	0	**4**	**0**

Scholars
Blackman, Andre Alexander-George; Castles, Louie; Collins, Joe; Cowan-Hall, Paris; Gbo, Guy Romain; Hughes, Jordan Gary; Mbuyi-Mutombo, Andrea; Pack, Marlon; Price, Geraint Rhys John; Ritchie, Matthew Thomas; Smith, Tommy Ben; Ward, Joel; Woodford, Ryan Joseph

PRESTON NE (66)

ADAMS, Dylan (D) 0 0
H: 5 8 W: 11 12 b.Liverpool 29-7-89
Source: Scholar.

2007–08	Preston NE	0	0		

ANYINSAH, Joe (M) 36 3
H: 5 8 W: 11 00 b.Bristol 8-10-84
Source: Scholar.

2001–02	Bristol C	0	0		
2002–03	Bristol C	0	0		
2003–04	Bristol C	0	0		
2004–05	Bristol C	7	0	**7**	**0**
2005–06	Preston NE	3	0		
2005–06	*Bury*	3	0	**3**	**0**
2006–07	Preston NE	3	0		
2007–08	Preston NE	0	0	**6**	**0**
2007–08	*Carlisle U*	12	3	**12**	**3**
2007–08	*Crewe Alex*	8	0	**8**	**0**

BROWN, Chris (F) 136 26
H: 6 3 W: 13 01 b.Doncaster 11-12-84
Source: Trainee. *Honours:* England Youth.

2002–03	Sunderland	0	0		
2003–04	Sunderland	0	0		
2003–04	*Doncaster R*	22	10	**22**	**10**
2004–05	Sunderland	37	5		
2005–06	Sunderland	13	1		
2005–06	*Hull C*	13	1	**13**	**1**
2006–07	Sunderland	16	3	**66**	**9**
2006–07	Norwich C	4	0		
2007–08	Norwich C	14	1	**18**	**1**
2007–08	Preston NE	17	5	**17**	**5**

CARTER, Darren (M) 147 12
H: 6 2 W: 12 11 b.Solihull 18-12-83
Source: Scholar. *Honours:* England Youth, Under-20.

2001–02	Birmingham C	13	1		
2002–03	Birmingham C	12	0		
2003–04	Birmingham C	5	0		
2004–05	Birmingham C	15	2	**45**	**3**
2004–05	*Sunderland*	10	1	**10**	**1**
2005–06	WBA	20	1		
2006–07	WBA	33	3	**53**	**4**
2007–08	Preston NE	39	4	**39**	**4**

CHAPLOW, Richard (M) 132 12
H: 5 9 W: 9 03 b.Accrington 2-2-85
Source: Scholar. *Honours:* England Youth, Under-20, Under-21.

2002–03	Burnley	5	0		
2003–04	Burnley	39	5		
2004–05	Burnley	21	2	**65**	**7**
2004–05	WBA	4	0		
2005–06	WBA	7	0		
2005–06	*Southampton*	11	1	**11**	**1**
2006–07	WBA	28	1		
2007–08	WBA	5	0	**44**	**1**
2007–08	Preston NE	12	3	**12**	**3**

CHILVERS, Liam (D) **202 6**
H: 6 2 W: 12 03 b.Chelmsford 6-11-81
Source: Scholar.

2000–01	Arsenal	0	0		
2000–01	*Northampton T*	7	0	**7**	**0**
2001–02	Arsenal	0	0		
2001–02	*Notts Co*	9	1	**9**	**1**
2002–03	Arsenal	0	0		
2002–03	*Colchester U*	6	0		
2003–04	Arsenal	0	0		
2003–04	*Colchester U*	32	0		
2004–05	Colchester U	41	1		
2005–06	Colchester U	34	2	**113**	**3**
2006–07	Preston NE	45	2		
2007–08	Preston NE	28	0	**73**	**2**

DAVIDSON, Callum (D) **311 16**
H: 5 10 W: 11 08 b.Stirling 25-6-76
Source: 'S' Form. *Honours:* Scotland Under-21, 17 full caps.

1994–95	St Johnstone	7	1		
1995–96	St Johnstone	2	0		
1996–97	St Johnstone	20	2		
1997–98	St Johnstone	15	1	**44**	**4**
1997–98	Blackburn R	1	0		
1998–99	Blackburn R	34	1		
1999–2000	Blackburn R	30	0	**65**	**1**
2000–01	Leicester C	28	1		
2001–02	Leicester C	30	0		
2002–03	Leicester C	30	1		
2003–04	Leicester C	13	0	**101**	**2**
2004–05	Preston NE	19	1		
2005–06	Preston NE	27	4		
2006–07	Preston NE	15	0		
2007–08	Preston NE	40	4	**101**	**9**

HART, Michael (M) **175 0**
H: 5 10 W: 11 06 b.Bellshill 10-2-80

1998–99	Aberdeen	14	0		
1999–2000	Aberdeen	3	0		
1999–2000	*Livingston*	3	0		
1999–2000	*Morton*	10	0	**10**	**0**
2000–01	Aberdeen	0	0		
2000–01	*Livingston*	22	0		
2001–02	*Livingston*	21	0		
2002–03	*Livingston*	11	0	**57**	**0**
2002–03	Aberdeen	8	0		
2003–04	Aberdeen	11	0		
2004–05	Aberdeen	32	0		
2005–06	Aberdeen	4	0		
2006–07	Aberdeen	34	0	**106**	**0**
2007–08	Preston NE	2	0	**2**	**0**

HAWLEY, Karl (F) **132 46**
H: 5 8 W: 12 02 b.Walsall 6-12-81
Source: Scholar.

2000–01	Walsall	0	0		
2001–02	Walsall	1	0		
2002–03	Walsall	0	0		
2002–03	*Raith R*	17	7		
2003–04	Walsall	0	0	**1**	**0**
2003–04	*Raith R*	11	2	**28**	**9**
2004–05	Carlisle U	0	0		
2005–06	Carlisle U	46	22		
2006–07	Carlisle U	32	12	**78**	**34**
2007–08	Preston NE	25	3	**25**	**3**

HENDERSON, Wayne (G) **73 0**
H: 5 11 W: 12 02 b.Dublin 16-9-83
Source: Scholar. *Honours:* Eire Youth, Under-21, 6 full caps.

2000–01	Aston Villa	0	0		
2001–02	Aston Villa	0	0		
2002–03	Aston Villa	0	0		
2003–04	Aston Villa	0	0		
2003–04	*Wycombe W*	3	0	**3**	**0**
2004–05	Aston Villa	0	0		
2004–05	*Notts Co*	11	0	**11**	**0**
2005–06	Aston Villa	0	0		
2005–06	Brighton & HA	32	0		
2006–07	Brighton & HA	20	0	**52**	**0**
2006–07	Preston NE	4	0		
2007–08	Preston NE	3	0	**7**	**0**

HILL, Matt (D) **302 6**
H: 5 7 W: 12 06 b.Bristol 26-3-81
Source: Trainee.

1998–99	Bristol C	3	0		
1999–2000	Bristol C	14	0		
2000–01	Bristol C	34	0		
2001–02	Bristol C	40	1		
2002–03	Bristol C	42	3		
2003–04	Bristol C	42	2		
2004–05	Bristol C	23	0	**198**	**6**
2004–05	Preston NE	14	0		
2005–06	Preston NE	26	0		
2006–07	Preston NE	38	0		
2007–08	Preston NE	26	0	**104**	**0**

JARRETT, Jason (M) **228 9**
H: 6 1 W: 13 10 b.Bury 14-9-79
Source: Trainee.

1998–99	Blackpool	2	0		
1999–2000	Blackpool	0	0	**2**	**0**
1999–2000	Wrexham	1	0	**1**	**0**
2000–01	Bury	25	2		
2001–02	Bury	37	2	**62**	**4**
2001–02	Wigan Ath	5	0		
2002–03	Wigan Ath	35	0		
2003–04	Wigan Ath	41	1		
2004–05	Wigan Ath	14	0	**95**	**1**
2004–05	*Stoke C*	2	0	**2**	**0**
2005–06	Norwich C	11	0	**11**	**0**
2005–06	*Plymouth Arg*	7	0	**7**	**0**
2005–06	*Preston NE*	10	1		
2006–07	Preston NE	5	0		
2006–07	*Hull C*	3	0	**3**	**0**
2006–07	*Leicester C*	13	0	**13**	**0**
2007–08	Preston NE	0	0	**15**	**1**
2007–08	*QPR*	2	0	**2**	**0**
2007–08	*Oldham Ath*	15	3	**15**	**3**

JONES, Billy (M) **161 8**
H: 5 11 W: 13 00 b.Shrewsbury 24-3-87
Source: Scholar. *Honours:* England Youth, Under-20.

2003–04	Crewe Alex	27	1		
2004–05	Crewe Alex	20	0		
2005–06	Crewe Alex	44	6		
2006–07	Crewe Alex	41	1	**132**	**8**
2007–08	Preston NE	29	0	**29**	**0**

LONERGAN, Andrew (G) **93 1**
H: 6 4 W: 13 02 b.Preston 19-10-83
Source: Scholar. *Honours:* Eire Youth, England Youth, Under-20.

2000–01	Preston NE	1	0		
2001–02	Preston NE	0	0		
2002–03	Preston NE	0	0		
2002–03	*Darlington*	2	0	**2**	**0**
2003–04	Preston NE	8	0		
2004–05	Preston NE	23	1		
2005–06	Preston NE	0	0		
2005–06	*Wycombe W*	2	0	**2**	**0**
2006–07	Preston NE	13	0		
2006–07	*Swindon T*	1	0	**1**	**0**
2007–08	Preston NE	43	0	**88**	**1**

MAWENE, Youl (D) **175 7**
H: 6 2 W: 12 06 b.Caen 16-7-79

1999–2000	Lens	6	0	**6**	**0**
2000–01	Derby Co	8	0		
2001–02	Derby Co	17	1		
2002–03	Derby Co	0	0		
2003–04	Derby Co	30	0	**55**	**1**
2004–05	Preston NE	46	2		
2005–06	Preston NE	30	1		
2006–07	Preston NE	0	0		
2007–08	Preston NE	38	3	**114**	**6**

McGRAIL, Chris (F) **3 0**
H: 6 0 W: 13 05 b.Preston 25-2-88
Source: Scholar.

2006–07	Preston NE	0	0		
2006–07	*Accrington S*	2	0		
2007–08	Preston NE	0	0		
2007–08	*Accrington S*	1	0	**3**	**0**

McKENNA, Paul (M) **378 28**
H: 5 7 W: 11 12 b.Eccleston 20-10-77
Source: Trainee.

1995–96	Preston NE	0	0		
1996–97	Preston NE	5	1		
1997–98	Preston NE	5	0		
1998–99	Preston NE	36	0		
1999–2000	Preston NE	24	2		
2000–01	Preston NE	44	5		
2001–02	Preston NE	38	4		
2002–03	Preston NE	41	3		
2003–04	Preston NE	39	6		
2004–05	Preston NE	39	3		
2005–06	Preston NE	41	2		
2006–07	Preston NE	33	2		
2007–08	Preston NE	33	0	**378**	**28**

MELLOR, Neil (F) **72 15**
H: 6 0 W: 13 05 b.Sheffield 4-11-82
Source: Scholar.

2001–02	Liverpool	0	0		
2002–03	Liverpool	3	0		
2003–04	Liverpool	0	0		
2003–04	*West Ham U*	16	2	**16**	**2**
2004–05	Liverpool	9	2		
2005–06	Liverpool	0	0		
2005–06	*Wigan Ath*	3	1	**3**	**1**
2006–07	Liverpool	0	0	**12**	**2**
2006–07	Preston NE	5	1		
2007–08	Preston NE	36	9	**41**	**10**

MURPHY, Andrew (G) **0 0**
H: 6 4 W: 14 00 b. 22-9-88
Source: Scholar.

2007–08	Preston NE	0	0		

NEAL, Chris (G) **1 0**
H: 6 2 W: 12 04 b.St Albans 23-10-85
Source: Scholar.

2004–05	Preston NE	1	0		
2005–06	Preston NE	0	0		
2006–07	Preston NE	0	0		
2007–08	*Morecambe*	0	0		
2007–08	Preston NE	0	0	**1**	**0**

NEAL, Lewis (M) **135 7**
H: 5 10 W: 11 02 b.Leicester 14-7-81
Source: Juniors.

1998–99	Stoke C	0	0		
1999–2000	Stoke C	0	0		
2000–01	Stoke C	1	0		
2001–02	Stoke C	11	0		
2002–03	Stoke C	16	0		
2003–04	Stoke C	19	1		
2004–05	Stoke C	23	1	**70**	**2**
2005–06	Preston NE	24	2		
2006–07	Preston NE	24	1		
2007–08	Preston NE	17	2	**65**	**5**

NICHOLLS, Kevin (M) **250 33**
H: 5 10 W: 11 13 b.Newham 2-1-79
Source: Trainee. *Honours:* England Youth.

1995–96	Charlton Ath	0	0		
1996–97	Charlton Ath	6	1		
1997–98	Charlton Ath	6	0		
1998–99	Charlton Ath	0	0	**12**	**1**
1998–99	*Brighton & HA*	4	1	**4**	**1**
1999–2000	Wigan Ath	8	0		
2000–01	Wigan Ath	20	0	**28**	**0**
2001–02	Luton T	42	7		
2002–03	Luton T	36	5		
2003–04	Luton T	21	2		
2004–05	Luton T	44	12		
2005–06	Luton T	32	5	**175**	**31**
2006–07	Leeds U	13	0	**13**	**0**
2007–08	Preston NE	18	0	**18**	**0**

NOWLAND, Adam (M) **171 15**
H: 5 11 W: 11 06 b.Preston 6-7-81
Source: Trainee.

1997–98	Blackpool	1	0		
1998–99	Blackpool	37	2		
1999–2000	Blackpool	21	3		
2000–01	Blackpool	10	0	**69**	**5**
2001–02	Wimbledon	7	0		
2002–03	Wimbledon	24	2		
2003–04	Wimbledon	25	3	**56**	**5**
2003–04	West Ham U	11	0		
2004–05	West Ham U	4	1	**15**	**1**
2004–05	*Gillingham*	3	1		
2004–05	Nottingham F	5	0		
2005–06	Nottingham F	0	0	**5**	**0**
2005–06	Preston NE	13	3		
2006–07	Preston NE	1	0		
2007–08	Preston NE	0	0	**14**	**3**
2007–08	*Gillingham*	5	0	**8**	**1**
2007–08	*Stockport Co*	4	0	**4**	**0**

ORMEROD, Brett (F) **314 74**
H: 5 11 W: 11 12 b.Blackburn 18-10-76
Source: Blackburn R Trainee, Accrington S.

1996–97	Blackpool	4	0		
1997–98	Blackpool	9	2		
1998–99	Blackpool	40	8		
1999–2000	Blackpool	13	5		
2000–01	Blackpool	41	17		
2001–02	Blackpool	21	13	**128**	**45**
2001–02	Southampton	18	1		
2002–03	Southampton	31	5		
2003–04	Southampton	22	5		
2004–05	Southampton	9	0		

2004–05 *Leeds U* 6 0 **6 0**
2004–05 *Wigan Ath* 6 2 **6 2**
2005–06 Southampton 19 1 **99 12**
2005–06 Preston NE 15 4
2006–07 Preston NE 29 8
2007–08 Preston NE 18 1 **62 13**
2007–08 *Nottingham F* 13 2 **13 2**

SEDGWICK, Chris (M) 398 27
H: 5 11 W: 11 10 b.Sheffield 28-4-80
Source: Trainee.
1997–98 Rotherham U 4 0
1998–99 Rotherham U 33 4
1999–2000 Rotherham U 38 5
2000–01 Rotherham U 21 2
2001–02 Rotherham U 44 1
2002–03 Rotherham U 43 1
2003–04 Rotherham U 40 2
2004–05 Rotherham U 20 2 **243 17**
2004–05 Preston NE 24 3
2005–06 Preston NE 46 4
2006–07 Preston NE 43 1
2007–08 Preston NE 42 2 **155 10**

ST LEDGER-HALL, Sean (D) 157 3
H: 6 0 W: 11 09 b.Solihull 28-12-84
Source: Scholar.
2002–03 Peterborough U 1 0
2003–04 Peterborough U 2 0
2004–05 Peterborough U 33 0
2005–06 Peterborough U 43 1 **79 1**
2006–07 Preston NE 41 1
2007–08 Preston NE 37 1 **78 2**

TROTMAN, Neal (D) 21 1
H: 6 3 W: 13 08 b.Levenshulme 11-3-87
Source: Burnley Scholar.
2006–07 Oldham Ath 1 0
2007–08 Oldham Ath 17 1 **18 1**
2007–08 Preston NE 3 0 **3 0**

WHALEY, Simon (M) 172 24
H: 5 10 W: 11 11 b.Bolton 7-6-85
Source: Scholar.
2002–03 Bury 2 0
2003–04 Bury 10 1
2004–05 Bury 38 3
2005–06 Bury 23 7 **73 11**
2005–06 Preston NE 16 3
2006–07 Preston NE 40 6
2007–08 Preston NE 43 4 **99 13**

QPR (67)

AGYEMANG, Patrick (F) 305 57
H: 6 1 W: 12 00 b.Walthamstow 29-9-80
Source: Trainee. *Honours:* Ghana 3 full caps, 1 goal.
1998–99 Wimbledon 0 0
1999–2000 Wimbledon 0 0
1999–2000 *Brentford* 12 0 **12 0**
2000–01 Wimbledon 29 4
2001–02 Wimbledon 33 4
2002–03 Wimbledon 33 5
2003–04 Wimbledon 26 7 **121 20**
2003–04 Gillingham 20 6
2004–05 Gillingham 13 2 **33 8**
2004–05 Preston NE 27 4
2005–06 Preston NE 42 6
2006–07 Preston NE 31 7
2007–08 Preston NE 22 4 **122 21**
2007–08 QPR 17 8 **17 8**

AINSWORTH, Gareth (M) 424 89
H: 5 10 W: 12 05 b.Blackburn 10-5-73
Source: Blackburn R Trainee.
1991–92 Preston NE 5 0
1992–93 Cambridge U 4 1 **4 1**
1992–93 Preston NE 26 0
1993–94 Preston NE 38 11
1994–95 Preston NE 16 1
1995–96 Preston NE 2 0
1995–96 Lincoln C 31 12
1996–97 Lincoln C 46 22
1997–98 Lincoln C 6 3 **83 37**
1997–98 Port Vale 40 5
1998–99 Port Vale 15 5 **55 10**
1998–99 Wimbledon 8 0
1999–2000 Wimbledon 2 2
2000–01 Wimbledon 12 2
2001–02 Wimbledon 2 0
2001–02 *Preston NE* 5 1 **92 13**
2002–03 Wimbledon 12 2 **36 6**
2002–03 *Walsall* 5 1 **5 1**
2002–03 Cardiff C 9 0 **9 0**
2003–04 QPR 29 6
2004–05 QPR 22 2
2005–06 QPR 43 9
2006–07 QPR 22 1
2007–08 QPR 24 3 **140 21**

BAILEY, Stefan (M) 18 0
H: 5 11 W: 12 08 b.Brent 10-11-87
Source: Scholar.
2004–05 QPR 2 0
2005–06 QPR 5 0
2006–07 QPR 10 0
2007–08 QPR 1 0 **18 0**

BALANTA, Angelo (F) 11 1
H: 5 10 W: 11 11 b.Colombia 1-7-90
Source: Scholar.
2007–08 QPR 11 1 **11 1**

BARKER, Chris (D) 339 3
H: 6 2 W: 13 08 b.Sheffield 2-3-80
Source: Alfreton.
1998–99 Barnsley 0 0
1999–2000 Barnsley 29 0
2000–01 Barnsley 40 0
2001–02 Barnsley 44 3 **113 3**
2002–03 Cardiff C 40 0
2003–04 Cardiff C 39 0
2004–05 *Stoke C* 4 0 **4 0**
2004–05 Cardiff C 39 0
2005–06 Cardiff C 41 0
2006–07 Cardiff C 0 0 **159 0**
2006–07 *Colchester U* 38 0 **38 0**
2007–08 QPR 25 0 **25 0**

BLACKSTOCK, Dexter (F) 125 30
H: 6 2 W: 13 00 b.Oxford 20-5-86
Source: Scholar. *Honours:* England Youth, Under-20, Under-21.
2004–05 Southampton 9 1
2004–05 *Plymouth Arg* 14 4 **14 4**
2005–06 Southampton 19 3 **28 4**
2005–06 *Derby Co* 9 3 **9 3**
2006–07 QPR 39 13
2007–08 QPR 35 6 **74 19**

BOLDER, Adam (M) 239 15
H: 5 9 W: 10 08 b.Hull 25-10-80
Source: Trainee.
1998–99 Hull C 1 0
1999–2000 Hull C 19 0 **20 0**
1999–2000 Derby Co 0 0
2000–01 Derby Co 2 0
2001–02 Derby Co 11 0
2002–03 Derby Co 45 6
2003–04 Derby Co 24 1
2004–05 Derby Co 36 2
2005–06 Derby Co 35 2
2006–07 Derby Co 13 0 **166 11**
2006–07 QPR 16 0
2007–08 QPR 24 2 **40 2**
2007–08 *Sheffield W* 13 2 **13 2**

BUZSAKY, Akos (M) 123 18
H: 5 11 W: 11 09 b.Hungary 7-5-82
Source: MTK, Porto. *Honours:* Hungary Under-21, 11 full caps, 1 goal.
2004–05 Plymouth Arg 15 1
2005–06 Plymouth Arg 34 4
2006–07 Plymouth Arg 36 3
2007–08 Plymouth Arg 11 0 **96 8**
2007–08 QPR 27 10 **27 10**

CAMP, Lee (G) 161 0
H: 5 11 W: 11 11 b.Derby 22-8-84
Source: Scholar. *Honours:* England Youth, Under-20, Under-21.
2002–03 Derby Co 1 0
2003–04 Derby Co 0 0
2003–04 *QPR* 12 0
2004–05 Derby Co 45 0
2005–06 Derby Co 40 0
2006–07 Derby Co 3 0 **89 0**
2006–07 *Norwich C* 3 0 **3 0**
2006–07 *QPR* 11 0
2007–08 QPR 46 0 **69 0**

COLE, Jake (G) 6 0
H: 6 2 W: 13 00 b.Hammersmith 11-9-85
Source: Scholar.
2005–06 QPR 3 0
2006–07 QPR 3 0
2007–08 QPR 0 0 **6 0**

CONNOLLY, Matthew (D) 41 3
H: 6 1 W: 11 03 b.Barnet 24-9-87
Source: Scholar. *Honours:* England Youth.
2005–06 Arsenal 0 0
2006–07 Arsenal 0 0
2006–07 *Bournemouth* 5 1 **5 1**
2007–08 Arsenal 0 0
2007–08 *Colchester U* 16 2 **16 2**
2007–08 QPR 20 0 **20 0**

CURTIS, John (D) 231 2
H: 5 10 W: 11 07 b.Nuneaton 3-9-78
Source: Trainee. *Honours:* England Schools, Youth, Under-21, B.
1995–96 Manchester U 0 0
1996–97 Manchester U 0 0
1997–98 Manchester U 8 0
1998–99 Manchester U 4 0
1999–2000 Manchester U 1 0 **13 0**
1999–2000 *Barnsley* 28 2 **28 2**
2000–01 Blackburn R 46 0
2001–02 Blackburn R 10 0
2002–03 Blackburn R 5 0 **61 0**
2002–03 *Sheffield U* 12 0 **12 0**
2003–04 Leicester C 15 0 **15 0**
2003–04 Portsmouth 6 0
2004–05 Portsmouth 1 0 **7 0**
2004–05 *Preston NE* 12 0 **12 0**
2004–05 Nottingham F 11 0
2005–06 Nottingham F 27 0
2006–07 Nottingham F 41 0 **79 0**
2007–08 QPR 4 0 **4 0**

DELANEY, Damien (D) 270 7
H: 6 3 W: 14 00 b.Cork 20-7-81
Source: Cork C. *Honours:* Eire 2 full caps.
2000–01 Leicester C 5 0
2001–02 Leicester C 3 0
2001–02 *Stockport Co* 12 1 **12 1**
2001–02 *Huddersfield T* 2 0 **2 0**
2002–03 Leicester C 0 0 **8 0**
2002–03 *Mansfield T* 7 0 **7 0**
2002–03 Hull C 30 1
2003–04 Hull C 46 2
2004–05 Hull C 43 1
2005–06 Hull C 46 0
2006–07 Hull C 37 1
2007–08 Hull C 22 0 **224 5**
2007–08 QPR 17 1 **17 1**

EPHRAIM, Hogan (F) 50 4
H: 5 9 W: 10 06 b.Islington 31-3-88
Source: Scholar. *Honours:* England Youth.
2004–05 West Ham U 0 0
2005–06 West Ham U 0 0
2006–07 West Ham U 0 0
2006–07 *Colchester U* 21 1 **21 1**
2007–08 West Ham U 0 0
2007–08 QPR 29 3 **29 3**

GOODE, Aaron (M) 0 0
H: 5 1 W: 11 00 b.London 18-12-88
2007–08 QPR 0 0

HALL, Fitz (D) 169 8
H: 6 3 W: 13 00 b.Leytonstone 20-12-80
Source: Barnet Trainee, Chesham U.
2001–02 Oldham Ath 4 1
2002–03 Oldham Ath 40 4 **44 5**
2003–04 Southampton 11 0 **11 0**
2004–05 Crystal Palace 36 2
2005–06 Crystal Palace 39 1 **75 3**
2006–07 Wigan Ath 24 0
2007–08 Wigan Ath 1 0 **25 0**
2007–08 QPR 14 0 **14 0**

HOWELL, Andrew (D) 0 0
H: 5 11 W: 12 01 b.Gt Yarmouth 18-3-89
Source: Scholar.
2005–06 QPR 0 0
2006–07 QPR 0 0
2007–08 QPR 0 0

JONES (DECEASED), Ray (F) 33 5
H: 6 4 W: 14 05 b.Newham 28-8-88
Source: Scholar. *Honours:* England Youth.
2005–06 QPR 2 0
2006–07 QPR 31 5
2007–08 QPR 0 0 **33 5**

LEIGERTWOOD, Mikele (D) **184 8**
H: 6 1 W: 11 04 b.Enfield 12-11-82
Source: Scholar.

2001–02	Wimbledon	1	0		
2001–02	*Leyton Orient*	8	0	**8**	**0**
2002–03	Wimbledon	28	0		
2003–04	Wimbledon	27	2	**56**	**2**
2003–04	Crystal Palace	12	0		
2004–05	Crystal Palace	20	1		
2005–06	Crystal Palace	27	0	**59**	**1**
2006–07	Sheffield U	19	0		
2007–08	Sheffield U	2	0	**21**	**0**
2007–08	QPR	40	5	**40**	**5**

MAHON, Gavin (M) **357 16**
H: 5 11 W: 13 07 b.Birmingham 2-1-77
Source: Trainee.

1995–96	Wolverhampton W	0	0		
1996–97	Hereford U	11	1		
1997–98	Hereford U	0	0		
1998–99	Hereford U	0	0	**11**	**1**
1998–99	Brentford	29	4		
1999–2000	Brentford	37	3		
2000–01	Brentford	40	1		
2001–02	Brentford	35	0	**141**	**8**
2001–02	Watford	6	0		
2002–03	Watford	17	0		
2003–04	Watford	32	2		
2004–05	Watford	43	0		
2005–06	Watford	38	3		
2006–07	Watford	34	1		
2007–08	Watford	19	0	**189**	**6**
2007–08	QPR	16	1	**16**	**1**

NARDIELLO, Daniel (F) **131 30**
H: 5 11 W: 11 04 b.Coventry 22-10-82
Source: Trainee. *Honours:* Wales 3 full caps.

1999–2000	Manchester U	0	0		
2000–01	Manchester U	0	0		
2001–02	Manchester U	0	0		
2002–03	Manchester U	0	0		
2003–04	Manchester U	0	0		
2003–04	*Swansea C*	4	0	**4**	**0**
2003–04	*Barnsley*	16	7		
2004–05	Manchester U	0	0		
2004–05	*Barnsley*	28	7		
2005–06	Barnsley	34	5		
2006–07	Barnsley	30	9		
2007–08	QPR	8	0	**8**	**0**
2007–08	*Barnsley*	11	2	**119**	**30**

NYGAARD, Marc (F) **244 39**
H: 6 5 W: 14 05 b.Copenhagen 1-9-76
Source: FC Copenhagen. *Honours:* Denmark Youth, Under-21, 6 full caps.

1995–96	Heerenveen	6	1		
1996–97	Heerenveen	20	5	**26**	**6**
1997–98	MVV	34	3	**34**	**3**
1998–99	Roda JC	30	10		
1999–2000	Roda JC	2	0		
2000–01	Roda JC	24	1		
2001–02	Roda JC	21	1	**77**	**12**
2002–03	Lommel	4	1	**4**	**1**
2002–03	Excelsior	8	1	**8**	**1**
2003–04	Catania	12	3	**12**	**3**
2003–04	Vicenza	4	0	**4**	**0**
2004–05	Brescia	10	0	**10**	**0**
2005–06	QPR	27	9		
2006–07	QPR	23	3		
2007–08	QPR	19	1	**69**	**13**

PICKENS, Matthew (G) **0 0**
H: 6 3 W: 13 00 b.Washington 5-4-82
Source: Chicago Fire.

2007–08	QPR	0	0

REHMAN, Zesh (D) **91 2**
H: 6 2 W: 12 08 b.Birmingham 14-10-83
Source: Scholar. *Honours:* England Youth, Pakistan 6 full caps.

2001–02	Fulham	0	0		
2002–03	Fulham	0	0		
2003–04	Fulham	1	0		
2003–04	*Brighton & HA*	11	2		
2004–05	Fulham	17	0		
2005–06	Fulham	3	0	**21**	**0**
2005–06	*Norwich C*	5	0	**5**	**0**
2006–07	QPR	25	0		
2006–07	*Brighton & HA*	8	0	**19**	**2**
2007–08	QPR	21	0	**46**	**0**

ROSE, Romone (M) **1 0**
H: 5 9 W: 11 05 b.Pennsylvania 19-1-90
Source: Scholar.

2007–08	QPR	1	0	**1**	**0**

ROWLANDS, Martin (M) **313 51**
H: 5 9 W: 10 10 b.Hammersmith 8-2-79
Source: Farnborough T. *Honours:* Eire Under-21, 3 full caps.

1998–99	Brentford	36	4		
1999–2000	Brentford	40	6		
2000–01	Brentford	32	2		
2001–02	Brentford	23	7		
2002–03	Brentford	18	1	**149**	**20**
2003–04	QPR	42	10		
2004–05	QPR	35	3		
2005–06	QPR	14	2		
2006–07	QPR	29	10		
2007–08	QPR	44	6	**164**	**31**

SHIMMIN, Dominic (D) **5 0**
H: 6 0 W: 12 06 b.Bermondsey 13-10-87
Source: Arsenal Scholar.

2004–05	QPR	0	0		
2005–06	QPR	2	0		
2006–07	QPR	1	0		
2007–08	QPR	0	0	**3**	**0**
2007–08	*Bournemouth*	2	0	**2**	**0**

STEWART, Damion (D) **107 7**
H: 6 3 W: 13 10 b.Jamaica 18-8-80
Source: Harbour View. *Honours:* Jamaica 37 full caps, 2 goals.

2005–06	Bradford C	23	1	**23**	**1**
2006–07	QPR	45	1		
2007–08	QPR	39	5	**84**	**6**

THOMAS, Sean (G) **0 0**
H: 6 1 W: 12 03 b.Edgware 5-9-87
Source: Scholar.

2005–06	QPR	0	0
2006–07	QPR	0	0
2007–08	QPR	0	0

TIMOSKA, Sampsa (D) **155 8**
H: 6 1 W: 11 11 b.Kokemaki 12-2-79
Honours: Finland Under-21, 2 full caps.

1998	MyPa	1	0		
1999	MyPa	14	0		
2000	MyPa	16	0		
2001	MyPa	19	1		
2002	MyPa	26	1		
2003	MyPa	18	1		
2004	MyPa	23	3		
2005	MyPa	17	2	**134**	**8**
2006–07	QPR	14	0		
2007–08	QPR	7	0	**21**	**0**

VINE, Rowan (F) **242 54**
H: 5 11 W: 12 10 b.Basingstoke 21-9-82
Source: Scholar.

2000–01	Portsmouth	2	0		
2001–02	Portsmouth	11	0		
2002–03	Portsmouth	0	0		
2002–03	*Brentford*	42	10	**42**	**10**
2003–04	Portsmouth	0	0		
2003–04	*Colchester U*	35	6	**35**	**6**
2004–05	Portsmouth	0	0	**13**	**0**
2004–05	*Luton T*	45	9		
2005–06	Luton T	31	10		
2006–07	Luton T	26	12	**102**	**31**
2006–07	Birmingham C	17	1		
2007–08	Birmingham C	0	0	**17**	**1**
2007–08	QPR	33	6	**33**	**6**

WALTON, Simon (D) **74 6**
H: 6 1 W: 13 05 b.Sherburn-in-Elmet 13-9-87
Source: Scholar. *Honours:* England Youth.

2004–05	Leeds U	30	3		
2005–06	Leeds U	4	0	**34**	**3**
2006–07	Charlton Ath	0	0		
2006–07	*Ipswich T*	19	3	**19**	**3**
2006–07	*Cardiff C*	6	0	**6**	**0**
2007–08	QPR	5	0	**5**	**0**
2007–08	*Hull C*	10	0	**10**	**0**

WARD, Nick (M) **28 2**
H: 6 0 W: 12 06 b.Perth 24-3-85
Honours: Australia Under-21.

2006–07	QPR	19	1		
2006–07	*Brighton & HA*	8	1	**8**	**1**
2007–08	QPR	1	0	**20**	**1**

READING (68)

ANDERSEN, Mikkel (G) **0 0**
H: 6 5 W: 12 08 b.Herlev 17-12-88
Source: AB Copenhagen. *Honours:* Denmark Youth.

2006–07	Reading	0	0
2007–08	Reading	0	0

BENNETT, Alan (D) **21 1**
H: 6 2 W: 12 08 b.Kilkenny 4-10-81
Honours: Eire Under-21, B, 2 full caps.

2006–07	Reading	0	0		
2007–08	Reading	0	0		
2007–08	*Southampton*	10	0	**10**	**0**
2007–08	*Brentford*	11	1	**11**	**1**

BIKEY, Andre (D) **64 4**
H: 6 0 W: 12 08 b.Douala 8-1-85
Source: Espanyol, Marco. *Honours:* Cameroon 10 full caps, 1 goal.

2003–04	Pacos de Ferreira	2	0	**2**	**0**
2004–05	Dep Aves	0	0		
2005	Shinnik	11	1	**11**	**1**
2005	Loko Moscow	9	0		
2006	Loko Moscow	5	0	**14**	**0**
2006–07	Reading	15	0		
2007–08	Reading	22	3	**37**	**3**

BOZANIC, Ollie (M) **0 0**
H: 6 0 W: 12 00 b.Melbourne 8-1-89
Source: Central Coast M. *Honours:* Australia Youth, Under-20.

2006–07	Reading	0	0
2007–08	Reading	0	0

BROWN, Aaron (D) **4 0**
H: 6 4 W: 14 07 b.Birmingham 23-6-83
Source: Tamworth.

2005–06	Reading	0	0		
2005–06	*Bournemouth*	4	0	**4**	**0**
2006–07	Reading	0	0		
2007–08	*Walsall*	0	0		
2007–08	Reading	0	0		

BYGRAVE, Adam (D) **15 0**
H: 5 9 W: 12 02 b.Walthamstow 24-2-89
Source: Scholar.

2007–08	Reading	0	0		
2007–08	*Gillingham*	15	0	**15**	**0**

CHURCH, Simon (F) **18 1**
H: 6 0 W: 13 04 b.Amersham 10-12-88
Source: Scholar. *Honours:* Wales Under-21.

2007–08	Reading	0	0		
2007–08	*Crewe Alex*	12	1	**12**	**1**
2007–08	*Yeovil T*	6	0	**6**	**0**

CISSE, Kalifa (M) **70 1**
H: 6 2 W: 12 11 b.Orleans 1-9-84
Source: Toulouse. *Honours:* Mali full caps.

2004–05	Estoril	6	0	**6**	**0**
2005–06	Boavista	15	0		
2006–07	Boavista	27	0	**42**	**0**
2007–08	Reading	22	1	**22**	**1**

CONVEY, Bobby (M) **92 7**
H: 5 8 W: 10 12 b.Philadelphia 27-5-83
Source: DC United. *Honours:* USA Youth, Under-21, 46 full caps, 1 goal.

2004–05	Reading	18	0		
2005–06	Reading	45	7		
2006–07	Reading	9	0		
2007–08	Reading	20	0	**92**	**7**

DAVIES, Scott (M) **0 0**
H: 5 11 W: 12 00 b.Dublin 10-3-88
Source: Scholar.

2006–07	Reading	0	0
2007–08	Reading	0	0

DE LA CRUZ, Ulises (D) **304 27**
H: 5 8 W: 12 10 b.Piqulucho 8-2-74
Source: Cruzeiro. *Honours:* Ecuador Youth, Under-23, 90 full caps, 5 goals.

1996	Aucas	32	3	**32**	**3**
1997	LDU Quito	38	4		
1998	LDU Quito	42	7		
1999	LDU Quito	22	4		
1999	Cruzeiro	4	0	**4**	**0**
2000	LDU Quito	30	5	**132**	**20**
2001–02	Hibernian	32	2	**32**	**2**
2002–03	Aston Villa	20	1		
2003–04	Aston Villa	28	0		
2004–05	Aston Villa	34	0		

2005–06	Aston Villa	7	0	**89**	**1**
2006–07	Reading	9	1		
2007–08	Reading	6	0	**15**	**1**

DOYLE, Kevin (F) **156** **57**
H: 5 11 W: 12 06 b.Adamstown 18-9-83
Source: Adamstown, Wexford, St Patrick's Ath. *Honours:* Eire Under-21, 18 full caps, 5 goals.

2004	Cork C	32	13		
2005	Cork C	11	7	**43**	**20**
2005–06	Reading	45	18		
2006–07	Reading	32	13		
2007–08	Reading	36	6	**113**	**37**

DUBERRY, Michael (D) **267** **6**
H: 6 1 W: 13 10 b.Enfield 14-10-75
Source: Trainee. *Honours:* England Under-21.

1993–94	Chelsea	1	0		
1994–95	Chelsea	0	0		
1995–96	Chelsea	22	0		
1995–96	*Bournemouth*	7	0	**7**	**0**
1996–97	Chelsea	15	1		
1997–98	Chelsea	23	0		
1998–99	Chelsea	25	0	**86**	**1**
1999–2000	Leeds U	13	1		
2000–01	Leeds U	5	0		
2001–02	Leeds U	3	0		
2002–03	Leeds U	14	0		
2003–04	Leeds U	19	3		
2004–05	Leeds U	4	0	**58**	**4**
2004–05	Stoke C	25	0		
2005–06	Stoke C	41	1		
2006–07	Stoke C	29	0	**95**	**1**
2006–07	Reading	8	0		
2007–08	Reading	13	0	**21**	**0**

FAE, Emerse (M) **114** **7**
H: 5 8 W: 11 00 b.Nantes 24-1-84
Honours: Ivory Coast 17 full caps, 1 goal.

2003–04	Nantes	25	1		
2004–05	Nantes	28	1		
2005–06	Nantes	29	4		
2006–07	Nantes	24	1	**106**	**7**
2007–08	Reading	8	0	**8**	**0**

FEDERICI, Adam (G) **2** **0**
H: 6 2 W: 14 02 b.Nowra 31-1-85
Honours: Australia Youth, Under-20, Under-21.

2005–06	Reading	0	0		
2006–07	Reading	2	0		
2007–08	Reading	0	0	**2**	**0**

GOLBOURNE, Scott (M) **55** **1**
H: 5 8 W: 11 08 b.Bristol 29-2-88
Source: Scholar. *Honours:* England Youth.

2004–05	Bristol C	9	0		
2005–06	Bristol C	5	0	**14**	**0**
2005–06	Reading	1	0		
2006–07	Reading	0	0		
2006–07	*Wycombe W*	34	1	**34**	**1**
2007–08	Reading	1	0	**2**	**0**
2007–08	*Bournemouth*	5	0	**5**	**0**

GUNNARSSON, Brynjar (M) **310** **29**
H: 6 1 W: 12 01 b.Reykjavik 16-10-75
Honours: Iceland Youth, Under-21, 65 full caps, 4 goals.

1995	KR	16	1		
1996	KR	18	0		
1997	KR	16	0	**50**	**1**
1998	Moss	5	2	**5**	**2**
1999–2000	Stoke C	22	1		
2000–01	Stoke C	46	5		
2001–02	Stoke C	23	5		
2002–03	Stoke C	40	5		
2003–04	Nottingham F	13	0	**13**	**0**
2003–04	*Stoke C*	3	0	**134**	**16**
2004–05	Watford	36	3	**36**	**3**
2005–06	Reading	29	4		
2006–07	Reading	23	3		
2007–08	Reading	20	0	**72**	**7**

HAHNEMANN, Marcus (G) **323** **0**
H: 6 3 W: 13 03 b.Seattle 15-6-72
Honours: USA 7 full caps.

1997	Colorado Rapids	25	0		
1998	Colorado Rapids	28	0		
1999	Colorado Rapids	13	0	**66**	**0**
1999–2000	Fulham	0	0		
2000–01	Fulham	2	0		
2001–02	Fulham	0	0	**2**	**0**
2001–02	*Rochdale*	5	0	**5**	**0**
2001–02	*Reading*	6	0		
2002–03	Reading	41	0		
2003–04	Reading	36	0		
2004–05	Reading	46	0		
2005–06	Reading	45	0		
2006–07	Reading	38	0		
2007–08	Reading	38	0	**250**	**0**

HALLS, John (M) **92** **3**
H: 6 0 W: 11 11 b.Islington 14-2-82
Source: Scholar. *Honours:* England Youth, Under-20.

2000–01	Arsenal	0	0		
2001–02	Arsenal	0	0		
2001–02	*Colchester U*	6	0	**6**	**0**
2002–03	Arsenal	0	0		
2003–04	Arsenal	0	0		
2003–04	Stoke C	34	0		
2004–05	Stoke C	22	0		
2005–06	Stoke C	13	2	**69**	**2**
2005–06	Reading	1	1		
2006–07	Reading	0	0		
2007–08	Reading	1	0	**2**	**1**
2007–08	*Preston NE*	4	0	**4**	**0**
2007–08	*Crystal Palace*	5	0	**5**	**0**
2007–08	*Sheffield U*	6	0	**6**	**0**

HAMER, Ben (G) **20** **0**
H: 5 11 W: 12 04 b.Chard 20-11-87
Source: Crawley T.

2006–07	Reading	0	0		
2007–08	Reading	0	0		
2007–08	*Brentford*	20	0	**20**	**0**

HARPER, James (M) **278** **24**
H: 5 10 W: 11 02 b.Chelmsford 9-11-80
Source: Trainee.

1999–2000	Arsenal	0	0		
2000–01	Arsenal	0	0		
2000–01	*Cardiff C*	3	0	**3**	**0**
2000–01	Reading	12	1		
2001–02	Reading	26	1		
2002–03	Reading	36	2		
2003–04	Reading	39	1		
2004–05	Reading	41	3		
2005–06	Reading	45	7		
2006–07	Reading	38	3		
2007–08	Reading	38	6	**275**	**24**

HENRY, James (M) **15** **4**
H: 6 1 W: 11 11 b.Readding 10-6-89
Source: Scholar. *Honours:* England Youth.

2006–07	Reading	0	0		
2006–07	*Nottingham F*	1	0	**1**	**0**
2007–08	Reading	0	0		
2007–08	*Bournemouth*	11	4	**11**	**4**
2007–08	*Norwich C*	3	0	**3**	**0**

HUNT, Steve (M) **249** **36**
H: 5 9 W: 10 10 b.Port Laoise 1-8-80
Source: Trainee. *Honours:* Eire Under-21, B, 11 full caps.

1999–2000	Crystal Palace	3	0		
2000–01	Crystal Palace	0	0	**3**	**0**
2001–02	Brentford	35	4		
2002–03	Brentford	42	7		
2003–04	Brentford	40	11		
2004–05	Brentford	19	3	**136**	**25**
2005–06	Reading	38	2		
2006–07	Reading	35	4		
2007–08	Reading	37	5	**110**	**11**

ILLUGASON, Viktor (F) **0** **0**
b.Iceland 25-1-90
Source: Scholar. *Honours:* Iceland Youth.

2007–08	Reading	0	0		

INGIMARSSON, Ivar (D) **413** **33**
H: 6 0 W: 12 07 b.Reykjavik 20-8-77
Honours: Iceland Youth, Under-21, 30 full caps.

1995	Valur	12	0		
1996	Valur	17	2		
1997	Valur	16	3	**45**	**5**
1998	IBV	18	1		
1999	IBV	18	4	**36**	**5**
1999–2000	Torquay U	4	1	**4**	**1**
1999–2000	Brentford	25	1		
2000–01	Brentford	42	3		
2001–02	Brentford	46	6	**113**	**10**
2002–03	Wolverhampton W	13	2		
2002–03	*Brighton & HA*	15	0	**15**	**0**
2003–04	Wolverhampton W	0	0	**13**	**2**
2003–04	Reading	25	1		
2004–05	Reading	44	3		
2005–06	Reading	46	2		
2006–07	Reading	38	2		
2007–08	Reading	34	2	**187**	**10**

KARACAN, Jem (M) **20** **1**
H: 5 10 W: 11 13 b.Lewisham 21-2-89
Source: Scholar.

2007–08	Reading	0	0		
2007–08	*Bournemouth*	13	1	**13**	**1**
2007–08	*Millwall*	7	0	**7**	**0**

KEBE, Jimmy (M) **39** **7**
H: 6 2 W: 11 07 b.Vitry-sur-Seine 19-1-84
Honours: Mali 8 full caps, 3 goals.

2005–06	Lens	0	0		
2006–07	*Chateauroux*	18	2	**18**	**2**
2007–08	Lens	0	0		
2007–08	*Boulogne*	16	5	**16**	**5**
2007–08	Reading	5	0	**5**	**0**

KITSON, Dave (F) **237** **94**
H: 6 3 W: 12 07 b.Hitchin 21-1-80
Source: Arlesey.

2000–01	Cambridge U	8	1		
2001–02	Cambridge U	33	9		
2002–03	Cambridge U	44	20		
2003–04	Cambridge U	17	10	**102**	**40**
2003–04	Reading	17	5		
2004–05	Reading	37	19		
2005–06	Reading	34	18		
2006–07	Reading	13	2		
2007–08	Reading	34	10	**135**	**54**

LITA, Leroy (F) **166** **53**
H: 5 7 W: 11 12 b.DR Congo 28-12-84
Source: Scholar. *Honours:* England Under-21.

2002–03	Bristol C	15	2		
2003–04	Bristol C	26	5		
2004–05	Bristol C	44	24	**85**	**31**
2005–06	Reading	26	11		
2006–07	Reading	33	7		
2007–08	Reading	14	1	**73**	**19**
2007–08	*Charlton Ath*	8	3	**8**	**3**

LITTLE, Glen (M) **358** **40**
H: 6 3 W: 13 00 b.Wimbledon 15-10-75
Source: Trainee.

1994–95	Crystal Palace	0	0		
1995–96	Crystal Palace	0	0		
1996–97	Glentoran	6	2	**6**	**2**
1996–97	Burnley	9	0		
1997–98	Burnley	24	4		
1998–99	Burnley	34	5		
1999–2000	Burnley	41	3		
2000–01	Burnley	34	3		
2001–02	Burnley	37	9		
2002–03	Burnley	33	5		
2002–03	*Reading*	6	1		
2003–04	Burnley	34	3	**246**	**32**
2003–04	*Bolton W*	4	0	**4**	**0**
2004–05	Reading	35	0		
2005–06	Reading	35	5		
2006–07	Reading	24	0		
2007–08	Reading	2	0	**102**	**6**

LONG, Shane (F) **62** **8**
H: 5 10 W: 11 02 b.Gortnahoe 22-1-87
Honours: Eire Youth, B, Under-21, 8 full caps, 3 goals.

2005	Cork C	1	0	**1**	**0**
2005–06	Reading	11	3		
2006–07	Reading	21	2		
2007–08	Reading	29	3	**61**	**8**

LYSKOV, Tom (M) **0** **0**

2007–08	Reading	0	0		

MATEJOVSKY, Marek (M) **103** **7**
H: 5 10 W: 11 00 b.Brandys nad Labem 20-12-81
Honours: Czech Republic 8 full caps, 1 goal.

2000–01	Jablonec	1	0		
2001–02	Jablonec	4	0		
2002–03	Jablonec	1	0	**6**	**0**
2003–04	Mlada Boleslav	0	0		
2004–05	Mlada Boleslav	28	1		
2005–06	Mlada Boleslav	26	5		
2006–07	Mlada Boleslav	29	0	**83**	**6**
2007–08	Reading	14	1	**14**	**1**

MURTY, Graeme (D) 423 9
H: 5 10 W: 11 10 b.Saltburn 13-11-74
Source: Trainee. *Honours:* Scotland B, 4 full caps.

1992–93	York C	0	0		
1993–94	York C	1	0		
1994–95	York C	20	2		
1995–96	York C	35	2		
1996–97	York C	27	2		
1997–98	York C	34	1	**117**	**7**
1998–99	Reading	9	0		
1999–2000	Reading	17	0		
2000–01	Reading	23	1		
2001–02	Reading	43	0		
2002–03	Reading	44	0		
2003–04	Reading	38	0		
2004–05	Reading	41	0		
2005–06	Reading	40	1		
2006–07	Reading	23	0		
2007–08	Reading	28	0	**306**	**2**

OSANO, Curtis (M) 0 0
H: 5 11 W: 11 04 b.Nakuru 8-3-87
Source: Scholar.

2005–06	Reading	0	0		
2006–07	Reading	0	0		
2007–08	Reading	0	0		

OSTER, John (M) 250 19
H: 5 9 W: 10 08 b.Boston 8-12-78
Source: Trainee. *Honours:* Wales Youth, Under-21, B, 13 full caps.

1996–97	Grimsby T	24	3		
1997–98	Everton	31	1		
1998–99	Everton	9	0	**40**	**1**
1999–2000	Sunderland	10	0		
2000–01	Sunderland	8	0		
2001–02	Sunderland	0	0		
2001–02	*Barnsley*	2	0	**2**	**0**
2002–03	Sunderland	3	0		
2002–03	*Grimsby T*	17	6	**41**	**9**
2003–04	Sunderland	38	5		
2004–05	Sunderland	9	0	**68**	**5**
2004–05	*Leeds U*	8	1	**8**	**1**
2004–05	Burnley	15	1	**15**	**1**
2005–06	Reading	33	1		
2006–07	Reading	25	1		
2007–08	Reading	18	0	**76**	**2**

PEARCE, Alex (D) 37 1
H: 6 0 W: 11 10 b.Wallingford 9-11-88
Source: Scholar. *Honours:* Scotland Youth, Under-21.

2006–07	Reading	0	0		
2006–07	*Northampton T*	15	1	**15**	**1**
2007–08	Reading	0	0		
2007–08	*Bournemouth*	11	0	**11**	**0**
2007–08	*Norwich C*	11	0	**11**	**0**

ROBSON-KANU, Hal (F) 8 3
H: 5 7 W: 11 08 b.Acton 21-5-89
Honours: England Youth.

2007–08	Reading	0	0		
2007–08	*Southend U*	8	3	**8**	**3**

ROSENIOR, Liam (D) 128 2
H: 5 10 W: 11 05 b.Wandsworth 9-7-84
Source: Scholar. *Honours:* England Youth, Under-20, Under-21.

2001–02	Bristol C	1	0		
2002–03	Bristol C	21	2		
2003–04	Bristol C	0	0	**22**	**2**
2003–04	Fulham	0	0		
2003–04	*Torquay U*	10	0	**10**	**0**
2004–05	Fulham	17	0		
2005–06	Fulham	24	0		
2006–07	Fulham	38	0		
2007–08	Fulham	0	0	**79**	**0**
2007–08	Reading	17	0	**17**	**0**

SHOREY, Nicky (D) 282 12
H: 5 9 W: 10 08 b.Romford 19-2-81
Source: Trainee. *Honours:* England B, 2 full caps.

1999–2000	Leyton Orient	7	0		
2000–01	Leyton Orient	8	0	**15**	**0**
2000–01	Reading	0	0		
2001–02	Reading	32	0		
2002–03	Reading	43	2		
2003–04	Reading	35	2		
2004–05	Reading	44	3		
2005–06	Reading	40	2		
2006–07	Reading	37	1		
2007–08	Reading	36	2	**267**	**12**

SIGURDSSON, Gylfi (M) 0 0
Source: Scholar.

2007–08	Reading	0	0		

SODJE, Sam (D) 120 15
H: 6 0 W: 12 00 b.Greenwich 29-5-79
Source: Stevenage B, Margate. *Honours:* Nigeria 2 full caps.

2004–05	Brentford	40	7		
2005–06	Brentford	43	5	**83**	**12**
2006–07	Reading	3	0		
2006–07	*WBA*	7	1	**7**	**1**
2007–08	Reading	0	0	**3**	**0**
2007–08	*Charlton Ath*	27	2	**27**	**2**

SONKO, Ibrahima (D) 204 13
H: 6 3 W: 13 07 b.Bignola 22-1-81
Source: St Etienne, Grenoble. *Honours:* Senegal Under-21, 1 full cap.

2002–03	Brentford	37	5		
2003–04	Brentford	43	3	**80**	**8**
2004–05	Reading	39	1		
2005–06	Reading	46	3		
2006–07	Reading	23	1		
2007–08	Reading	16	0	**124**	**5**

STACK, Graham (G) 41 0
H: 6 2 W: 12 07 b.Hampstead 26-9-81
Honours: Eire Youth, Under-21.

2000–01	Arsenal	0	0		
2001–02	Arsenal	0	0		
2002–03	Arsenal	0	0		
2003–04	Arsenal	0	0		
2004–05	Arsenal	0	0		
2004–05	*Millwall*	26	0	**26**	**0**
2005–06	Arsenal	0	0		
2005–06	Reading	1	0		
2006–07	Reading	0	0		
2006–07	*Leeds U*	12	0	**12**	**0**
2007–08	Reading	0	0	**1**	**0**
2007–08	*Wolverhampton W*	2	0	**2**	**0**

Scholars
Bignall, Nicholas; Bossman, Kelvin; Bryant, Mitchell Jon; Downes, Jahson; Frewen, Gary Christopher; Hateley, Tom; Kamdjo, Clovis; Kelly, Julian James; Kitteridge, Ross Harrison; Lyskov, Thomas Patrick; McCarthy, Alex; Mitchell, Ashley; Spence, Daniel; Vasilev, Radoslav

ROCHDALE (69)

BOWYER, George (M) 1 0
H: 6 0 W: 10 02 b.Stockport 11-11-90
Source: Scholar.

2007–08	Rochdale	1	0	**1**	**0**

BROWN, Gary (D) 38 0
H: 5 6 W: 10 00 b.Darwen 29-10-85
Source: Scholar.

2004–05	Rochdale	1	0		
2005–06	Rochdale	16	0		
2006–07	Rochdale	21	0		
2007–08	Rochdale	0	0	**38**	**0**

BUCKLEY, Will (F) 7 0
H: 6 0 W: 13 00 b.Burnley 12-8-88
Source: Curzon Ashton.

2007–08	Rochdale	7	0	**7**	**0**

CROOKS, Lee (M) 251 4
H: 6 2 W: 12 01 b.Wakefield 14-1-78
Source: Trainee. *Honours:* England Youth.

1994–95	Manchester C	0	0		
1995–96	Manchester C	0	0		
1996–97	Manchester C	15	0		
1997–98	Manchester C	5	0		
1998–99	Manchester C	34	1		
1999–2000	Manchester C	20	1		
2000–01	Manchester C	2	0	**76**	**2**
2000–01	*Northampton T*	3	0	**3**	**0**
2000–01	Barnsley	0	0		
2001–02	Barnsley	26	0		
2002–03	Barnsley	18	0		
2003–04	Barnsley	23	0	**67**	**0**
2004–05	Bradford C	32	1		
2005–06	Bradford C	15	0	**47**	**1**
2005–06	*Notts Co*	18	1	**18**	**1**
2006–07	Rochdale	31	0		
2007–08	Rochdale	9	0	**40**	**0**

D'LARYEA, Nathan (D) 7 0
H: 5 10 W: 12 02 b.Manchester 3-9-85
Source: Trainee.

2003–04	Manchester C	0	0		
2004–05	Manchester C	0	0		
2005–06	Manchester C	0	0		
2006–07	Manchester C	0	0		
2006–07	*Macclesfield T*	1	0	**1**	**0**
2007–08	Rochdale	6	0	**6**	**0**

DAGNALL, Chris (F) 111 34
H: 5 8 W: 12 03 b.Liverpool 15-4-86
Source: Scholar.

2003–04	Tranmere R	10	1		
2004–05	Tranmere R	23	6		
2005–06	Tranmere R	6	0	**39**	**7**
2005–06	Rochdale	21	3		
2006–07	Rochdale	37	17		
2007–08	Rochdale	14	7	**72**	**27**

DOOLAN, John (M) 444 22
H: 6 1 W: 13 00 b.Liverpool 7-5-74
Source: Trainee.

1992–93	Everton	0	0		
1993–94	Everton	0	0		
1994–95	Mansfield T	24	1		
1995–96	Mansfield T	42	2		
1996–97	Mansfield T	41	6		
1997–98	Mansfield T	24	1	**131**	**10**
1997–98	Barnet	17	0		
1998–99	Barnet	42	2		
1999–2000	Barnet	44	2		
2000–01	Barnet	31	3		
2001–02	Barnet	0	0		
2002–03	Barnet	0	0	**134**	**7**
2003–04	Doncaster R	39	0		
2004–05	Doncaster R	38	2	**77**	**2**
2005–06	Blackpool	19	0	**19**	**0**
2005–06	Rochdale	18	0		
2006–07	Rochdale	40	3		
2007–08	Rochdale	25	0	**83**	**3**

EVANS, Raphale (D) 1 0
H: 6 0 W: 14 07 b.Manchester 7-5-90

2007–08	Rochdale	1	0	**1**	**0**

HIGGINBOTHAM, Kallum (F) 33 3
H: 5 11 W: 10 10 b.Manchester 15-6-89

2007–08	Rochdale	33	3	**33**	**3**

HOLNESS, Marcus (D) 19 0
H: 6 0 W: 12 02 b.Swinton 8-12-88
Source: Scholar.

2007–08	Oldham Ath	0	0		
2007–08	Rochdale	19	0	**19**	**0**

JONES, Gary (M) 381 50
H: 5 11 W: 12 05 b.Birkenhead 3-6-77
Source: Caernarfon T.

1997–98	Swansea C	8	0	**8**	**0**
1997–98	Rochdale	17	2		
1998–99	Rochdale	20	0		
1999–2000	Rochdale	39	7		
2000–01	Rochdale	44	8		
2001–02	Rochdale	20	5		
2001–02	Barnsley	25	1		
2002–03	Barnsley	31	1		
2003–04	Barnsley	0	0	**56**	**2**
2003–04	Rochdale	26	4		
2004–05	Rochdale	39	8		
2005–06	Rochdale	42	4		
2006–07	Rochdale	27	3		
2007–08	Rochdale	43	7	**317**	**48**

KENNEDY, Tom (D) 186 7
H: 5 10 W: 11 01 b.Bury 24-6-85
Source: Scholar.

2002–03	Bury	0	0		
2003–04	Bury	27	0		
2004–05	Bury	46	1		
2005–06	Bury	33	4		
2006–07	Bury	37	0	**143**	**5**
2007–08	Rochdale	43	2	**43**	**2**

LE FONDRE, Adam (F) 116 37
H: 5 9 W: 11 04 b.Stockport 2-12-86
Source: Trainee.

2004–05	Stockport Co	20	4		
2005–06	Stockport Co	22	6		
2006–07	Stockport Co	21	7	**63**	**17**
2006–07	*Rochdale*	7	4		
2007–08	Rochdale	46	16	**53**	**20**

McARDLE, Rory (D) **88 3**
H: 6 1 W: 11 11 b.Doncaster 1-5-87
Source: Scholar. *Honours:* Northern Ireland Youth, Under-21.

2004–05	Sheffield W	0	0		
2005–06	Sheffield W	0	0		
2005–06	*Rochdale*	19	1		
2006–07	Sheffield W	1	0	**1**	**0**
2006–07	Rochdale	25	0		
2007–08	Rochdale	43	2	**87**	**3**

MUIRHEAD, Ben (M) **155 7**
H: 5 9 W: 11 02 b.Doncaster 5-1-83
Source: Trainee. *Honours:* England Youth.

1999–2000	Manchester U	0	0		
2000–01	Manchester U	0	0		
2001–02	Manchester U	0	0		
2002–03	Manchester U	0	0		
2002–03	Bradford C	8	0		
2003–04	Bradford C	28	2		
2004–05	Bradford C	40	1		
2005–06	Bradford C	32	1		
2006–07	Bradford C	4	0	**112**	**4**
2006–07	*Rochdale*	12	3		
2007–08	Rochdale	31	0	**43**	**3**

PERKINS, David (D) **58 4**
H: 5 6 W: 11 06 b.St Asaph 21-6-82

2006–07	Rochdale	18	0		
2007–08	Rochdale	40	4	**58**	**4**

PRENDERGAST, Rory (F) **59 2**
H: 5 8 W: 12 00 b.Pontefract 6-4-78
Source: Rochdale.

1995–96	Barnsley	0	0		
1996–97	Barnsley	0	0		
1997–98	Barnsley	0	0		
1998–99	York C	3	0	**3**	**0**
1998–99	Oldham Ath	0	0		
From Accrington S					
2005–06	Blackpool	24	0		
2006–07	Blackpool	5	0	**29**	**0**
2006–07	Rochdale	5	1		
2006–07	*Darlington*	8	0	**8**	**0**
2007–08	Rochdale	14	1	**19**	**2**

RAMSDEN, Simon (D) **153 6**
H: 6 0 W: 12 06 b.Bishop Auckland 17-12-81
Source: Scholar.

2000–01	Sunderland	0	0		
2001–02	Sunderland	0	0		
2002–03	Sunderland	0	0		
2002–03	*Notts Co*	32	0	**32**	**0**
2003–04	Sunderland	0	0		
2004–05	Grimsby T	25	0		
2005–06	Grimsby T	12	0	**37**	**0**
2005–06	Rochdale	15	1		
2006–07	Rochdale	34	3		
2007–08	Rochdale	35	2	**84**	**6**

RUNDLE, Adam (F) **185 19**
H: 5 8 W: 11 02 b.Durham 8-7-84
Source: Scholar.

2001–02	Darlington	12	0		
2002–03	Darlington	5	0	**17**	**0**
2002–03	Carlisle U	21	1		
2003–04	Carlisle U	23	0		
2004–05	Carlisle U	0	0	**44**	**1**
2004–05	Mansfield T	18	4		
2005–06	Mansfield T	35	5	**53**	**9**
2006–07	Rochdale	29	4		
2007–08	Rochdale	42	5	**71**	**9**

RUSSELL, Sam (G) **133 0**
H: 6 0 W: 10 13 b.Middlesbrough 4-10-82
Source: Scholar.

2000–01	Middlesbrough	0	0		
2001–02	Middlesbrough	0	0		
2002–03	Middlesbrough	0	0		
2002–03	*Darlington*	1	0		
2003–04	Middlesbrough	0	0		
2003–04	*Scunthorpe U*	10	0	**10**	**0**
2004–05	Darlington	46	0		
2005–06	Darlington	30	0		
2006–07	Darlington	31	0	**108**	**0**
2007–08	Rochdale	15	0	**15**	**0**

SPENCER, James (G) **111 0**
H: 6 3 W: 15 04 b.Stockport 11-4-85
Source: Trainee.

2001–02	Stockport Co	2	0		
2002–03	Stockport Co	1	0		
2003–04	Stockport Co	15	0		
2004–05	Stockport Co	24	0		
2005–06	Stockport Co	34	0		
2006–07	Stockport Co	15	0	**91**	**0**
2007–08	Rochdale	20	0	**20**	**0**

STANTON, Nathan (D) **299 0**
H: 5 9 W: 12 06 b.Nottingham 6-5-81
Source: Trainee. *Honours:* England Youth.

1997–98	Scunthorpe U	1	0		
1998–99	Scunthorpe U	4	0		
1999–2000	Scunthorpe U	34	0		
2000–01	Scunthorpe U	38	0		
2001–02	Scunthorpe U	42	0		
2002–03	Scunthorpe U	42	0		
2003–04	Scunthorpe U	33	0		
2004–05	Scunthorpe U	21	0		
2005–06	Scunthorpe U	22	0	**237**	**0**
2006–07	Rochdale	35	0		
2007–08	Rochdale	27	0	**62**	**0**

THOMPSON, Joe (M) **25 1**
H: 6 0 W: 9 07 b.Rochdale 5-3-89
Source: Scholar.

2005–06	Rochdale	1	0		
2006–07	Rochdale	13	0		
2007–08	Rochdale	11	1	**25**	**1**

THORPE, Lee (F) **402 93**
H: 6 0 W: 11 06 b.Wolverhampton 14-12-75
Source: Trainee.

1993–94	Blackpool	1	0		
1994–95	Blackpool	1	0		
1995–96	Blackpool	1	0		
1996–97	Blackpool	9	0	**12**	**0**
1997–98	Lincoln C	44	14		
1998–99	Lincoln C	38	8		
1999–2000	Lincoln C	42	16		
2000–01	Lincoln C	31	7		
2001–02	Lincoln C	37	13	**192**	**58**
2001–02	Leyton Orient	0	0		
2002–03	Leyton Orient	38	8		
2003–04	Leyton Orient	17	4	**55**	**12**
2003–04	*Grimsby T*	6	0	**6**	**0**
2003–04	Bristol R	10	1		
2004–05	Bristol R	25	3	**35**	**4**
2004–05	Swansea C	15	3		
2005–06	Swansea C	3	0	**18**	**3**
2005–06	*Peterborough U*	6	0	**6**	**0**
2005–06	*Torquay U*	10	3		
2006–07	Torquay U	41	8	**51**	**11**
2007–08	Brentford	19	4	**19**	**4**
2007–08	Rochdale	8	1	**8**	**1**

WARBURTON, Callum (M) **4 0**
H: 5 9 W: 11 00 b.Stockport 25-2-89
Source: Scholar.

2006–07	Rochdale	4	0		
2007–08	Rochdale	0	0	**4**	**0**

WHARTON, Ben (M) **1 0**
H: 6 1 W: 13 00 b.Stockport 17-6-90

2007–08	Rochdale	1	0	**1**	**0**

ROTHERHAM U (70)

BROGAN, Stephen (D) **55 3**
H: 5 7 W: 10 04 b.Rotherham 12-4-88
Source: Scholar.

2005–06	Rotherham U	3	0		
2006–07	Rotherham U	23	0		
2007–08	Rotherham U	29	3	**55**	**3**

CAHILL, Tom (F) **7 0**
H: 5 10 W: 12 08 b.Derby 21-11-86
Source: Matlock T.

2007–08	Rotherham U	7	0	**7**	**0**

CANN, Steven (G) **0 0**
H: 6 3 W: 13 01 b.South Africa 20-1-88
Source: Scholar. *Honours:* Wales Youth.

2006–07	Derby Co	0	0		
2007–08	Rotherham U	0	0		

COUGHLAN, Graham (D) **334 33**
H: 6 2 W: 13 07 b.Dublin 18-11-74
Source: Bray Wanderers.

1995–96	Blackburn R	0	0		
1996–97	Blackburn R	0	0		
1996–97	*Swindon T*	3	0	**3**	**0**
1997–98	Blackburn R	0	0		
1998–99	Livingston	6	0		
1999–2000	Livingston	29	0		
2000–01	Livingston	21	2	**56**	**2**
2001–02	Plymouth Arg	46	11		
2002–03	Plymouth Arg	42	5		
2003–04	Plymouth Arg	46	7		
2004–05	Plymouth Arg	43	2	**177**	**25**
2005–06	Sheffield W	33	4		
2006–07	Sheffield W	18	1	**51**	**5**
2006–07	*Burnley*	2	0	**2**	**0**
2007–08	Rotherham U	45	1	**45**	**1**

DUNCUM, Sam (M) **7 0**
H: 5 9 W: 11 02 b.Sheffield 18-2-87
Source: Scholar.

2004–05	Rotherham U	2	0		
2005–06	Rotherham U	1	0		
2006–07	Rotherham U	2	0		
2007–08	Rotherham U	2	0	**7**	**0**

GREEN, Jamie (F) **9 1**
H: 5 7 W: 10 07 b.Rossington 18-8-89
Source: Scholar.

2007–08	Rotherham U	9	1	**9**	**1**

HAGGARTY, David (M) **1 0**
H: 6 2 W: 13 07 b.Sheffield 28-3-91
Source: Scholar.

2007–08	Rotherham U	1	0	**1**	**0**

HARRISON, Danny (M) **168 9**
H: 5 11 W: 12 04 b.Liverpool 4-11-82
Source: Scholar.

2001–02	Tranmere R	1	0		
2002–03	Tranmere R	12	0		
2003–04	Tranmere R	32	2		
2004–05	Tranmere R	32	0		
2005–06	Tranmere R	35	2		
2006–07	Tranmere R	12	1	**124**	**5**
2007–08	Rotherham U	44	4	**44**	**4**

HARRISON, Simon (M) **0 0**
H: 5 9 W: 10 08 b.Nether Edge 24-12-88
Source: Scholar.

2007–08	Rotherham U	0	0		

HOLMES, Derek (F) **274 51**
H: 6 2 W: 13 00 b.Lanark 18-10-78
Source: Royal Albert.

1995–96	Hearts	0	0		
1996–97	Hearts	1	0		
1997–98	Hearts	1	1		
1997–98	Cowdenbeath	13	5	**13**	**5**
1998–99	Hearts	6	0	**8**	**1**
1999–2000	Ross Co	25	8		
2000–01	Ross Co	0	0	**25**	**8**
2001–02	Bournemouth	37	9		
2002–03	Bournemouth	29	3		
2003–04	Bournemouth	26	2		
2004–05	Bournemouth	23	2	**115**	**16**
2004–05	Carlisle U	0	0		
2005–06	Carlisle U	40	7		
2006–07	Carlisle U	36	3	**76**	**10**
2007–08	Rotherham U	37	11	**37**	**11**

HOLMES, Peter (M) **144 14**
H: 5 11 W: 11 13 b.Bishop Auckland 18-11-80
Source: Trainee. *Honours:* England Schools, Youth.

1997–98	Sheffield W	0	0		
1998–99	Sheffield W	0	0		
1999–2000	Sheffield W	0	0		
2000–01	Luton T	18	1		
2001–02	Luton T	7	1		
2002–03	Luton T	17	1		
2003–04	Luton T	16	3		
2004–05	Luton T	19	3		
2005–06	Luton T	23	2		
2006–07	Luton T	5	0	**105**	**11**
2006–07	*Chesterfield*	10	1	**10**	**1**
2006–07	*Lincoln C*	5	0	**5**	**0**
2007–08	Rotherham U	24	2	**24**	**2**

HUDSON, Mark (M) **205 25**
H: 5 10 W: 11 03 b.Bishop Auckland 24-10-80
Source: Trainee.

1999–2000	Middlesbrough	0	0		
2000–01	Middlesbrough	3	0		
2001–02	Middlesbrough	2	0		
2002–03	Middlesbrough	0	0	**5**	**0**
2002–03	*Carlisle U*	15	1	**15**	**1**
2002–03	Chesterfield	24	3		
2003–04	Chesterfield	35	2		
2004–05	Chesterfield	34	4	**93**	**9**
2005–06	Huddersfield T	29	3		

2006–07 Huddersfield T 32 3 **61 6**
2007–08 Rotherham U 31 9 **31 9**

HURST, Paul (D) 433 13
H: 5 4 W: 9 04 b.Sheffield 25-9-74
Source: Trainee.
1993–94 Rotherham U 4 0
1994–95 Rotherham U 13 0
1995–96 Rotherham U 40 1
1996–97 Rotherham U 30 3
1997–98 Rotherham U 30 0
1998–99 Rotherham U 32 2
1999–2000 Rotherham U 30 2
2000–01 Rotherham U 44 3
2001–02 Rotherham U 45 0
2002–03 Rotherham U 44 1
2003–04 Rotherham U 28 1
2004–05 Rotherham U 39 0
2005–06 Rotherham U 31 0
2006–07 Rotherham U 12 0
2007–08 Rotherham U 11 0 **433 13**

JOSEPH, Marc (D) 366 7
H: 6 0 W: 12 05 b.Leicester 10-11-76
Source: Trainee.
1995–96 Cambridge U 12 0
1996–97 Cambridge U 8 0
1997–98 Cambridge U 41 0
1998–99 Cambridge U 29 0
1999–2000 Cambridge U 33 0
2000–01 Cambridge U 30 0 **153 0**
2001–02 Peterborough U 44 2
2002–03 Peterborough U 17 0 **61 2**
2002–03 Hull C 23 0
2003–04 Hull C 32 1
2004–05 Hull C 29 0
2005–06 Hull C 5 0 **89 1**
2005–06 *Bristol C* 3 0 **3 0**
2005–06 Blackpool 16 0
2006–07 Blackpool 8 0 **24 0**
2007–08 Rotherham U 36 4 **36 4**

KERR, Natt (D) 3 0
H: 6 0 W: 10 10 b.Manchester 31-10-87
Source: Crewe Alex Scholar.
2006–07 Rotherham U 3 0
2007–08 Rotherham U 0 0 **3 0**

KING, Liam (D) 7 0
H: 5 9 W: 10 02 b.Rainworth 3-12-87
Source: Scholar.
2005–06 Rotherham U 0 0
2006–07 Rotherham U 6 0
2007–08 Rotherham U 1 0 **7 0**

MILLS, Pablo (D) 152 3
H: 5 9 W: 11 04 b.Birmingham 27-5-84
Source: Trainee. *Honours:* England Youth.
2002–03 Derby Co 16 0
2003–04 Derby Co 19 0
2004–05 Derby Co 22 0
2005–06 Derby Co 1 0 **58 0**
2005–06 *Milton Keynes D* 16 1 **16 1**
2005–06 *Walsall* 14 0 **14 0**
2006–07 Rotherham U 31 1
2007–08 Rotherham U 33 1 **64 2**

NEWSHAM, Mark (F) 48 7
H: 5 10 W: 9 11 b.Hatfield 24-3-87
Source: Scholar.
2004–05 Rotherham U 4 0
2005–06 Rotherham U 3 0
2006–07 Rotherham U 16 3
2007–08 Rotherham U 25 4 **48 7**

O'GRADY, Chris (F) 106 18
H: 6 3 W: 12 04 b.Nottingham 25-1-86
Source: Trainee. *Honours:* England Youth.
2002–03 Leicester C 1 0
2003–04 Leicester C 0 0
2004–05 Leicester C 0 0
2004–05 *Notts Co* 9 0 **9 0**
2005–06 Leicester C 13 1
2005–06 *Rushden & D* 22 4 **22 4**
2006–07 Leicester C 10 0 **24 1**
2006–07 Rotherham U 13 4
2007–08 Rotherham U 38 9 **51 13**

ROSS, Ian (M) 74 5
H: 5 10 W: 11 00 b.Sheffield 23-1-86
Source: Scholar. *Honours:* England Under-20.
2004–05 Sheffield U 0 0
2005–06 Sheffield U 0 0
2005–06 *Boston U* 14 4 **14 4**
2005–06 *Bury* 7 0 **7 0**
2006–07 Sheffield U 0 0
2006–07 *Notts Co* 36 1 **36 1**
2007–08 Sheffield U 0 0
2007–08 Rotherham U 17 0 **17 0**

SHARPS, Ian (D) 241 10
H: 6 3 W: 14 07 b.Warrington 23-10-80
Source: Trainee.
1998–99 Tranmere R 1 0
1999–2000 Tranmere R 0 0
2000–01 Tranmere R 0 0
2001–02 Tranmere R 29 0
2002–03 Tranmere R 30 3
2003–04 Tranmere R 27 1
2004–05 Tranmere R 44 1
2005–06 Tranmere R 39 1 **170 6**
2006–07 Rotherham U 38 2
2007–08 Rotherham U 33 2 **71 4**

STREETE, Theo (D) 10 1
H: 6 2 W: 13 05 b.Birmingham 23-11-87
Source: Scholar.
2006–07 Derby Co 0 0
2006–07 *Doncaster R* 6 1 **6 1**
2006–07 Rotherham U 4 0
2007–08 Rotherham U 0 0 **4 0**

TAYLOR, Ryan (F) 46 6
H: 6 2 W: 10 10 b.Rotherham 4-5-88
Source: Scholar.
2005–06 Rotherham U 1 0
2006–07 Rotherham U 10 0
2007–08 Rotherham U 35 6 **46 6**

TODD, Andrew (M) 81 10
H: 6 0 W: 11 03 b.Nottingham 22-2-79
Source: Eastwood T.
1995–96 Nottingham F 0 0
1996–97 Nottingham F 0 0
1997–98 Nottingham F 0 0
1998–99 Nottingham F 0 0
1998–99 Scarborough 1 0 **1 0**
From Etwd T, Wksop, Hucknall, Burton Alb
2006–07 Accrington S 46 10
2007–08 Rotherham U 13 0 **13 0**
2007–08 *Accrington S* 21 0 **67 10**

TONGE, Dale (D) 85 0
H: 5 10 W: 10 06 b.Doncaster 7-5-85
Source: Scholar.
2003–04 Barnsley 1 0
2004–05 Barnsley 14 0
2005–06 Barnsley 24 0
2006–07 Barnsley 6 0 **45 0**
2006–07 *Gillingham* 3 0 **3 0**
2007–08 Rotherham U 37 0 **37 0**

WARRINGTON, Andy (G) 216 0
H: 6 3 W: 12 13 b.Sheffield 10-6-76
Source: Trainee.
1994–95 York C 0 0
1995–96 York C 6 0
1996–97 York C 27 0
1997–98 York C 17 0
1998–99 York C 11 0 **61 0**
2003–04 Doncaster R 46 0
2004–05 Doncaster R 34 0
2005–06 Doncaster R 9 0
2006–07 Doncaster R 0 0 **89 0**
2006–07 Bury 20 0 **20 0**
2007–08 Rotherham U 46 0 **46 0**

YATES, Jamie (F) 23 3
H: 5 7 W: 10 11 b.Sheffield 24-12-88
Source: Scholar.
2006–07 Rotherham U 3 0
2007–08 Rotherham U 20 3 **23 3**

SCUNTHORPE U (71)

BARACLOUGH, Ian (M) 604 40
H: 6 1 W: 12 09 b.Leicester 4-12-70
Source: Trainee.
1988–89 Leicester C 0 0
1989–90 Leicester C 0 0
1989–90 *Wigan Ath* 9 2 **9 2**
1990–91 Leicester C 0 0
1990–91 *Grimsby T* 4 0
1991–92 Grimsby T 0 0
1992–93 Grimsby T 1 0 **5 0**
1992–93 Lincoln C 36 5
1993–94 Lincoln C 37 5 **73 10**
1994–95 Mansfield T 36 3
1995–96 Mansfield T 11 2 **47 5**
1995–96 Notts Co 35 2
1996–97 Notts Co 38 2
1997–98 Notts Co 38 6
1997–98 QPR 8 0
1998–99 QPR 43 1
1999–2000 QPR 45 0
2000–01 QPR 29 0 **125 1**
2001–02 Notts Co 33 3
2002–03 Notts Co 34 2
2003–04 Notts Co 34 0 **212 15**
2004–05 Scunthorpe U 45 3
2005–06 Scunthorpe U 38 3
2006–07 Scunthorpe U 33 1
2007–08 Scunthorpe U 17 0 **133 7**

BUTLER, Andy (D) 139 16
H: 6 0 W: 13 00 b.Doncaster 4-11-83
Source: Scholar.
2003–04 Scunthorpe U 35 2
2004–05 Scunthorpe U 37 10
2005–06 Scunthorpe U 16 1
2006–07 Scunthorpe U 11 1
2006–07 *Grimsby T* 4 0 **4 0**
2007–08 Scunthorpe U 36 2 **135 16**

BYRNE, Cliff (D) 162 3
H: 6 0 W: 12 11 b.Dublin 27-4-82
Honours: Eire Youth, Under-21.
1999–2000 Sunderland 0 0
2000–01 Sunderland 0 0
2001–02 Sunderland 0 0
2002–03 Sunderland 0 0
2002–03 *Scunthorpe U* 13 0
2003–04 Scunthorpe U 39 1
2004–05 Scunthorpe U 29 1
2005–06 Scunthorpe U 32 1
2006–07 Scunthorpe U 24 0
2007–08 Scunthorpe U 25 0 **162 3**

CROSBY, Andy (D) 619 39
H: 6 2 W: 13 13 b.Rotherham 3-3-73
Source: Leeds U Trainee.
1991–92 Doncaster R 22 0
1992–93 Doncaster R 29 0
1993–94 Doncaster R 0 0 **51 0**
1993–94 Darlington 25 0
1994–95 Darlington 35 0
1995–96 Darlington 45 1
1996–97 Darlington 42 1
1997–98 Darlington 34 1 **181 3**
1998–99 Chester C 41 4 **41 4**
1999–2000 Brighton & HA 36 3
2000–01 Brighton & HA 34 2
2001–02 Brighton & HA 2 0 **72 5**
2001–02 Oxford U 23 1
2002–03 Oxford U 46 6
2003–04 Oxford U 42 5 **111 12**
2004–05 Scunthorpe U 44 3
2005–06 Scunthorpe U 42 3
2006–07 Scunthorpe U 39 5
2007–08 Scunthorpe U 38 4 **163 15**

FORTE, Jonathan (M) 133 18
H: 6 0 W: 12 02 b.Sheffield 25-7-86
Source: Scholar. *Honours:* England Youth. Barbados 1 full cap.
2003–04 Sheffield U 7 0
2004–05 Sheffield U 22 1
2005–06 Sheffield U 1 0
2005–06 *Doncaster R* 13 4
2005–06 *Rotherham U* 11 4 **11 4**
2006–07 Sheffield U 0 0 **30 1**
2006–07 *Doncaster R* 41 5 **54 9**
2007–08 Scunthorpe U 38 4 **38 4**

GOODWIN, Jim (M) 187 13
H: 5 9 W: 12 01 b.Waterford 20-11-81
Source: Tramore. *Honours:* Eire Under-21, B, 1 full cap.
2001–02 Celtic 0 0
2002–03 Stockport Co 33 3
2003–04 Stockport Co 34 4
2004–05 Stockport Co 36 0 **103 7**
2005–06 Scunthorpe U 13 2
2006–07 Scunthorpe U 31 1
2007–08 Scunthorpe U 40 3 **84 6**

HAYES, Paul (F) 218 48
H: 6 0 W: 12 12 b.Dagenham 20-9-83
Source: Norwich C Scholar.
2002–03 Scunthorpe U 18 8
2003–04 Scunthorpe U 35 2
2004–05 Scunthorpe U 46 18

2005–06	Barnsley	45	6		
2006–07	Barnsley	30	5	**75**	**11**
2006–07	*Huddersfield T*	4	1	**4**	**1**
2007–08	Scunthorpe U	40	8	**139**	**36**

HORLOCK, Kevin (M) **472** **61**
H: 6 0 W: 12 00 b.Erith 1-11-72
Source: Trainee. *Honours:* Northern Ireland B, 32 full caps.

1991–92	West Ham U	0	0		
1992–93	West Ham U	0	0		
1992–93	Swindon T	14	1		
1993–94	Swindon T	38	0		
1994–95	Swindon T	38	1		
1995–96	Swindon T	45	12		
1996–97	Swindon T	28	8	**163**	**22**
1996–97	Manchester C	18	4		
1997–98	Manchester C	25	5		
1998–99	Manchester C	37	9		
1999–2000	Manchester C	38	10		
2000–01	Manchester C	14	2		
2001–02	Manchester C	42	7		
2002–03	Manchester C	30	0	**204**	**37**
2003–04	West Ham U	27	1	**27**	**1**
2004–05	Ipswich T	41	0		
2005–06	Ipswich T	17	0	**58**	**0**
2005–06	*Doncaster R*	13	0		
2006–07	Doncaster R	2	1		
2007–08	Doncaster R	0	0	**15**	**1**
2007–08	Scunthorpe U	0	0		
2007–08	*Mansfield T*	5	0	**5**	**0**

HURST, Kevan (M) **130** **10**
H: 5 10 W: 11 07 b.Chesterfield 27-8-85
Source: Sheffield U Scholar.

2003–04	*Boston U*	7	1	**7**	**1**
2004–05	Sheffield U	1	0		
2004–05	*Stockport Co*	14	1	**14**	**1**
2005–06	Sheffield U	0	0		
2005–06	*Chesterfield*	37	4		
2006–07	Sheffield U	0	0	**1**	**0**
2006–07	*Chesterfield*	25	3	**62**	**7**
2006–07	*Scunthorpe U*	13	0		
2007–08	Scunthorpe U	33	1	**46**	**1**

IRIEKPEN, Ezomo (D) **158** **10**
H: 6 1 W: 12 02 b.East London 14-5-82
Source: Trainee. *Honours:* England Youth.

1998–99	West Ham U	0	0		
1999–2000	West Ham U	0	0		
2000–01	West Ham U	0	0		
2001–02	West Ham U	0	0		
2002–03	West Ham U	0	0		
2002–03	*Leyton Orient*	5	1	**5**	**1**
2002–03	*Cambridge U*	13	1	**13**	**1**
2003–04	Swansea C	34	1		
2004–05	Swansea C	29	2		
2005–06	Swansea C	28	0		
2006–07	Swansea C	32	4	**123**	**7**
2007–08	Scunthorpe U	17	1	**17**	**1**

LILLIS, Josh (G) **4** **0**
H: 6 0 W: 12 08 b.Derby 24-6-87
Source: Scholar.

2006–07	Scunthorpe U	1	0		
2007–08	Scunthorpe U	3	0	**4**	**0**

MAY, Ben (F) **170** **24**
H: 6 3 W: 12 12 b.Gravesend 10-3-84
Source: Juniors.

2000–01	Millwall	0	0		
2001–02	Millwall	0	0		
2002–03	Millwall	10	1		
2002–03	*Colchester U*	6	0		
2003–04	Millwall	0	0		
2003–04	*Brentford*	41	7		
2004–05	Millwall	8	1		
2004–05	*Colchester U*	14	1	**20**	**1**
2004–05	Brentford	10	1	**51**	**8**
2005–06	Millwall	39	10		
2006–07	Millwall	13	2		
2007–08	Millwall	8	0	**78**	**14**
2007–08	Scunthorpe U	21	1	**21**	**1**

McBREEN, Daniel (F) **138** **31**
H: 6 1 W: 13 01 b.Newcastle, Aus 23-4-77
Source: Toronto-Awaba, Edgeworth.

2000–01	Newcastle U (Aus)	23	6		
2001–02	Newcastle U (Aus)	13	3	**36**	**9**
2002–03	Uni Craiova	13	1		
2003–04	Uni Craiova	20	2	**33**	**3**
2004–05	Falkirk	23	13		
2005–06	Falkirk	33	6	**56**	**19**
2006–07	Scunthorpe U	7	0		
2007–08	*St Johnstone*	6	0	**6**	**0**
2007–08	Scunthorpe U	0	0	**7**	**0**

McCANN, Grant (M) **254** **39**
H: 5 10 W: 11 00 b.Belfast 14-4-80
Source: Trainee. *Honours:* Northern Ireland Youth, Under-21, 16 full caps, 1 goal.

1998–99	West Ham U	0	0		
1999–2000	West Ham U	0	0		
2000–01	West Ham U	1	0		
2000–01	*Notts Co*	2	0	**2**	**0**
2000–01	*Cheltenham T*	30	3		
2001–02	West Ham U	3	0		
2002–03	West Ham U	0	0	**4**	**0**
2002–03	Cheltenham T	27	6		
2003–04	Cheltenham T	43	8		
2004–05	Cheltenham T	39	4		
2005–06	Cheltenham T	39	8		
2006–07	Cheltenham T	15	5	**193**	**34**
2006–07	Barnsley	22	1		
2007–08	Barnsley	19	3	**41**	**4**
2007–08	Scunthorpe U	14	1	**14**	**1**

MORRIS, Ian (D) **83** **9**
H: 6 0 W: 11 05 b.Dublin 27-2-87
Source: Scholar. *Honours:* Eire Under-21.

2003–04	Leeds U	0	0		
2004–05	Leeds U	0	0		
2005–06	Leeds U	0	0		
2005–06	*Blackpool*	30	3	**30**	**3**
2006–07	Leeds U	0	0		
2006–07	Scunthorpe U	28	3		
2007–08	Scunthorpe U	25	3	**53**	**6**

MURPHY, Joe (G) **197** **0**
H: 6 2 W: 13 06 b.Dublin 21-8-81
Source: Trainee. *Honours:* Eire Youth, Under-21, 1 full cap.

1999–2000	Tranmere R	21	0		
2000–01	Tranmere R	20	0		
2001–02	Tranmere R	22	0	**63**	**0**
2002–03	WBA	2	0		
2003–04	WBA	3	0		
2004–05	WBA	0	0	**5**	**0**
2004–05	*Walsall*	25	0		
2005–06	Sunderland	0	0		
2005–06	*Walsall*	14	0	**39**	**0**
2006–07	Scunthorpe U	45	0		
2007–08	Scunthorpe U	45	0	**90**	**0**

PATERSON, Martin (F) **70** **20**
H: 5 9 W: 10 11 b.Tunstall 13-5-87
Source: Scholar. *Honours:* Northern Ireland Youth, Under-21, 2 full caps.

2004–05	Stoke C	3	0		
2005–06	Stoke C	3	0		
2006–07	Stoke C	9	1	**15**	**1**
2006–07	*Grimsby T*	15	6	**15**	**6**
2007–08	Scunthorpe U	40	13	**40**	**13**

SPARROW, Matt (M) **270** **32**
H: 5 11 W: 10 06 b.Wembley 3-10-81
Source: Scholar.

1999–2000	Scunthorpe U	11	0		
2000–01	Scunthorpe U	11	4		
2001–02	Scunthorpe U	24	1		
2002–03	Scunthorpe U	42	9		
2003–04	Scunthorpe U	38	3		
2004–05	Scunthorpe U	44	5		
2005–06	Scunthorpe U	39	5		
2006–07	Scunthorpe U	29	4		
2007–08	Scunthorpe U	32	1	**270**	**32**

WILCOX, Joe (D) **0** **0**
H: 6 1 W: 11 05 b.Northampton 18-4-89
Source: Scholar.

2007–08	Scunthorpe U	0	0		

WILLIAMS, Marcus (D) **103** **0**
H: 5 8 W: 10 07 b.Doncaster 8-4-86
Source: Scholar.

2003–04	Scunthorpe U	1	0		
2004–05	Scunthorpe U	4	0		
2005–06	Scunthorpe U	29	0		
2006–07	Scunthorpe U	35	0		
2007–08	Scunthorpe U	34	0	**103**	**0**

WINN, Peter (M) **4** **0**
H: 6 0 W: 11 09 b.Cleethorpes 19-12-88
Source: Scholar.

2006–07	Scunthorpe U	0	0		
2007–08	Scunthorpe U	4	0	**4**	**0**

WRIGHT, Andrew (M) **2** **0**
H: 6 1 W: 13 07 b.Southport 15-1-85
Source: Scholar.

2001–02	Liverpool	0	0		
2002–03	Liverpool	0	0		
2003–04	Liverpool	0	0		
2004–05	Liverpool	0	0		
2005–06	Liverpool	0	0		
2006–07	Liverpool	0	0		

From West Virginia Univ.

2007–08	Scunthorpe U	2	0	**2**	**0**

SHEFFIELD U (72)

ABDI, Liban (M) **0** **0**
b.Somalia

2006–07	Sheffield U	0	0		
2007–08	Sheffield U	0	0		

ANNERSON, Jamie (G) **0** **0**
H: 6 2 W: 13 02 b.Sheffield 21-6-88
Source: Scholar. *Honours:* England Youth.

2005–06	Sheffield U	0	0		
2006–07	Sheffield U	0	0		
2007–08	*Rotherham U*	0	0		
2007–08	*Chesterfield*	0	0		
2007–08	Sheffield U	0	0		

ARMSTRONG, Chris (D) **198** **8**
H: 5 9 W: 11 00 b.Newcastle 5-8-82
Source: Scholar. *Honours:* England Under-20. Scotland B.

2000–01	Bury	22	1		
2001–02	Bury	11	0	**33**	**1**
2001–02	Oldham Ath	32	0		
2002–03	Oldham Ath	33	1	**65**	**1**
2003–04	Sheffield U	12	1		
2004–05	Sheffield U	0	0		
2005–06	Sheffield U	24	2		
2005–06	*Blackpool*	5	0	**5**	**0**
2006–07	Sheffield U	27	0		
2007–08	Sheffield U	32	3	**95**	**6**

ASHMORE, James (M) **8** **0**
H: 5 8 W: 11 00 b.Sheffield 2-3-86
Source: Scholar.

2004–05	Sheffield U	0	0		
2005–06	Sheffield U	0	0		
2006–07	Sheffield U	0	0		
2007–08	Sheffield U	0	0		
2007–08	*Macclesfield T*	8	0	**8**	**0**

BEATTIE, James (F) **323** **103**
H: 6 1 W: 13 06 b.Lancaster 27-2-78
Source: Trainee. *Honours:* England Under-21, 5 full caps.

1994–95	Blackburn R	0	0		
1995–96	Blackburn R	0	0		
1996–97	Blackburn R	1	0		
1997–98	Blackburn R	3	0	**4**	**0**
1998–99	Southampton	35	5		
1999–2000	Southampton	18	0		
2000–01	Southampton	37	11		
2001–02	Southampton	28	12		
2002–03	Southampton	38	23		
2003–04	Southampton	37	14		
2004–05	Southampton	11	3	**204**	**68**
2004–05	Everton	11	1		
2005–06	Everton	32	10		
2006–07	Everton	33	2	**76**	**13**
2007–08	Sheffield U	39	22	**39**	**22**

BENNETT, Ian (G) **383** **0**
H: 6 0 W: 12 10 b.Worksop 10-10-71
Source: Newcastle U Trainee.

1991–92	Peterborough U	7	0		
1992–93	Peterborough U	46	0		
1993–94	Peterborough U	19	0	**72**	**0**
1993–94	Birmingham C	22	0		
1994–95	Birmingham C	46	0		
1995–96	Birmingham C	24	0		
1996–97	Birmingham C	40	0		
1997–98	Birmingham C	45	0		
1998–99	Birmingham C	10	0		
1999–2000	Birmingham C	21	0		
2000–01	Birmingham C	45	0		
2001–02	Birmingham C	18	0		
2002–03	Birmingham C	10	0		
2003–04	Birmingham C	6	0		
2004–05	Birmingham C	0	0	**287**	**0**
2004–05	*Sheffield U*	5	0		
2004–05	*Coventry C*	6	0	**6**	**0**

2005–06 Leeds U 4 0
2006–07 Leeds U 0 0 **4 0**
2006–07 Sheffield U 2 0
2007–08 Sheffield U 7 0 **14 0**

BINNION, Travis (M) 0 0
H: 5 10 W: 11 02 b.Derby 10-11-86
Source: Scholar.
2005–06 Sheffield U 0 0
2006–07 Sheffield U 0 0
2007–08 Sheffield U 0 0

CARNEY, David (M) 67 9
H: 5 11 W: 11 00 b.Sydney 30-11-83
Source: Scholar. *Honours:* Australia Under-20, 12 full caps, 1 goal.
2000–01 Everton 0 0
2001–02 Everton 0 0
2002–03 Everton 0 0
2003–04 Oldham Ath 0 0
2004–05 Hamilton A 8 0 **8 0**
2005–06 Sydney FC 24 6
2006–07 Sydney FC 14 1 **38 7**
2007–08 Sheffield U 21 2 **21 2**

CHANOT, Maxime (D) 0 0
b.Nancy 21-11-89
Source: Scholar.
2007–08 Sheffield U 0 0

CRESSWELL, Ryan (D) 24 1
H: 5 9 W: 10 05 b.Rotherham 22-12-87
Source: Scholar.
2006–07 Sheffield U 0 0
2007–08 Sheffield U 0 0
2007–08 *Rotherham U* 3 0 **3 0**
2007–08 *Morecambe* 2 0 **2 0**
2007–08 *Macclesfield T* 19 1 **19 1**

DONNELLY, Martin (M) 0 0
b.Belfast 28-8-88
Source: Scholar. *Honours:* Northern Ireland Youth, Under-21.
2006–07 Sheffield U 0 0
2007–08 *Rochdale* 0 0
2007–08 Sheffield U 0 0

EHIOGU, Ugo (D) 390 21
H: 6 2 W: 14 10 b.Hackney 3-11-72
Source: Trainee. *Honours:* England Under-21, B, 4 full caps, 1 goal.
1990–91 WBA 2 0 **2 0**
1991–92 Aston Villa 8 0
1992–93 Aston Villa 4 0
1993–94 Aston Villa 17 0
1994–95 Aston Villa 39 3
1995–96 Aston Villa 36 1
1996–97 Aston Villa 38 3
1997–98 Aston Villa 37 2
1998–99 Aston Villa 25 2
1999–2000 Aston Villa 31 1
2000–01 Aston Villa 2 0 **237 12**
2000–01 Middlesbrough 21 3
2001–02 Middlesbrough 29 1
2002–03 Middlesbrough 32 3
2003–04 Middlesbrough 16 0
2004–05 Middlesbrough 10 0
2005–06 Middlesbrough 18 0
2006–07 Middlesbrough 0 0 **126 7**
2006–07 *Leeds U* 6 1 **6 1**
2006–07 Rangers 9 1
2007–08 Rangers 0 0 **9 1**
2007–08 Sheffield U 10 0 **10 0**

FATHI, Ahmed (M) 3 0
H: 5 9 W: 11 05 b.Egypt 11-10-84
Source: Ismaily SC. *Honours:* Egypt Youth, 11 full caps, 1 goal.
2006–07 Sheffield U 3 0
2007–08 Sheffield U 0 0 **3 0**

GEARY, Derek (D) 203 1
H: 5 6 W: 10 00 b.Dublin 19-6-80
Source: Rivermont BC.
1997–98 Sheffield W 0 0
1998–99 Sheffield W 0 0
1999–2000 Sheffield W 0 0
2000–01 Sheffield W 5 0
2001–02 Sheffield W 32 0
2002–03 Sheffield W 26 0
2003–04 Sheffield W 41 0 **104 0**
2004–05 Stockport Co 13 0 **13 0**
2004–05 Sheffield U 19 1
2005–06 Sheffield U 20 0
2006–07 Sheffield U 26 0
2007–08 Sheffield U 21 0 **86 1**

GERRARD, Paul (G) 320 1
H: 6 2 W: 13 11 b.Heywood 22-1-73
Source: Trainee. *Honours:* England Under-21.
1991–92 Oldham Ath 0 0
1992–93 Oldham Ath 25 0
1993–94 Oldham Ath 16 0
1994–95 Oldham Ath 42 0
1995–96 Oldham Ath 36 1 **119 1**
1996–97 Everton 5 0
1997–98 Everton 4 0
1998–99 Everton 0 0
1998–99 *Oxford U* 16 0 **16 0**
1999–2000 Everton 34 0
2000–01 Everton 32 0
2001–02 Everton 13 0
2002–03 Everton 2 0
2002–03 *Ipswich T* 5 0 **5 0**
2003–04 Everton 0 0 **90 0**
2003–04 *Sheffield U* 16 0
2003–04 *Nottingham F* 8 0
2004–05 Nottingham F 42 0
2005–06 Nottingham F 22 0
2006–07 Nottingham F 0 0 **72 0**
2006–07 Sheffield U 2 0
2007–08 *Blackpool* 0 0
2007–08 Sheffield U 0 0 **18 0**

GILLESPIE, Keith (M) 386 27
H: 5 10 W: 11 03 b.Larne 18-2-75
Source: Trainee. *Honours:* Northern Ireland Schools, Youth, Under-21, 81 full caps, 2 goals.
1992–93 Manchester U 0 0
1993–94 Manchester U 0 0
1993–94 *Wigan Ath* 8 4
1994–95 Manchester U 9 1 **9 1**
1994–95 Newcastle U 17 2
1995–96 Newcastle U 28 4
1996–97 Newcastle U 32 1
1997–98 Newcastle U 29 4
1998–99 Newcastle U 7 0 **113 11**
1998–99 Blackburn R 16 1
1999–2000 Blackburn R 22 2
2000–01 Blackburn R 18 0
2000–01 *Wigan Ath* 5 0 **13 4**
2001–02 Blackburn R 32 2
2002–03 Blackburn R 25 0 **113 5**
2003–04 Leicester C 12 0
2004–05 Leicester C 30 2 **42 2**
2005–06 Sheffield U 30 0
2006–07 Sheffield U 31 2
2007–08 Sheffield U 35 2 **96 4**

HENDRIE, Lee (M) 300 32
H: 5 10 W: 11 00 b.Birmingham 18-5-77
Source: Trainee. *Honours:* England Youth, Under-21, B, 1 full cap.
1993–94 Aston Villa 0 0
1994–95 Aston Villa 0 0
1995–96 Aston Villa 3 0
1996–97 Aston Villa 4 0
1997–98 Aston Villa 17 3
1998–99 Aston Villa 32 3
1999–2000 Aston Villa 29 1
2000–01 Aston Villa 32 6
2001–02 Aston Villa 29 2
2002–03 Aston Villa 27 4
2003–04 Aston Villa 32 2
2004–05 Aston Villa 29 5
2005–06 Aston Villa 16 1
2006–07 Aston Villa 1 0 **251 27**
2006–07 *Stoke C* 28 3 **28 3**
2007–08 Sheffield U 12 1 **12 1**
2007–08 *Leicester C* 9 1 **9 1**

HERNANDEZ, Stephen (G) 0 0
b.Doncaster 17-8-89
Source: Sheffield W.
2007–08 Sheffield U 0 0

HORSFIELD, Geoff (F) 314 78
H: 6 0 W: 11 07 b.Barnsley 1-11-73
1992–93 Scarborough 6 1
1993–94 Scarborough 6 0 **12 1**
From Witton Alb
1998–99 Halifax T 10 7 **10 7**
1998–99 Fulham 28 15
1999–2000 Fulham 31 7 **59 22**
2000–01 Birmingham C 34 7
2001–02 Birmingham C 40 11
2002–03 Birmingham C 31 5
2003–04 Birmingham C 3 0 **108 23**
2003–04 Wigan Ath 16 7 **16 7**
2003–04 WBA 20 7
2004–05 WBA 29 3
2005–06 WBA 18 4
2005–06 *Sheffield U* 3 0
2006–07 WBA 0 0 **67 14**
2006–07 Sheffield U 0 0
2006–07 *Leeds U* 14 2 **14 2**
2006–07 *Leicester C* 13 2 **13 2**
2007–08 Sheffield U 0 0 **3 0**
2007–08 *Scunthorpe U* 12 0 **12 0**

HULSE, Rob (F) 256 82
H: 6 1 W: 12 04 b.Crewe 25-10-79
Source: Trainee.
1998–99 Crewe Alex 0 0
1999–2000 Crewe Alex 4 1
2000–01 Crewe Alex 33 11
2001–02 Crewe Alex 41 12
2002–03 Crewe Alex 38 22 **116 46**
2003–04 WBA 33 10
2004–05 WBA 5 0 **38 10**
2004–05 *Leeds U* 13 6
2005–06 Leeds U 39 12 **52 18**
2006–07 Sheffield U 29 8
2007–08 Sheffield U 21 0 **50 8**

KAZIM-RICHARDS, Colin (F) 121 12
H: 6 1 W: 10 10 b.Leyton 26-8-86
Source: Scholar. *Honours:* Turkey Under-21, 7 full caps.
2004–05 Bury 30 3 **30 3**
2005–06 Brighton & HA 42 6
2006–07 Brighton & HA 1 0 **43 6**
2006–07 Sheffield U 27 1
2007–08 Fenerbahce 21 2 **21 2**
2007–08 Sheffield U 0 0 **27 1**
To Fenerbahce but retained by club.

KENNY, Paddy (G) 365 0
H: 6 1 W: 14 01 b.Halifax 17-5-78
Source: Bradford PA. *Honours:* Eire 7 full caps.
1998–99 Bury 0 0
1999–2000 Bury 46 0
2000–01 Bury 46 0
2001–02 Bury 41 0
2002–03 Bury 0 0 **133 0**
2002–03 Sheffield U 45 0
2003–04 Sheffield U 27 0
2004–05 Sheffield U 40 0
2005–06 Sheffield U 46 0
2006–07 Sheffield U 34 0
2007–08 Sheffield U 40 0 **232 0**

KERRY, Lloyd (M) 20 3
H: 6 2 W: 12 04 b.Chesterfield 22-1-88
Source: Scholar.
2006–07 Sheffield U 0 0
2006–07 *Torquay U* 7 1 **7 1**
2007–08 Sheffield U 0 0
2007–08 *Chesterfield* 13 2 **13 2**

KILGALLON, Matthew (D) 129 5
H: 6 1 W: 12 10 b.York 8-1-84
Source: Scholar. *Honours:* England Youth, Under-20, Under-21.
2000–01 Leeds U 0 0
2001–02 Leeds U 0 0
2002–03 Leeds U 2 0
2003–04 Leeds U 8 2
2003–04 *West Ham U* 3 0 **3 0**
2004–05 Leeds U 26 0
2005–06 Leeds U 25 1
2006–07 Leeds U 19 0 **80 3**
2006–07 Sheffield U 6 0
2007–08 Sheffield U 40 2 **46 2**

LAW, Nicky (M) 21 2
H: 5 10 W: 11 06 b.Nottingham 29-3-88
Source: Scholar. *Honours:* England Youth.
2005–06 Sheffield U 0 0
2006–07 Sheffield U 4 0
2006–07 *Yeovil T* 6 0 **6 0**
2007–08 Sheffield U 1 0 **5 0**
2007–08 *Bradford C* 10 2 **10 2**

LI TIE (M) 34 0
H: 6 0 W: 11 10 b.Liaoning 18-9-77
Source: Liaoning Bodao. *Honours:* China 87 full caps, 5 goals.
2002–03 Everton 29 0

2003–04	Everton	5	0		
2004–05	Everton	0	0		
2005–06	Everton	0	0	**34**	**0**
2006–07	Sheffield U	0	0		
2007–08	Sheffield U	0	0		

LUCKETTI, Chris (D) **592 21**
H: 6 1 W: 13 06 b.Rochdale 28-9-71
Source: Trainee.

1988–89	Rochdale	1	0		
1989–90	Rochdale	0	0	**1**	**0**
1990–91	Stockport Co	0	0		
1991–92	Halifax T	36	0		
1992–93	Halifax T	42	2	**78**	**2**
1993–94	Bury	27	1		
1994–95	Bury	39	3		
1995–96	Bury	42	1		
1996–97	Bury	38	0		
1997–98	Bury	46	2		
1998–99	Bury	43	1	**235**	**8**
1999–2000	Huddersfield T	26	0		
2000–01	Huddersfield T	40	1		
2001–02	Huddersfield T	2	0	**68**	**1**
2001–02	Preston NE	40	2		
2002–03	Preston NE	43	2		
2003–04	Preston NE	37	1		
2004–05	Preston NE	41	4		
2005–06	Preston NE	28	1	**189**	**10**
2005–06	*Sheffield U*	3	0		
2006–07	Sheffield U	8	0		
2007–08	Sheffield U	6	0	**17**	**0**
2007–08	*Southampton*	4	0	**4**	**0**

MONTGOMERY, Nick (M) **227 7**
H: 5 9 W: 11 08 b.Leeds 28-10-81
Source: Scholar. *Honours:* Scotland Under-21, B.

2000–01	Sheffield U	27	0		
2001–02	Sheffield U	31	2		
2002–03	Sheffield U	23	0		
2003–04	Sheffield U	36	3		
2004–05	Sheffield U	25	1		
2005–06	Sheffield U	39	1		
2006–07	Sheffield U	26	0		
2007–08	Sheffield U	20	0	**227**	**7**

MORGAN, Chris (D) **346 16**
H: 6 1 W: 12 03 b.Barnsley 9-11-77
Source: Trainee.

1996–97	Barnsley	0	0		
1997–98	Barnsley	11	0		
1998–99	Barnsley	19	0		
1999–2000	Barnsley	37	0		
2000–01	Barnsley	40	1		
2001–02	Barnsley	42	4		
2002–03	Barnsley	36	2	**185**	**7**
2003–04	Sheffield U	32	1		
2004–05	Sheffield U	41	2		
2005–06	Sheffield U	39	3		
2006–07	Sheffield U	24	1		
2007–08	Sheffield U	25	2	**161**	**9**

NAUGHTON, Kyle (M) **18 0**
b.Sheffield 11-11-88

2006–07	Sheffield U	0	0		
2007–08	*Gretna*	18	0	**18**	**0**
2007–08	Sheffield U	0	0		

NAYSMITH, Gary (D) **269 9**
H: 5 9 W: 12 01 b.Edinburgh 16-11-78
Source: Whitehill Welfare Colts. *Honours:* Scotland Schools, Under-21, B, 40 full caps, 1 goal.

1995–96	Hearts	1	0		
1996–97	Hearts	10	0		
1997–98	Hearts	16	2		
1998–99	Hearts	26	0		
1999–2000	Hearts	35	1		
2000–01	Hearts	9	0	**97**	**3**
2000–01	Everton	20	2		
2001–02	Everton	24	0		
2002–03	Everton	28	1		
2003–04	Everton	29	2		
2004–05	Everton	11	0		
2005–06	Everton	7	0		
2006–07	Everton	15	1	**134**	**6**
2007–08	Sheffield U	38	0	**38**	**0**

OLIVER, Dean (F) **1 0**
H: 6 0 W: 12 05 b.Derby 4-12-87
Source: Scholar.

2006–07	Sheffield U	0	0		
2006–07	*Torquay U*	1	0	**1**	**0**
2007–08	Sheffield U	0	0		

QUINN, Keith (M) **0 0**
b.Dublin 22-9-88
Source: Scholar. *Honours:* Eire Under-21.

2006–07	Sheffield U	0	0		
2007–08	Sheffield U	0	0		

QUINN, Stephen (M) **65 4**
H: 5 6 W: 9 08 b.Dublin 4-4-86
Source: Trainee. *Honours:* Eire Under-21.

2005–06	Sheffield U	0	0		
2005–06	*Milton Keynes D*	15	0	**15**	**0**
2005–06	*Rotherham U*	16	0	**16**	**0**
2006–07	Sheffield U	15	2		
2007–08	Sheffield U	19	2	**34**	**4**

ROBERTSON, Jordan (F) **43 9**
H: 6 0 W: 12 06 b.Sheffield 12-2-88
Source: Scholar.

2006–07	Sheffield U	0	0		
2006–07	*Torquay U*	9	2	**9**	**2**
2006–07	*Northampton T*	17	3	**17**	**3**
2007–08	Sheffield U	0	0		
2007–08	*Dundee U*	14	3	**14**	**3**
2007–08	*Oldham Ath*	3	1	**3**	**1**

S-LATEF, Zeyn (F) **0 0**
b.Sweden 22-7-90
Source: Scholar.

2007–08	Sheffield U	0	0		

SECK, Mamadou (M) **135 4**
H: 6 4 W: 12 13 b.Rufisgue 23-8-79
Honours: Senegal 6 full caps.

2000–01	Nimes	17	0		
2001–02	Nimes	24	0	**41**	**0**
2002–03	Ajaccio	20	2		
2003–04	Ajaccio	26	1		
2004–05	Ajaccio	28	1	**74**	**4**
2005–06	Kayseri	8	0	**8**	**0**
2005–06	Le Havre	7	0		
2006–07	Le Havre	4	0	**11**	**0**
2006–07	Sheffield U	0	0		
2007–08	Sheffield U	0	0		
2007–08	*Scunthorpe U*	1	0	**1**	**0**

SHARP, Billy (F) **129 66**
H: 5 9 W: 11 00 b.Sheffield 5-2-86
Source: Scholar.

2004–05	Sheffield U	2	0		
2004–05	*Rushden & D*	16	9	**16**	**9**
2005–06	Sheffield U	0	0		
2005–06	Scunthorpe U	37	23		
2006–07	Scunthorpe U	45	30	**82**	**53**
2007–08	Sheffield U	29	4	**31**	**4**

SHELTON, Luton (F) **38 10**
H: 5 11 W: 11 11 b.Jamaica 11-11-85
Source: Harbour View, Jamaica Youth, Under-20, Under-23, 27 full caps, 20 goals.

2006	Helsingborg	19	9	**19**	**9**
2006–07	Sheffield U	4	0		
2007–08	Sheffield U	15	1	**19**	**1**

SLAVKOVSKI, Goran (F) **0 0**
b.Skravlinge 8-4-89
Source: Internazionale.

2007–08	Sheffield U	0	0		

SPEED, Gary (M) **660 101**
H: 5 10 W: 12 10 b.Deeside 8-9-69
Source: Trainee. *Honours:* Wales Youth, Under-21, 85 full caps, 7 goals.

1988–89	Leeds U	1	0		
1989–90	Leeds U	25	3		
1990–91	Leeds U	38	7		
1991–92	Leeds U	41	7		
1992–93	Leeds U	39	7		
1993–94	Leeds U	36	10		
1994–95	Leeds U	39	3		
1995–96	Leeds U	29	2	**248**	**39**
1996–97	Everton	37	9		
1997–98	Everton	21	7	**58**	**16**
1997–98	Newcastle U	13	1		
1998–99	Newcastle U	38	4		
1999–2000	Newcastle U	36	9		
2000–01	Newcastle U	35	5		
2001–02	Newcastle U	29	5		
2002–03	Newcastle U	24	2		
2003–04	Newcastle U	38	3	**213**	**29**
2004–05	Bolton W	38	1		
2005–06	Bolton W	31	4		
2006–07	Bolton W	38	8		
2007–08	Bolton W	14	1	**121**	**14**
2007–08	Sheffield U	20	3	**20**	**3**

STAROSTA, Ben (D) **36 0**
H: 6 0 W: 12 00 b.Sheffield 7-1-87
Source: Scholar. *Honours:* Poland Youth.

2006–07	Sheffield U	0	0		
2007–08	Sheffield U	0	0		
2007–08	*Brentford*	21	0	**21**	**0**
2007–08	*Bradford C*	15	0	**15**	**0**

STEAD, Jon (F) **200 43**
H: 6 3 W: 13 03 b.Huddersfield 7-4-83
Source: Scholar. *Honours:* England Under-21.

2001–02	Huddersfield T	0	0		
2002–03	Huddersfield T	42	6		
2003–04	Huddersfield T	26	16	**68**	**22**
2003–04	Blackburn R	13	6		
2004–05	Blackburn R	29	2	**42**	**8**
2005–06	Sunderland	30	1		
2006–07	Sunderland	5	1	**35**	**2**
2006–07	*Derby Co*	17	3	**17**	**3**
2006–07	Sheffield U	14	5		
2007–08	Sheffield U	24	3	**38**	**8**

TONGE, Michael (M) **258 21**
H: 6 0 W: 11 10 b.Manchester 7-4-83
Source: Scholar. *Honours:* England Youth, Under-20, Under-21.

2000–01	Sheffield U	2	0		
2001–02	Sheffield U	30	3		
2002–03	Sheffield U	44	6		
2003–04	Sheffield U	46	4		
2004–05	Sheffield U	34	2		
2005–06	Sheffield U	30	3		
2006–07	Sheffield U	27	2		
2007–08	Sheffield U	45	1	**258**	**21**

TRAVIS, Nicky (M) **2 0**
H: 6 0 W: 12 01 b.Sheffield 12-3-87
Source: Scholar.

2004–05	Sheffield U	0	0		
2005–06	Sheffield U	0	0		
2006–07	Sheffield U	0	0		
2007–08	Sheffield U	0	0		
2007–08	*Chesterfield*	2	0	**2**	**0**

WEBBER, Danny (F) **154 40**
H: 5 10 W: 11 04 b.Manchester 28-12-81
Source: Trainee. *Honours:* England Youth, Under-20.

1998–99	Manchester U	0	0		
1999–2000	Manchester U	0	0		
2000–01	Manchester U	0	0		
2001–02	Manchester U	0	0		
2001–02	*Port Vale*	4	0	**4**	**0**
2001–02	*Watford*	5	2		
2002–03	Manchester U	0	0		
2002–03	*Watford*	12	2		
2003–04	Watford	27	5		
2004–05	Watford	28	12	**72**	**21**
2004–05	*Sheffield U*	7	3		
2005–06	Sheffield U	35	10		
2006–07	Sheffield U	22	3		
2007–08	Sheffield U	14	3	**78**	**19**

WEDGBURY, Samuel (M) **0 0**
b.Oldbury 26-2-89

2006–07	Sheffield U	0	0		
2007–08	Sheffield U	0	0		

SHEFFIELD W (73)

BEEVERS, Mark (D) **30 0**
H: 6 4 W: 13 00 b.Barnsley 21-11-89
Source: Scholar. *Honours:* England Youth.

2006–07	Sheffield W	2	0		
2007–08	Sheffield W	28	0	**30**	**0**

BODEN, Luke (F) **3 0**
H: 6 1 W: 12 00 b.Sheffield 26-11-88
Source: Scholar.

2006–07	Sheffield W	1	0		
2007–08	Sheffield W	2	0	**3**	**0**

BOWMAN, Matthew (F) **0 0**
H: 5 8 W: 11 11 b.Barnsley 31-1-90
Source: Scholar.

2006–07	Sheffield W	0	0		
2007–08	Sheffield W	0	0		

BRADLEY, Jason (F) **0 0**
H: 6 3 W: 13 00 b.Sheffield 16-3-89

2007–08	Sheffield W	0	0		

BULLEN, Lee (D) **387 87**
H: 6 1 W: 12 07 b.Edinburgh 29-3-71

1990–91	Meadowbank T	3	0	**3**	**0**
1991–92	Stenhousemuir	35	22		
1992–93	Stenhousemuir	35	24	**70**	**46**

From Stanmore, Golden, South China.

1997–98	Kalamata	18	4		
1998–99	Kalamata	27	7		
1999–2000	Kalamata	5	0	**50**	**11**
1999–2000	Dunfermline Ath	13	7		
2000–01	Dunfermline Ath	24	4		
2001–02	Dunfermline Ath	31	4		
2002–03	Dunfermline Ath	35	5		
2003–04	Dunfermline Ath	27	2	**130**	**22**
2004–05	Sheffield W	46	7		
2005–06	Sheffield W	28	0		
2006–07	Sheffield W	38	0		
2007–08	Sheffield W	22	1	**134**	**8**

BURCH, Rob (G) **8 0**
H: 6 2 W: 12 13 b.Yeovil 8-10-83
Source: Trainee. *Honours:* England Under-20.

2002–03	Tottenham H	0	0		
2003–04	Tottenham H	0	0		
2004–05	Tottenham H	0	0		
2004–05	*West Ham U*	0	0		
2005–06	Tottenham H	0	0		
2005–06	*Bristol C*	0	0		
2006–07	Tottenham H	0	0		
2006–07	*Barnet*	6	0	**6**	**0**
2007–08	Sheffield W	2	0	**2**	**0**

BURTON, Deon (F) **393 88**
H: 5 9 W: 11 09 b.Ashford 25-10-76
Source: Trainee. *Honours:* Jamaica 51 full caps, 9 goals.

1993–94	Portsmouth	2	0		
1994–95	Portsmouth	7	2		
1995–96	Portsmouth	32	7		
1996–97	Portsmouth	21	1		
1996–97	*Cardiff C*	5	2	**5**	**2**
1997–98	Derby Co	29	3		
1998–99	Derby Co	21	9		
1998–99	*Barnsley*	3	0	**3**	**0**
1999–2000	Derby Co	19	4		
2000–01	Derby Co	32	5		
2001–02	Derby Co	17	1		
2001–02	*Stoke C*	12	2	**12**	**2**
2002–03	Derby Co	7	3	**125**	**25**
2002–03	Portsmouth	15	4		
2003–04	Portsmouth	1	0	**78**	**14**
2003–04	*Walsall*	3	0	**3**	**0**
2003–04	*Swindon T*	4	1	**4**	**1**
2004–05	Brentford	40	10	**40**	**10**
2005–06	Rotherham U	24	12	**24**	**12**
2005–06	Sheffield W	17	3		
2006–07	Sheffield W	42	12		
2007–08	Sheffield W	40	7	**99**	**22**

CLARKE, Leon (F) **123 28**
H: 6 2 W: 14 02 b.Birmingham 10-2-85
Source: Scholar.

2003–04	Wolverhampton W	0	0		
2003–04	*Kidderminster H*	4	0	**4**	**0**
2004–05	Wolverhampton W	28	7		
2005–06	Wolverhampton W	24	1		
2005–06	*QPR*	1	0	**1**	**0**
2005–06	*Plymouth Arg*	5	0	**5**	**0**
2006–07	Wolverhampton W	22	5	**74**	**13**
2006–07	Sheffield W	10	1		
2006–07	*Oldham Ath*	5	3	**5**	**3**
2007–08	Sheffield W	8	3	**18**	**4**
2007–08	*Southend U*	16	8	**16**	**8**

ESAJAS, Etienne (F) **50 3**
H: 5 7 W: 10 03 b.Amsterdam 4-11-84
Source: Ajax.

2005–06	Vitesse	11	1		
2006–07	Vitesse	21	2	**32**	**3**
2007–08	Sheffield W	18	0	**18**	**0**

GILBERT, Peter (D) **120 1**
H: 5 11 W: 12 00 b.Newcastle 31-7-83
Source: Scholar. *Honours:* Wales Under-21.

2001–02	Birmingham C	0	0		
2002–03	Birmingham C	0	0		
2003–04	Birmingham C	0	0		
2003–04	Plymouth Arg	40	1		
2004–05	Plymouth Arg	38	0	**78**	**1**
2005–06	Leicester C	5	0	**5**	**0**
2005–06	Sheffield W	17	0		
2006–07	Sheffield W	6	0		
2006–07	*Doncaster R*	4	0	**4**	**0**
2007–08	Sheffield W	10	0	**33**	**0**

GRANT, Lee (G) **135 0**
H: 6 3 W: 13 01 b.Hemel Hempstead 27-1-83
Source: Scholar. *Honours:* England Youth, Under-21.

2000–01	Derby Co	0	0		
2001–02	Derby Co	0	0		
2002–03	Derby Co	29	0		
2003–04	Derby Co	36	0		
2004–05	Derby Co	2	0		
2005–06	Derby Co	0	0		
2005–06	*Burnley*	1	0	**1**	**0**
2005–06	*Oldham Ath*	16	0	**16**	**0**
2006–07	Derby Co	7	0	**74**	**0**
2007–08	Sheffield W	44	0	**44**	**0**

HINDS, Richard (D) **231 11**
H: 6 2 W: 12 02 b.Sheffield 22-8-80
Source: Schoolboy.

1998–99	Tranmere R	2	0		
1999–2000	Tranmere R	6	0		
2000–01	Tranmere R	29	0		
2001–02	Tranmere R	10	0		
2002–03	Tranmere R	8	0	**55**	**0**
2003–04	Hull C	39	1		
2004–05	Hull C	6	0	**45**	**1**
2004–05	*Scunthorpe U*	7	0		
2005–06	Scunthorpe U	42	6		
2006–07	Scunthorpe U	44	2	**93**	**8**
2007–08	Sheffield W	38	2	**38**	**2**

JEFFERS, Francis (F) **146 31**
H: 5 10 W: 11 02 b.Liverpool 25-1-81
Source: Trainee. *Honours:* England Schools, Youth, Under-21, 1 full cap, 1 goal.

1997–98	Everton	1	0		
1998–99	Everton	15	6		
1999–2000	Everton	21	6		
2000–01	Everton	12	6		
2001–02	Arsenal	6	2		
2002–03	Arsenal	16	2		
2003–04	Arsenal	0	0	**22**	**4**
2003–04	*Everton*	18	0	**67**	**18**
2004–05	Charlton Ath	20	3		
2005–06	Charlton Ath	0	0	**20**	**3**
2005–06	*Rangers*	8	0	**8**	**0**
2006–07	Blackburn R	10	0	**10**	**0**
2006–07	*Ipswich T*	9	4	**9**	**4**
2007–08	Sheffield W	10	2	**10**	**2**

JOHNSON, Jermaine (M) **120 16**
H: 5 11 W: 11 05 b.Kingston, Jamaica 25-6-80
Source: Tivoli Gardens. *Honours:* Jamaica 40 full caps, 5 goals.

2001–02	Bolton W	10	0		
2002–03	Bolton W	2	0		
2003–04	Bolton W	0	0	**12**	**0**
2003–04	Oldham Ath	20	5		
2004–05	Oldham Ath	19	4		
2005–06	Oldham Ath	0	0	**39**	**9**
2006–07	Bradford C	27	4	**27**	**4**
2006–07	Sheffield W	7	2		
2007–08	Sheffield W	35	1	**42**	**3**

KAY, James (D) **0 0**
H: 5 9 W: 11 07 b.Rotherham 9-2-89

2007–08	Sheffield W	0	0		

LEKAJ, Rocky (M) **2 0**
H: 5 10 W: 10 05 b.Kosovo 12-10-89
Source: Scholar. *Honours:* Norway Youth.

2006–07	Sheffield W	2	0		
2007–08	Sheffield W	0	0	**2**	**0**

LUNT, Kenny (M) **428 35**
H: 5 10 W: 10 05 b.Runcorn 20-11-79
Source: Trainee. *Honours:* England Schools, Youth.

1997–98	Crewe Alex	41	2		
1998–99	Crewe Alex	18	1		
1999–2000	Crewe Alex	43	3		
2000–01	Crewe Alex	46	1		
2001–02	Crewe Alex	45	5		
2002–03	Crewe Alex	46	7		
2003–04	Crewe Alex	45	7		
2004–05	Crewe Alex	46	5		
2005–06	Crewe Alex	43	4		
2006–07	Sheffield W	37	0		
2007–08	Sheffield W	4	0	**41**	**0**
2007–08	*Crewe Alex*	14	0	**387**	**35**

McALLISTER, Sean (M) **23 1**
H: 5 8 W: 10 07 b.Bolton 15-8-87
Source: Scholar.

2005–06	Sheffield W	2	0		
2006–07	Sheffield W	6	1		
2007–08	Sheffield W	8	0	**16**	**1**
2007–08	*Mansfield T*	7	0	**7**	**0**
2007–08	*Bury*	0	0		

McCLEMENTS, David (M) **0 0**
H: 5 7 W: 10 01 b.Ballymoney 14-1-89
Source: Scholar. *Honours:* Northern Ireland Youth.

2006–07	Sheffield W	0	0		
2007–08	Sheffield W	0	0		

McMENAMIN, Liam (D) **0 0**
H: 5 11 W: 10 11 b.Derry 10-4-89
Source: Scholar.

2007–08	Sheffield W	0	0		

O'BRIEN, Burton (M) **220 22**
H: 5 10 W: 11 09 b.South Africa 10-6-81
Source: S Form. *Honours:* Scotland Youth, Under-21.

1998–99	St Mirren	22	1	**22**	**1**
1998–99	Blackburn R	0	0		
1999–2000	Blackburn R	0	0		
2000–01	Blackburn R	0	0		
2001–02	Blackburn R	0	0		
2002–03	Livingston	28	1		
2003–04	Livingston	33	6		
2004–05	Livingston	38	8	**99**	**15**
2005–06	Sheffield W	44	2		
2006–07	Sheffield W	22	1		
2007–08	Sheffield W	33	3	**99**	**6**

O'DONNELL, Richard (G) **4 0**
H: 6 2 W: 13 05 b.Sheffield 12-9-88
Source: Scholar.

2007–08	Sheffield W	0	0		
2007–08	*Rotherham U*	0	0		
2007–08	*Oldham Ath*	4	0	**4**	**0**

SIMEK, Frankie (D) **114 2**
H: 6 0 W: 11 06 b.St Louis 13-10-84
Source: Trainee. *Honours:* USA 5 full caps.

2002–03	Arsenal	0	0		
2003–04	Arsenal	0	0		
2004–05	Arsenal	0	0		
2004–05	*QPR*	5	0	**5**	**0**
2004–05	*Bournemouth*	8	0	**8**	**0**
2005–06	Sheffield W	43	1		
2006–07	Sheffield W	41	1		
2007–08	Sheffield W	17	0	**101**	**2**

SMALL, Wade (M) **148 18**
H: 5 8 W: 11 05 b.Croydon 23-2-84
Source: Scholar.

2003–04	Wimbledon	27	1	**27**	**1**
2004–05	Milton Keynes D	44	10		
2005–06	Milton Keynes D	28	1	**72**	**11**
2006–07	Sheffield W	20	2		
2007–08	Sheffield W	29	4	**49**	**6**

SODJE, Akpo (F) **115 30**
H: 6 2 W: 12 08 b.Greenwich 31-1-81
Source: QPR, Stevenage B, Margate, Gravesend & N, Erith & Belvedere.

2004–05	Huddersfield T	7	0	**7**	**0**
2004–05	*Darlington*	7	1		
2005–06	Darlington	36	8	**43**	**9**
2006–07	Port Vale	43	14		
2007–08	Port Vale	3	0	**46**	**14**
2007–08	Sheffield W	19	7	**19**	**7**

SPURR, Tommy (D) **79 2**
H: 6 1 W: 11 05 b.Leeds 13-9-87
Source: Scholar.

2005–06	Sheffield W	2	0		
2006–07	Sheffield W	36	0		
2007–08	Sheffield W	41	2	**79**	**2**

TUDGAY, Marcus (F) **185 40**
H: 5 10 W: 12 04 b.Worthing 3-2-83
Source: Trainee.

2002–03	Derby Co	8	0		
2003–04	Derby Co	29	6		
2004–05	Derby Co	34	9		
2005–06	Derby Co	21	2	**92**	**17**
2005–06	Sheffield W	18	5		
2006–07	Sheffield W	40	11		
2007–08	Sheffield W	35	7	**93**	**23**

WALLWORK, Ronnie (M) **161** **10**
H: 5 10 W: 12 09 b.Manchester 10-9-77
Source: Trainee. *Honours:* England Youth, Under-20.

1994–95	Manchester U	0	0		
1995–96	Manchester U	0	0		
1996–97	Manchester U	0	0		
1997–98	Manchester U	1	0		
1997–98	*Carlisle U*	10	1	**10**	**1**
1997–98	*Stockport Co*	7	0	**7**	**0**
1998–99	Manchester U	0	0		
1999–2000	Manchester U	5	0		
2000–01	Manchester U	12	0		
2001–02	Manchester U	1	0	**19**	**0**
2002–03	WBA	27	0		
2003–04	WBA	5	0		
2003–04	*Bradford C*	7	4	**7**	**4**
2004–05	WBA	20	1		
2005–06	WBA	31	0		
2006–07	WBA	10	1		
2006–07	*Barnsley*	2	0	**2**	**0**
2007–08	WBA	0	0	**93**	**2**
2007–08	*Huddersfield T*	16	3	**16**	**3**
2007–08	Sheffield W	7	0	**7**	**0**

WATSON, Steve (D) **451** **29**
H: 6 0 W: 12 07 b.North Shields 1-4-74
Source: Trainee. *Honours:* England Youth, Under-21, B.

1990–91	Newcastle U	24	0		
1991–92	Newcastle U	28	1		
1992–93	Newcastle U	2	0		
1993–94	Newcastle U	32	2		
1994–95	Newcastle U	27	4		
1995–96	Newcastle U	23	3		
1996–97	Newcastle U	36	1		
1997–98	Newcastle U	29	1		
1998–99	Newcastle U	7	0	**208**	**12**
1998–99	Aston Villa	27	0		
1999–2000	Aston Villa	14	0	**41**	**0**
2000–01	Everton	34	0		
2001–02	Everton	25	4		
2002–03	Everton	18	5		
2003–04	Everton	24	5		
2004–05	Everton	25	0	**126**	**14**
2005–06	WBA	30	1		
2006–07	WBA	12	0	**42**	**1**
2006–07	*Sheffield W*	11	0		
2007–08	Sheffield W	23	2	**34**	**2**

WOOD, Richard (D) **118** **5**
H: 6 3 W: 12 13 b.Wakefield 5-7-85
Source: Scholar.

2002–03	Sheffield W	3	1		
2003–04	Sheffield W	12	0		
2004–05	Sheffield W	34	1		
2005–06	Sheffield W	30	1		
2006–07	Sheffield W	12	0		
2007–08	Sheffield W	27	2	**118**	**5**

SHREWSBURY T (74)

ASHTON, Neil (M) **146** **4**
H: 5 8 W: 12 04 b.Liverpool 15-1-85
Source: Scholar.

2002–03	Tranmere R	0	0		
2003–04	Tranmere R	1	0		
2004–05	Tranmere R	0	0	**1**	**0**
2004–05	*Shrewsbury T*	24	0		
2005–06	Shrewsbury T	44	1		
2006–07	Shrewsbury T	43	2		
2007–08	Shrewsbury T	15	0	**126**	**3**
2007–08	*Macclesfield T*	19	1	**19**	**1**

BEVAN, Scott (G) **57** **0**
H: 6 6 W: 15 10 b.Southampton 16-9-79
Source: Trainee.

1997–98	Southampton	0	0		
1998–99	Southampton	0	0		
1999–2000	Southampton	0	0		
2000–01	Southampton	0	0		
2001–02	Southampton	0	0		
2001–02	*Stoke C*	0	0		
2002–03	Southampton	0	0		
2002–03	*Huddersfield T*	30	0	**30**	**0**
2003–04	Southampton	0	0		
2003–04	*Wycombe W*	5	0	**5**	**0**
2003–04	Wimbledon	10	0	**10**	**0**
2004–05	Milton Keynes D	7	0		
2005–06	Milton Keynes D	0	0	**7**	**0**

From Kidderminster H.					
2007–08	Shrewsbury T	5	0	**5**	**0**

BRIGGS, Keith (D) **171** **11**
H: 6 0 W: 11 00 b.Glossop 11-12-81
Source: Trainee.

1999–2000	Stockport Co	7	1		
2000–01	Stockport Co	0	0		
2001–02	Stockport Co	32	0		
2002–03	Stockport Co	19	1		
2002–03	Norwich C	2	0		
2003–04	Norwich C	3	0		
2004–05	Norwich C	0	0	**5**	**0**
2004–05	*Crewe Alex*	3	0	**3**	**0**
2004–05	Stockport Co	16	2		
2005–06	Stockport Co	41	4		
2006–07	Stockport Co	20	2		
2007–08	Stockport Co	13	0	**148**	**10**
2007–08	Shrewsbury T	2	1	**2**	**1**
2007–08	*Mansfield T*	13	0	**13**	**0**

CONSTABLE, James (F) **37** **7**
H: 6 2 W: 12 12 b.Malmesbury 4-10-84
Source: Chippenham T.

2005–06	Walsall	17	3		
2006–07	Walsall	6	0	**23**	**3**
From Kidderminster H.					
2007–08	Shrewsbury T	14	4	**14**	**4**

COOKE, Andy (F) **358** **96**
H: 6 0 W: 12 07 b.Shrewsbury 20-1-74
Source: Newtown.

1994–95	Burnley	0	0		
1995–96	Burnley	23	5		
1996–97	Burnley	31	13		
1997–98	Burnley	34	16		
1998–99	Burnley	36	9		
1999–2000	Burnley	36	7		
2000–01	Burnley	11	2	**171**	**52**
2000–01	Stoke C	22	6		
2001–02	Stoke C	35	9		
2002–03	Stoke C	31	6		
2003–04	Stoke C	0	0	**88**	**21**
From Pusan Icons.					
2004–05	Bradford C	20	4		
2005–06	Bradford C	17	1	**37**	**5**
2005–06	*Darlington*	14	3	**14**	**3**
2006–07	Shrewsbury T	34	10		
2007–08	Shrewsbury T	14	5	**48**	**15**

DAVIES, Ben (M) **171** **27**
H: 5 7 W: 12 03 b.Birmingham 27-5-81
Source: Walsall trainee.

2000–01	Kidderminster H	3	0		
2001–02	Kidderminster H	9	0	**12**	**0**
2004–05	Chester C	44	2		
2005–06	Chester C	45	7	**89**	**9**
2006–07	Shrewsbury T	43	12		
2007–08	Shrewsbury T	27	6	**70**	**18**

GARNER, Glyn (G) **253** **0**
H: 6 2 W: 13 11 b.Pontypool 9-12-76
Source: Llanelli. *Honours:* Wales 1 full cap.

2000–01	Bury	0	0		
2001–02	Bury	7	0		
2002–03	Bury	46	0		
2003–04	Bury	46	0		
2004–05	Bury	27	0	**126**	**0**
2005–06	Leyton Orient	43	0		
2006–07	Leyton Orient	43	0	**86**	**0**
2007–08	Shrewsbury T	41	0	**41**	**0**

HALL, Danny (D) **106** **1**
H: 6 0 W: 12 02 b.Ashton-under-Lyne 14-11-83
Source: Scholar.

2002–03	Oldham Ath	2	0		
2003–04	Oldham Ath	31	1		
2004–05	Oldham Ath	21	0		
2005–06	Oldham Ath	10	0	**64**	**1**
2006–07	Shrewsbury T	27	0		
2007–08	Shrewsbury T	15	0	**42**	**0**
To Gretna January 2008.					

HERD, Ben (D) **122** **3**
H: 5 9 W: 10 12 b.Welwyn 21-6-85
Source: Scholar.

2002–03	Watford	0	0		
2003–04	Watford	0	0		
2004–05	Watford	0	0		
2005–06	Shrewsbury T	46	2		
2006–07	Shrewsbury T	31	1		
2007–08	Shrewsbury T	45	0	**122**	**3**

HIBBERT, Dave (F) **92** **16**
H: 6 2 W: 12 00 b.Eccleshall 28-1-86
Source: Scholar.

2004–05	Port Vale	9	2	**9**	**2**
2005–06	Preston NE	10	0		
2006–07	Preston NE	0	0	**10**	**0**
2006–07	*Rotherham U*	21	2	**21**	**2**
2006–07	*Bradford C*	8	0	**8**	**0**
2007–08	Shrewsbury T	44	12	**44**	**12**

HUMPHREY, Chris (M) **37** **0**
H: 5 10 W: 10 08 b.Walsall 19-9-87
Source: WBA Scholar.

2006–07	Shrewsbury T	12	0		
2007–08	Shrewsbury T	25	0	**37**	**0**

HUNT, David (M) **167** **6**
H: 5 11 W: 11 09 b.Dulwich 10-9-82
Source: Scholar.

2002–03	Crystal Palace	2	0	**2**	**0**
2003–04	Leyton Orient	38	1		
2004–05	Leyton Orient	27	0	**65**	**1**
2004–05	Northampton T	4	0		
2005–06	Northampton T	40	3		
2006–07	Northampton T	29	0	**73**	**3**
2007–08	Shrewsbury T	27	2	**27**	**2**

JONES, Luke (D) **14** **0**
H: 5 9 W: 11 09 b.Darwen 10-4-87
Source: Scholar.

2005–06	Blackburn R	0	0		
2006–07	Shrewsbury T	7	0		
2007–08	Shrewsbury T	7	0	**14**	**0**

KEMPSON, Darran (D) **50** **1**
H: 6 2 W: 13 00 b.Blackpool 6-12-84
Source: Scholar.

2004–05	Preston NE	0	0		
From Morecambe.					
2006–07	Crewe Alex	7	0	**7**	**0**
2006–07	*Bury*	12	0	**12**	**0**
2007–08	Shrewsbury T	23	0	**23**	**0**
2007–08	*Accrington S*	8	1	**8**	**1**

LANGMEAD, Kelvin (F) **176** **18**
H: 6 1 W: 12 00 b.Coventry 23-3-85
Source: Scholar.

2003–04	Preston NE	0	0		
2003–04	*Carlisle U*	11	1	**11**	**1**
2004–05	Preston NE	1	0	**1**	**0**
2004–05	*Kidderminster H*	10	1	**10**	**1**
2004–05	Shrewsbury T	28	3		
2005–06	Shrewsbury T	42	9		
2006–07	Shrewsbury T	45	3		
2007–08	Shrewsbury T	39	1	**154**	**16**

LESLIE, Steven (M) **23** **1**
H: 5 10 W: 11 02 b.Shrewsbury 5-11-87

2005–06	Shrewsbury T	1	0		
2006–07	Shrewsbury T	5	0		
2007–08	Shrewsbury T	17	1	**23**	**1**

MACKENZIE, Chris (G) **164** **1**
H: 5 11 W: 14 02 b.Northampton 14-5-72
Source: Corby T.

1994–95	Hereford U	22	0		
1995–96	Hereford U	38	1		
1996–97	Hereford U	0	0	**60**	**1**
1997–98	Leyton Orient	4	0		
1998–99	Leyton Orient	26	0	**30**	**0**
From Telford U					
2004–05	Chester C	24	0		
2005–06	Chester C	30	0	**54**	**0**
2006–07	Shrewsbury T	20	0		
2007–08	Shrewsbury T	0	0	**20**	**0**

MADJO, Guy (F) **25** **3**
H: 6 0 W: 13 05 b.Cameroon 1-6-84

2005–06	Bristol C	5	0	**5**	**0**
From Forest GR, Staff R, Crawley on loan					
2007–08	Cheltenham T	5	0	**5**	**0**
2007–08	Shrewsbury T	15	3	**15**	**3**

McINTYRE, Kevin (M) **168** **18**
H: 6 0 W: 11 10 b.Liverpool 23-12-77
Source: Trainee.

1996–97	Tranmere R	0	0		
1997–98	Tranmere R	2	0		
1998–99	Tranmere R	0	0		
1999–2000	Tranmere R	0	0		
2000–01	Tranmere R	0	0		
2001–02	Tranmere R	0	0	**2**	**0**
2004–05	Chester C	10	0	**10**	**0**
2004–05	Macclesfield T	23	0		
2005–06	Macclesfield T	44	5		

2006–07 Macclesfield T 44 9
2007–08 Macclesfield T 23 2 **134 16**
2007–08 Shrewsbury T 22 2 **22 2**

MEREDITH, James (D) 4 0
H: 6 0 W: 11 09 b.Albury 4-4-88
Source: Scholar.
2006–07 Derby Co 0 0
2006–07 *Chesterfield* 1 0 **1 0**
2007–08 Sligo R 0 0
2007–08 Shrewsbury T 3 0 **3 0**

MOSS, Darren (D) 229 14
H: 5 10 W: 11 00 b.Wrexham 24-5-81
Source: Trainee. *Honours:* Wales Youth, Under-21.
1998–99 Chester C 7 0
1999–2000 Chester C 35 0
2000–01 Chester C 0 0 **42 0**
2001–02 Shrewsbury T 31 2
2002–03 Shrewsbury T 40 2
2003–04 Shrewsbury T 0 0
2004–05 Shrewsbury T 26 6
2004–05 Crewe Alex 6 0
2005–06 Crewe Alex 31 0
2006–07 Crewe Alex 22 2 **59 2**
2007–08 Shrewsbury T 31 2 **128 12**

MURDOCK, Colin (D) 302 13
H: 6 2 W: 13 00 b.Ballymena 2-7-75
Source: Trainee. *Honours:* Northern Ireland Schools, Youth, B, 34 full caps, 1 goal.
1992–93 Manchester U 0 0
1993–94 Manchester U 0 0
1994–95 Manchester U 0 0
1995–96 Manchester U 0 0
1996–97 Manchester U 0 0
1997–98 Preston NE 27 1
1998–99 Preston NE 33 1
1999–2000 Preston NE 33 2
2000–01 Preston NE 37 0
2001–02 Preston NE 23 2
2002–03 Preston NE 24 0 **177 6**
2003–04 Hibernian 32 3
2004–05 Hibernian 5 0 **37 3**
2004–05 Crewe Alex 16 0 **16 0**
2005–06 Rotherham U 39 2
2006–07 Rotherham U 4 0 **43 2**
2007–08 Shrewsbury T 29 2 **29 2**

PUGH, Marc (M) 78 8
H: 5 11 W: 11 04 b.Burnley 2-4-87
Source: Scholar.
2005–06 Burnley 0 0
2005–06 Bury 6 1
2006–07 Bury 35 3 **41 4**
2007–08 Shrewsbury T 37 4 **37 4**

SYMES, Michael (F) 88 17
H: 6 3 W: 12 04 b.Gt Yarmouth 31-10-83
Source: Scholar.
2001–02 Everton 0 0
2002–03 Everton 0 0
2003–04 Everton 0 0
2003–04 *Crewe Alex* 4 1 **4 1**
2004–05 Bradford C 12 2
2004–05 *Darlington* 0 0
2005–06 Bradford C 3 1
2005–06 *Stockport Co* 1 0 **1 0**
2006–07 Bradford C 0 0 **15 3**
2006–07 Shrewsbury T 33 9
2007–08 Shrewsbury T 21 3 **54 12**
2007–08 *Macclesfield T* 14 1 **14 1**

TIERNEY, Marc (D) 98 1
H: 5 11 W: 11 04 b.Manchester 7-9-86
Source: Trainee.
2003–04 Oldham Ath 2 0
2004–05 Oldham Ath 11 0
2005–06 Oldham Ath 19 0
2006–07 Oldham Ath 5 0 **37 0**
2006–07 Shrewsbury T 18 0
2007–08 Shrewsbury T 43 1 **61 1**

SOUTHAMPTON (75)

BASEYA, Cedric (M) 4 0
H: 6 4 W: 14 07 b.Bretigny 19-12-87
Source: Scholar.
2006–07 Southampton 0 0
2007–08 Southampton 1 0 **1 0**
2007–08 *Crewe Alex* 3 0 **3 0**

BIALKOWSKI, Bartosz (G) 21 0
H: 6 3 W: 12 10 b.Braniewo 6-7-87
Honours: Poland Under-20, Under-21.
2004–05 Gornik Zabrze 7 0 **7 0**
2005–06 Southampton 5 0
2006–07 Southampton 8 0
2007–08 Southampton 1 0 **14 0**

CONDESSO, Feliciano (M) 0 0
H: 6 0 W: 11 13 b.Congo 6-4-87
2005–06 Southampton 0 0
2006–07 Southampton 0 0
2007–08 Southampton 0 0

DAVIES, Andrew (D) 108 3
H: 6 3 W: 14 08 b.Stockton 17-12-84
Source: Scholar. *Honours:* England Youth, Under-20, Under-21.
2002–03 Middlesbrough 1 0
2003–04 Middlesbrough 10 0
2004–05 Middlesbrough 3 0
2004–05 *QPR* 9 0 **9 0**
2005–06 Middlesbrough 12 0
2005–06 *Derby Co* 23 3 **23 3**
2006–07 Middlesbrough 23 0
2007–08 Middlesbrough 4 0 **53 0**
2007–08 Southampton 23 0 **23 0**

DAVIES, Kyle (M) 0 0
b.Oakland
2006–07 Southampton 0 0
2007–08 Southampton 0 0

DAVIS, Kelvin (G) 417 0
H: 6 1 W: 11 05 b.Bedford 29-9-76
Source: Trainee. *Honours:* England Youth, Under-21.
1993–94 Luton T 1 0
1994–95 Luton T 9 0
1994–95 *Torquay U* 2 0 **2 0**
1995–96 Luton T 6 0
1996–97 Luton T 0 0
1997–98 Luton T 32 0
1997–98 *Hartlepool U* 2 0 **2 0**
1998–99 Luton T 44 0 **92 0**
1999–2000 Wimbledon 0 0
2000–01 Wimbledon 45 0
2001–02 Wimbledon 40 0
2002–03 Wimbledon 46 0 **131 0**
2003–04 Ipswich T 45 0
2004–05 Ipswich T 39 0 **84 0**
2005–06 Sunderland 33 0 **33 0**
2006–07 Southampton 38 0
2007–08 Southampton 35 0 **73 0**

DUTTON-BLACK, Josh (M) 0 0
b.Oxford 29-12-87
Source: Oxford U, Southampton Scholar.
2005–06 Southampton 0 0
2006–07 Southampton 0 0
2007–08 Southampton 0 0

DYER, Nathan (M) 57 3
H: 5 5 W: 9 00 b.Trowbridge 29-11-87
Source: Scholar. *Honours:* England Youth.
2005–06 Southampton 17 0
2005–06 *Burnley* 5 2 **5 2**
2006–07 Southampton 18 0
2007–08 Southampton 17 1 **52 1**

EUELL, Jason (F) 335 78
H: 5 11 W: 11 13 b.Lambeth 6-2-77
Source: Trainee. *Honours:* England Youth, Under-21, Jamaica 3 full caps, 1 goal.
1995–96 Wimbledon 9 2
1996–97 Wimbledon 7 2
1997–98 Wimbledon 19 4
1998–99 Wimbledon 33 10
1999–2000 Wimbledon 37 4
2000–01 Wimbledon 36 19 **141 41**
2001–02 Charlton Ath 36 11
2002–03 Charlton Ath 36 10
2003–04 Charlton Ath 31 10
2004–05 Charlton Ath 26 2
2005–06 Charlton Ath 10 1
2006–07 Charlton Ath 0 0 **139 34**
2006–07 Middlesbrough 17 0
2007–08 Middlesbrough 0 0 **17 0**
2007–08 Southampton 38 3 **38 3**

GIALLOMBARDO, Andrew (M) 0 0
H: 5 9 W: 12 02 b.New York 15-3-89
Source: Scholar.
2006–07 Southampton 0 0
2007–08 Southampton 0 0

GILLETT, Simon (M) 46 2
H: 5 6 W: 11 07 b.London 6-11-85
Source: Trainee. *Honours:* Luxembourg full caps.
2003–04 Southampton 0 0
2004–05 Southampton 0 0
2005–06 Southampton 0 0
2005–06 *Walsall* 2 0 **2 0**
2006–07 Southampton 0 0
2006–07 *Blackpool* 31 1 **31 1**
2006–07 *Bournemouth* 7 1 **7 1**
2007–08 Southampton 2 0 **2 0**
2007–08 *Yeovil T* 4 0 **4 0**

HATCH, Jamie (M) 0 0
b.Hampshire 21-9-89
Source: Scholar.
2006–07 Southampton 0 0
2007–08 Southampton 0 0

IDIAKEZ, Inigo (M) 447 78
H: 6 0 W: 12 02 b.San Sebastian 8-11-73
Honours: Spain Under-21.
1992–93 Real Sociedad 1 0
1993–94 Real Sociedad B 25 13
1993–94 Real Sociedad 2 0
1994–95 Real Sociedad 26 4
1995–96 Real Sociedad 33 4
1996–97 Real Sociedad 31 4
1997–98 Real Sociedad 16 1
1998–99 Real Sociedad 29 7
1999–2000 Real Sociedad 27 4
2000–01 Real Sociedad 33 7
2001–02 Real Sociedad 34 2 **232 33**
2002–03 Oviedo 33 4 **33 4**
2003–04 Rayo Vallecano 29 5 **29 5**
2004–05 Derby Co 41 9
2005–06 Derby Co 42 11
2006–07 Derby Co 5 0 **88 20**
2006–07 Southampton 14 1
2006–07 *QPR* 5 1 **5 1**
2007–08 Southampton 21 1 **35 2**

IMUDIA, Jeffrey (D) 0 0
b.Nigeria
Honours: Everton Scholar.
2007–08 Southampton 0 0

JAMES, Lloyd (M) 0 0
H: 5 11 W: 11 01 b.Bristol 16-2-88
Source: Scholar. *Honours:* Wales Youth, Under-21.
2005–06 Southampton 0 0
2006–07 Southampton 0 0
2007–08 Southampton 0 0

JOHN, Stern (F) 345 128
H: 6 1 W: 12 13 b.Tunapuna 30-10-76
Honours: Trinidad & Tobago 101 full caps, 67 goals.
1998 Columbus Crew 27 26
1999 Columbus Crew 28 18 **55 44**
1999–2000 Nottingham F 17 3
2000–01 Nottingham F 29 2
2001–02 Nottingham F 26 13 **72 18**
2001–02 Birmingham C 15 7
2002–03 Birmingham C 30 5
2003–04 Birmingham C 29 4
2004–05 Birmingham C 3 0 **77 16**
2004–05 Coventry C 30 11
2005–06 Coventry C 25 10
2005–06 *Derby Co* 7 0 **7 0**
2006–07 Coventry C 23 5 **78 26**
2006–07 Sunderland 15 4
2007–08 Sunderland 1 1 **16 5**
2007–08 Southampton 40 19 **40 19**

LALLANA, Adam (M) 9 1
H: 5 8 W: 11 06 b.St Albans 10-5-88
Source: Scholar. *Honours:* England Youth.
2005–06 Southampton 0 0
2006–07 Southampton 1 0
2007–08 Southampton 5 1 **6 1**
2007–08 *Bournemouth* 3 0 **3 0**

LANCASHIRE, Oliver (D) 0 0
H: 6 1 W: 11 10 b.Basingstoke 13-12-88
Source: Scholar.
2006–07 Southampton 0 0
2007–08 Southampton 0 0

LICKA, Mario (M) 120 14
H: 5 10 W: 11 11 b.Ostrava 30-4-82
2002–03 Banik Ostrava 25 7
2003–04 Banik Ostrava 29 4

2004–05	Banik Ostrava	11	1	**65**	**12**
2005–06	Slovacko	28	1	**28**	**1**
2006–07	Southampton	15	1		
2007–08	Southampton	12	0	**27**	**1**

LUNDEKVAM, Claus (D) 410 3
H: 6 3 W: 13 05 b.Austevoll 22-2-73
Honours: Norway Youth, Under-21, 40 full caps, 2 goals.

1993	Brann	3	0		
1994	Brann	20	0		
1995	Brann	14	0		
1996	Brann	16	1	**53**	**1**
1996–97	Southampton	29	0		
1997–98	Southampton	31	0		
1998–99	Southampton	33	0		
1999–2000	Southampton	27	0		
2000–01	Southampton	38	0		
2001–02	Southampton	34	0		
2002–03	Southampton	33	0		
2003–04	Southampton	31	1		
2004–05	Southampton	34	0		
2005–06	Southampton	34	1		
2006–07	Southampton	33	0		
2007–08	Southampton	0	0	**357**	**2**

MAKIN, Chris (D) 409 7
H: 5 11 W: 11 02 b.Manchester 8-5-73
Source: Trainee. *Honours:* England Schools, Youth, Under-21.

1991–92	Oldham Ath	0	0		
1992–93	Oldham Ath	0	0		
1992–93	*Wigan Ath*	15	2	**15**	**2**
1993–94	Oldham Ath	27	1		
1994–95	Oldham Ath	28	1		
1995–96	Oldham Ath	39	2	**94**	**4**
1996–97	Marseille	29	0	**29**	**0**
1997–98	Sunderland	25	0		
1998–99	Sunderland	38	0		
1999–2000	Sunderland	34	1		
2000–01	Sunderland	23	0	**120**	**1**
2000–01	Ipswich T	10	0		
2001–02	Ipswich T	30	0		
2002–03	Ipswich T	33	0		
2003–04	Ipswich T	5	0	**78**	**0**
2004–05	Leicester C	21	0	**21**	**0**
2004–05	*Derby Co*	13	0	**13**	**0**
2005–06	Reading	12	0	**12**	**0**
2006–07	Southampton	22	0		
2007–08	Southampton	5	0	**27**	**0**

McGOLDRICK, David (F) 57 8
H: 6 1 W: 11 10 b.Nottingham 29-11-87
Source: Schoolboy.

2003–04	Notts Co	4	0		
2004–05	Notts Co	0	0		
2005–06	Southampton	1	0		
2005–06	*Notts Co*	6	0	**10**	**0**
2006–07	Southampton	9	0		
2006–07	*Bournemouth*	12	6	**12**	**6**
2007–08	Southampton	8	0	**18**	**0**
2007–08	*Port Vale*	17	2	**17**	**2**

McLAGGON, Kane (F) 0 0
b.Barry 21-9-90
Source: Scholar. *Honours:* Wales Youth.

2007–08	Southampton	0	0		

MILLS, Joseph (F) 0 0
H: 5 9 W: 11 00 b.Swindon 30-10-89
Source: Scholar.

2006–07	Southampton	0	0		
2007–08	Southampton	0	0		

OSTLUND, Alexander (D) 257 9
H: 5 11 W: 11 13 b.Akersborg 2-11-78
Honours: Sweden Under-21, 22 full caps.

1994	AIK Stockholm	3	1		
1995	AIK Stockholm	17	1		
1996	AIK Stockholm	2	0		
1997	Brommapojkarna	13	2	**13**	**2**
1998	AIK Stockholm	24	1	**46**	**3**
1998–99	Guimaraes	0	0		
1999	Norrkoping	11	1		
2000	Norrkoping	22	1		
2001	Norrkoping	21	1		
2002	Norrkoping	23	0	**77**	**3**
2003	Hammarby	20	0		
2004	Hammarby	25	0	**45**	**0**
2004–05	Feyenoord	16	0		
2005–06	Feyenoord	16	1	**32**	**1**
2005–06	Southampton	12	0		
2006–07	Southampton	20	0		
2007–08	Southampton	12	0	**44**	**0**

POKE, Michael (G) 4 0
H: 6 1 W: 13 12 b.Spelthorne 21-11-85
Source: Trainee.

2003–04	Southampton	0	0		
2004–05	Southampton	0	0		
2005–06	Southampton	0	0		
2005–06	*Oldham Ath*	0	0		
2005–06	*Northampton T*	0	0		
2006–07	Southampton	0	0		
2007–08	Southampton	4	0	**4**	**0**

POWELL, Darren (D) 231 11
H: 6 2 W: 13 07 b.Hammersmith 10-3-76
Source: Hampton.

1998–99	Brentford	33	2		
1999–2000	Brentford	36	2		
2000–01	Brentford	18	1		
2001–02	Brentford	41	1	**128**	**6**
2002–03	Crystal Palace	39	1		
2003–04	Crystal Palace	10	0		
2004–05	Crystal Palace	6	1	**55**	**2**
2004–05	*West Ham U*	5	1	**5**	**1**
2005–06	Southampton	25	1		
2006–07	Southampton	8	0		
2007–08	Southampton	10	1	**43**	**2**

RASIAK, Grzegorz (F) 225 89
H: 6 3 W: 13 03 b.Szczecin 12-1-79
Source: Warta, GKS. *Honours:* Poland 37 full caps, 8 goals.

2000–01	Odra	28	9	**28**	**9**
2001–02	Groclin	26	14		
2002–03	Groclin	22	10		
2003–04	Groclin	18	10	**66**	**34**
2003–04	Siena	0	0		
2004–05	Derby Co	35	16		
2005–06	Derby Co	6	2	**41**	**18**
2005–06	Tottenham H	8	0	**8**	**0**
2005–06	Southampton	13	4		
2006–07	Southampton	39	18		
2007–08	Southampton	23	6	**75**	**28**
2007–08	*Bolton W*	7	0	**7**	**0**

SAFRI, Youseff (M) 211 4
H: 5 9 W: 12 09 b.Casablanca 1-3-77
Source: Raja. *Honours:* Morocco 10 full caps.

2001–02	Coventry C	33	1		
2002–03	Coventry C	27	0		
2003–04	Coventry C	31	0	**91**	**1**
2004–05	Norwich C	18	1		
2005–06	Norwich C	30	1		
2006–07	Norwich C	35	1	**83**	**3**
2007–08	Southampton	37	0	**37**	**0**

SAGANOWSKI, Marek (F) 306 102
H: 5 10 W: 12 04 b.Lodz 31-10-78
Honours: Poland 26 full caps, 3 goals.

1994–95	Lodz	3	0		
1995–96	Lodz	29	11		
1996–97	Lodz	2	1		
1996–97	Hamburg	3	0	**3**	**0**
1996–97	Feyenoord	7	0	**7**	**0**
1997–98	Lodz	22	11		
1998–99	Lodz	15	1		
1999–2000	Lodz	24	6	**95**	**30**
2000–01	Plock	23	4	**23**	**4**
2001–02	Odra	27	2		
2002–03	Odra	3	0	**30**	**2**
2002–03	Legia	17	10		
2003–04	Legia	24	17		
2004–05	Legia	26	14	**67**	**41**
2005–06	Guimaraes	32	12	**32**	**12**
2006–07	Troyes	6	0	**6**	**0**
2006–07	Southampton	13	10		
2007–08	Southampton	30	3	**43**	**13**

SKACEL, Rudi (M) 190 39
H: 5 10 W: 12 01 b.Trutnov 17-7-79
Honours: Czech Republic Under-21, 4 full caps, 1 goal.

1998–99	Hradec Kralove	0	0		
1999–2000	Hradec Kralove	3	0		
2000–01	Hradec Kralove	0	0		
2001–02	Hradec Kralove	18	6	**21**	**6**
2001–02	Slavia Prague	12	3		
2002–03	Slavia Prague	28	8	**40**	**11**
2003–04	Marseille	20	1	**20**	**1**
2004–05	Panathinaikos	16	1	**16**	**1**
2005–06	Hearts	35	16	**35**	**16**
2006–07	Southampton	37	3		
2007–08	*Hertha Berlin*	5	0	**5**	**0**
2007–08	Southampton	16	1	**53**	**4**

SURMAN, Andrew (M) 127 16
H: 5 10 W: 11 06 b.Johannesburg 20-8-86
Source: Trainee. *Honours:* England Under-21.

2003–04	Southampton	0	0		
2004–05	Southampton	0	0		
2004–05	*Walsall*	14	2	**14**	**2**
2005–06	Southampton	12	2		
2005–06	*Bournemouth*	24	6	**24**	**6**
2006–07	Southampton	37	4		
2007–08	Southampton	40	2	**89**	**8**

THOMAS, Wayne (D) 392 13
H: 6 2 W: 14 12 b.Gloucester 17-5-79
Source: Trainee.

1995–96	Torquay U	6	0		
1996–97	Torquay U	12	0		
1997–98	Torquay U	21	1		
1998–99	Torquay U	44	1		
1999–2000	Torquay U	40	3	**123**	**5**
2000–01	Stoke C	34	0		
2001–02	Stoke C	40	2		
2002–03	Stoke C	41	0		
2003–04	Stoke C	39	3		
2004–05	Stoke C	35	2	**189**	**7**
2005–06	Burnley	16	1		
2006–07	Burnley	33	0		
2007–08	Burnley	1	0	**50**	**1**
2007–08	Southampton	30	0	**30**	**0**

THOMSON, Jake (M) 0 0
H: 5 11 W: 11 05 b.Southsea 12-5-89
Source: Scholar.

2006–07	Southampton	0	0		
2007–08	Southampton	0	0		

VIAFARA, John (M) 286 17
H: 6 0 W: 13 01 b.Robles 27-10-78
Honours: Colombia full caps.

1999	Pasto	44	2		
2000	America	27	0		
2001	America	10	0	**37**	**0**
2001	Pasto	18	0	**62**	**2**
2002	Once Caldas	37	2		
2003	Once Caldas	32	4		
2004	Once Caldas	17	3	**86**	**9**
2005–06	Portsmouth	14	1	**14**	**1**
2005–06	Real Sociedad	11	0	**11**	**0**
2006–07	Southampton	36	2		
2007–08	Southampton	40	3	**76**	**5**

VIGNAL, Gregory (D) 95 6
H: 5 9 W: 11 06 b.Montpellier 19-7-81
Source: Montpellier Herault SC.

2000–01	Liverpool	6	0		
2001–02	Liverpool	4	0		
2002–03	Liverpool	1	0	**11**	**0**
2002–03	Bastia	15	0	**15**	**0**
2003–04	*Rennes*	5	0	**5**	**0**
2004–05	*Rangers*	30	3	**30**	**3**
2005–06	Portsmouth	14	0		
2006–07	Portsmouth	0	0	**14**	**0**
2007–08	Southampton	20	3	**20**	**3**

WHITE, Jamie (F) 0 0
H: 5 8 W: 10 07 b.Southampton 21-9-89
Source: Scholar.

2006–07	Southampton	0	0		
2007–08	Southampton	0	0		

WRIGHT-PHILLIPS, Bradley (M) 110 18
H: 5 10 W: 10 07 b.Lewisham 12-3-85
Source: Scholar. *Honours:* England Youth, Under-20.

2002–03	Manchester C	0	0		
2003–04	Manchester C	0	0		
2004–05	Manchester C	14	1		
2005–06	Manchester C	18	1	**32**	**2**
2006–07	Southampton	39	8		
2007–08	Southampton	39	8	**78**	**16**

WRIGHT, Jermaine (M) 410 21
H: 5 9 W: 11 09 b.Greenwich 21-10-75
Source: Trainee. *Honours:* England Youth.

1992–93	Millwall	0	0		
1993–94	Millwall	0	0		
1994–95	Millwall	0	0		
1994–95	Wolverhampton W	6	0		
1995–96	Wolverhampton W	7	0		
1995–96	*Doncaster R*	13	0	**13**	**0**
1996–97	Wolverhampton W	3	0		
1997–98	Wolverhampton W	4	0	**20**	**0**
1997–98	Crewe Alex	5	0		
1998–99	Crewe Alex	44	5	**49**	**5**

1999–2000 Ipswich T 34 1
2000–01 Ipswich T 37 2
2001–02 Ipswich T 29 1
2002–03 Ipswich T 39 1
2003–04 Ipswich T 45 5 **184 10**
2004–05 Leeds U 35 3
2005–06 Leeds U 3 0 **38 3**
2005–06 *Millwall* 15 2 **15 2**
2005–06 *Southampton* 13 0
2006–07 Southampton 42 1
2007–08 Southampton 36 0 **91 1**

SOUTHEND U (76)

ADEMENO, Charles (F) 2 0
H: 5 10 W: 11 13 b.Milton Keynes 12-12-88
Source: Scholar.
2005–06 Southend U 1 0
2006–07 Southend U 1 0
2007–08 Southend U 0 0 **2 0**

BAILEY, Nicky (M) 133 21
H: 5 10 W: 12 06 b.Hammersmith 10-6-84
Source: Sutton U.
2005–06 Barnet 45 7
2006–07 Barnet 44 5 **89 12**
2007–08 Southend U 44 9 **44 9**

BARNARD, Lee (F) 44 12
H: 5 10 W: 10 10 b.Romford 18-7-84
Source: Trainee.
2002–03 Tottenham H 0 0
2002–03 *Exeter C* 3 0 **3 0**
2003–04 Tottenham H 0 0
2004–05 Tottenham H 0 0
2004–05 *Leyton Orient* 8 0 **8 0**
2004–05 *Northampton T* 5 0 **5 0**
2005–06 Tottenham H 3 0
2006–07 Tottenham H 0 0
2007–08 Tottenham H 0 0 **3 0**
2007–08 *Crewe Alex* 10 3 **10 3**
2007–08 Southend U 15 9 **15 9**

BARRETT, Adam (D) 340 32
H: 5 10 W: 12 00 b.Dagenham 29-11-79
Source: Leyton Orient Trainee.
1998–99 Plymouth Arg 1 0
1999–2000 Plymouth Arg 42 3
2000–01 Plymouth Arg 9 0 **52 3**
2000–01 Mansfield T 8 1
2001–02 Mansfield T 29 0 **37 1**
2002–03 Bristol R 45 1
2003–04 Bristol R 45 4 **90 5**
2004–05 Southend U 43 11
2005–06 Southend U 45 3
2006–07 Southend U 28 3
2007–08 Southend U 45 6 **161 23**

BLACK, Tommy (M) 200 19
H: 5 7 W: 11 10 b.Chigwell 26-11-79
Source: Trainee.
1998–99 Arsenal 0 0
1999–2000 Arsenal 1 0 **1 0**
1999–2000 *Carlisle U* 5 1 **5 1**
1999–2000 *Bristol C* 4 0 **4 0**
2000–01 Crystal Palace 40 4
2001–02 Crystal Palace 25 0
2002–03 Crystal Palace 36 6
2003–04 Crystal Palace 25 0
2004–05 Crystal Palace 0 0
2004–05 *Sheffield U* 4 1 **4 1**
2005–06 Crystal Palace 1 0
2005–06 *Gillingham* 17 5 **17 5**
2006–07 Crystal Palace 0 0 **127 10**
2006–07 *Bradford C* 4 0 **4 0**
2007–08 Southend U 38 2 **38 2**

CLARKE, Peter (D) 210 21
H: 6 0 W: 12 00 b.Southport 3-1-82
Source: Trainee. *Honours:* England Schools, Youth, Under-20, Under-21.
1998–99 Everton 0 0
1999–2000 Everton 0 0
2000–01 Everton 1 0
2001–02 Everton 7 0
2002–03 Everton 0 0
2002–03 *Blackpool* 16 3
2002–03 *Port Vale* 13 1 **13 1**
2003–04 Everton 1 0
2003–04 *Coventry C* 5 0 **5 0**
2004–05 Everton 0 0 **9 0**
2004–05 Blackpool 38 5
2005–06 Blackpool 46 6 **100 14**
2006–07 Southend U 38 2
2007–08 Southend U 45 4 **83 6**

COLLIS, Steve (G) 64 0
H: 6 3 W: 12 05 b.Harrow 18-3-81
Source: Barnet Juniors.
1999–2000 Barnet 0 0
2000–01 Nottingham F 0 0
2001–02 Nottingham F 0 0
2003–04 Yeovil T 11 0
2004–05 Yeovil T 9 0
2005–06 Yeovil T 23 0 **43 0**
2006–07 Southend U 1 0
2007–08 Southend U 20 0 **21 0**

FLAHAVAN, Darryl (G) 291 0
H: 5 11 W: 12 05 b.Southampton 9-9-77
Source: Trainee.
From Woking.
2000–01 Southend U 29 0
2001–02 Southend U 41 0
2002–03 Southend U 41 0
2003–04 Southend U 37 0
2004–05 Southend U 28 0
2005–06 Southend U 43 0
2006–07 Southend U 46 0
2007–08 Southend U 26 0 **291 0**

FORAN, Richie (F) 246 62
H: 6 1 W: 13 00 b.Dublin 16-6-80
Honours: Eire Under-21.
2000–01 Shelbourne 28 11 **28 11**
2001–02 Carlisle U 37 14
2002–03 Carlisle U 31 7
2003–04 Carlisle U 23 4 **91 25**
2003–04 *Oxford U* 4 0 **4 0**
2004–05 Motherwell 35 5
2005–06 Motherwell 32 11
2006–07 Motherwell 23 7 **90 23**
2006–07 Southend U 15 1
2007–08 Southend U 6 0 **21 1**
2007–08 *Darlington* 12 2 **12 2**

FRANCIS, Simon (D) 156 5
H: 6 0 W: 12 06 b.Nottingham 16-2-85
Source: Scholar. *Honours:* England Youth, Under-20.
2002–03 Bradford C 25 1
2003–04 Bradford C 30 0 **55 1**
2003–04 Sheffield U 5 0
2004–05 Sheffield U 6 0
2005–06 Sheffield U 1 0 **12 0**
2005–06 *Grimsby T* 5 0 **5 0**
2005–06 *Tranmere R* 17 1 **17 1**
2006–07 Southend U 40 1
2007–08 Southend U 27 2 **67 3**

GOWER, Mark (M) 226 37
H: 5 11 W: 11 12 b.Edmonton 5-10-78
Source: Trainee. *Honours:* England Schools, Youth.
1996–97 Tottenham H 0 0
1997–98 Tottenham H 0 0
1998–99 Tottenham H 0 0
1998–99 *Motherwell* 9 1 **9 1**
1999–2000 Tottenham H 0 0
2000–01 Tottenham H 0 0
2000–01 Barnet 14 1
2001–02 Barnet 0 0
2002–03 Barnet 0 0 **14 1**
2003–04 Southend U 40 6
2004–05 Southend U 38 6
2005–06 Southend U 40 6
2006–07 Southend U 43 8
2007–08 Southend U 42 9 **203 35**

HAMMELL, Steven (D) 270 5
H: 5 9 W: 11 11 b.Rutherglen 18-2-82
Honours: Scotland Under-21, 1 full cap.
1999–2000 Motherwell 4 0
2000–01 Motherwell 34 0
2001–02 Motherwell 38 1
2002–03 Motherwell 37 0
2003–04 Motherwell 37 1
2004–05 Motherwell 32 0
2005–06 Motherwell 33 0 **215 2**
2006–07 Southend U 39 1
2007–08 Southend U 16 2 **55 3**

HARROLD, Matt (F) 137 16
H: 6 1 W: 11 10 b.Leyton 25-7-84
Source: Harlow T.
2003–04 Brentford 13 2
2004–05 Brentford 19 0 **32 2**
2004–05 *Grimsby T* 6 2 **6 2**
2005–06 Yeovil T 42 9
2006–07 Yeovil T 5 0 **47 9**
2006–07 Southend U 36 3
2007–08 Southend U 16 0 **52 3**

HOOPER, Gary (M) 55 15
H: 5 10 W: 12 07 b.Loughton 26-1-88
Source: Grays Ath.
2006–07 Southend U 19 0
2006–07 *Leyton Orient* 4 2 **4 2**
2007–08 Southend U 13 2 **32 2**
2007–08 *Hereford U* 19 11 **19 11**

HUNT, Lewis (D) 157 2
H: 5 11 W: 12 09 b.Birmingham 25-8-82
Source: Scholar.
2000–01 Derby Co 0 0
2001–02 Derby Co 0 0
2002–03 Derby Co 10 0
2003–04 Derby Co 1 0 **11 0**
2003–04 *Southend U* 26 0
2004–05 Southend U 31 0
2005–06 Southend U 30 0
2006–07 Southend U 35 2
2007–08 Southend U 24 0 **146 2**

LIPTAK, Zoltan (D) 0 0
H: 6 4 W: 13 00 b.Hungary 10-12-84
Source: Lombard-Papa.
2007–08 Southend U 0 0

LOKANDO, Mbive (M) 0 0
H: 5 11 W: 10 12 b.Congo 18-9-89
Source: Scholar. *Honours:* DR Congo 1 full cap.
2007–08 Southend U 0 0

MACDONALD, Charlie (F) 50 5
H: 5 8 W: 12 10 b.Southwark 13-2-81
Source: Trainee.
1998–99 Charlton Ath 0 0
1999–2000 Charlton Ath 3 0
2000–01 Charlton Ath 3 0
2000–01 *Cheltenham T* 8 2 **8 2**
2001–02 Charlton Ath 2 1
2001–02 *Torquay U* 5 0 **5 0**
2001–02 *Colchester U* 4 1 **4 1**
2002–03 Charlton Ath 0 0
2003–04 Charlton Ath 0 0
2004–05 Charlton Ath 0 0
2005–06 Charlton Ath 0 0
2006–07 Charlton Ath 0 0 **8 1**
2007–08 Southend U 25 1 **25 1**

MAHER, Kevin (M) 390 22
H: 6 0 W: 12 13 b.Ilford 17-10-76
Source: Trainee. *Honours:* Eire Under-21.
1995–96 Tottenham H 0 0
1996–97 Tottenham H 0 0
1997–98 Tottenham H 0 0
1997–98 Southend U 18 1
1998–99 Southend U 34 4
1999–2000 Southend U 24 0
2000–01 Southend U 41 2
2001–02 Southend U 36 5
2002–03 Southend U 42 2
2003–04 Southend U 42 1
2004–05 Southend U 42 1
2005–06 Southend U 44 1
2006–07 Southend U 41 5
2007–08 Southend U 19 0 **383 22**
2007–08 *Gillingham* 7 0 **7 0**

MASTERS, Clark (G) 12 0
H: 6 3 W: 13 12 b.Hastings 31-5-87
Source: Scholar.
2005–06 Brentford 0 0
2006–07 Brentford 11 0
2007–08 Brentford 1 0 **12 0**
2007–08 Southend U 0 0

McCORMACK, Alan (M) 116 15
H: 5 8 W: 11 00 b.Dublin 10-1-84
Source: Stella Maris BC.
2002–03 Preston NE 0 0
2003–04 Preston NE 5 0
2003–04 *Leyton Orient* 10 0 **10 0**
2004–05 Preston NE 3 0
2004–05 *Southend U* 7 2
2005–06 Preston NE 0 0
2005–06 *Motherwell* 24 2 **24 2**
2006–07 Preston NE 3 0 **11 0**

2006–07 Southend U 22 3
2007–08 Southend U 42 8 **71 13**

MOUSSA, Franck (M) 21 0
H: 5 8 W: 10 08 b.Brussels 24-9-87
Source: Scholar.
2005–06 Southend U 1 0
2006–07 Southend U 4 0
2007–08 Southend U 16 0 **21 0**

REVELL, Alex (F) 124 18
H: 6 3 W: 13 00 b.Cambridge 7-7-83
Source: Scholar.
2000–01 Cambridge U 4 0
2001–02 Cambridge U 24 2
2002–03 Cambridge U 9 0
2003–04 Cambridge U 20 3 **57 5**
From Braintree T.
2006–07 Brighton & HA 38 7
2007–08 Brighton & HA 21 6 **59 13**
2007–08 Southend U 8 0 **8 0**

SCANNELL, Damian (M) 9 0
H: 5 10 W: 11 07 b.Croydon 28-4-85
Source: Eastleigh.
2007–08 Southend U 9 0 **9 0**

WILSON, Che (D) 212 2
H: 5 9 W: 11 04 b.Ely 17-1-79
Source: Trainee.
1997–98 Norwich C 0 0
1998–99 Norwich C 17 0
1999–2000 Norwich C 5 0 **22 0**
2000–01 Bristol R 37 0
2001–02 Bristol R 38 0
2002–03 Bristol R 0 0 **75 0**
From Cambridge C.
2003–04 Southend U 14 0
2004–05 Southend U 40 0
2005–06 Southend U 44 2
2006–07 Southend U 2 0
2006–07 *Brentford* 3 0 **3 0**
2006–07 *Rotherham U* 6 0 **6 0**
2007–08 Southend U 6 0 **106 2**

STOCKPORT CO (77)

ADAMSON, Chris (G) 33 0
H: 6 2 W: 13 07 b.Ashington 4-11-78
Source: Trainee.
1997–98 WBA 3 0
1998–99 WBA 0 0
1998–99 *Mansfield T* 2 0 **2 0**
1999–2000 WBA 9 0
1999–2000 *Halifax T* 7 0 **7 0**
2000–01 WBA 0 0
2001–02 WBA 0 0 **12 0**
2001–02 *Plymouth Arg* 1 0 **1 0**
From St Patrick's At
2004–05 Sheffield W 2 0
2005–06 Sheffield W 5 0
2006–07 Sheffield W 4 0 **11 0**
2007–08 Stockport Co 0 0

BLIZZARD, Dominic (M) 71 3
H: 6 2 W: 12 04 b.High Wycombe 2-9-83
Source: Scholar.
2001–02 Watford 0 0
2002–03 Watford 0 0
2003–04 Watford 2 1
2004–05 Watford 17 1
2005–06 Watford 10 0
2006–07 Watford 0 0 **29 2**
2006–07 *Stockport Co* 7 0
2006–07 *Milton Keynes D* 8 0 **8 0**
2007–08 Stockport Co 27 1 **34 1**

BOWLER, Michael (M) 13 0
H: 5 11 W: 12 00 b.Glossop 8-9-87
Source: Scholar.
2006–07 Stockport Co 8 0
2007–08 Stockport Co 5 0 **13 0**

COWARD, Chris (F) 0 0
H: 6 1 W: 11 07 b.Manchester 23-7-89
Source: Scholar.
2005–06 Stockport Co 0 0
2006–07 Stockport Co 0 0
2007–08 Stockport Co 0 0

DICKER, Gary (M) 98 5
H: 6 0 W: 12 00 b.Dublin 31-7-86
Honours: Eire Under-21.
2004 UCD 9 1
2005 UCD 31 2
2006 UCD 28 2 **68 5**
2006–07 Birmingham C 0 0
2007–08 Stockport Co 30 0 **30 0**

DICKINSON, Liam (F) 94 33
H: 6 4 W: 11 07 b.Salford 4-10-85
Source: Woodley Sports.
2005–06 Stockport Co 21 7
2006–07 Stockport Co 33 7
2007–08 Stockport Co 40 19 **94 33**

ELLIS, Dan (M) 5 0
H: 5 10 W: 12 07 b.Stockport 18-11-88
Source: Scholar.
2005–06 Stockport Co 3 0
2006–07 Stockport Co 2 0
2007–08 Stockport Co 0 0 **5 0**

FLOWERS, Craig (D) 0 0
H: 6 0 W: 12 00 b.Manchester 23-9-88
Source: Scholar.
2007–08 Stockport Co 0 0

GRIFFIN, Adam (D) 162 9
H: 5 7 W: 10 04 b.Salford 26-8-84
Source: Scholar.
2001–02 Oldham Ath 1 0
2002–03 Oldham Ath 0 0
2003–04 Oldham Ath 26 1
2004–05 Oldham Ath 35 2
2005–06 Oldham Ath 0 0 **62 3**
2005–06 *Oxford U* 9 0 **9 0**
2005–06 *Stockport Co* 21 2
2006–07 Stockport Co 42 3
2007–08 Stockport Co 28 1 **91 6**

HAVERN, Gianluca (F) 1 1
H: 6 1 W: 13 00 b.Manchester 24-9-88
Source: Scholar.
2006–07 Stockport Co 0 0
2007–08 Stockport Co 1 1 **1 1**

McNEIL, Matthew (F) 64 8
H: 6 5 W: 14 03 b.Macclesfield 14-7-76
Source: Burnley, Curzon Ashton, Altrincham, Woodley Sp, Stalybridge C, Woking, Runcorn, Hyde U.
2005–06 Macclesfield T 12 1
2006–07 Macclesfield T 35 5 **47 6**
2007–08 Stockport Co 17 2 **17 2**

McNULTY, Jim (D) 45 1
H: 6 1 W: 12 00 b.Liverpool 13-2-85
Source: Scholar. *Honours:* Scotland Youth.
2003–04 Wrexham 0 0
2004–05 Wrexham 0 0
2005–06 Wrexham 0 0
2006–07 Macclesfield T 15 0
2007–08 Macclesfield T 19 1 **34 1**
2007–08 Stockport Co 11 0 **11 0**

McSWEENEY, Leon (F) 11 1
H: 5 10 W: 10 11 b.Cork 19-2-83
Source: Cork C.
2001–02 Leicester C 0 0
2002–03 Leicester C 0 0
2003–04 Leicester C 0 0
2004–05 Leicester C 0 0
2005–06 Leicester C 0 0
2006–07 Leicester C 0 0
2007–08 Stockport Co 11 1 **11 1**

MORGAN-SMITH, Amari (F) 1 0
H: 6 0 W: 13 06 b.Wolverhampton 3-4-89
2007–08 Stockport Co 1 0 **1 0**

OWEN, Gareth (D) 126 1
H: 6 1 W: 11 07 b.Cheadle 21-9-82
Source: Scholar. *Honours:* Wales Youth.
2001–02 Stoke C 0 0
2002–03 Stoke C 0 0
2003–04 Stoke C 3 0
2003–04 *Oldham Ath* 15 1
2004–05 Stoke C 2 0 **5 0**
2004–05 *Torquay U* 5 0 **5 0**
2004–05 *Oldham Ath* 9 0
2005–06 Oldham Ath 17 0
2006–07 Oldham Ath 0 0 **41 1**
2006–07 *Stockport Co* 39 0
2007–08 Stockport Co 36 0 **75 0**

PILKINGTON, Anthony (M) 53 11
H: 5 11 W: 12 00 b.Manchester 3-11-87
Source: Atherton CW.
2006–07 Stockport Co 24 5
2007–08 Stockport Co 29 6 **53 11**

POOLE, David (M) 82 8
H: 5 8 W: 12 00 b.Manchester 25-11-84
Source: Trainee.
2002–03 Manchester U 0 0
2003–04 Manchester U 0 0
2004–05 Manchester U 0 0
2005–06 Yeovil T 25 2
2006–07 Yeovil T 4 0 **29 2**
2006–07 Stockport Co 31 4
2007–08 Stockport Co 22 2 **53 6**

PROUDLOCK, Adam (F) 203 39
H: 6 0 W: 13 07 b.Wellington 9-5-81
Source: Trainee.
1999–2000 Wolverhampton W 0 0
2000–01 *Clyde* 4 4 **4 4**
2000–01 Wolverhampton W 35 8
2001–02 Wolverhampton W 19 3
2001–02 *Nottingham F* 3 0 **3 0**
2002–03 Wolverhampton W 17 2
2002–03 *Tranmere R* 5 0 **5 0**
2002–03 *Sheffield W* 5 2
2003–04 Wolverhampton W 0 0 **71 13**
2003–04 Sheffield W 30 3
2004–05 Sheffield W 14 6
2005–06 Sheffield W 6 0 **55 11**
2005–06 Ipswich T 9 0
2006–07 Ipswich T 0 0 **9 0**
2006–07 Stockport Co 23 3
2007–08 Stockport Co 33 8 **56 11**

RAYNES, Michael (D) 80 1
H: 6 4 W: 12 00 b.Wythenshawe 15-10-87
Source: Scholar.
2004–05 Stockport Co 19 0
2005–06 Stockport Co 25 1
2006–07 Stockport Co 9 0
2007–08 Stockport Co 27 0 **80 1**

ROSE, Michael (D) 112 7
H: 5 11 W: 12 04 b.Salford 28-7-82
Source: Trainee.
1999–2000 Manchester U 0 0
2000–01 Manchester U 0 0
2001–02 Manchester U 0 0
From Hereford U
2004–05 Yeovil T 40 1
2005–06 Yeovil T 1 0 **41 1**
2005–06 *Cheltenham T* 3 0 **3 0**
2005–06 *Scunthorpe U* 15 0 **15 0**
2006–07 Stockport Co 25 3
2007–08 Stockport Co 28 3 **53 6**

ROWE, Tommy (M) 28 6
H: 5 11 W: 12 11 b.Manchester 1-5-89
Source: Scholar.
2006–07 Stockport Co 4 0
2007–08 Stockport Co 24 6 **28 6**

SMITH, James (D) 34 0
H: 5 10 W: 11 08 b.Liverpool 17-10-85
2004–05 Liverpool 0 0
2005–06 Liverpool 0 0
2006–07 Liverpool 0 0
2006–07 *Ross Co* 8 0 **8 0**
2007–08 Stockport Co 26 0 **26 0**

TANSEY, Greg (M) 16 0
H: 6 1 W: 12 03 b.Huyton 21-11-88
Source: Scholar.
2006–07 Stockport Co 3 0
2007–08 Stockport Co 13 0 **16 0**

TAYLOR, Jason (M) 96 5
H: 6 1 W: 11 03 b.Ashton-under-Lyne 28-1-87
Source: Scholar.
2005–06 Oldham Ath 0 0
2005–06 *Stockport Co* 9 0
2006–07 Stockport Co 45 1
2007–08 Stockport Co 42 4 **96 5**

TUNNICLIFFE, James (D) 11 0
H: 6 4 W: 12 03 b.Denton 17-1-89
Source: Scholar.
2005–06 Stockport Co 1 0
2006–07 Stockport Co 5 0
2007–08 Stockport Co 5 0 **11 0**

TURNBULL, Paul (F) **20 0**
H: 6 0 W: 12 07 b.Handforth 23-1-89
Source: Scholar.
2004–05 Stockport Co 1 0
2005–06 Stockport Co 0 0
2006–07 Stockport Co 0 0
2007–08 Stockport Co 19 0 **20 0**

VINCENT, James (M) **1 0**
H: 5 11 W: 11 00 b.Glssop 27-9-89
Source: Scholar.
2007–08 Stockport Co 1 0 **1 0**

WILLIAMS, Ashley (D) **165 3**
H: 6 0 W: 11 02 b.Wolverhampton 23-8-84
Source: Hednesford T. *Honours:* Wales 3 full caps.
2003–04 Stockport Co 10 0
2004–05 Stockport Co 44 1
2005–06 Stockport Co 36 1
2006–07 Stockport Co 46 1
2007–08 Stockport Co 26 0 **162 3**
2007–08 *Swansea C* 3 0 **3 0**

STOKE C (78)

BANGOURA, Sammy (F) **162 70**
H: 6 0 W: 12 02 b.Guinea 3-4-82
Source: Kindia, AS Kaloum. *Honours:* Guinea 11 full caps, 3 goals.
2000–01 Lokeren 30 13
2001–02 Lokeren 25 12
2002–03 Lokeren 29 16 **84 41**
2003–04 Standard Liege 20 5
2004–05 Standard Liege 30 15 **50 20**
2005–06 Stoke C 24 9
2006–07 Stoke C 4 0
2007–08 Stoke C 0 0 **28 9**
To Boavista August 2007

BROOMES, Marlon (D) **188 4**
H: 6 0 W: 12 12 b.Birmingham 28-11-77
Source: Trainee. *Honours:* England Schools, Youth, Under-21.
1994–95 Blackburn R 0 0
1995–96 Blackburn R 0 0
1996–97 Blackburn R 0 0
1996–97 *Swindon T* 12 1 **12 1**
1997–98 Blackburn R 4 0
1998–99 Blackburn R 13 0
1999–2000 Blackburn R 13 1
2000–01 Blackburn R 1 0
2000–01 *QPR* 5 0 **5 0**
2001–02 Blackburn R 0 0 **31 1**
2001–02 *Grimsby T* 15 0 **15 0**
2001–02 Sheffield W 19 0 **19 0**
2002–03 Preston NE 28 0
2003–04 Preston NE 30 0
2004–05 Preston NE 11 0 **69 0**
2005–06 Stoke C 37 2
2006–07 Stoke C 0 0
2007–08 Stoke C 0 0 **37 2**

BUXTON, Lewis (D) **130 1**
H: 6 1 W: 13 11 b.Newport (IW) 10-12-83
Source: School.
2000–01 Portsmouth 0 0
2001–02 Portsmouth 29 0
2002–03 Portsmouth 1 0
2002–03 *Exeter C* 4 0 **4 0**
2002–03 *Bournemouth* 17 0
2003–04 Portsmouth 0 0
2003–04 *Bournemouth* 26 0 **43 0**
2004–05 Portsmouth 0 0 **30 0**
2004–05 Stoke C 16 0
2005–06 Stoke C 32 1
2006–07 Stoke C 1 0
2007–08 Stoke C 4 0 **53 1**

CORT, Leon (D) **305 36**
H: 6 3 W: 13 01 b.Bermondsey 11-9-79
Source: Dulwich H.
1997–98 Millwall 0 0
1998–99 Millwall 0 0
1999–2000 Millwall 0 0
2000–01 Millwall 0 0
2001–02 Southend U 45 4
2002–03 Southend U 46 6
2003–04 Southend U 46 1 **137 11**
2004–05 Hull C 44 6
2005–06 Hull C 42 4 **86 10**
2006–07 Crystal Palace 37 7
2007–08 Crystal Palace 12 0 **49 7**
2007–08 Stoke C 33 8 **33 8**

CRESSWELL, Richard (F) **407 93**
H: 6 0 W: 11 08 b.Bridlington 20-9-77
Source: Trainee. *Honours:* England Under-21.
1995–96 York C 16 1
1996–97 York C 17 0
1996–97 *Mansfield T* 5 1 **5 1**
1997–98 York C 26 4
1998–99 York C 36 16 **95 21**
1998–99 Sheffield W 7 1
1999–2000 Sheffield W 20 1
2000–01 Sheffield W 4 0 **31 2**
2000–01 Leicester C 8 0 **8 0**
2000–01 *Preston NE* 11 2
2001–02 Preston NE 40 13
2002–03 Preston NE 42 16
2003–04 Preston NE 45 2
2004–05 Preston NE 46 16
2005–06 Preston NE 3 0 **187 49**
2005–06 Leeds U 16 5
2006–07 Leeds U 22 4 **38 9**
2007–08 Stoke C 43 11 **43 11**

DE LAET, Ritchie (D) **0 0**
H: 6 1 W: 12 02 b.Belgium 28-11-88
Source: Antwerp.
2007–08 Stoke C 0 0

DELAP, Rory (M) **358 26**
H: 6 3 W: 13 00 b.Sutton Coldfield 6-7-76
Source: Trainee. *Honours:* Eire Under-21, B, 11 full caps.
1992–93 Carlisle U 1 0
1993–94 Carlisle U 1 0
1994–95 Carlisle U 3 0
1995–96 Carlisle U 19 3
1996–97 Carlisle U 32 4
1997–98 Carlisle U 9 0 **65 7**
1997–98 Derby Co 13 0
1998–99 Derby Co 23 0
1999–2000 Derby Co 34 8
2000–01 Derby Co 33 3 **103 11**
2001–02 Southampton 28 2
2002–03 Southampton 24 0
2003–04 Southampton 27 1
2004–05 Southampton 37 2
2005–06 Southampton 16 0 **132 5**
2005–06 Sunderland 6 1
2006–07 Sunderland 6 0 **12 1**
2006–07 Stoke C 2 0
2007–08 Stoke C 44 2 **46 2**

DIAO, Salif (M) **165 1**
H: 6 1 W: 12 08 b.Kedougou 10-2-77
Honours: Senegal 39 full caps, 4 goals.
1996–97 Epinal 2 0 **2 0**
1996–97 Monaco 0 0
1997–98 Monaco 12 0
1998–99 Monaco 14 0
1999–2000 Monaco 1 0 **27 0**
2000–01 Sedan 26 0
2001–02 Sedan 22 0 **48 0**
2002–03 Liverpool 26 1
2003–04 Liverpool 3 0
2004–05 Liverpool 8 0
2004–05 *Birmingham C* 2 0 **2 0**
2005–06 Liverpool 0 0
2005–06 *Portsmouth* 11 0 **11 0**
2006–07 Liverpool 0 0 **37 1**
2006–07 Stoke C 27 0
2007–08 Stoke C 11 0 **38 0**

DICKINSON, Carl (D) **53 0**
H: 6 1 W: 12 04 b.Swadlincote 31-3-87
Source: Scholar.
2004–05 Stoke C 1 0
2005–06 Stoke C 5 0
2006–07 Stoke C 13 0
2006–07 *Blackpool* 7 0 **7 0**
2007–08 Stoke C 27 0 **46 0**

FULLER, Ricardo (F) **230 72**
H: 6 3 W: 12 10 b.Kingston, Jamaica 31-10-79
Source: Tivoli Gardens. *Honours:* Jamaica 33 full caps, 4 goals.
2000–01 Crystal Palace 8 0 **8 0**
2001–02 Hearts 27 8 **27 8**
From Tivoli Gardens.
2002–03 Preston NE 18 9
2003–04 Preston NE 38 17
2004–05 Preston NE 2 1 **58 27**
2004–05 Portsmouth 31 1 **31 1**
2005–06 Southampton 30 9
2005–06 *Ipswich T* 3 2 **3 2**
2006–07 Southampton 1 0 **31 9**
2006–07 Stoke C 30 10
2007–08 Stoke C 42 15 **72 25**

GARRETT, Robert (M) **24 0**
H: 5 7 W: 11 05 b.Belfast 5-5-88
Source: Scholar. *Honours:* Northern Ireland Youth, Under-21.
2005–06 Stoke C 2 0
2006–07 Stoke C 0 0
2006–07 *Wrexham* 10 0
2007–08 Stoke C 0 0 **2 0**
2007–08 *Wrexham* 12 0 **22 0**

GRIFFIN, Andy (D) **240 6**
H: 5 9 W: 10 10 b.Billinge 7-3-79
Source: Trainee. *Honours:* England Youth, Under-21.
1996–97 Stoke C 34 1
1997–98 Stoke C 23 1
1997–98 Newcastle U 4 0
1998–99 Newcastle U 14 0
1999–2000 Newcastle U 3 1
2000–01 Newcastle U 19 0
2001–02 Newcastle U 4 0
2002–03 Newcastle U 27 1
2003–04 Newcastle U 5 0 **76 2**
2004–05 Portsmouth 22 0
2005–06 Portsmouth 22 0
2006–07 Portsmouth 0 0 **44 0**
2006–07 *Stoke C* 33 2
2007–08 Derby Co 15 0 **15 0**
2007–08 Stoke C 15 0 **105 4**

HAZLEY, Matthew (M) **1 0**
H: 5 10 W: 12 03 b.Banbridge 30-12-87
Source: Scholar. *Honours:* Northern Ireland Youth, Under-21.
2005–06 Stoke C 1 0
2006–07 Stoke C 0 0
2007–08 Stoke C 0 0 **1 0**

HOULT, Russell (G) **407 0**
H: 6 3 W: 14 09 b.Ashby 22-11-72
Source: Trainee.
1990–91 Leicester C 0 0
1991–92 Leicester C 0 0
1991–92 *Lincoln C* 2 0
1991–92 *Blackpool* 0 0
1992–93 Leicester C 10 0
1993–94 Leicester C 0 0
1993–94 *Bolton W* 4 0 **4 0**
1994–95 Leicester C 0 0 **10 0**
1994–95 *Lincoln C* 15 0 **17 0**
1994–95 *Derby Co* 15 0
1995–96 Derby Co 41 0
1996–97 Derby Co 32 0
1997–98 Derby Co 2 0
1998–99 Derby Co 23 0
1999–2000 Derby Co 10 0 **123 0**
1999–2000 Portsmouth 18 0
2000–01 Portsmouth 22 0 **40 0**
2000–01 WBA 13 0
2001–02 WBA 45 0
2002–03 WBA 37 0
2003–04 WBA 44 0
2004–05 WBA 36 0
2005–06 WBA 1 0
2005–06 *Nottingham F* 8 0 **8 0**
2006–07 WBA 14 0 **190 0**
2006–07 Stoke C 0 0
2007–08 Stoke C 1 0 **1 0**
2007–08 *Notts Co* 14 0 **14 0**

LAWRENCE, Liam (M) **277 63**
H: 5 11 W: 12 06 b.Retford 14-12-81
Source: Trainee.
1999–2000 Mansfield T 2 0
2000–01 Mansfield T 18 4
2001–02 Mansfield T 32 2
2002–03 Mansfield T 43 10
2003–04 Mansfield T 41 18 **136 34**
2004–05 Sunderland 32 7
2005–06 Sunderland 29 3
2006–07 Sunderland 12 0 **73 10**
2006–07 Stoke C 27 5
2007–08 Stoke C 41 14 **68 19**

MATTEO, Dominic (D) **300** **4**
H: 6 1 W: 13 08 b.Dumfries 28-4-74
Source: Trainee. *Honours:* England Youth, Under-21, B, Scotland 6 full caps.

1992–93	Liverpool	0	0		
1993–94	Liverpool	11	0		
1994–95	Liverpool	7	0		
1994–95	*Sunderland*	1	0	**1**	**0**
1995–96	Liverpool	5	0		
1996–97	Liverpool	26	0		
1997–98	Liverpool	26	0		
1998–99	Liverpool	20	1		
1999–2000	Liverpool	32	0		
2000–01	Liverpool	0	0	**127**	**1**
2000–01	Leeds U	30	0		
2001–02	Leeds U	32	0		
2002–03	Leeds U	20	0		
2003–04	Leeds U	33	2	**115**	**2**
2004–05	Blackburn R	28	0		
2005–06	Blackburn R	6	0		
2006–07	Blackburn R	0	0	**34**	**0**
2006–07	Stoke C	9	1		
2007–08	Stoke C	14	0	**23**	**1**

PARKIN, Jon (F) **232** **60**
H: 6 4 W: 13 07 b.Barnsley 30-12-81
Source: Scholarship.

1998–99	Barnsley	2	0		
1999–2000	Barnsley	0	0		
2000–01	Barnsley	4	0		
2001–02	Barnsley	4	0	**10**	**0**
2001–02	*Hartlepool U*	1	0	**1**	**0**
2001–02	York C	18	2		
2002–03	York C	41	10		
2003–04	York C	15	2	**74**	**14**
2003–04	Macclesfield T	12	1		
2004–05	Macclesfield T	42	22		
2005–06	Macclesfield T	11	7	**65**	**30**
2005–06	Hull C	18	5		
2006–07	Hull C	29	6	**47**	**11**
2006–07	*Stoke C*	6	3		
2007–08	Stoke C	29	2	**35**	**5**

PERICARD, Vincent de Paul (F) **109** **17**
H: 6 1 W: 13 08 b.Efok 3-10-82
Source: Juventus.

2002–03	Portsmouth	32	9		
2003–04	Portsmouth	6	0		
2004–05	Portsmouth	0	0		
2005–06	Portsmouth	6	0	**44**	**9**
2005–06	*Sheffield U*	11	2	**11**	**2**
2005–06	*Plymouth Arg*	15	4	**15**	**4**
2006–07	Stoke C	29	2		
2007–08	Stoke C	5	0	**34**	**2**
2007–08	*Southampton*	5	0	**5**	**0**

PHILLIPS, Demar (M) **2** **0**
H: 5 6 W: 9 04 b.Kingston 23-9-83
Source: Waterhouse. *Honours:* Jamaica 27 full caps

2007–08	Stoke C	2	0	**2**	**0**

PUGH, Danny (M) **133** **9**
H: 6 0 W: 12 10 b.Manchester 19-10-82
Source: Scholar.

2000–01	Manchester U	0	0		
2001–02	Manchester U	0	0		
2002–03	Manchester U	1	0		
2003–04	Manchester U	0	0	**1**	**0**
2004–05	Leeds U	38	5		
2005–06	Leeds U	12	0	**50**	**5**
2006–07	Preston NE	45	4		
2007–08	Preston NE	7	0	**52**	**4**
2007–08	Stoke C	30	0	**30**	**0**

PULIS, Anthony (M) **20** **0**
H: 5 10 W: 10 10 b.Bristol 21-7-84
Source: Scholar. *Honours:* Wales Under-21.

2002–03	Portsmouth	0	0		
2003–04	Portsmouth	0	0		
2004–05	Portsmouth	0	0		
2004–05	Stoke C	0	0		
2004–05	*Torquay U*	3	0	**3**	**0**
2005–06	Stoke C	0	0		
2005–06	*Plymouth Arg*	5	0	**5**	**0**
2006–07	Stoke C	1	0		
2006–07	*Grimsby T*	9	0	**9**	**0**
2007–08	Stoke C	1	0	**2**	**0**
2007–08	*Bristol R*	1	0	**1**	**0**

ROONEY, Adam (F) **56** **14**
H: 5 10 W: 12 03 b.Dublin 21-4-87
Source: Scholar. *Honours:* Eire Youth, Under-21.

2005–06	Stoke C	5	4		
2006–07	Stoke C	10	0		
2006–07	*Yeovil T*	3	0	**3**	**0**
2007–08	Stoke C	0	0	**15**	**4**
2007–08	*Chesterfield*	22	7	**22**	**7**
2007–08	*Bury*	16	3	**16**	**3**

SHAWCROSS, Ryan (D) **41** **7**
H: 6 3 W: 13 13 b.Buckley 4-10-87
Source: Scholar. *Honours:* England Under-21.

2006–07	Manchester U	0	0		
2007–08	Manchester U	0	0		
2007–08	Stoke C	41	7	**41**	**7**

SHOTTON, Ryan (D) **0** **0**
H: 6 3 W: 13 05 b.Stoke 30-9-88
Source: Scholar.

2006–07	Stoke C	0	0
2007–08	Stoke C	0	0

SIDIBE, Mamady (F) **257** **36**
H: 6 4 W: 12 02 b.Bamako 18-12-79
Source: CA Paris. *Honours:* Mali 8 full caps, 3 goals.

2001–02	Swansea C	31	7	**31**	**7**
2002–03	Gillingham	30	3		
2003–04	Gillingham	41	5		
2004–05	Gillingham	35	2	**106**	**10**
2005–06	Stoke C	42	6		
2006–07	Stoke C	43	9		
2007–08	Stoke C	35	4	**120**	**19**

SIMONSEN, Steve (G) **223** **0**
H: 6 2 W: 12 08 b.South Shields 3-4-79
Source: Trainee. *Honours:* England Youth, Under-21.

1996–97	Tranmere R	0	0		
1997–98	Tranmere R	30	0		
1998–99	Tranmere R	5	0	**35**	**0**
1998–99	Everton	0	0		
1999–2000	Everton	1	0		
2000–01	Everton	1	0		
2001–02	Everton	25	0		
2002–03	Everton	2	0		
2003–04	Everton	1	0	**30**	**0**
2004–05	Stoke C	31	0		
2005–06	Stoke C	45	0		
2006–07	Stoke C	46	0		
2007–08	Stoke C	36	0	**158**	**0**

VASS, Adam (M) **0** **0**
H: 5 11 W: 11 00 b.Hungary 9-9-88
Source: Scholar. *Honours:* Hungary 2 full caps.

2006–07	Stoke C	0	0
2007–08	Stoke C	0	0

WHELAN, Glenn (M) **169** **13**
H: 5 11 W: 12 07 b.Dublin 13-1-84
Source: Scholar. *Honours:* Eire Youth, Under-21, B, 2 full caps.

2000–01	Manchester C	0	0		
2001–02	Manchester C	0	0		
2002–03	Manchester C	0	0		
2003–04	Manchester C	0	0		
2003–04	*Bury*	13	0	**13**	**0**
2004–05	Sheffield W	36	2		
2005–06	Sheffield W	43	1		
2006–07	Sheffield W	38	7		
2007–08	Sheffield W	25	2	**142**	**12**
2007–08	Stoke C	14	1	**14**	**1**

WILKINSON, Andy (D) **53** **0**
H: 5 11 W: 11 00 b.Stone 6-8-84
Source: Scholar.

2001–02	Stoke C	0	0		
2002–03	Stoke C	0	0		
2003–04	Stoke C	3	0		
2004–05	Stoke C	1	0		
2004–05	*Shrewsbury T*	9	0	**9**	**0**
2005–06	Stoke C	6	0		
2006–07	Stoke C	4	0		
2006–07	*Blackpool*	7	0	**7**	**0**
2007–08	Stoke C	23	0	**37**	**0**

SUNDERLAND (79)

ANDERSON, Russell (D) **289** **18**
H: 5 11 W: 10 09 b.Aberdeen 25-10-78
Source: Dyce J. *Honours:* Scotland Under-21, 11 full caps.

1996–97	Aberdeen	14	0		
1997–98	Aberdeen	26	0		
1998–99	Aberdeen	16	0		
1999–2000	Aberdeen	34	1		
2000–01	Aberdeen	0	0		
2001–02	Aberdeen	24	1		
2002–03	Aberdeen	33	2		
2003–04	Aberdeen	25	5		
2004–05	Aberdeen	31	1		
2005–06	Aberdeen	36	6		
2006–07	Aberdeen	35	2	**274**	**18**
2007–08	Sunderland	1	0	**1**	**0**
2007–08	*Plymouth Arg*	14	0	**14**	**0**

ARNAU, Caldentey (M) **22** **1**
H: 5 9 W: 11 07 b.Manacor 1-10-81
Source: Mallorca, Barcelona B.

2006–07	Sunderland	1	0		
2006–07	*Southend U*	2	0	**2**	**0**
2007–08	*Falkirk*	19	1	**19**	**1**
2007–08	Sunderland	0	0	**1**	**0**

BARDSLEY, Phillip (D) **59** **1**
H: 5 11 W: 11 13 b.Salford 28-6-85
Source: Trainee.

2003–04	Manchester U	0	0		
2004–05	Manchester U	0	0		
2005–06	Manchester U	8	0		
2005–06	*Burnley*	6	0	**6**	**0**
2006–07	Manchester U	0	0		
2006–07	*Rangers*	5	1	**5**	**1**
2006–07	*Aston Villa*	13	0	**13**	**0**
2007–08	Manchester U	0	0	**8**	**0**
2007–08	*Sheffield U*	16	0	**16**	**0**
2007–08	Sunderland	11	0	**11**	**0**

CARSON, Trevor (G) **0** **0**
H: 6 0 W: 14 11 b.Downpatrick 5-3-88
Source: Scholar. *Honours:* Northern Ireland Under-21.

2006–07	Sunderland	0	0
2007–08	Sunderland	0	0

CHANDLER, Jamie (M) **0** **0**
H: 5 7 W: 11 02 b.South Shields 24-3-89
Source: Scholar. *Honours:* England Youth.

2007–08	Sunderland	0	0

CHOPRA, Michael (F) **145** **51**
H: 5 9 W: 10 10 b.Newcastle 23-12-83
Source: Scholar. *Honours:* England Youth, Under-20, Under-21.

2000–01	Newcastle U	0	0		
2001–02	Newcastle U	0	0		
2002–03	Newcastle U	1	0		
2002–03	*Watford*	5	5	**5**	**5**
2003–04	Newcastle U	6	0		
2003–04	*Nottingham F*	5	0	**5**	**0**
2004–05	Newcastle U	1	0		
2004–05	*Barnsley*	39	17	**39**	**17**
2005–06	Newcastle U	13	1	**21**	**1**
2006–07	Cardiff C	42	22	**42**	**22**
2007–08	Sunderland	33	6	**33**	**6**

CLARKE, Clive (D) **243** **9**
H: 5 11 W: 12 03 b.Dublin 14-1-80
Source: Trainee. *Honours:* Eire Under-21, 2 full caps.

1996–97	Stoke C	0	0		
1997–98	Stoke C	0	0		
1998–99	Stoke C	2	0		
1999–2000	Stoke C	42	1		
2000–01	Stoke C	21	0		
2001–02	Stoke C	43	1		
2002–03	Stoke C	31	3		
2003–04	Stoke C	42	3		
2004–05	Stoke C	42	1	**223**	**9**
2005–06	West Ham U	2	0	**2**	**0**
2006–07	Sunderland	4	0		
2006–07	*Coventry C*	12	0	**12**	**0**
2007–08	Sunderland	0	0	**4**	**0**
2007–08	*Leicester C*	2	0	**2**	**0**

COLBACK, Jack (M) **0** **0**
H: 5 9 W: 11 05 b.Newcastle 24-10-89
Source: Scholar.

2007–08	Sunderland	0	0

COLE, Andy (F) **499 229**
H: 5 11 W: 12 11 b.Nottingham 15-10-71
Source: Trainee. *Honours:* England Schools, Youth, Under-21, B, 15 full caps, 1 goal. Football League.

1989–90	Arsenal	0	0		
1990–91	Arsenal	1	0		
1991–92	Arsenal	0	0	**1**	**0**
1991–92	*Fulham*	13	3		
1991–92	*Bristol C*	12	8		
1992–93	Bristol C	29	12	**41**	**20**
1992–93	Newcastle U	12	12		
1993–94	Newcastle U	40	34		
1994–95	Newcastle U	18	9	**70**	**55**
1994–95	Manchester U	18	12		
1995–96	Manchester U	34	11		
1996–97	Manchester U	20	6		
1997–98	Manchester U	33	15		
1998–99	Manchester U	32	17		
1999–2000	Manchester U	28	19		
2000–01	Manchester U	19	9		
2001–02	Manchester U	11	4	**195**	**93**
2001–02	Blackburn R	15	9		
2002–03	Blackburn R	34	7		
2003–04	Blackburn R	34	11	**83**	**27**
2004–05	Fulham	31	12	**44**	**15**
2005–06	Manchester C	22	9	**22**	**9**
2006–07	Portsmouth	18	3		
2006–07	*Birmingham C*	5	1	**5**	**1**
2007–08	Portsmouth	0	0	**18**	**3**
2007–08	Sunderland	7	0	**7**	**0**
2007–08	*Burnley*	13	6	**13**	**6**

COLLINS, Danny (D) **123 3**
H: 6 2 W: 11 13 b.Buckley 6-8-80
Source: Buckley T. *Honours:* Wales 7 full caps.

2004–05	Chester C	12	1	**12**	**1**
2004–05	Sunderland	14	0		
2005–06	Sunderland	23	1		
2006–07	Sunderland	38	0		
2007–08	Sunderland	36	1	**111**	**2**

CONNOLLY, David (F) **324 135**
H: 5 9 W: 11 00 b.Willesden 6-6-77
Source: Trainee. *Honours:* Eire Under-21, 41 full caps, 9 goals.

1994–95	Watford	2	0		
1995–96	Watford	11	8		
1996–97	Watford	13	2	**26**	**10**
1997–98	Feyenoord	10	2		
1998–99	Wolverhampton W	32	6	**32**	**6**
1999–2000	Excelsior	32	29	**32**	**29**
2000–01	Feyenoord	15	5	**25**	**7**
2001–02	Wimbledon	35	18		
2002–03	Wimbledon	28	24	**63**	**42**
2003–04	West Ham U	39	10	**39**	**10**
2004–05	Leicester C	44	13		
2005–06	Leicester C	5	4	**49**	**17**
2005–06	Wigan Ath	17	1		
2006–07	Wigan Ath	2	0	**19**	**1**
2006–07	Sunderland	36	13		
2007–08	Sunderland	3	0	**39**	**13**

COOK, Jordan (F) **0 0**
b.Hetton-le-Hole 20-3-90
Source: Scholar.

2007–08	Sunderland	0	0		

DENNEHY, Billy (F) **7 0**
H: 5 8 W: 11 10 b.Tralee 17-2-87
Honours: Eire Under-21.

2004–05	Sunderland	0	0		
2005–06	Sunderland	0	0		
2006–07	Sunderland	0	0		
2007–08	Sunderland	0	0		
2007–08	*Accrington S*	7	0	**7**	**0**

DONOGHUE, Gavin (D) **0 0**
H: 5 11 W: 13 07 b.Dublin 3-3-89
Source: Scholar.

2007–08	Sunderland	0	0		

DOWSON, David (F) **12 3**
H: 5 10 W: 12 00 b.Bishop Auckland 12-9-88
Source: Scholar.

2007–08	Sunderland	0	0		
2007–08	*Chesterfield*	12	3	**12**	**3**

EDWARDS, Carlos (M) **262 36**
H: 5 8 W: 11 02 b.Port of Spain 24-10-78
Source: Defence Force. *Honours:* Trinidad & Tobago 57 full caps, 1 goal.

2000–01	Wrexham	36	4		
2001–02	Wrexham	26	5		
2002–03	Wrexham	44	8		
2003–04	Wrexham	42	5		
2004–05	Wrexham	18	1	**166**	**23**
2005–06	Luton T	42	2		
2006–07	Luton T	26	6	**68**	**8**
2006–07	Sunderland	15	5		
2007–08	Sunderland	13	0	**28**	**5**

ETUHU, Dickson (M) **228 24**
H: 6 2 W: 13 04 b.Kano 8-6-82
Source: Scholar. *Honours:* Nigeria 5 full caps.

1999–2000	Manchester C	0	0		
2000–01	Manchester C	0	0		
2001–02	Manchester C	12	0	**12**	**0**
2001–02	Preston NE	16	3		
2002–03	Preston NE	39	6		
2003–04	Preston NE	31	3		
2004–05	Preston NE	35	3		
2005–06	Preston NE	13	2	**134**	**17**
2005–06	Norwich C	19	0		
2006–07	Norwich C	43	6	**62**	**6**
2007–08	Sunderland	20	1	**20**	**1**

FULOP, Marton (G) **68 0**
H: 6 6 W: 14 07 b.Budapest 3-5-83
Source: MTK, Elore, Bodajk. *Honours:* Hungary Under-21, 15 full caps.

2004–05	Tottenham H	0	0		
2004–05	*Chesterfield*	7	0	**7**	**0**
2005–06	Tottenham H	0	0		
2005–06	*Coventry C*	31	0	**31**	**0**
2006–07	Tottenham H	0	0		
2006–07	Sunderland	5	0		
2007–08	Sunderland	1	0	**6**	**0**
2007–08	*Leicester C*	24	0	**24**	**0**

GORDON, Craig (G) **172 0**
H: 6 4 W: 12 02 b.Edinburgh 31-12-82
Honours: Scotland Under-21, 31 full caps.

2000–01	Hearts	0	0		
2001–02	Hearts	0	0		
2002–03	Hearts	1	0		
2003–04	Hearts	29	0		
2004–05	Hearts	38	0		
2005–06	Hearts	36	0		
2006–07	Hearts	34	0	**138**	**0**
2007–08	Sunderland	34	0	**34**	**0**

HALFORD, Greg (D) **163 20**
H: 6 4 W: 12 10 b.Chelmsford 8-12-84
Source: Scholar. *Honours:* England Youth, Under-20.

2002–03	Colchester U	1	0		
2003–04	Colchester U	18	4		
2004–05	Colchester U	44	4		
2005–06	Colchester U	45	7		
2006–07	Colchester U	28	3	**136**	**18**
2006–07	Reading	3	0	**3**	**0**
2007–08	Sunderland	8	0	**8**	**0**
2007–08	*Charlton Ath*	16	2	**16**	**2**

HARTE, Ian (D) **251 29**
H: 5 11 W: 12 06 b.Drogheda 31-8-77
Source: Trainee. *Honours:* Eire 63 full caps, 11 goals.

1995–96	Leeds U	4	0		
1996–97	Leeds U	14	2		
1997–98	Leeds U	12	0		
1998–99	Leeds U	35	4		
1999–2000	Leeds U	33	6		
2000–01	Leeds U	29	7		
2001–02	Leeds U	36	5		
2002–03	Leeds U	27	3		
2003–04	Leeds U	23	1	**213**	**28**
2004–05	Levante	24	1		
2005–06	Levante	0	0		
2006–07	Levante	6	0	**30**	**1**
2007–08	Sunderland	8	0	**8**	**0**

HARTLEY, Peter (D) **13 0**
H: 6 0 W: 12 06 b.Hartlepool 3-4-88
Source: Scholar.

2006–07	Sunderland	1	0		
2007–08	Sunderland	0	0	**1**	**0**
2007–08	*Chesterfield*	12	0	**12**	**0**

HIGGINBOTHAM, Danny (D) **250 17**
H: 6 2 W: 13 01 b.Manchester 29-12-78
Source: Trainee.

1997–98	Manchester U	1	0		
1998–99	Manchester U	0	0		
1999–2000	Manchester U	3	0	**4**	**0**
2000–01	Derby Co	26	0		
2001–02	Derby Co	37	1		
2002–03	Derby Co	23	2	**86**	**3**
2002–03	Southampton	9	0		
2003–04	Southampton	27	0		
2004–05	Southampton	21	1		
2005–06	Southampton	37	3	**94**	**4**
2006–07	Stoke C	44	7		
2007–08	Stoke C	1	0	**45**	**7**
2007–08	Sunderland	21	3	**21**	**3**

JONES, Kenwyne (F) **124 36**
H: 6 2 W: 13 06 b.Trinidad & Tobago 5-10-84
Source: W Connection. *Honours:* Trindad & Tobago Youth, Under-23, 35 full caps, 3 goals.

2004–05	Southampton	2	0		
2004–05	*Sheffield W*	7	7	**7**	**7**
2004–05	*Stoke C*	13	3	**13**	**3**
2005–06	Southampton	34	4		
2006–07	Southampton	34	14		
2007–08	Southampton	1	1	**71**	**19**
2007–08	Sunderland	33	7	**33**	**7**

KAVANAGH, Graham (M) **473 69**
H: 5 10 W: 13 03 b.Dublin 2-12-73
Source: Home Farm. *Honours:* Eire Schools, Youth, Under-21, B, 16 full caps, 1 goal.

1991–92	Middlesbrough	0	0		
1992–93	Middlesbrough	10	0		
1993–94	Middlesbrough	11	2		
1993–94	*Darlington*	5	0	**5**	**0**
1994–95	Middlesbrough	7	0		
1995–96	Middlesbrough	7	1		
1996–97	Middlesbrough	0	0	**35**	**3**
1996–97	Stoke C	38	4		
1997–98	Stoke C	44	5		
1998–99	Stoke C	36	11		
1999–2000	Stoke C	45	7		
2000–01	Stoke C	43	8	**206**	**35**
2001–02	Cardiff C	43	13		
2002–03	Cardiff C	44	5		
2003–04	Cardiff C	27	7		
2004–05	Cardiff C	28	3	**142**	**28**
2004–05	Wigan Ath	11	0		
2005–06	Wigan Ath	35	0		
2006–07	Wigan Ath	2	0	**48**	**0**
2006–07	Sunderland	14	1		
2007–08	Sunderland	0	0	**14**	**1**
2007–08	*Sheffield W*	23	2	**23**	**2**

KAY, Michael (D) **0 0**
H: 6 0 W: 11 05 b.Shotley Bridge 12-9-89
Source: Scholar.

2007–08	Sunderland	0	0		

LEADBITTER, Grant (M) **92 10**
H: 5 9 W: 11 06 b.Sunderland 7-1-86
Source: Trainee. *Honours:* FA Schools, England Youth, Under-20, Under-21.

2002–03	Sunderland	0	0		
2003–04	Sunderland	0	0		
2004–05	Sunderland	0	0		
2005–06	Sunderland	12	0		
2005–06	*Rotherham U*	5	1	**5**	**1**
2006–07	Sunderland	44	7		
2007–08	Sunderland	31	2	**87**	**9**

LIDDLE, Michael (D) **0 0**
H: 5 6 W: 11 00 b.London 25-12-89
Source: Scholar.

2007–08	Sunderland	0	0		

M'VOTO, Jean-Yves (D) **0 0**
H: 6 4 W: 14 00 b.Paris 6-9-88
Source: Paris St Germain. *Honours:* France Youth.

2007–08	Sunderland	0	0		

McARDLE, Niall (D) **0 0**
H: 6 1 W: 11 09 b.Dublin 22-3-90
Source: Scholar.

2007–08	Sunderland	0	0		

McSHANE, Paul (D) **95 6**
H: 6 0 W: 11 05 b.Wicklow 6-1-86
Source: Trainee. *Honours:* Eire Youth, Under-21, 11 full caps.

2002–03	Manchester U	0	0		
2003–04	Manchester U	0	0		
2004–05	Manchester U	0	0		
2004–05	*Walsall*	4	1	**4**	**1**
2005–06	Manchester U	0	0		
2005–06	*Brighton & HA*	38	3	**38**	**3**
2006–07	WBA	32	2	**32**	**2**
2007–08	Sunderland	21	0	**21**	**0**

MILLER, Liam (M) **135 12**
H: 5 7 W: 10 05 b.Cork 13-2-81
Honours: Eire Under-21, 18 full caps, 1 goal.

1999–2000	Celtic	1	0		
2000–01	Celtic	0	0		
2001–02	Celtic	0	0		
2001–02	Aarhus	18	6	**18**	**6**
2002–03	Celtic	0	0		
2003–04	Celtic	25	2	**26**	**2**
2004–05	Manchester U	8	0		
2005–06	Manchester U	1	0	**9**	**0**
2005–06	*Leeds U*	28	1	**28**	**1**
2006–07	Sunderland	30	2		
2007–08	Sunderland	24	1	**54**	**3**

MURPHY, Daryl (F) **88 14**
H: 6 2 W: 13 12 b.Waterford 15-3-83
Honours: Eire Youth, Under-21, 8 full caps.

2000–01	Luton T	0	0		
2001–02	Luton T	0	0		
2005–06	Sunderland	18	1		
2005–06	*Sheffield W*	4	0	**4**	**0**
2006–07	Sunderland	38	10		
2007–08	Sunderland	28	3	**84**	**14**

NOSWORTHY, Nyron (D) **262 5**
H: 6 0 W: 12 08 b.Brixton 11-10-80
Source: Trainee. *Honours:* Jamaica 2 full caps.

1998–99	Gillingham	3	0		
1999–2000	Gillingham	29	1		
2000–01	Gillingham	10	0		
2001–02	Gillingham	29	0		
2002–03	Gillingham	39	2		
2003–04	Gillingham	27	2		
2004–05	Gillingham	37	0	**174**	**5**
2005–06	Sunderland	30	0		
2006–07	Sunderland	29	0		
2007–08	Sunderland	29	0	**88**	**0**

O'DONOVAN, Roy (F) **91 31**
H: 5 10 W: 11 07 b.Cork 10-8-85
Source: Scholar. *Honours:* Eire Under-21, B.

2002–03	Coventry C	0	0		
2003–04	Coventry C	0	0		
2004–05	Coventry C	0	0		
2005	Cork C	26	6		
2006	Cork C	29	11		
2007	Cork C	19	14	**74**	**31**
2007–08	Sunderland	17	0	**17**	**0**

PELTER, Jack (D) **0 0**
H: 6 01 W: 12 08 b.Barrow 30-7-80
Source: Canterbury U.

2007–08	Sunderland	0	0		

PRICA, Rade (F) **276 91**
H: 6 1 W: 12 08 b.Ljungby 30-6-80
Honours: Sweden Under-21, 14 full caps, 2 goals.

1995	Ljungby	6	1		
1996	Ljungby	20	6		
1997	Ljungby	11	8	**37**	**15**
1997	Helsingborg	0	0		
1998	Helsingborg	1	0		
1999	Helsingborg	17	6		
2000	Helsingborg	24	11		
2001	Helsingborg	25	7		
2002	Helsingborg	6	3	**73**	**27**
2002–03	Hansa Rostock	27	7		
2003–04	Hansa Rostock	27	3		
2004–05	Hansa Rostock	29	6		
2005–06	Hansa Rostock	29	4	**112**	**20**
2006–07	Aalborg	32	19		
2007–08	Aalborg	16	9	**48**	**28**
2007–08	Sunderland	6	1	**6**	**1**

REID, Andy (M) **221 30**
H: 5 9 W: 12 08 b.Dublin 29-7-82
Source: Trainee. *Honours:* Eire Youth, Under-21, 27 full caps, 4 goals.

1999–2000	Nottingham F	0	0		
2000–01	Nottingham F	14	2		
2001–02	Nottingham F	29	0		
2002–03	Nottingham F	30	1		
2003–04	Nottingham F	46	13		
2004–05	Nottingham F	25	5	**144**	**21**
2004–05	Tottenham H	13	1		
2005–06	Tottenham H	13	0	**26**	**1**
2006–07	Charlton Ath	16	2		
2007–08	Charlton Ath	22	5	**38**	**7**
2007–08	Sunderland	13	1	**13**	**1**

RICHARDSON, Jake (M) **0 0**
H: 5 8 W: 10 00 b.Watford 22-10-88

2006–07	Sunderland	0	0		
2007–08	Sunderland	0	0		

RICHARDSON, Kieran (M) **70 8**
H: 5 9 W: 11 13 b.Greenwich 21-10-84
Source: Scholar. *Honours:* England Under-21, 8 full caps, 2 goals.

2002–03	Manchester U	2	0		
2003–04	Manchester U	0	0		
2004–05	Manchester U	2	0		
2004–05	*WBA*	12	3	**12**	**3**
2005–06	Manchester U	22	1		
2006–07	Manchester U	15	1	**41**	**2**
2007–08	Sunderland	17	3	**17**	**3**

STAPLES, Daniel (G) **0 0**
Source: Scholar.

2007–08	Sunderland	0	0		

STOKES, Anthony (F) **50 17**
H: 5 11 W: 11 06 b.Dublin 25-7-88
Source: Scholar. *Honours:* Eire Youth, B, Under-21, 3 full caps.

2005–06	Arsenal	0	0		
2006–07	Arsenal	0	0		
2006–07	*Falkirk*	16	14	**16**	**14**
2006–07	Sunderland	14	2		
2007–08	Sunderland	20	1	**34**	**3**

VAN DER GOUW, Raimond (G) **493 1**
H: 6 3 W: 13 09 b.Oldenzaal 24-3-63

1985–86	Go Ahead	28	0		
1986–87	Go Ahead	34	0		
1987–88	Go Ahead	35	0	**97**	**0**
1988–89	Vitesse	36	0		
1989–90	Vitesse	34	0		
1990–91	Vitesse	31	0		
1991–92	Vitesse	34	0		
1992–93	Vitesse	34	0		
1993–94	Vitesse	34	0		
1994–95	Vitesse	34	0		
1995–96	Vitesse	21	0	**258**	**0**
1996–97	Manchester U	2	0		
1997–98	Manchester U	5	0		
1998–99	Manchester U	5	0		
1999–2000	Manchester U	14	0		
2000–01	Manchester U	10	0		
2001–02	Manchester U	1	0	**37**	**0**
2002–03	West Ham U	0	0		
2003–04	RKC Waalwijk	1	0	**1**	**0**
2004–05	Apeldoorn	29	0		
2005–06	Apeldoorn	33	0		
2006–07	Apeldoorn	38	1	**100**	**1**
2007–08	Sunderland	0	0		

VARGA, Stanislav (D) **297 34**
H: 6 5 W: 14 09 b.Lipany 8-10-72
Honours: Slovakia 54 full caps, 1 goal.

1993–94	Tatran Presov	12	2		
1994–95	Tatran Presov	25	2		
1995–96	Tatran Presov	21	2		
1996–97	Tatran Presov	22	3		
1997–98	Tatran Presov	26	1	**106**	**10**
1998–99	Slovan Bratislava	28	3		
1999–2000	Slovan Bratislava	28	9	**56**	**12**
2000–01	Sunderland	12	1		
2001–02	Sunderland	9	0		
2001–02	*WBA*	4	0	**4**	**0**
2002–03	Celtic	1	0		
2003–04	Celtic	35	6		
2004–05	Celtic	34	3		
2005–06	Celtic	10	1	**80**	**10**
2006–07	Sunderland	20	1		
2007–08	Sunderland	0	0	**41**	**2**
2007–08	*Burnley*	10	0	**10**	**0**

WAGHORN, Martyn (F) **3 0**
H: 5 9 W: 13 01 b.South Shields 23-1-90
Source: Scholar.

2007–08	Sunderland	3	0	**3**	**0**

WALLACE, Ross (M) **90 9**
H: 5 6 W: 9 12 b.Dundee 23-5-85
Source: Celtic S Form. *Honours:* Scotland Youth, Under-21, B.

2001–02	Celtic	0	0		
2002–03	Celtic	0	0		
2003–04	Celtic	8	1		
2004–05	Celtic	16	0		
2005–06	Celtic	11	0		
2006–07	Celtic	2	0	**37**	**1**
2006–07	Sunderland	32	6		
2007–08	Sunderland	21	2	**53**	**8**

WARD, Darren (G) **489 0**
H: 6 0 W: 13 09 b.Worksop 11-5-74
Source: Trainee. *Honours:* Wales Under-21, B, 5 full caps.

1992–93	Mansfield T	13	0		
1993–94	Mansfield T	33	0		
1994–95	Mansfield T	35	0	**81**	**0**
1995–96	Notts Co	46	0		
1996–97	Notts Co	38	0		
1997–98	Notts Co	44	0		
1998–99	Notts Co	43	0		
1999–2000	Notts Co	45	0		
2000–01	Notts Co	35	0	**251**	**0**
2000–01	Nottingham F	0	0		
2001–02	Nottingham F	46	0		
2002–03	Nottingham F	45	0		
2003–04	Nottingham F	32	0		
2004–05	Nottingham F	0	0	**123**	**0**
2004–05	Norwich C	1	0		
2005–06	Norwich C	0	0	**1**	**0**
2006–07	Sunderland	30	0		
2007–08	Sunderland	3	0	**33**	**0**

WEIR, Robbie (M) **0 0**
H: 5 9 W: 11 07 b.Belfast 12-12-88
Source: Scholar.

2007–08	Sunderland	0	0		

WHITEHEAD, Dean (M) **273 22**
H: 5 11 W: 12 06 b.Abingdon 12-1-82
Source: Trainee.

1999–2000	Oxford U	0	0		
2000–01	Oxford U	20	0		
2001–02	Oxford U	40	1		
2002–03	Oxford U	18	1		
2003–04	Oxford U	44	7	**122**	**9**
2004–05	Sunderland	42	5		
2005–06	Sunderland	37	3		
2006–07	Sunderland	45	4		
2007–08	Sunderland	27	1	**151**	**13**

WRIGHT, Stephen (D) **145 2**
H: 6 0 W: 12 06 b.Liverpool 8-2-80
Source: Trainee. *Honours:* England Youth, Under-21.

1997–98	Liverpool	0	0		
1998–99	Liverpool	0	0		
1999–2000	Liverpool	0	0		
1999–2000	*Crewe Alex*	23	0	**23**	**0**
2000–01	Liverpool	2	0		
2001–02	Liverpool	12	0	**14**	**0**
2002–03	Sunderland	26	0		
2003–04	Sunderland	22	1		
2004–05	Sunderland	39	1		
2005–06	Sunderland	2	0		
2006–07	Sunderland	3	0		
2007–08	Sunderland	0	0	**92**	**2**
2007–08	*Stoke C*	16	0	**16**	**0**

YORKE, Dwight (F) **474 148**
H: 5 10 W: 12 04 b.Canaan 3-11-71
Source: St Clair's, Tobago. *Honours:* Trinidad & Tobago 59 full caps, 16 goals.

1989–90	Aston Villa	2	0		
1990–91	Aston Villa	18	2		
1991–92	Aston Villa	32	11		
1992–93	Aston Villa	27	6		
1993–94	Aston Villa	12	2		
1994–95	Aston Villa	37	6		
1995–96	Aston Villa	35	17		
1996–97	Aston Villa	37	17		
1997–98	Aston Villa	30	12		
1998–99	Aston Villa	1	0	**231**	**73**
1998–99	Manchester U	32	18		
1999–2000	Manchester U	32	20		
2000–01	Manchester U	22	9		
2001–02	Manchester U	10	1	**96**	**48**
2002–03	Blackburn R	33	8		
2003–04	Blackburn R	23	4		
2004–05	Blackburn R	4	0	**60**	**12**

2004–05 Birmingham C 13 2 **13 2**
2005–06 Sydney 22 7 **22 7**
2006–07 Sunderland 32 5
2007–08 Sunderland 20 1 **52 6**

Scholars
Brown, David James; Cornforth, Joe Steven; Galer, Andrew Brian; Henderson, Jordan Brian; Hourihane, Conor; Hubbuck, Liam Keith; Hunter, Martin; Luscombe, Nathan John; Madden, Daniel Richard; Noble, Liam Thomas; Reed, Adam Michael; Scott, Gavin; Slegg, Adam

SWANSEA C (80)

ALLEN, Joe (M) 7 0
H: 5 6 W: 9 10 b.Carmarthen 14-3-90
Source: Scholar. *Honours:* Wales Under-21.
2006–07 Swansea C 1 0
2007–08 Swansea C 6 0 **7 0**

AMANKWAAH, Kevin (D) 154 2
H: 6 1 W: 12 12 b.Harrow 19-5-82
Source: Scholar. *Honours:* England Youth.
1999–2000 Bristol C 5 0
2000–01 Bristol C 14 0
2001–02 Bristol C 24 1
2002–03 Bristol C 1 0
2002–03 *Torquay U* 6 0 **6 0**
2003–04 Bristol C 5 0
2003–04 *Cheltenham T* 12 0 **12 0**
2004–05 Bristol C 5 0 **54 1**
2004–05 Yeovil T 15 0
2005–06 Yeovil T 38 1 **53 1**
2006–07 Swansea C 29 0
2007–08 Swansea C 0 0 **29 0**

AUSTIN, Kevin (D) 423 5
H: 6 1 W: 14 08 b.Hackney 12-2-73
Source: Saffron Walden. *Honours:* Trinidad & Tobago 1 full cap.
1993–94 Leyton Orient 30 0
1994–95 Leyton Orient 39 2
1995–96 Leyton Orient 40 1 **109 3**
1996–97 Lincoln C 44 1
1997–98 Lincoln C 46 0
1998–99 Lincoln C 39 1 **129 2**
1999–2000 Barnsley 3 0
2000–01 Barnsley 0 0 **3 0**
2000–01 *Brentford* 3 0 **3 0**
2001–02 Cambridge U 6 0 **6 0**
2002–03 Bristol R 33 0
2003–04 Bristol R 23 0 **56 0**
2004–05 Swansea C 42 0
2005–06 Swansea C 26 0
2006–07 Swansea C 30 0
2007–08 Swansea C 19 0 **117 0**

BAUZA, Guillem (F) 28 7
H: 5 11 W: 12 01 b.Palma de Mallorca 25-10-84
Source: Mallorca, Espanyol.
2007–08 Swansea C 28 7 **28 7**

BODDE, Ferrie (M) 194 17
H: 5 10 W: 12 06 b.Delft 4-5-82
2000–01 Den Haag 4 0
2001–02 Den Haag 27 3
2002–03 Den Haag 28 2
2003–04 Den Haag 27 1
2004–05 Den Haag 29 2
2005–06 Den Haag 19 2
2006–07 Den Haag 27 1 **161 11**
2007–08 Swansea C 33 6 **33 6**

BRITTON, Leon (M) 216 10
H: 5 6 W: 10 00 b.Merton 16-9-82
Source: Trainee. *Honours:* England Youth.
1999–2000 West Ham U 0 0
2000–01 West Ham U 0 0
2001–02 West Ham U 0 0
2002–03 West Ham U 0 0
2002–03 *Swansea C* 25 0
2003–04 Swansea C 42 3
2004–05 Swansea C 30 1
2005–06 Swansea C 38 4
2006–07 Swansea C 41 2
2007–08 Swansea C 40 0 **216 10**

BUTLER, Thomas (M) 160 9
H: 5 7 W: 12 00 b.Dublin 25-4-81
Source: Trainee. *Honours:* Eire Youth, Under-21, 2 full caps.
1998–99 Sunderland 0 0
1999–2000 Sunderland 1 0
2000–01 Sunderland 4 0
2000–01 *Darlington* 8 0 **8 0**
2001–02 Sunderland 7 0
2002–03 Sunderland 7 0
2003–04 Sunderland 12 0 **31 0**
2004–05 Dunfermline Ath 12 0 **12 0**
2004–05 Hartlepool U 9 1
2005–06 Hartlepool U 28 1 **37 2**
2006–07 Swansea C 30 1
2007–08 Swansea C 42 6 **72 7**

COLLINS, Matty (M) 2 0
H: 5 8 W: 10 10 b.Merthyr 31-3-86
Source: Trainee. *Honours:* Wales Youth, Under-21.
2002–03 Fulham 0 0
2003–04 Fulham 0 0
2004–05 Fulham 0 0
2005–06 Fulham 0 0
2006–07 Fulham 0 0
2007–08 Swansea C 0 0
2007–08 *Wrexham* 2 0 **2 0**

DE VRIES, Dorus (G) 204 0
H: 6 1 W: 12 08 b.Beverwijk 29-12-80
1999–2000 Telstar 1 0
2000–01 Telstar 27 0
2001–02 Telstar 27 0
2002–03 Telstar 26 0 **81 0**
2003–04 Den Haag 18 0
2004–05 Den Haag 32 0
2005–06 Den Haag 0 0 **50 0**
2006–07 Dunfermline Ath 27 0 **27 0**
2007–08 Swansea C 46 0 **46 0**

DUFFY, Darryl (F) 119 40
H: 5 11 W: 12 01 b.Glasgow 16-4-84
Honours: Scotland Under-21, B.
2003–04 Rangers 1 0 **1 0**
2004–05 Falkirk 35 17
2005–06 Falkirk 21 9 **56 26**
2005–06 Hull C 15 3
2006–07 Hull C 9 0 **24 3**
2006–07 *Hartlepool U* 10 5 **10 5**
2006–07 *Swansea C* 8 5
2007–08 Swansea C 20 1 **28 6**

EVANS, Scott (M) 0 0
H: 6 0 W: 11 07 b.Swansea 6-1-89
Source: Manchester C Scholar.
2006–07 Swansea C 0 0
2007–08 Swansea C 0 0

JONES, Chris (F) 7 0
H: 5 7 W: 10 00 b.Swansea 12-9-89
Honours: Wales Youth, Under-21.
2006–07 Swansea C 7 0
2007–08 Swansea C 0 0 **7 0**

KNIGHT, David (G) 5 0
H: 6 0 W: 11 07 b.Sunderland 15-1-87
Source: Scholar. *Honours:* England Youth.
2004–05 Middlesbrough 0 0
2005–06 Middlesbrough 0 0
2005–06 *Darlington* 3 0 **3 0**
2006–07 Middlesbrough 0 0
2006–07 *Oldham Ath* 2 0 **2 0**
2007–08 Swansea C 0 0

LAWRENCE, Dennis (D) 277 21
H: 6 7 W: 11 13 b.Trinidad 1-8-74
Source: Defence Force. *Honours:* Trinidad & Tobago 69 full caps, 4 goals.
2000–01 Wrexham 3 0
2001–02 Wrexham 32 2
2002–03 Wrexham 32 1
2003–04 Wrexham 45 5
2004–05 Wrexham 44 4
2005–06 Wrexham 39 2
2006–07 Wrexham 3 0 **198 14**
2006–07 Swansea C 39 5
2007–08 Swansea C 40 2 **79 7**

MACDONALD, Shaun (M) 16 0
H: 6 1 W: 11 04 b.Swansea 17-6-88
Source: Scholar. *Honours:* Wales Youth, Under-21.
2005–06 Swansea C 7 0
2006–07 Swansea C 8 0
2007–08 Swansea C 1 0 **16 0**

MONK, Garry (D) 162 2
H: 6 0 W: 12 10 b.Bedford 6-3-79
Source: Trainee.
1995–96 Torquay U 5 0
1996–97 Southampton 0 0
1997–98 Southampton 0 0
1998–99 Southampton 4 0
1998–99 *Torquay U* 6 0 **11 0**
1999–2000 Southampton 2 0
1999–2000 *Stockport Co* 2 0 **2 0**
2000–01 Southampton 2 0
2000–01 *Oxford U* 5 0 **5 0**
2001–02 Southampton 2 0
2002–03 Southampton 1 0
2002–03 *Sheffield W* 15 0 **15 0**
2003–04 Southampton 0 0 **11 0**
2003–04 Barnsley 17 0 **17 0**
2004–05 Swansea C 34 0
2005–06 Swansea C 33 1
2006–07 Swansea C 2 0
2007–08 Swansea C 32 1 **101 2**

O'LEARY, Kristian (M) 289 11
H: 5 11 W: 12 09 b.Port Talbot 30-8-77
Source: Trainee. *Honours:* Wales Youth.
1995–96 Swansea C 1 0
1996–97 Swansea C 12 1
1997–98 Swansea C 29 0
1998–99 Swansea C 19 2
1999–2000 Swansea C 20 0
2000–01 Swansea C 24 2
2001–02 Swansea C 31 2
2002–03 Swansea C 33 0
2003–04 Swansea C 34 0
2004–05 Swansea C 32 1
2005–06 Swansea C 15 1
2006–07 Swansea C 23 1
2006–07 *Cheltenham T* 5 1 **5 1**
2007–08 Swansea C 11 0 **284 10**

ORLANDI, Andrea (M) 76 5
H: 6 0 W: 12 01 b.Barcelona 3-8-84
2005–06 Alaves 0 0
2005–06 *Barcelona* 1 0
2005–06 *Barcelona B* 32 4
2006–07 *Barcelona B* 35 1 **1 0**
2007–08 Swansea C 8 0 **8 0**

PAINTER, Marcos (D) 58 0
H: 5 11 W: 12 04 b.Solihull 17-8-86
Source: Scholar. *Honours:* Eire Youth, Under-21.
2005–06 Birmingham C 4 0
2006–07 Birmingham C 1 0 **5 0**
2006–07 Swansea C 23 0
2007–08 Swansea C 30 0 **53 0**

PRATLEY, Darren (M) 117 11
H: 6 1 W: 10 12 b.Barking 22-4-85
Source: Scholar.
2001–02 Fulham 0 0
2002–03 Fulham 0 0
2003–04 Fulham 1 0
2004–05 Fulham 0 0
2004–05 *Brentford* 14 1
2005–06 Fulham 0 0 **1 0**
2005–06 *Brentford* 32 4 **46 5**
2006–07 Swansea C 28 1
2007–08 Swansea C 42 5 **70 6**

RANGEL, Angel (D) 77 4
H: 5 11 W: 11 09 b.Tortosa 28-10-82
Source: Tortosa, Reus Deportiu, Girona, Sant Andreu.
2006–07 Terrassa 34 2 **34 2**
2007–08 Swansea C 43 2 **43 2**

ROBINSON, Andy (M) 192 43
H: 5 8 W: 11 04 b.Birkenhead 3-11-79
Source: Cammell Laird.
2002–03 Tranmere R 0 0
2003–04 Swansea C 37 8
2004–05 Swansea C 37 8
2005–06 Swansea C 39 12
2006–07 Swansea C 39 7
2007–08 Swansea C 40 8 **192 43**

SCOTLAND, Jason (F) **161 64**
H: 5 8 W: 11 10 b.Morvant 18-2-79
Source: San Juan Jabloteh, Defence Force.
Honours: Trinidad & Tobago 28 full caps, 5 goals.
2003–04 Dundee U 21 4
2004–05 Dundee U 29 3 **50 7**
2005–06 St Johnstone 31 15
2006–07 St Johnstone 35 18 **66 33**
2007–08 Swansea C 45 24 **45 24**

TATE, Alan (D) **178 3**
H: 6 1 W: 13 05 b.Easington 2-9-82
Source: Scholar.
2000–01 Manchester U 0 0
2001–02 Manchester U 0 0
2002–03 Manchester U 0 0
2002–03 *Swansea C* 27 0
2003–04 Manchester U 0 0
2003–04 Swansea C 26 1
2004–05 Swansea C 23 0
2005–06 Swansea C 43 0
2006–07 Swansea C 38 1
2007–08 Swansea C 21 1 **178 3**

TUDUR JONES, Owain (M) **33 3**
H: 6 2 W: 12 00 b.Bangor 15-10-84
Source: Bangor C. *Honours:* Wales Under-21, 2 full caps.
2005–06 Swansea C 21 3
2006–07 Swansea C 4 0
2007–08 Swansea C 8 0 **33 3**

WATT, Steven (D) **7 1**
H: 6 2 W: 12 09 b.Aberdeen 1-5-85
Source: Trainee. *Honours:* Scotland Under-21, B.
2002–03 Chelsea 0 0
2003–04 Chelsea 0 0
2004–05 Chelsea 1 0
2005–06 Chelsea 0 0 **1 0**
2005–06 *Barnsley* 3 1 **3 1**
2005–06 Swansea C 2 0
2006–07 Swansea C 1 0
2007–08 Swansea C 0 0 **3 0**

WAY, Darren (M) **122 14**
H: 5 7 W: 11 00 b.Plymouth 21-11-79
Source: Norwich C Trainee.
2003–04 Yeovil T 39 5
2004–05 Yeovil T 45 7
2005–06 Yeovil T 15 1
2005–06 Swansea C 5 0
2006–07 Swansea C 9 0
2007–08 Swansea C 2 0 **16 0**
2007–08 *Yeovil T* 7 1 **106 14**

SWINDON T (81)

ADAMS, Steve (M) **179 7**
H: 6 0 W: 12 03 b.Plymouth 25-9-80
Source: Trainee.
1999–2000 Plymouth Arg 1 0
2000–01 Plymouth Arg 17 0
2001–02 Plymouth Arg 46 2
2002–03 Plymouth Arg 37 2
2003–04 Plymouth Arg 36 2
2004–05 Plymouth Arg 20 1 **157 7**
2004–05 Sheffield W 9 0
2005–06 Sheffield W 8 0
2006–07 Sheffield W 3 0 **20 0**
2007–08 Swindon T 2 0 **2 0**

ALJOFREE, Hasney (D) **230 9**
H: 6 0 W: 12 00 b.Manchester 11-7-78
Source: Trainee.
1996–97 Bolton W 0 0
1997–98 Bolton W 2 0
1998–98 Bolton W 4 0
1999–2000 Bolton W 8 0 **14 0**
2000–01 Dundee U 26 2
2001–02 Dundee U 27 2 **53 4**
2002–03 Plymouth Arg 19 1
2003–04 Plymouth Arg 24 0
2004–05 Plymouth Arg 12 1
2004–05 *Sheffield W* 2 0 **2 0**
2005–06 Plymouth Arg 37 1
2006–07 Plymouth Arg 25 0 **117 3**
2006–07 *Oldham Ath* 5 0 **5 0**
2007–08 Swindon T 39 2 **39 2**

ALLEN, Chris (M) **8 0**
H: 5 11 W: 11 10 b.Bristol 3-1-89
Source: Scholar.
2007–08 Swindon T 8 0 **8 0**

ARRIETA, Ibon (F) **4 0**
H: 5 10 W: 11 11 b.Guipozcoa 9-6-77
Source: Pollenca, Real Union, Huesca, Talavera, Chavez, Braga, Estoril, Racing, Logones, Maccabi Herzilya, Giannina, Melilla.
2007–08 Swindon T 4 0 **4 0**

BLACKBURN, Chris (M) **8 0**
H: 6 0 W: 12 00 b.Crewe 2-8-82
Source: Scholarship.
1999–2000 Chester C 1 0 **1 0**
From Morecambe.
2007–08 Swindon T 7 0 **7 0**

BREZOVAN, Peter (G) **72 0**
H: 6 6 W: 14 13 b.Bratislava 9-12-79
Source: PS Bratislava, Vinohrady, Devin, Slovan Breclav, Zigma Olomouc. *Honours:* Slovakia Under-21.
2002–03 Brno 10 0
2003–04 Brno 2 0
2004–05 Inter Bratislava 8 0 **8 0**
2005–06 Brno 7 0 **19 0**
2006–07 Swindon T 14 0
2007–08 Swindon T 31 0 **45 0**

CATON, Andy (M) **13 1**
H: 6 0 W: 12 03 b.Oxford 3-12-87
Source: Scholar.
2004–05 Swindon T 8 1
2005–06 Swindon T 0 0
2006–07 Swindon T 5 0
2007–08 Swindon T 0 0 **13 1**

COMMINGES, Miguel (D) **126 0**
H: 5 9 W: 11 03 b.Les Abymes 16-3-82
2002–03 Amiens 12 0 **12 0**
2003–04 Reims 29 0
2004–05 Reims 21 0
2005–06 Reims 11 0
2006–07 Reims 13 0 **74 0**
2007–08 Swindon T 40 0 **40 0**

CORR, Barry (F) **45 8**
H: 6 3 W: 12 07 b.Co Wicklow 2-4-85
Honours: Eire Youth.
2001–02 Leeds U 0 0
2002–03 Leeds U 0 0
2003–04 Leeds U 0 0
2004–05 Leeds U 0 0
2005–06 Sheffield W 16 0
2006–07 Sheffield W 1 0 **17 0**
2006–07 *Bristol C* 3 0 **3 0**
2006–07 *Swindon T* 8 3
2007–08 Swindon T 17 5 **25 8**

COX, Simon (M) **59 18**
H: 5 10 W: 10 12 b.Reading 28-4-87
Source: Scholar.
2005–06 Reading 2 0
2006–07 Reading 0 0
2006–07 *Brentford* 13 0 **13 0**
2006–07 *Northampton T* 8 3 **8 3**
2007–08 Reading 0 0 **2 0**
2007–08 Swindon T 36 15 **36 15**

EASTON, Craig (M) **172 13**
H: 5 11 W: 11 03 b.Bellshill 26-2-79
Source: Dundee U BC. *Honours:* Scotland Youth, Under-21.
1995–96 Dundee U 0 0
1996–97 Dundee U 2 0
1997–98 Dundee U 29 1
1998–99 Dundee U 30 1
1999–2000 Dundee U 0 0
2000–01 Dundee U 0 0
2001–02 Dundee U 0 0 **61 2**
2005–06 Leyton Orient 41 4
2006–07 Leyton Orient 30 1 **71 5**
2007–08 Swindon T 40 6 **40 6**

HAMMONDS, Kurt (M) **0 0**
b.Wakefield 6-12-90
Source: Scholar.
2007–08 Swindon T 0 0

HYDE, Jake (F) **0 0**
b.Slough
Source: Scholar.
2007–08 Swindon T 0 0

IFIL, Jerel (D) **189 2**
H: 6 1 W: 12 10 b.Wembley 27-6-82
Source: Academy.
1999–2000 Watford 0 0
2000–01 Watford 0 0
2001–02 Watford 0 0
2001–02 *Huddersfield T* 2 0 **2 0**
2002–03 Watford 1 0
2002–03 *Swindon T* 9 0
2003–04 Watford 10 0 **11 0**
2003–04 *Swindon T* 16 0
2004–05 Swindon T 35 0
2005–06 Swindon T 36 0
2006–07 Swindon T 40 1
2007–08 Swindon T 40 1 **176 2**

JOYCE, Ben (F) **3 1**
H: 5 8 W: 11 04 b.Plymouth 9-9-89
2007–08 Swindon T 3 1 **3 1**

KANYUKA, Patrick (D) **16 0**
H: 6 0 W: 12 06 b.Kinshasa 19-7-87
Source: QPR Juniors.
2004–05 QPR 1 0
2005–06 QPR 0 0
2006–07 QPR 11 0
2007–08 QPR 0 0 **12 0**
2007–08 Swindon T 4 0 **4 0**

KENNEDY, Callum (D) **0 0**
b.Chertsey 9-11-89
Source: Scholar.
2007–08 Swindon T 0 0

MACKLIN, Lloyd (M) **0 0**
b.Camberley 2-8-91
2007–08 Swindon T 0 0

McGOVERN, John-Paul (M) **156 12**
H: 5 10 W: 12 02 b.Glasgow 3-10-80
Source: Celtic BC.
2001–02 Celtic 0 0
2002–03 Celtic 0 0
2002–03 *Sheffield U* 15 1 **15 1**
2003–04 Celtic 0 0
2004–05 Sheffield W 46 6
2005–06 Sheffield W 7 0 **53 6**
2006–07 Milton Keynes D 44 3
2007–08 Milton Keynes D 3 0 **47 3**
2007–08 Swindon T 41 2 **41 2**

McNAMEE, Anthony (M) **115 4**
H: 5 6 W: 10 03 b.Kensington 13-7-84
Source: Scholar. *Honours:* England Youth, Under-20.
2001–02 Watford 7 1
2002–03 Watford 23 0
2003–04 Watford 2 0
2004–05 Watford 14 0
2005–06 Watford 38 1
2006–07 Watford 7 0
2006–07 *Crewe Alex* 5 0 **5 0**
2007–08 Watford 0 0 **91 2**
2007–08 Swindon T 19 2 **19 2**

MOHAMMED, Kaid (F) **118 32**
H: 5 11 W: 12 06 b.Cardiff 23-7-84
2003–04 Cwmbran T 29 3
2004–05 Cwmbran T 15 2
2004–05 Llanelli 3 1
2005–06 Carmarthen T 14 4
2005–06 Cwmbran T 11 7 **55 12**
2006–07 Llanelli 5 0 **8 1**
2006–07 Carmarthen T 30 15 **44 19**
2007–08 Swindon T 11 0 **11 0**

MORRIS, Samuel (M) **0 0**
b.Swindon
Source: Scholar.
2007–08 Swindon T 0 0

MORRISON, Sean (D) **2 0**
H: 6 4 W: 14 00 b.Plymouth 8-1-91
Source: Plymouth Arg.
2007–08 Swindon T 2 0 **2 0**

NICHOLAS, Andrew (D) **131 4**
H: 6 2 W: 12 08 b.Liverpool 10-10-83
Honours: Liverpool Trainee.
2003–04 Swindon T 31 1
2004–05 Swindon T 16 0
2004–05 *Chester C* 5 0 **5 0**
2005–06 Swindon T 33 0
2006–07 Swindon T 35 2
2007–08 Swindon T 11 1 **126 4**

PAYNTER, Billy (F) **226 45**
H: 6 1 W: 14 01 b.Liverpool 13-7-84
Source: Schoolboy.

2000–01	Port Vale	1	0		
2001–02	Port Vale	7	0		
2002–03	Port Vale	31	5		
2003–04	Port Vale	44	13		
2004–05	Port Vale	45	10		
2005–06	Port Vale	16	2	**144**	**30**
2005–06	Hull C	22	3	**22**	**3**
2006–07	Southend U	9	0		
2006–07	*Bradford C*	15	4	**15**	**4**
2007–08	Southend U	0	0	**9**	**0**
2007–08	Swindon T	36	8	**36**	**8**

PEACOCK, Lee (F) **462 118**
H: 6 0 W: 12 08 b.Paisley 9-10-76
Source: Trainee. *Honours:* Scotland Youth, Under-21.

1993–94	Carlisle U	1	0		
1994–95	Carlisle U	7	0		
1995–96	Carlisle U	22	2		
1996–97	Carlisle U	44	9		
1997–98	Carlisle U	2	0	**76**	**11**
1997–98	Mansfield T	32	5		
1998–99	Mansfield T	45	17		
1999–2000	Mansfield T	12	7	**89**	**29**
1999–2000	Manchester C	8	0	**8**	**0**
2000–01	Bristol C	35	13		
2001–02	Bristol C	31	15		
2002–03	Bristol C	37	12		
2003–04	Bristol C	41	14	**144**	**54**
2004–05	Sheffield W	29	4		
2005–06	Sheffield W	22	2	**51**	**6**
2005–06	Swindon T	15	2		
2006–07	Swindon T	42	10		
2007–08	Swindon T	37	6	**94**	**18**

POOK, Michael (M) **95 3**
H: 5 11 W: 11 10 b.Swindon 22-10-85
Source: Scholar.

2003–04	Swindon T	0	0		
2004–05	Swindon T	5	0		
2005–06	Swindon T	30	0		
2006–07	Swindon T	38	2		
2007–08	Swindon T	22	1	**95**	**3**

ROBERTS, Chris (F) **307 63**
H: 5 11 W: 12 08 b.Cardiff 22-10-79
Source: Trainee. *Honours:* Wales Youth, Under-21.

1997–98	Cardiff C	11	3		
1998–99	Cardiff C	4	0		
1999–2000	Cardiff C	8	0	**23**	**3**
2000–01	Exeter C	42	8		
2001–02	Exeter C	37	11	**79**	**19**
2001–02	Bristol C	4	0		
2002–03	Bristol C	44	13		
2003–04	Bristol C	38	6		
2004–05	Bristol C	8	1	**94**	**20**
2004–05	Swindon T	21	3		
2005–06	Swindon T	21	3		
2006–07	Swindon T	42	10		
2007–08	Swindon T	27	5	**111**	**21**

SCOTT, Mark (G) **0 0**
b.Fleet 3-1-91
Source: Scholar.

2007–08	Swindon T	0	0		

SMITH, Jack (D) **125 6**
H: 5 11 W: 11 05 b.Hemel Hempstead 14-10-83
Source: Scholar.

2001–02	Watford	0	0		
2002–03	Watford	1	0		
2003–04	Watford	17	2		
2004–05	Watford	7	0	**25**	**2**
2005–06	Swindon T	38	0		
2006–07	Swindon T	41	3		
2007–08	Swindon T	21	1	**100**	**4**

SMITH, Phil (G) **51 0**
H: 6 1 W: 13 11 b.Harrow 14-12-79
Source: Trainee.

1997–98	Millwall	0	0		
1998–99	Millwall	5	0	**5**	**0**

From Folkestone, Dover, Margate, Crawley

2006–07	Swindon T	31	0		
2007–08	Swindon T	15	0	**46**	**0**

STURROCK, Blair (F) **183 25**
H: 5 10 W: 12 09 b.Dundee 25-8-81
Source: Dundee U.

2000–01	Brechin C	27	6	**27**	**6**
2001–02	Plymouth Arg	19	1		
2002–03	Plymouth Arg	20	1		
2003–04	Plymouth Arg	24	0		
2004–05	Plymouth Arg	0	0	**63**	**2**
2004–05	Kidderminster H	22	5	**22**	**5**
2005–06	Rochdale	31	6		
2006–07	Rochdale	0	0	**31**	**6**
2006–07	Swindon T	19	3		
2007–08	Swindon T	21	3	**40**	**6**

VINCENT, Jamie (D) **364 10**
H: 5 10 W: 11 08 b.Wimbledon 18-6-75
Source: Trainee.

1993–94	Crystal Palace	0	0		
1994–95	Crystal Palace	0	0		
1994–95	*Bournemouth*	8	0		
1995–96	Crystal Palace	25	0		
1996–97	Crystal Palace	0	0	**25**	**0**
1996–97	Bournemouth	29	0		
1997–98	Bournemouth	44	3		
1998–99	Bournemouth	32	2	**113**	**5**
1998–99	Huddersfield T	7	0		
1999–2000	Huddersfield T	36	2		
2000–01	Huddersfield T	16	0	**59**	**2**
2000–01	Portsmouth	14	0		
2001–02	Portsmouth	34	1		
2002–03	Portsmouth	0	0		
2003–04	Portsmouth	0	0	**48**	**1**
2003–04	*Walsall*	12	0	**12**	**0**
2003–04	Derby Co	7	1		
2004–05	Derby Co	15	1	**22**	**2**
2005–06	Millwall	19	0	**19**	**0**
2005–06	Yeovil T	0	0		
2006–07	Swindon T	34	0		
2007–08	Swindon T	32	0	**66**	**0**

WELLS, Ben (M) **6 0**
H: 5 9 W: 10 07 b.Basingstoke 26-3-88
Source: Scholar.

2004–05	Swindon T	1	0		
2005–06	Swindon T	4	0		
2006–07	Swindon T	1	0		
2007–08	Swindon T	0	0	**6**	**0**

WILLIAMS, Ady (D) **435 21**
H: 6 2 W: 13 02 b.Reading 16-8-71
Source: Trainee. *Honours:* Wales 13 full caps, 1 goal.

1988–89	Reading	8	0		
1989–90	Reading	16	2		
1990–91	Reading	7	0		
1991–92	Reading	40	4		
1992–93	Reading	31	4		
1993–94	Reading	41	0		
1994–95	Reading	22	1		
1995–96	Reading	31	3		
1996–97	Wolverhampton W	6	0		
1997–98	Wolverhampton W	20	0		
1998–99	Wolverhampton W	0	0		
1999–2000	Wolverhampton W	1	0	**27**	**0**
1999–2000	*Reading*	15	1		
2000–01	Reading	5	0		
2001–02	Reading	35	1		
2002–03	Reading	38	1		
2003–04	Reading	33	1		
2004–05	Reading	11	0	**333**	**18**
2004–05	Coventry C	21	2		
2005–06	Coventry C	14	0	**35**	**2**
2005–06	*Millwall*	12	1	**12**	**1**
2006–07	Swindon T	27	0		
2007–08	Swindon T	1	0	**28**	**0**

WINTER, Jack (D) **0 0**
b.Hammersmith
Source: Scholar.

2007–08	Swindon T	0	0		

ZAABOUB, Sofiane (D) **76 2**
H: 5 11 W: 11 09 b.Melun 23-1-83
Source: Montereau, St Etienne, Modena, Sora, Real Jaen.

2005–06	FC Brussels	20	1	**20**	**1**
2006–07	Swindon T	27	1		
2007–08	Swindon T	29	0	**56**	**1**

TOTTENHAM H (82)

ALNWICK, Ben (G) **31 0**
H: 6 2 W: 13 12 b.Prudhoe 1-1-87
Source: Scholar. *Honours:* England Youth, Under-21.

2003–04	Sunderland	0	0		
2004–05	Sunderland	3	0		
2005–06	Sunderland	5	0		
2006–07	Sunderland	11	0	**19**	**0**
2006–07	Tottenham H	0	0		
2007–08	Tottenham H	0	0		
2007–08	*Luton T*	4	0	**4**	**0**
2007–08	*Leicester C*	8	0	**8**	**0**

ARCHIBALD-HENVILLE, Troy (D) **0 0**
H: 6 2 W: 13 03 b.Newham 4-11-88
Source: Scholar.

2007–08	Tottenham H	0	0		

ASSOU-EKOTTO, Benoit (M) **83 0**
H: 5 10 W: 10 12 b.Arras 24-3-84
Honours: Cameroon B.

2003–04	Lens	3	0		
2004–05	Lens	29	0		
2005–06	Lens	34	0	**66**	**0**
2006–07	Tottenham H	16	0		
2007–08	Tottenham H	1	0	**17**	**0**

BALE, Gareth (D) **48 7**
H: 6 0 W: 11 10 b.Cardiff 16-7-89
Source: Scholar. *Honours:* Wales Youth, Under-21, 11 full caps, 2 goals.

2005–06	Southampton	2	0		
2006–07	Southampton	38	5	**40**	**5**
2007–08	Tottenham H	8	2	**8**	**2**

BARCHAM, Andy (F) **25 1**
H: 5 8 W: 11 10 b.Basildon 16-12-86
Source: Scholar.

2005–06	Tottenham H	0	0		
2006–07	Tottenham H	0	0		
2007–08	Tottenham H	0	0		
2007–08	*Leyton Orient*	25	1	**25**	**1**

BENT, Darren (F) **217 86**
H: 5 11 W: 12 07 b.Wandsworth 6-2-84
Source: Scholar. *Honours:* England Youth, Under-21, 3 full caps.

2001–02	Ipswich T	5	1		
2002–03	Ipswich T	35	12		
2003–04	Ipswich T	37	16		
2004–05	Ipswich T	45	20	**122**	**49**
2005–06	Charlton Ath	36	18		
2006–07	Charlton Ath	32	13	**68**	**31**
2007–08	Tottenham H	27	6	**27**	**6**

BERBATOV, Dimitar (F) **273 121**
H: 6 2 W: 12 06 b.Blagoevgrad 30-1-81
Honours: Bulgaria 65 full caps, 39 goals.

1998–99	CSKA Sofia	11	3		
1999–2000	CSKA Sofia	27	14		
2000–01	CSKA Sofia	12	8	**50**	**25**
2000–01	Leverkusen	6	0		
2001–02	Leverkusen	24	8		
2002–03	Leverkusen	24	4		
2003–04	Leverkusen	33	16		
2004–05	Leverkusen	33	20		
2005–06	Leverkusen	34	21	**154**	**69**
2006–07	Tottenham H	33	12		
2007–08	Tottenham H	36	15	**69**	**27**

BERCHICHE, Yuri (D) **0 0**
b.Resideus 10-2-90
Source: Athletic Bilbao.

2007–08	Tottenham H	0	0		

BOATENG, Kevin-Prince (M) **55 4**
H: 6 0 W: 11 09 b.Berlin 6-3-87
Honours: Germany Under-21.

2005–06	Hertha Berlin	21	2		
2006–07	Hertha Berlin	21	2	**42**	**4**
2007–08	Tottenham H	13	0	**13**	**0**

BUTCHER, Callum (D) **0 0**
b.Rochford 26-2-91
Source: Scholar.

2007–08	Tottenham H	0	0		

BUTTON, David (G) **0 0**
H: 6 3 W: 13 00 b.Stevenage 27-2-89
Source: Scholar. *Honours:* England Youth.

2005–06	Tottenham H	0	0		
2006–07	Tottenham H	0	0		

2007–08 *Rochdale* 0 0
2007–08 Tottenham H 0 0

CERNY, Radek (G) 16 0
H: 6 1 W: 14 02 b.Prague 18-2-74
Source: Slavia Prague. *Honours:* Czech Republic 3 full caps.
2004–05 Tottenham H 3 0
2005–06 Tottenham H 0 0
2006–07 Tottenham H 0 0
2007–08 Tottenham H 13 0 **16 0**

CHIMBONDA, Pascal (D) 255 14
H: 5 10 W: 11 05 b.Les Abymes 21-2-79
Honours: France 1 full cap.
1999–2000 Le Havre 2 0
2000–01 Le Havre 32 1
2001–02 Le Havre 27 2
2002–03 Le Havre 24 2 **85 5**
2003–04 Bastia 31 1
2004–05 Bastia 36 3 **67 4**
2005–06 Wigan Ath 37 2
2006–07 Wigan Ath 1 0 **38 2**
2006–07 Tottenham H 33 1
2007–08 Tottenham H 32 2 **65 3**

DANIELS, Charlie (M) 33 2
H: 6 1 W: 12 12 b.Harlow 7-9-86
Source: Scholar.
2005–06 Tottenham H 0 0
2006–07 Tottenham H 0 0
2006–07 *Chesterfield* 2 0 **2 0**
2007–08 Tottenham H 0 0
2007–08 *Leyton Orient* 31 2 **31 2**

DAVIS, Jamie (M) 0 0
H: 5 7 W: 10 10 b.Braintree 25-10-88
Source: Scholar. *Honours:* England Youth.
2005–06 Tottenham H 0 0
2006–07 Tottenham H 0 0
2007–08 Tottenham H 0 0

DAWKINS, Simon (F) 0 0
H: 5 10 W: 11 01 b.Edgware 1-12-87
Source: Scholar.
2005–06 Tottenham H 0 0
2006–07 Tottenham H 0 0
2007–08 Tottenham H 0 0

DAWSON, Michael (D) 184 9
H: 6 2 W: 12 02 b.Northallerton 18-11-83
Source: School. *Honours:* England Youth, Under-21, B.
2000–01 Nottingham F 0 0
2001–02 Nottingham F 1 0
2002–03 Nottingham F 38 5
2003–04 Nottingham F 30 1
2004–05 Nottingham F 14 1 **83 7**
2004–05 Tottenham H 5 0
2005–06 Tottenham H 32 0
2006–07 Tottenham H 37 1
2007–08 Tottenham H 27 1 **101 2**

DERVITE, Dorian (D) 0 0
H: 6 3 W: 14 01 b.Lille 25-7-88
Honours: France Youth.
2006–07 Tottenham H 0 0
2007–08 Tottenham H 0 0

DIXON, Terry (F) 0 0
b.Holloway 15-1-90
Honours: Eire Youth, Under-21.
2006–07 Tottenham H 0 0
2007–08 Tottenham H 0 0

FORECAST, Tommy (G) 0 0
H: 6 6 W: 11 10 b.Newham 15-10-86
Source: Scholar.
2005–06 Tottenham H 0 0
2006–07 Tottenham H 0 0
2007–08 Tottenham H 0 0

GARDNER, Anthony (D) 155 6
H: 6 3 W: 14 00 b.Stone 19-9-80
Source: Trainee. *Honours:* England Under-21, 1 full cap.
1998–99 Port Vale 15 1
1999–2000 Port Vale 26 3 **41 4**
1999–2000 Tottenham H 0 0
2000–01 Tottenham H 8 0
2001–02 Tottenham H 15 0
2002–03 Tottenham H 12 1
2003–04 Tottenham H 33 0
2004–05 Tottenham H 17 0
2005–06 Tottenham H 17 0
2006–07 Tottenham H 8 0

2007–08 *Everton* 0 0
2007–08 Tottenham H 4 1 **114 2**

GHALY, Hossam (M) 79 3
H: 5 11 W: 12 04 b.Cairo 15-12-81
Honours: Egypt 21 full caps, 5 goals.
2003–04 Feyenoord 13 0
2004–05 Feyenoord 20 1
2005–06 Feyenoord 10 2 **43 3**
2005–06 Tottenham H 0 0
2006–07 Tottenham H 21 0
2007–08 Tottenham H 0 0 **21 0**
2007–08 *Derby Co* 15 0 **15 0**

GILBERTO (D) 276 32
H: 5 11 W: 12 04 b.Rio de Janeiro 28-2-77
Honours: Brazil 23 full caps, 1 goal.
1995 America 0 0
1996 Flamengo 17 0
1997 Flamengo 22 0 **39 0**
1998 Cruzeiro 28 2 **28 2**
1998–99 Internazionale 2 0 **2 0**
1999 Vasco da Gama 16 2
2000 Vasco da Gama 0 0
2001 Vasco da Gama 24 4 **40 6**
2002 Gremio 21 3
2003 Gremio 33 6 **54 9**
2004 Sao Caetano 6 0 **6 0**
2004–05 Hertha Berlin 33 6
2005–06 Hertha Berlin 23 2
2006–07 Hertha Berlin 30 5
2007–08 Hertha Berlin 15 1 **101 14**
2007–08 Tottenham H 6 1 **6 1**

GUNTER, Chris (D) 30 0
H: 5 11 W: 11 02 b.Newport 21-7-89
Source: Scholar. *Honours:* Wales Youth, Under-21, 6 full caps.
2006–07 Cardiff C 15 0
2007–08 Cardiff C 13 0 **28 0**
2007–08 Tottenham H 2 0 **2 0**

HAMED, Radwan (F) 0 0
b. 19-12-88
Source: Scholar.
2006–07 Tottenham H 0 0
2007–08 Tottenham H 0 0

HUDDLESTONE, Tom (M) 154 5
H: 6 2 W: 11 02 b.Nottingham 28-12-86
Source: Scholar. *Honours:* England Youth, Under-20, Under-21.
2003–04 Derby Co 43 0
2004–05 Derby Co 45 0 **88 0**
2005–06 Tottenham H 4 0
2005–06 *Wolverhampton W* 13 1 **13 1**
2006–07 Tottenham H 21 1
2007–08 Tottenham H 28 3 **53 4**

HUGHTON, Cian (D) 0 0
b.Enfield 25-1-89
Source: Scholar.
2007–08 Tottenham H 0 0

HUTCHINS, Daniel (M) 0 0
b.London 23-9-89
Source: Scholar.
2007–08 Tottenham H 0 0

HUTTON, Alan (D) 96 1
H: 6 1 W: 11 05 b.Glasgow 30-11-84
Honours: Scotland Under-21, 7 full caps.
2004–05 Rangers 10 0
2005–06 Rangers 19 0
2006–07 Rangers 33 1
2007–08 Rangers 20 0 **82 1**
2007–08 Tottenham H 14 0 **14 0**

JANSSON, Oscar (G) 0 0
b.Orebro
Source: Karlslund.
2007–08 Tottenham H 0 0

JENAS, Jermaine (M) 223 29
H: 5 11 W: 11 00 b.Nottingham 18-2-83
Source: Scholar. *Honours:* England Youth, Under-21, B, 18 full caps, 1 goal.
1999–2000 Nottingham F 0 0
2000–01 Nottingham F 1 0
2001–02 Nottingham F 28 4 **29 4**
2001–02 Newcastle U 12 0
2002–03 Newcastle U 32 6
2003–04 Newcastle U 31 2
2004–05 Newcastle U 31 1
2005–06 Newcastle U 4 0 **110 9**
2005–06 Tottenham H 30 6

2006–07 Tottenham H 25 6
2007–08 Tottenham H 29 4 **84 16**

KABOUL, Younes (D) 73 6
H: 6 2 W: 13 07 b.St-Julien-en-Genevois 4-1-86
Honours: France Under-21.
2004–05 Auxerre 12 1
2005–06 Auxerre 9 0
2006–07 Auxerre 31 2 **52 3**
2007–08 Tottenham H 21 3 **21 3**

KEANE, Robbie (F) 353 129
H: 5 9 W: 12 02 b.Dublin 8-7-80
Source: Trainee. *Honours:* Eire Youth, B, 81 full caps, 33 goals.
1997–98 Wolverhampton W 38 11
1998–99 Wolverhampton W 33 11
1999–2000 Wolverhampton W 2 2 **73 24**
1999–2000 Coventry C 31 12 **31 12**
2000–01 Internazionale 6 0 **6 0**
2000–01 Leeds U 18 9
2001–02 Leeds U 25 3
2002–03 Leeds U 3 1 **46 13**
2002–03 Tottenham H 29 13
2003–04 Tottenham H 34 14
2004–05 Tottenham H 35 11
2005–06 Tottenham H 36 16
2006–07 Tottenham H 27 11
2007–08 Tottenham H 36 15 **197 80**

KING, Ledley (D) 197 7
H: 6 2 W: 14 05 b.Bow 12-10-80
Source: Trainee. *Honours:* England Youth, B, Under-21, 19 full caps, 1 goal.
1998–99 Tottenham H 1 0
1999–2000 Tottenham H 3 0
2000–01 Tottenham H 18 1
2001–02 Tottenham H 32 0
2002–03 Tottenham H 25 0
2003–04 Tottenham H 29 1
2004–05 Tottenham H 38 2
2005–06 Tottenham H 26 3
2006–07 Tottenham H 21 0
2007–08 Tottenham H 4 0 **197 7**

LEE, Young-Pyo (D) 148 1
H: 5 8 W: 10 10 b.Hong Chung 23-4-77
Source: Anyang Cheetahs. *Honours:* South Korea 96 full caps, 5 goals.
2002–03 PSV Eindhoven 15 0
2003–04 PSV Eindhoven 32 0
2004–05 PSV Eindhoven 31 1 **78 1**
2005–06 Tottenham H 31 0
2006–07 Tottenham H 21 0
2007–08 Tottenham H 18 0 **70 0**

LENNON, Aaron (M) 120 8
H: 5 6 W: 10 03 b.Leeds 16-4-87
Source: Trainee. *Honours:* England Youth, Under-21, B, 9 full caps.
2003–04 Leeds U 11 0
2004–05 Leeds U 27 1 **38 1**
2005–06 Tottenham H 27 2
2006–07 Tottenham H 26 3
2007–08 Tottenham H 29 2 **82 7**

LIVERMORE, Jake (M) 5 0
b.Enfield 14-11-89
Source: Scholar.
2006–07 Tottenham H 0 0
2007–08 Tottenham H 0 0
2007–08 *Milton Keynes D* 5 0 **5 0**

MAGHOMA, Jacques (M) 0 0
H: 5 9 W: 11 06 b.Lubumbashi 23-10-87
Source: Scholar.
2005–06 Tottenham H 0 0
2006–07 Tottenham H 0 0
2007–08 Tottenham H 0 0

MALBRANQUE, Steed (M) 311 43
H: 5 7 W: 11 07 b.Mouscron 6-1-80
Honours: France Under-21.
1997–98 Lyon 2 0
1998–99 Lyon 21 0
1999–2000 Lyon 28 3
2000–01 Lyon 26 2 **77 5**
2001–02 Fulham 37 8
2002–03 Fulham 37 6
2003–04 Fulham 38 6
2004–05 Fulham 26 6
2005–06 Fulham 34 6 **172 32**
2006–07 Tottenham H 25 2
2007–08 Tottenham H 37 4 **62 6**

MARTIN, Joe (M) 1 0
H: 6 0 W: 12 13 b.Dagenham 29-11-88
Source: Scholar. *Honours:* England Youth.
2005–06 Tottenham H 0 0
2006–07 Tottenham H 0 0
2007–08 Tottenham H 0 0
2007–08 *Blackpool* 1 0 **1 0**

MASON, Ryan (M) 0 0
b.Enfield 13-6-91
2007–08 Tottenham H 0 0

McKENNA, Kieran (M) 0 0
H: 5 10 W: 10 07 b.London 14-5-86
Source: Academy. *Honours:* Northern Ireland Under-21.
2003–04 Tottenham H 0 0
2004–05 Tottenham H 0 0
2005–06 Tottenham H 0 0
2006–07 Tottenham H 0 0
2007–08 Tottenham H 0 0

MILLS, Leigh (D) 0 0
H: 6 2 W: 13 00 b.Winchester 8-2-88
Source: Scholar. *Honours:* England Youth.
2005–06 Tottenham H 0 0
2006–07 Tottenham H 0 0
2007–08 Tottenham H 0 0

O'HARA, Jamie (M) 50 8
H: 5 11 W: 12 04 b.South London 25-9-86
Source: Scholar. *Honours:* England Youth, Under-21.
2004–05 Tottenham H 0 0
2005–06 Tottenham H 0 0
2005–06 *Chesterfield* 19 5 **19 5**
2006–07 Tottenham H 0 0
2007–08 Tottenham H 17 1 **17 1**
2007–08 *Millwall* 14 2 **14 2**

OLSEN, Alex (F) 0 0
b.Gjovik 9-9-89
Source: Gjovik.
2006–07 Tottenham H 0 0
2007–08 Tottenham H 0 0

PEKHART, Tomas (F) 0 0
H: 6 3 W: 14 00 b.Susice 26-5-89
Honours: Czech Republic Youth.
2006–07 Tottenham H 0 0
2007–08 Tottenham H 0 0

RICARDO ROCHA (D) 173 5
H: 6 0 W: 12 08 b.Santo Tirso 3-10-78
Honours: Portugal 6 full caps.
2000–01 Braga 19 0
2001–02 Braga 25 2 **44 2**
2002–03 Benfica 27 0
2003–04 Benfica 25 0
2004–05 Benfica 25 0
2005–06 Benfica 26 0
2006–07 Benfica 12 3 **115 3**
2006–07 Tottenham H 9 0
2007–08 Tottenham H 5 0 **14 0**

RILEY, Chris (D) 0 0
b.London 2-2-88
Source: Scholar. *Honours:* England Youth.
2006–07 Tottenham H 0 0
2007–08 Tottenham H 0 0

ROBINSON, Paul (G) 232 1
H: 6 1 W: 14 07 b.Beverley 15-10-79
Source: Trainee. *Honours:* England Under-21, 41 full caps.
1996–97 Leeds U 0 0
1997–98 Leeds U 0 0
1998–99 Leeds U 5 0
1999–2000 Leeds U 0 0
2000–01 Leeds U 16 0
2001–02 Leeds U 0 0
2002–03 Leeds U 38 0
2003–04 Leeds U 36 0 **95 0**
2003–04 Tottenham H 0 0
2004–05 Tottenham H 36 0
2005–06 Tottenham H 38 0
2006–07 Tottenham H 38 1
2007–08 Tottenham H 25 0 **137 1**

ROSE, Daniel (M) 0 0
b.Doncaster 2-6-90
Source: Leeds U. *Honours:* England Youth.
2007–08 Tottenham H 0 0

SMITH, Adam (D) 0 0
b.London 29-4-91
Source: Scholar.
2007–08 Tottenham H 0 0

STALTERI, Paul (D) 205 8
H: 5 11 W: 11 13 b.Etobicoke 18-10-77
Source: Malton Bullets, Toronto Lynx.
Honours: Canada Youth, Under-20, Under-23, 67 full caps, 7 goals.
1999–2000 Werder Bremen 0 0
2000–01 Werder Bremen 31 1
2001–02 Werder Bremen 22 3
2002–03 Werder Bremen 33 0
2003–04 Werder Bremen 33 2
2004–05 Werder Bremen 31 0 **150 6**
2005–06 Tottenham H 33 1
2006–07 Tottenham H 6 1
2007–08 Tottenham H 3 0 **42 2**
2007–08 *Fulham* 13 0 **13 0**

TAARABT, Adel (M) 9 0
H: 5 9 W: 10 12 b.Berre-l'Etang 24-5-89
Honours: France Youth.
2006–07 Lens 1 0 **1 0**
2006–07 Tottenham H 2 0
2007–08 Tottenham H 6 0 **8 0**

TAINIO, Teemu (M) 205 19
H: 5 9 W: 11 09 b.Tornio 27-11-79
Honours: Finland Youth, Under-21, 43 full caps, 6 goals.
1996 Haka 20 4 **20 4**
1997–98 Auxerre 1 0
1998–99 Auxerre 13 1
1999–2000 Auxerre 25 3
2000–01 Auxerre 10 1
2001–02 Auxerre 28 3
2002–03 Auxerre 25 1
2003–04 Auxerre 22 3
2004–05 Auxerre 0 0 **124 12**
2005–06 Tottenham H 24 1
2006–07 Tottenham H 21 2
2007–08 Tottenham H 16 0 **61 3**

WOODGATE, Jonathan (D) 199 5
H: 6 2 W: 12 06 b.Middlesbrough 22-1-80
Source: Trainee. *Honours:* England Youth, Under-21, 7 full caps.
1996–97 Leeds U 0 0
1997–98 Leeds U 0 0
1998–99 Leeds U 25 2
1999–2000 Leeds U 34 1
2000–01 Leeds U 14 1
2001–02 Leeds U 13 0
2002–03 Leeds U 18 0 **104 4**
2002–03 Newcastle U 10 0
2003–04 Newcastle U 18 0 **28 0**
2004–05 Real Madrid 0 0
2005–06 Real Madrid 9 0 **9 0**
2006–07 Middlesbrough 30 0
2007–08 Middlesbrough 16 0 **46 0**
2007–08 Tottenham H 12 1 **12 1**

ZOKORA, Didier (D) 249 1
H: 5 10 W: 11 00 b.Abidjan 14-12-80
Honours: Ivory Coast 72 full caps, 1 goal.
2000–01 Genk 28 0
2001–02 Genk 30 0
2002–03 Genk 33 0
2003–04 Genk 33 1 **124 1**
2004–05 St Etienne 35 0
2005–06 St Etienne 31 0 **66 0**
2006–07 Tottenham H 31 0
2007–08 Tottenham H 28 0 **59 0**

Scholars
Asajile, Saulo; Butcher, Callum James; Casey, Chris; Clare, Mark James; Cox, Samuel Peter; Dalton, James; Fraser-Allen, Kyle; Hutton, David; Kasim, Yaser Safa; Mason, Ryan Glen; Mtandari, Takura Ndinadzo; Obika, Jonathan; Shehu, Ajet; Townsend, Andros

TRANMERE R (83)

ACHTERBERG, John (G) 291 0
H: 6 1 W: 14 03 b.Utrecht 8-7-71
Source: VV RUC, Utrecht.
1993–94 NAC 1 0
1994–95 NAC 2 0
1995–96 NAC 6 0 **9 0**
1996–97 Eindhoven 32 0 **32 0**
From Utrecht.
1998–99 Tranmere R 24 0
1999–2000 Tranmere R 26 0
2000–01 Tranmere R 25 0
2001–02 Tranmere R 25 0
2002–03 Tranmere R 38 0
2003–04 Tranmere R 45 0
2004–05 Tranmere R 39 0
2005–06 Tranmere R 19 0
2006–07 Tranmere R 4 0
2007–08 Tranmere R 5 0 **250 0**

AHMED, Adnan (M) 47 1
H: 5 10 W: 11 02 b.Burnley 7-6-84
Source: Scholar. *Honours:* Pakistan 8 full caps, 2 goals.
2003–04 Huddersfield T 1 0
2004–05 Huddersfield T 18 1
2005–06 Huddersfield T 13 0
2006–07 Huddersfield T 9 0 **41 1**
2007–08 Tranmere R 6 0 **6 0**

BEAHON, Thomas (M) 0 0
H: 5 8 W: 10 02 b.Wirral 18-9-88
Source: Scholar.
2006–07 Tranmere R 0 0
2007–08 Tranmere R 0 0

CANSDELL-SHERRIFF, Shane (D) 172 13
H: 5 11 W: 11 08 b.Sydney 10-11-82
Source: NSW Academy. *Honours:* Australia Youth, Under-23.
1999–2000 Leeds U 0 0
2000–01 Leeds U 0 0
2001–02 Leeds U 0 0
2002–03 Leeds U 0 0
2002–03 *Rochdale* 3 0 **3 0**
2003–04 Aarhus 29 4
2004–05 Aarhus 26 2
2005–06 Aarhus 27 1 **82 7**
2006–07 Tranmere R 43 3
2007–08 Tranmere R 44 3 **87 6**

CHORLEY, Ben (M) 185 7
H: 6 3 W: 13 02 b.Sidcup 30-9-82
Source: Scholar.
2001–02 Arsenal 0 0
2002–03 Arsenal 0 0
2002–03 *Brentford* 2 0 **2 0**
2002–03 Wimbledon 10 0
2003–04 Wimbledon 35 2 **45 2**
2004–05 Milton Keynes D 41 2
2005–06 Milton Keynes D 26 0
2006–07 Milton Keynes D 13 1 **80 3**
2006–07 *Gillingham* 27 1 **27 1**
2007–08 Tranmere R 31 1 **31 1**

COYNE, Danny (G) 377 0
H: 6 0 W: 13 00 b.Prestatyn 27-8-73
Source: Trainee. *Honours:* Wales Schools, Youth, Under-21, B, 16 full caps.
1991–92 Tranmere R 0 0
1992–93 Tranmere R 1 0
1993–94 Tranmere R 5 0
1994–95 Tranmere R 5 0
1995–96 Tranmere R 46 0
1996–97 Tranmere R 21 0
1997–98 Tranmere R 16 0
1998–99 Tranmere R 17 0
1999–2000 Grimsby T 44 0
2000–01 Grimsby T 46 0
2001–02 Grimsby T 45 0
2002–03 Grimsby T 46 0 **181 0**
2003–04 Leicester C 4 0 **4 0**
2004–05 Burnley 20 0
2005–06 Burnley 8 0
2006–07 Burnley 12 0 **40 0**
2007–08 Tranmere R 41 0 **152 0**

CURRAN, Craig (F) 39 6
H: 5 9 W: 11 09 b.Liverpool 23-9-89
Source: Scholar.
2006–07 Tranmere R 4 4
2007–08 Tranmere R 35 2 **39 6**

DAVIES, Steve (F) 60 5
H: 6 0 W: 12 00 b.Liverpool 29-12-87
Source: Scholar.
2005–06 Tranmere R 22 2
2006–07 Tranmere R 28 1
2007–08 Tranmere R 10 2 **60 5**

GOODISON, Ian (D) 246 3
H: 6 1 W: 13 04 b.St James, Jamaica 21-11-72
Source: Olympic Gardens. *Honours:* Jamaica 100 full caps, 9 goals.
1999–2000 Hull C 18 0
2000–01 Hull C 36 1
2001–02 Hull C 16 0
2002–03 Hull C 0 0 **70 1**
From Seba U.
2003–04 Tranmere R 12 0
2004–05 Tranmere R 44 1
2005–06 Tranmere R 38 1
2006–07 Tranmere R 40 0
2007–08 Tranmere R 42 0 **176 2**

GREENACRE, Chris (F) 360 105
H: 5 9 W: 12 09 b.Halifax 23-12-77
Source: Trainee.
1995–96 Manchester C 0 0
1996–97 Manchester C 4 0
1997–98 Manchester C 3 1
1997–98 *Cardiff C* 11 2 **11 2**
1997–98 *Blackpool* 4 0 **4 0**
1998–99 Manchester C 1 0
1998–99 *Scarborough* 12 2 **12 2**
1999–2000 Manchester C 0 0 **8 1**
1999–2000 Mansfield T 31 9
2000–01 Mansfield T 46 19
2001–02 Mansfield T 44 21 **121 49**
2002–03 Stoke C 30 4
2003–04 Stoke C 13 2
2004–05 Stoke C 32 1 **75 7**
2005–06 Tranmere R 45 16
2006–07 Tranmere R 44 17
2007–08 Tranmere R 40 11 **129 44**

HENRY, Paul (M) 2 0
H: 5 8 W: 11 06 b.Liverpool 28-1-88
Source: Scholar.
2005–06 Tranmere R 0 0
2006–07 Tranmere R 0 0
2007–08 Tranmere R 2 0 **2 0**

HOLMES, Daniel (D) 0 0
H: 5 10 W: 12 00 b.Wirral 6-1-89
Source: Scholar.
2007–08 Tranmere R 0 0

JENNINGS, Steven (M) 107 3
H: 5 7 W: 11 11 b.Liverpool 28-10-84
Source: Scholar.
2002–03 Tranmere R 0 0
2003–04 Tranmere R 4 0
2004–05 Tranmere R 11 0
2005–06 Tranmere R 38 1
2006–07 Tranmere R 2 0
2006–07 *Hereford U* 11 0 **11 0**
2007–08 Tranmere R 41 2 **96 3**

JOHNSTON, Michael (D) 0 0
H: 5 9 W: 12 03 b.Birkenhead 16-12-87
Source: Scholar.
2005–06 Tranmere R 0 0
2006–07 Tranmere R 0 0
2007–08 Tranmere R 0 0

JONES, Mike (M) 23 2
H: 5 11 W: 12 04 b.Birkenhead 15-8-87
Source: Scholar.
2005–06 Tranmere R 1 0
2006–07 Tranmere R 0 0
2006–07 *Shrewsbury T* 13 1 **13 1**
2007–08 Tranmere R 9 1 **10 1**

KAY, Antony (D) 212 17
H: 5 11 W: 11 08 b.Barnsley 21-10-82
Source: Trainee. *Honours:* England Youth.
1999–2000 Barnsley 0 0
2000–01 Barnsley 7 0
2001–02 Barnsley 1 0
2002–03 Barnsley 16 0
2003–04 Barnsley 43 3
2004–05 Barnsley 39 6
2005–06 Barnsley 36 1
2006–07 Barnsley 32 1 **174 11**
2007–08 Tranmere R 38 6 **38 6**

McLAREN, Paul (M) 420 21
H: 6 0 W: 13 04 b.High Wycombe 17-11-76
Source: Trainee.
1993–94 Luton T 1 0
1994–95 Luton T 0 0
1995–96 Luton T 12 1
1996–97 Luton T 24 0
1997–98 Luton T 43 0
1998–99 Luton T 23 0
1999–2000 Luton T 29 1
2000–01 Luton T 35 2 **167 4**
2001–02 Sheffield W 35 2
2002–03 Sheffield W 36 4
2003–04 Sheffield W 25 2 **96 8**
2004–05 Rotherham U 33 1
2005–06 Rotherham U 39 3 **72 4**
2006–07 Tranmere R 42 1
2007–08 Tranmere R 43 4 **85 5**

MOORE, Ian (F) 465 81
H: 5 11 W: 12 00 b.Birkenhead 26-8-76
Source: Trainee. *Honours:* England Youth, Under-21.
1994–95 Tranmere R 1 0
1995–96 Tranmere R 36 9
1996–97 Tranmere R 21 3
1996–97 *Bradford C* 6 0 **6 0**
1996–97 Nottingham F 5 0
1997–98 Nottingham F 10 1 **15 1**
1997–98 *West Ham U* 1 0 **1 0**
1998–99 Stockport Co 38 3
1999–2000 Stockport Co 38 10
2000–01 Stockport Co 17 7 **93 20**
2000–01 Burnley 27 5
2001–02 Burnley 46 11
2002–03 Burnley 44 8
2003–04 Burnley 40 9
2004–05 Burnley 35 4 **192 37**
2004–05 Leeds U 6 0
2005–06 Leeds U 20 0
2006–07 Leeds U 33 2 **59 2**
2007–08 Hartlepool U 24 6 **24 6**
2007–08 Tranmere R 17 3 **75 15**

MULLIN, John (M) 373 31
H: 6 0 W: 11 10 b.Bury 11-8-75
Source: School.
1992–93 Burnley 0 0
1993–94 Burnley 6 1
1994–95 Burnley 12 1
1995–96 Sunderland 10 1
1996–97 Sunderland 10 1
1997–98 Sunderland 6 0
1997–98 *Preston NE* 7 0 **7 0**
1997–98 *Burnley* 6 0
1998–99 Sunderland 9 2 **35 4**
1999–2000 Burnley 37 5
2000–01 Burnley 36 3
2001–02 Burnley 4 0 **101 10**
2001–02 Rotherham U 34 2
2002–03 Rotherham U 34 3
2003–04 Rotherham U 38 4
2004–05 Rotherham U 31 1
2005–06 Rotherham U 43 2 **180 12**
2006–07 Tranmere R 40 5
2007–08 Tranmere R 10 0 **50 5**

SHUKER, Chris (M) 216 29
H: 5 5 W: 9 03 b.Liverpool 9-5-82
Source: Scholarship.
1999–2000 Manchester C 0 0
2000–01 Manchester C 0 0
2000–01 *Macclesfield T* 9 1 **9 1**
2001–02 Manchester C 2 0
2002–03 Manchester C 3 0
2002–03 *Walsall* 5 0 **5 0**
2003–04 Manchester C 0 0 **5 0**
2003–04 *Rochdale* 14 1 **14 1**
2003–04 *Hartlepool U* 14 1 **14 1**
2003–04 Barnsley 9 0
2004–05 Barnsley 45 7
2005–06 Barnsley 46 10 **100 17**
2006–07 Tranmere R 46 6
2007–08 Tranmere R 23 3 **69 9**

STOCKDALE, Robbie (D) 228 3
H: 6 0 W: 11 03 b.Middlesbrough 30-11-79
Source: Trainee. *Honours:* England Under-21. Scotland B, 5 full caps.
1997–98 Middlesbrough 1 0
1998–99 Middlesbrough 19 0
1999–2000 Middlesbrough 11 1
2000–01 Middlesbrough 0 0
2000–01 *Sheffield W* 6 0 **6 0**
2001–02 Middlesbrough 28 1
2002–03 Middlesbrough 14 0
2003–04 Middlesbrough 2 0 **75 2**
2003–04 *West Ham U* 7 0 **7 0**
2003–04 *Rotherham U* 16 1
2004–05 Rotherham U 27 0 **43 1**
2004–05 Hull C 14 0
2005–06 Hull C 0 0 **14 0**
2005–06 *Darlington* 3 0 **3 0**
2006–07 Tranmere R 36 0
2007–08 Tranmere R 44 0 **80 0**

TAYLOR, Andy (D) 48 2
H: 5 11 W: 11 07 b.Blackburn 14-3-86
Source: Scholar. *Honours:* England Youth, Under-20, Under-21.
2004–05 Blackburn R 0 0
2005–06 Blackburn R 0 0
2005–06 *QPR* 3 0 **3 0**
2005–06 *Blackpool* 3 0 **3 0**
2006–07 Blackburn R 0 0
2006–07 *Crewe Alex* 4 0 **4 0**
2006–07 *Huddersfield T* 8 0 **8 0**
2007–08 Blackburn R 0 0
2007–08 Tranmere R 30 2 **30 2**

ZOLA, Calvin (F) 121 21
H: 6 3 W: 14 06 b.Kinshasa 31-12-84
Source: Scholar.
2001–02 Newcastle U 0 0
2002–03 Newcastle U 0 0
2003–04 Newcastle U 0 0
2003–04 *Oldham Ath* 25 5 **25 5**
2004–05 Tranmere R 15 2
2005–06 Tranmere R 22 4
2006–07 Tranmere R 29 5
2007–08 Tranmere R 30 5 **96 16**

WALSALL (84)

BOERTIEN, Paul (D) 162 3
H: 5 10 W: 11 02 b.Haltwhistle 21-1-79
Source: Trainee.
1996–97 Carlisle U 0 0
1997–98 Carlisle U 9 0
1998–99 Carlisle U 8 1 **17 1**
1998–99 Derby Co 1 0
1999–2000 Derby Co 2 0
1999–2000 *Crewe Alex* 2 0 **2 0**
2000–01 Derby Co 8 1
2001–02 Derby Co 32 0
2002–03 Derby Co 42 1
2003–04 Derby Co 18 0
2003–04 *Notts Co* 5 0 **5 0**
2004–05 Derby Co 0 0
2005–06 Derby Co 0 0
2006–07 Derby Co 11 0 **114 2**
2006–07 *Chesterfield* 4 0 **4 0**
2007–08 Walsall 20 0 **20 0**

BOSSU, Bertrand (G) 18 0
H: 6 7 W: 14 00 b.Calais 14-10-80
1999–2000 Barnet 0 0
2000–01 Barnet 0 0
2001–02 Barnet 0 0
2002–03 Barnet 0 0
From Hayes.
2003–04 Gillingham 4 0
2004–05 Gillingham 2 0 **6 0**
2004–05 *Torquay U* 2 0 **2 0**
2004–05 *Oldham Ath* 0 0
2005–06 Darlington 9 0 **9 0**
2006–07 Walsall 1 0
2007–08 Walsall 0 0 **1 0**

BRADLEY, Mark (D) 40 3
H: 6 0 W: 11 05 b.Dudley 14-1-88
Source: Scholar. *Honours:* Wales Youth, Under-21.
2004–05 Walsall 1 0
2005–06 Walsall 3 0
2006–07 Walsall 1 0
2007–08 Walsall 35 3 **40 3**

BRITTAIN, Martin (M) 18 0
H: 5 8 W: 10 07 b.Newcastle 29-12-84
Source: Trainee.
2003–04 Newcastle U 1 0
2004–05 Newcastle U 0 0
2005–06 Newcastle U 0 0 **1 0**
2006–07 Ipswich T 0 0
2006–07 *Yeovil T* 15 0 **15 0**
2007–08 Carlisle U 1 0 **1 0**
2007–08 Walsall 1 0 **1 0**

CARNEIRO, Carlos (F) 63 12
H: 6 1 W: 12 04 b.Pacos de Ferreira 8-1-75
2004–05 Gil Vicente 18 7

2005–06 Gil Vicente 31 4 **49 11**
2006–07 Panionios 11 1 **11 1**
2007–08 Walsall 3 0 **3 0**

CRADDOCK, Josh (M) 1 0
H: 5 11 W: 10 08 b.Wolverhampton 5-3-91
Source: Scholar.
2007–08 Walsall 1 0 **1 0**

DAVIES, Charlton (M) 0 0
b.Coleshill 24-1-89
Source: Scholar.
2007–08 Walsall 0 0

DEENEY, Troy (F) 36 1
H: 5 11 W: 12 00 b.Chelmsley 29-6-88
Source: Chelmsley T.
2006–07 Walsall 1 0
2007–08 Walsall 35 1 **36 1**

DEMONTAGNAC, Ishmel (F) 73 6
H: 5 10 W: 11 05 b.London 15-6-88
Source: Charlton Ath Scholar. *Honours:* England Youth.
2005–06 Walsall 24 2
2006–07 Walsall 19 1
2007–08 Walsall 30 3 **73 6**

DOBSON, Michael (D) 241 7
H: 6 0 W: 12 04 b.Isleworth 9-4-81
Source: Trainee.
1999–2000 Brentford 0 0
2000–01 Brentford 26 0
2001–02 Brentford 39 0
2002–03 Brentford 46 1
2003–04 Brentford 42 1
2004–05 Brentford 18 1
2005–06 Brentford 6 0 **177 3**
2005–06 *Reading* 1 0 **1 0**
2006–07 Walsall 39 3
2007–08 Walsall 24 1 **63 4**

GERRARD, Anthony (D) 121 4
H: 6 2 W: 13 07 b.Liverpool 6-2-86
Source: Scholar. *Honours:* Eire Youth.
2004–05 Everton 0 0
2004–05 *Walsall* 8 0
2005–06 Walsall 34 0
2006–07 Walsall 35 1
2007–08 Walsall 44 3 **121 4**

GILMARTIN, Rene (G) 2 0
H: 6 5 W: 13 06 b.Dublin 31-5-87
Source: St Patrick's BC. *Honours:* Eire Youth, Under-21.
2005–06 Walsall 2 0
2006–07 Walsall 0 0
2007–08 Walsall 0 0 **2 0**

HANNA, Christopher (F) 0 0
Source: Scholar.
2007–08 Walsall 0 0

HARRIS, Harry (F) 0 0
b.Aldridge 9-12-88
Source: Scholar.
2007–08 Walsall 0 0

INCE, Clayton (G) 215 0
H: 6 3 W: 13 03 b.Trinidad 13-7-72
Source: Defence Force. *Honours:* Trinidad & Tobago 63 full caps.
1999–2000 Crewe Alex 1 0
2000–01 Crewe Alex 1 0
2001–02 Crewe Alex 19 0
2002–03 Crewe Alex 43 0
2003–04 Crewe Alex 36 0
2004–05 Crewe Alex 23 0 **123 0**
2005–06 Coventry C 1 0 **1 0**
2006–07 Walsall 45 0
2007–08 Walsall 46 0 **91 0**

McDERMOTT, David (M) 14 0
H: 5 5 W: 10 00 b.Stourbridge 6-2-88
Source: Scholar.
2004–05 Walsall 0 0
2005–06 Walsall 1 0
2006–07 Walsall 0 0
2007–08 Walsall 13 0 **14 0**

MOONEY, Tommy (F) 638 185
H: 5 10 W: 13 05 b.Billingham 11-8-71
Source: Trainee.
1989–90 Aston Villa 0 0
1990–91 Scarborough 27 13
1991–92 Scarborough 40 8
1992–93 Scarborough 40 9 **107 30**
1993–94 Southend U 14 5 **14 5**
1993–94 *Watford* 10 2
1994–95 Watford 29 3
1995–96 Watford 42 6
1996–97 Watford 37 13
1997–98 Watford 45 6
1998–99 Watford 36 9
1999–2000 Watford 12 2
2000–01 Watford 39 19 **250 60**
2001–02 Birmingham C 33 13
2002–03 Birmingham C 1 0 **34 13**
2002–03 *Stoke C* 12 3 **12 3**
2002–03 *Sheffield U* 3 0 **3 0**
2002–03 *Derby Co* 8 0 **8 0**
2003–04 Swindon T 45 19 **45 19**
2004–05 Oxford U 42 15 **42 15**
2005–06 Wycombe W 45 17
2006–07 Wycombe W 42 12 **87 29**
2007–08 Walsall 36 11 **36 11**

MOORE, Stefan (F) 93 7
H: 5 10 W: 10 12 b.Birmingham 28-9-83
Source: Scholar. *Honours:* England Youth.
2000–01 Aston Villa 0 0
2001–02 Aston Villa 0 0
2001–02 *Chesterfield* 2 0 **2 0**
2002–03 Aston Villa 13 1
2003–04 Aston Villa 8 1
2004–05 Aston Villa 1 0 **22 2**
2004–05 *Millwall* 6 0 **6 0**
2004–05 *Leicester C* 7 0 **7 0**
2005–06 QPR 25 2
2006–07 QPR 3 0
2006–07 *Port Vale* 12 1 **12 1**
2007–08 QPR 11 1 **39 3**
2007–08 Walsall 5 1 **5 1**

N'DOUR, Alassane (D) 11 1
H: 6 1 W: 12 05 b.Dakar 12-12-81
Honours: Senegal full caps.
2003–04 WBA 2 0
2004–05 WBA 0 0
2005–06 WBA 0 0
2006–07 WBA 0 0
2007–08 WBA 0 0 **2 0**
2007–08 Walsall 9 1 **9 1**

NICHOLLS, Alex (F) 27 2
H: 5 10 W: 11 00 b.Stourbridge 9-12-87
Source: Scholar.
2005–06 Walsall 8 0
2006–07 Walsall 0 0
2007–08 Walsall 19 2 **27 2**

PICKEN, Allan (D) 2 0
H: 6 2 W: 13 12 b.Sydney 17-1-81
Source: Newcastle U Jets.
2006–07 Walsall 2 0
2007–08 Walsall 0 0 **2 0**

ROPER, Ian (D) 325 7
H: 6 3 W: 14 00 b.Nuneaton 20-6-77
Source: Trainee.
1994–95 Walsall 0 0
1995–96 Walsall 5 0
1996–97 Walsall 11 0
1997–98 Walsall 21 0
1998–99 Walsall 32 1
1999–2000 Walsall 34 1
2000–01 Walsall 25 0
2001–02 Walsall 27 0
2002–03 Walsall 40 0
2003–04 Walsall 33 0
2004–05 Walsall 26 0
2005–06 Walsall 25 0
2006–07 Walsall 27 4
2007–08 Walsall 19 1 **325 7**

SANSARA, Netan (D) 0 0
H: 6 0 W: 12 00 b.Walsall 3-8-89
Source: Scholar. *Honours:* England Youth.
2006–07 Walsall 0 0
2007–08 Walsall 0 0

SMITH, Emmanuel (D) 7 0
H: 6 2 W: 12 03 b.Birmingham 8-11-87
Source: Scholar.
2005–06 Walsall 0 0
2006–07 Walsall 3 0
2007–08 Walsall 4 0 **7 0**

SONKO, Edrissa (M) 154 26
H: 5 10 W: 11 05 b.Essau 23-3-80
Honours: Gambia 14 full caps, 7 goals.
2000–01 Roda JC 16 2
2001–02 Roda JC 9 2
2002–03 Roda JC 22 8
2003–04 Roda JC 18 2
2004–05 Roda JC 25 1
2005–06 Roda JC 18 5 **108 20**
2006–07 Xanthi 9 1 **9 1**
2007–08 Walsall 37 5 **37 5**

TAUNDRY, Richard (D) 21 0
H: 5 9 W: 12 10 b.Walsall 15-2-89
Source: Scholar.
2007–08 Walsall 21 0 **21 0**

WESTON, Rhys (D) 242 2
H: 6 1 W: 12 12 b.Kingston 27-10-80
Source: Trainee. *Honours:* Wales Schools, Youth, Under-21, 7 full caps.
1999–2000 Arsenal 1 0
2000–01 Arsenal 0 0 **1 0**
2000–01 Cardiff C 28 0
2001–02 Cardiff C 37 0
2002–03 Cardiff C 38 2
2003–04 Cardiff C 24 0
2004–05 Cardiff C 25 0
2005–06 Cardiff C 30 0 **182 2**
2006–07 Port Vale 15 0 **15 0**
2007–08 Walsall 44 0 **44 0**

WRACK, Darren (M) 379 48
H: 5 9 W: 12 02 b.Cleethorpes 5-5-76
Source: Trainee.
1994–95 Derby Co 16 1
1995–96 Derby Co 10 0 **26 1**
1996–97 Grimsby T 12 1
1996–97 *Shrewsbury T* 4 0 **4 0**
1997–98 Grimsby T 1 0 **13 1**
1998–99 Walsall 46 13
1999–2000 Walsall 44 4
2000–01 Walsall 28 4
2001–02 Walsall 43 4
2002–03 Walsall 43 6
2003–04 Walsall 27 6
2004–05 Walsall 43 7
2005–06 Walsall 7 0
2006–07 Walsall 18 1
2007–08 Walsall 37 1 **336 46**

WATFORD (85)

AINSWORTH, Lionel (F) 39 4
H: 5 9 W: 9 10 b.Nottingham 1-10-87
Source: Scholar. *Honours:* England Youth.
2005–06 Derby Co 2 0
2006–07 Derby Co 0 0 **2 0**
2006–07 *Bournemouth* 7 0 **7 0**
2006–07 *Wycombe W* 7 0 **7 0**
2007–08 Hereford U 15 4 **15 4**
2007–08 Watford 8 0 **8 0**

ALOI, Santiago (M) 0 0
H: 5 9 W: 11 00 b.Argentina 26-3-87
Source: River Plate.
2007–08 Watford 0 0

ASHIKODI, Moses (M) 30 2
H: 6 0 W: 11 09 b.Lagos 27-6-87
Honours: FA Schools, England Youth.
2002–03 Millwall 5 0
2003–04 Millwall 0 0 **5 0**
2004–05 West Ham U 0 0
2005–06 West Ham U 0 0
2005–06 *Gillingham* 4 0 **4 0**
2005–06 Rangers 1 0
2006–07 Rangers 0 0 **1 0**
2006–07 Watford 2 0
2006–07 *Bradford C* 8 2 **8 2**
2007–08 Watford 0 0 **2 0**
2007–08 *Swindon T* 10 0 **10 0**

AVINEL, Cedric (D) 2 0
H: 6 2 W: 13 03 b.Paris 11-9-86
2006–07 Creteil 1 0 **1 0**
2006–07 Watford 1 0
2007–08 Watford 0 0 **1 0**

BANGURA, Alhassan (M) 60 1
H: 5 11 W: 10 07 b.Freetown 24-1-88
Source: Scholar.
2004–05 Watford 2 0
2005–06 Watford 35 1
2006–07 Watford 16 0
2007–08 Watford 7 0 **60 1**

BROMBY, Leigh (D) **240 10**
H: 5 11 W: 11 06 b.Dewsbury 2-6-80
Honours: England Schools.

1998–99	Sheffield W	0	0		
1999–2000	Sheffield W	0	0		
1999–2000	*Mansfield T*	10	1	**10**	**1**
2000–01	Sheffield W	18	0		
2001–02	Sheffield W	26	1		
2002–03	Sheffield W	27	0		
2002–03	*Norwich C*	5	0	**5**	**0**
2003–04	Sheffield W	29	1	**100**	**2**
2004–05	Sheffield U	46	5		
2005–06	Sheffield U	35	1		
2006–07	Sheffield U	17	0		
2007–08	Sheffield U	11	0	**109**	**6**
2007–08	Watford	16	1	**16**	**1**

CAMPANA, Alex (M) **0 0**
H: 5 11 W: 12 01 b.Harrow 11-10-88
Source: Scholar.

2005–06	Watford	0	0		
2006–07	Watford	0	0		
2007–08	Watford	0	0		

CAVALLI, Johann (M) **119 13**
H: 5 6 W: 10 03 b.Ajaccio 12-9-81
Source: Nantes. *Honours:* France Youth.

2001–02	Lorient	3	0		
2002–03	Lorient	17	0		
2003–04	Creteil	30	6		
2003–04	Lorient	1	0	**21**	**0**
2004–05	Mallorca	0	0		
2004–05	Creteil	14	5	**44**	**11**
2005–06	Istres	35	1		
2006–07	Istres	16	1	**51**	**2**
2006–07	Watford	3	0		
2007–08	Watford	0	0	**3**	**0**

DEMERIT, Jay (D) **123 8**
H: 6 2 W: 12 13 b.Green Bay 4-12-79
Source: Chicago Fire, Univ of Illinois, Northwood. *Honours:* USA 7 full caps.

2004–05	Watford	24	3		
2005–06	Watford	32	2		
2006–07	Watford	32	2		
2007–08	Watford	35	1	**123**	**8**

DIAGOURAGA, Toumani (M) **57 2**
H: 6 2 W: 11 05 b.Corbeil-Essones 10-6-87
Source: Scholar.

2004–05	Watford	0	0		
2005–06	Watford	1	0		
2005–06	*Swindon T*	8	0	**8**	**0**
2006–07	Watford	0	0		
2006–07	*Rotherham U*	7	0	**7**	**0**
2007–08	Watford	0	0	**1**	**0**
2007–08	*Hereford U*	41	2	**41**	**2**

DOYLEY, Lloyd (D) **181 0**
H: 5 10 W: 12 13 b.Whitechapel 1-12-82
Source: Scholar.

2000–01	Watford	0	0		
2001–02	Watford	20	0		
2002–03	Watford	22	0		
2003–04	Watford	9	0		
2004–05	Watford	29	0		
2005–06	Watford	44	0		
2006–07	Watford	21	0		
2007–08	Watford	36	0	**181**	**0**

ELLINGTON, Nathan (F) **352 112**
H: 5 10 W: 13 01 b.Bradford 2-7-81
Source: Walton & Hersham.

1998–99	Bristol R	10	1		
1999–2000	Bristol R	37	4		
2000–01	Bristol R	42	15		
2001–02	Bristol R	27	15	**116**	**35**
2001–02	Wigan Ath	3	2		
2002–03	Wigan Ath	42	15		
2003–04	Wigan Ath	44	18		
2004–05	Wigan Ath	45	24	**134**	**59**
2005–06	WBA	31	5		
2006–07	WBA	34	9		
2007–08	WBA	3	0	**68**	**14**
2007–08	Watford	34	4	**34**	**4**

EUSTACE, John (M) **193 13**
H: 5 11 W: 11 12 b.Solihull 3-11-79
Source: Trainee.

1996–97	Coventry C	0	0		
1997–98	Coventry C	0	0		
1998–99	Coventry C	0	0		
1998–99	Dundee U	11	1	**11**	**1**
1999–2000	Coventry C	16	1		
2000–01	Coventry C	32	2		
2001–02	Coventry C	6	0		
2002–03	Coventry C	32	4	**86**	**7**
2002–03	*Middlesbrough*	1	0	**1**	**0**
2003–04	Stoke C	26	5		
2004–05	Stoke C	7	0		
2005–06	Stoke C	0	0		
2006–07	Stoke C	15	0		
2006–07	*Hereford U*	8	0	**8**	**0**
2007–08	Stoke C	26	0	**74**	**5**
2007–08	Watford	13	0	**13**	**0**

FRANCIS, Damien (M) **233 35**
H: 6 0 W: 11 10 b.Wandsworth 27-2-79
Source: Trainee. *Honours:* Jamaica 1 full cap.

1996–97	Wimbledon	0	0		
1997–98	Wimbledon	2	0		
1998–99	Wimbledon	0	0		
1999–2000	Wimbledon	9	0		
2000–01	Wimbledon	29	8		
2001–02	Wimbledon	23	1		
2002–03	Wimbledon	34	6	**97**	**15**
2003–04	Norwich C	41	7		
2004–05	Norwich C	32	7	**73**	**14**
2005–06	Wigan Ath	20	1	**20**	**1**
2006–07	Watford	32	3		
2007–08	Watford	11	2	**43**	**5**

HENDERSON, Darius (F) **228 56**
H: 6 3 W: 14 03 b.Sutton 7-9-81
Source: Trainee.

1999–2000	Reading	6	0		
2000–01	Reading	4	0		
2001–02	Reading	38	7		
2002–03	Reading	22	4		
2003–04	Reading	1	0	**71**	**11**
2003–04	*Brighton & HA*	10	2	**10**	**2**
2003–04	Gillingham	4	0		
2004–05	Gillingham	32	9	**36**	**9**
2004–05	*Swindon T*	6	5	**6**	**5**
2005–06	Watford	30	14		
2006–07	Watford	35	3		
2007–08	Watford	40	12	**105**	**29**

HOSKINS, Will (F) **95 25**
H: 5 11 W: 11 02 b.Nottingham 6-5-86
Source: Scholar. *Honours:* England Youth, Under-20.

2003–04	Rotherham U	4	2		
2004–05	Rotherham U	22	2		
2005–06	Rotherham U	23	4		
2006–07	Rotherham U	24	15	**73**	**23**
2006–07	Watford	9	0		
2007–08	Watford	1	0	**10**	**0**
2007–08	*Millwall*	10	2	**10**	**2**
2007–08	*Nottingham F*	2	0	**2**	**0**

JACKSON, Matt (D) **513 14**
H: 6 1 W: 14 00 b.Leeds 19-10-71
Source: School. *Honours:* England Schools, Under-21.

1990–91	Luton T	0	0		
1990–91	*Preston NE*	4	0	**4**	**0**
1991–92	Luton T	9	0	**9**	**0**
1991–92	Everton	30	1		
1992–93	Everton	27	3		
1993–94	Everton	38	0		
1994–95	Everton	29	0		
1995–96	Everton	14	0		
1995–96	*Charlton Ath*	8	0	**8**	**0**
1996–97	Everton	0	0	**138**	**4**
1996–97	*QPR*	7	0	**7**	**0**
1996–97	*Birmingham C*	10	0	**10**	**0**
1996–97	Norwich C	19	2		
1997–98	Norwich C	41	3		
1998–99	Norwich C	37	1		
1999–2000	Norwich C	38	0		
2000–01	Norwich C	26	0		
2001–02	Norwich C	0	0	**161**	**6**
2001–02	Wigan Ath	26	0		
2002–03	Wigan Ath	45	1		
2003–04	Wigan Ath	24	1		
2004–05	Wigan Ath	36	1		
2005–06	Wigan Ath	16	0		
2006–07	Wigan Ath	20	1		
2007–08	Wigan Ath	0	0	**167**	**4**
2007–08	*Blackpool*	3	0	**3**	**0**
2007–08	Watford	6	0	**6**	**0**

KABBA, Steven (F) **129 26**
H: 5 10 W: 11 03 b.Lambeth 7-3-81
Source: Trainee.

1999–2000	Crystal Palace	1	0		
2000–01	Crystal Palace	1	0		
2001–02	Crystal Palace	4	0		
2001–02	*Luton T*	3	0	**3**	**0**
2002–03	Crystal Palace	4	1	**10**	**1**
2002–03	*Grimsby T*	13	6	**13**	**6**
2002–03	Sheffield U	25	7		
2003–04	Sheffield U	1	0		
2004–05	Sheffield U	11	2		
2005–06	Sheffield U	34	9		
2006–07	Sheffield U	7	0	**78**	**18**
2006–07	Watford	11	0		
2007–08	Watford	14	1	**25**	**1**

LEE, Richard (G) **82 0**
H: 6 0 W: 12 06 b.Oxford 5-10-82
Source: Scholar. *Honours:* England Under-20.

2000–01	Watford	0	0		
2001–02	Watford	0	0		
2002–03	Watford	4	0		
2003–04	Watford	0	0		
2004–05	Watford	33	0		
2005–06	Watford	0	0		
2005–06	*Blackburn R*	0	0		
2006–07	Watford	10	0		
2007–08	Watford	35	0	**82**	**0**

LOACH, Scott (G) **22 0**
H: 6 1 W: 13 01 b.Nottingham 27-5-88
Source: Lincoln C.

2006–07	Watford	0	0		
2007–08	Watford	0	0		
2007–08	*Morecambe*	2	0	**2**	**0**
2007–08	*Bradford C*	20	0	**20**	**0**

MACKAY, Malky (D) **389 30**
H: 6 2 W: 14 07 b.Bellshill 19-2-72
Source: Queen's Park Youth. *Honours:* Scotland 5 full caps.

1990–91	Queen's Park	10	0		
1991–92	Queen's Park	27	3		
1992–93	Queen's Park	33	3	**70**	**6**
1993–94	Celtic	0	0		
1994–95	Celtic	1	0		
1995–96	Celtic	11	1		
1996–97	Celtic	20	1		
1997–98	Celtic	4	1		
1998–99	Celtic	1	1	**37**	**4**
1998–99	Norwich C	27	1		
1999–2000	Norwich C	21	0		
2000–01	Norwich C	38	1		
2001–02	Norwich C	44	3		
2002–03	Norwich C	37	6		
2003–04	Norwich C	45	4		
2004–05	Norwich C	0	0	**212**	**15**
2004–05	West Ham U	18	2		
2005–06	West Ham U	0	0	**18**	**2**
2005–06	Watford	38	3		
2006–07	Watford	14	0		
2007–08	Watford	0	0	**52**	**3**

MARIAPPA, Adrian (D) **47 0**
H: 5 10 W: 11 12 b.Harrow 3-10-86
Source: Scholar.

2005–06	Watford	3	0		
2006–07	Watford	19	0		
2007–08	Watford	25	0	**47**	**0**

McANUFF, Jobi (M) **266 31**
H: 5 11 W: 11 05 b.Edmonton 9-11-81
Source: Scholar. *Honours:* Jamaica 1 full cap.

2000–01	Wimbledon	0	0		
2001–02	Wimbledon	38	4		
2002–03	Wimbledon	31	4		
2003–04	Wimbledon	27	5	**96**	**13**
2003–04	West Ham U	12	1		
2004–05	West Ham U	1	0	**13**	**1**
2004–05	Cardiff C	43	2	**43**	**2**
2005–06	Crystal Palace	41	8		
2006–07	Crystal Palace	34	5	**75**	**13**
2007–08	Watford	39	2	**39**	**2**

O'TOOLE, John (M) **35 3**
H: 6 2 W: 13 07 b.Harrow 30-9-88
Honours: Eire Under-21.

2007–08	Watford	35	3	**35**	**3**

OSBORNE, Junior (D) **2 0**
H: 5 11 W: 11 13 b.Watford 12-2-88
Source: Scholar.

2004–05	Watford	1	0		
2005–06	Watford	1	0		
2006–07	Watford	0	0		
2007–08	Watford	0	0	**2**	**0**

PARKES, Jordan (D) **11 0**
H: 6 0 W: 12 00 b.Hemel Hempstead 26-7-89
Source: Scholar. *Honours:* England Youth.

2006–07	Watford	0	0		
2007–08	Watford	0	0		
2007–08	*Brentford*	1	0	**1**	**0**
2007–08	*Barnet*	10	0	**10**	**0**

POOM, Mart (G) **262 1**
H: 6 4 W: 14 02 b.Tallinn 3-2-72
Honours: Estonia 117 full caps.

1992–93	Flora Tallinn	11	0		
1993–94	Flora Tallinn	11	0		
1994–95	Portsmouth	0	0		
1995–96	Portsmouth	4	0		
1995–96	Flora Tallinn	7	0		
1996–97	Portsmouth	0	0	**4**	**0**
1996–97	Flora Tallinn	12	0	**41**	**0**
1996–97	Derby Co	4	0		
1997–98	Derby Co	36	0		
1998–99	Derby Co	17	0		
1999–2000	Derby Co	28	0		
2000–01	Derby Co	33	0		
2001–02	Derby Co	15	0		
2002–03	Derby Co	13	0	**146**	**0**
2002–03	Sunderland	4	0		
2003–04	Sunderland	43	1		
2004–05	Sunderland	11	0		
2005–06	Sunderland	0	0	**58**	**1**
2005–06	Arsenal	0	0		
2006–07	Arsenal	1	0	**1**	**0**
2007–08	Watford	12	0	**12**	**0**

PRISKIN, Tamas (F) **103 29**
H: 6 2 W: 13 03 b.Komarno 27-9-86
Honours: Hungary Under-21, 17 full caps, 6 goals.

2002–03	Gyor	3	0		
2003–04	Gyor	17	5		
2004–05	Gyor	23	8		
2005–06	Gyor	25	11	**68**	**24**
2006–07	Watford	16	2		
2007–08	Watford	14	1	**30**	**3**
2007–08	*Preston NE*	5	2	**5**	**2**

RINALDI, Douglas (D) **7 1**
H: 6 0 W: 12 03 b.Erval Seco 10-2-84
Source: Veranopolis.

2006–07	Watford	7	1		
2007–08	Watford	0	0	**7**	**1**

ROBINSON, Theo (M) **45 13**
H: 5 9 W: 10 03 b.Birmingham 22-1-89
Source: Scholar.

2005–06	Watford	1	0		
2006–07	Watford	1	0		
2007–08	Watford	0	0	**2**	**0**
2007–08	*Hereford U*	43	13	**43**	**13**

SADLER, Matthew (D) **73 0**
H: 5 11 W: 11 08 b.Birmingham 26-2-85
Source: Scholar. *Honours:* England Youth.

2001–02	Birmingham C	0	0		
2002–03	Birmingham C	2	0		
2003–04	Birmingham C	0	0		
2003–04	*Northampton T*	7	0	**7**	**0**
2004–05	Birmingham C	0	0		
2005–06	Birmingham C	8	0		
2006–07	Birmingham C	36	0		
2007–08	Birmingham C	5	0	**51**	**0**
2007–08	Watford	15	0	**15**	**0**

SHITTU, Dan (D) **255 27**
H: 6 2 W: 16 03 b.Lagos 2-9-80
Honours: Nigeria 12 full caps.

1999–2000	Charlton Ath	0	0		
2000–01	Charlton Ath	0	0		
2000–01	*Blackpool*	17	2	**17**	**2**
2001–02	Charlton Ath	0	0		
2001–02	QPR	27	2		
2002–03	QPR	43	7		
2003–04	QPR	20	0		
2004–05	QPR	34	4		
2005–06	QPR	45	4	**169**	**17**
2006–07	Watford	30	1		
2007–08	Watford	39	7	**69**	**8**

SMITH, Tommy (F) **350 65**
H: 5 8 W: 11 04 b.Hemel Hempstead 22-5-80
Source: Trainee. *Honours:* England Youth, Under-21.

1997–98	Watford	1	0		
1998–99	Watford	8	2		
1999–2000	Watford	22	2		
2000–01	Watford	43	11		
2001–02	Watford	40	11		
2002–03	Watford	35	7		
2003–04	Watford	0	0		
2003–04	Sunderland	35	4	**35**	**4**
2004–05	Derby Co	42	11		
2005–06	Derby Co	43	8		
2006–07	Derby Co	5	1	**90**	**20**
2006–07	Watford	32	1		
2007–08	Watford	44	7	**225**	**41**

STEWART, Jordan (D) **219 8**
H: 6 0 W: 12 09 b.Birmingham 3-3-82
Source: Trainee. *Honours:* England Youth, Under-21.

1999–2000	Leicester C	1	0		
1999–2000	*Bristol R*	4	0	**4**	**0**
2000–01	Leicester C	0	0		
2001–02	Leicester C	12	0		
2002–03	Leicester C	37	4		
2003–04	Leicester C	25	1		
2004–05	Leicester C	35	1	**110**	**6**
2005–06	Watford	35	0		
2006–07	Watford	31	0		
2007–08	Watford	39	2	**105**	**2**

WILLIAMS, Gareth (M) **223 12**
H: 6 1 W: 12 03 b.Glasgow 16-12-81
Source: Trainee. *Honours:* Scotland Youth, B, Under-21, 5 full caps.

1998–99	Nottingham F	0	0		
1999–2000	Nottingham F	2	0		
2000–01	Nottingham F	17	0		
2001–02	Nottingham F	44	0		
2002–03	Nottingham F	40	3		
2003–04	Nottingham F	39	6	**142**	**9**
2004–05	Leicester C	33	1		
2005–06	Leicester C	31	1		
2006–07	Leicester C	14	1	**78**	**3**
2006–07	Watford	3	0		
2007–08	Watford	0	0	**3**	**0**

WILLIAMSON, Lee (M) **274 14**
H: 5 10 W: 10 04 b.Derby 7-6-82
Source: Trainee.

1999–2000	Mansfield T	4	0		
2000–01	Mansfield T	15	0		
2001–02	Mansfield T	46	3		
2002–03	Mansfield T	40	0		
2003–04	Mansfield T	35	0		
2004–05	Mansfield T	4	0	**144**	**3**
2004–05	Northampton T	37	0	**37**	**0**
2005–06	Rotherham U	37	4		
2006–07	Rotherham U	19	5	**56**	**9**
2006–07	Watford	5	0		
2007–08	Watford	32	2	**37**	**2**

WBA (86)

ALBRECHTSEN, Martin (D) **279 7**
H: 6 1 W: 12 13 b.Copenhagen 31-3-80
Honours: Denmark Youth, Under-21, 4 full caps.

1998–99	Aalborg	9	1		
1999–2000	Aalborg	31	1		
2000–01	Aalborg	30	0		
2001–02	Aalborg	19	1	**89**	**3**
2001–02	FC Copenhagen	14	0		
2002–03	FC Copenhagen	27	0		
2003–04	FC Copenhagen	31	0	**72**	**0**
2004–05	WBA	24	0		
2005–06	WBA	31	1		
2006–07	WBA	31	1		
2007–08	WBA	32	2	**118**	**4**

BAKER, Lee (D) **0 0**
b.Redditch 20-1-89
Source: Scholar.

2007–08	WBA	0	0		

BARNETT, Leon (D) **91 6**
H: 6 0 W: 12 04 b.Stevenage 30-11-85
Source: Scholar.

2003–04	Luton T	0	0		
2004–05	Luton T	0	0		
2005–06	Luton T	20	0		
2006–07	Luton T	39	3	**59**	**3**
2007–08	WBA	32	3	**32**	**3**

BEATTIE, Craig (F) **74 16**
H: 6 0 W: 11 07 b.Glasgow 16-1-84
Honours: Scotland Under-21, 7 full caps, 1 goal.

2003–04	Celtic	10	1		
2004–05	Celtic	11	4		
2005–06	Celtic	14	6		
2006–07	Celtic	16	2	**51**	**13**
2007–08	WBA	21	3	**21**	**3**
2007–08	*Preston NE*	2	0	**2**	**0**

BEDNAR, Roman (F) **94 30**
H: 6 3 W: 13 03 b.Prague 26-3-83
Honours: Czech Republic Under-21, 1 full cap.

2001–02	Mlada Boleslav	0	0		
2002–03	Mlada Boleslav	0	0		
2003–04	Mlada Boleslav	0	0		
2004–05	Mlada Boleslav	25	6	**25**	**6**
2004–05	Kaunas	0	0		
2005–06	Hearts	22	7		
2006–07	Hearts	18	4	**40**	**11**
2007–08	WBA	29	13	**29**	**13**

BRUNT, Chris (M) **174 28**
H: 6 1 W: 13 04 b.Belfast 14-12-84
Source: Trainee. *Honours:* Northern Ireland Under-21, Under-23, 17 full caps.

2002–03	Middlesbrough	0	0		
2003–04	Middlesbrough	0	0		
2003–04	Sheffield W	9	2		
2004–05	Sheffield W	42	4		
2005–06	Sheffield W	44	7		
2006–07	Sheffield W	44	11		
2007–08	Sheffield W	1	0	**140**	**24**
2007–08	WBA	34	4	**34**	**4**

CESAR, Bostjan (D) **109 4**
H: 6 3 W: 13 10 b.Ljubljana 9-7-82
Honours: Slovenia 26 full caps, 2 goals.

2001–02	Dynamo Zagreb	18	0		
2002–03	Dynamo Zagreb	11	0		
2003–04	Dynamo Zagreb	11	0		
2004–05	Olimpija	9	0	**9**	**0**
2004–05	Dynamo Zagreb	11	1		
2005–06	Dynamo Zagreb	5	2	**56**	**3**
2005–06	Marseille	17	0		
2006–07	Marseille	7	0	**24**	**0**
2007–08	WBA	20	1	**20**	**1**

CLEMENT, Neil (D) **293 22**
H: 6 0 W: 12 03 b.Reading 3-10-78
Source: Trainee. *Honours:* England Schools, Youth.

1995–96	Chelsea	0	0		
1996–97	Chelsea	1	0		
1997–98	Chelsea	0	0		
1998–99	Chelsea	0	0		
1998–99	*Reading*	11	1	**11**	**1**
1998–99	*Preston NE*	4	0	**4**	**0**
1999–2000	Chelsea	0	0	**1**	**0**
1999–2000	*Brentford*	8	0	**8**	**0**
1999–2000	*WBA*	8	0		
2000–01	WBA	45	5		
2001–02	WBA	45	6		
2002–03	WBA	36	3		
2003–04	WBA	35	2		
2004–05	WBA	35	3		
2005–06	WBA	31	1		
2006–07	WBA	20	1		
2007–08	WBA	9	0	**264**	**21**
2007–08	*Hull C*	5	0	**5**	**0**

DANEK, Michal (G) **0 0**
H: 6 5 W: 15 00 b.Czech Republic 6-7-83
Source: Viktoria Plzen. *Honours:* Czech Republic Youth, Under-20, Under-21.

2007–08	WBA	0	0		

DANIELS, Luke (G) **2 0**
H: 6 1 W: 12 10 b.Bolton 5-1-88
Source: Manchester U Scholar.

2006–07	WBA	0	0		
2007–08	*Motherwell*	2	0	**2**	**0**
2007–08	WBA	0	0		

DAVIES, Curtis (D) **133 5**
H: 6 2 W: 11 13 b.Waltham Forest 15-3-85
Source: Scholar. *Honours:* England Under-21.

2003–04	Luton T	6	0		
2004–05	Luton T	44	1		
2005–06	Luton T	6	1	**56**	**2**
2005–06	WBA	33	2		
2006–07	WBA	32	0		

2007–08 WBA 0 0 **65 2**
2007–08 *Aston Villa* 12 1 **12 1**

GERA, Zoltan (M) 266 57
H: 6 0 W: 11 11 b.Pecs 22-4-79
Source: Hakarny. *Honours:* Hungary 53 full caps, 16 goals.
1999–2000 Pecsi 15 4 **15 4**
2000–01 Ferencvaros 32 7
2001–02 Ferencvaros 27 8
2002–03 Ferencvaros 26 6
2003–04 Ferencvaros 30 11 **115 32**
2004–05 WBA 38 6
2005–06 WBA 15 2
2006–07 WBA 40 5
2007–08 WBA 43 8 **136 21**

GREENING, Jonathan (M) 298 11
H: 5 11 W: 11 00 b.Scarborough 2-1-79
Source: Trainee. *Honours:* England Youth, Under-21.
1996–97 York C 5 0
1997–98 York C 20 2 **25 2**
1997–98 Manchester U 0 0
1998–99 Manchester U 3 0
1999–2000 Manchester U 4 0
2000–01 Manchester U 7 0 **14 0**
2001–02 Middlesbrough 36 1
2002–03 Middlesbrough 38 2
2003–04 Middlesbrough 25 1 **99 4**
2004–05 WBA 34 0
2005–06 WBA 38 2
2006–07 WBA 42 2
2007–08 WBA 46 1 **160 5**

HARTSON, John (F) 399 167
H: 6 0 W: 13 07 b.Swansea 5-4-75
Source: Trainee. *Honours:* Wales Under-21, 51 full caps, 14 goals.
1992–93 Luton T 0 0
1993–94 Luton T 34 6
1994–95 Luton T 20 5 **54 11**
1994–95 Arsenal 15 7
1995–96 Arsenal 19 4
1996–97 Arsenal 19 3 **53 14**
1996–97 West Ham U 11 5
1997–98 West Ham U 32 15
1998–99 West Ham U 17 4 **60 24**
1998–99 Wimbledon 14 2
1999–2000 Wimbledon 16 9
2000–01 Wimbledon 19 8 **49 19**
2000–01 Coventry C 12 6 **12 6**
2001–02 Celtic 31 19
2002–03 Celtic 27 18
2003–04 Celtic 15 8
2004–05 Celtic 38 25
2005–06 Celtic 35 18 **146 88**
2006–07 WBA 21 5
2007–08 WBA 0 0 **21 5**
2007–08 *Norwich C* 4 0 **4 0**

HODGKISS, Jared (M) 10 0
H: 5 6 W: 11 02 b.Stafford 15-11-86
Source: Scholar.
2005–06 WBA 1 0
2006–07 WBA 5 0
2007–08 WBA 4 0 **10 0**

HOEFKENS, Carl (D) 357 13
H: 6 1 W: 12 13 b.Lier 6-10-78
Honours: Belgium 21 full caps, 1 goal.
1996–97 Lierse 17 0
1997–98 Lierse 27 1
1998–99 Lierse 30 0
1999–2000 Lierse 31 0
2000–01 Lierse 27 0 **132 1**
2001–02 Lommel 33 3
2002–03 Lommel 22 0 **55 3**
2002–03 Westerlo 7 0 **7 0**
2003–04 Beerschot 32 4
2004–05 Beerschot 0 0 **32 4**
2005–06 Stoke C 44 3
2006–07 Stoke C 45 2 **89 5**
2007–08 WBA 42 0 **42 0**

KIELY, Dean (G) 656 0
H: 6 1 W: 13 10 b.Salford 10-10-70
Source: WBA School. *Honours:* England Schools, FA Schools, Youth, Eire B, 10 full caps.
1987–88 Coventry C 0 0
1988–89 Coventry C 0 0
1989–90 Coventry C 0 0
1989–90 *Ipswich T* 0 0
1989–90 *York C* 0 0
1990–91 York C 17 0
1991–92 York C 21 0
1992–93 York C 40 0
1993–94 York C 46 0
1994–95 York C 46 0
1995–96 York C 40 0 **210 0**
1996–97 Bury 46 0
1997–98 Bury 46 0
1998–99 Bury 45 0 **137 0**
1999–2000 Charlton Ath 45 0
2000–01 Charlton Ath 25 0
2001–02 Charlton Ath 38 0
2002–03 Charlton Ath 38 0
2003–04 Charlton Ath 37 0
2004–05 Charlton Ath 36 0
2005–06 Charlton Ath 3 0 **222 0**
2005–06 Portsmouth 15 0
2006–07 Portsmouth 0 0 **15 0**
2006–07 *Luton T* 11 0 **11 0**
2006–07 WBA 17 0
2007–08 WBA 44 0 **61 0**

KIM, Do-Heon (M) 163 23
H: 5 9 W: 11 07 b.Incheon 14-7-82
Source: Seongnam. *Honours:* South Korea 48 full caps, 8 goals.
2001 Suwon 15 0
2002 Suwon 20 2
2003 Suwon 34 4
2004 Suwon 19 1
2005 Suwon 1 0 **89 7**
2005 Seongnam 20 2
2006 Seongnam 25 6
2007 Seongnam 25 7 **70 15**
2007–08 WBA 4 1 **4 1**

KOREN, Robert (M) 273 62
H: 5 10 W: 11 03 b.Ljubljana 20-9-80
Honours: Slovenia Under-21, 30 full caps, 1 goal.
1999–2000 Dravograd 31 2
2000–01 Dravograd 31 9 **62 11**
2001–02 Publikum 31 5
2002–03 Publikum 32 12
2003–04 Publikum 15 5 **78 22**
2004 Lillestrom 23 1
2005 Lillestrom 26 8
2006 Lillestrom 26 10 **75 19**
2006–07 WBA 18 1
2007–08 WBA 40 9 **58 10**

MACDONALD, Sherjill (F) 112 26
H: 6 0 W: 12 06 b.Amsterdam 20-11-84
Source: Ajax youth. *Honours:* Holland Youth, Under-21.
2001–02 Anderlecht 11 1
2002–03 Anderlecht 9 0
2003–04 Anderlecht 6 0 **26 1**
2004–05 Heracles 17 4 **17 4**
2005–06 Hamburg II 22 4 **22 4**
2006–07 Apeldoorn 21 11 **21 11**
2006–07 WBA 9 0
2007–08 WBA 10 0 **19 0**
2007–08 Hereford U 7 6 **7 6**

MARTIS, Shelton (D) 69 2
H: 6 0 W: 11 11 b.Willemstad 29-11-82
Honours: Netherlands Antilles 1 full cap.
2002–03 Excelsior 12 0
2003–04 Excelsior 10 0 **22 0**
2005–06 Darlington 40 2
2006–07 Darlington 2 0 **42 2**
2007–08 WBA 2 0 **2 0**
2007–08 *Scunthorpe U* 3 0 **3 0**

MILLER, Ishmael (F) 51 9
H: 6 3 W: 14 00 b.Manchester 5-3-87
Source: Scholar.
2005–06 Manchester C 1 0
2006–07 Manchester C 16 0
2007–08 Manchester C 0 0 **17 0**
2007–08 WBA 34 9 **34 9**

MORRISON, James (M) 102 7
H: 5 10 W: 10 06 b.Darlington 25-5-86
Source: Trainee. *Honours:* England Youth, Under-20. Scotland 1 full cap.
2003–04 Middlesbrough 1 0
2004–05 Middlesbrough 14 0
2005–06 Middlesbrough 24 1
2006–07 Middlesbrough 28 2 **67 3**
2007–08 WBA 35 4 **35 4**

NARDIELLO, Michael (F) 0 0
H: 5 10 W: 11 09 b.Torquay 9-5-89
Source: Liverpool Scholar.
2006–07 WBA 0 0
2007–08 WBA 0 0

NICHOLSON, Stuart (F) 55 7
H: 5 10 W: 11 09 b.Newcastle 3-2-86
Source: Scholar. *Honours:* England Youth.
2005–06 WBA 4 0
2006–07 WBA 2 0
2006–07 *Bristol R* 22 6 **22 6**
2007–08 WBA 0 0 **6 0**
2007–08 *Shrewsbury T* 14 1 **14 1**
2007–08 *Wrexham* 13 0 **13 0**

PELE (D) 303 12
H: 6 1 W: 13 08 b.Albufeira 2-5-78
Honours: Cape Verde full caps.
1997–98 Imortal 15 0
1998–99 Imortal 20 0
1999–2000 Imortal 29 2
2000–01 Imortal 25 3
2001–02 Imortal 38 2 **127 7**
2002–03 Farense 28 2 **28 2**
2003–04 Belenenses 25 1
2004–05 Belenenses 33 1
2005–06 Belenenses 32 0 **90 2**
2006–07 Southampton 37 1 **37 1**
2007–08 WBA 21 0 **21 0**

PHILLIPS, Kevin (F) 425 201
H: 5 7 W: 11 00 b.Hitchin 25-7-73
Source: Baldock T. *Honours:* England B, 8 full caps.
1994–95 Watford 16 9
1995–96 Watford 27 11
1996–97 Watford 16 4 **59 24**
1997–98 Sunderland 43 29
1998–99 Sunderland 26 23
1999–2000 Sunderland 36 30
2000–01 Sunderland 34 14
2001–02 Sunderland 37 11
2002–03 Sunderland 32 6 **208 113**
2003–04 Southampton 34 12
2004–05 Southampton 30 10 **64 22**
2005–06 Aston Villa 23 4
2006–07 Aston Villa 0 0 **23 4**
2006–07 WBA 36 16
2007–08 WBA 35 22 **71 38**

ROBINSON, Paul (D) 398 12
H: 5 9 W: 11 12 b.Watford 14-12-78
Source: Trainee. *Honours:* England Under-21.
1996–97 Watford 12 0
1997–98 Watford 22 2
1998–99 Watford 29 0
1999–2000 Watford 32 0
2000–01 Watford 39 0
2001–02 Watford 38 3
2002–03 Watford 37 3
2003–04 Watford 10 0 **219 8**
2003–04 WBA 31 0
2004–05 WBA 30 1
2005–06 WBA 33 0
2006–07 WBA 42 2
2007–08 WBA 43 1 **179 4**

SLUSARSKI, Bartosz (F) 152 43
H: 6 1 W: 12 11 b.Szamocin 11-12-81
Honours: Poland Under-21, 2 full caps.
1999–2000 Lech Poznan 12 2
2000–01 Lech Poznan 0 0
2001–02 Lech Poznan 0 0
2001–02 Widzew Lodz 8 2 **8 2**
2002–03 Lech Poznan 28 8
2003–04 Lech Poznan 11 2 **51 12**
2003–04 Groclin 12 3
2004–05 Groclin 21 10
2005–06 Groclin 22 7
2006–07 Groclin 0 0 **55 20**
2006–07 *Uniao Leiria* 24 7 **24 7**
2007–08 WBA 1 0 **1 0**
2007–08 *Blackpool* 6 1 **6 1**
2007–08 *Sheffield W* 7 1 **7 1**

STEELE, Luke (G) 55 0
H: 6 2 W: 12 00 b.Peterborough 24-9-84
Source: Scholar. *Honours:* England Youth, Under-20.
2001–02 Peterborough U 2 0 **2 0**
2001–02 Manchester U 0 0
2002–03 Manchester U 0 0

2003–04 Manchester U 0 0
2004–05 Manchester U 0 0
2004–05 *Coventry C* 32 0
2005–06 Manchester U 0 0
2006–07 WBA 0 0
2006–07 *Coventry C* 5 0 **37 0**
2007–08 WBA 2 0 **2 0**
2007–08 *Barnsley* 14 0 **14 0**

TEIXEIRA, Felipe (F) 223 31
H: 5 9 W: 10 10 b.Paris 2-10-80
Honours: Portugal Under-21.
1998–99 Felgueiras 27 1
1999–2000 Felgueiras 27 5
2000–01 Felgueiras 31 9 **85 15**
2001–02 Istres 16 2 **16 2**
2002–03 Paris St Germain 8 2
2003–04 Paris St Germain 0 0
2003–04 *Uniao Leiria* 15 3 **15 3**
2004–05 Paris St Germain 10 0 **18 2**
2005–06 Academica 30 3
2006–07 Academica 29 1 **59 4**
2007–08 WBA 30 5 **30 5**

TININHO (D) 94 2
H: 5 9 W: 11 11 b.Beira 13-10-80
2004–05 Beira Mar 26 1
2005–06 Beira Mar 34 1
2006–07 Beira Mar 30 0 **90 2**
2007–08 WBA 1 0 **1 0**
2007–08 *Barnsley* 3 0 **3 0**

WORRALL, David (M) 1 0
H: 6 0 W: 11 03 b.Manchester 12-6-90
Source: Scholar.
2006–07 Bury 1 0
2007–08 Bury 0 0 **1 0**
2007–08 WBA 0 0

WEST HAM U (87)

ASHTON, Dean (F) 245 90
H: 6 2 W: 14 07 b.Crewe 24-11-83
Source: Schoolboy. *Honours:* England Youth, Under-20, Under-21, 1 full cap.
2000–01 Crewe Alex 21 8
2001–02 Crewe Alex 31 7
2002–03 Crewe Alex 39 9
2003–04 Crewe Alex 44 19
2004–05 Crewe Alex 24 17 **159 60**
2004–05 Norwich C 16 7
2005–06 Norwich C 28 10 **44 17**
2005–06 West Ham U 11 3
2006–07 West Ham U 0 0
2007–08 West Ham U 31 10 **42 13**

BELLAMY, Craig (F) 285 94
H: 5 9 W: 10 12 b.Cardiff 13-7-79
Source: Trainee. *Honours:* Wales Schools, Youth, Under-21, 51 full caps, 15 goals.
1996–97 Norwich C 3 0
1997–98 Norwich C 36 13
1998–99 Norwich C 40 17
1999–2000 Norwich C 4 2
2000–01 Norwich C 1 0 **84 32**
2000–01 Coventry C 34 6 **34 6**
2001–02 Newcastle U 27 9
2002–03 Newcastle U 29 7
2003–04 Newcastle U 16 4
2004–05 Newcastle U 21 7 **93 27**
2004–05 *Celtic* 12 7 **12 7**
2005–06 Blackburn R 27 13 **27 13**
2006–07 Liverpool 27 7 **27 7**
2007–08 West Ham U 8 2 **8 2**

BLACKMORE, David (G) 0 0
H: 6 1 W: 13 00 b.Chelmsford 23-3-89
Source: Scholar.
2006–07 West Ham U 0 0
2007–08 West Ham U 0 0

BOA MORTE, Luis (F) 285 46
H: 5 9 W: 12 06 b.Lisbon 4-8-77
Source: Sporting Lisbon, Lourihanense (loan). *Honours:* Portugal Youth, Under-21, 26 full caps, 1 goal.
1997–98 Arsenal 15 0
1998–99 Arsenal 8 0
1999–2000 Arsenal 2 0 **25 0**
1999–2000 Southampton 14 1
2000–01 Southampton 0 0 **14 1**
2000–01 *Fulham* 39 18
2001–02 Fulham 23 1
2002–03 Fulham 29 2
2003–04 Fulham 33 9
2004–05 Fulham 31 8
2005–06 Fulham 35 6
2006–07 Fulham 15 0 **205 44**
2006–07 West Ham U 14 1
2007–08 West Ham U 27 0 **41 1**

BOWYER, Lee (M) 373 56
H: 5 9 W: 10 12 b.Canning Town 3-1-77
Source: Trainee. *Honours:* England Youth, Under-21, 1 full cap.
1993–94 Charlton Ath 0 0
1994–95 Charlton Ath 5 0
1995–96 Charlton Ath 41 8 **46 8**
1996–97 Leeds U 32 4
1997–98 Leeds U 25 3
1998–99 Leeds U 35 9
1999–2000 Leeds U 33 5
2000–01 Leeds U 38 9
2001–02 Leeds U 25 5
2002–03 Leeds U 15 3 **203 38**
2002–03 West Ham U 10 0
2003–04 Newcastle U 24 2
2004–05 Newcastle U 27 3
2005–06 Newcastle U 28 1 **79 6**
2006–07 West Ham U 20 0
2007–08 West Ham U 15 4 **45 4**

COLE, Carlton (F) 128 18
H: 6 3 W: 14 02 b.Croydon 12-11-83
Source: Scholar. *Honours:* England Youth, Under-20, Under-21.
2000–01 Chelsea 0 0
2001–02 Chelsea 3 1
2002–03 Chelsea 13 3
2002–03 *Wolverhampton W* 7 1 **7 1**
2003–04 Chelsea 0 0
2003–04 *Charlton Ath* 21 4 **21 4**
2004–05 Chelsea 0 0
2004–05 *Aston Villa* 27 3 **27 3**
2005–06 Chelsea 9 0 **25 4**
2006–07 West Ham U 17 2
2007–08 West Ham U 31 4 **48 6**

COLLINS, James (D) 99 5
H: 6 2 W: 14 05 b.Newport 23-8-83
Source: Scholar. *Honours:* Wales Youth, Under-21, 24 full caps, 1 goal.
2000–01 Cardiff C 3 0
2001–02 Cardiff C 7 1
2002–03 Cardiff C 2 0
2003–04 Cardiff C 20 1
2004–05 Cardiff C 34 1 **66 3**
2005–06 West Ham U 14 2
2006–07 West Ham U 16 0
2007–08 West Ham U 3 0 **33 2**

COLLISON, Jack (M) 2 0
H: 6 0 W: 13 10 b.Watford 2-10-88
Source: Scholar. *Honours:* Wales Under-21, 2 full caps.
2007–08 West Ham U 2 0 **2 0**

DAILLY, Christian (D) 447 28
H: 6 1 W: 12 10 b.Dundee 23-10-73
Source: 'S' Form. *Honours:* Scotland Schools, Youth, Under-21, B, 67 full caps, 6 goals.
1990–91 Dundee U 18 5
1991–92 Dundee U 8 0
1992–93 Dundee U 14 4
1993–94 Dundee U 38 4
1994–95 Dundee U 33 4
1995–96 Dundee U 30 1 **141 18**
1996–97 Derby Co 36 3
1997–98 Derby Co 30 1
1998–99 Derby Co 1 0 **67 4**
1998–99 Blackburn R 17 0
1999–2000 Blackburn R 43 4
2000–01 Blackburn R 10 0 **70 4**
2000–01 West Ham U 12 0
2001–02 West Ham U 38 0
2002–03 West Ham U 26 0
2003–04 West Ham U 43 2
2004–05 West Ham U 3 0
2005–06 West Ham U 22 0
2006–07 West Ham U 14 0
2007–08 West Ham U 0 0 **158 2**
2007–08 *Southampton* 11 0 **11 0**
To Rangers January 2008.

DAVENPORT, Calum (D) 129 5
H: 6 4 W: 14 00 b.Bedford 1-1-83
Source: Trainee. *Honours:* England Youth, Under-20, Under-21.
1999–2000 Coventry C 0 0
2000–01 Coventry C 1 0
2001–02 Coventry C 3 0
2002–03 Coventry C 32 3
2003–04 Coventry C 33 0
2004–05 Coventry C 6 0 **75 3**
2004–05 *Southampton* 7 0 **7 0**
2004–05 Tottenham H 1 0
2004–05 *West Ham U* 10 0
2005–06 Tottenham H 4 0
2005–06 *Norwich C* 15 1 **15 1**
2006–07 Tottenham H 10 1 **15 1**
2006–07 West Ham U 6 0
2007–08 West Ham U 0 0 **16 0**
2007–08 *Watford* 1 0 **1 0**

DYER, Kieron (M) 283 32
H: 5 8 W: 10 01 b.Ipswich 29-12-78
Source: Trainee. *Honours:* England Youth, Under-21, B, 33 full caps.
1996–97 Ipswich T 13 0
1997–98 Ipswich T 41 4
1998–99 Ipswich T 37 5 **91 9**
1999–2000 Newcastle U 30 3
2000–01 Newcastle U 26 5
2001–02 Newcastle U 18 3
2002–03 Newcastle U 35 2
2003–04 Newcastle U 25 1
2004–05 Newcastle U 23 4
2005–06 Newcastle U 11 0
2006–07 Newcastle U 22 5
2007–08 Newcastle U 0 0 **190 23**
2007–08 West Ham U 2 0 **2 0**

ETHERINGTON, Matthew (M) 261 22
H: 5 10 W: 10 12 b.Truro 14-8-81
Source: School. *Honours:* England Youth, Under-21.
1996–97 Peterborough U 1 0
1997–98 Peterborough U 2 0
1998–99 Peterborough U 29 3
1999–2000 Peterborough U 19 3 **51 6**
1999–2000 Tottenham H 5 0
2000–01 Tottenham H 6 0
2001–02 *Bradford C* 13 1 **13 1**
2001–02 Tottenham H 11 0
2002–03 Tottenham H 23 1 **45 1**
2003–04 West Ham U 35 5
2004–05 West Ham U 39 4
2005–06 West Ham U 33 2
2006–07 West Ham U 27 0
2007–08 West Ham U 18 3 **152 14**

FAUBERT, Julien (M) 148 13
H: 5 10 W: 11 08 b.Le Havre 1-8-83
Honours: France 1 full cap, 1 goal.
2002–03 Cannes 26 1
2003–04 Cannes 19 3 **45 4**
2004–05 Bordeaux 36 1
2005–06 Bordeaux 34 5
2006–07 Bordeaux 26 3 **96 9**
2007–08 West Ham U 7 0 **7 0**

FERDINAND, Anton (D) 138 5
H: 6 2 W: 11 00 b.Peckham 18-2-85
Source: Trainee. *Honours:* England Youth, Under-20, Under-21.
2002–03 West Ham U 0 0
2003–04 West Ham U 20 0
2004–05 West Ham U 29 1
2005–06 West Ham U 33 2
2006–07 West Ham U 31 0
2007–08 West Ham U 25 2 **138 5**

FITZGERALD, Lorcan (D) 0 0
H: 5 9 W: 10 09 b.Republic of Ireland 3-1-89
Source: Scholar.
2005–06 West Ham U 0 0
2006–07 West Ham U 0 0
2007–08 West Ham U 0 0

GABBIDON, Daniel (D) 277 10
H: 6 0 W: 13 05 b.Cwmbran 8-8-79
Source: Trainee. *Honours:* Wales Youth, Under-21, 40 full caps.
1998–99 WBA 2 0
1999–2000 WBA 18 0
2000–01 WBA 0 0 **20 0**
2000–01 Cardiff C 43 3

2001–02	Cardiff C	44	3		
2002–03	Cardiff C	24	0		
2003–04	Cardiff C	41	3		
2004–05	Cardiff C	45	1	**197**	**10**
2005–06	West Ham U	32	0		
2006–07	West Ham U	18	0		
2007–08	West Ham U	10	0	**60**	**0**

GREEN, Rob (G) 287 0
H: 6 3 W: 14 09 b.Chertsey 18-1-80
Source: Trainee. *Honours:* England Youth, B, 1 full cap.

1997–98	Norwich C	0	0		
1998–99	Norwich C	2	0		
1999–2000	Norwich C	3	0		
2000–01	Norwich C	5	0		
2001–02	Norwich C	41	0		
2002–03	Norwich C	46	0		
2003–04	Norwich C	46	0		
2004–05	Norwich C	38	0		
2005–06	Norwich C	42	0	**223**	**0**
2006–07	West Ham U	26	0		
2007–08	West Ham U	38	0	**64**	**0**

HALES, Lee (M) 0 0
H: 5 9 W: 11 00 b.Sidcup 15-2-89
Source: Scholar. *Honours:* England Schools, Youth.

2005–06	West Ham U	0	0		
2006–07	West Ham U	0	0		
2007–08	West Ham U	0	0		

HINES, Zavon (F) 7 1
H: 5 10 W: 10 07 b.Jamaica 27-12-88
Source: Scholar.

2007–08	West Ham U	0	0		
2007–08	*Coventry C*	7	1	**7**	**1**

JEFFERY, Jack (F) 0 0
H: 5 8 W: 11 10 b.Gravesend 13-8-89
Source: Scholar.

2007–08	West Ham U	0	0		

KATAN, Yaniv (F) 229 40
H: 6 1 W: 12 13 b.Kiryat Ata 27-1-81
Honours: Israel 24 full caps, 5 goals.

1998–99	Maccabi Haifa	26	1		
1999–2000	Maccabi Haifa	36	3		
2000–01	Maccabi Haifa	35	5		
2001–02	Maccabi Haifa	19	5		
2002–03	Maccabi Haifa	32	6		
2003–04	Maccabi Haifa	28	7		
2004–05	Maccabi Haifa	32	8		
2005–06	Maccabi Haifa	15	5	**223**	**40**
2005–06	West Ham U	6	0		
2006–07	West Ham U	0	0		
2007–08	West Ham U	0	0	**6**	**0**

LJUNGBERG, Frederik (M) 320 58
H: 5 9 W: 11 00 b.Vittsjo 16-4-77
Honours: Sweden Under-21, 75 full caps, 14 goals.

1994	Halmstad	1	0		
1995	Halmstad	16	1		
1996	Halmstad	20	2		
1997	Halmstad	24	5		
1998	Halmstad	18	2	**79**	**10**
1998–99	Arsenal	16	1		
1999–2000	Arsenal	26	6		
2000–01	Arsenal	30	6		
2001–02	Arsenal	25	12		
2002–03	Arsenal	20	6		
2003–04	Arsenal	30	4		
2004–05	Arsenal	26	10		
2005–06	Arsenal	25	1		
2006–07	Arsenal	18	0	**216**	**46**
2007–08	West Ham U	25	2	**25**	**2**

McCARTNEY, George (D) 194 1
H: 5 11 W: 11 02 b.Belfast 29-4-81
Source: Trainee. *Honours:* Northern Ireland Schools, Youth, Under-21, 25 full caps, 1 goal.

1998–99	Sunderland	0	0		
1999–2000	Sunderland	0	0		
2000–01	Sunderland	2	0		
2001–02	Sunderland	18	0		
2002–03	Sunderland	24	0		
2003–04	Sunderland	41	0		
2004–05	Sunderland	36	0		
2005–06	Sunderland	13	0	**134**	**0**
2006–07	West Ham U	22	0		
2007–08	West Ham U	38	1	**60**	**1**

MILLER, Ashley (D) 0 0
Source: Scholar.

2007–08	West Ham U	0	0		

MULLINS, Hayden (D) 385 21
H: 5 11 W: 11 12 b.Reading 27-3-79
Source: Trainee. *Honours:* England Under-21.

1996–97	Crystal Palace	0	0		
1997–98	Crystal Palace	0	0		
1998–99	Crystal Palace	40	5		
1999–2000	Crystal Palace	45	10		
2000–01	Crystal Palace	41	1		
2001–02	Crystal Palace	43	0		
2002–03	Crystal Palace	43	2		
2003–04	Crystal Palace	10	0	**222**	**18**
2003–04	West Ham U	27	0		
2004–05	West Ham U	37	1		
2005–06	West Ham U	35	0		
2006–07	West Ham U	30	2		
2007–08	West Ham U	34	0	**163**	**3**

N'GALA, Bondz (D) 0 0
b.Newham 13-9-89
Source: Scholar.

2007–08	West Ham U	0	0		

NEILL, Lucas (D) 385 18
H: 6 0 W: 12 03 b.Sydney 9-3-78
Source: NSW Soccer Academy. *Honours:* Australia Under-20, Under-23, 41 full caps.

1995–96	Millwall	13	0		
1996–97	Millwall	39	3		
1997–98	Millwall	6	0		
1998–99	Millwall	35	6		
1999–2000	Millwall	31	1		
2000–01	Millwall	24	2		
2001–02	Millwall	4	1	**152**	**13**
2001–02	Blackburn R	31	1		
2002–03	Blackburn R	34	0		
2003–04	Blackburn R	32	2		
2004–05	Blackburn R	36	1		
2005–06	Blackburn R	35	1		
2006–07	Blackburn R	20	0	**188**	**5**
2006–07	West Ham U	11	0		
2007–08	West Ham U	34	0	**45**	**0**

NOBLE, Mark (M) 77 6
H: 5 11 W: 12 00 b.West Ham 8-5-87
Source: Scholar. *Honours:* England Youth, Under-21

2004–05	West Ham U	13	0		
2005–06	West Ham U	5	0		
2005–06	*Hull C*	5	0	**5**	**0**
2006–07	West Ham U	10	2		
2006–07	*Ipswich T*	13	1	**13**	**1**
2007–08	West Ham U	31	3	**59**	**5**

O'NEILL, Ryan (D) 0 0
Source: Scholar.

2007–08	West Ham U	0	0		

PANTSIL, John (D) 107 3
H: 5 10 W: 12 08 b.Berekum 15-6-81
Source: Liberty Professionals, Berkum Arsenals. *Honours:* Ghana Youth, Under-20, 45 full caps.

2002–03	Maccabi Tel Aviv	17	0		
2003–04	Maccabi Tel Aviv	29	0	**46**	**0**
2004–05	Hapoel Tel Aviv	15	1		
2005–06	Hapoel Tel Aviv	27	2	**42**	**3**
2006–07	West Ham U	5	0		
2007–08	West Ham U	14	0	**19**	**0**

PARKER, Scott (M) 222 16
H: 5 9 W: 11 10 b.Lambeth 13-10-80
Source: Trainee. *Honours:* England Schools, Youth, Under-21, 3 full caps.

1997–98	Charlton Ath	3	0		
1998–99	Charlton Ath	4	0		
1999–2000	Charlton Ath	15	1		
2000–01	Charlton Ath	20	1		
2000–01	*Norwich C*	6	1	**6**	**1**
2001–02	Charlton Ath	38	1		
2002–03	Charlton Ath	28	4		
2003–04	Charlton Ath	20	2	**128**	**9**
2003–04	Chelsea	11	1		
2004–05	Chelsea	4	0	**15**	**1**
2005–06	Newcastle U	26	1		
2006–07	Newcastle U	29	3	**55**	**4**
2007–08	West Ham U	18	1	**18**	**1**

QUASHIE, Nigel (M) 322 24
H: 6 0 W: 13 10 b.Peckham 20-7-78
Source: Trainee. *Honours:* England Youth, Under-21, B, Scotland 14 full caps, 1 goal.

1995–96	QPR	11	0		
1996–97	QPR	13	0		
1997–98	QPR	33	3		
1998–99	QPR	0	0	**57**	**3**
1998–99	Nottingham F	16	0		
1999–2000	Nottingham F	28	2	**44**	**2**
2000–01	Portsmouth	31	5		
2001–02	Portsmouth	35	2		
2002–03	Portsmouth	42	5		
2003–04	Portsmouth	21	1		
2004–05	Portsmouth	19	0	**148**	**13**
2004–05	Southampton	13	1		
2005–06	Southampton	24	4	**37**	**5**
2005–06	WBA	9	1		
2006–07	WBA	20	0	**29**	**1**
2006–07	West Ham U	7	0		
2007–08	West Ham U	0	0	**7**	**0**

REID, Kyel (M) 31 2
H: 5 10 W: 12 05 b.South London 26-11-87
Source: Scholar. *Honours:* England Youth.

2004–05	West Ham U	0	0		
2005–06	West Ham U	2	0		
2006–07	West Ham U	0	0		
2006–07	*Barnsley*	26	2	**26**	**2**
2007–08	West Ham U	1	0	**3**	**0**
2007–08	*Crystal Palace*	2	0	**2**	**0**

SEARS, Freddie (F) 7 1
H: 5 8 W: 10 01 b.Hornchurch 27-11-89
Source: Scholar. *Honours:* England Youth.

2007–08	West Ham U	7	1	**7**	**1**

SOLANO, Nolberto (M) 409 86
H: 5 8 W: 10 07 b.Callao 12-12-74
Honours: Peru 82 full caps, 20 goals.

1994–95	Sporting Cristal	38	12		
1995–96	Sporting Cristal	26	13		
1996–97	Sporting Cristal	11	7	**75**	**32**
1997–98	Boca Juniors	32	5	**32**	**5**
1998 99	Newcastle U	29	6		
1999–2000	Newcastle U	30	3		
2000–01	Newcastle U	33	6		
2001–02	Newcastle U	37	7		
2002–03	Newcastle U	31	7		
2003–04	Newcastle U	12	0		
2003–04	Aston Villa	10	0		
2004–05	Aston Villa	36	8		
2005–06	Aston Villa	3	0	**49**	**8**
2005–06	Newcastle U	29	6		
2006–07	Newcastle U	28	2		
2007–08	Newcastle U	1	0	**230**	**37**
2007–08	West Ham U	23	4	**23**	**4**

SPECTOR, Jonathan (D) 74 0
H: 6 0 W: 12 08 b.Arlington Heights 1-3-86
Source: Chicago Sockers. *Honours:* USA Youth, 12 full caps.

2003–04	Manchester U	0	0		
2004–05	Manchester U	3	0		
2005–06	Manchester U	0	0	**3**	**0**
2005–06	*Charlton Ath*	20	0	**20**	**0**
2006–07	West Ham U	25	0		
2007–08	West Ham U	26	0	**51**	**0**

SPENCE, Jordan (M) 0 0
b.Woodford 24-5-90
Source: Scholar. *Honours:* England Youth.

2007–08	West Ham U	0	0		

STANISLAS, Junior (M) 0 0
b.Eltham
Source: Scholar. *Honours:* England Youth.

2007–08	West Ham U	0	0		

STOKES, Tony (M) 25 0
H: 5 10 W: 11 10 b.East London 7-1-87
Source: Scholar.

2005–06	West Ham U	0	0		
2005–06	*Rushden & D*	19	0	**19**	**0**
2006–07	West Ham U	0	0		
2006–07	*Brighton & HA*	6	0	**6**	**0**
2007–08	West Ham U	0	0		

TOMKINS, James (D) 6 0
H: 6 3 W: 11 10 b.Basildon 29-3-89
Source: Scholar. *Honours:* England Schools, Youth.

2005–06	West Ham U	0	0		
2006–07	West Ham U	0	0		
2007–08	West Ham U	6	0	**6**	**0**

UPSON, Matthew (D) **201 6**
H: 6 1 W: 11 04 b.Stowmarket 18-4-79
Source: Trainee. *Honours:* England Youth, Under-21, 8 full caps.

1995–96	Luton T	0	0		
1996–97	Luton T	1	0	**1**	**0**
1996–97	Arsenal	0	0		
1997–98	Arsenal	5	0		
1998–99	Arsenal	5	0		
1999–2000	Arsenal	8	0		
2000–01	Arsenal	2	0		
2000–01	*Nottingham F*	1	0	**1**	**0**
2000–01	*Crystal Palace*	7	0	**7**	**0**
2001–02	Arsenal	14	0		
2002–03	Arsenal	0	0	**34**	**0**
2002–03	*Reading*	14	0	**14**	**0**
2002–03	Birmingham C	14	0		
2003–04	Birmingham C	30	0		
2004–05	Birmingham C	36	2		
2005–06	Birmingham C	24	1		
2006–07	Birmingham C	9	2	**113**	**5**
2006–07	West Ham U	2	0		
2007–08	West Ham U	29	1	**31**	**1**

WALKER, Jim (G) **416 0**
H: 5 11 W: 13 04 b.Sutton-in-Ashfield 9-7-73
Source: Trainee.

1991–92	Notts Co	0	0		
1992–93	Notts Co	0	0		
1993–94	Walsall	31	0		
1994–95	Walsall	4	0		
1995–96	Walsall	26	0		
1996–97	Walsall	36	0		
1997–98	Walsall	46	0		
1998–99	Walsall	46	0		
1999–2000	Walsall	43	0		
2000–01	Walsall	44	0		
2001–02	Walsall	43	0		
2002–03	Walsall	41	0		
2003–04	Walsall	43	0	**403**	**0**
2004–05	West Ham U	10	0		
2005–06	West Ham U	3	0		
2006–07	West Ham U	0	0		
2007–08	West Ham U	0	0	**13**	**0**

WIDDOWSON, Joe (D) **3 0**
H: 6 0 W: 12 00 b.Forest Gate 28-3-89
Source: Scholar.

2007–08	West Ham U	0	0		
2007–08	*Rotherham U*	3	0	**3**	**0**

WRIGHT, Richard (G) **319 0**
H: 6 2 W: 14 04 b.Ipswich 5-11-77
Source: Trainee. *Honours:* England Schools, Youth, Under-21, 2 full caps.

1994–95	Ipswich T	3	0		
1995–96	Ipswich T	23	0		
1996–97	Ipswich T	40	0		
1997–98	Ipswich T	46	0		
1998–99	Ipswich T	46	0		
1999–2000	Ipswich T	46	0		
2000–01	Ipswich T	36	0	**240**	**0**
2001–02	Arsenal	12	0	**12**	**0**
2002–03	Everton	33	0		
2003–04	Everton	4	0		
2004–05	Everton	7	0		
2005–06	Everton	15	0		
2006–07	Everton	1	0	**60**	**0**
2007–08	West Ham U	0	0		
2007–08	*Southampton*	7	0	**7**	**0**

ZAMORA, Bobby (F) **275 106**
H: 6 1 W: 11 11 b.Barking 16-1-81
Source: Trainee. *Honours:* England Under-21.

1999–2000	Bristol R	4	0	**4**	**0**
1999–2000	*Brighton & HA*	6	6		
2000–01	Brighton & HA	43	28		
2001–02	Brighton & HA	41	28		
2002–03	Brighton & HA	35	14	**125**	**76**
2003–04	Tottenham H	16	0	**16**	**0**
2003–04	West Ham U	17	5		
2004–05	West Ham U	34	7		
2005–06	West Ham U	34	6		
2006–07	West Ham U	32	11		
2007–08	West Ham U	13	1	**130**	**30**

Scholars
Ashman, Anthony Sean; Brookes, Antony Ross; Edgar, Anthony James; Fry, Matthew; Harvey, Thomas; Kearns, Daniel; Lee, Oliver Robert; Payne, Joshua James; Stech, Marek; Street, Adam Owen

WIGAN ATH (88)

AGHAHOWA, Julius (F) **109 32**
H: 5 10 W: 11 07 b.Benin City 12-2-82
Source: Esperance. *Honours:* Nigeria 32 full caps, 14 goals.

2000–01	Shakhtar Donetsk	8	7		
2001–02	Shakhtar Donetsk	17	7		
2002–03	Shakhtar Donetsk	10	1		
2003–04	Shakhtar Donetsk	17	6		
2004–05	Shakhtar Donetsk	14	7		
2005–06	Shakhtar Donetsk	8	0		
2006–07	Shakhtar Donetsk	15	4	**89**	**32**
2006–07	Wigan Ath	6	0		
2007–08	Wigan Ath	14	0	**20**	**0**

BOUAOUZAN, Rachid (M) **69 4**
H: 5 6 W: 11 02 b.Rotterdam 20-2-84

2003–04	Sparta Rotterdam	1	0		
2004–05	Sparta Rotterdam	10	1		
2005–06	Sparta Rotterdam	30	1		
2006–07	Sparta Rotterdam	28	2	**69**	**4**
2007–08	Wigan Ath	0	0		

BOYCE, Emmerson (D) **314 10**
H: 6 0 W: 12 03 b.Aylesbury 24-9-79
Source: Trainee. *Honours:* Barbados 1 full cap.

1997–98	Luton T	0	0		
1998–99	Luton T	1	0		
1999–2000	Luton T	30	1		
2000–01	Luton T	42	3		
2001–02	Luton T	37	0		
2002–03	Luton T	34	0		
2003–04	Luton T	42	4	**186**	**8**
2004–05	Crystal Palace	27	0		
2005–06	Crystal Palace	42	2	**69**	**2**
2006–07	Wigan Ath	34	0		
2007–08	Wigan Ath	25	0	**59**	**0**

BRAMBLE, Titus (D) **181 6**
H: 6 2 W: 13 10 b.Ipswich 31-7-81
Source: Trainee. *Honours:* England Under-21.

1998–99	Ipswich T	4	0		
1999–2000	Ipswich T	0	0		
1999–2000	*Colchester U*	2	0	**2**	**0**
2000–01	Ipswich T	26	1		
2001–02	Ipswich T	18	0	**48**	**1**
2002–03	Newcastle U	16	0		
2003–04	Newcastle U	29	0		
2004–05	Newcastle U	19	1		
2005–06	Newcastle U	24	2		
2006–07	Newcastle U	17	0	**105**	**3**
2007–08	Wigan Ath	26	2	**26**	**2**

BROWN, Michael (M) **372 32**
H: 5 9 W: 12 04 b.Hartlepool 25-1-77
Source: Trainee. *Honours:* England Under-21.

1994–95	Manchester C	0	0		
1995–96	Manchester C	21	0		
1996–97	Manchester C	11	0		
1996–97	*Hartlepool U*	6	1	**6**	**1**
1997–98	Manchester C	26	0		
1998–99	Manchester C	31	2		
1999–2000	Manchester C	0	0	**89**	**2**
1999–2000	*Portsmouth*	4	0	**4**	**0**
1999–2000	Sheffield U	24	3		
2000–01	Sheffield U	36	1		
2001–02	Sheffield U	36	5		
2002–03	Sheffield U	40	16		
2003–04	Sheffield U	15	2	**151**	**27**
2003–04	Tottenham H	17	1		
2004–05	Tottenham H	24	1		
2005–06	Tottenham H	9	0	**50**	**2**
2005–06	Fulham	7	0		
2006–07	Fulham	34	0	**41**	**0**
2007–08	Wigan Ath	31	0	**31**	**0**

CAMARA, Henri (F) **225 79**
H: 5 9 W: 10 08 b.Dakar 10-5-77
Honours: Senegal 52 full caps, 21 goals.

1999–2000	Neuchatel Xamax	20	12		
2000–01	Neuchatel Xamax	12	5	**32**	**17**
2000–01	Grasshoppers	11	3	**11**	**3**
2001–02	Sedan	25	8		
2002–03	Sedan	34	14	**59**	**22**
2003–04	Wolverhampton W	30	7		
2004–05	Wolverhampton W	0	0	**30**	**7**
2004–05	*Celtic*	18	8	**18**	**8**
2004–05	*Southampton*	13	4	**13**	**4**
2005–06	Wigan Ath	29	12		
2006–07	Wigan Ath	23	6		
2007–08	Wigan Ath	0	0	**52**	**18**
2007–08	*West Ham U*	10	0	**10**	**0**

COTTERILL, David (F) **96 9**
H: 5 9 W: 11 02 b.Cardiff 4-12-87
Source: Scholar. *Honours:* Wales Youth, Under-21, 11 full caps.

2004–05	Bristol C	12	0		
2005–06	Bristol C	45	7		
2006–07	Bristol C	5	1	**62**	**8**
2006–07	Wigan Ath	16	1		
2007–08	Wigan Ath	2	0	**18**	**1**
2007–08	*Sheffield U*	16	0	**16**	**0**

CYWKA, Thomasz (M) **4 0**
H: 5 10 W: 11 09 b.Gliwice 27-6-88
Source: Gwarek Zabrze. *Honours:* Poland Youth, Under-21.

2006–07	Wigan Ath	0	0		
2006–07	*Oldham Ath*	4	0	**4**	**0**
2007–08	Wigan Ath	0	0		

EDMAN, Erik (D) **257 3**
H: 5 10 W: 12 04 b.Huskvarna 11-11-78
Source: Habo. *Honours:* Sweden 55 full caps, 1 goal.

1997	Helsingborg	24	0		
1998	Helsingborg	25	0		
1999	Helsingborg	12	1	**61**	**1**
1999–2000	Torino	0	0		
1999–2000	Karlsruher	8	0	**8**	**0**
2000	AIK Stockholm	8	0		
2001	AIK Stockholm	13	0	**21**	**0**
2001–02	Heerenveen	33	1		
2002–03	Heerenveen	30	0	**63**	**1**
2004–05	Tottenham H	28	1		
2005–06	Tottenham H	3	0	**31**	**1**
2005–06	Rennes	26	0		
2006–07	Rennes	30	0		
2007–08	Rennes	12	0	**68**	**0**
2007–08	Wigan Ath	5	0	**5**	**0**

FIGUEROA, Maynor (D) **26 2**
H: 5 11 W: 12 02 b.Jutiapa 2-5-83
Honours: Honduras 53 full caps, 2 goals.

2000–01	Victoria La Ceiba	2	0		
2001–02	Victoria La Ceiba	22	2	**24**	**2**
2007–08	Wigan Ath	2	0	**2**	**0**

GRANQVIST, Andreas (D) **86 1**
H: 6 3 W: 13 03 b.Helsingborg 16-4-85
Honours: Sweden Under-21, 3 full caps.

2004	Helsingborg	21	0		
2005	Helsingborg	26	1		
2006	Helsingborg	25	0	**72**	**1**
2006–07	Wigan Ath	0	0		
2007–08	Wigan Ath	14	0	**14**	**0**

HAGEN, Erik (D) **205 7**
H: 6 1 W: 13 03 b.Veme 20-7-75
Honours: Norway 28 full caps, 3 goals.

1998	Stromsgodset	8	0		
1999	Stromsgodset	16	0	**24**	**0**
2000	Valerenga	23	0		
2001	Valerenga	29	2		
2002	Valerenga	21	0		
2003	Valerenga	14	0		
2004	Valerenga	26	2	**113**	**4**
2005	Zenit	28	0		
2006	Zenit	24	3		
2007	Zenit	15	0	**67**	**3**
2007–08	Wigan Ath	1	0	**1**	**0**

HESKEY, Emile (F) **434 105**
H: 6 2 W: 13 12 b.Leicester 11-1-78
Source: Trainee. *Honours:* England Youth, Under-21, B, 45 full caps, 5 goals.

1994–95	Leicester C	1	0		
1995–96	Leicester C	30	7		
1996–97	Leicester C	35	10		
1997–98	Leicester C	35	10		
1998–99	Leicester C	30	6		
1999–2000	Leicester C	23	7	**154**	**40**
1999–2000	Liverpool	12	3		
2000–01	Liverpool	36	14		
2001–02	Liverpool	35	9		
2002–03	Liverpool	32	6		
2003–04	Liverpool	35	7	**150**	**39**
2004–05	Birmingham C	34	10		
2005–06	Birmingham C	34	4	**68**	**14**
2006–07	Wigan Ath	34	8		
2007–08	Wigan Ath	28	4	**62**	**12**

KILBANE, Kevin (M) **436** **32**

H: 6 1 W: 13 05 b.Preston 1-2-77

Source: Trainee. *Honours:* Eire Under-21, 87 full caps, 7 goals.

1993–94	Preston NE	0	0		
1994–95	Preston NE	0	0		
1995–96	Preston NE	11	1		
1996–97	Preston NE	36	2	**47**	**3**
1997–98	WBA	43	4		
1998–99	WBA	44	6		
1999–2000	WBA	19	5	**106**	**15**
1999–2000	Sunderland	20	1		
2000–01	Sunderland	30	4		
2001–02	Sunderland	28	2		
2002–03	Sunderland	30	1		
2003–04	Sunderland	5	0	**113**	**8**
2003–04	Everton	30	3		
2004–05	Everton	38	1		
2005–06	Everton	34	0		
2006–07	Everton	2	0	**104**	**4**
2006–07	Wigan Ath	31	1		
2007–08	Wigan Ath	35	1	**66**	**2**

KING, Marlon (F) **309** **101**

H: 5 10 W: 12 10 b.Dulwich 26-4-80

Source: Trainee. *Honours:* Jamaica 13 full caps, 6 goals.

1998–99	Barnet	22	6		
1999–2000	Barnet	31	8	**53**	**14**
2000–01	Gillingham	38	15		
2001–02	Gillingham	42	17		
2002–03	Gillingham	10	4		
2003–04	Gillingham	11	4	**101**	**40**
2003–04	Nottingham F	24	5		
2004–05	Nottingham F	26	5		
2004–05	*Leeds U*	9	0	**9**	**0**
2005–06	Nottingham F	0	0	**50**	**10**
2005–06	Watford	41	21		
2006–07	Watford	13	4		
2007–08	Watford	27	11	**81**	**36**
2007–08	Wigan Ath	15	1	**15**	**1**

KIRKLAND, Christopher (G) **122** **0**

H: 6 5 W: 14 08 b.Leicester 2-5-81

Source: Trainee. *Honours:* England Youth, Under-21, 1 full cap.

1997–98	Coventry C	0	0		
1998–99	Coventry C	0	0		
1999–2000	Coventry C	0	0		
2000–01	Coventry C	23	0		
2001–02	Coventry C	1	0	**24**	**0**
2001–02	Liverpool	1	0		
2002–03	Liverpool	8	0		
2003–04	Liverpool	6	0		
2004–05	Liverpool	10	0		
2005–06	Liverpool	0	0		
2005–06	*WBA*	10	0	**10**	**0**
2006–07	Liverpool	0	0	**25**	**0**
2006–07	Wigan Ath	26	0		
2007–08	Wigan Ath	37	0	**63**	**0**

KOUMAS, Jason (M) **324** **61**

H: 5 10 W: 11 02 b.Wrexham 25-9-79

Source: Trainee. *Honours:* Wales 29 full caps, 9 goals.

1997–98	Tranmere R	0	0		
1998–99	Tranmere R	23	3		
1999–2000	Tranmere R	23	2		
2000–01	Tranmere R	39	10		
2001–02	Tranmere R	38	8		
2002–03	Tranmere R	4	2	**127**	**25**
2002–03	WBA	32	4		
2003–04	WBA	42	10		
2004–05	WBA	10	0		
2005–06	WBA	0	0		
2005–06	*Cardiff C*	44	12	**44**	**12**
2006–07	WBA	39	9	**123**	**23**
2007–08	Wigan Ath	30	1	**30**	**1**

KUPISZ, Tomasz (M) **0** **0**

b.Radom 2-1-90

Source: Piaseczno.

2006–07	Wigan Ath	0	0		
2007–08	Wigan Ath	0	0		

LANDZAAT, Denny (M) **373** **75**

H: 5 10 W: 11 00 b.Amsterdam 6-5-76

Honours: Holland 37 full caps, 1 goal.

1995–96	Ajax	1	0	**1**	**0**
1996–97	MVV	34	2		
1997–98	MVV	34	4		
1998–99	MVV	34	4	**102**	**10**
1999–2000	Willem II	25	3		
2000–01	Willem II	33	12		
2001–02	Willem II	34	16		
2002–03	Willem II	34	5		
2003–04	Willem II	13	2	**139**	**38**
2003–04	AZ	17	3		
2004–05	AZ	33	10		
2005–06	AZ	29	9	**79**	**22**
2006–07	Wigan Ath	33	2		
2007–08	Wigan Ath	19	3	**52**	**5**

To Feyenoord January 2008.

MELCHIOT, Mario (D) **321** **9**

H: 6 2 W: 11 09 b.Amsterdam 4-11-76

Honours: Holland 22 full caps.

1996–97	Ajax	23	0		
1997–98	Ajax	26	0		
1998–99	Ajax	24	1	**73**	**1**
1999–2000	Chelsea	5	0		
2000–01	Chelsea	31	0		
2001–02	Chelsea	37	2		
2002–03	Chelsea	34	0		
2003–04	Chelsea	23	2	**130**	**4**
2004–05	Birmingham C	34	1		
2005–06	Birmingham C	23	1	**57**	**2**
2006–07	Rennes	30	2	**30**	**2**
2007–08	Wigan Ath	31	0	**31**	**0**

MONTROSE, Lewis (M) **0** **0**

H: 6 0 W: 12 00 b.Manchester 17-11-88

Source: Scholar.

2006–07	Wigan Ath	0	0		
2007–08	Wigan Ath	0	0		

MOORE, Peter (D) **0** **0**

H: 5 8 W: 11 01 b.Liverpool 13-8-88

Source: Scholar.

2007–08	Wigan Ath	0	0		

NASH, Carlo (G) **243** **0**

H: 6 5 W: 14 01 b.Bolton 13-9-73

Source: Clitheroe.

1996–97	Crystal Palace	21	0		
1997–98	Crystal Palace	0	0	**21**	**0**
1998–99	Stockport Co	43	0		
1999–2000	Stockport Co	38	0		
2000–01	Stockport Co	8	0	**89**	**0**
2000–01	Manchester C	6	0		
2001–02	Manchester C	23	0		
2002–03	Manchester C	9	0	**38**	**0**
2003–04	Middlesbrough	1	0		
2004–05	Middlesbrough	2	0	**3**	**0**
2004–05	Preston NE	7	0		
2005–06	Preston NE	46	0		
2006–07	Preston NE	29	0	**82**	**0**
2007–08	Wigan Ath	0	0		
2007–08	*Stoke C*	10	0	**10**	**0**

OLEMBE, Salomon (M) **131** **7**

H: 5 7 W: 10 04 b.Yaounde 8-12-80

Honours: Cameroon full caps.

1997–98	Nantes	9	0		
1998–99	Nantes	29	1		
1999–2000	Nantes	22	2		
2000–01	Nantes	30	4		
2001–02	Nantes	13	0	**103**	**7**
2001–02	Marseille	8	0		
2002–03	Marseille	0	0	**8**	**0**
2003–04	Leeds U	12	0		
2004–05	Leeds U	0	0		
2005–06	Leeds U	0	0		
2006–07	Leeds U	0	0	**12**	**0**
2007–08	Wigan Ath	8	0	**8**	**0**

PALACIOS, Wilson (D) **23** **0**

H: 5 10 W: 11 11 b.La Ceiba 29-7-84

Source: Olimpia. *Honours:* Honduras 52 full caps, 4 goals.

2007–08	Birmingham C	7	0	**7**	**0**
2007–08	Wigan Ath	16	0	**16**	**0**

POLLITT, Mike (G) **495** **0**

H: 6 4 W: 15 03 b.Farnworth 29-2-72

Source: Trainee.

1990–91	Manchester U	0	0		
1990–91	*Oldham Ath*	0	0		
1991–92	Bury	0	0		
1992–93	Lincoln C	27	0		
1993–94	Lincoln C	30	0	**57**	**0**
1994–95	Darlington	40	0		
1995–96	Darlington	15	0	**55**	**0**
1995–96	Notts Co	0	0		
1996–97	Notts Co	8	0		
1997–98	Notts Co	2	0	**10**	**0**
1997–98	*Oldham Ath*	16	0	**16**	**0**
1997–98	*Gillingham*	6	0	**6**	**0**
1997–98	*Brentford*	5	0	**5**	**0**
1997–98	Sunderland	0	0		
1998–99	Rotherham U	46	0		
1999–2000	Rotherham U	46	0		
2000–01	Chesterfield	46	0	**46**	**0**
2001–02	Rotherham U	46	0		
2002–03	Rotherham U	41	0		
2003–04	Rotherham U	43	0		
2004–05	Rotherham U	45	0	**267**	**0**
2005–06	Wigan Ath	24	0		
2006–07	Wigan Ath	3	0		
2006–07	*Ipswich T*	1	0	**1**	**0**
2006–07	*Burnley*	4	0	**4**	**0**
2007–08	Wigan Ath	1	0	**28**	**0**

SAUNDERS, Russell (G) **0** **0**

H: 6 0 W: 12 02 b.Bury 3-1-89

Source: Scholar.

2007–08	Wigan Ath	0	0		

SCHARNER, Paul (D) **212** **23**

H: 6 3 W: 12 09 b.Scheibbs 11-3-80

Source: St Polten. *Honours:* Austria 15 full caps.

1998–99	FK Austria	4	0		
1999–2000	FK Austria	12	0		
2000–01	FK Austria	14	0		
2001–02	FK Austria	16	1		
2002–03	FK Austria	29	1		
2003–04	FK Austria	9	1	**84**	**3**
2003–04	Salzburg	13	2		
2004–05	Salzburg	5	1	**18**	**3**
2004	Brann	7	1		
2005	Brann	25	6	**32**	**7**
2005–06	Wigan Ath	16	3		
2006–07	Wigan Ath	25	3		
2007–08	Wigan Ath	37	4	**78**	**10**

SIBIERSKI, Antoine (M) **408** **79**

H: 6 2 W: 12 04 b.Lille 5-8-74

Honours: France Youth, Under-21, Under-23, B.

1992–93	Lille	6	0		
1993–94	Lille	22	1		
1994–95	Lille	36	7		
1995–96	Lille	33	9	**97**	**17**
1996–97	Auxerre	30	7		
1997–98	Auxerre	12	1	**42**	**8**
1998–99	Nantes	4	0		
1999–2000	Nantes	28	13	**32**	**13**
2000–01	Lens	27	5		
2001–02	Lens	25	6		
2002–03	Lens	37	12	**89**	**23**
2003–04	Manchester C	33	5		
2004–05	Manchester C	35	4		
2005–06	Manchester C	24	2		
2006–07	Manchester C	0	0	**92**	**11**
2006–07	Newcastle U	26	3	**26**	**3**
2007–08	Wigan Ath	30	4	**30**	**4**

SKOKO, Josip (M) **316** **32**

H: 5 9 W: 12 02 b.Mount Gambier 10-12-75

Honours: Australia Under-20, Under-23, 51 full caps, 9 goals.

1995–96	Hajduk Split	14	1		
1996–97	Hajduk Split	27	10		
1997–98	Hajduk Split	26	5		
1998–99	Hajduk Split	24	3		
1999–2000	Hajduk Split	15	0	**106**	**19**
1999–2000	Genk	9	1		
2000–01	Genk	28	3		
2001–02	Genk	32	2		
2002–03	Genk	29	1	**98**	**7**
2003–04	Genclerbirligi	28	2		
2004–05	Genclerbirligi	30	2	**58**	**4**
2005–06	Wigan Ath	5	0		
2005–06	*Stoke C*	9	2	**9**	**2**
2006–07	Wigan Ath	28	0		
2007–08	Wigan Ath	12	0	**45**	**0**

TAYLOR, Ryan (M) **142** **18**

H: 5 8 W: 10 04 b.Liverpool 19-8-84

Source: Scholar. *Honours:* England Youth, Under-21.

2001–02	Tranmere R	0	0		
2002–03	Tranmere R	25	1		
2003–04	Tranmere R	30	5		
2004–05	Tranmere R	43	8	**98**	**14**
2005–06	Wigan Ath	11	0		
2006–07	Wigan Ath	16	1		
2007–08	Wigan Ath	17	3	**44**	**4**

VALENCIA, Luis (M) **115 13**
H: 5 10 W: 12 04 b.Lago Agrio 5-8-85
Honours: Ecuador Under-21, Under-23, 29 full caps, 4 goals.

2003	El Nacional	42	5		
2004	El Nacional	14	4	**56**	**9**
2004–05	Villarreal	0	0		
2005–06	Villarreal	2	0	**2**	**0**
2005–06	*Recreativo*	4	0	**4**	**0**
2006–07	Wigan Ath	22	1		
2007–08	Wigan Ath	31	3	**53**	**4**

WEBSTER, Andy (D) **169 7**
H: 6 0 W: 11 13 b.Dundee 23-4-82
Honours: Scotland Under-21, B, 22 full caps, 1 goal.

1999–2000	Arbroath	4	0		
2000–01	Arbroath	13	1	**17**	**1**
2000–01	Hearts	4	0		
2001–02	Hearts	26	1		
2002–03	Hearts	21	1		
2003–04	Hearts	32	2		
2004–05	Hearts	35	1		
2005–06	Hearts	30	1	**148**	**6**
2006–07	Wigan Ath	4	0		
2007–08	Wigan Ath	0	0	**4**	**0**

Scholars
Ashworth, Luke Alexander; Barrie, Daniel James; Field, Lewis; Hampson, Matthew; Holt, Joseph; Kirkbride, Aidan; Mahon, Craig; McManaman, Callum Henry; Meace, Nicolas; Mustoe, Jordan David; Pearson, Andrew David; Postlethwaite, Neil; Prince, Adam

WOLVERHAMPTON W (89)

BAILEY, Matthew (M) **0 0**
H: 5 10 W: 9 11 b.Birmingham 24-9-88
Source: Scholar.

2006–07	Wolverhampton W	0	0		
2007–08	Wolverhampton W	0	0		

BENNETT, Elliott (M) **28 2**
H: 5 9 W: 10 11 b.Telford 18-12-88
Source: Scholar.

2006–07	Wolverhampton W	0	0		
2007–08	Wolverhampton W	0	0		
2007–08	*Crewe Alex*	9	1	**9**	**1**
2007–08	*Bury*	19	1	**19**	**1**

BENNETT, Kyle (M) **0 0**
b.Telford 9-9-90

2007–08	Wolverhampton W	0	0		

BOTHROYD, Jay (F) **186 33**
H: 6 3 W: 14 13 b.Islington 7-5-82
Source: Trainee. *Honours:* England Schools, Youth, Under-20, Under-21.

1999–2000	Arsenal	0	0		
2000–01	Coventry C	8	0		
2001–02	Coventry C	31	6		
2002–03	Coventry C	33	8	**72**	**14**
2003–04	*Perugia*	26	4	**26**	**4**
2004–05	Blackburn R	11	1	**11**	**1**
2005–06	Charlton Ath	18	2	**18**	**2**
2006–07	Wolverhampton W	33	9		
2007–08	Wolverhampton W	22	3	**55**	**12**
2007–08	*Stoke C*	4	0	**4**	**0**

BREEN, Gary (D) **505 13**
H: 6 3 W: 13 03 b.Hendon 12-12-73
Source: Charlton Ath. *Honours:* Eire Under-21, 63 full caps, 7 goals.

1991–92	Maidstone U	19	0	**19**	**0**
1992–93	Gillingham	29	0		
1993–94	Gillingham	22	0	**51**	**0**
1994–95	Peterborough U	44	1		
1995–96	Peterborough U	25	0	**69**	**1**
1995–96	Birmingham C	18	1		
1996–97	Birmingham C	22	1	**40**	**2**
1996–97	Coventry C	9	0		
1997–98	Coventry C	30	1		
1998–99	Coventry C	25	0		
1999–2000	Coventry C	21	0		
2000–01	Coventry C	31	1		
2001–02	Coventry C	30	0	**146**	**2**
2002–03	West Ham U	14	0	**14**	**0**
2003–04	Sunderland	32	4		
2004–05	Sunderland	40	2		
2005–06	Sunderland	35	1	**107**	**7**
2006–07	Wolverhampton W	40	1		
2007–08	Wolverhampton W	19	0	**59**	**1**

COLLINS, Lee (D) **16 0**
H: 6 1 W: 11 10 b.Telford 23-9-83
Source: Scholar. *Honours:* England Youth.

2006–07	Wolverhampton W	0	0		
2007–08	Wolverhampton W	0	0		
2007–08	*Hereford U*	16	0	**16**	**0**

COLLINS, Neill (D) **199 10**
H: 6 3 W: 12 07 b.Irvine 2-9-83
Honours: Scoland Under-21, B.

2000–01	Queen's Park	4	0		
2001–02	Queen's Park	28	0	**32**	**0**
2002–03	Dumbarton	33	2		
2003–04	Dumbarton	30	2	**63**	**4**
2004–05	Sunderland	11	0		
2005–06	Sunderland	1	0		
2005–06	*Hartlepool U*	22	0	**22**	**0**
2005–06	*Sheffield U*	2	0	**2**	**0**
2006–07	Sunderland	7	1	**19**	**1**
2006–07	Wolverhampton W	22	2		
2007–08	Wolverhampton W	39	3	**61**	**5**

CRADDOCK, Jody (D) **454 13**
H: 6 0 W: 12 04 b.Redditch 25-7-75
Source: Christchurch.

1993–94	Cambridge U	20	0		
1994–95	Cambridge U	38	0		
1995–96	Cambridge U	46	3		
1996–97	Cambridge U	41	1	**145**	**4**
1997–98	Sunderland	32	0		
1998–99	Sunderland	6	0		
1999–2000	Sunderland	19	0		
1999–2000	*Sheffield U*	10	0	**10**	**0**
2000–01	Sunderland	34	0		
2001–02	Sunderland	30	1		
2002–03	Sunderland	25	1	**146**	**2**
2003–04	Wolverhampton W	32	1		
2004–05	Wolverhampton W	42	1		
2005–06	Wolverhampton W	18	0		
2006–07	Wolverhampton W	34	4		
2007–08	Wolverhampton W	23	1	**149**	**7**
2007–08	*Stoke C*	4	0	**4**	**0**

DAVIES, Mark (M) **27 1**
H: 5 11 W: 11 08 b.Wolverhampton 18-2-88
Source: Scholar. *Honours:* England Youth.

2004–05	Wolverhampton W	0	0		
2005–06	Wolverhampton W	20	1		
2006–07	Wolverhampton W	7	0		
2007–08	Wolverhampton W	0	0	**27**	**1**

EASTWOOD, Freddy (F) **146 56**
H: 5 11 W: 12 04 b.Epsom 29-10-83
Source: West Ham U Trainee, Grays Ath. *Honours:* Wales 9 full caps, 4 goals.

2004–05	Southend U	33	19		
2005–06	Southend U	40	23		
2006–07	Southend U	42	11	**115**	**53**
2007–08	Wolverhampton W	31	3	**31**	**3**

EBANKS-BLAKE, Sylvan (F) **86 33**
H: 5 10 W: 13 04 b.Cambridge 29-3-86
Source: Scholar.

2004–05	Manchester U	0	0		
2005–06	Manchester U	0	0		
2006–07	Plymouth Arg	41	10		
2007–08	Plymouth Arg	25	11	**66**	**21**
2007–08	Wolverhampton W	20	12	**20**	**12**

EDWARDS, Dave (M) **132 17**
H: 5 11 W: 11 04 b.Shrewsbury 3-2-86
Source: Scholar. *Honours:* Wales Youth, Under-21, 5 full caps.

2002–03	Shrewsbury T	1	0		
2003–04	Shrewsbury T	0	0		
2004–05	Shrewsbury T	27	5		
2005–06	Shrewsbury T	30	2		
2006–07	Shrewsbury T	45	5	**103**	**12**
2007–08	Luton T	19	4	**19**	**4**
2007–08	Wolverhampton W	10	1	**10**	**1**

EDWARDS, Rob (D) **126 3**
H: 6 1 W: 11 10 b.Telford 25-12-82
Source: Trainee. *Honours:* Wales Youth, 15 full caps.

1999–2000	Aston Villa	0	0		
2000–01	Aston Villa	0	0		
2001–02	Aston Villa	0	0		
2002–03	Aston Villa	8	0		
2003–04	Aston Villa	0	0	**8**	**0**
2003–04	*Crystal Palace*	7	1	**7**	**1**
2003–04	*Derby Co*	11	1	**11**	**1**
2004–05	Wolverhampton W	17	0		
2005–06	Wolverhampton W	42	0		
2006–07	Wolverhampton W	33	0		
2007–08	Wolverhampton W	8	1	**100**	**1**

ELLIOTT, Stephen (F) **112 26**
H: 5 8 W: 11 07 b.Dublin 6-1-84
Source: School. *Honours:* Eire Youth, Under-21, 9 full caps, 1 goal.

2000–01	Manchester C	0	0		
2001–02	Manchester C	0	0		
2002–03	Manchester C	0	0		
2003–04	Manchester C	2	0	**2**	**0**
2004–05	Sunderland	42	15		
2005–06	Sunderland	15	2		
2006–07	Sunderland	24	5	**81**	**22**
2007–08	Wolverhampton W	29	4	**29**	**4**

ELOKOBI, George (D) **59 2**
H: 5 10 W: 13 02 b.Cameroon 31-1-86
Source: Dulwich Hamlet.

2004–05	Colchester U	0	0		
2004–05	*Chester C*	5	0	**5**	**0**
2005–06	Colchester U	12	1		
2006–07	Colchester U	10	0		
2007–08	Colchester U	17	1	**39**	**2**
2007–08	Wolverhampton W	15	0	**15**	**0**

FOLEY, Kevin (D) **195 4**
H: 5 9 W: 11 11 b.Luton 1-11-84
Source: Scholar. *Honours:* Eire B, Under-21.

2002–03	Luton T	2	0		
2003–04	Luton T	33	1		
2004–05	Luton T	39	2		
2005–06	Luton T	38	0		
2006–07	Luton T	39	0		
2007–08	Luton T	0	0	**151**	**3**
2007–08	Wolverhampton W	44	1	**44**	**1**

GLEESON, Stephen (M) **27 2**
H: 6 2 W: 11 00 b.Dublin 3-8-88
Source: Scholar. *Honours:* Eire Youth, Under-21, 2 full caps.

2006–07	Wolverhampton W	3	0		
2006–07	*Stockport Co*	14	2		
2007–08	Wolverhampton W	0	0	**3**	**0**
2007–08	*Hereford U*	4	0	**4**	**0**
2007–08	*Stockport Co*	6	0	**20**	**2**

GOBERN, Lewis (M) **29 4**
H: 5 10 W: 11 07 b.Birmingham 28-1-85
Source: Scholar.

2003–04	Wolverhampton W	0	0		
2004–05	Wolverhampton W	0	0		
2004–05	*Hartlepool U*	1	0	**1**	**0**
2005–06	Wolverhampton W	1	0		
2005–06	*Blackpool*	8	1	**8**	**1**
2005–06	*Bury*	7	1	**7**	**1**
2006–07	Wolverhampton W	12	2		
2007–08	Wolverhampton W	0	0	**13**	**2**

GRAY, Michael (D) **476 19**
H: 5 8 W: 10 07 b.Sunderland 3-8-74
Source: Trainee. *Honours:* England 3 full caps.

1992–93	Sunderland	27	2		
1993–94	Sunderland	22	1		
1994–95	Sunderland	16	0		
1995–96	Sunderland	46	4		
1996–97	Sunderland	34	3		
1997–98	Sunderland	44	2		
1998–99	Sunderland	37	2		
1999–2000	Sunderland	33	0		
2000–01	Sunderland	36	1		
2001–02	Sunderland	35	0		
2002–03	Sunderland	32	1		
2003–04	Sunderland	1	0	**363**	**16**
2003–04	Blackburn R	14	0		
2004–05	Blackburn R	9	0		
2004–05	*Leeds U*	10	0		
2005–06	Blackburn R	30	0		
2006–07	Blackburn R	11	0	**64**	**0**
2006–07	*Leeds U*	6	0	**16**	**0**
2007–08	Wolverhampton W	33	3	**33**	**3**

HENNESSEY, Wayne (G) **61 0**
H: 6 0 W: 11 06 b.Anglesey 24-1-87
Source: Scholar. *Honours:* Wales Schools, Youth, Under-21, 10 full caps.

2004–05	Wolverhampton W	0	0		
2005–06	Wolverhampton W	0	0		
2006–07	Wolverhampton W	0	0		
2006–07	*Bristol C*	0	0		

2006–07 *Stockport Co* 15 0 **15 0**
2007–08 Wolverhampton W 46 0 **46 0**

HENRY, Karl (M) 203 8
H: 6 0 W: 12 00 b.Wolverhampton 26-11-82
Source: Trainee. *Honours:* England Youth, Under-20.
1999–2000 Stoke C 0 0
2000–01 Stoke C 0 0
2001–02 Stoke C 24 0
2002–03 Stoke C 18 1
2003–04 Stoke C 20 0
2003–04 *Cheltenham T* 9 1 **9 1**
2004–05 Stoke C 34 0
2005–06 Stoke C 24 0 **120 1**
2006–07 Wolverhampton W 34 3
2007–08 Wolverhampton W 40 3 **74 6**

HUGHES, Liam (F) 4 0
H: 6 2 W: 11 09 b.Stourbridge 11-9-88
Source: Scholar.
2006–07 Wolverhampton W 0 0
2007–08 Wolverhampton W 0 0
2007–08 *Bury* 4 0 **4 0**

IKEME, Carl (G) 10 0
H: 6 2 W: 13 09 b.Sutton Coldfield 8-6-86
Source: Scholar.
2005–06 Wolverhampton W 0 0
2005–06 *Stockport Co* 9 0 **9 0**
2006–07 Wolverhampton W 1 0
2007–08 Wolverhampton W 0 0 **1 0**

JARVIS, Matthew (M) 136 13
H: 5 8 W: 11 10 b.Middlesbrough 22-5-86
Source: Scholar.
2003–04 Gillingham 10 0
2004–05 Gillingham 30 3
2005–06 Gillingham 35 3
2006–07 Gillingham 35 6 **110 12**
2007–08 Wolverhampton W 26 1 **26 1**

JONES, Daniel (D) 43 3
H: 6 2 W: 13 00 b.Wordsley 14-7-86
Source: Scholar.
2005–06 Wolverhampton W 1 0
2006–07 Wolverhampton W 8 0
2007–08 Wolverhampton W 1 0 **10 0**
2007–08 *Northampton T* 33 3 **33 3**

KEOGH, Andy (F) 162 36
H: 6 0 W: 11 00 b.Dublin 16-5-86
Source: Scholar. *Honours:* Eire Youth, B, Under-21, 7 full caps, 1 goal.
2003–04 Leeds U 0 0
2004–05 Leeds U 0 0
2004–05 *Bury* 4 2 **4 2**
2004–05 Scunthorpe U 25 3
2005–06 Scunthorpe U 45 11
2006–07 Scunthorpe U 28 7 **98 21**
2006–07 Wolverhampton W 17 5
2007–08 Wolverhampton W 43 8 **60 13**

KIGHTLY, Michael (F) 58 12
H: 5 10 W: 10 10 b.Basildon 24-1-86
Source: Scholar. *Honours:* England Under-21.
2002–03 Southend U 1 0
2003–04 Southend U 11 0
2004–05 Southend U 1 0 **13 0**
From Grays Ath.
2006–07 Wolverhampton W 24 8
2007–08 Wolverhampton W 21 4 **45 12**

LITTLE, Mark (D) 44 0
H: 6 1 W: 12 10 b.Worcester 20-8-88
Source: Scholar. *Honours:* England Youth.
2005–06 Wolverhampton W 0 0
2006–07 Wolverhampton W 26 0
2007–08 Wolverhampton W 1 0 **27 0**
2007–08 *Northampton T* 17 0 **17 0**

LOWE, Keith (D) 79 4
H: 6 2 W: 13 03 b.Wolverhampton 13-9-85
Source: Scholar.
2004–05 Wolverhampton W 11 0
2005–06 Wolverhampton W 3 0
2005–06 *Burnley* 16 0 **16 0**
2005–06 *QPR* 1 0 **1 0**
2005–06 *Swansea C* 4 0 **4 0**
2006–07 Wolverhampton W 0 0
2006–07 *Brighton & HA* 0 0
2006–07 *Cheltenham T* 16 1 **16 1**
2007–08 Wolverhampton W 0 0 **14 0**
2007–08 *Port Vale* 28 3 **28 3**

MULGREW, Charlie (D) 37 3
H: 6 2 W: 13 01 b.Glasgow 6-3-86
Honours: Scotland Youth, Under-21.
2002–03 Celtic 0 0
2003–04 Celtic 0 0
2004–05 Celtic 0 0
2005–06 Celtic 0 0
2005–06 *Dundee U* 13 2 **13 2**
2006–07 Wolverhampton W 6 0
2007–08 Wolverhampton W 0 0 **6 0**
2007–08 *Southend U* 18 1 **18 1**

MURRAY, Matt (G) 89 0
H: 6 4 W: 13 10 b.Solihull 2-5-81
Source: Trainee. *Honours:* England Youth, Under-21.
1997–98 Wolverhampton W 0 0
1998–99 Wolverhampton W 0 0
1999–2000 Wolverhampton W 0 0
2000–01 Wolverhampton W 0 0
2001–02 Wolverhampton W 0 0
2002–03 Wolverhampton W 40 0
2003–04 Wolverhampton W 1 0
2004–05 Wolverhampton W 1 0
2005–06 Wolverhampton W 1 0
2005–06 *Tranmere R* 2 0 **2 0**
2006–07 Wolverhampton W 44 0
2007–08 Wolverhampton W 0 0 **87 0**

O'CONNOR, Kevin (M) 10 1
H: 5 11 W: 12 02 b.Dublin 19-10-85
Source: Scholar. *Honours:* Eire Under-21.
2003–04 Wolverhampton W 0 0
2004–05 Wolverhampton W 0 0
2005–06 Wolverhampton W 0 0
2005–06 *Stockport Co* 7 1 **7 1**
2006–07 Wolverhampton W 3 0
2007–08 Wolverhampton W 0 0 **3 0**

OLOFINJANA, Seyi (M) 169 27
H: 6 4 W: 11 10 b.Lagos 30-6-80
Source: Kwara United Ilorin. *Honours:* Nigeria 20 full caps.
2003 Brann 25 9
2004 Brann 9 2 **34 11**
2004–05 Wolverhampton W 42 5
2005–06 Wolverhampton W 13 0
2006–07 Wolverhampton W 44 8
2007–08 Wolverhampton W 36 3 **135 16**

POTTER, Darren (M) 68 0
H: 6 0 W: 10 08 b.Liverpool 21-12-84
Source: Scholar. *Honours:* Eire Youth, B, Under-21, 5 full caps.
2001–02 Liverpool 0 0
2002–03 Liverpool 0 0
2003–04 Liverpool 0 0
2004–05 Liverpool 2 0
2005–06 Liverpool 0 0
2005–06 *Southampton* 10 0 **10 0**
2006–07 Liverpool 0 0 **2 0**
2006–07 Wolverhampton W 38 0
2007–08 Wolverhampton W 18 0 **56 0**

RILEY, Martin (D) 0 0
H: 6 0 W: 12 01 b.Wolverhampton 5-12-86
Source: Scholar. *Honours:* England Under-20.
2004–05 Wolverhampton W 0 0
2005–06 Wolverhampton W 0 0
2006–07 Wolverhampton W 0 0
2007–08 Wolverhampton W 0 0

ROSA, Denes (M) 198 29
H: 5 8 W: 10 05 b.Hungary 7-4-77
Honours: Hungary 10 full caps.
1996–97 BVSC 12 0
1997–98 BVSC 26 5
1998–99 BVSC 13 4
1999–2000 BVSC 0 0
1999–2000 Gyor 8 1
2000–01 Gyor 25 1
2001–02 BVSC 0 0 **51 9**
2001–02 Gyor 12 1 **45 3**
2002–03 Dunaferr 14 0 **14 0**
2002–03 Ujpest 9 1 **9 1**
2003–04 Ferencvaros 25 2
2004–05 Ferencvaros 27 8
2005–06 Ferencvaros 14 4 **66 14**
2005–06 Wolverhampton W 9 2
2006–07 Wolverhampton W 0 0
2006–07 *Cheltenham T* 4 0 **4 0**
2007–08 Wolverhampton W 0 0 **9 2**

SALMON, Mark (M) 9 0
H: 5 10 W: 10 07 b.Dublin 31-10-88
Source: Scholar.
2006–07 Wolverhampton W 0 0
2007–08 Wolverhampton W 0 0
2007–08 *Port Vale* 9 0 **9 0**

WARD, Darren (D) 308 11
H: 6 3 W: 11 04 b.Kenton 13-9-78
Source: Trainee.
1995–96 Watford 1 0
1996–97 Watford 7 0
1997–98 Watford 0 0
1998–99 Watford 1 0
1999–2000 Watford 9 1
1999–2000 *QPR* 14 0 **14 0**
2000–01 Watford 40 1
2001–02 Watford 1 0 **59 2**
2001–02 Millwall 14 0
2002–03 Millwall 39 1
2003–04 Millwall 46 3
2004–05 Millwall 43 0 **142 4**
2005–06 Crystal Palace 43 5
2006–07 Crystal Palace 20 0 **63 5**
2007–08 Wolverhampton W 30 0 **30 0**

WARD, Stephen (F) 119 14
H: 5 11 W: 12 02 b.Dublin 20-8-85
Honours: Eire Youth, Under-21, B.
2003 Bohemians 6 0
2004 Bohemians 16 2
2005 Bohemians 29 7
2006 Bohemians 21 2 **72 11**
2006–07 Wolverhampton W 18 3
2007–08 Wolverhampton W 29 0 **47 3**

WREXHAM (90)

AISTON, Sam (M) 271 10
H: 6 1 W: 14 00 b.Newcastle 21-11-76
Source: Newcastle U Trainee. *Honours:* England Schools.
1995–96 Sunderland 14 0
1996–97 Sunderland 2 0
1996–97 *Chester C* 14 0
1997–98 Sunderland 3 0
1998–99 Sunderland 1 0
1998–99 *Chester C* 11 0 **25 0**
1999–2000 Sunderland 0 0 **20 0**
1999–2000 *Stoke C* 6 0 **6 0**
1999–2000 *Shrewsbury T* 10 0
2000–01 Shrewsbury T 42 2
2001–02 Shrewsbury T 35 2
2002–03 Shrewsbury T 21 2
2003–04 Shrewsbury T 0 0
2004–05 Shrewsbury T 35 1 **143 7**
2005–06 Tranmere R 36 3 **36 3**
2006–07 Northampton T 21 0
2007–08 Northampton T 1 0 **22 0**
2007–08 Wrexham 19 0 **19 0**

BAYNES, Wes (M) 12 2
H: 5 11 W: 10 10 b.Chester 12-10-88
Source: Scholar.
2007–08 Wrexham 12 2 **12 2**

BOLLAND, Phil (D) 141 4
H: 6 4 W: 13 03 b.Liverpool 26-8-76
Source: Altrincham, Knowsley U, Trafford, Salford C, Altrincham, Southport.
2001–02 Oxford U 20 1 **20 1**
2001–02 Chester C 0 0
2002–03 Chester C 0 0
2003–04 Chester C 0 0
2004–05 Chester C 42 1
2005–06 Chester C 16 1
2005–06 Peterborough U 17 0 **17 0**
2006–07 Chester C 26 1
2007–08 Chester C 2 0 **86 3**
2007–08 Wrexham 18 0 **18 0**

CARVILL, Michael (F) 14 0
H: 5 10 W: 10 10 b.Belfast 3-4-88
Source: Scholar. *Honours:* Northern Ireland Youth, Under-21.
2005–06 Charlton Ath 0 0
2006–07 Charlton Ath 0 0
2006–07 Wrexham 6 0
2007–08 Wrexham 8 0 **14 0**

CROWELL, Matt (M) **93 4**
H: 5 11 W: 10 10 b.Bridgend 3-7-84
Source: Scholar. *Honours:* Wales Youth, Under-21.

2001–02	Southampton	0	0		
2002–03	Southampton	0	0		
2003–04	Wrexham	15	1		
2004–05	Wrexham	28	0		
2005–06	Wrexham	29	3		
2006–07	Wrexham	15	0		
2007–08	Wrexham	6	0	**93**	**4**

DARLINGTON, Alexander (F) **0 0**
H: 5 11 W: 10 07 b.Wales 26-12-88
Source: Scholar.

2007–08	Wrexham	0	0		

DONE, Matt (M) **66 1**
H: 5 10 W: 10 04 b.Oswestry 22-6-88
Source: Scholar.

2005–06	Wrexham	6	0		
2006–07	Wrexham	34	1		
2007–08	Wrexham	26	0	**66**	**1**

DUFFY, Robert (F) **35 1**
H: 6 1 W: 13 01 b.Swansea 2-12-82
Source: Juniors. *Honours:* Wales Under-18.

2001–02	Rushden & D	8	1		
2002–03	Rushden & D	12	0		
2003–04	Rushden & D	8	0		
2004–05	Rushden & D	1	0		
2005–06	Rushden & D	0	0		
2006–07	Rushden & D	0	0	**29**	**1**
From Stmfd, Cam U, Kett T, Steve, Ox U.					
2007–08	Wrexham	6	0	**6**	**0**

EVANS, Gareth (D) **25 0**
H: 6 1 W: 12 12 b.Wrexham 10-1-87
Source: Scholar.

2005–06	Wrexham	0	0		
2006–07	Wrexham	12	0		
2007–08	Wrexham	13	0	**25**	**0**

EVANS, Steve (D) **217 29**
H: 6 5 W: 13 05 b.Wrexham 26-2-79
Honours: Wales 6 full caps.

1999–2000	TNS	14	4		
2000–01	TNS	8	0		
2001–02	TNS	16	2		
2002–03	TNS	27	7		
2003–04	TNS	20	8		
2004–05	TNS	33	0		
2005–06	TNS	33	3	**151**	**24**
2006–07	Wrexham	35	2		
2007–08	Wrexham	31	3	**66**	**5**

FLEMING, Andy (M) **6 0**
H: 6 1 W: 12 00 b.Liverpool 1-4-87
Source: Scholar.

2006–07	Wrexham	2	0		
2007–08	Wrexham	4	0	**6**	**0**

HALL, Paul (M) **646 110**
H: 5 8 W: 12 00 b.Manchester 3-7-72
Source: Trainee. *Honours:* Jamaica 41 full caps, 9 goals.

1989–90	Torquay U	10	0		
1990–91	Torquay U	17	0		
1991–92	Torquay U	38	1		
1992–93	Torquay U	28	0	**93**	**1**
1992–93	Portsmouth	0	0		
1993–94	Portsmouth	28	4		
1994–95	Portsmouth	43	5		
1995–96	Portsmouth	46	10		
1996–97	Portsmouth	42	13		
1997–98	Portsmouth	29	5	**188**	**37**
1998–99	Coventry C	9	0		
1998–99	*Bury*	7	0	**7**	**0**
1999–2000	Coventry C	1	0	**10**	**0**
1999–2000	*Sheffield U*	4	1	**4**	**1**
1999–2000	*WBA*	4	0	**4**	**0**
1999–2000	Walsall	10	4		
2000–01	Walsall	42	6		
2001–02	Walsall	0	0		
2001–02	Rushden & D	34	8		
2002–03	Rushden & D	45	16		
2003–04	Rushden & D	33	2	**112**	**26**
2003–04	Tranmere R	9	2		
2004–05	Tranmere R	46	11	**55**	**13**
2005–06	Chesterfield	45	15		
2006–07	Chesterfield	46	5	**91**	**20**
2007–08	Walsall	19	1	**71**	**11**
2007–08	Wrexham	11	1	**11**	**1**

HOPE, Richard (D) **370 12**
H: 6 2 W: 12 06 b.Stockton 22-6-78
Source: Trainee.

1995–96	Blackburn R	0	0		
1996–97	Blackburn R	0	0		
1996–97	Darlington	20	0		
1997–98	Darlington	35	1		
1998–99	Darlington	8	0	**63**	**1**
1998–99	Northampton T	19	0		
1999–2000	Northampton T	17	0		
2000–01	Northampton T	33	0		
2001–02	Northampton T	43	6		
2002–03	Northampton T	23	1	**135**	**7**
2003–04	York C	36	2	**36**	**2**
2004–05	Chester C	28	0	**28**	**0**
2005–06	Shrewsbury T	42	2		
2006–07	Shrewsbury T	33	0	**75**	**2**
2007–08	Wrexham	33	0	**33**	**0**

JOHNSON, Josh (M) **29 1**
H: 5 5 W: 10 07 b.Carenage 16-4-81
Source: San Juan Jabloteh. *Honours:* Trinidad & Tobago Under-20, Under-21.

2006–07	Wrexham	22	1		
2007–08	Wrexham	7	0	**29**	**1**

JONES, Mark (M) **128 22**
H: 5 11 W: 10 12 b.Wrexham 15-8-83
Source: Scholar. *Honours:* Wales Under-21, 2 full caps.

2002–03	Wrexham	1	0		
2003–04	Wrexham	13	1		
2004–05	Wrexham	26	3		
2005–06	Wrexham	42	13		
2006–07	Wrexham	30	5		
2007–08	Wrexham	16	0	**128**	**22**

JONES, Michael (G) **11 0**
H: 6 4 W: 12 05 b.Liverpool 3-12-87
Source: Scholar.

2004–05	Wrexham	1	0		
2005–06	Wrexham	7	0		
2006–07	Wrexham	1	0		
2007–08	Wrexham	2	0	**11**	**0**

LLEWELLYN, Chris (F) **355 47**
H: 5 11 W: 11 06 b.Swansea 29-8-79
Source: Trainee. *Honours:* Wales Schools, Youth, Under-21, B, 6 full caps, 1 goal.

1996–97	Norwich C	0	0		
1997–98	Norwich C	15	4		
1998–99	Norwich C	31	2		
1999–2000	Norwich C	36	3		
2000–01	Norwich C	42	8		
2001–02	Norwich C	13	0		
2002–03	Norwich C	5	0	**142**	**17**
2002–03	*Bristol R*	14	3	**14**	**3**
2003–04	Wrexham	46	8		
2004–05	Wrexham	45	7		
2005–06	Hartlepool U	29	0	**29**	**0**
2006–07	Wrexham	39	9		
2007–08	Wrexham	40	3	**170**	**27**

MACKIN, Levi (M) **45 1**
H: 6 1 W: 11 04 b.Chester 4-4-86
Source: Scholar. *Honours:* Wales Under-21.

2003–04	Wrexham	1	0		
2004–05	Wrexham	10	0		
2005–06	Wrexham	17	0		
2006–07	Wrexham	8	0		
2007–08	Wrexham	9	1	**45**	**1**

MURTAGH, Conall (M) **67 5**
H: 6 0 W: 11 11 b.Belfast 29-6-85

2003–04	Hearts	0	0		
2004–05	Hearts	0	0		
2004–05	*Raith R*	11	1	**11**	**1**
2005–06	Connah's Quay N	27	3	**27**	**3**
2006–07	Rhyl	25	1	**25**	**1**
2007–08	Wrexham	4	0	**4**	**0**

PEJIC, Shaun (D) **174 0**
H: 6 0 W: 11 07 b.Hereford 16-11-82
Source: Trainee. *Honours:* Wales Youth, Under-21.

2000–01	Wrexham	1	0		
2001–02	Wrexham	12	0		
2002–03	Wrexham	27	0		
2003–04	Wrexham	21	0		
2004–05	Wrexham	35	0		
2005–06	Wrexham	26	0		
2006–07	Wrexham	33	0		
2007–08	Wrexham	19	0	**174**	**0**

PROCTOR, Michael (F) **229 52**
H: 5 11 W: 11 11 b.Sunderland 3-10-80
Source: Trainee.

1997–98	Sunderland	0	0		
1998–99	Sunderland	0	0		
1999–2000	Sunderland	0	0		
2000–01	Sunderland	0	0		
2000–01	*Halifax T*	12	4	**12**	**4**
2001–02	Sunderland	0	0		
2001–02	*York C*	41	14	**41**	**14**
2002–03	Sunderland	21	2		
2002–03	*Bradford C*	12	4	**12**	**4**
2003–04	Sunderland	17	1	**38**	**3**
2003–04	Rotherham U	17	6		
2004–05	Rotherham U	28	1	**45**	**7**
2004–05	*Swindon T*	4	2	**4**	**2**
2005–06	Hartlepool U	26	5		
2006–07	Hartlepool U	2	0	**28**	**5**
2006–07	*Wrexham*	9	2		
2007–08	Wrexham	40	11	**49**	**13**

REED, Jamie (F) **14 0**
H: 5 11 W: 11 07 b.Deeside 13-8-87
Source: Scholar.

2005–06	Wrexham	3	0		
2005–06	*Glentoran*	7	0	**7**	**0**
2006–07	Wrexham	4	0		
2007–08	Wrexham	0	0	**7**	**0**

ROBERTS, Neil (F) **325 56**
H: 5 10 W: 11 00 b.Wrexham 7-4-78
Source: Trainee. *Honours:* Wales Youth, Under-21, B, 4 full caps.

1996–97	Wrexham	0	0		
1997–98	Wrexham	34	8		
1998–99	Wrexham	22	3		
1999–2000	Wrexham	19	6		
1999–2000	Wigan Ath	9	1		
2000–01	Wigan Ath	34	6		
2001–02	*Hull C*	6	0	**6**	**0**
2001–02	Wigan Ath	17	4		
2002–03	Wigan Ath	37	6		
2003–04	Wigan Ath	28	2		
2004–05	Wigan Ath	0	0	**125**	**19**
2004–05	*Bradford C*	3	1	**3**	**1**
2004–05	Doncaster R	31	6		
2005–06	Doncaster R	30	2	**61**	**8**
2006–07	Wrexham	19	3		
2007–08	Wrexham	36	8	**130**	**28**

SONNER, Danny (M) **318 18**
H: 6 0 W: 12 03 b.Wigan 9-1-72
Source: Wigan Ath. *Honours:* Northern Ireland B, 13 full caps.

1990–91	Burnley	2	0		
1991–92	Burnley	3	0		
1992–93	Burnley	1	0	**6**	**0**
1992–93	*Bury*	5	3	**5**	**3**
From Erzgebirge Aue					
1996–97	Ipswich T	29	2		
1997–98	Ipswich T	23	1		
1998–99	Ipswich T	4	0	**56**	**3**
1998–99	Sheffield W	26	3		
1999–2000	Sheffield W	27	0	**53**	**3**
2000–01	Birmingham C	26	1		
2001–02	Birmingham C	15	1	**41**	**2**
2002–03	Walsall	24	4		
2003–04	Nottingham F	28	0		
2004–05	Nottingham F	0	0	**28**	**0**
2004–05	Peterborough U	15	0	**15**	**0**
2004–05	*Port Vale*	13	0		
2005–06	Port Vale	29	1		
2006–07	Port Vale	33	1	**75**	**2**
2007–08	Walsall	6	0	**30**	**4**
2007–08	Wrexham	9	1	**9**	**1**

SPANN, Silvio (M) **9 1**
H: 5 9 W: 11 11 b.Couva 21-8-81
Source: Doc's Khelwalaas, W Connection, Perugia, Sambenedettese, W Connection, Dynamo Zagreb, Yokohama, W Connection. Trinidad & Tobago 28 full caps, 1 goal.

2007–08	Wrexham	9	1	**9**	**1**

SPENDER, Simon (D) **97 5**
H: 5 11 W: 11 00 b.Mold 15-11-85
Source: Scholar. *Honours:* Wales Youth, Under-21.

2003–04	Wrexham	6	0		
2004–05	Wrexham	13	0		
2005–06	Wrexham	19	2		

2006–07 Wrexham 25 2
2007–08 Wrexham 34 1 **97 5**

TAYLOR, Neil (D) 26 0
H: 5 9 W: 10 02 b.Ruthin 7-2-89
Source: Scholar. *Honours:* Wales Youth, Under-21.
2007–08 Wrexham 26 0 **26 0**

TREMARCO, Carl (D) 62 1
H: 5 8 W: 11 11 b.Liverpool 11-10-85
Source: Scholar.
2003–04 Tranmere R 0 0
2004–05 Tranmere R 3 0
2005–06 Tranmere R 18 1
2006–07 Tranmere R 23 0
2007–08 Tranmere R 8 0 **52 1**
2007–08 Wrexham 10 0 **10 0**

UGARTE, Juan (F) 38 17
H: 5 10 W: 10 08 b.San Sebastian 7-11-80
2001–02 Real Sociedad 1 0
2002–03 Real Sociedad 0 0
2003–04 Real Sociedad 0 0 **1 0**
From Dorchester T
2004–05 Wrexham 30 17
2005–06 Crewe Alex 2 0 **2 0**
2005–06 *Wrexham* 2 0
2006–07 Wrexham 2 0
2007–08 Wrexham 1 0 **35 17**

WARD, Gavin (G) 338 1
H: 6 3 W: 14 12 b.Sutton Coldfield 30-6-70
Source: Aston Villa Trainee.
1988–89 Shrewsbury T 0 0
1989–90 WBA 0 0
1989–90 Cardiff C 2 0
1990–91 Cardiff C 1 0
1991–92 Cardiff C 24 0
1992–93 Cardiff C 32 0 **59 0**
1993–94 Leicester C 32 0
1994–95 Leicester C 6 0 **38 0**
1995–96 Bradford C 36 0 **36 0**
1995–96 Bolton W 5 0
1996–97 Bolton W 11 0
1997–98 Bolton W 6 0
1998–99 Bolton W 0 0 **22 0**
1998–99 *Burnley* 17 0 **17 0**
1998–99 Stoke C 6 0
1999–2000 Stoke C 46 0
2000–01 Stoke C 17 0
2001–02 Stoke C 10 0 **79 0**
2002–03 Walsall 7 0 **7 0**
2003–04 Coventry C 12 0 **12 0**
2003–04 *Barnsley* 1 0 **1 0**
2004–05 Preston NE 7 0
2005–06 Preston NE 0 0 **7 0**
2006–07 Tranmere R 38 1 **38 1**
2007–08 Chester C 0 0
2007–08 Wrexham 22 0 **22 0**

WHITLEY, Jeff (M) 277 14
H: 5 8 W: 11 06 b.Zambia 28-1-79
Source: Trainee. *Honours:* England Youth, Northern Ireland Under-21, B, 20 full caps, 2 goals.
1995–96 Manchester C 0 0
1996–97 Manchester C 23 1
1997–98 Manchester C 17 1
1998–99 Manchester C 8 1
1998–99 *Wrexham* 9 2
1999–2000 Manchester C 42 4
2000–01 Manchester C 31 1
2001–02 Manchester C 2 0
2001–02 *Notts Co* 6 0
2002–03 Manchester C 0 0 **123 8**
2002–03 *Notts Co* 12 0 **18 0**
2003–04 Sunderland 33 2
2004–05 Sunderland 35 0 **68 2**
2005–06 Cardiff C 34 1
2006–07 Cardiff C 0 0
2006–07 *Stoke C* 3 0 **3 0**
2006–07 *Wrexham* 11 1
2007–08 Cardiff C 0 0 **34 1**
2007–08 Wrexham 11 0 **31 3**

WILLIAMS, Danny (M) 277 19
H: 6 1 W: 13 00 b.Wrexham 12-7-79
Source: Trainee. *Honours:* Wales Under-21.
1996–97 Liverpool 0 0
1997–98 Liverpool 0 0
1998–99 Liverpool 0 0
1998–99 Wrexham 0 0
1999–2000 Wrexham 24 1
2000–01 Wrexham 15 2
2001–02 Kidderminster H 38 1
2002–03 Kidderminster H 45 2
2003–04 Kidderminster H 28 5 **111 8**
2003–04 Bristol R 6 1 **6 1**
2004–05 Wrexham 21 0
2005–06 Wrexham 45 4
2006–07 Wrexham 40 3
2007–08 Wrexham 15 0 **160 10**

WILLIAMS, Eifion (F) 332 75
H: 5 11 W: 11 02 b.Bangor 15-11-75
Source: Wolverhampton W trainee, Caernarfon T, Barry T. *Honours:* Wales Under-21, B.
1998–99 Torquay U 7 5
1999–2000 Torquay U 42 9
2000–01 Torquay U 37 9
2001–02 Torquay U 25 1 **111 24**
2001–02 Hartlepool U 8 4
2002–03 Hartlepool U 45 15
2003–04 Hartlepool U 41 13
2004–05 Hartlepool U 38 5
2005–06 Hartlepool U 36 7
2006–07 Hartlepool U 40 6 **208 50**
2007–08 Wrexham 13 1 **13 1**

WILLIAMS, Marc (F) 39 4
H: 5 10 W: 11 12 b.Colwyn Bay 27-7-88
Source: Scholar. *Honours:* Wales Youth, Under-21.
2005–06 Wrexham 4 0
2006–07 Wrexham 16 1
2007–08 Wrexham 19 3 **39 4**

WILLIAMS, Mike (D) 61 0
H: 5 11 W: 12 00 b.Colwyn Bay 27-10-86
Source: Scholar. *Honours:* Wales Youth, Under-21.
2005–06 Wrexham 12 0
2006–07 Wrexham 31 0
2007–08 Wrexham 18 0 **61 0**

WILLIAMS, Tony (G) 263 0
H: 6 2 W: 13 09 b.Maesteg 20-9-77
Source: Trainee. *Honours:* Wales Youth, Under-21.
1996–97 Blackburn R 0 0
1997–98 Blackburn R 0 0
1997–98 *QPR* 0 0
1998–99 Blackburn R 0 0
1998–99 *Macclesfield T* 4 0
1998–99 *Huddersfield T* 0 0
1998–99 *Bristol R* 9 0 **9 0**
1999–2000 Blackburn R 0 0
1999–2000 *Gillingham* 2 0 **2 0**
1999–2000 *Macclesfield T* 11 0 **15 0**
2000–01 Hartlepool U 41 0
2001–02 Hartlepool U 43 0
2002–03 Hartlepool U 46 0
2003–04 Hartlepool U 1 0 **131 0**
2003–04 *Swansea C* 0 0
2003–04 *Stockport Co* 15 0 **15 0**
2004–05 Grimsby T 46 0 **46 0**
2005–06 Carlisle U 11 0
2005–06 *Bury* 3 0 **3 0**
2006–07 Carlisle U 0 0 **11 0**
2006–07 *Wrexham* 9 0
2007–08 Wrexham 22 0 **31 0**

WYCOMBE W (91)

ANTWI, Will (D) 40 1
H: 6 2 W: 12 08 b.Epsom 19-10-82
Source: Scholar. *Honours:* Ghana 1 full cap.
2002–03 Crystal Palace 4 0
2003–04 Crystal Palace 0 0 **4 0**
From Aldershot T
2005–06 Wycombe W 5 0
2006–07 Wycombe W 25 1
2007–08 Wycombe W 6 0 **36 1**

BLOOMFIELD, Matt (M) 153 16
H: 5 9 W: 11 00 b.Felixstowe 8-2-84
Source: Scholar. *Honours:* England Youth, Under-20.
2001–02 Ipswich T 0 0
2002–03 Ipswich T 0 0
2003–04 Ipswich T 0 0
2003–04 Wycombe W 12 1
2004–05 Wycombe W 26 2
2005–06 Wycombe W 39 5
2006–07 Wycombe W 41 4
2007–08 Wycombe W 35 4 **153 16**

BOUCAUD, Andre (M) 49 2
H: 5 10 W: 11 02 b.Enfield 9-10-84
Source: Scholar. *Honours:* Trinidad & Tobago 6 full caps.
2001–02 Reading 0 0
2002–03 Reading 0 0
2002–03 *Peterborough U* 6 0
2003–04 Reading 0 0
2003–04 *Peterborough U* 8 1
2004–05 Peterborough U 22 1
2005–06 Peterborough U 3 0
2006–07 Peterborough U 0 0 **39 2**
From Kettering T.
2007–08 Wycombe W 10 0 **10 0**

BULLOCK, Martin (M) 452 20
H: 5 5 W: 10 07 b.Derby 5-3-75
Source: Eastwood T. *Honours:* England Under-21.
1993–94 Barnsley 0 0
1994–95 Barnsley 29 0
1995–96 Barnsley 41 1
1996–97 Barnsley 28 0
1997–98 Barnsley 33 0
1998–99 Barnsley 32 2
1999–2000 Barnsley 4 0
1999–2000 *Port Vale* 6 1 **6 1**
2000–01 Barnsley 18 1
2001–02 Barnsley 0 0 **185 4**
2001–02 Blackpool 43 2
2002–03 Blackpool 38 1
2003–04 Blackpool 44 1
2004–05 Blackpool 28 0 **153 4**
2005–06 Macclesfield T 40 7
2006–07 Macclesfield T 43 4 **83 11**
2007–08 Wycombe W 25 0 **25 0**

CADMORE, Tom (D) 0 0
b.Rickmansworth 26-1-88
Source: Scholar.
2005–06 Wycombe W 0 0
2006–07 Wycombe W 0 0
2007–08 Wycombe W 0 0

CHRISTON, Lewis (D) 8 0
H: 6 0 W: 12 02 b.Milton Keynes 24-1-89
Source: Scholar.
2005–06 Wycombe W 0 0
2006–07 Wycombe W 6 0
2007–08 Wycombe W 2 0 **8 0**

CROOKS, Leon (M) 63 0
H: 6 0 W: 11 12 b.Greenwich 21-11-85
Source: Scholar.
2004–05 Milton Keynes D 17 0
2005–06 Milton Keynes D 23 0
2006–07 Milton Keynes D 12 0 **52 0**
2006–07 Wycombe W 11 0
2007–08 Wycombe W 0 0 **11 0**

DALY, George (F) 2 0
H: 5 11 W: 10 11 b.Wycombe 25-10-90
Source: Scholar.
2007–08 Wycombe W 2 0 **2 0**

DOHERTY, Tom (M) 254 9
H: 5 8 W: 10 06 b.Bristol 17-3-79
Source: Trainee. *Honours:* Northern Ireland 9 full caps.
1997–98 Bristol C 30 2
1998–99 Bristol C 23 1
1999–2000 Bristol C 1 0
2000–01 Bristol C 0 0
2001–02 Bristol C 34 1
2002–03 Bristol C 38 0
2003–04 Bristol C 33 2
2004–05 Bristol C 29 1 **188 7**
2005–06 QPR 15 0
2005–06 *Yeovil T* 1 0 **1 0**
2006–07 QPR 0 0
2006–07 *Wycombe W* 26 2
2007–08 QPR 0 0 **15 0**
2007–08 Wycombe W 24 0 **50 2**

DUNCAN, Derek (M) 20 0
H: 5 10 W: 10 11 b.Newham 23-4-87
Source: Scholar.
2003–04 Leyton Orient 1 0
2004–05 Leyton Orient 15 0
2005–06 Leyton Orient 1 0
2006–07 Leyton Orient 3 0 **20 0**
2007–08 Wycombe W 0 0

GREGORY, Steven (D) 4 0
H: 6 1 W: 12 04 b.Aylesbury 19-3-87
Source: Scholar.
2005–06 Wycombe W 1 0
2006–07 Wycombe W 3 0
2007–08 Wycombe W 0 0 **4 0**

HOLT, Gary (M) 428 15
H: 6 0 W: 12 00 b.Irvine 9-3-73
Source: Celtic. *Honours:* Scotland 10 full caps, 1 goal.
1994–95 Stoke C 0 0
1995–96 Kilmarnock 26 0
1996–97 Kilmarnock 12 1
1997–98 Kilmarnock 27 2
1998–99 Kilmarnock 33 3
1999–2000 Kilmarnock 35 0
2000–01 Kilmarnock 19 3 **152 9**
2000–01 Norwich C 4 0
2001–02 Norwich C 46 2
2002–03 Norwich C 45 0
2003–04 Norwich C 46 1
2004–05 Norwich C 27 0 **168 3**
2005–06 Nottingham F 26 0
2006–07 Nottingham F 39 1 **65 1**
2007–08 Wycombe W 43 2 **43 2**

JOHNSON, Leon (D) 191 5
H: 6 1 W: 13 05 b.Shoreditch 10-5-81
Source: Scholarship.
1999–2000 Southend U 0 0
2000–01 Southend U 20 1
2001–02 Southend U 28 2 **48 3**
2002–03 Gillingham 18 0
2003–04 Gillingham 20 0
2004–05 Gillingham 8 0
2005–06 Gillingham 28 1
2006–07 Gillingham 24 1 **98 2**
2007–08 Wycombe W 45 0 **45 0**

KNIGHT, Leon (F) 264 78
H: 5 5 W: 9 06 b.Hackney 16-9-82
Source: Trainee. *Honours:* England Youth, Under-20.
1999–2000 Chelsea 0 0
2000–01 Chelsea 0 0
2000–01 *QPR* 11 0 **11 0**
2001–02 Chelsea 0 0
2001–02 *Huddersfield T* 31 16 **31 16**
2002–03 Chelsea 0 0
2002–03 *Sheffield W* 24 3 **24 3**
2003–04 Chelsea 0 0
2003–04 Brighton & HA 44 25
2004–05 Brighton & HA 39 4
2005–06 Brighton & HA 25 5 **108 34**
2005–06 Swansea C 17 8
2006–07 Swansea C 11 7 **28 15**
2006–07 *Barnsley* 9 0 **9 0**
2006–07 Milton Keynes D 16 1
2007–08 Milton Keynes D 17 4 **33 5**
2007–08 Wycombe W 20 5 **20 5**

LENNON, Neil (M) 345 21
H: 5 9 W: 13 02 b.Belfast 25-6-71
Source: Trainee. *Honours:* Northern Ireland Under-21, 39 full caps, 2 goals.
1987–88 Manchester C 1 0
1988–89 Manchester C 0 0
1989–90 Manchester C 0 0 **1 0**
1990–91 Crewe Alex 34 3
1991–92 Crewe Alex 0 0
1992–93 Crewe Alex 24 0
1993–94 Crewe Alex 33 4
1994–95 Crewe Alex 31 6
1995–96 Crewe Alex 25 2 **147 15**
1995–96 Leicester C 15 1
1996–97 Leicester C 35 1
1997–98 Leicester C 37 2
1998–99 Leicester C 37 1
1999–2000 Leicester C 31 1
2000–01 Leicester C 15 0
2001–02 Leicester C 0 0 **170 6**
2007–08 Nottingham F 18 0 **18 0**
2007–08 Wycombe W 9 0 **9 0**

MARTIN, Russell (M) 116 5
H: 6 0 W: 11 08 b.Brighton 4-1-86
2004–05 Wycombe W 7 0
2005–06 Wycombe W 23 3
2006–07 Wycombe W 42 2
2007–08 Wycombe W 44 0 **116 5**

MASSEY, Alan (D) 0 0
b.High Wycombe 11-1-89
Source: Scholar.
2006–07 Wycombe W 0 0
2007–08 Wycombe W 0 0

McCRACKEN, David (D) 215 9
H: 6 2 W: 11 06 b.Glasgow 16-10-81
Source: Dundee U BC. *Honours:* Scotland Under-21.
1999–2000 Dundee U 2 0
2000–01 Dundee U 9 1
2001–02 Dundee U 19 0
2002–03 Dundee U 25 1
2003–04 Dundee U 32 1
2004–05 Dundee U 24 2
2005–06 Dundee U 34 2
2006–07 Dundee U 33 1 **178 8**
2007–08 Wycombe W 37 1 **37 1**

McGLEISH, Scott (F) 535 167
H: 5 9 W: 11 09 b.Barnet 10-2-74
Source: Edgware T.
1994–95 Charlton Ath 6 0 **6 0**
1994–95 *Leyton Orient* 6 1
1995–96 Peterborough U 12 0
1995–96 *Colchester U* 15 6
1996–97 Peterborough U 1 0 **13 0**
1996–97 *Cambridge U* 10 7 **10 7**
1996–97 Leyton Orient 28 7
1997–98 Leyton Orient 8 0 **42 8**
1997–98 Barnet 37 13
1998–99 Barnet 36 8
1999–2000 Barnet 42 10
2000–01 Barnet 19 5 **134 36**
2000–01 Colchester U 21 5
2001–02 Colchester U 46 15
2002–03 Colchester U 43 8
2003–04 Colchester U 34 10 **159 44**
2004–05 Northampton T 44 13
2005–06 Northampton T 42 17
2006–07 Northampton T 25 12 **111 42**
2006–07 Wycombe W 14 5
2007–08 Wycombe W 46 25 **60 30**

OAKES, Stefan (M) 227 12
H: 6 1 W: 13 07 b.Leicester 6-9-78
Source: Trainee.
1997–98 Leicester C 0 0
1998–99 Leicester C 3 0
1999–2000 Leicester C 22 1
2000–01 Leicester C 13 0
2001–02 Leicester C 21 1
2002–03 Leicester C 5 0 **64 2**
2002–03 *Crewe Alex* 7 0 **7 0**
2003–04 Walsall 5 0 **5 0**
2003–04 Notts Co 14 0
2004–05 Notts Co 31 5 **45 5**
2005–06 Wycombe W 37 2
2006–07 Wycombe W 35 0
2007–08 Wycombe W 34 3 **106 5**

OBERSTELLER, Jack (D) 0 0
b. 10-10-88
Source: Millwall Scholar.
2007–08 Wycombe W 0 0

PALMER, Chris (M) 91 5
H: 5 7 W: 11 00 b.Derby 16-10-83
Source: Scholar.
2003–04 Derby Co 0 0
2004–05 Notts Co 25 4
2005–06 Notts Co 29 1 **54 5**
2006–07 Wycombe W 32 0
2007–08 Wycombe W 1 0 **33 0**
2007–08 *Darlington* 4 0 **4 0**

PHILLIPS, Matthew (M) 2 0
H: 6 0 W: 12 10 b.Aylesbury 13-3-91
Source: Scholar.
2007–08 Wycombe W 2 0 **2 0**

RICE, Robert (D) 1 0
H: 5 8 W: 11 11 b.Hendon 23-2-89
Source: Scholar.
2007–08 Wycombe W 1 0 **1 0**

SHEARER, Scott (G) 172 0
H: 6 3 W: 12 00 b.Glasgow 15-2-81
Source: Tower Hearts. *Honours:* Scotland B.
2000–01 Albion R 3 0
2001–02 Albion R 10 0
2002–03 Albion R 36 0 **49 0**
2003–04 Coventry C 30 0
2004–05 Coventry C 8 0 **38 0**
2004–05 *Rushden & D* 13 0 **13 0**
2005–06 Bristol R 45 0
2006–07 Bristol R 2 0 **47 0**
2006–07 *Shrewsbury T* 20 0 **20 0**
2007–08 Wycombe W 5 0 **5 0**

STOCKLEY, Sam (D) 427 6
H: 6 0 W: 12 08 b.Tiverton 5-9-77
Source: Trainee.
1996–97 Southampton 0 0
1996–97 Barnet 21 0
1997–98 Barnet 41 0
1998–99 Barnet 41 0
1999–2000 Barnet 34 1
2000–01 Barnet 45 1 **182 2**
2001–02 Oxford U 41 0
2002–03 Oxford U 0 0 **41 0**
2002–03 Colchester U 33 1
2003–04 Colchester U 44 0
2004–05 Colchester U 37 1
2005–06 Colchester U 27 1 **141 3**
2005–06 *Blackpool* 7 0 **7 0**
2006–07 Wycombe W 34 1
2007–08 Wycombe W 22 0 **56 1**

SUTTON, John (F) 172 56
H: 6 2 W: 13 11 b.Norwich 26-12-83
Source: Scholar. *Honours:* England Youth.
2001–02 Tottenham H 0 0
2002–03 Tottenham H 0 0
2002–03 *Carlisle U* 7 1 **7 1**
2002–03 Swindon T 1 0 **1 0**
2003–04 Raith R 21 13 **21 13**
2003–04 Millwall 4 0
2004–05 Millwall 0 0 **4 0**
2004–05 *Dundee* 32 10 **32 10**
2005–06 St Mirren 31 14
2006–07 St Mirren 33 12 **64 26**
2007–08 Wycombe W 43 6 **43 6**

TORRES, Sergio (M) 86 6
H: 6 2 W: 12 04 b.Mar del Plata 8-11-83
Source: Basingstoke T.
2005–06 Wycombe W 24 1
2006–07 Wycombe W 20 0
2007–08 Wycombe W 42 5 **86 6**

WILLIAMSON, Mike (D) 135 8
H: 6 4 W: 13 03 b.Stoke 8-11-83
Source: Trainee.
2001–02 Torquay U 3 0
2001–02 Southampton 0 0
2002–03 Southampton 0 0
2003–04 Southampton 0 0
2003–04 *Torquay U* 11 0 **14 0**
2003–04 *Doncaster R* 0 0
2004–05 Southampton 0 0
2004–05 *Wycombe W* 37 2
2005–06 Wycombe W 39 5
2006–07 Wycombe W 33 1
2007–08 Wycombe W 12 0 **121 8**

WOODMAN, Craig (D) 151 3
H: 5 9 W: 10 11 b.Tiverton 22-12-82
Source: Trainee.
1999–2000 Bristol C 0 0
2000–01 Bristol C 2 0
2001–02 Bristol C 6 0
2002–03 Bristol C 10 0
2003–04 Bristol C 21 0
2004–05 Bristol C 3 0
2004–05 *Mansfield T* 8 1 **8 1**
2004–05 *Torquay U* 22 1
2005–06 Bristol C 37 1
2005–06 *Torquay U* 2 0 **24 1**
2006–07 Bristol C 11 0 **90 1**
2007–08 Wycombe W 29 0 **29 0**

YOUNG, Jamie (G) 44 0
H: 5 11 W: 13 00 b.Brisbane 25-8-85
Source: Scholar. *Honours:* England Youth, Under-20.
2003–04 Reading 1 0
2004–05 Reading 0 0
2005–06 Reading 0 0 **1 0**
2005–06 *Rushden & D* 20 0 **20 0**
2006–07 Wycombe W 19 0
2007–08 Wycombe W 4 0 **23 0**

YEOVIL T (92)

ALCOCK, Craig (D) 9 0
H: 5 8 W: 11 00 b.Cornwall 8-12-87
Source: Youth.
2006–07 Yeovil T 1 0
2007–08 Yeovil T 8 0 **9 0**

BARRY, Anthony (M) 64 0
H: 5 7 W: 10 00 b.Liverpool 29-5-86
Source: Everton.
2004–05 Coventry C 0 0
From Accrington S.
2005–06 Yeovil T 4 0
2006–07 Yeovil T 24 0
2007–08 Yeovil T 36 0 **64 0**

BEHCET, Darren (M) 0 0
H: 6 0 W: 11 07 b.London 18-10-86
Source: Scholar.
2005–06 West Ham U 0 0
2006–07 Yeovil T 0 0
2007–08 Yeovil T 0 0

BIRCHAM, Marc (M) 269 10
H: 5 11 W: 11 06 b.Wembley 11-5-78
Source: Trainee. *Honours:* Canada 17 full caps, 1 goal.
1996–97 Millwall 6 0
1997–98 Millwall 4 0
1998–99 Millwall 28 0
1999–2000 Millwall 22 1
2000–01 Millwall 20 2
2001–02 Millwall 24 0 **104 3**
2002–03 QPR 36 2
2003–04 QPR 38 2
2004–05 QPR 35 1
2005–06 QPR 26 2
2006–07 QPR 17 0 **152 7**
2007–08 Yeovil T 13 0 **13 0**

BROWN, James (F) 0 0
H: 5 11 W: 12 00 b.Cramlingham
2007–08 Yeovil T 0 0

CLARKE, Tom (F) 1 0
H: 5 8 W: 9 13 b.Worthing 2-1-89
Source: Youth.
2006–07 Yeovil T 1 0
2007–08 Yeovil T 0 0 **1 0**

DEMPSEY, Gary (M) 151 10
H: 5 9 W: 10 04 b.Wexford 15-1-81
Source: Bray W, Waterford.
2002–03 Dunfermline Ath 31 1
2003–04 Dunfermline Ath 33 5
2004–05 Dunfermline Ath 17 0 **81 6**
2004–05 Aberdeen 4 0
2005–06 Aberdeen 24 0
2006–07 Aberdeen 26 2 **54 2**
2007–08 Yeovil T 16 2 **16 2**

DOMORAUD, Wilfried (F) 5 0
H: 6 0 W: 13 10 b.Maisons-Alfort 18-8-88
Source: Boulogne Billancourt, Nancy.
2007–08 Yeovil T 5 0 **5 0**

FITZGERALD, Rob (D) 0 0
Source: Hillingdon B.
2007–08 Yeovil T 0 0

FORBES, Terrell (D) 276 0
H: 5 11 W: 12 07 b.Southwark 17-8-81
Source: Trainee.
1999–2000 West Ham U 0 0
1999–2000 *Bournemouth* 3 0 **3 0**
2000–01 West Ham U 0 0
2001–02 QPR 43 0
2002–03 QPR 38 0
2003–04 QPR 30 0
2004–05 QPR 3 0 **114 0**
2004–05 Grimsby T 33 0 **33 0**
2005–06 Oldham Ath 39 0 **39 0**
2006–07 Yeovil T 46 0
2007–08 Yeovil T 41 0 **87 0**

GUYETT, Scott (D) 111 2
H: 6 2 W: 13 06 b.Ascot 20-1-76
Source: Brisbane C, Gresley R, Southport.
2001–02 Oxford U 22 0 **22 0**
From Chester C.
2004–05 Yeovil T 18 2
2005–06 Yeovil T 21 0
2006–07 Yeovil T 16 0
2007–08 Yeovil T 34 0 **89 2**

HUGHES, Jerahl (M) 1 0
H: 5 7 W: 10 00 b.Brighton 10-8-89
Source: Crystal Palace Scholar.
2007–08 Yeovil T 1 0 **1 0**

JONES, Nathan (M) 383 11
H: 5 6 W: 10 06 b.Rhondda 28-5-73
Source: Cardiff C Trainee, Maesteg Park, Ton Pentre, Merthyr T.
1995–96 Luton T 0 0
Badajoz, Numaicia
1997–98 Southend U 39 0
1998–99 Southend U 17 0
1998–99 *Scarborough* 9 0 **9 0**
1999–2000 Southend U 43 2 **99 2**
2000–01 Brighton & HA 40 4
2001–02 Brighton & HA 36 2
2002–03 Brighton & HA 28 1
2003–04 Brighton & HA 36 0
2004–05 Brighton & HA 19 0 **159 7**
2005–06 Yeovil T 43 0
2006–07 Yeovil T 42 1
2007–08 Yeovil T 31 1 **116 2**

KIRK, Andy (F) 314 103
H: 5 11 W: 11 01 b.Belfast 29-5-79
Honours: Northern Ireland Schools, Youth, Under-21, 8 full caps.
1995–96 Glentoran 1 1
1996–97 Glentoran 25 8
1997–98 Glentoran 25 9 **51 18**
1998–99 Hearts 5 0
1999–2000 Hearts 4 0
2000–01 Hearts 31 13
2001–02 Hearts 20 1
2002–03 Hearts 29 10
2003–04 Hearts 24 8 **113 32**
2004–05 Boston U 25 19 **25 19**
2004–05 Northampton T 8 7
2005–06 Northampton T 29 8
2006–07 Northampton T 44 7
2007–08 Northampton T 25 8 **106 30**
2007–08 Yeovil T 19 4 **19 4**

KNIGHTS, Darryl (F) 8 0
H: 5 7 W: 10 01 b.Ipswich 1-5-88
Source: Scholar. *Honours:* England Youth.
2004–05 Ipswich T 1 0
2005–06 Ipswich T 0 0
2006–07 Ipswich T 0 0 **1 0**
2006–07 *Yeovil T* 4 0
2007–08 Yeovil T 3 0 **7 0**

LYNCH, Mark (D) 78 0
H: 5 11 W: 11 03 b.Manchester 2-9-81
Source: Trainee.
1999–2000 Manchester U 0 0
2000–01 Manchester U 0 0
2001–02 Manchester U 0 0
2001–02 *St Johnstone* 20 0 **20 0**
2002–03 Manchester U 0 0
2003–04 Manchester U 0 0
2004–05 Sunderland 11 0 **11 0**
2005–06 Hull C 16 0
2006–07 Hull C 0 0 **16 0**
2006–07 Yeovil T 17 0
2007–08 Yeovil T 14 0 **31 0**

MAHER, Stephen (M) 7 0
H: 5 10 W: 11 01 b.Dublin 3-3-88
Source: Shelbourne.
2006–07 Yeovil T 1 0
2007–08 Yeovil T 6 0 **7 0**

MILDENHALL, Steve (G) 236 1
H: 6 4 W: 14 01 b.Swindon 13-5-78
Source: Trainee.
1996–97 Swindon T 1 0
1997–98 Swindon T 4 0
1998–99 Swindon T 0 0
1999–2000 Swindon T 5 0
2000–01 Swindon T 23 0 **33 0**
2001–02 Notts Co 26 0
2002–03 Notts Co 21 0
2003–04 Notts Co 28 0
2004–05 Notts Co 1 0 **76 0**
2004–05 Oldham Ath 6 0 **6 0**
2005–06 Grimsby T 46 1 **46 1**
2006–07 Yeovil T 46 0
2007–08 Yeovil T 29 0 **75 0**

MORRIS, Lee (F) 166 29
H: 5 10 W: 11 07 b.Blackpool 30-4-80
Source: Trainee. *Honours:* England Youth.
1997–98 Sheffield U 5 0
1998–99 Sheffield U 20 6
1999–2000 Sheffield U 1 0 **26 6**
1999–2000 Derby Co 3 0
2000–01 Derby Co 20 0
2000–01 *Huddersfield T* 5 1 **5 1**
2001–02 Derby Co 15 4
2002–03 Derby Co 30 8
2003–04 Derby Co 23 5 **91 17**
2003–04 Leicester C 0 0
2004–05 Leicester C 10 0
2005–06 Leicester C 0 0 **10 0**
2006–07 Yeovil T 33 5
2007–08 Yeovil T 1 0 **34 5**

OWUSU, Lloyd (F) 349 104
H: 6 2 W: 14 00 b.Slough 12-12-76
Source: Slough T. *Honours:* Ghana 2 full caps.
1998–99 Brentford 46 22
1999–2000 Brentford 41 12
2000–01 Brentford 33 10
2001–02 Brentford 44 20
2002–03 Sheffield W 32 4
2003–04 Sheffield W 20 5 **52 9**
2003–04 Reading 16 4
2004–05 Reading 25 6 **41 10**
2005–06 Brentford 42 12
2006–07 Brentford 7 0 **213 76**
2007–08 Yeovil T 43 9 **43 9**

PELTIER, Lee (F) 41 0
H: 5 10 W: 12 00 b.Liverpool 11-12-86
Source: Scholar.
2004–05 Liverpool 0 0
2005–06 Liverpool 0 0
2006–07 Liverpool 0 0
2006–07 *Hull C* 7 0 **7 0**
2007–08 Liverpool 0 0
2007–08 Yeovil T 34 0 **34 0**

ROSE, Matthew (D) 286 9
H: 5 11 W: 12 02 b.Dartford 24-9-75
Source: Trainee. *Honours:* England Under-21.
1994–95 Arsenal 0 0
1995–96 Arsenal 4 0
1996–97 Arsenal 1 0 **5 0**
1997–98 QPR 16 0
1998–99 QPR 29 0
1999–2000 QPR 29 1
2000–01 QPR 27 0
2001–02 QPR 39 3
2002–03 QPR 28 2
2003–04 QPR 20 0
2004–05 QPR 28 2
2005–06 QPR 15 0
2006–07 QPR 11 0 **242 8**
2006–07 Yeovil T 9 0
2007–08 Yeovil T 30 1 **39 1**

SKIVERTON, Terry (D) 190 20
H: 6 1 W: 13 06 b.Mile End 26-6-75
Source: Trainee.
1993–94 Chelsea 0 0
1994–95 Chelsea 0 0
1994–95 *Wycombe W* 10 0
1995–96 Chelsea 0 0
1995–96 Wycombe W 4 1
1996–97 Wycombe W 6 0 **20 1**
From Welling U
2003–04 Yeovil T 26 2
2004–05 Yeovil T 38 4
2005–06 Yeovil T 36 6
2006–07 Yeovil T 39 2
2007–08 Yeovil T 31 5 **170 19**

SMITH, Nathan (D) 7 0
H: 5 11 W: 12 00 b.Enfield 11-1-87
Source: Potters Bar T.
2007–08 Yeovil T 7 0 **7 0**

STEWART, Marcus (F) 579 190
H: 5 10 W: 11 00 b.Bristol 7-11-72
Source: Trainee. *Honours:* England Schools, Football League.
1991–92 Bristol R 33 5
1992–93 Bristol R 38 11
1993–94 Bristol R 29 5

1994–95	Bristol R	27	15		
1995–96	Bristol R	44	21	**171**	**57**
1996–97	Huddersfield T	20	7		
1997–98	Huddersfield T	41	15		
1998–99	Huddersfield T	43	22		
1999–2000	Huddersfield T	29	14	**133**	**58**
1999–2000	Ipswich T	10	2		
2000–01	Ipswich T	34	19		
2001–02	Ipswich T	28	6		
2002–03	Ipswich T	3	0	**75**	**27**
2002–03	Sunderland	19	1		
2003–04	Sunderland	40	14		
2004–05	Sunderland	43	16	**102**	**31**
2005–06	Bristol C	27	5		
2005–06	*Preston NE*	4	0	**4**	**0**
2006–07	Bristol C	0	0	**27**	**5**
2006–07	Yeovil T	31	8		
2007–08	Yeovil T	36	4	**67**	**12**

STREET, Jordan (D) **0** **0**
b.Southampton
Source: Scholar.

2007–08	Yeovil T	0	0		

WARNE, Paul (M) **392** **51**
H: 5 10 W: 11 07 b.Norwich 8-5-73
Source: Wroxham.

1997–98	Wigan Ath	25	2		
1998–99	Wigan Ath	11	1	**36**	**3**
1998–99	Rotherham U	19	8		
1999–2000	Rotherham U	43	10		
2000–01	Rotherham U	44	7		
2001–02	Rotherham U	25	0		
2002–03	Rotherham U	40	1		
2003–04	Rotherham U	35	1		
2004–05	Rotherham U	24	1	**230**	**28**
2004–05	*Mansfield T*	7	1	**7**	**1**
2005–06	Oldham Ath	40	9		
2006–07	Oldham Ath	46	9	**86**	**18**
2007–08	Yeovil T	33	1	**33**	**1**

WELSH, Ishmael (F) **21** **1**
H: 5 7 W: 10 11 b.Leicester 4-9-87
Source: West Ham U Scholar.

2006–07	Yeovil T	18	1		
2007–08	Yeovil T	3	0	**21**	**1**

WILLIAMS, Marvin (M) **76** **8**
H: 5 11 W: 11 06 b.London 12-8-87
Source: Scholar.

2005–06	Millwall	22	4		
2006–07	Millwall	29	3	**51**	**7**
2006–07	*Torquay U*	2	1	**2**	**1**
2007–08	Yeovil T	23	0	**23**	**0**

ALDERSHOT TOWN

Player	*Ht*	*Wt*	*Birthplace*	*D.O.B.*	*Source*
Bull Nikki (G)	6 1	11 03	Hastings	2 10 81	Hayes
Chalmers Lewis (M)	6 0	12 04	Manchester	4 2 86	Altrincham
Charles Anthony (D)	6 0	12 00	Isleworth	11 3 81	Barnet
Day Rhys (D)	6 1	12 08	Bridgend	31 8 82	Mansfield T
Donnelly Scott (M)	5 8	11 10	Hammersmith	25 12 87	QPR
Elvins Rob (F)	6 2	12 04	Alvechurch	17 9 86	WBA
Gier Rob (D)	5 9	11 07	Ascot	6 1 80	Woking
Grant Joel (M)	6 0	11 01	Hammersmith	27 8 87	Watford
Grant John (F)	5 11	11 00	Manchester	9 8 81	Halifax T
Harding Ben (M)	5 10	11 02	Carshalton	6 9 84	Milton Keynes D
Hudson Kirk (F)	6 0	10 10	Rochford	12 12 86	Bournemouth
Hylton Danny (F)	6 0	11 03	London	25 2 89	Youth
Jaimez-Ruiz Michael (G)	6 1	12 00	Merida	12 7 84	Northwood
Mendes Junior (F)	5 10	11 04	Ballam	15 9 76	Notts Co
Newman Ricky (D)	5 10	12 06	Guildford	5 8 70	Brentford
Scott Ryan (M)	5 10	12 07	Aldershot	27 12 86	Youth
Smith Dean (D)	5 10	10 10	Islington	13 8 86	Chelsea
Soares Louis (M)	5 11	11 05	Reading	8 1 85	Barnet
Straker Anthony (D)	5 9	11 11	Ealing	23 9 88	Crystal Palace
Williams Ryan (M)	5 4	11 02	Chesterfield	31 8 78	Bristol R
Winfield Dave (D)	6 3	13 08	Aldershot	24 3 88	Youth

EXETER CITY

Player	*Ht*	*Wt*	*Birthplace*	*D.O.B.*	*Source*
Basham Steve (F)	5 11	12 04	Southampton	2 12 77	Oxford U
Carlisle Wayne (M)	6 0	11 06	Lisburn	9 9 79	Leyton Orient
Cozic Bertrand (M)	5 10	12 06	Quimper	18 5 78	Team Bath
Edwards Rob (M)	6 0	12 07	Kendal	1 7 73	Blackpool
Elam Lee (M)	5 8	10 12	Bradford	24 9 76	Weymouth
Friend George (D)			Barnstaple	19 10 87	
Gill Matthew (M)	5 11	11 10	Cambridge	8 11 80	Notts Co
Harley Ryan (D)	5 9	11 00	Bristol	22 1 85	Weston-Super-Mare
Jones Paul (G)	6 3	13 00	Maidstone	28 6 86	Leyton Orient
Logan Richard (F)	6 0	12 05	Bury St Edmunds	4 1 82	Weymouth
Marriott Andy (G)	6 2	11 00	Sutton-in-Ashfield	11 10 70	Boston U
Moxey Dean (D)	5 11	12 00	Exeter	14 1 86	
Richardson Jon (D)	6 1	12 02	Nottingham	29 8 75	Forest Green R
Saunders Neil (M)			Barking	7 5 83	Team Bath
Seaborne Daniel (D)			Barnstaple	5 3 87	
Sercombe Liam (M)			Exeter	25 4 90	
Stansfield Adam (F)	5 11	11 02	Plymouth	10 9 78	Hereford U
Taylor Andrew (M)	5 9	12 10	Exeter	17 9 82	Northwich V
Taylor Matt (D)			Ormskirk	30 1 82	Team Bath
Tully Steve (D)	5 9	11 00	Paignton	10 2 80	Weymouth

ENGLISH LEAGUE PLAYERS – INDEX

REFEREEING AND THE LAWS OF THE GAME

For the second successive year there have been few if any changes to the Laws. In fact for the 2008–09 season there is only one, relating to Law 2 concerning the ball, and that is about the designation and logos on "FIFA-approved" footballs, where all official competitions have to use a ball bearing one of the three approved logos. There are various reminders underlined, perhaps the most important of these being that the referee still remains as the only one on the pitch who should stop the game in case of injury and not the players. Furthermore if in the opinion of the referee the player is only slightly injured, he is entitled to let play continue. The "football family" is asked to unite in eradicating simulation both in respect of fouls and feigning injury. FIFA is very much undecided about using technology to judge incidents and so it has forbidden the occupants of Technical Areas to have access to or be able to view pitchside monitors. Also all experiments relating to goal-line technology are postponed until further notice. However permission has been granted to conduct an experiment with two additional assistant referees in a tournament to be held during the season. This is expected to include the suggestion of Michele Platini to have them positioned behind each goal, to establish whether they can better see "ball over the line" incidents.

Although there were no real Law changes, referees were given strict instructions when they attended an Advanced Course for Elite and Premier Referees in Limassol, Cyprus in February 2008. It was stated that the referees must take strict action to prevent unfair play. Tackling was put under the microscope, especially high or reckless challenges that endanger opponents. Those where the foot was raised should, it was advocated, result in a red card because of its aggressive nature. Where an incident was missed by the referee and seen by his/her assistant, they were the ones marked out to make the necessary signals. It was further confirmed that holding and pushing in the penalty area would see the referee administer one warning, but for any subsequent infringement a yellow card should follow. Likewise, a penalty or free kick should be awarded.

The importance of high-quality refereeing has been acknowledged by UEFA who are continuing to bring young referees and their guides together on a regular basis. The 8th UEFA seminar for such talents occurred in May '08 at their headquarters in Nyon. The programme that began in 2001 has brought success in that three of the participants on former courses appeared at Euro 2008 as referees, including England's Howard Webb, whilst seven of the eight fourth officials selected for that competition had also attended those courses.

The vexed questions of dissent and players crowding around the referee, were not only dealt with at Limassol but preceded by the English FA in their "Respect" campaign earlier in the same month. They launched a five-year plan and a pilot scheme for amateur players in ten counties across England and Wales. There were three main prongs, namely – no player except the captain should approach and speak to the referee; in youth matches all spectators have to be on the touchlines and behind a roped off area three metres from the field of play; and participating clubs must sign up to a code of conduct with related sanctions. It is hoped that these measures will in some way help to recruit and keep qualified match officials. The FA have stated that in some areas 20% of games are played without a qualified referee, so that by 2012 their aim is to recruit 8000 new ones as well as to retain the existing 26,000 officials. Unfortunately at present there is a great deal of "wastage" and so each county has a "recruitment and retention" officer. It is part of their job to stress that anyone over the age of 14, male or female, can train to become a referee. The courses are organised by the County FAs and are modular based, whilst there are also mentoring schemes to help candidates to climb the proverbial ladder of success.

Some of those who have reached the top of those rungs are Howard Webb as referee and Darren Cann and Mark Mullarkey as assistants, who were the English represtatives at Euro 2008; Mike Dean, who refereed the FA Cup Final – Portsmouth v Cardiff City, and Mark Halsey, who refereed the Carling Cup Final between Chelsea and Spurs.

On the current National List of Referees, Peter Walton is a survivor at age 49, with his appeal against an imposed retirement through age, was upheld.

KEN GOLDMAN

NATIONAL LIST OF REFEREES FOR SEASON 2008–09

List 2007–08 season
Armstrong, P (Paul) – Berkshire
Atkinson, M (Martin) – W. Yorkshire
Attwell, SB (Stuart) – Warwickshire
Bates, A (Tony) – Staffordshire
Beeby, RJ (Richard) – Northamptonshire
Bennett, SG (Steve) – Kent
Booth, RJ (Russell) – Nottinghamshire
Boyeson, C (Carl) – E. Yorkshire
Bratt, SJ (Steve) – West Midlands
Clattenburg, M (Mark) – Tyne & Wear
Cook, SD (Steven) – Surrey
Crossley, PT (Phil) – Kent
Deadman, D (Darren) – Cambridgeshire
Dean, ML (Mike) – Wirral
Dorr, SJ (Steve) – Worcestershire
Dowd, P (Phil) – Staffordshire
Drysdale, D (Darren) – Lincolnshire
D'Urso, AP (Andy) – Essex
East, R (Roger) – Wiltshire
Evans, KG (Karl) – Gtr Manchester
Foster, D (David) – Tyne & Wear
Foy, CJ (Chris) – Merseyside
Friend, KA (Kevin) – Leicestershire
Graham F (Fred) – Essex
Haines, A (Andy) – Tyne & Wear
Hall, AR (Andy) – W. Midlands
Halsey, MR (Mark) – Lancashire
Haywood, M (Mark) – W. Yorkshire
Hegley, GK (Grant) – Hertfordshire
Hill, KD (Keith) – Hertfordshire
Horwood, GD (Graham) – Bedfordshire
Ilderton, EL (Eddie) – Tyne & Wear
Jones, MJ (Michael) – Cheshire
Joslin, PJ (Phil) – Nottinghamshire
Kettle, TM (Trevor) – Rutland
Knight, B (Barry) – Kent
Laws, G (Graham) – Tyne & Wear
Lee, R (Ray) – Essex
Lewis, GJ (Gary) – Cambridgeshire
Lewis, RL (Rob) – Shropshire
McDermid, D (Danny) – London
Marriner, AM (Andre) – W. Midlands
Mason, LS (Lee) – Lancashire
Mathieson, SW (Scott) – Cheshire
Mellin, PW (Paul) – Surrey
Miller, NS (Nigel) – Durham
Miller, P (Pat) – Bedfordshire
Moss, J (Jon) – W. Yorkshire
Oliver, CW (Clive) – Northumberland
Oliver, M (Michael) – Northumberland
Penn, AM (Andy) – W. Midlands
Penton, C (Clive) – Sussex
Pike, MS (Mike) – Cumbria
Probert, LW (Lee) – Wiltshire
Rennie, UD (Uriah) – S. Yorkshire
Riley, MA (Mike) – W. Yorkshire
Russell, MP (Mike) – Hertfordshire
Salisbury, G (Graham) – Lancashire
Shoebridge, RL (Rob) – Derbyshire
Singh, J (Jarnail) – Middlesex
Stroud, KP (Keith) – Hampshire
Styles, R (Rob) – Hampshire
Swarbrick, ND (Neil) – Lancashire
Tanner, SJ (Steve) – Somerset
Taylor, A (Anthony) – Gtr Manchester
Taylor, P (Paul) – Hertfordshire
Thorpe, M (Mike) – Suffolk
Walton, P (Peter) – Northamptonshire
Ward, GL (Gavin) – Surrey
Webb, HM (Howard) – S. Yorkshire
Webster, CH (Colin) – Tyne & Wear
Whitestone, D (Dean) – Northamptonshire
Wiley, AG (Alan) – Staffordshire
Williamson, IG (Iain) – Berkshire
Woolmer, KA (Andy) – Northamptonshire
Wright, KK (Kevin) – Cambridgeshire

Promoted to National List for 2008–09
Gibbs, P (Phil) – Midlands
Hooper, S (Simon) – Wiltshire
Langford, O (Oliver) – West Midlands
Linington, J (James) – Isle of Wight
Pawson, C (Craig) – Yorkshire
Phillips, D (David) – West Sussex
Sarginson, C (Chris) – Staffordshire
Scott, G (Graham) – Oxfordshire
Webb, D (David) – Co Durham

ASSISTANT REFEREES

List 2007–08 season
Artis, SG (Stephen) – Norfolk
Astley, MA (Mark) – Gtr Manchester
Atkin, W (Warren) – W. Sussex
Atkins, G (Graeme) – W. Yorkshire
Babski, DS (Dave) – Lincolnshire
Bannister, N (Nigel) – E. Yorkshire
Barnes, PW (Paul) – Cambridgeshire
Barratt, W (Wayne) – Worcestershire
Barrow, SJ (Simon) – Staffordshire
Beale, GA (Guy) – Somerset
Beck, SP (Simon) – Essex
Beevor, R (Richard) – Suffolk
Belbin, D (David) – Middlesex
Bennett, A (Andrew) – Devon
Bentley, IF (Ian) – Kent
Benton, DK (David) – S. Yorkshire
Berry, CJ (Carl) – Surrey
Beswick, G (Gary) – Co. Durham
Birkett, DJ (Dave) – Lincolnshire
Blackledge, M (Mike) – Cambridgeshire
Bond, DS (Darren) – Lancashire
Bramley, P (Philip) – W. Yorkshire
Brittain, GM (Gary) – S. Yorkshire
Brown, M (Mark) – E. Yorkshire
Brumwell, CA (Chris) – Cumbria
Bryan, DS (Dave) – Lincolnshire
Buck, D (David) – Kent
Bull, M (Michael) – Essex
Bull, W (William) – Hampshire
Burt, S (Stuart) – Northamptonshire
Burton, R (Roy) – Staffordshire
Bushell, DD (David) – London
Butler, AN (Andrew) – Lancashire
Cairns, MJ (Mike) – Somerset
Canadine, P (Paul) – S. Yorkshire
Cann, DJ (Darren) – Norfolk
Castle, S (Steve) – W. Midlands
Child, SA (Stephen) – Kent
Collin, J (Jake) – Merseyside
Comley, JG (Justin) – Berkshire
Cook, SJ (Steve) – Derbyshire
Cooke, SG (Stephen) – Nottinghamshire
Cooper, IJ (Ian) – Kent
Coote, DH (David) – Nottinghamshire
Cox, JL (James) – Worcestershire
Creighton, SW (Steve) – Berkshire
Cummins, SP (Steven) – Cheshire
Curry, PE (Paul) – Northumberland
Davies, A (Andy) – Hampshire
Davies, PP (Peter) – Cheshire
Denton, MJ (Michael) – Lancashire
Devine, JP (Jim) – Cleveland
Dexter, MC (Martin) – Leicestershire
Duncan, SAJ (Scott) – Tyne & Wear
Dunn, C (Carl) – Staffordshire
Evans, C (Craig) – Lincolnshire
Evans, IA (Ian) – W. Midlands
Evetts, GS (Gary) – Hertfordshire
Farries, J (John) – Oxfordshire

Fletcher, R (Russell) – Derbyshire
Flynn, J (John) – Wiltshire
Foley, MJ (Matt) – S. Yorkshire
Ford, D (Declan) – Leicestershire
Francis, CJ (Chris) – Cambridgeshire
Ganfield, RS (Ron) – Somerset
Garratt, AM (Andy) – W. Midlands
Gibbs, PN (Phil) – W. Midlands
George, M (Mike) – Norfolk
Gosling, IJ (Ian) – Kent
Graham, P (Paul) – Gtr Manchester
Green, RC (Russell) – Lancashire
Greenwood, AH (Alf) – Yorkshire
Grove, PJ (Peter) – W. Midlands
Grunnill, W (Wayne) – E. Yorkshire
Halliday, A (Andy) – London
Hambling, GS (Glenn) – Norfolk
Hamilton, IJ (Ian) – Gloucestershire
Handley, D (Darren) – Lancashire
Harrington, T (Tony) – Cleveland
Harwood, CN (Colin) – Gtr Manchester
Hay, J (John) – Lancashire
Haycock, KW (Ken) – W. Yorkshire
Hayto, JM (John) – Essex
Hendley, AR (Andy) – W. Midlands
Hewitt, RT (Richard) – N. Yorkshire
Heywood, M (Mark) – Cheshire
Hilton, G (Gary) – Lancashire
Hobbis, N (Nick) – W. Midlands
Holderness, BC (Barry) – Essex
Hooper, SA (Simon) – Wiltshire
Hopkins, JD (John) – Essex
Horton, AJ (Tony) – W. Midlands
Hutchinson, AD (Andrew) – Cheshire
Hutchinson, SM (Mark) – Nottinghamshire
Ihringova, A (Sasa) – Shropshire
Jerden, GJN (Gary) – Essex
Joyce, R (Ross) – Cleveland
Keane, PJ (Patrick) – W. Midlands
Kettlewell, PT (Paul) – Lancashire
Khatib, B (Billy) – Tyne & Wear
Kinseley, N (Nick) – Essex
Kirkup, PJ (Peter) – Northamptonshire
Knapp, SC (Simon) – S. Gloucestershire
Langford, O (Oliver) – W. Midlands
Laver, AA (Andrew) – Hampshire
Law, GC (Geoff) – Leicestershire
Lawson, KD (Keith) – Lincolnshire
Lawson, MR (Mark) – Northumberland
Ledger, S (Scott) – S. Yorkshire
Lennard, HW (Harry) – E. Sussex
Linington, JJ (James) – Isle of Wight
Long, SJ (Simon) – Suffolk
McCallum, DA (Dave) – Tyne & Wear
McCoy, MT (Michael) – Kent
McDonough, M (Mick – Tyne & Wear
McIntosh, WA (Wayne) – Lincolnshire
McLaughlin, M (Mathew) – Bedfordshire
Mackrell, EB (Eric) – Hampshire
Magill, JP (John) – Essex
Malone, B (Brendan) – Wiltshire
Margetts, DS (David) – Essex
Martin, PC (Paul) – Northamptonshire
Martin, RW (Rob) – S. Yorkshire
Mason, T (Tony) – Kent
Massey, T (Trevor) – Cheshire
Matadar, M (Mo) – Lancashire
Matthews, A (Adrian) – Wiltshire
Mattocks, KJ (Kevin) – Lancashire
Mellor, G (Glyn) – Derbyshire
Merchant, R (Rob) – Staffordshire
Metcalfe, RL (Lee) – Lancashire
Mohareb, D (Dean) – Cheshire
Mullarkey, M (Mike) – Devon
Murphy, ME (Michael) – W. Midlands
Murphy, N (Nigel) – Nottinghamshire
Naylor, D (Dave) – Nottinghamshire
Naylor, MA (Michael) – S. Yorkshire
Newbold, AM (Andrew) – Leicestershire
Newell, AC (Andy) – Lancashire
Nolan, I (Ian) – Lancashire
Norman, PV (Paul) – Dorset
Norris, P (Paul) – Cheshire
Pardoe, SA (Steve) – Cheshire
Parker, AR (Alan) – Derbyshire
Parry, B (Brian) – Co. Durham
Pawson, CL (Craig) – S. Yorkshire
Pearce, JE (John) – Norfolk
Phillips, D (David) – Sussex
Philpott, M (Mark) – Cornwall
Phipps, SJ (Stephen) – Oxfordshire
Pike, K (Kevin) – Dorset
Pollock, RM (Bob) – Merseyside
Porter, W (Wayne) – Lincolnshire
Procter-Green, SRM (Shaun) – Lincolnshire
Quinn, P (Peter) – Cleveland
Radford, N (Neil) – Worcestershire
Rayner, AE (Amy) – Leicestershire
Reeves, CL (Christopher) – E. Yorkshire
Richards, DC (Ceri) – Carmarthenshire
Richardson, D (David) – W. Yorkshire
Roberts, B (Bob) – Lancashire
Roberts, DJ (Danny) – Gtr Manchester
Rock, DK (David) – Hertfordshire
Rodda, A (Andrew – Devon
Ross, SJ (Stephen) – Lincolnshire
Rowbury, J (John) – Kent
Rowley, MD (Michael) – Berkshire
Rubery, SP (Steve) – Essex
Rushton, SJ (Steven) Staffordshire
Russell, GR (Geoff) – Northamptonshire
Sainsbury, A (Andrew) – Wiltshire
Saliy, O (Oleksandr) – London
Salt, RA (Richard) – N. Yorkshire
Sarginson, CD (Christopher) – Staffordshire
Scarr, IK (Ian) – W. Midlands
Scholes, MS (Mark) – Buckinghamshire
Scott, GD (Graham) – Oxfordshire
Scregg, AJ (Andrew) – Merseyside
Sharp, PR (Phil) – Hertfordshire
Sheffield, JA (Alan) – W. Midlands
Sheldrake, D (Darren) – Surrey
Siddall, I (Iain) – Lancashire
Simpson, J (Jeremy) – Lancashire
Simpson, P (Paul) – Co. Durham
Slaughter, A (Ashley) – Sussex
Smallwood, W (William) – Cheshire
Smedley, I (Ian) – Derbyshire
Smith, AN (Andrew) – W. Yorkshire
Smith, EI (Eamonn) – Surrey
Smith, N (Nigel) – Derbyshire
Smith, RH (Richard) – W. Midlands
Snartt, SP (Simon) – Gloucestershire
Stewart, M (Matt) – Essex
Stokes, JD (John) – Wirral
Storrie, D (David) – W. Yorkshire
Stott, GT (Gary) – Gtr Manchester
Street, DR (Duncan) – W. Yorkshire
Stretton, GS (Guy) – Leicestershire
Sutton, GJ (Gary) – Lincolnshire
Sutton, MA (Mark) – Derbyshire
Swabey, L (Lee) – Devon
Sygmuta, BC (Barry) – N. Yorkshire
Tattan, BJ (Brian) – Merseyside
Thompson, MF (Marvin) – Middlesex
Thompson, PI (Paul) – Derbyshire
Tierney, P (Paul) – Lancashire
Tincknell, SW (Steve) – Hertfordshire
Tingey, M (Mike) – Buckinghamshire
Tomlinson, SD (Stephen) – Hampshire
Turner, A (Andrew) – Devon
Turner, GB (Glenn) – Derbyshire
Tyas, J (Jason) – W. Yorkshire
Unsworth, D (David) – Gtr Manchester
Varley, PC (Paul) – W. Yorkshire
Vaughan, RG (Roger) – N. Somerset
Wallace, G (Garry) – Tyne & Wear
Waring, J (Jim) – Lancashire
Watts, AS (Adam) – Worcestershire
Waugh, J (Jock) – S. Yorkshire
Weaver, M (Mark) – W. Midlands
Webb, D (David) – Co. Durham
West, MG (Malcolm) – Cornwall
West, RJ (Richard) – E. Yorkshire
Whitton, RP (Rob) – Essex
Wigglesworth, RJ (Richard) – S. Yorkshire
Wilkinson, K (Keith) – Northumberland
Williams, MA (Andy) – Herefordshire
Woodward, IJ (Irvine) – E. Sussex
Yates, NA (Neil) – Lancashire
Yeo, KG (Keith) – Essex
Yerby, MS (Martin) – Kent
Young, GR (Gary) – Bedfordshire

TRANSFERS 2007–08

JUNE 2007	From	To	Fee in £
29 Bent, Darren	Charlton Athletic	Tottenham Hotspur	15,500,000
4 Bramble, Titus M.	Newcastle United	Wigan Athletic	undisclosed
20 Corr, Barry	Sheffield Wednesday	Swindon Town	undisclosed
27 Craig, Tony A.	Millwall	Crystal Palace	150,000
29 Earnshaw, Robert	Norwich City	Derby County	3,500,000
25 Forster, Nicholas	Hull City	Brighton & Hove Albion	75,000
27 Frampton, Andrew J.K.	Brentford	Millwall	undisclosed
11 Halford, Gregory	Reading	Sunderland	3,000,000
7 Hayter, James E.	AFC Bournemouth	Doncaster Rovers	200,000
18 Hibbert, David J.	Preston North End	Shrewsbury Town	undisclosed
1 Hreidarsson, Hermann	Charlton Athletic	Portsmouth	undisclosed
5 Hurst, Kevan	Sheffield United	Scunthorpe United	undisclosed
5 McAnuff, Joel J.	Crystal Palace	Watford	1,750,000
13 McCann, Gavin P.	Aston Villa	Bolton Wanderers	1,000,000
13 McCarthy, Patrick	Leicester City	Charlton Athletic	650,000
28 Nash, Carlo J.	Preston North End	Wigan Athletic	300,000
2 Odejayi, Olukayode	Cheltenham Town	Barnsley	200,000
13 O'Donnell, Daniel	Liverpool	Crewe Alexandra	nominal
7 Parker, Scott M.	Newcastle United	West Ham United	7,000,000
5 Sibierski, Antoine	Newcastle United	Wigan Athletic	undisclosed
1 Spencer, James M.	Stockport County	Rochdale	undisclosed
26 Weir-Daley, Spencer J.A.	Nottingham Forest	Notts County	undisclosed
21 Windass, Dean	Bradford City	Hull City	150,000
JULY 2007			
10 Aliadiere, Jeremie	Arsenal	Middlesbrough	1,500,000
3 Aljofree, Hasney	Plymouth Argyle	Swindon Town	undisclosed
5 Allott, Mark S.	Chesterfield	Oldham Athletic	undisclosed
17 Baird, Christopher P.	Southampton	Fulham	3,025,000
30 Barnett, Leon P.	Luton Town	West Bromwich Albion	2,500,000
3 Barton, Joseph A.	Manchester City	Newcastle United	5,800,000
11 Bellamy, Craig D.	Liverpool	West Ham United	7,500,000
20 Benayoun, Yossi S.	West Ham United	Liverpool	5,000,000
12 Best, Leon J.B.	Southampton	Coventry City	undisclosed
13 Blake, Robert J.	Leeds United	Burnley	250,000
24 Blinkhorn, Matthew D.	Blackpool	Morecambe	undisclosed
5 Borrowdale, Gary I.	Crystal Palace	Coventry City	undisclosed
31 Brown, Michael R.	Fulham	Wigan Athletic	2,500,000
16 Brown, Wayne L.	Colchester United	Hull City	450,000
23 Butcher, Richard T.	Peterborough United	Notts County	undisclosed
5 Cahill, Thomas	Matlock Town	Rotherham United	undisclosed
23 Campbell, Dudley J.	Birmingham City	Leicester City	2,100,000
20 Carlton, Daniel	Morecambe	Carlisle United	undisclosed
12 Charnock, Kieran J.	Northwich Victoria	Peterborough United	undisclosed
13 Chopra, Rocky M.	Cardiff City	Sunderland	5,000,000
16 Clemence, Stephen N.	Birmingham City	Leicester City	750,000
13 Cohen, Christopher D.	Yeovil Town	Nottingham Forest	1,000,000 combined
2 Coke, Giles C.	Mansfield Town	Northampton Town	undisclosed
20 Cook, Lee	Queens Park Rangers	Fulham	2,500,000
19 Crowther, Ryan J.	Stockport County	Liverpool	undisclosed
2 Cureton, Jamie	Colchester United	Norwich City	750,000
20 Davies, Aaron R.	Yeovil Town	Nottingham Forest	1,000,000 combined
25 Davis, Claude	Sheffield United	Derby County	3,000,000
17 Davis, Steven	Aston Villa	Fulham	4,000,000
25 Duffy, Darryl A.	Hull City	Swansea City	200,000
13 Eastwood, Freddy	Southend United	Wolverhampton Wanderers	1,500,000
31 Elliott, Marvin C.	Millwall	Bristol City	undisclosed
20 Elliott, Stephen W.	Sunderland	Wolverhampton Wanderers	undisclosed
26 Ellison, Kevin	Tranmere Rovers	Chester City	undisclosed
17 Etuhu, Dixon P.	Norwich City	Sunderland	1,500,000
18 Facey, Delroy M.	Rotherham United	Gillingham	undisclosed
9 Forte, Jonathan	Sheffield United	Scunthorpe United	undisclosed
14 Geremi	Chelsea	Newcastle United	undisclosed
18 Gray, Wayne W.	Yeovil Town	Leyton Orient	undisclosed
19 Harewood, Marlon A.	West Ham United	Aston Villa	4,500,000
16 Healy, David J.	Leeds United	Fulham	1,500,000
20 Helguson, Heidar	Fulham	Bolton Wanderers	2,000,000
9 Howarth, Christopher	Bolton Wanderers	Carlisle United	undisclosed
5 Howe, Jermaine R.	Kettering Town	Peterborough United	100,000
5 Hughes, Aaron W.	Aston Villa	Fulham	1,000,000
4 Hughes, Jeffrey	Lincoln City	Crystal Palace	250,000
5 Jagielka, Philip N.	Sheffield United	Everton	4,000,000
3 Jarvis, Matthew	Gillingham	Wolverhampton Wanderers	undisclosed
12 Jones, Billy	Crewe Alexandra	Preston North End	undisclosed
16 Kamara, Diomansky M.	West Bromwich Albion	Fulham	6,000,000
30 King, Simon D.R.	Barnet	Gillingham	200,000
16 Konchesky, Paul M.	West Ham United	Fulham	2,500,000
10 Koumas, Jason	West Bromwich Albion	Wigan Athletic	5,600,000
2 Kuszczak, Tomasz	West Bromwich Albion	Manchester United	undisclosed
3 Le Fondre, Adam J.	Stockport County	Rochdale	undisclosed
25 Ljungberg, Fredrik	Arsenal	West Ham United	undisclosed

20 Lockwood, Matthew D.	Leyton Orient	Nottingham Forest	undisclosed
30 McIndoe, Michael	Wolverhampton Wanderers	Bristol City	undisclosed
27 McShane, Paul D.	West Bromwich Albion	Sunderland	1,500,000
5 Mears, Tyrone	West Ham United	Derby County	1,000,000
5 Naysmith, Gary	Everton	Sheffield United	1,000,000
5 Nicholls, Kevin J.	Leeds United	Preston North End	700,000
11 Nugent, David J.	Preston North End	Portsmouth	4,500,000
18 Parkin, Jonathan	Hull City	Stoke City	270,000
3 Partridge, Richard J.	Rotherham United	Chester City	undisclosed
14 Pipe, David R.	Notts County	Bristol Rovers	50,000
14 Platt, Clive L.	Milton Keynes Dons	Colchester United	300,000
27 Price, Lewis P.	Ipswich Town	Derby County	undisclosed
6 Pugh, Marc	Bury	Shrewsbury Town	undisclosed
16 Reo-Coker, Nigel	West Ham United	Aston Villa	8,500,000
16 Richardson, Kieran E.	Manchester United	Sunderland	5,500,000
11 Ridley, Lee	Scunthorpe United	Cheltenham Town	undisclosed
4 Rocastle, Craig A.	Oldham Athletic	Port Vale	undisclosed
30 Russell, Darel F.R.G.	Stoke City	Norwich City	undisclosed
5 Sharp, William	Scunthorpe United	Sheffield United	2,000,000
31 Sinclair, Dean M.	Barnet	Charlton Athletic	125,000\
6 Smith, Ryan C.M.	Derby County	Millwall	150,000
9 Taylor-Fletcher, Gary	Huddersfield Town	Blackpool	undisclosed
9 Todd, Andrew J.J.	Blackburn Rovers	Derby County	750,000
31 Trundle, Lee C.	Swansea City	Bristol City	1,000,000
3 Ward, Darren P.	Crystal Palace	Wolverhampton Wanderers	500,000
19 Williams, Andrew	Hereford United	Bristol Rovers	undisclosed
16 Wilson, Kelvin J.	Preston North End	Nottingham Forest	300,000
20 Yeates, Mark	Tottenham Hotspur	Colchester United	100,000
27 Young, Luke P.	Charlton Athletic	Middlesbrough	2,500,000

TEMPORARY TRANSFERS

12 Antwi-Birago, Godwin – Liverpool – Hartlepool United; 17 Basey, Grant W. – Charlton Athletic – Brentford; 10 Connolly, Matthew T. – Arsenal – Colchester United; 25 Davies, Scott – Reading – Aldershot Town; 31 Dodds, Louis B. – Leicester City – Lincoln City; 18 Gilmartin, Rene – Walsall – Hednesford Town; 5 Guthrie, Danny S. – Liverpool – Bolton Wanderers; 12 Hammill, Adam J. – Liverpool – Southampton; 25 Harban, Thomas J. – Barnsley – Bradford City; 17 Heckingbottom, Paul – Barnsley – Bradford City; 27 Joynes, Nathan – Barnsley – Bradford City; 9 Lowe, Keith S. – Wolverhampton Wanderers – Port Vale; 31 Miller, Ian J. – Ipswich Town – Darlington; 25 Moore, Sammy – Ipswich Town – Brentford; 27 Nyatanga, Lewin J. – Derby County – Barnsley; 11 Richards, Justin D. – Peterborough United – Boston United; 19 Smith, James D. – Chelsea – Norwich City; 31 Turnbull, Ross – Middlesbrough – Cardiff City; 18 Wiles, Simon P. – Blackpool – Macclesfield Town; 10 Youga, Kelly A. – Charlton Athletic – Scunthorpe United

AUGUST 2007

2 Abbott, Pawel T.H.	Swansea City	Darlington	undisclosed
31 Alexander, Graham	Preston North End	Burnley	undisclosed
10 Aljofree, Hasney	Plymouth Argyle	Swindon Town	undisclosed
4 Bailey, Nicholas F.	Barnsley	Southend United	175,000
7 Baines, Leighton	Wigan Athletic	Everton	6,000,000
8 Batt, Shaun	Dagenham & Redbridge	Fisher Athletic	undisclosed
7 Beattie, James S.	Everton	Sheffield United	4,000,000
8 Bouazza, Hameur	Watford	Fulham	3,000,000
31 Bradbury, Lee	Southend United	AFC Bournemouth	undisclosed
15 Brunt, Christopher	Sheffield Wednesday	West Bromwich Albion	undisclosed
8 Butcher, Richard T.	Peterborough United	Notts County	undisclosed
30 Byfield, Darren	Millwall	Bristol City	undisclosed
3 Camp, Lee M.J.	Derby County	Queens Park Rangers	300,000
7 Campbell, Dudley J.	Birmingham City	Leicester City	undisclosed
31 Campbell-Ryce, Jamal	Southend United	Barnsley	undisclosed
17 Carlisle, Clarke J.	Watford	Burnley	undisclosed
10 Carter, Darren A.	West Bromwich Albion	Preston North End	undisclosed
7 Clemence, Stephen N.	Birmingham City	Leicester City	undisclosed
8 Cook, Lee	Queens Park Rangers	Fulham	undisclosed
10 Cranie, Martin J.	Southampton	Portsmouth	undisclosed
3 Cresswell, Richard P.W.	Leeds United	Stoke City	undisclosed
10 Dean, James	Northwich Victoria	Bury	undisclosed
31 Diarra, Lassana	Chelsea	Arsenal	undisclosed
31 Diop, Papa B.	Fulham	Portsmouth	undisclosed
16 Dyer, Kieron C.	Newcastle United	West Ham United	undisclosed
7 Edwards, David A.	Shrewsbury Town	Luton Town	undisclosed
30 Ellington, Nathan L.F.	West Bromwich Albion	Watford	undisclosed
3 Ellison, Kevin	Tranmere Rovers	Chester City	undisclosed
31 Faye, Abdoulaye D.	Bolton Wanderers	Newcastle United	undisclosed
31 Folan, Caleb C.	Wigan Athletic	Hull City	undisclosed
14 Foley, Kevin P.	Luton Town	Wolverhampton Wanderers	undisclosed
24 Foster, Stephen J.	Burnley	Barnsley	undisclosed
15 Garner, Joseph A.	Blackburn Rovers	Carlisle United	undisclosed
1 Griffin, Andrew	Portsmouth	Derby County	500,000
10 Gueret, Willy J.	Swansea City	Milton Keynes Dons	undisclosed
17 Hand, Jamie	Chester City	Lincoln City	undisclosed
31 Harte, Ian P.	Leeds United	Sunderland	undisclosed
6 Healy, David J.	Leeds United	Fulham	undisclosed
30 Higginbotham, Daniel J.	Stoke City	Sunderland	undisclosed
7 Hoefkens, Carl	Stoke City	West Bromwich Albion	750,000
31 Holmes, Ian D.	Matlock Town	Mansfield Town	undisclosed
10 Hughes, Andrew J.	Norwich City	Leeds United	undisclosed
31 Huntington, Paul	Newcastle United	Leeds United	undisclosed
8 Jacobson, Joseph M.	Cardiff City	Bristol Rovers	undisclosed
9 Jeffers, Francis	Blackburn Rovers	Sheffield Wednesday	undisclosed

30 John, Stern	Sunderland	Southampton	undisclosed
31 Johnson, Glen M.C.	Chelsea	Portsmouth	undisclosed
31 Johnson, Jemal J.	Wolverhampton Wanderers	Milton Keynes Dons	undisclosed
30 Jones, Kenwyne J.	Southampton	Sunderland	undisclosed
29 Knight, Zatyiah	Fulham	Aston Villa	undisclosed
31 Leigertwood, Mikele B.	Sheffield United	Queens Park Rangers	undisclosed
20 Lewis, Edward J.	Leeds United	Derby County	undisclosed
22 Martin, Richard W.	Brighton & Hove Albion	Manchester City	undisclosed
10 McCarthy, Patrick	Leicester City	Charlton Athletic	undisclosed
31 McGovern, Jon P.	Milton Keynes Dons	Swindon Town	undisclosed
10 McLeod, Izale M.	Milton Keynes Dons	Charlton Athletic	undisclosed
17 Mido	Tottenham Hotspur	Middlesbrough	undisclosed
7 Morrison, James C.	Middlesbrough	West Bromwich Albion	undisclosed
31 Murphy, Daniel B.	Tottenham Hotspur	Fulham	undisclosed
14 O'Brien, Andrew J.	Portsmouth	Bolton Wanderers	undisclosed
10 O'Donovan, Roy S.	Cork City	Sunderland	undisclosed
31 O'Neil, Gary	Portsmouth	Middlesbrough	undisclosed
10 Owen, Gareth J.	Oldham Athletic	Stockport County	undisclosed
9 Paterson, Martin A.	Stoke City	Scunthorpe United	undisclosed
31 Paynter, William P.	Southend United	Swindon Town	undisclosed
9 Pearce, Jason D.	Portsmouth	AFC Bournemouth	undisclosed
9 Pele	Southampton	West Bromwich Albion	1,000,000
3 Queudrue, Franck	Fulham	Birmingham City	2,500,000
8 Richards, Gary	Colchester United	Southend United	undisclosed
3 Ridgewell, Liam M.	Aston Villa	Birmingham City	2,000,000
31 Rosenior, Liam J.	Fulham	Reading	undisclosed
7 Safri, Youssef	Norwich City	Southampton	
31 Seol, Ki-Hyeon	Reading	Fulham	undisclosed
7 Sharp, Billy L.	Scunthorpe United	Sheffield United	undisclosed
3 Smith, Alan	Manchester United	Newcastle United	6,000,000
30 Sodje, Akpo	Port Vale	Sheffield Wednesday	undisclosed
31 Solano, Nolberto	Newcastle United	West Ham United	undisclosed
31 Stefanovic, Dejan	Portsmouth	Fulham	undisclosed
20 Swailes, Daniel	Macclesfield Town	Milton Keynes Dons	undisclosed
16 Thomas, Wayne	Burnley	Southampton	undisclosed
3 Walton, Simon W.	Charlton Athletic	Queens Park Rangers	200,000
7 Williams, Marvin T.	Millwall	Yeovil Town	undisclosed
24 Williams, Robert I.	Barnsley	Huddersfield Town	undisclosed
30 Yakubu, Ayegbeni	Middlesbrough	Everton	undisclosed
10 Young, Luke P.	Charlton Athletic	Middlesbrough	undisclosed

TEMPORARY TRANSFERS

31 Aiston, Sam J. – Northampton Town – Burton Albion; 23, Anderson – Everton – Barnsley; 7 Anderson, Paul – Liverpool – Swansea City; 10 Artus, Frankie – Bristol City – Exeter City; 10 Aspden, Curtis – Hull City – Harrogate Town; 30 Barnard, Lee J. – Tottenham Hotspur – Crewe Alexandra; 10 Bean, Marcus T. – Blackpool – Rotherham United; 10 Begovic, Asmir – Portsmouth – AFC Bournemouth; 17 Behcet, Darren – Yeovil Town – Dorchester Town; 1 Bennett, Alan J. – Reading – Southampton; 30 Bennett, Dean A. – Chester City – Kidderminster Harriers; 31 Bent, Marcus N. – Charlton Athletic – Wigan Athletic; 21 Bertrand, Ryan D. – Chelsea – Oldham Athletic; 24 Bradbury, Lee – Southend United – AFC Bournemouth; 24 Branston, Guy – Peterborough United – Rochdale; 30 Bullock, Lee – Hartlepool United – Mansfield Town; 10 Cadmore, Tom – Wycombe Wanderers – Hayes & Yeading United; 31 Camara, Henri – Wigan Athletic – West Ham United; 16 Carroll, Andrew T. – Newcastle United – Preston North End; 10 Carson, Scott P. – Liverpool – Aston Villa; 24 Caton, Andrew J. – Swindon Town – Swindon Supermarine; 9 Chamberlain, Scott D. – Brighton & Hove Albion – Eastbourne Borough; 10 Charles, Wesley D.D. – Brentford – Sutton United; 10 Christophe, Jean F. – Portsmouth – AFC Bournemouth; 20 Clapham, James R. – Wolverhampton Wanderers – Leeds United; 16 Clarke, Clive – Sunderland – Leicester City; 31 Clarke, Leon M. – Sheffield Wednesday – Southend United; 17 Cobbs, Sonny H. – Brighton & Hove Albion – Worthing; 17 Cork, Jack F.P. – Chelsea – Scunthorpe United; 31 Coulson, Michael – Barnsley – Northwich Victoria; 31 Cox, Simon – Reading – Swindon Town; 17 Craddock, Jody – Wolverhampton Wanderers – Stoke City; 4 Daniels, Charlie – Tottenham Hotspur – Leyton Orient; 31 Davies, Curtis E. – West Bromwich Albion – Aston Villa; 9 Diagouraga, Toumani – Watford – Hereford United; 31 Dickov, Paul – Manchester City – Crystal Palace; 16 Dickson, Christopher M. – Charlton Athletic – Crewe Alexandra; 10 Djourou, Johan – Arsenal – Birmingham City; 24 Doran, Peter J. – Walsall – Worcester City; 10 Ephraim, Hogan – West Ham United – Queens Park Rangers; 31 Feeney, Warren J. – Cardiff City – Swansea City; 31 Fojut, Jaroslaw – Bolton Wanderers – Luton Town; 24, Forde, David – Cardiff City – Luton Town; 15 Fulop, Marton – Sunderland – Leicester City; 31 Gallagher, Paul – Blackburn Rovers – Preston North End; 1 Gamble, Patrick J. – Nottingham Forest – Stalybridge Celtic; 10 Gargan, Sam J. – Brighton & Hove Albion – Worthing; 10 Garner, Joseph A. – Blackburn Rovers – Carlisle United; 3 Gaynor, Ross – Millwall – Fisher Athletic; 10 Giddings, Stuart J. – Coventry City – Oldham Athletic; 8 Gilbert, Kerrea K. – Arsenal – Southend United; 31 Gooding, Andrew M. – Coventry City – Burton Albion; 9 Gradel, Max – Leicester City – AFC Bournemouth; 24 Grant, Gavin – Millwall – Grays Athletic; 10 Green, Dominic A. – Dagenham & Redbridge – Thurrock; 10 Gregory, Steven M. – Wycombe Wanderers – Hayes & Yeading United; 13 Griffiths, Anthony J. – Doncaster Rovers – Halifax Town; 10 Hamer, Ben – Reading – Brentford; 17 Hardman, Lewis T. – Darlington – Whitby Town; 14 Hazley, Matthew – Stoke City – Stafford Rangers; 31 Henderson, Stephen – Bristol City – York City; 24 Holness, Marcus L. – Oldham Athletic – Ossett Town; 31 Idrizaj, Besian – Liverpool – Crystal Palace; 23 Jefferies, Michael J. – Macclesfield Town – Leek Town; 7 Jones, Daniel J. – Wolverhampton Wanderers – Northampton Town; 14 Jones, Richard G. – Manchester United – Yeovil Town; 31 Keogh, Richard J. – Bristol City – Huddersfield Town; 24 Kilkenny, Neil M. – Birmingham City – Oldham Athletic; 31 Kuqi, Shefki – Crystal Palace – Fulham; 1 Lewis, Joseph P. – Norwich City – Morecambe; 10 Logan, Conrad – Leicester City – Stockport County; 31 Maher, Stephen J. – Yeovil Town – Dorchester Town; 10 Maidens, Michael D. – Hartlepool United – Blyth Spartans; 9 Mancienne, Michael I. – Chelsea – Queens Park Rangers; 17 Marsh-Evans, Robert W. – Chester City – Droylsden; 12 Massey, Alan – Wycombe Wanderers – Wealdstone; 31 Masters, Clark J. – Brentford – Welling United; 31 McGoldrick, David J. – Southampton – Port Vale; 20 McGrail, Christopher – Preston North End – Accrington Stanley; 10 McKeown, James K. – Peterborough United – Kettering Town; 31 Miller, Ian – Ipswich Town – Darlington; 15 Miller, Ishmael – Manchester City – West Bromwich Albion; 31 Mills, Daniel J. – Manchester City – Charlton Athletic; 14 Mills, Matthew C.C. – Manchester City – Doncaster Rovers; 24 Mills, Pablo S.I. – Rotherham United – Crawley Town; 10 Montague, Ross P. – Brentford – Sutton United; 30 Mulligan, David – Scunthorpe United – Grimsby Town; 10 Murphy, Andrew – Preston North End – Northwich Victoria; 10 Myrie-Williams, Jennison – Bristol City – Cheltenham Town; 9 N'Dumbu-N'Sungu, Guy – Gillingham – Bradford City; 10 Newton, Sean – Chester City – Southport; 16 Nicholson, Stuart I. – West Bromwich Albion – Shrewsbury Town; 31 O'Callaghan, George – Ipswich Town – Brighton & Hove Albion; 10 O'Connor, Gareth – Burnley – AFC Bournemouth; 31 Odhiambo, Eric – Leicester City – Southend United; 24 O'Hara, Jamie

– Tottenham Hotspur – Millwall; 28 Oji, Samuel U.U. – Birmingham City – Leyton Orient; 8 Palmer, Christopher L. – Wycombe Wanderers – Darlington; 16 Palmer, James – Bristol Rovers – Tiverton Town; 2 Peltier, Lee A. – Liverpool – Yeovil Town; 10 Pentney, Carl – Leicester City – York City; 10 Pettigrew, Adrian R.J. – Chelsea – Brentford; 17 Reed, Jamie – Wrexham – Aberystwyth Town; 31 Reid, Reuben – Plymouth Argyle – Wycombe Wanderers; 17 Rigley, Alex – Swindon Town – Cirencester Town; 9 Robinson, Theo – Watford – Hereford United; 31 Rooney, Adam – Stoke City – Chesterfield; 31 Russell, Alexander J. – Bristol City – Northampton Town; 14 Ryan, James – Liverpool – Shrewsbury Town; 9 Sahar, Ben – Chelsea – Queens Park Rangers; 17 Sandell, Andrew C. – Bristol Rovers – Salisbury City; 10 Semple, Ryan D. – Lincoln City – Rushden & Diamonds; 9 Shawcross, Ryan J. – Manchester United – Stoke City; 31 Simpson, Jay-Alistaire F. – Arsenal – Millwall; 10 Skinner, Lloyd E. – Brighton & Hove Albion – Burgess Hill Town; 23 Smith, Adam – Peterborough United – Kings Lynn; 10 Smith, James – Liverpool – Stockport County; 31 Sodje, Samuel – Reading – Charlton Athletic; 9 Stack, Graham – Reading – Wolverhampton Wanderers; 1 Starosta, Ben M. – Sheffield United – Brenford; 24 Thomas, Sean I.S. – Queens Park Rangers – Wealdstone; 10 Tearney, Paul T. – Blackpool – Stockport County; 16 Travis, Nicholas – Sheffield United – Chesterfield; 10 Ujah, Curtis – Yeovil Town – Crawley Town; 31 Warburton, Callum S. – Rochdale – Kendal Town; 8 Weale, Christopher – Bristol City – Hereford United; 14 Welsh, Ishmael – Yeovil Town – Torquay United; 30 Westwood, Ashley M. – Chester City – Port Vale; 17 Winterton, Christopher C. – Brighton & Hove Albion – Burgess Hill Town; 31 Worley, Harry J. – Chelsea – Carlisle United; 31 Wright, Joshua W. – Charlton Athletic – Barnet; 3 Wright, Stephen J. – Sunderland – Stoke City; 31 Zakuani, Gabriel A. – Fulham – Stoke City; 2 Zebroski, Christopher – Millwall – Torquay United

SEPTEMBER 2007 TEMPORARY TRANSFERS

28 Alnwick, Ben – Tottenham Hotspur – Luton Town; 14 Annerson, Jamie – Sheffield United – Rotherham United; 20 Anyinsah, Joseph G. – Preston North End – Carlisle United; 14 Avinel, Cedric M. – Watford – Stafford Rangers; 8 Bennett, Dean A. – Chester City – Kidderminster Harriers; 14 Blackmore, David – West Ham United – Thurrock; 14 Boulding, Rory J.J. – Mansfield Town – Hucknall Town; 20 Cahill, Gary J. – Aston Villa – Sheffield United; 25 Carder-Andrews, Karle S. – Brentford – Margate; 21 Cattell, Stuart – Wycombe Wanderers – Oxford United; 17 Chamberlain, Scott D. – Brighton & Hove Albion – Bognor Regis Town; 24 Cisak, Alex – Leicester City – Oxford United; 14 Clarke, Tom – Yeovil Town – Bridgwater Town; 21 Clarke, Wayne J. – Darlington – Shildon; 29 Cole, James W. – Barnet – Wingate & Finchley; 28 Collins, Sam – Hull City – Swindon Town; 27 Collins, Sam C. – Milton Keynes Dons – Kettering Town; 28 Craney, Ian T.W. – Swansea City – Accrington Stanley; 21 Cresswell, Ryan – Sheffield United – Rotherham United; 21 Dailly, Christian – West Ham United – Southampton; 21 Davies, Gareth – Chesterfield – Stalybridge Celtic; 24 Davis, Sol S. – Luton Town – Peterborough United; 21 Dickson, Christopher M. – Charlton Athletic – Gillingham; 14 Douglas, Robert J. – Leicester City – Millwall; 14 Dyer, Bruce A. – Doncaster Rovers – Rotherham United; 21 Ellis, Mark I.I. – Bolton Wanderers – Torquay United; 14 Evans, Gareth D. – Wrexham – Northwich Victoria; 28 Fielding, Frank D. – Blackburn Rovers – Wycombe Wanderers; 28 Frizzell, Brewster – Hull City – North Ferriby United; 28 Garrett, Robert – Stoke City – Wrexham; 12 Gatting, Joe S. – Brighton & Hove Albion – Woking; 21 Gillett, Simon J. – Southampton – Yeovil Town; 6 Goode, Aaron M.O. – Queens Park Rangers – Kingstonian; 7 Grazioli, Giuliano – Barnet – AFC Wimbledon; 21 Hardman, Lewis – Darlington – Shildon; 17 Hastings, John J.D. – Milton Keynes Dons – Ebbsfleet United; 13 Hegarty, Nicholas – Grimsby Town – York City; 7 Hernandez, Stephen – Sheffield United – Worksop Town; 26 Heslop, Simon – Barnsley – Northwich Victoria; 18 Hoskins, William – Watford – Millwall; 28 Ifil, Phillip – Tottenham Hotspur – Southampton; 14 Johnson, Adam – Middlesbrough – Watford; 21 Johnson, Michael O. – Derby County – Sheffield Wednesday; 14 Jones, Zachariah S. – Blackburn Rovers – Stockport County; 21 Kavanagh, Graham A. – Sunderland – Sheffield Wednesday; 28 Kazimierczak, Przemyslaw – Bolton Wanderers – Wycombe Wanderers; 8 Kelly, Shaun – Chester City – Vauxhall Motors; 20 Laird, Scott – Plymouth Argyle – Torquay United; 21 Larrieu, Romain – Plymouth Argyle – Yeovil Town; 20 Leonard, Benjamin P. – Bury – Tamworth; 17 Loach, Scott J.J. – Watford – Stafford Rangers; 12 Lomax, Kelvin – Oldham Athletic – Rochdale; 21 MacKenzie, Christopher – Shrewsbury Town – Kidderminster Harriers; 28 Marsh-Evans, Robert W. – Chester City – Vauxhall Motors; 28 Mattis, Dwayne A.A. – Barnsley – Walsall; 28 May, Ben S. – Millwall – Scunthorpe United; 8 McAllister, Sean B. – Sheffield Wednesday – Mansfield Town; 21 Montague, Ross P. – Brentford – Welling United; 21 Nowland, Adam C. – Preston North End – Gillingham; 14 Page, Sam T. – Milton Keynes Dons – Walton & Hersham; 21 Potter, Alfie – Peterborough United – Grays Athletic; 14 Reet, Daniel – Mansfield Town – Alfreton Town; 21 Richards, Matthew – Ipswich Town – Brighton & Hove Albion; 21 Saunders, Russell – Wigan Athletic – Altrincham; 14 Shotton, Ryan – Stoke City – Altrincham; 12 Smart, Bally – Norwich City – Milton Keynes Dons; 27 Smith, Adam – Peterborough United – Boston United; 21 Stephens, Dale – Bury – Drolysden; 21 Taylor, Ryan – Rotherham United – Burton Albion; 28 Wallwork, Ronald – West Bromwich Albion – Huddersfield Town; 21 Wilson, Marc D. – Portsmouth – AFC Bournemouth

OCTOBER 2007 TEMPORARY TRANSFERS

11 Allison, Scott – Hartlepool United – Gateshead; 1 Andrews, Wayne M.H. – Coventry City – Leeds United; 21 Anyinsah, Joseph G. – Preston North End – Carlisle United; 4 Aspden, Curtis – Hull City – Harrogate Town; 19 Atkinson, Robert – Barnsley – Rochdale; 12 Atkinson, William H. – Hull City – Port Vale; 11 Bailey, Stefan K.L.K. – Queens Park Rangers – Oxford United; 19 Bardsley, Phillip A. – Manchester United – Sheffield United; 29 Bastians, Felix – Nottingham Forest – Chesterfield; 29 Bencherif, Hamza – Nottingham Forest – Lincoln City; 25 Bennett, Elliott – Wolverhampton Wanderers – Crewe Alexandra; 18 Beresford, Marlon – Luton Town – Oldham Athletic; 5 Betsy, Kevin – Bristol City – Yeovil Town; 5 Bradley, Jason – Sheffield Wednesday – Buxton; 25 Brkovic, Ahmet – Luton Town – Millwall; 1 Brooks-Meade, Corrin – Fulham – Darlington; 5 Bullock, Lee – Hartlepool United – Bury; 16 Butler, Martin N. – Walsall – Grimsby Town; 30 Buzsaky, Akos – Plymouth Argyle – Queens Park Rangers; 18 Campbell, Fraizer L. – Manchester United – Hull City; 26 Carayol, Mustapha – Milton Keynes Dons – Crawley Town; 8 Caton, Andrew J. – Swindon Town – North Leigh; 19 Church, Simon R. – Reading – Crewe Alexandra; 1 Clapham, James R. – Wolverhampton Wanderers – Leeds United; 14 Clarke, Tom – Yeovil Town – Bridgwater Town; 24 Colbeck, Philip J. – Bradford City – Darlington; 8 Cole, James W. – Barnet – Wingate & Finchley; 1 Coles, Daniel R. – Hull City – Hartlepool United; 25 Cooper, Kevin L. – Cardiff City – Tranmere Rovers; 5 Cotton, Jack M. – Lincoln City – Ilkeston Town; 5 Coward, Christopher D. – Stockport County – Northwich Victoria; 8 Cranie, Martin J. – Portsmouth – Queens Park Rangers; 9 Crow, Daniel – Peterborough United – Notts County; 26 Dark, Lewis K. – Brentford – Farnborough; 9 Davies, Andrew – Middlesbrough – Southampton; 1 De Vries, Mark – Leicester City – Leeds United; 11 Dean, James – Bury – Altrincham; 23 Doherty, Thomas – Queens Park Rangers – Wycombe Wanderers; 23 Douglas, Robert J. – Leicester City – Wycombe Wanderers; 26 Easter, Jermaine – Wycombe Wanderers – Plymouth Argyle; 12 Eckersley, Adam – Manchester United – Port Vale; 25 Emanuel, Lewis J. – Luton Town – Brentford; 4 Evans, Rhys K. – Blackpool – Bradford City; 5 Fogden, Wesley K. – Brighton & Hove Albion – Dorchester Town; 19 Gibson, Darron – Manchester United – Wolverhampton Wanderers; 8 Green, Matthew J. – Cardiff City – Darlington; 12 Hart, Daniel – Barnet – Northwood; 15 Hartson, John – West Bromwich Albion – Norwich City; 16 Heslop, Simon – Barnsley – Halifax Town; 2 Holness, Marcus L. – Oldham Athletic – Rochdale; 5 Jackson, Matthew A. – Watford – Blackpool; 2 Jarrett, Jason L. – Preston North End – Queens Park Rangers; 5 Jefferies, Michael J. – Macclesfield Town – Leek Town; 23 John, Collins – Fulham – Leicester City; 18 Karacan, Jem P. – Reading – AFC Bournemouth; 29 Kay, James – Sheffield Wednesday – Guiseley; 19 Kelly, Ashley C. – Oldham Athletic – Leigh RMI; 1 Keogh, Richard J. – Bristol City – Huddersfield Town; 23 Kishishev, Radostin – Leicester City – Leeds United; 19 Knights, Darryl J. – Yeovil Town – Cambridge United; 9 Lallana, Adam D. – Southampton – AFC Bournemouth; 5 Law, Joshua – Chesterfield – Alfreton Town; 5 Law, Nicholas – Sheffield United – Bradford City; 1 Legzdins, Adam R. – Birmingham City – Halifax Town; 11 Logan, Shaleum – Manchester City – Grimsby Town; 5 Martin, Lee R. – Manchester United – Plymouth Argyle; 4 Masters, Clark J. – Brentford – Welling United; 5 McBreen, Daniel J. – Scunthorpe United – York City; 17 McClements, David – Sheffield Wednesday – Hinckley United; 22 McKeown, James K. – Peterborough United – Worcester City; 30 Minto-St Aimie, Kieron L. – Queens Park Rangers – Oxford United; 19 Murphy, Andrew – Preston North End – Vauxhall Motors; 26 Obersteller, Jack – Wycombe Wanderers –

Grays Athletic; 4 Odhiambo, Eric – Leicester City – Southend United; 1 Oji, Samuel U. – Birmingham City – Leyton Orient; 8 Oliver, Dean – Sheffield United – Halifax Town; 15 Page, Sam T. – Milton Keynes Dons – Hendon; 8 Pearson, Michael T. – Oldham Athletic – Farsley Celtic; 11 Peatfield, Lee – Bury – Fleetwood Town; 1 Peters, Ryan V. – Brentford – Margate; 25 Potter, Luke A. – Barnsley – Stafford Rangers; 19 Puddy, Willem J.S. – Cheltenham Town – Stafford Rangers; 22 Pugh, Andrew J. – Gillingham – Welling United; 10 Rhodes, Jordan L. – Ipswich Town – Oxford United; 26 Rigby, Lloyd J. – Rochdale – Rossendale United; 4 Russell, Alexander J. – Bristol City – Northampton Town; 26 Schmeichel, Kasper P. – Manchester City – Cardiff City; 5 Sinclair, Dean M. – Charlton Athletic – Cheltenham Town; 12 Smith, Johann A.R. – Bolton Wanderers – Darlington; 29 Songo'o Franck S. – Portsmouth – Crystal Palace; 19 Taylor, Scott J. – Milton Keynes Dons – Rochdale; 26 Thomas, Anthony C. – Barnet – Cambridge City; 4 Thompson, Leslie – Bolton Wanderers – Stockport County; 5 Tunnicliffe, James – Stockport County – Northwich Victoria; 2 Vine, Rowan – Birmingham City – Queens Park Rangers; 25 Wainwright, Neil – Darlington – Shrewsbury Town; 19 Walker, James L.N. – Charlton Athletic – Yeovil Town; 5 Warburton, Callum S. – Rochdale – Kendal Town; 2 Wright, Joshua W. – Charlton Athletic – Barnet

NOVEMBER 2007 TEMPORARY TRANSFERS

9 Ademeno, Charles – Southend United – Welling United; 22 Ainsworth, Lionel – Hereford United – Watford; 22, Aiston, Sam J. – Northampton Town – Wrexham; 15 Ameobi, Tommy – Leeds United – Scunthorpe United; 22 Atkinson, Robert – Barnsley – Grimsby Town; 22 Baidoo, Shabazz K.K. – Queens Park Rangers – Gillingham; 30 Ball, Gary – Morecambe – Kendal Town; 22 Barcham, Andrew – Tottenham Hotspur – Leyton Orient; 22 Barnes, Ashley L. – Plymouth Argyle – Oxford United; 15 Baseya, Cedric – Southampton – Crewe Alexandra; 29 Belford, Cameron D. – Bury – Worcester City; 9 Bignot, Marcus J. – Queens Park Rangers – Millwall; 15 Branston, Guy – Peterborough United – Northampton Town; 13 Brooks-Meade, Corrin – Fulham – AFC Wimbledon; 1 Byron, Michael J. – Notts County – Hinckley United; 20 Camara, Mohamed – Derby County – Norwich City; 22 Carden, Paul A. – Accrington Stanley – Cambridge United; 30 Cobbs, Sonny H. – Brighton & Hove Albion – Dorchester Town; 2 Coles, Daniel R. – Hull City – Bristol Rovers; 2 Collins, Matthew J. – Swansea City – Wrexham; 9 Collins, Patrick – Darlington – Oxford United; 2 Cort, Leon T. – Crystal Palace – Stoke City; 9 Coward, Christopher D. – Stockport County – Ashton United; 1 Cresswell, Ryan – Sheffield United – Morecambe; 22 D'Agostino, Michael J. – Blackpool – Cheltenham Town; 9 Davies, Jamie – Morecambe – Leigh RMI; 22 Dennehy, Billy – Sunderland – Accrington Stanley; 19 Derry, Shaun – Leeds United – Crystal Palace; 23 Duncan, Derek – Wycombe Wanderers – Lewes; 22 Evans, Chedwyn M. – Manchester City – Norwich City; 22 Farquharson, Nicholas A. – Crewe Alexandra – Northwich Victoria; 22 Flynn, Matthew E. – Macclesfield Town – Warrington Town; 22 Flynn, Ryan – Liverpool – Hereford United; 8 Foulkes, Luke – Grimsby Town – Boston United; 16 Grant, Anthony P.S. – Chelsea – Luton Town; 22 Gray, David P. – Manchester United – Crewe Alexandra; 22 Green, Matthew J. – Cardiff City – Oxford United; 12 Hales, Lee A. – West Ham United – Rushden & Diamonds; 1 Halls, John – Reading – Preston North End; 20 Hastings, John – Milton Keynes Dons – Maidenhead United; 9 Havern, Gianluca – Stockport County – Ashton United; 9 Hessey, Sean P. – Chester City – Macclesfield Town; 6 Hill, Clinton – Stoke City – Crystal Palace; 22 Hinshelwood, Paul – Torquay United – Tiverton Town; 2 Hodge, Bryan – Blackburn Rovers – Millwall; 22 Hughes, Jeffrey – Crystal Palace – Peterborough United; 22 Hughes, Liam J. – Wolverhampton Wanderers – Bury; 2 Humphrey, Chris – Shrewsbury Town – Stafford Rangers; 30 Jeffery, Jack C. – West Ham United – Hampton & Richmond Borough; 22 Jones, Carl M. – York City – Gateshead; 22 Keogh, Richard J. – Bristol City – Carlisle United; 14 Langford, Andrew – Morecambe – Leek Town; 29 Ledgister, Aaron T. – Cheltenham Town – Weston-Super-Mare; 2 Lindfield, Craig A. – Liverpool – Notts County; 22 Liptak, Zoltan – Sheffield United – Stevenage Borough; 2 Loach, Scott J. – Watford – Stafford Rangers; 9 Logan, Shaleum – Manchester City – Scunthorpe United; 1 Macken, Jonathan P. – Derby County – Barnsley; 22 Madjo, Guy B. – Crawley Town – Cheltenham Town; 16 Malcolm, Robert – Derby County – Queens Park Rangers; 21 McEvilly, Lee – Accrington Stanley – Rochdale; 9 McMahon, Anthony – Middlesbrough – Blackpool; 22 Miller, Adam E. – Stevenage Borough – Gillingham; 16 Morgan, Dean – Luton Town – Southend United; 5 Noble, Matthew J. – Doncaster Rovers – Spennymoor Town; 9 Nowland, Adam C. – Preston North End – Stockport County; 22 Nutter, John R.W. – Stevenage Borough – Gillingham; 12 Oli, Dennis C. – Grays Athletic – Gillingham; 23 O'Loughlin, Charlie M. – Port Vale – Nantwich Town; 15 Palethorpe, Phillip J. – Chester City – Tamworth; 15 Pattison, Matthew J. – Newcastle United – Norwich City; 1 Potter, Alfie – Peterborough United – Havant & Waterlooville; 22 Power, Alan T.D. – Nottingham Forest – Grays Athletic; 2 Pugh, Daniel – Preston North End – Stoke City; 2 Ricketts, Michael B. – Oldham Athletic – Walsall; 22 Ridley, Lee – Cheltenham Town – Darlington; 7 Ross, Ian – Sheffield United – Rotherham United; 22 Salmon, Mark M. – Wolverhampton Wanderers – Port Vale; 21 Saynor, Ben K.G. – Bradford City – Leigh RMI; 9 Seanla, Stephane – Barnet – St Albans City; 22 Sharpe, Thomas R. – Nottingham Forest – Bury; 22 Shimmin, Dominic E. – Queens Park Rangers – AFC Bournemouth; 6 Sinclair, Scott A. – Chelsea – Queens Park Rangers; 22 Sleath, Daniel J. – Mansfield Town – Boston United; 21 Slusarski, Bartosz – West Bromwich Albion – Blackpool; 30 Stephens, Dale – Bury – Hyde United; 22 Stieber, Zoltan – Aston Villa – Yeovil Town; 22 Stokes, Anthony – West Ham United – Stevenage Borough; 22 Sweeney, Peter – Stoke City – Walsall; 2 Taylor, Martin – Birmingham City – Norwich City; 2 Threlfall, Robert R. – Liverpool – Hereford United; 22 Thurgood, Stuart A. – Grays Athletic – Gillingham; 20 Torpey, Stephen D.J. – Lincoln City – Farsley Celtic; 19 Tudor, Shane A. – Port Vale – Shrewsbury Town; 22 White, John – Colchester United – Stevenage Borough; 16 Wilson, Marc D. – Portsmouth – Luton Town

DECEMBER 2007

31 Scannell, Damian	Eastleigh	Southend United	undisclosed

TEMPORARY TRANSFERS

8 Aspden, Curtis – Hull City – Boston United; 9 Bignot, Marcus J. – Queens Park Rangers – Millwall; 20 Blackmore, David – West Ham United – Thurrock; 22 Bowditch, Dean – Ipswich Town – Northampton Town; 5 Brkovic, Ahmet – Luton Town – Millwall; 11 Brown, David P. – Nottingham Forest – Eastwood Town; 9 Brown, Junior – Crewe Alexandra – Kidsgrove Athletic; 3 Buckley, Kyle – Rochdale – Woodley Sports; 28 Campana, Alessandro – Watford – Wealdstone; 9 Carroll, Neil – Chester City – Leigh RMI; 21 Caton, Andrew J. – Swindon Town – Brackley Town; 7 Davies, Charlton – Walsall – Solihull Moors; 18 Dickson, Ryan A. – Plymouth Argyle – Brentford; 18 Donnelly-Jackson, Jamie – Chesterfield – Matlock Town; 13 Doughty, Philip M. – Blackpool – Macclesfield Town; 14 Erskine, Jacob – Dagenham & Redbridge – Tooting & Mitcham United; 6 Fogden, Wesley K. – Brighton & Hove Albion – Dorchester Town; 21 Gargan, Sam J. – Brighton & Hove Albion – Bognor Regis Town; 12 Golbourne, Julio S. – Reading – AFC Bournemouth; 14 Hanna, Christopher J. – Walsall – Hednesford Town; 21 Harris, Harry – Walsall – Hinckley United; 6 Hart, Gary J. – Brighton & Hove Albion – Havant & Waterlooville; 12 Henry, James – Reading – AFC Bournemouth; 3 Holness, Marcus L. – Oldham Athletic – Rochdale; 3 Hopkins, Damian L. – Bradford City – Ossett Albion; 10 Howard, Charlie S. – Gillingham – Bromley; 18 Husbands, Michael P. – Macclesfield Town – AFC Telford United; 24 Jevons, Phillip – Bristol City – Huddersfield Town; 27 Kelly, Ashley C. – Oldham Athletic – Barrow; 17 Klein-Davies, Joshua – Bristol Rovers – Yate Town; 9 Laird, Marc – Manchester City – Port Vale; 11 Liversedge, Nicholas – Darlington – Bishop Auckland; 14 Mason, Anthony – Plymouth Argyle – Bridgwater Town; 27 McAllister, Sean B. – Sheffield Wednesday – Bury; 3 Morgan, Luke W.M. – Bradford City – Ossett Albion; 24 Nolan, Edward W. – Blackburn Rovers – Hartlepool United; 10 O'Donnell, Richard M. – Sheffield Wednesday – Buxton; 17 Page, Sam T. – Milton Keynes Dons – Hendon; 12 Pearce, Alex – Reading – AFC Bournemouth; 9 Pearce, Krystian M.V. – Birmingham City – Notts County; 16 Reet, Daniel – Mansfield Town – Alfreton Town; 7 Sansara, Netan – Walsall – Solihull Moors; 13 Sinclair, Dean M. – Charlton Athletic – Cheltenham Town; 21 Sinclair, Emile A. – Nottingham Forest – Brentford; 17 Smith, Benjamin J. – Doncaster Rovers – Lincoln City; 3 Songo'o, Franck S. – Portsmouth – Crystal Palace; 17 Taylor, Andrew – Blackburn Rovers – Tranmere Rovers; 10 Wilkinson, David M. – Crystal Palace – Dover Athletic; 20 Yao, Sosthene A. – Cheltenham Town – Weston-Super-Mare; 3 Young, Neil A. – AFC Bournemouth – Weymouth

JANUARY 2008

31 Adebola, Bamberdele O.	Coventry City	Bristol City	250,000
3 Agyemang, Patrick	Preston North End	Queens Park Rangers	350,000
7 Ainsworth, Lionel	Hereford United	Watford	undisclosed
3 Akurang, Cliff D.	Histon	Barnet	undisclosed
21 Anelka, Nicolas	Bolton Wanderers	Chelsea	15,000,000
31 Aspden, Curtis	Hull City	Farsley Celtic	undisclosed
24 Bardsley, Philip A.	Manchester United	Sunderland	2,000,000
25 Barnard, Lee J.	Tottenham Hotspur	Southend United	undisclosed
31 Bevan, Scott A.	Kidderminster Harriers	Shrewsbury Town	undisclosed
8 Bolland, Philip C.	Chester City	Wrexham	Free
10 Brkovic, Ahmet	Luton Town	Millwall	Free
31 Bromby, Leigh	Sheffield United	Watford	600,000
10 Brown, Christopher	Norwich City	Preston North End	400,000
31 Brown, David P.	Nottingham Forest	Bradford City	Free
31 Bullock, Lee	Hartlepool United	Bradford City	undisclosed
7 Butler, Martin N.	Walsall	Grimsby Town	undisclosed
2 Buzsaky, Akos	Plymouth Argyle	Queens Park Rangers	500,000
30 Cahill, Gary J.	Aston Villa	Bolton Wanderers	4,500,000
10 Chaplow, Richard D.	West Bromwich Albion	Preston North End	800,000
7 Coles, Daniel R.	Hull City	Bristol Rovers	undisclosed
31 Collins, Sam	Hull City	Hartlepool United	undisclosed
4 Connolly, Matthew T.	Arsenal	Queens Park Rangers	1,000,000
31 Constable, James A.	Kidderminster Harriers	Shrewsbury Town	undisclosed
14 Cort, Leon T.	Crystal Palace	Stoke City	1,200,000
31 Cox, Simon	Reading	Swindon Town	Free
11 Coyne, Christopher	Luton Town	Colchester United	350,000
4 Craney, Ian T.W.	Swansea City	Accrington Stanley	85,000
31 Dann, Scott	Walsall	Coventry City	undisclosed
22 Danns, Neil A.	Birmingham City	Crystal Palace	600,000
10 Davies, Andrew	Middlesbrough	Southampton	1,000,000
17 Delaney, Damien	Hull City	Queens Park Rangers	600,000
24 Derry, Shaun	Leeds United	Crystal Palace	undisclosed
17 Diarra, Lassana	Arsenal	Portsmouth	5,500,000
11 Dickson, Ryan A.	Plymouth Argyle	Brentford	undisclosed
30 Dixon, Jonathan J.	Aldershot Town	Brighton & Hove Albion	56,000
23 Dobie, Scott	Nottingham Forest	Carlisle United	undisclosed
31 Dobson, Craig G.	Stevenage Borough	Milton Keynes Dons	undisclosed
4 Drummond, Stewart	Shrewsbury Town	Morecambe	15,000
28 D'Sane, Roscoe	Accrington Stanley	Torquay United	undisclosed
3 Easter, Jermaine	Wycombe Wanderers	Plymouth Argyle	210,000
10 Ebanks-Blake, Sylvan	Plymouth Argyle	Wolverhampton Wanderers	1,500,000
1 Eckersley, Adam	Manchester United	Port Vale	Free
14 Edwards, David	Luton Town	Wolverhampton Wanderers	675,000
31 Elder, Nathan	Brighton & Hove Albion	Brentford	35,000
31 Elding, Anthony L.	Stockport County	Leeds United	undisclosed
31 Elokobi, George N.	Colchester United	Wolverhampton Wanderers	undisclosed
2 Ephraim, Hogan	West Ham United	Queens Park Rangers	800,000
31 Eustace, John M.	Stoke City	Watford	undisclosed
22 Evans, Rhys K.	Blackpool	Millwall	Free
11 Folly, Yoann	Sheffield Wednesday	Plymouth Argyle	200,000
4 Forbes, Adrian E.	Blackpool	Millwall	undisclosed
28 Fox, Daniel J.	Walsall	Coventry City	300,000
28 Fuller, Barry M.	Stevenage Borough	Gillingham	undisclosed
14 Gosling, Daniel	Plymouth Argyle	Everton	1,000,000
21 Grabban, Lewis	Crystal Palace	Millwall	150,000
25 Gray, Andrew D.	Burnley	Charlton Athletic	1,500,000
11 Griffin, Andrew	Derby County	Stoke City	300,000
4 Hall, Fitz	Wigan Athletic	Queens Park Rangers	700,000
31 Hammond, Dean	Brighton & Hove Albion	Colchester United	250,000
3 Hatch, Liam M.	Barnet	Peterborough United	150,000
3 Hayles, Barrington	Plymouth Argyle	Leicester City	150,000
16 Hill, Clinton	Stoke City	Crystal Palace	200,000
4 Holness, Marcus L.	Oldham Athletic	Rochdale	Free
15 Horwood, Evan D.	Sheffield United	Carlisle United	undisclosed
3 Howard, Steven J.	Derby County	Leicester City	1,500,000
10 Ifil, Phillip	Tottenham Hotspur	Colchester United	undisclosed
31 Jackson, Simeon A.	Rushden & Diamonds	Gillingham	undisclosed
9 Jevons, Phillip	Bristol City	Huddersfield Town	undisclosed
9 Johnson, Bradley	Northampton Town	Leeds United	250,000
31 Kazimierczak, Przemyslaw	Bolton Wanderers	Darlington	Free
7 Kilkenny, Neil M.	Birmingham City	Leeds United	undisclosed
11 King, Mark	Blackburn Rovers	Accrington Stanley	undisclosed
25 King, Marlon F.	Watford	Wigan Athletic	5,000,000
7 Knight, Leon L.	Milton Keynes Dons	Wycombe Wanderers	undisclosed
9 Laird, Marc	Manchester City	Millwall	Free
31 Laird, Scott	Plymouth Argyle	Stevenage Borough	undisclosed
31 Lennon, Neil F.	Nottingham Forest	Wycombe Wanderers	Free
7 Lewis, Joseph	Norwich City	Peterborough United	400,000
28 Lewis, Stuart A.	Stevenage Borough	Gillingham	undisclosed
28 Macken, Jonathan P.	Derby County	Barnsley	100,000
25 Mackie, James	Exeter City	Plymouth Argyle	145,000
18 MacLean, Steven	Cardiff City	Plymouth Argyle	500,000
11 Madjo, Guy B.	Crawley Town	Shrewsbury Town	20,000
2 Mahon, Gavin A.	Watford	Queens Park Rangers	200,000
11 Marsh-Evans, Robert W.	Chester City	Leigh RMI	undisclosed

31 Martin, David	Crystal Palace	Millwall	undisclosed
11 Masters, Clark J.	Brentford	Southend United	undisclosed
18 May, Ben S.	Millwall	Scunthorpe United	100,000
16 McCann, Grant S.	Barnsley	Scunthorpe United	100,000
31 McCleary, Garath J.	Bromley	Nottingham Forest	undisclosed
18 McFadden, James	Everton	Birmingham City	5,750,000
4 McIntyre, Kevin	Macclesfield Town	Shrewsbury Town	50,000
18 McNamee, Anthony	Watford	Swindon Town	undisclosed
8 McPhee, Stephen	Hull City	Blackpool	200,000
31 Michalik, Lubomir	Bolton Wanderers	Leeds United	500,000
10 Miller, Adam E.	Stevenage Borough	Gillingham	undisclosed
11 Miller, Ian	Ipswich Town	Darlington	Free
31 Miller, Ishmael	Manchester City	West Bromwich Albion	undisclosed
31 Moore, Ian R.	Hartlepool United	Tranmere Rovers	Free
10 Mulligan, David	Scunthorpe United	Port Vale	undisclosed
4 Murray, Adam D.	Macclesfield Town	Oxford United	undisclosed
25 Murray, Glenn	Rochdale	Brighton & Hove Albion	300,000
30 Ndumbu-Nsungu, Guylain	Gillingham	Darlington	Free
31 Norris, David M.	Plymouth Argyle	Ipswich Town	2,000,000
7 Nutter, John R.W.	Stevenage Borough	Gillingham	undisclosed
11 Oakley, Matthew	Derby County	Leicester City	500,000
14 Oli, Dennis C.	Grays Athletic	Gillingham	undisclosed
4 Pattison, Matthew J.	Newcastle United	Norwich City	undisclosed
31 Peltier, Lee A.	Liverpool	Yeovil Town	undisclosed
13 Pugh, Daniel	Preston North End	Stoke City	500,000
24 Quinn, Alan	Sheffield United	Ipswich Town	400,000
31 Regan, Carl A.	Macclesfield Town	Milton Keynes Dons	undisclosed
31 Reid, Andrew M.	Charlton Athletic	Sunderland	4,000,000
30 Revell, Alexander D.	Brighton & Hove Albion	Southend United	150,000
25 Richards, Gary	Southend United	Gillingham	undisclosed
8 Ross, Ian	Sheffield United	Rotherham United	Free
30 Routledge, Wayne N.	Tottenham Hotspur	Aston Villa	1,250,000
25 Sadler, Matthew	Birmingham City	Watford	750,000
9 Savage, Robert W.	Blackburn Rovers	Derby County	1,500,000
17 Shawcross, Ryan J.	Manchester United	Stoke City	1,000,000
31 Silva De Franca, Anderson	Everton	Barnsley	undisclosed
11 Slater, Christopher J.	Chasetown	Port Vale	undisclosed
8 Speed, Gary A.	Bolton Wanderers	Sheffield United	250,000
31 Stubbs, Alan	Everton	Derby County	Free
10 Sweeney, Peter	Stoke City	Leeds United	250,000
18 Taylor, Andrew	Blackburn Rovers	Tranmere Rovers	undisclosed
31 Taylor, Cleveland	Scunthorpe United	Carlisle United	50,000
17 Taylor, Matthew S.	Portsmouth	Bolton Wanderers	4,500,000
9 Thurgood, Stuart A.	Grays Athletic	Gillingham	undisclosed
31 Trotman, Neal	Oldham Athletic	Preston North End	500,000
31 Vernon, Scott M.	Blackpool	Colchester United	undisclosed
11 Vine, Rowan	Birmingham City	Queens Park Rangers	1,000,000
8 Ward, Gavin J.	Chester City	Wrexham	Free
31 Whelan, Glenn D.	Sheffield Wednesday	Stoke City	undisclosed
3 Williams, Thomas A.	Wycombe Wanderers	Peterborough United	undisclosed
29 Woodgate, Jonathan S.	Middlesbrough	Tottenham Hotspur	8,000,000

TEMPORARY TRANSFERS

31 Ainge, Simon C. – Bradford City – Halifax Town; 20 Akins, Lucas – Huddersfield Town – Northwich Victoria; 1 Akurang, Cliff D. – Histon – Barnet; 7 Alnwick, Ben – Tottenham Hotspur – Leicester City; 10 Ameobi, Tomi – Leeds United – Scunthorpe United; 11 Anelka, Nicolas – Bolton Wanderers – Chelsea; 18 Ashikodi, Moses – Watford – Swindon Town; 30 Ashmore, James – Sheffield United – Macclesfield Town; 10 Ashton, Neil J. – Shrewsbury Town – Macclesfield Town; 18 Aspden, Curtis – Hull City – Farsley Celtic; 31 Atkinson, Robert – Barnsley – Grimsby Town; 27 Austin, Robert D. – Notts County – Eastwood Town; 31 Bailey, Matthew – Wolverhampton Wanderers – Kidderminster Harriers; 3 Ball, Gary – Morecambe – Kendal Town; 7 Barcham, Andrew – Tottenham Hotspur – Leyton Orient; 2 Barnes, Michael T. – Manchester United – Chesterfield; 4 Bastians, Felix – Nottingham Forest – Notts County; 31 Bates, Matthew D. – Middlesbrough – Norwich City; 1 Belford, Cameron D. – Bury – Worcester City; 3 Belt, Frank J. – Hull City – Bridlington Town; 4 Bennett, Dean A. – Chester City – Kidderminster Harriers; 31 Bennett, Elliott – Wolverhampton Wanderers – Bury; 4 Bertrand, Ryan D. – Chelsea – Norwich City; 31 Betsy, Kevin – Bristol City – Walsall; 7 Bradley, Jason – Sheffield Wednesday – Buxton; 18 Brooks-Meade, Corrin – Fulham – Carshalton Athletic; 31 Brown, David A. – Accrington Stanley – Rushden & Diamonds; 10 Bryant, Thomas J. – Gillingham – Folkestone Invicta; 1 Bullock, Lee – Hartlepool United – Bradford City; 3 Butcher, Lee A. – Tottenham Hotspur – AFC Wimbledon; 10 Button, David R. – Tottenham Hotspur – Grays Athletic; 21 Bygrave, Adam M. – Reading – Gillingham; 31 Bywater, Stephen – Derby County – Ipswich Town; 4 Camara, Mohamed – Derby County – Norwich City; 4 Campbell, Fraizer L. – Manchester United – Hull City; 27 Carayol, Mustapha – Milton Keynes Dons – Crawley Town; 3 Carden, Paul A. – Accrington Stanley – Cambridge United; 1 Chamberlain, Scott D. – Brighton & Hove Albion – Bognor Regis Town; 11 Christon, Lewis – Wycombe Wanderers – Woking; 30 Church, Simon R. – Reading – Yeovil Town; 10 Cisak, Alex – Leicester City – Tamworth; 30 Cole, Andrew A. – Sunderland – Burnley; 24 Collins, Lee H. – Wolverhampton Wanderers – Hereford United; 24 Collins, Sam C. – Milton Keynes Dons – Hendon; 31 Cook, Lee – Fulham – Charlton Athletic; 4 Cork, Jack F.P. – Chelsea – Scunthorpe United; 25 Coward, Christopher D. – Stockport County – Woodley Sports; 10 Cresswell, Ryan – Sheffield United – Macclesfield Town; 2 D'Agostino, Michael J. – Blackpool – Cheltenham Town; 7 Daniel, Colin – Crewe Alexandra – Grays Athletic; 18 Davenport, Callum R.P. – West Ham United – Watford; 11 Dean, James – Bury – Stalybridge Celtic; 31 Defoe, Jermaine C. – Tottenham Hotspur – Portsmouth; 3 Dennehy, Billy – Sunderland – Accrington Stanley; 1 Diagouraga, Toumani – Watford – Hereford United; 31 Dickov, Paul – Manchester City – Blackpool; 1 Domoraud, Wilfried – Yeovil Town – Weymouth; 21 Donnelly, Martin – Sheffield United – Rochdale; 18 Doughty, Philip M. – Blackpool – Accrington Stanley; 31 Drench, Steven M. – Morecambe – Southport; 25 Duffy, Robert J. – Oxford United – Wrexham; 31 Edge, Lewis J.S. – Blackpool – Northwich Victoria; 31 Elliott, Stuart – Hull City – Doncaster Rovers; 25 Ellis, Daniel J. – Stockport County – Droylsden; 1 Ellis, Mark I. – Bolton Wanderers – Torquay United; 10 Evans, Chedwyn M. – Manchester City – Norwich City; 4 Evans, Jonathan – Manchester United – Sunderland; 14 Fazenda, Miguel A.K. – West Bromwich Albion – Barnsley; 11 Fielding, Francis D. – Blackburn Rovers – Wycombe Wanderers; 17 Foran, Richard – Southend United – Darlington; 28 Frost, Stef – Notts County – Gainsborough Trinity; 31 Gallagher, Paul – Blackburn Rovers – Stoke City; 31 Gardner, Anthony – Tottenham Hotspur – Everton; 22 Gardner, Scott A. – Leeds United

– Farsley Celtic; 28 Garrett, Robert – Stoke City – Wrexham; 24 Gerrard, Paul W. – Sheffield United – Blackpool; 11 Ghaly, Hossam E.S. – Tottenham Hotspur – Derby County; 31 Gibb, Alistair S. – Hartlepool United – Notts County; 31 Gibbs, Kieran J.R. – Arsenal – Norwich City; 3 Gibson, Darron – Manchester United – Wolverhampton Wanderers; 11 Gradel, Max-Alain – Leicester City – AFC Bournemouth; 31 Grant, Anthony P.S. – Chelsea – Southend United; 19 Gray, Andrew D. – Burnley – Charlton Athletic; 17 Gregory, Steven M. – Wycombe Wanderers – Havant & Waterlooville; 17 Hadfield, Jordan – Macclesfield Town – Milton Keynes Dons; 8 Hales, Lee A. – West Ham United – Rushden & Diamonds; 31 Halford, Gregory – Sunderland – Charlton Athletic; 16 Hall, Asa – Birmingham City – Shrewsbury Town; 11 Hall, Paul A. – Walsall – Wrexham; 10 Halls, John – Reading – Crystal Palace; 28 Hamer, Ben – Reading – Brentford; 18 Hamilton-Omole, Marvin D. – Gillingham – Folkestone Invicta; 11 Harkin, Ruari B. – Charlton Athletic – Heybridge Swifts; 1 Hatch, Liam M.A. – Barnet – Peterborough United; 8 Hayes, Jonathan – Leicester City – Northampton Town; 1 Hayles, Barrington – Plymouth Argyle – Leicester City; 31 Henry, James – Reading – Norwich City; 31 Hernandez, Stephen – Sheffield United – Worksop Town; 16 Heslop, Simon – Barnsley – Halifax Town; 11 Hessey, Sean P. – Chester City – Macclesfield Town; 21 Hird, Adrian S. – Doncaster Rovers – Grimsby Town; 25 Hobbs, Jack – Liverpool – Scunthorpe United; 11 Holmes, Lee D. – Derby County – Walsall; 28 Hooper, Gary – Southend United – Hereford United; 31 Horsfield, Geoffrey M. – Sheffield United – Scunthorpe United; 1 Howard, Steven J. – Derby County – Leicester City; 8 Howe, Jermaine R. – Peterborough United – Rochdale; 23 Howland, David – Birmingham City – Port Vale; 10 Jalal, Shwan S. – Peterborough United – Morecambe; 31 Jarrett, Jason L. – Preston North End – Oldham Athletic; 31 Jarvis, Ryan – Norwich City – Notts County; 1 Jennings, James R. – Macclesfield Town – Altrincham; 31 Jones, Luke J. – Shrewsbury Town – Kidderminster Harriers; 1 Jutkiewicz, Lukas I.P. – Everton – Plymouth Argyle; 31 Kavanagh, Graham A. – Sunderland – Sheffield Wednesday; 10 Kenton, Darren E. – Leicester City – Leeds United; 23 Kerr, Nathaniel J. – Rotherham United – Northwich Victoria; 4 Kilkenny, Neil M. – Birmingham City – Leeds United; 16 Kitchen, Ashley – Mansfield Town – Gainsborough Trinity; 31 Knights, Darryl J. – Yeovil Town – Kidderminster Harriers; 30 Kyle, Kevin – Coventry City – Wolverhampton Wanderers; 1 Laird, Scott – Plymouth Argyle – Stevenage Borough; 6 Law, Joshua – Chesterfield – Alfreton Town; 5 Lawlor, Matthew – Blackpool – Farsley Celtic; 2 Lee, Kieran C. – Manchester United – Queens Park Rangers; 3 Legzdins, Adam R. – Birmingham City – Halifax Town; 18 Lindfield, Craig A. – Liverpool – Chester City; 1 Loach, Scott J. – Watford – Morecambe; 29 Loach, Scott J. – Watford – Bradford City; 4 Lynch, Ryan P. – Crewe Alexandra – Stafford Rangers; 25 Mackin, Levi A. – Wrexham – Droylsden; 1 Mahon, Gavin A. – Watford – Queens Park Rangers; 11 Martin, Lee R. – Manchester United – Sheffield United; 4 Martis, Shelton – West Bromwich Albion – Scunthorpe United; 18 Massey, Alan – Wycombe Wanderers – Hendon; 15 Masters, Clark J. – Southend United – Stevenage Borough; 8 Mayo, Paul – Notts County – Darlington; 18 McEvilly, Lee – Accrington Stanley – Cambridge United; 31 McKay, William – Leicester City – Hinckley United; 11 Medley, Luke – Bradford City – Cambridge City; 17 Mikaelsson, Tobias – Aston Villa – Port Vale; 24 Miles, John F. – Accrington Stanley – Milton Keynes Dons; 4 Mills, Daniel J. – Manchester City – Derby County; 14 Mills, Matthew C. – Manchester City – Doncaster Rovers; 11 Moloney, Brendon A. – Nottingham Forest – Chesterfield; 29 Moncur, Thomas J. – Fulham – Bradford City; 8 Morgan, Luke W.M. – Bradford City – Droylsden; 31 Mulgrew, Charles P. – Wolverhampton Wanderers – Southend United; 18 Murphy, Kieran – Milton Keynes Dons – Crawley Town; 25 Murtagh, Conal F. – Wrexham – Droylsden; 28 Myrie-Williams, Jennison – Bristol City – Tranmere Rovers; 24 Nardiello, Daniel A. – Queens Park Rangers – Barnsley; 29 Ndumbu-Nsungu, Guylain – Gillingham – Darlington; 31 Nyatanga, Lewin J. – Derby County – Barnsley; 11 Oakley, Matthew – Derby County – Leicester City; 25 Obersteller, Jack – Wycombe Wanderers – Grays Athletic; 8 O'Donnell, Richard M. – Sheffield Wednesday – Rotherham United; 16 O'Halloran, Stephen – Aston Villa – Southampton; 31 O'Loughlin, Charlie M. – Port Vale – Hinckley United; 17 Parkes, Jordan – Watford – Brentford; 31 Pearce, Alex – Reading – Norwich City; 31 Pearce, Krystian M.V. – Birmingham City – Port Vale; 29 Pentney, Carl – Leicester City – Ilkeston Town; 30 Peters, Jaime B. – Ipswich Town – Yeovil Town; 30 Pettigrew, Adrian R.J. – Chelsea – Rotherham United; 4 Power, Alan T.D. – Nottingham Forest – Grays Athletic; 24 Prosser, Luke B. – Port Vale – Leigh RMI; 18 Quinn, Alan – Sheffield United – Ipswich Town; 31 Randall, Mark L. – Arsenal – Burnley; 31 Rasiak, Grzegorz – Southampton – Bolton Wanderers; 17 Rayner, Simon – Torquay United – Boston United; 11 Reed, Jamie L. – Wrexham – Tamworth; 31 Reid, Reuben – Plymouth Argyle – Brentford; 17 Rice, Robert – Wycombe Wanderers – Wealdstone; 17 Richards, Matthew – Ipswich Town – Brighton & Hove Albion; 4 Ridley, Lee – Cheltenham Town – Lincoln City; 4 Rigby, Lloyd J. – Rochdale – Vauxhall Motors; 1 Robinson, Theo – Watford – Hereford United; 31 Robson-Kanu, Thomas H. – Reading – Southend United; 10 Rocastle, Craig A. – Port Vale – Gillingham; 3 Rooney, Adam – Stoke City – Chesterfield; 1 Ross, Ian – Sheffield United – Rotherham United; 11 Russell, Alexander J. – Bristol City – Cheltenham Town; 21 Sankofa, Osey O.K. – Charlton Athletic – Brentford; 29 Seck, Mamadou – Sheffield United – Scunthorpe United; 11 Sharpe, Thomas R. – Nottingham Forest – Halifax Town; 4 Shawcross, Ryan J. – Manchester United – Stoke City; 31 Sheehan, Alan – Leicester City – Leeds United; 1 Shotton, Ryan – Stoke City – Altrincham; 31 Showunmi, Enoch – Bristol City – Sheffield Wednesday; 2 Simpson, Jay-Alistaire F. – Arsenal – Millwall; 31 Sinclair, Robert J. – Luton Town – Salisbury City; 3 Slusarski, Bartosz – West Bromwich Albion – Blackpool; 4 Smith, Nathan A. – Chesterfield – Lincoln City; 25 Sorvel, Neil – Morecambe – Southport; 1 Speed, Gary A. – Bolton Wanderers – Sheffield United; 7 Spencer, Scott K. – Everton – Yeovil Town; 4 Stack, Graham – Reading – Wolverhampton Wanderers; 31 Stalteri, Paul – Tottenham Hotspur – Fulham; 21 Starosta, Ben M. – Sheffield United – Bradford City; 4 Stepien, Jordan – Bury – Nuneaton Borough; 2 Stieber, Zoltan – Aston Villa – Yeovil Town; 10 Symes, Michael – Shrewsbury Town – Macclesfield Town; 11 Taylforth, Sean J. – Bradford City – Droylsden; 31 Taylor, Gareth K. – Tranmere Rovers – Doncaster Rovers; 4 Teague, Andrew H. – Macclesfield Town – Tamworth; 22 Thompson, Alan – Leeds United – Hartlepool United; 3 Thompson, Leslie A. – Bolton Wanderers – Torquay United; 29 Threlfall, Robert R. – Liverpool – Hereford United; 1 Todd, Andrew J. – Rotherham United – Accrington Stanley; 31 Tyler, Mark R. – Peterborough United – Hull City; 18 Valentine, Ryan D. – Wrexham – Darlington; 29 Varga, Stanislav – Sunderland – Burnley; 4 Walker, James L. N. – Charlton Athletic – Yeovil Town; 30 Walton, Simon W. – Queens Park Rangers – Hull City; 31 Warner, Anthony R. – Fulham – Barnsley; 25 Watt, Philip A. – Lincoln City – Corby Town; 1 Welsh, John J. – Hull City – Chester City; 24 Wilkinson, David M. – Crystal Palace – Eastleigh; 1 Williams, Thomas A. – Wycombe Wanderers – Peterborough United; 25 Winterton, Christopher C. – Brighton & Hove Albion – Horsham YMCA; 11 Wright, Joshua W. – Charlton Athletic – Barnet; 3 Yeo, Simon J. – Chester City – Bury

FEBRUARY 2008

21 Defoe, Jermain C.	Tottenham Hotspur	Portsmouth	7,500,000
5 Mwaruwari, Benjani	Portsmouth	Manchester City	3,870,000
5 Taylor, Gareth K.	Tranmere Rovers	Doncaster Rovers	undisclosed

TEMPORARY TRANSFERS

21 Ademeno, Charles – Southend United – Rushden & Diamonds; 26 Andersen, Mikkel – Reading – Torquay United; 19 Anderson, Russell – Sunderland – Plymouth Argyle; 5 Arestidou, Andreas J. – Blackburn Rovers – Lancaster City; 12 Asafu-Adjaye, Edward Y.O. – Luton Town – Salisbury City; 29 Atkinson, William H. – Hull City – Mansfield Town; 25 Austin, Matthew S. – Notts County – Gainsborough Trinity; 8 Basham, Christopher P. – Bolton Wanderers – Rochdale; 15 Bastians, Felix – Nottingham Forest – Milton Keynes Dons; 28 Bedeau, Anthony C. – Torquay United – Weymouth; 4 Bentham, Craig M. – Bradford City – Farsley Celtic; 8 Bolder, Adam P. – Queens Park Rangers – Sheffield Wednesday; 11 Bowditch, Dean – Ipswich Town – Brighton & Hove Albion; 18 Boyle, Patrick – Everton – Crewe Alexandra; 8 Bridcutt, Liam R. – Chelsea – Yeovil Town; 15 Briggs, Keith – Shrewsbury Town – Mansfield Town; 14 Brooker, Stephen M.L. – Bristol City – Cheltenham Town; 29 Brooks-Meade, Corrin – Fulham – Cheshunt; 26 Broughton, Drewe O. – Milton Keynes Dons – Wrexham; 25 Brown, Wayne – Fulham – Brentford; 1 Cahill, Thomas – Rotherham United – Altrincham; 22 Clarke, Tom – Huddersfield Town – Halifax Town; 29 Clement, Neil – West Bromwich Albion – Hull City; 25 Cobbs, Sonny H. – Brighton & Hove Albion – Welling United; 11 Compton, Jack L.P. – West Bromwich Albion – Weymouth; 8 Cotterill, David – Wigan Athletic – Sheffield United; 14 Craddock, Thomas – Middlesbrough – Hartlepool United; 15 Crow, Daniel – Peterborough United –

Notts County; 11 Dark, Lewis K. – Brentford – Ramsgate; 14 Domoraud, Wilfried – Yeovil Town – Weston-Super-Mare; 21 Dowson, David – Sunderland – Chesterfield; 19 Duncum, Samuel – Rotherham United – York City; 15 Dutton-Black, Joshua R. – Southampton – Crawley Town; 1 Erskine, Jacob – Dagenham & Redbridge – Maidstone Unied; 27 Farquharson, Nicholas A. – Crewe Alexandra – Nantwich Town; 11 Flinders, Scott L. – Crystal Palace – Yeovil Town; 22 Flynn, Matthew E. – Macclesfield Town – Ashton United; 28 Fraser, James – Bristol Rovers – Tiverton Town; 22 Fulop, Marton – Sunderland – Stoke City; 28 Gall, Kevin A. – Carlisle United – Darlington; 25 Gargan, Sam J. – Brighton & Hove Albion – Welling United; 21 Gleeson, Stephen M. – Wolverhampton Wanderers – Hereford United; 15 Grant, Gavin – Millwall – Stevenage Borough; 15 Grundy, Aaron – Bury – FC United of Manchester; 14 Hall, Ryan – Crystal Palace – Dagenham & Redbridge; 26 Hand, Jamie – Lincoln City – Oxford United; 8 Hart, Daniel – Barnet – Wivenhoe Town; 21 Hartley, Peter – Sunderland – Chesterfield; 28 Henderson, Stephen – Bristol City – Weymouth; 28 Hendrie, Lee A. – Sheffield United – Leicester City; 10 Herd, Christopher – Aston Villa – Port Vale; 8 Hodge, Bryan – Blackburn Rovers – Darlington; 8 Holmes, Daniel – Tranmere Rovers – Southport; 8 Hoskins, William – Watford – Nottingham Forest; 22 Hoult, Russell – Stoke City – Notts County; 24 Howard, Michael A. – Morecambe – Oxford United; 22 Howell, Andrew – Queens Park Rangers – Wealdstone; 5 Hughes, Jerahl – Yeovil Town – Worthing; 29 Hughes, Liam J. – Wolverhampton Wanderers – Stafford Rangers; 15 Hurst, Paul – Rotherham United – Burton Albion; 25 Hyde, Jake M. – Swindon Town – Weymouth; 6 Jackson, Jamie D. – Chesterfield – Gainsborough Trinity; 22 Jeffery, Jack C. – West Ham United – Cambridge United; 22 John, Collins – Fulham – Watford; 29 Johnson, Michael O. – Derby County – Notts County; 15 Jones, Zachariah S. – Blackburn Rovers – Ashton United; 29 Kempson, Darran – Shrewsbury Town – Accrington Stanley; 29 Kennedy, Jason – Middlesbrough – Darlington; 15 Kerry, Lloyd – Sheffield United – Chesterfield; 14 Killock, Shane – Huddersfield Town – Hyde United; 1 King, Liam – Rotherham United – Altrincham; 28 Kirkup, Daniel – Carlisle United – Workington; 22 Lawlor, Matthew – Blackpool – Leigh RMI; 14 Lee, Graeme B. – Doncaster Rovers – Hartlepool United; 11 Little, Mark D. – Wolverhampton Wanderers – Northampton Town; 29 Livermore, David – Hull City – Oldham Athletic; 29 Livermore, Jake – Tottenham Hotspur – Milton Keynes Dons; 22 Logan, Shaleum – Manchester City – Stockport County; 19 Lunt, Kenny V. – Sheffield Wednesday – Crewe Alexandra; 8 MacDonald, Sherjill – West Bromwich Albion – Hereford United; 22 Mangan, Andrew F. – Bury – Accrington Stanley; 21 McGrail, Christopher – Preston North End – Vauxhall Motors; 29 McLeod, Izale M. – Charlton Athletic – Colchester United; 14 McLuckie, Philip – Morecambe – Workington; 11 Milsom, Robert S. – Fulham – Brentford; 26 Mohamed, Kaid – Swindon Town – Torquay United; 22 Moore, Luke – Aston Villa – West Bromwich Albion; 26 Morfaw, Alexandre – Scunthorpe United – Lincoln City; 11 Nelthorpe, Craig R. – Doncaster Rovers – Halifax Town; 29 Newton, Sean – Chester City – Droylsden; 15 Noble, Matthew J. – Doncaster Rovers – Guiseley; 29 O'Halloran, Stephen – Aston Villa – Leeds United; 21 Okuonghae, Magnus E. – Dagenham & Redbridge – Weymouth; 25 Palmer, Marcus J. – Hereford United – Gloucester City; 27 Parker, Ben B.C. – Leeds United – Darlington; 25 Patterson, Marlon – Dagenham & Redbridge – Grays Athletic; 22 Pearce, Ian A. – Fulham – Southampton; 8 Poke, Michael H. – Southampton – Torquay United; 29 Potter, Alfie – Peterborough United – AFC Wimbledon; 15 Pugh, Andrew J. – Gillingham – Maidstone United; 8 Pulis, Anthony J. – Stoke City – Bristol Rovers; 8 Randolph, Darren E. – Charlton Athletic – Bury; 21 Rendell, Scott – Cambridge United – Peterborough United; 29 Riggott, Christopher M. – Middlesbrough – Stoke City; 27 Roberts, Dale – Nottingham Forest – Rushden & Diamonds; 12 Roberts, Gary M. – Ipswich Town – Crewe Alexandra; 26 Robertson, Jordan – Sheffield United – Oldham Athletic; 8 Rooney, Adam – Stoke City – Bury; 22 Ruddy, John T.G. – Everton – Stockport County; 21 Sahar, Ben – Chelsea – Sheffield Wednesday; 28 Sinclair, Scott A. – Chelsea – Charlton Athletic; 19 Skinner, Lloyd E. – Brighton & Hove Albion – Worthing; 28 Smith, Dorian – Charlton Athletic – Tooting & Mitcham United; 21 Smith, Thomas J. – Ipswich Town – Stevenage Borough; 15 Sodje, Efetobore – Gillingham – Bury; 14 Steele, Luke D. – West Bromwich Albion – Stoke City; 16 Stone, Craig B.R. – Gillingham – Brentford; 27 Swaibu, Moses – Crystal Palace – Weymouth; 22 Taylor, Jamie – Dagenham & Redbridge – Grays Athletic; 18 Teague, Andrew H. – Macclesfield Town – Hyde United; 19 Teale, Gary – Derby County – Plymouth Argyle; 29 Thomas, Aswad – Charlton Athletic – Accrington Stanley; 21 Tomlinson, Stuart C. – Crewe Alexandra – Burton Albion; 29 Vaughan, Stephen J. – Chester City – Droylsden; 15 Walker, James L.N. – Charlton Athletic – Southend United; 28 Webb, Thomas J.J. – Colchester United – Folkestone Invicta; 16 Welsh, Ishmael – Yeovil Town – Forest Green Rovers; 12 Widdowson, Joseph – West Ham United – Rotherham United; 14 Woods, Martin P. – Doncaster Rovers – Yeovil Town

MARCH 2008 TEMPORARY TRANSFERS

27 Ameobi, Foluwashola – Newcastle United – Stoke City; 18 Anderson, Russell – Sunderland – Plymouth Argyle; 27 Andrews, Wayne M.H. – Coventry City – Bristol Rovers; 7 Annerson, James – Sheffield United – Chesterfield; 7 Anyinsah, Joseph G. – Preston North End – Crewe Alexandra; 27 Ashton, Nathan – Fulham – Millwall; 19 Bailey, Matthew – Crewe Alexandra – Weymouth; 7 Barnes, Ashley L. – Plymouth Argyle – Salisbury City; 27 Barnes, Michael T. – Manchester United – Shrewsbury Town; 4 Beattie, Craig – West Bromwich Albion – Preston North End; 27 Bell, David A. – Luton Town – Leicester City; 7 Bennett, Alan J. – Reading – Brentford; 2 Bennett, Elliott – Wolverhampton Wanderers – Bury; 4 Bentham, Craig M. – Bradford City – Farsley Celtic; 27 Begovic, Asmir – Portsmouth – Yeovil Town; 3 Blackburn, Christopher R. – Swindon Town – Weymouth; 7 Bolder, Adam P. – Queens Park Rangers – Sheffield Wednesday; 14 Bothroyd, Jay – Wolverhampton Wanderers – Stoke City; 19 Boyle, Patrick – Everton – Crewe Alexandra; 12 Brooker, Stephen M.L. – Bristol City – Cheltenham Town; 27 Brown, Aaron – Reading – Walsall; 27 Brown, David A. – Accrington Stanley – Northwich Victoria; 27 Brown, Junior – Crewe Alexandra – Witton Albion; 21 Burgess, Kevin M. – Darlington – Whitby Town; 27 Button, David R. – Tottenham Hotspur – Rochdale; 2 Cahill, Thomas – Rotherham United – Altrincham; 20 Charles, Wesley D.D. – Brentford – Ebbsfleet United; 27 Christon, Lewis – Wycombe Wanderers – AFC Wimbledon; 10 Christophe, Jean F. – Portsmouth – Yeovil Town; 25 Cobbs, Sonny H. – Brighton & Hove Albion – Welling United; 14 Cogan, Barry C. – Gillingham – Grays Athletic; 4 Constantine, Leon – Leeds United – Oldham Athletic; 14 Corden, Wayne – Leyton Orient – Notts County; 27 Craig, Tony A. – Crystal Palace – Millwall; 27 Daniel, Colin – Crewe Alexandra – Leek Town; 27 Devaux, Thomas – Colchester United – Heybridge Swifts; 18 Domoraud, Wilfried – Yeovil Town – Weston-Super-Mare; 14 Douglas, Robert J. – Leicester City – Plymouth Argyle; 27 Downes, Aiden – Everton – Yeovil Town; 26 Dowson, David – Sunderland – Chesterfield; 21 Duffy, Richard – Portsmouth – Coventry City; 20 Duncum, Samuel – Rotherham United – York City; 29 Ehui, Ismael – Fulham – Carshalton Athletic; 28 Erskine, Emmanuel J. – Dagenham & Redbridge – Maidstone United; 5 Etuhu, Kelvin – Manchester City – Leicester City; 27 Facey, Delroy M. – Gillingham – Wycombe Wanderers; 8 Fagan, Craig – Derby County – Hull City; 27 Farquharson, Nicholas A. – Crewe Alexandra – Nuneaton Borough; 7 Fitzgerald, Lorcan – West Ham United – Cheshunt; 28 Fitzpatrick, Jordan P. – Hereford United – Bromsgrove Rovers; 12 Flinders, Scott L. – Crystal Palace – Yeovil Town; 27 Flinders, Scott L. – Crystal Palace – Blackpool; 31 Fogden, Wesley K. – Brighton & Hove Albion – Bognor Regis Town; 28 Foley, Sam – Cheltenham Town – Bath City; 7 Freedman, Douglas A. – Crystal Palace – Leeds United; 7 Frost, Stef – Notts County – Matlock Town; 25 Gargan, Sam J. – Brighton & Hove Albion – Welling United; 27 Gleeson, Stephen M. – Wolverhampton Wanderers – Stockport County; 4 Goode, Aaron M.O. – Queens Park Rangers – Wealdstone; 15 Grant, Gavin – Millwall – Stevenage Borough; 7 Groves, Matt – Bristol Rovers – Chippenham Town; 27 Hall, Ryan – Crystal Palace – Crawley Town; 14 Halls, John – Reading – Sheffield United; 27 Hanson, Mitchell G.B. – Derby County – Port Vale; 9 Hart, Daniel – Barnet – Wivenhoe Town; 26 Hartley, Peter – Sunderland – Chesterfield; 27 Hawkins, Colin J. – Coventry City – Chesterfield; 14 Heath, Matthew P. – Leeds United – Colchester United; 30 Henderson, Stephen – Bristol City – Weymouth; 14 Hird, Christopher – Aston Villa – Wycombe Wanderers; 27 Hines, Zavon – West Ham United – Coventry City; 9 Hodge, Bryan – Blackburn Rovers – Darlington; 27 Holmes, Ian D. – Mansfield Town – AFC Telford United; 20 Holt, Grant – Nottingham Forest – Blackpool; 3 Hooper, Gary – Southend United – Hereford United; 21 Horlock, Kevin – Scunthorpe United – Mansfield Town; 6 Hoult, Russell – Stoke City – Notts County; 27 Hughes, Jeffrey – Crystal Palace – Bristol Rovers; 14 Hughes, Jerahl – Yeovil Town – Worthing; 16 Hurst, Paul – Rotherham United – Burton Albion; 7 Ide, Charles J. – Brentford – Lewes; 27 Igoe, Samuel – Bristol Rovers – Hereford United; 27 Jackson, Jamie D. – Chesterfield

– Matlock Town; 23 Jeffery, Jack C. – West Ham United – Cambridge United; 25 John, Collins – Fulham – Watford; 28 Jones, Craig N. – Hereford United – Bromsgrove Rovers; 7 Jones, Daniel J. – Wolverhampton Wanderers – Northampton Town; 3 Jones, Luke J. – Shrewsbury Town – Kidderminster Harriers; 27 Jones, Stephen G. – Burnley – Crewe Alexandra; 20 Karacan, Jem P. – Reading – Millwall; 29 Kempson, Darran – Shrewsbury Town – Accrington Stanley; 10 Keogh, Richard J. – Bristol City – Cheltenham Town; 17 Kerry, Lloyd – Sheffield United – Chesterfield; 17 Killock, Shane – Huddersfield Town – Hyde United; 2 King, Liam – Rotherham United – Altrincham; 25 Konstantopoulos, Dimitrios – Coventry City – Nottingham Forest; 14 Kuqi, Shefki – Crystal Palace – Ipswich Town; 27 Lawlor, Matthew – Blackpool – Leigh RMI; 29 Ledgister, Aaron T. – Cheltenham Town – Bath City; 19 Lee, Graeme B. – Doncaster Rovers – Shrewsbury Town; 27 Lee, Thomas E. – Macclesfield Town – Rochdale; 5 Lita, Leroy – Reading – Charlton Athletic; 13 Little, Mark D. – Wolverhampton Wanderers – Northampton Town; 27 Logan, Shaleum – Manchester City – Stockport County; 27 Lowe, Ryan – Crewe Alexandra – Stockport County; 27 Lucketti, Christopher J. – Sheffield United – Southampton; 4 Lunt, Kenny V. – Sheffield Wednesday – Crewe Alexandra; 10 Lynch, Ryan P. – Crewe Alexandra – Altrincham; 7 Maher, Kevin A. – Southend United – Gillingham; 27 Martin, Joseph J. – Tottenham Hotspur – Blackpool; 3 McClements, David – Sheffield Wednesday – Buxton; 26 Mitchell, Scott – Peterborough United – Stevenage Borough; 1 Moncur, Thomas J. – Fulham – Bradford City; 27 Montrose, Lewis – Wigan Athletic – Rochdale; 7 Morgan, Dean – Luton Town – Crewe Alexandra; 27 Moult, Jake O. – Plymouth Argyle – Kidderminster Harriers; 4 Nash, Carlo J. – Wigan Athletic – Stoke City; 27 Nelthorpe, Craig R. – Doncaster Rovers – Darlington; 30 Newton, Sean – Chester City – Droylsden; 17 Noble, Matthew J. – Doncaster Rovers – Guiseley; 28 O'Donnell, Richard M. – Sheffield Wednesday – Oldham Athletic; 7 Ormerod, Brett R. – Preston North End – Nottingham Forest; 27 Owens, Graeme A. – Middlesbrough – Chesterfield; 30 Parker, Ben B.C. – Leeds United – Darlington; 14 Parkes, Jordan – Watford – Barnet; 27 Patterson, Marlon – Dagenham & Redbridge – Grays Athletic; 3 Pearce, Krystian M.V. – Birmingham City – Port Vale; 27 Pearson, Stephen – Derby County – Stoke City; 14 Pericard, Vincent D.P. – Stoke City – Southampton; 27 Perry, Christopher J. – Luton Town – Southampton; 7 Priskin, Tamas – Watford – Preston North End; 6 Prosser, Luke B. – Port Vale – Leigh RMI; 20 Racon, Therry – Charlton Athletic – Brighton & Hove Albion; 7 Rae, Michael E. – Hartlepool United – Southport; 10 Randolph, Darren E. – Charlton Athletic – Bury; 27 Reid, Kyel – West Ham United – Crystal Palace; 27 Reid, Paul M. – Barnsley – Carlisle United; 19 Rigters, Maceo – Blackburn Rovers – Norwich City; 27 Roberts, Mark A. – Accrington Stanley – Northwich Victoria; 27 Rochester, Kraig – Dagenham & Redbridge – Dulwich Hamlet; 10 Rooney, Adam – Stoke City – Bury; 27 Ruddy, John T.G. – Everton – Stockport County; 25 Sahar, Ben – Chelsea – Sheffield Wednesday; 28 Saunders, Russell – Wigan Athletic – Gainsborough Trinity; 14 Schmeichel, Kasper P. – Manchester City – Coventry City; 7 Seanla, Stephane – Barnet – Wivenhoe Town; 3 Showunmi, Enoch – Bristol City – Sheffield Wednesday; 27 Simmonds, Donovan – Coventry City – Gillingham; 7 Simmonds, James R. – Chelsea – Dover Athletic; 21 Simpson, Daniel P. – Manchester United – Ipswich Town; 27 Sinclair, Scott A. – Chelsea – Crystal Palace; 28 Sleath, Daniel J. – Mansfield Town – Gainsborough Trinity; 27 Slusarski, Bartosz – West Bromwich Albion – Sheffield Wednesday; 20 Smith, Johann – Bolton Wanderers – Stockport County; 29 Smith, Thomas J. – Ipswich Town – Stevenage Borough; 17 Sodje, Efetobore – Gillingham – Bury; 7 Songo'o, Franck S. – Portsmouth – Sheffield Wednesday; 7 Spencer, Scott K. – Everton – Macclesfield Town; 20 Steele, Luke D. – West Bromwich Albion – Barnsley; 27 Tansey, Gregory J. – Stockport County – Altrincham; 14 Taylforth, Sean J. – Bradford City – Guiseley; 27 Taylor, Jamie – Dagenham & Redbridge – Grays Athletic; 18 Teague, Andrew H. – Macclesfield Town – Hyde United; 11 Tejan-Sie, Thomas M. – Dagenham & Redbridge – Billericay Town; 29 Thomas, Aswad – Charlton Athletic – Accrington Stanley; 13 Thurgood, Stuart A. – Gillingham – Grays Athletic; 13 Timlin, Michael – Fulham – Swindon Town; 27 Turnbull, Paul – Stockport County – Altrincham; 21 Wainwright, Neil – Darlington – Mansfield Town; 4 Waite, Jamie – Bradford City – Droylsden; 17 Welsh, Ishmael – Yeovil Town – Forest Green Rovers; 4 Westlake, Ian J. – Leeds United – Brighton & Hove Albion; 4 Weston, Curtis J. – Leeds United – Scunthorpe United; 7 Worley, Harry J. – Chelsea – Leicester City; 20 Wright, Richard I. – West Ham United – Southampton; 27 Wylde, Michael J. – Cheltenham Town – Kidderminster Harriers

APRIL 2008 TEMPORARY TRANSFERS

1 Adamson, Chris – Stockport County – Northwich Victoria; 16 Andersen, Mikkel – Reading – Rushden & Diamonds; 10 Annerson, James – Sheffield United – Chesterfield; 15 Bailey, Matthew – Crewe Alexandra – Weymouth; 4 Bennett, Alan J. – Reading – Brentford; 7 Bennett, Elliott – Wolverhampton Wanderers – Bury; 7 Bolder, Adam P. – Queens Park Rangers – Sheffield Wednesday; 14 Bothroyd, Jay – Wolverhampton Wanderers – Stoke City; 22 Burgess, Kevin M. – Darlington – Whitby Town; 30 Carayol, Mustapha – Milton Keynes Dons – Crawley Town; 14 Cogan, Barry C. – Gillingham – Grays Athletic; 27 Craig, Tony A. – Crystal Palace – Millwall; 20 Crow, Daniel – Peterborough United – Notts County; 26 Ellis, Mark I. – Bolton Wanderers – Torquay United; 2 Goode, Aaron M.O. – Queens Park Rangers – Wealdstone; 30 Hall, Ryan – Crystal Palace – Crawley Town; 14 Halls, John – Reading – Sheffield United; 13 Hart, Daniel – Barnet – Wivenhoe Town; 13 Heath, Matthew P. – Leeds United – Colchester United; 14 Hurst, Paul – Rotherham United – Burton Albion; 20 Karacan, Jem P. – Reading – Millwall; 13 Keogh, Richard J. – Bristol City – Cheltenham Town; 19 Lee, Thomas E. – Macclesfield Town – Rochdale; 1 Lita, Leroy – Reading – Charlton Athletic; 10 Lynch, Ryan P. – Crewe Alexandra – Altrincham; 18 Martin, Alan – Leeds United – Hinckley United; 4 Morgan, Dean – Luton Town – Crewe Alexandra; 30 Murphy, Kieran – Milton Keynes Dons – Crawley Town; 28 Nelthorpe, Craig R. – Doncaster Rovers – Darlington; 14 Parkes, Jordan – Watford – Barnet; 9 Pearce, Krystian M.V. – Birmingham City – Port Vale; 6 Rae, Michael E. – Hartlepool United – Southport; 29 Reid, Kyel – West Ham United – Crystal Palace; 14 Rooney, Adam – Stoke City – Bury; 7 Sahar, Ben – Chelsea – Sheffield Wednesday; 4 Simmonds, James R. – Chelsea – Dover Athletic; 28 Sinclair, Robert J. – Luton Town – Salisbury City; 5 Smith, Thomas J. – Ipswich Town – Stevenage Borough; 21 Sodje, Efetobore – Gillingham – Bury; 7 Songo'o, Franck S. – Portsmouth – Sheffield Wednesday; 15 Taylforth, Sean J. – Bradford City – Guiseley; 25 Teague, Andrew H. – Macclesfield Town – Hyde United; 14 Thurgood, Stuart A. – Gillingham – Grays Athletic; 24 Turnbull, Paul – Stockport County – Altrincham; 6 Westlake, Ian J. – Leeds United – Brighton & Hove Albion; 20 Wright, Richard I. – West Ham United – Southampton

MAY 2008

30 Earnshaw, Robert	Derby County	Nottingham Forest	2,650,000
8 Griffith, Anthony	Doncaster Rovers	Port Vale	undisclosed
14 Heath, Matthew P.	Leeds United	Colchester United	Free
28 O'Grady, Christopher	Rotherham United	Oldham Athletic	undisclosed
22 Rendell, Scott	Cambridge United	Peterborough United	undisclosed
23 Steele, Luke D.	WBA	Barnsley	Free
20 Walker, James L.N.	Charlton Athletic	Southend United	undisclosed
6 Worley, Harry J.	Chelsea	Leicester City	Free

TEMPORARY TRANSFERS

3 Basham, Christopher P. – Bolton Wanderers – Rochdale; 30 Ellington, Nathan L.F. – Watford – Derby County; 4 Facey, Delroy M. – Gillingham – Wycombe Wanderers; 4 Holmes, Ian D. – Mansfield Town – AFC Telford United; 2 Howe, Jermaine R. – Peterborough United – Rochdale; 2 Parker, Ben B.C. – Leeds United – Darlington; 1 Pentney, Carl – Leicester City – Fisher Athletic; 7 Robson-Kanu, Thomas H. – Reading – Southend United; 2 Sheehan, Alan – Leicester City – Leeds United; 4 Zebroski, Christopher – Millwall – Torquay United

THE NEW FOREIGN LEGION 2007–08

	From	*To*	*Fee in £*
MAY 2007			
18 Cisse, Kalifa	Boavista	Reading	650,000
25 Fabianski, Lukosz	Legia Warsaw	Arsenal	undisclosed
12 Lucas	Gremio	Liverpool	undisclosed
30 Muntari, Sulley	Udinese	Portsmouth	undisclosed
JUNE 2007			
19 Granqvist, Andreas	Helsingborg	Wigan Athletic	undisclosed
29 Kapo, Olivier	Juventus	Birmingham City	3,000,000
29 Rozehnal, David	Paris St Germain	Newcastle United	2,900,000
9 Taarabt, Adel	Lens	Tottenham Hotspur	undisclosed
JULY 2007			
16 Alonso, Mikel	Real Sociedad	Bolton Wanderers	loan
2 Anderson	Porto	Manchester United	undisclosed
13 Babel, Ryan	Ajax	Liverpool	11,500,000
13 Bianchi, Rolando	Reggina	Manchester City	8,800,000
1 Cid, Gerald	Bordeaux	Bolton Wanderers	undisclosed
3 De Ridder, Daniel	Celta Vigo	Birmingham City	Free
1 Dzemaili, Blerim	Zurich	Bolton Wanderers	undisclosed
2 Eduardo	Dinamo Zagreb	Arsenal	undisclosed
1 Faubert, Julien	Bordeaux	West Ham United	6,100,000
14 Gelson	Sion	Manchester City	undisclosed
17 Geovanni	Cruzeiro	Manchester City	Free
1 Hargreaves, Owen	Bayern Munich	Manchester United	undisclosed
5 Kaboul, Younes	Auxerre	Tottenham Hotspur	undisclosed
4 Kingson, Richard	Hammarby	Birmingham City	Free
10 Malouda, Florent	Lyon	Chelsea	13,500,000
5 Mvuemba, Arnold	Rennes	Portsmouth	undisclosed
2 Nani	Sporting Lisbon	Manchester United	undisclosed
26 Petrov, Martin	Atletico Madrid	Manchester City	4,700,000
20 Pienaar, Steven	Borussia Dortmund	Everton	loan
1 Pizarro, Claudio	Bayern Munich	Chelsea	Free
30 Prince-Boateng, Kevin	Hertha Berlin	Tottenham Hotspur	undisclosed
2 Rigters, Maceo	NAC Breda	Blackburn Rovers	undisclosed
12 Sagna, Bacary	Auxerre	Arsenal	undisclosed
28 Santa Cruz, Roque	Bayern Munich	Blackburn Rovers	3,500,000\
6 Schmitz, Rafael	Lille	Birmingham City	loan
4 Torres, Fernando	Atletico Madrid	Liverpool	20,000,000
4 Tuncay	Fenerbahce	Middlesbrough	Free
11 Utaka, John	Rennes	Portsmouth	undisclosed
6 Voronin, Andriy	Leverkusen	Liverpool	Free
27 Wilhelmsson, Christian	Nantes	Bolton Wanderers	loan
AUGUST 2007			
10 Alex	PSV Eindhoven	Chelsea	Free
23 Belletti, Juliano	Barcelona	Chelsea	undisclosed
31 Beye, Habib	Marseille	Newcastle United	undisclosed
3 Bojinov, Valeri	Fiorentina	Manchester City	undisclosed
3 Braaten, Daniel	Rosenborg	Bolton Wanderers	undisclosed
4 Cacapa, Claudio	Lyon	Newcastle United	Free
2 Corluka, Vedran	Dinamo Zagreb	Manchester City	undisclosed
2 Elano	Shakhtar Donetsk	Manchester City	8,000,000
2 Fae, Emerse	Nantes	Reading	2,500,000
17 Feilhaber, Benny	Hamburg	Derby County	1,000,000
2 Garrido, Javier	Real Sociedad	Manchester City	1,500,000\
6 Jose Enrique	Villarreal	Newcastle United	6,300,000
31 Palacios, Wilson	Olimpia	Birmingham City	loan
31 Plessis, Damian	Lyon	Liverpool	undisclosed
31 Salifou, Moustapha	Wil	Aston Villa	undisclosed
31 Shawky, Mohamed	Al-Ahly	Middlesbrough	650,000
21 Wessels, Stefan	Cologne	Everton	Free
JANUARY 2008			
29 Andreasen, Leon	Werder Bremen	Fulham	2,000,000
31 Alves, Afonso	Heerenveen	Middlesbrough	12,000,000
18 Aubey, Lucien	Lens	Portsmouth	loan
31 Caicedo, Felipe	Basle	Manchester City	5,200,000
4 Castillo, Nery	Shakhtar Donetsk	Manchester City	loan\
4 Cohen, Tamir	Maccabi Netanya	Bolton Wanderers	650,000
10 Fernandes, Manuel	Valencia	Everton	loan
22 Figueroa, Maynor	Dep Olimpia	Wigan Athletic	loan
31 Gilberto	Hertha Berlin	Tottenham Hotspur	2,000,000
31 Hagen, Erik	Zenit	Wigan Athletic	loan
22 Hangeland, Brede	FC Copenhagen	Fulham	2,500,000
31 Johnson, Eddie	Kansas City Wizards	Fulham	3,000,000
31 Kebe, Jimmy	Lens	Reading	undisclosed
11 Matejovsky, Marek	Mlada Boleslav	Reading	1,400,000
25 Prica, Rade	Aalborg	Sunderland	2,000,000
14 Skrtel, Martin	Zenit	Liverpool	6,500,000
31 Sterjovski, Mile	Genclerbirligi	Derby County	300,000
17 Steinsson, Gretar	AZ	Bolton Wanderers	3,500,000
8 Villa, Emanuel	UAG Tecos	Derby County	2,000,000
21 Zarate, Mauro	Al-Saad	Birmingham City	loan
MARCH 2008			
7 Lamine, Diatta	Besiktas	Newcastle United	Free
18 Vogel, Johann	Real Betis	Blackburn Rovers	Free

Three players signed in earlier seasons made their debut: Armand Traore (Arsenal), Martin Olsson (Blackburn Rovers) and Ali Al-Habsi (Bolton Wanderers).

THE THINGS THEY SAID . . .

Before a kick was taken in earnest for the four full-time professional divisions in the country, Leeds United had some good news and a lot of bad. The first was being back in the League, the second they were to start life in League One with a big handicap. Chairman Ken Bates commented:
"We are delighted we are back in the League. We are surprised it has taken this long. We intend to appeal against the 15-point deduction because we have still to have an explanation for that."

Jose Mourinho in the wake of quitting as The Special One at Chelsea:
"From a professional and personal point of view, I'm feeling great. I'm glad to have left. I am proud of what I did at Chelsea, not only in terms of results, but the mark I left on the country."

Defeat for England in Moscow against Russia brought the Euro 2008 qualification in some doubt again, but Football Association chief executive Brian Barwick was as undeterred as ever:
"The real issue at the moment is to just gather our thoughts after the last five days of football and then push it on into the Croatia match. We do need some help from elsewhere now, but of course we are behind Steve [McClaren]."

In the aftermath of defeat by Croatia at Wembley and when Steve McClaren had been seen disappearing down the tunnel under an umbrella and clearly sinking in the reign:
"Ultimately I take responsibility. I pick the team. I said over 12 games I'll be judged and I will be. That is my job." (Sadly it was only his until the next day.)

Tinkerman supreme Rafa Benitez on a somewhat rare day of feeling content about his Liverpool team's showing following the 3-0 win against Newcastle United:
"I must be happy with a performance like that. Three goals, three points, nothing conceded and I was able to rest key players."

Sir Alex Ferguson's fair assessment of Manchester United's win in the Champions League against Chelsea:
"I think this has got the makings of our best team ever. I think we deserved to win the game. In the first half we were frustrated and we should have been three up, but they scored right on half-time. They got a lucky break there and I thought Chelsea were the better side in the second half."

Paul Jewell on the relegation of Derby County who had broken most of the wrong kind of records for the Premier League:
"I've never had a relegation as a manager and it isn't pleasant, but I've had two promotions from the Championship and I know what it takes."

Then the caring, sharing manager of Everton none other than David Moyes announced as Manager of the Month for February 2008:
"I'd like to thank everyone at the club especially the players not only for the month of February but the previous ones, too. They are playing tremendously well and we are making progress."

After retaining the Premiership title in 2007–08, a confident Sir Alex Ferguson was already thinking towards the possibility of a double with the Champions League looming:
"The great thing is we are bouncing into the final. We can look forward to it."

Referee Rob Styles, for once a whistler seeing red – facially of course – admitting he was in error in awarding Chelsea a penalty at Liverpool in the 1-1 draw. His punishment was a weekend off:
"All referees enter into matches hoping not to make any mistakes but understanding that they may happen. What none of us want is for any mistake to potentially affect the result of the match. Yesterday, in mistakenly awarding a penalty, I accept that I may have affected the result of the match and for that I apologise."

England skipper John Terry in the run-up towards that fateful, soggy evening at Wembley against Croatia, after beating Israel 3-0:
"This was a vital win for us. We answered a lot of questions. If we beat Russia on Wednesday we could be on a roll. It was a wonderful performance full of little cameos like Michael Owen's goal, Gareth Barry's performance in midfield and then, of course, Micah Richards in defence. Everyone answered the call."

Howard Wilkinson – actually the last English-born manager to win the championship in the highest echelon of League football in the country – confirming that the League Managers' Association were looking into the credentials of Avram Grant at Chelsea:
"Speaking with my LMA hat on, all I can do is reiterate that we are in favour of coach education and preparation and therefore mandatory qualifications. At the moment it is very difficult to comment on the Avram Grant situation, because the Premier League have not clarified this situation vis-à-vis him and vis-à-vis Chelsea."

Portsmouth manager Harry Redknapp after the record-breaking aggregate score in the Premier League when his team beat Reading 7-4:
"It was an amazing game. There was some flat defending obviously. I thought the first half was the best we've played all season. Today we've played with one striker and we scored seven goals, so it's not systems. We've let four goals in by playing a 4-5-1 so systems it blows out of the water."

FIFA supremo Sepp Blatter for once giving England some glimmer of hope of staging the World Cup sometime at least in the future:
"I am advocating we open the market – it will give a better competition. We are not in a very comfortable situation in South America. We only have one bidder and if we maintain this rotation system as we have now, that could be the case again. It would be better to have three or four associations trying to get the number one competition of the world."

Steven Gerrard, the Liverpool and England international midfield player, voicing his opinion on the vexed question of numbers of foreign players in the Premier League:
"I think there is a risk that there are too many foreign players coming over, which will affect our national team eventually, if it's not doing so now. I'm sure it [a quota] will definitely help our national team, if that's the case and we want as many home grown players in the league as possible."

Modest David Healy, the Irish international striker, on breaking the European Championship qualifying goalscoring record with his 13th goal in the competition against Denmark:
"It was all about winning this game rather than me setting the record. That goal is for the whole team. We never know when we are beaten. I'm just proud to wear this jersey and it was another phenomenal night."

Before his appointment as England coach, Fabio Capello expressed his thoughts over the failure to qualify for the finals of Euro 2008. Perhaps this was what convinced the FA to give him the job?:
"As coaches, we all ask ourselves how England, with the players they have, failed. I have seen some of England's games. Against Russia in Moscow they defended on the edge of the area for 90 minutes despite holding a 1-0 lead. Against Croatia, they all pushed up and lost 3-2 when a draw would have qualified them.

"The difference in attitude between these games is too great. It is clear the shirt weighs heavy even for these winners. In these situations the coach's role is fundamental and he needs to be more psychologist than tactician or technician."

Arsène Wenger, the Arsenal manager, challenged his team to prove the critics wrong about their ability to win the Premier League after a fairly comfortable 2-0 win over West Ham United:
"We want to keep going, it's a marathon, we want to be consistent. We are highly focused and that is a good ingredient because we know we have the quality."

Kevin Blackwell when he was still manager of Luton Town and with a financial deadline looming reported an attempt by the club's administrator to boost funds after their FA Cup meeting:
"The administrator asked Liverpool about donating their share of the gate money. They probably said – we have to pay players £100,000 a week. You must be joking! Otherwise we will be like you."

Being a manager of a football club is a transitional occupation from job to job, but departure is always accompanied by surprise as Sam Allardyce, eight months into the role at Newcastle United, revealed:
"I am disappointed obviously but I would like to wish everyone at Newcastle all the best for the future and I hope things go very well. It was a shock – I didn't expect it."

After scoring his first hat-trick in the 6-0 win over Newcastle United, the Manchester United and Portuguese international Cristiano Ronaldo said:
"It's a special day for me. I'm very happy to win the game and go to the top of the League. This is the most important thing. If we keep playing like we did in the second half I am sure we will be the best team."

Robbie Keane's 100th goal for Tottenham Hotspur, against his former Republic of Ireland colleague Roy Keane in charge of Sunderland, brought this response from his manager Juande Ramos:
"I think it's a great achievement for him, the club and the Spurs family."

Arsenal manager Arsène Wenger on the shock departure from the Carling Cup at the hands of north London rivals Spurs and underlining that a defeat, is a defeat, is a defeat:
"I feel defeat is painful. Overall, I think everything went against us and we were a bit naïve. Of course they were better than us. We have to accept that. I feel sorry for the young players that gave absolutely everything. It is always better to win. Big scores like that do not really have a big meaning."

And the Arsenal boss was still very much with his keen eye on youth as he prepared to add the FA Cup's youngest debutant to his ranks, aged 15 and with Gillingham, as the Kent club's chairman Paul Scally reported:
"We have agreed in principle a deal for Luke Freeman to go to Arsenal. We are still waiting on some of the finer details to be concluded but we are confident that it will happen very soon. Arsenal have gone about their business in a fair and commendable way."

The chance of a return of the fixture between old enemies England and Scotland was given short shrift by incoming Scotland manager George Burley, as explained by SFA chief executive Gordon Smith:
"Unfortunately the proposed date of May 28 does not fit in with the new national team manager's plans for the forthcoming World Cup campaign, so it won't go ahead."

New England boss Fabio Capello reported after his initial test on the international field, a friendly against Switzerland, and said he was moved by the atmosphere at Wembley:
"I am very happy now that I know what it is to be England manager."

He also dismissed the notion that the players were nervous because of a fear-factor he has instilled into the team:
"I have never hit anyone, so I don't see why they should be scared. If anything I think they had something at the back of their mind about failing to qualify for the Euro 2008 finals. We played some good football in places and created a lot of goalscoring chances which we didn't take and defensively we have played solidly. The last ten minutes again we didn't play football as we were concerned about the result."

Premier League chief executive Richard Scudamore on the proposal that they want to extend the competition to include a 39th match abroad each season:
"The international round is an exciting and innovative proposal that needs careful consideration before being introduced. However, this concept recognises the truly global appeal of the Barclays Premier League whilst understanding that the traditions of the English game have always underpinned our success."

While reaction to the 39ers was pretty negative in this country, the first foreign reponse came from Australia and Asia – before their u-turn – and the former's chairman Frank Lowy was not convinced at all:
"The bottom line is the Federation rejects the notion of another country playing a round of their domestic competition in Australia and intruding on the development of the Hyundai A-League and the game in the country."

There was plenty of the old magic about the FA Cup in 2007–08 with some outstanding performances given by many of the minnows. However the giant-killing was not confined to the lower echelons of the professional game, as illustrated by Barnsley's performance against Liverpool at Anfield, and the comments of manager Simon Davey:
"Fantastic. We came here and said we would enjoy the game and we have enjoyed the day. We had a gameplan and to be fair there was no coming back from that when we scored at the last. Credit to the players, now they have got their rewards – they are in the next round."

As AC Milan suffered their first defeat in the San Siro against visiting English opposition, Arsenal manager Arsène Wenger watched with justifiable pride:
"Fabregas was outstanding but tonight it is very difficult to single one out. I believe the whole team defended well and attacked well. It was a complete team performance."

After Fernando Torres became the first Livepool player to strike 20 Premier League goals since Robbie Fowler in 1996, manager Rafa Benitez was quick to sing his praises:
"He is a fantastic player working for the team and scoring a lot of goals thanks to his team-mates so we have to be very pleased with him. "

Chelsea's win over a somewhat tinkered Manchester United threatened to derail the champions elect from taking the Premiership again and Avram Grant was understandably delighted with the outcome:
"We did what we needed to do. I think we have put them under pressure."

From the same encounter, Sir Alex Ferguson put an entirely different emphasis on the affair:
"First of all, if a game is going to be decided on penalties, then we've got no chance on the last few weeks. Starting at Middlesbrough, their player dives and saves the ball from Ronaldo six yards away from the referee – a clear penalty but we don't get it. Then Rooney is through and the linesman – the same one as today – flags offside when he is five yards onside. Today he has given a penalty kick in a major game like that."

Fabio Capello talking about the need to transfer club success in the country into the national team:
"This is my toughest job, understanding why this happens and solving the problem. Because looking at the performance of the English teams in the Champions League, then at the moment the Premier League is the best in the world. Absolutely. I can't perform miracles, these are the players we have and I can only call up the players we have."

It takes a proper professional to put penalty shoot-outs in perspective and Ryan Giggs, on the Champions League final after eclipsing Sir Bobby Charlton's appearance record for Manchester United, did just that:
"I want more nights like this again but I don't think you can beat '99. Penalties can be a lottery. It's how close the teams have been all season."

PFA chief executive Gordon Taylor commenting on the famous "6-5 special" that Sepp Blatter is keen on FIFA implementing for the Premier League and tending to favour the UEFA plan instead:
"We are very much aware of the decreasing number of players qualified to play for England and it is one of the reasons why we have the embarrassment of not having England at Euro 2008. But in Europe you cannot discriminate on the grounds of nationality. So we have to really look at the UEFA proposal and say that not only should we have eight players in a squad of 25 that have been developed in a country or club irrespective of nationality, but to have them on the field of play. I am not saying it should be eight but the figure should at least be four to encourage clubs to develop players for the future generation."

ENGLISH LEAGUE HONOURS 1888 TO 2008

FA PREMIER LEAGUE

MAXIMUM POINTS: *a* 126; *b* 114.
**Won or placed on goal average (ratio), goal difference or most goals scored. ††Not promoted after play-offs.*

	First	*Pts*	*Second*	*Pts*	*Third*	*Pts*
1992–93*a*	Manchester U	84	Aston Villa	74	Norwich C	72
1993–94*a*	Manchester U	92	Blackburn R	84	Newcastle U	77
1994–95*a*	Blackburn R	89	Manchester U	88	Nottingham F	77
1995–96*b*	Manchester U	82	Newcastle U	78	Liverpool	71
1996–97*b*	Manchester U	75	Newcastle U*	68	Arsenal*	68
1997–98*b*	Arsenal	78	Manchester U	77	Liverpool	65
1998–99*b*	Manchester U	79	Arsenal	78	Chelsea	75
1999–2000*b*	Manchester U	91	Arsenal	73	Leeds U	69
2000–01	Manchester U	80	Arsenal	70	Liverpool	69
2001–02	Arsenal	87	Liverpool	80	Manchester U	77
2002–03	Manchester U	83	Arsenal	78	Newcastle U	69
2003–04	Arsenal	90	Chelsea	79	Manchester U	75
2004–05	Chelsea	95	Arsenal	83	Manchester U	77
2005–06	Chelsea	91	Manchester U	83	Liverpool	82
2006–07	Manchester U	89	Chelsea	83	Liverpool*	68
2007–08	Manchester U	87	Chelsea	85	Arsenal	83

FOOTBALL LEAGUE CHAMPIONSHIP

MAXIMUM POINTS: 138

	First	*Pts*	*Second*	*Pts*	*Third*	*Pts*
2004–05	Sunderland	94	Wigan Ath	87	Ipswich T††	85
2005–06	Reading	106	Sheffield U	90	Watford	81
2006–07	Sunderland	88	Birmingham C	86	Derby Co	84
2007–08	WBA	81	Stoke C	79	Hull C	75

FIRST DIVISION

MAXIMUM POINTS: 138

	First	*Pts*	*Second*	*Pts*	*Third*	*Pts*
1992–93	Newcastle U	96	West Ham U*	88	Portsmouth††	88
1993–94	Crystal Palace	90	Nottingham F	83	Millwall††	74
1994–95	Middlesbrough	82	Reading††	79	Bolton W	77
1995–96	Sunderland	83	Derby Co	79	Crystal Palace††	75
1996–97	Bolton W	98	Barnsley	80	Wolverhampton W††	76
1997–98	Nottingham F	94	Middlesbrough	91	Sunderland††	90
1998–99	Sunderland	105	Bradford C	87	Ipswich T††	86
1999–2000	Charlton Ath	91	Manchester C	89	Ipswich T	87
2000–01	Fulham	101	Blackburn R	91	Bolton W	87
2001–02	Manchester C	99	WBA	89	Wolverhampton W††	86
2002–03	Portsmouth	98	Leicester C	92	Sheffield U††	80
2003–04	Norwich C	94	WBA	86	Sunderland††	79

FOOTBALL LEAGUE CHAMPIONSHIP 1

MAXIMUM POINTS: 138

	First	*Pts*	*Second*	*Pts*	*Third*	*Pts*
2004–05	Luton T	98	Hull C	86	Tranmere R††	79
2005–06	Southend U	82	Colchester U	79	Brentford††	76
2006–07	Scunthorpe U	91	Bristol C	85	Blackpool	83
2007–08	Swansea C	92	Nottingham F	82	Doncaster R	80

SECOND DIVISION

MAXIMUM POINTS: 138

	First	*Pts*	*Second*	*Pts*	*Third*	*Pts*
1992–93	Stoke C	93	Bolton W	90	Port Vale††	89
1993–94	Reading	89	Port Vale	88	Plymouth Arg*††	85
1994–95	Birmingham C	89	Brentford††	85	Crewe Alex††	83
1995–96	Swindon T	92	Oxford U	83	Blackpool††	82
1996–97	Bury	84	Stockport Co	82	Luton T††	78
1997–98	Watford	88	Bristol C	85	Grimsby T	72
1998–99	Fulham	101	Walsall	87	Manchester C	82
1999–2000	Preston NE	95	Burnley	88	Gillingham	85
2000–01	Millwall	93	Rotherham U	91	Reading††	86
2001–02	Brighton & HA	90	Reading	84	Brentford*††	83
2002–03	Wigan Ath	100	Crewe Alex	86	Bristol C††	83
2003–04	Plymouth Arg	90	QPR	83	Bristol C††	82

FOOTBALL LEAGUE CHAMPIONSHIP 2

MAXIMUM POINTS: 138

	First	*Pts*	*Second*	*Pts*	*Third*	*Pts*
2004–05	Yeovil T	83	Scunthorpe U*	80	Swansea C	80
2005–06	Carlisle U	86	Northampton T	83	Leyton Orient	81
2006–07	Walsall	89	Hartlepool U	88	Swindon T	85
2007–08	Milton Keynes D	97	Peterborough U	92	Hereford U	88

THIRD DIVISION

MAXIMUM POINTS: *a* 126; *b* 138.

	First	*Pts*	*Second*	*Pts*	*Third*	*Pts*
1992–93*a*	Cardiff C	83	Wrexham	80	Barnet	79
1993–94*a*	Shrewsbury T	79	Chester C	74	Crewe Alex	73
1994–95*a*	Carlisle U	91	Walsall	83	Chesterfield	81
1995–96*b*	Preston NE	86	Gillingham	83	Bury	79
1996–97*b*	Wigan Ath*	87	Fulham	87	Carlisle U	84
1997–98*b*	Notts Co	99	Macclesfield T	82	Lincoln C	72
1998–99*b*	Brentford	85	Cambridge U	81	Cardiff C	80
1999–2000*b*	Swansea C	85	Rotherham U	84	Northampton T	82
2000–01	Brighton & HA	92	Cardiff C	82	Chesterfield¶	80

	First	Pts	Second	Pts	Third	Pts
2001–02	Plymouth Arg	102	Luton T	97	Mansfield T	79
2002–03	Rushden & D	87	Hartlepool U	85	Wrexham	84
2003–04	Doncaster R	92	Hull C	88	Torquay U*	81

¶9pts deducted for irregularities.

FOOTBALL LEAGUE

MAXIMUM POINTS: *a* 44; *b* 60

	First	Pts	Second	Pts	Third	Pts
1888–89*a*	Preston NE	40	Aston Villa	29	Wolverhampton W	28
1889–90*a*	Preston NE	33	Everton	31	Blackburn R	27
1890–91*a*	Everton	29	Preston NE	27	Notts Co	26
1891–92*b*	Sunderland	42	Preston NE	37	Bolton W	36

FIRST DIVISION to 1991–92

MAXIMUM POINTS: *a* 44; *b* 52; *c* 60; *d* 68; *e* 76; *f* 84; *g* 126; *h* 120; *k* 114.

	First	Pts	Second	Pts	Third	Pts
1892–93*c*	Sunderland	48	Preston NE	37	Everton	36
1893–94*c*	Aston Villa	44	Sunderland	38	Derby Co	36
1894–95*c*	Sunderland	47	Everton	42	Aston Villa	39
1895–96*c*	Aston Villa	45	Derby Co	41	Everton	39
1896–97*c*	Aston Villa	47	Sheffield U*	36	Derby Co	36
1897–98*c*	Sheffield U	42	Sunderland	37	Wolverhampton W*	35
1898–99*d*	Aston Villa	45	Liverpool	43	Burnley	39
1899–1900*d*	Aston Villa	50	Sheffield U	48	Sunderland	41
1900–01*d*	Liverpool	45	Sunderland	43	Notts Co	40
1901–02*d*	Sunderland	44	Everton	41	Newcastle U	37
1902–03*d*	The Wednesday	42	Aston Villa*	41	Sunderland	41
1903–04*d*	The Wednesday	47	Manchester C	44	Everton	43
1904–05*d*	Newcastle U	48	Everton	47	Manchester C	46
1905–06*e*	Liverpool	51	Preston NE	47	The Wednesday	44
1906–07*e*	Newcastle U	51	Bristol C	48	Everton*	45
1907–08*e*	Manchester U	52	Aston Villa*	43	Manchester C	43
1908–09*e*	Newcastle U	53	Everton	46	Sunderland	44
1909–10*e*	Aston Villa	53	Liverpool	48	Blackburn R*	45
1910–11*e*	Manchester U	52	Aston Villa	51	Sunderland*	45
1911–12*e*	Blackburn R	49	Everton	46	Newcastle U	44
1912–13*e*	Sunderland	54	Aston Villa	50	Sheffield W	49
1913–14*e*	Blackburn R	51	Aston Villa	44	Middlesbrough*	43
1914–15*e*	Everton	46	Oldham Ath	45	Blackburn R*	43
1919–20*f*	WBA	60	Burnley	51	Chelsea	49
1920–21*f*	Burnley	59	Manchester C	54	Bolton W	52
1921–22*f*	Liverpool	57	Tottenham H	51	Burnley	49
1922–23*f*	Liverpool	60	Sunderland	54	Huddersfield T	53
1923–24*f*	Huddersfield T*	57	Cardiff C	57	Sunderland	53
1924–25*f*	Huddersfield T	58	WBA	56	Bolton W	55
1925–26*f*	Huddersfield T	57	Arsenal	52	Sunderland	48
1926–27*f*	Newcastle U	56	Huddersfield T	51	Sunderland	49
1927–28*f*	Everton	53	Huddersfield T	51	Leicester C	48
1928–29*f*	Sheffield W	52	Leicester C	51	Aston Villa	50
1929–30*f*	Sheffield W	60	Derby Co	50	Manchester C*	47
1930–31*f*	Arsenal	66	Aston Villa	59	Sheffield W	52
1931–32*f*	Everton	56	Arsenal	54	Sheffield W	50
1932–33*f*	Arsenal	58	Aston Villa	54	Sheffield W	51
1933–34*f*	Arsenal	59	Huddersfield T	56	Tottenham H	49
1934–35*f*	Arsenal	58	Sunderland	54	Sheffield W	49
1935–36*f*	Sunderland	56	Derby Co*	48	Huddersfield T	48
1936–37*f*	Manchester C	57	Charlton Ath	54	Arsenal	52
1937–38*f*	Arsenal	52	Wolverhampton W	51	Preston NE	49
1938–39*f*	Everton	59	Wolverhampton W	55	Charlton Ath	50
1946–47*f*	Liverpool	57	Manchester U*	56	Wolverhampton W	56
1947–48*f*	Arsenal	59	Manchester U*	52	Burnley	52
1948–49*f*	Portsmouth	58	Manchester U*	53	Derby Co	53
1949–50*f*	Portsmouth*	53	Wolverhampton W	53	Sunderland	52
1950–51*f*	Tottenham H	60	Manchester U	56	Blackpool	50
1951–52*f*	Manchester U	57	Tottenham H*	53	Arsenal	53
1952–53*f*	Arsenal*	54	Preston NE	54	Wolverhampton W	51
1953–54*f*	Wolverhampton W	57	WBA	53	Huddersfield T	51
1954–55*f*	Chelsea	52	Wolverhampton W*	48	Portsmouth*	48
1955–56*f*	Manchester U	60	Blackpool*	49	Wolverhampton W	49
1956–57*f*	Manchester U	64	Tottenham H*	56	Preston NE	56
1957–58*f*	Wolverhampton W	64	Preston NE	59	Tottenham H	51
1958–59*f*	Wolverhampton W	61	Manchester U	55	Arsenal*	50
1959–60*f*	Burnley	55	Wolverhampton W	54	Tottenham H	53
1960–61*f*	Tottenham H	66	Sheffield W	58	Wolverhampton W	57
1961–62*f*	Ipswich T	56	Burnley	53	Tottenham H	52
1962–63*f*	Everton	61	Tottenham H	55	Burnley	54
1963–64*f*	Liverpool	57	Manchester U	53	Everton	52
1964–65*f*	Manchester U*	61	Leeds U	61	Chelsea	56
1965–66*f*	Liverpool	61	Leeds U*	55	Burnley	55
1966–67*f*	Manchester U	60	Nottingham F*	56	Tottenham H	56
1967–68*f*	Manchester C	58	Manchester U	56	Liverpool	55
1968–69*f*	Leeds U	67	Liverpool	61	Everton	57
1969–70*f*	Everton	66	Leeds U	57	Chelsea	55
1970–71*f*	Arsenal	65	Leeds U	64	Tottenham H*	52
1971–72*f*	Derby Co	58	Leeds U*	57	Liverpool*	57

	First	Pts	Second	Pts	Third	Pts
1972–73*f*	Liverpool	60	Arsenal	57	Leeds U	53
1973–74*f*	Leeds U	62	Liverpool	57	Derby Co	48
1974–75*f*	Derby Co	53	Liverpool*	51	Ipswich T	51
1975–76*f*	Liverpool	60	QPR	59	Manchester U	56
1976–77*f*	Liverpool	57	Manchester C	56	Ipswich T	52
1977–78*f*	Nottingham F	64	Liverpool	57	Everton	55
1978–79*f*	Liverpool	68	Nottingham F	60	WBA	59
1979–80*f*	Liverpool	60	Manchester U	58	Ipswich T	52
1980–81*f*	Aston Villa	60	Ipswich T	56	Arsenal	53
1981–82*g*	Liverpool	87	Ipswich T	83	Manchester U	78
1982–83*g*	Liverpool	82	Watford	71	Manchester U	70
1983–84*g*	Liverpool	80	Southampton	77	Nottingham F*	74
1984–85*g*	Everton	90	Liverpool*	77	Tottenham H	77
1985–86*g*	Liverpool	88	Everton	86	West Ham U	84
1986–87*g*	Everton	86	Liverpool	77	Tottenham H	71
1987–88*h*	Liverpool	90	Manchester U	81	Nottingham F	73
1988–89*k*	Arsenal*	76	Liverpool	76	Nottingham F	64
1989–90*k*	Liverpool	79	Aston Villa	70	Tottenham H	63
1990–91*k*	Arsenal†	83	Liverpool	76	Crystal Palace	69
1991–92*g*	Leeds U	82	Manchester U	78	Sheffield W	75

No official competition during 1915–19 and 1939–46; Regional Leagues operated. †2 pts deducted.

SECOND DIVISION to 1991–92

MAXIMUM POINTS: ***a*** **44;** ***b*** **56;** ***c*** **60;** ***d*** **68;** ***e*** **76;** ***f*** **84;** ***g*** **126;** ***h*** **132;** ***k*** **138.**

	First	Pts	Second	Pts	Third	Pts
1892–93*a*	Small Heath	36	Sheffield U	35	Darwen	30
1893–94*b*	Liverpool	50	Small Heath	42	Notts Co	39
1894–95*c*	Bury	48	Notts Co	39	Newton Heath*	38
1895–96*c*	Liverpool*	46	Manchester C	46	Grimsby T*	42
1896–97*c*	Notts Co	42	Newton Heath	39	Grimsby T	38
1897–98*c*	Burnley	48	Newcastle U	45	Manchester C	39
1898–99*d*	Manchester C	52	Glossop NE	46	Leicester Fosse	45
1899–1900*d*	The Wednesday	54	Bolton W	52	Small Heath	46
1900–01*d*	Grimsby T	49	Small Heath	48	Burnley	44
1901–02*d*	WBA	55	Middlesbrough	51	Preston NE*	42
1902–03*d*	Manchester C	54	Small Heath	51	Woolwich A	48
1903–04*d*	Preston NE	50	Woolwich A	49	Manchester U	48
1904–05*d*	Liverpool	58	Bolton W	56	Manchester U	53
1905–06*e*	Bristol C	66	Manchester U	62	Chelsea	53
1906–07*e*	Nottingham F	60	Chelsea	57	Leicester Fosse	48
1907–08*e*	Bradford C	54	Leicester Fosse	52	Oldham Ath	50
1908–09*e*	Bolton W	52	Tottenham H*	51	WBA	51
1909–10*e*	Manchester C	54	Oldham Ath*	53	Hull C*	53
1910–11*e*	WBA	53	Bolton W	51	Chelsea	49
1911–12*e*	Derby Co*	54	Chelsea	54	Burnley	52
1912–13*e*	Preston NE	53	Burnley	50	Birmingham	46
1913–14*e*	Notts Co	53	Bradford PA*	49	Woolwich A	49
1914–15*e*	Derby Co	53	Preston NE	50	Barnsley	47
1919–20*f*	Tottenham H	70	Huddersfield T	64	Birmingham	56
1920–21*f*	Birmingham*	58	Cardiff C	58	Bristol C	51
1921–22*f*	Nottingham F	56	Stoke C*	52	Barnsley	52
1922–23*f*	Notts Co	53	West Ham U*	51	Leicester C	51
1923–24*f*	Leeds U	54	Bury*	51	Derby Co	51
1924–25*f*	Leicester C	59	Manchester U	57	Derby Co	55
1925–26*f*	Sheffield W	60	Derby Co	57	Chelsea	52
1926–27*f*	Middlesbrough	62	Portsmouth*	54	Manchester C	54
1927–28*f*	Manchester C	59	Leeds U	57	Chelsea	54
1928–29*f*	Middlesbrough	55	Grimsby T	53	Bradford PA*	48
1929–30*f*	Blackpool	58	Chelsea	55	Oldham Ath	53
1930–31*f*	Everton	61	WBA	54	Tottenham H	51
1931–32*f*	Wolverhampton W	56	Leeds U	54	Stoke C	52
1932–33*f*	Stoke C	56	Tottenham H	55	Fulham	50
1933–34*f*	Grimsby T	59	Preston NE	52	Bolton W*	51
1934–35*f*	Brentford	61	Bolton W*	56	West Ham U	56
1935–36*f*	Manchester U	56	Charlton Ath	55	Sheffield U*	52
1936–37*f*	Leicester C	56	Blackpool	55	Bury	52
1937–38*f*	Aston Villa	57	Manchester U*	53	Sheffield U	53
1938–39*f*	Blackburn R	55	Sheffield U	54	Sheffield W	53
1946–47*f*	Manchester C	62	Burnley	58	Birmingham C	55
1947–48*f*	Birmingham C	59	Newcastle U	56	Southampton	52
1948–49*f*	Fulham	57	WBA	56	Southampton	55
1949–50*f*	Tottenham H	61	Sheffield W*	52	Sheffield U*	52
1950–51*f*	Preston NE	57	Manchester C	52	Cardiff C	50
1951–52*f*	Sheffield W	53	Cardiff C*	51	Birmingham C	51
1952–53*f*	Sheffield U	60	Huddersfield T	58	Luton T	52
1953–54*f*	Leicester C*	56	Everton	56	Blackburn R	55
1954–55*f*	Birmingham C*	54	Luton T*	54	Rotherham U	54
1955–56*f*	Sheffield W	55	Leeds U	52	Liverpool*	48
1956–57*f*	Leicester C	61	Nottingham F	54	Liverpool	53
1957–58*f*	West Ham U	57	Blackburn R	56	Charlton Ath	55
1958–59*f*	Sheffield W	62	Fulham	60	Sheffield U*	53
1959–60*f*	Aston Villa	59	Cardiff C	58	Liverpool*	50
1960–61*f*	Ipswich T	59	Sheffield U	58	Liverpool	52
1961–62*f*	Liverpool	62	Leyton Orient	54	Sunderland	53

	First	*Pts*	*Second*	*Pts*	*Third*	*Pts*
1962–63*f*	Stoke C	53	Chelsea*	52	Sunderland	52
1963–64*f*	Leeds U	63	Sunderland	61	Preston NE	56
1964–65*f*	Newcastle U	57	Northampton T	56	Bolton W	50
1965–66*f*	Manchester C	59	Southampton	54	Coventry C	53
1966–67*f*	Coventry C	59	Wolverhampton W	58	Carlisle U	52
1967–68*f*	Ipswich T	59	QPR*	58	Blackpool	58
1968–69*f*	Derby Co	63	Crystal Palace	56	Charlton Ath	50
1969–70*f*	Huddersfield T	60	Blackpool	53	Leicester C	51
1970–71*f*	Leicester C	59	Sheffield U	56	Cardiff C*	53
1971–72*f*	Norwich C	57	Birmingham C	56	Millwall	55
1972–73*f*	Burnley	62	QPR	61	Aston Villa	50
1973–74*f*	Middlesbrough	65	Luton T	50	Carlisle U	49
1974–75*f*	Manchester U	61	Aston Villa	58	Norwich C	53
1975–76*f*	Sunderland	56	Bristol C*	53	WBA	53
1976–77*f*	Wolverhampton W	57	Chelsea	55	Nottingham F	52
1977–78*f*	Bolton W	58	Southampton	57	Tottenham H*	56
1978–79*f*	Crystal Palace	57	Brighton & HA*	56	Stoke C	56
1979–80*f*	Leicester C	55	Sunderland	54	Birmingham C*	53
1980–81*f*	West Ham U	66	Notts Co	53	Swansea C*	50
1981–82*g*	Luton T	88	Watford	80	Norwich C	71
1982–83*g*	QPR	85	Wolverhampton W	75	Leicester C	70
1983–84*g*	Chelsea*	88	Sheffield W	88	Newcastle U	80
1984–85*g*	Oxford U	84	Birmingham C	82	Manchester C	74
1985–86*g*	Norwich C	84	Charlton Ath	77	Wimbledon	76
1986–87*g*	Derby Co	84	Portsmouth	78	Oldham Ath††	75
1987–88*h*	Millwall	82	Aston Villa*	78	Middlesbrough	78
1988–89*k*	Chelsea	99	Manchester C	82	Crystal Palace	81
1989–90*k*	Leeds U*	85	Sheffield U	85	Newcastle U††	80
1990–91*k*	Oldham Ath	88	West Ham U	87	Sheffield W	82
1991–92*k*	Ipswich T	84	Middlesbrough	80	Derby Co	78

No official competition during 1915–19 and 1939–46; Regional Leagues operated.

THIRD DIVISION to 1991–92

MAXIMUM POINTS: 92; 138 FROM 1981–82.

	First	*Pts*	*Second*	*Pts*	*Third*	*Pts*
1958–59	Plymouth Arg	62	Hull C	61	Brentford*	57
1959–60	Southampton	61	Norwich C	59	Shrewsbury T*	52
1960–61	Bury	68	Walsall	62	QPR	60
1961–62	Portsmouth	65	Grimsby T	62	Bournemouth*	59
1962–63	Northampton T	62	Swindon T	58	Port Vale	54
1963–64	Coventry C*	60	Crystal Palace	60	Watford	58
1964–65	Carlisle U	60	Bristol C*	59	Mansfield T	59
1965–66	Hull C	69	Millwall	65	QPR	57
1966–67	QPR	67	Middlesbrough	55	Watford	54
1967–68	Oxford U	57	Bury	56	Shrewsbury T	55
1968–69	Watford*	64	Swindon T	64	Luton T	61
1969–70	Orient	62	Luton T	60	Bristol R	56
1970–71	Preston NE	61	Fulham	60	Halifax T	56
1971–72	Aston Villa	70	Brighton & HA	65	Bournemouth*	62
1972–73	Bolton W	61	Notts Co	57	Blackburn R	55
1973–74	Oldham Ath	62	Bristol R*	61	York C	61
1974–75	Blackburn R	60	Plymouth Arg	59	Charlton Ath	55
1975–76	Hereford U	63	Cardiff C	57	Millwall	56
1976–77	Mansfield T	64	Brighton & HA	61	Crystal Palace*	59
1977–78	Wrexham	61	Cambridge U	58	Preston NE*	56
1978–79	Shrewsbury T	61	Watford*	60	Swansea C	60
1979–80	Grimsby T	62	Blackburn R	59	Sheffield W	58
1980–81	Rotherham U	61	Barnsley*	59	Charlton Ath	59
1981–82	Burnley*	80	Carlisle U	80	Fulham	78
1982–83	Portsmouth	91	Cardiff C	86	Huddersfield T	82
1983–84	Oxford U	95	Wimbledon	87	Sheffield U*	83
1984–85	Bradford C	94	Millwall	90	Hull C	87
1985–86	Reading	94	Plymouth Arg	87	Derby Co	84
1986–87	Bournemouth	97	Middlesbrough	94	Swindon T	87
1987–88	Sunderland	93	Brighton & HA	84	Walsall	82
1988–89	Wolverhampton W	92	Sheffield U*	84	Port Vale	84
1989–90	Bristol R	93	Bristol C	91	Notts Co	87
1990–91	Cambridge U	86	Southend U	85	Grimsby T*	83
1991–92	Brentford	82	Birmingham C	81	Huddersfield T	78

FOURTH DIVISION (1958–1992)

MAXIMUM POINTS: 92; 138 FROM 1981–82.

	First	*Pts*	*Second*	*Pts*	*Third*	*Pts*	*Fourth*	*Pts*
1958–59	Port Vale	64	Coventry C*	60	York C	60	Shrewsbury T	58
1959–60	Walsall	65	Notts Co*	60	Torquay U	60	Watford	57
1960–61	Peterborough U	66	Crystal Palace	64	Northampton T*	60	Bradford PA	60
1961–62†	Millwall	56	Colchester U	55	Wrexham	53	Carlisle U	52
1962–63	Brentford	62	Oldham Ath*	59	Crewe Alex	59	Mansfield T*	57
1963–64	Gillingham*	60	Carlisle U	60	Workington	59	Exeter C	58
1964–65	Brighton & HA	63	Millwall*	62	York C	62	Oxford U	61
1965–66	Doncaster R*	59	Darlington	59	Torquay U	58	Colchester U*	56
1966–67	Stockport Co	64	Southport*	59	Barrow	59	Tranmere R	58
1967–68	Luton T	66	Barnsley	61	Hartlepools U	60	Crewe Alex	58

	First	*Pts*	*Second*	*Pts*	*Third*	*Pts*	*Fourth*	*Pts*
1968–69	Doncaster R	59	Halifax T	57	Rochdale*	56	Bradford C	56
1969–70	Chesterfield	64	Wrexham	61	Swansea C	60	Port Vale	59
1970–71	Notts Co	69	Bournemouth	60	Oldham Ath	59	York C	56
1971–72	Grimsby T	63	Southend U	60	Brentford	59	Scunthorpe U	57
1972–73	Southport	62	Hereford U	58	Cambridge U	57	Aldershot*	56
1973–74	Peterborough U	65	Gillingham	62	Colchester U	60	Bury	59
1974–75	Mansfield T	68	Shrewsbury T	62	Rotherham U	59	Chester*	57
1975–76	Lincoln C	74	Northampton T	68	Reading	60	Tranmere R	58
1976–77	Cambridge U	65	Exeter C	62	Colchester U*	59	Bradford C	59
1977–78	Watford	71	Southend U	60	Swansea C*	56	Brentford	56
1978–79	Reading	65	Grimsby T*	61	Wimbledon*	61	Barnsley	61
1979–80	Huddersfield T	66	Walsall	64	Newport Co	61	Portsmouth*	60
1980–81	Southend U	67	Lincoln C	65	Doncaster R	56	Wimbledon	55
1981–82	Sheffield U	96	Bradford C*	91	Wigan Ath	91	Bournemouth	88
1982–83	Wimbledon	98	Hull C	90	Port Vale	88	Scunthorpe U	83
1983–84	York C	101	Doncaster R	85	Reading*	82	Bristol C	82
1984–85	Chesterfield	91	Blackpool	86	Darlington	85	Bury	84
1985–86	Swindon T	102	Chester C	84	Mansfield T	81	Port Vale	79
1986–87	Northampton T	99	Preston NE	90	Southend U	80	Wolverhampton W††	79
1987–88	Wolverhampton W	90	Cardiff C	85	Bolton W	78	Scunthorpe U††	77
1988–89	Rotherham U	82	Tranmere R	80	Crewe Alex	78	Scunthorpe U††	77
1989–90	Exeter C	89	Grimsby T	79	Southend U	75	Stockport Co††	74
1990–91	Darlington	83	Stockport Co*	82	Hartlepool U	82	Peterborough U	80
1991–92†*	Burnley	83	Rotherham U*	77	Mansfield T	77	Blackpool	76

†*Maximum points:* 88 owing to Accrington Stanley's resignation.
†**Maximum points:* 126 owing to Aldershot being expelled (and only 23 teams started the competition).

THIRD DIVISION—SOUTH (1920–1958)

1920–21 SEASON AS THIRD DIVISION. MAXIMUM POINTS: ***a*** **84;** ***b*** **92.**

	First	*Pts*	*Second*	*Pts*	*Third*	*Pts*
1920–21*a*	Crystal Palace	59	Southampton	54	QPR	53
1921–22*a*	Southampton*	61	Plymouth Arg	61	Portsmouth	53
1922–23*a*	Bristol C	59	Plymouth Arg*	53	Swansea T	53
1923–24*a*	Portsmouth	59	Plymouth Arg	55	Millwall	54
1924–25*a*	Swansea T	57	Plymouth Arg	56	Bristol C	53
1925–26*a*	Reading	57	Plymouth Arg	56	Millwall	53
1926–27*a*	Bristol C	62	Plymouth Arg	60	Millwall	56
1927–28*a*	Millwall	65	Northampton T	55	Plymouth Arg	53
1928–29*a*	Charlton Ath*	54	Crystal Palace	54	Northampton T*	52
1929–30*a*	Plymouth Arg	68	Brentford	61	QPR	51
1930–31*a*	Notts Co	59	Crystal Palace	51	Brentford	50
1931–32*a*	Fulham	57	Reading	55	Southend U	53
1932–33*a*	Brentford	62	Exeter C	58	Norwich C	57
1933–34*a*	Norwich C	61	Coventry C*	54	Reading*	54
1934–35*a*	Charlton Ath	61	Reading	53	Coventry C	51
1935–36*a*	Coventry C	57	Luton T	56	Reading	54
1936–37*a*	Luton T	58	Notts Co	56	Brighton & HA	53
1937–38*a*	Millwall	56	Bristol C	55	QPR*	53
1938–39*a*	Newport Co	55	Crystal Palace	52	Brighton & HA	49
1939–46	Competition cancelled owing to war. Regional Leagues operated.					
1946–47*a*	Cardiff C	66	QPR	57	Bristol C	51
1947–48*a*	QPR	61	Bournemouth	57	Walsall	51
1948–49*a*	Swansea T	62	Reading	55	Bournemouth	52
1949–50*a*	Notts Co	58	Northampton T*	51	Southend U	51
1950–51*b*	Nottingham F	70	Norwich C	64	Reading*	57
1951–52*b*	Plymouth Arg	66	Reading*	61	Norwich C	61
1952–53*b*	Bristol R	64	Millwall*	62	Northampton T	62
1953–54*b*	Ipswich T	64	Brighton & HA	61	Bristol C	56
1954–55*b*	Bristol C	70	Leyton Orient	61	Southampton	59
1955–56*b*	Leyton Orient	66	Brighton & HA	65	Ipswich T	64
1956–57*b*	Ipswich T*	59	Torquay U	59	Colchester U	58
1957–58*b*	Brighton & HA	60	Brentford*	58	Plymouth Arg	58

THIRD DIVISION—NORTH (1921–1958)

MAXIMUM POINTS: ***a*** **76;** ***b*** **84;** ***c*** **80;** ***d*** **92.**

	First	*Pts*	*Second*	*Pts*	*Third*	*Pts*
1921–22*a*	Stockport Co	56	Darlington*	50	Grimsby T	50
1922–23*a*	Nelson	51	Bradford PA	47	Walsall	46
1923–24*b*	Wolverhampton W	63	Rochdale	62	Chesterfield	54
1924–25*b*	Darlington	58	Nelson*	53	New Brighton	53
1925–26*b*	Grimsby T	61	Bradford PA	60	Rochdale	59
1926–27*b*	Stoke C	63	Rochdale	58	Bradford PA	55
1927–28*b*	Bradford PA	63	Lincoln C	55	Stockport Co	54
1928–29*b*	Bradford C	63	Stockport Co	62	Wrexham	52
1929–30*b*	Port Vale	67	Stockport Co	63	Darlington*	50
1930–31*b*	Chesterfield	58	Lincoln C	57	Wrexham*	54
1931–32*c*	Lincoln C*	57	Gateshead	57	Chester	50
1932–33*b*	Hull C	59	Wrexham	57	Stockport Co	54
1933–34*b*	Barnsley	62	Chesterfield	61	Stockport Co	59
1934–35*b*	Doncaster R	57	Halifax T	55	Chester	54
1935–36*b*	Chesterfield	60	Chester*	55	Tranmere R	55
1936–37*b*	Stockport Co	60	Lincoln C	57	Chester	53
1937–38*b*	Tranmere R	56	Doncaster R	54	Hull C	53
1938–39*b*	Barnsley	67	Doncaster R	56	Bradford C	52

	First	Pts	Second	Pts	Third	Pts
1939–46	Competition cancelled owing to war. Regional Leagues operated.					
1946–47*b*	Doncaster R	72	Rotherham U	60	Chester	56
1947–48*b*	Lincoln C	60	Rotherham U	59	Wrexham	50
1948–49*b*	Hull C	65	Rotherham U	62	Doncaster R	50
1949–50*b*	Doncaster R	55	Gateshead	53	Rochdale*	51
1950–51*d*	Rotherham U	71	Mansfield T	64	Carlisle U	62
1951–52*d*	Lincoln C	69	Grimsby T	66	Stockport Co	59
1952–53*d*	Oldham Ath	59	Port Vale	58	Wrexham	56
1953–54*d*	Port Vale	69	Barnsley	58	Scunthorpe U	57
1954–55*d*	Barnsley	65	Accrington S	61	Scunthorpe U*	58
1955–56*d*	Grimsby T	68	Derby Co	63	Accrington S	59
1956–57*d*	Derby Co	63	Hartlepools U	59	Accrington S*	58
1957–58*d*	Scunthorpe U	66	Accrington S	59	Bradford C	57

PROMOTED AFTER PLAY-OFFS

(NOT ACCOUNTED FOR IN PREVIOUS SECTION)

1986–87 Aldershot to Division 3.
1987–88 Swansea C to Division 3.
1988–89 Leyton Orient to Division 3.
1989–90 Sunderland to Division 1; Notts Co to Division 2; Cambridge U to Division 3.
1990–91 Notts Co to Division 1; Tranmere R to Division 2; Torquay U to Division 3.
1991–92 Blackburn R to Premier League; Peterborough U to Division 1.
1992–93 Swindon T to Premier League; WBA to Division 1; York C to Division 2.
1993–94 Leicester C to Premier League; Burnley to Division 1; Wycombe W to Division 2.
1994–95 Huddersfield T to Division 1.
1995–96 Leicester C to Premier League; Bradford C to Division 1; Plymouth Arg to Division 2.
1996–97 Crystal Palace to Premier League; Crewe Alex to Division 1; Northampton T to Division 2.
1997–98 Charlton Ath to Premier League; Colchester U to Division 2.
1998–99 Watford to Premier League; Scunthorpe U to Division 2.
1999–2000 Peterborough U to Division 2
2000–01 Walsall to Division 1; Blackpool to Division 2
2001–02 Birmingham C to Premier League; Stoke C to Division 1; Cheltenham T to Division 2
2002–03 Wolverhampton W to Premier League; Cardiff C to Division 1; Bournemouth to Division 2
2003–04 Crystal Palace to Premier League; Brighton & HA to Division 1; Huddersfield T to Division 2
2004–05 West Ham U to Premier League; Sheffield W to Championship; Southend U to Championship 1
2005–06 Watford to Premier League; Barnsley to Championship; Cheltenham T to Championship 1
2006–07 Derby Co to Premier League; Blackpool to Championship; Bristol R to Championship 1
2007–08 Hull C to Premier League; Doncaster R to Championship; Stockport Co to Championship 1

LEAGUE TITLE WINS

FA PREMIER LEAGUE – Manchester U 10, Arsenal 3, Chelsea 2, Blackburn R 1.

FOOTBALL LEAGUE CHAMPIONSHIP – Sunderland 2, Reading 1, WBA 1.

LEAGUE DIVISION 1 – Liverpool 18, Arsenal 10, Everton 9, Sunderland 8, Aston Villa 7, Manchester U 7, Newcastle U 5, Sheffield W 4, Huddersfield T 3, Leeds U 3, Manchester C 3, Portsmouth 3, Wolverhampton W 3, Blackburn R 2, Burnley 2, Derby Co 2, Nottingham F 2, Preston NE 2, Tottenham H 2; Bolton W, Charlton Ath, Chelsea, Crystal Palace, Fulham, Ipswich T, Middlesbrough, Norwich C, Sheffield U, WBA 1 each.

FOOTBALL LEAGUE CHAMPIONSHIP 1 – Luton T 1, Scunthorpe U 1, Southend U 1, Swansea C 1.

LEAGUE DIVISION 2 – Leicester C 6, Manchester C 6, Birmingham C (one as Small Heath) 5, Sheffield W 5, Derby Co 4, Liverpool 4, Preston NE 4, Ipswich T 3, Leeds U 3, Middlesbrough 3, Notts Co 3, Stoke C 3, Aston Villa 2, Bolton W 2, Burnley 2, Bury 2, Chelsea 2, Fulham 2, Grimsby T 2, Manchester U 2, Millwall 2, Norwich C 2, Nottingham F 2, Tottenham H 2, WBA 2, West Ham U 2, Wolverhampton W 2; Blackburn R, Blackpool, Bradford C, Brentford, Brighton & HA, Bristol C, Coventry C, Crystal Palace, Everton, Huddersfield T, Luton T, Newcastle U, QPR, Oldham Ath, Oxford U, Plymouth Arg, Reading, Sheffield U, Sunderland, Swindon T, Watford, Wigan Ath 1 each.

FOOTBALL LEAGUE CHAMPIONSHIP 2 – Carlisle U 1, Milton Keynes D 1, Walsall 1, Yeovil T 1.

LEAGUE DIVISION 3 – Brentford 2, Carlisle U 2, Oxford U 2, Plymouth Arg 2, Portsmouth 2, Preston NE 2, Shrewsbury T 2; Aston Villa, Blackburn R, Bolton W, Bournemouth, Bradford C, Brighton & HA, Bristol R, Burnley, Bury, Cambridge U, Cardiff C, Coventry C, Doncaster R. Grimsby T, Hereford U, Hull C, Leyton Orient, Mansfield T, Northampton T, Notts Co, Oldham Ath, QPR, Reading, Rotherham U, Rushden & D Southampton, Sunderland, Swansea C, Watford, Wigan Ath, Wolverhampton W, Wrexham 1 each.

LEAGUE DIVISION 4 – Chesterfield 2, Doncaster R 2, Peterborough U 2; Brentford, Brighton & HA, Burnley, Cambridge U, Darlington, Exeter C, Gillingham, Grimsby T, Huddersfield T, Lincoln C, Luton T, Mansfield T, Millwall, Northampton T, Notts Co, Port Vale, Reading, Rotherham U, Sheffield U, Southend U, Southport, Stockport Co, Swindon T, Walsall, Watford, Wimbledon, Wolverhampton W, York C 1 each.

TO 1957–58

DIVISION 3 (South) – Bristol C 3, Charlton Ath 2, Ipswich T 2, Millwall 2, Notts Co 2, Plymouth Arg 2, Swansea T 2; Brentford, Brighton & HA, Bristol R, Cardiff C, Coventry C, Crystal Palace, Fulham, Leyton Orient, Luton T, Newport Co, Norwich C, Nottingham F, Portsmouth, QPR, Reading, Southampton 1 each.

DIVISION 3 (North) – Barnsley 3, Doncaster R 3, Lincoln C 3, Chesterfield 2, Grimsby T 2, Hull C 2, Port Vale 2, Stockport Co 2; Bradford C, Bradford PA, Darlington, Derby Co, Nelson, Oldham Ath, Rotherham U, Scunthorpe U, Stoke C, Tranmere R, Wolverhampton W 1 each.

RELEGATED CLUBS

1891–92 League extended. Newton Heath, Sheffield W and Nottingham F admitted. *Second Division formed* including Darwen.
1892–93 In Test matches, Sheffield U and Darwen won promotion in place of Notts Co and Accrington S.
1893–94 In Tests, Liverpool and Small Heath won promotion. Newton Heath and Darwen relegated.
1894–95 After Tests, Bury promoted, Liverpool relegated.
1895–96 After Tests, Liverpool promoted, Small Heath relegated.
1896–97 After Tests, Notts Co promoted, Burnley relegated.
1897–98 Test system abolished after success of Stoke C and Burnley. League extended. Blackburn R and Newcastle U elected to First Division. *Automatic promotion and relegation introduced.*

FA PREMIER LEAGUE TO DIVISION 1

1992–93 Crystal Palace, Middlesbrough, Nottingham F
1993–94 Sheffield U, Oldham Ath, Swindon T
1994–95 Crystal Palace, Norwich C, Leicester C, Ipswich T
1995–96 Manchester C, QPR, Bolton W
1996–97 Sunderland, Middlesbrough, Nottingham F
1997–98 Bolton W, Barnsley, Crystal Palace
1998–99 Charlton Ath, Blackburn R, Nottingham F
1999–2000 Wimbledon, Sheffield W, Watford
2000–01 Manchester C, Coventry C, Bradford C
2001–02 Ipswich T, Derby Co, Leicester C
2002–03 West Ham U, WBA, Sunderland
2003–04 Leicester C, Leeds U, Wolverhampton W.

FA PREMIER LEAGUE TO CHAMPIONSHIP

2004–05 Crystal Palace, Norwich C, Southampton
2005–06 Birmingham C, WBA, Sunderland
2006–07 Sheffield U, Charlton Ath, Watford
2007–08 Reading, Birmingham C, Derby Co

DIVISION 1 TO DIVISION 2

1898–99 Bolton W and Sheffield W
1899–1900 Burnley and Glossop
1900–01 Preston NE and WBA
1901–02 Small Heath and Manchester C
1902–03 Grimsby T and Bolton W
1903–04 Liverpool and WBA
1904–05 League extended. Bury and Notts Co, two bottom clubs in First Division, re-elected.
1905–06 Nottingham F and Wolverhampton W
1906–07 Derby Co and Stoke C
1907–08 Bolton W and Birmingham C
1908–09 Manchester C and Leicester Fosse
1909–10 Bolton W and Chelsea
1910–11 Bristol C and Nottingham F
1911–12 Preston NE and Bury
1912–13 Notts Co and Woolwich Arsenal
1913–14 Preston NE and Derby Co
1914–15 Tottenham H and Chelsea*
1919–20 Notts Co and Sheffield W
1920–21 Derby Co and Bradford PA
1921–22 Bradford C and Manchester U
1922–23 Stoke C and Oldham Ath
1923–24 Chelsea and Middlesbrough
1924–25 Preston NE and Nottingham F
1925–26 Manchester C and Notts Co
1926–27 Leeds U and WBA
1927–28 Tottenham H and Middlesbrough
1928–29 Bury and Cardiff C
1929–30 Burnley and Everton
1930–31 Leeds U and Manchester U
1931–32 Grimsby T and West Ham U
1932–33 Bolton W and Blackpool
1933–34 Newcastle U and Sheffield U
1934–35 Leicester C and Tottenham H
1935–36 Aston Villa and Blackburn R
1936–37 Manchester U and Sheffield W
1937–38 Manchester C and WBA
1938–39 Birmingham C and Leicester C
1946–47 Brentford and Leeds U
1947–48 Blackburn R and Grimsby T
1948–49 Preston NE and Sheffield U
1949–50 Manchester C and Birmingham C
1950–51 Sheffield W and Everton
1951–52 Huddersfield T and Fulham
1952–53 Stoke C and Derby Co
1953–54 Middlesbrough and Liverpool
1954–55 Leicester C and Sheffield W
1955–56 Huddersfield T and Sheffield U
1956–57 Charlton Ath and Cardiff C
1957–58 Sheffield W and Sunderland
1958–59 Portsmouth and Aston Villa
1959–60 Luton T and Leeds U
1960–61 Preston NE and Newcastle U
1961–62 Chelsea and Cardiff C
1962–63 Manchester C and Leyton Orient
1963–64 Bolton W and Ipswich T
1964–65 Wolverhampton W and Birmingham C
1965–66 Northampton T and Blackburn R
1966–67 Aston Villa and Blackpool
1967–68 Fulham and Sheffield U
1968–69 Leicester C and QPR
1969–70 Sunderland and Sheffield W
1970–71 Burnley and Blackpool
1971–72 Huddersfield T and Nottingham F
1972–73 Crystal Palace and WBA
1973–74 Southampton, Manchester U, Norwich C
1974–75 Luton T, Chelsea, Carlisle U
1975–76 Wolverhampton W, Burnley, Sheffield U
1976–77 Sunderland, Stoke C, Tottenham H
1977–78 West Ham U, Newcastle U, Leicester C
1978–79 QPR, Birmingham C, Chelsea
1979–80 Bristol C, Derby Co, Bolton W
1980–81 Norwich C, Leicester C, Crystal Palace
1981–82 Leeds U, Wolverhampton W, Middlesbrough
1982–83 Manchester C, Swansea C, Brighton & HA
1983–84 Birmingham C, Notts Co, Wolverhampton W
1984–85 Norwich C, Sunderland, Stoke C
1985–86 Ipswich T, Birmingham C, WBA
1986–87 Leicester C, Manchester C, Aston Villa
1987–88 Chelsea**, Portsmouth, Watford, Oxford U
1988–89 Middlesbrough, West Ham U, Newcastle U
1989–90 Sheffield W, Charlton Ath, Millwall
1990–91 Sunderland and Derby Co
1991–92 Luton T, Notts Co, West Ham U
1992–93 Brentford, Cambridge U, Bristol R
1993–94 Birmingham C, Oxford U, Peterborough U
1994–95 Swindon T, Burnley, Bristol C, Notts Co
1995–96 Millwall, Watford, Luton T
1996–97 Grimsby T, Oldham Ath, Southend U
1997–98 Manchester C, Stoke C, Reading
1998–99 Bury, Oxford U, Bristol C
1999–2000 Walsall, Port Vale, Swindon T
2000–01 Huddersfield T, QPR, Tranmere R
2001–02 Crewe Alex, Barnsley, Stockport Co
2002–03 Sheffield W, Brighton & HA, Grimsby T
2003–04 Walsall, Bradford C, Wimbledon

***Relegated after play-offs.*
**Subsequently re-elected to Division 1 when League was extended after the War.*

FOOTBALL LEAGUE CHAMPIONSHIP TO FOOTBALL LEAGUE CHAMPIONSHIP 1

2004–05 Gillingham, Nottingham F, Rotherham U
2005–06 Crewe Alex, Millwall, Brighton & HA
2006–07 Southend U, Luton T, Leeds U
2007–08 Leicester C, Scunthorpe U, Colchester U

DIVISION 2 TO DIVISION 3

1920–21 Stockport Co
1921–22 Bradford PA and Bristol C
1922–23 Rotherham Co and Wolverhampton W
1923–24 Nelson and Bristol C
1924–25 Crystal Palace and Coventry C
1925–26 Stoke C and Stockport Co
1926–27 Darlington and Bradford C
1927–28 Fulham and South Shields
1928–29 Port Vale and Clapton Orient
1929–30 Hull C and Notts Co
1930–31 Reading and Cardiff C
1931–32 Barnsley and Bristol C
1932–33 Chesterfield and Charlton Ath
1933–34 Millwall and Lincoln C
1934–35 Oldham Ath and Notts Co
1935–36 Port Vale and Hull C
1936–37 Doncaster R and Bradford C
1937–38 Barnsley and Stockport Co
1938–39 Norwich C and Tranmere R
1946–47 Swansea T and Newport Co
1947–48 Doncaster R and Millwall
1948–49 Nottingham F and Lincoln C
1949–50 Plymouth Arg and Bradford PA
1950–51 Grimsby T and Chesterfield
1951–52 Coventry C and QPR
1952–53 Southampton and Barnsley
1953–54 Brentford and Oldham Ath
1954–55 Ipswich T and Derby Co

1955–56 Plymouth Arg and Hull C
1956–57 Port Vale and Bury
1957–58 Doncaster R and Notts Co
1958–59 Barnsley and Grimsby T
1959–60 Bristol C and Hull C
1960–61 Lincoln C and Portsmouth
1961–62 Brighton & HA and Bristol R
1962–63 Walsall and Luton T
1963–64 Grimsby T and Scunthorpe U
1964–65 Swindon T and Swansea T
1965–66 Middlesbrough and Leyton Orient
1966–67 Northampton T and Bury
1967–68 Plymouth Arg and Rotherham U
1968–69 Fulham and Bury
1969–70 Preston NE and Aston Villa
1970–71 Blackburn R and Bolton W
1971–72 Charlton Ath and Watford
1972–73 Huddersfield T and Brighton & HA
1973–74 Crystal Palace, Preston NE, Swindon T
1974–75 Millwall, Cardiff C, Sheffield W
1975–76 Oxford U, York C, Portsmouth
1976–77 Carlisle U, Plymouth Arg, Hereford U
1977–78 Blackpool, Mansfield T, Hull C
1978–79 Sheffield U, Millwall, Blackburn R
1979–80 Fulham, Burnley, Charlton Ath
1980–81 Preston NE, Bristol C, Bristol R
1981–82 Cardiff C, Wrexham, Orient
1982–83 Rotherham U, Burnley, Bolton W
1983–84 Derby Co, Swansea C, Cambridge U
1984–85 Notts Co, Cardiff C, Wolverhampton W
1985–86 Carlisle U, Middlesbrough, Fulham
1986–87 Sunderland**, Grimsby T, Brighton & HA
1987–88 Huddersfield T, Reading, Sheffield U**
1988–89 Shrewsbury T, Birmingham C, Walsall
1989–90 Bournemouth, Bradford C, Stoke C
1990–91 WBA and Hull C
1991–92 Plymouth Arg, Brighton & HA, Port Vale
1992–93 Preston NE, Mansfield T, Wigan Ath, Chester C
1993–94 Fulham, Exeter C, Hartlepool U, Barnet
1994–95 Cambridge U, Plymouth Arg, Cardiff C, Chester C, Leyton Orient
1995–96 Carlisle U, Swansea C, Brighton & HA, Hull C
1996–97 Peterborough U, Shrewsbury T, Rotherham U, Notts Co
1997–98 Brentford, Plymouth Arg, Carlisle U, Southend U
1998–99 York C, Northampton T, Lincoln C, Macclesfield T
1999–2000 Cardiff C, Blackpool, Scunthorpe U, Chesterfield
2000–01 Bristol R, Luton T, Swansea C, Oxford U
2001–02 Bournemouth, Bury, Wrexham, Cambridge U
2002–03 Cheltenham T, Huddersfield T, Mansfield T Northampton T
2003–04 Grimsby T, Rushden & D, Notts Co, Wycombe W

FOOTBALL LEAGUE CHAMPIONSHIP 1 TO FOOTBALL LEAGUE CHAMPIONSHIP 2

2004–05 Torquay U, Wrexham, Peterborough U, Stockport Co
2005–06 Hartlepool U, Milton Keynes D, Swindon T, Walsall
2006–07 Chesterfield, Bradford C, Rotherham U, Brentford
2007–08 Bournemouth, Gillingham, Port Vale, Luton T

DIVISION 3 TO DIVISION 4

1958–59 Stockport Co, Doncaster R, Notts Co, Rochdale
1959–60 York C, Mansfield T, Wrexham, Accrington S
1960–61 Tranmere R, Bradford C, Colchester U, Chesterfield
1961–62 Torquay U, Lincoln C, Brentford, Newport Co
1962–63 Bradford PA, Brighton & HA, Carlisle U, Halifax T
1963–64 Millwall, Crewe Alex, Wrexham, Notts Co
1964–65 Luton T, Port Vale, Colchester U, Barnsley
1965–66 Southend U, Exeter C, Brentford, York C
1966–67 Swansea T, Darlington, Doncaster R, Workington
1967–68 Grimsby T, Colchester U, Scunthorpe U, Peterborough U (demoted)
1968–69 Northampton T, Hartlepool, Crewe Alex, Oldham Ath
1969–70 Bournemouth, Southport, Barrow, Stockport Co
1970–71 Reading, Bury, Doncaster R, Gillingham
1971–72 Mansfield T, Barnsley, Torquay U, Bradford C
1972–73 Rotherham U, Brentford, Swansea C, Scunthorpe U
1973–74 Cambridge U, Shrewsbury T, Southport, Rochdale
1974–75 Bournemouth, Tranmere R, Watford, Huddersfield T
1975–76 Aldershot, Colchester U, Southend U, Halifax T
1976–77 Reading, Northampton T, Grimsby T, York C
1977–78 Port Vale, Bradford C, Hereford U, Portsmouth
1978–79 Peterborough U, Walsall, Tranmere R, Lincoln C
1979–80 Bury, Southend U, Mansfield T, Wimbledon
1980–81 Sheffield U, Colchester U, Blackpool, Hull C
1981–82 Wimbledon, Swindon T, Bristol C, Chester
1982–83 Reading, Wrexham, Doncaster R, Chesterfield
1983–84 Scunthorpe U, Southend U, Port Vale, Exeter C
1984–85 Burnley, Orient, Preston NE, Cambridge U
1985–86 Lincoln C, Cardiff C, Wolverhampton W, Swansea C
1986–87 Bolton W**, Carlisle U, Darlington, Newport Co
1987–88 Rotherham U**, Grimsby T, York C, Doncaster R
1988–89 Southend U, Chesterfield, Gillingham, Aldershot
1989–90 Cardiff C, Northampton T, Blackpool, Walsall
1990–91 Crewe Alex, Rotherham U, Mansfield T
1991–92 Bury, Shrewsbury T, Torquay U, Darlington

*** Relegated after play-offs.*

APPLICATIONS FOR RE-ELECTION

FOURTH DIVISION

Eleven: Hartlepool U.
Seven: Crewe Alex.
Six: Barrow (lost League place to Hereford U 1972), Halifax T, Rochdale, Southport (lost League place to Wigan Ath 1978), York C.
Five: Chester C, Darlington, Lincoln C, Stockport Co, Workington (lost League place to Wimbledon 1977).
Four: Bradford PA (lost League place to Cambridge U 1970), Newport Co, Northampton T.
Three: Doncaster R, Hereford U.
Two: Bradford C, Exeter C, Oldham Ath, Scunthorpe U, Torquay U.
One: Aldershot, Colchester U, Gateshead (lost League place to Peterborough U 1960), Grimsby T, Swansea C, Tranmere R, Wrexham, Blackpool, Cambridge U, Preston NE.
Accrington S resigned and Oxford U were elected 1962.
Port Vale were forced to re-apply following expulsion in 1968.
Aldershot expelled March 1992. Maidstone U resigned August 1992.

THIRD DIVISIONS NORTH & SOUTH

Seven: Walsall.
Six: Exeter C, Halifax T, Newport Co.
Five: Accrington S, Barrow, Gillingham, New Brighton, Southport.
Four: Rochdale, Norwich C.
Three: Crystal Palace, Crewe Alex, Darlington, Hartlepool U, Merthyr T, Swindon T.
Two: Aberdare Ath, Aldershot, Ashington, Bournemouth, Brentford, Chester, Colchester U, Durham C, Millwall, Nelson, QPR, Rotherham U, Southend U, Tranmere R, Watford, Workington.
One: Bradford C, Bradford PA, Brighton & HA, Bristol R, Cardiff C, Carlisle U, Charlton Ath, Gateshead, Grimsby T, Mansfield T, Shrewsbury T, Torquay U, York C.

LEAGUE STATUS FROM 1986–87

RELEGATED FROM LEAGUE

1986–87 Lincoln C
1987–88 Newport Co
1988–89 Darlington
1989–90 Colchester U
1990–91 —
1991–92 —
1992–93 Halifax T
1993–94 —
1994–95 —
1995–96 —
1996–97 Hereford U
1997–98 Doncaster R
1998–99 Scarborough
1999–2000 Chester C
2000–01 Barnet
2001–02 Halifax T
2002–03 Shrewsbury T, Exeter C
2003–04 Carlisle U, York C
2004–05 Kidderminster H, Cambridge U
2005–06 Oxford U, Rushden & D
2006–07 Boston U, Torquay U
2007–08 Mansfield T, Wrexham

PROMOTED TO LEAGUE

1986–87 Scarborough
1987–88 Lincoln C
1988–89 Maidstone U
1989–90 Darlington
1990–91 Barnet
1991–92 Colchester U
1992–93 Wycombe W
1993–94 —
1994–95 —
1995–96 —
1996–97 Macclesfield T
1997–98 Halifax T
1998–99 Cheltenham T
1999–2000 Kidderminster H
2000–01 Rushden & D
2001–02 Boston U
2002–03 Yeovil T, Doncaster R
2003–04 Chester C, Shrewsbury T
2004–05 Barnet, Carlisle U
2005–06 Accrington S, Hereford U
2006–07 Dagenham & R, Morecambe
2007–08 Aldershot T, Exeter C

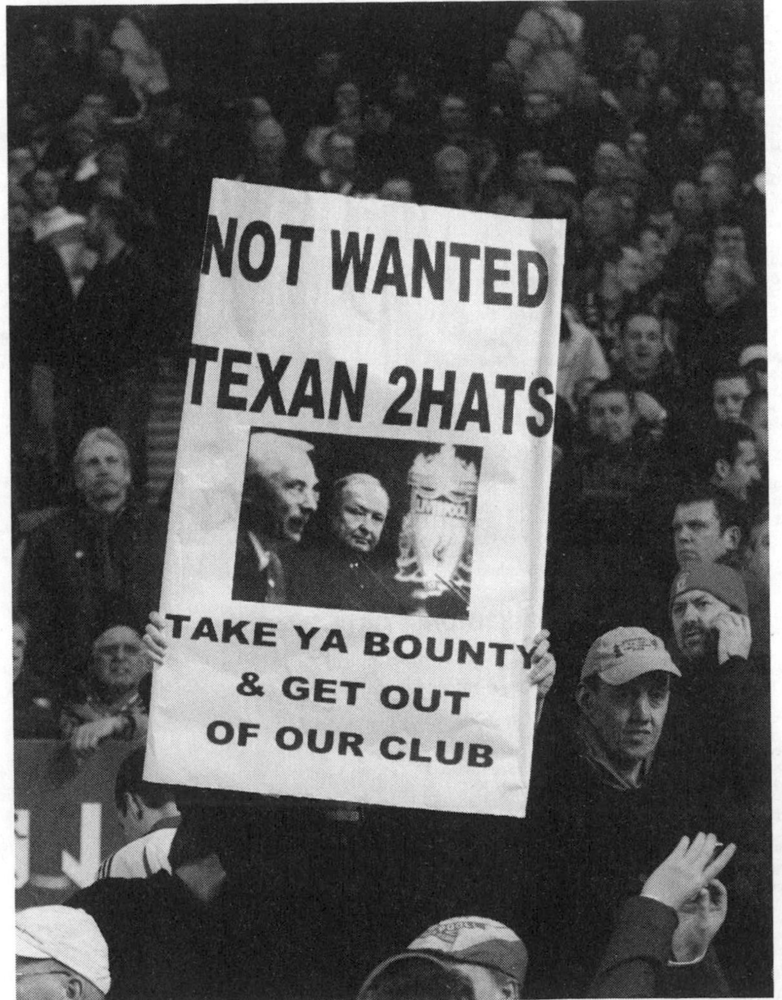

Liverpool fans demonstrate against the club's owners at the match against West Ham at Anfield in March. (Action Images/Jason Cairnduff/Livepic)

LEAGUE ATTENDANCES SINCE 1946–47

Season	*Matches*	*Total*	*Div. 1*	*Div. 2*	*Div. 3 (S)*	*Div. 3 (N)*
1946–47	1848	35,604,606	15,005,316	11,071,572	5,664,004	3,863,714
1947–48	1848	40,259,130	16,732,341	12,286,350	6,653,610	4,586,829
1948–49	1848	41,271,414	17,914,667	11,353,237	6,998,429	5,005,081
1949–50	1848	40,517,865	17,278,625	11,694,158	7,104,155	4,440,927
1950–51	2028	39,584,967	16,679,454	10,780,580	7,367,884	4,757,109
1951–52	2028	39,015,866	16,110,322	11,066,189	6,958,927	4,880,428
1952–53	2028	37,149,966	16,050,278	9,686,654	6,704,299	4,708,735
1953–54	2028	36,174,590	16,154,915	9,510,053	6,311,508	4,198,114
1954–55	2028	34,133,103	15,087,221	8,988,794	5,996,017	4,051,071
1955–56	2028	33,150,809	14,108,961	9,080,002	5,692,479	4,269,367
1956–57	2028	32,744,405	13,803,037	8,718,162	5,622,189	4,601,017
1957–58	2028	33,562,208	14,468,652	8,663,712	6,097,183	4,332,661
		Total	*Div. 1*	*Div. 2*	*Div. 3*	*Div. 4*
1958–59	2028	33,610,985	14,727,691	8,641,997	5,946,600	4,276,697
1959–60	2028	32,538,611	14,391,227	8,399,627	5,739,707	4,008,050
1960–61	2028	28,619,754	12,926,948	7,033,936	4,784,256	3,874,614
1961–62	2015	27,979,902	12,061,194	7,453,089	5,199,106	3,266,513
1962–63	2028	28,885,852	12,490,239	7,792,770	5,341,362	3,261,481
1963–64	2028	28,535,022	12,486,626	7,594,158	5,419,157	3,035,081
1964–65	2028	27,641,168	12,708,752	6,984,104	4,436,245	3,512,067
1965–66	2028	27,206,980	12,480,644	6,914,757	4,779,150	3,032,429
1966–67	2028	28,902,596	14,242,957	7,253,819	4,421,172	2,984,648
1967–68	2028	30,107,298	15,289,410	7,450,410	4,013,087	3,354,391
1968–69	2028	29,382,172	14,584,851	7,382,390	4,339,656	3,075,275
1969–70	2028	29,600,972	14,868,754	7,581,728	4,223,761	2,926,729
1970–71	2028	28,194,146	13,954,337	7,098,265	4,377,213	2,764,331
1971–72	2028	28,700,729	14,484,603	6,769,308	4,697,392	2,749,426
1972–73	2028	25,448,642	13,998,154	5,631,730	3,737,252	2,081,506
1973–74	2027	24,982,203	13,070,991	6,326,108	3,421,624	2,163,480
1974–75	2028	25,577,977	12,613,178	6,955,970	4,086,145	1,992,684
1975–76	2028	24,896,053	13,089,861	5,798,405	3,948,449	2,059,338
1976–77	2028	26,182,800	13,647,585	6,250,597	4,152,218	2,132,400
1977–78	2028	25,392,872	13,255,677	6,474,763	3,332,042	2,330,390
1978–79	2028	24,540,627	12,704,549	6,153,223	3,374,558	2,308,297
1979–80	2028	24,623,975	12,163,002	6,112,025	3,999,328	2,349,620
1980–81	2028	21,907,569	11,392,894	5,175,442	3,637,854	1,701,379
1981–82	2028	20,006,961	10,420,793	4,750,463	2,836,915	1,998,790
1982–83	2028	18,766,158	9,295,613	4,974,937	2,943,568	1,552,040
1983–84	2028	18,358,631	8,711,448	5,359,757	2,729,942	1,557,484
1984–85	2028	17,849,835	9,761,404	4,030,823	2,667,008	1,390,600
1985–86	2028	16,488,577	9,037,854	3,551,968	2,490,481	1,408,274
1986–87	2028	17,379,218	9,144,676	4,168,131	2,350,970	1,715,441
1987–88	2030	17,959,732	8,094,571	5,341,599	2,751,275	1,772,287
1988–89	2036	18,464,192	7,809,993	5,887,805	3,035,327	1,791,067
1989–90	2036	19,445,442	7,883,039	6,867,674	2,803,551	1,891,178
1990–91	2036	19,508,202	8,618,709	6,285,068	2,835,759	1,768,666
1991–92	2064*	20,487,273	9,989,160	5,809,787	2,993,352	1,694,974
		Total	*FA Premier*	*Div. 1*	*Div. 2*	*Div. 3*
1992–93	2028	20,657,327	9,759,809	5,874,017	3,483,073	1,540,428
1993–94	2028	21,683,381	10,644,551	6,487,104	2,972,702	1,579,024
1994–95	2028	21,856,020	11,213,168	6,044,293	3,037,752	1,560,807
1995–96	2036	21,844,416	10,469,107	6,566,349	2,843,652	1,965,308
1996–97	2036	22,783,163	10,804,762	6,931,539	3,195,223	1,851,639
1997–98	2036	24,692,608	11,092,106	8,330,018	3,503,264	1,767,220
1998–99	2036	25,435,542	11,620,326	7,543,369	4,169,697	2,102,150
1999-2000	2036	25,341,090	11,668,497	7,810,208	3,700,433	2,161,952
2000–01	2036	26,030,167	12,472,094	7,909,512	3,488,166	2,160,395
2001–02	2036	27,756,977	13,043,118	8,352,128	3,963,153	2,398,578
2002–03	2036	28,343,386	13,468,965	8,521,017	3,892,469	2,460,935
2003–04	2036	29,197,510	13,303,136	8,772,780	4,146,495	2,975,099
		Total	*FA Premier*	*Championship*	*Championship 1*	*Championship 2*
2004–05	2036	29,245,870	12,878,791	9,612,761	4,270,674	2,483,644
2005–06	2036	29,089,084	12,871,643	9,719,204	4,183,011	2,315,226
2006–07	2036	29,541,949	13,058,115	10,057,813	4,135,599	2,290,422
2007–08	2036	29,914,212	13,708,875	9,397,036	4,412,023	2,396,278

**Figures include matches played by Aldershot.*
Football League official total for their three divisions in 2001–02 was 14,716,162.

ENGLISH LEAGUE ATTENDANCES 2007–08

FA BARCLAYCARD PREMIERSHIP ATTENDANCES

	Average Gate			*Season 2007–08*	
	2006–07	2007–08	+/–%	Highest	Lowest
Arsenal	60,045	60,070	+0.04	60,161	59,442
Aston Villa	36,214	40,029	+10.53	42,640	32,288
Birmingham City	22,274	26,181	+17.54	29,252	22,089
Blackburn Rovers	21,275	23,944	+12.55	30,316	19,316
Bolton Wanderers	23,606	20,901	–11.46	25,414	17,014
Chelsea	41,542	41,397	–0.35	41,837	39,447
Derby County	25,945	32,432	+25.00	33,087	30,048
Everton	36,739	36,955	+0.59	40,049	31,885
Fulham	22,279	23,774	+6.71	25,357	20,774
Liverpool	43,563	43,532	–0.07	44,459	42,308
Manchester City	39,997	42,126	+5.32	47,321	38,261
Manchester United	75,826	75,691	–0.18	76,013	75,055
Middlesbrough	27,730	26,708	-3.69	33,952	22,920
Newcastle United	50,686	51,321	+1.25	52,307	49,948
Portsmouth	19,862	19,914	+0.26	20,556	17,108
Reading	23,829	23,585	–1.02	24,374	21,379
Sunderland	31,887	43,344	+35.93	47,802	37,369
Tottenham Hotspur	35,739	35,967	+0.64	36,178	35,504
West Ham United	34,719	34,601	–0.34	34,980	33,629
Wigan Athletic	18,159	19,046	+4.88	25,133	14,007

TOTAL ATTENDANCES: 13,708,875 (380 games)
Average 36,076 (+4.99%)

HIGHEST: 76,013 Manchester United v West Ham United
LOWEST: 14,007 Wigan Athletic v Middlesbrough
HIGHEST AVERAGE: 75,691 Manchester United
LOWEST AVERAGE: 19,046 Wigan Athletic

FOOTBALL LEAGUE: CHAMPIONSHIP ATTENDANCES

	Average Gate			*Season 2007–08*	
	2006–07	2007–08	+/–%	Highest	Lowest
Barnsley	12,733	11,425	–10.3	18,257	8,531
Blackpool	6,877	8,861	+28.8	9,640	7,214
Bristol City	12,818	16,276	+27.0	19,332	12,474
Burnley	11,956	12,365	+3.4	16,843	9,779
Cardiff City	15,219	13,939	–8.4	18,840	11,006
Charlton Athletic	26,195	23,191	–11.5	26,337	20,737
Colchester United	5,466	5,509	+0.8	6,300	4,450
Coventry City	20,342	19,123	–6.0	27,992	14,036
Crystal Palace	17,541	16,031	–8.6	23,950	13,048
Hull City	18,758	18,025	–3.9	24,350	14,822
Ipswich Town	22,445	21,935	–2.3	29,656	17,938
Leicester City	23,206	23,509	+1.3	31,892	19,264
Norwich City	24,545	24,527	–0.1	25,497	23,176
Plymouth Argyle	13,012	13,000	–0.1	17,511	10,451
Preston North End	14,430	12,647	–12.4	17,807	10,279
Queens Park Rangers	12,936	13,959	+7.9	18,309	10,514
Scunthorpe United	5,669	6,434	+13.5	8,801	4,407
Sheffield United	30,512	25,631	–16.0	31,760	23,161
Sheffield Wednesday	23,638	21,418	–9.4	36,208	17,211
Southampton	23,556	21,254	–9.8	31,957	17,741
Stoke City	15,749	16,823	+6.8	26,609	11,147
Watford	18,750	16,876	–10.0	18,698	15,021
West Bromwich Albion	20,472	22,311	+9.0	27,493	18,310
Wolverhampton Wanderers	20,968	23,499	+12.1	27,883	20,763

TOTAL ATTENDANCES: 9,397,036 (552 games)
Average 17,024 (–6.6%)

HIGHEST: 36,208 Sheffield Wednesday v Norwich City
LOWEST: 4,407 Scunthorpe United v Blackpool
HIGHEST AVERAGE: 25,631 Sheffield United
LOWEST AVERAGE: 5,509 Colchester United

Premiership and Football League attendance averages and highest crowd figures for 2007–08 are unofficial.

FOOTBALL LEAGUE: CHAMPIONSHIP 1 ATTENDANCES

	Average Gate 2006–07	2007–08	+/–%	*Season 2007–08* Highest	Lowest
AFC Bournemouth	6,028	5,504	–8.7	9,632	3,489
Brighton & Hove Albion	6,048	5,937	–1.8	8,691	4,395
Bristol Rovers	5,480	6,850	+25.0	11,883	3,933
Carlisle United	7,907	7,835	–0.9	16,668	5,477
Cheltenham Town	4,359	4,310	–1.1	7,043	3,169
Crewe Alexandra	5,462	4,932	–9.7	6,786	3,929
Doncaster Rovers	7,746	7,978	+3.0	15,001	5,967
Gillingham	6,282	6,077	–3.3	8,719	4,402
Hartlepool United	5,096	4,507	–11.6	7,784	3,217
Huddersfield Town	10,573	9,391	–11.2	16,413	6,004
Leeds United	21,613	26,543	+22.8	38,256	19,095
Leyton Orient	4,857	5,210	+7.3	7,602	3,082
Luton Town	8,580	6,492	–24.3	9,297	5,417
Millwall	9,234	8,691	–5.9	13,895	6,520
Northampton Town	5,573	5,409	–2.9	7,260	4,555
Nottingham Forest	20,612	19,964	–3.1	28,520	15,860
Oldham Athletic	6,334	5,326	–15.9	10,054	3,633
Port Vale	4,725	4,417	–6.5	7,908	2,869
Southend United	10,024	8,173	–18.5	9,828	6,844
Swansea City	12,720	13,520	+6.3	19,010	10,135
Swindon Town	7,419	7,170	–3.4	13,270	4,840
Tranmere Rovers	6,930	6,504	–6.1	11,008	5,006
Walsall	5,643	5,620	–0.4	10,102	4,309
Yeovil Town	5,765	5,468	–5.2	9,527	4,319

TOTAL ATTENDANCES:	4,412,023 (552 games) Average 7,993 (+6.7%)
HIGHEST:	38,256 Leeds United v Gillingham
LOWEST:	2,869 Port Vale v Yeovil Town
HIGHEST AVERAGE:	26,543 Leeds United
LOWEST AVERAGE:	4,310 Cheltenham Town

FOOTBALL LEAGUE: CHAMPIONSHIP 2 ATTENDANCES

	Average Gate 2006–07	2007–08	+/–%	*Season 2007–08* Highest	Lowest
Accrington Stanley	2,260	1,634	–27.7	2,898	1,149
Barnet	2,279	2,147	–5.8	3,074	1,303
Bradford City	8,694	13,659	+57.1	15,510	13,019
Brentford	5,600	4,469	–20.2	6,246	3,155
Bury	2,588	2,601	+0.5	6,271	1,690
Chester City	2,473	2,479	+0.2	3,849	1,566
Chesterfield	4,235	4,103	–3.1	6,300	3,274
Dagenham & Redbridge	1,756	2,007	+14.3	3,451	1,328
Darlington	3,814	3,818	+0.1	6,965	2,628
Grimsby Town	4,379	4,115	–6.0	5,829	2,537
Hereford United	3,328	3,421	+2.8	6,020	2,271
Lincoln City	5,176	4,078	–21.2	5,286	3,189
Macclesfield Town	2,863	2,298	–19.7	3,585	1,378
Mansfield Town	3,176	2,821	–11.2	5,271	1,606
Milton Keynes Dons	6,034	9,456	+56.7	17,250	6,483
Morecambe	1,598	2,812	+76.0	4,761	1,634
Notts County	4,974	4,732	–4.9	10,027	3,421
Peterborough United	4,662	5,995	+28.6	10,400	4,200
Rochdale	2,898	3,057	+5.5	4,692	2,278
Rotherham United	4,763	4,201	–11.8	6,709	2,979
Shrewsbury Town	4,730	5,659	+19.6	7,707	4,499
Stockport County	5,514	5,643	+2.3	8,838	4,477
Wrexham	5,030	4,234	–15.8	7,687	2,805
Wycombe Wanderers	4,983	4,747	–4.7	6,202	3,821

TOTAL ATTENDANCES:	2,396,278 (552 games) Average 4,341 (+4.6%)
HIGHEST:	17,250 Milton Keynes Dons v Morecambe
LOWEST:	1,149 Accrington Stanley v Brentford
HIGHEST AVERAGE:	13,659 Bradford City
LOWEST AVERAGE:	1,634 Accrington Stanley

LEAGUE CUP FINALISTS 1961–2008

Played as a two-leg final until 1966. All subsequent finals at Wembley until 2000, then at Millennium Stadium, Cardiff.

Year	*Winners*	*Runners-up*	*Score*
1961	Aston Villa	Rotherham U	0-2, 3-0 (aet)
1962	Norwich C	Rochdale	3-0, 1-0
1963	Birmingham C	Aston Villa	3-1, 0-0
1964	Leicester C	Stoke C	1-1, 3-2
1965	Chelsea	Leicester C	3-2, 0-0
1966	WBA	West Ham U	1-2, 4-1
1967	QPR	WBA	3-2
1968	Leeds U	Arsenal	1-0
1969	Swindon T	Arsenal	3-1 (aet)
1970	Manchester C	WBA	2-1 (aet)
1971	Tottenham H	Aston Villa	2-0
1972	Stoke C	Chelsea	2-1
1973	Tottenham H	Norwich C	1-0
1974	Wolverhampton W	Manchester C	2-1
1975	Aston Villa	Norwich C	1-0
1976	Manchester C	Newcastle U	2-1
1977	Aston Villa	Everton	0-0, 1-1 (aet), 3-2 (aet)
1978	Nottingham F	Liverpool	0-0 (aet), 1-0
1979	Nottingham F	Southampton	3-2
1980	Wolverhampton W	Nottingham F	1-0
1981	Liverpool	West Ham U	1-1 (aet), 2-1

MILK CUP

1982	Liverpool	Tottenham H	3-1 (aet)
1983	Liverpool	Manchester U	2-1 (aet)
1984	Liverpool	Everton	0-0 (aet), 1-0
1985	Norwich C	Sunderland	1-0
1986	Oxford U	QPR	3-0

LITTLEWOODS CUP

1987	Arsenal	Liverpool	2-1
1988	Luton T	Arsenal	3-2
1989	Nottingham F	Luton T	3-1
1990	Nottingham F	Oldham Ath	1-0

RUMBELOWS LEAGUE CUP

1991	Sheffield W	Manchester U	1-0
1992	Manchester U	Nottingham F	1-0

COCA-COLA CUP

1993	Arsenal	Sheffield W	2-1
1994	Aston Villa	Manchester U	3-1
1995	Liverpool	Bolton W	2-1
1996	Aston Villa	Leeds U	3-0
1997	Leicester C	Middlesbrough	1-1 (aet), 1-0 (aet)
1998	Chelsea	Middlesbrough	2-0 (aet)

WORTHINGTON CUP

1999	Tottenham H	Leicester C	1-0
2000	Leicester C	Tranmere R	2-1
2001	Liverpool	Birmingham C	1-1 (aet)
Liverpool won 5-4 on penalties			
2002	Blackburn R	Tottenham H	2-1
2003	Liverpool	Manchester U	2-0

CARLING CUP

2004	Middlesbrough	Bolton W	2-1
2005	Chelsea	Liverpool	3-2 (aet)
2006	Manchester U	Wigan Ath	4-0
2007	Chelsea	Arsenal	2-1
2008	Tottenham H	Chelsea	2-1 (aet)

LEAGUE CUP WINS

Liverpool 7, Aston Villa 5, Chelsea 4, Nottingham F 4, Tottenham H 4, Leicester C 3, Arsenal 2, Manchester C 2, Manchester U 2, Norwich C 2, Wolverhampton W 2, Birmingham C 1, Blackburn R 1, Leeds U 1, Luton T 1, Middlesbrough 1, Oxford U 1, QPR 1, Sheffield W 1, Stoke C 1, Swindon T 1, WBA 1.

APPEARANCES IN FINALS

Liverpool 10, Aston Villa 7, Arsenal 6, Chelsea 6, Manchester U 6, Nottingham F 6, Tottenham H 6, Leicester C 5, Norwich C 4, Manchester C 3, Middlesbrough 3, WBA 3, Birmingham C 2, Bolton W 2, Everton 2, Leeds U 2, Luton T 2, QPR 2, Sheffield W 2, Stoke C 2, West Ham U 2, Wolverhampton W 2, Blackburn R 1, Newcastle U 1, Oldham Ath 1, Oxford U 1, Rochdale 1, Rotherham U 1, Southampton 1, Sunderland 1, Swindon T 1, Tranmere R 1, Wigan Ath 1.

APPEARANCES IN SEMI-FINALS

Arsenal 13, Liverpool 13, Aston Villa 12, Tottenham H 12, Chelsea 10, Manchester U 10, West Ham U 7, Nottingham F 6, Blackburn R 5, Leeds U 5, Leicester C 5, Manchester C 5, Middlesbrough 5, Norwich C 5, Birmingham C 4, Bolton W 4, Everton 4, Sheffield W 4, WBA 4, Burnley 3, Crystal Palace 3, Ipswich T 3, QPR 3, Sunderland 3, Swindon T 3, Wolverhampton W 3, Bristol C 2, Coventry C 2, Luton T 2, Oxford U 2, Plymouth Arg 2, Southampton 2, Stoke C 2, Tranmere R 2, Watford 2, Wimbledon 2, Blackpool 1, Bury 1, Cardiff C 1, Carlisle U 1, Chester C 1, Derby Co 1, Huddersfield T 1, Newcastle U 1, Oldham Ath 1, Peterborough U 1, Rochdale 1, Rotherham U 1, Sheffield U 1, Shrewsbury T 1, Stockport Co 1, Walsall 1, Wigan Ath 1, Wycombe W 1.

CARLING CUP 2007–08

▪ *Denotes player sent off.*

FIRST ROUND

Monday, 13 August 2007

Peterborough U (2) 2 *(Rasiak 21 (og), Boyd 26)*
Southampton (1) 1 *(Rasiak 37)* 4087
Peterborough U: Jalal; Newton (Westwood), Day, Hyde, Morgan, Blackett, Whelpdale (Lee), Keates, Boyd (Crow), McLean, Low.
Southampton: Bialkowski; Wright J, Skacel, Bennett, Makin, Safri, Dyer, Licka (McGoldrick), Rasiak (Saganowski), Wright-Phillips, Surman (Vignal).

Tuesday, 14 August 2007

Accrington S (0) 0
Leicester C (1) 1 *(Wesolowski 4)* 2029
Accrington S: Arthur; Cavanagh, Richardson, Proctor, Williams, Roberts, Miles, Boco, McEvilly (Whalley), Mullin, Harris.
Leicester C: Henderson; Sheehan, Kenton (Stearman), N'Gotty, McAuley, Clemence, Kishishev, Campbell (Odhiambo), Hume (De Vries), Fryatt, Wesolowski.

Barnsley (0) 2 *(Ferenczi 65, Reid 77)*
Darlington (0) 1 *(Wright 70)* 3780
Barnsley: Muller; Kozluk (McCann), Souza, Reid, Nyatanga, Howard, Werling, Johnson (Togwell), Odejayi, Mostto (Ferenczi), Ricketts.
Darlington: Stockdale; Purdie, Brackstone, Ravenhill, White, Foster, Joachim, Palmer (Cummins), Wright, Abbott (Harty), McBride (Blundell).

Blackpool (0) 1 *(Burgess 75)*
Huddersfield T (0) 0 6395
Blackpool: Rachubka; Barker, Hills (Hoolahan), Fox, Jackson, Evatt (Gorkss), Taylor-Fletcher, Southern, Morrell, Parker (Burgess), Crainey.
Huddersfield T: Glennon; Sinclair (Hardy), Skarz, Collins, Mirfin, Clarke N, Worthington, Brandon, Kamara (Booth), Beckett, Schofield.

Brentford (0) 0
Bristol C (2) 3 *(Elliott 16, Jevons 42, 86)* 2213
Brentford: Hamer; O'Connor (Smith), Basey, Starosta, Mackie, Pettigrew, Brooker (Peters), Mousinho, Ide, Connell (Tillen), Moore.
Bristol C: Weale; Keogh, McAllister (Orr), Fontaine, Vasko, Russell, Murray, Elliott (Skuse), Jevons, Showunmi (Trundle), Betsy.

Bristol R (0) 1 *(Disley 64)*
Crystal Palace (1) 1 *(Freedman 31)* 5566
Bristol R: Phillips; Lescott, Carruthers, Campbell, Anthony, Elliott, Pipe (Rigg), Disley, Walker, Williams (Lambert), Haldane (Jacobson).
Crystal Palace: Flinders; Butterfield, Craig, Watson (Lawrence), Hudson, Fonte, Green (Grabban), Soares, Freedman, Kuqi, Martin (Morrison).
aet; Bristol R won 4-1 on penalties.

Bury (0) 0
Carlisle U (1) 1 *(Graham 12)* 2213
Bury: Provett; Parrish, Buchanan, Challinor, Morgan, Futcher, Scott, Barry-Murphy (Baker), Hurst (Mangan), Dean (Bishop), Adams.
Carlisle U: Westwood; Arnison, Aranalde, Thirlwell, Livesey, Raven, Gall, Bridge-Wilkinson, Garner (Carlton), Graham, Smith J (Hackney).

Cardiff C (0) 1 *(Johnson 110)*
Brighton & HA (0) 0 3726
Cardiff C: Turnbull; Gunter, Capaldi, Rae, Purse, Johnson, Whittingham (Ledley), McPhail, MacLean, Feeney (Green), Parry (Ramsey).
Brighton & HA: Kuipers; Whing, Lynch (Rents), Butters, Elphick, El-Abd, Cox, Hammond, Forster, Revell (Savage), Fraser (Reid).
aet.

Chester C (0) 0
Nottingham F (0) 0 2720
Chester C: Danby; Vaughan, Wilson, Grant (Roberts), Butler, Linwood, Hand, Hughes, Lowndes (Holroyd), Yeo, Ellison (Rutherford).
Nottingham F: Smith; Chambers, Bennett, Clingan, Morgan, Wilson, Lennon, Bastians (Thornhill), Dobie (Agogo), Holt (Sinclair), Commons.
aet; Nottingham F won 4-2 on penalties.

Coventry C (0) 3 *(Adebola 47, Best 67, Simpson 78)*
Notts Co (0) 0 6735
Coventry C: Marshall; Osbourne, Borrowdale, Doyle, Page, Hawkins, Cairo (Birchall), Hughes S, Adebola (Simpson), Best, Gray (Tabb).
Notts Co: Pilkington; Tann (Silk), McCann, Smith, Canoville, Hunt, Butcher, MacKenzie, Lee, Dudfield (Weir-Daley), Sam (Weston).

Dagenham & R (0) 1 *(Strevens 73)*
Luton T (1) 2 *(Spring 42 (pen), Talbot 68)* 1754
Dagenham & R: Roberts; Foster, Griffiths, Rainford (Huke), Uddin, Boardman, Saunders, Southam, Moore, Nurse (Strevens), Sloma.
Luton T: Brill; Jackson, Emanuel, Edwards, Coyne, Keane, Morgan (McVeigh), Hutchison, Talbot, Parkin (Furlong), Spring.

Doncaster R (1) 4 *(Hayter 23, Wellens 55, Heffernan 59, McCammon 73)*
Lincoln C (0) 1 *(Forrester 80)* 5084
Doncaster R: Sullivan; O'Connor, Roberts G (McDaid), Wilson, Lockwood, Greer, Coppinger (Guy), Wellens, Hayter, Heffernan (McCammon), Woods.
Lincoln C: Marriott; Amoo, Green, Brown, Moses, Kerr, Frecklington (Dodds), Wright (Warlow), Forrester, Torpey (Stallard), N'Guessan.

Grimsby T (0) 1 *(North 101)*
Burnley (0) 1 *(Gray 108)* 2431
Grimsby T: Barnes; Bennett, Newey, Hunt (Jones), Fenton, Whittle, Till (Bore), Bolland, Rankin (North), Toner, Boshell.
Burnley: Jensen; Duff, Jordan, Mahon, Foster, Unsworth (Harley), O'Connor J, Jones, Lafferty (Blake), Akinbiyi (Gray), Spicer.
aet; Burnley won 4-2 on penalties.

Hereford U (4) 4 *(Ainsworth 8, 24, 41, Easton 35)*
Yeovil T (0) 1 *(Owusu 50)* 2085
Hereford U: Brown; McClenahan, Rose, Diagouraga (Taylor), Beckwith, Broadhurst, Ainsworth (Johnson), Smith, Robinson, Benjamin (Guinan), Easton.
Yeovil T: Mildenhall; Lynch (Alcock), Jones N (Rose), Peltier, Guyett, Forbes, Williams (Cochrane), Barry, Owusu, Morris, Warne.

Macclesfield T (0) 0
Leeds U (0) 1 *(Westlake 78)* 3422
Macclesfield T: Lee; Regan, McIntyre, Edghill, Dimech, Dunfield, Murray (Wiles), Reid L, Husbands (Evans), Green, Thomas.
Leeds U: Ankergren; Gardner, Lewis, Howson, Heath, Parker, Prutton (Weston), Douglas, Elliott (Beckford), Kandol, Carole (Westlake).

Milton Keynes D (2) 3 *(Knight 16, Bruce 22 (og), Gallen 120 (pen))*
Ipswich T (1) 3 *(Lee 45 (pen), Garvan 98, Murphy 52 (og))* 7496
Milton Keynes D: Abbey; Stirling, Lewington, Howell (Gallen), O'Hanlon, Murphy, McGovern (Dyer), Wright, Knight, Wilbraham, Navarro (Edds).
Ipswich T: Alexander; Wright, Walters, Garvan, De Vos, Bruce, Miller, Harding, Lee (Legwinski), Counago (Clarke), Roberts (Haynes).
aet; Milton Keynes D won 5-3 on penalties.

Northampton T (1) 2 *(Bradley Johnson 38, Kirk 62)*
Millwall (0) 0 1735
Northampton T: Bunn; Crowe, Jackman (Jones), Hughes, Doig, Gilligan, Bradley Johnson, Henderson, Hubertz (Brett Johnson), Kirk (Larkin), Holt.
Millwall: Day; Senda, Frampton, Dunne, Robinson, Whitbread, Smith, Spiller, Alexander (Barron), May, Harris.

Norwich C (5) 5 *(Cureton 3, 16, Lappin 21, Fotheringham 25, Russell 31)*
Barnet (0) 2 *(Puncheon 66, Birchall 74)* 13,971
Norwich C: Marshall; Otsemobor, Drury (Martin), Shackell, Doherty, Russell, Croft, Fotheringham, Cureton (Dublin), Brown (Strihavka), Lappin.
Barnet: Harrison; Hendon (Porter), Nicolau, Carew, Devera, Burton, Bishop■, Leary (Seanla), Birchall, Thomas, Puncheon.

Oldham Ath (2) 4 *(Kilkenny 20, Kamudimba Kalala 27, Smalley 82, Davies 86)*
Mansfield T (0) 1 *(Mullins 72)* 3155
Oldham Ath: Crossley; Eardley, Giddings, Kilkenny (McDonald), Thompson, Gregan, Allott, Kamudimba Kalala (Taylor), Ricketts (Smalley), Davies, Liddell.
Mansfield T: Muggleton; Mullins, Jelleyman, Dawson, Buxton, McIntosh, Arnold, Bell, McAliskey (Boulding R), Boulding M, Martin (Sleath).

Plymouth Arg (2) 2 *(Bullock 41 (og), Hodges 45)*
Wycombe W (0) 1 *(Oakes 76)* 5474
Plymouth Arg: McCormick; Connolly, Sawyer, Laird, Timar, Seip, Reid (Dickson), Summerfield, Ebanks-Blake (Barnes), Chadwick (Fallon), Hodges.
Wycombe W: Shearer; Williams (McGleish), Woodman, Bloomfield, Johnson, McCracken, Bullock, Oakes, Sutton, Torres, Martin.

Port Vale (1) 1 *(Rodgers 33 (pen))*
Wrexham (1) 1 *(Proctor 10)* 2916
Port Vale: Anyon; McGregor, Talbot (Miles), Hulbert (Edwards), Pilkington, Lowe, Whitaker, Rocastle, Willock (Richards), Rodgers, Tudor.
Wrexham: Michael Jones; Spender, Valentine, Williams D (Murtagh), Hope, Pejic, Llewellyn, Mackin, Proctor (Johnson), Roberts (Marc Williams), Done.
aet; Wrexham won 5-3 on penalties.

Preston NE (0) 1 *(Pugh 73)*
Morecambe (1) 2 *(Bentley 6, Artell 84)* 7703
Preston NE: Henderson; Jones, Hill, Nicholls, St Ledger-Hall, Mawene, Whaley (Carroll), Carter (Sedgwick), Ormerod, Mellor (Hawley), Pugh.
Morecambe: Lewis; Yates, Adams, Stanley, Bentley, Artell, Thompson (Hunter), Sorvel, Twiss (Curtis), Baker, McLachlan (Burns).

QPR (0) 1 *(Rowlands 68)*
Leyton Orient (0) 2 *(Demetriou 55, Boyd 64 (pen))* 5260
QPR: Camp; Bignot (Curtis), Rehman (Stewart), Cullip, Mancienne, Bolder, Rowlands, Bailey, Nygaard, Moore (St Aimie), Ward.
Leyton Orient: Nelson; Thelwell, Demetriou, Chambers, Mkandawire, Palmer, Melligan (Daniels), Terry, Boyd (Echanomi), Gray, Corden.

Rochdale (0) 2 *(Perkins 83, Prendergast 101)*
Stoke C (1) 2 *(Shawcross 4, Cresswell 120)* 2369
Rochdale: Spencer; Ramsden, Kennedy, Jones, D'Laryea, McArdle, Muirhead, Perkins, Murray, Dagnall (Le Fondre), Rundle (Prendergast).
Stoke C: Hoult; Wright, Dickinson, Pulis, Shawcross, Higginbotham (Wilkinson), Eustace, Delap (Sweeney), Sidibe, Parkin (Cresswell), Lawrence.
aet; Rochdale won 4-2 on penalties.

Scunthorpe U (0) 1 *(Paterson 51)*
Hartlepool U (0) 2 *(Foley 70, 85)* 2965
Scunthorpe U: Lillis; Byrne, Williams, Youga, Iriekpen (Butler), Crosby, Taylor (Forte), Sparrow (Goodwin), Hayes, Paterson, Hurst.
Hartlepool U: Budtz; McCunnie (Gibb■), Robson, Liddle, Nelson, Antwi, Brown, Boland, Barker (Porter), Moore (Foley), Sweeney.

Sheffield U (2) 3 *(Stead 14, 45, Webber 56)*
Chesterfield (1) 1 *(Lester 16)* 11,170
Sheffield U: Kenny; Geary, Armstrong, Carney, Bromby, Kilgallon, Leigertwood, Tonge, Stead (Horsfield), Webber (Shelton), Naysmith (Quinn A).
Chesterfield: Roche; Picken, Robertson, Kovacs, Downes, Niven, Ward (Smith), Winter, Lester, Allison (Lowry), Leven.

Shrewsbury T (0) 1 *(Kempson 106)*
Colchester U (0) 0 3069
Shrewsbury T: Esson; Herd, Tierney, Drummond (Hunt), Kempson, Langmead, Humphrey, Ryan, Onibuje (Cooke) (Hibbert), Symes, Leslie.
Colchester U: Gerken; White (Webb), Granville, Jackson, Baldwin, Elokobi, Duguid, Guttridge (Izzet), Platt, Yeates, McLeod K (Wordsworth).
aet.

Southend U (1) 4 *(Bradbury 11, 108 (pen), 117, Barrett 104)*
Cheltenham T (0) 1 *(Finnigan 70)* 3084
Southend U: Collis; Gilbert (Hunt), Wilson, Bailey, Clarke P, Barrett, Campbell-Ryce, Moussa, Bradbury, Hooper (MacDonald), Gower (Black).
Cheltenham T: Higgs; Gill J, Ridley, Bird, Duff, Gallinagh, Lindegaard, Finnigan, Reid (Gill B), Connor (Vincent), Yao (Ledgister).
aet.

Stockport Co (0) 1 *(McNeil 84)*
Tranmere R (0) 0 3499
Stockport Co: Logan C; James Smith, Tierney, Taylor, Williams, Owen, Poole (Pilkington), Dicker (Blizzard), Elding, McNeil, Griffin (Dickinson).
Tranmere R: Coyne; Stockdale, Cansdell-Sherriff, Jennings, Chorley, Goodison, McLaren, Shuker (Curran), Davies, Greenacre (Taylor G), Zola.

Swansea C (1) 2 *(Anderson 22, Scotland 90)*
Walsall (0) 0 6943
Swansea C: De Vries; Austin, Painter, O'Leary, Tate, Monk, Britton (Scotland), Craney, Allen, Bauza (Duffy), Anderson (Robinson).
Walsall: Ince; Fox, Boertien, Dann, Gerrard, Dobson, Wrack, Sonner, Mooney, Carneiro (Nicholls), Hall.

Swindon T (0) 0
Charlton Ath (0) 2 *(Ambrose 52, Reid 63 (pen))* 6175
Swindon T: Brezovan; Smith J, Aljofree, Easton, Ifil, Tozer, Roberts (Pook), Adams, Sturrock (Arrieta), Peacock, Comminges (Zaaboub).
Charlton Ath: Weaver; Moutaouakil, Powell, Fortune, Bougherra, Semedo, Sam, Reid (Sinclair D), Bent (Iwelumo), McLeod (Dickson), Ambrose.

Watford (2) 3 *(Priskin 22, Rinaldi 36, Campana 71)*
Gillingham (0) 0 8166
Watford: Lee; Mariappa, Parkes (Forbes), Bangura, Jackson (Osborne), Avinel, Rinaldi, Kabba, Priskin (Campana), Hoskins, McNamee.
Gillingham: Royce; Southall, Armstrong, Stone, Sodje■, King, Bentley, Crofts, Mulligan (Facey), Graham (Pugh), Brown (Cogan).

WBA (1) 1 *(Beattie 22)*
Bournemouth (0) 0 10,250
WBA: Kiely; Hodgkiss, Robinson, Pele, Cesar, Albrechtsen, Teixeira (Worrall), Morrison, Ellington, Beattie (Nicholson), Greening.
Bournemouth: Moss; Pearce J, Cummings, Christophe, Young, Gowling, Gradel (Cooper), Anderton, Vokes, Osei-Kuffour (Pitman), O'Connor (Garry).

Wednesday, 15 August 2007

Crewe Alex (0) 0

Hull C (1) 3 *(Bridges 44, Garcia 55, McPhee 70)* 2862

Crewe Alex: Williams; Woodards, Jones B, Roberts GS, McCready, Baudet, Rix, Moore (Carrington), Miller, Pope, Schumacher (Bopp).
Hull C: Duke; Doyle, Delaney, Featherstone, Brown (Ricketts), Turner, Garcia (Marney), Livermore, Bridges (Ashbee), McPhee, Elliott.

Wolverhampton W (0) 2 *(Eastwood 46, Craddock 49)*

Bradford C (0) 1 *(Nix 77)* 9625

Wolverhampton W: Stack; Foley, Mulgrew (Clapham), Henry, Craddock, Edwards R, Kightly, Potter, Keogh, Eastwood, Bennett (Ward S).
Bradford C: Ricketts; Williams, Heckingbottom, Evans P, Wetherall, Bower, Colbeck, Johnson, Conlon (Ndumbu-Nsungu), Daley (Rhodes), Nix.

Thursday, 16 August 2007

Rotherham U (1) 1 *(Harrison D 34)*

Sheffield W (1) 3 *(Whelan 45, Burton 49, Small 55)* 6416

Rotherham U: Warrington; Tonge, Hurst, Harrison D, Sharps, Coughlan, Todd (Duncum), Holmes P, Holmes D (Newsham), O'Grady, Brogan (Joseph).
Sheffield W: Grant; Simek, Spurr, Whelan, Wood, Watson, Lunt, Small, Tudgay (Clarke), Burton, Johnson J.

SECOND ROUND

Tuesday, 28 August 2007

Birmingham C (2) 2 *(O'Connor 27, McSheffrey 38)*

Hereford U (0) 1 *(Robinson 74)* 10,185

Birmingham C: Kingson; Parnaby, Sadler, Nafti (Aluko), Kelly, Ridgewell, Larsson, Danns, Vine, O'Connor, McSheffrey.
Hereford U: Brown; McClenahan, Rose, Diagouraga, Beckwith, Broadhurst, Ainsworth, Smith (Taylor), Robinson, Benjamin (Guinan), Easton.

Bristol R (0) 1 *(Williams 72)*

West Ham U (2) 2 *(Bellamy 31, 45)* 10,831

Bristol R: Phillips; Lescott, Carruthers, Campbell, Anthony, Elliott, Pipe, Disley (Igoe), Walker, Lambert (Williams), Jacobson (Haldane).
West Ham U: Wright; Neill, McCartney (Collins), Gabbidon, Ferdinand, Mullins, Dyer (Noble), Bowyer, Zamora, Bellamy (Cole), Boa Morte.

Burnley (0) 3 *(Gray 59, Blake 76, Akinbiyi 90)*

Oldham Ath (0) 0 7317

Burnley: Jensen; Jordan, McCann, Gudjonsson (O'Connor J), Carlisle, Caldwell, Spicer, Jones (Mahon), Blake (Akinbiyi), Gray, Elliott.
Oldham Ath: Crossley; Eardley, Bertrand, McDonald, Thompson, Gregan, Smalley (Liddell), Kamudimba Kalala, Ricketts (Wolfenden), Davies, Taylor (Trotman).

Cardiff C (0) 1 *(Whittingham 90)*

Leyton Orient (0) 0 6150

Cardiff C: Turnbull; Gunter, Capaldi, Rae, Purse (Blake), Johnson, Parry, McPhail, Hasselbaink, Fowler (MacLean), Whittingham.
Leyton Orient: Nelson; Terry, Palmer, Demetriou, Mkandawire, Thelwell, Daniels, Thornton■, Melligan (Chambers), Gray, Echanomi (Boyd).

Carlisle U (0) 0

Coventry C (1) 2 *(Mifsud 21, 56)* 5744

Carlisle U: Westwood; Arnison, Aranalde, Thirlwell (McDermott), Livesey, Raven, Brittain, Lumsdon, Carlton, Graham (Gall), Hackney (Smith J).
Coventry C: Marshall; Borrowdale, Osbourne, Doyle, Page (Hall), Ward (Turner), Cairo, Hughes S, Adebola (Simpson), Mifsud, Tabb.

Charlton Ath (2) 4 *(Todorov 35, Zheng Zhi 42 (pen), Sam 74, McCarthy 90)*

Stockport Co (0) 3 *(Proudlock 54, Elding 62, Blizzard 69)* 8022

Charlton Ath: Randolph; Faye, Powell, Semedo, McCarthy, Fortune, Sam, Racon (Ambrose), Todorov, McLeod (Iwelumo), Zheng Zhi.
Stockport Co: Logan C; Bowler (Griffin), Tierney, Taylor, Williams, Owen, Proudlock, Blizzard, Elding, McNeil (Pilkington), Dicker.

Derby Co (0) 2 *(Camara 63, Fagan 101)*

Blackpool (0) 2 *(Gorkss 86, 120)* 8658

Derby Co: Bywater; Beardsley (Todd), McEveley, Jones, Moore, Leacock, Teale, Malcolm, Fagan, Earnshaw (Howard), Camara (Pearson).
Blackpool: Evans; Barker, Gorkss, Fox, Michael Jackson, Evatt, Forbes, Flynn (Southern), Vernon (Morrell), Parker, Hills (Hoolahan).
aet; Blackpool won 7-6 on penalties.

Luton T (2) 3 *(Bell 16, Furlong 43, 75)*

Sunderland (0) 0 4401

Luton T: Forde; Jackson (Keane), Goodall, Robinson, Coyne, Perry, Morgan (McVeigh), Bell, Furlong, Talbot (Andrew), Spring.
Sunderland: Ward; Halford■, Wallace, Miller, Nosworthy, Anderson, Leadbitter, Etuhu (O'Donovan), Stokes (Yorke), Chopra, Murphy (Connolly).

Milton Keynes D (1) 2 *(Broughton 12, McGovern 78)*

Sheffield U (1) 3 *(Lucketti 20, Law 55, Horsfield 104)* 7943

Milton Keynes D: Abbey; Edds (Wilbraham), Murphy, Carayol (Dyer), Diallo, Swailes, Stirling, Navarro, Broughton, Gallen (Wright), McGovern.
Sheffield U: Kenny; Geary, Kilgallon, Leigertwood, Lucketti, Morgan, Carney (Tonge), Law (Horsfield), Stead, Sharp (Shelton), Quinn A.
aet.

Nottingham F (0) 0

Leicester C (0) 0

abandoned due to injury to Clarke (Leicester C).

Peterborough U (0) 0

WBA (2) 2 *(Gera 33, Ellington 45)* 4917

Peterborough U: Jalal; Newton, Day, Strachan (Keates), Westwood, Blackett, Whelpdale (Potter), Lee, Crow, McLean, Low.
WBA: Kiely; Hodgkiss, Clement, Chaplow, Cesar, Albrechtsen, Gera, Teixeira (Koren), Beattie (Tininho), Ellington (MacDonald), Greening.

Plymouth Arg (1) 2 *(Ebanks-Blake 15, Summerfield 90)*

Doncaster R (0) 0 5133

Plymouth Arg: McCormick; Connolly, Hodges, Buzsaky (Summerfield), Timar, Seip, Norris, Abdou, Ebanks-Blake, Chadwick (Reid), Halmosi (Djordjic).
Doncaster R: Sullivan; O'Connor, Roberts G (Wilson), Lockwood, Mills, Woods, Guy (McCammon), Wellens, Hayter, Heffernan (Greer), McDaid.

Portsmouth (1) 3 *(Pamarot 43, 80, Nugent 84)*

Leeds U (0) 0 8502

Portsmouth: Ashdown; Cranie, Traore, Hughes (Mvuemba), Pamarot, Distin (Hreidarsson), Utaka, Pedro Mendes, Mwaruwari (O'Neil), Nugent, Kranjcar.
Leeds U: Ankergren; Richardson, Parker, Douglas (Delph), Heath, Rui Marques, Prutton (Bayly), Howson, Ameobi, Kandol (Beckford), Carole.

Rochdale (1) 1 *(Murray 9)*

Norwich C (0) 1 *(Dublin 49)* 2990

Rochdale: Spencer; Ramsden, Kennedy, Doolan, Branston, McArdle, Muirhead, Jones, Murray (Le Fondre), Dagnall, Rundle (Prendergast).
Norwich C: Marshall; Otsemobor, Murray (Chadwick), Shackell, Doherty, Russell, Martin, Brellier (Croft), Huckerby, Dublin (Brown), Lappin.
aet; Norwich C won 4-3 on penalties.

Sheffield W (0) 2 *(Burton 68, Folly 120)*
Hartlepool U (0) 1 *(Moore 55)* 8751
Sheffield W: Burch; Simek, Spurr, Whelan, Hinds, Wood, O'Brien (Boden), Johnson J, Tudgay (Bullen), Burton, Lunt (Folly).
Hartlepool U: Budtz; McCunnie, Humphreys, Liddle, Nelson, Antwi, Boland (Foley), Brown (Monkhouse), Barker, Moore (Porter), Robson.
aet.

Shrewsbury T (0) 0
Fulham (0) 1 *(Kamara 59)* 6223
Shrewsbury T: Esson; Moss, Tierney, Kempson, Murdock, Ryan, Humphrey, Hunt (Hall D), Hibbert (Onibuje), Symes, Leslie.
Fulham: Warner; Volz (Omozusi), Konchesky, Davis, Pearce, Bocanegra, Davies, Smertin, Kamara, Healy (John), Dempsey.

Southend U (1) 2 *(MacDonald 20, Harrold 55)*
Watford (0) 0 5554
Southend U: Flahavan; Francis, Hunt, Moussa (Hooper), Richards, Barrett, Bailey, McCormack (Lokando), Harrold, MacDonald, Black.
Watford: Lee; Mariappa, Parkes (O'Toole), Bangura, Jackson, Avinel, McNamee, Campana, Priskin, Hoskins, Rinaldi.

Swansea C (0) 0
Reading (0) 1 *(Lita 105)* 12,027
Swansea C: De Vries; Rangel, Austin, O'Leary (Duffy), Monk, Lawrence, Robinson (Britton), Craney, Bauza (Scotland), Allen, Anderson.
Reading: Federici; Halls (Golbourne), De la Cruz, Sodje■, Duberry, Harper, Convey (Cox), Cisse, Lita (Pearce), Kitson, Fae.
aet.

Wigan Ath (0) 0
Hull C (1) 1 *(Elliott 31)* 5440
Wigan Ath: Pollitt; Melchiot, Boyce (Koumas), Brown, Hall, Granqvist, Skoko, Cotterill, Folan, Camara (Aghahowa), Kilbane.
Hull C: Myhill; Dawson, Delaney, Hughes, Brown, Turner, Featherstone, Livermore (Ashbee), Bridges (Windass), McPhee (Marney), Elliott.

Wolverhampton W (0) 1 *(Keogh 84 (pen))*
Morecambe (0) 3 *(Baker 62 (pen), Newby 92, Thompson 105)* 11,296
Wolverhampton W: Stack; Foley, Edwards R, Bennett (Kightly), Henry, Gray, Collins N, Gleeson (Potter), Keogh, Eastwood, Mulgrew (Rosa).
Morecambe: Lewis; Yates, Adams, Artell, Bentley, Stanley, Baker, Sorvel (Newby), Twiss (Blinkhorn), Allen (Hunter), Thompson.
aet.

Wrexham (0) 0
Aston Villa (1) 5 *(Maloney 30, 72, Moore 52, Reo-Coker 62, Harewood 78)* 8221
Wrexham: Michael Jones; Spender, Valentine, Mackin, Evans S, Pejic, Mark Jones, Murtagh (Marc Williams), Williams E (Taylor), Proctor (Johnson), Llewellyn.
Aston Villa: Taylor; Gardner, Barry, Reo-Coker (Petrov), Mellberg, Cahill, Agbonlahor, Osbourne, Harewood, Moore, Maloney.

Wednesday, 29 August 2007
Bristol C (0) 1 *(Orr 69)*
Manchester C (1) 2 *(Mpenza 17, Bianchi 81)* 14,541
Bristol C: Weale; Orr (Jevons), McAllister, Johnson, Carey, Fontaine, Murray, Wilson (Sproule), Trundle, Elliott, McIndoe.
Manchester C: Hart; Jihai, Ball, Gelson, Corluka, Onuoha, Logan, Ireland, Bianchi (Dickov), Mpenza, Geovanni (Dabo).

Middlesbrough (0) 2 *(Rochemback 53, Lee 66)*
Northampton T (0) 0 11,686
Middlesbrough: Jones; Young (Boateng), Taylor, Johnson, Davies (Hines), Wheater, Rochemback, Cattermole, Tuncay, Lee, Downing (Mido).
Northampton T: Bunn; Crowe, Jones, Burnell (Aiston), Doig, Hughes, Dyer (Brett Johnson), Bradley Johnson, Hubertz, Henderson, Holt (Larkin).

Newcastle U (0) 2 *(Owen 57, Martins 86)*
Barnsley (0) 0 30,523
Newcastle U: Given; Jose Enrique, N'Zogbia, Smith (Edgar), Taylor, Cacapa, Solano, Geremi, Ameobi, Owen (Martins), Emre (Butt).
Barnsley: Muller; Kozluk, Werling, Souza, Nyatanga, Togwell, Devaney (Butterfield), Mattis (Coulson), Ricketts, Mostto (Christensen), McCann.

Tuesday, 18 September 2007
Nottingham F (1) 2 *(Smith 1, Tyson 64)*
Leicester C (1) 3 *(Sheehan 31, Stearman 88, Clemence 90)* 15,519
Nottingham F: Smith; Chambers, Bennett, Wilson, Morgan, Clingan, Lennon (Perch), Cohen, Agogo, Tyson (Holt), Commons.
Leicester C: Fulop; N'Gotty (Stearman), Sheehan, Clemence, McAuley, Kisnorbo, Wesolowski (Chambers J), Campbell (Fryatt), De Vries, Hume, Mattock.

THIRD ROUND

Tuesday, 25 September 2007
Arsenal (0) 2 *(Bendtner 83, Denilson 89)*
Newcastle U (0) 0 60,004
Arsenal: Fabianski; Hoyte J, Traore, Diarra, Senderos, Song Billong, Eboue (Diaby), Walcott, Denilson, Eduardo (Merida), Bendtner.
Newcastle U: Given; Beye, Jose Enrique, Diagne-Faye, Taylor, Rozehnal, Milner (Butt), Smith, Martins, Ameobi (Emre), N'Zogbia.

Blackpool (0) 2 *(Hoolahan 81, Jackson 118)*
Southend U (1) 1 *(Harrold 7 (pen))* 5022
Blackpool: Evans; Coid, Hills (Morrell), Fox, Barker, Gorkss, Taylor-Fletcher (Jackson), Flynn, Vernon, Parker (Hoolahan), Welsh.
Southend U: Collis; Hunt, Barrett, Maher, Clarke P, Richards, Black (Francis), Bailey, Harrold (Moussa), MacDonald (Foran), McCormack.
aet.

Burnley (0) 0
Portsmouth (0) 1 *(Nugent 69)* 8202
Burnley: Kiraly; Duff, Jordan, Unsworth (Blake), Carlisle, Caldwell, O'Connor J (Alexander), Mahon, Lafferty (Jones), Akinbiyi, Spicer.
Portsmouth: Ashdown; Lauren, Pamarot, Hughes, Traore, Distin, Mvuemba (Diop), Pedro Mendes, Mwaruwari (Utaka), Nugent, Taylor.

Luton T (1) 3 *(Robinson 43, Spring 105, Talbot 117)*
Charlton Ath (1) 1 *(Sinclair 4)* 4534
Luton T: Brill; Jackson, Goodall, Robinson, Fojut, Perry, Morgan (Currie), Bell (Brkovic), Furlong, McVeigh (Talbot), Spring.
Charlton Ath: Randolph; Moutaouakil, Sankofa, Holland, McCarthy, Bougherra, Ambrose (Fortune), Sinclair D, Todorov (Arter), McLeod, Racon (Varney).
aet.

Manchester C (0) 1 *(Samaras 90)*
Norwich C (0) 0 20,938
Manchester C: Hart; Logan, Ball, Dunne, Onuoha, Gelson (Etuhu), Ireland, Geovanni (Evans), Samaras, Bianchi, Jihai.
Norwich C: Marshall; Otsemobor, Lappin, Murray, Doherty, Russell, Croft, Rossi Jarvis, Brown, Cureton, Spillane.

Reading (1) 2 *(Convey 28, Halls 64)*
Liverpool (1) 4 *(Benayoun 23, Torres 50, 72, 86)* 23,563
Reading: Federici; Halls (Kitson), Shorey, Bikey, Duberry, Harper, De la Cruz, Convey (Hunt), Lita, Long (Henry), Fae.
Liverpool: Itandje; Finnan, Fabio Aurelio (Riise), Leto, Carragher, Arbeloa, Lucas (Hobbs), Sissoko, Torres, Crouch (Gerrard), Benayoun.

Sheffield U (2) 5 *(Sharp 18, 33, Shelton 52, 72, Hendrie 67)*
Morecambe (0) 0 8853
Sheffield U: Kenny; Geary (Bromby), Naysmith, Montgomery (Armstrong), Lucketti, Kilgallon, Quinn A, Hendrie (Tonge), Shelton, Sharp, Quinn S.
Morecambe: Lewis; Yates, Adams (Grand), Artell, Bentley, Stanley, Baker (Hunter), Sorvel (Thompson), Twiss (Newby), Blinkhorn, Allen.

WBA (1) 2 *(Miller 33, 87 (pen))*
Cardiff C (4) 4 *(Fowler 4, 27 (pen), Hasselbaink 23, Sinclair 30)* 14,085
WBA: Kiely; Hodgkiss, Tininho, Pele (Greening), Martis, Albrechtsen, Morrison, Chaplow (Teixeira), Beattie (MacDonald), Miller, Brunt.
Cardiff C: Oakes; McNaughton (Gunter), Capaldi, Rae, Johnson, Loovens, Ledley, McPhail, Hasselbaink, Fowler (Parry), Sinclair (Whittingham).

Wednesday, 26 September 2007
Aston Villa (0) 0
Leicester C (0) 1 *(Fryatt 76)* 25,956
Aston Villa: Taylor; Mellberg, Barry, Reo-Coker, Davies (Berger), Knight, Petrov, Osbourne (Young), Agbonlahor, Harewood (Moore), Maloney.
Leicester C: Fulop; N'Gotty, Chambers J, Clemence, McAuley, Kisnorbo, Kishishev (Maybury), Stearman, Hume (Campbell), Fryatt (Kenton), Mattock.

Blackburn R (0) 3 *(Bentley 66, Derbyshire 82 (pen), Santa Cruz 90)*
Birmingham C (0) 0 9205
Blackburn R: Friedel; Emerton, Olsson (Warnock), Tugay, Ooijer, Samba, Bentley, Dunn, Derbyshire (Rigters), Roberts (Santa Cruz), Mokoena.
Birmingham C: Kingson (Doyle); Parnaby, Sadler, Johnson, Martin Taylor, Jaidi (Schmitz), De Ridder (Palacios), Danns, Forssell, O'Connor, Vine.

Fulham (0) 1 *(Healy 78)*
Bolton W (0) 2 *(Guthrie 57, Giannakopoulos 112)* 10,500
Fulham: Keller; Baird (Healy), Konchesky, Davis, Hughes, Bocanegra, Seol, Murphy, Bouazza (Kamara), Dempsey, Davies.
Bolton W: Al-Habsi; Hunt, Cid, McCann, Michalik, Meite, Alonso, Wilhelmsson, Braaten (Giannakopoulos), Davies, Guthrie (Teimourian).
aet.

Hull C (0) 0
Chelsea (1) 4 *(Sinclair 37, Kalou 48, 81, Sidwell 52)* 23,543
Hull C: Myhill; Ricketts, Delaney (Dawson), Ashbee, Turner, Brown, Okocha, Livermore, McPhee, Elliott (Garcia), Pedersen (Featherstone).
Chelsea: Cudicini; Belletti, Cole A (Bridge), Essien (Makelele), Terry, Ben-Haim, Wright-Phillips (Cole J), Sidwell, Pizarro, Kalou, Sinclair.

Manchester U (0) 0
Coventry C (1) 2 *(Mifsud 27, 70)* 74,055
Manchester U: Kuszczak; Bardsley (Brown), Simpson, O'Shea, Pique, Evans (Carrick), Eagles, Martin (Campbell), Anderson, Dong, Nani.
Coventry C: Marshall; Osbourne (McNamee), Borrowdale, Hughes S, Turner, Ward, Simpson, Doyle, Best (Adebola), Mifsud, Tabb.

Sheffield W (0) 0
Everton (0) 3 *(McFadden 59, 84, Yakubu 85)* 16,463
Sheffield W: Grant; Simek, Gilbert, Whelan, Wood, Hinds, Small, Johnson J (Burton), Tudgay, Jeffers (Sodje), Kavanagh (Lunt).
Everton: Wessels; Hibbert (Neville), Nuno Valente (Baines), Jagielka, Lescott, Stubbs, Osman, Pienaar, Yakubu (Anichebe), McFadden, Carsley.

Tottenham H (0) 2 *(Bale 72, Huddlestone 75)*
Middlesbrough (0) 0 32,280
Tottenham H: Robinson; Chimbonda, Bale, Huddlestone, Kaboul, Dawson, Lennon, Jenas (Zokora), Berbatov, Defoe (Keane), Tainio.
Middlesbrough: Jones; Young (Davies), Taylor, Wheater, Riggott, Boateng, Rochemback (Owens), Cattermole, Lee, Shawky (Craddock), Downing.

West Ham U (0) 1 *(Ashton 90)*
Plymouth Arg (0) 0 25,774
West Ham U: Wright; Neill, McCartney, Mullins, Gabbidon, Collins, Ljungberg (Bowyer), Parker (Noble), Cole (Reid), Ashton, Boa Morte.
Plymouth Arg: McCormick; Connolly, Sawyer (Chadwick), Buzsaky, Timar, Seip, Norris, Nalis, Ebanks-Blake (Fallon), Hayles, Halmosi.

FOURTH ROUND

Tuesday, 30 October 2007
Coventry C (0) 1 *(Tabb 68)*
West Ham U (0) 2 *(Hall 71 (og), Cole 90)* 23,968
Coventry C: Marshall; McNamee, Hall, Doyle, Turner, De Zeeuw, Osbourne, Gray (Simpson), Best (Kyle), Mifsud, Tabb.
West Ham U: Wright; Neill, McCartney, Noble (Pantsil), Ferdinand (Gabbidon), Upson, Bowyer, Mullins (Spector), Cole, Boa Morte, Etherington.

Wednesday, 31 October 2007
Bolton W (0) 0
Manchester C (0) 1 *(Elano 86 (pen))* 15,510
Bolton W: Jaaskelainen; O'Brien J (Michalik), Samuel, McCann, O'Brien A (Campo), Meite, Nolan, Alonso, Diouf, Giannakopoulos (Braaten), Guthrie.
Manchester C: Isaksson; Corluka, Ball, Dunne, Richards (Onuoha), Johnson, Ireland, Hamann (Gelson), Elano, Samaras, Garrido (Vassell).

Chelsea (2) 4 *(Lampard 20, 29, 90, Shevchenko 87)*
Leicester C (1) 3 *(McAuley 6, Campbell 69, Cort 74)* 40,037
Chelsea: Cudicini; Belletti, Paulo Ferreira (Malouda), Sidwell, Ben Haim (Essien), Alex, Wright-Phillips, Lampard, Pizarro, Shevchenko, Sinclair (Kalou).
Leicester C: Fulop; Stearman, N'Gotty, Chambers J, McAuley, Kisnorbo, Kenton, Newton (Porter) (Maybury), Cort, Fryatt (Campbell), Sheehan.

Liverpool (0) 2 *(El Zhar 48, Gerrard 66)*
Cardiff C (0) 1 *(Purse 65)* 41,780
Liverpool: Itandje; Arbeloa, Fabio Aurelio, Lucas (Mascherano), Carragher, Hobbs, El Zhar (Kewell), Gerrard, Crouch, Leto (Benayoun), Babel.
Cardiff C: Oakes; McNaughton (Gunter), Capaldi, Rae, Purse, Johnson, Ledley, McPhail (Whittingham), Hasselbaink (Thompson), Fowler, Parry.

Luton T (0) 0
Everton (0) 1 *(Cahill 101)* 8944
Luton T: Brill; Goodall, Fojut, Robinson, Coyne, Perry, Currie (Morgan), Bell, Furlong (Andrew), Edwards (McVeigh), Spring.
Everton: Wessels; Lescott, Nuno Valente, Jagielka, Stubbs, Carsley, Osman, Neville, McFadden (Vaughan), Anichebe (Cahill), Pienaar (Gravesen).
aet.

Portsmouth (0) 1 *(Kanu 90)*
Blackburn R (1) 2 *(McCarthy 11, Pedersen 77)* 11,788
Portsmouth: James; Johnson, Pamarot (Nugent), Davis, Campbell, Distin, Kranjcar, Diop (Taylor), Mwaruwari (Kanu), Utaka, Pedro Mendes.

Blackburn R: Friedel; Mokoena (Emerton), Berner, Khizanishvili, Nelsen, Samba, Bentley (Derbyshire), Dunn, Santa Cruz, McCarthy (Treacy), Pedersen.

Sheffield U (0) 0

Arsenal (1) 3 *(Eduardo 8, 50, Denilson 69)* 16,971

Sheffield U: Bennett; Bromby, Armstrong, Montgomery, Lucketti, Morgan, Carney, Tonge (Gillespie), Stead (Quinn A), Sharp, Quinn S (Webber).
Arsenal: Fabianski; Hoyte J, Gibbs, Silva, Diarra, Song Bilong, Diaby (Perez), Denilson, Eduardo (Barazite), Bendtner, Walcott (Lansbury).

Tottenham H (1) 2 *(Keane 18, Chimbonda 58)*

Blackpool (0) 0 32,196

Tottenham H: Robinson; Chimbonda, Lee, Zokora, Kaboul (Tainio), Dawson, Lennon, Jenas, Berbatov (Bent), Keane (Defoe), Malbranque.
Blackpool: Rachubka; Barker, Crainey, Flynn (Welsh), Jackson (Coid), Gorkss, Taylor-Fletcher, Fox, Vernon (Morrell), Parker, Hoolahan.

QUARTER-FINALS

Wednesday, 12 December 2007

West Ham U (1) 1 *(Cole 12)*

Everton (1) 2 *(Osman 40, Yakubu 88)* 28,377

West Ham U: Green; Neill, McCartney, Mullins, Gabbidon, Upson, Ljungberg, Parker, Cole (Pantsil), Ashton, Boa Morte (Reid).
Everton: Howard; Neville, Lescott, Yobo, Jagielka, Carsley, Osman, Pienaar, Yakubu, Cahill, Arteta.

Tuesday, 18 December 2007

Blackburn R (1) 2 *(Santa Cruz 42, 60)*

Arsenal (2) 3 *(Diaby 6, Eduardo 29, 104)* 16,207

Blackburn R: Friedel; Reid, Warnock (Khizanishvili), Dunn (Mokoena), Nelsen, Samba, Bentley, Savage, Santa Cruz, Derbyshire (McCarthy), Pedersen.
Arsenal: Fabianski; Hoyte J, Traore, Denilson■, Senderos, Song Billong, Randall (Barazite) (Perez), Diarra, Eduardo (Gibbs), Bendtner, Diaby.
aet.

Manchester C (0) 0

Tottenham H (1) 2 *(Defoe 5, Malbranque 82)* 38,564

Manchester C: Hart; Corluka, Garrido (Ball), Dunne, Richards, Johnson, Vassell (Mpenza), Hamann (Geovanni), Elano, Bianchi, Petrov.
Tottenham H: Robinson; Chimbonda, Lee, Zokora■, Kaboul, Boateng, Lennon (O'Hara), Jenas, Berbatov, Defoe (Tainio), Malbranque (Huddlestone).

Wednesday, 19 December 2007

Chelsea (0) 2 *(Lampard 59, Shevchenko 90)*

Liverpool (0) 0 41,366

Chelsea: Cech; Belletti, Bridge, Mikel (Ballack), Ben Haim, Ricardo Carvalho, Essien, Lampard, Kalou, Shevchenko (Sidwell), Sinclair (Cole J).
Liverpool: Itandje; Arbeloa, Fabio Aurelio, Xabi Alonso (El Zhar), Carragher, Hobbs, Sissoko, Lucas, Crouch■, Voronin, Babel (Benayoun).

SEMI-FINALS FIRST LEG

Tuesday, 8 January 2008

Chelsea (1) 2 *(Wright-Phillips 26, Lescott 90 (og))*

Everton (0) 1 *(Yakubu 64)* 41,178

Chelsea: Hilario; Belletti, Bridge, Mikel■, Alex, Ricardo Carvalho, Wright-Phillips, Ballack, Pizarro (Paulo Ferreira), Cole J (Sidwell), Malouda (Ben-Haim).
Everton: Howard; Hibbert, Lescott, Yobo, Jagielka, Carsley, McFadden, Neville, Johnson, Yakubu (Anichebe), Cahill.

Wednesday, 9 January 2008

Arsenal (0) 1 *(Walcott 79)*

Tottenham H (1) 1 *(Jenas 37)* 53,136

Arsenal: Fabianski; Hoyte J, Traore, Silva, Djourou (Sagna), Senderos, Walcott (Randall), Denilson, Van Persie (Eduardo), Bendtner, Diaby.
Tottenham H: Cerny; Chimbonda, Lee, O'Hara, Dawson, King, Lennon, Jenas, Berbatov, Keane (Defoe), Malbranque (Boateng).

SEMI-FINALS SECOND LEG

Tuesday, 22 January 2008

Tottenham H (2) 5 *(Jenas 3, Bendtner 27 (og), Keane 48, Lennon 60, Malbranque 90)*

Arsenal (0) 1 *(Adebayor 70)* 35,979

Tottenham H: Cerny; Chimbonda, Lee, Tainio, Dawson, King, Lennon (Huddlestone), Jenas, Berbatov (Defoe), Keane (Boateng), Malbranque.
Arsenal: Fabianski; Sagna, Traore (Eduardo), Silva, Hoyte J, Gallas, Hleb, Denilson (Fabregas), Walcott (Adebayor), Bendtner, Diaby.

Wednesday, 23 January 2008

Everton (0) 0

Chelsea (0) 1 *(Cole J 69)* 37,086

Everton: Howard; Neville, Nuno Valente, Jagielka, Lescott, Carsley (Anichebe), Osman, Cahill, Johnson, Fernandes (Vaughan), Arteta.
Chelsea: Cech; Belletti, Bridge, Makelele, Alex, Ricardo Carvalho, Wright-Phillips, Sidwell, Anelka (Ben Haim), Cole J (Pizarro), Malouda (Cole A).

CARLING CUP FINAL

Sunday, 24 February 2008

(at Wembley Stadium, attendance 87,660)

Tottenham H (0) 2 **Chelsea (1) 1**

aet.

Tottenham H: Robinson; Hutton, Chimbonda (Huddlestone), Zokora, Woodgate, King, Lennon, Jenas, Berbatov, Keane (Kaboul), Malbranque (Tainio).

Scorers: Berbatov 70 (pen), Woodgate 94.

Chelsea: Cech; Belletti, Bridge, Mikel (Cole J), Terry, Ricardo Carvalho, Essien (Ballack), Lampard, Drogba, Anelka, Wright-Phillips (Kalou).

Scorer: Drogba 39.

Referee: M. Halsey (Lancashire).

JOHNSTONE'S PAINT TROPHY 2007–08

▪ *Denotes player sent off.*

NORTHERN SECTION FIRST ROUND

Tuesday, 4 September 2007

Accrington S (2) 2 *(D'Sane 8, Proctor 29 (pen))*
Oldham Ath (0) 3 *(Liddell 55, Davies 56, Wolfenden 73)* 1465

Accrington S: Dunbavin; Richardson, Edwards, Proctor, Williams, Roberts, Miles (McGrail), Boco (Whalley), Brown, Mullin, D'Sane (McGivern).
Oldham Ath: Crossley; Thompson, Bertrand, McDonald (Lomax), Trotman, Gregan, Allott, Kamudimba Kalala (Wolfenden), Liddell, Davies, Taylor.

Chester C (0) 1 *(Partridge 61)*
Crewe Alex (1) 1 *(Lowe 37)* 2126

Chester C: Danby (Ward); Vaughan, Wilson, Hughes, Butler, Linwood, Partridge, Grant (Roberts), Murphy, Yeo (Lowndes), Ellison.
Crewe Alex: Tomlinson; Woodards (Lynch), Jones B, Schumacher, O'Donnell, Baudet, Lowe, Bopp, Pope (Miller), Farquharson (Carrington), Rix.
Chester C won 4-3 on penalties.

Chesterfield (0) 1 *(Allison 72)*
Hartlepool U (1) 3 *(Foley 34, Brown 51, 59)* 2127

Chesterfield: Roche; Picken (Law), Robertson, Jackson (Algar), Kovacs, Niven, Gray, Winter (O'Hare), Allison, Rooney, Lowry.
Hartlepool U: Budtz; Nelson, Clark, Liddle, Brown (McCunnie), Antwi, Humphreys, Gibb, Barker (Mackay), Porter, Robson (Foley).

Doncaster R (3) 5 *(McCammon 16, 41, Guy 24, Woods 64, Harban 78 (og))*
Bradford C (0) 1 *(Nix 70)* 4710

Doncaster R: Sullivan (Smith); O'Connor (Hird), Roberts G, Woods, Mills, Roberts S, Green, Guy, Heffernan, McCammon (Dyer), McDaid.
Bradford C: Saynor; Harban, Heckingbottom, Phelan (Joynes), Clarke, Ainge (O'Brien), Colbeck, Bentham, Conlon (Thorne), Nix, Taylforth.

Grimsby T (1) 4 *(Fenton 45, Toner 49, Rankin 53, Till 68)*
Huddersfield T (1) 1 *(Collins 45)* 1204

Grimsby T: Barnes; Mulligan, Newey, Hunt, Fenton, Whittle, Till (Bore), Boshell (Clarke), Rankin (North), Taylor, Toner.
Huddersfield T: Glennon; Hardy, Skarz, Holdsworth, Keogh, Clarke N (Clarke T), Brandon, Collins, Kamara, Beckett (Akins), Schofield (Young).

Mansfield T (0) 0
Rotherham U (0) 1 *(Sharps 49)* 1578

Mansfield T: Muggleton; Wood, Jelleyman, Dawson (Martin), Buxton, Mullins, Hamshaw (Boulding R), Holmes, McAliskey (Reet), Arnold, Sleath.
Rotherham U: Warrington; Joseph (Duncum), Tonge, Harrison D, Sharps (Hurst), Coughlan, Taylor (Todd), Bean, Holmes D, Newsham, Brogan.

Tranmere R (0) 0
Morecambe (0) 1 *(Burns 55)* 2557

Tranmere R: Achterberg; Stockdale (Goodison), Tremarco, Jennings, Chorley, Kay, Ahmed, Shuker (Jones), Curran, Greenacre, Davies.
Morecambe: Drench; Yates (Langford), Howard, Burns, Grand, Artell, Hunter, Allen, Blinkhorn, Newby, Twiss (Lloyd).

Tuesday, 18 September 2007

Wrexham (0) 0
Macclesfield T (0) 1 *(Husbands 67 (pen))* 1503

Wrexham: Williams A; Mike Williams (Pejic), Valentine (Marc Williams), Spann, Evans S, Hope, Crowell, Carvill, Williams E (Proctor▪), Llewellyn▪, Done.
Macclesfield T: Brain; Regan, Jennings (Flynn), Hadfield, Morley, McNulty, Wiles, Reid L, Gritton (Evans), Husbands, Thomas (Reid I).

SOUTHERN SECTION FIRST ROUND

Monday, 3 September 2007

Notts Co (0) 0
Leyton Orient (1) 1 *(Echanomi 43)* 900

Notts Co: Sandercombe; Silk, McCann, Hunt, Tann, Somner, Smith, MacKenzie (Parkinson), Weir-Daley (Frost), Dudfield (Sam), Mayo.
Leyton Orient: Morris; Thelwell, Daniels, Chambers, Mkandawire, Oji, Melligan (Terry), Thornton, Boyd, Echanomi, Demetriou.

Tuesday, 4 September 2007

Bournemouth (2) 2 *(Bradbury 3, 8)*
Walsall (0) 0 2206

Bournemouth: Begovic; Young, Cummings, Telfer, Perrett, Gowling, O'Connor (Pitman), Anderton (Hollands), Bradbury, Osei-Kuffour, Gradel.
Walsall: Ince; Weston, Boertien (McDermott), Fox, Roper, Gerrard, Hall (Deeney), Carneiro (Nicholls), Butler, Demontagnac, Wrack.

Luton T (1) 2 *(Hutchison 12, Peschisolido 48)*
Northampton T (0) 0 2532

Luton T: Brill; Keane, Goodall, Robinson, Fojut, Perry, Hutchison, Bell (McVeigh), Talbot (Peschisolido), Andrew (Morgan), Brkovic.
Northampton T: Bunn; Hughes, May, Jones, Doig (Crowe), Dolman, Bradley Johnson, Dyer (Gilligan), Hubertz (Kirk), Larkin, Russell.

Nottingham F (1) 2 *(Chambers 33, 49)*
Peterborough U (0) 3 *(Lee 48, Chambers 51 (og), Boyd 72)* 3102

Nottingham F: Smith; Chambers, Bennett, Power (Lennon), Breckin, Morgan, Perch, Bastians, Agogo (Sinclair), Tyson, Commons.
Peterborough U: Tyler; Newton, Day, Westwood, Blackett, Charnock, Low, Hyde, Boyd, McLean, Lee (Strachan).

Southend U (1) 2 *(Foran 20, McCormack 60)*
Dagenham & R (0) 2 *(Saunders 48, Moore 85)* 5215

Southend U: Collis; Hunt, Barrett, Bailey, Clarke P, Richards, Black, McCormack, Harrold (MacDonald), Odhiambo (Hooper), Foran.
Dagenham & R: Roberts; Huke, Griffiths, Rainford, Uddin (Smith), Okuonghae, Saunders, Southam, Benson (Nurse), Taylor (Moore), Sloma.
Dagenham & R won 7-6 on penalties.

Swansea C (1) 3 *(Anderson 16, Scotland 64, Whitbread 78 (og))*
Millwall (1) 2 *(May 20, Simpson 53)* 5721

Swansea C: De Vries; Rangel (Amankwaah), Austin, O'Leary, Monk, Lawrence, Anderson, Craney (Pratley), Bauza (Scotland), Duffy, Butler.
Millwall: Day (Edwards); Senda, Frampton, Dunne (Kilbey), Robinson, Whitbread, Barron, O'Hara▪, May (Alexander), Simpson, Hackett.

Swindon T (2) 4 *(Arrieta 26, Cox 42, Blackburn 68, 81)*
Brentford (1) 1 *(Shakes 11)* 3118

Swindon T: Brezovan; Tozer, Almeida, Allen, Kennedy, Blackburn, McGovern (Macklin), Adams, Cox, Arrieta (Mohamed), Comminges.
Brentford: Simon Brown; O'Connor, Osborne, Basey, Pettigrew, Heywood (Pead), Shakes, Smith (Ide), Moore, Connell, Poole (Peters).

Yeovil T (0) 1 *(Owusu 53)*
Shrewsbury T (0) 0 1669
Yeovil T: Mildenhall; Alcock, Jones N, Peltier (Knights), Guyett, Forbes, Barry, Warne, Owusu (Rose), Stewart, Jones R.
Shrewsbury T: MacKenzie; Moss (Herd), Tierney (Leslie), Ryan, Kempson, Langmead, Humphrey, Hall D, Nicholson, Symes, Ashton.

NORTHERN SECTION SECOND ROUND

Tuesday, 9 October 2007

Carlisle U (2) 4 *(Gall 11, 53, Bridge-Wilkinson 37, Graham 54)*
Chester C (1) 2 *(Partridge 19, Holroyd 70)* 3154
Carlisle U: Westwood; Arnison, Aranalde, Anyinsah (Hackney), Livesey, Raven, Lumsdon, Bridge-Wilkinson, Graham (Carlton), Gall, Smith J.
Chester C: Danby; Marples, Sandwith, Dinning, Bolland, Linwood, Partridge (Rutherford), Hughes (Holroyd), McManus, Yeo, Wilson (Rule).

Darlington (0) 0
Leeds U (0) 1 *(Huntington 48)* 7891
Darlington: Oakes; Purdie, Ryan, Ravenhill (Cummins), Foster, White, Joachim, Keltie, Blundell, Wright (Green), Barrau (Wainwright).
Leeds U: Lucas; Richardson, Parker, Howson, Huntington, Heath (Clapham), Weston, Thompson (Da Costa), De Vries, Andrews (Ameobi), Westlake.

Lincoln C (1) 2 *(Stallard 4 (pen), 77)*
Hartlepool U (1) 5 *(Porter 28, 50, 75, Mackay 69, Moore 71)* 936
Lincoln C: Marriott; Amoo, Green (Wright), Bencherif, Beevers, Kerr, Hand (N'Guessan), Warlow (Forrester), Stallard, Ryan, Frecklington.
Hartlepool U: Lee-Barrett; McCunnie, Elliott, Clark, Antwi, Liddle (Gibb), Sweeney, Robson, Barker (Porter), Moore, Brown (Mackay).

Macclesfield T (0) 0
Stockport Co (0) 1 *(Tierney 59)* 2248
Macclesfield T: Brain; Reid I (Jennings), McNulty, Morley, Dimech, Hadfield, Wiles, Reid L, Gritton, Green (Evans), McIntyre.
Stockport Co: Logan C; Bowler, Tierney, Taylor, Williams, Owen (Raynes), Thompson (Rowe), Turnbull, Elding (Proudlock), Dickinson, Pilkington.

Morecambe (0) 2 *(Hunter 48, Newby 61)*
Port Vale (2) 2 *(Miller 5, Rodgers 30)* 1644
Morecambe: Drench; Yates (Burns), Howard, Artell, Grand, Sorvel, Hunter, Curtis, Blinkhorn (Jarvis), Newby, Twiss (Lloyd).
Port Vale: Anyon; Miller, Richards (Glover), Hulbert, Pilkington, Westwood, Tudor, Rocastle, Rodgers, McGoldrick (Willock), Edwards.
Morecambe won 4-2 on penalties.

Rochdale (1) 1 *(Prendergast 45)*
Bury (0) 3 *(Hurst 57, 84, Rouse 82)* 2376
Rochdale: Russell; Ramsden (Doolan), Kennedy, Jones, Branston, Holness, Prendergast, Perkins, Murray, Le Fondre (Higginbotham), Rundle (Thompson).
Bury: Provett; Anane (Scott), Parrish, Adams, Challinor, Haslam, Baker, Barry-Murphy, Hurst (Dorney), Dean (Rouse), Buchanan.

Rotherham U (1) 1 *(O'Grady 18)*
Grimsby T (0) 1 *(Till 50)* 2362
Rotherham U: Annerson; Tonge, Hurst, Harrison D, Sharps, Cresswell, Yates (Cahill), Holmes P (Brogan), Newsham, O'Grady (Holmes D), Bean.
Grimsby T: Barnes; Bennett, Newey, Bolland, Fenton, Whittle, Till, Clarke (Jones), North (Taylor), Toner, Boshell.
Grimsby T won 4-2 on penalties.

Tuesday, 23 October 2007

Doncaster R (0) 3 *(Price 54, Green 74, Woods 87)*
Oldham Ath (0) 0 4608
Doncaster R: Sullivan; O'Connor, Roberts G (Woods), Mills, Greer, Stock, Green, Wellens (Roberts S), Price (Hayter), Guy, McDaid.
Oldham Ath: Beresford; Eardley, Bertrand, Kilkenny, Hazell, Gregan (Thompson), Allott, Kamudimba Kalala, Ricketts (Wolfenden), Davies, Taylor (Smalley).

SOUTHERN SECTION SECOND ROUND

Tuesday, 9 October 2007

Brighton & HA (1) 2 *(Robinson 21, Cox 47)*
Barnet (0) 1 *(Birchall 74)* 1995
Brighton & HA: Kuipers; Whing, Richards, O'Callaghan (Fraser), Elphick, El-Abd, Cox (Martot), Hammond, Savage, Revell (Elder), Robinson.
Barnet: Harrison; Devera (Seanla), Nicolau, Bishop, O'Cearuill, Burton, Carew (Thomas), Porter, Norville (Hatch), Birchall, Puncheon.

Bristol R (0) 0
Bournemouth (0) 1 *(Osei-Kuffour 49)* 3313
Bristol R: Phillips; Green, Carruthers, Campbell, Hinton, Anthony (Elliott), Pipe (Haldane), Lines, Williams, Lambert (Walker), Rigg.
Bournemouth: Moss; Telfer, Pearce J, Hollands, Wilson, Lallana (Pitman) (O'Connor), Cooper, Anderton, Bradbury, Osei-Kuffour (Newman), Vokes.

Gillingham (1) 4 *(Dickson 17, 74, 80, Bentley 88)*
Luton T (3) 3 *(Furlong 26, 43, Spring 45 (pen))* 1417
Gillingham: Stillie; Jupp, Armstrong, Stone, Sodje, King, Southall, Bentley, Mulligan (Nowland), Dickson, Cogan (Graham).
Luton T: Brill; Jackson, Emanuel, Hutchison (O'Leary), Fojut, Perry, Edwards (Brkovic), McVeigh, Furlong, Andrew (Talbot), Spring.

Hereford U (0) 0
Yeovil T (0) 0 1859
Hereford U: Ingham; McClenahan, Rose (Smith), Diagouraga (Gwynne), Beckwith, McCombe, Webb, Taylor, Johnson, Benjamin, Easton (Robinson).
Yeovil T: Larrieu; Lynch, Jones N (Alcock), Rose (Jones R), Guyett, Forbes, Barry, Warne (Gillett), Owusu, Stewart, Betsy.
Yeovil T won 4-2 on penalties.

Leyton Orient (0) 0
Dagenham & R (0) 1 *(Strevens 74)* 2397
Leyton Orient: Morris; Terry, Palmer, Chambers (Purches), Oji, Saah, Melligan (Daniels), Demetriou, Ibehre, Gray (Echanomi), Corden.
Dagenham & R: Roberts; Huke, Griffiths, Rainford, Smith, Boardman, Taiwo (Graham), Southam, Taylor (Moore), Strevens, Sloma.

Milton Keynes D (1) 3 *(Wright 25, 52, Cameron 85)*
Peterborough U (1) 1 *(McLean 16)* 5087
Milton Keynes D: Gueret; Stirling, Lewington, Howell (Edds), O'Hanlon, Swailes, Cameron, Wright (Carayol), Broughton (Taylor), Johnson, Smart.
Peterborough U: Jalal; Blanchett, Hyde (Lee), Gnapka, Westwood, Charnock, Whelpdale (Day), Strachan, Boyd, McLean (Mackail-Smith), Howe.

Swansea C (2) 2 *(Bauza 29, Anderson 33)*
Wycombe W (0) 0 5922
Swansea C: De Vries; Amankwaah, Austin, Bodde (Allen), Monk, Painter (Lawrence), O'Leary, Pratley (Feeney), Anderson, Bauza, Orlandi.
Wycombe W: Kazimierczak; Antwi, Martin (Duncan), Williams, Johnson (Christon), McCracken, Bloomfield, Boucaud, Sutton, Reid, Woodman.

Swindon T (0) 1 *(Sturrock 56)*

Cheltenham T (2) 3 *(Myrie-Williams 21, Reid 24, Tozer 68 (og))* 3765

Swindon T: Brezovan; Adams, Mohamed (Roberts), Easton (Allen), Blackburn, Tozer, McGovern, Pook (Cox), Sturrock, Comminges, Zaaboub.
Cheltenham T: Higgs; Gallinagh, Wright, Bird, Duff, Townsend, Connolly (Gill B), Sinclair, Connor (Caines), Reid, Myrie-Williams (Yao).

NORTHERN QUARTER-FINALS

Tuesday, 13 November 2007

Carlisle U (0) 0

Stockport Co (0) 3 *(Proudlock 49, McNeil 68, Elding 74)* 3395

Carlisle U: Westwood; Raven, Aranalde (Hackney), Anyinsah (Gall), Livesey, Murphy, Lumsdon, Bridge-Wilkinson, Graham, Carlton (Garner), Smith J.
Stockport Co: Logan C; Bowler, Griffin, Briggs (Rowe), Raynes, Tansey (Rose), Turnbull, Dickinson, Elding, McNeil, Proudlock.

Grimsby T (2) 2 *(Boshell 13, Mills 44 (og))*

Doncaster R (1) 2 *(Guy 25, Heffernan 79 (pen))* 4011

Grimsby T: Barnes; Clarke (Bore), Hegarty, Hunt, Fenton, Bennett, Till (Whittle), Bolland, North, Jones (Jarman), Boshell.
Doncaster R: Smith; Roberts S (McCammon), Hird (Nelthorpe), Greer, Mills, Green, Woods, Wilson, Coppinger (Wellens), Heffernan, Guy.
Grimsby T won 5-4 on penalties.

Hartlepool U (1) 1 *(Barker 13)*

Morecambe (0) 1 *(Newby 48 (pen))* 2776

Hartlepool U: Budtz; McCunnie, Humphreys, Boland (Gibb), Nelson, Antwi, Moore, Sweeney, Barker, Mackay (Porter), Robson (Foley).
Morecambe: Davies; Yates, Adams (Grand), Artell, Lloyd, Burns, Howard, Allen, Twiss, Newby, Hunter.
Morecambe won 4-2 on penalties.

Leeds U (1) 1 *(Constantine 8)*

Bury (2) 2 *(Futcher 24, Bishop 29)* 18,809

Leeds U: Lucas; Madden, Parker, Howson, Huntington, Rui Marques, Prutton (Douglas), Da Costa■, De Vries (Heath), Constantine, Carole (Kandol).
Bury: Provett; Scott, Parrish, Futcher, Challinor, Haslam, Adams (Baker), Woodthorpe, Bishop (Mangan), Barry-Murphy, Buchanan (Hurst).

SOUTHERN QUARTER-FINALS

Tuesday, 13 November 2007

Bournemouth (0) 0

Milton Keynes D (2) 2 *(Andrews 6 (pen), Swailes 14)* 3247

Bournemouth: Moss (Stewart); Telfer, Golbourne, Hollands, Pearce A, Gowling, Cooper, Pitman (McQuoid), Vokes, Osei-Kuffour, Karacan.
Milton Keynes D: Gueret; Diallo, Lewington, Andrews, O'Hanlon, Swailes, Wright, Navarro, Gallen (Cameron), Wilbraham (Broughton), Johnson (Smart).

Gillingham (2) 4 *(Armstrong 17, Brown 29, Dickson 60 (pen), Oli 70)*

Dagenham & R (0) 0 2904

Gillingham: Stillie; Clohessy, Armstrong, Stone, Cox, King, Howard (Bentley), Brown, Cogan (Freeman), Dickson, Hamilton (Oli).
Dagenham & R: Roberts; Huke, Griffiths, Rainford■, Uddin, Boardman, Taiwo, Southam, Benson (Taylor), Strevens (Nurse), Moore (Sloma).

Swansea C (1) 1 *(Bauza 41)*

Yeovil T (0) 0 6644

Swansea C: De Vries; Amankwaah, Austin, Allen, Monk, Tate, Orlandi, Pratley, Bauza (Bodde), Duffy (Scotland), Anderson (Butler).
Yeovil T: Mildenhall; Alcock, Jones N, Peltier, Skiverton, Forbes, Barry (Maher), Walker, Owusu, Stewart (Domoraud) (Hughes), Dempsey.

Wednesday, 14 November 2007

Brighton & HA (2) 4 *(Martot 13, Forster 37, 87, Savage 90)*

Cheltenham T (1) 1 *(Connor 45)* 2490

Brighton & HA: Kuipers; Lynch, Richards, O'Callaghan (Whing), Butters, El-Abd, Cox, Fraser (Hammond), Forster, Elder (Savage), Martot.
Cheltenham T: Higgs; Gill J (Gallinagh), Wylde, Bird, Ridley, Caines, Connolly (Gill B), Sinclair, Gillespie, Connor, Spencer (Vincent).

NORTHERN SEMI-FINALS

Tuesday, 8 January 2008

Morecambe (1) 2 *(Blinkhorn 10, Newby 90)*

Bury (0) 0 2434

Morecambe: Loach; Yates, Adams (Howard), Grand, Bentley, Stanley, Thompson, Drummond, Twiss, Blinkhorn (Newby), Curtis.
Bury: Provett; Parrish, Haslam (Dorney), Adams, Challinor, Futcher, Barry-Murphy, Woodthorpe, Hurst (Mangan), Bishop, Buchanan.

Stockport Co (0) 1 *(Pilkington 61)*

Grimsby T (0) 2 *(Clarke 59, Raynes 79 (og))* 3679

Stockport Co: Logan C; James Smith (Taylor), Rose, Dicker, Raynes, Tunnicliffe, Poole (McSweeney), Turnbull, Elding, Dickinson, Pilkington.
Grimsby T: Barnes; Bennett, Newey, Hunt, Fenton, Atkinson, Clarke, Bolland, North, Jones, Hegarty.

SOUTHERN SEMI-FINALS

Tuesday, 8 January 2008

Gillingham (0) 1 *(Stone 84)*

Milton Keynes D (0) 1 *(Johnson 85)* 3717

Gillingham: Royce; Clohessy, Nutter, Stone, King, Bygrave, Southall, Cogan (Howard), Mulligan, Facey (Griffiths), Brown (Cumbers).
Milton Keynes D: Gueret; Stirling, Lewington, Howell, O'Hanlon, Diallo, Johnson, Navarro, Broughton, Baldock (Taylor), Wright.
Milton Keynes Dons won 5-4 on penalties.

Swansea C (1) 1 *(Duffy 9)*

Brighton & HA (0) 0 6066

Swansea C: De Vries; Rangel, Painter, O'Leary, Monk, Lawrence, Orlandi, Allen (Britton), Duffy (Pratley), Bauza, Anderson (Butler).
Brighton & HA: Kuipers; Lynch (Rents), Fogden, Loft (Hart), Elphick, El-Abd, Cox, Fraser, Forster, Revell (Elder), Martot.

SOUTHERN FINAL FIRST LEG

Tuesday, 19 February 2008

Swansea C (0) 0

Milton Keynes D (0) 1 *(Johnson 69)* 10,125

Swansea C: De Vries; Rangel, Painter, O'Leary, Tate, Monk, Robinson (Butler), Way, Brandy, Bauza (Duffy), Anderson (MacDonald).
Milton Keynes D: Gueret; Diallo, Lewington, Andrews, O'Hanlon, Swailes, Cameron (Stirling), Navarro, Gallen (Carbon), Johnson, Dyer (Baldock).

SOUTHERN FINAL SECOND LEG

Monday, 25 February 2008

Milton Keynes D (0) 0

Swansea C (1) 1 *(Scotland 20 (pen))* 9757

Milton Keynes D: Gueret; Diallo (Broughton), Lewington, Andrews, O'Hanlon, Swailes, Cameron (Stirling), Navarro, Johnson, Gallen, Dyer.
Swansea C: De Vries; Rangel, Painter (Austin), Way, Tate, Monk, Butler (MacDonald), Pratley, Scotland, Brandy (Duffy), Robinson.
Milton Keynes D won 5-4 on penalties.

NORTHERN FINAL FIRST LEG

Tuesday, 26 February 2008

Morecambe (0) 0

Grimsby T (0) 1 *(Bolland 69)* 3207

Morecambe: Davies; Yates, Adams, Artell, McStay, Stanley, Baker, Thompson, Twiss (Newby), Blinkhorn (Curtis), Hunter.

Grimsby T: Barnes; Atkinson, Bennett, Boshell, Fenton, Newey, Hegarty, Bolland, North (Jones), Till, Clarke.

NORTHERN FINAL SECOND LEG

Tuesday, 4 March 2008

Grimsby T (0) 0

Morecambe (0) 0 7417

Grimsby T: Barnes; Atkinson, Newey, Hunt, Fenton, Boshell, Hegarty, Bolland, North (Bore), Till (Jones), Clarke.

Morecambe: Davies; Yates, Adams, Artell, Bentley, Stanley, Baker (Twiss), Sorvel, Blinkhorn (Curtis), Thompson, Hunter (Drummond).

JOHNSTONE'S PAINT TROPHY FINAL

Sunday, 30 March 2008

(at Wembley Stadium, attendance 56,618)

Grimsby T (0) 0 Milton Keynes D (0) 2

Grimsby T: Barnes; Clarke, Newey, Hunt (Toner), Fenton, Atkinson, Hegarty, Bolland, North (Bore), Till (Jones), Boshell.

Milton Keynes D: Gueret; Stirling, Lewington, Andrews, O'Hanlon, Swailes, Cameron (Baldock), Navarro, Gallen (Wilbraham), Johnson (Wright), Dyer.

Scorers: Andrews 74 (pen), O'Hanlon 81.

Referee: P. Joslin (Nottinghamshire).

FOOTBALL LEAGUE COMPETITION ATTENDANCES

LEAGUE CUP ATTENDANCES

Season	*Attendances*	*Games*	*Average*
1960–61	1,204,580	112	10,755
1961–62	1,030,534	104	9,909
1962–63	1,029,893	102	10,097
1963–64	945,265	104	9,089
1964–65	962,802	98	9,825
1965–66	1,205,876	106	11,376
1966–67	1,394,553	118	11,818
1967–68	1,671,326	110	15,194
1968–69	2,064,647	118	17,497
1969–70	2,299,819	122	18,851
1970–71	2,035,315	116	17,546
1971–72	2,397,154	123	19,489
1972–73	1,935,474	120	16,129
1973–74	1,722,629	132	13,050
1974–75	1,901,094	127	14,969
1975–76	1,841,735	140	13,155
1976–77	2,236,636	147	15,215
1977–78	2,038,295	148	13,772
1978–79	1,825,643	139	13,134
1979–80	2,322,866	169	13,745
1980–81	2,051,576	161	12,743
1981–82	1,880,682	161	11,681
1982–83	1,679,756	160	10,498
1983–84	1,900,491	168	11,312
1984–85	1,876,429	167	11,236
1985–86	1,579,916	163	9,693
1986–87	1,531,498	157	9,755
1987–88	1,539,253	158	9,742
1988–89	1,552,780	162	9,585
1989–90	1,836,916	168	10,934
1990–91	1,675,496	159	10,538
1991–92	1,622,337	164	9,892
1992–93	1,558,031	161	9,677
1993–94	1,744,120	163	10,700
1994–95	1,530,478	157	9,748
1995–96	1,776,060	162	10,963
1996–97	1,529,321	163	9,382
1997–98	1,484,297	153	9,701
1998–99	1,555,856	153	10,169
1999–2000	1,354,233	153	8,851
2000–01	1,501,304	154	9,749
2001–02	1,076,390	93	11,574
2002-03	1,242,478	92	13,505
2003-04	1,267,729	93	13,631
2004-05	1,313,693	93	14,216
2005-06	1,072,362	93	11,531
2006-07	1,098,403	93	11,811
2007-08	1,332,841	94	14,179

CARLING CUP 2007–08

Round	*Aggregate*	*Games*	*Average*
One	178,543	36	4,960
Two	220,574	25	8,823
Three	362,977	16	22,686
Four	191,194	8	23,899
Quarter-finals	124,514	4	31,129
Semi-finals	167,379	4	41,845
Final	87,660	1	87,660
Total	1,332,841	94	14,179

JOHNSTONE'S PAINT TROPHY 2007–08

Round	*Aggregate*	*Games*	*Average*
One	41,733	16	2,608
Two	50,974	16	3,186
Area Quarter-finals	44,276	8	5,535
Area Semi-finals	15,896	4	3,974
Area finals	30,506	4	7,627
Final	56,618	1	56,618
Total	240,003	49	4,898

FA CUP FINALS 1872–2008

1872 and 1874–92	Kennington Oval	1911	Replay at Old Trafford
1873	Lillie Bridge	1912	Replay at Bramall Lane
1886	Replay at Derby (Racecourse Ground)	1915	Old Trafford, Manchester
1893	Fallowfield, Manchester	1920–22	Stamford Bridge
1894	Everton	1923–2000	Wembley
1895–1914	Crystal Palace	1970	Replay at Old Trafford
1901	Replay at Bolton	2001–2006	Millennium Stadium, Cardiff
1910	Replay at Everton	2007 to date	Wembley

Year	*Winners*	*Runners-up*	*Score*
1872	Wanderers	Royal Engineers	1-0
1873	Wanderers	Oxford University	2-0
1874	Oxford University	Royal Engineers	2-0
1875	Royal Engineers	Old Etonians	2-0 (after 1-1 draw aet)
1876	Wanderers	Old Etonians	3-0 (after 1-1 draw aet)
1877	Wanderers	Oxford University	2-1 (aet)
1878	Wanderers*	Royal Engineers	3-1
1879	Old Etonians	Clapham R	1-0
1880	Clapham R	Oxford University	1-0
1881	Old Carthusians	Old Etonians	3-0
1882	Old Etonians	Blackburn R	1-0
1883	Blackburn Olympic	Old Etonians	2-1 (aet)
1884	Blackburn R	Queen's Park, Glasgow	2-1
1885	Blackburn R	Queen's Park, Glasgow	2-0
1886	Blackburn R†	WBA	2-0 (after 0-0 draw)
1887	Aston Villa	WBA	2-0
1888	WBA	Preston NE	2-1
1889	Preston NE	Wolverhampton W	3-0
1890	Blackburn R	The Wednesday	6-1
1891	Blackburn R	Notts Co	3-1
1892	WBA	Aston Villa	3-0
1893	Wolverhampton W	Everton	1-0
1894	Notts Co	Bolton W	4-1
1895	Aston Villa	WBA	1-0
1896	The Wednesday	Wolverhampton W	2-1
1897	Aston Villa	Everton	3-2
1898	Nottingham F	Derby Co	3-1
1899	Sheffield U	Derby Co	4-1
1900	Bury	Southampton	4-0
1901	Tottenham H	Sheffield U	3-1 (after 2-2 draw)
1902	Sheffield U	Southampton	2-1 (after 1-1 draw)
1903	Bury	Derby Co	6-0
1904	Manchester C	Bolton W	1-0
1905	Aston Villa	Newcastle U	2-0
1906	Everton	Newcastle U	1-0
1907	The Wednesday	Everton	2-1
1908	Wolverhampton W	Newcastle U	3-1
1909	Manchester U	Bristol C	1-0
1910	Newcastle U	Barnsley	2-0 (after 1-1 draw)
1911	Bradford C	Newcastle U	1-0 (after 0-0 draw)
1912	Barnsley	WBA	1-0 (aet, after 0-0 draw)
1913	Aston Villa	Sunderland	1-0
1914	Burnley	Liverpool	1-0
1915	Sheffield U	Chelsea	3-0
1920	Aston Villa	Huddersfield T	1-0 (aet)
1921	Tottenham H	Wolverhampton W	1-0
1922	Huddersfield T	Preston NE	1-0
1923	Bolton W	West Ham U	2-0
1924	Newcastle U	Aston Villa	2-0
1925	Sheffield U	Cardiff C	1-0
1926	Bolton W	Manchester C	1-0
1927	Cardiff C	Arsenal	1-0
1928	Blackburn R	Huddersfield T	3-1
1929	Bolton W	Portsmouth	2-0
1930	Arsenal	Huddersfield T	2-0
1931	WBA	Birmingham	2-1
1932	Newcastle U	Arsenal	2-1
1933	Everton	Manchester C	3-0
1934	Manchester C	Portsmouth	2-1
1935	Sheffield W	WBA	4-2

Year	*Winners*	*Runners-up*	*Score*
1936	Arsenal	Sheffield U	1-0
1937	Sunderland	Preston NE	3-1
1938	Preston NE	Huddersfield T	1-0 (aet)
1939	Portsmouth	Wolverhampton W	4-1
1946	Derby Co	Charlton Ath	4-1 (aet)
1947	Charlton Ath	Burnley	1-0 (aet)
1948	Manchester U	Blackpool	4-2
1949	Wolverhampton W	Leicester C	3-1
1950	Arsenal	Liverpool	2-0
1951	Newcastle U	Blackpool	2-0
1952	Newcastle U	Arsenal	1-0
1953	Blackpool	Bolton W	4-3
1954	WBA	Preston NE	3-2
1955	Newcastle U	Manchester C	3-1
1956	Manchester C	Birmingham C	3-1
1957	Aston Villa	Manchester U	2-1
1958	Bolton W	Manchester U	2-0
1959	Nottingham F	Luton T	2-1
1960	Wolverhampton W	Blackburn R	3-0
1961	Tottenham H	Leicester C	2-0
1962	Tottenham H	Burnley	3-1
1963	Manchester U	Leicester C	3-1
1964	West Ham U	Preston NE	3-2
1965	Liverpool	Leeds U	2-1 (aet)
1966	Everton	Sheffield W	3-2
1967	Tottenham H	Chelsea	2-1
1968	WBA	Everton	1-0 (aet)
1969	Manchester C	Leicester C	1-0
1970	Chelsea	Leeds U	2-1 (aet)
	(after 2-2 draw, after extra time)		
1971	Arsenal	Liverpool	2-1 (aet)
1972	Leeds U	Arsenal	1-0
1973	Sunderland	Leeds U	1-0
1974	Liverpool	Newcastle U	3-0
1975	West Ham U	Fulham	2-0
1976	Southampton	Manchester U	1-0
1977	Manchester U	Liverpool	2-1
1978	Ipswich T	Arsenal	1-0
1979	Arsenal	Manchester U	3-2
1980	West Ham U	Arsenal	1-0
1981	Tottenham H	Manchester C	3-2
	(after 1-1 draw, after extra time)		
1982	Tottenham H	QPR	1-0
	(after 1-1 draw, after extra time)		
1983	Manchester U	Brighton & HA	4-0
	(after 2-2 draw, after extra time)		
1984	Everton	Watford	2-0
1985	Manchester U	Everton	1-0 (aet)
1986	Liverpool	Everton	3-1
1987	Coventry C	Tottenham H	3-2 (aet)
1988	Wimbledon	Liverpool	1-0
1989	Liverpool	Everton	3-2 (aet)
1990	Manchester U	Crystal Palace	1-0
	(after 3-3 draw, after extra time)		
1991	Tottenham H	Nottingham F	2-1 (aet)
1992	Liverpool	Sunderland	2-0
1993	Arsenal	Sheffield W	2-1 (aet)
	(after 1-1 draw, after extra time)		
1994	Manchester U	Chelsea	4-0
1995	Everton	Manchester U	1-0
1996	Manchester U	Liverpool	1-0
1997	Chelsea	Middlesbrough	2-0
1998	Arsenal	Newcastle U	2-0
1999	Manchester U	Newcastle U	2-0
2000	Chelsea	Aston Villa	1-0
2001	Liverpool	Arsenal	2-1
2002	Arsenal	Chelsea	2-0
2003	Arsenal	Southampton	1-0
2004	Manchester U	Millwall	3-0
2005	Arsenal	Manchester U	0-0 (aet)
	(Arsenal won 5-4 on penalties)		
2006	Liverpool	West Ham U	3-3 (aet)
	(Liverpool won 3-1 on penalties)		
2007	Chelsea	Manchester U	1-0 (aet)
2008	Portsmouth	Cardiff C	1-0

** Won outright, but restored to the Football Association. † A special trophy was awarded for third consecutive win.*

FA CUP WINS

Manchester U 11, Arsenal 10, Tottenham H 8, Aston Villa 7, Liverpool 7, Blackburn R 6, Newcastle U 6, Everton 5, The Wanderers 5, WBA 5, Bolton W 4, Chelsea 4, Manchester C 4, Sheffield U 4, Wolverhampton W 4, Sheffield W 3, West Ham U 3, Bury 2, Nottingham F 2, Old Etonians 2, Portsmouth 2, Preston NE 2, Sunderland 2, Barnsley 1, Blackburn Olympic 1, Blackpool 1, Bradford C 1, Burnley 1, Cardiff C 1, Charlton Ath 1, Clapham R 1, Coventry C 1, Derby Co 1, Huddersfield T 1, Ipswich T 1, Leeds U 1, Notts Co 1, Old Carthusians 1, Oxford University 1, Royal Engineers 1, Southampton 1, Wimbledon 1.

APPEARANCES IN FINALS

Manchester U 18, Arsenal 17, Liverpool 13, Newcastle U 13, Everton 12, Aston Villa 10, WBA 10, Tottenham H 9, Blackburn R 8, Chelsea 8, Manchester C 8, Wolverhampton W 8, Bolton W 7, Preston NE 7, Old Etonians 6, Sheffield U 6, Sheffield W 6, Huddersfield T 5, *The Wanderers 5, West Ham U 5, Derby Co 4, Leeds U 4, Leicester C 4, Oxford University 4, Portsmouth 4, Royal Engineers 4, Southampton 4, Sunderland 4, Blackpool 3, Burnley 3, Cardiff C 3, Nottingham F 3, Barnsley 2, Birmingham C 2, *Bury 2, Charlton Ath 2, Clapham R 2, Notts Co 2, Queen's Park (Glasgow) 2, *Blackburn Olympic 1, *Bradford C 1, Brighton & HA 1, Bristol C 1, *Coventry C 1, Crystal Palace 1, Fulham 1, *Ipswich T 1, Luton T 4, Middlesbrough 1, Millwall 1, *Old Carthusians 1, QPR 1, Watford 1, *Wimbledon 1.
* *Denotes undefeated.*

APPEARANCES IN SEMI-FINALS

Arsenal 25, Manchester U 25, Everton 23, Liverpool 22, WBA 20, Aston Villa 19, Blackburn R 18, Chelsea 17, Newcastle U 17, Tottenham H 17, Sheffield W 16, Wolverhampton W 14, Bolton W 13, Derby Co 13, Sheffield U 13, Nottingham F 12, Sunderland 12, Southampton 11, Manchester C 10, Preston NE 10, Birmingham C 9, Burnley 8, Leeds U 8, Leicester C 8, Huddersfield T 7, West Ham U 7, Old Etonians 6, Fulham 6, Oxford University 6, Portsmouth 6, Notts Co 5, The Wanderers 5, Watford 5, Cardiff C 4, Luton T 4, Millwall 4, Queen's Park (Glasgow) 4, Royal Engineers 4, Barnsley 3, Blackpool 3, Clapham R 3, Crystal Palace (professional club) 3, Ipswich T 3, Middlesbrough 3, Norwich C 3, Old Carthusians 3, Oldham Ath 3, Stoke C 3, The Swifts 3, Blackburn Olympic 2, Bristol C 2, Bury 2, Charlton Ath 2, Grimsby T 2, Swansea T 2, Swindon T 2, Wimbledon 2, Bradford C 1, Brighton & HA 1, Cambridge University 1, Chesterfield 1, Coventry C 1, Crewe Alex 1, Crystal Palace (amateur club) 1, Darwen 1, Derby Junction 1, Glasgow R 1, Hull C 1, Marlow 1, Old Harrovians 1, Orient 1, Plymouth Arg 1, Port Vale 1, QPR 1, Reading 1, Shropshire W 1, Wycombe W 1, York C 1.

FA CUP ATTENDANCES 1969–2008

	1st Round	*2nd Round*	*3rd Round*	*4th Round*	*5th Round*	*6th Round*	*Semi-finals & Final*	*Total*	*No. of matches*	*Average per match*
2007–08	175,195	99,528	704,300	356,404	276,903	142,780	256,210	2,011,320	152	13,232
2006–07	168,884	113,924	708,628	478,924	340,612	230,064	177,810	2,218,846	158	14,043
2005–06	188,876	107,456	654,570	388,339	286,225	163,449	177,723	1,966,638	160	12,291
2004–05	161,197	98,702	602,152	477,472	339,082	127,914	193,233	1,999,752	146	13,697
2003–04	162,738	117,967	624,732	347,964	292,521	156,780	167,401	1,870,103	149	12,551
2002–03	189,905	104,103	577,494	404,599	242,483	156,244	175,498	1,850,326	150	12,336
2001–02	198,369	119,781	566,284	330,434	249,190	173,757	171,278	1,809,093	148	12,224
2000–01	171,689	122,061	577,204	398,241	256,899	100,663	177,778	1,804,535	151	11,951
1999–2000	181,485	127,728	514,030	374,795	182,511	105,443	214,921	1,700,913	158	10,765
1998–99	191,954	132,341	609,486	431,613	359,398	181,005	202,150	2,107,947	155	13,599
1997–98	204,803	130,261	629,127	455,557	341,290	192,651	172,007	2,125,696	165	12,883
1996–97	209,521	122,324	651,139	402,293	199,873	67,035	191,813	1,843,998	151	12,211
1995–96	185,538	115,669	748,997	391,218	274,055	174,142	156,500	2,046,199	167	12,252
1994–95	219,511	125,629	640,017	438,596	257,650	159,787	174,059	2,015,249	161	12,517
1993–94	190,683	118,031	691,064	430,234	172,196	134,705	228,233	1,965,146	159	12,359
1992–93	241,968	174,702	612,494	377,211	198,379	149,675	293,241	2,047,670	161	12,718
1991–92	231,940	117,078	586,014	372,576	270,537	155,603	201,592	1,935,340	160	12,095
1990–91	194,195	121,450	594,592	530,279	276,112	124,826	196,434	2,038,518	162	12,583
1989–90	209,542	133,483	683,047	412,483	351,423	123,065	277,420	2,190,463	170	12,885
1988–89	212,775	121,326	690,199	421,255	206,781	176,629	167,353	1,966,318	164	12,173
1987–88	204,411	104,561	720,121	443,133	281,461	119,313	177,585	2,050,585	155	13,229
1986–87	209,290	146,761	593,520	349,342	263,550	119,396	195,533	1,877,400	165	11,378
1985–86	171,142	130,034	486,838	495,526	311,833	184,262	192,316	1,971,951	168	11,738
1984–85	174,604	137,078	616,229	320,772	269,232	148,690	242,754	1,909,359	157	12,162
1983–84	192,276	151,647	625,965	417,298	181,832	185,382	187,000	1,941,400	166	11,695
1982–83	191,312	150,046	670,503	452,688	260,069	193,845	291,162	2,209,625	154	14,348
1981–82	236,220	127,300	513,185	356,987	203,334	124,308	279,621	1,840,955	160	11,506
1980–81	246,824	194,502	832,578	534,402	320,530	288,714	339,250	2,756,800	169	16,312
1979–80	267,121	204,759	804,701	507,725	364,039	157,530	355,541	2,661,416	163	16,328
1978–79	243,773	185,343	880,345	537,748	243,683	263,213	249,897	2,604,002	166	15,687
1977–78	258,248	178,930	881,406	540,164	400,751	137,059	198,020	2,594,578	160	16,216
1976–77	379,230	192,159	942,523	631,265	373,330	205,379	258,216	2,982,102	174	17,139
1975–76	255,533	178,099	867,880	573,843	471,925	206,851	205,810	2,759,941	161	17,142
1974–75	283,956	170,466	914,994	646,434	393,323	268,361	291,369	2,968,903	172	17,261
1973–74	214,236	125,295	840,142	747,909	346,012	233,307	273,051	2,779,952	167	16,646
1972–73	259,432	169,114	938,741	735,825	357,386	241,934	226,543	2,928,975	160	18,306
1971–72	277,726	236,127	986,094	711,399	486,378	230,292	248,546	3,158,562	160	19,741
1970–71	329,687	230,942	956,683	757,852	360,687	304,937	279,644	3,220,432	162	19,879
1969–70	345,229	195,102	925,930	651,374	319,893	198,537	390,700	3,026,765	170	17,805

THE FA CUP 2007–08

PRELIMINARY AND QUALIFYING ROUNDS

EXTRA PRELIMINARY ROUND

Guisborough Town v Norton & Stockton Ancients 1-3
West Auckland Town v Bedlington Terriers 2-1
Winterton Rangers v Armthorpe Welfare 3-2
Glasshoughton Welfare v Liversedge 1-1, 3-4
Horden CW v Sunderland Nissan 2-1
Thackley v Ashington 0-1
Darlington Railway Athletic v Yorkshire Amateur 6-0
Whitley Bay v Dunston Federation 0-1
Hall Road Rangers v Tadcaster Albion 6-1
Spennymoor Town v North Shields 3-0
Hebburn Town v Tow Law Town 1-3
Crook Town v Sunderland RCA 2-2, 3-0
Morpeth Town v Seaham Red Star 3-0
Pontefract Collieries v Selby Town 0-0, 0-1
Thornaby v South Shields 2-3
Jarrow Roofing Boldon CA v West Allotment Celtic 2-1
Brandon United v Durham City 0-5
Washington v Pickering Town 1-3
Esh Winning v Whickham 1-0
Ryton v Silsden 3-4
Billingham Synthonia v Northallerton Town 2-1
Bottesford Town v Shildon 1-2
Team Northumbria v Consett 0-11
Chester-Le-Street Town v Bishop Auckland 1-1, 2-1
Ashton Town v Ramsbottom United 4-2
Daisy Hill v Congleton Town 0-4
Rossington Main v Atherton Collieries 2-2, 0-5
Chadderton v Winsford United 3-4
Holker Old Boys v St Helens Town 2-3
Blackpool Mechanics v Maine Road 1-3
Formby v Oldham Town 2-3
Squires Gate v Penrith Town 1-3
Flixton v Bootle 2-1
Trafford v Atherton LR 1-0
Hallam v Nelson 2-0
Salford City v Padiham 6-3
Abbey Hey v Bacup Borough 1-2
Brodsworth MW v Parkgate 2-3
Glossop North End v Eccleshall 2-0
Highgate United v Shirebrook Town 2-1
Castle Vale v Brierly Hill & Withymoor 3-3, 0-4
Loughborough Dynamo v Stapenhill 1-1, 2-1
Tividale v Mickleover Sports 1-4
Nuneaton Griff v Rainworth MW 0-3
Pegasus Juniors v New Mills 0-0, 1-5
Glapwell v Dudley Town 2-2, 5-0
Shifnal Town v Arnold Town 1-1, 1-1
Shifnal Town won 6-5 on penalties.
Ledbury Town v Boldmere St Michaels 2-6
Oadby Town v Racing Club Warwick 1-0
Teversal v Coventry Sphinx 2-2, 2-2
Teversal won 6-5 on penalties.
Market Drayton Town v Studley 1-1, 4-0
Long Eaton United v Bridgnorth Town 2-1
Coalville Town v Rocester 1-2
Gornal Athletic v Meir KA 0-3
Norton United v Oldbury United 1-1, 0-1
Westfields v Friar Lane & Epworth 3-2
Borrowash Victoria v Biddulph Victoria 0-1
Cradley Town v Gedling Town 1-3
Cadbury Athletic v Alvechurch 1-1, 0-6
South Normanton Athletic v Lye Town 1-0
Barwell v Newcastle Town 1-1, 2-1
Tipton Town v Leek CSOB 1-1, 4-0
Colesville Town v Wellington 1-1, 2-3
Wroxham v Hadleigh United 3-0
Walsham Le Willows v Stowmarket Town 3-0
St Ives Town v Cornard United 3-2
Bourne Town v Haverhill Rovers 2-3
Mildenhall Town v Leiston 3-0
Holbeach United v Wisbech Town 2-1
Dereham Town v Fakenham Town 12-0
Felixstowe & Walton United v Debenham LC 2-2, 0-2
Long Melford v Blackstones 0-2
Needham Market v Lowestoft Town 4-1
Soham Town Rangers v St Neots Town 5-2
Deeping Rangers v Lincoln Moorlands Railway 5-0
Yaxley v March Town United 1-0
Brimsdown Rovers v Burnham Ramblers 1-2
Saffron Walden Town v Wootton Blue Cross 2-2, 6-1
Daventry United v Raunds Town 0-2
Northampton Spencer v Clapton 3-2
Clacton v Desborough Town 1-1, 3-2
Biggleswade United v Broxbourne Borough V&E 1-1, 1-2
Welwyn Garden City v Bowers & Pitsea 3-1
Bedfont v Oxhey Jets 0-2
Tring Athletic v Ruislip Manor 2-1
Hertford Town v Cogenhoe United 1-0
Long Buckby v Hoddesdon Town 3-1
Barkingside v Stewarts & Lloyds 5-3
Halstead Town v Wellingborough Town 2-2, 0-2
London Colney v Langford 0-1
Bedfont Green v Stanway Rovers 2-2, 1-2
Cockfosters v Southend Manor 3-2
Tiptree United v Sawbridgeworth Town 2-2, 4-2
Barking v Harefield United 4-0
Leverstock Green v Stotfold 0-3
Harringey Borough v Wembley 2-2, 0-3
North Greenford United v Royston Town 5-0
Tunbridge Wells v Chessington & Hook United 3-4
Three Bridges v Wealden 1-0
Camberley Town v Worthing United 2-0
Frimley Green v Colliers Wood United 1-2
Dorking v Selsey 0-1
Whitehawk v VCD Athletic 0-1
Redhill v Sidley United 3-1
Farnham Town v Ringmer 1-4
Raynes Park Vale v Deal Town 3-3, 2-4
Westfield v Banstead Athletic 0-2
Eastbourne United v Sevenoaks Town 1-3
Erith Town v Cobham 3-1
Lordswood v Bookham 1-1, 2-1
Herne Bay v East Grinstead Town 0-0, 3-1
Epsom & Ewell v Crowborough Athletic 1-7
Merstham v Hythe Town 2-3
Saltdean United removed v Croydon w.o.
Peacehaven & Telscombe v East Preston 1-2
Pagham v Hailsham Town 1-1, 0-2
Wick v Chertsey Town 2-2, 0-3
Thamesmead Town v Egham Town 4-1
Shoreham v Horley Town 0-1
Hassocks v Rye United 1-0
Mile Oak v Guildford City 0-2
VT v Cowes Sports 5-0
Fareham Town v Carterton 1-1, 3-0
Bournemouth v Beaconsfield SYCOB 2-3
Henley Town v Westbury United 3-2
Christchurch v Aylesbury Vale 6-1
Sandhurst Town v Newport Pagnell Town 2-0
Kidlington v Schrivenham 1-1, 2-1
Buckingham Town v Chalfont St Peter 1-3
Bemerton Heath Harlequins v Reading Town 5-3
Brockenhurst v Witney United 2-0
Abingdon Town v Ardley United 2-1
Flackwell Heath v Moneyfields 1-2
Thame United v Downton 1-2
Holmer Green v Melksham Town 0-1
North Leigh v Devizes Town 4-0
New Milton Town v AFC Totton 1-5
Bicester Town v Milton United 1-1, 1-0
Hungerford Town v Calne Town 0-0, 3-0
Minehead v Harrow Hill 4-0
Saltash United v Almondsbury Town 2-1
Shortwood United v Bishop Sutton 1-0
Shepton Mallet v Radstock Town 2-2, 2-0
Bitton v Bideford 2-0
Street v Wimborne Town 2-5
Barnstaple Town v Clevedon United 4-0
Liskeard Athletic v Shaftsbury 2-2, 3-0
Tavistock v Bodmin Town 1-3
Keynsham Town v St Blazey 1-2
Poole Town v Dawlish Town 0-2
Torrington removed v Hamworthy United w.o.
Hallen v Fairford Town 4-2
Bridport v Welton Rovers 0-5
Chard Town v Sherborne Town 1-3
Odd Down v Bristol Manor Farm 2-0

Falmouth Town v Frome Town 1-2
Potton United v Romford 3-2
AFC Emley v Darwen 3-0
Woodbridge Town v Great Yarmouth Town 5-0
Stansted v Hullbridge Sports 2-0
Hamble ASSC v Alton Town 1-0
Dinnington Town v Maltby Main 2-1
Marlow United v Cove 1-2
London APSA v Sporting Bengal United 4-3

PRELIMINARY ROUND

Jarrow Roofing Boldon CA v Norton & Stockton Ancients 1-0
Chester-Le-Street Town v Billingham Synthonia 2-1
Winterton Rangers v Morpeth Town 1-0
Selby Town v Pickering Town 4-0
Marske United v Horden CW 1-1, 1-2
Wakefield v West Auckland Town 1-1, 0-1
Ashington v Newcastle Blue Star 1-3
Liversedge v Dunston Federation 2-0
Bridlington Town v Newcastle Benfield 1-2
Durham City v Silsden 2-2, 3-0
Spennymoor Town v Garforth Town 3-2
Shildon v Goole 5-4
Brigg Town v South Shields 4-0
Tow Law Town v Billingham Town 0-0, 2-3
Hall Road Rangers v Crook Town 1-0
Esh Winning v Harrogate Railway Athletic 1-4
Consett v Darlington Railway Athletic 4-0
Ossett Albion v Bradford (Park Avenue) 0-1
Cheadle Town v Ashton Town 3-0
Chorley v Warrington Town 2-0
Atherton Collieries v Bacup Borough 3-1
Parkgate v Alsager Town 2-1
Clitheroe v St Helens Town 3-2
Colwyn Bay v Congleton Town 2-2, 5-1
Maine Road v Skelmersdale United 0-3
Winsford United v Penrith Town 1-3
Radcliffe Borough v Lancaster City 3-0
Colne v Nantwich Town 1-3
Rossendale United v Dinnington Town 0-2
Hallam v AFC Emley 2-2, 2-1
Flixton v Salford City 1-0
Cammell Laird v Sheffield 2-0
Bamber Bridge v Oldham Town 2-0
Stocksbridge Park Steels v Curzon Ashton 3-2
Leamington v Shifnal Town 1-0
Bromyard Town v Shepshed Dynamo 1-4
Retford United v Tipton Town 1-2
Rushall Olympic v Boldmere St Michaels 3-0
Pelshall Villa v Quorn 1-6
Causeway United v Westfields 1-1, 3-2
Glapwell v Stone Dominoes 1-0
Mickleover Sports v Long Eaton United 0-0, 4-3
Bolehall Swifts v Alvechurch 1-3
Brierley Hill & Withymoor v Staveley MW 1-0
Sutton Coldfield Town v Romulus 1-1, 4-4
Sutton Coldfield Town won 7-6 on penalties.
Evesham United v Gresley Rovers 1-0
Loughborough Dynamo v Market Drayton Town 1-1, 0-4
New Mills v Atherstone Town 1-3
Rocester v Wellington 1-0
Southam United v Stratford Town 0-2
Stourbridge v Highgate United 2-1
Barwell v Biddulph Victoria 0-4
Chasetown v Oadby Town 4-1
South Normanton Athletic v Bedworth United 1-1, 0-1
Teversal v Rainworth MW 0-0, 1-2
Barnt Green Spartak v Willenhall Town 3-2
Tie ordered to be replayed. 1-3
Carlton Town v Pilkington XXX 2-1
Meir KA v Gedling Town 1-1, 0-5
Oldbury United v Kidsgrove Athletic 1-3
Belper Town v Stourport Swifts 3-3, 5-2
Malvern Town v Glossop North End 3-0
Deeping Rangers v Dereham Town 0-0, 1-0
Diss Town v Kirkley & Pakefield 0-1
Ipswich Wanderers v Needham Market 1-10
Ely City v Boston Town 0-1
Yaxley v Soham Town Rangers 0-3
Spalding United v Norwich United 5-1
Blackstones v Grantham Town 0-0, 1-2
Walsham Le Willows v Haverhill Rovers 0-0, 2-4
Mildenhall Town v St Ives Town 2-1
Holbeach United v Newmarket Town 2-0
Debenham LC v Gorleston 2-0

Woodbridge Town v Wroxham 0-2
AFC Sudbury v Bury Town 2-3
Stanway Rovers v Saffron Walden Town 0-3
Wivenhoe Town v Concord Rangers 0-4
Tilbury v Great Wakering Rovers 0-4
Hillingdon Borough v Barking 0-0, 1-1
Hillingdon Borough won 4-3 on penalties.
Tring Athletic v Hertford Town 4-4, 0-2
Enfield Town v AFC Hayes 2-1
Rothwell Town v Canvey Island 2-1
Dunstable Town v Wingate & Finchley 3-1
Aveley v Berkhamsted Town 2-1
Harwich & Parkeston v Ilford 2-0
Northwood v Uxbridge 1-0
Bedford v Broxbourne Borough V&E 0-3
Arlesey Town v Brentwood Town 0-1
Langford v Potters Bar Town 0-0, 1-5
Waltham Forest v Wellingborough Town 1-1, 1-0
Wembley v Ware 1-4
Leighton Town v Clacton 3-1
Maldon Town v Eton Manor 5-0
Stotfold v Potton United 7-2
Welwyn Garden City v Cockfosters 1-1, 1-0
Oxhey Jets v Burnham Ramblers 1-4
Tiptree United v London APSA 2-0
Tie awarded to London APSA; Tiptree United removed.
Raunds Town v Edgware Town 1-5
Long Buckby v Barton Rovers 1-1, 0-5
Witham Town v Waltham Abbey 2-3
Stansted v St Margaretsbury 4-1
Northampton Spencer v North Greenford United 2-1
Redbridge v Woodford United 1-2
Corinthian Casuals v Deal Town 1-2
Arundel v Molesey 1-1, 2-1
Walton & Hersham v Hassocks 3-0
Burgess Hill Town v Banstead Athletic 7-0
Dartford v Leatherhead 3-0
Slade Green v Croydon 1-6
Ringmer v Chatham Town 1-4
Selsey v Lordswood 1-0
Sittingbourne v Chertsey Town 1-0
Camberley Town v Ash United 0-0, 3-0
Metropolitan Police v Croydon Athletic 0-1
Eastbourne Town v Kingstonian 2-1
Colliers Wood United v Faversham Town 7-6
Redhill v Dover Athletic 0-1
Herne Bay v Guildford City 2-0
Erith & Belvedere v Ashford Town 2-0
Dulwich Hamlet v Three Bridges 2-0
Horley Town v East Preston 0-0, 1-1
Horley Town won 6-5 on penalties.
Walton Casuals v Sevenoaks Town 1-3
Thamesmead Town v Whitstable Town 3-1
Erith Town v VCD Athletic 1-0
Littlehampton Town v Chipstead 3-2
Tooting & Mitcham United v Cray Wanderers 1-2
Crowborough Athletic v Hailsham Town 1-1, 1-1
Crowborough Athletic won 6-5 on penalties.
Hythe Town v Whyteleafe 2-1
Godalming Town v Worthing 2-2, 0-3
Horsham YMCA v Chessington & Hook United 4-1
Wootton Bassett Town v Bracknell Town 2-1
Slough Town v Fleet Town 1-4
Windsor & Eton v Marlow 1-1, 3-0
Melksham Town v Bicester Town 4-0
Burnham v Brockenhurst 1-1, 0-3
Christchurch v Didcot Town 2-4
Chalfont St Peter v Hamble ASSC 1-0
Winchester City v Moneyfields 0-2
Fareham Town v Sandhurst Town 3-3, 0-0
Sandhurst Town won 4-3 on penalties.
Beaconsfield SYCOB v Hungerford Town 0-0, 3-0
Farnborough v Chesham United 0-2
Aylesbury United v Newport (IW) 4-2
Henley Town v Bemerton Heath Harlequins 3-2
Abingdon Town v AFC Totton 2-3
Downton v Abingdon United 1-1, 2-5
Cove v Gosport Borough 1-6
Andover v Oxford City 3-4
North Leigh v VT 1-1, 1-2
Corsham Town v Lymington Town 2-1
Kidlington v Thatcham Town 2-3
Slimbridge withdrew v Bitton w.o.
Brislington v Wimborne Town 0-5
Dawlish Town v Bishop's Cleeve 1-2

Shepton Mallet v Hallen	0-2
Shortwood United v Frome Town	2-1
Cinderford Town v Elmore	3-2
Paulton Rovers v St Blazey	1-1, 3-0
Bridgwater Town v Minehead	3-1
Barnstaple Town v Truro City	0-6
Sherborne Town v Liskeard Athletic	3-2
Willand Rovers v Hamworthy United	2-3
Bodmin Town v Ilfracombe Town	4-0
Saltash United v Taunton Town	2-3
Welton Rovers v Odd Down	1-0
Trafford v FC United of Manchester	2-5
Woodley Sports v Mossley	1-1, 2-1
Barkingside v Hanwell Town	2-1

FIRST QUALIFYING ROUND

Bradford (Park Avenue) w.o. v Scarborough removed	
West Auckland Town v Winterton Rangers	3-2
Newcastle Benfield v Newcastle Blue Star	2-1
Whitby Town v Shildon	3-2
Chester-Le-Street Town v Harrogate Railway Athletic	1-1, 0-3
Consett v Ossett Town	3-0
Hall Road Rangers v Billingham Town	2-3
Gateshead v Selby Town	6-1
Liversedge v North Ferriby United	1-0
Spennymoor Town v Brigg Town	2-1
Horden CW v Jarrow Roofing Boldon CA	1-1, 2-1
Durham City v Guiseley	1-3
Dinnington Town v Penrith Town	2-2, 2-1
Flixton v Bamber Bridge	2-2, 1-3
Fleetwood Town v FC United of Manchester	2-1
Witton Albion v Prescot Cables	1-2
Hallam v Woodley Sports	0-1
Frickley Athletic v Stocksbridge Park Steels	1-2
Nantwich Town v Ashton United	3-2
Chorley v Clitheroe	2-2, 1-1
Clitheroe won 4-3 on penalties.	
Colwyn Bay v Parkgate	2-1
Skelmersdale United v Marine	2-0
Radcliffe Borough v Cammell Laird	4-1
Atherton Collieries v Cheadle Town	2-5
Worksop Town v Kendal Town	0-1
Stourbridge v Leamington	2-0
Kidsgrove Athletic v Willenhall Town	2-0
Rushall Olympic v Atherstone Town	4-1
Rocester v Chasetown	0-1
Belper Town v Causeway United	3-0
Bromsgrove Rovers v Shepshed Dynamo	1-1, 2-0
Glapwell v Rugby Town	3-2
Quorn v Alvechurch	5-0
Halesowen Town v Malvern Town	4-0
Biddulph Victoria v Rainworth MW	1-3
Sutton Coldfield Town v Ilkeston Town	2-1
Carlton Town v Matlock Town	2-4
Hednesford Town v Stratford Town	0-0, 1-0
Evesham United v Tipton Town	1-1, 2-0
Brierley Hill & Withymoor v Market Drayton Town	1-2
Bedworth United v Eastwood Town	2-1
Gedling Town v Mickleover Sports	3-1
Leek Town v Buxton	1-2
Holbeach United v Debenham LC	0-2
Kirkley & Pakefield v Wroxham	2-1
Boston Town v Soham Town Rangers	0-4
Bury Town v Deeping Rangers	2-0
Lincoln United v King's Lynn	0-3
Grantham Town v Needham Market	1-1
Replay abandoned after 69 minutes; floodlight failure.	1-0
Stamford v Spalding United	5-0
Mildenhall Town v Haverhill Rovers	1-1, 0-0
Haverhill Rovers won 5-4 on penalties.	
Hemel Hempstead Town v East Thurrock United	4-0
Hillingdon Borough v Northampton Spencer	1-0
Dunstable Town v Waltham Abbey	1-0
Hertford Town v Barkingside	3-3, 1-3
Edgware Town v Potters Bar Town	2-0
Chelmsford City v Burnham Ramblers	5-0
Barton Rovers v Corby Town	0-0, 1-3
Harwich & Parkeston v Woodford United	0-0, 1-3
Rothwell Town v Enfield Town	1-1, 2-2
Enfield Town won 4-3 on penalties.	
Broxbourne Borough V&E v Bedford Town	1-1, 0-2
Saffron Walden Town v Maldon Town	1-2
AFC Hornchurch v Cheshunt	3-1
Welwyn Garden City v Billericay Town	2-8
Hendon v Aveley	1-1, 3-2
Boreham Wood v Northwood	1-0
Ware v Great Wakering Rovers	0-0, 5-4
Stotfold v Stansted	4-2
Wealdstone v Waltham Forest	1-0
Harrow Borough v Hitchin Town	2-3
Harlow Town v Concord Rangers	2-0
Brackley Town v Staines Town	0-0, 0-0
Staines Town won 5-4 on penalties.	
Heybridge Swifts v Leyton	4-3
Ashford Town (Middlesex) v Leighton Town	0-1
London APSA v Brentwood Town	0-4
Dulwich Hamlet v Deal Town	2-2, 3-1
Hythe Town v Littlehampton Town	3-1
Burgess Hill Town v Dover Athletic	0-2
Herne Bay v Sevenoaks Town	1-0
Worthing v Croydon	0-0, 1-0
Horsham v Arundel	7-1
Chatham Town v Margate	0-3
Dartford v Sittingbourne	1-1, 5-1
Folkstone Invicta v Horsham YMCA	1-1, 2-0
Horley Town v Erith Town	0-1
Croydon Athletic v Tonbridge Angels	1-1, 2-4
Cray Wanderers v AFC Wimbledon	2-6
Maidstone United v Erith & Belvedere	3-0
Eastbourne Town v Walton & Hersham	1-1, 1-2
Camberley Town v Colliers Wood United	4-2
Thamesmead Town v Carshalton Athletic	2-4
Crowborough Athletic v Selsey	2-1
Hastings United v Ramsgate	0-1
VT v Bashley	1-1, 3-4
Didcot Town v Windsor & Eton	0-1
Sandhurst Town v Chalfont St Peter	1-6
Banbury United v Aylesbury United	1-4
Fleet Town v Gosport Borough	0-0, 3-1
Oxford City v Swindon Supermarine	4-2
Abingdon United v AFC Totton	1-1, 1-4
Corsham Town v Melksham Town	1-0
Moneyfields v Thatcham Town	1-0
Chesham United v Henley Town	5-1
Brockenhurst v Wootton Bassett Town	1-1, 5-1
Beaconsfield SYCOB v Chippenham Town	1-1, 0-2
Mangotsfield United v Taunton Town	3-0
Yate Town v Gloucester City	1-5
Tiverton Town v Shortwood United	0-3
Hamworthy United v Bishop's Cleeve	3-3, 1-0
Bridgwater Town v Paulton Rovers	0-2
Hallen v Sherborne Town	2-0
Cirencester Town v Cinderford Town	1-1, 2-1
Team Bath v Bodmin Town	2-0
Welton Rovers v Truro City	0-2
Clevedon Town v Wimborne Town	4-0
Bitton v Merthyr Tydfil	2-4

SECOND QUALIFYING ROUND

Liversedge v Kendal Town	0-3
Consett v Workington	0-2
Barrow v Colwyn Bay	5-0
Billingham Town v Fleetwood Town	0-4
Skelmersdale United v Southport	0-1
Prescot Cables v Guiseley	1-1, 0-1
Dinnington Town v Cheadle Town	2-1
Harrogate Railway Athletic v Leigh RMI	4-1
Bradford (Park Avenue) v Whitby Town	4-0
Stalybridge Celtic v Hyde United	1-0
Bamber Bridge v Burscough	2-1
Gainsborough Trinity v Stocksbridge Park Steels	6-1
Harrogate Town v Nantwich Town	2-2, 2-1
West Auckland Town v Newcastle Benfield	1-0
Gateshead v Vauxhall Motors	1-3
Clitheroe v Spennymoor Town	8-2
Blyth Spartans v Radcliffe Borough	2-1
Horden CW v Woodley Sports	0-5
Cambridge City v Chasetown	1-1, 1-2
Kettering Town v Redditch United	3-1
Bromsgrove Rovers v Nuneaton Borough	1-1, 0-2
Rainworth MW v Kidsgrove Athletic	2-0
Matlock Town v AFC Telford United	3-1
Stourbridge v King's Lynn	0-5
Soham Town Rangers v Solihull Moors	0-3
Hinckley United v Grantham Town	4-2
Boston United v Buxton	4-1
Quorn v Evesham United	1-3
Tamworth v Worcester City	1-0
Hednesford Town v Alfreton Town	0-0, 2-1
Rushall Olympic v Sutton Coldfield Town	2-0

Glapwell v Market Drayton Town 4-4, 2-1
Belper Town v Hucknall Town 2-1
Halesowen Town v Bedworth United 2-1
Stamford v Gedling Town 3-1
Horsham v Bury Town 3-2
Hayes & Yeading United v Herne Bay 2-2, 3-0
Dulwich Hamlet v Chalfont St Peter 2-1
Crowborough Athletic v Staines Town 1-5
Boreham Wood v Bedford Town 3-3, 3-2
Ware v Thurrock 3-2
Haverhill Rovers v Hitchin Town 1-1, 0-5
Dartford v Camberley Town 2-2, 0-0
Dartford won 4-1 on penalties.
Fisher Athletic v Margate 3-4
Hemel Hempstead Town v Chelmsford City 0-2
Welling United v Barkingside 2-1
Billericay Town v Maidstone United 2-0
Tonbridge Angels v Maldon Town 2-2, 3-0
Dunstable Town v Lewes 0-2
St Albans City v Bishop's Stortford 1-2
Kirkley & Pakefield v Leighton Town 1-2
Brentwood Town v Harlow Town 2-0
Chesham United v Stotfold 1-1, 1-2
Worthing v Walton & Hersham 3-0
Hampton & Richmond Borough v Braintree Town 3-1
Hendon v AFC Hornchurch 1-1, 1-2
Sutton United v Woodford United 1-1, 2-0
Debenham LC v AFC Wimbledon 1-5
Ramsgate v Corby Town 0-1
Folkestone Invicta v Windsor & Eton 0-0, 1-0
Hythe Town v Dover Athletic 2-1
Enfield Town v Hillingdon Borough 2-2, 1-2
Erith Town v Heybridge Swifts 0-3
Aylesbury United v Bromley 1-1, 2-4
Carshalton Athletic v Wealdstone 0-1
Eastbourne Borough v Edgware Town 2-0
Merthyr Tydfil v AFC Totton 2-2,0-0
Merthyr Tydfil won 4-3 on penalties.
Brockenhurst v Maidenhead United 0-6
Oxford City v Weston-Super-Mare 3-4
Bognor Regis Town v Havant & Waterlooville 1-2
Chippenham Town v Hallen 2-0
Dorchester Town v Paulton Rovers 1-1, 0-2
Gloucester City v Shortwood United 0-2
Basingstoke Town v Newport County 0-1
Truro City v Bath City 0-1
Corsham Town v Bashley 1-2
Moneyfields v Team Bath 1-8
Hamworthy United v Eastleigh 1-3
Cirencester Town v Clevedon Town 0-1
Fleet Town v Mangotsfield United 2-0

THIRD QUALIFYING ROUND

Harrogate Railway Athletic v Matlock Town 3-2
Harrogate Town v Clitheroe 2-0
Barrow v Fleetwood Town 2-1
West Auckland Town v Bamber Bridge 2-2, 1-5
Dinnington Town v Bradford (Park Avenue) 1-7
Belper Town v Southport 0-3
Gainsborough Trinity v Blyth Spartans 1-0
Stalybridge Celtic v Workington 0-5
Kendal Town v Woodley Sports 4-0
Guiseley v Vauxhall Motors 2-3
Rushall Olympic v Hednesford Town 2-0
Chasetown v Rainworth MW 2-0
Tamworth v King's Lynn 2-1
Boston United v Hinckley United 4-1
Evesham United v Halesowen Town 3-0
Glapwell v Corby Town 0-3
Kettering Town v Solihull Moors 1-2
Nuneaton Borough v Stamford 4-1
Wealdstone v Bishop's Stortford 1-0
Brentwood Town v Staines Town 0-3
Heybridge Swifts v Billericay Town 2-2, 0-2
Leighton Town v Boreham Wood 3-1
AFC Hornchurch v Dulwich Hamlet 2-1
Hitchin Town v Margate 4-3
Eastbourne Borough v Welling United 2-1
Hayes & Yeading United v Chelmsford City 1-0
AFC Wimbledon v Horsham 0-0, 1-1
Horsham won 5-4 on penalties.
Lewes v Sutton United 1-0
Folkestone Invicta v Hillingdon Borough 1-0
Worthing v Hampton & Richmond Borough 0-2
Hythe Town v Ware 1-3
Bromley v Dartford 1-0
Stotfold v Tonbridge Angels 0-5
Team Bath v Weston-Super-Mare 1-0
Eastleigh v Clevedon Town 5-0
Havant & Waterlooville v Fleet Town 2-1
Merthyr Tydfil v Paulton Rovers 2-0
Newport County v Bath City 1-2
Maidenhead United v Shortwood United 3-0
Chippenham Town v Bashley 5-1

FOURTH QUALIFYING ROUND

Evesham United v Halifax Town 0-0, 1-2
Corby Town v Droylsden 1-2
Kendal Town v Altrincham 0-1
Rushden & Diamonds v Solihull Moors 5-0
Burton Albion v Tamworth 2-1
Histon v Bamber Bridge 4-1
Stafford Rangers v Cambridge United 1-1, 1-5
Southport v Northwich Victoria 1-3
Farsley Celtic v Barrow 1-1, 1-2
Bradford (Park Avenue) v Gainsborough Trinity 0-4
Workington v Boston United 1-0
York City v Rushall Olympic 6-0
Kidderminster Harriers v Vauxhall Motors 3-1
Harrogate Railway Athletic v Harrogate Town 2-1
Chasetown v Nuneaton Borough 2-1
Weymouth v Hitchin Town 1-1, 1-0
AFC Hornchurch v Team Bath 0-1
Maidenhead United v Hayes & Yeading United 1-0
Salisbury City v Stevenage Borough 0-0, 0-1
Merthyr Tydfil v Oxford United 1-2
Hampton & Richmond Borough v Wealdstone 1-0
Bath City v Torquay United 0-2
Crawley Town v Aldershot Town 1-1, 0-1
Chippenham Town v Horsham 2-3
Eastleigh v Forest Green Rovers 3-3, 1-4
Eastbourne Borough v Bromley 2-1
Ware v Tonbridge Angels 3-1
Folkestone Invicta v Billericay Town 0-2
Grays Athletic v Lewes 1-1, 0-2
Woking v Staines Town 0-1
Ebbsfleet United v Exeter City 1-3
Havant & Waterlooville v Leighton Town 3-0

THE E.ON FA CUP 2007–08

COMPETITION PROPER

▪ *Denotes player sent off.*

FIRST ROUND

Friday, 9 November 2007

Hereford U (0) 0

Leeds U (0) 0 5924

Hereford U: Brown; Rose, Threlfall, Diagouraga, McCombe, Broadhurst (Taylor), Ainsworth, Smith, Robinson, Benjamin (Guinan), Easton.
Leeds U: Ankergren; Huntington, Parker, Douglas, Heath, Rui Marques, Weston (Da Costa), Howson, Beckford, Kandol (Constantine), Carole (Clapham).

Saturday, 10 November 2007

Accrington S (2) 2 *(Cavanagh 12, Mullin 25)*

Huddersfield T (1) 3 *(Kamara 45, 83, Beckett 89)* 2202

Accrington S: Dunbavin; Cavanagh, Williams, Proctor, Roberts, Webb, Richardson (McEvilly), Harris, D'Sane (Whalley), Mullin, Brown (Miles).
Huddersfield T: Glennon; Sinclair, Skarz (Beckett), Holdsworth, Mirfin, Clarke N, Kamara, Wallwork, Cadamarteri, Booth, Schofield (Collins).

Altrincham (1) 1 *(Senior 45)*

Millwall (0) 2 *(Dunne 53 (pen), Hoskins 62)* 2457

Altrincham: Coburn; Lane▪, Scott, Sedgemore, Tinson, Shotton, Lawton, O'Neill (Logan), Little, Senior (McFadden), Peyton (Munroe).
Millwall: Pidgeley; Dunne, Bignot, Hodge, Robinson, Whitbread, Simpson, Brkovic, Alexander, Hoskins, Bakayogo.

Barnet (0) 2 *(Yakubu 61, Hatch 63)*

Gillingham (1) 1 *(Graham 27)* 2843

Barnet: Harrison; Devera, Gillet, Carew▪, Yakubu, Burton, Bishop, Wright (Leary), Hatch, Birchall (Nicolau), Puncheon.
Gillingham: Royce; Southall, King, Lomas (Crofts), Cox, Sodje (Freeman), Cogan, Bentley, Facey (Mulligan), Graham, Brown.

Barrow (1) 1 *(Rapley 19)*

Bournemouth (1) 1 *(Karacan 45)* 2203

Barrow: Deasy; Woodyatt, Butler, Sheridan, Jones, McNulty, Henney, Bond, Rapley, Rogan (Thompson), Brown.
Bournemouth: Moss; Telfer, Golbourne, Hollands, Pearce J, Gowling, Cooper, Vokes, Pitman (McQuoid), Osei-Kuffour, Karacan.

Billericay T (1) 1 *(Semanshia 26)*

Swansea C (0) 2 *(Bauza 59, 83)* 2334

Billericay T: McMahon; McSweeney, Kerrigan, Hunter, Heffer, Blewitt, Semanshia (Lay), Dormer, Flack, Boot (Woods-Garness), Abbott (Hodges).
Swansea C: Knight; Rangel, Austin, O'Leary, Monk, Tate, Anderson, Britton, Bauza, Duffy (Scotland), Orlandi (Allen).

Bradford C (1) 1 *(Thorne 28)*

Chester C (0) 0 4069

Bradford C: Ricketts; Williams, Heckingbottom, Evans P (Phelan), Wetherall, Clarke, Daley (Rhodes), Johnson, Thorne (Conlon), Ndumbu-Nsungu▪, Nix.
Chester C: Danby; Marples, Wilson, Dinning, Butler, Linwood, Grant (Rutherford), Hughes, Lowndes (McManus), Yeo, Ellison.

Bury (1) 4 *(Scott 22, Bishop 80, 85, 90)*

Workington (0) 1 *(Berkeley 75)* 2641

Bury: Provett; Parrish, Woodthorpe, Scott, Challinor, Haslam, Baker, Stephens (Buchanan), Hurst (Mangan), Bishop, Adams (Barry-Murphy).
Workington: Collin; Hewson (Edmondson), Rowntree (Wright A), Anthony, May, Gray, Johnston, Hopper, Berkeley, Reed, Nicholson (Wright J).

Cambridge U (0) 2 *(Boylan 62, Fortune-West 85)*

Aldershot T (1) 1 *(Dixon 31)* 3547

Cambridge U: Potter; Gleeson, Pitt, Albrighton (Hoyte), Peters, Morrison, Knights (Hyem), Wolleaston, Rendell (Fortune-West), Boylan, Reed.
Aldershot T: Bull; Gier, Starkey, Davies▪, Day, Newman (Charles), Soares (Chalmers), Harding, Dixon, Elvins (John Grant), Joel Grant.

Carlisle U (0) 1 *(Aranalde 85 (pen))*

Grimsby T (1) 1 *(Bolland 28)* 5128

Carlisle U: Westwood; Raven, Aranalde, Bridge-Wilkinson, Livesey, Murphy, Hackney (Smith J), Gall, Garner, Graham (Carlton), Lumsdon.
Grimsby T: Barnes; Clarke, Newey▪, Hegarty, Fenton, Bennett, Bolland (Till), Boshell (Toner), Butler (Whittle), Jones, Hunt.

Cheltenham T (0) 1 *(Gillespie 78)*

Brighton & HA (0) 1 *(Loft 90)* 2984

Cheltenham T: Higgs; Gill J, Wright, Bird, Duff, Caines, Connolly, Spencer, Connor (Yao), Gillespie, Vincent (Reid).
Brighton & HA: Kuipers; Whing, Richards, Fraser (Loft), Elphick (Butters), El-Abd, Cox, Hammond, Forster, Savage, Robinson (Elder).

Chesterfield (1) 1 *(Lester 29)*

Tranmere R (1) 2 *(Greenacre 37 (pen), Kay 84)* 4296

Chesterfield: Roche; Picken, Robertson, Downes, Gray, Niven, Leven, Bastians (Smith), Lester, Fletcher, Rooney.
Tranmere R: Coyne; Stockdale, Cansdell-Sherriff, Jennings, Kay, Goodison, McLaren, Shuker, Taylor G (Curran▪), Greenacre (Zola), Tremarco.

Crewe Alex (1) 2 *(McCready 3, Cox 65)*

Milton Keynes D (0) 1 *(Johnson 69 (pen))* 3049

Crewe Alex: Williams; Woodards (Bennett), Jones B, Cox, McCready, Baudet, Rix, Roberts GS, Church, Lowe (Schumacher), Moore.
Milton Keynes D: Abbey; Edds, Lewington, Johnson (Baldock), O'Hanlon, Swailes, Wright, Navarro, Broughton (Wilbraham), Gallen, Smart (Cameron).

Darlington (1) 1 *(Blundell 8)*

Northampton T (1) 1 *(Larkin 26)* 2964

Darlington: Stockdale; Austin, Brackstone (Abbott), Keltie, Foster, White, Purdie (Barrau), Joachim, Blundell, Wright, Cummins.
Northampton T: Bunn; Crowe, Jackman, Hughes, Doig (Bradley Johnson), Dolman, Gilligan, Burnell, Hubertz (Kirk), Larkin, Holt.

Eastbourne B (0) 0

Weymouth (0) 4 *(Louis 54, Beavon 81, 85, 88)* 2711

Eastbourne B: Hook; Baker, Austin, Harding (Budd), Lovett, Mart, Pullan, Armstrong, Atkin (Tait), Crabb M, Ramsay (Crabb N).
Weymouth: Stewart; Hart, Doe, Young, Kitamirike, Coutts (Louis), Crittenden, Vernazza, Beavon (Platt), McCallum (Phillips), Robinson.

Exeter C (2) 4 *(Carlisle 18, Mackie 40, Basham 60 (pen), Taylor M 67)*

Stevenage B (0) 0 3513

Exeter C: Marriott; Richardson, Friend, Taylor M, Edwards, Gill, Carlisle, Cozic, Basham (Stansfield), Mackie (Logan), Moxey (Elam).
Stevenage B: Julian; Fuller (Hakim), Nutter, Arber (Gaia), Oliver, Lewis, Molesley, Henry, Dobson (Wilson), Morison, McMahon.

Halifax T (0) 0

Burton Alb (1) 4 *(Clare 26, 63, McGrath 47, 73)* 1936

Halifax T: Legzdins; Scott, Doughty (Wright), Kearney, Young, Belle (Taylor), Torpey, Griffith■, Stamp (Bushell), Shaw, Heslop.
Burton Alb: Poole; Brayford (Goodfellow), Webster, McGrath, Greaves, James, Corbett, Simpson (Gooding), Clare, Harrad (Edwards), Gilroy.

Hampton & R (0) 0

Dagenham & R (0) 3 *(Benson 68, Huke 83, Strevens 90)* 2252

Hampton & R: Lovett; Harper (Mcauley), Inns, Jeffrey, Lake (Paris), Barnett, Wells, Frost (Harris), Matthews, Godfrey, Hodges.
Dagenham & R: Roberts; Foster, Griffiths, Rainford, Boardman, Smith (Strevens), Huke, Southam, Benson, Moore, Sloma (Uddin).

Harrogate RA (0) 2 *(Littlefair 65, Haigh 69)*

Droylsden (0) 0 884

Harrogate RA: McLaughlin; Haigh, Morgan R, Thirkall, Lowe, Conway, Riley, Littlefair, Jones, Smith, Ryan S (Ryan L).
Droylsden: Phillips; Roche, McGuire, Lynch (Smith), Morris, Cryan (Talbot), Burke, Murphy (Daly), Denham, Murray, Fearns.

Horsham (1) 4 *(Brake 45, Carney 62, 83, Farrell 90)*

Maidenhead U (0) 1 *(Lee 64 (pen))* 3379

Horsham: Mansfield; Myall, Brake, Graves, Hemsley, Carney, Mingle, Taylor, Austin (Farrell), Rook, Charman■.
Maidenhead U: Wells; Sterling, Clarke, Daly, Smith (Newman), Nisbet, Lee, Brown, Williams, Yashwa (James), Benjamin (Makofo).

Leyton Orient (1) 1 *(Gray 16)*

Bristol R (0) 1 *(Lambert 81)* 3157

Leyton Orient: Nelson; Purches, Daniels, Chambers, Mkandawire, Thelwell, Melligan (Thornton), Terry (Echanomi), Boyd, Gray, Demetriou (Corden).
Bristol R: Phillips; Green, Jacobson (Walker), Campbell, Coles, Elliott, Lines (Hinton), Carruthers, Lambert, Rigg (Williams), Igoe.

Lincoln C (1) 1 *(Wilson 38 (og))*

Nottingham F (1) 1 *(McGugan 25)* 7361

Lincoln C: Marriott; Green, Croft, Hone, Moses, Kerr, Dodds, Frecklington (Amoo), Wright, Forrester, N'Guessan (Warlow).
Nottingham F: Smith; Chambers, Bennett, Wilson, Breckin, Clingan, Cohen, McGugan (Thornhill), Agogo (Davies), Tyson, Commons.

Luton T (0) 1 *(Andrew 79)*

Brentford (1) 1 *(Ide 20)* 4167

Luton T: Brill; Jackson, Fojut (Goodall), Robinson, Coyne, Perry, Currie, Bell, Furlong (Andrew), Edwards (Talbot), Spring.
Brentford: Simon Brown; Starosta, O'Connor, Moore, Heywood, Pettigrew, Pead, Shakes, Ide (Charles), Thorpe, Poole.

Mansfield T (2) 3 *(Boulding M 33, Boulding R 40, Holmes 82)*

Lewes (0) 0 2607

Mansfield T: Muggleton; Mullins, Jelleyman, Dawson, Buxton, Bell (Kitchen), Hamshaw, D'Laryea, Boulding R (Holmes), Boulding M (McAliskey), Martin.
Lewes: Williams; Conroy, Barness (Legge), Kennett (Drury), Robinson, Simpemba■, Cade, Wormull, Booth, Binns (Griffiths), Holloway.

Morecambe (0) 0

Port Vale (2) 2 *(Pilkington 6, Willock 22)* 2730

Morecambe: Drench; Yates, Adams, Stanley, Bentley, Grand, Baker, Sorvel (Hunter), Curtis, Newby, Thompson (Blinkhorn).
Port Vale: Anyon; McGregor, Talbot, Laird, Pilkington, Lowe, Whitaker, Rocastle, Rodgers (Lawrie), Willock (Tudor), Edwards (Miles).

Notts Co (0) 3 *(Dudfield 48, 88, Sam 73)*

Histon (0) 0 4344

Notts Co: Pilkington; Canoville, Mayo, Butcher, Tann, Pearce, Silk, MacKenzie (Somner), Lindfield (Sam), Dudfield (Weir-Daly), Parkinson.
Histon: Naisbitt; Pope (Mitchell-King), Okay (Kennedy N), Kennedy J, Langston, Ada, Gwillim, Cambridge, Murray, Wright (Barker), Knight-Percival.

Oldham Ath (1) 2 *(Trotman 32, Davies 49)*

Doncaster R (0) 2 *(Hayter 63, 86)* 4280

Oldham Ath: Crossley; Eardley, Taylor, Kilkenny, Trotman, Stam, Allott, McDonald, Smalley, Hughes (Alessandra), Davies.
Doncaster R: Sullivan; O'Connor, Roberts G (Roberts S), Greer, Lockwood (Guy), Stock, Green, Wellens, Hayter, Coppinger (Price), Woods.

Oxford U (2) 3 *(Jeannin 7, Odubade 45 (pen), Anaclet 86)*

Northwich Vic (1) 1 *(Williams 39)* 2972

Oxford U: Turley; Foster, Day (Anaclet), Trainer, Quinn, Collins, Pettefer, Bailey, St Aimie (Fisher), Odubade, Jeannin.
Northwich Vic: Tynan; Brown, Williams (Maylett), Rusk, Taylor (Townson), Welch, Carr, Battersby (Tait), Steele, Horrocks, Wilson.

Peterborough U (2) 4 *(Mackail-Smith 2, 41, 53, McLean 88)*

Wrexham (0) 1 *(Roberts 66)* 4266

Peterborough U: Tyler; Gnapka, Day, Hyde, Morgan, Westwood, Whelpdale (Low), Keates (Lee), Boyd, McLean, Mackail-Smith (Howe).
Wrexham: Williams A; Spender, Valentine, Spann, Evans G, Hope (Pejic), Garrett, Collins (Roberts), Williams E (Marc Williams), Llewellyn, Done.

Rushden & D (2) 3 *(Jackson 6, 58, Challinor 45)*

Macclesfield T (0) 1 *(Gritton 76)* 1759

Rushden & D: Nicholls; Osano, Howell, Foster, Gulliver, Hope, Kelly, Challinor, Jackson (Malcolm), McAllister (Rankine), Burgess.
Macclesfield T: Lee; Regan, McIntyre, McNulty, Dimech, Dunfield (Tolley), Murray, Reid L (Wiles), Gritton, Evans, Thomas (Green).

Southend U (2) 2 *(Bailey 1, Harrold 24 (pen))*

Rochdale (1) 1 *(Le Fondre 12)* 5180

Southend U: Collis; Hunt, Hammell, Maher, Clarke P, Barrett, Moussa, Bailey, Harrold, Hooper (MacDonald), Gower.
Rochdale: Russell; D'Laryea, Stanton, Jones, Crooks (Prendergast), McArdle, Higginbotham, Perkins, Murray (Rundle), Le Fondre, Kennedy.

Stockport Co (0) 1 *(McNeil 47)*

Staines T (0) 1 *(Charles-Smith 76)* 3460

Stockport Co: Adamson; Bowler (Tansey), Tierney, Taylor, Owen, Raynes, Turnbull, Dickinson, Elding (Proudlock), McNeil, Griffin (Rose).
Staines T: Allaway; Nugent, Sargent, Risbridger, Gordon, Flitter, Cook (Newton), Toppin, Charles-Smith, Nwokeji, Clarke (Scarlett).

Team Bath (0) 0

Chasetown (2) 2 *(Thomas 11, Holland 30)* 2067

Team Bath: Chitty; Lock, Lamb, Smith, Green, El-Abd, Townley, Dillon (Canham M), Canham S, Llewellyn (Abbott), Thomson (Flurry).
Chasetown: Evans; Slater, Branch M, Steane, Thomas, Williams, Branch J, Parsons, Perrow (Smith D), Perry, Holland.

Walsall (1) 2 *(Ricketts 10, Demontagnac 66)*

Shrewsbury T (0) 0 4972

Walsall: Ince; Weston, Fox, Bradley, Gerrard, Dann, Sonko (Demontagnac), Hall (McDermott), Mooney, Ricketts (Deeney), Wrack.
Shrewsbury T: Garner; Moss (Herd), Tierney, Drummond, Murdock, Langmead, Hall D, Leslie, Nicholson, Symes, Pugh.

Ware (0) 0

Kidderminster H (0) 2 *(Blackwood 76, Constable 80)* 982

Ware: Woods; Hammonds, Bardle, Spendlove (Stevens), Blower (Horsey), Wolf■, Berry, Burton, Ellerbeck (Neilsen), Frendo, Gudgeon.
Kidderminster H: MacKenzie; Bignot, Blackwood, McGrath, Creighton, Whitehead■, Smikle (Hurren), Penn, Christie (Richards), Constable (Harkness), Ferrell.

Wycombe W (0) 1 *(Bloomfield 83)*

Swindon T (0) 2 *(Roberts 66, Paynter 72)* 3332

Wycombe W: Fielding; Martin, Williams, Bloomfield, Johnson, McCracken (Stockley), Bullock (Sutton), Torres, Oakes, McGleish, Holt.
Swindon T: Brezovan; Smith J (Adams), Aljofree, Easton, Tozer, Comminges (Roberts), Pook, Corr, Sturrock (Paynter), Peacock, Zaaboub.

York C (0) 0

Havant & W (1) 1 *(Harkin 24)* 2001

York C: Evans; Craddock, Robinson, Elliott (Wroe), McGurk, Kelly (Rhodes), Brayson (Brodie), Panther, Farrell, Sodje, Woolford.
Havant & W: Scriven; Smith, Poate, Collins, Jordan, Sharp, Harkin, Oatway (Wilkinson), Slabber (Pacquette), Baptiste, Taggart (Gregory).

Sunday, 11 November 2007

Forest Green R (2) 2 *(Fleetwood 32, 45)*

Rotherham U (0) 2 *(Brogan 57 (pen), O'Grady 84)* 2102

Forest Green R: Robinson; Hardiker (Preece), Tonkin, Clist, Jones, Giles, Lawless, Pitman (Smith), Fleetwood, Beesley, Afful (Carey-Bertram).
Rotherham U: Warrington; Tonge, Brogan, Harrison D, Sharps, Coughlan, Mills (Hurst), Hudson, Taylor (Yates), O'Grady, Newsham.

Gainsborough T (0) 0

Hartlepool U (2) 6 *(Barker 8, 25, Liddle 51, Moore 70, Brown 76, Porter 82)* 2402

Gainsborough T: Sollitt; Wood, Drury, Anson, Parker, Pell, Collery (Wiggins-Thomas), McMahon, Hall, Clayton (Smith), Needham (Mallon).
Hartlepool U: Budtz; McCunnie, Humphreys, Liddle (Antwi), Nelson, Clark, Moore, Sweeney, Barker (Monkhouse), Mackay (Porter), Brown.

Torquay U (2) 4 *(Todd 43, 64, Stevens 45, 89)*

Yeovil T (1) 1 *(Stewart 20)* 3718

Torquay U: Rice; Robertson, Nicholson, Mansell, Todd, Ellis, Stevens, Hargreaves, Benyon (Hill), Sills, Zebroski.
Yeovil T: Mildenhall; Alcock (Dempsey), Jones N, Forbes, Guyett, Skiverton, Barry, Peltier (Lynch), Owusu, Walker (Warne), Stewart.

FIRST ROUND REPLAYS

Tuesday, 20 November 2007

Bournemouth (1) 3 *(Golbourne 43, Gradel 90 (pen), Hollands 120)*

Barrow (0) 2 *(Rogan 55, Walker 63)* 2969

Bournemouth: Stewart; Telfer, Golbourne, Hollands■, Cooper, Gowling, Cummings (McQuoid), Karacan (Pearce J), Bradbury, Pitman, Gradel.
Barrow: Deasy; Woodyatt, McNulty, Bond, Butler, Jones, Henney, Sheridan (Fowler), Walker (Thompson), Rogan (Rapley), Brown.

Brighton & HA (1) 2 *(El-Abd 18, Hammond 67 (pen))*

Cheltenham T (0) 1 *(Gillespie 65)* 3711

Brighton & HA: Kuipers; Whing, Richards, O'Callaghan (Fraser), Butters (Lynch), El-Abd, Cox, Hammond, Forster, Savage, Robinson (Martot).
Cheltenham T: Higgs; Gill J, Wright, Gill B (Reid), Duff, Caines, Connolly, Bird, Gillespie (Yao), Connor, Spencer.

Grimsby T (0) 1 *(Jones 62)*

Carlisle U (0) 0 2008

Grimsby T: Montgomery; Clarke, Newey, Hunt, Fenton, Bennett, Till (Taylor), Bolland (Hegarty), North, Jones, Toner.
Carlisle U: Westwood; Raven, Aranalde, Bridge-Wilkinson, Livesey, Murphy, Gall (Carlton), Lumsdon, Garner, Graham, Smith J (Hackney).

Leeds U (0) 0

Hereford U (1) 1 *(Ainsworth 3)* 11,315

Leeds U: Ankergren (Lucas); Richardson, Parker, Howson, Heath, Huntington, Carole (Weston), Hughes, Beckford, Kandol, Westlake (Constantine).
Hereford U: Brown; Rose, Threlfall, Diagouraga, Beckwith, McCombe, Ainsworth, Smith, Robinson, Benjamin, Easton (Taylor).

Northampton T (2) 2 *(Kirk 36, Bradley Johnson 41)*

Darlington (0) 1 *(Wright 90)* 2895

Northampton T: Bunn; Crowe, Jackman, Burnell, Dolman, Hughes, Bradley Johnson, Larkin, Hubertz (Aiston), Kirk, Holt (Jones).
Darlington: Stockdale; Wiseman, Brackstone, Ravenhill, Foster, White (Burgess), Joachim, Keltie (Cummins), Wright, Blundell, Purdie (Abbott).

Rotherham U (0) 0

Forest Green R (1) 3 *(Giles 28, Clist 54, Fleetwood 87)* 2754

Rotherham U: Warrington; Tonge, Brogan (Todd), Harrison D, Sharps, Coughlan, Hudson, Yates (Newsham), O'Grady (Holmes P), Taylor, Hurst.
Forest Green R: Robinson; Preece, Tonkin (Hardiker), Clist, Jones, Giles, Lawless, Pitman (Smith), Fleetwood, Beesley (Rigoglioso), Stonehouse.

Thursday, 22 November 2007

Staines T (1) 1 *(Toppin 78)*

Stockport Co (0) 1 *(McNeil 78)* 2860

Staines T: Allaway; Nugent, Fliter, Cook, Sargent, Gordon, Risbridger, Toppin, Nwokeji, Clarke (Newton), Charles-Smith (Asombang).
Stockport Co: Adamson; Rose (Pilkington), Tansey, Taylor, Raynes, Owen, Griffin (Rowe), Proudlock, Elding (Poole), McNeil, Turnbull.
aet; Staines T won 4-3 on penalties

Tuesday, 27 November 2007

Brentford (0) 0

Luton T (1) 2 *(Coyne 36, Fojut 61)* 2643

Brentford: Masters; O'Connor, Charles, Moore, Heywood, Mackie (Osborne), Ide, Pead (Smith), Thorpe, Connell (Shakes), Poole.
Luton T: Brill; Jackson, Fojut, Hutchison (Currie), Coyne, Perry, Edwards (Keane), Bell, Talbot (McVeigh), Andrew, Spring.

Bristol R (1) 3 *(Hinton 2, Lambert 90 (pen), Disley 111)*

Leyton Orient (1) 3 *(Boyd 28, 92 (pen), Gray 55)* 3742

Bristol R: Phillips; Lescott, Carruthers (Igoe), Campbell, Hinton, Jacobson, Pipe, Disley, Lambert, Williams, Haldane (Lines).
Leyton Orient: Morris; Purches, Daniels, Chambers, Mkandawire, Saah, Corden■, Terry, Boyd (Melligan), Gray (Ibehre■), Demetriou.
aet; Bristol R won 6-5 on penalties.

Doncaster R (1) 1 *(McCammon 26)*

Oldham Ath (1) 2 *(Kilkenny 45, McDonald 49)* 4340

Doncaster R: Sullivan; O'Connor, McDaid, Greer, Lockwood, Stock, Woods (Price), Wellens, Hayter, McCammon (Coppinger), Guy (Nelthorpe).
Oldham Ath: Crossley; Eardley, Taylor, Kilkenny, Trotman■, Stam, Allott, McDonald, Smalley, Davies, Wolfenden (Hazell).

Nottingham F (1) 3 *(Commons 35, Tyson 49, 61)*

Lincoln C (0) 1 *(Forrester 71)* 6783

Nottingham F: Smith; Chambers, Bennett (Perch), Wilson, Morgan, Clingan, Cohen, McGugan, Tyson, Davies, Commons (Agogo).
Lincoln C: Marriott; Croft, Green, Hone, Moses (Watt), Kerr, Dodds (N'Guessan), Frecklington, Forrester, Wright, Warlow (John-Lewis).

SECOND ROUND

Friday, 30 November 2007

Horsham (0) 1 *(Taylor 85 (pen))*

Swansea C (1) 1 *(Bauza 41)* 2731

Horsham: Seuke; Myall, Hemsley, Mingle, Graves, Brake, Carney, Taylor, Rook, Charman, Austin (Farrell).
Swansea C: De Vries; Rangel, Austin, O'Leary, Monk, Tate, Orlandi (Robinson), Bauza, Allen, Feeney (Duffy), Butler (Britton).

Saturday, 1 December 2007

Bradford C (0) 0

Tranmere R (2) 3 *(Jennings 7, Greenacre 37, 68)* 6379

Bradford C: Ricketts; Williams, O'Brien, Evans P (Penford), Wetherall, Clarke, Daley, Phelan, Thorne, Ndumbu-Nsungu (Conlon), Nix (Taylforth).
Tranmere R: Coyne; Stockdale (Chorley), Taylor A, Jennings (Mullin), Kay, Goodison, McLaren, Shuker, Zola (Taylor G), Greenacre, Cansdell-Sherriff.

Bristol R (2) 5 *(Williams 33, Disley 35, Hinton 51, Lambert 54, 87)*

Rushden & D (1) 1 *(Kelly 11)* 4816

Bristol R: Phillips; Lescott, Carruthers, Campbell, Hinton, Pipe, Igoe, Disley (Parrinello), Williams (Groves), Lambert, Haldane (Lines).
Rushden & D: Bastock; Osano, Howell, Woodhouse (Hales), Gulliver, Hope, Challinor, Burgess, Jackson (Tomlin), McAllister (Rankine), Kelly.

Burton Alb (0) 1 *(Stride 86)*

Barnet (1) 1 *(Hatch 19)* 2769

Burton Alb: Poole; Brayford, Webster, Simpson, Greaves, James (Stride), Corbett, McGrath, Goodfellow (Edwards), Harrad, Gilroy.
Barnet: Harrison; Devera, Gillet, Bishop, Yakubu, Burton (O'Cearuill), Carew, Wright, Hatch, Birchall (Thomas), Nicolau■.

Bury (0) 1 *(Adams 79)*

Exeter C (0) 0 2725

Bury: Provett; Parrish, Haslam, Scott, Morgan, Futcher, Adams (Baker), Woodthorpe, Mangan (Hughes), Bishop, Buchanan.
Exeter C: Jones; Richardson (Elam), Edwards, Taylor M, Seaborne, Gill, Carlisle (Stansfield), Taylor A, Basham (Logan), Mackie, Moxey.

Cambridge U (1) 1 *(Rendell 26 (pen))*

Weymouth (0) 0 4552

Cambridge U: Potter; Gleeson, Pitt (Knights), Morrison, Peters, Hoyte, Carden, Wolleaston (Convery), Rendell, Boylan (Fortune-West), Reed.
Weymouth: Matthews; Doe, Hart, Browning (Crittenden), Young, Roberts, Lombarti, Vernazza (Douglas), McCallum (Carmichael), Beavon, Robinson.

Dagenham & R (1) 3 *(Benson 33, 90, Strevens 85)*

Kidderminster H (1) 1 *(Creighton 14)* 1493

Dagenham & R: Roberts; Foster, Griffiths, Huke, Uddin, Boardman, Strevens, Southam, Benson, Moore (Nurse), Sloma.
Kidderminster H: Bevan; Bignot (Barnes-Homer), Blackwood, Whitehead, Creighton, Hurren, Russell (Christie), Penn, Richards, Ferrell, Bennett.

Hereford U (1) 2 *(McCombe 45, Robinson 85)*

Hartlepool U (0) 0 3801

Hereford U: Brown; Collins, Threlfall (McClenahan), Diagouraga, Beckwith, McCombe, Gwynne (Johnson), Smith, Robinson, Benjamin (Guinan), Taylor.
Hartlepool U: Budtz; Nolan (Monkhouse), Humphreys, Boland, Nelson, Antwi, McCunnie (Liddle), Sweeney, Barker, Moore (Mackay), Brown.

Huddersfield T (0) 3 *(Jevons 53, 62, Beckett 85)*

Grimsby T (0) 0 6729

Huddersfield T: Glennon; Sinclair, Skarz, Holdsworth, Mirfin, Clarke N, Kamara (Collins), Wallwork, Jevons (Cadamarteri), Booth (Beckett), Schofield.
Grimsby T: Montgomery; Bennett (Bore), Newey, Atkinson, Fenton, Hird, Till (Taylor), Hunt, North (Bolland), Jones, Toner.

Millwall (0) 2 *(Brkovic 50, Hoskins 55)*

Bournemouth (0) 1 *(Cooper 74)* 4495

Millwall: Pidgeley; Bignot, Bakayogo (Gaynor) (Akinfenwa), Senda, Robinson, Whitbread, Hodge, Brkovic, Harris, Hoskins, Fuseini.
Bournemouth: Stewart; Telfer, Cummings, Hollands (Pitman), Pearce J, Gowling, Cooper, Karacan, Bradbury, Osei-Kuffour (Bartley), Gradel.

Northampton T (1) 1 *(Kirk 8)*

Walsall (1) 1 *(Mooney 4)* 3887

Northampton T: Bunn; Crowe (Jones), Jackman, Gilligan, Dolman, Hughes, Bradley Johnson, Larkin (Burnell), Hubertz (Henderson), Kirk, Holt.
Walsall: Ince; Weston, Fox, Bradley, Gerrard, Dann, Sonko (Hall), Demontagnac (Nicholls), Mooney, Ricketts, Wrack.

Notts Co (0) 0

Havant & W (0) 1 *(Taggart 87)* 3810

Notts Co: Pilkington; Canoville, Mayo, Somner, Tann, Hunt, Silk (Lee), MacKenzie (Butcher), Sam, Dudfield, Weston (Weir-Daley).
Havant & W: Scriven; Gregory, Sharp, Collins, Poate, Smith, Harkin, Oatway (Wilkinson), Pacquette (Taggart), Baptiste, Potter (Gurney).

Oldham Ath (1) 1 *(Hughes 41)*

Crewe Alex (0) 0 3900

Oldham Ath: Crossley; Eardley, Taylor, Kilkenny, Hazell, Stam, Allott, McDonald, Smalley, Davies, Hughes.
Crewe Alex: Williams; Woodards, Jones B, Cox, McCready, Bailey M, Rix, Roberts GS (Bennett), Church, Lowe (Maynard), Moore (Baseya).

Oxford U (0) 0

Southend U (0) 0 5162

Oxford U: Turley; Clarke, Jeannin, Trainer, Quinn, Foster, Anaclet, Hutchinson, Twigg (Odubade), Barnes, Green (Ledgister).
Southend U: Collis; Francis, Hammell, Maher, Clarke P, Barrett, Hunt, Bailey, McCormack, Morgan (MacDonald), Gower.

Staines T (0) 0

Peterborough U (3) 5 *(Mackail-Smith 10, 23, 53, 62, McLean 18)* 2460

Staines T: Allaway; Nugent (Thompson), Sargent, Risbridger, Gordon, Flitter, Clarke, Toppin, Charles-Smith (Asombang), Nwokeji, Cook (Newton).
Peterborough U: Tyler; Lee, Day, Gnapka, Morgan, Westwood, Whelpdale (Low), Hyde (Keates), Boyd (Hughes), McLean, Mackail-Smith.

Swindon T (1) 3 *(McGovern 12, Aljofree 69, Sturrock 88)*

Forest Green R (0) 2 *(Fleetwood 54, Beesley 66)* 7588

Swindon T: Brezovan; Smith J, Tozer, Easton, Comminges, Aljofree, McGovern, Pook, Roberts (Allen), Paynter, Corr (Sturrock).
Forest Green R: Robinson; Hardiker, Tonkin, Clist, Jones, Giles, Lawless (Afful), Pitman (Smith), Fleetwood (Carey-Bertram), Beesley, Stonehouse.

Torquay U (0) 0

Brighton & HA (0) 2 *(Forster 63, 90)* 4010

Torquay U: Rice; Robertson, Nicholson, Mansell, Todd, Woods, Stevens (Bedeau), Hargreaves, Benyon (Welsh), Sills, Phillips (Hill).
Brighton & HA: Kuipers; Whing, Richards, Fraser (Martot), Lynch, El-Abd, Cox, Hammond, Forster, Savage, Robinson (Loft).

Sunday, 2 December 2007

Harrogate RA (0) 2 *(Davidson 61, 84)*

Mansfield T (1) 3 *(Jelleyman 38, Boulding M 51, 77)* 1486

Harrogate RA: McLaughlin; Haigh, Lowe, Jones (Conway), Morgan R, Riley (Blair), Littlefair, Ryan S, Marshall, Smith (Davidson), Morgan M.
Mansfield T: Muggleton; Mullins, Martin, Dawson (D'Laryea), Buxton, John-Baptiste, Hamshaw, Bell, Boulding R (Brown), Boulding M, Jelleyman.

Port Vale (1) 1 *(Rodgers 18)*

Chasetown (1) 1 *(Branch M 44)* 5875

Port Vale: Anyon; Miller, Talbot, Laird, Pilkington, Westwood, Edwards, Rocastle, Rodgers, Willock, Whitaker.
Chasetown: Evans; Branch J, Branch M, Slater, Thomas, Williams, Steane, Hawkins (Smith S), Perry, Perrow (Smith D), Holland.

Tuesday, 11 December 2007

Luton T (0) 1 *(Andrew 54)*

Nottingham F (0) 0 5758

Luton T: Brill; Jackson, Fojut, Robinson, Coyne, Perry, Currie, Bell (Grant), Edwards, Andrew, Spring.
Nottingham F: Smith; Chambers (Davies), Lockwood, Lennon, Breckin, Wilson, Cohen, McGugan (Commons), Tyson (Agogo), Holt, Perch.

SECOND ROUND REPLAYS

Monday, 10 December 2007

Swansea C (4) 6 *(Pratley 21, Britton 38, Scotland 42, Bodde 43, Robinson 56, Feeney 79)*

Horsham (2) 2 *(Farrell 20, 23)* 5911

Swansea C: De Vries; Rangel, Austin, Bodde, Tate, Lawrence, Britton (Bauza), Pratley, Scotland (Feeney), Anderson (Orlandi), Robinson.
Horsham: Seuke; Myall (Salaam), Brake, Mingle, Hemsley, Graves, Carney, Taylor, Farrell, Austin, Charman (French).

Tuesday, 11 December 2007

Barnet (0) 1 *(Birchall 83)*

Burton Alb (0) 0 1379

Barnet: Harrison; Devera, Gillet (Nicolau), Bishop, Yakubu, O'Cearuill, Carew, Leary (Porter), Grazioli (Thomas), Birchall, Puncheon.
Burton Alb: Poole; Brayford, Webster, McGrath, Greaves, James, Corbett, Simpson, Edwards, Harrad, Gilroy (Stride).

Chasetown (0) 1 *(Smith D 89)*

Port Vale (0) 0 1986

Chasetown: Evans; Branch J, Williams, Steane, Slater, Thomas, Branch M, Hawkins (Smith S), Perrow (Smith D), Perry, Holland.
Port Vale: Anyon; McGregor, Talbot (Richards), Salmon, Pilkington, Lowe, Laird, Harsley, Rodgers, Willock, Whitaker.

Southend U (2) 3 *(MacDonald 5, 90, Morgan 45 (pen))*

Oxford U (0) 0 2740

Southend U: Collis; Hunt, Francis, Maher, Clarke P, Richards, Bailey (Moussa), McCormack (Black), Morgan, MacDonald, Gower.
Oxford U: Turley; Clarke, Day (Weedon), Trainer, Quinn, Foster, Ledgister (Duffy), Hutchinson, Barnes (Fisher), Odubade, Twigg.

Walsall (0) 1 *(Ricketts 85 (pen))*

Northampton T (0) 0 3086

Walsall: Ince; Weston, Fox, Bradley, Gerrard, Dann, Hall (Deeney), Sonko (Demontagnac), Mooney (Nicholls), Ricketts, Wrack.
Northampton T: Bunn; Jones, Jackman (Branston), Gilligan (Dyer), Dolman, Hughes, Larkin, Burnell, Hubertz, Henderson, Holt.

THIRD ROUND

Saturday, 5 January 2008

Aston Villa (0) 0

Manchester U (0) 2 *(Ronaldo 81, Rooney 89)* 33,630

Aston Villa: Carson; Mellberg, Bouma (Gardner), Reo-Coker, Davies, Laursen, Petrov (Maloney), Young, Agbonlahor, Carew (Moore), Barry.
Manchester U: Van der Sar; Brown, Evra, Carrick, Ferdinand, Vidic, Ronaldo, Anderson, Park (Rooney), Saha (Hargreaves), Giggs (O'Shea).

Barnsley (0) 2 *(Foster 78, Coulson 81)*

Blackpool (1) 1 *(Fox 32)* 8276

Barnsley: Muller (Letheren); Souza, Van Homoet, Hassell, Foster, Howard, Campbell-Ryce (Coulson), Togwell, Odejayi, Mostto, McCann (Devaney).
Blackpool: Rachubka; Hills, Crainey, Fox, Michael Jackson, Evatt, Taylor-Fletcher (Jorgensen), Flynn, Vernon (Morrell), Burgess, Welsh (Hoolahan).

Blackburn R (0) 1 *(Bentley 85)*

Coventry C (1) 4 *(Mifsud 34, 90, Ward 64 (pen), Adebola 83)* 14,421

Blackburn R: Friedel; Emerton (Pedersen), Berner, Tugay, Khizanishvili, Samba, Bentley, Mokoena, Rigters (Nelsen), McCarthy, Treacy (Derbyshire).
Coventry C: Konstantopoulos; Borrowdale, Osbourne, Doyle, Turner, Ward, Hughes M, Best, Adebola, Mifsud, Tabb.

Bolton W (0) 0

Sheffield U (1) 1 *(Carney 42)* 15,286

Bolton W: Al Habsi; Hunt (Dzemaili), O'Brien J, Cid, O'Brien A (Meite), Michalik, Cohen, Guthie, Diouf (Wilhelmsson), Braaten, Gianniakopoulos.
Sheffield U: Kenny; Geary (Gillespie), Armstrong, Montgomery, Bromby, Kilgallon, Hendrie (Sharp), Carney, Shelton (Hulse), Stead, Quinn S.

Brighton & HA (1) 1 *(Revell 23)*

Mansfield T (2) 2 *(Hamshaw 10, Holmes 45)* 5857

Brighton & HA: Kuipers; Lynch, Elphick, Reid, Butters (Rents), El-Abd, Cox, Fraser (Loft), Forster, Revell, Robinson (Elder).
Mansfield T: Muggleton; Mullins, Jelleyman, Dawson, Buxton, Martin, Hamshaw, D'Laryea, Holmes (Boulding R), Brown (Sleath), Arnold (Bell).

Bristol C (1) 1 *(Fontaine 18)*

Middlesbrough (1) 2 *(Downing 37, Wheater 72)* 15,895

Bristol C: Basso; Orr, McAllister, Johnson, Fontaine, Vasko, Sproule, Elliott, Noble (Trundle), Byfield (Showunmi), Wilson (Murray).
Middlesbrough: Schwarzer; Young, Pogatetz, Wheater, Huth, Johnson (Tuncay), Rochemback, Arca, Hutchinson (Lee), Cattermole, Downing.

Charlton Ath (1) 1 *(Zheng Zhi 2)*

WBA (1) 1 *(Miller 34)* 12,682

Charlton Ath: Weaver; Bougherra, Youga, Holland, McCarthy, Moutaoukil, Sam, Ambrose (Basey), Varney (Iwelumo), Zheng Zhi, McLeod (Dickson).
WBA: Kiely; Hoefkens, Albrechtsen, Koren (Morrison), Cesar, Barnett (Pele), Gera (MacDonald), Teixeira, Miller, Brunt, Greening.

Chasetown (1) 1 *(McNaughton 17 (og))*

Cardiff C (1) 3 *(Whittingham 45, Ramsey 60, Parry 73)* 2420

Chasetown: Evans; Thomas, Branch J, Holland (Spacey), Slater, Williams, Hawkins, Steane, Perry (Edwards), Perrow (Smith D), Branch M.
Cardiff C: Oakes; McNaughton, Capaldi, Rae, Johnson, Loovens, Ledley, Ramsey (Blake), MacLean, Whittingham, Parry.

Chelsea (1) 1 *(Camp 28 (og))*

QPR (0) 0 41,289

Chelsea: Hilario; Paulo Ferreira, Cole A, Mikel, Alex, Ben Haim, Wright-Phillips (Cole J), Sidwell, Pizarro (Ballack), Kalou, Sinclair (Drogba).
QPR: Camp; Hall, Barker, Mahon, Connolly, Stewart, Ainsworth (Agyemang), Buzsaky (Lee), Blackstock, Rowlands, Ephraim (Balanta).

Colchester U (1) 1 *(Sheringham 43 (pen))*

Peterborough U (1) 3 *(McLean 4, Boyd 46, Lee 73)* 4003

Colchester U: Gerken; White, Elokobi, Guttridge, Baldwin, Virgo, Jackson, Yeates, Lisbie, Sheringham (Guy), McLeod K (Duguid).
Peterborough U: Tyler; Newton, Lee, Hughes, Morgan, Charnock, Whelpdale (Gnapka), Hyde, Boyd, McLean, Mackail-Smith (Howe).

Everton (0) 0

Oldham Ath (1) 1 *(McDonald 45)* 33,086

Everton: Wessels; Hibbert, Baines (Lescott), Jagielka, Stubbs, Carsley, Pienaar, Gravesen (Anichebe), Johnson, Vaughan (Yakubu), McFadden.
Oldham Ath: Crossley; Eardley, Lomax (Thompson), McDonald, Hazell, Stam, Smalley, Kamudimba Kalala, Hughes, Davies, Allott.

Huddersfield T (1) 2 *(Beckett 4, Brandon 81)*

Birmingham C (1) 1 *(O'Connor 19)* 13,410

Huddersfield T: Glennon; Sinclair, Williams (Skarz), Holdsworth, Mirfin, Berrett, Kamara (Jevons), Collins, Brandon, Beckett, Schofield.
Birmingham C: Maik Taylor; Kelly, Queudrue, Muamba, Jaidi, Ridgewell, Larsson, De Ridder, Forssell (Jerome), O'Connor, McSheffrey.

Ipswich T (0) 0

Portsmouth (0) 1 *(Nugent 51)* 23,446

Ipswich T: Alexander; Wright, Sito (Naylor), Garvan, Wilnis, Bruce, Haynes, Williams (Lee), Clarke (Peters), Counago, Trotter■.
Portsmouth: James; Johnson, Hreidarsson, Diop, Campbell, Distin, Mvuemba, Pedro Mendes (Nugent), Kanu, Utaka, Kranjcar.

Norwich C (0) 1 *(Doherty 80)*

Bury (0) 1 *(Bishop 71)* 19,815

Norwich C: Marshall; Croft (Bertrand), Camara, Doherty, Dublin, Russell, Huckerby, Fotheringham, Martin (Ryan Jarvis), Cureton, Pattison (Otsemobor).
Bury: Provett; Haslam, Parrish, Futcher, Challinor, Barry-Murphy, Baker, Woodthorpe, Adams (Hurst), Bishop, Buchanan.

Plymouth Arg (2) 3 *(Abdou 23, Halmosi 26, Ebanks-Blake 58)*

Hull C (0) 2 *(Windass 51, 60)* 12,419

Plymouth Arg: McCormick; Connolly, Hodges (Sawyer), Abdou, Doumbe, Seip, Summerfield (Chadwick), Nalis, Ebanks-Blake (Jutkiewicz), Easter, Halmosi.
Hull C: Myhill; Doyle (Atkinson), Delaney, Marney, Turner, Collins, France, Barmby, Folan, Elliott (Windass), Livermore (Garcia).

Preston NE (0) 1 *(Whaley 47)*

Scunthorpe U (0) 0 4616

Preston NE: Lonergan; Davidson, Hill, Whaley, Chilvers, Mawene, Neal, Carter, Mellor (Ormerod), Hawley, McKenna.
Scunthorpe U: Murphy (Lillis); Byrne, Williams (Forte), Cork, Crosby, Martis, Sparrow, Morris, Hayes (Ameobi), Paterson, Hurst.

Southampton (2) 2 *(Surman 16, Vignal 36)*

Leicester C (0) 0 20,094

Southampton: Davis; Wright J, Vignal, Thomas, Powell, Safri, Hammill (McGoldrick), Euell, Rasiak, Wright-Phillips, Surman.
Leicester C: Henderson; Stearman, Sheehan, Wesolowski, McAuley, Kisnorbo, Kenton (King), Fryatt (N'Gotty), Howard, Hayles, Hume.

Southend U (1) 5 *(MacDonald 11, Morgan 64, 90, Francis 77, Bailey 89)*

Dagenham & R (1) 2 *(Nurse 32, Strevens 58)* 6393

Southend U: Flahavan; Hunt, Hammell, Francis, Clarke P, Barrett, Bailey, McCormack, Harrold (Hooper), MacDonald, Morgan.
Dagenham & R: Roberts■; Foster, Griffiths, Huke, Uddin (Smith), Boardman, Saunders (Thompson), Southam, Nurse, Strevens, Sloma (Taylor).

Sunderland (0) 0

Wigan Ath (1) 3 *(Scharner 19, McShane 56 (og), Cotterill 76)* 20,821

Sunderland: Gordon; McShane, Collins, Whitehead (Leadbitter), Nosworthy, Evans, O'Donovan, Kavanagh, Murphy, Waghorn (Cole), Richardson (Connolly).
Wigan Ath: Pollitt; Boyce, Kilbane, Skoko, Scharner, Granqvist, Olembe, Koumas, Heskey (Brown), Sibierski (Aghahowa), Taylor (Cotterill).

Swansea C (0) 1 *(Robinson 74)*

Havant & W (0) 1 *(Baptiste 87)* 8761

Swansea C: De Vries; Austin, Amankwaah, Britton, Tate■, Painter, Butler (Orlandi), Pratley, Scotland (Bauza), Allen (Duffy), Robinson.
Havant & W: Scriven; Gregory, Warner, Harkin (Taggart), Poate■, Smith, Oatway (Wilkinson), Collins, Pacquette (Slabber), Baptiste, Potter.

Swindon T (0) 1 *(Sturrock 60)*

Barnet (0) 1 *(Birchall 85)* 5944

Swindon T: Brezovan; Comminges, Vincent, Easton, Ifil, Aljofree, McGovern, Sturrock (Roberts), Paynter, Peacock, Zaaboub (Mohamed).
Barnet: Beckwith; Devera, Nicolau, Bishop, Yakubu, Gillet, Carew (Thomas), Leary, Porter, Akurang (Birchall), Puncheon.

Tottenham H (1) 2 *(Berbatov 28, 50 (pen))*

Reading (1) 2 *(Hunt 25, 78)* 35,243

Tottenham H: Robinson; Chimbonda, Lee, Zokora, Dawson, King, Lennon, Jenas, Berbatov, Keane (Taarabt), Malbranque (Huddlestone■).
Reading: Federici; De la Cruz, Rosenior, Cisse, Duberry (Pearce), Bikey, Convey, Hunt, Lita, Long, Fae.

Tranmere R (0) 2 *(Jennings 75, Taylor G 78)*

Hereford U (0) 2 *(Smith 65, Benjamin 76)* 6909

Tranmere R: Coyne; Stockdale, Taylor A, Jennings, Kay, Chorley, Curran, McLaren, Zola (Jones), Taylor G, Cansdell-Sherriff.
Hereford U: Brown; McClenahan, Taylor, Diagouraga, Beckwith, Collins, Gwynne (McCombe), Smith, Robinson, Benjamin, Johnson (Rose).

Walsall (0) 0
Millwall (0) 0 4358
Walsall: Ince; Weston, Fox, Nicholls, Roper, Dann, Wrack, Bradley, Demontagnac (Sonko), Ricketts (Brittain), Deeney.
Millwall: Pidgeley; Bignot, Frampton (Barron), Simpson, Robinson, Whitbread, Hodge, Gaynor, Akinfenwa, Forbes (May), Fuseini.

Watford (1) 2 *(Shittu 28, 65)*
Crystal Palace (0) 0 10,480
Watford: Lee; Doyley, Stewart, Francis, Shittu (Mariappa), DeMerit, McAnuff, Williamson, Henderson (Priskin), King (Ellington), Smith.
Crystal Palace: Flinders; Hills, Lawrence, Watson, Hudson, Fonte (Hill), Bostock (Moses), Fletcher, Scowcroft, Morrison (Hall), Scannell.

West Ham U (0) 0
Manchester C (0) 0 33,806
West Ham U: Green; Neill (Spector), McCartney, Mullins (Bowyer), Ferdinand, Upson, Pantsil, Noble, Cole, Ashton, Etherington (Reid).
Manchester C: Hart; Onuoha, Ball, Dunne, Richards, Corluka, Ireland (Etuhu), Hamann, Vassell (Bianchi), Castillo (Gelson), Petrov.

Wolverhampton W (0) 2 *(Kightly 69, Collins N 88)*
Cambridge U (1) 1 *(Rendell 42 (pen))* 15,340
Wolverhampton W: Hennessey; Foley, Gray, Potter, Collins N, Ward D, Jarvis (Edwards R), Gibson, Keogh (Eastwood), Bothroyd, Ward S (Kightly).
Cambridge U: Potter; Gleeson, Reed (Boylan), Albrighton, Coulson, Morrison, Convery (Fortune-West), Brown (Pitt), Rendell, Wolleaston, Carden.

Sunday, 6 January 2008
Burnley (0) 0
Arsenal (1) 2 *(Eduardo 9, Bendtner 75)* 16,709
Burnley: Kiraly; Alexander, Harley, McCann, Caldwell, Varga, O'Connor J (Gudjonsson), Blake (Jones), Lafferty■, Gray (Akinbiyi), Elliott.
Arsenal: Lehmann; Sagna, Traore (Hoyte J), Silva, Toure, Senderos, Eboue, Denilson, Eduardo, Bendtner, Diaby.

Derby Co (2) 2 *(Miller 38, Barnes 45)*
Sheffield W (2) 2 *(Beevers 9, Tudgay 23)* 20,612
Derby Co: Price; Mears (Johnson), Mills, Oakley, Moore, Todd, Teale (Macken), Barnes, Fagan, Miller, Lewis.
Sheffield W: Grant; Bullen, Spurr, Whelan, Beevers, Hinds, Esajas, Johnson J, Jeffers (Burton), Tudgay, O'Brien.

Fulham (1) 2 *(Healy 40, Murphy 73)*
Bristol R (1) 2 *(Coles 3, Hinton 65)* 13,634
Fulham: Niemi; Volz (Seol), Konchesky, Smertin (Davis), Bocanegra, Stefanovic, Davies, Murphy, Dempsey, Healy, Bouazza (Baird).
Bristol R: Phillips; Lescott, Jacobson, Coles, Hinton, Elliott, Pipe, Lines, Williams (Rigg), Lambert (Walker), Igoe (Carruthers).

Luton T (0) 1 *(Riise 77 (og))*
Liverpool (0) 1 *(Crouch 74)* 10,226
Luton T: Brill; Keane, Goodall, Bell, Coyne, Perry, Currie, Edwards, Talbot, Andrew, Spring.
Liverpool: Itandje; Finnan, Riise, Xabi Alonso (Mascherano), Carragher, Hyypia, Benayoun (El Zhar), Lucas, Crouch, Kuyt, Babel (Voronin).

Stoke C (0) 0
Newcastle U (0) 0 22,861
Stoke C: Simonsen; Wilkinson, Dickinson, Pugh, Cort, Shawcross, Lawrence, Eustace (Pulis), Sidibe (Parkin), Fuller (Pericard), Cresswell.
Newcastle U: Given; Rozehnal, Jose Enrique, Butt, Taylor, Diagne-Faye, Duff (Lua-Lua), Smith, Owen, Viduka (Carroll), N'Zogbia.

THIRD ROUND REPLAYS

Tuesday, 15 January 2008
Bury (1) 2 *(Futcher 18, Bishop 61)*
Norwich C (0) 1 *(Dublin 86)* 4146
Bury: Provett; Scott, Woodthorpe, Barry-Murphy (Dorney), Haslam, Futcher, Baker, Stephens, Adams, Bishop, Buchanan (Anane).
Norwich C: Marshall; Spillane, Bertrand, Shackell, Doherty, Russell, Huckerby (Camara), Fotheringham, Ryan Jarvis (Dublin), Cureton, Pattison (Croft).

Liverpool (1) 5 *(Babel 45, Gerrard 52, 64, 72, Hyypia 57)*
Luton T (0) 0 41,446
Liverpool: Itandje; Arbeloa, Riise, Xabi Alonso, Carragher, Hyypia, Pennant, Gerrard (Lucas), Torres (Fabio Aurelio), Crouch (Kuyt), Babel.
Luton T: Brill; Goodall, Jackson, Robinson (O'Leary), Keane, Hutchison, Currie, Bell (McVeigh), Talbot, Andrew (Furlong), Spring.

Millwall (1) 2 *(May 15, Alexander 49)*
Walsall (0) 1 *(Nicholls 61)* 4645
Millwall: Pidgeley; Senda, Barron, Simpson (Forbes), Robinson, Frampton, Gaynor (Bakayogo), Brammer, Alexander, May, Fuseini.
Walsall: Ince; Weston, Taundry, Bradley (Boertien), Gerrard, Dann, Wrack (Dobson), Deeney, Nicholls, Demontagnac (Brittain), Sonko.

Reading (0) 0
Tottenham H (1) 1 *(Keane 15)* 22,130
Reading: Federici; De la Cruz, Shorey (Hunt), Ingimarsson, Pearce (Cox), Harper, Rosenior, Cisse, Lita, Long, Convey.
Tottenham H: Cerny; Chimbonda, Gunter, Boateng, Kaboul (Stalteri), Dawson, Tainio (O'Hara), Jenas, Keane, Defoe (Lennon), Malbranque.

WBA (1) 2 *(Bednar 14, Morrison 51)*
Charlton Ath (0) 2 *(Ambrose 64, Dickson 90)* 12,691
WBA: Kiely; Hoefkens, Albrechtsen, Morrison, Barnett, Pele, Gera (Koren), Teixeira (Brunt), Bednar, Miller (MacDonald), Greening.
Charlton Ath: Weaver; Moutaouakil, Youga, Holland (Dickson), McCarthy, Bougherra, Sam, Ambrose (Thomas), Varney, Zheng Zhi, McLeod (Iwelumo).
aet; WBA won 4-3 on penalties.

Wednesday, 16 January 2008
Havant & W (3) 4 *(Monk 4 (og), Collins 25, Baptiste 37, Jordan 65)*
Swansea C (1) 2 *(Bauza 39, Scotland 48)* 4400
Havant & W: Scriven; Gregory, Poate, Collins, Warner, Smith (Jordan), Potter, Oatway (Wilkinson), Pacquette (Slabber), Baptiste, Harkin.
Swansea C: De Vries; Rangel, Painter (Duffy), Britton, Monk, Lawrence, Anderson (Butler), Pratley, Scotland, Bauza, Robinson.

Hereford U (0) 1 *(Johnson 72)*
Tranmere R (0) 0 6471
Hereford U: Brown; McClenahan, Rose, Diagouraga, Beckwith, Collins, Johnson, Smith, Robinson, Benjamin, Taylor.
Tranmere R: Coyne; Stockdale, Taylor A, Jennings (Mullin), Kay, Chorley, McLaren, Myrie-Williams, Taylor G, Zola, Cansdell-Sherriff (Curran).

Manchester C (0) 1 *(Elano 73)*
West Ham U (0) 0 27,809
Manchester C: Hart; Corluka, Ball, Dunne, Richards, Castillo (Bianchi), Ireland, Hamann, Elano, Vassell (Gelson), Petrov.
West Ham U: Green; Neill, McCartney, Noble, Ferdinand, Upson, Ljungberg (Faubert), Bowyer, Ashton, Boa Morte (Cole), Etherington.

Newcastle U (2) 4 *(Owen 8, Cacapa 31, Milner 68, Duff 76)*
Stoke C (0) 1 *(Lawrence 89)* 35,108

Newcastle U: Given; Carr, Jose Enrique, Emre■, Cacapa (Rozehnal), Taylor, Milner, Duff, Owen, Viduka (Carroll), N'Zogbia (LuaLua).
Stoke C: Simonsen; Zakuani, Pugh, Delap (Dickinson), Cort, Shawcross, Lawrence, Eustace (Pulis), Parkin (Diao), Fuller, Cresswell.

Tuesday, 22 January 2008
Barnet (0) 1 *(Paynter 53 (og))*
Swindon T (1) 1 *(Paynter 42)* 2810

Barnet: Beckwith; Devera, Nicolau (O'Cearuill), Porter, Yakubu, Gillet, Bishop, Leary■, Birchall (Thomas), Akurang (Grazioli), Puncheon.
Swindon T: Brezovan; Comminges, Vincent, Pook, Ifil, Aljofree, McGovern, Sturrock (Corr), Paynter, Peacock, Zaaboub (Roberts).
aet; Barnet won 2-0 on penalties.

Bristol R (0) 0
Fulham (0) 0 11,882

Bristol R: Phillips; Lescott, Jacobson, Campbell, Hinton, Elliott (Disley), Pipe, Coles, Williams (Rigg), Lambert, Lines.
Fulham: Warner; Baird, Konchesky, Hughes, Bocanegra, Stefanovic■, Volz, Bullard, Dempsey, Healy, Brown (Seol).
aet; Bristol R won 5-3 on penalties.

Sheffield W (1) 1 *(Watson 10)*
Derby Co (0) 1 *(Miller 47)* 18,020

Sheffield W: Grant; Bullen, Spurr, Whelan, Beevers, Hinds, Watson (Lunt), Johnson J, Tudgay, Sodje (Clarke), Small (Burton).
Derby Co: Price; Edworthy, Nyatanga, Leacock (Moore), Davis, Todd, Teale (Earnshaw), Pearson, Fagan, Miller, Barnes (Lewis).
aet; Derby Co won 4-2 on penalties.

FOURTH ROUND

Friday, 25 January 2008
Southend U (0) 0
Barnsley (1) 1 *(Campbell-Ryce 22)* 7212

Southend U: Flahavan; Hunt, Hammell, Bailey, Clarke P, Barrett, Francis, McCormack, Black, Hooper (Barnard), Gower.
Barnsley: Muller; Tininho, Van Homoet (Kozluk), Hassell, Souza, Foster, Campbell-Ryce, Howard, Ferenczi, Nardiello (Odejayi), Ricketts (Togwell).

Saturday, 26 January 2008
Arsenal (0) 3 *(Adebayor 51, 83, Butt 89 (og))*
Newcastle U (0) 0 60,046

Arsenal: Lehmann; Hoyte J, Clichy, Flamini, Senderos, Gallas, Diaby (Silva), Fabregas, Adebayor, Walcott (Hleb), Rosicky (Eduardo).
Newcastle U: Given; Carr, Jose Enrique (Rozehnal), Butt, Cacapa, Taylor, Milner, Duff (LuaLua), Owen, Smith, N'Zogbia.

Barnet (0) 0
Bristol R (0) 1 *(Lambert 49)* 5190

Barnet: Harrison; Devera, Nicolau (Birchall), Porter, Yakubu, Gillet, Wright, Bishop, Carew (Thomas), Akurang (Grazioli), Puncheon.
Bristol R: Phillips; Lescott, Jacobson, Campbell, Hinton, Coles, Pipe (Igoe), Disley, Williams (Rigg), Lambert (Walker), Lines.

Coventry C (1) 2 *(Hughes S 16, Mifsud 52)*
Millwall (1) 1 *(Simpson 42)* 17,268

Coventry C: Konstantopoulos; Borrowdale, Osbourne, Doyle, Davis, Ward, Gray, Hughes S, Adebola (Simpson), Mifsud (Best), Tabb.
Millwall: Evans; Senda, Barron, Forbes (Brammer), Robinson, Frampton, Dunne, Simpson, Alexander, Grabban, Fuseini (Harris).

Derby Co (0) 1 *(Earnshaw 55)*
Preston NE (3) 4 *(Hawley 14, 45, Whaley 33, Mellor 90 (pen))* 17,344

Derby Co: Price; Edworthy, Nyatanga■, Savage, Davis, Todd (Barnes), Ghaly, Pearson, Villa (Earnshaw), Miller, Lewis (Teale).
Preston NE: Lonergan; St Ledger-Hall, Davidson (Hill), Whaley (Nicholls), Chilvers, Mawene, Sedgwick, Carter, Brown, Hawley (Mellor), McKenna.

Liverpool (2) 5 *(Lucas 27, Benayoun 44, 56, 59, Crouch 90)*
Havant & W (2) 2 *(Pacquette 8, Skrtel 31 (og))* 42,566

Liverpool: Itandje; Finnan, Riise, Mascherano (Gerrard), Skrtel, Hyypia (Carragher), Pennant, Lucas, Benayoun (Kuyt), Crouch, Babel.
Havant & W: Scriven; Smith, Warner (Taggart), Jordan, Sharp, Collins, Potter, Wilkinson (Oatway), Pacquette (Slabber), Baptiste, Harkin.

Mansfield T (0) 0
Middlesbrough (1) 2 *(Lee 17, Buxton 87 (og))* 6258

Mansfield T: Muggleton; Martin, Jelleyman, Dawson, Mullins, Buxton, Hamshaw, Bell (Arnold), Brown (McAliskey), Boulding M, D'Laryea.
Middlesbrough: Schwarzer; Young, Pogatetz (Boateng), Wheater, Huth, Johnson (Downing), Rochemback, Arca, Lee (Mido), Aliadiere, Cattermole.

Oldham Ath (0) 0
Huddersfield T (1) 1 *(Beckett 10)* 12,749

Oldham Ath: Crossley; Eardley, Hazell, McDonald, Trotman, Stam, Allott, Kamudimba Kalala (Wolfenden), Smalley, Davies, Taylor.
Huddersfield T: Glennon; Sinclair, Williams, Holdsworth, Page, Clarke N, Collins, Worthington, Jevons (Kamara), Beckett (Mirfin), Schofield.

Peterborough U (0) 0
WBA (2) 3 *(Bednar 7, Koren 15, Phillips 58 (pen))* 12,701

Peterborough U: Lewis; Newton, Day, Keates (Mitchell), Morgan■, Charnock, Whelpdale, Lee, Boyd, McLean, Mackail-Smith.
WBA: Kiely; Hoefkens, Robinson, Koren, Cesar, Albrechtsen, Morrison, Teixeira, Bednar (Phillips), Beattie (MacDonald), Greening (Brunt).

Portsmouth (2) 2 *(Diarra 34, Kranjcar 45)*
Plymouth Arg (1) 1 *(Clark 5)* 19,612

Portsmouth: James; Johnson, Hreidarsson, Diarra, Pamarot, Distin, Lauren (Davis), Pedro Mendes (Hughes), Mwaruwari, Nugent (Mvuemba), Kranjcar.
Plymouth Arg: McCormick; Connolly, Sawyer, Clark (Folly), Timar, Doumbe, Norris, Nalis, Fallon, Easter (Jutkiewicz), Halmosi.

Southampton (0) 2 *(Surman 71, Rasiak 80)*
Bury (0) 0 25,449

Southampton: Davis; Thomas, Vignal, Wright J, Davies (Idiakez), Powell (Skacel), Hammill (John), Euell, Rasiak, Wright-Phillips, Surman.
Bury: Provett; Scott, Woodthorpe, Barry-Murphy (Mangan), Haslam, Futcher, Baker, Stephens, Adams, Bishop, Buchanan (Dorney).

Watford (0) 1 *(O'Toole 70)*
Wolverhampton W (1) 4 *(Keogh 5, 90, Elliott 58, Bothroyd 68)* 12,719

Watford: Lee; Doyley, Sadler, Bangura, DeMerit, Mackay (Mariappa), McAnuff, Kabba, Priskin (Smith), Ellington, O'Toole.
Wolverhampton W: Hennessey; Foley, Edwards R, Potter, Collins N, Ward D, Jarvis (Gray), Henry (Kightly), Keogh, Bothroyd (Gibson), Elliott.

Wigan Ath (0) 1 *(Sibierski 87)*
Chelsea (0) 2 *(Anelka 53, Wright-Phillips 82)* 14,166

Wigan Ath: Kirkland; Melchiot, Kilbane, Palacios (Sibierski), Bramble, Scharner, Valencia, Brown, Heskey (Aghahowa), Bent, Taylor (Koumas).
Chelsea: Cech; Belletti, Bridge, Makelele, Alex, Ricardo Carvalho, Wright-Phillips, Sidwell, Anelka (Pizarro), Cole J, Malouda (Paulo Ferreira).

Sunday, 27 January 2008

Hereford U (0) 1 *(Robinson 77)*

Cardiff C (1) 2 *(McNaughton 45, Thompson 67 (pen))* 6855

Hereford U: Brown; McClenahan, Rose, Diagouraga, Beckwith, Collins, Johnson, Smith, Robinson, Benjamin (Gwynne), Taylor (Easton).
Cardiff C: Oakes; McNaughton, Capaldi, Rae, Johnson, Loovens, Ledley, McPhail, Thompson (Hasselbaink), Whittingham, Parry.

Manchester U (1) 3 *(Tevez 38, Ronaldo 69 (pen), 88)*

Tottenham H (1) 1 *(Keane 24)* 75,369

Manchester U: Van der Sar; O'Shea, Evra (Simpson), Carrick (Scholes), Ferdinand, Brown, Ronaldo, Hargreaves, Rooney, Tevez (Anderson), Giggs.
Tottenham H: Cerny; Tainio (Defoe), Lee (Gunter), Huddlestone, Dawson▪, O'Hara, Lennon (Boateng), Jenas, Berbatov, Keane, Malbranque.

Sheffield U (2) 2 *(Shelton 12, Stead 24)*

Manchester C (0) 1 *(Sturridge 48)* 20,900

Sheffield U: Kenny; Geary, Naysmith, Martin, Bromby, Morgan, Gillespie, Speed, Shelton (Tonge), Stead (Sharp), Quinn S.
Manchester C: Hart; Corluka, Ball, Dunne, Onuoha, Gelson, Vassell, Hamann (Ireland), Elano (Sturridge), Mpenza (Geovanni), Petrov.

FIFTH ROUND

Saturday, 16 February 2008

Bristol R (0) 1 *(Lambert 84)*

Southampton (0) 0 11,920

Bristol R: Phillips; Lescott, Jacobson, Campbell, Hinton, Coles, Pipe, Disley, Williams (Rigg), Lambert, Lines.
Southampton: Davis; Ostlund, Wright J, Idiakez (Wright-Phillips), Davies, Powell, Viafara (Hammill), Euell, John, Saganowski (McGoldrick), Surman.

Cardiff C (2) 2 *(Whittingham 2, Hasselbaink 11)*

Wolverhampton W (0) 0 15,339

Cardiff C: Enckleman; McNaughton, Capaldi, Rae, Johnson, Loovens, Ramsey, McPhail (Blake), Hasselbaink (Thompson), Whittingham (Sinclair), Parry.
Wolverhampton W: Hennessey; Foley (Gibson), Gray, Olofinjana (Eastwood), Breen, Craddock, Potter, Henry, Kyle (Elliott), Bothroyd, Keogh.

Chelsea (1) 3 *(Lampard 18, 60, Kalou 70)*

Huddersfield T (1) 1 *(Collins 45)* 41,324

Chelsea: Cudicini; Paulo Ferreira, Bridge, Mikel, Terry, Ben Haim, Sidwell (Shevchenko), Lampard (Essien), Pizarro (Anelka), Kalou, Sinclair.
Huddersfield T: Glennon; Sinclair, Williams, Holdsworth, Page, Clarke N, Collins, Brandon, Jevons (Kamara), Beckett (Booth), Berrett (Schofield).

Coventry C (0) 0

WBA (1) 5 *(Brunt 12, Bednar 59, 69 (pen), Miller 76, Gera 78)* 28,163

Coventry C: Marshall; Osbourne, Hall, Doyle▪, De Zeeuw (Birchall), Ward, Hughes M, Simpson (Thornton), Best, Mifsud, Tabb.
WBA: Kiely; Hoefkens, Robinson, Pele, Barnett, Albrechtsen, Gera (Beattie), Texeira (Kim), Bednar (Miller), Brunt, Morrison.

Liverpool (1) 1 *(Kuyt 32)*

Barnsley (0) 2 *(Foster 57, Howard 90)* 42,449

Liverpool: Itandje; Finnan, Riise, Xabi Alonso, Carragher, Hyypia, Benayoun, Lucas (Gerrard), Crouch, Kuyt, Babel (Kewell).
Barnsley: Steele; Souza, Kozluk (Van Homoet), Hassell, Foster, Howard, Leon (Campbell-Ryce), Anderson, Ferenczi, Nardiello (Odejayi), Devaney.

Manchester U (3) 4 *(Rooney 16, Fletcher 20, 74, Nani 38)*

Arsenal (0) 0 75,550

Manchester U: Van der Sar; Brown, Evra, Carrick, Ferdinand, Vidic, Fletcher, Anderson (Scholes), Rooney (Saha), Park, Nani.
Arsenal: Lehmann; Hoyte J, Traore, Silva, Toure, Gallas, Eboue▪, Fabregas (Flamini), Eduardo (Senderos), Bendtner, Hleb (Adebayor).

Sunday, 17 February 2008

Preston NE (0) 0

Portsmouth (0) 1 *(Carter 90 (og))* 11,840

Preston NE: Lonergan; Jones, Davidson, Whaley, Chilvers, Mawene, Sedgwick (Chaplow), Carter, Brown, Hawley (Mellor), McKenna.
Portsmouth: James; Johnson, Hreidarsson, Diarra, Campbell, Distin, Kranjcar, Diop, Kanu, Utaka, Muntari (Baros).

Sheffield U (0) 0

Middlesbrough (0) 0 22,210

Sheffield U: Kenny; Geary, Naysmith, Tonge, Morgan, Kilgallon, Stead (Carney), Martin (Armstrong), Beattie (Hulse), Sharp, Quinn S.
Middlesbrough: Schwarzer; Young, Grounds, Wheater, Pogatetz, O'Neil, Rochemback, Arca (Boateng), Aliadiere, Mido (Afonso Alves), Downing.

FIFTH ROUND REPLAY

Wednesday, 27 February 2008

Middlesbrough (0) 1 *(Kenny 114 (og))*

Sheffield U (0) 0 28,108

Middlesbrough: Schwarzer; Young, Grounds, Hines, Pogatetz, Boateng, Rochemback (Johnson), Arca (O'Neil), Afonso Alves (Tuncay), Mido, Downing.
Sheffield U: Kenny; Geary, Naysmith, Speed, Morgan, Kilgallon, Stead (Martin) (Shelton), Tonge, Beattie, Sharp (Hulse), Quinn S.
aet.

SIXTH ROUND

Saturday, 8 March 2008

Barnsley (0) 1 *(Odejayi 66)*

Chelsea (0) 0 22,410

Barnsley: Steele; Souza, Van Homoet, Foster, Kozluk, Howard, Campbell-Ryce, Hassell, Ferenczi, Odejayi (Coulson), Devaney (Togwell).
Chelsea: Cudicini; Belletti (Pizarro), Bridge, Essien, Terry, Ricardo Carvalho, Wright-Phillips, Ballack, Anelka, Cole J, Malouda (Kalou).

Manchester U (0) 0

Portsmouth (0) 1 *(Muntari 78 (pen))* 75,463

Manchester U: Van der Sar (Kuszczak▪); Brown, Evra, Hargreaves (Carrick), Ferdinand, Vidic, Ronaldo, Scholes, Rooney, Tevez (Anderson), Nani.
Portsmouth: James; Johnson, Hreidarsson, Diarra, Campbell, Distin, Kranjcar (Hughes), Diop, Kanu (Baros), Utaka (Lauren), Muntari.

Sunday, 9 March 2008

Bristol R (1) 1 *(Coles 31)*

WBA (2) 5 *(Morrison 16, Miller 30, 69, 85, Phillips 73)* 12,011

Bristol R: Phillips; Lescott, Jacobson, Campbell, Hinton, Coles, Pipe (Walker), Disley, Williams (Igoe), Lambert, Lines (Haldane).
WBA: Kiely; Hodgkiss, Robinson, Koren, Barnett, Albrechtsen, Morrison (Kim), Brunt (Gera), Bednar (Phillips), Miller, Greening.

Middlesbrough (0) 0

Cardiff C (2) 2 *(Whittingham 9, Johnson 23)* 32,896

Middlesbrough: Schwarzer; Young, Pogatetz, Wheater, Huth, O'Neil (Johnson), Rochemback, Arca, Afonso Alves (Mido), Tuncay, Downing.
Cardiff C: Enckelman; McNaughton (Blake), Capaldi, Rae, Johnson, Loovens, Ramsey, McPhail, Hasselbaink (Thompson), Whittingham, Parry (Sinclair).

SEMI-FINALS (AT WEMBLEY)

Saturday, 5 April 2008

WBA (0) 0

Portsmouth (0) 1 *(Kanu 54)* 83,584

WBA: Kiely; Hoefkens, Robinson, Koren, Albrechtsen, Clement, Gera (Kim), Morrison (Brunt), Phillips, Bednar (Miller), Greening.

Portsmouth: James; Johnson, Hreidarsson, Diop, Campbell, Distin, Kranjcar, Diarra, Baros (Nugent), Kanu (Davis), Muntari.

Sunday, 6 April 2008

Barnsley (0) 0

Cardiff C (1) 1 *(Ledley 9)* 82,752

Barnsley: Steele; Souza, Kozluk (Butterfield), Foster, Van Homoet, Howard, Campbell-Ryce, Hassell, Ferenczi (Coulson), Odejayi, Devaney (Leon).

Cardiff C: Enckelman; McNaughton (Ramsey), Capaldi, Rae, Johnson, Loovens, Ledley, McPhail, Hasselbaink (Scimeca), Whittingham, Sinclair (Thompson).

THE FA CUP FINAL

Saturday, 17 May 2008

(at Wembley Stadium, attendance 89,874)

Portsmouth (1) 1 Cardiff C (0) 0

Portsmouth: James; Johnson, Hreidarsson, Diarra, Campbell, Distin, Utaka (Nugent), Pedro Mendes (Diop), Kranjcar, Kanu (Baros), Muntari.

Scorer: Kanu 37.

Cardiff C: Enckelman; McNaughton, Capaldi, Rae (Sinclair), Johnson, Loovens, Ledley, McPhail, Hasselbaink (Thompson), Whittingham (Ramsey), Parry.

Referee: M. Dean (Wirral).

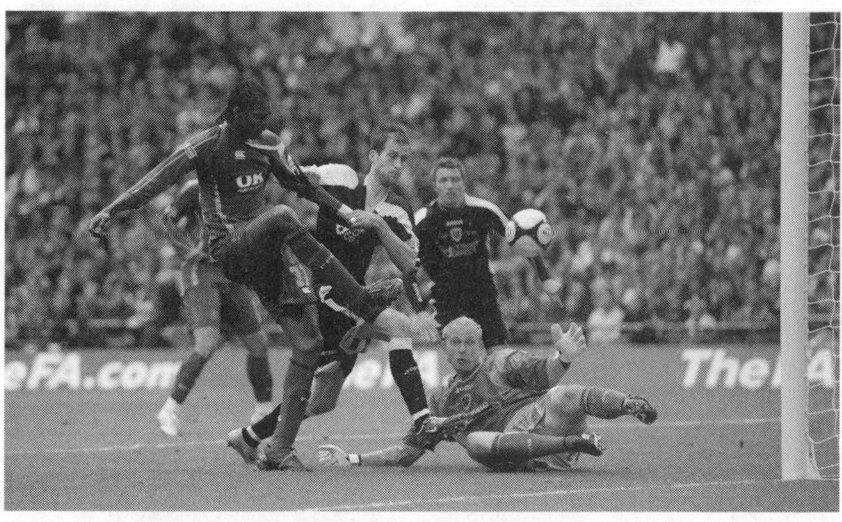

Despite the close attention of the Cardiff City defence, Nwankwo Kanu of Portsmouth scores the winning goal in the FA Cup Final at Wembley. The 1-0 victory was Portsmouth's first FA Cup Final success since 1939.
(Action Images/Tony O'Brien/Livepic)

BLUE SQUARE 2007–08

Any final League table scarcely reveals everything that happened during a season and the Blue Square Premier in 2007–08 was no exception. It might be imagined at a glance that Aldershot Town were runaway winners with the rest nowhere as one famous commentator said on the occasion of a foot race.

True the Shots finished with 31 record wins and similar chart-topping 101 points, some 15 to spare at the end, but they made anything but a scintillating start to the campaign losing two of their first three home games including a 3-0 drubbing at the Recreation Ground at the hands of Torquay United.

In fact it was Torquay who looked the more settled team in the early stages losing just twice in the opening 14 games. Neighbours Exeter City were as competitive as ever though with a tendency to draw too many games. Other early challengers included Stevenage Borough who topped the table in mid-September as the strengths and weaknesses were exposed up and down the country.

One of the key factors to Aldershot's ultimate success was their ability to avoid drawn matches. In fact six of their eight such occurred in the last nine games when the title was relentlessly being wound up. Their crucial period came with four games, three away, in which they dropped just two points.

Anyway, it was Cambridge United who caught Torquay United for runners-up position on goal difference. They, too, made a useful start unbeaten until losing to Forest Green Rovers on 29 September, unlucky thirteen for them. Never lower than the top five positions, Cambridge won five of their last six matches, while Torquay were taking just one point out of a possible 12.

It might be argued that Torquay had Trophy thoughts at this time. Their Wembley opponents Ebbsfleet United had a different agenda it seems. Winning only two of their last nine matches, the Kent club were concentrating on the final which they won.

The play-offs paired Exeter and Torquay, two west country teams. United snatched the lead away at the death, Cambridge meanwhile were to fight back at Burton Albion after going two goals behind. However there was a sensation at Torquay in the return match, United apparently coasting 1-0 until Exeter overran them with four goals in the last 20 minutes. Off to a flier at home Cambridge beat Burton 2-1. But it was Exeter who prevailed at Wembley in the final 1-0 against Cambridge to return to the Football League after an absence of five years. In Aldershot's case of course it was 16 years and time spent in the lower reaches of the non-league pyramid system.

Burton had never managed more than three wins in a row at any time, Stevenage falling away badly in the second half of the season, but Histon in their first season were a revelation and but for drawing six of their last ten unbeaten matches might well have made the play-offs.

Forest Green's best sequence was eight without defeat to mid-November but again had a poor second half despite the prolific scoring of Stuart Fleetwood. But perhaps the biggest surprise was the failure of Oxford United, expected to be strong contenders. Ninth was obtained only by winning their last five games. Grays Athletic crucially put the skids under Torquay in early March and lost just two of the last 14.

Salisbury City, another new name, gave more than a good account of themselves and were never outclassed, but Kidderminster Harriers had a disappointing season, a seven-match unbeaten run coming too late into early April. For York City a mid-season haul from the depths was not sustained – 10 without defeat at the time.

Crawley Town were capable of some notable wins but lacked consistency, Woking won just three of their last 15 but stayed out of trouble. Rushden & Diamonds had one run of four successive wins, but far below their ambitions and Weymouth only escaped the drop in the last six games.

Northwich Victoria, Halifax Town and Altrincham also survived, Halifax despite a ten-point penalty, though post-season their problems began in earnest. Not so fortunate were Farsley Celtic, Stafford Rangers and Droylsden, relegated after toiling much of the season.

The revival of a cup competition enlivened matters, too, as the Setanta Shield gave Aldershot a double of their own, beating Rushden & Diamonds in a dramatic penalty shoot-out on their own ground!

BLUE SQUARE PREMIER ATTENDANCES BY CLUB 2007–08

	Aggregate 2007–08	*Average 2007–08*	*Highest Attendance 2007–08*
Oxford United	108,750	4,728	5,900 v Crawley Town
Exeter City	85,206	3,705	7,839 v Torquay United
Cambridge United	81,675	3,551	7,125 v Histon
Torquay United	71,879	3,125	6,021 v Exeter City
Aldershot Town	69,710	3,031	5,980 v Weymouth
York City	51,940	2,258	3,136 v Cambridge United
Stevenage Borough	51,166	2,225	4,533 v Cambridge United
Burton Albion	41,079	1,786	2,881 v Exeter City
Woking	40,353	1,754	4,356 v Aldershot Town
Rushden & Diamonds	36,487	1,586	2,405 v Stevenage Borough
Kidderminster Harriers	35,786	1,556	2,027 v Torquay United
Salisbury City	35,488	1,543	2,633 v Torquay United
Weymouth	32,463	1,411	2,995 v Exeter City
Halifax Town	31,011	1,348	2,875 v York City
Forest Green Rovers	27,104	1,178	2,382 v Torquay United
Altrincham	27,053	1,176	4,154 v Farsley Celtic
Ebbsfleet United	25,002	1,087	1,852 v Oxford United
Histon	24,454	1,063	3,721 v Cambridge United
Crawley Town	23,955	1,042	1,940 v Aldershot Town
Grays Athletic	21,144	919	1,460 v Stevenage Borough
Northwich Victoria	20,888	908	1,875 v Droylsden
Stafford Rangers	19,394	843	1,853 v Farsley Celtic
Farsley Celtic	16,187	704	1,603 v York City
Droylsden	14,800	643	1,178 v Altrincham

BLUE SQUARE PREMIER FINAL LEAGUE TABLE

			Home					Away					Total						
		P	*W*	*D*	*L*	*F*	*A*	*W*	*D*	*L*	*F*	*A*	*W*	*D*	*L*	*F*	*A*	*GD*	*Pts*
1	Aldershot T	46	18	2	3	44	21	13	6	4	38	27	31	8	7	82	48	34	101
2	Cambridge U	46	14	6	3	36	17	11	5	7	32	24	25	11	10	68	41	27	86
3	Torquay U	46	15	3	5	39	21	11	5	7	44	36	26	8	12	83	57	26	86
4	Exeter C	46	13	9	1	44	26	9	8	6	39	32	22	17	7	83	58	25	83
5	Burton Alb	46	15	3	5	48	31	8	9	6	31	25	23	12	11	79	56	23	81
6	Stevenage B	46	13	5	5	47	25	11	2	10	35	30	24	7	15	82	55	27	79
7	Histon	46	10	7	6	42	36	10	5	8	34	31	20	12	14	76	67	9	72
8	Forest Green R	46	11	6	6	45	34	8	8	7	31	25	19	14	13	76	59	17	71
9	Oxford U	46	10	8	5	32	21	10	3	10	24	27	20	11	15	56	48	8	71
10	Grays Ath	46	11	6	6	35	23	8	7	8	23	24	19	13	14	58	47	11	70
11	Ebbsfleet U	46	14	3	6	40	29	5	9	9	25	32	19	12	15	65	61	4	69
12	Salisbury C	46	12	7	4	35	22	6	7	10	35	38	18	14	14	70	60	10	68
13	Kidderminster H	46	12	5	6	38	23	7	5	11	36	34	19	10	17	74	57	17	67
14	York C	46	8	5	10	33	34	9	6	8	38	40	17	11	18	71	74	−3	62
15	Crawley T*	46	12	5	6	47	31	7	4	12	26	36	19	9	18	73	67	6	60
16	Rushden & D	46	7	10	6	26	22	8	4	11	29	33	15	14	17	55	55	0	59
17	Woking	46	7	9	7	28	27	5	8	10	25	34	12	17	17	53	61	−8	53
18	Weymouth	46	7	5	11	24	34	4	8	11	29	39	11	13	22	53	73	−20	46
19	Northwich Vic	46	6	7	10	30	36	5	4	14	22	42	11	11	24	52	78	−26	44
20	Halifax T†	46	8	10	5	30	29	4	6	13	31	41	12	16	18	61	70	−9	42
21	Altrincham	46	6	6	11	32	44	3	8	12	24	38	9	14	23	56	82	−26	41
22	Farsley Celtic	46	6	5	12	27	38	4	4	15	21	48	10	9	27	48	86	−38	39
23	Stafford R	46	2	4	17	16	48	3	6	14	26	51	5	10	31	42	99	−57	25
24	Droylsden	46	4	5	14	27	45	1	4	18	19	58	5	9	32	46	103	−57	24

* Crawley Town deducted 6 points; † Halifax Town deducted 10 points.

BLUE SQUARE PREMIER LEADING GOALSCORERS 2007–08

	League	*FA Cup*	*Trophy*	*Total*
Stuart Fleetwood *(Forest Green Rovers)*	28	6	2	36
Steve Morison *(Stevenage Borough)*	22	0	1	23
Colin Little *(Altrincham)*	21	1	1	23
John Grant *(Aldershot Town)*	20	0	5	25
Jon Shaw *(Halifax Town)*	20	1	4	25
Daryl Clare *(Burton Albion)*	19	2	3	24
Tim Sills *(Torquay United)*	19	0	2	21
Richard Logan *(Exeter City)*	18	0	0	18
Chris Zebroski *(Torquay United loan)*	18	0	0	18
Scott Rendell *(Cambridge United)*	17	4	2	23
Mark Beesley *(Cambridge United)*	17	2	0	19
(Includes 10 League and 2 FA Cup goals for Forest Green Rovers.)				
Iyseden Christie *(Kidderminster Harriers)*	17	0	0	17

BLUE SQUARE PREMIER LEAGUE PLAY-OFFS

SEMI-FINALS FIRST LEG

Thursday, 1 May 2008

Exeter C (0) 1 *(Carlisle 76)*

Torquay U (1) 2 *(Sills 37, Zebroski 90)* 8276

Exeter C: Jones; Friend, Tully, Seaborne (Logan), Edwards, Taylor M, Harley, Gill, Stansfield (Watson), Moxey, Carlisle (Elam).
Torquay U: Rayner; Robertson, Nicholson, Mansell, Woods, Todd, Adams (D'Sane), Hargreaves, Phillips (Hill), Sills, Zebroski.

Friday, 2 May 2008

Burton Alb (0) 2 *(Clare 66 (pen), Stride 69)*

Cambridge U (0) 2 *(McEvilly 78 (pen), 84)* 5757

Burton Alb: Poole; Brayford, Hurst, Simpson, James, Stride, Corbett, McGrath, Clare, Harrad, Gilroy (Webster).
Cambridge U: Potter; Gleeson (Farrell), Reed (Pitt), Albrighton, Morrison, Hatswell, Carden, Wolleaston, Vieira, Beesley (McEvilly), Brown.

SEMI-FINALS SECOND LEG

Monday, 5 May 2008

Torquay U (0) 1 *(Hill 59)*

Exeter C (0) 4 *(Harley 70, Watson 81 (pen), Logan 89, Carlisle 90)* 6015

Torquay U: Rayner; Robertson, Nicholson, Mansell, Woods (D'Sane), Todd, Adams, Hargreaves, Zebroski, Sills (Phillips), Hill.
Exeter C: Jones; Friend (Carlisle), Tully, Seaborne, Edwards, Taylor M, Gill, Cozic (Harley), Stansfield (Watson), Logan, Moxey.

Tuesday, 6 May 2008

Cambridge U (1) 2 *(Wolleaston 1, 62)*

Burton Alb (1) 1 *(Clare 14)* 7276

Cambridge U: Potter; Gleeson, Pitt, Albrighton, Peters, Hatswell, Carden, Wolleaston, Vieira (Boylan), McEvilly (Fortune-West), Brown (Reed).
Burton Alb: Poole; Brayford, Webster, Simpson, James, Stride, Corbett, McGrath, Clare, Harrad, Farrell (Williams).

FINAL (at Wembley)

Sunday, 18 May 2008

Exeter C (1) 1 *(Edwards 22)* **Cambridge U (0) 0** 42,511

Exeter C: Jones; Friend, Tully, Seaborne, Edwards, Taylor M, Harley, Gill, Stansfield (Watson), Logan, Moxey.
Cambridge U: Potter; Gleeson (Fortune-West), Pitt, Albrighton, Peters, Hatswell, Carden, Wolleaston, Boylan (Vieira), McEvilly, Brown (Reed).
Referee: C. Pawson (Sheffield).

BLUE SQUARE SETANTA SHIELD

NORTHERN Section

FIRST ROUND

AFC Telford United v Solihull Moors	3-2
Alfreton Town v Hucknall Town	3-0
Barrow v Leigh RMI	4-0
Burscough v Vauxhall Motors	2-0
Gainsborough Trinity v Boston United	1-2
Stalybridge Celtic v Blyth Spartans	0-0

Blyth Spartans won 4-3 on penalties.

SECOND ROUND

AFC Telford United v Redditch United	2-0
Alfreton Town v Hinckley United	1-2
Harrogate Town v Blyth Spartans	3-2
Kettering Town v Boston United	2-0
Southport v Burscough	3-2
Tamworth v Hyde United	3-2
Workington v Barrow	2-2

Barrow won 7-6 on penalties.

Worcester City v Nuneaton Borough	1-2

THIRD ROUND

Kettering Town v Hinckley United	2-4
Nuneaton Borough v AFC Telford United	4-2
Southport v Barrow	2-3
Tamworth v Harrogate Town	3-1

FOURTH ROUND

Barrow v Northwich Victoria	0-2
Burton Albion v Tamworth	2-1
Cambridge United v Rushden & Diamonds	0-1
Droylsden v Farsley Celtic	2-1
Hinckley United v Kidderminster Harriers	1-2
Histon v Halifax Town	1-2
Nuneaton Borough v Altrincham	2-1
Stafford Rangers v York City	0-2

FIFTH ROUND

Droylsden v Burton Albion	0-2
Nuneaton Borough v Halifax Town	0-1
York City v Northwich Victoria	3-3

Northwich Victoria won 3-2 on penalties.

Kidderminster Harriers v Rushden & Diamonds	1-3

QUARTER-FINALS

Northwich Victoria v Rushden & Diamonds	0-4
Halifax Town v Burton Albion	3-1

SEMI-FINAL

Rushden & Diamonds v Halifax Town	1-0

SOUTHERN Section

FIRST ROUND

Basingstoke Town v Hampton & Richmond Borough	1-3
Bath City v Weston Super Mare	3-2
Bromley v Sutton United	2-1
Cambridge City v Thurrock	1-3
Dorchester Town v Eastleigh	3-2
Maidenhead United v Hayes & Yeading United	3-0

SECOND ROUND

Hampton & Richmond Borough v Dorchester Town	5-2
Bishop's Stortford v Thurrock	0-1
Eastbourne Borough v Bognor Regis Town	3-0
Havant & Waterlooville v Lewes	2-3
Maidenhead United v Bromley	1-2
Newport County v Bath City	3-2
St Albans City v Braintree Town	1-1

St Albans City won 5-4 on penalties.

Welling United v Fisher Athletic	2-1

THIRD ROUND

St Albans City v Thurrock	2-1
Eastbourne Borough v Lewes	7-2
Bromley v Welling United	1-2
Hampton & Richmond Borough v Newport County	2-1

FOURTH ROUND

Aldershot Town v Oxford United	1-0
Eastbourne Borough v Crawley Town	1-2
Exeter City v Ebbsfleet United	2-3
Hampton & Richmond Borough v Forest Green Rovers	0-1
St Albans City v Torquay United	2-0
Salisbury City v Weymouth	1-2
Welling United v Grays Athletic	1-3
Woking v Stevenage Borough	2-1

FIFTH ROUND

Weymouth v Ebbsfleet United	4-0
Woking v Forest Green Rovers	1-0
Crawley Town v Grays Athletic	4-0
St Albans City v Aldershot Town	0-4

QUARTER-FINALS

Crawley Town v Aldershot Town	2-6
Woking v Weymouth	3-0

SEMI-FINAL

Aldershot Town v Woking	2-2

Aldershot Town won 4-3 on penalties.

FINAL

at Aldershot

Attendance 3174

Aldershot Town (0) 3 *(Mendes 71, Hudson 95, Donnelly 107)*
Rushden & Diamonds (0) 3 *(Burgess 73, 109 (pen), Rankine 120)*
aet; Aldershot Town won 4-3 on penalties.

Aldershot: Jaimez-Ruiz; Smith, Straker, Donnelly, Newman, Winfield (Gier), Hudson, Chalmers (Harding), John Grant (Hylton), Mendes, Joel Grant.

Rushden & Diamonds: Roberts; Osano (El Kholti), Howell, Hope, Gulliver, Shaw (Gooding), Challinor, Woodhouse, Kelly (Tomlin), Rankine, Burgess.

Penalties: Gooding missed; Donnelly scored; Howell scored; Harding scored; Burgess scored; Newman scored; Woodhouse scored; Hudson scored; Hope saved.

Referee: S. Hooper (Wiltshire).

BLUE SQUARE NORTH & SOUTH 2007–08

BLUE SQUARE NORTH FINAL LEAGUE TABLE

			Home					Away					Total						
		P	*W*	*D*	*L*	*F*	*A*	*W*	*D*	*L*	*F*	*A*	*W*	*D*	*L*	*F*	*A*	*GD*	*Pts*
1	Kettering T	42	17	1	3	57	19	13	6	2	36	15	30	7	5	93	34	59	97
2	AFC Telford U	42	14	4	3	45	21	10	4	7	25	22	24	8	10	70	43	27	80
3	Stalybridge Celtic	42	12	4	5	47	24	13	0	8	41	27	25	4	13	88	51	37	79
4	Southport	42	10	8	3	38	21	12	3	6	39	29	22	11	9	77	50	27	77
5	Barrow	42	13	4	4	40	18	8	9	4	30	21	21	13	8	70	39	31	76
6	Harrogate T	42	10	6	5	25	16	11	5	5	30	25	21	11	10	55	41	14	74
7	Nuneaton B	42	12	6	3	32	17	7	8	6	26	23	19	14	9	58	40	18	71
8	Burscough	42	8	8	5	33	30	11	0	10	29	28	19	8	15	62	58	4	65
9	Hyde U	42	12	2	7	45	32	8	1	12	39	34	20	3	19	84	66	18	63
10	Boston U	42	12	3	6	39	22	5	5	11	26	35	17	8	17	65	57	8	59
11	Gainsborough Trinity	42	8	8	5	35	26	7	4	10	27	39	15	12	15	62	65	–3	57
12	Worcester C	42	8	7	6	27	30	6	5	10	21	38	14	12	16	48	68	–20	54
13	Redditch U	42	10	4	7	28	24	5	4	12	13	34	15	8	19	41	58	–17	53
14	Workington	42	8	4	9	25	20	5	7	9	27	36	13	11	18	52	56	–4	50
15	Tamworth	42	9	6	6	31	20	4	5	12	22	39	13	11	18	53	59	–6	50
16	Alfreton T	42	7	5	9	27	26	5	6	10	22	28	12	11	19	49	54	–5	47
17	Solihull Moors	42	7	5	9	29	36	5	6	10	21	40	12	11	19	50	76	–26	47
18	Blyth Spartans	42	7	2	12	27	31	5	8	8	25	31	12	10	20	52	62	–10	46
19	Hinckley U	42	7	4	10	24	28	4	8	9	24	41	11	12	19	48	69	–21	45
20	Hucknall T	42	4	4	13	25	36	7	2	12	28	39	11	6	25	53	75	–22	39
21	Vauxhall Motors	42	5	4	12	26	47	2	3	16	16	53	7	7	28	42	100	–58	28
22	Leigh	42	5	4	12	21	38	1	4	16	15	49	6	8	28	36	87	–51	26

BLUE SQUARE SOUTH FINAL LEAGUE TABLE

			Home					Away					Total						
		P	*W*	*D*	*L*	*F*	*A*	*W*	*D*	*L*	*F*	*A*	*W*	*D*	*L*	*F*	*A*	*GD*	*Pts*
1	Lewes	42	14	4	3	37	13	13	4	4	44	26	27	8	7	81	39	42	89
2	Eastbourne B	42	12	6	3	42	15	11	5	5	41	23	23	11	8	83	38	45	80
3	Hampton & Richmond B	42	10	8	3	49	23	11	6	4	38	26	21	14	7	87	49	38	77
4	Fisher Ath	42	10	3	8	35	36	12	2	7	30	25	22	5	15	65	61	4	71
5	Braintree T	42	13	4	4	30	14	6	8	7	22	28	19	12	11	52	42	10	69
6	Eastleigh	42	9	7	5	34	29	10	3	8	42	33	19	10	13	76	62	14	67
7	Havant & Waterlooville	42	14	3	4	33	16	5	7	9	26	37	19	10	13	59	53	6	67
8	Bath C	42	10	8	3	30	12	7	7	7	29	24	17	15	10	59	36	23	66
9	Newport Co	42	9	5	7	37	27	9	7	5	27	22	18	12	12	64	49	15	66
10	Bishop's Stortford	42	9	6	6	43	32	9	4	8	29	28	18	10	14	72	60	12	64
11	Bromley	42	11	3	7	44	29	8	4	9	33	37	19	7	16	77	66	11	64
12	Thurrock	42	13	4	4	39	26	5	5	11	24	38	18	9	15	63	64	–1	63
13	Hayes & Yeading U	42	7	9	5	40	35	7	3	11	27	38	14	12	16	67	73	–6	54
14	Cambridge C	42	8	7	6	43	32	6	3	12	28	40	14	10	18	71	72	–1	52
15	Basingstoke	42	8	6	7	33	34	4	8	9	21	41	12	14	16	54	75	–21	50
16	Welling U	42	6	5	10	23	34	7	2	12	18	30	13	7	22	41	64	–23	46
17	Maidenhead U	42	2	6	13	24	34	9	6	6	32	25	11	12	19	56	59	–3	45
18	Bognor Regis T	42	6	5	10	21	31	5	6	10	28	36	11	11	20	49	67	–18	44
19	St Albans C	42	5	5	11	21	35	5	7	9	22	34	10	12	20	43	69	–26	42
20	Weston Super Mare	42	6	4	11	28	38	3	6	12	24	47	9	10	23	52	85	–33	37
21	Dorchester T	42	5	4	12	17	33	3	6	12	19	37	8	10	24	36	70	–34	34
22	Sutton U	42	2	3	16	13	45	3	6	12	19	41	5	9	28	32	86	–54	24

BLUE SQUARE NORTH & SOUTH PLAY-OFFS

BLUE SQUARE NORTH

SEMI-FINALS FIRST LEG

Barrow 2 *(Tait 72, Rogan 82)* **AFC Telford 0**
Southport 1 *(Blakeman 36)* **Stalybridge C 0**

SEMI-FINALS SECOND LEG

AFC Telford 0 **Barrow 2** *(Reynolds 33 (og), Tait 78)*
Stalybridge C 2 *(Winn 31, Payne 70)* **Southport 1** *(Sykes 87)*
Stalybridge C won 5-3 on penalties.

FINAL

Barrow 1 *(Henney 58)* **Stalybridge C 0** 2530

BLUE SQUARE SOUTH

SEMI-FINALS FIRST LEG

Braintree T 0 **Eastbourne B 2** *(Tait 31, 68)*
Fisher Ath 1 *(Tomlin 59)* **Hampton & Richmond B 1** *(Hodges 34)*

SEMI-FINALS SECOND LEG

Eastbourne B 3 *(Tait 43, Crabb N 86, Atkins 90)*
Braintree T 0
Hampton & Richmond B 0 **Fisher Ath 0**
Hampton & Richmond B won 4-2 on penalties.

FINAL

Eastbourne B 2 *(Crabb N 85, Armstrong 90)*
Hampton & Richmond B 0 1077

BLUE SQUARE NORTH RESULTS 2007–08

	Alfreton T	AFC Telford U	Barrow	Blyth Spartans	Boston U	Burscough	Gainsborough Trinity	Harrogate T	Hinckley U	Hucknall T	Hyde U	Kettering T	Leigh RMI	Nuneaton B	Redditch U	Solihull Moors	Southport	Stalybridge C	Tamworth	Vauxhall M	Worcester C	Workington
Alfreton T	—	0-1	0-0	1-1	2-1	1-2	3-1	1-2	0-0	2-1	0-3	1-2	1-0	1-3	0-0	0-0	1-2	3-4	1-2	4-0	3-1	2-0
AFC Telford U	3-0	—	0-2	3-1	1-1	1-0	2-1	3-1	3-0	1-0	2-1	0-1	6-1	0-0	1-0	4-0	1-5	3-0	4-1	3-2	1-1	3-3
Barrow	2-1	4-0	—	1-1	1-0	4-1	4-1	2-2	0-1	2-1	1-0	1-1	1-2	0-1	2-0	5-1	1-0	1-3	2-0	4-1	1-0	1-1
Blyth Spartans	2-0	1-2	2-3	—	2-1	1-4	1-1	0-1	1-3	1-2	0-2	2-0	2-0	1-0	2-4	1-2	1-0	0-1	1-1	0-2	6-0	0-2
Boston U	2-1	2-1	2-1	3-2	—	0-1	0-1	0-1	1-1	2-3	2-1	0-1	5-1	1-1	3-0	2-0	1-2	3-1	1-0	5-1	2-2	2-0
Burscough	1-1	1-3	2-1	2-2	2-1	—	2-2	2-1	1-1	2-1	3-2	1-1	5-2	2-0	0-2	2-2	1-1	0-2	2-3	0-0	2-1	0-1
Gainsborough Trinity	2-2	1-1	1-1	4-0	1-3	0-1	—	0-1	2-2	4-1	3-3	3-1	2-1	1-1	3-0	0-2	0-3	2-1	1-0	3-0	1-1	1-1
Harrogate T	0-1	1-0	2-2	0-1	3-2	0-1	3-1	—	1-1	0-0	2-1	0-0	0-0	1-2	2-0	1-0	1-0	2-0	3-2	2-0	0-1	1-1
Hinckley U	1-0	1-1	1-2	1-1	0-1	1-0	1-2	2-3	—	2-1	2-1	0-0	3-1	0-0	1-2	0-1	2-3	0-3	2-0	0-1	2-4	2-1
Hucknall T	2-2	0-2	0-1	0-3	1-2	0-2	0-1	0-1	1-1	—	1-4	0-2	3-0	2-2	1-2	2-2	1-2	0-3	3-1	2-0	5-0	1-3
Hyde U	0-2	1-0	2-1	2-4	2-1	1-0	3-0	2-2	5-2	4-2	—	0-3	1-1	2-0	4-0	3-0	1-3	1-3	1-2	6-3	3-1	1-2
Kettering T	1-1	3-0	3-1	1-0	3-0	0-1	2-1	3-1	5-2	3-2	0-2	—	3-0	3-2	2-0	6-1	5-2	0-1	2-1	6-0	3-0	3-1
Leigh RMI	1-0	0-3	1-2	0-2	2-2	2-1	1-3	0-2	2-1	2-0	1-5	1-4	—	1-3	0-1	1-1	0-1	1-3	0-0	3-1	0-1	2-1
Nuneaton B	1-0	2-0	0-0	1-1	2-2	2-3	2-2	1-2	4-0	2-1	1-0	1-1	1-0	—	1-0	2-1	0-2	2-1	1-0	2-0	1-1	3-0
Redditch U	1-1	0-1	0-5	1-0	3-1	3-1	1-0	1-3	3-2	0-1	3-1	0-2	1-1	0-0	—	0-1	1-1	0-2	3-1	2-0	3-0	2-0
Solihull Moors	0-3	2-0	1-1	0-1	1-3	1-3	3-1	3-1	0-2	2-2	1-4	1-3	1-0	3-1	0-0	—	4-1	0-4	1-0	1-1	2-3	2-2
Southport	1-0	1-1	1-1	2-1	2-2	1-0	3-0	0-0	4-0	5-0	2-1	0-1	2-0	2-2	1-1	3-2	—	2-3	2-2	3-2	0-1	1-1
Stalybridge C	3-1	1-2	2-2	0-0	3-0	2-4	5-1	3-2	2-1	0-3	3-1	0-1	3-1	0-2	6-0	4-0	2-2	—	0-0	4-1	1-0	3-0
Tamworth	0-1	0-0	0-0	3-0	1-1	4-2	2-2	1-1	3-0	4-0	2-1	1-2	2-0	1-2	1-0	0-2	1-3	2-0	—	1-1	0-2	2-0
Vauxhall M	3-2	1-3	0-2	2-2	1-0	2-0	0-3	0-1	0-1	0-3	3-4	0-6	2-2	0-0	2-0	3-2	1-2	2-5	1-3	—	1-1	2-5
Worcester C	1-1	0-3	1-1	2-2	2-1	2-1	0-1	1-1	2-1	0-1	0-2	2-3	3-1	0-4	1-0	0-0	2-1	2-1	3-3	1-0	—	2-2
Workington	1-2	0-1	0-1	2-0	0-1	0-1	1-2	0-1	1-1	1-3	2-0	1-1	2-1	2-0	1-1	1-1	2-3	1-0	5-0	1-0	1-0	—

BLUE SQUARE SOUTH RESULTS 2007–08

	Basingstoke T	Bath C	Bishop's Stortford	Bognor Regis T	Braintree T	Bromley	Cambridge C	Dorchester T	Eastbourne B	Eastleigh	Fisher Ath	Hampton & Richmond B	Havant & Waterlooville	Hayes & Yeading	Lewes	Maidenhead U	Newport Co	St Albans C	Sutton U	Thurrock	Welling U	Weston Super Mare
Basingstoke T	—	0-4	1-2	3-2	2-2	1-1	2-1	1-0	2-3	3-4	1-5	1-2	2-3	1-1	1-1	0-0	3-1	3-1	1-0	3-0	2-1	0-0
Bath C	0-1	—	4-0	0-0	0-0	1-1	2-0	1-0	0-0	2-0	0-1	2-0	1-1	2-2	1-1	2-0	1-1	3-0	2-3	3-1	2-0	1-0
Bishop's Stortford	0-0	1-1	—	5-3	3-4	2-0	4-0	0-0	2-1	2-2	1-2	6-2	4-1	0-1	1-5	2-1	0-0	3-4	3-1	1-0	1-2	2-2
Bognor Regis T	1-1	1-3	0-2	—	2-1	1-2	2-0	0-0	0-2	0-3	0-1	2-4	1-1	3-0	0-5	1-2	0-2	1-0	1-1	3-1	0-0	2-0
Braintree T	2-1	2-0	2-1	3-2	—	2-1	0-1	1-0	1-0	0-2	2-3	3-0	1-0	0-1	3-0	1-1	0-0	0-0	1-0	0-0	2-1	4-0
Bromley	3-2	1-1	3-1	2-1	4-0	—	3-1	0-1	1-3	1-2	1-2	0-2	2-1	2-1	1-2	1-1	2-2	3-4	1-0	8-1	2-0	3-1
Cambridge C	3-0	2-2	2-4	2-2	0-0	1-2	—	2-2	1-1	1-1	3-2	1-2	2-0	1-4	1-3	3-0	0-2	4-0	4-1	2-2	3-1	5-1
Dorchester T	1-0	1-1	0-4	1-1	0-1	2-3	3-2	—	0-4	0-1	2-1	0-1	0-1	1-0	1-3	2-1	2-3	0-3	0-0	0-1	0-0	1-2
Eastbourne B	6-0	0-0	1-1	3-0	2-0	1-2	0-1	4-1	—	3-2	4-0	0-0	2-2	3-1	0-2	2-1	0-0	4-0	3-0	1-0	1-0	2-2
Eastleigh	1-1	4-4	0-0	1-0	2-1	1-4	1-0	3-1	1-2	—	3-0	1-1	1-1	1-4	3-0	3-2	0-2	1-1	1-2	0-0	3-1	3-2
Fisher Ath	4-1	2-1	0-1	3-1	2-0	0-3	1-1	1-1	0-4	1-4	—	0-3	4-2	4-2	0-3	0-1	1-3	0-0	4-2	2-0	3-2	3-1
Hampton & Richmond B	2-2	0-0	1-1	1-1	3-0	3-2	2-2	4-0	0-2	3-1	0-2	—	1-1	4-1	6-0	1-1	1-0	4-1	2-2	2-3	4-0	5-1
Havant & Waterlooville	1-1	1-0	1-2	2-0	0-0	1-0	2-1	4-0	2-1	1-0	1-0	0-3	—	4-1	1-2	0-3	2-0	3-1	2-0	3-0	1-0	1-1
Hayes & Yeading	1-1	3-0	2-2	0-2	3-3	6-1	3-1	2-2	1-1	2-4	2-1	0-0	3-1	—	2-1	1-4	1-3	2-1	3-3	1-1	0-1	2-2
Lewes	4-0	1-0	1-0	0-1	0-0	2-2	3-1	2-0	2-2	3-2	1-0	1-2	4-0	2-1	—	0-0	1-0	0-2	4-0	1-0	2-0	3-0
Maidenhead U	1-2	0-1	5-0	1-2	0-1	2-3	1-1	3-1	1-2	0-5	2-3	1-2	3-3	0-1	0-0	—	2-3	0-0	1-1	1-2	0-1	0-0
Newport Co	2-0	2-3	1-0	2-2	2-0	3-1	4-1	3-2	1-1	1-2	1-2	2-2	0-1	1-1	1-3	1-1	—	2-0	2-0	1-4	0-1	5-0
St Albans C	4-1	1-2	1-2	1-1	1-1	1-0	0-2	0-3	2-3	3-2	0-1	1-1	1-0	2-0	1-1	0-3	0-0	—	1-2	0-5	1-2	0-3
Sutton U	1-2	0-4	0-1	0-2	0-3	2-2	0-3	1-3	1-5	0-0	0-2	2-1	1-3	1-2	0-3	2-3	0-1	0-0	—	1-0	1-2	0-3
Thurrock	1-1	1-0	1-0	1-0	1-1	2-1	5-2	3-1	3-2	4-1	0-0	0-5	0-2	2-0	2-3	2-3	3-0	1-1	2-1	—	2-0	3-2
Welling U	0-1	1-0	2-1	2-3	0-2	3-1	2-6	1-1	1-0	3-1	0-1	1-3	1-1	1-2	0-4	0-2	1-2	0-0	0-0	2-2	—	2-1
Weston Super Mare	3-3	0-2	0-4	3-2	1-2	0-1	0-1	1-0	1-2	0-3	1-1	2-2	3-1	3-1	1-2	1-2	2-2	0-3	3-0	3-1	0-3	—

ALDERSHOT TOWN

FL Championship 2

Ground: Recreation Ground, High Street, Aldershot, Hampshire GU11 1TW. *Tel:* (01252) 320 211.
Year Formed: 1992 (formerly 1926). *Record Gate:* 7,500 (2000 v Brighton & Hove Albion, FA Cup 1st rd) (in Football League 19,138). *Nickname:* Shots. *Manager:* Gary Waddock. *Secretary:* Graham Hortop. *Colours:* Red shirts with blue trim, red shorts, red stockings with blue trim.

ALDERSHOT TOWN 2007–08 LEAGUE RECORD

Match No.	Date	Venue	Opponents	Result		H/T Score	Lg. Pos.	Goalscorers	Attendance
1	Aug 11	A	Kidderminster H	W	2-1	0-0	—	Davies 46, John Grant 58	1976
2	Aug 15	H	Torquay U	L	0-3	0-2	—		3139
3	Aug 18	H	Droylsden	W	3-1	0-1	9	John Grant 58, Chalmers 67, Harding 82	1773
4	Aug 24	A	Histon	W	2-1	2-0	—	Davies 2 31, 39	1614
5	Aug 27	H	Crawley T	L	0-1	0-0	—		2457
6	Sept 1	A	Altrincham	W	2-1	2-1	4	Dixon 24, Soares 78	991
7	Sept 4	A	Forest Green R	W	3-2	2-1	—	John Grant 2 11, 55, Dixon 27	1103
8	Sept 8	H	Northwich Vic	W	5-0	2-0	1	Day 28, Davies 2 37, 60, John Grant 62, Elvins 90	2002
9	Sept 15	A	Oxford U	W	3-2	2-0	2	John Grant 2 (1 pen) 15 (p), 43, Chalmers 83	5811
10	Sept 18	H	York C	W	2-0	0-0	—	Davies 57, Elvins 73	2402
11	Sept 22	H	Farsley C	W	4-3	1-0	1	Elvins 30, John Grant 2 47, 84, Newman 60	2334
12	Sept 25	A	Cambridge U	D	1-1	0-1	—	Winfield 87	3610
13	Oct 2	H	Exeter C	W	2-0	0-0	—	Soares 78, Joel Grantl 81	2943
14	Oct 6	A	Stevenage Bor	L	1-3	0-2	3	Day (pen) 48	3070
15	Oct 9	H	Ebbsfleet U	W	2-0	0-0	—	Day (pen) 71, Soares 86	2399
16	Oct 13	A	Burton Alb	L	0-2	0-1	2		1564
17	Oct 20	H	Halifax T	W	1-0	0-0	2	Dixon 90	2389
18	Nov 2	A	Weymouth	W	2-0	1-0	—	Elvins 33, Dixon 70	1782
19	Nov 17	H	Rushden & D	W	2-1	1-0	1	John Grant 25, Harding 50	3110
20	Nov 22	H	Grays Ath	W	3-2	3-0	—	Harding 3, Dixon 40, Joel Grant 45	2034
21	Dec 2	A	Salisbury C	W	4-0	2-0	—	John Grant 3 13, 81, 90, Harding 31	1786
22	Dec 8	H	Stafford R	W	4-3	3-2	1	Soares 10, John Grant 21, Dixon 44, Davies 78	2669
23	Dec 26	A	Woking	W	1-0	0-0	—	Hudson 78	4356
24	Dec 29	A	Grays Ath	L	1-2	0-1	1	Dixon 65	1210
25	Jan 1	H	Woking	W	2-1	2-0	1	Hudson 20, Newman 27	4728
26	Jan 5	A	Northwich Vic	W	2-1	1-0	1	Hudson 36, Joel Grant 49	871
27	Jan 19	H	Forest Green R	L	0-1	0-1	1		2895
28	Jan 26	A	York C	L	0-2	0-1	1		3092
29	Jan 29	H	Oxford U	W	1-0	0-0	—	John Grant 65	2754
30	Feb 9	A	Farsley C	W	3-1	1-0	1	Hylton 32, Hudson 2 62, 90	662
31	Feb 12	H	Cambridge U	D	0-0	0-0	—		3259
32	Feb 17	H	Stevenage Bor	W	3-1	3-0	1	Joel Grant 9, John Grant (pen) 18, Hylton 30	3261
33	Mar 1	H	Kidderminster H	W	2-1	1-1	1	Hylton 5, Harding 66	2835
34	Mar 3	A	Torquay U	W	2-1	1-0	—	Hylton 6, Davies 90	4510
35	Mar 11	H	Histon	W	3-1	2-0	—	Davies 12, Hudson 2 32, 65	2177
36	Mar 22	H	Altrincham	W	2-1	1-1	1	Charles 23, Davies 68	2991
37	Mar 24	A	Crawley T	W	1-0	1-0	1	Chalmers 7	1940
38	Mar 27	A	Droylsden	D	2-2	0-1	—	Mendes 57, Roche (og) 81	733
39	Mar 29	A	Stafford R	W	2-1	1-0	1	Elvins 41, John Grant 65	981
40	Apr 5	H	Salisbury C	W	2-1	1-0	1	Elvins 3, Hylton 82	3388
41	Apr 8	A	Ebbsfleet U	D	2-2	0-1	—	John Grant 2 56, 71	1439
42	Apr 12	H	Burton Alb	W	1-0	1-0	1	Elvins 36	5791
43	Apr 15	A	Exeter C	D	1-1	1-1	—	Donnelly 42	5005
44	Apr 19	A	Halifax T	D	0-0	0-0	1		1545
45	Apr 22	H	Weymouth	D	0-0	0-0	—		5980
46	Apr 26	A	Rushden & D	D	1-1	0-0	1	John Grant (pen) 72	2197

Final League Position: 1

GOALSCORERS

League (82): John Grant 20 (3 pens), Davies 10, Dixon 7, Elvins 7, Hudson 7, Harding 5, Hylton 5, Joel Grant 4, Soares 4, Chalmers 3, Day 3 (2 pens), Newman 2, Charles 1, Donnelly 1, Mendes 1, Winfield 1, own goal 1.
FA Cup (3): Dixon 2, Soares 1.
Trophy (16): John Grant 5, Dixon 2, Hudson 2, Mendes 2, Charles 1, Davies 1, Harding 1, Soares 1, Winfield 1.

Bull 44	Smith 6 + 2	Straker 43	Davies 24 + 5	Day 32 + 4	Charles 35	Soares 30 + 7	Chalmers 41 + 1	Grant John 32 + 2	Elvins 29 + 8	Harding 46	Hudson 18 + 17	Gier 38	Dixon 18 + 3	Winfield 18 + 6	Hylton 9 + 14	Newman 14 + 13	Grant Joel 20 + 10	Simmons — + 1	Mendes 3 + 3	Donnelly 2 + 6	Jaimez-Ruiz 2 + 1	Scott 1	Williams 1	*Match No.*
1	2	3	4	5	6	7	8^1	9	10	11	12													1
1		3	4^2	5	6	7	8	9	10	11	12	2^1	13											2
1		3	4	5	6^1	7^2	8	9	10^3	11	14	2	13	12										3
1		3	4	5	6	12	8^2	9	13	11	7^1	2	10											4
1		3	4	5	6	12	8	9		11	7	2^1	10											5
1		3	4	5	6	7	8		10^1	11		2	9^2		12	13								6
1		3■	4	5	6	7	8	9		11^1		2	10^2	12		13								7
1			4^1	5^3	3	7	8	9^2	10	11	12	2		6	13	14								8
1		3	4		6^1	7	8	9	10^2	11	12	2		5		13								9
1		3	4	5		7	8^1	9	10	11		2		6		12								10
1		3	4	5^1		7	8	9	10	11		2		6		12								11
1	12	3	4^2	5		7	8	9	10	11		2^1		6			13							12
1	2	3	4^1	5		7	8^2	9	10	11				6		13	12							13
1	2	3	4^1	5		7	8		10	11	13		12	6			9^2							14
1	2	3	12	5		7	8^1		10	4	11^2		9^3	6	14	13								15
1		3		5		7	8		10	4	11^1	2	9^3	6^2	12	13	14							16
1		3		5^1		7^2	8		10^3	11	12	2	9	6	14	4	13							17
1		3	4	5		7		12	10^2	8	13	2	9^1			6	11							18
1		6		5	3		8	9		7	12	2	10^2	4^1			11	13						19
1		3		5	6		8	9	12	4	7^1	2	10				11							20
1		3		5	6	7^1	8	9	14	4	13	2	10^3			12	11^2							21
1		3	12		6	7^1	8	9	13	4	14	2	10^2			5	11^3							22
1		3	7^1	5	6		8		10	4	12	2	9^2		13		11							23
1		3^2	7■	5	6		8		10^3	4	13	2^1	9	12	14		11							24
1		3		5^1	6		13	9		8^2	7	2	10^3	12	14	4	11							25
1	12	3			6		8	9		4	7	2^1	10^3	13	14	5	11^2							26
1	2	3		5^1	6	7		9	12	8			10		13	4^2	11							27
1	2	3	4^1	5		7	8	9		11			10^2	6	13		12							28
1		3	12		6	7	8	9		4		2^1		5	10		11							29
1		3		12	6		8	9	14	4	7	2^1		5	10^3	13	11^2							30
1		3	12	13	6■		8	9	10^1	4	7	2		5			11^2							31
1		3		5		12	8	9		4	7	2		6	10^1		11							32
1		3	12	5	6	13	8		10^3	4	7^1	2^2			9		11		14					33
1			7	5	3	12	8^1		10	4	13	2		6	9^3		11^2		14					34
1		3^1	4	5	6	14	8		10^3	11	7	2		12	9^2	13								35
1		3	7^2	5	6	12	8		13	4	11^3	2^1			10		14		9					36
1		3	7^2		6	2	8		12	4	14				10^1	5	11^3		9	13				37
1		3^1	4■	12	6	2	8	14		11^2	7				10^3	5	13		9					38
1			4^1	5	3	7	8	9^2	10	11		2		6	13					12				39
1		3		5	6	7	8^2	9^3	10	4	11	2^1			12	14				13				40
1		3			6	7	8^2	9	10	4	11	2^1				5	12			13				41
1		3			6	7^1	8	9	10	4	13	2				5	11^2			12				42
1		3			6	7		9	10	4	11	2				5				8				43
		3			6			9	10^3	4	12	2			14	5	13			7	1	8^1	11^2	44
1^G		3		12	6^1	7	8	9	10	4	11	2^2				5	13				15			45
		3■			6	7	8	9	10^2	4		2				5^1	11		13	12	1			46

FA Cup

Fourth Qualifying Round	Crawley T	(a)	1-1
		(h)	1-0
First Round	Cambridge U	(a)	1-2

Trophy

First Round	Hayes & Yeading	(a)	5-0
Second Round	Woking	(a)	4-2
Third Round	Braintree T	(h)	3-0
Fourth Round	Tamworth	(h)	2-1
Semi-Final	Ebbsfleet U	(a)	1-3
		(h)	1-1

ALTRINCHAM

Blue Square Premier

Ground: Moss Lane, Altrincham WA15 8AP. *Tel:* (0161) 928 1045. *Year Formed:* 1903. *Record Gate:* 10,275 (1991 Altrincham Boys v Sunderland Boys, ESFA Shield). *Nickname:* The Robins. *Manager:* Graham Heathcote. *Secretary:* Graham Heathcote. *Colours:* Red and white striped shirts, black shorts, red stockings.

ALTRINCHAM 2007–08 LEAGUE RECORD

Match No.	Date	Venue	Opponents	Result		H/T Score	Lg. Pos.	Goalscorers	Attendance
1	Aug 11	H	Exeter C	L	1-4	1-0	—	Munroe [31]	1318
2	Aug 14	A	Halifax T	D	2-2	2-2	—	Little [33], Sedgemore [37]	1401
3	Aug 18	A	Forest Green R	L	1-3	1-1	22	O'Neil [35]	738
4	Aug 25	H	Grays Ath	L	0-1	0-0	23		807
5	Aug 27	A	Stafford R	D	1-1	1-1	—	Lawton [15]	986
6	Sept 1	H	Aldershot T	L	1-2	1-2	22	Tinson [45]	991
7	Sept 4	A	York C	D	2-2	1-1	—	Tinson [44], O'Neill [90]	2079
8	Sept 8	H	Oxford U	L	1-3	0-1	21	Sedgemore [77]	1298
9	Sept 15	A	Woking	L	0-2	0-1	21		1391
10	Sept 18	H	Cambridge U	L	0-3	0-2	—		982
11	Sept 22	H	Droylsden	W	3-2	1-1	21	Little 2 [42, 62], Senior [71]	1187
12	Sept 29	A	Crawley T	W	1-0	0-0	21	Peyton [82]	1104
13	Oct 6	H	Rushden & D	L	1-2	0-2	21	Senior [54]	941
14	Oct 9	H	Burton Alb	D	0-0	0-0	—		1012
15	Oct 13	A	Salisbury C	D	3-3	2-0	21	Dean [35], Sedgemore (pen) [38], Senior [68]	1257
16	Oct 20	H	Ebbsfleet U	L	1-3	0-3	21	Little (pen) [67]	861
17	Nov 3	A	Histon	L	0-1	0-1	21		814
18	Nov 17	H	Weymouth	W	3-2	1-1	21	Senior 2 [7, 66], Shotton [47]	960
19	Nov 20	A	Farsley C	D	1-1	0-1	—	Little [67]	645
20	Nov 26	A	Stevenage Bor	L	1-2	1-1	—	Oliver (og) [16]	1662
21	Dec 1	H	Histon	L	1-2	0-1	—	Lane [60]	911
22	Dec 26	H	Northwich Vic	L	1-2	1-2	—	Senior [3]	1851
23	Dec 29	H	Stevenage Bor	L	1-5	1-2	21	White (og) [34]	763
24	Jan 1	A	Northwich Vic	W	2-1	0-0	21	Shotton [56], O'Neill [87]	1447
25	Jan 5	A	Oxford U	L	0-4	0-2	21		3950
26	Jan 8	H	Kidderminster H	W	2-1	0-0	—	Cahill [64], Peyton [76]	788
27	Jan 19	H	York C	D	2-2	1-0	20	Little 2 [41, 53]	1210
28	Jan 26	A	Cambridge U	L	1-2	0-1	20	Little [81]	3595
29	Jan 31	H	Woking	D	2-2	0-1	—	Little [57], Shotton [71]	905
30	Feb 9	A	Droylsden	W	2-0	0-0	20	Lawton [46], Little [72]	1178
31	Feb 12	H	Farsley C	D	0-0	0-0	—		4154
32	Feb 16	A	Rushden & D	L	0-1	0-1	20		1364
33	Feb 26	A	Torquay U	D	1-1	0-1	—	Peyton (pen) [72]	2310
34	Mar 1	A	Exeter C	L	1-2	0-2	20	Little [90]	3501
35	Mar 4	H	Halifax T	D	3-3	1-2	—	Little 2 (1 pen) [30, 49 (p)], O'Neill [68]	903
36	Mar 8	H	Forest Green R	W	1-0	0-0	19	Battersby [87]	956
37	Mar 11	H	Crawley T	L	2-3	0-0	—	Little 2 [75, 90]	715
38	Mar 15	A	Grays Ath	L	0-1	0-1	20		810
39	Mar 22	A	Aldershot T	L	1-2	1-1	21	Little [14]	2991
40	Mar 24	H	Stafford R	W	2-0	2-0	19	Little 2 [13, 42]	1135
41	Mar 29	H	Torquay U	D	1-1	0-0	19	Little [65]	1163
42	Apr 5	A	Kidderminster H	D	1-1	1-1	20	Little [7]	1535
43	Apr 8	A	Burton Alb	L	1-2	0-0	—	Young [81]	1295
44	Apr 12	H	Salisbury C	W	3-1	0-1	18	Shotton 2 [56, 61], Senior [78]	1242
45	Apr 19	A	Ebbsfleet U	L	0-2	0-1	20		911
46	Apr 26	A	Weymouth	D	2-2	1-2	21	Little [27], Senior [79]	1728

Final League Position: 21

GOALSCORERS

League (56): Little 21 (2 pens), Senior 8, Shotton 5, O'Neill 4, Peyton 3 (1 pen), Sedgemore 3 (1 pen), Lawton 2, Tinson 2, Battersby 1, Cahill 1, Dean 1, Lane 1, Munroe 1, Young 1, own goals 2.
FA Cup (2): Little 1, Senior 1.
Trophy (1): Little 1.

Coburn 37	Lane 32 + 7	Munroe 12 + 4	Sedgemore 18 + 4	Tinson 45	Aspinall 8 + 4	Lawton 45	Owen 11 + 2	Little 34 + 5	O'Neill 23 + 19	Whalley 9 + 5	Berkeley — + 2	Potts — + 13	Senior 28 + 10	Coo — + 1	Rose 1 + 1	Peyton 41 + 2	Acton 8	Scott 14 + 5	Thornley — + 1	McFadden 4 + 3	Logan 9 + 10	Clancy 1 + 3	Shotton 34	Saunders 1	Dean 3	Jennings 9	Toulson 13 + 2	King 16	Cahill 6 + 5	Young 21 + 1	Battersby 4 + 7	Roca — + 7	Lynch 8	Tansey 5	Turnbull 6	*Match No.*
1	2	3	4	5	6	7	8	9^{1}	10^{2}	11^{3}	12	13	14																							1
1	2	3	4	5	6	7■	8	9^{3}	12	11^{1}		14	10^{2}	13																						2
1	2	6^{1}	4	5			8^{2}	9	7	11	14	13	10^{3}		12	3																				3
	2	3		5	12	7	8	9■	10^{3}	11^{2}		13				4	1	6^{1}	14																	4
	2		4	5	6	7	8^{1}			11		12	9^{2}		10	3	1			13																5
1	2	3	4	5	6	7			10	12		13	9^{3}			11^{1}				14	8^{2}															6
1	2	3	4^{1}	5	6^{3}	7			10	8		12	13			11					9^{2}	14														7
1	2	3■	4	5	6	7^{2}		9^{3}	10	8^{1}		12	13			11					14															8
1	2		4	5	6	7		9	10^{2}			14	13			3^{1}					8^{3}	12	11													9
	2		4^{2}	5		7	8	14	10^{3}	11			13			3^{1}	1				9	12	6													10
	2		14	5		7	8	9		11^{3}		12	10			13					6	3^{2}	4	1^{1}												11
	2	13		5		7	8	9^{2}	14			12	10^{3}			11	1	3		4^{1}			6													12
	2			5		7	8	9^{3}	14			12	10			11^{1}	1	3		6^{2}	13		4													13
	2		4	5		7		9	13			12	10^{2}			11	1	3			8^{1}		6													14
	2	12	4	5		7			10				9			11	1	3					6		8^{1}											15
1	2^{1}	13	4	5^{2}		7		14		12			10			11^{3}		3			8		6		9											16
1	2	12	4	5	13	7			10				9					3			8		6^{1}		11^{2}											17
1		3	4	5		7	14	9^{2}	10^{3}				8^{1}			11		2		12	13		6													18
1	2^{2}	3	4	5		7	8^{1}	9	12				10			11		6			13															19
1	2	3	4^{1}	5		7		9	10	12			8			11		6^{2}			13															20
1	2		4^{1}	5		7		9	10^{2}	12			8			11		3			13		6													21
1	2	3^{1}	13	5	6^{2}	7		9	12	14			10■			11		4^{3}			8															22
1	2	3^{1}	4	5	12	7		9	10^{2}							11		6		8	13															23
1	2		14	5		7^{3}		9	13							11		12					6			3^{1}	4^{2}	8	10							24
1	2			5		7			13							11				9^{2}	14		6			3	4	8^{1}	10^{3}	12						25
1				5		7		14	13				9^{3}			11		12					6			3	2^{1}	8	10^{2}	4						26
1				5		7		14	13				10^{2}			11							2			3	4	8^{1}	9^{3}	6	12					27
1	12			5^{1}		7		9	14				10^{3}			11							2			3	4	8		6^{2}	13					28
1	13					7		9	12				10^{3}			11					14		6			3	4	8^{2}		5	2^{1}					29
1				5		7		9^{2}	12				10^{1}			11					13		6			3	2	8		4						30
1				5		7		9	12				10			11^{1}							2			3	4^{2}	8	13	6						31
1				5		7		9	13				14			11^{2}							2			3	4^{1}	8	10^{3}	6	12					32
1	2			5		7			12							11							6				4	9	10^{1}	3	8					33
1	2^{1}			5		7		12	10							11							6				4	9^{3}	13	3	8^{2}	14				34
1	12			5		7		9	10				8^{3}			11							6					4^{2}	14	3	2^{1}	13				35
1	2			5		7		9	10^{3}							11							6^{1}				4^{2}	8	12	3	14	13				36
	2^{2}			5		7		9	10■							11	1						6				13	8^{3}	14	4	12		3^{1}			37
1	2			5		7		9					13			11							6				4^{1}	8^{2}		10		12	3			38
1	2^{1}		12	5		7		9	10^{2}				8^{3}			11							6							4	13	14	3			39
1	12			5		7	14	9	10^{2}				8^{1}			11		13					6					4^{3}		3			2			40
1	14			5		7	8^{3}	9	12				13			11^{2}							6							3			2^{1}	4	10	41
1	12			5		7		9	10^{2}				13			11^{3}		14					6							3			8^{1}	2	4	42
1				5		7		9	14				10^{3}			11^{2}							6							3	12	13	2	4^{1}	8	43
1	14			5		7		9	10^{3}				12			11		13					6							3			2^{1}	4	8^{2}	44
1	2			5	13	7		9	14				10^{3}			11							6							3		12		4^{1}	8^{2}	45
1	2			5		7		9	10^{2}				8			13		4■					6				12			3					11^{1}	46

FA Cup

Fourth Qualifying Round	Kendal T	(a)	1-0
First Round	Millwall	(h)	1-2

Trophy

First Round	York C	(h)	1-3

BURTON ALBION

Blue Square Premier

Ground: Eton Park, Princess Way, Burton-on-Trent DE14 2RU. *Tel:* (01283) 565 938. *Year Formed:* 1950.
Record Gate: 5,806 (1964 v Weymouth, Southern League Cup Final). *Nickname:* Brewers. *Manager:* Nigel Clough.
Secretary: Tony Kirkland. *Colours:* All yellow with black trim.

BURTON ALBION 2007–08 LEAGUE RECORD

Match No.	*Date*	*Venue*	*Opponents*	*Result*		*H/T Score*	*Lg. Pos.*	*Goalscorers*	*Attendance*
1	Aug 11	A	Histon	D	2-2	0-0	—	McGrath [46], Clare [90]	1265
2	Aug 14	H	York C	W	4-3	1-1	—	Greaves [26], Harrad [83], McGrath [87], Holmes [90]	1892
3	Aug 19	H	Oxford U	L	1-2	1-1	12	Clare [11]	2259
4	Aug 23	A	Weymouth	W	2-1	2-1	—	Corbett [40], Harrad [45]	1404
5	Aug 27	H	Farsley C	W	1-0	0-0	—	Gilroy [79]	1521
6	Sept 1	A	Crawley T	D	1-1	0-1	8	Webster [58]	906
7	Sept 4	A	Northwich Vic	W	2-0	1-0	—	Webster [24], Gilroy [63]	845
8	Sept 10	H	Torquay U	W	3-1	2-0	—	Brayford [14], Gooding [32], Harrad [83]	2086
9	Sept 15	A	Rushden & D	D	0-0	0-0	5		1807
10	Sept 18	H	Ebbsfleet U	D	1-1	0-1	—	Gilroy [86]	1594
11	Sept 22	H	Woking	W	2-0	2-0	5	Clare 2 (1 pen) [17 (p), 32]	1501
12	Sept 25	A	Droylsden	W	2-0	0-0	—	Greaves [74], Harrad [78]	665
13	Oct 2	A	Halifax T	D	2-2	0-1	—	Goodfellow [67], Clare [90]	1206
14	Oct 6	H	Salisbury C	W	4-3	1-2	4	Gilroy [25], Greaves [80], Taylor [88], Clare (pen) [90]	1362
15	Oct 9	A	Altrincham	D	0-0	0-0	—		1012
16	Oct 13	H	Aldershot T	W	2-0	1-0	3	Webster [10], Greaves [51]	1564
17	Oct 18	A	Stevenage Bor	D	3-3	1-1	—	Clare [27], Harrad 2 [76, 79]	1843
18	Nov 3	H	Kidderminster H	L	0-2	0-1	5		1864
19	Nov 17	A	Exeter C	W	4-1	1-1	4	Harrad 2 [33, 89], Clare 2 [53, 58]	3823
20	Nov 23	H	Cambridge U	L	1-2	1-0	—	Harrad [17]	2263
21	Dec 8	H	Forest Green R	D	1-1	1-1	5	Harrad [45]	1489
22	Dec 26	A	Stafford R	W	3-0	3-0	—	Greaves [35], Edwards 2 [44, 45]	1679
23	Dec 29	A	Cambridge U	D	0-0	0-0	5		3382
24	Jan 1	H	Stafford R	W	2-1	1-1	4	Goodfellow [34], Edwards [66]	2465
25	Jan 7	A	Torquay U	W	2-1	1-1	—	Webster [23], Harrad [51]	2359
26	Jan 19	H	Northwich Vic	W	4-1	2-1	4	Webster 2 [2, 74], Corbett [30], Harrad [60]	2165
27	Jan 26	A	Ebbsfleet U	L	1-2	0-1	4	Clare [90]	1385
28	Jan 29	H	Rushden & D	W	2-1	1-1	—	Clare [11], Goodfellow [77]	1460
29	Feb 9	A	Woking	L	1-2	0-2	4	McGrath [88]	1493
30	Feb 12	H	Droylsden	W	3-0	2-0	—	Clare 2 [8, 19], Holmes [54]	1501
31	Feb 16	A	Salisbury C	L	0-2	0-0	5		1433
32	Mar 1	H	Histon	L	1-3	0-2	6	Edwards [80]	1508
33	Mar 4	A	York C	D	0-0	0-0	—		1882
34	Mar 8	A	Oxford U	W	3-0	2-0	6	Clare [20], Gilroy 2 [27, 84]	4392
35	Mar 11	A	Grays Ath	D	0-0	0-0	—		496
36	Mar 16	H	Weymouth	W	2-1	0-1	5	McGrath [68], Brayford [76]	1501
37	Mar 22	H	Crawley T	W	1-0	0-0	5	Clare [59]	1559
38	Mar 24	A	Farsley C	W	1-0	1-0	3	Williams [14]	696
39	Mar 31	A	Forest Green R	L	1-3	0-2	—	Clare [71]	943
40	Apr 5	H	Grays Ath	L	2-3	2-1	6	Stuart (og) [34], Williams [41]	1582
41	Apr 8	H	Altrincham	W	2-1	0-0	—	Harrad [68], Brayford [90]	1295
42	Apr 12	A	Aldershot T	L	0-1	0-1	6		5791
43	Apr 15	H	Halifax T	W	2-1	0-0	—	Clare [74], Goodfellow [89]	1607
44	Apr 18	H	Stevenage Bor	W	3-0	0-0	—	Brayford 2 [58, 81], Clare (pen) [77]	2160
45	Apr 22	A	Kidderminster H	L	1-4	0-3	—	Harrad [79]	1761
46	Apr 26	H	Exeter C	D	4-4	1-1	5	Clare [9], Williams [70], Harrad 2 [80, 83]	2881

Final League Position: 5

GOALSCORERS

League (79): Clare 19 (3 pens), Harrad 16, Gilroy 6, Webster 6, Brayford 5, Greaves 5, Edwards 4, Goodfellow 4, McGrath 4, Williams 3, Corbett 2, Holmes 2, Gooding 1, Taylor 1, own goal 1.
FA Cup (7): Clare 2, McGrath 2, Harrad 1, Stride 1, own goal 1.
Trophy (8): Clare 3 (1 pen), Edwards 2, McGrath 2, Brayford 1.
Play-Offs (3): Clare 2 (1 pen), Stride 1.

Poole 32	Brayford 45	Webster 33 + 4	Greaves 30 + 5	James 29 + 1	Shaw 2 + 3	Corbett 33 + 3	McGrath 46	Clare 33 + 6	Edwards 23 + 9	Farrell 17 + 4	Harrad 26 + 20	Gilroy 32 + 3	Holmes 10 + 11	Goodfellow 15 + 20	Hall — + 2	Gooding 11 + 1	Austin 5 + 6	Aiston 4 + 1	Stride 16 + 8	Taylor 3 + 2	Simpson 25	Deeney 13 + 1	Clough — + 1	Hurst 16	Tomlinson 1	Williams 6 + 3	Match No.
1	2^{1}	3	4	5^{2}	6	7	8	9	10	11	12	13															1
1	2	5■	4^{1}		6	7	8	9	10^{3}	3	14	11^{2}	12	13													2
1	2		4		13	5	7	9	10^{2}	3	12	11	8^{1}	6													3
1	2	5	4		13	7^{1}	8^{2}	9^{3}	10	3	14	11	6	12													4
1	2	5	4		14		8	12	9^{1}	3	10^{2}	11^{3}	7	6	13												5
1	2	5	4				8	9^{1}	10	3^{2}	12	11	13	6		7											6
1	2	3	4^{1}				8		10^{3}		9	11	5	13	14	6	12	7^{2}									7
1	2	3	4^{1}			13	8		10^{3}		9	11	5			6	14	7^{2}	12								8
1	2	3				7	8		10	12	9		5			6		11^{1}	4								9
1	2	3	4			13	8	14	10^{3}		9	11	5^{1}			6		7^{2}	12								10
1	2		4			7	8	9^{3}		3	10	11^{2}	5	13		6^{1}		12		14							11
1	2	3	4				8	9^{3}		7^{1}	14	11^{2}	12	13		6			5	10							12
1	2	3	4			7^{2}	8	14	12		9	11		13		6			5^{1}	10^{3}							13
1	2	3	4■				8	9	10^{3}	13	12	11^{2}	5^{1}	7		6				14							14
1	2	3		12		7	8	9		11^{1}	13			6		4			5	10^{2}							15
1	2	3	4	5		7	8	9^{3}	10^{1}		12	11^{2}		13			14		6								16
1	2	3	4	5		7	8	9	10^{2}		13	11^{1}		12					6								17
1	2	3		5		7	8	9	10		12	11				6	4^{1}										18
1	2	3	4	5		7	8	9^{3}	14		10	11^{2}	12			13					6^{1}						19
1		3	4	5		2	8	9■			10	11		7^{1}					12		6						20
	2	3	4	5		7	8		9^{2}		10	11^{1}		12					13		6	1					21
1	2^{1}	3	4	5		7	8	13	9	11	10^{2}			12							6						22
	2	3	4	5		7	8			9^{1}	10	12							6		11	1					23
	2	12		5		13	8^{2}	9^{3}	10	3^{1}	14	11		7					6		4	1					24
	2	3	4	5		7	8			9^{2}	10		12	13					6^{1}		11	1					25
1	2^{1}	3	14	5		7	8	9^{3}		11^{2}	10		12	13					6		4						26
1	2^{1}	3	4	5		7	8	13		9^{2}	10			12					6		11						27
1	2	3		5		7	8	9^{2}	14	13	10^{3}	11^{1}		12			6				4						28
1	2		4^{1}	5		7	8	9	13	11	10^{2}		12	6			3										29
1	2			5		7	8^{2}	9	13	3^{1}	10	11^{3}	12	4			6						14				30
1^{6}	2		4	5		7	8	9			10	13	6^{1}	11^{2}			12					15		3			31
	2			5		7	8	9	10^{1}		12	11	13				6				4^{2}			3	1		32
	2		4	5		7	8	12	13		10^{2}	11		6^{1}							9	1		3			33
	2		4	5		7	8	9^{3}	10^{2}		14	11^{1}	13	12							6	1		3			34
	2	3	4			7	8	9	10^{2}		13		12						6		5^{1}	1		11			35
	2	12	4^{1}			7^{2}	8	9	10^{3}		14	11		13					6		5	1		3			36
	2	13	12	5			8	9	10^{3}		14	11^{2}		7					6^{1}		4	1		3			37
	2	11	4^{1}	5			8	9^{2}	14	12	6			13							7	1		3		10^{3}	38
	2	12	4	5			8	9	13		10^{2}	11									6	1		3		7^{1}	39
	2	11		5			8	9			12	7							6		4	1		3^{1}		10	40
	2	5	12			7	8	9^{1}			10	11		13					14		6	1		3^{3}		4^{2}	41
1	2	6		5		7	8		9^{2}		10^{3}			11			12		14		4			3^{1}		13	42
1	2	6	12	5^{3}		7	8	9^{1}			13			11					14		4			3^{2}		10	43
1	2	6		5		7	8	9^{3}			13	11^{1}		12					14		4			3		10^{2}	44
1	2	6	13	5		7^{1}	8	9^{3}			10	11^{2}		12							4			3		14	45
1	2			5^{1}			8	9^{2}	14		10	11		7			12		6		4			3		13^{3}	46

FA Cup

Fourth Qualifying Round	Tamworth	(h)	2-1
First Round	Halifax T	(a)	4-0
Second Round	Barnet	(h)	1-1
		(a)	0-1

Trophy

First Round	Colwyn Bay	(a)	2-1
Second Round	Vauxhall M	(a)	4-1
Third Round	Histon	(h)	1-1
		(a)	1-0
Fourth Round	Ebbsfleet U	(h)	0-0
		(a)	0-1

Play-Offs

Semi-Final	Cambridge U	(h)	2-2
		(a)	1-2

CAMBRIDGE UNITED — Blue Square Premier

Ground: Abbey Stadium, Newmarket Road, Cambridge CB5 8LN. *Tel:* (01223) 566 500. *Year Formed:* 1912.
Record Gate: 14,000 (1970 v Chelsea, Friendly). *Nickname:* The U's. *Manager:* Gary Brabin.
Secretary: Andrew Pincher. *Colours:* Navy and sky blue shirts, sky blue shorts, sky blue stockings.

CAMBRIDGE UNITED 2007–08 LEAGUE RECORD

Match No.	Date	Venue	Opponents	Result		H/T Score	Lg. Pos.	Goalscorers	Attendance
1	Aug 11	A	York C	W	2-1	0-1	—	Hoyte 51, Boylan (pen) 56	3136
2	Aug 16	H	Oxford U	W	2-1	0-1	—	Fortune-West 50, Boylan 90	3327
3	Aug 21	H	Farsley C	W	5-1	3-0	—	Wolleaston 2, Fortune-West 3 10, 27, 80, Albrighton 88	2845
4	Aug 25	A	Woking	D	0-0	0-0	2		1805
5	Aug 27	H	Ebbsfleet U	D	1-1	0-1	—	Rendell 90	2974
6	Aug 31	A	Weymouth	D	2-2	0-1	—	Fortune-West 63, Rendell 70	1502
7	Sept 4	H	Grays Ath	W	1-0	0-0	—	Rendell 48	2793
8	Sept 8	A	Exeter C	D	1-1	0-1	4	Rendell 55	3197
9	Sept 15	H	Crawley T	W	2-1	0-1	4	Fortune-West 47, Wolleaston 51	2975
10	Sept 18	A	Altrincham	W	3-0	2-0	—	Pitt 17, Gleeson 21, Rendell 58	982
11	Sept 22	A	Stevenage Bor	W	2-1	1-0	4	Convery 42, Rendell 62	4533
12	Sept 25	H	Aldershot T	D	1-1	1-0	—	Rendell 21	3610
13	Sept 29	A	Forest Green R	L	1-3	0-1	4	Boylan 90	1179
14	Oct 6	H	Halifax T	D	2-2	1-1	5	Robinson 24, Wolleaston 55	3027
15	Oct 9	H	Rushden & D	W	1-0	0-0	—	Rendell 80	3005
16	Oct 13	A	Stafford R	D	1-1	1-1	5	Pitt 14	741
17	Oct 20	H	Salisbury C	D	1-1	1-0	5	Rendell 11	3868
18	Nov 3	A	Torquay U	W	2-1	1-1	4	Boylan 40, Wolleaston 87	3368
19	Nov 17	H	Northwich Vic	W	2-1	1-0	3	Rendell 2 41, 79	4044
20	Nov 23	A	Burton Alb	W	2-1	0-1	—	Reed 50, Rendell 68	2263
21	Dec 6	A	Kidderminster H	L	0-1	0-0	—		1314
22	Dec 26	H	Histon	W	1-0	0-0	—	Albrighton 54	7125
23	Dec 29	H	Burton Alb	D	0-0	0-0	4		3382
24	Jan 1	A	Histon	L	0-1	0-0	5		3721
25	Jan 19	A	Grays Ath	L	1-2	1-0	5	Rendell 26	1403
26	Jan 22	H	Droylsden	W	5-0	2-0	—	Rendell 3 10, 69, 75, Wolleaston 32, McEvilly 61	2000
27	Jan 26	H	Altrincham	W	2-1	1-0	5	McEvilly 23, Convery 85	3595
28	Jan 29	H	Exeter C	L	0-1	0-1	—		2769
29	Feb 9	H	Stevenage Bor	W	2-1	0-0	5	Pitt 64, Rendell 89	3772
30	Feb 12	A	Aldershot T	D	0-0	0-0	—		3259
31	Feb 16	A	Halifax T	W	2-1	1-1	3	Beesley 45, McEvilly 56	1402
32	Feb 23	H	Forest Green R	W	2-0	1-0	3	Hatswell 5, Preece (og) 64	4797
33	Mar 1	H	York C	W	2-0	1-0	3	Boylan 2 45, 50	3666
34	Mar 4	A	Oxford U	W	2-1	1-1	—	Boylan 2 16, 57	4422
35	Mar 8	A	Farsley C	L	1-2	0-0	2	Boylan 51	868
36	Mar 15	H	Woking	W	1-0	1-0	2	Boylan (pen) 45	3778
37	Mar 18	A	Crawley T	L	1-2	1-1	—	Boylan 21	1024
38	Mar 22	H	Weymouth	D	0-0	0-0	2		2914
39	Mar 24	A	Ebbsfleet U	L	1-2	1-1	4	Hatswell 34	1388
40	Mar 29	H	Kidderminster H	L	0-3	0-1	4		3999
41	Apr 5	A	Droylsden	W	2-0	1-0	3	Farrell 9, Beesley 52	634
42	Apr 8	A	Rushden & D	W	2-1	0-0	—	Beesley 2 65, 73	2358
43	Apr 12	H	Stafford R	L	1-2	1-1	3	Farrell 6	3310
44	Apr 19	A	Salisbury C	W	2-0	2-0	4	Jeffrey 31, Beesley 41	1710
45	Apr 22	H	Torquay U	W	2-0	2-0	—	Beesley 2 41, 45	4100
46	Apr 26	A	Northwich Vic	W	2-0	1-0	2	Vieira 2 23, 84	1512

Final League Position: 2

GOALSCORERS

League (68): Rendell 17, Boylan 11 (2 pens), Beesley 7, Fortune-West 6, Wolleaston 5, McEvilly 3, Pitt 3, Albrighton 2, Convery 2, Farrell 2, Hatswell 2, Vieira 2, Gleeson 1, Hoyte 1, Jeffrey 1, Reed 1, Robinson 1, own goal 1.
FA Cup (10): Rendell 4 (3 pens), Boylan 2, Knight 2, Fortune-West 1, Wolleaston 1.
Trophy (5): Rendell 2, Boylan 1, Fortune-West 1, Hoyte 1.
Play-Offs (4): McEvilly 2 (1 pen), Wolleaston 2.

Potter 44	Gleeson 40	Pitt 40 + 6	Albrighton 37 + 1	Hoyte 11	Morrison 39 + 1	Quinton 12 + 3	Convery 13 + 9	Fortune-West 17 + 6	Boylan 24 + 8	Brown 13 + 1	Peters 26 + 7	Reed 28 + 10	Smith 1 + 13	Wolleaston 44	Rendell 23 + 6	Hyem — + 5	Willmott 1 + 14	Robinson 2 + 2	Coulson 9 + 4	Knights 4	McShane 1	Carden 17	Hatswell 18	McEvilly 13 + 1	Farrell 7 + 6	Beesley 13 + 4	Jeffrey 4 + 6	Vieira 4 + 6	Collins — + 1	McCarthy 1	*Match No.*
1	2	3^{3}	4	5^{1}	6	7	8^{2}	9	10	11	12	13	14																		1
1	2	3	4	5^{1}	6	7		9^{3}	10		12	11^{2}	13	8	14																2
1	2	3	4	5^{1}	6	7^{2}		9	10	11^{3}	12	14	13	8																	3
1	2^{1}	3	4		6	7^{2}		9	10^{3}	11	5	13	12	8	14																4
1	2	3	4	5^{1}	6			9^{3}	10		7	11^{2}	12	8	14	13															5
1	2	3^{2}	4	5		7^{1}		9	10^{3}		6	11	13	8	14	12															6
1	2	3	4	5^{1}	6	7	13	9^{2}			12	11		8	10																7
1	2	3	4	5^{1}	6	7^{3}	14	9			12	11^{2}	13	8	10																8
1	2	14	4		6	11^{2}	7^{1}	9			5	3	12	8	10^{3}		13														9
1	2	3	4		6	12	8	9			5	11^{1}		7	10^{2}		13														10
1	2	3	4		6	13	8^{2}	9			5	11	12	7^{1}	10^{3}		14														11
1	2	3	4		6	13	8	9			5	11^{1}	12	7^{2}	10^{3}			14■													12
1	2	3^{2}	4	5^{1}	6		8	9^{3}	14		12	13	11	7	10																13
1	2	3		5^{1}	6	7^{2}	13		14		4	11		8	10^{3}			9	12												14
1	2	3	4		6	7	8^{1}	9^{2}	14		5	12		11	13			10^{3}													15
1	2	3	4		6	7	8^{1}	13	10^{3}		5		12	11	9^{2}			14													16
1	2	3	4		6	7^{1}		9			5	12	13	11	10					8^{2}											17
	2	3^{1}	4		6			14	10		5	11	12^{2}	8	9	13				7^{3}	1										18
1		3^{2}		5	6		8^{1}	14	10		4	11		7	9	13	12			2^{3}											19
1	2	12	4		6		8^{1}	13	10^{2}		5	3		7	9							11									20
1	2	12		6				10^{2}	13		5	3^{1}		8	9		14		4	11^{3}		7									21
1	2	3	4		6			12	10^{1}	11	5	7		8	9																22
1	2	3	4		6		12	13	10^{2}	11^{1}	5	7		8	9																23
1	2	3	4		6			10	14	7	5^{1}	11		8^{2}	9^{3}		13		12												24
1	2	13	4		6		8^{2}			11		3^{1}		7	9		12						5	10							25
1	2	3	4		6		12			11^{1}		7^{2}		8	9^{3}		14						5	10	13						26
1	2	3^{2}	4		6		8^{1}					11		7	9^{3}	12	14						5	10	13						27
1	2	14	4		6		12					3^{3}		7	9							8^{1}	5	10	13	11^{2}					28
1	2	3^{1}			6		12				5			8	13							11	4	10	7	9^{2}					29
1	2	3			6				12		5	13		8	9							7	4	10^{1}		11^{2}					30
1	2	3	12		6						5■	11		8	9^{2}				13				4	10		7^{1}					31
1		3	4		6				10^{2}			11		8^{1}					2			7	5	9	12		13				32
1		3	4						10^{2}			11		6					2			7	5	9	12	8^{1}	13				33
1	2	3	4						10^{2}					8					5			7	6	9	12	11^{1}	13				34
1	2	3^{2}	4				12		10		5			8					6			7		9^{3}	11^{1}	13		14			35
1	2	3	4		6		14		10^{2}		5^{1}			8					12			7		9^{3}		13		11			36
1	2	3	4		6		8^{2}		10		5^{1}			7			13					11				9^{3}	14		12		37
1	2	3	4		6				10					7			13					11	5			9^{1}	8^{2}	12			38
1■	2	3^{2}	4		6^{1}				10^{G}	12	15	13		8					7				5				9	11			39
		3			6^{1}				14		5	11		8			12		4			7	2			13	10^{2}	9^{3}		1	40
1		3			6				10^{2}	11				8			12		5			7	4		2^{1}	9		13			41
1		3	4		6				10^{3}	11^{1}		13		8								7^{2}	5		2	9	12	14			42
1	2	3^{2}	4		6				10^{3}			12		8								7	5		11^{1}	9	13	14			43
1	2	3^{2}	4		12				14	11		7		8			13						5		6^{1}	10	9^{3}				44
1	2	3	4		6				10^{1}	11		7		8									5	12		9^{2}		13			45
1	2	12								11	5	3^{1}					4		6			7		10^{2}	8	13		9			46

FA Cup

Fourth Qualifying Round	Stafford R	(a)	1-1
		(h)	5-1
First Round	Aldershot T	(h)	2-1
Second Round	Weymouth	(h)	1-0
Third Round	Wolverhampton W	(a)	1-2

Trophy

First Round	Kings Lynn	(h)	5-0
Second Round	Histon	(a)	0-2

Play-Offs

Semi-Final	Burton Alb	(a)	2-2
		(h)	2-1
Final *(at Wembley)*	Exeter C		0-1

CRAWLEY TOWN

Blue Square Premier

Ground: Broadfield Ground, Broadfield Stadium, Brighton Road, West Sussex RH11 9RX. *Tel:* (01293) 410 000.
Year Formed: 1896. *Record Gate:* 4,522 (2004 v Weymouth, Dr Martens League). *Nickname:* The Reds.
Manager: Steve Evans. *Secretary:* Barry Munn. *Colours:* All red.

CRAWLEY TOWN 2007–08 LEAGUE RECORD

Match No.	*Date*	*Venue*	*Opponents*	*Result*		*H/T Score*	*Lg. Pos.*	*Goalscorers*	*Attendance*
1	Aug 11	H	Stevenage Bor	W	2-1	2-0	—	Madjo 2 [11, 37]	1257
2	Aug 14	A	Exeter C	L	0-2	0-1	—		3726
3	Aug 18	A	Salisbury C	L	1-4	0-2	17	Madjo [71]	1317
4	Aug 25	H	Northwich Vic	W	2-1	1-1	13	Vieira 2 [45, 53]	793
5	Aug 27	A	Aldershot T	W	1-0	0-0	—	Pittman [53]	2457
6	Sept 1	H	Burton Alb	D	1-1	1-0	12	Madjo [21]	906
7	Sept 4	A	Rushden & D	D	1-1	1-0	—	Madjo [13]	1534
8	Sept 8	H	Droylsden	W	5-0	2-0	8	Madjo (pen) [13], Thompson [45], Stevens [57], Mills [65], Joseph-Dubois [77]	825
9	Sept 15	A	Cambridge U	L	1-2	1-0	11	Madjo (pen) [12]	2975
10	Sept 18	H	Woking	W	5-3	3-1	—	Madjo 2 (1 pen) [9 (p), 83], Pittman 2 [33, 45], Pinault [62]	959
11	Sept 22	H	Forest Green R	W	3-0	0-0	7	Stevens [54], Bulman [68], Cook [79]	982
12	Sept 25	A	Ebbsfleet U	L	0-1	0-0	—		932
13	Sept 29	H	Altrincham	L	0-1	0-0	8		1104
14	Oct 6	A	Kidderminster H	D	1-1	0-1	10	Madjo [70]	1462
15	Oct 9	H	Histon	W	1-0	1-0	—	Pinault [32]	886
16	Oct 12	A	Weymouth	W	2-1	1-1	—	Cook [37], Madjo [47]	1333
17	Oct 20	H	Stafford R	D	1-1	1-0	13	Cook [41]	1025
18	Nov 3	A	Halifax T	L	0-3	0-2	15		1197
19	Nov 17	H	Torquay U	L	2-3	0-3	16	Vieira [49], Robertson (og) [74]	1848
20	Nov 24	H	Farsley C	W	4-1	1-1	15	Pittman (pen) [39], Vieira 2 [59, 70], Pinault [90]	803
21	Dec 1	A	York C	D	1-1	0-0	—	Pittman [61]	2212
22	Dec 26	A	Oxford U	L	0-1	0-0	—		5900
23	Dec 29	A	Farsley C	W	5-1	2-0	16	Blackburn [8], Joseph-Dubois [44], Thompson [56], Evans [59], Cook [60]	471
24	Jan 1	H	Oxford U	W	2-0	0-0	15	Cook 2 (1 pen) [67, 70 (p)]	1630
25	Jan 5	A	Droylsden	W	2-1	0-1	14	Cook 2 (1 pen) [74, 86 (p)]	423
26	Jan 19	H	Rushden & D	W	4-1	3-0	14	Pittman [11], Cook 3 [33, 37, 63]	1226
27	Jan 26	A	Woking	D	1-1	1-1	14	James [12]	1697
28	Feb 10	A	Forest Green R	L	0-1	0-0	15		1044
29	Feb 14	H	Ebbsfleet U	L	1-2	1-2	—	Cook [4]	986
30	Mar 1	A	Stevenage Bor	L	1-3	1-2	17	Pittman [41]	1717
31	Mar 4	H	Exeter C	D	2-2	1-1	—	Allen 2 (1 pen) [19, 60 (p)]	841
32	Mar 8	H	Salisbury C	D	1-1	0-0	16	Pittman [90]	948
33	Mar 11	A	Altrincham	W	3-2	0-0	—	Pittman [58], Thompson [72], Pinault [84]	715
34	Mar 15	A	Northwich Vic	L	0-2	0-0	16		585
35	Mar 18	H	Cambridge U	W	2-1	1-1	—	James [13], Bulman [58]	1024
36	Mar 22	A	Burton Alb	L	0-1	0-0	15		1559
37	Mar 24	H	Aldershot T	L	0-1	0-1	16		1940
38	Mar 27	H	Kidderminster H	L	0-4	0-4	—		595
39	Mar 29	A	Grays Ath	L	1-2	1-0	16	Pittman [45]	853
40	Apr 5	H	York C	W	6-1	3-1	15	Pittman 2 [18, 81], Hall [29], Joseph-Dubois 2 [30, 86], Cook [90]	862
41	Apr 8	A	Histon	L	0-3	0-1	—		601
42	Apr 12	H	Weymouth	D	1-1	1-1	16	Murphy [40]	943
43	Apr 15	H	Grays Ath	W	2-1	0-0	—	Carayol [46], Cook [87]	755
44	Apr 19	A	Stafford R	W	3-1	2-1	16	Thompson [20], Carayol [38], Cook (pen) [57]	470
45	Apr 22	H	Halifax T	L	0-4	0-2	—		817
46	Apr 26	A	Torquay U	W	2-1	1-0	15	Hall [17], Cook [85]	3121

Final League Position: 15

GOALSCORERS

League (73): Cook 16 (3 pens), Pittman 12 (1 pen), Madjo 11 (3 pens), Vieira 5, Joseph-Dubois 4, Pinault 4, Thompson 4, Allen 2 (1 pen), Bulman 2, Carayol 2, Hall 2, James 2, Stevens 2, Blackburn 1, Evans 1, Mills 1, Murphy 1, own goal 1.
FA Cup (1): Carayol 1.
Trophy (12): Cook 4 (1 pen), Vieira 4, Bulman 2, Pitman 2.

Bayes 45	Wilson 31 + 4	Bull 20	Pinault 38 + 3	Ujah 2	Stevens 43	Scully 3	Thompson 42 + 2	Pittman 32 + 4	Madjo 17 + 1	Cook 36 + 4	Thomas 12 + 6	Evans 2 + 11	Vieira 11 + 11	Judge 1 + 1	Bulman 42 + 2	Lovegrove 1 + 1	Mills 14	Joseph-Dubois 9 + 22	Krause 24 + 3	Blackburn 15 + 9	Carayol 13 + 13	Njome-Ndebi 1 + 1	Watson 11	Murphy 20 + 3	James 10 + 2	Shimmin 2	Dutton-Black 1 + 2	Knowles 1	Allen 2	Hall 5 + 2	Carter — + 3	Raynor — + 1	*Match No.*
1	2	3	4	5^1	6	7^2	8	9^3	10	11	12	13	14																				1
1	2^1	3	4		6	7	8	9^3	10	11^2	5		14	12	13																		2
1		3		5■	6	7^2	8		10	11^1	12	13	9	2	4																		3
1		3			6		8	9^3	12	13		7^2	10		4	2	5	11^1	14														4
1		2			6		8	9■	10^1	11		13	7^2		4		5	12	3														5
1		2	4		6		8		10	11^1			9		7		5	12	3														6
1	13	2	4		6		8	9^3	10^2	11^1		12			7		5	14	3														7
1	12	2^1	4		6		8^2	9^3	10	11		13			7		5	14	3														8
1	2■		4		6		8	9^3	10	11^2			13		7		5	14	3^1	12													9
1		2^1	4		6		8	9^3	10	11			13		7^2	12	5	14	3														10
1	12	2	4		6		8	9^3	10	11^2		13	14		7		5		3^1														11
1	2	3	4		6		8	9^2	10	11^1			12		7		5	13															12
1	2	3^1	4		6		8	9^3	10	11		12	13		7^2		5	14															13
1		2	4		6		8	9	10	11					7		5		3														14
1		2	4^1		6		8	9^3	10	11^2		14			7		5	13	3	12													15
1	12	2	4		6		8	9^1	10	11^2		13			7^3		5	14	3														16
1	2		4		6			9^2	10	11		7^1	12		8		5	13	3														17
1	5	2^1	4		6		8	9	10^2						7			11^3	3	14	12	13											18
1		3^1	4^2		6		8	14					9		7			12		13	11	10^3	2	5									19
1	2		4		6		8	9^1					10					12		7	11		3	5									20
1	2		4^1		6		8	9^3		13			10		12			14		7	11^2		3	5									21
1	2		13		6		8	9		11			10		7^3			14		4^2	12		3^1	5									22
1	2	3	4		6		8^1			11		13			7			10^3	12	9^2	14		5										23
1	2	3	4		6		8	12^2		11		14			9			10^1		7^3	13		5										24
1	2	3^1	4		6		8	14		11			12		9			10^3		7^2	13		5										25
1	2		4		6		8	9		11^2			13		7^1				14		10^3		5	3	12								26
1	2		4		6		8			11			12		7^1			13			9^2		3	5	10								27
1	2		12		6		8	9^3		11			10^2		4			14			7		3^1	5	13								28
1	2		4^3				8	14		11	12		9		7						10		3^1	13	6	5^2							29
1■	2				6			9		11	12		10^1		4				3■	7	14				8	5^2	13^3						30
	2				6		12	9		11^2	3				7					8^1	13			5	4			1	10				31
1	2		13		6		8^1	9		11^3	3				7						14			5	4		12		10^2				32
1	2		4		6		8	9^2			3				7			13			12			5	10		11^1						33
1	2		4		6		8	9			3				7					12	11			5^1	10								34
1	2		4		6		8	9^2		11^3	3				7^1			13	5	12				14	10								35
1	2^1		4^2		6		8^3	9		11	5				7			12	3	13	14				10								36
1			4		6		13	9		11	2				7			14	3	5^1	12			8^2	10^3								37
1	2^1		4		6		8	9		11^3	5				7			14	3	13	10^2			12									38
1			4		6		8^2	9		13	12				7			10	3	2				5^1						11			39
1			4				8	9^2		13	2				7			10^3	3	5^1	14			6						11	12		40
1	2		4				8				6				7			10	3	11				5						9			41
1	2		4		6		8			11					7			10^1	3		12			5						9			42
1	2		4		6		8			11	12				7				3	10^1	9			5									43
1	2		4		6		8			11					7				3	9^1	10^2			5						12	13		44
1	2		4		6		8			11					7				3■	9^1	10			5						12			45
1	2		4		6		8^3			11	3^1				7					13	10^2			5						9	14	12	46

FA Cup
Fourth Qualifying Round

Aldershot T	(h)	1-1
	(a)	0-1

Trophy

First Round	Bromley	(h)	1-0
Second Round	Eastleigh	(h)	2-1
Third Round	Droylsden	(h)	8-0
Fourth Round	Torquay U	(a)	1-4

DROYLSDEN

Blue Square North

Ground: Butchers Arms Ground, Market Street, Droylsden M43 7AW. *Tel:* (0161) 370 1426. *Year Formed:* 1892. *Record Gate:* 15,000 (1921 v Hyde, Cheshire League). *Nickname:* The Bloods. *Manager:* Dave Pace. *Secretary:* Alan Slater. *Colours:* Red shirts, black shorts, red stockings.

DROYLSDEN 2007–08 LEAGUE RECORD

Match No.	Date	Venue	Opponents	Result		H/T Score	Lg. Pos.	Goalscorers	Attendance
1	Aug 11	H	Salisbury C	D	0-0	0-0	—		821
2	Aug 14	A	Northwich Vic	D	3-3	2-2	—	Cryan 34, Denham 45, McGuire 55	1875
3	Aug 18	A	Aldershot T	L	1-3	1-0	20	Fearnes 25	1773
4	Aug 25	H	Exeter C	L	2-3	0-1	20	Banim 46, McGuire 90	847
5	Aug 27	A	Halifax T	L	0-3	0-2	—		1302
6	Sept 1	H	Grays Ath	L	1-2	0-0	21	Daly 63	592
7	Sept 4	H	Stevenage Bor	L	0-3	0-0	—		671
8	Sept 8	A	Crawley T	L	0-5	0-2	22		825
9	Sept 15	H	Weymouth	L	1-3	0-1	22	Banim 60	578
10	Sept 18	A	Kidderminster H	L	1-3	1-1	—	Banim 43	1305
11	Sept 22	A	Altrincham	L	2-3	1-1	23	Banim 2 (2 pens) 9, 78	1187
12	Sept 25	H	Burton Alb	L	0-2	0-0	—		665
13	Sept 29	A	Torquay U	L	1-2	1-0	23	Ellis (og) 42	3321
14	Oct 6	H	Oxford U	W	3-1	1-0	23	Daly 15, Banim (pen) 61, McGuire 85	1074
15	Oct 9	H	Farsley C	L	0-3	0-1	—		624
16	Oct 13	A	Ebbsfleet U	L	0-2	0-0	23		788
17	Oct 20	H	Histon	L	0-1	0-0	23		497
18	Nov 3	A	Woking	D	1-1	1-1	23	Lynch 38	1284
19	Nov 17	H	Stafford R	D	1-1	0-1	23	Denham 58	612
20	Nov 24	H	Forest Green R	W	5-3	2-3	22	McGuire 2 8, 63, Denham 2 17, 90, Daly 73	450
21	Dec 8	H	Rushden & D	L	1-4	0-2	23	Banim (pen) 60	417
22	Dec 26	A	York C	L	1-2	1-1	—	Burberry 6	3042
23	Dec 29	A	Forest Green R	L	2-3	0-2	24	Denham 54, Fearns 62	1226
24	Jan 1	H	York C	L	3-4	2-0	24	Banim 2 28, 89, Fearns 40	1015
25	Jan 5	H	Crawley T	L	1-2	1-0	24	Bull (og) 40	423
26	Jan 19	A	Stevenage Bor	L	0-5	0-2	24		2320
27	Jan 22	A	Cambridge U	L	0-5	0-2	—		2000
28	Jan 26	H	Kidderminster H	W	1-0	1-0	23	Banim 16	629
29	Feb 9	H	Altrincham	L	0-2	0-0	24		1178
30	Feb 12	A	Burton Alb	L	0-3	0-2	—		1501
31	Feb 16	A	Oxford U	L	0-1	0-1	24		4331
32	Mar 1	A	Salisbury C	L	1-3	0-2	24	Burberry 81	1307
33	Mar 4	H	Northwich Vic	L	1-3	1-0	—	Daly (pen) 12	424
34	Mar 20	A	Grays Ath	L	1-3	1-1	—	Johnson 14	862
35	Mar 24	H	Halifax T	W	2-0	1-0	24	McGuire 6, Fearns 53	887
36	Mar 27	H	Aldershot T	D	2-2	1-0	—	Fearns 2 17, 61	733
37	Mar 29	A	Rushden & D	D	0-0	0-0	24		1186
38	Apr 1	H	Torquay U	L	1-2	0-2	—	Mackin 70	476
39	Apr 3	A	Exeter C	D	1-1	0-0	—	Talbot 49	3071
40	Apr 5	H	Cambridge U	L	0-2	0-1	24		634
41	Apr 8	A	Farsley C	W	2-1	1-1	—	Lynch 12, Fearns 86	480
42	Apr 15	A	Weymouth	L	1-2	1-1	—	McGuire 34	1102
43	Apr 17	H	Ebbsfleet U	D	1-1	0-0	—	Denham 73	252
44	Apr 19	A	Histon	L	0-2	0-1	23		1177
45	Apr 22	H	Woking	D	1-1	1-0	—	Fearns 35	301
46	Apr 26	A	Stafford R	L	1-2	0-1	24	Newton 51	685

Final League Position: 24

GOALSCORERS

League (46): Banim 10 (4 pens), Fearns 8, McGuire 7, Denham 6, Daly 4 (1 pen), Burberry 2, Lynch 2, Cryan 1, Johnson 1, Mackin 1, Newton 1, Talbot 1, own goals 2.
FA Cup (2): Banim 1 (pen), Fearns 1.
Trophy (3): Banim 2 (1 pen), Fearns 1.

Phillips 44	Murray 19	Morris 18 + 3	Cryan 37 + 3	Robinson 4	Murphy 17 + 13	Denham 35 + 2	McGuire 36	Fearns 30 + 9	Daly 24 + 2	Tandy 9 + 11	Warner 12 + 3	Banim 27 + 4 / Johnson 3	Gibson 5 + 6	Hotte 3	Lynch 21 + 10	Marsh-Evans 2 + 1	Norton — + 1	Burke 5 / Williams — + 1	Salmon 2 + 15	Halford 33 + 2	Smith 1 + 1	Talbot 4 + 14	Stephens 5 + 2	Senior 2	Roche 20 + 1	Burberry 22 + 4	Dugdale 8 + 6	Wilson — + 1	Woods — + 1	Tayforth 1 + 1	Murtagh 6	Mackin 12	Ellis 3 + 9	Strong 13 + 1	Munroe 7 + 4	Newton 14 + 1	Vaughan 2	*Match No.*
1	2^{1}	3■	4	5	6	7	8	9^{2}	10	11^{3}	12	13	14																									1
1			4	5	6^{1}	7^{2}	8	9^{3}	10	11	3	14	13	2	12																							2
1			4	5	6^{2}	7	8	9^{3}	10	11^{1}		14		2	13	3	12																					3
1			4			7	8	9	10^{3}	13		11	12	2^{1}	6	3^{2}		5	14																			4
1	2	3^{2}	4	5	6	7^{1}	8	9^{3}	10	12		14	11						13																			5
1		3	4		6		8	9^{3}	10^{2}		5	11	14			12		7	13	2^{1}																		6
1	2	3	4		6	7^{3}	8	12	10^{2}		5	9	14						13	11^{1}																		7
1	2	3	4				8■	9^{3}	10■	13	5^{1}	7^{2}	11		14				12	6																		8
1	2	3	4		6			14		12	5^{1}	9	11^{2}		7				13	8	10^{3}																	9
1		3^{2}	4		6	7		14		13	5	9			8			11	10^{3}	2^{1}		12																10
1		3^{2}	4			7		13		14	5	9	6^{1}		8			11	10^{3}	2			12															11
	2		4		12	7	8		10	11^{3}		9^{2}	3		6^{1}					5		14	13	1														12
	2		4		13	7^{2}	8		10	11^{1}	12	9			3					5			6	1														13
1	2		4			7	8	12	10^{1}	11		9			6					3			5															14
1	2	13	4			7	8	14	10^{3}	11		9	12		3^{1}					5			6^{2}															15
1	2	12	4		13	7^{3}	3	9	10^{2}	11^{1}		8							14	5			6															16
1	2	3^{2}	4		13	7	8	9	12		5^{1}	10			14					6			11^{3}															17
1	2	3			6	12	8	9^{3}				10^{2}			11^{1}			5	13	4	14				7													18
1	2	3	4			7	8	9^{3}	10^{2}		5	11^{1}							13			12			6	14												19
1	2	3^{1}	4			7	8		10^{3}	13	5	9			12				14						6	11^{2}												20
1	2	3	4			7			10^{3}	13	5^{1}	9			8					12		14			6■	11^{2}												21
1	2	3^{3}	4		6	7	8	12		13		9^{1}							14	5					11	10^{2}												22
1	2	3^{2}	4		6	7	8	9^{3}		13		10^{1}							12	5		14				11												23
1	2		4		12	7^{2}	8	9^{3}		11^{1}	13	10							14	5						6	3											24
1		3	4					9	12		11^{2}	10			6				13	5		7^{3}				8^{1}	2	14										25
1		3	4^{1}					9		12		10^{3}			7^{2}					5■		14			2	8	6		13	11								26
1	2	3			6	7^{3}		9				10			11^{2}				14			13			5	8	4^{1}			12								27
1		12	4		6		8^{1}		10^{2}			9								5					2	11					3	7	13					28
1			12			7	8	9^{3}				10								3					2^{1}	14	6				4^{2}	11	13	5				29
1			4		13	12	8^{2}		10			9^{1}								2^{3}					3■	11					6	7		5	14			30
1			4				8^{1}	14	10			9			12					2						11					6	7^{3}	13	5^{2}	3			31
1			4^{3}		6^{1}		8	9	10						12					2						11							13	5	3	14	7^{2}	32
1						7^{1}	9	14	10■						13					2						11					8^{3}		12	5	3	4	6^{2}	33
1			12			7	8	9				10^{3}			14					4^{1}					2	13					11^{2}	6		5		3		34
1			13			7	8	9^{2}	10^{1}											6		12			2	11						4		5■		3		35
1			4		12	7	8^{1}	9^{2}	10■						13					5					2	11						6				3		36
1			4		14	7		9^{1}				10^{2}			8							13^{3}			2	11	12					6		5		3		37
1			4		13	7									8^{1}					5		14			2	11^{2}	9					6	10^{3}		12	3		38
1					12	7		9^{2}							8^{1}					5		10^{3}				11	13					6	14	4	2	3		39
1			4		12	7	8	9^{3}	10^{2}													13			2	11^{1}	14					6		5		3		40
1					12	7	11^{2}	9^{3}							10^{1}					5		13			2	8						6		14	4	3		41
1			4		8	7	2	9				10^{3}						13		5							12						14	6^{1}	11	3^{2}		42
1			4^{1}		6	7	8	9							11^{2}							10^{3}			2	13	5						14		12	3		43
1					4^{2}	7^{3}	10	9							11					5^{1}		14			12	8	6						13		2	3		44
1			4			11^{3}	8	9							10^{2}					3		12			2		14						7^{1}	5	13	6		45
1			4		12■		6	9							7^{1}					14		11^{2}			3	8	13						10^{3}	5		2		46

FA Cup

Fourth Qualifying Round	Corby T	(a)	2-1
First Round	Harrogate RA	(a)	0-2

Trophy

First Round	Redditch U	(h)	2-1
Second Round	Cambridge C	(h)	1-0
Third Round	Crawley T	(a)	0-8

EBBSFLEET UNITED

Blue Square Premier

Ground : Stonebridge Road, Northfleet, Kent DA11 9BA. *Tel:* (01474) 533 796. *Year Formed:* 1946. *Record Gate:* 12,036 (1963 v Sunderland, FA Cup 4th rd). *Nickname:* The Fleet. *Manager:* Liam Daish. *Secretary:* Roly Edwards. *Colours:* Red shirts, white shorts, red stockings.

EBBSFLEET UNITED 2007–08 LEAGUE RECORD

Match No.	Date	Venue	Opponents	Result		H/T Score	Lg. Pos.	Goalscorers	Attendance
1	Aug 11	H	Northwich Vic	W	2-1	1-0	—	Moore[3], Eribenne[67]	1045
2	Aug 14	A	Salisbury C	L	1-2	1-1	—	Debolla (pen)[4]	1310
3	Aug 18	A	Rushden & D	W	1-0	1-0	7	Purcell[33]	1456
4	Aug 25	H	Halifax T	W	1-0	0-0	7	Long[50]	931
5	Aug 27	A	Cambridge U	D	1-1	1-0	—	Moore[42]	2974
6	Sept 1	H	Stevenage Bor	L	0-1	0-1	11		1201
7	Sept 4	H	Histon	L	0-1	0-0	—		866
8	Sept 8	A	Weymouth	L	0-2	0-1	15		1140
9	Sept 15	H	Kidderminster H	W	5-4	3-0	14	Eribenne 2[4,45], Debolla 2[12,61], Coleman Luke[86]	812
10	Sept 18	A	Burton Alb	D	1-1	1-0	—	Moore[13]	1594
11	Sept 22	A	Exeter C	D	1-1	1-0	14	Bostwick[38]	2923
12	Sept 25	H	Crawley T	W	1-0	0-0	—	Nade[78]	932
13	Sept 29	A	Farsley C	D	1-1	1-1	13	Long[23]	582
14	Oct 6	H	Torquay U	W	2-1	0-0	9	Moore[77], Long[87]	1368
15	Oct 9	A	Aldershot T	L	0-2	0-0	—		2399
16	Oct 13	H	Droylsden	W	2-0	0-0	9	Nade[52], Eribenne[79]	788
17	Oct 20	A	Altrincham	W	3-1	3-0	8	Purcell[30], Nade[35], Lane (og)[37]	861
18	Nov 3	H	Forest Green R	L	0-2	0-1	9		930
19	Nov 17	A	Oxford U	D	0-0	0-0	10		4655
20	Nov 24	H	Stafford R	W	2-1	0-0	8	Purcell[58], Long[76]	1055
21	Nov 29	A	Woking	L	0-1	0-1	—		1255
22	Dec 8	H	York C	L	1-2	0-1	9	McPhee[79]	933
23	Dec 26	A	Grays Ath	D	1-1	0-1	—	Akinde[77]	813
24	Dec 29	A	Stafford R	W	1-0	0-0	9	Akinde[90]	653
25	Jan 1	H	Grays Ath	W	4-1	2-0	9	Barrett[29], Long 2[42,87], Bostwick[76]	1396
26	Jan 5	H	Weymouth	W	4-1	3-0	8	Long 2[2,27], Eribenne[41], Bostwick[90]	952
27	Jan 26	H	Burton Alb	W	2-1	1-0	7	Barrett[13], Akinde[68]	1385
28	Feb 9	H	Exeter C	D	1-1	1-0	8	McPhee (pen)[18]	1617
29	Feb 14	A	Crawley T	W	2-1	2-1	—	Akinde[15], Wilson (og)[33]	986
30	Feb 16	A	Torquay U	L	1-3	0-1	9	Nade[72]	2704
31	Mar 1	A	Northwich Vic	D	3-3	0-1	10	Smith[63], Long[70], Eribenne[88]	1045
32	Mar 4	H	Salisbury C	W	2-1	2-0	—	Eribenne 2[31,36]	670
33	Mar 11	H	Rushden & D	L	0-3	0-1	—		546
34	Mar 18	A	Histon	L	2-3	2-1	—	Akinde[24], Long[45]	552
35	Mar 21	A	Stevenage Bor	L	1-3	0-2	—	Bostwick[64]	2016
36	Mar 24	H	Cambridge U	W	2-1	1-1	10	McPhee (pen)[29], Akinde[65]	1388
37	Mar 29	A	York C	W	1-0	1-0	10	Long[9]	2256
38	Apr 1	A	Kidderminster H	L	1-2	1-2	—	Hearn[27]	1450
39	Apr 5	H	Woking	D	1-1	0-0	12	Long[72]	1175
40	Apr 8	H	Aldershot T	D	2-2	1-0	—	Moore[14], McPhee[88]	1439
41	Apr 10	A	Halifax T	L	0-1	0-0	—		1063
42	Apr 15	H	Farsley C	W	3-1	0-1	—	Smith[53], Moore[66], Hearn[80]	810
43	Apr 17	A	Droylsden	D	1-1	0-0	—	Eribenne[53]	252
44	Apr 19	H	Altrincham	W	2-0	1-0	9	McPhee[40], Long[53]	911
45	Apr 22	A	Forest Green R	D	2-2	1-1	—	Moore[42], Long[69]	822
46	Apr 26	H	Oxford U	L	1-3	0-3	11	Purcell[50]	1852

Final League Position: 11

GOALSCORERS

League (65): Long 14, Eribenne 9, Moore 7, Akinde 6, McPhee 5 (2 pens), Bostwick 4, Nade 4, Purcell 4, Debolla 3 (1 pen), Barrett 2, Hearn 2, Smith 2, Coleman Luke 1, own goals 2.
FA Cup (1): Moore 1.
Trophy (13): McPhee 6, Akinde 1, Barrett 1, Bostwick 1, Long 1, McCarthy 1, Moore 1, Opinel 1.

Tynan 7	Ricketts 22 + 7	Purcell 21 + 11	Hawkins 37 + 1	Smith 21 + 2	MacDonald 5 + 2	Debolla 13 + 3	Barrett 26 + 8	Moore 39 + 5	Eribenne 17 + 12	Long 43 + 1	McPhee 43 + 1	Opinel 32 + 2	Nade 20 + 13	McCarthy 27 + 1	Coleman Liam 2 + 12	Starkey 1 + 1	Bostwick 40 + 3	Goodkind 7 + 1	Slatter 4 + 2	Cronin 38	Coleman Luke — + 4	Hastings 5 + 2	Maskell — + 1	Akinde 15 + 4	Bull 6 + 3	Hearn 6 + 7	Charles 8 + 1	Mott 1	*Match No.*
1	2[1]	3[2]	4	5■	6	7	8	9[3]	10	11	12	13	14																1
1		12	2			7[2]	8	9	10	11[3]	6	3[1]	14	5	13	4													2
1		3	2			7[2]		9	10[3]	8	6	11	14	5	13	12	4[1]												3
1		3	4			7[1]		9	10[3]	11[2]	6		14	5	12		8	2	13										4
1		3[2]	4	12		7		9	10[3]	11	6		14	5			8	2[1]	13										5
1		3	6			8[1]		9	10	11	2		12	5■	13		4		7[2]										6
1		3	4			12		9	10[1]	11	5		8[2]		13		6	2	7										7
		11[2]				8[1]		9	12	13	10	3	14	5	6[3]		4	2	7	1									8
			4			13			10[3]	11	6	3	9	5	12		8	2[1]	7[2]	1	14								9
			4			7[1]	12	9		11	6	3	10	5			8			1	13	2[2]							10
			4			7	12	9[3]	13	11	6	3	10	5			2[1]	14		1		8[2]							11
			4			7		9	10[1]	11	2	3	8	5			6			1		12							12
	14		4			7	13	9[1]		11[2]	2	3	8[3]	5			6			1	12	10							13
	12		4			7	8	6		11	2	3	10	5						1		9[1]							14
	2[1]		4			7	8[2]	9		11	6	3	10	5			13			1		12							15
			4			12	8[1]	9[2]	14	11	5	3	10				6	2		1	13	7[3]							16
	12	3[1]	4	13			8	9		11	5	2	10[2]				7■	6		1									17
	13			5			8[2]	9	10[3]	11	2	3	7	6[1]	14		4			1			12						18
	2	12	3	5				9	10	11	7		8[1]	6			4			1									19
		11[1]	2	5			12	9	10■	8	7	3		6			4			1									20
		11	2	5			12	10[3]		8	7	3[2]	9	6	13		4[1]			1				14					21
	2	11	4	5			13	9[3]		8	7	3[1]	10		12		6[2]			1				14					22
	2	13[3]	3	5				9	10[2]	11	7	14		6■	4[1]		8			1				12					23
	2		4	5			8	9		11	10	3					7			1				6					24
	2	14	4	5			8	9[3]	13	11	7[1]	3			12		6			1				10[2]					25
	2	14	4[1]	5			8	9	10[3]	11[2]		3		12	13		6			1				7					26
	2	13		5			8	9[2]	12	11	7	3		6			4			1				10[1]					27
	2			5			8	9	12	11	7	3		6			4[1]			1				10					28
	2			5			8	9[2]	12	11[3]	4	3	10[1]	6			13			1				7	14				29
		13		5			8[1]	9[3]		11[2]	7	3	14	6	12		4			1				10	2				30
	12	11	2	5	6■			13	14	8	7		9[1]				4			1				10[3]	3[2]				31
	2[1]		4				8	9	10[2]	11	7	3	13	5			6			1					12				32
	2	13	4		6		8	12	10[3]	11	7		14				5[1]			1				9[2]	3				33
		14	4		12		8[3]	9[2]		11	2	3	7	5[1]			6			1				10		13			34
	13	14	4		6[1]		8[2]	9[3]		11	2	3					7			1				10		5	12		35
	2	11[2]	4					13		8	7	3	12				6			1				10[1]		9	5		36
	2	11[2]	4				12	13		8[1]	7		9				6			1					3	10	5		37
	2	11	4				12	13		8	7		9[2]				6[1]			1					3	10	5		38
	2	11	4				7[1]	9		8	10	3					6			1						12	5		39
	2	11	4				8[1]	9		10	7	3					6			1						12	5		40
	2	11[3]		4			8[2]	9		10[1]	7	3■	13				6			1					14	12	5		41
	2	11	4	5			8[1]	9[2]	13		7		14				12			1				10[3]		6	3		42
	2[1]	11	12	5	6		4		10[2]				9				7							13	3	8		1	43
		12	3	5			8[2]	9	14	11[1]	2			4			7			1				10[3]		13	6		44
	13		4	5			8	9[2]	14	11[1]	2	3		6			7			1				10[3]		12			45
	2	11		5	12		8	9	14	10[3]	7	3		6[1]			4[2]			1						13			46

FA Cup

Fourth Qualifying Round	Exeter C	(h)	1-3

Trophy

First Round	Cashalton Ath	(h)	4-1
Second Round	Dorchester T	(a)	2-0
Third Round	Weymouth	(h)	1-0
Fourth Round	Burton Alb	(a)	0-0
		(h)	1-0
Semi-Final	Aldershot T	(h)	3-1
		(a)	1-1
Final *(at Wembley)*	Torquay U		1-0

EXETER CITY

FL Championship 2

Ground: St James Park, Exeter EX4 6PX. *Tel:* (01392) 411 243. *Year Formed:* 1904.
Record Gate: 20,984 (1931 v Sunderland, FA Cup 6th rd replay). *Nickname:* The Grecians.
Manager: Paul Tisdale. *Secretary:* Sally Cooke. *Colours:* Red and white shirts, white shorts, white stockings.

EXETER CITY 2007–08 LEAGUE RECORD

Match No.	Date	Venue	Opponents	Result		H/T Score	Lg. Pos.	Goalscorers	Attendance
1	Aug 11	A	Altrincham	W	4-1	0-1	—	Taylor M [66], Logan [69], Basham [89], Elam [90]	1318
2	Aug 14	H	Crawley T	W	2-0	1-0	—	Stansfield [14], Thomas (og) [57]	3726
3	Aug 20	H	York C	D	1-1	1-0	—	Logan (pen) [36]	4242
4	Aug 25	A	Droylsden	W	3-2	1-0	1	Moxey 2 [15, 50], Elam [89]	847
5	Aug 27	H	Weymouth	D	0-0	0-0	—		4773
6	Sept 1	A	Kidderminster H	L	0-4	0-2	9		1860
7	Sept 4	A	Oxford U	D	2-2	0-1	—	Logan 2 [78, 90]	4560
8	Sept 8	H	Cambridge U	D	1-1	1-0	10	Mackie [11]	3197
9	Sept 15	A	Farsley C	W	2-0	1-0	6	Stansfield [10], Logan (pen) [78]	1128
10	Sept 18	H	Forest Green R	D	3-3	2-0	—	Logan 2 [11, 74], Mackie [29]	2753
11	Sept 22	H	Ebbsfleet U	D	1-1	0-1	8	Mackie [81]	2923
12	Sept 25	A	Woking	D	1-1	1-0	—	Lorraine (og) [22]	1448
13	Oct 2	A	Aldershot T	L	0-2	0-0	—		2943
14	Oct 6	H	Grays Ath	W	1-0	1-0	8	Logan [10]	2783
15	Oct 9	H	Salisbury C	W	4-2	2-1	—	Logan 3 [9, 45, 70], Taylor M [49]	2903
16	Oct 13	A	Northwich Vic	D	0-0	0-0	7		1061
17	Oct 20	H	Rushden & D	D	2-2	1-0	9	Hatswell (og) [14], Mackie [65]	3106
18	Nov 3	A	Stafford R	W	5-1	2-1	8	Carlisle [22], Taylor M 2 [26, 87], Mackie [60], Basham (pen) [90]	914
19	Nov 17	H	Burton Alb	L	1-4	1-1	8	Mackie [30]	3823
20	Nov 24	A	Histon	D	2-2	1-1	9	Moxey [30], Mackie [65]	973
21	Dec 8	A	Halifax T	W	3-0	1-0	8	Logan (pen) [3], Elam [48], Mackie [74]	1160
22	Dec 26	H	Torquay U	W	4-3	2-0	—	Mackie 2 [23, 62], Moxey [34], Carlisle [56]	7839
23	Dec 29	H	Histon	W	2-1	0-1	7	Mackie [66], Cambridge (og) [75]	3350
24	Jan 1	A	Torquay U	L	0-1	0-0	8		6021
25	Jan 20	H	Oxford U	W	2-0	2-0	8	Stansfield 2 [29, 36]	3301
26	Jan 26	A	Forest Green R	D	1-1	1-1	8	Carlisle [16]	2325
27	Jan 29	A	Cambridge U	W	1-0	1-0	—	Seaborne [36]	2769
28	Feb 2	H	Stevenage Bor	W	4-0	3-0	—	Taylor M [24], Basham [32], Stansfield 2 [35, 55]	3436
29	Feb 9	A	Ebbsfleet U	D	1-1	0-1	6	Gill [50]	1617
30	Feb 12	H	Woking	D	2-2	2-0	—	Taylor M 2 [17, 37]	3586
31	Feb 16	A	Grays Ath	W	2-0	2-0	6	Carlisle [22], Stansfield [29]	1089
32	Feb 23	H	Farsley C	W	2-1	2-0	5	Seaborne [22], Taylor M [34]	3339
33	Mar 1	H	Altrincham	W	2-1	2-0	5	Stansfield [25], Gill [34]	3501
34	Mar 4	A	Crawley T	D	2-2	1-1	—	Edwards [13], Moxey [80]	841
35	Mar 10	A	York C	L	2-3	1-2	—	Basham [45], Logan [85]	1567
36	Mar 22	H	Kidderminster H	W	1-0	0-0	6	Gill [58]	3812
37	Mar 24	A	Weymouth	L	1-3	0-1	6	Taylor M [63]	2995
38	Mar 29	H	Halifax T	W	1-0	0-0	6	Logan [61]	3096
39	Apr 3	H	Droylsden	D	1-1	0-0	—	Logan (pen) [76]	3071
40	Apr 5	A	Stevenage Bor	W	1-0	1-0	5	Basham [10]	2146
41	Apr 8	A	Salisbury C	L	0-2	0-1	—		2037
42	Apr 12	H	Northwich Vic	W	2-1	1-1	5	Logan 2 [7, 59]	3562
43	Apr 15	H	Aldershot T	D	1-1	1-1	—	Stansfield [39]	5005
44	Apr 19	A	Rushden & D	W	2-0	1-0	5	Stansfield [9], Harley [63]	1572
45	Apr 22	H	Stafford R	W	4-1	2-0	—	Moxey 3 [1, 35, 47], Watson [54]	4079
46	Apr 26	A	Burton Alb	D	4-4	1-1	4	Moxey [3], Stansfield [47], Friend [87], Logan [90]	2881

Final League Position: 4

GOALSCORERS

League (83): Logan 18 (4 pens), Mackie 11, Stansfield 11, Moxey 9, Taylor M 9, Basham 5 (1 pen), Carlisle 4, Elam 3, Gill 3, Seaborne 2, Edwards 1, Friend 1, Harley 1, Watson 1, own goals 4.
FA Cup (7): Mackie 2, Taylor M 2, Basham 1 (pen), Carlisle 1, own goal 1.
Trophy (3): Basham 1, Mackie 1, Moxey 1.
Play-Offs (6): Carlisle 2, Edwards 1, Harley 1, Logan 1, Watson 1 (pen).

Marriott 39	Friend 27 + 3	Tully 38 + 1	Artus 8 + 2	Edwards 46	Taylor M 40	Taylor A 19 + 1	Mackie 21 + 3	Stansfield 36 + 5	Logan 28 + 13	Moxey 43 + 2	Sercombe 4 + 3	Elam 9 + 14	Basham 15 + 17	Richardson 15 + 4	Gill 43	Cozic 10 + 5	Carlisle 24 + 8	Seaborne 24	Jones 7	Harley 9 + 3	Watson 1 + 8	*Match No.*
1	2	3	4	5	6	7^1	8^2	9	10^3	11	12	13	14									1
1	2	3	4	5	6		8	9	10	11	7^1			12								2
1	2	3	4	5	6		7^2	8	9^1	10		12	13	11								3
1	2	3		5	6		7	8^1	9^2	10		12	13	11	4							4
1	2	3	4	5	6^1		8	9	10^2	11		12	13		7							5
1	2^1	3	4	5	6		8	9	10^2	11		12	13		7							6
1		3	12	5	6		8	9	14	11		13	10^3	2^1	4	7^2						7
1		3	4^1	5	6		8	9	10^2	11		12	13	2	7							8
1		3	4^2	5	6		12	9	14	11	8^1	7	10^3	13	2							9
1		3	4^1	5	6		8	9	10^2	11		12		2	7	13						10
1	12	3	13	5	6^1		8	9^3	10	11		7		2^2	4		14					11
1	2	3		5			8	9	12	11		7		6	4	10^1						12
1	2	3		5			8^3	9	13	11^1		7	14	4	6	10^2	12					13
1	2	3		5			8	9^2	10^1	11			12	4	7	6	13					14
1	2			5	6		13	9	10^2	11		7^1		3	4	8	12					15
1	2			5	6		12	9	10	11^1		7^2		3	4	8	13					16
1	2^1			5	6		9	12	10^2	11			13	3	4	8	7					17
1	2	12		5	6		8		13	11			9^2	3	4^1	10	7					18
1	2			5	6		8^2	13	12	11			9	3	4	10^1	7					19
1				5	8	11	10		13	3		12	9^2	2	4		7^1	6				20
		2		3^1	6	8	9	14	10^3	11^2		12		13	4		7	5	1			21
		3		5	6	7	8	12		11			9^1		4		2	10■	1			22
	2	3		5	6	7	8		12	11			9^1		4		10		1			23
		3		5	6^1	7	8	13	14	11		10^2	9^3	12	4		2		1			24
1	2	3		5		6		9		11			10		8		7	4				25
1	2	3		5		6		9	12	11			10^1		8		7	4				26
1	2^1	3		5	6	7		9		11		12			8		10	4				27
1		3		5	6^1	7		9^3	13	11		12	10^2		8	14	2	4				28
1	12	3		5	6	7		9		11			10^1		8		2	4				29
1		3		5	6	7		9	12	11			10^1		8^2	13	2	4				30
1	2	3		5		6		9	10	11					8		7	4				31
1	13	3		5	6	7		9^2	10^1	11			12		8		2	4				32
1		3		5	6	7		9^1	10	11		12			8		2	4				33
1		3		5	6	7^2			10	11		9^1	12		8		2	4		13		34
1	2	3		9^3	6	7^1			10	11^2		13	12		8		4	5		14		35
1		3		5	6	7		9^1	10	11			12		8		2	4				36
1		3■		5	6	7^1		9^3	10^2	11			13		8		2	4		12	14	37
1				5	6			9^2	10^1	11	2		13		8		7	3		4	12	38
1				5	6			9^1	10	11	2		12		8		7^2	4		3	13	39
1	2	3		5	6			9	10				11^1		8			4		7	12	40
1	2	3		5^2	6			9^3	10	12					8	13	7^1	4		11	14	41
1	2	3		5	6			9^2	10	11					8^1	12		4		7	13	42
1	2	3		5	6			9	10^3	13			14		8		12	4		7^1	11^2	43
	2	3		5	6			9^2		11			10^1		8		12	4	1	7	13	44
	2	3		5	6			9^3	10	11	13				8^2		12	4^1	1	7	14	45
	2	3		5	6	13		9	14	11	12	10^3			8^2	4^1			1	7		46

FA Cup

Fourth Qualifying Round	Ebbsfleet U	(a)	3-1
First Round	Stevenage B	(h)	4-0
Second Round	Bury	(a)	0-1

Trophy

First Round	Salisbury C	(h)	3-0
Second Round	Rushden & D	(a)	0-3

Play-Offs

Semi-Finals	Torquay U	(h)	1-2
		(a)	4-1
Final *(at Wembley)*	Cambridge U		1-0

FARSLEY CELTIC

Blue Square North

Ground: Throstle Nest, Newlands, Farsley, Pudsey, Leeds LS28 5BE. *Tel:* (0113) 255 7292. *Year Formed:* 1908. *Record Gate:* 3,900. *Nickname:* Villagers or Little Celts. *Manager:* John Deacey. *Secretary:* Josh Greaves. *Colours:* Blue shirts, blue shorts, white stockings.

FARSLEY CELTIC 2007–08 LEAGUE RECORD

Match No.	Date	Venue	Opponents	Result		H/T Score	Lg. Pos.	Goalscorers	Attendance
1	Aug 11	H	Stafford R	W	1-0	1-0	—	Reeves [13]	825
2	Aug 14	A	Rushden & D	L	0-1	0-1	—		1502
3	Aug 21	A	Cambridge U	L	1-5	0-3	—	Grant [65]	2845
4	Aug 25	H	Salisbury C	D	2-2	1-1	15	Whitman [17], Grant [68]	475
5	Aug 27	A	Burton Alb	L	0-1	0-0	—		1521
6	Sept 1	H	Northwich Vic	W	2-1	0-1	19	Bambrook [84], Whitman [89]	502
7	Sept 4	H	Kidderminster H	D	1-1	1-0	—	Iqbal [2]	492
8	Sept 8	A	Histon	W	2-1	0-0	14	Reeves 2 [47, 59]	714
9	Sept 15	H	Exeter C	L	0-2	0-1	18		1128
10	Sept 18	A	Stevenage Bor	L	0-4	0-1	—		2186
11	Sept 22	A	Aldershot T	L	3-4	0-1	19	Grant [52], Heath [55], Downes (pen) [79]	2334
12	Sept 29	H	Ebbsfleet U	D	1-1	1-1	20	Downes (pen) [12]	582
13	Oct 4	A	Woking	L	0-2	0-0	—		1535
14	Oct 9	A	Droylsden	W	3-0	1-0	—	Iqbal [22], Bambrook 2 [70, 76]	624
15	Oct 14	H	Oxford U	L	0-1	0-0	20		1219
16	Oct 20	A	Forest Green R	D	2-2	0-1	20	Heath (pen) [60], Knowles [67]	969
17	Nov 3	H	York C	L	1-4	1-2	20	Stamer [29]	1603
18	Nov 17	A	Grays Ath	L	0-1	0-1	20		724
19	Nov 20	H	Altrincham	D	1-1	1-0	—	Reeves [13]	645
20	Nov 24	A	Crawley T	L	1-4	1-1	20	Knowles [37]	803
21	Dec 12	H	Torquay U	L	1-2	0-1	—	Stamer [78]	717
22	Dec 26	H	Halifax T	W	3-0	1-0	—	Stamer [28], Knowles [61], Torpey [64]	1501
23	Dec 29	H	Crawley T	L	1-5	0-2	20	Grant [74]	471
24	Jan 1	A	Halifax T	L	0-2	0-1	20		1538
25	Jan 5	H	Histon	L	1-3	1-2	20	Downes (pen) [9]	400
26	Jan 19	A	Kidderminster H	L	1-2	1-0	21	Reeves [17]	1475
27	Jan 24	H	Stevenage Bor	D	0-0	0-0	—		501
28	Feb 9	H	Aldershot T	L	1-3	0-1	21	Reeves [70]	662
29	Feb 12	A	Altrincham	D	0-0	0-0	—		4154
30	Feb 16	H	Woking	W	3-0	2-0	21	Bentham [20], Reeves [38], Torpey [50]	479
31	Feb 23	A	Exeter C	L	1-2	0-2	21	McNiven D [64]	3339
32	Mar 1	A	Stafford R	W	2-0	1-0	19	Torpey [26], Krief (pen) [62]	1853
33	Mar 4	H	Rushden & D	L	0-1	0-0	—		475
34	Mar 8	H	Cambridge U	W	2-1	0-0	20	Reeves [64], Krief [69]	868
35	Mar 11	A	Weymouth	D	0-0	0-0	—		951
36	Mar 15	A	Salisbury C	D	1-1	0-0	19	Reeves [46]	1081
37	Mar 22	A	Northwich Vic	L	0-4	0-2	20		651
38	Mar 24	H	Burton Alb	L	0-1	0-1	21		696
39	Mar 29	H	Weymouth	W	4-2	1-1	20	Stamer [37], McNiven D [67], Jackson [76], Reeves [88]	459
40	Apr 5	A	Torquay U	W	1-0	1-0	18	Rayner (og) [16]	2406
41	Apr 8	H	Droylsden	L	1-2	1-1	—	Reeves [16]	480
42	Apr 12	A	Oxford U	L	1-5	0-2	19	Bambrook [47]	4266
43	Apr 15	A	Ebbsfleet U	L	1-3	1-0	—	McNiven D [25]	810
44	Apr 19	H	Forest Green R	L	0-2	0-1	22		628
45	Apr 22	A	York C	L	1-4	0-2	—	Bambrook [75]	1886
46	Apr 26	H	Grays Ath	L	1-3	1-1	22	Downes (pen) [34]	379

Final League Position: 22

GOALSCORERS

League (48): Reeves 11, Bambrook 5, Downes 4 (4 pens), Grant 4, Stamer 4, Knowles 3, McNiven D 3, Torpey 3, Heath 2 (1 pen), Iqbal 2, Krief 2 (1 pen), Whitman 2, Bentham 1, Jackson 1, own goal 1.
FA Cup (2): Reeves 2.
Trophy (6): Tuck 2, Bambrook 1, Billy 1, Knowles 1, own goal 1.

Cuss 4	McNiven S 28 + 3	Lloyd 3	Knowles 28 + 8	Iqbal 40	Crossley 20	Allanson 7 + 14	Bambrook 30 + 9	Grant 12 + 8	Sugden 2 + 1	Reeves 43 + 1	Jackson 26 + 5	Dunne 1 + 3	Whitman 3 + 10	Sutcliffe 2 / McNiven D 6 + 6	Law 2	Stamer 21 + 8	Camfield — + 5	Watson 17 + 10	Tuck 7 + 9	Downes 35 + 1	Smith — + 1	Billy 12 + 3	Wilberforce 4 + 1	Heath 4 + 9	Serrant C 7	Morgan 15	Serrant R 10 + 2	Pearson 7	Torpey 17 + 5	Krief 17 + 2	Hotte 2	Bentham 16	Aspden 21	Lawlor 1	Santos 17	Gardner 3	Prendergast 16 + 1	*Match No.*
1	2	3	4■	5	6	7^{1}	8	9	10^{2}	11^{3}	12	13	14																									1
	2	3		5	6	13	8	9^{3}		11	4^{1}	7^{2}	12	1	10	14																						2
	2^{2}	7	4	5	6		8	9	10^{3}	11	3^{1}			1		14	12	13																				3
1			4	5	6	7^{2}	8	9		11			10^{3}		2^{1}	3	12	13	14																			4
1			4	5	6	14	8	9	12	11			10^{2}			7^{3}		3^{1}		2	13																	5
1			4	5	6^{2}	13	8	9^{3}		11	14		12			3		7^{1}		2		10																6
			13	5	6	7^{1}	8	14		9	4		10^{3}			3		12		2		11^{2}	1															7
			4	5	6		8			9^{1}	10		12			3		7^{2}		2		11	1	13														8
			4^{1}	5	6	13	8	14		9	7					3		10^{3}		2		11^{2}	1	12														9
				5	6^{2}	13	8	14		9	7		12			3^{1}		10^{3}		2		11	1		4													10
			4^{1}	5		13	14	9		10	6					3^{2}	12			2		11		8^{3}	7	1												11
			4	5		7	8	9		10^{3}	14						12	13		2		11		6^{2}		1	3^{1}											12
			4	5^{2}	6	7	8	9		11		13					12	14		2^{1}				10^{3}	3	1												13
			4	5	6	12	8	13		9^{2}									7^{1}	2		11	15		3	1^{6}		10										14
	12		4^{1}		6	7^{2}	8	14		9^{3}						13			10	2		11			3	1		5										15
	2		4		6	7^{1}				9^{2}	13	14	12							5		11		10^{3}	3	1		8										16
	14			5	6		8	12		9			13			4^{1}		7^{2}		2		11			3	1		10^{3}										17
	4		6	5		12		9^{3}		10	8		14			7				2		11^{1}				1	13	3^{2}										18
			4^{3}	5	6		8^{1}	12		9■	2		13			3^{2}				7		14				1	11	10										19
	12		4^{2}	5	6	14		9			2■		13			3^{1}				7^{3}						1	11	8	10									20
	2		4^{1}	5	6		13			9^{2}						11		14	8	3		12				1	7		10^{3}									21
	2		4^{2}	5	6	13	8									9^{3}		12	11	7		14				1	3^{1}		10									22
	2		4	5	6^{1}	13	8^{2}	14		9									7	11						1	3		10^{3}	12								23
	2		4	5		12	8	9		14	6^{1}								11^{2}	7				13		1	3		10^{3}									24
	2		4	5■		13	8			10						9^{3}			14	7						1	3^{1}		12		6	11^{2}						25
	2		4	5		14	8			9	12					10^{3}		13		6											3^{1}	7	1	11^{2}				26
	2		4^{1}	5			8			9	3					10														12		11	1		6	7		27
	2		13	5			12			9	4					10^{3}				3									14	7^{1}		8^{2}	1		6		11	28
				5			14			9	2							12	13								3^{1}		10^{3}	4		8	1		6	7^{2}	11	29
	2			5						9^{2}	3							12	13										10	4		8	1		6	7^{1}	11	30
	2		12^{2}	5						9	3			14		13		7											10^{3}	4		8	1		6^{1}		11	31
	2			5			12			9	3							7											10^{1}	4		8	1		6		11	32
	2^{1}		12	5						9	3			13		14		7^{2}											10^{3}	4		8	1		6■		11■	33
	2		13	5			12			9	3					11^{1}		7		4									10^{2}	6		8	1					34
	2		12				8			9	5							11■		3									10^{1}	4		7	1		6			35
	2			5						9	3									7									10	4		8	1		6		11	36
	2^{1}		13	5			14			9	3			12						7^{2}									10^{3}	4		8	1		6		11	37
	2^{1}			5			10			9	3			14		13			12	7^{2}										4		8	1		6		11^{3}	38
			12	5			10^{3}			9	2			14		3^{1}		7^{2}		13										4		8	1		6		11	39
			3	5^{1}			12			9^{3}	2			10^{2}				7		4				14					13			8	1		6		11	40
	2		4				8			9	3^{1}			10		7^{3}			14	5				13			12^{2}						1		6		11	41
	2		4■				14			9^{2}				10				3^{1}	13	5				12					8^{3}	7			1		6		11	42
	2						8			9				10				7	14	5^{1}				13			3^{3}		12	4			1		6^{2}		11	43
	2			5			8^{1}			9				10		14		6	7^{2}	3				12					13	4			1				11^{3}	44
	2		7	5			8			9				10^{2}				6^{1}		3				13					11	4			1				12	45
	2^{1}		7	5			8			9				12		13			14	3^{2}									10	4			1		6		11^{3}	46

FA Cup
Fourth Qualifying Round

	Barrow	(h)	1-1
		(a)	1-2

Trophy

First Round	Gateshead	(h)	4-1
Second Round	Alfreton T	(a)	2-0
Third Round	York C	(h)	0-2

FOREST GREEN ROVERS Blue Square Premier

Ground: The Lawn, Nympsfield Road, Forest Green, Nailsworth GL6 0ET. *Tel:* (01453) 834 860.
Year Formed: 1890. *Record Gate:* 3,002 (1999 v St Albans City, FA Umbro Trophy). *Nickname:* Rovers.
Manager: Jim Harvey. *Secretary:* David Honeybill. *Colours:* Black and white striped shirts, black shorts, red stockings.

FOREST GREEN ROVERS 2007–08 LEAGUE RECORD

Match No.	Date	Venue	Opponents	Result		H/T Score	Lg. Pos.	Goalscorers	Attendance
1	Aug 11	A	Oxford U	L	0-1	0-0	—		5521
2	Aug 14	H	Weymouth	W	3-2	3-1	—	Clist 5, Carey-Bertram 25, Fleetwood 27	865
3	Aug 18	H	Altrincham	W	3-1	1-1	5	Carey-Bertram 5, Clist 47, Dodgson 50	738
4	Aug 24	A	York C	W	2-0	0-0	—	Jones 50, Fleetwood 77	2294
5	Aug 27	H	Torquay U	D	2-2	2-1	—	Beesley 2 20, 22	2382
6	Sept 1	A	Woking	D	1-1	0-0	6	Fleetwood (pen) 84	1499
7	Sept 4	H	Aldershot T	L	2-3	1-2	—	Fleetwood 2, Jones 81	1103
8	Sept 8	A	Grays Ath	W	1-0	1-0	6	Dodgson 33	746
9	Sept 13	H	Salisbury C	L	0-3	0-2	—		1082
10	Sept 18	A	Exeter C	D	3-3	0-2	—	Fleetwood 2 53, 90, Dodgson 55	2753
11	Sept 22	A	Crawley T	L	0-3	0-0	15		982
12	Sept 25	H	Stevenage Bor	W	4-2	1-1	—	Beesley 2 21, 71, Fleetwood 2 49, 63	719
13	Sept 29	H	Cambridge U	W	3-1	1-0	7	Fleetwood 3 37, 50, 72	1179
14	Oct 6	A	Stafford R	W	3-1	0-1	6	Fleetwood 2 56, 85, Beesley 89	754
15	Oct 9	H	Northwich Vic	W	4-1	1-0	—	Fleetwood 2 6, 72, Beesley 47, Smith 74	859
16	Oct 12	A	Rushden & D	W	2-1	1-0	—	Beesley 2 32, 88	1381
17	Oct 20	H	Farsley C	D	2-2	1-0	6	Giles 2 45, 86	969
18	Nov 3	A	Ebbsfleet U	W	2-0	1-0	6	Fleetwood 2 40, 47	930
19	Nov 17	H	Histon	W	3-1	2-0	5	Stonehouse 10, Fleetwood 2 20, 52	1306
20	Nov 24	A	Droylsden	L	3-5	3-2	5	Carey-Bertram 3 6, 21, 45	450
21	Dec 8	A	Burton Alb	D	1-1	1-1	6	Fleetwood 39	1489
22	Dec 26	H	Kidderminster H	D	2-2	1-1	—	Beesley 21, Giles 74	2106
23	Dec 29	H	Droylsden	W	3-2	2-0	6	Fleetwood 2 7, 78, Murray (og) 34	1226
24	Jan 1	A	Kidderminster H	L	0-1	0-0	6		1852
25	Jan 5	H	Grays Ath	L	1-2	0-1	7	Clist 62	975
26	Jan 19	A	Aldershot T	W	1-0	1-0	6	Beesley 1	2895
27	Jan 26	H	Exeter C	D	1-1	1-1	6	Jones 45	2325
28	Feb 2	A	Salisbury C	D	0-0	0-0	—		1478
29	Feb 10	H	Crawley T	W	1-0	0-0	7	Lawless 73	1044
30	Feb 13	A	Stevenage Bor	D	0-0	0-0	—		1630
31	Feb 16	H	Stafford R	L	1-2	1-1	7	Brough 35	1093
32	Feb 23	A	Cambridge U	L	0-2	0-1	8		4797
33	Mar 1	H	Oxford U	D	0-0	0-0	9		1624
34	Mar 4	A	Weymouth	W	6-0	3-0	—	Fleetwood 2 4, 45, Jones 36, Rigoglioso 3 52, 78, 81	783
35	Mar 8	A	Altrincham	L	0-1	0-0	8		956
36	Mar 15	H	Halifax T	W	2-0	2-0	7	Fleetwood 2 3, 5	690
37	Mar 18	H	York C	L	1-2	0-2	—	Rigoglioso 70	734
38	Mar 21	H	Woking	W	2-1	1-1	—	Rigoglioso 30, Fleetwood 86	1143
39	Mar 24	A	Torquay U	L	0-1	0-1	8		3071
40	Mar 31	H	Burton Alb	W	3-1	2-0	—	Rigoglioso 19, Afful 2 36, 74	943
41	Apr 5	A	Halifax T	D	1-1	0-0	7	Carey-Bertram 74	1094
42	Apr 8	A	Northwich Vic	D	1-1	0-1	—	Carey-Bertram 53	651
43	Apr 12	H	Rushden & D	L	0-1	0-0	8		1177
44	Apr 19	A	Farsley C	W	2-0	1-0	8	Preece 23, Stonehouse 70	628
45	Apr 22	H	Ebbsfleet U	D	2-2	1-1	—	Lawless 36, Smith 89	822
46	Apr 26	A	Histon	D	2-2	1-2	8	Fleetwood 25, Jones 72	2103

Final League Position: 8

GOALSCORERS

League (76): Fleetwood 28 (1 pen), Beesley 10, Carey-Bertram 7, Rigoglioso 6, Jones 5, Clist 3, Dodgson 3, Giles 3, Afful 2, Lawless 2, Smith 2, Stonehouse 2, Brough 1, Preece 1, own goal 1.
FA Cup (14): Fleetwood 6, Beesley 2, Carey-Bertram 1, Clist 1, Dodgson 1, Forbes 1, Giles 1, Lawless 1.
Trophy (5): Fleetwood 2 (1 pen), Giles 1, Lawless 1, Stonehouse 1.

Robinson 32 + 1	James 4 + 3	Tonkin 37 + 1	Clist 39	Jones 37 + 2	Preece 17 + 18	Lawless 32	Brough 31 + 2	Fleetwood 41	Beesley 19 + 4	Stonehouse 24 + 11	Afful 20 + 22	Pitman 29 + 2	Dodgson 16 + 12	Giles 30 + 3	Carey-Bertram 13 + 11	Hardiker 31 + 3	Smith 11 + 14	Burton 14 + 1	Rigoglioso 18 + 9	Welsh 11 + 5	Match No.
1	2^{1}	3	4	5	6	7	8	9	10^{2}	11^{3}	12	13	14								1
1	14	3	4	12	6	2	8	9		13	7		11^{2}	5^{1}	10^{3}						2
1		3	4	5		7	8^{1}	9^{2}		13	14		11	6	10^{3}	2	12				3
		3	4	5	13	7	8	9^{2}	14	11	12			6	10^{3}	2^{1}		1			4
		3	4	5		7		9	8^{1}	11	12			6	10^{2}	2		1	13		5
1		3	4	5	12		7	9		11	13		14	6	10^{3}	2^{1}			8^{2}		6
1	12	3^{2}	4	5	14		8	9		11	7^{3}		10	6^{1}		2	13				7
1	2^{1}		4	5	12		8	9	14	11	7^{2}		10^{3}	6		3	13				8
1	2		4	5			8^{2}	9	12	11	7		10	6^{1}		3	13				9
1	2^{1}	3	4	5				9	10	13	11	8^{3}	12^{2}	6		7	14				10
1		3	4	5			12	9	10	13	7	8	11^{2}	6		2^{1}					11
1		3	4	2	5			9^{3}	10	13	7	8^{1}	11^{2}	6	14		12				12
1	12	3	4	2	5			9^{3}	10^{2}		7	8	11^{1}	6	13		14				13
1		3	4	2	5			9	10	13	7^{2}	8^{3}	11	6^{1}		12	14				14
1		3	4	2	5			9	10^{2}	11^{3}			7^{1}	6	12	14	8		13		15
1		3^{2}	4	5	13			9	10		7^{1}	8^{3}	11	6	12	2	14				16
1		3	4	5^{1}				9	10		7	8^{2}	11^{3}	6	14	2	13		12		17
1		3	4	2	5	7		9^{3}	10^{2}		12	11^{1}		6	14		8		13		18
1		3	4	2	5	7		9^{2}	10^{3}	11	12	8^{1}		6		13			14		19
1		3	4	5	2	7^{2}			10	11	12	8^{1}		6	9^{3}		13		14		20
1		3	4	5	12	7		9	10^{3}	11	13			6	14	2^{1}			8^{2}		21
1		3	4	5	12	7		9	10	11	13		8^{2}	6		2^{1}					22
1		3	4	5	6	7^{1}	13	9	14	11	12	8^{2}				2			10^{3}		23
1		3	4	5^{2}	13	7^{1}	8	9	10^{3}	11		2			14	6			12		24
1			4	5	6		8	9	10	11^{1}	13	7^{3}	12			2	14		3^{2}		25
1		3	4	5	12	7	8	9	10^{3}	13	14	6^{2}				2^{1}	11				26
1^{6}		3		5		7	8	9	10^{2}	11	12	6		13		2	4^{1}	15			27
1		3	4	5	6	7	8			12		9		11	10^{1}	2					28
1		3	4	5	12	7	8^{1}	9^{3}			13	11		6	14	2			10^{2}		29
1		3	4	5		7	8	9		12	13	11^{1}		6		2			10^{2}		30
1		3		5	14	7	8	9			12	4^{1}	13^{3}	6		2			10^{2}	11	31
1		3	4		5	2	8	9			12	11		6	10^{1}					7	32
		3	4		6		8	9			12	5	13		10^{3}	2	11^{2}	1	14	7^{1}	33
		3	4	5	14	7^{1}	8	9			12	11^{2}		6		2^{3}		1	10	13	34
15		3	4	5	13	7^{6}	8	9				11		6		2■		1■	10^{1}	12^{2}	35
1		3	4	5	14	2	8	9		12	11^{2}		13	6					10^{3}	7^{1}	36
1		3	4	5		7	8	9			12		13	6^{1}		2			10	11^{2}	37
		3^{1}	4			7	8	9		12	11	6^{2}	14			5	13	1	10	2^{3}	38
			4	5	14	2	8^{1}	9■		11	7	12	13			3		1	10^{3}	6^{2}	39
			4		12	2	8			11	7	6^{2}	13		10^{3}	5	14	1	9^{1}	3	40
		12	4		13	2	8^{2}			11	7	6^{3}		14	10	5	9	1		3^{1}	41
		3■				2	8			11	7		4^{2}	12	10	5^{1}	6	1	9	13	42
					6	2	8	9		11	7		5^{1}		12		4	1	10	3	43
		3		14	6	2	8	9		11^{2}	7^{1}	5	12				4	1	10^{3}	13	44
				5	13	2	8	9		3	11	4^{2}	7^{1}		14		6	1	12	10^{3}	45
				5	6^{1}	2	8	9		11	12	4			10^{2}		3	1	7	13	46

FA Cup

Fourth Qualifying Round	Eastleigh	(a)	3-3
		(h)	4-1
First Round	Rotherham U	(h)	2-2
		(a)	3-0
Second Round	Swindon T	(a)	2-3

Trophy

First Round	Sutton U	(a)	4-1
Second Round	Stafford R	(a)	1-2

GRAYS ATHLETIC — Blue Square Premier

Ground: Recreation Ground, Bridge Road, Grays RM17 6BZ. *Tel:* (01375) 391 649. *Year Formed:* 1890.
Record Gate: 9,500 (1959 v Chelmsford City, FA Cup). *Nickname:* The Blues. *Manager:* Mick Woodward.
Secretary: Phil O'Reilly. *Colours:* All sky blue.

GRAYS ATHLETIC 2007–08 LEAGUE RECORD

Match No.	Date	Venue	Opponents	Result		H/T Score	Lg. Pos.	Goalscorers	Attendance
1	Aug 12	A	Torquay U	D	0-0	0-0	—		4012
2	Aug 15	H	Woking	D	1-1	0-0	—	Watson [87]	1004
3	Aug 18	H	Kidderminster H	W	5-1	4-0	10	Kedwell 3 (1 pen) [9, 22 (p), 35], Watson [24], O'Connor [68]	1017
4	Aug 25	A	Altrincham	W	1-0	0-0	9	Ashton [54]	807
5	Aug 27	H	Histon	L	0-1	0-0	—		1290
6	Sept 1	A	Droylsden	W	2-1	0-0	5	McAllister [55], O'Connor [85]	592
7	Sept 4	A	Cambridge U	L	0-1	0-0	—		2793
8	Sept 8	H	Forest Green R	L	0-1	0-1	12		746
9	Sept 11	H	Oxford U	D	0-0	0-0	—		1201
10	Sept 15	A	Stafford R	W	2-0	2-0	8	Hearn [35], Grant [45]	649
11	Sept 22	H	York C	L	0-2	0-1	13		1014
12	Sept 25	A	Rushden & D	D	1-1	0-1	—	Murray [58]	1345
13	Sept 29	H	Stevenage Bor	L	0-2	0-1	15		1460
14	Oct 6	A	Exeter C	L	0-1	0-1	17		2783
15	Oct 9	H	Weymouth	L	0-2	0-0	—		779
16	Oct 16	A	Halifax T	D	0-0	0-0	—		1104
17	Oct 20	H	Northwich Vic	W	3-1	1-1	15	Murray 2 [27, 58], Hearn [80]	590
18	Nov 3	A	Salisbury C	W	1-0	1-0	13	Day [7]	1226
19	Nov 10	A	Woking	W	1-0	0-0	—	Watson [83]	1118
20	Nov 17	H	Farsley C	W	1-0	1-0	9	O'Connor [36]	724
21	Nov 22	A	Aldershot T	L	2-3	0-3	—	Grant [53], Cumbers [87]	2034
22	Dec 26	H	Ebbsfleet U	D	1-1	1-0	—	Kedwell [20]	813
23	Dec 29	H	Aldershot T	W	2-1	1-0	11	Obersteller [43], Watson [52]	1210
24	Jan 1	A	Ebbsfleet U	L	1-4	0-2	13	Power [64]	1396
25	Jan 5	A	Forest Green R	W	2-1	1-0	13	Cumbers [45], Watson [82]	975
26	Jan 19	H	Cambridge U	W	2-1	0-1	11	Standing 2 [46, 71]	1403
27	Jan 26	A	Oxford U	D	0-0	0-0	12		4891
28	Feb 9	A	York C	L	0-2	0-0	13		2531
29	Feb 16	H	Exeter C	L	0-2	0-2	14		1089
30	Feb 23	A	Stevenage Bor	D	0-0	0-0	14		1856
31	Mar 1	H	Torquay U	W	2-0	1-0	12	Ashton [40], Kedwell [90]	1018
32	Mar 8	A	Kidderminster H	L	0-1	0-1	14		1262
33	Mar 11	H	Burton Alb	D	0-0	0-0	—		496
34	Mar 15	H	Altrincham	W	1-0	1-0	12	O'Connor [36]	810
35	Mar 20	H	Droylsden	W	3-1	1-1	—	Kedwell 2 [11, 64], Cogan [87]	862
36	Mar 24	A	Histon	D	2-2	1-1	13	Taylor S [44], Taylor J [59]	711
37	Mar 29	H	Crawley T	W	2-1	0-1	12	Kedwell 2 (2 pens) [76, 84]	853
38	Apr 1	H	Stafford R	W	5-1	3-0	—	Taylor J 2 [7, 63], Kedwell (pen) [24], Cogan 2 [27, 68]	512
39	Apr 5	A	Burton Alb	W	3-2	1-2	10	Cogan 2 [26, 50], Taylor J [52]	1582
40	Apr 8	A	Weymouth	D	1-1	1-0	—	Taylor J [33]	817
41	Apr 12	H	Halifax T	D	3-3	1-1	11	Taylor J 2 [40, 47], Taylor S [86]	1204
42	Apr 15	A	Crawley T	L	1-2	0-0	—	Goulding [84]	755
43	Apr 19	A	Northwich Vic	L	0-1	0-0	13		769
44	Apr 22	H	Salisbury C	D	1-1	1-1	—	Kedwell [4]	507
45	Apr 24	H	Rushden & D	W	3-0	2-0	—	Taylor J [16], Kedwell [36], Taylor S [68]	542
46	Apr 26	A	Farsley C	W	3-1	1-1	10	Taylor J [17], Goulding [71], Kedwell [79]	379

Final League Position: 10

GOALSCORERS

League (58): Kedwell 13 (4 pens), Taylor J 9, Cogan 5, Watson 5, O'Connor 4, Murray 3, Taylor S 3, Ashton 2, Cumbers 2, Goulding 2, Grant 2, Hearn 2, Standing 2, Day 1, McAllister 1, Obersteller 1, Power 1.
FA Cup (1): O'Connor 1.
Trophy (5): O'Connor 3 (1 pen), Kedwell 2.

Flitney 30	Sambrook 22 + 1	Cooksey 18 + 1	Thurgood 24 + 1	Stuart 43	Ashton 39 + 1	Murray 23	Hearn 12 + 3	O'Connor 34 + 12	Kedwell 35 + 7	Marshall 3 + 8	Lawson 5 + 4	Watson 12 + 12 / Cogan 10 + 3	McAllister 5 + 4	Oli 16 + 1 / Saunders 1 + 1	Day 8 + 9	Gross 25 + 2	Barnard 4	Grant 9 + 6 / Goulding 2 + 7	Haverson 2 + 1	Potter — + 1 / Barnes — + 1	Knowles 5	Downer 29	Kamara — + 1	Oberstellar 9 + 3	Cumbers 1 + 4	Selley 3 + 1 / Whincup — + 1	Gaia 8	Power 4 + 1	Standing 9 + 6	Button 1	Mawer 4 + 1	Taylor S 11 + 7	Daniel — + 1	McCafferty 10 + 6	Taylor J 13 + 4	Patterson 7 + 2	Eyre 10 + 1	*Match No.*
1	2	3	4^{1}	5	6	7	8	9^{2}	10^{3}	11	12	13	14																									1
1	2	3	4^{1}	5	6	7	8	9^{3}	10^{2}	11		14	13	12																								2
1	2	3^{1}		5	6	7	8	14	10	13	4	9^{3}		11^{2}	12																							3
1	2	3		5	6		8	13	10^{3}		7^{1}	9^{2}	14	11		12	4																					4
1	2	3		5	6		8	14	10	12	7^{1}	9^{3}		11	13		4^{2}																					5
1	2	3^{1}		5	6		8^{2}	9	14				10^{3}	11	13	7	4	12																				6
1	2	3		5	6	7		9	14				10^{3}	11^{1}	13	4	8^{2}	12																				7
1	2	$3^{\blacksquare}$	4	5	6	7^{2}		9^{3}	10	12	8^{1}			11		13		14																				8
1	2		4	5	6		8	9^{2}	10^{3}		12	13	14	11^{1}		3		7																				9
1	2		4	5	6	7	8	12				13	10^{2}	11		3		9^{1}																				10
1	2		4	$5^{\blacksquare}$	6	7	8	14	12	13			10^{3}	11^{2}		3^{1}		9																				11
1	2	3	4		6	7	12	14	10	11^{2}	13			8				9^{3}	5^{1}																			12
1	2	3	4		6	5	8^{2}	14	10	12	11^{1}			7				9^{3}	13																			13
1	2		4		6^{1}	7	12	9^{3}				14	10	11^{2}		3		8	5	13																		14
1		11^{1}	4	5	6	2	8	9^{3}	10	12	13	14				3		7^{2}																				15
		3	4	5	6	7		13	10			9^{2}		11		8					1	2^{1}	12															16
	12	11^{2}		5	6	7	8	14	10^{3}	13				4		3		9			1	2^{1}																17
1		11		5	6	7		9	10			12		8^{1}	4							2		3														18
1		11		5	6	7		9	10^{2}			12		8^{1}	4			13				2		3														19
1		11	12	5	6	7		9^{2}	10	13		8^{3}			4^{1}			14				2		3														20
1		11^{3}		5	6	7		9	10^{2}			12			4^{1}			8				2		3	13	14												21
1				5	6	7		9	10^{1}			11^{2}			3			12				2			13	8	4											22
1	2			5		7^{2}		9	10			6^{3}			12							3		11	14	8^{1}	4	13										23
1	2^{1}			5				9	10^{3}			6			13							3		11^{2}	14	8	4	7	12									24
1		13		5	6	7		9^{2}				8			12							$2^{\blacksquare}$		14	11		3	4^{1}	10^{3}									25
				5	6	7		9	10^{1}			11^{2}															2	4	8	1	3	12	13					26
1	2			5	3	7		9^{1}	10			12															6	11^{2}	8			4		13				27
1				5	6	7		14	10			13			3							4		11^{2}					8		2^{1}	9^{3}		12				28
1		3		5	6			9	14			13			8							2		11^{2}			4		7^{1}			10^{3}		12				29
1	2			5	6^{1}			9	10						12							3		11			4		7			8^{2}			13			30
1				5	6			9	12			11				3						2		13					7			8^{1}		14	10^{3}	4^{2}		31
1	4			5	6^{1}			13	10			8^{2}			12	3						2		14					11						7	9^{3}		32
1^{G}	2			5			12	9							8^{1}	3						4										7		6	10	11	15	33
	2^{1}		4	5	12			9^{2}	14			13				3						6										7		8	10^{3}	11	1	34
			4	5	6			9	10			14				3						2							12			7^{2}		8^{1}	13	11^{3}	1	35
			4	5	6			7	10			8^{3}		12		3						2^{1}							13			11^{2}			9	14	1	36
			4^{1}	5	6			9	10^{2}			8				3		12				2							13			11^{3}		7	14		1	37
			4	5	6^{3}			9^{1}	10^{2}			11				3		13		12		2										14		7	8		1	38
			4	5	6			9^{2}	10			11				3						2										12		7	8^{1}	13	1	39
			4	5	6			9	10			7^{1}				3		12				2												8	11		1	40
			4	5	6			9	10^{3}			7				3		14				2							12			13		8^{1}	11^{2}		1	41
			4	5	$6^{\blacksquare}$			9	10^{2}			8^{3}				3		14				2							7^{1}			13		12	11		1	42
			4	5				9	12			8				3		11^{1}				6				15					2	13		7	10^{2}		1^{G}	43
			4	5	6^{1}			13	10			8				3		11^{3}			1	2									7			12	14	9^{2}		44
	2^{1}		4^{3}	5				11^{2}	10			13				3		12			1	6										14		7	9	8		45
			4	5				11	10			7^{2}		2^{1}		3		13			1	6							14		12	8^{3}			9			46

FA Cup
Fourth Qualifying Round — Lewes (h) 1-1; (a) 0-2

Trophy
First Round — Lewes (h) 3-0
Second Round — York C (a) 1-1; (h) 1-4

HALIFAX TOWN

Unibond One North

Ground: The Shay Stadium, Shay Syke, Halifax, West Yorkshire HX1 2YS. *Tel:* (01422) 341 222.
Year Formed: 1911. *Record Gate:* 36,885 (1953 v Tottenham Hotspur, FA Cup 5th rd).
Nickname: The Shaymen. *Manager:* Jim Vince. *Secretary:* Jenna Helliwell. *Colours:* All blue.

HALIFAX TOWN 2007–08 LEAGUE RECORD

Match No.	Date	Venue	Opponents	Result		H/T Score	Lg. Pos.	Goalscorers	Attendance
1	Aug 11	A	Weymouth	L	1-2	0-0	—	Kearney [76]	1612
2	Aug 14	H	Altrincham	D	2-2	2-2	—	Campbell 2 [8, 22]	1401
3	Aug 18	H	Histon	D	0-0	0-0	18		1280
4	Aug 25	A	Ebbsfleet U	L	0-1	0-0	19		931
5	Aug 27	H	Droylsden	W	3-0	2-0	—	Campbell 3 (1 pen) [5, 35, 71 (p)]	1302
6	Sept 1	A	Oxford U	D	1-1	0-0	18	Torpey (pen) [74]	4926
7	Sept 6	A	Stafford R	W	3-2	1-0	—	Killeen [35], Shaw 2 [75, 80]	927
8	Sept 11	H	Woking	W	1-0	0-0	—	Griffith [62]	1304
9	Sept 14	A	Torquay U	L	1-3	0-0	—	Shaw (pen) [62]	2727
10	Sept 18	H	Northwich Vic	W	3-1	2-0	—	Shaw 2 [33, 36], Killeen [48]	1256
11	Sept 22	H	Rushden & D	D	1-1	1-0	10	Torpey [23]	1384
12	Sept 27	A	York C	L	2-3	1-0	—	Griffith [17], Forrest [52]	2134
13	Oct 2	H	Burton Alb	D	2-2	1-0	—	Shaw [39], Stride (og) [66]	1206
14	Oct 6	A	Cambridge U	D	2-2	1-1	15	Shaw (pen) [18], Belle [83]	3027
15	Oct 9	A	Kidderminster H	L	0-1	0-0	—		1365
16	Oct 16	H	Grays Ath	D	0-0	0-0	—		1104
17	Oct 20	A	Aldershot T	L	0-1	0-0	18		2389
18	Nov 3	H	Crawley T	W	3-0	2-0	16	Heslop [27], Shaw [30], Griffith [48]	1197
19	Nov 17	A	Stevenage Bor	W	3-2	0-2	14	Stamp [51], Heslop [53], Shaw [58]	2421
20	Nov 24	H	Salisbury C	D	1-1	0-0	14	Belle [76]	1237
21	Dec 8	H	Exeter C	L	0-3	0-1	18		1160
22	Dec 26	A	Farsley C	L	0-3	0-1	—		1501
23	Dec 29	A	Salisbury C	L	0-1	0-0	18		1212
24	Jan 1	H	Farsley C	W	2-0	1-0	17	Jackson (og) [10], Shaw [50]	1538
25	Jan 5	A	Woking	L	0-1	0-1	18		1299
26	Jan 26	A	Northwich Vic	D	2-2	2-2	18	Nelthorpe [4], Shaw [36]	1024
27	Feb 9	A	Rushden & D	D	2-2	1-1	18	Nelthorpe [3], Campbell [81]	1472
28	Feb 12	H	York C	D	2-2	1-1	—	Joynes [27], Whitehouse [80]	2875
29	Feb 16	H	Cambridge U	L	1-2	1-1	18	Heslop [15]	1402
30	Feb 23	H	Stafford R	D	0-0	0-0	18		1103
31	Mar 1	H	Weymouth	W	2-1	0-1	18	Campbell [61], Heslop [78]	971
32	Mar 4	A	Altrincham	D	3-3	2-1	—	Shaw 2 (1 pen) [6, 67 (p)], Campbell (pen) [35]	903
33	Mar 8	A	Histon	W	3-1	2-0	18	Clarke [32], Davies [37], Griffith [53]	622
34	Mar 11	H	Torquay U	W	3-2	2-0	—	Shaw 2 [9, 49], Doughty [43]	894
35	Mar 15	A	Forest Green R	L	0-2	0-2	17		690
36	Mar 22	H	Oxford U	L	0-3	0-1	18		1369
37	Mar 24	A	Droylsden	L	0-2	0-1	20		887
38	Mar 29	A	Exeter C	L	0-1	0-0	21		3096
39	Apr 5	H	Forest Green R	D	1-1	0-0	22	Stamp [77]	1094
40	Apr 8	H	Kidderminster H	L	1-6	1-4	—	Shaw (pen) [45]	1097
41	Apr 10	H	Ebbsfleet U	W	1-0	0-0	—	Heslop [70]	1063
42	Apr 12	A	Grays Ath	D	3-3	1-1	20	Taylor [45], Forrest [50], Shaw (pen) [89]	1204
43	Apr 15	A	Burton Alb	L	1-2	0-0	—	Stamp [90]	1607
44	Apr 19	H	Aldershot T	D	0-0	0-0	21		1545
45	Apr 22	A	Crawley T	W	4-0	2-0	—	Killeen [22], Shaw 2 [44, 73], Murphy (og) [90]	817
46	Apr 26	H	Stevenage Bor	L	1-2	0-2	20	Shaw (pen) [64]	2229

Final League Position: 20

GOALSCORERS

League (61): Shaw 20 (6 pens), Campbell 8 (2 pens), Heslop 5, Griffith 4, Killeen 3, Stamp 3, Belle 2, Forrest 2, Nelthorpe 2, Torpey 2 (1 pen), Clarke 1, Davies 1, Doughty 1, Joynes 1, Kearney 1, Taylor 1, Whitehouse 1, own goals 3.
FA Cup (2): Shaw 1, Heslop 1.
Trophy (8): Shaw 4, Heslop 1, Nelthorpe 1, Quinn 1, Sharpe 1.

Mawson 16	Scott 11 + 1	Doughty 31 + 7	Kearney 38 + 3	Quinn 32 + 1	Bushell 8 + 6	Forrest 22 + 6	Campbell 15 + 15	Killeen 33 + 7	Stamp 13 + 10	Belle 16 + 3	Taylor 10 + 14	Torpey 16 + 6	Toulson 16 + 3	Wright 34 + 3	Griffith 35 + 2	Shaw 36 + 1	Young 10 + 1	Dadson — + 2	Legzdins 30	Bailey 2 + 2	Oliver 2	Heslop 28 + 2	Gray — + 7	Joynes 5	Harban 4 + 2	Sharpe 1	O'Callaghan 1	Nelthorpe 6 + 1	Ainge 11 + 1	Whitehouse — + 4	Davies 10 + 1	Clarke 7	Gaia 6 + 3	Atherton 1	*Match No.*
1	2	3	4	5	6	7¹	8	9²	10³	11	12	13	14																						1
1	2	3	4	5	6	12	8	9	10²	11	7¹	13																							2
1	2	3	4	5	6	14	8	9²	10³	11	7¹	13		12																					3
1	2	3	4	5	6	14	8	13	10³	11¹		12		7	9²																				4
1		14	13	5	6²	7¹	8³	9	12	4		10	2	3	11																				5
1		3¹	4	5		13	8	9		11		12	2	7	6	10²																			6
1	12		4	5¹	13		8	9		6		11²	2	3	7	10																			7
1	2¹	12	4		14	13	8³	9		5		10²	6	3	7	11																			8
1			4	5		7		9¹	10²	6	13	12	2	3	8	11																			9
1			4	5	14	12	8³	9¹		6	13	10²	2	3	7	11																			10
1		13	4	5		7¹	8³			6	14	10²	2	3	11	9	12																		11
1			4	5		7			9²	6	12	10	2	3	8	11¹		13																	12
			4	5	12	7²					8	10¹	2	3	11	9	6	14	1	13³															13
		3²	4	5¹	12			9		2	11			13	8	10▮	6		1	7															14
			4	5	12			9	13	6	11		14	7	8▮		2¹		1	3³	10²														15
			4	5	6			9	12		11	10	2	3			7		1		8¹														16
		14	4	5	11			9²	8	13	7	10³	2¹	3▮			6		1			12													17
		3	4	12					10²	5	13	7¹	2▮		8	9	6		1			11													18
	2²	3	4▮	5	8¹			12	10³			7	13			9	6		1			11	14												19
	2²	3		5¹				9		12	13	7	4	11³		10	6		1			8	14												20
		3						9²	10	6	13	7³	2	12	8	11	5¹		1			4	14												21
	2		4					13	10²		12	7	6	3	8¹	9	5		1			11													22
	2	3	4					9	12		6²		7	5	8¹	10			1			11	13												23
	2	3	4	5¹			13	9³		12		7²		6	8▮	10			1			11	14												24
	2	3	4	5			13	9				7¹		6		10			1			11	12	8²											25
		3	4				13	9²								10			1	12		7	14	8▮	2¹	5	6	11³							26
		3	4	5			13	9	12						8	10			1			7			2			11²	6¹						27
		3	4¹	5			12								8	10			1			7		9	2			11²	6	13					28
		3	4	5			13	12							8	10			1			7		9	2¹			11³	6²	14					29
		3	4	5			13	12							8¹	10			1			7		9²				11			2	6			30
		3	4²			8	9	12						5	13	10			1			7						11¹			2	6			31
		3				7¹	8	9						5	4	10			1			11						12			2	6			32
		3		5		7¹	12	9						4	8	10			1			11									2	6			33
		3	14	6¹		7³	13	9						5	8	10			1			11			12²						4	2			34
		3	4³			7²	14	9						5	8	10			1			11								13	6	2¹	12		35
		3				7	13	9			12			2¹	8	10²			1			11									4	6	5		36
1		11²	4	5¹		7	10³	9			14			3	8							13							12		2		6		37
1		3¹	4²			7³		9			14			5	8	10						11			12				2	13			6		38
1		13	4²			7¹	8	9	12					3	6	10						11							2				5		39
1		12	4			7¹	8²	9	13		14			3	6	10³						11							2				5		40
		3	14			7	12	9						5	6	10			1			11							2¹		8³		13	4²	41
		3²	4	6		7		13	10³		9			5	12	14			1			11¹							2		8				42
		3	4	6²		7			12		9¹			5	8	10			1			11							2▮				13		43
		12	4	2		7²	14	9³	8		13			3	6	10			1			11											5¹		44
		3	4	6		7¹	12	9	13					5	8	10²			1			11							2						45
		3	4¹	6		7²	13	9³	14					5	8	10			1			11							2		12				46

FA Cup

Fourth Qualifying Round	Evesham U	(a)	0-0
		(h)	2-1
First Round	Burton Alb	(h)	0-4

Trophy

First Round	Leamington	(h)	2-1
Second Round	Bishop's Stortford	(a)	2-2
		(h)	4-1
Third Round	Rushden & D	(h)	0-2

HISTON

Blue Square Premier

Ground: Glassworld Stadium, Bridge Road, Impington, Cambridge CB24 9PH. *Tel:* (01223) 237 373. *Year Formed:* 1904. *Record Gate:* 3,800. *Nickname:* The Stutes. *Manager:* Steve Fallon. *Secretary:* Lisa Baldwin. *Colours:* Red shirts, black shorts, black stockings.

HISTON 2007–08 LEAGUE RECORD

Match No.	Date	Venue	Opponents	Result		H/T Score	Lg. Pos.	Goalscorers	Attendance
1	Aug 11	H	Burton Alb	D	2-2	0-0	—	Wright [63], Nightingale [88]	1265
2	Aug 14	A	Stevenage Bor	L	1-2	0-1	—	Dillon [74]	2073
3	Aug 18	A	Halifax T	D	0-0	0-0	19		1280
4	Aug 24	H	Aldershot T	L	1-2	0-2	—	Akurang [65]	1614
5	Aug 27	A	Grays Ath	W	1-0	0-0	—	Akurang [48]	1290
6	Sept 1	H	Salisbury C	W	2-0	0-0	14	Wright 2 [81, 84]	803
7	Sept 4	A	Ebbsfleet U	W	1-0	0-0	—	Murray [50]	866
8	Sept 8	H	Farsley C	L	1-2	0-0	13	Barker [56]	714
9	Sept 15	A	Northwich Vic	W	3-1	2-0	10	Akurang (pen) [3], Warhurst (og) [12], Kennedy J [81]	641
10	Sept 18	H	Torquay U	L	4-5	0-3	—	Knight-Percival [52], Akurang 3 (2 pens) [54, 82 (p), 88 (p)]	763
11	Sept 20	H	Oxford U	W	1-0	1-0	—	Murray [28]	1257
12	Sept 25	A	Stafford R	D	1-1	1-0	—	Kennedy J [3]	705
13	Sept 29	H	Weymouth	D	2-2	1-1	11	Knight-Percival [2], Kennedy J [46]	891
14	Oct 6	A	York C	W	4-1	1-1	7	Murray [43], Knight-Percival [55], Wright [86], Akurang [90]	2199
15	Oct 9	A	Crawley T	L	0-1	0-1	—		886
16	Oct 14	H	Kidderminster H	W	2-1	1-0	8	Akurang [28], Okay [54]	1051
17	Oct 20	A	Droylsden	W	1-0	0-0	7	Knight-Percival [71]	497
18	Nov 3	H	Altrincham	W	1-0	1-0	7	Wright [23]	814
19	Nov 17	A	Forest Green R	L	1-3	0-2	7	Langston [56]	1306
20	Nov 24	H	Exeter C	D	2-2	1-1	7	Langston 2 [45, 67]	973
21	Dec 1	A	Altrincham	W	2-1	1-0	—	Akurang [33], Wright [74]	911
22	Dec 4	A	Rushden & D	W	3-2	2-2	—	Akurang [28], Gwillim [41], Kennedy J [68]	1351
23	Dec 8	H	Woking	L	0-1	0-0	7		887
24	Dec 26	A	Cambridge U	L	0-1	0-0	—		7125
25	Dec 29	A	Exeter C	L	1-2	1-0	8	Barker [45]	3350
26	Jan 1	H	Cambridge U	W	1-0	0-0	7	Mitchell-King [53]	3721
27	Jan 5	A	Farsley C	W	3-1	2-1	6	Knight-Percival [23], Murray 2 [24, 81]	400
28	Jan 28	A	Torquay U	L	0-1	0-0	—		2482
29	Feb 9	A	Oxford U	L	0-3	0-2	11		4851
30	Feb 16	H	York C	W	3-1	2-1	10	Midson 2 [4, 50], Knight-Percival [15]	1021
31	Feb 23	A	Weymouth	W	1-0	0-0	9	Murray [53]	1121
32	Feb 26	H	Stafford R	D	3-3	1-0	—	Wright 2 [45, 58], Okay [81]	527
33	Mar 1	A	Burton Alb	W	3-1	2-0	8	Wright 2 [4, 27], Midson [87]	1508
34	Mar 4	H	Stevenage Bor	L	1-4	1-1	—	Mitchell-King [41]	916
35	Mar 8	H	Halifax T	L	1-3	0-2	9	Murray [61]	622
36	Mar 11	A	Aldershot T	L	1-3	0-2	—	Murray [63]	2177
37	Mar 15	H	Rushden & D	W	2-1	0-0	9	Murray [65], Andrews [90]	767
38	Mar 18	H	Ebbsfleet U	W	3-2	1-2	—	Wright [9], Mitchell-King [75], Andrews [79]	552
39	Mar 21	A	Salisbury C	D	3-3	2-1	—	Wright [26], Gwillim (pen) [28], Murray [52]	1483
40	Mar 24	H	Grays Ath	D	2-2	1-1	7	Knight-Percival [10], Gwillim (pen) [79]	711
41	Mar 29	A	Woking	D	3-3	1-1	7	Knight-Percival [6], Midson [61], Gwillim [70]	1310
42	Apr 1	H	Northwich Vic	D	1-1	0-0	—	Murray [68]	704
43	Apr 8	H	Crawley T	W	3-0	1-0	—	Murray 2 [44, 50], Langston [61]	601
44	Apr 12	A	Kidderminster H	D	1-1	0-1	7	Wright [52]	1540
45	Apr 19	H	Droylsden	W	2-0	1-0	7	Wright 2 [37, 76]	1177
46	Apr 26	H	Forest Green R	D	2-2	2-1	7	Midson [15], Nightingale [33]	2103

Final League Position: 7

GOALSCORERS

League (76): Wright 15, Murray 13, Akurang 10 (3 pens), Knight-Percival 8, Midson 5, Gwillim 4 (2 pens), Kennedy J 4, Langston 4, Mitchell-King 3, Andrews 2, Barker 2, Nightingale 2, Okay 2, Dillon 1, own goal 1.
FA Cup (4): Barker 1, Knight-Percival 1, Murray 1, Wright 1.
Trophy (8): Knight-Percival 3, Wright 2, Kennedy J 1, Murray 1, Nightingale 1.

Osborn 10	Haniver 5 + 5	Okay 41 + 2	Kennedy J 45	Mitchell-King 40	Ada 32 + 4	Nightingale 10 + 8	Barker 11 + 25	Murray 39 + 2	Wright 30 + 11	Knight-Percival 43 + 1	Kennedy N 1 + 10	Dillon 1 + 2	Cambridge 36 + 5	Gwillim 42 + 2	Pope 28	Akurang 19	Naisbitt 36	Hipperson 4 + 2	Langston 16 + 8	Midson 17 + 2	Andrews — + 3	*Match No.*
1	2	3	4	5	6	7	8	9	10^1	11	12											1
1	2	3	4	5	6	7^1	8	9	10^2	11	12	13										2
1	2	3	4	5	6	12	8	7^1	13		10^3	9^2	11	14								3
1	2^1	3	4	5	6		8		13	11			7	12	9	10^2						4
1	12	3	4^1	5	6		9^2		14	11	13		8	7	2	10^3						5
1		3	4^1	5	6	12	9^2	13	14	11			8	7	2	10^3						6
1	12	3	4^1	5	6		13	9		11^2			8	7	2	10						7
1	12	3	4^2	5	6		13	9		11^3		14	8	7	2^1	10						8
1	12	3^1	4	5	6		13	9	14	11^2			8	7	2	10^3						9
1		3	4	5■	6		12	9		11			8	7	2^1	10						10
		3	4^2		6		13	9		11			8	7	2	10	1	5^1	12			11
		3^1	4		6		12	9^3	13	11			8	7	2	10^2	1	5■	14			12
		3	4		6			9	12	11			8	7	2^1	10	1		5			13
		3	4	5^1	6		13	9^3	14	11^2			8	7	2	10	1		12			14
		3	4	5	6		12	9^2	13	11			8	7	2^1	10	1					15
		3	4		6			9	12	11			8	7	2	10^1	1		5			16
			4				12	9	10^1	11			8	7	2	3■	1	5	6			17
		3	4		6		12	9	10^1	11			8	7	2		1		5			18
		3	4	5	6^3		12	9	13	11^1			8^2	7	2	10	1		14			19
		3	4	5			12		9	11			8	7	2	10^1	1		6			20
		3	4	5	12	13	14		9^2	11			8^3	7	2^1	10	1		6			21
		3	4	5				12	9	11			8^1	7	2	10	1		6			22
			4	5			12	3	9^2	11	13		8	7	2	10^1	1		6			23
		3	4	6				9	10	11			8	7	2		1		5			24
		3	4	5^2			9		10	11	12		8	7	2^1		1	13	6			25
		3	4	5			12	9	10^1	11			8	7	2		1		6			26
	12	3^1		5		13	4	9	10	11^2			8	7	2		1		6			27
	2^1	3	4	5	6	12	8^3	9	10		14		11^2	7			1			13		28
		3	4	5	6	13	8^3	9	10	14			11^2	7	2^1		1			12		29
		13	4^2	5	6		12	9	10^3	11	14		8^1	7	2		1			3		30
			4	5	6		12	9	10	11			8	7	2		1			3^1		31
		12	4	5	6		13	9	10	11			8^1	7	2^3		1	14		3^2		32
		2	4	5	6			9	10	11			8	7			1			3		33
		3	4	5		7		9		11	12		8^1	2			1	6		10		34
		3	4	5	6		13	9	10^2	11			8^1	2			1			7	12	35
		3	4	5	6			9	10	11			8	2			1			7		36
		3	4	5	6	7^2	14	9	10	11^3				2^1			1		12	8	13	37
		3	4	5	6			9	10	11			8^1	2			1			7	12	38
		3^1	4^2	5	6	13	8^3	9	10	11			14	2			1		12	7		39
		3	4	5	6	12	13	9	10	11^2			8^1	2			1			7		40
		3	4	5	6^1	7		9	10	11				2			1		12	8		41
		3	4	5	6^2	7	12	9	10^1	11				2			1		13	8		42
		3	4^2	5		7^1	14	9	10^3	11	13		12	2			1		6	8		43
		3^1	4	5	12	7^2	14	9	10	11			13	2			1		6	8^3		44
		3^1	4^2	5	12	7^3	13	9	10	11			14	2			1		6	8		45
		3^1	4	5	12	7^2		9	10^3	11	14		13	2			1		6	8		46

FA Cup

Fourth Qualifying Round	Bamber Bridge	(h)	4-1
First Round	Notts Co	(a)	0-3

Trophy

First Round	Retford U	(h)	5-2
Second Round	Cambridge U	(h)	2-0
Third Round	Burton Alb	(a)	1-1
		(h)	0-1

KIDDERMINSTER HARRIERS Blue Square Premier

Ground: Aggborough Stadium, Hoo Road, Kidderminster DY10 1NB. *Tel:* (01562) 823 951. *Year Formed:* 1886. *Record Gate:* 9,155 (1948 v Hereford U). *Nickname:* Harriers. *Manager:* Mark Yates. *Secretary:* Roger Barlow. *Colours:* Red shirts, white shorts, red stockings.

KIDDERMINSTER HARRIERS 2007–08 LEAGUE RECORD

Match No.	Date	Venue	Opponents	Result		H/T Score	Lg. Pos.	Goalscorers	Attendance
1	Aug 11	H	Aldershot T	L	1-2	0-0	—	Creighton [77]	1976
2	Aug 14	A	Stafford R	W	3-1	1-1	—	Richards 2 (1 pen) [26, 84 (p)], Hurren [65]	1126
3	Aug 18	A	Grays Ath	L	1-5	0-4	15	Christie (pen) [49]	1017
4	Aug 24	H	Stevenage Bor	L	0-2	0-2	—		1692
5	Aug 27	A	Rushden & D	W	1-0	0-0	—	Penn [60]	1653
6	Sept 1	H	Exeter C	W	4-0	2-0	13	Constable 3 [27, 59, 63], Penn [41]	1860
7	Sept 4	A	Farsley C	D	1-1	0-1	—	Penn [70]	492
8	Sept 8	H	York C	W	3-0	2-0	9	Richards 2 [16, 89], Bennett [30]	1589
9	Sept 15	A	Ebbsfleet U	L	4-5	0-3	13	Goodhind (og) [59], Constable 3 [67, 72, 90]	812
10	Sept 18	H	Droylsden	W	3-1	1-1	—	Harkness [33], Constable [49], Creighton [55]	1305
11	Sept 22	H	Torquay U	L	2-5	0-3	12	Constable 2 [67, 78]	2027
12	Sept 29	A	Salisbury C	W	1-0	1-0	12	Blackwood [38]	1621
13	Oct 2	A	Northwich Vic	D	1-1	1-0	—	Richards [36]	481
14	Oct 6	H	Crawley T	D	1-1	1-0	11	Constable [45]	1462
15	Oct 9	H	Halifax T	W	1-0	0-0	—	Belle (og) [71]	1365
16	Oct 14	A	Histon	L	1-2	0-1	10	Barnes-Homer [90]	1051
17	Oct 20	H	Weymouth	L	0-2	0-0	11		1374
18	Nov 3	A	Burton Alb	W	2-0	1-0	10	Penn [19], Bignot [61]	1864
19	Nov 17	H	Woking	D	1-1	1-0	11	Richards (pen) [37]	1426
20	Nov 24	H	Oxford U	L	0-2	0-1	12		2025
21	Dec 6	H	Cambridge U	W	1-0	0-0	—	Christie [59]	1314
22	Dec 26	A	Forest Green R	D	2-2	1-1	—	Christie (pen) [8], Russell [46]	2106
23	Dec 29	A	Oxford U	D	0-0	0-0	12		5380
24	Jan 1	H	Forest Green R	W	1-0	0-0	11	Russell [57]	1852
25	Jan 5	A	York C	D	2-2	2-2	11	McGrath [2], Christie [24]	2423
26	Jan 8	A	Altrincham	L	1-2	0-0	—	Christie [56]	788
27	Jan 19	H	Farsley C	W	2-1	0-1	10	Constable [51], Penn [90]	1475
28	Jan 26	A	Droylsden	L	0-1	0-1	13		629
29	Feb 2	H	Northwich Vic	D	0-0	0-0	—		1282
30	Feb 9	A	Torquay U	L	0-1	0-1	12		3012
31	Feb 23	H	Salisbury C	L	1-2	1-2	13	Penn [11]	1497
32	Mar 1	A	Aldershot T	L	1-2	1-1	15	Barnes-Homer [3]	2835
33	Mar 4	H	Stafford R	W	6-0	4-0	—	Knights [14], Christie 2 [21, 57], Russell 2 [25, 90], Barnes-Homer (pen) [36]	1240
34	Mar 8	H	Grays Ath	W	1-0	1-0	11	Knights [23]	1262
35	Mar 13	A	Stevenage Bor	L	1-2	0-1	—	Christie [52]	1326
36	Mar 22	A	Exeter C	L	0-1	0-0	16		3812
37	Mar 24	H	Rushden & D	W	2-0	1-0	14	Christie [16], Creighton [50]	1477
38	Mar 27	A	Crawley T	W	4-0	4-0	—	Christie 2 [6, 8], Barnes-Homer [21], Russell [42]	595
39	Mar 29	A	Cambridge U	W	3-0	1-0	11	Barnes-Homer 2 [27, 66], Christie (pen) [85]	3999
40	Apr 1	H	Ebbsfleet U	W	2-1	2-1	—	Christie [4], Penn [12]	1450
41	Apr 5	H	Altrincham	D	1-1	1-1	11	Christie (pen) [45]	1535
42	Apr 8	A	Halifax T	W	6-1	4-1	—	Penn 4 [15, 22, 38, 80], Christie [36], Ferrell (pen) [67]	1097
43	Apr 12	H	Histon	D	1-1	1-0	9	Christie [8]	1540
44	Apr 19	A	Weymouth	L	1-2	0-0	11	Russell [61]	1205
45	Apr 22	H	Burton Alb	W	4-1	3-0	—	Knights 2 [18, 42], Christie [21], Hurren [89]	1761
46	Apr 26	A	Woking	L	0-3	0-1	13		2310

Final League Position: 13

GOALSCORERS

League (74): Christie 17 (4 pens), Constable 11, Penn 11, Barnes-Homer 6 (1 pen), Richards 6 (2 pens), Russell 6, Knights 4, Creighton 3, Hurren 2, Bennett 1, Bignot 1, Blackwood 1, Ferrell 1 (pen), Harkness 1, McGrath 1, own goals 2.
FA Cup (6): Barnes-Homer 1, Blackwood 1, Constable 1, Creighton 1, McGrath 1, Richards 1.
Trophy (4): Constable 1, Harkness 1, Kenna 1, Russell 1 (pen).

Bevan 17	Kenna 26 + 2	Bignot 25 + 3	Ferrell 31 + 7	Creighton 44	Hurren 31 + 3	Smikle 8 + 20	Penn 42	Richards 22 + 4	Constable 24	Blackwood 27	McGrath 10 + 21	Christie 24 + 14	Barnes-Homer 17 + 17	Munday 3	Russell 24 + 6	Harkness 15 + 3	Whitehead 16 + 1	Bennett 33 + 2	Coleman 8 + 2	MacKenzie 21	Jeannin 17 + 1	Bailey 2 + 1	Knights 12 + 5	Jones 6	Wylde 1 + 1	*Match No.*
1	2	3	4[1]	5	6	7	8	9	10[2]	11[3]	12	13	14													1
1	2	3	12	5	6	7		9[3]	10[2]		11[1]	13	14	4	8											2
1	13	2[1]	14	5	6	7[2]	8	9[3]	10	11		12		4		3										3
1	2	13		5	6	7	8	9[3]	10	11[2]		14	12			3[1]	4									4
1	2	12	7	5	6		8	9[2]	10[1]	11		13				3	4									5
1	2		7	5	6		8[1]	9[2]	10[3]	11		13	14			3	4	12								6
1	2		7	5	6	13	8	9[2]	10	11		12				3[1]		4								7
1	6	2	7	5[1]	12	13	8	9	10[3]	11		14				3		4[2]								8
	6	2[1]	7[3]	5	13		8	9	10	11	14		12			3[2]		4	1							9
	2		7	5	12■		8[1]	9	10[3]	11[2]			14		13	3	4	6	1							10
	2		7[1]	5			8	9	10	11					12	3	6	4		1						11
		2	7[1]	5		12	8	9	10	11						3	4	6		1						12
		2	7[2]	5			8	9	10	11	12		13			3[1]	6	4		1						13
		2		5	6	12	8	9	10	11						3	4	7[1]		1						14
		2[1]	13	5	6		8	9	10	11	12					3[2]	4	7		1						15
		2[1]	12	5■	6		8	9	10[3]	11	13		14			3	4	7[2]		1						16
		2[1]	7			13	8	9		11	14	12	10[3]	5		3	4	6[2]		1						17
		2	11	5		7	8	9[2]		3	10[1]	13	12				6	4■		1						18
		2	4	5	6	7[1]	8	9	10	3	11	12								1						19
1		2[1]	7	5	6[2]		8	9	10■	3	13[3]	14	12		11		4									20
1		2	7	5	11		8	9[1]		3		10	12		4[2]		6		13							21
1		2	4	5	6	12	8	13	10	3	11[1]	9[2]			7											22
1	2		4	5	6		8	13	10[1]	3	11	9[2]	12		7											23
1		2	7	5	6	12	8	9[3]	10[2]	3	11[1]	13	14		4											24
1	2	3		5[1]	6	14				11[2]	7	9	10		4[3]	13	12	8								25
1	12	2[1]	4	5	6		8	13	10[2]	3	11	9			14			7[3]								26
1	2		7	5			8	13	10	3	11[1]	9[2]			4		6	12								27
1		2[3]	7	5		13			10	11[2]	12	9	14		8[1]		6	4			3					28
	2		4	5			8[2]				13	9	12		14			11[3]		1	3	7[1]	10	6		29
	2		4	5	6[2]	7[1]						9	14		10[3]			11		1	3	13	12	8		30
	2		7[1]	5			8				12	9	13		14			6		1	3	11[2]	10[3]	4		31
		2	4[1]	5		7[2]	8				10[3]	12	11		13			9		1	3		14	6		32
	2			5		13	8[2]				14	9	11		7	12		4		1	3[1]		10[3]	6		33
	2[1]	12		5			8				13	9	11		7			4		1	3		10[2]	6		34
	2			5	6		8				12	9	11		7			4		1	3		10[1]			35
	2		7[2]	5	6	13	8[1]				12	9	11[3]		10			4		1	3		14			36
	2			5	6	12	8				13	9	11[2]		7			4		1	3		10[1]			37
	2			5	6	13	8[1]				12	9[2]	11		7			4	15	1[G]	3		10			38
		2	12	5	6	13	8				14	9	11[3]		7[1]			4	1		3		10[2]			39
	2		12	5	6	13	8[2]				14	9	11		7[3]			4	1		3		10[1]			40
	2		12	5	6	13	8					9	11		7[2]			4	1		3		10[1]			41
	2		7	5[1]	6	14	8[2]				13	9	11		10[3]			4	1		3				12	42
	2		7		6	12	8					9	11[2]		10			4[1]	1		3		13		5	43
		2	7[1]	5	6		8					9	11		10			4		1	3		12			44
		2	4[1]	5	6	14	8				13	9[3]	11		7[2]	12		3	1				10			45
		2[1]	4[2]	5	6	14	8				13	9	11[3]		7			3		1	12		10			46

FA Cup

Fourth Qualifying Round	Vauxhall M	(h)	3-1
First Round	Ware	(a)	2-0
Second Round	Dagenham & R	(a)	1-3

Trophy

First Round	Guiseley	(a)	2-1
Second Round	Weymouth	(a)	0-0
		(h)	2-2

NORTHWICH VICTORIA   Blue Square Premier

Ground: Victoria Stadium, Wincham Avenue, Northwich, Cheshire CW9 6GB. *Tel:* (01606) 815 200.
Year Formed: 1874. *Record Gate:* 12,000 (1977 v Watford, FA Cup 4th rd). *Nickname:* The Vics.
Manager: Dino Maamria. *Secretary:* Derek Nuttall. *Colours:* Green and white hooped shirts, white shorts, white stockings.

NORTHWICH VICTORIA 2007–08 LEAGUE RECORD

Match No.	Date	Venue	Opponents	Result		H/T Score	Lg. Pos.	Goalscorers	Attendance
1	Aug 11	A	Ebbsfleet U	L	1-2	0-1	—	Rusk 50	1045
2	Aug 14	H	Droylsden	D	3-3	2-2	—	Tait 12, Williams C 18, Welch 60	1875
3	Aug 18	H	Torquay U	L	1-3	0-2	21	Tait 78	1117
4	Aug 25	A	Crawley T	L	1-2	1-1	21	Rusk 43	793
5	Aug 27	H	York C	L	0-1	0-0	—		1302
6	Sept 1	A	Farsley C	L	1-2	1-0	23	Tait 22	502
7	Sept 4	H	Burton Alb	L	0-2	0-1	—		845
8	Sept 8	A	Aldershot T	L	0-5	0-2	24		2002
9	Sept 15	H	Histon	L	1-3	0-2	24	Coulson 51	641
10	Sept 18	A	Halifax T	L	1-3	0-2	—	Coulson 65	1256
11	Sept 22	A	Salisbury C	L	0-2	0-1	24		1350
12	Sept 29	H	Woking	L	1-3	0-2	24	Brown R 84	550
13	Oct 2	H	Kidderminster H	D	1-1	0-1	—	Williams C 52	481
14	Oct 6	A	Weymouth	L	0-2	0-1	24		1106
15	Oct 9	A	Forest Green R	L	1-4	0-1	—	Giles (og) 58	859
16	Oct 13	H	Exeter C	D	0-0	0-0	24		1061
17	Oct 20	A	Grays Ath	L	1-3	1-1	24	Williams D (pen) 12	590
18	Nov 3	H	Stevenage Bor	L	0-2	0-1	24		669
19	Nov 17	A	Cambridge U	L	1-2	0-1	24	Steele 46	4044
20	Nov 24	H	Rushden & D	W	1-0	1-0	24	Steele 19	601
21	Dec 1	A	Stafford R	D	0-0	0-0	—		886
22	Dec 8	H	Oxford U	W	1-0	1-0	24	Steele 37	911
23	Dec 26	A	Altrincham	W	2-1	2-1	—	Akins 17, Brown R 42	1851
24	Dec 29	A	Rushden & D	L	0-1	0-1	22		1519
25	Jan 1	H	Altrincham	L	1-2	0-0	22	Welch 49	1447
26	Jan 5	H	Aldershot T	L	1-2	0-1	22	Byrom 75	871
27	Jan 19	A	Burton Alb	L	1-4	1-2	22	Burns 32	2165
28	Jan 26	H	Halifax T	D	2-2	2-2	22	Burns 2 15, 45	1024
29	Feb 2	A	Kidderminster H	D	0-0	0-0	—		1282
30	Feb 9	H	Salisbury C	L	0-1	0-0	22		673
31	Feb 23	A	Woking	W	3-2	1-1	22	Welch 2 6, 90, Steele 74	2672
32	Mar 1	H	Ebbsfleet U	D	3-3	1-0	22	Steele 2 39, 69, Williams D (pen) 50	1045
33	Mar 4	A	Droylsden	W	3-1	0-1	—	Steele 2 57, 75, Byrom 64	424
34	Mar 15	H	Crawley T	W	2-0	0-0	22	Stamp 52, Steele 54	585
35	Mar 18	H	Weymouth	D	2-2	0-0	—	Steele 48, Stamp 73	636
36	Mar 22	H	Farsley C	W	4-0	2-0	22	Stamp 39, Crowell 45, Byrne 66, Steele 90	651
37	Mar 25	A	York C	D	1-1	0-1	—	Byrne 74	1941
38	Mar 29	A	Oxford U	W	1-0	1-0	22	Steele 10	4673
39	Apr 1	A	Histon	D	1-1	0-0	—	Byrom 88	704
40	Apr 5	H	Stafford R	W	4-3	3-2	19	Steele 19, Roberts 32, Belle 45, Byrne (pen) 52	971
41	Apr 8	H	Forest Green R	D	1-1	1-0	—	Brown D 37	651
42	Apr 12	A	Exeter C	L	1-2	1-1	22	Byrom 11	3562
43	Apr 15	A	Torquay U	L	0-1	0-1	—		2270
44	Apr 19	H	Grays Ath	W	1-0	0-0	19	Carr 90	769
45	Apr 22	A	Stevenage Bor	W	2-1	1-0	—	Carr 12, Byrom 59	1596
46	Apr 26	H	Cambridge U	L	0-2	0-1	19		1512

Final League Position: 19

GOALSCORERS

League (52): Steele 13, Byrom 5, Welch 4, Burns 3, Byrne 3 (1 pen), Tait 3, Stamp 3, Brown R 2, Carr 2, Coulson 2, Rusk 2, Williams C 2, Williams D 2 (2 pens), Akins 1, Belle 1, Roberts 1, Crowell 1, Brown D 1, own goal 1.
FA Cup (4): Tait 1, Townson 1, Williams D 1, own goal 1.
Trophy (1): Steele 1.

Murphy 2	Birch 9 + 2 / Roberts 9	Brown R 38	Rusk 15 + 1	Sharp 7 / Barker — + 4	Welch 33 + 2	Strong 16 + 2 / Bowler 5	Battersby 18 + 2	Tait 13 + 3 / Belle 16	Townson 7 + 6 / Stamp 0 + 6	Carr 33 + 8	Byrne 17 + 11	Williams C 12 + 2 / Roddy — + 1	Maamria 6 + 5	Speight 1 + 3 / Allan — + 2	Connett 19 + 1	Wilson 21 + 5	Steele 23 + 6	Maylett 11 + 5	Coulson 6	Scales — + 1	Evans 1 / Brown D 8 + 1	Warhurst 2 / Mullan 15 + 4	Heslop 6	Johnson — + 1 / Edge 4	Tunnicliffe 2 + 1	Coward — + 1 / Crowell 14 + 1	Tynan 21	Williams D 15 + 2	Taylor 1	Horrocks 9 + 6	Kerr 13	Morning 3 + 3	Akins 10	Farquharson 2 + 1 / Meadowcroft 8 + 1	Burns 7 + 12	Hanley 1 + 6	Byrom 21	*Match No.*
1	2	3	4[1]	5[2]	6	7	8[3]	9	10■	11	12	13	14																									1
1	2	3	4	5[2]	6	7[1]		9		11	12	8	10	13																								2
	2	3	4		6		12	9		11	5[1]	7	13	10	1	8[2]																						3
	2[1]	3	4		6	12	8	9[3]		11[2]		7	14		1	5	13	10																				4
	2		4	5	6	7		9	13	11		8	12		1		10[2]	3[1]																				5
	2		4	5	13	3		9	12	11		8[1]	10[2]		1	6		7																				6
	2	3	4	5[1]		6	8	9[3]	13	11	7[2]				1	12		14	10																			7
	12		4[2]	5	6[1]	2	8			11		14	10		1	3		7[3]	9	13																		8
	13	3				6	8	9[3]		11[1]	12		10		1	14			7[2]		2■	5	4															9
		3		5[1]		6	8	9[3]	13	2	14		10[2]		1	12			11			4	7															10
	2	3				6	8	13	12	11	5[1]	9[2]			1	7			10				4															11
	2[1]	3				6	8	14	10	11	13	7[3]			1	12		4[2]	9				5															12
		3				6	8	9[3]	10	11	12[2]	7	14		1	5		4[1]					2	13														13
		3				6[1]	8	9[3]	10	11		7[2]			1	2	13	4					5		12	14												14
		3			12	6	8	9[2]	10	11			7		1	2	13	4							5[1]													15
		3			5	6	8		10	11		4				2	9	12									1	7[1]										16
		3	12		6[2]	5	8[1]	14	13	11		7				4	9	10[3]									1	2										17
			4		6[1]			9[3]	10	11		7[2]				8	14	12							5		1	2	3	13								18
		3	4		6	5	8									7	9	11									1	2		10								19
		3	4		6	12				11[1]						2	9	13									1	7[2]		8[3]	5	14	10					20
			4		6		8			11						2	9										1	7[1]		3[2]	5	13	10	12				21
		3			6		8■			11						4	9	12									1	7[1]		2	5		10					22
		3	4		6		8			11	2																1	7		5■		12	10	9[1]				23
		3	4		6					11	12			13		2[1]											1	7			5	8	10	9[2]				24
		3■	4		6		13			11	12			14		8■	9[3]										1	7[1]			5	2	10[2]					25
				14	6	2	8[1]			11	4																1	7			5	3[2]	10[3]		12	13	9	26
				13	6	8[2]		2		11[1]		12										4					1			3	5		10[3]		9	14	7	27
				14	6	3[1]		5		12												11		1		7				4[2]	2		10[3]		9	13	8	28
		3			6			5								11						7		1		4							10[1]	2	9	12	8	29
		3			6	2[1]		5		12							13	11[3]				7[2]		1		4				14					9	10	8	30
		3		12	6			5		2	13						10					14		1				7[1]		4[2]	11				9[3]		8	31
		3						5		11	4[1]					12	10					13					1	7[2]		6	2				9[3]	14	8	32
		3			6	2		5	10[3]		7[1]					4	9					11[2]					1			12					14	13	8	33
		11			6			5	10	7[2]	3[1]					4	9[3]					13				12	1							2	14		8	34
		7						6	10		11[1]					2	9					3				4	1							5	12		8	35
		7[1]			2			6	10[2]		11				15		9					3				4	1[G]			12				5	13		8	36
		3			2			6	10	12	7				1		9[2]					11				4								5	13		8[1]	37
	6	3			2			5	10[3]	12	7[1]				1		9[2]				14	11				4									13		8	38
	6	7[2]			2			5		14	11[3]				1		9				10	3				4[1]				13					12		8	39
	6	7			2			5		12	11				1		9				10	3[1]				4											8	40
	7	2			6			5		12	11■				1		9				10[2]	3				4[1]									13		8	41
	11	2[2]			6			5		7					1		9				10[3]	3				4[1]				13				14	12		8	42
	6	7			2					11[2]	13						9				10[3]	3				4[1]	1	12						5	14		8	43
	5	7								13	11[3]						9				10	3[1]				4[2]	1	12			6			2	14		8	44
	3	7								11	12			13			9				10[2]					4	1	6[1]			2			5			8	45
	5	11			2					3	4			13			14				10[3]	12					1	7[1]			6				9[2]		8	46

FA Cup

Fourth Qualifying Round	Southport	(a)	3-1
First Round	Oxford U	(a)	1-3

Trophy

First Round	Vauxhall M	(a)	1-2

OXFORD UNITED

Blue Square Premier

Ground: The Kassam Stadium, Grenoble Road, Oxford OX4 4XP. *Tel:* (01865) 337 500. *Year Formed:* 1893.
Record Gate: 22,730 (1964 v Preston NE, FA Cup 6th rd). *Nickname:* The U's. *Manager:* Darren Patterson.
Secretary: Mick Brown. *Colours:* Yellow with navy trim shirts, navy shorts, navy stockings.

OXFORD UNITED 2007–08 LEAGUE RECORD

Match No.	*Date*	*Venue*	*Opponents*	*Result*		*H/T Score*	*Lg. Pos.*	*Goalscorers*	*Atten-dance*
1	Aug 11	H	Forest Green R	W	1-0	0-0	—	Twigg (pen) 90	5521
2	Aug 16	A	Cambridge U	L	1-2	1-0	—	Twigg 41	3327
3	Aug 19	A	Burton Alb	W	2-1	1-1	8	Twigg 12, Odubade 57	2259
4	Aug 25	H	Stafford R	W	2-1	1-0	6	Trainer 2 45, 46	4617
5	Aug 27	A	Stevenage Bor	D	0-0	0-0	—		3024
6	Sept 1	H	Halifax T	D	1-1	0-0	10	Duffy 51	4926
7	Sept 4	H	Exeter C	D	2-2	1-0	—	Duffy 2 (2 pens) 15, 67	4560
8	Sept 8	A	Altrincham	W	3-1	1-0	5	Shaw 39, Day 86, Odubade 90	1298
9	Sept 11	A	Grays Ath	D	0-0	0-0	—		1201
10	Sept 15	H	Aldershot T	L	2-3	0-2	7	Jeannin 46, Shaw 55	5811
11	Sept 20	A	Histon	L	0-1	0-1	—		1257
12	Sept 25	H	Salisbury C	W	2-1	1-0	—	Odubade 19, Duffy (pen) 78	4231
13	Sept 30	H	York C	D	1-1	1-0	9	Corcoran 37	4944
14	Oct 6	A	Droylsden	L	1-3	0-1	13	Odubade 88	1074
15	Oct 11	H	Torquay U	D	3-3	3-0	—	Hutchinson 15, Odubade 2 18, 45	4633
16	Oct 14	A	Farsley C	W	1-0	0-0	11	Trainer 54	1219
17	Oct 20	H	Woking	D	0-0	0-0	10		4713
18	Nov 1	A	Rushden & D	L	0-5	0-3	—		1990
19	Nov 17	H	Ebbsfleet U	D	0-0	0-0	13		4655
20	Nov 24	A	Kidderminster H	W	2-0	1-0	11	Green 31, Barnes 69	2025
21	Dec 8	A	Northwich Vic	L	0-1	0-1	12		911
22	Dec 26	H	Crawley T	W	1-0	0-0	—	Trainer 47	5900
23	Dec 29	H	Kidderminster H	D	0-0	0-0	13		5380
24	Jan 1	A	Crawley T	L	0-2	0-0	14		1630
25	Jan 5	H	Altrincham	W	4-0	2-0	12	McAllister 22, Duffy 2 (1 pen) 41 (p), 55, Fisher 81	3950
26	Jan 8	H	Weymouth	L	0-1	0-1	—		3996
27	Jan 12	A	Salisbury C	L	1-3	0-2	—	Odubade 78	2016
28	Jan 20	A	Exeter C	L	0-2	0-2	15		3301
29	Jan 26	H	Grays Ath	D	0-0	0-0	15		4891
30	Jan 29	A	Aldershot T	L	0-1	0-0	—		2754
31	Feb 9	H	Histon	W	3-0	2-0	14	Green 2 33, 83, Howard 45	4851
32	Feb 16	H	Droylsden	W	1-0	1-0	12	Quinn 31	4331
33	Mar 1	A	Forest Green R	D	0-0	0-0	13		1624
34	Mar 4	H	Cambridge U	L	1-2	1-1	—	Green 18	4422
35	Mar 8	H	Burton Alb	L	0-3	0-2	15		4392
36	Mar 15	A	Stafford R	W	1-0	1-0	15	Green 11	962
37	Mar 22	A	Halifax T	W	3-0	1-0	13	Murray (pen) 37, Richards 57, Gaia (og) 84	1369
38	Mar 24	H	Stevenage Bor	W	2-1	1-0	12	Trainer 27, Green 71	4456
39	Mar 29	H	Northwich Vic	L	0-1	0-1	14		4673
40	Apr 5	A	Weymouth	W	1-0	0-0	13	Trainer 76	1635
41	Apr 8	A	Torquay U	L	2-3	1-1	—	McAllister 1, Murray (pen) 87	2241
42	Apr 12	H	Farsley C	W	5-1	2-0	13	Odubade 3, Trainer 40, Green 2 72, 90, Murray (pen) 82	4266
43	Apr 15	A	York C	W	1-0	0-0	—	Anaclet 48	1808
44	Apr 19	A	Woking	W	2-1	1-0	10	Odubade 20, Trainer 77	1857
45	Apr 22	H	Rushden & D	W	1-0	0-0	—	Odubade 85	4631
46	Apr 26	A	Ebbsfleet U	W	3-1	3-0	9	Green 2 1, 28, Trainer 20	1852

Final League Position: 9

GOALSCORERS

League (56): Green 10, Odubade 10, Trainer 9, Duffy 6 (4 pens), Murray 3 (3 pens), Twigg 3 (1 pen), McAllister 2, Shaw 2, Anaclet 1, Barnes 1, Corcoran 1, Day 1, Fisher 1, Howard 1, Hutchinson 1, Jeannin 1, Quinn 1, Richards 1, own goal 1.
FA Cup (5): Rhodes 2, Anaclet 1, Jeannin 1, Odubadé 1 (pen).
Trophy (0).

Turley 45	Quinn 42	Anaclet 30 + 2	Trainer 41	Day 36 + 3	Gnohere 7 + 1	Standing 3 + 3	Hutchinson 22 + 6	Duffy 14 + 6	Semple — + 1	Ledgister 6 + 3	Jeannin 27 + 1	Pettefer 15 + 8	Twigg 5 + 5	Hand 13	Odubade 28 + 13	Corcoran 14 + 2	Foster 30 + 2	Robinson 2 + 7	Rose 4 + 15	Shaw 10	Tardif 1 + 1	Willmott 5 + 2	Gilchrist 3	Rhodes 3 + 1	Bailey 3	Fisher 1 + 9	St Aimie 2	Collins 1	Benjamin — + 2	Clarke 13 + 5	Green 16 + 4	Barnes 1 + 2	Taylor — + 3	Murray 21	McAllister 9 + 8	Weedon 1 + 1	Howard 17	Richards 10 + 5	Blackwood 5 + 2	*Match No.*
1	2	3	4	5	6	7^{1}	8	9^{2}		10^{3}	11	12	13		14																									1
1	2	3	4	5	6		8	9^{3}			11	7^{1}	10^{2}		13		12	14																						2
1	2	3	4	5			8^{1}			13	11	12	9^{2}		10^{3}	6	7	14																						3
1	2	3	4	5		7^{1}	8	13			11		9^{3}		10^{2}	6		14	12																					4
1	2	3^{1}	4	5	12		8^{2}	14			11	7	9^{3}		10	6			13																					5
1	2	3	4	5				9^{3}			11	7^{2}			12	6	13	14	8	10^{1}																					6
1^{6}	2	3	4	5		7^{1}		9^{2}			11				12	6		13	8	10	15																			7
	2		4	5	6		8^{1}	9^{3}			11	12			10	3		14	13	7^{2}	1																			8
1	2		4^{1}	5	6	12	8	14			11	7			10^{3}	3		13		9^{2}																				9
1	2	12	4	5	6^{1}		13	9^{3}			11	7			14	3		10^{2}		8																				10
1	2	3	4	5	6	12	8^{1}	14			11				10			9^{3}	13	7^{2}																				11
1	2	3	4	5			8	9			11				10	6			12	7^{1}																				12
1	2^{1}	3	4	5			8^{2}	9^{3}			11	13	14		10	6				7		12																		13
1	2		4	5^{2}	6^{1}		8				11	12	13		10		7			9		3																		14
1			4	12			8^{2}				11	7			10	2	3^{1}			9		5	6	13																15
1			4	13			12				3	7			10^{3}		2		11^{2}			5	6	8	9^{1}	14														16
1	2		4	5		12	13				11	7^{2}			10		3					6^{1}		9^{3}	8	14														17
1	2		4	5							11^{3}	14			12		8					6	3^{1}	9	10	13	7^{2}													18
1	2	3^{1}	4				8	12■			11	7			10^{3}		6									13	9^{2}	5	14											19
1	2	3^{2}	4				8				11	7■	12		10^{3}		6					13								5	9^{1}	14								20
1	2	3^{1}		5			8			14	11■		9		13	12	6													4	7^{3}	10^{2}								21
1	2		4	5^{1}			8	9		7^{2}	3	11	13		10		6													12										22
1	2		4				8	9^{2}		7^{1}	3	11			10	6														5		13	12							23
1	2■		4	5			8	14		9^{3}	3	7^{2}			10	13	6													11^{1}			12							24
1			4	5				9^{3}		7^{2}	3	12			8^{1}	2	6									14				13				11	10					25
1	2		4	5^{1}				9		7^{2}	3	14			10		6									13				12				8	11^{3}					26
1	2		4^{2}				14	9^{3}			3^{1}	11			10	5	6									13				7				8		12				27
1		3	4	5				9		13	12	11					6		7^{2}							10^{3}			14	2						8^{1}				28
1	2	3	4				14								10^{1}		5		12											6	8^{2}		13	7			11	9^{3}		29
1	2	3^{2}	4	12			8								14		7		13											5^{1}	10^{3}			11			6	9		30
1	2	13		5			8								10^{2}		3									14				12	7^{3}			6			4^{1}	9	11	31
1	2	3^{1}		5			8								14		6		12												10^{3}			7	13		4	9	11^{2}	32
1	2	3^{2}							13					8			5													4	12			7	10^{1}		6	9	11	33
1	2	3^{1}		5										8	12		6														9			4	10		7	13	11^{2}	34
1	2		4^{2}											8	11^{1}		3		13											6■	9^{3}			7	10		5	14	12	35
1	2	3	4^{1}	5										11			6		12												10			8	13		7	9^{2}		36
1	2	3	4	5										8			6									12					10^{2}			7	13		11	9^{1}		37
1	2	3^{1}	4	5										7			6		12												10			8	13			9^{2}	11	38
1	2	3	4	5										7^{1}	14		6■														10^{3}			8	13		11	9^{2}	12	39
1	2	3	4	5										7	12															6	10^{1}			8	13		11	9^{2}		40
1	2	3	4	5										7	12		8														9^{1}			11	10^{2}		6	13		41
1	2	3	4^{1}	5			8								9^{2}		7		12												14			11	10^{3}		6	13		42
1	2	3	4	5										8	10^{1}															6	9^{2}			7	13		11	12		43
1	2	3	4	5			13							8	10^{3}				12											6	14			7	9^{2}		11^{1}			44
1	2	3	4^{1}	5										8	10		6		12												13			7	9^{2}		11			45
1	2	3^{2}	4	5										8	10		6^{1}		13											12	9^{3}			7	14		11			46

FA Cup

Fourth Qualifying Round	Merthyr T	(a)	2-1
First Round	Northwich Vic	(h)	3-1
Second Round	Southend U	(h)	0-0
		(a)	0-3

Trophy

First Round	Tonbridge A	(h)	0-0
		(a)	0-1

RUSHDEN & DIAMONDS Blue Square Premier

Ground: Nene Park, Irthlingborough, Northants NN9 5QF. *Tel:* (01933) 652 000. *Year Formed:* 1992.
Record Gate: 6,431 (1999 v Leeds U, FA Cup 3rd rd). *Nickname:* The Diamonds. *Manager:* Garry Hill.
Secretary: Matt Wild. *Colours:* White shirts, white shorts, white stockings.

RUSHDEN & DIAMONDS 2007–08 LEAGUE RECORD

Match No.	*Date*	*Venue*	*Opponents*	*Result*		*H/T Score*	*Lg. Pos.*	*Goalscorers*	*Attendance*
1	Aug 11	A	Woking	D	1-1	0-0	—	Woodhouse [51]	1576
2	Aug 14	H	Farsley C	W	1-0	1-0	—	Hatswell [29]	1502
3	Aug 18	H	Ebbsfleet U	L	0-1	0-1	13		1456
4	Aug 25	A	Torquay U	L	2-3	0-0	14	Rankine [69], Howell (pen) [90]	3017
5	Aug 27	H	Kidderminster H	L	0-1	0-0	—		1653
6	Aug 30	A	York C	W	3-2	1-1	—	Kelly [87] (og), Burgess [38], Rankine [76]	2044
7	Sept 4	H	Crawley T	D	1-1	0-1	—	Jackson [83]	1534
8	Sept 8	A	Salisbury C	D	1-1	0-0	17	Challinor [48]	1538
9	Sept 15	H	Burton Alb	D	0-0	0-0	19		1807
10	Sept 18	A	Weymouth	W	2-1	1-1	—	Jackson [10], Malcolm [83]	1252
11	Sept 22	A	Halifax T	D	1-1	0-1	16	Jackson (pen) [90]	1384
12	Sept 25	H	Grays Ath	D	1-1	1-0	—	Jackson [9]	1345
13	Sept 29	H	Stafford R	D	1-1	0-0	16	Jackson [84]	1533
14	Oct 6	A	Altrincham	W	2-1	2-0	14	Rankine [36], Jackson [45]	941
15	Oct 9	A	Cambridge U	L	0-1	0-0	—		3005
16	Oct 12	H	Forest Green R	L	1-2	0-1	—	Jackson [68]	1381
17	Oct 20	A	Exeter C	D	2-2	0-1	16	Jackson 2 [52, 56]	3106
18	Nov 1	H	Oxford U	W	5-0	3-0	—	Jackson 2 [4, 65], Day (og) [9], McAllister [14], St Aimie (og) [53]	1990
19	Nov 17	A	Aldershot T	L	1-2	0-1	15	Jackson [62]	3110
20	Nov 24	A	Northwich Vic	L	0-1	0-1	17		601
21	Dec 4	H	Histon	L	2-3	2-2	—	Hope [30], Jackson [43]	1351
22	Dec 8	A	Droylsden	W	4-1	2-0	17	Hatswell [36], Rankine 2 (1 pen) [45, 62 (p)], Jackson (pen) [52]	417
23	Dec 26	H	Stevenage Bor	D	0-0	0-0	—		2405
24	Dec 29	H	Northwich Vic	W	1-0	1-0	15	Hatswell [45]	1519
25	Jan 1	A	Stevenage Bor	L	1-2	0-0	16	Rankine [84]	2702
26	Jan 5	H	Salisbury C	D	0-0	0-0	16		1380
27	Jan 19	A	Crawley T	L	1-4	0-3	17	Shaw [85]	1226
28	Jan 26	H	Weymouth	W	3-2	1-1	17	Shaw [2], Jackson 2 [62, 75]	1448
29	Jan 29	A	Burton Alb	L	1-2	1-1	—	Burgess [42]	1460
30	Feb 9	H	Halifax T	D	2-2	1-1	17	Shaw (pen) [42], Gulliver [90]	1472
31	Feb 16	H	Altrincham	W	1-0	1-0	17	Rankine [12]	1364
32	Mar 1	H	Woking	W	2-1	1-1	14	Challinor [34], Rankine [72]	1335
33	Mar 4	A	Farsley C	W	1-0	0-0	—	Challinor [73]	475
34	Mar 11	A	Ebbsfleet U	W	3-0	1-0	—	Challinor [21], Rankine [81], Tomlin [90]	546
35	Mar 15	A	Histon	L	1-2	0-0	13	Ademeno [77]	767
36	Mar 22	H	York C	D	1-1	0-0	14	Hope [61]	1423
37	Mar 24	A	Kidderminster H	L	0-2	0-1	15		1477
38	Mar 29	H	Droylsden	D	0-0	0-0	15		1186
39	Apr 8	H	Cambridge U	L	1-2	0-0	—	Rankine [75]	2358
40	Apr 12	A	Forest Green R	W	1-0	0-0	15	Burgess [62]	1177
41	Apr 15	A	Stafford R	W	1-0	1-0	—	Rankine [5]	436
42	Apr 17	H	Torquay U	W	2-1	1-1	—	Rankine [44], Challinor [69]	1276
43	Apr 19	H	Exeter C	L	0-2	0-1	15		1572
44	Apr 22	A	Oxford U	L	0-1	0-0	—		4631
45	Apr 24	A	Grays Ath	L	0-3	0-2	—		542
46	Apr 26	H	Aldershot T	D	1-1	0-0	16	Smith [65]	2197

Final League Position: 16

GOALSCORERS

League (55): Jackson 16 (2 pens), Rankine 12 (1 pen), Challinor 5, Burgess 3, Hatswell 3, Shaw 3 (1 pen), Hope 2, Ademeno 1, Gulliver 1, Howell 1 (pen), Malcolm 1, McAllister 1, Smith 1, Tomlin 1, Woodhouse 1, own goals 3.
FA Cup (9): Jackson 2, Kelly 2, Burgess 1, Challinor 1, Gulliver 1, Rankine 1, own goal 1.
Trophy (8): Tomlin 3, Brown 1, Burgess 1, Gulliver 1, Hales 1, Kelly 1.

Bastock 19	Osano 42	Hatswell 22 + 1	Woodhouse 28 + 1	Gulliver 31 + 3	Hope 36 + 1	Challinor 35 + 10	Howell 40 + 3	Tomlin 15 + 19	Rankine 27 + 15	Shaw 15 + 17	Watson 3 + 1	Jackson 22 + 6	Semple 2 + 2	Lambley — + 3	Burgess 35 + 4	Foster 20	El Kholti 9 + 4	Rusk 6	Malcolm 2 + 6	Kelly 19 + 6	Nicholls 8	McAllister 7 + 2	Hales 4 + 3	Roberts 13	Gooding 10 + 3	Brown 2	Corcoran 14	Ademeno 4 + 3	Platt 7 + 3	Smith 3 + 5	Margarson 3	Andersen 3	Beecroft — + 3	Nunn — + 1	*Match No.*
1	2	3[1]	4[2]	5	6	7	8	9[3]	10	11	12	13	14																						1
1	2	3	4		6	7	8	9[3]	10[2]	12	5	13	11[1]	14																					2
1	2	5	4	12	6	7	8	9[3]	13	14	3[1]	10	11[2]																						3
1	2	3[1]	4■	5	6	7	8	14	10	13		9[3]			12	11[2]																			4
1	2	3[2]		5[1]	6	11[3]	8	14	10	4		9	13		12	7																			5
1	2	3	4		6	7[1]	8	12	10	14		13			9[2]	11[3]	5																		6
1	2	3	4		6	7[2]	8[3]	14	10	13	5[1]	12			9	11																			7
1	2	3	4■	5	6	7	12	13	10[2]	14		9[3]			11	8[1]																			8
1	2	3		5	6	7		12	10			13			8	4		11[1]	9[2]																9
1	2	3		5		7	8	12	10			9[2]			11[1]	4		6	13																10
1	2	3[2]		5	13	7	8	9	10[3]			11				4		6[1]	14	12															11
1	2	3			6	7	8	9[1]	10			11[2]			4	5			13	12															12
	2	3			6	12	8	14	13			9			5	4[1]		11	10[3]	7[2]	1														13
	2	3			6	7	8	12	10[3]	13		9[2]			11	4			14	5[1]	1														14
	2	3			6	7	8	14	10[3]	12		9			13	5		4[1]		11[2]	1														15
		5			6	7	8		12	13		9			11	4		2[2]	14	3[3]	1	10[1]													16
		3[1]		5	6	7	8		14	13		9			11	4	12			2[2]	1	10[2]													17
	2			5	6	7	8		14	12		9[2]			11	4[1]			13	3	1	10[3]													18
	2		13	5[1]	6	7[3]	8	9	12			10			4	3[2]				11	1		14												19
	2		4	5	6	7[1]	8	12	13			9				3[3]				11	1	10[2]	14												20
1	2	12		5	6[1]	7	8	13	14			9			3	4				11[2]		10[3]													21
1	2	3	4	5		7[1]	8		10	12		9[2]			11[3]	6				14		13													22
1	2	3	4	5		12	8	9[2]				10			7					11		13	6[1]												23
1	2	3	4	5		7	8		12			9			11	6						10[1]													24
1	2	3	4	5		12	8	9[1]	13						7					11		10[2]	6												25
1	2	3	4[1]	5		12	8	9	10			13			7					11[2]			6												26
1	2		4	5	6	14	8	9[2]	10	12		7			11[1]					13			3[3]												27
	2			5	6	7	8	9[2]	13	11		10			3					4[1]			12	1											28
	2		4	5	6	7[1]	3	9[3]	12	11[2]		10			8					14				1	13										29
	2			5	6	7	8	12	10	4					3					11[1]				1	13	9[2]									30
	2		4	5		13	8	14	10	11[1]					6					7[2]				1	12	9[3]	3								31
	2		4	12	6	7	8		10[3]	13					9					11[1]				1	3[2]		5	14							32
	2[1]		4	5	6	7		14	10[3]	11					12		8							1	9[2]		3	13							33
	2				6	7[1]	8	12	14	11					4					9[2]				1	3		5	10[3]	13						34
	2			13	6[1]	7[3]	8	12	9	10					4					11				1	3[2]		5	14							35
	2		4		6	7[2]	8		14	3					9		12			11[1]				1			5	10[3]	13						36
	2		4[2]	5		12		14	10	11[1]							3			13				1	7		6	9[3]	8						37
			4	5	6	13	12	9	14						11		3[1]							1	8		2	10[3]	7[2]						38
			4	5	6	7[1]	8	9	10	11					3									1			2			12					39
	2		4		6	13	8		10[3]	12					11		3							1	7[1]		5		9[2]	14					40
	2		4[2]	5		7	12		10	13					11		3[1]								8		6		9[3]	14	1				41
	2		4	5	6	7[2]	8		10	11					3		13												9[1]	12		1			42
	2		4[2]		6[1]	14	8	9	10[3]						11		3								7		5			12		1	13		43
	2		4	5	6	7	8	14		12					11		13										3[1]		9[2]	10[3]		1			44
	2			5	6[1]	7[2]	8			11				13			3								4[3]				9	10	1		14	12	45
	2[1]		4	5	6		8			11				12	7		3[2]										10		13	9[3]	1		14		46

FA Cup

Fourth Qualifying Round			
	Solihull M	(h)	5-0
First Round	Macclesfield T	(h)	3-1
Second Round	Bristol R	(a)	1-5

Trophy

First Round	Bamber Bridge	(a)	3-2
Second Round	Exeter C	(h)	3-0
Third Round	Halifax T	(a)	2-0
Fourth Round	York C	(h)	0-1

SALISBURY CITY

Blue Square Premier

Ground: The Raymond McEnhill Stadium, Partridge Way, Old Sarum, Salisbury SP4 6PU. *Tel:* (01722) 326 454. *Year Formed:* 1947. *Record Gate:* 8,902 (1948 v Weymouth, Western League). *Nickname:* The Whites. *Manager:* Nick Holmes. *Secretary:* Alec Hayter. *Colours:* White shirts, black shorts, white stockings.

SALISBURY CITY 2007–08 LEAGUE RECORD

Match No.	*Date*	*Venue*	*Opponents*	*Result*		*H/T Score*	*Lg. Pos.*	*Goalscorers*	*Attendance*
1	Aug 11	A	Droylsden	D	0-0	0-0	—		821
2	Aug 14	H	Ebbsfleet U	W	2-1	1-1	—	Matthews ^{41}, Tubbs ^{51}	1310
3	Aug 18	H	Crawley T	W	4-1	2-0	2	Tubbs (pen) ^{31}, Matthews ^{37}, Sandell ^{58}, Feeney ^{76}	1317
4	Aug 25	A	Farsley C	D	2-2	1-1	10	Sandell ^{38}, Cook ^{88}	475
5	Aug 27	H	Woking	W	2-1	2-0	—	Tubbs ^{13}, Clarke D ^{33}	2093
6	Sept 1	A	Histon	L	0-2	0-0	7		803
7	Sept 4	A	Torquay U	L	0-4	0-2	—		3215
8	Sept 8	H	Rushden & D	D	1-1	0-0	11	Brown ^{90}	1538
9	Sept 13	A	Forest Green R	W	3-0	2-0	—	Brown ^{2}, Giles (og) ^{38}, Matthews ^{90}	1082
10	Sept 18	H	Stafford R	W	1-0	1-0	—	Brown ^{30}	1302
11	Sept 22	H	Northwich Vic	W	2-0	1-0	6	Oliver ^{12}, Tubbs ^{47}	1350
12	Sept 25	A	Oxford U	L	1-2	0-1	—	Cook ^{55}	4231
13	Sept 29	H	Kidderminster H	L	0-1	0-1	6		1621
14	Oct 6	A	Burton Alb	L	3-4	2-1	12	Tubbs 2 (1 pen) $^{36 (p), 62}$, Matthews ^{43}	1362
15	Oct 9	A	Exeter C	L	2-4	1-2	—	Matthews ^{34}, Feeney ^{76}	2903
16	Oct 13	H	Altrincham	D	3-3	0-2	12	Brown 2 $^{71, 90}$, Oliver ^{88}	1257
17	Oct 20	A	Cambridge U	D	1-1	0-1	12	Brown ^{87}	3868
18	Nov 3	H	Grays Ath	L	0-1	0-1	14		1226
19	Nov 17	A	York C	W	3-1	1-1	12	Tubbs ^{5}, Turk ^{60}, Brown ^{77}	2303
20	Nov 24	A	Halifax T	D	1-1	0-0	13	Turk ^{57}	1237
21	Dec 2	H	Aldershot T	L	0-4	0-2	—		1786
22	Dec 8	A	Stevenage Bor	L	1-3	1-2	15	Henry (og) ^{4}	1808
23	Dec 26	H	Weymouth	D	1-1	0-0	—	Brown ^{46}	1687
24	Dec 29	H	Halifax T	W	1-0	0-0	14	Feeney ^{76}	1212
25	Jan 1	A	Weymouth	W	3-0	0-0	12	Tubbs 2 (1 pen) $^{51, 84 (p)}$, Brown ^{65}	2002
26	Jan 5	A	Rushden & D	D	0-0	0-0	15		1380
27	Jan 12	H	Oxford U	W	3-1	2-0	—	Barnes ^{31}, Brown 2 $^{43, 79}$	2016
28	Jan 19	H	Torquay U	D	0-0	0-0	12		2633
29	Jan 26	A	Stafford R	W	5-1	3-0	10	Tubbs 2 $^{4, 24}$, Fowler ^{44}, Matthews ^{71}, Feeney ^{90}	706
30	Feb 2	H	Forest Green R	D	0-0	0-0	—		1478
31	Feb 9	A	Northwich Vic	W	1-0	0-0	9	Turk ^{83}	673
32	Feb 16	H	Burton Alb	W	2-0	0-0	8	Fowler ^{70}, Matthews ^{84}	1433
33	Feb 23	A	Kidderminster H	W	2-1	2-1	7	Feeney ^{25}, Matthews ^{29}	1497
34	Mar 1	H	Droylsden	W	3-1	2-0	7	Feeney ^{19}, Turk ^{45}, Clarke D ^{90}	1307
35	Mar 4	A	Ebbsfleet U	L	1-2	0-2	—	Clarke D ^{89}	670
36	Mar 8	A	Crawley T	D	1-1	0-0	7	Sandell ^{68}	948
37	Mar 15	H	Farsley C	D	1-1	0-0	8	Iqbal (og) ^{87}	1081
38	Mar 21	H	Histon	D	3-3	1-2	—	Clarke D ^{15}, Cook ^{68}, Tubbs ^{90}	1483
39	Mar 24	A	Woking	L	2-3	1-1	9	Sinclair ^{30}, Feeney ^{51}	2829
40	Mar 27	H	Stevenage Bor	W	1-0	0-0	—	Tubbs ^{90}	1211
41	Apr 5	A	Aldershot T	L	1-2	0-1	9	Feeney ^{61}	3388
42	Apr 8	H	Exeter C	W	2-0	1-0	—	Turk ^{9}, Tubbs (pen) ^{87}	2037
43	Apr 12	A	Altrincham	L	1-3	1-0	10	Tubbs ^{16}	1242
44	Apr 19	H	Cambridge U	L	0-2	0-2	12		1710
45	Apr 22	A	Grays Ath	D	1-1	1-1	—	Bond ^{27}	507
46	Apr 26	H	York C	W	3-0	2-0	12	Bond ^{34}, Tubbs ^{37}, Feeney ^{80}	1400

Final League Position: 12

GOALSCORERS

League (70): Tubbs 16 (4 pens), Brown 11, Feeney 9, Matthews 8, Turk 5, Clarke D 4, Cook 3, Sandell 3, Bond 2, Fowler 2, Oliver 2, Barnes 1, Sinclair 1, own goals 3.
FA Cup (0).
Trophy (0).

Clarke R 46	Bass 36	Robinson 43	Cook 42	Bond 17 + 2	Fowler 25 + 5	Turk 43	Clarke D 30 + 3	Matthews 26 + 6	Tubbs 33 + 9	Prince 3 + 7	Sales — + 2	Brown 12 + 22	Feeney 23 + 19	Bartlett 31 + 4	Sandell 32 + 1	Oliver 9 + 1	Clay 5 + 6	Herring 11 + 2	Richards 2 + 4	Barnes 7 + 3	Beswetherick 1 + 1	Assau-Adjaye 14	Sinclair 15 + 1	Knight — + 1	Barron — + 2	Widdrington — + 1	*Match No.*
1	2	3	4	5	6	7	8	9^{1}	10^{2}	11^{3}	12	13	14														1
1	2	3	4	5	6	7	8	9^{3}	10^{2}	11^{1}	14	13		12													2
1	2	3	4	5	6	7	8^{2}	9	10^{3}			14	12	13	11^{1}												3
1	2	3	4	5	6^{1}	7	8	9	10^{2}	12		13			11												4
1	2	3	4	5	6	7	8^{1}	9	10					12	11												5
1	2^{1}	3	4	5	6	7	8^{2}	9	10	13					11	12											6
1	2	3	4	5	6	7	8^{1}	9	10^{2}			13	12		11												7
1	2^{1}	3	4		6■	7	8^{3}	9	10^{2}	12		13	14		11	5											8
1	2	3	4			7		9	14			10^{3}	13	6^{1}	11	5	12	8^{2}									9
1	2	3	4			7	8^{1}	9	14			10^{3}	12	13	11^{2}	5		6									10
1	2	3^{1}	4			7	12	9	10^{3}			14	13	6	11^{2}	5	8										11
1	2^{1}		4		6	7		9	10^{3}			14	13	3	11^{2}	5	8■	12									12
1	2	3	4^{1}	12	6	7^{2}		9	10	11^{3}		13	14	8		5											13
1	2	3	4	12		7■	8	9	10^{2}				11^{1}	6		5			13								14
1	2^{1}	3	4		6		8	9	10	13		12	11	7^{2}		5											15
1	2^{1}	3		5	6^{2}		8		10	12		7	9	11		4	13										16
1		3	4				8	9	10^{2}			13	7	2	11		12	6^{1}		5							17
1		3	4			7	8	9	10^{2}			13	11^{1}	6	2		12				5						18
1		3	4			7			10^{1}			12	8	2^{2}	11		9	6	13^{3}	5	14						19
1		3	4	5	12	7		9				13	10		11^{2}		8	6^{1}	2								20
1		3	4	5	8	7^{1}		9	12	13			10	2	11				6^{2}								21
1		3	4		6	7		9		13		12	10^{1}	8	2		11^{2}			5							22
1	2	3	4			7	8^{2}	9^{3}	14			10	13	6	11		12	5^{1}									23
1	2	3	4			7	8	9^{3}	13			10^{2}	14	6	11		12	5^{1}									24
1	2	3^{1}	4		14	7	8^{2}		10			9	13	5	11			6^{3}		12							25
1	2	3	4		12	7	8^{1}	13	10^{3}			9^{2}	14	5	11			6■									26
1	2	3			6	7	8^{1}	13	10^{2}			9	12		11					5		4					27
1	2	3	4		6	7		13	10			9^{2}	12	8^{1}	11							5					28
1	2	3	4		6	7		13	10^{1}			9^{2}	12	8	11							5					29
1	2	3^{1}	4		6	7		13	10^{2}			9	12	8	11							5					30
1	2		4		6	7		12	10^{1}			9^{2}	13	3	11							5	8				31
1	2		4		6	7	8	9	10^{1}				12	3								5	11				32
1	2	3	4			7		9					10	6	11							5	8				33
1	2	3		5		7^{1}	12	9				13	10	4^{2}	11			14				6^{3}	8				34
1	2	3		5^{1}	6	7^{2}	13	9^{3}	14			12	10		11							4	8				35
1	2	3	4		6	7			13				10	8	12					9^{2}		5	11^{1}				36
1	2^{1}	3	4			7	8		13				10	6	11					9^{2}		5	12				37
1	2^{1}	3	4		12	7	8		13				10		11					9^{2}		5	6				38
1	2	3	4		12	7	8		10^{2}				9	6						13		5	11^{1}				39
1		3	4			7	8		10				9	6	2							5	11				40
1		3	4	5		7	8		10				9	2	11^{1}					12			6				41
1		3	4	5	6	7	8		10			12	9^{1}	2									11				42
1		3	4	5	6^{2}	7	8^{3}		10			12	9	2									11^{1}	13	14		43
1	2	3	4		6■	7	8		10			12	9^{2}	5^{1}									11		13		44
1	2	3	4	5		7	8^{2}		10			13	9					6^{1}	12				11				45
1	2	3^{3}	4	5		7	8^{2}		10			13	9					6^{1}	14				11			12	46

FA Cup
Fourth Qualifying Round Stevenage B (h) 0-0
(a) 0-1

Trophy
First Round Exeter C (a) 0-3

STAFFORD RANGERS Blue Square North

Ground: Marston Road, Stafford ST16 3BX. *Tel:* (01785) 602 430. *Year formed:* 1876.
Record gate: 8,536 (1975 v Rotherham U, FA Cup 3rd rd). *Nickname:* The Boro. *Manager:* Steve Bull.
Secretary: Michael Hughes. *Colours:* Black and white striped shirts, black shorts, black stockings.

STAFFORD RANGERS 2007–08 LEAGUE RECORD

Match No.	Date	Venue	Opponents	Result		H/T Score	Lg. Pos.	Goalscorers	Attendance
1	Aug 11	A	Farsley C	L	0-1	0-1	—		825
2	Aug 14	H	Kidderminster H	L	1-3	1-1	—	Arnolin 45	1126
3	Aug 18	H	Woking	L	0-1	0-0	24		642
4	Aug 25	A	Oxford U	L	1-2	0-1	24	McAughtrie 78	4617
5	Aug 27	H	Altrincham	D	1-1	1-1	—	Adaggio (pen) 20	986
6	Sept 1	A	Torquay U	L	0-2	0-1	24		2980
7	Sept 6	H	Halifax T	L	2-3	0-1	—	Adaggio 47, McNiven 51	927
8	Sept 10	A	Stevenage Bor	L	0-3	0-0	—		2424
9	Sept 15	H	Grays Ath	L	0-2	0-2	23		649
10	Sept 18	A	Salisbury C	L	0-1	0-1	—		1302
11	Sept 22	A	Weymouth	W	3-1	2-0	22	Adaggio 15, McNiven 2 41, 59	1217
12	Sept 25	H	Histon	D	1-1	0-1	—	Grayson 74	705
13	Sept 29	A	Rushden & D	D	1-1	0-0	22	Adaggio 78	1533
14	Oct 6	H	Forest Green R	L	1-3	1-0	22	Adaggio 17	754
15	Oct 9	A	York C	L	0-2	0-2	—		1784
16	Oct 13	H	Cambridge U	D	1-1	1-1	22	Grayson 28	741
17	Oct 20	A	Crawley T	D	1-1	0-1	22	Smith 90	1025
18	Nov 3	H	Exeter C	L	1-5	1-2	22	Street 45	914
19	Nov 17	A	Droylsden	D	1-1	1-0	22	Sangare 45	612
20	Nov 24	A	Ebbsfleet U	L	1-2	0-0	23	Grayson 50	1055
21	Dec 1	H	Northwich Vic	D	0-0	0-0	—		886
22	Dec 8	A	Aldershot T	L	3-4	2-3	22	McNiven 8, Flynn 35, Grayson 67	2669
23	Dec 26	H	Burton Alb	L	0-3	0-3	—		1679
24	Dec 29	H	Ebbsfleet U	L	0-1	0-0	23		653
25	Jan 1	A	Burton Alb	L	1-2	1-1	23	McNiven 41	2465
26	Jan 5	H	Stevenage Bor	L	1-2	0-2	23	Richards 51	688
27	Jan 26	H	Salisbury C	L	1-5	0-3	24	Adaggio 46	706
28	Feb 9	H	Weymouth	W	2-1	1-0	23	Grayson 29, Shaw 86	591
29	Feb 16	A	Forest Green R	W	2-1	1-1	22	Grayson 12, Street 67	1093
30	Feb 23	A	Halifax T	D	0-0	0-0	23		1103
31	Feb 26	A	Histon	D	3-3	0-1	—	Grayson 70, Jarrett (pen) 89, Djoumin 90	527
32	Mar 1	H	Farsley C	L	0-2	0-1	23		1853
33	Mar 4	A	Kidderminster H	L	0-6	0-4	—		1240
34	Mar 8	A	Woking	D	2-2	1-1	23	Arnolin (pen) 30, Grayson 58	1133
35	Mar 15	H	Oxford U	L	0-1	0-1	23		962
36	Mar 22	H	Torquay U	L	0-2	0-0	23		905
37	Mar 24	A	Altrincham	L	0-2	0-2	23		1135
38	Mar 29	H	Aldershot T	L	1-2	0-1	23	Wellecomm 62	981
39	Apr 1	A	Grays Ath	L	1-5	0-3	—	Jarrett 75	512
40	Apr 5	A	Northwich Vic	L	3-4	2-3	23	Grayson (pen) 23, Flynn 29, Wellecomm 59	971
41	Apr 8	H	York C	L	0-4	0-0	—		455
42	Apr 12	A	Cambridge U	W	2-1	1-1	23	Grayson 9, Smith 64	3310
43	Apr 15	H	Rushden & D	L	0-1	0-1	—		436
44	Apr 19	H	Crawley T	L	1-3	1-2	24	Wellecomm 13	470
45	Apr 22	A	Exeter C	L	1-4	0-2	—	Reid 90	4079
46	Apr 26	H	Droylsden	W	2-1	1-0	23	Grayson 13, Wellecomm 69	685

Final League Position: 23

GOALSCORERS

League (42): Grayson 11 (1 pen), Adaggio 6 (1 pen), McNiven 5, Wellecomm 4, Arnolin 2 (1 pen), Flynn 2, Jarrett 2 (1 pen), Smith 2, Street 2, Djoumin 1, McAughtrie 1, Reid 1, Richards 1, Sangare 1, Shaw 1.
FA Cup (2): Grayson 1 (pen), Street 1.
Trophy (8): McNiven 3 (1 pen), Draper 1, Flynn 1, Sangare 1, Jarrett 1, Street 1.

Alcock 32	Sutton 39 + 1	Stones 9 + 1	McAughtrie 6	Daniel 42 + 2	Sangare 24 + 2	Flynn 38 + 3	Street 25 + 6	Grayson 34 + 8	McNiven 20 + 3	Olaoye 5 + 3	Adaggio 16 + 8	Arnolin 12 + 5	Hazley 11 + 4	Hopkinson 9 + 6	Richards 6 + 3	Murray 16 / Meakin-Richards 1	Manak — + 3	Duggan 2 / Hughes 3	Oldfield 7 + 3	Draper 26 + 6	Avinel 8	Loach 11 / Wellecomm 9 + 2	Smith 8 + 9	Hamilton 1 + 4	Youngs 1 + 2	Puddy 1 / Loukes 7 + 2	Robinson — + 2	Potter 6 / Dodd 3 + 1	Humphrey 4	Mawene 16 + 2	Ingram 6 + 3	Lynch 2	Jarrett 10 + 6	Gibson 13	Shaw 1 + 5	Djoumin 7 + 1	Reid 9 + 3	*Match No.*
1	2	3[1]	4	5	6	7	8[2]	9	10	11	12	13																										1
1	2	3	4	5	6	7		9	10		13	8[2]	11[1]	12																								2
1	2	3	4	5	6[1]	7		9	10		13	8[2]	11[3]	14	12																							3
1	2	3	4	5		7	8[2]	9[3]	10		14	6[1]	13			11	12																					4
1	2	3	4	5		7	8[1]	12	10		9		11[2]			6	13																					5
	2	3	4	5		7	8[1]	12	10[2]		9			11		6	13	1																				6
	2	3		5	6	7	12[2]	13	10		9	11[3]	14	4[1]		8		1																				7
1	2	3[2]		5	6	7[1]	13	9[3]	14		10		11■			4			12	8																		8
1	2	13		5	6[1]	7	12	9	10		11					3				8[2]	4																	9
	12	3		5	6	7	8[2]	9[3]	13		10					4			14	11[1]	2	1																10
	2			5	6		8	12	10[1]		9					3			7	4	11	1																11
	2			5	6	13	8	12	10		9					3			11[2]	7[1]	4	1																12
	2			5	6	7	8	12	10[1]		9					3			11		4	1																13
	2			5[1]	6■	7	8[3]	9			10					11			4[2]	13	3	1	12	14														14
	2					7		9			10	3[2]			12	5			8	6	4[1]	1		13	11													15
	2			5	6	7		9			10					11			8[1]	4	3	1	12															16
	2[1]			5	6	11	8	9			10				3				4[2]	7			14		13[3]	1	12											17
				5■	6	7[1]	8	9	12							11				13		1	10[3]		14			2	3	4[2]								18
	2				6	7[1]	8	9	10[2]							3			12			1	13					5	11	4								19
	2			5	6	7	8[3]	12	10							3[1]				14		1	9[2]				13	4	11									20
	2			5	6[1]	7		9	10						12					8		1	13					3	11	4[2]								21
1	2			5	6	7		9	10			13		12						8			11[2]					3		4[1]								22
1	2			5		7■	8[1]	9	10					14	6					11[3]				12				3		4[2]	13							23
1	2			5			8	9	10	12		4[1]			3					11			7[2]	13						6								24
1	2			5	6[1]			9	10	12		11		13	3					7										4	8[2]							25
1				5	6[1]		12	9	10	14			11[3]		3					8										7[2]	4	2	13					26
1	2			5[1]	12	13	8		10	11[3]	14		9[2]		4					6												3	7					27
1	2			5		7	8	9		11	14	10[3]		6[2]																	12		4	3[1]	13			28
1	2[1]			5	12	7	8	9		11[3]	14	10	13	6																			4[2]	3				29
1	2			5		7	8	9			10[3]	6[1]	12	11[2]						13													4	3	14			30
1	2			5		7	8	9				4[1]	11[3]							6													10	3[2]	12	13	14	31
1	2			5			8	9					11[2]			7[1]		10		6													12		4	3	13	32
1	2			5		7[1]	8	9										10[2]		11													4	6	13	3	12	33
1	2			5		7	8	9		10[2]		4[1]								11													13		12	3	6	34
1	2			5		12		13			10[3]		3	11				9[2]		7			14							4			8			6[1]		35
1	2			5	6	7	8	9[2]			13		11[1]	10[3]						14		4								12				3				36
1	2[1]			5		7					10	14	3[2]	11[3]						8		9	13							12				4		6		37
1	2			5		7														8		9	10[1]			6				4			12	3			11	38
1	2			5		7[1]						12								4		9	10			8		13		6[3]			14	3[2]			11	39
1	2[1]			12	6	7	13	9														10				8		5[2]		4[3]			14	3			11	40
1				5		7		9						14						12		10	13			4[1]				2	3			11[3]		6	8[2]	41
1				5	6	7		9				12								8		14	10[3]			13				2	3[2]		4[1]				11	42
1				5	6	7		9												8		13	10[2]			12				2	4		3[1]				11	43
1	2■			13		7	12	9												8		10				6		5		3	4[1]						11[2]	44
1				5		7	8	9						4								10				2		6[1]			12			3			11	45
1	2			5		7		9														10	12	11[1]		8							4	6		3		46

FA Cup

Fourth Qualifying Round	Cambridge U	(h)	1-1
		(a)	1-5

Trophy

First Round	Ossett T	(h)	3-1
Second Round	Forest Green R	(h)	2-1
Third Round	Tamworth	(h)	2-2
		(a)	1-2

STEVENAGE BOROUGH Blue Square Premier

Ground: Broadhall Way Stadium, Broadhall Way, Stevenage, Hertfordshire SG2 8RH. *Tel:* (01438) 223 223.
Year Formed: 1976. *Record Gate:* 6,489 (1997 v Kidderminster Harriers, Conference). *Nickname:* The Boro.
Manager: Graham Westley. *Secretary:* Roger Austin. *Colours:* Red and white shirts, black shorts, white stockings.

STEVENAGE BOROUGH 2007–08 LEAGUE RECORD

Match No.	*Date*	*Venue*	*Opponents*	*Result*		*H/T Score*	*Lg. Pos.*	*Goalscorers*	*Attendance*
1	Aug 11	A	Crawley T	L	1-2	0-2	—	Martin [66]	1257
2	Aug 14	H	Histon	W	2-1	1-0	—	Morison [43], Arber [90]	2073
3	Aug 18	H	Weymouth	W	3-0	1-0	4	Nutter [16], Morison [66], Miller [74]	2016
4	Aug 24	A	Kidderminster H	W	2-0	2-0	—	McMahon [19], Miller [30]	1692
5	Aug 27	H	Oxford U	D	0-0	0-0	—		3024
6	Sept 1	A	Ebbsfleet U	W	1-0	1-0	2	Dobson [30]	1201
7	Sept 4	A	Droylsden	W	3-0	0-0	—	McMahon [54], Dobson [64], Nutter (pen) [84]	671
8	Sept 10	H	Stafford R	W	3-0	0-0	—	Morison [47], Miller [60], Allen [87]	2424
9	Sept 15	A	York C	W	2-0	0-0	1	Morison [46], McMahon [81]	2052
10	Sept 18	H	Farsley C	W	4-0	1-0	—	Morison 2 [27, 55], Dobson [80], Lewis S [90]	2186
11	Sept 22	H	Cambridge U	L	1-2	0-1	3	Miller (pen) [68]	4533
12	Sept 25	A	Forest Green R	L	2-4	1-1	—	McMahon [17], Gaia [47]	719
13	Sept 29	A	Grays Ath	W	2-0	1-0	2	Morison [32], Arber (pen) [80]	1460
14	Oct 6	H	Aldershot T	W	3-1	2-0	2	Winfield (og) [24], Arber (pen) [45], Dobson [46]	3070
15	Oct 9	H	Woking	D	1-1	1-1	—	Dobson [5]	3007
16	Oct 14	A	Torquay U	L	2-4	1-2	4	Dobson [38], Bramble [85]	3744
17	Oct 18	H	Burton Alb	D	3-3	1-1	—	Morison [31], Miller [48], Cole [78]	1843
18	Nov 3	A	Northwich Vic	W	2-0	1-0	3	Lewis S [29], McMahon [68]	669
19	Nov 17	H	Halifax T	L	2-3	2-0	6	Dobson [14], Morison [25]	2421
20	Nov 26	H	Altrincham	W	2-1	1-1	—	Dobson 2 [28, 66]	1662
21	Dec 8	H	Salisbury C	W	3-1	2-1	3	Henry [3], Stokes [17], Dobson [69]	1808
22	Dec 26	A	Rushden & D	D	0-0	0-0	—		2405
23	Dec 29	A	Altrincham	W	5-1	2-1	3	Morison 2 [9, 90], Berry [45], Lewis S [67], McMahon [86]	763
24	Jan 1	H	Rushden & D	W	2-1	0-0	3	Burke [89], Arber (pen) [90]	2702
25	Jan 5	A	Stafford R	W	2-1	2-0	3	Morison 2 [9, 41]	688
26	Jan 19	H	Droylsden	W	5-0	2-0	2	Arber [32], Willock [44], McMahon [52], Morison 2 (1 pen) [63 (p), 79]	2320
27	Jan 24	A	Farsley C	D	0-0	0-0	—		501
28	Feb 2	A	Exeter C	L	0-4	0-3	—		3436
29	Feb 9	A	Cambridge U	L	1-2	0-0	3	Oliver [77]	3772
30	Feb 13	H	Forest Green R	D	0-0	0-0	—		1630
31	Feb 17	A	Aldershot T	L	1-3	0-3	4	Grant [63]	3261
32	Feb 23	H	Grays Ath	D	0-0	0-0	4		1856
33	Mar 1	H	Crawley T	W	3-1	2-1	4	Vincenti [7], Grant [38], Morison [83]	1717
34	Mar 4	A	Histon	W	4-1	1-1	—	Morison 2 (1 pen) [44 (p), 73], Grant [86], Laird [90]	916
35	Mar 8	A	Weymouth	L	0-1	0-1	4		930
36	Mar 13	H	Kidderminster H	W	2-1	1-0	—	Morison [15], Grant [72]	1326
37	Mar 21	H	Ebbsfleet U	W	3-1	2-0	—	Berry [37], Westwood [42], Morison [50]	2016
38	Mar 24	A	Oxford U	L	1-2	0-1	5	Martin [68]	4456
39	Mar 27	A	Salisbury C	L	0-1	0-0	—		1211
40	Apr 1	H	York C	W	3-2	1-2	—	Grant [27], Westwood [48], Cole [60]	1117
41	Apr 5	H	Exeter C	L	0-1	0-1	—		2146
42	Apr 8	A	Woking	W	2-0	1-0	—	Morison [3], Oliver [73]	1210
43	Apr 12	H	Torquay U	L	1-3	0-0	4	Grant (pen) [52]	2673
44	Apr 18	A	Burton Alb	L	0-3	0-0	—		2160
45	Apr 22	H	Northwich Vic	L	1-2	0-1	—	Moore [70]	1596
46	Apr 26	A	Halifax T	W	2-1	2-0	6	Morison [27], Grant [45]	2229

Final League Position: 6

GOALSCORERS

League (82): Morison 22 (2 pens), Dobson 10, Grant 7 (1 pen), McMahon 7, Arber 5 (3 pens), Miller 5 (1 pen), Lewis S 3, Berry 2, Cole 2, Martin 2, Nutter 2 (1 pen), Oliver 2, Westwood 2, Allen 1, Bramble 1, Burke 1, Gaia 1, Henry 1, Laird 1, Moore 1, Stokes 1, Vincenti 1, Willock 1, own goal 1.
FA Cup (1): Molesley 1.
Trophy (1): Morison 1.

Julian 43	Fuller 22 + 2	Nutter 13 + 1 / Grant 12 + 2	Arber 27	Henry 33 + 3	Martin 33	Miller 16	Lewis S 21 + 1	Bramble 4 + 7	Morison 43	Cole 22 + 5	Allen 1 + 12	Dobson 24 + 2 / Smith 15	McMahon 27 + 10	Wilson 17 + 7	John — + 5	Gaia 6 + 3	Molesley 5 + 6	Anderson 1 + 5	Eames — + 1	Oliver 14 + 2	Hakim 1 + 2	Batt — + 2 / Mitchell 5 + 1	White 4	Stokes 2 + 1 / Masters 3	Liptak 2	Berry 8 + 6	Lewis J 8	Laird 11 + 4	Burke — + 2	Murray 12 + 1	Westwood 20	O'Sullivan 1 + 6	Willock 6 + 3	Vincenti 11 + 1	Moore 11 + 1	Rankin 2 + 4	Buchanan — + 1	*Match No.*
1	2	3	4	5	6	7	8	9^1	10	11^2	12	13																										1
1	2	3	4	5	6	7	8	9^2	10	11^1	13	12																										2
1	2	3	4	5	6	7^1	8		10		12	9^2	11	13																								3
1	2	3	4	5	6	7^2	8		10		13	9^1	11	12																								4
1	2	3	4	5	6	7	8		10			9	11																									5
1	2	3	4	5	6	7^2	8		10		13	9^1	11		12																							6
1	2	3^1	4	5	6	7	8■		10^3		14	9^2	11	13		12																						7
1	2	3	4	5^1	6	7^3	8		10		14	9^2	11		13	12																						8
1	2	3^1	4	5	6	7	8		10		14	9^2	11^3		13	12																						9
1	2		4	5	6^1	7^2	8	13	10^3		14	9	11			3	12																					10
1	2		4	5		7	8■	14	10^3	12	13	9^2	11	6^1		3																						11
1	2		4			7		9		14	10^3	8^1	11^2	3		5	6	13	12																			12
1	2		4	5		7^1		12	10^2	11		9	8			3	6	13																				13
1	2		4	5	6				10	11^2		9^1	7	12		3	8	13																				14
1	2	12	4	5	6		13	14	10	11		9	7^3			3^1	8^2																					15
1	2	3	4	5	6	7^2	8	13	10	11^3		9^1	14	12																								16
1	2	3	4		6	7^1	8		10	11		9	12							5																		17
1	2	3	4	12			8	9^2				7	11				6	13		5	10^1																	18
1		3	4	5	6■	7^2	8^1		10			9^3	11				12			2	13	14																19
1	12		4^1	2			8		10			9	6							5	13		3	11^2	7													20
1	2			5					10	12		9^2	4							6		13	3	11^3	7	14	8^1											21
1			4	5	6		8		10			9	11^1							2			3			12	7											22
1			4	5			8		10			9	11							2			3			6	7											23
1	13		4	5	6^1		8		10			9	12							3						11^3	7^2	2	14									24
1	2		4				8		10			9	6^1							3				12		11^2	7	5	13									25
1	2		4				8	14	10			9^2	6^1															3		12	5	13	7^3	11				26
1	2		4					14	10				12	7													8^2	3^1		6	5	13	9^3	11				27
1			4	12					10	14	13		11^3	2												7^1	8^2	9		3	5				6			28
1				2					10	11^3	14									5						7^1	8	9^2		3	6	12			4	13		29
1				5	6				10	11^1				8						3								12		2	4				7	9^2	13	30
1		12		5	6				10	11^1				7						3										2	4	13			8	9^2		31
1		9^3			6				10	11^1		4		3	13															2	5	14		7	8^2	12		32
1		9^1			6				10	11^3		8	13	2	12															3	5			7	4^2	14		33
1		7			4				10	11^2		6	13	2														12		3	5			9	8^1			34
1		7			4				10	11		6	13	2																3	5			9^1	8^2	12		35
1		9							10	11^1		3	8	2			12											4			5		13	7	6^2			36
1				12	6				10	11^2		4	8	3				13								9^1				2	5			7				37
1		14		5	6				10^3	12		2	8	13				9^2								7^1		3			4			11				38
1		9		5	6				10	11^2		8		4								12				13				3	2			7^1				39
1		9^2		5	6				10	11		4		7								8						12		2^1	3		13					40
1		9^1		5	6				10	11		4		7^2			12			13		8						3^3			2		14					41
1				5	6				10■			3	11^2				14			2		8				7^1					4	13	9^3		12			42
1		9		5	6^2					11		3	13				12			2		8									4		10	7^1				43
		7^2		5	6				10	11		4	14	12								8		1		13		3			2^1		9^3					44
		7^3		5	6^2				10	11		3	13	2						12				1		14		4^1					9		8			45
		7^1		5	8				10			3	4	2										1		12		14			6	9^3		13	11^2			46

FA Cup

Fourth Qualifying Round	Salisbury C	(a)	0-0
		(h)	1-0
First Round	Exeter C	(a)	0-4

Trophy

First Round	Dorchester T	(a)	1-2

TORQUAY UNITED

Blue Square Premier

Ground: Plainmoor Ground, Torquay, Devon TQ1 3PS. *Tel:* (01803) 328 666. *Year Formed:* 1899.
Record Gate: 21,908 (2005 v Huddersfield T, FA Cup 4th rd). *Nickname:* The Gulls. *Manager:* Paul Buckle.
Secretary: Deborah Hancox. *Colours:* Yellow shirts, yellow shorts, yellow stockings.

TORQUAY UNITED 2007–08 LEAGUE RECORD

Match No.	*Date*	*Venue*	*Opponents*	*Result*		*H/T Score*	*Lg. Pos.*	*Goalscorers*	*Attendance*
1	Aug 12	H	Grays Ath	D	0-0	0-0	—		4012
2	Aug 15	A	Aldershot T	W	3-0	2-0	—	Sills [6], Stevens [45], Zebroski [56]	3139
3	Aug 18	A	Northwich Vic	W	3-1	2-0	1	Sills [11], Phillips 2 [26, 90]	1117
4	Aug 25	H	Rushden & D	W	3-2	0-0	3	Sills [51], Phillips (pen) [54], Zebroski [67]	3017
5	Aug 27	A	Forest Green R	D	2-2	1-2	—	Hargreaves [10], Robertson [66]	2382
6	Sept 1	H	Stafford R	W	2-0	1-0	1	Todd [44], Benyon [81]	2980
7	Sept 4	H	Salisbury C	W	4-0	2-0	—	Todd [15], Phillips (pen) [40], Sills 2 [81, 90]	3215
8	Sept 10	A	Burton Alb	L	1-3	0-2	—	Benyon [77]	2086
9	Sept 14	H	Halifax T	W	3-1	0-0	—	Robertson [49], Sills [79], Hockley [86]	2727
10	Sept 18	A	Histon	W	5-4	3-0	—	Sills [28], Mullings [33], Zebroski 2 (1 pen) [43, 68 (p)], Todd [90]	763
11	Sept 22	A	Kidderminster H	W	5-2	3-0	2	Hinshelwood [13], Sills [37], Zebroski 2 [40, 60], Phillips [75]	2027
12	Sept 25	H	Weymouth	W	3-2	0-1	—	Zebroski [52], Phillips [72], Hill [89]	3548
13	Sept 29	H	Droylsden	W	2-1	0-1	1	Sills [79], Phillips [90]	3321
14	Oct 6	A	Ebbsfleet U	L	1-2	0-0	1	Ellis [82]	1368
15	Oct 11	A	Oxford U	D	3-3	0-3	—	Welsh [58], Zebroski [79], Sills [89]	4633
16	Oct 14	H	Stevenage Bor	W	4-2	2-1	1	Zebroski 2 [32, 42], Julian (og) [53], Phillips [56]	3744
17	Oct 21	A	York C	W	1-0	0-0	1	Todd [51]	2483
18	Nov 3	H	Cambridge U	L	1-2	1-1	2	Benyon [41]	3368
19	Nov 17	A	Crawley T	W	3-2	3-0	2	Mansell [6], Ellis [13], Sills [39]	1848
20	Nov 24	H	Woking	W	2-0	1-0	2	Benyon [23], Hargreaves [60]	3275
21	Dec 12	A	Farsley C	W	2-1	1-0	—	Zebroski [6], Stevens [59]	717
22	Dec 26	A	Exeter C	L	3-4	0-2	—	Todd [50], Phillips [71], Nicholson [78]	7839
23	Dec 29	A	Woking	W	1-0	0-0	2	Sills (pen) [60]	2181
24	Jan 1	H	Exeter C	W	1-0	0-0	2	Sills [75]	6021
25	Jan 7	H	Burton Alb	L	1-2	1-1	—	Zebroski [45]	2359
26	Jan 19	A	Salisbury C	D	0-0	0-0	3		2633
27	Jan 28	H	Histon	W	1-0	0-0	—	Sills [76]	2482
28	Feb 9	H	Kidderminster H	W	1-0	1-0	2	Ellis [45]	3012
29	Feb 12	A	Weymouth	D	0-0	0-0	—		1970
30	Feb 16	H	Ebbsfleet U	W	3-1	1-0	2	Mohamed 2 [35, 85], Zebroski [55]	2704
31	Feb 26	H	Altrincham	D	1-1	1-0	—	Zebroski [44]	2310
32	Mar 1	A	Grays Ath	L	0-2	0-1	2		1018
33	Mar 3	H	Aldershot T	L	1-2	0-1	—	Phillips [63]	4510
34	Mar 11	A	Halifax T	L	2-3	0-2	—	Phillips 2 [66, 74]	894
35	Mar 22	A	Stafford R	W	2-0	0-0	4	Sills [48], D'Sane [90]	905
36	Mar 24	H	Forest Green R	W	1-0	1-0	-2	D'Sane (pen) [31]	3071
37	Mar 29	A	Altrincham	D	1-1	0-0	2	Hill [56]	1163
38	Apr 1	A	Droylsden	W	2-1	2-0	—	Sills [1], D'Sane [28]	476
39	Apr 5	H	Farsley C	L	0-1	0-1	2		2406
40	Apr 8	H	Oxford U	W	3-2	1-1	—	Zebroski 2 [40, 78], Sills (pen) [80]	2241
41	Apr 12	A	Stevenage Bor	W	3-1	0-0	2	Hargreaves [64], Zebroski [69], Sills (pen) [85]	2673
42	Apr 15	H	Northwich Vic	W	1-0	1-0	—	Zebroski [40]	2270
43	Apr 17	A	Rushden & D	L	1-2	1-1	—	Benyon [6]	1276
44	Apr 19	H	York C	D	0-0	0-0	2		2165
45	Apr 22	A	Cambridge U	L	0-2	0-2	—		4100
46	Apr 26	H	Crawley T	L	1-2	0-1	3	Sills [87]	3121

Final League Position: 3

GOALSCORERS

League (83): Sills 19 (3 pens), Zebroski 18 (1 pen), Phillips 12 (2 pens), Benyon 5, Todd 5, D'Sane 3 (1 pen), Ellis 3, Hargreaves 3, Hill 2, Mohamed 2, Robertson 2, Stevens 2, Hinshelwood 1, Hockley 1, Mansell 1, Mullings 1, Nicholson 1, Welsh 1, own goal 1.
FA Cup (6): Stevens 3, Todd 2, Phillips 1.
Trophy (11): Phillips 3, D'Sane 2 (1 pen), Hargreaves 2, Mohamed 2, Sills 2.
Play-Offs (3): Hill 1, Sills 1, Zebroski 1.

Rayner 30	Robertson 23	Nicholson 46	Mansell 34	Woods 21	Todd 42	Bedeau 13 + 10	Hargreaves 38	Phillips 35 + 7	Sills 43 + 1	Hill 4 + 9	Stevens 18 + 11	Benyon 5 + 17	Zebroski 43 + 3	Welsh 5 + 13	Wring — + 7	Hockley 23 + 6	Hinshelwood 7	Mullings 3 + 3	Ellis 22	Laird 2	Rice 9	Poke 4	Thompson — + 1	Mohamed 5 + 5	Adams 11 + 1	D'Sane 14 + 5	Andersen 3	Banim 3 + 5	*Match No.*
1	2	3	4	5	6	7[1]	8	9	10[2]	11[3]	12	13	14																1
1	2	3	4	5	6	7[1]	8	9	10[3]		12	13	11[2]	14															2
1	2	3	4	5	6		8	9	10[2]		7[1]		11	13	12														3
1	2	3	4[1]	5	6		8	9	10[3]		7	13	11[2]	14		12													4
1	2	3		5	6		8	9[1]	10		11[2]	12	7	13		4													5
1	2	3		5	6	13	8	9	10[3]		7[1]	14	11[2]	12		4													6
1	2	3		5	6	12	8[1]	9[3]	10		7	14	11[2]	13		4													7
1		3	4■	5	6	12		9[2]	10[3]		7[1]	13	11	14		8	2												8
1	2	3		5	6	7[1]		9[2]	10		8	13	11	12		4													9
1	2[1]	3		5[2]	6	7		9[3]	10	13		14	11	12		4		8■											10
1		3			6	7		13	10[3]	12			9	11[2]	14	4	2		5[1]	8									11
1		3				7		9[3]	10	5	12		11	13	14	4	2[1]		6	8[2]									12
1		3	8[3]		6	7		9	10		12		11	13	14	4	2[1]		5[2]										13
1		3		5	6	7[1]	8	9[3]	10		12	13	11		14	4[2]			2										14
1		3	4	5	6	12	8	9	10		7[2]		11	13					2[1]										15
1		3	4	5	6	2	8	9	10[2]		12	13	11	7[1]															16
1		3	4[1]	5	6	7	8	9	10	12			11	2[2]		13													17
1	2	3	4			7[1]	8		10	12	14	9[3]	11	6[2]	13				5										18
	2	3	4		6		8		10	13	7[1]	9[2]	11	12					5		1								19
	2	3	4		6		8	12	10		7	9[1]	11[2]		13				5		1								20
	2	3[1]	4	5	6	13	8	9	10		7[3]	14	11[2]			12					1								21
	2[1]	3	4	5	6	12	8	9	10		13		11	7[2]							1								22
		3	4	5	6		8	9	10		7		11			2					1								23
		3	4	5	6		8	9	10		7		11			2					1								24
		3		5	6	12	8	9[2]	10		7[1]	13	11			4[3]	2	14			1								25
		3		5	6		8		10		7	9[1]	11			4	2					1	12						26
		3	4		6		8	12	10				11						5			1		2	7	9[1]			27
		3	4		6	12	8	14	10[2]				11			13			5			1		2[1]	7	9[3]			28
		3	2		6		8	9[2]	10		12		11						5			1		7[1]	4	13			29
		3	4		6		8	7[1]	10			13	11						5		1			12	2	9[2]			30
		3	4		6		8	12	10			13	11						5					7[1]	2	9[2]	1		31
		3		5	6		8	9	10		12		11[2]			2[1]			4					13		7[3]	1	14	32
		3	4		6		8	9[3]	10		12		11[2]			2			5					7[1]		14	1	13	33
		3	4		6		8	9	10[3]		7[1]		11[2]			2			5		1			12		14		13	34
1		3[1]	4		6		8	9[3]	10				11[2]			12			5					13	2	14		7	35
1		3	4		6		8	9[3]	14		7[2]		12						5					13	2	10		11[1]	36
1		3	4		6		8	9		11		12	7						5						2	10[1]			37
1	2	3	4		6	7	8		10	12			11[1]												5	9			38
1	2	3	4			7[3]	8	12	10				11					13	6						5[2]	9[1]		14	39
1	2	3	4		6		8	9	10				11			12									5[1]	7			40
1	2	3	4		6		8	9	10	12			11			5										7[1]			41
1	2	3	4		6		8	9	10	12			11			5										7[1]			42
1	2	3	4					14		11		9[3]	12			5	7	8[2]	6							13		10[1]	43
1	2	3	4		6		8	9	10[1]				11			5										7		12	44
1	2	3	4[1]		6	13	8	9	10	14			11[3]			5		12								7[2]			45
1	2[1]	3			6	12		9[3]	10		7	14	11			4		8[2]	5						13				46

FA Cup

Fourth Qualifying Round	Bath C	(a)	2-0
First Round	Yeovil T	(h)	4-1
Second Round	Brighton & HA	(h)	0-2

Play-Offs

Semi-Final	Exeter C	(a)	2-1
		(h)	1-4

Trophy

First Round	Bashley	(h)	1-0
Second Round	Newport Co	(a)	2-1
Third Round	AFC Wimbledon	(a)	2-0
Fourth Round	Crawley T	(h)	4-1
Semi-Final	York C	(h)	2-0
		(a)	0-1
Final *(at Wembley)*	Ebbsfleet U		0-1

WEYMOUTH

Blue Square Premier

Ground: Wessex Stadium, Radipole Road, Weymouth, Dorset DT4 9XJ. *Tel:* (01305) 785 558. *Year formed:* 1890. *Record gate:* 6,680 (2005 v Nottingham F, FA Cup 1st rd replay). *Nickname:* The Terras. *Manager:* John Hollins. *Secretary:* Pete Saxby. *Colours:* Claret and sky blue.

WEYMOUTH 2007–08 LEAGUE RECORD

Match No.	*Date*	*Venue*	*Opponents*	*Result*		*H/T Score*	*Lg. Pos.*	*Goalscorers*	*Attendance*
1	Aug 11	H	Halifax T	W	2-1	0-0	—	Coutts ^{56}, Robinson ^{88}	1612
2	Aug 14	A	Forest Green R	L	2-3	1-3	—	Coutts ^{36}, Weatherstone ^{48}	865
3	Aug 18	A	Stevenage Bor	L	0-3	0-1	16		2016
4	Aug 23	H	Burton Alb	L	1-2	1-2	—	Robinson ^{18}	1404
5	Aug 27	A	Exeter C	D	0-0	0-0	—		4773
6	Aug 31	H	Cambridge U	D	2-2	1-0	—	Louis 2 $^{39, 84}$	1502
7	Sept 4	A	Woking	D	1-1	0-0	—	Louis ^{50}	1532
8	Sept 8	H	Ebbsfleet U	W	2-0	1-0	18	Beavon ^{38}, Louis ^{85}	1140
9	Sept 15	A	Droylsden	W	3-1	1-0	16	Beavon ^{14}, Crittenden ^{52}, Coutts ^{90}	578
10	Sept 18	H	Rushden & D	L	1-2	1-1	—	Louis ^{33}	1252
11	Sept 22	H	Stafford R	L	1-3	0-2	9	Crittenden ^{55}	1217
12	Sept 25	A	Torquay U	L	2-3	1-0	—	Crittenden ^{4}, Platt ^{55}	3548
13	Sept 29	A	Histon	D	2-2	1-1	18	Robinson ^{31}, Vickers ^{61}	891
14	Oct 6	H	Northwich Vic	W	2-0	1-0	18	McCallum ^{45}, Louis ^{58}	1106
15	Oct 9	A	Grays Ath	W	2-0	0-0	—	Coutts ^{51}, Louis ^{68}	779
16	Oct 12	H	Crawley T	L	1-2	1-1	—	Crittenden ^{10}	1333
17	Oct 20	A	Kidderminster H	W	2-0	0-0	14	Vickers ^{53}, McCallum ^{60}	1374
18	Nov 2	H	Aldershot T	L	0-2	0-1	—		1782
19	Nov 17	A	Altrincham	L	2-3	1-1	17	Shotton (og) ^{14}, Platt ^{51}	960
20	Nov 24	H	York C	L	1-2	0-0	18	McCallum ^{84}	1566
21	Dec 26	A	Salisbury C	D	1-1	0-0	—	Jombarti ^{54}	1687
22	Dec 29	A	York C	L	0-2	0-0	19		2546
23	Jan 1	H	Salisbury C	L	0-3	0-0	19		2002
24	Jan 5	A	Ebbsfleet U	L	1-4	0-3	19	McCallum ^{74}	952
25	Jan 8	A	Oxford U	W	1-0	1-0	—	McCallum ^{39}	3996
26	Jan 19	H	Woking	L	0-1	0-0	19		1310
27	Jan 26	A	Rushden & D	L	2-3	1-1	19	Doe ^{25}, Malcolm ^{48}	1448
28	Feb 9	A	Stafford R	L	1-2	0-1	19	McCallum ^{73}	591
29	Feb 12	H	Torquay U	D	0-0	0-0	—		1970
30	Feb 23	H	Histon	L	0-1	0-0	19		1121
31	Mar 1	A	Halifax T	L	1-2	1-0	21	Robinson ^{29}	971
32	Mar 4	H	Forest Green R	L	0-6	0-3	—		783
33	Mar 8	H	Stevenage Bor	W	1-0	1-0	21	Vernazza ^{39}	930
34	Mar 11	H	Farsley C	D	0-0	0-0	—		951
35	Mar 16	A	Burton Alb	L	1-2	1-0	21	Coutts ^{18}	1501
36	Mar 18	A	Northwich Vic	D	2-2	0-0	—	Hyde ^{74}, Coutts ^{78}	636
37	Mar 22	A	Cambridge U	D	0-0	0-0	19		2914
38	Mar 24	H	Exeter C	W	3-1	1-0	18	Blackburn ^{36}, Weatherstone ^{65}, Malcolm ^{87}	2995
39	Mar 29	A	Farsley C	L	2-4	1-1	18	Bedeau ^{11}, Weatherstone ^{54}	459
40	Apr 5	H	Oxford U	L	0-1	0-0	21		1635
41	Apr 8	H	Grays Ath	D	1-1	0-1	—	Weatherstone (pen) ^{58}	817
42	Apr 12	A	Crawley T	D	1-1	1-1	21	Weatherstone ^{24}	943
43	Apr 15	H	Droylsden	W	2-1	1-1	—	Beavon ^{10}, Robinson ^{77}	1102
44	Apr 19	H	Kidderminster H	W	2-1	0-0	18	Blackburn ^{64}, Douglas ^{88}	1205
45	Apr 22	A	Aldershot T	D	0-0	0-0	—		5980
46	Apr 26	H	Altrincham	D	2-2	2-1	18	Scott (og) ^{6}, Malcolm ^{45}	1728

Final League Position: 18

GOALSCORERS

League (53): Louis 7, Coutts 6, McCallum 6, Robinson 5, Weatherstone 5 (1 pen), Crittenden 4, Beavon 3, Malcolm 3, Blackburn 2, Platt 2, Vickers 2, Bedeau 1, Doe 1, Douglas 1, Hyde 1, Jombarti 1, Vernazza 1, own goals 2.
FA Cup (6): Beavon 3, Louis 1, Roberts J 1, Robinson 1.
Trophy (3): Malcolm 2, Louis 1.

Matthews 22	Critchell 34 + 1	Roberts J 20 + 2	Browning 16 + 3	Weatherstone 24 + 3	Coutts 33 + 8	Crittenden 25 + 12	Vernazza 27 + 2	Platt 13 + 7	Beavon 31 + 8	Robinson 42 + 1	McCallum 10 + 14	Louis 16 + 5	Douglas 2 + 14	Phillips 4 + 11	Bernard 9	Vickers 10 + 2	Convery 4 + 1	Kitamirike 18	Jombarti 11 + 1	Doe 30 + 4	Stewart 8	Young 3	Hart 1	Domoraud 4	Gross 2 + 1	Malcolm 8 + 11	Challis 16 + 2	Ngala 2	Compton 3	Anzite 3 + 1	Okuonghae 5	Henderson 16	Swaibu 1	Bedeau 9	Blackburn 12 + 1	Hyde 3 + 2	Roberts D — + 1	Bailey 9	Match No.
1	2	3	4	5	6[1]	7	8	9[2]	10[3]	11	12	13	14																									1
1	2	3	4[2]	5	6[1]	7	8	9[3]	10	11	12		13	14																								2
1	2	3	4[1]	5	6[2]	7	8			11	12	9[3]	14		10	13																								3
1				5	6[3]		8[2]	13	10	11		12	9■	7[1]	3	4		2	14																					4
1	2		4■	5	6		13	12	10[3]	11	14	9[2]				3		7	8[1]																					5
1	2[1]			5	6[2]	13	8	12	10[3]	11	14	9				4		3	7																					6
1	2			5	6[1]	12	8[2]	9	10[3]	11	14	7		13				3	4																					7
1		3	4	5	6[3]	12		9[2]	10	11		7		13				2	8[1]	14																				8
1	2	3	4		6	12		9[2]	10	11		7[3]		14				5	8[1]	13																				9
	2	3	4[2]	5		7		9[3]	10	11	13	8		14		12		6[1]			1																			10
1	2			5	6[2]	7	8	9[1]	10		13	11		12		4		3																						11
1		3[1]			6	7[2]	8	13		11	10	9		12		5		2		4																				12
	12	3			6		8	9[1]		11	10	7				5		2		4	1																			13
		3			6	7	8	12	13	11	10[3]	9[2]	14		4[1]	5				2	1																			14
		5			6	7	8		13	11	10[2]	9[1]	12		3	4				2	1																			15
		5			6[1]	7	8		14	11	10[3]	9[2]	13	12	3	4				2	1																			16
		3			6	7	8■		12	11	10	9[1]			5	4				2	1																			17
					6	7[2]	8	9	14	11	10[3]	12		13				5		2	1	4	3[1]																	18
					13	7[2]	8	9	10	11[3]	14	4		12	3[1]			5		2	1	6																		19
1		12			13	7	8	9	10		14	11[3]		4	3[2]			5[1]		2		6																		20
1	2	3	13			7	8	9[1]	10[3]	11	12	14		6[2]					4	5																				21
1	2		4[1]		6		8[2]	9		11	10[3]	14	12	13				5	7	3																				22
1	2	3	4[1]		6[3]	7		12	10[2]	11	14		13						8	5				9																23
1	2[1]	3		5[2]		7				11	13							6	10	4				9	8	12															24
1	2	13	4		6				14	11	10[2]							5	7	3				9[3]	8[1]		12														25
1	2		4		6[1]			12	14	11	10[2]								8	5				9[3]		13	3	7														26
1			4		13		8		10[3]	11			14	7[2]				5		2					12	9	3[1]	6														27
1	2		4	12	6[2]	13	8		10	11	14				3[1]			5		7						9[3]																28
1	2	3		4[1]		7	8		10	12										5						13	6		11[2]	9									29
1	2	3[1]		5[3]	13	7[2]	8		10											14						12	6		9	11	4								30
	2		4	12		7			10[3]	11											13■						14	3[1]		8		5	1	6[2]	9					31
	2	5[1]	6[3]		13	7[2]	8			11																14	3				4	1		9	12	10			32
	2				13	7	8		10[2]	11																12	3				5	1		9	6	4[1]			33
	2				12	7	8		10	11																13	3[1]				4	1		9	5	6[2]			34
	2			12	6		8		10	11										5						13	3			7[1]		1[G]		9[2]	4		15		35
	2[1]			5	6	13[3]	8[2]		10	11										7						14	3					1		9	4	12			36
	2[1]			5	6	14			10[3]	11										7						13	3					1		9	4	12[2]		8	37
	2			8	6[1]	7				11										5						10				12		1		9	4			3	38
	2			8	6	7[2]			12	11							13			5[1]						9						1		10	4			3	39
	2[2]			8	6[1]	12			10	11			13				7			5						9						1			4			3	40
	2			8	12	7[1]			10	11							4			3						9[2]	13					1			5			6	41
	2			8	6[2]	13			10	11			12				7			9							3[1]					1			5			4	42
	2			8	6				10	11			12				7■			9							3					1			5			4[1]	43
	2		4[2]	8	6	13			10	11			12							9							3					1			7			5[1]	44
	2	3	14	8	6[2]	13			10[3]	11			12							5						9	7					1						4[1]	45
	2■	4	13	8	6[1]	12	14		10[2]	11			9[3]							5						7	3					1							46

FA Cup

Fourth Qualifying Round — Hitchin T — (h) 1-1; (a) 1-0

First Round — Eastbourne B — (a) 4-0

Second Round — Cambridge U — (a) 0-1

Trophy

First Round — Wealdstone — (a) 1-0

Second Round — Kidderminster H — (h) 0-0; (a) 2-2

Third Round — Ebbsfleet U — (a) 0-1

WOKING

Blue Square Premier

Ground: Kingfield Sports Ground, Kingfield, Woking, Surrey GU22 9AA. *Tel:* (01483) 772 470. *Year Formed:* 1889. *Record Gate:* 6,084 (1997 v Coventry City, FA Cup 3rd rd). *Nickname:* The Cards. *Manager:* Kim Grant. *Secretary:* Phil Ledger. *Colours:* Red and white shirts, black shorts, red stockings.

WOKING 2007–08 LEAGUE RECORD

Match No.	Date	Venue	Opponents	Result		H/T Score	Lg. Pos.	Goalscorers	Attendance
1	Aug 11	H	Rushden & D	D	1-1	0-0	—	Morgan 49	1576
2	Aug 15	A	Grays Ath	D	1-1	0-0	—	Pattison 85	1004
3	Aug 18	A	Stafford R	W	1-0	0-0	11	Morgan 54	642
4	Aug 25	H	Cambridge U	D	0-0	0-0	12		1805
5	Aug 27	A	Salisbury C	L	1-2	0-2	—	Sole 83	2093
6	Sept 1	H	Forest Green R	D	1-1	0-0	15	Sole (pen) 55	1499
7	Sept 4	H	Weymouth	D	1-1	0-0	—	Sole 56	1532
8	Sept 11	A	Halifax T	L	0-1	0-0	—		1304
9	Sept 15	H	Altrincham	W	2-0	1-0	17	Tinson (og) 40, Bunce 90	1391
10	Sept 18	A	Crawley T	L	3-5	1-3	—	Gatting (pen) 17, Hutchinson 72, Hakin 90	959
11	Sept 22	A	Burton Alb	L	0-2	0-2	18		1501
12	Sept 25	H	Exeter C	D	1-1	0-1	—	Morgan 87	1448
13	Sept 29	A	Northwich Vic	W	3-1	2-0	17	Pattison 3, Gatting 22, Hakin 83	550
14	Oct 4	H	Farsley C	W	2-0	0-0	—	Quamina 56, Morgan 80	1535
15	Oct 9	A	Stevenage Bor	D	1-1	1-1	—	Ruby 18	3007
16	Oct 13	H	York C	L	0-3	0-1	16		1557
17	Oct 20	A	Oxford U	D	0-0	0-0	17		4713
18	Nov 3	H	Droylsden	D	1-1	1-1	18	Sole 18	1284
19	Nov 10	H	Grays Ath	L	0-1	0-0	—		1118
20	Nov 17	A	Kidderminster H	D	1-1	0-1	18	Sole 85	1426
21	Nov 24	A	Torquay U	L	0-2	0-1	19		3275
22	Nov 29	H	Ebbsfleet U	W	1-0	1-0	—	Pattison 20	1255
23	Dec 8	A	Histon	W	1-0	0-0	13	Sole (pen) 60	887
24	Dec 26	H	Aldershot T	L	0-1	0-0	—		4356
25	Dec 29	H	Torquay U	L	0-1	0-0	17		2181
26	Jan 1	A	Aldershot T	L	1-2	0-2	18	Sole (pen) 48	4728
27	Jan 5	H	Halifax T	W	1-0	1-0	17	Sole 27	1299
28	Jan 19	A	Weymouth	W	1-0	0-0	16	Morgan 80	1310
29	Jan 26	H	Crawley T	D	1-1	1-1	16	Morgan 45	1697
30	Jan 31	A	Altrincham	D	2-2	1-0	—	Quamina 39, Morgan 56	905
31	Feb 9	H	Burton Alb	W	2-1	2-0	16	Marum 20, Hutchinson 23	1493
32	Feb 12	A	Exeter C	D	2-2	0-2	—	Pattison 58, Morgan 89	3586
33	Feb 16	A	Farsley C	L	0-3	0-2	15		479
34	Feb 23	H	Northwich Vic	L	2-3	1-1	15	Morgan 31, Marum 88	2672
35	Mar 1	A	Rushden & D	L	1-2	1-1	16	Pattison 3	1335
36	Mar 8	H	Stafford R	D	2-2	1-1	17	Pattison 17, Norville 55	1133
37	Mar 15	A	Cambridge U	L	0-1	0-1	18		3778
38	Mar 21	A	Forest Green R	L	1-2	1-1	—	Batt 40	1143
39	Mar 24	H	Salisbury C	W	3-2	1-1	17	Morgan 28, Sole (pen) 71, Norville 90	2829
40	Mar 29	H	Histon	D	3-3	1-1	17	Ruby 4, Norville 52, Sole 55	1310
41	Apr 5	A	Ebbsfleet U	D	1-1	0-0	17	Sole 90	1175
42	Apr 8	H	Stevenage Bor	L	0-2	0-1	—		1216
43	Apr 12	A	York C	W	3-2	1-1	17	Norville 42, Sole 2 (2 pens) 64, 70	2246
44	Apr 19	H	Oxford U	L	1-2	0-1	17	Sole 58	1857
45	Apr 22	A	Droylsden	D	1-1	0-1	—	Pattison 65	301
46	Apr 26	H	Kidderminster H	W	3-0	1-0	17	Pattison 2 24, 60, Quamina 55	2310

Final League Position: 17

GOALSCORERS

League (53): Sole 14 (6 pens), Morgan 10, Pattison 9, Norville 4, Quamina 3, Gatting 2 (1 pen), Hakin 2, Hutchinson 2, Marum 2, Ruby 2, Batt 1, Bunce 1, own goal 1.
FA Cup (0).
Trophy (3): James 1, Morgan 1, Norville 1.

Gindre 30	Ruby 22 + 4	Bunce 41	Lorraine 34	Hutchinson 33	Gasson 42 + 1	Gray 21 + 8	Quamina 37 + 1	Sole 24 + 16	Morgan 39 + 3	Pattison 40 + 2	Charles 1 + 4	Lambu 30 + 11	Maledon 8 + 10	Warner 15 + 1	McCarthy 1	Shin — + 1	Green 18 + 3	Gibbs 3 + 1	Harusha 1 + 1	James 18	Gatting 13 + 2	Hakin 3 + 4	Marum 8 + 18	Christon 1 + 1	Norville 13 + 3	Batt 10 + 3	Yorkie — + 1	*Match No.*
1	2	3	4	5	6	7	8	9^1	10	11	12																	1
1	2	3	4	5	6	7^1	8	9^2	10	11	13	12																2
1	2	3	4	5	6		8	9^1	10^2	11■	12	7	13															3
1^6	2	3	4	5	6		8	9^1	10		12	7	11	15														4
	2		4		6	12	8	13	10	11	9^3	7^1	3^2		1	14	5											5
1	2	3	4		6		8	9	5	11		7						10										6
1	2	3	4		6	14	8^2	9	10	11		7^1	12				13	5^3										7
1	2	3	4		6			9	10	11		7^1	5				13	8^2	12									8
1		3	4	5	6			12	10^3			7	14				11		8^1	2	9^2	13						9
1	13	3	4■	5	6			14	10^3	11^2		7^1					8			2	9	12						10
1	2■	3		5	6		8	12	13	11^1		7	14							4	9^3	10^2						11
1		3	4	5	6		8		10	11^1		7								2	12	9						12
1	2	3	4		6		8		10^1	11		7						13		5	9^2	12						13
1	2	3	4		6		8	14	13	11^1		7	12							5	9^2	10^3						14
1	2	3	4		6	14	8	12	10^3	11^2		7	13							5	9^1							15
1	2	3	4		6	14	8	12	10	11^2		7^1								5	9^3	13						16
1		3	4	5	6		8		10	11^1		7					12			2	9^2		13					17
1		3	4	5	6	7^1		9^2		11		2	12							8	10		13					18
		3	4	5	6		8^1		10^2	11		7	12	1						2	9		13					19
			4	5	6		8^1	12	10	11		7^2	13	1			3			2	9^3		14					20
1			4^1	5	6		8	9^3	10■	11		7^2	13				3			2	14		12					21
1	2	3			6		8	9		11		12	4^1				7			5	10^2		13					22
1	2	3		5	6	7		9^1		11							8			4	10		12					23
1		3	4	5	6	7^2	13	9^3	10	11^1		12					8			2			14					24
1		3	4	5	6		8^1	13	10	11		12					7^2			2			9					25
1		3	4	5	6		8	9^2	10	11^1		12					7			2			13					26
1		3	4■	5	6	7	8	9^1	10^2	13		2					11						12					27
1		3		5	6	7	8	12	10	11^2		4					2^1						14	13	9^3			28
1		3		5	6	7	8	9	10	11		2											12		4^1			29
1		3		5	6	12	8	9	10	11		2^1											13	4	7^2			30
	2	3	4	5		7	8^1			11		12		1			6						10^2		9	13		31
	2	3	4	5		7^1	8		13	11		12		1			6^3						10^2		9	14		32
	2^1	3	4	5		7		12	10	11		13		1			8^2								9	6		33
1		3		5	6	12	8	9	10	11^1		4											13		7^2	2		34
	2	3	4^3	5	6	7^1	8	12	10	11				1									9^2		13	14		35
	12	3		5■	6	7	8	13	10^2	11				1			4^1						14		9^3	2		36
	2	3	4		6	7	8	13	10	11		5^1		1									9^2		12			37
		3		5	6	7	8	9	10	11				1									12		4^1	2		38
		3		5	6	7^2	8	12	10	13		11		1			4^1						9^3		14	2		39
	2	3		5	6	7	8	9	10	11^1		12		1											4			40
		3	4	5	6	7		12	10			11^1	8	1											9	2		41
	12		4	5	6	7		9	10			13	11	1			3^1						14		8^3	2^2		42
			4	5	12	7	8	9	10	11		2^1		1									13		6^2	3		43
		3	4		6	7	8	9	10	11		5		1									2					44
1	2	3			6	12	8	9	10	11		13	4										7^2			5^1		45
1	13	3	4		6	12	8	9^2	10^3	11		7	2													5^1	14	46

FA Cup
Fourth Qualifying Round
Staines T (h) 0-1

Trophy
First Round Hemel Hempstead T (a) 1-0
Second Round Aldershot T (h) 2-4

YORK CITY

Blue Square Premier

Ground: KitKat Crescent, York YO30 7AQ. *Tel:* (01904) 624 447. *Year Formed:* 1922.
Record Gate: 28,123 (1938 v Huddersfield T, FA Cup 6th rd). *Nickname:* Minster Men.
Manager: Colin Walker. *Secretary:* Nick Barrett. *Colours:* Red shirts, navy shorts, navy stockings.

YORK CITY 2007–08 LEAGUE RECORD

Match No.	Date	Venue	Opponents	Result		H/T Score	Lg. Pos.	Goalscorers	Attendance
1	Aug 11	H	Cambridge U	L	1-2	1-0	—	Farrell (pen) [38]	3136
2	Aug 14	A	Burton Alb	L	3-4	1-1	—	Woolford [45], Sodje [48], Farrell (pen) [52]	1892
3	Aug 20	A	Exeter C	D	1-1	0-1	—	Sodje [87]	4242
4	Aug 24	H	Forest Green R	L	0-2	0-0	—		2294
5	Aug 27	A	Northwich Vic	W	1-0	0-0	—	Brayson [90]	1302
6	Aug 30	H	Rushden & D	L	2-3	1-1	—	Brodie [20], Woolford [54]	2044
7	Sept 4	H	Altrincham	D	2-2	1-1	—	Brodie [45], Brayson [51]	2079
8	Sept 8	A	Kidderminster H	L	0-3	0-2	20		1589
9	Sept 15	H	Stevenage Bor	L	0-2	0-0	20		2052
10	Sept 18	A	Aldershot T	L	0-2	0-0	—		2402
11	Sept 22	A	Grays Ath	W	2-0	1-0	20	Sodje [44], Elliott [65]	1014
12	Sept 27	H	Halifax T	W	3-2	0-1	—	Sodje [58], Woolford [61], Meechan [70]	2134
13	Sept 30	A	Oxford U	D	1-1	0-1	19	Sodje [81]	4944
14	Oct 6	H	Histon	L	1-4	1-1	19	Wroe [29]	2199
15	Oct 9	H	Stafford R	W	2-0	2-0	—	Elliott [36], McBreen [39]	1784
16	Oct 13	A	Woking	W	3-0	1-0	18	Sodje 2 [4, 49], Woolford [71]	1557
17	Oct 21	H	Torquay U	L	0-1	0-0	19		2483
18	Nov 3	A	Farsley C	W	4-1	2-1	19	McBreen [8], Brayson [23], Farrell 2 [81, 87]	1603
19	Nov 17	H	Salisbury C	L	1-3	1-1	19	Brayson [35]	2303
20	Nov 24	A	Weymouth	W	2-1	0-0	16	Kelly [53], Farrell [61]	1566
21	Dec 1	H	Crawley T	D	1-1	0-0	—	Sodje [79]	2212
22	Dec 8	A	Ebbsfleet U	W	2-1	1-0	14	Sodje [26], Woolford [50]	933
23	Dec 26	H	Droylsden	W	2-1	1-1	—	Farrell (pen) [23], Kelly [53]	3042
24	Dec 29	H	Weymouth	W	2-0	0-0	10	Woolford [51], McGurk [74]	2546
25	Jan 1	A	Droylsden	W	4-3	0-2	10	Panther [70], Farrell [87], Brodie 2 [89, 90]	1015
26	Jan 5	H	Kidderminster H	D	2-2	2-2	10	Sodje [31], Farrell [34]	2423
27	Jan 19	A	Altrincham	D	2-2	0-1	13	Woolford 2 [63, 65]	1210
28	Jan 26	H	Aldershot T	W	2-0	1-0	11	Brodie [7], Woolford [86]	3092
29	Feb 9	H	Grays Ath	W	2-0	0-0	10	Wroe (pen) [53], Fortune-West [72]	2531
30	Feb 12	A	Halifax T	D	2-2	1-1	—	Sodje [33], Woolford [72]	2875
31	Feb 16	A	Histon	L	1-3	1-2	11	Wroe (pen) [19]	1021
32	Mar 1	A	Cambridge U	L	0-2	0-1	11		3666
33	Mar 4	H	Burton Alb	D	0-0	0-0	—		1882
34	Mar 10	H	Exeter C	W	3-2	2-1	—	Woolford [31], Parslow [41], Sodje [69]	1567
35	Mar 18	A	Forest Green R	W	2-1	2-0	—	Wroe [16], Robinson [40]	734
36	Mar 22	A	Rushden & D	D	1-1	0-0	10	Brodie [55]	1423
37	Mar 25	H	Northwich Vic	D	1-1	1-0	—	Brodie [11]	1941
38	Mar 29	H	Ebbsfleet U	L	0-1	0-1	13		2256
39	Apr 1	A	Stevenage Bor	L	2-3	2-1	—	Wroe 2 (1 pen) [25, 31 (p)]	1117
40	Apr 5	A	Crawley T	L	1-6	1-3	14	Woolford [27]	862
41	Apr 8	A	Stafford R	W	4-0	0-0	—	Woolford [53], Brodie [58], Elliott [78], Robinson [90]	455
42	Apr 12	H	Woking	L	2-3	1-1	14	Sodje 2 [3, 67]	2246
43	Apr 15	H	Oxford U	L	0-1	0-0	—		1808
44	Apr 19	A	Torquay U	D	0-0	0-0	14		2165
45	Apr 22	H	Farsley C	W	4-1	2-0	—	Woolford [11], Fortune-West [20], Brodie 2 [84, 90]	1886
46	Apr 26	A	Salisbury C	L	0-3	0-2	14		1400

Final League Position: 14

GOALSCORERS

League (71): Sodje 14, Woolford 14, Brodie 10, Farrell 8 (3 pens), Wroe 6 (3 pens), Brayson 4, Elliott 3, Fortune-West 2, Kelly 2, McBreen 2, Robinson 2, McGurk 1, Meechan 1, Panther 1, Parslow 1.
FA Cup (6): Farrell 3, Sodje 2, Wroe 1.
Trophy (12): Farrell 3 (1 pen), Wroe 3, Brodie 2 (1 pen), Lloyd 1, Parslow 1, Woolford 1, own goal 1.

Evans 36	Purkiss 33 + 4	Robinson 28 + 3	Jones 2	McGurk 46	Elliott 32 + 4	Brayson 16 + 6	Panther 36 + 4	Beardsley 4 + 4	Farrell 13 + 7	Woolford 45 + 1	Greenwood 4 + 3	Brodie 21 + 18	Sodje 29 + 16	Meechan 3 + 4	Craddock 25 + 5	Parslow 30 + 1	Hutchinson 2 + 1	Kelly 25 + 2	Henderson 7	Hegarty 2	Wroe 21 + 8	Fry — + 4	McBreen 5	Lloyd 11 + 4	Rusk 10 + 4	Fortune-West 7 + 6	Duncum 1 + 1	Hall 1 + 1	Mimms 3 + 1	Shepherd — + 3	McWilliams 4 + 1	Boyes — + 3	Beadle 4	*Match No.*
1	2	3	4	5	6■	7[1]	8	9[2]	10[3]	11	12	13	14																					1
1	2	3	4	5		13	8	14	11[1]	7	6	9[3]	10[2]	12																				2
1	12	3		5		13	8	14		11	6	9[3]	10		2[1]	4	7[2]																	3
1	13	3		5			8[2]	9[3]	12	11		14	10	7[1]	2	6	4																	4
1	12	3		5	6	7			14	11	8	10	9[3]		2[1]	4[2]	13																	5
1	2	3		5	6	7[1]	8[2]	14	10	11	13	9[3]	12					4																6
	2	3		5	6	7	8		9	11		10[1]	12					4	1															7
	2[3]	3		5	6	12	8		13	11	7[1]	10[2]	9		14			4	1															8
		3		5[1]		7	8			11		9[2]	13		2	12		4	1	10	6													9
		3		5			8	9[1]		11		12	10		2			4	1	6	7													10
	2	3■		5	6	12	8	9[3]		11		14■	10[2]		13			4	1		7[1]													11
	2			5	6	7	8			11			10[2]	12	3			4	1		9[1]	13												12
	2	3		5	6	9	8[2]			11			10	7[1]				4	1		13	12												13
1	2	3		5	4	10	13			11			12	7[1]				6			8[2]	14	9[3]											14
1		3		5	6	7	8			11		12	10[1]	13	2			4					9[2]											15
1		3		5	6	7	8			11		13	10[1]		2			4				12	9[2]											16
1		3		5	6	7	8			11		13	10	12	2			4[1]					9[2]											17
1		3		5	6	7[1]	8		13	11[2]		14	10[3]		2			4			12		9											18
1		3		5	6[3]	9	8		10	11	12	13	14		2[1]			4[2]			7													19
1	12	3		5	13	9[2]	8		10[3]	11			14		2[1]	4		6			7													20
1		3		5	13	9[3]	8	12	10	11			14		6[1]	4		2			7[2]													21
1	2[1]	3[2]		5	6		8		10	11			9		13	4		7			12													22
1	2			5	6[1]		8		10	11		13	9[2]			4		3			12			7										23
1	2			5	6		8		10	11		13	9[2]			4		3			12			7[1]										24
1	2			5	6[1]	12	8		10	11		14	9[3]			4		3			13			7[2]										25
1	2			5	6	13	8[2]		10[3]	11		14	9		12	3		4[1]			7													26
1	2			5	6	9[2]	8			11		13	10[1]		3	4					7			12										27
1				5	6		8		12	11		9[1]			2	4					7			10	3									28
1	2			5	6		8[2]			11[1]		10[3]	13		3	4					9			7	12	14								29
1	2			5	6[2]		12		14	11			10[3]		3[1]	4					7			8	13	9								30
1	2			5	6				13	11		14	12		3	4					7			8[2]	10[1]	9[3]								31
1	2			5	6		12		10	11		13	9[2]		3[3]	4		14			7			8[1]										32
1	2	3[1]		5			8[2]			13		10	14			6		4			7				11	9[3]	12							33
1	2	3		5[1]	13		8[3]			11		10	9			4		12			6				14		7[2]							34
1	2	3[2]		5	6					11		10[3]	12			4		8			9			13	7[1]	14								35
1	2	3[3]		5	6		14			11		10	9		12	4		8[1]						13	7[2]									36
1	2[2]	3		5	6[1]		8			11		10	9		7	4					12					13								37
1	2	3		5	13		8[1]			11		10[3]	9			4					7				12	14		6[2]						38
	2[2]	12		5	6					11		10	13		3	4					9			7[1]	8[3]	14			1					39
	2			5	6					11		10[3]	13		4	3					9			7[2]	8[1]	14		12	1					40
1	2	3		5	6		8			11		10[2]	9[3]		7	4[1]					13			12								14		41
1■	2			5	6■		8[1]			11		10	9[2]		7■	3								4					15	12[6]	13			42
	2			5			8			11		10[2]	9			4										7			1	13	3	12	6[1]	43
1	2	12		5			8			11[3]		13	14		3	4									7	10[2]					9[1]		6	44
1	2			5			8			11[1]		12	9[2]			4									7	10				13	3		6	45
1	2	13		5						11		9	12			4		3							7[1]	10[3]					8[2]	14	6	46

FA Cup

Fourth Qualifying Round	Rushall O	(h)	6-0
First Round	Havant & W	(h)	0-1

Trophy

First Round	Altrincham	(a)	3-1
Second Round	Grays Ath	(h)	1-1
		(a)	4-1
Third Round	Farsley C	(a)	2-0
Fourth Round	Rushden & D	(a)	1-0
Semi-Final	Torquay U	(a)	0-2
		(h)	1-0

REVIEW OF THE SCOTTISH SEASON 2007–08

As with the rest of the UK, the Euro 2008 finals had a somewhat detached appeal, but also served to duly note the quality of opposition likely in the qualifying stages of the 2010 World Cup. For Scotland, Group 9 features four opponents: Holland, Iceland, Macedonia and Norway. On the face of it this is a less demanding programme than the one for the European Championship. However, the sting in the tail is provided by less opportunity to qualify because though there is one fewer team than in the other groups, overall only eight runners up will be eligible for the play-offs from nine sections.

This is the future; the brave attempt to reach the Euro 2008 finals was highly commendable and of all the British involvement, Scotland were in easily the most difficult group with formidable opponents in Italy and France the finalists in the 2006 World Cup no less. Alex McLeish was disappointed enough to decide to resign, head for Birmingham City and be replaced by George Burley.

However, there was a European finalist as Rangers reached the last stage of the UEFA Cup having at one time had thoughts of an unprecedented quadruple of Scottish Premier League, European glory and two domestic cup competitions. Events conspired against them and the fixture list provided too many matches in too short a space of time. Rangers were not afforded the luxury given to their final opponents Zenit St Petersburg, who were allowed dispensation to postpone Russian League commitments until after the final. It should not be forgotten that Rangers had started their continental adventure in the second qualifying round of the Champions League.

Naturally European involvement did not confine itself to Ibrox. Celtic joined Rangers in the third qualifying round and came through after beating Spartak Moscow on penalties. But in the UEFA Cup, Dunfermline Athletic were held by Swedish entry Hacken and were narrowly beaten in the return leg. In came Aberdeen in the first round to face the Ukrainian club Dnepr. At Pittodrie it finished goalless, but the Dons also drew away and progressed on away goals.

Meanwhile the lines were drawn for the group stage of the Champions League, Celtic in a tough one with AC Milan and Benfica included. Rangers, too, faced formidable opponents including Barcelona and Lyon. The group stage of the UEFA Cup interested Aberdeen, of course, but a 3-0 defeat in Greece against Panathinaikos was a distinct omen, although they finished with a splendid 4-0 win over FC Copenhagen to finish a creditable third.

Celtic in the Champions League were full value for runners-up in Group D, Rangers third in their section and afforded a place in the UEFA Cup where the third round proved a knock-out for Aberdeen 5-1 at Bayern Munich. Rangers thus fought on to the ultimate game itself.

There it was weary Rangers who lost 2-0 to Zenit and then with their lead in the SPL eroded until the last day there was all to play for with Celtic level on points but with a superior goal difference. It was academic in the unravelling because Rangers lost at Aberdeen while Celtic were beating Dundee United. For their part, Celtic would point with some justification to two wins in the previous couple of months over their rivals.

There was silverware consolation for Rangers in both CIS Insurance Cup and the Scottish Cup, though both were hard-earned final struggles. Dundee United pushed them to penalties in the former and Queen of the South flying the Scottish League flag recovered from being two goals down to level before Rangers edged home. Rangers were forced to penalties before disposing of St Johnstone, the League Challenge Cup winners in the Scottish Cup semi-final.

In fact it was a new look Scottish Cup, the qualifying competition of old being scrapped in favour of leading clubs outside the Scottish League. These were the winners of the East of Scotland League, the South of Scotland League and four teams from the Scottish Junior ranks, including its cup winners.

With third place the battleground for Europe, Motherwell after early tussles with Dundee United, secured it. Yet it had been Hibernian whose unbeaten record had lasted the longest, before failing to maintain this encouraging start. Aberdeen finished fourth and could claim to have ended Rangers' championship hopes at the final reckoning.

Falkirk again finished seventh, but it was a disappointing season for Hearts who missed the cut. Inverness Caley who began badly improved to finish ninth and St Mirren moved up one place from 2006–07, leaving Kilmarnock slipping six places from the previous season. But the tragedy was Gretna whose dream, fairytale rise suddenly became a nightmare with their owner Brookes Mileson taken ill, the funding ceasing, ten points being deducted and even worse to follow. The Scottish League relegated them to the Third Division and then the administrators pulled the plug leaving a vacancy in the competition.

Replacing Gretna in the SPL were Hamilton Academical who held off the challenge from Dundee fairly comfortably in the end, though the Dees had chances to catch them. Down from the First Division initially went Stirling Albion, but Clyde survived the challengers from the Second Division. Ross County won promotion and because of the unfortunate position in which Gretna found themselves, there was an unexpected lift up for Airdrie United, too.

East Fife were runaway winners of the Third Division and despite finishing fourth Abroath saw off Cowdenbeath and then Stranraer to accompany them. However, the disappointment was again brief for Stranraer. Berwick Rangers, struggling most of the season were early casualties from the Second Division.

There was tragedy in the sudden death of Phil O'Donnell at Motherwell who collapsed after being substituted. He was 35 years old. Yet in the aftermath of it the entire football community came together in a remarkable display of sportsmanship which did much to enhance the reputation of the game.

The vacancy left by the demise of Gretna was filled by Annan Athletic who join the Third Division after a vote by the 29 clubs in the Scottish Football League. Three rounds of votes were required before Annan's place was confirmed. The Dumfries and Galloway side held off the challenge from Cove Rangers, Spartans, Preston Athletic and Edinburgh City.

ANNAN ATHLETIC — Third Division

Year Formed: 1942. *Ground & Address:* Galabank, North Street, Annan. *Telephone:* 01461 204108.
Website: www.annanathleticfc.com
Ground capacity: 3500 (500 seated). *Chairman:* Henry McClelland. *Secretary:* Alan Irving. *Manager:* Harry Cairney.
Club colours: Black and gold striped shirts, black shorts, black stockings with gold trim.

SCOTTISH LEAGUE TABLES 2007–08

CLYDESDALE BANK SCOTTISH PREMIER LEAGUE

			Home					*Away*					*Total*						
		P	*W*	*D*	*L*	*F*	*A*	*W*	*D*	*L*	*F*	*A*	*W*	*D*	*L*	*F*	*A*	*GD*	*Pts*
1	Celtic	38	14	4	1	42	7	14	1	4	42	19	28	5	5	84	26	58	89
2	Rangers	38	18	0	1	50	10	9	5	5	34	23	27	5	6	84	33	51	86
3	Motherwell	38	9	4	6	30	26	9	2	8	20	20	18	6	14	50	46	4	60
4	Aberdeen	38	11	5	4	33	21	4	3	11	17	37	15	8	15	50	58	–8	53
5	Dundee U	38	9	6	4	26	14	5	4	10	27	33	14	10	14	53	47	6	52
6	Hibernian	38	10	5	4	34	22	4	5	10	15	23	14	10	14	49	45	4	52
7	Falkirk	38	8	6	5	21	16	5	4	10	24	33	13	10	15	45	49	–4	49
8	Hearts	38	8	4	7	27	26	5	5	9	20	29	13	9	16	47	55	–8	48
9	Inverness CT	38	9	2	8	32	28	4	2	13	19	34	13	4	21	51	62	–11	43
10	St Mirren	38	7	4	8	17	27	3	7	9	9	27	10	11	17	26	54	–28	41
11	Kilmarnock	38	7	5	7	26	23	3	5	11	13	29	10	10	18	39	52	–13	40
12	Gretna*	38	4	3	11	18	34	1	5	14	14	49	5	8	25	32	83	–51	13

** Gretna deducted 10 points.*

IRN-BRU SCOTTISH FOOTBALL LEAGUE FIRST DIVISION

			Home					*Away*					*Total*						
		P	*W*	*D*	*L*	*F*	*A*	*W*	*D*	*L*	*F*	*A*	*W*	*D*	*L*	*F*	*A*	*GD*	*Pts*
1	Hamilton A	36	14	4	0	29	3	9	3	6	33	24	23	7	6	62	27	35	76
2	Dundee	36	13	3	2	34	13	7	6	5	24	17	20	9	7	58	30	28	69
3	St Johnstone	36	10	7	1	38	21	5	6	7	22	24	15	13	8	60	45	15	58
4	Queen of the S	36	9	6	3	29	20	5	4	9	18	23	14	10	12	47	43	4	52
5	Dunfermline Ath	36	7	5	6	19	20	6	7	5	17	21	13	12	11	36	41	–5	51
6	Partick Th	36	7	8	3	23	15	4	4	10	17	24	11	12	13	40	39	1	45
7	Livingston	36	8	4	6	29	26	2	5	11	26	40	10	9	17	55	66	–11	39
8	Morton	36	4	5	9	22	29	5	5	8	18	29	9	10	17	40	58	–18	37
9	Clyde	36	5	3	10	22	32	4	7	7	18	27	9	10	17	40	59	–19	37
10	Stirling Alb	36	3	7	8	22	33	1	5	12	19	38	4	12	20	41	71	–30	24

IRN-BRU SCOTTISH FOOTBALL LEAGUE SECOND DIVISION

			Home					*Away*					*Total*						
		P	*W*	*D*	*L*	*F*	*A*	*W*	*D*	*L*	*F*	*A*	*W*	*D*	*L*	*F*	*A*	*GD*	*Pts*
1	Ross Co	36	11	4	3	45	23	11	3	4	33	21	22	7	7	78	44	34	73
2	Airdrie U	36	11	3	4	32	12	9	3	6	32	22	20	6	10	64	34	30	66
3	Raith R	36	8	3	7	28	27	11	0	7	32	23	19	3	14	60	50	10	60
4	Alloa Ath	36	12	1	5	32	27	4	7	7	25	29	16	8	12	57	56	1	56
5	Peterhead	36	10	2	6	37	25	6	5	7	28	29	16	7	13	65	54	11	55
6	Brechin C	36	7	7	4	35	23	6	6	6	28	25	13	13	10	63	48	15	52
7	Ayr U	36	6	2	10	26	32	7	5	6	25	30	13	7	16	51	62	–11	46
8	Queen's Park	36	6	3	9	23	26	7	2	9	25	25	13	5	18	48	51	–3	44
9	Cowdenbeath	36	5	4	9	20	33	5	3	10	27	40	10	7	19	47	73	–26	37
10	Berwick R	36	2	6	10	25	42	1	1	16	15	59	3	7	26	40	101	–61	16

IRN-BRU SCOTTISH FOOTBALL LEAGUE THIRD DIVISION

			Home					*Away*					*Total*						
		P	*W*	*D*	*L*	*F*	*A*	*W*	*D*	*L*	*F*	*A*	*W*	*D*	*L*	*F*	*A*	*GD*	*Pts*
1	East Fife	36	14	2	2	40	8	14	2	2	37	16	28	4	4	77	24	53	88
2	Stranraer	36	10	3	5	29	21	9	5	4	36	22	19	8	9	65	43	22	65
3	Montrose	36	9	3	6	31	22	8	5	5	28	14	17	8	11	59	36	23	59
4	Arbroath	36	6	7	5	24	20	8	3	7	30	27	14	10	12	54	47	7	52
5	Stenhousemuir	36	6	5	7	23	27	7	4	7	27	32	13	9	14	50	59	–9	48
6	Elgin C	36	9	2	7	35	33	4	6	8	21	35	13	8	15	56	68	–12	47
7	Albion R	36	4	7	7	29	35	5	3	10	22	33	9	10	17	51	68	–17	37
8	Dumbarton	36	7	5	6	17	19	2	5	11	14	29	9	10	17	31	48	–17	37
9	East Stirling	36	6	3	9	32	35	4	1	13	16	36	10	4	22	48	71	–23	34
10	Forfar Ath	36	6	3	9	20	26	2	6	10	15	36	8	9	19	35	62	–27	33

ABERDEEN Premier League

Year Formed: 1903. *Ground & Address:* Pittodrie Stadium, Pittodrie St, Aberdeen AB24 5QH. *Telephone:* 01224 650400. *Fax:* 01224 644173. *E-mail:* davidj@afc.co.uk. *Website:* www.afc.co.uk
Ground Capacity: all seated: 21,421. *Size of Pitch:* 115yd × 72yd.
Chairman: Stewart Milne. *Executive Director:* Duncan Fraser. *Director of Football:* Willie Miller. *Secretary:* David Johnston. *Operations Manager:* John Morgan.
Manager: Jimmy Calderwood. *Assistant Manager:* Jimmy Nicholl. *U-19 Manager:* Neil Cooper. *Physios:* David Wylie, John Sharp. *Reserve Team Coach:* Sandy Clark.
Previous Grounds: None.
Record Attendance: 45,061 v Hearts, Scottish Cup 4th rd, 13 Mar 1954.
Record Transfer Fee received: £1.75 million for Eoin Jess to Coventry City (February 1996).
Record Transfer Fee paid: £1m+ for Paul Bernard from Oldham Athletic (September 1995).
Record Victory: 13-0 v Peterhead, Scottish Cup, 9 Feb 1923.
Record Defeat: 0-8 v Celtic, Division 1, 30 Jan 1965.
Most Capped Player: Alex McLeish, 77 (Scotland).
Most League Appearances: 556: Willie Miller, 1973-90.
Most League Goals in Season (Individual): 38: Benny Yorston, Division I, 1929-30.
Most Goals Overall (Individual): 199: Joe Harper, 1969-72; 1976-81.

ABERDEEN 2007–08 LEAGUE RECORD

Match No.	Date	Venue	Opponents	Result		H/T Score	Lg. Pos.	Goalscorers	Attendance
1	Aug 4	A	Dundee U	L	0-1	0-0	—		12,496
2	12	H	Hearts	D	1-1	1-1	8	Nicholson [19]	13,134
3	19	H	Celtic	L	1-3	1-0	1	Brewster [24]	16,232
4	25	A	Hibernian	D	3-3	2-1	9	Brewster 2 [18, 37], Jamie Smith [57]	15,280
5	Sept 1	A	Kilmarnock	W	1-0	0-0	8	Miller [54]	5814
6	15	H	Motherwell	L	1-2	0-2	9	Jamie Smith [65]	10,154
7	23	A	Rangers	L	0-3	0-0	10		49,046
8	29	H	Gretna	W	2-0	2-0	8	Diamond [16], Jamie Smith [18]	10,279
9	Oct 7	H	St Mirren	W	4-0	1-0	8	Severin 2 (2 pens) [43, 71], Miller 2 [63, 88]	12,841
10	21	A	Inverness CT	W	2-1	1-0	6	Young [8], Tokely (og) [62]	6023
11	28	H	Falkirk	D	1-1	1-0	7	Severin (pen) [45]	10,399
12	Nov 3	H	Dundee U	W	2-0	1-0	5	Aluko [45], Miller [90]	11,964
13	11	A	Hearts	L	1-4	1-2	7	De Visscher [38]	17,122
14	24	A	Celtic	L	0-3	0-2	7		58,296
15	Dec 2	H	Hibernian	W	3-1	1-1	6	Miller [33], Clark [47], Young [86]	10,110
16	8	H	Kilmarnock	W	2-1	0-1	6	Nicholson (pen) [63], Miller [75]	10,207
17	15	A	Motherwell	L	0-3	0-3	6		5320
18	23	H	Rangers	D	1-1	1-1	6	Miller [45]	17,798
19	26	A	Gretna	D	1-1	0-0	6	Lovell [86]	1740
20	29	A	St Mirren	W	1-0	0-0	5	Lovell [85]	5025
21	Jan 2	H	Inverness CT	W	1-0	0-0	5	Nicholson (pen) [83]	13,372
22	5	A	Falkirk	D	0-0	0-0	4		5457
23	19	A	Dundee U	L	0-3	0-0	5		8579
24	26	H	Hearts	L	0-1	0-0	5		14,000
25	Feb 10	H	Celtic	L	1-5	0-3	5	Miller [62]	14,651
26	17	A	Hibernian	L	1-3	1-0	8	Diamond [18]	13,825
27	24	A	Kilmarnock	L	1-3	0-2	9	Mackie [86]	6113
28	27	H	Motherwell	D	1-1	1-0	—	Diamond [28]	8240
29	Mar 1	A	Rangers	L	1-3	1-1	8	Lovell [28]	50,066
30	15	H	Gretna	W	3-0	1-0	8	Maguire [40], Miller (pen) [71], Nicholson [73]	9025
31	22	H	St Mirren	D	1-1	1-1	8	Mair [29]	9779
32	29	A	Inverness CT	W	4-3	2-2	8	Aluko [7], Nicholson [45], Miller [53], Maguire [90]	5655
33	Apr 7	H	Falkirk	W	2-1	1-0	—	Maguire 2 [22, 82]	11,484
34	19	A	Celtic	L	0-1	0-0	6		55,766
35	26	H	Hibernian	W	2-1	0-0	6	Mackie [63], Miller (pen) [70]	8387
36	May 3	H	Dundee U	W	2-1	1-0	6	Foster [30], Touzani [48]	10,312
37	10	A	Motherwell	L	1-2	0-0	6	Aluko [67]	8574
38	22	H	Rangers	W	2-0	0-0	—	Miller [63], Mackie [77]	17,509

Final League Position: 4

Honours

League Champions: Division I 1954-55. Premier Division 1979-80, 1983-84, 1984-85; *Runners-up:* Division I 1910-11, 1936-37, 1955-56, 1970-71, 1971-72. Premier Division 1977-78, 1980-81, 1981-82, 1988-89, 1989-90, 1990-91, 1992-93, 1993-94.
Scottish Cup Winners: 1947, 1970, 1982, 1983, 1984, 1986, 1990; *Runners-up:* 1937, 1953, 1954, 1959, 1967, 1978, 1993, 2000.
League Cup Winners: 1955-56, 1976-77, 1985-86, 1989-90, (Coca-Cola cup) 1995-96; *Runners-up:* 1946-47, 1978-79, 1979-80, 1987-88, 1988-89, 1992-93, 1999-2000.
Drybrough Cup Winners: 1971, 1980.

European: *European Cup:* 12 matches (1980-81, 1984-85, 1985-86); *Cup Winners' Cup:* 39 matches (1967-68, 1970-71, 1978-79, 1982-83 winners, 1983-84 semi-finals, 1986-87, 1990-91, 1993-94); *UEFA Cup:* 56 matches (*Fairs Cup:* 1968-69. *UEFA Cup:* 1971-72, 1972-73, 1973-74, 1977-78, 1979-80, 1981-82, 1987-88, 1988-89, 1989-90, 1991-92, 1994-95, 1996-97, 2000-01, 2002-03, 2007-08).

Club colours: Shirt, Shorts, Stockings: Red.

Goalscorers: *League (50):* Miller 12 (2 pens), Nicholson 5 (2 pens), Maguire 4, Aluko 3, Brewster 3, Diamond 3, Lovell 3, Mackie 3, Severin 3 (3 pens), Jamie Smith 3, Young 2, Clark 1, De Visscher 1, Foster 1, Mair 1, Touzani 1, own goal 1.
Scottish Cup (12): Considine 3, Jamie Smith 3, De Visscher 2, Diamond 1, Lovell 1, Mackie 1, Nicholson 1.
CIS Cup (6): Nicholson 3 (2 pens), Considine 1, Miller 1, Young 1.

Soutar D 13	Hart M 18	Foster R 27 + 6	McNamara J 12 + 5	Considine A 21 + 1	Severin S 33 + 2	Smith Jamie 16 + 1	Nicholson B 38	Miller L 32 + 4	Mackie D 13 + 6	Clark C 17 + 1	Lovell S 7 + 15	De Visscher J 13 + 9	Mair L 15 + 3	Diamond Z 26	Brewster C 2 + 1	Maguire C 14 + 14	Touzani K 8 + 6	Young D 21 + 3	Langfield J 25	Byrne R 11 + 2	Aluko S 10 + 10	Smith D 1 + 2	Smith Jonathan — + 1	Duff S 6 + 4	Maybury A 13	Bus D 3 + 3	Walker J 3 + 5	Match No.
1	2	3	4^{3}	5	6	7	8	9	10^{1}	11^{2}	12	13	14															1
1	2	12	4		6	7	8		10	11^{3}	9^{2}		3^{1}	5	14	13												2
1	2	13	4	5	6	7^{2}	8	12	10	11				3^{3}	9^{1}		14											3
1	2	12	4	5	6^{3}	7	8	13	9	11				3^{1}	10^{2}			14										4
1	2	3	4	5		7	8	9	12	6	10^{2}						13	11^{1}										5
1	2	12	4^{1}		6	7	8	9^{3}	14	3	10			5		13		11^{2}										6
	2	3		5^{3}	6	7^{2}	8	9		11		13		4		10^{1}	14	12	1									7
	2			5	6	7	8	9	12	11^{2}		10^{1}	13	4				3	1									8
	2	3	14	5	6^{3}		8	9	10^{1}		12	7^{2}		4		13		11	1									9
		3	4		6^{1}		8	9	10^{2}		13	11^{3}	2	5			14	7	1	12								10
	2	3	4		6		8	9		11^{2}		7^{1}		5		14		10^{3}	1	13	12							11
	2		13	5			8	12				7	6			10^{3}	4^{2}	11	1	3	9^{1}	14						12
	2	3			6		8^{1}	9		12	14	11^{3}	4	5		10^{2}		7	1		13							13
	2				6	7^{2}	8	9^{3}		11^{1}	14	13	10	5		12			1	3	4							14
	2	3			12		8	9		11^{3}	13	14	4			10^{2}	7^{1}	6	1	5								15
	2	3			13		8	9		11	12		5			10^{2}		7	1	4	6^{1}							16
	2	12			6^{3}		8	9		11	10			5		14	4^{2}	7^{1}	1	3	13							17
	2	3		5^{1}	6^{2}	10	8	9		11^{3}			14	4		12	13		1	7								18
	2^{3}	3				10	8	9			12		7			13	4^{1}	6	1	5	11^{2}	14						19
		3			6	9	8	10		11	13		5					7^{2}	1	4	12	2^{1}						20
		3			6	7	8	9		11	12	13	2					4^{2}	1	5	10^{1}							21
		3			6	9	8	10^{3}		11	12	13	2^{2}	5				7^{1}	1	4			14					22
			12	5^{3}	6	9	8		13		10		2^{1}	4		14		7	1	3	11^{2}							23
		3	4	5	6^{2}	9^{3}	8	10			14	7		2		12		11^{1}	1					13				24
		12^{2}	4	14	6		8^{1}	9	10					5^{3}		13		11	1						2	3	7	25
					6		8	9			12	11^{2}	3^{3}	5		7^{1}			1		10			14	2	4	13	26
1		3			6		8	9^{3}	10			14	4	5		13					12			2	7^{2}		11^{1}	27
1		3		5	6		8	13	10^{1}		9^{2}	7		4		11^{3}					14				2		12	28
1		3		5	6		8	9			10	7		4		11^{1}					12				2			29
1		3	14	5	6^{3}		8	9			12	11		4		10^{1}	7^{2}				13				2			30
1		3	12	5	6		8	9	10				4^{2}			7^{1}					11				2^{3}	13	14	31
1		3	4	5	6		8	9	10^{2}							12					11			13	2	7^{1}		32
1		7	3^{1}	5	6		8	9	12			13		4		10^{3}					11			14	2^{2}			33
		10		5	6		8	9				7^{1}		4				11	1		12			3	2			34
		3		5	6^{3}		8	9	12					4		10^{1}	14	7^{2}	1					11	2		13	35
		3		5	6		8^{2}	9			14	7^{3}				10^{1}	4	11	1					2		13	12	36
		3		5^{1}	6		8	9	10^{3}							14	4		1		13			7	2	12	11^{2}	37
		3			6	12	8^{3}	9	10^{2}			13		5		7^{1}	4	14	1					11	2			38

AIRDRIE UNITED — First Division

Year Formed: 2002. *Ground & Address:* Shyberry Excelsior Stadium, Broomfield Park, Craigneuk Avenue, Airdrie ML6 8QZ. *Telephone:* (Stadium) 01236 622000. *Postal Address:* 60 St Enoch Square, Glasgow G1 4AG.
E-mail: enquiries@airdrieunitedfc.com. *Website:* www.airdrieunited.com
Ground Capacity: all seated: 10,000. *Size of Pitch:* 112yd × 76yd.
Chairman: James Ballantyne. *Secretary:* Ann Marie Ballantyne. *Commercial Manager:* Nicola Dickson (tel: 07956 632296; fax 01236 626002).
Manager: Kenny Black. *Management team:* Jimmy Boyle, Michael McLaughlin, John Donnelly.
Record Attendance: 5704 v Morton, Second Division, 15 May 2004.
Record Victory: 7-0 v Dundee, First Division, 11 March 2006.
Record Defeat: 1-6 v Morton, Second Division, 1 Nov 2003.
Most League Appearances: 101: Mark McGeown, 2002-05.
Most League Goals in Season (Individual): 18: Jerome Vareille, 2002-03.
Most Goals Overall (Individual): 28: Jerome Vareille, 2002-04.

AIRDRIE UNITED 2007–08 LEAGUE RECORD

Match No.	Date	Venue	Opponents	Result		H/T Score	Lg. Pos.	Goalscorers	Attendance
1	Aug 4	H	Raith R	L	0-1	0-1	—		1645
2	11	A	Alloa Ath	W	6-0	3-0	4	McKeown 2 (1 pen) 19 (p), 38, Noble 31, Russell 48, McDonald 51, Holmes 71	801
3	18	A	Berwick R	L	0-2	0-2	6		678
4	25	H	Queen's Park	W	1-0	0-0	4	Noble 53	1148
5	Sept 1	A	Ross Co	D	1-1	1-1	4	Noble 31	2094
6	15	H	Peterhead	D	1-1	0-1	4	Russell 55	936
7	22	H	Brechin C	W	2-1	0-0	3	Prunty 53, Waddell 75	872
8	29	A	Cowdenbeath	D	1-1	0-1	4	Noble 55	493
9	Oct 6	H	Ayr U	D	0-0	0-0	5		1269
10	20	A	Raith R	L	1-2	1-0	6	McKeown 21	1727
11	27	H	Berwick R	W	4-0	3-0	5	Russell 17, Noble 34, McKeown 2 (1 pen) 42 (p), 61	850
12	Nov 3	A	Queen's Park	W	1-0	1-0	4	Russell 38	1211
13	10	H	Ross Co	L	0-1	0-0	5		1062
14	Dec 1	A	Peterhead	W	1-0	1-0	4	Russell 36	685
15	8	H	Cowdenbeath	W	3-1	2-1	4	McDougall 18, Noble 36, Russell 79	823
16	15	A	Brechin C	L	2-4	1-1	4	Noble 33, Russell 50	434
17	26	H	Alloa Ath	W	2-0	1-0	4	Noble 5, McDonald 48	934
18	29	A	Berwick R	W	4-2	4-0	3	McKeown (pen) 2, Russell 2 15, 25, McDonald 26	672
19	Jan 2	H	Queen's Park	W	3-2	0-2	3	McDonald 47, Russell 57, McDougall 89	1244
20	5	H	Peterhead	W	2-0	0-0	3	Watt 2 80, 87	892
21	19	A	Ross Co	L	2-3	1-1	3	McDonald 1, Noble 58	2319
22	26	A	Alloa Ath	W	2-1	1-0	3	Russell 19, Prunty 61	769
23	Feb 2	H	Raith R	W	3-0	0-0	3	Smith 50, Prunty 68, Russell 75	1252
24	9	A	Cowdenbeath	W	1-0	0-0	2	Noble 60	475
25	16	H	Brechin C	L	1-2	0-0	2	Noble 87	997
26	27	A	Ayr U	D	1-1	1-0	—	McDonald 44	1098
27	Mar 1	A	Queen's Park	W	2-0	0-0	2	Russell 2 62, 80	913
28	5	H	Berwick R	W	3-0	2-0	—	Russell 3 10, 11, 62	611
29	15	A	Raith R	L	0-1	0-1	2		1458
30	19	H	Ayr U	L	0-2	0-0	—		737
31	22	A	Peterhead	W	4-1	2-0	2	Noble 32, Russell 33, Watt 2 48, 53	550
32	Apr 5	A	Brechin C	L	1-2	1-1	2	Noble 3	466
33	9	H	Ross Co	W	2-0	1-0	—	Noble 23, Russell 56	724
34	15	H	Cowdenbeath	W	4-0	2-0	—	Andreoni 20, Holmes 36, Prunty 60, Waddell 79	735
35	19	H	Alloa Ath	D	1-1	0-1	2	Prunty 59	928
36	26	A	Ayr U	W	2-1	1-1	2	Gillies 8, Andreoni (pen) 76	1328

Final League Position: 2

Honours
League Champions: Second Division 2003-04. *Runners-up:* Second Division 2007-08.
Bell's League Challenge Cup runners-up: 2003-04.

Club colours: Shirt: White with red diamond. Shorts: White with two red horizontal stripes. Stockings: White with red hoops.

Goalscorers: *League* (64): Russell 19, Noble 14, McDonald 6, McKeown 6 (3 pens), Prunty 5, Watt 4, Andreoni 2 (1 pen), Holmes 2, McDougall 2, Waddell 2, Gillies 1, Smith 1.
Play-offs (4): Russell 2, Donnelly 1, Prunty 1.
Scottish Cup (5): McDonald 1, McKeown 1, Noble 1, Russell 1, Watt 1.
CIS Cup (1): McKenna 1.
Challenge Cup (7): Russell 4 (1 pen), Noble 1, own goals 2.

Robertson S 34	Soutar W 1 + 1	Smyth M 28	Smith D 30 + 2	Lovering P 30	McDonald K 33	Sharp J 8	Russell A 32	McKeown S 15	Holmes G 17 + 2	Waddell R 29 + 3	McKenna S 29 + 1	Noble S 29 + 5	McDougall S 8 + 9	Watt K 2 + 21	Gillies D 1 + 15	Prunty B 17 + 15	Hollis L 2 + 1	Donnelly R 24 + 1	Brady C 1 + 3	Andreoni M 16 + 1	Campbell S 7 + 1	McMennamin C 1 + 1	Craig F 1	McCarry M 1	Byrne P — + 1	Match No.
1	2^{1}	3	4^{3}	5	6^{2}	7	8	9	10	11	12	13	14													1
1		3	4	5	6		8^{2}	9	10	11^{1}	2	7^{3}	12	14	13											2
1	14	3	4	5	6^{1}		8	9	10	11^{2}	2^{3}	7	12		13											3
1		3	4	5	6		8^{1}	9^{2}	10	11	2	7	13			12										4
1		3	4	5	6		8^{2}	9	10	11^{1}	2	7	12			13										5
1		3	4	5	6		8	9	10	11^{1}	2	7^{2}	13			12										6
1		3	4	5	6	7	8■		10	11	2	12				9^{1}										7
1		3■	4	5	6	7			10	11^{1}	2	8	12		13	9^{2}										8
1			4	5	6	7	3	9	10	11^{1}	2		12			8										9
1^{G}		3		5	6^{2}	7	8	9	10		2	12	13			11^{1}	15	4								10
1		3	4	5^{2}	6	7^{1}	8^{3}	9		11	2	10			14	13		12								11
1		3	4^{1}	5	6	7	8	9	12	11	2	10^{2}				13										12
1		3		5	6	7		9	10	11	2	4			12	8^{1}										13
1		3	13	5	6		8		10	11^{2}	2	4^{1}	7^{3}	14		12		9								14
1			4	5	6		8^{3}	10		11	2	9^{2}	7^{1}	14	13	12		3								15
1		3		5^{3}	6		8	9		11^{2}	2	10^{1}	7	14	13	12		4								16
1		3	4		6		8	9		11^{2}	2	10^{1}	7	13		12		5								17
1		3	4		6		8	9^{2}			2	10^{1}	11	12		7		5	13							18
1		5	3		11		9		10^{1}		2		7	12		8		4		6						19
1		5	7^{3}	3^{2}	4		9			13	2	12	11	14		10^{1}		6		8						20
1		5	12	3	4		9^{2}			11	2	10	7^{1}			13		6		8						21
1			7		6		9			3	4	11^{1}		12		10		5		8	2					22
1		5	7	3	4		9^{3}		13	11^{1}	2	10		14		12		6		8^{2}						23
1		2	6	5	3		10^{2}			8		11		13	12	9^{1}		4		7						24
1		5	7	3^{1}	4		9			11	2^{3}	10		13	14	8^{2}		6		12						25
1		4	6	5	3		10			9	2	11^{1}		13		12		8		7^{2}						26
1		5	7	3	4		9^{2}			11	2	10^{3}		14	13	12		6			8^{1}					27
1			7		4		9^{2}			3	2	10		11^{1}	13	12		5	14	6^{3}	8					28
1			7	3	4					11	6	10^{1}		12	13	9		5		8^{2}	2^{3}	14				29
1			7	3^{2}	4		9			11	6	10		13		12		5		8	2^{1}					30
1			7	3	4^{2}		9			11^{3}	2	10		12	13	8^{1}		5	14	6						31
1		5		3^{1}			9		10^{2}	11		8		13	12	7		4		6	2					32
1		5	2	3			9		10^{2}			11		12	13	8^{1}		4		6	7					33
		5	7	3^{1}	4		9		10	12		11^{3}		13		8	1	2		6^{2}	14					34
1		5	2	3^{2}	4		9^{1}		10	12		11		13		8		6		7						35
			2							9		12		6	11^{1}		1	4	5	7		8	3	10^{2}	13	36

ALBION ROVERS Third Division

Year Formed: 1882. *Ground & Address:* Cliftonhill Stadium, Main St, Coatbridge ML5 3RB. *Telephone/Fax:* 01236 606334.
Ground capacity: 1249 (seated 489). *Size of Pitch:* 110yd × 72yd.
Chairman and Secretary: Frank Meade ACMA. *General Manager:* John Reynolds. *Commercial Manager:* Patrick Rollink.
Manager: Paul Martin. *Assistant Manager:* Graham Diamond. *Physio:* Derek Kelly.
Club Nickname(s): The Wee Rovers. *Previous Grounds:* Cowheath Park, Meadow Park, Whifflet.
Record Attendance: 27,381 v Rangers, Scottish Cup 2nd rd, 8 Feb 1936.
Record Transfer Fee received: £40,000 from Motherwell for Bruce Cleland.
Record Transfer Fee paid: £7000 for Gerry McTeague to Stirling Albion, September 1989.
Record Victory: 12-0 v Airdriehill, Scottish Cup, 3 Sept 1887.
Record Defeat: 1-11 v Partick Th, League Cup, 11 Aug 1993.
Most Capped Player: Jock White, 1 (2), Scotland.
Most League Appearances: 399: Murdy Walls, 1921-36.
Most League Goals in Season (Individual): 41: Jim Renwick, Division II, 1932-33.
Most Goals Overall (Individual): 105: Bunty Weir, 1928-31.

ALBION ROVERS 2007–08 LEAGUE RECORD

Match No.	Date	Venue	Opponents	Result		H/T Score	Lg. Pos.	Goalscorers	Attendance
1	Aug 4	A	Montrose	W	1-0	0-0	—	Hunter [66]	415
2	11	H	Stranraer	W	3-2	2-1	2	Wright (pen) [4], Hunter [33], Donnelly (pen) [89]	306
3	18	H	Stenhousemuir	D	1-1	0-1	2	Wright [74]	339
4	25	A	Dumbarton	L	0-2	0-1	4		644
5	Sept 1	H	East Stirling	L	2-3	2-0	6	Wright 2 [6, 30]	488
6	15	A	Elgin C	L	2-3	1-0	8	Wright [37], Benton [48]	310
7	22	A	Arbroath	L	0-1	0-1	8		579
8	Oct 6	A	East Fife	L	0-4	0-1	9		639
9	9	H	Forfar Ath	W	2-1	0-1	—	Adam [49], Wright [72]	272
10	20	H	Montrose	L	1-3	0-1	9	McKenzie [56]	239
11	Nov 3	A	Stenhousemuir	W	1-0	0-0	8	Wright [89]	362
12	10	H	Dumbarton	W	2-0	1-0	5	Hunter [45], Walker P [49]	512
13	Dec 1	H	Elgin C	L	3-4	1-1	7	Hunter 2 [10, 63], Wright [77]	186
14	8	A	East Stirling	W	5-4	1-3	5	Gemmell 4 [34, 47, 63, 75], Chisholm [54]	239
15	15	H	Arbroath	W	5-2	2-2	5	Walker P 2 [10, 90], Wright (pen) [25], Watson [53], Hunter [84]	240
16	26	A	Stranraer	L	1-3	0-1	6	Wright [71]	322
17	29	H	East Fife	L	1-4	0-0	6	Gemmell [70]	472
18	Jan 2	A	Dumbarton	L	0-2	0-0	7		634
19	5	H	Stenhousemuir	D	3-3	1-1	7	McKenzie 2 [8, 90], Hunter [61]	282
20	19	H	East Stirling	D	2-2	1-2	6	Hunter [7], McKenzie [79]	296
21	Feb 2	A	Montrose	L	1-2	0-2	7	Donnelly [72]	430
22	9	H	Forfar Ath	D	0-0	0-0	7		232
23	16	A	Arbroath	W	4-1	1-0	7	Gemmell 3 (1 pen) [24, 58 (p), 85], Ferry [72]	503
24	23	A	Stenhousemuir	D	2-2	2-0	7	Walker P [4], Gemmell [37]	389
25	26	A	Forfar Ath	L	0-1	0-0	—		270
26	Mar 1	H	Dumbarton	L	0-1	0-0	7		329
27	5	A	Elgin C	D	1-1	0-1	—	Walker P [79]	301
28	8	A	East Fife	D	0-0	0-0	7		873
29	15	H	Montrose	L	0-3	0-1	7		279
30	18	H	Stranraer	D	1-1	1-1	—	Barr [1]	238
31	22	H	Elgin C	D	1-1	1-1	7	Gemmell (pen) [37]	212
32	29	A	East Stirling	L	0-3	0-0	7		262
33	Apr 5	H	Arbroath	L	0-2	0-0	7		264
34	12	A	Forfar Ath	W	4-1	2-0	7	Martin W 3 [5, 17, 56], Barr [48]	331
35	19	A	Stranraer	L	0-3	0-1	7		172
36	26	H	East Fife	D	2-2	0-0	7	Gemmell [61], Barr [68]	404

Final League Position: 7

Honours
League Champions: Division II 1933-34, Second Division 1988-89; *Runners-up:* Division II 1913-14, 1937-38, 1947-48.
Scottish Cup Runners-up: 1920.

Club colours: Shirt: Primrose yellow. Shorts: Red. Stockings: Red.

Goalscorers: *League* (51): Gemmell 11 (2 pens), Wright 10 (2 pens), Hunter 8, Walker P 5, McKenzie 4, Barr 3, Martin W 3, Donnelly 2 (1 pen), Adam 1, Benton 1, Chisholm 1, Ferry 1, Watson 1.
Scottish Cup (9): Hunter 4, Gemmell 2, Adams 1, Martin 1, Walker P 1.
CIS Cup (2): Chisholm 1, Hunter 1.
Challenge Cup (1): McKenzie 1.

Scott D 32	Watson G 15 + 9	Benton A 32	Smith B 7 + 5	Reid A 26 + 5	Donnelly C 23 + 2	Donald B 23	McKenzie J 23 + 2	Hunter R 14 + 3	Adam C 14	Walker P 25 + 6	Chisholm I 15 + 9	Friel S 2 + 2	McGeough J 2 + 3	Dimilta D 1 + 6	Wright K 19	Thompson L 1	McStay J 1 + 2	Walker R 22 + 2	McGowan M 18	Gemmell J 20 + 1	Martin A 4 + 8	Buckley R 20	Hughes C 10	Martin W 6 + 2	Ferry D 9	Barr R 9 + 1	McDougal J — + 4	Connell P — + 1	Mitchell T 3	Match No.
1	2	3	4	5	6	7	8^2	9	10	11^1	12	13																		1
1	2	3		5	6	7	8^3	9		12	11	14	4^2	13	10^1															2
		3		5	6		8	9^1		11	4	7	12		10	1	2													3
1	2	3	4	5	6	7				11^2	8^3	9^1	14	13	10			12												4
1	12	3	4		6	7^1	8			13	14		9^3	11	10^2			2	5											5
1	13	3	4	12	6	7^1	8^2		10^3		11		14		9			2	5											6
1	2^1	3	12	5^3	6		8	9	10	14	13				11^2			4	7											7
1	13	3		5	6■	7	8^2	9^1	10		14				11^3			2	4	12										8
1		3	12	5		7	8	9^1	10						11			2	4	6										9
1		3	11	5^2	6	7^1	8^3	9	10	14				13				2	4		12									10
1		3	13	5	12	7^1	8	9^3	10	11^2	14				6■			4	2											11
1		3	4	5	12	7	8^1	9^3	10	13	14							6	2	11^2										12
1		3	4	5			8^1	9	10	12	13			14	7^2			6		11		2^3								13
1		3					8	9^1	10	11	4			12	6			5		7		2								14
1	12	3		5	6^1			13	10	11	7				8^2			4		9		2								15
1	14	3		5		7^1	12	9	10	11	8^3				6		13	4				2^2								16
1	12	3		5		7^1		13	10	11^2	8				6			4		9		2								17
1	12	4		5		6		13	11	7^2	8				9			3		10		2^1								18
1	2	5		3		6	10	9		7	8				11			4												19
1		5		3		6	10	9		7	8			12				4		11		2^1								20
1		4		12	5	7	11			6	8^2				9			3^1		10			2	13						21
1				12	4	6^2	8^1			10	13				11				3	9		2	5		7					22
1	12	5		13	4	6^2				7^3					11^1				3	9	14	2	8		10					23
1	10	5			7	6				11								4	3■	9		2	8							24
1	10	5		4	3	6				7	11									9		2	8							25
1	12	5		13	4	6^1				7	11								3	9		2	8		10^2					26
1	8	5			6					11	10^1								3	9	12	2	4			7^2	13			27
1	7	4		8	3					11	12^2								5	10	9^3	2		14		6^1	13			28
1	8	5		6■	4		12			10									3		11^1	2		9^2		7	13			29
1		5			6		8			11								4	3	9	12	2		10		7^1				30
1		5		2	3		8			11								4		9	12			10^1	6	7				31
1	10^2	5■		3			8			11								4			12	2		9■	6	7^1		13		32
	6		12	5			8			11									3	9■	13	2	4^1		10	7^2			1	33
	10		12	5		6	8												3		11	2		9^1	4	7			1	34
	10			5	3	6											14	13			11^1	2^2	4	9	8	7^3	12		1	35
1	11	5		2	3		8^2			10^1								4		9	12		6		7	13				36

ALLOA ATHLETIC Second Division

Year Formed: 1878. *Ground & Address:* Recreation Park, Clackmannan Rd, Alloa FK10 1RY. *Telephone:* 01259 722695. *Fax:* 01259 210886. *E-mail:* fcadmin@alloaathletic.co.uk. *Website:* www.alloaathletic.co.uk
Ground Capacity: total: 3100, seated: 400. *Size of Pitch:* 110yd × 75yd.
Honorary President: George Ormiston. *Chairman:* Robert Hopkins. *Secretary:* Ewen G. Cameron.
Manager: Allan Maitland. *Assistant Manager:* James Ward. *Head of Youth Development:* Hugh McCann. *Sports Therapist:* Vanessa Smith. *Physios:* Vanessa Smith & Stuart Murphy.
Club Nickname(s): The Wasps. *Previous Grounds:* West End Public Park, Gabberston Park, Belleview Park.
Record Attendance: 13,000 v Dunfermline Athletic, Scottish Cup 3rd rd replay, 26 Feb 1939.
Record Transfer Fee received: £100,000 for Martin Cameron to Bristol Rovers.
Record Transfer Fee paid: £26,000 for Ross Hamilton from Stenhousemuir.
Record Victory: 9-0 v Selkirk, Scottish Cup First Round, 28 November 2005.
Record Defeat: 0-10 v Dundee, Division II, 8 Mar 1947 v Third Lanark, League Cup, 8 Aug 1953.
Most Capped Player: Jock Hepburn, 1, Scotland.
Most League Goals in Season (Individual): 49: 'Wee' Willie Crilley, Division II, 1921-22.

ALLOA ATHLETIC 2007–08 LEAGUE RECORD

Match No.	Date	Venue	Opponents	Result	H/T Score	Lg. Pos.	Goalscorers	Attendance
1	Aug 4	A	Peterhead	W 4-1	2-1	—	Brown 3 30, 32, 71, McKeown (pen) 57	808
2	11	H	Airdrie U	L 0-6	0-3	5		801
3	18	A	Raith R	L 1-2	0-0	7	Brown 85	1978
4	25	H	Brechin C	D 2-2	1-1	8	Ferguson B 2 42, 58	449
5	Sept 1	A	Ayr U	L 0-2	0-0	10		1237
6	15	H	Queen's Park	W 2-0	2-0	8	Ferguson A 11, Townsley 27	555
7	22	H	Cowdenbeath	W 3-2	1-1	6	Townsley 15, Wilson 50, Forrest 72	613
8	29	A	Ross Co	D 2-2	0-1	7	Andrew 66, Grant 74	2115
9	Oct 6	A	Berwick R	W 3-0	1-0	3	Grant 33, Andrew 49, Wilson 89	454
10	20	H	Peterhead	W 2-0	1-0	3	Coakley 44, Ferguson B 73	456
11	27	H	Raith R	W 2-1	1-0	3	Agnew 10, Ferguson B 64	1053
12	Nov 3	A	Brechin C	D 0-0	0-0	3		443
13	10	H	Ayr U	W 2-1	1-1	3	Wilson 3, Buist 61	711
14	Dec 1	A	Queen's Park	L 0-1	0-0	3		652
15	8	H	Ross Co	W 3-1	2-0	3	Brown 4, Agnew 21, Townsley 64	523
16	15	A	Cowdenbeath	W 4-1	2-0	3	Brown 3 22, 62, 69, Ferguson B 26	356
17	26	A	Airdrie U	L 0-2	0-1	3		934
18	29	A	Raith R	L 2-3	1-1	4	Ferguson A 14, McKeown (pen) 90	1896
19	Jan 2	H	Brechin C	L 0-4	0-3	4		655
20	5	H	Queen's Park	L 1-2	1-0	4	Ferguson A 22	534
21	12	H	Berwick R	W 2-1	1-0	—	Brown 38, Wilson 78	441
22	19	A	Ayr U	L 1-3	1-1	4	Keenan (og) 2	971
23	26	H	Airdrie U	L 1-2	0-1	4	Scott 77	769
24	Feb 9	A	Ross Co	L 1-6	0-3	6	Coakley 85	2272
25	16	H	Cowdenbeath	W 3-2	0-0	6	Andrew 49, Brown (pen) 83, Scott 89	542
26	23	H	Raith R	W 2-0	0-0	6	Coakley 49, Buist 66	712
27	26	A	Peterhead	D 2-2	1-1	—	McAulay 44, Ferguson B (pen) 62	590
28	Mar 1	A	Brechin C	D 0-0	0-0	5		451
29	8	A	Berwick R	W 2-1	1-0	—	Ferguson B 2 (1 pen) 2, 87 (p)	332
30	15	H	Peterhead	W 2-0	0-0	4	Grant 47, McAulay 48	445
31	22	A	Queen's Park	D 1-1	1-1	4	McAulay 26	549
32	29	H	Ayr U	L 1-2	0-1	4	Grant 88	493
33	Apr 5	A	Cowdenbeath	D 1-1	0-0	5	Brown 86	272
34	12	H	Ross Co	W 2-0	0-0	4	Ferguson A 2 86, 90	452
35	19	A	Airdrie U	D 1-1	1-0	4	McAulay 21	928
36	26	H	Berwick R	W 2-1	1-0	4	Agnew 11, Ferguson A 57	629

Final League Position: 4

Honours
League Champions: Division II 1921-22; Third Division 1997-98. *Runners-up:* Division II 1938-39. Second Division 1976-77, 1981-82, 1984-85, 1988-89, 1999-2000, 2001-02.
Bell's League Challenge Winners: 1999-2000; *Runners-up:* 2001-02.

Club colours: Shirt: Gold with black trim. Shorts: Black with gold stripe. Stockings: Gold with black hoop on top.

Goalscorers: *League* (57): Brown 11 (1 pen), Ferguson B 8 (2 pens), Ferguson A 6, Grant 4, McAulay 4, Wilson 4, Agnew 3, Andrew 3, Coakley 3, Townsley 3, Buist 2, McKeown 2 (2 pens), Scott 2, Forrest 1, own goal 1.
Play-offs (5): Coakley 1, Ferguson B 1, Forrest 1, Scott 1, own goal 1.
Scottish Cup (1): Coakley 1.
CIS Cup (1): Mackie 1.
Challenge Cup (0).

Jellema R 34	Clark R 14 + 1	Townsley C 31	McKeown S 25 + 4	Fleming D 22	Buist S 22 + 2	Grant J 26 + 3	Ferguson B 31 + 2	Brown G 18 + 5	Agnew S 27 + 3	Ferguson A 5 + 7	Creer A 2 + 1	Andrew J 16 + 12	Mackie C — + 5	Forrest F 26 + 1	Kelly F 1 + 6	Wilson D 25	Fairbairn B 2 + 10	McClune D 20 + 6	Coleman P — + 1	Ure M —	Hodge S 14 + 3	Coakley A 13 + 3	Scott A 9 + 8	Barker S — + 1	Kerr H — + 3	McLeod P 1	Hay J 1 + 2	McAulay K 11 + 1	Foster A — + 1	O'Neill M — + 1	*Match No.*
1^{G}	2	3	4	5	6	7	8	9^{2}	10^{1}	11	15	12	13																		1
	2^{2}	3	4	5	6	7^{3}	8	9	10^{1}		1	11	12	13	14																2
		3	4	5	6	7	8^{1}	13			1	9^{2}	12	2	10	11^{3}	14														3
1		3	4^{2}	5	6	7	8	9				10^{1}	12	2		11	13														4
1		3	4	5	6^{3}	7	8	9^{1}	10^{2}			12	13	2		11		14													5
1	2	3	4	5			8		10^{2}	11^{1}		9		6	12	7			13												6
1	2	3^{2}	4	5			8		10^{1}			9		6	14	7					13	11^{3}	12								7
1	2^{1}	3	4	5		12	8		10^{3}			9		6	13	7						11^{2}		14							8
1		3	4	5		7	8		10^{3}			9^{2}		2	14	6	12					11^{1}			13						9
1		3	4	5	12	7	8		10^{1}			9^{3}		2		6	14	13				11^{2}									10
1		3	4	5	6		8	14	10^{3}			9^{2}		2		7	12	13				11^{1}									11
1		3	4	5	6		8	12	10^{3}			11^{1}		2	14	7	9^{2}	13													12
1		3	4	5	6	12	8^{1}		10			9^{2}		2		7	11^{3}	13			14										13
1		3	4			7		9^{3}	10^{2}	14		12		2		8	13	6			5					11^{1}					14
1	2	3	4			7		8^{1}	9	13		10^{2}		6		11	12	5													15
1	2	3	4	5		7	8	9^{2}		12				6		11^{1}	13	10													16
1	2^{3}	3	4	5			8	9^{2}	10^{1}	13		14		6		7	12	11													17
1		3	4	5	6		8	9		11^{1}				7		2	12	10													18
1		4	6^{1}	3	2		8	11^{2}	10	9		13		5		7		12													19
1	2	4		3		6	10		13	9^{1}		11		5		7		8^{2}					12								20
1	2	4			5	6	11	9^{3}	10^{2}							7		8^{1}			3		14		13		12				21
1	2	3			4	7	11^{2}	10^{3}	13			9^{1}				6		8			5■				14		12				22
1	2^{2}	4	13	3	5	6	8	9	10							7						11^{1}	12								23
1	3		2		4	6	8	9^{3}	12							7					5	13	11^{2}				10^{1}	14			24
1	3	4			2	6		12	10■			11^{2}				7		8			5	9^{1}	13								25
1					3	6	8	9^{1}				13		5		7		2			4	12	10					11^{2}			26
1			13		3	6	8		10^{3}			12		5		7^{2}		2			4	9	14					11^{1}			27
1			13		5	7	8		11			12		4				2			3	10^{1}	6					9^{2}			28
1			6		3	12	8		10			13		5■				2			4	9^{3}	7^{1}					11^{2}	14		29
1	14	5	12		3	6	8^{1}		10			13						2			4	9^{3}	7					11^{2}			30
1		5	8^{1}		3	6	12		10			13						2			4	9^{2}	7					11^{3}		14	31
1		5			3	6	8		10■			12						2			4	9^{1}	7					11			32
1		2		5		7	6^{1}	12				10		4				8			3		9					11			33
1		4	8	3		6	14	9^{1}	10^{3}	13				5				2				12	7^{2}					11			34
1		4	7		14	6	8^{3}	9^{1}	10^{2}	12				5				2			3		13					11			35
1		4	7	3		8	6^{1}	9^{2}	10^{3}	13				5				2			14		12					11			36

ARBROATH Second Division

Year Formed: 1878. *Ground & Address:* Gayfield Park, Arbroath DD11 1QB. *Telephone:* 01241 872157. *Fax:* 01241 431125. *E-mail:* AFCwebmaster@arbroathfc.co.uk. *Website:* www.arbroathfc.co.uk
Ground Capacity: 8488. *Size of Pitch:* 115yd × 71yd.
President: John D. Christison. *Secretary:* Dr Gary Callon. *Administrator:* Mike Cargill.
Manager: John McGlashan. *Assistant Manager:* Robbie Raeside. *Physio:* Jim Crosby.
Club Nickname(s): The Red Lichties. *Previous Grounds:* None.
Record Attendance: 13,510 v Rangers, Scottish Cup 3rd rd, 23 Feb 1952.
Record Transfer Fee received: £120,000 for Paul Tosh to Dundee (Aug 1993).
Record Transfer Fee paid: £20,000 for Douglas Robb from Montrose (1981).
Record Victory: 36-0 v Bon Accord, Scottish Cup 1st rd, 12 Sept 1885.
Record Defeat: 1-9 v Celtic, League Cup 3rd rd, 25 Aug 1993.
Most Capped Player: Ned Doig, 2 (5), Scotland.
Most League Appearances: 445: Tom Cargill, 1966-81.
Most League Goals in Season (Individual): 45: Dave Easson, Division II, 1958-59.
Most Goals Overall (Individual): 120: Jimmy Jack, 1966-71.

ARBROATH 2007–08 LEAGUE RECORD

Match No.	Date	Venue	Opponents	Result	H/T Score	Lg. Pos.	Goalscorers	Attendance
1	Aug 4	A	Stenhousemuir	L 0-1	0-1	—		498
2	11	H	East Fife	L 2-3	1-2	8	Scott B [41], Watson [90]	768
3	18	H	Dumbarton	D 1-1	1-0	8	Scott B [25]	647
4	25	A	Montrose	D 3-3	1-1	9	Brazil [40], Tosh [49], Sellars [60]	1073
5	Sept 1	H	Elgin C	W 4-0	3-0	8	Watson [13], Sellars 2 (1 pen) [16, 41 (p)], Tosh [89]	525
6	15	A	Forfar Ath	W 3-1	2-0	6	Sellars (pen) [12], Tosh [16], Scott B [87]	615
7	22	H	Albion R	W 1-0	1-0	5	Scott B [42]	579
8	29	A	East Stirling	W 3-2	2-2	3	Raeside [21], Sellars [27], Tosh [88]	407
9	Oct 6	A	Stranraer	D 1-1	0-1	4	Scott [90]	320
10	20	H	Stenhousemuir	D 2-2	0-1	4	Tosh [54], Watson [78]	529
11	Nov 3	A	Dumbarton	D 1-1	1-1	4	Bishop [27]	637
12	10	H	Montrose	D 0-0	0-0	4		957
13	16	H	Stranraer	D 2-2	1-1	—	Rennie [1], Scott B [51]	528
14	Dec 1	H	Forfar Ath	L 3-4	2-1	4	Campbell [21], Webster [38], Hegarty (pen) [50]	621
15	8	A	Elgin C	W 3-1	1-1	4	Reilly [29], Webster [60], Watson [87]	422
16	15	A	Albion R	L 2-5	2-2	4	Sellars [36], Scott (og) [38]	240
17	26	A	East Fife	W 2-0	1-0	4	Ferguson [28], Scott B [74]	907
18	Jan 2	A	Montrose	L 0-5	0-4	4		1470
19	19	H	Elgin C	W 2-0	2-0	5	Watson [12], Sellars [31]	486
20	26	H	East Fife	L 0-1	0-1	5		872
21	Feb 2	A	Stenhousemuir	W 3-0	0-0	5	Watson [79], Brazil [81], Scott B [85]	426
22	9	A	East Stirling	W 1-0	1-0	5	Brazil [40]	368
23	16	H	Albion R	L 1-4	0-1	5	Raeside [63]	503
24	23	A	Dumbarton	L 1-2	1-1	5	Scott B [42]	511
25	27	H	East Stirling	W 2-0	0-0	—	Brazil (pen) [57], Scott B [72]	421
26	Mar 1	H	Montrose	W 2-1	2-0	4	Scott B [11], McBride [35]	959
27	5	H	Dumbarton	D 0-0	0-0	—		441
28	8	A	Stranraer	W 3-0	1-0	4	Raeside [17], Watson [57], Deasley [74]	269
29	11	A	Forfar Ath	L 0-1	0-1	—		566
30	15	H	Stenhousemuir	W 1-0	1-0	4	Brazil (pen) [45]	513
31	22	H	Forfar Ath	D 1-1	0-1	4	Smith [77]	723
32	29	A	Elgin C	L 1-2	0-1	4	Tosh [84]	624
33	Apr 5	A	Albion R	W 2-0	0-0	4	Sellars [73], McBride [87]	264
34	12	H	East Stirling	L 0-1	0-1	4		501
35	19	A	East Fife	L 1-2	1-0	4	Lunan [21]	1340
36	26	H	Stranraer	D 0-0	0-0	4		431

Final League Position: 4

Honours
League Runners-up: Division II 1934-35, 1958-59, 1967-68, 1971-72; Second Division 2000-01; Third Division 1997-98.
Scottish Cup: Quarter-finals 1993.

Club colours: Shirt: Maroon with white trim. Shorts: White. Stockings: Maroon.

Goalscorers: *League* (54): Scott B 11, Sellars 8 (2 pens), Watson 7, Tosh 6, Brazil 5 (2 pens), Raeside 3, McBride 2, Webster 2, Bishop 1, Campbell 1, Deasley 1, Ferguson 1, Hegarty 1 (pen), Lunan 1, Reilly 1, Rennie 1, Smith 1, own goal 1.
Play-offs (5): Raeside 2, Black 1, Sellars 1, Watson 1.
Scottish Cup (5): Scott B 2, Sellars 1, Watson 1, Webster 1.
CIS Cup (5): Brazil 2, Scott B 2, Sellars 1.
Challenge Cup (3): McKay 1, Reilly 1, Tosh 1.

Morrison S 4	McMullan K 29 + 3	Smith N 10 + 4	Webster K 9 + 8	Ferguson S 16 + 1	Raeside R 30	Bishop J 24 + 1	Tully C 23	Tosh P 19 + 12	Reilly A 13 + 13	Watson P 22 + 8	Scott B 19 + 9	Rennie S 10 + 3	Hegarty C 12	MacKay S 1 + 2	Wight C 15	Brazil A 27 + 4	Sellars B 24	Clark B 1 + 5	Campbell A 13 + 3	Black R 18	Fellows G 5	Scott D — + 4	Hill D 17	Masson T — + 3	Rattray A 13	Marvin P 1 + 1	McBride S 9 + 3	Lunan P 8	Deasley B 4 + 4	Pepper J — + 1	*Match No.*
1	2^{2}	3	4	5	6	7	8	9	10^{1}	11	12	13																			1
1		3^{3}	12	5	6^{2}	7	8	9	10	13	11	2	4^{1}	14																	2
	12	3	13	5^{1}	6	7	8^{3}	14	10^{2}		4■	2	11		1	9															3
	2	3^{1}	4		6	7		12	13	11		5	8■		1	9^{2}	10														4
	2	3		5	6	7^{1}	8	13		11^{3}	4^{2}	12			1	9	10	14													5
	2	13	12		6		8	9^{1}		11	3		4^{3}		1	10^{2}	7	14	5												6
	2	3			6		8	9^{1}		13	7		4		1	12	10	11^{2}	5												7
	2		4^{3}		6		8	13	14	11	7^{2}		3^{1}	12	1	9	10		5												8
	2		12		6		8	9^{1}	13	11^{2}	4■			3^{3}	1	7	10	14	5												9
1	2		4		6	7		12	14	11	8^{1}	13	3			9^{3}	10		5^{2}												10
	2		4^{1}		6	7		9	12	11	13	5			1	8^{2}	10			3											11
	2		13		6	7		9	10^{2}	11^{1}		3			1	4	8	12		5											12
	2		4		6	7		9^{2}		12	8	3	11^{1}		1	13				5	10										13
	2^{2}		4		6	7			13	11	8^{1}		3		1	9	10		5			12									14
	2		4^{2}	5	6	7			10	13	8^{1}	3	11		1		9					12									15
	11		4	5^{3}	6	7			10	12	8^{2}	2	3^{1}		1		9	14				13									16
	2■			5	6	7	8	9	10^{2}	11	12				1	4^{1}					3	13									17
			12	5	3^{2}	4	7	10	6	9^{3}	13		2^{1}		1	11			14		8										18
	2			3	4		6	12	8^{1}	11						9	10		5	7^{2}			1	13							19
	2^{3}		14	3	4		6	8	11^{1}		12					9^{2}	10			7			1		5	13					20
	2			3	4		6	8^{1}	13	11^{3}	12					9^{2}	10			7			1	14	5						21
	2			3	4		6	8		11^{1}	13					9^{2}	10			7			1		5		12				22
	2^{3}		14	3^{2}	4	12	6^{1}	8			13					9				7	10		1		5		11				23
				5	3	4■		13	14	12	8					10^{3}	11			7^{1}			1		2		9^{2}	6			24
	7	13		3			5	14			8^{3}					9^{2}	10		2^{1}				1		4		11	6	12		25
	2	6^{1}		12		5		13			8					9^{2}	10			3			1		4		11	7			26
	2^{3}	6^{1}				5		14		13	8					12				3	10		1		4		11	7	9^{2}		27
	2			3^{1}	4				12	11	14					9	10		13	6			1		5^{2}			7	8^{3}		28
	2^{3}				4		5	13	14	6^{2}	8					12	10			3			1				11	7	9^{1}		29
	2	12			4	5	6	9	3	11^{3}	8^{1}					7	10^{2}		13				1						14		30
	2^{1}	7			4	5	6	9		8						10				3			1	12			11				31
	2				4	5	6	13	8^{2}	12						9	10		7	3			1				11^{1}				32
	12	7				5	6	8^{3}	14	11^{2}						9	10		2	3			1		4^{1}		13				33
	2	13				5	6^{1}	8^{3}	14	10						9			7^{2}	3			1		4		12		11		34
	12				4	5			11	10		2^{1}				9^{2}			8	3			1		6			7	13		35
1						5	4	9^{3}	14		10^{1}	2							8^{2}						6	11	3	7	12	13	36

AYR UNITED Second Division

Year Formed: 1910. *Ground & Address:* Somerset Park, Tryfield Place, Ayr KA8 9NB. *Telephone:* 01292 263435.
E-mail: info@ayrunitedfc.co.uk. *Website:* ayrunitedfc.co.uk
Ground Capacity: 10,185, seated: 1549. *Size of Pitch:* 110yd × 72yd.
Chairman and Managing Director: Lachlan Cameron.
Manager: Brian Reid. *Assistant Manager:* Scott MacKenzie. *Physio:* Karen MacLellan.
Club Nickname(s): The Honest Men. *Previous Grounds:* None.
Record Attendance: 25,225 v Rangers, Division I, 13 Sept 1969.
Record Transfer Fee received: £300,000 for Steven Nicol to Liverpool (Oct 1981).
Record Transfer Fee paid: £90,000 for Mark Campbell from Stranraer (March 1999).
Record Victory: 11-1 v Dumbarton, League Cup, 13 Aug 1952.
Record Defeat: 0-9 in Division I v Rangers (1929); v Hearts (1931); B Division v Third Lanark (1954).
Most Capped Player: Jim Nisbet, 3, Scotland.
Most League Appearances: 459: John Murphy, 1963-78.
Most League League and Cup Goals in Season (Individual): 66: Jimmy Smith, 1927-28.
Most League and Cup Goals Overall (Individual): 213: Peter Price, 1955-61.

AYR UNITED 2007–08 LEAGUE RECORD

Match No.	Date	Venue	Opponents	Result		H/T Score	Lg. Pos.	Goalscorers	Attendance
1	Aug 4	A	Ross Co	L	0-2	0-1	—		2164
2	11	H	Queen's Park	L	2-3	1-1	10	McLaren 12, Moore 84	1262
3	18	A	Brechin C	D	2-2	1-1	10	Moore 8, Stevenson 77	419
4	25	H	Berwick R	W	4-0	3-0	6	Stevenson 23, Moore 2 39, 62, Williams 45	1142
5	Sept 1	H	Alloa Ath	W	2-0	0-0	5	Swift 75, Stevenson 86	1237
6	15	A	Cowdenbeath	D	1-1	1-0	5	Williams 40	462
7	22	A	Raith R	W	3-2	2-0	4	Williams 11, Robertson 19, Stevenson 59	1762
8	29	H	Peterhead	L	1-2	1-1	6	Williams 4	1345
9	Oct 6	A	Airdrie U	D	0-0	0-0	6		1269
10	20	H	Ross Co	L	1-4	0-4	7	Williams (pen) 77	1075
11	27	H	Brechin C	W	2-1	1-0	6	Stevenson 34, Swift 50	1181
12	Nov 3	A	Berwick R	D	1-1	1-0	6	Stevenson 7	473
13	10	A	Alloa Ath	L	1-2	1-1	7	Williams 33	711
14	Dec 1	H	Cowdenbeath	L	1-4	1-1	8	Williams 21	989
15	8	A	Peterhead	L	0-3	0-0	8		540
16	15	H	Raith R	L	0-3	0-2	8		1040
17	26	A	Queen's Park	D	1-1	1-0	9	Lowing 45	809
18	29	A	Brechin C	L	1-5	0-1	9	Stevenson 63	545
19	Jan 2	H	Berwick R	W	4-0	2-0	9	Henderson 4, Williams 2 31, 78, Stevenson 73	1059
20	5	A	Cowdenbeath	L	0-2	0-1	9		297
21	19	H	Alloa Ath	W	3-1	1-1	9	Williams 45, Wardlaw 80, Stevenson 90	971
22	26	H	Queen's Park	W	3-1	1-1	7	Williams 14, Stevenson 48, Anderson 85	1242
23	Feb 9	H	Peterhead	L	0-3	0-1	9		1102
24	16	A	Raith R	W	2-1	2-0	7	Williams 2 14, 39	1513
25	23	H	Brechin C	L	0-3	0-2	7		1102
26	27	H	Airdrie U	D	1-1	0-1	—	Forrest 67	1098
27	Mar 1	A	Berwick R	W	1-0	0-0	7	Stevenson 85	424
28	11	A	Ross Co	W	4-2	3-0	—	Wardlaw 30, Williams 31, Stevenson 2 45, 51	1627
29	15	H	Ross Co	L	0-2	0-0	7		1079
30	19	A	Airdrie U	W	2-0	0-0	—	McLeod 54, Stevenson 70	737
31	22	H	Cowdenbeath	D	1-1	0-0	7	Easton 90	1011
32	29	A	Alloa Ath	W	2-1	1-0	7	Wardlaw 2, Forrest 78	493
33	Apr 5	H	Raith R	L	0-1	0-0	7		1209
34	12	A	Peterhead	L	1-4	0-2	7	Lowing 72	661
35	19	A	Queen's Park	W	3-1	1-0	7	Stevenson 45, Williams 2 54, 84	1092
36	26	H	Airdrie U	L	1-2	1-1	7	Forrest 3	1328

Final League Position: 7

Honours
League Champions: Division II 1911-12, 1912-13, 1927-28, 1936-37, 1958-59, 1965-66. Second Division 1987-88, 1996-97;
Runners-up: Division II 1910-11, 1955-56, 1968-69.
Scottish Cup: Semi-finals 2002.
League Cup: Runners-up: 2001-02.
B&Q Cup Runners-up: 1990-91, 1991-92.

Club colours: Shirt: White with black trim. Shorts: Black. Stockings: White with black.

Goalscorers: *League* (51): Williams 16 (1 pen), Stevenson 15, Moore 4, Forrest 3, Wardlaw 3, Lowing 2, Swift 2, Anderson 1, Easton 1, Henderson 1, McLaren 1, McLeod 1, Robertson 1.
Scottish Cup (1): Williams 1.
CIS Cup (0).
Challenge Cup (6): Williams 3 (1 pen), Stevenson 2, Moore 1.

McGeown M 31 + 1	Swift S 13	Henderson M 30 + 1	Hamilton D 7 + 3	Lowing D 16 + 1	Forrest E 34	Stevenson R 33	Dunn D 14 + 4	McLaren A 3 + 5	Wardlaw G 16 + 12	Moore M 13 + 1	Robertson C 21 + 5	Casey M 7 + 5	Williams A 32 + 2	Higgins C 1	Vareille J 16 + 7	Pettigrew C 13 + 3	Weaver P 17 + 5	Corr B 5	Baldacchino R 4	Campbell M 12	Woodburn A 2 + 4	Marshall C 4 + 3	Keenan D 15	Anderson I 5 + 1	Stewart F — + 1	Easton W 8 + 3	McGowan N 16	McLeod P 6 + 7	Staunton M 2	Kinneard L — + 1	*Match No.*
1	2	3	4	5^{1}	6	7	8^{2}	9	10^{3}	11	12	13	14																		1
1	2	3	4^{3}	5^{2}	6	7	13	9■	12	10		8^{1}		11	14																2
1	2	3	4		6	7		9^{1}		10	11	8	12			5															3
1	2^{2}	3	4		6	7	8		12	10^{3}	11		9^{1}		13	5	14														4
1	2	3	4		6	7	8^{1}		13	10	11^{3}	14	9^{2}		12	5															5
	2	3	4		6	7	8		12	10^{1}	11		9			5		1													6
	2	3	12		6	7	8^{3}		13	10^{2}	11	14	9		4^{1}	5		1													7
	2	3	12		6	7	8		13	10	11		9■		4^{2}	5^{1}		1													8
	2	3	12	5	6	7	8^{2}		14	10	4	13	9^{3}		11^{1}			1													9
15	2		4^{1}	5	6	7	8			11	3	10^{2}	9		12		13	1^{6}													10
1	2			5	6	7^{2}	8			11	3	4	10		9^{1}	13	12														11
1	2			5	6	7	8^{1}			11	3	4	9		10		12														12
1	2^{1}	12		5	6	7				13	3	4	9^{2}		10		11		8												13
1		3		5	6	7	12		13	11^{2}	2	4■	9				8		10^{1}												14
1		3		5	6	7	12		10■		8^{1}		9			4	11^{2}			2	13										15
1		3		5	6	7	8^{3}				9	12			10	2	11^{2}			4^{1}	14	13									16
1		3		5■	6	7	12				9		11			2			10^{1}			8	4								17
1		3			6	7	8		13		4^{2}		11		14	5	12		10^{3}			9^{1}	2								18
1		4		5	2	6^{2}	9		13		3		11		12							8	7	10^{1}							19
1^{6}		4		5	2	6	9^{2}		13		3		11									7^{1}	8	10	15	12					20
1		4			2^{1}	7			10				11		9	12							8	6		5	3				21
1		3			2	7■			10^{1}				11		6^{2}	13							8	9		5	4	12			22
1		4		5	2■				10				11		6							12	7	8^{1}		9^{2}	3	13			23
1		5		3					9		12		10			7	6				13		8			11^{2}	4^{1}		2		24
1		4		9■					10		3		11			6^{1}	7					12	8				5	13	2^{2}		25
1		4			2	7			10		3■		11		6		9						8				5				26
1		5			2	6			9^{2}				10		7^{1}		11			4			8			12	3	13			27
1		4			2	6			9^{2}				10				7			5			8	12		11^{1}	3	13			28
1		3			2	6			10^{2}				11		13		7			4			8			9^{1}	5	12			29
1		4			2	6			9^{1}				10		7		11			5			8				3	12			30
1		3			2	6			13		14		11		9^{2}		8^{1}			4^{3}			7			12	5	10			31
1		4			2	6		13	11		12		10		7^{2}		8			5^{1}							3	9			32
1		3■			2	7		12	6				11		9^{1}		8			4							5	10			33
1				12	2	6		13	7^{3}		4^{2}		10			11	8			5	14						3^{1}	9			34
1					2	6		13	9^{2}		12		11^{1}				8			4	7^{3}					5	3	10		14	35
1		3			2	7		12					11				8			4	6					9^{1}	5	10			36

BERWICK RANGERS Third Division

Year Formed: 1881. *Ground & Address:* Shielfield Park, Tweedmouth, Berwick-upon-Tweed TD15 2EF. *Telephone:* 01289 307424. *Fax:* 01289 309424. *Email:* dennis@mccleary133.fsnet.co.uk. *Website:* berwickrangers.net
Ground Capacity: 4131, seated: 1366. *Size of Pitch:* 110yd × 70yd.
Chairman: Robert L. Wilson. *Vice-Chairman:* Moray McLaren. *Company Secretary:* Ross Hood. *Football Secretary:* Dennis McCleary. *Treasurer:* Lyndsay Flannigan.
Manager: Alan McGonigal. *Coach:* Ian Smith. *Physios:* Ian Smith, Ian Oliver. *Ground/Kit:* Ian Oliver.
Club Nickname(s): The Borderers, The Wee Gers. *Previous Grounds:* Bull Stob Close, Pier Field, Meadow Field, Union Park, Old Shielfield.
Record Attendance: 13,283 v Rangers, Scottish Cup 1st rd, 28 Jan 1967.
Record Victory: 8-1 v Forfar Ath, Division II, 25 Dec 1965; v Vale of Leithen, Scottish Cup, Dec 1966.
Record Defeat: 1-9 v Hamilton A, First Division, 9 Aug 1980.
Most League Appearances: 435: Eric Tait, 1970-87.
Most League Goals in Season (Individual): 33: Ken Bowron, Division II, 1963-64.
Most Goals Overall (Individual): 115: Eric Tait, 1970-87.

BERWICK RANGERS 2007–08 LEAGUE RECORD

Match No.	Date	Venue	Opponents	Result		H/T Score	Lg. Pos.	Goalscorers	Attendance
1	Aug 4	H	Cowdenbeath	D	1-1	1-0	—	Greenhill G [25]	778
2	11	A	Raith R	L	1-3	1-1	7	Little [30]	2020
3	18	H	Airdrie U	W	2-0	2-0	4	McLeish [7], Gemmill [28]	678
4	25	A	Ayr U	L	0-4	0-3	9		1142
5	Sept 1	A	Peterhead	L	3-4	1-2	9	Swanson [25], Gemmill 2 (1 pen) [69, 78 (p)]	462
6	15	H	Brechin C	D	3-3	2-0	10	Diack [20], McLeish [30], Greenhill D [67]	487
7	22	H	Ross Co	L	0-1	0-1	10		495
8	29	A	Queen's Park	L	0-1	0-0	10		537
9	Oct 6	H	Alloa Ath	L	0-3	0-1	12		454
10	20	A	Cowdenbeath	L	1-3	0-0	10	Diack [75]	319
11	27	A	Airdrie U	L	0-4	0-3	10		850
12	Nov 3	H	Ayr U	D	1-1	0-1	10	Diack [49]	473
13	10	H	Peterhead	L	1-2	1-1	10	Gemmill [11]	422
14	Dec 1	A	Brechin C	D	2-2	1-0	10	Little [36], Davison [65]	345
15	8	H	Queen's Park	D	1-1	0-1	10	Greenhill D [74]	455
16	15	A	Ross Co	L	1-2	0-0	10	Swanson [65]	2027
17	26	H	Raith R	W	2-1	1-1	10	Diack [20], Little [56]	570
18	29	H	Airdrie U	L	2-4	0-4	10	Swanson (pen) [56], Diack [66]	672
19	Jan 2	A	Ayr U	L	0-4	0-2	10		1059
20	5	H	Brechin C	D	2-2	0-1	10	Diack 2 [85, 89]	421
21	12	A	Alloa Ath	L	1-2	0-1	—	Anderson [89]	441
22	19	A	Peterhead	L	2-9	1-5	10	Diack 2 [14, 88]	590
23	26	A	Raith R	L	0-3	0-1	10		1466
24	Feb 9	A	Queen's Park	L	1-3	0-1	10	Little [47]	511
25	16	H	Ross Co	L	0-4	0-3	10		449
26	Mar 1	H	Ayr U	L	0-1	0-0	10		424
27	5	A	Airdrie U	L	0-3	0-2	—		611
28	8	H	Alloa Ath	L	1-2	0-1	—	Tolmie [54]	332
29	11	H	Cowdenbeath	L	4-5	2-3	—	Little 2 [32, 45], Greenhill D [70], Fairbairn [72]	259
30	15	A	Cowdenbeath	W	2-1	1-1	10	Gemmill 2 [30, 63]	284
31	22	A	Brechin C	L	0-5	0-2	10		424
32	29	H	Peterhead	D	2-2	0-0	10	Little [52], McLaren (pen) [86]	377
33	Apr 5	A	Ross Co	L	0-4	0-2	10		2579
34	15	H	Queen's Park	L	1-4	1-3	—	Ayre [39]	325
35	19	H	Raith R	L	2-5	2-1	10	McLaren [12], Gemmill [27]	545
36	26	A	Alloa Ath	L	1-2	0-1	10	Thomson [54]	629

Final League Position: 10

Honours
League Champions: Second Division 1978-79. Third Division 2006-07; *Runners-up:* Second Division 1993-94. Third Division 1999-2000.
Scottish Cup: Quarter-finals 1953-54, 1979-80.
League Cup: Semi-finals 1963-64.
Bell's League Challenge: Quarter-finals 2004-05.

Club colours: Shirt: Black with broad gold vertical stripes. Shorts: black with white trim. Stockings: Black with gold tops.

Goalscorers: *League* (40): Diack 9, Gemmill 7 (1 pen), Little 7, Greenhill D 3, Swanson 3 (1 pen), McLaren 2 (1 pen), McLeish 2, Anderson 1, Ayre 1, Davison 1, Fairbairn 1, Greenhill G 1, Thomson 1, Tolmie 1.
Scottish Cup (0).
CIS Cup (5): Bolochoweckyj 1, Diack 1, Gemmill 1 (pen), Wood 1, own goal 1.
Challenge Cup (2): Swanson 1, Thomson 1.

O'Connor G 18	Manson R 9 + 2	Bolochoweckyj M 12 + 4	Thomson I 30 + 3	Horn R 19 + 3	McGroarty C 12	Fraser S 14 + 2	Greenhill G 2 + 1	Diack I 22	Wood G 11 + 4	Little I 25 + 1	Greenhill D 22 + 10	Gemmill S 21 + 6	Swanson D 11 + 3	Lennox T 11 + 4	McLeish K 21 + 4	Noble S 5 + 2	Smith J 15	McMullan P 20 + 3	Stevenson M — + 12	Davison K 5	Staunton M 3	Flockhart C 9 + 1	Murdoch S 4	Fairbairn B 13	McLean A 2 + 2	Coult L 1 + 6	Anderson C — + 1	Henderson R 1	Logan P 8	Ayre K 9	Howat A 8 + 3	McNicoll G 6 + 1	Tolmie B 12	Callaghan S 10	McGlynn G 1	McLaren F 4 + 1	*Match No.*
1	2	3	4	5	6	7	8[1]	9[2]	10	11	12	13																									1
1	2	3	12	5	6	7	8[1]	9[2]	10	11		4[3]	14	13																							2
1		3	4	5	6	7	12	9[2]	13	11[3]		10		2	8[1]	14																					3
1		3	4	5	6	7		9	12	11[1]		10[2]	13	2	8																						4
1		3	13	5[3]	6[1]	7[2]		9	10	11■	14	12	8		2		4																				5
1		3	4	5[1]		7		9	10		12	11[3]	8	2	6[2]			13	14																		6
1	13	3[2]	4			7		9[1]	10	11	12	6[3]	8	2	5				14																		7
1	2	3	12		6	7[1]		9		11[2]	13	10[3]	8		4		5		14																		8
1	2[1]	13	4		6			9[2]	10		7	12	11	3			5	8[3]	14																		9
1			4	5	6	7		9			8[1]	13	11[2]	2	12	10[3]	3		14																		10
1		12		5[1]		7[2]		9		11[3]	13	10	8	2	4	6	3	14																			11
1		3	4					9[1]		11	13	10	8[2]	2	6		7	5	12																		12
1		3[1]	4			12		9		11		10	8■	2	6		7	5																			13
1			4	5		7		9	10	11	8						6	3		2																	14
1			4	5		7[1]		8	9[2]	10	11				12	13	3	6		2																	15
1			4	5		7			10	11	9		8	2				3		6																	16
1		3	4					9[2]	10[1]	11	8		2		12	5		7	13	6																	17
1		3	4			12		9		11[3]	8	14	13			5	6[1]	10		7[2]	2																18
		12[2]	6			5[1]		9		7	8	10			13	11[3]		3	14		4	1	2														19
			4					9		8	11	10[1]			2		5	3[2]				1	6	7	13	12											20
								9		8	11				2		5				4	1	6	7	3	10[1]	12										21
				13[3]	3			9			11	10[1]			8		5		12			1	6	7	2[2]	14		4■									22
			6	4[1]	3			10			11[2]				2		5							7■	13				1	8	9	12					23
			6	3	5[2]					10	12				7		4	13											1	8	11		2[1]	9			24
	2	13	6	4	11				5	9	12							3											1	8[1]	10[2]			7			25
	2		6							9	7	12[2]						3								13			1	8	10[1]	4	5	11			26
	2		6							9[2]	8	10[1]						3						7		12			1		13	4	5	11			27
			6							12	11[2]	10			2[3]				14			13		7					1■	8	9[1]	4	5	3			28
	12		6							9	8	10			2[1]			3						7								4	5	11	1		29
	2		8	12						10	7	11[2]						5						6[1]					1		13	3	4	9			30
	2[3]		7	12							8	11		14	9			5	13			1		6							10[2]	3[1]	4				31
			6	4						9	11	10[1]			2			3				1		7						8			5			12	32
			6	4					14		11[2]	10[1]		13	2			3■				1		7		12				8			5			9[3]	33
			6	4					12		11			14	2							1		7		13				8	10[2]		5[1]	3[3]		9	34
			6	4							12	10[2]			2			3				1		7						8	13		5[1]	11		9	35
			8	4							6	10		2				3	12										1		7[1]		5	11		9	36

BRECHIN CITY — Second Division

Year Formed: 1906. *Ground & Address:* Glebe Park, Trinity Rd, Brechin, Angus DD9 6BJ. *Telephone:* 01356 622856.
Fax (to Secretary): 01356 625524. *Website:* www.brechincity.com
Ground Capacity: total: 3960, seated: 1519. *Size of Pitch:* 110yd × 67yd.
Chairman: David Birse. *Vice-Chairman:* Hugh Campbell Adamson. *Secretary:* Ken Ferguson.
Manager: Michael O'Neill. *Physio:* Tom Gilmartin.
Club Nickname(s): The City. *Previous Grounds:* Nursery Park.
Record Attendance: 8122 v Aberdeen, Scottish Cup 3rd rd, 3 Feb 1973.
Record Transfer Fee received: £100,000 for Scott Thomson to Aberdeen (1991) and Chris Templeman to Morton (2004).
Record Transfer Fee paid: £16,000 for Sandy Ross from Berwick Rangers (1991).
Record Victory: 12-1 v Thornhill, Scottish Cup 1st rd, 28 Jan 1926.
Record Defeat: 0-10 v Airdrieonians, Albion R and Cowdenbeath, all in Division II, 1937-38.
Most League Appearances: 459: David Watt, 1975-89.
Most League Goals in Season (Individual): 26: Ronald McIntosh, Division II, 1959-60.
Most Goals Overall (Individual): 131: Ian Campbell, 1977-85.

BRECHIN CITY 2007–08 LEAGUE RECORD

Match No.	Date	Venue	Opponents	Result	H/T Score	Lg. Pos.	Goalscorers	Attendance
1	Aug 4	A	Queen's Park	L 0-3	0-1	—		768
2	11	H	Peterhead	D 2-2	2-0	9	Russell 9, Smith D 36	448
3	18	H	Ayr U	D 2-2	1-1	9	Johnston 33, Russell 86	419
4	25	A	Alloa Ath	D 2-2	1-1	10	Russell 2 9, 46	449
5	Sept 1	H	Cowdenbeath	D 1-1	0-1	8	King 90	448
6	15	A	Berwick R	D 3-3	0-2	9	Geddes 49, Smith D 52, Callaghan S (pen) 59	487
7	22	A	Airdrie U	L 1-2	0-0	9	Murie (pen) 81	872
8	29	H	Raith R	L 0-1	0-1	9		669
9	Oct 6	A	Ross Co	L 1-2	0-0	9	Gribben 66	2022
10	20	H	Queen's Park	W 2-1	2-0	9	Gribben 7, Johnston 9	511
11	27	A	Ayr U	L 1-2	0-1	9	King 82	1181
12	Nov 3	H	Alloa Ath	D 0-0	0-0	9		443
13	10	A	Cowdenbeath	L 0-1	0-0	9		363
14	Dec 1	H	Berwick R	D 2-2	0-1	9	King 60, Callaghan S (pen) 72	345
15	8	A	Raith R	D 1-1	1-0	9	Smith D 40	1475
16	15	H	Airdrie U	W 4-2	1-1	9	White 21, Callaghan S 66, Smith C 68, King 80	434
17	26	A	Peterhead	W 2-1	1-1	8	Smith C 43, Kula (og) 59	720
18	29	H	Ayr U	W 5-1	1-0	7	Fusco 2, Walker S 50, Smith C 66, Byers 67, Callaghan S (pen) 70	545
19	Jan 2	A	Alloa Ath	W 4-0	3-0	6	King 15, Byers 2 29, 87, Smith C 33	655
20	5	A	Berwick R	D 2-2	1-0	7	King 26, Smith C 66	421
21	19	H	Cowdenbeath	L 0-1	0-1	8		432
22	26	H	Peterhead	W 3-1	2-0	6	Paton 10, King 2 36, 58	501
23	Feb 2	A	Queen's Park	W 3-2	0-2	6	Diack 57, Walker S 71, Smith D 75	491
24	9	H	Raith R	W 3-2	2-1	5	Byers 1, Diack 2 2, 68	656
25	16	A	Airdrie U	W 2-1	0-0	5	Smith D 57, King 79	997
26	23	A	Ayr U	W 3-0	2-0	5	Weaver (og) 11, Paton 19, Walker N 90	1102
27	26	H	Ross Co	L 1-2	1-1	—	Paton 34	561
28	Mar 1	H	Alloa Ath	D 0-0	0-0	6		451
29	15	H	Queen's Park	L 0-1	0-1	6		465
30	18	A	Ross Co	D 0-0	0-0	—		1648
31	22	H	Berwick R	W 5-0	2-0	6	Smith D 24, Nelson A 27, Ward 47, King 66, Smith C 83	424
32	29	A	Cowdenbeath	W 2-0	0-0	5	Smith D 82, Nelson A 85	259
33	Apr 5	H	Airdrie U	W 2-1	1-1	4	Paton 8, Walker N 87	466
34	12	A	Raith R	D 1-1	1-0	5	Diack 12	1995
35	19	A	Peterhead	L 0-2	0-1	6		926
36	26	H	Ross Co	D 3-3	1-1	6	Smith D 40, Janczyk 51, Dyer 60	586

Final League Position: 6

Honours
League Champions: C Division 1953-54. Second Division 1982-83, 1989-90, 2004-05. Third Division 2001-02. *Runners-up:* Second Division 1992-93, 2002-03. Third Division 1995-96. Second Division 2004-05.
Bell's League Challenge: Runners-up 2002-03. Semi-finals 2001-02.

Club colours: Shirt, Shorts, Stockings: Red with white trimmings.

Goalscorers: *League* (63): King 10, Smith D 8, Smith C 6, Byers 4, Callaghan S 4 (3 pens), Diack 4, Paton 4, Russell 4, Gribben 2, Johnston 2, Nelson A 2, Walker N 2, Walker S 2, Dyer 1, Fusco 1, Geddes 1, Janczyk 1, Murie 1 (pen), Ward 1, White 1, own goals 2.
Scottish Cup (5): Byers 2, King 2, Callaghan 1 (pen).
CIS Cup (0).
Challenge Cup (7): Johnson 2, Russell 2 (1 pen), Janczyk 1, Nelson A 1, Smith 1.

Nelson C 35	Murie D 22	McNicholl G 1	Byers K 29 + 2	Walker S 26 + 2	Nelson A 20 + 3	Hughes C 3	Janczyk N 18 + 4	Johnston M 12 + 3	Russell I 4	Smith D 35	King C 32 + 4	McCluskey C 1 + 1	Callaghan B 1 + 1	Walker R 16 + 10	White D 28 + 1	Callaghan S 17 + 1	Geddes C 4 + 7	Fusco G 14 + 4	Smith C 9 + 12	Dyer W 23 + 2	Gribben D 6 + 2	Rusin L — + 1	Ward J 13 + 1	Paton M 15 + 1	Diack I 10 + 3	Walker N 2 + 11	*Match No.*
1■	2	3^{6}	4	5	6	7^{2}	8^{1}	9	10	11	13	15	12														1
	2^{2}		14	5	6		8^{3}	9	10	11	12	1	7^{1}	13	3	4											2
1			4	5	6^{2}		8	9	10	11^{1}	12			2	3	7	13										3
1	2		4	5	6^{2}		8^{1}	9	10	11	12				3	7	13										4
1	2		4^{2}	5	12		8^{1}	9		11	7				3	6	10^{3}	13	14								5
1	2			5	6		8^{1}	9		11	7				3	4	10^{2}	13	12								6
1	2			5	6		8^{2}	9		11^{1}	7			12	3	10	13			4							7
1			4^{1}	5		7		13		11	8^{2}			12	3	6	9		10	2							8
1				5		2	13	12		10	11			8^{2}	4	7^{3}	9^{1}		14	6	3						9
1	2		4	5	12			9		11^{1}	8			13	6	7^{2}	14			3	10^{3}						10
1	2^{2}		4^{1}	5			8	9		11	7			12	6		13			3	10						11
1	2		4	5			8^{1}	9		11	7^{2}				6	12	13			3	10						12
1	2		4	5	6^{1}			9		11	7				8		12^{2}			3	10	13					13
1	2		12		6^{3}			9■		11	7			13	5	3		8	14	4^{2}	10^{1}						14
1	2^{1}		4		6			13		11	10			5	7	3		8	9^{2}	12							15
1	2		4		6					11	10			3	5	8		7	9^{1}		12						16
1	2		4	12	6					11	10			3	8	5		7	9^{1}								17
1	2		4	5^{3}	6		13			11^{1}	10^{2}				3	8		7	9		12		14				18
1	2		8	5	6					11	10				4	3		7	9								19
1	2		8	5	6					11	10				4	3		7	9								20
1	2^{3}		6	4	7^{2}					9	11			14	3	5^{1}		8	10	12				13			21
1	2^{1}		6				8			9	11			12	4			7		5			3	10			22
1			6	13			7			11	9			2	4			8^{1}		5			3^{2}	10^{3}	12	14	23
1			7				6			11	10			2	5				13	3			4	8^{2}	9^{1}	12	24
1	2		7				6			11	10				5				12	3			4	8	9^{1}		25
1	2		6^{3}				8			9	11			14	4				12	5			3	7^{2}	10^{1}	13	26
1	2^{1}		6	3			7^{2}			9	8			12	4				13	5^{3}				10	11	14	27
1			6	3			7^{1}			9	8			2	4			12		5				10	11^{2}	13	28
1				4	14		7^{1}			9	11^{2}			2				8^{3}	13	5			3	10	12	6	29
1			8	5	6					11	7			2						3			4	10^{1}	9	12	30
1			6	4	7		12			9	8^{1}			2					13	5			3	11^{3}	10^{2}	14	31
1				4	7					9	8			2				13	11^{2}	5			3	10^{1}	12	6	32
1			7	5						11^{1}	10			2				6		3			4	8	9	12	33
1			7	5	11		13				10			2				6^{2}	14	3			4	8^{3}	9^{1}	12	34
1			7	5	6■					11	10			2^{2}	12					3^{1}			4	8	9	13	35
1			6				8			9	11^{1}			2	4			7	12	5			3	10^{2}		13	36

CELTIC — Premier League

Year Formed: 1888. *Ground & Address:* Celtic Park, Glasgow G40 3RE. *Telephone:* 0871 226 1888. *Fax:* 0141 551 8106. *E-mail:* customerservices@celticfc.co.uk. *Website:* www.celticfc.net
Ground Capacity: all seated: 60,355. *Size of Pitch:* 105m × 68m.
Chairman: Rt Hon Dr John Reid, MP. *Chief Executive:* Peter Lawwell. *Commercial Manager:* Adrian Filby. *Secretary:* Robert Howat.
Manager: Gordon Strachan. *Assistant Manager:* Garry Pendrey. *Head Youth Coach:* Willie McStay. *Physio:* Tim Williamson. *Club Doctor:* Derek McCormack. *Kit Manager:* John Clark.
Club Nickname(s): The Bhoys. *Previous Grounds:* None.
Record Attendance: 92,000 v Rangers, Division I, 1 Jan 1938.
Record Transfer Fee received: £4,700,000 for Paolo Di Canio to Sheffield W (August 1997).
Record Transfer Fee paid: £6,000,000 for Chris Sutton from Chelsea (July 2000).
Record Victory: 11-0 Dundee, Division I, 26 Oct 1895.
Record Defeat: 0-8 v Motherwell, Division I, 30 Apr 1937.
Most Capped Player: Pat Bonner 80, Republic of Ireland.
Most League Appearances: 486: Billy McNeill, 1957-75.
Most League Goals in Season (Individual): 50: James McGrory, Division I, 1935-36.
Most Goals Overall (Individual): 397: James McGrory, 1922-39.

Honours
League Champions: (42 times) Division I 1892-93, 1893-94, 1895-96, 1897-98, 1904-05, 1905-06, 1906-07, 1907-08, 1908-09, 1909-10, 1913-14, 1914-15, 1915-16, 1916-17, 1918-19, 1921-22, 1925-26, 1935-36, 1937-38, 1953-54, 1965-66, 1966-67, 1967-68, 1968-69, 1969-70, 1970-71, 1971-72, 1972-73, 1973-74. Premier Division 1976-77, 1978-79, 1980-81, 1981-82,

CELTIC 2007–08 LEAGUE RECORD

Match No.	Date	Venue	Opponents	Result	H/T Score	Lg. Pos.	Goalscorers	Attendance
1	Aug 5	H	Kilmarnock	D 0-0	0-0	—		50,591
2	11	A	Falkirk	W 4-1	1-1	4	Milne (og) 30, Miller 76, Nakamura 79, Vennegoor 81	6329
3	19	A	Aberdeen	W 3-1	0-1	2	Donati 61, Miller 2 85, 90	16,232
4	25	H	Hearts	W 5-0	2-0	2	Nakamura 2 9, 79, Donati 22, Brown S 61, Vennegoor (pen) 63	57,042
5	Sept 2	A	St Mirren	W 5-1	2-0	2	Brown S 22, NcDonald 25, Vennegoor 53, Miranda (og) 56, McManus 74	7519
6	15	H	Inverness CT	W 5-0	2-0	1	Vennegoor 2 15, 59, Donati 41, Nakamura 56, McGuire (og) 70	56,020
7	23	A	Hibernian	L 2-3	1-2	2	McGeady 26, Caldwell 66	16,125
8	29	H	Dundee U	W 3-0	1-0	1	McDonald 3 7, 67, 72	57,006
9	Oct 7	A	Gretna	W 2-1	0-1	1	Killen 86, McDonald 90	6011
10	20	A	Rangers	L 0-3	0-1	1		50,428
11	27	H	Motherwell	W 3-0	1-0	1	McDonald 3 (1 pen) 42, 59, 88 (p)	57,633
12	Nov 3	A	Kilmarnock	W 2-1	2-0	1	McDonald 2 34, 36	8260
13	24	H	Aberdeen	W 3-0	2-0	1	Vennegoor 14, McGeady 27, McDonald 49	58,296
14	Dec 1	A	Hearts	D 1-1	0-0	1	McDonald 73	16,454
15	8	H	St Mirren	D 1-1	0-0	1	Riordan 85	56,088
16	11	H	Falkirk	W 4-0	2-0	—	McDonald (pen) 9, McGeady 3 41, 67, 82	54,411
17	16	A	Inverness CT	L 2-3	2-1	1	Vennegoor 2 24, 26	7004
18	22	H	Hibernian	D 1-1	0-1	1	Jarosik 78	57,465
19	26	A	Dundee U	W 2-0	0-0	1	Vennegoor 68, McManus 74	12,357
20	29	H	Gretna	W 3-0	1-0	1	McDonald 35, Brown S 49, McGuffie (og) 89	57,250
21	Jan 19	H	Kilmarnock	W 1-0	0-0	2	Corrigan (og) 64	56,618
22	27	A	Falkirk	W 1-0	1-0	2	McDonald 45	6803
23	Feb 10	A	Aberdeen	W 5-1	3-0	2	Nakamura 17, McGeady 34, McDonald 2 (1 pen) 44 (p), 48, Robson 74	14,651
24	16	H	Hearts	W 3-0	1-0	2	Vennegoor 14, McDonald 51, Hinkel 76	56,738
25	24	A	St Mirren	W 1-0	0-0	2	Nakamura 87	7213
26	27	H	Inverness CT	W 2-1	1-0	—	McDonald 45, Samaras 61	56,787
27	Mar 1	A	Hibernian	W 2-0	0-0	2	Naylor 64, Samaras 75	15,735
28	12	H	Dundee U	D 0-0	0-0	—		54,352
29	23	A	Gretna	W 3-0	1-0	2	McDonald 42, Vennegoor 70, Samaras 88	3561
30	29	A	Rangers	L 0-1	0-1	2		50,325
31	Apr 5	H	Motherwell	L 0-1	0-1	2		58,624
32	13	A	Motherwell	W 4-1	3-1	—	McManus 17, McDonald 30, Vennegoor 2 43, 57	9771
33	16	H	Rangers	W 2-1	1-0	—	Nakamura 20, Vennegoor 90	58,964
34	19	H	Aberdeen	W 1-0	0-0	1	Samaras 56	55,766
35	27	H	Rangers	W 3-2	2-2	1	McDonald 2 4, 43, Robson (pen) 70	58,662
36	May 3	A	Motherwell	W 2-1	0-0	1	McDonald 62, Samaras 79	9158
37	11	H	Hibernian	W 2-0	1-0	1	McManus 37, McDonald 87	58,515
38	22	A	Dundee U	W 1-0	0-0	—	Vennegoor 72	13,613

Final League Position: 1

1985-86, 1987-88, 1997-98, 2000-01, 2001-02, 2003-04, 2005-06, 2006-07, 2007-08. *Runners-up:* 27 times.
Scottish Cup Winners: (34 times) 1892, 1899, 1900, 1904, 1907, 1908, 1911, 1912, 1914, 1923, 1925, 1927, 1931, 1933, 1937, 1951, 1954, 1965, 1967, 1969, 1971, 1972, 1974, 1975, 1977, 1980, 1985, 1988, 1989, 1995, 2001, 2004, 2005, 2007. *Runners-up:* 18 times.
League Cup Winners: (13 times) 1956-57, 1957-58, 1965-66, 1966-67, 1967-68, 1968-69, 1969-70, 1974-75, 1982-83, 1997-98, 1999-2000, 2000-01, 2005-06. *Runners-up:* 13 times.

European: *European Cup:* 122 matches (1966-67 winners, 1967-68, 1968-69, 1969-70 runners-up, 1970-71, 1971-72, 1972-73, 1973-74 semi-finals, 1974-75, 1977-78, 1979-80, 1981-82, 1982-83, 1986-87, 1988-89, 1998-99, 2001-02, 2002-03, 2003-04, 2005-06, 2006-07, 2007-08). *Cup Winners' Cup:* 39 matches (1963-64 semi-finals, 1965-66 semi-finals, 1975-76, 1980-81, 1984-85, 1985-86, 1989-90, 1995-96). *UEFA Cup:* 73 matches (*Fairs Cup:* 1962-63, 1964-65. *UEFA Cup:* 1976-77, 1983-84, 1987-88, 1991-92, 1992-93, 1993-94, 1996-97, 1997-98, 1998-99, 1999-2000, 2000-01, 2001-02, 2002-03 runners-up, 2003-04 quarter-finals).

Club colours: Shirt: Emerald green and white hoops. Shorts: White with emerald green trim. Stockings: White.

Goalscorers: *League* (84): McDonald 25 (3 pens), Vennegoor 15 (1 pen), Nakamura 7, McGeady 6, Samaras 5, McManus 4, Brown S 3, Donati 3, Miller 3, Robson 2 (1 pen), Caldwell 1, Hinkel 1, Jarosik 1, Killen 1, Naylor 1, Riordan 1, own goals 5.
Scottish Cup (9): McDonald 3, Vennegoor 3, Caldwell 1, Nakamura 1, Samaras 1.
CIS Cup (2): McDonald 1, Vennegoor 1.

Brown M 8	Wilson M 8 + 3	Naylor L 33	Donati M 22 + 3	Kennedy J 5 + 2	McManus S 37	Hartley P 23 + 4	Brown S 31 + 4	Zurawski M 1 + 4	Vennegoor J 31 + 1	McGeady A 35 + 1	Nakamura S 24 + 2	Killen C 2 + 18	Miller K 1 + 1	Boruc A 30	Caldwell G 35	McDonald S 35 + 1	Riordan D 2 + 6	Sno E 3 + 9	McGowan P — + 1	Perrier Doumbe2	O'Brien J — + 1	Jarosik J 6 + 2	O'Dea D 3 + 3	Pressley S 5	Conroy R 2	Balde B 4	Hinkel A 16	Caddis P — + 2	Robson B 9 + 6	Samaras G 5 + 10	Hutchinson B — + 2	Sheridan C — + 1	Match No.
1	2	3	4^{1}	5	6	7	8	9^{2}	10	11	12	13																					1
1	2	3	4^{1}	5	6	12	8		10	11	7		9																				2
	2	3	4		6		8		10	11	7		12	1	5	9^{1}																	3
	2	3	4		6		8	14	10^{2}	11^{1}	7	13		1	5	9^{3}	12																4
	2	3	12		6	7	8	14	10^{2}			13		1	5	9^{3}	11	4^{1}															5
	2	3	4		6		8^{1}		10^{2}	11	7	13		1	5	9^{3}		12	14														6
		3	4^{2}		6	7	8		10	11		12		1	5	9^{1}	13			2													7
		3	4^{2}		6	7	8	14	10^{1}	11		12		1	5	9^{3}		13		2													8
		3	4^{3}	12^{2}	6	2^{1}	8			11	7	10		1	5	9					13	14											9
		3	4	12	6^{1}		8			13	7^{2}			1	5	9		11				10	2										10
		3	12	5	6	4	8			11	7^{1}	10		1	2	9																	11
		3		5	6	4	8		10	11				1	2	9						7											12
1		3	4^{3}	5	6		8	12	10^{2}	11		13			2	9^{1}		14				7											13
					6	4	8		10^{1}	11		12		1	2	9						7	3	5									14
1					6	4	8		10^{3}	11		14			2	9	13	12				7^{1}	3^{2}	5									15
1			4		6	7	8^{3}		10^{2}	11		13			2	9		14					12	5^{1}	3								16
1			4		6	7	8		10	11		13			2	9^{2}	12							5^{1}	3								17
1		3	4^{1}		6	7	8		10	11					2	9	13					12		5^{2}									18
1		3	12		6	4	8		10	11					2	9						7^{1}				5							19
		3	4^{2}		6	12	8		10	11				1	2	9	7^{1}	13								5							20
		3	4		6	11	8		10^{1}		7^{3}	12		1	5	9	13	14									2^{2}						21
		5	4		6	3^{2}	8		10	11	7^{1}	14		1	2	9^{3}		12										13					22
		3			6	4	8		10^{3}	11	7^{2}	14		1	5	9^{1}											2		13	12			23
		3	4^{2}		6		8		10^{1}	11	7			1	5	9^{3}											2		13	12	14		24
		3	4		6^{1}		8			11	13	14		1	5	9							12				2		7^{2}	10^{3}			25
		3	4		6		8			11	7	12		1	5	9^{1}											2			10			26
		3	4^{2}		6	13	8		10^{1}	11	7^{3}			1	5	9											2		14	12			27
		3			6		8		12	11	7			1	5	9		4^{2}									2		13	10^{1}			28
		3			6	13	8^{2}		10	11	7			1	5	9^{1}		14									2		4^{3}	12			29
		3			6	4^{2}	8		10^{1}	11	7			1	5	12											2		13	9			30
		3	4^{2}		6		8		10	11	7			1	5	9^{1}											2^{3}		13	12	14		31
		3			6	4			10^{1}	11	7	13		1	5	9^{2}											2		8	12			32
	12	3^{1}			6	4			10	11	7			1	5	9											2		8^{2}	13			33
	3		4		6					11	7	13		1		9^{2}										5	2^{1}	12	8	10			34
		3			6^{1}	4^{3}	14		10^{2}	11	7			1	5	9							12				2		8	13			35
	14	3^{3}				4	12		10^{2}	11	7^{1}			1	5	9										6	2		8	13			36
	2	3			6	4	12		10^{1}	11	7			1	5	9^{2}													8			13	37
	13	3^{2}			6	4	12		10^{3}	11	7^{1}			1	5	9											2		8	14			38

CLYDE — First Division

Year Formed: 1877. *Ground & Address:* Broadwood Stadium, Cumbernauld, G68 9NE. *Telephone:* 01236 451511.
E-mail: info@clydefc.co.uk. *Website:* www.clydefc.co.uk
Ground Capacity: all seated: 8200. *Size of Pitch:* 112yd × 76yd.
Chairman: Len McGuire. *Secretary:* John D. Taylor.
Manager: John Brown. *Physio:* Ian McKinlay.
Club Nickname(s): The Bully Wee. *Previous Grounds:* Barrowfield Park 1877-97, Shawfield Stadium 1897-1986.
Record Attendance: 52,000 v Rangers, Division I, 21 Nov 1908.
Record Transfer Fee received: £175,000 for Scott Howie to Norwich City (Aug 1993).
Record Transfer Fee paid: £14,000 for Harry Hood from Sunderland (1966).
Record Victory: 11-1 v Cowdenbeath, Division II, 6 Oct 1951.
Record Defeat: 0-11 v Dumbarton, Scottish Cup 4th rd, 22 Nov, 1879; v Rangers, Scottish Cup 4th rd, 13 Nov 1880.
Most Capped Player: Tommy Ring, 12, Scotland.
Most League Appearances: 420: Brian Ahern, 1971-81; 1987-88.
Most League Goals in Season (Individual): 32: Bill Boyd, 1932-33.

CLYDE 2007–08 LEAGUE RECORD

Match No.	Date	Venue	Opponents	Result		H/T Score	Lg. Pos.	Goalscorers	Attendance
1	Aug 4	A	Morton	L	2-3	2-2	—	Masterton 10, Higgins 45	3818
2	11	H	Hamilton A	L	0-2	0-1	9		1152
3	18	A	Partick Th	L	0-4	0-2	10		3175
4	25	H	St Johnstone	W	1-0	0-0	9	Ruari MacLennan 70	1274
5	Sept 1	H	Dundee	L	1-2	1-0	9	Higgins 4	1606
6	15	A	Queen of the S	D	1-1	0-1	10	McGregor 49	1730
7	22	H	Dunfermline Ath	W	2-1	1-0	7	Masterton 19, McGowan D 65	1558
8	29	A	Livingston	L	2-4	1-2	9	McGowan D 15, Imrie (pen) 85	1492
9	Oct 6	A	Stirling A	W	2-0	2-0	7	Arbuckle 38, McGregor 45	946
10	20	H	Morton	L	0-1	0-1	7		1306
11	27	A	St Johnstone	D	1-1	0-0	7	Imrie 75	2782
12	Nov 3	H	Partick Th	L	1-2	0-0	10	Imrie (pen) 88	1979
13	11	A	Dundee	W	1-0	0-0	7	Dixon (og) 86	3727
14	Dec 1	H	Queen of the S	D	0-0	0-0	7		1008
15	8	A	Dunfermline Ath	D	1-1	1-1	7	McGowan D 3	3505
16	15	H	Livingston	W	2-1	1-1	7	McKeown 43, McGregor 75	910
17	26	A	Hamilton A	D	0-0	0-0	9		1750
18	29	H	St Johnstone	L	1-3	1-2	9	Bradley 14	1149
19	Jan 2	A	Partick Th	D	1-1	1-1	9	Arbuckle 26	3299
20	5	A	Queen of the S	L	1-3	1-0	9	McGowan M (pen) 15	1513
21	19	H	Dundee	D	1-1	0-0	9	Arbuckle 72	1328
22	26	H	Hamilton A	L	2-3	2-1	9	Arbuckle 3, Imrie 15	1214
23	Feb 2	H	Stirling A	L	1-3	0-0	9	Fagan (pen) 79	960
24	9	A	Morton	W	2-1	0-0	8	Ruari MacLennan 89, McKeown 90	2276
25	23	H	Dunfermline Ath	L	1-2	0-2	8	Clarke (pen) 68	1124
26	Mar 1	H	Partick Th	L	1-4	1-3	9	McKeown 10	1717
27	8	A	Livingston	D	0-0	0-0	—		1258
28	11	H	Morton	D	1-1	0-1	—	Clarke 56	1270
29	15	A	Stirling A	D	1-1	1-0	9	Albertz 45	1075
30	22	H	Queen of the S	L	1-4	0-2	9	Masterton (pen) 69	1210
31	25	A	St Johnstone	W	2-1	1-0	—	Bradley 30, Albertz 51	1686
32	29	A	Dundee	L	0-2	0-1	8		4037
33	Apr 5	H	Livingston	W	3-2	2-1	8	Clarke 19, Ruari MacLennan 2 24, 48	1155
34	12	A	Dunfermline Ath	L	1-2	1-0	8	Clarke 44	3129
35	19	A	Hamilton A	L	0-2	0-2	9		4940
36	26	H	Stirling A	W	3-0	1-0	9	McSwegan 44, Clarke 2 (1 pen) 46, 83 (p)	1489

Final League Position: 9

Honours

League Champions: Division II 1904-05, 1951-52, 1956-57, 1961-62, 1972-73. Second Division 1977-78, 1981-82, 1992-93, 1999-2000.

Runners-up: Division II 1903-04, 1905-06, 1925-26, 1963-64. Second Division 2003-04.

Scottish Cup Winners: 1939, 1955, 1958; *Runners-up:* 1910, 1912, 1949.

Bell's League Challenge: Quarter-finals 2004-05. *League Challenge Cup Runners-up:* 2006-07.

Club colours: Shirt: White with red and black trim. Shorts: Black. Stockings: White.

Goalscorers: *League* (40): Clarke 6 (2 pens), Arbuckle 4, Imrie 4 (2 pens), Ruari MacLennan 4, Masterton 3 (1 pen), McGowan D 3, McGregor 3, McKeown 3, Albertz 2, Bradley 2, Higgins 2, Fagan 1 (pen), McGowan M 1 (pen), McSwegan 1, own goal 1.

Play-offs (9): Clarke 3, McSwegan 2, Arbuckle 1, Gibson J 1, Gibson W 1, Masterton 1.

Scottish Cup (2): Arbuckle 1, Imrie 1.

CIS Cup (0).

Challenge Cup (2): Ruari MacLennan 1, Masterton 1.

Hutton D 36	McGowan M 28 + 4	McGregor N 33	Masterton S 20 + 6	Higgins C 32	Potter C 4	Smith C 20 + 7	Bradley K 17 + 10	Arbuckle G 16 + 11	Imrie D 19	Wilson M 15 + 4	MacLennan Ruari 27 + 4	McGowan D 20 + 8	Thomson D — + 1	McKenna S 1 + 7	Traub A 1	Connolly S — + 1	Doherty M — + 1	Kirkup D 6 + 1	Cardell J 8	Bestvina D 22 + 1	McKeown C 16 + 1	MacLennan Roddy 3 + 5	Campbell I 4	Gibson B 12 + 1	Fagan S 2 + 1	Clarke P 11	Gibson J 4 + 3	McKay D 7 + 5	McSwegan G 5 + 1	Albertz J 7	McCusker M — + 3	Match No.
1	2	5	7	3	4	6^{1}	8	10	11	9^{2}	12	13																				1
1^{6}	5	2■	8	4	3	7^{1}	9	10^{2}	11	6		12	15	13																		2
1	2		8	3	5	9	6^{2}	11	10	7^{3}	12	13			4^{1}	14																3
1	2	4	8	3	5	9^{1}	13	14	11	12	7	6^{2}		10^{3}																		4
1	4^{1}	2	7	3		6		13	11		9^{2}	10^{3}		14			12	5	8■													5
1	8^{1}	2	7	4		6	12		11		9	10						5		3												6
1	12	2	6	4		5			10		8^{1}	7^{2}		13				9	11	3												7
1		2	6^{1}	4		5■		12	10		8■	7						9	11	3												8
1	11	2	6	4			12	8	10	5^{2}		7^{3}		13				14	9^{1}	3												9
1	11^{2}	2	6	4		14		8^{3}	10	5	13	7							9	3^{1}	12											10
1	11	2	6	4			12	13	10	3	8	7^{1}							9^{2}		5											11
1	5^{1}	3	7	4		14	12	13	9	8^{3}	11	10^{2}							6		2											12
1	11	2	6	4		12	14	13	10	3^{1}	8	7^{2}							9^{3}		5											13
1	11			4		3	7^{2}		10		8	12		13				6		2	5	9^{1}										14
1	11	2		4		7	13	12	10■		8	9^{2}						6^{1}		3	5											15
1	11	2	6^{1}	4		7	3	10			8	9		12							5											16
1	11	2		4		6	7	9		10	8^{1}	12								3	5											17
1	2	3		4		9^{1}	6	10		8■	7	11^{2}		13						12	5											18
1	2	3		5			7^{1}	11	9		8	10								4	6	12										19
1	9	2		4		12	7^{2}	11	10	13	8	5^{1}								3^{3}	6	14										20
1	2	4	8	5		10	7	11	6		9										3											21
1	2	4	8	3		6^{1}		10	11		9	7									5	12										22
1	2^{1}	4	8	3^{3}			13	10			9^{2}	14									5		6	7	12	11						23
1	9^{1}	4	14				7	12			13	10								2	3		5^{3}	6	8^{2}	11						24
1	13	3	14				6					9								2^{1}	4		5^{3}	7	8^{2}	10	12	11				25
1	2	4	8^{1}	3		13	12				9										5	14		6		10	7^{3}	11^{2}				26
1	11	2	14	4		8	7^{1}			6^{2}		9								5		10^{3}		3			13	12				27
1	11	2	12	4		8	7^{2}			6^{1}		13								5		10^{3}				9	3	14				28
1	14	2	12			6	13				8	7								5			4■	3				10^{3}	9^{2}	11^{1}		29
1	7^{3}	2	4			6		12			8									5		14		3				10	9^{1}	11^{2}	13	30
1	7^{2}	2		4		12	6	10^{3}			8									5				3		9		13		11^{1}	14	31
1	7^{2}	2		4			6	11^{1}		13	8^{3}									5				3		10		12		9	14	32
1		3	12	4						7	8									2				5		11	13	6	10^{1}	9^{2}		33
1		3		4		12		11^{2}		7	8	14								2				5		10		6^{3}	13	9^{1}		34
1		2■		4		11	7^{3}	12		6^{2}	8									5				13		10	3	14	9^{1}			35
1	13		2	3				14		12	8									4				5		11	7^{1}	6	10^{3}	9^{2}		36

COWDENBEATH Third Division

Year Formed: 1881. *Ground & Address:* Central Park, Cowdenbeath KY4 9EY. *Telephone:* 01383 610166. *Fax:* 01383 512132.
E-mail: bluebrazil@cowdenbeathfc.com. *Website:* www.cowdenbeathfc.com
Ground Capacity: total: 5268, seated: 1622. *Size of Pitch:* 107yd × 66yd.
Chairman: Gordon McDougall. *Secretary:* Tom Ogilvie. *Commercial Managers:* Joe MacNamara and Susan Welsh.
Manager: Brian Welsh. *Assistant Manager:* Danny Lennon. *First Team Coaches:* S. McLeish, M. Renwick. *Physio:* Neil Bryson.
Previous Grounds: North End Park, Cowdenbeath.
Record Attendance: 25,586 v Rangers, League Cup quarter-final, 21 Sept 1949.
Record Transfer Fee received: £30,000 for Nicky Henderson to Falkirk (March 1994).
Record Victory: 12-0 v Johnstone, Scottish Cup 1st rd, 21 Jan 1928.
Record Defeat: 1-11 v Clyde, Division II, 6 Oct 1951.
Most Capped Player: Jim Paterson, 3, Scotland.
Most League and Cup Appearances: 491 Ray Allan 1972-75, 1979-89.
Most League Goals in Season (Individual): 54, Rab Walls, Division II, 1938-39.
Most Goals Overall (Individual): 127, Willie Devlin, 1922-26, 1929-30.

COWDENBEATH 2007–08 LEAGUE RECORD

Match No.	Date	Venue	Opponents	Result		H/T Score	Lg. Pos.	Goalscorers	Attendance
1	Aug 4	A	Berwick R	D	1-1	0-1	—	McBride 58	778
2	11	H	Ross Co	D	2-2	0-0	6	Dalziel 66, Howatt 82	320
3	18	A	Peterhead	L	2-4	1-1	8	McConalogue 41, Bavidge (og) 58	680
4	25	H	Raith R	W	1-0	1-0	5	Deasley 38	1935
5	Sept 1	A	Brechin C	D	1-1	1-0	7	Docherty 35	448
6	15	H	Ayr U	D	1-1	0-1	7	Dalziel 68	462
7	22	A	Alloa Ath	L	2-3	1-1	8	Gilfillan 16, Scullion 63	613
8	29	H	Airdrie U	D	1-1	1-0	8	Clarke 6	493
9	Oct 6	A	Queen's Park	W	1-0	0-0	8	Clarke (pen) 51	614
10	20	H	Berwick R	W	3-1	0-0	4	Clarke 3 68, 80, 90	319
11	27	H	Peterhead	L	0-2	0-2	7		293
12	Nov 3	A	Raith R	L	0-2	0-2	7		2357
13	10	H	Brechin C	W	1-0	0-0	6	McBride 64	363
14	Dec 1	A	Ayr U	W	4-1	1-1	5	Scullion 29, Hill 59, Ramsay 65, Armstrong J 75	989
15	8	A	Airdrie U	L	1-3	1-2	6	McConalogue 3	823
16	15	H	Alloa Ath	L	1-4	0-2	7	Scullion 89	356
17	29	A	Peterhead	L	0-1	0-0	8		639
18	Jan 2	H	Raith R	L	1-4	1-1	8	Manson 22	1896
19	5	H	Ayr U	W	2-0	1-0	8	McQuade 10, Dempster 76	297
20	19	A	Brechin C	W	1-0	1-0	6	Dempster (pen) 38	432
21	26	H	Ross Co	L	2-4	0-2	8	Clarke 71, Dempster 89	362
22	Feb 9	H	Airdrie U	L	0-1	0-0	8		475
23	16	A	Alloa Ath	L	2-3	0-0	9	Manson 53, Gates 57	542
24	23	H	Peterhead	L	0-4	0-1	9		244
25	Mar 1	A	Raith R	L	2-3	1-2	9	Fahey (og) 35, McQuade 62	1607
26	4	A	Ross Co	L	1-4	0-1	—	McBride (pen) 81	1511
27	11	A	Berwick R	W	5-4	3-2	—	McLaughlin 4 1, 4, 75, 90, Ramsay 44	259
28	15	H	Berwick R	L	1-2	1-1	9	Drough 8	284
29	18	H	Queen's Park	L	2-4	1-1	—	Dempster (pen) 17, Gilfillan 86	317
30	22	A	Ayr U	D	1-1	0-0	9	Dempster 47	1011
31	29	H	Brechin C	L	0-2	0-0	9		259
32	Apr 1	A	Queen's Park	W	3-2	2-0	—	Gates 32, McQuade 35, McLaughlin 78	431
33	5	H	Alloa Ath	D	1-1	0-0	9	McQuade 66	272
34	15	A	Airdrie U	L	0-4	0-2	—		735
35	19	A	Ross Co	L	0-3	0-2	9		3716
36	26	H	Queen's Park	W	1-0	0-0	9	McLaughlin 48	369

Final League Position: 9

Honours
League Champions: Division II 1913-14, 1914-15, 1938-39; *Champions:* Third Division 2005-06. *Runners-up:* Division II 1921-22, 1923-24, 1969-70. Second Division 1991-92. *Runners-up:* Third Division 2000-01.
Scottish Cup: Quarter-finals 1931.
League Cup: Semi-finals 1959-60, 1970-71.

Club colours: Shirt: Royal blue with white cuffs and collar. Shorts: White. Stockings: White.

Goalscorers: *League* (47): Clarke 6 (1 pen), McLaughlin 6, Dempster 5 (2 pens), McQuade 4, McBride 3 (1 pen), Scullion 3, Dalziel 2, Gates 2, Gilfillan 2, Manson 2, McConalogue 2, Ramsay 2, Armstrong J 1, Deasley 1, Docherty 1, Drough 1, Hill 1, Howatt 1, own goals 2.
Play-offs (2): McQuade 1, Scullion 1 (pen).
Scottish Cup (1): Clarke 1 (pen).
CIS Cup (3): Clarke 1, Dalziel 1, O'Neil 1.
Challenge Cup (0).

Hay D 36	Baxter M 8	Armstrong J 19	O'Neil J 20+10	Adamson K 27+2	Galloway M 12	Scullion P 26+4	Matusik O 1+2	McConalogue S 12+3 / McLaughlin D 8+4	Clarke P 10+2	McBride M 17+13	Dalziel S 6+10	Lennon D 2+1	Howatt A 2+8	Anton C 4+2 / Tomana M 6	Bryan T —+1	Hill D 26+1	Deasley B 5+1	Gilfillan B 22+1	Armstrong D 13	Docherty M 4+1 / Lynch M 2	Mackle S 2+1	Boyle M —+1 / McCay D —+1	Ramsay M 20+1	Hannah D 3	McQuade P 14+3	Manson S 3+4	Dempster J 11+2	Tennerazzo G 3	Linton S 4+2	Young C —+1 / Ferguson J —+1	Robertson J 6+4	Bingham D 6+2	Shields J 12	Ried J 1	Gates S 12+1	Drough D 4+2	Shanks C 7+4	Match No.
1	2	3	4[3]	5	6	7	8[1]	9[2]	10	11	12	13	14																									1
1		3	4	5	6	7		9[2]	10	11[1]	8		13■	2	12																							2
1		3	4[3]	5	6	7	14	9		13	12	8		2		11[1]	10[2]																					3
1	2	3		5	6	7		12		11	9		10				8[1]	4																				4
1	2	3		5	6			9[2]		10	13		14			12	11[3]	4	7[1]	8																		5
1	2	3		5	6	7		9[1]		11	12		13				10	4		8[2]																		6
1	2	3	12	5	6[3]	7		14	13	11[2]	10						9[1]	4		8																		7
1	2	3	4[1]		6	7			10	12	13					11	14	5		8[3]	9[2]																	8
1	2	3	4		6	7			10	11[2]	13					8		5		12	9[1]																	9
1				5[1]	6	7	13	9[2]	10	11	8			2		3		4			12																	10
1			4[3]	5	6[1]	7		9[2]	10	12	11		13	2		3		8				14																11
1		3	4[3]	12	6[1]	7		13	10	11	9[2]		14			5		2					8															12
1		3	4[1]	5		7		9[2]	10	11	13			12		6		2					8															13
1		3	13	5		7[3]		9[1]	10	14			12			4		6	11[2]				8	2														14
1		3	13	5		7[1]		9[3]	10	12	14					2		6	11[2]				8	4														15
1		3[1]	4			12		9		11	13		10[2]			6		5	2				7	8														16
1		3	14	5[3]		7		9		11[1]	12		13			4		6	2				8		10[2]													17
1		3	8	5		6■				12				14		4		7[2]	2[1]				11		13	9[3]	10											18
1		3	7	5						8						4							6[3]		11[2]	9[1]	10	2	14	12	13							19
1		3	7	5						8						4			2				6		9	12	10					11[1]						20
1		4	8	12		13			14	7[1]						3			2				6		11[3]		10					9[2]	5					21
1			7	4		6[3]				12						11			3				5		10[2]	8[1]	9				14	13		2				22
1			6	3		8				13						5[3]		14	4				7		9[1]	12						10	2		11[2]			23
1			8[2]	5		7				13								4■	3				6		10							11[1]	2		9	12		24
1			6[3]			10		9[2]		7[1]									4						13				3		14	12	8		11	5	2	25
1						10[2]		14		13								4	2						7				3		6	9[3]	8		11[1]	5	12	26
1			8[3]			14		9								5							7			13	12		3			10[1]	6		11[2]	4	2	27
1			13	5		8		11		12						4							6[2]				10						7[1]		9	3	2	28
1			13					10[3]				7[2]				4		3					6		14	12	11				8		5[1]		9		2	29
1	2[1]		13	5				14						8[2]		4		3					6				11[3]				10		7■		9		12	30
1			13	5				12						8[1]		4		3[3]					6		11		10[2]				7				9	14	2	31
1				3		14		13						8[3]		5		4[1]					7		10		9[2]				6		2		11		12	32
1			13	5		8		10						7		4		3[1]					6[2]		11[3]		14						2		9		12	33
1			6[1]	3		4		11		12				7		5									10[3]		9[2]				14		8		13		2	34
1			12	3		8		10		13				7[2]		5				4					9			2	14		6[1]				11[3]			35
1			8	4		7[1]		10		9										3		13	12		11[3]			6[2]	5	14							2	36

DUMBARTON

Third Division

Year Formed: 1872. *Ground:* Strathclyde Homes Stadium, Dumbarton G82 1JJ. *Telephone:* 01389 762569. *Fax:* 01389 762629. *E-mail:* dumbarton.footballclub@btopenworld.com. *Website:* www.dumbartonfootballclub.com
Ground Capacity: total: 2050. *Size of Pitch:* 110yd × 75yd.
Chairman: Neil Rankine. *Club Secretary:* David Prophet. *Company Secretary:* Gilbert Lawrie.
Manager: Jim Chapman. *Assistant Manager:* Jim Clark. *Physio:* Lindsay Smart.
Club Nickname(s): The Sons. *Previous Grounds:* Broadmeadow, Ropework Lane, Townend Ground, Boghead Park.
Record Attendance: 18,000 v Raith Rovers, Scottish Cup, 2 Mar 1957.
Record Transfer Fee received: £125,000 for Graeme Sharp to Everton (March 1982).
Record Transfer Fee paid: £50,000 for Charlie Gibson from Stirling Albion (1989).
Record Victory: 13-1 v Kirkintilloch Central. 1st rd, 1 Sept 1888.
Record Defeat: 1-11 v Albion Rovers, Division II; 30 Jan, 1926: v Ayr United, League Cup, 13 Aug 1952.
Most Capped Player: James McAulay, 9, Scotland.
Most League Appearances: 297: Andy Jardine, 1957-67.
Most Goals in Season (Individual): 38: Kenny Wilson, Division II, 1971-72. *(League and Cup):* 46 Hughie Gallacher, 1955-56.
Most Goals Overall (Individual): 169: Hughie Gallacher, 1954-62 (including C Division 1954-55). *(League and Cup):* 202 Hughie Gallacher, 1954-62

DUMBARTON 2007–08 LEAGUE RECORD

Match No.	Date	Venue	Opponents	Result	H/T Score	Lg. Pos.	Goalscorers	Attendance
1	Aug 4	H	Elgin C	W 1-0	0-0	—	Tiernan ^{71}	640
2	11	A	East Stirling	L 2-3	2-2	6	Tiernan 2 $^{12, 15}$	306
3	18	A	Arbroath	D 1-1	0-1	6	Hamilton ^{79}	647
4	25	H	Albion R	W 2-0	1-0	3	Coyne 2 (1 pen) $^{12, 62 (p)}$	644
5	Sept 1	A	Stranraer	L 0-2	0-1	5		343
6	15	H	Stenhousemuir	L 1-2	1-1	7	Campbell ^{3}	907
7	22	H	East Fife	D 1-1	0-1	7	Tiernan ^{66}	692
8	29	A	Montrose	W 1-0	0-0	6	Campbell ^{53}	545
9	Oct 6	H	Forfar Ath	D 0-0	0-0	5		668
10	20	A	Elgin C	L 1-2	0-2	6	O'Byrne ^{80}	541
11	Nov 3	H	Arbroath	D 1-1	1-1	7	McPhee ^{3}	637
12	10	A	Albion R	L 0-2	0-1	8		512
13	Dec 1	A	Stenhousemuir	L 1-2	1-1	9	McPhee ^{45}	403
14	8	H	Stranraer	L 0-2	0-1	9		478
15	15	A	East Fife	L 0-2	0-1	9		674
16	18	H	East Stirling	W 3-1	2-0	—	McPhee ^{11}, Geggan ^{44}, Hamilton ^{90}	303
17	22	H	Montrose	L 1-3	0-2	9	Campbell ^{90}	510
18	29	A	Forfar Ath	L 1-3	1-2	9	Gentile ^{40}	422
19	Jan 2	H	Albion R	W 2-0	0-0	9	Tiernan ^{53}, McPhee ^{63}	634
20	19	A	Stranraer	L 0-2	0-0	9		214
21	Feb 2	H	Elgin C	L 1-4	0-3	9	Coyne (pen) ^{61}	514
22	9	A	Montrose	L 1-3	0-2	9	Moore ^{76}	458
23	16	H	East Fife	L 0-3	0-2	9		688
24	23	H	Arbroath	W 2-1	1-1	9	Canning 2 $^{37, 61}$	511
25	Mar 1	A	Albion R	W 1-0	0-0	8	Canning ^{74}	329
26	5	A	Arbroath	D 0-0	0-0	—		441
27	15	A	Elgin C	L 1-2	0-1	9	Moore ^{70}	551
28	18	H	Stenhousemuir	W 1-0	1-0	—	McNaught ^{42}	389
29	22	A	Stenhousemuir	D 1-1	1-0	8	Geggan ^{11}	449
30	25	A	East Stirling	D 1-1	0-1	—	McNaught ^{86}	359
31	29	H	Stranraer	L 0-1	0-0	8		512
32	Apr 5	A	East Fife	L 1-2	0-1	8	Tiernan ^{64}	639
33	8	H	Forfar Ath	D 0-0	0-0	—		282
34	12	H	Montrose	D 0-0	0-0	8		463
35	19	H	East Stirling	W 1-0	1-0	8	Brittain ^{11}	612
36	26	A	Forfar Ath	D 1-1	0-0	8	Hamilton ^{69}	400

Final League Position: 8

Honours
League Champions: Division I 1890-91 (shared with Rangers), 1891-92. Division II 1910-11, 1971-72. Second Division 1991-92; *Runners-up:* First Division 1983-84. Division II 1907-08. Third Division 2001-02.
Scottish Cup Winners: 1883; *Runners-up:* 1881, 1882, 1887, 1891, 1897.

Club colours: Shirt: Gold with black sleeves and black panel down sides. Shorts: Black with three gold panels. Stockings: Black.

Goalscorers: *League* (31): Tiernan 6, McPhee 4, Campbell 3, Canning 3, Coyne 3 (2 pens), Hamilton 3, Geggan 2, McNaught 2, Moore 2, Brittain 1, Gentile 1, O'Byrne 1.
Scottish Cup (3): McPhee 2, MacFarlane 1.
CIS Cup (0).
Challenge Cup (2): Campbell 2.

Nugent A 8 + 1	Geggan A 28	Craig D 7	Hamilton C 19 + 9	Russell R 21 + 7	O'Byrne M 30	Canning M 29	Tiernan F 22 + 4	McFarlane D 10 + 1	Campbell R 15 + 1	Coyne T 16 + 12	McQuilken P 4 + 7	Shaw P 2	Gentile C 10 + 9	McNaught D 6 + 12	Henderson N 13	Hasswell K 6 + 2	McPhee B 17 + 6	Crawford D 26	Potter C 23	Brittain C 20 + 1	McLaughlin J 3 + 1	Kerr S 2 + 3	McKillen R 1 + 1	Ferry D — + 1	Yule J 2	Evans G 8 + 1	Stokes M 6	Lennon G 16	Mackie C 2 + 2	Moore M 7	Orrstarm A 6 + 1	Wright K 1	Brannon K 2 + 5	Cusack L 5	Canning M 2	Pierman F 1	Match No.
1	2	3	4	5	6	7	8	9	10[1]	11	12																										1
	2	3	4[2]	5	6	7[1]	8	9	10	11		1	12	13																							2
1	2■	3	4	5	6		8	9	10[1]	11	12				7																						3
1		3	4	5	6	7	8	9	10[1]	11	12				2																						4
1		3	4[2]	5	6	7	8	9[3]	13	11	12		14		10	2[1]																					5
1	2	3			6	7		9	10	11	12				4	5	8[1]																				6
1	2	3		5		7	8[2]	9	10	12	13				4	6	11[1]																				7
	2		13	5	6	7	8	9[1]	10	12			14		4[3]	3	11[2]	1																			8
	2			5	6	7	8			11			12	10[1]	4	3	9	1																			9
			4	10	6	7		12	9				8[3]	14	3[2]		11[1]	1	2	5	13																10
	2		4[1]	5	6	7	12	9	10	13					8		11[2]	1		3																	11
	2		4[1]	13	6	7	8	9	10				14		3■		11[3]	1		5[2]		12															12
	2		4	5	6[2]	7	8			11							9	1		3[1]	10	12	13														13
	2[3]		4[2]	5	6	7	8		10	13	12						9	1	11[1]		3			14													14
			12	5	6	7	8		10	13	11		4[2]		9			1	2		3[1]																15
	2		12	5	6		8		10		9[1]		3		7		11	1	4																		16
	2		4[2]		6				10	12	9[1]		5	13	7■	14	11	1	8				3[3]														17
			12		6	7	8		10[1]	11[2]			9			3[3]	13	1	5	14		4			2												18
			6	9		3	7			14	11[1]		4[3]			13	10	1	8	5[2]		12			2												19
1	8		14	13		4	6			12				10[2]			9[1]		2	3		7				5	11[3]										20
	8		14	5		7	9			12			2[1]	11[3]			6[2]	1								4		3	13	10							21
1	2		6[1]	5		3	13			9[2]							14		8							7■		4	12	10[3]	11						22
	6					4	7[3]					1	13	14			12		2	5							9	3	11[1]	10	8[2]						23
	6			12	4	7	8						13	14				1	2	5							9[1]	3		10[3]	11[2]						24
	7			13	5	6	8							14			12	1	2	3							11[2]	4		9[3]	10[1]						25
	7				5	6	8											1	2	3							11■	4		9	10						26
	7		8	11[2]	5	6				12							13	1	2	3[3]						14		4		9	10[1]						27
	8		6	9	4	7				12			13	11[2]				1	2	5								3	10[1]								28
	8		7	12	5	6				9[3]			10[2]	13				1	2	3								4				11[1]	14				29
	9		7[2]	8[1]	5	6				10			11	12				1	2[3]	3								4			13		14				30
	8		6		4		12			10			11■	13			9[3]	1	7[2]	5							7[1]	3					14				31
	6		14		4		8			10[1]				12			11[2]	1	7	5						2		3					13	9[3]			32
	6		12	14	4								13	10				1	8[1]	5						2		3					11	9[3]	7[2]		33
	6			12	4		13			10				9[2]				1	7	5						2		3					14	11[3]	8[1]		34
			12	6	4	7				10[2]				13			14	1	8	5						2		3					11[3]	9[1]			35
15			7		5	6				12				13			9[1]	1[6]	8	3						2		4						10		11[2]	36

DUNDEE — First Division

Year Formed: 1893. *Ground & Address:* Dens Park Stadium, Sandeman St, Dundee DD3 7JY. *Telephone:* 01382 889966. *Fax:* 01382 832284. *E-mail:* dfc@dundeefc.co.uk. *Website:* www.dundeefc.co.uk
Ground Capacity: all seated: 11,760. *Size of Pitch:* 101m × 66m.
Chairman: Bob Brannan. *Chief Executive:* David MacKinnon. *Club Secretary:* Laura Hayes (tel: 01382 826104; mob: 07855 410 929). *Email:* laura@dundeefc.co.uk
Manager: Alex Rae. *Assistant Manager:* Davie Farrell. *Youth Development Coach:* Gordon Wallace. *Community Coach:* Gavin Timley. *Physio:* Karen Gibson.
Club Nickname(s): The Dark Blues or The Dee. *Previous Grounds:* Carolina Port 1893-98.
Record Attendance: 43,024 v Rangers, Scottish Cup, 1953.
Record Transfer Fee received: £500,000 for Tommy Coyne to Celtic (March 1989).
Record Transfer Fee paid: £200,000 for Jim Leighton (Feb 1992).
Record Victory: 10-0 Division II v Alloa, 9 Mar 1947 and v Dunfermline Ath, 22 Mar 1947.
Record Defeat: 0-11 v Celtic, Division I, 26 Oct 1895.
Most Capped Player: Alex Hamilton, 24, Scotland.
Most League Appearances: 341: Doug Cowie, 1945-61.
Most League Goals in Season (Individual): 52: Alan Gilzean, 1960-64.
Most Goals Overall (Individual): 113: Alan Gilzean 1960-64.

DUNDEE 2007–08 LEAGUE RECORD

Match No.	Date	Venue	Opponents	Result	H/T Score	Lg. Pos.	Goalscorers	Attendance
1	Aug 4	A	Livingston	W 2-0	1-0	—	Robertson 2 [17, 58]	2865
2	11	H	Queen of the S	W 2-1	1-1	1	Davidson 2 (1 pen) [13 (p), 75]	4023
3	18	A	St Johnstone	D 1-1	0-0	3	Daquin [77]	6279
4	25	H	Partick Th	W 3-0	2-0	2	Swankie [8], Davidson [16], McDonald [56]	4354
5	Sept 1	A	Clyde	W 2-1	0-1	2	McHale [52], O'Brien [64]	1606
6	15	H	Dunfermline Ath	D 1-1	1-1	2	McDonald [23]	5173
7	22	A	Stirling A	D 2-2	1-1	2	Davidson [32], Palenik [69]	1595
8	29	H	Morton	W 2-1	1-1	2	Palenik [2], Sturm [74]	3952
9	Oct 6	A	Hamilton A	L 0-2	0-0	2		3197
10	20	H	Livingston	W 4-1	1-1	2	Davidson 2 [20, 68], Zemlik [61], Lyle [73]	3639
11	27	A	Partick Th	D 1-1	0-1	2	Lyle (pen) [55]	2589
12	Nov 3	H	St Johnstone	W 2-1	0-1	2	Davidson [59], McDonald [90]	5518
13	11	H	Clyde	L 0-1	0-0	2		3727
14	24	H	Hamilton A	W 1-0	1-0	—	Robertson [12]	4375
15	Dec 1	A	Dunfermline Ath	W 1-0	0-0	2	McDonald [72]	4123
16	8	H	Stirling A	W 3-1	0-0	2	Robertson [56], McDonald [60], Lyle [66]	3590
17	15	A	Morton	W 2-0	1-0	2	McDonald [13], Lyle [89]	2569
18	26	A	Queen of the S	L 1-2	1-1	2	Palenik [20]	1980
19	29	H	Partick Th	W 1-0	0-0	2	McDonald [90]	4548
20	Jan 2	A	St Johnstone	D 1-1	0-0	2	McDonald [49]	6072
21	5	H	Dunfermline Ath	D 0-0	0-0	2		4607
22	19	A	Clyde	D 1-1	0-0	2	Palenik [90]	1328
23	26	H	Queen of the S	L 2-3	1-0	2	McMenamin 2 [9, 90]	3926
24	Feb 9	A	Livingston	D 1-1	1-1	2	Antoine-Curier (pen) [44]	1746
25	16	H	Morton	W 2-0	2-0	2	Antoine-Curier [6], Swankie [8]	4103
26	23	A	Stirling A	W 6-1	2-0	2	Antoine-Curier 2 [14, 57], McMenamin [36], Ellis (og) [49], Davidson [66], Lyle [78]	1419
27	Mar 1	H	St Johnstone	W 3-2	1-0	2	Antoine-Curier [40], McMenamin 2 [74, 90]	6192
28	11	H	Livingston	W 2-0	0-0	—	Antoine-Curier 2 [48, 61]	3715
29	15	A	Hamilton A	L 0-1	0-1	2		5078
30	22	A	Dunfermline Ath	W 1-0	0-0	2	Daquin [50]	3881
31	29	H	Clyde	W 2-0	1-0	2	O'Brien [8], McDonald [73]	4037
32	Apr 1	A	Partick Th	L 0-1	0-0	—		2326
33	5	A	Morton	W 2-1	1-1	2	Antoine-Curier [25], Lyle [80]	2741
34	12	H	Stirling A	W 3-0	0-0	2	MacKenzie [55], Swankie [58], Robertson [90]	4129
35	19	A	Queen of the S	L 0-1	0-1	2		3005
36	26	H	Hamilton A	D 1-1	0-1	2	McMenamin [90]	3146

Final League Position: 2

Honours
League Champions: Division I 1961-62. First Division 1978-79, 1991-92, 1997-98. Division II 1946-47; *Runners-up:* Division I 1902-03, 1906-07, 1908-09, 1948-49, 1980-81. First Division 2007-08.
Scottish Cup Winners: 1910; *Runners-up:* 1925, 1952, 1964, 2003.
League Cup Winners: 1951-52, 1952-53, 1973-74; *Runners-up:* 1967-68, 1980-81. *(Coca-Cola Cup):* 1995-96.
B&Q (Centenary) Cup Winners: 1990-91; *Runners-up:* 1994-95.

European: *European Cup:* 8 matches (1962-63 semi-finals). *Cup Winners' Cup:* 2 matches: (1964-65).
UEFA Cup: 22 matches: (*Fairs Cup:* 1967-68 semi-finals. *UEFA Cup:* 1971-72, 1973-74, 1974-75, 2003-04).

Club colours: Shirt: Navy with white and red shoulder and sleeve flashes. Shorts: White with navy/red piping. Stockings: Navy, top with two white hoops.

Goalscorers: *League* (58): McDonald 9, Antoine-Curier 8 (1 pen), Davidson 8 (1 pen), Lyle 6 (1 pen), McMenamin 6, Robertson 5, Palenik 4, Swankie 3, Daquin 2, O'Brien 2, MacKenzie 1, McHale 1, Sturm 1, Zemlik 1, own goal 1.
Scottish Cup (5): Daquin 1, McDonald 1, McHale 1, Malone 1, Robertson 1.
CIS Cup (5): Lyle 1 (pen), McDonald 1, Swankie 1, Robertson 1, Zemlik 1.
Challenge Cup (1): Sturm 1.

Roy L 5	Worrell D 21 + 1	MacKenzie G 33	Robertson S 29 + 1	Dixon P 26 + 4	McDonald K 34	Griffin D 4 + 3	Daquin F 22 + 9	Davidson B 18 + 9	Swankie G 26 + 4	Palenik M 22	Sturm J 9 + 10	O'Brien D 9 + 9	McHale P 15 + 10	Zemlik J 7 + 10	Samson C 30 + 1	Lyle D 13 + 13	Corrigan M 4	Rae A — + 1	Malone E 25	McMenamin C 12	Deasley B 1	Cowan D 12	Antoine-Curier M 11	Clark B — + 2	Noubissie P 7 + 2	White M 1	*Match No.*
1	2	3	4	5	6	7	8	9^{1}	10	11	12																1
1	2		4	5	6	7	8^{1}	9	10^{2}	3		12	13	11													2
1	2	3	4	5	6		8	9^{1}	10^{2}	11	13	12		7■													3
	2	3	4	5^{1}	6	12	8	9	10	11^{3}	7^{2}	13	14		1												4
	2	3	4	5	6^{1}		8	9^{3}		11	14	7	12	10^{2}	1	13											5
	2	3	4	5	6		8^{2}	9	10^{3}	11	7^{1}		14	13	1	12											6
	2	3^{1}	4	5	6	13	8^{3}	9	10^{2}	11			14	12	1	7											7
		3	4	5	6^{3}	7	8	9^{1}	10	2	13		14	11^{2}	1	12											8
		3	4	5	6	12	8	14	10	11^{1}			9^{3}	7^{2}	1	13	2										9
	2	3	4	5	6^{2}		8	9^{3}	10		14		13	11^{1}	1	12	7										10
	2		4	5	6^{2}	3^{1}	8	9^{3}	10		14		12		1	11	7	13									11
		3	4	5^{2}	6		8^{1}	9	13	11	14		12		1	10^{3}	2		7								12
	2	3	4^{2}	5			12		10	11	9^{1}	13	6		1	8			7								13
	2	3	4	14	6^{2}		13	9^{1}	10^{3}	11			8	12	1	7			5								14
	2	3	4		6			9^{2}	10	11	13		8	12	1	7^{1}			5								15
	2	3	4^{2}		6		13		10	11	8		7	9^{1}	1	12			5								16
	2	3	4	12	6			13	10^{1}	11	9^{2}		7		1	8			5								17
	2	3^{3}	4	12	6			13	10^{1}	11	8^{2}		7	14	1	9■			5								18
	2^{2}	3	4		6		13	9^{1}	10	11	8		7	12	1				5								19
	2	5^{1}	7	12	4			13	11	6	10^{2}		8	14	1	9^{3}			3								20
	2		7	5	8		6	10^{1}	9^{2}	3	12			13	1	11			4								21
	2	4	7				6	11	9^{2}	3	10^{1}	13	8	12	1				5								22
	3^{1}	2	5		7		12	9	8^{2}			13	6^{3}	14	1				4	10	11						23
1		5	7		4		12	13		6■		11^{2}	8^{1}						3	9		2	10				24
1^{6}		5	7	3	4		13		11				8^{2}		15	12			6	9		2	10^{1}				25
		5	7	3	4		14	12	11				8^{3}		1	13			6	9^{1}		2	10^{2}				26
		3	8^{1}	5	7		6^{2}			4		13			1	12			9	11		2	10				27
		3		4	9		7	12			13	6^{3}			1				5	11^{2}		2	10^{1}	14	8		28
	12	5^{1}		3	4			14				11^{2}	7		1	13			6	9		2	10■		8^{3}		29
		5		3	4		7	12				11			1	10^{1}			6	9		2			8		30
		3		5	7		6	10^{1}	12			9			1	11^{2}			4			7		13	8		31
		4		5	7		6		12			8^{1}			1	10			9			2	11		3		32
		5		3	4		7^{2}		12			11^{1}			1	13			6	9		2	10		8		33
	2	3	14	5	8		6^{3}		9^{2}			13			1	12			4	11			10^{1}		7		34
		4	8^{2}	3	6		7^{1}		9^{3}			14			1	12			5	10		2	11		13		35
		3^{2}	7^{3}	5^{1}	8		12		9			6	13						4	10		2	11		14	1	36

DUNDEE UNITED — Premier League

Year Formed: 1909 (1923). *Ground & Address:* Tannadice Park, Tannadice St, Dundee DD3 7JW. *Telephone:* 01382 833166. *Fax:* 01382 889398. *E-mail:* enquiries@dundeeunited.co.uk. *Website:* www.dundeeunitedfc.co.uk
Ground Capacity: total: 14,223 all seated: stands: east 2868, west 2096, south 2201, Fair Play 1601, George Fox 5151, executive boxes 292. *Size of Pitch:* 110yd × 72yd.
Chairman: Eddie Thompson, OBE. *Secretary:* Spence Anderson. *Commercial Manager:* Bill Campbell.
Manager: Craig Levein. *Assistant Manager:* Peter Houston. *First Team Coach:* Tony Docherty. *Coach:* Graeme Liveston. *Goalkeeping Coach:* Scott Thomson. *Youth Coach:* Stevie Campbell. *Youth Development:* Graeme Liveston. *Physio:* Jeff Clarke. *Stadium Manager:* Ron West.
Club Nickname(s): The Terrors. *Previous Grounds:* None.
Record Attendance: 28,000 v Barcelona, Fairs Cup, 16 Nov 1966.
Record Transfer Fee received: £4,000,000 for Duncan Ferguson from Rangers (July 1993).
Record Transfer Fee paid: £750,000 for Steven Pressley from Coventry C (July 1995).
Record Victory: 14-0 v Nithsdale Wanderers, Scottish Cup 1st rd, 17 Jan 1931.
Record Defeat: 1-12 v Motherwell, Division II, 23 Jan 1954.
Most Capped Player: Maurice Malpas, 55, Scotland.
Most League Appearances: 618, Maurice Malpas, 1980-2000.
Most Appearances in European Matches: 76, Dave Narey (record for Scottish player).
Most League Goals in Season (Individual): 41: John Coyle, Division II, 1955-56.
Most Goals Overall (Individual): 158: Peter McKay, 1947-54.

DUNDEE UNITED 2007–08 LEAGUE RECORD

Match No.	*Date*	*Venue*	*Opponents*	*Result*	*H/T Score*	*Lg. Pos.*	*Goalscorers*	*Attendance*
1	Aug 4	H	Aberdeen	W 1-0	0-0	—	Robertson D [90]	12,496
2	13	A	Kilmarnock	L 1-2	0-0	—	Hunt [50]	5557
3	18	H	Hibernian	D 0-0	0-0	6		8405
4	25	A	Inverness CT	W 3-0	0-0	5	Dillon [47], Robson 2 (2 pens) [58, 81]	4178
5	Sept 1	H	Falkirk	W 2-0	0-0	4	Hunt [58], Robson [84]	6864
6	16	H	St Mirren	W 2-0	1-0	4	Hunt [38], Robertson J [68]	6128
7	22	A	Gretna	L 2-3	1-2	4	Buaben [9], Wilkie [65]	1627
8	29	A	Celtic	L 0-3	0-1	4		57,006
9	Oct 6	H	Motherwell	W 1-0	0-0	4	Dods [78]	6286
10	20	A	Hearts	W 3-1	2-0	4	Robertson J 2 [14, 25], Robson (pen) [89]	16,661
11	28	H	Rangers	W 2-1	1-0	3	Wilkie [28], Robson (pen) [54]	12,129
12	Nov 3	A	Aberdeen	L 0-2	0-1	4		11,964
13	10	H	Kilmarnock	W 2-0	1-0	4	Hunt [8], Buaben [90]	6065
14	24	A	Hibernian	D 2-2	0-0	4	Robertson D 2 [66, 74]	14,440
15	Dec 1	H	Inverness CT	L 0-1	0-1	4		5846
16	8	A	Falkirk	L 0-3	0-2	5		4803
17	15	A	St Mirren	W 3-0	0-0	4	Robertson D [49], Hunt [77], Flood [90]	3490
18	22	H	Gretna	L 1-2	1-2	4	Hunt [29]	6304
19	26	H	Celtic	L 0-2	0-0	4		12,357
20	29	A	Motherwell	L 3-5	1-3	4	Robertson D [36], Hunt 2 [75, 90]	5227
21	Jan 2	H	Hearts	W 4-1	1-1	4	Robson 3 (2 pens) [23, 70 (p), 88 (p)], Hunt [84]	7557
22	5	A	Rangers	L 0-2	0-2	5		48,559
23	19	H	Aberdeen	W 3-0	0-0	3	Hunt [50], Robson 2 [77, 84]	8579
24	26	A	Kilmarnock	W 2-1	1-0	3	Robson [30], Conway [66]	4803
25	Feb 9	H	Hibernian	D 1-1	1-0	3	Hunt (pen) [13]	6635
26	16	A	Inverness CT	D 1-1	0-0	4	Buaben [68]	4087
27	23	H	Falkirk	D 0-0	0-0	4		6835
28	27	H	St Mirren	D 1-1	0-0	—	Dillon [69]	6037
29	Mar 6	A	Gretna	W 3-0	1-0	—	Kenneth [16], Gomis [51], Robertson D [64]	507
30	12	A	Celtic	D 0-0	0-0	—		54,352
31	22	H	Motherwell	W 2-0	0-0	3	Swanson [76], De Vries [89]	6779
32	29	A	Hearts	L 0-1	0-1	3		16,871
33	Apr 6	H	Rangers	D 3-3	1-1	4	Kalvenes [37], Hunt [51], Cuellar (og) [65]	11,214
34	20	H	Hibernian	D 1-1	0-0	4	Hunt (pen) [60]	7404
35	26	A	Motherwell	D 2-2	1-1	4	Craigan (og) [45], Wilkie [86]	5027
36	May 3	A	Aberdeen	L 1-2	0-1	4	Swanson [49]	10,312
37	10	A	Rangers	L 1-3	0-2	4	De Vries [76]	50,293
38	22	H	Celtic	L 0-1	0-0	—		13,613

Final League Position: 5

Honours
League Champions: Premier Division 1982-83. Division II 1924-25, 1928-29; *Runners-up:* Division II 1930-31, 1959-60. First Division Runners-up 1995-96.
Scottish Cup Winners: 1994; *Runners-up:* 1974, 1981, 1985, 1987, 1988, 1991, 2005.
League Cup Winners: 1979-80, 1980-81; *Runners-up:* 1981-82, 1984-85, 1997-98, 2007-08.
Summer Cup Runners-up: 1964-65. *Scottish War Cup Runners-up:* 1939-40.

European: *European Cup:* 8 matches (1983-84, semi-finals). *Cup Winners' Cup:* 10 matches (1974-75, 1988-89, 1994-95). *UEFA Cup:* 86 matches (*Fairs Cup:* 1966-67, 1969-70, 1970-71. *UEFA Cup:* 1975-76, 1977-78, 1978-79, 1979-80, 1980-81, 1981-82, 1982-83, 1984-85, 1985-86, 1986-87 runners-up, 1987-88, 1989-90, 1990-91, 1993-94, 1997-98, 2005-06).

Club colours: Shirts: Tangerine. Shorts: Tangerine. Stockings: Tangerine.

Goalscorers: *League* (53): Hunt 13 (2 pens), Robson 11 (6 pens), Robertson D 6, Buaben 3, Robertson J 3, Wilkie 3, De Vries 2, Dillon 2, Swanson 2, Conway 1, Dods 1, Flood 1, Gomis 1, Kalvenes 1, Kenneth 1, own goals 2.
Scottish Cup (5): Conway 1, Dods 1, Gomis 1, Kalvenes 1, Robson 1.
CIS Cup (8): Hunt 5 (1 pen), De Vries 1, Robertson J 1, Wilkie 1.

Szamotulski G 18	Dillon S 33	Kalvenes C 18 + 1	Kenneth G 14 + 5	Dods D 33	Flood W 33 + 3	Robertson D 16 + 4	Robb S 3 + 9	Gomis M 36	Hunt N 34 + 2	Robson B 21	Conway C 7 + 8	Buaben P 20 + 4	Duff S 4 + 5	Wilkie L 31	Kerr M 24 + 6	Goodwillie D — + 2	Robertson J 12 + 2	Cameron G 1 + 2	McLean E 5 + 1	Daly J 3 + 6	Milligan F — + 1	Russell J — + 2	Grainger D 12 + 2	Odhiambo E 1 + 3	Swanson D 4 + 8	Zaluska L 15	De Vries M 11 + 3	O'Brien J 5 + 5	Kovacevic M 4	*Match No.*
1	2	3	4	5	6■	7	8^{1}	9	10	11^{3}	12^{2}	13	14																	1
1	2	3■		5		7		9	10^{2}	11	4^{1}	8	12	6		13														2
1	2	3		5	6^{3}	14		9	10	11	8^{1}	13		4	7^{2}	12														3
1	2	3	4	5			12	9	10	11		8		6^{1}	7															4
1	2	3		5	6			9■	10^{1}	11		7		4	12		8													5
1	2	3^{3}		5	6	7^{1}	12		10	11^{2}		8	13	4			9	14												6
1	2		13	5	6^{2}		12	9^{1}	10	11		7	3	4			8													7
1	2			5	6^{3}	7^{1}	13	9^{2}	10	3		11	12	4			8	14												8
1	2	3		5	6		8^{1}	9	10	11		7		4			12													9
1■	2	3		5	6^{G}		13	9^{1}	10	11		8		4	12		7^{2}		15											10
	2	3		5	6			7	10	11		8^{1}		4	12		9		1											11
1	2	3	14	5	6^{1}		12	7^{2}	10	11■		8		4■	13		9^{3}													12
1	2	3	4	5	12			7	10			8			6		9■			11^{1}										13
1	2■	3	12	5	6	7^{2}	13	9				8		4	11					10^{1}										14
1			4	5	6^{2}	7	8^{1}	11					12	10	3		9^{3}	2			13	14								15
1	2			5	6	12		7	10	11			3	4	8^{1}		9													16
	2		4	5	6	7^{1}		8	10	11		9	3		12				1											17
	2		4	5	6^{1}	9		7	10	11	13	8^{2}	3				12		1											18
1	2			5	6	7^{1}		11	10	3	12	8		4			9													19
1	2		12	5	6	13		7	10	11^{3}	14	8^{1}		4	3		9^{2}													20
1	2		14	5	6^{2}	9^{1}		7	10	11				4^{3}	8								3	13	12					21
	2^{1}			5	6			7	10	11	13			4	8				1				3	9^{2}	12					22
	2		4		6			7	10	11	9^{3}	13		5^{1}	8				1				3	14	12^{2}					23
	2		4	5	6			7^{1}	10	11	9^{2}	12			8								3			1	13			24
	2	14		5	6^{2}			7	10		8			4	11								3^{3}		13	1	12	9^{1}		25
	2		4		6^{2}			7	12			8		5	11								3		13	1	9^{1}	10		26
	2	3		5	12			7	10			6		4	8										11^{1}	1	9			27
	2			5	6			7	10					4	8								3		11^{1}	1	9	12		28
	2	3	4	5	6^{2}	7		11	10^{3}		12	8			13									14		1		9^{1}		29
			4		12	7^{1}			13		10^{3}	8		5	11					14			3			1	9^{2}	6	2	30
		3	4		6			7	10					5^{1}	8								12		13	1	9	11^{2}	2	31
		3	4■		6			7	10^{2}		11^{1}			5	8					14					12■	1	9	13	2^{3}	32
	2	3		5	6	7		11	10					4	8					12						1	9^{1}			33
	2	3^{2}		5	6	11		7^{3}	10		14			4	8					12			13			1	9^{1}			34
	2			5	6	7^{1}		11	10		13			4	8^{2}					9^{3}			3			1	14	12		35
	2			5	6			7^{3}	10^{1}					4	11^{2}					14		12	3		8	1	9	13		36
				5	6^{1}	7	13	11^{2}	10					4	8								2		12	1	9	14	3^{3}	37
	2		4	5	6	12	13	11	10						7^{2}					14			3		8^{1}	1	9^{3}			38

DUNFERMLINE ATHLETIC — First Division

Year Formed: 1885. *Ground & Address:* East End Park, Halbeath Rd, Dunfermline KY12 7RB. *Telephone:* 01383 724295. *Fax:* 01383 723468. *Ticket office telephone:* 0870 300 1201. *E-mail:* enquiries@dafc.co.uk. *Website:* www.dafc.co.uk
Ground Capacity: all seated: 11,780. *Size of Pitch:* 115yd × 71yd.
Chairman: John Yorkston. *Chief Executive:* William Hodgins. *Commercial Director:* Wilma Cameron. *Commercial Manager:* Karen Brown.
Manager: Jim McIntyre. *Assistant Manager:* Gerry McCabe. *Physio:* Gerry Docherty. *First Team Coach:* Steven Wright.
Head of Youth: Hamish French.
Club Nickname(s): The Pars. *Previous Grounds:* None.
Record Attendance: 27,816 v Celtic, Division I, 30 Apr 1968.
Record Transfer Fee received: £650,000 for Jackie McNamara to Celtic (Oct 1995).
Record Transfer Fee paid: £540,000 for Istvan Kozma from Bordeaux (Sept 1989).
Record Victory: 11-2 v Stenhousemuir, Division II, 27 Sept 1930.
Record Defeat: 1-11 v Hibernian, Scottish Cup, 3rd rd replay, 26 Oct 1889.
Most Capped Player: Colin Miller 16 (61), Canada.
Most League Appearances: 497: Norrie McCathie, 1981-96.
Most League Goals in Season (Individual): 53: Bobby Skinner, Division II, 1925-26.
Most Goals Overall (Individual): 154: Charles Dickson, 1954-64.

DUNFERMLINE ATHLETIC 2007–08 LEAGUE RECORD

Match No.	Date	Venue	Opponents	Result		H/T Score	Lg. Pos.	Goalscorers	Attendance
1	Aug 4	A	Hamilton A	L	1-2	1-1	—	Burchill 18	3383
2	11	H	Morton	L	0-1	0-1	8		4748
3	19	A	Livingston	D	1-1	0-0	8	Morrison O 89	2493
4	25	H	Stirling A	W	2-1	0-0	6	Hamilton 55, Harper 87	3921
5	Sept 2	H	St Johnstone	D	0-0	0-0	6		4946
6	15	A	Dundee	D	1-1	1-1	7	Hamilton 14	5173
7	22	A	Clyde	L	1-2	0-1	9	Burchill 73	1558
8	29	H	Partick Th	W	1-0	1-0	6	Burchill 9	4351
9	Oct 6	A	Queen of the S	W	1-0	1-0	4	McManus 30	2026
10	20	H	Hamilton A	L	0-5	0-3	5		3846
11	27	A	Stirling A	L	0-3	0-1	6		1590
12	Nov 3	H	Livingston	L	0-4	0-1	8		3473
13	10	A	St Johnstone	D	0-0	0-0	9		3317
14	Dec 1	H	Dundee	L	0-1	0-0	9		4123
15	8	H	Clyde	D	1-1	1-1	9	Burchill 9	3505
16	15	A	Partick Th	D	1-1	0-0	9	Burchill 62	2176
17	22	H	Queen of the S	W	2-0	1-0	8	Burchill 32, Phinn 78	3324
18	26	A	Morton	W	1-0	1-0	5	Glass (pen) 15	2604
19	29	H	Stirling A	W	2-1	2-0	5	Burchill 1, Simmons 45	4023
20	Jan 2	A	Livingston	W	2-0	2-0	4	Hamilton 9, Burchill 10	2339
21	5	A	Dundee	D	0-0	0-0	4		4607
22	19	H	St Johnstone	L	0-1	0-1	6		4230
23	26	H	Morton	W	2-0	0-0	5	Simmons 51, Glass 83	2100
24	Feb 9	A	Hamilton A	L	0-3	0-3	5		2044
25	16	H	Partick Th	D	1-1	1-0	5	Crawford 11	3315
26	23	A	Clyde	W	2-1	2-0	5	Simmons 12, Burchill 36	1124
27	Mar 1	H	Livingston	D	1-1	1-1	5	Burke 12	3208
28	11	H	Hamilton A	D	1-1	1-1	—	Glass (pen) 10	2444
29	15	A	Queen of the S	D	1-1	1-1	5	Morrison S 25	2114
30	22	H	Dundee	L	0-1	0-0	6		3881
31	25	A	Stirling A	W	3-2	1-2	—	Harper 3 25, 76, 85	698
32	29	A	St Johnstone	D	1-1	0-1	5	Crawford 77	2372
33	Apr 5	A	Partick Th	W	1-0	1-0	5	Crawford 45	2280
34	12	H	Clyde	W	2-1	0-1	4	Glass (pen) 48, McIntyre 68	3129
35	19	A	Morton	L	0-3	0-1	5		2495
36	26	H	Queen of the S	W	4-0	0-0	5	Thomson S 48, Williamson 55, Burchill 2 62, 85	3444

Final League Position: 5

Honours
League Champions: First Division 1988-89, 1995-96. Division II 1925-26. Second Division 1985-86; *Runners-up:* First Division 1986-87, 1993-94, 1994-95, 1999-2000. Division II 1912-13, 1933-34, 1954-55, 1957-58, 1972-73. Second Division 1978-79.
Scottish Cup Winners: 1961, 1968; *Runners-up:* 1965, 2004, 2007.
League Cup Runners-up: 1949-50, 1991-92, 2005-06.
League Challenge Cup Runners-up: 2007-08.

European: *Cup Winners' Cup:* 14 matches (1961-62, 1968-69 semi-finals). *UEFA Cup:* 32 matches (*Fairs Cup:* 1962-63, 1964-65, 1965-66, 1966-67, 1969-70. *UEFA Cup:* 2004-05, 2007-08).

Club colours: Shirt: White and black stripes. Shorts: White. Stockings: Black.

Goalscorers: *League* (36): Burchill 11, Glass 4 (3 pens), Harper 4, Crawford 3, Hamilton 3, Simmons 3, Burke 1, McIntyre 1, McManus 1, Morrison O 1, Morrison S 1, Phinn 1, Thomson S 1, Williamson 1.
Scottish Cup (1): Wilson 1.
CIS Cup (1): Simmons 1.
Challenge Cup (9): Burchill 4, Glass 2 (1 pen), Morrison O 2, Wilson 1.

McKenzie R 2	Shields G 8+1	McGuire P 1+1	Harper K 12+3	Wilson S 27+2	Young D 15+1	Glass S 31	Simmons S 25+6	McManus T 9+9	Burchill M 28+5	Muirhead S 12	Morrison O 5+6	Hamilton J 17+4	Crawford S 28+6	Bamba S 13+2	Thomson S 22+2	Morrison S 16+3	Murdoch S 4+1	Phinn N 12+7	Gallacher P 30	Woods C 25	Labonte A 2	Ryan B 7+1	Williamson I 1+9	McIntyre J 6+11	Harris J 7+2	McBride S 1+2	Murphy D 12	McGlinchey M 6+2	Ross G 1	Burke A 11+2	Willis P —+3	Thomson R —	Dearden S —+1	*Match No.*
1	2	3■	6[3]	4	7	9	8[1]	11[2]	10	5	12	13	14																					1
1	2		6		7[3]	8■	13	9	10[1]	5	12	14	11[2]	3	4																			2
	2		6	4	7		8[2]	11[1]	14		9	12	10[3]	3■		5	1	13																3
	2	12	6	3	7	8					9[1]	11	10		4	5■			1															4
			6	4	7	8	12	13	14		9[3]	11[2]	10	3	5[1]				1	2														5
					7	5	13	12	11[1]		9	10	8	4					1	2	3	6[2]												6
					2	5	7[2]	12	11		9[1]	10	8	3			15		1[6]		4	6	13											7
				4	2[1]	5	7	6[3]	11[2]			10	9	3	12			8	1				13	14										8
				4		8		9[1]	11[2]	5	12	10[3]	7	3				6	1	2			13	14										9
				4	13	9		6	11	5	12	10[1]	8[3]	3				7[2]	1	2		14												10
				4		8		10		5	12		11	3			1	7[2]		2		6			13	9[1]								11
				4		8	12	10	11	9[2]			7[3]	3			1	14		2[1]		6				13	5							12
				4		8	7	10[1]	11	9[3]		14	12	3			1			2		6[2]					5	13						13
					8[2]	9	6		10			11	7[1]	3[3]		14			1	5			13		2		4	12						14
				3		8	6	13	10			11	7[2]		4	9[1]			1	2						12	5							15
			2	3[3]		8	7	12	10[2]			11	9[1]		4	14			1				13				5	6						16
						8	7[1]		10[2]			11			4			12	1	2		6	13	14	3		5	9[3]						17
						8	7		10			11	12		4				1	2		6			3		5	9[1]						18
						7[1]	8	13	10[2]			11[3]	12		6	9			1	2				14	5		3	4						19
				12			4		9			10[2]	8		6	11			1	2				13	5		3	7[1]						20
				12			7		10			11[2]	8		3[1]	9			1	2			13	14	4		5	6[3]						21
			12	6	8[1]		4		9			10	14		2	11			1					13	5[3]		3■		7[2]					22
			7[3]	3		8	4		9			10	14		5[2]			12	1	2				11[1]	13		6							23
			7	5		8	4[1]	13	9		14		10[2]	6		3		12	1	2										11[3]				24
			7■	3		8	4		9				10		5	6		12	1	2										11[1]				25
				5		8	3	12	10[2]				11[1]		4	9		6	1	2										7	13			26
			7[1]	3		8	4	13	9				10[2]		5	6		12	1	2										11[3]	14			27
	12		13	3		8	4		9				10[3]		5[1]	6		7[2]	1	2				14						11				28
	4		12	3		8	6[1]		10				11[2]			5		7	1	2				13						9				29
	5			3		8	4		9				10		12	6		7[3]	1	2[1]			13	14						11[2]				30
			7	3	2		4		9[2]	11[1]			10		5	6		8	1					13						12				31
	2		7	3	6	8	4[1]			11			9		5				1					10						12				32
	2[1]			3	4	8	12		13	6			9		5	14		7	1					10[2]						11[3]				33
				3	7	8	6[1]		13	5			10		4				1	2			12	11[2]						9				34
				3	8[3]	9	14		13	5			10[2]	12	4			6	1	2				7						11[1]				35
				3		8[3]			9					12	5	6		4	1	2			7[2]	10[1]						11	13		14	36

EAST FIFE — Second Division

Year Formed: 1903. *Ground & Address:* Bayview Stadium, Harbour View, Methil, Fife KY8 3RW. *Telephone:* 01333 426323. *Fax:* 01333 426376. *E-mail:* office@eastfife.org. *Website:* www.eastfife.org
Ground Capacity: all seated: 2000. *Size of Pitch:* 115yd × 75yd.
Chairman: William Gray. *Secretary:* James Stevenson.
Manager: David Baikie. *Assistant Manager:* Graeme Irons. *Physio:* Brian McNeil.
Club Nickname(s): The Fifers. *Previous Ground:* Bayview Park.
Record Attendance: 22,515 v Raith Rovers, Division I, 2 Jan 1950.
Record Transfer Fee received: £150,000 for Paul Hunter from Hull C (March 1990).
Record Transfer Fee paid: £70,000 for John Sludden from Kilmarnock (July 1991).
Record Victory: 13-2 v Edinburgh City, Division II, 11 Dec 1937.
Record Defeat: 0-9 v Hearts, Division I, 5 Oct 1957.
Most Capped Player: George Aitken, 5 (8), Scotland.
Most League Appearances: 517: David Clarke, 1968-86.
Most League Goals in Season (Individual): 41: Jock Wood, Division II; 1926-27 and Henry Morris, Division II, 1947-48.
Most Goals Overall (Individual): 225: Phil Weir, 1922-35.

EAST FIFE 2007–08 LEAGUE RECORD

Match No.	*Date*	*Venue*	*Opponents*	*Result*		*H/T Score*	*Lg. Pos.*	*Goalscorers*	*Attendance*
1	Aug 4	H	East Stirling	W	3-1	0-0	—	Nicholas [46], McDonald [77], Stewart [86]	692
2	11	A	Arbroath	W	3-2	2-1	1	Tosh (og) [10], Nicholas [28], Fotheringham [60]	768
3	18	A	Elgin C	W	3-2	1-1	1	Tweed [7], Walker [64], Gordon [90]	557
4	25	H	Stranraer	W	3-1	2-0	1	Fotheringham 2 [26, 45], McManus [71]	614
5	Sept 1	H	Forfar Ath	W	3-0	1-0	1	Blackadder [34], Cameron 2 [76, 88]	729
6	15	A	Montrose	L	1-3	0-2	1	Cameron (pen) [69]	612
7	22	A	Dumbarton	D	1-1	1-0	1	McManus [15]	692
8	29	H	Stenhousemuir	W	7-0	0-0	1	McManus 4 [47, 63, 68, 79], Walker [50], Smart 2 [53, 58]	540
9	Oct 6	H	Albion R	W	4-0	1-0	1	Cameron (pen) [40], McManus [73], Linn [77], Smart [88]	639
10	20	A	East Stirling	W	2-0	1-0	1	Cameron (pen) [41], McManus [58]	428
11	Nov 3	H	Elgin C	W	4-0	1-0	1	McManus [2], Smart [61], Walker [65], Linn [78]	635
12	10	A	Stranraer	W	2-0	1-0	1	McManus [15], O'Reilly [85]	487
13	Dec 1	H	Montrose	W	2-0	2-0	1	Fotheringham [26], McManus [42]	785
14	8	A	Forfar Ath	W	2-0	1-0	1	Tweed [4], Linn [46]	489
15	15	H	Dumbarton	W	2-0	1-0	1	McDonald [3], McGowan [83]	674
16	22	A	Stenhousemuir	L	1-2	1-1	1	McDonald [10]	755
17	26	H	Arbroath	L	0-2	0-1	1		907
18	29	A	Albion R	W	4-1	0-0	1	Cameron [59], O'Reilly [81], Gordon [86], Stewart [90]	472
19	Jan 2	H	Stranraer	W	2-1	0-0	1	O'Reilly [50], McDonald [84]	1029
20	5	A	Elgin C	W	2-1	1-0	1	Fotheringham [45], Stewart [85]	572
21	12	A	Montrose	W	1-0	1-0	—	Smart [11]	908
22	19	H	Forfar Ath	W	3-0	3-0	1	Linn [4], Davison [16], Fotheringham [24]	710
23	26	A	Arbroath	W	1-0	1-0	1	Templeman [36]	872
24	Feb 2	H	East Stirling	W	1-0	0-0	1	Cameron (pen) [90]	829
25	9	H	Stenhousemuir	L	0-1	0-0	1		753
26	16	A	Dumbarton	W	3-0	2-0	1	McDonald [20], Smart 2 [40, 89]	688
27	23	H	Elgin C	W	2-0	0-0	1	Stewart [63], Mackay (og) [67]	728
28	Mar 1	A	Stranraer	W	2-0	1-0	1	McManus [1], Linn [85]	260
29	8	H	Albion R	D	0-0	0-0	1		873
30	15	A	East Stirling	W	3-0	2-0	1	McManus 2 [6, 12], McDonald [76]	791
31	22	H	Montrose	D	0-0	0-0	1		773
32	29	A	Forfar Ath	W	3-2	0-1	1	McManus [74], McDonald [81], Templeman [86]	501
33	Apr 5	H	Dumbarton	W	2-1	1-0	1	Templeman [42], Cameron [58]	639
34	12	A	Stenhousemuir	W	1-0	1-0	1	Blackadder [42]	501
35	19	H	Arbroath	W	2-1	0-1	1	McManus 2 (1 pen) [69 (p), 80]	1340
36	26	A	Albion R	D	2-2	0-0	1	Linn [79], Fotheringham [85]	404

Final League Position: 1

Honours
League Champions: Division II 1947-48. Third Division 2007-08. *Runners-up:* Division II 1929-30, 1970-71. Second Division 1983-84, 1995-96. Third Division 2002-03.
Scottish Cup Winners: 1938; *Runners-up:* 1927, 1950.
League Cup Winners: 1947-48, 1949-50, 1953-54.

Club colours: Shirt: Gold and black. Shorts: White. Stockings: Black.

Goalscorers: *League* (77): McManus 17 (1 pen), Cameron 8 (4 pens), Fotheringham 7, McDonald 7, Smart 7, Linn 6, Stewart 4, O'Reilly 3, Templeman 3, Walker 3, Blackadder 2, Gordon 2, Nicholas 2, Tweed 2, Davison 1, McGowan 1, own goals 2.
Scottish Cup (4): Cameron 2 (1 pen), Smart 1, Tweed 1.
CIS Cup (2): McDonald 1, O'Reilly 1.
Challenge Cup (2): O'Reilly 1, Walker 1.

McCulloch W 14	Guy G 7 + 4	Fotheringham K 34	Young L 24 + 3	Smart J 33	Tweed S 31	Blackadder R 22 + 3	Stewart P 33 + 1	O'Reilly C 12 + 17	Nicholas S 5 + 11	Cameron D 36	McDonald G 33 + 1	Walker P 6 + 2	Gordon K 8 + 24	Linton S 1	McManus P 24 + 3	Fox S 11	Greenhill G 10 + 3	Martin J — + 4	Linn B 24 + 4	McGowan J 2	Davison K 3 + 4	Templeman C 12 + 1	Wight C 11	Muir D — + 1	Match No.
1	2[1]	3	4	5	6	7[2]	8	9[3]	10	11	12	13	14												1
1		3	4[2]	5	6	13	8	12	10[1]	7	2		14	11	9[3]										2
1		3		5	6	7	8	9[1]	10	11	2	4[2]	13		12										3
		3		5	6	7	8	9[1]	12	11	2		13		10[2]	1	4								4
		3		5	6	7	8	9		11	2		12		10[1]	1	4[2]	13							5
		3	4	5[3]	6	7	8	9[2]	10[1]	11	2	14	12		13	1									6
1		3	4	5	6	14	8[3]	9[1]	12	11[2]	2				10		7	13							7
	2[3]	3	12	5	6	14	8	13		11		4	10[2]		9	1	7[1]								8
1	2	3		5	6	7	8[3]	13		11		4[1]	10[2]		9			14	12						9
1		3	14	5	6	7	8			4	2	11[2]	12		9[3]			13	10[1]						10
		3	4	5	6		8	13		11	2	7	12		9[1]	1			10[2]						11
		3	4	5	6		8	12		11	2[2]	7[1]			9	1	13		10						12
		3	4	5	6	7	8	12		11	2		13		9[1]	1			10[2]						13
		3	4	5	6■	7	8	13		11	2		12		9[2]	1			10[1]						14
	2	3	4			7	8	12		11	5		13		9[1]	1			10[2]	6					15
	2		4	5	6	7[1]	8	9		11	3		12			1			10						16
	2	3[2]	4	5	6		8	12	14	11	7		13		9[1]	1			10[3]						17
1		3	4	5	6	7	8	9		11	2		12						10[1]						18
1		7	6[1]	3	4	9	8	10		5	2		13						11[2]		12				19
1	12	6	7	4	5[1]	11[3]	8	9	14	3	2		13						10[2]						20
1	12	7	9	3			8	10[2]	13	5	2		6						11	4[1]					21
1		7	9	3	4		8	13	14	5	2		12						11[3]		6[1]	10[2]			22
1		6	11	4	5		8	14	13	3	2		12						10[2]		7[1]	9[3]			23
1		7	9	3	4		8	13		5	2		12						11[2]		6[1]	10			24
1		6	8	3	4		7	13		5	2				9				11[2]		12	10[1]			25
		7		3	4	9	8	14		5	2		6[1]		11[3]				13		12	10[2]	1		26
		7	6[1]		4	9	2			5	3				11		12		8			10	1		27
		5	8			11	2[3]			3	4		7		10[2]		6		12		13	9[1]	1	14	28
		7	12	3	4	9	8	14		5	2		13		11[3]				6[2]			10[1]	1		29
		6[1]	7	4	5	11[3]	8		14	3	2		12		9		13		10[2]				1		30
		7[1]		3	4	9	12	10[3]	13	5	2		6[2]		14		8		11				1		31
			8	4	5	11				3	2		7		9		6[1]		10			12	1		32
	12	7	6	3	4[1]				9[3]	5	2		14		10		8[2]		13			11	1		33
	13	5		4		7[1]	8	14		3	2		12		9[3]		6[2]		11			10	1		34
		6		4	5		7	13	14	3	2		12		9[2]		8[1]		11			10[3]	1		35
	2[1]	6		4			8		12	3	5		7		9				11			10	1		36

EAST STIRLINGSHIRE Third Division

Year Formed: 1880. *Ground & Address:* Firs Park, Firs St, Falkirk FK2 7AY. *Telephone:* 01324 623583. *Fax:* 01324 637 862.
E-mail: lestshire@aol.com. *Website:* www.eaststirlingshire.com
Ground Capacity: total: 1880, seated: 200. *Size of Pitch:* 112yd × 72yd.
Chairman: A. Mackin. *Vice Chairman:* Douglas Morrison. *Chief Executive/Secretary:* Leslie G. Thomson.
Manager: Jim McInally. *Physio:* David Jenkins.
Club Nickname(s): The Shire. *Previous Grounds:* Burnhouse, Randyford Park, Merchiston Park, New Kilbowie Park.
Record Attendance: 12,000 v Partick Th, *Scottish Cup* 3rd rd, 21 Feb 1921.
Record Transfer Fee received: £35,000 for Jim Docherty to Chelsea (1978).
Record Transfer Fee paid: £6,000 for Colin McKinnon from Falkirk (March 1991).
Record Victory: 11-2 v Vale of Bannock, *Scottish Cup* 2nd rd, 22 Sept 1888.
Record Defeat: 1-12 v Dundee United, Division II, 13 Apr 1936.
Most Capped Player: Humphrey Jones, 5 (14), Wales.
Most League Appearances: 415: Gordon Russell, 1983-2001.
Most League Goals in Season (Individual): 36: Malcolm Morrison, Division II, 1938-39.

EAST STIRLINGSHIRE 2007–08 LEAGUE RECORD

Match No.	Date	Venue	Opponents	Result		H/T Score	Lg. Pos.	Goalscorers	Attendance
1	Aug 4	A	East Fife	L	1-3	0-0	—	Savage 58	692
2	11	H	Dumbarton	W	3-2	2-2	7	McBride K 19, Brand 2 41, 60	306
3	18	H	Forfar Ath	W	2-1	2-1	5	Kelly (pen) 27, Brand 33	329
4	25	A	Stenhousemuir	W	3-0	2-0	2	Simpson 2 6, 29, Savage 87	520
5	Sept 1	A	Albion R	W	3-2	0-2	2	Donnelly (og) 73, Kelly (pen) 85, Simpson 90	488
6	15	H	Stranraer	L	2-3	1-0	3	Moffat 27, Savage 47	331
7	22	A	Elgin C	L	0-6	0-2	4		399
8	29	H	Arbroath	L	2-3	2-2	5	Savage 2, Colquhoun 40	407
9	Oct 6	A	Montrose	L	1-3	0-2	6	Savage 61	407
10	20	H	East Fife	L	0-2	0-1	7		428
11	Nov 3	A	Forfar Ath	W	2-0	0-0	5	Simpson 86, Donaldson 89	322
12	10	H	Stenhousemuir	D	1-1	0-1	6	Savage 77	528
13	Dec 1	A	Stranraer	L	1-2	1-1	8	Doyle 2	241
14	8	H	Albion R	L	4-5	3-1	8	Brand 2 2, 61, Ure 27, Savage 32	239
15	15	H	Elgin C	W	3-1	1-1	7	Brand 3 26, 64, 71	291
16	18	A	Dumbarton	L	1-3	0-2	—	Brand 61	303
17	29	H	Montrose	L	0-3	0-0	8		295
18	Jan 2	A	Stenhousemuir	L	0-3	0-3	8		477
19	5	H	Forfar Ath	W	4-1	0-1	8	Brand 60, Savage 72, Donaldson 82, McBride K 90	263
20	19	A	Albion R	D	2-2	2-1	8	Donaldson 36, McKenzie 39	296
21	Feb 2	A	East Fife	L	0-1	0-0	8		829
22	9	H	Arbroath	L	0-1	0-1	8		368
23	23	A	Forfar Ath	L	0-1	0-0	8		344
24	27	A	Arbroath	L	0-2	0-0	—		421
25	Mar 1	H	Stenhousemuir	L	3-4	2-2	9	Brand 17, Simpson 28, Savage 64	369
26	4	H	Stranraer	L	1-3	0-0	—	Brownlie 58	235
27	8	A	Montrose	L	0-2	0-0	9		410
28	15	H	East Fife	L	0-3	0-2	10		791
29	19	A	Elgin C	L	0-3	0-0	—		357
30	22	A	Stranraer	L	1-2	1-1	10	Donaldson 7	152
31	25	H	Dumbarton	D	1-1	1-0	—	Bolochoweckyj 10	359
32	29	H	Albion R	W	3-0	0-0	10	Bolochoweckyj 46, Oates 69, McBride K 72	262
33	Apr 5	H	Elgin C	D	0-0	0-0	10		426
34	12	A	Arbroath	W	1-0	1-0	10	Nicholls 35	501
35	19	A	Dumbarton	L	0-1	0-1	10		612
36	26	H	Montrose	W	3-1	1-0	9	Rodgers 40, Savage 65, Bolochoweckyj 80	551

Final League Position: 9

Honours
League Champions: Division II 1931-32; C Division 1947-48. *Runners-up:* Division II 1962-63. Second Division 1979-80. Division Three 1923-24.

Club colours: Shirt: Black with white. Shorts: Black with white. Stockings: Black with white hoops.

Goalscorers: *League* (48): Brand 11, Savage 10, Simpson 5, Donaldson 4, Bolochoweckyj 3, McBride K 3, Kelly 2 (2 pens), Brownlie 1, Colquhoun 1, Doyle 1, McKenzie 1, Moffat 1, Nicholls 1, Oates 1, Rodgers 1, Ure 1, own goal 1.
Scottish Cup (7): Savage 2, Brand 1, Donaldson 1, Kelly 1 (pen), Simpson 1, Ure 1.
CIS Cup (1): McBride K 1 (pen).
Challenge Cup (5): Simpson 3, Struthers 2.

Hill D 14	Doyle P 14 + 2	McBride K 28 + 2	Kelly G 15 + 5	King D 25 + 2	Thywissen C 26 + 3	McKenzie M 12 + 14	Brand A 30	Savage J 25 + 3	McLaren G 2 + 1	Ure D 30 + 4	Struthers K 1 + 5	Moffat G 12 + 2	Donaldson C 25 + 4	Simpson S 11 + 12	McBride P 5 + 7	Carr R 2 + 2	Oates S 21 + 5	Upton S — + 1	Brownlie P 16 + 7	Gibb S 24 + 1	Colquhoun D 1	McShane J — + 1	Brown M 7	Rodgers A 13	Mitchell T 1	Smith A 3	O'Connor G 13	Richardson D 2	Bolochoweckyj M 9	Black C 2 + 2	Nicholls D 6	McIntyre N 1	*Match No.*
1	2	3	4	5	6	7	8	9	10^{1}	11^{2}	12	13																					1
1	12	3	4^{2}	5	6	7^{1}	8	9	10		13	2	11																				2
1	2^{2}	3	4	5	6		8	9	13	11		10	7^{1}	12																			3
1	2	3	4	5	6		8	9		11			7	10^{1}	12																		4
1	2	3	4	5	6		8	9		11	12		7^{1}	10																			5
1	12	3■	4	5	6		8^{3}	9		11^{2}		2	7^{1}	10		14	13																6
1	2■		4	5^{2}	6			9		11	8	3	7	10^{1}				13	12														7
1		3	4	5	6			9		11		2		13			12		7^{1}	8	10^{2}												8
1		3	4	5	6			9		11	13	2^{1}		12			7^{2}		10	8													9
1	2	3	4^{1}	5	6			9			12		8^{2}	10^{3}		13	11		7			14											10
1	2	3			6			9		12		7	8	10		5			4^{1}	11													11
1	2	3			6	13	8	9		12		7^{2}	11	10		5^{1}				4													12
1	2	3		12	6^{1}	7	8	9^{2}		11			10				13		4	5													13
1	2	3		5^{1}		7	8	9		11			10	13			12		6^{2}	4													14
	2		12		6	7	8	9^{2}		11			10	13			5		4^{1}	3			1										15
	2	13	12		6	7^{3}	8	9		11			10	14			3^{2}		4^{1}	5			1										16
	2			12	6^{1}	7	8	9■		11		4^{3}	10^{2}	13			5		14	3			1										17
	4^{1}	3	12		5	7	8			11			10	9^{2}			13		6	2			1										18
		3	6		5	7^{1}	8	9		11			10^{2}	13			4		12	2			1										19
		3	6		5	7^{2}	8			11			10^{1}	13	9		4		12	2			1										20
		9^{2}		5	4	12	8	10^{3}		14			6^{1}		13		3		7	2			1	11									21
		11		3	5	12	8	9^{2}		14					13		4		6	2^{1}				10	1	7^{3}							22
		6		3	5	7^{1}	8^{2}	13		11				12	9^{3}		4		14					10		2	1						23
		3	14	4		12		9		11^{3}		2		13	10^{1}		5■		6					7^{2}		8	1						24
			12	3	5	13	8	9		11		2■	14	7^{1}					6^{3}	4				10^{2}			1						25
				3	5	12	8	9^{2}		11			14	7^{1}	13		2		6	4^{3}				10			1						26
			11^{1}		4	14	8^{2}			9		2	12	6^{3}	13		5		7	3				10			1						27
		14	6		5	7^{2}	10	9^{3}		11				12	13				8^{1}	2							1	3	4				28
		3	8^{1}	6	13	12	10			11			7		9^{2}		4			2							1		5				29
		3^{2}		6		13	8			11			7		10^{1}		4		12	2				9			1		5				30
		3		6	13		8			11			7^{2}		12		4			2				9^{1}			1		5		10		31
		3		6^{1}		12	8			11		14	7^{2}				4			2^{3}				9			1		5	13	10		32
		3		6		13	8^{3}			11			12				4			2				9^{2}			1	7^{1}	5	14	10		33
		3		6		13	8	9^{1}		11^{2}			7				4		12								1		5	2	10		34
		5		7^{3}		14	8	12		9			6^{2}				3			13				10					4	2^{1}	11	1	35
		2^{1}		6	14	13	8	12		11			7				4			3				9^{2}			1		5		10^{3}		36

ELGIN CITY — Third Division

Year Formed: 1893. *Ground and Address:* Borough Briggs, Borough Briggs Road, Elgin IV30 1AP.
Telephone: 01343 551114. *Fax:* 01343 547921. *E-mail:* elgincityfc@ukonline.co.uk. *Website:* www.elgincity.com
Ground Capacity: 3927, seated 478, standing 3449. *Size of pitch:* 111yd × 72yd.
Chairman: Derek W. Shewan. *Secretary:* Ian A. Allan. *Administrator:* Audrey Fanning.
Manager: Robbie Williamson. *Assistant Manager:* Kenny Gilbert. *Director of Football:* Graham Tatters. *Physios:* Billy Belcher and Leigh Thomas.
Previous names: 1893-1900 Elgin City, 1900–03 Elgin City United, 1903– Elgin City.
Club Nickname(s): City or Black & Whites. *Previous Grounds:* Association Park 1893-95; Milnfield Park 1895-1909; Station Park 1909-19; Cooper Park 1919-21.
Record Attendance: 12,608 v Arbroath, Scottish Cup, 17 Feb 1968.
Record Transfer Fee received: £32,000 for Michael Teasdale to Dundee (Jan 1994).
Record Transfer Fee paid: £10,000 to Fraserburgh for Russell McBride (July 2001).
Record Victory: 18-1 v Brora Rangers, North of Scotland Cup, 6 Feb 1960.
Record Defeat: 1-14 v Hearts, Scottish Cup, 4 Feb 1939.
Most League Appearances: 191: David Hind, 2001-08.
Most League Goals in Season (Individual): 20: Martin Johnston, 2005-06.
Most Goals Overall (Individual): 39: Martin Johnston, 2005-07.

ELGIN CITY 2007–08 LEAGUE RECORD

Match No.	Date	Venue	Opponents	Result		H/T Score	Lg. Pos.	Goalscorers	Attendance
1	Aug 4	A	Dumbarton	L	0-1	0-0	—		640
2	11	H	Montrose	L	0-2	0-0	9		479
3	18	H	East Fife	L	2-3	1-1	9	Martin [39], Smith [73]	557
4	25	A	Forfar Ath	L	0-4	0-1	10		328
5	Sept 1	A	Arbroath	L	0-4	0-3	10		525
6	15	H	Albion R	W	3-2	0-1	10	Shallicker 2 [85, 88], Kaczan [90]	310
7	22	H	East Stirling	W	6-0	2-0	9	Shallicker 3 (1 pen) [33 (p), 40, 52], Frizzel 2 [60, 80], Nicolson [62]	399
8	29	A	Stranraer	D	3-3	2-1	9	Shallicker [15], Smith [39], Kaczan [78]	270
9	Oct 6	A	Stenhousemuir	W	3-2	0-1	7	Dickson [57], Sutherland [60], Tansley [78]	378
10	12	A	Montrose	D	0-0	0-0	—		623
11	20	H	Dumbarton	W	2-1	2-0	5	Smith [18], Frizzel [33]	541
12	Nov 3	A	East Fife	L	0-4	0-1	6		635
13	10	H	Forfar Ath	D	2-2	1-1	7	Martin 2 [45, 68]	472
14	Dec 1	A	Albion R	W	4-3	1-1	5	Shallicker [30], Campbell [60], Dickson [70], Frizzel [80]	186
15	8	H	Arbroath	L	1-3	1-1	6	Bishop (og) [2]	422
16	15	A	East Stirling	L	1-3	1-1	8	Martin [25]	291
17	29	H	Stenhousemuir	W	2-0	0-0	7	Shallicker [47], Martin [75]	456
18	Jan 2	A	Forfar Ath	W	1-0	0-0	7	Smith [65]	332
19	5	H	East Fife	L	1-2	0-1	6	Smith [75]	572
20	19	A	Arbroath	L	0-2	0-2	7		486
21	26	H	Montrose	W	2-1	1-1	6	Charlesworth 2 [26, 79]	449
22	Feb 2	A	Dumbarton	W	4-1	3-0	6	Frizzel [1], Charlesworth 2 (1 pen) [32 (p), 44], O'Donoghue [52]	514
23	9	A	Stranraer	D	0-0	0-0	6		191
24	23	A	East Fife	L	0-2	0-0	6		728
25	27	H	Stranraer	L	0-5	0-3	—		336
26	Mar 1	H	Forfar Ath	W	3-1	0-0	6	Campbell [47], Mackay 2 (1 pen) [65 (p), 75]	452
27	5	H	Albion R	D	1-1	1-0	—	Crooks [10]	301
28	8	A	Stenhousemuir	D	2-2	0-1	6	Frizzel [72], Shallicker [90]	291
29	15	H	Dumbarton	W	2-1	1-0	6	O'Donoghue [25], Shallicker [71]	551
30	19	H	East Stirling	W	3-0	0-0	—	Kaczan [53], Shallicker [57], Frizzel [62]	357
31	22	A	Albion R	D	1-1	1-1	5	Campbell [27]	212
32	29	H	Arbroath	W	2-1	1-0	5	Shallicker [17], Campbell [68]	624
33	Apr 5	A	East Stirling	D	0-0	0-0	5		426
34	12	H	Stranraer	L	2-3	1-1	5	Sutherland 2 [43, 62]	619
35	19	A	Montrose	L	2-3	1-1	5	Mackay [42], Kaczan [89]	492
36	26	H	Stenhousemuir	L	1-5	1-3	6	Crooks [35]	582

Final League Position: 6

Honours
Scottish Cup: Quarter-finals 1968.
Highland League Champions: winners 15 times.
Scottish Qualifying Cup (North): winners 7 times.
North of Scotland Cup: winners 17 times.
Highland League Cup: winners 5 times.
Inverness Cup: winners twice.

Club colours: Shirt: Black and white vertical stripes. Shorts: Black. Stockings: Red.

Goalscorers: *League* (56): Shallicker 12 (1 pen), Frizzel 7, Martin 5, Smith 5, Campbell 4, Charlesworth 4 (1 pen), Kaczan 4, Mackay 3 (1 pen), Sutherland 3, Crooks 2, Dickson 2, O'Donoghue 2, Nicolson 1, Tansley 1, own goal 1.
Scottish Cup (0).
CIS Cup (1): Charlesworth 1.
Challenge Cup (1): Nicolson 1.

Malin J 2	Campbell C 27 + 3	Dickson H 15	Frizzel C 30 + 6	Dempsie A 27 + 2	Hind D 25 + 5	Gibert K 25 + 1	Nicolson M 30	Shallicker D 18 + 5	Charlesworth M 6 + 6	O'Donoghue R 27 + 5	Martin W 10 + 1	Smith M 21 + 5	Kaczan P 29 + 3	Ross D 8 + 12	Dunn S 2	Ridgers A 31	Lewis A — + 1	Sutherland Z 31 + 1	Tansley A — + 2	Bowden M 1	Crooks J 7 + 4	Mackay S 10 + 2	Niven D 14	Cameron B — + 1	Match No.
1	2	3	4	5	6[2]	7	8	9[1]	10	11	12■	13													1
1	2	3	4	5	6	7			10[1]	11		12	8	9											2
	2	3	13	5		7	8		12	11	10[1]	6	4	9[2]	1										3
	2	3	12	5	13	7	8			11	10[1]	6	4	9[2]	1										4
	2	3	4[3]	5■	13	7[1]	8	12		11[2]		6	9			1	14	10							5
	2	3[3]	4		6	7	8[1]	9	13	12		5	14	10[2]		1		11							6
	2[3]	3	4	12	6	7[1]	8	9[2]	13			11	5	14		1		10							7
	2	3	4[1]	13	6	7■	8	9[2]		12		5	10			1		11							8
	2	3	4	5	6		8			12		10	7[1]	9[2]		1		11	13						9
	2	3	4	5	6		8	9[1]				10	7	12		1		11							10
	2	3	4[2]	5	6		8	9[1]		13		7	11	12		1		10							11
	14	3[2]	12	5	13	7	8			11	9[3]	6	2	10[1]		1		4							12
		3	12	5	6	7	8	13		11	4[2]	9		10[1]				2		1					13
	12	3	13	5	6	7	2	9[2]		11	8[1]	4■				1		10							14
	2	3■	12	5	6	7	8■	9[2]		11[3]	10[1]		14	13		1		4							15
	2		4	5	6	7		9		11	8[2]		10	12		1		3[1]	13						16
			4	5	6	7	8	9	12		3[1]	10	2			1		11							17
			11	3	4	6	2	9		12	8	10[1]	5			1		7							18
			11	3	4	6	2	9	12		8[1]	10	5			1		7							19
	13		8[2]	3	4[1]	6	2	9	12	11		10	5[3]	14		1		7							20
	10		11[1]	3	13	6	2	12	9[2]	4		8	5			1		7							21
	11		9[3]	5	14	7	2		10[1]	3		8	4	13		1		6[2]			12				22
	10		11				2		9	4		8	5			1		7				3	6		23
			9		8[3]		2	13	10[2]	11		14	4	7[1]		1		6			12	5	3		24
			10		6	12	2			8		7[1]	5			1		11			9	3	4		25
	11		10	3		6				4		8	5			1		12			9[1]	7	2		26
	11		10	3		6				4			5			1		7			9	8	2		27
	8		10	3			2	12		6			5	13		1		7			9[1]	11[2]	4		28
	8		10[1]	3			2	9		6			5			1		7			12	11	4		29
	3		11		8	6	2	9[2]		10[1]		12	5	14		1		7[3]			13		4		30
	3		11		8	6	2			10		12	5			1		7			9[1]		4		31
	8		11	3	4	6		9[1]		10			5			1		7				12	2		32
	8		11	3	4	6[2]		9		10			5[1]	13		1		7				12	2		33
	8		11	3	4		2	9		10						1		7				6	5		34
	8		10	5	3		2[2]			11			12	13		1		6			9[1]	7	4		35
	8		11		6		2			10			5[1]	12		1		7[2]			9	3	4	13	36

FALKIRK Premier League

Year Formed: 1876. *Ground & Address:* The Falkirk Stadium, Westfield, Falkirk FK2 9DX. *Telephone:* 01324 624121. *Fax:* 01324 612418. *Website:* www.falkirkfc.co.uk
Ground Capacity: seated: 6123. *Size of Pitch:* 110yd × 72yd.
Chairman: Campbell Christie. *Managing Director:* George Craig. *Head of Development:* Eddie May. *Secretary:* Alex Blackwood.
Head Coach: John Hughes. *Assistant Coach:* Brian Rice. *Director of Football:* Alex Totten. *Youth Co-ordinator:* Ian McIntyre.
Club Nickname(s): The Bairns. *Previous Grounds:* Randyford 1876-81; Blinkbonny Grounds 1881-83; Brockville Park 1883-2003.
Record Attendance: 23,100 v Celtic, Scottish Cup 3rd rd, 21 Feb 1953.
Record Transfer Fee received: £380,000 for John Hughes to Celtic (Aug 1995).
Record Transfer Fee paid: £225,000 to Chelsea for Kevin McAllister (Aug 1991).
Record Victory: 12-1 v Laurieston, Scottish Cup 2nd rd, 23 Sept 1893.
Record Defeat: 1-11 v Airdrieonians, Division I, 28 Apr 1951.
Most Capped Player: Alex Parker, 14 (15), Scotland.
Most League Appearances: (post-war): 353: George Watson, 1975-87.
Most League Goals in Season (Individual): 43: Evelyn Morrison, Division I, 1928-29.
Most Goals Overall (Individual): 86: Dougie Moran, 1957-61 and 1964-67.

FALKIRK 2007–08 LEAGUE RECORD

Match No.	Date	Venue	Opponents	Result		H/T Score	Lg. Pos.	Goalscorers	Attendance
1	Aug 4	A	Gretna	W	4-0	2-0	—	Higdon 2 14, 24, Moutinho 66, Latapy 74	2731
2	11	H	Celtic	L	1-4	1-1	5	Higdon 5	6329
3	18	A	Rangers	L	2-7	1-2	8	Arnau 44, Barrett 72	46,061
4	25	H	St Mirren	L	0-1	0-0	8		5339
5	Sept 1	A	Dundee U	L	0-2	0-0	9		6864
6	15	H	Hibernian	D	1-1	0-1	10	Moutinho 47	6298
7	22	H	Motherwell	W	1-0	0-0	8	Latapy 74	5245
8	29	A	Inverness CT	L	2-4	1-3	9	Milne 28, Arfield 47	4011
9	Oct 6	A	Hearts	L	2-4	0-2	9	Barrett 87, Moutinho 89	15,800
10	20	H	Kilmarnock	D	1-1	1-1	10	Finnigan 2	5143
11	28	A	Aberdeen	D	1-1	0-1	11	Cregg 68	10,399
12	Nov 3	H	Gretna	W	2-0	1-0	10	Barr 41, Barrett 50	4843
13	24	H	Rangers	L	1-3	0-1	11	Moutinho 62	6627
14	Dec 1	A	St Mirren	W	5-1	3-0	10	Moutinho 2 5, 41, Thomson 14, Barrett 82, Finnigan 85	4133
15	8	H	Dundee U	W	3-0	2-0	9	Moutinho 5, Barrett 41, Higdon 66	4803
16	11	A	Celtic	L	0-4	0-2	—		54,411
17	15	A	Hibernian	D	1-1	0-1	9	Barrett 80	12,391
18	22	A	Motherwell	W	3-0	0-0	8	Higdon 2 49, 60, Cregg 65	5247
19	26	H	Inverness CT	W	1-0	1-0	7	Aafjes 35	5265
20	29	H	Hearts	W	2-1	0-1	7	Finnigan 78, Higdon 81	6614
21	Jan 2	A	Kilmarnock	W	1-0	1-0	6	Finnigan 11	5956
22	5	H	Aberdeen	D	0-0	0-0	6		5457
23	19	A	Gretna	L	0-2	0-1	6		1609
24	27	H	Celtic	L	0-1	0-1	6		6803
25	Feb 9	A	Rangers	L	0-2	0-1	7		48,601
26	16	H	St Mirren	W	4-0	1-0	6	Arfield 2 6, 58, Cregg 2 61, 71	5803
27	23	A	Dundee U	D	0-0	0-0	6		6835
28	27	H	Hibernian	L	0-2	0-1	—		5928
29	Mar 1	H	Motherwell	D	0-0	0-0	6		5108
30	15	A	Inverness CT	W	1-0	0-0	6	Clarke 86	4012
31	22	A	Hearts	D	0-0	0-0	6		16,682
32	29	H	Kilmarnock	D	0-0	0-0	6		5154
33	Apr 7	A	Aberdeen	L	1-2	0-1	—	Finnigan 49	11,484
34	19	H	Gretna	D	0-0	0-0	8		4490
35	26	A	St Mirren	L	0-1	0-0	8		3574
36	May 5	H	Hearts	W	2-1	1-0	—	Scobbie 45, Finnigan 52	4638
37	10	H	Inverness CT	W	2-1	1-0	7	Higdon 28, Finnigan 68	5631
38	17	A	Kilmarnock	L	1-2	1-1	7	Moutinho 11	5475

Final League Position: 7

Honours
League Champions: Division II 1935-36, 1969-70, 1974-75. First Division 1990-91, 1993-94, 2002-03, 2004-05. Second Division 1979-80; *Runners-up:* Division I 1907-08, 1909-10. First Division 1985-86, 1988-89. Division II 1904-05, 1951-52, 1960-61.
Scottish Cup Winners: 1913, 1957; *Runners-up:* 1997. *League Cup Runners-up:* 1947-48. *B&Q Cup Winners:* 1993-94. *League Challenge Cup Winners:* 1997-98, 2004-05.

Club colours: Shirt: Navy blue with white seams. Shorts: Navy. Stockings: Navy with two white hoops.

Goalscorers: *League* (45): Higdon 8, Moutinho 8, Finnigan 7, Barrett 6, Cregg 4, Arfield 3, Latapy 2, Aafjes 1, Arnau 1, Barr 1, Clarke 1, Milne 1, Scobbie 1, Thomson 1.
Scottish Cup (3): Arnau 1, Barr 1, Barrett 1.
CIS Cup (2): Higdon 1, Thomson 1.

Krul T 22	Ross J 23	Scobbie T 29 + 3	Cregg P 36	Barr D 33	Milne K 24 + 4	Moutinho P 29 + 8	Thomson S 17 + 1	Higdon M 24 + 4	Latapy R 12 + 20	Arnau13 + 6	Arfield S 31 + 4	Wallner R — + 2	Moffat K — + 3	Craig L — + 6	Barrett G 26 + 7	Finnigan C 19 + 12	Aafjes J 23 + 3	Holden D 20	Allison B 1 + 2	Mitchell C 3 + 2	Olejnik R 12 + 1	Bradley S 1 + 2	McBride K 15	Clarke B 1 + 7	Stewart M — + 3	Robertson D — + 1	Supple S 4	*Match No.*
1	2	3	4	5	6	7^{3}	8	9	10^{2}	11^{1}	12	13	14															1
1	2	3	4	5	6■	7	8^{3}	9	10^{2}	11^{1}	12			14	13													2
1	2	3	4	5	6	7^{2}	8	9^{1}	10	11^{3}	14				12	13												3
1	2	3	4	5	6	7	8^{1}	9	10^{2}		11			12	13													4
1	2		4	5		7	8^{2}	9	10		14			13	11^{3}	12	6	3^{1}										5
1	2^{1}	13	4■	5■	6	7	8	14	10	11^{2}					9^{3}		12	3										6
1		3			6	7^{2}	8	9	10	11^{1}	4				12	13	2	5										7
1		3^{1}	4	5	6	7^{3}		9	10^{2}		8	13			14	11		2	12									8
1		3	4	5	6	7	12	9^{2}	10^{1}	11^{3}	8				14	13		2										9
1			4	5	6	12	8	9	13		7				11^{1}	10^{2}	3	2										10
1			4	5	6^{2}	14		9^{3}		11^{1}	7			12	8	10	2	3	13									11
1			4	5	6	7^{2}		12	11^{3}		8		13	14	10	9^{1}	2	3										12
1			4	5	6	12	8	13	10^{1}		7				11	9^{2}	2	3										13
1		12	4	5	6	7	8	9^{3}			11^{2}			13	10	14	2	3^{1}										14
1			4^{3}	5	6	7^{1}	8	9^{2}	12	14	11				10	13	2	3										15
1		12	4^{2}	5■	6	7	8	9^{3}	14	13	11				10^{1}		2	3										16
1	2	3	4			7^{1}	8	9^{2}	12		11				10	13	5	6										17
1	2	3	4	5		7^{2}	8^{3}	9	13		11				10^{1}	12		6		14								18
1	2	3	4		13	7	8	9^{3}	12		11^{2}				10^{1}	14	5	6										19
1	2	3	4^{1}			7	8	9	12		11				10^{2}	13	5	6										20
1■	2	3	4	5		7^{1}	8	9	12^{2}	14	11					10^{3}		6			13							21
	2	3	4	5	13			9^{3}	12	11	7■				8^{2}	10^{1}	14	6			1							22
1	2	3	4^{1}	5	13	7^{2}			14	11					9	10		6^{3}				12	8					23
	2	3	4	5	12	7			13	11	8				9^{3}	14		6^{1}			1		10^{2}					24
	2	3	4	5	6^{1}	7^{2}			12		9				10	11	8				1			13				25
	2	3	4	5	6	7^{1}					11				9^{2}	10^{3}					1	13	8	12	14			26
	2	3	4	5	6	7			12		11^{1}				9						1		8	10^{2}		13		27
	2^{1}	3	4	5	6	13			10^{2}		11				9		12				1	7^{3}	8	14				28
		3	4	5	6	7^{1}					11				9	10	2				1		8	12				29
		3	4^{1}	5	6	7^{3}			12	13	11				9	10^{2}	2				1		8	14				30
	2	3	4	5	6	12				13	11				9	10^{1}	8				1		7^{2}					31
	2	3^{2}	4^{3}	5	6^{1}	12			13	14	7				9	10	8				1		11					32
	2^{3}	3	4	5	6^{2}	12		13	14		7				9	10^{1}	11				1		8					33
	2	3^{3}		5		7		9^{2}	14	11	8				10^{1}	13	6						4	12			1	34
	2^{1}	3	4	5		12		9^{2}		11■	6					10	7^{3}			14			8	13			1	35
		3	4	5		7^{1}		9	12		11					10	6			2			8				1	36
		3	4	5		7^{2}		9	12		11^{1}		13			10^{3}	6			2			8		14		1	37
		3	4^{1}			7^{3}		9	12	11					13	10^{2}	5		6	2	1		8		14			38

FORFAR ATHLETIC Third Division

Year Formed: 1885. *Ground & Address:* Station Park, Carseview Road, Forfar. *Telephone:* 01307 463576/462259. *Fax:* 01307 466956. *E-mail:* pat@ramsayladders.co.uk. *Website:* www.forfarathletic.co.uk
Ground Capacity: total: 4602, seated: 739. *Size of Pitch:* 115yd × 69yd.
Chairman: Neill Wilson. *Secretary:* David McGregor.
Manager: Dick Campbell.
Club Nickname(s): Loons. *Previous Grounds:* None.
Record Attendance: 10,780 v Rangers, Scottish Cup 2nd rd, 2 Feb 1970.
Record Transfer Fee received: £65,000 for David Bingham to Dunfermline Ath (September 1995).
Record Transfer Fee paid: £50,000 for Ian McPhee from Airdrieonians (1991).
Record Victory: 14-1 v Lindertis, Scottish Cup 1st rd, 1 Sept 1988.
Record Defeat: 2-12 v King's Park, Division II, 2 Jan 1930.
Most League Appearances: 484: Ian McPhee, 1978-88 and 1991-98.
Most League Goals in Season (Individual): 45: Dave Kilgour, Division II, 1929-30.
Most Goals Overall: 124: John Clark, 1978-91.

FORFAR ATHLETIC 2007–08 LEAGUE RECORD

Match No.	Date		Venue	Opponents	Result		H/T Score	Lg. Pos.	Goalscorers	Attendance
1	Aug	4	A	Stranraer	L	0-3	0-1	—		377
2		11	H	Stenhousemuir	L	0-1	0-1	10		349
3		18	A	East Stirling	L	1-2	1-2	10	Ovenstone 33	329
4		25	H	Elgin C	W	4-0	1-0	8	Duell 12, Stuart 2 48, 64, Lunan 67	328
5	Sept	1	A	East Fife	L	0-3	0-1	9		729
6		15	H	Arbroath	L	1-3	0-2	9	Duell 90	615
7		22	H	Montrose	L	1-4	1-3	10	Grady 9	584
8	Oct	6	A	Dumbarton	D	0-0	0-0	10		668
9		9	A	Albion R	L	1-2	1-0	—	Kilgallon 17	272
10		20	H	Stranraer	D	1-1	1-0	10	Rattray 35	332
11	Nov	3	H	East Stirling	L	0-2	0-0	10		322
12		10	A	Elgin C	D	2-2	1-1	10	Fotheringham 15, Kilgallon 56	472
13		24	A	Stenhousemuir	L	0-4	0-3	—		212
14	Dec	1	A	Arbroath	W	4-3	1-2	10	Stuart 23, Lunan 46, Kerrigan 80, Tulloch 88	621
15		8	H	East Fife	L	0-2	0-1	10		489
16		15	A	Montrose	W	1-0	1-0	10	Rattray 32	588
17		29	H	Dumbarton	W	3-1	2-1	10	Fotheringham 2, Smith 39, Lunan 79	422
18	Jan	2	H	Elgin C	L	0-1	0-0	10		332
19		5	A	East Stirling	L	1-4	1-0	10	McCallum 21	263
20		19	A	East Fife	L	0-3	0-3	10		710
21		26	H	Stenhousemuir	L	1-2	0-1	10	Kerrigan 53	293
22	Feb	2	A	Stranraer	L	1-2	0-1	10	Duell 78	147
23		9	A	Albion R	D	0-0	0-0	10		232
24		16	H	Montrose	D	1-1	0-1	10	Ovenstone 86	554
25		23	H	East Stirling	W	1-0	0-0	10	Lombardi 69	344
26		26	H	Albion R	W	1-0	0-0	—	Anton 59	270
27	Mar	1	A	Elgin C	L	1-3	0-0	10	Graham 56	452
28		11	H	Arbroath	W	1-0	1-0	—	Kilgannon 4	566
29		15	H	Stranraer	W	1-0	0-0	8	Fraser J 53	342
30		22	A	Arbroath	D	1-1	1-0	9	McNally 31	723
31		29	H	East Fife	L	2-3	1-0	9	Ovenstone 9, Stuart 79	501
32	Apr	5	A	Montrose	D	2-2	1-1	9	Fraser J 42, Geddes 84	590
33		8	A	Dumbarton	D	0-0	0-0	—		282
34		12	H	Albion R	L	1-4	0-2	9	Graham 54	331
35		19	A	Stenhousemuir	L	0-2	0-1	9		387
36		26	H	Dumbarton	D	1-1	0-0	10	Ovenstone 71	400

Final League Position: 10

Honours
League Champions: Second Division 1983-84. Third Division 1994-95; *Runners-up:* 1996-97. C Division 1948-49.
Scottish Cup: Semi-finals 1982.
League Cup: Semi-finals 1977-78.
Bell's League Challenge: Semi-finals 2004-05.

Club colours: Shirt: Sky blue with navy side panels, shoulder/sleeve bands. Shorts: Navy with sky blue side trim. Stockings: Sky blue with navy band on top.

Goalscorers: *League* (35): Ovenstone 4, Stuart 4, Duell 3, Kilgannon 3, Lunan 3, Fotheringham 2, Fraser J 2, Graham 2, Kerrigan 2, Rattray 2, Anton 1, Geddes 1, Grady 1, Lombardi 1, McCallum 1, McNally 1, Smith 1, Tulloch 1.
Scottish Cup (1): Mackay 1.
CIS Cup (0).
Challenge Cup (3): Lombardi 1, Lunan 1, Tulloch 1.

Wood S 33	Smith E 30 + 3	Ovenstone J 32 + 2	Grady S 6 + 5	Beith G 4 + 3	Dunn D 10	Kerrigan S 21 + 6	Fotheringham M 17 + 5	Lumsden C 9 + 1	Tulloch S 18 + 2	Duell B 23 + 5	Fraser J 21 + 2	Lombardi M 14 + 5	McNally S 32	Stuart M 16 + 7	Watson S — + 2	Allison M 3 + 1	Lunan P 14	Kilgannon S 15 + 2	Reid A 3 + 1	Mackie C 4 + 1	McCallum N 6 + 6	Fraser G 3	Rattray A 7	Anderson C — + 2	Anton C 9 + 2	Stephen N 13	Donachie B 15	Geddes C 6 + 6	Cruickshank A 2 + 3	Graham M 10	Match No.
1	2	3	4	5	6	7^{1}	8	9	10	11^{2}	12	13																			1
1	2	3	14	5	6^{3}			8	10	11^{1}	7	9^{2}	4	12	13																2
1		3	14	5^{2}			8	9^{1}	10^{3}	12		11	2	13		4	6	7													3
1	2	3	14	12			8		10^{1}	11^{2}		13	4	9^{3}		5	6	7													4
1	2	3		14		12	8^{1}		10	11		13	4■	9^{3}		5	6■	7^{2}													5
	2	3	12	5	6	7		13	8	9		10^{2}		11^{1}				4	1												6
	12	3	4		6	7	8	9	5^{1}	11^{2}		10	2		13				1												7
1	2	3	4		6	7	8						5					11		10	12	9^{1}									8
1	2	3			6	7	8^{1}				12		5				4	11		9	13	10^{2}									9
1	2	3	4	13		7	12				8		5				6^{1}	9^{2}		10			11								10
1	2	3	11			7	8^{3}		14				4			12	6	9		10^{2}	13		5^{1}								11
1		3	12			7	8^{2}	9	10	13	6		2				4	11			5^{1}										12
1	13	3^{2}				7		5	6	11	8		2				4	10		12	9^{1}										13
1	2	3				7			10	11	8		4	9			6						5								14
1	2	3■	4^{1}				12	9	10	11	7			8			6						5								15
1	2					7	8^{1}	9	10	11	6			3			4				12		5								16
1	2	12				7	8^{2}	9^{1}	10	11	6		3	4			5				13										17
1	3	5				10^{1}	8^{2}		4	9■	6		2	11			7				12			13							18
1	3	5					8^{1}		11		6	13	2	10			7■				9^{2}		4	12							19
1	5	4^{1}				13			12		8		2	9^{2}							10		3		6	7	11				20
1	2					10			3	13	8		5	11^{1}				12			9^{2}				7	4	6				21
1	2	12				10			3^{1}	7	8		5								9^{2}				11■	4	6	13			22
1	3	5				10	12■			7^{1}	8		2	11^{2}				13								4	6	9			23
1	3	5				10				7^{1}		13	2	11				8								4	6	9^{2}	12		24
1	3	5				10				13		11^{2}	2	7				8								4	6	9^{1}	12		25
1	12	5				10^{1}	11					7^{2}	2					8							3	4	6	9	13		26
1	3	5					10^{1}				8		2					11							12	4	6	9		7	27
1	3	5				13				7		9	2					11^{1}				8			12	4	6			10^{2}	28
1	3	5				14				7	8	9^{1}	2	13											11^{2}	4	6	12		10^{3}	29
1	3	5			4	12				7	8^{1}	9	2												11		6			10	30
1	3	5			4					7	8	9	2	12											11^{1}		6			10	31
1	3	5				14				7^{1}	8	9^{3}	2	12											11^{2}	4	6	13		10	32
1	5	4					14			6	8■	10^{3}	2	12											9^{1}	3	7	13		11^{2}	33
1	3	5				8^{1}	12			7		9	2	11												4	6■	13		10^{2}	34
1^{6}	3	5			4		6			7			2	8					15									11	9	10	35
		5			4	11^{3}	6		3	14	8	7■	2	12					1									13	9^{2}	10^{1}	36

GRETNA

Year Formed: 1946. *Ground & Address:* Raydale Park, Dominion Rd, Gretna DG16 5AP. Currently playing home games at Motherwell. *Telephone:* 01461 337602. *Fax:* 01461 338047. *E-mail:* info@gretnafootballclub.co.uk. *Website:* www.gretnafootballclub.co.uk
Ground Capacity: 2200.
Club Shop: Alan Watson, 01387 251550.
President: Brian Fulton. *Chairman:* Ron MacGregor. *Secretary:* Helen MacGregor. *Managing Director:* Brookes Mileson. *Chief Executive:* Graeme Muir. *Director of Club Development:* Mick Wadsworth.
Record Attendance: 3000 v Dundee U, Scottish Cup, 17 Jan 2005.
Record Victory: 20-0 v Silloth, 1962.
Record Defeat: 0-6 v Worksop Town, 1994-95 and 0-6 v Bradford (Park Avenue) 1999-2000.
Most League Appearances: 200: Gavin Skelton, 2002-08.
Most League Goals in Season (Individual): 38: Kenny Deuchar, 2004-05.
Most Goals Overall (Individual): 60: Kenny Deuchar, 2004-07.

GRETNA 2007–08 LEAGUE RECORD

Match No.	*Date*	*Venue*	*Opponents*	*Result*	*H/T Score*	*Lg. Pos.*	*Goalscorers*	*Attendance*
1	Aug 4	H	Falkirk	L 0-4	0-2	—		2731
2	11	A	Hibernian	L 2-4	1-0	12	Yantorno 17, McMenamin 49	13,795
3	18	A	Hearts	D 1-1	0-0	11	Yantorno 79	16,407
4	25	H	Motherwell	L 1-2	1-1	11	Osman 18	3758
5	Sept 1	A	Rangers	L 0-4	0-1	11		49,689
6	15	H	Kilmarnock	L 1-2	0-2	11	Skelton 90	1516
7	22	H	Dundee U	W 3-2	2-1	11	Cowan 2 14, 36, Jenkins 86	1627
8	29	A	Aberdeen	L 0-2	0-2	12		10,279
9	Oct 7	H	Celtic	L 1-2	1-0	12	Yantorno 37	6011
10	20	A	St Mirren	L 0-1	0-1	12		3339
11	27	H	Inverness CT	L 0-4	0-2	12		1096
12	Nov 3	A	Falkirk	L 0-2	0-1	12		4843
13	10	H	Hibernian	L 0-1	0-0	12		2666
14	25	H	Hearts	D 1-1	0-1	12	Kingston (og) 49	1544
15	Dec 1	A	Motherwell	L 0-3	0-1	12		6431
16	15	A	Kilmarnock	D 3-3	1-1	12	Skelton 5, Grainger (pen) 51, Horwood 57	5122
17	22	A	Dundee U	W 2-1	2-1	12	Deuchar 12, Deverdics 42	6304
18	26	H	Aberdeen	D 1-1	0-0	12	Jenkins 90	1740
19	29	A	Celtic	L 0-3	0-1	12		57,250
20	Jan 5	A	Inverness CT	L 0-3	0-3	12		3919
21	16	H	Rangers	L 1-2	0-1	—	Deuchar 46	6137
22	19	H	Falkirk	W 2-0	1-0	12	Deuchar 33, Murray 50	1609
23	Feb 9	A	Hearts	L 0-2	0-2	12		16,138
24	13	A	Hibernian	L 2-4	0-2	—	Skelton 81, Deuchar 88	12,087
25	16	H	Motherwell	L 1-3	0-1	12	McGill 50	2877
26	24	A	Rangers	L 2-4	0-2	12	Deuchar 2 71, 89	48,375
27	27	H	Kilmarnock	W 4-2	3-0	—	Deverdics 27, Meynell 39, Barr 44, Buscher 59	1545
28	Mar 6	H	Dundee U	L 0-3	0-1	—		507
29	15	A	Aberdeen	L 0-3	0-1	12		9025
30	23	H	Celtic	L 0-3	0-1	12		3561
31	29	A	St Mirren	L 0-2	0-1	12		3577
32	Apr 5	H	Inverness CT	L 1-2	0-0	12	Barr 80	431
33	9	H	St Mirren	D 0-0	0-0	—		751
34	19	A	Falkirk	D 0-0	0-0	12		4490
35	26	A	Kilmarnock	D 1-1	0-0	12	Barr 74	4086
36	May 3	A	Inverness CT	L 1-6	1-2	12	Hogg 27	3639
37	10	A	St Mirren	D 0-0	0-0	12		3163
38	13	H	Hearts	W 1-0	0-0	—	Skelton 90	1090

Final League Position: 12

Honours
League Champions: First Division 2006-07. Second Division 2005-06. Third Division 2004-05.
Bell's League Challenge: Quarter-finals 2004-05.
Scottish Cup Runners-up: 2006.

European: *UEFA Cup:* 2 matches (2006-07).

Club colours: Shirt: White with black detail. Shorts: White. Stockings: White topped with black hoops.

Goalscorers: *League* (32): Deuchar 6, Skelton 4, Barr 3, Yantorno 3, Cowan 2, Deverdics 2, Jenkins 2, Buscher 1, Grainger 1 (pen), Hogg 1, Horwood 1, McGill 1, McMenamin 1, Meynell 1, Murray 1, Osman 1, own goal 1.
Scottish Cup (2): Horwood 1, Yantorno 1.
CIS Cup (3): Barr 1, Jenkins 1, Yantorno 1.

Fleming G 28	Barr C 22 + 4	Grainger D 9 + 1	Jenkins A 16 + 4	Innes C 21	Osman A 16 + 2	Murray P 31 + 1	Graham D 2 + 8	Yantorno F 21	McMenamin C 7 + 5	Skelton G 37 + 1	Deuchar K 11 + 4	Paartalu E 3 + 6	Deverdics N 20 + 5	Baldacchino R 4 + 4	Collin A 18 + 1	Cowan D 10 + 1	McLaren F — + 3	Buscher M 8 + 9	Horwood E 15	McGill B 15 + 5	Grady J 6 + 2	Caig T 7	McGuffie R 5 + 4	Hogg S 4 + 7	Makinwa H 7 + 6	Canning M — + 1	Naughton K 18	Hall D 14 + 1	Wilkinson B 7 + 6	Griffiths R 9 + 3	Meynell R 14 + 2	Kissock J 10 + 1	Schultz-Eklund E — + 1	Krysiak A 3 + 1	Taylor N — + 6	Fisher N — + 1	*Match No.*
1	2	3	4^{1}	5	6	7^{2}	8^{3}	9	10	11	12	13	14																								1
1	2	3	4	5	6^{3}	7	8^{2}	9	10^{1}	11	12	14		13																							2
1	2		4	5	6^{1}	7^{2}	12	9	10	11	14	13	3^{3}		8																						3
1	2▮		4	5	6	7^{2}	12	9^{3}	10	3	14		11^{1}		8	13																					4
1			4^{2}	5	6^{3}	7		9	10	3		14	11^{1}		2	8	13	12																			5
1	2			5	6^{1}	7	13	9	10^{3}	11		12			4			14	3	8^{2}																	6
1			12	5		7		9^{2}	10	11		6	8^{1}		4	2		13	3																		7
1			4^{2}	5		7		9	12	11		8	10^{1}		6	2^{3}		13	3		14																8
1	2	12	4	5		7		9^{3}	13	11		14			8^{1}	6			3		10^{2}																9
1	2▮	3	4	5		7	12	9^{3}	14	11						6^{1}		13	8		10^{2}																10
		3	4			7	12	9	14	11						2^{1}		10^{3}	6		13	1	5	8^{2}													11
1		3	4^{3}			7	12	9	13	11		8						10^{1}	6		2^{2}		5	14													12
1		3	4	5		7^{2}	12	9		11									6	8^{1}	10		2	13													13
1		3	14	5		7^{3}	12	9		11					4			13	6		8^{2}		2^{1}		10												14
1	2	3^{3}		5		7		9		11					4		13	14	6		10^{1}		12		8^{2}												15
1		3	4^{1}	5		7				11	10		14		8	2	13		6^{3}				12		9^{2}												16
	12		14	5		7		9		11	10		8^{2}		6	2^{1}			3			1	13		4^{3}												17
			13	5		7^{3}		9		11	10		8^{2}		4	2			3	14		1	12		6^{1}												18
			4			7^{2}		9		11	10		8^{1}		5	2			6	12		1	3		13												19
	2		4^{1}	5	12	7		9		11	10				3				6	13		1			8^{2}												20
	2^{2}		4		6^{1}	7		9		11	10				5			12				1			14	13	8^{3}	3									21
			4	5		7		9^{1}		11	10				6			8				1			12		3	2									22
1	12			5		7^{3}				11	10				4^{1}			8									3	2▮	14	6^{2}	13	9					23
1▮	2					7				8	10		12		5^{G}			11		13							3			4^{2}	6^{1}	9	15				24
	2					7				11	10		13	12				8^{2}		4					14		3	5			6^{3}	9^{1}		1			25
1	2					7^{1}				11	10		8^{3}	14				13		4							3	5	12		6	9^{2}					26
1	2			5						11			10^{3}					7^{2}		8					12		3	6	13	14	4	9^{1}					27
1	2			5		12				11			8^{1}		13			10^{3}		7							3	6	14		4	9^{2}					28
					6^{1}					12			10	11						7				13	9^{2}		3	5	8^{3}	2	4			1	14		29
1	12				6	2				11			10^{1}	8						7^{3}					13		3	5	9^{2}	14	4						30
1	12				6	7				11			10	8^{3}						4							2	5^{2}	9^{1}		3	13			14		31
1	2				6	7^{1}				11			10^{2}							8				13			3		12	5	4	9^{3}			14		32
1	2				6	7^{1}				11			12							8				13			3		10^{2}	5	4	9^{3}			14		33
1	2				6					11			10	13						8^{2}				14			3	12	7^{1}	5	4	9^{3}					34
	2				12					11			10	8^{2}						13				7^{1}			3	5	4	6	14	9^{3}		1			35
1	2				6					11			9							10^{3}				8^{2}			3	7^{1}	12	5	4				13	14	36
1	2				6	7^{2}				11			10							9				13			3	5	8^{1}	12	4						37
1^{G}	2				8					11			10							7				9^{1}			3	6		5	4			15	12		38

HAMILTON ACADEMICAL Premier League

Year Formed: 1874. *Ground:* New Douglas Park, Cadzow Avenue, Hamilton ML3 0FT. *Telephone:* 01698 368652. *Fax:* 01698 285422. *E-mail:* scott@acciesfc.co.uk. *Website:* www.acciesfc.co.uk
Ground Capacity: 6078. *Size of Pitch:* 115yd × 75yd.
Chairman: Ronnie MacDonald. *Vice-Chairman:* Les Gray. *Chief Executive:* George W. Fairley. *Commercial:* Arthur Lynch/John Vint. *Secretary:* Scott A. Struthers BA. *Commercial Manager:* Derek McQuade.
Manager: Billy Reid. *Assistant Manager:* John McCormack. *First Team Coach:* Stuart Taylor. *Goalkeeper Coach:* Brian Potter. *Physio:* Alan Rankin. *Sports Science Coach:* Ross Hughes. *Sports Therapist:* Avril Downs.
Club Nickname(s): The Accies. *Previous Grounds:* Bent Farm, South Avenue, South Haugh, Douglas Park, Cliftonhill Stadium, Firhill Stadium.
Record Attendance: 28,690 v Hearts, Scottish Cup 3rd rd, 3 Mar 1937.
Record Transfer Fee received: £380,000 for Paul Hartley to Millwall (July 1996).
Record Transfer Fee paid: £60,000 for Paul Martin from Kilmarnock (Oct 1988) and for John McQuade from Dumbarton (Aug 1993).
Record Victory: 11-1 v Chryston, Lanarkshire Cup, 28 Nov 1885.
Record Defeat: 1-11 v Hibernian, Division I, 6 Nov 1965.
Most Capped Player: Colin Miller, 29, Canada, 1988-94.
Most League Appearances: 452: Rikki Ferguson, 1974-88.
Most League Goals in Season (Individual): 35: David Wilson, Division I; 1936-37.
Most Goals Overall (Individual): 246: David Wilson, 1928-39.

HAMILTON ACADEMICAL 2007–08 LEAGUE RECORD

Match No.	Date	Venue	Opponents	Result	H/T Score	Lg. Pos.	Goalscorers	Attendance
1	Aug 4	H	Dunfermline Ath	W 2-1	1-1	—	Taylor [4], Offiong (pen) [47]	3383
2	11	A	Clyde	W 2-0	1-0	2	Offiong (pen) [45], Elebert [80]	1152
3	18	H	Queen of the S	W 1-0	1-0	1	Offiong [17]	1764
4	25	A	Morton	W 2-0	0-0	1	Offiong 2 (1 pen) [52, 66 (p)]	3188
5	Sept 1	A	Partick Th	W 3-0	2-0	1	Offiong 2 [26, 29], Taylor [46]	3075
6	15	H	Stirling A	W 4-0	1-0	1	Neil [26], Gilhaney [56], McCarthy [60], Wake [85]	1749
7	22	H	Livingston	D 1-1	1-0	1	Taylor [36]	1835
8	29	A	St Johnstone	L 1-4	1-0	1	Taylor [3]	2713
9	Oct 6	H	Dundee	W 2-0	0-0	1	McLaughlin [83], McLeod [90]	3197
10	20	A	Dunfermline Ath	W 5-0	3-0	1	McArthur [4], McCarthy [18], Offiong [30], Winters 2 [46, 53]	3846
11	27	H	Morton	W 1-0	1-0	1	McCarthy [5]	2562
12	Nov 3	A	Queen of the S	L 1-2	1-0	1	McCarthy [1]	1646
13	10	H	Partick Th	W 2-0	1-0	1	Offiong [24], Swailes [77]	2755
14	24	A	Dundee	L 0-1	0-1	—		4375
15	Dec 1	A	Stirling A	W 4-2	2-0	1	Mensing 2 [27, 69], Wallner [40], Offiong [55]	1045
16	8	A	Livingston	L 0-2	0-0	1		1452
17	15	H	St Johnstone	W 1-0	1-0	1	McArthur [11]	1922
18	26	H	Clyde	D 0-0	0-0	1		1750
19	29	A	Morton	W 3-1	3-1	1	Offiong [12], Graham [31], Mensing [45]	2642
20	Jan 2	H	Queen of the S	W 1-0	0-0	1	McArthur [71]	2298
21	5	H	Stirling A	D 0-0	0-0	1		1410
22	19	A	Partick Th	L 0-3	0-2	1		2409
23	26	A	Clyde	W 3-2	1-2	1	Offiong 2 [43, 77], Mensing [56]	1214
24	Feb 9	H	Dunfermline Ath	W 3-0	3-0	1	Offiong 3 (1 pen) [13 (p), 34, 43]	2044
25	16	A	St Johnstone	L 1-2	1-0	1	Gilhaney [31]	2973
26	23	H	Livingston	W 3-1	1-0	1	Stevenson [7], Stewart (og) [49], McLaughlin [64]	1800
27	Mar 1	A	Queen of the S	D 2-2	1-2	1	Grady [22], McCarthy [90]	2133
28	8	H	Morton	W 3-0	1-0	—	Graham [36], Stevenson (pen) [54], Gibson [70]	1980
29	11	A	Dunfermline Ath	D 1-1	1-1	—	Offiong [39]	2444
30	15	H	Dundee	W 1-0	1-0	1	McArthur [18]	5078
31	22	A	Stirling A	W 1-0	1-0	1	McCarthy [3]	975
32	29	H	Partick Th	D 0-0	0-0	1		2150
33	Apr 5	H	St Johnstone	W 2-0	1-0	1	Stevenson [5], Elebert [56]	1825
34	12	A	Livingston	W 3-1	2-0	1	Offiong [25], McArthur [39], Mensing [46]	2107
35	19	H	Clyde	W 2-0	2-0	1	Stevenson (pen) [21], Offiong [43]	4940
36	26	A	Dundee	D 1-1	1-0	1	Waterworth [38]	3146

Final League Position: 1

Honours
League Champions: First Division 1985-86, 1987-88, 2007-08; Third Division 2000-01. *Runners-up:* Division II 1903-04, 1952-53, 1964-65; Second Division 1996-97, 2003-04.
Scottish Cup Runners-up: 1911, 1935. *League Cup:* Semi-finalists three times. *League Challenge Cup:* Runners-up 2006.
B&Q Cup Winners: 1991-92, 1992-93.

Club colours: Shirt: Red and white hoops. Shorts: White. Stockings: White.

Goalscorers: *League* (62): Offiong 19 (4 pens), McCarthy 6, McArthur 5, Mensing 5, Stevenson 4 (2 pens), Taylor 4, Elebert 2, Gilhaney 2, Graham 2, McLaughlin 2, Winters 2, Gibson 1, Grady 1, McLeod 1, Neil 1, Swailes 1, Wake 1, Wallner 1, Waterworth 1, own goal 1.
Scottish Cup (1): McLaughlin 1.
CIS Cup (8): Offiong 2 (1 pen), Wake 2, McArthur 1, McCarthy 1, McLeod 1, Winters 1.
Challenge Cup (1): Taylor 1.

Halliwell B 23	Elebert D 29	Swailes C 14 + 5	McLaughlin M 33	Easton B 36	Taylor S 8 + 5	McLeod P 1 + 6	McArthur J 33 + 1	Gilhaney M 24 + 11	Neil A 30	Offiong R 34	Parratt T 17 + 1	McCarthy J 27 + 8	Wake B — + 19	Cerny T 13 + 2	Gibson J 4 + 11	Teggart N 1	Winters D 10 + 4	Stevenson T 12 + 4	Evans G 1	Davison K — + 1	Wallner R 4	Mensing S 17	Graham D 17 + 3	Barrau X 2 + 2	Twigg G 2 + 1	Waterworth A 1 + 9	Grady J 1 + 4	Potter B — + 1	Gillespie G 1	Potter T — + 1	Gow G 1	Kirkpatrick J — + 1	*Match No.*
1	2	3^{1}	4	5	6	7^{2}	8	9	10	11^{3}	12	13	14																				1
	2		4^{3}	5	6^{2}	12	8	9	11	10	3	13		1	14	7^{1}																	2
1^{6}	2		4	5	6		8	9	10	11^{2}	3	12	13	15			7^{1}																3
1	2	3	4^{1}	5		14	8	9	10	11^{2}	6^{3}	7	13		12																		4
1	2		4	5	6	12	8	9^{1}	10	11^{2}	3	7^{3}	13		14																		5
1	2	12	4^{1}	5	6		8	9	10	11^{3}	3	7^{2}	14				13																6
1	2		4	5	6^{1}	14	8	9	10	11^{2}	3	7^{3}	13				12																7
1		3	4	5	6^{1}	14	8	9		11^{2}	2	7	12		13		10^{3}																8
1	2		4	5	12	14	8	9		11^{2}	3	6	13				7^{3}	10^{1}															9
1	2^{1}	12	4	5			8	9	10	11^{2}	3	6^{3}	13				7	14															10
1		3	4	5			8	9	10	11^{1}		7	12				6		2														11
1		3	4	5			8	9^{2}	10	11		7	12		2		6^{1}			13													12
1		3	4	5	14		8	9^{3}	10	11^{2}		6	13		12		7^{1}	2															13
1	2^{3}	3	4	5	14		8	9^{1}	10	11^{2}		6	13				12				7												14
1		3	4	5			8^{1}	9^{3}	10	11^{2}		6	13		12						7	2	14										15
1		3	4	5			8	9^{2}	10	11		6	12								7^{1}	2	13										16
1	2		4	5			8	14	10	11^{2}		6	13		12		7					3^{1}	9^{3}										17
1	2		4	5			8	13	10	11^{1}		6	12				7^{2}					3	9										18
1	2		4	5			8	14	10	11^{2}	3^{3}	6	13		12							7	9^{1}										19
1^{6}	5		6	3			8	13	10	9^{2}	2	4		15			7^{1}						11	12									20
	5		6	3^{3}			8	12	10		2^{2}	4	14	1				13					7	11	9^{1}								21
1	5		6	3			7	13	10^{1}	8	2^{2}	4					14				9		11^{3}		12								22
1		3	4	5			12	9	6	10	2^{2}				7^{3}							8	13	14	11^{1}								23
1	5	6		3			8^{1}	11	10	9^{2}	2	12						14				4^{3}	7			13							24
1	5		6	3			8	11	10^{1}	9^{2}	2^{3}	12										4	7			14	13						25
	5^{1}	12	6	3			8	11	10^{2}	9^{3}		13		1				2				4	7				14						26
	4	3	5	2			8	13		10		14		1				6^{2}				9^{3}	7			12	11^{1}						27
	5^{2}	14	6	3				11		9^{3}	2^{1}	4		1	12			10				8	7			13							28
	5		6	3			8	12	10	9^{3}		4^{2}		1				13				2	7	11^{1}		14							29
	5		6	3			8	11^{3}	10	9^{2}		12		1				2				4	7^{1}			13	14						30
	5		6	3	14		8	11	10^{1}	9^{3}		4		1	12			2					7^{2}				13						31
	5		6	3	12		8	11		9		4		1	10^{1}			2					7										32
	5		6	3			8	13	10	9^{1}		11		1	14			2^{2}				4	7^{3}			12							33
	5	6		3	7^{1}		8	12	10	9^{2}		11		1				2				4				13							34
	5	14	6	3			8	12	10^{1}	9^{2}		7		1				2^{3}				4	11			13							35
	4	5		3								7		1^{6}	6			2				8				10		15	9^{2}	13	11^{1}	12	36

HEART OF MIDLOTHIAN Premier League

Year Formed: 1874. *Ground & Address:* Tynecastle Stadium, Gorgie Rd, Edinburgh EH11 2NL. *Telephone:* 0871 663 1874. *Fax:* 0131 200 7222. *E-mail:* hearts@homplc.co.uk. *Website:* www.heartsfc.co.uk
Ground Capacity: 17,402. *Size of Pitch:* 100m × 64m.
Chairman: Roman Romanov. *Managing Director:* Campbell Ogilvie.
Manager: Laszlo Csaba. *Coach:* Stephen Frail. *Physio:* Alan Rae.
Club Nickname(s): Hearts, Jambos. *Previous Grounds:* The Meadows 1874, Powderhall 1878, Old Tynecastle 1881, (Tynecastle Park, 1886).
Record Attendance: 53,396 v Rangers, Scottish Cup 3rd rd, 13 Feb 1932.
Record Transfer Fee received: £2,100,000 for Alan McLaren from Rangers (October 1994).
Record of Transfer paid: £850,000 for Mirsad Beslija to Celtic (January 2006).
Record Victory: 21-0 v Anchor, EFA Cup, 30 Oct 1880.
Record Defeat: 1-8 v Vale of Leven, Scottish Cup, 1888.
Most Capped Player: Bobby Walker, 29, Scotland.
Most League Appearances: 515: Gary Mackay, 1980-97.
Most League Goals in Season (Individual): 44: Barney Battles, 1930-31.
Most Goals Overall (Individual): 214: John Robertson, 1983-98.

HEART OF MIDLOTHIAN 2007–08 LEAGUE RECORD

Match No.	Date	Venue	Opponents	Result		H/T Score	Lg. Pos.	Goalscorers	Attendance
1	Aug 6	H	Hibernian	L	0-1	0-1	—		16,436
2	12	A	Aberdeen	D	1-1	1-1	9	Stewart 45	13,134
3	18	H	Gretna	D	1-1	0-0	9	Driver 73	16,407
4	25	A	Celtic	L	0-5	0-2	10		57,042
5	Sept 3	A	Motherwell	W	2-0	1-0	—	Kingston 24, Velicka 90	5081
6	15	H	Rangers	W	4-2	2-0	7	Driver 13, Tall 27, Stewart (pen) 66, Ivaskevicius 70	15,948
7	22	A	Inverness CT	L	1-2	1-0	7	Black (og) 34	4918
8	30	A	St Mirren	W	3-1	1-0	6	Driver 40, Stewart (pen) 56, Velicka 83	4233
9	Oct 6	H	Falkirk	W	4-2	2-0	5	Ksanavicius 5, Zaliukas 27, Velicka 58, Nade 68	15,800
10	20	H	Dundee U	L	1-3	0-2	7	Kingston 90	16,661
11	27	A	Kilmarnock	L	1-3	0-0	8	Tall 90	6373
12	Nov 4	A	Hibernian	D	1-1	0-1	8	Nade 46	17,015
13	11	H	Aberdeen	W	4-1	2-1	6	Driver 3, Velicka 14, Tall 54, Nade 62	17,122
14	25	A	Gretna	D	1-1	1-0	6	Kingston 27	1544
15	Dec 1	H	Celtic	D	1-1	0-0	7	Velicka (pen) 90	16,454
16	8	H	Motherwell	L	1-2	1-0	7	Driver 12	16,633
17	15	A	Rangers	L	1-2	0-1	8	Velicka 56	48,392
18	22	H	Inverness CT	L	2-3	0-1	9	Berra 62, Velicka (pen) 90	16,202
19	26	H	St Mirren	L	0-1	0-1	10		16,476
20	29	A	Falkirk	L	1-2	1-0	10	Palazuelos 28	6614
21	Jan 2	A	Dundee U	L	1-4	1-1	10	Berra 37	7557
22	5	H	Kilmarnock	D	1-1	0-1	11	Velicka 63	14,346
23	19	H	Hibernian	W	1-0	1-0	10	Velicka 20	17,131
24	26	A	Aberdeen	W	1-0	0-0	9	Nade 55	14,000
25	Feb 9	H	Gretna	W	2-0	2-0	8	Velicka 2 (1 pen) 3, 42 (p)	16,138
26	16	A	Celtic	L	0-3	0-1	9		56,738
27	23	A	Motherwell	W	1-0	1-0	7	Craigan (og) 12	5925
28	27	H	Rangers	L	0-4	0-2	—		16,173
29	Mar 1	A	Inverness CT	W	3-0	2-0	7	Karipidis 22, Elliot 2 33, 47	4489
30	15	A	St Mirren	D	1-1	0-0	7	Mikoliunas 87	4557
31	22	H	Falkirk	D	0-0	0-0	7		16,682
32	29	H	Dundee U	W	1-0	1-0	7	Kingston 27	16,871
33	Apr 5	A	Kilmarnock	D	0-0	0-0	7		5901
34	19	H	St Mirren	W	3-2	2-1	7	Jonsson 28, Glen 42, Kingston 81	15,259
35	26	H	Inverness CT	W	1-0	0-0	7	Glen 80	15,423
36	May 5	A	Falkirk	L	1-2	0-1	—	Cesnauskis 77	4638
37	10	H	Kilmarnock	L	0-2	0-0	8		10,512
38	13	A	Gretna	L	0-1	0-0	—		1090

Final League Position: 8

Honours
League Champions: Division I 1894-95, 1896-97, 1957-58, 1959-60. First Division 1979-80; *Runners-up:* Division I 1893-94, 1898-99, 1903-04, 1905-06, 1914-15, 1937-38, 1953-54, 1956-57, 1958-59, 1964-65. Premier Division 1985-86, 1987-88, 1991-92; *Runners-up:* 2005-06. First Division 1977-78, 1982-83.
Scottish Cup Winners: 1891, 1896, 1901, 1906, 1956, 1998;, 2006; *Runners-up:* 1903, 1907, 1968, 1976, 1986, 1996.
League Cup Winners: 1954-55, 1958-59, 1959-60, 1962-63; *Runners-up:* 1961-62, 1996-97.

European: *European Cup:* 8 matches (1958-59, 1960-61, 2006-07). *Cup Winners' Cup:* 10 matches (1976-77, 1996-97, 1998-99). *UEFA Cup:* 47 matches (*Fairs Cup:* 1961-62, 1963-64, 1965-66. *UEFA Cup:* 1984-85, 1986-87, 1988-89, 1990-91, 1992-93, 1993-94, 2000-01, 2003-04, 2004-05, 2006-07).

Club colours: Shirt: Maroon. Shorts: White. Stockings: Maroon.

Goalscorers: *League* (47): Velicka 11 (3 pens), Driver 5, Kingston 5, Nade 4, Stewart 3 (2 pens), Tall 3, Berra 2, Elliot 2, Glen 2, Cesnauskis 1, Ivaskevicius 1, Jonsson 1, Karipidis 1, Ksanavicius 1, Mikoliunas 1, Palazuelos 1, Zaliukas 1, own goals 2.
Scottish Cup (2): Cesnauskis 1, Velicka 1.
CIS Cup (8): Elliot 2, Velicka 2, Berra 1, Kingston 1, Nade 1 (pen), own goal 1.

Banks S 28	Neilson R 33	Wallace L 16+5	Tall I 12	Zaliukas M 21+5	Karipidis C 15+1	Mikoliunas S 14+11	Stewart M 23+4	Beniusis R 1+7	Ksanavicius A 17+5	Driver A 23+2	Jonsson E 25+3	Makela J 1+4	Pospisil M —+8	Berra C 35	Palazuelos R 24+5	Ivaskevicius K 8+9	Velicka A 16+4	Kingston L 16+2	Goncalves J 23	McCann N —+3	Elliot C 14+10	Nade C 17+7	Basso A 7	Kancelskis T 1	Pinilla M —+2	Kurskis E 3	Cesnauskis D 10+3	Screpis F 3+2	Mole J 2+4	Glen G 5+1	Thomson J 5	Robinson S —+1	McGowan R —+1	Match No.
1	2	3	4[1]	5	6	7[2]	8	9[3]	10	11	12	13	14																					1
1	2	3		5		13	8		12	11[1]	4	14		6	7	9[2]	10[3]																	2
1	2	3		5			8		11	13	4[1]	14		6	7[2]	9	10[3]	12																3
1	2			3	12	7	8		10	14				4		9[3]		6[2]	5[1]	13	11													4
1	2		4	3			7[2]		11[3]					5	13	14	12	8	6		10	9[1]												5
1	2	3	4	5[2]			8		10	11[1]				6	13	12		7			14	9[3]												6
1	2	3	4	5			12		10[3]	11[1]			14	6		7	9[2]	8			13													7
	2		4	14			8[3]		10[1]	11	7			5			13	6	3		12	9[2]	1											8
1	2			5			8[3]		10[1]	11	3			6	14		9[2]	7			12	13		4										9
1	2			5			8		12	11[1]	7			6		14		4	3[3]		10■	9[2]			13									10
	2		4	10			8[2]	12		11	13	6[1]		5	7				3			9■	1											11
	2		4				8		7[3]	11	6		13	5			10[2]		3		14	9[1]	1		12									12
1	2[1]		4	12			8	14	7	11	6			5			10[2]	13	3			9[3]												13
	2			5			8■		10	11	7[2]			6	13		12	4	3			9[1]	1											14
	2		4	5[2]		14			10	11				6	7[3]		12	8	3		13	9[1]	1											15
	2			5		7[1]	8		9	11	4[3]			6		14	10[2]		3		13	12				1								16
	2			5		7[1]		14		11	4			6	8[3]	12	10[2]		3		9	13				1								17
	2	3		5		14			9[1]	11	4		13	6	8	7[3]	10				12[2]					1■								18
1	2	3	4			13	12			11	6[1]		14	5	8	7[2]	10					9[3]												19
1	2	3	4	5[3]		13	8			11	14		12	6	9	10[2]					7[1]													20
1	2	3■		5■		7[3]	8■			11[1]			14	6	4		10				9[2]	13					12							21
1	2				6	12			7[1]		8		14	5	4		10[2]		3		9■	13					11[3]							22
1	2	12			6	13	8[1]			11	7			5	4[3]		10		3			14					9[2]							23
1	2				6	7[3]	8	13	12		11			5	4		10[2]		3	14		9[1]												24
1	2				6	12	8[3]		9[2]	11				5	4		10		3	14	13						7[1]							25
1	2				6	12			9[2]	11	8			5	4		10		3			13					7[1]							26
1	2	3		14	6	12		13			8			5	11				4		10[3]	9[2]					7[1]							27
1	2	11		14	6	12			13		8[3]			5	4				3[2]		10	9					7[1]							28
1	2	3			6	7[2]		14		11[1]	8			5	4	12					10	9[3]						13						29
1	2	3			6	7	13	14		11[1]	8[2]			5	4						10						12		9[3]					30
1	2	3		5		7	8		12					6	4			9[3]			10[2]						11[1]	14	13					31
	2	13		5		7[2]	8				4			6	11	12		9[1]	3			10	1											32
	2		4			7	13							5	6	11[1]		8[2]	3		14	9	1					10[3]		12				33
1		13			6	7					8	12		5	4			11	3[2]			9[1]							14	10[3]	2			34
1		12		13	6	7					8			5	4				3		10[2]						11[1]			9[3]	2	14		35
1		13			6	7[2]					8			5	4			11	3		10[3]						14		12	9[1]	2			36
1		3		5	6		8[2]				4[1]					12		10									11	7	13	9	2			37
1		3		5[3]	6		8								12	13		4									11[2]	7[1]	10	9■	2		14	38

HIBERNIAN — Premier League

Year Formed: 1875. *Ground & Address:* Easter Road Stadium, Albion Rd, Edinburgh EH7 5QG. *Telephone:* 0131 661 2159. *Fax:* 0131 659 6488. *E-mail:* club@hibernianfc.co.uk. *Website:* www.hibernianfc.co.uk
Ground Capacity: total: 17,400. *Size of Pitch:* 112yd × 74yd.
Chairman: Rod Petrie. *Chief Executive:* Scott Lindsay. *Club Secretary:* Garry O'Hagan. *Marketing & Communications Director:* Ian Spence.
Manager: Mixu Paatelainen. *Assistant Manager:* Donald Park. *Goalkeeping Coach:* Gordon Marshall. *Reserve Team Coach:* Gareth Evans. *Physio:* Colin McLelland.
Club Nickname(s): Hibees. *Previous Grounds:* Meadows 1875-78, Powderhall 1878-79, Mayfield 1879-80, First Easter Road 1880-92, Second Easter Road 1892-.
Record Attendance: 65,860 v Hearts, Division I, 2 Jan 1950.
Record Victory: 22-1 v 42nd Highlanders, 3 Sept 1881.
Record Defeat: 0-10 v Rangers, 24 Dec 1898.
Most Capped Player: Lawrie Reilly, 38, Scotland.
Most League Appearances: 446: Arthur Duncan.
Most League Goals in Season (Individual): 42: Joe Baker, 1959-60.
Most Goals Overall (Individual): 364: Gordon Smith, 1941-1959.

HIBERNIAN 2007–08 LEAGUE RECORD

Match No.	Date	Venue	Opponents	Result	H/T Score	Lg. Pos.	Goalscorers	Attendance
1	Aug 6	A	Hearts	W 1-0	1-0	—	Kerr [2]	16,436
2	11	H	Gretna	W 4-2	0-1	2	Zemmama 2 [64, 82], Fletcher [66], McCann [90]	13,795
3	18	A	Dundee U	D 0-0	0-0	3		8405
4	25	H	Aberdeen	D 3-3	1-2	4	Zemmama [5], Fletcher [70], Shiels [84]	15,280
5	Sept 1	H	Inverness CT	W 1-0	1-0	3	Fletcher (pen) [2]	13,258
6	15	A	Falkirk	D 1-1	1-0	4	Donaldson (pen) [5]	6298
7	23	H	Celtic	W 3-2	2-1	3	Fletcher [5], Gathuessi [41], Shiels [87]	16,125
8	29	H	Kilmarnock	W 4-1	2-0	3	Donaldson 3 (2 pens) [12, 31 (p), 78 (p)], Antoine-Curier [65]	13,662
9	Oct 6	A	Rangers	W 1-0	0-0	2	Murphy [61]	50,440
10	20	A	Motherwell	L 1-2	1-2	3	Fletcher (pen) [31]	7071
11	27	H	St Mirren	L 0-1	0-1	4		13,884
12	Nov 4	H	Hearts	D 1-1	1-0	3	Berra (og) [18]	17,015
13	10	A	Gretna	W 1-0	0-0	3	Fletcher [52]	2666
14	24	H	Dundee U	D 2-2	0-0	3	Benjelloun [77], Antoine-Curier (pen) [82]	14,440
15	Dec 2	A	Aberdeen	L 1-3	1-1	3	Fletcher [24]	10,110
16	8	A	Inverness CT	L 0-2	0-1	4		4224
17	15	H	Falkirk	D 1-1	1-0	5	Donaldson (pen) [21]	12,391
18	22	A	Celtic	D 1-1	1-0	5	Murphy [20]	57,465
19	26	A	Kilmarnock	L 1-2	0-1	5	Shiels (pen) [90]	6372
20	29	H	Rangers	L 1-2	0-1	6	Zemmama [88]	16,217
21	Jan 5	A	St Mirren	L 1-2	0-2	8	Antoine-Curier [89]	4212
22	19	A	Hearts	L 0-1	0-1	8		17,131
23	Feb 9	A	Dundee U	D 1-1	0-1	9	Rankin [46]	6635
24	13	H	Gretna	W 4-2	2-0	—	Nish [10], Fletcher 3 (1 pen) [19, 58, 90 (p)]	12,087
25	17	H	Aberdeen	W 3-1	0-1	5	Zemmama [49], Shiels [55], Fletcher [90]	13,825
26	23	H	Inverness CT	W 2-0	2-0	5	Nish [3], Fletcher [5]	12,552
27	27	A	Falkirk	W 2-0	1-0	—	Ross (og) [12], Rankin [52]	5928
28	Mar 1	H	Celtic	L 0-2	0-0	5		15,735
29	12	H	Motherwell	W 1-0	0-0	—	Nish [52]	11,692
30	15	H	Kilmarnock	W 2-0	1-0	3	Morais [29], Fletcher [73]	12,486
31	22	A	Rangers	L 1-2	0-1	4	Shiels [90]	50,117
32	29	A	Motherwell	L 0-1	0-1	5		6580
33	Apr 5	H	St Mirren	W 2-0	2-0	5	Nish [4], Zemmama [5]	12,343
34	20	A	Dundee U	D 1-1	0-0	5	Shiels [57]	7404
35	26	A	Aberdeen	L 1-2	0-0	5	Shiels [54]	8387
36	May 4	H	Rangers	D 0-0	0-0	5		15,520
37	11	A	Celtic	L 0-2	0-1	5		58,515
38	22	H	Motherwell	L 0-2	0-1	—		10,754

Final League Position: 6

Honours
League Champions: Division I 1902-03, 1947-48, 1950-51, 1951-52. First Division 1980-81, 1998-99. Division II 1893-94, 1894-95, 1932-33; *Runners-up:* Division I 1896-97, 1946-47, 1949-50, 1952-53, 1973-74, 1974-75.
Scottish Cup Winners: 1887, 1902; *Runners-up:* 1896, 1914, 1923, 1924, 1947, 1958, 1972, 1979, 2001.
League Cup Winners: 1972-73, 1991-92, 2006-07; *Runners-up:* 1950-51, 1968-69, 1974-75, 1993-94, 2003-04.

European: *European Cup:* 6 matches (1955-56 semi-finals). *Cup Winners' Cup:* 6 matches (1972-73). *UEFA Cup:* 63 matches (*Fairs Cup:* 1960-61 semi-finals, 1961-62, 1962-63, 1965-66, 1967-68, 1968-69, 1970-71. *UEFA Cup:* 1973-74, 1974-75, 1975-76, 1976-77, 1978-79, 1989-90, 1992-93, 2001-02, 2005-06).

Club colours: Shirt: Green with white sleeves and collar. Shorts: White with green stripe. Stockings: White with green trim.

Goalscorers: *League* (49): Fletcher 13 (3 pens), Shiels 7 (1 pen), Zemmama 6, Donaldson 5 (4 pens), Nish 4, Antoine-Curier 3 (1 pen), Murphy 2, Rankin 2, Benjelloun 1, Gathuessi 1, Kerr 1, McCann 1, Morais 1, own goals 2.
Scottish Cup (3): Shiels 3.
CIS Cup (4): Antoine-Curier 1, Donaldson 1, Fletcher 1, Morais 1.

Ma-Kalambay Y 29	McCann K 19	Murphy D 17	Hogg C 34	Jones R 30	Kerr B 23 + 3	Beuzelin G 25 + 2	Donaldson C 11 + 6	Fletcher S 29 + 3	Zemmama M 18 + 10	Stevenson L 18 + 3	Benjelloun A 5 + 10	O'Brien A 6 + 17	Morais F 19 + 9	Gathuessi T 18 + 5	Joneleit T — + 2	Shiels D 14 + 8	Antoine-Curier M 8 + 5	McCormack D 2 + 2	Chisholm R 13 + 5	Campbell R 2 + 3	Noubissie P 4	McNeil A 9 + 1	Gray D — + 2	Murray I 14 + 1	Rankin J 15 + 2	Hanlon P 5 + 2	Nish C 13 + 2	Zarabi A 7	Canning M 11	*Match No.*
1	2	3	4	5	6	7	8^{1}	9^{2}	10^{3}	11	12	13	14																	1
1	8	3	4	5^{1}	6^{3}	7		13	14		9	11	10^{2}	2	12															2
1	2	3	4	5	6	7^{2}		9	10^{1}	11	12	8		13																3
1	2	3^{1}	4	5	6	7		9	10	11^{2}	13	8^{3}		12		14														4
1		3	4	5	6	7		9	10^{2}	11^{3}	8^{1}	14	12	2		13														5
1		3	4	5	6	7^{3}	8■	13		11		12	10^{1}	2	14		9^{2}													6
1	2^{3}	3	4	5	6	7		9^{1}	14	11^{2}			13	8		12	10													7
1	11	3		5	6	7^{1}	8	9^{2}				14	4^{3}	12			13	2	10											8
1	2	3	4	5	6	7	8^{1}	9^{3}	13			14	12				10^{2}		11											9
1	2	3	4	5	6		8^{2}	9^{1}	13	11^{3}		14	7■				12		10											10
1	2^{3}	3	4	5	6		9		7^{1}	11		12				13■	10^{2}		8	14										11
1	2	3	4	5	6	7	12	9^{3}	13	11		14	8^{2}				10^{1}													12
1	2		4	5	6	7^{2}	12	9		11		14	8^{3}	3			10^{1}		13											13
1	2	3	4	5	6			9	10	11	12	7^{2}					13		8^{1}											14
1	2	3	4		6	7^{3}		9	10^{1}	11	13		12	5		14	8^{2}													15
1	2	3	4		6	12	8	9		11^{2}		13	7^{1}				14	10			5^{3}									16
		3	4	5		7	8	9^{1}	13	11	14		10^{3}	2■			12^{2}				6	1								17
1	2	3^{3}	4	5	6	7			10^{1}	11^{2}	9	13	12					14	8											18
1	2^{3}		4	5	6	7	8		10^{2}	11		13		14		12			9		3^{1}									19
1			4	5	6	12	8^{3}		14	11		13	7^{2}	2		9			10		3^{1}									20
1			4	5	6^{3}	7	8^{1}			11		3	14	2^{2}			9	13	10				12							21
1	2		4	5	6	7		12	10^{2}		8^{1}		11^{3}			9							14	3	13					22
1	2^{1}		4			7		9	13				5^{2}	12		8								11	6	3	10			23
1			4		12	7^{1}		9				14	6^{2}	2		11^{3}			13					5	8		10	3		24
1			4	5				9	10^{1}			13	12	2		11								6	8		7^{2}	3		25
1			4	5		7		9	10^{1}				12	2		11^{2}								13	6	14	8	3^{3}		26
1^{6}			4		13			9	10^{2}					2		11				12		15		7	6	5	8^{1}		3	27
			4		6^{3}	7^{1}		9	14			13		2					12			1		8	11		10^{2}	3	5	28
1			4	5	6^{1}			9	10^{2}		13		3^{3}						12					7■	11	14	8		2	29
1			4	5				9	10^{2}	13			6^{1}			12			11						7	3	8		2	30
1			4	5				9^{3}	13		14		7^{1}			12			6^{2}					11	8		10	3	2	31
			4	5			13		10		12		2^{2}			9						1		6	7^{1}	11	8		3	32
			4^{1}				14	9	10	13				2		7^{2}			12			1		6	11		8^{3}	3	5	33
						7		9	10		12			2		11						1		6	4		8^{1}	3	5	34
				5		7	13	9^{1}			10		8^{2}	2■		11						1		3	4		12■		6	35
	2			5			12	9				13	7^{2}			11			6	10^{1}		1		3	8				4	36
			4	5	12	7		9					8^{2}			10				11^{1}		1		3■	2		13		6■	37
			4	5		7^{3}		9^{2}		12		11		2		10			6^{1}	13		1			14	3	8			38

INVERNESS CALEDONIAN THISTLE

Premier League

Year Formed: 1994. *Ground & Address:* Tulloch Caledonian Stadium, East Longman, Inverness IV1 1FF. *Telephone:* 01463 222880. *Fax:* 01463 227479. *E-mail:* jim.falconer@ictfc.co.uk. *Website:* www.ictfc.co.uk
Ground Capacity (seated): 7780. *Size of Pitch:* 115yd × 75yd.
Chairman: George Fraser. *President:* John MacDonald. *Chief Executive:* Mike Smith. *Secretary:* Jim Falconer.
Commercial Manager: Darren Mackintosh. *Football and Community Development Manager:* Danny MacDonald.
Manager: Craig Brewster. *Assistant Manager:* Malky Thomson. *First Team Coach:* John Docherty. *Physio:* David Brandie.
Record Attendance: 7753 v Rangers, SPL, 20 January 2008.
Record Victory: 8-1, v Annan Ath, Scottish Cup 3rd rd, 24 January 1998.
Record Defeat: 1-5, v Morton, First Division, 12 November 1999 and v Airdrieonians, First Division, 15 April 2000.
Most League Appearances: 440: Ross Tokely, 1995-2008.
Most League Goals in Season: 27: Iain Stewart, 1996-97; Denis Wyness, 2002-03.
Most Goals Overall (Individual): 118: Denis Wyness, 2000-03, 2005-08.

INVERNESS CALEDONIAN THISTLE 2007–08 LEAGUE RECORD

Match No.	Date	Venue	Opponents	Result	H/T Score	Lg. Pos.	Goalscorers	Attendance
1	Aug 4	H	Rangers	L 0-3	0-1	—		7711
2	11	A	Motherwell	L 1-2	0-0	11	Tokely 82	4259
3	18	A	St Mirren	L 1-2	0-1	12	Cowie 58	3309
4	25	H	Dundee U	L 0-3	0-0	12		4178
5	Sept 1	A	Hibernian	L 0-1	0-1	12		13,258
6	15	A	Celtic	L 0-5	0-2	12		56,020
7	22	H	Hearts	W 2-1	0-1	12	Wyness 64, Brewster 90	4918
8	29	H	Falkirk	W 4-2	3-1	11	Wyness 2 7, 54, Duncan 18, Black 32	4011
9	Oct 6	A	Kilmarnock	D 2-2	1-1	10	Ford (og) 22, Cowie 61	4456
10	21	H	Aberdeen	L 1-2	0-1	11	Wyness 58	6023
11	27	A	Gretna	W 4-0	2-0	10	Wyness (pen) 2, Cowie 31, Wilson 73, McBain 75	1096
12	Nov 3	A	Rangers	L 0-2	0-1	11		48,898
13	10	H	Motherwell	L 0-3	0-1	11		3608
14	24	H	St Mirren	W 1-0	1-0	10	Cowie 6	3699
15	Dec 1	A	Dundee U	W 1-0	1-0	9	Black 20	5846
16	8	H	Hibernian	W 2-0	1-0	8	Niculae 2 42, 78	4224
17	16	H	Celtic	W 3-2	1-2	7	Rankin (pen) 42, Proctor 57, Cowie 61	7004
18	22	A	Hearts	W 3-2	1-0	7	Duncan 22, Rankin (pen) 53, Bayne 90	16,202
19	26	A	Falkirk	L 0-1	0-1	8		5265
20	29	H	Kilmarnock	W 3-1	1-0	8	Niculae 2 42, 76, Cowie 52	4169
21	Jan 2	A	Aberdeen	L 0-1	0-0	8		13,372
22	5	H	Gretna	W 3-0	3-0	7	Niculae 2 34, 43, Rankin (pen) 40	3919
23	20	H	Rangers	L 0-1	0-0	7		7753
24	Feb 9	A	St Mirren	D 1-1	1-0	6	Munro 28	3609
25	16	H	Dundee U	D 1-1	0-0	4	Paatelainen 84	4087
26	20	A	Motherwell	L 1-3	1-3	—	Cowie 19	4526
27	23	A	Hibernian	L 0-2	0-2	8		12,552
28	27	A	Celtic	L 1-2	0-1	—	Niculae 70	56,787
29	Mar 1	H	Hearts	L 0-3	0-2	9		4489
30	15	H	Falkirk	L 0-1	0-0	9		4012
31	22	A	Kilmarnock	L 1-4	1-1	9	Black (pen) 14	5100
32	29	H	Aberdeen	L 3-4	2-2	9	Bus (og) 21, Duncan 40, McBain 57	5655
33	Apr 5	A	Gretna	W 2-1	0-0	9	McBain 71, Cowie 73	431
34	19	H	Kilmarnock	W 3-0	1-0	9	Imrie 10, Lilley (og) 71, Niculae 79	3420
35	26	A	Hearts	L 0-1	0-0	9		15,423
36	May 3	H	Gretna	W 6-1	2-1	9	Imrie 1, McAllister 24, Wilson 51, Cowie 70, Tokely 89, Vigurs 90	3639
37	10	A	Falkirk	L 1-2	0-1	9	Wilson (pen) 90	5631
38	17	H	St Mirren	D 0-0	0-0	9		3783

Final League Position: 9

Honours
Scottish Cup: Semi-finals 2003, 2004; Quarter-finals 1996.
League Champions: First Division 2003-04. Third Division 1996-97; *Runners-up:* Second Division 1998-99.
Bell's League Challenge Cup Winners: 2003-04. *Runners-up:* 1999-2000.

Club colours: Shirts: Royal blue with red. Shorts: Royal blue with red. Stockings: Royal blue.

Goalscorers: *League* (51): Cowie 9, Niculae 8, Wyness 5 (1 pen), Black 3 (1 pen), Duncan 3, McBain 3, Rankin 3 (3 pens), Wilson 3 (1 pen), Imrie 2, Tokely 2, Bayne 1, Brewster 1, McAllister 1, Munro 1, Paatelainen 1, Proctor 1, Vigurs 1, own goals 3.
Scottish Cup (0).
CIS Cup (7): Bayne 2, Niculae 2, Wyness 2, Wilson 1.

Fraser M 36	Tokely R 34 + 1	Hastings R 31 + 2	Munro G 33	McCaffrey S 7	McBain R 31 + 2	Wilson B 13 + 12	Black I 31 + 2	Wyness D 19 + 5	Rankin J 11 + 4	McAllister R 3 + 7	Cowie D 35 + 2	Hart R — + 7	McDonald D — + 5	Duncan R 33 + 1	Niculae M 33 + 2	Bayne G 9 + 17	McGuire P 23 + 1	Brewster C 1 + 1	Proctor D 16 + 5	Morgan A — + 3	Malkowski Z 2	Vigurs I 1 + 3	Paatelainen M 4 + 7	Imrie D 12 + 3	Kerr G — + 1	*Match No.*
1	2	3	4	5	6²	7	8	9	10³	11¹	12	13	14													1
1	2	3	4	5	6		8	9¹			11		13	7	10²	12										2
1	2	3¹	4	5		12	8²	13	7		11			6	10	9										3
1	2		4	5	6	12	8¹		10		3		13	7	9	11²										4
1	2		4	5¹	6	7³	8	13	14		11			3	9²		12	10								5
1	2		4		6	7¹	8	9³	12		10²		14	5	11		3		13							6
1	2		4		6	7¹	8	9			11			3	10²		5	13		12						7
1	2	12	4		6	7²	8¹	9			11			3	10³	14	5			13						8
1	2	13	4		6	7²	8	9³			11		14	3	10¹	12	5									9
	2	3	4		6	13	8²	9			7			11	10³	14	5¹		12		1					10
1	2	3	4		6	12	8¹	9			7			11	10²	13	5³		14							11
1	2	3	4	5	6		8³	9¹			14			11	12	10			7²	13						12
1	2■	3	4	5	6³	12	8¹	9²	14		7			11	13	10■										13
1		3	4		6	7¹		9²	12	13	8			11	10		5		2							14
1		3¹	4		6	12	8		10³		7			11	9²	13	5		2			14				15
1		3	4		6¹	13	8		10		7			11²	9	12	5		2							16
1	12	3	4		6¹	14	8		10		7³			11	9²	13	5		2■							17
1	2	3	4		6¹	13	8²		10		7			11	9	12	5									18
1	2	3	4		6¹	13	8		10		7²			11	9	12	5									19
1	2	3	4				8	12	6		7			11	10	9¹	5²		13							20
1	2	3	4				8		10¹		7	12		6	9	11	5									21
1	2	3²	4		13		8	9	10		7¹			6	11³	14			5				12			22
1	2	3	4		6	12	8				7			11	10				5				9¹			23
1	2	3	4		6	13	8	9²			7			5	10				11¹					12		24
1	2	3	4		6		8²				7			11	10¹	12	5						13	9		25
1	2	3	4		6¹		13	9			11			7		10	5						12	8²		26
1	2	3	4				8				11			7¹	9	10	5						12	6		27
1	2	3	4		12		8¹	13			7			5	10		6						9²	11		28
1	2	3	4				8²	12		14	7³			6	10		5		13				9¹	11		29
1	2	3	4		6³		8	9¹		13	7²			11	10	12	5							14		30
1	2		4		6²		8			14		12		11	10³	9	5		7			3¹		13		31
1	2²	3	4■		6						8	12		11■	10		5		7				13	9¹		32
1	2	3			6	7		9²		13	11	12					5		4				10¹	8		33
1	2	3	4²		6	7¹		9		13	8	12			10³				5				14	11		34
1	2	3			6	7²		9¹		14	8			4	10³	12			5				13	11		35
	2	3			6	7²	8³			9¹	4				10	12			5		1	13		11	14	36
1	2	3			6	7	8¹			11²	4			12	10³	13			5			14		9		37
1	2	3			6	7³	12	9¹			8	14		4	10²	13			5■					11		38

KILMARNOCK — Premier League

Year Formed: 1869. *Ground & Address:* Rugby Park, Kilmarnock KA1 2DP. *Telephone:* 01563 545300. *Fax:* 01563 522181. *Website:* www.kilmarnockfc.co.uk
Ground Capacity: all seated: 18,128. *Size of Pitch:* 115yd × 74yd.
Chairman: Michael Johnston. *Secretary:* Kirsten Callaghan..
Manager: Jim Jefferies. *Assistant Manager:* Billy Brown. *Physio:* A. MacQueen.
Club Nickname(s): Killie. *Previous Grounds:* Rugby Park (Dundonald Road); The Grange; Holm Quarry; Present ground since 1899.
Record Attendance: 35,995 v Rangers, Scottish Cup, 10 Mar 1962.
Record Transfer Fee received: £400,000 for Kris Boyd to Rangers (2006).
Record Transfer Fee paid: £300,000 for Paul Wright from St Johnstone (1995).
Record Victory: 11-1 v Paisley Academical, Scottish Cup, 18 Jan 1930 (15-0 v Lanemark, Ayrshire Cup, 15 Nov 1890).
Record Defeat: 1-9 v Celtic, Division I, 13 Aug 1938.
Most Capped Player: Joe Nibloe, 11, Scotland.
Most League Appearances: 481: Alan Robertson, 1972-88.
Most League Goals in Season (Individual): 34: Harry 'Peerie' Cunningham 1927-28; Andy Kerr 1960-61.
Most Goals Overall (Individual): 148: Willy Culley, 1912-23.

KILMARNOCK 2007–08 LEAGUE RECORD

Match No.	Date	Venue	Opponents	Result		H/T Score	Lg. Pos.	Goalscorers	Attendance
1	Aug 5	A	Celtic	D	0-0	0-0	—		50,591
2	13	H	Dundee U	W	2-1	0-0	—	Gibson 79, Nish 87	5557
3	18	A	Motherwell	W	2-1	0-1	4	Lilley 60, Dodds 90	4985
4	25	H	Rangers	L	1-2	0-0	6	Invincibile 61	11,544
5	Sept 1	H	Aberdeen	L	0-1	0-0	6		5814
6	15	A	Gretna	W	2-1	2-0	6	Gibson 4, Jarvis 36	1516
7	22	H	St Mirren	D	0-0	0-0	6		5596
8	29	A	Hibernian	L	1-4	0-2	7	Nish 76	13,662
9	Oct 6	H	Inverness CT	D	2-2	1-1	7	Koudou 1, Nish 56	4456
10	20	A	Falkirk	D	1-1	1-1	8	Wright 10	5143
11	27	H	Hearts	W	3-1	0-0	5	Wales 55, Nish (pen) 72, Gibson 77	6373
12	Nov 3	H	Celtic	L	1-2	0-2	7	Wright 55	8260
13	10	A	Dundee U	L	0-2	0-1	8		6065
14	24	H	Motherwell	L	0-1	0-0	8		5016
15	Dec 1	A	Rangers	L	0-2	0-1	8		48,055
16	8	A	Aberdeen	L	1-2	1-0	10	Fernandez 27	10,207
17	15	H	Gretna	D	3-3	1-1	10	Invincibile 27, Fernandez 53, Nish 73	5122
18	22	A	St Mirren	D	0-0	0-0	10		4217
19	26	H	Hibernian	W	2-1	1-0	9	Nish 36, Taouil 75	6372
20	29	A	Inverness CT	L	1-3	0-1	9	Nish (pen) 87	4169
21	Jan 2	H	Falkirk	L	0-1	0-1	9		5956
22	5	A	Hearts	D	1-1	1-0	9	Di Giacomo 45	14,346
23	19	A	Celtic	L	0-1	0-0	11		56,618
24	26	H	Dundee U	L	1-2	0-1	11	Hay 83	4803
25	Feb 9	A	Motherwell	L	0-1	0-0	11		6618
26	17	H	Rangers	L	0-2	0-1	11		10,546
27	24	H	Aberdeen	W	3-1	2-0	11	Bryson 2 14, 75, Wright 41	6113
28	27	A	Gretna	L	2-4	0-3	—	Ford 72, Gibson 83	1545
29	Mar 1	H	St Mirren	W	1-0	1-0	10	Invincibile 25	5352
30	15	A	Hibernian	L	0-2	0-1	10		12,486
31	22	H	Inverness CT	W	4-1	1-1	10	Wright 38, Bryson 2 50, 56, Flannigan 64	5100
32	29	A	Falkirk	D	0-0	0-0	10		5154
33	Apr 5	H	Hearts	D	0-0	0-0	10		5901
34	19	A	Inverness CT	L	0-3	0-1	10		3420
35	26	H	Gretna	D	1-1	0-0	11	Fernandez 57	4086
36	May 3	A	St Mirren	L	0-1	0-0	11		3690
37	10	A	Hearts	W	2-0	0-0	11	Murray 74, Di Giacomo 83	10,512
38	17	H	Falkirk	W	2-1	1-1	11	Taouil 24, Di Giacomo 81	5475

Final League Position: 11

Honours
League Champions: Division I 1964-65. Division II 1897-98, 1898-99; *Runners-up:* Division I 1959-60, 1960-61, 1962-63, 1963-64. First Division 1975-76, 1978-79, 1981-82, 1992-93. Division II 1953-54, 1973-74. Second Division 1989-90.
Scottish Cup Winners: 1920, 1929, 1997; *Runners-up:* 1898, 1932, 1938, 1957, 1960.
League Cup Runners-up: 1952-53, 1960-61, 1962-63, 2000-01, 2006-07.

European: *European Cup:* 4 matches (1965-66). *Cup Winners' Cup:* 4 matches (1997-98). *UEFA Cup:* 24 matches (*Fairs Cup:* 1964-65, 1966-67, 1969-70, 1970-71. *UEFA Cup:* 1998-99, 1999-2000, 2001-02).

Club colours: Shirt: Blue and white vertical stripes. Shorts: White. Stockings: White.

Goalscorers: *League* (39): Nish 7 (2 pens), Bryson 4, Gibson 4, Wright 4, Di Giacomo 3, Fernandez 3, Invincibile 3, Taouil 2, Dodds 1, Flannigan 1, Ford 1, Hay 1, Jarvis 1, Koudou 1, Lilley 1, Murray 1, Wales 1.
Scottish Cup (3): Hamill 2, Nish 1 (pen).
CIS Cup (3): Naismith 1, Nish 1, Wright 1.

Combe A 37	Fowler J 34	Hay G 26	Lilley D 23 + 1	Wright F 25	Ford S 28	Naismith S 4	O'Leary R 16 + 3	Nish C 20 + 2	Johnston A 14 + 8	Hamill J 29 + 3	Dodds R 6 + 3	Gibson W 9 + 14	Fernandez D 16 + 13	Wales G 16 + 8	Locke G 7 + 10	Murray G 8 + 3	Invincibile D 27	Koudou A 2 + 4	Jarvis R 4 + 5	Clancy T 10 + 1	Bryson C 16 + 3	Flannigan I 7 + 1	Taouil M 19 + 3	Skora E — + 1	Morgan A — + 3	Corrigan M 7	Di Giacomo P 4 + 6	Dalglish P 3 + 3	Harpur C 1	Cox D — + 2	Match No.
1	2^{1}	3^{2}	4	5	6	7	8	9	10^{3}	11	12	13	14																		1
1			4	5	6	7	8	9	10	11	2^{1}	13	12	3^{2}																	2
1			4	5	6	7	8	9	10^{3}	11	14	2^{1}	3^{2}	13	12																3
1			4	5	6	7	8	9	13	11^{2}			14	10^{3}	3^{1}	12	2														4
1			4	5	3			9	10		7	11	12	6^{2}		2		13	8^{1}												5
1	6		4	3			5^{1}	9	10		7	11^{3}	13		14	2			8^{2}	12											6
1	2		4	5	6			9	10		7^{1}	8^{3}	13		12				11^{2}	3	14										7
1	2		4	5	6		8■	13	10^{1}	11		14			3			9^{3}	7^{2}		12										8
1	2		4	5	6			9		11		8			13			10^{1}	12		7	3^{2}									9
1	2		12	5	6^{1}		8	9^{3}		11		4		10	13		7				3^{2}		14								10
1	4	3	2^{1}	5	6		12	9		11		8^{2}		10^{3}			7						13	14							11
1	2	3		5	6^{3}		8	9		11^{2}		4^{1}		10	13		7		14		12										12
1	2	3		5	6		8	9^{3}			13	14		10	12		7				4^{2}	11^{1}									13
1	2		4		6			9^{3}			8	12	13	10		3	7^{1}	14		11^{2}			5								14
1	2				6		8	12		11^{2}	4^{1}		13	10		5	7			3			9								15
1	2			5^{2}			8	9		11		13	6	10			7^{1}		12	3			4								16
1	2	3					8	9		11		12	10^{2}	4	6^{1}		7		13				5								17
1	2	3			6		8	9		11		4^{2}	10^{1}	12			7		13				5								18
1	2	3			6		8	9	14	11			10^{2}	7	12			13			4^{1}		5^{3}								19
1	2	3			6		8	9	13	11			10^{2}	7				12			4^{1}		5								20
1	2	3		5■	6			9	13	11			10^{1}	8			7						4^{2}		12						21
1	2	3			6			9	12	11		13			8^{1}		7			5						4	10^{2}				22
1	2	3		5	6					11		12	13				7^{2}				8^{1}		9			4	10				23
1	2	3		5	6				10^{1}	11		12	14	13			7				8^{3}					4	9^{2}				24
1	2	3	4■		6		12			11				10^{2}	13		7				8^{3}				14	5	9^{1}				25
1	2	3		5	6				10^{1}	11		13	12		4^{3}		7				8		9^{2}				14				26
1	2	3	4	5					10^{2}	11			13				7				8		9^{1}			6		12			27
	2	3		5	6				10^{1}	11^{3}		13	14				7				8		9			4^{2}		12	1		28
1	2	3	4	5					10^{3}	11		14				12	7				8		9^{2}			6^{1}	13				29
1	2	3	4	5						11		13	10^{1}	12		6^{2}	7^{3}				8		9				14				30
1	2	3	4	5					13	12			10				7			6	8^{3}	11^{1}	9^{2}		14						31
1	2	3	4	5					13				8^{1}	12			7			6	11	10	9^{2}								32
1	2	3	4	5■						14			10^{2}	13	8^{1}		7			6	11	12	9^{3}								33
1	2	3	4				5			13			8^{3}	10^{1}	11^{2}		7			6		9					14	12			34
1	2	3	4		6					11			9	13		12	7			5^{1}		8						10^{2}			35
1	2	3	4		6^{1}		12		10^{3}	11			9	14		5	7					8^{2}	13								36
1	2	3	4		6				10^{1}	11			9^{3}		13	5							7^{2}				12	8		14	37
1	2	3	4		6				14	11			9^{2}			5	7						10^{3}				12	8^{1}		13	38

LIVINGSTON First Division

Year Formed: 1974. *Ground:* Almondvale Stadium, Alderton Road, Livingston EH54 7DN. *Telephone:* 01506 417000. *Fax:* 01506 418888. *Email:* info@livingstonfc.co.uk. *Website:* www.livingstonfc.co.uk
Ground Capacity: 10,005 (all seated). *Size of Pitch:* 107yd × 75yd.
Chairman: Pearse Flynn. *Chief Executive:* Vivien Kyles. *General Manager:* David Hay. *Secretary:* M. Kaplan.
Team Manager: Roberto Landi. *Physios:* Arthur Duncan, Marie McPhail.
Club Nickname: Livi Lions. *Previous Grounds:* None.
Record Attendance: 10,024 v Celtic, Premier League, 18 Aug 2001.
Record Transfer Fee received: £1,000,000 for D. Fernandez to Celtic (June 2002).
Record Transfer Fee paid: £120,000 for Wes Hoolahan from Shelbourne (December 2005).
Record Victory: 7-0 v Queen of the South, Scottish Cup, 29 Jan 2000.
Record Defeat: 0-8 v Hamilton A. Division II, 14 Dec 1974.
Most Capped Player (under 18): I. Little.
Most League Appearances: 446: Walter Boyd, 1979-89.
Most League Goals in Season (Individual): 21: John McGachie, 1986-87. *(Team):* 69; Second Division, 1986-87.
Most Goals Overall (Individual): 64: David Roseburgh, 1986-93.

LIVINGSTON 2007–08 LEAGUE RECORD

Match No.	Date	Venue	Opponents	Result	H/T Score	Lg. Pos.	Goalscorers	Attendance
1	Aug 4	H	Dundee	L 0-2	0-1	—		2865
2	11	A	Partick Th	L 0-3	0-2	10		2481
3	19	H	Dunfermline Ath	D 1-1	0-0	9	MacKay (pen) 81	2493
4	25	A	Queen of the S	L 0-1	0-0	10		1830
5	Sept 1	A	Stirling A	D 3-3	1-0	10	Pesir 32, Dorrans 54, Snodgrass 89	972
6	15	H	Morton	W 4-0	3-0	8	Fox 9, Dorrans 2 41, 42, MacKay (pen) 67	1911
7	22	A	Hamilton A	D 1-1	0-1	8	Craig 54	1835
8	29	H	Clyde	W 4-2	2-1	5	Pesir 23, MacKay (pen) 42, Craig 64, Fox 65	1492
9	Oct 6	H	St Johnstone	L 0-2	0-0	8		1776
10	20	A	Dundee	L 1-4	1-1	8	Pesir 14	3639
11	27	H	Queen of the S	D 2-2	1-1	9	Dorrans 21, Pesir 54	1355
12	Nov 3	A	Dunfermline Ath	W 4-0	1-0	6	Craig 2 44, 49, Tinkler 68, Kennedy 90	3473
13	10	H	Stirling A	W 4-3	3-0	5	Dorrans 3 24, 34, 74, MacKay 33	1610
14	14	H	Partick Th	L 0-4	0-2	—		1492
15	Dec 1	A	Morton	D 2-2	2-2	6	Dorrans 10, Kennedy 42	2228
16	8	H	Hamilton A	W 2-0	0-0	5	Snodgrass 2 52, 72	1452
17	15	A	Clyde	L 1-2	1-1	5	Dorrans 8	910
18	22	A	St Johnstone	L 2-5	1-2	6	McMenamin 14, Pesir 90	2217
19	29	A	Queen of the S	L 0-1	0-0	8		1719
20	Jan 2	H	Dunfermline Ath	L 0-2	0-2	8		2339
21	5	H	Morton	W 6-1	2-0	8	MacKay (pen) 17, Pesir 2 36, 58, Walker 71, McMenamin 72, Griffiths 88	1367
22	19	A	Stirling A	W 4-1	2-1	7	Dorrans 35, Craig 39, Snodgrass 2 58, 65	848
23	Feb 9	H	Dundee	D 1-1	1-1	7	Snodgrass 26	1746
24	23	A	Hamilton A	L 1-3	0-1	7	Snodgrass 70	1800
25	Mar 1	A	Dunfermline Ath	D 1-1	1-1	7	Dorrans 23	3208
26	4	A	Partick Th	L 1-2	1-1	—	Griffiths 37	1372
27	8	H	Clyde	D 0-0	0-0	—		1258
28	11	A	Dundee	L 0-2	0-0	—		3715
29	15	H	St Johnstone	L 0-2	0-1	7		1543
30	22	A	Morton	D 1-1	0-1	7	Snodgrass 59	2449
31	29	H	Stirling A	W 2-1	1-1	7	Griffiths 36, Snodgrass 47	1125
32	Apr 1	H	Queen of the S	W 1-0	0-0	—	Griffiths 85	952
33	5	A	Clyde	L 2-3	1-2	7	Weir 29, Tinkler 71	1155
34	12	H	Hamilton A	L 1-3	0-2	7	MacKay (pen) 86	2107
35	19	H	Partick Th	W 1-0	1-0	7	Fox 30	1601
36	26	A	St Johnstone	L 2-5	0-1	7	Griffiths 63, Davidson 80	2571

Final League Position: 7

Honours
League Champions: First Division 2000-01. Second Division 1986-87, 1998-99. Third Division 1995-96; *Runners-up:* Second Division 1982-83. First Division 1987-88.
Scottish Cup: Semi-finals 2004.
League Cup Winners: 2003-04. Semi-finals 1984-85. *B&Q Cup:* Semi-finals 1992-93, 1993-94, 2001.
Bell's League Challenge Runners-up: 2000-01.

European: *UEFA Cup:* 4 matches (2002-03).

Club colours: Shirt: Gold with black sleeves and side panels. Shorts: Black. Stockings: Gold with black trim.

Goalscorers: *League* (55): Dorrans 11, Snodgrass 9, Pesir 7, MacKay 6 (5 pens), Craig 5, Griffiths 5, Fox 3, Kennedy 2, McMenamin 2, Tinkler 2, Davidson 1, Walker 1, Weir 1.
Scottish Cup (7): MacKay 2 (1 pen), Craig 1, Dorrans 1, Jacobs 1, McMenamin 1, Raliukonis 1.
CIS Cup (7): Craig 2, MacKay 2 (1 pen), Mitchell 1, Snodgrass 1, own goal 1.
Challenge Cup (0).

Liberda M 14	MacKay D 33 + 1	Tinkler M 18 + 1	Noubissie P 5 + 3	James C 26 + 3	McPake J 19	Dorrans G 34	Kennedy J 18	Snodgrass R 27 + 4	Weir S 3 + 12	Craig S 20 + 8	Fox L 28 + 4	Hamill J 2 + 2	McCaffrey D 28	Pesir T 14 + 6	Mitchell S 9	Matthews L 4 + 2	Griffiths L 13 + 5	Quitongo J — + 2	Makel L 18	Hottek J — + 1	Raliukonis J 9	McMenamin C 8 + 2	Stewart C 21	Jacobs K 2 + 4	Walker A 6 + 2	MacDonald C 7 + 3	Malone C 4 + 2	Davidson M 3 + 3	Sinclair D 2	Lunn M 1	Smith G — + 1	Halliday A — + 1	*Match No.*
1	2	3	4	5^{2}	6	7■	8	9	10	11^{1}	12	13■																					1
1	2	3	7	5^{2}	6		8	9^{1}	13	4			11	12		10																	2
1	2		7^{2}	12	6	10	8			13	4	11	3^{1}	14	5	9^{3}																	3
1	2		3^{2}	5	6	7	8		14	12	4	11^{3}	13	10	9^{1}																		4
1	2	3	14	13		7	8	9	10		4^{3}		5	11^{1}	6^{2}		12																5
1	2	3	12			7^{2}	8	9	13	11^{1}	4		5	10^{3}	6		14																6
1	2	3				7	8	9	12	11^{1}	4		5	10	6																		7
1	2	3	13	12		7^{3}	8	9■		11	4^{2}		5^{1}	10	6			14															8
1	2	3	9^{1}			7	8		12	11	6		5	10	4^{2}			13															9
1		3		4		6	7^{1}			10	11		5	9^{2}	2	12			8	13													10
1	13	3		5		9	8	12		11^{3}	7^{2}		6	10	2^{1}	14			4														11
1	2	3				7^{1}	8	9		11	12		5	10					4		6												12
1	2	3				7	8	9					5	10		11^{1}			6		4	12											13
1	2	3		5		7		9^{1}		12	6			11					4		8	10											14
	2			3		7	8	12		13			5	9^{2}					4		6	10	1	11^{1}									15
	2			5		7	8	9^{3}		13	12		3	11					4^{1}		6	10^{2}	1	14									16
	2			5		7	8	9^{1}		13	12		6	11^{2}					4		3	10	1										17
	2			5		7	8	12		11	6		4	13							3^{2}	10	1	9^{1}									18
	2			5		7	8^{2}	13		9^{1}	11		6	12					4		3	10	1										19
	2	5^{1}				7		11		10	8		3	13					4^{3}		6	9^{2}	1	14	12								20
	2			3		7		11	13	9^{2}	8		6^{1}	10^{3}			14					12	1		4	5							21
	2			3	4	7		11^{3}	12	10^{2}	8						13		6			9^{1}	1		14	5							22
	2			3	4	7		11		9	10						12		6				1		8^{1}	5							23
	2			3	4	7		11	13	12^{2}	10^{1}						9		6				1			5	8						24
	2			3	4	7		11			10						9		6				1	12		5	8^{1}						25
	2			3	4	7		11	13		10						9^{2}		6				1	12		5	8^{1}						26
	2			3	4	7		11			10		5				9		6				1		8^{1}		12						27
	2	12		3	4			11			10		5				9		6				1		8^{1}			7■					28
	2			3	4	7		11			10^{1}		5				9		6				1		8		12						29
	2	6^{2}		3	4	7		11		10^{1}			5				9						1		8■	13		12■					30
	2	6		3	4	7		11		10	8		5				9						1										31
	2	6^{1}		3	4	7		11		10	8		5				9						1					12					32
	2	5^{2}		6	3	7		11	12	9	8		4				10^{1}						1			13							33
	2	6^{3}		3^{1}	4	7		11	13	10	8		5				9^{2}						1			14		12					34
	2			3	4	7		11^{2}	12	13	8		5				9^{1}						1					10	6				35
					4	7^{2}			10		8	13	5				9^{3}									2	3^{1}	11	6	1	12	14	36

MONTROSE

Third Division

Year Formed: 1879. *Ground & Address:* Links Park, Wellington St, Montrose DD10 8QD. *Telephone:* 01674 673200.
Fax: 01674 677311. *E-mail:* montrosefootballclub@tesco.net. *Website:* www.montrosefc.co.uk
Ground Capacity: total: 3292, seated: 1338. *Size of Pitch:* 113yd × 70yd.
Chairman: Brian Winton. *Secretary:* Malcolm J. Watters.
Manager: Jim Weir. *Physio:* Brian Duncan.
Club Nickname(s): The Gable Endies. *Previous Grounds:* None.
Record Attendance: 8983 v Dundee, Scottish Cup 3rd rd, 17 Mar 1973.
Record Transfer Fee received: £50,000 for Gary Murray to Hibernian (Dec 1980).
Record Transfer Fee paid: £17,500 for Jim Smith from Airdrieonians (Feb 1992).
Record Victory: 12-0 v Vale of Leithen, Scottish Cup 2nd rd, 4 Jan 1975.
Record Defeat: 0-13 v Aberdeen, 17 Mar 1951.
Most Capped Player: Alexander Keillor, 2 (6), Scotland.
Most League Appearances: 432: David Larter, 1987-98.
Most League Goals in Season (Individual): 28: Brian Third, Division II, 1972-73.

MONTROSE 2007–08 LEAGUE RECORD

Match No.	Date	Venue	Opponents	Result		H/T Score	Lg. Pos.	Goalscorers	Attendance
1	Aug 4	H	Albion R	L	0-1	0-0	—		415
2	11	A	Elgin C	W	2-0	0-0	5	Baird 2 [66, 75]	479
3	18	A	Stranraer	L	0-1	0-0	7		272
4	25	H	Arbroath	D	3-3	1-1	7	Baird [24], Stein [81], Rodgers [89]	1073
5	Sept 1	A	Stenhousemuir	W	4-0	2-0	4	Stein [19], Andreoni [20], Baird 2 [54, 63]	398
6	15	H	East Fife	W	3-1	2-0	4	Gibson [44], Gates 2 [45, 59]	612
7	22	A	Forfar Ath	W	4-1	3-1	3	Baird [24], Stein [27], Wood [45], Gibson [55]	584
8	29	H	Dumbarton	L	0-1	0-0	4		545
9	Oct 6	H	East Stirling	W	3-1	2-0	3	Baird 2 (1 pen) [17 (p), 28], Rodgers [67]	407
10	12	H	Elgin C	D	0-0	0-0	—		623
11	20	A	Albion R	W	3-1	1-0	2	Rodgers [43], Stein [70], Dobbins [86]	239
12	Nov 6	H	Stranraer	L	2-4	0-3	—	Andreoni [51], Stein [75]	321
13	10	A	Arbroath	D	0-0	0-0	2		957
14	Dec 1	A	East Fife	L	0-2	0-2	3		785
15	8	H	Stenhousemuir	W	1-0	1-0	3	Doris [43]	365
16	15	H	Forfar Ath	L	0-1	0-1	3		588
17	22	A	Dumbarton	W	3-1	2-0	3	Baird 2 (1 pen) [11 (p), 66], Wood [13]	510
18	29	A	East Stirling	W	3-0	0-0	3	Black [48], Wood [52], Rodgers [79]	295
19	Jan 2	H	Arbroath	W	5-0	4-0	2	Gardiner [16], Wood 2 [28, 64], Black [35], Gibson [45]	1470
20	5	A	Stranraer	W	2-0	0-0	2	Baird 2 (1 pen) [75 (p), 86]	187
21	12	H	East Fife	L	0-1	0-1	—		908
22	19	A	Stenhousemuir	D	0-0	0-0	2		346
23	26	A	Elgin C	L	1-2	1-1	2	McLeod [14]	449
24	Feb 2	H	Albion R	W	2-1	2-0	2	Baird [10], Doris [45]	430
25	9	H	Dumbarton	W	3-1	2-0	2	Wood [5], Hunter 2 [29, 69]	458
26	16	A	Forfar Ath	D	1-1	1-0	2	Hunter [45]	554
27	23	H	Stranraer	L	0-2	0-1	2		514
28	Mar 1	A	Arbroath	L	1-2	0-2	3	Hunter [76]	959
29	8	H	East Stirling	W	2-0	0-0	3	Wood [54], Stewart [90]	410
30	15	A	Albion R	W	3-0	1-0	2	Gibson [35], Baird 2 (1 pen) [73 (p), 83]	279
31	22	A	East Fife	D	0-0	0-0	3		773
32	29	H	Stenhousemuir	W	2-1	1-1	3	Doris [42], Lyle (og) [50]	510
33	Apr 5	H	Forfar Ath	D	2-2	1-1	3	Baird (pen) [6], Doris [55]	590
34	12	A	Dumbarton	D	0-0	0-0	3		463
35	19	H	Elgin C	W	3-2	1-1	3	Baird 2 (1 pen) [11, 67 (p)], Stein [90]	492
36	26	A	East Stirling	L	1-3	0-1	3	King (og) [27]	551

Final League Position: 3

Honours
League Champions: Second Division 1984-85; *Runners-up:* Second Division 1990-91. Third Division 1994-95.
Scottish Cup: Quarter-finals 1973, 1976.
League Cup: Semi-finals 1975-76.
B&Q Cup: Semi-finals 1992-93.
League Challenge Cup: Semi-finals 1996-97.

Club colours: Shirt: Royal blue. Shorts: Royal blue. Stockings: White.

Goalscorers: *League* (59): Baird 18 (6 pens), Wood 7, Stein 6, Doris 4, Gibson 4, Hunter 4, Rodgers 4, Andreoni 2, Black 2, Gates 2, Dobbins 1, Gardiner 1, McLeod 1, Stewart 1, own goals 2.
Play-offs (1): Wood 1.
Scottish Cup (2): Baird 1, Rogers 1.
CIS Cup (3): Gibson 1, Stein 1, Wood 1.
Challenge Cup (6): Baird 3 (1 pen), Wood 2, Stein 1.

Peat M 33	McLeod C 33	Cumming S 19 + 2	Gibson K 33	McGowne K 3	Dobbins I 19 + 1	Donachie B 2 + 4	Thomson S 13 + 1	Rodgers A 8 + 14	Baird J 28 + 6	Stein J 22 + 10	Wood G 23 + 1	Gates S 7 + 8	Stewart P 2 + 15	Gardiner R 31 + 1	Davidson H 22 + 3	McKenzie S 3 + 2	Andreoni M 11 + 1	Doris R 21 + 4	Mitchell C 5	Black S 20 + 4	Stephen N 1	Maitland J 2 + 8	Buchan J 13	Heggerty C 8	Hunter R 5 + 5	McLaren F — + 4	Forsythe C 9	Nicol D — + 1	*Match No.*
1	2	3	4	5	6	7	8^{1}	9	10^{3}	11^{2}	12	13	14																1
1	2	3	4		6		8	9^{1}	12	11^{2}	10^{3}	13	14	5	7														2
1	2	3	4		6		8^{3}	13	10	11^{1}	9^{2}	12	14	5	7														3
1^{G}	2	3^{1}	4	5	6			13	10	11	9■	7^{2}		8	12	15													4
1^{G}	2		4		6		13	9	10	11^{1}		7^{2}	12	5	3	15	8												5
1	2		4		6	12		13	10^{2}	11^{3}	9	7	14	5	3		8^{1}												6
	2		4		6	12		13	10^{2}	11	9	7^{3}	14	5	3	1	8^{1}												7
1	2	12	4		6			13	10^{3}	11	9	7^{2}	14	5	3^{1}		8												8
1	2	3	4		6	13		9	10^{3}	11		12	14	5	7^{1}		8^{2}												9
1	2	3	4^{2}		6	13		9	10	11^{1}		12		5	7		8												10
1	2	3	4		6			9^{1}	10^{2}	11		13		5	7		8	12											11
1	2				6	7^{2}		12	10	11		14		3^{1}	4		13	9	8	5^{3}									12
1	2		4		6			9	10^{1}	11				3	5		7	12	8										13
1	2		4^{1}				8	9^{3}	12	11^{2}		14			6		7	10	3	13	5								14
1	2	14	4				8	13		11^{1}	10^{2}	6^{3}		3	7			9	5	12									15
1	2		4		6			14	12	11^{2}	10	8^{1}		3^{3}	7			9	5	13									16
1	2	3	4				8	12	10^{1}	13	9			5			7^{3}	11		6^{2}		14							17
1	2	3	4^{3}		14		8	12	10^{1}	13	11			5			6	7		9^{2}									18
1	3	2	7		8^{1}		5	13	11	14	10^{2}			4				6		9^{3}		12							19
1	4	2	6		8		3		10	12	9			5				7		11^{1}									20
1	3	2^{1}	7		8^{3}		5	13	11	6	10			4	12^{2}					9		14							21
1	4		6		2		3	12	10	7	9			5				13		11^{1}		8^{2}							22
1	4		6^{2}	10^{1}	2		3^{3}	12		13	9		14	5				7		11		8							23
1	3		7				5^{1}		11^{2}	12	10			4				6		9			2	8	13				24
1	3	2	7						11	13	10^{1}			5				6^{2}		9^{3}		14	4	8	12				25
1	4	2	6						10	12				3				7		11^{1}			5	8	9^{2}	13			26
1	3	2^{3}	7						11				14	5				6		9		12	4^{2}	8^{1}	10	13			27
1	4	2^{1}	6						10^{3}		9			5	14			7		11			8		13	12	3^{2}		28
1	3		8						12		10		14	4^{3}	7^{2}			6		9			2		11^{1}	13	5		29
1	4		6						12	13	9^{2}		14	5	8			7		11^{3}			2		10^{1}		3		30
1	3		7						11^{2}	13	10^{1}		12		8			6		9			2	4			5		31
1	3		7						11		10^{1}		12		8			6^{2}		9			2	4	13		5		32
1	4		6^{1}						10^{2}	9				13	8			7		11		12	2	5■			3		33
1		4							11^{2}	10			8	3	7			6		9^{1}		12	2		13		5		34
		2							11^{3}	9			6^{1}	4	8	1		10		12		13	3	7^{2}			5	14	35
		5	6						13	11^{3}	9^{2}		14	4	8	1		12		10			2		7^{1}		3		36

MORTON First Division

Year Formed: 1874. *Ground & Address:* Cappielow Park, Sinclair St, Greenock. *Telephone:* 01475 723571. *Fax:* 01475 781084. *E-mail:* info@gmfc.net. *Website:* www.gmfc.net
Ground Capacity: total: 11,612, seated: 6062. *Size of Pitch:* 110yd × 71yd.
Chairman: Douglas Rae. *Chief Executive:* Gillian Donaldson. *Company Secretary:* Mary Davidson. *Commercial Manager:* Susan Gregory.
Manager: Davie Irons. *Assistant Manager:* Martin Clark. *Physios:* Paul Kelly, Bruce Coyle.
Club Nickname(s): The Ton. *Previous Grounds:* Grant Street 1874, Garvel Park 1875, Cappielow Park 1879, Ladyburn Park 1882, (Cappielow Park 1883).
Record Attendance: 23,500 v Celtic, 29 April 1922.
Record Transfer Fee received: £350,000 for Neil Orr to West Ham U.
Record Transfer Fee paid: £150,000 for Alan Mahood from Nottingham Forest (August 1998).
Record Victory: 11-0 v Carfin Shamrock, Scottish Cup 1st rd, 13 Nov 1886.
Record Defeat: 1-10 v Port Glasgow Ath, Division II, 5 May, 1894 and v St Bernards, Division II, 14 Oct 1933.
Most Capped Player: Jimmy Cowan, 25, Scotland.
Most League Appearances: 358: David Hayes, 1969-84.
Most League Goals in Season (Individual): 58: Allan McGraw, Division II, 1963-64.

MORTON 2007–08 LEAGUE RECORD

Match No.	Date	Venue	Opponents	Result	H/T Score	Lg. Pos.	Goalscorers	Attendance
1	Aug 4	H	Clyde	W 3-2	2-2	—	Weatherson [29], McAlistair [42], Stevenson (pen) [57]	3818
2	11	A	Dunfermline Ath	W 1-0	1-0	3	Weatherson [21]	4748
3	18	A	Stirling A	D 0-0	0-0	4		1538
4	25	H	Hamilton A	L 0-2	0-0	4		3188
5	Sept 1	H	Queen of the S	L 0-1	0-0	5		2813
6	15	A	Livingston	L 0-4	0-3	6		1911
7	22	H	St Johnstone	D 2-2	1-1	6	Russell [15], Stevenson [63]	2922
8	29	A	Dundee	L 1-2	1-1	8	Graham [42]	3952
9	Oct 6	H	Partick Th	W 4-2	2-0	5	Weatherson 3 [8, 11, 49], McAnespie [47]	3329
10	20	A	Clyde	W 1-0	1-0	4	Weatherson [15]	1306
11	27	A	Hamilton A	L 0-1	0-1	4		2562
12	Nov 3	H	Stirling A	D 1-1	1-0	5	Russell [8]	2850
13	10	A	Queen of the S	W 3-1	1-1	4	Weatherson [24], Russell (pen) [77], Millar [90]	2110
14	Dec 1	H	Livingston	D 2-2	2-2	5	Millar [7], Russell [38]	2228
15	8	A	St Johnstone	D 2-2	1-0	6	Anderson (og) [3], Weatherson [82]	2517
16	15	H	Dundee	L 0-2	0-1	6		2569
17	22	A	Partick Th	D 1-1	0-0	5	McAlistair [52]	3611
18	26	H	Dunfermline Ath	L 0-1	0-1	7		2604
19	29	H	Hamilton A	L 1-3	1-3	7	Russell [18]	2642
20	Jan 2	A	Stirling A	W 2-1	0-0	7	Harding [60], McGuffie [81]	1256
21	5	A	Livingston	L 1-6	0-2	7	Russell (pen) [89]	1367
22	19	H	Queen of the S	L 0-3	0-0	8		2521
23	26	A	Dunfermline Ath	L 0-2	0-0	8		2100
24	Feb 9	H	Clyde	L 1-2	0-0	9	Millar [52]	2276
25	16	A	Dundee	L 0-2	0-2	9		4103
26	23	H	St Johnstone	L 1-2	1-2	9	Weatherson [16]	2564
27	Mar 1	H	Stirling A	W 2-1	1-0	8	Jenkins [22], Russell [72]	2355
28	8	A	Hamilton A	L 0-3	0-1	—		1980
29	11	A	Clyde	D 1-1	1-0	—	McGregor (og) [26]	1270
30	15	H	Partick Th	D 0-0	0-0	8		2787
31	22	H	Livingston	D 1-1	1-0	8	McAlister [30]	2449
32	29	A	Queen of the S	D 0-0	0-0	9		1808
33	Apr 5	H	Dundee	L 1-2	1-1	9	McAlister [8]	2741
34	12	A	St Johnstone	L 2-3	0-2	9	Wake [49], Russell (pen) [73]	2341
35	19	H	Dunfermline Ath	W 3-0	1-0	8	Wake [14], Harding [59], Finlayson [73]	2495
36	26	A	Partick Th	W 3-0	2-0	8	Wake 2 [14, 56], Finlayson [45]	4915

Final League Position: 8

Honours
League Champions: First Division 1977-78, 1983-84, 1986-87. Division II 1949-50, 1963-64, 1966-67. Second Division 1994-95, 2006-07. Third Division 2002-03. *Runners-up:* Division 1 1916-17, Division II 1899-1900, 1928-29, 1936-37.
Scottish Cup Winners: 1922; *Runners-up:* 1948. *League Cup Runners-up:* 1963-64.
B&Q Cup Runners-up: 1992-93.

European: *UEFA Cup:* 2 matches (*Fairs Cup:* 1968-69).

Club colours: Shirt: Royal blue with 3½ inch white hoops. Shorts: White with royal blue panel down side. Stockings: Royal blue with white tops.

Goalscorers: *League* (40): Weatherson 9, Russell 8 (3 pens), McAlister 4, Wake 4, Millar 3, Finlayson 2, Harding 2, Stevenson 2 (1 pen), Graham 1, Jenkins 1, McAnespie 1, McGuffie 1, own goals 2.
Scottish Cup (7): Finlayson 1, McAlistair 1, McLaughlin 1, Miller 1, Russell 1, Templeman 1, Weatherston 1.
CIS Cup (0).
Challenge Cup (7): Graham 2, Templeman 2, Linn 1, McAlistair 1, own goal 1.

Robinson L 20	Weatherson P 33 + 2	Walker A 12 + 1	Millar C 23 + 2	Harding R 34	Greacen S 34	Finlayson K 29 + 3	Stevenson J 12 + 11	McAlister J 36	Templeman C 7 + 10	McAnespie K 10 + 4	Shields J 17 + 2	Keenan D 6 + 2	Graham B 3 + 10	Linn B 1 + 2	Coakley A — + 2	Gardyne M 3 + 7	Russell I 24 + 6	Adams J —	McGurn D 16	McLaughlin S 23 + 1	MacGregor D 15 + 2	McGuffie R 16 + 1	Smith B 5	Jenkins A 8 + 1	Wake B 4 + 7	Paartalu E 5	Match No.
1	2	3	4	5	6	7	8[1]	9	10[3]	11[2]	12	13	14														1
1	2	3	4	5	6		8	9	10			7	11[1]	12													2
1	2	3	4	5	6	12	8[1]	9	10		11	7															3
1	2	3[1]	4[2]	5	6	13	8[3]	9	10	12	7■	11			14												4
1	2		4[1]	5	6	7[3]	14	9	13	11		3		8[2]		12	10										5
1	2			5	6	7[1]	8[2]	9	12		3	4			13	10	11										6
1	2	3[3]		5	6	13	8	9	10		12	7[1]		14		4[2]	11										7
1	2	3		5	6	7	8	9	10		4		11														8
	2[2]			5	6	7	8	9	12	3	4		13				10[1]		1	11							9
	2[3]		12	5	6	7	8[1]	9		11	4		14			13	3[2]		1	10							10
	2		12	5	6	7[2]	8[1]	9	14	3	4					13	11[3]		1	10							11
	2	12	4	5	6	7	13	9	14	11[2]	8[3]					10[1]	3		1								12
	2	3	4	5	6	7	14	9		13	8[1]	12					10[3]		1	11[2]							13
	2[1]	3[2]	4	5	6	7		9	12		8		14			13	10[3]		1	11							14
	2	3[3]	4	5	6	7		9	12	13	11[1]					14	10		1	8[2]							15
	2	3[3]	4	5	6	7		9	13		8		14			12	10[2]		1	11[1]							16
	2			5	6	7		9	12	11	3						10[1]		1	8	4						17
	2			5	6	7		9	13	4[1]	3		12			14	10[3]		1	8[2]	11						18
	2			5	6		12	9	10	13	3		11[1]				7		1	4[2]	8						19
1	9			4	5	7	12	11		6[1]	2						10				3	8					20
1	9[2]			4	5	7■	13	11		6[1]	2		14				10			12	3[3]	8					21
	10		5	4			6[1]	9					12				11		1	7	2	8	3				22
	12		10	4	5	7		11					13				9[2]		1	3	2[1]	8	6				23
	10		8		3	6		9									12		1	5		4	2	7	11[1]		24
1	2		7■			10		11									9[1]			3	5	6	4	8	12		25
1	10			2	4	5	14	8									12			9	13	6[3]	3[2]	7	11[1]		26
	11		7	4	3	8		9									10[2]		1	2	12	5[1]		6	13		27
	9[3]		4	6	5	7[1]	12	11									13		1	3	2	8[2]		10	14		28
1	9		4	6	5			11					12				10[1]			3	2	7		8			29
1	10[3]		6[1]	4	3	5	11[2]	9									13			8	2	12		7	14		30
1	9			6	5	7	12	11[1]									10[2]			3	2	4		8	13		31
1	11		6	5	4	7		10												3	2	8				9	32
1	9[1]		4	6	5	7[3]	14	11									12			3	2[2]	8			13	10	33
1	9[2]		4	6	5	7[3]	14	11									12			3[1]	2	8			13	10	34
1		5	7	2	3	6		9									11					4			10	8	35
1	12	3[1]	4	2	5	7[2]		11									10					6		13	9	8	36

MOTHERWELL Premier League

Year Formed: 1886. *Ground & Address:* Fir Park Stadium, Motherwell ML1 2QN. *Telephone:* 01698 333333. *Fax:* 01698 338001.
E-mail: info@motherwellfc.co.uk. *Website:* www.motherwellfc.co.uk
Ground Capacity: all seated: 13,742. *Size of Pitch:* 110yd × 75yd.
Chairman: John Boyle. *Chief Executive:* Ian Stillie. *Secretary:* Stewart Robertson.
Manager: Mark McGhee. *Assistant Manager:* Scott Leitch. *Physios:* John Porteous, R. Mayberry.
Club Nickname(s): The Well. *Previous Grounds:* Roman Road, Dalziel Park.
Record Attendance: 35,632 v Rangers, Scottish Cup 4th rd replay, 12 Mar 1952.
Record Transfer Fee received: £1,750,000 for Phil O'Donnell to Celtic (September 1994).
Record Transfer Fee paid: £500,000 for John Spencer from Everton (Jan 1999).
Record Victory: 12-1 v Dundee U, Division II, 23 Jan 1954.
Record Defeat: 0-8 v Aberdeen, Premier Division, 26 Mar 1979.
Most Capped Player: Tommy Coyne, 13, Republic of Ireland.
Most League Appearances: 626: Bobby Ferrier, 1918-37.
Most League Goals in Season (Individual): 52: Willie McFadyen, Division I, 1931-32.
Most Goals Overall (Individual): 283: Hugh Ferguson, 1916-25.

MOTHERWELL 2007–08 LEAGUE RECORD

Match No.	Date	Venue	Opponents	Result	H/T Score	Lg. Pos.	Goalscorers	Attendance
1	Aug 4	A	St Mirren	W 1-0	1-0	—	McGarry 3	5257
2	11	H	Inverness CT	W 2-1	0-0	3	O'Donnell 85, McCormack (pen) 90	4259
3	18	H	Kilmarnock	L 1-2	1-0	5	Clarkson 23	4985
4	25	A	Gretna	W 2-1	1-1	3	Lasley 8, Porter 62	3758
5	Sept 3	H	Hearts	L 0-2	0-1	—		5081
6	15	A	Aberdeen	W 2-1	2-0	5	Quinn 34, Porter 37	10,154
7	22	A	Falkirk	L 0-1	0-0	5		5245
8	29	H	Rangers	D 1-1	1-0	5	Porter 24	10,009
9	Oct 6	A	Dundee U	L 0-1	0-0	6		6286
10	20	H	Hibernian	W 2-1	2-1	5	McCormack 2 35, 37	7071
11	27	A	Celtic	L 0-3	0-1	6		57,633
12	Nov 3	H	St Mirren	D 1-1	1-1	6	Porter 29	5123
13	10	A	Inverness CT	W 3-0	1-0	5	Clarkson 2 15, 53, Smith D 87	3608
14	24	A	Kilmarnock	W 1-0	0-0	5	O'Donnell 46	5016
15	Dec 1	H	Gretna	W 3-0	1-0	5	Clarkson 2 44, 74, Porter 61	6431
16	8	A	Hearts	W 2-1	0-1	3	Porter 53, Zaliukas (og) 67	16,633
17	15	H	Aberdeen	W 3-0	3-0	3	McCormack 2 (1 pen) 8 (p), 45, McGarry 12	5320
18	22	H	Falkirk	L 0-3	0-0	3		5247
19	26	A	Rangers	L 1-3	0-1	3	Quinn 65	49,823
20	29	H	Dundee U	W 5-3	3-1	3	Hughes 11, Porter 14, McCormack 17, Clarkson 2 55, 56	5227
21	Jan 19	A	St Mirren	L 1-3	1-2	4	Clarkson 11	4291
22	Feb 9	H	Kilmarnock	W 1-0	0-0	4	Clarkson 90	6618
23	16	A	Gretna	W 3-1	1-0	3	Porter 25, McCormack 2 47, 90	2877
24	20	H	Inverness CT	W 3-1	3-1	—	Clarkson 2 7, 42, Porter 10	4526
25	23	H	Hearts	L 0-1	0-1	3		5925
26	27	A	Aberdeen	D 1-1	0-1	—	Smith D 83	8240
27	Mar 1	A	Falkirk	D 0-0	0-0	3		5108
28	12	A	Hibernian	L 0-1	0-0	—		11,692
29	22	A	Dundee U	L 0-2	0-0	5		6779
30	29	H	Hibernian	W 1-0	1-0	4	Clarkson 3	6580
31	Apr 5	A	Celtic	W 1-0	1-0	3	Lappin 33	58,624
32	13	H	Celtic	L 1-4	1-3	—	McCormack 24	9771
33	26	H	Dundee U	D 2-2	1-1	3	Porter 2 17, 50	5027
34	May 3	H	Celtic	L 1-2	0-0	3	Porter 60	9158
35	7	A	Rangers	L 0-1	0-0	—		48,238
36	10	H	Aberdeen	W 2-1	0-0	3	Smith D 61, Porter 81	8574
37	17	H	Rangers	D 1-1	0-1	3	Porter 50	10,445
38	22	A	Hibernian	W 2-0	1-0	—	Lappin 4, Murphy J (pen) 80	10,754

Final League Position: 3

Honours
League Champions: Division I 1931-32. First Division 1981-82, 1984-85. Division II 1953-54, 1968-69; *Runners-up:* Premier Division 1994-95. Division I 1926-27, 1929-30, 1932-33, 1933-34. Division II 1894-95, 1902-03. *Scottish Cup:* 1952, 1991; *Runners-up:* 1931, 1933, 1939, 1951.
League Cup Winners: 1950-51. *Runners-up:* 1954-55, 2004-05. *Scottish Summer Cup:* 1944, 1965.

European: *Cup Winners' Cup:* 2 matches (1991-92). *UEFA Cup:* 6 matches (1994-95, 1995-96).

Club colours: Shirt: Amber with claret hoop and trimmings. Shorts: Amber. Stockings: Amber with claret trim.

Goalscorers: *League* (50): Porter 14, Clarkson 12, McCormack 9 (2 pens), Smith D 3, Lappin 2, McGarry 2, O'Donnell 2, Quinn 2, Hughes 1, Lasley 1, Murphy J 1 (pen), own goal 1.
Scottish Cup (4): Porter 2, McCormack 1 (pen), Smith D 1.
CIS Cup (8): McCormack 2, Porter 2, Clarkson 1, Lasley 1, McLean 1, Quinn 1.

Smith G 36	Quinn P 31	Paterson J 20	Reynolds M 38	Craigan S 38	Fitzpatrick M 19 + 10	Lasley K 25 + 7	McGarry S 27 + 4	Porter C 34 + 3	Clarkson D 34 + 1	O'Donnell P 15 + 3	Mensing S — + 1	Smith D 4 + 18	Murphy D — + 3	McCormack R 30 + 6	Grabban L — + 6	Hughes S 29 + 2	Kinniburgh W — + 2	McLean B 6 + 3	Grehan M — + 1	Hammell S 15	Lappin S 7 + 7	Murphy J — + 16	Malcolm R 8	Daniels L 2	McHugh R — + 1	*Match No.*
1	2	3	4	5	6	7	8^{2}	9	10^{3}	11^{1}	12	13	14													1
1	2	3	4	5	6	7	8	9^{1}	10	11				12												2
1	2	3	4	5	6	7	8^{1}	9^{2}	10	11		13		12												3
1	2	3	4	5	6	7	8^{1}	12	10	11^{2}			13	9												4
1	2	3	4	5		7^{1}	8	12	10	11^{2}				9	13	6										5
1	2	3	4	5	12	14	8	9	10^{2}	11^{1}				7^{3}	13	6										6
1	2	3	4	5	6^{2}	7^{1}	8	9	10					12		11						13				7
1	2	3	4	5	12	7	8^{1}	9	10^{2}					11		6						13				8
1	2	3	4	5		7	8^{3}	9	10^{1}	14		13		11^{2}	12	6										9
1	2	3	4	5		7	8	9	10	12				11^{2}	13	6^{1}										10
1	2^{3}	3^{2}	4	5		7	8	9	10	12				11	14	6^{1}	13									11
1	2	3	4	5	12	7^{1}	8	9	10^{2}	11		13		6												12
1	2	3	4	5^{3}		7	8^{1}	9	10	11		12		6^{2}	13		14									13
1	2	3	4	5	13	7^{2}	8^{1}	9	10	11				6^{3}		12						14				14
1	2	3^{2}	4	5	12	13	8^{1}	9	10	11		14		7^{3}		6										15
1	2	3	4	5			8	9	10	7				11		6										16
1	2	3	4	5	12	13	8^{1}	9	10^{3}	11^{2}		14		7		6										17
1	2	3	4	5		14	8	9	10^{2}	11^{1}		12		7		6^{3}						13				18
1	2	3	4	5			8^{1}	9	10^{2}	11		12		7		6						13				19
1	2	3	4	5	13	12	8^{1}	9	10^{3}	11^{2}		14		7		6										20
1	2		4	5	6	7	8^{1}	9^{3}	10					11^{2}		3		13	14			12				21
1	2		4	5	6	7^{1}	8^{2}		10			13		9^{3}		11				3	12	14				22
1	2		4	5	6	12		9^{2}	10			7		8		11^{1}				3	13					23
1	2		4	5	6	7	13	9^{3}	10			11^{1}		8^{2}						3	12	14				24
1	2		4	5^{3}	6	7		9	10^{1}			13		8		11^{2}				3	12	14				25
1	2		4	5	12	7		9	10^{3}			13		8^{2}		6				3	11^{1}	14				26
1	2		4	5	6	7		9	10^{1}			12		8		11				3						27
1			4	5	6		8^{1}	9	10			13		7		11				3	12		2^{2}			28
1			4	5	6	7^{2}	13^{3}	9	10					8		11				3^{1}	12	14	2			29
1	2		4	5	6	7^{2}	13	9	10^{1}					12		8					3		11			30
1	2^{2}		4	5	6			9						10^{1}		8		13		3	11	12	7■			31
1	2		4	5	6^{2}		12	9^{3}					14	10		8		7		3	11^{1}	13				32
1	2		4	5	12	13		9	10					7^{2}		8^{1}		14		3	11^{3}		6			33
			4	5	6	7^{3}		9	10^{2}			11^{1}		12		13		2		3		14	8	1		34
1			4	5	6	7^{2}	8^{1}	14	12			13		9^{3}		11		2			10		3			35
1			4	5	6^{1}		8^{2}	9	10			12		13^{3}		7		2		3	14		11			36
1			4	5	12	7	8	9	10^{2}			11^{1}				6		2		3		13				37
			4	5		7	8	9^{2}				12		10^{3}		6		2		3^{1}	11	13		1	14	38

PARTICK THISTLE — First Division

Year Formed: 1876. *Ground & Address:* Firhill Stadium, 80 Firhill Rd, Glasgow G20 7AL. *Telephone:* 0141 579 1971. *Fax:* 0141 945 1525. *E-mail:* mail@ptfc.co.uk. *Website:* www.ptfc.co.uk
Ground Capacity: total: 13,141, seated: 10,921. *Size of Pitch:* 105yd × 68yd.
Chairman: Allan Cowan. *Secretary:* Antonia Kerr.
Manager: Ian McCall. *Assistant Manager:* Gardner Spiers. *Physio:* George Hannah.
Club Nickname(s): The Jags. *Previous Grounds:* Jordanvale Park; Muirpark; Inchview; Meadowside Park.
Record Attendance: 49,838 v Rangers, Division I, 18 Feb 1922. *Ground Record:* 54,728, Scotland v Ireland, 25 Feb 1928.
Record Transfer Fee received: £200,000 for Mo Johnston to Watford.
Record Transfer Fee paid: £85,000 for Andy Murdoch from Celtic (Feb 1991).
Record Victory: 16-0 v Royal Albert, Scottish Cup 1st rd, 17 Jan 1931.
Record Defeat: 0-10 v Queen's Park, Scottish Cup, 3 Dec 1881.
Most Capped Player: Alan Rough, 51 (53), Scotland.
Most League Appearances: 410: Alan Rough, 1969-82.
Most League Goals in Season (Individual): 41: Alex Hair, Division I, 1926-27.

PARTICK THISTLE 2007–08 LEAGUE RECORD

Match No.	*Date*	*Venue*	*Opponents*	*Result*		*H/T Score*	*Lg. Pos.*	*Goalscorers*	*Attendance*
1	Aug 4	A	Stirling A	D	1-1	0-0	—	Donnelly [60]	2215
2	11	H	Livingston	W	3-0	2-0	4	Strachan 2 [18, 24], Buchanan [55]	2481
3	18	H	Clyde	W	4-0	2-0	2	Chaplain [18], Buchanan [37], Twaddle [61], Higgins (og) [72]	3175
4	25	A	Dundee	L	0-3	0-2	3		4354
5	Sept 1	H	Hamilton A	L	0-3	0-2	3		3075
6	15	A	St Johnstone	L	1-2	0-0	4	Buchanan [86]	2895
7	22	H	Queen of the S	W	2-0	1-0	3	Buchanan [11], McKinlay [81]	2419
8	29	A	Dunfermline Ath	L	0-1	0-1	4		4351
9	Oct 6	A	Morton	L	2-4	0-2	6	Storey [74], Twaddle [89]	3329
10	20	H	Stirling A	D	1-1	1-1	6	Buchanan [18]	2071
11	27	H	Dundee	D	1-1	1-0	5	Keegan [40]	2589
12	Nov 3	A	Clyde	W	2-1	0-0	4	Chaplain [51], Harkins [74]	1979
13	10	A	Hamilton A	L	0-2	0-1	6		2755
14	14	A	Livingston	W	4-0	2-0	—	Chaplain [7], Buchanan 2 [39, 62], Roberts [79]	1492
15	Dec 1	H	St Johnstone	D	2-2	1-0	4	Roberts [39], Chaplain [65]	2388
16	8	A	Queen of the S	W	2-1	0-1	3	Buchanan 2 [63, 68]	1753
17	15	H	Dunfermline Ath	D	1-1	0-0	3	Buchanan [85]	2176
18	22	H	Morton	D	1-1	0-0	4	Di Giacomo [74]	3611
19	29	A	Dundee	L	0-1	0-0	4		4548
20	Jan 2	H	Clyde	D	1-1	1-1	6	Roberts [34]	3299
21	5	A	St Johnstone	L	0-2	0-0	6		2490
22	19	H	Hamilton A	W	3-0	2-0	5	McKinlay 2 [24, 35], Buchanan (pen) [55]	2409
23	Feb 9	A	Stirling A	L	0-1	0-1	6		1306
24	16	A	Dunfermline Ath	D	1-1	0-1	6	McKeown [73]	3315
25	23	H	Queen of the S	D	0-0	0-0	6		2599
26	Mar 1	A	Clyde	W	4-1	3-1	6	Grey 2 [14, 78], Roberts [29], Chaplain [37]	1717
27	4	H	Livingston	W	2-1	1-1	—	McKeown [15], Grey [63]	1372
28	15	A	Morton	D	0-0	0-0	6		2787
29	22	H	St Johnstone	D	0-0	0-0	5		2309
30	29	A	Hamilton A	D	0-0	0-0	6		2150
31	Apr 1	H	Dundee	W	1-0	0-0	—	Roberts [88]	2326
32	5	H	Dunfermline Ath	L	0-1	0-1	6		2280
33	8	H	Stirling A	W	1-0	0-0	—	Keegan [90]	1267
34	16	A	Queen of the S	L	0-2	0-0	—		1702
35	19	A	Livingston	L	0-1	0-1	6		1601
36	26	H	Morton	L	0-3	0-2	6		4915

Final League Position: 6

Honours
League Champions: First Division 1975-76, 2001-02. Division II 1896-97, 1899-1900, 1970-71; Second Division 2000-01; *Runners-up:* First Division 1991-92. Division II 1901-02.
Scottish Cup Winners: 1921; *Runners-up:* 1930; *Semi-finals:* 2002.
League Cup Winners: 1971-72; *Runners-up:* 1953-54, 1956-57, 1958-59.
Bell's League Challenge: Quarter-finals 2004-05.

European: *Fairs Cup:* 4 matches (1963-64). *UEFA Cup:* 2 matches (1972-73). *Intertoto Cup:* 4 matches 1995-96.

Club colours: Shirt: Red and yellow halves with black sleeves. Shorts: Black. Stockings: Black.

Goalscorers: *League* (40): Buchanan 11 (1 pen), Chaplain 5, Roberts 5, Grey 3, McKinlay 3, Keegan 2, McKeown 2, Strachan 2, Twaddle 2, Di Giacomo 1, Donnelly 1, Harkins 1, Storey 1, own goal 1.
Scottish Cup (6): Buchanan 3, Grey 1, Roberts 1, Twaddle 1.
CIS Cup (2): Harkins 1, Murray 1.
Challenge Cup (4): Di Giacomo 1, Harkins 1, Keegan 1, own goal 1.

Tuffey J 25 + 1	Robertson J 30	Archibald A 27	Twaddle M 32 + 1	Harkins G 24 + 5	Rowson D 34	Donnelly S 8 + 10	Storey S 31 + 4	Roberts M 23 + 6	Buchanan L 19 + 3	Murray S 13 + 16	Chaplain S 25 + 5	Connor S — + 1	Strachan A 3 + 1	McStay R 12 + 8	Keegan P 4 + 17	McKinlay K 18 + 8	Gibson J 4 + 4	Di Giacomo P 4 + 2	Hinchcliffe C 11	Cameron G 3	Kinniburgh W 18 + 1	McKeown S 13 + 1	Mooc V 3	Grey D 10 + 1	Little R 2 + 1	Ardalany P — + 1	Eaglesham G — + 2	Match No.
1	2	3	4	5^{1}	6	7	8	9	10^{2}	11	12	13																1
1		3	4	5	6	7^{1}	2	9^{2}	12	10	13		11	8														2
1		3	4	5	6		2		10	11	7^{2}		9^{1}	8	12	13												3
1		3▪	4	5	6		2		10	11	7^{2}		13	8^{1}	14		12	9^{3}										4
1	2		4	5	6		3		10	11^{3}	7			8^{2}	14	12	13	9^{1}										5
1	2	3	4	5^{3}	6		8	9	13	11				7^{1}	14		12	10^{2}										6
	2	3		5	6	13	8	9^{3}	10	11^{1}	7^{2}				14	12	4		1									7
	2	3	4	14	6^{3}		8	9	10	13	7^{1}				12	11^{2}	5		1									8
	2	3	4	5	6		8	9^{3}	10^{2}	11^{1}				12	13		7	14	1									9
	2	3	4		6		8	13	10	11			5^{2}	12	14	9^{3}	7^{1}		1									10
	2	3	4	5	6		8	13	10^{2}	14	7^{3}			12	9				1	11^{1}								11
	2	3	4	5	6		8	12	10^{2}	13	7			14	9^{1}				1	11^{3}								12
	2	3	4	5^{3}	6		8	12	10^{1}	13	11				9^{2}	14			1	7								13
	2	3	4	5	6	12		9^{2}	10	13	11			8^{1}		7			1									14
15	2^{1}	3	4	13	6		12	9	10		11			7^{2}		5			1^{G}		8							15
1	2	3	4		6		12	9	10		7			11^{1}		8					5							16
1	2	3	4		6	13	8^{1}	9^{3}	10	14	7^{2}			12		11					5							17
1	2	3	4	5^{3}	6		12	9	10^{2}	14	11					7^{1}		13			8							18
	2	3	4	5	6		13	12	10		11^{2}					8		9^{1}	1		7▪							19
	2	4	12	3	8		7^{3}	11	10	13	6▪			14		5^{2}			1			9^{1}						20
1	2	6	3	12	8		7^{1}	10	13	11				9^{2}		4	14				5^{3}							21
1	2	6	3	11^{2}	8	14	5	10	9^{1}	12	7					4^{3}						13						22
1	2		3	14	8	10	6			13	7^{3}			12	9^{2}	4					5	11^{1}						23
1		6	3		8	10	2			12	13			7^{2}	14	4^{1}					5	11	9^{3}					24
1		6	3	4	8	9^{1}	2	10^{3}		13	7				12						5	11^{2}		14				25
1	2^{1}	4	5	12	8	13	7	11^{2}			6				14						3	9		10^{3}				26
1		6	3	2	8	13	4	10^{2}			7^{1}				14	12					5	11		9^{3}				27
1	2	4	5		8		6	11^{1}		13	7^{2}				12	14					3	9		10^{3}				28
1	3	4	5	8	7	12	2^{2}	11		9^{1}						14					13	6		10^{3}				29
1	5		3	7	8	13	2	10			12					4					6	11^{1}		9^{2}				30
1	3		5	8	7	11	2	13		12	6					9^{1}					4			10^{2}				31
1	5		3^{1}	11	8	14	2	10		12	7^{2}					13					6	4		9^{3}				32
1	4					10	2			9^{3}				8	12	5						6	7^{1}	11^{2}	3	14	13	33
1	4		3		8	7	2	11		12	13				14	6^{1}					5	9^{2}		10^{3}				34
1	5			11		14	2				7			10^{3}	13	3					6	8	9^{2}		4^{1}		12	35
1	5		3	11	8		2	10^{3}		4^{1}	7			13	14						6^{2}			9	12			36

PETERHEAD — Second Division

Year Formed: 1891. *Ground and Address:* Balmoor Stadium, Lord Catto Park, Peterhead AB42 1EU.
Telephone: 01779 478256. *Fax:* 01779 490682. *E-mail:* shona@peterheadfc.org.uk. *Website:* www.peterheadfc.org.uk
Ground Capacity: 3250, seated 1000.
Chairman: Rodger Morrison. *General Manager:* Dave Watson. *Secretary:* George Moore.
Manager: Neil Cooper. *First Team Coach:* Dave McGinlay.
Club Nickname(s): Blue Toon. *Previous Ground:* Recreation Park.
Record Attendance: 6310 friendly v Celtic, 1948.
Record Victory: 17-0 v Fort William, 1998-99 (in Highland League).
Record Defeat: 0-13 v Aberdeen, Scottish Cup, 1923-24.
Most League Appearances: 135: Martin Johnston, 2000-05.
Most League Goals in Season (Individual): 21: Iain Stewart, 2002-03; 21, Scott Michie, 2004-05.
Most Goals Overall (Individual): 58: Iain Stewart, 2000-05.

PETERHEAD 2007–08 LEAGUE RECORD

Match No.	Date	Venue	Opponents	Result		H/T Score	Lg. Pos.	Goalscorers	Attendance
1	Aug 4	H	Alloa Ath	L	1-4	1-2	—	Anderson [36]	808
2	11	A	Brechin C	D	2-2	0-2	8	Bavidge 2 [76, 90]	448
3	18	H	Cowdenbeath	W	4-2	1-1	5	Mackay [31], Bavidge [67], Kozmanski 2 [72, 73]	680
4	25	A	Ross Co	L	0-1	0-1	7		2056
5	Sept 1	H	Berwick R	W	4-3	2-1	6	Sharp [14], Bavidge 3 [30, 54, 68]	462
6	15	A	Airdrie U	D	1-1	1-0	6	Mackay [33]	936
7	22	H	Queen's Park	W	1-0	1-0	5	McKay [23]	681
8	29	A	Ayr U	W	2-1	1-1	3	Cowie [45], Bavidge [63]	1345
9	Oct 6	H	Raith R	L	0-1	0-1	4		885
10	20	A	Alloa Ath	L	0-2	0-1	5		456
11	27	A	Cowdenbeath	W	2-0	2-0	4	Bagshaw [10], MacDonald [17]	293
12	Nov 3	H	Ross Co	L	1-2	0-1	5	Sharp [55]	815
13	10	A	Berwick R	W	2-1	1-1	4	Kozmanski [38], Bavidge [59]	422
14	Dec 1	H	Airdrie U	L	0-1	0-1	6		685
15	8	H	Ayr U	W	3-0	0-0	5	Bagshaw [58], Mann (pen) [87], McKay [90]	540
16	15	A	Queen's Park	D	1-1	1-1	5	Buchan [28]	491
17	22	A	Raith R	D	2-2	1-1	5	Lumsden (og) [19], Istead [65]	1454
18	26	H	Brechin C	L	1-2	1-1	5	McKay [26]	720
19	29	H	Cowdenbeath	W	1-0	0-0	5	Bagshaw [52]	639
20	Jan 2	A	Ross Co	L	1-5	1-2	5	Mann [14]	2213
21	5	A	Airdrie U	L	0-2	0-0	5		892
22	19	H	Berwick R	W	9-2	5-1	5	Bavidge 2 [9, 19], Mann [21], McKay 3 [25, 51, 89], MacDonald [29], Sharp [49], McAllister [84]	590
23	26	A	Brechin C	L	1-3	0-2	5	Mann (pen) [71]	501
24	Feb 9	A	Ayr U	W	3-0	1-0	4	MacDonald [44], Mann 2 (2 pens) [89, 90]	1102
25	16	H	Queen's Park	W	1-0	1-0	4	Mann [18]	715
26	23	A	Cowdenbeath	W	4-0	1-0	4	Adamson (og) [19], Mann [48], Good [57], Bavidge [72]	244
27	26	H	Alloa Ath	D	2-2	1-1	—	Mann (pen) [31], Sharp [90]	590
28	Mar 1	H	Ross Co	D	1-1	1-1	4	Bavidge [30]	792
29	8	H	Raith R	W	1-0	1-0	—	McKay [43]	751
30	15	A	Alloa Ath	L	0-2	0-0	5		445
31	22	H	Airdrie U	L	1-4	0-2	5	Anderson [84]	550
32	29	A	Berwick R	D	2-2	0-0	6	Bavidge [76], Mann [83]	377
33	Apr 5	A	Queen's Park	L	0-2	0-2	6		522
34	12	H	Ayr U	W	4-1	2-0	6	Ross 2 [15, 47], Anderson [24], Bavidge [63]	661
35	19	H	Brechin C	W	2-0	1-0	5	Mann [20], McKay [75]	926
36	26	A	Raith R	W	5-2	0-1	5	Bavidge [53], Mann (pen) [56], Ross 2 [68, 76], Sharp [80]	1349

Final League Position: 5

Honours
Third Division Runners up: 2004-05.
Scottish Cup: Quarter-finals 2001.
Highland League Champions: winners 5 times.
Scottish Qualifying Cup (North): winners 6 times.
North of Scotland Cup: winners 5 times.
Aberdeenshire Cup: winners: 20 times.

Club colours: Shirt: Royal blue with white; Shorts: Royal blue; Stockings: Royal blue tops with white hoops.

Goalscorers: *League* (65): Bavidge 15, Mann 12 (6 pens), McKay 8, Sharp 5, Ross 4, Anderson 3, Bagshaw 3, Kozmanski 3, MacDonald 3, Mackay 2, Buchan 1, Cowie 1, Good 1, Istead 1, McAllister 1, own goals 2.
Scottish Cup (0).
CIS Cup (1): Istead 1.
Challenge Cup (1): Cowie 1.

Will J 2	Munro H 2 + 3	Donald D 23 + 3	Sharp G 33 + 1	MacDonald C 33 + 1	Mann B 32	Anderson S 26 + 3	McKay S 30 + 2	Istead S 12 + 12	Bavidge M 30 + 2	Soane S 8 + 1	Bagshaw A 10 + 18	Keith M 1 + 1	Buchan J 22 + 1	Mackay S 16 + 2	Leask P 1	Kula M 33	Kozmanski K 11 + 12	Kelly D 3 + 3	Gilfillan B — + 1	Cowie D 8 + 5	Ballard D — + 1	Good I 11 + 1	Monroe D 12 + 2	McAllister R 4	Smith S 13	McVitie N 13	Ross D 7 + 1	Bruce S — + 1	*Match No.*
1	2^{3}	3	4	5	6	7	8^{1}	9^{2}	10	11	13	12	14																1
1			4	5	6	7	8	9^{1}	10	12		11^{2}	2	3			13												2
	14	3	4		6	7	8^{2}		10		12		2	5		1	9^{3}	11^{1}	13										3
		3^{3}	4	14	6	7	8^{1}	13	10		12		2	5		1	9^{2}			11									4
	12		4^{2}	5	6	7			10		11^{1}		2	3		1	9			8	13								5
		13	12	5	6	7	8		10		11^{1}		2	4		1	9^{2}	3											6
			4^{1}	5	6	7	8		10		12		2	3		1	9■	11											7
	14	3^{3}	4^{2}	5	6^{1}	7		13	10		9		2	11		1				8		12							8
		3^{1}	4	5	6	7			10		9		2	8		1	12			11									9
			4	5	6	7	13	12	10		8		2	3		1	9^{2}			11^{1}									10
		14	4	5	6	7	8^{3}	9^{2}	10		11^{1}		2	3		1	12	13											11
			4	5	6	7	8	9^{2}	10		11^{1}		2	3		1	12			13									12
	11^{1}	13	4	5	6	7	3	9^{2}	10				2	14		1	8^{3}			12									13
		3	4	5	6		8	9	12	11	13		7			1	10^{1}					2^{2}							14
		3	4	5	6	13	8	9	10^{1}	11^{2}	12		7			1						2							15
		3	4	5	6	12	8^{2}	9^{3}		11	10^{1}		7			1	13					2	14						16
			4	5		7	8	9		11^{2}	12		2	3		1	10^{1}			13		6							17
			2	5	6	7^{2}	8	9		11^{1}	13		4			1	10					3	12						18
			4^{1}	5	6	7	8	9^{2}			10■		2			1	13			12		3	11						19
			7	5	4	6^{2}	10	11	13				2	12		1						3^{1}	8	9					20
			7^{2}	5	4		13	12■	9^{1}	8	14		2	3		1				6			10	11^{3}					21
		2	7	5	4^{2}	12	9		10^{1}		14		6	3		1		13					8^{3}	11					22
		2	6	4	3		5		10^{2}		13		7	9		1	12			8^{1}				11					23
		2	6	4	3	11	9	12	10^{1}							1							7		5	8			24
		2	7	5	4	9^{1}	10		11							1	12						8		3	6			25
		2	8		3	9	11^{2}	13	10		12					1						4	7^{1}		5	6			26
		2	7	5	4	10^{1}	11	13	9^{2}		12					1							8		3	6			27
		2	7	5	4	10■	11		9							1							8		3	6			28
		2	7^{2}	5	4		9	13	10		12					1							8		3	6	11^{1}		29
		2	7	5			11^{2}	13	9		12					1						4	8^{1}		3	6	10		30
		2		5		8	9	13	11							1	12					4	7^{1}		3	6	10^{2}		31
		2		5	4■			12	9		13			7		1	11^{1}			8					3	6	10^{2}		32
		2	7	4			9	12	10	8^{6}	11^{2}					1■						3			5	6^{1}	13	15	33
		2	7	5	4	10^{1}	11^{2}		9^{3}		13				1		14			12					3	6	8		34
		2	7^{1}	5	4	8	9		11							1	12								3	6	10		35
		2	7^{1}	5	4	10^{3}	11		9		12					1	14	13							3	6	8^{2}		36

QUEEN OF THE SOUTH First Division

Year Formed: 1919. *Ground & Address:* Palmerston Park, Dumfries DG2 9BA. *Telephone and Fax:* 01387 254853. *E-mail:* admin@qosfc.com. *Website:* www.qosfc.co.uk
Ground Capacity: total: 7412, seated: 3509. *Size of Pitch:* 112yd × 73yd.
Chairman: David Rae. *Vice-Chairman:* Thomas Harkness. *Club Secretary:* Eric Moffat. *Commercial Manager:* Margaret Heuchan.
Manager: Gordon Chisholm. *First Team Coach:* Stevie Morrison. *Physio:* John Kerr.
Club Nickname(s): The Doonhamers. *Previous Grounds:* None.
Record Attendance: 26,552 v Hearts, Scottish Cup 3rd rd, 23 Feb 1952.
Record Transfer Fee received: £250,000 for Andy Thomson to Southend U (1994).
Record Transfer Fee paid: £30,000 for Jim Butter from Alloa Athletic (1995).
Record Victory: 11-1 v Stranraer, Scottish Cup 1st rd, 16 Jan 1932.
Record Defeat: 2-10 v Dundee, Division I, 1 Dec 1962.
Most Capped Player: Billy Houliston, 3, Scotland.
Most League Appearances: 731: Allan Ball, 1963-82.
Most League Goals in Season (Individual): 37: Jimmy Gray, Division II, 1927-28.
Most Goals in Season: 41: Jimmy Rutherford, 1931-32.
Most Goals Overall (Individual): 250: Jim Patterson, 1949-63.

QUEEN OF THE SOUTH 2007–08 LEAGUE RECORD

Match No.	Date	Venue	Opponents	Result		H/T Score	Lg. Pos.	Goalscorers	Attendance
1	Aug 4	H	St Johnstone	D	3-3	2-1	—	Dobbie 2 3, 54, MacFarlane 27	2255
2	11	A	Dundee	L	1-2	1-1	7	O'Connor 35	4023
3	18	A	Hamilton A	L	0-1	0-1	7		1764
4	25	H	Livingston	W	1-0	0-0	5	Scally 54	1830
5	Sept 1	A	Morton	W	1-0	0-0	4	O'Connor 47	2813
6	15	H	Clyde	D	1-1	1-0	3	Dobbie (pen) 23	1730
7	22	A	Partick Th	L	0-2	0-1	5		2419
8	29	H	Stirling A	D	2-2	0-1	7	O'Connor 48, Dobbie 74	1484
9	Oct 6	H	Dunfermline Ath	L	0-1	0-1	9		2026
10	20	A	St Johnstone	L	0-2	0-1	9		2710
11	27	A	Livingston	D	2-2	1-1	10	O'Connor 17, Dobbie 56	1355
12	Nov 3	H	Hamilton A	W	2-1	0-1	7	Tosh 66, Halliwell (og) 68	1646
13	10	H	Morton	L	1-3	1-1	8	Tosh 3	2110
14	Dec 1	A	Clyde	D	0-0	0-0	8		1008
15	8	H	Partick Th	L	1-2	1-0	8	Dobbie 13	1753
16	15	A	Stirling A	W	3-1	1-1	8	Dobbie 28, Tosh 75, O'Neill (pen) 89	883
17	22	A	Dunfermline Ath	L	0-2	0-1	9		3324
18	26	H	Dundee	W	2-1	1-1	8	Burns 43, Worrell (og) 62	1980
19	29	H	Livingston	W	1-0	0-0	6	O'Neill 83	1719
20	Jan 2	A	Hamilton A	L	0-1	0-0	5		2298
21	5	H	Clyde	W	3-1	0-1	5	Dobbie 62, Burns 73, Tosh (pen) 83	1513
22	19	A	Morton	W	3-0	0-0	4	Dobbie 3 65, 73, 84	2521
23	26	A	Dundee	W	3-2	0-1	4	O'Connor 2 57, 61, Burns 62	3926
24	Feb 9	H	St Johnstone	W	3-1	1-0	4	McQuilken 13, O'Connor 2 54, 87	2229
25	16	H	Stirling A	W	3-1	2-1	4	Burns 2 8, 40, Thomson 52	2335
26	23	A	Partick Th	D	0-0	0-0	4		2599
27	Mar 1	H	Hamilton A	D	2-2	2-1	4	Dobbie 2 30, 35	2133
28	11	A	St Johnstone	L	1-2	0-0	—	Dobbie 57	1853
29	15	H	Dunfermline Ath	D	1-1	1-1	4	Harris 8	2114
30	22	A	Clyde	W	4-1	2-0	4	Dobbie 2 29, 64, Tosh (pen) 33, Bestvina (og) 88	1210
31	29	H	Morton	D	0-0	0-0	4		1808
32	Apr 1	A	Livingston	L	0-1	0-0	—		952
33	5	A	Stirling A	D	0-0	0-0	4		641
34	16	H	Partick Th	W	2-0	0-0	—	Stewart 57, Harris 74	1702
35	19	H	Dundee	W	1-0	1-0	4	Gilmour 42	3005
36	26	A	Dunfermline Ath	L	0-4	0-0	4		3444

Final League Position: 4

Honours
League Champions: Division II 1950-51. Second Division 2001-02. *Runners-up:* Division II 1932-33, 1961-62, 1974-75. Second Division 1980-81, 1985-86.
Scottish Cup Runners-up: 2007-08.
League Cup: semi-finals 1950-51, 1960-61.
B&Q Cup: semi-finals 1991-92. *League Challenge Cup Winners:* 2002-03; *Runners-up:* 1997-98.

Club colours: Shirt: Royal blue with white sleeves. Shorts: White with blue piping. Stockings: Royal blue.

Goalscorers: *League* (47): Dobbie 16 (1 pen), O'Connor 8, Burns 5, Tosh 5 (2 pens), Harris 2, O'Neill 2 (1 pen), Gilmour 1, MacFarlane 1, McQuilken 1, Scally 1, Stewart 1, Thomson 1, own goals 3.
Scottish Cup (19): O'Connor 5, Dobbie 4, Burns 2, Stewart 2, Thomson 2, Tosh 2, McCann 1, own goal 1.
CIS Cup (0).
Challenge Cup (0).

MacDonald J 34	Paton E 16 + 4	Aitken A 26	Burns P 26 + 2	McQuilken J 30 + 2	Atkin L 2	MacFarlane N 27 + 1	Scally N 17	O'Connor S 32	Dobbie S 28 + 8	Gilmour B 14 + 10	Bingham D 4 + 11	Robertson S 9 + 5	Mole J 2 + 6	O'Neill J 5 + 18	Tosh S 28	Harris R 26	Thomson J 29 + 1	Lauchlan J 6	Adams J — + 1	McGowan N 2 + 1	Nixon D 2	Campbell R 1 + 3	Stewart J 6 + 10	McCann R 14	Reid C 8	Grindlay S 2	*Match No.*
1	2	3	4^{2}	5	6	7	8	9^{3}	10	11^{1}	12	13	14														1
1	2	3	4	5	6	7	8	9	10^{1}	11			12														2
1	2	3	4	5^{2}		7	8		13	14	11^{3}		12	9	10^{1}	6											3
1			4	5		7^{3}	8	9	10^{2}		12		13	14	11^{1}	3	6	2									4
1	2		4	5		7^{3}	8	9	10^{2}		14		13		11^{1}		6	3	12								5
1	2		4	5		7^{2}	8	9^{3}	10^{1}	14	13		12		11		6	3									6
1	2		4^{2}	5		7	8	9	10^{3}	14	13				11		6	3^{1}		12							7
1	2			5		7	8	9	12	11^{1}	10^{3}	14		13	4^{2}		6			3							8
1		3	14	5			8	9^{1}	10	13	11^{3}	7		12		2	6			4^{2}							9
1	2		13	5			8	9^{3}	12	11	14	7^{1}		6^{2}		3	4				10						10
1		3		5		7	8	9	10			4		13	11	6^{2}	12				2^{1}						11
1				5		7	8	9	10^{1}	13	12	4	6^{2}		11	3	2										12
1				5		7	2	9	13	12	10^{2}	6^{3}	8^{1}	14	11	3	4										13
1	2	3	4	13			8	9^{1}	10	11^{2}	12				6	5	7										14
1	2	3		5			8	9	10^{2}	11^{1}	13	12			7	4	6										15
1	2	3	4^{1}				8	9	10^{2}	11	13			12	7	5	6										16
1	2	3	4	5		12	8^{1}	9^{3}	10	11^{2}	14			13	6		7										17
1	2	3	4	5		7		9^{1}	10	11^{2}		13		12	8		6										18
1	2	3	4	13		7		9	10^{1}	11^{2}				12	8	5	6										19
1	2	5	10	3					12	14		4		9^{2}	8^{3}	7	6					13	11^{1}				20
1	2	4	9			6		10	12	7^{2}					8	3	5					13	11^{1}				21
1	13	3	8	5		7		10^{3}	12					14	6	9	4						11^{1}	2^{2}			22
1		3	8	5		7		11	10^{1}						6	9	4						12	2			23
1		4	9	7		6		10^{2}	11^{1}					13	8	3	5						12	2			24
1		4	9	7^{1}		6		10	11^{2}						8	3	5					12	13	2			25
1		5	11	7		4		9	10^{2}					12	8	3^{1}	6■						13	2			26
1		4	9	3		6		10	11^{1}					7	8■								12	2	5		27
1	13	5		7		4		9^{1}	10^{3}	14		11^{2}		8		3							12	2	6		28
1		4	9	7		6		10	11						8	3								2	5		29
1		5	11	7		4		9^{1}	10						8	3	6						12	2			30
1		3	9	8		7		10^{1}	11					13		6	4						12	2^{2}	5		31
1		5	11■			4			10	12				13		3	6					7^{1}	9^{2}	2	8		32
1	13	5		7		4^{3}			10	11		14		12	8^{2}	3^{1}	6						9	2			33
				7^{2}		6		10^{1}	11	13				14	8	3	5	4					12	2^{3}	9	1	34
1		4	9					10^{2}	12	7		8		13		2	5						11^{1}	6	3		35
	14		11^{2}	3				9^{3}	10^{1}	7		4		13	8		6	5					12		2	1	36

QUEEN'S PARK — Second Division

Year Formed: 1867. *Ground & Address:* Hampden Park, Mount Florida, Glasgow G42 9BA. *Telephone:* 0141 632 1275.
Fax: 0141 636 1612. *E-mail:* secretary@queensparkfc.co.uk. *Website:* queensparkfc.co.uk
Ground Capacity: all seated: 52,000. *Size of Pitch:* 115yd × 75yd.
President: James M. Hastie. *Secretary:* Alistair MacKay. *Treasurer:* David Gordon.
Coach: Gardner Speirs. *Physio:* R. C. Findlay.
Club Nickname(s): The Spiders. *Previous Grounds:* 1st Hampden (Recreation Ground); (Titwood Park was used as an interim measure between 1st & 2nd Hampdens); 2nd Hampden (Cathkin); 3rd Hampden.
Record Attendance: 95,772 v Rangers, Scottish Cup, 18 Jan 1930.
Record for Ground: 149,547 Scotland v England, 1937.
Record Transfer Fee received: Not applicable due to amateur status.
Record Transfer Fee paid: Not applicable due to amateur status.
Record Victory: 16-0 v St. Peters, Scottish Cup 1st rd, 29 Aug 1885.
Record Defeat: 0-9 v Motherwell, Division I, 26 Apr 1930.
Most Capped Player: Walter Arnott, 14, Scotland.
Most League Appearances: 532: Ross Caven, 1982-2002.
Most League Goals in Season (Individual): 30: William Martin, Division I, 1937-38.
Most Goals Overall (Individual): 163: James B. McAlpine, 1919-33.

QUEEN'S PARK 2007–08 LEAGUE RECORD

Match No.	Date	Venue	Opponents	Result	H/T Score	Lg. Pos.	Goalscorers	Attendance
1	Aug 4	H	Brechin C	W 3-0	1-0	—	Canning [14], Trouten 2 (2 pens) [73, 79]	768
2	11	A	Ayr U	W 3-2	1-1	1	Kettlewell [14], Canning [71], Trouten [90]	1262
3	18	H	Ross Co	W 3-2	1-1	1	Sinclair [14], Canning [76], Dunn [84]	815
4	25	A	Airdrie U	L 0-1	0-0	1		1148
5	Sept 1	H	Raith R	L 2-5	0-2	2	Cairney [49], Trouten (pen) [51]	1015
6	15	A	Alloa Ath	L 0-2	0-2	3		555
7	22	A	Peterhead	L 0-1	0-1	7		681
8	29	H	Berwick R	W 1-0	0-0	5	Ferry [70]	537
9	Oct 6	H	Cowdenbeath	L 0-1	0-0	7		614
10	20	A	Brechin C	L 1-2	0-2	8	Canning [82]	511
11	27	A	Ross Co	D 1-1	1-0	8	Ferry [4]	2323
12	Nov 3	H	Airdrie U	L 0-1	0-1	8		1211
13	10	A	Raith R	W 2-0	0-0	8	Cairney 2 [49, 90]	1860
14	Dec 1	H	Alloa Ath	W 1-0	0-0	7	Trouten [88]	652
15	8	A	Berwick R	D 1-1	1-0	7	McGrady [25]	455
16	15	H	Peterhead	D 1-1	1-1	6	Kettlewell [25]	491
17	26	H	Ayr U	D 1-1	0-1	6	Ferry [76]	809
18	29	H	Ross Co	L 0-1	0-0	6		657
19	Jan 2	A	Airdrie U	L 2-3	2-0	6	Trouten (pen) [7], Cairney [17]	1244
20	5	A	Alloa Ath	W 2-1	0-1	6	Canning [62], Trouten [79]	534
21	19	H	Raith R	L 0-1	0-1	7		743
22	26	A	Ayr U	L 1-3	1-1	9	Keenan (og) [21]	1242
23	Feb 2	H	Brechin C	L 2-3	2-0	9	Cairney [1], Trouten (pen) [30]	491
24	9	H	Berwick R	W 3-1	1-0	7	Cairney [21], Ferry [65], McGrady [90]	511
25	16	A	Peterhead	L 0-1	0-1	8		715
26	23	A	Ross Co	L 2-3	1-2	8	Ferry [45], Trouten [62]	2162
27	Mar 1	H	Airdrie U	L 0-2	0-0	8		913
28	15	A	Brechin C	W 1-0	1-0	8	Dunn [38]	465
29	18	A	Cowdenbeath	W 4-2	1-1	8	Kettlewell [18], Ferry [51], Trouten 2 (2 pens) [72, 83]	317
30	22	H	Alloa Ath	D 1-1	1-1	8	Trouten [43]	549
31	29	A	Raith R	W 1-0	0-0	8	Ferry [64]	1368
32	Apr 1	H	Cowdenbeath	L 2-3	0-2	—	Ferry [54], Quinn [84]	431
33	5	H	Peterhead	W 2-0	2-0	8	Ferry [8], Quinn [12]	522
34	15	A	Berwick R	W 4-1	3-1	—	Cairney [10], Quinn 2 [43, 44], McLeish (og) [49]	325
35	19	H	Ayr U	L 1-3	0-1	8	Kettlewell [61]	1092
36	26	A	Cowdenbeath	L 0-1	0-0	8		369

Final League Position: 8

Honours
League Champions: Division II 1922-23. B Division 1955-56. Second Division 1980-81. Third Division 1999-2000.
Scottish Cup Winners: 1874, 1875, 1876, 1880, 1881, 1882, 1884, 1886, 1890, 1893; *Runners-up:* 1892, 1900.
League Cup: —.
FA Cup runners-up: 1884, 1885.

Club colours: Shirt: White and black hoops. Shorts: White. Stockings: Black with white tops.

Goalscorers: *League* (48): Trouten 12 (7 pens), Ferry 9, Cairney 7, Canning 5, Kettlewell 4, Quinn 4, Dunn 2, McGrady 2, Sinclair 1, own goals 2.
Scottish Cup (3): Ferry 2, Trouten 1.
CIS Cup (3): Canning 1, Dunlop 1, Trouten 1.
Challenge Cup (1): Canning 1.

Cairns M 18	Paton P 34	Agostini D 30	Kettlewell S 27 + 1	Dunlop M 25	Sinclair R 17	Trouten A 33	Cairney P 35	Ronald P 10 + 10	Canning S 27 + 3	Ferry M 34	Bowers R 2 + 7	Quinn T 18 + 10	McGrady S 17 + 15	Molloy S 6 + 5	Dunn R 9 + 9	Ure M 9 + 2	Reilly S 11 + 3	Murray S 5 + 1	Boslen A 1 + 1	Torrence D — + 3	Cowie A 12	Neill J 11	Terry Z 1	Brough J 4 + 1	Match No.
1	2	3	4	5	6	7	8^{2}	9^{1}	10^{3}	11	12	13	14												1
1	2	3	4	5	6■	7	8^{1}		10	11^{2}		9	13	12											2
1	2	3	4	5	6	7	8		10^{2}	11		9^{1}	13		12										3
1	2	3	4	5	6	7	8^{2}	13	10	11^{3}		9^{1}	14		12										4
1	2	3	4	5	6	7■	8	9^{1}	10^{3}	11^{2}		13	12	14											5
1	2	3	4■	5		7	8^{2}		10	11	12	13	9^{3}	6^{1}		14									6
1	2			5		7	8			11	6	10	9	12		4	3^{1}								7
1	2	3		5	6^{1}	7	8		10	11	4^{2}	9	13			12									8
1	2	3		5		7	8^{2}	9^{1}	10	11	13	6	12			4									9
	2	3	4	5			8	9	10	11		7	12			6^{1}		1							10
1	2		4	5			8	9^{1}	10	11			7^{2}	6	12				3	13					11
1	2	3	4	5		7	8	12	10	11		13	9^{1}	6^{2}											12
1^{G}	2	3	4	5		7	8	9^{1}	10	11		12	6^{2}					15	13						13
	2	3	4	5		7	8	9^{1}	10	11		12	6^{2}		13			1							14
	2	3	4^{1}		6	7	8	12		11		9	10	5				1							15
			4	5	6	7■	8	13	12	11		10^{1}	9	3		2^{2}		1							16
		3^{3}	4	5	6		8	9	10	11		7^{1}		13	12	2^{2}	14				1				17
	2	3^{1}	4	5	6	7	8^{3}	9^{2}	10	11				14	13		12				1				18
	2	5^{1}	7	3	4	6	8		10	11			13		9^{2}		12	1							19
1	2	5	7^{1}	3	4	6	8	12	10	11			13		9^{2}										20
1	2	5		3	4	6	8^{2}	7^{1}	10	11		13	9		12										21
1	2	5	7	3	4	6	8^{2}	13	10	11■			12		9^{1}										22
1	2	4	7	5		6	8		9			11	12		10^{1}		3								23
1	2	4	7	5		6	8			9		11	12		10^{1}		3								24
1	2	5	7	3		6	8		12	11		10^{1}			9		4								25
	2	5	7	3^{2}		6	8		13	11		14	9^{1}		12		4				1	10^{3}			26
	2	5	7			6		14	3	11^{3}	13	8	9^{1}		12		4				1	10^{2}			27
	2		6		4	7	8	12		9					10^{1}	5	3				1	11			28
	2		8■		4	7	6			11		13	12		10^{1}	5	3				1	9^{2}			29
	2				5	6	8	13	7	11			12		9^{1}	3^{2}	4					10	1		30
	2	5	7			6	8	12^{2}	3	11	13		9				4				1	10^{1}			31
	2	5				6	8		7	11		12	9			3	4^{2}				1	10^{1}		13	32
	2	4				6	7		5	9	12	11	10^{1}								1	8		3	33
	2	5				6	8		3	11		9	7^{1}							12	1	10		4	34
	2	5	12			6	8^{1}		3	11		9	7^{2}							13	1	10		4	35
	2	4	6			7	8				12	10	9	5							1	11^{1}		3	36

RAITH ROVERS — Second Division

Year Formed: 1883. *Ground & Address:* Stark's Park, Pratt St, Kirkcaldy KY1 1SA. *Telephone:* 01592 263514. *Fax:* 01592 642833. *E-mail:* office@raithroversfc.com. *Website:* www.raithroversfc.com
Ground Capacity: all seated: 10,104. *Size of Pitch:* 113yd × 70yd.
Chairman: David Somerville. *General Manager:* Bob Mullen. *Commercial Manager:* John Drysdale.
Manager: John McGlynn. *Assistant Manager:* Gary Kirk. *Coach:* Shaun Dennis. *Physio:* Lesley Mackie
Club Nickname: Rovers. *Previous Grounds:* Robbie's Park.
Record Attendance: 31,306 v Hearts, Scottish Cup 2nd rd, 7 Feb 1953.
Record Transfer Fee received: £900,000 for S. McAnespie to Bolton Wanderers (Sept 1995).
Record Transfer Fee paid: £225,000 for Paul Harvey from Airdrieonians (1996).
Record Victory: 10-1 v Coldstream, Scottish Cup 2nd rd, 13 Feb 1954.
Record Defeat: 2-11 v Morton, Division II, 18 Mar 1936.
Most Capped Player: David Morris, 6, Scotland.
Most League Appearances: 430: Willie McNaught, 1946-51.
Most League Goals in Season (Individual): 38: Norman Haywood, Division II, 1937-38.
Most Goals Overall (Individual): 154: Gordon Dalziel (League), 1987-94.

RAITH ROVERS 2007–08 LEAGUE RECORD

Match No.	Date	Venue	Opponents	Result	H/T Score	Lg. Pos.	Goalscorers	Attendance
1	Aug 4	A	Airdrie U	W 1-0	1-0	—	Andrews [10]	1645
2	11	H	Berwick R	W 3-1	1-1	2	Tod [26], Borris [64], Andrews [78]	2020
3	18	H	Alloa Ath	W 2-1	0-0	2	Fleming (og) [53], Tod [81]	1978
4	25	A	Cowdenbeath	L 0-1	0-1	2		1935
5	Sept 1	A	Queen's Park	W 5-2	2-0	1	Weir 3 (1 pen) [32, 45 (p), 63], Silvestro [66], Hislop [70]	1015
6	15	H	Ross Co	L 0-2	0-0	1		2101
7	22	H	Ayr U	L 2-3	0-2	2	Hislop 2 (1 pen) [89, 90 (p)]	1762
8	29	A	Brechin C	W 1-0	1-0	2	Carcary [5]	669
9	Oct 6	A	Peterhead	W 1-0	1-0	2	Sloan [27]	885
10	20	H	Airdrie U	W 2-1	0-1	2	Weir (pen) [65], Sloan [85]	1727
11	27	A	Alloa Ath	L 1-2	0-1	2	Sloan [73]	1053
12	Nov 3	H	Cowdenbeath	W 2-0	2-0	2	Hislop [16], Goodwillie [29]	2357
13	10	H	Queen's Park	L 0-2	0-0	2		1860
14	Dec 1	A	Ross Co	W 3-2	1-0	2	Hislop 2 (1 pen) [2, 59 (p)], Weir [88]	2627
15	8	H	Brechin C	D 1-1	0-1	2	Andrews [69]	1475
16	15	A	Ayr U	W 3-0	2-0	2	Andrews [21], Campbell [39], Sloan [53]	1040
17	22	H	Peterhead	D 2-2	1-1	1	Goodwillie 2 [11, 80]	1454
18	26	A	Berwick R	L 1-2	1-1	1	Davidson [21]	570
19	29	H	Alloa Ath	W 3-2	1-1	1	Goodwillie [5], Sloan [79], Hislop [84]	1896
20	Jan 2	A	Cowdenbeath	W 4-1	1-1	1	Sloan [10], Hislop [66], Templeton [68], Weir [84]	1896
21	5	H	Ross Co	L 0-1	0-1	2		2319
22	19	A	Queen's Park	W 1-0	1-0	2	Templeton [24]	743
23	26	H	Berwick R	W 3-0	1-0	2	Campbell [34], Hislop [69], Weir [83]	1466
24	Feb 2	A	Airdrie U	L 0-3	0-0	2		1252
25	9	A	Brechin C	L 2-3	1-2	3	Walker R (og) [23], Carcary [90]	656
26	16	H	Ayr U	L 1-2	0-2	3	Templeton [66]	1513
27	23	A	Alloa Ath	L 0-2	0-0	3		712
28	Mar 1	H	Cowdenbeath	W 3-2	2-1	3	Goodwillie [23], Davidson 2 [25, 80]	1607
29	8	A	Peterhead	L 0-1	0-1	—		751
30	15	H	Airdrie U	W 1-0	1-0	3	Goodwillie [21]	1458
31	22	A	Ross Co	W 3-2	2-2	3	Templeton [25], Goodwillie 2 [28, 67]	2973
32	29	H	Queen's Park	L 0-1	0-0	3		1368
33	Apr 5	A	Ayr U	W 1-0	0-0	3	Carcary [90]	1209
34	12	H	Brechin C	D 1-1	0-1	3	Weir [71]	1995
35	19	A	Berwick R	W 5-2	1-2	3	Weir 2 [42, 67], Carcary [72], Sloan [80], Bryce [87]	545
36	26	H	Peterhead	L 2-5	1-0	3	Goodwillie (pen) [21], Bryce [61]	1349

Final League Position: 3

Honours
League Champions: First Division: 1992-93, 1994-95. Division II 1907-08, 1909-10 (shared), 1937-38, 1948-49; *Runners-up:* Division II 1908-09, 1926-27, 1966-67. Second Division 1975-76, 1977-78, 1986-87.
Scottish Cup Runners-up: 1913. *League Cup Winners: (Coca-Cola Cup):* 1994-95. *Runners-up:* 1948-49.

European: *UEFA Cup:* 6 matches (1995-96).

Club colours: Shirt: Navy blue with white sleeves. Shorts: White with navy and red trim. Stockings: Navy blue with white turnover.

Goalscorers: *League* (60): Weir 10 (2 pens), Goodwillie 9 (1 pen), Hislop 9 (2 pens), Sloan 7, Andrews 4, Carcary 4, Templeton 4, Davidson 3, Bryce 2, Campbell 2, Tod 2, Borris 1, Silvestro 1, own goals 2.
Play-offs (2): Weir 2 (1 pen).
Scottish Cup (6): Carcary 2, Hislop 2, Davidson 1, Weir 1.
CIS Cup (4): Carcary 2, Tod 1, Weir 1.
Challenge Cup (1): Tod 1.

Fahey C 19 + 1	Wilson C 36	Davidson I 30	Pelosi M 19	Tod A 17 + 7	Andrews M 19	Borris R 19 + 8	Silvestro C 17 + 1	Weir G 20 + 11	Sloan R 30 + 4	Hislop S 28 + 6	Winter C 16 + 10	Carcary D 7 + 21	Renton K 16 + 1	Darling J — + 2	Helley J — + 4	Campbell M 25 + 1	Dingwall J 17 + 2	Lumsden T 7 + 2	Walker A 6 + 1	Goodwillie D 20 + 1	Watley M — + 1	Templeton G 15	Henderson N 11 + 3	Brown M 1	Bryce L — + 4	Main D 1	*Match No.*
1	2	3^{1}	4	5	6	7^{2}	8	$9^{\blacksquare}$	10	11	12	13															1
1^{6}	2		4	5	6	7	8		10^{2}	11	3	9^{1}	15	12	13												2
	2			5	6	7	8	9^{2}	10^{1}		11		1	12	13	4	3										3
	2	3	4	5^{1}	6	7		9	10^{2}	12	8	13	1			11											4
1	2	3	4		6	7^{1}	8	9^{2}	12	11	5	10			13												5
1	2	3	4	14	6	7^{1}	8^{2}	9	12	11^{3}	5	10				13											6
1	2	3	4	5	6		8	9^{1}	13	11	7^{2}	12				10											7
1	2	3	4	13	6		8	9	10^{1}	11^{2}	12	7				5											8
1	2	3	4	5	6		8^{2}	9^{1}	10	11	12					7	13										9
1	2	3	4	5	6			9^{1}	10	11	7	12^{2}				8		13									10
1	2	3	4^{1}	5^{2}				9	10	11	8					6	12	7	13								11
1	2	3			6	7^{1}		13	10	11		12				5	4		8	9^{2}							12
1	2	3^{1}			6	7^{2}		14	10	11	12	13				5	4^{3}		8	9							13
1	2	3			6	7		12	10	11^{2}	13					5	4		8	9^{1}							14
1	2	3		13	6	7^{2}		12	10	11						5	4		8	9^{1}							15
1	2	3			6	7^{2}		12	10	11	14	13				5	4		8^{3}	9^{1}							16
1	2	3				7^{2}		13	10	11		12				5	4	6	8^{1}	9							17
1	2	3		14		7		13	10	11^{2}	12	8^{1}				5	4	6		9^{3}							18
	2	3		12		7^{1}		9^{2}	10	13	6		1			5	4	8^{3}		11	14						19
	2	8		4		14		10	6^{3}	12	7	13	1			3	5			11^{1}		9^{2}					20
	2	8		5		13		9	7	10	6	14	1			4^{1}	3^{3}	12^{2}				11					21
	2	4			5	12			6	9	13	7^{2}	1		14		3			10		11^{1}	8^{3}				22
	2	6^{1}			5	14		13	7	9	12		1			4	3			10^{2}		11^{3}	8				23
	2			14	5	7^{1}		12	6	9^{3}		13	1			4	3			10^{2}		11	8				24
	2			12	5	14			7	9^{1}	8^{3}	13	1			4	3			10^{2}		11	6				25
	2		3	4		14	6	9	11	12		13^{3}	1					5^{1}		10^{2}		7	8				26
	2	5	3			13	6	10	11	9^{1}			1					4		12		7^{2}	8				27
1	2	7	3	5			8	9		12	10^{2}	14				4		6^{1}		11^{3}			13				28
	2	6	3	5			8	11	13	10	7	12								9^{1}			4^{2}	1			29
1	2	5	3	4^{2}		7^{3}	6	13	8	9		12								10		11^{1}	14				30
1	2	5	3			7^{3}	6^{1}		8	9	13	14				4				10		11^{2}	12				31
	2	5	3			$7^{\blacksquare}$	6	12	8	9		13	1			4				10^{1}		11^{2}					32
	2	8	5	4			7	10^{1}	9	12		14	1			3						11^{2}	6^{3}		13		33
	2	5	3	4			6^{1}	10	11	9		12	1									7^{2}	8		13		34
	2	5		4^{1}		12		10	11	9	8^{2}	13	1				3					7^{3}	6		14		35
15	2					7	13				6	11	1^{G}			5	3			9^{1}		10	8^{2}		12	4	36

RANGERS — Premier League

Year Formed: 1873. *Ground & Address:* Ibrox Stadium, 150 Edmiston Drive, Glasgow G51 2XD.
Telephone: 0871 702 1972. *Fax:* 0870 600 1978. *Website:* www.rangers.co.uk
Ground Capacity: all seated: 51,082. *Size of Pitch:* 105m × 68m.
Executive Chairman: Sir David Murray. *Chief Executive:* Martin Bain. *Head of Football Administration:* Andrew Dickson.
Manager: Walter Smith. *Assistant Manager:* Ally McCoist. *Physio:* David Henderson.
Club Nickname(s): The Gers. *Previous Grounds:* Flesher's Haugh, Burnbank, Kinning Park, Old Ibrox.
Record Attendance: 118,567 v Celtic, Division I, 2 Jan 1939.
Record Transfer Fee received: £8,500,000 for Gio Van Bronckhorst to Arsenal (2001).
Record Transfer Fee paid: £12 million for Tore Andre Flo from Chelsea (November 2000).
Record Victory: 14-2 v Blairgowrie, Scottish Cup 1st rd, 20 Jan, 1934. *Record Defeat:* 2-10 v Airdrieonians; 1886.
Most Capped Player: Ally McCoist, 60, Scotland.
Most League Appearances: 496: John Greig, 1962-78.
Most League Goals in Season (Individual): 44: Sam English, Division I, 1931-32.
Most Goals Overall (Individual): 355: Ally McCoist; 1985-98.

Honours
League Champions: (51 times) Division I 1890-91 (shared), 1898-99, 1899-1900, 1900-01, 1901-02, 1910-11, 1911-12, 1912-13, 1917-18, 1919-20, 1920-21, 1922-23, 1923-24, 1924-25, 1926-27, 1927-28, 1928-29, 1929-30, 1930-31, 1932-33, 1933-34, 1934-35, 1936-37, 1938-39, 1946-47, 1948-49, 1949-50, 1952-53, 1955-56, 1956-57, 1958-59, 1960-61, 1962-63, 1963-64, 1974-75. Premier Division: 1975-76, 1977-78, 1986-87, 1988-89, 1989-90, 1990-91, 1991-92, 1992-93, 1993-94, 1994-95, 1995-96, 1996-97, 1998-99, 1999-2000, 2002-03, 2004-05; *Runners-up:* 26 times.

RANGERS 2007–08 LEAGUE RECORD

Match No.	*Date*	*Venue*	*Opponents*	*Result*	*H/T Score*	*Lg. Pos.*	*Goalscorers*	*Attendance*
1	Aug 4	A	Inverness CT	W 3-0	1-0	—	Ferguson 2 $^{16, 90}$, Novo ^{64}	7711
2	11	H	St Mirren	W 2-0	0-0	1	Ferguson ^{52}, Cousin ^{80}	47,772
3	18	H	Falkirk	W 7-2	2-1	1	Cousin 2 $^{2, 54}$, Whittaker ^{34}, Boyd ^{75}, Darcheville 2 $^{88, 89}$, Broadfoot ^{90}	46,061
4	25	A	Kilmarnock	W 2-1	0-0	1	Beasley ^{52}, Darcheville ^{76}	11,544
5	Sept 1	H	Gretna	W 4-0	1-0	1	Boyd ^{38}, Webster ^{63}, Cuellar ^{81}, Collin (og) ^{83}	49,689
6	15	A	Hearts	L 2-4	0-2	2	Cousin (pen) ^{49}, Beasley ^{74}	15,948
7	23	H	Aberdeen	W 3-0	0-0	1	McCulloch ^{46}, Naismith ^{65}, Boyd ^{88}	49,046
8	29	A	Motherwell	D 1-1	0-1	2	Boyd (pen) ^{67}	10,009
9	Oct 6	H	Hibernian	L 0-1	0-0	3		50,440
10	20	H	Celtic	W 3-0	1-0	2	Novo 2 (1 pen) $^{28, 79 (p)}$, Ferguson ^{57}	50,428
11	28	A	Dundee U	L 1-2	0-1	2	Cousin (pen) ^{51}	12,129
12	Nov 3	H	Inverness CT	W 2-0	1-0	2	Boyd ^{1}, Cuellar ^{63}	48,898
13	24	A	Falkirk	W 3-1	1-0	2	Cuellar ^{20}, Darcheville ^{55}, Boyd ^{90}	6627
14	Dec 1	H	Kilmarnock	W 2-0	1-0	2	Darcheville ^{4}, Whittaker ^{55}	48,055
15	15	H	Hearts	W 2-1	1-0	2	McCulloch ^{18}, Kurskis (og) ^{89}	48,392
16	23	A	Aberdeen	D 1-1	1-1	2	Adam ^{30}	17,798
17	26	H	Motherwell	W 3-1	1-0	2	Cousin ^{42}, Porter (og) ^{70}, Boyd ^{90}	49,823
18	29	A	Hibernian	W 2-1	1-0	2	Naismith ^{12}, Cousin ^{59}	16,217
19	Jan 5	H	Dundee U	W 2-0	2-0	1	Naismith ^{9}, Ferguson ^{40}	48,559
20	16	A	Gretna	W 2-1	1-0	—	Ferguson ^{45}, Cousin ^{74}	6137
21	20	A	Inverness CT	W 1-0	0-0	1	Darcheville ^{89}	7753
22	26	H	St Mirren	W 4-0	3-0	1	Burke ^{27}, Boyd ^{32}, Whittaker 2 $^{37, 81}$	49,198
23	Feb 9	H	Falkirk	W 2-0	1-0	1	Boyd ^{23}, Naismith ^{89}	48,601
24	17	A	Kilmarnock	W 2-0	1-0	1	Cuellar ^{25}, Boyd (pen) ^{63}	10,546
25	24	H	Gretna	W 4-2	2-0	1	Cousin ^{13}, Naismith ^{22}, Burke ^{60}, Boyd ^{88}	48,375
26	27	A	Hearts	W 4-0	2-0	—	Darcheville 2 $^{25, 44}$, Novo 2 $^{53, 70}$	16,173
27	Mar 1	H	Aberdeen	W 3-1	1-1	1	Dailly ^{38}, Adam ^{50}, Boyd ^{83}	50,066
28	22	H	Hibernian	W 2-1	1-0	1	Darcheville ^{40}, Novo ^{79}	50,117
29	29	H	Celtic	W 1-0	1-0	1	Thomson ^{45}	50,325
30	Apr 6	A	Dundee U	D 3-3	1-1	1	Weir ^{44}, Novo ^{58}, Boyd ^{67}	11,214
31	16	A	Celtic	L 1-2	0-1	—	Novo ^{55}	58,964
32	27	A	Celtic	L 2-3	2-2	2	Weir ^{17}, Cousin ^{29}	58,662
33	May 4	A	Hibernian	D 0-0	0-0	2		15,520
34	7	H	Motherwell	W 1-0	0-0	—	Ferguson ^{74}	48,238
35	10	H	Dundee U	W 3-1	2-0	2	Novo 2 $^{7, 18}$, Darcheville ^{90}	50,293
36	17	A	Motherwell	D 1-1	1-0	2	Dailly ^{29}	10,445
37	19	A	St Mirren	W 3-0	2-0	—	Boyd ^{4}, Darcheville 2 $^{24, 69}$	7449
38	22	A	Aberdeen	L 0-2	0-0	—		17,509

Final League Position: 2

Scottish Cup Winners: (32 times) 1894, 1897, 1898, 1903, 1928, 1930, 1932, 1934, 1935, 1936, 1948, 1949, 1950, 1953, 1960, 1962, 1963, 1964, 1966, 1973, 1976, 1978, 1979, 1981, 1992, 1993, 1996, 1999, 2000, 2002, 2003, 2008; *Runners-up:* 17 times.
League Cup Winners: (25 times) 1946-47, 1948-49, 1960-61, 1961-62, 1963-64, 1964-65, 1970-71, 1975-76, 1977-78, 1978-79, 1981-82, 1983-84, 1984-85, 1986-87, 1987-88, 1988-89, 1990-91, 1992-93, 1993-94, 1996-97, 1998-99, 2001-02, 2002-03, 2004-05, 2007-08; *Runners-up:* 6 times.

European: *European Cup:* 137 matches (1956-57, 1957-58, 1959-60 semi-finals, 1961-62, 1963-64, 1964-65, 1975-76, 1976-77, 1978-79, 1987-88, 1989-90, 1990-91, 1991-92, 1992-93 final pool, 1993-94, 1994-95, 1995-96; 1996-97, 1997-98, 1999-2000, 2000-01, 2003-04, 2005-06, 2007-08).
Cup Winners' Cup: 54 matches (1960-61 runners-up, 1962-63, 1966-67 runners-up, 1969-70, 1971-72 winners, 1973-74, 1977-78, 1979-80, 1981-82, 1983-84).
UEFA Cup: 77 matches (*Fairs Cup:* 1967-68, 1968-69 semi-finals, 1970-71. *UEFA Cup:* 1982-83, 1984-85, 1985-86, 1986-87, 1988-89, 1997-98, 1998-99, 1999-2000, 2000-01, 2002-03, 2004-05, 2006-07, 2007-08 runners-up).

Club colours: Shirt: Royal blue with red and white trim. Shorts: White with red and blue trim. Stockings: Black with red tops.

Goalscorers: *League* (84): Boyd 14 (2 pens), Darcheville 12, Cousin 10 (2 pens), Novo 10 (1 pen), Ferguson 7, Naismith 5, Cuellar 4, Whittaker 4, Adam 2, Beasley 2, Burke 2, Dailly 2, McCulloch 2, Weir 2, Broadfoot 1, Thomson 1, Webster 1, own goals 3.
Scottish Cup (14): Boyd 6 (1 pen), Burke 2, McCulloch 2, Novo 2 (1 pen), Beasley 1, Hutton 1.
CIS Cup (10): Boyd 5 (1 pen), Novo 2, Cuellar 1, Darcheville 1, Ferguson 1.

McGregor A 31	Hutton A 20	Papac S 22	Cuellar C 36	Weir D 37	Ferguson B 37 + 1	Hemdani B 12	Thomson K 25 + 1	Boyd K 17 + 11	Beasley D 8 + 3	McCulloch L 19 + 3	Novo N 10 + 18	Cousin D 20 + 6	Darcheville J 14 + 16	Whittaker S 29 + 1	Broadfoot K 14 + 1	Webster A 1	Naismith S 12 + 9	Faye A 2 + 2	Adam C 12 + 4	Burke C 10 + 1	Buffel T — + 1	Davis S 11 + 1	Dailly C 12 + 1	Alexander N 7 + 1	Furman D — + 1	Fleck J — + 1	Match No.
1	2	3	4	5	6	7	8	9^{1}	10	11	12																1
1	2	3	4	5	6		8	9^{2}	10	11	12	13	7^{1}														2
1	2	3	4	5	6		8	12		11^{1}	10^{3}	9^{2}	13	7	14												3
1	2	3	4	5	6		8	9	7^{2}		13	10^{1}	12	11													4
1	2	3	4		6		8	9^{2}	7^{3}		13	10^{1}	12	11		5	14										5
1	2	3	4	5	13		8	9^{2}	7		14	10^{3}	12	11				6^{1}									6
1	2	3	4	5	6		8^{3}	13		11		10^{1}	12	7			9^{2}	14									7
1	2	3	4	5	6		8	9	13	11			12^{2}	7^{1}			10^{3}		14								8
1	2	3	4	5	6	7	8^{2}	9^{3}		13		14		11^{1}			12		10								9
1	2	3	4	5	6		8		12	11	9^{2}	10^{1}					13		7								10
1	2	3	4	5	6		8	13	7	10	12	9^{2}						11^{1}									11
1	2	3	4	5	6	7		9^{2}	8	11	10^{1}	12	13														12
1	2	3	4	5	6		8	13	7	11		10^{1}	9^{2}				12										13
1	2		4	5	6		8	9		11			10^{1}	3			7		12								14
1	2		4	5	6	7		9^{1}		11			12	3			10^{2}		8	13							15
1	2		4	5	6		8	12		10■		9^{1}		3			7		11								16
1	2		4	5	6		8	12				9^{1}		3			10^{2}		11	7	13						17
1	2		4	5	6	7	8					9^{1}	12	3			10			11							18
1	2		4	5	6	7	8	13			12	9^{2}		3			10^{1}			11							19
1		3	4	5	6	7						9	12	2			10^{1}		8	11							20
1		3	4	5	6	7					13	9^{2}	12	2			10^{1}		8	11							21
1	2		4	5	6	7		9		13	14		10^{1}	3			12		8^{2}	11^{3}							22
1			4	5	6	7		9^{1}		8	13		10^{2}	3	2		12			11							23
1		3	4	5	6	7		9		8	12		10^{2}		2		13			11^{1}							24
1			4	5	6			13			12	9^{2}	10^{1}	3	2		7			11		8					25
1			4	5	6		13				12		10^{1}	3	2		7		9			11^{2}	8				26
1			4	5	6			9		13	12			3	2				10^{2}	7^{1}		11	8				27
1		3	4	5	6		8			9^{2}	12		10^{1}	13	2							11	7				28
1			4	5	6		8^{2}			9	12		10^{1}	3	2		14		13			11^{3}	7				29
1		3	4	5	6		8^{1}	9^{2}		11	10		12	2			13						7				30
1■		3	4■	5	6					9	12	13	10^{2}	8	2^{1}							11	7	15			31
		3		5^{1}	6	7^{2}					9	10	13	11■	2			12				8	4	1			32
		3^{1}	4	5	6		8	12			9	10^{2}	13		2							11	7	1			33
			4	5	6		8	9^{2}			7^{3}	13	10^{1}	3	2				12			11	14	1			34
		3	4	5	6		8^{1}				9	10^{2}	13	11	2								7	1	12		35
			4	5	6			14		11^{1}	9^{3}	10	13	3	2				8^{2}			12	7	1			36
				5	6		7	9	12		10^{1}	13	8^{2}	3	2							11	4	1			37
			4	5	6		8	13			12■	9^{1}	10^{2}	3					11^{3}			7	2	1		14	38

ROSS COUNTY — First Division

Year Formed: 1929. *Ground & Address:* Victoria Park, Dingwall IV15 9QW. *Telephone:* 01349 860860. *Fax:* 01349 866277.
E-mail: donnie@rosscountyfootballclub.co.uk. *Website:* www.rosscountyfootballclub.co.uk
Ground Capacity: 6700. *Size of Ground:* 105×68m.
Chairman: Roy MacGregor. *Secretary:* Donnie MacBean.
Manager: Derek Adam. *Director of Football:* George Adams. *Coaches:* Derek Adams and (*Head of Youth*) David Kirkwood. *Physio:* Douglas Sim.
Club Nickname(s): The Staggies.
Record Attendance: 6600, benefit match v Celtic, 31 August 1970.
Record Transfer Fee Received: £200,000 for Neil Tarrant to Aston Villa (April 1999).
Record Transfer Fee Paid: £25,000 for Barry Wilson from Southampton (Oct. 1992).
Record Victory: 11-0 v St Cuthbert Wanderers, Scottish Cup, 11 Dec 1993.
Record Defeat: 1-10 v Inverness Thistle, Highland League.
Most League Appearances: 157: David Mackay, 1995-2001.
Most League Goals in Season: 22: Derek Adams, 1996-97.
Most League Goals (Overall): 44: Steven Ferguson, 1996-2002.

ROSS COUNTY 2007–08 LEAGUE RECORD

Match No.	*Date*	*Venue*	*Opponents*	*Result*		*H/T Score*	*Lg. Pos.*	*Goalscorers*	*Attendance*
1	Aug 4	H	Ayr U	W	2-0	1-0	—	Barrowman [4], Petrie [60]	2164
2	11	A	Cowdenbeath	D	2-2	0-0	3	Barrowman [46], Adams [52]	320
3	18	A	Queen's Park	L	2-3	1-1	3	Anderson [25], McCulloch [88]	815
4	25	H	Peterhead	W	1-0	1-0	3	Higgins [24]	2056
5	Sept 1	H	Airdrie U	D	1-1	1-1	3	Barrowman [39]	2094
6	15	A	Raith R	W	2-0	0-0	2	Petrie 2 [73, 83]	2101
7	22	A	Berwick R	W	1-0	1-0	1	Barrowman (pen) [8]	495
8	29	H	Alloa Ath	D	2-2	1-0	1	Brady [41], Moore [79]	2115
9	Oct 6	H	Brechin C	W	2-1	0-0	1	Petrie [50], Shields [67]	2022
10	20	A	Ayr U	W	4-1	4-0	1	Adams [10], Petrie 2 [24, 31], Barrowman [26]	1075
11	27	H	Queen's Park	D	1-1	0-1	1	Boyd [85]	2323
12	Nov 3	A	Peterhead	W	2-1	1-0	1	Petrie 2 [41, 61]	815
13	10	A	Airdrie U	W	1-0	0-0	1	Shields [80]	1062
14	Dec 1	H	Raith R	L	2-3	0-1	1	Barrowman [47], Scott [90]	2627
15	8	A	Alloa Ath	L	1-3	0-2	1	Dowie [77]	523
16	15	H	Berwick R	W	2-1	0-0	1	Higgins [54], Shields [76]	2027
17	29	A	Queen's Park	W	1-0	0-0	2	Barrowman [49]	657
18	Jan 2	H	Peterhead	W	5-1	2-1	2	Keddie [25], Barrowman 2 [45, 56], Shields [70], Moore [72]	2213
19	5	A	Raith R	W	1-0	1-0	1	Higgins [34]	2319
20	19	H	Airdrie U	W	3-2	1-1	1	Barrowman 2 [25, 90], Golabek [55]	2319
21	26	A	Cowdenbeath	W	4-2	2-0	1	Armstrong J (og) [1], Armstrong D (og) [31], Scott [48], Barrowman [77]	362
22	Feb 9	H	Alloa Ath	W	6-1	3-0	1	Golabek [22], Barrowman [32], Higgins [36], Keddie [61], Shields [65], Dowie [90]	2272
23	16	A	Berwick R	W	4-0	3-0	1	Strachan [20], Horn (og) [23], Barrowman 2 [27, 71]	449
24	23	H	Queen's Park	W	3-2	2-1	1	Gardyne [5], Barrowman [27], Lawson [83]	2162
25	26	A	Brechin C	W	2-1	1-1	—	Higgins 2 [1, 50]	561
26	Mar 1	A	Peterhead	D	1-1	1-1	1	Higgins [19]	792
27	4	H	Cowdenbeath	W	4-1	1-0	—	Keddie [39], Higgins [55], Barrowman [62], Winters [89]	1511
28	11	H	Ayr U	L	2-4	0-3	—	Higgins [62], Gardyne [78]	1627
29	15	A	Ayr U	W	2-0	0-0	1	Barrowman [52], Gardyne [69]	1079
30	18	H	Brechin C	D	0-0	0-0	—		1648
31	22	H	Raith R	L	2-3	2-2	1	Barrowman [16], Scott [20]	2973
32	Apr 5	H	Berwick R	W	4-0	2-0	1	Shields [6], Barrowman 2 (1 pen) [45, 64 (p)], Lawson [82]	2579
33	9	A	Airdrie U	L	0-2	0-1	—		724
34	12	A	Alloa Ath	L	0-2	0-0	1		452
35	19	H	Cowdenbeath	W	3-0	2-0	1	Barrowman 2 [2, 55], Higgins [28]	3716
36	26	A	Brechin C	D	3-3	1-1	1	Gardyne [10], Barrowman [79], Winters [83]	586

Final League Position: 1

Honours
League Champions: Second Division 2007-08. Third Division 1998-99.
Bell's League Challenge Cup Winners: 2006-07; *Runners up:* 2004-05.

Club colours: Shirt: Navy blue with white trim. Shorts: White with navy side panels. Stockings: Navy blue with two white hoops.

Goalscorers: *League* (78): Barrowman 24 (2 pens), Higgins 10, Petrie 8, Shields 6, Gardyne 4, Keddie 3, Scott 3, Adams 2, Dowie 2, Golabek 2, Lawson 2, Moore 2, Winters 2, Anderson 1, Boyd 1, Brady 1, McCulloch 1, Strachan 1, own goals 3.
Scottish Cup (14): Shields 4, Barrowman 2 (1 pen), Dowie 2, Higgins 2, Boyd 1, Golabek 1, Keddie 1, Scott 1.
CIS Cup (4): Barrowman 3, Dowie 1.
Challenge Cup (2): Barrowman 1 (pen), Keddie 1.

Bullock T 24	McCulloch M 30	Keddie A 27 + 1	Scott M 21 + 10	Golabek S 26	Dowie A 33 + 1	Brady D 14 + 3	Adams D 11	Barrowman A 32 + 1	Petrie S 15 + 9	Moore D 7 + 12	Robertson H — + 4	Higgins S 23 + 11	Niven D — + 1	Anderson I 3 + 4	Malin J 8	Campbell I 10	Shields D 17 + 8	Boyd S 21 + 2	Lawson P 24	Miller G 19 + 1	Gunn C 2 + 13	Strachan A 10 + 8	Gardyne M 9 + 7	Winters D 2 + 4	Creer A 4	Girvan G 2	Sancho B 2	Grant R — + 1	Match No.
1	2	3	4	5	6	7■	8^{3}	9^{2}	10^{1}	11	12	13	14																1
1	2	3	4^{1}	5	6	7	8	9	10	11				12															2
	2	3	4^{1}	5	6	7^{2}	8	9	10^{3}	14	13	12		11	1														3
	2	3	4	5	6	12	8^{1}	9^{2}	13	14		10		7	1	11^{3}													4
	2	3	4	5	6	13	8^{2}	9		14		11		7^{1}	1	10^{3}	12												5
	2	3	13		6	7	8		10^{3}			11^{1}		14	1	5	12	4	9^{2}										6
	2	3	14		6	7	8	9^{3}	10^{1}			13			1	5	12	4	11^{2}										7
	2	3	13		6^{2}	7^{1}	8	9	10^{3}	12		14			1	5		4	11										8
1	2	3	4^{1}				8	9^{2}	10^{3}	11		14		13		5	12	6	7										9
1	2	3	13		6^{3}	7	8^{2}	9	10^{1}	14						4	12	11	5										10
1	2	3	12			7^{2}	8^{1}	9^{3}	10	13		11		14		5		6	4										11
1	2		4	5	6	7		9^{1}	10^{2}			13				11^{3}	12	3	8	14									12
1	2		4	5	6	7^{1}		9^{3}	10^{2}			13				11	12	3	8		14								13
1	2		4	5	6	7		9	10^{1}			13					11^{2}	3	8		12								14
1	2		4	5	6	7		9	10^{2}	12		14					11^{3}	8	3^{1}		13								15
1	2	3	4	5^{1}	6			9^{3}	14	12		10^{2}					11		8	7	13								16
1	2	3	4^{1}	5	6			9^{2}	13		12	10^{3}					11		8	7	14								17
1	6	5	12	3	4^{1}			10		13		11^{2}					9^{3}		7	2	14	8							18
1	6	5	12	3	4			10		13		11^{1}					9		7■	2		8^{2}							19
1	6	5	7	3	4			10	13			11^{2}					9^{1}			2	12	8							20
1	7^{2}	4	6	5	3			11			13	9^{1}					10^{3}	2		8		14	12						21
1		5	7	3	4	6^{2}		10	14			8^{3}					9	13		2		11^{1}	12						22
1	6^{2}	5		3	4	13		10	14			8^{1}							7	2		11^{3}	9	12					23
1		5^{1}	6	3	4			10		13		8						12	7	2	14	11^{3}	9^{2}						24
		4	6^{1}	5	3			11				8^{2}					10^{3}	9	7	2	14	13	12		1				25
		5	13	3^{1}	4			10		12		8					9	11	6	2			7^{2}		1				26
		5			4			10		3		8^{3}					9^{2}	11	6	2	13	7^{1}	12	14	1				27
		5	14		4			10		3^{3}		8					9^{2}	11	6	2	13	7^{1}	12		1				28
1	9	4	13	5	3			11				7^{3}					12	8	6^{2}	2		14	10^{1}						29
1	11	5^{1}		3	4				13			8^{3}					10^{2}	6	7	2	12	14	9						30
1	11		6^{1}	3	4			10	14			8^{3}						5	7	2	13	12	9^{2}						31
1	6			3	4			10	11^{3}			8^{1}					9^{2}	5	7	2		14	13	12					32
1	6			3	4	7		10	11^{3}			8^{1}					9^{2}	5		2		13	12	14					33
	6^{1}	5	7		12					3		13			1						9^{2}	11	8	10		2	4		34
1	6	12	7	3	4			10^{3}	14			8					9^{2}	5^{1}		2		13	11						35
	7		6		3			13		5^{2}		12			1						10^{1}	9	8^{3}	11		2	4	14	36

ST JOHNSTONE First Division

Year Formed: 1884. *Ground & Address:* McDiarmid Park, Crieff Road, Perth PH1 2SJ. *Telephone:* 01738 459090. *Fax:* 01738 625 771. *Clubcall:* 0898 121559. *Email:* karin@perthsaints.co.uk *Website:* www.perthstjohnstonefc.co.uk
Ground Capacity: all seated: 10,673. *Size of Pitch:* 115yd × 75yd.
Chairman: G.S. Brown. *Secretary and Managing Director:* Stewart Duff. *Sales Executives:* Paul Smith and Susan Weir.
Manager: Derek McInnes. *Coach:* Tony Docherty. *Youth Coach:* Tommy Campbell.
Club Nickname(s): Saints. *Previous Grounds:* Recreation Grounds, Muirton Park.
Record Attendance: (McDiarmid Park): 10,545 v Dundee, Premier Division, 23 May 1999.
Record Transfer Fee received: £1,750,000 for Calum Davidson to Blackburn R (March 1998).
Record Transfer Fee paid: £400,000 for Billy Dodds from Dundee (1994).
Record Victory: 9-0 v Albion R, League Cup, 9 Mar 1946.
Record Defeat: 1-10 v Third Lanark, Scottish Cup, 24 Jan 1903.
Most Capped Player: Nick Dasovic, 26, Canada.
Most League Appearances: 298: Drew Rutherford, 1976-85.
Most League Goals in Season (Individual): 36: Jimmy Benson, Division II, 1931-32.
Most Goals Overall (Individual): 140: John Brogan, 1977-83.

ST JOHNSTONE 2007–08 LEAGUE RECORD

Match No.	Date	Venue	Opponents	Result		H/T Score	Lg. Pos.	Goalscorers	Attendance
1	Aug 4	A	Queen of the S	D	3-3	1-2	—	Sheerin 2 (2 pens) [31, 87], Hardie [89]	2255
2	11	H	Stirling A	D	2-2	1-2	5	Hardie [20], Rutkiewicz [63]	2996
3	18	H	Dundee	D	1-1	0-0	5	Stewart [46]	6279
4	25	A	Clyde	L	0-1	0-0	7		1274
5	Sept 2	A	Dunfermline Ath	D	0-0	0-0	8		4946
6	15	H	Partick Th	W	2-1	0-0	5	Deuchar [72], Quinn [75]	2895
7	22	A	Morton	D	2-2	1-1	4	Jackson [20], Sheerin (pen) [57]	2922
8	29	H	Hamilton A	W	4-1	0-1	3	Sheerin [48], Jackson 2 [63, 79], Deuchar [72]	2713
9	Oct 6	A	Livingston	W	2-0	0-0	3	Deuchar [62], Jackson [77]	1776
10	20	H	Queen of the S	W	2-0	1-0	3	Deuchar [11], Jackson [66]	2710
11	27	H	Clyde	D	1-1	0-0	3	Deuchar [83]	2782
12	Nov 3	A	Dundee	L	1-2	1-0	3	Sheerin (pen) [18]	5518
13	10	H	Dunfermline Ath	D	0-0	0-0	3		3317
14	Dec 1	A	Partick Th	D	2-2	0-1	3	Sheerin (pen) [89], Deuchar [90]	2388
15	8	H	Morton	D	2-2	0-1	4	Sheerin (pen) [55], Milne [58]	2517
16	15	A	Hamilton A	L	0-1	0-1	4		1922
17	22	H	Livingston	W	5-2	2-1	3	Jackson 2 [22, 72], Craig [41], Quinn [56], MacDonald [78]	2217
18	26	A	Stirling A	D	0-0	0-0	3		1556
19	29	A	Clyde	W	3-1	2-1	3	Jackson [21], MacDonald (pen) [28], Moon [90]	1149
20	Jan 2	H	Dundee	D	1-1	0-0	3	Milne [67]	6072
21	5	H	Partick Th	W	2-0	0-0	3	McCaffrey [61], Milne [73]	2490
22	19	A	Dunfermline Ath	W	1-0	1-0	3	Jackson [44]	4230
23	26	H	Stirling A	W	2-1	1-0	3	Jackson [5], Moon [74]	2482
24	Feb 9	A	Queen of the S	L	1-3	0-1	3	Jackson [77]	2229
25	16	H	Hamilton A	W	2-1	0-1	3	Craig [77], MacDonald [81]	2973
26	23	A	Morton	W	2-1	2-1	3	Milne 2 [29, 40]	2564
27	Mar 1	A	Dundee	L	2-3	0-1	3	Morris [72], Jackson [80]	6192
28	11	H	Queen of the S	W	2-1	0-0	—	MacDonald 2 [76, 87]	1853
29	15	A	Livingston	W	2-0	1-0	3	Quinn 2 [24, 56]	1543
30	22	A	Partick Th	D	0-0	0-0	3		2309
31	25	H	Clyde	L	1-2	0-1	—	Wilson [61]	1686
32	29	H	Dunfermline Ath	D	1-1	1-0	3	McManus [36]	2372
33	Apr 5	A	Hamilton A	L	0-2	0-1	3		1825
34	12	H	Morton	W	3-2	2-0	3	Jackson 2 [23, 27], James [86]	2341
35	23	A	Stirling A	L	1-3	1-2	—	James [15]	430
36	26	H	Livingston	W	5-2	1-0	3	Moon [45], Sheerin 2 (2 pens) [57, 60], Milne 2 [64, 81]	2571

Final League Position: 3

Honours
League Champions: First Division 1982-83, 1989-90, 1996-97. Division II 1923-24, 1959-60, 1962-63; *Runners-up:* Division II 1931-32. Second Division 1987-88.
Scottish Cup: Semi-finals 1934, 1968, 1989, 1991.
League Cup: Runners-up: 1969-70, 1998-99.
League Challenge Cup Winners: 2007-08; *Runners-up:* 1996-97.

European: *UEFA Cup:* 10 matches (1971-72, 1999-2000).

Club colours: Shirt: Royal blue with white trim. Shorts: White. Stockings: Royal blue with white hoops.

Goalscorers: *League* (60): Jackson 14, Sheerin 9 (8 pens), Milne 7, Deuchar 6, MacDonald 5 (1 pen), Quinn 4, Moon 3, Craig 2, Hardie 2, James 2, McCaffrey 1, McManus 1, Morris 1, Rutkiewicz 1, Stewart 1, Wilson 1.
Scottish Cup (9): Craig 2 (1 pen), Jackson 2, McBreen 1, MacDonald 1, Milne 1, Quinn 1, Sheerin 1 (pen).
CIS Cup (0).
Challenge Cup (13): Deuchar 4, Jackson 3, MacDonald 2, Sheerin 2 (2 pens), Quinn 1, Weatherson 1.

Main A 34	Lawrie A 4+3	James K 4+1	Weatherston D 9+18	Stanic G 29	McManus A 29+2	McInnes D 14	Hardie M 6+2	MacDonald P 22+11	Stewart J 4+4	Sheerin P 33+3	Daal D 3+5	Jackson A 26+8	McCluskey J 1+3	Rutkiewicz K 20	Anderson S 27+1	Dyer W —+1	Irvine G 33	Moon K 8+12	Quinn R 20+1	Deuchar K 10	McLaren W 6+1	Milne S 17+5	Craig L 19	McBreen D 3+3	McCaffrey S 1	Cameron G 4+1	Lynch S 1	Morris J 4+1	Wilson B 2+4	Cuthbert K 2	Monaghan A —+1	Kerr S 1+1	Fairbairn J —+1	Match No.
1	2	3	4^3	5	6	7	8	9^2	10^1	11	12	13	14																					1
1	2		4	5	6	7	8	9^2	12	11	10^1	13		3																				2
1	2		4^2		6	7	8■	9^1	10^3	11		14	12	3	5	13																		3
1			4^2	5	6	7		13	10^3	11	9^1	12	8		3		2	14																4
1			13		6	7^2	8	12	10^1	11		14		3	5		2		4	9^3														5
1			12	5	6	7^1			13	11	14	10^2		3	4		2		8	9^3														6
1			13	5^3	6	7^2				11		10		3	4		2	12	8^1	9	14													7
1				5	6	7		12		11		10^1			4		2		3	9	8													8
1				5	6	7		12		11		10			3		2		4	8^1	9													9
1			12	5	6	7		14		11		8			3		2	13^3	4^2	9	10^1													10
1			12	5	6	7^3		13		11		10^2	14		4		2		3	9	8^1													11
1			13	5	6	7		12		11		10^1			4		2		3	9	8^2													12
1			12	5	6	7		13		11		9^2			4		2		10	8	3^1													13
1	13		14	5			8	9^3		11		4^1		6	3		2^2		7	10		12												14
1	13			5	6	7^1		9^2	14	11		12		3■	4		2		8			10^3												15
1			12	5^1	6			9	13	11		10^2			7		2	4	8				3											16
1			12	5	6			8		11	13	9^1			7		2		4			10^2	3											17
1	12		13	5	6			9		11^2	14	10			4		2		7^1			8^3	3											18
1	2			5	6			9		13	8^1	10^2		3			4	7				12	11											19
1				3	6			7		11	14	9^3		5	4^1		2	12				10	8^2	13										20
1			13	3				8^1		11		12		5			2	7				10	6	9^2	4									21
1				3	12			7		11^1		9		5	6		2					10	8			4								22
1			13	3	14			7^2		11		9		5	6		2^3	12				10	8			4^1								23
1		5	14	3	4			9		8^2		10					2	6^1	12			11^3	7			13								24
1			11^2	3				10		12		9		5	6		2	14	7^3			13	8			4^1								25
1		12		5	3			9^2		8		10		4^1			2	14	7^3			11	6	13										26
1			14	5	4			11^3		7		9		3			2		8^1			10					6^2	13	12					27
1			13		6			8		11		9^3		5	3^1		2	14	7			10						4^2	12					28
1			14		5			10^3		11		9^2			3		2	12	8			13	6					4	7^1					29
1					4			11^3		13		9		3	5^2		2	12	7^1			10	8					6	14					30
1			11^3		6		13	12		3^2				5	14		2	10				9	8			4^1			7					31
1			14	3^1	6			7^3		11		9^2		5			2	12				8	10					4	13					32
				3	6^1		12	7^2		11		9		5	4		2	8				13	10							1				33
1		5	7^1	3			8	14		11		9^3			4		2	12				10^2	6	13										34
1		6■	7					14		11		12^2			5		2	4				8^1	10	9^3								3	13	35
			7	3^1	6					11					5		2^2	4				8	10	9						1	13	12		36

ST MIRREN Premier League

Year Formed: 1877. *Ground & Address:* St Mirren Park, Love St, Paisley PA3 2EA. *Telephone:* 0141 889 2558. *Fax:* 0141 848 6444. *E-mail:* commercial@saintmirren.net *Website:* www.saintmirren.net
Ground Capacity: 10,476 (all seated). *Size of Pitch:* 105yd × 68yd.
Chairman: Stewart Gilmour. *Vice-Chairman:* George Campbell. *General Manager:* Brian Caldwell (tel: 0141 8892558; fax: 0141 8406139). *Commercial Manager:* Campbell Kennedy. *Secretary:* Allan Marshall.
Manager: Gus MacPherson. *Assistant Manager:* Andy Millen. *Youth Development Officer:* David Longwell.
Club Nickname(s): The Buddies. *Previous Grounds:* Short Roods 1877-79, Thistle Park Greenhill 1879-83, Westmarch 1883-94.
Record Attendance: 47,438 v Celtic, League Cup, 20 Aug 1949.
Record Transfer Fee received: £850,000 for Ian Ferguson to Rangers (1988).
Record Transfer Fee paid: £400,000 for Thomas Stickroth from Bayer Uerdingen (1990).
Record Victory: 15-0 v Glasgow University, Scottish Cup 1st rd, 30 Jan 1960.
Record Defeat: 0-9 v Rangers, Division I, 4 Dec 1897.
Most Capped Player: Godmundor Torfason, 29, Iceland.
Most League Appearances: 351: Tony Fitzpatrick, 1973-88.
Most League Goals in Season (Individual): 45: Dunky Walker, Division I, 1921-22.
Most Goals Overall (Individual): 221: David McCrae, 1923-34.

ST MIRREN 2007–08 LEAGUE RECORD

Match No.	Date	Venue	Opponents	Result	H/T Score	Lg. Pos.	Goalscorers	Attendance
1	Aug 4	H	Motherwell	L 0-1	0-1	—		5257
2	11	A	Rangers	L 0-2	0-0	10		47,772
3	18	H	Inverness CT	W 2-1	1-0	7	Miranda 19, Corcoran 55	3309
4	25	A	Falkirk	W 1-0	0-0	7	Mehmet 90	5339
5	Sept 2	H	Celtic	L 1-5	0-2	7	Miranda 75	7519
6	16	A	Dundee U	L 0-2	0-1	8		6128
7	22	A	Kilmarnock	D 0-0	0-0	9		5596
8	30	H	Hearts	L 1-3	0-1	10	Corcoran 78	4233
9	Oct 7	A	Aberdeen	L 0-4	0-1	11		12,841
10	20	H	Gretna	W 1-0	1-0	9	Mehmet 35	3339
11	27	A	Hibernian	W 1-0	1-0	9	Mehmet 13	13,884
12	Nov 3	A	Motherwell	D 1-1	1-1	9	Kean 45	5123
13	24	A	Inverness CT	L 0-1	0-1	9		3699
14	Dec 1	H	Falkirk	L 1-5	0-3	11	Mehmet 50	4133
15	8	A	Celtic	D 1-1	0-0	11	McGinn 74	56,088
16	15	H	Dundee U	L 0-3	0-0	11		3490
17	22	H	Kilmarnock	D 0-0	0-0	11		4217
18	26	A	Hearts	W 1-0	1-0	11	McGinn 17	16,476
19	29	H	Aberdeen	L 0-1	0-0	11		5025
20	Jan 5	H	Hibernian	W 2-1	2-0	10	Maxwell 4, Mason 43	4212
21	19	H	Motherwell	W 3-1	2-1	9	Corcoran 9, Maxwell 2 38, 49	4291
22	26	A	Rangers	L 0-4	0-3	10		49,198
23	Feb 9	H	Inverness CT	D 1-1	0-1	10	Mehmet 74	3609
24	16	A	Falkirk	L 0-4	0-1	10		5803
25	24	H	Celtic	L 0-1	0-0	10		7213
26	27	A	Dundee U	D 1-1	0-0	—	Dorman 88	6037
27	Mar 1	A	Kilmarnock	L 0-1	0-1	11		5352
28	15	H	Hearts	D 1-1	0-0	11	Hamilton 59	4557
29	22	A	Aberdeen	D 1-1	1-1	11	Dorman 10	9779
30	29	H	Gretna	W 2-0	1-0	11	Dargo 27, Mehmet 49	3577
31	Apr 5	A	Hibernian	L 0-2	0-2	11		12,343
32	9	A	Gretna	D 0-0	0-0	—		751
33	19	A	Hearts	L 2-3	1-2	11	McCay 20, Mason 78	15,259
34	26	H	Falkirk	W 1-0	0-0	10	Dorman 82	3574
35	May 3	H	Kilmarnock	W 1-0	0-0	10	Haining 90	3690
36	10	H	Gretna	D 0-0	0-0	10		3163
37	17	A	Inverness CT	D 0-0	0-0	10		3783
38	19	H	Rangers	L 0-3	0-2	—		7449

Final League Position: 10

Honours
League Champions: First Division 1976-77, 1999-2000, 2005-06; *Runners-up:* 2004-05. Division II 1967-68; *Runners-up:* 1935-36.
Scottish Cup Winners: 1926, 1959, 1987. *Runners-up:* 1908, 1934, 1962.
League Cup Runners-up: 1955-56.
League Challenge Cup Winners: 2005-06.
B&Q Cup Runners-up: 1993-94. *Anglo-Scottish Cup:* 1979-80.

European: *Cup Winners' Cup:* 4 matches (1987-88). *UEFA Cup:* 10 matches (1980-81, 1983-84, 1985-86).

Club colours: Shirt: Black and white vertical stripes. Shorts: White with black trim. Stockings: White with two black hoops. Change colours: Predominantly red.

Goalscorers: *League* (26): Mehmet 6, Corcoran 3, Dorman 3, Maxwell 3, Mason 2, McGinn 2, Miranda 2, Dargo 1, Haining 1, Hamilton 1, Kean 1, McCay 1.
Scottish Cup (6): Dorman 2, Mehmet 2 (1 pen), Barron 1, Corcoran 1.
CIS Cup (0).

Smith C 28	Van Zanten D 29	Reid A 10 + 2	Mason G 31	Haining W 29	Potter J 31	Murray H 27 + 2	Brady G 16 + 2	Mehmet B 32 + 5	Kean S 15 + 17	Corcoran M 18 + 8	Brittain R 2 + 4	Burke A 7 + 3	McGinn S 10 + 15	McCay R 10 + 2	Miranda F 20 + 4	Birchall C 5 + 4	O'Donnell S 5 + 5	Millen A 8 + 1	Maxwell I 17	Molloy C — + 5	Barron D 18	Dargo C 15 + 1	Dorman A 18	Hamilton J 7 + 8	Howard M 10	Docherty M — + 1	McAusland M — + 1	*Match No.*
1	2	3	4	5	6^{3}	7	8^{1}	9^{2}	10	11	12	13	14															1
1	2	3^{1}	4	5	6	7	8^{2}	14	10^{3}	9	12		13	11														2
1	2	12	4	5	6	7		13	10^{3}	11	8^{1}	14		3	9^{2}													3
1	2		4	5	6	7	8	9	10	11					3													4
1	2	3	4^{2}	5	6	7^{3}	8	12	10^{1}	11	14				9	13												5
1	2		4^{3}	5	6	7	8^{1}	9	10	11^{2}			14	13	3■	12												6
1	2	3^{1}	4	5	6	7		9^{2}	13				12	10		11	8											7
1	2		4	5^{1}	6	7		9^{3}	12	13			14	3	11	10	8^{2}											8
1	2		4	5	6	7		12	10^{2}	13				3	9	8	11^{1}											9
1	2		4	5		7		9	12	11^{3}		8^{1}	14		3	10^{2}	13	6										10
1	2		4	5		7	8	9	10			6^{1}	12		11			3										11
1	2		4	5		7	8^{1}	9	10	13		6^{2}			11	12		3										12
1	2		4^{2}	5■		7	8^{1}	9	10	11					3	12	13	6										13
1	2		4		6	7^{3}	8^{1}	9	10	12			13		3	11^{2}	14	5										14
1	2	3	4			7	12	9^{3}	14	11			8^{1}	13	10^{2}			5	6									15
1	2	3	4			7■		9	12	10			8^{1}		11^{2}			5	6	13								16
1	2	12	4				8	9	14	11^{3}		7			13			5	6		3^{1}	10^{2}						17
1	2	3	4		6	12		9	10^{2}	13		8^{1}	7		11				5									18
1	2	3	4		6			9	10^{2}	13		7^{1}	8		11				5	12								19
1	2		4	5	6		8^{1}	9^{3}	10			11^{2}	12		13				3		7	14						20
1	2			5	6	7		9	12	11									3		4	10^{1}	8					21
1	2			5■	6	7^{2}	8	9^{1}	12	11		14	13						3		4		10^{3}					22
1	2				6	7		9		11			8^{1}						3		5	10	4	12				23
	2				6	7	13	9		11			8^{1}						3		5	10	4^{2}	12	1			24
	2		4^{2}	5	6	7		9	12	13									3		11	10^{1}	8		1			25
	2		4^{2}	5	6			9	13	11									3		8	10^{1}	7	12	1			26
1	2		4^{3}	5	6	7^{1}		9	10	11			14		13				3^{2}				8	12				27
1	2		4		6^{1}	13		14					8^{2}		11			12	3		5	9^{3}	7	10				28
1	2		4	5	6	7		9^{1}	12						3						8■		11	10				29
1		2		5^{3}	6	7	8	9	13										3^{1}			11	4	10^{2}		12	14	30
1		2^{3}		5	6	7^{1}	8	9	14		12								3		11	10^{2}	4	13				31
				5	6		8^{1}		12	11^{2}	7^{3}		13	2						14	3	10	4	9	1			32
			4^{3}	5	6		8^{1}	9		14			12	7^{2}					3		2	10	11	13	1			33
			4	5	6			9^{3}	14				10^{2}	11^{1}	12					13	8	7	3	2	1			34
			4	5	6			9	12				7^{1}		3		14			13	2	10^{2}	8	11^{3}	1			35
			4	5	6			9	14				12	8^{1}	3		13				2	11^{3}	7	10^{2}	1			36
			4^{1}	5	6	7		9					13	3			11^{2}				2	10	8	12	1			37
			4	5	6	7		9					11^{1}		3		10				2		8	12	1			38

STENHOUSEMUIR Third Division

Year Formed: 1884. *Ground & Address:* Ochilview Park, Gladstone Rd, Stenhousemuir FK5 4QL. *Telephone:* 01324 562992. *Fax:* 01324 562980. *E-mail:* info@stenhousemuirfc.com. *Website:* www.stenhousemuirfc.com
Ground Capacity (total): 3746. *Size of Pitch:* 110yd × 72yd.
Chairman: David O. Reid. *Secretary:* Margaret Kilpatrick. *Commercial Manager:* Brian McGinlay.
Manager: John Coughlin. *Assistant Manager:* Matt Kerr. *Community Coach:* Steven Ferguson. *Physio:* Alain Davidson.
Club Nickname(s): The Warriors. *Previous Grounds:* Tryst Ground 1884-86, Goschen Park 1886-90.
Record Attendance: 12,500 v East Fife, Scottish Cup 4th rd, 11 Mar 1950.
Record Transfer Fee received: £70,000 for Euan Donaldson to St Johnstone (May 1995).
Record Transfer Fee paid: £20,000 to Livingston for Ian Little (June 1995).
Record Victory: 9-2 v Dundee U, Division II, 16 Apr 1937.
Record Defeat: 2-11 v Dunfermline Ath, Division II, 27 Sept 1930.
Most League Appearances: 434: Jimmy Richardson, 1957-73.
Most League Goals in Season (Individual): 32: Robert Taylor, Division II, 1925-26.

STENHOUSEMUIR 2007–08 LEAGUE RECORD

Match No.	Date	Venue	Opponents	Result		H/T Score	Lg. Pos.	Goalscorers	Attendance
1	Aug 4	H	Arbroath	W	1-0	1-0	—	Dempster (pen) 36	498
2	11	A	Forfar Ath	W	1-0	1-0	3	Ferguson 10	349
3	18	A	Albion R	D	1-1	1-0	3	Dempster (pen) 18	339
4	25	H	East Stirling	L	0-3	0-2	5		520
5	Sept 1	H	Montrose	L	0-4	0-2	7		398
6	15	A	Dumbarton	W	2-1	1-1	5	Hampshire 4, Desmond 89	907
7	22	H	Stranraer	L	1-4	0-0	6	Dempster (pen) 49	356
8	29	A	East Fife	L	0-7	0-0	7		540
9	Oct 6	H	Elgin C	L	2-3	1-0	8	Dempster 2 (1 pen) 35, 50 (p)	378
10	20	A	Arbroath	D	2-2	1-0	8	Hampshire 17, Ferguson 46	529
11	Nov 3	H	Albion R	L	0-1	0-0	9		362
12	10	A	East Stirling	D	1-1	1-0	9	Dempster 4	528
13	24	H	Forfar Ath	W	4-0	3-0	—	Dillon 2 21, 30, Thomson 38, Gilbride 53	212
14	Dec 1	H	Dumbarton	W	2-1	1-1	6	Thomson 23, Dempster (pen) 77	403
15	8	A	Montrose	L	0-1	0-1	7		365
16	15	A	Stranraer	W	3-2	2-0	6	McEwan 5, Hampshire 15, Tyrrell 55	225
17	22	H	East Fife	W	2-1	1-1	4	Lyle 36, Ferguson 60	755
18	29	A	Elgin C	L	0-2	0-0	5		456
19	Jan 2	H	East Stirling	W	3-0	3-0	5	Dalziel 2 (1 pen) 13 (p), 18, Lyle 30	477
20	5	A	Albion R	D	3-3	1-1	4	Ferguson 30, Gilbride 51, Dalziel 64	282
21	19	H	Montrose	D	0-0	0-0	4		346
22	26	A	Forfar Ath	W	2-1	1-0	4	Dillon 20, Dalziel 56	293
23	Feb 2	H	Arbroath	L	0-3	0-0	4		426
24	9	A	East Fife	W	1-0	0-0	4	Dalziel 47	753
25	16	H	Stranraer	D	1-1	1-1	4	Dalziel 28	381
26	23	H	Albion R	D	2-2	0-2	4	Dalziel 2 (1 pen) 48, 77 (p)	389
27	Mar 1	A	East Stirling	W	4-3	2-2	5	Lyle 8, Tyrrell 36, Hamilton 77, Harty 86	369
28	8	H	Elgin C	D	2-2	1-0	5	McLaughlin 25, Dalziel 73	291
29	15	A	Arbroath	L	0-1	0-1	5		513
30	18	A	Dumbarton	L	0-1	0-1	—		389
31	22	H	Dumbarton	D	1-1	0-1	6	Harty 80	449
32	29	A	Montrose	L	1-2	1-1	6	Harty 22	510
33	Apr 5	A	Stranraer	L	1-3	1-0	6	Mailey 28	135
34	12	H	East Fife	L	0-1	0-1	6		501
35	19	H	Forfar Ath	W	2-0	1-0	6	Gibson 6, Harty (pen) 84	387
36	26	A	Elgin C	W	5-1	3-1	5	Love 3 6, 41, 65, Ferguson 23, Tyrrell 50	582

Final League Position: 5

Honours
League Champions: Third Division runners-up: 1998-99.
Scottish Cup: Semi-finals 1902-03. Quarter-finals 1948-49, 1949-50, 1994-95.
League Cup: Quarter-finals 1947-48, 1960-61, 1975-76.
League Challenge Cup: Winners: 1995-96.

Club colours: Shirt: Maroon with dark blue trim. Shorts: White. Stockings: Maroon.

Goalscorers: *League* (50): Dalziel 9 (2 pens), Dempster 7 (5 pens), Ferguson 5, Harty 4 (1 pen), Dillon 3, Hampshire 3, Love 3, Lyle 3, Tyrrell 3, Gilbride 2, Thomson 2, Desmond 1, Gibson 1, Hamilton 1, Mailey 1, McEwan 1, McLaughlin 1.
Scottish Cup (0).
CIS Cup (1): Lyle 1.
Challenge Cup (1): Dempster 1.

Hillcoat J 11	Lyle W 30 + 2	Smith J 17	Hamilton R 15 + 10	McEwan C 31 + 3	Tyrrell P 35	McCulloch S 9 + 1	Dempster J 17	Murdoch T 6 + 4	Hampshire S 19 + 4	Dillon J 18 + 4	Menzies C 8 + 13	Ferguson S 17 + 2	McLaughlin B 14 + 9	Gilbride A 30 + 1	Thomson A 6 + 2	Lindsay A 6 + 3	Love R 2 + 2	Flynn M 2	Desmond S 1 + 3	Johnstone S 1	Thom G 5 + 2	McManus S 2 + 4	Sideserf M 1	Felvus B — + 1	Brown A 24	Lennon G 10	Galloway R 6 + 1	Quitongo J 3 + 7	Gibson G 13 + 5	Dalziel S 15	McKeown J 1	Mailey P 12	Harty I 8 + 1	Lister J 1	Stewart M — + 1	*Match No.*
1	2	3	4[1]	5	6	7	8	9	10■	11	12																									1
1	2	3	4	5			8	9[2]		11	13	6[1]	12	7	10																					2
1	2	3	4[3]	5	6		8	9[2]	10	11[1]	14		12	7		13																				3
1	2	3		5[1]	6		8	9[2]	10	12	14		13	7	4	11[3]																				4
1	2	3	4[3]	5	6			9	10	11[1]	14		12	7	8[2]		13																			5
1	2	3	13	5	6		8		10	11[3]	12			7		9[1]		4[2]	14																	6
1	2	3		5	6		8		10	11	12			7		9[2]		4[1]	13																	7
1	2	3	4■	13	6	7[2]	8[1]	12	10		9	5■		11																						8
		3		12	6[1]		8		10		2		7[2]	5					13	1	4	9[3]	11	14												9
	2	3	13	5	6		8[2]	12	10[1]	4		11	9												1	7										10
	2		12	5	6		8[2]	13	10[3]	11[1]	7		9	4	14										1	3										11
	2		4	5	6		8	9[1]	10[2]	11			13	3							7				1		12									12
			4	5	6		8[3]	14		10[2]	12	11		3	9										1	7[1]	2	13								13
	13		4	5	6		8		14	11	12[2]	7		3	9[3]										1	10	2[1]									14
	14		4[2]	5	6		8		13	11[3]		10		3	9										1	2	7[1]	12								15
	2		12	5	6		8[2]		10[1]	11		9		3	13										1	7	4									16
	2		9	5	6		8		10[1]			7		11											1	4	3		12							17
	2		9[2]	5	6		8[3]		10			11	12	3							14				1	7■	4[1]		13							18
	3			2	6				10			8	11	5							4	12			1				7	9[1]						19
	3			2	6				10[1]			8	11[2]	5							13	12			1	4			7	9						20
1	3		12		6				10			8		5												4		7[1]	11	9	2					21
1	3			2	6	14			10[2]	11		8		5														12	7[1]	9[3]		4	13			22
1	3			2	6	8				11[2]	13		12	5								14						10[1]	7[3]	9		4				23
	5			2	8	4					12		9	7		11[1]									1				6	10		3				24
	3			2	8	5			14		13	12[2]	11	6[3]		10[1]									1				7	9		4				25
	7[2]		12	2	6	3			10	11			8	5[1]											1			13		9		4				26
	7		12	2	8	6			14	3[2]			11	4											1				13	9[3]		5[1]	10			27
	3		8[1]	2	6								11	4		12									1				7	9		5	10			28
	3	5	8[3]	2	6					14	13		11	12											1				7	9[2]		4[1]	10■			29
		3	12	13	7	5				9	2[1]		11	4		6[3]									1			14	10[2]					8		30
	11	5	7[3]	2	6	3[1]				12		8										10[2]			1			14	13			4	9			31
	5	4		2	7							8	9[2]	6											1			13	12	10		3[1]	11			32
		5	11[2]		6						3	8	12			13					2■				1				7	9[1]		4	10			33
	7[1]	5	12	2[3]	6						3	8	11[2]				13					14			1					9■		4	10			34
	7	5	12	2	6[1]					14	3		13	4			10[2]								1			11[3]	9				8			35
	2			3	6						10	12		5			11		7[2]		4				1				8[1]	9					13	36

STIRLING ALBION — Second Division

Year Formed: 1945. *Ground & Address:* Forthbank Stadium, Springkerse Industrial Estate, Stirling FK7 7UJ. *Telephone:* 01786 450399. *Fax:* 01786 448400. *Email:* stirlingalbion@btconnect.com *Website:* www.stirlingalbionfc.co.uk
Ground Capacity: 3808, seated: 2508. *Size of Pitch:* 110yd × 74yd.
Chairman: Peter McKenzie. *Secretary:* Mrs Marlyn Hallam.
Manager: Allan Moore. *Assistant Manager:* John O'Neill. *Physio:* Andy Myles.
Club Nickname(s): The Binos. *Previous Grounds:* Annfield 1945-92.
Record Attendance: 26,400 (at Annfield) v Celtic, Scottish Cup 4th rd, 14 Mar 1959; 3808 v Aberdeen, Scottish Cup 4th rd, 15 February 1996 (Forthbank).
Record Transfer Fee received: £90,000 for Stephen Nicholas to Motherwell (Mar 1999).
Record Transfer Fee paid: £25,000 for Craig Taggart from Falkirk (Aug 1994).
Record Victory: 20-0 v Selkirk, Scottish Cup 1st rd, 8 Dec 1984.
Record Defeat: 0-9 v Dundee U, Division I, 30 Dec 1967.
Most League Appearances: 504: Matt McPhee, 1967-81.
Most League Goals in Season (Individual): 27: Joe Hughes, Division II, 1969-70.
Most Goals Overall (Individual): 129: Billy Steele, 1971-83.

STIRLING ALBION 2007–08 LEAGUE RECORD

Match No.	Date	Venue	Opponents	Result		H/T Score	Lg. Pos.	Goalscorers	Attendance
1	Aug 4	H	Partick Th	D	1-1	0-0	—	McKenna 74	2215
2	11	A	St Johnstone	D	2-2	2-1	6	McKenna 2 31, 45	2996
3	18	H	Morton	D	0-0	0-0	6		1538
4	25	A	Dunfermline Ath	L	1-2	0-0	8	Aitken (pen) 73	3921
5	Sept 1	H	Livingston	D	3-3	0-1	7	Tinkler (og) 64, McKenna 2 66, 75	972
6	15	A	Hamilton A	L	0-4	0-1	9		1749
7	22	H	Dundee	D	2-2	1-1	10	Bell 5, McKenna 50	1595
8	29	A	Queen of the S	D	2-2	1-0	10	Easton 17, McBride 88	1484
9	Oct 6	H	Clyde	L	0-2	0-2	10		946
10	20	A	Partick Th	D	1-1	1-1	10	Bell 44	2071
11	27	H	Dunfermline Ath	W	3-0	1-0	8	Cramb 33, Bell 75, McKenna 83	1590
12	Nov 3	A	Morton	D	1-1	0-1	9	Ellis 61	2850
13	10	A	Livingston	L	3-4	0-3	10	Bell 46, McBride 52, Cramb 53	1610
14	Dec 1	H	Hamilton A	L	2-4	0-2	10	Cramb 51, Aitken (pen) 71	1045
15	8	A	Dundee	L	1-3	0-0	10	Bell 89	3590
16	15	H	Queen of the S	L	1-3	1-1	10	Aitken (pen) 19	883
17	26	H	St Johnstone	D	0-0	0-0	10		1556
18	29	A	Dunfermline Ath	L	1-2	0-2	10	Aitken 58	4023
19	Jan 2	H	Morton	L	1-2	0-0	10	Aitken 62	1256
20	5	A	Hamilton A	D	0-0	0-0	10		1410
21	19	H	Livingston	L	1-4	1-2	10	Paartalu 28	848
22	26	A	St Johnstone	L	1-2	0-1	10	Aitken 51	2482
23	Feb 2	A	Clyde	W	3-1	0-0	10	Taggart 54, Aitken 2 (1 pen) 66 (p), 78	960
24	9	H	Partick Th	W	1-0	1-0	10	Allison 13	1306
25	16	A	Queen of the S	L	1-3	1-2	10	Aitken 16	2335
26	23	H	Dundee	L	1-6	0-2	10	Cramb 68	1419
27	Mar 1	A	Morton	L	1-2	0-1	10	Rodriguez 90	2355
28	15	H	Clyde	D	1-1	0-1	10	Aitken (pen) 65	1075
29	22	H	Hamilton A	L	0-1	0-1	10		975
30	25	H	Dunfermline Ath	L	2-3	2-1	—	Aitken (pen) 11, Bell 41	698
31	29	A	Livingston	L	1-2	1-1	10	Rodriguez 14	1125
32	Apr 5	H	Queen of the S	D	0-0	0-0	10		641
33	8	A	Partick Th	L	0-1	0-0	—		1267
34	12	A	Dundee	L	0-3	0-0	10		4129
35	23	H	St Johnstone	W	3-1	2-1	—	Aitken 2 (2 pens) 30, 32, Rodriguez 69	430
36	26	A	Clyde	L	0-3	0-1	10		1489

Final League Position: 10

Honours
League Champions: Division II 1952-53, 1957-58, 1960-61, 1964-65. Second Division 1976-77, 1990-91, 1995-96; *Runners-up:* Division II 1948-49, 1950-51. Third Division 2003-04.
League Cup: Semi-finals 1961-62.

Club colours: All red.

Goalscorers: *League* (41): Aitken 13 (8 pens), McKenna 7, Bell 6, Cramb 4, Rodriguez 3, McBride 2, Allison 1, Easton 1, Ellis 1, Paartalu 1, Taggart 1, own goal 1.
Scottish Cup (6): Aitken 2 (1 pen), Walker 2, Cramb 1, McKenna 1.
CIS Cup (1): McKenna 1.
Challenge Cup (1): Harris 1.

Hogarth M 24	Nugent P 31	Graham A 26	Tomana M 2 + 11	Forsyth R 18	Ellis L 33	Murphy P 8 + 2	Bell S 26 + 1	Gribben D 1 + 2	Lilley D 12 + 12	Taggart N 24 + 6	Walker N 6 + 3	Devine S 13 + 4	McKenna D 30 + 5	Aitken C 32 + 2	Hay C 9 + 5	Cramb C 10 + 13	Harris R 11 + 6	Reid C 13	McBride J 14 + 5	Easton W 6 + 1	Christie S 12	Paartalu E 10	Rodriguez J 10 + 1	Allison B 3	Churchill G — + 1	Moffat K — + 3	Lithgow A 2 + 1	McKay R 4	Malloy C 5	Muir G 1 + 5	Corr L — + 2	*Match No.*
1	2	3	4	5	6	7^2	8	9^3	10	11^1	12	13	14																			1
1	2	3			6	7	8	12	10^1	11^2		5	9	4	13																	2
1	2	3	12		6	7	8	13	10	11^1		5	9^2	4																		3
1	2	3	14		6	7^3	8		10	11^2		5	9^1	4		12	13															4
1	2	3			6		8		10^3	12			9	4		14	13	5	7^2	11^1												5
1	2^1	3			6	7^2	8		10^3	11			9	4		14		5	12	13												6
1	2	3		5	6		8		12		7		9	4		10^1				11												7
1		3^3		5	6		8		14	12	7^2		9	4	13			2	11	10^1												8
1		3^3	14	5	6		8		10^2		7^1		9	4		13		2	12	11												9
	2		12	5	6		8		13				9	14		10^2	4^3	3	7	11^1	1											10
	2		14	5	6		8		13	11^3			9^2	12		10	4	3	7^1		1											11
	2			5	6				12	11^2		13	9▮	7		10^1	4	3	8		1											12
	2			5	6		8		10	11						9	7▮	3	4		1											13
	2		14	5	6		8			11^3		13	7	4		12	10^1	3	9^2		1											14
1		3	13	5	6^1		8				14	11^2	9	7	12	10^3		2	4													15
1		3	14	5			8		12	13			11	6	2^3	10^1	7	4		9^2												16
1	2	3		5			8		12		9^1	4	10	6	7			11														17
1	2	3	14	5	9^1		8		10	12			7	6	4^2		13	11^3														18
1	2	5	11^2	3	4		8^1		10^3	13	14		9	6	7		12															19
	2	5		3	4				10		11^1		9	6	7		12				1	8										20
	2	5^3		11	4				13	14		3	9^2	6	7^1				12		1	8	10									21
1	2			3	5				13	11^3	7^1		9	6^2			12		8			10		4	14							22
1	2			5	4				13	9			10^3	8^2	12		6^1		7			11		3		14						23
1		5							13	11^2		3	9	6	2		7^1		10			8		4		12						24
1	2	5	14		4					9^2			10	6	3^3	12	7^1		11			8				13						25
1	2^1	4	12		3	14			10	11			9^2	6^3	7	13						8					5					26
1	2				5^2					11			10	6		12			7			8	13				4^1	3	9			27
1	2	5^3			4		12		14	11^2			13	6		9			7^1				10					3	8			28
1	2				4		7			11^2			12	6^3		9^1			14			5	10					3	8	13		29
1	2				4		7			11		12	10^2	6		13						5	9					3^1	8			30
1	2	5			4		7^1			11^3		3	10^2	6		13							9						8	12	14	31
	2	5			4	8	7			11^2		3	10^1	6		12					1		9							13		32
	2	3^3			4	7	6			9^1		5	12	8		11^2					1		10				14			13		33
	2	5			4	8^3	7			11^2		3	13	6	14						1		9							10^1	12	34
	2	5			4		7			11		3	9^2	6		13	8^1				1		10							12		35
	2	4			5	14	7			9		3^1	10^3	8		13	6^2		12		1		11									36

STRANRAER — Second Division

Year Formed: 1870. *Ground & Address:* Stair Park, London Rd, Stranraer DG9 8BS. *Telephone:* 01776 703271. *Fax:* 01776 889514. *E-mail:* grodgers_sfc@yahoo.co.uk. *Website:* www.stranraerfc.org
Ground Capacity: 5600, seated: 1830. *Size of Pitch:* 110yd × 70yd.
Chairman: Nigel Redhead. *Secretary:* Barney Duffy. *Commercial Manager:* Ian Alldred.
Manager: Derek Ferguson. *Physio:* Walter Cannon.
Club Nickname(s): The Blues. *Previous Grounds:* None.
Record Attendance: 6500 v Rangers, Scottish Cup 1st rd, 24 Jan 1948.
Record Transfer Fee received: £90,000 for Mark Campbell to Ayr U (1999).
Record Transfer Fee paid: £15,000 for Colin Harkness from Kilmarnock (Aug 1989).
Record Victory: 7-0 v Brechin C, Division II, 6 Feb 1965.
Record Defeat: 1-11 v Queen of the South, Scottish Cup 1st rd, 16 Jan 1932.
Most League Appearances: 301: Keith Knox, 1986-90; 1999-2001.
Most League Goals in Season (Individual): 59: Tommy Sloan.

STRANRAER 2007–08 LEAGUE RECORD

Match No.	Date	Venue	Opponents	Result		H/T Score	Lg. Pos.	Goalscorers	Attendance
1	Aug 4	H	Forfar Ath	W	3-0	1-0	—	Gillies 20, White 68, Mullen 72	377
2	11	A	Albion R	L	2-3	1-2	4	Gillies (pen) 35, Keogh 52	306
3	18	H	Montrose	W	1-0	0-0	—	Mullen 67	272
4	25	A	East Fife	L	1-3	0-2	6	Cashmore 65	614
5	Sept 1	H	Dumbarton	W	2-0	1-0	3	Mullen 17, Tade 84	343
6	15	A	East Stirling	W	3-2	0-1	2	Tade 59, Savage (og) 73, Mitchell 78	331
7	22	A	Stenhousemuir	W	4-1	0-0	2	Gibson 51, Tade 54, Mullen 63, White 77	356
8	29	H	Elgin C	D	3-3	1-2	2	Mullen 2 43, 89, Gibson (pen) 51	270
9	Oct 6	H	Arbroath	D	1-1	1-0	2	Mullen 27	320
10	20	A	Forfar Ath	D	1-1	0-1	3	Mullen 56	332
11	Nov 6	A	Montrose	W	4-2	3-0	—	Mullen 16, Gibson 34, Tade 41, Stewart 55	321
12	10	H	East Fife	L	0-2	0-1	3		487
13	16	A	Arbroath	D	2-2	1-1	—	Stewart 45, Kane 81	528
14	Dec 1	H	East Stirling	W	2-1	1-1	2	Tade 26, Stewart 90	241
15	8	A	Dumbarton	W	2-0	1-0	2	Stewart 16, Mitchell 87	478
16	15	H	Stenhousemuir	L	2-3	0-2	2	Stewart 2 52, 87	225
17	26	H	Albion R	W	3-1	1-0	2	Mullen 26, Nicoll 85, Mitchell 88	322
18	Jan 2	A	East Fife	L	1-2	0-0	3	Nicoll 67	1029
19	5	H	Montrose	L	0-2	0-0	3		187
20	19	H	Dumbarton	W	2-0	0-0	3	Tade 58, Cashmore 83	214
21	Feb 2	H	Forfar Ath	W	2-1	1-0	3	Tade 14, Gibson 77	147
22	9	H	Elgin C	D	0-0	0-0	3		191
23	16	A	Stenhousemuir	D	1-1	1-1	3	Mullen 30	381
24	23	A	Montrose	W	2-0	1-0	3	Bonar 44, McConalogue 52	514
25	27	A	Elgin C	W	5-0	3-0	—	Mitchell 1, Tade 38, McColm 43, McConalogue 65, Mullen 90	336
26	Mar 1	H	East Fife	L	0-2	0-1	2		260
27	4	A	East Stirling	W	3-1	0-0	—	Thywissen (og) 49, McColm 55, Cashmore 88	235
28	8	H	Arbroath	L	0-3	0-1	2		269
29	15	A	Forfar Ath	L	0-1	0-0	3		342
30	18	A	Albion R	D	1-1	1-1	—	Mitchell 9	238
31	22	H	East Stirling	W	2-1	1-1	2	Tade 21, Mullen 78	152
32	29	A	Dumbarton	W	1-0	0-0	2	Tade 66	512
33	Apr 5	H	Stenhousemuir	W	3-1	0-1	2	Gibson (pen) 74, McKinstry 75, Tade 90	135
34	12	A	Elgin C	W	3-2	1-1	2	Tade 10, Cochrane 83, Gibson 87	619
35	19	H	Albion R	W	3-0	1-0	2	McConalogue 28, White 75, Dobbins 85	172
36	26	A	Arbroath	D	0-0	0-0	2		431

Final League Position: 2

Honours
League Champions: Second Division 1993-94, 1997-98; *Runners-up:* 2004-05. Third Division 2003-04.
Qualifying Cup Winners: 1937.
Scottish Cup: Quarter-finals 2003
League Challenge Cup Winners: 1996-97.

Club colours: Shirt: Blue with white side panels. Shorts: Blue with white side panels. Stockings: Blue with two white hoops.

Goalscorers: *League* (65): Mullen 13, Tade 12, Gibson 6 (2 pens), Stewart 6, Mitchell 5, Cashmore 3, McConalogue 3, White 3, Gillies 2 (1 pen), McColm 2, Nicoll 2, Bonar 1, Cochrane 1, Dobbins 1, Kane 1, Keogh 1, McKinstry 1, own goals 2.
Play-offs (5): Tade 2, Gibson 1 (pen), McConalogue 1, Mullen 1.
Scottish Cup (2): Keogh 1 (pen), Tade 1.
CIS Cup (1): Keogh 1.
Challenge Cup (0).

Black S 32	McKinstry J 29 + 2	Keogh P 3 + 2	Bonar S 22	White A 30 + 5	Kane J 28 + 3	McLaughlin G 26 + 3	Tade G 31 + 1	Mullen M 28 + 4	Gillies R 5 + 1	Gibson A 33 + 1	Cochrane J — + 9	Cashmore I 8 + 21	Caddis R — + 5	McCusker M 3 + 4	Ferguson A 4 + 1	Thomas M 5 + 1	Mitchell D 31	Beggs S — + 1	McColm S 5 + 5	McGowan N 8	Coakley A 1 + 3	Stewart M 8	Creaney J 9 + 3	McLoughlin J — + 1	Paddy G 2	Paisley R — + 1	Nicoll K 2 + 3	Payne S 1	Noble S 14 + 2	McConalogue S 12 + 3	Dobbins I 13	Gribben D 3 + 6	*Match No.*
1	2	3	4	5	6	7	8^{3}	9^{2}	10^{1}	11	13	12	14																				1
1	2	3	4	5	6	7	8	9^{2}	10^{3}	11^{1}		13	12	14																			2
1^{6}			4	5	6	7		12	10	11		8^{1}	13	9^{2}	15	2	3																3
	13		4	5	6	7	12		10	11^{3}		8		9^{1}	1	2^{2}	3	14															4
1	2		4^{3}	12	6	7	8	9	13	11		10^{2}		14		5^{1}	3																5
1	2	12	4	13	6	7	8	9^{3}	10^{1}	11		14				5^{2}	3																6
1	2	3	4	12	6	7	8	9^{3}		11		13		14		5^{1}	10^{7}																7
	2		4^{2}	5	6	7	8	9		11		10^{1}	13	12	1		3																8
	2		4	5	6	7	8	9		11		12		10^{1}	1		3																9
	2		4	5	6	7	8	9		11		10^{1}			1		3		12														10
1	2			5	6	7	8	9^{1}		11		13					4			3	12	10^{2}											11
1	2■			5	6	7				11^{3}		12					8				10^{1}	9	3^{2}	13	4	14							12
1		14	4^{1}	5	6	7	8			11		13^{3}					10			3^{2}	12	9	2										13
1			4	5	6	7	8	9^{1}		11		13					2			3	12	10^{2}											14
1			4	5	6	7	8	9^{2}		11^{1}		13					2			3		10					12						15
1			4^{2}	5		7		9		11	13						2			3		10			8		12	6^{1}					16
1	13		4	5	6■	7	8	9^{2}		11^{1}		14					2			3		10^{3}					12						17
1	2		8	6^{2}		7	5	10		12■		13					3			4		11^{1}					9						18
1	2		8	3^{1}	4	6	7	9			12	11					10			5													19
1	2^{2}		8	3		6	7	9^{3}			14	11				12	5										4^{1}		13	10			20
1	2		8^{2}	3	13	5	11	9^{3}		7		10^{1}					6													12	4	14	21
1	2		6^{3}	3	12	5^{1}	11	9		7		13					8												14		4	10^{2}	22
1	2		6	3	5		11	9^{1}		7	13	12																	8		4	10^{2}	23
1	2		7^{1}	5	4		9	14		6		13					8^{2}		10				12						3	11^{3}			24
1	2^{2}			3	6	13■	11	12		7		14					8		9^{1}										5	10^{3}	4		25
1	2			3^{3}	8		11	9^{1}		7							6		12				14						5	10^{2}	4	13	26
1	2			3	6	12	11^{1}			7		13					8		9^{2}										5	10^{3}	4	14	27
1	2			3	6	5		13		7			12				8		9^{3}										11^{2}	10^{1}	4	14	28
1	2			3	6^{1}		11	9^{2}		7							8		10^{3}				12						5	14	4■	13	29
1	2			5		4	11	9^{1}		7							8		12				3						6	10			30
1	2				12	5	11	9^{3}		7		13					8		14				3						6^{1}	10^{2}	4		31
1	2			12	7		9	10^{2}		6	13						8^{1}						5						4	11	3		32
1	2			13	6^{2}		11	9^{3}		7	14	12					8						3						5	10^{1}	4		33
1	2			8		12	11	9^{2}		7	13						6^{1}						3						5	14	4	10^{3}	34
1	2			8	6^{2}		11	9^{3}		7	14	13							12				3						5	10^{1}	4		35
1	2			8	6	4	11	9^{1}		7		13											3						5	10^{2}		12	36

SCOTTISH LEAGUE PLAY-OFFS 2007–08

SCOTTISH DIVISION 1 SEMI-FINALS FIRST LEG

Wednesday, 30 April 2008

Alloa Ath (1) 2 *(Scott 31, Coakley 83)*

Clyde (0) 1 *(Masterton 62)* 1026

Alloa Ath: Jellema; McClune, Fleming, Townsley, Forrest, Grant, Scott (Coakley), McKeown, Ferguson A (Ferguson B), Agnew, Brown (McAuley).
Clyde: Hutton; McGregor, Gibson B, Higgins, Bestvina, Masterton (Gibson J), McKay (Bradley), Ruari MacLennan, Arbuckle (McGowan D), Clarke, McGowan M.

Raith R (0) 0

Airdrie U (2) 2 *(Russell 31, 39)* 2841

Raith R: Fahey; Wilson, Pelosi, Campbell, Davidson, Silvestro, Borris (Templeton), Henderson, Hislop (Weir), Goodwillie, Sloan.
Airdrie U: Robertson; Smith, Lovering (Waddle), McDonald, Smyth, Donnelly, Andreoni, Prunty (Watt), Russell, Holmes, Noble (Gillies).

SCOTTISH DIVISION 1 SEMI-FINALS SECOND LEG

Saturday, 3 May 2008

Airdrie U (1) 2 *(Prunty 10, Donnelly 77)*

Raith R (1) 2 *(Weir 18 (pen), 88)* 2077

Airdrie U: Robertson; Smith, Lovering, McDonald, Smyth, Donnelly, Andreoni, Prunty (Watt), Russell (Gillies), Holmes, Noble (Waddle).
Raith R: Brown; Wilson, Pelosi, Campbell, Davidson, Tod, Henderson, Silvestro (Carcary), Weir, Goodwillie (Bryce), Sloan.

Clyde (1) 5 *(Gibson J 30, Arbuckle 64, Gibson B 68, McSwegan 84, Clarke 111)*

Alloa Ath (2) 3 *(Ferguson B 40, Forrest 42, Bestvina 46 (og))* 1648

Clyde: Hutton; Higgins, Bestvina (McGowan M), Gibson B, Masterton, Wilson, Gibson J (McKay), Ruari MacLennan, Bradley (McSwegan), Arbuckle, Clarke.
Alloa Ath: Jellema; McClune, Townsley, Forrest, Fleming, Grant, Ferguson B (Scott), McKeown, McAuley, Brown (Ferguson A), Agnew (Hodge).
aet.

SCOTTISH DIVISION 1 FINAL FIRST LEG

Wednesday, 7 May 2008

Airdrie U (0) 0

Clyde (0) 1 *(Clarke 77)* 1878

Airdrie U: Robertson; Smith, Lovering, McDonald, Smyth, Donnelly (Waddle), Andreoni, Prunty (Watt), Russell, Holmes, Noble (Gillies).
Clyde: Hutton; Masterton, Gibson B, Higgins, Gibson J, Wilson (Albertz), Bradley (McSwegan), Ruari MacLennan, Arbuckle (McKay), Clarke, McGowan M.

SCOTTISH DIVISION 1 FINAL SECOND LEG

Saturday, 10 May 2008

Clyde (0) 2 *(McSwegan 47, Clarke 65)*

Airdrie U (0) 0 2561

Clyde: Hutton; McGregor, Higgins (McGowan M), Masterton, Ruari MacLennan, Wilson, Gibson J, Gibson B, Bradley, McSwegan (Arbuckle) (McKay), Clarke.
Airdrie U: Robertson; Campbell (Watt), Smyth (Smith), Andreoni, Lovering, McDonald, Waddle, Holmes, Noble, Prunty, Russell.

SCOTTISH DIVISION 2 SEMI-FINALS FIRST LEG

Wednesday, 30 April 2008

Arbroath (0) 1 *(Watson 58)*

Cowdenbeath (0) 1 *(Scullion 75 (pen))* 638

Arbroath: Hill; Rennie (McMullen), Black, Rattray, Bishop, Tully, Lunan, Reilly (Scott B), Brazil, Sellars, Watson.
Cowdenbeath: Hay; Shields, Adamson, Shanks, Hill (Linton), O'Neil, Ramsey, Scullion, McLaughlin, McQuade (Gates), Tomana.

Montrose (1) 1 *(Wood 27)*

Stranraer (0) 1 *(McConalogue 54)* 678

Montrose: Peat; Buchan, McLeod (Black), Cumming, Forsyth (Gardiner), Doris, Gibson, Davidson, Stein, Wood, Baird■.
Stranraer: Black; McKinstry, Kane, Noble, Creaney, Gibson, White, Bonar (Gribben) (Cashmore), Tade, Mullen (Cochrane), McConalogue.

SCOTTISH DIVISION 2 SEMI-FINALS SECOND LEG

Saturday, 3 May 2008

Cowdenbeath (0) 1 *(McQuade 71)*

Arbroath (0) 2 *(Black 83, Raeside 115)* 778

Cowdenbeath: Hay; Shields, Shanks, Hill, Adamson, Scullion, O'Neil (McQuade), Tomana (Robertson), Ramsey, McLaughlin, Gates (Linton).
Arbroath: Hill; McMullen, Raeside, Bishop, Black, Lunan, Tully (Rennie), Campbell (McBride), Scott B (Watson), Brazil, Sellars.
aet.

Stranraer (0) 3 *(Tade 68, Mullen 79, Gibson 88 (pen))*

Montrose (0) 0 484

Stranraer: Black; McKinstry, Creaney, Kane, Noble, Mitchell (Bonar), Gibson, White, Mullen (Cashmore), McConalogue (Cochrane), Tade.
Montrose: Peat; Buchan, Gardiner (Hunter), McLeod, Cumming, Gibson, Doris, Davidson, Wood (Stewart), Baird, Stein (Black).

SCOTTISH DIVISION 2 FINAL FIRST LEG

Wednesday, 7 May 2008

Arbroath (1) 2 *(Raeside 43, Sellars 60)*

Stranraer (0) 0 1016

Arbroath: Hill; Rennie (McMullan), Black, Raeside, Bishop, Tully, Lunan (Masson), Campbell (Reilly), Brazil, Sellars, Watson.
Stranraer: Black; Kane, Creaney, Dobbins, Noble, Mitchell, Gibson, White, Mullen (Cashmore), McConalogue, Tade.

SCOTTISH DIVISION 2 FINAL SECOND LEG

Saturday, 10 May 2008

Stranraer (0) 1 *(Tade 63)*

Arbroath (0) 0 680

Stranraer: Black; Kane, Noble (Nicoll), Dobbins, McLaughlin (Cochrane), Mitchell, McKinistry, White, Mullen, McConalogue, Tade.
Arbroath: Hill; Rennie, Black, Raeside, Bishop, Tully■, Lunan, Campbell (Rattray), Brazil (Reilly), Sellars, Watson (McMullan).

SCOTTISH LEAGUE HONOURS 1890 to 2008

*On goal average (ratio)/difference. †Held jointly after indecisive play-off. ‡Won on deciding match. ††Held jointly. ¶Two points deducted for fielding ineligible player. Competition suspended 1940–45 during war; Regional Leagues operating. ‡‡Two points deducted for registration irregularities. §Not promoted after play-offs.

PREMIER LEAGUE

	First	Pts	Second	Pts	Third	Pts
			Maximum points: 108			
1998–99	Rangers	77	Celtic	71	St Johnstone	57
1999–2000	Rangers	90	Celtic	69	Hearts	54
			Maximum points: 114			
2000–01	Celtic	97	Rangers	82	Hibernian	66
2001–02	Celtic	103	Rangers	85	Livingston	58
2002–03	Rangers*	97	Celtic	97	Hearts	63
2003–04	Celtic	98	Rangers	81	Hearts	68
2004–05	Rangers	93	Celtic	92	Hibernian*	61
2005–06	Celtic	91	Hearts	74	Rangers	73
2006–07	Celtic	84	Rangers	72	Aberdeen	65
2007–08	Celtic	89	Rangers	86	Motherwell	60

PREMIER DIVISION

	First	Pts	Second	Pts	Third	Pts
			Maximum points: 72			
1975–76	Rangers	54	Celtic	48	Hibernian	43
1976–77	Celtic	55	Rangers	46	Aberdeen	43
1977–78	Rangers	55	Aberdeen	53	Dundee U	40
1978–79	Celtic	48	Rangers	45	Dundee U	44
1979–80	Aberdeen	48	Celtic	47	St Mirren	42
1980–81	Celtic	56	Aberdeen	49	Rangers*	44
1981–82	Celtic	55	Aberdeen	53	Rangers	43
1982–83	Dundee U	56	Celtic*	55	Aberdeen	55
1983–84	Aberdeen	57	Celtic	50	Dundee U	47
1984–85	Aberdeen	59	Celtic	52	Dundee U	47
1985–86	Celtic*	50	Hearts	50	Dundee U	47
			Maximum points: 88			
1986–87	Rangers	69	Celtic	63	Dundee U	60
1987–88	Celtic	72	Hearts	62	Rangers	60
			Maximum points: 72			
1988–89	Rangers	56	Aberdeen	50	Celtic	46
1989–90	Rangers	51	Aberdeen*	44	Hearts	44
1990–91	Rangers	55	Aberdeen	53	Celtic*	41
			Maximum points: 88			
1991–92	Rangers	72	Hearts	63	Celtic	62
1992–93	Rangers	73	Aberdeen	64	Celtic	60
1993–94	Rangers	58	Aberdeen	55	Motherwell	54
			Maximum points: 108			
1994–95	Rangers	69	Motherwell	54	Hibernian	53
1995–96	Rangers	87	Celtic	83	Aberdeen*	55
1996–97	Rangers	80	Celtic	75	Dundee U	60
1997–98	Celtic	74	Rangers	72	Hearts	67

FIRST DIVISION

	First	Pts	Second	Pts	Third	Pts
			Maximum points: 52			
1975–76	Partick Th	41	Kilmarnock	35	Montrose	30
			Maximum points: 78			
1976–77	St Mirren	62	Clydebank	58	Dundee	51
1977–78	Morton*	58	Hearts	58	Dundee	57
1978–79	Dundee	55	Kilmarnock*	54	Clydebank	54
1979–80	Hearts	53	Airdrieonians	51	Ayr U*	44
1980–81	Hibernian	57	Dundee	52	St Johnstone	51
1981–82	Motherwell	61	Kilmarnock	51	Hearts	50
1982–83	St Johnstone	55	Hearts	54	Clydebank	50
1983–84	Morton	54	Dumbarton	51	Partick Th	46
1984–85	Motherwell	50	Clydebank	48	Falkirk	45
1985–86	Hamilton A	56	Falkirk	45	Kilmarnock	44
			Maximum points: 88			
1986–87	Morton	57	Dunfermline Ath	56	Dumbarton	53
1987–88	Hamilton A	56	Meadowbank Th	52	Clydebank	49
			Maximum points: 78			
1988–89	Dunfermline Ath	54	Falkirk	52	Clydebank	48
1989–90	St Johnstone	58	Airdrieonians	54	Clydebank	44
1990–91	Falkirk	54	Airdrieonians	53	Dundee	52
			Maximum points: 88			
1991–92	Dundee	58	Partick Th*	57	Hamilton A	57
1992–93	Raith R	65	Kilmarnock	54	Dunfermline Ath	52
1993–94	Falkirk	66	Dunfermline Ath	65	Airdrieonians	54
			Maximum points: 108			
1994–95	Raith R	69	Dunfermline Ath*	68	Dundee	68
1995–96	Dunfermline Ath	71	Dundee U*	67	Morton	67
1996–97	St Johnstone	80	Airdieonians	60	Dundee*	58
1997–98	Dundee	70	Falkirk	65	Raith R*	60

	First	*Pts*	*Second*	*Pts*	*Third*	*Pts*
1998–99	Hibernian	89	Falkirk	66	Ayr U	62
1999–2000	St Mirren	76	Dunfermline Ath	71	Falkirk	68
2000–01	Livingston	76	Ayr U	69	Falkirk	56
2001–02	Partick Th	66	Airdrieonians	56	Ayr U	52
2002–03	Falkirk	81	Clyde	72	St Johnstone	67
2003–04	Inverness CT	70	Clyde	69	St Johnstone	57
2004–05	Falkirk	75	St Mirren*	60	Clyde	60
2005–06	St Mirren	76	St Johnstone	66	Hamilton A	59
2006–07	Gretna	66	St Johnstone	65	Dundee*	53
2007–08	Hamilton A	76	Dundee	69	St Johnstone	58

SECOND DIVISION

Maximum points: 52

	First	*Pts*	*Second*	*Pts*	*Third*	*Pts*
1975–76	Clydebank*	40	Raith R	40	Alloa Ath	35

Maximum points: 78

	First	*Pts*	*Second*	*Pts*	*Third*	*Pts*
1976–77	Stirling A	55	Alloa Ath	51	Dunfermline Ath	50
1977–78	Clyde*	53	Raith R	53	Dunfermline Ath	48
1978–79	Berwick R	54	Dunfermline Ath	52	Falkirk	50
1979–80	Falkirk	50	East Stirling	49	Forfar Ath	46
1980–81	Queen's Park	50	Queen of the S	46	Cowdenbeath	45
1981–82	Clyde	59	Alloa Ath*	50	Arbroath	50
1982–83	Brechin C	55	Meadowbank Th	54	Arbroath	49
1983–84	Forfar Ath	63	East Fife	47	Berwick R	43
1984–85	Montrose	53	Alloa Ath	50	Dunfermline Ath	49
1985–86	Dunfermline Ath	57	Queen of the S	55	Meadowbank Th	49
1986–87	Meadowbank Th	55	Raith R*	52	Stirling A*	52
1987–88	Ayr U	61	St Johnstone	59	Queen's Park	51
1988–89	Albion R	50	Alloa Ath	45	Brechin C	43
1989–90	Brechin C	49	Kilmarnock	48	Stirling A	47
1990–91	Stirling A	54	Montrose	46	Cowdenbeath	45
1991–92	Dumbarton	52	Cowdenbeath	51	Alloa Ath	50
1992–93	Clyde	54	Brechin C*	53	Stranraer	53
1993–94	Stranraer	56	Berwick R	48	Stenhousemuir*	47

Maximum points: 108

	First	*Pts*	*Second*	*Pts*	*Third*	*Pts*
1994–95	Morton	64	Dumbarton	60	Stirling A	58
1995–96	Stirling A	81	East Fife	67	Berwick R	60
1996–97	Ayr U	77	Hamilton A	74	Livingston	64
1997–98	Stranraer	61	Clydebank	60	Livingston	59
1998–99	Livingston	77	Inverness CT	72	Clyde	53
1999–2000	Clyde	65	Alloa Ath	64	Ross Co	62
2000–01	Partick Th	75	Arbroath	58	Berwick R*	54
2001–02	Queen of the S	67	Alloa Ath	59	Forfar Ath	53
2002–03	Raith R	59	Brechin C	55	Airdrie U	54
2003–04	Airdrie U	70	Hamilton A	62	Dumbarton	60
2004–05	Brechin C	72	Stranraer	63	Morton	62
2005–06	Gretna	88	Morton§	70	Peterhead*§	57
2006–07	Morton	77	Stirling A	69	Raith R§	62
2007–08	Ross Co	73	Airdrie U	66	Raith R§	60

THIRD DIVISION

Maximum points: 108

	First	*Pts*	*Second*	*Pts*	*Third*	*Pts*
1994–95	Forfar Ath	80	Montrose	67	Ross Co	60
1995–96	Livingston	72	Brechin C	63	Inverness CT	57
1996–97	Inverness CT	76	Forfar Ath*	67	Ross Co	67
1997–98	Alloa Ath	76	Arbroath	68	Ross Co*	67
1998–99	Ross Co	77	Stenhousemuir	64	Brechin C	59
1999–2000	Queen's Park	69	Berwick R	66	Forfar Ath	61
2000–01	Hamilton A*	76	Cowdenbeath	76	Brechin C	72
2001–02	Brechin C	73	Dumbarton	61	Albion R	59
2002–03	Morton	72	East Fife	71	Albion R	70
2003–04	Stranraer	79	Stirling A	77	Gretna	68
2004–05	Gretna	98	Peterhead	78	Cowdenbeath	51
2005–06	Cowdenbeath*	76	Berwick R§	76	Stenhousemuir§	73
2006–07	Berwick R	75	Arbroath§	70	Queen's Park	68
2007–08	East Fife	88	Stranraer	65	Montrose§	59

FIRST DIVISION to 1974–75

Maximum points: a 36; *b* 44; *c* 40; *d* 52; *e* 60; *f* 68; g 76; *h* 84.

1890–91*a*	Dumbarton††	29	Rangers††	29	Celtic	21
1891–92*b*	Dumbarton	37	Celtic	35	Hearts	34
1892–93*a*	Celtic	29	Rangers	28	St Mirren	20
1893–94*a*	Celtic	29	Hearts	26	St Bernard's	23
1894–95*a*	Hearts	31	Celtic	26	Rangers	22
1895–96*a*	Celtic	30	Rangers	26	Hibernian	24
1896–97*a*	Hearts	28	Hibernian	26	Rangers	25
1897–98*a*	Celtic	33	Rangers	29	Hibernian	22
1898–99*a*	Rangers	36	Hearts	26	Celtic	24
1899–1900*a*	Rangers	32	Celtic	25	Hibernian	24
1900–01*c*	Rangers	35	Celtic	29	Hibernian	25
1901–02*a*	Rangers	28	Celtic	26	Hearts	22
1902–03*b*	Hibernian	37	Dundee	31	Rangers	29
1903–04*d*	Third Lanark	43	Hearts	39	Celtic*	38
1904–05*d*	Celtic‡	41	Rangers	41	Third Lanark	35

	First	Pts	Second	Pts	Third	Pts
1905–06e	Celtic	49	Hearts	43	Airdrieonians	38
1906–07f	Celtic	55	Dundee	48	Rangers	45
1907–08f	Celtic	55	Falkirk	51	Rangers	50
1908–09f	Celtic	51	Dundee	50	Clyde	48
1909–10f	Celtic	54	Falkirk	52	Rangers	46
1910–11f	Rangers	52	Aberdeen	48	Falkirk	44
1911–12f	Rangers	51	Celtic	45	Clyde	42
1912–13f	Rangers	53	Celtic	49	Hearts*	41
1913–14g	Celtic	65	Rangers	59	Hearts*	54
1914–15g	Celtic	65	Hearts	61	Rangers	50
1915–16g	Celtic	67	Rangers	56	Morton	51
1916–17g	Celtic	64	Morton	54	Rangers	53
1917–18f	Rangers	56	Celtic	55	Kilmarnock*	43
1918–19f	Celtic	58	Rangers	57	Morton	47
1919–20h	Rangers	71	Celtic	68	Motherwell	57
1920–21h	Rangers	76	Celtic	66	Hearts	50
1921–22h	Celtic	67	Rangers	66	Raith R	51
1922–23g	Rangers	55	Airdrieonians	50	Celtic	46
1923–24g	Rangers	59	Airdrieonians	50	Celtic	46
1924–25g	Rangers	60	Airdrieonians	57	Hibernian	52
1925–26g	Celtic	58	Airdrieonians*	50	Hearts	50
1926–27g	Rangers	56	Motherwell	51	Celtic	49
1927–28g	Rangers	60	Celtic*	55	Motherwell	55
1928–29g	Rangers	67	Celtic	51	Motherwell	50
1929–30g	Rangers	60	Motherwell	55	Aberdeen	53
1930–31g	Rangers	60	Celtic	58	Motherwell	56
1931–32g	Motherwell	66	Rangers	61	Celtic	48
1932–33g	Rangers	62	Motherwell	59	Hearts	50
1933–34g	Rangers	66	Motherwell	62	Celtic	47
1934–35g	Rangers	55	Celtic	52	Hearts	50
1935–36g	Celtic	66	Rangers*	61	Aberdeen	61
1936–37g	Rangers	61	Aberdeen	54	Celtic	52
1937–38g	Celtic	61	Hearts	58	Rangers	49
1938–39g	Rangers	59	Celtic	48	Aberdeen	46
1946–47e	Rangers	46	Hibernian	44	Aberdeen	39
1947–48e	Hibernian	48	Rangers	46	Partick Th	36
1948–49e	Rangers	46	Dundee	45	Hibernian	39
1949–50e	Rangers	50	Hibernian	49	Hearts	43
1950–51e	Hibernian	48	Rangers*	38	Dundee	38
1951–52e	Hibernian	45	Rangers	41	East Fife	37
1952–53e	Rangers*	43	Hibernian	43	East Fife	39
1953–54e	Celtic	43	Hearts	38	Partick Th	35
1954–55e	Aberdeen	49	Celtic	46	Rangers	41
1955–56f	Rangers	52	Aberdeen	46	Hearts*	45
1956–57f	Rangers	55	Hearts	53	Kilmarnock	42
1957–58f	Hearts	62	Rangers	49	Celtic	46
1958–59f	Rangers	50	Hearts	48	Motherwell	44
1959–60f	Hearts	54	Kilmarnock	50	Rangers*	42
1960–61f	Rangers	51	Kilmarnock	50	Third Lanark	42
1961–62f	Dundee	54	Rangers	51	Celtic	46
1962–63f	Rangers	57	Kilmarnock	48	Partick Th	46
1963–64f	Rangers	55	Kilmarnock	49	Celtic*	47
1964–65f	Kilmarnock*	50	Hearts	50	Dunfermline Ath	49
1965–66f	Celtic	57	Rangers	55	Kilmarnock	45
1966–67f	Celtic	58	Rangers	55	Clyde	46
1967–68f	Celtic	63	Rangers	61	Hibernian	45
1968–69f	Celtic	54	Rangers	49	Dunfermline Ath	45
1969–70f	Celtic	57	Rangers	45	Hibernian	44
1970–71f	Celtic	56	Aberdeen	54	St Johnstone	44
1971–72f	Celtic	60	Aberdeen	50	Rangers	44
1972–73f	Celtic	57	Rangers	56	Hibernian	45
1973–74f	Celtic	53	Hibernian	49	Rangers	48
1974–75f	Rangers	56	Hibernian	49	Celtic	45

SECOND DIVISION to 1974–75

Maximum points: a 76; b 72; c 68; d 52; e 60; f 36; g 44.

	First	Pts	Second	Pts	Third	Pts
1893–94f	Hibernian	29	Cowlairs	27	Clyde	24
1894–95f	Hibernian	30	Motherwell	22	Port Glasgow	20
1895–96f	Abercorn	27	Leith Ath	23	Renton	21
1896–97f	Partick Th	31	Leith Ath	27	Kilmarnock*	21
1897–98f	Kilmarnock	29	Port Glasgow	25	Morton	22
1898–99f	Kilmarnock	32	Leith Ath	27	Port Glasgow	25
1899–1900f	Partick Th	29	Morton	28	Port Glasgow	20
1900–01f	St Bernard's	25	Airdrieonians	23	Abercorn	21
1901–02g	Port Glasgow	32	Partick Th	31	Motherwell	26
1902–03g	Airdrieonians	35	Motherwell	28	Ayr U*	27
1903–04g	Hamilton A	37	Clyde	29	Ayr U	28
1904–05g	Clyde	32	Falkirk	28	Hamilton A	27
1905–06g	Leith Ath	34	Clyde	31	Albion R	27
1906–07g	St Bernard's	32	Vale of Leven*	27	Arthurlie	27
1907–08g	Raith R	30	Dumbarton*‡‡	27	Ayr U	27
1908–09g	Abercorn	31	Raith R*	28	Vale of Leven	28
1909–10g	Leith Ath‡	33	Raith R	33	St Bernard's	27
1910–11g	Dumbarton	31	Ayr U	27	Albion R	25
1911–12g	Ayr U	35	Abercorn	30	Dumbarton	27

	First	*Pts*	*Second*	*Pts*	*Third*	*Pts*
1912–13*d*	Ayr U	34	Dunfermline Ath	33	East Stirling	32
1913–14*g*	Cowdenbeath	31	Albion R	27	Dunfermline Ath*	26
1914–15*d*	Cowdenbeath*	37	St Bernard's*	37	Leith Ath	37
1921–22*a*	Alloa Ath	60	Cowdenbeath	47	Armadale	45
1922–23*a*	Queen's Park	57	Clydebank¶	50	St Johnstone¶	45
1923–24*a*	St Johnstone	56	Cowdenbeath	55	Bathgate	44
1924–25*a*	Dundee U	50	Clydebank	48	Clyde	47
1925–26*a*	Dunfermline Ath	59	Clyde	53	Ayr U	52
1926–27*a*	Bo'ness	56	Raith R	49	Clydebank	45
1927–28*a*	Ayr U	54	Third Lanark	45	King's Park	44
1928–29*b*	Dundee U	51	Morton	50	Arbroath	47
1929–30*a*	Leith Ath*	57	East Fife	57	Albion R	54
1930–31*a*	Third Lanark	61	Dundee U	50	Dunfermline Ath	47
1931–32*a*	East Stirling*	55	St Johnstone	55	Raith R*	46
1932–33*c*	Hibernian	54	Queen of the S	49	Dunfermline Ath	47
1933–34*c*	Albion R	45	Dunfermline Ath*	44	Arbroath	44
1934–35*c*	Third Lanark	52	Arbroath	50	St Bernard's	47
1935–36*c*	Falkirk	59	St Mirren	52	Morton	48
1936–37*c*	Ayr U	54	Morton	51	St Bernard's	48
1937–38*c*	Raith R	59	Albion R	48	Airdrieonians	47
1938–39*c*	Cowdenbeath	60	Alloa Ath*	48	East Fife	48
1946–47*d*	Dundee	45	Airdrieonians	42	East Fife	31
1947–48*e*	East Fife	53	Albion R	42	Hamilton A	40
1948–49*e*	Raith R*	42	Stirling A	42	Airdrieonians*	41
1949–50*e*	Morton	47	Airdrieonians	44	Dunfermline Ath*	36
1950–51*e*	Queen of the S*	45	Stirling A	45	Ayr U*	36
1951–52*e*	Clyde	44	Falkirk	43	Ayr U	39
1952–53*e*	Stirling A	44	Hamilton A	43	Queen's Park	37
1953–54*e*	Motherwell	45	Kilmarnock	42	Third Lanark*	36
1954–55*e*	Airdrieonians	46	Dunfermline Ath	42	Hamilton A	39
1955–56*b*	Queen's Park	54	Ayr U	51	St Johnstone	49
1956–57*b*	Clyde	64	Third Lanark	51	Cowdenbeath	45
1957–58*b*	Stirling A	55	Dunfermline Ath	53	Arbroath	47
1958–59*b*	Ayr U	60	Arbroath	51	Stenhousemuir	46
1959–60*b*	St Johnstone	53	Dundee U	50	Queen of the S	49
1960–61*b*	Stirling A	55	Falkirk	54	Stenhousemuir	50
1961–62*b*	Clyde	54	Queen of the S	53	Morton	44
1962–63*b*	St Johnstone	55	East Stirling	49	Morton	48
1963–64*b*	Morton	67	Clyde	53	Arbroath	46
1964–65*b*	Stirling A	59	Hamilton A	50	Queen of the S	45
1965–66*b*	Ayr U	53	Airdrieonians	50	Queen of the S	47
1966–67*a*	Morton	69	Raith R	58	Arbroath	57
1967–68*b*	St Mirren	62	Arbroath	53	East Fife	49
1968–69*b*	Motherwell	64	Ayr U	53	East Fife*	48
1969–70*b*	Falkirk	56	Cowdenbeath	55	Queen of the S	50
1970–71*b*	Partick Th	56	East Fife	51	Arbroath	46
1971–72*b*	Dumbarton*	52	Arbroath	52	Stirling A	50
1972–73*b*	Clyde	56	Dumfermline Ath	52	Raith R*	47
1973–74*b*	Airdrieonians	60	Kilmarnock	58	Hamilton A	55
1974–75*a*	Falkirk	54	Queen of the S*	53	Montrose	53

Elected to First Division: 1894 Clyde; 1895 Hibernian; 1896 Abercorn; 1897 Partick Th; 1899 Kilmarnock; 1900 Morton and Partick Th; 1902 Port Glasgow and Partick Th; 1903 Airdrieonians and Motherwell; 1905 Falkirk and Aberdeen; 1906 Clyde and Hamilton A; 1910 Raith R; 1913 Ayr U and Dumbarton.

RELEGATED FROM PREMIER LEAGUE

1998–99 Dunfermline Ath
1999–2000 *No relegation due to League reorganization*
2000–01 St Mirren
2001–02 St Johnstone
2002–03 *No relegated team*
2003–04 Partick Th
2004–05 Dundee
2005–06 Livingston
2006–07 Dunfermline Ath
2007–08 Gretna

RELEGATED FROM PREMIER DIVISION

1974–75 *No relegation due to League reorganization*
1975–76 Dundee, St Johnstone
1976–77 Hearts, Kilmarnock
1977–78 Ayr U, Clydebank
1978–79 Hearts, Motherwell
1979–80 Dundee, Hibernian
1980–81 Kilmarnock, Hearts
1981–82 Partick Th, Airdrieonians
1982–83 Morton, Kilmarnock
1983–84 St Johnstone, Motherwell
1984–85 Dumbarton, Morton
1985–86 *No relegation due to League reorganization*
1986–87 Clydebank, Hamilton A
1987–88 Falkirk, Dunfermline Ath, Morton
1988–89 Hamilton A
1989–90 Dundee
1990–91 *None*
1991–92 St Mirren, Dunfermline Ath
1992–93 Falkirk, Airdrieonians
1993–94 *See footnote*
1994–95 Dundee U
1995–96 Partick Th, Falkirk
1996–97 Raith R
1997–98 Hibernian

RELEGATED FROM DIVISION 1

1974–75 *No relegation due to League reorganization*
1975–76 Dunfermline Ath, Clyde
1976–77 Raith R, Falkirk
1977–78 Alloa Ath, East Fife
1978–79 Montrose, Queen of the S
1979–80 Arbroath, Clyde
1980–81 Stirling A, Berwick R
1981–82 East Stirling, Queen of the S
1991–92 Montrose, Forfar Ath
1992–93 Meadowbank Th, Cowdenbeath
1993–94 *See footnote*
1994–95 Ayr U, Stranraer
1995–96 Hamilton A, Dumbarton
1996–97 Clydebank, East Fife
1997–98 Partick Th, Stirling A
1998–99 Hamilton A, Stranraer

1982–83 Dunfermline Ath, Queen's Park
1983–84 Raith R, Alloa Ath
1984–85 Meadowbank Th, St Johnstone
1985–86 Ayr U, Alloa Ath
1986–87 Brechin C, Montrose
1987–88 East Fife, Dumbarton
1988–89 Kilmarnock, Queen of the S
1989–90 Albion R, Alloa Ath
1990–91 Clyde, Brechin C
1999–2000 Clydebank
2000–01 Morton, Alloa Ath
2001–02 Raith R
2002–03 Alloa Ath, Arbroath
2003–04 Ayr U, Brechin C
2004–05 Partick Th, Raith R
2005–06 Stranraer, Brechin C
2006–07 Airdrie U, Ross Co
2007–08 Stirling A

RELEGATED FROM DIVISION 2

1994–95 Meadowbank Th, Brechin C
2000–01 Queen's Park, Stirling A
1995–96 Forfar Ath, Montrose
2001–02 Morton
1996–97 Dumbarton, Berwick R
2002–03 Stranraer, Cowdenbeath
1997–98 Stenhousemuir, Brechin C
2003–04 East Fife, Stenhousemuir
1998–99 East Fife, Forfar Ath
2004–05 Arbroath, Berwick R
1999–2000 Hamilton A**
2005–06 Dumbarton
2006–07 Stranraer, Forfar Ath
2007–08 Cowdenbeath, Berwick R

RELEGATED FROM DIVISION 1 (TO 1973–74)

1921–22 *Queen's Park, Dumbarton, Clydebank
1922–23 Albion R, Alloa Ath
1923–24 Clyde, Clydebank
1924–25 Third Lanark, Ayr U
1925–26 Raith R, Clydebank
1926–27 Morton, Dundee U
1927–28 Dunfermline Ath, Bo'ness
1928–29 Third Lanark, Raith R
1929–30 St Johnstone, Dundee U
1930–31 Hibernian, East Fife
1931–32 Dundee U, Leith Ath
1932–33 Morton, East Stirling
1933–34 Third Lanark, Cowdenbeath
1934–35 St Mirren, Falkirk
1935–36 Airdrieonians, Ayr U
1936–37 Dunfermline Ath, Albion R
1937–38 Dundee, Morton
1938–39 Queen's Park, Raith R
1946–47 Kilmarnock, Hamilton A
1947–48 Airdrieonians, Queen's Park
1948–49 Morton, Albion R
1949–50 Queen of the S, Stirling A
1950–51 Clyde, Falkirk
1951–52 Morton, Stirling A
1952–53 Motherwell, Third Lanark
1953–54 Airdrieonians, Hamilton A
1954–55 *No clubs relegated*
1955–56 Stirling A, Clyde
1956–57 Dunfermline Ath, Ayr U
1957–58 East Fife, Queen's Park
1958–59 Queen of the S, Falkirk
1959–60 Arbroath, Stirling A
1960–61 Ayr U, Clyde
1961–62 St Johnstone, Stirling A
1962–63 Clyde, Raith R
1963–64 Queen of the S, East Stirling
1964–65 Airdrieonians, Third Lanark
1965–66 Morton, Hamilton A
1966–67 St Mirren, Ayr U
1967–68 Motherwell, Stirling A
1968–69 Falkirk, Arbroath
1969–70 Raith R, Partick Th
1970–71 St Mirren, Cowdenbeath
1971–72 Clyde, Dunfermline Ath
1972–73 Kilmarnock, Airdrieonians
1973–74 East Fife, Falkirk

*Season 1921–22 – only 1 club promoted, 3 clubs relegated. ***15pts deducted for failing to field a team.*

Scottish League Championship wins: Rangers 51, Celtic 42, Aberdeen 4, Hearts 4, Hibernian 4, Dumbarton 2, Dundee 1, Dundee U 1, Kilmarnock 1, Motherwell 1, Third Lanark 1.

At the end of the 1993–94 season four divisions were created assisted by the admission of two new clubs Ross County and Caledonian Thistle. Only one club was promoted from Division 1 and Division 2. The three relegated from the Premier joined with teams finishing second to seventh in Division 1 to form the new Division 1. Five relegated from Division 1 combined with those who finished second to sixth to form a new Division 2 and the bottom eight in Division 2 linked with the two newcomers to form a new Division 3. At the end of the 1997–98 season the nine clubs remaining in the Premier Division plus the promoted team from Division 1 formed a breakaway Premier League. At the end of the 1999–2000 season two teams were added to the Scottish League. There was no relegation from the Premier League but two promoted from the First Division and three from each of the Second and Third Divisions. One team was relegated from the First Division and one from the Second Division, leaving 12 teams in each division. In season 2002–03, Falkirk were not promoted to the Premier League due to the failure of their ground to meet League rules. Inverness CT were promoted after a previous refusal in 2003–04 because of ground sharing. At the end of 2005–06 the Scottish League introduced play-offs for the team finishing second from the bottom of Division 1 against the winners of the second, third and fourth finishing teams in Division 2 and with a similar procedure for Division 2 and Division 3.

LEAGUE CHALLENGE FINALS 1991–2008

Year	*Winners*	*Runners-up*	*Score*
1990–91	Dundee	Ayr U	3-2
1991–92	Hamilton A	Ayr U	1-0
1992–93	Hamilton A	Morton	3-2
1993–94	Falkirk	St Mirren	3-0
1994–95	Airdrieonians	Dundee	3-2
1995–96	Stenhousemuir	Dundee U	0-0
	(Stenhousemuir won 5-4 on penalties)		
1996–97	Stranraer	St Johnstone	1-0
1997–98	Falkirk	Queen of the South	1-0
1998–99	no competition		
1999–2000	Alloa Ath	Inverness CT	4-4
	(Alloa Ath won 5-4 on penalties)		
2000–01	Airdrieonians	Livingston	2-2
	(Airdrieonians won 3-2 on penalties)		
2001–02	Airdrieonians	Alloa Ath	2-1
2002–03	Queen of the S	Brechin C	2-0
2003–04	Inverness CT	Airdrie U	2-0
2004–05	Falkirk	Ross Co	2-1
2005–06	St Mirren	Hamilton A	2-1
2006–07	Ross Co	Clyde	1-1
	(Ross Co won 5-4 on penalties)		
2007–08	St Johnstone	Dunfermline Ath	3-2

SCOTTISH LEAGUE CUP FINALS 1946–2008

Season	*Winners*	*Runners-up*	*Score*
1946–47	Rangers	Aberdeen	4-0
1947–48	East Fife	Falkirk	4-1 after 0-0 draw
1948–49	Rangers	Raith R	2-0
1949–50	East Fife	Dunfermline Ath	3-0
1950–51	Motherwell	Hibernian	3-0
1951–52	Dundee	Rangers	3-2
1952–53	Dundee	Kilmarnock	2-0
1953–54	East Fife	Partick Th	3-2
1954–55	Hearts	Motherwell	4-2
1955–56	Aberdeen	St Mirren	2-1
1956–57	Celtic	Partick Th	3-0 after 0-0 draw
1957–58	Celtic	Rangers	7-1
1958–59	Hearts	Partick Th	5-1
1959–60	Hearts	Third Lanark	2-1
1960–61	Rangers	Kilmarnock	2-0
1961–62	Rangers	Hearts	3-1 after 1-1 draw
1962–63	Hearts	Kilmarnock	1-0
1963–64	Rangers	Morton	5-0
1964–65	Rangers	Celtic	2-1
1965–66	Celtic	Rangers	2-1
1966–67	Celtic	Rangers	1-0
1967–68	Celtic	Dundee	5-3
1968–69	Celtic	Hibernian	6-2
1969–70	Celtic	St Johnstone	1-0
1970–71	Rangers	Celtic	1-0
1971–72	Partick Th	Celtic	4-1
1972–73	Hibernian	Celtic	2-1
1973–74	Dundee	Celtic	1-0
1974–75	Celtic	Hibernian	6-3
1975–76	Rangers	Celtic	1-0
1976–77	Aberdeen	Celtic	2-1
1977–78	Rangers	Celtic	2-1
1978–79	Rangers	Aberdeen	2-1
1979–80	Dundee U	Aberdeen	3-0 after 0-0 draw
1980–81	Dundee U	Dundee	3-0
1981–82	Rangers	Dundee U	2-1
1982–83	Celtic	Rangers	2-1
1983–84	Rangers	Celtic	3-2
1984–85	Rangers	Dundee U	1-0
1985–86	Aberdeen	Hibernian	3-0
1986–87	Rangers	Celtic	2-1
1987–88	Rangers	Aberdeen	3-3
		(Rangers won 5-3 on penalties)	
1988–89	Rangers	Aberdeen	3-2
1989–90	Aberdeen	Rangers	2-1
1990–91	Rangers	Celtic	2-1
1991–92	Hibernian	Dunfermline Ath	2-0
1992–93	Rangers	Aberdeen	2-1
1993–94	Rangers	Hibernian	2-1
1994–95	Raith R	Celtic	2-2
		(Raith R won 6-5 on penalties)	
1995–96	Aberdeen	Dundee	2-0
1996–97	Rangers	Hearts	4-3
1997–98	Celtic	Dundee U	3-0
1998–99	Rangers	St Johnstone	2-1
1999–2000	Celtic	Aberdeen	2-0
2000–01	Celtic	Kilmarnock	3-0
2001–02	Rangers	Ayr U	4-0
2002–03	Rangers	Celtic	2-1
2003–04	Livingston	Hibernian	2-0
2004–05	Rangers	Motherwell	5-1
2005–06	Celtic	Dunfermline Ath	3-0
2005–06	Celtic	Dunfermline Ath	3-0
2006–07	Hibernian	Kilmarnock	5-1
2007–08	Rangers	Dundee U	2-2
		(Rangers won 3-2 on penalties)	

SCOTTISH LEAGUE CUP WINS

Rangers 25, Celtic 13, Aberdeen 5, Hearts 4, Dundee 3, East Fife 3, Hibernian 3, Dundee U 2, Livingston 1, Motherwell 1, Partick Th 1, Raith R 1.

APPEARANCES IN FINALS

Rangers 31, Celtic 26, Aberdeen 12, Hibernian 9, Dundee 6, Dundee U 6, Hearts 6, Kilmarnock 5, Partick Th 4, Dunfermline Ath 3, East Fife 3, Motherwell 3, Raith R 2, St Johnstone 2, Ayr U 1, Falkirk 1, Livingston 1, Morton 1, St Mirren 1, Third Lanark 1.

CIS SCOTTISH LEAGUE CUP 2007–08

■ *Denotes player sent off.*

FIRST ROUND

Tuesday, 7 August 2007

Berwick R (1) 3 *(Gemmill 15 (pen), Bolochoweckyj 105, Wood 111)*

Stenhousemuir (0) 1 *(Lyle 90)* 346

Berwick R: O'Connor; Manson, Bolochoweckyj, Fraser (Greenhill D), Horn, McGroarty, Thomson, McLeish, McMullan (Swanson), Gemmill, Wood.
Stenhousemuir: Hillcoat; Lyle, Smith, Thomson (Thom), McKeown, Tyrrell (Menzies), McCulloch■, Dempster, Murdoch, Hampshire, Dillon (McLaughlin).
aet.

Brechin C (0) 0

Stirling Alb (1) 1 *(McKenna 31)* 403

Brechin C: Nelson C; Murie (Callaghan B), Walker R, Callaghan S (Ward), White, Walker S, Byers, Janczyk (King), Johnston, Russell, Smith D.
Stirling Alb: Hogarth; Nugent, Forsyth (Devine), Tomana (Walker), Graham, Ellis, Aitken, Bell, McKenna, Cramb (Gribben), Taggart.

Clyde (0) 0

Raith R (1) 3 *(Tod 21, Carcary 70, Weir 80)* 913

Clyde: Hutton; McGregor, Smith, Masterton (Ruari MacLennan), Potter, Higgins, Wilson, Bradley, Arbuckle, Imrie, McGowan M (McGowan D).
Raith R: Fahey; Wilson, Andrews, Pelosi, Campbell, Silvestro, Carcary (Darling), Tod, Weir (Helley), Sloan, Winter.

Cowdenbeath (0) 2 *(Clarke 69, Dalziel 77)*

Dumbarton (0) 0 266

Cowdenbeath: Hay; Baxter, Armstrong J, McBride■, Armstrong D, Hill, O'Neil (Scullion), Galloway, McConalogue (Dalziel), Clarke (Howatt), Anderson.
Dumbarton: Nugent■; Geggan, Hasswell, Tiernan (Gentile), O'Byrne, Craig, Hamilton, Campbell (Coyne), McFarlane (McQuilken), Canning, Russell.

Dundee (0) 2 *(Zemlik 47, Swankie 52)*

Morton (0) 0 2942

Dundee: Roy; Worrell, Griffin, McDonald, Dixon, Palenik, Robertson, Daquin (O'Brien), Swankie, Zemlik (Lyle), Sturm.
Morton: Robinson; Weatherson, Greacen, Finlayson (Shields), Harding (Graham), Walker, Millar (Keenan), Stevenson, McAnespie, McAlister, Templeman.

Forfar Ath (0) 0

Peterhead (1) 1 *(Istead 15)* 388

Forfar Ath: Wood; McNulty, Ovenstone, Beith, Smith, Dunn, Fraser, Grady (Stuart), Duell, Lumsden (Lombardi), Tulloch.
Peterhead: Will; Buchan, MacDonald, Sharp, McKay, Mann, Anderson, Keith, Mackay, Istead, Bavidge.

Hamilton A (1) 2 *(Offiong 30, McLeod 76)*

East Stirling (0) 1 *(McBride K 57 (pen))* 554

Hamilton A: Cerny; Parratt, Elebert, McJimpsey (Gibson), McCarthy, Easton, Wake (Gilhaney), McArthur, Davison (McLeod), Offiong, Neil.
East Stirling: Hill; Doyle, McBride K, McKenzie, Moffat, Thywissen, Brownlie, Brand, McBride P, McLaren (Kelly), Savage (Struthers■).

Livingston (3) 5 *(Craig 3, Snodgrass 36, MacKay 39, 83 (pen), Lowing 75 (og))*

Ayr U (0) 0 914

Livingston: Liberda; MacKay, Tinkler, Kennedy, James, McPake, Fox (Torrance), Dorrans, Snodgrass (Pesir), Hamill (Weir), Craig.
Ayr U: McGeown; Swift, Henderson, Hamilton, Lowing, Forrest, Stevenson, Casey, McLaren (Williams), Moore (Wardlaw), Dunn.

Queen's Park (2) 2 *(Canning 26, Trouten 40)*

Alloa Ath (0) 1 *(Mackie 65)* 429

Queen's Park: Cairns; Paton, Agostini, Kettlewell (Quinn), Sinclair, Canning, Dunlop, Trouten, Ronald (McGrady), Cairney, Ferry.
Alloa Ath: Creer; Clark, Fleming, Ferguson A (Mackie), Buist, McKeown, Grant, Fairbairn (Kelly), Brown, Agnew (Andrew), Ferguson B.

Ross Co (1) 3 *(Dowie 23, Barrowman 72, 90)*

Elgin C (1) 1 *(Charlesworth 44)* 817

Ross Co: Bullock; McCulloch, Keddie, Gunn (Shields), Golabek, Dowie, Scott, Adams, Moore (Higgins), Petrie, Barrowman.
Elgin C: Dunn; Campbell, Dickson, O'Donoghue, Dempsie■, Hind, Gibert, Martin (Smith), Kaczan, Ross, Charlesworth.

Wednesday, 8 August 2007

Arbroath (4) 4 *(Brazil 1, 6, Scott B 20, Sellars 22)*

Albion R (0) 2 *(Hunter 80, Chisholm 88)* 575

Arbroath: Morrison; Rennie (Black), Ferguson, Raeside (McMullan), Tully, Smith, Hegarty, Brazil (Watson), Scott B, Sellars, Reilly.
Albion R: Scott; Watson G, Reid, Donnelly, Benton (Chisholm), Donald (Friel), Dimilta, McKenzie (Wright), Hunter, Adams, Walker P.

East Fife (0) 1 *(McDonald 63)*

Queen of the S (0) 0 693

East Fife: McCulloch; McDonald, Linton, Fotheringham, Smart, Tweed, Walker (McManus), Stewart, Young, Gordon (O'Reilly), Cameron.
Queen of the S: Grindlay; Paton, Harris■, Aitken, Lauchlan, MacFarlane, Scally, Tosh, Dobbie (O'Connor), Gilmour (McQuilken), Bingham (Mole).

Partick Th (1) 2 *(Harkins 14, Murray 88)*

Airdrie U (0) 1 *(McKenna 61)* 2025

Partick Th: Tuffey; Storey, Twaddle, Chaplain (Donnelly), Harkins, Archibald, Connor (Strachan), Rowson, Murray, Roberts, Buchanan (McStay).
Airdrie U: Robertson; McKenna, Smyth, McKeown, Lovering (Sharp), Smith, McDonald, McDougall, Holmes, Waddell (Noble), Russell.

Stranraer (0) 1 *(Keogh 54)*

Montrose (2) 2 *(Stein 17, Gibson 34)* 289

Stranraer: Black; McKinstry (Cashmore), White, Kane (Cochrane), Keogh, McLaughlan, Tade, Bonar, Mullen, Gilles, Gibson (Caddis).
Montrose: Peat; Cumming, Thomson■, McLeod, Dobbins, Gardiner, Davidson, Gibson (Donachie), Rogers (Baird), Wood, Stein.

SECOND ROUND

Tuesday, 28 August 2007

Berwick R (1) 2 *(Diack 10, Parratt 65 (og))*

Hamilton A (1) 3 *(Winters 15, Wake 55, 75)* 402

Berwick R: O'Connor; Noble, Bolochoweckyj, Greenhill D (Gemmill), Horn, Smith J, McLeish, Lennox (McMullan), Diack, Swanson (Thomson), Wood.
Hamilton A: Halliwell; McArthur, Parratt, Gibson, Swailes, Elebert, Stevenson (Neil), McCarthy, Gilhaney (McLeod), Offiong (Wake), Winters.

Dundee (1) 2 *(Robertson 33, Lyle 88 (pen))*

Livingston (1) 2 *(Mitchell 8, Craig 49)* 2355

Dundee: Samson; Worrell, MacKenzie, McDonald, Dixon, Palenik, Robertson, Daquin, Davidson (Lyle), Zemlik (Sturm), Swankie (O'Brien).
Livingston: Liberda; Mitchell, McCaffrey, Kennedy, McPake, MacKay, Fox, Dorrans, Snodgrass, Pesir, Craig (Weir) (Griffiths).
aet; Dundee won 6-5 on penalties.

Gretna (0) 3 *(Barr 52, Yantorno 85, Jenkins 88)*
Cowdenbeath (1) 1 *(O'Neil 13)* 342
Gretna: Fleming; Barr, Skelton, Osman, Cowan, Grainger (Collin), Paartalu (Deverdics), Jenkins, Yantorno, McMenamin, Graham (McLaren).
Cowdenbeath: Hay; Baxter, Armstrong J, Armstrong D, Adamson, Scullion, Gilfillan, O'Neil (Howatt), Galloway, Deasley (Hill), Dalziel (McConalogue).

Inverness CT (1) 3 *(Niculae 34, 74, Wyness 64)*
Arbroath (0) 1 *(Scott B 71)* 1264
Inverness CT: Fraser; Tokely, McBain (Morgan), Black, Watt, McCaffrey, Wilson (Rankin), Duncan, Wyness, Niculae (McAllister), Cowie.
Arbroath: Morrison; McKay, Bishop, Scott B, Ferguson, Raeside (Rennie), Tully, Hegarty (Webster), Watson (Reilly), Sellars, Tosh.

Montrose (0) 1 *(Wood 83)*
Falkirk (1) 2 *(Higdon 17, Thomson 60)* 720
Montrose: McKenzie; Davidson, Gardiner, McLeod, Dobbins, Andreoni, Gates (Wood), Gibson, Baird (Stewart), Rodgers, Stein.
Falkirk: Krul; Ross, Holden, Barr, Milne (Latapy), Thomson, Cregg, Craig, Arfield, Higdon, Moutinho (Moffat).

Partick Th (0) 0
St Johnstone (0) 0 1769
Partick Th: Tuffey; Storey, Twaddle, McStay (Chaplain), Harkins, Archibald, Strachan (Connor), Rowson, Di Giacomo (Keegan), Murray, Buchanan.
St Johnstone: Main; Irvine, Anderson, Weatherston (McCluskey), Stanic, McManus, Moon (MacDonald), McInnes, Hardie, Stewart (Jackson), Sheerin.
aet; Partick T won 5-4 on penalties.

Peterhead (0) 0
Kilmarnock (1) 3 *(Nish 30, Wright 48, Naismith 55)* 1055
Peterhead: Kula; Buchan, Mackay, Sharp, MacDonald, Mann, Anderson, Kelly, Istead (Bagshaw), Kozmanski (Munro), Bavidge.
Kilmarnock: Combe; Wright, Hay (Lilley), Johnston, Murray, O'Leary, Invincible (Gibson), Jarvis, Nish (Koudou), Naismith, Dodds.

Queen's Park (0) 1 *(Dunlop 62)*
Hibernian (0) 2 *(Morais 56, Fletcher 58)* 2343
Queen's Park: Cairns; Paton, Agostini, Kettlewell, Dunlop, Sinclair, Dunn (Ronald), Cairney, Trouten, Canning, Ferry.
Hibernian: Ma Kalambay; McCann (O'Brien), Stevenson, McCormack, Joneleit, Kerr, Chisholm, Morais, Benjelloun, Shiels (Beuzelin), Donaldson (Fletcher).

St Mirren (0) 0
East Fife (0) 1 *(O'Reilly 63)* 1782
St Mirren: Smith; Van Zanten, Potter, Brittain (Reid), Mason (O'Donnell), Haining, Murray, Burke (Kean), Mehmet, Miranda, Corcoran.
East Fife: McCulloch; McDonald, Fotheringham, Walker (O'Reilly), Smart, Tweed, Blackadder, Stewart, Gordon, Nicholas (Martin), Cameron.

Stirling Alb (0) 0
Hearts (1) 2 *(Ellis 39 (og), Kingston 53)* 2061
Stirling Alb: Hogarth; Nugent, Devine (McKenna), Aitken, Graham, Ellis, Murphy, Bell, Lilley (Hay), Cramb, Easton (Tomana).
Hearts: Banks; Neilson, Goncalves, Zaliukas (Karipidis), Berra, Tall, Kingston, Stewart, Mikoliunas (Ksanavicius), Elliot (Velicka), Driver.

Wednesday, 29 August 2007

Dundee U (0) 2 *(Hunt 65 (pen), Robertson J 88)*
Ross Co (0) 1 *(Barrowman 78)* 3114
Dundee U: Szamotulski; Dillon, Kalvenes, Kenneth, Dods, Flood, Robertson D, Buaben (Kerr), Robertson J, Hunt, Gomis.
Ross Co: Bullock; McCulloch (Brady), Keddie, Anderson (Moore), Golabek, Dowie, Scott (Webb), Adams, Campbell, Higgins, Barrowman.

Motherwell (1) 3 *(McLean 45, McCormack 74, Porter 90)*
Raith R (0) 1 *(Carcary 48)* 3571
Motherwell: Smith G; Kinniburgh, Corrigan, Lasley, McLean, Reynolds, Smith D (McGarry), Mensing, McCormack (Clarkson), Porter, Paterson.
Raith R: Fahey; Wilson, Andrews, Pelosi, Campbell, Silvestro, Weir, Borris (Sloan), Hislop, Carcary (Davidson), Winter.

THIRD ROUND

Tuesday, 25 September 2007

Falkirk (0) 0
Dundee U (0) 1 *(Wilkie 60)* 2804
Falkirk: Krul; Holden, Scobbie, Milne, Barr, Cregg, Arfield, Thomson (Latapy), Arnau (Moutinho), Barrett (Finnigan), Higdon.
Dundee U: Szamoutulski; Dillon, Dods, Wilkie, Flood, Buaben, Kerr, Gomis (Robertson D), Robson, Robertson J, Hunt.

Hamilton A (2) 2 *(McCarthy 16, McArthur 37)*
Kilmarnock (0) 0 2627
Hamilton A: Halliwell; Parratt, Elebert, McArthur, Swailes, Gibson, McCarthy (Easton), Stevenson, Gilhaney, Offiong (Wake), Winters.
Kilmarnock: Combe; Murray, Wright, Fowler, Lilley, Ford, Dodds (Finnigan), Johnston (Jarvis), Nish, Bryson (Fernandez■), Gibson.

Hearts (1) 4 *(Nade 34 (pen), Berra 97, Elliot 100, 102)*
Dunfermline Ath (0) 1 *(Simmons 84)* 10,500
Hearts: Banks; Neilson, Goncalves, Jonsson, Berra, Kancelskis, Kingston, Stewart (Palazuelos), Nade (Velicka), Elliot, Ivaskevicius (Ksanavicius).
Dunfermline Ath: Gallacher; Young, Woods, Williamson (Ryan), Bamba, Simmons, Glass, Phinn (Morrison O), Crawford, McManus, McBride (Hamilton).
aet.

Inverness CT (1) 3 *(Bayne 21, Wilson 67, Wyness 80)*
Gretna (0) 0 1794
Inverness CT: Malkowski; Tokely, Bayne (McDonald), Morgan, McCaffrey, Wilson (Rankin), Duncan, Munro, Hastings, Brewster (Wyness), Cowie.
Gretna: Fleming; Jenkins, Horwood (Skelton), McGill, Grainger, Collin, Paartalu, Hogg, McLaren (Yantorno), McMenamin (Grady), Buscher.

Wednesday, 26 September 2007

Dundee (0) 1 *(McDonald 71)*
Celtic (1) 2 *(McDonald 27, Vennegoor 60)* 8535
Dundee: Samson; Worrell (Griffin), Palenik, McDonald, Dixon, MacKenzie, McHale (Davidson), Daquin, Swankie, Zemlik■, Robertson.
Celtic: Boruc; Kennedy, Naylor, Donati, Caldwell, McManus, Sno, Brown S, McDonald, Vennegoor, Riordan.

East Fife (0) 0
Rangers (2) 4 *(Novo 14, Boyd 35, 66 (pen), Cuellar 54)* 7413
East Fife: McCulloch; McDonald, Fotheringham, Gordon (Walker), Smart, Tweed, Blackadder (O'Reilly), Stewart, Young, McManus (Nicholas), Cameron.
Rangers: Carroll; Whittaker, Broadfoot, Faye, Ehiogu, Cuellar, Adam (Emslie), Burke, Novo (Buffel), Boyd (Cousin), Gow.

Hibernian (1) 2 *(Donaldson 11, Antoine-Curier 85)*
Motherwell (3) 4 *(Clarkson 17, Lasley 20, McCormack 24, Porter 83)* 8641
Hibernian: Ma Kalambay; Gathuessi, Murphy, Hogg (McCann), Jones, Kerr, Shiels (Morais), Beuzelin, Antoine-Curier, Donaldson, Stevenson (Zemmama).
Motherwell: Smith; Quinn, Paterson, Lasley, Craigan, Reynolds, Hughes, McGarry (Fitzpatrick), McCormack, Clarkson (Mensing), Porter (Grabban).

Partick Th (0) 0
Aberdeen (1) 2 *(Young 42, Considine 64)* 3337
Partick Th: Hinchcliffe; Robertson, Twaddle, Harkins, Archibald, Rowson, McKinlay (Keegan), Storey (Donnelly), Roberts, Murray (Gibson), Buchanan.
Aberdeen: Langfield; Hart, Foster, Nicholson, Considine, Severin, De Visscher (Smith D), Clark, Miller, Jamie Smith, Young.

QUARTER-FINALS

Wednesday, 31 October 2007

Aberdeen (3) 4 *(Nicholson 10 (pen), 21 (pen), 78, Miller 45)*
Inverness CT (0) 1 *(Bayne 68)* 7270
Aberdeen: Langfield; Hart, Byrne, McNamara, Diamond, Mair, Jamie Smith (Foster), Nicholson, Aluko (Considine), Miller, Young (Clark).
Inverness CT: Fraser; Tokely, Hastings, Munro, McCaffrey, McBain (Rankin), Wilson (Niculae), Duncan, Wyness (Morgan), Bayne, Cowie.

Celtic (0) 0
Hearts (0) 2 *(Velicka 77, 86)* 21,492
Celtic: Boruc; Caldwell, Naylor (Sno), Donati, Kennedy, McManus, Hartley, Brown S, McDonald, Vennegoor (Killen), McGeady.
Hearts: Basso; Neilson, Goncalves, Tall, Zaliukas (Jonsson), Berra, Palazuelos, Stewart, Ksanavicius (Mikoliunas), Elliot (Velicka), Driver.

Dundee U (1) 3 *(Hunt 10, 77, 85)*
Hamilton A (0) 1 *(Offiong 79 (pen))* 4567
Dundee U: Szamotulski; Dillon, Kalvenes, Wilkie, Dods, Flood, Gomis (Kerr), Buaben, Robertson J (Robb), Hunt, Robson.
Hamilton A: Halliwell; Evans (Gibson), Easton, McArthur, McLaughlin, Swailes, Winters (Wake), McCarthy (Taylor), Neil, Gilhaney, Offiong.

Motherwell (0) 1 *(Quinn 90)*
Rangers (1) 2 *(Novo 22, Boyd 53)* 9236
Motherwell: Smith; Quinn, Paterson, Fitzpatrick, Craigan, Reynolds, Maguire, Lasley (Porter), McCormack, Clarkson, O'Donnell.
Rangers: McGregor; Hutton, Papac, Cuellar, Weir, Ferguson, Beasley, Thomson, Boyd (Cousin), Novo, McCulloch.

SEMI-FINALS

Wednesday, 30 January 2008

Rangers (0) 2 *(Ferguson 50, Darchville 69)*
Hearts (0) 0 31,989
Rangers: McGregor; Whittaker, Papac, Cuellar, Weir, Ferguson, Hemdani, Adam, McCulloch, Darchville (Novo), Burke.
Hearts: Banks; Neilson, Goncalves (Wallace), Palazuelos, Karipidis, Berra, Jonsson, Stewart, Nade (Beniusis), Ksanavicius, Mikoliunas (Driver).

Tuesday, 5 February 2008

Aberdeen (1) 1 *(Considine 19)*
Dundee U (1) 4 *(Dods 23, Kalvenes 60, Conway 65, Gomis 77)* 12,046
Aberdeen: Langfield; McNamara (Bus), Considine (Aluko), Nicholson, Diamond, Severin, Young, Walker, Foster, Miller■, Mackie.
Dundee U: Zaluska; Flood (Dillon), Kalvenes, Wilkie, Dods, Kerr, Gomis (Buaben), Robertson D, De Vries, Hunt, Conway.

FINAL (at Hampden Park)

Sunday, 16 March 2008

Dundee U (1) 2 *(Hunt 34, De Vries 96)*
Rangers (0) 2 *(Boyd 85, 113)* 50,019
Dundee U: Zaluska; Kovacevic, Kalvenes, Kenneth, Wilkie, Flood, Gomis, Kerr, Hunt (Conway), De Vries, Buaben (Robertson D).
Rangers: McGregor; Broadfoot, Papac (Boyd), Cuellar, Weir, Ferguson, Hemdani (Darcheville), Dailly, McCulloch, Davis, Burke (Whittaker).
aet; Rangers won 3-2 on penalties.
Referee: K. Clark.

SCOTTISH LEAGUE ATTENDANCES 2007–08

PREMIER LEAGUE

	Average	Highest	Lowest
Aberdeen	11,994	17,798	8,240
Celtic	56,675	58,964	50,591
Dundee U	8,291	13,613	5,846
Falkirk	5,554	6,803	4,490
Gretna	2,289	6,137	431
Hearts	15,930	17,131	10,512
Hibernian	13,845	17,015	10,754
Inverness CT	4,753	7,753	3,420
Kilmarnock	6,181	11,544	4,086
Motherwell	6,599	10,445	4,259
Rangers	49,072	50,440	46,061
St Mirren	4,519	7,519	3,163

FIRST DIVISION

	Average	Highest	Lowest
Clyde	1,301	1,979	910
Dundee	4,264	6,192	3,146
Dunfermline Ath	3,667	4,946	2,100
Hamilton A	2,469	5,078	1,410
Livingston	1,694	2,865	952
Morton	2,731	3,818	2,228
Partick Th	2,598	4,915	1,267
Queen of the S	1,965	3,005	1,484
St Johnstone	2,959	6,279	1686
Stirling A	1,166	2,215	430

SECOND DIVISION

	Average	Highest	Lowest
Airdrie U	981	1,645	611
Alloa Ath	602	1,053	441
Ayr U	1,137	1,345	971
Berwick R	479	778	259
Brechin C	489	669	345
Cowdenbeath	518	1,935	244
Peterhead	694	926	462
Queen's Park	712	1,211	431
Raith R	1,761	2,357	1,349
Ross Co	2,247	3,716	1,511

THIRD DIVISION

	Average	Highest	Lowest
Albion R	311	512	186
Arbroath	611	959	421
Dumbarton	560	907	282
East Fife	772	1,340	540
East Stirling	377	791	235
Elgin C	471	624	301
Forfar Ath	410	615	270
Montrose	596	1,470	321
Stenhousemuir	418	755	212
Stranraer	255	487	135

LEAGUE CHALLENGE CUP 2007–08

■ *Denotes player sent off.*

FIRST ROUND NORTH EAST

Tuesday, 14 August 2007

Dundee (0) 1 *(Sturm 59)*

Ross Co (2) 2 *(Barrowman 12 (pen), Keddie 43)* 1471

Dundee: Samson; Forsyth, Clark (Milne), Rae, MacKenzie, Griffin, O'Brien■, McHale, Lyle, Deasley (Worrell), Sturm.
Ross Co: Bullock (Cartis); McCulloch, Golabek, Anderson (Higgins), Dowie, Keddie, Scott, Adams, Barrowman, Petrie (Moore), Brady.

Elgin C (0) 1 *(Nicolson 88)*

Brechin C (1) 4 *(Russell 9, 60 (pen), Janczyk 70, Johnson 74)* 228

Elgin C: Malin; Campbell (Charlesworth), Dickson, Kaczan, Nicolson, Hind, Gibert, O'Donoghue (Duguid), Ross (Lewis), Smith, Frizzel.
Brechin C: McCluskey; Walker R, White, Nelson A (Geddes), Callaghan S, Ward (Byers), Walker S, Janczyk, Smith D, Russell (Smith C), Johnson.

Forfar Ath (1) 3 *(Lombardi 26, Tulloch 85, Lunan 104)*

East Fife (0) 2 *(Walker 53, O'Reilly 69)* 319

Forfar Ath: Reid; McNally, Ovenstone, Stuart (Grady), Allison, Smith (Lumsden), Lunan, Fraser (Kilgannon), Tulloch, Fotheringham, Lombardi.
East Fife: McCulloch; McDonald, Tweed, Gordon, Linton, Smart, Fotheringham■, Blackadder, O'Reilly (Stewart), Walker (Cameron), McManus (Nicholas).
aet.

Montrose (2) 5 *(Baird 11 (pen), 32, 59, Wood 50, 52)*

Stirling Alb (0) 1 *(Harris 51)* 251

Montrose: Peat; Cumming, Thomson, Dobbins, McLeod, Gardiner, Gates (Donachie), Davidson, Wood, Baird (Rogers), Stein (Stewart).
Stirling Alb: Christie; Hay (Walker), Devine, Aitken, Ellis, Murphy, Tomana (Bell), Harris, Cramb, Gribben (McKenna), Taggart.

Peterhead (0) 1 *(Cowie 90)*

Cowdenbeath (0) 0 438

Peterhead: Kula; Buchan, MacDonald, Sharp, Mackay (Donald), Mann, Anderson, Soane (Cowie), Bavidge, Kozmanski, McKay.
Cowdenbeath: Hay; Baxter, Armstrong J, Bryan (Matusik), Hill, Galloway, Armstrong D, Clarke (McBride), Scullion, Adamson, Dalziel.

Raith R (0) 1 *(Tod 89)*

St Johnstone (1) 1 *(Sheerin 14 (pen))* 1801

Raith R: Renton; Wilson, Andrews, Borris (Darling), Pelosi, Tod, Silvestro■, Winter, Sloan, Weir, Hislop (Campbell).
St Johnstone: Main; Lawrie, McManus, Weatherston, Stanic, McInnes, Anderson (Dyer), Hardie, Sheerin, McCluskey (MacDonald), Stewart (Daal).
aet; St Johnstone won 5-4 on penalties.

Wednesday, 15 August 2007

Arbroath (1) 2 *(McKay 40, Reilly 81)*

Alloa Ath (0) 0 526

Arbroath: Wight; McMullan (Rennie), Bishop, Webster, Black, Campbell, Watson, Hegarty (Reilly), McKay, Sellars, Effern (Scott B).
Alloa Ath: Creer; McBuglie, Townsley, Fairbairn (Wilson), Fleming, Buist■, McKeown, Ferguson B, Andrew, Agnew (Kelly), Brown (Mackie).

FIRST ROUND SOUTH WEST

Tuesday, 14 August 2007

Albion R (0) 1 *(McKenzie 90)*

Berwick R (0) 1 *(Swanson 73)* 152

Albion R: Scott (Thompson); Watson G (Dimilta), Benton, Chisholm, Reid, Donnelly, Donald (Friel), McKenzie, Wright, Walker P, Hunter.
Berwick R: Flockhart; Lennox, Bolochoweckyj, Greenhill D (Manson), Noble, Smith J, Lucas, McLeish, McMullan (Haynes), Wood, Swanson (Diack).
aet; Berwick R won 4-3 on penalties.

Clyde (1) 1 *(Masterton 13)*

Queen of the S (0) 0 621

Clyde: Hutton; McGregor, Smith (Dougherty), Bradley, Potter, Higgins, Masterton, Ruari MacLennan (Wilson), McGowan, Imrie, Arbuckle.
Queen of the S: Grindlay; Paton, Lauchlan, O'Neill, McQuilken, MacFarlane, McGowan (Aitken), Tosh, Dobbie (Mole J), Gilmour (Bingham), O'Connor.

East Stirling (1) 4 *(Simpson 32, 48, Struthers 71, 88)*

Dumbarton (1) 2 *(Campbell 31, 53)* 130

East Stirling: Mitchell; Moffat, Thywissen, McShane (McLaren), Carr, Doyle, Kelly (McGregor), Simpson, McBride P, Ure, Struthers.
Dumbarton: Nugent; Farro, Aitkin, Gentile, McLennan, Yule (Hasswell), McNaught (Thompson), McQuilken, Orr, Campbell (Cavanagh), McAlpine.

Hamilton A (1) 1 *(Taylor 17)*

Ayr U (0) 2 *(Moore 60, Stevenson 76)* 611

Hamilton A: Halliwell; Wroe, Evans, Taylor (Elebert), Gibson, Stevenson, Easton (Gilhaney), McCarthy, Davison, McLeod, Teggart (Wake).
Ayr U: Corr; Swift, Robertson, Vareille, Pettigrew, Forrest, Stevenson, Weaver, Williams, Dunn, Wardlaw (Moore).

Morton (1) 1 *(Graham 26)*

Livingston (0) 0 1658

Morton: McGurn; Weatherson, Walker, Millar, Harding, Keenan, Shields (Black), McAlister, Templeman, Graham (Greacen), Linn (Coakley).
Livingston: Liberda; Mitchell (Snodgrass), McCaffrey, McPake, MacKay, Noubissie (Weir), Dorrans, Kennedy, Matthews (Pesir), Fox, Hamill.

Queen's Park (0) 1 *(Canning 64)*

Stranraer (0) 0 387

Queen's Park: Cairns; Paton, Agostini, Kettlewell, Dunlop, Molloy, Trouten, Quinn (Cairney), Ferry, Canning, Dunn (McGrady).
Stranraer: Black; McKinstry (Caddis), Kane, Cashmore, White (Tade), Thomas, McLauchlan, Bonar, Gillies, Mitchell, McCusker (Mullen).

Stenhousemuir (0) 1 *(Dempster 59)*

Airdrie U (1) 3 *(McEwan 16 (og), Lyle 82 (og), Noble 85)* 386

Stenhousemuir: Hillcoat; Lyle, Smith, Hamilton (Flynn), McEwan, Tyrrell, Gilbride, Dempster, Dillon, Murdock (Lindsay), Hampshire (Thomson).
Airdrie U: Robertson; McKenna, Smyth, Noble, Lovering, Smith, McDonald, McKeown, Waddell (McDougall), Holmes (Gillies), Russell.

SECOND ROUND

Tuesday, 4 September 2007

Airdrie U (2) 5 *(Russell 15, 61, 85 (pen), 86, McDonald 26)*
Arbroath (1) 1 *(Tosh 37)* 754

Airdrie U: Robertson; McKenna, Smyth, McKeown, Lovering, Smith, McDonald, Noble (Prunty), Holmes, Waddell (McDougall), Russell.
Arbroath: Morrison; McMullan, Rennie■, Webster (Reilly), Ferguson, Tully, Watson, Hegarty, Scott D (Scott B), McKay (Smith), Tosh.

East Stirling (1) 1 *(Simpson 33)*
Queen's Park (0) 0 332

East Stirling: Hill; Moffat, McBride K, Donaldson, King, Thywissen, Kelly, Brand, Simpson, Ure, Savage (Struthers).
Queen's Park: Cairns; Paton, Agostini, Kettlewell, Dunlop, Sinclair, Quinn (Bowers), Cairney, Canning, McGrady, Ferry.

Forfar Ath (0) 0
Ayr U (1) 2 *(Williams 32, Stevenson 57)* 333

Forfar Ath: Reid; Smith, Ovenstone, Stuart (Grady), Allison, Tulloch, Fotheringham■, Kerrigan, Duell, Lombardi (Watson), Beith.
Ayr U: Corr; Pettigrew, Henderson, Hamilton, Robertson, Forrest, Stevenson, Dunn, Lowing, Williams, Moore (Wardlaw).

Montrose (0) 1 *(Stein 103)*
Brechin C (0) 2 *(Johnston 104, Nelson A 111)* 705

Montrose: McKenzie; Davidson, Gardner, Andreoni, McLeod, Dobbins, Gates (Stewart), Gibson, Rodgers (Wood), Baird, Stein.
Brechin C: McCluskey; Murie, Callaghan S, Fusco (Janczyk), White, Walker S, King, Nelson A, Geddes (Smith C), Johnston, Byers.
aet.

Partick Th (1) 3 *(Harkins 26, Di Giacomo 82, Keegan 90)*
Berwick R (0) 1 *(Thomson 78)* 1226

Partick Th: Tuffey; Storey, Twaddle, Rowson, Harkins, Archibald, Strachan (McKinlay), McStay (Gibson), Di Giacomo, Buchanan (Keegan), Murray.
Berwick R: Flockhart; Bolochoweckyj, Fraser, Greenhill B (Little), Smith, McGroarty, Thomson (McLeish), Wood, McMullan (Diack), Gemmill, Swanson.

Peterhead (0) 0
Morton (1) 1 *(McAlister 18)* 623

Peterhead: Kula; Buchan, MacDonald, Munro (McKay), MacKay, Mann, Anderson, Cowie, Bagshaw (Monroe), Kozminski, Bavidge.
Morton: Robinson; Shields, Greacen, Finlayson, Weatherson, McAnespie, Keenan, Stevenson (Graham), Gardyne, McAlister, Linn (Millar).

Wednesday, 5 September 2007

Clyde (0) 1 *(Ruari MacLennan 46)*
Dunfermline Ath (1) 4 *(Burchill 26, 74, Morrison O 57, 90)* 796

Clyde: Hutton; McGregor, Smith (McKenna), Masterton, Kirkup, Higgins, Cardle (Bradley), Ruari MacLennan, Imrie, McGowan M, McGowan D.
Dunfermline Ath: Murdoch; Woods, Labonte, Ryan, Wilson, Simmons, Glass, Crawford, McManus, Burchill, Morrison O.

Ross Co (0) 0
St Johnstone (1) 2 *(Deucher 14, Jackson 49)* 838

Ross Co: Cartis; McCulloch, Keddie, Scott (Higgins), Golabek (Anderson), Dowie, Lawson, Adams, Brady, Petrie (Shields), Barrowman.
St Johnstone: Cuthbert; Irvine, McManus, Weatherston, Dyer, Anderson, McInnes, McCluskey, Deucher, Jackson, Sheerin.

QUARTER-FINALS

Tuesday, 18 September 2007

Airdrie U (0) 0
Dunfermline Ath (0) 2 *(Burchill 54, 81)* 931

Airdrie U: Robertson; McKenna, Smyth, McKeown■, Lovering (Noble), Smith, McDonald, Prunty (McDougall), Holmes, Waddell, Russell.
Dunfermline Ath: Murdoch; Williamson (McCulloch), Labonte, Ryan, Muirhead (Young), Woods■, Glass, Simmons, McManus, Burchill, Morrison O.

Ayr U (0) 2 *(Williams 86 (pen), 120)*
Partick Th (0) 1 *(Forrest 65 (og))* 1081

Ayr U: Corr; Forrest, Pettigrew (Weaver), Stevenson, Robertson, Henderson, Vareille (Wardlaw), Dunn, Moore (Hamilton), Williams, Swift.
Partick Th: Tuffey; Robertson, Twaddle, Rowson, Harkins, Archibald, Strachan (Roberts), Gibson, Keegan (Murray), Buchanan, McKinlay (Storey).
aet.

East Stirling (0) 0
Morton (0) 4 *(Templeman 49, 82, Moffat 61 (og), Linn 83)* 478

East Stirling: Hill; Moffat, McBride K, Donaldson, King, Thywissen, Kelly, Oates (Carr), Simpson (Struthers), Ure (Doyle), Savage.
Morton: Robinson; Weatherson (Shields), Greacen, Walker, Harding, Graham (Linn), Keenan, Stevenson, Gardyne, McAlister, Templeman (Coakley).

Tuesday, 25 September 2007

St Johnstone (4) 4 *(Deuchar 21, 42, Jackson 36, Weatherston 43)*
Brechin C (0) 1 *(Smith 57)* 1159

St Johnstone: Cuthbert; Irvine, McManus, Weatherston (Doris), Stanic, Moon, Anderson, McLaren, Deuchar (Daal), Jackson (Stewart), Sheerin.
Brechin C: McCluskey; Walker R, Walker S, Callaghan B, Murie, Hughes, Fusco (Janczyk), Nelson A, Geddes (Connolly), King, Johnston (Smith C).

SEMI-FINALS

Tuesday, 2 October 2007

Dunfermline Ath (0) 1 *(Glass 83)*
Ayr U (0) 0 1744

Dunfermline Ath: Gallacher; Thomson (McBride), McManus, Simmons (Hamilton), Bamba, Wilson, Glass, Phinn, McIntyre (Burchill), Williamson, Morrison O.
Ayr U: Corr; Swift, Forrest, Stevenson, Lowing, Henderson, Vareille (Hamilton), Robertson, Wardlaw, Moore, Dunn.

Morton (1) 1 *(Graham 12)*
St Johnstone (1) 3 *(Jackson 10, MacDonald 65, Quinn 87)* 1886

Morton: Robinson; Weatherson, Greacen, Finlayson, McLaughlin (McAnespie), Walker, Stevenson, Shields, Graham (Harding), McAlister, Templeman (Linn).
St Johnstone: Cuthbert; Irvine, McManus, McInnes, Stanic, Anderson, Quinn, McLaren (Moon), Deuchar (Stewart), Jackson (MacDonald), Sheerin.

FINAL (at East End Park)

Sunday, 25 November 2007

Dunfermline Ath (1) 2 *(Wilson 37, Glass 70 (pen))*
St Johnstone (3) 3 *(Sheerin 13 (pen), MacDonald 19, Deuchar 30)* 6446

Dunfermline Ath: Gallacher; Woods (Young), Wilson, Bamber, Murphy, Ryan, Simmons (Harris), Glass, Crawford, Burchill, McGlinchey (Hamilton).
St Johnstone: Main; Irvine, McManus, Anderson (Rutkiewicz), Stanic, Quinn, McInnes, MacDonald (Hardie), Deuchar, Jackson (Milne), Sheerin.
Referee: Eddie Smith.

SCOTTISH CUP FINALS 1874–2008

Year	*Winners*	*Runners-up*	*Score*
1874	Queen's Park	Clydesdale	2-0
1875	Queen's Park	Renton	3-0
1876	Queen's Park	Third Lanark	2-0 after 1-1 draw
1877	Vale of Leven	Rangers	3-2 after 0-0 and 1-1 draws
1878	Vale of Leven	Third Lanark	1-0
1879	Vale of Leven*	Rangers	
1880	Queen's Park	Thornlibank	3-0
1881	Queen's Park†	Dumbarton	3-1
1882	Queen's Park	Dumbarton	4-1 after 2-2 draw
1883	Dumbarton	Vale of Leven	2-1 after 2-2 draw
1884	Queen's Park‡	Vale of Leven	
1885	Renton	Vale of Leven	3-1 after 0-0 draw
1886	Queen's Park	Renton	3-1
1887	Hibernian	Dumbarton	2-1
1888	Renton	Cambuslang	6-1
1889	Third Lanark§	Celtic	2-1
1890	Queen's Park	Vale of Leven	2-1 after 1-1 draw
1891	Hearts	Dumbarton	1-0
1892	Celtic¶	Queen's Park	5-1
1893	Queen's Park	Celtic	2-1
1894	Rangers	Celtic	3-1
1895	St Bernard's	Renton	2-1
1896	Hearts	Hibernian	3-1
1897	Rangers	Dumbarton	5-1
1898	Rangers	Kilmarnock	2-0
1899	Celtic	Rangers	2-0
1900	Celtic	Queen's Park	4-3
1901	Hearts	Celtic	4-3
1902	Hibernian	Celtic	1-0
1903	Rangers	Hearts	2-0 after 1-1 and 0-0 draws
1904	Celtic	Rangers	3-2
1905	Third Lanark	Rangers	3-1 after 0-0 draw
1906	Hearts	Third Lanark	1-0
1907	Celtic	Hearts	3-0
1908	Celtic	St Mirren	5-1
1909	••		
1910	Dundee	Clyde	2-1 after 2-2 and 0-0 draws
1911	Celtic	Hamilton A	2-0 after 0-0 draw
1912	Celtic	Clyde	2-0
1913	Falkirk	Raith R	2-0
1914	Celtic	Hibernian	4-1 after 0-0 draw
1920	Kilmarnock	Albion R	3-2
1921	Partick Th	Rangers	1-0
1922	Morton	Rangers	1-0
1923	Celtic	Hibernian	1-0
1924	Airdrieonians	Hibernian	2-0
1925	Celtic	Dundee	2-1
1926	St Mirren	Celtic	2-0
1927	Celtic	East Fife	3-1
1928	Rangers	Celtic	4-0
1929	Kilmarnock	Rangers	2-0
1930	Rangers	Partick Th	2-1 after 0-0 draw
1931	Celtic	Motherwell	4-2 after 2-2 draw
1932	Rangers	Kilmarnock	3-0 after 1-1 draw
1933	Celtic	Motherwell	1-0
1934	Rangers	St Mirren	5-0
1935	Rangers	Hamilton A	2-1
1936	Rangers	Third Lanark	1-0
1937	Celtic	Aberdeen	2-1
1938	East Fife	Kilmarnock	4-2 after 1-1 draw
1939	Clyde	Motherwell	4-0
1947	Aberdeen	Hibernian	2-1
1948	Rangers	Morton	1-0 after 1-1 draw
1949	Rangers	Clyde	4-1
1950	Rangers	East Fife	3-0
1951	Celtic	Motherwell	1-0
1952	Motherwell	Dundee	4-0
1953	Rangers	Aberdeen	1-0 after 1-1 draw
1954	Celtic	Aberdeen	2-1
1955	Clyde	Celtic	1-0 after 1-1 draw
1956	Hearts	Celtic	3-1
1957	Falkirk	Kilmarnock	2-1 after 1-1 draw
1958	Clyde	Hibernian	1-0
1959	St Mirren	Aberdeen	3-1
1960	Rangers	Kilmarnock	2-0
1961	Dunfermline Ath	Celtic	2-0 after 0-0 draw
1962	Rangers	St Mirren	2-0
1963	Rangers	Celtic	3-0 after 1-1 draw

Year	*Winners*	*Runners-up*	*Score*
1964	Rangers	Dundee	3-1
1965	Celtic	Dunfermline Ath	3-2
1966	Rangers	Celtic	1-0 after 0-0 draw
1967	Celtic	Aberdeen	2-0
1968	Dunfermline Ath	Hearts	3-1
1969	Celtic	Rangers	4-0
1970	Aberdeen	Celtic	3-1
1971	Celtic	Rangers	2-1 after 1-1 draw
1972	Celtic	Hibernian	6-1
1973	Rangers	Celtic	3-2
1974	Celtic	Dundee U	3-0
1975	Celtic	Airdrieonians	3-1
1976	Rangers	Hearts	3-1
1977	Celtic	Rangers	1-0
1978	Rangers	Aberdeen	2-1
1979	Rangers	Hibernian	3-2 after 0-0 and 0-0 draws
1980	Celtic	Rangers	1-0
1981	Rangers	Dundee U	4-1 after 0-0 draw
1982	Aberdeen	Rangers	4-1 (aet)
1983	Aberdeen	Rangers	1-0 (aet)
1984	Aberdeen	Celtic	2-1 (aet)
1985	Celtic	Dundee U	2-1
1986	Aberdeen	Hearts	3-0
1987	St Mirren	Dundee U	1-0 (aet)
1988	Celtic	Dundee U	2-1
1989	Celtic	Rangers	1-0
1990	Aberdeen	Celtic	0-0 (aet)
		(Aberdeen won 9-8 on penalties)	
1991	Motherwell	Dundee U	4-3 (aet)
1992	Rangers	Airdrieonians	2-1
1993	Rangers	Aberdeen	2-1
1994	Dundee U	Rangers	1-0
1995	Celtic	Airdrieonians	1-0
1996	Rangers	Hearts	5-1
1997	Kilmarnock	Falkirk	1-0
1998	Hearts	Rangers	2-1
1999	Rangers	Celtic	1-0
2000	Rangers	Aberdeen	4-0
2001	Celtic	Hibernian	3-0
2002	Rangers	Celtic	3-2
2003	Rangers	Dundee	1-0
2004	Celtic	Dunfermline Ath	3-1
2005	Celtic	Dundee U	1-0
2006	Hearts	Gretna	1-1 (aet)
		(Hearts won 4-2 on penalties)	
2007	Celtic	Dunfermline Ath	1-0
2008	Rangers	Queen of the S	3-2

*Vale of Leven awarded cup, Rangers failing to appear for replay after 1-1 draw.
†After Dumbarton protested the first game, which Queen's Park won 2-1.
‡Queen's Park awarded cup, Vale of Leven failing to appear.
§Replay by order of Scottish FA because of playing conditions in first match, won 3-0 by Third Lanark.
¶After mutually protested game which Celtic won 1-0.
••Owing to riot, the cup was withheld after two drawn games – between Celtic and Rangers 2-2 and 1-1.

SCOTTISH CUP WINS

Celtic 34, Rangers 32, Queen's Park 10, Aberdeen 7, Hearts 7, Clyde 3, Kilmarnock 3, St Mirren 3, Vale of Leven 3, Dunfermline Ath 2, Falkirk 2, Hibernian 2, Motherwell 2, Renton 2, Third Lanark 2, Airdrieonians 1, Dumbarton 1, Dundee 1, Dundee U 1, East Fife 1, Morton 1, Partick Th 1, St Bernard's 1.

APPEARANCES IN FINAL

Celtic 53, Rangers 49, Aberdeen 15, Hearts 13, Queen's Park 12, Hibernian 11, Dundee U 8, Kilmarnock 8, Vale of Leven 7, Clyde 6, Dumbarton 6, Motherwell 6, St Mirren 6, Third Lanark 6, Dundee 5, Dunfermline Ath 5, Renton 5, Airdrieonians 4, East Fife 3, Falkirk 3, Hamilton A 2, Morton 2, Partick Th 2, Albion R 1, Cambuslang 1, Clydesdale 1, Gretna 1, Queen of the S 1, Raith R 1, St Bernard's 1, Thornlibank 1.

TENNENT'S SCOTTISH CUP 2007–08

▪ *Denotes player sent off.*

FIRST ROUND

Brora Rangers v Cove Rangers	0-5
Civil Service Strollers v Selkirk	1-2
Clachnacuddon v Edinburgh City	2-2, 0-1
Coldstream v Dalbeattie Star	0-4
Culter v Hawick Royal Albert	7-0
Fort William v Spartans 0-6	
Fraserburgh v Huntly	1-1, 0-2
Girvan v Forres Mechanics	2-0
Glasgow University v Buckie Thistle	1-2
Golspie Sutherland v Preston Athletic	3-1
Lossiemouth v Whitehill Welfare	1-3
Newton Stewart v Linlithgow Rose	0-6
Rothes v Nairn County	1-4
St Cuthbert's Wanderers v Pollok	2-6
Vale of Leithen v Gala Fairydean	3-1
Wick Academy v Deveronvale	0-5
Wigtown & Bladnoch v Burntisland Shipyard	3-5

SECOND ROUND

Albion Rovers v Burntisland Shipyard	8-0
Annan Athletic v Huntly	2-5
Arbroath v Elgin City	5-0
Buckie Thistle v Nairn County	4-1
Cove Rangers v Keith	3-0
Culter v Vale of Leithen	2-1
Edinburgh City v East Stirling	1-2
Edinburgh University v Deveronvale	3-1
Forfar Athletic v Dumbarton	1-1, 0-3
Girvan v Stranraer	1-2
Inverurie Loco Works v East Fife	0-2
Linlithgow Rose v Spartans	4-1
Montrose v Pollok	2-2, 1-0
Selkirk v Dalbeattie Star	0-2
Threave Rovers v Stenhousemuir	1-0
Whitehill Welfare v Golspie Sutherland	6-1

THIRD ROUND

Saturday, 24 November 2007

Airdrie U (0) 1 *(McKeown 57)*

Queen's Park (0) 1 *(Ferry 70)* 1013

Airdrie U: Robertson; McKenna, Lovering (McDougall), McDonald, Smyth, Donnelly, Noble (Prunty), McKeown, Russell, Holmes, Waddell.
Queen's Park: Murray; Paton, Dunlop, Ronald, Sinclair, Trouten, Kettlewell, Cairney, Dunn (Quinn), Canning, Ferry.

Albion R (0) 1 *(Gemmell 75)*

East Stirling (3) 5 *(Kelly 20 (pen), Ure 35, Savage 45, Brand 69, Donaldson 88)* 425

Albion R: Scott; Reid (Donnelly), McGowan, Walker R, Benton, Donald▪, Wright, McKenzie (Smith), Hunter, Adams, Gemmell.
East Stirling: Hill; Gibb, McBride K, Doyle, Thywissen, Kelly (Brownlie), McKenzie, Brand, Savage (Simpson), Donaldson, Ure.

Arbroath (0) 0

Cowdenbeath (1) 1 *(Clarke 5 (pen))* 595

Arbroath: Wight; Rennie, Black, Raeside (Campbell), Bishop, Hegarty, Scott B (Reilly), Tosh▪, Sellars, Watson (Brazil), McMullan.
Cowdenbeath: Hay; Scullion (Howatt), Adamson, Hannah, Armstrong J, Hill, Ramsey, Gilfillan, McConalogue, McBride (O'Neil), Clarke.

Brechin C (0) 1 *(Callaghan S 74 (pen))*

East Fife (1) 1 *(Smart 44)* 652

Brechin C: Nelson C; Murie, Walker S, Hughes (Walker R), Callaghan S, Byers (Fusco), Nelson A, Smith D, King, Johnson, Gribben.
East Fife: Fox; McDonald, Smart, Tweed, Cameron, Young, Fotheringham▪, Stewart, Walker (O'Reilly), McManus, Linn.

Clyde (1) 2 *(Arbuckle 8, Imrie 90)*

Montrose (0) 0 821

Clyde: Hutton; McGregor, Smith, Higgins, McKeown, Roddy MacLennan (McGowan D), Cardell (Valentin), Ruari MacLennan, Arbuckle, Imrie, McGowan M.
Montrose: Peat; Cumming, Gardiner, McLeod, Dobbins, Davidson, Doris (Gates), Gibson (Maitland), Wood, Black (Rogers), Stein.

Cove R (0) 1 *(McKibben 90)*

Edinburgh Univ (0) 0 480

Cove R: Windrum; Tindal, Livingstone, Watson E, Fraser G, McKenzie, Stephen, McKibben, Watt, O'Driscoll (Henderson), Coutts.
Edinburgh Univ: Bennet; Cathcart, Cook, Fusco▪, Thompson, Irvine (Beck-Friif), Beesley, Redman, Hazeldine (Munro), McKinnon, Maxwell.

Culter (1) 1 *(Mountford 18)*

Huntly (2) 3 *(Cormie 22, 38, McWilliam 60)* 975

Culter: Perry; Simm, Rathay (Campbell A), Wilson, Craib, Pressley (Farmer), Brown, Mountford, Shand (Stewart P), Craik, Rinto.
Huntly: Bremner; Murray (Corser), Bissett, Redpath, Morrison, Gairns, McWilliam, Guild, Cormie, Gauld (Robertson), McGowan (Maitland).

Dumbarton (2) 2 *(McFarlane 5, McPhee 36)*

Berwick R (0) 0 524

Dumbarton: Crawford; Geggan, Canning, O'Byrne, Potter, McPhee (Kerr), Tiernan (Hamilton), Henderson, Russell, Campbell (Coyne), McFarlane.
Berwick R: O'Connor; Fraser, Bolochoweckyj, Smith J, McMullan, McLeish, Thomson, Greenhill D, Little, Diack, Wood (Stevenson).

Linlithgow Rose (1) 1 *(McArthur 2)*

Dalbeattie Star (0) 0 1519

Linlithgow Rose: Logan; Gallacher, McDermott, Donnelly, Hogg, Bradley, Tyrell (MacSween), McArthur, Carrigan, Herd (Burnett), Courts (Feeney).
Dalbeattie Star: Wright; Steele, McBeth, McMinn, Laurie, Cluckie (Harkness), Redpath, McClymont, Neilson, Parker, Sloan.

Livingston (1) 4 *(Raliukonis 33, MacKay 57 (pen), 56, Jacobs 63)*

Alloa Ath (0) 0 819

Livingston: Stewart; MacKay, James, Makel (Fox), Tinkler (McCaffrey), Raliukonis, Dorrans, Kennedy, McMenamin, Pesir (Craig), Jacobs.
Alloa Ath: Jellema; Buist, Fleming, Townsley, Forrest, McKeown, Wilson, McClune, Andrew (Brown), Agnew (Kelly), Fairbairn (Grant).

Morton (2) 3 *(Russell 21, McLaughlin 23, Templeman 90)*

Buckie Th (1) 2 *(Macrae 45, Stewart G 68)* 1833

Morton: McGurn; Finlayson, Harding, Greacen, Walker, McLaughlin, Millar, McAnespie (Gardyne), McAlister, Weatherson, Russell (Templeman).
Buckie Th: Main; Shewan, Mackinnon, Matheson (Davidson N), Duncan, Small, Neill (Macdonald), Macrae, Stewart G, Bruce (Low A), MacMillan.

Partick Th (1) 2 *(Roberts 45, Buchanan 56)*

Ayr U (1) 1 *(Williams 19)* 2260

Partick Th: Hinchcliffe; Robertson, Harkins, Archibald, Twaddle, McKinlay, McStay (Murray), Rowson, Chaplain, Buchanan, Roberts (Donnelly).
Ayr U: McGeown; Forrest, Henderson, Robertson, Lowing, Weaver, Stevenson, Casey (Wardlaw), Baldacchino, Williams, Moore.

Peterhead (0) 0

Queen of the S (2) 5 *(Dobbie 27, 89, O'Connor 44, 57, Burns 90)* 695

Peterhead: Kula; Buchan, Good, Mann, MacDonald, Anderson (Istead), Sharp, Cowie, McKay (Donald), Bavidge, Kozminski.
Queen of the S: MacDonald; Paton, Harris, Scally, Aitken, Thomson, Gilmour (Robertson), Tosh, Burns, O'Connor (O'Neill), Dobbie.

Ross Co (2) 4 *(Shields 16, 56, Scott 43, Higgins 88)*

Whitehill Welfare (0) 0 1208

Ross Co: Bullock; McCulloch (Miller), Golabek, Brady, Dowie, Boyd, Lawson, Scott, Shields (Higgins), Keddie, Campbell (Gunn).
Whitehill Welfare: McGurk; Cornett, Lee, Johnston, Woodburn, Kidd, Swanson (Calvey) (Wilkes), Pryde, Gormley, Doig (McDonagh), Christie.

Stranraer (0) 0

Stirling Alb (3) 6 *(Aitken 15 (pen), 81, McKenna 20, Cramb 44, Walker 48, 68)* 326

Stranraer: Black; McKinstry■, White, Paddy, Payne, Keogh (Cashmore), McLaughlan, Creaney, Coakley (McColm), Mitchell, Gibson (Bonar).
Stirling Alb: Christie; Nugent, Forsyth, Ellis, Reid, McBride, Bell (Easton), Aitken, McKenna, Cramb (Walker), Taggart (Hay).

Threave R (0) 0

Raith R (1) 5 *(Davidson 29, Carcary 62, 72, Hislop 77, 89)* 629

Threave R: Parker; Stenton (Struthers), Kerr (Gault), Fingland, Patterson, Green, Baty, Wilby, Warren, Rogerson, Donley (McGinley).
Raith R: Fahey; Wilson, Dingwall, Campbell (Lumsden), Andrews, Sloan (Winter), Borris, Davidson, Hislop, Weir (Tod), Carcary.

THIRD ROUND REPLAYS

Tuesday, 4 December 2007

Queen's Park (0) 2 *(Trouten 75, Ferry 90)*

Airdrie U (2) 4 *(McDonald 15, Noble 17, Russell 97, Watt 109)* 579

Queen's Park: Murray; Paton, Agostini, Quinn (Ferry), Boslen, Kettlewell, Cairney, Trouten, McGrady (Molloy), Dunn, Canning (Ronald).
Airdrie U: Robertson; Donnelly, Smyth, McKeown, McKenna, McDougall (Watt), Holmes (Smith), McDonald, Waddell, Russell, Noble (Prunty).
aet.

Wednesday, 5 December 2007

East Fife (1) 1 *(Cameron 25 (pen))*

Brechin C (1) 2 *(Byers 20, King 83)* 659

East Fife: Fox; McDonald, Smart, Tweed, Cameron, Blackadder, Greenhill (Martin), Stewart, O'Reilly (Gordon), McManus, Linn.
Brechin C: Nelson C; Murie, White, Walker R, Callaghan S, Fusco, King, Nelson A, Smith D, Smith C (Hughes), Byers.

FOURTH ROUND

Saturday, 12 January 2008

Celtic (1) 3 *(Vennegoor 37, McDonald 70, Nakamura 75)*

Stirling Alb (0) 0 27,923

Celtic: Boruc; Hinkel, Naylor, Donati, Caldwell, McManus, Nakamura (O'Brien), Brown S (Hartley), McDonald (Killen), Vennegoor, McGeady.
Stirling Alb: Christie; Nugent, Ellis, Graham, Devine, Hay, McBride (Lilley), Atkin, Forsyth, Harris (Walker), McKenna (Rodriguez).

Falkirk (1) 2 *(Barr 5, Arnau 73)*

Aberdeen (2) 2 *(Smith 4, Lovell 10)* 5798

Falkirk: Krul; Ross, Barr, Barrett, Holden, Scobbie, Arfield (Latapy), McBride, Finnigan, Moutinho, Arnau.
Aberdeen: Langfield; Mair, Severin, Smith, Diamond, Byrne, Nicholson, Foster, Lovell (Aluko), Miller (Young), Clark.

Hamilton A (0) 0

Brechin C (0) 0 1023

Hamilton A: Cerny; Parratt, Gibson, McCarthy, Elebert, Swailes, Graham, McArthur, Twigg (Barrau), Stevenson (Neil), Gilhaney (Winters).
Brechin C: Nelson C; Murie (Walker R), Callaghan S, White, Walker S, Nelson A, Fusco, Byers, Smith C, King, Smith D.

Hearts (1) 2 *(Cesnauskas 10, Velicka 52)*

Motherwell (0) 2 *(Porter 64, 78)* 13,651

Hearts: Kurskis; Neilson, Goncalves, Palazuelos, Karipidis, Berra, Cesnauskis (Mikoliunas), Stewart, Ksanavicius (Pospisil), Velicka, Driver (Wallace).
Motherwell: Smith G; Quinn, Paterson, McGarry (Smith D), Craigan, Reynolds, Clarkson (Fitzpatrick), Lasley, Porter, McCormack, Hughes.

Hibernian (1) 3 *(Shiels 5, 53, 84)*

Inverness CT (0) 0 12,578

Hibernian: Ma-Kalambay; McCann, Hanlon (McCormack), Jones, Hogg, Kerr, Morais■, Beuzelin, Zemmama (O'Brien), Benjelloun (Antoine-Curier), Shiels.
Inverness CT: Fraser; Tokely, Hastings, Black (McDonald), McGuire■, Munro, Cowie (Proctor), Duncan, Bayne (Wyness), Niculae, McBain.

Morton (0) 2 *(Finlayson 64, McAlister 75)*

Gretna (1) 2 *(Yantorno 13, Horwood 49)* 2848

Morton: McGurn; MacGregor, McLaughlin (Stevenson), Smith, Harding, Millar (Greacen), Finlayson, McGuffie, Weatherson, Russell, McAlister.
Gretna: Caig; Barr, Innes, Osman (Jenkins), Hall, Horwood, Skelton, Deverdics (McLaren), Yantorno (McGill), Deuchar, Murray.

Queen of the S (3) 4 *(Dobbie 16, Thomson 22, O'Connor 40, McArthur 72 (og))*

Linlithgow Rose (0) 0 3062

Queen of the S: MacDonald; McCann, Harris, Aitken, Thomson, MacFarlane (O'Neill), Gilmour, Tosh (Paton), Burns, O'Connor, Dobbie (Stewart).
Linlithgow Rose: Logan; Gallacher, McDermott, Donnelly, Hogg, Bradley, Dick (Burnett), McArthur, MacSween (Feeney), Carrigan, Herd (Donaldson).

St Mirren (2) 3 *(Corcoran 17, Barron 38, Mehmet 70)*

Dumbarton (0) 0 2814

St Mirren: Smith; Barron, Maxwell, Van Zanten (McGinn), Haining, Potter, Burke (Dorman), Mason, Dargo, Mehmet (Kean), Corcoran.
Dumbarton: Crawford (Nugent); Yule (Geggan), Potter, Canning, Hasswell (Russell), Hamilton, Tiernan, Evans, Brittain, McPhee, Kerr.

Tuesday, 15 January 2008

Huntly (0) 1 *(Reid 77)*

Dundee (1) 3 *(McDonald 29, Malone 81, Daquin 90)* 2000

Huntly: Gray S; Murray, Bissett, Redford, Morrison, Gray M, Guild, Robertson, Dorrat (Maitland), Cormie (Reid), Munro (Cunningham).
Dundee: Samson; Worrell, Dixon (O'Brien), McDonald, Palenik, Malone, Robertson, McHale, Zemlik (Lyle), Davidson (Sturm), Daquin.

Livingston (2) 2 *(Craig 4, McMenamin 31)*

Cowdenbeath (0) 0 830

Livingston: Stewart; MacKay, James, McPake, McDonald, Walker (Makel), Dorrans, Fox, McMenamin, Craig (Griffiths), Snodgrass (Jacobs).
Cowdenbeath: Hay; Armstrong D, Adamson, Armstrong J, Hill, O'Neil, Ramsay, McBride, McQuade (Robertson), Bingham (Scullion), Manson (Young).

St Johnstone (1) 3 *(Jackson 19, Milne 49, Sheerin 57 (pen))*

Raith R (0) 1 *(Weir 80)* 2113

St Johnstone: Main; Irvine, Stanic, Moon, Rutkiewicz (Anderson), McCaffrey (McManus), MacDonald (Weatherston), Craig, Jackson, Milne, Sheerin.
Raith R: Renton; Wilson, Dingwall, Tod, Andrews, Winter, Sloan (Borris), Davidson, Weir, Hislop (Carcary), Templeton.

Wednesday, 16 January 2008

Clyde (0) 0

Dundee U (0) 1 *(Robson 57)* 1550

Clyde: Hutton; McGregor, Smith, Higgins, McKeown, Masterton (McGowan D), Bradley, Ruari MacLennan, Arbuckle, Imrie, McGowan M.
Dundee U: McLean; Dillon, Dods, Grainger, Wilkie, Flood, Gomis, Kerr, Robertson J (Odhiambo), Hunt, Robson.

Tuesday, 22 January 2008

Partick Th (0) 2 *(Buchanan 68, 87)*

Dunfermline Ath (0) 1 *(Wilson 49)* 2434

Partick Th: Tuffey; Harkins (Keegan), Archibald, Twaddle, Robertson, Storey, Rowson, McKinlay (Murray), Buchanan, Roberts, Chaplain.
Dunfermline Ath: Gallacher; Woods, Thomson, Morrison S, Wilson, Harper (McManus), Simmons, McIntyre, Glass, Burchill, Hamilton.

Wednesday, 23 January 2008

Cove R (0) 2 *(Watt 63, 76 (pen))*

Ross Co (4) 4 *(Shields 10, Dowie 30, Boyd 33, Barrowman 40 (pen))* 1200

Cove R: Windrum; Bain, Livingstone, Watson E, Fraser G, McKenzie, Stephen, Coutts, Watt, Henderson (O'Driscoll), McKibben (Tindal) (Reid).
Ross Co: Bullock; Boyd, Golabek, Dowie (Strachan), Lawson, Keddie, McCulloch, Scott (Miller), Watson, Shields, Barrowman (Petrie).

Rangers (4) 6 *(McCulloch 25, 50, Hutton 28, Boyd 30, 45, 62 (pen))*

East Stirling (0) 0 34,024

Rangers: Smith; Hutton, Whittaker, Gow, Papac, Broadfoot, Hemdani (Fleck), Adam, Boyd (Naismith), Darchville (Buffel), McCulloch.
East Stirling: Brown; Gibb, Kelly (Donaldson), Thywissen, McBride K, Brand, McKenzie (Simpson), Oates, Brownlie, Ure, Savage (King).

Monday, 28 January 2008

Airdrie U (0) 0

Kilmarnock (2) 2 *(Hamill 25, Nish 37 (pen))* 3258

Airdrie U: Robertson; Donnelly, Smyth, McKenna, Lovering, McDonald, Smith■, Andreoni (Watt), Russell, Noble (Prunty), Waddle.
Kilmarnock: Harpur; Corrigan, Wright, Gibson (Bryson), Fowler, Ford, Hay, Morgan (Invincibile), Nish (Fernandez), Wales, Hamill.

FOURTH ROUND REPLAYS

Tuesday, 22 January 2008

Aberdeen (2) 3 *(Jamie Smith 19, 55, De Visscher 43)*

Falkirk (0) 1 *(Barrett 61)* 8547

Aberdeen: Langfield; McNamara (Smith D), Considine, Nicholson, Diamond, Severin, Young, De Visscher (Jonathan Smith), Jamie Smith, Lovell (Maguire), Miller.
Falkirk: Krul (Olejnik); Ross, Barr, Milne, Holden, Arfield, Arnau (Bradley), McBride, Moutinho (Cregg), Finnigan, Barrett.

Motherwell (0) 1 *(McCormack 23 (pen))*

Hearts (0) 0 8300

Motherwell: Smith G; Quinn, Paterson, Fitzpatrick, Craigan, Reynolds, Lasley, Hughes, Porter (Smith D), McCormack, Clarkson.
Hearts: Banks; Neilson, Goncalves, Jonsson, Karipidis, Berra, Mikoliunas, Stewart, Cesnauskis (Nade), Velicka, Palazuelos.

Monday, 28 January 2008

Brechin C (0) 2 *(King 48, Byers 112)*

Hamilton A (1) 1 *(McLaughlin 12)* 696

Brechin C: Nelson C; Walker R, Dyer, Ward, White, Fusco, Byers, Janczyk (Callaghan S), Paton, King, Smith D.
Hamilton A: Cerny; Love (Gibson), Easton, Stevenson, Swailes■, McLaughlin, Winters (Graham), McArthur, Offiong, Neil, Barrau (Gilhaney).
aet; Brechin C subsequently removed for fielding two ineligible players.

Gretna (0) 0

Morton (0) 3 *(Weatherson 67, 70, Millar 78)* 1167

Gretna: Caig; Hall, Naughton, Murray (McGill), Collin, Innes, Jenkins, Skelton, Makinwa (Deverdics), Deuchar, Buscher.
Morton: McGurn; Millar, Greacen, Harding, Smith (MacGregor), Finlayson, McLaughlin, McGuffie, McAlistair, Weatherson (Stevenson), Graham (Russell).

FIFTH ROUND

Saturday, 2 February 2008

Aberdeen (0) 1 *(Diamond 62)*

Hamilton A (0) 0 6441

Aberdeen: Langfield; Duff (Maybury), Foster, Considine, Diamond, Severin, De Visscher (Young), Nicholson, Mackie (Lovell), Miller, Walker.
Hamilton A: Halliwell; Parratt, McLaughlin, Stevenson, Easton, Graham (Waterworth), Mensing, McArthur, McCarthy, Gilhaney (Grady), Offiong.

Kilmarnock (0) 1 *(Hamill 66)*

Celtic (1) 5 *(McDonald 22, 67, Caldwell 52, Vennegoor 58, Samaras 85)* 6491

Kilmarnock: Combe; Corrigan, Wright, Gibson (Fernandez), Fowler, Ford, Hay, Bryson, Invincibile (Di Giacomo), Wales, Hamill.
Celtic: Boruc; Caddis, Naylor, Donati, Caldwell, McManus (O'Dea), Nakamura, Brown S (Sno), McDonald (Samaras), Vennegoor, McGeady.

Livingston (0) 0

Partick Th (0) 0 2110

Livingston: Stewart; MacKay, James, McPake, McCaffrey (MacDonald), Makel, Dorrans, Walker (Griffiths), Craig, Fox, Snodgrass.
Partick Th: Tuffey; Robertson, Twaddle, Storey, Kinniburgh, Archibald, Chaplain, Rowson, Buchanan (McStay), Donnelly (Keegan), Harkins (Murray).

Morton (0) 0

Queen of the S (0) 2 *(O'Connor 46, Stewart 87)* 3506

Morton: McGurn; Smith (Russell), McLaughlin, Harding, Greacen, Millar, Finlayson, McGuffie, Weatherson, Wake, McAlister.
Queen of the S: MacDonald; McCann, Harris, MacFarlane, Aitken, Thomson, McQuilken, Tosh, O'Connor (O'Neill), Dobbie (Stewart), Burns.

St Mirren (0) 0

Dundee U (0) 0 3945

St Mirren: Smith; Van Zanten, Maxwell, Barron, Haining, Dorman, Mason (Murray), Potter, Dargo (Kean), Mehmet, Corcoran.
Dundee U: Zaluska; Dillon, Grainger, Wilkie, Dods, Kerr, Gomis (Swanson), Flood, Hunt (Odhiambo), Conway (De Vries), Buaben.

Sunday, 3 February 2008

Hibernian (0) 0

Rangers (0) 0 11,513

Hibernian: Ma Kalambay; McCann, Hanlon, Hogg, Jones, Kerr, Shiels, Murray, Zemmama (O'Brien), Fletcher (Donaldson), Rankin.
Rangers: McGregor■; Broadfoot, Papac, Cuellar, Weir, Ferguson (Boyd), Hemdani (Alexander), Adam, McCulloch, Naysmith (Darcheville), Burke.

Monday, 11 February 2008

Motherwell (0) 1 *(Smith D 61)*

Dundee (0) 2 *(McHale 49, Robertson 55)* 5733

Motherwell: Smith G; McLean, Hammell (Murphy J), Lasley (Smith D), Craigan, Reynolds, McGarry (Lappin), Hughes, McCormack, Clarkson, Fitzpatrick.
Dundee: Roy; Cowan, MacKenzie■, Palenik, Malone, Robertson, McHale, McDonald■, Swankie (Dixon), Lyle (Daquin), Davidson (Sturm).

Tuesday, 12 February 2008

Ross Co (0) 0

St Johnstone (1) 1 *(Craig 14)* 2385

Ross Co: Bullock; Miller, Golabek, Dowie, Keddie, Brady (Lawson), Scott, Higgins, Shields (Petrie), Barrowman, Strachan (Moore).
St Johnstone: Main; Irvine, Stanic (McManus), Cameron, Rutkiewicz, Anderson, Milne (Weatherston), Craig, Jackson, MacDonald (Moon), Sheerin.

FIFTH ROUND REPLAYS

Tuesday, 12 February 2008

Partick Th (0) 1 *(Twaddle 83)*

Livingston (1) 1 *(Dorrans 41)* 2554

Partick Th: Tuffey; Robertson (McKinlay), Storey (Kinniburgh), Harkins, Archibald, Twaddle, Chaplain, Rowson, Murray, Donnelly, Buchanan (Keegan).
Livingston: Stewart; MacKay, McPake, MacDonald, James, Dorrans, Craig, Walker, Makel, Fox, Snodgrass (Weir).
aet; Partick Th won 5-4 on penalties.

Wednesday, 13 February 2008

Dundee U (0) 0

St Mirren (0) 1 *(Dorman 48)* 3723

Dundee U: Zaluska; Flood, Kalvenes (Odhiambo), Wilkie (Dillon), Dods, Kerr, Robertson D (Swanson), Conway, De Vries, Hunt, Gomis.
St Mirren: Howard; Barron, Maxwell, Dorman, Haining, Potter, Van Zanten, Murray, Mehmet, Dargo (Kean), Corcoran.

Sunday, 9 March 2008

Rangers (1) 1 *(Burke 39)*

Hibernian (0) 0 33,837

Rangers: Alexander; Broadfoot, Whittaker, Cuellar, Dailly, Ferguson, Thomson, Davis, Naismith (Novo), McCulloch (Boyd), Burke.
Hibernian: Ma-Kalambay; Gatthuessi, Zarabi, Hogg, Jones, Kerr (Benjelloun), Murray, Rankin, Fletcher, Shiels (Morais), O'Brien.

QUARTER-FINALS

Saturday, 8 March 2008

Queen of the S (0) 2 *(Dobbie 52, McCann 90)*

Dundee (0) 0 6278

Queen of the S: MacDonald; McCann, Thomson, Aitken, Harris, Burns, MacFarlane, Tosh, McQuilken, O'Connor, Dobbie (Stewart).
Dundee: Samson; Worrell, Palenik, Malone, Dixon, Cowan, McHale, Noubissie (Clark), Daquin (O'Brien), Zemlik (Sturm), Davidson.

St Johnstone (1) 1 *(Craig 32 (pen))*

St Mirren (0) 1 *(Dorman 73)* 6094

St Johnstone: Main; Irvine, Stanic, Anderson (James), Rutkiewicz, McManus, Morris, Craig, Jackson, Milne, MacDonald (Sheerin).
St Mirren: Smith; Van Zanten, Maxwell (Kean), Haining, Potter, Murray (McGinn), Dorman, Mason, Corcoran (Miranda), Dargo, Mehmet.

Sunday, 9 March 2008

Aberdeen (0) 1 *(De Visscher 79)*

Celtic (0) 1 *(Vennegoor 90)* 10,909

Aberdeen: Soutar; Maybury, Foster, Considine, Diamond, Severin, De Visscher, Touzani, Miller, Maguire, Jamie Smith (Aluko).
Celtic: Boruc; Hinkel, O'Dea, Sno (Donati), Caldwell, McManus, Nakamura, Hartley, McDonald (Samaras), Vennegoor, McGeady.

Wednesday, 19 March 2008

Rangers (0) 1 *(Boyd 69)*

Partick Th (0) 1 *(Grey 67)* 36,724

Rangers: McGregor; Broadfoot, Whittaker, Cuellar, Dailly, Davis, Naismith (McCulloch), Thomson, Boyd, Novo, Adam (Burke).
Partick Th: Tuffey; Storey, Robertson, Archibald, Twaddle, Chaplain (McStay), Rowson, Roberts, Harkins, Grey (Murray), Donnelly (McKinlay).

QUARTER-FINAL REPLAYS

Tuesday, 18 March 2008

Celtic (0) 0

Aberdeen (0) 1 *(Mackie 69)* 33,506

Celtic: Boruc; Hinkel, Naylor, Donati, Caldwell (Riordan), McManus, Nakamura, Brown S, McDonald (Samaras), Vennegoor, McGeady.
Aberdeen: Soutar; Maybury, McNamara (Walker), Considine, Diamond (Mair), Severin, Touzani (Aluko), Nicholson, Miller, Mackie, Foster.

St Mirren (0) 1 *(Mehmet 70 (pen))*

St Johnstone (3) 3 *(Quinn 13, Jackson 20, MacDonald 28)* 4596

St Mirren: Smith; Van Zanten, Maxwell, Millen (McGinn), Haining, Mason, Dorman, Barron (Kean), Mehmet, Dargo, Corcoran (Miranda).
St Johnstone: Main; Irvine, Sheerin, Craig, Rutkiewicz, McManus, Quinn (Wilson), Morris, Jackson (Moon), Milne, MacDonald (James).

Sunday, 13 April 2008

Partick Th (0) 0

Rangers (2) 2 *(Novo 27, Burke 40)* 9909

Partick Th: Tuffey; Storey (Murray), Donnelly (McKinlay), Robertson, Twaddle, Chaplain, Archibald, Rowson, Gray, Roberts (Keegan), Harkins.
Rangers: McGregor; Smith, Whittaker, Cuellar, Weir, Dailly, Naismith, Thomson, Boyd (Cousin), Novo (McCulloch), Burke.

SEMI-FINAL (at Hampden Park)

Saturday, 12 April 2008

Queen of the S (1) 4 *(Tosh 22, Burns 49, O'Connor 56, Stewart 60)*

Aberdeen (1) 3 *(Considine 36, 59, Nicholson 53)* 24,008

Queen of the S: MacDonald; McCann (Paton), Thomson, Aitken, Harris, Burns, Tosh, MacFarlane, McQuilken, O'Connor, Dobbie (Stewart).
Aberdeen: Soutar; Maybury (Young), McNamara (Mackie), Diamond, Considine, Severin, Foster, Nicholson, Miller, Maguire, Aluko.

Sunday, 20 April 2008

St Johnstone (0) 1 *(McBreen 94)*

Rangers (0) 1 *(Novo 103 (pen))* 26,180

St Johnstone: Main; Irvine, Rutkiewicz, McManus, Stanic (Anderson), Milne, Morris, Hardie (Sheerin), Craig, Jackson, MacDonald (McBreen).
Rangers: Alexander; Whittaker, Smith S (Broadfoot), Cuellar, Dailly, Hemdani, Naismith (Davis), Thomson, Novo, Cousin, Burke (Buffel).
aet; Rangers won 4-3 on penalties.

FINAL (at Hampden Park)

Saturday, 24 May 2008

Queen of the S (0) 2 *(Tosh 50, Thomson 53)*

Rangers (2) 3 *(Boyd 33, 72, Beasley 43)* 48,821

Queen of the S: MacDonald; McCann (Robertson), Thomson, Aitken, Harris, McQuilken (Stewart), MacFarlane, Tosh, Burns, Dobbie (O'Neill), O'Connor.
Rangers: Alexander; Whittaker, Papac, Cuellar, Weir, Ferguson, McCulloch, Thomson, Boyd, Darcheville (Fleck), Beasley (Davis).
Referee: S. Dougal (Scotland).

WELSH FOOTBALL 2007–08

Talk about the biter being bitten. Eighty-one years after winning the FA Cup through a goalkeeping mistake, Cardiff City lost in the final of the world's most famous knockout competition. For Dan Lewis, read Peter Enckelman. In 1927, the Arsenal goalkeeper let a speculative shot by Hughie Ferguson slip under his body and over the line; in 2008, a hopeful cross was fumbled by the Cardiff keeper and Kanu popped in the winner for Portsmouth. In a season of shocks which saw another Championship side, Barnsley, beat both Liverpool and Chelsea, the Bluebirds had deservedly won a rare opportunity to strengthen their unique claim to fame as the only club to have taken the FA Cup out of England. Sadly, the final proved a game too far with Cardiff running out of steam and ideas against a poor Pompey team. A lingering interest in the play-offs had inevitably taken its toll on a small squad but the disappointing display failed to dampen the spirits of the thousands of Cardiff supporters who flocked to the home of English football for only the second FA Cup final to be staged at the new stadium. It was a day to remember – if not for the result then certainly for the occasion.

The Bluebirds eventually finished mid-table in the Championship – six points off the last play-off place – and as the building of their new stadium opposite Ninian Park continues apace, they can also look forward to the reintroduction of local derbies against their rivals from down the road at Swansea. Robert Martinez's astute style of management, mixing British with foreign and particularly Spanish talent, produced a side which hit the front early on and rarely looked back. The Swans may have been embarrassingly dumped out of the FA Cup by Havant and Waterlooville after a replay but their breathtaking league form swept them to promotion as League One champions – after the Leeds points deduction farce was settled. Swansea eventually finished 10 points clear of runners-up Nottingham Forest and the statistics reflected their domination of the division: they won most games (27, jointly with Leeds United), scored most goals (82) and had the biggest goal difference (40).

As Swansea reached the second tier of English football for the first time in nearly a quarter of a century, Wrexham bade farewell to the Football League after a stay of 87 years. Their 2-0 defeat at Hereford in late April merely confirmed the inevitable: the Red Dragons were simply not good enough. Having escaped relegation on the last day of the previous season, they struggled from the outset and although new manager Brian Little attempted to stop the rot by bringing in a coachload of players, it all ended in tears. As the club's official website stated: "It's over . . . the sands of time have finally run out for us." After agreeing a new two-year contract, Little immediately set about clearing the decks with very few players escaping the axe.

With Wales suffering just three defeats in 13 games during the season, manager John Toshack will be reasonably confident that his much trumpeted youngsters can make their mark in the 2010 World Cup qualifying campaign. As usual, they face a formidable group of opponents with Euro 2008 finalists Germany and semi-finalists Russia looking the favourites to go through. But Toshack will have been heartened by a six-match unbeaten run which was ended only in June by Holland, another team who performed well in the summer. Four successive clean sheets against Germany, Norway, Luxembourg and Iceland – and the emergence of keepers Wayne Hennessy, of Wolves, and Hull's Boaz Myhill – augur well for the qualifiers which begin with a home game against Azerbaijan in Cardiff in September. The defence would be further strengthened by the return of the injured West Ham duo of Danny Gabbidon and James Collins and if skipper Craig Bellamy can recapture his best form after injury and Simon Davies and Jason Koumas are able to capitalise on their clubs' successful survival campaigns in the Premier League, then Wales might just surprise one or two teams.

It proved another indifferent season for the three teams competing in the English pyramid with Newport and Colwyn Bay both failing to reach the play-offs in the Blue Square South and Unibond First Division South respectively and Merthyr making slight progress by finishing 13th in the Southern League's Premier Division – a place higher than the previous season.

The dreaded away-goals rule put paid to the hopes of three of the four clubs who represented Wales in Europe. Llanelli made history by becoming the first Welsh team to win an Intertoto Cup match when they beat Vetra 5-3 in the second leg of their first round tie but an aggregate score of 6-6 meant the Lithuanians went through and a hat-trick by striker Rhys Griffiths counted for nothing. The New Saints also made their mark in the record books by winning their first ever European game. The Latvian side Ventspils were beaten 3-2 at home in the first leg of the first qualifying round tie but they turned the tables with a 2-1 victory in the return leg while Rhyl suffered the same fate against Haka in their UEFA Cup first qualifying round game after winning 3-1 at Belle Vue and then losing 2-0 in Finland. Carmarthen were completely outclassed at the same stage in the same competition when they were hammered 8-0 at home by Brann in the first leg. The Norwegians completed the rout with a 6-3 drubbing in the return fixture to create an aggregate score of 14-3 – a record defeat for a Welsh Premier side in Europe.

Llanelli narrowly missed out on the domestic treble when, having won the Welsh Premier League and the League Cup, they surprisingly lost 4-2 to Bangor City in the Welsh Cup Final – having already been beaten 1-0 by Newport in the final of the FAW Premier Cup. As Llanelli make their debut in the Champions League, The New Saints, who slipped to second in the table, will join Bangor in the UEFA Cup while Rhyl qualified for the Intertoto Cup by finishing third.

Despite Wrexham's relegation, the mood in Welsh football is encouragingly upbeat. With the support of the Welsh Assembly Government, the FAW has stepped up its campaign to mount a joint bid with Scotland to stage Euro 2016 and the Under-21 conveyor belt is working overtime as Premiership managers start to sit up and take out their cheque books. Cardiff full-back Chris Gunter joined fellow Welsh international Gareth Bale at Spurs and then Manchester United and Arsenal were involved in a tug-of-war for the £5 million signature of Aaron Ramsey, the 17-year-old Bluebird who came on as a substitute in the FA Cup Final. Arsène Wenger eventually emerged triumphant and he knows a thing or two about developing prodigiously talented teenagers. One of them, Cesc Fabregas, helped Spain to win Euro 2008 and even though Ramsey has yet to make his full international debut, he will surely have some part to play in the latest Welsh attempt to reach the finals of a major competition for the first time since 1958. This young Gunner really is one for the future.

GRAHAME LLOYD

VAUXHALL MASTERFIT RETAILERS WELSH PREMIER LEAGUE 2007–08

		Home					Away					Total						
	P	W	D	L	F	A	W	D	L	F	A	W	D	L	F	A	GD	Pts
1 Llanelli	34	13	2	2	52	13	14	2	1	47	22	27	4	3	99	35	64	85
2 The New Saints	34	15	1	1	53	11	10	2	5	32	19	25	3	6	85	30	55	78
3 Rhyl	34	12	2	3	29	12	9	4	4	31	12	21	6	7	60	24	36	69
4 Port Talbot Town	34	10	5	2	36	18	7	3	7	21	30	17	8	9	57	48	9	59
5 Bangor City	34	8	7	2	34	16	7	3	7	28	15	15	10	9	62	31	31	55
6 Carmarthen Town	34	7	6	4	31	22	8	3	6	28	25	15	9	10	59	47	12	54
7 Neath Athletic	34	9	4	4	31	23	6	5	6	26	29	15	9	10	57	52	5	54
8 Haverfordwest County	34	9	3	5	36	25	5	2	10	25	34	14	5	15	61	59	2	47
9 Aberystwyth Town	34	8	3	6	35	23	5	4	8	22	22	13	7	14	57	45	12	46
10 Welshpool Town	34	6	4	7	23	27	6	6	5	26	25	12	10	12	49	52	–3	46
11 Airbus UK Broughton	34	7	4	6	19	18	4	5	8	17	26	11	9	14	36	44	–8	42
12 NEWI Cefn Druids	34	9	1	7	33	29	3	1	13	12	37	12	2	20	45	66	–21	38
13 Newtown	34	6	5	6	28	26	3	5	9	19	40	9	10	15	47	66	–19	37
14 Caernarfon Town	34	5	4	8	20	32	5	2	10	22	42	10	6	18	42	74	–32	36
15 Connah's Quay Nomads	34	7	3	7	21	30	2	4	11	21	55	9	7	18	42	85	–43	34
16 Porthmadog	34	1	4	12	19	38	6	2	9	29	32	7	6	21	48	70	–22	27
17 Caersws	34	2	3	12	20	43	4	5	8	17	29	6	8	20	37	72	–35	26
18 Llangefni Town	34	5	0	12	21	35	2	3	12	18	47	7	3	24	39	82	–43	24

PREVIOUS WELSH LEAGUE WINNERS

1993	Cwmbran Town	1997	Barry Town	2001	Barry Town	2005	TNS
1994	Bangor City	1998	Barry Town	2002	Barry Town	2006	TNS
1995	Bangor City	1999	Barry Town	2003	Barry Town	2007	TNS
1996	Barry Town	2000	TNS	2004	Rhyl	2008	Llanelli

FAW PREMIER CUP

FIRST ROUND
Connah's Quay Nomads 1, Carmarthen Town 1
Carmarthen Town won 3-2 on penalties.
Porthmadog 2, Port Talbot Town 7
Haverfordwest County 3, Airbus UK Broughton 1
Bangor City 3, Aberystwyth Town 0

SECOND ROUND
Haverfordwest County 0, Welshpool Town 2
Newport County 1, Bangor City 0
Llanelli 4, Rhyl 1
Carmarthen Town 2, Port Talbot Town 1

QUARTER-FINALS
Carmarthen Town 3, TNS 1
Llanelli 4, Wrexham 2
Newport County 1, Swansea City 0
Welshpool Town 0, Cardiff City 1

SEMI-FINALS
Cardiff City 1, Newport County 1
Newport County won 5-4 on penalties.
Llanelli 1, Carmarthen Town 0

FAW PREMIER LEAGUE CUP FINAL

11 March 2008 (at Spytty Park) 1889

Newport County (0) 1 Llanelli (0) 0

Newport County: James; Jenkins, Searle, Davies, Jarman, Cochlin, Bowen, Gurney, Griffin (Clarke 75), Hughes, Evans (Fowler 80), Dodds.
Scorer: Hughes 82.

Llanelli: Harrison; Phillips, Lloyd (Mark Jones 71), Mumford, Jones S, Pritchard (Follows 87), Jones C (Matthew Jones 87), Corbisiero, Griffiths, Holloway, Legg.

Referee: L. Evans.

MACWHIRTER WELSH LEAGUE 2007–08

DIVISION ONE	P	W	D	L	F	A	GD	Pts
Goytre United	34	25	3	6	101	30	71	78
Dinas Powys	34	25	1	8	92	34	58	76
Ton Pentre	34	22	7	5	102	33	69	73
ENTO Aberaman Ath	34	21	6	7	75	40	35	69
Bryntirion Athletic	34	20	5	9	82	35	47	65
Afan Lido	34	17	11	6	58	31	27	62
Newport YMCA	34	19	4	11	88	70	18	61
Caerleon	34	16	7	11	60	42	18	55
Cambrian & Clydach	34	13	10	11	59	47	12	49
Bridgend Town	34	13	6	15	84	68	16	45
Caldicot Town	34	13	3	18	54	65	–11	42
Taffs Well	34	11	7	16	53	70	–17	40
Pontardawe Town	34	11	6	17	47	55	–8	39
Cwmbran Town	34	10	8	16	56	50	6	38
Croesyceiliog	34	9	5	20	60	80	–20	32
Maesteg Park	34	7	6	21	43	83	–40	27
Pontypridd Town	34	3	4	27	38	116	–78	13
Garw	34	1	1	32	14	217	–203	4

HUWS GRAY-FITLOCK CYMRU ALLIANCE LEAGUE 2007–08

	P	W	D	L	F	A	GD	Pts
Prestatyn Town	32	24	4	4	93	29	64	76
Bala Town	32	19	4	9	71	42	29	61
Flint Town Utd	32	16	10	6	62	42	20	58
Llandudno Town	32	16	8	8	58	36	22	56
Holyhead Hotspur	32	15	9	8	76	53	23	54
Gap Queens Park*	32	15	10	7	82	47	35	52
Glantraeth	32	15	6	11	64	55	9	51
Denbigh Town	32	13	7	12	52	50	2	46
Guilsfield	32	12	5	15	57	62	–5	41
Llanfairpwll	32	10	10	12	59	71	–12	40
Mynydd Isa	32	10	9	13	45	51	–6	39
Llandyrnog United	32	10	8	14	54	69	–15	38
Ruthin Town	32	10	6	16	41	63	–22	36
Buckley Town*	32	8	9	15	45	80	–35	30
Penrhyncoch	32	6	8	18	38	66	–28	26
Lex XI*	32	6	7	19	44	85	–41	22
Gresford Athletic	32	4	6	22	32	72	–40	18

** points deducted*

VAUXHALL MASTERFIT WELSH PREMIER LEAGUE RESULTS 2007–08

	Aberystwyth Town	Airbus UK	Bangor City	Caernarfon Town	Caersws	Carmarthen Town	Connah's Quay Nomads	Haverfordwest County	Llanelli	Llangefni Town	Neath Athletic	NEWI Cefn Druids	Newtown	Porthmadog	Port Talbot Town	Rhyl	The New Saints	Welshpool Town
Aberystwyth Town	—	0-0	2-1	4-0	2-1	0-2	6-1	2-3	1-2	3-0	1-2	1-0	2-2	2-1	2-4	0-0	5-1	2-3
Airbus UK	1-1	—	1-0	1-2	0-2	0-1	0-0	3-1	0-1	1-3	2-1	3-2	1-1	2-0	1-0	0-2	2-0	1-1
Bangor City	1-0	5-0	—	5-1	1-1	1-1	3-2	2-0	1-1	2-2	1-1	5-1	2-2	2-0	0-0	1-2	1-2	1-0
Caernarfon Town	1-0	0-3	0-4	—	2-0	2-1	1-1	1-2	3-4	1-0	1-2	1-1	0-0	2-4	3-1	0-1	1-7	1-1
Caersws	1-1	2-3	1-0	0-1	—	1-2	3-4	1-2	0-5	1-1	2-2	1-2	1-0	2-4	1-4	2-7	1-2	0-3
Carmarthen Town	0-3	2-1	2-1	1-1	1-3	—	8-0	2-1	1-2	2-2	1-1	4-1	2-1	0-0	0-0	0-0	0-3	5-2
Connah's Quay Nomads	1-2	1-0	0-7	1-0	1-0	4-3	—	1-1	0-1	2-0	2-0	2-1	1-1	1-2	0-1	0-5	1-3	3-3
Haverfordwest County	3-1	4-0	0-1	1-1	1-0	2-2	6-2	—	1-4	5-1	1-2	3-0	2-3	3-2	2-1	1-1	0-4	1-0
Llanelli	1-0	1-0	0-2	5-1	1-1	4-1	4-0	4-2	—	5-0	3-3	1-0	5-0	1-2	8-0	2-1	4-0	3-0
Llangefni Town	3-0	0-3	0-1	1-2	0-1	0-3	1-2	2-1	1-5	—	4-2	2-0	2-3	1-4	4-1	0-3	0-3	0-1
Neath Athletic	2-2	2-1	1-0	3-2	2-2	1-2	4-0	2-1	0-2	2-0	—	3-0	2-0	2-1	0-2	1-1	2-2	2-5
NEWI Cefn Druids	0-2	4-1	1-6	5-1	4-0	3-1	5-2	1-0	2-5	2-1	0-2	—	3-0	1-1	0-1	1-4	1-0	0-2
Newtown	1-2	1-1	2-2	3-1	2-2	0-1	4-1	1-4	3-5	2-1	3-0	1-0	—	4-2	0-0	0-2	0-0	1-2
Porthmadog	2-6	2-2	0-0	1-3	0-1	1-2	3-3	0-2	2-4	2-4	0-2	1-2	2-3	—	1-2	1-0	0-1	1-1
Port Talbot Town	2-1	0-0	0-0	2-1	3-1	2-0	2-1	2-2	0-1	3-1	3-3	5-1	5-1	4-2	—	1-2	1-0	1-1
Rhyl	0-0	2-1	1-2	3-1	2-1	2-1	1-0	2-0	1-2	4-1	1-0	1-0	2-1	1-0	5-0	—	0-1	1-1
The New Saints	1-0	0-0	2-1	4-0	6-0	0-3	3-1	6-2	3-0	7-1	3-1	3-0	6-0	4-1	2-1	1-0	—	2-0
Welshpool Town	2-1	0-1	2-0	2-4	1-1	2-2	1-1	2-1	3-3	3-0	1-2	0-1	2-1	0-3	1-3	1-0	0-3	—

WELSH CUP 2007–08

PRELIMINARY ROUND SOUTH
Abertillery Excelsiors v Cwmamman United 2-3
Cwmaman Institute v Cwmffrwdr Sports 6-1
Llanwern v Monmouth Town 6-3
Risca United v Goytre United 2-2
Goytre United won 5-4 on penalties.
Seven Sisters v Porthcawl Town 1-1
Seven Sisters won 4-3 on penalties.
Ystradgynlais v Aberbargoed Buds 1-2

PRELIMINARY ROUND MID
Four Crosses v Carno 3-5
Kerry v Knighton Town 1-2
Llanidloes Town v Montgomery Town 0-1
Newbridge on Wye v Newcastle Emlyn 3-4

PRELIMINARY ROUND NORTH
Chirk AAA v Amlwch Town 2-2
Chirk AAA won 4-2 on penalties.
Corwen v Holywell Town 2-1
CPD Llanberis v Castell Alun Colts 3-0
CPD Nantlle Vale v Llandudno Junction 1-0
Nefyn United v Llangollen Town 4-1
Rhos Aelwyd v Halkyn United 3-4

FIRST ROUND SOUTH
Bridgend Town v Garden Village 3-1
Bryntirion Athletic v Pontypridd Town 6-1
Caerau Ely v Garw Athletic 7-0
Caerleon v Treharris 4-0
Cwmaman Institute v Llangeinor 4-2
Cwmamman United v AFC Llwydcoed 3-0
Dinas Powys v Penrhiwceiber 3-0
Ely Rangers v Llantwit Fadre 1-4
Goytre United v Pontardawe Town 3-0
Llansawel v ENTO Aberaman Athletic 2-5
Llanwern v Barry Town 4-2
Maesteg Park v Seven Sisters 2-1
Merthyr Saints v Cwmbran Town 2-0
Newport YMCA v Goytre 2-0
Pentwyn Dynamoes v Cwmbran Celtic 3-1
Pontyclun v Cambrian & Clydach Vale 1-2
Taffs Well v Caldicot 3-2
Ton Pentre v Aberbargoed Buds 3-0
Tredegar Town v Cardiff Corinthians 1-1
Cardiff Corinthians won 4-3 on penalties.
Troedyrhiw v Croesyceiliog 3-7
West End v Bettws 2-1
N.B: Briton Ferry w.o. v UW Aberystwyth withdrew.

FIRST ROUND MID
Carno v Penrhyncoch 1-4
Guilsfield v Presteigne St Andrews 2-1
Montgomery Town v Llanfyllyn Town 2-1
Llanhaedr v Berriew 3-2
Newcastle Emlyn v Knighton Town 4-1

FIRST ROUND NORTH
Bala Town v Denbigh Town 6-3
Bodedern v Llanfair PG 0-2
Brickfield Rangers v Brymbo 0-12
CPD Llanberis v Llanwrst United 4-3
Coedpoeth United v Mold Alexandra 0-1
Conwy United v CPD Glynceiriog 4-0
Corwen v Lex XI 3-1
CPD Nantlle Vale v Chirk AAA 0-2
Glan Conwy v Llanrug United 1-3
Halkyn United v Ruthin Town 2-1
Hawarden Rangers v Buckley Town 3-0
Holyhead Hotspurs v Cefn United 3-2
Llandymog United v Penycae 3-1
Mynydd Isa v Glantreath 3-1
Nefyn United v Gresford Athletic 2-0
Prestatyn v Llandudno Town 1-2
Pwllheli v GAP Queens Park 3-4
Tywyn & Bryncrug v Rhydmwyn 6-6
Tywyn & Bryncrug won 5-4 on penalties.

SECOND ROUND
Aberystwyth Town v Newcastle Emlyn 3-0
Afan Lido v Croesyceiliog 3-1
Bangor City v Llandymog United 3-0
Bridgend Town v Bryntirion Athletic 1-2
Brymbo v Halkyn United 4-0
Caerau Ely v Goytre United 3-2
Caerleon v Taffs Well 2-1
Caernarfon Town v Llanfair PG 2-1
Caersws v Mold Alexandra 9-0
Cardiff Corinthians v Ton Pentre 2-3
Connah's Quay Nomads v The New Saints 3-1
Corwen v Mynydd Isa 1-3
CPD Llanberis v Newtown 1-5
Cwmaman Institute v ENTO Aberaman Athletic 0-3
Cwmamman United v Dinas Powys 0-5
GAP Queens Park v Penrhyncoch 3-1
Guilsfield Athletic v Airbus UK Broughton 3-2
Haverfordwest County v Llantwit Fadre 1-0
Holyhead Hotspurs v Bala Town 2-1
Llandudno Town v NEWI Cefn Druids 1-2
Llangefni Town v Hawarden Rangers 5-0
Llanrug United v Llanrhaedr 5-1
Maesteg Park v Briton Ferry 2-0
Merthyr Saints v Carmarthen Town 1-2
Neath Athletic v Llanwern 6-0
Nefyn United v Chirk AAA 2-0
Newport YMCA v Cambrian & Clydach Vale 4-1
Pentwyn Dynamoes v Llanelli 3-7
Porthmadog v Welshpool Town 0-2
Rhyl v Montgomery Town 10-0
Tywyn & Bryncrug v Conwy United 3-2
West End v Port Talbot Town 1-2

THIRD ROUND
Aberystwyth Town v Neath Athletic 3-1
Bryntirion Athletic v Dinas Powys 4-2
Caerleon v Brymbo 2-0
Caersws v Bangor City 2-3
ENTO Aberaman Athletic v Caerau Ely 3-1
GAP Queens Park v Afan Lido 3-1
Haverfordwest County v Ton Pentre 3-0
Llangefni Town v Mynydd Isa 3-0
Llanrug United v Llanelli 3-5
Nefyn United v Caernarfon Town 1-3
NEWI Cefn Druids v Holyhead Hotspurs 3-0
Newport YMCA v Carmarthen Town 2-1
Newtown v Maesteg Park 2-1
Rhyl v Port Talbot Town 1-0
Tywyn & Bryncrug v Welshpool Town 1-3
Connah's Quay Nomads v Guilsfield Athletic 0-2

FOURTH ROUND
Aberystwyth Town v Bangor City 0-0
Bangor City won 3-2 on penalties.
Bryntirion Athletic v Welshpool Town 1-2
GAP Queens Park v Caerleon 2-0
Guilsfield Athletic v Caernarfon Town 1-0
Haverfordwest County v Rhyl 1-2
NEWI Cefn Druids v ENTO Aberaman Athletic 0-0
NEWI Cefn Druids won 5-3 on penalties.
Newport YMCA v Llangefni Town 1-1
Newport YMCA won 4-3 on penalties.
Newtown AFC v Llanelli 1-2

QUARTER-FINALS
Guilsfield Athletic v Bangor City 0-6
Newport YMCA v Welshpool Town 3-2
Rhyl v GAP Queens Park 3-2
NEWI Cefn Druids v Llanelli 3-6

SEMI-FINALS
Llanelli v Rhyl 5-2
Newport YMCA v Bangor City 1-3

FINAL (at Newtown) **1510**
4 May 2008

Bangor C (1) 4 Llanelli (0) 2 *aet*
Bangor C: Smith; Swanick, Hoy■, Johnston, Webber (Noon 73), Seargeant, Limbert, Walsh (Killackey 73), Davies, Stott, Edwards (Beatie 57).
Scorers: Stott 20, Seargeant 90, Limbert 97 (pen), Noon 99.
Llanelli: Roberts; Phillips, Mumford, Thomas■, Corbisiero (Evans 46), Griffiths R■, Holloway, Pritchard, Jones C (Mark Jones 62), Legg, Matthew Jones (Wanless 97).
Scorers: Swanick 48 (og), Griffiths R 56.
Referee: P. Southall.

■ *Denotes player sent off.*

PREVIOUS WELSH CUP WINNERS

1878	Wrexham Town	1909	Wrexham	1950	Swansea Town	1981	Swansea City
1879	White Star Newtown	1910	Wrexham	1951	Merthyr Tydfil	1982	Swansea City
1880	Druids	1911	Wrexham	1952	Rhyl	1983	Swansea City
1881	Druids	1912	Cardiff City	1953	Rhyl	1984	Shrewsbury Town
1882	Druids	1913	Swansea Town	1954	Flint Town United	1985	Shrewsbury Town
1883	Wrexham	1914	Wrexham	1955	Barry Town	1986	Wrexham
1884	Oswestry United	1915	Wrexham	1956	Cardiff City	1987	Merthyr Tydfil
1885	Druids	1920	Cardiff City	1957	Wrexham	1988	Cardiff City
1886	Druids	1921	Wrexham	1958	Wrexham	1989	Swansea City
1887	Chirk	1922	Cardiff City	1959	Cardiff City	1990	Hereford United
1888	Chirk	1923	Cardiff City	1960	Wrexham	1991	Swansea City
1889	Bangor	1924	Wrexham	1961	Swansea Town	1992	Cardiff City
1890	Druids	1925	Wrexham	1962	Bangor City	1993	Cardiff City
1891	Shrewsbury Town	1926	Ebbw Vale	1963	Borough United	1994	Barry Town
1892	Chirk	1927	Cardiff City	1964	Cardiff City	1995	Wrexham
1893	Wrexham	1928	Cardiff City	1965	Cardiff City	1996	TNS
1894	Chirk	1929	Connah's Quay	1966	Swansea Town	1997	Barry Town
1895	Newtown	1930	Cardiff City	1967	Cardiff City	1998	Bangor City
1896	Bangor	1931	Wrexham	1968	Cardiff City	1999	Inter Cable-Tel
1897	Wrexham	1932	Swansea Town	1969	Cardiff City	2000	Bangor City
1898	Druids	1933	Chester	1970	Cardiff City	2001	Barry Town
1899	Druids	1934	Bristol City	1971	Cardiff City	2002	Barry Town
1900	Aberystwyth	1935	Tranmere Rovers	1972	Wrexham	2003	Barry Town
1901	Oswestry United	1936	Crewe Alexandra	1973	Cardiff City	2004	Rhyl
1902	Wellington Town	1937	Crewe Alexandra	1974	Cardiff City	2005	TNS
1903	Wrexham	1938	Shrewsbury Town	1975	Wrexham	2006	Rhyl
1904	Druids	1939	South Liverpool	1976	Cardiff City	2007	Carmarthen Town
1905	Wrexham	1940	Wellington Town	1977	Shrewsbury Town	2008	Bangor C
1906	Wellington Town	1947	Chester	1978	Wrexham		
1907	Oswestry United	1948	Lovell's Athletic	1979	Shrewsbury Town		
1908	Chester	1949	Merthyr Tydfil	1980	Newport County		

THE LOOSEMORES OF CARDIFF CHALLENGE CUP 2007–08

GROUP 1	*P*	*W*	*D*	*L*	*F*	*A*	*GD*	*Pts*
Llangefni Town	4	4	0	0	10	4	6	12
Porthmadog	4	1	1	2	8	8	0	4
Caernarfon Town	4	0	1	3	7	13	–6	1
GROUP 2	*P*	*W*	*D*	*L*	*F*	*A*	*GD*	*Pts*
Rhyl	4	3	1	0	10	3	7	10
Bangor City	4	2	1	1	8	2	6	7
Connah's Quay Nomads	4	0	0	4	2	15	–13	0
GROUP 3	*P*	*W*	*D*	*L*	*F*	*A*	*GD*	*Pts*
TNS	4	3	0	1	7	4	3	9
NEWI Cefn Druids	4	2	1	1	3	2	1	7
Airbus UK	4	0	1	3	2	6	–4	1
GROUP 4	*P*	*W*	*D*	*L*	*F*	*A*	*GD*	*Pts*
Welshpool Town	4	2	2	0	8	5	3	8
Caersws	4	2	1	1	10	6	4	7
Newtown	4	0	1	3	3	10	–7	1
GROUP 5	*P*	*W*	*D*	*L*	*F*	*A*	*GD*	*Pts*
Carmarthen Town	4	3	1	0	17	4	13	10
Aberystwyth Town	4	2	1	1	10	5	5	7
Haverfordwest County	4	0	0	4	3	21	–18	0
GROUP 6	*P*	*W*	*D*	*L*	*F*	*A*	*GD*	*Pts*
Llanelli	4	3	0	1	12	7	5	9
Neath Athletic	4	2	0	2	7	9	–2	6
Port Talbot Town	4	1	0	3	8	11	–3	2

Port Talbot Town deducted one point for fielding ineligible players.

QUARTER-FINALS

Carmarthen Town v Aberystwyth Town	0-3
Llanelli v Welshpool Town	2-0
Llangefni Town v Rhyl	2-5
TNS v Bangor City	1-2

SEMI-FINALS FIRST LEG

Aberystwyth Town v Llanelli	2-1
Rhyl v Bangor City	1-1

SEMI-FINALS SECOND LEG

Llanelli v Aberystwyth Town	1-0
Bangor City v Rhyl	0-2

FINAL

27 April 2008

Llanelli 2 *(Mumford 15, Holloway 40)*

Rhyl 0 510

Llanelli: Roberts; Phillips, Lloyd, Mumford, Wanless (Holland 55), Holloway, Pritchard, Mark Jones, Legg, Evans, Matthew Jones.

Rhyl: Kendall; Ruffer, Graves, Connolly, Horan, O'Neill (Garside 55), Jones, Wilson, Hunt, Sharp, Roberts.

Referee: S. Hames.

NORTHERN IRISH FOOTBALL 2007–08

Northern Ireland domestic football is entering a year of dramatic change – indeed, experiencing a revolution. The 16-club Premier League has been abandoned and a Premier Invitation League established, consisting of 12 teams selected on a points system covering facilities, playing record and financial situation.

Irish FA officials are confident this will be the much needed injection required to stimulate the game, generate greater crowd pulling appeal and with £400,000 prize money – the winners collecting £50,000 – a competitive element should be ensured. Others are not so sure, contending it could perhaps be the same mix as before, the usual teams dominating, just a cash enhanced stereotyped version of the old. We shall see.

The restructuring, carried out with scrupulous fairness, was not, however, without controversy. Portadown, the provincial club with the largest support, now embarking on a £2m ground investment programme, submitted their application 14 minutes after the March 31 deadline and were ruled out. They will compete in the Intermediate League hoping to gain promotion at the first attempt. Donegal Celtic, pipped to the post by Bangor and Institute, appealed against exclusion to an independent panel. This was also rejected so Donegal Celtic will also figure in the lower division.

Controversy still exists over the five-year saga of the proposed new multi-purpose national stadium at the Maze. With so much uncertainty, Linfield, owners of Windsor Park, international venue for more than 100 years, and the Irish FA have entered talks for a possible joint approach to the Government whose grant aid is required for the refurbishing of the stadium either on a temporary or, more preferably, a permanent basis. Once Windsor Park could accommodate 58,000 plus, currently it is limited to 14,000, due to health and safety regulations and there is a need for a 22,000 all-seated arena which would make the running of international football financially viable to counteract escalating costs and reduced revenue.

From a playing viewpoint, it was a case of so near yet so far in the European Championship qualifiers, finishing behind Spain and Sweden. There were victories over Liechtenstein, Denmark, disastrous back-to-back away defeats in Latvia and Iceland and finally overwhelmed by Spain at Las Palmas, Gran Canaria.

Manager Nigel Worthington, who has reshuffled his coaching staff from Under-21 to Under-17 level, is confident they can make an impact in the forthcoming World Cup qualifiers against the Czech Republic, Poland, Slovakia, Slovenia and San Marino, commencing in September.

After studying the Czechs and Poles in the Euro 2008 finals, he delivered this verdict: "Each team possesses quality players, some world-class but they don't frighten me. Obviously, we'll treat them with the respect they deserve, but I believe we can pick up points, particularly at Windsor Park which we have made a fortress again.

"Visiting teams don't relish playing there because of the passion we display against a backcloth of a huge crowd, the Green and White Army."

There is a heritage about Windsor, a tradition. Everyone who plays there in a green jersey is filled with pride.

Linfield, with a glitterati of talent, including striker Glenn Ferguson, who has scored more than 500 goals in a distinguished career, again swept the boards, winning the Irish Premier Division title, Irish Cup, CIS Insurance Cup, and are one of the favourites for the Setanta All-Ireland Cup which this season has been split into two calendar segments instead of being completed. They were a class apart, with David Jeffrey, known as The Special One by the fans, in May collecting the Manager of the Year Trophy, international goalkeeper Alan Mannus, Ulster Footballer of the Year, while Michael Gault was nominated by the football writers as Player of the Year.

Glentoran, under Alan McDonald, former Northern Ireland and QPR centre-back, were runners-up, while Cliftonville, among the early pacesetters, stumbled at the final hurdles due to fatigue, physically and mentally, after almost nine months of constant football – an impossibility for semi-professionals.

A new dawn breaks but what lies beyond the horizon remains to be seen.

DR MALCOLM BRODIE MBE

CARNEGIE IRISH PREMIER LEAGUE

	P	W	D	L	F	A	GD	Pts
Linfield	30	23	5	2	71	18	53	74
Glentoran	30	22	5	3	69	24	45	71
Cliftonville	30	18	6	6	55	32	23	60
Lisburn Distillery	30	17	7	6	50	28	22	58
Portadown	30	15	2	13	44	39	5	47
Ballymena United	30	12	8	10	42	41	1	44
Crusaders	30	12	7	11	45	47	–2	43
Newry City	30	13	4	13	45	52	–7	53
Coleraine	30	11	7	12	41	50	–9	40
Dungannon Swifts	30	9	9	12	38	44	–6	36
Donegal Celtic	30	9	8	13	39	47	–8	35
Glenavon	30	9	3	18	37	51	–14	30
Larne	30	7	4	19	44	71	–27	25
Institute	30	5	8	17	23	41	–18	23
Limavady United	30	6	5	19	26	57	–31	23
Armagh City	30	5	6	19	29	56	–27	21

No promotion or relegation. New invitational 12 club Premier League for 2008–09. Competing clubs as above, minus Donegal Celtic, Larne, Limavady United, Armagh City and Portadown, plus Bangor. Portadown's application submitted too late. They lost a subsequent appeal as did Donegal Celtic.

CARNEGIE IRISH LEAGUE FIRST DIVISION

	P	W	D	L	F	A	GD	Pts
Loughgall	22	15	4	3	42	21	21	49
Dundela	22	12	3	7	38	28	10	39
Bangor	22	10	7	5	43	33	10	37
Ballyclare Comrades	22	10	6	6	28	17	11	36
Tobermore United	22	10	5	7	41	32	9	35
Carrick Rangers	22	10	3	9	34	30	4	33
Banbridge Town	22	10	2	10	38	38	0	32
Ards	22	8	3	11	32	28	4	27
Coagh United	22	7	6	9	27	35	–8	27
HW Welders	22	6	8	8	10	27	–8	26
Lurgan Celtic	22	5	3	14	22	44	–22	18
Portstewart	22	1	6	15	19	50	–31	9

CARNEGIE IRISH LEAGUE SECOND DIVISION

	P	W	D	L	F	A	GD	Pts
Dergview	22	17	3	2	65	18	47	54
Ballymoney United	22	14	6	2	44	20	24	48
Ballinamallard United	22	12	6	4	47	15	32	42
Glebe Rangers	22	13	3	6	47	25	22	42
Annagh United	22	12	3	7	33	24	9	39
PSNI	22	9	3	10	37	35	2	30
Wakehurst	22	8	6	8	32	27	5	30
Oxford United Stars	22	9	2	11	33	37	–4	29
Brantwood	22	6	3	13	26	44	–18	21
Queens University	22	4	5	13	25	45	–20	17
Chimney Corner	22	4	3	15	25	75	–50	15
Moyola Park	22	2	1	19	18	67	–49	7

CARNEGIE IRISH RESERVE LEAGUE

	P	W	D	L	F	A	GD	Pts
Donegal Celtic	30	21	5	4	63	34	29	68
Ballymena United	30	20	5	5	72	32	40	65
Linfield Swifts	30	17	6	7	80	44	36	57
Coleraine	30	17	5	8	61	43	18	56
Cliftonville Olympic	30	15	7	8	34	28	6	52
Crusaders	30	14	6	10	59	46	13	48
Lisburn Distillery II	30	13	8	9	54	40	14	47
Glentoran II	30	11	9	10	40	37	3	42
Portadown	30	11	5	14	61	58	3	38
Armagh City	30	11	4	15	43	54	–11	37
Glenavon	30	10	6	14	47	62	–15	36
Dungannon Swifts	30	8	11	11	47	54	–7	35
Limavady United	30	9	5	16	45	64	–19	32
Institute	30	9	2	19	36	57	–21	29
Newry City	30	9	0	21	35	36	–1	27
Larne Olympic	30	2	2	26	17	105	–88	8

IRISH LEAGUE CHAMPIONSHIP WINNERS

1891 Linfield
1892 Linfield
1893 Linfield
1894 Glentoran
1895 Linfield
1896 Distillery
1897 Glentoran
1898 Linfield
1899 Distillery
1900 Belfast Celtic
1901 Distillery
1902 Linfield
1903 Distillery
1904 Linfield
1905 Glentoran
1906 Cliftonville
Distillery
1907 Linfield
1908 Linfield
1909 Linfield
1910 Cliftonville
1911 Linfield
1912 Glentoran
1913 Glentoran
1914 Linfield
1915 Belfast Celtic
1920 Belfast Celtic
1921 Glentoran
1922 Linfield
1923 Linfield
1924 Queen's Island
1925 Glentoran
1926 Belfast Celtic
1927 Belfast Celtic
1928 Belfast Celtic
1929 Belfast Celtic
1930 Linfield
1931 Glentoran
1932 Linfield
1933 Belfast Celtic
1934 Linfield
1935 Linfield
1936 Belfast Celtic
1937 Belfast Celtic
1938 Belfast Celtic
1939 Belfast Celtic
1940 Belfast Celtic
1948 Belfast Celtic
1949 Linfield
1950 Linfield
1951 Glentoran
1952 Glenavon
1953 Glentoran
1954 Linfield
1955 Linfield
1956 Linfield
1957 Glentoran
1958 Ards
1959 Linfield
1960 Glenavon
1961 Linfield
1962 Linfield
1963 Distillery
1964 Glentoran
1965 Derry City
1966 Linfield
1967 Glentoran
1968 Glentoran
1969 Linfield
1970 Glentoran
1971 Linfield
1972 Glentoran
1973 Crusaders
1974 Coleraine
1975 Linfield
1976 Crusaders
1977 Glentoran
1978 Linfield
1979 Linfield
1980 Linfield
1981 Glentoran
1982 Linfield
1983 Linfield
1984 Linfield
1985 Linfield
1986 Linfield
1987 Linfield
1988 Glentoran
1989 Linfield
1990 Portadown
1991 Portadown
1992 Glentoran
1993 Linfield
1994 Linfield
1995 Crusaders
1996 Portadown
1997 Crusaders
1998 Cliftonville
1999 Glentoran
2000 Linfield
2001 Linfield
2002 Portadown
2003 Glentoran
2004 Linfield
2005 Glentoran
2006 Linfield
2007 Linfield
2008 Linfield

FIRST DIVISION

1996 Coleraine
1997 Ballymena United
1998 Newry Town
1999 Distillery
2000 Omagh Town
2001 Ards
2002 Lisburn Distillery
2003 Dungannon Swifts
2004 Loughgall
2005 Armagh City
2006 Crusaders
2007 Institute
2008 Loughgall

SETANTA SPORTS CUP

GROUP 1	P	W	D	L	F	A	Pts
Drogheda United	3	2	1	0	7	2	7
Cork City	3	2	1	0	4	0	7
Cliftonville	3	0	1	2	2	5	1
Dungannon Swifts	3	0	1	2	0	6	1

GROUP 2	P	W	D	L	F	A	Pts
Linfield	3	2	0	1	6	4	6
St Patrick's Athletic	3	1	1	1	5	5	4
Derry City	3	1	1	1	4	4	4
Glentoran	3	0	2	1	5	7	2

REMAINING FIXTURES GROUP 1
Drogheda United v Dungannon Swifts; Cliftonville v Cork City; Drogheda United v Cork City; Dungannon Swifts v Cliftonville; Cliftonville v Drogheda United; Cork City v Dungannon Swifts.

REMAINING FIXTURES GROUP 2
Derry City v Glentoran; Linfield v St Patrick's Athletic; Linfield v Glentoran; St Patrick's Athletic v Derry City; Glentoran v St Patrick's Athletic; Derry City v Linfield.

SETANTA SPORTS CUP WINNERS

2004–05 Linfield
2005–06 Drogheda United
2006–07 Drogheda United

CIS INSURANCE IRISH LEAGUE CUP

GROUP TABLES

GROUP A	P	W	D	L	F	A	GD	Pts
Linfield	6	5	1	0	13	2	11	16
Dungannon Swifts	6	3	1	2	7	6	1	10
Glenavon	6	1	1	4	8	13	–5	4
Ballymena United	6	1	1	4	7	14	–7	4

GROUP B	P	W	D	L	F	A	GD	Pts
Glentoran	6	6	0	0	19	6	13	18
Lisburn Distillery	6	3	1	2	9	8	1	10
Larne	6	1	1	4	11	13	–2	4
Armagh City	6	1	0	5	5	17	–12	3

GROUP C	P	W	D	L	F	A	GD	Pts
Cliftonville	6	4	2	0	12	5	7	14
Crusaders	6	3	1	2	11	12	–1	10
Donegal Celtic	6	1	2	3	8	10	–2	5
Limavady United	6	1	1	4	10	14	–4	4

GROUP D	P	W	D	L	F	A	GD	Pts
Portadown	6	5	1	0	12	6	6	16
Newry City	6	4	1	1	8	5	3	13
Coleraine	6	0	2	4	7	11	–4	2
Institute	6	0	2	4	6	11	–5	2

QUARTER-FINALS
Linfield v Lisburn Distillery 5-1
Glentoran v Dungannon Swifts 1-0
Cliftonville v Newry City 3-3
(Newry City won 6-5 on penalties).
Portadown v Crusaders 3-4

SEMI-FINALS
Crusaders v Glentoran 1-0
Linfield v Newry City 1-1
(Linfield won 4-3 on penalties).

CIS INSURANCE IRISH LEAGUE CUP FINAL
(at Windsor Park, 2 February 2008)

Crusaders 2 *(Rainey 54, Brown 77)*
Linfield 3 *(Thompson 46, Ferguson 86, 89)* 6000

Crusaders: Kerr; Magowan (Owens 90), McBride, Doherty, Smyth, Coates, Morrow, Coulter, Brown, Rainey, Emerson (McAllister 68).

Linfield: Mannus; Murphy, Curran, Lindsay, McAreavey, O'Kane, Thompson, Ervin (Dickson 80), Mulgrew (Kearaney 60), Stewart, Downey (Ferguson 66).

Ferguson's career total goals now 502.

Referee: D. Malcolm (Bangor).

JJB SPORTS IRISH CUP 2007–08

FIFTH ROUND

Institute v Dunmurry Rec	6-0
Banbridge Town v Abbey Villa	2-3
Ards v Brantwood	1-1, 0-1
Limavady United v Dungannon Swifts	1-1, 1-2
Newry City v Ballymena United	2-2, 0-0
(Newry City won 4-2 on penalties.)	
Killyleagh YC v Downpatrick	0-1
Glenavon v Bangor	1-2
Armagh City v Crusaders	1-5
Loughgall v Linfield	0-3
Larne v Cliftonville	2-3
Donegal Celtic v Carrick Rangers	3-0
Portadown v Newington YC	1-0
Ballyclare Comrades v Ballymoney United	0-0, 1-0
Dundela v Portstewart	0-0
Coleraine v Tobermore United	1-0
Glentoran v Lisburn Distillery	0-0, 3-1

SIXTH ROUND

Ballyclare Comrades v Institute	2-2, 0-2
Coleraine v Brantwood	5-1
Dungannon Swifts v Glentoran	0-2
Newry City v Dundela	1-1, 1-0
Cliftonville v Crusaders	1-0
Donegal Celtic v Abbey Villa	1-0
Linfield v Bangor	3-0
Portadown v Downpatrick	2-1

QUARTER-FINALS

Institute v Coleraine	0-0, 1-5
Cliftonville v Portadown	4-3
Glentoran v Donegal Celtic	1-2
Newry City v Linfield	1-1, 0-4

SEMI-FINALS

Donegal Celtic v Coleraine	1-1, 1-2
Linfield v Cliftonville	2-1

JJB SPORTS IRISH CUP FINAL 2007–08

(at Windsor Park, 3 May 2008).

Coleraine (1) 1
Linfield (0) 2 8543

Coleraine: O'Hare; Watt (Dooley 75), McVey, McLaughlin P, Clanaghan, Hunter, McCallion, Neill, Carson, Tolan, Patton.
Scorer: McLaughlin P 19.

Linfield: Mannus; Lindsay, Murphy, Bailie, O'Kane, Mulgrew, Gault, McAreavey (Dickson 46), Kearney (Curran 87), Ferguson, Thompson.
Scorers: Thompson 49, 52.

Referee: D. Malcolm (Bangor).

IRISH CUP FINALS (from 1946–47)

1946–47 Belfast Celtic 1, Glentoran 0
1947–48 Linfield 3, Coleraine 0
1948–49 Derry City 3, Glentoran 1
1949–50 Linfield 2, Distillery 1
1950–51 Glentoran 3, Ballymena U 1
1951–52 Ards 1, Glentoran 0
1952–53 Linfield 5, Coleraine 0
1953–54 Derry City 1, Glentoran 0
1954–55 Dundela 3, Glenavon 0
1955–56 Distillery 1, Glentoran 0
1956–57 Glenavon 2, Derry City 0
1957–58 Ballymena U 2, Linfield 0
1958–59 Glenavon 2, Ballymena U 0
1959–60 Linfield 5, Ards 1
1960–61 Glenavon 5, Linfield 1
1961–62 Linfield 4, Portadown 0
1962–63 Linfield 2, Distillery 1
1963–64 Derry City 2, Glentoran 0
1964–65 Coleraine 2, Glenavon 1
1965–66 Glentoran 2, Linfield 0
1966–67 Crusaders 3, Glentoran 1
1967–68 Crusaders 2, Linfield 0
1968–69 Ards 4, Distillery 2
1969–70 Linfield 2, Ballymena U 1
1970–71 Distillery 3, Derry City
1971–72 Coleraine 2, Portadown 1
1972–73 Glentoran 3, Linfield 2
1973–74 Ards 2, Ballymena U 1
1974–75 Coleraine 1:0:1, Linfield 1:0:0
1975–76 Carrick Rangers 2, Linfield 1
1976–77 Coleraine 4, Linfield 1
1977–78 Linfield 3, Ballymena U 1
1978–79 Cliftonville 3, Portadown 2
1979–80 Linfield 2, Crusaders 0
1980–81 Ballymena U 1, Glenavon 0
1981–82 Linfield 2, Coleraine 1
1982–83 Glentoran 1:2, Linfield 1:1
1983–84 Ballymena U 4, Carrick Rangers 1
1984–85 Glentoran 1:1, Linfield 1:0
1985–86 Glentoran 2, Coleraine 1
1986–87 Glentoran 1, Larne 0
1987–88 Glentoran 1, Glenavon 0
1988–89 Ballymena U 1, Larne 0
1989–90 Glentoran 3, Portadown 0
1990–91 Portadown 2, Glenavon 1
1991–92 Glenavon 2, Linfield 1
1992–93 Bangor 1:1:1, Ards 1:1:0
1993–94 Linfield 2, Bangor 0
1994–95 Linfield 3, Carrick Rangers 1
1995–96 Glentoran 1, Glenavon 0
1996–97 Glenavon 1, Cliftonville 0
1997–98 Glentoran 1, Glenavon 0
1998–99 *Portadown awarded trophy after Cliftonville were eliminated for using an ineligible player in semi-final.*
1999–2000 Glentoran 1, Portadown 0
2000–01 Glentoran 1, Linfield 0
2001–02 Linfield 2, Portadown 1
2002–03 Coleraine 1, Glentoran 0
2003–04 Glentoran 1, Coleraine 0
2004–05 Portadown 5, Larne 1
2005–06 Linfield 2, Glentoran 1
2006–07 Linfield 2, Dungannon Swifts 2 *(aet; Linfield won 3-2 on penalties).*
2007–08 Linfield 2, Coleraine 1

CREST WEAR COUNTY ANTRIM SHIELD

SEMI-FINALS

Cliftonville 1 *(F Murphy 48 (pen))*
Glentoran 2 *(Hamilton 33, Nixon 66)* 2238
(at Windsor Park).

Ballymena United 1 *(Flynn 70)*
Crusaders 2 *(Rainey 48, 81)* 545
(at Ballymena).

COUNTY ANTRIM SHIELD FINAL

(at Windsor Park, 30 October 2007)

Crusaders 1 *(Morrow (90)*
Glentoran 2 *(Scullion 64, Berry 71)* 3370

Crusaders: Hogg; Magowan, McBride, Doherty, Spence, Coates, Coulter (Tumilty 31), Lockhart, Reilly (McAllister 69), Rainey, Morrow.

Glentoran: Morris; Nixon, Hill, Leeman, Ward S, Hamill (Ward M 83), Halliday, Hamilton, Scullion, Berry, Fordyce.

Referee: D. Best (Carnmoney).

ULSTER CUP WINNERS

1949 Linfield	1962 Linfield	1975 Coleraine	1988 Glentoran	2001 *No competition*
1950 Larne	1963 Crusaders	1976 Glentoran	1989 Glentoran	2002 *No competition*
1951 Glentoran	1964 Linfield	1977 Linfield	1990 Portadown	2003 Dungannon Swifts
1952	1965 Coleraine	1978 Linfield	1991 Bangor	*(Confined to*
1953 Glentoran	1966 Glentoran	1979 Linfield	1992 Linfield	*First Division clubs)*
1954 Crusaders	1967 Linfield	1980 Ballymena U	1993 Crusaders	2004 *No competition*
1955 Glenavon	1968 Coleraine	1981 Glentoran	1994 Bangor	2005 *No competition*
1956 Linfield	1969 Coleraine	1982 Glentoran	1995 Portadown	2006 *No competition*
1957 Linfield	1970 Linfield	1983 Glentoran	1996 Portadown	2007 *No competition*
1958 Distillery	1971 Linfield	1984 Linfield	1997 Coleraine	2008 *No competition*
1959 Glenavon	1972 Coleraine	1985 Coleraine	1998 Ballyclare Comrades	
1960 Linfield	1973 Ards	1986 Coleraine	1999 Distillery	
1961 Ballymena U	1974 Linfield	1987 Larne	2000 *No competition*	

ROLL OF HONOUR SEASON 2007–08

Competition	*Winner*	*Runner-up*
Carnegie Premier Division	Linfield	Glentoran
Carnegie First Division	Loughgall	Dundela
JJB Sports Irish Cup	Linfield	Coleraine
CIS Insurance Irish League Cup	Linfield	Crusaders
County Antrim Shield	Glentoran	Crusaders
Steel & Sons Cup	Dundela	Ballyclare Comrades
County Antrim Junior Shield	Ballywalter Rec	Malachans II
WKD Intermediate Cup	Loughgall	Ards
Irish Junior Cup	Immaculata	High Street
Mid-Ulster Cup	Loughgall	Banbridge Town
North West Senior Cup	Coleraine	Tobermore United
The Harry Cavan Youth Cup	Lisburn Distillery III	Portadown III
George Wilson Memorial Cup	Cliftonville Olympic	Linfield Swifts
Irish League Youth Cup	Ards	Cliftonville
Carnegie Irish League Cup	Loughgall	Bangor

AWARDS

ULSTER FOOTBALLER OF THE YEAR
(Castlereagh Glentoran Supporters Award)
Alan Mannus *(Linfield)*

NORTHERN IRELAND PLAYER OF THE YEAR
(Football Writers Association)
Michael Gault *(Linfield)*

YOUNG PLAYER
Aaron Smyth *(Cliftonville)*

MANAGER OF THE YEAR
David Jeffrey *(Linfield)*

OUTSTANDING NON SENIOR TEAM
Loughgall

INTERNATIONAL PERSONALITY
David Healy *(Fulham)*

SUNDAY LIFE LEADING SCORER

Premier Division
Peter Thompson *(Linfield)* 44

First Division
Matt Burrows *(Dundela)* 56

TEAM OF THE YEAR
Mannus *(Linfield)*
Smyth *(Cliftonville)*
Murphy *(Linfield)*
Leeman *(Glentoran)*
R. Scannell *(Cliftonville)*
McMullan *(Cliftonville)*
Gault *(Linfield)*
Johnston *(Cliftonville)*
Carson *(Coleraine)*
Thompson *(Linfield)*
Hamilton *(Glentoran)*

CHAMPIONS LEAGUE REVIEW 2007–08

A Champions League final involving two English teams was a clear indication of the strength of the Premier League. There was drama aplenty, too, in Moscow in yet another match decided by penalties. In such circumstances there has to be a hero and a fall guy. United goalkeeper Erwin Van der Sar fell into the former category, John Terry the latter.

When the dust settled it had produced Manchester United's third European Cup success and for Chelsea an unwanted hat-trick of runners-up in the season, Premier League, Carling Cup and then the Champions League final.

Cristiano Ronaldo had given Manchester United the lead after 26 minutes and they were the better side for most of the half. But Frank Lampard had equalised just before half-time. Both sides had their chances, the woodwork even denying Chelsea a couple of times. Then in injury time tempers flared and resulted in Didier Drogba becoming only the second player to be sent off in a Champions League final.

Naturally withdrawn from the list of penalty takers, his place in the line-up went to Terry. Surprisingly, however, it was Ronaldo who missed from the spot, his hesitating run-up and subsequent poor shot saved by Petr Cech. But it was Terry who could have settled it but slipped on his run-up and though the goalkeeper went the wrong way, the ball scraped the foot of the post and went wide. And when Nicolas Anelka had his effort saved by Van der Sar it was all over.

So much for the final. The competition itself of course began in mid-July as usual, though the first two qualifying rounds are virtually ignored by the media and sadly it seems in a strange way by UEFA, too. Only the third such round receives much attention and the British contingent made a useful start with Arsenal, Liverpool and Rangers winning the first leg games, Celtic drawing away to Spartak Moscow. All three moved on, Celtic needing a penalty shoot-out.

Those fortunate enough to be exempt until the group stage included Manchester United and Chelsea. In a not-too difficult section, Chelsea won half and drew the other half of their matches. While Manchester United in a more exacting group dropped just two points, Liverpool had to fight their way through after a disastrous opening, Arsenal finished second and Rangers third in Group E went into the UEFA Cup to acquit themselves well. Celtic having to contend with AC Milan were worthy survivors, too.

The measure of Liverpool's task is underlined by their defeat at home to Marseille and then losing to Besiktas in Turkey. The change in their fortunes was so marked that their 8-0 return leg success over Besiktas rated as a record score in the Champions League.

Plenty of big names headed the various sections – Porto, Real Madrid, Barcelona, Internazionale and Sevilla. The first knock-out round was the end of the road for Celtic against Barcelona, but perhaps the shocks were starting to happen with Arsenal pulling off an outstanding 2-0 win over AC Milan in Italy, Manchester United edging Lyon, Roma beating Real Madrid home and away and both Schalke and Fenerbahce coming through via penalties against Sevilla and Porto respectively. Chelsea eased in via Olympiakos, Liverpool outstandingly over Internazionale.

The quarter-final round fashioned another excellent performance by Manchester United 2-0 at Roma, but Chelsea lost the first leg late on to Fenerbahce. Meanwhile Liverpool held Arsenal at the Emirates. Barcelona took a narrow lead away to Schalke. In the return matches, Chelsea left it late to dispose of the Turkish team, Liverpool hit Arsenal late and decisively 4-2 and both Manchester United and Barcelona had 1-0 wins of their own.

Chelsea have had problems with Liverpool in Europe before, but this time held them at Anfield. United did well enough to leave Barcelona with a goalless draw. Though Liverpool pushed Chelsea to extra time, it was 3-2 against them at the end. One goal was enough for United, too.

Chelsea captain John Terry in despair at his penalty miss in the Champions League Final penalty shoot-out against Manchester United. (Action Images/Michael Regan/Livepic)

EUROPEAN CUP

EUROPEAN CUP FINALS 1956–1992

Year	Winners	Runners-up	Venue	Attendance	Referee
1956	Real Madrid 4	Reims 3	Paris	38,000	Ellis (E)
1957	Real Madrid 2	Fiorentina 0	Madrid	124,000	Horn (Ho)
1958	Real Madrid 3	AC Milan 2 *(aet)*	Brussels	67,000	Alsteen (Bel)
1959	Real Madrid 2	Reims 0	Stuttgart	80,000	Dutsch (WG)
1960	Real Madrid 7	Eintracht Frankfurt 3	Glasgow	135,000	Mowat (S)
1961	Benfica 3	Barcelona 2	Berne	28,000	Dienst (Sw)
1962	Benfica 5	Real Madrid 3	Amsterdam	65,000	Horn (Ho)
1963	AC Milan 2	Benfica 1	Wembley	45,000	Holland (E)
1964	Internazionale 3	Real Madrid 1	Vienna	74,000	Stoll (A)
1965	Internazionale 1	Benfica 0	Milan	80,000	Dienst (Sw)
1966	Real Madrid 2	Partizan Belgrade 1	Brussels	55,000	Kreitlein (WG)
1967	Celtic 2	Internazionale 1	Lisbon	56,000	Tschenscher (WG)
1968	Manchester U 4	Benfica 1 *(aet)*	Wembley	100,000	Lo Bello (I)
1969	AC Milan 4	Ajax 1	Madrid	50,000	Ortiz (Sp)
1970	Feyenoord 2	Celtic 1 *(aet)*	Milan	50,000	Lo Bello (I)
1971	Ajax 2	Panathinaikos 0	Wembley	90,000	Taylor (E)
1972	Ajax 2	Internazionale 0	Rotterdam	67,000	Helies (F)
1973	Ajax 1	Juventus 0	Belgrade	93,500	Guglovic (Y)
1974	Bayern Munich 1	Atletico Madrid 1	Brussels	49,000	Loraux (Bel)
Replay	Bayern Munich 4	Atletico Madrid 0	Brussels	23,000	Delcourt (Bel)
1975	Bayern Munich 2	Leeds U 0	Paris	50,000	Kitabdjian (F)
1976	Bayern Munich 1	St Etienne 0	Glasgow	54,864	Palotai (H)
1977	Liverpool 3	Moenchengladbach 1	Rome	57,000	Wurtz (F)
1978	Liverpool 1	FC Brugge 0	Wembley	92,000	Corver (Ho)
1979	Nottingham F 1	Malmo 0	Munich	57,500	Linemayr (A)
1980	Nottingham F 1	Hamburg 0	Madrid	50,000	Garrido (P)
1981	Liverpool 1	Real Madrid 0	Paris	48,360	Palotai (H)
1982	Aston Villa 1	Bayern Munich 0	Rotterdam	46,000	Konrath (F)
1983	Hamburg 1	Juventus 0	Athens	80,000	Rainea (R)
1984	Liverpool 1	Roma 1	Rome	69,693	Fredriksson (Se)
	(aet; Liverpool won 4-2 on penalties)				
1985	Juventus 1	Liverpool 0	Brussels	58,000	Daina (Sw)
1986	Steaua Bucharest 0	Barcelona 0	Seville	70,000	Vautrot (F)
	(aet; Steaua won 2-0 on penalties)				
1987	Porto 2	Bayern Munich 1	Vienna	59,000	Ponnet (Bel)
1988	PSV Eindhoven 0	Benfica 0	Stuttgart	70,000	Agnolin (I)
	(aet; PSV won 6-5 on penalties)				
1989	AC Milan 4	Steaua Bucharest 0	Barcelona	97,000	Tritschler (WG)
1990	AC Milan 1	Benfica 0	Vienna	57,500	Kohl (A)
1991	Red Star Belgrade 0	Marseille 0	Bari	56,000	Lanese (I)
	(aet; Red Star won 5-3 on penalties)				
1992	Barcelona 1	Sampdoria 0 *(aet)*	Wembley	70,827	Schmidhuber (G)

UEFA CHAMPIONS LEAGUE FINALS 1993–2008

Year	Winners	Runners-up	Venue	Attendance	Referee
1993	Marseille* 1	AC Milan 0	Munich	64,400	Rothlisberger (Sw)
1994	AC Milan 4	Barcelona 0	Athens	70,000	Don (E)
1995	Ajax 1	AC Milan 0	Vienna	49,730	Craciunescu (R)
1996	Juventus 1	Ajax 1	Rome	67,000	Vega (Sp)
	(aet; Juventus won 4-2 on penalties)				
1997	Borussia Dortmund 3	Juventus 1	Munich	59,000	Puhl (H)
1998	Real Madrid 1	Juventus 0	Amsterdam	47,500	Krug (G)
1999	Manchester U 2	Bayern Munich 1	Barcelona	90,000	Collina (I)
2000	Real Madrid 3	Valencia 0	Paris	78,759	Braschi (I)
2001	Bayern Munich 1	Valencia 1	Milan	71,500	Jol (Ho)
	(aet; Bayern Munich won 5-4 on penalties)				
2002	Real Madrid 2	Leverkusen 1	Glasgow	52,000	Meier (Sw)
2003	AC Milan 0	Juventus 0	Manchester	63,215	Merk (G)
	(aet; AC Milan won 3-2 on penalties)				
2004	Porto 3	Monaco 0	Gelsenkirchen	52,000	Nielsen (D)
2005	Liverpool 3	AC Milan 3	Istanbul	65,000	González (Sp)
	(aet; Liverpool won 3-2 on penalties)				
2006	Barcelona 2	Arsenal 1	Paris	79,500	Hauge (N)
2007	AC Milan 2	Liverpool 1	Athens	74,000	Fandel (G)
2008	Manchester U 1	Chelsea 1	Moscow	69,552	Michel (Slo)
	(aet; Manchester U won 6-5 on penalties)				

**Subsequently stripped of title.*

UEFA CHAMPIONS LEAGUE 2007–08

■ *Denotes player sent off.*

FIRST QUALIFYING ROUND FIRST LEG

Tuesday, 17 July 2007

Apoel (1) 2 *(Michail 42, Machlas 61)*

BATE Borisov (0) 0 10,971

Apoel: Morphis; Kontis, Michail, Kapsis, Florea, Satsias (Sapanis 74), Makridis, Tavares (Pinto 67), Machlas (Barreto 90), Fernandes, Nuno Morais.
BATE Borisov: Fedorovich; Likhtarovich, Platonov P (Platonov D 57), Radkov, Rodionov, Stasevich (Zhavnerchik 68), Ermakovich, Kazantsev, Bliznyuk (Vishnyakov 77), Filipenko, Sakharov■.

Lenkoran (0) 1 *(Ramazanov 58)*

Dinamo Zagreb (0) 1 *(Etto 63)* 16,000

Lenkoran: Arhayev; Amirguliyev, Guliyev E■, Bakhshiev, Zutautas, Abdullayev (Mamedov 79), Sultanov (Bamba 84), Ramazanov (Gurbanov A 88), Juninho, Todorov, Djambazov.
Dinamo Zagreb: Koch; Pokrivac (Chago 85), Cale, Sammir (Etto 58), Corluka, Tadic (Mandzukic 46), Sokota, Carlos, Drpic, Modric, Vukojevic.

Linfield (0) 0

Elfsborg (0) 0 2009

Linfield: Mannus; Douglas, O'Kane, Gault, Murphy, McAreavey (Mouncey 77), Curran, Dickson (Ferguson 87), Mulgrew, Thompson (Stewart 80), Bailie.
Elfsborg: Wiland; Augustsson, Bjorck, Karlsson, Andersson, Ishizaki (Alexandersson 89), Berglund (Keene 68), Svensson A, Svensson M (Avdic 52), Holmen, Mobaeck.

Murata (1) 1 *(Protti 43)*

Tampere (0) 2 *(Niemi 68, 88)* 2686

Murata: Scalabrelli; Albani, Bollini (Donati 72), D'Orsi, Vitaioli, Aldair (Gasperoni B 46), Valentini C, Protti, Teodorani, Agostini, Vannoni (Manuel Marani 84).
Tampere: Kaven; Jarvinen, Lindstrom, Niemi, Ojanpera, Savolainen, Kujala, Pohja, Hynynen (Saarinen 89), Wiss, Aho (Petrescu 52).

Olimpi (0) 0

Astana (0) 0 2900

Olimpi: Merlani; Chichveishvili, Orbeladze, Makhviladze, Navalovsky, Akouassaga, Silagadze (Koshkadze 66), Dvalishvili, Getsadze, Dvali (Massouanga 56), Zivkovic (Djikia 46).
Astana: Boychenko; Kumisbeckov, Kuchma, Zhalmagambetov, Kenzhesariev (Kukeev 73), Chichulin, Sergienko, Suchkov, Bulatov, Todorov (Aliyev 90), Kochkaev (Tlekhugov 46).

The New Saints (1) 3 *(Wilde 14, Baker 54, Hogan 90)*

Ventspils (1) 2 *(Rimkus 26, 89)* 649

The New Saints: Harrison; Courtney, King, Baker, Holmes, Toner (Morgan 46), Ruscoe (Leah 81), Hogan, Wilde, Beck, Wood (Taylor 85).
Ventspils: Davidovs; Soleicuks, Sernetskiy, Dubenskiy, Ndeki, Zizilevs, Tigirlas (Zangareyev 69), Kacanovs, Rimkus, Menteshashvili, Kolesnicenko (Kosmacovs 65).

Zeta (2) 3 *(Korac 34 (pen), Tumbasevic 36, Stjepanovic 59)*

Kaunas (0) 1 *(Kvartskhelia 68)* 3000

Zeta: Ivanovic S; Korac (Pelicic Z 76), Vuckovic, Radulovic, Kaluderovic M, Tumbasevic, Ivanovic B, Markovic (Boljevic 89), Igumanovic, Cetkovic, Stjepanovic (Marinkovic 89).
Kaunas: Stonys; Radzius, Mrowiec, Mendy, Baguzis (Grigalevicius 59), Manchkhava, Ksanavicius (Zubavicius 67), Beniusis (Cinikas 76), Kvartskhelia, Valkanov■, Rafael.

Wednesday, 18 July 2007

Derry City (0) 0

Pyunik (0) 0 2285

Derry City: Jennings; McCallion, Hargan, Hutton, McCourt, Farren (Hynes 85), Molloy, Morrow (McHugh 67), Oman, Martyn, McGlynn (Deery 57).
Pyunik: Kasparov; Mkrtchian (Sahakian 78), Tadevosian, Hovsepian, Yedigarian, Nazarian, Cre (Hzeina 46), Pachajian, Arzumanian, Dokhoian, Ghazarian (Henrik Mkhitarian 62).

Domzale (1) 1 *(Jankovic 44)*

SK Tirana (0) 0 824

Domzale: Nemec; Elsner, Aljancic, Varga, Zinko, Brezic, Jankovic (Dvorancic 60), Ljubijankic, Kirm, Juninho (Jusufi 67), Grabic (Peskar 85).
SK Tirana: Hidi; Sina, Capja, Dede, Xhafa, Abazaj, Duro K, Sefa (Bakalli 69), Hajdari (Deliallisi 78), Mukaj, Fortuzi (Merkoci 69).

F91 Dudelange (1) 1 *(Di Gregorio 45 (pen))*

Zilina (0) 2 *(Jez 48 (pen), Lietava 73)* 1221

F91 Dudelange: Joubert; Borbiconi, Mouny, Bellini, Franceschi, Gruszczynski (Coquelet 79), Guthleber, Di Gregorio (Hug 79), Hammami (Walder 67), Joly, Remy.
Zilina: Kuciak; Breska (Vladavic 69), Jez, Vomacka, Hubocan, Strba, Leitner, Devaty, Nemec (Lietava 59), Porazik (Styvar 84), Pekarik.

Hafnarfjordur (2) 4 *(Bjarnason 14, Vilhjalmsson 16, 58, Olafsson S 52)*

HB Torshavn (1) 1 *(Nielsen T 44 (og))* 1422

Hafnarfjordur: Larusson; Gardarsson, Siim (Asgeirsson 77), Nielsen T, Bjarnason, Gudmundsson M, Saevarsson, Vidarsson, Gudmundsson T, Olafsson S (Gudnason A 74), Vilhjalmsson.
HB Torshavn: Vatnhamar; Olavsstovu (Joensen H 71), Horg, Lag, Nolsoe, Akselsen, Flotum (Jespersen 60), Nielsen, Borg, Kuljic, Jacobsen C.

Marsaxlokk (0) 0

Sarajevo (4) 6 *(Rascic 5, 9, Obuca 20, 65, Maksimovic 42, Bucan 87)* 321

Marsaxlokk: Gauci; Licari, Bajada, Sciberras, Tellus, Wellman, Sammut, Pullicino, Webb, Magro, Pace.
Sarajevo: Alaim; Milosevic, Hadzic, Bucan, Grujic, Maksimovic, Ihtijarevic, Muharemovic, Obuca, Basic, Rascic.

Pobeda (0) 0

Levadia (0) 1 *(Nahk 53)* 1200

Pobeda: Tofiloski; Krstevski, Itoua, Georgiev (Obradovic 58), Savic, Jovanovic (Nestoroski 70), Gesovski (Aceski 16), Kapinkovski, Stojkovic■, Nacev, Dameski.
Levadia: Kotenko; Kalimullin, Smirnov, Teniste (Malov 51), Leitan, Vassiljev (Nahk 46), Sisov, Lemsalu, Dmitrijev, Kink, Zelinski (Cepauskas 64).

Sheriff (1) 2 *(Kuchuk 45, Gorodetchil 71)*

Ranger's (0) 0 8800

Sheriff: Pascenco; Arbanas (Gumenyuk 60), Chinwo, Wallace, Tarkhnishvili (Suvorov 75), Thiago, Corneencov, Balima (Gorodetchil 69), Kuchuk, Nadson, Bulgaru.
Ranger's: Rodriguez■; Porta, Pimentel F, Venturi, Albanell■, Pimentel M, Somoza, Da, Cacador (Martinez 90), Walker (Contrer 16), Moreira (Perez 71).

FIRST QUALIFYING ROUND SECOND LEG

Tuesday, 24 July 2007

Astana (1) 3 *(Kuchma 12, Tlekhugov 55, Zhalmagambetov 84)*

Olimpi (0) 0 6000

Astana: Boychenko; Kumisbeckov, Kuchma, Zhalmagambetov, Kenzhesariev, Chichulin (Aksenov 84), Sergienko (Kukeev 90), Suchkov, Suyumagambetov (Tlekhugov 46), Bulatov, Todorov.
Olimpi: Merlani; Chichveishvili (Dvali 51), Orbeladze, Getsadze, Navalovsky, Akouassaga, Silagadze, Zivkovic, Kebadze (Koshkadze 66), Djikia■, Kakhelishvili (Dvalishvili 70).

BATE Borisov (1) 3 *(Stasevich 14, Platonov D 74, Bliznyuk 104)*

Apoel (0) 0 5500

BATE Borisov: Fedorovich; Likhtarovich, Rodionov, Radkov, Zhavnerchik, Stasevich (Sivakov 72), Ermakovich (Bliznyuk 80), Filipenko, Kazantsev, Krivets, Khagush (Platonov D 64).
Apoel: Morphis; Elia (Ze Carlos 81), Kontis, Kapsis, Makridis, Michail, Tavares (Sapanis 25), Nuno Morais, Machlas, Fernandes, Pinto (Louka 68).
aet.

Dinamo Zagreb (0) 3 *(Vugrinec 56, Mandzukic 99, Tadic 116)*

Lenkoran (1) 1 *(Juninho 16)* 9240

Dinamo Zagreb: Koch; Mandzukic, Chago (Vugrinec 46) (Tomic 73), Sammir, Carlos, Etto, Drpic (Cale 46), Modric, Schildenfeld, Vukojevic, Tadic.
Lenkoran: Arhayev; Zutautas, Amirguliyev, N'tiamoah■, Abdullayev (Bamba 85), Mamedov (Gurbanov 49), Todorov, Bakhshiev, Juninho, Ramazanov, Djambazov.
aet.

Kaunas (3) 3 *(Beniusis 6, Kvartskhelia 16, Ksanavicius 20)*

Zeta (1) 2 *(Stjepanovic 34, Cetkovic 89)* 1500

Kaunas: Kello; Radzius (Screpis 69), Mrowiec, Mendy, Baguzis, Manchkhava, Ksanavicius (Klimek 46), Beniusis, Kvartskhelia, Pehlic, Rafael.
Zeta: Ivanovic S (Mustur 76); Igumanovic, Boljevic (Vuckovic 46), Radulovic, Kaluderovic M, Korac, Ivanovic B, Markovic, Tumbasevic, Cetkovic (Durovic 90), Stjepanovic.

Ranger's (0) 0

Sheriff (0) 3 *(Balima 68, Kajkut 77, Suvorov 89)* 280

Ranger's: Gonzalez I; Porta, Venturi, Pimentel F, Perez, Pimentel M, Somoza (Combarros 82), Gonzalez J, Cacador (Martinez 78), Walker, Moreira (Peire 66).
Sheriff: Pascenco; Arbanas, Chinwo, Wallace (Derme 80), Thiago, Balima, Corneencov, Rouamba, Kuchuk (Kajkut 67), Nadson (Suvorov 72), Bulgaru.

Sarajevo (1) 3 *(Mesic 42, Saraba 60, Turkovic 76)*

Marsaxlokk (0) 1 *(Frendo 65)* 8000

Sarajevo: Alaim; Milosevic, Hadzic, Kurto (Saraba 46), Bucan, Mesic, Grujic, Maksimovic (Janjos 79), Muharemovic, Basic, Rascic (Turkovic 64).
Marsaxlokk: Debono; Licari, Bajada, Sciberras (Mizzi 81), Frendo, Wellman, Sammut, Tellus, Magro, Pace, Templeman.

Wednesday, 25 July 2007

Elfsborg (1) 1 *(Svensson M 32)*

Linfield (0) 0 1023

Elfsborg: Wiland; Bjorck, Augustsson, Karlsson, Andersson, Ishizaki, Berglund (Alexandersson 83), Svensson A (Avdic 60), Svensson M (Keene 49), Holmen, Mobaeck.
Linfield: Mannus; Douglas (Mouncey 76), Dickson, Gault, McAreavey, O'Kane, Curran (Ferguson 74), Thompson, Lindsam, Mulgrew (Stewart 64), Bailie.

HB Torshavn (0) 0

Hafnarfjordur (0) 0 655

HB Torshavn: Vatnhamar; Jacobsen R, Horg, Lag, Nolsoe, Akselsen, Flotum (Joensen P 76), Nielsen, Olavsstovu (Leifsson 82), Jespersen (Dam 82), Kuljic.
Hafnarfjordur: Larusson; Gardarsson, Siim, Nielsen (Helgason 83), Bjarnason, Gudmundsson M, Saevarsson, Vidarsson, Gudmundsson T (Gudnason A 79), Olafsson S (Asgeirsson 70), Vilhjalmsson.

Levadia (0) 0

Pobeda (0) 0 2297

Levadia: Kotenko; Kalimullin, Andrejev (Zelinski 46), Kink, Leitan (Cepauskas 77), Lemsalu, Sisov, Nahk, Dmitrijev, Smirnov (Dovydenas 90), Malov.
Pobeda: Tofiloski; Krstevski, Itoua, Georgiev (Nestoroski 84), Jovanovic, Kapinkovski, Loncar (Siskov 46), Aceski, Obradovic, Nacev, Dameski■.

Pyunik (1) 2 *(Avetisian 28, Ghazarian 67)*

Derry City (0) 0 5300

Pyunik: Kasparov; Mkrtchian, Tadevosian, Hovsepian, Nazarian (Yedigarian 59), Hamlet Mkhitarian, Pachajian, Arzumanian, Avetisian (Henrik Mkhitarian 70), Ghazarian (Sahakian 81), Dokhoyan.
Derry City: Jennings; McCallion, Deery (Higgins 82), McCourt (Farren 65), Kelly, Molloy (O'Halloran 40), Martyn, Morrow, Oman, McHugh, Brennan.

SK Tirana (0) 1 *(Duro K 74)*

Domzale (1) 2 *(Ljubijankic 30, 77)* 8000

SK Tirana: Hidi; Sina (Sefa 70), Abazaj, Dede, Xhafa, Bakalli, Capja, Deliallisi, Duro K, Mukaj, Fortuzi (Merkoci 61).
Domzale: Nemec; Elsner, Aljancic, Zinko, Brezic, Zahora (Apatic 88), Jankovic (Peskar 73), Ljubijankic, Kirm, Juninho (Varga 13), Grabic.

Tampere (2) 2 *(Petrescu 7, Niemi 21)*

Murata (0) 0 5368

Tampere: Kaven; Jarvinen, Lindstrom (Myntti 67), Niemi, Ojanpera, Savolainen, Kujala, Pohja, Hynynen (Saarinen 46), Petrescu (Nwoke 80), Wiss.
Murata: Scalabrelli; Albani, Bollini (Conti 72), D'Orsi, Vitaioli, Gasperoni A (Molinari 84), Valentini C, Teodorani, Zaboul (Bacciocchi 71), Agostini, Vannoni.

Ventspils (1) 2 *(Ndeki 17, Kacanovs 53)*

The New Saints (0) 1 *(Naylor 90)* 1500

Ventspils: Davidovs; Ndeki, Sernetskiy (Slesarcuks 90), Dubenskiy, Tigirlas, Zizilevs, Cilinsek, Kacanovs, Rimkus, Menteshashvili (Mysikov 90), Kolesnicenko (Kosmacovs 70).
The New Saints: Harrison; Courtney, King, Baker, Holmes, Lamb (Carter 57), Ruscoe, Hogan (Naylor 72), Wilde (Morgan 64), Beck, Wood.

Zilina (3) 5 *(Devaty 8, Lietava 11, Styvar 29, 75, Vomacka 66)*

F91 Dudelange (1) 4 *(Di Gregorio 40, Hammami 49, Guthleber 71, Lukic 82)* 5822

Zilina: Kuciak; Breska (Vladavic 46), Hubocan, Vomacka, Lietava (Nemec 59), Strba, Leitner, Devaty, Jez, Styvar (Pecalka 89), Pekarik.
F91 Dudelange: Joubert; Walder, Mouny, Bigard, Franceschi, Gruszczynski (Lukic 73), Guthleber, Di Gregorio (Zeghdane 81), Hammami, Remy, Bellini (Coquelet 61).

SECOND QUALIFYING ROUND FIRST LEG

Tuesday, 31 July 2007

Debrecen (0) 0

Elfsborg (0) 1 *(Mobaeck 65)* 10,000

Debrecen: Balogh; Bernath, Demjen (Czvitkovics 88), Leandro, Vukmir, Komlosi, Dombi (Sandor 40), Meszaros, Stojkov (Rudolf 74), Kovemaha, Dzsudzsak.
Elfsborg: Wiland; Augustsson, Berglund (Alexandersson 59), Karlsson, Andersson, Bjorck, Ishizaki (Bajrami 79), Svensson A (Avdic 19), Keene, Holmen, Mobaeck.

FC Copenhagen (1) 1 *(Allback 9)*

Beitar Jerusalem (0) 0 21,336

FC Copenhagen: Christiansen; Gravgaard, Jensen, Norregaard, Hangeland, Kvist, Hutchinson, Silberbauer, Nordstrand (Ailton 65), Gronkjaer, Allback (Antonsson 69).
Beitar Jerusalem: Kale; Alvarez, Alberman, Benado, Gershon, Boateng■, Zandberg, Ziv (Afek 84), Itzhaki, Tamuz (Mirosevic 60), Tal.

Genk (1) 1 *(Cornelis 23)*

Sarajevo (1) 2 *(Rascic 15, Muharemovic 86)* 11,090

Genk: Bailly; Vrancken, Cornelis, Mikulic, Matoukou (Ljubojevic 74), Caillet, Haroun, Alex (Dahmane 64), Bosnjak, Soetaers, Toth.
Sarajevo: Alaim; Milosevic, Hadzic (Dzakmic 73), Babic, Bucan (Turkovic 68), Grujic, Maksimovic, Muharemovic, Rascic (Mesic 77), Basic, Saraba.

Pyunik (0) 0

Shakhtar Donetsk (1) 2 *(Gladkiy 45, Brandao 48)* 8000

Pyunik: Kasparov (Lopez 44); Arzumanian, Dokhoyan, Hovsepian, Yedigarian, Hamlet Mkhitarian, Mkrtchian, Nazarian (Henrik Mkhitarian 46), Avetisian (Sahakian 46), Ghazarian, Pachajian.
Shakhtar Donetsk: Pyatov; Gladkiy (Lucarelli 52), Brandao (Fomin), Duljaj (Pryiomov 53), Kucher, Lewandowski, Fernandinho, Jadson, Rat, Srna, Chygrynskiy.

Rangers (0) 2 *(Weir 55, Novo 72)*

Zeta (0) 0 36,145

Rangers: McGregor; Hutton■, Papac, Cuellar, Weir, Ferguson, Hemdani, Darcheville (Sebo 83), Boyd (Broadfoot 63), McCulloch, Adam (Novo 46).
Zeta: Ivanovic S; Korac, Vuckovic, Radulovic (Durovic 77), Kaluderovic M, Tumbasevic, Ivanovic B, Markovic, Igumanovic, Cetkovic (Boljevic 83), Stjepanovic.

Tampere (1) 1 *(Petrescu 15)*

Levski (0) 0 8126

Tampere: Kaven; Jarvinen, Lindstrom, Niemi, Ojanpera (Nwoke 85), Savolainen, Kujala, Pohja, Hynynen (Aho 63), Petrescu (Hjelm 90), Saarinen.
Levski: Petkov; Bardon (Jayeoba 90), Milanov, Tomasic, Domovchiyski, Eromoigbe, Wagner, Telkiyski, Tasevski (Ivanov M 63), Yovov (Dimitrov 57), Benzoukane.

Zaglebie (0) 0

Steaua (0) 1 *(Goian 55)* 7300

Zaglebie: Vaclavik; Bartczak G, Tiago Gomes, Stasiak, Arboleda, Golinski (Kolendowicz 75), Iwanski, Bartczak M, Rui Miguel (Lobodzinski 46), Nunes, Wlodarczyk (Chalbinski 57).
Steaua: Cernea; Marin, Goian, Golanski (Nesu 73), Rada, Radoi, Neaga, Nicolita (Badoi 77), Lovin, Dica, Croitoru (Petre O 87).

Wednesday, 1 August 2007

Astana (1) 1 *(Kuchma 26)*

Rosenborg (1) 3 *(Kone 3, 61, Iversen 56 (pen))* 7000

Astana: Boychenko; Kumisbeckov, Kuchma, Chichulin, Kenzhesariev, Bulatov, Sergienko (Kukeev 61), Aliyev (Tlekhugov 70), Suchkov, Kochkaev (Suyumagambetov 50), Shishkin.
Rosenborg: Hirschfeld; Koppinen, Dorsin, Tettey, Basma, Strand (Stoor 75), Kone (Jamtfall 83), Ya (Storflor 36), Iversen, Riseth, Sapara.

Besiktas (0) 1 *(Ibrahim T 73)*

Sheriff (0) 0 17,871

Besiktas: Rustu; Serdar K, Cisse (Koray 68), Bobo, Ibrahim K, Ricardinho (Mehmet 86), Serdar O, Tello, Ibrahim T, Ibrahim U, Delgado (Batuhan 46).
Sheriff: Pascenco; Gnanou, Arbanas, Wallace, Tarkhnishvili, Balima, Corneencov (Demalde 43), Thiago (Kajkut 75), Kuchuk, Mamah, Rouamba.

Domzale (0) 1 *(Zezelj 87)*

Dinamo Zagreb (1) 2 *(Sokota 7, Modric 50 (pen))* 2787

Domzale: Nemec; Brezic, Aljancic, Varga, Elsner, Kirm, Jankovic (Zezelj 66), Ljubijankic, Zahora, Zinko, Grabic (Jusufi 79).
Dinamo Zagreb: Koch; Sokota (Tadic 83), Cale, Schildenfeld, Sammir, Pokrivac (Chago 80), Etto, Carlos, Guela (Mikic 75), Vukojevic, Modric.

Hafnarfjordur (1) 1 *(Vilhjalmsson 18)*

BATE Borisov (1) 3 *(Likhtarovic 31, Rodionov 50, Bliznyuk 61)* 1587

Hafnarfjordur: Larusson; Gardarsson, Siim, Nielsen T, Bjarnason, Gudmundsson M (Snorrason 84), Saevarsson, Vidarsson (Asgeirsson 70), Gudmundsson T, Olafsson S (Gunnlaugsson 70), Vilhjalmsson.
BATE Borisov: Fedorovich; Likhtarovic (Sivakov 72), Filipenko, Radkov, Kazantsev, Khagush, Ermakovich, Rodionov (Platonov D 73), Bliznyuk (Zhavnerchik 65), Krivets, Stasevich.

Red Star Belgrade (1) 1 *(Koroman 35)*

Levadia (0) 0 18,886

Red Star Belgrade: Randelovic; Lukas (Molina 64), Andelkovic, Gueye, Castillo, Tutoric, Milijas, Koroman, Barcos (Dordevic 46), Basta (Bronowicki 74), Milovanovic.
Levadia: Kotenko; Kalimullin, Cepauskas, Kink (Sadrin 85), Leitan (Dovydenas 89), Lemsalu, Sisov, Smirnov, Dmitrijev, Malov, Zelinski (Saag 63).

Ventspils (0) 0

Salzburg (2) 3 *(Aufhauser 20, 27, 83 (pen))* 4100

Ventspils: Davidovs; Ndeki, Slesarcuks (Sernentskiy 53) (Grebis 85), Dubenskiy, Kosmacovs, Tigirlas, Cilinsek, Kacanovs, Rimkus, Zizilevs, Kolesnicenko (Mysikov 76).
Salzburg: Ochs; Pitak, Dudic, Steinhofer, Carboni, Kovac (Leitgeb 74), Zickler (Lokvenc 74), Aufhauser, Vargas, Vonlanthen (Jezek 85), Sekagya.

Zilina (0) 0

Slavia Prague (0) 0 9600

Zilina: Kuciak; Breska (Ancic 70), Pecalka, Jez, Porazik, Strba, Leitner, Devaty (Belak 90), Styvar (Lietava 59), Szorad, Pekarik.
Slavia Prague: Vaniak; Tavares, Brabec, Aracic■, Kalivoda (Suchy 85), Krajcik, Vlcek, Janda (Smicer 63), Sourek, Senkerik (Svec 46), Drizdal.

SECOND QUALIFYING ROUND SECOND LEG

Tuesday, 7 August 2007

Beitar Jerusalem (0) 1 *(Itzhaki 60)*

FC Copenhagen (1) 1 *(Allback 97)* 16,800

Beitar Jerusalem: Kale; Alberman (Azriel 100), Gershon, Itzhaki, Zandberg, Ziv, Romulo (Tamuz 62), Benado, Tal, Alvarez, Mirosevic (Bruchyan 46).
FC Copenhagen: Christiansen; Allback (Almeida 100), Gravgaard, Gronkjaer, Hangeland, Kvist, Silberbauer, Norregaard, Jensen, Wurtz (Antonsson 110), Hutchinson.
aet.

Dinamo Zagreb (2) 3 *(Vukojevic 18, Sokota 22, Sammir 60)*

Domzale (1) 1 *(Zahora 27)* 14,550

Dinamo Zagreb: Koch; Cale, Carlos Santos, Schildenfeld, Etto, Modric, Sammir (Mikic 82), Vukojevic, Mandzukic, Guela (Chago 46), Sokota (Drpic 64).
Domzale: Nemec; Aljanic, Varga, Elsner, Kirm, Brezic, Zinko, Zahora (Zezelj 62), Apatic (Grabic 43), Jankovic (Knezovic 73), Ljubijankic.

Levski (0) 0

Tampere (1) 1 *(Niemi 40)* 11,704

Levski: Petkov; Milanov (Jayeoba 46), Stojchev (Borimirov 42), Benzoukane, Wagner, Eromoigbe, Ivanov M, Telkiyski, Bardon (Koprivarov 75), Yovov, Domovchiniyski.
Tampere: Kaven; Lindstrom, Jarvinen, Ojanpera, Kujala, Wiss, Savolainen, Pohja, Petrescu, Saarinen (Hynynen 78), Niemi (Nwoke 64).

Zeta (0) 0

Rangers (0) 1 *(Beasley 81)* 11,000

Zeta: Ivanovic S; Tumbasevic (Vuckovic 84), Igumanovic, Kaluderovic M, Radulovic, Cetkovic, Ivanovic B (Boljevic 71), Markovic, Durovic (Knezevic 56), Stjepanovic, Korac.
Rangers: McGregor; Broadfoot, Papac, Cuellar, Weir, Ferguson, Hemdani, Thomson (Adam 87), Darcheville (Novo 61), Beasley, McCulloch.

Wednesday, 8 August 2007

BATE Borisov (0) 1 *(Platonov P 90)*

Hafnarfjordur (1) 1 *(Gudmundsson T 33)* 5300

BATE Borisov: Fedorovich; Radkov, Khagush, Filipenko, Kazantsev, Likhtarovich, Ermakovich, Krivets (Platonov P 63), Stasevich (Zhavnerchik 88), Bliznyuk (Platonov D 82), Rodionov■.
Hafnarfjordur: Larusson; Helgason■, Bjarnason, Saevarsson, Gardarsson (Nielsen T 78), Vidarsson, Olafsson S (Asgeirsson 63), Gudmundsson M, Gunnlaugsson B, Gudmundsson T (Valgardsson 76), Vilhjalmsson.

Elfsborg (0) 0

Debrecen (0) 0 11,952

Elfsborg: Wiland; Karlsson, Andersson, Bjorck, Augustsson, Svensson A (Avdic 66), Holmen, Ishizaki, Svensson M, Mobaeck (Floren 86), Keene (Berglund 81).
Debrecen: Balogh; Szucs, Vukmir, Komlosi, Bernath (Sandor 82), Leandro, Meszaros, Dzsudzsak, Demjen (Kerekes 72), Kouemaha■, Stojkov (Rudolf 55).

Levadia (1) 2 *(Malov 33, Nahk 68)*

Red Star Belgrade (1) 1 *(Burzanovic 37)* 3600

Levadia: Kotenko; Kalimullin, Shishov, Lemsalu, Leitan, Nahk, Dmitrijev, Malov, Smirnov (Teniste 57), Zelinski (Cepauskas 84), Kink (Saag 64).
Red Star Belgrade: Randelovic, Andelkovic, Tutoric, Gueye, Koroman, Lucas, Basta (Bronowicki 61), Milovanovic, Castillo, Barcos (Milijas 72), Burzanovic (Trajkovic 55).

Rosenborg (4) 7 *(Kone 1, 33, 49, 52, Iversen 6, Traore 17, Sapara 61)*

Astana (1) 1 *(Suchkov 22)* 12,827

Rosenborg: Hirschfeld; Koppinen, Basma, Dorsin, Strand (Stoor 46), Riseth (Skjelbred 46), Tettey, Traore, Sapara (Jamtfall 64), Kone, Iversen.
Astana: Kuznetsov; Kumisbeckov, Kuchma, Zhalmagambetov, Kenzhesariev, Bulatov, Chichulin, Sergienko, Suchkov (Suyumagambetov 46), Todorov, Kochkaev.

Salzburg (1) 4 *(Aufhauser 9, Dudic 48, Ilic 77, Leitgeb 90)*

Ventspils (0) 0 11,665

Salzburg: Ochs; Dudic, Miyamoto, Sekagya, Carboni, Jezek (Ilic 71), Steinhofer (Alex 78), Leitgeb, Aufhauser, Lokvenc, Vonlanthen (Janocko 56).
Ventspils: Vanins; Ndeki, Cilinsek, Tigirlas, Dubenskiy, Kacanovs, Menteshashvili, Kolesnicenko (Kosmacovs 58), Zizilevs, Rimkus (Butriks 75), Slesarcuks (Grebis 46).

Sarajevo (0) 0

Genk (0) 1 *(Mikulic 57)* 21,000

Sarajevo: Alaim; Milosevic, Hadzic, Muharemovic, Saraba, Basic, Maksimovic (Repuh 83), Dzakmic, Grujic, Rascic (Babic 77), Bucan (Turkovic 60).
Genk: Bailly; Mikulic, Matoukou (Ljubojevic 69), De Decker (Alex 37), Caillet, Cornelis, Vrancken, Bosnjak, Soetaers (Vandooren 76), Toth, Barda.

Sheriff (0) 0

Besiktas (0) 3 *(Bobo 57, 69, Koray 90)* 13,000

Sheriff: Pascenco; Chinwo, Mamah■, Tarkhnishvili, Gnanou, Rouamba (Gumenyuk 30), Corneencov (Demalde 71), Balima, Arbanas, Kuchuk, Thiago (Suvorov 64).
Besiktas: Hakan; Serdar K, Ibrahim U, Ibrahim T, Ibrahim K (Baki 46), Delgado (Ricardinho 68), Tello, Cisse, Serdar O, Koray, Bobo (Nobre 74).

Shakhtar Donetsk (1) 2 *(Brandao 40, Gladkiy 49)*

Pyunik (1) 1 *(Ghazarian 32)* 18,000

Shakhtar Donetsk: Pyatov; Fomin (Jadson 38), Hubschmann, Rat, Yezerskiy, Duljaj, Lewandowski, Tkachenko (Srna 57), Pryiomov, Luiz Adriano (Gladkiy 38), Brandao.
Pyunik: Lopez; Tadevosian, Hovsepian, Dokhoyan, Arzumanian, Yedigarian■, Mkrtchian, Ghazarian (Nazarian 57), Pachajyan (Gharabaghtsian 88), Henrik Mkhitarian, Hzeina (Sahakian 75).

Slavia Prague (0) 0

Zilina (0) 0 11,222

Slavia Prague: Vaniak; Brabec, Drizdal, Tavares, Janda, Smicer (Svec 79), Suchy, Krajcik, Kalivoda (Volesak 95), Vlcek, Senkerik (Necid 70).
Zilina: Kuciak; Vomacka, Leitner, Pekarik, Pecalka, Strba, Devaty, Jez, Lietava (Styvar 55), Porazik (Belak 74), Breska (Vladavic 116).
aet; Slavia Prague won 4-3 on penalties.

Steaua (1) 2 *(Nicolita 37, Zaharia 82)*

Zaglebie (1) 1 *(Stasiak 29)* 16,287

Steaua: Zapata; Golanski, Rada, Radoi, Marin, Petre O, Nicolita (Bicfalvy 90), Lovin, Croitoru (Badoi 71), Dica, Neaga (Zaharia 80).
Zaglebie: Vaclavik; Tiago Gomes, Stasiak, Arboleda, Bartczak G, Iwanski, Bartczak M, Lobodzinski, Pietron (Kolendowicz 71), Golinski, Chalbinski (Wlodarczyk 58) (Rui Miguel 72).

THIRD QUALIFYING ROUND FIRST LEG

Tuesday, 14 August 2007

Benfica (1) 2 *(Rui Costa 25, 85)*

FC Copenhagen (1) 1 *(Hutchinson 35)* 55,722

Benfica: Quim; Luis Filipe, Luisao (Adu 37), Leo, David Luiz, Petit, Katsouranis, Rui Costa, Nuno Assis (Nuno Gomes 74), Cardozo, Bergessio (Fabio Coentrao 46).
FC Copenhagen: Christiansen; Jensen, Hangeland, Gravgaard, Norregaard (Sionko 89), Wurtz, Silberbauer, Gronkjaer, Hutchinson, Kvist, Allback (Nordstrand 78).

Lazio (0) 1 *(Mutarelli 54)*

Dinamo Bucharest (1) 1 *(Danciulescu 21)* 35,172

Lazio: Ballotta; Stendardo (De Silvestri 46), Scaloni, Zauri, Cribari (Kolarov 22), Mutarelli■, Mauri (Del Nero 63), Ledesma, Behrami■, Rocchi, Pandev.
Dinamo Bucharest: Lobont; Nastase (Goian■ 31), Pulhac, Blay, Radu, Zicu (Oprita 8) (Chiacu 72), Cristea, Ropotan, Izvoreanu, Niculescu, Danciulescu.

Rangers (0) 1 *(Novo 90)*

Red Star Belgrade (0) 0 35,364

Rangers: McGregor; Hutton, Buffel, Cuellar, Weir, Ferguson, Hemdani, Thomson, Darcheville (Cousin 65), Beasley (Novo 65), McCulloch.
Red Star Belgrade: Randelovic; Andelkovic, Tutoric, Bronowicki, Gueye, Milijas, Koroman, Lucas, Castillo, Raskovic (Molina 70), Dordevic (Milovanovic 83).

Valencia (1) 3 *(Vicente 7, Silva 58, Morientes 70)*

Elfsborg (0) 0 46,320

Valencia: Canizares; Albiol, Marchena, Caneira, Moretti, Albelda, Baraja, Vicente (Morientes 59), Joaquin (Angulo 81), Silva, Villa (Gavilan 78).
Elfsborg: Wiland; Karlsson, Bjorck, Augustsson, Ilola (Avdic 76), Svensson A, Holmen, Ishizaki, Svensson M (Alexandersson 69), Mobaeck, Keene (Berglund 63).

Wednesday, 15 August 2007

Ajax (0) 0

Slavia Prague (0) 1 *(Kalivoda 75 (pen))* 30,092

Ajax: Stekelenburg; Heitinga, Stam, Vermaelen, Colin, Emanuelson, Gabri, Bakircioglu, Huntelaar, Suarez (Urzaiz 72), Rommedahl (Sarpong 82).
Slavia Prague: Vaniak; Brabec, Svec, Drizdal, Tavares, Janda (Belaid 86), Suchy, Krajcik, Kalivoda (Volesak 80), Vlcek (Gaucho 89), Senkerik.

BATE Borisov (1) 2 *(Radkov 39, Bliznyuk 90)*

Steaua (0) 2 *(Goian 59, Dica 84)* 5300

BATE Borisov: Fedorovich; Radkov, Khagush, Filipenko, Kazantsev, Likhtarovich (Krivets 53), Platonov P (Sivakov 83), Ermakovich (Zhavnerchik 69), Stasevich, Platonov D, Bliznyuk.
Steaua: Zapata; Goian, Golanski, Rada (Lovin 61), Radoi, Marin, Nicolita (Zaharia 74), Plesan, Croitoru (Bicfalvi 54), Dica, Neaga.

Fenerbahce (1) 1 *(Alex 33)*

Anderlecht (0) 0 37,919

Fenerbahce: Serdar; Lugano, Roberto Carlos, Onder, Deniz, Edu, Tumer (Ugur 59), Mehmet, Alex (Ali 83), Kezman, Deivid.
Anderlecht: Zitka; Deschacht, Juhasz, Wasilewski, Biglia, Polak, Hassan, Goor, De Man, Tchite (Mpenza 78), Boussoufa (Legear 83).

Salzburg (1) 1 *(Zickler 10 (pen))*

Shakhtar Donetsk (0) 0 23,690

Salzburg: Ochs; Dudic, Miyamoto, Sekagya, Carboni, Kovac, Steinhofer, Leitgeb, Aufhauser, Zickler (Lokvenc 85), Vonlanthen (Pitak 90).
Shakhtar Donetsk: Pyatov; Kucher, Ilsinho (Lewandowski 82), Rat, Chygrynskiy, Duljaj, Fernandinho, Jadson (Vukic 70), Srna, Gladkiy, Brandao (Lucarelli 74).

Sarajevo (0) 0

Dynamo Kiev (1) 1 *(Shatskikh 12)* 21,000

Sarajevo: Alaim; Milosevic, Hadzic, Muharemovic, Saraba, Basic, Maksimovic, Dzakmic (Repuh 46), Grujic, Rascic (Mesic 66), Bucan (Turkovic 58).
Dynamo Kiev: Shovkovskiy; Diakhate, Nesmachni, Gavrancic, Markovic, Correa, Michael, Mikhalik, Gusev (Ninkovic 64), Rebrov (Bangoura 83), Shatskikh (Kleber 67).

Sevilla (0) 2 *(Luis Fabiano 48, Kanoute 68)*

AEK Athens (0) 0 34,852

Sevilla: Palop; Dragutinovic, Boulahrouz (Renato 46), Hinkel, Fazio, Jesus Navas, Poulsen, Diego Capel, Maresca (Keita 46), Luis Fabiano (Marti 70), Kanoute.
AEK Athens: Moretto; Edson (Kafes 61), Arruabarrena, Geraldo, Dellas, Nsaliwa, Zikos (Tozser 90), Rivaldo (Kone 66), Manduca, Lyberopoulos, Julio Cesar.

Sparta Prague (0) 0

Arsenal (0) 2 *(Fabregas 72, Hleb 90)* 19,586

Sparta Prague: Postulka; Repka (Brezinsky 36), Kladrubsky, Pospech, Kadlec, Horvath (Limbersky 86), Abraham, Husek, Dosek, Rezek (Matusovic 59), Kulic.
Arsenal: Lehmann; Sagna, Clichy, Flamini, Toure, Gallas, Eboue, Fabregas, Hleb, Van Persie, Rosicky (Song Billong 80).

Spartak Moscow (1) 1 *(Pavlyuchenko 42)*

Celtic (1) 1 *(Hartley 21)* 67,000

Spartak Moscow: Pletikosa; Stranzl, Soava, Shishkin, Mozart, Titov, Torbinskiy, Kovac, Bystrov (Kalynychenko 76), Pavlyuchenko, Welliton.
Celtic: Brown M; Wilson, Naylor, Donati (Sno 74), Kennedy, McManus, Hartley, Brown S, McDonald (Caldwell 79), Vennegoor (McGeady 82), Nakamura.

Tampere (0) 0

Rosenborg (2) 3 *(Koppinen 19, Kone 21, 83)* 16,400

Tampere: Kaven; Lindstrom, Jarvinen, Kujala, Savolainen, Wiss, Pohja, Hynynen (Nwoke 71), Petrescu (Hjelm 87), Saarinen, Niemi.
Rosenborg: Hirschfeld; Koppinen, Stoor, Basma, Dorsin (Kvarme 85), Riseth, Tettey, Traore (Ya Konan 90), Sapara, Kone, Iversen (Storflor 26).

Toulouse (0) 0

Liverpool (1) 1 *(Voronin 43)* 30,380

Toulouse: Douchez; Fofana, Mathieu, Ebondo (Sissoko 83), Paulo Cesar (Gignac 69), Cetto, Sirieix, Emana Edzimbi, Dieuze, Elmander, Bergougnoux (Mansare 46).
Liverpool: Reina; Finnan, Arbeloa, Mascherano, Carragher, Hyypia, Benayoun (Riise 59), Gerrard (Sissoko 65), Crouch, Voronin (Torres 78), Babel.

Werder Bremen (0) 2 *(Hugo Almeida 46, Jensen 85)*

Dinamo Zagreb (1) 1 *(Balaban 45)* 25,474

Werder Bremen: Wiese; Pasanen, Naldo, Baumann, Andreasen (Jensen 46), Schulz, Mertesacker, Diego, Carlos Alberto (Harnik 74), Sanogo, Schindler (Hugo Almeida 46).
Dinamo Zagreb: Koch; Schildenfeld, Drpic, Pokrivac, Etto, Modric, Mikic, Sammir (Guela 89), Vukojevic, Balaban (Vrdoljak 80), Sokota (Mandzukic 38).

Zurich (0) 1 *(Alphonse 90)*

Besiktas (1) 1 *(Delgado 3)* 14,000

Zurich: Leoni; Von Bergen, Stahel, Rochat, Tihinen, Aegerter (Okonkwo 46), Clederson (Hassli 84), Abdi, Alphonse, Raffael, Chikhaoui.
Besiktas: Hakan; Serdar K, Gokhan, Ibrahim U, Ibrahim T, Delgado (Burak 78), Ricardinho (Koray 62), Cisse, Serdar O, Ali (Ibrahim A 46), Bobo.

THIRD QUALIFYING ROUND SECOND LEG

Tuesday, 28 August 2007

Dinamo Bucharest (1) 1 *(Bratu 27)*

Lazio (0) 3 *(Rocchi 47 (pen), 66, Pandev 54)* 40,164

Dinamo Bucharest: Lobont; Nastase, Pulhac, Blay, Radu, Margaritescu (Niculescu 59), Cristea, Ropotan, Danciulescu (Munteanu 71), Bratu, Oprita (Chiacu 59).
Lazio: Ballotta; Stendardo (Scaloni 35), Zauri, Cribari, De Silvestri, Ledesma, Mudingayi, Manfredini, Rocchi, Pandev, Del Nero (Belleri 85).

Liverpool (1) 4 *(Crouch 19, Hyypia 49, Kuyt 87, 90)*

Toulouse (0) 0 43,118

Liverpool: Reina; Arbeloa, Riise, Mascherano, Agger (Finnan 80), Hyypia, Benayoun, Sissoko (Lucas 68), Crouch, Kuyt, Leto (Babel 75).
Toulouse: Douchez; Fofana, Mathieu (Sissoko 82), Paulo Cesar, Ilunga, Cetto, Sirieix, Emana Edzimbi (Fabinho 77), Dieuze, Elmander, Gignac (Bergougnoux 54).

Red Star Belgrade (0) 0

Rangers (0) 0 40,104

Red Star Belgrade: Randelovic; Andelkovic, Tutoric, Gueye, Basta, Milijas (Raskovic 74), Koroman, Burzanovic (Barcos 71), Lucas, Castillo, Dordevic.
Rangers: McGregor; Hutton, Papac, Cuellar, Weir, Ferguson, Hemdani, Thomson, Darcheville (Cousin 70), McCulloch, Whittaker (Beasley 79).

Wednesday, 29 August 2007

Anderlecht (0) 0

Fenerbahce (1) 2 *(Kezman 3, Alex 77)* 20,722

Anderlecht: Zitka; Deschacht, Van Damme (Goor 78), Juhasz, Pareja, Wasilewski (Legear 78), Biglia, Polak, Hassan, Tchite, Boussoufa (Thereau 59).
Fenerbahce: Volkan; Lugano, Roberto Carlos, Onder, Deniz, Edu, Tumer (Kazim-Richards 66), Mehmet, Alex (Selcuk 78), Kezman, Deivid (Wederson 90).

Arsenal (1) 3 *(Rosicky 8, Fabregas 82, Eduardo 90)*

Sparta Prague (0) 0 58,462

Arsenal: Almunia; Hoyte J, Clichy, Silva, Toure, Senderos, Diaby (Fabregas 68), Walcott, Eduardo, Van Persie (Adebayor 68), Rosicky (Denilson 73).
Sparta Prague: Postulka; Repka, Kladrubsky (Limbersky 77), Pospech, Kadlec, Horvath, Abraham, Husek, Dosek, Rezek (Kolar 73), Kulic (Zofcak 46).

Besiktas (0) 2 *(Delgado 55, 63)*

Zurich (0) 0 22,773

Besiktas: Hakan; Serdar K, Gokhan, Ibrahim U, Ibrahim T, Delgado (Ali 75), Tello (Batuhan 90), Ricardinho (Ibrahim A 77), Cisse, Serdar O, Bobo.
Zurich: Leoni; Stahel (Schonbachler 79), Rochat, Barmettler, Schneider (Kollar 67), Tihinen, Okonkwo, Abdi, Raffael, Eudis (Hassli 67), Chikhaoui.

Celtic (1) 1 *(McDonald 27)*

Spartak Moscow (1) 1 *(Pavlyuchenko 45)* 57,644

Celtic: Boruc; Wilson, Naylor (O'Dea 110), Donati, Caldwell, McManus, Nakamura, Brown S, McDonald (Zurawski 97), Vennegoor, McGeady (Riordan 104).
Spartak Moscow: Pletikosa; Stranzl■, Soava, Shishkin, Mozart, Titov, Torbinskiy (Boyarintsev 100), Kovac, Bystrov (Kalynychenko 105), Pavlyuchenko, Welliton (Dedura 88).
aet; Celtic won 4-3 on penalties.

Dynamo Kiev (1) 3 *(Bangoura 3, 76, Rebrov 90 (pen))*

Sarajevo (0) 0 16,100

Dynamo Kiev: Shovkovskiy; Diakhate, Gavrancic, Markovic, Ghioane, Correa (Belkevich 77), Michael (Rotan 81), Gusev, El-Kaddouri, Bangoura (Rebrov 82), Shatskikh.
Sarajevo: Alaim; Milosevic, Hadzic, Saraba, Babic, Basic, Repuh (Obuca 46), Dzakmic, Grujic, Mesic, Rascic.

Dinamo Zagreb (2) 2 *(Vukojevic 21, Modric 40 (pen))*

Werder Bremen (2) 3 *(Diego 13 (pen), 70 (pen), Sanogo 38)* 34,175

Dinamo Zagreb: Koch; Carlos Santos, Schildenfeld, Drpic, Pokrivac (Vugrinec 62), Etto (Guela 78), Modric, Sammir (Mikic 75), Vukojevic, Balaban, Mandzukic.
Werder Bremen: Wiese; Pasanen, Naldo, Baumann, Schulz (Tosic 81), Mertesacker, Vranjes, Diego, Jensen, Sanogo (Rosenberg 76), Hugo Almeida (Harnik 68).

Elfsborg (1) 1 *(Alexandersson 31)*

Valencia (1) 2 *(Helguera 5, Villa 90)* 13,148

Elfsborg: Wiland; Karlsson (Andersson 74), Mobaeck (Floren 19), Bjorck, Augustsson, Ilola (Svensson M 64), Svensson A, Avdic, Alexandersson, Keene, Berglund.
Valencia: Hildebrand; Albiol, Marchena, Caneira, Helguera, Moretti (Alexis 85), Obayan, Gavilan, Joaquin, Silva (Villa 62), Morientes (Arizmendi 57).

FC Copenhagen (0) 0

Benfica (1) 1 *(Katsouranis 16)* 39,711

FC Copenhagen: Christiansen; Jensen, Hangeland, Gravgaard, Norregaard, Wurtz (Sionko 58), Silberbauer, Hutchinson, Kvist, Nordstrand (Ailton 73), Allback.
Benfica: Quim; Luis Felipe, Leo, Nelson (Nuno Assis 46), Petit, Katsouranis, Rui Costa, Miguelito, Di Maria (Romeo Ribeiro 73), Cardozo, Nuno Gomes (Bergessio 90).

Rosenborg (1) 2 *(Sapara 45, Ya Konan 49)*

Tampere (0) 0 14,123

Rosenborg: Hirschfeld; Koppinen (Skjelbred 46), Basma, Dorsin, Strand (Stoor 30), Riseth, Tettey, Traore, Sapara (Iversen 76), Kone, Ya Konan.
Tampere: Kaven; Lindstrom, Jarvinen (Nwoke 74), Ojanpera, Kujala, Wiss, Savolainen, Pohja, Petrescu (Hjelm 86), Saarinen (Aho 46), Niemi.

Shakhtar Donetsk (1) 3 *(Lucarelli 9, Nery Castillo 78 (pen), Brandao 87)*

Salzburg (1) 1 *(Meyer 5)* 25,500

Shakhtar Donetsk: Pyatov; Kucher, Ilsinho (Duljaj 72), Rat, Chygrynskiy, Fernandinho, Jadson, Lewandowski (Nery Castillo 57), Srna, Gladkiy (Brandao 55), Lucarelli.
Salzburg: Ochs; Miyamoto, Meyer, Sekagya, Carboni, Kovac, Steinhofer, Leitgeb, Aufhauser (Lokvenc 89), Zickler, Vonlanthen.

Slavia Prague (1) 2 *(Vlcek 22, 86)*

Ajax (1) 1 *(Suarez 33)* 17,330

Slavia Prague: Vaniak; Brabec, Svec, Drizdal, Tavares, Janda, Smicer (Ivana 14) (Necid 81), Suchy, Krajcik, Kalivoda (Volesak 76), Vlcek.
Ajax: Stekelenburg; Heitinga, Stam, Vermaelen, Colin, Emanuelson (Vertonghen 59), Delorge, Gabri (Urzaiz 78), Bakircioglu (Rommedahl 65), Huntelaar, Suarez.

Steaua (1) 2 *(Zaharia 12, Neaga 54)*

BATE Borisov (0) 0 24,254

Steaua: Zapata; Goian, Rada, Nesu, Marin, Petre O, Nicolita, Lovin (Bicfalvi 65), Dica, Neaga (Croitoru 69), Zaharia (Badea 53).
BATE Borisov: Fedorovich; Radkov, Sakharov (Zhavnerchik 65), Filipenko, Kazantsev, Likhtarovich, Platonov P, Ermakovich (Radevich 77), Stasevich (Vishnyakov 83), Platonov D, Bliznyuk.

Monday, 3 September 2007

AEK Athens (0) 1 *(Rivaldo 82 (pen))*

Sevilla (3) 4 *(Luis Fabiano 32, 45, Keita 41, Kerzhakov 53)* 37,777

AEK Athens: Moretto; Edson Ramos, Geraldo, Papastathopoulos, Nsaliwa (Tozser 46), Zikos (Paulis 62), Rivaldo, Manduca, Bourbos, Lyberopoulos, Julio Cesar (Pappas 46).
Sevilla: Palop; Dragutinovic, Daniel Alves, Escude (Mosquera 59), Fazio, Jesus Navas, Poulsen (Maresca 62), Diego Capel, Keita, Kerzhakov, Luis Fabiano (De Mul 46).

GROUP STAGE

GROUP A

Tuesday, 18 September 2007

Marseille (0) 2 *(Rodriguez 76, Cisse 90)*

Besiktas (0) 0 44,576

Marseille: Mandanda; Taiwo, Rodriguez, Faty, Bonnart, Ziani, Zenden (Valbuena 76), Cana, Nasri (M'Bami 88), Cisse, Niang (Gragnic 86).
Besiktas: Hakan; Serdar K (Ibrahim K 26), Diatta, Ibrahim U, Ibrahim T, Delgado (Higuain 75), Tello, Ricardinho (Koray 44), Cisse, Serdar O, Bobo.

Porto (1) 1 *(Lucho Gonzalez 8 (pen))*

Liverpool (1) 1 *(Kuyt 18)* 41,208

Porto: Nuno; Bruno Alves, Fucile, Joao Paulo, Paulo Assuncao, Quaresma, Lucho Gonzalez, Bosingwa, Raul Meireles (Mariano Gonzalez 64), Sektioui (Farias 64), Lisandro Lopez.
Liverpool: Reina; Finnan, Arbeloa, Mascherano, Carragher, Hyypia, Pennant■, Gerrard, Torres (Voronin 76), Kuyt, Babel (Fabio Aurelio 85).

Wednesday, 3 October 2007

Besiktas (0) 0

Porto (0) 1 *(Quaresma 90)* 32,145

Besiktas: Hakan; Serdar K (Ali 71), Gokhan, Ibrahim U, Ibrahim T, Delgado, Tello, Cisse, Serdar O, Ibrahim A (Higuain 67), Bobo (Nobre 28).
Porto: Helton; Bruno Alves, Stepanov, Fucile, Paulo Assuncao, Quaresma, Lucho Gonzalez, Bosingwa, Raul Meireles (Leandro Lima 88), Sektioui (Cech 66), Lisandro Lopez (Adriano 75).

Liverpool (0) 0

Marseille (0) 1 *(Valbuena 77)* 41,355

Liverpool: Reina; Finnan, Fabio Aurelio (Voronin 70), Leto (Riise 52), Carragher, Hyypia, Gerrard, Sissoko, Torres, Crouch (Kuyt 75), Benayoun.
Marseille: Mandanda; Taiwo, Rodriguez, Bonnart, Givet, Ziani, Cheyrou, Zenden (Arrache 88), Cana, Valbuena (Oruma 84), Niang (Cisse 70).

Wednesday, 24 October 2007

Besiktas (1) 2 *(Hyypia 13 (og), Bobo 82)*

Liverpool (0) 1 *(Gerrard 85)* 25,837

Besiktas: Hakan; Serdar K (Koray 42), Gokhan, Ibrahim U, Ibrahim T, Delgado (Higuain 62), Tello, Cisse, Serdar O, Ali, Bobo (Diatta 86).
Liverpool: Reina; Finnan, Riise, Mascherano (Lucas 76), Carragher, Hyypia (Crouch 83), Pennant (Benayoun 59), Gerrard, Voronin, Kuyt, Babel.

Marseille (0) 1 *(Niang 69)*

Porto (0) 1 *(Lucho Gonzalez 79 (pen))* 46,458

Marseille: Mandanda; Faty, Zubar, Bonnart, Givet (Taiwo 68), Cheyrou, Zenden (Arrache 55), Cana, Valbuena, Cisse (Ayew Pele 88), Niang.
Porto: Helton; Bruno Alves, Stepanov, Fucile, Paulo Assuncao, Quaresma, Lucho Gonzalez, Mariano Gonzalez (Helder Postiga 46), Bosingwa, Raul Meireles (Leandro Lima 72), Lisandro Lopez.

Tuesday, 6 November 2007

Liverpool (2) 8 *(Crouch 19, 89, Benayoun 32, 53, 56, Gerrard 69, Babel 78, 81)*

Besiktas (0) 0 41,143

Liverpool: Reina; Arbeloa, Fabio Aurelio (Babel 63), Mascherano, Carragher, Hyypia, Benayoun, Gerrard (Lucas 73), Crouch, Voronin (Kewell 72), Riise.
Besiktas: Hakan; Serdar K (Higuain 62), Diatta, Ibrahim U, Ibrahim T, Mehmet (Ricardinho 78), Delgado, Cisse, Serdar O (Ali 46), Koray, Bobo.

Porto (1) 2 *(Sektioui 27, Lisandro Lopez 78)*

Marseille (0) 1 *(Niang 47)* 42,217

Porto: Helton; Bruno Alves, Stepanov, Cech (Helder Postiga 59), Fucile, Paulo Assuncao, Quaresma, Bosingwa, Raul Meireles (Bolatti 68), Sektioui (Mariano Gonzalez 87), Lisandro Lopez.
Marseille: Mandanda; Taiwo, Rodriguez, Bonnart, Givet, M'Bami (Cheyrou 84), Cana, Nasri, Valbuena, Ayew Pele (Arrache 77), Niang (Cisse 63).

Wednesday, 28 November 2007

Besiktas (1) 2 *(Tello 27, Bobo 88)*

Marseille (0) 1 *(Taiwo 65)* 19,448

Besiktas: Rustu; Baki, Ibrahim U, Ibrahim T, Delgado, Tello, Ricardinho (Ibrahim A 66), Cisse (Koray 20), Serdar O (Nobre 74), Ali, Bobo.
Marseille: Mandanda; Rodriguez, Zubar (Taiwo 46), Bonnart, Givet, Cheyrou, Zenden (Ayew Pele 55), Cana, Nasri (Cisse 26), Valbuena, Niang.

Liverpool (1) 4 *(Torres 19, 78, Gerrard 84 (pen), Crouch 87)*

Porto (1) 1 *(Lisandro Lopez 33)* 41,095

Liverpool: Reina; Finnan, Arbeloa, Mascherano, Carragher, Hyypia, Benayoun (Crouch 71), Gerrard, Torres, Voronin (Kewell 63), Babel (Kuyt 85).
Porto: Helton; Bruno Alves, Stepanov, Cech, Paulo Assuncao (Helder Postiga 81), Quaresma, Lucho Gonzalez, Mariano Gonzalez (Sektioui 77), Bosingwa, Kazmierczak (Raul Meireles 65), Lisandro Lopez.

Tuesday, 11 December 2007

Marseille (0) 0

Liverpool (2) 4 *(Gerrard 4, Torres 10, Kuyt 47, Babel 90)* 53,097

Marseille: Mandanda; Taiwo, Rodriguez, Bonnart, Givet (Faty 46), Ziani, Cheyrou (Nasri 34), Zenden (Cisse 46), Cana, Valbuena, Niang.
Liverpool: Reina; Arbeloa, Riise, Mascherano, Carragher, Hyypia, Benayoun, Gerrard, Torres (Babel 77), Kuyt (Lucas 86), Kewell (Fabio Aurelio 67).

Porto (1) 2 *(Lucho Gonzalez 44, Quaresma 62)*

Besiktas (0) 0 39,608

Porto: Helton; Bruno Alves, Pedro Emanuel, Bosingwa, Fucile (Cech 75), Paulo Assuncao, Quaresma, Lucho Gonzalez (Bolatti 81), Raul Meireles, Sektioui (Helder Postiga 74), Lisandro Lopez.
Besiktas: Rustu; Baki, Ibrahim U, Ibrahim T, Burak (Ibrahim A 45), Delgado, Tello (Higuain 84), Cisse, Serdar O, Ali, Bobo.

Group A Final Table	*P*	*W*	*D*	*L*	*F*	*A*	*Pts*
Porto	6	3	2	1	8	7	11
Liverpool	6	3	1	2	18	5	10
Marseille	6	2	1	3	6	9	7
Besiktas	6	2	0	4	4	15	6

GROUP B

Tuesday, 18 September 2007

Chelsea (0) 1 *(Shevchenko 53)*

Rosenborg (1) 1 *(Koppinen 24)* 24,973

Chelsea: Cech; Belletti, Cole A (Ben Haim 74), Makelele, Terry, Alex, Cole J (Wright-Phillips 74), Essien, Kalou, Shevchenko, Malouda.
Rosenborg: Hirschfeld; Koppinen, Basma (Kvarme 46), Dorsin, Strand, Riseth, Skjelbred (Iversen 85), Tettey, Traore, Sapara (Ya Konan 69), Kone.

Schalke (0) 0

Valencia (0) 1 *(Villa 63)* 53,951

Schalke: Neuer; Westermann, Bordon, Rafinha (Grossmuller 73), Pander, Ernst, Rakitic, Jones, Asamoah (Ozil 61), Halil Altintop (Lovenkrands 73), Kuranyi.
Valencia: Canizares; Albiol, Marchena, Helguera, Miguel, Moretti, Albelda, Silva, Villa (Sunny 90), Morientes (Arizmendi 80), Angulo (Joaquin 75).

Wednesday, 3 October 2007

Rosenborg (0) 0

Schalke (0) 2 *(Jones 62, Kuranyi 89)* 21,361

Rosenborg: Hirschfeld; Koppinen, Basma, Dorsin (Ya Konan 79), Strand, Riseth, Skjelbred (Kone 68), Tettey, Traore, Sapara, Iversen.
Schalke: Neuer; Westermann, Bordon, Rafinha, Howedes, Ernst, Rakitic (Grossmuller 74), Jones (Varela 84), Bajramovic, Lovenkrands (Asamoah 64), Kuranyi.

Valencia (1) 1 *(Villa 9)*

Chelsea (1) 2 *(Cole J 21, Drogba 70)* 52,000

Valencia: Hildebrand; Albiol, Marchena, Helguera, Miguel, Moretti, Albelda (Baraja 75), Joaquin (Arizmendi 88), Silva, Villa, Morientes (Zigic 69).
Chelsea: Cech; Paulo Ferreira, Cole A, Makelele, Terry, Ricardo Carvalho, Essien (Sidwell 83), Mikel (Alex 88), Drogba, Cole J, Malouda (Kalou 85).

Wednesday, 24 October 2007

Chelsea (1) 2 *(Malouda 4, Drogba 47)*

Schalke (0) 0 40,910

Chelsea: Cech; Paulo Ferreira, Bridge, Makelele, Alex, Ricardo Carvalho, Essien (Mikel 70), Lampard, Drogba, Cole J (Shevchenko 89), Malouda (Kalou 84).
Schalke: Neuer; Westermann, Bordon, Rodriguez (Bajramovic 81), Rafinha, Ernst, Jones, Grossmuller (Azaouagh 77), Larsen, Lovenkrands, Asamoah (Rakitic 61).

Rosenborg (0) 2 *(Kone 53, Riseth 61)*

Valencia (0) 0 21,119

Rosenborg: Hirschfeld; Kvarme, Dorsin, Strand (Stoor 86), Riseth, Skjelbred, Tettey, Traore, Sapara, Kone (Storflor 80), Iversen.
Valencia: Canizares; Albiol, Marchena (Baraja 67), Helguera, Miguel (Angulo 78), Moretti, Albelda, Gavilan (Zigic 67), Joaquin, Silva, Morientes.

Tuesday, 6 November 2007

Schalke (0) 0

Chelsea (0) 0 53,951

Schalke: Neuer; Westermann, Bordon, Rafinha, Krstajic, Rakitic, Jones, Ozil (Lovenkrands 60), Bajramovic, Larsen, Asamoah.
Chelsea: Cech (Cudicini 46); Belletti (Mikel 64), Bridge, Makelele, Alex, Ricardo Carvalho, Essien, Lampard, Drogba, Cole J, Malouda (Wright-Phillips 78).

Valencia (0) 0

Rosenborg (1) 2 *(Iversen 31, 58)* 29,725

Valencia: Hildebrand; Caneira, Helguera, Miguel, Moretti (Angulo 63), Manuel Fernandes, Albelda, Joaquin (Zigic 63), Silva, Villa, Morientes (Vicente 46).
Rosenborg: Hirschfeld; Stoor, Kvarme, Dorsin, Riseth, Skjelbred (Storflor 80), Tettey, Traore, Sapara (Ya Konan 84), Kone, Iversen.

Wednesday, 28 November 2007

Rosenborg (0) 0

Chelsea (3) 4 *(Drogba 8, 20, Alex 40, Cole J 73)* 21,582

Rosenborg: Hirschfeld; Stoor, Kvarme, Dorsin (Basma 86), Riseth, Skjelbred, Tettey, Traore (Strand 57), Sapara, Kone (Ya Konan 63), Iversen.
Chelsea: Cudicini; Belletti, Cole A, Makelele, Terry, Alex, Essien, Lampard (Pizarro 76), Drogba (Shevchenko 68), Cole J, Wright-Phillips (Kalou 69).

Valencia (0) 0

Schalke (0) 0 29,232

Valencia: Canizares; Marchena, Caneira (Albiol 43), Helguera, Miguel, Albelda■, Vicente (Silva 72), Joaquin, Edu, Villa, Morientes (Manuel Fernandes 35).
Schalke: Neuer; Westermann, Bordon, Rafinha, Krstajic, Ernst, Rakitic (Grossmuller 66), Jones (Bajramovic 71), Ozil, Halil Altintop (Asamoah 80), Kuranyi.

Tuesday, 11 December 2007

Chelsea (0) 0

Valencia (0) 0 41,139

Chelsea: Cech; Paulo Ferreira (Belletti 72), Bridge, Essien, Terry, Ben Haim, Wright-Phillips, Lampard (Cole J 62), Shevchenko (Makelele 46), Kalou, Pizarro.
Valencia: Canizares; Albiol, Marchena, Helguera, Miguel (Manuel Fernandes 65), Moretti, Obayan, Vicente (Mata 75), Silva, Villa (Arizmendi 50), Morientes.

Schalke (3) 3 *(Asamoah 12, Rafinha 19, Kuranyi 36)*

Rosenborg (1) 1 *(Kone 23)* 53,951

Schalke: Neuer; Westermann, Bordon, Rodriguez, Rafinha, Ernst, Ozil (Kobiashvili 86), Grossmuller, Bajramovic, Asamoah (Howedes 90), Kuranyi (Halil Altintop 88).
Rosenborg: Hirschfeld; Stoor, Basma, Kvarme, Strand (Traore 61), Riseth, Skjelbred, Tettey, Sapara, Kone (Ya Konan 77), Iversen.

Group B Final Table	P	W	D	L	F	A	Pts
Chelsea	6	3	3	0	9	2	12
Schalke	6	2	2	2	5	4	8
Rosenborg	6	2	1	3	6	10	7
Valencia	6	1	2	3	2	6	5

GROUP C

Tuesday, 18 September 2007

Olympiakos (0) 1 *(Galletti 55)*

Lazio (0) 1 *(Zauri 77)*

Olympiakos: Nikopolidis; Patsatzoglou (Kovacevic 80), Domi, Zewlakow, Antzas, Torosidis, Stoltidis, Galletti, Djordjevic, Ledesma, Lua Lua.
Lazio: Ballotta; Stendardo, Zauri, Cribari, De Silvestri (Scaloni 81), Mauri (Mutarelli 61), Ledesma, Mudingayi, Manfredini (Del Nero 70), Rocchi, Pandev.
Behind closed doors.

Real Madrid (1) 2 *(Raul 16, Van Nistelrooy 74)*

Werder Bremen (1) 1 *(Sanogo 17)* 63,500

Real Madrid: Casillas; Sergio Ramos, Cannavaro, Marcelo, Metzelder, Gago, Guti (Drenthe 77), Sneijder, Raul (Robben 84), Van Nistelrooy, Higuain (Robinho 69).
Werder Bremen: Wiese; Pasanen, Naldo, Baumann, Tosic, Mertesacker, Vranjes, Diego, Jensen, Rosenberg (Hugo Almeida 69), Sanogo.

Wednesday, 3 October 2007

Lazio (1) 2 *(Pandev 32, 75)*

Real Madrid (1) 2 *(Van Nistelrooy 9, 61)* 80,246

Lazio: Ballotta; Stendardo, Zauri, Cribari, Mutarelli, Mauri (Del Nero 78), Ledesma, Mudingayi, Behrami (Scaloni 66), Rocchi (Makinwa 66), Pandev.
Real Madrid: Casillas; Sergio Ramos, Cannavaro, Marcelo, Heinze, Diarra, Guti, Sneijder (Drenthe 88), Raul (Saviola 83), Robben (Higuain 78), Van Nistelrooy.

Werder Bremen (1) 1 *(Hugo Almeida 32)*

Olympiakos (0) 3 *(Stoltidis 73, Patsatzoglou 82, Kovacevic 87)* 37,500

Werder Bremen: Vander; Pasanen, Naldo, Fritz (Borowski 62), Tosic, Mertesacker, Diego, Jensen, Frings, Rosenberg (Sanogo 77), Hugo Almeida.
Olympiakos: Nikopolidis; Patsatzoglou, Domi (Julio Cesar 19), Raul Bravo, Antzas, Torosidis (Pantos 86), Stoltidis, Galletti (Kovacevic 72), Djordjevic, Ledesma, Lua Lua.

Wednesday, 24 October 2007

Real Madrid (1) 4 *(Raul 2, Robinho 68, 83, Balboa 90)*

Olympiakos (1) 2 *(Galletti 7, Julio Cesar 47)* 64,477

Real Madrid: Casillas; Michel Salgado (Higuain 64), Sergio Ramos, Marcelo, Metzelder, Gago, Guti, Sneijder (Balboa 82), Raul (Miguel Torres 88), Robinho, Van Nistelrooy.
Olympiakos: Nikopolidis; Patsatzoglou, Julio Cesar, Raul Bravo (Zewlakow 75), Antzas, Torosidis■, Stoltidis, Galletti, Djordjevic, Ledesma (Nunez 86), Lua Lua (Kovacevic 72).

Werder Bremen (1) 2 *(Sanogo 28, Hugo Almeida 54)*

Lazio (0) 1 *(Manfredini 82)* 36,587

Werder Bremen: Wiese; Pasanen (Tosic 46), Naldo, Fritz, Mertesacker, Diego, Jensen, Frings, Borowski (Andreasen 73), Sanogo (Rosenberg 64), Hugo Almeida.
Lazio: Ballotta; Stendardo, Kolarov, Zauri, Mutarelli, Meghni (Del Nero 51), Mudingayi, Manfredini, Behrami, Rocchi (Tare 82), Pandev (Makinwa 69).

Tuesday, 6 November 2007

Lazio (0) 2 *(Rocchi 57, 68)*

Werder Bremen (0) 1 *(Diego 88 (pen))* 28,236

Lazio: Ballotta; Stendardo, Zauri (De Silvestri 18), Cribari■, Mutarelli, Meghni (Manfredini 74), Ledesma, Mudingayi, Behrami, Rocchi, Makinwa (Scaloni 87).
Werder Bremen: Wiese; Pasanen, Naldo, Baumann (Jensen 31), Fritz (Harnik 76), Andreasen, Mertesacker, Diego■, Borowski, Rosenberg, Hugo Almeida.

Olympiakos (0) 0

Real Madrid (0) 0 33,500

Olympiakos: Nikopolidis; Patsatzoglou, Julio Cesar (Mendrinos 74), Zewlakow, Raul Bravo (Archubi 53), Stoltidis, Galletti, Djordjevic, Pantos, Kovacevic (Konstantinou 80), Lua Lua.
Real Madrid: Casillas; Sergio Ramos, Cannavaro, Marcelo, Heinze, Diarra, Gago, Sneijder, Raul (Balboa 82), Robinho (Saviola 82), Van Nistelrooy.

Wednesday, 28 November 2007

Lazio (1) 1 *(Pandev 30)*

Olympiakos (1) 2 *(Galletti 35, Kovacevic 64)* 39,996

Lazio: Ballotta; Stendardo, Kolarov (De Silvestri 63), Siviglia, Mutarelli (Meghni 71), Mauri, Ledesma, Mudingayi, Behrami (Scaloni 78), Rocchi, Pandev.
Olympiakos: Nikopolidis; Patsatzoglou (Mendrinos 75), Zewlakow, Antzas, Torosides, Stoltidis, Galletti, Djordjevic (Mitroglou 90), Ledesma, Pantos, Lua Lua (Kovacevic 56).

Werder Bremen (2) 3 *(Rosenberg 4, Sanogo 40, Hunt 58)*

Real Madrid (1) 2 *(Robinho 14, Van Nistelrooy 71)* 36,350

Werder Bremen: Vander; Pasanen, Naldo, Baumann, Fritz (Tosic 6), Mertesacker, Vranjes, Jensen, Rosenberg, Hunt (Harnik 76), Sanogo (Carlos Alberto 87).
Real Madrid: Casillas; Pepe, Sergio Ramos, Marcelo, Metzelder, Diarra, Gago (Higuain 61), Guti, Raul, Robinho (Robben 75), Van Nistelrooy.

Tuesday, 11 December 2007

Olympiakos (1) 3 *(Stoltidis 12, 74, Kovacevic 70)*

Werder Bremen (0) 0 30,297

Olympiakos: Nikopolidis; Patsatzoglou (Mendrinos 23), Zewlakow, Antzas, Torosidis, Stoltidis, Galletti (Nunez 85), Ledesma, Pantos, Kovacevic (Mitroglou 82), Lua Lua.
Werder Bremen: Wiese; Pasanen, Naldo, Baumann (Tosic 82), Fritz, Vranjes (Hunt 58), Diego, Jensen, Borowski, Rosenberg, Sanogo (Hugo Almeida 67).

Real Madrid (3) 3 *(Baptista 13, Raul 15, Robinho 36)*

Lazio (0) 1 *(Pandev 80)* 70,559

Real Madrid: Casillas; Pepe, Sergio Ramos, Cannavaro, Marcelo, Diarra, Baptista, Sneijder (Guti 46), Raul, Robinho (Robben 46), Van Nistelrooy (Higuain 73).
Lazio: Ballotta; Scaloni, Siviglia, Cribari, De Silvestri, Mutarelli, Meghni (Manfredini 63), Ledesma (Baronio 46), Mudingayi, Rocchi, Pandev (Makinwa 82).

Group C Final Table	*P*	*W*	*D*	*L*	*F*	*A*	*Pts*
Real Madrid	6	3	2	1	13	9	11
Olympiakos	6	3	2	1	11	7	11
Werder Bremen	6	2	0	4	8	13	6
Lazio	6	1	2	3	8	11	5

GROUP D

Tuesday, 18 September 2007

AC Milan (2) 2 *(Pirlo 9, Inzaghi 24)*

Benfica (0) 1 *(Nuno Gomes 90)* 38,362

AC Milan: Dida; Kaladze, Nesta, Jankulovski, Oddo (Bonera 81), Gattuso, Seedorf (Emerson 75), Pirlo, Kaka, Ambrosini, Inzaghi (Gilardino 84).
Benfica: Quim; Luis Filipe, Edcarlos, Leo, Miguel Vitor (Binya 73), Katsouranis, Rui Costa (Nuno Assis 87), Pereira, Di Maria, Rodriguez, Cardozo (Nuno Gomes 63).

Shakhtar Donetsk (2) 2 *(Brandao 5, Lucarelli 8)*

Celtic (0) 0 26,100

Shakhtar Donetsk: Pyatov; Hubschmann, Kucher, Ilsinho, Rat, Fernandinho (Duljaj 86), Jadson (Nery Castillo 65), Lewandowski, Srna, Brandao, Lucarelli (Gladkiy 70).
Celtic: Boruc; Wilson, Naylor, Donati, Caldwell, McManus, Hartley, Brown S, McDonald (Killen 68), Vennegoor (Zurawski 85), Nakamura (McGeady 65).

Wednesday, 3 October 2007

Benfica (0) 0

Shakhtar Donetsk (1) 1 *(Jadson 42)* 34,647

Benfica: Quim; Edcarlos, Luisao, Leo, Nelson (Nuno Gomes 46), Katsouranis, Rui Costa, Pereira, Di Maria (Binya 61), Rodriguez, Cardozo.
Shakhtar Donetsk: Pyatov; Kucher, Ilsinho (Duljaj 79), Rat, Chygrynskiy, Fernandinho, Jadson (Nery Castillo 77), Lewandowski (Hubschmann 87), Srna, Brandao, Lucarelli.

Celtic (0) 2 *(McManus 63, McDonald 90)*

AC Milan (0) 1 *(Kaka 68 (pen))* 58,643

Celtic: Boruc; Perrier Doumbe (Kennedy 79), Naylor, Donati, Caldwell, McManus, Hartley, Brown S, McDonald, Jarosik (Nakamura 84), McGeady (Killen 84).
AC Milan: Dida (Kalac 90); Nesta, Jankulovski, Bonera, Oddo, Gattuso, Seedorf (Gourcuff 55), Pirlo, Kaka, Ambrosini, Inzaghi (Gilardino 77).

Wednesday, 24 October 2007

AC Milan (2) 4 *(Gilardino 6, 14, Seedorf 62, 69)*

Shakhtar Donetsk (0) 1 *(Lucarelli 51)* 36,850

AC Milan: Kalac; Kaladze, Nesta, Favalli (Bonera 61), Oddo, Gattuso, Seedorf, Pirlo, Kaka, Ambrosini (Emerson 82), Gilardino (Serginho 75).
Shakhtar Donetsk: Pyatov; Kucher (Hubschmann 17), Ilsinho, Rat, Chygrynskiy, Fernandinho, Jadson (Nery Castillo 63), Lewandowski, Srna, Brandao (Gladkiy 75), Lucarelli.

Benfica (0) 1 *(Cardozo 87)*

Celtic (0) 0 38,512

Benfica: Quim; Luisao, Leo, Katsouranis, Rui Costa, Pereira, Binya, Nuno Assis (Di Maria 82), Rodriguez (Luis Filipe 84), Cardozo, Bergessio (Adu 62).
Celtic: Boruc; Kennedy, Naylor, Donati (Sno 63), Caldwell, McManus, Hartley, Brown S, Killen (McDonald 74), Jarosik, McGeady.

Tuesday, 6 November 2007

Celtic (1) 1 *(McGeady 45)*

Benfica (0) 0 58,691

Celtic: Boruc; Caldwell, Naylor, Hartley, Kennedy, McManus, Jarosik (Donati 66), Brown S (Sno 89), McDonald, Vennegoor (Killen 66), McGeady.
Benfica: Quim; Luis Filipe, Edcarlos, Luisao, Leo, Katsouranis, Rui Costa (Bergessio 77), Pereira (Di Maria 61), Binya■, Rodriguez, Cardozo (Nuno Gomes 77).

Shakhtar Donetsk (0) 0

AC Milan (0) 3 *(Inzaghi 66, 90, Kaka 72)* 25,700

Shakhtar Donetsk: Pyatov; Hubschmann, Ilsinho, Rat (Willian 73), Chygrynskiy, Yezerskiy, Fernandinho, Jadson, Srna, Brandao (Gladkiy 84), Lucarelli (Nery Castillo 77).
AC Milan: Dida; Kaladze, Nesta, Bonera, Gattuso, Seedorf (Maldini 71), Pirlo, Kaka, Ambrosini, Serginho (Brocchi 85), Gilardino (Inzaghi 63).

Wednesday, 28 November 2007

Benfica (1) 1 *(Pereira 20)*

AC Milan (1) 1 *(Pirlo 15)* 46,034

Benfica: Quim; Luis Filipe (Di Maria 74), Luisao, Leo, David Luiz (Adu 88), Petit, Katsouranis, Rui Costa, Pereira, Rodriguez, Nuno Gomes (Cardozo 75).
AC Milan: Dida; Kaladze, Nesta, Bonera, Gattuso, Seedorf (Oddo 73), Pirlo, Kaka, Serginho (Maldini 46), Brocchi (Gourcuff 51), Gilardino.

Celtic (1) 2 *(Jarosik 45, Donati 90)*

Shakhtar Donetsk (1) 1 *(Brandao 4)* 59,396

Celtic: Boruc; Caldwell, Naylor (Donati 16), Hartley, Kennedy (Pressley 41), McManus, Jarosik, Brown S, McDonald, Vennegoor (Killen 79), McGeady.
Shakhtar Donetsk: Pyatov; Hubschmann, Kucher, Ilsinho (Yezerskiy 84), Rat, Chygrynskiy, Jadson, Lewandowski, Srna, Brandao, Lucarelli (Gladkiy 88).

Tuesday, 4 December 2007

AC Milan (0) 1 *(Inzaghi 70)*

Celtic (0) 0 38,409

AC Milan: Kalac; Cafu, Simic (Kaladze 30), Favalli, Bonera, Gattuso, Seedorf (Gourcuff 69), Pirlo (Brocchi 74), Kaka, Ambrosini, Inzaghi.
Celtic: Boruc; Caldwell, O'Dea, Donati (Sno 71), Pressley, McManus, Hartley, Brown S, McDonald (Vennegoor 65), Jarosik (Zurawski 78), McGeady.

Shakhtar Donetsk (1) 1 *(Lucarelli 30 (pen))*

Benfica (2) 2 *(Cardozo 6, 22)* 24,200

Shakhtar Donetsk: Pyatov; Kucher, Ilsinho (Willian 67), Rat, Chygrynskiy, Fernandinho, Jadson, Lewandowski (Hubschmann 57), Srna, Brandao, Lucarelli (Gladkiy 74).
Benfica: Quim; Luisao, Leo, Nelson, David Luiz, Petit, Katsouranis, Rui Costa, Pereira (Luis Filipe 83), Di Maria (Nuno Assis 67), Cardozo (Nuno Gomes 90).

Group D Final Table	*P*	*W*	*D*	*L*	*F*	*A*	*Pts*
AC Milan	6	4	1	1	12	5	13
Celtic	6	3	0	3	5	6	9
Benfica	6	2	1	3	5	6	7
Shakhtar Donetsk	6	2	0	4	6	11	6

GROUP E

Wednesday, 19 September 2007

Barcelona (1) 3 *(Clerc 21 (og), Messi 82, Henry 90)*
Lyon (0) 0 76,689

Barcelona: Victor Valdes; Gabi Milito, Marquez, Abidal, Xavi (Giovanni Dos Santos 79), Ronaldinho (Iniesta 66), Zambrotta, Deco, Toure Yaya, Henry, Messi (Bojan Krkic 88).
Lyon: Vercoutre; Clerc, Reveillere, Squillaci, Bodmer, Kallstrom (Keita 83), Juninho Pernambucano, Belhadj (Baros 62), Toulalan, Benzema (Ben Arfa 76), Govou.

Rangers (0) 2 *(Adam 62, Darcheville 75 (pen))*
Stuttgart (0) 1 *(Gomez 56)* 49,795

Rangers: McGregor; Hutton, Papac, Cuellar, Weir, Ferguson, Hemdani, Thomson, Darcheville (Novo 83), Adam (Beasley 67), Whittaker (Faye 86).
Stuttgart: Schafer; Osorio, Tasci, Fernando Meira, Boka, Pardo, Hilbert, Da Silva (Ewerthon 70), Khedira (Basturk 78), Cacau, Gomez.

Tuesday, 2 October 2007

Lyon (0) 0
Rangers (1) 3 *(McCulloch 23, Cousin 48, Beasley 53)* 38,076

Lyon: Vercoutre; Grosso, Reveillere (Clerc 81), Anderson, Squillaci, Bodmer (Ben Arfa 60), Kallstrom, Juninho Pernambucano, Baros (Keita 60), Benzema, Govou.
Rangers: McGregor; Hutton, Papac, Cuellar, Weir, Ferguson, Hemdani, Thomson, Cousin (Whittaker 66), McCulloch (Novo 81), Beasley (Adam 90).

Stuttgart (0) 0
Barcelona (0) 2 *(Puyol 53, Messi 67)* 51,300

Stuttgart: Schafer; Osorio (Marica 63), Tasci, Fernando Meira, Boka, Farnerud (Magnin 76), Pardo, Hilbert, Khedira (Meissner 76), Cacau, Gomez.
Barcelona: Victor Valdes; Marquez (Puyol 7) (Sylvinho 64), Thuram, Abidal, Oleguer, Xavi, Iniesta, Ronaldinho (Bojan Krkic 82), Deco, Henry, Messi.

Tuesday, 23 October 2007

Rangers (0) 0
Barcelona (0) 0 49,957

Rangers: McGregor; Hutton, Papac, Cuellar, Weir, Ferguson, Adam, Thomson, Novo (Beasley 72), Cousin, McCulloch.
Barcelona: Victor Valdes; Milito, Puyol, Thuram, Abidal, Xavi, Iniesta, Ronaldinho, Gudjohnsen, Henry (Giovanni Dos Santos 82), Messi.

Stuttgart (0) 0
Lyon (0) 2 *(Fabio Santos 56, Benzema 79)* 51,300

Stuttgart: Schafer; Osorio, Tasci, Fernando Meira, Meissner (Khedira 62), Farnerud, Basturk (Ewerthon 71), Pardo, Hilbert, Cacau, Gomez.
Lyon: Vercoutre; Grosso, Reveillere, Anderson, Squillaci, Kallstrom, Juninho Pernambucano, Ben Arfa (Keita 74), Fabio Santos, Benzema (Bodmer 84), Govou (Clerc 85).

Wednesday, 7 November 2007

Barcelona (2) 2 *(Henry 6, Messi 43)*
Rangers (0) 0 82,887

Barcelona: Victor Valdes; Gabi Milito, Puyol (Oleguer 85), Thuram, Abidal, Xavi, Iniesta (Gudjohnsen 71), Ronaldinho (Bojan Krkic 77), Toure Yaya, Henry, Messi.
Rangers: McGregor; Hutton, Papac, Cuellar, Weir, Ferguson, Hemdani, Beasley (Novo 69), Cousin (Naismith 78), McCulloch, Adam (Darcheville 62).

Lyon (3) 4 *(Kallstrom 15, Ben Arfa 37, 38, Juninho Pernambucano 90)*
Stuttgart (1) 2 *(Gomez 16, 56)* 38,215

Lyon: Vercoutre; Grosso, Reveillere, Anderson, Squillaci, Kallstrom, Juninho Pernambucano, Ben Arfa (Keita 70), Fabio Santos, Benzema (Belhadj 82), Govou (Clerc 90).
Stuttgart: Schafer; Beck (Osorio 77), Tasci, Fernando Meira, Delpierre, Magnin (Farnerud 81), Basturk, Hitzlsperger, Khedira, Cacau (Marica 58), Gomez.

Tuesday, 27 November 2007

Lyon (1) 2 *(Juninho Pernambucano 7, 80 (pen))*
Barcelona (1) 2 *(Iniesta 3, Messi 58 (pen))* 38,113

Lyon: Vercoutre; Grosso, Reveillere, Anderson, Squillaci, Juninho Pernambucano, Ben Arfa (Remy 82), Fabio Santos (Kallstrom 68), Toulalan, Fred (Keita 60), Govou.
Barcelona: Victor Valdes; Gabi Milito, Puyol, Abidal, Xavi, Iniesta, Zambrotta (Marquez 82), Toure Yaya, Gudjohnsen (Ronaldinho 71), Messi, Bojan Krkic.

Stuttgart (1) 3 *(Cacau 45, Pardo 62, Marica 85)*
Rangers (1) 2 *(Adam 27, Ferguson 70)* 51,300

Stuttgart: Schafer; Beck, Fernando Meira, Delpierre, Magnin, Hitzlsperger, Pardo, Hilbert (Ewerthon 83), Khedira (Da Silva 46), Cacau (Tasci 88), Marica.
Rangers: McGregor; Hutton, Papac, Cuellar, Weir, Ferguson, Hemdani, Thomson, Darcheville (Cousin 82), Beasley (Naismith 49), McCulloch (Adam 26).

Wednesday, 12 December 2007

Barcelona (1) 3 *(Giovanni Dos Santos 36, Eto'o 57, Ronaldinho 67)*
Stuttgart (1) 1 *(Da Silva 3)* 52,651

Barcelona: Jorquera; Gabi Milito, Marquez, Puyol, Sylvinho, Thuram, Xavi (Marc Crosas 70), Ronaldinho, Gudjohnsen (Bojan Krkic 52), Eto'o (Iniesta 62), Giovanni Dos Santos.
Stuttgart: Schafer; Osorio, Tasci, Fernando Meira, Boka, Delpierre, Farnerud (Hilbert 58), Basturk (Meissner 72), Da Silva, Ewerthon, Marica (Fischer 71).

Rangers (0) 0
Lyon (1) 3 *(Govou 16, Benzema 85, 88)* 50,260

Rangers: McGregor; Hutton, Papac (Darcheville■ 71), Cuellar, Weir, Ferguson, Hemdani (Boyd 84), Thomson, Cousin (Naismith 46), McCulloch, Whittaker.
Lyon: Vercoutre; Clerc, Grosso, Anderson, Squillaci, Kallstrom, Juninho Pernambucano (Baros 85), Ben Arfa (Bodmer 68), Toulalan, Benzema, Govou (Reveillere 77).

Group E Final Table	*P*	*W*	*D*	*L*	*F*	*A*	*Pts*
Barcelona	6	4	2	0	12	3	14
Lyon	6	3	1	2	11	10	10
Rangers	6	2	1	3	7	9	7
Stuttgart	6	1	0	5	7	15	3

GROUP F

Wednesday, 19 September 2007

Roma (1) 2 *(Perrotta 9, Totti 70)*
Dynamo Kiev (0) 0 40,000

Roma: Doni; Juan (Ferrari 82), Mexes, Cassetti, Aquilani (Pizarro 83), Taddei, De Rossi, Perrotta, Tonetto, Mancini (Giuly 61), Totti.
Dynamo Kiev: Shovkovskiy; Fedorov, Gavrancic, Markovic, Michael (Rebrov 56), Mikhalik, Gusev (Correa 71), El-Kaddouri, Ayila, Bangoura (Diogo Rincon 46), Shatskikh.

Sporting Lisbon (0) 0
Manchester United (0) 1 *(Ronaldo 62)* 39,514

Sporting Lisbon: Stojkovic; Anderson Polga, Ronny (Pereirinha 74), Tonel, Miguel Veloso, Abel, Izmailov (Vukcevic 56), Joao Moutinho, Romagnoli (Purovic 68), Yannick, Liedson.
Manchester United: Van der Sar; Brown, Evra, Carrick, Ferdinand, Vidic, Nani, Scholes, Ronaldo (Tevez 87), Rooney (Saha 72), Giggs (Anderson 76).

Tuesday, 2 October 2007

Dynamo Kiev (1) 1 *(Vaschchuk 29)*
Sporting Lisbon (2) 2 *(Tonel 14, Anderson Polga 38)* 34,000

Dynamo Kiev: Shovkovskiy; Vaschchuk, Gavrancic, Ghioane (Gusev 56), Correa, Diogo Rincon, Mikhalik, El-Kaddouri, Ayila, Shatskikh, Milevski (Kleber 58).
Sporting Lisbon: Stojkovic; Anderson Polga, Ronny, Tonel, Miguel Veloso, Abel, Vukcevic (Izmailov 68), Joao Moutinho, Romagnoli (Paredes 77), Yannick (Gladstone 90), Liedson.

Manchester United (0) 1 *(Rooney 70)*

Roma (0) 0 73,652

Manchester United: Kuszczak; O'Shea, Evra, Carrick, Ferdinand, Vidic, Ronaldo, Scholes, Saha (Tevez 66), Rooney (Anderson 85), Nani (Giggs 80).
Roma: Curci; Juan, Mexes, Cicinho, Aquilani (Pizarro 62), De Rossi, Perrotta, Tonetto, Mancini (Vucinic 74), Totti, Giuly (Esposito 80).

Tuesday, 23 October 2007

Dynamo Kiev (1) 2 *(Diogo Rincon 34, Bangoura 78)*

Manchester United (3) 4 *(Ferdinand 10, Rooney 18, Ronaldo 41, 68 (pen))* 42,000

Dynamo Kiev: Shovkovskiy; Diakhate, Nesmachni, Gavrancic, Ghioane (Belkevich 46), Correa (Rotan 83), Diogo Rincon, Gusev, Ayila, Bangoura, Shatskikh (Milevski 46).
Manchester United: Van der Sar (Kuszczak 80); Brown, O'Shea, Anderson, Ferdinand, Vidic, Ronaldo, Fletcher, Rooney, Tevez (Nani 73), Giggs (Simpson 80).

Roma (1) 2 *(Juan 15, Vucinic 70)*

Sporting Lisbon (1) 1 *(Liedson 18)* 26,893

Roma: Doni; Panucci, Juan, Mexes, Cassetti, Pizarro, De Rossi, Tonetto, Mancini (Cicinho 87), Totti (Vucinic 35), Giuly (Brighi 73).
Sporting Lisbon: Tiago; Ronny (Purovic 77), Tonel, Miguel Veloso, Abel, Izmailov (Celsinho 81), Vukcevic (Paredes 71), Joao Moutinho, Romagnoli, Yannick, Liedson.

Wednesday, 7 November 2007

Manchester United (2) 4 *(Pique 31, Tevez 37, Rooney 76, Ronaldo 88)*

Dynamo Kiev (0) 0 75,017

Manchester United: Van der Sar (Kuszczak 46); Pique (Evans 73), Evra, Carrick, Simpson, Vidic, Ronaldo, Fletcher, Rooney, Tevez (Saha 68), Nani.
Dynamo Kiev: Shovkovskiy; Fedorov, Diakhate, Vashchuk, Markovic, Ghioane, Correa, Rotan (Diogo Rincon 46), Gusev (Rebrov 46), El-Kaddouri, Milevski (Bangoura 76).

Sporting Lisbon (1) 2 *(Liedson 22, 64)*

Roma (1) 2 *(Cassetti 4, Anderson Polga 90 (og))* 32,273

Sporting Lisbon: Tiago; Anderson Polga, Ronny, Tonel, Miguel Veloso, Abel, Izmailov (Pereirinha 89), Joao Moutinho, Romagnoli, Yannick (Vukcevic 63), Liedson.
Roma: Doni; Cicinho, Juan, Mexes (Ferrari 46), Cassetti, Pizarro, De Rossi, Perrotta (Esposito 80), Mancini, Vucinic, Giuly (Brighi 90).

Tuesday, 27 November 2007

Dynamo Kiev (0) 1 *(Bangoura 64)*

Roma (3) 4 *(Vucinic 4, 36, 78, Giuly 32)* 11,000

Dynamo Kiev: Rybka; Nesmachni, Vashchuk, Gavrancic, Ghioane, Rotan (Belkevich 46), Diogo Rincon (Milevski 69), Gusev, Ninkovic (Shatskikh 55), Dopilka, Bangoura.
Roma: Doni; Panucci, Juan, Ferrari, Cassetti, Pizarro, Taddei (Esposito 46), De Rossi (Barusso 61), Tonetto, Vucinic (Cicinho 84), Giuly.

Manchester United (0) 2 *(Tevez 61, Ronaldo 90)*

Sporting Lisbon (1) 1 *(Abel 21)* 75,162

Manchester United: Kuszczak; O'Shea, Evra, Carrick, Ferdinand, Vidic, Ronaldo, Anderson, Saha (Hargreaves 79), Fletcher (Tevez 46), Nani (Giggs 46).
Sporting Lisbon: Rui Patricio; Had, Anderson Polga, Tonel, Miguel Veloso, Abel, Izmailov (Farnerud 82), Joao Moutinho, Romagnoli (Vukcevic 68), Purovic (Pereirinha 82), Liedson.

Wednesday, 12 December 2007

Roma (0) 1 *(Mancini 71)*

Manchester United (1) 1 *(Pique 34)* 29,490

Roma: Doni; Cicinho, Mexes, Antunes, Ferrari, Pizarro, Taddei (De Rossi 46), Barusso (Vucinic 62), Mancini, Totti, Esposito (Giuly 62).
Manchester United: Kuszczak; Pique, O'Shea (Brown 54), Carrick, Evans, Simpson, Eagles, Fletcher, Saha, Rooney (Dong 72), Nani.

Sporting Lisbon (1) 3 *(Anderson Polga 35 (pen), Joao Moutinho 67, Liedson 88)*

Dynamo Kiev (0) 0 19,402

Sporting Lisbon: Rui Patricio; Anderson Polga, Ronny (Miguel Veloso 61), Tonel, Abel, Adrien Silva, Izmailov, Farnerud (Vukcevic 68), Joao Moutinho, Purovic (Paez 86), Liedson.
Dynamo Kiev: Lutsenko; Nesmachni, Gavrancic, Markovic, Ghioane, Gusev, Ninkovic, Dopilka, Rebrov (Belkevich 80), Bangoura (Kravets 57), Shatskikh.

Group F Final Table	*P*	*W*	*D*	*L*	*F*	*A*	*Pts*
Manchester United	6	5	1	0	13	4	16
Roma	6	3	2	1	11	6	11
Sporting Lisbon	6	2	1	3	9	8	7
Dynamo Kiev	6	0	0	6	4	19	0

GROUP G

Wednesday, 19 September 2007

Fenerbahce (1) 1 *(Deivid 43)*

Internazionale (0) 0 52,500

Fenerbahce: Volkan; Lugano, Roberto Carlos, Onder, Deniz, Edu Dracena, Wederson, Mehmet, Alex, Kezman (Semih 67), Deivid.
Internazionale: Julio Cesar; Zanetti, Maxwell, Rivas, Samuel, Stankovic, Dacourt (Jimenez 70), Cambiasso, Solari (Figo 57), Ibrahimovic, Suazo (Crespo 72).

PSV Eindhoven (0) 2 *(Lazovic 59, Perez 80)*

CSKA Moscow (0) 1 *(Vagner Love 89)* 35,100

PSV Eindhoven: Gomes; Salcido, Da Costa, Alcides, Simons, Mendez (Kromkamp 71), Culina, Addo, Lazovic, Koevermans (Farfan 75), Afellay (Perez 28).
CSKA Moscow: Mandrikin; Semberas, Ignashevich, Berezutski A, Berezutski V, Krasic, Zhirkov, Cearense, Rahimic (Ratinho 78), Vagner Love, Jo.

Tuesday, 2 October 2007

CSKA Moscow (0) 2 *(Krasic 49, Vagner Love 53 (pen))*

Fenerbahce (1) 2 *(Alex 9, Deivid 85)* 27,000

CSKA Moscow: Mandrikin; Semberas, Ignashevich, Berezutski A, Berezutski V, Krasic, Zhirkov, Cearense (Aldonin 90), Rahimic, Vagner Love, Jo.
Fenerbahce: Volkan; Lugano (Gokhan 77), Roberto Carlos, Onder, Deniz (Yasin 72), Edu Dracena (Kazim-Richards 72), Wederson, Mehmet, Alex, Kezman, Deivid.

Internazionale (2) 2 *(Ibrahimovic 15 (pen), 31)*

PSV Eindhoven (0) 0 34,238

Internazionale: Julio Cesar; Zanetti, Maxwell, Samuel, Chivu■, Stankovic, Figo, Cambiasso, Solari (Bolzoni 70), Ibrahimovic, Crespo (Suazo■ 61).
PSV Eindhoven: Gomes; Kromkamp (Bakkal 69), Salcido, Alcides, Simons, Mendez (Koevermans 56), Culina, Addo, Lazovic, Perez, Farfan (Aissati 75).

Tuesday, 23 October 2007

CSKA Moscow (1) 1 *(Jo 32)*

Internazionale (0) 2 *(Crespo 52, Samuel 80)* 24,000

CSKA Moscow: Mandrikin; Ignashevich, Berezutski A (Grigoriev 46), Berezutski V, Krasic, Zhirkov, Cearense (Ratinho 42) (Janczyk 76), Aldonin, Rahimic, Daniel Carvalho, Jo.
Internazionale: Julio Cesar; Cordoba, Zanetti, Maxwell, Samuel, Figo, Vieira (Stankovic 17), Dacourt (Solari 77), Cambiasso, Ibrahimovic, Crespo (Cruz 62).

PSV Eindhoven (0) 0

Fenerbahce (0) 0 36,200

PSV Eindhoven: Gomes; Kromkamp, Salcido, Marcellis, Simons, Mendez (Zonneveld 58), Addo (Koevermans 58), Bakkal (Aissati 78), Lazovic, Perez, Farfan.
Fenerbahce: Volkan; Lugano, Roberto Carlos, Deniz, Edu Dracena, Gokhan, Wederson, Mehmet, Alex (Ali 35), Semih (Kazim-Richards 72), Deivid■.

Wednesday, 7 November 2007

Fenerbahce (2) 2 *(Marcellis 28 (og), Semih 30)*

PSV Eindhoven (0) 0 46,229

Fenerbahce: Volkan; Roberto Carlos, Yasin, Deniz, Edu Dracena, Gokhan (Onder 88), Wederson, Kazim-Richards (Appiah 86), Mehmet, Alex (Ali 71), Semih.
PSV Eindhoven: Gomes; Kromkamp (Zonneveld 46), Salcido, Alcides, Marcellis, Simons, Mendez, Van der Leegte (Bakkal 80), Lazovic, Perez (Koevermans 63), Farfan.

Internazionale (2) 4 *(Ibrahimovic 32, 75, Cambiasso 34, 67)*

CSKA Moscow (2) 2 *(Jo 23, Vagner Love 31)* 22,384

Internazionale: Julio Cesar; Cordoba, Zanetti, Maxwell (Solari 66), Maicon, Samuel, Chivu, Dacourt, Cambiasso, Ibrahimovic (Suazo 84), Crespo (Cruz 63).
CSKA Moscow: Akinfeev; Berezutski A, Berezutski V (Ratinho 69), Grigoriev, Krasic, Zhirkov, Cearense (Taranov 83), Rahimic, Daniel Carvalho, Vagner Love, Jo (Aldonin 46).

Tuesday, 27 November 2007

CSKA Moscow (0) 0

PSV Eindhoven (1) 1 *(Farfan 39)* 14,000

CSKA Moscow: Akinfeev; Semberas, Ignashevich, Berezutski A, Berezutski V, Zhirkov, Cearense (Odiah 73), Aldonin, Rahimic (Grigoriev 86), Ramon (Caner 61), Janczyk.
PSV Eindhoven: Gomes; Salcido, Alcides, Rajkovic, Marcellis, Zonneveld, Mendez, Bakkal (Culina 77), Lazovic (Perez 84), Farfan (Koevermans 81), Afellay.

Internazionale (0) 3 *(Cruz 55, Ibrahimovic 66, Jimenez 90)*

Fenerbahce (0) 0 24,203

Internazionale: Julio Cesar; Cordoba, Zanetti, Maxwell (Jimenez 72), Maicon, Samuel, Chivu, Stankovic (Materazzi 89), Cambiasso, Ibrahimovic (Suazo 78), Cruz.
Fenerbahce: Volkan; Lugano, Roberto Carlos, Edu Dracena, Gokhan, Wederson, Mehmet (Appiah 62), Alex, Selcuk, Semih (Kazim-Richards 66), Deivid (Tumer 83).

Wednesday, 12 December 2007

Fenerbahce (2) 3 *(Alex 32, Ugur 45, 90)*

CSKA Moscow (1) 1 *(Edu Dracena 31 (og))* 45,745

Fenerbahce: Volkan; Lugano, Roberto Carlos (Wederson 90), Edu Dracena, Gokhan, Mehmet, Alex, Selcuk, Ugur (Kezman 90), Semih (Kazim-Richards 70), Deivid.
CSKA Moscow: Akinfeev; Semberas, Ignashevich, Berezutski A, Ratinho (Taranov 77), Grigoriev, Zhirkov, Aldonin, Caner (Odiah 46), Ramon (Mamaev 46), Janczyk.

PSV Eindhoven (0) 0

Internazionale (0) 1 *(Cruz 64)* 35,000

PSV Eindhoven: Gomes; Salcido, Alcides, Marcellis, Zonneveld, Simons, Mendez■, Culina, Lazovic (Jonathan 84), Farfan (Perez 62), Afellay (Aissati 65).
Internazionale: Julio Cesar; Cordoba, Maxwell (Zanetti 86), Materazzi, Rivas, Chivu (Cambiasso 68), Solari, Bolzoni, Cruz (Puccio 75), Crespo, Suazo.

Group G Final Table	*P*	*W*	*D*	*L*	*F*	*A*	*Pts*
Internazionale	6	5	0	1	12	4	15
Fenerbahce	6	3	2	1	8	6	11
PSV Eindhoven	6	2	1	3	3	6	7
CSKA Moscow	6	0	1	5	7	14	1

GROUP H

Wednesday, 19 September 2007

Arsenal (1) 3 *(Fabregas 27, Van Persie 59, Eduardo 90)*

Sevilla (0) 0 59,992

Arsenal: Almunia; Sagna, Clichy, Flamini, Toure, Senderos, Hleb, Fabregas, Adebayor (Eduardo 83), Van Persie (Diarra 88), Rosicky (Diaby 50).
Sevilla: Palop; Dragutinovic, Daniel Alves, Escude, Fazio, Jesus Navas, Poulsen, Diego Capel (Renato 67), Marti (Keita 66), Luis Fabiano (Kerzhakov 46), Kanoute.

Slavia Prague (1) 2 *(Senkerik 13, Belaid 63)*

Steaua (1) 1 *(Goian 33)* 15,723

Slavia Prague: Vaniak; Brabec (Janda 43), Drizdal, Tavares, Latka (Hubacek 46), Pudil, Suchy, Krajcik, Belaid (Volesak 81), Vlcek, Senkerik.
Steaua: Zapata; Goian, Rada, Marin, Petre O, Cristocea (Croitoru 53), Nicolita, Lovin (Surdu 62), Badoi, Dica, Iacob (Badea 71).

Tuesday, 2 October 2007

Sevilla (2) 4 *(Kanoute 8, Luis Fabiano 27, Escude 58, Kone 69)*

Slavia Prague (1) 2 *(Pudil 19, Kalivoda 90)* 31,000

Sevilla: Palop; Dragutinovic, Daniel Alves, Escude, Boulahrouz, Adriano (Hinkel 81), Jesus Navas (Duda 75), Poulsen, Keita, Luis Fabiano (Kone 64), Kanoute.
Slavia Prague: Vaniak; Hubacek, Svec, Drizdal (Ivana 46), Sourek, Janda (Kalivoda 63), Pudil, Suchy, Krajcik, Belaid (Volesak 70), Vlcek.

Steaua (0) 0

Arsenal (0) 1 *(Van Persie 76)* 15,000

Steaua: Zapata; Rada, Emeghara, Baciu, Marin, Petre O, Nicolita, Badea (Iacob 60), Dica, Neaga (Zaharia 77), Surdu (Badoi 84).
Arsenal: Almunia; Sagna, Clichy, Flamini, Toure, Senderos, Eboue (Silva 73), Fabregas, Adebayor, Van Persie, Hleb.

Tuesday, 23 October 2007

Arsenal (3) 7 *(Fabregas 5, 58, Hubacek 24 (og), Walcott 41, 55, Hleb 51, Bendtner 89)*

Slavia Prague (0) 0 59,621

Arsenal: Almunia; Sagna, Clichy, Flamini (Silva 63), Toure, Gallas, Eboue, Fabregas, Adebayor (Rosicky 64), Walcott, Hleb (Bendtner 63).
Slavia Prague: Vaniak; Hubacek, Svec, Tavares (Belaid 63), Pudil, Suchy, Krajcik, Kalivoda (Jablonsky 46), Vlcek, Senkerik, Ivana (Volesak 56).

Sevilla (2) 2 *(Kanoute 5, Luis Fabiano 17)*

Steaua (0) 1 *(Petre 63)* 28,945

Sevilla: Palop; Dragutinovic, Daniel Alves, Mosquera, Adriano, Jesus Navas, Poulsen, Diego Capel (Marti 85), Keita, Luis Fabiano, Kanoute (Renato 71).
Steaua: Zapata; Goian, Rada, Emeghara, Marin, Petre O, Nicolita, Croitoru, Dica (Badea 46), Iacob (Zaharia 71), Surdu (Neaga 46).

Wednesday, 7 November 2007

Slavia Prague (0) 0

Arsenal (0) 0 18,000

Slavia Prague: Vorel; Brabec, Hubacek, Svec, Drizdal, Tavares, Smicer (Kalivoda 64), Pudil (Jablonsky 90), Suchy, Krajcik, Senkerik (Ivana 77).
Arsenal: Almunia; Diarra, Clichy, Silva, Song Billong, Gallas, Denilson, Walcott, Eduardo (Eboue 81), Bendtner (Adebayor 78), Diaby.

Steaua (0) 0

Sevilla (1) 2 *(Renato 25, 65)* 7984

Steaua: Zapata; Goian, Rada, Emeghara, Nesu, Petre O, Nicolita, Lovin, Croitoru (Badea 46), Dica, Iacob (Surdu 61).
Sevilla: Palop; Dragutinovic, Daniel Alves, Mosquera, Adriano, Jesus Navas (Hinkel 89), Poulsen C, Renato, De Mul (Diego Capel 63), Keita, Kanoute (Luis Fabiano 69).

Tuesday, 27 November 2007

Sevilla (2) 3 *(Keita 24, Luis Fabiano 34, Kanoute 89 (pen))*

Arsenal (1) 1 *(Eduardo 11)* 35,529

Sevilla: Palop; Dragutinovic, Daniel Alves, Jesus Navas, Poulsen, Fazio, Keita, Adriano (Marti 90), Luis Fabiano (Kerzhakov 75), Crespo (Mosquera 64), Kanoute.
Arsenal: Almunia; Hoyte J (Sagna 66), Traore, Silva, Toure, Senderos, Eboue (Walcott 78), Fabregas (Rosicky 56), Eduardo, Bendtner, Denilson.

Steaua (1) 1 *(Badea 12)*

Slavia Prague (0) 1 *(Senkerik 78)* 8287

Steaua: Zapata; Goian, Rada, Emeghara, Nesu, Petre O, Lovin (Bicfalvi 65), Croitoru (Surdu 76), Badea (Cristocea 89), Dica, Neaga.
Slavia Prague: Vaniak; Brabec, Hubacek, Svec (Belaid 29), Tavares, Pudil, Suchy, Krajcik, Volesak (Sourek 61), Gaucho (Necid 77), Senkerik.

Wednesday, 12 December 2007

Arsenal (2) 2 *(Diaby 8, Bendtner 42)*

Steaua (0) 1 *(Zaharia 68)* 59,786

Arsenal: Lehmann; Sagna (Eboue 71), Traore, Song-Billong, Senderos, Gallas, Walcott, Denilson, Van Persie (Eduardo 65), Bendtner, Diaby (Diarra 71).
Steaua: Zapata; Goian, Rada, Emeghara, Nesu, Petre O, Cristocea (Surdu 57), Lovin, Badea (Golanski 81), Dica, Neaga (Zaharia 64).

Slavia Prague (0) 0

Sevilla (0) 3 *(Luis Fabiano 66, Kanoute 69, Daniel Alves 87)* 11,689

Slavia Prague: Vaniak; Brabec, Hubacek, Tavares, Smicer (Jablonsky 46), Pudil (Gaucho 74), Suchy, Krajcik, Belaid, Volesak (Necid 66), Ivana.
Sevilla: De Sanctis; Dragutinovic, Daniel Alves, Mosquera, Lolo, Jesus Navas, Renato (Maresca 64), Diego Capel, Marti, Kanoute (Duda 70), Kone (Luis Fabiano 59).

Group H Final Table	*P*	*W*	*D*	*L*	*F*	*A*	*Pts*
Sevilla	6	5	0	1	14	7	15
Arsenal	6	4	1	1	14	4	13
Slavia Prague	6	1	2	3	5	16	5
Steaua	6	0	1	5	4	10	1

KNOCK-OUT STAGE

KNOCK-OUT ROUND FIRST LEG

Tuesday, 19 February 2008

Liverpool (0) 2 *(Kuyt 85, Gerrard 90)*

Internazionale (0) 0 41,999

Liverpool: Reyna; Finnan, Fabio Aurelio, Mascherano, Carragher, Hyypia, Lucas (Crouch 64), Gerrard, Torres, Kuyt, Babel (Pennant 72).
Internazionale: Julio Cesar; Cordoba (Burdisso 76), Zanetti, Maxwell, Maicon, Materazzi■, Chivu, Stankovic, Cambiasso, Ibrahimovic, Cruz (Vieira 55).

Olympiakos (0) 0

Chelsea (0) 0 31,302

Olympiakos: Nikopolidis; Julio Cesar, Zewlakow, Antzas, Torosidis, Stoltidis, Galletti (Leonardo 83), Djordjevic (Belluschi 76), Ledesma, Pantos, Kovacevic (Nunez 87).
Chelsea: Cech; Belletti, Cole A, Makelele, Alex, Ricardo Carvalho, Essien, Ballack (Lampard 86), Drogba, Cole J (Kalou 75), Malouda (Anelka 75).

Roma (1) 2 *(Pizarro 24, Mancini 58)*

Real Madrid (1) 1 *(Raul 8)* 59,617

Roma: Doni; Panucci (Tonetto 67), Mexes, Juan (Ferrari 76), Cassetti, De Rossi, Pizarro (Aquilani 62), Perrotta, Giuly, Mancini, Totti.
Real Madrid: Casillas; Sergio Ramos, Cannavaro, Heinze, Miguel Torres, Diarra (Drenthe 79), Guti, Gago, Robben (Julio Baptista 79), Raul, Van Nistelrooy.

Schalke (1) 1 *(Kuranyi 4)*

Porto (0) 0 53,951

Schalke: Neuer; Westermann, Bordon, Rafinha, Krstajic, Kobiashvili, Ernst, Rakitic (Grossmuller 76), Jones, Asamoah (Halil Altintop 80), Kuranyi (Sanchez 89).
Porto: Helton; Bruno Alves, Pedro Emanuel, Jorge Fucile (Mariano Gonzalez 85), Joao Paulo, Paulo Assuncao, Quaresma, Lucho Gonzalez, Raul Meireles, Lisandro Lopez, Farias (Sektioui 56).

Wednesday, 20 February 2008

Arsenal (0) 0

AC Milan (0) 0 60,082

Arsenal: Lehmann; Sagna, Clichy, Flamini, Toure (Senderos 7), Gallas, Eboue (Walcott 90), Fabregas, Adebayor, Eduardo (Bendtner 74), Hleb.
AC Milan: Kalac; Maldini, Kaladze, Nesta (Jankulovski 50), Oddo, Gattuso, Seedorf (Emerson 86), Pirlo, Kaka, Ambrosini, Pato (Gilardino 77).

Celtic (2) 2 *(Vennegoor 16, Robson 38)*

Barcelona (1) 3 *(Messi 18, 79, Henry 52)* 56,395

Celtic: Boruc; Caddis (Wilson 61), Naylor, Hartley (Donati 65), Caldwell, McManus, Nakamura, Robson, McDonald, Vennegoor (Samaras 55), McGeady.
Barcelona: Victor Valdes; Gabi Milito, Marquez, Puyol, Abidal, Iniesta, Ronaldinho (Eto'o 73), Deco (Xavi 66), Toure Yaya, Henry (Gudjohnsen 88), Messi.

Fenerbahce (1) 3 *(Kezman 16, Lugano 56, Semih 87)*

Sevilla (1) 2 *(Edu Dracena 23 (og), Escude 67)* 46,210

Fenerbahce: Volkan; Lugano, Roberto Carlos (Wederson 68), Edu Dracena, Gokhan, Mehmet, Alex, Selcuk, Ugur (Kazim-Richards 79), Kezman (Semih 84), Deivid.
Sevilla: Palop; Dragutinovic, Daniel Alves, Escude, Duda (Diego Capel 63), Adriano, Jesus Navas, Poulsen C, Keita, Luis Fabiano, Kanoute.

Lyon (0) 1 *(Benzema 54)*

Manchester United (0) 1 *(Tevez 87)* 39,219

Lyon: Coupet; Clerc (Ben Arfa 78), Grosso, Reveillere, Squillaci, Boumsong, Kallstrom, Juninho Pernambucano (Bodmer 74), Toulalan, Benzema (Fred 83), Govou.
Manchester United: Van der Sar; Brown, Evra, Hargreaves (Carrick 78), Ferdinand, Vidic, Anderson, Scholes (Nani 65), Rooney, Ronaldo, Giggs (Tevez 65).

KNOCK-OUT ROUND SECOND LEG

Tuesday, 4 March 2008

AC Milan (0) 0

Arsenal (0) 2 *(Fabregas 84, Adebayor 90)* 81,879

AC Milan: Kalac; Maldini, Kaladze, Nesta, Oddo, Gattuso, Pirlo, Kaka, Ambrosini, Pato, Inzaghi (Gilardino 69).
Arsenal: Almunia; Sagna, Clichy, Flamini, Senderos, Gallas, Eboue (Walcott 72), Fabregas, Adebayor, Hleb (Silva 90), Diaby.

Barcelona (1) 1 *(Xavi 3)*

Celtic (0) 0 75,326

Barcelona: Victor Valdes; Puyol, Sylvinho, Thuram, Xavi (Gudjohnsen 82), Ronaldinho, Zambrotta, Deco, Toure Yaya (Edmilson 68), Eto'o, Messi (Henry 38).
Celtic: Boruc; Wilson, Naylor, Donati (Sno 46), Caldwell, McManus, Nakamura, Hartley (McDonald 78), Brown S, Vennegoor (Samaras 55), McGeady.

Manchester United (1) 1 *(Ronaldo 41)*

Lyon (0) 0 75,521

Manchester United: Van der Sar; Brown, Evra, Carrick, Ferdinand, Vidic, Ronaldo (Hargreaves 90), Anderson (Tevez 70), Rooney, Fletcher, Nani.
Lyon: Coupet; Clerc, Cris, Grosso, Squillaci, Kallstrom (Fred 79), Juninho Pernambucano, Ben Arfa, Toulalan, Benzema, Govou (Keita 68).

Sevilla (3) 3 *(Daniel Alves 5, Keita 10, Kanoute 41)*

Fenerbahce (1) 2 *(Deivid 29, 79)* 38,626

Sevilla: Palop; Dragutinovic, Daniel Alves, Escude, Adriano, Jesus Navas (Kone 105), Poulsen C (Maresca 91), Diego Capel, Keita, Luis Fabiano (Renato 78), Kanoute.
Fenerbahce: Volkan; Lugano, Edu Dracena, Gokhan, Wederson, Mehmet, Alex (Ali 112), Selcuk (Semih 63), Ugur (Kazim-Richards 111), Kezman, Deivid.
aet; Fenerbahce won 3-2 on penalties.

Wednesday, 5 March 2008

Chelsea (2) 3 *(Ballack 5, Lampard 25, Kalou 48)*

Olympiakos (0) 0 37,721

Chelsea: Cudicini; Paul Ferreira, Cole A, Makelele, Terry, Ricardo Carvalho, Ballack, Lampard (Essien 76), Drogba, Kalou (Malouda 71), Cole J (Wright-Phillips 79).
Olympiakos: Nikopolidis; Patsatzoglou, Julio Cesar, Zewlakow, Antzas, Torosidis (Sisic 75), Stoltidis, Djordjevic (Leonardo 57), Ledesma (Belluschi 54), Pantos, Kovacevic.

Porto (0) 1 *(Lisandro Lopez 86)*

Schalke (0) 0 45,316

Porto: Helton; Bruno Alves, Pedro Emanuel, Bosingwa (Mariano Gonzalez 54), Fucile■, Paulo Assuncao, Quaresma, Lucho Gonzalez, Raul Meireles (Cech 97), Sektioui (Farias 58), Lisandro Lopez.
Schalke: Neuer; Westermann, Bordon (Howedes 114), Rafinha, Krstajic, Kobiashvili, Ernst, Jones, Grossmuller (Rakitic 111), Halil Altintop, Kuranyi (Asamoah 79).
aet; Schalke won 4-1 on penalties.

Real Madrid (0) 1 *(Raul 75)*

Roma (0) 2 *(Taddei 73, Vucinic 90)* 71,569

Real Madrid: Casillas; Michel Salgado (Miguel Torres 64), Pepe■, Cannavaro, Heinze, Diarra (Drenthe 61), Gago, Guti, Julio Baptista (Soldado 85), Raul, Robinho.
Roma: Doni; Cicinho (Panucci 87), Juan, Mexes, Aquilani, Taddei, De Rossi, Perrotta (Pizarro 77), Tonetto, Mancini (Vucinic 65), Totti.

Tuesday, 11 March 2008

Internazionale (0) 0

Liverpool (0) 1 *(Torres 63)* 71,501

Internazionale: Julio Cesar; Zanetti, Maicon, Burdisso■, Rivas, Chivu, Stankovic (Jimenez 84), Vieira (Pele 77), Cambiasso, Ibrahimovic (Suazo 80), Cruz.
Liverpool: Reina; Carragher, Fabio Aurelio, Mascherano (Pennant 87), Skrtel, Hyypia, Lucas, Gerrard, Torres, Kuyt (Riise 81), Babel (Benayoun 61).

QUARTER-FINALS FIRST LEG

Tuesday, 1 April 2008

Roma (0) 0

Manchester United (1) 2 *(Ronaldo 39, Rooney 66)* 60,931

Roma: Doni; Panucci, Mexes, Cassetti, Pizarro, Aquilani (Esposito 77), Taddei (Giuly 59), De Rossi, Tonetto (Cicinho 68), Mancini, Vucinic.
Manchester United: Van der Sar; Brown, Evra, Carrick, Ferdinand, Vidic (O'Shea 33), Ronaldo, Anderson (Hargreaves 55), Rooney (Tevez 84), Scholes, Park.

Schalke (0) 0

Barcelona (1) 1 *(Bojan Krkic 12)* 53,951

Schalke: Neuer; Westermann, Bordon, Rafinha, Krstajic, Pander, Kobiashvili, Ernst, Asamoah (Larsen 73), Halil Altintop (Lovenkrands 89), Kuranyi (Sanchez 60).
Barcelona: Victor Valdes; Gabi Milito, Puyol, Abidal, Xavi, Iniesta, Zambrotta, Toure Yaya (Marquez 74), Eto'o (Giovanni Dos Santos 82), Henry, Bojan Krkic (Sylvinho 86).

Wednesday, 2 April 2008

Arsenal (1) 1 *(Adebayor 23)*

Liverpool (1) 1 *(Kuyt 25)* 60,041

Arsenal: Almunia; Toure, Clichy, Flamini, Senderos, Gallas, Eboue (Bendtner 67), Fabregas, Adebayor, Van Persie (Walcott 46), Hleb.
Liverpool: Reina; Carragher, Fabio Aurelio, Xabi Alonso (Lucas 77), Skrtel, Hyypia, Gerrard, Mascherano, Torres (Voronin 86), Kuyt, Babel (Benayoun 58).

Fenerbahce (0) 2 *(Kazim-Richards 64, Deivid 80)*

Chelsea (1) 1 *(Deivid 12 (og))* 49,055

Fenerbahce: Volkan; Lugano, Onder, Edu Dracena, Wederson, Mehmet, Alex, Ugur (Kazim-Richards 54), Maldonado, Kezman (Semih 72), Deivid.
Chelsea: Cudicini; Essien, Cole A, Makelele, Terry, Ricardo Carvalho, Ballack, Lampard (Mikel 76), Drogba, Cole J (Anelka 86), Malouda.

QUARTER-FINALS SECOND LEG

Tuesday, 8 April 2008

Chelsea (1) 2 *(Ballack 3, Lampard 88)*

Fenerbahce (0) 0 38,369

Chelsea: Cudicini (Hilario 26); Essien, Cole A, Makelele, Terry, Ricardo Carvalho, Ballack, Lampard, Drogba, Kalou (Belletti 58), Cole J (Malouda 85).
Fenerbahce: Volkan; Lugano, Edu Dracena, Gokhan, Wederson (Ali 89), Mehmet, Alex, Maldonado (Kezman 60), Semih (Ugur 75), Kazim-Richards, Deivid.

Liverpool (1) 4 *(Hyypia 30, Torres 69, Gerrard 86 (pen), Babel 90)*

Arsenal (1) 2 *(Diaby 13, Adebayor 84)* 41,985

Liverpool: Reina; Carragher, Fabio Aurelio, Xabi Alonso, Skrtel, Hyypia, Gerrard, Mascherano, Torres (Riise 87), Kuyt (Arbeloa 90), Crouch (Babel 78).
Arsenal: Almunia; Toure, Clichy, Flamini (Silva 42), Senderos, Gallas, Eboue (Van Persie 72), Fabregas, Adebayor, Hleb, Diaby (Walcott 72).

Wednesday, 9 April 2008

Barcelona (1) 1 *(Toure Yaya 43)*

Schalke (0) 0 72,113

Barcelona: Victor Valdes; Puyol, Thuram, Abidal, Xavi, Iniesta, Zambrotta, Toure Yaya (Marquez 81), Eto'o, Henry (Gudjohnsen 90), Bojan Krkic (Giovanni Dos Santos 73).
Schalke: Neuer; Westermann, Bordon, Rafinha (Larsen 77), Krstajic, Kobiashvili (Grossmuller 32), Ernst, Jones, Asamoah (Sanchez 69), Halil Altintop, Kuranyi.

Manchester United (0) 1 *(Tevez 70)*

Roma (0) 0 74,423

Manchester United: Van der Sar; Brown, Silvestre, Carrick (O'Shea 74), Ferdinand, Pique, Park, Hargreaves, Anderson (Neville 81), Tevez, Giggs (Rooney 74).
Roma: Doni; Panucci, Juan, Mexes, Cassetti (Tonetto 57), Pizarro (Giuly 69), Taddei (Esposito 81), De Rossi, Perrotta, Mancini, Vucinic.

SEMI-FINALS FIRST LEG

Tuesday, 22 April 2008

Liverpool (1) 1 *(Kuyt 43)*

Chelsea (0) 1 *(Riise 90 (og))* 42,180

Liverpool: Reina; Arbeloa, Fabio Aurelio (Riise 62), Xabi Alonso, Carragher, Skrtel, Gerrard, Mascherano, Torres, Kuyt, Babel (Benayoun 76).
Chelsea: Cech; Paulo Ferreira, Cole A, Makelele, Terry, Ricardo Carvalho, Ballack (Anelka 86), Lampard, Drogba, Cole J (Kalou 63), Malouda.

Wednesday, 23 April 2008

Barcelona (0) 0

Manchester United (0) 0 95,949

Barcelona: Victor Valdes; Gabi Milito, Marquez, Abidal, Xavi, Iniesta, Zambrotta, Deco (Henry 77), Toure Yaya, Eto'o, Messi (Bojan Krkic 62).
Manchester United: Van der Sar; Brown, Evra, Carrick, Ferdinand, Hargreaves, Ronaldo, Scholes, Rooney (Nani 76), Tevez (Giggs 85), Park.

SEMI-FINALS SECOND LEG

Tuesday, 29 April 2008

Manchester United (1) 1 *(Scholes 14)*

Barcelona (0) 0 75,061

Manchester United: Van der Sar; Brown, Evra (Silvestre 90), Carrick, Ferdinand, Hargreaves, Ronaldo, Scholes (Fletcher 77), Nani (Giggs 77), Tevez, Park.
Barcelona: Victor Valdes; Gabi Milito, Puyol, Abidal, Xavi, Iniesta (Henry 61), Zambrotta, Deco, Toure Yaya (Gudjohnsen 88), Eto'o (Bojan Krkic 72), Messi.

Wednesday, 30 April 2008

Chelsea (1) 3 *(Drogba 33, 105, Lampard 98 (pen))*

Liverpool (0) 2 *(Torres 64, Babel 117)* 38,900

Chelsea: Cech; Essien, Cole A, Makelele, Terry, Ricardo Carvalho, Ballack, Lampard (Shevchenko 119), Drogba, Kalou (Malouda 70), Cole J (Anelka 91).
Liverpool: Reina; Arbeloa, Riise, Xabi Alonso, Carragher, Skrtel (Hyypia 22), Gerrard, Mascherano, Torres (Babel 98), Kuyt, Benayoun (Pennant 78).
aet.

UEFA CHAMPIONS LEAGUE FINAL 2008

Wednesday, 21 May 2008

Manchester United (1) 1 *(Ronaldo 26)* **Chelsea (1) 1** *(Lampard 45)*

(in Moscow, 69,552)

Manchester United: Van der Sar; Brown (Anderson 120), Evra, Carrick, Ferdinand, Vidic, Hargreaves, Scholes (Giggs 87), Rooney (Nani 101), Tevez, Ronaldo.

Chelsea: Cech; Essien, Cole A, Makelele (Belletti 120), Terry, Ricardo Carvalho, Ballack, Lampard, Drogba■, Cole J (Anelka 99), Malouda (Kalou 92).

aet; Manchester United won 6-5 on penalties: Tevez scored; Ballack scored; Carrick scored; Belletti scored; Ronaldo saved; Lampard scored; Hargreaves scored; Cole A scored; Nani scored; Terry hit post; Anderson scored; Kalou scored; Giggs scored; Anelka saved.

Referee: L. Michel (Slovakia).

Manchester United goalkeeper Edwin Van der Sar saves Nicolas Anelka's penalty to win the EUFA Champions League for Manchester United against Chelsea in Moscow. (Chelsea FC/PA Photos/Darren Walsh)

EUROPEAN CUP-WINNERS' CUP FINALS 1961–99

Year	Winners	Runners-up	Venue	Attendance	Referee
1961	Fiorentina 2	Rangers 0 *(1st Leg)*	Glasgow	80,000	Steiner (A)
	Fiorentina 2	Rangers 1 *(2nd Leg)*	Florence	50,000	Hernadi (H)
1962	Atletico Madrid 1	Fiorentina 1	Glasgow	27,389	Wharton (S)
Replay	Atletico Madrid 3	Fiorentina 0	Stuttgart	38,000	Tschenscher (WG)
1963	Tottenham Hotspur 5	Atletico Madrid 1	Rotterdam	49,000	Van Leuwen (Ho)
1964	Sporting Lisbon 3	MTK Budapest 3 *(aet)*	Brussels	3000	Van Nuffel (Bel)
Replay	Sporting Lisbon 1	MTK Budapest 0	Antwerp	19,000	Versyp (Bel)
1965	West Ham U 2	Munich 1860 0	Wembley	100,000	Szolt (H)
1966	Borussia Dortmund 2	Liverpool 1 *(aet)*	Glasgow	41,657	Schwinte (F)
1967	Bayern Munich 1	Rangers 0 *(aet)*	Nuremberg	69,480	Lo Bello (I)
1968	AC Milan 2	Hamburg 0	Rotterdam	53,000	Ortiz (Sp)
1969	Slovan Bratislava 3	Barcelona 2	Basle	19,000	Van Ravens (Ho)
1970	Manchester C 2	Gornik Zabrze 1	Vienna	8,000	Schiller (A)
1971	Chelsea 1	Real Madrid 1 *(aet)*	Athens	42,000	Scheurer (Sw)
Replay	Chelsea 2	Real Madrid 1 *(aet)*	Athens	35,000	Bucheli (Sw)
1972	Rangers 3	Moscow Dynamo 2	Barcelona	24,000	Ortiz (Sp)
1973	AC Milan 1	Leeds U 0	Salonika	45,000	Mihas (Gr)
1974	Magdeburg 2	AC Milan 0	Rotterdam	4000	Van Gemert (Ho)
1975	Dynamo Kiev 3	Ferencvaros 0	Basle	13,000	Davidson (S)
1976	Anderlecht 4	West Ham U 2	Brussels	58,000	Wurtz (F)
1977	Hamburg 2	Anderlecht 0	Amsterdam	65,000	Partridge (E)
1978	Anderlecht 4	Austria/WAC 0	Paris	48,679	Adlinger (WG)
1979	Barcelona 4	Fortuna Dusseldorf 3 *(aet)*	Basle	58,000	Palotai (H)
1980	Valencia 0	Arsenal 0	Brussels	36,000	Christov (Cz)
	(aet; Valencia won 5-4 on penalties)				
1981	Dynamo Tbilisi 2	Carl Zeiss Jena 1	Dusseldorf	9000	Lattanzi (I)
1982	Barcelona 2	Standard Liege 1	Barcelona	100,000	Eschweiler (WG)
1983	Aberdeen 2	Real Madrid 1 *(aet)*	Gothenburg	17,804	Menegali (I)
1984	Juventus 2	Porto 1	Basle	60,000	Prokop (EG)
1985	Everton 3	Rapid Vienna 1	Rotterdam	50,000	Casarin (I)
1986	Dynamo Kiev 3	Atletico Madrid 0	Lyon	39,300	Wohrer (A)
1987	Ajax 1	Lokomotiv Leipzig 0	Athens	35,000	Agnolin (I)
1988	Mechelen 1	Ajax 0	Strasbourg	39,446	Pauly (WG)
1989	Barcelona 2	Sampdoria 0	Berne	45,000	Courtney (E)
1990	Sampdoria 2	Anderlecht 0	Gothenburg	20,103	Galler (Sw)
1991	Manchester U 2	Barcelona 1	Rotterdam	42,000	Karlsson (Se)
1992	Werder Bremen 2	Monaco 0	Lisbon	16,000	D'Elia (I)
1993	Parma 3	Antwerp 1	Wembley	37,393	Assenmacher (G)
1994	Arsenal 1	Parma 0	Copenhagen	33,765	Krondl (CzR)
1995	Zaragoza 2	Arsenal 1	Paris	42,424	Ceccarini (I)
1996	Paris St Germain 1	Rapid Vienna 0	Brussels	37,500	Pairetto (I)
1997	Barcelona 1	Paris St Germain 0	Rotterdam	45,000	Merk (G)
1998	Chelsea 1	Stuttgart 0	Stockholm	30,216	Braschi (I)
1999	Lazio 2	Mallorca 1	Villa Park	33,021	Benko (A)

INTER-CITIES FAIRS CUP FINALS 1958–71

(Winners in italics)

Year	First Leg	Attendance	Second Leg	Attendance
1958	London 2 Barcelona 2	45,466	*Barcelona* 6 London 0	62,000
1960	Birmingham C 0 Barcelona 0	40,500	*Barcelona* 4 Birmingham C 1	70,000
1961	Birmingham C 2 Roma 2	21,005	*Roma* 2 Birmingham C 0	60,000
1962	Valencia 6 Barcelona 2	65,000	Barcelona 1 *Valencia* 1	60,000
1963	Dynamo Zagreb 1 Valencia 2	40,000	*Valencia* 2 Dynamo Zagreb 0	55,000
1964	*Zaragoza* 2 Valencia 1	50,000	(in Barcelona)	
1965	*Ferencvaros* 1 Juventus 0	25,000	(in Turin)	
1966	Barcelona 0 Zaragoza 1	70,000	Zaragoza 2 *Barcelona* 4	70,000
1967	Dynamo Zagreb 2 Leeds U 0	40,000	Leeds U 0 *Dynamo Zagreb* 0	35,604
1968	Leeds U 1 Ferencvaros 0	25,368	Ferencvaros 0 *Leeds U* 0	70,000
1969	Newcastle U 3 Ujpest Dozsa 0	60,000	Ujpest Dozsa 2 *Newcastle U* 3	37,000
1970	Anderlecht 3 Arsenal 1	37,000	*Arsenal* 3 Anderlecht 0	51,612
1971	Juventus 0 Leeds U 0 *(abandoned 51 minutes)*	42,000		
	Juventus 2 Leeds U 2	42,000	*Leeds U* 1* Juventus 1	42,483

UEFA CUP FINALS 1972–97

(Winners in italics)

Year	First Leg	Attendance	Second Leg	Attendance
1972	Wolverhampton W 1 Tottenham H 2	45,000	*Tottenham H* 1 Wolverhampton W 1	48,000
1973	Liverpool 0 Moenchengladbach 0			
	(abandoned 27 minutes)	44,967		
	Liverpool 3 Moenchengladbach 0	41,169	Moenchengladbach 2 *Liverpool* 0	35,000
1974	Tottenham H 2 Feyenoord 2	46,281	*Feyenoord* 2 Tottenham H 0	68,000
1975	Moenchengladbach 0 Twente 0	45,000	Twente 1 *Moenchengladbach* 5	24,500
1976	Liverpool 3 FC Brugge 2	56,000	FC Brugge 1 *Liverpool* 1	32,000
1977	Juventus 1 Athletic Bilbao 0	75,000	Athletic Bilbao 2 *Juventus* 1*	43,000
1978	Bastia 0 PSV Eindhoven 0	15,000	*PSV Eindhoven* 3 Bastia 0	27,000
1979	Red Star Belgrade 1 Moenchengladbach 1	87,500	*Moenchengladbach* 1 Red Star Belgrade 0	45,000
1980	Moenchengladbach 3 Eintracht Frankfurt 2	25,000	*Eintracht Frankfurt* 1* Moenchengladbach 0	60,000
1981	Ipswich T 3 AZ 67 Alkmaar 0	27,532	AZ 67 Alkmaar 4 *Ipswich T* 2	28,500
1982	Gothenburg 1 Hamburg 0	42,548	Hamburg 0 *Gothenburg* 3	60,000
1983	Anderlecht 1 Benfica 0	45,000	Benfica 1 *Anderlecht* 1	80,000
1984	Anderlecht 1 Tottenham H 1	40,000	*Tottenham H* 1[1] Anderlecht 1	46,258
1985	Videoton 0 Real Madrid 3	30,000	*Real Madrid* 0 Videoton 1	98,300
1986	Real Madrid 5 Cologne 1	80,000	Cologne 2 *Real Madrid* 0	15,000
1987	Gothenburg 1 Dundee U 0	50,023	Dundee U 1 *Gothenburg* 1	20,911
1988	Espanol 3 Bayer Leverkusen 0	42,000	*Bayer Leverkusen* 3[2] Espanol 0	22,000
1989	Napoli 2 Stuttgart 1	83,000	Stuttgart 3 *Napoli* 3	67,000
1990	Juventus 3 Fiorentina 1	45,000	Fiorentina 0 *Juventus* 0	32,000
1991	Internazionale 2 Roma 0	68,887	Roma 1 *Internazionale* 0	70,901
1992	Torino 2 Ajax 2	65,377	*Ajax* 0* Torino 0	40,000
1993	Borussia Dortmund 1 Juventus 3	37,000	*Juventus* 3 Borussia Dortmund 0	62,781
1994	Salzburg 0 Internazionale 1	47,500	*Internazionale* 1 Salzburg 0	80,326
1995	Parma 1 Juventus 0	23,000	Juventus 1 *Parma* 1	80,750
1996	Bayern Munich 2 Bordeaux 0	62,000	Bordeaux 1 *Bayern Munich* 3	36,000
1997	Schalke 1 Internazionale 0	56,824	Internazionale 1 *Schalke* 0[3]	81,670

**won on away goals* [1]*aet; Tottenham H won 4-3 on penalties* [2]*aet; Bayer Leverkusen won 3-2 on penalties*
[3]*aet; Schalke won 4-1 on penalties*

UEFA CUP FINALS 1998–2008

Year	Winners	Runners-up	Venue	Attendance	Referee
1998	Internazionale 3	Lazio 0	Paris	42,938	Nieto (Sp)
1999	Parma 3	Marseille 0	Moscow	61,000	Dallas (S)
2000	Galatasaray 0	Arsenal 0	Copenhagen	38,919	Nieto (Sp)
	(aet; Galatasaray won 4-1 on penalties)				
2001	Liverpool 5	Alaves 4	Dortmund	65,000	Veissiere (F)
	(aet; Liverpool won on sudden death)				
2002	Feyenoord 3	Borussia Dortmund 2	Rotterdam	45,000	Pereira (P)
2003	Porto 3	Celtic 2	Seville	52,972	Michel (Slo)
	(aet)				
2004	Valencia 2	Marseille 0	Gothenburg	40,000	Collina (I)
2005	CSKA Moscow 3	Sporting Lisbon 1	Lisbon	48,000	Poll (E)
2006	Sevilla 4	Middlesbrough 0	Eindhoven	36,500	Fandel (G)
2007	Sevilla 2	Espanyol 2	Glasgow	50,670	Busacca (Sw)
	(aet; Sevilla won 3-1 on penalties)				
2008	Zenit St Petersburg 2	Rangers 0	Manchester	43,878	Fröjdfeldt (Sw)

UEFA CUP 2007–08

■ *Denotes player sent off.*

FIRST QUALIFYING ROUND FIRST LEG

Thursday, 19 July 2007

Aktobe (0) 1 *(Khayrullin 85)*

Mattersburg (0) 0 13,000

Aktobe: Dehkanov; Assanbayev, Fokine (Logvienko 75), Golovskoy, Badlo, Shkurin, Kosolapov, Smakov, Mytrofanov, Khayrullin, Pushkarev (Bogomolov 46).
Mattersburg: Almer; Pollhuber (Burger 83), Sedloski, Cem, Csizmadia, Kovrig, Mravac, Jancker, Wagner, Kuhbauer, Schmidt.

Artmedia (1) 1 *(Durica M 21 (pen))*

Zimbru (0) 1 *(Zhdanov 70 (pen))* 2151

Artmedia: Kamenar; Borbely, Burak (Durica P 77), Cisovsky, Guede (Gajdos 71), Dosoudil■, Mraz (Obzera 55), Kozak, Halenar, Oravec, Durica M.
Zimbru: Calancea; Gibalyuk, Lomidze■, Berbinschi, Stan V, Andronic, Frantuz (Erhan 46), Zhdanov (Krioutchikhine 84), Kovalchuk (Nikulin 65), Savinov, Cojocari.

B36 (1) 1 *(Hojsted 41)*

Ekranas (2) 3 *(Luksys 11, Paulauskas 45, Pogreban 67)* 2000

B36: Mikkelsen; Alex, Jacobsen H, Jacobsen K, Matras, Thorleifsson (Skorini 58), Midjord, Thomassen (Gunnarsson A 89), Davy, Benjaminsen, Hojsted (Rubeksen 83).
Ekranas: Stefanovic; Gardzijauskas, Kavaliauskas, Paulauskas, Rahn, Pogreban, Tomkevicius (Galkevicius 75), Skroblas, Luksys (Varnas 87), Bicka (Saulenas 85), Sidlauskas.

Banants (0) 1 *(Kakosian 68)*

Young Boys (1) 1 *(Mangane 17)* 5000

Banants: Radaca; Cherevko, Hakobian, Grigorian, Simonian, Melkonian (Muradian 86), Jenebian (Bareghamian 55), Kakosian, Khachatrian (Sargsian 81), Melikian, Balabekian.
Young Boys: Wolfli; Schneuwly M (Haberli 46), Yapi-Yapo, Tiago, Portillo, Mangane, Raimondi, Regazzoni (Kallio 61), Joao Paulo (Frimpong 83), Schwegler, Varela.

Belchatow (0) 2 *(Pietrasiak 51, 82)*

Ameri (0) 0 3000

Belchatow: Lech; Kowalczyk, Pietrasiak, Popek, Strak, Cecot, Stolarczyk, Jarzebowski, Costly Molina (Ujek 82), Rachwal, Wrobel (Marciniak 88).
Ameri: Kvachakia; Didava, Bolkvadze, Chikviladze, Davitnidze (Kobauri 90), Dobrovolski, Davitashvili (Tatanashvili 61), Dolidze (Shalamberidze 75), Jeladze, Khvadagiani, Gotsiridze.

Bezanija (1) 2 *(Dalovic 37, Durovski 57 (pen))*

Besa (0) 2 *(Ishaka 49, Endene 90)* 500

Bezanija: Pavlovic B; Stanceski (Mihajlovic 63), Baranin, Vanic, Pavlovic V, Putincanin, Ilic, Dalovic, Osmanovic, Durovski (Milic 77), Vukajlovic (Nikolic 46).
Besa: Zendeli; Endene (Kaja 90), Krasniqi, Veliaj (Alikaj 60), Dragusha, Ramadan, Bikoula, Belisha, Xhihani, Fortunat (Nuhiji 72), Ishaka.

Buducnost (0) 1 *(Scepanovic 59)*

Hajduk Split (1) 1 *(Hrgovic M 28)* 2500

Buducnost: Vujadinovic; Vukcevic, Lakic, Perisic, Vukovic, Raicevic (Bozovic D 46), Delic, Sekulic (Milic B 77), Mugosa (Scepanovic 46), Vlahovic, Durisic.
Hajduk Split: Balic; Rukavina (Cubrilo 86), Gal, Gabric (Musa 86), Buljat, Zivkovic, Pelaic, Hrgovic M, Kalinic, Cernat, Andric (Damjanovic 74).

Carmarthen Town (0) 0

Brann (5) 8 *(Winters 8, 30, 45, Helstad 17, 28, Sigurdsson K 70, Solli 83, Bjornsson 90)* 769

Carmarthen Town: Thomas N; Hancock, Smothers■, Palmer, Warton, Thomas C, Walters, Ramasut, Fowler, Hicks, Cotterall.
Brann: Thorbjornsen; Bjarnason, Dahl, Hanstveit, Helstad (Bjornsson 58), Huseklepp (Gashi 74), Sigurdsson K, Andresen (Jaiteh 46), Solli, Winters, Vaagan Moen.

Dungannon Swifts (1) 1 *(McAllister 17)*

Suduva (0) 0 500

Dungannon Swifts: Wells; McConkey, Gallagher, Montgomery, Hegarty, Curran, McCabe, McMinn, Campbell (McGinn 74), McCluskey, McAllister (Baron 89).
Suduva: Klevinskas S; Sobol, Skinderis, Klevinskas G, Mikuckis, Feldmann (Urbsys 46), Miklinevicius, Maciulevicius, Potapov, Viller, Braga (Juska 69).

Dynamo Tbilisi (0) 2 *(Merebashvili 66 (pen), Akieremy 72)*

Vaduz (0) 0 500

Dynamo Tbilisi: Ebang; Krsko, Kashia S, Zelic, Merebashvili, Kobakhidze (Spasojevic 81), Digmelashvili, Khmaladze, Odikadze (Peikrishvili 55), Akieremy (Khutsishvili 86), Dobcs.
Vaduz: Sommer; Langlet (Rohrer 77), Maggetti, Reinmann (Akdemir 71), Alastra, Ritzberger, Sturm, Polverino, Dzombic, Grossklaus (Wieczorek 67), Cerrone.

Flora (0) 0

Valerenga (1) 1 *(Lange 31)* 1500

Flora: Aksalu; Hurt (Ahjupera 65), Talimaa (Taska 73), Allas, Barengrub, Vunk, Kams, Reim, Zahovaiko, Vanna (Sirevicius 76), Sidorenkov.
Valerenga: Arason; Forsund, Jepsen, Holm T, Grindheim, Johnsen, Lange, Storbaek, Jalland (Mathisen 61), Sorensen (Roberts 79), Berre.

Glentoran (0) 0

AIK Stockholm (1) 5 *(Figueiredo 21, 62, Valdemarin 68, Stephenson 73, Johnson 84)* 2033

Glentoran: Dougherty; Nixon, Fitzgerald, Hill (Morgan 69), Leeman, Smyth, Ward S, Hamill (Carson 69), Halliday, Hamilton, Berry (Ward M 80).
AIK Stockholm: Orlund; Karlsson, Tamandi, Johansson, Ivan (Mendes 76), Arnefjord, Johnson, Tjernstrom (Bengtsson 82), Pavey, Figueiredo (Valdemarin 66), Stephenson.

Gorica (0) 1 *(Matavz 83)*

Rabotnicki (0) 2 *(Suler 79 (og), Velkoski 90)* 1250

Gorica: Simcic; Osterc (Djukic 62), Dedic, Lerant, Demirovic, Jogan, Suler, Kovacevic, Matavz, Zivec, Velikonja (Cvijanovic 74).
Rabotnicki: Madzovski; Bozinovski, Lazarevski, Demiri, Stanisic, Ignatov (Velkoski 85), Osmani (Milisavljevic 5), Kovacevic, Mihajlovic, Pejcic, Trickovski (Selim 80).

HJK Helsinki (1) 2 *(Bah 24, Sorsa 90)*

Etzella (0) 0 4000

HJK Helsinki: Wallen; Halsti, Smith, Kamara (Aijala 87), Bah, Aalto I, Savolainen, Samura, Raitala, Zeneli (Parikka 51), Vuorinen (Sorsa 63).
Etzella: Diederich; Binsfeld (Engeldinger 88), Leweck C, Hoffmann, Plein, Rocha, Fernandes, Da Luz, Ferreira, Fevry (Da Mota 9) (Bombele 84), Mannon.

Hacken (1) 1 *(Heden 12)*

KR Reykjavik (0) 1 *(Petursson 69)* 7230

Hacken: Hysen; Lind, Heden, Lucic (Forsell 50), Henriksson, Jarlegren, Olofsson (Larsson 64), Skulason, Williams, Rishoft (Holster 80), Mambo Mumba.
KR Reykjavik: Magnusson S; Kristjansson S, Kristinsson, Jonsson G, Magnusson K, Marteinsson, Fridgeirsson, Petursson, Einarsson, Gunnarsson, Olfasson.

Helsingborg (2) 6 *(Omotoyossi 28, Dahl 30, Larsson 59, 64, Karekezi 80, Andersson C 84)*

Trans (0) 0 5075

Helsingborg: Andersson D; Andersson C, Tamboura, Beloufa, Jakobsson, Skulasson, Stefanidis (Unkuri 84), Larsson, Dahl (Chansa 78), Wahlstedt, Omotoyossi (Karekezi 74).
Trans: Usoltsev; Lepik (Popov 80), Kulik, Gorskov, Kazakov, Gorjatsov, Tarassenkov, Lipartov, Gruznov, Ivanov (Paitsev 70), Dobrovolskiy.

Keflavik (2) 3 *(Steinarsson 27, Troest 34 (og), Samuelsen 57)*

Midtjylland (2) 2 *(Dadu 9, Afriyie 20)* 827

Keflavik: Johannsson; Mete, Antoniusson, Kristjansson (Gustafsson 82), Kotilainen, Jorgensen, Milicevic, Jonasson (Einarsson 82), Steinarsson (Saevarsson 68), Samuelsen, Sigurdsson B.
Midtjylland: Raska; Troest, Afriyie, Poulsen C, Olsen D, Oluwafemi, Reid (Klimpl 70), Larsen, Dadu (Babatunde 75), Thygesen, Poulsen S (Madsen 61).

Libertas (0) 1 *(Pari 77)*

Drogheda United (1) 1 *(Zayed 44)* 250

Libertas: Ceccoli; Macerata, Gazzi, Sottili, Simoncini (Pari 53), Cevoli, Santini, Semprini, Fambri, Tarini, Cavalli (Nanni 71).
Drogheda United: Connor; Tambouras, Shelley, Gray (Webb 67), Ristila, Gartland, Robinson, Whelan, Zayed (Grant 71), Byrne, O'Keeffe (Baker 79).

Lillestrom (2) 2 *(Occean 19, Sundgot 44 (pen))*

Kaerjeng (1) 1 *(Andresen 45 (og))* 1563

Lillestrom: Fredrikson; Rambekk, Stefanutto, Andresen, Johansen, Brenne, Sogard (Myklebust 63), Mouelhi (Kiesenebner 63), Occean (Strand 77), Riise, Sundgot.
Kaerjeng: Silva Costa; Leite, Marinelli (Muslic 84), Da Costa, Facques, Ramdedovic, Kivunghe, Boulahfari (Thill 77), Pace (Mateos 35), Rolandi, Matos.

MKT Araz (0) 0

Groclin (0) 0 2000

MKT Araz: Kovalyov; Gashimov, Barisev, Doros, Yunisoglu, Vishtalyuk, Poladov (Jabbarov 77), Mammadov J (Guliyev 83), Mammadov E (Ismaylov 65), Abbasov, Danayev.
Groclin: Przyrowski; Koziol, Cumbev, Lazarevski, Muszalik (Majewski 60), Jodlowiec (Piechniak 59), Lato, Ivanovski (Klodawski 68), Sikora, Telichowski, Sokolowski.

MTK Budapest (1) 2 *(Pinter 20, Urban 57)*

Mika (1) 1 *(Cleber 45)* 1500

MTK Budapest: Vegh; Patkai, Bori, Horvath, Kanta (Szabo 84), Lambulic, Pinter, Pollak, Pal (Ladaczki 77), Urban, Zsidai.
Mika: Hakobian; Alex, Petikian, Thiago (Davtian 69), Shahgeldian, Antonian (Scanion 59), Ristic, Fursin, Kleber (Tales 82), Cleber, Mikaelian.

Metalurgs Liepaja (1) 1 *(Ferreira De Oli 5)*

Dynamo Brest (0) 1 *(Sokol 77)* 2500

Metalurgs Liepaja: Spole; Zuravljovs, Karlsons, Zirnis, Ferreira De Oli, Ivanovs, Solonicins, Surnins, Tamosauskas, Kalonas, Kruglak (Kamess 59) (Kets 81).
Dynamo Brest: Tsygalko; Shchigolev, Kots, Tsevan (Demidovich 85), Ishmakov, Mozolevskiy, Panasyuk, Kozak, Volodko, Sokol, Chistyi (Goginashvili 69).

Moravce (0) 3 *(Gibala 51, 78, Greguska 71)*

Alma-Ata (0) 1 *(Larin 82)* 2880

Moravce: Peskovic; Greguska, Choma, Ciz, Pavlenda, Kuracka, Cernak, Ondrejka (Farkas 90), Hozl (Gibala 46), Chren (Pelegrini 86), Juska.
Alma-Ata: Bogdan; Kovalev, Kirov, Utabaev, Vorotnikov, Shakhmetov, Larin, Berco, Byakov, Borovskiy (Rodionov 70), Irismetov (Kenzhekhanov 79).

MyPa (0) 1 *(Hyyrynen 11)*

EB/Streymur (0) 0 1500

MyPa: Korhonen; Pulkkinen, Fofana (Kuparinen 75), Tanska, Huttunen, Karhu, Kansikas, Peltonen (Manso 62), Puhakainen, Muinonen (Kangaskolkka 62), Hyyrynen.
EB/Streymur: Torgard; Olsen B, Djurhuus (Hansen G 84), Eliasen S, Potemkin (Anghel 58), Dam, Samuelesen R, Bo, Hansen A (Eliasen H 68), Szekeres, Samuelesen H.

Omonia (1) 2 *(Kaiafas 43, Chailis 46)*

Rudar (0) 0 13,000

Omonia: Georgallides; Torrao, Chailis, Veiga, Ba (Grozdanovski 55), Georgiou, Kaiafas, Weisheimer (Kaseke 64), Kakoyiannis, Mguni, Magno (Vakouftsis 74).
Rudar: Mijatovic; Vranes, Ramovic (Basic 61), Vukovic, Sekulic, Damjanovic, Karadzic, Minic (Lujinovic 79), Reljic S, Bojovic, Lukovac (Durakovic 81).

Otaci (1) 1 *(Malitskiy 29)*

Honved (0) 1 *(Guei-Guei 51)* 2000

Otaci: Ersov; Butelschi, Mekang, Sangare, Dolgov, Matiura, Groshev, Tcaciuc O, Taranu (Studzinskiy 79), Malitskiy (Poungoue 75), Savchuk (Kristofovich 46).
Honved: Toth I; Mogyorosi (Schindler 63), Toth B, Hercegfalvi, Brou (Genito 46), Pomper, Ivancsics (Koos 69), Smiljanic, Dobos, Baranyos, Guei-Guei.

Rhyl (2) 3 *(Moran 26, Hunt 36, Garside 47)*

Haka (1) 1 *(Lehtinen 15)* 1787

Rhyl: Gann; Powell M, Brewerton (Desormeaux 90), Connolly, Horan, Ruffer, Garside, Kelly, Hunt (Cameron 80), Moran, Graves (Roberts C 76).
Haka: Dovbnya; Kangaskorpi, Fowler, Okkonen, Holopainen, Strandvall, Innanen, Kauppila, Manninen (Mattila■ 72), Parviainen, Lehtinen.

Ried (1) 3 *(Drechsel 2, Brenner 87, Salihi 90)*

Neftchi (1) 1 *(Aliyev 14)* 2500

Ried: Berger; Jank, Kujabi (Erbek 53), Brenner, Drechsel, Rzasa, Kovacevic (Toth 46), Dospel, Damjanovic, Pichorner, Djokic (Salihi 73).
Neftchi: Micovic; Melikov, Bayramov (Boret 73), Guliyev R, Allahverdiyev, Sadykov RA, Sadykov RF, Tagizade, Aliyev (Subasic 61), Adamia (Yusifov 89), Mammadov.

Santa Coloma (0) 1 *(Juli Fernandez 57)*

Maccabi Tel Aviv (0) 0 500

Santa Coloma: Ricardo Fernandez; Urbani M (Aguirre 74), Gil, Juli Fernandez, Da Cunha, Victor Rodriguez, Maicon (Meza 87), Ayala, Urbani N (Toscano 68), Alvarez, Garcia.
Maccabi Tel Aviv: Solomon; Peretz, Shitrit, Shpungin (Edri 85), Mishaelof, Martinovic, Yeini, Nimni, Biton (Ron 90), Kamanan, Mesika.

Siroki (3) 3 *(Celson 24, 33, Ronielle 44)*

Koper (1) 1 *(Viler 8)* 3500

Siroki: Vasilj; Ronielle, Hannich (Kozul 53), Juric (Sakic 72), Vidic, Zelenika, Karoglan, Topic, Bubalo S, Silic, Celson (Bubalo I 85).
Koper: Hasic; Bozic M, Mejac, Rajcevic, Viler, Handanagic, Plut (Sucevic 88), Galun, Bordon (Secic 64), Bozicic (Bozic R 90), Volas.

Skonto Riga (1) 1 *(Pereplyotkin 27)*

Dynamo Minsk (1) 1 *(Rak 11)* 2000

Skonto Riga: Piedels; Kozans, Astafjevs (Semjonovs 68), Piacek, Gamezardashvili, Sluka, Pereplyotkin, Cauna (Visnakovs 72), Blanks (Kalnins 77), Morozs, Dirnbach.
Dynamo Minsk: Tumilovich; Pavlyukovich, Rak, Temrioukov, Nudny (Gigevich 75), Pankov, Khatskevich (Kislyak 68), Martinovich, Veretilo, Putilo (Yanushkevich 81), Marcio.

Slaven (2) 6 *(Posavec 18 (pen), Sehic 29, 47, Vrucina 60, 82, Bosnjak 90)*

Teuta (1) 2 *(Xhafa 10, Brahja 65)* 2500

Slaven: Ivesa; Sopic, Caval, Vrucina, Kristic, Bozac, Poldrugac, Radeljic, Kresinger (Juric 46), Posavec (Poljak 61), Sehic (Bosnjak 74).
Teuta: Kapllani; Vrapi, Vila, Xhafa, Buna, Hodo (Blloku 85), Kapaj■, Pashaj (Brahja 50), Kuli (Fagu 46), Mancaku, Devolli.

Sliema Wanderers (0) 0

Litex (1) 3 *(Popov I 22, 56, Beto 53)* 500

Sliema Wanderers: Bonello; Anonam (Nwoko 79), Azzopardi, Said, Chetcuti, Ciantar (Baldacchino 75), Madzar, Mattocks (Scerri 72), Pace, Woods, Bartolo.
Litex: Todorov; Popov R, Boudarene, Nikolov, Venkov, Uras, Nikolov, Tom, Popov I (Genchev 69), Sandrinho (Bibishkov 78), Zlatinov (Manolev 60).

St Patrick's Ath (0) 0

Odense (0) 0 2800

St Patrick's Ath: Ryan; Brennan, Rogers, Murphy, Maguire, Guy (O'Connor 90), Gibson (Foley-Sheridan 88), Fahey, Paisley, Keane (Mulcahy 63), Quigley.
Odense: Onyszko; Borring, Laursen, Hansen, Christensen A, Helveg, Christensen K (Timm 80), Bechara (Andreasen 69), Jensen, Bolanos, Absalonsen.

Vardar (0) 0

Anorthosis (0) 1 *(Deyanov 88)* 4000

Vardar: Georgievski; Braga, Sekuloski, Bojovic, Ristevski, Peev (Ze Carlos 59), Perendija■, Stjepanovic, Kirovski (Kostovski 80), Emurlahu (Petrov 89), Mojsov.
Anorthosis: Beqaj; Panagi (Luis Loureiro 57), Lambrou, Katsavakis, Ndikumana, Zlogar, Poursaitidis, Fabinho, Sosin (Belic 46), Pahars (William 75), Deyanov.

Vojvodina (2) 5 *(Despotovic 21, 42, 89 (pen), Duric 60, Kacar 84)*

Hibernians (0) 1 *(Doffo 86 (pen))* 3500

Vojvodina: Kahriman; Popovic, Markovic, Stosic, Stojcev (Drakulic 60), Pekaric, Cotra (Kacar 56), Duric, Lerinc (Sarac 79), Buac, Despotovic.
Hibernians: Muscat; Miwtoff, Julio Cesar, Pulis, Xuereb, Agius, Failla, Doffo, Scerri, Cohen (Soler 74), Nwoko.

Zrinjski (0) 1 *(Matko 68)*

Partizan Belgrade (2) 6 *(Diarra 32, 60, 63, Maletic 40, Jovetic 48, Lazetic 80)* 9000

Zrinjski: Maric; Duric (Karadza 24), Dzidic I (Landeka 24), Nikolic, Joldic, Dzidic D (Matko 65), Zurzinov, Pezo, Selimovic, Smajic, Rajovic.
Partizan Belgrade: Bozovic; Jovetic (Marinkovic N 76), Rukavina, Diarra (Lazetic 67), Sikimic, Lazarevic, Lazic P, Juca, Mihajlov, Moreira (Zajic 81), Maletic.
Partizan Belgrade allowed to play in the second leg while disqualification hearing was being conducted; club also fined for conduct of their supporters.

FIRST QUALIFYING ROUND SECOND LEG

Tuesday, 31 July 2007

Kaerjeng (0) 1 *(Boulahfari 49)*

Lillestrom (0) 0 3000

Kaerjeng: Silva Costa; Leite, Da Costa (Martins 72), Rolandi, Facques, Ramdedovic, Kivunghe, Boulahfari (Marinelli 82), Bianchini (Scholer 24), Matos, Mateos.
Lillestrom: Muller; Kippe, Stefanutto (Kiesenebner 77), Andresen, Strand (Sundgot 64), Mouelhi, Sogard, Essediri (Rambekk 64), Occean, Riise, Brenne.

Thursday, 2 August 2007

AIK Stockholm (2) 4 *(Ozkan 7, Karlsson 24, Gerndt 88, Johnson 89)*

Glentoran (0) 0 8707

AIK Stockholm: Orlund; Karlsson, Arnefjord, Johansson, Tamandi, Pavey, Stephenson, Ozkan (Gerndt 67), Johnson, Figueiredo (Bengtsson 67), Valdemarin (Mendes 67).
Glentoran: Dougherty; Nixon, Neill, Hill (McMenamin 72), Leeman, Fitzgerald, Ward S, Ward M (Hamill 84), Halliday (Morgan 83), Hamilton, Carson.

Almaty (0) 1 *(Irismetov 58)*

Moravce (0) 1 *(Cernak 77)* 15,000

Almaty: Bogdan; Vorotnikov, Utabaev (Rodionov 70), Shakhmetov (Klimov 75), Kirov, Kovalev■, Larin, Borovskiy (Irismetov 46), Byakov, Kenzhekhanov, Berco.
Moravce: Peskovic; Greguska, Choma, Ciz, Pavlenda, Kuracka, Cernak, Ondrejka (Balat 81), Gibala (Chren 60), Hozl, Juska (Farkas 70).

Ameri (2) 2 *(Tatanashvili 12, Davitashvili 46)*

Belchatow (0) 0 2000

Ameri: Kvachakia; Elbakidze, Didava, Jeladze (Dolidze 70), Davitnidze, Khvadagiani, Dekanosidze, Bolkvadze (Kobauri 101), Davitashvili (Gotsiridze 76), Tatanashvili, Dobrovolski.
Belchatow: Lech; Rachwal, Grodzicki (Marciniak 103), Popek, Strak, Cecot, Stolarczyk, Wrobel, Costly Molina (Nowak 46), Jarzebowski, Ujek (Tosik 98).
aet; Belchatow won 4-2 on penalties.

Anorthosis (0) 1 *(Zlogar 53)*

Vardar (0) 0 3500

Anorthosis: Beqaj; Panagi, Lambrou, Katsavakis, Ndikumana, Zlogar (Loureiro 76), Poursaitidis, Fabinho, Sosin (Belic 62), Deyanov, Pahars (Frousos 70).
Vardar: Georgievski; Braga, Sekuloski■, Bojovic, Tonev, Mojsov, Ristevski (Petrov 79), Peev, Kirovski (Kostovski 46), Emurlahu (Milosavljev 46), Stjepanovic.

Besa (0) 0

Bezanija (0) 0 3500

Besa: Zendeli; Ramadan, Arapi, Bikoula, Hoxha■, Belisha, Ishaka, Alikaj (Fortunat 83), Krasniqi (Endene 46), Veliaj (Kaja 90), Xhihani.
Bezanija: Jankovic■; Stanceski, Vanic, Pavlovic V, Baranin, Djalovic, Durovski (Pavlovic B 74), Putincanin, Osmanovic (Milic 84), Mihajlovic, Vukajlovic.

Brann (4) 6 *(Vaagan Moen 9, Bjornsson 19, Winters 27, 32, Sigurdsson K 56, Hanstveit 57)*

Carmarthen Town (1) 3 *(Thomas D 36, Hicks 47, 90)* 4597

Brann: Thorbjornsen; Dahl, Hanstveit, Bjarnason, Sigurdsson K, Bjornsson, Vaagan Moen (Guntveit 58), Huseklepp, Jaiteh, Bakke, Winters.
Carmarthen Town: Thomas N; Hancock, Hughes, Warton (Brace 71), Palmer, Thomas C, Thomas D (Davies M 74), Ramasut (Hicks 46), Fowler, Walters, Cotterrall.

Drogheda United (1) 3 *(Keegan 11, 48, Byrne 57)*

Libertas (0) 0 3250

Drogheda United: Connor; Shelley, Webb, Tambouras, Byrne (Bradley 63), Keegan, Gartland, Robinson (Baker 60), Ristila, Zayed, Keddy (O'Keeffe 75).
Libertas: Ceccoli; Sottili, Cevoli, Valentini, Gazzi, Macerata, Tarini, Nanni (Toccaceli 79), Semprini (Pari 58), Fambri, Santini (Angelini 89).

Dynamo Brest (0) 1 *(Sokol 47)*

Metalurgs (1) 2 *(Kruglak 40, Karlsons 50)* 10,000

Dynamo Brest: Tsygalko; Shchigolev■, Kots■, Tsevan (Zhersh 67), Shcherbo (Goginashvili 53), Sokol, Panasyuk, Kozak, Volodko, Mozolevskiy (Trotsyuk 82), Chistiyi.
Metalurgs: Spole; Surnins, Klava, Zirnis, Ferreira De Oli, Ivanovs, Solonicins, Karlsons, Kruglak (Zuravlovs 90), Tamosauskas, Kalonas (Kamess 90).

Dynamo Minsk (0) 2 *(Rak 57, 74)*

Skonto Riga (0) 0 3000

Dynamo Minsk: Lesko; Pankov, Veretilo, Pavlyukovich, Martinovich, Temrioukov, Khatskevich (Pavlyuchek 90), Putilo (Kislyak 87), Mbanangoye, Nudny (Gigevich 71), Rak.
Skonto Riga: Piedels; Kozans, Gamezardashvili (Gailus 46), Astafjevs (Cauna 78), Piacek, Sluka, Pereplyotkin, Visnakovs, Blanks, Morozs, Dirnbach.

EB/Streymur (0) 1 *(Potemkin 86)*
MyPa (0) 1 *(Kuparinen 70)* 250
EB/Streymur: Torgard; Bo, Olsen B, Eliasen S, Dam, Samuelsen R, Djurhuus, Szekeres (Kwiecinski 65), Anghel (Eliasen H 79), Samuelsen H, Hansen A (Potemkin 67).
MyPa: Korhonen; Pulkkinen, Agboh, Huttunen, Miranda, Kansikas, Fofana (Puhakainen 63), Kuparinen (Mustafi 79), Muinonen (Manso 63), Kangaskolkka, Peltonen.

Ekranas (0) 3 *(Sidlauskas 51, Luksys 77, 87)*
B36 (0) 2 *(Midjord 85, Benjaminsen 86 (pen))* 1250
Ekranas: Skrupskis; Skroblas (Rahn 46), Paulauskas, Rimavicius, Sidlauskas (Saulenas 90), Gardzijauskas, Bicka, Tomkevicius (Galkevicius 71), Luksys, Kavaliauskas, Pogreban.
B36: Mikkelsen; Alex (Midjord 71), Benjaminsen, Gunnarsson J, Jacobsen K, Jacobsen H, Skorini, Thomassen, Hojsted, Matras, Davy.

Etzella (0) 0
HJK Helsinki (1) 1 *(Fernandes 26 (og))* 300
Etzella: Flick; Plein, Leweck C, Ferreira, Fernandes, Engeldinger, Da Luz, Binsfeld, Pinto (Reiter 46), Da Mota (Bombele 69), Mannon.
HJK Helsinki: Wallen; Aalto I, Medjoudi, Nurmela (Aijala 83), Raitala, Halsti, Savolainen (Aho 60), Smith, Samura, Vuroinen (Parikka 73), Bah.

Groclin (0) 1 *(Klodawski 88)*
MKT Araz (0) 0 3000
Groclin: Przyrowski; Mynar, Lazarevski (Klodawski 81), Telichowski, Koziol, Jodlowiec, Piechniak (Rocki 70), Lato, Majewski, Sikora (Sokolowski 90), Slusarski.
MKT Araz: Kovalyov; Gashimov, Vyshtalyuk, Mammadov J (Guliyev 84), Yunisoglu, Poladov, Barisev, Danayev, Abbasov, Mammadov E (Ismaylov 74), Doros■.

Hajduk Split (0) 1 *(Damjanovic 46)*
Buducnost (0) 0 10,000
Hajduk Split: Balic; Zivkovic, Pelaic, Hrgovic M, Pandza, Damjanovic (Ljubicic 88), Cernat, Andric, Rubil, Kalinic (Bartolovic 79), Rukavina.
Buducnost: Vujadinovic; Vukcevic, Lakic, Perisic, Durisic, Raicevic (Tuzovic 62), Delic (Bozovic D 8), Vukovic, Vlahovic, Scepanovic (Mugosa 70), Milic B.

Haka (0) 2 *(Innanen 62, Popovich 64)*
Rhyl (0) 0 1565
Haka: Dovbnya; Kangaskorpi, Okkonen, Holopainen, Innanen, Kauppila, Manninen (Strandvall 64), Fowler, Parviainen, Lehtinen (Mahlakaarto 90), Popovich.
Rhyl: Gann; Powell M (Holt 90), Roberts C (Jones 84), Connolly, Horan, Ruffer, Garside (Cameron 75), Kelly, Hunt, Graves, Moran.

Hibernians (0) 0
Vojvodina (1) 2 *(Xuereb 30 (og), Despotovic 62)* 350
Hibernians: Muscat; Pulis, Xuereb, Cassar (Soler 87), Mintoff, Faillia, Doffo■, Cohen, Agius, Scerri, Julio Cesar (Vella 63).
Vojvodina: Kahriman (Brkic 81); Kacar, Pekaric, Sarac, Stosic (Miroslav Milutinovic 66), Duric, Popovic, Lerinc, Tadic, Buac (Smiljanic 85), Despotovic.

Honved (1) 1 *(Guei-Guei 14)*
Otaci (0) 1 *(Mekang 50)* 3023
Honved: Toth I; Pomper, Smiljanic, Vincze Z, Schindler, Ivancsics, Dobos (Brou 90), Baranyos, Genito, Guei-Guei (Diego 65), Hercegfalvi (Koos 46).
Otaci: Ersov; Lupascu■, Mekang, Sangare, Dolgov, Tcaciuc O (Savchuk 73), Muhovicov, Groshev, Matiura, Studzinskiy (Taranu 78), Poungoue (Butelschi 103).
aet; Honved won 5-4 on penalties.

KR Reykjavik (0) 0
Hacken (0) 1 *(De Oliveira 83)* 2500
KR Reykjavik: Magnusson S; Jonsson G, Marteinsson, Einarsson (Petursson 88), Magnusson K, Larusson (Hjartarson 68), Kristinsson, Kristjansson S, Hauksson, Gunnarsson (Juliusson 46), Takefusa.
Hacken: Kallqvist; Lind, Marek (Friberg 79), Forsell, Ljung (Mambo Mumba 46), Ze Antonio, Jarlegren, Skulasson, Henriksson, Williams (Olofsson 76), De Oliveira.

Koper (1) 2 *(Volas 34, Mejac 82)*
Siroki (3) 3 *(Karoglan 18, Bozic R 25 (og), Ronielle 36)* 300
Koper: Hasic; Rajcevic, Galun (Klun 85), Ibeji, Bozic M, Bozic R (Mejac 28), Secic, Viler, Bozicic, Bordon (Plut 46), Volas.
Siroki: Vasilj; Vidic, Topic, Juric, Karoglan, Silic, Zelenika, Hannich (Sakic 71), Ronielle (Bubalo I 78), Bubalo S (Zovko 63), Da Costa.

Litex (1) 4 *(Boudarene 28, Beto 48, 60, Popov I 59)*
Sliema Wanderers (0) 0 3000
Litex: Todorov; Popov R, Venkov, Uras, Boudarene (Jelenkovic 46), Nikolov (Genchev 46), Tom, Sandrinho, Beto, Dudu (Bibishkov 46), Popov I.
Sliema Wanderers: Bonello; Azzopardi, Said, Ciantar, Chetcuti, Pace, Mattocks (Muscat 6), Bartolo (Turner 74), Woods, Anonam, Nwoko (Scerri 67).

Maccabi Tel Aviv (2) 4 *(Mesika 12, 25, Shivhon 63, Kamanan 71)*
Santa Coloma (0) 0 2500
Maccabi Tel Aviv: Solomon; Shpungin, Martinovic, Shivhon (Biton 65), Haddad A, Shitrit■, Nimni (Edri 75), Mesika, Yeini, Kamanan, Peretz (Gan 65).
Santa Coloma: Ricardo Fernandez; Gil, Juli Fernandez, Da Cunha (Meza 54), Victor Rodriguez, Ayala, Alvarez, Urbani M (Costa 88), Garcia, Urbani N, Maicon (Toscano 46).

Mattersburg (1) 4 *(Jancker 22, Wagner 62, Csizmadia 67, Kovrig 90)*
Aktobe (0) 2 *(Bogomolov 71, Kosolapov 77)* 4000
Mattersburg: Almer; Sedloski, Mravac■, Csizmadia, Morz, Kuhbauer, Kovrig, Schmidt, Atan, Jancker, Wagner.
Aktobe: Denkanov; Badlo, Kosolapov, Smakov, Shkurin, Fokine (Bogomolov 46), Logvinenko, Mytrofanov (Kiselev 87), Khayrullin, Golovskoy, Assanbayev.

Midtjylland (0) 2 *(Poulsen S 68, Dadu 75)*
Keflavik (1) 1 *(Sigurdsson B 11)* 6125
Midtjylland: Raska; Troest, Afriyie (Olsen C 41), Jessen, Klimpl, Oluwafemi (Poulsen C 82), Madsen (Olsen D 57), Kristensen, Dadu, Thygesen, Poulsen S.
Keflavik: Gudmundsson; Antoniusson, Jorgensen (Kotilainen 62), Milicevic, Mete, Saevarsson, Jonasson (Gustafsson 77), Sigurdsson B, Steinarsson, Samuelsen, Kristjansson (Thorsteinsson 83).

Mika (1) 1 *(Adamian A 26)*
MTK Budapest (0) 0 5000
Mika: Hakobian; Petikian, Antonian, Fursin, Ristic, Thiago, Cleber, Kleber (Davtian 69), Alex, Adamian A (Meytikhanian 83), Tales (Mikaelian 52).
MTK Budapest: Vegh; Horvath, Lambulic, Pollak, Pinter, Patkai (Szabo 73), Ladoczki (Hrepka 46), Zsidai, Kanta, Pal, Urban (Simon A 83).

Neftchi (2) 2 *(Subasic 14, Sadykov RF 21)*
Ried (0) 1 *(Salihi 85)* 25,000
Neftchi: Micovic; Melikov, Sadykov RF, Guliyev R, Sadykov RA, Mammadov (Nabiyev 82), Tagizade■, Aliyev (Boret 63), Adamia, Subasic (Allahverdiyev 80), Bayramov.
Ried: Berger; Jank, Glasner, Rzasa, Brenner, Toth (Salihi 46), Erbek, Drechsel, Hackmair (Kovacevic 75), Pichorner, Djokic (Riegler 87).

Odense (3) 5 *(Andreasen 20, Christensen K 29, 73, Borring 45, Nymann 89)*
St Patrick's Ath (0) 0 5306
Odense: Onyszko; Laursen, Christensen A, Helveg (Troest 46), Sorensen, Andreasen (Nymann 79), Timm, Hansen, Bolanos (Radonjic 70), Borring, Christensen K.
St Patrick's Ath: Ryan; Brennan, Maguire, Quigley (Foley-Sheridan 79), Rogers, Kirby, Fahey, Keane (Paisley 16), Murphy (O'Connor 59), Gibson, Guy.

Partizan Belgrade (3) 5 *(Maletic 4, Moreira 32, Jovetic 37, 51, 71)*
Zrinjski (0) 0 10,238
Partizan Belgrade: Bozovic; Rukavina, Rnic, Mihajlov, Obradovic, Juca, Moreira, Lazic D (Lazic P 68), Diarra (Veselinovic 56), Maletic, Jovetic (Marinkovic 75).
Zrinjski: Maric; Basic (Suton 65), Karadza, Brankovic, Sunjic, Dragicevic, Landeka, Smajic, Duric (Pezo 55), Matko (Selimovic 72), Rajovic.
Partizan Belgrade expelled from the competition after crowd trouble in the first leg; Zrinjski qualify for next round.

Rabotnicki (1) 2 *(Velkoski 44, Demiri 68)*
Gorica (0) 1 *(Demirovic 85 (pen))* 2500
Rabotnicki: Madzovski; Lazarevski, Stanisic, Kovacevic, Bozinovski, Demiri (Babatunde 90), Mihajlovic, Ignatov (Nedzipi 78), Velkoski, Trickovski (Selim 84), Milisavljevic.
Gorica: Simcic; Lerant, Komel, Zivec (Krsic 82), Suler, Kovacevic, Dedic, Demirovic, Cvijanovic, Matavz (Velikonja 67), Djukic (Osterc 46).

Rudar (0) 0
Omonia (1) 2 *(Mguni 34, Ricardo Sousa 75)* 300
Rudar: Mijatovic; Vukovic■, Damjanovic, Bojovic, Sekulic, Karadzic (Nestorovic 61), Reljic S, Vranes, Ramovic (Lujinovic 35), Minic, Lukovac (Brasanac 55).
Omonia: Georgallides; Veiga, Kakoyiannis, Dobrasinovic (Kaseke 70), Kaiafas, Georgiou, Torrao, Magno, Weisheimer (Ricardo Sousa 59), Mguni (Chailis 80), Ba.

Suduva (1) 4 *(Grigas 29, Urbsys 50, 55, 84)*
Dungannon Swifts (0) 0 1500
Suduva: Klevinskas S; Grigas, Klevinskas G, Mikuckis, Sobol, Miklinevicius, Maciulevicius (Slavickas G 70), Urbsys (Potapov 84), Viller■, Juska (Jasaitis 46), Braga.
Dungannon Swifts: Nelson; McConkey (Baron 81), Gallagher, McMinn, Fitzpatrick G, Curran, McCabe, Fitzpatrick T (Magennis 64), Campbell, Hegarty (McManus 64), McAllister.

Teuta (1) 2 *(Kuli 45, 74)*
Slaven (0) 2 *(Kresinger 64, Vrucina 70)* 1000
Teuta: Kapllani; Brahja (Stafa 90), Vrapi, Buna, Devolli, Hodo, Vila, Kuli, Blloku (Likmeta 88), Sula (Hashani 27), Xhafa.
Slaven: Ivesa (Rodic 46); Bosnjak, Kristic, Poldrugac, Radeljic, Posavec (Delic 75), Sopic, Poljak, Juric (Jajalo 40), Kresinger, Vrucina.

Trans (0) 0
Helsingborg (2) 3 *(Wahlstedt 18, Svanback 32, Unkuri 76)* 164
Trans: Usoltsev; Lepik, Kulik (Kitto 77), Dobrovolskiy, Kazakov, Gorjatsov, Tarassenkov, Ivanov (Smirnov 55), Paitsev (Dubokin 69), Lipartov, Gruznov.
Helsingborg: Andersson D; Andersson C, Wahlstedt, Ronningberg, Jakobsson, Svanback, Dahl (Landgren 46), Mariga, Skulasson (Chansa 66), Unkuri, Omotoyossi (Astrom 62).

Vaduz (0) 0
Dynamo Tbilisi (0) 0 755
Vaduz: Sommer; Akdemir (Polverino 57), Reinmann, Ritzberger, Cerrone, Maggetti, Wieczorek, Sturm, Sutter, Gaspar (Rohrer 70), Grossklaus.
Dynamo Tbilisi: Ebang; Kashia G, Krsko, Kashia S, Zelic, Khmaladze, Peikrishvili (Odikadze 76), Merebashvili, Kobakhidze, Digmelashvili (Khutsishvili 89), Akieremy (Spasojevic 90).

Valerenga (0) 1 *(Berre 90)*
Flora (0) 0 4290
Valerenga: Bolthof; Jepsen, Storbaek, Johnsen (Horn 38), Waehler, Holm T, Dos Santos, Jalland, Berre, Fellah (Lange 50) (Forsund 74), Holm D.
Flora: Aksalu; Talimaa (Hurt 58), Allas, Barengrub, Vanna, Vunk (Sirevicius 85), Sidorenkov, Kams (Ahjupera 73), Reim, Hakola, Zahovaiko.

Young Boys (3) 4 *(Joao Paulo 11, 41, Tiago 21, Schneuwly M 58)*
Banants (0) 0 5478
Young Boys: Collaviti; Tiago, Zayatte (Portillo 63), Schwegler, Raimondi, Regazzoni (Schneuwly M 46), Yakin (Schneuwly C 67), Varela, Yapi-Yapo, Joao Paulo, Frimpong.
Banants: Radaca; Simonyan, Cherevko, Arakelyan, Grigorian, Jenebyan (Karapetian 36), Kakosian, Khachatrian (Bareghamian 43), Melkonian, Balabekian (Muradian 72), Hakobian.

Zimbru (1) 2 *(Kovalchuk 34, Zhdanov 60 (pen))*
Artmedia (0) 2 *(Guede 73, Borbely 90)* 2500
Zimbru: Calancea; Armas (Andronic 68), Berbinschi, Krioutchikhine, Savinov, Stan V (Boyko 58), Frantuz (Levandovschi 62), Cojocari, Gibalyuk, Kovalchuk, Zhdanov.
Artmedia: Kamenar; Cisovsky, Burak, Guede, Mraz (Durica P■ 67), Durica M, Gajdos (Cvirik 87), Borbely, Fodrek (Obzera 62), Kozak, Halenar.

SECOND QUALIFYING ROUND FIRST LEG

Thursday, 16 August 2007

Atletico Madrid (1) 3 *(Maxi Rodriguez 38, Forlan 62, Aguero 70)*
Vojvodina (0) 0 42,000
Atletico Madrid: Leo Franco; Seitaridis, Pernia, Luis Perea, Ibanez, Raul Garcia, Maxi Rodriguez (Jurado 81), Maniche, Forlan, Aguero (Luis Garcia 75), Simao (Reyes 64).
Vojvodina: Markovic; Kahriman, Pekaric, Stosic, Duric, Miroslav Milutinovic■, Kacar (Trivunovic 66), Popovic (Milan Milutinovic 79), Tadic, Buac (Smiljanic 62), Despotovic.

Basle (1) 2 *(Ergic 24, Caicedo 54)*
Mattersburg (1) 1 *(Nakata 20 (og))* 9203
Basle: Costanzo; Majstorovic, Nakata, Marque, Zanni, Huggel, Chipperfield, Ergic, Carlitos (Frei 86), Caicedo, Eduardo (Derdiyok 69).
Mattersburg: Almer; Sedloski, Csizmadia, Morz, Kuhbauer, Kovrig, Schmidt, Atan■, Jancker (Burger 83), Wagner, Naumoski (Pauschenwein 27).

Besa (0) 0
Litex (3) 3 *(Popov I 13, 20, Beto 32)* 4000
Besa: Zendeli; Bikoula, Duro, Krasniqi, Veliaj (Arapi 46), Ramadan, Mertiri, Xhihani (Kaja 60), Ishaka, Alikaj, Endene (Nuhiji 46).
Litex: Todorov; Benkov, Uras, Manolev, Nikolov, Popov R, Tom (Jelenkovic 46), Boudarene (Dudu 46), Sandrinho, Beto, Popov I (Bibishkov 46).

Brann (1) 2 *(Bjornsson 24, Winters 49)*
Suduva (0) 1 *(Negreiros 56 (pen))* 7400
Brann: Thorbjornsen; Dahl, Hanstveit, Bjarnason, Bjornsson, Andresen, Solli, Huseklepp (Sjohage 86), Bakke (El-Fakiri 81), Sigurdsson K, Winters.
Suduva: Klevinskas S; Klevinskas G, Mikuckis, Klimavicius, Sobol, Skinderis, Miklinevicius, Maciulevicius (Slavickas V 46), Urbsys, Jasaitis (Potapov 80), Braga (Negreiros 46).

Cluj (0) 1 *(Trica 70 (pen))*
Anorthosis (1) 3 *(Zlogar 42, William 48, Sosin 59)* 8000
Cluj: Stancioiu; Tony (Manuel Jose 70), Sandberg, Panin (Fredy Martins 46), Cadu, Muresan, Trica, Culio, Leao (Fabbiani 52), Semedo, Didi Magalhaes.
Anorthosis: Beqaj; Katsavakis, Konstantinou, Ndikumana (Loumpoutis 65), Zlogar, Poursaitidis, Fabinho (Belic 77), Panagi, Deanov (Loureiro 59), Sosin, William.

Dnepr (0) 1 *(Nazarenko 81)*
Belchatow (1) 1 *(Ujek 16)* 16,000
Dnepr: Kernozenko; Gritsay (Lepa 61), Shershun, Rusol, Denisov, Shelayev, Andrienko, Kravchenko, Nazarenko, Samodin (Karnilenka 66), Vorobei.
Belchatow: Kozik; Popek, Cecot, Stolarczyk, Kowalczyk, Herrera (Wrobel 49), Strak, Jarzebowski, Rachwal, Ujek (Grodzicki 87), Dziedzic (Nowak 70).

Drogheda United (0) 1 *(Zayed 54)*
Helsingborg (1) 1 *(Larsson 34)* 4500
Drogheda United: Connor; Webb, Gavin, Gartland, Shelley, Robinson, Keddy (Cahill 51), Byrne, Ristila (Grant 46), Baker (Keegan 78), Zayed.
Helsingborg: Andersson D; Jakobsson, Andersson C, Ronningberg, Tamboura, Svanback, Dahl, Mariga, Wahlstedt, Omotoyossi, Larsson.

Dunfermline Athletic (1) 1 *(Hamilton 1)*
Hacken (0) 1 *(Henriksson 57)* 6017
Dunfermline Athletic: McKenzie (Murdock 10); Shields, Wilson, Bamba, Young, Thomson S (Morrison S 46), Simmons (Morrison O 77), Harper, Glass, Burchill, Hamilton.
Hacken: Kallqvist; Williams, Lind, Heden, Forsell, Marek, Ze Antonio, Mambo Mumba, Skulason, Henriksson, Larsson (Olofsson 86).

Dynamo Minsk (0) 1 *(Putilo 73)*
Odense (0) 1 *(Laursen 90)* 1000
Dynamo Minsk: Lesko; Pankov, Pavlyukovich, Veretilo, Martinovich, Khatskevich (Kislyak 72), Yurchenko (Temrioukov 79), Putilo (Pavlyuchek 86), Mbanangoye, Nudny, Rak.
Odense: Onyszko; Laursen, Christensen A, Helveg, Sorensen, Bechara, Hansen, Bolanos (Nymann 79), Borring, Nielsen D (Jacobsen 69), Absalonsen (Radonjic 90).

Dynamo Tbilisi (0) 0
Rapid Vienna (2) 3 *(Fabiano 21, Hofmann 39, Bazina 54)* 4000
Dynamo Tbilisi: Ebang (Loria 37); Kashia G, Krsko, Kashia S, Zelic, Khmaladze, Merebashvili, Odikadze, Kobakhidze (Spasojevic 46), Peikrishvili (Khutsishvili 78), Akieremy.
Rapid Vienna: Payer; Tokic, Patocka, Katzer, Thonhofer, Heikkinen (Dober 67), Hofmann (Sara 67), Kavlak (Bilic 67), Boskovic, Bazina, Fabiano.

Ekranas (1) 1 *(Bicka 45 (pen))*
Valerenga (0) 1 *(Dos Santos 77)* 1500
Ekranas: Skrupskis; Rahn, Skroblas, Paulauskas, Rimavicius, Kavaliauskas, Bicka (Gardzijauskas 67), Tomkevicius (Saulenas 82), Luksys, Varnas, Pogreban.
Valerenga: Arason; Jepsen, Storbaek, Thomassen■, Horn, Johnsen, Dos Santos, Mila (Holm T 46), Holm D (Roberts 74), Sorensen (Jalland 46), Berre.

FK Austria (2) 4 *(Ertl 9, Kuljic 21, 66, Lasnik 47)*
Jablonec (2) 3 *(Zelenka 28, 35, Baranek 76)* 5020
FK Austria: Safar; Majstorovic, Bak, Ertl, Schiemer, Blanchard, Lasnik, Sulimani (Okotie 79), Acimovic (Sariyar 57), Aigner (Lafata 75), Kuljic.
Jablonec: Spit; Krejci, Homola, Fukal, Vacha (Zabojnik 89), Hamouz, Elias, Kordula (Valenta 70), Baranek, Rilke, Zelenka (Nulicek 79).

HJK Helsinki (1) 2 *(Samura 15, 55)*
Aalborg (1) 1 *(Risgard 37)* 2375
HJK Helsinki: Wallen; Aalto I, Raitala, Halsti, Kamara, Savolainen, Nurmela (Parikka 88), Smith, Haapala, Samura (Sorsa 78), Bah.
Aalborg: Jensen; Jakobsen M, Pedersen, Califf, Olesen, Lindstrom (Kristensen 76), Johansson, Risgard, Enevoldsen (Caca 22), Curth (Mota 68), Nomvethe.

Hajduk Split (0) 0
Sampdoria (1) 1 *(Campagnaro 44)* 32,500
Hajduk Split: Balic; Buljat, Zivkovic, Sablic (Pandza 46), Damjanovic (Linic 80), Cernat, Andric, Hrgovic M, Rubil (Bartolovic 58), Kalinic, Rukavina.
Sampdoria: Castellazzi; Accardi (Campagnaro 42), Lucchini, Sala, Pieri (Ziegler 77), Zenoni, Volpi, Sammarco, Delvecchio, Bellucci, Caracciolo (Montella 63).

Haka (0) 1 *(Parviainen 50)*
Midtjylland (2) 2 *(Kristensen 13, 43)* 1649
Haka: Dovbnya; Kangaskorpi, Okkonen, Fowler, Innanen (Mahlakaarto 86), Kauppila, Manninen (Strandvall 61), Parviainen, Lehtinen (Matilla 86), Popovich, Holopainen.
Midtjylland: Raska; Troest, Afriyie, Klimpl, Jessen, Thygesen, Poulsen, Oluwafemi, Flinta, Kristensen, Babatunde.

Hammarby (1) 2 *(Guara 35, Castro-Tello 49)*
Fredrikstad (0) 1 *(Kvisvik 75)* 5524
Hammarby: Lekstrom; Johansson, Monteiro, Jensen, Traore, Chanko, Andersson, Zengin (Davies 87), Laitinen, Castro-Tello (Eguren 79), Guara (Sosseh 84).
Fredrikstad: Shaaban; Czwartek, Gerrbrand, Piiroja, Sjoberg (Multaharjo 46), Wehrman, Kvisvik, Bjorkoy, West (Ramberg 58), Elyounoussi, Johansson (Hoas 76).

Honved (0) 0
Hamburg (0) 0 9000
Honved: Toth I; Mogyorosi, Brou, Smiljanic, Vincze Z, Ivancsics, Baranyos, Magasfoldi (Diego 70), Genito, Guei-Guei (Koos 85), Hercegfalvi (Abass 78).
Hamburg: Rost; Atouba, Reinhardt, Kompany, De Jong, Jarolim, Trochowski, Demel, Zidan (Guerrero 66), Olic (Ben-Hatira 76), Castelen.

Kaerjeng (0) 0
Standard Liege (0) 3 *(Mbokani 59, Witsel 81, 86)* 7112
Kaerjeng: Silva Costa; Leite, Facques, Ramdedovic, Da Costa, Matos, Mukenge (Scholer 67), Rolandi (Martins 75), Kivunghe, Boulafari, Mateos (Bianchini 83).
Standard Liege: Renard; Bonfim, Camozzato (Mulemo 85), Sarr, Dupre, Toama (Jovanovic 77), Fellaini, Witsel, Dembele, Mbokani, De Camargo (Lukunku 71).

Lokomotiv Sofia (1) 3 *(Dafchev 19, Baldovaliev 61, Djilas 84)*
Otelul (0) 1 *(Semeghin 74)* 2000
Lokomotiv Sofia: Golubovic; Markov, Dobrev, Varbanov, Savic, Dafchev (Zlatinski 89), Koilov (Ivanov 70), Orachev, Karadzhinhov, Antunovic (Djilas 81), Baldovaliev.
Otelul: Giurgiu; Grybauskas, Nogo, Ilie (Carja 55), Sarghi (Ngapounu 69), Semeghin, Paraschiv, Gado, Kim, Labukas (Ratnikov 55), Jula.

Maccabi Tel Aviv (1) 1 *(Kamanan 42)*
Erciyesspor (1) 1 *(Ilhan 5)* 4000
Maccabi Tel Aviv: Jevric; Yifrah, Shpungin, Martinovic, Nimny (Shivhon 58), Mesika, Yeini, Roman, Haddad R (Azran 64), Kamanan (Malul 72), Peretz.
Erciyesspor: Yusuf; Huseyin, Kemal, Adem (Ilker 78), Kamil, Aydin, Osman (Emrah 45), Ramazan, Ilhan, Koksal, Burhan.

Metalurgs Liepaja (2) 3 *(Karlsons 20, Ivanovs 44, Tamosauskas 63)*
AIK Stockholm (0) 2 *(Ivanovs 49 (og), Ivan 61)* 3100
Metalurgs Liepaja: Spole; Klava (Kruglak 59), Zirnis, Ferreira De Oli, Ivanovs, Rubins, Bleidelis, Tamosauskas, Surnins, Solonicins, Karlsons.
AIK Stockholm: Orlund; Karlsson, Johansson, Arnefjord, Jonsson, Tjernstrom, Stephenson (Pavey 62), Ozkan (Mendes 81), Johnson, Ivan, Valdemarin (Batata 62).

Mika (1) 2 *(Shahgeldian 8, Alex 80)*
Artmedia (0) 1 *(Fodrek 66)* 9000
Mika: Hakobian; Petikian, Alex, Fursin, Antonian (Meloian 46), Ristic, Thiago, Cleber, Shahgeldian (Davtian 63), Adamian (Mikaelian 38), Kleber.
Artmedia: Sninsky; Kamenar, Farkas, Guede, Cisovsky, Urbanek (Mraz 57), Durica M (Cvirik 86), Obzera, Gajdos (Piroska 46), Fodrek, Kozak.

Moravce (0) 0

Zenit (1) 2 *(Hagen 38, Ionov 90)* 3368

Moravce: Peskovic; Pavlenda, Hozl, Klabal, Choma, Ciz, Ondrejka (Balat 46), Juska (Pelegriny 83), Kuracka, Greguska, Gibala.
Zenit: Malafeev (Contofalsky 60); Kim, Lombaerts, Hagen, Anyukov, Sirl, Zyryanov, Denisov (Ionov 75), Timoshchuk, Dominguez, Pogrebnyak (Maksimov 75).

MyPa (0) 0

Blackburn Rovers (1) 1 *(Santa Cruz 6)* 2012

MyPa: Korhonen; Pulkkinen, Huttunen, Miranda, Kansikas, Agboh, Kuparinen (Manso 65), Muinonen (Puhakainen 53), Mustafi, Hyyrynen, Peltonen (Nykanen 79).
Blackburn Rovers: Friedel; Ooijer, Warnock, Dunn (Tugay 72), Nelsen, Samba, Bentley, Savage, Santa Cruz, Roberts (Derbyshire 65), Pedersen (Emerton 72).

Omonia (1) 1 *(Kaiafas 14)*

CSKA Sofia (1) 1 *(Nei 1)* 20,000

Omonia: Georgallides; Veiga, Georgiou, Kakoyiannis, Dobrasinovic (Kaseke 40), Kaiafas, Torrao (Theodotou 23), Ba (Ricardo Sousa 77), Weisheimer, Magno, Mguni.
CSKA Sofia: Ivanov; Tunchev, Vujadinovic, Iliev V■, Todorov, Yanchev, Petre (Lanzaat 68), Kabous, Dimitrov, Amuneke (Garces 65), Nei (Chigozie 82).

Rabotnicki (0) 0

Zrinjski (0) 0 1000

Rabotnicki: Madzovski; Lazarevski (Gjoreski 73), Demiri, Stanisic, Babatunde, Kovacevic, Milisavljevic, Ignatov (Ilijoski 76), Nedzipi, Trickovski, Pejcic (Velkovski 64).
Zrinjski: Maric; Nikolic, Dzidic D, Karadza, Landeka, Smajic (Joldic 83), Juric■, Ivankovic, Suton, Selimovic (Basic 72), Rajovic (Zizovic 66).

Ried (0) 1 *(Dospel 66)*

Sion (0) 1 *(Saborio 90)* 2000

Ried: Berger; Jank, Glasner, Rzasa, Toth (Kujabi 56), Erbek, Drechsel, Brenner, Hackmair, Pichorner (Dospel 56), Damjanovic (Salihi 81).
Sion: Vailati; Nwaneri, Paito, Vanczak, Buhler, Beto (Zakrzewski 68), Geiger, Chedli, Obradovic, Dominguez, Saborio.

Siroki (0) 0

Hapoel Tel Aviv (2) 3 *(Abedi 14, Asulin 32, Dos Santos 74)* 3500

Siroki: Bandovic; Vidic, Topic, Juric (Kozul 46), Silic, Zelenika (Sakic 73), Ronielle (Hannich 46), Marciano, Karoglan, Bubalo S, Celson.
Hapoel Tel Aviv: Enyeama; Dos Santos, Antebi, Bondarv, Duani, Dego (Oved 90), Badir, Abedi (Natcho 85), Mazuwa, Asulin, Sabag (Fabio Junior 69).

Slaven (1) 1 *(Posavec 16)*

Galatasaray (1) 2 *(Ayhan 42, Volkan 73)* 3500

Slaven: Ivesa; Bosnjak, Kristic, Radeljic, Poldrugac, Sopic, Poljak (Delic 61), Jajalo (Somoci 46), Posavec, Sehic, Vrucina (Kresinger 79).
Galatasaray: Orkun; Song, Ugur, Volkan, Servet, Hasan Sas (Baris 52), Ayhan, Sabri (Okan 83), Mehmet G (Mehmet T 89), Hakan Sukur, Umit K.

Tobol (0) 0

Groclin (1) 1 *(Muszalik 2)* 8000

Tobol: Pryadkin; Irismetov, Mukanov, Dimitrov, Nurdauletov, Nurgaliev (Ostapenko 70), Zhumaskaliev, Skorykh, Yurin (Meshkov 46), Baltiev, Bakaev (Urazov 83).
Groclin: Przyrowski; Mynar, Lazarevski, Koziol, Jodlowiec, Piechniak (Rocki 90), Sokolowski, Lato, Muszalik (Majewski 73), Slusarski, Babnic (Cumbev 69).

Uniao Leiria (0) 0

Maccabi Netanya (0) 0 1945

Uniao Leiria: Fernando; Eder, Renato, Laranjeiro, Eder Gaucho, Alhandra (N'Gal 58), Faria, Sougou, Marco Soares, Paulo Cesar, Tonito (Cadu Da Silva 69).
Maccabi Netanya: Shtruber; Marin, Saban, Ben Dayan, Hermon, Taga (Yampolski 87), Bundea (Rozental 76), Cohen T, Cohen A, Shechter, Awudu.

Young Boys (0) 1 *(Tiago 70)*

Lens (0) 1 *(Monterrubio 74)* 13,411

Young Boys: Wolfli; Tiago, Mangane, Schwegler, Zayatte■, Yakin (Frimpong 85), Raimondi, Varela, Yapi-Yapo, Regazzoni (Schneuwly M 77), Joao Paulo (Kallio 90).
Lens: Runje; Coulibaly, Aubey, Bisevac, Akale, Kovacevic, Demont, Sable (Keita 87), Kalou (Boukari 90), Monterrubio, Dindane (Carriere 75).

SECOND QUALIFYING ROUND SECOND LEG

Thursday, 30 August 2007

AIK Stockholm (1) 2 *(Batata 43, 54)*

Metalurgs Liepaja (0) 0 7528

AIK Stockholm: Orlund; Johansson, Tamandi, Jonsson, Tjernstrom, Pavey, Stephenson (Karlsson 46), Johnson, Batata (Mendes 86), Ivan (Bengtsson 89), Valdemarin.
Metalurgs Liepaja: Spole; Klava (Torres 80), Zirnis, Ferreira De Oli, Ivanovs, Rubins, Bleidelis, Tamosauskas, Surnins, Solonicins (Kruglak 64), Karlsons.

Aalborg (3) 3 *(Enevoldsen 7, Johansson 26, Curth 43)*

HJK Helsinki (0) 0 3902

Aalborg: Zaza; Jakobsen M, Califf, Olesen, Johansson (Caca 89), Risgard, Enevoldsen (Augustinussen 67), Prica, Curth (Lindstrom 60), Nomvethe, Kristensen.
HJK Helsinki: Wallen; Aalto I, Raitala, Halsti, Kamara, Savolainen, Nurmela, Smith (Vuorinen 55), Haapala (Parikka 90), Sorsa (Samura 69), Bah.

Anorthosis (0) 0

Cluj (0) 0 15,000

Anorthosis: Beqaj; Katsavakis, Ndikumana, Lambrou, Zlogar, Poursaitidis, Fabinho (Nicolaou 46), Panagi, Deanov (Loumpoutis 46), Sosin (Laban 79), William.
Cluj: Stancioiu; Tony, Panin, Cadu, Galiassi, Manuel Jose, Muresan, Trica (Minteuan 69), Deac (Culio 58), Fabbiani, Didi Magalhaes (Semedo 46).

Artmedia (1) 2 *(Obzera 5, 71)*

Mika (0) 0 1400

Artmedia: Hyll; Guede, Dosoudil, Urbanek, Burak, Durica M (Farkas 66), Obzera (Gajdos 90), Borbely, Fodrek, Kozak, Halenar (Piroska 75).
Mika: Hakobian; Petikian, Mikaelian, Alex, Fursin (Meloian 46), Antonian, Ristic, Thiago (Davtian 68), Cleber, Shahgeldian (Tales 73), Kleber.

Belchatow (2) 2 *(Stolarczyk 10 (pen), Nowak 21)*

Dnepr (4) 4 *(Kravchenko 7, Shelayev 32, Samodin 33, Karnilenka 40)* 4000

Belchatow: Lech; Stolarczyk, Pietrasiak, Kowalczyk, Herrera (Cecot 46), Strak, Gargula, Rachwal, Nowak (Sanchez 75), Ujek (Wrobel 46), Dziedzic.
Dnepr: Kernozenko; Shershun, Rusol, Denisov, Shelayev, Kankava (Gritsay 66), Andrienko, Kravchenko, Nazarenko (Bartulovic 80), Karnilenka, Samodin (Lepa 77).

Blackburn Rovers (0) 2 *(Bentley 48, Roberts 90)*

MyPa (0) 0 13,490

Blackburn Rovers: Friedel; Ooijer, Warnock (Olsson 77), Tugay, Nelsen, Mokoena, Emerton, Bentley, Rigters (Derbyshire 76), Roberts, Pedersen.
MyPa: Korhonen; Pulkkinen, Huttunen, Miranda, Kansikas, Agboh, Kuparinen, Muinonen (Peltonen 73), Leilei (Puhakainen 46), Mustafi, Kangaskolkka (Helenius 60).

CSKA Sofia (1) 2 *(Nei 17, Chilikov 88)*
Omonia (1) 1 *(Magno 8)* 3000
CSKA Sofia: Ivanov; Tunchev, Vujadinovic, Lanzaat, Todorov, Yanchev, Petre (Garces 66), Chigozie, Marquinos, Dimitrov (Chilikov 85), Nei (Kabous 89).
Omonia: Georgallides; Theodotou (Lima 73), Veiga■, Georgiou, Kakoyiannis, Dobrasinovic, Kaiafas, Ba■, Weisheimer (Ricardo Sousa 63), Magno (Kaseke 82), Mguni.

Erciyesspor (2) 3 *(Ilhan 7, Koksal 14, Alaattin 72)*
Maccabi Tel Aviv (1) 1 *(Haddad R 40)* 20,000
Erciyesspor: Yusuf; Huseyin, Kemal, Adem (Ramazan 76), Kamil, Aydin, Ilker, Emrah (Alaattin 58), Ilhan, Koksal, Burhan (Omer 87).
Maccabi Tel Aviv: Jevric; Shpungin, Haddad A, Nimny, Mesika, Yeyni, Kapiloto, Roman, Haddad R (Shivhon 71), Azran (Peretz 64), Kamanan (Biton 78).

Fredrikstad (0) 1 *(Bjorkoy 85)*
Hammarby (0) 1 *(Eguren 90 (pen))* 7548
Fredrikstad: Shaaban; Czwartek, Gerrbrand, Piiroja, Sjoberg (West 90), Ramberg (Kouadio 65), Wehrman, Kvisvik, Bjorkoy, Elyounoussi, Johansson (Hoas 72).
Hammarby: Lekstrom; Johansson, Monteiro, Sleyman, Gunnarsson, Traore, Andersson, Zengin, Castro-Tello (Jensen 78), Juliusson (Eguren 46), Guara (Davies 90).

Galatasaray (2) 2 *(Umit K 9, Hakan Sukur 37)*
Slaven (1) 1 *(Poljak 36 (pen))* 22,000
Galatasaray: Orkun; Song, Ugur, Volkan (Baris 46), Servet, Lincoln, Hasan Sas, Ayhan, Sabri, Hakan Sukur (Serkan 88), Umit K (Okan 90).
Slaven: Ivesa; Bosnjak (Posavec 65), Bozac, Radeljic, Poldrugac, Sopic, Poljak, Jajalo, Radicek, Kresinger (Tepuric 74), Sehic (Vrucina 52).

Groclin (2) 2 *(Sikora 5, 20)*
Tobol (0) 0 2500
Groclin: Przyrowski; Mynar (Piechniak 59), Lazarevski, Telichowski, Koziol, Jodlowiec, Sokolowski, Lato (Klodawski 65), Majewski (Muszalik 77), Ivanovski, Sikora.
Tobol: Petuhkov; Irismetov, Mukanov, Dimitrov, Nurdauletov, Meshkov, Nurgaliev (Yurin 72), Zhumaskaliev, Skorykh (Kharabara 46), Baltiev, Bakaev (Ostapenko 65).

Hacken (1) 1 *(Skulason 27)*
Dunfermline Athletic (0) 0 2712
Hacken: Hysen; Lind, Heden, Lucic, Marek, Ljung (Forsell 32), Mambo Mumba, Skulason, Henriksson, Larsson (Olofsson 82), De Oliveira (Holster 90).
Dunfermline Athletic: Gallacher; Shields (Simmons 76), Wilson, Bamba, Morrison S (McManus 52), Young, Harper, Glass, Morrison O (Burchill 67), Crawford, Hamilton■.

Hamburg (2) 4 *(Guerrero 10, 39, Choupo-Moting 90, Smiljanic 50 (og))*
Honved (0) 0 42,090
Hamburg: Rost; Atouba, Reinhardt, Mathijsen, Kompany, Jarolim, Demel, Van der Vaart (Ben-Hatira 76), Guerrero (Choupo-Moting 60), Olic (Trochowski 66), Castelen.
Honved: Toth I; Mogyorosi, Brou, Smiljanic, Vincze Z, Vincze G (Abass 68), Diego, Baranyos, Magasfoldi (Ivancsics 49), Guei-Guei (Toth M 79), Hercegfalvi.

Hapoel Tel Aviv (1) 3 *(Asulin 41, Badir 50, Natcho 75)*
Siroki (0) 0 3500
Hapoel Tel Aviv: Enyeama; Dos Santos, Antebi, Bondarv, Duani, Dego (Oved 55), Badir (Tai Chen 67), Abedi, Mazuwa, Asulin, Fabio Junior (Natcho 62).
Siroki: Bandovic; Kozul (Bozic 65), Vidic, Topic, Juric (Marciano 59), Silic, Zelenika, Lago (Sakic 75), Ronielle, Karoglan, Bubalo S.

Helsingborg (0) 3 *(Jakobsson 52, Omotoyossi 68, Karekezi 90)*
Drogheda United (0) 0 4767
Helsingborg: Andersson D; Jakobsson, Andersson C, Ronningberg, Tamboura, Svanback, Dahl (Mariga 86), Skulasson, Wahlstedt, Omotoyossi (Karekezi 86), Larsson.
Drogheda United: Connor; Byrne, Webb, Gavin, Gartland, Shelley, Robinson (Whelan 79), Keddy (Bates 55), Keegan, Cahill, Zayed (O'Keeffe 74).

Jablonec (0) 1 *(Rilke 82)*
FK Austria (1) 1 *(Sariyar 89)* 5710
Jablonec: Spit; Zabojnik, Flachbart (Rilke 46), Homola, Fukal, Vacha (Krejci 88), Hamouz, Elias (Valenta 61), Baranek, Zelenka, Svatek.
FK Austria: Safar; Majstorovic, Bak, Ertl, Schiemer, Blanchard, Lasnik (Lafata 65), Sariyar, Acimovic (Gercaliu 88), Standfest, Kuljic (Aigner 81).

Lens (2) 5 *(Dindane 13, 58, Akale 16, Carriere 67, Feindouno 89)*
Young Boys (1) 1 *(Varela 32)* 31,055
Lens: Runje; Ramos, Hilton, Laurenti, Bisevac, Carriere (Keita 69), Akale, Kovacevic, Sable (Feindouno 75), Monterrubio, Dindane (Boukari 73).
Young Boys: Wolfli; Tiago, Portillo, Kallio, Yakin (Schneuwly C 73), Raimondi, Varela (Kavak 64), Hochstrasser (Frimpong 60), Regazzoni, Joao Paulo, Schneuwly M.

Litex (1) 3 *(Genchev 13, Beto 69, Dudu 79)*
Besa (0) 0 2000
Litex: Todorov; Cichero, Venkov, Bandalovski, Nikolov (Cambon 78), Genchev, Tom, Dudu, Sandrinho, Bibishkov (Hazurov 65), Popov I (Beto 60).
Besa: Dura; Lila, Kaja, Okshtuni, Arapi, Hoxha, Krasniqi, Veliaj, Ramadan, Xhihani, Nuhiji (Alikaj 90).

Maccabi Netanya (0) 0
Uniao Leiria (0) 1 *(N'Gal 84)* 2000
Maccabi Netanya: Shtruber; Marin, Strul, Saban, Ben Dayan, Taga, Bundea (Rozental 77), Cohen T, Cohen A (Yampolski 67), Shechter, Awudu.
Uniao Leiria: Fernando; Hugo Costa (Bruno Miguel 46), Renato (Alhandra 50), Larangeiro, Eder Gaucho, Hugo Faria, Sougou (N'Gal 60), Tiago, Paulo Cesar, Cadu Da Silva, Joao Paulo.

Mattersburg (0) 0
Basle (3) 4 *(Caicedo 21, Ergic 36, Streller 40, Carlitos 52)* 4600
Mattersburg: Almer; Pollhuber, Pauschenwein, Csizmadia, Morz (Kauten 89), Kuhbauer, Schmidt, Jancker (Malic 67), Wagner, Burger, Naumoski (Lindner 83).
Basle: Costanzo; Majstorovic, Nakata, Marque, Zanni, Huggel, Chipperfield, Ergic, Carlitos (Frei 83), Streller (Derdiyok 73), Caicedo (Eduardo 58).

Midtjylland (3) 5 *(Flinta 16, Olsen D 27, Dadu 34, Troest 67, Roll 85)*
Haka (1) 2 *(Popovich 33, Kauppila 72)* 4707
Midtjylland: Raska; Troest, Afriyie, Klimpl, Jessen, Thygesen, Olsen D (Madsen 64), Oluwafemi (Roll 62), Flinta, Dadu, Kristensen (Olsen C 60).
Haka: Dovbnya; Kangaskorpi, Viljanen, Okkonen, Fowler, Innanen (Mahlakaarto 84), Kauppila, Manninen (Strandvall 56), Leitinen (Matilla 64), Popovich, Holopainen.

Odense (1) 4 *(Nielsen D 38, 55, Absalonsen 77, 79)*
Dynamo Minsk (0) 0 6416
Odense: Onyszko; Laursen, Christensen A, Helveg, Sorensen, Bechara (Andreasen 63), Hansen, Bolanos (Bisgaard 74), Borring, Nielsen D (Jacobsen 83), Absalonsen.
Dynamo Minsk: Lesko; Pankov, Pavlyuchek, Veretilo, Martinovich, Khatskevich, Yurchenko (Kislyak 60), Mbanangoye (Marcio 80), Nudny (Rekish 84), Edu, Rak.

Otelul (0) 0

Lokomotiv Sofia (0) 0 12,000

Otelul: Bors; Nogo (Carja 19), Ngapounu (Ilie 83), Semeghin, Zhelev, Parashiv, Gado, Kim, Szekely, Labukas (Ratnikov 60), Jula.
Lokomotiv Sofia: Golubovic; Markov, Dobrev, Varbanov, Savic, Ivanov, Davchev, Orachev, Karadzhinov (Koilov 83), Antunovic (Djilas 62), Baldovaliev (Paskov 72).

Rapid Vienna (1) 5 *(Bazina 31, Bilic 55, Hofmann 60, 76 (pen), Kavlak 75)*

Dynamo Tbilisi (0) 0 12,600

Rapid Vienna: Payer; Patocka (Eder 58), Hiden, Katzer, Dober, Heikkinen (Kulovits 46), Hofmann, Kavlak, Boskovic (Hoffer 58), Bilic, Bazina.
Dynamo Tbilisi: Loria; Kashia G, Krsko, Zelic, Khmaladze, Merebashvili, Doves, Peikrishvili, Digmelashvili (Kobakhidze 57), Khutsishvili, Akieremy (Spasojevic 63).

Sampdoria (1) 1 *(Montella 34 (pen))*

Hajduk Split (0) 1 *(Hrgovic M 82)* 21,000

Sampdoria: Mirante; Lucchini, Maggio, Sala, Campagnaro, Pieri (Zenoni 89), Volpi, Palombo, Sammarco, Montella (Caracciolo 72), Bellucci (Delvecchio 80).
Hajduk Split: Tomic; Buljat, Zivkovic, Pelaic, Cernat, Ljubicic, Hrgovic M, Linic, Rubil (Peraic 46), Kalinic (Rukavina 78), Bartolovic (Verpakovskis 46).

Sion (2) 3 *(Obradovic 40, Zakrzewski 44, Dominguez 47)*

Ried (0) 0 4500

Sion: Vailati; Kali, Nwaneri, Paito, Vanczak, Buhler, Chedli (Reset 60), Ahoueya (Alioui 29), Obradovic, Dominguez, Zakrzewski (Saborio 73).
Ried: Berger; Jank, Glasner, Rzasa, Dospel, Toth (Kujabi 56), Erbek, Brenner, Hackmair, Damjanovic (Djokic 35), Salihi (Muslic 73).

Standard Liege (0) 1 *(De Camargo 89)*

Kaerjeng (0) 0 6000

Standard Liege: Aragon; Bonfim (Onyewu 46), Mulemo (Dachelet 90), Sarr, Dupre, Defour (Villano 62), Walasiak, Papassarantis, Dembele, De Camargo, Lukunku.
Kaerjeng: Silva Costa (Dunkel 70); Leite, Facques, Ramdedovic, Da Costa, Matos, Mukenge (Boulahfari 64), Rolandi, Kivunghe (Scholer 81), Pace, Marinelli.

Suduva (0) 3 *(Urbsys 46, Maciulevicius 78, Braga 84)*

Brann (2) 4 *(Vaagan Moen 37, Bjornsson 45, Solli 57, Huseklepp 63)* 1300

Suduva: Klevinskas S; Mikuckis, Klimavicius, Sobol (Slavickas G 46), Skinderis, Miklinevicius, Maciulevicius, Urbsys (Potapov■ 81), Slavickas V, Jasaitis (Braga 74), Negreiros.
Brann: Opdal; Dahl, Hanstveit, Bjarnason, Bjornsson, Jaiteh, El-Fakiri, Solli (Guntveit 66), Vaagan Moen (Huseklepp 53), Sigurdsson K, Winters (Sjohage 79).

Valerenga (3) 6 *(Grindheim 5, 45, Sorensen 42, Horn 67, Storbaek 81, Brix 90)*

Ekranas (0) 0 2939

Valerenga: Arason; Jepsen, Storbaek, Horn, Johnsen (Mathisen 46), Waehler, Mila, Jalland, Grindheim (Brix 57), Holm D (Roberts 65), Sorensen.
Ekranas: Stefanovic; Rahn, Paulauskas, Rimavicius (Skroblas 54), Gardzijauskas, Kavaliauskas, Bicka, Tomkevicius, Luksys, Varnas (Saulenas 70), Pogreban (Savenas 54).

Vojvodina (1) 1 *(Buac 38)*

Atletico Madrid (0) 2 *(Luis Garcia 53, Raul Garcia 74)* 5000

Vojvodina: Kahriman; Kizito, Pekaric, Stosic (Radosavljevic 44), Duric, Kacar, Popovic, Trivunovic (Miroslav Milutinovic 81), Tadic (Aleksic 58), Buac, Despotovic.
Atletico Madrid: Abbiati; Antonio Lopez, Eller (Seitaridis 61), Ze Castro, Luis Perea, Cleber Santana, Raul Garcia, Forlan (Jurado 67), Luis Garcia, Reyes (Simao 53), Mista.

Zenit (1) 3 *(Pogrebnyak 10, Maksimov 61, Kim 71)*

Moravce (0) 0 15,000

Zenit: Contofalsky; Kim, Lombaerts, Hagen, Anyukov, Sirl (Ho Lee 68), Zyryanov (Maksimov 46), Denisov, Timoshchuk (Radimov 46), Ionov, Pogrebnyak.
Moravce: Peskovic; Pavlenda, Hozl (Farkas 58), Choma, Ciz (Zembera 75), Cernak, Ondrejka, Juska (Chren 68), Kuracka, Greguska, Gibala.

Zrinjski (1) 1 *(Ivankovic 36)*

Rabotnicki (1) 2 *(Milisavljevic 33, Stanisic 90)* 3000

Zrinjski: Maric; Nikolic, Dzidic D, Karadza, Landeka■, Smajic (Matko 54), Ivankovic, Zizovic (Duric 74), Suton, Joldic■, Rajovic (Selimovic 46).
Rabotnicki: Madzovski; Lazarevski, Demiri, Babatunde, Kovacevic, Vajs, Milisavljevic (Ilijoski 65), Mihajlovic (Gligorov 12), Nedzipi (Stanisic 90), Velkovski, Trickovski.

FIRST ROUND FIRST LEG

Tuesday, 18 September 2007

Litex (0) 0

Hamburg (0) 1 *(Castelen 75)* 8000

Litex: Todorov; Cichero, Venkov, Nikolov, Popov R, Tom, Boudarene, Dudu (Manolev 69), Sandrinho, Bibishkov, Popov I (Beto 80).
Hamburg: Rost; Atouba, Reinhardt, Mathijsen, De Jong, Jarolim, Trochowski, Demel, Van der Vaart (Zidan 89), Guerrero (Olic 79), Castelen (Ben-Hatira 85).

Wednesday, 19 September 2007

Lens (0) 1 *(Dindane 71)*

FC Copenhagen (1) 1 *(Allback 5)* 24,539

Lens: Runje; Coulibaly, Laurenti, Bisevac, Carriere, Akale (Monterrubio 55), Kovacevic, Demont, Sable (Keita 46), Pieroni, Monnet-Paquet (Dindane 55).
FC Copenhagen: Christiansen; Jensen, Hangeland, Gravgaard (Sionko 71), Norregaard, Wurtz, Silberbauer, Gronkjaer, Hutchinson, Kvist, Allback (Nordstrand 71).

Thursday, 20 September 2007

AEK Athens (1) 3 *(Geraldo 3, Rivaldo 58, Kone 82)*

Salzburg (0) 0 25,520

AEK Athens: Macho; Edson Ramos, Arruabarrena, Geraldo, Dellas, Kafes (Kone 51), Nsaliwa, Rivaldo (Blanco 61), Manu, Lyberopoulos, Julio Cesar (Tozser 30).
Salzburg: Ochs; Dudic, Meyer (Vargas■ 46), Sekagya, Carboni, Kovac (Jezek 60), Pitak, Steinhofer, Leitgeb, Zickler, Rakic (Lokvenc 56).

Aberdeen (0) 0

Dnepr (0) 0 15,431

Aberdeen: Langfield; Hart, Considine, Diamond, McNamara (Foster 62), Severin, Jamie Smith, Nicholson, Young (Lovell 71), Miller, Clark (Mair 90).
Dnepr: Kernozenko; Gritsay, Shershun, Rusol, Denisov, Shelayev, Andrienko, Kravchenko (Lepa 61), Nazarenko, Samodin (Kankava 66), Vorobei (Karnilenka 90).

Anderlecht (1) 1 *(Serhat 11)*

Rapid Vienna (0) 1 *(Hofmann 80)* 14,821

Anderlecht: Zitka; Deschacht, Van Damme, Pareja, Wasilewski, Biglia, Polak, Hassan, Goor (Boussoufa 86), Serhat, Mpenza (Legear 67).
Rapid Vienna: Payer; Tokic, Patocka, Hiden, Thonhofer, Heikkinen, Hofmann (Eder 88), Kavlak (Korkmaz 61), Boskovic, Bilic, Bazina (Hoffer 75).

Aris Salonika (1) 1 *(Papadopoulos 7)*

Zaragoza (0) 0 20,000

Aris Salonika: Chalkias; Neto, Ronaldo, Marco Aurelio, Papadopoulos, Nebegleras, Toni Calvo (Javito 59), Ronald Garcia, Ivic (Kouloucheris 81), Koke, Felipe (Siston 49).
Zaragoza: Lopez Vallejo; Diogo (Gabi 71), Ayala, Juanfran, Pavon, Luccin, D'Alessandro (Diego Milito 71), Matuzalem, Zapater, Sergio Garcia, Oliveira.

Artmedia (0) 1 *(Urbanek 47)*
Panathinaikos (0) 2 *(Papadopoulos 62 (pen), N'Doye 90)* 3981
Artmedia: Hyll; Farkas (Durica M 79), Guede, Dosoudil, Cisovsky, Urbanek, Obzera (Piroska 79), Borbely■, Fodrek, Kozak, Halenar (Mraz 87).
Panathinaikos: Malarz; Enakarhire, Goumas, Vintra, Marcelo, Karagounis (N'Doye 74), Tziolis, Nilsson, Dimoutsos (Simao 90), Papadopoulos, Salpigidis (Romero 81).

Atletico Madrid (2) 4 *(Mista 13, Forlan 17, Luis Garcia 82, 90)*
Erciyesspor (0) 0 27,500
Atletico Madrid: Abbiati; Antonio Lopez, Eller, Ze Castro, Luis Perea, Cleber Santana (Raul Garcia 80), Jurado (Simao 23), Maniche, Forlan, Luis Garcia, Mista (Aguero 69).
Erciyesspor: Yusuf; Huseyin, Kemal, Kamil (Osman 69), Ilker (Kazim 84), Mustafa, Ramazan, Ilhan, Koksal, Emre, Burhan (Emrah 74).

Bayern Munich (1) 1 *(Toni 34)*
Belenenses (0) 0 62,000
Bayern Munich: Kahn; Lucio, Demichelis, Jansen, Lell, Ribery (Schlaudraff 84), Ze Roberto, Van Bommel, Schweinsteiger (Hamit Altintop 73), Toni (Wagner 63), Podolski.
Belenenses: Costinha; Rodrigo Alvim, Rolando, Hugo Alcantara, Devic, Ruben Amorim, Silas (Joao Paulo 63), Jose Pedro, Roncatto, Evandro Paulista (Fernando 54), Candido Costa (Amaral 46).

Brann (0) 0
FC Brugge (0) 1 *(Sterchele 85)* 10,471
Brann: Opdal; Guntveit (Huseklepp 68), Hanstveit, Bjarnason, Walde, Bjornsson, El-Fakiri, Andresen (Bakke 56), Solli, Vaagan Moen, Helstad (Karadas 56).
FC Brugge: Stijnen; Klukowski, Clement, Kucera, Priske, Englebert, Blondel, Simaeys, Geraerts, Sonck (Sterchele 78), Salou (Leko 82).

Dinamo Bucharest (1) 1 *(Niculescu 9)*
Elfsborg (2) 2 *(Keene 12, 31)* 10,000
Dinamo Bucharest: Lobont; Pulhac, Goian, Radu, Galliquio, Munteanu (Izvoreanu 69), Cristea, Ropotan, Niculescu (Margaritescu 46), Danciulescu, Oprita (Bratu 46).
Elfsborg: Wiland; Karlsson, Andersson, Mobaeck, Bjorck, Augustsson, Ilola, Svensson A, Ishizaki (Bajrami 90), Alexandersson (Avdic 83), Keene (Berglund 80).

Dynamo Zagreb (0) 0
Ajax (0) 1 *(Rommedahl 62)* 30,000
Dynamo Zagreb: Koch; Cale, Schildenfeld, Drpic, Pokrivac, Etto, Modric, Sammir, Vukojevic (Guela 69), Balaban, Vugrinec (Sokota 46).
Ajax: Stekelenburg; Heitinga, Stam, Vermaelen, Ogararu, Van der Wiel, Emanuelson, Maduro, Gabri, Huntelaar (Luque 83), Rommedahl (Suarez 77).

Empoli (1) 2 *(Piccolo 45, Antonini 49 (pen))*
Zurich (0) 1 *(Alphonse 74)* 2000
Empoli: Bassi; Piccolo, Rincon (Raggi 84), Marzoratti, Iacoponi (Eder 84), Abate, Marchisio, Antonini (Vanigli 86), Prevete, Pozzi, Volpato.
Zurich: Leoni; Konde, Stahel, Rochat, Barmettler, Schneider, Okonkwo, Abdi, Raffael, Chikhaoui, Hassli (Alphonse 70).

Everton (1) 1 *(Lescott 24)*
Metalist Kharkiv (0) 1 *(Edmar 78)* 37,120
Everton: Wessels; Hibbert, Baines, Yobo, Lescott, Carsley (Jagielka 79), Osman, Neville, Johnson, Yakubu (Anichebe 65), McFadden.
Metalist Kharkiv: Goryainov; Babych■, Gancarczyk■, Obradovic, Gueye, Bordian, Valyayev, Slyusar, Rykun (Edmar 67), Devic, Nwoga (Antonov 59) (Mahdoufi 77).

FK Austria (1) 2 *(Kuljic 41, Lasnik 62)*
Valerenga (0) 0 5500
FK Austria: Safar; Bak, Gercaliu (Majstorovic 71), Schiemer, Blanchard, Lasnik (Sulimani 81), Sariyar, Acimovic, Standfest, Aigner, Kuljic (Mair 85).
Valerenga: Arason; Jepsen, Storbaek, Thomassen, Horn, Johnsen, Dos Santos, Mila (Thorvaldsson 46), Grindheim, Holm D, Berre.

Getafe (0) 1 *(Uche 90)*
Twente (0) 0 10,000
Getafe: Abbondanzieri; Cata Diaz, Belenguer, Licht, Cortes, Celestini, Casquero (Sousa 81), Granero (Braulio 69), Kepa (Albin 46), Uche, Pablo Hernandez.
Twente: Boschker; Wielaert, Heubach (Zomer 61), Braafheid■, Engelaar, Wilkshire, Wellenberg, El Ahmadi, Denneboom (Brama 64), N'Kufo, Huysegems (Elia 87).

Groclin (0) 0
Red Star Belgrade (1) 1 *(Basta 19)* 5000
Groclin: Przyrowski; Mynar, Telichowski, Koziol, Jodlowiec, Piechniak, Sokolowski, Lato (Babnic 78), Majewski (Muszalik 64), Ivanovski (Rocki 67), Sikora.
Red Star Belgrade: Radivojevic; Andelkovic (Bogdanovic 90), Tutoric, Bronowicki, Gueye, Basta, Milijas, Lucas, Castillo, Barcos (Dordjevic F 75), Salas.

Groningen (1) 1 *(Lovre 25)*
Fiorentina (0) 1 *(Semioli 66)* 19,344
Groningen: Van Loo; Silva, Sankoh, Kruiswijk, Stenman, Lovre, Levchenko, Meerdink, Lindgren, Nevland (Kolder 90), Nijland (Van de Laak 73).
Fiorentina: Frey; Kroldrup, Gamberini, Ujfalusi, Pasqual, Semioli, Pazienza (Kuzmanovic 46), Liverani, Montolivo, Mutu, Vieri (Pazzini 57).

Hammarby (0) 2 *(Andersson 49, 65)*
Braga (0) 1 *(Linz 58)* 6971
Hammarby: Hellstrom; Johansson, Monteiro, Sleyman, Traore, Chanko, Andersson, Zengin, Laitinen (Gunnarsson 90), Castro-Tello (Saarenpaa 72), Guara (Juliusson 88).
Braga: Dani; Paulo Jorge, Carlos Fernandes, Frechaut, Joao Pereira, Andres Madrid, Vandinho (Jailson 88), Jorginho, Wender (Hussain 83), Linz, Lenny (Joao Pinto 61).

Hapoel Tel Aviv (0) 0
AIK Stockholm (0) 0 9000
Hapoel Tel Aviv: Enyeama; Dos Santos, Antebi, Bondarv, Duani, Natcho (Oved 68), Badir, Abedi (Peretz 87), Mazuwa, Asulin, Fabio Junior (Sabag 74).
AIK Stockholm: Orlund; Arnefjord, Tamandi, Jonsson, Carlsson, Monsalvo (Rubarth 71), Tjernstrom, Pavey (Daniel Mendes 90), Stephensson, Johnsson, Ivan (Valdemarin 65).

Heerenveen (3) 5 *(Bradley 20, 60, Sibon 30, 35, Bak Nielsen 59)*
Helsingborg (0) 3 *(Larsson 53, 70 (pen), Omotoyossi 58)* 15,000
Heerenveen: Vandenbussche; Bak Nielsen, Breuer, Dingsdag, Zuiverloon, Bradley (Prager 72), Beerens, Pranjic, Roorda (Poulsen 76), Sulejmani, Sibon (Matusiak 66).
Helsingborg: Andersson D; Jakobsson, Beloufa (Castan 46), Andersson C, Tamboura, Dahl, Lantz (Wahlstedt 46), Skulasson, Kolar (Unkuri 87), Omotoyossi, Larsson.

Larissa (2) 2 *(Bakayoko 33, Cleyton 35)*
Blackburn Rovers (0) 0 8126
Larissa: Kotsolis S; Dabizas, Forster, Katsiaros, Kyriakidis, Galitsios, Cleyton (Kalantzis 85), Sarmiento, Fotakis, Alexandrou (Gikas 77), Bakayoko (Venetis 90).
Blackburn Rovers: Friedel; Emerton, Warnock, Dunn, Nelsen (Khizanishvili 57), Ooijer, Bentley, Savage, Santa Cruz, McCarthy (Tugay 78), Pedersen (Derbyshire 62).

Leverkusen (2) 3 *(Kiessling 19, 78, Rolfes 32)*

Uniao Leiria (1) 1 *(Joao Paulo 29)* 16,331

Leverkusen: Adler; Haggui, Friedrich, Vidal, Castro, Rolfes, Barnetta, Gresko■, Schneider (Barbarez 56), Gekas (Sarpei 82), Kiessling.
Uniao Leiria: Fernando; Lukasiewicz (Faria■ 49), Eder, Bruno Miguel, Laranjeiro, Eder Gaucho, Alhandra (Sougou 61), Tiago, Paulo Cesar, Cadu Da Silva (Tonito 66), Joao Paulo.

Lokomotiv Sofia (0) 1 *(Dafchev 51)*

Rennes (1) 3 *(Leroy 40, 90, Cheyrou 75)* 1800

Lokomotiv Sofia: Golubovic; Dobrev, Varbanov, Savic (Adelino 46), Dafchev, Koilov (Atanasov 61), Orachev, Karadzhinov, Paskov, Antunovic (Zlatinski 74), Baldovaliev.
Rennes: Pouplin; Edman, Fanni, Hansson, Jeunechamp (Marveaux 64), Leroy, Cheyrou, M'Bia Etoundi, Sorlin, Wiltord (Briand 64), Thomert (Emerson 78).

Midtjylland (1) 1 *(Babatunde 30)*

Lokomotiv Moscow (0) 3 *(Samedov 58, Bilyaletdinov 70, Sychev 90)* 5885

Midtjylland: Raska; Troest, Afriyie, Klimpl, Poulsen C, Madsen (Olsen D 66), Thygesen, Poulsen S, Oluwafemi, Kristensen (Dadu 77), Babatunde (Olsen C 73).
Lokomotiv Moscow: Pelizzoli; Ivanovic, Sennikov, Gurenko, Efimov, Maminov, Asatiani, Yanbaev (Samedov 51), Bilyaletdinov, Odemwingie, Sychev.

Mlada Boleslav (0) 0

Palermo (0) 1 *(Jankovic 90)* 4110

Mlada Boleslav: Miller; Rolko, Kopic, Rajnoch, Matejovsky, Vorisek, Hrdlicka, Taborsky (Reznicek 89), Sedlacek, Mendy (Kalina 67), Kysela.
Palermo: Agliardi; Zaccardo, Diana, Barzagli, Rinaudo, Tedesco (Simplicio 86), Migliaccio, Jankovic, Brienza (Caserta 58), Bresciano (Amauri 69), Cavani.

Nuremberg (0) 0

Rapid Bucharest (0) 0 40,066

Nuremberg: Blazek; Wolf, Pinola, Reinhardt, Galasek, Misimovic, Mintal, Kristiansen (Benko 86), Kluge (Engelhardt 64), Mnari (Kennedy 74), Charisteas.
Rapid Bucharest: Andrade; Perja, Sapunaru, Maftei, Grigorie (Dica 64), Maldarasanu, Grigore, Bozovic, Cesinha (Mazilu 90), Boya, Buga (Burdujan 46).

Pacos Ferreira (0) 0

AZ (0) 1 *(Pocognoli 89)* 5000

Pacos Ferreira: Pecanha; Roversio, Luiz Carlos, Mangualde, Valdir, Edson (Pedrinha 71), Cristiano, Fernando Pilar (Carioca 71), Dede, Filipe Anunciacao, Ricardinho (Renato Queiros 84).
AZ: Waterman; Jaliens, Opdam (Pocognoli 73), Donk, De Zeeuw, Steinsson, Martens, Agustien, Jenner (El Hamdaoui 80), Ari, Dembele (Pelle 58).

Rabotnicki (0) 1 *(Milisavljevic 53)*

Bolton Wanderers (0) 1 *(Meite 84)* 16,000

Rabotnicki: Madzovski; Demiri, Stanisic, Babatunde, Bozinovski, Vajs, Osmani (Pejcic 65), Gligorov, Milisavljevic (Velkovski 71), Nedzipi, Trickovski (Selim 89).
Bolton Wanderers: Jaaskelainen; Hunt (O'Brien J 75), Gardner, McCann (O'Brien A 63), Cid (Braaten 63), Meite, Nolan, Speed, Anelka, Davies, Diouf.

Sampdoria (1) 2 *(Delvecchio 17, Bellucci 58)*

Aalborg (1) 2 *(Johansson 18, Prica 54)* 15,000

Sampdoria: Castellazzi; Gastaldello, Bastrini (Pieri 82), Zenoni (Volpi 64), Ziegler, Palombo, Franceschini, Sammarco, Delvecchio (Montella 55), Bellucci, Caracciolo.
Aalborg: Zaza; Jakobsen M, Pedersen, Califf, Olesen, Johansson, Augustinussen, Risgard, Enevoldsen, Prica, Curth.

Sarajevo (0) 1 *(Milosevic 90)*

Basle (1) 2 *(Carlitos 11, Ergic 63)* 10,000

Sarajevo: Fejzic; Milosevic, Hadzic (Maksimovic 46), Saraba, Babic, Muharemovic, Basic, Repuh (Janjos 72), Dzakmic (Turkovic 46), Grujic, Rascic.
Basle: Costanzo; Majstorovic, Nakata, Marque, Zanni, Huggel, Chipperfield (Frei 72), Ergic, Carlitos, Streller (Eduardo 85), Caicedo (Degen 65).

Sion (3) 3 *(Dominguez 7, Vanczak 10, Song 31 (og))*

Galatasaray (1) 2 *(Lincoln 39, Linderoth 67)* 15,000

Sion: Vailati; Kali (Mijadinoski 71), Nwaneri, Alioui (Geiger 50), Paito, Vanczak, Buhler, Chedli, Obradovic, Dominguez, Adeshina (Zakrzewski 62).
Galatasaray: Orkun; Song, Ugur, Volkan, Servet, Linderoth, Lincoln, Hasan Sas, Carrusca (Ayhan 38), Hakan Sukur (Ismael 88), Nonda (Umit K 61).

Sochaux (0) 0

Panionios (1) 2 *(Djebbour 27, Fernandez 55)* 9469

Sochaux: Richert; Afolabi, Perquis (Daf 82), Pichot, Pitau, N'Daw, Sene, Dalmat, Pancrate, Vargas (Dagano 46), Birsa (Quercia 46).
Panionios: Kresic; Maniatis, Pletsch, Majstorovic, Spyropoulos, Makos, Kumordzi, Goundoulakis (Wagner 90), Fernandez (Gaspar 82), Djebbour, Kodi (Kapetanos 75).

Sparta Prague (0) 0

Odense (0) 0 17,247

Sparta Prague: Postulka; Repka, Kladrubsky, Pospech, Kadlec, Horvath, Kisel (Petrzela 63), Abraham, Dosek (Rezek 67), Slepicka, Matusovic.
Odense: Onyszko; Laursen, Christensen A, Helveg, Sorensen, Troest, Andreasen, Bisgaard (Nymann 74), Borring, Timm (Jacobsen 90), Nielsen D (Bechara 88).

Spartak Moscow (3) 5 *(Pavlyuchenko 6, 13, 19, Welliton 55, Titov 57)*

Hacken (0) 0 15,000

Spartak Moscow: Pletikosa; Geder, Soava, Shishkin, Dedura, Mozart (Sabitov 61), Titov, Torbinskiy, Bystrov (Boyarintsev 68), Pavlyuchenko, Welliton (Dzyuba 59).
Hacken: Hysen; Lind, Lucic, Forsell, Marek, Ze Antonio, Mambo Mumba (Friberg 85), Skulason (Holster 72), Henriksson, Larsson (Ljung 65), De Oliveira.

Tampere United (1) 2 *(Wiss 7, Petrescu 68)*

Bordeaux (0) 3 *(Cavenaghi 47, 90, Micoud 89)* 5300

Tampere United: Kaven; Lindstrom, Myntti, Aho (Hynynen 64), Jarvinen, Ojanpera, Kujala, Wiss, Pohja, Petrescu, Nwoke.
Bordeaux: Rame; Jemmali, Diawara, Bregerie, Marange, Tremoulinas (Wendel 65), Fernando (Micoud 64), Ducasse, Cavenaghi, Obertan, Chamakh.

Tottenham Hotspur (4) 6 *(Kaboul 5, Dawson 40, Keane 42, Bent 43, Defoe 65, 90)*

Anorthosis (0) 1 *(Zlogar 81)* 35,780

Tottenham Hotspur: Cerny; Chimbonda, Assou-Ekotto (Bale 79), Zokora, Kaboul, Dawson, Lennon, Huddlestone, Keane (Defoe 62), Bent, Malbranque (Taarabt 69).
Anorthosis: Beqaj; Katsavakis, Nicolaou (Panagi 58), Loumpoutis, Lambrou, Zlogar (Deanov 81), Poursaitidis, Fabinho (Pahars 64), Skopelitis, Sosin, William.

Toulouse (0) 0

CSKA Sofia (0) 0 14,201

Toulouse: Douchez; Fofana, Congre, Ilunga, Cetto, Batiles, Sirieix, Emana Edzimbi, Dieuze, Mansare (Bergougnoux 58), Elmander (Gignac 77).
CSKA Sofia: Ivanov; Tunchev, Vujadinovic, Iliev V, Todorov, Yanchev, Chigozie (Garces 89), Kabous, Marquinos (Iliev G 65), Dimitrov (Amuneke 76), Nei.

Villarreal (2) 4 *(Nihat 5, 50, Senna 17, Tomasson 53)*

BATE Borisov (0) 1 *(Zhavnerchik 67)* 15,000

Villarreal: Diego Lopez; Godin, Javi Venta, Angel, Fuentes, Cani, Matias Fernandez, Senna (Mavuba 55), Bruno Soriano, Tomasson (Rossi 62), Nihat (Josico 75).
BATE Borisov: Fedorovich; Radkov, Khagush, Sakharov (Nekhaychik 68), Kazantsev, Likhtarovich (Zhavnerchik 62), Platonov P, Ermakovich, Krivets, Platonov D, Bliznyuk (Sivakov 73).

Zenit (1) 3 *(Arshavin 38, 65, Kim 86)*

Standard Liege (0) 0 19,500

Zenit: Contofalsky; Kim, Lombaerts, Hagen, Anyukov, Sirl, Zyryanov, Timoshchuk, Dominguez, Pogrebnyak, Arshavin.
Standard Liege: Renard; Bonfim, Onyewu, Camozzato, Sarr, Defour, Toama, Fellaini, Witsel (Dufer 82), Mbokani (Lukunku 79), De Camargo.

FIRST ROUND SECOND LEG

Tuesday, 2 October 2007

Panathinaikos (2) 3 *(Papadopoulos 44 (pen), 45, 74 (pen))*

Artmedia (0) 0 6200

Panathinaikos: Malarz; Sarriegi, Morris, Vintra, Romero (Seric 62), Karagounis (Ivanschitz 69), Tziolis, Nilsson, Dimoutsos, Papadopoulos, N'Doye (Mantzios 62).
Artmedia: Hyll; Guede, Dosoudil, Cisovsky, Urbanek, Burak■, Obzera (Mraz 64), Fodrek (Gajdos 77), Kozak, Halenar, Piroska (Farkas 46).

Thursday, 4 October 2007

AIK Stockholm (0) 0

Hapoel Tel Aviv (0) 1 *(Oved 63)* 9082

AIK Stockholm: Westberg; Johansson, Arnefjord, Tamandi (Stephenson 71), Jonsson, Monsalvo (Bengtsson 84), Tjernstrom, Pavey, Johnson, Ivan, Valdemarin.
Hapoel Tel Aviv: Enyeama; Dos Santos, Antebi, Manzur (Tai Chen 85), Duani, Badir, Oved (Natcho 88), Abedi, Mazuwa, Asulin (Dego 42), Fabio Junior.

AZ (0) 0

Pacos Ferreira (0) 0 13,418

AZ: Waterman; Jaliens, Opdam, Donk, De Zeeuw, Steinsson, Martens (Mendes da Silva 77), Agustien, Jenner, Ari, Dembele (Cziommer 57).
Pacos Ferreira: Pecanha; Luiz Carlos, Mangualde, Ferreira, Tiago, Edson (Carioca 81), Fernando Pilar (Edson Di 81), Dede, Filipe Anunciacao, Renato Queiros (Furtado 69), Ricardinho.

Aalborg (0) 0

Sampdoria (0) 0 10,398

Aalborg: Zaza; Jakobsen M, Pedersen (Olfers 81), Califf, Olesen, Johansson, Augustinussen, Risgard, Enevoldsen (Lindstrom 87), Prica, Nomvethe (Curth 70).
Sampdoria: Castellazzi; Lucchini, Sala (Delvecchio 81), Campagnaro, Ziegler (Pieri 84), Volpi, Palombo, Sammarco, Bellucci, Caracciolo, Cassano (Montella 61).

Ajax (0) 2 *(Huntelaar 101, 120)*

Dynamo Zagreb (1) 3 *(Modric 34 (pen), Mandzukic 94, 96)* 44,678

Ajax: Stekelenburg; Heitinga, Stam, Van der Wiel (Ogararu 62), Colin (Delorge 33), Emanuelson, Maduro (Urzaiz 105), Gabri, Huntelaar, Suarez, Rommedahl.
Dynamo Zagreb: Koch; Cale, Schildenfeld (Carlos 106), Drpic, Pokrivac, Etto, Modric, Sammir (Guela 69), Vukojevic, Tadic (Mikic 78), Mandzukic.
aet.

Anorthosis (0) 1 *(Fabinho 59)*

Tottenham Hotspur (0) 1 *(Keane 78)* 8000

Anorthosis: Nagy; Tripotseris, Nicolaou, Konstantinou, Ndikumana, Zlogar (Skopelitis 46), Fabinho (Pahars 62), Laban (Deanov 83), Panagi, Frousos, William.
Tottenham Hotspur: Robinson; Stalteri, Lee (Keane 75), Zokora, Dawson, Gardner, Boateng (Bale 69), Huddlestone, Bent (Taarabt 85), Defoe, Malbranque.

BATE Borisov (0) 0

Villarreal (1) 2 *(Cani 24, Angel 77)* 6000

BATE Borisov: Fedorovich; Radkov, Khagush, Sakharov, Filipenko, Likhtarovich, Ermakovich (Zhavnerchik 85), Krivets, Stasevich, Bliznyuk (Platonov P 86), Rodionov (Platonov D 72).
Villarreal: Diego Lopez; Godin, Capdevila (Angel 70), Javi Venta, Fuentes (Cygan 46), Cani, Matias Fernandez, Soriano, Mavuba, Guille Franco (Cazorla 73), Tomasson.

Basle (4) 6 *(Carlitos 9, 10, Streller 19, 29, Huggel 75, Caicedo 90)*

Sarajevo (0) 0 15,124

Basle: Costanzo; Majstorovic, Nakata, Marque, Zanni, Huggel, Frei, Carlitos (Degen 46), Streller (Derdiyok 62), Caicedo, Eduardo (Burgmeier 73).
Sarajevo: Fejzic; Milosevic, Zukic (Kurto 46), Muharemovic, Basic, Maksimovic, Grujic, Janjos (Skoro 79), Mesic (Handzic 80), Rascic, Bucan.

Belenenses (0) 0

Bayern Munich (0) 2 *(Toni 60, Hamit Altintop 77)* 4000

Belenenses: Costinha; Rodrigo Alvim, Rolando, Hugo Alcantara, Devic (Mendonca 72), Ruben Amorim, Silas, Jose Pedro, Weldon (Joao Paulo 79), Roncatto, Candido Costa (Amaral 16).
Bayern Munich: Rensing; Lucio, Demichelis, Jansen, Lell, Ribery (Schlaudraff 68), Hamit Altintop, Ze Roberto (Ottl 73), Van Bommel, Schweinsteiger (Kroos 81), Toni.

Blackburn Rovers (1) 2 *(Derbyshire 45 (pen), Warnock 51)*

Larissa (1) 1 *(Cleyton 17)* 20,741

Blackburn Rovers: Friedel; Emerton, Warnock, Tugay, Ooijer, Samba, Bentley, Mokoena (Pedersen 65), Santa Cruz, Derbyshire (McCarthy 68), Dunn (Savage 77).
Larissa: Kotsolis S; Dabizas, Forster, Katsiaros, Kyriakidis, Galitsios (Kalatantzis 77), Cleyton, Sarmiento, Fotakis, Alexandrou (Kotsios 56), Bakayoko (Gikas 90).

Bolton Wanderers (0) 1 *(Anelka 68)*

Rabotnicki (0) 0 18,932

Bolton Wanderers: Jaaskelainen; O'Brien J, Michalik, Alonso (Giannakopoulos 46), O'Brien A, Cid, Guthrie, Wilhelmsson, Braaten (Diouf 75), Davies (Anelka 66), McCann.
Rabotnicki: Pacovski; Demiri, Stanisic, Babatunde (Bozinovski 75), Kovacevic, Vajs, Osmani (Velkovski 46), Gligorov, Milisavljevic, Nedzipi, Trickovski (Pejcic 63).

Bordeaux (0) 1 *(Chamakh 50)*

Tampere United (0) 1 *(Ojanpera 51)* 8445

Bordeaux: Rame; Jemmali, Bregerie, Marange, Planus (Diawara 46), Tremoulinas, Diarra (Micoud 66), Ducasse, Cavenaghi (Alonso 74), Obertan, Chamakh.
Tampere United: Kaven; Lindstrom, Myntti, Aho, Jarvinen, Ojanpera, Kujala, Savolainen, Pohja, Nwoke (Hjelm 80), Niemi.

Braga (0) 4 *(Wender 46, Jorginho 68, Linz 80 (pen), Castanheira 90)*

Hammarby (0) 0 9301

Braga: Dani; Paulo Jorge, Frechaut, Joao Pereira, Ze Manel (Hussain 64), Cesar Peixoto, Andres Madrid, Vandinho, Jorginho (Jailson 76), Wender (Castanheira 85), Linz.
Hammarby: Moussan; Johansson, Sleyman, Saarenpaa, Traore, Chanko, Eguren, Andersson, Zengin (Castro-Tello 74), Laitinen, Guara (Davies 79).

CSKA Sofia (0) 1 *(Nei 65 (pen))*

Toulouse (0) 1 *(Gignac 90)* 18,000

CSKA Sofia: Ivanov; Vujandinovic, Iliev V, Lanzaat, Todorov, Yanchev, Kabous, Marquinos (Garces 59), Dimitrov (Kotev 87), Amuneke (Chigozie■ 73), Nei.
Toulouse: Douchez; Congre, Ebondo, Ilunga, Cetto, Batiles (Bergougnoux 65), Sirieix (Gignac 78), Emana Edzimbi, Dieuze (Arribage 90), Mansare, Elmander.

Dnepr (0) 1 *(Vorobei 75)*
Aberdeen (1) 1 *(Mackie 28)* 26,275
Dnepr: Kernozenko; Shershun, Rusol, Denisov, Shelayev, Kankava (Kravchenko 58), Andrienko, Nazarenko, Lipa, Samodin (Karnilenka 74), Vorobei.
Aberdeen: Langfield; Hart, Nicholson, Diamond, Considine, Severin, Jamie Smith (Mair 46), Clark, Mackie (Lovell 71), Foster, Young.

Elfsborg (0) 0
Dinamo Bucharest (1) 1 *(Danciulescu 31 (pen))* 6827
Elfsborg: Wiland; Karlsson, Andersson, Mobaeck, Bjorck (Bajrami 81), Augustsson, Ilola, Svensson A, Alexandersson (Ishizaki 73), Svensson M, Keene (Berglund 78).
Dinamo Bucharest: Lobont; Pulhac, Moti, Radu, Galliquio, Margaritescu (Ropotan 89), Munteanu, Cristea, Danciulescu, Bratu (Ganea 80), Oprita (Chiacu 65).

Erciyesspor (0) 0
Atletico Madrid (3) 5 *(Aguero 6, 43, Jurado 13, Maxi Rodriguez 53 (pen), Forlan 79)* 8000
Erciyesspor: Kaya; Huseyin, Adem, Kamil, Aydin, Omer (Emre 46), Kazim (Ilker 73), Ilhan, Koksal (Ali 86), Alaattin, Burhan.
Atletico Madrid: Abbiati; Antonio Lopez, Pernia, Eller (Pablo Ibanez 46), Ze Castro, Cleber Santana, Raul Garcia (Reyes 61), Maxi Rodriguez, Jurado, Luis Garcia, Aguero (Forlan 46).

FC Brugge (0) 1 *(Clement 76)*
Brann (2) 2 *(Helstad 14, Winters 39)* 14,570
FC Brugge: Stijnen; Klukowski, Clement, Kucera (Leko 46), Priske, Englebert (Sterchele 46), Blondel, Simaeys■, Geraerts, Sonck, Salou.
Brann: Opdal; Dahl, Corrales, Bjarnason, Andresen, Solli, Huseklepp (Guntveit 82), Bakke, Sigurdsson K (Karadas 46), Helstad, Winters (El-Fakiri 55).

FC Copenhagen (0) 2 *(Allback 76, Gronkjaer 112 (pen))*
Lens (1) 1 *(Carriere 14)* 23,861
FC Copenhagen: Christiansen; Jensen, Hangeland, Gravgaard■, Norregaard (Nordstrand 60), Silberbauer (Wurtz 72), Gronkjaer, Hutchinson, Kvist, Sionko, Allback (Jorgensen 101).
Lens: Runje; Coulibaly, Aubey, Bisevac, Carriere, Akale (Dindane 74), Keita (Kovacevic 81), Lacourt, Demont, Sable, Pieroni (Monterrubio 92).
aet.

Fiorentina (0) 1 *(Mutu 59)*
Groningen (0) 1 *(Nevland 56)* 26,925
Fiorentina: Frey; Kroldrup, Gamberini, Ujfalusi, Pasqual, Donadel (Kuzmanovic 98), Semioli, Liverani (Santana 57), Montolivo, Mutu, Vieri (Pazzini 82).
Groningen: Van Loo; Silva, Sankoh, Kruiswijk, Stenman, Lovre, Levchenko, Meerdink, Lindgren, Berg (Van de Laak 45), Nevland (Kolder 101).
aet; Fiorentina won 4-3 on penalties.

Galatasaray (3) 5 *(Umit K 22, 28, Lincoln 36, Arda 67, Ismael 90)*
Sion (0) 1 *(Nwaneri 88)* 22,600
Galatasaray: Orkun; Song, Ugur, Volkan, Servet, Linderoth (Ismael 88), Baris, Lincoln (Nonda 82), Arda (Hasan Sas 73), Hakan Sukur, Umit K.
Sion: Vailati; Kali, Nwaneri, Alioui (Reset 69), Paito, Vanczak, Buhler, Beto (Geiger 69), Obradovic, Dominguez, Adeshina (Saborio 77).

Hacken (0) 1 *(Henriksson 84)*
Spartak Moscow (1) 3 *(Titov 7, Bazhenov 80, Dzyuba 90)* 1103
Hacken: Hysen; Lucic (Lind 69), Jarlegren, Forsell, Marek, Ljung (Friberg 75), Mambo Mumba, Skulason, Henriksson, Larsson, De Oliveira (Olofsson 69).
Spartak Moscow: Pletikosa; Kudryashov, Dedura, Mozart, Boyarintsev, Titov (Sabitov 61), Kovac, Kalynychenko (Bazhenov 76), Parshivlyuk, Pavlyuchenko (Welliton 58), Dzyuba.

Hamburg (1) 3 *(Guerrero 40, 52, Van der Vaart 72)*
Litex (1) 1 *(Popov R 38)* 38,200
Hamburg: Rost; Atouba, Reinhardt, Mathijsen, De Jong, Jarolim, Trochowski, Demel, Van der Vaart (Zidan 74), Guerrero (Choupo-Moting 73), Olic (Ben-Hatira 79).
Litex: Todorov; Cichero, Venkov, Manolev (Dudu 67), Nikolov, Popov R, Tom (Genchev 77), Boudarene (Bibishkov 77), Sandrinho, Beto, Popov I.

Helsingborg (3) 5 *(Larsson 19, Dahl 37, Omotoyossi 45, 80, Makondele 51)*
Heerenveen (0) 1 *(Sibon 89)* 6296
Helsingborg: Andersson D; Jakobsson, Castan, Andersson C (Landgren 90), Tamboura, Dahl (Kolar 90), Skulasson, Wahlstedt, Omotoyossi (Unkuri 84), Makondele, Larsson.
Heerenveen: Vandenbussche; Bak Nielsen, Breuer, Dingsdag, Zuiverloon, Bradley (Sibon 58), Beerens, Pranjic, Roorda, Afonso Alves (Prager 76), Sulejmani (Matusiak 68).

Lokomotiv Moscow (2) 2 *(Bilyaletdinov 10, Maminov 15)*
Midtjylland (0) 0 9800
Lokomotiv Moscow: Pelizzoli; Spahic, Ivanovic, Sennikov (Yanbaev 46), Gurenko, Efimov (Rodolfo 43), Maminov (Samedov 58), Asatiani, Bilyaletdinov, Odemwingie, Sychev.
Midtjylland: Raska; Troest, Afriyie, Klimpl, Thygesen, Oluwafemi (Roll 61), Poulsen S (Jessen 57), Poulsen C, Dadu, Olsen D, Babatunde (Kristensen 46).

Metalist Kharkiv (1) 2 *(Edmar 21, Mahdoufi 52)*
Everton (0) 3 *(Lescott 48, McFadden 72, Anichebe 88)* 27,500
Metalist Kharkiv: Goryainov; Obradovic, Gueye, Bordian (Nwoga 85), Valyayev, Edmar, Slyusar, Mahdoufi, Rykun, Devic (Zezeto 90), Jakobia (Danilov 74).
Everton: Howard; Neville, Lescott, Yobo (Baines 76), Stubbs, Jagielka (Anichebe 62), Osman, Pienaar, Yakubu, McFadden (Hibbert 90), Arteta.

Odense (0) 0
Sparta Prague (0) 0 10,565
Odense: Onyszko; Laursen, Christensen A, Helveg, Sorensen, Troest, Andreasen, Bisgaard, Borring, Tim (Jacobsen 46) (Saeternes 101), Nielsen D (Bechara 38).
Sparta Prague: Postulka; Repka, Kladrubsky, Brezinsky, Pospech, Kadlec, Ludovic (Kolar 66), Kisel, Abraham (Horvath 91), Slepicka (Dosek 74), Kulic.
aet; Sparta Prague won 4-3 on penalties.

Palermo (0) 0
Mlada Boleslav (0) 1 *(Sedlacek 90)* 6335
Palermo: Agliardi; Capuano, Cassani, Barzagli, Rinaudo, Tedesco (Diana 71), Migliaccio, Bresciano (Caserta 88), Simplicio, Cavani, Amauri (Jankovic 83).
Mlada Boleslav: Miller; Rolko, Kopic, Rajnoch, Matejovsky, Polacek (Kalina 53), Vorisek, Taborsky (Vanecek 73), Sedlacek, Mendy, Kysela (Holub 79).
aet; Mlada Boleslav won 4-2 on penalties.

Panionios (0) 0
Sochaux (0) 1 *(Kumordzi 53 (og))* 9000
Panionios: Kresic; Maniatis, Pletsch, Majstorovic, Spyropoulos, Makos (Skoufalis 83), Kumordzi, Goundoulakis, Fernandez (Berthe 90), Djebbour, Kodi (Nikolaou 46).
Sochaux: Richert; Afolabi, Perquis, Pichot, Pitau, N'Daw, Isabey, Jokic (Pancrate 80), Dalmat (Quercia 35), Dagano (Erding 66), Birsa.

Rapid Bucharest (1) 2 *(Cesinha 15, Lazar 90)*
Nuremberg (1) 2 *(Kluge 22, Misimovic 55)* 11,000
Rapid Bucharest: Andrade; Sapunaru, Constantin, Maftei, Grigorie (Mazilu 59), Maldarasanu, Grigore (Lazar 46), Bozovic, Cesinha, Boya (Burdujan 63), Buga.
Nuremberg: Blazek; Wolf, Spiranovic, Reinhardt, Galasek, Misimovic, Mintal (Charisteas 71), Kristiansen, Kluge (Kennedy 85), Mnari (Schmidt 68), Saenko.

Rapid Vienna (0) 0

Anderlecht (1) 1 *(Akin 23)* 17,400

Rapid Vienna: Payer; Tokic (Harding 74), Patocka, Hiden, Thonhofer, Heikkinen, Hofmann, Korkmaz (Kavlak 21), Boskovic, Bilic, Bazina (Fabiano 59).
Anderlecht: Zitka; Deschacht, Van Damme, Juhasz (Wasilewski 73), Pareja, Biglia, Polak, Hassan, De Man, Akin (Frutos 77), Legear (Boussoufa 80).

Red Star Belgrade (1) 1 *(Castillo 42)*

Groclin (0) 0 20,000

Red Star Belgrade: Randelovic; Andelkovic, Tutoric, Gueye, Basta, Milijas, Koroman (Trisovic 90), Lucas, Molina, Castillo (Bogdanovic 46), Jestrovic (Barcos 66).
Groclin: Przyrowski; Mynar, Lazarevski, Telichowski (Batata 79), Cumbev, Jodlowiec, Piechniak, Lato, Rocki (Ivanovski 54), Majewski (Babnic 64), Sikora.

Rennes (1) 1 *(Marveaux 25)*

Lokomotiv Sofia (2) 2 *(Antunovic 37, 41)* 16,208

Rennes: Luzi; Borne, Hansson, Jeunechamp, Cheyrou, M'Bia, Sorlin, Marveaux, Pagis (Briand 75), Kembo Ekoko (Leroy 46), Badiane (Thomert 46).
Lokomotiv Sofia: Golubovic; Donchev, Markov, Dobrev, Savic, Dafchev, Koilov (Zlatinski 85), Orachev, Karadzhinov, Atanasov (Baldovaliev 71), Antunovic (Djilas 80).

Salzburg (1) 1 *(Lokvenc 19)*

AEK Athens (0) 0 15,500

Salzburg: Ochs; Bodnar, Dudic, Meyer, Carboni, Jezek, Steinhofer, Leitgeb (Janocko 64), Aufhauser, Lokvenc, Vonlanthen (Rakic 60).
AEK Athens: Macho; Edson Ramos, Arruabarrena, Geraldo, Dellas, Kafes, Nsaliwa, Tozser (Kone 88), Rivaldo (Papastathopoulos 67), Manduca (Blanco 50), Lyberopoulos.

Standard Liege (1) 1 *(Contofalsky 36 (og))*

Zenit (0) 1 *(Pogrebnyak 81)* 25,000

Standard Liege: Aragon; Bonfim, Onyewu▪, Camozzato, Sarr, Xavier (Mbokani 46), Defour, Toama (Dembele 72), Fellaini, Witsel, De Camargo (Lukunku 80).
Zenit: Contofalsky; Skrtel, Kim, Lombaerts, Anyukov, Sirl (Maksimov 89), Zyryanov (Radimov 77), Denisov (Dominguez 72), Timoshchuk, Pogrebnyak▪, Arshavin.

Twente (1) 3 *(Wielaert 29, Engelaar 117, Zomer 120)*

Getafe (0) 2 *(Belenguer 101, Granero 103)* 13,200

Twente: Boschker; Wielaert, Zomer, Heubach, Engelaar, Wilkshire, Wellenberg, El Ahmadi (Brama 105), Denneboom (Elia 105), N'Kufo▪, Hersi (Arnautovic 110).
Getafe: Abbondanzieri; Cata Diaz, Belenguer, Licht, Celestini, Mario Cotelo (Sousa 82), Nacho, Braulio (Uche 46), De la Red, Manu Del Moral, Pablo Hernandez (Granero 7).
aet.

Uniao Leiria (2) 3 *(Cadu Da Silva 3, Joao Paulo 13, Laranjeiro 90)*

Leverkusen (1) 2 *(Papadopoulos 11, Kiessling 87)* 1800

Uniao Leiria: Fernando; Hugo Costa, Laranjeiro, Eder Gaucho, Alhandra (Marco Soares 54), Sougou, Tiago, Cadu Da Silva, Maciel (N'Gal 61), Tonito (Zongo 72), Joao Paulo.
Leverkusen: Adler; Haggui, Friedrich, Sarpei, Vidal (Sinkiewicz 90), Castro, Rolfes, Barnetta (Dum 90), Kiessling, Papadopoulos (Schwegler 46), Barbarez.

Valerenga (0) 2 *(Dos Santos 51, Bak 87 (og))*

FK Austria (1) 2 *(Kuljic 22, Acimovic 90)* 3868

Valerenga: Arason; Jepsen, Storbaek, Thomassen, Johnsen (Horn 60), Dos Santos, Jalland, Grindheim (Holm T 66), Holm D, Berre, Thorvaldsson (Mila 46).
FK Austria: Safar (Fornezzi 46); Troyansky, Bak, Gercaliu (Majstorovic 81), Schiemer, Blanchard, Sariyar, Acimovic, Standfest, Lafata (Metz 75), Kuljic.

Zaragoza (1) 2 *(Oliveira 19, Sergio Garcia 75)*

Aris Salonika (0) 1 *(Javito 63)* 33,100

Zaragoza: Cesar; Cuartero (Gabi 65), Ayala, Juanfran, Sergio, Luccin, Aimar, D'Alessandro, Zapater, Oliveira (Sergio Garcia 61), Diego Milito.
Aris Salonika: Chalkias; Neto, Ronaldo, Marco Aurelio, Papadopoulos, Nebegieras, Toni Calvo (Javito 58), Ronald Garcia, Siston (Vangeli 88), Ivic, Koke (Kouloucheris 81).

Zurich (1) 3 *(Kollar 37, Abdi 78, Alphonse 82)*

Empoli (0) 0 13,600

Zurich: Leoni; Stahel (Lampi 27), Rochat, Barmettler, Tihinen, Kollar, Okonkwo, Abdi, Alphonse (Hassli 82), Raffael (Konde 75), Chikhaoui.
Empoli: Bassi; Piccolo, Ascoli (Antonini 61), Rincon▪, Marzoratti, Abate, Marianini, Vannucchi (Pozzi 46), Giacomazzi, Marchisio (Giovinco 46), Volpato.

GROUP STAGE

GROUP A

Thursday, 25 October 2007

Everton (1) 3 *(Cahill 14, Osman 50, Anichebe 85)*

Larissa (0) 1 *(Cleyton 65)* 33,777

Everton: Howard; Hibbert, Baines, Yobo, Lescott, Carsley, Osman, Pienaar (Stubbs 87), McFadden (Gravesen 65), Cahill (Anichebe 65), Arteta.
Larissa: Kotsoliss; Venetidis, Dabizas, Forster (Venetis 79), Kyriakidis (Labropoulos 75), Galitsios, Cleyton, Sarmiento, Fotakis, Parra (Kalantzis 58), Bakayoko.

Zenit (1) 1 *(Timoshchuk 43 (pen))*

AZ (1) 1 *(Ari 20)* 19,000

Zenit: Contofalsky; Skrtel, Kim, Lombaerts, Anyukov, Sirl, Zyryanov, Timoshchuk, Dominguez (Maksimov 81), Fatih, Arshavin.
AZ: Waterman; Jaliens, Opdam, Donk, Mendes da Silva (El Hamdaoui 59), Cziommer (Medunjanin 90), Martens (Pocognoli 49), Koenders, Agustien, Ari▪, Dembele.

Thursday, 8 November 2007

Larissa (0) 2 *(Alexandrou 58, Fotakis 62)*

Zenit (1) 3 *(Pogrebnyak 39, Zyryanov 70, Fatih 78)* 14,508

Larissa: Kotsolis S; Kotsios, Venetidis (Katsiaros 46), Dabizas, Kyriakidis (Labropoulos 83), Galitsios, Cleyton, Sarmiento, Fotakis, Alexandrou (Kalantzis 74), Bakayoko.
Zenit: Contofalsky; Skrtel, Kim, Lombaerts, Anyukov, Ricksen (Radimov 72), Sirl, Zyryanov, Timoshchuk, Pogrebnyak (Fatih 72), Arshavin (Dominguez 46).

Nuremberg (0) 0

Everton (0) 2 *(Arteta 83 (pen), Anichebe 88)* 44,000

Nuremberg: Blazek; Glauber (Benko 86), Wolf, Schmidt (Kennedy 77), Reinhardt, Galasek, Misimovic, Mintal, Kluge, Mnari, Saenko (Pagenburg 85).
Everton: Howard; Neville, Nuno Valente, Yobo, Lescott, Carsley, Osman, Pienaar (Hibbert 90), Yakubu (Anichebe 75), Cahill (Jagielka 90), Arteta.

Thursday, 29 November 2007

AZ (0) 1 *(Dembele 77)*

Larissa (0) 0 16,800

AZ: Waterman (Romero 32); Jaliens, Opdam, Pocognoli, De Zeeuw, Steinsson, Mendes da Silva, Cziommer (Jenner 74), Agustien, Medunjanin (Pelle 65), Dembele.
Larissa: Kotsolis S; Kotsios■, Dabizas, Katsiaros, Kyriakidis (Bachramis 82), Galitsios, Cleyton, Sarmiento, Fotakis, Alexandrou (Kozlej 82), Kalantzis (Parra 69).

Zenit (0) 2 *(Pogrebnyak 76, Ionov 79)*

Nuremberg (1) 2 *(Charisteas 25, Benko 84)* 21,500

Zenit: Contofalsky; Skrtel, Kim, Lombaerts (Ionov 73), Anyukov, Sirl, Zyryanov, Timoshchuk, Dominguez (Radimov 80), Pogrebnyak, Arshavin.
Nuremberg: Blazek; Beauchamp, Wolf, Reinhardt, Galasek, Misimovic, Mintal (Kristiansen 75), Engelhardt (Benko 82), Kluge, Charisteas, Adler (Saenko 46).

Wednesday, 5 December 2007

Everton (0) 1 *(Cahill 85)*

Zenit (0) 0 38,407

Everton: Howard; Neville, Baines, Jagielka, Lescott, Carsley, Pienaar, Cahill, Johnson (Vaughan 81), McFadden (Anichebe 64), Arteta.
Zenit: Malafeev; Skrtel, Kim, Lombaerts■, Anyukov (Ho Lee 78), Sirl, Zyryanov, Timoshchuk, Dominguez (Gorshkov 46), Pogrebnyak (Hagen 61), Arshavin.

Nuremberg (0) 2 *(Mintal 83, 85)*

AZ (1) 1 *(De Zeeuw 29)* 35,020

Nuremberg: Blazek; Beauchamp, Wolf, Reinhardt, Galasek, Misimovic (Kristiansen 90), Engelhardt, Kluge, Charisteas, Adler (Saenko 62), Benko (Mintal 38).
AZ: Waterman; Jaliens, Opdam (Koenders 74), Pocognoli, De Zeeuw, Steinsson, Mendes Da Silva, Cziommer (Jenner 80), Agustien, Dembele, Pelle.

Thursday, 20 December 2007

AZ (1) 2 *(Pelle 16, Jaliens 65)*

Everton (2) 3 *(Johnson 2, Jagielka 44, Vaughan 79)* 16,578

AZ: Waterman; Jaliens, Opdam, Pocognoli (Agustien 77), De Zeeuw (Jenner 65), Steinsson, Vormer, Mendes da Silva, Cziommer (El Hamdaoui 66), Dembele, Pelle.
Everton: Wessels; Hibbert, Nuno Valente, Gravesen (Rodwell 80), Lescott, Carsley, Jagielka, Pienaar (Vidarsson 69), Johnson (Vaughan 68), Anichebe, McFadden.

Larissa (1) 1 *(Kozlej 11)*

Nuremberg (1) 3 *(Saenko 44, Mintal 57, Charisteas 73)* 2863

Larissa: Kipouros; Dabizas, Venetis, Katsiaros, Kyriakidis, Gikas (Cleyton 61), Galitsios, Bachramis (Bakayoko 77), Parra (Alexandrou 72), Kalantzis, Kozlej.
Nuremberg: Blazek; Beauchamp, Glauber, Wolf, Reinhardt, Galasek, Misimovic, Mintal, Kluge, Charisteas, Saenko.

Group A Final Table	*P*	*W*	*D*	*L*	*F*	*A*	*Pts*
Everton	4	4	0	0	9	3	12
Nuremberg	4	2	1	1	7	6	7
Zenit	4	1	2	1	6	6	5
AZ	4	1	1	2	5	6	4
Larrisa	4	0	0	4	4	10	0

GROUP B

Thursday, 25 October 2007

Lokomotiv Moscow (1) 3 *(Bilyaletdinov 27, Odemwingie 61, 64)*

Atletico Madrid (1) 3 *(Aguero 16, 85, Forlan 47)* 17,000

Lokomotiv Moscow: Pelizzoli; Rodolfo, Spahic, Ivanovic, Sinnikov, Gurenko (Maminov 90), Efimov (Yanbaev 60), Bilyaletdinov, Odemwingie, Sychev, Samedov (Cocis 81).
Atletico Madrid: Abbiati; Antonio Lopez, Pernia, Eller, Pablo Ibanez, Cleber Santana (Maxi Rodriguez 65), Raul Garcia, Jurado (Maniche 75), Forlan, Aguero, Simao (Luis Garcia 69).

Panathinaikos (1) 3 *(Goumas 11, Papadopoulos 73, Salpigidis 77)*

Aberdeen (0) 0 8154

Panathinaikos: Malarz; Morris, Goumas, Fyssas, Marcelo, Tziolis, Ivanschitz (Seric 81), Nilsson, Dimoutsos, Salpigidis (Mantzios 81), N'Doye (Papadopoulos 59).
Aberdeen: Langfield; Hart, McNamara (De Visscher 75), Diamond, Considine (Mair 61), Severin (Aluko 86), Nicholson, Foster, Young, Miller, Clark.

Thursday, 8 November 2007

Aberdeen (1) 1 *(Diamond 27)*

Lokomotiv Moscow (1) 1 *(Ivanovic 45)* 18,843

Aberdeen: Langfield; Hart, Considine, Foster, Diamond, Severin, Nicholson, Clark (Maguire 66), Aluko (De Visscher 81), Miller (Lovell 85), Young.
Lokomotiv Moscow: Pelizzoli; Rodolfo, Spahic, Ivanovic, Sennikov, Gurenko, Asatiani, Bilyaletdinov, Odemwingie, Sychev, Samedov (Cocis 79).

FC Copenhagen (0) 0

Panathinaikos (1) 1 *(N'Doye 15)* 25,142

FC Copenhagen: Christiansen; Jensen, Hangeland, Antonsson, Wurtz (Norregaard 56), Gronkjaer, Hutchinson, Kvist, Sionko (Silberbauer 56), Nordstrand, Allback.
Panathinaikos: Galinovic; Enakarhire, Goumas, Fyssas, Vintra, Marcelo, Karagounis (Seric 87), Tziolis, Ivanschitz (Dimoutsos 67), Papadopoulos (Salpigidis 76), N'Doye.

Thursday, 29 November 2007

Atletico Madrid (1) 2 *(Forlan 45 (pen), Simao 61)*

Aberdeen (0) 0 30,000

Atletico Madrid: Abbiati; Antonio Lopez, Pernia, Eller, Pablo Ibanez, Motta, Cleber Santana, Maxi Rodriguez (Maniche 71), Forlan (Mista 70), Luis Garcia, Aguero (Simao 46).
Aberdeen: Langfield; Hart, Byrne, McNamara (Clark 34), Diamond, Severin (Maguire 76), Jamie Smith (De Visscher 44), Foster, Young, Miller, Touzani.

Lokomotiv Moscow (0) 0

FC Copenhagen (0) 1 *(Nordstrand 62 (pen))* 11,000

Lokomotiv Moscow: Pelizzoli; Rodolfo (Cocis 85), Spahic■, Ivanovic, Gurenko, Maminov, Asatiani, Bilyaletdinov, Odemwingie (Samedov 46), Sychev, Traore.
FC Copenhagen: Christiansen; Hangeland, Gravgaard, Antonsson, Wendt, Norregaard, Wurtz (Sionko 32), Hutchinson, Kvist, Nordstrand (Ailton 79), Allback.

Wednesday, 5 December 2007

FC Copenhagen (0) 0

Atletico Madrid (1) 2 *(Simao 21, Aguero 62)* 33,034

FC Copenhagen: Christiansen; Jensen, Hangeland, Gravgaard, Wendt, Norregaard, Wurtz (Sionko 54), Hutchinson (Jorgensen 83), Kvist, Nordstrand (Ailton 53), Allback.
Atletico Madrid: Abbiati; Antonio Lopez, Pernia, Eller, Pablo Ibanez, Motta, Cleber Santana (Maniche 73), Forlan (Raul Garcia 72), Luis Garcia, Aguero, Simao (Maxi Rodriguez 67).

Panathinaikos (0) 2 *(Salpigidis 70, 74)*

Lokomotiv Moscow (0) 0 7013

Panathinaikos: Galinovic; Sarriegi, Morris, Fyssas, Simao, Vintra, Romero (Ninis 82), Tziolis, Dimoutsos (Karagounis 66), Papadopoulos, N'Doye (Salpigidis 63).
Lokomotiv Moscow: Pelizzoli; Ivanovic, Sennikov, Gurenko, Maminov (Fomin 82), Cocis, Asatiani, Yanbaev, Bilyaletdinov, Traore (Korchagin 86), Samedov (Kuznetsov 64).

Thursday, 20 December 2007

Aberdeen (0) 4 *(Jamie Smith 47, 55, Antonsson 71 (og), Foster 82)*

FC Copenhagen (0) 0 20,446

Aberdeen: Langfield; Hart, Byrne, Diamond, Considine, Severin, Jamie Smith (Maguire 74), Nicholson, Clark, Aluko (Foster 59), Miller.

FC Copenhagen: Christiansen; Gravgaard, Antonsson, Wendt, Norregaard (Silberbauer 61), Wurtz (Ailton 56), Gronkjaer (Nordstrand 70), Hutchinson, Kvist, Sionko, Allback.

Atletico Madrid (0) 2 *(Raul Garcia 74, Simao 90)*

Panathinaikos (1) 1 *(Salpigidis 34)* 14,000

Atletico Madrid: Abbiati; Antonio Lopez, Eller, Ze Castro (Reyes 61), Luis Perea, Cleber Santana (Simao 46), Raul Garcia■, Luis Garcia, Maxi Rodriguez, Forlan, Aguero (Pablo Ibanez 90).
Panathinaikos: Malarz; Sarriegi, Morris, Fyssas, Simao (Dimoutsos 85), Vintra, Marcelo, Romero (Ivanschitz 68), Tziolis, Papadopoulos, Salpigidis (Mantzios 79).

Group B Final Table	P	W	D	L	F	A	Pts
Atletico Madrid	4	3	1	0	9	4	10
Panathinaikos	4	3	0	1	7	2	9
Aberdeen	4	1	1	2	5	6	4
FC Copenhagen	4	1	0	3	1	7	3
Lokomotiv Moscow	4	0	2	2	4	7	2

GROUP C

Thursday, 25 October 2007

Elfsborg (1) 1 *(Mobaeck 15)*

AEK Athens (0) 1 *(Pappas 49)* 4175

Elfsborg: Wiland; Karlsson, Andersson, Mobaeck, Bjorck, Augustsson, Ilola, Svensson A, Ishizaki (Berglund 88), Alexandersson, Svensson M (Keene 78).
AEK Athens: Moretto; Arruabarrena, Geraldo, Papastathopoulos, Nsaliwa (Kafes 62), Tozser, Manduca, Blanco, Manu (Pappas 46), Bourbos, Julio Cesar (Kone 76).

Villarreal (0) 1 *(Capdevila 87)*

Fiorentina (0) 1 *(Vieri 47)* 18,662

Villarreal: Diego Lopez; Godin, Capdevila, Angel, Fuentes, Josico (Cazorla 63), Cani (Nihat 63), Matias Fernandez, Senna, Tomasson (Pires 79), Rossi.
Fiorentina: Frey; Kroldrup, Dainelli, Balzaretti, Ujfalusi, Pazienza, Liverani, Jorgensen (Vanden Borre 58), Kuzmanovic (Donadel 74), Mutu, Vieri (Osvaldo 65).

Thursday, 8 November 2007

Fiorentina (2) 6 *(Jorgensen 4, 78, Vieri 5, Donadel 62, Kroldrup 65, Di Carmine 87)*

Elfsborg (1) 1 *(Ishizaki 41)* 18,732

Fiorentina: Frey; Kroldrup, Vanden Borre (Pasqual 69), Balzaretti, Ujfalusi, Donadel, Semioli, Pazienza, Jorgensen, Osvaldo (Kuzmanovic 63), Vieri (Di Carmine 82).
Elfsborg: Wiland; Karlsson, Andersson, Mobaeck (Bajrami 81), Bjorck, Augustsson, Ilola, Svensson A, Ishizaki, Alexandersson (Avdic 77), Keene (Svensson M 21).

Mlada Boleslav (0) 1 *(Mendy 90)*

Villarreal (1) 2 *(Nihat 33, Cazorla 56)* 4900

Mlada Boleslav: Miller; Kopic, Rajnoch, Prochazka, Kalina (Vanecek 46), Matejovsky, Vorisek, Hrdlicka (Taborsky 83), Sedlacek (Reznicek 58), Mendy, Kysela.
Villarreal: Diego Lopez; Josemi, Godin, Cygan, Angel (Capdevila 83), Josico, Cazorla, Matias Fernandez, Mavuba, Tomasson, Nihat (Guille Franco 73).

Thursday, 29 November 2007

AEK Athens (1) 1 *(Balzaretti 34 (og))*

Fiorentina (1) 1 *(Osvaldo 29)* 26,386

AEK Athens: Moretto; Edson Ramos, Arruabarrena, Dellas, Papastathopoulos, Nsaliwa (Kafes 71), Kone (Manduca 55), Tozser, Blanco, Manu, Julio Cesar (Pappas 82).
Fiorentina: Frey; Kroldrup, Dainelli, Balzaretti, Pasqual, Liverani, Montolivo, Jorgensen, Kuzmanovic (Gobbi 82), Osvaldo, Vieri (Pazzini 86).

Elfsborg (1) 1 *(Svensson M 31)*

Mlada Boleslav (0) 3 *(Toborsky 67, Mendy 79, Vorisek 90)* 3631

Elfsborg: Wiland; Karlsson, Andersson, Mobaeck, Bjorck (Bajrami 84), Augustsson, Ilola (Avdic 70), Svensson A, Ishizaki, Svensson M, Keene (Berglund 74).
Mlada Boleslav: Pizanowski; Kopic, Reznicek (Taborsky 46), Rajnoch, Prochazka, Matejovsky, Vorisek, Hrdlicka, Vanecek (Kalina 47), Mendy, Kysela (Polacek 90).

Wednesday, 5 December 2007

Mlada Boleslav (0) 0

AEK Athens (0) 1 *(Nsaliwa 46)* 4670

Mlada Boleslav: Pizanowski; Kopic, Reznicek (Taborsky 53), Rajnoch, Prochazka, Matejovsky, Vorisek, Hrdlicka, Sedlacek (Holub 76), Mendy, Kysela (Vanecek 63).
AEK Athens: Moretto; Edson Ramos, Arruabarrena, Geraldo, Dellas, Nsaliwa, Tozser, Rivaldo (Papastathopoulos 89), Blanco (Manduca 46), Manu (Julio Cesar 75), Lyberopoulos.

Villarreal (1) 2 *(Tomasson 2, 51)*

Elfsborg (0) 0 10,000

Villarreal: Diego Lopez; Godin, Capdevila (Javi Venta 75), Cygan, Angel, Cazorla, Matias Fernandez, Senna (Soriano 78), Mavuba, Tomasson, Nihat (Guille Franco 69).
Elfsborg: Wiland; Floren, Andersson, Mobaeck, Augustsson, Svensson A, Avdic, Bajrami (Karlsson 90), Ishizaki, Svensson M (Falk-Olander 85), Keene (Berglund 90).

Thursday, 20 December 2007

AEK Athens (0) 1 *(Rivaldo 68)*

Villarreal (1) 2 *(Mavuba 40, Tomasson 69)* 16,380

AEK Athens: Macho; Edson Ramos, Arruabarrena, Geraldo, Papastathopoulos, Nsaliwa (Kafes 46), Kone (Manduca 60), Tozser, Rivaldo (Pappas 82), Lyberopoulos, Julio Cesar.
Villarreal: Diego Lopez; Josemi, Cygan, Javi Venta, Fuentes, Cazorla (Cani 46), Matias Fernandez, Soriano, Mavuba, Tomasson (Angel 89), Rossi (Guille Franco 69).

Fiorentina (1) 2 *(Mutu 44 (pen), Vieri 67)*

Mlada Boleslav (0) 1 *(Rajnoch 60)* 11,140

Fiorentina: Lupatelli; Kroldrup, Dainelli, Ujfalusi, Pasqual, Donadel (Pazienza 48), Semoli, Liverani, Gobbi, Mutu (Osvaldo 76), Pazzini (Vieri 62).
Mlada Boleslav: Pizanowski; Rolko, Kopic, Rajnoch, Prochazka, Kalina (Holub 65), Vorisek, Hrdlicka (Vanecek 80), Sedlacek, Mendy, Kysela (Taborsky 46).

Group C Final Table	P	W	D	L	F	A	Pts
Villarreal	4	3	1	0	7	3	10
Fiorentina	4	2	2	0	10	4	8
AEK Athens	4	1	2	1	4	4	5
Mlada Boleslav	4	1	0	3	5	6	3
Elfsborg	4	0	1	3	3	12	1

GROUP D

Thursday, 25 October 2007

Basle (0) 1 *(Streller 55)*

Rennes (0) 0 11,407

Basle: Costanzo; Hodel, Majstrovic, Marque, Zanni, Huggel, Chipperfield, Ergic, Carlitos (Frei 86), Streller (Eduardo 89), Caicedo (Degen 60).
Rennes: Luzi; Fanni, Hansson, Jeunechamp, Cheyrou, M'Bia (Borne 59), Didot (Wiltord 65), Sorlin, Marveaux, Pagis, Briand.

Brann (0) 0

Hamburg (0) 1 *(Kompany 61)* 13,029

Brann: Opdal; Dahl, Hanstveit, Bjarnason, Jaiteh (Huseklepp 46), El-Fakiri, Solli, Vaagan Moen (Bjornsson 85), Bakke (Karadas 46), Sigurdsson K, Helstad.
Hamburg: Rost; Atouba, Reinhardt, Mathijsen, Kompany, Boateng, Jarolim, Trochowski (Benjamin 87), Demel, Zidan (Choupo-Moting 90), Olic.

Thursday, 8 November 2007

Dynamo Zagreb (0) 0

Basle (0) 0 28,000

Dynamo Zagreb: Koch; Cale (Santos 70), Schildenfeld, Drpic, Pokrivac, Etto, Modric, Vukojevic, Mandzukic, Guela (Sammir 62), Sokota (Tadic 74).
Basle: Costanzo; Hodel, Majstorovic, Marque, Zanni, Chipperfield (Frei 73), Ergic, Degen, Streller, Caicedo (Burgmeier 76), Eduardo.

Rennes (0) 1 *(Cheyrou 88 (pen))*

Brann (1) 1 *(Karadas 24)* 11,291

Rennes: Luzi; Mensah, Fanni, Hansson, Jeunechamp (Emerson 66), Leroy, Cheyrou, Didot, Marveaux, Pagis, Briand (Kembo Ekoko 81).
Brann: Opdal; Dahl, Hanstveit, Bjarnason, El-Fakiri■, Solli, Huseklepp (Guntveit 55), Bakke, Sigurdsson K, Karadas (Vaagan Moen 55), Helstad.

Thursday, 29 November 2007

Brann (1) 2 *(Bjarnason 45 (pen), Bakke 72)*

Dynamo Zagreb (0) 1 *(Vukojevic 49)* 9962

Brann: Opdal; Dahl, Corrales, Hanstveit, Bjarnason, Solli, Vaagan Moen, Huseklepp (Bjornsson 90), Bakke, Karadas (Guntveit 85), Helstad.
Dynamo Zagreb: Koch; Cale, Schildenfeld■, Drpic, Pokrivac, Etto, Modric, Sammir (Santos 46), Vukojevic (Guela 79), Balaban (Tadic 60), Mandzukic.

Hamburg (1) 3 *(Van der Vaart 30, Choupo-Moting 83, Zidan 90 (pen))*

Rennes (0) 0 36,472

Hamburg: Rost; Reinhardt, Mathijsen, Kompany, Boateng, Benjamin, De Jong (Demel 69), Trochowski, Van der Vaart (Zidan 85), Olic (Choupo-Moting 80), Castelen.
Rennes: Pouplin; Edman (Thomert 46), Borne, Fanni (Badiane 80), Hansson, Leroy, Cheyrou, Sorlin, Marveaux, Wiltord (Emerson 58), Briand.

Wednesday, 5 December 2007

Basle (1) 1 *(Carlitos 40)*

Brann (0) 0 13,731

Basle: Costanzo; Majstorovic, Nakata, Marque, Zanni, Huggel, Ergic, Carlitos, Caicedo (Degen 68), Eduardo, Derdiyok.
Brann: Opdal; Dahl, Guntveit (Sjohage 50), Corrales (Bjornsson 46), Hanstveit, Bjarnason, Solli, Vaagan Moen, Huseklepp, Karadas, Helstad.

Dynamo Zagreb (0) 0

Hamburg (0) 2 *(De Jong 87, Trochowski 90 (pen))* 27,000

Dynamo Zagreb: Koch; Cale, Santos, Drpic, Pokrivac (Sokota 89), Etto, Modric, Sammir (Vrdoljak 76), Vukojevic, Balaban (Tadic 59), Mandzukic.
Hamburg: Rost; Atouba, Reinhardt, Mathijsen, Kompany, Boateng, De Jong, Jarolim, Van der Vaart (Trochowski 88), Olic (Choupo-Moting 84), Castelen (Demel 76).

Thursday, 20 December 2007

Hamburg (0) 1 *(Olic 72)*

Basle (0) 1 *(Ergic 58)* 48,917

Hamburg: Rost; Atouba, Reinhardt, Mathijsen, Kompany (Castelen 71), Boateng, De Jong, Jarolim, Trochowski (Guerrero 62), Van der Vaart, Olic.
Basle: Costanzo; Hodel, Majstorovic, Marque, Zanni■, Huggel, Ba, Ergic, Carlitos (Caicedo 81), Degen (Morganella 51), Eduardo (Derdiyok 85).

Rennes (0) 1 *(M'Bia 88)*

Dynamo Zagreb (0) 1 *(Vukojevic 55)* 11,846

Rennes: Pouplin; Mensah, Fanni, Hansson, Leroy (Kembo Ekoko 65), Cheyrou, M'Bia, Sorlin, Wiltord (Thomert 64), Pagis, Briand (Moreira 76).
Dynamo Zagreb: Koch; Cale (Sokota 88), Santos, Drpic, Pokrivac, Etto, Modric, Sammir (Guela 65), Vukojevic, Tadic (Balaban 77), Mandzukic.

Group D Final Table	*P*	*W*	*D*	*L*	*F*	*A*	*Pts*
Hamburg	4	3	1	0	7	1	10
Basle	4	2	2	0	3	1	8
Brann	4	1	1	2	3	4	4
Dynamo Zagreb	4	0	2	2	2	5	2
Rennes	4	0	2	2	2	6	2

GROUP E

Thursday, 25 October 2007

Leverkusen (1) 1 *(Kiessling 35)*

Toulouse (0) 0 15,276

Leverkusen: Adler; Haggui, Friedrich, Sarpei, Vidal, Castro, Rolfes, Barnetta, Gekas (Freier 59) (Papadopoulos 90), Kiessling, Barbarez (Sinkiewicz 79).
Toulouse: Douchez; Congre, Ebondo, Paulo Cesar, Ilunga, Cetto, Sirieix (Dieuze 87), Fabinho (Bergougnoux 74), Emana Edzimbi, Mansare, Gignac (Dupuis 90).

Sparta Prague (1) 1 *(Slepicka 24)*

Zurich (1) 2 *(Konde 38, Alphonse 62)* 6007

Sparta Prague: Postulka; Repka, Brezinsky, Kadlec, Limbersky (Nadenicek 82), Ludovic, Kisel, Dosek, Slepicka, Rezek (Petrzela 72), Matusovic.
Zurich: Leoni; Konde, Stahel, Rochat, Schneider, Tihinen, Kollar, Abdi, Alphonse (Lampi 87) (Eudis 90), Raffael (Hassli■ 77), Chikhaoui.

Thursday, 8 November 2007

Spartak Moscow (0) 2 *(Pavlyuchenko 63 (pen), Mozart 77 (pen))*

Leverkusen (0) 1 *(Freier 89)* 23,000

Spartak Moscow: Pletikosa; Geder, Stranzl, Ivanov, Mozart, Titov, Torbinskiy (Boyarintsev 82), Kovac, Kalynychenko (Shishkin 86), Pavlyuchenko, Welliton (Dedura 88).
Leverkusen: Adler; Haggui, Friedrich, Sarpei, Vidal (Dum 80), Castro, Rolfes, Barnetta, Gekas (Freier 68), Kiessling (Bulykin 80), Barbarez.

Toulouse (1) 2 *(Elmander 14, Mansare 80)*

Sparta Prague (0) 3 *(Kisel 67, 88, Dosek 68)* 15,572

Toulouse: Douchez; Congre, Arribage, Ebondo, Paulo Cesar (Bergougnoux 88), Ilunga, Sirieix (Batiles 77), Emana Edzimbi, Dieuze, Mansare, Elmander (Gignac 65).
Sparta Prague: Grigar; Repka, Kladrubsky, Pospech (Horvath 65), Kadlec, Limbersky, Kisel, Slepicka (Dosek 57), Rezek, Matusovic (Zeman 84), Kulic.

Thursday, 29 November 2007

Sparta Prague (0) 0

Spartak Moscow (0) 0 6307

Sparta Prague: Grigar; Repka, Kladrubsky, Pospech, Kadlec, Zabavnik, Horvath, Kisel, Dosek, Slepicka, Rezek (Limbersky 80).
Spartak Moscow: Pletikosa; Geder, Stranzl, Soava, Ivanov, Dedura, Titov, Torbinskiy, Covalciuc, Welliton (Bazhenov 87), Dzyuba (Prudnikov 78).

Zurich (1) 2 *(Tihinen 42, Raffael 69 (pen))*

Toulouse (0) 0 10,600

Zurich: Leoni; Lampi, Konde, Rochat, Schneider, Tihinen, Okonkwo, Abdi, Alphonse (Eudis 62), Raffael (Schonbachler 89), Chikhaoui (Stahel 90).
Toulouse: Douchez; Fofana, Arribage, Ebondo, Ilunga, Fabinho (Sissoko 56), Emana Edzimbi, Dieuze, Mansare (Bergougnoux 77), Elmander (Santos 69), Gignac.

Thursday, 6 December 2007

Leverkusen (0) 1 *(Friedrich 71)*

Sparta Prague (0) 0 17,771

Leverkusen: Adler; Haggui, Friedrich, Sarpei, Castro, Rolfes, Barnetta, Freier (Schneider 65) (Gresko 83), Ramelow■, Gekas (Sinkiewicz 78), Kiessling.
Sparta Prague: Grigar; Repka, Kladrubsky, Pospech, Kadlec, Zabavnik (Brezinski 89), Horvath, Kisel, Dosek, Slepicka, Rezek (Matusovic 73).

Spartak Moscow (0) 1 *(Titov 57)*
Zurich (0) 0 20,000
Spartak Moscow: Pletikosa; Stranzl, Shishkin, Ivanov (Soava 46), Dedura, Titov, Torbinskiy, Covalciuc, Pavlyuchenko, Bazhenov (Boyarintsev 71), Dzyuba (Welliton 58).
Zurich: Guatelli; Konde, Stahel, Rochat, Schneider, Tihinen, Aegerter (Gashi 81), Okonkwo, Alphonse, Raffael, Chikhaoui.

Wednesday, 19 December 2007

Toulouse (1) 2 *(Santos 41, 53)*
Spartak Moscow (0) 1 *(Dzyuba 61 (pen))* 14,608
Toulouse: Riou; Fofana, Arribage, Ilunga, M'Bengue, Batiles (Sissoko 90), Sirieix (Capoue 46), Emana Edzimbi, Dieuze, Bergougnoux, Santos (Dupuis 81).
Spartak Moscow: Kohmich; Geder, Stranzl, Soava, Kudryashav, Shishkin, Covalciuc, Parshivlyuk, Welliton, Prudnikov (Bystrov 83), Dzyuba.

Zurich (0) 0
Leverkusen (2) 5 *(Gresko 18, Bulykin 22, 57, Barnetta 50, Kiessling 80)* 20,100
Zurich: Leoni; Konde, Stahel, Rochat, Barmettler, Schneider, Aegerter (Okonkwo 64), Abdi, Alphonse (Eudis 63), Raffael (Schonbachler 85), Chikhaoui.
Leverkusen: Fernandez; Haggui, Friedrich (Callsen-Bracker 28), Sarpei, Sinkiewicz (Faty 60), Rolfes, Barnetta, Gresko, Kiessling, Bulykin (Gekas 78), Barbarez.

Group E Final Table	*P*	*W*	*D*	*L*	*F*	*A*	*Pts*
Leverkusen	4	3	0	1	8	2	9
Spartak Moscow	4	2	1	1	4	3	7
Zurich	4	2	0	2	4	7	6
Sparta Prague	4	1	1	2	4	5	4
Toulouse	4	1	0	3	4	7	3

GROUP F

Thursday, 25 October 2007

Bolton Wanderers (0) 1 *(Diouf 66)*
Braga (0) 1 *(Jailson 87)* 10,848
Bolton Wanderers: Jaaskelainen; Hunt, Gardner (Teimourian 82), Meite, O'Brien A, Cid, Guthrie (Diouf 61), Speed, Anelka, Davies, McCann.
Braga: Paulo Santos; Rodriguez, Paulo Jorge, Joao Pereira, Castanheira (Stelvio 68), Cesar Peixoto, Andres Madrid (Jailson 76), Vandinho, Jorginho, Wender (Ze Manel 67), Linz.

Red Star Belgrade (1) 2 *(Koroman 16, Milijas 74)*
Bayern Munich (1) 3 *(Klose 20, 85, Kroos 90)* 41,000
Red Star Belgrade: Randelovic; Andelkovic, Tutoric, Gueye, Basta (Bajalica 46), Milijas, Koroman, Lucas, Molina (Bogdanovic 90), Castillo, Barcos (Burzanovic 69).
Bayern Munich: Rensing; Lucio, Lahm, Jansen, Lell, Hamit Altintop (Schlaudraff 71), Ze Roberto, Van Bommel (Kroos 81), Schweinsteiger, Podolski, Klose.

Thursday, 8 November 2007

Aris Salonika (0) 3 *(Papazoglou 76, 89, Koke 90)*
Red Star Belgrade (0) 0 16,000
Aris Salonika: Chalkias; Neto, Ronaldo, Vangeli, Papadopoulos, Nebegleras, Ronald Garcia, Ivic (Calvo 66), Koke, Felipe (Siston 80), Javito (Papazoglou 53).
Red Star Belgrade: Randelovic; Andelkovic, Tutoric, Bronowicki, Gueye (Burzanovic 83), Basta, Milijas, Koroman, Lucas (Bogdanovic 69), Molina (Jestrovic 79), Castillo.

Bayern Munich (1) 2 *(Podolski 31, 49)*
Bolton Wanderers (1) 2 *(Gardner 8, Davies 82)* 66,000
Bayern Munich: Kahn; Lucio, Van Buyten, Jansen, Lell, Ribery (Kroos 61), Ottl, Van Bommel, Schweinsteiger (Hamit Altintop 73), Podolski (Toni 58), Klose.
Bolton Wanderers: Al Habsi; Michalik, Gardner, McCann, O'Brien A, Cid, Nolan, Alonso (Giannakopoulos 56), Braaten (Teimourian 77), Davies, Guthrie.

Thursday, 29 November 2007

Bolton Wanderers (0) 1 *(Giannakopoulos 90)*
Aris Salonika (1) 1 *(Toni Calvo 44)* 10,229
Bolton Wanderers: Jaaskelainen; Hunt, Cid, McCann (Alonso 13), O'Brien A, Meite, Nolan, Wilhelmsson (Diouf 65), Davies (Anelka 65), Guthrie, Giannakopoulos.
Aris Salonika: Chalkias; Neto, Ronaldo, Karabelas, Papadopoulos, Nebegleras, Toni Calvo (Javito 61), Ronaldo Garcia (Gogolos 83), Siston, Prittas, Koke (Kyriakos 87).

Braga (0) 1 *(Linz 66)*
Bayern Munich (0) 1 *(Klose 47)* 12,000
Braga: Paulo Santos; Rodriguez, Paulo Jorge, Frechaut, Joao Pereira, Roberto Brum, Vandinho (Joao Pinto 52), Stelvio (Jailson 58), Jorginho, Wender (Andres Madrid 69), Linz.
Bayern Munich: Kahn; Lucio, Demichelis, Lahm, Lell, Ribery (Sagnol 90), Hamit Altintop (Sosa 81), Ze Roberto, Van Bommel, Toni, Klose (Schlaudraff 67).

Thursday, 6 December 2007

Aris Salonika (1) 1 *(Ronaldo 26)*
Braga (1) 1 *(Linz 6)* 14,000
Aris Salonika: Chalkias; Neto, Ronaldo, Marco Aurelio, Papadopoulos, Nebegleras, Ronald Garcia, Siston (Calvo 79), Ivic, Koke, Javito (Felipe 79).
Braga: Paulo Santos; Rodriguez, Carlos Fernandes, Frechaut, Anilton, Joao Pereira, Roberto Brum, Cesar Peixoto (Joao Pinto 53), Jorginho (Jailson 73), Wender, Linz.

Red Star Belgrade (0) 0
Bolton Wanderers (1) 1 *(McCann 45)* 45,000
Red Star Belgrade: Randelovic; Tutoric, Bronowicki (Andelkovic 81), Bajalica, Basta, Milijas (Burzanovic 74), Koroman, Lucas, Molina, Milovanovic, Jestrovic (Djordjevic F 64).
Bolton Wanderers: Al Habsi; Hunt, Samuel, Teimourian, Michalik, Meite, McCann, Speed, Braaten (Sinclair 88), Wilhelmsson, Giannakopoulos.

Wednesday, 19 December 2007

Bayern Munich (2) 6 *(Toni 25, 38, 64, 66, Lell 78, Lahm 81)*
Aris Salonika (0) 0 64,000
Bayern Munich: Kahn; Lucio, Demichelis, Lahm, Lell (Sagnol 79), Ribery, Ze Roberto, Van Bommel (Ottl 62), Schweinsteiger, Toni, Klose (Podolski 62).
Aris Salonika: Chalkias; Ronaldo, Marco Aurelio, Vangeli, Papadopoulos, Nebegleras, Ronald Garcia (Karabelas 86), Ivic (Javito 46), Prittas, Koke (Siston 71), Felipe.

Braga (1) 2 *(Linz 11, Wender 66)*
Red Star Belgrade (0) 0 10,000
Braga: Paulo Santos; Rodriguez, Paulo Jorge, Carlos Fernandes, Frechaut, Joao Pereira, Roberto Brum (Andres Madrid 89), Vandinho, Jorginho (Jailson 73), Wender (Cesar Peixoto 71), Linz.
Red Star Belgrade: Banovic; Andgelkovic, Dordjevic V, Bajalica, Basta (Lucas 18), Milijas, Koroman, Milovanovic, Castillo, Barcos (Dordjevic F 89), Salas (Molina 60).

Group F Final Table	*P*	*W*	*D*	*L*	*F*	*A*	*Pts*
Bayern Munich	4	2	2	0	12	5	8
Braga	4	1	3	0	5	3	6
Bolton Wanderers	4	1	3	0	5	4	6
Aris Salonika	4	1	2	1	5	8	5
Red Star Belgrade	4	0	0	4	2	9	0

GROUP G

Thursday, 25 October 2007

Anderlecht (1) 2 *(Frutos 36, 71)*

Hapoel Tel Aviv (0) 0 16,586

Anderlecht: Zitka; Deschacht, Juhasz, Pareja, Wasilewski, Biglia, Polak, Hassan, Goor (Van Damme 69), Frutos (De Man 86), Legear (Thereau 83).
Hapoel Tel Aviv: Enyeama; Dos Santos, Antebi, Manzur, Duani, Natcho, Badir (Abedi 69), Oved (Srur 53), Mazuwa, Asulin (Sabag 62), Fabio Junior.

Tottenham Hotspur (1) 1 *(Defoe 19)*

Getafe (1) 2 *(De la Red 21, Braulio 70)* 36,240

Tottenham Hotspur: Cerny; Chimbonda, Lee, Zokora (Tainio 73), Kaboul, Gardner (Dawson 43), Lennon, Huddlestone, Berbatov, Defoe, Malbranque (Keane 71).
Getafe: Ustari (Abbondanzieri 46); Cata Diaz, Belenguer, Signorino, Cortes, Nacho, Albin, Casquero (Sousa 62), Granero (Mario Cotelo 76), Braulio, De la Red.

Thursday, 8 November 2007

Aalborg (0) 1 *(Lindstrom 86)*

Anderlecht (0) 1 *(Wasilewski 59)* 10,300

Aalborg: Zaza; Jakobsen M, Pedersen, Califf, Olesen, Johansson (Enevoldsen 60), Augustinussen, Risgard, Prica, Curth, Nomvethe (Lindstrom 78).
Anderlecht: Zitka; Deschacht, Juhasz, Pareja, Wasilewski, Biglia, Polak, Hassan (Legear 82), Goor, Akin (Van Damme 88), Frutos.

Hapoel Tel Aviv (0) 0

Tottenham Hotspur (2) 2 *(Keane 26, Berbatov 31)* 10,000

Hapoel Tel Aviv: Enyeama; Tai Chen, Dos Santos, Shaish■, Bakshi (Manzur 46), Natcho, Dego (Antebi 58), Badir, Abutbul (Abedi 46), Mazuwa, Fabio Junior.
Tottenham Hotspur: Robinson; Chimbonda, Lee, Zokora, Stalteri, Dawson, Lennon, Jenas (Boateng 68), Berbatov, Keane (Bent 68), Malbranque (Defoe 56).

Thursday, 29 November 2007

Getafe (0) 1 *(Pablo Hernandez 90 (pen))*

Hapoel Tel Aviv (2) 2 *(Badir 5, Dego 31)* 5000

Getafe: Ustari; Contra, Cata Diaz, Belenguer (Sousa 67), Signorino, De la Red, Albin, Casquero (Braulio 46), Pablo Hernandez, Granero, Kepa (Mario Del Moral 46).
Hapoel Tel Aviv: Enyeama; Dos Santos, Antebi, Bondarv, Duani, Srur (Oved 82), Dego (Asulin 86), Badir, Abedi (Natcho 75), Abutbul, Fabio Junior.

Tottenham Hotspur (0) 3 *(Berbatov 46, Malbranque 51, Bent 66)*

Aalborg (2) 2 *(Enevoldsen 2, Risgard 37)* 29,758

Tottenham Hotspur: Robinson; Chimbonda, Bale, Zokora, Lee (Huddlestone 46), Dawson, Lennon, Jenas (Bent 46), Berbatov (Boateng 74), Keane, Malbranque.
Aalborg: Zaza; Jakobsen M, Pedersen, Califf, Olesen, Johansson, Augustinussen, Risgard, Enevoldsen (Curth 74), Prica, Nomvethe (Lindstrom 61).

Thursday, 6 December 2007

Aalborg (0) 1 *(Prica 90)*

Getafe (1) 2 *(Pablo Hernandez 11, Granero 78)* 10,634

Aalborg: Zaza; Jakobsen M, Pedersen (Olfers 58), Califf, Olesen, Johansson, Augustinussen, Risgard (Nomvethe 58), Enevoldsen (Lindstrom 77), Prica, Curth.
Getafe: Abbondanzieri; Contra, Cata Diaz, Belenguer (Mario Cotelo 81), Licht, Celestini (Cortes 60), De la Red, Pablo Hernandez, Granero, Braulio, Mario Del Moral (Albin 76).

Anderlecht (0) 1 *(Goor 68)*

Tottenham Hotspur (0) 1 *(Berbatov 71 (pen))* 22,500

Anderlecht: Zitka; Deschacht, Van Damme, Juhasz, Wasilewski, Biglia, Polak, Hassan, Goor, Mpenza (Baseggio 72), Frutos (Thereau 55).
Tottenham Hotspur: Robinson; Chimbonda, Lee (Stalteri 81), Zokora, Dawson, Huddlestone, Lennon, Jenas, Keane (Berbatov 59), Bent (Defoe 72), Malbranque.

Wednesday, 19 December 2007

Getafe (1) 2 *(Pablo Hernandez 6, Celestini 50)*

Anderlecht (0) 1 *(Thereau 90)* 7000

Getafe: Abbondanzieri; Contra, Cata Diaz, Belenguer, Licht, Celestini (Casquero 70), De la Red, Pablo Hernandez (Mario Cotelo 60), Granero, Braulio (Kepa 77), Mario Del Moral.
Anderlecht: Zitka; Deschacht, Van Damme, Juhasz, Wasilewski (Mpenza 53), Biglia, Polak, Hassan, Goor, Thereau, Legear (De Man 75).

Hapoel Tel Aviv (1) 1 *(Fabio Junior 45)*

Aalborg (1) 3 *(Risgard 27, Jakobsen M 50 (pen), Enevoldsen 66)* 2000

Hapoel Tel Aviv: Enyeama; Antebi, Bondarv, Duani, Natcho, Dego (Srur 70), Oved, Abutbul, Mazuwa, Asulin (Sabag 76), Fabio Junior (Lousky 87).
Aalborg: Zaza; Jakobsen, Califf, Jacobsen M, Olfers (Olsen 78), Olesen, Johansson (Vilakazi 90), Caca (Lindstrom 59), Risgard, Enevoldsen, Curth.

Group G Final Table	*P*	*W*	*D*	*L*	*F*	*A*	*Pts*
Getafe	4	3	0	1	7	5	9
Tottenham Hotspur	4	2	1	1	7	5	7
Anderlecht	4	1	2	1	5	4	5
Aalborg	4	1	1	2	7	7	4
Hapoel Tel Aviv	4	1	0	3	3	8	3

GROUP H

Thursday, 25 October 2007

Bordeaux (0) 2 *(Cavengahi 53, Chamakh 64)*

Galatasaray (1) 1 *(Nonda 21 (pen))* 10,863

Bordeaux: Rame; Jemmali (Planus 28), Diawara, Marange, Tremoulinas (Wendel 75), Fernando (Diarra 61), Micoud, Ducasse, Chalme, Cavenaghi, Chamakh.
Galatasaray: Orkun; Song, Ugur (Carrusca 78), Volkan, Servet, Linderoth (Serkan 86), Baris (Mehmet T 72), Hasan Sas, Arda, Nonda, Umit K.

Helsingborg (0) 1 *(Larsson 83)*

Panionios (1) 1 *(Goundoulakis 45)* 6451

Helsingborg: Andersson D; Jakobsson, Andersson C (Landgren 85), Ronningberg, Tamboura, Dahl, Skulasson (Lantz 46), Wahlstedt, Omotoyossi, Makondele, Larsson.
Panionios: Kresic; Maniatis, Berthe, Majstorovic, Spyropoulos, Kapetanos (Pletsch 85), Makos (Skoufalis 88), Kumordzi, Goundoulakis, Nikolaou, Djebbour (Kondi 72).

Thursday, 8 November 2007

FK Austria (1) 1 *(Kuljic 5)*

Bordeaux (1) 2 *(Chamakh 45, Wendel 88 (pen))* 20,100

FK Austria: Safar; Troyansky, Bak, Gercaliu, Metz, Schiemer, Sariyar, Acimovic (Lasnik 82), Standfest, Lafata (Sulimani 64), Kuljic (Mair 74).
Bordeaux: Rame; Diawara, Planus, Tremoulinas, Fernando, Micoud, Wendel, Ducasse, Chalme, Obertan (Bellion 77), Chamakh.

Galatasaray (1) 2 *(Nonda 44, 90)*

Helsingborg (2) 3 *(Larsson 31, Omotoyossi 39, Andersson C 75)* 22,000

Galatasaray: Aykut; Song, Volkan, Servet, Linderoth, Baris, Lincoln, Hasan Sas, Sabri (Arda 44), Hakan Sukur (Umit K 64), Nonda.
Helsingborg: Andersson D; Jakobsson, Andersson C (Lantz 87), Ronningberg, Tamboura, Dahl (Beloufa 90), Skulasson, Wahlstedt, Omotoyossi, Makondele (Svanback 66), Larsson.

Thursday, 29 November 2007

Helsingborg (0) 3 *(Skulasson 48, Omotoyossi 66, 70)*

FK Austria (0) 0 8243

Helsingborg: Andersson D; Tamboura, Jakobsson, Andersson C, Wahlstedt, Ronningberg, Dahl (Lantz 71), Skulasson (Chansa 85), Omotoyossi (Karekezi 89), Makondele, Larsson.
FK Austria: Fornezzi; Troyansky (Ertl 82), Bak, Gercaliu, Metz (Sulimani 84), Schiemer, Acimovic, Standfest, Aigner, Lafata, Okotie (Mair 72).

Panionios (0) 0

Galatasaray (0) 3 *(Serkan 50, Song 63 (pen), Hakan Sukur 82)* 7500

Panionios: Tabasis; Maniatis, Pletsch, Majstorovic, Spyropoulos, Aravidis (Koutsopoulos 66), Makos■, Kumordzi (Skoufalis 65), Goundoulakis (Kondi 80), Fernandez, Djebbour.
Galatasaray: Orkun; Song, Ugur, Volkan, Servet, Linderoth (Hakan Sukur 46), Lincoln, Hasan Sas, Mehmet T, Arda (Mehmet G 80), Serkan (Sabri 86).

Thursday, 6 December 2007

Bordeaux (1) 2 *(Chamakh 12, Jussie 69)*

Helsingborg (1) 1 *(Larsson 17)* 12,000

Bordeaux: Rame; Henrique, Marange, Planus, Tremoulinas (Alonso 62), Fernando, Ducasse (Diarra 61), Chalme, Jussie, Obertan, Chamakh (Cavenaghi 73).
Helsingborg: Andersson D; Tamboura■, Jakobsson, Andersson C, Wahlstedt, Ronningberg, Lantz, Skulason (Chansa 85), Omotoyossi (Svanback 71), Makondele, Larsson.

FK Austria (0) 0

Panionios (0) 1 *(Majstorovic 90)* 12,000

FK Austria: Fornezzi; Majstorovic, Bak, Ertl (Sulimani 64), Schiemer, Blanchard, Lasnik (Mair 71), Sariyar, Acimovic, Standfest, Okotie (Lafata 80).
Panionios: Konig; Maniatis, Berthe, Pletsch, Majstorovic, Spyropoulos, Kumordzi (Gaspar 87), Goundoulakis, Nikolaou (Fernandez 73), Skoufalis (Koutsopoulos 85), Djebbour.

Wednesday, 19 December 2007

Galatasaray (0) 0

FK Austria (0) 0 7320

Galatasaray: Orkun; Song, Ugur, Volkan, Servet, Baris (Umit K 61), Mehmet, Sabri (Serkan 82), Arda, Hakan Sukur (Hasan Sas 62), Nonda.
FK Austria: Fornezzi; Troyansky (Schiemer 86), Majstorovic, Metz, Ertl, Blanchard, Lasnik, Sariyar, Acimovic, Mair (Aigner 75), Lafata (Okotie 79).

Panionios (2) 2 *(Djebbour 6, Makos 20)*

Bordeaux (1) 3 *(Cavenaghi 40, 75, Moimbe 87)* 7000

Panionios: Konig; Maniatis (Aravidis 78), Berthe, Pletsch, Majstorovic, Spyropoulos, Makos, Kumordzi (Gaspar 90), Goundoulakis, Skoufalis (Fernandez 55), Djebbour.
Bordeaux: Valverde; Jemmali (Traore 19), Bregerie, Marange, Tremoulinas (Moimbe 81), Ecuele, Ducasse, Lavie, Cavenaghi, Jussie (Perea 57), Obertan.

Group H Final Table	*P*	*W*	*D*	*L*	*F*	*A*	*Pts*
Bordeaux	4	4	0	0	9	5	12
Helsingborg	4	2	1	1	8	5	7
Galatasaray	4	1	1	2	6	5	4
Panionios	4	1	1	2	4	7	4
FK Austria	4	0	1	3	1	6	1

KNOCK-OUT STAGE

THIRD ROUND FIRST LEG

Wednesday, 13 February 2008

AEK Athens (0) 1 *(Blanco 90)*

Getafe (0) 1 *(De la Red 87)* 13,080

AEK Athens: Moretto; Arruabarrena, Dellas, Papastathopoulos, Kafes, Nsaliwa, Zikos, Pappas (Blanco 82), Rivaldo, Manduca (Manu 66), Lyberopoulos (Kallon 75).
Getafe: Abbondanzieri; Contra, Diaz, Belenguer, Signorino, Celestini, Gavilan (Cortes 61), Casquero (De la Red 68), Hernandez, Braulio, Uche (Del Moral 78).

Anderlecht (0) 2 *(Polak 79, Mpenza 90)*

Bordeaux (0) 1 *(Jussie 68 (pen))* 20,000

Anderlecht: Zitka; Van Damme, Juhasz, Pareja, Wasilewski, Biglia, Polak, Chatelle (Legear 84), Goor, Boussoufa, Serhat (Mpenza 90).
Bordeaux: Rame; Henrique, Jurietti, Diawara, Diarra, Alonso (Wendel 61), Ducasse, Chalme, Jussie (Micoud 81), Obertan, Chamakh (Cavenaghi 61).

Brann (0) 0

Everton (0) 2 *(Osman 59, Anichebe 88)* 16,207

Brann: Opdal; Dahl (Thwaite 89), Hanstveit, Bjarnason, El-Fakiri (Huseklepp 75), Solli, Vaagan Moen, Bakke, Sigurdsson K, Karadas (Demba-Nyren 69), Helstad.
Everton: Howard; Neville, Lescott, Jagielka, Yobo, Carsley, Osman, Fernandes (Hibbert 89), Johnson (Anichebe 76), Yakubu (Baines 90), Cahill.

Galatasaray (0) 0

Leverkusen (0) 0 22,000

Galatasaray: Orkun; Emre, Ugur, Volkan (Lincoln 84), Servet, Baris, Mehmet, Ayhan (Hakan Balta 65), Arda, Hakan Sukur (Nonda 78), Umit K.
Leverkusen: Adler; Friedrich, Sarpei, Vidal (Schwegler 86), Castro, Callsen-Bracker, Rolfes, Barnetta, Schneider (Freier 62), Kiessling, Barbarez.

Marseille (0) 3 *(Cheyrou 61, Taiwo 68, Niang 79)*

Spartak Moscow (0) 0 31,790

Marseille: Mandanda; Taiwo, Faty (Kabore 46), Bonnart, Givet, Cheyrou, Cana, Nasri, Valbuena (Zenden 77), Cisse, Niang (Oruma 83).
Spartak Moscow: Pletikosa; Stranzl, Kudryashov, Mozart, Pavlenko (Prudnikov 83), Titov, Kovac, Maidana (Dineev 65), Bystrov (Pavlyuchenko 69), Parshivlyuk, Welliton.

PSV Eindhoven (2) 2 *(Simons 7 (pen), Lazovic 33)*

Helsingborg (0) 0 22,000

PSV Eindhoven: Gomes; Kromkamp, Salcido, Alcides (Rajkovic 65), Marcellis, Zonneveld, Simons, Dzsudzsak, Bakkal, Lazovic (Koevermans 71), Afellay.
Helsingborg: Andersson D; Landgren, Jakobsson, Andersson C, Lantz, Skulasson, Kolar (Unkuri 77), Ekstrand, Omotoyossi (Olsson 88), Makondele, Larsson.

Rangers (0) 0

Panathinaikos (0) 0 45,203

Rangers: McGregor; Broadfoot, Papac, Cuellar, Weir, Ferguson, Hemdani, Adam (Cousin 67), Novo (Burke 81), McCulloch, Davis.
Panathinaikos: Galinovic; Morris, Goumas, Simao, Vintra, Mattos, Karagounis, Tziolis, Nilsson, Salpingidis (Helder Postiga 66), N'Doye.

Sporting Lisbon (1) 2 *(Vukcevic 9, 58)*

Basle (0) 0 16,639

Sporting Lisbon: Rui Patricio; Anderson Polga, Tonel, Grimi, Veloso, Abel, Izmailov (Pereirinha 72), Vukcevic (Tiui 72), Joao Moutinho, Romagnoli, Liedson.
Basle: Costanzo (Crayton 46); Hodel, Majstorovic, Marque, Degen (Cabral 64), Huggel, Ba, Ergic, Carlitos, Eduardo, Derdiyok.

Werder Bremen (2) 3 *(Naldo 4, Jensen 27, Hugo Almeida 90 (pen))*

Braga (0) 0 25,690

Werder Bremen: Wiese; Naldo, Baumann, Fritz, Mertesacker, Diego (Ozil 74), Owomoyela, Jensen, Rosenberg, Hunt (Borowski 59), Hugo Almeida.
Braga: Santos; Rodriguez, Paulo Jorge, Fernandes, Contreras (Stelvio 62), Frechaut, Joao Pereira, Vandinho, Jorginho (Jailson 78), Linz, Matheus (Wender 68).

Zenit (0) 1 *(Pogrebnyak 64)*

Villarreal (0) 0 21,500

Zenit: Malafeev; Krizanac, Kim, Anyukov, Sirl, Shirokov, Syryanov, Fayzulin, Timoshchuk, Pogrebnyak, Arshavin.
Villarreal: Diego Lopez; Rodriguez, Josemi, Godin, Capdevila, Josico, Cazorla (Tomasson 75), Cani, Soriano (Cygan 82), Franco, Kahveci (Rossi 66).

Thursday, 14 February 2008

Aberdeen (2) 2 *(Walker 24, Aluko 41)*

Bayern Munich (1) 2 *(Klose 29, Hamit Altintop 54)* 20,047

Aberdeen: Langfield; Maybury, Mair, Considine, Diamond, Severin, Walker (Touzani 87), Nicholson, Aluko, Miller, Mackie (Lovell 68).
Bayern Munich: Rensing; Lucio, Demichelis, Jansen, Lell (Lahm 46), Hamit Altintop, Ze Roberto (Podolski 66), Ottl, Schweinsteiger, Toni, Klose (Schlaudraff 80).

Benfica (1) 1 *(Makukula 43)*

Nuremberg (0) 0 25,000

Benfica: Quim; Luisao, Leo, Nelson, Petit, Katsouranis, Rui Costa, Nuno Assis (David Luiz 85), Rodriguez (Adu 85), Cardozo (Di Maria 60), Makukula.
Nuremberg: Blazek; Glauber, Wolf, Pinola, Reinhardt, Galasek, Engelhardt, Kluge, Saenko, Adler (Kristiansen 46), Koller.

Bolton Wanderers (0) 1 *(Diouf 74)*

Atletico Madrid (0) 0 26,163

Bolton Wanderers: Jaaskelainen; Hunt, Samuel, Campo, O'Brien A, Cahill, Nolan, Guthrie (Giannakopoulos 59), Taylor, Davies, Diouf.
Atletico Madrid: Abbiati; Antonio Lopez, Pernia, Luis Perea, Pablo Ibanez, Santana, Maxi Rodriguez, Reyes (Aguero■ 59), Simao (Jurado 72), Forlan, Mista (Miguel 88).

Rosenborg (0) 0

Fiorentina (1) 1 *(Mutu 16)* 16,000

Rosenborg: Jarstein; Stoor, Nordvik, Kvarme, Demidov, Strand (Storflor 81), Skjelbred, Traore, Sapara, Kone, Iversen (Konan 46).
Fiorentina: Frey; Kroldrup, Gamberini, Ujfalusi, Semioli, Montolivo, Gobbi (Pasqual 46), Jorgensen, Kuzmanovic (Santana 85), Mutu, Pazzini (Cacia 72).

Slavia Prague (0) 1 *(Strihavka 69)*

Tottenham Hotspur (2) 2 *(Berbatov 4, Keane 30)* 11,134

Slavia Prague: Vaniak; Brabec, Hubacek, Drizdal, Tavares, Latka, Pudil (Ivana 46), Suchy (Volesak 83), Jarolim (Kalivoda 59), Cerny, Strihavka.
Tottenham Hotspur: Cerny; Chimbonda, Tainio (O'Hara 59), Huddlestone, Woodgate, Zokora, Lennon, Jenas, Berbatov, Keane (Bent 66), Malbranque.

Zurich (0) 1 *(Rochat 87)*

Hamburg (0) 3 *(Jarolim 49, Olic 67, Trochowski 77)* 16,800

Zurich: Leoni; Stahel, Rochat, Barmettler (Lampi 69), Tihinen, Aegerter, Okonkwo, Djuric, Abdi (Vasquez 86), Chikhaoui (Tahirovic 75), Hassli.
Hamburg: Rost; Reinhardt, Mathijsen, Kompany, Benjamin, De Jong, Jarolim (Brecko 86), Trochowski, Demel, Van der Vaart (Guerrero 32), Olic (Zidan 82).

THIRD ROUND SECOND LEG

Thursday, 21 February 2008

Atletico Madrid (0) 0

Bolton Wanderers (0) 0 30,000

Atletico Madrid: Abbiati; Antonio Lopez, Pernia, Luis Perea, Pablo Ibanez (Mista 67), Santana, Luis Garcia (Miguel 54), Maxi Rodriguez, Jurado, Reyes, Forlan.
Bolton Wanderers: Jaaskelainen; Hunt, Samuel, McCann (Campo 58), O'Brien A, Cahill, Nolan, O'Brien J (Meite 85), Taylor, Davies, Giannakopoulos (Diouf 59).

Basle (0) 0

Sporting Lisbon (2) 3 *(Pereirinha 2, Liedson 41, 51)* 16,360

Basle: Crayton; Hodel, Majstorovic, Marque, Zanni, Degen, Huggel (Ba 46), Ergic (Perovic 71), Carlitos, Eduardo (Frei 59), Derdiyok.
Sporting Lisbon: Rui Patricio; Anderson Polga (Gladstone 55), Tonel, Grimi (Ronny 68), Veloso, Abel, Pereirinha, Joao Moutinho, Romagnoli (Farnerud 60), Tiui, Liedson.

Bayern Munich (2) 5 *(Lucio 12, Van Buyten 36, Podolski 71, 77, Van Bommel 85)*

Aberdeen (0) 1 *(Lovell 83)* 66,000

Bayern Munich: Kahn; Sagnol, Lucio, Van Buyten, Jansen, Hamit Altintop (Schweinsteiger 75), Ottl, Van Bommel, Kroos (Sosa 69), Toni (Klose 65), Podolski.
Aberdeen: Langfield; Maybury, Foster, Considine, Diamond, Severin, Walker (Maguire 62), Nicholson, Aluko (Lovell 79), Miller, Mackie (De Visscher 72).

Bordeaux (0) 1 *(Cavenaghi 71)*

Anderlecht (1) 1 *(Chatelle 34)* 20,127

Bordeaux: Rame; Henrique, Diawara, Marange, Tremoulinas■, Alonso (Micoud 52), Ducasse, Chalme■, Bellion (Cavenaghi 53), Obertan (Wendel 77), Chamakh.
Anderlecht: Zitka; Van Damme, Juhasz (De Man 90), Pareja, Wasilewski, Biglia, Polak, Chatelle (Mpenza 60), Gillet, Boussoufa, Serhat.

Braga (0) 0

Werder Bremen (0) 1 *(Klasnic 78)* 6000

Braga: Kieszek; Rodriguez, Paulo Jorge, Fernandes, Joao Pereira, Brum, Manel (Joao Tomas 46), Cesar Peixoto, Stelvio (Vandinho 61), Wender (Matheus 46), Linz.
Werder Bremen: Wiese; Naldo, Baumann, Fritz, Mertesacker, Ozil (Vranjes 57), Owomoyela, Jensen, Borowski (Boenisch 79), Rosenberg (Klasnic 69), Hugo Almeida.

Everton (2) 6 *(Yakubu 36, 54, 72, Johnson 41, 90, Arteta 70)*

Brann (0) 1 *(Vaagan Moen 60)* 32,834

Everton: Howard; Neville, Nuno Valente, Jagielka, Lescott, Carsley (Fernandes 46), Pienaar, Cahill (Hibbert 46), Johnson, Yakubu (Anichebe 74), Arteta.
Brann: Opdal; Dahl, Hanstveit, Bjarnason (Karadas 65), El-Fakiri (Huseklepp 60), Solli, Vaagan Moen, Bakke, Sigurdsson K, Demba-Nyren (Winters 72), Helstad.

Fiorentina (1) 2 *(Liverani 38, Cacia 81)*

Rosenborg (0) 1 *(Kone 88)* 23,139

Fiorentina: Frey; Kroldrup, Dainelli, Ujfalusi, Pasqual, Donadel, Semioli, Liverani (Kuzmanovic 82), Montolivo (Jorgensen 64), Mutu, Pazzini (Cacia 72).
Rosenborg: Jarstein; Basma (Lago 54), Nordvik, Kvarme, Demidov, Skjelbred, Tettey, Sapara, Kone (Pelu 90), Konan (Iversen 71), Storflor.

Getafe (1) 3 *(Granero 45, Contra 82 (pen), Braulio 84)*

AEK Athens (0) 0 8000

Getafe: Ustari; Contra, Belenguer, Mario, Licht, Celestini (Casquero 69), De la Red, Alvin (Uche 59), Fernandez (Cortes 78), Granero, Braulio.
AEK Athens: Moretto; Edson Ramos, Arruabarrena, Dellas, Papastathopoulos, Kafes (Blanco 65), Nsaliwa, Zikos, Lagos (Manduca 57), Rivaldo, Kallon (Lyberopoulos 72).

Hamburg (0) 0

Zurich (0) 0 33,586

Hamburg: Rost; Reinhardt, Mathijsen, Kompany, Benjamin, De Jong, Jarolim, Trochowski (Fillinger 82), Demel (Boateng 78), Guerrero (Choupo-Moting 62), Olic.
Zurich: Leoni; Lampi, Stahel, Rochat, Barmettler, Aegerter, Okonkwo (Konde 46), Djuric, Abdi (Hassli 60), Alphonse (Tahirovic 58), Chikhaoui.

Helsingborg (0) 1 *(Castan 81)*
PSV Eindhoven (0) 2 *(Zonneveld 47, Lazovic 65)* 10,194
Helsingborg: Andersson D; Tamboura (Landgren 46), Jakobsson, Andersson C, Lantz (Chansa 77), Skulasson, Kolar, Ekstrand (Castan 46), Omotoyossi, Makondele, Larsson.
PSV Eindhoven: Gomes; Salcido, Alcides, Marcellis, Zonneveld, Simons, Mendez, Dzsudzsak (Rajkovic 78), Bakkal, Lazovic (Koevermans 68), Afellay (Aissati 72).

Leverkusen (3) 5 *(Barbarez 11, 21, Kiessling 13, Haggui 55, Schneider 60 (pen))*
Galatasaray (0) 1 *(Ahmed 87 (pen))* 22,500
Leverkusen: Fernandez; Haggui, Friedrich, Sarpei, Vidal, Castro, Rolfes, Barnetta, Schneider (Dum 76), Kiessling (Gekas 71), Barbarez (Schwegler 66).
Galatasaray: Orkun; Emre, Volkan, Servet, Baris, Mehmet (Lincoln 46), Ayhan (Ahmed 68), Arda, Hakan Sukur, Serkan (Sabri 46), Umit K.

Nuremberg (0) 2 *(Charisteas 59, Saenko 66)*
Benfica (0) 2 *(Cardozo 89, Di Maria 90)* 42,890
Nuremberg: Blazek; Glauber, Wolf, Pinola, Reinhardt, Galasek, Engelhardt, Mnari (Abardonado 87), Charisteas, Saenko, Koller.
Benfica: Quim; Luis Filipe, EdCarlos (Sepsi 70), Luisao, Leo, Petit, Katsouranis, Rui Costa, Maxi Pereira (Cardozo 70), Nuno Assis (Di Maria 81), Makukula.

Panathinaikos (1) 1 *(Goumas 12)*
Rangers (0) 1 *(Novo 81)* 14,452
Panathinaikos: Galinovic; Morris, Goumas, Vintra, Mattos, Karagounis, Tziolis (Gonzalez 83), Ivanschitz, Nilsson (Papadopoulos 86), Helder Postiga (N'Doye 62), Salpingidis.
Rangers: McGregor; Broadfoot, Papac (Dailly 66), Cuellar, Weir, Ferguson, Hemdani (Burke 69), Adam (Naismith 66), Boyd, Novo, Davis.

Spartak Moscow (1) 2 *(Pavlenko 39, Pavlyuchenko 85)*
Marseille (0) 0 16,000
Spartak Moscow: Pletikosa; Stranzl, Kudryashov, Mozart, Pavlenko, Titov (Bystrov 76), Kovac, Maidana, Parshivlyuk (Dedura 89), Pavlyuchenko, Welliton (Dzuba 72).
Marseille: Mandanda; Taiwo, Bonnart, Givet, Kabore (Oruma 9), M'Bami, Cana, Nasri (Zenden 60), Valbuena, Cisse, Niang (Ziani 79).

Tottenham Hotspur (1) 1 *(O'Hara 7)*
Slavia Prague (0) 1 *(Krajcik 51)* 34,224
Tottenham Hotspur: Robinson; Chimbonda (Malbranque 61), Tainio, Zokora, Woodgate, Kaboul, Lennon (Jenas 70), Huddlestone, Berbatov (Keane 46), Bent, O'Hara.
Slavia Prague: Vorel; Brabec, Hubacek, Drizdal (Volesak 81), Latka, Pudil, Suchy, Krajcik (Belaid 87), Kalivoda (Ivana 46), Cerny, Strihavka.

Villarreal (0) 2 *(Franco 75, Tomasson 90)*
Zenit (1) 1 *(Pogrebnyak 31)* 18,000
Villarreal: Diego Lopez; Rodriguez, Godin, Capdevila, Angel, Josico (Franco 46), Pires, Cazorla, Senna (Soriano 63), Tomasson, Rossi (Kahveci 51).
Zenit: Malafeev; Kim, Lombaerts (Krizanac 34), Anyukov, Sirl■, Shirokov■, Zyryanov, Fayzulin (Ho Lee 90), Timoshchuk, Pogrebnyak, Arshavin (Gorshkov 86).

FOURTH ROUND FIRST LEG

Thursday, 6 March 2008

Anderlecht (0) 0
Bayern Munich (2) 5 *(Hamit Altintop 9, Toni 45, Podolski 57, Klose 67, Ribery 86)* 21,750
Anderlecht: Zitka; Van Damme, Juhasz, Pareja, Wasilewski■, Biglia, Polak, Chatelle (Hassan 62), Gillet, Boussoufa, Serhat (Goor 69).
Bayern Munich: Rensing; Sagnol, Van Buyten, Demichelis, Lahm, Hamit Altintop (Jose Sosa 58), Ottl, Van Bommel, Schweinsteiger (Ribery 46), Toni (Klose 46), Podolski.

Benfica (0) 1 *(Mantorras 76)*
Getafe (1) 2 *(De la Red 25, Hernandez 66)* 25,000
Benfica: Quim; EdCarlos, Luisao (Zoro 29), Leo, Nelson, Sepsi, Katsouranis, Rui Costa, Di Maria (Mantorras 62), Rodriguez, Cardozo■.
Getafe: Ustari; Contra, Diaz, Belenguer, Licht, De la Red (Celestini 73), Albin, Casquero, Hernandez, Granero (Cotelo 46), Braulio (Del Moral 61).

Bolton Wanderers (1) 1 *(McCann 25)*
Sporting Lisbon (0) 1 *(Vukcevic 69)* 25,664
Bolton Wanderers: Al Habsi; Hunt, Gardner, Campo (Teimourian 84), O'Brien A, Cahill, O'Brien J (Guthrie 66), McCann, Helguson (Giannakopoulos 55), Davies, Taylor.
Sporting Lisbon: Rui Patricio, Anderson Polga, Tonel, Grimi, Miguel Veloso, Abel (Romagnoli 46), Izmailov (Gladstone 84), Vukcevic, Pereirinha, Joao Moutinho, Tiui (Silva 79).

Fiorentina (0) 2 *(Kuzmanovic 70, Montolivo 81)*
Everton (0) 0 32,934
Fiorentina: Frey; Dainelli, Gamberini, Ujfalusi, Pasqual, Donadel, Montolivo, Jorgensen, Kuzmanovic (Gobbi 76), Osvaldo (Santana 74), Vieri (Pazzini 67).
Everton: Howard; Hibbert (Johnson 73), Lescott, Yobo, Jagielka, Carsley, Osman (Arteta 56), Neville, Yakubu, Cahill, Pienaar.

Leverkusen (0) 1 *(Gekas 77)*
Hamburg (0) 0 22,500
Leverkusen: Adler; Haggui, Friedrich, Sarpei, Castro, Rolfes, Barnetta, Schneider (Vidal 75), Gekas (Callsen-Bracker 88), Kiessling, Barbarez (Freier 67).
Hamburg: Rost; Reinhardt, Mathijsen, Kompany, Benjamin, De Jong, Jarolim, Demel (Boateng 56), Van der Vaart, Guerrero (Zidane 79), Olic (Trochowski 76).

Marseille (1) 3 *(Cisse 38, 55, Niang 48)*
Zenit (0) 1 *(Arshavin 82)* 30,000
Marseille: Mandanda; Taiwo, Faty (Zubar 44), Bonnart, Givet, Cheyrou, M'Bami, Nasri (Kabore 88), Valbuena, Cisse, Niang (Zenden 62).
Zenit: Malafeev; Krizanac, Kim, Anyukov (Radimov 81), Ricksen (Denisov 70), Zyryanov, Fayzulin, Timoshchuk, Gorshkov, Pogrebnyak, Arshavin.

Rangers (1) 2 *(Cousin 45, Davis 48)*
Werder Bremen (0) 0 45,959
Rangers: McGregor; Broadfoot, Papac, Cuellar, Weir, Ferguson, Hemdani, Dailly, Cousin (McCulloch 75), Adam, Davis.
Werder Bremen: Wiese; Pasanen (Boenisch 64), Naldo, Baumann, Fritz, Mertesacker, Vranjes (Hugo Almeida 60), Diego, Jensen, Rosenberg, Hunt.

Tottenham Hotspur (0) 0
PSV Eindhoven (1) 1 *(Farfan 34)* 33,259
Tottenham Hotspur: Robinson; Chimbonda, Gilberto (O'Hara 46), Zokora, Woodgate, King (Taarabt 73), Lennon, Jenas (Huddlestone 64), Berbatov, Keane, Malbranque.
PSV Eindhoven: Gomes; Kromkamp, Salcido, Alcides, Marcellis, Simons, Mendez, Culina, Koevermans (Lazovic 78), Farfan (Dzsudzsak 85), Afellay (Bakkal 90).

FOURTH ROUND SECOND LEG

Wednesday, 12 March 2008

Bayern Munich (1) 1 *(Lucio 8)*
Anderlecht (2) 2 *(Serhat 20, Yakobenko 35)* 63,000
Bayern Munich: Rensing; Sagnol, Lucio, Lahm, Breno, Ottl (Schlaudraff 73), Van Bommel, Jose Sosa, Kroos (Ribery 46), Podolski, Klose (Hamit Altintop 87).
Anderlecht: Zitka (Schollen 46); Deschacht, Sare, Juhasz, Biglia, Hassan, Goor, Gillet, De Man, Yakobenko (Boussoufa 66), Serhat (Gillis 90).

Everton (1) 2 *(Johnson 16, Arteta 67)*
Fiorentina (0) 0 38,026
Everton: Howard; Neville, Lescott, Yobo, Jagielka, Carsley, Osman, Pienaar (Anichebe 106), Johnson (Gravesen 119), Yakubu, Arteta.
Fiorentina: Frey; Dainelli, Gamberini, Ujfalusi, Pasqual, Donadel, Montolivo, Jorgensen (Santana 106), Kuzmanovic (Gobbi 90), Osvaldo, Vieri (Pazzini 46).
aet; Fiorentina won 4-2 on penalties.

Getafe (0) 1 *(Albin 77)*
Benfica (0) 0 14,000
Getafe: Abbondanzieri; Contra, Licht, Tena, Celestini, Cotelo (Cortes 74), Gavilan (Fuertes 79), De la Red, Albin, Casquero, Kepa (Signorino 69).
Benfica: Quim; EdCarlos (Sepsi 74), Leo, Nelson, Petit, Katsouranis, Rui Costa, Maxi Pereira (Di Maria 59), Rodriguez, Nuno Gomes (Mantorras 66), Makukula.

Hamburg (0) 3 *(Trochowski 53, Guerrero 64, Van der Vaart 80)*
Leverkusen (1) 2 *(Barbarez 18, Gekas 55)* 38,083
Hamburg: Rost; Atouba (Boateng 61), Reinhardt, Mathijsen, Odjidja-Ofoe (Trochowski 46), Brecko, Jarolim, Demel, Van der Vaart, Guerrero, Olic (Sam 76).
Leverkusen: Adler; Haggui, Friedrich, Sarpei, Vidal (Bulykin 87), Castro, Rolfes, Barnetta, Gekas (Callsen-Bracker 82), Kiessling, Barbarez (Schwegler 72).

PSV Eindhoven (0) 0
Tottenham Hotspur (0) 1 *(Berbatov 81)* 33,000
PSV Eindhoven: Gomes; Kromkamp, Salcido, Alcides, Marcellis, Simons, Mendez (Bakkal 112), Culina, Koevermans (Lazovic 72), Farfan, Afellay (Dzsudzsak 82).
Tottenham Hotspur: Robinson; Chimbonda, Lee (Bent 46), Zokora, Woodgate, King (Lennon 61), Huddlestone, Jenas, Berbatov, Keane (O'Hara 86), Malbranque.
aet; PSV Eindhoven won 6-5 on penalties.

Zenit (1) 2 *(Pogrebnyk 39, 78)*
Marseille (0) 0 21,500
Zenit: Malafeev; Anyukov, Krizanac, Sirl, Shirokov, Zyryanov, Fayzulin (Fatih 75), Denisov, Timoshchuk, Pogrebnyk, Arshavin.
Marseille: Mandanda; Taiwo, Bonnart, Givet (Ayew 89), Cheyrou, M'Bami, Cana, Nasri, Valbuena, Cisse, Niang.

Thursday, 13 March 2008

Sporting Lisbon (0) 1 *(Pereirinha 85)*
Bolton Wanderers (0) 0 22,031
Sporting Lisbon: Rui Patricio; Anderson Polga, Tonel, Grimi, Abel, Izmailov (Gladstone 87), Vukcevic (Tiui 66), Pereirinha, Joao Moutinho, Romagnoli (Silva 75), Liedson.
Bolton Wanderers: Al Habsi; Hunt, Samuel, Teimourian (Braaten 71), Cahill, Meite, O'Brien J, Guthrie, Helguson (Woolfe 76), Vaz Te, Giannakopoulos.

Werder Bremen (0) 1 *(Diego 58)*
Rangers (0) 0 33,660
Werder Bremen: Wiese; Boenisch, Naldo, Mertesacker, Diego, Owomoyela (Harnik 78), Jensen, Borowski, Rosenberg, Hunt, Hugo Almeida (Sanogo 66).
Rangers: McGregor; Broadfoot, Papac, Cuellar, Weir, Ferguson, Hemdani, Dailly, Novo (McCulloch 78), Adam (Whittaker 57), Davis.

QUARTER-FINALS FIRST LEG

Thursday, 3 April 2008

Bayern Munich (1) 1 *(Toni 26)*
Getafe (0) 1 *(Contra 90)* 62,000
Bayern Munich: Kahn; Lucio, Demichelis, Lahm, Jansen (Lell 80), Ribery, Ze Roberto, Van Bommel (Ottl 86), Schweinsteiger, Toni (Klose 80), Podolski.
Getafe: Ustari; Mario, Signorino, Cortes, Tena, De la Red, Alvin, Casquero (Celestini 73), Hernandez, Granero (Contra 78), Uche (Del Moral 68).

Fiorentina (0) 1 *(Mutu 56)*
PSV Eindhoven (0) 1 *(Koevermans 63)* 34,317
Fiorentina: Frey; Gamberini, Ujfalusi, Liverani (Vieri 76), Montolivo, Gobbi, Jorgensen, Kuzmanovic (Donadel 67), Santana (Osvaldo 90), Mutu, Pazzini.
PSV Eindhoven: Gomes (Roorda 59); Kromkamp, Salcido, Rajkovic, Marcellis, Simons, Mendes, Culina, Koevermans (Lazovic 64), Farfan (Vayrynen 90), Afellay.

Leverkusen (1) 1 *(Kiessling 33)*
Zenit (1) 4 *(Arshavin 20, Pogrebnyak 53, Anyukov 61, Denisov 65)* 19,500
Leverkusen: Adler; Haggui, Friedrich, Vidal (Sinkiewicz 74), Castro, Rolfes, Barnetta, Gresko (Sarpei 66), Schneider (Barbarez 62), Gekas, Kiessling.
Zenit: Malafeev; Krizanac, Anyukov, Sirl, Shirokov, Syryanov, Fayzulin, Timoschuk, Pogrebnyak, Arshavin, Denisov.

Rangers (0) 0
Sporting Lisbon (0) 0 48,923
Rangers: McGregor; Broadfoot, Papac, Cuellar, Weir, Ferguson, Hemdani, Thomson, McCulloch, Darcheville (Novo 72), Davis.
Sporting Lisbon: Rui Patricio; Anderson Polga, Tonel, Grimi, Miguel Veloso, Abel, Izmailov (Pereirinha 70), Vukcevic (Silva 76), Joao Moutinho, Romagnoli, Liedson.

QUARTER-FINALS SECOND LEG

Thursday, 10 April 2008

Getafe (1) 3 *(Contra 44, Casquero 92, Braulio 94)*
Bayern Munich (0) 3 *(Ribery 89, Toni 115, 120)* 14,225
Getafe: Abbondanzieri; Contra (Mario Cotelo 66), Licht, Cortes, Tena, Celestini, Gavilan, De la Red■, Casquero, Del Moral (Braulio 61), Uche (Belenguer 21).
Bayern Munich: Kahn; Lucio, Demichelis, Lahm, Lell (Jansen 46), Ribery, Ze Roberto (Podolski 75), Van Bommel, Schweinsteiger (Jose Sosa 64), Toni, Klose.
aet.

PSV Eindhoven (0) 0
Fiorentina (1) 2 *(Mutu 38, 53)* 35,000
PSV Eindhoven: Gomes; Kromkamp, Salcido, Rajkovic, Marcellis, Simons, Mendez (Zonneveld 82), Culina (Vayrynen 78), Dzsudzsak, Bakkal (Lazovic 46), Koevermans.
Fiorentina: Frey; Gamberini, Ujfalusi, Donadel, Liverani, Montolivo, Gobbi, Jorgensen, Santana (Kuzmanovic 78), Mutu (Osvaldo 86), Pazzini (Vieri 73).

Sporting Lisbon (0) 0
Rangers (0) 2 *(Darchville 60, Whittaker 90)* 31,155
Sporting Lisbon: Rui Patricio; Tonel, Grimi (Tiui 76), Miguel Veloso, Gladstone (Pereirinha 70), Abel, Izmailov (Djalo 62), Vukcevic, Joao Moutinho, Romagnoli, Liedson.
Rangers: McGregor; Broadfoot, Papac, Cuellar, Dailly, Ferguson, Hemdani, Thomson, McCulloch (Whittaker 77), Darchville (Cousin 72), Davis.

Zenit (0) 0
Leverkusen (1) 1 *(Bulykin 18)* 21,500
Zenit: Malafeev; Krizanac, Anyukov, Sirl, Shirokov, Zyryanov, Fayzulin (Radimov 87), Timoshchuk, Pogrebnyak, Arshavin, Denisov.
Leverkusen: Adler; Haggui, Sarpei, Sinkiewicz, Castro, Callsen-Bracker, Freier (Kiessling 69), Dum (Gekas 75), Schwegler (Rolfes 59), Schneider, Bulykin.

SEMI-FINALS FIRST LEG

Thursday, 24 April 2008

Bayern Munich (1) 1 *(Ribery 18)*
Zenit (0) 1 *(Lucio 60 (og))* 66,000
Bayern Munich: Kahn (Rensing 67); Lucio, Demichelis, Lahm (Kroos 80), Jansen, Ribery, Ze Roberto, Van Bommel, Schweinsteiger (Lell 66), Podolski, Klose.
Zenit: Malafeev; Krizanac, Ricksen, Sirl, Shirokov, Zyryanov, Fayzulin, Timoshchuk, Pogrebnyak, Arshavin, Denisov.

Rangers (0) 0
Fiorentina (0) 0 49,199
Rangers: Alexander; Broadfoot, Papac, Cuellar, Weir, Dailly, Hemdani, Davis, Novo (Buffel 59), Darcheville (Cousin 60), Whittaker.
Fiorentina: Frey; Gamberini, Ujfalusi, Liverani, Montolivo, Gobbi, Jorgensen, Kuzmanovic, Santana, Mutu, Pazzini (Vieri 80).

Zenit (2) 4 *(Pogrebnyak 4, 73, Zyryanov 39, Fayzulin 54)*
Bayern Munich (0) 0 21,500
Zenit: Malafeev; Krizanac, Anyukov, Shirokov, Zyryanov, Fayzulin, Timoshchuk, Gershkov, Dominguez (Ho Lee 89), Pogrebnyak, Denisov (Ionov 90).
Bayern Munich: Kahn; Lucio, Demichelis, Lahm, Jansen (Lell 46), Ribery, Ze Roberto (Podolski 46), Van Bommel, Schweinsteiger, Toni, Klose (Jose Sosa 62).

SEMI-FINALS SECOND LEG

Thursday, 1 May 2008
Fiorentina (0) 0
Rangers (0) 0 39,130
Fiorentina: Frey; Gamberini, Ujfalusi, Donadel (Kuzmanovic 42), Liverani, Montolivo, Gobbi, Jorgensen, Santana (Semioli 94), Mutu, Pazzini (Vieri 79).
Rangers: Alexander; Broadfoot, Papac, Cuellar, Weir, Ferguson, Hemdani, Thomson, Davis (Novo 81), Darchville (Cousin■ 65), Whittaker.
aet; Rangers won 4-2 on penalties.

UEFA CUP FINAL 2008

Wednesday, 14 May 2007
(at City of Manchester Stadium, Manchester, 47,726)

Zenit (0) 2 *(Denisov 72, Zyryanov 90)* **Rangers (0) 0**

Zenit: Malafeev; Krizanac, Anyukov, Sirl, Shirokov, Zyryanov, Fayzulin (Kim 90), Timoshchuk, Fatih, Arshavin, Denisov.

Rangers: Alexander; Broadfoot, Papac (Novo 77), Cuellar, Weir, Ferguson, Hemdani (McCulloch 80), Thomson, Darcheville, Davis, Whittaker (Boyd 86).

Referee: Frojdfeldt (Sweden).

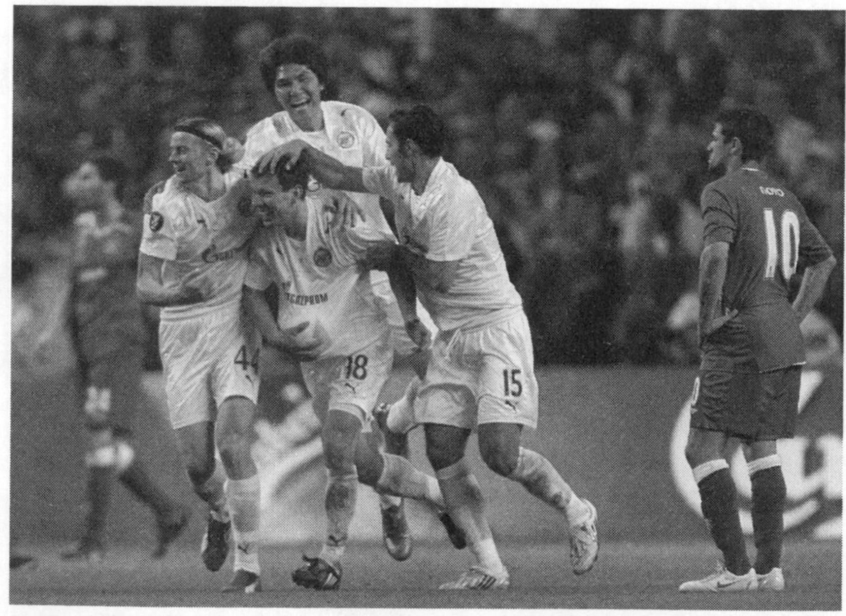

Zenit St Petersburg's Konstatin Zyryanov (18) celebrates with his team mates after scoring his side's second goal in the last minute of the 2-0 UEFA Cup Final defeat of Rangers at the City of Manchester Stadium.
(EMPICS Sport/PA Photos/Mike Egerton)

UEFA CHAMPIONS LEAGUE 2008–09

Champions League 2008–09 participating clubs (provisional)

IOC	*Stage*	*Club*
ENG1	Grp	Manchester United FC
ESP1	Grp	Real Madrid CF
ESP2	Grp	Villarreal CF
ESP3	Q3	FC Barcelona
ESP4	Q3	Club Atlético de Madrid
ENG2	Grp	Chelsea FC
ENG3	Q3	Arsenal FC
ENG4	Q3	Liverpool FC
ITA1	Grp	FC Internazionale Milano
ITA2	Grp	AS Roma
ITA3	Q3	Juventus
ITA4	Q3	ACF Fiorentina
FRA1	Grp	Olympique Lyonnais
FRA2	Grp	FC Girondins de Bordeaux
FRA3	Q3	Olympique de Marseille
GER1	Grp	FC Bayern München
GER2	Grp	Werder Bremen
GER3	Q3	FC Schalke 04
POR1	Grp	FC Porto
POR2	Grp	Sporting Clube de Portugal
POR3	Q3	Vitória SC
ROU1	Grp	CFR 1907 Cluj
ROU2	Q3	FC Steaua Bucureşti
NED1	Grp	PSV Eindhoven
NED2	Q3	FC Twente
RUS1	Grp	FC Zenit St. Petersburg
RUS2	Q3	FC Spartak Moskva
SCO1	Grp	Celtic FC
SCO2	Q2	Rangers FC
UKR1	Q3	FC Shakhtar Donetsk
UKR2	Q2	FC Dynamo Kyiv
BEL1	Q3	R. Standard de Liège
BEL2	Q2	RSC Anderlecht
CZE1	Q3	SK Slavia Praha
CZE2	Q2	AC Sparta Praha
TUR1	Q3	Galatasaray AS
TUR2	Q2	Fenerbahçe SK
GRE1	Q3	Olympiacos CFP
GRE2	Q2	Panathinaikos FC
BUL	Q3	PFC Levski Sofia
SUI	Q2	FC Basel 1893
NOR	Q2	SK Brann
ISR	Q2	Beitar Jerusalem FC
SCG	Q2	FK Partizan
DEN	Q2	Aalborg BK
AUT	Q2	SK Rapid Wien
POL	Q2	Wisla Kraków
HUN	Q2	MTK Budapest
SVK	Q1	FC Artmedia Petržalka
CRO	Q1	NK Dinamo Zagreb
CYP	Q1	Anorthosis Famagusta FC
SWE	Q1	IFK Göteborg
SVN	Q1	NK Domžale
BIH	Q1	FK Modriča
LVA	Q1	FK Ventspils
LTU	Q1	FBK Kaunus
FIN	Q1	Tampere United
MDA	Q1	FC Sheriff
IRL	Q1	Drogheda United FC
GEO	Q1	FC Dinamo Tbilisi
MKD	Q1	FK Rabotnicki
ISL	Q1	Valur Reykjavík
BLR	Q1	FC BATE Borisov
ALB	Q1	KS Dinamo Tirana
EST	Q1	FC Levadia Tallinn
ARM	Q1	FC Pyunik
AZE	Q1	FC Inter Bakı
KAZ	Q1	FK Aktobe
NIR	Q1	Linfield FC
WAL	Q1	Llanelli AFC
FRO	Q1	NSÍ Runavík
LUX	Q1	F91 Dudelange
MLT	Q1	Valetta FC
MNE	Q1	FK Budućnost Podgorica
AND	Q1	FC Santa Coloma
SMR	Q1	S.S. Murata

UEFA CUP 2008–09

UEFA Cup 2008–09 participating clubs

IOC	*Round*	*Club*
ESP	1st	Valencia CF[1]
ESP	1st	Sevilla FC
ESP	1st	Real Racing Club Santander
ENG	1st	Portsmouth FC[1]
ENG	1st	Everton FC
ENG	1st	Tottenham Hotspur FC[3]
ENG	Q1	Manchester City FC[4]
ITA	1st	AC Milan
ITA	1st	UC Sampdoria
ITA	1st	Udinese Calcio
FRA	1st	AS Nancy-Lorraine
FRA	1st	AS Saint-Etienne
FRA	1st	Paris Saint-Germain FC[3]
GER	1st	Hamburger SV
GER	1st	VfL Wolfsburg
GER	1st	BV Borussia Dortmund[2]
GER	Q1	Hertha BSC Berlin[4]
POR	1st	SL Benfica
POR	1st	CS Marítimo
POR	1st	Vitória FC
ROU	1st	FC Rapid Bucureşti
ROU	1st	FC Dinamo 1848 Bucureşti
ROU	1st	AFC Unirea Valahorum Urziceni
ROU	1st	FCU Politehnica Timisoara
NED	1st	Feyenoord[1]
NED	1st	AFC Ajax
NED	1st	SC Heerenveen
NED	1st	NEC Nijmegen
RUS	1st	PFC CSKA Moskva[1]
RUS	Q2	FC Moskva
SCO	1st	Motherwell FC
SCO	Q2	Queen of the South FC[2]
UKR	1st	FC Metalist Kharkiv
UKR	Q2	FC Dnipro Dnipropetrovsk
BEL	1st	Club Brugge KV[1]
BEL	Q2	KAA Gent[2]
CZE	1st	FC Baník Ostrava
CZE	Q2	FC Slovan Liberec[2]
TUR	1st	Kayserispor
TUR	Q2	Beşiktaş JK
GRE	Q2	AEK Athens FC
GRE	Q2	Aris Thessaloniki FC[2]
BUL	Q2	PFC Litex Lovech[1]
BUL	Q2	PFC Lokomotiv Sofia
BUL	Q1	PFC Cherno More Varna
SUI	Q2	BSC Young Boys
SUI	Q2	FC Zürich
SUI	Q1	AC Bellinzona[2]
NOR	Q2	Lillestrøm SK[1]
NOR	Q2	Stabæk IF
NOR	Q1	Viking FC
ISR	Q2	Maccabi Netanya FC
ISR	Q1	Hapoel Kiryat Shmona FC
ISR	Q1	Hapoel Tel-Aviv FC[2]
SRB	Q2	FK Crvena Zvezda
SRB	Q1	FK Vojvodina
SRB	Q1	FK Borac
DEN	Q1	Brøndby IF[1]
DEN	Q1	FC Midtjylland
DEN	Q1	FC København
DEN	Q1	FC Nordsjælland[4]
AUT	Q1	FC Salzburg
AUT	Q1	FK Austria Wien
POL	Q1	Legia Warszawa[1]
POL	Q1	KKS Lech Poznań
HUN	Q1	Debreceni VSC
HUN	Q1	Győri ETO FC
SVK	Q1	MŠK Žilina
SVK	Q1	FC Spartak Trnava[2]
CRO	Q1	NK Slaven Koprivnica
CRO	Q1	HNK Hajduk Split[2]
CYP	Q1	APOEL FC[1]
CYP	Q1	AC Omonia
SWE	Q1	Kalmar FC[1]
SWE	Q1	Djurgårdens IF FF
SVN	Q1	NK IB Ljubljana[1]
SVN	Q1	FC Koper
BIH	Q1	NK Zrinjski[1]
BIH	Q1	NK Široki Brijeg
LVA	Q1	SK Liepājas Metalurgs
LVA	Q1	JFK Olimps[2]
LTU	Q1	FK Suduva
LTU	Q1	FK Vetra[2]
FIN	Q1	FC Haka
FIN	Q1	FC Honko Espoo[2]
MDA	Q1	FC Dacia Chisinau
MDA	Q1	FC Nistru Otaci[2]
IRL	Q1	Cork City FC[1]
IRL	Q1	Saint Patrick's Athletic FC
GEO	Q1	FC Zestafoni[1]
GEO	Q1	FC WIT Georgia
LIE	Q1	FC Vaduz[1]
MKD	Q1	FK Milano
MKD	Q1	FK Pelister
ISL	Q1	FH Hafnarfjördur[1]
ISL	Q1	ÍA Akranes
BLR	Q1	FC MTZ-RIPO Minsk[1]
BLR	Q1	FC Gomel
ALB	Q1	KS Vllaznia[1]
ALB	Q1	FK Partizani
EST	Q1	FC Flora[1]
EST	Q1	FC TVMK Tallinn
ARM	Q1	FC Ararat Yerevan[1]
ARM	Q1	FC Banants
AZE	Q1	FK Khazar Lenkoran[1]
AZE	Q1	FK Olimpik Baku
KAZ	Q1	FC Tobol Kostanay[1]
KAZ	Q1	FC Shakhtyor Karagandy
NIR	Q1	Glentoran FC
NIR	Q1	Cliftonville FC
WAL	Q1	Bangor City FC
WAL	Q1	The New Saints FC
FRO	Q1	EB Streymur
FRO	Q1	B36 Tórshavn
LUX	Q1	CS Grevenmacher[1]
LUX	Q1	FC Racing Union Luxembourg
MLT	Q1	Birkirkara FC[1]
MLT	Q1	Marsaxlokk FC
MNE	Q1	FK Mogren[1]
MNE	Q1	FK Zeta
AND	Q1	UE Sant Julià[1]
SMR	Q1	AC Juvenes-Dogana[2]
TBC	Q2	11 Teams as winners of UEFA Intertoto Cup

[1] domestic cup winners, [2] losing domestic cup finalists, [3] domestic league cup winners, [4] Fair Play winners

SUMMARY OF APPEARANCES

EUROPEAN CUP AND CHAMPIONS LEAGUE (1955–2008)

ENGLISH CLUBS
19 Manchester U
18 Liverpool
12 Arsenal
6 Chelsea
4 Everton, Leeds U
3 Derby Co, Wolverhampton W, Aston Villa, Newcastle U, Nottingham F
1 Burnley, Tottenham H, Ipswich T, Manchester C, Blackburn R

SCOTTISH CLUBS
26 Rangers
23 Celtic
3 Aberdeen, Hearts
1 Dundee, Dundee U, Kilmarnock, Hibernian

WELSH CLUBS
6 Barry T
3 TNS
1 Cwmbran T, Rhyl

NORTHERN IRELAND CLUBS
23 Linfield
11 Glentoran
3 Crusaders, Portadown
1 Glenavon, Ards, Distillery, Derry C, Coleraine, Cliftonville

REPUBLIC OF IRELAND CLUBS
7 Shamrock R, Dundalk
6 Shelbourne, Waterford
4 Bohemians
3 Drumcondra, St Patrick's Ath, Derry C*
2 Sligo R, Limerick, Athlone T, Cork City
1 Cork Hibs, Cork Celtic

Winners: Celtic 1966–67; Manchester U 1967–68, 1998–99; 2007–08; Liverpool 1976–77, 1977–78, 1980–81, 1983–84, 2004–05; Nottingham F 1978–79, 1979–80; Aston Villa 1981–82

Finalists: Celtic 1969–70; Leeds U 1974–75; Liverpool 1984–85, 2006–07; Arsenal 2005–06; Chelsea 2007–08

EUROPEAN CUP-WINNERS' CUP (1960–99)

ENGLISH CLUBS
6 Tottenham H
5 Manchester U, Liverpool, Chelsea
4 West Ham U
3 Arsenal, Everton
2 Manchester C
1 Wolverhampton W, Leicester C, WBA, Leeds U, Sunderland, Southampton, Ipswich T, Newcastle U

SCOTTISH CLUBS
10 Rangers
8 Aberdeen, Celtic
3 Hearts
2 Dunfermline Ath, Dundee U
1 Dundee, Hibernian, St Mirren, Motherwell, Airdrieonians, Kilmarnock

WELSH CLUBS
14 Cardiff C
8 Wrexham
7 Swansea C
3 Bangor C
1 Borough U, Newport Co, Merthyr Tydfil, Barry T, Llansantfraid, Cwmbran T

NORTHERN IRELAND CLUBS
9 Glentoran
5 Glenavon
4 Ballymena U, Coleraine
3 Crusaders, Linfield
2 Ards, Bangor
1 Derry C, Distillery, Portadown, Carrick Rangers, Cliftonville

REPUBLIC OF IRELAND CLUBS
6 Shamrock R
4 Shelbourne
3 Limerick, Waterford, Dundalk, Bohemians
2 Cork Hibs, Galway U, Derry C*, Cork City
1 Cork Celtic, St Patrick's Ath, Finn Harps, Home Farm, University College Dublin, Bray W, Sligo R

Winners: Tottenham H 1962–63; West Ham U 1964–65; Manchester C 1969–70; Chelsea 1970–71, 1997–98; Rangers 1971–72; Aberdeen 1982–83; Everton 1984–85; Manchester U 1990–91; Arsenal 1993–94

Finalists: Rangers 1960–61, 1966–67; Liverpool 1965–66; Leeds U 1972–73; West Ham U 1975–76; Arsenal 1979–80, 1994–95

EUROPEAN FAIRS CUP & UEFA CUP (1955–2008)

ENGLISH CLUBS
13 Leeds U
12 Liverpool
10 Aston Villa, Ipswich T, Newcastle U
9 Arsenal
8 Everton, Tottenham H
7 Manchester U
6 Southampton, Chelsea, Blackburn R
5 Nottingham F, Manchester C
4 Birmingham C, Wolverhampton W, WBA
3 Sheffield W
2 Stoke C, Derby Co, QPR, Leicester C, Middlesbrough, West Ham U, Bolton W
1 Burnley, Coventry C, Millwall, Norwich C, London Rep XI, Watford, Fulham

SCOTTISH CLUBS
19 Dundee U
16 Hibernian, Aberdeen, Rangers
15 Celtic
13 Hearts
7 Kilmarnock, Dunfermline Ath
5 Dundee
3 St Mirren
2 Partick T, Motherwell, St Johnstone
1 Morton, Raith R, Livingston, Gretna

WELSH CLUBS
5 TNS
4 Bangor C
3 Inter Cardiff (formerly Inter Cable-Tel), Cwmbran T, Rhyl
2 Newtown, Carmarthen T, Barry T
1 Afan Lido, Haverfordwest, Llanelli

NORTHERN IRELAND CLUBS
17 Glentoran
9 Linfield
8 Coleraine, Portadown
7 Glenavon
3 Crusaders
1 Ards, Ballymena U, Bangor, Dungannon Swifts

EIRE CLUBS
12 Bohemians
7 Shelbourne
6 Dundalk
5 Shamrock R, Cork City
4 Derry C*, St Patrick's Ath
3 Finn Harps, Longford T, Drogheda U
2 Drumcondra
1 Cork Hibs, Athlone T, Limerick, Galway U, Bray Wanderers

Winners: Leeds U 1967–68, 1970–71; Newcastle U 1968–69; Arsenal 1969–70; Tottenham H 1971–72, 1983–84; Liverpool 1972–73, 1975–76, 2000–01; Ipswich T 1980–81

Finalists: London 1955–58, Birmingham C 1958–60, 1960–61; Leeds U 1966–67; Wolverhampton W 1971–72; Tottenham H 1973–74; Dundee U 1986–87; Celtic 2002–03; Middlesbrough 2005–06; Rangers 2007–08

** Now play in League of Ireland*

INTERTOTO CUP 2007

▪ *Denotes player sent off.*

FIRST ROUND, FIRST LEG

Sant Julia 2, Slavija 3
Tobol 3, Zestaponi 0
Valur 0, Cork City 2
Zagreb 2, Vllaznia 1
Achnas 1, Makedonija 0
Baku 1, Dacia 1
Differdange 0, Slovan 2
Hammarby 1, KI 0
Cliftonville 1, Dinaburg 1
Shakhtyor 4, Ararat 1
Gloria 2, Grbalj 1
Birkirkara 0, Maribor 3
Vetra 3, Llanelli 1
Honka 0, VMK 0

FIRST ROUND, SECOND LEG

Slavija 3, Sant Julia 2
Zestaponi 2, Tobol 0
Cork City 0, Valur 1
Vllaznia 1, Zagreb 0
Makedonija 2, Achnas 0
Dacia 4, Baku 2
Slovan 3, Differdange 0
KI 1, Hammarby 2
Dinaburg 0, Cliftonville 1
Ararat 2, Shakhtyor 0
Grbalj 1, Gloria 1
Maribor 2, Birkirkara 1
Llanelli 5, Vetra 3
VMK 2, Honka 4

SECOND ROUND, FIRST LEG

Maccabi Haifa 0, Gloria 2
Dacia 0, St Gallen 1
Gent 2, Cliftonville 0
Cork City 1, Hammarby 1
ZTE 0, Rubin 3
Rapid Vienna 3, Slovan 1
Slavija 0, Otelul 0
Makedonija 0, Chernomore 4
Maribor 2, Kula 0
Chernomorets 4, Shakhtyor 2
Tobol 1, Liberec 1
Honka 2, Aalborg 2
Vetra v Legia match cancelled.
Trabzonspor 6, Vllaznia 0

SECOND ROUND, SECOND LEG

Gloria 3, Maccabi Haifa 4
St Gallen 0, Dacia 5
Cliftonville 0, Gent 4
Hammarby 1, Cork City 0
Rubin 2, ZTE 0
Slovan 1, Rapid Vienna 0
Otelul 3, Slavija 0
Chernomore 3, Makedonija 0
Kula 5, Maribor 0
Shakhtyor 0, Chernomorets 2
Liberec 0, Tobol 2
Aalborg 1, Honka 1
Legia v Vetra match cancelled.
Vllaznia 0, Trabzonspor 4

THIRD ROUND, FIRST LEG

Chernomore 0, Sampdoria 1
Gloria 2, Atletico Madrid 1
Otelul 2, Trabzonspor 1
Chernomorets 0, Lens 0
Rapid Vienna 3, Rubin 1
Dacia 1, Hamburg 1
Gent 1, Aalborg 1
Vetra 0, Blackburn Rovers 2
Hammarby 0, Utrecht 0
Tobol 1, OFI Crete 0
Kula 1, Leiria 0

THIRD ROUND, SECOND LEG

Sampdoria 1, Chernomore 0
Atletico Madrid 1, Gloria 0
Trabzonspor 1, Otelul 2
Lens 3, Chernomorets 1
Rubin 0, Rapid Vienna 0
Hamburg 4, Dacia 0
Aalborg 2, Gent 1
Blackburn Rovers 4, Vetra 0
Utrecht 1, Hammarby 1
OFI Crete 0, Tobol 1
Leiria 4, Kula 1
Legia expelled because of crowd trouble.
Eleven winners qualify for UEFA Cup Second Qualifying Round.

Vetra (0) 0

Blackburn Rovers (1) 2 *(McCarthy 30, Derbyshire 81)* 5200

Blackburn Rovers: Friedel; Ooijer, Warnock, Tugay (Mokoena 46), Nelsen, Samba, Bentley (Derbyshire 65), Savage, Roberts, McCarthy (Rigters 65), Pedersen.

Blackburn Rovers (1) 4 *(Pedersen 25, Roberts 48, McCarthy 54, Samba 55)*

Vetra (0) 0 *Milosevski*▪ 11,854

Blackburn Rovers: Friedel; Ooijer, Warnock, Mokoena (Dunn 53), Nelsen, Samba, Bentley, Savage, Roberts (Rigters 57), McCarthy (Derbyshire 57), Pedersen.

WORLD CLUB CHAMPIONSHIP

Played annually up to 1974 and intermittently since then between the winners of the European Cup and the winners of the South American Champions Cup — known as the Copa Libertadores. In 1980 the winners were decided by one match arranged in Tokyo in February 1981 which remained the venue until 2004, when the match was superseded by the FIFA Club World Championship. AC Milan replaced Marseille who had been stripped of their European Cup title in 1993.

1960 Real Madrid beat Penarol 0-0, 5-1
1961 Penarol beat Benfica 0-1, 5-0, 2-1
1962 Santos beat Benfica 3-2, 5-2
1963 Santos beat AC Milan 2-4, 4-2, 1-0
1964 Inter-Milan beat Independiente 0-1, 2-0, 1-0
1965 Inter-Milan beat Independiente 3-0, 0-0
1966 Penarol beat Real Madrid 2-0, 2-0
1967 Racing Club beat Celtic 0-1, 2-1, 1-0
1968 Estudiantes beat Manchester United 1-0, 1-1
1969 AC Milan beat Estudiantes 3-0, 1-2
1970 Feyenoord beat Estudiantes 2-2, 1-0
1971 Nacional beat Panathinaikos* 1-1, 2-1
1972 Ajax beat Independiente 1-1, 3-0
1973 Independiente beat Juventus* 1-0
1974 Atlético Madrid* beat Independiente 0-1, 2-0
1975 Independiente and Bayern Munich could not agree dates; no matches.
1976 Bayern Munich beat Cruzeiro 2-0, 0-0
1977 Boca Juniors beat Borussia Moenchengladbach* 2-2, 3-0
1978 Not contested
1979 Olimpia beat Malmö* 1-0, 2-1
1980 Nacional beat Nottingham Forest 1-0
1981 Flamengo beat Liverpool 3-0
1982 Penarol beat Aston Villa 2-0
1983 Gremio Porto Alegre beat SV Hamburg 2-1
1984 Independiente beat Liverpool 1-0
1985 Juventus beat Argentinos Juniors 4-2 on penalties after a 2-2 draw
1986 River Plate beat Steaua Bucharest 1-0
1987 FC Porto beat Penarol 2-1 after extra time
1988 Nacional (Uru) beat PSV Eindhoven 7-6 on penalties after 1-1 draw
1989 AC Milan beat Atletico Nacional (Col) 1-0 after extra time
1990 AC Milan beat Olimpia 3-0
1991 Red Star Belgrade beat Colo Colo 3-0
1992 Sao Paulo beat Barcelona 2-1
1993 Sao Paulo beat AC Milan 3-2
1994 Velez Sarsfield beat AC Milan 2-0
1995 Ajax beat Gremio Porto Alegre 4-3 on penalties after 0-0 draw
1996 Juventus beat River Plate 1-0
1997 Borussia Dortmund beat Cruzeiro 2-0
1998 Real Madrid beat Vasco da Gama 2-1
1999 Manchester U beat Palmeiras 1-0
2000 Boca Juniors beat Real Madrid 2-1
2001 Bayern Munich beat Boca Juniors 1-0 after extra time
2002 Real Madrid beat Olimpia 2-0
2003 Boca Juniors beat AC Milan 3-1 on penalties after 1-1 draw
2004 Porto beat Once Caldas 8-7 on penalties after 0-0 draw

*European Cup runners-up; winners declined to take part.

EUROPEAN SUPER CUP

Played annually between the winners of the European Champions' Cup and the European Cup-Winners' Cup (UEFA Cup from 2000). AC Milan replaced Marseille in 1993–94.

EUROPEAN SUPER CUP 2007

31 August 2007, Monaco (attendance 18,000)

AC Milan (0) 3 *(Inzaghi 55, Jankulovski 62, Kaka 87)* **Sevilla (1) 1** *(Renato 14)*

AC Milan: Dida; Oddo, Kaladze, Nesta, Jankulovski, Ambrosini, Pirlo, Gattuso (Emerson 73), Kaka, Seedorf (Brocchi 89), Inzaghi (Gilardino 88).

Sevilla: Palop; Daniel Alves, Escude (Luis Fabiano 84), Marti (Kerzhakov 65), Dragutinovic, Jesus Navas, Poulsen, Duda (Maresca 74), Renato, Keita, Kanoute.

Referee: K. Plautz (Austria).

PREVIOUS MATCHES

1972 Ajax beat Rangers 3-1, 3-2
1973 Ajax beat AC Milan 0-1, 6-0
1974 Not contested
1975 Dynamo Kiev beat Bayern Munich 1-0, 2-0
1976 Anderlecht beat Bayern Munich 4-1, 1-2
1977 Liverpool beat Hamburg 1-1, 6-0
1978 Anderlecht beat Liverpool 3-1, 1-2
1979 Nottingham F beat Barcelona 1-0, 1-1
1980 Valencia beat Nottingham F 1-0, 1-2
1981 Not contested
1982 Aston Villa beat Barcelona 0-1, 3-0
1983 Aberdeen beat Hamburg 0-0, 2-0
1984 Juventus beat Liverpool 2-0
1985 Juventus v Everton not contested due to UEFA ban on English clubs
1986 Steaua Bucharest beat Dynamo Kiev 1-0
1987 FC Porto beat Ajax 1-0, 1-0
1988 KV Mechelen beat PSV Eindhoven 3-0, 0-1
1989 AC Milan beat Barcelona 1-1, 1-0
1990 AC Milan beat Sampdoria 1-1, 2-0
1991 Manchester U beat Red Star Belgrade 1-0
1992 Barcelona beat Werder Bremen 1-1, 2-1
1993 Parma beat AC Milan 0-1, 2-0
1994 AC Milan beat Arsenal 0-0, 2-0
1995 Ajax beat Zaragoza 1-1, 4-0
1996 Juventus beat Paris St Germain 6-1, 3-1
1997 Barcelona beat Borussia Dortmund 2-0, 1-1
1998 Chelsea beat Real Madrid 1-0
1999 Lazio beat Manchester U 1-0
2000 Galatasaray beat Real Madrid 2-1
2001 Liverpool beat Bayern Munich 3-2
2002 Real Madrid beat Feyenoord 3-1
2003 AC Milan beat Porto 1-0
2004 Valencia beat Porto 2-1
2005 Liverpool beat CSKA Moscow 3-1
2006 Sevilla beat Barcelona 3-0
2007 AC Milan beat Sevilla 3-1

FIFA CLUB WORLD CUP 2007

Formerly known as the FIFA Club World Championship, this tournament is played annually between the champion clubs from all 6 continental confederations, although since 2007 the champions of Oceania must play a qualifying play-off against the champion club of the permanent host country Japan.

FIFA CLUB WORLD CUP 2007

PLAY-OFF FOR QUARTER-FINALS

Sepahan (2) 3 *(Emad Mohammed 3, 4, Abdul Wahab Abu Al Hail 47)*, **Waitakere United (0) 1** *(Aghily 74 (og))*
att: 24,788 in Tokyo.

QUARTER-FINALS

Etoile Sportive Du Sahel (0) 1 *(Narry 85)*, **Pachuca (0) 0**
att: 34,934 in Tokyo.
Sepahan (0) 1 *(Karimi 80)*, **Urawa Red Diamonds (1) 3** *(Nagai 32, Washington 54, Aghily 70 (og))*
att: 33,263 in Tokyo.

SEMI-FINALS

Urawa Red Diamonds (0) 0, AC Milan (0) 1 *(Seedorf 68)*
att: 67,005 in Yokohama.
Etoile Sportive Du Sahel (0) 0, Boca Juniors (1) 1 *(Cardozo 37)*
att: 37,255 in Tokyo.

MATCH FOR 3RD PLACE

Etoil Sportive Du Sahel (1) 2 *(Frej 5 (pen), Chermiti 75)*, **Urawa Red Diamonds (1) 2** *(Washington 35, 70)*
att: 53,363 in Yokohama.
Urawa Red Diamonds won 4-2 on penalties.

FIFA CLUB WORLD CUP FINAL 2007

Sunday 16 December, Yokohama, Japan (attendance 68,263)

Boca Juniors (1) 2 *(Palacio 22, Ledesma 85)*

AC Milan (1) 4 *(Inzaghi 21, 71, Nesta 50, Kaka 61)*

Boca Juniors: Caranta; Morel Rodriguez, Ibarra, Battaglia, Palermo, Palacio, Gonzalez (Ledesma■ 67), Cardozo (Gracian 68), Maidana, Banega, Paletta.

AC Milan: Dida; Maldini, Kaladze■, Gattuso (Emerson 65), Inzaghi (Cafu 76), Seedorf (Brocchi 87), Nesta, Pirlo, Kaka, Ambrosini, Bonera.

Referee: Rodriguez (Mexico).

PREVIOUS MATCHES

2000 Corinthians beat Vaso de Gama 4-3 on penalties after 0-0 draw
2005 Sao Paulo beat Liverpool 1-0
2006 Internacional beat Barcelona 1-0
2007 AC Milan beat Boca Juniors 4-2

■ *Denotes player sent off.*

INTERNATIONAL DIRECTORY

The latest available information has been given regarding numbers of clubs and players registered with FIFA, the world governing body. Where known, official colours are listed. With European countries, League tables show a number of signs. * indicates relegated teams, + play-offs, *+ relegated after play-offs, ++ promoted.

There are 207 member associations. The four home countries, England, Scotland, Northern Ireland and Wales, are dealt with elsewhere in the Yearbook; but basic details appear in this directory. The following countries are not members of FIFA: Gibraltar, Kosovo, and Northern Cyprus.

EUROPE

ALBANIA

The Football Association of Albania, Rruga Labinoti, Pallati Perballe Shkolles 'Gjuhet e Huaja'.
Founded: 1930; *National Colours:* Red shirts, black shorts, red stockings.

International matches 2007
Macedonia (h) 0-1, Slovenia (h) 0-0, Bulgaria (a) 0-0, Luxembourg (h) 2-0, Luxembourg (a) 3-0, Malta (h) 3-0, Holland (h) 0-1, Slovenia (a) 0-0, Bulgaria (h) 1-1, Belarus (h) 2-4, Romania (a) 1-6.

League Championship wins (1930–37; 1945–2008)
SK Tirana 23 (including 17 Nentori 8); Dinamo Tirana 17; Partizani Tirana 15; Vllaznia 9; Elbasan 2 (including Labinoti 1); Flamurtari 1; Skenderbeu 1; Teuta 1.

Cup wins (1948–2008)
Partizani Tirana 15; Dinamo Tirana 13; SK Tirana 13 (including 17 Nentori 8); Vllaznia 6; Teuta 3; Elbasan 2 (including Labinoti 1); Flamurtari 2; Apolonia 1, Besa 1.

Final League Table 2007–08

	P	*W*	*D*	*L*	*F*	*A*	*Pts*
Dinamo Tirana	33	21	7	5	56	14	70
Partizani	33	18	11	4	47	22	65
Besa	33	17	5	11	45	36	56
Elbasan	33	13	13	7	40	24	52
Shkumbini	33	14	8	11	35	28	50
SK Tirana	33	14	7	12	46	36	49
Vllaznia	33	12	9	12	46	46	45
Flamurtari	33	10	14	9	35	37	44
Teuta+	33	9	8	16	32	45	35
Kastrioti*+	33	10	5	18	24	43	35
Beselidhja*	33	9	7	17	31	52	34
Skenderbeu*	33	3	2	28	26	80	11

Top scorer: Sinani (Vllaznia) 20.
Cup Final: Vllaznia 2, SK Tirana 0.

ANDORRA

Federacio Andorrana de Futbol, Avinguda Carlemany 67, 3er Pis, Apartado postal 65, Escaldes-Engordany, Principat D'Andorra.
Founded: 1994; *National Colours:* Yellow shirts, red shorts, blue stockings.

International matches 2007
Armenia (h) 0-0, England (h) 0-3, Russia (a) 0-4, Israel (h) 0-2, Estonia (a) 1-2, Croatia (h) 0-6, Macedonia (a) 0-3, Estonia (h) 0-2, Russia (h) 0-1.

League Championship wins (1996–2008)
Santa Coloma 4; Principat 3; Encamp 2; Ranger's 2; Constelacio 1; St Julia 1.

Cup wins (1991–2008)
Santa Coloma 7; Principat 6; Constelacio 1; Lusitanos 1; St Julia 1.

Qualifying League Table 2007–08

	P	*W*	*D*	*L*	*F*	*A*	*Pts*
Santa Coloma	14	11	3	0	58	4	36
Ranger's	14	10	3	1	37	16	33
St Julia	14	9	3	2	46	11	30
Lusitanos	14	9	0	5	34	13	27
Principat	14	5	2	7	20	33	17
Engordany	14	3	1	10	17	61	10
Inter	14	2	1	11	11	32	7
Casa Benfica	14	0	1	13	4	57	1

Championship Play-Offs

	P	*W*	*D*	*L*	*F*	*A*	*Pts*
Santa Coloma	20	14	5	1	69	10	44
St Julia	20	12	5	3	59	19	41
Ranger's	20	12	4	4	47	30	40
Lusitanos	20	10	1	9	44	29	31

Relegation Play-Offs

	P	*W*	*D*	*L*	*F*	*A*	*Pts*
Principat	20	9	3	8	33	37	30
Inter	20	6	2	12	23	37	20
Engordany+	20	4	1	15	21	79	13
Casa Benfica*	20	2	1	17	13	68	7

Cup Final: St Julia 6, Lusitanos 1.

ARMENIA

Football Federation of Armenia, Saryan 38, Yerevan, 375 010, Armenia.
Founded: 1992; *National Colours:* Red shirts, blue shorts, orange stockings.

International matches 2007
Panama (a) 1-1, Andorra (a) 0-0, Poland (a) 0-1, Kazakhstan (a) 2-1, Poland (h) 1-0, Portugal (h) 1-1, Cyprus (a) 1-3, Malta (a) 1-0, Serbia (h) 0-0, Belgium (a) 0-3, Portugal (a) 0-1, Kazakhstan (h) 0-1.

League Championship wins (1992–2007)
Pyunik 10 (including Homenetmen 3); Shirak Gyumri 4*; Ararat Yerevan 2*; Araks 2 (including Tsement); FC Yerevan 1.
*Includes one unofficial title.

Cup wins (1992–2008)
Mika 5; Ararat Yerevan 5; Pyunik 3; Tsement 2; Banants 2.

Final League Table 2007

	P	*W*	*D*	*L*	*F*	*A*	*Pts*
Pyunik	28	18	3	7	58	22	57
Banants	28	16	4	8	56	26	52
Mika	28	14	8	6	42	24	50
Ararat	28	15	4	9	49	42	49
Grandzasar	28	11	6	11	35	31	39
Shirak	28	9	7	12	27	37	34
Ulysses	28	8	6	14	21	46	30
Kilikia	28	1	2	25	10	70	5

Newly promoted Lernayin withdrew. No clubs relegated.
Play-Off: Ulysses 4, Dinamo 2.
Top scorer: Pizelli (Ararat) 25.
Cup Final: Ararat 2, Banants 1.

AUSTRIA

Oesterreichischer Fussball-Bund, Ernst-Happel Stadion – Sektor A/F, Postfach 340, Meierestrasse 7, Wien 1021.
Founded: 1904; *National Colours:* White shirts, black shorts, white stockings.

International matches 2007
Malta (a) 1-1, Ghana (h) 1-1, France (a) 0-1, Scotland (h) 0-1, Paraguay (h) 0-0, Czech Republic (h) 1-1, Japan (h) 0-0, Chile (h) 0-2, Switzerland (a) 1-3, Ivory Coast (h) 3-2, England (h) 0-1, Tunisia (h) 0-0.

League Championship wins (1912–2008)
Rapid Vienna 32; FK Austria (formerly Amateure) 23; Tirol-Svarowski-Innsbruck 10; Admira-Energie-Wacker 8; First Vienna 6; Austria Salzburg 4; Wiener Sportklub 3; Sturm Graz 2; WAC 1; FAC 1; Hakoah 1; Linz ASK 1; WAF 1; Voest Linz 1; Graz 1; WAC 1; Wacker 1.

Cup wins (1919–2007)
FK Austria (formerly Amateure) 26; Rapid Vienna 14; TS Innsbruck (formerly Wacker Innsbruck) 7; Admira-Energie-Wacker (formerly Sportklub Admira & Admira-Energie) 5; Graz 4; First Vienna 3; WAC 3; Sturm Graz 3; Linz ASK 1; Wacker Vienna 1; WAF 1; Wiener Sportklub 1; Kremser 1; Stockerau 1; Ried 1; Karnten 1; WAC 1; Kremser 1, Horn 1.

Final League Table 2007–08

	P	*W*	*D*	*L*	*F*	*A*	*Pts*
Rapid Vienna	36	21	6	9	69	36	69
Salzburg	36	18	9	9	63	42	63

FK Austria	36	15	13	8	46	33	58
Sturm Graz	36	15	11	10	60	41	56
Mattersburg	36	13	14	9	55	43	58
Linz	36	14	11	11	54	47	53
Ried	36	10	8	18	38	53	38
Rheindorf	36	8	12	16	37	64	36
Karnten	36	8	9	19	26	58	33
Wacker Innsbruck*	36	6	11	19	32	63	29

Wacker Innsbruck formerly Tirol and Karnten formally Pasching.
Top scorer: Zickler (Salzburg) 16.
Cup Final: Horn 1, 2, Feldkirchen 1, 1.

AZERBAIJAN

Association of Football Federations of Azerbaijan, 42 Gussi Gadjiev Street, Baku 370 009.
Founded: 1992; *National Colours:* White shirts, blue shorts, white stockings.

International matches 2007

Uzbekistan (a) 0-0, Uzbekistan (h) 1-0, Kazakhstan (a) 0-1, Kyrgyzstan (h) 1-0, Poland (a) 0-5, Finland (h) 1-0, Poland (h) 1-3, Kazakhstan (a) 1-1, Tajikistan (a) 3-2, Georgia (h) 1-1, Portugal (h) 0-2, Serbia (h) 1-6, Finland (a) 1-2, Belgium (h) 0-1.

League Championship wins (1992–2008)

Neftchi 5; Kapaz 3; Shamkir 3; Karabakh 1; Turan 1; Baku 1; Xazar 1; Inter 1.
Includes one unofficial title for Shamkir in 2002.

Cup wins (1992–2008)

Neftchi 5; Kapaz 4; Karabakh 2; Xazar 2; Inshatchi 1; Shafa 1; Baku 1.

Final League Table 2007–08

	P	*W*	*D*	*L*	*F*	*A*	*Pts*
Inter	26	18	4	4	55	18	58
Olimpik	26	17	7	2	29	7	58
Neftchi	26	16	7	3	42	18	55
Xazar	26	14	10	2	44	16	52
Karabakh	26	11	8	7	25	16	41
Kabala	26	11	3	12	33	36	36
Simurq	26	9	9	8	31	25	36
Baku	26	8	11	7	35	26	35
Standard	26	8	8	10	36	26	32
Masalli	26	8	6	12	30	40	30
Karvan	26	6	5	15	23	36	23
Turan	26	4	6	16	21	49	18
Ganclarbirliyi*	26	4	2	20	21	68	14
ABN-Barda*	26	2	6	18	12	56	12

MTK Araz dissolved; ABN-Barda replaced them. MTK Araz later reinstated to Second Division.
Top scorer: Mammadov (Inter) 19.
Cup Final: Xazar 2, Inter 0.

BELARUS

Belarus Football Federation, Kirova Street 8/2, Minsk 220 600, Belarus.
Founded: 1992; *National Colours:* Red shirts, green shorts, red stockings.

International matches 2007

Iran (a) 2-2, Luxembourg (a) 2-1, Bulgaria (h) 0-2, Bulgaria (a) 1-2, Israel (h) 2-1, Romania (h) 1-3, Slovenia (a) 0-1, Luxembourg (h) 0-1, Israel (a) 1-2, Albania (a) 4-2, Holland (h) 2-1.

League Championship wins (1992–2007)

Dynamo Minsk 7; BATE Borisov 4; Slavia Mozyr (formerly MPKC Mozyr) 2; Dnepr Mogilev 1; Belshina 1; Gomel 1; Shakhtyor 1.

Cup wins (1992–2008)

Belshina 3; Dynamo Minsk 3; Slavia Mozyr (formerly MPKC Mozyr) 2; MTZ-RIPA 2; Neman 1; Dynamo 93 Minsk 1; Lokomotiv 96 1; Gomel 1; Shakhtyor 1; BATE Borisov 1; Dynamo Brest 1.

Final League Table 2007

	P	*W*	*D*	*L*	*F*	*A*	*Pts*
BATE Borisov	26	18	2	6	50	25	56
Gomel	26	12	8	6	49	28	44
Shakhtyor	26	12	8	6	41	27	44
Torpedo Zhodino	26	11	10	5	28	21	43
MTZ-RIPA	26	11	9	6	32	25	42
Neman	26	9	9	8	23	22	36
Naftan	26	9	9	8	28	30	36
FK Viebsk#	26	9	8	9	25	28	35
Dynamo Minsk	26	8	11	7	27	28	35
Smorgon	26	6	8	12	15	29	26
Daryda	26	7	4	15	27	46	25
Dynamo Brest	26	6	7	13	23	31	25
Dnepr	26	5	8	13	21	33	23
FK Minsk*	26	4	9	13	18	34	21

 # Formerly Lokomotiv.
Top scorer: Vasilyuk (Gomel) 24.
Cup Final: MTZ-RIPA 2, Shakhtyor 1.

BELGIUM

Union Royale Belge Des Societes De Football Association, 145 Avenue Houba de Strooper, B-1020 Bruxelles.
Founded: 1895; *National Colours:* All red.

International matches 2007

Czech Republic (h) 0-2, Portugal (a) 0-4, Portugal (h) 1-2, Finland (a) 0-2, Serbia (h) 3-2, Kazakhstan (a) 2-2, Finland (h) 0-0, Armenia (h) 3-0, Poland (a) 0-2, Azerbaijan (a) 1-0.

League Championship wins (1896–2008)

Anderlecht 29; Club Brugge 13; Union St Gilloise 11; Standard Liege 9; Beerschot 7; RC Brussels 6; FC Liege 5; Daring Brussels 5; Antwerp 4; Mechelen 4; Lierse SK 4; Cercle Brugge 3; Beveren 2; Genk 2; RWD Molenbeek 1.

Cup wins (1912–14; 1927; 1935; 1954–2008)

Club Brugge 10; Anderlecht 9; Standard Liege 5; Beerschot (became Germinal) 2; Waterschei (became Racing Genk) 2; Beveren 2; Gent 2; Antwerp 2; Lierse SK 2; Racing Genk 2; Union St Gilloise 2; Cercle Brugge 2; Mechelen 1; FC Liege 1; Ekeren (became Germinal) 1; Westerlo 1; La Louviere 1; Zulte-Waregem 1; Daring 1; Germinal 1; Tournai 1; Racing 1; Waregem 1.

Final League Table 2007–08

	P	*W*	*D*	*L*	*F*	*A*	*Pts*
Standard Liege	34	22	11	1	61	19	77
Anderlecht	34	21	7	6	59	31	70
FC Brugge	34	20	7	7	45	30	67
CS Brugge	34	17	9	8	62	33	60
Beerschot	34	16	7	11	46	34	55
Gent	34	14	10	10	57	46	52
Waregem	34	13	8	13	47	54	47
Charleroi	34	13	7	14	41	45	46
Westerlo	34	12	9	13	43	37	45
Genk	34	12	9	13	54	55	45
Mouscron	34	12	6	16	38	43	42
Lokeren	34	9	15	10	32	33	42
Mechelen	34	10	10	14	45	52	40
Roeselare	34	9	11	14	36	55	38
Verbroedering	34	9	6	19	33	59	33
Mons	34	7	12	15	37	45	33
St Truiden*	34	6	9	19	32	58	27
FC Brussels*	34	4	7	23	27	66	19

Top scorer: Akpala (Charleroi) 18.
Cup Final: Anderlecht 3, Gent 2.

BOSNIA-HERZEGOVINA

Football Federation of Bosnia & Herzegovina, Ferhadija 30, Sarajevo 71000.
Founded: 1992; *National Colours:* White shirts, blue shorts, white stockings.

International matches 2007

Norway (a) 2-1, Turkey (h) 3-2, Malta (h) 1-0, Croatia (h) 3-5, Hungary (a) 0-1, Moldova (h) 0-1, Greece (a) 2-3, Norway (h) 0-2, Turkey (a) 0-1.

League Championship wins (1998–2008)

Zeljeznicar 3; Siroki 2; Sarajevo 2; Brotnjo 1; Leotar 1; Zrinjski 1; Modrica 1.

Cup wins (1998–2008)

Sarajevo 3; Zeljeznicar 3; Modrica 1; Orasje 1; Siroki 1; Zrinjski 1.

Final League Table 2007–08

	P	*W*	*D*	*L*	*F*	*A*	*Pts*
Modrica	30	18	1	11	57	45	55
Siroki	30	17	3	10	44	29	54
Celik	30	16	4	10	38	32	52
Zrinjski	30	15	4	11	46	27	49
Sarajevo	30	14	6	10	42	29	48
Sloboda	30	15	2	13	44	38	47
Zeljeznicar	30	14	3	13	47	35	45
Slavija	30	14	2	14	39	44	44
Velez	30	14	2	14	39	46	44
Laktasi	30	13	4	13	42	40	43

Posusje	30	13	4	13	42	46	43
Orasje	30	13	3	14	50	45	42
Travnik	30	13	3	14	35	39	42
Leotar	30	13	2	15	38	45	41
Jedinstvo*	30	12	4	14	28	43	40
Zepce*	30	2	1	27	25	73	7

Top scorers 2006–07: Benic (Borac), Nikolic (Modrica) 19.
Cup Final: Sloboda 2, 1, Zrinjski 1, 2.
Zrinjski won 4-1 on penalties.

BULGARIA

Bulgarian Football Union, Karnigradska Street 19, BG-1000 Sofia.
Founded: 1923; *National Colours:* White shirts, green shorts, white stockings.

International matches 2007
Latvia (n) 2-0, Cyprus (n) 3-0, Albania (h) 0-0, Belarus (a) 2-0, Belarus (h) 2-1, Wales (h) 0-1, Holland (a) 0-2, Luxembourg (h) 3-0, Albania (a) 1-1, Romania (h) 1-0, Slovenia (a) 2-0.

League Championship wins (1925–2008)
CSKA Sofia 31; Levski Sofia 25; Slavia Sofia 7; Vladislav Varna 3; Lokomotiv Sofia 3; Litex 2; Botev Plovdiv (includes Trakija) 2; AC 23 Sofia 1; SC Sofia 1; Sokol Varna 1; Spartak Plovdiv 1; Tichka Varna 1; JSZ Sofia 1; Beroe Stara Zagora 1; Etur 1; Lokomotiv Plovdiv 1.

Cup wins (1946–2008)
Levski Sofia 24; CSKA Sofia 18; Slavia Sofia 7; Lokomotiv Sofia 4; Litex 3; Botev Plovdiv (includes Trakija) 2; Spartak Plovdiv 1; Septemvri Sofia 1; Marek Dupnica 1; Spartak Varna 1; Sliven 1.

Final League Table 2007–08

	P	*W*	*D*	*L*	*F*	*A*	*Pts*
CSKA Sofia	30	24	6	0	53	11	78
Levski Sofia	30	19	5	6	56	19	62
Lokomotiv Sofia	30	16	9	5	47	28	57
Litex	30	16	8	6	51	26	56
Cherno Varna	30	13	9	8	39	28	48
Chernomorets	30	13	8	9	39	32	47
Slavia Sofia	30	13	8	9	38	28	47
Pirin	30	13	7	10	33	29	46
Lokomotiv Plovdiv	30	12	7	11	37	28	43
Vihren	30	9	6	15	26	29	33
Spartak	30	8	7	15	21	34	31
Botev Plovdiv	30	8	6	16	36	54	30
Belasitsa	30	7	5	18	23	43	26
Beroe*	30	6	8	16	23	39	26
Vidima*	30	4	6	20	17	61	18
Marek*	30	5	3	22	16	66	18

Top scorer: Hristov (Botev Plovdiv) 19.
Cup Final: Litex 1, Cherno Varna 0.

CROATIA

Croatian Football Federation, Rusanova 13, Zagreb, 10 3000, Croatia.
Founded: 1912; *National Colours:* Red & white shirts, white shorts, blue stockings.

International matches 2007
Norway (h) 2-1, Macedonia (h) 2-1, Estonia (a) 1-0, Russia (h) 0-0, Bosnia (a) 5-3, Estonia (h) 2-0, Andorra (a) 6-0, Israel (h) 1-0, Slovakia (h) 3-0, Macedonia (a) 0-2, England (a) 3-2.

League Championship wins (1941–46; 1992–2008)
Dinamo Zagreb (formerly Croatia Zagreb) 10; Hajduk Split 8; Gradjanski 1; Concordia 1; Zagreb 1.

Cup wins (1992–2008)
Dinamo Zagreb (formerly Croatia Zagreb) 9; Hajduk Split 4; Rijeka 2, Inker Zapresic 1; Osijek 1.

Final League Table 2007–08

	P	*W*	*D*	*L*	*F*	*A*	*Pts*
Dinamo Zagreb	33	26	4	3	91	34	79
Slaven	33	16	6	11	45	29	54
Osijek	33	16	6	11	43	34	54
Rijeka	33	14	11	8	53	41	53
Hajduk Split	33	14	10	9	57	41	52
Zagreb	33	11	11	11	51	40	44
Varteks	33	11	7	15	46	33	40
Cibalia	33	11	7	15	40	48	40
Zadar	33	11	7	15	49	61	40
Sibenik	33	9	12	12	34	52	39
Inter+	33	8	9	16	27	59	33
Medimurje*	33	3	6	24	37	81	15

Top scorer: Terkes (Zadar) 21.
Cup Final: Dinamo Zagreb 3, 0, Hajduk Split 0, 0.

CYPRUS

Cyprus Football Association, 1 Stasinos Str., Engomi, P.O. Box 25071, Nicosia 2404.
Founded: 1934; *National Colours:* Blue shirts, white shorts, blue stockings.

International matches 2007
Hungary (h) 2-1, Bulgaria (h) 0-3, Slovakia (h) 1-3, Czech Republic (a) 0-1, San Marino (a) 1-0, Armenia (h) 3-1, San Marino (h) 3-0, Wales (h) 3-1, Republic of Ireland (a) 1-1, Germany (a) 0-4, Czech Republic (h) 0-2.

League Championship wins (1935–2008)
Omonia 19; Apoel 19; Anorthosis 13; AEL 5; EPA 3; Olympiakos 3; Apollon 3; Pezoporikos 2; Cetinkaya 1; Trast 1.

Cup wins (1935–2008)
Apoel 19; Omonia 12; Anorthosis 10; AEL 6; EPA 5; Apollon 5; Trast 3; Cetinkaya 2; Olympiakos 1; Pezoporikos 1; Salamina 1; AEK 1.

Final League Table 2007–08

	P	*W*	*D*	*L*	*F*	*A*	*Pts*
Anorthosis	26	19	7	0	49	13	64
Apoel	26	16	5	5	51	19	53
Omonia	26	14	6	6	36	22	48
AEK	26	12	5	9	34	32	41
Apollon	26	10	9	7	40	33	39
Apop	26	10	7	9	35	35	37
ENP	26	10	6	10	28	30	36
Ethnikos Achnas	26	11	1	14	34	35	34
Doxa	26	9	7	10	38	40	34
Alki	26	7	6	13	32	40	27
Aris	26	7	6	13	24	35	27
AEL	26	7	6	13	28	38	27
NEA Salamina*	26	6	6	14	28	54	24
Olympiakos*	26	3	5	18	23	54	14

Play-Offs League Table 2007–08

Group A	*P*	*W*	*D*	*L*	*F*	*A*	*Pts*
Anorthosis	32	20	12	0	58	19	72
Apoel	32	18	7	7	58	28	61
Omonia	32	14	10	8	42	31	52
AEK	32	14	8	10	46	42	50
Group B	*P*	*W*	*D*	*L*	*F*	*A*	*Pts*
Apollon	32	12	11	9	49	41	47
ENP	32	13	7	12	42	45	46
Ethnikos Achnas	32	13	4	15	44	43	43
Apop	32	11	9	12	47	49	42
Group C	*P*	*W*	*D*	*L*	*F*	*A*	*Pts*
AEL	32	11	7	14	39	45	40
Alki	32	11	7	14	41	44	40
Doxa	32	10	9	13	43	48	39
Aris*	32	8	6	18	31	48	30

Top scorer 2006–07: Solari (Apoel) 20.
Top scorers: Da Costa (Doxa), Sosin (Anorthosis) 16.
Cup Final: Apoel 2, Anorthosis 0.

CZECH REPUBLIC

Football Association of Czech Republic, Diskarska 100, Prague 6 16017 – Strahov, Czech Republic.
Founded: 1901; *National Colours:* Red shirts, white shorts, blue stockings.

International matches 2007
Belgium (a) 2-0, Germany (h) 1-2, Cyprus (h) 1-0, Wales (a) 0-0, Austria (a) 1-1, San Marino (a) 3-0, Republic of Ireland (h) 1-0, Germany (a) 3-0, Slovakia (h) 3-1, Cyprus (a) 2-0.

League Championship wins (1925–93)
Sparta Prague 19; Dukla Prague (prev. UDA, now Marila Pribram) 11; Slavia Prague 9; Slovan Bratislava (formerly NV Bratislava) 8; Spartak Trnava 5; Banik Ostrava 3; Inter-Bratislava 1; Spartak Hradec Kralove 1; Viktoria Zizkov 1; Zbrojovka Brno 1; Bohemians 1; Vitkovice 1.

Cup wins (1961–93)
Dukla Prague 8; Sparta Prague 8; Slovan Bratislava 5; Spartak Trnava 4; Banik Ostrava 3; Lokomotiva Kosice 2; TJ Gottwaldov 1; Dunajska Streda 1; Kosice 1.
From 1993–94, there were two separate countries; the Czech Republic and Slovakia.

League Championship wins (1994–2008)
Sparta Prague 10; Slovan Liberec 2; Slavia Prague 2; Banik Ostrava 1.

Cup wins (1994–2008)
Sparta Prague 4; Slavia Prague 4; Viktoria Zizkov 2; Spartak Hradec Kralove 1; Jablonec 1; Slovan Liberec 1; Teplice 1; Banik Osrava 1.

Final League Table 2007–08

	P	W	D	L	F	A	Pts
Slavia Prague	30	17	9	4	45	24	60
Sparta Prague	30	17	6	7	53	26	57
Banik Ostrava	30	15	10	5	51	28	55
Brno	30	16	7	7	43	32	55
Teplice	30	16	5	9	40	27	53
Slovan Liberec	30	12	8	10	35	31	44
Mlada	30	11	9	10	37	36	42
Zlin	30	10	8	12	28	31	38
Viktoria Plzen	30	10	8	12	32	37	38
Viktoria Zizkov	30	10	7	13	35	48	37
Sigma Olomouc	30	8	12	10	20	26	36
Jablonec	30	8	9	13	24	32	33
Ceske	30	8	8	14	27	35	32
Kladno	30	6	9	15	31	45	27
Bohemians*	30	5	11	14	24	40	26
Siad*	30	4	8	18	31	58	20

Top scorer 2006–07: Pecka (Mlada Boleslav) 16.
Top scorer: Sverkos (Banik Ostrava) 15.
Cup Final: Sparta Prague 0, Slovan Liberec 0.
Sparta Prague won 4-3 on penalties.

DENMARK

Danish Football Association, Idraettens Hus, Brondby Stadion 20, DK-2605, Brondby.
Founded: 1889; *National Colours:* Red shirts, white shorts, red stockings.

International matches 2007
Australia (a) 3-1, Spain (a) 1-2, Germany (a) 1-0, Sweden (h) 0-3, Latvia (a) 2-0, Republic of Ireland (h) 0-4, Sweden (a) 0-0, Liechtenstein (h) 4-0, Spain (h) 1-3, Lativa (h) 3-1, Northern Ireland (a) 1-2, Iceland (h) 3-0.

League Championship wins (1913–2008)
KB Copenhagen 15; Brondby 10; B 93 Copenhagen 9; AB (Akademisk) 9; B 1903 Copenhagen 7; Frem 6; FC Copenhagen 6; Esbjerg BK 5; Vejle BK 5; AGF Aarhus 5; Hvidovre 3; OB Odense 3; AaB Aalborg 3; B 1909 Odense 2; Koge BK 2; Lyngby 2; Silkeborg 1; Herfolge 1.

Cup wins (1955–2008)
AGF Aarhus 9; Vejle BK 6; Brondby 6; OB Odense 5; Randers Freja 4; Lyngby 3; FC Copenhagen 3; B 1909 Odense 2; Aab Aalborg 2; Esbjerg BK 2; Frem 2; B 1903 Copenhagen 2; B 93 Copenhagen 1; KB Copenhagen 1; Vanlose 1; Hvidovre 1; B1913 Odense 1, AB (Akademisk) 1, Viborg 1; Silkeborg 1.

Final League Table 2007–08

	P	W	D	L	F	A	Pts
Aalborg	33	22	5	6	60	38	71
Midtjylland	33	18	8	7	53	36	62
FC Copenhagen	33	17	9	7	51	29	57
Odense	33	12	16	5	46	27	52
Horsens	33	14	10	9	47	43	52
Randers	33	13	8	12	41	33	47
Esbjerg	33	13	6	14	59	54	45
Brondby	33	11	10	12	44	44	43
Nordsjaelland	33	11	10	12	47	51	43
Aarhus	33	7	8	18	33	51	29
Viborg*	33	5	5	23	29	68	20
Lyngby*	33	3	9	21	33	69	18

Cup Final: Brondby 3, Esbjerg 2.

ENGLAND

The Football Association, 25 Soho Square, London W1D 4FA.
Founded: 1863; *National Colours:* White shirts with navy blue collar, navy shorts, white stockings.

ESTONIA

Estonian Football Association, Rapia 8/10, Tallinn 11312.
Founded: 1921; *National Colours:* Blue shirts, black shorts, white stockings.

International matches 2007
Poland (h) 0-4, Slovenia (a) 0-1, Russia (h) 0-2, Israel (a) 0-4, Croatia (h) 0-1, England (h) 0-3, Andorra (h) 2-1, Croatia (a) 0-2, Macedonia (a) 1-1, England (a) 0-3, Montenegro (h) 0-1, Saudi Arabia (a) 0-2, Andorra (a) 2-0, Uzbekistan (a) 0-0.

League Championship wins (1921–40; 1992–2007)
Sport 9; Flora Tallinn 7; Levadia Tallinn (includes Levadia Maardu) 6; Estonia 5; Tallinn JK 2; Norma 2; Lantana (formerly Nikol) 2; Kalev 2; Olimpia 1; VMK Tallinn 1.

Cup wins (1993–2008)
Levadia Tallinn (includes Levadia Maardu) 5; Flora Tallinn 3; Sadam 2; VMV Tallinn 2; Lantana (formerly Nikol) 1; Trans 1; Levadia Tallinn (pre-2004) 1; Norma 1.

Final League Table 2007

	P	W	D	L	F	A	Pts
Levadia Tallinn	36	29	4	3	126	20	91
Flora	36	26	5	5	108	30	83
VMK	36	25	4	7	116	36	79
Trans	36	25	3	8	89	28	78
Maag	36	18	8	10	54	40	62
Kalev	36	13	4	19	44	77	43
Tulevik	36	11	4	21	43	80	37
Vaprus	36	8	1	27	35	96	25
Kuressaare+	36	5	3	28	25	94	18
Ajax*	36	1	2	33	14	153	5

Top scorer: Lipartov (Trans) 30.
Cup Final: Flora 3, Maag 1.

FAEROE ISLANDS

Fotboltssamband Foroya, The Faeroes' Football Assn., Gundalur, P.O. Box 3028, FR-110, Torshavn.
Founded: 1979; *National Colours:* White shirts, blue shorts, white stockings.

International matches 2007
Ukraine (h) 0-2, Georgia (a) 1-3, Italy (h) 1-2, Scotland (h) 0-2, Lithuania (a) 1-2, France (h) 0-6, Ukraine (a) 0-5, Italy (a) 1-3.

League Championship wins (1942–2007)
HB Torshavn 19; KI Klaksvik 17; B36 Torshavn 8; TB Tvoroyri 7; GI Gotu 6; B68 Toftir 3; SI Sorvag 1; IF Fuglafjordur 1; B71 Sandur 1; VB Vagur 1; NSI Runavik 1.

Cup wins (1955–2007)
HB Torshavn 26; GI Gotu 6; KI Klaksvik 5; TB Tvoroyri 5; B36 Torshavn 5; NSI Runavik 2; EB/Streymur 2; VB Vagur 1; B71 Sandur 1.

Final League Table 2007

	P	W	D	L	F	A	Pts
NSI	27	19	4	4	52	24	61
EB/Streymur	27	17	3	7	58	33	54
B36	27	15	7	5	47	23	52
HB	27	15	4	8	59	34	49
GI	27	11	5	11	46	53	38
Skala	27	10	4	13	27	40	34
KI	27	9	6	12	44	47	33
B71	27	9	5	13	39	49	32
AB*	27	4	5	18	30	55	17
VB*	27	2	5	20	27	71	11

Top scorer: Sylla (B36) 18.
Cup Final: EB/Streymur 4, HB 3.

FINLAND

Suomen Palloliitto Finlands Bollfoerbund, Urheilukatu 5, P.O. Box 191, Helsinki 00251.
Founded: 1907; *National Colours:* White shirts, blue shorts, white stockings.

International matches 2007
Azerbaijan (a) 0-1, Serbia (h) 0-2, Belgium (h) 2-0, Kazakhstan (h) 2-1, Serbia (a) 0-0, Poland (h) 0-0, Belgium (a) 0-0, Spain (h) 0-0, Azerbaijan (h) 2-1, Portugal (a) 0-0.

League Championship wins (1908–2007)
HJK Helsinki 21; Haka Valkeakoski 9; HPS Helsinki 9; TPS Turku 8; HIFK Helsinki 7; Tampere United (includes IKIssat and Ilves) 5; KuPS Kuopio 5; Kuusysi Lahti 5; KIF Helsinki 4; AIFK Turku 3; Reipas Lahti 3; VIFK Vaasa 3; Jazz Pori 2; KTP Kotka 2; OPS Oulu 2; VPS Vaasa 2; Unitas Helsinki 1; PUS Helsinki 1; Sudet Viipuri 1; HT Helsinki 1; Pyrkiva Turku 1; KPV Kokkola 1; TPV Tampere 1; MyPa Anjalankoski 1.

Cup wins (1955–2007)
Haka Valkeakoski 12; HJK Helsinki 9; Reipas Lahti 7; KTP Kotka 4; MyPa Anjalankoski 3; Tampere United (includes Ilves) 3; KuPS Kuopio 2; Kuusysi Lahti 2; Mikkeli 2; TPS Turku 2; PPojat 1; Drott (renamed Jaro) 1;

HPS Helsinki 1; AIFK Turku 1; RoPS Rovaniemi 1; Jokerit (formerly PK-35) 1; Allianssi (formerly Atlantis) 1.

Final League Table 2007

	P	*W*	*D*	*L*	*F*	*A*	*Pts*
Tampere U	26	16	6	4	45	27	54
Haka	26	13	7	6	39	23	46
TPS Turku	26	13	4	9	43	33	43
Honka	26	10	11	5	34	25	41
MyPa	26	11	7	8	29	26	40
Mariehamn	26	9	10	7	31	30	37
HJK Helsinki	26	7	13	6	31	25	34
Lahti	26	9	6	11	38	34	33
Inter	26	9	6	11	32	28	33
VPS	26	7	11	8	26	35	32
Jaro	26	7	7	12	30	41	28
KooTeePee	26	7	5	14	27	38	26
Viikingit+	26	5	8	13	25	44	23
Oulu*	26	5	7	14	28	49	22

Top scorer: Vieira (Lahti) 14.
Cup Final: Tampere U 3, Honka 3.
Tampere U won 3-1 on penalties.

FRANCE

Federation Francaise De Football, 60 Bis Avenue d'Iena, Paris 75116.
Founded: 1919; *National Colours:* Blue shirts, white shorts, red stockings.

International matches 2007
Argentina (h) 0-1, Lithuania (a) 1-0, Austria (h) 1-0, Ukraine (h) 2-0, Georgia (h) 1-0, Slovakia (a) 1-0, Italy (a) 0-0, Scotland (h) 0-1, Faeroes (a) 6-0, Ukraine (h) 2-0, Morocco (h) 2-2, Ukraine (a) 2-2.

League Championship wins (1933–2008)
Saint Etienne 10; Olympique Marseille 8; Nantes 8; AS Monaco 7; Lyon 7; Stade de Reims 6; Girondins de Bordeaux 5; OGC Nice 4; Lille OSC (includes Olympique Lillois) 3; Paris St Germain 2; FC Sete 2; Sochaux 2; Racing Club Paris 1; Roubaix-Tourcoing 1; Strasbourg 1; Auxerre 1; Lens 1.

Cup wins (1918–2008)
Olympique Marseille 10; Paris St Germain 7; Saint Etienne 6; AS Monaco 5; Lille OSC 5; Racing Club Paris 5; Red Star 5; Auxerre 4; Lyon 4; Girondins de Bordeaux 3; OGC Nice 3; Nantes 3; Strasbourg 3; CAS Genereaux 2; Nancy 2; Sedan 2; FC Sete 2; Stade de Reims 2; SO Montpellier 2; Stade Rennes 2; Metz 2; Sochaux 2; AS Cannes 1; Club Français 1; Excelsior Roubaix 1; Le Havre 1; Olympique de Pantin 1; CA Paris 1; Toulouse 1; Bastia 1; Lorient 1.

Final League Table 2007–08

	P	*W*	*D*	*L*	*F*	*A*	*Pts*
Lyon	38	24	7	7	74	37	79
Bordeaux	38	22	9	7	65	38	75
Marseille	38	17	11	10	58	45	62
Nancy	38	15	15	8	44	30	60
St Etienne	38	16	10	12	47	34	58
Rennes	38	16	10	12	47	44	58
Lille	38	13	18	7	45	32	57
Nice	38	13	16	9	35	30	55
Le Mans	38	14	11	13	46	49	53
Lorient	38	12	16	10	32	35	52
Caen	38	13	12	13	48	53	51
Monaco	38	13	8	17	40	48	47
Valenciennes	38	12	9	17	42	40	45
Sochaux	38	10	14	14	34	43	44
Auxerre	38	12	8	18	33	52	44
Paris St Germain	38	10	13	15	37	45	43
Toulouse	38	9	15	14	36	42	42
Lens*	38	9	13	16	43	52	40
Strasbourg*	38	9	8	21	34	55	35
Metz*	38	5	9	24	28	64	24

Top scorer 2006–07: Pauleta (Paris St Germain) 15.
Top scorer: Benzema (Lyon) 20.
Cup Final: Lyon 1, Paris St Germain 0.

GEORGIA

Georgian Football Federation, 76a Tchavtchavadze Avenue, Tbilisi 380062.
Founded: 1990; *National Colours:* All white.

International matches 2007
Turkey (h) 1-0, Scotland (a) 1-2, Faeroes (h) 3-1, Lithuania (a) 0-1, France (a) 0-1, Luxembourg (a) 0-0, Ukraine (h) 1-1, Azerbaijan (a) 1-1, Italy (a) 0-2, Scotland (h) 2-0, Qatar (a) 2-1, Lithuania (h) 0-2.

League Championship wins (1990–2008)
Dinamo Tbilisi 13; Torpedo Kutaisi 3; WIT Georgia 1; Sioni 1; Olimpi 1.

Cup wins (1990–2008)
Dinamo Tbilisi 8; Lokomotivi 3; Torpedo Kutaisi 2; Ameri 2; Dynamo Batumi 1; Guria 1; Zestafoni 1.

Final League Table 2007–08

	P	*W*	*D*	*L*	*F*	*A*	*Pts*
Dinamo Tbilisi	26	23	1	2	67	18	70
WIT	26	19	3	4	45	14	60
Zestafoni	26	18	5	3	56	16	59
Olimpi	26	16	4	6	26	16	52
Ameri	26	15	3	8	48	27	48
Meskheti	26	11	6	9	29	30	39
Mglebi	26	10	3	13	27	33	33
Sioni	26	9	5	12	34	35	32
Borjomi	26	9	4	13	32	39	31
Lokomotivi	26	7	6	13	27	35	27
Spartaki+	26	5	8	13	15	28	23
Merani*	26	6	1	19	15	54	19
Dynamo Batumi*	26	4	4	18	16	51	16
Dila Gori*	26	1	5	20	12	53	8

Torpedo Kutaisi and Chikhura relegated for financial reasons.
Top scorer 2006–07: Iashvili (Dinamo Tbilisi) 21.
Top scorer: Khutsishvili (Dinamo Tbilisi) 16.
Cup Final: Zestafoni 2, Ameri 1.

GERMANY

Deutscher Fussball-Bund, Otto-Fleck-Schneise 6, Postfach 710265, Frankfurt Am Main 60492.
Founded: 1900; *National Colours:* White shirts, black shorts, white stockings.

International matches 2007
Switzerland (h) 3-1, Czech Republic (a) 2-1, Denmark (h) 0-1, San Marino (h) 6-0, Slovakia (h) 2-1, England (a) 2-1, Wales (a) 2-0, Romania (h) 3-1, Republic of Ireland (a) 0-0, Czech Republic (h) 0-3, Cyprus (h) 4-0, Wales (h) 0-0.

League Championship wins (1903–2008)
Bayern Munich 21; 1.FC Nuremberg 9; Schalke 04 7; Borussia Dortmund 6; SV Hamburg 6; Borussia Moenchengladbach 5; VfB Stuttgart 5; 1.FC Kaiserslautern 4; Werder Bremen 4; VfB Leipzig 3; SpVgg Furth 3; 1.FC Cologne 3; Viktoria Berlin 2; Hertha Berlin 2; Hannover 96 2; Dresden SC 2; Munich 1860 1; Union Berlin 1; FC Freiburg 1; Phoenix Karlsruhe 1; Karlsruher FV 1; Holstein Kiel 1; Fortuna Dusseldorf 1; Rapid Vienna 1; VfR Mannheim 1; Rot-Weiss Essen 1; Eintracht Frankfurt 1; Eintracht Brunswick 1.

Cup wins (1935–2008)
Bayern Munich 14; Werder Bremen 5; 1.FC Cologne 4; Eintracht Frankfurt 4; Schalke 04 4; 1.FC Nuremberg 4; SV Hamburg 3; Moenchengladbach 3; VfB Stuttgart 3; Dresden SC 2; Fortuna Dusseldorf 2; Karlsruhe SC 2; Munich 1860 2; Borussia Dortmund 2; 1.FC Kaiserslautern 2; First Vienna 1; VfB Leipzig 1; Kickers Offenbach 1; Rapid Vienna 1; Rot-Weiss Essen 1; SW Essen 1; Bayer Uerdingen 1; Hannover 96 1; Leverkusen 1.

Final League Table 2007–08

	P	*W*	*D*	*L*	*F*	*A*	*Pts*
Bayern Munich	34	22	10	2	68	21	76
Werder Bremen	34	20	6	8	75	45	66
Schalke	34	18	10	6	55	32	64
Hamburg	34	14	12	8	47	26	54
Wolfsburg	34	15	9	10	58	46	54
Stuttgart	34	16	4	14	57	57	52
Leverkusen	34	15	6	13	57	40	51
Hannover	34	13	10	11	54	56	49
Eintracht Frankfurt	34	12	10	12	43	50	46
Hertha	34	12	8	14	39	44	44
Karlsruher	34	11	10	13	38	53	43
Bochum	34	10	11	13	48	54	41
Borussia Dortmund	34	10	10	14	50	62	40
Arminia	34	8	10	16	35	60	34
Nuremberg*	34	7	10	17	35	51	31
Hansa Rostock*	34	8	6	20	30	52	30
Duisburg*	34	8	5	21	36	55	29

Top scorer: Toni (Bayern Munich) 24.
Cup Final: Bayern Munich 2, Borussia Dortmund 1.

GIBRALTAR

Gibraltar Football Association, 32a Rosia Road, Gibraltar.
Founded: 1905.

League Championship wins (1896–2008)
Prince of Wales 19; Glacis United 17; Britannia 14; Gibraltar United 11; Lincoln 8; Manchester United 7; Europa 6; Newcastle (formerly Lincoln) 5; St Theresas 3; Chief Construction 2; Exiles 2; Gibraltar FC 2; Jubilee 2; South United 2; Albion 1; Athletic 1; Commander of the Yard 1; Royal Soverign 1; St Joseph's 1.

Cup wins (1896–2008)
St Joseph's 7; Europa 5; Glacis United 5; Lincoln 5; Newcastle (formerly Lincoln) 4; Britannia 3; Gibraltar United 3; Manchester United 3; AARA 1; Gibraltar FC 1; HMS Hood 1; Lincoln ABG 1; Lincoln Reliance 1; Manchester United Reserves 1; Prince of Wales 1; St Theresas 1; 2nd Battalion RGS 1; 2nd Battalion The King's Regiment 1; 4th Battalion Royal Scots 1; RAF Gibraltar 1; RAF New Camp 1.

Final League Table 2007–08

	P	*W*	*D*	*L*	*F*	*A*	*Pts*
Lincoln	16	11	5	0	48	17	38
Gibraltar U	16	5	7	4	23	21	22
Glacis U	15	4	5	6	17	26	17
St Joseph's	16	4	3	9	18	34	15
Manchester U	15	2	6	7	17	25	12

Lincoln formerly Newcastle.
Cup Final: Lincoln 3, Laguna 0.

GREECE

Hellenic Football Federation, Singrou Avenue 137, Nea Smirni, 17121 Athens.
Founded: 1926; *National Colours:* Blue shirts, white shorts, blue stockings.

International matches 2007
South Korea (n) 0-1, Turkey (h) 1-4, Malta (a) 1-0, Hungary (h) 2-0, Moldova (h) 2-1, Spain (h) 2-3, Norway (a) 2-2, Bosnia (h) 3-2, Turkey (a) 1-0, Malta (h) 5-0, Hungary (a) 2-1.

League Championship wins (1928–2008)
Olympiakos 36; Panathinaikos 19; AEK Athens 11; Aris Salonika 3; PAOK Salonika 2; Larisa 1.

Cup wins (1932–2008)
Olympiakos 23; Panathinaikos 16; AEK Athens 13; PAOK Salonika 4; Panionios 2; Larisa 2; Aris Salonika 1; Ethnikos 1; Iraklis 1; Kastoria 1; OFI Crete 1.

Final League Table 2007–08

	P	*W*	*D*	*L*	*F*	*A*	*Pts*
Olympiakos	30	21	7	2	58	23	70
AEK Athens	30	22	2	6	65	17	68
Panathinaikos	30	20	6	4	44	18	66
Aris Salonika	30	14	8	8	33	20	50
Panionios	30	13	6	11	39	42	45
Larissa	30	11	12	7	35	30	45
Asteras	30	11	11	8	28	24	44
Xanthi	30	10	6	14	33	39	36
PAOK Salonika	30	10	5	15	29	35	35
Iraklis	30	8	11	11	28	34	35
Levadiakos	30	10	3	17	31	51	33
OFI Crete	30	9	5	16	39	49	32
Ergotelis	30	7	9	14	28	42	30
Atromitos*	30	8	5	17	23	36	29
Veria*	30	5	8	17	21	44	23
Apollon*	30	5	8	17	27	57	22

Apollon one point deducted for ineligible player.

Champions League Qualifying Play-Offs 2007–08

	P	*W*	*D*	*L*	*F*	*A*	*Pts*
Panathinaikos (+7)	6	4	2	0	14	5	21
AEK Athens (+8)	6	2	2	2	10	11	16
Aris Salonika (+2)	6	1	2	3	9	9	7
Panionios	6	1	2	3	7	15	5

Top scorer 2006–07: Lymberopoulos (AEK Athens) 18.
Top scorer: Blanco (AEK Athens) 19.
Cup Final: Olympiakos 2, Aris Salonika 0.

HOLLAND

Koninklijke Nederlandsche Voetbalbond, Woudenbergseweg 56–58, Postbus 515, NL-3700 AM, Zeist.
Founded: 1889; *National Colours:* Orange shirts, black shorts, orange stockings.

International matches 2007
Russia (h) 4-1, Romania (h) 0-0, Slovenia (a) 1-0, South Korea (a) 2-0, Thailand (a) 3-1, Switzerland (a) 1-2, Bulgaria (h) 2-0, Albania (a) 1-0, Romania (a) 0-1, Slovenia (h) 2-0, Luxembourg (h) 1-0, Belarus (a) 1-2.

League Championship wins (1898–2008)
Ajax Amsterdam 29; PSV Eindhoven 21; Feyenoord 14; HVV The Hague 8; Sparta Rotterdam 6; Go Ahead Deventer 4; HBS The Hague 3; Willem II Tilburg 3; RAP Amsterdam 2; RCH Heemstede 2; Heracles 2; ADO The Hague 2; Quick The Hague 1; BVV Den Bosch 1; NAC Breda 1; Eindhoven 1; Enschede 1; Volewijckers Amsterdam 1; Limburgia 1; Rapid JC Den Heerlen 1; DOS Utrecht 1; DWS Amsterdam 1; Haarlem 1; SVV Schiedam 1; Be Quick Groningen 1; AZ 67 Alkmaar 1.

Cup wins (1899–2008)
Ajax Amsterdam 17; Feyenoord 11; PSV Eindhoven 8; Quick The Hague 4; AZ 67 Alkmaar 3; Sparta Rotterdam 3; Utrecht 3; HFC Haarlem 3; DFC 2; Fortuna Geleen 2; Haarlem 2; HBS The Hague 2; RCH Haarlem 2; Roda JC 2; VOC 2; Wageningen 2; Willem II Tilburg 2; FC Den Haag (includes ADO) 2; Twente Enschede 2; Concordia Delft 1; CVV 1; Eindhoven 1; HVV The Hague 1; Longa 1; Quick Nijmegen 1; RAP Amsterdam 1; Roermond 1; Schoten 1; Velocitas Breda 1; Velocitas Groningen 1; VSV 1; VUC 1; VVV Groningen 1; ZFC Zaandam 1; NAC Breda 1.

Final League Table 2007–08

	P	*W*	*D*	*L*	*F*	*A*	*Pts*
PSV Eindhoven	34	21	9	4	65	24	72
Ajax	34	20	9	5	94	45	69
NAC Breda	34	19	6	9	48	40	63
Twente	34	17	11	6	52	32	62
Heerenveen	34	18	6	10	88	48	60
Feyenoord	34	18	6	10	64	41	60
Groningen	34	15	6	13	53	54	51
NEC Nijmegen	34	14	7	13	49	50	49
Roda JC	34	12	11	11	55	55	47
Utrecht	34	13	7	14	59	55	46
AZ	34	11	10	13	48	53	43
Vitesse	34	12	7	15	46	55	43
Sparta	34	9	7	18	52	76	34
Heracles	34	8	8	18	34	64	32
Willem II	34	8	7	19	40	49	31
De Graafschap+	34	7	9	18	33	64	30
VVV Venlo*+	34	7	8	19	44	76	29
Excelsior*	34	7	6	21	32	75	27

Play-Offs: Heerenveen qualify for UEFA Cup, Twente to Champions League, Ajax and NEC Nijmegen to UEFA Cup.
Top scorer: Huntelaar (Ajax) 33.
Cup Final: Feyenoord 2, Roda JC 0.

HUNGARY

Hungarian Football Federation, Robert Karoly krt 61-65, Robert Haz Budapest 1134.
Founded: 1901; *National Colours:* Red shirts, white shorts, green stockings.

International matches 2007
Cyprus (a) 1-2, Latvia (n) 2-0, Moldova (h) 2-0, Greece (a) 0-2, Norway (a) 0-4, Italy (h) 3-1, Bosnia (h) 1-0, Turkey (a) 0-3, Malta (h) 2-0, Poland (a) 1-0, Moldova (a) 0-3, Greece (h) 1-2.

League Championship wins (1901–2008)
Ferencvaros 28; MTK-Hungaria Budapest 23; Ujpest 20; Kispest Honved 13; Vasas Budapest 6; Csepel 4; Raba Gyor 3; Debrecen 3; BTC 2; Nagyvarad 1; Vac 1; Dunaferr 1; Zalaegerszeg 1.

Cup wins (1910–2008)
Ferencvaros 20; MTK-Hungaria Budapest 12; Ujpest 8; Kispest Honved 6; Raba Gyor 4; Vasas Budapest 4; Debrecen 3; Diösgyör 2; Bocskai 1; III Ker 1; Soroksar 1; Szolnoki MAV 1; Siofok Banyasz 1; Bekescsaba 1; Pecsi 1; Matav 1; Fehervar 1.
Cup not regularly held until 1964.

Final League Table 2007–08

	P	*W*	*D*	*L*	*F*	*A*	*Pts*
MTK	30	20	6	4	67	23	66
Debrecen	30	19	7	4	67	29	64
Gyor	30	16	10	4	64	35	58
Ujpest	30	16	7	7	58	40	55
Fehervar	30	17	3	10	48	32	54

Rakoczi	30	14	9	7	48	38	51
Zalaegerszeg	30	13	7	10	55	39	46
Honved	30	12	7	11	45	36	43
Vasas	30	12	5	13	41	45	41
Nyiregyhaza	30	11	7	12	34	37	40
Paksi	30	9	10	11	51	51	37
Rakospalotai	30	7	9	14	42	60	30
Diosgyor	30	5	13	12	43	63	28
Siofok	30	6	9	15	33	46	27
Tatabanya*	30	2	4	24	34	93	10
Matav*	30	2	5	23	10	73	0

Matav Sopron licence revoked during winter break; eleven points deducted and remaining matches awarded 3-0 against them.
Top scorer: Urban (MTK) 11.
Cup Final: Debrecen 7, 2, Honved 0, 1.

ICELAND

Knattspyrnusamband Island, Laugardal, 104 Reykjavik.
Founded: 1929; *National Colours;* All blue.

International matches 2007
Spain (a) 0-1, Liechtenstein (h) 1-1, Sweden (a) 0-5, Canada (h) 1-1, Spain (h) 1-1, Northern Ireland (h) 2-1, Latvia (h) 2-4, Liechtenstein (a) 0-3, Denmark (a) 0-3.

League Championship wins (1912–2007)
KR 24; Valur 20; Fram 18; IA Akranes 18; Vikingur 5; IBK Keflavik 4; IBV Vestmannaeyjar 3; FH Hafnarfjordur 3; KA Akureyri 1.

Cup wins (1960–2007)
KR 10; Valur 9; IA Akranes 9; Fram 7; IBV Vestmannaeyjar 4; IBK Keflavik 4; Fylkir 2; IBA Akureyri 1; Vikingur 1; FH Hafnarfjordur 1.

Final League Table 2007

	P	*W*	*D*	*L*	*F*	*A*	*Pts*
Valur	18	11	5	2	41	20	38
FH	18	11	4	3	42	26	37
IA	18	8	6	4	34	27	30
Fylkir	18	8	5	5	23	18	29
Breidblik	18	5	9	4	29	20	24
Keflavik	18	5	6	7	26	32	21
Fram	18	3	7	8	25	31	16
KR	18	3	7	8	17	30	16
HK	18	4	4	10	17	35	16
Vikingur*	18	3	5	10	15	30	14

League extended to 12 clubs 2008.
Top scorer: Gardarsson (Fram) 13.
Cup Final: FH 2, Fjolnir 0.

REPUBLIC OF IRELAND

The Football Association of Ireland (Cumann Peile Na H-Eireann), 80 Merrion Square, South Dublin 2.
Founded: 1921; *National Colours:* Green shirts, white shorts, green and white stockings.

League Championship wins (1922–2007)
Shamrock Rovers 15; Shelbourne 13; Dundalk 9; Bohemians 9; Cork Athletic (formerly Cork United) 7; St Patrick's Athletic 7; Waterford 6; Drumcondra 5; St James's Gate 2; Sligo Rovers 2; Limerick 2; Athlone Town 2; Derry City 2; Cork City 2; Dolphin 1; Cork Hibernians 1; Cork Celtic 1; Drogheda United 1.

Cup wins (1922–2007)
Shamrock Rovers 24; Dundalk 9; Shelbourne 7; Bohemians 6; Drumcondra 5; Cork Athletic (formerly Cork United) 4; Derry City 4; Cork City 2; St James's Gate 2; St Patrick's Athletic 2; Cork Hibernians 2; Limerick 2; Waterford 2; Sligo 2; Bray Wanderers 2; Longford Town 2; Alton United 1; Athlone Town 1; Fordsons 1; Cork 1; Transport 1; Finn Harps 1; Home Farm 1; UCD 1; Galway United 1; Drogheda United 1.

Final League Table 2007

	P	*W*	*D*	*L*	*F*	*A*	*Pts*
Drogheda United	33	19	11	3	48	24	68
St Patrick's Ath	33	18	7	8	54	29	61
Bohemians	33	16	10	7	35	17	58
Cork City	33	15	10	8	44	32	55
Shamrock Rovers	33	14	9	10	36	26	51
Sligo Rovers	33	12	5	16	34	45	41
Derry City	33	8	13	12	30	31	37
Galway United	33	7	14	12	28	35	35
Bray Wanderers	33	8	10	15	30	48	34
UCD	33	7	10	16	31	44	31
Waterford United*+	33	7	9	17	23	47	30
Longford Town*	33	9	8	16	34	49	29

Longford Town six points deducted for breach of licence.
Top scorer: Mooney (Longford Town) 19.
Cup Final: Cork City 1, Longford Town 0.

ISRAEL

Israel Football Association, Ramat-Gan Stadium, 299 Aba Hilell Street, Ramat-Gan 52134.
Founded: 1948; *National Colours:* Blue shirts, white shorts, blue stockings.

International matches 2007
Ukraine (h) 1-1, England (h) 0-0, Estonia (h) 4-0, Macedonia (a) 2-1, Andorra (a) 2-0, Belarus (a) 1-2, England (a) 0-3, Croatia (a) 0-1, Belarus (h) 2-1, Russia (h) 2-1, Macedonia (h) 1-0.

League Championship wins (1932–2008)
Maccabi Tel Aviv 18; Hapoel Tel Aviv 10; Maccabi Haifa 10; Hapoel Petah Tikva 6; Beitar Jerusalem 6; Maccabi Netanya 5; Hakoah Ramat Gan 2; Hapoel Beersheba 2; Bnei Yehouda 1; British Police 1; Hapoel Kfar Saba 1; Hapoel Ramat Gan 1; Hapoel Haifa 1.

Cup wins (1928–2008)
Maccabi Tel Aviv 22; Hapoel Tel Aviv 13; Beitar Jerusalem 6; Maccabi Haifa 5; Hapoel Haifa 3; Hapoel Kfar Saba 3; Beitar Tel Aviv 2; Bnei Yehouda 2; Hakoah Ramat Gan 2; Hapoel Petah Tikva 2; Maccabi Petah Tikva 2; Maccabi Hashmonai Jerusalem 1; British Police 1; Gunners 1; Hapoel Jerusalem 1; Hapoel Yehud 1; Hapoel Lod 1; Maccabi Netanya 1; Hapoel Beersheba 1; Hapoel Ramat Gan 1; Hapoel Bnei Sakhnin 1.

Final League Table 2007–08

	P	*W*	*D*	*L*	*F*	*A*	*Pts*
Beitar Jerusalem	33	20	7	6	61	23	67
Maccabi Netanya	33	16	10	7	40	24	58
Ironi	33	15	11	7	43	34	56
Bnei Sakhnin	33	15	10	8	35	29	55
Maccabi Haifa	33	13	8	12	38	27	47
Maccabi Tel Aviv	33	11	8	14	43	43	41
Hapoel Tel Aviv	33	12	5	16	35	40	41
Ashdod	33	11	6	16	36	52	39
Bnei Yehouda	33	11	5	17	31	43	38
Maccabi Petah Tikva	33	10	7	16	28	39	37
Hapoel Kfar Saba*	33	9	10	14	37	54	37
Maccabi Herzlia*	33	7	9	17	32	51	30

Top scorer: Yeboah (Hapoel Kfar Saba) 15.
Cup Final: Beitar Jerusalem 0, Hapoel Tel Aviv 0.
Beitar Jerusalem won 5-4 on penalties.

ITALY

Federazione Italiana Giuoco Calcio, Via Gregorio Allegri 14, Roma 00198.
Founded: 1898; *National Colours:* Blue shirts, white shorts, blue stockings.

International matches 2007
Scotland (h) 2-0, Faeroes (a) 2-1, Lithuania (a) 2-0, Hungary (a) 1-3, France (h) 0-0, Ukraine (a) 2-1, Georgia (h) 2-0, South Africa (h) 2-0, Scotland (a) 2-1, Faeroes (h) 3-1.

League Championship wins (1898–2008)
Juventus 27 (excludes two titles revoked); AC Milan 17; Internazionale 16 (includes one title awarded); Genoa 9; Torino 7 (excludes one title revoked); Pro Vercelli 7; Bologna 7; AS Roma 3; Fiorentina 2; Lazio 2; Napoli 2; Casale 1; Novese 1; Cagliari 1; Verona 1; Sampdoria 1.

Cup wins (1928–2008)
AS Roma 9; Juventus 9; Fiorentina 6; AC Milan 5; Internazionale 5; Torino 5; Sampdoria 4; Lazio 4; Napoli 3; Parma 3; Bologna 2; Atalanta 1; Genoa 1; Vado 1; Venezia 1; Vicenza 1.

Final League Table 2007–08

	P	*W*	*D*	*L*	*F*	*A*	*Pts*
Internazionale	38	25	10	3	69	26	85
Roma	38	24	10	4	72	37	82
Juventus	38	20	12	6	72	37	72
Fiorentina	38	19	9	10	55	39	66
AC Milan	38	18	10	10	66	38	64
Sampdoria	38	17	9	12	56	46	60
Udinese	38	16	9	13	48	53	57
Napoli	38	14	8	16	50	53	50
Atalanta	38	12	12	14	52	56	48
Genoa	38	13	9	16	44	52	48
Palermo	38	12	11	15	47	57	47
Lazio	38	11	13	14	47	51	46

Siena	38	9	17	12	40	45	44
Cagliari	38	11	9	18	40	56	42
Torino	38	8	16	14	36	49	40
Reggina	38	9	13	16	37	56	40
Catania	38	8	13	17	33	45	37
Empoli*	38	9	9	20	29	52	36
Parma*	38	7	13	18	42	62	34
Livorno*	38	6	12	20	35	60	30

Top scorer: Del Piero (Juventus) 21.
Cup Final: Roma 2, Internazionale 1.

KAZAKHSTAN

The Football Union of Kazakhstan, Satpayev Street, 29/3 Almaty 480 072, Kazakhstan.
Founded: 1914; *National Colours:* Blue shirts, blue shorts, yellow stockings.

International matches 2007
China (a) 1-2, Kyrgyzstan (h) 2-0, Azerbaijan (h) 1-0, Uzbekistan (h) 1-1, Serbia (h) 2-1, Armenia (h) 1-2, Azerbaijan (h) 1-1, Finland (a) 1-2, Tajikistan (h) 1-1, Belgium (h) 2-2, Poland (a) 1-3, Portugal (h) 1-2, Armenia (a) 1-0, Serbia (a) 0-1.

League Championship wins (1992–2007)
Irtysh (includes Ansat) 5; Yelimai 3; Astana (includes Zhenis) 3; Aqtobe 3; Kairat 2; Taraz 1.

Cup wins (1992–2007)
Kairat 5; Astana (includes Zhenis) 3; Dostyk 1; Vostok 1; Yelimai 1; Irtysh 1; Kaisar 1; Taraz 1; Almaty 1; Tobol 1.

Final League Table 2007

	P	*W*	*D*	*L*	*F*	*A*	*Pts*
Aqtobe	30	22	6	2	55	12	72
Tobol	30	19	7	4	60	20	64
Shakhtyor	30	17	7	6	45	23	58
Yertis	30	16	4	10	34	27	52
Jetisu	30	13	7	10	33	32	46
Almaty	30	13	5	12	35	32	44
Vostok	30	12	5	13	30	38	41
Astana	30	11	8	11	34	25	41
Ordabasy	30	9	11	10	28	29	38
Qaysar	30	10	7	13	27	37	37
Yesil Bogatyr	30	8	13	9	24	28	37
Yekibastuzets*	30	8	8	14	28	38	32
Qayrat	30	9	3	18	23	43	30
Atyrau	30	8	6	16	29	39	30
Oqjetpes	30	8	5	17	26	56	29
Taraz*	30	3	6	21	18	50	15

Yekibastuzets relegated for disciplinary reasons; Oqjetpes not relegated.
Top scorer: Irismetov (Almaty) 17.
Cup Final: Tobol 3, Ordabasy 0.

KOSOVO

Football Federation Kosova, Agim Ramadani 45, Prishtina, Kosovo 10000.

League Championship wins (1945–2008)
Prishtina 11; Vellaznimi 9; Trepca 6; Liria 5; Buduqnosti 4; Red Star 3; Rudari 3; Besa 3; Fushe-Kosova 2; Jedinstvo 2; Kosova Prishtina 2; Obiliqi 2; Slloga 2; Besiana 1; Drita 1; Dukagjini 1; KNI Ramiz Sadiku 1; KXEK Kosova 1; Proletari 1; Rudniku 1.

Cup wins (1992–2008)
Flamurtari 2; Liria 2; Prishtina 2; Besa 1; Besiana 1; Drita 1; Gjilani 1; KEK-u 1; Kosova Prishtina 1; Trepca 1; Vellaznimi 1.

Final League Table 2007–08

	P	*W*	*D*	*F*	*L*	*A*	*Pts*
Prishtina	30	20	5	5	61	19	65
Vellaznimi	30	19	4	7	65	32	61
Besa	30	18	4	8	77	43	58
Gjilani	30	16	8	6	48	25	56
Hysi	30	13	6	11	32	30	45
Flamurtari	30	12	7	11	52	55	43
Korriku	30	12	5	13	46	54	41
Kosova	30	11	7	12	44	34	40
Trepca	30	10	10	10	40	36	40
Trepca 89	30	11	6	13	52	47	39
Drenica	30	11	6	13	33	43	39
Drita	30	10	8	12	39	48	38
Fushe*+	30	10	7	13	40	45	37
Besiana+	30	10	7	13	31	49	37
Shqiponjja*	30	4	5	21	33	87	17
KEK-u*	30	3	5	22	22	68	14

Cup Final 2006–07: Liria 0, Flamurtari 0.
Liria won 3-0 on penalties.
Cup Final: Vellaznimi 2, Trepca 89 0.

LATVIA

Latvian Football Federation, Augsiela 1, LV-1009, Riga.
Founded: 1921; *National Colours:* Carmine red shirts, white shorts, carmine red stockings.

International matches 2007
Bulgaria (n) 0-2, Hungary (n) 0-2, Liechtenstein (a) 0-1, Spain (h) 0-2, Denmark (h) 0-2, Moldova (h) 1-2, Northern Ireland (h) 1-0, Spain (a) 0-2, Iceland (a) 4-2, Denmark (a) 1-3, Liechtenstein (h) 4-1, Sweden (a) 1-2.

League Championship wins (1922–2007)
Skonto Riga 14; ASK Riga 9; RFK Riga 8; Olympija Liepaya 7; Sarkanais Metalurgs Liepaya 7; VEF Riga 6; Energija Riga 4; Elektrons Riga 3; Torpedo Riga 3; Daugava Liepaya 2; ODO Riga 2; Khimikis Daugavpils 2; RAF Yelgava 2; Keisermezhs Riga 2; FK Ventspils 2; Dinamo Riga 1; Zhmilyeva Team 1; Darba Rezervi 1; RER Riga 1; Starts Brotseni 1; Venta Ventspils 1; Yurnieks Riga 1; Alta Riga 1; Gauja Valmiera 1; Metalurgs Liepaya 1.

Cup wins (1937–2007)
Elektrons Riga 7; Skonto Riga 7; Sarkanais Metalurgs Liepaya 5; FK Ventspils 4; ODO Riga 3; VEF Riga 3; ASK Riga 3; Tseltnieks Riga 3; RAF Yelgava 3; RFK Riga 2; Daugava Liepaya 2; Starts Brotseni 2; Selmash Liepaya 2; Yurnieks Riga 2; Khimikis Daugavpils 2; Rigas Vilki 1; Dinamo Liepaya 1; Dinamo Riga 1; RER Riga 1; Voulkan Kouldiga 1; Baltika Liepaya 1; Venta Ventspils 1; Pilots Riga 1; Lielupe Yurmala 1; Energija Riga 1; Torpedo Riga 1; Daugava SKIF Riga 1; Tseltnieks Daugavpils 1; Olympija Riga 1; FK Riga 1; Metalurgs Liepaya 1.

Final League Table 2007

	P	*W*	*D*	*L*	*F*	*A*	*Pts*
FK Ventspils	28	18	6	4	59	16	60
Metalurgs Liepaya	28	18	4	6	42	21	58
FK Riga	28	17	6	5	48	28	57
Skonto Riga	28	16	7	5	54	27	55
Daugava Daugavpils	28	9	6	13	33	38	33
Jurmala	28	7	5	16	28	51	26
Dinaburg	28	6	2	20	23	58	20
Olimps Riga	28	2	2	24	15	63	8

Ditton changed name to Daugava; no relegation: League extended to ten clubs.
Top scorer: Rimkus (FK Ventspils) 20.
Cup Final 2006–07: FK Ventspils 3, Olimps 0.
Cup Final: Ventspils 3, Olimps Riga 0.

LIECHTENSTEIN

Liechtensteiner Fussball-Verband, Malbuner Huus Altenbach 11, Postfach 165, 9490 Vaduz.
Founded: 1934; *National Colours:* Blue shirts, red shorts, blue stockings.

International matches 2007
Northern Ireland (h) 1-4, Latvia (h) 1-0, Iceland (a) 1-1, Spain (h) 0-2, Northern Ireland (a) 1-3, Denmark (a) 0-4, Sweden (h) 0-3, Iceland (h) 3-0, Latvia (a) 1-4.
Liechtenstein has no national league. Teams compete in Swiss regional leagues.

Cup wins (1937–2008)
Vaduz 37; Balzers 11; Triesen 8; Eschen/Mauren 4; Schaan 3.
Cup Final: Vaduz 4, Balzers 0.

LITHUANIA

Lithuanian Football Federation, Seimyniskiu str. 15, 2005 Vilnius.
Founded: 1922; *National Colours:* Yellow shirts, green shorts, yellow stockings.

International matches 2007
Mali (a) 1-3, France (h) 0-1, Ukraine (a) 0-1, Georgia (h) 1-0, Italy (h) 0-2, Turkmenistan (h) 2-1, Scotland (a) 1-3, Faeroes (h) 2-1, France (a) 0-2, Ukraine (h) 2-0, Georgia (a) 2-0.

League Championship wins (1990–2007)
FBK Kaunas 8 (including Zalgiris Kaunas 1); Zalgiris Vilnius 3; Kareda 2; Inkaras Kaunas 2; Ekranas Panevezys 2; Sirijus Klaipeda 1; ROMAR Mazeikiai 1.

Cup wins (1990–2008)
Zalgiris Vilnius 5; FBK Kaunas 4; Kareda 2; Ekranas Panevezys 2; Atlantas 2; Sirijus Klaipeda 1; Lietuvos Makabi Vilnius 1; Inkaras Kaunas 1; Suduva 1.

Final League Table 2007

	P	W	D	L	F	A	Pts
FBK Kaunas	36	25	8	3	91	26	83
Suduva	36	20	8	8	66	34	68
Ekranas	36	19	9	8	83	36	66
Zalgiris	36	18	10	8	64	34	64
Vetra	36	18	7	11	55	30	61
Atlantas	36	13	6	17	54	45	45
FK Vilnius	36	13	6	17	54	63	45
Siauliai	36	13	6	17	47	50	45
Silute	36	6	4	26	28	86	22
Interas*	36	2	2	32	16	154	8

Top scorer: Luksys (Ekranas) 26.
Cup Final: FBK Kaunas 2, Vetra 1.

LUXEMBOURG

Federation Luxembourgeoise De Football (F.L.F.), 68 Rue De Gasperich, Luxembourg 1617.
Founded: 1908; *National Colours:* All red.

International matches 2007
Gambia (h) 2-1, Belarus (h) 1-2, Romania (a) 0-3, Albania (a) 0-2, Albania (h) 0-3, Georgia (h) 0-0, Slovenia (h) 0-3, Bulgaria (a) 0-3, Belarus (a) 1-0, Romania (h) 0-2, Holland (a) 0-1.

League Championship wins (1910–2008)
Jeunesse Esch 27; Spora Luxembourg 11; Stade Dudelange 10; F91 Dudelange 7; Red Boys Differdange 6; Union Luxembourg 6; Avenir Beggen 6; US Hollerich-Bonnevoie 5; Fola Esch 5; Aris Bonnevoie 3; Progres Niedercorn 3; Sporting Club 2; Racing Club 1; National Schifflange 1; Grevenmacher 1.

Cup wins (1922–2008)
Red Boys Differdange 15; Jeunesse Esch 12; Union Luxembourg 10; Spora Luxembourg 8; Avenir Beggen 7; Stade Dudelange 4; Progres Niedercorn 4; Grevenmacher 4; Fola Esch 3; F91 Dudelange 3; Alliance Dudelange 2; US Rumelange 2; Aris Bonnevoie 1; US Dudelange 1; Jeunesse Hautcharage 1; National Schifflange 1; Racing Club 1; SC Tetange 1; Swift Hesperange 1; Etzella Ettelbruck 1; CS Petange 1.

Final League Table 2007–08

	P	W	D	L	F	A	Pts
F91 Dudelange	26	23	2	1	74	12	71
Union Luxembourg	26	14	8	4	50	28	50
Jeunesse Esch	26	13	6	7	51	39	45
Etzella	26	13	5	8	54	48	44
Avenir Beggen	26	11	4	11	41	38	37
Grevenmacher	26	10	6	10	45	36	36
Differdange	26	11	2	13	43	43	35
Hamm Benfica	26	9	5	12	32	48	32
Hesperange	26	8	7	11	36	44	31
Kaerjeng	26	8	6	12	30	40	30
Progres	26	7	7	12	31	46	28
FC Wiltz 71*+	26	6	7	13	33	48	25
Victoria Rosport*	26	6	6	14	29	56	24
Petange*	26	4	7	15	27	50	19

Cup Final: Grevenmacher 4, Victoria Rosport 1.

MACEDONIA

Football Association of Macedonia, VIII-ma Udarna Brigada 31-A, Skopje 1000.
Founded: 1948; *National Colours:* All red.

International matches 2007
Albania (a) 1-0, Croatia (a) 1-2, Israel (h) 1-2, Nigeria (h) 0-0, Russia (a) 0-3, Estonia (h) 1-1, Andorra (h) 3-0, Croatia (h) 2-0, Israel (a) 0-1.

League Championship wins (1993–2008)
Vardar 5; Sileks 3; Sloga Jugomagnat 3; Rabotnicki 3; Pobeda 2.

Cup wins (1993–2008)
Vardar 5; Sloga Jugomagnat 3; Sileks 2; Pelister 1; Pobeda 1; Cement 1; Baskimi 1; Makedonija 1; Rabotnicki 1.

Final League Table 2007–08

	P	W	D	L	F	A	Pts
Rabotnicki	33	24	7	2	51	11	79
Milano	33	21	3	9	74	36	66
Pelister	33	17	7	9	42	27	58
Vardar	33	12	11	10	45	40	47
Renova	33	13	8	12	34	34	47
Pobeda	33	12	9	12	48	48	45
Makedonija	33	13	5	15	34	42	44
Napredok	33	11	9	13	38	49	42
Sileks+	33	10	11	12	33	36	40
Baskimi+	33	8	6	19	40	63	30
Shkendija*	33	7	5	21	26	57	26
Cement*	33	5	9	19	24	46	24

Top scorer: Gligorevski (Milano) 15.
Cup Final: Rabotnicki 2, Milano 0.

MALTA

Malta Football Association, 280 St Paul Street, Valletta VLT07.
Founded: 1900; *National Colours:* Red shirts, white shorts, red stockings.

International matches 2007
Austria (h) 1-1, Moldova (a) 1-1, Greece (h) 0-1, Norway (a) 0-4, Bosnia (a) 0-1, Albania (a) 0-3, Turkey (h) 2-2, Armenia (h) 0-1, Hungary (a) 0-2, Moldova (h) 2-3, Greece (a) 0-5, Norway (h) 1-4.

League Championship wins (1910–2008)
Sliema Wanderers 26; Floriana 25; Valletta 19; Hibernians 9; Hamrun Spartans 7; Rabat Ajax 2; Birkirkara 2; St George's 1; KOMR 1; Marsaxlokk 1.

Cup wins (1935–2008)
Sliema Wanderers 19; Floriana 18; Valletta 11; Hibernians 8; Hamrun Spartans 6; Birkirkara 4; Gzira United 1; Melita 1; Zurrieq 1; Rabat Ajax 1.

Qualifying League Table 2007–08

	P	W	D	L	F	A	Pts
Valletta	18	10	6	2	40	16	36
Marsaxlokk	18	10	3	5	35	26	33
Sliema Wanderers	18	9	5	4	31	18	32
Floriana	18	8	4	6	33	28	28
Birkirkara	18	7	6	5	27	18	27
Hamrun Spartans	18	7	6	5	30	29	27
Hibernians	18	6	7	5	22	19	25
Msida St Joseph	18	6	3	9	25	35	21
Pieta Hotspurs	18	5	0	13	21	40	15
Mqabba	18	2	0	16	15	50	6

Championship Table 2007–08

	P	W	D	L	F	A	Pts
Valletta	28	17	7	4	58	27	40
Marsaxlokk	28	16	3	9	56	40	35
Birkirkara	28	13	8	7	46	26	34
Sliema Wanderers	28	15	5	8	47	33	34
Floriana	28	10	6	12	40	42	22
Hamrun Spartans	28	7	7	14	42	60	15

Promotion/Relegation Table 2007–08

	P	W	D	L	F	A	Pts
Hibernians	24	10	8	6	35	27	26
Msida St Joseph	24	10	4	10	41	46	24
Pieta Hotspurs*	24	6	0	18	27	53	11
Mqabba*	24	3	2	19	24	62	8

Top scorer: Monesterolo (Valletta) 19.
Cup Final: Birkirkara 2, Hamrun Spartans 1.

MOLDOVA

Football Association of Moldova, 39 Tricolorului Str, 2012, Chisinau.
Founded: 1990; *National Colours:* Red shirts, blue shorts, red stockings.

International matches 2007
Romania (a) 0-2, Malta (h) 1-1, Hungary (a) 0-2, Greece (a) 1-2, Latvia (a) 2-1, Norway (h) 0-1, Bosnia (a) 1-0, Turkey (h) 1-1, Malta (a) 3-2, Hungary (h) 3-0.

League Championship wins (1992–2008)
Zimbru Chisinau 8; Sheriff 8; Constructorul 1.

Cup wins (1992–2008)
Zimbru Chisinau 5; Sheriff 5; Tiligul 3; Constructorul 2; Comrat 1; Nistru Otaci 1.

Final League Table 2007–08

	P	W	D	L	F	A	Pts
Sheriff	30	26	3	1	68	8	81
Dacia	30	19	5	6	60	28	62
Otaci	30	17	8	5	34	17	59
Tiraspol	30	16	7	7	36	21	55
Zimbru Chisinau	30	13	13	4	43	21	52
Iscra-Stali	30	9	8	13	23	34	35
Tiligul	30	7	8	15	16	36	29
Olimpia	30	7	6	17	24	46	27
Dinamo	30	7	5	18	30	57	26
Steaua	30	5	3	22	21	55	18
Politehnica	30	3	6	21	7	39	15
Rapid	16	6	4	6	19	15	22

Withdrew November; results annulled.
Top scorer: Picusciac (Tiraspol) 11, (Sheriff) 3.
Cup Final: Sheriff 1, Otaci 0.

MONTENEGRO

Football Association of Montenegro.
Founded: 1931.

International matches 2007
Japan (a) 0-2, Colombia (n) 0-1, Slovenia (h) 1-1, Sweden (h) 1-2, Estonia (a) 1-0.

League Championship wins (2006–08)
Buducnost 1; Zeta 1.

Cup wins (2006–08)
Mogren 1; Rudar 1.

Final League Table 2007–08

	P	W	D	L	F	A	Pts
Buducnost	33	18	12	3	43	13	66
Zeta	33	19	9	5	56	28	66
Mogren	33	19	9	5	46	21	66
Grbalj	33	14	13	6	40	25	55
Rudar	33	14	10	9	38	26	52
Lovcen	33	11	10	12	28	30	43
Decic	33	10	8	15	26	37	38
Petrovac	33	8	12	13	36	46	36
Kom	33	9	9	15	29	49	36
Bokelj*+	33	8	8	17	24	38	32
Sutjeska+	33	5	11	17	19	44	23
Mladost*	33	4	7	22	16	44	19

Sutjeska three points deducted.
Cup Final 2006–07: Rudar 2, Sutjeska 1.
Cup Final: Mogren 1, Buducnost 1.
Mogren won 6-5 on penalties.

NORTHERN CYPRUS

League Championship wins (1956–63; 1969–74; 1976–2008)
Cetinkaya 12; Gonyeli 8; Magusa 7; Dogan 6; Yenicami 5; BAF Ulku 4; Kucuk 3; Akincilar 1; Binatli 1.

Cup wins (1956-2007)
Cetinkaya 16; Kucuk 6; Gonyeli 6; Magusa 5; Yenicami 5; Turk Ocagi 4; Binatli 1; Dogan 1; Genclik 1; Lefke 1; Yalova 1.

Final League Table 2007–08

	P	W	D	L	F	A	Pts
Gonyeli	26	22	4	0	73	14	70
Kucuk	26	15	8	3	63	34	53
Magusa	26	13	5	8	44	34	44
Bostanci	26	13	4	9	45	33	43
Cihangir	26	13	3	10	48	36	42
Tatlisu	26	11	5	10	46	38	38
Cetinkaya	26	11	5	10	44	50	38
Yeni	26	10	3	13	34	47	33
Ozankoy	26	9	5	12	31	39	32
Turk Ocagi	26	8	6	12	36	41	30
Lapta	26	9	3	14	34	47	30
Yenicami*	26	7	5	14	34	60	26
Iskele*	26	4	6	16	40	68	18
Hamitkoy*	26	5	2	19	35	66	17

Top scorer: Jacques (Gonyeli) 25.
Cup Final: Gronyeli 5, Esentepe 1.

NORTHERN IRELAND

Irish Football Association Ltd, 20 Windsor Avenue, Belfast BT9 6EE.
Founded: 1880; *National Colours:* Green shirts, white shorts, green stockings.

NORWAY

Norges Fotballforbund, Ullevaal Stadion, Sognsveien 75J, Serviceboks 1, Oslo 0855.
Founded: 1902; *National Colours:* Red shirts, white shorts, blue stockings.

International matches 2007
Croatia (a) 1-2, Bosnia (h) 1-2, Turkey (a) 2-2, Malta (h) 4-0, Hungary (h) 4-0, Argentina (h) 2-1, Moldova (a) 1-0, Greece (h) 2-2, Bosnia (a) 2-0, Turkey (h) 1-2, Malta (a) 4-1.

League Championship wins (1938–2007)
Rosenborg Trondheim 20; Fredrikstad 9; Viking Stavanger 8; Lillestrom 5; Valerenga 5; Larvik Turn 3; Brann Bergen 3; Lyn Oslo 2; IK Start 2; Freidig 1; Fram 1; Skeid Oslo 1; Strömsgodset Drammen 1; Moss 1.

Cup wins (1902–2007)
Odd Grenland 12; Fredrikstad 11; Rosenborg Trondheim 9; Lyn Oslo 8; Skeid Oslo 8; Rosenborg Trondheim 8; Sarpsborg 6; Brann Bergen 6; Viking Stavanger 5; Lillestrom 5; Orn Horten 4; Strömsgodset Drammen 4; Frigg 3; Mjondalen 3; Valerenga 3; Bodo/Glimt 2; Mercantile 2; Tromso 2; Molde 2; Grane Nordstrand 1; Kvik Halden 1; Sparta 1; Gjovik/Lyn 1; Moss 1; Bryne 1; Stabaek 1.
(Known as the Norwegian Championship for HM The King's Trophy).

Final League Table 2007

	P	W	D	L	F	A	Pts
Brann	26	17	3	6	59	39	54
Stabaek	26	14	6	6	53	35	48
Viking	26	13	6	7	50	40	47
Lillestrom	26	13	7	6	47	28	44
Rosenborg	26	12	5	9	53	39	41
Tromso	26	12	4	10	45	44	40
Valerenga	26	10	6	10	34	34	36
Fredrikstad	26	9	9	8	37	40	36
Lyn	26	10	4	12	43	46	34
Stromsgodset	26	8	6	12	34	47	30
Aalesunds	26	9	3	14	40	56	30
Odd*+	26	8	3	15	33	43	27
Start*	26	6	8	12	34	44	26
Sandefjord*	26	4	4	18	26	53	16

Top scorer: Helstad (Brann) 22.
Cup Final: Lillestrom 2, Haugesund 0.

POLAND

Polish Football Association, Polski Zwiazek Pilki Noznej, Miodowa 1, Warsaw 00-080.
Founded: 1919; *National Colours:* White shirts, red shorts, white stockings.

International matches 2007
Estonia (a) 4-0, Slovakia (h) 2-2, Azerbaijan (h) 5-0, Armenia (h) 1-0, Azerbaijan (a) 3-1, Armenia (a) 0-1, Russia (a) 2-2, Portugal (a) 2-2, Finland (a) 0-0, Kazakhstan (h) 3-1, Hungary (h) 0-1, Belgium (h) 2-0, Serbia (a) 2-2.

League Championship wins (1921–2008)
Gornik Zabrze 14; Ruch Chorzow 14; Wisla Krakow 12; Legia Warsaw 8; Cracovia 5; Lech Poznan 5; Pogon Lwow 4; Widzew Lodz 4; Warta Poznan 2; Polonia Bytom 2; Stal Mielec 2; LKS Lodz 2; Polonia Warsaw 2; Zaglebie Lubin 2; Garbarnia Krakow 1; Slask Wroclaw 1; Szombierki Bytom 1.

Cup wins (1951–2008)
Legia Warsaw 13; Gornik Zabrze 6; Zaglebie Sosnowiec 4; Lech Poznan 4; GKS Katowice 3; Ruch Chorzow 3; Amica Wronki 3; Wisla Krakow 3; Slask Wroclaw 2; Polonia Warsaw 2; Groclin 2; Gwardia Warsaw 1; LKS Lodz 1; Stal Rzeszow 1; Arka Gdynia 1; Lechia Gdansk 1; Widzew Lodz 1; Miedz Legnica 1; Wisla Plock 1.

Final League Table 2007–08

	P	W	D	L	F	A	Pts
Wisla	30	24	5	1	68	18	77
Legia	30	20	3	7	48	17	63
Groclin	30	18	6	6	52	24	60
Lech	30	17	6	7	55	32	57
Zaglebie Lubin	30	15	7	8	43	30	52
Korona	30	15	6	9	38	32	51
Cracovia	30	11	6	13	30	32	39
Gornik Zabrze	30	11	6	13	34	39	39
GKS Belchatow	30	9	11	10	26	32	38
Ruch	30	8	10	12	35	41	34
Lodzki	30	7	9	14	25	31	30
Odra	30	8	5	17	28	47	29
Polonia	30	7	7	16	22	45	28
Jagiellonia	30	7	6	17	27	57	27
Widzew*	30	5	11	14	27	42	26
Zaglebie Sosnowiec*	30	4	4	22	19	58	16

Widzew and Zaglebie Sosnowiec relegated an additional level due to corruption.
Top scorer: Brozek (Wisla) 23.
Cup Final: Legia 0, Wisla 0.
Legia won 4-3 on penalties.

PORTUGAL

Federacao Portuguesa De Futebol, Praca De Alegria N.25, Apartado 21.100, P-1127, Lisboa 1250-004.
Founded: 1914; *National Colours:* Red shirts, green shorts, red stockings.

International matches 2007
Brazil (a) 2-0, Belgium (h) 4-0, Serbia (a) 1-1, Belgium

(a) 2-1, Kuwait (a) 1-1, Armenia (a) 1-1, Poland (h) 2-2, Serbia (h) 1-1, Azerbaijan (a) 2-0, Kazakhstan (a) 2-1, Armenia (h) 1-0, Finland (h) 0-0.

League Championship wins (1935–2008)
Benfica 31; FC Porto 23; Sporting Lisbon 18; Belenenses 1; Boavista 1.

Cup wins (1939–2008)
Benfica 24; Sporting Lisbon 15; FC Porto 13; Boavista 5; Belenenses 3; Vitoria Setubal 3; Academica Coimbra 1; Leixoes 1; Sporting Braga 1; Estrela Amadora 1; Beira Mar 1.

Final League Table 2007–08

	P	*W*	*D*	*L*	*F*	*A*	*Pts*
Porto	30	24	3	3	60	13	69
Sporting Lisbon	30	16	7	7	46	28	55
Guimaraes	30	15	8	7	35	31	53
Benfica	30	13	13	4	45	21	52
Maritimo	30	14	4	12	39	28	46
Setubal	30	11	12	7	37	33	45
Braga	30	10	11	9	32	34	41
Belenenses	30	11	10	9	35	33	40
Boavista	30	8	12	10	32	41	36
Nacional	30	9	8	13	23	28	35
Naval	30	9	7	14	26	45	34
Academica	30	6	14	10	31	38	32
Amadora	30	6	13	11	29	41	31
Leixoes	30	4	14	12	27	37	26
Ferreira	30	6	7	17	31	49	25
Uniao Leiria*	30	3	7	20	25	53	13

Porto six points deducted for corruption 2003–04. Uniao Leiria three points for the same reason and Boavista relegated in the same affair. Belenenses three points deducted for an ineligible player.
Top scorer: Lisandro Lopez (Porto) 24.
Cup Final: Sporting Lisbon 2, Porto 0.

ROMANIA

Federatia Romana De Fotbal, House of Football, Str. Serg. Serbanica Vasile 12, Bucharest 73412.
Founded: 1909; *National Colours:* All yellow.

International matches 2007
Moldova (h) 2-0, Holland (a) 0-0, Luxembourg (h) 3-0, Slovenia (a) 2-1, Slovenia (h) 2-0, Turkey (h) 2-0, Belarus (a) 3-1, Germany (a) 1-3, Holland (h) 1-0, Luxembourg (a) 2-0, Bulgaria (a) 0-1, Albania (h) 6-1.

League Championship wins (1910–2008)
Steaua Bucharest 23; Dinamo Bucharest 18; Venus Bucharest 8; Chinezul Timisoara 6; UT Arad 6; Ripensia Timisoara 4; Uni Craiova 4; Petrolul Ploiesti 3; Rapid Bucharest 3; Olimpia Bucharest 2; Colentina Bucharest 2; Arges Pitesti 2; ICO Oradea 1; Romano-Americana Bucharest 1; Prahova Ploiesti 1; Coltea Brasov 1; Juventus Bucharest 1; Metalochimia Resita 1; United Ploiesti 1; Unirea Tricolor 1; Cluj 1.

Cup wins (1934–2008)
Steaua Bucharest 21; Rapid Bucharest 13; Dinamo Bucharest 12; Uni Craiova 6; UT Arad 2; Ripensia Timisoara 2; Politehnica Timisoara 2; Petrolul Ploiesti 2; Metalochimia Resita 1; Universitata Cluj (includes Stiinta) 1; CFR Turnu Severin 1; Chimia Ramnicu Vilcea 1; Jiul Petrosani 1; Progresul Bucharest 1; Progresul Oradea (formerly ICO) 1; Ariesul Turda 1; Gloria Bistrita 1; Cluj 1.

Final League Table 2007–08

	P	*W*	*D*	*L*	*F*	*A*	*Pts*
Cluj	34	23	7	4	52	22	76
Steaua (–7)	34	23	6	5	51	19	68
Rapid Bucharest	34	18	7	9	52	31	61
Dinamo Bucharest	34	17	10	7	55	36	61
Unirea	34	16	13	5	42	24	61
Timisoara	34	16	9	9	57	44	57
Otelul	34	14	5	15	48	48	47
Vaslui	34	11	12	11	42	35	45
Uni Craiova	34	12	7	15	42	48	43
Gloria	34	11	9	14	34	40	42
Iasi	34	11	8	15	37	41	41
Pandurii	34	11	7	16	36	43	40
Farul	34	10	10	14	25	38	40
Buzau	34	10	7	17	30	56	37
Ceahlaul*	34	10	6	18	33	46	36
Dacia*	34	7	10	17	26	43	31
UT Arad*	34	6	8	20	30	52	26
Uni Cluj* (–6)	34	4	11	19	32	58	17

Ceahlaul not relegated as Delta did not obtain a licence.
Top scorer: Danciulescu (Dinamo Bucharest) 20.
Cup Final: Cluj 2, Unirea 1.

RUSSIA

Football Union of Russia; Luzhnetskaya Naberezyhnaja 8, Moscow 119 992.
Founded: 1912; *National Colours:* All white.

International matches 2007
Holland (a) 1-4, Estonia (a) 2-0, Andorra (h) 4-0, Croatia (a) 0-0, Poland (h) 2-2, Macedonia (h) 3-0, England (a) 0-3, England (h) 2-1, Israel (a) 1-2, Andorra (a) 1-0.

League Championship wins (1936–2007)
Spartak Moscow 21; Dynamo Kiev 13; Dynamo Moscow 11; CSKA Moscow 10; Torpedo Moscow 3; Dinamo Tbilisi 2; Zenit St Petersburg (formerly Zenit Leningrad) 2; Dnepr Dnepropetrovsk 2; Lokomotiv Moscow 2; Saria Voroshilovgrad 1; Ararat Erevan 1; Dynamo Minsk 1; Spartak Vladikavkaz 1.

Cup wins (1936–2008)
Spartak Moscow 13; Dynamo Kiev 9; CSKA Moscow 9; Torpedo Moscow 7; Dynamo Moscow 7; Lokomotiv Moscow 7; Shakhtar Donetsk 4; Dinamo Tbilisi 2; Ararat Erevan 2; Zenit St Petersburg (formerly Zenit Leningrad) 2; Karpaty Lvov 1; SKA Rostov 1; Metalist Kharkov 1; Dnepr 1; Terek Groznyi 1.

Final League Table 2007	*P*	*W*	*D*	*L*	*F*	*A*	*Pts*
Zenit	30	18	7	5	54	32	61
Spartak Moscow	30	17	8	5	50	30	59
CSKA Moscow	30	14	11	5	43	24	53
FK Moscow	30	15	7	8	40	32	52
Saturn	30	11	12	7	34	28	45
Dynamo Moscow	30	11	8	11	37	35	41
Lokomotiv Moscow	30	11	8	11	39	42	41
Amkar	30	10	11	9	30	27	41
Khimki	30	9	10	11	32	33	37
Rubin	30	10	5	15	31	39	35
Tomsk	30	8	11	11	37	35	35
Spartak Nalchik	30	8	9	13	29	38	33
Krylia Sovekov	30	8	8	14	35	46	32
Luch-Energia	30	8	8	14	26	39	32
Kuban*	30	7	11	12	27	38	32
Rostov*	30	2	12	16	18	44	18

Top scorers: Adamov (FK Moscow) 14, Pavlyuchenko (Spartak Moscow) 14.
Cup Final: CSKA Moscow 2, Amkar 2.
CSKA Moscow won 4-1 on penalties.

SAN MARINO

Federazione Sammarinese Giuoco Calcio, Viale Campo dei Giudei, 14; Rep. San Marino 47890.
Founded: 1931; *National Colours:* All light blue.

International matches 2007
Republic of Ireland (h) 1-2, Wales (a) 0-3, Germany (a) 0-6, Cyprus (h) 0-1, Czech Republic (h) 0-3, Cyprus (a) 0-3, Slovakia (a) 0-7, Wales (h) 1-2, Slovakia (h) 0-5.

League Championship wins (1986–2008)
Tre Fiori 4; Domagnono 4; Faetano 3; Folgore Falciano 3; Murata 3; La Fiorita 2; Montevito 1; Libertas 1; Cosmos 1; Pennarossa 1.

Cup wins (1937–2008)
Libertas 10; Domagnono 8; Juvenes 5; Tre Fiore 5; Tre Penne 5; Cosmos 4; Caetano 3; Murata 3; Dogana 2; Pennarossa 2; La Fiorita 1.

Qualifying League Table 2007–08

Group A	*P*	*W*	*D*	*L*	*F*	*A*	*Pts*
Tre Penne	21	13	5	3	51	22	43
Tre Fiore	21	10	6	5	35	26	36
Juvenes/Dogana	21	10	6	5	31	18	36
Cailungo	21	10	6	5	37	24	36
Pennarossa	21	7	4	10	33	42	25
Folgore/Falciano	21	6	4	11	21	37	22
Domagnono	21	4	5	12	36	54	17
Fiorentino	21	1	1	19	17	60	4

Group B	*P*	*W*	*D*	*L*	*F*	*A*	*Pts*
Murata	20	12	7	1	46	15	43
La Fiorita	20	12	6	2	39	24	42
Faetano	20	11	4	5	45	18	37
Virtus	20	9	7	4	34	23	34
Cosmos	20	6	5	9	21	33	23
Libertas	20	5	6	9	27	36	21
San Giovanni	20	1	2	17	15	56	5

Play-Offs: Tre Fiore 1, Faetano 0; La Fiorita 0, Juvenes/Dogana 0 (3-4 pens); Tre Penne 1, Juvenes/Dogana 5; Murata 2, Tre Fiore 2 (4-1 pens); Tre Penne 1, Faetano 2; Tre Fiore 1, La Fiorita 0; Juvenes/Dogana 0, Murata 2; Faetano 2, Tre Fiore 1; Juvenes/Dogana 1, Faetano 0.
Final: Murata 1, Juvenes/Dogana 0.
Cup Final: Murata 1, Juvenes/Dogana 0.

SCOTLAND

The Scottish Football Association Ltd, Hampden Park, Glasgow G42 9AY.
Founded: 1873; *National Colours:* Dark blue shirts, white shorts, dark blue stockings.

SERBIA

Football Association of Serbia, Terazije 35, P.O. Box 263, 11000 Beograd.
Founded: 1919; *National Colours:* Blue shirts, white shorts, red stockings.

International matches 2007
Kazakhstan (a) 1-2, Portugal (h) 1-1, Finland (a) 2-0, Belgium (a) 2-3, Finland (h) 0-0, Portugal (a) 1-1, Armenia (a) 0-0, Azerbaijan (a) 6-1, Poland (h) 2-2, Kazakhstan (h) 1-0.

League Championship wins (1923–2008)
Red Star Belgrade 25; Partizan Belgrade 20; Hajduk Split 9; Gradjanski Zagreb 5; BSK Belgrade 5; Dinamo Zagreb 4; Jugoslavija Belgrade 2; Concordia Zagreb 2; FC Sarajevo 2; Vojvodina Novi Sad 2; HASK Zagreb 1; Zeljeznicar 1; Obilic 1.

Cup wins (1947–2008)
Red Star Belgrade 22; Partizan Belgrade 10; Hajduk Split 9; Dinamo Zagreb 8; BSK Belgrade (includes OFK) 2; Rijeka 2; Velez Mostar 2; Vardar Skopje 1; Borac Banjaluka 1; Sartid 1; Zeleznik 1.

Final League Table 2007–08

	P	*W*	*D*	*L*	*F*	*A*	*Pts*
Partizan Belgrade	33	24	8	1	63	23	80
Red Star Belgrade	33	21	12	0	65	22	75
Vojvodina	33	18	8	7	53	33	62
Borac	33	12	10	11	29	33	46
Napredak	33	11	8	14	25	33	41
Cukaricki	33	10	10	13	31	32	40
Mladost	33	8	14	11	32	41	38
Hajduk Kula	33	8	13	12	25	31	37
OFK Belgrade	33	9	9	15	31	45	36
Smederevo*+	33	10	6	17	33	44	36
Banat*	33	6	10	17	34	57	28
Bezanija*	33	5	4	24	31	58	17

Bezanija two points deducted.
Top scorer: Jestrovic (Red Star Belgrade) 13.
Cup Final: Partizan Belgrade 3, Zemun 0.

SLOVAKIA

Slovak Football Association, Junacka 6, 83280 Bratislava, Slovakia.
Founded: 1993; *National Colours:* All blue and white.

International matches 2007
Poland (a) 2-2, Cyprus (a) 3-1, Republic of Ireland (a) 0-1, Germany (a) 1-2, France (h) 0-1, Republic of Ireland (h) 2-2, Wales (h) 2-5, San Marino (h) 7-0, Croatia (a) 0-3, Czech Republic (a) 1-3, San Marino (a) 5-0.

League Championship wins (1939–44; 1994–2008)
Slovan Bratislava 8; Zilina 4; Kosice 2; Inter Bratislava 2; Artmedia Petrzalka 2; Bystrica 1; OAP Bratislava 1; Ruzomberok 1.

Cup wins (1994–2008)
Inter Bratislava 3; Slovan Bratislava 3; Artmedia Petrzalka 2; Humenne 1; Spartak Trnava 1; Koba Senec 1; Matador Puchov 1; Bystrica 1; Ruzomberok 1; ViOn Zlate 1.

Final League Table 2007–08

	P	*W*	*D*	*L*	*F*	*A*	*Pts*
Artmedia	33	27	3	3	77	30	84
Zilina	33	22	7	4	75	30	73
Nitra	33	17	6	10	40	26	57
Spartak Trnava	33	15	7	11	52	40	52
Slovan Bratislava	33	15	6	12	46	37	51
Kosice	33	13	6	14	45	44	45
Ruzomberok	33	10	14	9	46	43	44
Bystrica	33	10	9	14	41	37	39
Dubnica	33	7	12	14	34	53	33
Senec	33	6	10	17	30	51	28
Moravce	33	6	7	20	22	66	25
Trencin*	33	3	7	23	26	77	16

Top scorer: Halenar (Artmedia) 16.
Cup Final: Artmedia 1, Spartak Trnava 0.

SLOVENIA

Football Association of Slovenia, Nogometna zveza Slovenije, Cerinova 4, P.P. 3986, 1001 Ljubljana, Slovenia.
Founded: 1920; *National Colours:* White shirts with green sleeves, white shorts, white stockings.

International matches 2007
Estonia (h) 1-0, Albania (a) 0-0, Holland (h) 0-1, Romania (h) 1-2, Romania (a) 0-2, Montenegro (a) 1-1, Luxembourg (a) 3-0, Belarus (h) 1-0, Albania (h) 0-0, Holland (a) 0-2, Bulgaria (h) 0-2.

League Championship wins (1992–2008)
Maribor 7; SCT Olimpija 4; Gorica 4; Domzale 2.

Cup wins (1992–2008)
Maribor 5; SCT Olimpija 4; Gorica 2; Koper 2; Mura 1; Rudar 1; Publikum 1; Interblock 1.

Final League Table 2007–08

	P	*W*	*D*	*L*	*F*	*A*	*Pts*
Domzale	36	22	10	4	69	28	76
Koper	36	18	10	8	68	50	64
Gorica	36	16	9	11	61	50	57
Maribor	36	14	10	12	55	46	52
Interblock	36	14	8	14	49	42	50
Primorje	36	14	6	16	52	41	48
Nafta	36	12	11	13	43	56	47
Celje	36	13	6	17	42	51	45
Drava+	36	13	5	18	45	64	44
Livar*	36	4	5	27	39	95	17

Top scorer: Zahora (Domzale) 22.
Cup Final: Interblock 2, Maribor 1.

SPAIN

Real Federacion Espanola De Futbol, Ramon y Cajal, s/n, Apartado Postale 385, Madrid 28230.
Founded: 1913; *National Colours:* Red shirts, blue shorts, blue stockings with red, blue and yellow border.

International matches 2007
England (a) 1-0, Denmark (h) 2-1, Iceland (h) 1-0, Latvia (a) 2-0, Liechtenstein (a) 2-0, Greece (a) 3-2, Iceland (a) 1-1, Latvia (h) 2-0, Denmark (a) 3-1, Finland (a) 0-0, Sweden (h) 3-0, Northern Ireland (h) 1-0.

League Championship wins (1929–36; 1940–2008)
Real Madrid 31; Barcelona 18; Atletico Madrid 9; Athletic Bilbao 8; Valencia 6; Real Sociedad 2; Real Betis 1; Sevilla 1; La Coruna 1.

Cup wins (1994–2008)
Barcelona 24; Athletic Bilbao 23; Real Madrid 17; Atletico Madrid 9; Valencia 7; Real Zaragoza 6; Espanyol 4; Sevilla 4; Real Union de Irun 3; La Coruna 2; Real Sociadad (includes Ciclista) 2; Real Betis 2; Arenas 1; Racing de Irun 1; Vizcaya Bilbao 1; Real Sociedad 1; Mallorca 1.

Final League Table 2007–08

	P	*W*	*D*	*L*	*F*	*A*	*Pts*
Real Madrid	38	27	4	7	84	36	87
Villarreal	38	24	5	9	63	40	77
Barcelona	38	19	10	9	76	43	67
Atletico Madrid	38	19	7	12	66	47	64
Sevilla	38	20	4	14	75	49	64
Santander	38	17	9	12	42	41	60
Mallorca	38	15	14	9	69	54	59
Almeria	38	14	10	14	42	45	52
La Coruna	38	15	7	16	46	47	52
Valencia	38	15	6	17	48	62	51
Athletic Bilbao	38	13	11	14	40	43	50
Espanyol	38	13	9	16	43	53	48
Betis	38	12	11	15	45	51	47
Getafe	38	12	11	15	44	48	47
Valladolid	38	11	12	15	42	57	45
Recreativo	38	11	11	16	40	60	44
Osasuna	38	12	7	19	37	44	43
Zaragoza*	38	10	12	16	50	61	42
Murcia*	38	7	9	22	36	65	30
Levante*	38	7	5	26	33	75	26

Top scorer: Guiza (Mallorca) 27.
Cup Final: Valencia 3, Getafe 1.

SWEDEN

Svenska Fotbollfoerbundet, Box 1216, S-17123 Solna.
Founded: 1904; *National Colours:* Yellow shirts, blue shorts, yellow stockings.

International matches 2007
Venezuela (a) 0-2, Ecuador (a) 1-2, Ecuador (a) 1-1, Egypt (a) 0-2, Northern Ireland (a) 1-2, Denmark (a) 3-0, Iceland (h) 5-0, USA (h) 1-0, Denmark (h) 0-0, Montenegro (a) 2-1, Liechtenstein (a) 3-0, Northern Ireland (h) 1-1, Spain (a) 0-3, Latvia (h) 2-1.

League Championship wins (1896–2007)
IFK Gothenburg 19; Malmo FF 15; Orgryte 14; IFK Norrköping 12; Djurgaarden 11; AIK Stockholm 10; GAIS Gothenburg 6; IF Helsingborg 6; IF Elfsborg 5; Oster Vaxjo 4; Halmstad 4; Atvidaberg 2; IFK Eskilstuna 1; IF Gavic Brynas 1; IF Gothenburg 1; Fassbergs 1; IK Sleipner 1; Hammarby 1.

Cup wins (1941–2007)
Malmo FF 14; AIK Stockholm 7; IFK Norrköping 6; IFK Gothenburg 4; Djurgaarden 4; Helsingborg 3; Kalmar 3; Atvidaberg 2; IF Elfsborg 2; GAIS Gothenburg 1; IF Raa 1; Landskrona 1; Oster Vaxjo 1; Degerfors 1; Halmstad 1; Orgryte 1.

Final League Table 2007

	P	*W*	*D*	*L*	*F*	*A*	*Pts*
IFK Gothenburg	26	14	7	5	45	23	49
Kalmar	26	15	3	8	43	32	48
Djurgaarden	26	13	7	6	39	24	46
Elfsborg	26	10	10	6	39	30	40
AIK	26	10	8	8	30	27	38
Hammarby	26	11	3	12	35	31	36
Halmstad	26	9	9	8	33	41	36
Helsingborg	26	9	8	9	49	37	35
Malmo	26	9	7	10	29	28	34
Gefle	26	9	7	10	29	30	34
GAIS Gothenburg	26	7	8	11	24	37	29
Orebro	26	6	7	13	28	45	25
Trelleborg	26	5	8	13	22	38	23
Brommapojkarna*	26	5	8	13	21	43	23

League extended to 16 clubs in 2008.
Top scorers: Berg (IFK Gothenburg) 14, Omotoyossi (Helsingborg) 14.
Cup Final: Kalmar 3, IFK Gothenburg 0.

SWITZERLAND

Schweizerisher Fussballverband, Postfach 3000, Berne 15.
Founded: 1895; *National Colours:* Red shirts, white shorts, red stockings.

International matches 2007
Germany (a) 1-3, Jamaica (a) 2-0, Colombia (a) 1-3, Argentina (h) 1-1, Holland (h) 2-1, Chile (n) 2-1, Japan (n) 3-4, Austria (h) 3-1, USA (h) 0-1, Nigeria (h) 0-1.

League Championship wins (1898–2008)
Grasshoppers 26; Servette 17; FC Basle 12; Young Boys Berne 11; FC Zurich 11; Lausanne 7; La Chaux-de-Fonds 3; FC Lugano 3; Winterthur 3; FC Aarau 3; Neuchatel Xamax 2; Sion 2; St Gallen 2; FC Anglo-American Club 1; FC Brühl 1; Cantonal-Neuchatel 1; Biel-Bienne 1; Bellinzona 1; FC Etoile La Chaux-de-Fonds 1; Lucerne 1.

Cup wins (1926–2008)
Grasshoppers 18; FC Sion 10; Lausanne 9; FC Basle 9; Servette 7; FC Zurich 7; La Chaux-de-Fonds 6; Young Boys Berne 6; FC Lugano 3; Lucerne 2; FC Grenchen 1; St Gallen 1; Urania Geneva 1; Young Fellows Zurich 1; FC Aarau 1; Wil 1.

Final League Table 2007–08

	P	*W*	*D*	*L*	*F*	*A*	*Pts*
Basle	36	22	8	6	73	39	74
Young Boys	36	21	7	8	82	49	70
Zurich	36	15	11	10	58	43	56
Grasshoppers	36	15	9	12	57	49	54
Aarau	36	11	14	11	47	48	47
Lucerne	36	10	14	12	40	49	44
Sion	36	11	10	15	48	51	43
Neuchatel Xamax	36	10	11	15	48	55	41
St Gallen+	36	9	7	20	39	69	34
Thun*	36	6	9	21	30	70	27

Top scorer: Yakin (Young Boys) 24.
Cup Final: Basle 4, Bellinzona 1.

TURKEY

Turkiye Futbol Federasyonu, Konaklar Mah. Ihlamurlu Sok. 9, 4 Levent, Istanbul 80620.
Founded: 1923; *National Colours:* All white.

International matches 2007
Georgia (a) 0-1, Greece (a) 4-1, Norway (h) 2-2, Bosnia (a) 2-3, Brazil (a) 0-0, Romania (a) 0-2, Malta (a) 2-2, Hungary (h) 3-0, Moldova (a) 1-1, Greece (h) 0-1, Norway (a) 2-1, Bosnia (h) 1-0.

League Championship wins (1959–2008)
Fenerbahce 17; Galatasaray 17; Besiktas 10; Trabzonspor 6.

Cup wins (1963–2008)
Galatasaray 14; Besiktas 7; Trabzonspor 7; Fenerbahce 4; Goztepe Izmir 2; Altay Izmir 2; Ankaragucu 2; Genclerbirligi 2; Kocaelispor 2; Eskisehirspor 1; Bursapor 1; Sakaryaspor 1; Kayseri 1.

Final League Table 2007–08

	P	*W*	*D*	*L*	*F*	*A*	*Pts*
Galatasaray	34	24	7	3	64	23	79
Fenerbahce	34	22	7	5	72	37	73
Besiktas	34	23	4	7	58	32	73
Sivas	34	23	4	7	57	29	73
Kayseri	34	15	10	9	50	31	55
Trabzonspor	34	14	7	13	44	39	49
Denizli	34	13	6	15	48	48	45
Ankaragucu	34	11	10	13	36	44	43
Gaziantep	34	11	10	13	36	45	43
Ankara	34	10	11	13	35	38	41
Genclerbirligi OFTAS	34	10	10	14	30	36	40
Istanbul	34	10	8	16	44	47	38
Bursa	34	9	11	14	31	40	38
Konya	34	10	6	18	37	64	36
Genclerbirligi	34	9	8	17	44	51	35
Vestel*	34	7	8	19	42	62	29
Rize*	34	7	8	19	32	64	29
Kasimpasa*	34	8	5	21	26	56	29

Top scorer: Semih (Fenerbahce) 17.
Cup Final: Kayseri 0, Genclerbirligi 0.
Kayseri won 11-10 on penalties.

UKRAINE

Football Federation of Ukraine, Laboratorna Str. 1, P.O. Box 293, Kiev 03150.
Founded: 1991; *National Colours:* All yellow and blue.

International matches 2007
Israel (a) 1-1, Faeroes (a) 2-0, Lithuania (h) 1-0, France (a) 0-2, Uzbekistan (h) 2-1, Georgia (a) 1-1, Italy (h) 1-2, Scotland (a) 1-3, Faeroes (h) 5-0, Lithuania (a) 0-2, France (h) 2-2.

League Championship wins (1992–2008)
Dynamo Kiev 12; Shakhtar Donetsk 4; Tavriya Simferopol 1.

Cup wins (1992–2008)
Dynamo Kiev 9; Shakhtar Donetsk 6; Chernomorets Odessa 2.

Final League Table 2007–08

	P	*W*	*D*	*L*	*F*	*A*	*Pts*
Shakhtar Donetsk	30	24	2	4	75	24	74
Dynamo Kiev	30	22	5	3	65	26	71
Metalist	30	19	6	5	51	27	63
Dnepro	30	18	5	7	40	27	59
Tavriya	30	13	8	9	38	40	47
Arsenal Kiev	30	11	9	10	42	36	42
Chernomorets	30	11	5	14	27	33	38
Vorskla	30	9	9	12	28	30	36
Metalurg Zapor	30	9	9	12	24	32	36
Karpaty	30	9	6	15	29	41	33
Zorya	30	9	4	17	24	43	31
Metalurg Donetsk	30	6	13	11	34	39	31
Krivbas	30	7	9	14	29	39	30
Kharkiv	30	6	9	15	20	32	27
Naftovyk*	30	6	8	16	18	38	26
Zakarpattja*	30	3	9	18	17	54	18

Top scorer: Devic (Metalist) 19.
Cup Final: Shakhtar Donetsk 2, Dynamo Kiev 0.

WALES

The Football Association of Wales Limited, Plymouth Chambers, 3 Westgate Street, Cardiff, CF10 1DP.
Founded: 1876; *National Colours:* All red.

SOUTH AMERICA

ARGENTINA

Asociacion Del Futbol Argentina, Viamonte 1366/76, 1053 Buenos Aires.
Founded: 1893; *National Colours:* Light blue and white vertical striped shirts, dark blue shorts, white stockings.
International matches 2007
France (a) 1-0, Chile (h) 0-0, Switzerland (a) 1-1, Algeria (a) 4-3, USA (n) 4-1, Colombia (n) 4-2, Paraguay (n) 1-0, Peru (n) 4-0, Mexico (n) 3-0, Brazil (n) 0-3, Norway (a) 1-2, Australia (a) 1-0, Chile (h) 2-0, Venezuela (a) 2-0, Bolivia (h) 3-0, Colombia (a) 1-2.

BOLIVIA

Federacion Boliviana De Futbol, Av. Libertador Bolivar No. 1168, Casilla de Correo 484, Cochabamba, Bolivia.
Founded: 1925; *National Colours:* Green shirts, white shorts, green stockings.
International matches 2007
South Africa (a) 1-0, Republic of Ireland (h) 1-1, Paraguay (h) 0-0, Venezuela (a) 2-2, Uruguay (n) 0-1, Peru (n) 2-2, Ecuador (a) 0-1, Peru (a) 0-2, Uruguay (a) 0-5, Colombia (h) 0-0, Argentina (a) 0-3, Venezuela (a) 3-5.

BRAZIL

Confederacao Brasileira De Futebol, Rua Victor Civita 66, Bloco 1-Edificio 5-5 Andar, Barra da Tijuca, Rio De Janeiro 22775-040.
Founded: 1914; *National Colours:* Yellow shirts with green collar and cuffs, blue shorts, white stockings with green and yellow border.
International matches 2007
Portugal (a) 0-2, Chile (h) 4-0, Ghana (h) 1-0, England (a) 1-1, Turkey (a) 0-0, Mexico (n) 0-2, Chile (n) 3-0, Ecuador (n) 1-0, Chile (n) 6-1, Uruguay (n) 2-2, Argentina (n) 3-0, Algeria (a) 2-0, USA (a) 4-2, Mexico (a) 3-1, Colombia (a) 0-0, Ecuador (h) 5-0, Peru (a) 1-1, Uruguay (h) 2-1.

CHILE

Federacion De Futbol De Chile, Avda. Quillin No. 5635, Casilla postal 3733, Correo Central, Santiago de Chile.
Founded: 1895; *National Colours:* Red shirts with blue collar and cuffs, blue shorts, white stockings.
International matches 2007
Venezuela (a) 1-0, Brazil (a) 0-4, Costa Rica (h) 1-1, Argentina (a) 0-0, Cuba (h) 3-0, Cuba (h) 2-0, Haiti (a) 0-0, Costa Rica (a) 0-2, Jamaica (a) 1-0, Ecuador (n) 3-2, Brazil (n) 0-3, Mexico (n) 0-0, Brazil (n) 1-6, Switzerland (n) 2-3, Austria (a) 2-0, Argentina (a) 0-2, Peru (h) 2-0, Uruguay (a) 2-2, Paraguay (h) 0-3.

COLOMBIA

Federacion Colombiana De Futbol, Avenida 32, No. 16–22 piso 4o. Apartado Aereo 17602, Santafe de Bogota.
Founded: 1924; *National Colours:* Yellow shirts, blue shorts, red stockings.
International matches 2007
Uruguay (h) 1-3, Switzerland (h) 3-1, Paraguay (h) 2-0, Panama (a) 4-0, Montenegro (n) 1-0, Japan (a) 0-0, Ecuador (h) 3-1, Paraguay (n) 0-5, Argentina (n) 2-4, USA (n) 1-0, Mexico (a) 1-0, Peru (a) 2-2, Paraguay (h) 1-0, Brazil (h) 0-0, Bolivia (a) 0-0, Venezuela (h) 1-0, Argentina (h) 2-1.

ECUADOR

Federacion Ecuatoriana del Futbol, km 4 1/2 via a la Costa (Avda. del Bombero), PO Box 09-01-7447 Guayaquil.
Founded: 1925; *National Colours:* Yellow shirts, blue shorts, red stockings.
International matches 2007
Sweden (h) 2-1, Sweden (h) 1-1, USA (a) 1-3, Mexico (a) 2-4, Republic of Ireland (h) 1-1, Peru (a) 1-2, Peru (h) 2-0, Colombia (a) 1-3, Chile (n) 2-3, Mexico (n) 1-2, Brazil (n) 0-1, Bolivia (h) 1-0, El Salvador (h) 5-1, Honduras (a) 1-2, Venezuela (h) 0-1, Brazil (a) 0-5, Paraguay (a) 1-5, Peru (h) 5-1.

PARAGUAY

Asociacion Paraguaya de Futbol, Estadio De Los Defensores del Chaco, Calles Mayor Martinez 1393, Asuncion.
Founded: 1906; *National Colours:* Red and white shirts, blue shorts, blue stockings.
International matches 2007
Mexico (a) 1-2, Colombia (a) 0-2, Austria (a) 0-0, Mexico (a) 1-0, Bolivia (a) 0-0, Colombia (n) 5-0, USA (n) 3-1, Argentina (n) 0-1, Mexico (a) 0-6, Venezuela (h) 1-1, Venezuela (a) 2-3, Colombia (a) 0-1, Peru (a) 0-0, Uruguay (h) 1-0, Ecuador (h) 5-1, Chile (a) 3-0.

PERU

Federacion Peruana De Futbol, Av. Aviacion 2085, San Luis, Lima 30.
Founded: 1922; *National Colours:* White shirts with red stripe, white shorts with red lines, white stockings with red line.
International matches 2007
Japan (a) 0-2, Ecuador (h) 2-1, Peru (h) 2-0, Uruguay (n) 3-0, Venezuela (n) 0-2, Bolivia (n) 2-2, Argentina (n) 0-4, Costa Rica (a) 1-1, Colombia (h) 2-2, Bolivia (h) 2-0, Paraguay (h) 0-0, Chile (a) 0-2, Brazil (h) 1-1, Ecuador (a) 1-5.

URUGUAY

Asociacion Uruguaya De Futbol, Guayabo 1531, 11200 Montevideo.
Founded: 1900; *National Colours:* Sky blue shirts with white collar/cuffs, black shorts and stockings with sky blue borders.
International matches 2007
Colombia (a) 3-1, South Korea (a) 2-0, Australia (a) 2-1, Peru (n) 0-3, Bolivia (n) 1-0, Venezuela (a) 0-0, Venezuela (a) 4-1, Brazil (n) 2-2, Mexico (n) 1-3, South Africa (a) 0-0, Bolivia (h) 5-0, Paraguay (a) 0-1, Chile (h) 2-2, Brazil (a) 1-2.

VENEZUELA

Federacion Venezolana De Futbol, Avda. Santos Erminy Ira, Calle las Delicias Torre Mega II, P.H. Sabana Grande, Caracas 1050.
Founded: 1926; *National Colours:* Burgundy shirts, white shorts and stockings.
International matches 2007
Sweden (h) 2-0, Chile (h) 0-1, Mexico (a) 1-3, Cuba (h) 3-1, New Zealand (h) 5-0, Honduras (h) 2-1, Canada (h) 2-2, Bolivia (h) 2-2, Peru (h) 2-0, Uruguay (h) 0-0, Uruguay (h) 1-4, Paraguay (a) 1-1, Paraguay (h) 3-2, Panama (h) 1-1, Ecuador (a) 1-0, Argentina (h) 0-2, Colombia (a) 0-1, Bolivia (h) 5-3.

ASIA

AFGHANISTAN

Afghanistan Football Federation, PO Box 5099, Kabul.
Founded: 1933; *National Colours*: All white with red lines.
International matches 2007
Syria (a) 0-3, Syria (n) 1-2.

BAHRAIN

Bahrain Football Association, P.O. Box 5464, Manama.
Founded: 1957; *National Colours:* All red.
International matches 2007
Yemen (h) 4-0, Saudi Arabia (a) 1-2, Iraq (h) 1-1, Qatar (a) 2-1, Oman (a) 0-1, UAE (n) 2-2, Vietnam (n) 3-5, Indonesia (a) 1-2, South Korea (h) 2-1, Saudi Arabia (a) 0-4, Jordan (h) 1-3, Singapore (h) 3-1, Libya (h) 2-0, Malaysia (h) 4-1, Malaysia (a) 0-0.

BANGLADESH

Bangladesh Football Federation, Bangabandhu National Stadium-1, Dhaka 1000.
Founded: 1972; *National Colours:* Orange shirts, white shorts, green stockings.
International matches 2007
Syria (n) 0-2, India (a) 0-1, Cambodia (n) 1-1, Krgyzstan (n) 0-3, Takikistan (h) 1-1, Takikistan (a) 0-5.

BHUTAN

Bhutan Football Federation, P.O. Box 365, Thimphu.
National Colours: All yellow and red.

BRUNEI DARUSSALAM

The Football Association of Brunei Darussalam, P.O. Box 2010, 1920 Bandar Seri Begawan BS 8674.
Founded: 1959; *Number of Clubs:* 22; *Number of Players:* 830; *National Colours:* Yellow shirts, black shorts, black and white stockings.
Telephone: 00673-2/382 761; *Fax:* 00673-2/382 760.

BURMA

Myanmar Football Federation, Youth Training Centre, Thingankyun Township, Yangon.
Founded: 1947; *National Colours:* Red shirts, white shorts, red stockings.
International matches 2007
Thailand (a) 1-1, Malaysia (a) 0-0, Philippines (h) 0-0, Lesotho (h) 1-0, Laos (h) 1-0, China (a) 0-7, China (n) 0-4.

CAMBODIA

Cambodian Football Federation, Chaeng Maeng Village, Rd. Kab Srov, Sangkat Samrong Krom, Khan Dangkor, Phnom-Penh .
Founded: 1933; *National Colours:* All blue.
International matches 2007
Malaysia (a) 0-6, India (a) 0-6, Kyrgyzstan (n) 3-4, Bangladesh (n) 1-1, Syria (n) 1-5, Turkmenistan (h) 0-1, Turkmenistan (a) 1-4.

CHINA PR

Football Association of The People's Republic of China, 9 Tiyuguan Road, Beijing 100763.
Founded: 1924; *National Colours:* All white.
International matches 2007
Kazakhstan (h) 2-1, Australia (h) 0-2, Uzbekistan (n) 3-1, Thailand (a) 0-1, USA (a) 1-4, Malaysia (a) 5-1, Iran (h) 2-2, Uzbekistan (a) 0-3, Burma (h) 7-0, Burma (a) 4-0.

CHINESE TAIPEI

Chinese Taipei Football Association, 2F No. Yu Men St., Taipei, Taiwan 104.
Founded: 1936; *National Colours:* Blue shirts and shorts, white stockings.
International matches 2007
Uzbekistan (h) 0-1, Guam (a) 10-0, Hong Kong (a) 1-1, Macao (a) 7-2, Uzbekistan (a) 0-9, Uzbekistan (h) 0-2.

GUAM

Guam Football Association, P.O.Box 5093, Agana, Guam 96932.
Founded: 1975; *National Colours:* Blue shirts, white shorts, blue stockings.
International matches 2007
Chinese Taipei (a) 0-10, Hong Kong (a) 1-15, Mongolia (a) 2-5.

HONG KONG

The Hong Kong Football Association Ltd, 55 Fat Kwong Street, Homantin, Kowloon, Hong Kong.
Founded: 1914; *National Colours:* All red.
International matches 2007
Indonesia (a) 0-3, Macao (h) 2-1, Chinese Taipei (h) 1-1, Guam (h) 15-1, South Korea (a) 0-1, Timor-Leste (a) 3-2, Timor-Leste (h) 8-1, Turkmenistan (h) 0-0, Turkmenistan (a) 0-3.

INDIA

All India Football Federation, Nehru Stadium (West Stand), Fatorda Margao-Goa 403 602.
Founded: 1937; *National Colours:* Sky blue shirts, navy blue shorts, sky and navy blue stockings.
International matches 2007
Cambodia (h) 6-0, Bangladesh (h) 1-0, Syria (h) 2-3, Kyrgyzstan (h) 3-0, Syria (h) 1-0, Libya (a) 1-4, Libya (h) 2-2.

INDONESIA

Football Association of Indonesia, Gelora Bung Karno, Pintu X-XI, Jakarta 10270.
Founded: 1930; *National Colours:* Red shirts, white shorts, red stockings.
International matches 2007
Laos (h) 3-1, Vietnam (a) 1-1, Singapore (a) 2-2, Hong Kong (h) 3-0, Jamaica (h) 2-1, Oman (h) 0-1, Bahrain (h) 2-1, Saudi Arabia (h) 1-2, South Korea (h) 0-1, Syria (h) 1-4, Syria (a) 0-7.

IRAN

IR Iran Football Federation, No. 16-4th deadend, Pakistan Street, PO Box 15316-6967 Shahid Beheshti Avenue, Tehran 15316.
Founded: 1920; *National Colours:* All white.
International matches 2007
UAE (a) 2-0, Belarus (h) 2-2, Qatar (a) 1-0, Mexico (a) 0-4, Iraq (h) 0-0, Palestine (h) 2-0, Jordan (a) 2-0, Iraq (h) 2-1, Jamaica (h) 8-1, Uzbekistan (h) 2-1, China (a) 2-2, Malaysia (a) 2-0, South Korea (h) 0-0.

IRAQ

Iraqi Football Association, Olympic Committee Building, Palestine Street, PO Box 484, Baghdad.
Founded: 1948; *National Colours:* All black.
International matches 2007
Qatar (a) 1-0, Bahrain (a) 1-1, Saudi Arabia (a) 0-1, Jordan (a) 1-1, Jordan (a) 0-0, Iran (a) 0-0, Palestine (h) 1-0, Syria (a) 3-0, Iran (a) 1-2, South Korea (a) 0-3, Uzbekistan (n) 0-2, Thailand (a) 1-1, Australia (h) 3-1, Oman (a) 0-0, Vietnam (h) 2-0, South Korea (h) 0-0, Saudi Arabia (h) 1-0, Qatar (a) 2-3, Palestine (a) 7-0, Palestine (n) 0-0, South Korea (n) 1-0, Thailand (n) 1-2, Uzbekistan (n) 3-1, Thailand (n) 0-1.

JAPAN

Japan Football Association, JFA House, 3-10-15, Hongo, Bunkyo-ku, Tokyo 113-0033.
Founded: 1921; *National Colours:* Blue shirts, white shorts, blue stockings.
International matches 2007
Peru (h) 2-0, Montenegro (h) 2-0, Colombia (h) 0-0, Qatar (h) 1-1, UAE (a) 3-1, Vietnam (a) 4-1, Australia (h) 1-1, Saudi Arabia (h) 2-3, South Korea (a) 0-0, Cameroon (h) 2-0, Austria (a) 0-0, Switzerland (n) 4-3, Egypt (h) 4-1.

JORDAN

Jordan Football Association, P.O. Box 962024 Al Hussein Sports City, 11196 Amman.
Founded: 1949; *National Colours:* All white and red.
International matches 2007
Iraq (h) 1-1, Iraq (h) 0-0, Syria (h) 0-1, Libya (h) 3-0, Iran (h) 0-2, Bahrain (a) 3-1, Kyrgyzstan (a) 0-2, Kyrgyzstan (h) 2-0, Oman (a) 3-0.

KOREA, NORTH

Football Association of The Democratic People's Rep. of Korea, Kumsong-dong, Kwangbok Street, Mangyongdae Distr, PO Box 56, Pyongyang FNJ-PRK.
Founded: 1945; *National Colours:* All white.
International matches 2007
Mongolia (h) 7-0, Macao (a) 7-1, Hong Kong (h) 1-0, Singapore (a) 1-2, Oman (n) 2-2, UAE (a) 0-1, Saudi Arabia (n) 1-1, Mongolia (a) 4-1, Mongolia (h) 5-1, Iraq (n) 0-1, Uzbekistan (n) 2-2, Thailand (n) 0-1.

KOREA, SOUTH

Korea Football Association, 1-131 Sinmunno, 2-ga, Jongno-Gu, Seoul 110-062.
Founded: 1928; *National Colours:* Red shirts, blue shorts, red stockings.
International matches 2007
Greece (n) 1-0, Uruguay (h) 0-2, Holland (h) 0-2, Iraq (h) 3-0, Uzbekistan (h) 2-1, Saudi Arabia (h) 1-1, Bahrain (a) 1-2, Indonesia (a) 1-0, Iran (h) 0-0, Iraq (a) 0-0, Japan (h) 0-0.

KUWAIT

Kuwait Football Association, P.O. Box 2029, Udiliya, Block 4 Al-Ittihad Street, Safat 13021.
Founded: 1952; *National Colours:* All blue.
International matches 2007
Portugal (h) 1-1, Egypt (h) 1-1, Yemen (h) 1-1, Oman (h) 1-2, UAE (a) 2-3.

KYRGYZSTAN

Football Federation of Kyrgyz Republic, PO Box 1484, Kurenkeeva Street 195, Bishkek 720040, Kyrgyzstan.
Founded: 1992; *National Colours:* Red shirts, white shorts, red stockings.
International matches 2007
Kazakhzstan (a) 0-2, Uzbekistan (h) 0-6, Azerbaijan (a) 0-1, Cambodia (n) 4-3, Syria (n) 1-4, Bangladesh (n) 3-0, India (a) 0-3, Jordan (h) 2-0, Jordan (a) 0-2.

LAOS

Federation Lao de Football, National Stadium, Kounboulo Street, PO Box 3777, Vientiane 856-21, Laos.
Founded: 1951; *National Colours:* All red.
International matches 2007
Indonesia (a) 1-3, Singapore (a) 0-11, Vietnam (a) 0-9, Lesotho (a) 1-3, Burma (a) 0-1.

LEBANON

Federation Libanaise De Football-Association, P.O. Box 4732, Verdun Street, Bristol, Radwan Centre Building, Beirut.
Founded: 1933; *National Colours:* Red shirts, white shorts, red stockings.
International matches 2007
Syria (h) 0-1, Jordan (a) 0-3, UAE (a) 1-1, India (h) 4-1, India (a) 2-2.

MACAO

Associacao De Futebol De Macau (AFM), Ave. da Amizade 405, Seng Vo Kok, 13 Andar "A", Macau.
Founded: 1939; *National Colours:* All green.
International matches 2007
Hong Kong (a) 1-2, Mongolia (h) 0-0, South Korea (h) 1-7, Chinese Taipei (h) 2-7, Thailand (a) 1-6, Thailand (h) 1-7.

MALAYSIA

Football Association of Malaysia, 3rd Floor, Wisma Fam, Jalan, SSA/9, Kelana Jaya Selangor Darul Ehsan 47301.
Founded: 1933; *National Colours:* All yellow and black.
International matches 2007
Philippines (h) 4-0, Burma (h) 0-0, Thailand (a) 0-1, Singapore (h) 1-1, Singapore (a) 1-1, Sri Lanka (a) 4-1, Sri Lanka (a) 1-2, Cambodia (h) 6-0, UAE (h) 1-3, Jamaica (h) 0-2, China (h) 1-5, Uzbekistan (h) 0-5, Iran (h) 0-2, Bahrain (a) 1-4, Bahrain (h) 0-0.

MALDIVES REPUBLIC

Football Association of Maldives, National Stadium G. Banafsaa Magu 20-04, Male.
Founded: 1982; *National Colours:* Red shirts, Green shorts, white stockings.
International matches 2007
Oman (a) 0-1, Yemen (a) 0-3, Yemen (h) 2-0.

MONGOLIA

Mongolia Football Federation, PO Box 259 Ulaan-Baatar 210646.
National Colours: White shirts, red shorts, white stockings.
International matches 2007
Macao (a) 0-0, South Korea (a) 0-7, Guam (h) 5-2, North Korea (h) 1-4, North Korea (a) 1-5.

NEPAL

All-Nepal Football Association, AMFA House, Ward No. 4, Bishalnagar, PO Box 12582, Kathmandu.
Founded: 1951; *National Colours:* All red.
International matches 2007
Oman (a) 0-2, Oman (h) 0-2.

OMAN

Oman Football Association, P.O. Box 3462, Ruwi Postal Code 112.
Founded: 1978; *National Colours:* All white.
International matches 2007
Qatar (a) 1-1, UAE (a) 2-1, Kuwait (a) 2-1, Yemen (h) 2-1, Bahrain (h) 1-0, UAE (a) 0-1, Indonesia (a) 1-0, North Korea (n) 2-2, Saudi Arabia (n) 1-1, Australia (a) 1-1, Thailand (a) 0-2, Iraq (h) 0-0, Qatar (a) 1-1, Maldives (h) 1-0, Nepal (h) 2-0, Nepal (a) 2-0, Kenya (h) 2-2, Kenya (h) 1-1, Jordan (h) 0-3, Tajikistan (h) 4-2.

PAKISTAN

Pakistan Football Federation, 6 National Hockey Stadium, Feroze Pure Road, Lahore, Pakistan.
Founded: 1948; *National Colours:* All green and white.
International matches 2007
Iraq (n) 0-7, Iraq (n) 0-0.

PALESTINE

Palestinian Football Federation, Al-Yarmouk, Gaza.
Founded: 1928; *National Colours:* White shirts, black shorts, white stockings.
International matches 2007
Iraq (a) 0-1, Iran (a) 0-2, Singapore (h) 0-4, Singapore (a) 0-3.

PHILIPPINES

Philippine Football Federation, Room 405, Building V, Philsports Complex, Meralco Avenue, Pasig City, Metro Manila.
Founded: 1907; *National Colours:* All blue.
International matches 2007
Singapore (a) 1-4, Malaysia (a) 0-4, Thailand (a) 0-4, Burma (a) 0-0.

QATAR

Qatar Football Association, 7th Floor, QNOC Building, Cornich, P.O. Box 5333, Doha.
Founded: 1960; *National Colours:* All white.
International matches 2007
Oman (h) 1-1, Iraq (h) 0-1, Saudi Arabia (a) 1-1, Bahrain (h) 1-2, Iran (h) 0-1, Turkmenistan (h) 1-0, Thailand (a) 0-2, Japan (a) 1-1, Vietnam (a) 1-1, UAE (h) 1-2, Oman (h) 1-1, Iraq (h) 3-2, Sri Lanka (a) 1-0, Sri Lanka (h) 5-0, Georgia (h) 1-2, Ivory Coast (h) 1-6.

SAUDI ARABIA

Saudi Arabian Football Federation, Al Mather Quarter (Olympic Complex), Prince Faisal Bin Fahad Street, P.O. Box 5844, Riyadh 11432.
Founded: 1959; *National Colours:* White shirts, green shorts, white stockings.
International matches 2007
Gambia (h) 3-0, Syria (h) 2-1, Bahrain (h) 2-1, Qatar (h) 1-1, Iraq (h) 1-0, UAE (a) 0-1, UAE (n) 2-0, Singapore (a) 2-1, Oman (n) 1-1, North Korea (n) 1-1, South Korea (a) 1-1, Indonesia (a) 2-1, Bahrain (h) 4-0, Uzbekistan (h) 2-1, Japan (h) 3-2, Iraq (h) 0-1, Ghana (h) 5-0, Namibia (h) 1-0, Estonia (h) 2-0, Libya (a) 1-2, Egypt (a) 1-2, Syria (h) 1-3.

SINGAPORE

Football Association of Singapore, Jalan Besar Stadium, 100 Tyrwhitt Road, Singapore 207542.
Founded: 1892; *National Colours:* All red.
International matches 2007
Philippines (h) 4-1, Vietnam (h) 0-0, Laos (h) 11-0, Indonesia (h) 2-2, Malaysia (a) 1-1, Malaysia (h) 1-1, Thailand (h) 2-1, Thailand (a) 1-1, North Korea (h) 2-1, Saudi Arabia (h) 1-2, Australia (h) 0-3, UAE (h) 1-1, Bahrain (a) 1-3, Palestine (a) 4-0, Palestine (h) 3-0, Takijistan (h) 2-0, Takijistan (a) 1-1.

SRI LANKA

Football Federation of Sri Lanka, 100/9, Independence Avenue, Colombo 07.
Founded: 1939; *National Colours:* All white.
International matches 2007
Malaysia (h) 1-4, Malaysia (h) 2-1, Qatar (h) 0-1, Qatar (a) 0-5.

SYRIA

Syrian Football Federation, PO Box 421, Maysaloon Street, Damascus.
Founded: 1936; *National Colours:* All red.
International matches 2007
Saudi Arabia (a) 1-2, Libya (a) 1-0, Jordan (a) 1-0, Iraq (h) 0-3, Bangladesh (n) 2-0, Kyrgyzstan (n) 4-1, India (a) 3-2, Cambodia (n) 5-1, India (a) 0-1, Afghanistan (h) 3-0, Afghanistan (a) 2-1, Indonesia (a) 4-1, Indonesia (h) 7-0, Saudi Arabia (a) 3-1.

TAJIKISTAN

Tajikistan Football Federation, 22 Shotemur Ave., Dushanbe 734 025.
Founded: 1991; *National Colours:* All white.
International matches 2007
Azerbaijan (h) 2-3, Kazakhstan (a) 1-1, Bangladesh (a) 1-1, Bangladesh (h) 5-0, Singapore (a) 0-2, Singapore (h) 1-1, Oman (a) 2-4.

THAILAND

The Football Association of Thailand, Gate 3, Rama I Road, Patumwan, Bangkok 10330.
Founded: 1916; *National Colours:* All red.
International matches 2007
Burma (h) 1-1, Philippines (h) 4-0, Malaysia (h) 1-0, Vietnam (a) 2-0, Vietnam (h) 0-0, Singapore (a) 1-2, Singapore (h) 1-1, China (h) 1-0, Holland (h) 1-3, Qatar (h) 2-0, Iraq (h) 1-1, Oman (h) 2-0, Australia (h) 0-4, UAE (h) 1-1, Macao (h) 6-1, Macao (a) 7-1, Yemen (a) 1-1, Yemen (h) 1-0, Uzbekistan (h) 3-2, Iraq (h) 2-1, North Korea (h) 1-0, Iraq (h) 1-0.

TIMOR-LESTE

Federacao Futebol Timor-Leste, Rua 12 de Novembro Str., Cruz, Dili.
Founded: 2002; *National Colours:* Red shirts, black shorts, red stockings.
International matches 2007
Hong Kong (h) 2-3, Hong Kong (a) 1-8.

TURKMENISTAN

Football Association of Turkmenistan, 32 Belinskiy Street, Stadium Kopetdag, Ashgabat 744 001.
Founded: 1992; *National Colours:* Green shirts, white shorts, green stockings.
International matches 2007
Qatar (a) 0-1, Lithuania (a) 1-2, Cambodia (a) 1-0, Cambodia (h) 4-1, Hong Kong (a) 0-0, Hong Kong (h) 3-0.

UNITED ARAB EMIRATES

United Arab Emirates Football Association, P.O. Box 916, Abu Dhabi.
Founded: 1971; *National Colours:* All white.

International matches 2007
Iran (h) 0-2, Oman (h) 1-2, Yemen (h) 2-1, Kuwait (h) 3-2, Saudi Arabia (h) 1-0, Oman (h) 1-0, Malaysia (a) 3-1, Saudi Arabia (a) 0-2, Bahrain (a) 2-2, North Korea (h) 1-0, Vietnam (a) 0-2, Japan (h) 1-3, Qatar (a) 2-1, Singapore (a) 1-1, Lebanon (h) 1-1, Thailand (a) 1-1, Vietnam (a) 1-0, Tunisia (h) 0-1, Vietnam (h) 5-0, Egypt (a) 0-3, Benin (n) 0-1, Togo (n) 0-5.

UZBEKISTAN

Uzbekistan Football Federation, Massiv Almazar Furkat Street 15/1, 700003 Tashkent, Uzbekistan.
Founded: 1946; *National Colours:* All white.
International matches 2007
Azerbaijan (h) 0-0, Azerbaijan (a) 0-1, Kyrgyzstan (a) 6-0, Kazakhstan (a) 1-1, Chinese Taipei (a) 1-0, China (n) 1-3, Iraq (n) 2-0, South Korea (a) 1-2, Iran (a) 1-2, Malaysia (a) 5-0, China (h) 3-0, Saudi Arabia (a) 1-2, Ukraine (a) 1-2, Chinese Taipei (h) 9-0, Chinese Taipei (a) 2-0, Estonia (h) 0-0, Thailand (a) 2-3, North Korea (a) 2-2, Iraq (a) 1-3.

VIETNAM

Vietnam Football Federation, 18 Ly van Phuc, Dong Da District, Hanoi 844.
Founded: 1962; *National Colours:* All red.
International matches 2007
Singapore (a) 0-0, Indonesia (h) 1-1, Laos (h) 9-0, Thailand (h) 0-2, Thailand (a) 0-0, Jamaica (h) 3-0, Bahrain (h) 5-3, UAE (h) 2-0, Qatar (h) 1-1, Japan (h) 1-4, Iraq (a) 0-2, UAE (h) 0-1, UAE (a) 0-5.

YEMEN

Yemen Football Association, Quarter of Sport – Al Jeraf, Behind the Stadium of Ali Mushsen, Al Moreissy in the Sport, Al-Thawra City.
Founded: 1962; *National Colours:* All green.
International matches 2007
Eritrea (h) 4-1, Bahrain (n) 0-4, Kuwait (a) 1-1, UAE (a) 1-2, Oman (a) 1-2, Maldives (h) 3-0, Maldives (a) 0-2, Thailand (h) 1-1, Thailand (a) 0-1.

CONCACAF

ANGUILLA

Anguilla Football Association, P.O. Box 1318, The Valley, Anguilla, BWI.
National Colours: Turquoise, white, orange and blue shirts and shorts, turquoise and orange stockings.

ANTIGUA & BARBUDA

The Antigua/Barbuda Football Association, Newgate Street, P.O. Box 773, St John's.
Founded: 1928; *National Colours:* Red, black, yellow and blue shirts, black shorts and stockings.
International matches 2007
St Kitts & Nevis (a) 0-3, St Kitts & Nevis (h) 2-0.

ARUBA

Arubaanse Voetbal Bond, Ferguson Street, Z/N P.O. Box 376, Oranjestad, Aruba.
Founded: 1932; *National Colours:* Yellow shirts, blue shorts, yellow and blue stockings.

BAHAMAS

Bahamas Football Association, Plaza on the Way, West Bay Street, P.O. Box N 8434, Nassau, NP.
Founded: 1967; *National Colours:* Yellow shirts, black shorts, yellow stockings.

BARBADOS

Barbados Football Association, Hildor No. 4, 10th Avenue, P.O. Box 1362, Belleville-St. Michael, Barbados.
Founded: 1910; *National Colours:* Royal blue and gold shirts, gold shorts, white, gold and blue stockings.
International matches 2007
Trinidad & Tobago (a) 1-1, Haiti (h) 0-2, Martinique (h) 2-3, Guatemala (h) 0-0.

BELIZE

Belize National Football Association, 26 Hummingbird Highway, Belmopan, P.O. Box 1742, Belize City.
Founded: 1980; *National Colours:* Red, white and black shirts, black shorts, red and black stockings.
International matches 2007
El Salvador (a) 1-2, Guatemala (h) 0-1, Nicaragua (h) 2-4.

BERMUDA

The Bermuda Football Association, 48 Cedar Avenue, Hamilton HM12.
Founded: 1928; *National Colours:* All blue.
International matches 2007
Haiti (h) 0-2, Haiti (h) 0-3, Canada (h) 0-3, St Kitts & Nevis (h) 1-2, St Kitts & Nevis (h) 4-2.

BRITISH VIRGIN ISLANDS

British Virgin Islands Football Association, P.O. Box 29, Road Town, Tortola, BVI.
National Colours: Gold and green shirts, green shorts, and stockings.
International matches 2007
Saint Martin (a) 1-0.

US VIRGIN ISLANDS

USVI Soccer Federation Inc., 54, Castle Coakley, PO Box 2346, Kingshill, St Croix 00851.
National Colours: Royal blue and gold shirts, royal blue shorts and stockings.

CANADA

The Canadian Soccer Association, Place Soccer Canada, 237 Metcalfe Street, Ottawa, ONT K2P 1R2.
Founded: 1912; *National Colours:* All red.
International matches 2007
Bermuda (a) 3-0, Venezuela (a) 2-2, Costa Rica (n) 2-1, Guadeloupe (n) 1-2, Haiti (n) 2-0, Guatemala (n) 3-0, USA (a) 1-2, Iceland (a) 1-1, Costa Rica (h) 1-1, South Africa (a) 0-2.

CAYMAN ISLANDS

Cayman Islands Football Association, PO Box 178 GT, Truman Bodden Sports Complex, Olympic Way Off Walkers Rd, George Town, Grand Cayman, Cayman Islands WI.
Founded: 1966; *National Colours:* Red and white shirts, blue and white shorts, white and red stockings.

COSTA RICA

Federacion Costarricense De Futbol, Costado Norte Estatua Leon Cortes, San Jose 670-1000.
Founded: 1921; *National Colours:* Red shirts, blue shorts, white stockings.
International matches 2007
Trinidad & Tobago (h) 4-0, Honduras (h) 3-1, Panama (h) 0-1, El Salvador (a) 2-0, Panama (h) 1-1, New Zealand (h) 4-0, Chile (a) 1-1, Chile (h) 2-0, Canada (n) 1-2, Haiti (n) 1-1, Guadeloupe (n) 1-0, Mexico (n) 0-1, Peru (h) 1-1, Honduras (h) 0-0, Canada (a) 1-1, El Salvador (a) 2-2, Haiti (h) 1-1, Panama (a) 1-1.

CUBA

Asociacion de Futbol de Cuba, Calle 13 No. 661, Esq. C. Vedado, ZP 4, La Habana.
Founded: 1924; *National Colours:* All red, white and blue.
International matches 2007
Guadeloupe (h) 1-2, St Vincent & the G (h) 3-0, Guyana (h) 0-0, Trinidad & Tobago (a) 1-3, Guadeloupe (h) 2-1, Venezuela (a) 1-3, Chile (a) 0-3, Chile (a) 0-2, Mexico (n) 1-2, Panama (n) 2-2, Honduras (n) 0-5.

DOMINICA

Dominica Football Association, 33 Great Marlborough Street, Roseau.
Founded: 1970; *National Colours:* Emerald green shirts, black shorts, green stockings.
International matches 2007
Guadeloupe (a) 0-2, Guadeloupe (a) 0-0.

DOMINICAN REPUBLIC

Federacion Dominicana De Futbol, Centro Olimpico Juan Pablo Duarte, Ensanche Miraflores, Apartado De Correos No. 1953, Santo Domingo.
Founded: 1953; *National Colours:* Navy blue shirts, white shorts, red stockings.

EL SALVADOR

Federacion Salvadorena De Futbol, Primera Calle Poniente No. 2025, San Salvador CA1029.
Founded: 1935; *National Colours:* All blue.
International matches 2007
Belize (h) 2-1, Nicaragua (h) 2-1, Guatemala (h) 0-0, Costa Rica (h) 0-2, Guatemala (h) 0-1, Honduras (h) 0-2,

Honduras (h) 0-2, Haiti (h) 0-1, Trinidad & Tobago (n) 2-1, Guatemala (n) 0-1, USA (a) 0-4, Honduras (h) 2-0, Ecuador (a) 1-5, Costa Rica (h) 2-2, Trinidad & Tobago (h) 0-0, Jamaica (a) 0-3.

GRENADA

Grenada Football Association, P.O. Box 326, National Stadium, Queens Park, St George's, Grenada, W.I.
Founded: 1924; *National Colours:* Green and yellow striped shirts, red shorts, yellow stockings.

GUADELOUPE

Ligue Guadeloupeenne de Football, Rue de la Ville D'Orly, Bergevin, 97110, Pointe-a-Pitre.
Not affiliated to FIFA.
International matches 2007
Martinique (a) 0-3, Cuba (h) 2-1, Guyana (h) 3-4, St Vincent & the G (h) 1-0, Haiti (h) 1-3, Cuba (h) 1-2, Dominica (h) 2-0, Dominica (h) 0-0, Haiti (n) 1-1, Canada (n) 2-1, Costa Rica (n) 0-1, Honduras (n) 2-1, Mexico (n) 0-1.

GUATEMALA

Federacion Nacional de Futbol de Guatemala, 2a Calle 15-57, Zona 15, Boulevard Vista Hermosa, Guatemala City 01009.
Founded: 1946; *National Colours:* Blue shirts, white shorts, blue stockings.
International matches 2007
Nicaragua (h) 1-0, Belize (h) 1-0, El Salvador (a) 0-0, Panama (h) 0-2, El Salvador (a) 1-0, Barbados (a) 0-0, USA (a) 0-0, USA (a) 0-1, El Salvador (n) 1-0, Trinidad & Tobago (n) 1-1, Canada (n) 0-3, Panama (a) 1-2, Mexico (h) 3-2, Honduras (h) 0-1, Jamaica (a) 0-2.

GUYANA

Guyana Football Federation, 159 Rupununi Street, Bel Air Park, P.O. Box 10727, Georgetown.
Founded: 1902; *National Colours:* Green shirts and shorts, yellow stockings.
International matches 2007
St Vincent & the G (h) 0-2, Guadeloupe (h) 4-3, Cuba (h) 0-0.

HAITI

Federation Haitienne De Football, 128 Avenue Christiophe, P.O. Box 2258, Port-Au-Prince.
Founded: 1904; *National Colours:* Blue shirts, red shorts, blue stockings.
International matches 2007
Bermuda (h) 2-0, Bermuda (h) 3-0, Martinique (h) 1-0, Barbados (h) 2-0, Trinidad & Tobago (a) 1-3, Guadeloupe (h) 3-1, Trinidad & Tobago (a) 2-1, Panama (h) 3-0, El Salvador (a) 1-0, Honduras (a) 3-1, Chile (a) 0-0, Trinidad & Tobago (a) 0-1, St Vincent & the G (h) 3-0, Guadeloupe (h) 1-1, Costa Rica (h) 1-1, Canada (h) 0-2, Costa Rica (a) 1-1.

HONDURAS

Federacion Nacional Autonoma De Futbol De Honduras, Colonia Florencia Norte, Ave Roble, Edificio Plaza America, Ave. Roble 1 y 2 Nivel, Tegucigalpa, D.C.
Founded: 1951; *National Colours:* All white.
International matches 2007
Costa Rica (h) 1-3, Panama (h) 1-1, Nicaragua (h) 9-1, El Salvador (h) 2-0, El Salvador (h) 2-0, Haiti (h) 1-3, Venezuela (a) 1-2, Trinidad & Tobago (h) 3-1, Panama (n) 2-3, Mexico (n) 2-1, Cuba (n) 5-0, Guadeloupe (n) 1-2, El Salvador (a) 0-2, Costa Rica (h) 0-0, Ecuador (h) 2-1, Panama (h) 1-0, Guatemala (h) 1-0.

JAMAICA

Jamaica Football Federation Ltd, 20 St Lucia Crescent, Kingston 5.
Founded: 1910; *National Colours:* Gold shirts, black shorts, gold stockings.
International matches 2007
Switzerland (h) 0-2, Panama (h) 1-1, Chile (h) 0-1, Indonesia (a) 1-2, Vietnam (a) 0-3, Malaysia (a) 2-0, Iran (a) 1-8, El Salvador (h) 3-0, Guatemala (h) 2-0.

MARTINIQUE

2, Rue Saint John Perse, Nome Tartenson, BP 307, 97203 Fort de France.
Not affiliated to FIFA.
International matches 2007
Guadeloupe (h) 3-0, Haiti (h) 0-1, Trinidad & Tobago (a) 1-5, Barbados (h) 3-2.

MEXICO

Federacion Mexicana De Futbol Asociacion, A.C., Colima No. 373, Colonia Roma Mexico DF 06700.
Founded: 1927; *National Colours:* Green shirts with white collar, white shorts, red stockings.
International matches 2007
USA (a) 0-2, Venezuela (h) 3-1, Paraguay (h) 2-1, Ecuador (h) 4-2, Iran (h) 4-0, Paraguay (h) 0-1, Cuba (n) 2-1, Honduras (n) 1-2, Panama (n) 1-0, Costa Rica (n) 1-0, Guadeloupe (n) 1-0, USA (a) 1-2, Brazil (n) 2-0, Ecuador (n) 2-1, Chile (n) 0-0, Paraguay (n) 6-0, Argentina (n) 0-3, Uruguay (n) 3-1, Colombia (h) 0-1, Brazil (h) 1-3, Nigeria (h) 2-2, Guatemala (h) 2-3.

MONSERRAT

Monserrat Football Association Inc., P.O. Box 505, Woodlands, Monserrat.
National Colours: Green shirts with black and white stripes, green shorts with white stripes, green stockings with black and white stripes.

NETHERLANDS ANTILLES

Nederlands Antiliaanse Voetbal Unie, Bonamweg 49, Curacao, NA.
Founded: 1921; *National Colours:* White shirts with red and blue stripes, red shorts with blue and white stripes, white stockings with red stripes.

NICARAGUA

Federacion Nicaraguense De Futbol, Hospital Pautista 1, Cuadra avajo, 1 cuada al Sur y 1/2, Cuadra Abajo, Managua 976.
Founded: 1931; *National Colours:* Blue shirts, white shorts, blue stockings.
International matches 2007
Guatemala (h) 0-1, El Salvador (a) 1-2, Belize (h) 4-2, Honduras (h) 1-9.

PANAMA

Federacion Panamena De Futbol, Estadio Rommel Fernandez, Puerta 24, Ave. Jose Aeustin Araneo, Apartado Postal 8-391, Zona 8, Panama.
Founded: 1937; *National Colours:* All red.
International matches 2007
Armenia (h) 1-1, Trinidad & Tobago (h) 2-1, Honduras (h) 1-1, Costa Rica (h) 1-0, Guatemala (h) 2-0, Costa Rica (h) 1-1, Haiti (h) 0-3, Jamaica (a) 1-1, Colombia (h) 0-4, Honduras (n) 3-2, Cuba (n) 2-2, Mexico (n) 0-1, USA (a) 1-2, Guatemala (h) 2-1, Venezuela (a) 1-1, Honduras (a) 0-1, Costa Rica (h) 1-1.

PUERTO RICO

Federacion Puertorriquena De Futbol, P.O. Box 193590 San Juan 00919.
Founded: 1940; *National Colours:* Red, blue and white shirts and shorts, red and blue stockings.

SAINT KITTS & NEVIS

St Kitts & Nevis Football Association, P.O. Box 465, Warner Park, Basseterre, St Kitts, W.I.
Founded: 1932; *National Colours:* Green and yellow shirts, red shorts, yellow stockings.
International matches 2007
Antigua (h) 3-0, Antigua (a) 0-2, Bermuda (a) 2-1, Bermuda (a) 2-4.

SAINT LUCIA

St Lucia National Football Association, PO Box 255, Sans Souci, Castries, St Lucia.
Founded: 1979; *National Colours:* White shirts and shorts with yellow, blue and black stripes, white, blue and yellow stockings.

SAINT MARTIN

Comite de Football des Iles du Nord, PO Box 811, S-M 97059.
Not affiliated to FIFA.
International matches 2007
British Virgin Islands (h) 0-1.

SAINT VINCENT & THE GRENADINES

St Vincent & The Grenadines Football Federation, Sharpe Street, PO Box 1278, Saint George.
Founded: 1979; *National Colours:* Green shirts with yellow border, blue shorts, yellow stockings.
International matches 2007
Guyana (h) 2-0, Cuba (h) 0-3, Guadeloupe (h) 0-1, Haiti (h) 0-3.

SURINAM

Surinaamse Voetbal Bond, Letitia Vriesde Laan 7, P.O. Box 1223, Paramaribo.
Founded: 1920; *National Colours:* White, green and red shirts, green and white shirts and stockings.

TRINIDAD & TOBAGO

Trinidad & Tobago Football Federation, 24–26 Dundonald Street, PO Box 400, Port of Spain.
Founded: 1908; *National Colours:* Red shirts, black shorts, white stockings.
International matches 2007
Barbados (h) 1-1, Martinique (h) 5-1, Haiti (h) 3-1, Cuba (h) 3-1, Haiti (h) 1-2, Panama (a) 1-2, Costa Rica (a) 0-4, Haiti (h) 1-0, Honduras (a) 1-3, El Salvador (n) 1-2, USA (a) 0-2, Guatemala (n) 1-1, El Salvador (a) 0-0.

TURKS & CAICOS

Turks & Caicos Islands Football Association, P.O. Box 626, Tropicana Plaza, Leeward Highway, Providenciales.
National Colours: All white.

USA

US Soccer Federation, US Soccer House, 1801–1811 S. Prairie Avenue, Chicago, Illinois 60616.
Founded: 1913; *National Colours:* White shirts, blue shorts, white stockings.
International matches 2007
Mexico (h) 2-0, Ecuador (h) 3-1, Guatemala (h) 0-0, China (h) 4-1, Guatemala (h) 1-0, Trinidad & Tobago (h) 2-0, El Salvador (h) 4-0, Panama (h) 2-1, Canada (h) 2-1, Mexico (h) 2-1, Argentina (n) 1-4, Paraguay (n) 1-3, Colombia (n) 0-1, Sweden (a) 0-1, Brazil (h) 2-4, Switzerland (a) 1-0, South Africa (a) 1-0.

OCEANIA

AMERICAN SAMOA

American Samoa Football Association, P.O. Box 282, Pago Pago AS 96799.
National Colours: Navy blue shirts, white shorts, red stockings.
International matches 2007
Solomon Islands (h) 1-12, Samoa (a) 0-7, Vanuatu (h) 0-15, Tonga (h) 0-4.

AUSTRALIA

Soccer Australia Ltd, Level 3, East Stand, Stadium Australia, Edwin Flack Avenue, Homebush, NSW 2127.
Founded: 1961; *National Colours:* All green with gold trim.
International matches 2007
Denmark (n) 1-3, China (a) 2-0, Uruguay (h) 1-2, Singapore (a) 3-0, Oman (h) 1-1, Iraq (h) 1-3, Thailand (a) 4-0, Japan (a) 1-1, Argentina (h) 0-1, Nigeria (n) 1-0.

COOK ISLANDS

Cook Islands Football Association, Victoria Road, Tupapa, P.O. Box 29, Avarua, Rarotonga, Cook Islands.
Founded: 1971; *National Colours:* Green shirts with white sleeves, green shorts, white stockings.
International matches 2007
Fiji (a) 0-4, New Caledonia (a) 0-3, Tuvalu (h) 4-1, Tahiti (h) 0-1.

FIJI

Fiji Football Association, PO Box 2514, Government Buildings, Suva.
Founded: 1938; *National Colours:* White shirts, blue shorts and stockings.
International matches 2007
Tuvalu (h) 16-0, Cook Islands (h) 4-0, Tahiti (h) 4-0, New Caledonia (h) 1-1, Vanuatu (h) 3-0, New Caledonia (h) 0-1, New Zealand (h) 0-2, New Caledonia (h) 3-3, New Caledonia (a) 0-4.

NEW CALEDONIA

Federation Caledonienne de Football, 7 bis, Rue Suffren Quartien latin, BP 560, 99845 Noumea, New Caledonia.
Founded: 1928; *National Colours:* Grey shirts, red shorts, grey stockings.
International matches 2007
Tahiti (h) 1-0, Tuvalu (h) 1-0, Cook Islands (h) 3-0, Fiji (a) 1-1, Solomon Islands (h) 3-2, Fiji (a) 1-0, Fiji (a) 3-3, Fiji (h) 4-0.

NEW ZEALAND

New Zealand Soccer Inc., PO Box 301 043, Albany, Auckland, New Zealand.
Founded: 1891; *National Colours:* All white.
International matches 2007
Costa Rica (a) 0-4, Venezuela (a) 0-5, Fiji (a) 2-0, Vanuatu (a) 2-1, Vanuatu (h) 4-1.

PAPUA NEW GUINEA

Papua New Guinea Football Association, PO Box 957, Room II Level I, Haus Tisa, Lae.
Founded: 1962; *National Colours:* Red and yellow shirts, black shorts, yellow stockings.

SAMOA

The Samoa Football Soccer Federation, P.O. Box 960, Apia.
Founded: 1968; *National Colours:* Blue, white and red shirts, blue and white shorts, red and blue stockings.
International matches 2007
Vanuatu (h) 0-4, American Samoa (h) 7-0, Tonga (h) 2-1, Solomon Islands (h) 0-3.

SOLOMON ISLANDS

Solomon Islands Football Federation, PO Box 854, Honiara, Solomon Islands.
Founded: 1978; *National Colours:* Gold and blue shirts, blue and white shorts, white and blue stockings.
International matches 2007
American Samoa (a) 12-1, Tonga (a) 4-0, Vanuatu (h) 2-0, Samoa (a) 3-0, New Caledonia (a) 2-3, Vanuatu (h) 0-2.

TAHITI

Federation Tahitienne de Football, Rue Coppenrath Stade de Fautana, PO Box 50858 Pirae 98716.
Founded: 1989; *National Colours:* Red shirts, white shorts, red stockings.
International matches 2007
New Caledonia (a) 0-1, Tuvalu (a) 1-1, Fiji (a) 0-4, Cook Islands (a) 1-0.

TONGA

Tonga Football Association, Tungi Arcade, Taufa'Ahau Road, P.O. Box 852, Nuku'Alofa, Tonga.
Founded: 1965; *National Colours:* Red shirts, white shorts, red stockings.
International matches 2007
Solomon Islands (h) 0-4, Samoa (a) 1-2, American Samoa (a) 4-0, Vanuatu (h) 1-4.

TUVALU

Not affiliated to FIFA.
International matches 2007
Fiji (a) 0-16, New Caledonia (a) 0-1, Tahiti (h) 1-1, Cook Islands (a) 1-4.

VANUATU

Vanuatu Football Federation, P.O. Box 266, Port Vila, Vanuatu.
Founded: 1934; *National Colours:* Gold and black shirts, black shorts, gold and black stockings.
International matches 2007
Samoa (a) 4-0, American Samoa (a) 15-0, Solomon Islands (a) 0-2, Tonga (a) 4-1, Fiji (a) 0-3, Solomon Islands (a) 2-0, New Zealand (h) 1-2, New Zealand (a) 1-4.

AFRICA

ALGERIA

Federation Algerienne De Foot-ball, Chemin Ahmed Ouaked, Boite Postale No. 39, Dely-Ibrahim-Alger.
Founded: 1962; *National Colours:* Green shirts, white shorts, green stockings.
International matches 2007

Libya (h) 2-1, Cape Verde Islands (h) 2-0, Cape Verde Islands (a) 2-2, Argentina (h) 3-4, Guinea (h) 0-2, Brazil (h) 0-2, Gambia (a) 1-2, Mali (h) 3-2.

ANGOLA

Federation Angolaise De Football, Compl. da Cidadela Desportiva, B.P. 3449, Luanda.
Founded: 1979; *National Colours:* Red shirts, black shorts, red stockings.
International matches 2007
Eritrea (h) 6-1, Congo (h) 0-0, Eritrea (a) 1-1, Swaziland (h) 3-0, Lesotho (h) 2-0, Botswana (a) 0-0, Congo DR (a) 1-3, Kenya (a) 1-2, Ivory Coast (h) 2-1, Guinea (a) 0-3.

BENIN

Federation Beninoise De Football, Stade Rene Pleven d'Akpakpa, B.P. 965, Cotonou 01.
Founded: 1962; *National Colours:* Green shirts, Yellow shorts, red stockings.
International matches 2007
Senegal (a) 1-2, Chad (h) 0-1, Mali (a) 1-1, Mali (h) 0-0, Togo (h) 4-1, Gabon (h) 2-2, Sierra Leone (a) 2-0, UAE (h) 1-0, Ghana (a) 2-4.

BOTSWANA

Botswana Football Association, P.O. Box 1396, Gabarone.
Founded: 1970; *National Colours:* Blue, white and black striped shirts, blue, white and black shorts and stockings.
International matches 2007
Namibia (h) 1-0, Burundi (h) 1-0, Libya (a) 0-0, Burundi (a) 0-1, Mauritania (h) 2-1, Zambia (h) 0-0, Namibia (h) 1-0, Angola (h) 0-0, South Africa (a) 0-1, Egypt (a) 0-0.

BURKINA FASO

Federation Burkinabe De Foot-Ball, 01 B.P. 57, Ouagadougou 01.
Founded: 1960; *National Colours:* All green, red and white.
International matches 2007
Mozambique (h) 1-1, Zimbabwe (a) 1-1, Mozambique (a) 1-3, Mali (h) 0-1, Tanzania (h) 0-1, Mali (h) 2-3, Senegal (a) 1-5.

BURUNDI

Federation De Football Du Burundi, Bulding Nyogozi, Boulevard de l'Uprona, B.P. 3426, Bujumbura.
Founded: 1948; *National Colours:* Red and white shirts, white and red shorts, green stockings.
International matches 2007
Botswana (a) 0-1, Rwanda (a) 0-1, Botswana (h) 1-0, Egypt (h) 0-0, Mauritania (a) 1-2, Somalia (h) 3-0, Kenya (h) 1-0, Eritrea (h) 2-1, Sudan (h) 1-2, Uganda (h) 0-2.

CAMEROON

Federation Camerounaise De Football, B.P. 1116, Yaounde.
Founded: 1959; *National Colours:* Green shirts, red shorts, yellow stockings.
International matches 2007
Togo (a) 2-2, Liberia (h) 3-1, Liberia (a) 2-1, Rwanda (h) 2-1, Japan (a) 0-2, Guinea Equatorial (a) 0-1.

CAPE VERDE ISLANDS

Federacao Cabo-Verdiana De Futebol, Praia Cabo Verde, FCF CX, P.O. Box 234, Praia.
Founded: 1982; *National Colours:* Blue and white shirts and shorts, blue and red stockings.
International matches 2007
Algeria (a) 0-2, Algeria (h) 2-2, Gambia (h) 0-0, Guinea (a) 0-4, Gambia (h) 0-0, Guinea-Bissau (a) 0-0.

CENTRAL AFRICAN REPUBLIC

Federation Centrafricaine De Football, Immeuble Soca Constructa, B.P. 344, Bangui.
Founded: 1937; *National Colours:* Blue and white shirts, white shorts, blue stockings.
International matches 2007
Chad (a) 2-3, Congo (a) 1-4, Chad (a) 0-1, Guinea Equatorial (a) 1-1.

CHAD

Federation Tchadienne de Football, B.P. 886, N'Djamena.
Founded: 1962; *National Colours:* Blue shirts, yellow shorts, red stockings.
International matches 2007
Benin (a) 1-0, Central African Rep (h) 3-2, Gabon (h) 1-2, Central African Rep (h) 1-0, South Africa (h) 0-3, South Africa (a) 0-4, Zambia (a) 1-1, Congo (h) 1-1.

COMOROS

Comoros FA, BP 798, Moroni.
Founded: 1979.
International matches 2007
Madagascar (a) 0-3, Madagascar (a) 2-6, Madagascar (h) 0-4.

CONGO

Federation Congolaise De Football, 80 Rue Eugene-Etienne, Centre Ville, PO Box 11, Brazzaville.
Founded: 1962; *National Colours:* Green shirts, yellow shorts, red stockings.
International matches 2007
Guinea Equatorial (h) 2-1, Gabon (h) 2-2, Central African Rep (h) 4-1, Gabon (a) 1-0, Zambia (h) 0-0, Angola (a) 0-0, Congo DR (h) 2-1, Zambia (a) 0-3, South Africa (h) 1-1, Chad (a) 1-1.

CONGO DR

Federation Congolaise De Football-Association, Av. de l'Enseignemt 210, C/Kasa-Vubu, Kinshasa 1.
Founded: 1919; *National Colours:* Blue and yellow shirts, yellow and blue shorts, white and blue stockings.
International matches 2007
Ethiopia (h) 2-0, Congo (a) 1-2, Ethiopia (a) 0-1, Namibia (a) 1-1, Madagascar (a) 0-0, Angola (h) 3-1, Libya (h) 1-1.

DJIBOUTI

Federation Djiboutienne de Football, Stade el Haoj Hassan Gouled, B.P. 2694, Djibouti.
Founded: 1977; *National Colours:* Green shirts, white shorts, blue stockings.
International matches 2007
Somalia (h) 1-0, Uganda (h) 0-7, Eritrea (h) 2-3, Rwanda (h) 0-9.

EGYPT

Egyptian Football Association, 5 Gabalaya Street, Guezira, El Borg Post Office, Cairo.
Founded: 1921; *National Colours:* Red shirts, white shorts, black stockings.
International matches 2007
Sweden (h) 2-0, Mauritania (h) 3-0, Mauritania (a) 1-1, Kuwait (a) 1-1, Ivory Coast (h) 0-0, Burundi (a) 0-0, Botswana (h) 1-0, Japan (a) 1-4, UAE (h) 3-0, Sudan (h) 5-0, Libya (h) 0-0, Saudi Arabia (h) 2-1.

ERITREA

The Eritrean National Football Federation, Sematat Avenue 29–31, P.O. Box 3665, Asmara.
National Colours: Blue shirts, red shorts, green stockings.
International matches 2007
Yemen (a) 1-4, Angola (a) 1-6, Sudan (h) 1-0, Sudan (h) 1-1, Angola (h) 1-1, Kenya (h) 1-0, Swaziland (a) 0-0, Sudan (a) 0-1, Sudan (a) 0-1, Rwanda (h) 1-2, Djibouti (a) 3-2, Uganda (h) 3-2, Buruni (a) 1-2.

ETHIOPIA

Ethiopia Football Federation, Addis Ababa Stadium, P.O. Box 1080, Addis Ababa.
Founded: 1943; *National Colours:* Green shirts, yellow shorts, red stockings.
International matches 2007
Congo DR (a) 0-2, Congo DR (h) 1-0, Libya (a) 1-3, Namibia (h) 2-3, Sudan (h) 0-0.

GABON

Federation Gabonaise De Football, B.P. 181, Libreville.
Founded: 1962; *National Colours:* Green, yellow and blue shirts, blue and yellow shorts, white stockings with tri-colour trims.
International matches 2007
Congo (a) 2-2, Guinea Equatorial (a) 1-1, Chad (a) 2-1, Congo (h) 0-1, Madagascar (a) 2-0, Benin (a) 2-2, Ivory Coast (h) 0-0.

GAMBIA

Gambia Football Association, Independence Stadium, Bakau, P.O. Box 523, Banjul.
Founded: 1952; *National Colours:* All red, blue and white.

International matches 2007
Saudi Arabia (a) 0-3, Luxembourg (a) 1-2, Guinea (h) 0-2, Guinea (a) 2-2, Cape Verde Islands (a) 0-0, Algeria (h) 2-1, Cape Verde Islands (a) 0-0, Sierra Leone (h) 2-1.

GHANA

Ghana Football Association, National Sports Council, P.O. Box 1272, Accra.
Founded: 1957; *National Colours:* All yellow.
International matches 2007
Nigeria (h) 4-1, Austria (a) 1-1, Brazil (a) 0-1, Senegal (h) 0-0, Morocco (h) 2-0, Saudi Arabia (a) 0-5, Togo (h) 2-0, Benin (h) 4-2.

GUINEA

Federation Guineenne De Football, P.O. Box 3645, Conakry.
Founded: 1959; *National Colours:* Red shirts, yellow shorts, green stockings.
International matches 2007
Ivory Coast (a) 0-1, Gambia (a) 2-0, Gambia (h) 2-2, Algeria (a) 2-0, Tunisia (a) 1-1, Cape Verde Islands (h) 4-0, Senegal (a) 1-3, Angola (a) 3-0.

GUINEA-BISSAU

Federacao De Football Da Guinea-Bissau, Alto Bandim (Nova Sede), PO Box 375 Bissau 1035.
Founded: 1974; *National Colours:* Red, green and yellow shirts, green and yellow shorts, red, green and yellow stockings.
International matches 2007
Sierra Leone (a) 0-1, Sierra Leone (h) 0-0, Sierra Leone (h) 2-0, Cape Verde Islands (h) 0-0.

GUINEA, EQUATORIAL

Federacion Ecuatoguineana De Futbol, c/P Patricio Lumumba (Estadio La Paz), Malabo 1071.
Founded: 1986; *National Colours:* All red.
International matches 2007
Congo (a) 1-2, Gabon (h) 1-1, Rwanda (h) 3-1, Rwanda (a) 0-2, Central African Rep (h) 1-1.

IVORY COAST

Federation Ivoirienne De Football, 01 PO Box 1202, Abidjan 01.
Founded: 1960; *National Colours:* Orange shirts, black shorts, green stockings.
International matches 2007
Guinea (h) 1-0, Mauritius (a) 3-0, Madagascar (a) 3-0, Madagascar (h) 5-0, Egypt (a) 0-0, Gabon (a) 0-0, Austria (a) 2-3, Angola (a) 1-2, Qatar (a) 6-1.

KENYA

Kenya Football Federation, Nyayo National Stadium, P.O. Box 40234, Nairobi.
Founded: 1960; *National Colours:* All red.
International matches 2007
Swaziland (h) 2-0, Nigeria (h) 0-1, Swaziland (a) 0-0, Rwanda (h) 2-0, Eritrea (a) 0-1, Angola (h) 2-1, Oman (a) 2-2, Oman (a) 1-1, Burundi (a) 0-1, Somalia (h) 2-0, Uganda (a) 1-1.

LESOTHO

Lesotho Football Association, P.O. Box 1879, Maseru-100, Lesotho.
Founded: 1932; *National Colours:* Blue shirts, green shorts, white stockings.
International matches 2007
Swaziland (h) 0-1, Swaziland (a) 1-0, Niger (h) 3-1, Zimbabwe (a) 1-1, Niger (a) 0-2, Uganda (h) 0-0, Angola (a) 0-2, Namibia (h) 3-2, Burma (a) 0-1, Laos (a) 3-1, Nigeria (a) 0-2.

LIBERIA

Liberia Football Association, Broad and Center Streets, PO Box 10-1066, Monrovia 1000.
Founded: 1936; *National Colours:* Blue shirts, white shorts, red stockings.
International matches 2007
Cameroon (a) 1-3, Cameroon (h) 1-2, Guinea Equatorial (h) 0-0, Rwanda (a) 0-4.

LIBYA

Libyan Football Federation, Asayadi Street, Near Janat Al-Areet, P.O. Box 5137, Tripoli.
Founded: 1963; *National Colours:* Green and black shirts, black shorts and stockings.
International matches 2007
Algeria (a) 1-2, Mauritania (h) 0-0, Namibia (h) 2-1, Botswana (a) 0-0, Namibia (a) 0-1, Ethiopia (h) 3-1, Sudan (a) 0-1, Congo DR (a) 1-1, Bahrain (a) 0-2, Saudi Arabia (h) 2-1, Egypt (a) 0-0.

MADAGASCAR

Federation Malagasy de Football, Immeuble Preservatrice Vie-Lot IBF-9B, Rue Rabearivelo-Antsahavola, PO Box 4409, Antananarivo 101.
Founded: 1961; *National Colours:* Red and green shirts, white and green shorts, green and white stockings.
International matches 2007
Ivory Coast (h) 0-3, Zimbabwe (h) 0-1, Seychelles (h) 5-0, Ivory Coast (a) 0-5, Gabon (h) 0-2, Congo DR (h) 0-0, Comoros (h) 3-0, Comoros (h) 6-2, Comoros (a) 4-0.

MALAWI

Football Association of Malawi, Mpira House, Old Chileka Road, P.O. Box 865, Blantyre.
Founded: 1966; *National Colours:* Red shirts, white shorts, red and black stockings.
International matches 2007
South Africa (h) 0-0, Swaziland (a) 0-1, Senegal (h) 2-3, Morocco (h) 0-1, Namibia (h) 1-0, Zimbabwe (a) 1-3, Swaziland (a) 3-0.

MALI

Federation Malienne De Football, Avenue du Mali, Hamdallaye ACI 2000, PO Box 1020, Bamako 12582.
Founded: 1960; *National Colours:* Green shirts, yellow shorts, red stockings.
International matches 2007
Lithuania (h) 3-1, Benin (h) 1-1, Benin (a) 0-0, Burkina Faso (a) 1-0, Sierra Leone (h) 6-0, Burkina Faso (h) 3-2, Togo (a) 2-0, Senegal (a) 2-3, Algeria (a) 2-3.

MAURITANIA

Federation De Foot-Ball De La Rep. Islamique. De Mauritanie, B.P. 566, Nouakchott.
Founded: 1961; *National Colours:* Green and yellow shirts, yellow shorts, green stockings.
International matches 2007
Libya (a) 0-0, Egypt (a) 0-3, Egypt (h) 1-1, Botswana (a) 1-2, Burundi (h) 2-1.

MAURITIUS

Mauritius Football Association, Chancery House, 2nd Floor Nos. 303–305, 14 Lislet Geoffroy Street, Port Louis.
Founded: 1952; *National Colours:* All red.
International matches 2007
Ivory Coast (h) 0-3, Sudan (h) 1-2, Swaziland (a) 0-0, South Africa (h) 0-2, Sudan (a) 0-3, Tunisia (a) 0-2, Seychelles (h) 3-0, Seychelles (h) 1-1.

MOROCCO

Federation Royale Marocaine De Football, 51 Bis Av. Ibn Sina, PO Box 51, Agdal, Rabat 10 000.
Founded: 1955; *National Colours:* All green white and red.
International matches 2007
Tunisia (h) 1-1, Zimbabwe (a) 1-1, Zimbabwe (h) 2-0, Malawi (a) 1-1, Ghana (a) 0-2, Namibia (h) 2-0, France (a) 2-2, Senegal (h) 3-0.

MOZAMBIQUE

Federacao Mocambicana De Futebol, Av. Samora Machel 11-2, Caixa Postal 1467, Maputo.
Founded: 1978; *National Colours:* Red shirts, black shorts, red and black stockings.
International matches 2007
Burkina Faso (a) 1-1, Seychelles (h) 2-0, Zimbabwe (h) 0-0, Burkina Faso (h) 3-1, Senegal (h) 0-0, Zimbabwe (h) 0-0, Tanzania (a) 1-0, Zambia (a) 0-3.

NAMIBIA

Namibia Football Association, Abraham Mashego Street 8521, Katurua Council of Churches in Namibia, P.O. Box 1345, Windhoek 9000, Namibia.
Founded: 1990; *National Colours:* All red.
International matches 2007
Botswana (a) 0-1, Libya (a) 1-2, Zambia (h) 2-1, Libya (h) 1-0, Congo DR (h) 1-1, Malawi (a) 2-1, Botswana (a) 0-1, Lesotho (h) 3-2, Ethiopia (a) 3-2, Morocco (a) 0-2, Saudi Arabia (a) 0-1, Tunisia (a) 0-2.

NIGER

Federation Nigerienne De Football, Rue de la Tapoa, PO Box 10299, Niamey.
Founded: 1967; *National Colours:* Orange shirts, white shorts, green stockings.
International matches 2007
Lesotho (a) 1-3, Lesotho (h) 2-0, Nigeria (h) 1-3, Uganda (a) 1-3.

NIGERIA

Nigeria Football Association, Plot 2033, Olusegun, Obasanjo Way, Zone 7, Wuse Abuja, PO Box 5101 Garki, Abuja, Nigeria.
Founded: 1945; *National Colours:* All green and white.
International matches 2007
Ghana (a) 1-4, Uganda (h) 1-0, Kenya (a) 1-0, Uganda (a) 1-2, Niger (a) 3-1, Macedonia (a) 0-0, Lesotho (h) 2-0, Mexico (a) 2-2, Australia (a) 0-1, Switzerland (a) 1-0.

RWANDA

Federation Rwandaise De Football Amateur, B.P. 2000, Kigali.
Founded: 1972; *National Colours:* Red, green and yellow shirts, green shorts, red stockings.
International matches 2007
Guinea Equatorial (a) 1-3, Burundi (h) 1-0, Guinea Equatorial (h) 2-0, Kenya (a) 0-2, Cameroon (a) 1-2, Liberia (h) 4-0, Eritrea (a) 2-1, Uganda (h) 0-2, Djibouti (a) 9-0, Uganda (h) 1-0, Sudan (h) 2-2.

SENEGAL

Federation Senegalaise De Football, Stade Leopold Sedar Senghor, Route De L'Aeroport De Yoff, B.P. 130 21, Dakar.
Founded: 1960; *National Colours:* All white and green.
International matches 2007
Benin (h) 2-1, Tanzania (h) 4-0, Tanzania (a) 1-1, Malawi (a) 3-2, Mozambique (a) 0-0, Ghana (a) 1-1, Burkina Faso (h) 5-1, Guinea (h) 3-1, Mali (h) 3-2, Morocco (a) 0-3.

SEYCHELLES

Seychelles Football Federation, P.O. Box 843, People's Stadium, Victoria-Mahe, Seychelles.
Founded: 1979; *National Colours:* Red and green shirts and shorts, red stockings.
International matches 2007
Tunisia (h) 0-3, Mozambique (a) 0-2, Madagascar (a) 0-5, Tunisia (a) 0-4, Sudan (h) 0-2, Mauritius (a) 0-3, Mauritius (a) 1-1.

ST THOMAS AND PRINCIPE

Federation Santomense De Futebol, Rua Ex-Joao de Deus No. QXXIII-426/26, PO Box 440, Sao Tome.
Founded: 1975; *National Colours:* Green and red shirts, yellow shorts, green stockings.

SIERRA LEONE

Sierra Leone Football Association, 21 Battery Street, Kingtorn, P.O. Box 672, National Stadium, Brookfields, Freetown.
Founded: 1967; *National Colours:* Green and blue shirts, green, blue and white shorts and stockings.
International matches 2007
Togo (a) 1-3, Togo (h) 0-1, Mali (a) 0-6, Benin (h) 0-2, Guinea-Bissau (h) 1-0, Guinea-Bissau (a) 0-0, Guinea-Bissau (a) 0-2, Gambia (a) 1-2.

SOMALIA

Somali Football Federation, PO Box 222, Mogadishu BN 03040.
Founded: 1951; *National Colours:* Sky blue and white shirts and shorts, white and sky blue stockings.
International matches 2007
Djibouti (a) 0-1, Burundi (a) 0-3, Kenya (a) 0-2.

SOUTH AFRICA

South African Football Association, First National Bank Stadium, PO Box 910, Johannesburg 2000, South Africa.
Founded: 1991; *National Colours:* White shirts with yellow striped sleeves, white shorts with yellow stripes, white stockings.
International matches 2007
Swaziland (h) 1-1, Chad (a) 3-0, Bolivia (h) 0-1, Malawi (a) 0-0, Mauritius (a) 2-0, Chad (h) 4-0, Congo (a) 1-1, Scotland (a) 0-1, Zambia (h) 1-3, Uruguay (h) 0-0, Botswana (h) 1-0, Italy (a) 0-2, Zambia (h) 0-0, USA (h) 0-1, Canada (h) 2-0.

SUDAN

Sudan Football Association, Bladia Street, Khartoum.
Founded: 1936; *National Colours:* Red shirts, white shorts, black stockings.
International matches 2007
Mauritius (a) 2-1, Eritrea (a) 0-1, Eritrea (a) 1-1, Mauritius (h) 3-0, Seychelles (a) 2-0, Libya (h) 1-0, Tunisia (h) 3-2, Eritrea (h) 1-0, Eritrea (h) 1-0, Ethiopia (a) 0-0, Burundi (a) 2-1, Rwanda (a) 2-2.

SWAZILAND

National Football Association of Swaziland, Sigwaca House, Plot 582, Sheffield Road, PO Box 641, Mbabane H100.
Founded: 1968; *National Colours:* Blue shirts, gold shorts, red stockings.
International matches 2007
South Africa (a) 1-1, Lesotho (h) 0-1, Kenya (a) 0-2, Mauritius (h) 0-0, Malawi (h) 1-0, Kenya (h) 0-0, Angola (a) 0-3, Eritrea (h) 0-0, Malawi (h) 0-3.

TANZANIA

Football Association of Tanzania, Uhuru/Shaurimoyo Road, Karume Memorial Stadium, P.O. Box 1574, Ilala/Dar Es Salaam.
Founded: 1930; *National Colours:* Green, yellow and blue shirts, black shorts, green stockings with horizontal stripe.
International matches 2007
Senegal (a) 0-4, Uganda (a) 1-1, Senegal (h) 1-1, Zambia (h) 1-1, Burkina Faso (a) 1-0, Uganda (h) 1-0, Mozambique (h) 0-1, Zambia (h) 1-0.

TOGO

Federation Togolaise De Football, C.P. 5, Lome.
Founded: 1960; *National Colours:* White shirts, green shorts, red stockings with yellow and green stripes.
International matches 2007
Cameroon (h) 2-2, Sierra Leone (h) 3-1, Sierra Leone (a) 1-0, Benin (a) 1-4, Zambia (h) 3-1, Mali (h) 0-2, Ghana (a) 0-2, UAE (h) 5-0.

TUNISIA

Federation Tunisienne De Football, Maison des Federations Sportives, Cite Olympique, Tunis 1003.
Founded: 1956; *National Colours:* Red shirts, white shorts, red stockings.
International matches 2007
Morocco (a) 1-1, Seychelles (a) 3-0, Seychelles (h) 4-0, Mauritius (h) 2-0, Guinea (h) 1-1, Sudan (a) 2-3, UAE (a) 1-0, Namibia (h) 2-0, Austria (a) 0-0.

UGANDA

Federation of Uganda Football Associations, Plot No. 879, Kyadondo Block 8, Mengo Wakaliga Road, P.O. Box 22518, Kampala.
Founded: 1924; *National Colours:* All yellow, red and white.
International matches 2007
Nigeria (a) 0-1, Tanzania (h) 1-1, Nigeria (h) 2-1, Lesotho (a) 0-0, Tanzania (a) 0-1, Nigeria (h) 3-1, Djibouti (a) 7-0, Rwanda (a) 2-0, Eritrea (a) 2-3, Kenya (h) 1-1, Rwanda (a) 0-1, Burundi (a) 2-0.

ZAMBIA

Football Association of Zambia, Football House, Alick Nkhata Road, P.O. Box 34751, Lusaka.
Founded: 1929; *National Colours:* White and green shirts, green and white shorts, white and green stockings.
International matches 2007
Congo (a) 0-0, Namibia (a) 1-2, Congo (h) 3-0, Tanzania (a) 1-1, Chad (h) 1-1, Botswana (a) 0-0, Togo (a) 1-3, South Africa (a) 3-1, Mozambique (h) 3-0, South Africa (a) 0-0, Tanzania (a) 0-1.

ZIMBABWE

Zimbabwe Football Association, P.O. Box CY 114, Causeway, Harare.
Founded: 1965; *National Colours:* All green and gold.
International matches 2007
Morocco (h) 1-1, Madagascar (a) 1-0, Mozambique (a) 0-0, Lesotho (h) 1-1, Burkina Faso (h) 1-1, Morocco (a) 0-2, Mozambique (a) 0-0, Malawi (h) 3-1.

THE WORLD CUP 1930–2006

Year	Winners		Runners-up		Venue	Attendance	Referee
1930	Uruguay	4	Argentina	2	Montevideo	90,000	Langenus (B)
1934	Italy*	2	Czechoslovakia	1	Rome	50,000	Eklind (Se)
1938	Italy	4	Hungary	2	Paris	45,000	Capdeville (F)
1950	Uruguay	2	Brazil	1	Rio de Janeiro	199,854	Reader (E)
1954	West Germany	3	Hungary	2	Berne	60,000	Ling (E)
1958	Brazi	5	Sweden	2	Stockholm	49,737	Guigue (F)
1962	Brazil	3	Czechoslovakia	1	Santiago	68,679	Latychev (USSR)
1966	England*	4	West Germany	2	Wembley	93,802	Dienst (Sw)
1970	Brazil	4	Italy	1	Mexico City	107,412	Glockner (EG)
1974	West Germany	2	Holland	1	Munich	77,833	Taylor (E)
1978	Argentina*	3	Holland	1	Buenos Aires	77,000	Gonella (I)
1982	Italy	3	West Germany	1	Madrid	90,080	Coelho (Br)
1986	Argentina	3	West Germany	2	Mexico City	114,580	Filho (Br)
1990	West Germany	1	Argentina	0	Rome	73,603	Mendez (Mex)
1994	Brazil*	0	Italy	0	Los Angeles	94,194	Puhl (H)
	(Brazil won 3-2 on penalties)						
1998	France	3	Brazil	0	St-Denis	75,000	Belqola (Mor)
2002	Brazil	2	Germany	0	Yokohama	69,029	Collina (I)
2006	Italy	1	France	1	Berlin	69,000	Elizondo (Arg)
	(Italy won 5-3 on penalties)						

*(*After extra time)*

GOALSCORING AND ATTENDANCES IN WORLD CUP FINAL ROUNDS

Venue	*Matches*	*Goals (av)*	*Attendance (av)*
1930, Uruguay	18	70 (3.9)	434,500 (24,138)
1934, Italy	17	70 (4.1)	395,000 (23,235)
1938, France	18	84 (4.6)	483,000 (26,833)
1950, Brazil	22	88 (4.0)	1,337,000 (60,772)
1954, Switzerland	26	140 (5.4)	943,000 (36,270)
1958, Sweden	35	126 (3.6)	868,000 (24,800)
1962, Chile	32	89 (2.8)	776,000 (24,250)
1966, England	32	89 (2.8)	1,614,677 (50,458)
1970, Mexico	32	95 (2.9)	1,673,975 (52,311)
1974, West Germany	38	97 (2.5)	1,774,022 (46,684)
1978, Argentina	38	102 (2.7)	1,610,215 (42,374)
1982, Spain	52	146 (2.8)	2,064,364 (38,816)
1986, Mexico	52	132 (2.5)	2,441,731 (46,956)
1990, Italy	52	115 (2.2)	2,515,168 (48,368)
1994, USA	52	141 (2.7)	3,567,415 (68,604)
1998, France	64	171 (2.6)	2,775,400 (43,366)
2002, Japan/S. Korea	64	161 (2.5)	2,705,566 (42,274)
2006, Germany	64	147 (2.3)	3,354,646 (52,416)

LEADING GOALSCORERS

Year	*Player*	*Goals*
1930	Guillermo Stabile (Argentina)	8
1934	Angelo Schiavio (Italy), Oldrich Nejedly (Czechoslovakia), Edmund Conen (Germany)	4
1938	Leonidas da Silva (Brazil)	8
1950	Ademir (Brazil)	9
1954	Sandor Kocsis (Hungary)	11
1958	Just Fontaine (France)	13
1962	Valentin Ivanov (USSR), Leonel Sanchez (Chile), Garrincha, Vava (both Brazil), Florian Albert (Hungary), Drazen Jerkovic (Yugoslavia)	4
1966	Eusebio (Portugal)	9
1970	Gerd Muller (West Germany)	10
1974	Grzegorz Lato (Poland)	7
1978	Mario Kempes (Argentina)	6
1982	Paolo Rossi (Italy)	6
1986	Gary Lineker (England)	6
1990	Salvatore Schillaci (Italy)	6
1994	Oleg Salenko (Russia) Hristo Stoichkov (Bulgaria)	6
1998	Davor Suker (Croatia)	6
2002	Ronaldo (Brazil)	8
2006	Miroslav Klose (Germany)	5

EUROPEAN FOOTBALL CHAMPIONSHIP

(formerly EUROPEAN NATIONS' CUP)

Year	*Winners*		*Runners-up*		*Venue*	*Attendance*
1960	USSR	2	Yugoslavia	1	Paris	17,966
1964	Spain	2	USSR	1	Madrid	120,000
1968	Italy After 1-1 draw	2	Yugoslavia	0	Rome	60,000 75,000
1972	West Germany	3	USSR	0	Brussels	43,437
1976	Czechoslovakia *(Czechoslovakia won on penalties)*	2	West Germany	2	Belgrade	45,000
1980	West Germany	2	Belgium	1	Rome	47,864
1984	France	2	Spain	0	Paris	48,000
1988	Holland	2	USSR	0	Munich	72,308
1992	Denmark	2	Germany	0	Gothenburg	37,800
1996	Germany *(Germany won on sudden death)*	2	Czech Republic	1	Wembley	73,611
2000	France *(France won on sudden death)*	2	Italy	1	Rotterdam	50,000
2004	Greece	1	Portugal	0	Lisbon	62,865
2008	Spain	1	Germany	0	Vienna	51,428

WORLD CUP 2010 QUALIFYING COMPETITION

SOUTH AMERICA

Buenos Aires, 13 October 2007, 55,000

Argentina (2) 2 *(Riquelme 27, 45)* **Chile (0) 0**

Argentina: Abbondanzieri; Zanetti, Milito, Demichelis, Heinze, Riquelme, Cambiasso, Mascherano, Maxi Rodriguez (Gago 68), Tevez (Aguero 74), Messi (Saviola 84).
Chile: Bravo; Alvarez■, Riffo, Vidal, Ponce, Fernandez, Iturra (Maldonado 63), Gonzalez, Fierro (Droguett 37), Suazo, Rubio (Salas 46).
Referee: Vazquez (Uruguay).

Montevideo, 13 October 2007, 25,200

Uruguay (2) 5 *(Suarez 5, Forlan 38, Abreu 48, Sanchez 68, Bueno 83)* **Bolivia (0) 0**

Uruguay: Carini; Fucile, Godin, Garcia, Perez, Scotti, Pereira, Rodriguez, Abreu (Bueno 73), Suarez (Regueiro 66), Forlan (Sanchez 66).
Bolivia: Galarza; Raldes, Santos, Soliz (Cabrera 46), Hoyos (Suarez 75), Alvarez, Lima, Vaca, Nacho■, Moreno M, Moreno J (Cardozo 59).
Referee: Selman (Chile).

Bogota, 14 October 2007, 41,000

Colombia (0) 0 Brazil (0) 0

Colombia: Julio; Zuniga, Velez, Mosquera, Moreno W, Amaya, Ferreira (Ramirez 55), Sanchez, Castrillon (Grisales 55), Garcia (Perea 81), Renteria.
Brazil: Julio Cesar; Maicon, Juan, Lucio, Ronaldinho, Kaka (Alves 84), Gilberto Silva, Gilberto, Mineiro, Vagner Love (Josue 70), Robinho (Julio Baptista 62).
Referee: Amarilla (Paraguay).

Quito, 14 October 2007, 29,644

Ecuador (0) 0 Venezuela (0) 1 *(Rey 68)*

Ecuador: Viteri; Hurtado I, Espinoza, Bagui (Quiroz 76), Mendez, Castillo, Lara (Ayovi 46), Valencia (Borja 71), De la Cruz, Tenorio C, Benitez.
Venezuela: Vega; Rouga, Rojas, Rey, Cichero, Vallenilla, Arango (Guerra 65), Vera, Paez (Gonzalez 77), Mea (Vielma 77), Maldonado.
Referee: Ortube (Bolivia).

Lima, 14 October 2007, 50,000

Peru (0) 0 Paraguay (0) 0

Peru: Butron; Acasiete, Vargas, Galliquio (Maestri 73), Rodriguez, Vilchez, Solano, De La Haza, Quinteros (Jayo 88), Farfan, Pizarro.
Paraguay: Villar; Morel, Caceres J, Da Silva, Caniza, Vera, Baretto (Britez 87), Riveros, Caceres V, Cabanas (Achucarro 76), Valdez (Cardozo 69).
Referee: Simon (Brazil).

Maracaibo, 16 October 2007, 10,600

Venezuela (0) 0 Argentina (2) 2 *(Milito 16, Messi 43)*

Venezuela: Vega; Rojas (Arismendi 66), Vallenilla (Rosales 46), Rey, Cichero, Rouga, Arango, Seijas (Guerra 53), Paez, Mea, Maldonado.
Argentina: Abbondanzieri; Ibarra (Gago 63), Milito, Demichelis, Zanetti, Burdisso (Diaz 73), Riquelme, Cambiasso, Mascherano, Messi, Tevez (Denis 80).
Referee: Simon (Brazil).

La Paz, 17 October 2007, 19,469

Bolivia (0) 0 Colombia (0) 0

Bolivia: Galarza; Santos, Gatty, Raldes, Verduguez, Reyes L■, Mojica, Campos (Cabrera 55), Arce (Gutierrez R 72), Andaveris (Vaca 46), Limberg Gutierrez.
Colombia: Julio; Arizala, Mosquera, Vallejo, Moreno W, Amaya, Sanchez, Ferreira (Ramirez 55), Anchico (Banguero 85), Valencia (Castrillon 63), Renteria.
Referee: Reinoso (Ecuador).

Rio de Janeiro, 17 October 2007, 87,000

Brazil (1) 5 *(Vagner Love 19, Ronaldinho 62, Kaka 77, 85, Elano 83)* **Ecuador (0) 0**

Brazil: Julio Cesar; Juan, Maicon, Lucio, Mineiro, Gilberto Silva, Gilberto, Ronaldinho, Kaka (Diego 89), Vagner Love (Elano 76), Robinho.
Ecuador: Viteri; Hurtado I, Bagui, Espinoza, Ayovi (Guerron 77), Mendez, De la Cruz, Castillo, Urrutia, Quiroz (Tenorio C 46), Benitez (Lara 82).
Referee: Larrionda (Uruguay).

Santiago, 17 October 2007, 58,000

Chile (1) 2 *(Suazo 11, Fernandez 52)* **Peru (0) 0**

Chile: Bravo; Droguett, Riffo, Vidal, Ponce, Fernandez, Iturra, Gonzalez, Fierro (Fuentes 89), Suazo (Rubio 83), Salas (Jimenez 87).
Peru: Butron; Vilchez (Cruzado 73), Vargas, Galliquio, Acasiete, Rodriguez, De La Haza (Quinteros 46), Jayo, Solano, Pizarro, Farfan.
Referee: Ruiz (Colombia).

Asuncion, 17 October 2007, 23,200

Paraguay (1) 1 *(Valdez 15)* **Uruguay (0) 0**

Paraguay: Villar; Morel, Caceres J, Da Silva, Caniza, Riveros, Caceres V, Vera, Barreto (Santana 86), Cabanas (Achucarro 79), Valdez (Cardozo 66).
Uruguay: Carini; Godin, Fucile, Lugano, Rodriguez (Bueno 79), Perez (Gonzalez A 68), Garcia, Pereira, Scotti, Forlan, Suarez (Sanchez 62).
Referee: Baldassi (Argentina).

Buenos Aires, 17 November 2007, 43,308

Argentina (1) 3 *(Aguero 41, Riquelme 57, 74)*
Bolivia (0) 0

Argentina: Abbondanzieri; Milito, Zanetti, Demichelis, Ibarra, Mascherano, Cambiasso (Gago 69), Riquelme, Messi, Tevez (Denis 82), Aguero (Maxi Rodriguez 75).
Bolivia: Arias; Luis Gutierrez, Hoyos, Raldes, Garcia, Vaca, Mendez, Suarez, Moreno (Gutierrez R 61), Limberg Gutierrez (Arce 61), Cabrera (Moreno 80).
Referee: Rivera (Peru).

Bogota, 17 November 2007, 28,273

Colombia (0) 1 *(Bustos 82)* **Venezuela (0) 0**

Colombia: Julio; Mosquera, Bustos, Velez, Moreno W, Ramirez (Torres 46), Castrillon, Amaya, Sanchez (Grisales 71), Renteria, Garcia (Moreno T 50).
Venezuela: Morales; Rojas, Vielma, Rey, Vallenilla, Rouga, Arango, Paez (Vera 67), Mea, Maldonado (Guerra 56), Fedor (Cichero 79).
Referee: Selman (Chile).

Asuncion, 17 November 2007, 30,000

Paraguay (2) 5 *(Valdez 10, Riveros 28, 88, Santa Cruz 51, Ayala 83)* **Ecuador (0) 1** *(Kaviedes 80)*

Paraguay: Villar; Da Silva, Caceres J, Morel (Veron 77), Barreto, Vera, Caceres V, Riveros, Santa Cruz (Ayala 74), Valdez (Bonet 60), Cabanas.
Ecuador: Elizaga; Montano, Guagua, Bagui, Espinoza, Ayovi, Urrutia (Campos 46), Castillo, Mendez, Ordonez (Kaviedes 63), Benitez (Caicedo 74).
Referee: Lopes (Brazil).

Lima, 18 November 2007, 45,847

Peru (0) 1 *(Vargas 72)* **Brazil (1) 1** *(Kaka 40)*

Peru: Penny; Acasiete, Salas, Rodriguez, Vargas, Lobaton (De La Haza 66), Jayo (Mendoza 63), Solano, Pizarro, Guerrero (Palacios 46), Farfan.
Brazil: Julio Cesar; Maicon, Juan, Lucio, Mineiro, Julio Baptista, Gilberto Silva, Ronaldinho, Kaka, Robinho (Elano 74), Vagner Love (Luis Fabiano 69).
Referee: Torres (Paraguay).

Montevideo, 18 November 2007, 45,000

Uruguay (1) 2 *(Suarez 42, Abreu 81)*
Chile (0) 2 *(Salas 59, 69 (pen))*

Uruguay: Carini; Godin, Fucile, Lugano, Rodriguez, Gargano, Perez (Arevalo 46), Scotti (Pereira 61), Abreu, Sanchez (Gonzalez I 65), Suarez.
Chile: Bravo; Alvarez (Fuentes 60), Jara, Droguett, Riffo, Vidal, Ponce, Fernandez, Suazo (Moya 72), Salas, Rubio (Villanueva 46).
Referee: Pezzotta (Argentina).

San Cristobal, 20 November 2007, 24,000

Venezuela (2) 5 *(Arismendi 20, 40, Guerra 81, Maldonado 89, 90)*
Bolivia (2) 3 *(Arce 27, Moreno M 19, 77)*

Venezuela: Morales; Rey, Cichero, Rojas, Arango, Vera (Mea 59), Seijas (Perez 73), Paez (Guerra 78), Rosales, Maldonado, Arismendi.
Bolivia: Arias; Raldes, Luis Gutierrez, Gatty, Vaca (Lima 46), Mendez, Garcia, Gomez, Mojica (Limberg Gutierrez 70), Arce, Moreno M (Moreno J 79).
Referee: Fagundes (Brazil).

Bogota, 21 November 2007, 45,000

Colombia (0) 2 *(Bustos 62, Moreno D 82)*
Argentina (1) 1 *(Messi 36)*

Colombia: Julio; Velez, Moreno W, Bustos, Mosquera, Ferreira (Torres 46), Castrillon (Grisales 46), Sanchez, Amaya, Renteria, Moreno T (Moreno D 72).
Argentina: Abbondanzieri; Milito, Demichelis, Zanetti, Ibarra, Gago, Cambiasso (Maxi Rodrigues 74), Mascherano, Riquelme, Messi, Tevez■.
Referee: Larrionda (Uruguay).

Quito, 21 November 2007, 28,557

Ecuador (3) 5 *(Ayovi 10, 48, Kaviedes 24, Mendez 44, 62)*
Peru (0) 1 *(Mendoza 86)*

Ecuador: Elizaga (Villafuerte 66); Espinoza, De Jesus, Ambrosi, Hurtado I, Quiroz, Mendez, Castillo, Ayovi, Kaviedes (Urrutia 68), Benitez (Montero 84).
Peru: Penny; Salas, Vilchez (Solis 9), Acasiete, Gomez, Palacios, Bazalar (Mendoza 58), Lobaton, Garcia, Mostto, Pizarro (Farfan 58).
Referee: Chandia (Chile).

Sao Paulo, 21 November 2007, 70,000

Brazil (1) 2 *(Luis Fabiano 44, 64)* **Uruguay (1) 1** *(Abreu 8)*

Brazil: Julio Cesar; Maicon (Alves 86), Juan, Alex, Ronaldinho (Josue 60), Mineiro, Kaka, Gilberto Silva, Gilberto, Robinho (Vagner Love 73), Luis Fabiano.
Uruguay: Carini; Lugano, Godin, Fucile, Rodriguez, Maxi Pereira, Gonzalez I (Bueno 82), Gonzalez A, Gargano, Suarez (Sanchez 71), Abreu.
Referee: Baldassi (Argentina).

Santiago, 21 November 2007, 52,320

Chile (0) 0

Paraguay (2) 3 *(Cabanas 24, Da Silva 45, 57)*

Chile: Bravo; Riffo, Ponce, Droguett, Alvarez, Maldonado, Iturra (Jimenez 46), Fernandez, Suazo, Salas, Rubio (Villanueva 46).
Paraguay: Villa; Morel, Da Silva, Caceres J, Vera, Santana, Riveros (Barreto 80), Caceres V, Bonet, Valdez (Achucarro 67), Cabanas (Santa Cruz 57).
Referee: Ruiz (Colombia).

Lima, 14 June 2008, 25,000

Peru (1) 1 *(Marino 40)* **Colombia (1) 1** *(Rodallega 8)*

Peru: Butron; Neyra (Rengifo 76), Vilchez, Vargas, Rodriguez, Prado, Hidalgo (Cominges 59), Torres, Marino, Solano, Guerrero.
Colombia: Julio; Bustos, Zapata, Velez (Zuniga 72), Moreno W, Vargas (Grisales 60), Guarin, Torres (Portocarrero 86), Sanchez, Rodallega, Perea.
Referee: Torres (Paraguay).

Montevideo, 14 June 2008, 25,000

Uruguay (1) 1 *(Lugano 12)* **Venezuela (0) 1** *(Vargas 56)*

Uruguay: Carini; Caceres, Lugano, Godin, Gargano, Perez, Pereira (Silva 76), Gonzalez I, Forlan (Sanchez 65), Abreu, Suarez (Bueno 65).
Venezuela: Vega; Hernandez, Rey, Vielma, Rojas (Seijas 79), Mea, Chacon, Vargas (Rondon 74), Rincon, Arango, Maldonado (Boada 87).
Referee: A. Intriago (Ecuador).

Buenos Aires, 15 June 2008, 41,167

Argentina (0) 1 *(Palacio 89)* **Ecuador (0) 1** *(Urrutia 69)*

Argentina: Abbondanzieri; Demichelis, Burdisso, Zanetti, Heinze, Veron (Palacio 85), Maxi Rodriguez (Gago 46), Riquelme, Mascherano (Cruz 63), Aguero, Messi.
Ecuador: Cevallos; De Jesus, Mina, Hurtado I, Espinoza, Castillo, Ayovi (Bolanos 85), Valencia, Urrutia, Tenorio C (De la Cruz 88), Guerron (Benitez 88).
Referee: Artube (Bolivia).

La Paz, 15 June 2008, 27,722

Bolivia (0) 0 **Chile (1) 2** *(Medel 28, 76)*

Bolivia: Galarza; Alvarez (Gatty 46), Raldes, Hoyos (Saucedo 78), Luis Gutierrez, Reyes A, Reyes L, Campos (Botero 65), Moreno, Limberg Gutierrez, Arce.
Chile: Bravo; Cereceda, Medel, Jara, Fuentes, Morales (Villanueva 55), Fuenzalida (Estrada 46), Carmona, Beausejour (Gonzalez 58), Sanchez, Suazo.
Referee: Rivera (Peru).

Asuncion, 15 June 2008, 38,000

Paraguay (1) 2 *(Santa Cruz 26, Cabanas 49)*

Brazil (0) 0

Paraguay: Villar; Caniza, Caceres J, Veron■, Da Silva, Barreto, Vera, Santana, Cabanas (Torres 74), Valdez (Caceres V 52), Santa Cruz (Cardozo 81).
Brazil: Julio Cesar; Juan, Maicon, Lucio, Josue (Anderson 46), Gilberto Silva, Gilberto, Diego (Julio Baptista 69), Mineiro (Adriano 60), Robinho, Luis Fabiano.
Referee: Larrionda (Uruguay).

La Paz, 18 June 2008, 8561

Bolivia (2) 4 *(Botero 23, 70, Garcia 25, Moreno 76)*
Paraguay (0) 2 *(Santa Cruz 66, Valdez 82)*

Bolivia: Arias; Gatty, Raldes, Luis Gutierrez, Torrico, Garcia (Ronald Gutierrez 46), Vaca, Reyes A (Rivero 67), Reyes L, Moreno, Botero (Saucedo 73).
Paraguay: Bobadilla; Morel, Da Silva, Caceres J, Vera (Zeballos 46), Riveros, Caceres V, Bonet, Barreto, Cardozo (Valdez 62), Cabanas (Santa Cruz 62).
Referee: Gaciba (Brazil).

Montevideo, 17 June 2008, 20,016

Uruguay (2) 6 *(Forlan 8, 37 (pen), 56, Bueno 61, 69, Abreu 90)* **Peru (0) 0**

Uruguay: Castillo; Silva, Lugano, Godin, Caceres, Rodriguez, Perez (Eguren 69), Gonzalez I (Suarez 72), Gargano, Forlan, Bueno (Abreu 79).
Peru: Butron; Villalta, Vargas (Rengifo 46), Rodriguez, Prado, Hidalgo (Salas 67), Cevasco, Torres, Solano, Marino (Cruzado 71), Guerrero.■.
Referee: Pozo (Chile).

Belo Horizonte, 18 June 2008, 65,000

Brazil (0) 0 **Argentina (0) 0**

Brazil: Julio Cesar; Maicon, Lucio, Juan, Mineiro, Julio Baptista, Gilberto Silva, Gilberto, Anderson (Diego 34) (Alves 79), Adriano (Luis Fabiano 70), Robinho.
Argentina: Abbondanzieri; Zanetti, Heinze, Coloccini, Burdisso, Riquelme (Battaglia 83), Mascherano, Gutierrez, Gago, Messi (Palacio 90), Cruz (Aguero 67).
Referee: Ruiz (Colombia).

Quito, 18 June 2008, 25,000

Ecuador (0) 0 **Colombia (0) 0**

Ecuador: Cevallos; Hurtado I, Ambrosi, Urrutia (Guerron 46), Tenorio C (Caicedo 81), Benitez, De Jesus, Castillo, Ayovi (Bolanos 72), Valencia, Espinoza.
Colombia: Agustin; Moreno W, Mosquera, Gonzalez, Escobar (Moreno D 54), Guarin, Rodallega, Amaya, Torres (Hernandez 63), Soto (Sanchez 80), Zuniga.
Referee: Baldassi (Argentina).

Puerto La Cruz, 19 June 2008, 38,000

Venezuela (0) 2 *(Maldonado 59, Arango 80)*

Chile (0) 3 *(Suazo 54 (pen), 90, Jara 73)*

Venezuela: Vega; Vielma, Rojas, Rey, Hernandez, Arango, Vargas (Rincon 59), Mea (Seijas 80), Chacon, Rondon (Arismendi 55), Maldonado.
Chile: Bravo; Medel, Jara, Fuentes, Cereceda (Ponce 76), Beausejor (Gonzalez 59), Morales (Gazale 60), Estrada, Carmona, Suazo, Sanchez.
Referee: Silvera (Uruguay).

OCEANIA

GROUP A
Tahiti 0, New Caledonia 1; Fiji 16, Tuvalu 0; New Caledonia 1, Tuvalu 0; Fiji 4, Cook Islands 0; Tahiti 1, Tuvalu 1; New Caledonia 3, Cook Islands 0; Cook Islands 4, Tuvalu 1; Fiji 4, Tahiti 0; Fiji 1, New Caledonia 1; Tahiti 1, Cook Islands 0.
Fiji and New Caledonia qualify.

GROUP B
Solomon Islands 12, American Samoa 1; Samoa 0, Vanuatu 4; Solomon Islands 4, Tonga 0; Samoa 7, American Samoa 0; Vanuatu 15, American Samoa 0; Samoa 2, Tonga 1; Tonga 4, American Samoa 0; Solomon Islands 2, Vanuatu 0; Samoa 0, Solomon Islands 3; Vanuatu 4, Tonga 1.
Solomon Islands and Vanuatu qualify.

SEMI-FINALS
Solomon Islands 2, New Caledonia 3; Fiji 3, Vanuatu 0.

THIRD PLACE
Vanuatu 2, Solomon Islands 0.

FINAL
Fiji 0, New Caledonia 1.

FINAL ROUND
Fiji 0, New Zealand 2; Vanuatu 1, New Zealand 2; Fiji 3, New Caledonia 3; New Zealand 4, Vanuatu 1; New Caledonia 4, Fiji 0; Vanuatu 1, New Caledonia 1; New Caledonia 3, Vanuatu 0; New Caledonia v Fiji; Fiji v Vanuatu; New Zealand v New Caledonia; Vanuatu v Fiji; New Zealand v Fiji.

ASIA

FIRST ROUND
Bangladesh 1, Tajikistan 1; Tajikistan 5, Bangladesh 0; Thailand 6, Macao 1; Macao 1, Thailand 7; Vietnam 0, UAE 1; UAE 5, Vietnam 0; Oman 2, Nepal 0; Nepal 0, Oman 2; Syria 3, Afganistan 0; Afganistan 1, Syria 2; Palestine 0, Singapore 4; Singapore v Palestine awarded to Singapore 3-0; Lebanon 4, India 1; India 2, Lebanon 2; Yemen 3, Maldives 0; Maldives 2, Yemen 0; Cambodia 0, Turkmenistan 1; Turkmenistan 4, Cambodia 1; Uzbekistan 9, Taiwan 0; Taiwan 0, Uzbekistan 2; Kyrgyzstan 2, Jordan 0; Jordan 2, Kyrgyzstan 0 – Jordan won 6-5 on penalties; Mongolia 1, North Korea 4; North Korea 5, Mongolia 1; Timor-Leste 2, Hong Kong 3; Hong Kong 8, Timor-Leste 1; Sri Lanka 0, Qatar 1; Qatar 5, Sri Lanka 0; China 7, Myanmar 0; Myanmar 0, China 4; Bahrain 4, Malaysia 1; Malaysia 0, Bahrain 0; Pakistan 0, Iraq 7; Iraq 0, Pakistan 0.

SECOND ROUND
Singapore 2, Tajikistan 0; Tajikistan 1, Singapore 1; Indonesia 1, Syria 4; Syria 7, Indonesia 0; Yemen 1, Thailand 1; Thailand 1, Yemen 0; Hong Kong 0, Turkmenistan 0; Turkmenistan 3, Hong Kong 0.

GROUP 1
Australia 3, Qatar 0; Iraq 1, China 1; China 0, Australia 0; Qatar 2, Iraq 0; Australia 1, Iraq 0; Qatar 0, China 0; China 0, Qatar 1; Iraq 1, Australia 0. China 1, Iraq 2; Qatar1, Australia 3; Australia 0, China 1; Iraq 0, Qatar 1.

GROUP 2
Japan 4, Thailand 1; Oman 0, Bahrain 1; Thailand 0, Oman 1; Bahrain 1, Japan 0; Japan 3, Oman 0; Thailand 2, Bahrain 3; Oman 1, Japan 1; Bahrain 1, Thailand 1. Thailand 0, Japan 3; Bahrain 1, Oman 1; Japan 1, Bahrain 0; Oman 2, Thailand 1.

GROUP 3
South Korea 4, Turkmenistan 0; Jordan 0, North Korea 1; North Korea 0, South Korea 0; Turkmenistan 0, Jordan 2; South Korea 2, Jordan 2; Turkmenistan 0, North Korea 0; North Korea 1, Turkmenistan 0; Jordan 0, South Korea 1; North Korea 2, Jordan 0; Turkmenistan 1, South Korea 3; South Korea 0, North Korea 0; Jordan 2, Turkmenistan 0.

GROUP 4
Lebanon 0, Uzbekistan 1; Saudi Arabia 2, Singapore 0; Uzbekistan 3, Saudi Arabia 0; Singapore 2, Lebanon 0; Singapore 3, Uzbekistan 7; Saudi Arabia 4, Lebanon 1; Uzbekistan 1, Singapore 0; Lebanon 1, Saudi Arabia 2; Singapore 0, Saudi Arabia 2; Uzbekistan 3, Lebanon 0; Lebanon 1, Singapore 2; Saudi Arabia 4, Uzbekistan 0.

GROUP 5
Iran 0, Syria 0; UAE 2, Kuwait 0; Syria 1, UAE 1; Kuwait 2, Iran 2; Iran 0, UAE 0; Syria 1, Kuwait 0; UAE 0, Iran 1; Kuwait 4, Syria 2; Kuwait 2, UAE 3; Syria 0, Iran 2; Iran 2, Kuwait 0; UAE 1, Syria 3.

CONCACAF

FIRST ROUND
Dominican Republic v Puerto Rico not played; Puerto Rico 1, Dominican Republic 0; US Virgin Islands v Grenada not played; Grenada 10, US Virgin Islands 0; Surinam v Monserrat not played; Monserrat 1, Surinam 7; Bermuda 1, Cayman Islands 1; Cayman Islands 1, Bermuda 3; Belize 3, St Kitts & Nevis 1; St Kitts & Nevis 1, Belize 1; Nicaragua 0, Netherlands Antilles 1; Netherlands Antilles 2, Nicaragua 0; Dominica 1, Barbados 1; Barbados 1, Dominica 0; Aruba 0, Antigua & Barbuda 3; Antigua & Barbuda 1, Aruba 0; Turks & Caicos 2, St Lucia 1; St Lucia 2, Turks & Caicos 0; El Salvador 12, Anguilla 0; Anguilla 0, El Salvador 4; Bahamas 1, British Virgin Islands 1; British Virgin Islands 2, Bahamas 2.

SECOND ROUND
Honduras 4, Puerto Rico 0; Puerto Rico 2, Honduras 2; Belize 0, Mexico 2; Mexico 7, Belize 0; Surinam 1, Guyana 0; Guyana 1, Surinam 2; Grenada 2, Costa Rica 2; Costa Rica 3, Grenada 0; Guatemala 6, St Lucia 0; St Lucia 1, Guatemala 3; St Vincent & the Grenadines 0, Canada 3; Canada 4, St Vincent & the Grenadines 1; Trinidad & Tobago 1, Bermuda 2; Bermuda 0, Trinidad & Tobago 2; Haiti 0, Netherlands Antilles 0; Netherlands Antilles 0, Haiti 1; USA 8, Barbados 0; Barbados 0, USA 1; Panama 1, El Salvador 0; El Salvador 3, Panama 1; Antigua & Barbuda 3, Cuba 4; Cuba 4, Antigua & Barbuda 0; Jamaica 7, Bahamas 0; Bahamas 0, Jamaica 6.

AFRICA

FIRST ROUND
Madagascar 6, Comoros 2; Comoros 0, Madagascar 4; Sierra Leone 1, Guinea-Bissau 0; Guinea-Bissau 0, Sierra Leone 0; Djibouti 1, Somalia 0; Somalia v Djibouti not played.

GROUP 1
Tanzania 1, Mauritius 1; Cameroon 2, Cape Verde Islands 0; Cape Verde Islands 1, Tanzania 0; Mauritius 0, Cameroon 3; Tanzania 0, Cameroon 0; Mauritius 0, Cape Verde Islands 1; Cameroon 2, Tanzania 1; Cape Verde Islands 3, Mauritius 1.

GROUP 2
Namibia 2, Kenya 1; Guinea 0, Zimbabwe 0; Kenya 2, Guinea 0; Zimbabwe 2, Namibia 0; Kenya 2, Zimbabwe 0; Namibia 1, Guinea 2; Guinea 4, Namibia 0; Zimbabwe 0, Kenya 0.

GROUP 3
Uganda 1, Niger 0; Angola 3, Benin 0; Niger 1, Angola 2; Benin 4, Uganda 1; Uganda 3, Angola 1; Niger 0, Benin 2; Angola 0, Uganda 0; Benin 2, Niger 0.

GROUP 4
Equatorial Guinea 2, Sierra Leone 0; Nigeria 2, South Africa 0; South Africa 4, Equatorial Guinea 1; Sierra Leone 0, Nigeria 1; Sierra Leone 1, South Africa 0; Equatorial Guinea 0, Nigeria 1; Nigeria 2, Equatorial Guinea 0; South Africa 0, Sierra Leone 0.

GROUP 5
Gabon v Lesotho not played; Ghana 3, Libya 0; Libya 1, Gabon 0; Lesotho 2, Ghana 3; Gabon 2, Ghana 0; Lesotho 0, Libya 1; Ghana 2, Gabon 0; Libya 4, Lesotho 0.

GROUP 6
Senegal 1, Algeria 0; Liberia 1, Gambia 1; Algeria 3, Liberia 0; Gambia 0, Senegal 0; Gambia 1, Algeria 0; Liberia 2, Senegal 2; Algeria 1, Gambia 0; Senegal 3, Liberia 1.

GROUP 7
Botswana 0, Madagascar 0; Ivory Coast 1, Mozambique 0; Madagascar 0, Ivory Coast 0; Mozambique 1, Botswana 2; Botswana 1, Ivory Coast 1; Madagascar 1, Mozambique 1; Ivory Coast 4, Botswana 0; Mozambique 3, Madagascar 0.

GROUP 8
Rwanda 3, Mauritania 0; Morocco 3, Ethiopia 0; Mauritania 1, Morocco 4; Ethiopia 1, Rwanda 2; Mauritania 0, Ethiopia 1; Rwanda 3, Morocco 1; Ethiopia 6, Mauritania 1; Morocco 2, Rwanda 0.

GROUP 9
Burundi 1, Seychelles 0; Tunisia 1, Burkina Faso 2; Seychelles 0, Tunisia 2; Burkina Faso 2, Burundi 0; Seychelles 2, Burkina Faso 3; Burundi 0, Tunisia 1; Burkina Faso 4, Seychelles 1; Tunisia 2, Burundi 1.

GROUP 10
Sudan v Chad not played; Mali 4, Congo 2; Chad 1, Mali 2; Congo 1, Sudan 0; Chad 2, Congo 1; Sudan 3, Mali 2; Congo 2, Chad 0; Mali 3, Sudan 0.

GROUP 11
Togo 1, Zambia 0; Swaziland 2, Togo 1; Swaziland0, Zambia 0; Zambia 1, Swaziland 0.

GROUP 12
Malawi 8, Djibouti 1; Egypt 2, Congo DR 1; Djibouti 0, Egypt 4; Congo DR 1, Malawi 0; Djibouti 0, Congo DR 6; Malawi 1, Egypt 0; Egypt 2, Malawi 0; Congo DR 5, Djibouti 1.

WORLD CUP 2010 QUALIFYING COMPETITION
(Remaining fixtures)

EUROPE

GROUP 1
06.09.08 Albania v Sweden; Hungary v Denmark; Malta v Portugal.
10.09.08 Albania v Malta; Portugal v Denmark; Sweden v Hungary.
11.10.08 Hungary v Albania; Denmark v Malta; Sweden v Portugal.
15.10.08 Portugal v Albania; Malta v Hungary.
11.02.09 Malta vAlbania.
28.03.09 Albania v Hungary; Malta v Denmark; Portugal v Sweden.
01.04.09 Denmark v Albania; Hungary v Malta.
06.06.09 Albania v Portugal; Sweden v Denmark.
10.06.09 Sweden v Malta.
05.09.09 Denmark v Portugal; Hungary v Sweden.
09.09.09 Albania v Denmark; Malta v Sweden; Hungary v Portugal.
10.10.09 Denmark v Sweden; Portugal v Hungary.
14.10.09 Sweden v Albania; Denmark v Hungary; Portugal v Malta.

GROUP 2
06.09.08 Luxembourg v Greece; Israel v Switzerland; Moldova v Latvia.
10.09.08 Latvia v Greece; Moldova v Israel; Switzerland v Luxembourg.
11.10.08 Greece v Moldova; Luxembourg v Israel; Switzerland v Latvia.
15.10.08 Greece v Switzerland; Latvia v Israel; Luxembourg v Moldova.
28.03.09 Israel v Greece; Luxembourg v Latvia; Moldova v Switzerland.
01.04.09 Greece v Israel; Latvia v Luxembourg; Switzerland v Moldova.
05.09.09 Switzerland v Greece; Israel v Latvia; Moldova v Luxembourg.
09.09.09 Moldova v Greece; Israel v Luxembourg; Latvia v Switzerland.
10.10.09 Greece v Latvia; Israel v Moldova; Luxembourg v Switzerland.
14.10.09 Greece v Luxembourg; Switzerland v Israel; Latvia v Moldova.

GROUP 3
06.09.08 Slovakia v Northern Ireland; Poland v Slovenia.
10.09.08 Northern Ireland v Czech Republic; San Marino v Poland; Slovenia v Slovakia.
11.10.08 Slovenia v Northern Ireland; Poland v Czech Republic; San Marino v Slovakia.
15.10.08 Northern Ireland v San Marino; Slovakia v Poland; Czech Republic v Slovenia.
19.11.08 San Marino v Czech Republic.
11.02.09 San Marino v Northern Ireland.
28.03.09 Northern Ireland v Poland; Slovenia v Czech Republic.
01.04.09 Northern Ireland v Slovenia; Poland v San Marino; Czech Republic v Slovakia.
06.06.09 Slovakia v San Marino.
19.08.09 Slovenia v San Marino.
05.09.09 Poland v Northern Ireland; Slovakia v Czech Republic.
09.09.09 Northern Ireland v Slovakia; Slovenia v Poland; Czech Republic v San Marino.
10.10.09 Czech Republic v Poland; Slovakia v Slovenia.
14.10.09 San Marino v Slovenia; Czech Republic v Northern Ireland; Poland v Slovakia.

GROUP 4
06.09.08 Liechtenstein v Germany; Wales v Azerbaijan.
10.09.08 Azerbaijan v Liechtenstein; Russia v Wales; Finland v Germany.
11.10.08 Germany v Russia; Wales v Liechtenstein; Finland v Azerbaijan.
15.10.08 Germany v Wales; Russia v Finland.
28.03.09 Germany v Liechtenstein; Wales v Finland; Russia v Azerbaijan.
01.04.09 Liechtenstein v Russia; Wales v Germany.
06.06.09 Azerbaijan v Wales; Finland v Liechtenstein.
10.06.09 Finland v Russia.
19.08.09 Azerbaijan v Germany.
05.09.09 Azerbaijan v Finland; Russia v Liechtenstein.
09.09.09 Wales v Russia; Germany v Azerbaijan; Liechtenstein v Finland.
10.10.09 Liechtenstein v Azerbaijan; Finland v Wales; Russia v Germany.
14.10.09 Azerbaijan v Russia; Germany v Finland; Liechtenstein v Wales.

GROUP 5
06.09.08 Armenia v Turkey; Belgium v Estonia; Spain v Bosnia.
10.09.08 Spain v Armenia; Turkey v Belgium; Bosnia v Estonia.
11.10.08 Belgium v Armenia; Turkey v Bosnia; Estonia v Spain.
15.10.08 Bosnia v Armenia; Belgium v Spain; Estonia v Turkey.
28.03.09 Armenia v Estonia; Belgium v Bosnia; Spain v Turkey.
01.04.09 Estonia v Armenia; Bosnia v Belgium; Turkey v Spain.
05.09.09 Armenia v Bosnia; Spain v Belgium; Turkey v Estonia.
09.09.09 Armenia v Belgium; Bosnia v Turkey; Spain v Estonia.
10.10.09 Armenia v Spain; Belgium v Turkey; Estonia v Bosnia.
14.10.09 Turkey v Armenia; Estonia v Belgium; Bosnia v Spain.

GROUP 6

20.08.08 Kazakhstan v Andorra.
06.09.08 Andorra v England; Ukraine v Belarus; Croatia v Kazakhstan.
10.09.08 Andorra v Belarus; Croatia v England; Kazakhstan v Ukraine.
11.10.08 England v Kazakhstan; Ukraine v Croatia.
15.10.08 Croatia v Andorra; Belarus v England.
01.04.09 Andorra v Croatia; Kazakhstan v Belarus; England v Ukraine.
06.06.09 Belarus v Andorra; Kazakhstan v England; Croatia v Ukraine.
10.06.09 England v Andorra.
19.08.09 Belarus v Croatia.
05.09.09 Ukraine v Andorra; Croatia v Belarus.
09.09.09 Andorra v Kazakhstan; Belarus v Ukraine; England v Croatia.
10.09.09 Ukraine v Kazakhstan.
10.10.09 Belarus v Kazakhstan; Ukraine v England.
14.10.09 Andorra v Ukraine; England v Belarus; Kazakhstan v Croatia.

GROUP 7

06.09.08 Serbia v Faeroes; Austria v France; Romania v Lithuania.
10.09.08 Faeroes v Romania; France v Serbia; Lithuania v Austria.
11.10.08 Faeroes v Austria; Romania v France; Serbia v Lithuania.
15.10.08 Lithuania v Faeroes; Austria v Serbia.
28.03.09 Lithuania v France; Romania v Serbia.
01.04.09 France v Lithuania; Austria v Romania.
06.06.09 Lithuania v Romania; Serbia v Austria.
10.06.09 Faeroes v Serbia.
19.08.09 Faeroes v France.
05.09.09 Austria v Faeroes; France v Romania.
09.09.09 Faeroes v Lithuania; Serbia v France; Romania v Austria.
10.10.09 France v Faeroes; Austria v Lithuania; Serbia v Romania.
14.10.09 Romania v Faeroes; France v Austria; Lithuania v Serbia.

GROUP 8

06.09.08 Montenegro v Bulgaria; Georgia v Eire; Cyprus v Italy.
10.09.08 Italy v Georgia; Montenegro v Eire.
11.10.08 Bulgaria v Italy; Georgia v Cyprus.
15.10.08 Georgia v Bulgaria; Eire v Cyprus; Italy v Montenegro.
11.02.09 Eire v Georgia.
28.03.09 Eire v Bulgaria; Cyprus v Georgia; Montenegro v Italy.
01.04.09 Georgia v Montenegro; Bulgaria v Cyprus; Italy v Eire.
06.06.09 Bulgaria v Eire; Cyprus v Montenegro.
05.09.09 Bulgaria v Montenegro; Georgia v Italy; Cyprus v Eire.
09.09.09 Italy v Bulgaria; Montenegro v Cyprus.
10.10.09 Montenegro v Georgia; Cyprus v Bulgaria; Eire v Italy.
14.10.09 Bulgaria v Georgia; Eire v Montenegro; Italy v Cyprus.

GROUP 9

06.09.08 Norway v Iceland; Macedonia v Scotland.
10.09.08 Iceland v Scotland; Macedonia v Holland.
11.10.08 Holland v Iceland; Scotland v Norway.
15.10.08 Iceland v Macedonia; Norway v Holland.
28.03.09 Holland v Scotland.
01.04.09 Scotland v Iceland; Holland v Macedonia.
06.06.09 Iceland v Holland; Macedonia v Norway.
10.06.09 Macedonia v Iceland; Holland v Norway.
19.08.09 Norway v Scotland.
05.09.09 Iceland v Norway; Scotland v Macedonia.
09.09.09 Norway v Macedonia; Scotland v Holland.

SOUTH AMERICA

06.09.08 Argentina v Paraguay; Chile v Brazil; Colombia v Uruguay; Ecuador v Bolivia; Peru v Venezuela.
10.09.08 Brazil v Bolivia; Chile v Colombia; Paraguay v Venezuela; Peru v Argentina; Uruguay v Ecuador.
11.10.08 Argentina v Uruguay; Bolivia v Peru; Colombia v Paraguay; Ecuador v Chile; Venezuela v Brazil.
15.10.08 Chile v Argentina; Brazil v Colombia; Venezuela v Ecuador; Paraguay v Peru; Bolivia v Uruguay.
28.03.09 Colombia v Bolivia; Ecuador v Brazil; Peru v Chile; Uruguay v Paraguay; Argentina v Venezuela.
01.04.09 Bolivia v Argentina; Venezuela v Colombia; Ecuador v Paraguay; Brazil v Peru; Chile v Uruguay.
06.06.09 Uruguay v Brazil; Paraguay v Chile; Argentina v Colombia; Peru v Ecuador; Bolivia v Venezuela.
10.06.09 Ecuador v Argentina; Chile v Bolivia; Brazil v Paraguay; Colombia v Peru; Venezuela v Uruguay.
05.09.09 Paraguay v Bolivia; Argentina v Brazil; Colombia v Ecuador; Peru v Uruguay; Chile v Venezuela.
09.09.09 Paraguay v Argentina; Brazil v Chile; Uruguay v Colombia; Bolivia v Ecuador; Venezuela v Peru.
10.10.09 Bolivia v Brazil; Colombia v Chile; Venezuela v Paraguay; Argentina v Peru; Ecuador v Uruguay.
14.10.09 Uruguay v Argentina; Peru v Bolivia; Paraguay v Colombia; Chile v Ecuador; Brazil v Venezuela.

EURO 2008 QUALIFYING COMPETITION

GROUP A

Brussels, 16 August 2006, 15,495

Belgium (0) 0 Kazakhstan (0) 0

Belgium: Stijnen; Vermaelen, Simons, Van Buyten, Kompany (Huysegems 38), Van Damme (Pieroni 60), Hoefkens (Vanden Borre 74), Goor, Buffel, Geraerts, Dembele.
Kazakhstan: Loria; Kuchma, Smakov, Azovskiy Y, Karpovich (Travin 54), Sergienko, Khokhlov, Byakov, Baltiev, Zhalmagambetov, Zhumaskaliyev.
Referee: Courtney (Northern Ireland).

Bydgoszcz, 2 September 2006, 17,000

Poland (0) 1 *(Gargula 89)*

Finland (0) 3 *(Litmanen 54, 76 (pen), Vayrynen 84)*

Poland: Dudek; Wasilewski, Glowacki■, Bak, Michal Zewlakow, Blaszczykowski (Jelen 46), Szymkowiak (Smolarek 46), Radomski, Krzynowek, Zurawski, Frankowski (Gargula 73).
Finland: Jaaskelainen; Tihinen, Hyypia, Kallio, Tainio, Pasanen, Heikkinen, Kolkka (Nurmela 78), Litmanen (Forssell 86), Johansson (Eremenko Jr 66), Vayrynen.
Referee: Duhamel (France).

Belgrade, 2 September 2006, (*behind closed doors*)

Serbia (0) 1 *(Zigic 72)* **Azerbaijan (0) 0**

Serbia: Stojkovic; Markovic, Stepanov, Krstajic, Lukovic, Duljaj, Koroman (Ilic 64), Stankovic, Lazovic (Ergic 74), Pantelic (Ljuboja 81), Zigic.
Azerbaijan: Veliyev; Gashimov, Ruslan Abbasov, Kerimov, Sokolov, Bakhshiev, Ladaga (Dzavadov 77), Muzika (Gurbanov I 62), Imamaliev, Chertoganov, Izmailov (Musaev 72).
Referee: Kircher (Germany).

Erevan, 6 September 2006, 8000

Armenia (0) 0 Belgium (1) 1 *(Van Buyten 41)*

Armenia: Kasparov; Hovsepian, Arzumanian, Dokhoyan, Melikian, Khachatrian, Aleksanian, Mkrtchian (Arm Karamian 76), Mkhitarian (Petrosian 81), Melkonian, Shahgeldian (Aram Hakobian 72).
Belgium: Stijnen; Hoefkens, Simons, Van Damme, Van Buyten, Daerden (De Decker 66), Englebert, Collen (Vanden Borre 59), Geraerts, Dembele (Defour 77), Pieroni.
Referee: Lehner (Austria).

Baku, 6 September 2006, 18,000

Azerbaijan (1) 1 *(Ladaga 16)*

Kazakhstan (1) 1 *(Byakov 36)*

Azerbaijan: Veliyev; Kerimov, Sokolov (Muzika 58), Ruslan Abbasov (Melikov 46), Ladaga, Sultanov (Musaev 65), Chertoganov, Imamaliev, Dzavadov, Gurbanov I, Gomes.
Kazakhstan: Loria; Azovskiy Y, Kuchma, Zhalmagambetov, Smakov, Karpovich (Travin 66), Sergienko, Khokhlov, Byakov, Baltiev, Zhumaskaliyev (Utabayev 74).
Referee: Szabo (Hungary).

Helsinki, 6 September 2006, 38,015

Finland (1) 1 *(Johansson 22)*

Portugal (1) 1 *(Nuno Gomes 42)*

Finland: Jaaskelainen; Kallio, Hyypia, Tihinen, Pasanen, Kolkka (Eremenko Jr 81), Tainio, Vayrynen, Litmanen, Heikkinen, Johansson (Kuqi S 63).
Portugal: Ricardo; Caneira, Ricardo Costa■, Ricardo Carvalho, Nuno Valente, Costinha, Petit, Deco (Tiago 85), Nani (Ricardo Rocha 56), Ronaldo, Nuno Gomes (Joao Moutinho 75).
Referee: Plautz (Austria).

Warsaw, 6 September 2006, 15,000

Poland (1) 1 *(Matusiak 30)* **Serbia (0) 1** *(Lazovic 71)*

Poland: Kowalewski; Golanski (Wasilewski 72), Jop, Bak, Michal Zewlakow, Jelen (Blaszczykowski 73), Lewandowski, Radomski, Krzynowek, Zurawski, Matusiak.
Serbia: Stojkovic; Markovic, Stepanov, Bisevac, Krstajic, Duljaj (Ergic 67), Kovacevic N, Stankovic, Trisovic (Lazovic 60), Pantelic (Koroman 82), Zigic.
Referee: Poll (England).

Erevan, 7 October 2006, 7500

Armenia (0) 0 Finland (0) 0

Armenia: Kasparov; Hovsepian, Arzumanian, Dokhoyan, Melikian, Melkonian, Tigranian, Aleksanian (Aram Hakobian 54), Arm Karamian (Mkrtchian 46), Shahgeldian, Manucharian (Ara Hakobian 78).
Finland: Jaaskelainen; Pasanen, Hyypia, Tihinen, Vayrynen (Nurmela 73), Litmanen, Kolkka, Kuqi S (Forssell 66), Kallio, Johansson (Riihilahti 83), Heikkinen.
Referee: Skomina (Slovenia).

Almaty, 7 October 2006, 18,000

Kazakhstan (0) 0 Poland (0) 1 *(Smolarek 52)*

Kazakhstan: Loria; Azovskiy Y, Kuchma, Zhalmagambetov, Smakov, Karpovich (Travin 59), Sergienko (Larin 81), Khokhlov, Byakov, Zhumaskaliyev, Utabayev (Ashirbekov 68).
Poland: Kowalewski; Bronowicki, Golanski, Blaszczykowski (Grzelak 87), Bak, Smolarek, Sobolewski, Zurawski (Matusiak 71), Rasiak, Radomski, Lewandowski (Kazmierczak 30).
Referee: Trivkovic (Croatia).

Porto, 7 October 2006, 20,000

Portugal (2) 3 *(Ronaldo 25, 63, Ricardo Carvalho 31)*

Azerbaijan (0) 0

Portugal: Ricardo; Miguel, Ricardo Carvalho, Ricardo Rocha, Nuno Valente (Caneira 46), Costinha, Maniche (Tiago 64), Deco, Ronaldo (Nani 73), Nuno Gomes, Simao Sabrosa.
Azerbaijan: Veliyev; Gashimov, Pereira, Sokolov, Kerimov, Ladaga, Chertoganov, Imamaliev, Muzika (Gurbanov I 66), Sultanov (Izmailov 64), Gomes (Dzavadov 76).
Referee: Halsey (England).

Belgrade, 7 October 2006, 35,000

Serbia (0) 1 *(Zigic 54)* **Belgium (0) 0**

Serbia: Stojkovic; Markovic, Vidic, Krstajic, Dragutinovic, Kovacevic N, Stankovic, Koroman (Ergic 71), Trisovic (Lazovic 58), Pantelic (Duljaj 90), Zigic.
Belgium: Stijnen; Kompany, Hoefkens, Simons, Vermaelen, Van Buyten, Geraerts, Mudingayi (Pieroni 75), Goor (Vandenbergh 84), Mpenza E, Dembele (Mpenza M 62).
Referee: Messina (Italy).

Brussels, 11 October 2006, 12,000

Belgium (1) 3 *(Simons 24 (pen), Vandenbergh 47, Dembele 82)* **Azerbaijan (0) 0**

Belgium: Stijnen; Simons, Vermaelen, Vanden Borre (Mpenza M 77), Leonard, Van Buyten, Hoefkens, Geraerts, Goor, Mpenza E (Dembele■ 70), Vandenbergh (Pieroni 86).
Azerbaijan: Veliyev; Gashimov (Nadyrov 77), Sokolov, Kerimov, Pereira, Ladaga, Muzika■ (Gurbanov I 33), Sultanov (Dzavadov 55), Imamaliev, Chertoganov, Gomes.
Referee: Lajuks (Latvia).

Almaty, 11 October 2006, 17,000

Kazakhstan (0) 0 Finland (1) 2 *(Litmanen 27, Hyypia 65)*

Kazakhstan: Loria; Smakov, Kuchma, Zhalmagambetov, Azovskiy Y, Baltiev, Khokhlov, Travin (Azovskiy M 82), Sergienko (Larin 76), Zhumaskaliyev (Ashirbekov 63), Byakov.
Finland: Jaaskelainen; Pasanen, Hyypia, Tihinen, Litmanen, Kolkka, Ilola, Vayrynen (Riihilahti 90), Nurmela, Forssell (Kuqi S 72), Kallio.
Referee: Briakos (Greece).

Chorzow, 11 October 2006, 40,000
Poland (2) 2 *(Smolarek 9, 18)*
Portugal (0) 1 *(Nuno Gomes 90)*
Poland: Kowalewski; Bronowicki, Golanski, Bak, Lewandowski, Blaszczykowski (Krzynowek 65), Smolarek, Sobolewski, Radomski, Zurawski, Rasiak (Matusiak 73).
Portugal: Ricardo; Miguel, Nuno Valente, Ricardo Carvalho, Ricardo Rocha, Deco (Maniche 83), Petit (Nani 68), Costinha (Tiago 46), Simao Sabrosa, Nuno Gomes, Ronaldo.
Referee: Stark (Germany).

Belgrade, 11 October 2006, 20,000
Serbia (0) 3 *(Stankovic 54 (pen), Lazovic 62, Zigic 90)*
Armenia (0) 0
Serbia: Stojkovic; Dragutinovic, Stepanov, Krstajic, Duljaj, Kovacevic N, Stankovic, Koroman (Ergic 72), Trisovic (Ilic 46), Pantelic (Lazovic 46), Zigic.
Armenia: Kasparov; Hovsepian, Arzumanian, Dokhoyan, Nazarian■, Melikian, Melkonian, Mkrtchian, Aram Hakobian (Minasian 69), Manucharian (Tigranian 79), Shahgeldian (Erzrumian 65).
Referee: Kasnaferis (Greece).

Brussels, 15 November 2006, 37,578
Belgium (0) 0 Poland (1) 1 *(Matusiak 19)*
Belgium: Stijnen; Vermaelen, Simons, Van Buyten, Hoefkens, Leonard (Mudingayi 80), Vanden Borre (Huysegems 46), Goor, Geraerts, Mpenza E, Vandenbergh (Pieroni 62).
Poland: Boruc; Dudka (Murawski 79), Bronowicki, Wasilewski, Bak, Michal Zewlakow, Sobolewski, Blaszczykowski, Smolarek, Zurawski (Gargula 62), Matusiak (Kazmierczak 89).
Referee: Dougal (Scotland).

Helsinki, 15 November 2006, 9445
Finland (1) 1 *(Nurmela 10)* **Armenia (0) 0**
Finland: Jaaskelainen; Hyypia, Nyman, Tihinen, Heikkinen, Kallio, Kolkka, Eremenko Jr (Kuqi S 88), Vayrynen (Ilola 47), Johansson, Nurmela.
Armenia: Kasparov; Dokhoyan (Aleksanian 52), Hovsepian, Tadevosian, Pachajian, Mkhitarian (Ara Hakobian 75), Khachatrian, Mkrtchian, Art Karamian, Zebelian (Arm Karamian 78), Shahgeldian.
Referee: Thomson (Scotland).

Coimbra, 15 November 2006, 27,000
Portugal (2) 3 *(Simao Sabrosa 8, 86, Ronaldo 30)*
Kazakhstan (0) 0
Portugal: Ricardo; Luis Miguel, Paulo Ferreira, Ricardo Carvalho, Tonel (Jorge Andrade 77), Tiago, Deco (Martins 63), Meireles, Ronaldo (Quaresma 58), Simao Sabrosa, Nuno Gomes.
Kazakhstan: Loria; Kuchma, Zhalmagambetov, Smakov, Azovskiy Y, Travin, Sergienko (Larin 74), Khokhlov, Byakov, Baltiev, Zhumaskaliyev.
Referee: Rogalla (Switzerland).

Almaty, 24 March 2007, 15,000
Kazakhstan (0) 2 *(Ashirbekov 47, Zhumaskaliyev 61)*
Serbia (0) 1 *(Zigic 68)*
Kazakhstan: Loria; Smakov, Kuchma, Zhalmagambetov, Irismetov, Skorykh, Sergienko (Chichulin 58), Baltiyev, Suyumagambetov (Finonchenko 80), Zhumaskaliyev, Ashirbekov (Byakov 71).
Serbia: Stojkovic; Markovic, Stepanov, Vidic, Tosic D, Kovacevic N, Ergic (Koroman 70), Jankovic, Krasic, Pantelic (Lazovic 69), Zigic■.
Referee: Hrinak (Slovakia).

Warsaw, 24 March 2007, 12,000
Poland (3) 5 *(Bak 3, Dudka 6, Lobodzinski 34, Krzynowek 58, Kazmierczak 84)*
Azerbaijan (0) 0
Poland: Boruc; Wasilewski, Dudka, Bak, Michal Zewlakow, Lobodzinski, Gargula, Lewandowski, Krzynowek (Jelen 79), Zurawski, Matusiak (Kazmierczak 69).
Azerbaijan: Hasanzade; Karimov, Samir Abbasov, Pereira, Bakhshiev, Gurbanov I, Imamaliev (Aghakishiyev 65), Kerimov (Javadov 67), Chertoganov, Gomes (Ladaga 62), Subasic.
Referee: Jakobsson (Iceland).

Lisbon, 24 March 2007, 47,009
Portugal (0) 4 *(Nuno Gomes 53, Ronaldo 55, 75, Quaresma 69)* **Belgium (0) 0**
Portugal: Ricardo; Miguel, Ricardo Carvalho, Jorge Andrade, Paulo Ferreira, Tiago, Petit (Fernando Meira 76), Joao Moutinho, Ronaldo (Hugo Viana 78), Nuno Gomes, Quaresma (Nani 70).
Belgium: Stijnen; Hoefkens (Sterchele 64), Clement, Van Buyten, Van der Heyden, Fellaini, Mudingayi, De Man, Defour, Martens (Chatelle 56), Mpenza M (Van Damme 81).
Referee: Vassaras (Greece).

Baku, 28 March 2007, 14,000
Azerbaijan (0) 1 *(Imamaliev 82)* **Finland (0) 0**
Azerbaijan: Veliyev; Pereira, Ladaga (Imamaliev 66), Guliyev R, Kerimov, Samir Abbasov, Sultanov (Gurbanov I 76), Gomes (Nadyrov 10), Aghakishiyev, Subasic, Chertoganov.
Finland: Jaaskelainen; Pasanen, Hyypia, Tihinen, Vayrynen, Litmanen, Kolkka (Kuqi S 85), Kallio, Eremenko Jr, Johansson (Forssell 86), Heikkinen.
Referee: Messina (Italy).

Kielce, 28 March 2007, 15,000
Poland (1) 1 *(Zurawski 26)* **Armenia (0) 0**
Poland: Boruc; Dudka, Bak, Wasilewski, Michal Zewlakow, Krzynowek (Jelen 83), Blaszczykowski, Lewandowski, Gargula, Zurawski, Kazmierczak (Sobolewski 61).
Armenia: Berezovski; Shahgeldian (Mkhitarian 75), Nazarian (Manucharian 46), Hovsepian, Khachatrian, Dokhoyan, Melikian, Art Karamian (Melkonian 68), Pachajyan, Arzumanian, Zebelian.
Referee: Mallenco (Spain).

Belgrade, 28 March 2007, 51,300
Serbia (1) 1 *(Jankovic 37)* **Portugal (1) 1** *(Tiago 5)*
Serbia: Stojkovic; Tosic D (Lazovic 84), Vidic, Dragutinovic, Krstajic, Duljaj, Jankovic (Koroman 64), Kovacevic N, Krasic, Stankovic (Markovic 78), Pantelic.
Portugal: Ricardo; Paulo Ferreira, Jorge Andrade, Luis Miguel (Caneira 72), Ricardo Carvalho, Petit, Joao Moutinho (Meireles 77), Tiago, Ronaldo, Nuno Gomes (Quaresma 82), Simao Sabrosa.
Referee: Layec (France).

Baku, 2 June 2007, 30,000
Azerbaijan (1) 1 *(Subasic 6)*
Poland (0) 3 *(Smolarek 63, Krzynowek 66, 90)*
Azerbaijan: Veliyev; Kerimov, Abbasov S, Chertoganov, Guliyev R, Abbasov R, Imamaliev (Gasimov 70), Guliyev E, Gurbanov A (Gurbanov I 65), Mamedov (Javadov 53), Subasic.
Poland: Boruc; Wasilewski, Dudka, Bak, Michal Zewlakow, Blaszczykowski (Lobodzinski 57), Lewandowski, Krzynowek, Smolarek, Rasiak (Sobolewski 81), Zurawski (Saganowski 57).
Referee: Kapitanis (Cyprus).

Brussels, 2 June 2007, 46,000
Belgium (0) 1 *(Fellaini 55)*
Portugal (1) 2 *(Nani 43, Helder Postiga 64)*
Belgium: Stijnen; Hoefkens (De Man 46), Clement, Simons, Vermaelen, Defour, Mudingayi (Geraerts 76), Fellaini, Vertonghen, Mpenza E, Sterchele (De Mul 61).
Portugal: Ricardo; Miguel (Bosingwa 53), Jorge Andrade, Fernando Meira, Paulo Ferreira, Deco, Petit, Tiago, Quaresma, Helder Postiga (Hugo Almeida■ 79), Nani (Duda 86).
Referee: Hansson (Sweden).

Helsinki, 2 June 2007, 33,615
Finland (0) 0 Serbia (1) 2 *(Jankovic 3, Jovanovic 86)*
Finland: Jaaskelainen; Kallio, Hyypia, Tihinen, Pasanen, Heikkinen, Ilola, Vayrynen, Tainio (Kolkka 28), Forssell (Johansson 63), Kuqi S (Litmanen 70).
Serbia: Stojkovic; Dragutinovic, Krstagic, Vidic, Rukavina, Stankovic, Kovacevic N, Kuzmanovic, Jankovic (Lazovic 68), Pantelic (Jovanovic 60), Krasic (Duljaj 85).
Referee: Gonzalez (Spain).

Almaty, 2 June 2007, 17,100

Kazakhstan (0) 1 *(Baltiyev 88 (pen))*

Armenia (2) 2 *(Arzumainian 31, Hovsepian 39 (pen))*

Kazakhstan: Loria; Smakov, Kuchma, Zhalmagambetov, Irismetov, Chichulin, Sergienko (Byakov 36), Baltiyev, Suyumagambetov, Zhumaskaliyev (Kornienko 78), Kukeyev (Tleshev 57).
Armenia: Kasparov; Hovsepian, Arzumainian, Tadevosian, Mkrtchian, Minasian, Arakelian (Aram Hakobian 80), Voskanian, Melikian, Mkhitarian (Shahgeldian 75), Melkonian (Arm Karamian 90).
Referee: Kralovec (Czech Republic).

Erevan, 6 June 2007, 13,500

Armenia (0) 1 *(Mkhitarian 66)* **Poland (0) 0**

Armenia: Kasparov; Hovsepian, Arzumanian, Melikian, Minasian (Pachajyan 78), Tadevosian, Mkrtchian, Voskanian, Arakelian, Mkhitarian (Arm Karamian 70), Shahgeldian (Aram Hakobian 46).
Poland: Boruc; Dudka, Bronowicki, Wasilewski, Michal Zewlakow, Lewandowski, Bak (Sobolewski 65), Smolarek (Zurawski 60), Krzynowek, Lobodzinski (Blaszczykowski 60), Saganowski.
Referee: Balaj (Romania).

Helsinki, 6 June 2007, 34,188

Finland (1) 2 *(Johansson 27, Eremenko Jr 71)*

Belgium (0) 0

Finland: Jaaskelainen; Kallio, Pasanen, Nyman, Tihinen, Kolkka (Nurmela 88), Heikkinen, Eremenko, Vayrynen, Eremenko Jr (Forssell 89), Johansson.
Belgium: Stijnen; Vermaelen (Maertens 46), Simons, Clement, De Man, Van Damme, Vertonghen, Fellaini■, Defour, De Mul (Haroun 55), Mpenza E (Sterchele 86).
Referee: Clattenburg (England).

Almaty, 6 June 2007, 11,800

Kazakhstan (0) 1 *(Baltiyev 53)*

Azerbaijan (1) 1 *(Nadyrov 30)*

Kazakhstan: Loria; Smakov, Kuchma, Zhalmagambetov■, Irismetov, Chichulin, Baltiyev, Karpovich, Ostapenko (Tleshev 79), Byakov, Zhumaskaliyev (Utabayev 90).
Azerbaijan: Hasanzade; Gashimov, Guliyev E, Guliyev R, Abbasov S, Sultanov (Gurbanov A 74), Chertoganov, Abbasov R, Subasic, Nadyrov (Mamedov 84), Kerimov (Imamaliev 58).
Referee: Wimes (Luxembourg).

Erevan, 22 August 2007, 8000

Armenia (1) 1 *(Arzumanian 12)*

Portugal (1) 1 *(Ronaldo 37)*

Armenia: Berezovskiy; Arakelyan, Tadevosian, Arzumanian, Hovsepian, Pachajian, Voskanian, Mkhitarian (Ghazarian 59), Art Karamian (Melikian 70), Mkrtchian, Melkonian (Khachatrian 90).
Portugal: Ricardo; Jorge Andrade (Bruno Alves 76), Fernando Meira, Paulo Ferreira, Miguel, Raul Meireles, Deco, Tiago, Helder Postiga (Nuno Gomes 61), Ronaldo, Simao Sabrosa (Quaresma 63).
Referee: Bo Larsen (Denmark).

Brussels, 22 August 2007, 19,202

Belgium (2) 3 *(Dembele 10, 88, Mirallas 30)*

Serbia (0) 2 *(Kuzmanovic 73, 90)*

Belgium: Stijnen; Vermaelen, Hoefkens, Kompany, Defour (Mpenza M 86), Goor, Simons, Geraerts, Mudingayi, Dembele (Lombaerts 90), Mirallas (Vanden Borre 67).
Serbia: Stojkovic; Dragutinovic, Krstajic, Rukavina, Vidic, Kovacevic N, Jankovic, Kuzmanovic, Koroman (Krasic 56), Pantelic (Jovanovic 56), Lazovic (Smiljanic 70).
Referee: Hauge (Norway).

Tampere, 22 August 2007, 13,000

Finland (1) 2 *(Eremenko Jr 13, Tainio 61)*

Kazakhstan (1) 1 *(Byakov 23)*

Finland: Jaaskelainen; Kallio, Pasanen, Heikkinen, Tihinen, Hyypia, Eremenko (Sjolund 46), Kolkka (Nurmela 88), Eremenko Jr, Johansson, Tainio (Riihilahti 76).
Kazakhstan: Loria; Azovskiy Y, Kuchma, Smakov, Irismetov, Skorykh (Chichulin 69), Larin (Ashirbekov 78), Baltiev, Zhumaskaliyev, Byakov, Ostapenko (Suyumagambetov 70).
Referee: Kassai (Hungary).

Lisbon, 8 September 2007, 55,000

Portugal (0) 2 *(Maniche 50, Ronaldo 73)*

Poland (1) 2 *(Lewandowski 44, Krzynowek 88)*

Portugal: Ricardo; Caneira (Miguel 12), Bruno Alves, Fernando Meira, Bosingwa, Deco, Petit, Maniche, Nuno Gomes (Quaresma 69), Ronaldo, Simao Sabrosa (Joao Moutinho 81).
Poland: Boruc; Jop, Zewlakow, Dudka, Wasilewski, Bronowicki (Golanski 55), Blaszczykowski, Lewandowski, Krzynowek, Zurawski (Matusiak 56), Smolarek (Lobodzinski 73).
Referee: Rosetti (Italy).

Belgrade, 8 September 2007, 15,000

Serbia (0) 0 Finland (0) 0

Serbia: Stojkovic; Dragutinovic, Rukavina, Ivanovic, Tosic D (Tosic Z 53), Krasic, Stankovic, Kovacevic N, Jankovic (Jovanovic 54), Kuzmanovic, Lazovic (Zigic 62).
Finland: Jaaskelainen; Pasanen, Quivasto, Hyypia, Tihinen, Eremenko (Forssell 74), Tainio, Nurmela, Heikkinen, Johansson (Wiss 78), Sjolund.
Referee: Braamhaar (Holland).

Helsinki, 12 September 2007, 34,088

Finland (0) 0 Poland (0) 0

Finland: Jaaskelainen; Pasanen, Hyypia, Quivasto, Tihinen, Eremenko, Tainio, Heikkinen (Wiss 89), Kolkka, Johansson (Forssell 72), Sjolund.
Poland: Boruc; Jop, Golanski, Dudka, Michal Zewlakow, Blaszczykowski, Sobolewski, Lewandowski, Krzynowek, Smolarek (Zurawski 80), Rasiak (Saganowski 65).
Referee: Fandel (Germany).

Almaty, 12 September 2007, 18,000

Kazakhstan (1) 2 *(Byakov 39, Smakov 77 (pen))*

Belgium (2) 2 *(Geraerts 13, Mirallas 24)*

Kazakhstan: Loria; Azovskiy Y (Lyapkin 66), Kuchma, Irismetov, Karpovich, Byakov, Larin (Suyumagambetov 73), Smakov, Skorykh, Ostapenko, Zhumaskaliev.
Belgium: Stijnen; Kompany, Vermaelen, Hoefkens, Defour, Goor (Mpenza M 84), Simons, Geraerts (Haroun 77), Fellaini, Mirallas (Vertonghen 63), Dembele.
Referee: Tudor (Romania).

Lisbon, 12 September 2007, 53,000

Portugal (1) 1 *(Simao Sabrosa 11)*

Serbia (0) 1 *(Ivanovic 88)*

Portugal: Ricardo; Fernando Meira, Paulo Ferreira, Bruno Alves, Bosingwa, Petit, Deco (Joao Moutinho 77), Maniche (Raul Meireles 83), Nuno Gomes (Quaresma 65), Ronaldo, Simao Sabrosa.
Serbia: Stojkovic; Dragutinovic■, Rukavina, Ivanovic, Vidic, Tosic Z (Pantelic 61), Krasic (Zigic 61), Kovacevic, Stankovic, Kuzmanovic (Duljaj 71), Jovanovic.
Referee: Merk (Germany).

Erevan, 13 October 2007, 10,000

Armenia (0) 0 Serbia (0) 0

Armenia: Berezovskiy; Arakelian, Tadevosian, Hovsepian, Dokhoyan, Arzumanian, Pachajian, Mkhitarian (Aram Hakobian 82), Voskanian (Khachatrian 70), Art Karamian, Melkonian (Zebelian 62).
Serbia: Stojkovic; Ivanovic, Tosic D, Stepanov, Rukavina, Kuzmanovic (Tosic Z 61), Krasic (Jankovic 73), Stankovic, Kovacevic N, Pantelic (Lazovic 62), Zigic.
Referee: Johannesson (Sweden).

Baku, 13 October 2007, 30,000

Azerbaijan (0) 0

Portugal (2) 2 *(Bruno Alves 12, Hugo Almeida 45)*

Azerbaijan: Veliyev; Yunisoglu, Kerimov■, Abbasov S, Aliyev E, Guliyev E, Imamaliev (Gashimov 7), Chertoganov, Gurbanov I (Mamedov 56), Subasic, Aliyev S (Gurbanov A 73).

Portugal: Ricardo; Bruno Alves, Miguel Veloso, Miguel (Jorge Ribeiro 75), Ricardo Carvalho, Paulo Ferreira, Maniche, Deco, Quaresma (Nani 70), Hugo Almeida, Ronaldo.
Referee: Bebek (Croatia).

Brussels, 13 October 2007, 4131
Belgium (0) 0 Finland (0) 0

Belgium: Stijnen; Kompany, Van Buyten, Lombaerts, Simons, Haroun (Goor 67), Mudingayi, Gregoire (Sonck 67), Gillet, Dembele, Mirallas (Sterchele 84).
Finland: Jaaskelainen; Pasanen, Hyypia, Tihinen, Kallio, Eremenko Jr, Riihilahti, Kolkka, Eremenko, Sjolund (Nurmela 90), Johansson (Kuqi 90).
Referee: Kapitanis (Cyprus).

Warsaw, 13 October 2007, 12,000
Poland (1) 3 *(Smolarek 56, 64, 65)*
Kazakhstan (1) 1 *(Byakov 20)*

Poland: Boruc; Bak, Jop, Dudka, Bronowicki, Michal Zewlakow (Wasilewski 46), Lewandowski, Krzynowek, Lobodzinski (Kosowski 79), Smolarek, Saganowski (Zurawski 46).
Kazakhstan: Loria; Kuchma, Lyapkin, Baltiev, Larin (Suyumagambetov 73), Byakov (Ashirbekov 85), Nurdauletov, Smakov, Skorykh (Karpovich 81), Zhumaskaliev, Ostapenko.
Referee: Berntsen (Norway).

Baku, 17 October 2007, 9000
Azerbaijan (1) 1 *(Aliyev S 26)*
Serbia (4) 6 *(Tosic D 4, Zigic 22, 42, Jankovic 41, Smiljanic 45, Lazovic 84)*

Azerbaijan: Veliyev (Hasanzade 46), Gashimov, Guliyev R, Abbasov S, Guliyev E, Abbasov R, Imamaliev (Ismailov 67), Chertoganov (Bakhshiyev 46), Gurbanov A, Subasic, Aliyev S.
Serbia: Stojkovic; Bisevac, Tosic D, Ivanovic, Rukavina, Tosic Z, Kovacevic N (Smiljanic 65), Jankovic (Lazovic 68), Duljaj, Kuzmanovic, Zigic (Pantelic 73).
Referee: Einwaller (Austria).

Brussels, 17 October 2007, 14,812
Belgium (0) 3 *(Sonck 63, Dembele 69, Geraerts 76)*
Armenia (0) 0

Belgium: Stijnen; Van Buyten (Kompany 60), Lombaerts (Vertonghen 83), Defour, Goor, Geraerts, Simons, Swerts, Fellaini, Mirallas (Sonck 46), Dembele.
Armenia: Kasparov; Arakelian, Tadevosian (Mkrtchian 82), Hovespian, Dokhoyan, Arzumanian, Art Karamian, Pachajian, Khachatrian (Aram Hakobian 57), Voskanian, Melkonian (Zebelian 70).
Referee: Valgeirsson (Iceland).

Almaty, 17 October 2007, 18,500
Kazakhstan (0) 1 *(Byakov 90)*
Portugal (0) 2 *(Makukula 84, Ronaldo 89)*

Kazakhstan: Loria; Zhalmaganbetov, Kuchma, Irismetov, Byakov, Larin (Lyapkin 37), Karpovich (Nurdauletov 89), Smakov, Skorykh, Ostapenko, Zhumaskaliev.
Portugal: Ricardo; Bruno Alves, Paulo Ferreira, Miguel Veloso, Ricardo Carvalho, Miguel, Maniche (Nani 59), Quaresma (Joao Moutinho 85), Deco, Hugo Almeida (Makukula 63), Ronaldo.
Referee: Wegereef (Holland).

Helsinki, 17 November 2007, 10,325
Finland (0) 2 *(Forssell 79, Kuqi 86)*
Azerbaijan (0) 1 *(Gurbanov M 63)*

Finland: Jaaskelainen; Pasanen, Hyypia, Tihinen, Kallio (Vayrynen 66), Eremenko (Kuqi 80), Tainio, Kolkka, Johansson (Litmanen 59), Sjolund, Forssell.
Azerbaijan: Veliyev; Nduka (Aliyev E 46), Guliyev R (Ladaga 61), Yunisoglu, Abbasov S, Maharramov, Gurbanov M, Sadikhov, Ramazanov, Subasic, Tagizade.
Referee: Hamer (Luxembourg).

Chorzow, 17 November 2007, 47,000
Poland (1) 2 *(Smolarek 45, 49)* **Belgium (0) 0**

Poland: Boruc; Bak, Michal Zewlakow, Wasilewski, Bronowicki, Lewandowski, Krzynowek, Sobolewski, Lobodzinski (Blaszczykowski 46), Smolarek (Kosowski 85), Zurawski (Murawski 82).
Belgium: Stijnen; Van Buyten, Kompany, Defour (Pieroni 61), Goor, Gillet, Haroun (Geraerts 84), Felliani, Vertonghen, Mirallas (Huysegems 77), Dembele.
Referee: Bo Larsen (Denmark).

Leiria, 17 November 2007, 23,000
Portugal (1) 1 *(Hugo Almeida 42)* **Armenia (0) 0**

Portugal: Ricardo; Fernando Meira, Caneira, Miguel Veloso, Bruno Alves, Bosingwa, Quaresma (Manuel Fernandes 61), Maniche, Hugo Almeida (Makukula 68), Simao Sabrosa (Nani 77), Ronaldo.
Armenia: Berezovskiy; Dokhoyan, Arzumanian, Arakelian, Tadevosian, Hovsepian, Pachajian, Khachatrian (Mkhitarian 59), Voskanian, Art Karamian (Mkrtchian 76), Melkonian (Manucharian 63).
Referee: Riley (England).

Erevan, 21 November 2007, 8000
Armenia (0) 0 Kazakhstan (0) 1 *(Ostapenko 64)*

Armenia: Berezovskiy; Arakelian (Khachatrian 56), Tadevosian, Hovsepian, Dokhoyan, Arzumanian, Pachajian, Mkhitarian, Voskanian (Ghazarian 80), Art Karamian, Melkonian (Manucharian 59).
Kazakhstan: Loria; Zhalmagambetov, Kuchma, Irismetov, Baltiev, Larin (Lyapkin 61), Nurdauletov, Byakov, Skorykh, Ostapenko, Zhumaskaliev.
Referee: Fautrel (France).

Baku, 21 November 2007, 17,000
Azerbaijan (0) 0 Belgium (0) 1 *(Pieroni 53)*

Azerbaijan: Veliyev; Kerimov (Mamedov 87), Guliyev R, Melikov, Abbasov S, Maharramov (Ponomarev 77), Gurbanov M, Sadikhov, Tagizade (Gomesh 71), Subasic, Ramazanov.
Belgium: Vandenbussche; Van Damme, Van Buyten, Gregoire (Goor 69), Gillet, Geraerts (Defour 46), Swerts, Fellaini, Vertonghen, Dembele, Pieroni (Mirallas 82).
Referee: Kenan (Israel).

Oporto, 21 November 2007, 50,000
Portugal (0) 0 Finland (0) 0

Portugal: Ricardo; Caneira, Miguel Veloso, Bruno Alves, Pepe, Fernando Meira, Quaresma (Nani 84), Maniche (Raul Meireles 73), Bosingwa, Nuno Gomes (Makukula 77), Ronaldo.
Finland: Jaaskelainen; Pasanen, Hyypia, Tihinen, Kallio, Tainio (Eremenko 69), Heikkenen, Kolkka (Johansson 75), Forssell, Sjolund, Litmanen (Vayrynen 67).
Referee: Michel (Slovakia).

Belgrade, 21 November 2007, 20,000
Serbia (0) 2 *(Zigic 69, Lazovic 71)*
Poland (1) 2 *(Murawski 28, Matusiak 47)*

Serbia: Avramov; Rukavina, Ivanovic, Krstajic (Tosic D 64), Dragutinovic, Kuzmanovic, Duljaj (Lazovic 46), Krasic (Jankovic 76), Kovacevic, Zigic, Jovanovic.
Poland: Fabianski; Bak (Michal Zewlakow 77), Wasilewski, Jop, Bronowicki, Wawrzyniak, Lewandowski, Kosowski (Zahorski 19), Murawski, Lobodzinski, Rasiak (Matusiak 46).
Referee: Busacca (Switzerland).

Belgrade, 24 November 2007, 5000
Serbia (0) 1 *(Ostapenko 79 (og))*
Kazakhstan (0) 0

Serbia: Avramov; Stepanov, Ivanovic, Tutoric, Andjelkovic, Kacar, Krasic (Jankovic 24), Duljaj, Zigic (Fejsa 80), Despotovic, Jovanovic (Babovic 63).
Kazakhstan: Loria; Lyapkin (Zhumaskaliev 83), Zhalmagambetov, Irismetov, Baltiev (Ashirbekov 86), Byakov, Nurdauletov, Karpovich, Skorykh, Smakov, Suyumagambetov (Ostapenko 73).
Referee: Cantalejo (Spain).

Group A Table	*P*	*W*	*D*	*L*	*F*	*A*	*Pts*
Poland	14	8	4	2	24	12	28
Portugal	14	7	6	1	24	10	27
Serbia	14	6	6	2	22	11	24
Finland	14	6	6	2	13	7	24
Belgium	14	5	3	6	14	16	18
Kazakhstan	14	2	4	8	11	21	10
Armenia	12	2	3	7	4	13	9
Azerbaijan	12	1	2	9	6	28	5

Armenia v Azerbaijan and return match not played.

GROUP B

Toftir, 16 August 2006, 2114
Faeroes (0) 0
Georgia (3) 6 *(Kankava 16, Iashvili 18, Arveladze 37, 62, 82, Kobiashvili 51 (pen))*
Faeroes: Mikkelsen; Joensen J, Danielsen, Johannesen O, Jorgensen (Hansen P 45), Benjaminsen, Borg, Nielsen, Samuelsen S (Samuelsen H 60), Jacobsen C, Jacobsen R (Fredriksberg 71).
Georgia: Chanturia; Shashiashvili, Asatiani, Kandelaki (Kvirkvelia 66), Kobiashvili, Aladashvili (Gakhokidze 71), Gogua (Ionanidze 56), Kankava, Mujiri, Iashvili, Arveladze.
Referee: Ross (Northern Ireland).

Tbilisi, 2 September 2006, 65,000
Georgia (0) 0
France (2) 3 *(Malouda 7, Saha 16, Henry 46)*
Georgia: Chanturia; Khizanishvili, Kobiashvili, Asatiani, Kankava, Aladashvili (Kandelaki 39), Gogua, Iashvili (Kvirkvelia 46), Demetradze (Menteshashvili 82), Mujiri, Arveladze.
France: Coupet; Sagnol, Thuram, Gallas, Abidal, Vieira, Makelele (Mavuba 58), Ribery (Govou 69), Malouda, Saha (Wiltord 86), Henry.
Referee: Wegereef (Holland).

Naples, 2 September 2006, 60,000
Italy (1) 1 *(Inzaghi 30)* **Lithuania (1) 1** *(Danilevicius 21)*
Italy: Buffon; Oddo, Cannavaro, Barzagli, Grosso, Pirlo, De Rossi (Marchionni 61), Gattuso, Perrotta (Gilardino 72), Cassano, Inzaghi (Di Michele 86).
Lithuania: Karcemarskas; Stankevicius, Dziaukstas, Skerla, Preiksaitis, Zvirgzdauskas, Savenas (Kalonas 65), Mikoliunas (Tamosauskas 82), Cesnauskis, Poskus (Labukas 79), Danilevicius.
Referee: Hansson (Sweden).

Celtic Park, 2 September 2006, 50,059
Scotland (5) 6 *(Fletcher D 7, McFadden 10, Boyd 24 (pen), 38, Miller 30 (pen), O'Connor 85)*
Faeroes (0) 0
Scotland: Gordon; Dailly, Weir, Pressley, Naysmith, Fletcher D (Teale 46), Hartley, Quashie (Severin 84), Miller (O'Connor 61), Boyd, McFadden.
Faeroes: Mikkelsen; Hansen P, Johannesen O, Danielsen, Joensen J, Benjaminsen, Johnsson (Samuelsen S 76), Borg, Fredriksberg (Thorleifson 60), Jacobsen C, Jacobsen R (Nielsen 84).
Referee: Yegorov (Russia).

Saint Denis, 6 September 2006, 78,831
France (2) 3 *(Govou 2, 55, Henry 18)*
Italy (1) 1 *(Gilardino 20)*
France: Coupet; Sagnol, Gallas, Thuram, Abidal, Ribery (Saha 88), Vieira, Makelele, Malouda, Govou (Wiltord 75), Henry.
Italy: Buffon; Zambrotta, Cannavaro, Barzagli, Grosso, Semioli (Di Michele 54), Pirlo, Gattuso, Perrotta, Cassano (Inzaghi 73), Gilardino (De Rossi 87).
Referee: Fandel (Germany).

Kaunas, 6 September 2006, 6500
Lithuania (0) 1 *(Miceika 85)*
Scotland (0) 2 *(Dailly 46, Miller 62)*
Lithuania: Karcemarskas; Stankevicius, Dziaukstas, Skerla, Zvirgzdauskas, Savenas (Tamosauskas 50), Kalonas, Mikoliunas (Labukas 66), Preiksaitis (Miceika 81), Poskus, Danilevicius.
Scotland: Gordon; Dailly, Weir, Caldwell G, Naysmith, Pressley, Fletcher D, Quashie (Boyd 43), McFadden (Alexander G 21), Hartley (Severin 88), Miller.
Referee: Hrinek (Slovakia).

Kiev, 6 September 2006, 40,000
Ukraine (1) 3 *(Shevchenko 31, Rotan 61, Rusol 80)*
Georgia (1) 2 *(Arveladze 38, Demetradze 61)*
Ukraine: Shovkovskyi; Nesmachni, Rusol, Tymoschuk, Rotan, Shelayev, Gusev, Rebrov (Voronin 57), Gusin (Yezerskiy 46), Tkachenko (Vorobei 63), Shevchenko.
Georgia: Chanturia; Kobiashvili, Asatiani, Khizanishvili, Imedashvili (Kandelaki 35), Kankava, Gogua, Kvirkvelia (Mujiri 85), Menteshashvili (Ashvetia 81), Demetradze, Arveladze.
Referee: Jara (Czech Republic).

Torshavn, 7 October 2006, 1982
Faeroes (0) 0 **Lithuania (0) 1** *(Skerla 89)*
Faeroes: Mikkelsen; Mortensen, Danielsen, Thomassen, Benjaminsen, Hansen P (Hansen A 90), Borg, Djurhuus, Samuelsen S (Fredriksberg 73), Jacobsen R (Nielsen 81), Jacobsen C.
Lithuania: Karcemarskas; Stankevicius, Paulauskas, Skerla, Zvirgzdauskas, Savenas (Kalonas 46), Miceika, Cesnauskis, Mikoliunas (Kavaliauskas 62), Danilevicius, Poskus (Beniusis 70).
Referee: Buttimer (Republic of Ireland).

Rome, 7 October 2006, 49,149
Italy (0) 2 *(Oddo 71 (pen), Toni 79)* **Ukraine (0) 0**
Italy: Buffon; Oddo, Cannavaro, Materazzi, Zambrotta, Gattuso, Pirlo, De Rossi, Iaquinta (Camoranesi 76), Toni (Inzaghi 85), Del Piero (Di Natale 62).
Ukraine: Shovkovskyi; Rusol, Shershun, Yezerskiy, Nesmachni, Nazarenko (Kalynychenko 59), Gusev, Shelayev, Tymoschuk, Vorobei (Milevski 73), Voronin.
Referee: Vassaras (Greece).

Glasgow, 7 October 2006, 57,000
Scotland (0) 1 *(Caldwell G 67)* **France (0) 0**
Scotland: Gordon; Dailly, Alexander G, Pressley, Weir, Ferguson B, Fletcher D, Caldwell G, McFadden (O'Connor 72), Hartley, McCulloch (Teale 58).
France: Coupet; Abidal, Thuram, Boumsong, Sagnol, Ribery (Wiltord 74), Vieira, Makelele, Malouda, Trezeguet (Saha 62), Henry.
Referee: Busacca (Switzerland).

Sochaux, 11 October 2006, 19,314
France (2) 5 *(Saha 1, Henry 22, Anelka 77, Trezeguet 78, 84)*
Faeroes (0) 0
France: Landreau; Sagnol (Clerc 79), Gallas, Thuram, Escude, Ribery, Vieira, Toulalan, Malouda, Saha (Trezeguet 61), Henry (Anelka 61).
Faeroes: Mikkelsen; Djurhuus, Mortensen, Danielsen, Samuelsen S, Jacobsen R, Benjaminsen, Thomassen, Borg (Fredriksberg 87), Jacobsen C, Hansen P (Nielsen 47).
Referee: Corpodean (Romania).

Tbilisi, 11 October 2006, 50,000
Georgia (1) 1 *(Shashiashvili 26)*
Italy (1) 3 *(De Rossi 18, Camoranesi 63, Perrotta 71)*
Georgia: Lomaia; Khizanishvili, Khizaneishvili, Kaladze, Shashiashvili, Kankava (Iashvili 70), Tskitishvili (Kandelaki 74), Menteshashvili, Martsvaladze (Gigiadze 85), Kvirkvelia, Ashvetia.
Italy: Buffon; Oddo, Cannavaro (Materazzi 74), Nesta, Pirlo (Mauri 64), De Rossi, Perrotta, Zambrotta, Camoranesi (Iaquinta 87), Toni, Di Natale.
Referee: Riley (England).

Kiev, 11 October 2006, 55,000
Ukraine (0) 2 *(Kucher 60, Shevchenko 90 (pen))*
Scotland (0) 0
Ukraine: Shovkovskyi; Nesmachni, Sviderskyi, Kucher, Rusol, Tymoschuk, Shelayev, Gusev (Milevski 62), Kalynychenko (Vorobei 76), Shevchenko, Voronin (Shershun 90).
Scotland: Gordon; Neilson (McManus 89), Alexander G, Ferguson B, Weir, Pressley■, Fletcher D, Caldwell, Miller, Hartley, McFadden (Boyd 73).
***Referee:* Hansson (Sweden).**

Toftir, 24 March 2007, 717
Faeroes (0) 0 **Ukraine (1) 2** *(Yezerskiy Y 20, Gusev 57)*
Faeroes: Mikkelsen; Olsen (Hansen T 74), Djurhuus, Danielsen, Samuelsen S (Holst 66), Jacobsen R, Benjaminsen, Thomassen (Joensen S 78), Borg, Jacobsen C, Johannesen O.
Ukraine: Shovkovskyi; Yezerskiy Y, Chygrynskiy, Rusol, Nesmachni, Gusev (Vorobei 65), Tymoschuk (Shelayev 82), Mikhalik, Kalynychenko, Bielik, Voronin (Nazarenko 72).
Referee: Skomina (Slovenia).

Kaunas, 24 March 2007, 10,000
Lithuania (0) 0
France (0) 1 *(Anelka 73)*
Lithuania: Karcemarskas; Klimavacius, Skerla, Zvirgzdauskas, Paulauskas, Semberas, Morinas (Beniusis 82), Savenas (Kalonas 77), Stankevicius, Poskus (Radzinevicius 86), Danilevicius.
France: Coupet; Sagnol, Thuram, Gallas, Abidal, Malouda (Diaby 89), Makelele, Toulalan, Diarra, Govou (Cisse 62), Anelka.
Referee: Webb (England).

Glasgow, 24 March 2007, 50,850
Scotland (1) 2 *(Boyd 11, Beattie 89)*
Georgia (1) 1 *(Arveladze 41)*
Scotland: Gordon; Alexander G, Naysmith, Ferguson B, Weir, McManus, Teale (Brown 60), Hartley, Boyd (Beattie 76), Miller (Maloney 90), McCulloch.
Georgia: Lomaia; Shashiashvili, Khizanishvili, Sulukvadze, Eliava, Burduli (Siradze 57), Tskitishvili (Mujiri 90), Menteshashvili (Gogua 46), Kobiashvili, Demetradze, Arveladze.
Referee: Vollquartz (Denmark).

Tbilisi, 28 March 2007, 15,000
Georgia (2) 3 *(Siradze 26, Iashvili 45, 90 (pen))*
Faeroes (0) 1 *(Jacobsen R 56)*
Georgia: Lomaia; Kvirkvelia, Tskitishvili, Iashvili, Kobiashvili (Menteshashvili 61), Mujiri, Kankava, Salukvadze, Demetradze, Shashiashvili, Siradze.
Faeroes: Mikkelsen; Olsen, Djurhuus, Danielsen, Jacobsen R, Benjaminsen■, Thomassen, Borg (Samuelsen S 90), Jacobsen C, Flotum (Holst 43), Johannesen O.
Referee: Saliy (Kazakhstan).

Bari, 28 March 2007, 37,500
Italy (1) 2 *(Toni 12, 70)* **Scotland (0) 0**
Italy: Buffon; Oddo, Cannavaro, Materazzi, Zambrotta, Gattuso, De Rossi, Camoranesi, Perrotta (Pirlo 77), Di Natale (Del Piero 66), Toni (Quagliarella 87).
Scotland: Gordon; Alexander G, Naysmith, Weir, McManus, Ferguson B, Teale (Maloney 66), Hartley, Brown (Beattie 86), McCulloch (Boyd 81), Miller.
Referee: De Bleeckere (Belgium).

Odessa, 28 March 2007, 33,600
Ukraine (0) 1 *(Gusev 47)* **Lithuania (0) 0**
Ukraine: Shovkovskyi; Nesmachni, Kucher, Yezerskiy Y, Rusol, Gusev (Vorobei 79), Tymoschuk, Kalynychenko (Chygrynskiy 82), Mikhalik (Shelayev 70), Shevchenko, Voronin.
Lithuania: Grybauskas; Semberas, Klimavicius, Paulauskas, Stankevicius, Skerla, Zvirgzdauskas, Savenas (Kalonas 51), Morinas (Gedgaudas 56), Poskus (Radzinevicius 64), Danilevicius.
Referee: Meyer (Germany).

Torshavn, 2 June 2007, 6040
Faeroes (0) 1 *(Jacobsen R 77)* **Italy (1) 2** *(Inzaghi 12, 48)*
Faeroes: Mikkelsen; Danielsen, Johannesen O, Jacobsen J, Djurhuus, Borg (Samuelsen S 61), Olsen, Thomassen, Jacobsen C, Jacobsen R, Flotum (Holst 57).
Italy: Buffon; Oddo, Materazzi (Barzagli 76), Cannavaro, Tonetto, Gattuso, Pirlo, Diana, Rocchi (Quagliarella 82), Del Piero, Inzaghi (Lucarelli 59).
Referee: Malek (Poland).

Paris, 2 June 2007, 79,500
France (0) 2 *(Ribery 57, Anelka 71)* **Ukraine (0) 0**
France: Coupet; Abidal, Gallas, Clerc, Thuram, Makelele, Malouda, Toulalan, Nasri (Diarra 81), Ribery, Anelka (Cisse 77).
Ukraine: Shovkovskyi; Nesmachny, Yezerskiy (Levchenko 78), Rusol, Chygrynskiy, Gay, Tymoschuk, Gusev, Mikhalik, Kalynychenko (Rotan 64), Voronin (Vorobei 72).
Referee: Cantalejo (Spain).

Kaunas, 2 June 2007, 6000
Lithuania (0) 1 *(Mikoliunas 78)* **Georgia (0) 0**
Lithuania: Karcemarskas; Semberas, Stankevicius, Skerla, Zvirgzdauskas, Klimavicius, Paulauskas, Savenas (Kalonas 55), Morinas (Mikoliunas 62), Danilevicius, Beniusis (Labukas 75).
Georgia: Lomaia; Khizaneishvili, Kaladze, Eliava, Kobiashvili, Khizanishvili, Tskitishvili (Mujiri 80), Menteshashvili (Martsvaladze 64), Kvirkvelia, Iashvili, Demetradze.
Referee: Circhetta (Switzerland).

Toftir, 6 June 2007, 4100
Faeroes (0) 0 **Scotland (2) 2** *(Maloney 31, O'Connor 35)*
Faeroes: Mikkelsen; Danielsen, Jacobsen J, Johannesen O (Djurhuss 36) (Samuelsen S 77), Benjaminsen, Thomassen, Borg (Flotum 82), Olsen, Jacobsen R, Jacobsen C, Holst.
Scotland: Gordon; Alexander G, Weir, McManus, Naysmith, Hartley, Ferguson B, Fletcher (Teale 68), Maloney (Adam 77), O'Connor, Boyd (Naismith 83).
Referee: Germanakos (Greece).

Auxerre, 6 June 2007, 20,000
France (1) 1 *(Nasri 33)* **Georgia (0) 0**
France: Landreau; Abidal, Clerc, Gallas, Makelele, Malouda (Cisse 65), Toulalan, Nasri, Ribery (Govou 90), Anelka (Benzema 90), Thuram.
Georgia: Lomaia; Khizaneishvili, Kaladze, Khizanishvili, Ghvinianidze, Salukvadze (Mujiri 12), Eliava (Martsvaladze 62), Kvirkverlia, Kankava (Shashiashvili 89), Burduli, Iashvili.
Referee: Batista (Portugal).

Kaunas, 6 June 2007, 7000
Lithuania (0) 0 **Italy (2) 2** *(Quagliarella 31, 45)*
Lithuania: Grybauskas; Semberas, Stankevicius, Skerla, Zvirgzdauskas, Klimavicius, Paulauskas (Gedgaudas 46), Savenas (Labukas 60), Kalonas, Morinas (Mikoliunas 39), Danilevicus.
Italy: Buffon; Oddo, Cannavaro, Materazzi, Zambrotta, Pirlo, De Rossi (Gattuso 65), Perrotta (Ambrosini 71), Quagliarella, Inzaghi, Di Natale (Del Piero 74).
Referee: Vink (Holland).

Tbilisi, 8 September 2007, 25,000
Georgia (0) 1 *(Siradze 89)* **Ukraine (1) 1** *(Shelayev 9)*
Georgia: Lomaia; Salukvadze, Gvininanidze, Kaladze, Asatiani, Menteshashvili (Tatanashvili 79), Tskitishvili, Jakobia (Kenia 62), Iashvili (Siradze 62), Martsvaladze, Demetradze.
Ukraine: Shovkovskiy; Rusol, Kucher, Yezerskiy, Gusev, Timoshchuk, Rotan (Gay 80), Nazarenko, Shelayev (Gladkiy 90), Voronin (Kalinichenko 72), Shevchenko.
Referee: Hamer (Luxembourg).

Milan, 8 September 2007, 80,000
Italy (0) 0 **France (0) 0**
Italy: Buffon; Barzagli, Oddo, Cannavaro, Pirlo, De Rossi, Camoranesi (Perrotta 58), Gattuso, Zambrotta, Inzaghi (Lucarelli 65), Del Piero (Di Natale 83).
France: Landreau; Abidal, Thuram, Escude, Ribery (Toulalan 86), Malouda, Diarra, Makelele, Vieira, Henry, Anelka.
Referee: Michel (Slovakia).

Hampden Park, 8 September 2007, 51,349
Scotland (1) 3 *(Boyd 31, McManus 77, McFadden 83)*
Lithuania (0) 1 *(Danilevicius 61 (pen))*
Scotland: Gordon; Hutton, McEveley, Brown, Weir, McManus, Teale (McFadden 69), Fletcher D, Boyd, McCulloch (Maloney 76), O'Connor (Beattie 76).
Lithuania: Karcemarskas; Klimavicius, Stankevicius (Jankauskas 56), Skerla, Zvirgzdauskas, Semberas, Kalonas, Cesnauskis, Velicka (Ksanavicius 46), Danilevicius, Morinas (Mikoliunas 46).
Referee: Skomina (Slovenia).

Paris, 12 September 2007, 42,000
France (0) 0 **Scotland (0) 1** *(McFadden 64)*
France: Landreau; Abidal (Benzema 77), Thuram, Escude, Ribery, Diarra, Malouda, Vieira (Nasri 69), Makelele, Trezeguet, Anelka.
Scotland: Gordon; Alexander G, Hutton, Ferguson B, Weir, McManus, Hartley, Brown, McFadden (O'Connor 76), McCulloch, Fletcher D (Pearson 26).
Referee: Plautz (Austria).

Kaunas, 12 September 2007, 4000
Lithuania (1) 2 *(Jankauskas 8, Danilevicius 53)*
Faeroes (0) 1 *(Jacobsen R 90)*
Lithuania: Karcemarskas; Alunderis, Skerla, Klimavicius, Semberas, Ksanavicius, Ivaskevicius, Mikoliunas (Velicka 32), Jankauskas (Kucys 86), Danilevicius, Cesnauskis (Kalonas 31).
Faeroes: Mikkelsen; Danielsen, Samuelsen S, Benjaminsen, Thomassen, Jacobsen R, Olsen (Hansen P 63), Borg, Jacobsen C (Flotum 84), Jacobsen J, Holst (Samuelson H 74).
Referee: Georgiev (Bulgaria).

Kiev, 12 September 2007, 41,500
Ukraine (0) 1 *(Shevchenko 71)*
Italy (1) 2 *(Di Natale 41, 77)*
Ukraine: Shovkovskiy; Kucher, Yezerskiy, Rusol, Gay, Timoshchuk, Nazarenko, Kalinichenko (Voronin 60), Shelayev (Gladkiy 69), Gusev (Milevsky 88), Shevchenko.
Italy: Buffon; Cannavaro, Barzagli, Panucci, Ambrosini, Zambrotta, Pirlo, Camoranesi (Oddo 78), Perrotta (Aquilani 68), Iaquinta, Di Natale.
Referee: Webb (England).

Torshavn, 13 October 2007, 8076
Faeroes (0) 0
France (2) 6 *(Anelka 7, Henry 8, Benzema 49, 79, Rothen 65, Ben Arfa 90)*
Faeroes: Mikkelsen; Elttor (Midjord 51), Jacobsen R, Thomassen (Jespersen 77), Samuelsen S (Flotum 85), Benjaminsen, Hansen E, Olsen, Jacobsen C, Jacobsen J, Holst.
France: Landreau; Sagna, Evra, Abidal, Thuram, Rothen, Toulalan, Makelele (Diarra 72), Ribery (Ben Arfa 62), Henry, Anelka (Benzema 46).
Referee: Rossi (San Marino).

Genoa, 13 October 2007, 23,057
Italy (1) 2 *(Pirlo 44, Grosso 84)* **Georgia (0) 0**
Italy: Buffon; Oddo, Barzagli, Panucci, Grosso, Ambrosini (Mauri 88), Gattuso, Pirlo, Quagliarella (Foggia 72), Di Natale, Toni.
Georgia: Lomaia; Kvirkvelia, Shashiashvili (Siradze 60), Khizanishvili, Salukvadze, Asatiani, Tskitishvili, Kankava, Menteshashvili, Demetradze (Jakobia 85), Mchedlidze (Kenia 60).
Referee: Davila (Spain).

Hampden Park, 13 October 2007, 51,366
Scotland (2) 3 *(Miller 4, McCulloch 10, McFadden 68)*
Ukraine (1) 1 *(Shevchenko 24)*
Scotland: Gordon; Hutton, Naysmith, Ferguson B, Weir, McManus, Pearson, Brown (Maloney 76), McFadden (O'Connor 80), Miller, McCulloch (Dailly 60).
Ukraine: Shovkovskiy; Chigrinskiy, Nesmachny, Kucher, Yezerskiy, Timoshchuk (Shelayev 73), Gusev (Rotan 46), Voronin, Vorobei (Nazarenko 62), Gladkiy, Shevchenko.
Referee: Vink (Holland).

Nantes, 17 October 2007, 36,350
France (0) 2 *(Henry 80, 81)* **Lithuania (0) 0**
France: Landreau; Abidal, Thuram, Gallas, Makelele, Toulalan, Ribery, Malouda, Diarra (Ben Arfa 70), Benzema, Henry.
Lithuania: Karcemarskas; Dedura, Zvirgzdauskas, Klimavicius, Skerla, Kucys (Velicka 84), Ksanavicius (Labukas 77), Kalonas (Savenas 64), Jankauskas, Danilevicius, Morinas.
Referee: Kassai (Hungary).

Tbilisi, 17 October 2007, 55,500
Georgia (1) 2 *(Mchedlidze 16, Siradze 64)*
Scotland (0) 0
Georgia: Makaridze; Kvirkvelia, Shashiashvili, Khizanishvili, Salukvadze, Menteshashvili, Kankava, Asatiani, Siradze (Jakobia 89), Kenia (Kandelaki 79), Mchedlidze (Kvakhadze 85).
Scotland: Gordon; Alexander G, Murty, Ferguson B, Weir, McManus, Pearson (Boyd 66), Fletcher D, Maloney, Miller (Beattie 66), McFadden.
Referee: Kircher (Germany).

Kiev, 17 October 2007, 3000
Ukraine (3) 5 *(Kalinichenko 42, 49, Gusev 43, 45, Vorobei 64)*
Faeroes (0) 0
Ukraine: Pyatov; Chigrinskiy, Rusol, Nesmachny, Timoshchuk (Gritsay 69), Kalinichenko, Gusev (Vorobei 62), Gay, Nazarenko, Gladkiy (Milevsky 46), Voronin.
Faeroes: Mikkelsen; Danielsen, Hansen O, Hansen E, Davidsen, Samuelsen S, Jacobsen R, Thomassen (Hansen T 8), Jacobsen C (Samuelsen H 89), Holst (Flotum 75), Jacobsen J.
Referee: Jakov (Israel).

Kaunas, 17 November 2007, 3000
Lithuania (1) 2 *(Savenas 41, Danilevicius 67)*
Ukraine (0) 0
Lithuania: Karcemarskas; Dedura, Paulauskas, Zvirgzdauskas, Klimavicius, Stankevicius, Skerla, Savenas, Papeckys (Morinas 17), Danilevicius (Velicka 82), Jankauskas (Kalonas 90).
Ukraine: Shovkovskiy (Pyatov 44); Vashchuk, Chigrinskiy, Yezerskiy, Gay, Shelayev (Nazarenko 72), Rotan, Timoshchuk, Gusev, Shevchenko, Voronin (Milevsky 69).
Referee: Malcolm (Northern Ireland).

Hampden Park, 17 November 2007, 53,301
Scotland (0) 1 *(Ferguson B 65)*
Italy (1) 2 *(Toni 2, Panucci 90)*
Scotland: Gordon; Hutton, Naysmith, Ferguson B, Weir, McManus, Hartley, Brown (Miller 74), McFadden, McCulloch (Boyd 90), Fletcher D.
Italy: Buffon; Cannavaro, Barzagli, Panucci, Ambrosini, Pirlo, Camoranesi (Chiellini 83), Gattuso (De Rossi 87), Zambrotta, Toni, Di Natale (Iaquinta 68).
Referee: Gonzalez (Spain).

Tbilisi, 21 November 2007, 2000
Georgia (0) 0
Lithuania (0) 2 *(Ksanavicius 52, Kalonas 90)*
Georgia: Makaridze; Kvirkvelia, Salukvadze, Kaladze, Kenia, Menteshashvili (Martsvaladze 33), Kankava, Tskitishvili, Asatiani, Siradze (Gelashvili 80), Mchedlidze.
Lithuania: Karcemarskas; Skerla, Dedura, Paulauskas, Zvirgzdauskas, Alunderis, Stankevicius, Savenas (Kalonas 67), Ksanavicius, Jankauskas (Velicka 56), Danilevicius (Morinas 76).
Referee: Stavrev (Macedonia).

Modena, 21 November 2007, 19,000
Italy (3) 3 *(Benjaminsen 10 (og), Toni 36, Chiellini 41)*
Faeroes (0) 1 *(Jacobsen R 83)*
Italy: Amelia; Oddo, Cannavaro (Bonera 53), Grosso, Chiellini, Ambrosini (Quagliarella 58), De Rossi, Perrotta, Iaquinta, Palladino, Toni (Gilardino 74).
Faeroes: Mikkelsen; Danielsen, Hansen E, Davidsen, Jacobsen R, Benjaminsen, Samuelsen S (Thorleifson 75), Olsen, Jacobsen C, Holst (Flotum 86), Jacobsen J.
Referee: Meyer (Germany).

Kiev, 21 November 2007, 30,000
Ukraine (1) 2 *(Voronin 13, Shevchenko 47)*
France (2) 2 *(Henry 20, Govou 34)*
Ukraine: Pyatov; Gritsay, Fedorov, Romanchuk (Yezerskiy 81), Vashchuk, Rotan, Gay, Timoshchuk, Gusev (Milevsky 90), Shevchenko, Voronin (Shelayev 85).
France: Frey; Thuram, Gallas, Abidal, Clerc, Ribery (Ben Arfa 89), Makelele, Diarra, Govou, Benzema (Nasri 46), Henry.
Referee: Ovrebo (Norway).

Group B Table	*P*	*W*	*D*	*L*	*F*	*A*	*Pts*
Italy	12	9	2	1	22	9	29
France	12	8	2	2	25	5	26
Scotland	12	8	0	4	21	12	24
Ukraine	12	5	2	5	18	16	17
Lithuania	12	5	1	6	11	13	16
Georgia	12	3	1	8	16	19	10
Faeroes	12	0	0	12	4	43	0

GROUP C

Budapest, 2 September 2006, 10,500
Hungary (0) 1 *(Gera 90 (pen))*
Norway (3) 4 *(Solskjaer 15, 54, Stromstad 32, Pedersen 41)*
Hungary: Kiraly; Feher C, Low, Juhasz (Vanczak 66), Eger, Sowunmi (Torghelle 80), Molnar, Dardai, Horvath (Kiss 61), Gera, Huszti.
Norway: Myhre; Rambekk, Hagen, Hangeland, Johnsen M, Stromstad (Braaten 62), Andresen, Haestad (Larsen 85), Pedersen, Solskjaer, Carew (Iversen 76).
Referee: Vink (Holland).

Ta'Qali, 2 September 2006, 4000
Malta (1) 2 *(Pace 6, Michael Mifsud 85)*
Bosnia (3) 5 *(Barbarez 4, Hrgovic 10, 46, Muslimovic 48, 50)*
Malta: Haber; Ciantar (Woods 45), Azzopardi, Said, Dimech, Agius (Sciberras 82), Mattocks (Pullicino 65), Michael Mifsud, Schembri, Pace, Sammut.
Bosnia: Hasagic; Berberovic, Music, Spahic, Bajramovic, Papac (Milenkovic 61), Barbarez (Grujic 66), Misimovic, Muslimovic, Hrgovic, Bartolovic (Beslija 53).
Referee: Vejlgaard (Denmark).

Chisinau, 2 September 2006, 10,500
Moldova (0) 0 Greece (0) 1 *(Liberopoulos 77)*
Moldova: Pascenco; Lascencov, Corneencov, Testimitanu, Epureanu (Clescenco 65), Rebeja, Covalciuc, Olexici, Berco, Rogaciov (Dadu 78), Ivanov.
Greece: Nikopolidis; Seitaridis, Fyssas, Dellas (Anatolakis 89), Kyrgiakos, Katsouranis, Basinas, Zagorakis (Salpigidis 46), Karagounis, Charisteas (Liberopoulos 46), Amanatidis.
Referee: Trefoloni (Italy).

Zenica, 6 September 2006, 18,000
Bosnia (0) 1 *(Misimovic 64)*
Hungary (1) 3 *(Huszti 36 (pen), Gera 46, Dardai 49)*
Bosnia: Hasagic; Spahic■, Music (Muslimovic 46), Papac, Barbarez, Kerkez, Bajramovic, Hrgovic (Beslija 73), Bartolovic (Trivunovic 63), Misimovic, Bolic.
Hungary: Kiraly; Feher C (Kiss 82), Low (Juhasz 65), Torghelle (Kabat 90), Eger, Toth B, Molnar, Dardai, Huszti, Gera, Vanczak.
Referee: Kapitanis (Cyprus).

Oslo, 6 September 2006, 23,848
Norway (0) 2 *(Stromstad 73, Iversen 79)* **Moldova (0) 0**
Norway: Myhre; Hagen, Hangeland, Johnsen M (Iversen 65), Stromstad (Larsen 90), Andresen, Pedersen, Rambekk, Haestad, Carew, Johnsen F (Solksjaer 46).
Moldova: Pascenco; Lascencov (Clescenco 77), Corneencov, Testimitanu, Rebeja, Epureanu, Covalciuc, Ivanov, Berco■, Rogaciov (Dadu 72), Olexici.
Referee: Ristoskov (Bulgaria).

Frankfurt, 6 September 2006
Turkey (0) 2 *(Nihat 56, Tumer 77)* **Malta (0) 0**
Turkey: Rustu; Mehmet T, Can, Gokhan Z, Marco Aurelio, Fatih (Nihat 46), Basturk (Arda 46), Tumer, Ergun, Hakan Sukur (Nuri 85), Hamit Altintop.
Malta: Haber; Ciantar, Wellman, Said, Dimech, Agius (Sciberras 87), Sammut (Pullicino 81), Michael Mifsud, Woods, Schembri (Scerri 89), Pace.
Played behind closed doors.
Referee: Vazquez (Spain).

Athens, 7 October 2006, 25,000
Greece (1) 1 *(Katsouranis 33)* **Norway (0) 0**
Greece: Nikopolidis; Seitaridis, Fyssas, Anatolakis, Kyrgiakos, Basinas, Katsouranis, Karagounis (Patsatzoglou 90), Giannakopoulos (Charisteas 46), Samaras, Liberopoulos (Amanatidis 71).
Norway: Myhre; Rambekk (Arst 85), Hagen, Hangeland, Riise J, Stromstad (Braaten 61), Andresen, Haestad, Pedersen, Iversen, Solskjaer.
Referee: Michel (Slovakia).

Budapest, 7 October 2006, 9500
Hungary (0) 0
Turkey (1) 1 *(Tuncay 41)*
Hungary: Kiraly; Feher C, Vanczak, Juhasz, Eger, Toth B, Halmosi (Kabat 46) (Komlosi 76), Dardai, Torghelle (Szabics 83), Gera, Huszti.
Turkey: Rustu; Hamit Altintop, Servet, Gokhan Z, Aurelio, Gokdeniz (Huseyin 63), Arda (Mehmet T 90), Ibrahim U, Sabri, Tuncay (Can 90), Hakan Sukur.
Referee: Hamer (Luxembourg).

Chisinau, 7 October 2006, 11,000
Moldova (2) 2 *(Rogaciov 13, 32 (pen))*
Bosnia (0) 2 *(Misimovic 62, Grlic 68)*
Moldova: Pascenco; Lascencov, Catinsus, Gatcan (Clescenco 90), Epureanu, Olexici, Testimitanu, Rebeja, Ivanov, Iepureanu (Corneencov 72), Rogaciov (Dadu 71).
Bosnia: Hasagic; Trivunovic, Papac, Vidic, Silic, Bajramovic (Grujic 77), Hrgovic (Smajic 86), Barbarez, Misimovic, Damjanovic (Grlic 46), Bartolovic.
Referee: Piccirillo (France).

Zenica, 11 October 2006, 10,000
Bosnia (0) 0 Greece (1) 4 *(Charisteas 8 (pen), Patsatzoglou 82, Samaras 85, Katsouranis 90)*
Bosnia: Hasagic (Tolja 46); Silic (Ibricic 69), Bajic, Bajramovic, Papac■, Grlic (Grujic 61), Misimovic, Barbarez, Hrgovic, Bartolovic, Skoro.
Greece: Nikopolidis; Anatolakis, Kyrgiakos, Fyssas, Seitaridis (Patsatzoglou 57), Katsouranis, Karagounis (Alexopoulos 36), Giannakopoulos (Amanatidis 89), Basinas, Samaras, Charisteas.
Referee: Kalugin (Russia).

Ta'Qali, 11 October 2006, 5000
Malta (1) 2 *(Schembri 14, 53)* **Hungary (1) 1** *(Torghelle 19)*
Malta: Haber; Scicluna, Wellman, Said, Dimech, Mallia (Cohen 64), Sammut, Pace, Schembri (Scerri 72), Michael Mifsud, Agius (Pullicino 82).
Hungary: Kiraly; Feher C (Halmosi 76), Toth B, Juhasz, Vanczak■, Leandro (Kiss 46), Huszti, Dardai, Torghelle, Szabics (Czvitkovics 60), Gera.
Referee: Ver Eecke (Belgium).

Frankfurt, 11 October 2006, 200
Turkey (3) 5 *(Hakan Sukur 35, 37 (pen), 43, 73, Tuncay 68)*
Moldova (0) 0
Turkey: Rustu; Servet, Hamit Altintop, Gokhan Z, Marco Aurelio, Gokdeniz (Tumer 60), Arda (Nihat 72), Ibrahim U, Sabri, Tuncay, Hakan Sukur (Halil Altintop 81).
Moldova: Pascenco; Epureanu (Corneencov 46), Catinsus, Olexici, Gatcan, Iepureanu (Dadu 63), Covalciuc, Ivanov, Rebeja, Rogaciov, Romanenco.
Played behind closed doors.
Referee: Vollquartz (Denmark).

Athens, 24 March 2007, 31,405
Greece (1) 1 *(Kyrgiakos 5)* **Turkey (1) 4** *(Tuncay 27, Gokhan U 55, Tumer 70, Gokdeniz 81)*
Greece: Nikopolidis; Dellas, Kyrgiakos, Seitaridis, Fyssas (Torosidis 56), Katsouranis, Basinas, Karagounis, Giannakopoulos (Amanatidis 72), Charisteas (Gekas 63), Samaras.
Turkey: Volkan D; Servet, Hamit Altintop, Gokhan Z, Ibrahim U (Volkan Y 19), Mehmet A, Tumer (Gokdeniz 80), Sabri, Gokhan U (Huseyin 57), Hakan Sukur, Tuncay.
Referee: Stark (Germany).

Chisinau, 24 March 2007, 10,000
Moldova (0) 1 *(Epureanu 85)* **Malta (0) 1** *(Mallia 73)*
Moldova: Pascenco; Golovatenco, Epureanu, Olexici, Bordian, Rebeja, Comlenoc (Dadu■ 85), Namasco, Frunza, Bugaev, Zmeu (Ivanov 63).
Malta: Haber; Said, Briffa, Dimech■, Agius, Michael Mifsud (Sciberras 90), Woods (Sammut 77), Mallia, Schembri (Bogdanovic 70), Scicluna, Pace.
Referee: Aliyev (Azerbaijan).

Oslo, 24 March 2007, 16,987
Norway (0) 1 *(Carew 50 (pen))*
Bosnia (2) 2 *(Misimovic 18, Muslimovic 33)*
Norway: Myhre; Hagen, Hangeland, Riise J, Stromstad (Grindheim 62), Andresen, Carew, Pedersen, Haestad, Johnsen F (Iversen 46), Storbaek (Brenne 79).
Bosnia: Guso; Berberovic (Music 58), Nadarevic (Radeljic 46), Bajic, Krunic, Danjanovic, Muslimovic, Misimovic, Ibisevic, Custovic (Maletic 82), Hrgovic.
Referee: Riley (England).

Budapest, 28 March 2007, 5000
Hungary (1) 2 *(Priskin 9, Gera 63)* **Moldova (0) 0**
Hungary: Vegh; Csizmadia, Bodor, Juhasz, Balogh B (Vasko 36), Toth B, Vadocz, Tozser, Priskin (Tisza 88), Hajnal (Huszti 64), Gera.
Moldova: Pascenco; Golovatenco, Cojocari, Olexici, Epureanu, Ivanov (Namasco 46), Corneencov, Bordian, Comleonoc (Zmeu 66), Frunza (Alexeev 46), Bugaev.
Referee: Ingvarsson (Sweden).

Ta'Qali, 28 March 2007, 15,000
Malta (0) 0 Greece (0) 1 *(Basinas 66 (pen))*
Malta: Haber; Azzopardi, Said, Briffa■, Scicluna, Agius, Mallia (Barbara 90), Sammut, Pace, Michael Mifsud, Schembri (Bogdanovic 71).
Greece: Chalkias; Dellas (Anatolakis 83), Vintra, Kyrgiakos, Kapsis, Torosidis, Basinas, Karagounis, Katsouranis, Gekas (Samaras 90), Salpigidis (Liberopoulos 64).
Referee: Garcia (Portugal).

Frankfurt, 28 March 2007
Turkey (0) 2 *(Hamit Altintop 72, 90)*
Norway (2) 2 *(Brenne 31, Andresen 40)*
Turkey: Volkan D; Sabri, Servet, Emre A, Hamit Altintop, Tumer (Volkan Y 46), Emre B, Gokdeniz (Mehmet Y 79), Mehmet A, Hakan Sukur (Huseyin 90), Tuncay.
Norway: Myhre; Riise J, Hagen, Hangeland, Storbaek, Stromstad, Andresen, Haestad (Skjelbred 57), Brenne (Nevland 85), Helstad (Holm 63), Carew.
Played behind closed doors.
Referee: Farina (Italy).

Sarajevo, 2 June 2007, 14,000
Bosnia (2) 3 *(Muslimovic 27, Dzeko 47, Custovic 90)*
Turkey (2) 2 *(Hakan Sukur 13, Sabri 39)*
Bosnia: Guso; Bajic, Music, Radeljic, Danjanovic, Rahimic, Hrgovic, Misimovic, Maletic (Custovic 83), Muslimovic (Pandza 90), Dzeko (Zeba 61).
Turkey: Rustu; Hamit A, Servet, Gokhan Z, Ibrahim U, Mehmet A, Sabri (Umit K 77), Gokdeniz (Huseyin 46), Arda (Basturk 63), Tuncay, Hakan Sukur.
Referee: Frojdfeldt (Sweden).

Iraklion, 2 June 2007, 24,000
Greece (2) 2 *(Gekas 16, Seitaridis 29)* **Hungary (0) 0**
Greece: Chalkias; Seitaridis, Torosidis, Anatolakis (Patsatzoglou 53), Kyrgiakos, Katsouranis, Karagounis, Basinas, Gekas, Amanatidis (Liberopoulos 88), Charisteas (Giannakopoulos 80).
Hungary: Vegh; Csizmadia, Bodor (Vanczak 39), Juhasz, Balogh B, Toth B, Vadocz (Szelesi 76), Tozser, Priskin (Dzsudzsak 80), Hajnal, Gera.
Referee: Larsen (Denmark).

Oslo, 2 June 2007, 16,364
Norway (1) 4 *(Haestad 31, Helstad 73, Iversen 79, Riise JA 90)* **Malta (0) 0**
Norway: Opdal; Storbaek, Hagen, Hangeland, Riise J, Riise B, Andresen, Haestad (Braaten 83), Iversen, Carew (Helstad 72), Pedersen (Brenne 62).
Malta: Muscat; Azzopardi, Said, Wellmen, Scicluna, Agius, Sammut (Woods 46), Mallia, Pace, Michael Mifsud (Barbara 83), Schembri (Bogdanovic 70).
Referee: Granat (Poland).

Sarajevo, 6 June 2007, 15,000
Bosnia (1) 1 *(Muslimovic 6)* **Malta (0) 0**
Bosnia: Guso; Music (Muharemovic 90), Hrgovic, Pandza, Radeljic, Maletic (Bartolovic 80), Danjanovic, Misimovic, Rahimic, Muslimovic, Dzeko (Zeba 57).
Malta: Muscat; Azzopardi, Said, Bogdanovic (Schembri 65), Dimech, Agius, Briffa, Michael Mifsud, Woods (Mallia 70), Sammut, Pace (Barbara 82).
Referee: Richards (Wales).

Iraklion, 6 June 2007, 22,000
Greece (1) 2 *(Charisteas 30, Liberopoulos 90)*
Moldova (0) 1 *(Frunza 80)*
Greece: Nikopolidis; Seitaridis, Goumas, Kyrgiakos, Patsatzoglou (Giannakopoulos 83), Torosidis, Karagounis, Katsouranis, Amanatidis (Samaras 71), Charisteas, Gekas (Liberopoulos 63).
Moldova: Calancea; Epureanu, Golovatenco, Katinsus, Namasco, Bordian, Comleonoc (Tigirlas 82), Josan, Gatcan, Alexeev (Frunza 64), Bugaev (Zmeu 50).
Referee: Wegereef (Holland).

Oslo, 6 June 2007, 19,198
Norway (1) 4 *(Iversen 22, Braaten 57, Carew 60, 78)*
Hungary (0) 0
Norway: Opdal; Storbaek, Hagen, Hangeland, Riise J, Riise B, Andresen, Grindheim (Haestad 46), Iversen (Braaten 46), Carew, Pedersen (Helstad 82).
Hungary: Vegh; Szelesi, Juhasz, Balogh B, Vanczak, Buzsaky (Vadocz 83), Toth B, Tozser, Gera, Priskin (Tisza 71), Hajnal.
Referee: Gonzalez (Spain).

Szekesfehervar, 8 September 2007, 11,000
Hungary (1) 1 *(Gera 39 (pen))* **Bosnia (0) 0**
Hungary: Fulop; Szelesi, Juhasz, Vasko, Vanczak, Tozser, Dzsudzsak (Halmosi 90), Vass, Hajnal (Csizmadia 72), Feczesin (Filkor 89), Gera.
Bosnia: Guso; Bajic, Radeljic, Berberovic, Maletic (Bozic 79), Rahimic, Hrgovic (Custovic 84), Misimovic, Ibisevic (Dzeko 67), Muslimovic, Blatnjak.
Referee: Trefoloni (Italy).

Ta'Qali, 8 September 2007, 18,000
Malta (1) 2 *(Said 41, Schembri 76)*
Turkey (1) 2 *(Halil Altintop 45, Servet 78)*
Malta: Haber; Azzopardi, Scicluna, Dimech, Said, Pace, Briffa (Sammut 88), Woods (Mallia 83), Michael Mifsud, Agius, Schembri (Scerri 90).
Turkey: Hakan; Servet, Ibrahim T, Ibrahim U, Hamit Altintop, Sabri (Gokdeniz 52), Arda (Ayhan 30), Emre B, Hakan Sukur, Halil Altintop, Tuncay (Deniz 66).
Referee: Meissner (Austria).

Chisinau, 8 September 2007, 15,000
Moldova (0) 0 Norway (0) 1 *(Iversen 49)*
Moldova: Pascenco; Lascencov, Rebeja, Olexici (Rogaciov 78), Bordiyan, Epureanu, Gatcan (Suvorov 66), Comleonoc, Zmeu, Bugaiov, Frunza.
Norway: Opdal; Waehler (Riseth 66), Storbaek, Riise J, Hangeland, Pedersen, Andresen, Riise B, Grindheim, Carew, Iversen (Helstad 68).
Referee: Malek (Poland).

Sarajevo, 12 September 2007, 4000
Bosnia (0) 0 Moldova (1) 1 *(Bugaiov 22)*
Bosnia: Guso; Bajic, Radeljic (Ibisevic 46), Nadarevic, Berberovic, Zeba (Damjanovic 47), Maletic (Custovic 78), Rahimic, Muslimovic, Dzeko, Blatnjak.
Moldova: Calancea; Rebeja, Lascencov, Golovatenco, Epureanu, Bordiyan, Gatcan (Josan 85), Corneencov, Comleonoc (Namasco 63), Bugaiov, Doros (Rogaciov 73).
Referee: Hyytia (Finland).

Oslo, 12 September 2007, 24,080
Norway (2) 2 *(Carew 15, Riise J 39)*
Greece (2) 2 *(Kyrgiakos 7, 30)*
Norway: Opdal; Storbaek, Riise J, Hangeland, Hagen, Pedersen, Andresen, Solli (Helstad 70), Riise B (Kippe 90), Carew, Iversen (Riseth 80).
Greece: Chalkias; Kyrgiakos, Torosidis, Seitaridis (Antzas 64), Dellas, Patsatzoglou, Katsouranis, Basinas (Samaras 76), Karagounis, Salpigidis (Lyberopoulos 46), Gekas.
Referee: Busacca (Switzerland).

Istanbul, 12 September 2007, 28,020
Turkey (0) 3 *(Gokhan U 68, Mehmet A 72, Halil Altintop 90)*
Hungary (0) 0
Turkey: Hakan; Servet, Emre A, Ibrahim U, Gokdeniz (Halil Altintop 61), Hamit Altintop, Mehmet A, Ayhan (Serdar 67), Nihat (Emre B 46), Gokhan U, Tuncay.
Hungary: Fulop (Balogh J 71); Juhasz, Csizmadia, Vasko, Vanczak, Szelesi, Dzsudzsak (Halmosi 82), Vass, Hajnal, Priskin (Toth B 66), Gera■.
Referee: Dougal (Scotland).

Athens, 13 October 2007, 15,000

Greece (1) 3 *(Charisteas 10, Gekas 57, Lyberopoulos 72)*

Bosnia (0) 2 *(Hrgovic 54, Ibisevic 90)*

Greece: Nikopolidis; Torosidis, Dellas, Kyrgiakos, Patsatzoglou, Katsouranis, Basinas, Karagounis, Amanatidis (Giannakopoulos 71), Gekas (Antzas 79), Charisteas (Lyberopoulos 69).
Bosnia: Guso; Bajic, Nadarevic, Berberovic, Misimovic (Salihovic 82), Vladavic, Krunic (Ibisevic 46), Rahimic, Hrgovic■, Muslimovic, Blatnjak (Merzic 62).
Referee: Gilewski (Poland).

Budapest, 13 October 2007, 7633

Hungary (1) 2 *(Feczesin 34, Tozser 77)* **Malta (0) 0**

Hungary: Fulop; Juhasz, Balogh B, Vasko, Szelesi, Dzsudzsak (Leandro 87), Vass, Tozser, Filkor (Buzsaky 74), Gera, Feczesin (Rajczi 82).
Malta: Haber; Said, Azzopardi, Scicluna, Dimech, Briffa, Mallia, Woods (Bajada 90), Michael Mifsud, Sammut (Nwoko 65), Schembri (Scerri 82).
Referee: Nalbandyan (Armenia).

Chisinau, 13 October 2007, 10,500

Moldova (1) 1 *(Frunza 11)* **Turkey (0) 1** *(Umit K 62)*

Moldova: Calancea; Golovatenco, Bordiyan, Epureanu, Gatcan (Olexici 89), Savinov, Josan, Corneencov, Comleonoc, Zmeu (Namasco 67), Frunza (Calincov 87).
Turkey: Hakan (Volkan 18); Selcuk (Umit K 46), Gokhan Z, Servet, Ibrahim U, Arda (Tumer 70), Emre B, Mehmet T, Mehmet A, Gokhan U, Tuncay.
Referee: Atkinson (England).

Sarajevo, 17 October 2007, 15,000

Bosnia (0) 0 **Norway (1) 2** *(Hagen 5, Riise B 75)*

Bosnia: Guso; Bajic, Nadarevic, Berberovic, Maletic (Muharemovic 78), Krunic, Misimovic, Merzic, Muslimovic (Dzeko 46), Blatnjak (Ibisevic 46), Salihovic.
Norway: Opdal; Storbaek, Riise J, Hangeland, Hagen, Andresen, Solli, Riise B (Bjorkoy 90), Pedersen, Grindheim (Rushfeldt 58), Helstad (Braaten 76).
Referee: Lannoy (France).

Ta'Qali, 17 October 2007, 10,000

Malta (0) 2 *(Scerri 71, Michael Mifsud 84)*

Moldova (3) 3 *(Bugaev 24 (pen), Frunza 31, 35)*

Malta: Haber; Said, Dimech, Scicluna (Cohen 46), Azzopardi, Pace, Briffa (Nwoko 90), Mallia, Michael Mifsud, Woods, Schembri (Scerri 46).
Moldova: Pascenco; Stroenco, Golovatenco■, Lascencov, Bordiyan, Josan, Comleonoc (Namasco 69), Gatcan (Zmeu 77), Corneencov, Bugaev, Frunza (Doros 83).
Referee: Ishchenko (Ukraine).

Istanbul, 17 October 2007, 24,000

Turkey (0) 0 **Greece (0) 1** *(Amanatidis 79)*

Turkey: Volkan; Servet, Gokhan Z, Ibrahim U, Emre B (Arda 72), Hamit Altintop, Mehmet A, Gokdeniz (Hakan Sukur 65), Gokhan U, Umit K (Tumer 46), Tuncay.
Greece: Chalkias; Antzas, Torosidis, Dellas, Seitaridis, Kyrgiakos, Karagounis, Basinas, Gekas (Lyberopoulos 57), Amanatidis, Charisteas (Samaras 59).
Referee: Gonzalez (Spain).

Athens, 17 November 2007, 31,332

Greece (1) 5 *(Gekas 32, 72, 74, Basinas 54, Amanatidis 61)*

Malta (0) 0

Greece: Nikopolidis; Torosidis (Spyropoulos 48), Kyrgiakos, Dellas, Patsatzoglou, Katsouranis, Basinas, Karagounis (Tziolis 70), Giannakopoulos (Lyberopoulos 46), Amanatidis, Gekas.
Malta: Haber; Azzopardi, Said, Mifsud J, Pace, Briffa, Pullicino, Nwoko, Sammut (Cohen 61), Michael Mifsud (Sciberras 78), Schembri (Scerri 68).
Referee: Kaldma (Estonia).

Chisinau, 17 November 2007, 6483

Moldova (2) 3 *(Bugaev 13, Josan 23, Olexici 86)*

Hungary (0) 0

Moldova: Namasco; Rebeja, Lascencov, Bordiyan, Epureanu, Cebotari (Bulgaru 50), Namasco, Calincov (Alekseev 64), Josan, Zmeu (Olexici 90), Bugaev.
Hungary: Fulop; Szelesi, Vasko, Csizmadia, Vanczak, Vadocz (Balogh B 39), Tozser (Buzsaky 38), Dzsudzsak (Feczesin 71), Hajnal, Gera, Priskin.
Referee: Kralovec (Czech Republic).

Oslo, 17 November 2007, 23,783

Norway (1) 1 *(Hagen 12)*

Turkey (1) 2 *(Emre B 31, Nihat 59)*

Norway: Opdal; Hagen, Storbaek (Rushfeldt 88), Riise J, Hangeland, Riise B, Pedersen, Haestad (Skjelbred 68), Tettey, Carew, Iversen (Helstad 84).
Turkey: Volkan; Emre A, Servet, Ibrahim K (Gokhan G 15), Emre B, Arda (Tuncay 87), Hamit Altintop, Mehmet A, Hakan, Nihat, Semih (Yusuf 67).
Referee: Merk (Germany).

Budapest, 21 November 2007, 32,300

Hungary (1) 1 *(Buzsaky 7)*

Greece (1) 2 *(Vanczak 22 (og), Basinas 56 (pen))*

Hungary: Fulop; Szelesi, Vasko, Juhasz, Vanczak, Vass, Buzsaky, Halmosi (Feczesin 83), Tozser (Leandro 86), Hajnal (Filkor 79), Priskin.
Greece: Chalkias (Nikopolidis 46); Kyrgiakos, Vintra, Kapsis, Patsatzoglou, Katsouranis, Basinas, Tziolis (Samaras 46), Karagounis, Salpigidis, Gekas (Amanatidis 84).
Referee: Styles (England).

Ta'Qali, 21 November 2007, 6000

Malta (0) 1 *(Michael Mifsud 53)*

Norway (3) 4 *(Iversen 25, 28 (pen), 45, Pedersen 75)*

Malta: Haber; Azzopardi, Wellmann, Dimech, Briffa, Pullicino, Pace, Woods (Barbara 84), Michael Mifsud (Scerri 89), Nwoko (Cohen 87), Schembri■.
Norway: Opdal; Storbaek, Riise J, Hangeland, Hagen, Pedersen, Riise B (Haestad 76), Skjelbred, Riseth, Carew (Helstad 68), Iversen (Rushfeldt 84).
Referee: Baskakov (Russia).

Istanbul, 21 November 2007, 22,000

Turkey (1) 1 *(Nihat 43)*

Bosnia (0) 0

Turkey: Rustu; Servet, Emre A, Gokhan G, Mehmet A, Hamit Altintop, Arda (Tuncay 76), Emre B, Hakan, Nihat (Gokdeniz 90), Semih (Sabri 61).
Bosnia: Guso; Bajic, Nadarevic, Berberovic, Krunic, Ibricic (Ibisevic 75), Rahimic, Merzic (Muharemovic 89), Misimovic, Maletic, Dzeko (Salihovic 83).
Referee: Braamhaar (Holland).

Group C Table	*P*	*W*	*D*	*L*	*F*	*A*	*Pts*
Greece	12	10	1	1	25	10	31
Turkey	12	7	3	2	25	11	24
Norway	12	7	2	3	27	11	23
Bosnia	12	4	1	7	16	22	13
Moldova	12	3	3	6	12	19	12
Hungary	12	4	0	8	11	22	12
Malta	12	1	2	9	10	31	5

GROUP D

Teplice, 2 September 2006, 16,204

Czech Republic (0) 2 *(Lafata 76, 89)*

Wales (0) 1 *(Jiranek 85 (og))*

Czech Republic: Cech; Ujfalusi, Jiranek, Rozehnal, Jankulovski, Stajner (Sionko 46), Galasek (Kovac R 87), Rosicky, Plasil, Kulic (Lafata 75), Koller.
Wales: Jones P; Delaney (Cotterill 78), Ricketts (Earnshaw 79), Robinson, Gabbidon, Collins J, Davies S, Fletcher (Ledley 47), Bellamy, Nyatanga, Giggs.
Referee: Eriksson (Sweden).

Stuttgart, 2 September 2006, 53,198

Germany (0) 1 *(Podolski 57)* **Republic of Ireland (0) 0**

Germany: Lehmann; Lahm, Friedrich A, Friedrich M, Jansen, Schneider (Borowski 83), Frings, Ballack, Schweinsteiger, Podolski (Neuville 76), Klose.
Republic of Ireland: Given; Carr, Finnan, Andy O'Brien, Dunne, O'Shea, Duff (McGeady 77), Reid S, Keane, Doyle K (Elliott 79), Kilbane (Alan O'Brien 83).
Referee: Kantalejo (Spain).

Bratislava, 2 September 2006, 4783

Slovakia (3) 6 *(Skrtel 9, Mintal 33, 56, Sebo 43, 49, Karhan 52)* **Cyprus (0) 1** *(Yiasoumis 90)*

Slovakia: Contofalsky; Zabavnik (Holosko 46), Skrtel, Durica, Cech, Hlinka, Karhan, Svento, Mintal, Nemeth (Krajcik 46), Sebo (Hodur 56).
Cyprus: Morfis; Theodotou, Lambrou, Louka (Theofilou 67), Michael, Charalambides, Makrides, Garpozis (Krassas 46), Okkas, Yiasoumis, Alexandrou (Elia 46).
Referee: Oriekhov (Ukraine).

Serravalle, 6 September 2006, 5019

San Marino (0) 0 Germany (6) 13 *(Podolski 11, 43, 64, 72, Schweinsteiger 28, 47, Klose 30, 45, Ballack 35, Hitzlsperger 66, 73, Friedrich M 87, Schneider 90 (pen))*

San Marino: Simoncini A; Albani, Della Valle, Bacciocchi, Palazzi, Valentini C, Vannucci (Simoncini D 68), Michele Marani (Masi 78), Domeniconi (Bonini 46), Manuel Marani, Selva A.
Germany: Lehmann; Jansen, Friedrich A, Lahm, Schweinsteiger, Frings (Hitzlsperger 62), Ballack (Odonkor 46), Schneider, Friedrich M, Klose (Asamoah 46), Podolski.
Referee: Selcuk (Turkey).

Bratislava, 6 September 2006, 27,683

Slovakia (0) 0

Czech Republic (2) 3 *(Sionko 10, 21, Koller 57)*

Slovakia: Contofalsky; Hlinka, Skrtel, Durica, Valachovic (Hodur 46), Svento, Cech (Nemeth 24), Krajcik, Karhan, Mintal, Sebo (Holosko 46).
Czech Republic: Cech; Jankulovski, Jiranek, Ujfalusi, Rozehnal, Polak (Kovac R 72), Galasek, Sionko (Stajner 77), Rosicky, Plasil, Koller.
Referee: Bennett (England).

Nicosia, 7 October 2006, 12,000

Cyprus (2) 5 *(Konstantinou M 10, 50 (pen), Garpozis 16, Charalambides 60, 75)*

Republic of Ireland (2) 2 *(Ireland 8, Dunne 44)*

Cyprus: Morfis; Satsias, Lambrou, Louka, Theodotou, Michael (Charalambides 46), Garpozis (Charalambous 77), Makrides, Okkas (Yiasoumis 86), Konstantinou M, Aloneftis.
Republic of Ireland: Kenny; Finnan, O'Shea, Andy O'Brien (Lee 71), Dunne■, Kilbane, McGeady (Alan O'Brien 80), Ireland (Douglas 83), Morrison, Keane, Duff.
Referee: Batista (Portugal).

Liberec, 7 October 2006, 9514

Czech Republic (4) 7 *(Kulic 15, Polak 22, Baros 28, 68, Koller 43, 52, Jarolim 49)* **San Marino (0) 0**

Czech Republic: Cech; Ujfalusi, Grygera, Rozehnal (Zapotocny 46), Jankulovski, Jarolim, Polak, Rosicky (Plasil 63), Baros, Kulic (Lafata 46), Koller.
San Marino: Valentini F; Albani, Della Valle, Bacciocchi, Andreini (Mariotti 82), Valentini C, Vannucci, Masi (Crescentini 69), Domeniconi, Moretti (Michele Marani 54), Selva A.
Referee: Aliyev (Azerbaijan).

Cardiff, 7 October 2006, 28,493

Wales (1) 1 *(Bale 37)* **Slovakia (3) 5** *(Svento 14, Mintal 32, 38, Karhan 51, Vittek 59)*

Wales: Jones P; Duffy, Bale, Gabbidon, Nyatanga, Robinson, Edwards (Ledley 58), Koumas, Davies S (Cotterill 88), Bellamy, Earnshaw (Parry 46).
Slovakia: Contofalsky; Kozak, Kratochvil, Petras M, Varga, Karhan (Krajcik 67), Mintal (Hodur 71), Vittek (Holosko 77), Petras P, Svento, Durica.
Referee: Egmond (Holland).

Dublin, 11 October 2006, 35,500

Republic of Ireland (0) 1 *(Kilbane 62)*

Czech Republic (0) 0

Republic of Ireland: Henderson; Kelly, Finnan, O'Shea, McShane, Carsley, Reid A (Quinn A 72), Douglas, Keane, Kilbane (Alan O'Brien 79), Duff.
Czech Republic: Cech; Polak, Ujfalusi, Kovac R, Jankulovski, Jiranek, Rosicky, Plasil (Grygera 85), Rozehnal, Koller, Baros (Jarolim 82).
Referee: Layec (France).

Bratislava, 11 October 2006, 21,582

Slovakia (0) 1 *(Varga 58)* **Germany (3) 4** *(Podolski 13, 72, Ballack 25, Schweinsteiger 36)*

Slovakia: Contofalsky; Petras P (Holosko 73), Varga, Skrtel, Durica, Karhan, Petras M, Svento, Kozak (Hodur 65), Mintal, Vittek.
Germany: Lehmann; Friedrich A, Friedrich M, Fritz, Lahm, Ballack, Frings, Schneider (Odonkor 75), Schweinsteiger (Trochowski 77), Klose, Podolski (Hanke 85).
Referee: Hauge (Norway).

Cardiff, 11 October 2006, 20,456

Wales (2) 3 *(Koumas 33, Earnshaw 39, Bellamy 72)*

Cyprus (0) 1 *(Okkas 83)*

Wales: Price; Duffy (Edwards 78), Bale, Gabbidon, Nyatanga, Robinson, Morgan, Koumas (Ledley 76), Earnshaw, Bellamy (Parry 90), Davies S.
Cyprus: Morfis; Theodotou, Lambrou, Louka, Satsias (Yiasoumis 84), Michael (Charalambides 46), Garpozis (Charalambous 46), Makrides, Aloneftis, Konstantinou M, Okkas.
Referee: Granat (Poland).

Nicosia, 15 November 2006, 15,000

Cyprus (1) 1 *(Okkas 43)* **Germany (1) 1** *(Ballack 16)*

Cyprus: Georgiallides; Elia, Lambrou, Louka, Theodotou (Charalambous 79), Makrides, Charalambides, Michael (Krassas 68), Okkas (Nicolaou 72), Aloneftis, Konstantinou M.
Germany: Hildebrand; Friedrich A, Lahm, Schweinsteiger, Frings, Ballack, Fritz, Friedrich M, Odonkor (Hitzlsperger 79), Klose, Neuville (Hanke 62).
Referee: Frojdfeldt (Sweden).

Dublin, 15 November 2006, 34,018

Republic of Ireland (3) 5 *(Simoncini D 7 (og), Doyle K 24, Robbie Keane 31, 58 (pen), 85)*

San Marino (0) 0

Republic of Ireland: Given; Finnan, O'Shea, Dunne, McShane, Carsley (Douglas 50), Reid A, Doyle K (McGeady 63), Keane, Duff, Kilbane (Lee 79).
San Marino: Valentini F; Bugli, Albani, Bacciocchi, Simoncini D (Bonini 81), Vannucci (Crescentini 72), Valentini C, Andreini, Mariotti (Michele Marani 59), Manuel Marani, Selva A.
Referee: Isaksen (Faeroes).

Serravalle, 7 February 2007, 3294

San Marino (0) 1 *(Manuel Marani 86)*

Republic of Ireland (0) 2 *(Kilbane 49, Ireland 90)*

San Marino: Simoncini A; Valentini C, Manuel Marani, Albani, Simoncini D, Muccioli, Bonini (Vannucci 76), Domeniconi (Bugli 88), Michele Marani, Selva A, Gasperoni A (Andreini 66).
Republic of Ireland: Henderson; Finnan, Harte (Hunt 74), Dunne, O'Shea (McShane 46), Carsley, Duff, Ireland, Keane, Long (Stokes 80), Kilbane.
Referee: Rasmussen (Denmark).

Nicosia, 24 March 2007, 2696

Cyprus (1) 1 *(Aloneftis 43)*

Slovakia (0) 3 *(Vittek 54, Skrtel 67, Jakubko 77)*

Cyprus: Morfis■; Satsias, Lambrou, Louka, Theodotou (Georgiallides 43), Michael, Charalambidis, Garpozis (Charalambous 66), Makrides (Elia 58), Yiasoumis, Aloneftis.
Slovakia: Cantofalsky; Singlar (Sofcak 46), Skrtel, Durica, Gresko, Borbely, Krajcik, Svento, Sapara (Kozak 68), Vittek, Jakubko (Sestak 79).
Referee: Lehner (Austria).

Prague, 24 March 2007, 17,821

Czech Republic (0) 1 *(Baros 77)*

Germany (1) 2 *(Schweinsteiger 42, Kuranyi 62)*

Czech Republic: Cech; Ujfalusi (Vlcek 84), Jiranek, Rozehnal, Jankulovski, Sionko (Plasil 46), Rosicky, Galasek (Kulic 67), Polak, Koller, Baros.
Germany: Lehmann; Lahm, Mertesacker, Metzelder, Jansen, Schneider, Frings, Ballack, Schweinsteiger, Podolski (Hitzlsperger 89), Kuranyi.
Referee: Rosetti (Italy).

Dublin, 24 March 2007, 72,539

Republic of Ireland (1) 1 *(Ireland 39)* **Wales (0) 0**

Republic of Ireland: Given; Finnan, O'Shea, Dunne, McShane, Carsley, Douglas (Hunt 80), Ireland (Doyle K 59), Keane (McGeady 89), Kilbane, Duff.
Wales: Coyne; Ricketts, Bale (Collins D 74), Collins J, Evans, Nyatanga, Ledley (Fletcher 46), Robinson (Easter 90), Davies S, Bellamy, Giggs.
Referee: Hauge (Norway).

Liberec, 28 March 2007, 9310

Czech Republic (1) 1 *(Kovac R 22)* **Cyprus (0) 0**

Czech Republic: Cech; Ujfalusi, Grygera (Kovac R 12) (Jiranek 27), Rozehnal, Jankulovski, Galasek, Rosicky, Polak, Jarolim, Koller, Baros (Plasil 77).
Cyprus: Georgiallides; Satsias, Lambrou, Theodotou, Paraskevas, Elia (Charalambous 76), Charalampidis (Krassas 75), Makrides, Yiasoumis (Chaili 72), Okkas, Aloneftis.
Referee: Bebek (Croatia).

Dublin, 28 March 2007, 71,297

Republic of Ireland (1) 1 *(Doyle K 12)* **Slovakia (0) 0**

Republic of Ireland: Given; O'Shea, Finnan, McShane, Dunne, Carsley, Ireland (Hunt 70), McGeady (Quinn A 87), Kilbane, Duff, Doyle K (Long 74).
Slovakia: Contofalsky; Singlar (Sestak 80), Skrtel, Klimpl, Gresko, Svento (Michalik 86), Zofcak, Borbely, Sapara (Holosko 72), Vittek, Jakubko.
Referee: Baskakov (Russia).

Cardiff, 28 March 2007, 18,752

Wales (2) 3 *(Giggs 3, Bale 20, Koumas 63 (pen))*
San Marino (0) 0

Wales: Coyne; Ricketts, Evans (Nyatanga 63), Collins J, Bale, Fletcher, Koumas, Davies S, Giggs (Parry 73), Bellamy, Easter (Cotterill 46).
San Marino: Simoncini A; Valentini C (Toccaceli 85), Andreini, Albani, Muccioli, Bacciocchi, Negri (Nanni 79), Domeniconi (Bugli 67), Manuel Marani, Selva A, Gasperoni A.
Referee: Tchagharyan (Armenia).

Nuremberg, 2 June 2007, 43,967

Germany (1) 6 *(Kuranyi 45, Jansen 52, Frings 56 (pen), Gomez 63, 65, Fritz 67)* **San Marino (0) 0**

Germany: Lehmann; Lahm (Helmes 70), Mertesacker, Metzelder, Jansen, Frings, Hilbert (Fritz 59), Hitzlsperger, Schneider, Klose, Kuranyi (Gomez 59).
San Marino: Simoncini A; Simoncini D■, Della Valle, Albani, Valentini C, Vannucci, Bugli (Vitaioli 85), Bacciocchi, Negri (Bonini 68), Gasperoni A, Manuel Marani (Domeniconi 77).
Referee: Asumaa (Finland).

Cardiff, 2 June 2007, 30,714

Wales (0) 0 Czech Republic (0) 0

Wales: Hennessey; Ricketts, Nyatanga, Gabbidon, Collins J, Robinson, Ledley, Koumas, Davies S, Giggs (Earnshaw 89), Bellamy.
Czech Republic: Cech; Ujfalusi, Kovac R, Rozehnal, Jankulovski, Polak (Jarolim 65), Sivok (Matejovsky 83), Rosicky, Plasil, Koller, Baros (Kulic 46).
Referee: Allaerts (Belgium).

Hamburg, 6 June 2007, 51,500

Germany (2) 2 *(Durica 10 (og), Hitzlsperger 43)*

Slovakia (1) 1 *(Metzelder 20 (og))*

Germany: Lehmann; Jansen, Lahm, Mertesacker, Metzelder, Fritz, Frings, Hitzlsperger, Schneider (Rolfes 90), Klose (Trochowski 74), Kuranyi (Gomez 65).
Slovakia: Contofalsky; Skrtel, Mansyk, Durica, Klimpl, Svento, Strba (Oravec 83), Krajcik, Sapara (Holosko 65), Sestak (Zofcak 65), Vittek.
Referee: Benquerenca (Portugal).

Serravalle, 22 August 2007, 522

San Marino (0) 0 Cyprus (0) 1 *(Okkas 53)*

San Marino: Simoncini A; Della Valle, Albani, Vannucci, Valentini C, Bollini G (Ciacci 77), Bugli, Bonini (Nanni 84), Bollini F (Andreini 63), Manuel Marani, Selva A.
Cyprus: Georgallides; Marangos (Nicolaou 24), Theodotou, Christou, Michael, Lambrou, Aloneftis, Yiasoumi (Charalambides 55), Konstantinou, Okkas, Garpozis (Charalambous 86).
Referee: Janku (Albania).

Serravalle, 8 September 2007, 3412

San Marino (0) 0

Czech Republic (1) 3 *(Rosicky 33, Jankulovski 75, Koller 90)*

San Marino: Simoncini A; Bollini G (Mariotti 85), Vannucci, Della Valle■, Valentini C, Simoncini D, Bugli (Vitaioli 67), Bonini, Bollini F (Andreini 58), Selva A, Manuel Marani.
Czech Republic: Cech; Ujfalusi, Rozehnal, Jankulovski, Galasek (Plasil 82), Kovac R, Jarolim (Polak 69), Rosicky, Kulic (Vlcek 56), Fenin, Koller.
Referee: Filipovic (Serbia).

Bratislava, 8 September 2007, 12,360

Slovakia (1) 2 *(Klimpl 37, Cech 90)*

Republic of Ireland (1) 2 *(Ireland 7, Doyle K 57)*

Slovakia: Senecky; Durica, Cech, Klimpl, Mintal, Hamsyk, Krajcik, Sapara (Sebo 71), Gresko, Sestak (Obzera 65), Holosko.
Republic of Ireland: Given; Kelly, O'Shea, Dunne, McShane, Carsley, Kilbane, Ireland (Douglas 76), Doyle K (Murphy 89), McGeady (Gibson 61), Keane.
Referee: Farina (Italy).

Millennium Stadium, 8 September 2007, 31,000

Wales (0) 0 Germany (1) 2 *(Klose 5, 60)*

Wales: Hennessey; Ricketts, Gabbidon, Bale, Nyatanga, Robinson, Ledley (Earnshaw 46), Davies S (Crofts 79), Koumas (Fletcher 67), Collins J, Eastwood.
Germany: Lehmann; Metzelder, Mertesacker, Jansen, Friedrich A, Hitzlsperger, Hilbert, Pander (Trochowski 46), Schweinsteiger, Kuranyi (Podolski 73), Klose (Helmes 87).
Referee: Gonzalez (Spain).

Nicosia, 12 September 2007, 600

Cyprus (2) 3 *(Makrides 15, Aloneftis 41, 90)*

San Marino (0) 0

Cyprus: Georgallides; Okkarides, Elia (Theodotou 76), Christou, Makrides, Charalambous (Garpozis 65), Nicolaou, Michael, Konstantinou, Aloneftis, Okkas (Yiasoumi 46).
San Marino: Valentini F; Albani (Benedettini 81), Vannucci, Valentini C, Bollini G, Andreini, Vitaioli, Bugli, Bonini (Mariotti 73), Michele Marani (Nanni 87), Selva A.
Referee: Kulbakou (Belarus).

Prague, 12 September 2007, 16,648

Czech Republic (1) 1 *(Jankulovski 15)*

Republic of Ireland (0) 0

Czech Republic: Cech; Ujfalusi, Rozehnal, Jankulovski, Polak, Plasil, Sionko (Vlcek 74), Kovac R, Rosicky, Galasek (Sivok 46), Baros (Jarolim 89).
Republic of Ireland: Given; Kelly, O'Shea (Hunt■ 38), Dunne, McShane, Kilbane, Duff, Reid A, Carsley (Keogh A 82), Keane, McGeady (Long 62).
Referee: Vassaras (Greece).

Trnava, 12 September 2007, 5486

Slovakia (1) 2 *(Mintal 12, 57)*

Wales (3) 5 *(Eastwood 22, Bellamy 34, 41, Durica 78 (og), Davies S 90)*

Slovakia: Senecky; Durica, Klimpl, Cech, Petras P, Mintal, Sapara, Hamsyk, Gresko (Zofcak 64), Sestak (Obzera 46), Holosko.
Wales: Hennessey; Bale, Ricketts, Collins J, Gabbidon, Morgan, Ledley (Vaughan 85), Robinson, Bellamy, Eastwood (Fletcher 73), Davies S.
Referee: Duhamel (France).

Nicosia, 13 October 2007, 8500

Cyprus (0) 3 *(Okkas 59, 68, Charalambides 79)*

Wales (1) 1 *(Collins J 21)*

Cyprus: Georgallides; Okkarides, Elia (Charalambides 63), Christou, Michael (Yiasoumi 46), Satsias (Marangos 71), Makrides, Aloneftis, Okkas, Garpozis, Nicolaou.
Wales: Coyne; Gabbidon, Bale, Ricketts (Easter 73), Nyatanga, Robinson, Davies S, Ledley, Collins J (Morgan 44), Bellamy, Eastwood (Earnshaw 58).
Referee: Bertolini (Switzerland).

Dublin, 13 October 2007, 67,495

Republic of Ireland (0) 0 Germany (0) 0

Republic of Ireland: Given; Kelly, O'Brien J, Dunne, Finnan, Carsley, Kilbane (Murphy 90), Reid A, Doyle K (Long 70), Keane, Keogh A (McGeady 80).
Germany: Lehmann; Mertesacker, Jansen, Friedrich A, Metzelder, Fritz, Trochowski (Castro 90), Schweinsteiger (Rolfes 18), Frings, Kuranyi, Gomez (Podolski 64).
Referee: Hansson (Sweden).

Dubnica, 13 October 2007, 2576

Slovakia (3) 7 *(Hamsyk 25, Sestak 32, 57, Sapara 37, Skrtel 51, Holosko 54, Durica 76 (pen))*

San Marino (0) 0

Slovakia: Contofalsky; Cech, Skrtel, Durica, Krajcik, Szabo, Kozak, Hamsyk, Sapara (Hesek 79), Holosko (Sebo 71), Sestak (Vascak 60).
San Marino: Valentini F; Andreini, Vitaioli, Albani, Vannucci, Della Valle, Valentini C, Bollini G (Benedettini 57), Nanni, Bugli (Bonifazzi 68), Manuel Marani (De Luigi 85).
Referee: Wilmes (Luxembourg).

Munich, 17 October 2007, 66,400

Germany (0) 0

Czech Republic (2) 3 *(Sionko 2, Matejovsky 23, Plasil 63)*

Germany: Hildebrand; Metzelder (Fritz 46), Mertesacker, Friedrich A, Jansen, Frings, Schweinsteiger (Gomez 65), Trochowski (Rolfes 46), Kuranyi, Podolski, Odonkor.
Czech Republic: Cech; Rozehnal, Ujfalusi, Galasek, Pudil (Kulic 73), Plasil, Matejovsky, Kovac R, Sionko (Vlcek 58), Pospech, Koller (Fenin 79).
Referee: Webb (England).

Dublin, 17 October 2007, 45,500

Republic of Ireland (0) 1 *(Finnan 90)*

Cyprus (0) 1 *(Okkarides 80)*

Republic of Ireland: Given; Finnan, O'Shea, McShane, O'Brien J (Miller 46), Kilbane, Reid A, Doyle K, Keane, Hunt (Murphy 73), Keogh A (McGeady 63).
Cyprus: Georgallides; Okkarides, Elia■, Christou, Makrides (Theofilou 86), Charalambides, Satsias (Marangos 69), Nicolaou, Yiasoumi (Michael 73), Okkas, Garpozis.
Referee: Vuorela (Finland).

Serravalle, 17 October 2007, 1182

San Marino (0) 1 *(Selva A 73)*

Wales (2) 2 *(Earnshaw 13, Ledley 36)*

San Marino: Simoncini A; Andreini, Albani■, Vannucci (Bugli 76), Valentini C, Della Valle, Simoncini D, Bonifazi (Bonini 62), Muccioli, Selva A, De Luigi (Vitaioli 80).
Wales: Price; Gabbidon, Bale, Eardley, Nyatanga, Robinson, Ledley, Earnshaw, Bellamy, Davies S, Vaughan (Ricketts 62).
Referee: Zammit (Malta).

Prague, 17 November 2007, 15,651

Czech Republic (1) 3 *(Grygera 14, Kulic 77, Rosicky 83)*

Slovakia (0) 1 *(Kadlec 79 (og))*

Czech Republic: Blazek; Grygera (Kadlec 46), Rozehnal, Kovac R, Rosicky, Polak (Matejovsky 85), Galasek, Plasil, Baros (Kulic 70), Koller, Pospech.
Slovakia: Contofalsky; Michalik, Cech, Skrtel, Strba, Krajcik, Kozak, Sapara, Hamsyk (Holosko 58), Mintal (Sestak 68), Kisel (Halenar 88).
Referee: Asumaa (Finland).

Hannover, 17 November 2007, 45,016

Germany (2) 4 *(Fritz 2, Klose 20, Podolski 53, Hitzlsperger 82)*

Cyprus (0) 0

Germany: Lehmann; Lahm, Friedrich A, Metzelder, Mertesacker, Fritz (Hilbert 77), Trochowski (Borowski 66), Hitzlsperger, Podolski, Klose, Gomez (Hanke 73).
Cyprus: Georgallides; Theodotou (Nicolaou 28), Christou, Lambrou, Charalambides (Theofilou 46), Satsias, Makrides, Konstantinou (Yiasoumi 69), Aloneftis, Okkas, Garpozis.
Referee: Rasmussen (Denmark).

Millennium Stadium, 17 November 2007, 24,619

Wales (1) 2 *(Koumas 23, 89 (pen))*

Republic of Ireland (1) 2 *(Keane 31, Doyle K 60)*

Wales: Hennessey; Gunter, Gabbidon, Eardley (Cotterill 81), Collins J, Robinson (Edwards 37), Fletcher, Ledley, Koumas, Eastwood (Easter 59), Davies S.
Republic of Ireland: Given; O'Shea, Finnan, McShane, Carsley, Kilbane, Reid A (Potter 87), Miller (Hunt 59), Doyle K, Keane, McGeady.
Referee: Oriekhov (Ukraine).

Nicosia, 21 November 2007, 8000

Cyprus (0) 0 Czech Republic (1) 2 *(Pudil 11, Koller 74)*

Cyprus: Georgallides; Christou, Lambrou, Charalambides (Yiasoumi 62), Nicolaou (Charalambous 56), Satsias, Makrides (Michael 84), Konstantinou M, Aloneftis, Okkas, Garpozis.
Czech Republic: Zitka; Kadlec, Rozehnal, Plasil (Kladrubsky 87), Matejovsky, Galasek, Pudil, Kovac R, Kulic (Baros 57), Pospech, Koller (Fenin 76).
Referee: Paniashvili (Georgia).

Frankfurt, 21 November 2007, 49,292

Germany (0) 0 Wales (0) 0

Germany: Lehmann; Lahm, Metzelder, Mertesacker, Fritz, Castro (Hilbert 57), Borowski, Hitzlsperger (Rolfes 46), Podolski, Klose, Gomez (Neuville 71).
Wales: Hennessey; Gunter, Ricketts, Gabbidon, Nyatanga, Collins J, Fletcher, Davies S, Edwards (Crofts 90), Earnshaw (Easter 56), Ledley.
Referee: Balaj (Romania).

Serravalle, 21 November 2007, 500

San Marino (0) 0

Slovakia (1) 5 *(Michalik 42, Holosko 51, Hamsyk 53, Cech 57, 83)*

San Marino: Valentini F; Bollini G (Berretti 61), Vannucci, Valentini C, Simoncini D, Della Valle, Muccioli, Michele Marani, Mauro Marani (Andreini 84), Manuel Marani, Selva A (De Luigi 50).
Slovakia: Senecky; Cech, Hubocan, Michalik, Krajcik (Petras P 63), Kozak, Kisel (Szabo 46), Hamsyk, Borbely, Holosko, Sestak (Halenar 75).
Referee: Sipailo (Latvia).

Group D Table	*P*	*W*	*D*	*L*	*F*	*A*	*Pts*
Czech Republic	12	9	2	1	27	5	29
Germany	12	8	3	1	35	7	27
Republic of Ireland	12	4	5	3	17	14	17
Slovakia	12	5	1	6	33	23	16
Wales	12	4	3	5	18	19	15
Cyprus	12	4	2	6	17	24	14
San Marino	12	0	0	12	2	57	0

GROUP E

Tallinn, 16 August 2006, 7500

Estonia (0) 0 Macedonia (0) 1 *(Sedloski 73)*

Estonia: Poom; Jaager, Stepanov, Piiroja, Kruglov, Dmitrijev, Terehhov, Klavan, Lindpere, Sidorenkov (Teever 67), Viikmae (Barengrub 90).
Macedonia: Nikolovski; Lazarevski, Petrov (Vasoski 87), Sedloski, Mitreski I, Noveski, Sumulikoski, Jancevski, Pandev (Tasevski 82), Naumoski (Stojkov 71), Maznov.
Referee: Jakobsson (Iceland).

Old Trafford, 2 September 2006, 56,290
England (3) 5 *(Crouch 5, 66, Gerrard 13, Defoe 38, 47)*
Andorra (0) 0
England: Robinson; Neville P (Lennon 65), Cole A, Hargreaves, Terry, Brown, Gerrard, Lampard, Crouch, Defoe (Johnson A 71), Downing (Richardson 64).
Andorra: Koldo; Lima A, Txema, Ayala, Sonejee, Javi Sanchez (Juli Sanchez 46), Sivera (Garcia 77), Vieira, Silva, Pujol (Jimenez 49), Ruiz.
Referee: Brugger (Austria).

Tallinn, 2 September 2006, 7800
Estonia (0) 0 Israel (1) 1 *(Colautti 8)*
Estonia: Poom; Jaager, Stepanov, Piiroja, Kruglov, Terehhov, Klavan, Dmitrijev (Teever 85), Viikmae (Vassiljev 69), Neemelo (Barengrub 85), Oper.
Israel: Awat; Gershon, Ben Haim, Badir, Tal, Zandberg (Ben Shushan 60), Afek, Ziv, Colautti, Benayoun, Katan (Alberman 72).
Referee: Verbist (Belgium).

Nijmegen, 6 September 2006, 5000
Israel (3) 4 *(Benayoun 9, Ben Shushan 11, Gershon 43 (pen), Tamuz Temile 69)* **Andorra (0) 1** *(Fernandez 84)*
Israel: Awat; Afek, Ben Haim, Gershon, Ziv, Tal, Badir (Alberman 76), Benayoun (Golan 69), Ben Shushan, Katan (Tamuz Temile 62), Colautti.
Andorra: Koldo; Bernaus, Txema, Lima A, Ayala, Silva■, Sonejee, Vieira (Moreno 67), Jimenez, Pujol (Garcia 46), Ruiz (Fernandez 54).
Referee: Zrnic (Bosnia).

Skopje, 6 September 2006, 16,500
Macedonia (0) 0 England (0) 1 *(Crouch 46)*
Macedonia: Nikolovski; Noveski, Petrov, Sedloski, Mitreski I, Lazarevski, Jancevski (Tasevski 52), Sumulikoski, Naumoski (Sakiri 74), Maznov (Stojkov 56), Pandev.
England: Robinson; Neville P, Cole A, Hargreaves, Terry, Ferdinand, Gerrard, Lampard (Carrick 84), Crouch (Johnson A 87), Defoe (Lennon 76), Downing.
Referee: Layec (France).

Moscow, 6 September 2006, 29,000
Russia (0) 0 Croatia (0) 0
Russia: Akinfeev; Ignashevich, Anyukov, Kolodin, Berezutski A, Izmailov, Aldonin, Semshov, Bilyaletdinov, Pavlyuchenko (Pogrebnyak 53), Arshavin.
Croatia: Pletikosa; Kovac R, Corluka, Sabljic, Seric, Kovac N, Modric, Kranjcar, Rapaic (Petric 58), Klasnic (Babic 88), Eduardo (Leko J 71).
Referee: Gonzalez (Spain).

Zagreb, 7 October 2006, 20,000
Croatia (2) 7 *(Petric 12, 37, 48, 50, Klasnic 58, Balaban 62, Modric 83)* **Andorra (0) 0**
Croatia: Pletikosa; Simic, Simunic, Kovac R, Corluka, Kovac N (Leko J 69), Modric, Klasnic, Kranjcar, Petric (Balaban 60), Eduardo (Babic 64).
Andorra: Koldo; Ayala, Rubio, Sonejee, Fernandez, Escura, Garcia (Jimenez 68), Vieira, Juli Sanchez (Toscano 53), Pujol, Sivera (Ruiz 60).
Referee: Zammit (Malta).

Old Trafford, 7 October 2006, 72,062
England (0) 0 Macedonia (0) 0
England: Robinson; Neville G, Cole A, Carrick, Terry, King, Gerrard, Lampard, Crouch, Rooney (Defoe 74), Downing (Wright-Phillips 70).
Macedonia: Nikolovski; Noveski, Petrov, Sedloski, Lazarevski, Mitreski I, Mitreski A, Sumulikoski, Maznov, Naumoski (Stojkov 46), Pandev (Tasevski 83).
Referee: Merk (Germany).

Moscow, 7 October 2006, 22,000
Russia (1) 1 *(Arshavin 5)* **Israel (0) 1** *(Ben Shushan 84)*
Russia: Akinfeev; Berezutski V, Ignashevich, Anyukov, Berezutski A, Smertin, Aldonin, Arshavin, Bilyaletdinov (Kerzhakov A 30), Zhirkov (Semshov 77), Pogrebnyak (Izmailov 57).
Israel: Awat; Ben Haim, Gershon (Ben-Yosef 46), Keise, Saban (Ben Shushan 46), Afek, Badir, Tal, Benayoun (Tamuz Temile 75), Alberman, Colautti.
Referee: Meyer (Germany).

La Vella, 11 October 2006, 300
Andorra (0) 0
Macedonia (3) 3 *(Pandev 13, Noveski 16, Naumoski 31)*
Andorra: Koldo; Txema, Ayala, Sonejee, Rubio, Garcia, Vieira, Pujol (Jimenez 87), Bernaus, Sivera■, Toscano (Ruiz 34).
Macedonia: Nikolovski; Noveski, Mitreski I, Sedloski, Petrov (Sakiri 80), Mitreski A, Sumulikoski, Lazarevski, Naumoski, Pandev (Tasevski 55), Maznov.
Referee: Silagava (Georgia).

Zagreb, 11 October 2006, 38,000
Croatia (0) 2 *(Eduardo 61, Neville G 69 (og))*
England (0) 0
Croatia: Pletikosa; Simic, Simunic, Kovac R, Corluka, Rapaic (Olic 76), Kovac N, Modric, Kranjcar (Babic 89), Eduardo (Leko J 81), Petric.
England: Robinson; Neville G, Cole A, Ferdinand, Terry, Carragher (Wright-Phillips 73), Carrick, Lampard, Crouch (Richardson 72), Rooney, Parker (Defoe 72).
Referee: Rosetti (Italy).

St Petersburg, 11 October 2006, 21,500
Russia (0) 2 *(Pogrebnyak 78, Sychev 90)* **Estonia (0) 0**
Russia: Akinfeev; Berezutski A, Berezutski V, Ignashevich, Anyukov, Bystrov, Titov, Bilyaletdinov (Saenko 90), Aldonin (Sychev 74), Arshavin, Kerzhakov A (Pogrebnyak 46).
Estonia: Poom; Allas (Purje 80), Jaager, Stepanov, Piiroja■, Kruglov, Terehhov (Rahn 81), Dmitrijev, Klavan, Teever (Gussev 80), Oper.
Referee: Braamhaar (Holland).

Tel Aviv, 15 November 2006, 45,000
Israel (1) 3 *(Colautti 8, 89, Benayoun 68)*
Croatia (2) 4 *(Srna 35 (pen), Eduardo 39, 54, 72)*
Israel: Awat; Afek, Ben Haim, Ben-Yosef, Keise, Alberman, Badir (Tamuz Temile 46), Tal, Katan (Ben Shushan 59), Benayoun, Colautti.
Croatia: Runje; Corluka, Simic, Kovac R, Simunic, Srna (Olic 88), Kovac N, Modric, Kranjcar (Babic 70), Eduardo (Leko J 81), Petric.
Referee: Gonzalez (Spain).

Skopje, 15 November 2006, 16,000
Macedonia (0) 0 Russia (2) 2 *(Bystrov 18, Arshavin 32)*
Macedonia: Nikoloski; Noveski, Petrov, Sedloski, Mitreski I, Lazarevski, Sumulikoski, Sakiri (Tasevski 35), Mitreski A (Jancevski 46) (Grozdanoski 71), Maznov, Stojkov.
Russia: Akinfeev; Berezutski V, Berezutski A, Kolodin, Bystrov, Bilyaletdinov, Semshov, Zhirkov, Titov, Arshavin (Pavlyuchenko 90), Pogrebnyak (Sychev 57).
Referee: Allaerts (Belgium).

Zagreb, 24 March 2007, 20,000
Croatia (0) 2 *(Srna 58, Eduardo 88)*
Macedonia (1) 1 *(Sedloski 38)*
Croatia: Pletikosa; Simic, Simunic, Corluka, Rapaic (Srna 46), Babic, Balaban (Budan 79), Kovac N, Modric, Kranjcar, Eduardo.
Macedonia: Nikolovski; Noveski, Popov R, Sedloski■, Lazarevski, Mitreski A (Jancevski 77), Sumulikoski, Maznov (Vajs 71), Naumoski (Tasevski 60), Pandev, Vasoski.
Referee: Plautz (Austria).

Tallinn, 24 March 2007, 11,000
Estonia (0) 0 Russia (0) 2 *(Kerzhakov A 66, 78)*
Estonia: Poom; Sisov (Neemelo 80), Lemsalu, Kruglov, Sidorenkov, Dmitrijev, Leetma (Kink 69), Lindpere, Klavan, Oper, Terehhov (Kams 52).
Russia: Akinfeev; Shishkin, Ignashevich, Anyukov, Torbinsky, Bilyaletdinov, Zurianov, Zhirkov, Bystrov (Saenko 90), Kerzhakov A (Sychev 83), Arshavin.
Referee: Ceferin (Slovenia).

Tel Aviv, 24 March 2007, 35,000
Israel (0) 0 England (0) 0
Israel: Awat; Ben Haim, Gershon, Ziv, Benado, Shpungin, Badir, Benayoun, Ben Shushan (Alberman 87), Tamuz Temile (Barda 75), Balali (Sahar 69).
England: Robinson; Neville P (Richards 72), Carragher, Gerrard, Ferdinand, Terry, Hargreaves, Lampard, Johnson A (Defoe 80), Rooney, Lennon (Downing 83).
Referee: Ovrebo (Norway).

Barcelona, 28 March 2007, 12,800
Andorra (0) 0 England (0) 3 *(Gerrard 54, 76, Nugent 90)*
Andorra: Koldo; Sonejee, Lima A, Ayala, Bernaus, Escura, Vieira, Garcia, Ruiz (Fernandez 88), Jimenez (Martinez 69), Toscano (Moreno 90).
England: Robinson; Richards (Dyer 61), Cole A, Hargreaves, Terry, Ferdinand, Lennon, Gerrard, Johnson A (Nugent 79), Rooney (Defoe 61), Downing.
Referee: Paixao (Portugal).

Tel Aviv, 28 March 2007, 23,658
Israel (2) 4 *(Tal 19, Colautti 29, Sahar 77, 80)*
Estonia (0) 0
Israel: Awat; Shpungin, Ben Haim, Gershon, Ziv, Tal (Toema 87), Badir, Benayoun, Ben Shushan (Alberman 70), Tamuz Temile (Sahar 64), Colautti.
Estonia: Poom; Sisov, Lemsalu, Barengrub, Oper, Kruglov, Dmitrijev, Rahn (Kink 39), Lindpere (Kams 80), Klavan, Neemelo (Konsa 61).
Referee: Cuneyt (Turkey).

Tallinn, 2 June 2007, 10,000
Estonia (0) 0 Croatia (1) 1 *(Eduardo 32)*
Estonia: Poom; Jaager, Stepanov, Piiroja, Kruglov, Dmitrijev, Lindpere (Kink 78), Klaven, Vassiljev, Konsa (Neemelo 71), Voskoboinikov.
Croatia: Pletikosa; Simunic, Kovac R, Corluka, Babic, Kovac N, Srna, Modric, Kranjcar (Leko J 74), Petric (Olic 53), Eduardo.
Referee: Kassai (Hungary).

Skopje, 2 June 2007, 14,500
Macedonia (1) 1 *(Stojkov 13)*
Israel (2) 2 *(Itzhaki 11, Colautti 44)*
Macedonia: Nikolovski; Noveski, Petrov, Lazarevski (Grozdanovski 46), Mitreski I, Vasoski, Naumoski (Ristic 46), Sumulikoski, Tasevski, Pandev (Polozani 55), Stojkov.
Israel: Awat; Shpungin, Keinan, Benado, Ziv, Tal, Badir, Alberman, Balali (Sahar 61), Colautti (Golan 81), Itzhaki (Zandberg 76).
Referee: Kircher (Germany).

St Petersburg, 2 June 2007, 21,500
Russia (2) 4 *(Kerzhakov A 8, 16, 49, Sychev 71)*
Andorra (0) 0
Russia: Malafeev; Berezutski V, Ignashevich, Berezutski A (Anyukov 46), Bystrov, Zurianov, Torbinsky, Semshov, Zhirkov (Budianski 57), Arshavin, Kerzhakov A (Sychev 54).
Andorra: Koldo; Txema, Oscar (Juli Sanchez 57), Bernaus, Ayala, Escura, Vieira, Pujol, Jimenez (Xavi 73), Ruiz, Moreno (Somoza 88).
Referee: Skjerven (Norway).

La Vella, 6 June 2007, 680
Andorra (0) 0
Israel (1) 2 *(Tamuz Temile 37, Colautti 53)*
Andorra: Koldo; Lima I, Txema (Sonejee 61), Lima A, Ayala, Escura, Garcia, Vieira, Bernaus, Ruiz, Toscano (Juli Sanchez 77).
Israel: Awat; Ziv, Benado, Yehiel, Ben Dayan, Tal, Benayoun, Alberman (Badir 71), Tamuz Temile (Katan 77), Colautti (Golan 86), Itzhaki.
Referee: Stokes (Republic of Ireland).

Zagreb, 6 June 2007, 35,000
Croatia (0) 0 Russia (0) 0
Croatia: Pletikosa; Corluka, Simic, Kovac R, Simunic, Srna (Leko J 8), Kovac N, Modric, Kranjcar (Petric 66), Eduardo, Olic (Babic 83).
Russia: Malafeev; Berezutski V, Ignashevich, Berezutski A, Bystrov (Saenko 61), Anyukov, Zhirkov, Semshov, Budianski (Torbinsky 46), Arshavin, Kerzhakov A (Sychev 73).
Referee: Lubos (Slovakia).

Tallinn, 6 June 2007, 11,000
Estonia (0) 0
England (1) 3 *(Cole J 37, Crouch 54, Owen 62)*
Estonia: Poom; Jaager, Stepanov, Kruglov, Klavan, Dmitrijev, Lindpere, Vassilijev, Konsa (Neemelo 46), Voskoboinikov, Terehhov (Kink 64).
England: Robinson; Brown, Bridge, Gerrard, Terry, King, Beckham (Dyer 68), Lampard, Crouch, Owen (Jenas 88), Cole J (Downing 75).
Referee: Gilewski (Poland).

Tallinn, 22 August 2007, 7500
Estonia (1) 2 *(Piiroja 34, Zelinski 90)*
Andorra (0) 1 *(Silva 87)*
Estonia: Poom; Jaager, Piiroja, Stepanov, Kruglov, Klavan■, Dmitrijev, Reim, Lindpere, Zelinski■, Voskoboinikov (Kink 46).
Andorra: Koldo; Txema, Lima I, Lima A, Sivera (Toscano 53), Escura, Ayala (Garcia 90), Vieira, Sonejee, Silva, Pujol (Sanchez 80).
Referee: McCourt (Northern Ireland).

Zagreb, 8 September 2007, 20,000
Croatia (2) 2 *(Eduardo 39, 45)*
Estonia (0) 0
Croatia: Pletikosa; Corluka, Simunic, Simic, Kovac R, Srna (Babic 82), Modric, Kranjcar (Rakitic 60), Kovac N, Petric (Olic 70), Eduardo.
Estonia: Londak; Stepanov, Allas, Rooba U (Anniste 84), Rahn, Kruglov, Piiroja, Dmitrijev, Lindpere (Reim 90), Oper, Kink (Saag 80).
Referee: Laperriere (Switzerland).

Wembley, 8 September 2007, 85,372
England (1) 3 *(Wright-Phillips 20, Owen 49, Richards 66)*
Israel (0) 0
England: Robinson; Richards, Cole A, Gerrard (Neville P 71), Terry, Ferdinand, Wright-Phillips (Bentley 83), Barry, Heskey (Johnson A 71), Owen, Cole J.
Israel: Awat; Gershon, Shpungin, Benado (Golan 58), Ben Haim, Badir, Tal, Benayoun, Itzhaki (Tamuz 46), Ziv, Katan (Zandberg 73).
Referee: Vink (Holland).

Moscow, 8 September 2007, 26,000
Russia (1) 3 *(Berezutski V 8, Arshavin 84, Kerzhakov A 88)*
Macedonia (0) 0
Russia: Gabulov■; Ignashevich, Berezutski A, Berezutski V, Zyryanov, Bistrov (Anyukov 89), Semshov, Bilyaletdinov, Arshavin, Sychev (Malafeev 70), Pavlyuchenko (Kerzhakov A 66).
Macedonia: Milosevski; Sedloski, Lazarevski, Vasoski (Toleski 87), Mitreski I, Mitreski A (Trajanov 46), Popov G, Tasevski, Pandev, Sumulikoski, Stojkov (Maznov 46).
Referee: Ovrebo (Norway).

La Vella, 12 September 2007, 200
Andorra (0) 0
Croatia (3) 6 *(Srna 34, Petric 38, 44, Kranjcar 49, Eduardo 55, Rakitic 64)*
Andorra: Koldo; Txema, Lima A, Sivera (Andorra 59), Ayala, Vieira, Sonejee, Jimenez, Garcia■, Silva (Moreno 57), Ruiz (Somoza 82).
Croatia: Runje; Corluka, Kovac R, Knezevic, Leko J, Srna, Kranjcar, Babic, Modric (Pranjic 46), Petric (Balaban 46), Eduardo (Rakitic 62).
Referee: Thual (France).

Wembley, 12 September 2007, 86,106
England (2) 3 *(Owen 7, 31, Ferdinand 84)*
Russia (0) 0
England: Robinson; Richards, Cole A, Gerrard, Terry, Ferdinand, Wright-Phillips, Barry, Heskey (Crouch 80), Owen (Downing 90), Cole J (Neville P 88).

Russia: Malafeev; Ignashevich, Anyukov (Kerzhakov A 80), Berezutski V, Berezutski A, Zyryanov, Zhirkov, Bilyaletdinov, Semshov (Bistrov 40), Arshavin, Sychev (Pavlyuchenko 63).
Referee: Hansson (Sweden).

Skopje, 12 September 2007, 5000
Macedonia (1) 1 *(Maznov 30)* **Estonia (1) 1** *(Piiroja 17)*
Macedonia: Milosevski; Lazarevski, Vasoski, Sedloski, Noveski, Grozdanovski, Trajanov (Polozani 46), Tasevski, Sumulikoski, Stojkov (Toleski 81), Maznov.
Estonia: Londak; Jaager, Stepanov, Rahn (Reim 62), Kruglov, Piiroja, Klavan, Dmitrijev, Lindpere, Oper (Anniste 90), Saag (Kink 79).
Referee: Trattou (Cyprus).

Zagreb, 13 October 2007, 16,000
Croatia (0) 1 *(Eduardo 52)* **Israel (0) 0**
Croatia: Pletikosa; Corluka, Simunic, Simic, Kovac R, Srna, Modric, Leko J, Kranjcar (Pranjic 46), Olic (Rakitic 81), Eduardo.
Israel: Davidovich; Antebi, Meshumar, Ben Haim, Gershon, Alberman, Cohen T, Baruchian (Toema 58), Benayoun, Barda (Ohayon 78), Balili (Tamuz 67).
Referee: Stark (Germany).

Wembley, 13 October 2007, 86,655
England (3) 3 *(Wright-Phillips 11, Rooney 32, Rahn 33 (og))*
Estonia (0) 0
England: Robinson; Richards, Cole A (Neville P 49), Gerrard, Campbell, Ferdinand (Lescott 46), Wright-Phillips, Barry, Rooney, Owen (Lampard 70), Cole J.
Estonia: Poom; Piiroja, Jaager, Stepanov, Kruglov, Rahn, Klavan, Dmitrijev, Lindpere, Saag, Kink (Viikmae 62).
Referee: Vollquartz (Denmark).

Skopje, 17 October 2007, 18,000
Macedonia (2) 3 *(Naumoski 30, Sedloski 44, Pandev 59)*
Andorra (0) 0
Macedonia: Pachovski; Lazarevski, Noveski, Sedloski, Mitreski I, Pandev, Tasevski (Trajanov 84), Popov G, Sumulikoski, Maznov (Ristic 62), Naumoski (Polozani 75).
Andorra: Koldo; Lima I, Fernandez, Escura, Ayala, Vieira, Toscano (Riera 82), Jimenez (Somoza 78), Sonejee, Pujol, Ruiz (Andorra 63).
Referee: Malzinskas (Lithuania).

Moscow, 17 October 2007, 84,700
Russia (0) 2 *(Pavlyuchenko 70 (pen), 73)*
England (1) 1 *(Rooney 29)*
Russia: Gabulov; Ignashevich, Anyukov, Berezutski V (Torbinskiy 46), Berezutski A, Zyryanov, Zhirkov, Bilyaletdinov, Semshov, Arshavin (Kolodin 90), Kerzhakov A (Pavlyuchenko 58).
England: Robinson; Richards, Lescott (Lampard 79), Gerrard, Campbell, Ferdinand, Wright-Phillips (Crouch 80), Barry, Rooney, Owen, Cole J (Downing 81).
Referee: Cantalejo (Spain).

La Vella, 17 November 2007, 200
Andorra (0) 0 **Estonia (1) 2** *(Oper 31, Lindpere 60)*
Andorra: Koldo; Lima I (Ruiz 81), Sivera, Lima A, Rubio, Garcia (Vieira 46), Ayala, Sonejee, Jimenez, Pujol, Moreno (Toscano 70).
Estonia: Londak; Jaager, Stepanov, Kruglov (Vassiljev 84), Piiroja, Klavan, Dmitrijev, Reim (Teniste 68), Lindpere, Oper (Kink 46), Saag.
Referee: Collum (Scotland).

Tel Aviv, 17 November 2007, 27,563
Israel (1) 2 *(Barda 10, Golan 90)*
Russia (0) 1 *(Bilyaletdinov 61)*
Israel: Awat; Keinan, Shpungin, Ben Haim, Alberman, Cohen T, Barda, Itzhaki (Ben Shushan 62), Ziv, Buzaglo (Ohayon 64), Sahar (Golan 69).
Russia: Gabulov; Ignashevich, Anyukov, Berezutski V (Pogrebnyak 68), Berezutski A, Zyryanov, Zhirkov, Bilyaletdinov, Semshov (Torbinskiy 30), Arshavin, Pavlyuchenko (Sychev 52).
Referee: Farina (Italy).

Skopje, 17 November 2007, 18,000
Macedonia (0) 2 *(Maznov 71, Naumoski 79)*
Croatia (0) 0
Macedonia: Milosevski; Noveski, Lazarevski, Mitreski I, Sedloski (Grncarov 89), Tasevski, Grozdanovski, Popov G, Sumulikoski, Naumoski (Polozani 78), Maznov.
Croatia: Pletikosa; Corluka, Simunic, Simic, Kovac R, Srna, Modric, Kranjcar (Vukojevic 75), Kovac N, Petric (Mandzukic 42), Eduardo (Olic 54).
Referee: De Bleeckere (Belgium).

La Vella, 21 November 2007, 1000
Andorra (0) 0 **Russia (1) 1** *(Sychev 39)*
Andorra: Koldo (Gomes 46); Escura, Lima I, Lima A, Sivera, Bernaus, Vieira (Andorra 50), Sonejee (Riera 83), Jimenez, Ruiz, Pujol.
Russia: Gabulov; Anyukov, Berezutski V (Torbinskiy 38), Berezutski A, Kolodin, Zyrynaov, Zhirkov, Bilyaletdinov, Kerzhakov A, Arshavin■, Sychev.
Referee: Hauge (Norway).

Wembley, 21 November 2007, 88,091
England (0) 2 *(Lampard 56 (pen), Crouch 65)*
Croatia (2) 3 *(Kranjcar 8, Olic 14, Petric 77)*
England: Carson; Lescott, Bridge, Gerrard, Campbell, Richards, Wright-Phillips (Beckham 46), Barry (Defoe 46), Crouch, Lampard, Cole J (Bent D 80).
Croatia: Pletikosa; Corluka, Simunic, Simic, Kovac R, Srna, Modric, Kranjcar (Pranjic 75), Kovac N, Olic (Rakitic 84), Eduardo (Petric 69).
Referee: Frojdfeldt (Sweden).

Tel Aviv, 21 November 2007, 2736
Israel (1) 1 *(Barda 35)* **Macedonia (0) 0**
Israel: Awat; Keinan, Ben Haim, Shpungin, Cohen T, Ohayon, Itzhaki (Baruchian 72), Barda, Ziv, Colautti (Sahar 55), Buzaglo (Ben Shushan 46).
Macedonia: Milosevski; Lazarevski, Noveski, Mitreski I, Sedloski, Popov G, Tasevski (Polozani 46), Grozdanovski (Georgievski 66), Sumulikoski, Stojkov, Maznov (Ristic 60).
Referee: Mikulski (Poland).

Group E Table	*P*	*W*	*D*	*L*	*F*	*A*	*Pts*
Croatia	12	9	2	1	28	8	29
Russia	12	7	3	2	18	7	24
England	12	7	2	3	24	7	23
Israel	12	7	2	3	20	12	23
Macedonia	12	4	2	6	12	12	14
Estonia	12	2	1	9	5	21	7
Andorra	12	0	0	12	2	42	0

GROUP F

Riga, 2 September 2006, 7500
Latvia (0) 0
Sweden (1) 1 *(Kallstrom 38)*
Latvia: Kolinko; Stepanovs, Astafjevs, Zirnis (Karlsons 83), Laizans (Visnakovs 86), Smirnovs, Bleidelis, Verpakovskis, Rubins, Prohorenkovs (Pahars 57), Klava.
Sweden: Shaaban; Nilsson, Mellberg, Hansson, Edman, Linderoth, Alexandersson, Kallstrom (Anders Svensson 71), Ljungberg, Ibrahimovic, Elmander (Wilhelmsson 81).
Referee: Ceferin (Slovenia).

Belfast, 2 September 2006, 14,500
Northern Ireland (0) 0 **Iceland (3) 3** *(Thorvaldsson 13, Hreidarsson 20, Gudjohnsen E 37)*
Northern Ireland: Taylor; Baird, Capaldi (Duff 76), Davis, Hughes, Craigan, Gillespie, Clingan, Quinn (Feeney 83), Healy, Elliott (Lafferty 63).
Iceland: Arason; Steinsson, Sigurdsson I, Ingimarsson, Hreidarsson, Gunnarsson B (Gislason 75), Arnason (Danielsson 55), Gudjonsson J, Gudjohnsen E, Sigurdsson H (Jonsson H 64), Thorvaldsson.
Referee: Skjerven (Norway).

Badajoz, 2 September 2006, 14,876
Spain (2) 4 *(Fernando Torres 20, David Villa 45, 62, Luis Garcia 66)* **Liechtenstein (0) 0**
Spain: Casillas; Sergio Ramos, Puyol, Pablo, Pernia, Albelda (Oubina 69), Xabi Alonso, Fabregas (Iniesta 63), Raul, Fernando Torres, David Villa (Luis Garcia 63).
Liechtenstein: Jehle; Telser (Fischer 56), Maierhofer, Hasler, Martin Stocklasa, Burgmeier, Buchel M, Ritzberger, D'Elia, Beck T (Beck R 69), Frick M (Rohrer 86).
Referee: Bozinovski (Macedonia).

Reykjavik, 6 September 2006, 10,007
Iceland (0) 0 Denmark (2) 2 *(Rommedahl 5, Tomasson 33)*
Iceland: Arason; Steinsson, Sigurdsson I, Hreidarsson, Ingimarsson, Jonsson H (Gunnarsson V 66), Gunnarsson B (Gislason 76), Arnason (Vidarsson 82), Gudjonsson J, Gudjohnsen E, Thorvaldsson.
Denmark: Sorensen T; Jacobsen, Gravgaard, Agger, Poulsen, Kahlenberg (Jensen C 82), Gravesen (Jensen D 70), Kristiansen, Tomasson, Jorgensen (Helveg 90), Rommedahl.
Referee: Ivanov (Russia).

Belfast, 6 September 2006, 14,500
Northern Ireland (1) 3 *(Healy 20, 64, 80)*
Spain (1) 2 *(Xavi 14, David Villa 52)*
Northern Ireland: Carroll (Taylor 12); Duff, Hughes, Craigan, Evans, Gillespie, Clingan, Davis, Baird, Healy (Feeney 85), Lafferty (Quinn 54).
Spain: Casillas; Sergio Ramos (Michel Salgado 46), Puyol, Pablo, Antonio Lopez, Albelda (Fabregas 29), Xavi, Xabi Alonso, Fernando Torres (Luis Garcia 63), David Villa, Raul.
Referee: De Bleeckere (Belgium).

Gothenburg, 6 September 2006, 17,735
Sweden (1) 3 *(Allback 2, 69, Rosenberg 89)*
Liechtenstein (1) 1 *(Frick M 27)*
Sweden: Shaaban; Nilsson, Hansson, Lucic, Edman, Linderoth, Alexandersson, Kallstrom (Anders Svensson 57), Ljungberg, Allback, Elmander (Rosenberg 82).
Liechtenstein: Jehle; Hasler, Ritter, Maierhofer (D'Elia 89), Buchel M, Martin Stocklasa, Fischer (Buchel R 55), Frick D, Ritzberger, Beck T (Burgmeier 42), Frick M.
Referee: Banari (Moldova).

Copenhagen, 7 October 2006, 41,482
Denmark (0) 0 Northern Ireland (0) 0
Denmark: Sorensen T (Christiansen 68); Jacobsen, Gravgaard, Agger, Jensen N (Bendtner 73), Jensen D, Poulsen, Kahlenberg, Tomasson, Jorgensen, Lovenkrands (Jensen C 55).
Northern Ireland: Taylor; Duff, Hughes, Craigan, Baird, Clingan (Johnson 56), Davis, Evans, Gillespie, Lafferty (Jones 63), Healy (Feeney 84).
Referee: Plautz (Austria).

Riga, 7 October 2006, 7500
Latvia (3) 4 *(Karlsons 14, Verpakovskis 15, 25, Visnakovs 52)*
Iceland (0) 0
Latvia: Kolinko; Stepanovs, Astafjevs, Zirnis, Laizans, Klava (Kacanovs 82), Smirnovs, Bleidelis (Visnakovs 46), Verpakovskis (Pahars 57), Solonicins, Karlsons.
Iceland: Arason; Steinsson, Sigurdsson K, Gislason, Ingimarsson, Sigurdsson H (Hallfredsson 71), Hreidarsson, Gunnarsson B, Gudjohnsen E, Gudjonsson J (Gunnarsson V 46), Arnason (Danielsson 42).
Referee: Kelly (Republic of Ireland).

Solna, 7 October 2006, 33,056
Sweden (1) 2 *(Elmander 10, Allback 82)* **Spain (0) 0**
Sweden: Shaaban; Nilsson, Mellberg, Hansson, Edman, Linderoth, Alexandersson, Ljungberg (Wilhelmsson 56), Anders Svensson (Kallstrom 75), Elmander (Andersson D 77), Allback.
Spain: Casillas; Sergio Ramos, Puyol, Juanito, Capdevila (Puerta 52), Albelda, Angulo (Luis Garcia 59), Fabregas (Iniesta 46), Xavi, David Villa, Fernando Torres.
Referee: Bennett (England).

Reykjavik, 11 October 2006, 8725
Iceland (1) 1 *(Vidarsson 6)*
Sweden (1) 2 *(Kallstrom 8, Wilhelmsson 59)*
Iceland: Arason; Ingimarsson, Steinsson, Hreidarsson, Sigurdsson K, Sigurdsson I (Jonsson H 51), Gudjonsson J (Baldvinsson 81), Vidarsson, Hallfredsson, Sigurdsson H, Gudjohnsen E.
Sweden: Shaaban; Nilsson, Antonsson, Hansson, Edman, Alexandersson, Andersson D, Kallstrom, Wilhelmsson, Allback (Rosenberg 79), Elmander (Majstorovic 90).
Referee: Gilewski (Poland).

Vaduz, 11 October 2006, 2700
Liechtenstein (0) 0
Denmark (2) 4 *(Jensen D 29, Gravgaard 32, Tomasson 51, 64)*
Liechtenstein: Jehle; Telser, Hasler, Ritter, Martin Stocklasa, Fischer (D'Elia 80), Beck T, Frick M, Burgmeier (Frick D 62), Buchel M, Oehri.
Denmark: Christiansen; Poulsen, Gravgaard, Agger, Jensen N, Jacobsen, Jensen D (Sorensen D 46), Kahlenberg (Jensen C 64), Tomasson, Jorgensen, Rommedahl (Krohn-Dehli 78).
Referee: Richards (Wales).

Belfast, 11 October 2006, 14,500
Northern Ireland (1) 1 *(Healy 35)* **Latvia (0) 0**
Northern Ireland: Taylor; Baird, Evans, Craigan, Hughes, Davis, Gillespie, Johnson, Lafferty (Quinn 88), Healy (Feeney 90), Clingan.
Latvia: Kolinko; Stepanovs, Astafjevs, Zirnis, Laizans, Kacanovs, Solonicins (Visnakovs 85), Smirnovs (Gorkss 46), Verpakovskis (Kalnins 78), Karlsons, Pahars.
Referee: Fleischer (Germany).

Vaduz, 24 March 2007, 4340
Liechtenstein (0) 1 *(Burgmeier 89)*
Northern Ireland (0) 4 *(Healy 52, 75, 83, McCann 90)*
Liechtenstein: Jehle; Oehri (Telser 68), Martin Stocklasa, Ritter, Michael Stocklasa, Buchel M, Buchel R (Frick D 88), Burgmeier, Beck T, Frick M, Rohrer (Buchel S 84).
Northern Ireland: Taylor; Duff, Johnson, Evans, Hughes, Craigan, Brunt (McCann 68), Davis, Lafferty (Feeney 56), Healy (Jones 84), Gillespie.
Referee: Oriekhov (Ukraine).

Madrid, 24 March 2007, 80,000
Spain (2) 2 *(Morientes 34, David Villa 45)*
Denmark (0) 1 *(Gravgaard 49)*
Spain: Casillas; Javi Navarro, Marchena, Capdevila, Angel, Xavi (Xabi Alonso 60), Iniesta, Silva, Albelda, Morientes (Fernando Torres 64), David Villa (Angulo 76).
Denmark: Sorensen T; Agger, Gravgaard, Jacobsen, Jensen N■, Poulsen, Jensen D, Kahlenberg (Gronkjaer 60), Rommedahl, Jorgensen (Andreasen 38) (Bendtner 73), Tomasson.
Referee: Busacca (Switzerland).

Vaduz, 28 March 2007, 1680
Liechtenstein (1) 1 *(Frick M 17)* **Latvia (0) 0**
Liechtenstein: Jehle; Telser, Martin Stocklasa, Hasler, Michael Stocklasa, Buchel M, Buchel R, Burgmeier, Frick M, Beck T (Fischer 76), Rohrer (Buchel S 90).
Latvia: Kolinko; Kacanovs, Gorkss (Prohorenkovs 79), Stepanovs, Klava, Bleidelis, Morozs (Pereplyotkin 61), Laizans, Visnakovs, Verpakovskis (Karlsons 46), Pahars.
Referee: Gumienny (Belgium).

Belfast, 28 March 2007, 14,500
Northern Ireland (1) 2 *(Healy 31, 58)*
Sweden (1) 1 *(Elmander 26)*
Northern Ireland: Taylor; Duff, Hughes, Craigan, Evans, Johnson, McCann, Davis, Brunt (Sproule 90), Healy (Webb 89), Feeney (Lafferty 79).
Sweden: Isaksson; Nilsson, Mellberg (Majstorovic 69), Hansson, Edman, Alexandersson (Wilhelmsson 61), Andersson D, Anders Svensson (Kallstrom 46), Ljungberg, Ibrahimovic, Elmander.
Referee: Braamhaar (Holland).

Mallorca, 28 March 2007, 20,000
Spain (0) 1 *(Iniesta 80)* **Iceland (0) 0**

Spain: Casillas; Sergio Ramos, Marchena, Puyol, Capdevila (Angulo 46), Iniesta, Albelda (Xabi Alonso 78), Xavi, Silva, David Villa, Morientes (Fernando Torres 43).
Iceland: Arason; Sigurdsson K, Bjarnason O, Ingimarsson, Gunnarsson G, Steinsson, Vidarsson (Sigurdsson H 83), Gunnarsson B, Hallfredsson (Sigurdsson I 74), Gunnarsson V (Gislason 56), Gudjonsen.
Referee: Duhamel (France).

Copenhagen, 2 June 2007, 42,083
Denmark (1) 3 *(Agger 34, Tomasson 62, Andreasen 75)*
Sweden (3) 3 *(Elmander 7, 26, Hansson 23)*

Denmark: Sorensen T; Gravgaard, Agger, Jacobsen, Poulsen■, Kristiansen (Andreasen 34), Jensen D (Gronkjaer 63), Kahlenberg (Bendtner 47), Rommedahl, Tomasson, Jorgensen.
Sweden: Isaksson; Nilsson, Mellberg, Hansson, Alexandersson, Wilhelmsson, Linderoth, Anders Svensson, Ljungberg, Allback (Bakircioglu 80), Elmander (Rosenberg 74).
Match abandoned 89 minutes; awarded to Sweden 3-0.
Referee: Fandel (Germany).

Reykjavik, 2 June 2007, 5139
Iceland (1) 1 *(Gunnarsson B 27)*
Liechtenstein (0) 1 *(Rohrer 69)*

Iceland: Arason; Steinsson, Sigurdsson K, Ingimarsson, Gunnarsson G, Gislason, Hallfredsson (Bjarnason T 82), Gunnarsson B, Gudjohnsen E, Gunnarsson V (Sigurdsson H 72), Gudmundsson M (Saevarsson 70).
Liechtenstein: Jehle; Michael Stocklasa, Hasler, Martin Stocklasa, Buchel R, Beck T (Beck R 87), Frick M, Burgmeier (Frick D 78), Steuble, Rohrer, Ritzberger.
Referee: Kaldma (Estonia).

Riga, 2 June 2007, 8000
Latvia (0) 0 Spain (1) 2 *(David Villa 45, Xavi 60)*

Latvia: Kolinko; Zirnis, Ivanovs, Zakresevskis, Klava, Bleidelis (Pereplyotkin 86), Astafjevs, Laizans, Rubins (Solonicins 65), Verpakovskis, Karlsons (Cauna 89).
Spain: Casillas; Sergio Ramos, Puyol, Marchena, Capdevila, Angulo (Joaquin 46), Albelda (Xabi Alonso 67), Xavi, Iniesta, Luis Garcia (Soldado 55), David Villa.
Referee: Thomson (Scotland).

Riga, 6 June 2007, 7500
Latvia (0) 0 Denmark (2) 2 *(Rommedahl 15, 17)*

Latvia: Kolinko; Zirnis, Klava, Ivanovs, Stepanovs, Rubins (Cauna 75), Astafjevs, Laizans, Bleidelis (Solonicins 66), Verpakovskis, Karlsons (Pahars 61).
Denmark: Sorensen T; Jacobsen, Laursen M, Agger, Jensen N, Jensen D, Jorgensen, Tomasson, Rommedahl (Kahlenberg 46), Bendtner (Wurtz 60), Gronkjaer.
Referee: Trefoloni (Italy).

Vaduz, 6 June 2007, 5739
Liechtenstein (0) 0 Spain (2) 2 *(David Villa 8, 14)*

Liechtenstein: Jehle; Michael Stocklasa (Telser 29), Hasler, Martin Stocklasa, Ritzberger, Buchel R, Burgmeier, Polverino, Rohrer (Frick D 59), Frick M, Beck T (Beck R 82).
Spain: Reina; Javi Navarro, Marchena, Sergio Ramos, Capdevila (Antonio Lopez 52), Xabi Alonso, Iniesta, Joaquin, Fabregas (Luis Garcia 67), Silva (Soldado 77), David Villa.
Referee: Ivanov (Russia).

Stockholm, 6 June 2007, 33,358
Sweden (3) 5 *(Allback 11, 51, Anders Svensson 42, Mellberg 45, Rosenberg 50)*
Iceland (0) 0

Sweden: Isaksson; Alexandersson, Mellberg, Hansson, Nilsson (Schlebrugge 57), Wilhelmsson, Linderoth (Andersson D 62), Anders Svensson, Ljungberg, Rosenberg, Allback (Ibrahimovic 73).
Iceland: Arason; Steinsson (Sigurdsson K 90), Gunnarsson G, Bjarnason O, Ingimarsson, Bjarnason T, Vidarsson, Hallfredsson (Jonsson H 53), Gunnarsson B, Sigurdsson H, Saevarsson (Gudmundsson M 65).
Referee: Hamer (Luxembourg).

Windsor Park, 22 August 2007, 20,322
Northern Ireland (2) 3 *(Healy 5, 35, Lafferty 56)*
Liechtenstein (0) 1 *(Frick M 89)*

Northern Ireland: Taylor; McCartney, Duff, Baird, Craigan, Brunt (Elliott 62), Davis, Clingan, Gillespie (Jones 85), Lafferty (Feeney 75), Healy.
Liechtenstein: Jehle; Michael Stocklasa (Oehri 39), Martin Stocklasa, Telser, Biedermann (Buchel S 62), Rohrer (Beck R 74), Buchel R, Frick M, Frick D, D'Elia, Polverino.
Referee: Matejek (Czech Republic).

Reykjavik, 8 September 2007, 9483
Iceland (1) 1 *(Hallfredsson 40)* **Spain (0) 1** *(Iniesta 86)*

Iceland: Arason; Hreidarsson, Steinsson, Sigurdsson R, Hallfredsson, Gudjonsson J (Adalsteinsson 79), Sigurdsson K, Arnason, Ingimarsson, Vidarsson (Skulason 69), Thorvaldsson (Bjornsson 88).
Spain: Casillas; Marchena, Juanito, Sergio Ramos, Pernia (Albelda 26), Silva, Joaquin (Luis Garcia 69), Xavi, Xabi Alonso■, Villa, Torres (Iniesta 57).
Referee: Stark (Germany).

Riga, 8 September 2007, 7500
Latvia (0) 1 *(Baird 56 (og))* **Northern Ireland (0) 0**

Latvia: Vanins; Zirnis, Klava, Ivanovs, Gorkss, Laizans, Bleidelis, Astafjevs, Rubins, Verpakovskis (Blanks 90), Karlsons (Rimkus 72).
Northern Ireland: Taylor; Evans, Baird, McCartney, Duff, Clingan, Elliott (Brunt 66), Davis, Gillespie, Lafferty (Feeney 72), Healy.
Referee: Proenca (Portugal).

Stockholm, 8 September 2007, 33,082
Sweden (0) 0 Denmark (0) 0

Sweden: Isaksson; Edman, Hansson, Mellberg, Linderoth, Wilhelmsson (Bakircioglu 57), Alexandersson, Anders Svensson (Kallstrom 69), Nilsson, Ibrahimovic (Prica 89), Elmander.
Denmark: Sorensen T; Andreasen (Lovenkrands 81), Agger, Helveg, Laursen M, Kahlenberg (Bendtner 54), Jensen N, Jensen D, Gronkjaer, Tomasson (Gravgaard 90), Rommedahl.
Referee: De Bleeckere (Belgium).

Aarhus, 12 September 2007, 20,005
Denmark (4) 4 *(Nordstrand 3, 36, Laursen M 12, Tomasson 18)*
Liechtenstein (0) 0

Denmark: Sorensen T; Andreasen, Laursen M, Agger (Gravgaard 28), Helveg, Jensen N, Gronkjaer (Kahlenberg 46), Hansen, Nordstrand, Tomasson (Lovenkrands 68), Rommedahl.
Liechtenstein: Jehle; Martin Stocklasa, Burgmeier, Telser, Oehri (Beck T 46), Rohrer, Ritzberger (Frick D 46), Buchel R, Frick M (Beck R 84), D'Elia, Polverino.
Referee: Clattenburg (England).

Reykjavik, 12 September 2007, 2500
Iceland (1) 2 *(Bjornsson 6, Gillespie 90 (og))*
Northern Ireland (0) 1 *(Healy 72)*

Iceland: Arason; Hreidarsson, Steinsson, Bjornsson (Gudjohnsen E 53), Sigurdsson R, Hallfredsson, Sigurdsson K, Arnason (Asgeirsson 88), Vidarsson, Ingimarsson, Thorvaldsson (Skulason 79).
Northern Ireland: Taylor; Baird, McCartney, Duff, Evans, Davis (McCann 79), Clingan, Brunt (Jones 83), Healy, Gillespie, Feeney.
Referee: Baskakov (Russia).

Oviedo, 12 September 2007, 25,000
Spain (1) 2 *(Xavi 13, Torres 86)*
Latvia (0) 0

Spain: Casillas; Pernia, Marchena, Juanito, Sergio Ramos, Xavi, Albelda, Silva (Fabregas 70), Joaquin (Angulo 79), Torres, Villa (Iniesta 50).
Latvia: Vanins; Zirnis, Klava, Ivanovs, Gorkss, Laizans, Bleidelis, Astafjevs, Rubins, Verpakovskis (Blanks 90), Karlsons (Pahars 64).
Referee: Yefet (Israel).

Aarhus, 13 October 2007, 19,849

Denmark (0) 1 *(Tomasson 88)*

Spain (2) 3 *(Tamudo 14, Sergio Ramos 40, Riera 89)*

Denmark: Sorensen T; Andreasen (Bendtner 46), Laursen U, Laursen M, Helveg, Gronkjaer (Kahlenberg 66), Jensen D (Perez 79), Poulsen C, Jensen N, Rommedahl, Tomasson.
Spain: Casillas; Marchena, Capdevila, Sergio Ramos, Raul Albiol, Joaquin (Riera 69), Albelda (Pablo Ibanez 64), Iniesta, Xavi, Fabregas (Luis Garcia 78), Tamudo.
Referee: Michel (Slovakia).

Reykjavik, 13 October 2007, 5865

Iceland (1) 2 *(Gudjohnsen E 4, 52)*

Latvia (3) 4 *(Klava 27, Laizans 31, Verpakovskis 37, 46)*

Iceland: Arason; Jonsson H, Steinsson (Arnason 25), Gunnarsson B, Sigurdsson R, Gudjonsson J, Ingimarsson, Hallfredsson, Sigurdsson K (Bjornsson 88), Gudjohnsen E, Thorvaldsson (Sigurdsson H 65).
Latvia: Vanins; Gorkss, Zirnis, Klava, Ivanovs, Solonicins, Laizans, Astafjevs, Visnakovs (Zigajevs 90), Verpakovskis (Pahars 78), Karlsons (Rimkus 59).
Referee: Dean (England).

Vaduz, 13 October 2007, 4131

Liechtenstein (0) 0

Sweden (2) 3 *(Ljungberg 19, Wilhelmssson 29, Anders Svensson 56)*

Liechtenstein: Jehle; Hasler, Buchel M (Gerster 61), Telser, Rohrer, Oehri, Burgmeier (Steuble 59), Frick M, Beck T, Frick D (Fischer 60), Buchel R.
Sweden: Isaksson; Hansson, Majstorovic, Edman, Concha, Linderoth (Andersson D 70), Wilhelmsson, Anders Svensson, Ljungberg (Kallstrom 39), Allback, Elmander (Rosenberg 60).
Referee: Dondarini (Italy).

Copenhagen, 17 October 2007, 19,004

Denmark (2) 3 *(Tomasson 7 (pen), Laursen U 27, Rommedahl 90)*

Latvia (0) 1 *(Gorkss 80)*

Denmark: Sorensen T; Helveg, Laursen U (Andreasen 32), Laursen M, Sorensen C, Jensen D, Poulsen C (Gronkjaer 71), Kahlenberg, Rommedahl, Bendtner, Tomasson.
Latvia: Vanins; Gorkss, Zirnis, Klava, Ivanovs, Astafjevs, Visnakovs (Zigajevs 78), Laizans, Solonicins, Rimkus (Butriks 63), Pahars (Kacanovs 90).
Referee: Cuneyt (Turkey).

Vaduz, 17 October 2007, 2589

Liechtenstein (1) 3 *(Frick M 27, Beck T 80, 83)*

Iceland (0) 0

Liechtenstein: Jehle; Hasler, Martin Stocklasa, Burgmeier, Telser, Gerster, Rohrer (Beck R 69), Oehri, Buchel R, Frick M (D'Elia 90), Fischer (Beck T 61).
Iceland: Arason; Jonsson H (Skulason 71), Gunnarsson B (Asgeirsson 85), Sigurdsson R, Vidarsson, Ingimarsson, Hallfredsson, Sigurdsson K, Gudjonsson J (Bjornsson 57), Gudjohnsen E, Thorvaldsson.
Referee: Zografos (Greece).

Stockholm, 17 October 2007, 33,112

Sweden (1) 1 *(Mellberg 15)*

Northern Ireland (0) 1 *(Lafferty 72)*

Sweden: Isaksson; Edman, Concha, Hansson, Mellberg, Linderoth, Kallstrom (Johansson 85), Wilhelmsson (Nilsson 42), Anders Svensson, Ibrahimovic, Elmander (Allback 73).
Northern Ireland: Taylor; Hughes, McCartney (Capaldi 87), McAuley, Craigan, Clingan, Brunt, Sproule, Davis, Lafferty, Healy.
Referee: Layec (France).

Riga, 17 November 2007, 4800

Latvia (2) 4 *(Karlsons 14, Verpakovskis 30, Laizans 63, Visnakovs 87)*

Liechtenstein (1) 1 *(Zirnis 13 (og))*

Latvia: Vanins; Ivanovs, Gorkss, Zirnis, Klava, Rubins, Astafjevs, Laizans, Bleidelis (Visnakovs 82), Verpakovskis (Rimkus 77), Karlsons (Pahars 71).
Liechtenstein: Jehle; Hasler, Martin Stocklasa, Burgmeier, Gerster, Rohrer (Frick D 72), Ritzberger, D'Elia, Buchel R (Buchel M 80), Frick M, Fischer (Beck R 71).
Referee: Moen (Norway).

Windsor Park, 17 November 2007, 14,500

Northern Ireland (0) 2 *(Feeney 62, Healy 80)*

Denmark (0) 1 *(Bendtner 51)*

Northern Ireland: Taylor; McAuley, Evans, Hughes, Craigan, Clingan, Brunt, Davis, Gillespie (Sproule 74), Feeney (Baird 85), Healy.
Denmark: Sorensen T; Laursen M, Andreasen, Sorensen C, Kroldrup, Priske (Wurtz 72), Poulsen C, Kahlenberg (Sorensen D 46), Jorgensen (Poulsen S 79), Bendtner, Rommedahl.
Referee: Vink (Holland).

Madrid, 17 November 2007, 75,000

Spain (2) 3 *(Capdevila 14, Iniesta 39, Sergio Ramos 65)*

Sweden (0) 0

Spain: Casillas; Puyol, Capdevila, Marchena, Sergio Ramos, Xavi, Albelda, Iniesta (Joaquin 52), Silva (Riera 66), Fabregas, Villa (Tamudo 52).
Sweden: Isaksson; Mellberg, Edman, Hansson, Wilhelmsson (Bakircioglu 79), Ljungberg, Andersson D (Kallstrom 46), Anders Svensson, Nilsson, Rosenberg (Allback 60), Ibrahimovic.
Referee: Rosetti (Italy).

Copenhagen, 21 November 2007, 15,393

Denmark (2) 3 *(Bendtner 34, Tomasson 44, Kahlenberg 59)*

Iceland (0) 0

Denmark: Sorensen T; Laursen U, Sorensen C, Kroldrup, Poulsen C, Kvist, Jensen D, Jorgensen (Kahlenberg 54), Tomasson, Rommedahl (Poulsen S 73), Bendtner (Larsen 84).
Iceland: Arason; Steinsson, Hreidarsson, Gunnarsson B, Sigurdsson R, Gislason, Sigurdsson K (Gardarsson 8), Hallfredsson (Jonsson E 73), Bjarnason T, Thorvaldsson, Gunnarsson V (Asgeirsson 84).
Referee: Benquerenca (Portugal).

Gran Canaria, 21 November 2007, 30,000

Spain (0) 1 *(Xavi 52)* **Northern Ireland (0) 0**

Spain: Reina; Sergio Ramos, Pernia, Pablo Ibanez, Raul Albiol, Xavi (Villa 67), Iniesta, Marcos Senna, Silva, Fabregas (Joaquin 47), Guiza (Tamudo 57).
Northern Ireland: Taylor; McAuley, Baird, Hughes, Craigan, Clingan, Sproule (Robinson 61), Brunt (Lafferty 59), Davis, Feeney (Paterson 72), Healy.
Referee: Fandel (Germany).

Stockholm, 21 November 2007, 26,128

Sweden (1) 2 *(Allback 2, Kallstrom 57)*

Latvia (1) 1 *(Laizans 26)*

Sweden: Isaksson; Edman, Majstorovic, Mellberg, Ljungberg, Anders Svensson, Kallstrom, Nilsson, Wilhelmsson, Ibrahimovic, Allback.
Latvia: Kolinko; Zirnis, Ivanovs, Stepanovs, Gorkss, Bleidelis (Visnakovs 43), Astafjevs (Solonicins 49), Laizans, Rubins, Karlsons (Pahars 62), Verpakovskis.
Referee: Stark (Germany).

Group F Table	*P*	*W*	*D*	*L*	*F*	*A*	*Pts*
Spain	12	9	1	2	23	8	28
Sweden	12	8	2	2	23	9	26
Northern Ireland	12	6	2	4	17	14	20
Denmark	12	6	2	4	21	11	20
Latvia	12	4	0	8	15	17	12
Iceland	12	2	2	8	10	27	8
Liechtenstein	12	2	1	9	9	32	7

GROUP G

Minsk, 2 September 2006, 23,000

Belarus (2) 2 *(Kalachev 2, Romashchenko 24)*

Albania (1) 2 *(Skela 7 (pen), Hasi 86)*

Belarus: Khomutovski; Kulchi, Korytko, Omelyanchuk, Shtaniuk, Hleb V (Bulyga 64), Kalachev (Lanko 84), Kovba, Romashchenko, Hleb A, Kutuzov.

Albania: Lika; Dallku, Hasi, Aliaj (Curri 46), Beqiri, Haxhi, Lala (Mukaj 84), Cana, Skela (Kapllani 73), Tare, Bogdani.
Referee: Asumaa (Finland).

Luxembourg, 2 September 2006, 8000
Luxembourg (0) 0 Holland (1) 1 *(Mathijsen 18)*
Luxembourg: Joubert; Strasser, Hoffmann, Reiter, Kintziger, Bettmer, Joachim, Lombardelli (Federspiel 83), Mutsch, Remy, Ferreira (Huss 88).
Holland: Van der Sar; Heitinga, Ooijer (Emanuelson 46), Mathijsen, De Cler, Schaars (Vennegoor of Hesselink 46), Janssen, Landzaat, Huntelaar, Van Persie (Babel 77), Kuyt.
Referee: Ferreira (Portugal).

Constanta, 2 September 2006, 15,000
Romania (1) 2 *(Rosu 40, Marica 55)*
Bulgaria (0) 2 *(Petrov M 82, 84)*
Romania: Lobont; Contra, Rat, Tamas■, Chivu, Codrea, Petre F (Nicolita 71), Dica (Cocis 59), Marica, Mutu, Rosu (Marin 79).
Bulgaria: Petkov G; Tunchev, Angelov S, Topuzakov, Vagner, Petrov S, Kishishev (Yankov 47), Petrov M, Jankovic, Berbatov (Bozhinov 62), Peev (Georgiev 47).
Referee: Farina (Italy).

Tirana, 6 September 2006, 10,000
Albania (0) 0 Romania (0) 2 *(Dica 65, Mutu 75 (pen))*
Albania: Beqaj; Beqiri, Dallku, Cana, Hasi, Skela (Aliaj 64), Lala (Mukaj 78), Tare, Bogdani (Kastrati 62), Haxhi, Curri.
Romania: Lobont; Contra, Rat, Ghionea, Chivu, Codrea, Petre F, Dica, Marica (Ganea 78), Mutu (Nicolita 85), Rosu (Margaritescu 89).
Referee: Benquerenca (Portugal).

Sofia, 6 September 2006, 16,543
Bulgaria (0) 3 *(Bozhinov 58, Petrov M 72, Telkiyski 81)*
Slovenia (0) 0
Bulgaria: Ivankov; Angelov S, Vagner, Tunchev, Topuzakov, Petrov S, Yankov, Georgiev (Telkiyski 53), Petrov M, Bozhinov (Yovov 60), Jankovic (Kishishev 69).
Slovenia: Mavric B; Ilic, Knavs, Jokic, Cesar, Zlogar, Koren (Lavric 76), Komac, Acimovic, Birsa (Semler 80), Novakovic.
Referee: Larsen (Denmark).

Eindhoven, 6 September 2006, 30,089
Holland (1) 3 *(Van Persie 33, 78, Kuyt 90)* **Belarus (0) 0**
Holland: Van der Sar; Heitinga (Boulahrouz 67), Ooijer, Mathijsen, Van Bronckhorst, De Jong, Sneijder, Landzaat (Schaars 68), Huntelaar (Babel 76), Van Persie, Kuyt.
Belarus: Khomutovski; Yurevich, Shtaniuk, Omelyanchuk, Lentsevich, Kalachev (Lanko 73), Kovba, Korytko (Strakhanovich 46), Romashchenko (Kontsevoy 69), Hleb A, Kornilenko.
Referee: Webb (England).

Sofia, 7 October 2006, 30,547
Bulgaria (1) 1 *(Petrov M 12)* **Holland (0) 1** *(Van Persie 62)*
Bulgaria: Ivankov; Angelov S, Gargorov, Iliev, Vagner, Kishishev, Yankov (Jankovic 82), Yovov (Telkiyski 54), Petrov S, Petrov M (Bozhinov 64), Berbatov.
Holland: Van der Sar; Boulahrouz, Ooijer, Mathijsen, Van Bronckhorst, De Jong, Landzaat, Sneijder (Schaars 90), Van Persie, Kuyt (Babel 16), Robben.
Referee: Ovrebo (Norway).

Bucharest, 7 October 2006, 12,000
Romania (2) 3 *(Mutu 7, Marica 10, Goian 76)*
Belarus (1) 1 *(Kornilenko 20)*
Romania: Coman; Rat, Tamas, Chivu, Petre F, Marica (Niculescu 90), Mutu (Buga 72), Rosu, Goian, Marin, Dica (Cocis 88).
Belarus: Gayev; Kulchi (Strakhanovich 65), Lentsevich, Omelyanchuk, Shtaniuk, Kalachev (Hleb V 50), Hleb A, Gurenko, Romashchenko, Kornilenko (Korytko 66), Yurevich.
Referee: Mallenco (Spain).

Celje, 7 October 2006, 3500
Slovenia (2) 2 *(Novakovic 30, Koren 44)*
Luxembourg (0) 0
Slovenia: Mavric B; Ilic, Mavric M, Cesar, Jokic, Ceh, Acimovic (Komac 75), Birsa, Koren, Novakovic, Lavric (Burgic 85).
Luxembourg: Joubert (Gillet 72); Kintziger, Hoffmann, Reiter, Peters, Strasser, Bettmer, Joachim (Huss 66), Lombardelli (Leweck C 42), Remy, Mutsch.
Referee: Kallis (Cyprus).

Minsk, 11 October 2006, 23,000
Belarus (1) 4 *(Kovba 18, Kornilenko 52, 60, Korytko 85)*
Slovenia (2) 2 *(Cesar 19, Lavric 43)*
Belarus: Gayev; Omelyanchuk, Shtaniuk, Gurenko, Kulchi, Kovba, Kalachev, Romashchenko (Korytko 50), Hleb A, Hleb V (Strakhanovich 69), Kornilenko (Kontsevoy 90).
Slovenia: Mavric B; Ilic, Jokic, Cesar, Mavric M, Koren, Acimovic (Komac 70), Zlogar, Birsa, Novakovic (Burgic 82), Lavric.
Referee: Kassai (Hungary).

Amsterdam, 11 October 2006, 40,000
Holland (2) 2 *(Van Persie 15, Beqaj 42 (og))*
Albania (0) 1 *(Curri 67)*
Holland: Van der Sar; Boulahrouz, Ooijer, Mathijsen, Van Bronckhorst (Emanuelson 68), De Jong (Schaars 50), Sneijder (De Cler 80), Landzaat, Babel, Van Persie, Robben.
Albania: Beqaj; Dede, Dallku, Aliaj (Murati 65), Hasi, Haxhi, Curri, Skela, Lala (Mukaj 46), Tare, Bogdani (Berisha 79).
Referee: Yefet (Israel).

Luxembourg, 11 October 2006, 3156
Luxembourg (0) 0
Bulgaria (1) 1 *(Tunchev 26)*
Luxembourg: Gillet; Reiter, Strasser, Kintziger, Peters (Payal 61), Bettmer, Mutsch, Remy, Joachim (Huss 52), Lombardelli (Leweck C 69), Ferreira.
Bulgaria: Ivankov; Angelov S, Tunchev, Topuzakov, Vagner, Yankov (Kishishev 77), Lazarov (Yovov 46), Petrov S, Telkiyski, Bozhinov (Jankovic 68), Berbatov.
Referee: Panic (Bosnia).

Shkoder, 24 March 2007, 12,000
Albania (0) 0 Slovenia (0) 0
Albania: Beqai; Dallku, Beqiri, Dede, Cana, Haxhi, Lala, Duro, Mukaj (Berisha 86), Kapllani (Bushi 58), Bogdani (Salihi 89).
Slovenia: Handanovic S; Mavric M, Jokic, Cesar, Ilic, Koren, Zlogar, Komac (Cipot 90), Ceh (Acimovic 80), Lavric, Rakovic (Birsa 63).
Referee: Attard (Malta).

Rotterdam, 24 March 2007, 49,000
Holland (0) 0 Romania (0) 0
Holland: Stekelenburg; Jaliens, Bouma, Mathijsen, Van Bronckhorst, Landzaat (Emanuelson 79), Sneijder, Babel, Van der Vaart (Seedorf 86), Huntelaar, Robben.
Romania: Lobont; Contra, Goian, Tamas, Rat (Radu 78), Cocis, Nicolita, Radoi, Codrea (Rosu 87), Marica (Niculae 64), Mutu.
Referee: Merk (Germany).

Luxembourg, 24 March 2007, 2000
Luxembourg (0) 1 *(Sagramola 68)*
Belarus (1) 2 *(Kalachev 25, Kutuzov 54)*
Luxembourg: Joubert; Strasser, Hoffmann, Reiter, Kintziger, Peters, Bettmer, Payal (Ferreira 67), Lombardelli (Bigard 58), Remy, Collette (Sagramola 64).
Belarus: Zhevnov; Yurevich, Shtaniuk, Kulchi, Korytko, Strakhanovich (Chelyadinski 58), Hleb A, Kalachev, Hleb V, Kornilenko (Bliznyuk 74), Kutuzov (Radkov 80).
Referee: Whitby (Wales).

Sofia, 28 March 2007, 25,000
Bulgaria (0) 0 Albania (0) 0
Bulgaria: Ivankov; Kishishev, Tunchev, Tomasic, Vagner, Yankov, Petrov S, Peev (Bozhinov 65), Yovov (Telkiyski 46), Jankovic (Todorov 46), Berbatov.
Albania: Beqaj; Dallku, Dede, Beqiri, Curri, Lala, Duro (Bulku 68), Haxhi (Kapllani 54), Cana, Berisha (Bushaj 79), Bogdani.
Referee: Eriksson (Sweden).

Piatra Neamt, 28 March 2007, 12,000
Romania (1) 3 *(Mutu 26, Contra 56, Marica 90)*
Luxembourg (0) 0
Romania: Lobont; Contra, Tamas (Stoica 87), Goian, Radu, Radoi, Zicu, Rosu (Cristea 53), Cocis, Niculae (Marica 65), Mutu.
Luxembourg: Joubert; Strasser, Bigard, Hoffmann, Reiter, Peters, Bettmer (Payal 50), Lombardelli (Ferreira 81), Remy, Mutsch, Collette (Sagramola 49).
Referee: Lajuks (Latvia).

Celje, 28 March 2007, 9500
Slovenia (0) 0 Holland (0) 1 *(Van Bronckhorst 86)*
Slovenia: Handanovic S; Ilic, Jokic, Mavric M, Cesar, Ceh, Komac, Koren, Acimovic (Sukalo 61), Lavric (Birsa 83), Rakovic (Novakovic 65).
Holland: Van der Sar; Heitinga (De Zeeuw 74), Mathijsen, Bouma, Emanuelson, Afellay (Seedorf 85), Babel (Koevermans 73), Van Bronckhorst, Kuyt, Sneijder, Robben.
Referee: Gonzalez (Spain).

Tirana, 2 June 2007, 3000
Albania (1) 2 *(Kapllani 38, Haxhi 57)*
Luxembourg (0) 0
Albania: Beqaj; Curri, Dallku, Dede, Skela, Cana, Haxhi (Vangaeli 74), Duro, Berisha (Mukaj 46), Bushaj (Salihi 76), Kapllani.
Luxembourg: Joubert; Kinziger, Bigard (Da Mota 60), Hoffmann, Peters, Strasser, Bettmer, Payal (Ferreira 82), Collette (Sagramola 69), Remy, Mutsch.
Referee: Silagava (Georgia).

Minsk, 2 June 2007, 29,000
Belarus (0) 0
Bulgaria (1) 2 *(Berbatov 28, 46)*
Belarus: Zhevnov; Omelyanchuk (Strakhanovich 72), Shtaniuk, Tigorev, Kulchi, Kalachev, Korytko, Kovba, Hleb A, Kornilenko (Vasilyuk 59), Kutuzov (Hleb V 46).
Bulgaria: Ivankov; Tunchev, Tomasic, Angelov S (Domovchiyski 90), Vagner, Telkiyski, Kishishev, Petrov S, Yovov (Manchev 80), Petrov M (Genkov 90), Berbatov.
Referee: Jara (Czech Republic).

Celje, 2 June 2007, 6000
Slovenia (0) 1 *(Vrsic 90)*
Romania (0) 2 *(Tamas 52, Nicolita 69)*
Slovenia: Handanovic S; Ilic, Mavric M, Cesar■, Jokic, Sukalo (Vrsic 83), Komac, Ceh, Koren (Birsa 52), Rakovic (Novakovic 61), Lavric.
Romania: Lobont; Contra, Tamas, Chivu, Rat, Nicolita, Codrea, Rosu (Zicu 63), Stoica (Niculae■ 74), Marica (Muresan 78), Mutu.
Referee: Dougal (Scotland).

Sofia, 6 June 2007, 10,227
Bulgaria (2) 2 *(Petrov M 10, Yankov 40)*
Belarus (1) 1 *(Vasilyuk 5 (pen))*
Bulgaria: Ivankov; Kishishev, Tunchev, Tomasic, Vagner, Yankov (Sirakov 90), Petrov S, Telkiyski, Yovov (Angelov S 68), Berbatov, Petrov M (Manchev 84).
Belarus: Zhevnov; Shtaniuk, Radkov, Tigorev, Yurevich, Kalachev (Kutuzov 44), Korytko, Kovba, Hleb A, Strakhanovich (Hleb V 64), Vasilyuk (Kornilenko 55).
Referee: Jakobsson (Iceland).

Luxembourg, 6 June 2007, 4325
Luxembourg (0) 0
Albania (2) 3 *(Skela 25, Kapllani 36, 72)*
Luxembourg: Joubert; Strasser, Bigard (Lombardelli 46), Hoffmann, Kintziger, Payal (Da Mota 64), Peters, Bettmer, Remy, Mutsch, Collette (Sagramola 79).
Albania: Beqaj; Dede, Haxhi, Dallku, Curri, Skela (Duro 60), Cana, Mukaj (Xhafaj 77), Kapllani, Bushaj (Berisha 67), Bogdani.
Referee: Malzinskas (Latvia).

Timisoara, 6 June 2007, 22,000
Romania (1) 2 *(Mutu 40, Contra 70)* **Slovenia (0) 0**
Romania: Lobont; Rat, Tamas, Goian, Contra, Zicu (Rosu 60), Chivu, Codrea (Plesan 78), Petre F (Nicolita 75), Marica, Mutu.
Slovenia: Handanovic S; Mavric M, Morec, Jokic (Filekovic 84), Ilic, Ceh, Komac, Vrsic, Zlogar (Sukalo 77), Lavric, Birsa (Novakovic 54).
Referee: Yefet (Israel).

Minsk, 8 September 2007, 19,320
Belarus (1) 1 *(Romashchenko 20)*
Romania (2) 3 *(Mutu 16, 77 (pen), Dica 42)*
Belarus: Khomutovsky; Tigorev, Radkov, Plaskonny, Stasevich, Kalachev (Skvernyuk 78), Hleb A, Romashchenko, Korytko, Karnilenka, Rodionov (Vasilyuk 61).
Romania: Lobont; Chivu, Rat, Goian, Marin, Nicolita, Codrea (Trica 90), Petre O, Dica (Munteanu 67), Mutu, Radu (Petre F 56).
Referee: Frojdfeldt (Sweden).

Amsterdam, 8 September 2007, 50,000
Holland (1) 2 *(Sneijder 23, Van Nistelrooy 58)*
Bulgaria (0) 0
Holland: Van der Sar; Melchiot (Boulahrouz 65), Mathijsen, Heitinga, De Zeeuw (De Jong 81), Bouma, Van Bronckhorst, Sneijder (Seedorf 73), Babel, Van Persie, Van Nistelrooy.
Bulgaria: Ivankov; Angelov S, Tomasic, Wagner (Yankov 78), Kishishev, Tunchev, Telkijski (Dimitrov 68), Petrov S, Petrov M, Peev (Popov 62), Berbatov.
Referee: Cantalejo (Spain).

Luxembourg, 8 September 2007, 2012
Luxembourg (0) 0
Slovenia (2) 3 *(Lavric 7, 47, Novakovic 37)*
Luxembourg: Joubert; Hoffmann, Bigard, Bettmer, Strasser, Peters, Mutsch, Ferreira, Lombardelli (Payal 46), Huss (Kitenge 63), Peiffer (Da Mota 52).
Slovenia: Handanovic; Kirm (Komac 64), Brecko, Morec, Kokot, Zlogar (Cipot 82), Koren, Stevanovic, Vrsic (Mihelic 78), Novakovic, Lavric.
Referee: Berezka (Ukraine).

Tirana, 12 September 2007, 19,600
Albania (0) 0 Holland (0) 1 *(Van Nistelrooy 90)*
Albania: Beqaj; Dallku, Curri, Dede, Vangeli, Mukaj, Lala, Cana■, Duro (Haxhi 69), Kapllani (Bushi 46), Bogdani (Bulku 83).
Holland: Van der Sar; Melchiot, Mathijsen, De Zeeuw (Van der Vaart 49), Bouma, Ooijer, Van Bronckhorst, Sneijder, Babel, Van Persie, Van Nistelrooy.
Referee: Riley (England).

Sofia, 12 September 2007, 8000
Bulgaria (2) 3 *(Berbatov 27, 28, Petrov M 54 (pen))*
Luxembourg (0) 0
Bulgaria: Petkov; Angelov S, Tunchev, Tomasic, Kishishev, Zanev, Petrov S (Yankov 60), Petrov M (Yovov 66), Popov I (Kouchev 74), Dimitrov, Berbatov.
Luxembourg: Joubert; Hoffmann, Bigard, Kintziger, Bettmer (Da Mota 83), Remy, Peters, Mutsch, Strasser, Huss (Payal 46), Peiffer (Collette 46).
Referee: Bulent (Turkey).

Celje, 12 September 2007, 4000

Slovenia (1) 1 *(Lavric 3 (pen))* **Belarus (0) 0**

Slovenia: Handanovic S; Cipot, Kirm, Morec, Ilic (Brecko 82), Koren, Stevanovic (Zinko 75), Jokic, Lavric, Birsa (Vrsic 66), Novakovic.
Belarus: Gaev; Radkov■, Plaskonny, Tigorev, Hleb A, Korytko (Kashevski 90), Stasevich, Romashchenko, Kalachev, Bliznyuk (Filipenko 74), Karnilenka (Rodionov 46).
Referee: Banari (Moldova).

Gomel, 13 October 2007, 14,000

Belarus (0) 0 Luxembourg (0) 1 *(Leweck 90)*

Belarus: Zhevnov (Khomutovsky 62); Filipenko, Omelyanchuk, Plaskonny, Stasevich (Kalachev 62), Korytko, Romashchenko, Hleb A, Skvernyuk, Karnileka, Voronkov.
Luxembourg: Joubert; Lang, Kintziger, Wagner, Bettmer, Lombardelli (Leweck F 45), Remy, Peters, Payal (Ferreira 79), Mutsch, Kitenge (Da Mota 61).
Referee: Svendsen (Denmark).

Constanta, 13 October 2007, 13,000

Romania (0) 1 *(Goian 71)* **Holland (0) 0**

Romania: Lobont; Chivu, Ogararu, Tamas, Rat, Goian, Nicolita, Codrea, Petre F, Marica (Niculae 70), Mutu.
Holland: Stekelenburg; Bouma, Ooijer (Koevermans 84), Mathijsen, Heitinga (Jaliens 68), De Zeeuw, Van der Vaart, Van Bronckhorst, Seedorf, Van Nistelrooy, Robben (Babel 79).
Referee: Vassaras (Greece).

Celje, 13 October 2007, 4625

Slovenia (0) 0 Albania (0) 0

Slovenia: Handanovic S; Morec, Cipot, Brecko, Kirm, Jokic (Ilic 77), Koren, Zlogar, Birsa (Mihelic 82), Novakovic (Rusic 61), Lavric.
Albania: Beqaj; Dede, Rrustemi, Curri, Vangeli, Skela (Hyka 90), Lala, Bulku, Haxhi (Mukaj 60), Duro (Bushaj 77), Bogdani.
Referee: Gomes (Portugal).

Tirana, 17 October 2007, 9200

Albania (1) 1 *(Kishishev 32 (og))*

Bulgaria (0) 1 *(Berbatov 87)*

Albania: Beqaj; Dede, Dallku, Curri, Vangeli, Skela, Lala, Haxhi (Mukaj 46), Duro, Bogdani, Salihi (Bulku 73).
Bulgaria: Petkov; Angelov S, Wagner, Kishishev, Iliev V, Tomasic, Telkijski (Georgiev 46), Petrov S (Yankov 46), Petrov M, Popov I (Yovov 72), Berbatov.
Referee: Stuchlik (Austria).

Eindhoven, 17 October 2007, 35,000

Holland (1) 2 *(Sneijder 14, Huntelaar 87)*

Slovenia (0) 0

Holland: Stekelenburg; De Zeeuw, Jaliens, Bouma, Heitinga, Emanuelson, Seedorf, Van der Vaart (Robben 29) (Babel 63), Sneijder, Huntelaar, Van Persie (Ooijer 60).
Slovenia: Handanovic S; Brecko (Ljubijankic 85), Kirm (Jokic 82), Morec, Ilic, Cesar, Komac, Zlogar, Koren, Birsa (Novakovic 68), Lavric.
Referee: Rizzoli (Italy).

Luxembourg, 17 October 2007, 3584

Luxembourg (0) 0

Romania (1) 2 *(Petre F 42, Marica 61)*

Luxembourg: Gillet; Kintziger, Hoffmann, Wagner, Lang, Bettmer (Ferreira 49), Remy, Peters, Payal (Leweck F 68), Mutsch, Kitenge (Da Mota 57).
Romania: Lobont; Chivu (Petre O 87), Tamas, Rat, Ogararu, Goian, Margaritescu, Petre F, Niculae (Bratu 76), Dica (Cristea 68), Marica.
Referee: Brych (Germany).

Tirana, 17 November 2007, 5000

Albania (2) 2 *(Bogdani 39, Kapllani 43)*

Belarus (2) 4 *(Romashchenko 33, 63 (pen), Kutuzov 45, 54)*

Albania: Beqaj; Rrustemi (Vangeli 38), Dallku, Curri, Dede, Lala (Bushaj 75), Cana, Duro, Skela, Kapllani (Salihi 74), Bogdani.
Belarus: Zhevnov; Plaskonny (Skvernyuk 65), Omelyanchuk, Filipenko, Kirenkin, Romashchenko, Kalachev (Korytko 75), Hleb A, Kulchy, Bulyga, Kutuzov (Karnilenka 90).
Referee: Bulent (Turkey).

Sofia, 17 November 2007, 15,000

Bulgaria (1) 1 *(Dimitrov 6)* **Romania (0) 0**

Bulgaria: Ivankov; Zanev, Tunchev, Tomasic, Milanov, Petrov M (Lazarov 90), Georgiev, Petrov S, Berbatov, Yovov (Telkijski 83), Dimitrov.
Romania: Lobont; Chivu, Rat, Ogararu, Goian, Tamas (Cocis 58), Petre O, Codrea (Trica 82), Nicolita, Mazilu (Marica 65), Niculae.
Referee: Plautz (Austria).

Rotterdam, 17 November 2007, 49,000

Holland (1) 1 *(Koevermans 43)* **Luxembourg (0) 0**

Holland: Van der Sar; Bouma, Melchiot, Mathijsen, De Zeeuw, Van der Vaart, Van Bronckhorst, Sneijder, Seedorf (Emanuelson 77), Koevermans (Babel 84), Van Nistelrooy (Kuyt 46).
Luxembourg: Joubert; Kintziger, Hoffmann, Wagner, Bettmer (Leweck F 66), Strasser, Remy, Peters, Payal, Mutsch, Kitenge (Joachim 49).
Referee: Hansson (Sweden).

Minsk, 21 November 2007, 12,000

Belarus (0) 2 *(Bulyga 49, Korytko 65)*

Holland (0) 1 *(Van der Vaart 90)*

Belarus: Zhevnov; Kirenkin, Omelyanchuk (Stasevich 90), Filipenko, Korytko, Romashchenko, Hleb A (Kashevski 46), Skvernyuk, Kulchy, Bulyga (Karnilenka 87), Kutuzov.
Holland: Stekelenburg; Mathijsen, De Zeeuw (De Jong 69), Ooijer, Bouma, Melchiot, Van Bronckhorst (Engelaar 66), Sneijder (Kuyt 46), Van der Vaart, Babel, Koevermans.
Referee: Layec (France).

Bucharest, 21 November 2007, 25,000

Romania (1) 6 *(Dica 22, 72 (pen), Tamas 53, Niculae 61, 66, Marica 67 (pen))*

Albania (0) 1 *(Kapllani 65)*

Romania: Lobont; Tamas (Constantin 78), Rat, Ogararu, Goian, Margaritescu, Petre F (Bucur 65), Cocis, Dica, Marica (Mazilu 74), Niculae.
Albania: Beqaj; Dede■, Lila, Curri■, Vangeli (Kapllani 40), Duro (Hyka 78), Skela, Lala, Bulku, Haxhi, Bogdani (Bakaj 82).
Referee: Trivkovic (Croatia).

Celje, 21 November 2007, 4000

Slovenia (0) 0

Bulgaria (0) 2 *(Georgiev 81, Berbatov 84)*

Slovenia: Handanovic S; Morec, Cesar, Brecko, Kirm, Stevanovic (Komac 56), Jokic■, Koren, Zolgar, Birsa (Ilic 49), Lavric (Novakovic 65).
Bulgaria: Ivankov; Angelov S, Tunchev, Tomasic, Milanov (Todorov 46), Georgiev, Petrov S (Telkijski 46), Petrov M, Dimitrov, Yovov (Lazarov 76), Berbatov.
Referee: Webb (England).

Group G Table	*P*	*W*	*D*	*L*	*F*	*A*	*Pts*
Romania	12	9	2	1	26	7	29
Holland	12	8	2	2	15	5	26
Bulgaria	12	7	4	1	18	7	25
Belarus	12	4	1	7	17	23	13
Albania	12	2	5	5	12	18	11
Slovenia	12	3	2	7	9	16	11
Luxembourg	12	1	0	11	2	23	3

EURO 2008

One goal is often not considered comfortable for the winners. But for the final, the gulf between the two teams was more of an ocean. Spain attacking in droves like bees in search of their hive, swarm all round the Germans, making them at times seemed incredibly awkward and out of touch with play surrounding them. But the Spaniards had to be satisfied with a superb effort from Fernando Torres who first undertook, then overtook Phillip Lahm before skipping over Jens Lehmann to clip the ball in for the 33rd minute winner. Overall the best team won Euro 2008.

Statistically, they scored 12 goals in the tournament, had 117 shots and contributed 3,415 passes. Midfield player Xavi Hernandez was considered the player of the finals, too. Yet any firm conclusion drawn from the opening group matches would have been highly misleading. Turkey looked anything but knock-out stage material in losing to Portugal, Italy looked fortunate to get nil against a rampant Holland and Russia were run ragged by a fluent Spanish team. However, Greece the holders were well beaten by Sweden. In addition to all this both hosts lost their opening fixtures, the Swiss to the Czech Republic, Austria to Croatia.

The Portuguese again caught the attention with a 3-1 win over the Czech Republic, but Turkey had to battle hard and late before edging the Swiss. Croatia gave a clever exhibition to make the Germans look much less than the team which had beaten Poland in their opener. At least Austria at the death salvaged a draw against the Poles to give them a chance against their near neighbours. Once again the Dutch produced a fluid performance to make the French look decidedly weak, though the victims were denied an obvious penalty. Italy, the reigning World Cup holders, were only saved when Romania missed a penalty in the dying moments. Russia piled on the agony for Greece and Spain were unable to repeat the dynamism of their first match in beating the Swedes.

But the last group games produced the fireworks. Turkey, two goals down to the Czechs and seemingly preparing to pack their bags, found stamina and spirit and not a little football to win through, the Germans nervously beat target-missing Austria, but Holland resting key players still found space against Romania. Then there was the repeat of the 2006 World Cup final, but it was Italy who prevailed as the French finished with ten players.

Taking stock before the last eight carried on, it is interesting to note that Holland produced the finest goal thus far and the most blatantly off-side one – in the same match against Italy. And despite the efforts of the authorities to say differently, a player off the field of play is in no position to play an opponent onside. However, Wesley Sneijder, the finisher of a classic move, provided easily the most thrilling goal of the group stage.

To underline the situation, three of the teams who topped their group did not survive the quarter-finals. The draw for the semi-finals could have been better handled by a group of eleven-plus examination sitting school children, since the entire tournament is mapped out before a ball is kicked. So we had a repeat of the Spain v Russia opener! Perhaps UEFA had too much to think about with organising the Intertoto Cup at the same time as Euro 2008 was under way.

But there was the same kind of walkover for the Spaniards as in the previous match, though on this occasion, the Russians hardly had a kick. The day before the Germans played the late, late scoring Turks at their own game. Having gone behind, Germany levelled but when Turkey snatched the lead with a few minutes to spare, at least extra time appeared inevitable. But Phillip Lahm, who only minutes before had been skinned for the equaliser, atoned with the winner.

Overall the standard of play was pleasingly high. Most favoured the lone, isolated striker but the variations on a theme of 4-5-1 did not curtail the attacking intentions, though often the spearhead found himself overwhelmed by numbers and when chances arose, his finishing left much to be desired. Those teams with a more fluid approach to forward movement looked far more at ease. Discipline was reasonable, too, with three dismissals. True, there was plenty of simulated "death" from the briefest of tackles, but no bouts of fisticuffs.

One match might easily have been called off at half-time because of a waterlogged pitch. Interesting to note what would have happened had it been abandoned. Yes, you guessed it – a penalty shoot-out!

Spanish striker Fernando Torres powers past Germany's Phillip Lahm and delicately chips goalkeeper Jens Lehmann to score the winning goal in the Euro 2008 final in Vienna. (Action Images/Tony O'Brien/Livepic)

EURO 2008 FINALS

▪ *Denotes player sent off.*

GROUP A

Geneva, 7 June 2008, 29,106

Portugal (0) 2 *(Pepe 61, Raul Meireles 90)*

Turkey (0) 0

Portugal: Ricardo; Bosingwa, Paulo Ferreira, Joao Moutinho, Pepe, Ricardo Carvalho, Ronaldo, Petit, Nuno Gomes (Nani 69), Deco (Fernando Meira 90), Simao (Raul Meireles 83).
Turkey: Volkan; Hamit Altintop (Semih 75), Hakan Balta, Mehmet Aurelio, Gokhan Z (Emre A 55), Servet, Kazim-Richards, Erding (Sabri 46), Emre B, Nihat, Tuncay.
Referee: H. Fandel (Germany).

Basle, 7 June 2008, 39,730

Switzerland (0) 0

Czech Republic (0) 1 *(Sverkos 70)*

Switzerland: Benaglio; Lichtsteiner (Vonlanthen 75), Magnin, Inler, Muller, Senderos, Behrami (Derdiyok 83), Fernandes, Frei (Yakin 46), Streller, Barnetta.
Czech Republic: Cech; Grygera, Sionko (Vlcek 83), Galasek, Ujfalusi, Rozehnal, Jankulovski, Polak, Jarolim (Kovac 87, Koller (Sverkos 56), Plasil.
Referee: R. Rosetti (Italy).

Geneva, 11 June 2008, 29,016

Czech Republic (1) 1 *(Sionko 17)*

Portugal (1) 3 *(Deco 8, Ronaldo 63, Quaresma 90)*

Czech Republic: Cech; Grygera, Jankulovski, Polak, Ujfalusi, Rozehnal, Galasek (Koller 73), Sionko, Matejovsky (Vlcek 68), Baros, Plasil (Jarolim 85).
Portugal: Ricardo; Bosingwa, Paulo Ferreira, Petit, Pepe, Ricardo Carvalho, Joao Moutinho (Fernando Meira 75), Ronaldo, Deco, Nuno Gomes (Hugo Almeida 79), Simao (Quaresma 80).
Referee: K. Vassaras (Greece).

Basle, 11 June 2008, 39,730

Switzerland (1) 1 *(Yakin 32)*

Turkey (0) 2 *(Semih 57, Arda 90)*

Switzerland: Benaglio; Lichtsteiner, Magnin, Inler, Muller, Senderos, Behrami, Fernandes (Cabanas 76), Yakin (Gygax 85), Barnetta (Vonlanthen 66), Derdiyok.
Turkey: Volkan; Hamit Altintop, Emre A, Servet, Hakan Balta, Mehmet Aurelio, Tumer (Mehmet T 46), Gokdeniz (Semih 46), Tuncay, Arda, Nihat (Kazim-Richards 85).
Referee: L. Michel (Slovakia).

Basle, 15 June 2008, 39,730

Switzerland (0) 2 *(Yakin 71, 83 (pen))*

Portugal (0) 0

Switzerland: Zuberbuhler; Lichtsteiner (Grichting 85), Magnin, Fernandes, Muller, Senderos, Behrami, Inler, Yakin, Derdiyok, Vonlanthen.
Portugal: Ricardo; Miguel, Paulo Ferreira (Ribeiro 41), Raul Meireles, Bruno Alves, Pepe, Fernando Meira, Miguel Veloso (Joao Moutinho 70), Quaresma, Helder Postiga (Hugo Almeida 74), Nani.
Referee: K. Plautz (Austria).

Geneva, 15 June 2008, 29,016

Turkey (0) 3 *(Arda 75, Nihat 87, 89)*

Czech Republic (1) 2 *(Koller 34, Plasil 62)*

Turkey: Volkan▪; Hamit Altintop, Hakan Balta, Mehmet Aurelio, Servet, Emre G (Emre A 62), Mehmet T (Kazim-Richards 57), Arda, Semih (Sabri 46), Tuncay, Nihat.
Czech Republic: Cech; Grygera, Jankulovski, Sionko (Vlcek 84), Ujfalusi, Rozehnal, Galasek, Matejovsky (Jarolim 39), Koller, Plasil (Kadlec 80), Polak.
Referee: P. Frojdfeldt (Sweden).

Group A Table	P	W	D	L	F	A	Pts
Portugal	3	2	0	1	5	3	6
Turkey	3	2	0	1	5	5	6
Switzerland	3	1	0	2	3	3	3
Czech Republic	3	1	0	2	4	6	3

GROUP B

Vienna, 8 June 2008, 51,428

Austria (0) 0

Croatia (1) 1 *(Modric 4 (pen))*

Austria: Macho; Prodl, Pogatetz, Aufhauser, Stranzl, Saumel (Vastic 61), Standfest, Ivanschitz, Harnik, Linz (Kienast 74), Gercaliu (Korkmaz 69).
Croatia: Pletikosa; Corluka, Pranjic, Kovac N, Kovac R, Simunic, Srna, Modric, Olic (Vukojevic 83), Petric (Budan 72), Kranjcar (Knezevic 61).
Referee: P. Vink (Holland).

Klagenfurt, 8 June 2008, 30,461

Germany (1) 2 *(Podolski 20, 72)*

Poland (0) 0

Germany: Lehmann; Lahm, Jansen, Frings, Metzelder, Mertesacker, Fritz (Schweinsteiger 56), Ballack, Gomez (Hitzlsperger 74), Klose (Kuryani 90), Podolski.
Poland: Boruc; Wasilewski, Golanski (Saganowski 74), Dudka, Michal Zewlakow, Bak, Lobodzinski (Piszczek 66), Uralsk (Guerreiro 46), Lewandowski, Smolarek, Krzynowek.
Referee: T. Ovrebo (Norway).

Vienna, 12 June 2008, 51,428

Austria (0) 1 *(Vastic 90 (pen))*

Poland (1) 1 *(Guerreiro 30)*

Austria: Macho; Garics, Pogatetz, Aufhauser (Saumel 74), Prodl, Stranzl, Leitgeb, Ivanschitz (Vastic 64), Harnik, Linz (Kienast 64), Korkmaz.
Poland: Boruc; Wasilewski, Michal Zewlakow, Lewandowski, Jop (Golanski 46), Bak, Dudka, Guerreiro (Murawski 85), Smolarek, Saganowski (Lobodzinski 83), Krzynowek.
Referee: H. Webb (England).

Klagenfurt, 12 June 2008, 30,461

Croatia (1) 2 *(Srna 24, Olic 63)*

Germany (0) 1 *(Podolski 79)*

Croatia: Pletikosa; Corluka, Pranjic, Kovac N, Kovac R, Simunic, Srna (Leko J 80), Rakitic, Modric, Olic (Petric 72), Kranjcar.
Germany: Lehmann; Lahm, Jansen (Odonkor 46), Frings, Metzelder, Mertesacker, Fritz (Kuranyi 82), Ballack, Gomez (Schweinsteiger▪ 65), Klose, Podolski.
Referee: F. De Bleeckere (Belgium).

Vienna, 16 June 2008, 51,428

Austria (0) 0

Germany (0) 1 *(Ballack 49)*

Austria: Macho; Garics, Pogatetz, Aufhauser (Saumel 64), Hiden (Leitgeb 55), Stranzl, Fuchs, Harnik (Kienast 67), Ivanschitz, Hoffer, Korkmaz.
Germany: Lehmann; Friedrich A, Lahm, Frings, Mertesacker, Metzelder, Fritz (Borowski 90), Ballack, Gomez (Hitzlsperger 60), Klose, Podolski (Neuville 83).
Referee: M. Gonzalez (Spain).

Klagenfurt, 16 June 2008, 30,461

Poland (0) 0

Croatia (0) 1 *(Klasnic 53)*

Poland: Boruc; Wasilewski, Wawrzyniak, Lobodzinski (Smolarek 55), Michal Zewlakow, Dudka, Murawski, Guerreiro, Lewandowski (Kokoszka 46), Saganowski (Zahorski 68), Krzynowek.
Croatia: Runje; Simic, Pranjic, Vukojevic, Vejic, Knezevic (Corluka 27), Leko J, Pokrivac, Klasnic (Kalinic 74), Petric (Kranjcar 75), Rakitic.
Referee: K. Vassaras (Greece).

Group B Table	P	W	D	L	F	A	Pts
Croatia	3	3	0	0	4	1	9
Germany	3	2	0	1	4	2	6
Austria	3	0	1	2	1	3	1
Poland	3	0	1	2	1	4	1

GROUP C

Berne, 9 June 2008, 30,777

Holland (2) 3 *(Van Nistelrooy 26, Sneijder 31, Van Bronckhorst 80)*

Italy (0) 0

Holland: Van der Sar; Mathijsen, Van Bronckhorst, De Jong, Engelaar, Boulahrouz (Heitinga 77), Ooijer, Van der Vaart, Sneijder, Van Nistelrooy (Van Persie 70), Kuyt (Afellay 81).
Italy: Buffon; Panucci, Zambrotta, Pirlo, Barzagli, Materazzi (Grosso 55), Gattuso, Camoranesi (Cassano 75), Di Natale (Del Piero 64), Toni, Ambrosini.
Referee: P. Frojdfeldt (Sweden).

Zurich, 9 June 2008, 30,585

Romania (0) 0

France (0) 0

Romania: Lobont; Contra, Rat, Radoi (Dica 90), Tamas, Goian, Cocis (Codrea 63), Chivu, Nicolita, Niculae D, Mutu (Niculae M 79).
France: Coupet; Sagnol, Abidal, Makelele, Thuram, Gallas, Ribery, Toulalan, Anelka (Gomis 72), Benzema (Nasri 77), Malouda.
Referee: M. Gonzalez (Spain).

Berne, 13 June 2008, 30,777

Holland (1) 4 *(Kuyt 10, Van Persie 59, Robben 72, Sneijder 90)*

France (0) 1 *(Henry 71)*

Holland: Van der Sar; Boulahrouz, Van Bronckhorst, Engelaar (Robben 46), Ooijer, Mathijsen, De Jong, Kuyt (Van Persie 55), Van Nistelrooy, Sneijder, Van der Vaart (Bouma 78).
France: Coupet; Sagnol, Evra, Makelele, Thuram, Gallas, Ribery, Toulalan, Govou (Anelka 75), Henry, Malouda (Gomis 60).
Referee: H. Fandel (Germany).

Zurich, 13 June 2008, 30,585

Italy (0) 1 *(Panucci 56)*

Romania (0) 1 *(Mutu 55)*

Italy: Buffon; Zambrotta, Grosso, Pirlo, Panucci, Chiellini, De Rossi, Camoranesi (Ambrosini 84), Del Piero (Quagliarella 77), Toni, Perrotta (Cassano 58).
Romania: Lobont; Contra, Rat, Petre F (Nicolita 60), Tamas, Goian, Radoi (Dica 26), Codrea, Chivu, Niculae D, Mutu (Cocis 87).
Referee: T. Henning (Norway).

Zurich, 17 June 2008, 30,585

France (0) 0

Italy (1) 2 *(Pirlo 25 (pen), De Rossi 82)*

France: Coupet; Clerc, Evra, Makelele, Abidal■, Gallas, Ribery (Nasri 10) (Boumsong 26), Toulalan, Govou (Anelka 66), Benzema, Henry.
Italy: Buffon; Zambrotta, Grosso, Pirlo (Ambrosini 55), Panucci, Chiellini, Gattuso (Aquilani 82), De Rossi, Toni, Cassano, Perrotta (Camoranesi 64).
Referee: L. Michel (Slovakia).

Berne, 17 June 2008, 30,777

Holland (0) 2 *(Huntelaar 54, Van Persie 87)*

Romania (0) 0

Holland: Stekelenburg; Boulahrouz (Melchiot 58), De Cler, Engelaar, Heitinga, Bouma, Afellay, De Zeeuw, Huntelaar (Vennegoor of Hesselink 82), Van Persie, Robben (Kuyt 62).
Romania: Lobont; Contra, Rat, Codrea (Dica 72), Tamas, Ghionea, Cocis, Chivu, Nicolita (Petre F 82), Niculae M (Niculae D 59), Mutu.
Referee: M. Busacca (Switzerland).

Group C Table	*P*	*W*	*D*	*L*	*F*	*A*	*Pts*
Holland	3	3	0	0	9	1	9
Italy	3	1	1	1	3	4	4
Romania	3	0	2	1	1	3	2
France	3	0	1	2	1	6	1

GROUP D

Salzburg, 10 June 2008, 31,063

Greece (0) 0

Sweden (0) 2 *(Ibrahimovic 67, Hansson 72)*

Greece: Nikopolidis; Seitaridis, Torosidis, Kyrgiakos, Dellas (Spiropoulos 69), Antzas, Katsouranis, Basinas, Charisteas, Karagounis, Gekas (Samaras 46).
Sweden: Isaksson; Alexandersson (Stoor 74), Nilsson, Andersson D, Mellberg, Hansson, Wilhelmsson (Rosenberg 78), Anders Svensson, Ibrahimovic (Elmander 71), Larsson H, Ljungberg.
Referee: M. Busacca (Switzerland).

Innsbruck, 10 June 2008, 30,772

Spain (2) 4 *(Villa 20, 45, 75, Fabregas 90)*

Russia (0) 1 *(Pavlyuchenko 86)*

Spain: Casillas; Sergio Ramos, Capdevila, Marcos Senna, Puyol, Marchena, Silva (Xabi Alonso 76), Xavi, Villa, Torres (Fabregas 53), Iniesta (Cazorla 62).
Russia: Akinfeev; Anyukov, Zhirkov, Semak, Shirokov, Kolodin, Sychev (Bystrov 46) (Adamov 70), Bilyaletdinov, Zyryanov, Semshov (Torbinski 57), Pavlyuchenko.
Referee: K. Plautz (Austria).

Salzburg, 14 June 2008, 31,063

Greece (0) 0

Russia (1) 1 *(Zyryanov 34)*

Greece: Nikopolidis; Petridis (Karagounis 39), Torosidis, Basinas, Dellas, Krygiakos, Katsouranis, Patsatzoglou, Amanatidis (Giannakopoulos 79), Liberopoulos (Gekas 60), Charisteas.
Russia: Akinfeev; Anyukov, Zhirkov (Berezutski V 87), Kolodin, Ignashevich, Semak, Torbinsky, Semshov, Bilyaletdinov (Saenko 69), Pavlyuchenko, Zyryanov.
Referee: R. Rosetti (Italy).

Innsbruck, 14 June 2008, 30,772

Sweden (1) 1 *(Ibrahimovic 34)*

Spain (1) 2 *(Torres 15, Villa 90)*

Sweden: Isaksson; Stoor, Nilsson, Andersson D, Mellberg, Hansson, Elmander (Larsson S 79), Anders Svensson, Ibrahimovic (Rosenberg 46), Larsson H (Kallstrom 86), Ljungberg.
Spain: Casillas; Sergio Ramos, Capdevila, Xavi (Fabregas 59), Puyol (Albiol 24), Marchena, Marcos Senna, Iniesta (Santi Cazorla 59), Torres, Villa, Silva.
Referee: P. Vink (Holland).

Salzburg, 18 June 2008, 30,883

Greece (1) 1 *(Charisteas 42)*

Spain (0) 2 *(De la Red 61, Guiza 88)*

Greece: Nikopolidis; Vintra, Spiropoulos, Katsouranis, Dellas, Kyrgiakos (Antzas 62), Basinas, Salpigidis (Giannakopoulos 86), Amanatidis, Charisteas, Karagounis (Tziolis 74).
Spain: Reina; Arbeloa, Fernando Navarro, Xabi Alonso, Albiol, Juanito, Sergio Garcia, De la Red, Guiza, Fabregas, Iniesta (Santi Cazorla 58).
Referee: H. Webb (England).

Innsbruck, 18 June 2008, 30,772

Russia (1) 2 *(Pavlychenko 24, Arshavin 50)*

Sweden (0) 0

Russia: Akinfeev; Anyukov, Zhirkov, Semshov, Ignashevich, Kolodin, Semak, Bilyaletdinov (Saenko 66), Arshavin, Pavlyuchenko (Bystrov 90), Syryanov.
Sweden: Isaksson; Stoor, Nilsson (Allback 79), Andersson D (Kallstrom 56), Mellberg, Hansson, Elmander, Anders Svensson, Larsson H, Ibrahimovic, Ljungberg.
Referee: F. De Bleeckere (Belgium).

Group D Table	*P*	*W*	*D*	*L*	*F*	*A*	*Pts*
Spain	3	3	0	0	8	3	9
Russia	3	2	0	1	4	4	6
Sweden	3	1	0	2	3	4	3
Greece	3	0	0	3	1	5	0

QUARTER-FINALS

Basle, 19 June 2008, 39,374

Portugal (1) 2 *(Nuno Gomes 40, Helder Postiga 86)*

Germany (2) 3 *(Schweinsteiger 22, Klose 26, Ballack 62)*

Portugal: Ricardo; Bosingwa, Paulo Ferreira, Joao Moutinho (Raul Meireles 31), Pepe, Ricardo Carvalho, Petit (Helder Postiga 73), Deco, Nuno Gomes (Nani 67), Ronaldo, Simao.
Germany: Lehmann; Friedrich A, Lahm, Rolfes, Metzelder, Mertesacker, Hitzlsperger (Borowski 73), Ballack, Schweinsteiger (Fritz 83), Klose, Podolski.
Referee: P. Frojdfeldt (Sweden).

Vienna, 20 June 2008, 51,428

Croatia (0) 1 *(Klasnik 119)*

Turkey (0) 1 *(Semih 120)*

Croatia: Pletikosa; Corluka, Pranjic, Kovac N, Kovac R, Simunic, Srna, Modric, Olic (Klasnik 97), Kranjcar (Petric 64), Ratitic.
Turkey: Rustu; Hamit Altintop, Hakan Balta, Sabri, Emre A, Gokhan Z, Arda, Kazim-Richards (Ugur 61), Mehmet T (Semih 76), Nihat (Gokdeniz 117), Tuncay.
aet; Turkey won 3-1 on penalties: Modric missed; Arda scored; Srna scored; Semih scored; Ratitic missed; Hamit Altintop scored; Petric saved.
Referee: R. Rosetti (Italy).

Basle, 21 June 2008, 38,374

Holland (0) 1 *(Van Nistelrooy 86)*

Russia (0) 3 *(Pavlyuchenko 56, Torbinski 112, Arshavin 116)*

Holland: Van der Sar; Boulahrouz (Heitinga 54), Van Bronckhorst, Engelaar (Afellay 61), Ooijer, Mathijsen, De Jong, Kuyt (Van Persie 46), Van Nistelrooy, Sneijder, Van der Vaart.
Russia: Akinfeev; Anyukov, Zhirkov, Semchov (Bilyaletdinov 69), Ignashevich, Kolodin, Semak, Zyryanov, Saenko (Torbinski 81), Pavlyuchenko (Sychev 115), Arshavin.
aet.
Referee: L. Michel (Slovakia).

Vienna, 22 June 2008, 51,428

Spain (0) 0

Italy (0) 0

Spain: Casillas; Sergio Ramos, Capdevila, Xavi (Fabregas 59), Puyol, Marchena, Senna, Iniesta (Santi Cazorla 59), Silva, Torres, Villa.
Italy: Buffon; Zambrotta, Grosso, Di Rossi, Panucci, Chiellini, Aquilani, Ambrosini, Toni, Cassano (Di Natale 75), Perrotta (Camoranesi 58).
aet; Spain won 4-2 on penalties: Villa scored; Grosso scored; Santi Cazorla scored; Di Rossi saved; Senna scored; Camoranesi scored; Guiza saved; Di Natale saved; Fabregas scored.
Referee: H. Fandel (Germany).

SEMI-FINALS

Basle, 25 June 2008, 39,374

Germany (1) 3 *(Schweinsteiger 27, Klose 79, Lahm 90)*

Turkey (1) 2 *(Ugur 22, Semih 86)*

Germany: Lehmann; Friedrich A, Lahm, Rolfes (Frings 46), Metzelder, Mertesacker, Schweinsteiger, Hitzlsperger, Klose (Jansen 90), Ballack, Podolski.
Turkey: Rustu; Sabri, Hakan Balta, Ugur (Gokdeniz 84), Gokhan Z, Mehmet T, Mehmet Aurelio, Ayhan (Erdinc 81), Semih, Hamit Altintop, Kazim-Richards (Tumer 90).
Referee: M. Bussaca (Switzerland).

Vienna, 26 June 2008, 51,428

Russia (0) 0

Spain (0) 3 *(Xavi 50, Guiza 73, Silva 82)*

Russia: Akinfeev; Anyukov, Zhirkov, Semchov (Bilyaletdinov 56), Ignashevich, Berezutski V, Semak, Zyryanov, Pavlyuchenko, Arshavin, Saenko (Sychev 57).
Spain: Casillas; Sergio Ramos, Capdevila, Xavi (Xabi Alonso 69), Puyol, Marchena, Senna, Iniesta, Torres (Guiza 69), Villa (Fabregas 34), Silva.
Referee: F. De Bleeckere (Belgium).

EURO 2008 FINAL

Vienna, 29 June 2008, 51,428

Germany (0) 0 **Spain (1) 1**

Germany: Lehmann; Friedrich A, Lahm (Jansen 46), Frings, Metzelder, Mertesacker, Hitzlsperger (Kuranyi 58), Ballack, Klose (Gomes 79), Schweinsteiger, Podolski.

Spain: Casillas; Sergio Ramos, Capdevila, Senna, Puyol, Marchena, Iniesta, Xavi, Torres (Guiza 78), Fabregas (Xabi Alonso 63), Silva (Santi Cazorla 66).

Scorer: Torres 33.

Referee: R. Rossetti (Italy).

EURO 2008 STATISTICS

Total attendances at Finals – 1,149,353.

Average number of goals per game – 2.48.

Number of red cards – 3.

Number of yellow cards – 122.

BRITISH AND IRISH INTERNATIONAL RESULTS 1872–2008

Note: In the results that follow, wc=World Cup, ec=European Championship, ui=Umbro International Trophy. tf = Tournoi de France. For Ireland, read Northern Ireland from 1921. *After extra time.

ENGLAND v SCOTLAND

Played: 110; England won 45, Scotland won 41, Drawn 24. Goals: England 192, Scotland 169.

			E	*S*
1872	30 Nov	Glasgow	0	0
1873	8 Mar	Kennington Oval	4	2
1874	7 Mar	Glasgow	1	2
1875	6 Mar	Kennington Oval	2	2
1876	4 Mar	Glasgow	0	3
1877	3 Mar	Kennington Oval	1	3
1878	2 Mar	Glasgow	2	7
1879	5 Apr	Kennington Oval	5	4
1880	13 Mar	Glasgow	4	5
1881	12 Mar	Kennington Oval	1	6
1882	11 Mar	Glasgow	1	5
1883	10 Mar	Sheffield	2	3
1884	15 Mar	Glasgow	0	1
1885	21 Mar	Kennington Oval	1	1
1886	31 Mar	Glasgow	1	1
1887	19 Mar	Blackburn	2	3
1888	17 Mar	Glasgow	5	0
1889	13 Apr	Kennington Oval	2	3
1890	5 Apr	Glasgow	1	1
1891	6 Apr	Blackburn	2	1
1892	2 Apr	Glasgow	4	1
1893	1 Apr	Richmond	5	2
1894	7 Apr	Glasgow	2	2
1895	6 Apr	Everton	3	0
1896	4 Apr	Glasgow	1	2
1897	3 Apr	Crystal Palace	1	2
1898	2 Apr	Glasgow	3	1
1899	8 Apr	Birmingham	2	1
1900	7 Apr	Glasgow	1	4
1901	30 Mar	Crystal Palace	2	2
1902	3 Mar	Birmingham	2	2
1903	4 Apr	Sheffield	1	2
1904	9 Apr	Glasgow	1	0
1905	1 Apr	Crystal Palace	1	0
1906	7 Apr	Glasgow	1	2
1907	6 Apr	Newcastle	1	1
1908	4 Apr	Glasgow	1	1
1909	3 Apr	Crystal Palace	2	0
1910	2 Apr	Glasgow	0	2
1911	1 Apr	Everton	1	1
1912	23 Mar	Glasgow	1	1
1913	5 Apr	Chelsea	1	0
1914	14 Apr	Glasgow	1	3
1920	10 Apr	Sheffield	5	4
1921	9 Apr	Glasgow	0	3
1922	8 Apr	Aston Villa	0	1
1923	14 Apr	Glasgow	2	2
1924	12 Apr	Wembley	1	1
1925	4 Apr	Glasgow	0	2
1926	17 Apr	Manchester	0	1
1927	2 Apr	Glasgow	2	1
1928	31 Mar	Wembley	1	5
1929	13 Apr	Glasgow	0	1
1930	5 Apr	Wembley	5	2
1931	28 Mar	Glasgow	0	2
1932	9 Apr	Wembley	3	0
1933	1 Apr	Glasgow	1	2
1934	14 Apr	Wembley	3	0
1935	6 Apr	Glasgow	0	2
1936	4 Apr	Wembley	1	1
1937	17 Apr	Glasgow	1	3
1938	9 Apr	Wembley	0	1
1939	15 Apr	Glasgow	2	1
1947	12 Apr	Wembley	1	1
1948	10 Apr	Glasgow	2	0
1949	9 Apr	Wembley	1	3
wc1950	15 Apr	Glasgow	1	0
1951	14 Apr	Wembley	2	3
1952	5 Apr	Glasgow	2	1
1953	18 Apr	Wembley	2	2
wc1954	3 Apr	Glasgow	4	2
1955	2 Apr	Wembley	7	2
1956	14 Apr	Glasgow	1	1
1957	6 Apr	Wembley	2	1
1958	19 Apr	Glasgow	4	0
1959	11 Apr	Wembley	1	0
1960	9 Apr	Glasgow	1	1
1961	15 Apr	Wembley	9	3
1962	14 Apr	Glasgow	0	2
1963	6 Apr	Wembley	1	2
1964	11 Apr	Glasgow	0	1
1965	10 Apr	Wembley	2	2
1966	2 Apr	Glasgow	4	3
ec1967	15 Apr	Wembley	2	3
ec1968	24 Jan	Glasgow	1	1
1969	10 May	Wembley	4	1
1970	25 Apr	Glasgow	0	0
1971	22 May	Wembley	3	1
1972	27 May	Glasgow	1	0
1973	14 Feb	Glasgow	5	0
1973	19 May	Wembley	1	0
1974	18 May	Glasgow	0	2
1975	24 May	Wembley	5	1
1976	15 May	Glasgow	1	2
1977	4 June	Wembley	1	2
1978	20 May	Glasgow	1	0
1979	26 May	Wembley	3	1
1980	24 May	Glasgow	2	0
1981	23 May	Wembley	0	1
1982	29 May	Glasgow	1	0
1983	1 June	Wembley	2	0
1984	26 May	Glasgow	1	1
1985	25 May	Glasgow	0	1
1986	23 Apr	Wembley	2	1
1987	23 May	Glasgow	0	0
1988	21 May	Wembley	1	0
1989	27 May	Glasgow	2	0
ec1996	15 June	Wembley	2	0
ec1999	13 Nov	Glasgow	2	0
ec1999	17 Nov	Wembley	0	1

ENGLAND v WALES

Played: 99; England won 64, Wales won 14, Drawn 21. Goals: England 242, Wales 90.

			E	*W*
1879	18 Jan	Kennington Oval	2	1
1880	15 Mar	Wrexham	3	2
1881	26 Feb	Blackburn	0	1
1882	13 Mar	Wrexham	3	5
1883	3 Feb	Kennington Oval	5	0
1884	17 Mar	Wrexham	4	0

			E	*W*
1885	14 Mar	Blackburn	1	1
1886	29 Mar	Wrexham	3	1
1887	26 Feb	Kennington Oval	4	0
1888	4 Feb	Crewe	5	1
1889	23 Feb	Stoke	4	1
1890	15 Mar	Wrexham	3	1
1891	7 May	Sunderland	4	1
1892	5 Mar	Wrexham	2	0
1893	13 Mar	Stoke	6	0
1894	12 Mar	Wrexham	5	1
1895	18 Mar	Queen's Club, Kensington	1	1
1896	16 Mar	Cardiff	9	1
1897	29 Mar	Sheffield	4	0
1898	28 Mar	Wrexham	3	0
1899	20 Mar	Bristol	4	0
1900	26 Mar	Cardiff	1	1
1901	18 Mar	Newcastle	6	0
1902	3 Mar	Wrexham	0	0
1903	2 Mar	Portsmouth	2	1
1904	29 Feb	Wrexham	2	2
1905	27 Mar	Liverpool	3	1
1906	19 Mar	Cardiff	1	0
1907	18 Mar	Fulham	1	1
1908	16 Mar	Wrexham	7	1
1909	15 Mar	Nottingham	2	0
1910	14 Mar	Cardiff	1	0
1911	13 Mar	Millwall	3	0
1912	11 Mar	Wrexham	2	0
1913	17 Mar	Bristol	4	3
1914	16 Mar	Cardiff	2	0
1920	15 Mar	Highbury	1	2
1921	14 Mar	Cardiff	0	0
1922	13 Mar	Liverpool	1	0
1923	5 Mar	Cardiff	2	2
1924	3 Mar	Blackburn	1	2
1925	28 Feb	Swansea	2	1
1926	1 Mar	Crystal Palace	1	3
1927	12 Feb	Wrexham	3	3
1927	28 Nov	Burnley	1	2
1928	17 Nov	Swansea	3	2
1929	20 Nov	Chelsea	6	0
1930	22 Nov	Wrexham	4	0
1931	18 Nov	Liverpool	3	1
1932	16 Nov	Wrexham	0	0
1933	15 Nov	Newcastle	1	2
1934	29 Sept	Cardiff	4	0
1936	5 Feb	Wolverhampton	1	2
1936	17 Oct	Cardiff	1	2
1937	17 Nov	Middlesbrough	2	1
1938	22 Oct	Cardiff	2	4
1946	13 Nov	Manchester	3	0
1947	18 Oct	Cardiff	3	0
1948	10 Nov	Aston Villa	1	0
WC1949	15 Oct	Cardiff	4	1
1950	15 Nov	Sunderland	4	2
1951	20 Oct	Cardiff	1	1
1952	12 Nov	Wembley	5	2
WC1953	10 Oct	Cardiff	4	1
1954	10 Nov	Wembley	3	2
1955	27 Oct	Cardiff	1	2
1956	14 Nov	Wembley	3	1
1957	19 Oct	Cardiff	4	0
1958	26 Nov	Aston Villa	2	2
1959	17 Oct	Cardiff	1	1
1960	23 Nov	Wembley	5	1
1961	14 Oct	Cardiff	1	1
1962	21 Oct	Wembley	4	0
1963	12 Oct	Cardiff	4	0
1964	18 Nov	Wembley	2	1
1965	2 Oct	Cardiff	0	0
EC1966	16 Nov	Wembley	5	1
EC1967	21 Oct	Cardiff	3	0
1969	7 May	Wembley	2	1
1970	18 Apr	Cardiff	1	1
1971	19 May	Wembley	0	0
1972	20 May	Cardiff	3	0
WC1972	15 Nov	Cardiff	1	0
WC1973	24 Jan	Wembley	1	1
1973	15 May	Wembley	3	0
1974	11 May	Cardiff	2	0
1975	21 May	Wembley	2	2
1976	24 Mar	Wrexham	2	1
1976	8 May	Cardiff	1	0
1977	31 May	Wembley	0	1
1978	3 May	Cardiff	3	1
1979	23 May	Wembley	0	0
1980	17 May	Wrexham	1	4
1981	20 May	Wembley	0	0
1982	27 Apr	Cardiff	1	0
1983	23 Feb	Wembley	2	1
1984	2 May	Wrexham	0	1
WC2004	9 Oct	Old Trafford	2	0
WC2005	3 Sept	Cardiff	1	0

ENGLAND v IRELAND

Played: 98; England won 75, Ireland won 7, Drawn 16. Goals: England 323, Ireland 81.

			E	*I*
1882	18 Feb	Belfast	13	0
1883	24 Feb	Liverpool	7	0
1884	23 Feb	Belfast	8	1
1885	28 Feb	Manchester	4	0
1886	13 Mar	Belfast	6	1
1887	5 Feb	Sheffield	7	0
1888	31 Mar	Belfast	5	1
1889	2 Mar	Everton	6	1
1890	15 Mar	Belfast	9	1
1891	7 Mar	Wolverhampton	6	1
1892	5 Mar	Belfast	2	0
1893	25 Feb	Birmingham	6	1
1894	3 Mar	Belfast	2	2
1895	9 Mar	Derby	9	0
1896	7 Mar	Belfast	2	0
1897	20 Feb	Nottingham	6	0
1898	5 Mar	Belfast	3	2
1899	18 Feb	Sunderland	13	2
1900	17 Mar	Dublin	2	0
1901	9 Mar	Southampton	3	0
1902	22 Mar	Belfast	1	0
1903	14 Feb	Wolverhampton	4	0
1904	12 Mar	Belfast	3	1
1905	25 Feb	Middlesbrough	1	1
1906	17 Feb	Belfast	5	0
1907	16 Feb	Everton	1	0
1908	15 Feb	Belfast	3	1
1909	13 Feb	Bradford	4	0
1910	12 Feb	Belfast	1	1
1911	11 Feb	Derby	2	1
1912	10 Feb	Dublin	6	1
1913	15 Feb	Belfast	1	2
1914	14 Feb	Middlesbrough	0	3
1919	25 Oct	Belfast	1	1
1920	23 Oct	Sunderland	2	0
1921	22 Oct	Belfast	1	1
1922	21 Oct	West Bromwich	2	0
1923	20 Oct	Belfast	1	2
1924	22 Oct	Everton	3	1
1925	24 Oct	Belfast	0	0
1926	20 Oct	Liverpool	3	3
1927	22 Oct	Belfast	0	2

			E	*I*
1928	22 Oct	Everton	2	1
1929	19 Oct	Belfast	3	0
1930	20 Oct	Sheffield	5	1
1931	17 Oct	Belfast	6	2
1932	17 Oct	Blackpool	1	0
1933	14 Oct	Belfast	3	0
1935	6 Feb	Everton	2	1
1935	19 Oct	Belfast	3	1
1936	18 Nov	Stoke	3	1
1937	23 Oct	Belfast	5	1
1938	16 Nov	Manchester	7	0
1946	28 Sept	Belfast	7	2
1947	5 Nov	Everton	2	2
1948	9 Oct	Belfast	6	2
wc1949	16 Nov	Manchester	9	2
1950	7 Oct	Belfast	4	1
1951	14 Nov	Aston Villa	2	0
1952	4 Oct	Belfast	2	2
wc1953	11 Nov	Everton	3	1
1954	2 Oct	Belfast	2	0
1955	2 Nov	Wembley	3	0
1956	10 Oct	Belfast	1	1
1957	6 Nov	Wembley	2	3
1958	4 Oct	Belfast	3	3
1959	18 Nov	Wembley	2	1
1960	8 Oct	Belfast	5	2
1961	22 Nov	Wembley	1	1
1962	20 Oct	Belfast	3	1
1963	20 Nov	Wembley	8	3
1964	3 Oct	Belfast	4	3
1965	10 Nov	Wembley	2	1
EC1966	20 Oct	Belfast	2	0
EC1967	22 Nov	Wembley	2	0
1969	3 May	Belfast	3	1
1970	21 Apr	Wembley	3	1
1971	15 May	Belfast	1	0
1972	23 May	Wembley	0	1
1973	12 May	Everton	2	1
1974	15 May	Wembley	1	0
1975	17 May	Belfast	0	0
1976	11 May	Wembley	4	0
1977	28 May	Belfast	2	1
1978	16 May	Wembley	1	0
EC1979	7 Feb	Wembley	4	0
1979	19 May	Belfast	2	0
EC1979	17 Oct	Belfast	5	1
1980	20 May	Wembley	1	1
1982	23 Feb	Wembley	4	0
1983	28 May	Belfast	0	0
1984	24 Apr	Wembley	1	0
wc1985	27 Feb	Belfast	1	0
wc1985	13 Nov	Wembley	0	0
EC1986	15 Oct	Wembley	3	0
EC1987	1 Apr	Belfast	2	0
wc2005	26 Mar	Old Trafford	4	0
wc2005	7 Sept	Belfast	0	1

SCOTLAND v WALES

Played: 103; Scotland won 60, Wales won 20, Drawn 23. Goals: Scotland 238, Wales 116.

			S	*W*
1876	25 Mar	Glasgow	4	0
1877	5 Mar	Wrexham	2	0
1878	23 Mar	Glasgow	9	0
1879	7 Apr	Wrexham	3	0
1880	3 Apr	Glasgow	5	1
1881	14 Mar	Wrexham	5	1
1882	25 Mar	Glasgow	5	0
1883	12 Mar	Wrexham	3	0
1884	29 Mar	Glasgow	4	1
1885	23 Mar	Wrexham	8	1
1886	10 Apr	Glasgow	4	1
1887	21 Mar	Wrexham	2	0
1888	10 Mar	Edinburgh	5	1
1889	15 Apr	Wrexham	0	0
1890	22 Mar	Paisley	5	0
1891	21 Mar	Wrexham	4	3
1892	26 Mar	Edinburgh	6	1
1893	18 Mar	Wrexham	8	0
1894	24 Mar	Kilmarnock	5	2
1895	23 Mar	Wrexham	2	2
1896	21 Mar	Dundee	4	0
1897	20 Mar	Wrexham	2	2
1898	19 Mar	Motherwell	5	2
1899	18 Mar	Wrexham	6	0
1900	3 Feb	Aberdeen	5	2
1901	2 Mar	Wrexham	1	1
1902	15 Mar	Greenock	5	1
1903	9 Mar	Cardiff	1	0
1904	12 Mar	Dundee	1	1
1905	6 Mar	Wrexham	1	3
1906	3 Mar	Edinburgh	0	2
1907	4 Mar	Wrexham	0	1
1908	7 Mar	Dundee	2	1
1909	1 Mar	Wrexham	2	3
1910	5 Mar	Kilmarnock	1	0
1911	6 Mar	Cardiff	2	2
1912	2 Mar	Tynecastle	1	0
1913	3 Mar	Wrexham	0	0
1914	28 Feb	Glasgow	0	0
1920	26 Feb	Cardiff	1	1
1921	12 Feb	Aberdeen	2	1
1922	4 Feb	Wrexham	1	2
1923	17 Mar	Paisley	2	0
1924	16 Feb	Cardiff	0	2
1925	14 Feb	Tynecastle	3	1
1925	31 Oct	Cardiff	3	0
1926	30 Oct	Glasgow	3	0
1927	29 Oct	Wrexham	2	2
1928	27 Oct	Glasgow	4	2
1929	26 Oct	Cardiff	4	2
1930	25 Oct	Glasgow	1	1
1931	31 Oct	Wrexham	3	2
1932	26 Oct	Edinburgh	2	5
1933	4 Oct	Cardiff	2	3
1934	21 Nov	Aberdeen	3	2
1935	5 Oct	Cardiff	1	1
1936	2 Dec	Dundee	1	2
1937	30 Oct	Cardiff	1	2
1938	9 Nov	Edinburgh	3	2
1946	19 Oct	Wrexham	1	3
1947	12 Nov	Glasgow	1	2
wc1948	23 Oct	Cardiff	3	1
1949	9 Nov	Glasgow	2	0
1950	21 Oct	Cardiff	3	1
1951	14 Nov	Glasgow	0	1
wc1952	18 Oct	Cardiff	2	1
1953	4 Nov	Glasgow	3	3
1954	16 Oct	Cardiff	1	0
1955	9 Nov	Glasgow	2	0
1956	20 Oct	Cardiff	2	2
1957	13 Nov	Glasgow	1	1
1958	18 Oct	Cardiff	3	0
1959	4 Nov	Glasgow	1	1
1960	20 Oct	Cardiff	0	2
1961	8 Nov	Glasgow	2	0
1962	20 Oct	Cardiff	3	2
1963	20 Nov	Glasgow	2	1
1964	3 Oct	Cardiff	2	3
EC1965	24 Nov	Glasgow	4	1
EC1966	22 Oct	Cardiff	1	1

			S	W				S	W
1967	22 Nov	Glasgow	3	2	wc1977	12 Oct	Liverpool	2	0
1969	3 May	Wrexham	5	3	1978	17 May	Glasgow	1	1
1970	22 Apr	Glasgow	0	0	1979	19 May	Cardiff	0	3
1971	15 May	Cardiff	0	0	1980	21 May	Glasgow	1	0
1972	24 May	Glasgow	1	0	1981	16 May	Swansea	0	2
1973	12 May	Wrexham	2	0	1982	24 May	Glasgow	1	0
1974	14 May	Glasgow	2	0	1983	28 May	Cardiff	2	0
1975	17 May	Cardiff	2	2	1984	28 Feb	Glasgow	2	1
1976	6 May	Glasgow	3	1	wc1985	27 Mar	Glasgow	0	1
wc1976	17 Nov	Glasgow	1	0	wc1985	10 Sept	Cardiff	1	1
1977	28 May	Wrexham	0	0	1997	27 May	Kilmarnock	0	1
					2004	18 Feb	Cardiff	0	4

SCOTLAND v IRELAND

Played: 93; Scotland won 62, Ireland won 15, Drawn 16. Goals: Scotland 257, Ireland 81.

			S	I				S	I
1884	26 Jan	Belfast	5	0	1934	20 Oct	Belfast	1	2
1885	14 Mar	Glasgow	8	2	1935	13 Nov	Edinburgh	2	1
1886	20 Mar	Belfast	7	2	1936	31 Oct	Belfast	3	1
1887	19 Feb	Glasgow	4	1	1937	10 Nov	Aberdeen	1	1
1888	24 Mar	Belfast	10	2	1938	8 Oct	Belfast	2	0
1889	9 Mar	Glasgow	7	0	1946	27 Nov	Glasgow	0	0
1890	29 Mar	Belfast	4	1	1947	4 Oct	Belfast	0	2
1891	28 Mar	Glasgow	2	1	1948	17 Nov	Glasgow	3	2
1892	19 Mar	Belfast	3	2	1949	1 Oct	Belfast	8	2
1893	25 Mar	Glasgow	6	1	1950	1 Nov	Glasgow	6	1
1894	31 Mar	Belfast	2	1	1951	6 Oct	Belfast	3	0
1895	30 Mar	Glasgow	3	1	1952	5 Nov	Glasgow	1	1
1896	28 Mar	Belfast	3	3	1953	3 Oct	Belfast	3	1
1897	27 Mar	Glasgow	5	1	1954	3 Nov	Glasgow	2	2
1898	26 Mar	Belfast	3	0	1955	8 Oct	Belfast	1	2
1899	25 Mar	Glasgow	9	1	1956	7 Nov	Glasgow	1	0
1900	3 Mar	Belfast	3	0	1957	5 Oct	Belfast	1	1
1901	23 Feb	Glasgow	11	0	1958	5 Nov	Glasgow	2	2
1902	1 Mar	Belfast	5	1	1959	3 Oct	Belfast	4	0
1902	9 Aug	Belfast	3	0	1960	9 Nov	Glasgow	5	2
1903	21 Mar	Glasgow	0	2	1961	7 Oct	Belfast	6	1
1904	26 Mar	Dublin	1	1	1962	7 Nov	Glasgow	5	1
1905	18 Mar	Glasgow	4	0	1963	12 Oct	Belfast	1	2
1906	17 Mar	Dublin	1	0	1964	25 Nov	Glasgow	3	2
1907	16 Mar	Glasgow	3	0	1965	2 Oct	Belfast	2	3
1908	14 Mar	Dublin	5	0	1966	16 Nov	Glasgow	2	1
1909	15 Mar	Glasgow	5	0	1967	21 Oct	Belfast	0	1
1910	19 Mar	Belfast	0	1	1969	6 May	Glasgow	1	1
1911	18 Mar	Glasgow	2	0	1970	18 Apr	Belfast	1	0
1912	16 Mar	Belfast	4	1	1971	18 May	Glasgow	0	1
1913	15 Mar	Dublin	2	1	1972	20 May	Glasgow	2	0
1914	14 Mar	Belfast	1	1	1973	16 May	Glasgow	1	2
1920	13 Mar	Glasgow	3	0	1974	11 May	Glasgow	0	1
1921	26 Feb	Belfast	2	0	1975	20 May	Glasgow	3	0
1922	4 Mar	Glasgow	2	1	1976	8 May	Glasgow	3	0
1923	3 Mar	Belfast	1	0	1977	1 June	Glasgow	3	0
1924	1 Mar	Glasgow	2	0	1978	13 May	Glasgow	1	1
1925	28 Feb	Belfast	3	0	1979	22 May	Glasgow	1	0
1926	27 Feb	Glasgow	4	0	1980	17 May	Belfast	0	1
1927	26 Feb	Belfast	2	0	wc1981	25 Mar	Glasgow	1	1
1928	25 Feb	Glasgow	0	1	1981	19 May	Glasgow	2	0
1929	23 Feb	Belfast	7	3	wc1981	14 Oct	Belfast	0	0
1930	22 Feb	Glasgow	3	1	1982	28 Apr	Belfast	1	1
1931	21 Feb	Belfast	0	0	1983	24 May	Glasgow	0	0
1931	19 Sept	Glasgow	3	1	1983	13 Dec	Belfast	0	2
1932	12 Sept	Belfast	4	0	1992	19 Feb	Glasgow	1	0
1933	16 Sept	Glasgow	1	2					

WALES v IRELAND

Played: 93; Wales won 43, Ireland won 27, Drawn 23. Goals: Wales 187, Ireland 131.

			W	I				W	I
1882	25 Feb	Wrexham	7	1	1886	27 Feb	Wrexham	5	0
1883	17 Mar	Belfast	1	1	1887	12 Mar	Belfast	1	4
1884	9 Feb	Wrexham	6	0	1888	3 Mar	Wrexham	11	0
1885	11 Apr	Belfast	8	2	1889	27 Apr	Belfast	3	1

			W	I
1890	8 Feb	Shrewsbury	5	2
1891	7 Feb	Belfast	2	7
1892	27 Feb	Bangor	1	1
1893	8 Apr	Belfast	3	4
1894	24 Feb	Swansea	4	1
1895	16 Mar	Belfast	2	2
1896	29 Feb	Wrexham	6	1
1897	6 Mar	Belfast	3	4
1898	19 Feb	Llandudno	0	1
1899	4 Mar	Belfast	0	1
1900	24 Feb	Llandudno	2	0
1901	23 Mar	Belfast	1	0
1902	22 Mar	Cardiff	0	3
1903	28 Mar	Belfast	0	2
1904	21 Mar	Bangor	0	1
1905	18 Apr	Belfast	2	2
1906	2 Apr	Wrexham	4	4
1907	23 Feb	Belfast	3	2
1908	11 Apr	Aberdare	0	1
1909	20 Mar	Belfast	3	2
1910	11 Apr	Wrexham	4	1
1911	28 Jan	Belfast	2	1
1912	13 Apr	Cardiff	2	3
1913	18 Jan	Belfast	1	0
1914	19 Jan	Wrexham	1	2
1920	14 Feb	Belfast	2	2
1921	9 Apr	Swansea	2	1
1922	4 Apr	Belfast	1	1
1923	14 Apr	Wrexham	0	3
1924	15 Mar	Belfast	1	0
1925	18 Apr	Wrexham	0	0
1926	13 Feb	Belfast	0	3
1927	9 Apr	Cardiff	2	2
1928	4 Feb	Belfast	2	1
1929	2 Feb	Wrexham	2	2
1930	1 Feb	Belfast	0	7
1931	22 Apr	Wrexham	3	2
1931	5 Dec	Belfast	0	4
1932	7 Dec	Wrexham	4	1
1933	4 Nov	Belfast	1	1
1935	27 Mar	Wrexham	3	1
1936	11 Mar	Belfast	2	3
1937	17 Mar	Wrexham	4	1
1938	16 Mar	Belfast	0	1
1939	15 Mar	Wrexham	3	1
1947	16 Apr	Belfast	1	2
1948	10 Mar	Wrexham	2	0
1949	9 Mar	Belfast	2	0
WC1950	8 Mar	Wrexham	0	0
1951	7 Mar	Belfast	2	1
1952	19 Mar	Swansea	3	0
1953	15 Apr	Belfast	3	2
WC1954	31 Mar	Wrexham	1	2
1955	20 Apr	Belfast	3	2
1956	11 Apr	Cardiff	1	1
1957	10 Apr	Belfast	0	0
1958	16 Apr	Cardiff	1	1
1959	22 Apr	Belfast	1	4
1960	6 Apr	Wrexham	3	2
1961	12 Apr	Belfast	5	1
1962	11 Apr	Cardiff	4	0
1963	3 Apr	Belfast	4	1
1964	15 Apr	Cardiff	2	3
1965	31 Mar	Belfast	5	0
1966	30 Mar	Cardiff	1	4
EC1967	12 Apr	Belfast	0	0
EC1968	28 Feb	Wrexham	2	0
1969	10 May	Belfast	0	0
1970	25 Apr	Swansea	1	0
1971	22 May	Belfast	0	1
1972	27 May	Wrexham	0	0
1973	19 May	Everton	0	1
1974	18 May	Wrexham	1	0
1975	23 May	Belfast	0	1
1976	14 May	Swansea	1	0
1977	3 June	Belfast	1	1
1978	19 May	Wrexham	1	0
1979	25 May	Belfast	1	1
1980	23 May	Cardiff	0	1
1982	27 May	Wrexham	3	0
1983	31 May	Belfast	1	0
1984	22 May	Swansea	1	1
WC2004	8 Sept	Cardiff	2	2
WC2005	8 Oct	Belfast	3	2
2007	6 Feb	Belfast	0	0

OTHER BRITISH INTERNATIONAL RESULTS 1908–2008

ENGLAND

		v ALBANIA	E	A
WC1989	8 Mar	Tirana	2	0
WC1989	26 Apr	Wembley	5	0
WC2001	28 Mar	Tirana	3	1
WC2001	5 Sept	Newcastle	2	0

		v ANDORRA	E	A
EC2006	2 Sept	Old Trafford	5	0
EC2007	28 Mar	Barcelona	3	0

		v ARGENTINA	E	A
1951	9 May	Wembley	2	1
1953	17 May	Buenos Aires	0	0
(abandoned after 21 mins)				
WC1962	2 June	Rancagua	3	1
1964	6 June	Rio de Janeiro	0	1
WC1966	23 July	Wembley	1	0
1974	22 May	Wembley	2	2
1977	12 June	Buenos Aires	1	1
1980	13 May	Wembley	3	1
WC1986	22 June	Mexico City	1	2
1991	25 May	Wembley	2	2
WC1998	30 June	St Etienne	2	2
2000	23 Feb	Wembley	0	0
WC2002	7 June	Sapporo	1	0
2005	12 Nov	Geneva	3	2

		v AUSTRALIA	E	A
1980	31 May	Sydney	2	1
1983	11 June	Sydney	0	0
1983	15 June	Brisbane	1	0
1983	18 June	Melbourne	1	1
1991	1 June	Sydney	1	0
2003	12 Feb	West Ham	1	3

		v AUSTRIA	E	A
1908	6 June	Vienna	6	1
1908	8 June	Vienna	11	1
1909	1 June	Vienna	8	1
1930	14 May	Vienna	0	0
1932	7 Dec	Chelsea	4	3
1936	6 May	Vienna	1	2
1951	28 Nov	Wembley	2	2
1952	25 May	Vienna	3	2
WC1958	15 June	Boras	2	2
1961	27 May	Vienna	1	3
1962	4 Apr	Wembley	3	1
1965	20 Oct	Wembley	2	3
1967	27 May	Vienna	1	0
1973	26 Sept	Wembley	7	0
1979	13 June	Vienna	3	4
WC2004	4 Sept	Vienna	2	2
WC2005	8 Oct	Old Trafford	1	0
2007	16 Nov	Vienna	1	0

		v AZERBAIJAN	E	A
WC2004	13 Oct	Baku	1	0
WC2005	30 Mar	Newcastle	2	0

		v BELGIUM	E	B
1921	21 May	Brussels	2	0
1923	19 Mar	Highbury	6	1
1923	1 Nov	Antwerp	2	2
1924	8 Dec	West Bromwich	4	0

			E	*B*
1926	24 May	Antwerp	5	3
1927	11 May	Brussels	9	1
1928	19 May	Antwerp	3	1
1929	11 May	Brussels	5	1
1931	16 May	Brussels	4	1
1936	9 May	Brussels	2	3
1947	21 Sept	Brussels	5	2
1950	18 May	Brussels	4	1
1952	26 Nov	Wembley	5	0
WC1954	17 June	Basle	4	4*
1964	21 Oct	Wembley	2	2
1970	25 Feb	Brussels	3	1
EC1980	12 June	Turin	1	1
WC1990	27 June	Bologna	1	0*
1998	29 May	Casablanca	0	0
1999	10 Oct	Sunderland	2	1

v BOHEMIA

			E	*B*
1908	13 June	Prague	4	0

v BRAZIL

			E	*B*
1956	9 May	Wembley	4	2
WC1958	11 June	Gothenburg	0	0
1959	13 May	Rio de Janeiro	0	2
WC1962	10 June	Vina del Mar	1	3
1963	8 May	Wembley	1	1
1964	30 May	Rio de Janeiro	1	5
1969	12 June	Rio de Janeiro	1	2
WC1970	7 June	Guadalajara	0	1
1976	23 May	Los Angeles	0	1
1977	8 June	Rio de Janeiro	0	0
1978	19 Apr	Wembley	1	1
1981	12 May	Wembley	0	1
1984	10 June	Rio de Janeiro	2	0
1987	19 May	Wembley	1	1
1990	28 Mar	Wembley	1	0
1992	17 May	Wembley	1	1
1993	13 June	Washington	1	1
UI1995	11 June	Wembley	1	3
TF1997	10 June	Paris	0	1
2000	27 May	Wembley	1	1
WC2002	21 June	Shizuoka	1	2
2007	1 June	Wembley	1	1

v BULGARIA

			E	*B*
WC1962	7 June	Rancagua	0	0
1968	11 Dec	Wembley	1	1
1974	1 June	Sofia	1	0
EC1979	6 June	Sofia	3	0
EC1979	22 Nov	Wembley	2	0
1996	27 Mar	Wembley	1	0
EC1998	10 Oct	Wembley	0	0
EC1999	9 June	Sofia	1	1

v CAMEROON

			E	*C*
WC1990	1 July	Naples	3	2*
1991	6 Feb	Wembley	2	0
1997	15 Nov	Wembley	2	0
2002	26 May	Kobe	2	2

v CANADA

			E	*C*
1986	24 May	Burnaby	1	0

v CHILE

			E	*C*
WC1950	25 June	Rio de Janeiro	2	0
1953	24 May	Santiago	2	1
1984	17 June	Santiago	0	0
1989	23 May	Wembley	0	0
1998	11 Feb	Wembley	0	2

v CHINA

			E	*C*
1996	23 May	Beijing	3	0

v CIS

			E	*C*
1992	29 Apr	Moscow	2	2

v COLOMBIA

			E	*C*
1970	20 May	Bogota	4	0
1988	24 May	Wembley	1	1
1995	6 Sept	Wembley	0	0
WC1998	26 June	Lens	2	0
2005	31 May	New Jersey	3	2

v CROATIA

			E	*C*
1996	24 Apr	Wembley	0	0
2003	20 Aug	Ipswich	3	1
EC2004	21 June	Lisbon	4	2
EC2006	11 Oct	Zagreb	0	2
EC2007	21 Nov	Wembley	2	3

v CYPRUS

			E	*C*
EC1975	16 Apr	Wembley	5	0
EC1975	11 May	Limassol	1	0

v CZECHOSLOVAKIA

			E	*C*
1934	16 May	Prague	1	2
1937	1 Dec	Tottenham	5	4
1963	29 May	Bratislava	4	2
1966	2 Nov	Wembley	0	0
WC1970	11 June	Guadalajara	1	0
1973	27 May	Prague	1	1
EC1974	30 Oct	Wembley	3	0
EC1975	30 Oct	Bratislava	1	2
1978	29 Nov	Wembley	1	0
WC1982	20 June	Bilbao	2	0
1990	25 Apr	Wembley	4	2
1992	25 Mar	Prague	2	2

v CZECH REPUBLIC

			E	*C*
1998	18 Nov	Wembley	2	0

v DENMARK

			E	*D*
1948	26 Sept	Copenhagen	0	0
1955	2 Oct	Copenhagen	5	1
WC1956	5 Dec	Wolverhampton	5	2
WC1957	15 May	Copenhagen	4	1
1966	3 July	Copenhagen	2	0
EC1978	20 Sept	Copenhagen	4	3
EC1979	12 Sept	Wembley	1	0
EC1982	22 Sept	Copenhagen	2	2
EC1983	21 Sept	Wembley	0	1
1988	14 Sept	Wembley	1	0
1989	7 June	Copenhagen	1	1
1990	15 May	Wembley	1	0
EC1992	11 June	Malmo	0	0
1994	9 Mar	Wembley	1	0
WC2002	15 June	Niigata	3	0
2003	16 Nov	Old Trafford	2	3
2005	17 Aug	Copenhagen	1	4

v ECUADOR

			E	*Ec*
1970	24 May	Quito	2	0
WC2006	25 June	Stuttgart	1	0

v EGYPT

			E	*Eg*
1986	29 Jan	Cairo	4	0
WC1990	21 June	Cagliari	1	0

v ESTONIA

			E	*Es*
EC2007	6 June	Tallinn	3	0
EC2007	13 Oct	Wembley	3	0

v FIFA

			E	*FIFA*
1938	26 Oct	Highbury	3	0
1953	21 Oct	Wembley	4	4
1963	23 Oct	Wembley	2	1

v FINLAND

			E	*F*
1937	20 May	Helsinki	8	0
1956	20 May	Helsinki	5	1
1966	26 June	Helsinki	3	0
WC1976	13 June	Helsinki	4	1
WC1976	13 Oct	Wembley	2	1
1982	3 June	Helsinki	4	1
WC1984	17 Oct	Wembley	5	0
WC1985	22 May	Helsinki	1	1
1992	3 June	Helsinki	2	1
WC2000	11 Oct	Helsinki	0	0
WC2001	24 Mar	Liverpool	2	1

v FRANCE

			E	*F*
1923	10 May	Paris	4	1
1924	17 May	Paris	3	1
1925	21 May	Paris	3	2
1927	26 May	Paris	6	0
1928	17 May	Paris	5	1

			E	F
1929	9 May	Paris	4	1
1931	14 May	Paris	2	5
1933	6 Dec	Tottenham	4	1
1938	26 May	Paris	4	2
1947	3 May	Highbury	3	0
1949	22 May	Paris	3	1
1951	3 Oct	Highbury	2	2
1955	15 May	Paris	0	1
1957	27 Nov	Wembley	4	0
EC1962	3 Oct	Sheffield	1	1
EC1963	27 Feb	Paris	2	5
WC1966	20 July	Wembley	2	0
1969	12 Mar	Wembley	5	0
WC1982	16 June	Bilbao	3	1
1984	29 Feb	Paris	0	2
1992	19 Feb	Wembley	2	0
EC1992	14 June	Malmo	0	0
TF1997	7 June	Montpellier	1	0
1999	10 Feb	Wembley	0	2
2000	2 Sept	Paris	1	1
EC2004	13 June	Lisbon	1	2
2008	26 Mar	Paris	0	1

		v GEORGIA	E	G
WC1996	9 Nov	Tbilisi	2	0
WC1997	30 Apr	Wembley	2	0

		v GERMANY	E	G
1930	10 May	Berlin	3	3
1935	4 Dec	Tottenham	3	0
1938	14 May	Berlin	6	3
1991	11 Sept	Wembley	0	1
1993	19 June	Detroit	1	2
EC1996	26 June	Wembley	1	1*
EC2000	17 June	Charleroi	1	0
WC2000	7 Oct	Wembley	0	1
WC2001	1 Sept	Munich	5	1
2007	22 Aug	Wembley	1	2

		v EAST GERMANY	E	EG
1963	2 June	Leipzig	2	1
1970	25 Nov	Wembley	3	1
1974	29 May	Leipzig	1	1
1984	12 Sept	Wembley	1	0

		v WEST GERMANY	E	WG
1954	1 Dec	Wembley	3	1
1956	26 May	Berlin	3	1
1965	12 May	Nuremberg	1	0
1966	23 Feb	Wembley	1	0
WC1966	30 July	Wembley	4	2*
1968	1 June	Hanover	0	1
WC1970	14 June	Leon	2	3*
EC1972	29 Apr	Wembley	1	3
EC1972	13 May	Berlin	0	0
1975	12 Mar	Wembley	2	0
1978	22 Feb	Munich	1	2
WC1982	29 June	Madrid	0	0
1982	13 Oct	Wembley	1	2
1985	12 June	Mexico City	3	0
1987	9 Sept	Dusseldorf	1	3
WC1990	4 July	Turin	1	1*

		v GREECE	E	G
EC1971	21 Apr	Wembley	3	0
EC1971	1 Dec	Piraeus	2	0
EC1982	17 Nov	Salonika	3	0
EC1983	30 Mar	Wembley	0	0
1989	8 Feb	Athens	2	1
1994	17 May	Wembley	5	0
WC2001	6 June	Athens	2	0
WC2001	6 Oct	Old Trafford	2	2
2006	16 Aug	Old Trafford	4	0

		v HOLLAND	E	H
1935	18 May	Amsterdam	1	0
1946	27 Nov	Huddersfield	8	2
1964	9 Dec	Amsterdam	1	1
1969	5 Nov	Amsterdam	1	0
1970	14 Jun	Wembley	0	0
1977	9 Feb	Wembley	0	2
1982	25 May	Wembley	2	0
1988	23 Mar	Wembley	2	2
EC1988	15 June	Dusseldorf	1	3
WC1990	16 June	Cagliari	0	0
2005	9 Feb	Villa Park	0	0
WC1993	28 Apr	Wembley	2	2
WC1993	13 Oct	Rotterdam	0	2
EC1996	18 June	Wembley	4	1
2001	15 Aug	Tottenham	0	2
2002	13 Feb	Amsterdam	1	1
2006	15 Nov	Amsterdam	1	1

		v HUNGARY	E	H
1908	10 June	Budapest	7	0
1909	29 May	Budapest	4	2
1909	31 May	Budapest	8	2
1934	10 May	Budapest	1	2
1936	2 Dec	Highbury	6	2
1953	25 Nov	Wembley	3	6
1954	23 May	Budapest	1	7
1960	22 May	Budapest	0	2
WC1962	31 May	Rancagua	1	2
1965	5 May	Wembley	1	0
1978	24 May	Wembley	4	1
WC1981	6 June	Budapest	3	1
WC1982	18 Nov	Wembley	1	0
EC1983	27 Apr	Wembley	2	0
EC1983	12 Oct	Budapest	3	0
1988	27 Apr	Budapest	0	0
1990	12 Sept	Wembley	1	0
1992	12 May	Budapest	1	0
1996	18 May	Wembley	3	0
1999	28 Apr	Budapest	1	1
2006	30 May	Old Trafford	3	1

		v ICELAND	E	I
1982	2 June	Reykjavik	1	1
2004	5 June	City of Manchester	6	1
EC2007	24 Mar	Tel Aviv	0	0

		v REPUBLIC OF IRELAND	E	RI
1946	30 Sept	Dublin	1	0
1949	21 Sept	Everton	0	2
WC1957	8 May	Wembley	5	1
WC1957	19 May	Dublin	1	1
1964	24 May	Dublin	3	1
1976	8 Sept	Wembley	1	1
EC1978	25 Oct	Dublin	1	1
EC1980	6 Feb	Wembley	2	0
1985	26 Mar	Wembley	2	1
EC1988	12 June	Stuttgart	0	1
WC1990	11 June	Cagliari	1	1
EC1990	14 Nov	Dublin	1	1
EC1991	27 Mar	Wembley	1	1
1995	15 Feb	Dublin	0	1

(abandoned after 27 mins)

		v ISRAEL	E	I
1986	26 Feb	Ramat Gan	2	1
1988	17 Feb	Tel Aviv	0	0
EC2007	24 Mar	Tel Aviv	0	0
EC2007	8 Sept	Wembley	3	0

		v ITALY	E	I
1933	13 May	Rome	1	1
1934	14 Nov	Highbury	3	2
1939	13 May	Milan	2	2
1948	16 May	Turin	4	0
1949	30 Nov	Tottenham	2	0
1952	18 May	Florence	1	1
1959	6 May	Wembley	2	2
1961	24 May	Rome	3	2
1973	14 June	Turin	0	2
1973	14 Nov	Wembley	0	1
1976	28 May	New York	3	2
WC1976	17 Nov	Rome	0	2
WC1977	16 Nov	Wembley	2	0
EC1980	15 June	Turin	0	1
1985	6 June	Mexico City	1	2
1989	15 Nov	Wembley	0	0
WC1990	7 July	Bari	1	2

			E	*I*
WC1997	12 Feb	Wembley	0	1
TF1997	4 June	Nantes	2	0
WC1997	11 Oct	Rome	0	0
2000	15 Nov	Turin	0	1
2002	27 Mar	Leeds	1	2

		v JAMAICA	*E*	*J*
2006	3 June	Old Trafford	6	0

		v JAPAN	*E*	*J*
UI1995	3 June	Wembley	2	1
2004	1 June	City of Manchester	1	1

		v KUWAIT	*E*	*K*
WC1982	25 June	Bilbao	1	0

		v LIECHTENSTEIN	*E*	*L*
EC2003	29 Mar	Vaduz	2	0
EC2003	10 Sept	Old Trafford	2	0

		v LUXEMBOURG	*E*	*L*
1927	21 May	Esch-sur-Alzette	5	2
WC1960	19 Oct	Luxembourg	9	0
WC1961	28 Sept	Highbury	4	1
WC1977	30 Mar	Wembley	5	0
WC1977	12 Oct	Luxembourg	2	0
EC1982	15 Dec	Wembley	9	0
EC1983	16 Nov	Luxembourg	4	0
EC1998	14 Oct	Luxembourg	3	0
EC1999	4 Sept	Wembley	6	0

		v MACEDONIA	*E*	*M*
EC2002	16 Oct	Southampton	2	2
EC2003	6 Sept	Skopje	2	1
EC2006	6 Sept	Skopje	1	0
EC2006	7 Oct	Old Trafford	0	0

		v MALAYSIA	*E*	*M*
1991	12 June	Kuala Lumpur	4	2

		v MALTA	*E*	*M*
EC1971	3 Feb	Valletta	1	0
EC1971	12 May	Wembley	5	0
2000	3 June	Valletta	2	1

		v MEXICO	*E*	*M*
1959	24 May	Mexico City	1	2
1961	10 May	Wembley	8	0
WC1966	16 July	Wembley	2	0
1969	1 June	Mexico City	0	0
1985	9 June	Mexico City	0	1
1986	17 May	Los Angeles	3	0
1997	29 Mar	Wembley	2	0
2001	25 May	Derby	4	0

		v MOLDOVA	*E*	*M*
WC1996	1 Sept	Chisinau	3	0
WC1997	10 Sept	Wembley	4	0

		v MOROCCO	*E*	*M*
WC1986	6 June	Monterrey	0	0
1998	27 May	Casablanca	1	0

		v NEW ZEALAND	*E*	*NZ*
1991	3 June	Auckland	1	0
1991	8 June	Wellington	2	0

		v NIGERIA	*E*	*N*
1994	16 Nov	Wembley	1	0
WC2002	12 June	Osaka	0	0

		v NORWAY	*E*	*N*
1937	14 May	Oslo	6	0
1938	9 Nov	Newcastle	4	0
1949	18 May	Oslo	4	1
1966	29 June	Oslo	6	1
WC1980	10 Sept	Wembley	4	0
WC1981	9 Sept	Oslo	1	2
WC1992	14 Oct	Wembley	1	1
WC1993	2 June	Oslo	0	2
1994	22 May	Wembley	0	0
1995	11 Oct	Oslo	0	0

		v PARAGUAY	*E*	*P*
WC1986	18 June	Mexico City	3	0
2002	17 Apr	Liverpool	4	0
WC2006	10 June	Frankfurt	1	0

		v PERU	*E*	*P*
1959	17 May	Lima	1	4
1962	20 May	Lima	4	0

		v POLAND	*E*	*P*
1966	5 Jan	Everton	1	1
1966	5 July	Chorzow	1	0
WC1973	6 June	Chorzow	0	2
WC1973	17 Oct	Wembley	1	1
WC1986	11 June	Monterrey	3	0
WC1989	3 June	Wembley	3	0
WC1989	11 Oct	Katowice	0	0
EC1990	17 Oct	Wembley	2	0
EC1991	13 Nov	Poznan	1	1
WC1993	29 May	Katowice	1	1
WC1993	8 Sept	Wembley	3	0
WC1996	9 Oct	Wembley	2	1
WC1997	31 May	Katowice	2	0
EC1999	27 Mar	Wembley	3	1
EC1999	8 Sept	Warsaw	0	0
WC2004	8 Sept	Katowice	2	1
WC2005	12 Oct	Old Trafford	2	1

		v PORTUGAL	*E*	*P*
1947	25 May	Lisbon	10	0
1950	14 May	Lisbon	5	3
1951	19 May	Everton	5	2
1955	22 May	Oporto	1	3
1958	7 May	Wembley	2	1
WC1961	21 May	Lisbon	1	1
WC1961	25 Oct	Wembley	2	0
1964	17 May	Lisbon	4	3
1964	4 June	São Paulo	1	1
WC1966	26 July	Wembley	2	1
1969	10 Dec	Wembley	1	0
1974	3 Apr	Lisbon	0	0
EC1974	20 Nov	Wembley	0	0
EC1975	19 Nov	Lisbon	1	1
WC1986	3 June	Monterrey	0	1
1995	12 Dec	Wembley	1	1
1998	22 Apr	Wembley	3	0
EC2000	12 June	Eindhoven	2	3
2002	7 Sept	Villa Park	1	1
2004	18 Feb	Faro	1	1
EC2004	24 June	Lisbon	2	2*
WC2006	1 July	Gelsenkirchen	0	0

		v ROMANIA	*E*	*R*
1939	24 May	Bucharest	2	0
1968	6 Nov	Bucharest	0	0
1969	15 Jan	Wembley	1	1
WC1970	2 June	Guadalajara	1	0
WC1980	15 Oct	Bucharest	1	2
WC1981	29 April	Wembley	0	0
WC1985	1 May	Bucharest	0	0
WC1985	11 Sept	Wembley	1	1
1994	12 Oct	Wembley	1	1
WC1998	22 June	Toulouse	1	2
EC2000	20 June	Charleroi	2	3

		v RUSSIA	*E*	*R*
EC2007	12 Sept	Wembley	3	0
EC2007	17 Oct	Moscow	1	2

		v SAN MARINO	*E*	*SM*
WC1992	17 Feb	Wembley	6	0
WC1993	17 Nov	Bologna	7	1

		v SAUDI ARABIA	*E*	*SA*
1988	16 Nov	Riyadh	1	1
1998	23 May	Wembley	0	0

		v SERBIA-MONTENEGRO	*E*	*S-M*
2003	3 June	Leicester	2	1

		v SLOVAKIA	*E*	*S*
EC2002	12 Oct	Bratislava	2	1
EC2003	11 June	Middlesbrough	2	1

		v SOUTH AFRICA	*E*	*SA*
1997	24 May	Old Trafford	2	1
2003	22 May	Durban	2	1

		v SOUTH KOREA	*E*	*SK*
2002	21 May	Seoguipo	1	1

		v SPAIN	E	S
1929	15 May	Madrid	3	4
1931	9 Dec	Highbury	7	1
WC1950	2 July	Rio de Janeiro	0	1
1955	18 May	Madrid	1	1
1955	30 Nov	Wembley	4	1
1960	15 May	Madrid	0	3
1960	26 Oct	Wembley	4	2
1965	8 Dec	Madrid	2	0
1967	24 May	Wembley	2	0
EC1968	3 Apr	Wembley	1	0
EC1968	8 May	Madrid	2	1
1980	26 Mar	Barcelona	2	0
EC1980	18 June	Naples	2	1
1981	25 Mar	Wembley	1	2
WC1982	5 July	Madrid	0	0
1987	18 Feb	Madrid	4	2
1992	9 Sept	Santander	0	1
EC 1996	22 June	Wembley	0	0
2001	28 Feb	Villa Park	3	0
2004	17 Nov	Madrid	0	1
2007	7 Feb	Old Trafford	0	1

		v SWEDEN	E	S
1923	21 May	Stockholm	4	2
1923	24 May	Stockholm	3	1
1937	17 May	Stockholm	4	0
1947	19 Nov	Highbury	4	2
1949	13 May	Stockholm	1	3
1956	16 May	Stockholm	0	0
1959	28 Oct	Wembley	2	3
1965	16 May	Gothenburg	2	1
1968	22 May	Wembley	3	1
1979	10 June	Stockholm	0	0
1986	10 Sept	Stockholm	0	1
WC1988	19 Oct	Wembley	0	0
WC1989	6 Sept	Stockholm	0	0
EC1992	17 June	Stockholm	1	2
UI1995	8 June	Leeds	3	3
EC1998	5 Sept	Stockholm	1	2
EC1999	5 June	Wembley	0	0
2001	10 Nov	Old Trafford	1	1
WC2002	2 June	Saitama	1	1
2004	31 Mar	Gothenburg	0	1
WC2006	20 June	Cologne	2	2

		v SWITZERLAND	E	S
1933	20 May	Berne	4	0
1938	21 May	Zurich	1	2
1947	18 May	Zurich	0	1
1948	2 Dec	Highbury	6	0
1952	28 May	Zurich	3	0
WC1954	20 June	Berne	2	0
1962	9 May	Wembley	3	1
1963	5 June	Basle	8	1
EC1971	13 Oct	Basle	3	2
EC1971	10 Nov	Wembley	1	1
1975	3 Sept	Basle	2	1
1977	7 Sept	Wembley	0	0
WC1980	19 Nov	Wembley	2	1
WC1981	30 May	Basle	1	2
1988	28 May	Lausanne	1	0
1995	15 Nov	Wembley	3	1
EC1996	8 June	Wembley	1	1
1998	25 Mar	Berne	1	1
EC2004	17 June	Coimbra	3	0
2008	6 Feb	Wembley	2	1

		v TRINIDAD & TOBAGO	E	Tr
WC2006	15 June	Nuremberg	2	0
2008	2 June	Port of Spain	3	0

		v TUNISIA	E	T
1990	2 June	Tunis	1	1
WC1998	15 June	Marseilles	2	0

		v TURKEY	E	T
WC1984	14 Nov	Istanbul	8	0
			E	T
WC1985	16 Oct	Wembley	5	0
EC1987	29 Apr	Izmir	0	0
EC1987	14 Oct	Wembley	8	0
EC1991	1 May	Izmir	1	0
EC1991	16 Oct	Wembley	1	0
WC1992	18 Nov	Wembley	4	0
WC1993	31 Mar	Izmir	2	0
EC2003	2 Apr	Sunderland	2	0
EC2003	11 Oct	Istanbul	0	0

		v UKRAINE	E	U
2000	31 May	Wembley	2	0
2004	18 Aug	Newcastle	3	0

		v URUGUAY	E	U
1953	31 May	Montevideo	1	2
WC1954	26 June	Basle	2	4
1964	6 May	Wembley	2	1
WC1966	11 July	Wembley	0	0
1969	8 June	Montevideo	2	1
1977	15 June	Montevideo	0	0
1984	13 June	Montevideo	0	2
1990	22 May	Wembley	1	2
1995	29 Mar	Wembley	0	0
2006	1 Mar	Liverpool	2	1

		v USA	E	USA
WC1950	29 June	Belo Horizonte	0	1
1953	8 June	New York	6	3
1959	28 May	Los Angeles	8	1
1964	27 May	New York	10	0
1985	16 June	Los Angeles	5	0
1993	9 June	Foxboro	0	2
1994	7 Sept	Wembley	2	0
2005	28 May	Chicago	2	1
2008	28 May	Wembley	2	0

		v USSR	E	USSR
1958	18 May	Moscow	1	1
WC1958	8 June	Gothenburg	2	2
WC1958	17 June	Gothenburg	0	1
1958	22 Oct	Wembley	5	0
1967	6 Dec	Wembley	2	2
EC1968	8 June	Rome	2	0
1973	10 June	Moscow	2	1
1984	2 June	Wembley	0	2
1986	26 Mar	Tbilisi	1	0
EC1988	18 June	Frankfurt	1	3
1991	21 May	Wembley	3	1

		v YUGOSLAVIA	E	Y
1939	18 May	Belgrade	1	2
1950	22 Nov	Highbury	2	2
1954	16 May	Belgrade	0	1
1956	28 Nov	Wembley	3	0
1958	11 May	Belgrade	0	5
1960	11 May	Wembley	3	3
1965	9 May	Belgrade	1	1
1966	4 May	Wembley	2	0
EC1968	5 June	Florence	0	1
1972	11 Oct	Wembley	1	1
1974	5 June	Belgrade	2	2
EC1986	12 Nov	Wembley	2	0
EC1987	11 Nov	Belgrade	4	1
1989	13 Dec	Wembley	2	1

SCOTLAND

		v ARGENTINA	*S*	*A*
1977	18 June	Buenos Aires	1	1
1979	2 June	Glasgow	1	3
1990	28 Mar	Glasgow	1	0

		v AUSTRALIA	*S*	*A*
wc1985	20 Nov	Glasgow	2	0
wc1985	4 Dec	Melbourne	0	0
1996	27 Mar	Glasgow	1	0
2000	15 Nov	Glasgow	0	2

		v AUSTRIA	*S*	*A*
1931	16 May	Vienna	0	5
1933	29 Nov	Glasgow	2	2
1937	9 May	Vienna	1	1
			S	*A*
1950	13 Dec	Glasgow	0	1
1951	27 May	Vienna	0	4
wc1954	16 June	Zurich	0	1
1955	19 May	Vienna	4	1
1956	2 May	Glasgow	1	1
1960	29 May	Vienna	1	4
1963	8 May	Glasgow	4	1
(abandoned after 79 mins)				
wc1968	6 Nov	Glasgow	2	1
wc1969	5 Nov	Vienna	0	2
EC1978	20 Sept	Vienna	2	3
EC1979	17 Oct	Glasgow	1	1
1994	20 Apr	Vienna	2	1
wc1996	31 Aug	Vienna	0	0
wc1997	2 Apr	Celtic Park	2	0
2003	30 Apr	Glasgow	0	2
2005	17 Aug	Graz	2	2
2007	30 May	Vienna	1	0

		v BELARUS	*S*	*B*
wc1997	8 June	Minsk	1	0
wc1997	7 Sept	Aberdeen	4	1
wc2005	8 June	Minsk	0	0
wc2005	8 Oct	Glasgow	0	1

		v BELGIUM	*S*	*B*
1947	18 May	Brussels	1	2
1948	28 Apr	Glasgow	2	0
1951	20 May	Brussels	5	0
EC1971	3 Feb	Liège	0	3
EC1971	10 Nov	Aberdeen	1	0
1974	2 June	Brussels	1	2
EC1979	21 Nov	Brussels	0	2
EC1979	19 Dec	Glasgow	1	3
EC1982	15 Dec	Brussels	2	3
EC1983	12 Oct	Glasgow	1	1
EC1987	1 Apr	Brussels	1	4
EC1987	14 Oct	Glasgow	2	0
wc2001	24 Mar	Glasgow	2	2
wc2001	5 Sept	Brussels	0	2

		v BOSNIA	*S*	*B*
EC1999	4 Sept	Sarajevo	2	1
EC1999	5 Oct	Glasgow	1	0

		v BRAZIL	*S*	*B*
1966	25 June	Glasgow	1	1
1972	5 July	Rio de Janeiro	0	1
1973	30 June	Glasgow	0	1
wc1974	18 June	Frankfurt	0	0
1977	23 June	Rio de Janeiro	0	2
wc1982	18 June	Seville	1	4
1987	26 May	Glasgow	0	2
wc1990	20 June	Turin	0	1
wc1998	10 June	Saint-Denis	1	2

		v BULGARIA	*S*	*B*
1978	22 Feb	Glasgow	2	1
EC1986	10 Sept	Glasgow	0	0
EC1987	11 Nov	Sofia	1	0
EC1990	14 Nov	Sofia	1	1
EC1991	27 Mar	Glasgow	1	1
2006	11 May	Kobe	5	1

		v CANADA	*S*	*C*
1983	12 June	Vancouver	2	0
1983	16 June	Edmonton	3	0
1983	20 June	Toronto	2	0
1992	21 May	Toronto	3	1
2002	15 Oct	Easter Road	3	1

		v CHILE	*S*	*C*
1977	15 June	Santiago	4	2
1989	30 May	Glasgow	2	0

		v CIS	*S*	*C*
EC1992	18 June	Norrkoping	3	0

		v COLOMBIA	*S*	*C*
1988	17 May	Glasgow	0	0
1996	30 May	Miami	0	1
1998	23 May	New York	2	2

		v COSTA RICA	*S*	*CR*
wc1990	11 June	Genoa	0	1

		v CROATIA	*S*	*C*
wc2000	11 Oct	Zagreb	1	1
wc2001	1 Sept	Glasgow	0	0
2008	26 Mar	Glasgow	1	1

		v CYPRUS	*S*	*C*
wc1968	17 Dec	Nicosia	5	0
wc1969	11 May	Glasgow	8	0
wc1989	8 Feb	Limassol	3	2
wc1989	26 Apr	Glasgow	2	1

		v CZECHOSLOVAKIA	*S*	*C*
1937	22 May	Prague	3	1
1937	8 Dec	Glasgow	5	0
wc1961	14 May	Bratislava	0	4
wc1961	26 Sept	Glasgow	3	2
wc1961	29 Nov	Brussels	2	4*
1972	2 July	Porto Alegre	0	0
wc1973	26 Sept	Glasgow	2	1
wc1973	17 Oct	Prague	0	1
wc1976	13 Oct	Prague	0	2
wc1977	21 Sept	Glasgow	3	1

		v CZECH REPUBLIC	*S*	*C*
EC1999	31 Mar	Glasgow	1	2
EC1999	9 June	Prague	2	3
2008	30 May	Prague	1	3

		v DENMARK	*S*	*D*
1951	12 May	Glasgow	3	1
1952	25 May	Copenhagen	2	1
1968	16 Oct	Copenhagen	1	0
EC1970	11 Nov	Glasgow	1	0
EC1971	9 June	Copenhagen	0	1
wc1972	18 Oct	Copenhagen	4	1
wc1972	15 Nov	Glasgow	2	0
EC1975	3 Sept	Copenhagen	1	0
EC1975	29 Oct	Glasgow	3	1
wc1986	4 June	Nezahualcayotl	0	1
1996	24 Apr	Copenhagen	0	2
1998	25 Mar	Glasgow	0	1
2002	21 Aug	Glasgow	0	1
2004	28 Apr	Copenhagen	0	1

		v ECUADOR	*S*	*E*
1995	24 May	Toyama	2	1

		v EGYPT	*S*	*E*
1990	16 May	Aberdeen	1	3

		v ESTONIA	*S*	*E*
wc1993	19 May	Tallinn	3	0
wc1993	2 June	Aberdeen	3	1
wc1997	11 Feb	Monaco	0	0
wc1997	29 Mar	Kilmarnock	2	0
EC1998	10 Oct	Edinburgh	3	2
EC1999	8 Sept	Tallinn	0	0
2004	27 May	Tallinn	1	0

		v FAEROES	*S*	*F*
EC1994	12 Oct	Glasgow	5	1
EC1995	7 June	Toftir	2	0
EC1998	14 Oct	Aberdeen	2	1
EC1999	5 June	Toftir	1	1
EC2002	7 Sept	Toftir	2	2
EC2003	6 Sept	Glasgow	3	1
EC2006	2 Sept	Celtic Park	6	0
EC2007	6 June	Toftir	2	0

		v FINLAND	*S*	*F*
1954	25 May	Helsinki	2	1
WC1964	21 Oct	Glasgow	3	1
WC1965	27 May	Helsinki	2	1
1976	8 Sept	Glasgow	6	0
1992	25 Mar	Glasgow	1	1
EC1994	7 Sept	Helsinki	2	0
EC1995	6 Sept	Glasgow	1	0
1998	22 Apr	Edinburgh	1	1

		v FRANCE	*S*	*F*
1930	18 May	Paris	2	0
1932	8 May	Paris	3	1
1948	23 May	Paris	0	3
1949	27 Apr	Glasgow	2	0
1950	27 May	Paris	1	0
1951	16 May	Glasgow	1	0
WC1958	15 June	Orebro	1	2
1984	1 June	Marseilles	0	2
WC1989	8 Mar	Glasgow	2	0
WC1989	11 Oct	Paris	0	3
1997	12 Nov	St Etienne	1	2
2000	29 Mar	Glasgow	0	2
2002	27 Mar	Paris	0	5
EC2006	7 Oct	Glasgow	1	0
EC2007	12 Sept	Paris	1	0

		v GEORGIA	*S*	*G*
EC2007	24 Mar	Glasgow	2	1
EC2007	17 Oct	Tblisi	0	2

		v GERMANY	*S*	*G*
1929	1 June	Berlin	1	1
1936	14 Oct	Glasgow	2	0
EC1992	15 June	Norrkoping	0	2
1993	24 Mar	Glasgow	0	1
1998	28 Apr	Bremen	1	0
EC2003	7 June	Glasgow	1	1
EC2003	10 Sept	Dortmund	1	2

		v EAST GERMANY	*S*	*EG*
1974	30 Oct	Glasgow	3	0
1977	7 Sept	East Berlin	0	1
EC1982	13 Oct	Glasgow	2	0
EC1983	16 Nov	Halle	1	2
1985	16 Oct	Glasgow	0	0
1990	25 Apr	Glasgow	0	1

		v WEST GERMANY	*S*	*WG*
1957	22 May	Stuttgart	3	1
1959	6 May	Glasgow	3	2
1964	12 May	Hanover	2	2
WC1969	16 Apr	Glasgow	1	1
WC1969	22 Oct	Hamburg	2	3
1973	14 Nov	Glasgow	1	1
1974	27 Mar	Frankfurt	1	2
WC1986	8 June	Queretaro	1	2

		v GREECE	*S*	*G*
EC1994	18 Dec	Athens	0	1
EC1995	16 Aug	Glasgow	1	0

		v HOLLAND	*S*	*H*
1929	4 June	Amsterdam	2	0
1938	21 May	Amsterdam	3	1
1959	27 May	Amsterdam	2	1
1966	11 May	Glasgow	0	3
1968	30 May	Amsterdam	0	0
1971	1 Dec	Rotterdam	1	2
WC1978	11 June	Mendoza	3	2
1982	23 Mar	Glasgow	2	1
1986	29 Apr	Eindhoven	0	0
EC1992	12 June	Gothenburg	0	1
1994	23 Mar	Glasgow	0	1
1994	27 May	Utrecht	1	3
EC1996	10 June	Birmingham	0	0
2000	26 Apr	Arnhem	0	0
EC2003	15 Nov	Glasgow	1	0
EC2003	19 Nov	Amsterdam	0	6

		v HONG KONG XI	*S*	*HK*
†2002	23 May	Hong Kong	4	0

†match not recognised by FIFA

		v HUNGARY	*S*	*H*
1938	7 Dec	Glasgow	3	1
1954	8 Dec	Glasgow	2	4
1955	29 May	Budapest	1	3
1958	7 May	Glasgow	1	1
1960	5 June	Budapest	3	3
1980	31 May	Budapest	1	3
1987	9 Sept	Glasgow	2	0
2004	18 Aug	Glasgow	0	3

		v ICELAND	*S*	*I*
WC1984	17 Oct	Glasgow	3	0
WC1985	28 May	Reykjavik	1	0
EC2002	12 Oct	Reykjavik	2	0
EC2003	29 Mar	Glasgow	2	1

		v IRAN	*S*	*I*
WC1978	7 June	Cordoba	1	1

		v REPUBLIC OF IRELAND	*S*	*RI*
WC1961	3 May	Glasgow	4	1
WC1961	7 May	Dublin	3	0
1963	9 June	Dublin	0	1
1969	21 Sept	Dublin	1	1
EC1986	15 Oct	Dublin	0	0
EC1987	18 Feb	Glasgow	0	1
2000	30 May	Dublin	2	1
2003	12 Feb	Glasgow	0	2

		v ISRAEL	*S*	*I*
WC1981	25 Feb	Tel Aviv	1	0
WC1981	28 Apr	Glasgow	3	1
1986	28 Jan	Tel Aviv	1	0

		v ITALY	*S*	*I*
1931	20 May	Rome	0	3
WC1965	9 Nov	Glasgow	1	0
WC1965	7 Dec	Naples	0	3
1988	22 Dec	Perugia	0	2
WC1992	18 Nov	Glasgow	0	0
WC1993	13 Oct	Rome	1	3
WC2005	26 Mar	Milan	0	2
WC2005	3 Sept	Glasgow	1	1
EC2007	28 Mar	Bari	0	2
EC2007	17 Nov	Glasgow	3	1

		v JAPAN	*S*	*J*
1995	21 May	Hiroshima	0	0
2006	13 May	Saitama	0	0

		v LATVIA	*S*	*L*
WC1996	5 Oct	Riga	2	0
WC1997	11 Oct	Glasgow	2	0
WC2000	2 Sept	Riga	1	0
WC2001	6 Oct	Glasgow	2	1

		v LITHUANIA	*S*	*L*
EC1998	5 Sept	Vilnius	0	0
EC1999	9 Oct	Glasgow	3	0
EC2003	2 Apr	Kaunas	0	1
EC2003	11 Oct	Glasgow	1	0
EC2006	6 Sept	Kaunas	2	1
EC2007	8 Sept	Glasgow	3	1

		v LUXEMBOURG	*S*	*L*
1947	24 May	Luxembourg	6	0
EC1986	12 Nov	Glasgow	3	0
EC1987	2 Dec	Esch	0	0

		v MALTA	*S*	*M*
1988	22 Mar	Valletta	1	1
1990	28 May	Valletta	2	1
WC1993	17 Feb	Glasgow	3	0
WC1993	17 Nov	Valletta	2	0
1997	1 June	Valletta	3	2

		v MOLDOVA	*S*	*M*
EC2004	13 Oct	Chisinau	1	1
EC2005	4 June	Glasgow	2	0

		v MOROCCO	*S*	*M*
WC1998	23 June	St Etienne	0	3

		v NEW ZEALAND	*S*	*NZ*
WC1982	15 June	Malaga	5	2
2003	27 May	Tynecastle	1	1

		v NIGERIA	*S*	*N*
2002	17 Apr	Aberdeen	1	2

		v NORWAY	*S*	*N*
1929	28 May	Oslo	7	3
1954	5 May	Glasgow	1	0
1954	19 May	Oslo	1	1
1963	4 June	Bergen	3	4
1963	7 Nov	Glasgow	6	1
1974	6 June	Oslo	2	1
EC1978	25 Oct	Glasgow	3	2
EC1979	7 June	Oslo	4	0
WC1988	14 Sept	Oslo	2	1
WC1989	15 Nov	Glasgow	1	1
1992	3 June	Oslo	0	0
WC1998	16 June	Bordeaux	1	1
2003	20 Aug	Oslo	0	0
WC2004	9 Oct	Glasgow	0	1
WC2005	7 Sept	Oslo	2	1

		v PARAGUAY	*S*	*P*
WC1958	11 June	Norrkoping	2	3

		v PERU	*S*	*P*
1972	26 Apr	Glasgow	2	0
WC1978	3 June	Cordoba	1	3
1979	12 Sept	Glasgow	1	1

		v POLAND	*S*	*P*
1958	1 June	Warsaw	2	1
1960	4 June	Glasgow	2	3
WC1965	23 May	Chorzow	1	1
WC1965	13 Oct	Glasgow	1	2
1980	28 May	Poznan	0	1
1990	19 May	Glasgow	1	1
2001	25 Apr	Bydgoszcz	1	1

		v PORTUGAL	*S*	*P*
1950	21 May	Lisbon	2	2
1955	4 May	Glasgow	3	0
1959	3 June	Lisbon	0	1
1966	18 June	Glasgow	0	1
EC1971	21 Apr	Lisbon	0	2
EC1971	13 Oct	Glasgow	2	1
1975	13 May	Glasgow	1	0
EC1978	29 Nov	Lisbon	0	1
EC1980	26 Mar	Glasgow	4	1
WC1980	15 Oct	Glasgow	0	0
WC1981	18 Nov	Lisbon	1	2
WC1992	14 Oct	Glasgow	0	0
WC1993	28 Apr	Lisbon	0	5
2002	20 Nov	Braga	0	2

		v ROMANIA	*S*	*R*
EC1975	1 June	Bucharest	1	1
EC1975	17 Dec	Glasgow	1	1
1986	26 Mar	Glasgow	3	0
EC1990	12 Sept	Glasgow	2	1
EC1991	16 Oct	Bucharest	0	1
2004	31 Mar	Glasgow	1	2

		v RUSSIA	*S*	*R*
EC1994	16 Nov	Glasgow	1	1
EC1995	29 Mar	Moscow	0	0

		v SAN MARINO	*S*	*SM*
EC1991	1 May	Serravalle	2	0
EC1991	13 Nov	Glasgow	4	0
EC1995	26 Apr	Serravalle	2	0
EC1995	15 Nov	Glasgow	5	0
WC2000	7 Oct	Serravalle	2	0
WC2001	28 Mar	Glasgow	4	0

		v SAUDI ARABIA	*S*	*SA*
1988	17 Feb	Riyadh	2	2

		v SLOVENIA	*S*	*Sl*
WC2004	8 Sept	Glasgow	0	0
WC2005	12 Oct	Celje	3	0

		v SOUTH AFRICA	*S*	*SA*
2002	20 May	Hong Kong	0	2
2007	22 Aug	Aberdeen	1	0

		v SOUTH KOREA	*S*	*SK*
2002	16 May	Busan	1	4

		v SPAIN	*S*	*Sp*
WC1957	8 May	Glasgow	4	2
WC1957	26 May	Madrid	1	4
1963	13 June	Madrid	6	2
1965	8 May	Glasgow	0	0
EC1974	20 Nov	Glasgow	1	2
EC1975	5 Feb	Valencia	1	1
1982	24 Feb	Valencia	0	3
WC1984	14 Nov	Glasgow	3	1
WC1985	27 Feb	Seville	0	1
1988	27 Apr	Madrid	0	0
2004	3 Sept	Valencia	1	1

Match abandoned afer 60 minutes; floodlight failure.

		v SWEDEN	*S*	*Sw*
1952	30 May	Stockholm	1	3
1953	6 May	Glasgow	1	2
1975	16 Apr	Gothenburg	1	1

			S	*Sw*
1977	27 Apr	Glasgow	3	1
WC1980	10 Sept	Stockholm	1	0
WC1981	9 Sept	Glasgow	2	0
WC1990	16 June	Genoa	2	1
1995	11 Oct	Stockholm	0	2
WC1996	10 Nov	Glasgow	1	0
WC1997	30 Apr	Gothenburg	1	2
2004	17 Nov	Edinburgh	1	4

		v SWITZERLAND	*S*	*Sw*
1931	24 May	Geneva	3	2
1948	17 May	Berne	1	2
1950	26 Apr	Glasgow	3	1
WC1957	19 May	Basle	2	1
WC1957	6 Nov	Glasgow	3	2
1973	22 June	Berne	0	1
1976	7 Apr	Glasgow	1	0
EC1982	17 Nov	Berne	0	2
EC1983	30 May	Glasgow	2	2
EC1990	17 Oct	Glasgow	2	1
EC1991	11 Sept	Berne	2	2
WC1992	9 Sept	Berne	1	3
WC1993	8 Sept	Aberdeen	1	1
WC1996	18 June	Birmingham	1	0
2006	1 Mar	Glasgow	1	3

		v TRINIDAD & TOBAGO	*S*	*TT*
2004	30 May	Edinburgh	4	1

		v TURKEY	*S*	*T*
1960	8 June	Ankara	2	4

		v UKRAINE	*S*	*U*
EC2006	11 Oct	Kiev	0	2
EC2007	13 Oct	Glasgow	3	1

		v URUGUAY	*S*	*U*
WC1954	19 June	Basle	0	7
1962	2 May	Glasgow	2	3
1983	21 Sept	Glasgow	2	0
WC1986	13 June	Nezahualcoyotl	0	0

		v USA	*S*	*USA*
1952	30 Apr	Glasgow	6	0
1992	17 May	Denver	1	0
1996	26 May	New Britain	1	2
1998	30 May	Washington	0	0
2005	11 Nov	Glasgow	1	1

		v USSR	*S*	*USSR*
1967	10 May	Glasgow	0	2
1971	14 June	Moscow	0	1
WC1982	22 June	Malaga	2	2
1991	6 Feb	Glasgow	0	1

		v YUGOSLAVIA	*S*	*Y*
1955	15 May	Belgrade	2	2
1956	21 Nov	Glasgow	2	0
WC1958	8 June	Vasteras	1	1
1972	29 June	Belo Horizonte	2	2
WC1974	22 June	Frankfurt	1	1
1984	12 Sept	Glasgow	6	1
WC1988	19 Oct	Glasgow	1	1
WC1989	6 Sept	Zagreb	1	3

		v ZAIRE	*S*	*Z*
WC1974	14 June	Dortmund	2	0

WALES

		v ALBANIA	*W*	*A*
EC1994	7 Sept	Cardiff	2	0
EC1995	15 Nov	Tirana	1	1

		v ARGENTINA	*W*	*A*
1992	3 June	Tokyo	0	1
2002	13 Feb	Cardiff	1	1

		v ARMENIA	*W*	*A*
WC2001	24 Mar	Erevan	2	2
WC2001	1 Sept	Cardiff	0	0

		v AUSTRIA	*W*	*A*
1954	9 May	Vienna	0	2
			W	*A*
EC1955	23 Nov	Wrexham	1	2
EC1974	4 Sept	Vienna	1	2
1975	19 Nov	Wrexham	1	0
1992	29 Apr	Vienna	1	1
EC2005	26 Mar	Cardiff	0	2
EC2005	30 Mar	Vienna	0	1

		v AZERBAIJAN	*W*	*A*
EC2002	20 Nov	Baku	2	0
EC2003	29 Mar	Cardiff	4	0
WC2004	4 Sept	Baku	1	1
WC2005	12 Oct	Cardiff	2	0

		v BELARUS	*W*	*B*
EC1998	14 Oct	Cardiff	3	2
EC1999	4 Sept	Minsk	2	1
WC2000	2 Sept	Minsk	1	2
WC2001	6 Oct	Cardiff	1	0

		v BELGIUM	*W*	*B*
1949	22 May	Liège	1	3
1949	23 Nov	Cardiff	5	1
EC1990	17 Oct	Cardiff	3	1
EC1991	27 Mar	Brussels	1	1
WC1992	18 Nov	Brussels	0	2
WC1993	31 Mar	Cardiff	2	0
WC1997	29 Mar	Cardiff	1	2
WC1997	11 Oct	Brussels	2	3

		v BOSNIA	*W*	*B*
2003	12 Feb	Cardiff	2	2

		v BRAZIL	*W*	*B*
WC1958	19 June	Gothenburg	0	1
1962	12 May	Rio de Janeiro	1	3
1962	16 May	São Paulo	1	3
1966	14 May	Rio de Janeiro	1	3
1966	18 May	Belo Horizonte	0	1
1983	12 June	Cardiff	1	1
1991	11 Sept	Cardiff	1	0
1997	12 Nov	Brasilia	0	3
2000	23 May	Cardiff	0	3
2006	5 Sept	Cardiff	0	2

		v BULGARIA	*W*	*B*
EC1983	27 Apr	Wrexham	1	0
EC1983	16 Nov	Sofia	0	1
EC1994	14 Dec	Cardiff	0	3
EC1995	29 Mar	Sofia	1	3
2006	15 Aug	Swansea	0	0
2007	22 Aug	Burgas	1	0

		v CANADA	*W*	*C*
1986	10 May	Toronto	0	2
1986	20 May	Vancouver	3	0
2004	30 May	Wrexham	1	0

		v CHILE	*W*	*C*
1966	22 May	Santiago	0	2

		v COSTA RICA	*W*	*CR*
1990	20 May	Cardiff	1	0

		v CROATIA	*W*	*C*
2002	21 Aug	Varazdin	1	1

		v CYPRUS	*W*	*C*
WC1992	14 Oct	Limassol	1	0
WC1993	13 Oct	Cardiff	2	0
2005	16 Nov	Limassol	0	1
EC2006	11 Oct	Cardiff	3	1
EC2007	13 Oct	Nicosia	1	3

		v CZECHOSLOVAKIA	*W*	*C*
WC1957	1 May	Cardiff	1	0
WC1957	26 May	Prague	0	2
EC1971	21 Apr	Swansea	1	3
EC1971	27 Oct	Prague	0	1
WC1977	30 Mar	Wrexham	3	0
WC1977	16 Nov	Prague	0	1
WC1980	19 Nov	Cardiff	1	0
WC1981	9 Sept	Prague	0	2
EC1987	29 Apr	Wrexham	1	1
EC1987	11 Nov	Prague	0	2
WC1993	28 Apr	Ostrava†	1	1
WC1993	8 Sept	Cardiff†	2	2

†*Czechoslovakia played as RCS (Republic of Czechs and Slovaks).*

		v CZECH REPUBLIC	*W*	*CR*
2002	27 Mar	Cardiff	0	0
EC2006	2 Sept	Teplice	1	2
EC2007	2 June	Cardiff	0	0

		v DENMARK	*W*	*D*
WC1964	21 Oct	Copenhagen	0	1
WC1965	1 Dec	Wrexham	4	2
EC1987	9 Sept	Cardiff	1	0
EC1987	14 Oct	Copenhagen	0	1
			W	*D*
1990	11 Sept	Copenhagen	0	1
EC1998	10 Oct	Copenhagen	2	1
EC1999	9 June	Liverpool	0	2

		v ESTONIA	*W*	*E*
1994	23 May	Tallinn	2	1

		v FINLAND	*W*	*F*
EC1971	26 May	Helsinki	1	0
EC1971	13 Oct	Swansea	3	0
EC1987	10 Sept	Helsinki	1	1
EC1987	1 Apr	Wrexham	4	0
WC1988	19 Oct	Swansea	2	2
WC1989	6 Sept	Helsinki	0	1
2000	29 Mar	Cardiff	1	2
EC2002	7 Sept	Helsinki	2	0
EC2003	10 Sept	Cardiff	1	1

		v FAEROES	*W*	*F*
WC1992	9 Sept	Cardiff	6	0
WC1993	6 June	Toftir	3	0

		v FRANCE	*W*	*F*
1933	25 May	Paris	1	1
1939	20 May	Paris	1	2
1953	14 May	Paris	1	6
1982	2 June	Toulouse	1	0

		v GEORGIA	*W*	*G*
EC1994	16 Nov	Tbilisi	0	5
EC1995	7 June	Cardiff	0	1

		v GERMANY	*W*	*G*
EC1995	26 Apr	Dusseldorf	1	1
EC1995	11 Oct	Cardiff	1	2
2002	14 May	Cardiff	1	0
EC2007	8 Sept	Cardiff	0	2
EC2007	21 Nov	Frankfurt	0	0

		v EAST GERMANY	*W*	*EG*
WC1957	19 May	Leipzig	1	2
WC1957	25 Sept	Cardiff	4	1
WC1969	16 Apr	Dresden	1	2
WC1969	22 Oct	Cardiff	1	3

		v WEST GERMANY	*W*	*WG*
1968	8 May	Cardiff	1	1
1969	26 Mar	Frankfurt	1	1
1976	6 Oct	Cardiff	0	2
1977	14 Dec	Dortmund	1	1
EC1979	2 May	Wrexham	0	2
EC1979	17 Oct	Cologne	1	5
WC1989	31 May	Cardiff	0	0
WC1989	15 Nov	Cologne	1	2
EC1991	5 June	Cardiff	1	0
EC1991	16 Oct	Nuremberg	1	4

		v GREECE	*W*	*G*
WC1964	9 Dec	Athens	0	2
WC1965	17 Mar	Cardiff	4	1

		v HOLLAND	*W*	*H*
WC1988	14 Sept	Amsterdam	0	1
WC1989	11 Oct	Wrexham	1	2
1992	30 May	Utrecht	0	4
WC1996	5 Oct	Cardiff	1	3
WC1996	9 Nov	Eindhoven	1	7
2008	1 June	Rotterdam	0	2

		v HUNGARY	*W*	*H*
WC1958	8 June	Sanviken	1	1
WC1958	17 June	Stockholm	2	1
1961	28 May	Budapest	2	3
EC1962	7 Nov	Budapest	1	3
EC1963	20 Mar	Cardiff	1	1
EC1974	30 Oct	Cardiff	2	0
EC1975	16 Apr	Budapest	2	1
1985	16 Oct	Cardiff	0	3
2004	31 Mar	Budapest	2	1
2005	9 Feb	Cardiff	2	0

		v ICELAND	*W*	*I*
WC1980	2 June	Reykjavik	4	0
WC1981	14 Oct	Swansea	2	2
WC1984	12 Sept	Reykjavik	0	1
WC1984	14 Nov	Cardiff	2	1
1991	1 May	Cardiff	1	0
2008	28 May	Reykjavik	1	0

		v IRAN	*W*	*I*
1978	18 Apr	Teheran	1	0

		v REPUBLIC OF IRELAND	*W*	*RI*
1960	28 Sept	Dublin	3	2
1979	11 Sept	Swansea	2	1
1981	24 Feb	Dublin	3	1
1986	26 Mar	Dublin	1	0
1990	28 Mar	Dublin	0	1
1991	6 Feb	Wrexham	0	3
1992	19 Feb	Dublin	1	0
1993	17 Feb	Dublin	1	2
1997	11 Feb	Cardiff	0	0

			W	*RI*
EC2007	24 Mar	Dublin	0	1
EC2007	17 Nov	Cardiff	2	2

		v ISRAEL	*W*	*I*
WC1958	15 Jan	Tel Aviv	2	0
WC1958	5 Feb	Cardiff	2	0
1984	10 June	Tel Aviv	0	0
1989	8 Feb	Tel Aviv	3	3

		v ITALY	*W*	*I*
1965	1 May	Florence	1	4
WC1968	23 Oct	Cardiff	0	1
WC1969	4 Nov	Rome	1	4
1988	4 June	Brescia	1	0
1996	24 Jan	Terni	0	3
EC1998	5 Sept	Liverpool	0	2
EC1999	5 June	Bologna	0	4
EC2002	16 Oct	Cardiff	2	1
EC2003	6 Sept	Milan	0	4

		v JAMAICA	*W*	*J*
1998	25 Mar	Cardiff	0	0

		v JAPAN	*W*	*J*
1992	7 June	Matsuyama	1	0

		v LATVIA	*W*	*L*
2004	18 Aug	Riga	2	0

		v LIECHTENSTEIN	*W*	*L*
2006	14 Nov	Swansea	4	0

		v KUWAIT	*W*	*K*
1977	6 Sept	Wrexham	0	0
1977	20 Sept	Kuwait	0	0

		v LUXEMBOURG	*W*	*L*
EC1974	20 Nov	Swansea	5	0
EC1975	1 May	Luxembourg	3	1
EC1990	14 Nov	Luxembourg	1	0
EC1991	13 Nov	Cardiff	1	0
2008	26 Mar	Luxembourg	2	0

		v MALTA	*W*	*M*
EC1978	25 Oct	Wrexham	7	0
EC1979	2 June	Valletta	2	0
1988	1 June	Valletta	3	2
1998	3 June	Valletta	3	0

		v MEXICO	*W*	*M*
WC1958	11 June	Stockholm	1	1
1962	22 May	Mexico City	1	2

		v MOLDOVA	*W*	*M*
EC1994	12 Oct	Kishinev	2	3
EC1995	6 Sept	Cardiff	1	0

		v NEW ZEALAND	*W*	*NZ*
2007	26 May	Wrexham	2	2

		v NORWAY	*W*	*N*
EC1982	22 Sept	Swansea	1	0
EC1983	21 Sept	Oslo	0	0
1984	6 June	Trondheim	0	1
1985	26 Feb	Wrexham	1	1
1985	5 June	Bergen	2	4
1994	9 Mar	Cardiff	1	3
WC2000	7 Oct	Cardiff	1	1
WC2001	5 Sept	Oslo	2	3
2004	27 May	Oslo	0	0
2008	6 Feb	Wrexham	3	0

		v PARAGUAY	*W*	*P*
2006	1 Mar	Cardiff	0	0

		v POLAND	*W*	*P*
WC1973	28 Mar	Cardiff	2	0
WC1973	26 Sept	Katowice	0	3
1991	29 May	Radom	0	0
WC2000	11 Oct	Warsaw	0	0
WC2001	2 June	Cardiff	1	2
WC2004	13 Oct	Cardiff	2	3
WC2005	7 Sept	Warsaw	0	1

		v PORTUGAL	*W*	*P*
1949	15 May	Lisbon	2	3
1951	12 May	Cardiff	2	1
2000	2 June	Chaves	0	3

		v QATAR	*W*	*Q*
2000	23 Feb	Doha	1	0

		v ROMANIA	*W*	*R*
EC1970	11 Nov	Cardiff	0	0
EC1971	24 Nov	Bucharest	0	2
1983	12 Oct	Wrexham	5	0
WC1992	20 May	Bucharest	1	5
WC1993	17 Nov	Cardiff	1	2

		v RUSSIA	*W*	*R*
EC2003	15 Nov	Moscow	0	0
EC2003	19 Nov	Cardiff	0	1

		v SAN MARINO	*W*	*SM*
WC1996	2 June	Serravalle	5	0
WC1996	31 Aug	Cardiff	6	0
EC2007	28 Mar	Cardiff	3	0
EC2007	17 Oct	Serravalle	2	1

		v SAUDI ARABIA	*W*	*SA*
1986	25 Feb	Dahran	2	1

		v SERBIA-MONTENEGRO	*W*	*SM*
EC2003	20 Aug	Belgrade	0	1
EC2003	11 Oct	Cardiff	2	3

		v SLOVAKIA	*W*	*S*
EC2006	7 Oct	Cardiff	1	5
EC2007	12 Sept	Trnava	5	2

		v SLOVENIA	*W*	*Sl*
2005	17 Aug	Swansea	0	0

		v SPAIN	*W*	*S*
WC1961	19 Apr	Cardiff	1	2
WC1961	18 May	Madrid	1	1
1982	24 Mar	Valencia	1	1
WC1984	17 Oct	Seville	0	3
WC1985	30 Apr	Wrexham	3	0

		v SWEDEN	*W*	*S*
WC1958	15 June	Stockholm	0	0
1988	27 Apr	Stockholm	1	4
1989	26 Apr	Wrexham	0	2
1990	25 Apr	Stockholm	2	4
1994	20 Apr	Wrexham	0	2

		v SWITZERLAND	*W*	*S*
1949	26 May	Berne	0	4
1951	16 May	Wrexham	3	2
1996	24 Apr	Lugano	0	2
EC1999	31 Mar	Zurich	0	2
EC1999	9 Oct	Wrexham	0	2

		v TRINIDAD & TOBAGO	*W*	*TT*
2006	27 May	Graz	2	1

		v TUNISIA	*W*	*T*
1998	6 June	Tunis	0	4

		v TURKEY	*W*	*T*
EC1978	29 Nov	Wrexham	1	0
EC1979	21 Nov	Izmir	0	1
WC1980	15 Oct	Cardiff	4	0
WC1981	25 Mar	Ankara	1	0
WC1996	14 Dec	Cardiff	0	0
WC1997	20 Aug	Istanbul	4	6

		v REST OF UNITED KINGDOM	*W*	*UK*
1951	5 Dec	Cardiff	3	2
1969	28 July	Cardiff	0	1

		v UKRAINE	*W*	*U*
WC2001	28 Mar	Cardiff	1	1
WC2001	6 June	Kiev	1	1

		v USA	*W*	*USA*
2003	27 May	San Jose	0	2

		v URUGUAY	*W*	*U*
1986	21 Apr	Wrexham	0	0

		v USSR	*W*	*USSR*
WC1965	30 May	Moscow	1	2
WC1965	27 Oct	Cardiff	2	1
WC1981	30 May	Wrexham	0	0
WC1981	18 Nov	Tbilisi	0	3
1987	18 Feb	Swansea	0	0

		v YUGOSLAVIA	*W*	*Y*
1953	21 May	Belgrade	2	5
1954	22 Nov	Cardiff	1	3

			W	*Y*
EC1976	24 Apr	Zagreb	0	2
EC1976	22 May	Cardiff	1	1
EC1982	15 Dec	Titograd	4	4
EC1983	14 Dec	Cardiff	1	1
1988	23 Mar	Swansea	1	2

NORTHERN IRELAND

		v ALBANIA	*NI*	*A*
WC1965	7 May	Belfast	4	1
WC1965	24 Nov	Tirana	1	1
EC1982	15 Dec	Tirana	0	0
EC1983	27 Apr	Belfast	1	0
WC1992	9 Sept	Belfast	3	0
WC1993	17 Feb	Tirana	2	1
WC1996	14 Dec	Belfast	2	0
WC1997	10 Sept	Zurich	0	1

		v ALGERIA	*NI*	*A*
WC1986	3 June	Guadalajara	1	1

		v ARGENTINA	*NI*	*A*
WC1958	11 June	Halmstad	1	3

		v ARMENIA	*NI*	*A*
WC1996	5 Oct	Belfast	1	1
WC1997	30 Apr	Erevan	0	0
EC2003	29 Mar	Erevan	0	1
EC2003	10 Sept	Belfast	0	1

		v AUSTRALIA	*NI*	*A*
1980	11 June	Sydney	2	1
1980	15 June	Melbourne	1	1
1980	18 June	Adelaide	2	1

		v AUSTRIA	*NI*	*A*
WC1982	1 July	Madrid	2	2
EC1982	13 Oct	Vienna	0	2
EC1983	21 Sept	Belfast	3	1
EC1990	14 Nov	Vienna	0	0
EC1991	16 Oct	Belfast	2	1
EC1994	12 Oct	Vienna	2	1
EC1995	15 Nov	Belfast	5	3
WC2004	13 Oct	Belfast	3	3
WC2005	12 Oct	Vienna	0	2

		v AZERBAIJAN	*NI*	*A*
WC2004	9 Oct	Baku	0	0
WC2005	3 Sept	Belfast	2	0

		v BARBADOS	*NI*	*B*
2004	30 May	Waterford	1	1

		v BELGIUM	*NI*	*B*
WC1976	10 Nov	Liège	0	2
WC1977	16 Nov	Belfast	3	0
1997	11 Feb	Belfast	3	0

		v BRAZIL	*NI*	*B*
WC1986	12 June	Guadalajara	0	3

		v BULGARIA	NI	B
WC1972	18 Oct	Sofia	0	3
WC1973	26 Sept	Sheffield	0	0
EC1978	29 Nov	Sofia	2	0
EC1979	2 May	Belfast	2	0
WC2001	28 Mar	Sofia	3	4
WC2001	2 June	Belfast	0	1
2008	6 Feb	Belfast	0	1

		v CANADA	NI	C
1995	22 May	Edmonton	0	2
1999	27 Apr	Belfast	1	1
2005	9 Feb	Belfast	0	1

		v CHILE	NI	C
1989	26 May	Belfast	0	1
1995	25 May	Edmonton	1	2

		v COLOMBIA	NI	C
1994	4 June	Boston	0	2

		v CYPRUS	NI	C
EC1971	3 Feb	Nicosia	3	0
EC1971	21 Apr	Belfast	5	0
WC1973	14 Feb	Nicosia	0	1
WC1973	8 May	London	3	0
2002	21 Aug	Belfast	0	0

		v CZECHOSLOVAKIA	NI	C
WC1958	8 June	Halmstad	1	0
WC1958	17 June	Malmo	2	1*

**After extra time*

		v CZECH REPUBLIC	NI	C
WC2001	24 Mar	Belfast	0	1
WC2001	6 June	Teplice	1	3

		v DENMARK	NI	D
EC1978	25 Oct	Belfast	2	1
EC1979	6 June	Copenhagen	0	4
1986	26 Mar	Belfast	1	1
EC1990	17 Oct	Belfast	1	1
EC1991	13 Nov	Odense	1	2
WC1992	18 Nov	Belfast	0	1
WC1993	13 Oct	Copenhagen	0	1
WC2000	7 Oct	Belfast	1	1
WC2001	1 Sept	Copenhagen	1	1
EC2006	7 Oct	Copenhagen	0	0
EC2007	17 Nov	Belfast	2	1

		v ESTONIA	NI	E
2004	31 Mar	Tallinn	1	0
2006	1 Mar	Belfast	1	0

		v FAEROES	NI	F
EC1991	1 May	Belfast	1	1
EC1991	11 Sept	Landskrona	5	0

		v FINLAND	NI	F
WC1984	27 May	Pori	0	1
WC1984	14 Nov	Belfast	2	1
EC1998	10 Oct	Belfast	1	0
EC1998	9 Oct	Helsinki	1	4
2003	12 Feb	Belfast	0	1
2006	16 Aug	Helsinki	2	1

		v FRANCE	NI	F
1928	21 Feb	Paris	0	4
1951	12 May	Belfast	2	2
1952	11 Nov	Paris	1	3
WC1958	19 June	Norrkoping	0	4
1982	24 Mar	Paris	0	4
WC1982	4 July	Madrid	1	4
1986	26 Feb	Paris	0	0
1988	27 Apr	Belfast	0	0
1999	18 Aug	Belfast	0	1

		v GEORGIA	NI	G
2008	26 Mar	Belfast	4	1

		v GERMANY	NI	G
1992	2 June	Bremen	1	1
1996	29 May	Belfast	1	1
WC1996	9 Nov	Nuremberg	1	1
WC1997	20 Aug	Belfast	1	3
EC1999	27 Mar	Belfast	0	3
EC1999	8 Sept	Dortmund	0	4
2005	4 June	Belfast	1	4

		v WEST GERMANY	NI	WG
WC1958	15 June	Malmo	2	2
WC1960	26 Oct	Belfast	3	4
WC1961	10 May	Hamburg	1	2
1966	7 May	Belfast	0	2
1977	27 Apr	Cologne	0	5
EC1982	17 Nov	Belfast	1	0
EC1983	16 Nov	Hamburg	1	0

		v GREECE	NI	G
WC1961	3 May	Athens	1	2
WC1961	17 Oct	Belfast	2	0
1988	17 Feb	Athens	2	3
EC2003	2 Apr	Belfast	0	2
EC2003	11 Oct	Athens	0	1

		v HOLLAND	NI	H
1962	9 May	Rotterdam	0	4
WC1965	17 Mar	Belfast	2	1
WC1965	7 Apr	Rotterdam	0	0
WC1976	13 Oct	Rotterdam	2	2
WC1977	12 Oct	Belfast	0	1

		v HONDURAS	NI	H
WC1982	21 June	Zaragoza	1	1

		v HUNGARY	NI	H
WC1988	19 Oct	Budapest	0	1
WC1989	6 Sept	Belfast	1	2
2000	26 Apr	Belfast	0	1

		v ICELAND	NI	I
WC1977	11 June	Reykjavik	0	1
WC1977	21 Sept	Belfast	2	0
WC2000	11 Oct	Reykjavik	0	1
WC2001	5 Sept	Belfast	3	0
EC2006	2 Sept	Belfast	0	3
EC2007	12 Sept	Reykjavik	1	2

		v REPUBLIC OF IRELAND	NI	RI
EC1978	20 Sept	Dublin	0	0
EC1979	21 Nov	Belfast	1	0
WC1988	14 Sept	Belfast	0	0
WC1989	11 Oct	Dublin	0	3
WC1993	31 Mar	Dublin	0	3
WC1993	17 Nov	Belfast	1	1
EC1994	16 Nov	Belfast	0	4
EC1995	29 Mar	Dublin	1	1
1999	29 May	Dublin	1	0

		v ISRAEL	NI	I
1968	10 Sept	Jaffa	3	2
1976	3 Mar	Tel Aviv	1	1
WC1980	26 Mar	Tel Aviv	0	0
WC1981	18 Nov	Belfast	1	0
1984	16 Oct	Belfast	3	0
1987	18 Feb	Tel Aviv	1	1

		v ITALY	NI	I
WC1957	25 Apr	Rome	0	1
1957	4 Dec	Belfast	2	2
WC1958	15 Jan	Belfast	2	1
1961	25 Apr	Bologna	2	3
1997	22 Jan	Palermo	0	2
2003	3 June	Campobasso	0	2

		v LATVIA	NI	L
WC1993	2 June	Riga	2	1
WC1993	8 Sept	Belfast	2	0
EC1995	26 Apr	Riga	1	0
EC1995	7 June	Belfast	1	2
EC2006	11 Oct	Belfast	1	0
EC2007	8 Sept	Riga	0	1

		v LIECHTENSTEIN	*NI*	*L*
EC1994	20 Apr	Belfast	4	1
EC1995	11 Oct	Eschen	4	0
2002	27 Mar	Vaduz	0	0
EC2007	24 Mar	Vaduz	4	1
EC2007	22 Aug	Belfast	3	1

		v LITHUANIA	*NI*	*L*
WC1992	28 Apr	Belfast	2	2
WC1993	25 May	Vilnius	1	0

		v LUXEMBOURG	*NI*	*L*
2000	23 Feb	Luxembourg	3	1

		v MALTA	*NI*	*M*
WC1988	21 May	Belfast	3	0
WC1989	26 Apr	Valletta	2	0
2000	28 Mar	Valletta	3	0
WC2000	2 Sept	Belfast	1	0
WC2001	6 Oct	Valletta	1	0
2005	17 Aug	Ta'Qali	1	1

		v MEXICO	*NI*	*M*
1966	22 June	Belfast	4	1
1994	11 June	Miami	0	3

		v MOLDOVA	*NI*	*M*
EC1998	18 Nov	Belfast	2	2
EC1999	31 Mar	Chisinau	0	0

		v MOROCCO	*NI*	*M*
1986	23 Apr	Belfast	2	1

		v NORWAY	*NI*	*N*
1922	25 May	Bergen	1	2
EC1974	4 Sept	Oslo	1	2
EC1975	29 Oct	Belfast	3	0
1990	27 Mar	Belfast	2	3
1996	27 Mar	Belfast	0	2
2001	28 Feb	Belfast	0	4
2004	18 Feb	Belfast	1	4

		v POLAND	*NI*	*P*
EC1962	10 Oct	Katowice	2	0
EC1962	28 Nov	Belfast	2	0
1988	23 Mar	Belfast	1	1
1991	5 Feb	Belfast	3	1
2002	13 Feb	Limassol	1	4
EC2004	4 Sept	Belfast	0	3
EC2005	30 Mar	Warsaw	0	1

		v PORTUGAL	*NI*	*P*
WC1957	16 Jan	Lisbon	1	1
WC1957	1 May	Belfast	3	0
WC1973	28 Mar	Coventry	1	1
WC1973	14 Nov	Lisbon	1	1
WC1980	19 Nov	Lisbon	0	1
WC1981	29 Apr	Belfast	1	0
EC1994	7 Sept	Belfast	1	2
EC1995	3 Sept	Lisbon	1	1
WC1997	29 Mar	Belfast	0	0
WC1997	11 Oct	Lisbon	0	1
2005	15 Nov	Belfast	1	1

		v ROMANIA	*NI*	*R*
WC1984	12 Sept	Belfast	3	2
WC1985	16 Oct	Bucharest	1	0
1994	23 Mar	Belfast	2	0
2006	27 May	Chicago	0	2

		v ST KITTS & NEVIS	*NI*	*SK*
2004	2 June	Basseterre	2	0

		v SERBIA-MONTENEGRO	*NI*	*SM*
2004	28 Apr	Belfast	1	1

		v SLOVAKIA	*NI*	*S*
1998	25 Mar	Belfast	1	0

		v SOUTH AFRICA	*NI*	*SA*
1924	24 Sept	Belfast	1	2

		v SPAIN	*NI*	*S*
1958	15 Oct	Madrid	2	6
1963	30 May	Bilbao	1	1
1963	30 Oct	Belfast	0	1
EC1970	11 Nov	Seville	0	3
EC1972	16 Feb	Hull	1	1
WC1982	25 June	Valencia	1	0
1985	27 Mar	Palma	0	0
WC1986	7 June	Guadalajara	1	2
WC1988	21 Dec	Seville	0	4
WC1989	8 Feb	Belfast	0	2
WC1992	14 Oct	Belfast	0	0
WC1993	28 Apr	Seville	1	3
1998	2 June	Santander	1	4
2002	17 Apr	Belfast	0	5
EC2002	12 Oct	Albacete	0	3
EC2003	11 June	Belfast	0	0
EC2006	6 Sept	Belfast	3	2
EC2007	21 Nov	Las Palmas	0	1

		v SWEDEN	*NI*	*S*
EC1974	30 Oct	Solna	2	0
EC1975	3 Sept	Belfast	1	2
WC1980	15 Oct	Belfast	3	0
WC1981	3 June	Solna	0	1
1996	24 Apr	Belfast	1	2
EC2007	28 Mar	Belfast	2	1
EC2007	17 Oct	Stockholm	1	1

		v SWITZERLAND	*NI*	*S*
WC1964	14 Oct	Belfast	1	0
WC1964	14 Nov	Lausanne	1	2
1998	22 Apr	Belfast	1	0
2004	18 Aug	Zurich	0	0

		v THAILAND	*NI*	*T*
1997	21 May	Bangkok	0	0

		v TRINIDAD & TOBAGO	*NI*	*TT*
2004	6 June	Bacolet	3	0

		v TURKEY	*NI*	*T*
WC1968	23 Oct	Belfast	4	1
WC1968	11 Dec	Istanbul	3	0
EC1983	30 Mar	Belfast	2	1
EC1983	12 Oct	Ankara	0	1
WC1985	1 May	Belfast	2	0
WC1985	11 Sept	Izmir	0	0
EC1986	12 Nov	Izmir	0	0
EC1987	11 Nov	Belfast	1	0
EC1998	5 Sept	Istanbul	0	3
EC1999	4 Sept	Belfast	0	3

		v UKRAINE	*NI*	*U*
WC1996	31 Aug	Belfast	0	1
WC1997	2 Apr	Kiev	1	2
EC2002	16 Oct	Belfast	0	0
EC2003	6 Sept	Donetsk	0	0

		v URUGUAY	*NI*	*U*
1964	29 Apr	Belfast	3	0
1990	18 May	Belfast	1	0
2006	21 May	New Jersey	0	1

		v USSR	*NI*	*USSR*
WC1969	19 Sept	Belfast	0	0
WC1969	22 Oct	Moscow	0	2
EC1971	22 Sept	Moscow	0	1
EC1971	13 Oct	Belfast	1	1

		v YUGOSLAVIA	*NI*	*Y*
EC1975	16 Mar	Belfast	1	0
EC1975	19 Nov	Belgrade	0	1
WC1982	17 June	Zaragoza	0	0
EC1987	29 Apr	Belfast	1	2
EC1987	14 Oct	Sarajevo	0	3
EC1990	12 Sept	Belfast	0	2
EC1991	27 Mar	Belgrade	1	4
2000	16 Aug	Belfast	1	2

REPUBLIC OF IRELAND

		v ALBANIA	RI	A
WC1992	26 May	Dublin	2	0
WC1993	26 May	Tirana	2	1
EC2003	2 Apr	Tirana	0	0
EC2003	7 June	Dublin	2	1

		v ALGERIA	RI	A
1982	28 Apr	Algiers	0	2

		v ANDORRA	RI	A
WC2001	28 Mar	Barcelona	3	0
WC2001	25 Apr	Dublin	3	1

		v ARGENTINA	RI	A
1951	13 May	Dublin	0	1
†1979	29 May	Dublin	0	0
1980	16 May	Dublin	0	1
1998	22 Apr	Dublin	0	2

†*Not considered a full international.*

		v AUSTRALIA	RI	A
2003	19 Aug	Dublin	2	1

		v AUSTRIA	RI	A
1952	7 May	Vienna	0	6
1953	25 Mar	Dublin	4	0
1958	14 Mar	Vienna	1	3
1962	8 Apr	Dublin	2	3
EC1963	25 Sept	Vienna	0	0
EC1963	13 Oct	Dublin	3	2
1966	22 May	Vienna	0	1
1968	10 Nov	Dublin	2	2
EC1971	30 May	Dublin	1	4
EC1971	10 Oct	Linz	0	6
EC1995	11 June	Dublin	1	3
EC1995	6 Sept	Vienna	1	3

		v BELGIUM	RI	B
1928	12 Feb	Liège	4	2
1929	30 Apr	Dublin	4	0
1930	11 May	Brussels	3	1
WC1934	25 Feb	Dublin	4	4
1949	24 Apr	Dublin	0	2
1950	10 May	Brussels	1	5
1965	24 Mar	Dublin	0	2
1966	25 May	Liège	3	2
WC1980	15 Oct	Dublin	1	1
WC1981	25 Mar	Brussels	0	1
EC1986	10 Sept	Brussels	2	2
EC1987	29 Apr	Dublin	0	0
WC1997	29 Oct	Dublin	1	1
WC1997	16 Nov	Brussels	1	2

		v BOLIVIA	RI	B
1994	24 May	Dublin	1	0
1996	15 June	New Jersey	3	0
2007	26 May	Boston	1	1

		v BRAZIL	RI	B
1974	5 May	Rio de Janeiro	1	2
1982	27 May	Uberlandia	0	7
1987	23 May	Dublin	1	0
2004	18 Feb	Dublin	0	0
2008	6 Feb	Dublin	0	1

		v BULGARIA	RI	B
WC1977	1 June	Sofia	1	2
WC1977	12 Oct	Dublin	0	0
EC1979	19 May	Sofia	0	1
EC1979	17 Oct	Dublin	3	0
WC1987	1 Apr	Sofia	1	2
WC1987	14 Oct	Dublin	2	0
2004	18 Aug	Dublin	1	1

		v CAMEROON	RI	C
WC2002	1 June	Niigata	1	1

		v CANADA	RI	C
2003	18 Nov	Dublin	3	0

		v CHILE	RI	C
1960	30 Mar	Dublin	2	0
1972	21 June	Recife	1	2
1974	12 May	Santiago	2	1
1982	22 May	Santiago	0	1
1991	22 May	Dublin	1	1
2006	24 May	Dublin	0	1

		v CHINA	RI	C
1984	3 June	Sapporo	1	0
2005	29 Mar	Dublin	1	0

		v COLOMBIA	RI	C
2008	29 May	Fulham	1	0

		v CROATIA	RI	C
1996	2 June	Dublin	2	2
EC1998	5 Sept	Dublin	2	0
EC1999	4 Sept	Zagreb	0	1
2001	15 Aug	Dublin	2	2
2004	16 Nov	Dublin	1	0

		v CYPRUS	RI	C
WC1980	26 Mar	Nicosia	3	2
WC1980	19 Nov	Dublin	6	0
WC2001	24 Mar	Nicosia	4	0
WC2001	6 Oct	Dublin	4	0
WC2004	4 Sept	Dublin	3	0
WC2005	8 Oct	Nicosia	1	0
EC2006	7 Oct	Nicosia	2	5
EC2007	17 Oct	Dublin	1	1

		v CZECHOSLOVAKIA	RI	C
1938	18 May	Prague	2	2
EC1959	5 Apr	Dublin	2	0
EC1959	10 May	Bratislava	0	4
WC1961	8 Oct	Dublin	1	3
WC1961	29 Oct	Prague	1	7
EC1967	21 May	Dublin	0	2
EC1967	22 Nov	Prague	2	1
WC1969	4 May	Dublin	1	2
WC1969	7 Oct	Prague	0	3
1979	26 Sept	Prague	1	4
1981	29 Apr	Dublin	3	1
1986	27 May	Reykjavik	1	0

		v CZECH REPUBLIC	RI	C
1994	5 June	Dublin	1	3
1996	24 Apr	Prague	0	2
1998	25 Mar	Olomouc	1	2
2000	23 Feb	Dublin	3	2
2004	31 Mar	Dublin	2	1
EC2006	11 Oct	Dublin	1	1
EC2007	12 Sept	Prague	0	1

		v DENMARK	RI	D
WC1956	3 Oct	Dublin	2	1
WC1957	2 Oct	Copenhagen	2	0
WC1968	4 Dec	Dublin	1	1
		(*abandoned after 51 mins*)		
WC1969	27 May	Copenhagen	0	2
WC1969	15 Oct	Dublin	1	1
EC1978	24 May	Copenhagen	3	3
EC1979	2 May	Dublin	2	0
WC1984	14 Nov	Copenhagen	0	3
WC1985	13 Nov	Dublin	1	4
WC1992	14 Oct	Copenhagen	0	0
WC1993	28 Apr	Dublin	1	1
2002	27 Mar	Dublin	3	0
2007	22 Aug	Copenhagen	4	0

		v ECUADOR	RI	E
1972	19 June	Natal	3	2
2007	23 May	New Jersey	1	1

		v EGYPT	RI	E
WC1990	17 June	Palermo	0	0

		v ENGLAND	RI	E
1946	30 Sept	Dublin	0	1
1949	21 Sept	Everton	2	0
WC1957	8 May	Wembley	1	5
WC1957	19 May	Dublin	1	1
1964	24 May	Dublin	1	3
1976	8 Sept	Wembley	1	1
EC1978	25 Oct	Dublin	1	1
EC1980	6 Feb	Wembley	0	2

			RI	E
1985	26 Mar	Wembley	1	2
EC1988	12 June	Stuttgart	1	0
WC1990	11 June	Cagliari	1	1
EC1990	14 Nov	Dublin	1	1
EC1991	27 Mar	Wembley	1	1
1995	15 Feb	Dublin	1	0

(*abandoned after 27 mins*)

		v ESTONIA	*RI*	*E*
WC2000	11 Oct	Dublin	2	0
WC2001	6 June	Tallinn	2	0

		v FAEROES	*RI*	*F*
EC2004	13 Oct	Dublin	2	0
EC2005	8 June	Toftir	2	0

		v FINLAND	*RI*	*F*
WC1949	8 Sept	Dublin	3	0
WC1949	9 Oct	Helsinki	1	1
1990	16 May	Dublin	1	1
2000	15 Nov	Dublin	3	0
2002	21 Aug	Helsinki	3	0

		v FRANCE	*RI*	*F*
1937	23 May	Paris	2	0
1952	16 Nov	Dublin	1	1
WC1953	4 Oct	Dublin	3	5
WC1953	25 Nov	Paris	0	1
WC1972	15 Nov	Dublin	2	1
WC1973	19 May	Paris	1	1
WC1976	17 Nov	Paris	0	2
WC1977	30 Mar	Dublin	1	0
WC1980	28 Oct	Paris	0	2
WC1981	14 Oct	Dublin	3	2
1989	7 Feb	Dublin	0	0
WC2004	9 Oct	Paris	0	0
WC2005	7 Sept	Dublin	0	1

		v GEORGIA	*RI*	*G*
EC2003	29 Mar	Tbilisi	2	1
EC2003	11 June	Dublin	2	0

		v GERMANY	*RI*	*G*
1935	8 May	Dortmund	1	3
1936	17 Oct	Dublin	5	2
1939	23 May	Bremen	1	1
1994	29 May	Hanover	2	0
WC2002	5 June	Ibaraki	1	1
EC2006	2 Sept	Stuttgart	0	1
EC2007	13 Oct	Dublin	0	0

		v WEST GERMANY	*RI*	*WG*
1951	17 Oct	Dublin	3	2
1952	4 May	Cologne	0	3
1955	28 May	Hamburg	1	2
1956	25 Nov	Dublin	3	0
1960	11 May	Dusseldorf	1	0
1966	4 May	Dublin	0	4
1970	9 May	Berlin	1	2
1975	1 Mar	Dublin	1	0†
1979	22 May	Dublin	1	3
1981	21 May	Bremen	0	3†
1989	6 Sept	Dublin	1	1

†*v West Germany 'B'*

		v GREECE	*RI*	*G*
2000	26 Apr	Dublin	0	1
2002	20 Nov	Athens	0	0

		v HOLLAND	*RI*	*N*
1932	8 May	Amsterdam	2	0
1934	8 Apr	Amsterdam	2	5
1935	8 Dec	Dublin	3	5
1955	1 May	Dublin	1	0
1956	10 May	Rotterdam	4	1
WC1980	10 Sept	Dublin	2	1
WC1981	9 Sept	Rotterdam	2	2
EC1982	22 Sept	Rotterdam	1	2
EC1983	12 Oct	Dublin	2	3
EC1988	18 June	Gelsenkirchen	0	1
WC1990	21 June	Palermo	1	1
1994	20 Apr	Tilburg	1	0
WC1994	4 July	Orlando	0	2
EC1995	13 Dec	Liverpool	0	2
1996	4 June	Rotterdam	1	3
WC2000	2 Sept	Amsterdam	2	2

			RI	*N*
WC2001	1 Sept	Dublin	1	0
2004	5 June	Amsterdam	1	0
2006	16 Aug	Dublin	0	4

		v HUNGARY	*RI*	*H*
1934	15 Dec	Dublin	2	4
1936	3 May	Budapest	3	3
1936	6 Dec	Dublin	2	3
1939	19 Mar	Cork	2	2
1939	18 May	Budapest	2	2
WC1969	8 June	Dublin	1	2
WC1969	5 Nov	Budapest	0	4
WC1989	8 Mar	Budapest	0	0
WC1989	4 June	Dublin	2	0
1991	11 Sept	Gyor	2	1

		v ICELAND	*RI*	*I*
EC1962	12 Aug	Dublin	4	2
EC1962	2 Sept	Reykjavik	1	1
EC1982	13 Oct	Dublin	2	0
EC1983	21 Sept	Reykjavik	3	0
1986	25 May	Reykjavik	2	1
WC1996	10 Nov	Dublin	0	0
WC1997	6 Sept	Reykjavik	4	2

		v IRAN	*RI*	*I*
1972	18 June	Recife	2	1
WC2001	10 Nov	Dublin	2	0
WC2001	15 Nov	Tehran	0	1

		v N. IRELAND	*RI*	*NI*
EC1978	20 Sept	Dublin	0	0
EC1979	21 Nov	Belfast	0	1
WC1988	14 Sept	Belfast	0	0
WC1989	11 Oct	Dublin	3	0
WC1993	31 Mar	Dublin	3	0
WC1993	17 Nov	Belfast	1	1
EC1994	16 Nov	Belfast	4	0
EC1995	29 Mar	Dublin	1	1
1999	29 May	Dublin	0	1

		v ISRAEL	*RI*	*I*
1984	4 Apr	Tel Aviv	0	3
1985	27 May	Tel Aviv	0	0
1987	10 Nov	Dublin	5	0
EC2005	26 Mar	Tel Aviv	1	1
EC2005	4 June	Dublin	2	2

		v ITALY	*RI*	*I*
1926	21 Mar	Turin	0	3
1927	23 Apr	Dublin	1	2
EC1970	8 Dec	Rome	0	3
EC1971	10 May	Dublin	1	2
1985	5 Feb	Dublin	1	2
WC1990	30 June	Rome	0	1
1992	4 June	Foxboro	0	2
WC1994	18 June	New York	1	0
2005	17 Aug	Dublin	1	2

		v JAMAICA	*RI*	*J*
2004	2 June	Charlton	1	0

		v LATVIA	*RI*	*L*
WC1992	9 Sept	Dublin	4	0
WC1993	2 June	Riga	2	1
EC1994	7 Sept	Riga	3	0
EC1995	11 Oct	Dublin	2	1

		v LIECHTENSTEIN	*RI*	*L*
EC1994	12 Oct	Dublin	4	0
EC1995	3 June	Eschen	0	0
WC1996	31 Aug	Eschen	5	0
WC1997	21 May	Dublin	5	0

		v LITHUANIA	*RI*	*L*
WC1993	16 June	Vilnius	1	0
WC1993	8 Sept	Dublin	2	0
WC1997	20 Aug	Dublin	0	0
WC1997	10 Sept	Vilnius	2	1

		v LUXEMBOURG	*RI*	*L*
1936	9 May	Luxembourg	5	1
WC1953	28 Oct	Dublin	4	0
WC1954	7 Mar	Luxembourg	1	0

			RI	L
EC1987	28 May	Luxembourg	2	0
EC1987	9 Sept	Dublin	2	1

v MACEDONIA

			RI	M
WC1996	9 Oct	Dublin	3	0
WC1997	2 Apr	Skopje	2	3
EC1999	9 June	Dublin	1	0
EC1999	9 Oct	Skopje	1	1

v MALTA

			RI	M
EC1983	30 Mar	Valletta	1	0
EC1983	16 Nov	Dublin	8	0
WC1989	28 May	Dublin	2	0
WC1989	15 Nov	Valletta	2	0
1990	2 June	Valletta	3	0
EC1998	14 Oct	Dublin	5	0
EC1999	8 Sept	Valletta	3	2

v MEXICO

			RI	M
1984	8 Aug	Dublin	0	0
WC1994	24 June	Orlando	1	2
1996	13 June	New Jersey	2	2
1998	23 May	Dublin	0	0
2000	4 June	Chicago	2	2

v MOROCCO

			RI	M
1990	12 Sept	Dublin	1	0

v NIGERIA

			RI	N
2002	16 May	Dublin	1	2
2004	29 May	Charlton	0	3

v NORWAY

			RI	N
WC1937	10 Oct	Oslo	2	3
WC1937	7 Nov	Dublin	3	3
1950	26 Nov	Dublin	2	2
1951	30 May	Oslo	3	2
1954	8 Nov	Dublin	2	1
1955	25 May	Oslo	3	1
1960	6 Nov	Dublin	3	1
1964	13 May	Oslo	4	1
1973	6 June	Oslo	1	1
1976	24 Mar	Dublin	3	0
1978	21 May	Oslo	0	0
WC1984	17 Oct	Oslo	0	1
WC1985	1 May	Dublin	0	0
1988	1 June	Oslo	0	0
WC1994	28 June	New York	0	0
2003	30 Apr	Dublin	1	0

v PARAGUAY

			RI	P
1999	10 Feb	Dublin	2	0

v POLAND

			RI	P
1938	22 May	Warsaw	0	6
1938	13 Nov	Dublin	3	2
1958	11 May	Katowice	2	2
1958	5 Oct	Dublin	2	2
1964	10 May	Kracow	1	3
1964	25 Oct	Dublin	3	2
1968	15 May	Dublin	2	2
1968	30 Oct	Katowice	0	1
1970	6 May	Dublin	1	2
1970	23 Sept	Dublin	0	2
1973	16 May	Wroclaw	0	2
1973	21 Oct	Dublin	1	0
1976	26 May	Poznan	2	0
1977	24 Apr	Dublin	0	0
1978	12 Apr	Lodz	0	3
1981	23 May	Bydgoszcz	0	3
1984	23 May	Dublin	0	0
1986	12 Nov	Warsaw	0	1
1988	22 May	Dublin	3	1
EC1991	1 May	Dublin	0	0
EC1991	16 Oct	Poznan	3	3
2004	28 Apr	Bydgoszcz	0	0

v PORTUGAL

			RI	P
1946	16 June	Lisbon	1	3
1947	4 May	Dublin	0	2
1948	23 May	Lisbon	0	2
1949	22 May	Dublin	1	0
1972	25 June	Recife	1	2
1992	7 June	Boston	2	0
EC1995	26 Apr	Dublin	1	0
EC1995	15 Nov	Lisbon	0	3
1996	29 May	Dublin	0	1
WC2000	7 Oct	Lisbon	1	1
WC2001	2 June	Dublin	1	1
2005	9 Feb	Dublin	1	0

v ROMANIA

			RI	R
1988	23 Mar	Dublin	2	0
WC1990	25 June	Genoa	0	0*
WC1997	30 Apr	Bucharest	0	1
WC1997	11 Oct	Dublin	1	1
2004	27 May	Dublin	1	0

v RUSSIA

			RI	R
1994	23 Mar	Dublin	0	0
1996	27 Mar	Dublin	0	2
2002	13 Feb	Dublin	2	0
EC2002	7 Sept	Moscow	2	4
EC2003	6 Sept	Dublin	1	1

v SAN MARINO

			RI	SM
EC2006	15 Nov	Dublin	5	0
EC2007	7 Feb	Serravalle	2	1

v SAUDI ARABIA

			RI	SA
WC2002	11 June	Yokohama	3	0

v SERBIA

			RI	S
2008	24 May	Dublin	1	1

v SCOTLAND

			RI	S
WC1961	3 May	Glasgow	1	4
WC1961	7 May	Dublin	0	3
1963	9 June	Dublin	1	0
1969	21 Sept	Dublin	1	1
EC1986	15 Oct	Dublin	0	0
EC1987	18 Feb	Glasgow	1	0
2000	30 May	Dublin	1	2
2003	12 Feb	Glasgow	2	0

v SLOVAKIA

			RI	S
EC2007	28 Mar	Dublin	1	0
EC2007	8 Sept	Bratislava	2	2

v SOUTH AFRICA

			RI	SA
2000	11 June	New Jersey	2	1

v SPAIN

			RI	S
1931	26 Apr	Barcelona	1	1
1931	13 Dec	Dublin	0	5
1946	23 June	Madrid	1	0
1947	2 Mar	Dublin	3	2
1948	30 May	Barcelona	1	2
1949	12 June	Dublin	1	4
1952	1 June	Madrid	0	6
1955	27 Nov	Dublin	2	2
EC1964	11 Mar	Seville	1	5
EC1964	8 Apr	Dublin	0	2
WC1965	5 May	Dublin	1	0
WC1965	27 Oct	Seville	1	4
WC1965	10 Nov	Paris	0	1
EC1966	23 Oct	Dublin	0	0
EC1966	7 Dec	Valencia	0	2
1977	9 Feb	Dublin	0	1
EC1982	17 Nov	Dublin	3	3
EC1983	27 Apr	Zaragoza	0	2
1985	26 May	Cork	0	0
WC1988	16 Nov	Seville	0	2
WC1989	26 Apr	Dublin	1	0
WC1992	18 Nov	Seville	0	0
WC1993	13 Oct	Dublin	1	3
WC2002	16 June	Suwon	1	1

v SWEDEN

			RI	S
WC1949	2 June	Stockholm	1	3
WC1949	13 Nov	Dublin	1	3
1959	1 Nov	Dublin	3	2
1960	18 May	Malmo	1	4
EC1970	14 Oct	Dublin	1	1
EC1970	28 Oct	Malmo	0	1
1999	28 Apr	Dublin	2	0
2006	1 Mar	Dublin	3	0

		v SWITZERLAND	RI	S
1935	5 May	Basle	0	1
1936	17 Mar	Dublin	1	0
1937	17 May	Berne	1	0
1938	18 Sept	Dublin	4	0
1948	5 Dec	Dublin	0	1
EC1975	11 May	Dublin	2	1
EC1975	21 May	Berne	0	1
			RI	*S*
1980	30 Apr	Dublin	2	0
WC1985	2 June	Dublin	3	0
WC1985	11 Sept	Berne	0	0
1992	25 Mar	Dublin	2	1
EC2002	16 Oct	Dublin	1	2
EC2003	11 Oct	Basle	0	2
WC2004	8 Sept	Basle	1	1
WC2005	12 Oct	Dublin	0	0

		v TRINIDAD & TOBAGO	RI	TT
1982	30 May	Port of Spain	1	2

		v TUNISIA	RI	T
1988	19 Oct	Dublin	4	0

		v TURKEY	RI	T
EC1966	16 Nov	Dublin	2	1
EC1967	22 Feb	Ankara	1	2
EC1974	20 Nov	Izmir	1	1
EC1975	29 Oct	Dublin	4	0
1976	13 Oct	Ankara	3	3
1978	5 Apr	Dublin	4	2
1990	26 May	Izmir	0	0
EC1990	17 Oct	Dublin	5	0
EC1991	13 Nov	Istanbul	3	1
EC2000	13 Nov	Dublin	1	1
EC2000	17 Nov	Bursa	0	0
2003	9 Sept	Dublin	2	2

		v URUGUAY	RI	U
1974	8 May	Montevideo	0	2
1986	23 Apr	Dublin	1	1

		v USA	RI	USA
1979	29 Oct	Dublin	3	2
1991	1 June	Boston	1	1
1992	29 Apr	Dublin	4	1
1992	30 May	Washington	1	3
1996	9 June	Boston	1	2
2000	6 June	Boston	1	1
2002	17 Apr	Dublin	2	1

		v USSR	RI	USSR
WC1972	18 Oct	Dublin	1	2
WC1973	13 May	Moscow	0	1
EC1974	30 Oct	Dublin	3	0
EC1975	18 May	Kiev	1	2
WC1984	12 Sept	Dublin	1	0
WC1985	16 Oct	Moscow	0	2
EC1988	15 June	Hanover	1	1
1990	25 Apr	Dublin	1	0

		v WALES	RI	W
1960	28 Sept	Dublin	2	3
1979	11 Sept	Swansea	1	2
1981	24 Feb	Dublin	1	3
1986	26 Mar	Dublin	0	1
1990	28 Mar	Dublin	1	0
1991	6 Feb	Wrexham	3	0
1992	19 Feb	Dublin	0	1
1993	17 Feb	Dublin	2	1
1997	11 Feb	Cardiff	0	0
EC2007	24 Mar	Dublin	1	0
EC2007	17 Nov	Cardiff	2	2

		v YUGOSLAVIA	RI	Y
1955	19 Sept	Dublin	1	4
1988	27 Apr	Dublin	2	0
EC1998	18 Nov	Belgrade	0	1
EC1999	1 Sept	Dublin	2	1

Republic of Ireland and Tottenham Hotspur striker Robbie Keane in typical celebratory mood.
(EMPICS Sport/PA Photos/Mike Egerton)

OTHER BRITISH AND IRISH INTERNATIONAL MATCHES 2007–08

FRIENDLIES

Wembley, 22 August 2007, 86,133

England (1) 1 *(Lampard 9)*

Germany (2) 2 *(Kuranyi 26, Pander 40)*

England: Robinson (James 46); Richards, Shorey, Carrick (Barry 55), Ferdinand (Brown 46), Terry, Beckham, Lampard, Smith (Crouch 57), Owen (Dyer 57), Cole J (Wright-Phillips 70).
Germany: Lehmann; Friedrich A, Mertesacker, Metzelder, Lahm, Odonkor (Hilbert 54), Schneider (Castro 90), Hitzlsperger, Pander, Trochowski (Rolfes 72), Kuranyi.
Referee: M. Puscaba (Switzerland).

Vienna, 16 November 2007, 39,432

Austria (0) 0

England (1) 1 *(Crouch 44)*

Austria: Macho (Manninger 26); Garics, Stanzl (Hiden 86), Schiemer, Gercaliu, Standfest (Kavlak 78), Aufhauser, Sariyar (Harnik 65), Weissenberger (Kienast 46), Ivanschitz, Kuljic (Leitgeb 46).
England: Carson; Richards, Bridge, Gerrard (Barry 46), Lescott, Campbell (Brown 46), Beckham (Bentley 62), Lampard, Crouch (Smith 76), Owen (Defoe 34), Cole J (Young 46).
Referee: N. Vollquartz (Denmark).

Wembley, 6 February 2008, 86,857

England (1) 2 *(Jenas 40, Wright-Phillips 62)*

Switzerland (0) 1 *(Derdiyok 58)*

England: James; Brown, Cole A (Bridge 74), Barry (Hargreaves 74), Ferdinand, Upson, Bentley, Jenas (Wright-Phillips 57), Rooney (Young 87), Gerrard, Cole J (Crouch 57).
Switzerland: Benaglio; Senderos (Grichting 55), Gygax (Derdiyok 46), Barnetta, Spycher, Yakin H (Margairaz 64), Inler, Lichsteiner (Behrami 46), Nkufo (Vonlanthen 46), Fernandes (Huggel 84), Eggimann.
Referee: F. Bryche (Germany).

Paris, 26 March 2008, 78,500

France (1) 1 *(Ribery 32 (pen))*

England (0) 0

France: Coupet; Abidal, Gallas, Makelele, Toulalan, Clerc, Thuram, Ribery, Trezeguet (Gouvou 64), Anelka (Cisse 80), Malouda.
England: James; Brown (Johnson G 63), Cole A, Hargreaves, Ferdinand, Terry (Lescott 46), Beckham (Bentley 63), Barry, Rooney (Owen 46), Gerrard (Crouch 46), Cole J (Downing 46).
Referee: F. Meyer (Germany).

Wembley, 28 May 2008, 71,233

England (1) 2 *(Terry 38, Gerrard 59)*

USA (0) 0

England: James; Brown (Johnson G 57), Cole A (Bridge 82), Hargreaves, Ferdinand, Terry, Beckham (Bentley 46), Lampard (Barry 57), Rooney (Cole J 78), Defoe (Crouch 68), Gerrard.
USA: Howard (Guzan 46); Cherundolo (Hejduk 46), Onyewu, Bocanegra, Pearce, Dempsey, Bradley, Clark (Edu 78), Beasley (Lewis 68), Johnson (Jaqua 89), Wolff (Adu 68).
Referee: K. Vassaras (Greece).

Port of Spain, 2 June 2008, 25,001

Trinidad & Tobago (0) 0

England (2) 3 *(Barry 12, Defoe 16, 49)*

Trinidad & Tobago: Ince; Cupid (Smith 46), Lawrence, Hislop, Farrier, Edwards, Hyland (Yorke 76), Whitley, Daniel (Connell 76), John (Forbes 74), Jones K (Roberts D 11) (Telesford 46).
England: James (Hart 46); Johnson G, Bridge (Warnock 84), Gerrard, Ferdinand (Jagielka 46), Woodgate, Beckham (Bentley 46), Barry, Ashton (Crouch 46), Defoe (Walcott 69), Downing (Young A 57).
Referee: E. Wijngaarde (Surinam).

Aberdeen, 22 August 2007, 13,723

Scotland (0) 1 *(Boyd 71)*

South Africa (0) 0

Scotland: Gordon; Hutton, Anderson, McManus, McEveley, Brown (Teale 72), Caldwell (Robson 56), Fletcher D, McFadden (Pearson 46), O'Connor (Beattie 68), Miller (Boyd 68).
South Africa: Fernandez; Nzama (Mere 83), Mokoena, Mhlongo, Carnell, Pienaar (Modise 76), Zothwane, Sibaya, Buckley (Sheppard 76), Nkosi (Fanteni 75), Zuma (Nomvethe 14).
Referee: M. Atkinson (England).

Glasgow, 26 March 2008, 28,821

Scotland (1) 1 *(Miller 30)*

Croatia (1) 1 *(Kranjcar 10)*

Scotland: Gordon; Hutton, Naysmith (McEveley 62), Caldwell (Anderson 70), McManus, Fletcher D (Alexander 90), Hartley, Brown (Teale 66), Maloney (Boyd 72), Miller, Fletcher S (Rae 46).
Croatia: Pletikosa; Kovac R (Knezevic 73), Corluka (Simic 85), Simunic, Srna (Leko 63), Kovac N (Vukojevic 46), Modric, Kranjcar, Pranjic, Petric (Klasnic 58), Olic (Budan 57).
Referee: T. Hauge (Norway).

Prague, 30 May 2008, 11,314

Czech Republic (0) 3 *(Sionko 60, 90, Kadlec 84)*

Scotland (0) 1 *(Clarkson 85)*

Czech Republic: Cech; Pospech (Sivok 74), Ujfalusi (Rozehnal 46), Kovac, Jankulovski (Kadlec 46), Sionko, Polak, Matejovsky (Jarolim 46), Galasek, Skacel (Plasil 46), Koller (Sverkos 46).
Scotland: Gordon; McNaughton (Berra 90), McManus (Dailly 57), Caldwell G, Naysmith, Robson (McCormack 82), Hartley, Fletcher D, Rae (Clarkson 71), Morrison (Maloney 68), Miller.
Referee: E. Braamhaar (Holland).

Burgas, 22 August 2007, 15,000

Bulgaria (0) 0

Wales (1) 1 *(Eastwood 45)*

Bulgaria: Ivankov; Kishishev (Yankov 52), Wagner (Zanev 54), Tomasic, Angelov S, Petrov S, Tunchev, Telkiyski (Popov I 46), Yovov (Genkov 66), Chillikov (Dimitrov 46), Petrov M.
Wales: Hennessey; Bale (Eardley 46), Ricketts (Collins D 46), Gabbidon, Morgan (Evans S 46), Nyatanga, Crofts, Davies S (Nardiello 66), Eastwood (Earnshaw 46), Vaughan, Ledley (Jones M 61).
Referee: M. Germanakos (Greece).

Wrexham, 6 February 2008, 7000

Wales (1) 3 *(Fletcher 15, Koumas 62, 89)*

Norway (0) 0

Wales: Hennessey (Price 46); Gunter, Ricketts (Eardley 59), Fletcher, Morgan, Nyatanga, Robinson (Crofts 66), Eastwood (Cotterill 59), Koumas, Davies S (Davies C 59), Ledley (Edwards D 46).
Norway: Opdal; Kah, Hangeland (Kippe 61), Riise, Stromstad (Grindheim 46), Andresen, Carew (Haestad 46), Pedersen, Braaten, Storbaek, Nevland (Bjorkoy 77).
Referee: D. McKeon (Republic of Ireland).

Luxembourg, 26 March 2008, 3000

Luxembourg (0) 0

Wales (1) 2 *(Eastwood 37, 46)*

Luxembourg: Joubert; Kintziger, Hoffmann, Wagner, Strasser, Leweck (Da Mota 66), Gerson (Lukic 90), Joachim (Kitenge 53), Remy, Mutsch, Lang (Peters 46).
Wales: Price (Myhill 46); Eardley (Duffy 65), Ricketts, Williams A, Morgan, Nyatanga, Eastwood, Fletcher (Cotterill 75), Koumas (Nardiello 84), Davies S, Easter (Tudur-Jones 46).
Referee: B. Kuipers (Holland).

Reykjavik, 28 May 2008, 5322

Iceland (0) 0

Wales (1) 1 *(Evans C 44)*

Iceland: Sturuson (Torgeirsson 46); Saevarsson B, Thorarinsson, Gunnarsson A (Saevarsson J 76), Sigurdsson J, Palmason, Sigurdsson K, Jonsson (Sigurdsson H 60), Hallfredsson (Bjarnason 70), Thordarson (Danielsson 61), Thorvaldsson (Smarason 81).
Wales: Hennessey; Gunter, Williams A, Morgan, Nyatanga, Collison (Tudur-Jones 60), Fletcher (Evans C 41), Koumas (Crofts 89), Edwards D (Bellamy 62), Ledley (Eardley 49), Eastwood (Vokes 49).
Referee: A. McCourt (Northern Ireland).

Rotterdam, 1 June 2008, 49,000

Holland (1) 2 *(Robben 35, Sneijder 54)*

Wales (0) 0

Holland: Van der Sar; Ooijer, Mathijsen (Vennegoor of Hesselink 80), Heitinga (Melchiot 46), Van Bronckhorst (De Cler 46), De Zeeuw (Kuyt 46), Englelaar (De Jong 46), Van der Vaart (Afellay 67), Sneijder, Van Nistelrooy, Robben.
Wales: Hennessey; Gunter, Williams A, Morgan, Nyatanga (Collison 47), Ricketts (Crofts 78), Robinson, Edwards D (Evans C 57), Ledley (Eardley 88), Koumas (Vokes 73), Eastwood (Bellamy 57).
Referee: F. Brych (Germany).

Copenhagen, 22 August 2007, 30,000

Denmark (0) 0

Republic of Ireland (2) 4 *(Keane 29, 40, Long 54, 66)*

Denmark: Christiansen; Bogelund (Kahlenberg 46), Gravgaard (Kristiansen 46), Agger, Jensen N (Kvist 46), Wurtz (Lovenkrands 68), Rommedahl, Jensen D (Laursen 46), Gronkjaer, Bendtner, Tomasson (Nordstrand 59).
Republic of Ireland: Henderson; Carr, Finnan (Kilbane 62), Potter (Kelly 67), O'Shea, Dunne, Reid A (Gibson 46), Hunt (Keogh A 46), Keane (Murphy 58), Doyle K (Long 46), McGeady.
Referee: T. Einwaller (Austria).

Dublin, 6 February 2008, 30,000

Republic of Ireland (0) 0

Brazil (0) 1 *(Robinho 67)*

Republic of Ireland: Given; Kelly, Kilbane, Miller (Potter 46), O'Shea, Dunne, Duff, Carsley, Keane, Doyle (Hunt 72), McGeady.
Brazil: Julio Cesar; Leonardo, Anderson Silva, Alex, Richarlyson, Josue (Lucas 83), Gilberto Silva, Diego (Anderson 78), Robinho, Luis Fabiano (Rafael Sobis 84), Baptista.
Referee: R. Rogalla (Switzerland).

Croke Park, 24 May 2008, 42,500

Republic of Ireland (0) 1 *(Keogh A 90)*

Serbia (0) 1 *(Pantelic 75)*

Republic of Ireland: Kiely; Kelly, McShane, Dunne, Delaney, Duff, Whelan, Miller, Hunt (Keogh A 80), Keane (Murphy D 69), Doyle (Long 86).
Serbia: Stojkovic; Rukavina, Ivanovic, Rajkovic, Dragutinovic, Babovic (Markovic 80), Smiljanic, Kuzmanovic, Jankovic, Ilic (Kacar 86), Lazovic (Pantelic 69).
Referee: L. Evans (Wales).

Fulham, 29 May 2008, 15,000

Republic of Ireland (1) 1 *(Keane 3)*

Colombia (0) 0

Republic of Ireland: Kiely; O'Shea, Dunne, McShane, Delaney, Miller, Whelan, McGeady, Keogh A (Hoolahan 90), Doyle (Murphy D 85), Keane.
Colombia: Zapata R; Zapata C, Bustos (Vallejo 46), Perea L (Morena 66), Gonzalez (Armero 70), Guarin, Sanchez, Escobar (Sota 63), Torres (Hernandez 73), Perea E, Garcia (Polo 65).
Referee: M. Clattenburg (England).

Belfast, 6 February 2008, 11,000

Northern Ireland (0) 0

Bulgaria (1) 1 *(Evans 38 (og))*

Northern Ireland: Taylor (Mannus 83); McAuley, McCartney (Baird 46), Hughes, Evans (Craigan 46), Clingan, Gillespie (Thompson 78), Johnson (Davis 46), Healy, Lafferty (Paterson 60), Brunt.
Bulgaria: Petkov G (Ivankov 46); Angelov M, Venkov (Zanev 73), Tunchev (Karaslavov 66), Tomasic, Milanov, Petrov S, Yanchev (Dimitrov 46), Georgiev, Berbatov (Domovchiyski 82), Lazarov (Popov I 66).
Referee: D. McDonald (Scotland).

Belfast, 26 March 2008, 15,000

Northern Ireland (3) 4 *(Lafferty 25, 36, Healy 33, Kobiashvili 87 (og))*

Georgia (0) 1 *(Healy 55 (og))*

Northern Ireland: Taylor (Mannus 80); Baird, Hughes, Craigan (McAuley 57), Evans, Gillespie, Johnson (O'Connor 46), Davis (Gault 70), Elliott, Healy (Thompson 70), Lafferty (Feeney 46).
Georgia: Makaridze; Salukvadze, Kaladze, Kenia (Khidasheli 81), Shashiashvili (Jakobia 81), Kobiashvili, Tskitishvili (Eliava 90), Kankava, Kvakhadze, Kvirkevlia, Iashvili.
Referee: L. Wilmes (Luxembourg).

B INTERNATIONALS

Airdrie, 21 November 2007, 3133

Scotland (0) 1 *(Howard 83)*

Republic of Ireland (0) 1 *(Byrne 65)*

Scotland: Smith; McNaughton, Armstrong, Berra, Dodds, Stewart (Broadfoot), Whittaker, Thomson, Iwelumo (Fletcher), Howard, Wallace (Adam).
Republic of Ireland: Doyle C (Connor); Goodwin, Bruce, Gartland (Bennett), Dillon, Walters (Bell), Whelan (Byrne R), Doyle M, Hoolahan, O'Donovan (Ward S), Hunt (Yeates).

BRITISH & IRISH INTERNATIONAL MANAGERS

England
Walter Winterbottom 1946–1962 (after period as coach); Alf Ramsey 1963–1974; Joe Mercer (caretaker) 1974; Don Revie 1974–1977; Ron Greenwood 1977–1982; Bobby Robson 1982–1990; Graham Taylor 1990–1993; Terry Venables (coach) 1994–1996; Glenn Hoddle 1996–1999; Kevin Keegan 1999–2000; Sven-Goran Eriksson 2001–2006; Steve McClaren 2006–07; Fabio Capello from January 2008.

Northern Ireland
Peter Doherty 1951–1952; Bertie Peacock 1962–1967; Billy Bingham 1967–1971; Terry Neill 1971–1975; Dave Clements (player-manager) 1975–1976; Danny Blanchflower 1976–1979; Billy Bingham 1980–1994; Bryan Hamilton 1994–1998; Lawrie McMenemy 1998–1999; Sammy McIlroy 2000–2003; Lawrie Sanchez 2004–2007; Nigel Worthington from June 2007.

Scotland (since 1967)
Bobby Brown 1967–1971; Tommy Docherty 1971–1972; Willie Ormond 1973–1977; Ally MacLeod 1977–1978; Jock Stein 1978–1985; Alex Ferguson (caretaker) 1985–1986 Andy Roxburgh (coach) 1986–1993; Craig Brown 1993–2001; Berti Vogts 2002–2004; Walter Smith 2004–2007; Alex McLeish 2007; George Burley from January 2008.

Wales (since 1974)
Mike Smith 1974–1979; Mike England 1980–1988; David Williams (caretaker) 1988; Terry Yorath 1988–1993; John Toshack 1994 for one match; Mike Smith 1994–1995; Bobby Gould 1995–1999; Mark Hughes 1999–2004; John Toshack from November 2004.

Republic of Ireland
Liam Tuohy 1971–1972; Johnny Giles 1973–1980 (after period as player-manager); Eoin Hand 1980–1985; Jack Charlton 1986–1996; Mick McCarthy 1996–2002; Brian Kerr 2003–2006; Steve Staunton 2006–07; Giovanni Trapattoni from February 2008.

New England manager Fabio Capello gets his feet under the table on his first day in office.
(The FA/Action Images/Michael Regan/Pool pic Livepic)

INTERNATIONAL APPEARANCES 1872–2008

This is a list of full international appearances by Englishmen, Irishmen, Scotsmen and Welshmen in matches against the Home Countries and against foreign nations. It does not include unofficial matches against Commonwealth and Empire countries. The year indicated refers to the player's international debut season; i.e. 2005 is the 2004–05 season.
As at July 2008.

ENGLAND

Abbott, W. 1902 (Everton) 1
A'Court, A. 1958 (Liverpool) 5
Adams, T. A. 1987 (Arsenal) 66
Adcock, H. 1929 (Leicester C) 5
Alcock, C. W. 1875 (Wanderers) 1
Alderson, J. T. 1923 (C Palace) 1
Aldridge, A. 1888 (WBA, Walsall Town Swifts) 2
Allen, A. 1888 (Aston Villa) 1
Allen, A. 1960 (Stoke C) 3
Allen, C. 1984 (QPR, Tottenham H) 5
Allen, H. 1888 (Wolverhampton W) 5
Allen, J. P. 1934 (Portsmouth) 2
Allen, R. 1952 (WBA) 5
Alsford, W. J. 1935 (Tottenham H) 1
Amos, A. 1885 (Old Carthusians) 2
Anderson, R. D. 1879 (Old Etonians) 1
Anderson, S. 1962 (Sunderland) 2
Anderson, V. A. 1979 (Nottingham F, Arsenal, Manchester U) 30
Anderton, D. R. 1994 (Tottenham H) 30
Angus, J. 1961 (Burnley) 1
Armfield, J. C. 1959 (Blackpool) 43
Armitage, G. H. 1926 (Charlton Ath) 1
Armstrong, D. 1980 (Middlesbrough, Southampton) 3
Armstrong, K. 1955 (Chelsea) 1
Arnold, J. 1933 (Fulham) 1
Arthur, J. W. H. 1885 (Blackburn R) 7
Ashcroft, J. 1906 (Woolwich Arsenal) 3
Ashmore, G. S. 1926 (WBA) 1
Ashton, C. T. 1926 (Corinthians) 1
Ashton, D. 2008 (West Ham U) 1
Ashurst, W. 1923 (Notts Co) 5
Astall, G. 1956 (Birmingham C) 2
Astle, J. 1969 (WBA) 5
Aston, J. 1949 (Manchester U) 17
Athersmith, W. C. 1892 (Aston Villa) 12
Atyeo, P. J. W. 1956 (Bristol C) 6
Austin, S. W. 1926 (Manchester C) 1

Bach, P. 1899 (Sunderland) 1
Bache, J. W. 1903 (Aston Villa) 7
Baddeley, T. 1903 (Wolverhampton W) 5
Bagshaw, J. J. 1920 (Derby Co) 1
Bailey, G. R. 1985 (Manchester U) 2
Bailey, H. P. 1908 (Leicester Fosse) 5
Bailey, M. A. 1964 (Charlton Ath) 2
Bailey, N. C. 1878 (Clapham Rovers) 19
Baily, E. F. 1950 (Tottenham H) 9
Bain, J. 1877 (Oxford University) 1
Baker, A. 1928 (Arsenal) 1
Baker, B. H. 1921 (Everton, Chelsea) 2
Baker, J. H. 1960 (Hibernian, Arsenal) 8
Ball, A. J. 1965 (Blackpool, Everton, Arsenal) 72
Ball, J. 1928 (Bury) 1
Ball, M. J. 2001 (Everton) 1
Balmer, W. 1905 (Everton) 1
Bamber, J. 1921 (Liverpool) 1
Bambridge, A. L. 1881 (Swifts) 3
Bambridge, E. C. 1879 (Swifts) 18
Bambridge, E. H. 1876 (Swifts) 1
Banks, G. 1963 (Leicester C, Stoke C) 73
Banks, H. E. 1901 (Millwall) 1
Banks, T. 1958 (Bolton W) 6
Bannister, W. 1901 (Burnley, Bolton W) 2
Barclay, R. 1932 (Sheffield U) 3
Bardsley, D. J. 1993 (QPR) 2
Barham, M. 1983 (Norwich C) 2
Barkas, S. 1936 (Manchester C) 5
Barker, J. 1935 (Derby Co) 11
Barker, R. 1872 (Herts Rangers) 1
Barker, R. R. 1895 (Casuals) 1
Barlow, R. J. 1955 (WBA) 1
Barmby, N. J. 1995 (Tottenham H, Middlesbrough, Everton, Liverpool) 23
Barnes, J. 1983 (Watford, Liverpool) 79
Barnes, P. S. 1978 (Manchester C, WBA, Leeds U) 22
Barnet, H. H. 1882 (Royal Engineers) 1
Barrass, M. W. 1952 (Bolton W) 3
Barrett, A. F. 1930 (Fulham) 1
Barrett, E. D. 1991 (Oldham Ath, Aston Villa) 3
Barrett, J. W. 1929 (West Ham U) 1
Barry, G. 2000 (Aston Villa) 20
Barry, L. 1928 (Leicester C) 5
Barson, F. 1920 (Aston Villa) 1
Barton, J. 1890 (Blackburn R) 1
Barton, J. 2007 (Manchester C) 1
Barton, P. H. 1921 (Birmingham) 7
Barton, W. D. 1995 (Wimbledon, Newcastle U) 3
Bassett, W. I. 1888 (WBA) 16
Bastard, S. R. 1880 (Upton Park) 1
Bastin, C. S. 1932 (Arsenal) 21
Batty, D. 1991 (Leeds U, Blackburn R, Newcastle U, Leeds U) 42
Baugh, R. 1886 (Stafford Road, Wolverhampton W) 2
Bayliss, A. E. J. M. 1891 (WBA) 1
Baynham, R. L. 1956 (Luton T) 3
Beardsley, P. A. 1986 (Newcastle U, Liverpool, Newcastle U) 59
Beasant, D. J. 1990 (Chelsea) 2
Beasley, A. 1939 (Huddersfield T) 1
Beats, W. E. 1901 (Wolverhampton W) 2
Beattie, J. S. 2003 (Southampton) 5
Beattie, T. K. 1975 (Ipswich T) 9
Beckham, D. R. J. 1997 (Manchester U, Real Madrid, LA Galaxy) 102
Becton, F. 1895 (Preston NE, Liverpool) 2
Bedford, H. 1923 (Blackpool) 2
Bell, C. 1968 (Manchester C) 48
Bennett, W. 1901 (Sheffield U) 2
Benson, R. W. 1913 (Sheffield U) 1
Bent, D. A. 2006 (Charlton Ath, Tottenham H) 3
Bentley, D. M. 2008 (Blackburn R) 6
Bentley, R. T. F. 1949 (Chelsea) 12
Beresford, J. 1934 (Aston Villa) 1
Berry, A. 1909 (Oxford University) 1
Berry, J. J. 1953 (Manchester U) 4
Bestall, J. G. 1935 (Grimsby T) 1
Betmead, H. A. 1937 (Grimsby T) 1
Betts, M. P. 1877 (Old Harrovians) 1
Betts, W. 1889 (Sheffield W) 1
Beverley, J. 1884 (Blackburn R) 3
Birkett, R. H. 1879 (Clapham Rovers) 1
Birkett, R. J. E. 1936 (Middlesbrough) 1
Birley, F. H. 1874 (Oxford University, Wanderers) 2
Birtles, G. 1980 (Nottingham F) 3
Bishop, S. M. 1927 (Leicester C) 4
Blackburn, F. 1901 (Blackburn R) 3
Blackburn, G. F. 1924 (Aston Villa) 1

Blenkinsop, E. 1928 (Sheffield W) 26
Bliss, H. 1921 (Tottenham H) 1
Blissett, L. L. 1983 (Watford, AC Milan) 14
Blockley, J. P. 1973 (Arsenal) 1
Bloomer, S. 1895 (Derby Co, Middlesbrough) 23
Blunstone, F. 1955 (Chelsea) 5
Bond, R. 1905 (Preston NE, Bradford C) 8
Bonetti, P. P. 1966 (Chelsea) 7
Bonsor, A. G. 1873 (Wanderers) 2
Booth, F. 1905 (Manchester C) 1
Booth, T. 1898 (Blackburn R, Everton) 2
Bould, S. A. 1994 (Arsenal) 2
Bowden, E. R. 1935 (Arsenal) 6
Bower, A. G. 1924 (Corinthians) 5
Bowers, J. W. 1934 (Derby Co) 3
Bowles, S. 1974 (QPR) 5
Bowser, S. 1920 (WBA) 1
Bowyer, L. D. 2003 (Leeds U) 1
Boyer, P. J. 1976 (Norwich C) 1
Boyes, W. 1935 (WBA, Everton) 3
Boyle, T. W. 1913 (Burnley) 1
Brabrook, P. 1958 (Chelsea) 3
Bracewell, P. W. 1985 (Everton) 3
Bradford, G. R. W. 1956 (Bristol R) 1
Bradford, J. 1924 (Birmingham) 12
Bradley, W. 1959 (Manchester U) 3
Bradshaw, F. 1908 (Sheffield W) 1
Bradshaw, T. H. 1897 (Liverpool) 1
Bradshaw, W. 1910 (Blackburn R) 4
Brann, G. 1886 (Swifts) 3
Brawn, W. F. 1904 (Aston Villa) 2
Bray, J. 1935 (Manchester C) 6
Brayshaw, E. 1887 (Sheffield W) 1
Bridge W. M. 2002 (Southampton, Chelsea) 30
Bridges, B. J. 1965 (Chelsea) 4
Bridgett, A. 1905 (Sunderland) 11
Brindle, T. 1880 (Darwen) 2
Brittleton, J. T. 1912 (Sheffield W) 5
Britton, C. S. 1935 (Everton) 9
Broadbent, P. F. 1958 (Wolverhampton W) 7
Broadis, I. A. 1952 (Manchester C, Newcastle U) 14
Brockbank, J. 1872 (Cambridge University) 1
Brodie, J. B. 1889 (Wolverhampton W) 3
Bromilow, T. G. 1921 (Liverpool) 5
Bromley-Davenport, W. E. 1884 (Oxford University) 2
Brook, E. F. 1930 (Manchester C) 18
Brooking, T. D. 1974 (West Ham U) 47
Brooks, J. 1957 (Tottenham H) 3
Broome, F. H. 1938 (Aston Villa) 7
Brown, A. 1882 (Aston Villa) 3
Brown, A. 1971 (WBA) 1
Brown, A. S. 1904 (Sheffield U) 2
Brown, G. 1927 (Huddersfield T, Aston Villa) 9
Brown, J. 1881 (Blackburn R) 5
Brown, J. H. 1927 (Sheffield W) 6
Brown, K. 1960 (West Ham U) 1
Brown, W. 1924 (West Ham U) 1
Brown, W. M. 1999 (Manchester U) 17
Bruton, J. 1928 (Burnley) 3
Bryant, W. I. 1925 (Clapton) 1
Buchan, C. M. 1913 (Sunderland) 6
Buchanan, W. S. 1876 (Clapham R) 1
Buckley, F. C. 1914 (Derby Co) 1
Bull, S. G. 1989 (Wolverhampton W) 13
Bullock, F. E. 1921 (Huddersfield T) 1
Bullock, N. 1923 (Bury) 3
Burgess, H. 1904 (Manchester C) 4
Burgess, H. 1931 (Sheffield W) 4
Burnup, C. J. 1896 (Cambridge University) 1
Burrows, H. 1934 (Sheffield W) 3
Burton, F. E. 1889 (Nottingham F) 1
Bury, L. 1877 (Cambridge University, Old Etonians) 2
Butcher, T. 1980 (Ipswich T, Rangers) 77
Butler, J. D. 1925 (Arsenal) 1
Butler, W. 1924 (Bolton W) 1
Butt, N. 1997 (Manchester U, Newcastle U) 39
Byrne, G. 1963 (Liverpool) 2
Byrne, J. J. 1962 (C Palace, West Ham U) 11
Byrne, R. W. 1954 (Manchester U) 33

Callaghan, I. R. 1966 (Liverpool) 4
Calvey, J. 1902 (Nottingham F) 1
Campbell, A. F. 1929 (Blackburn R, Huddersfield T) 8
Campbell, S. 1996 (Tottenham H, Arsenal, Portsmouth) 73
Camsell, G. H. 1929 (Middlesbrough) 9
Capes, A. J. 1903 (Stoke) 1
Carr, J. 1905 (Newcastle U) 2
Carr, J. 1920 (Middlesbrough) 2
Carr, W. H. 1875 (Owlerton, Sheffield) 1
Carragher, J. L. 1999 (Liverpool) 34
Carrick, M. 2001 (West Ham U, Tottenham H, Manchester U) 14
Carson, S. P. 2008 (Liverpool) 2
Carter, H. S. 1934 (Sunderland, Derby Co) 13
Carter, J. H. 1926 (WBA) 3
Catlin, A. E. 1937 (Sheffield W) 5
Chadwick, A. 1900 (Southampton) 2
Chadwick, E. 1891 (Everton) 7
Chamberlain, M. 1983 (Stoke C) 8
Chambers, H. 1921 (Liverpool) 8
Channon, M. R. 1973 (Southampton, Manchester C) 46
Charles, G. A. 1991 (Nottingham F) 2
Charlton, J. 1965 (Leeds U) 35
Charlton, R. 1958 (Manchester U) 106
Charnley, R. O. 1963 (Blackpool) 1
Charsley, C. C. 1893 (Small Heath) 1
Chedgzoy, S. 1920 (Everton) 8
Chenery, C. J. 1872 (C Palace) 3
Cherry, T. J. 1976 (Leeds U) 27
Chilton, A. 1951 (Manchester U) 2
Chippendale, H. 1894 (Blackburn R) 1
Chivers, M. 1971 (Tottenham H) 24
Christian, E. 1879 (Old Etonians) 1
Clamp, E. 1958 (Wolverhampton W) 4
Clapton, D. R. 1959 (Arsenal) 1
Clare, T. 1889 (Stoke) 4
Clarke, A. J. 1970 (Leeds U) 19
Clarke, H. A. 1954 (Tottenham H) 1
Clay, T. 1920 (Tottenham H) 4
Clayton, R. 1956 (Blackburn R) 35
Clegg, J. C. 1872 (Sheffield W) 1
Clegg, W. E. 1873 (Sheffield W, Sheffield Albion) 2
Clemence, R. N. 1973 (Liverpool, Tottenham H) 61
Clement, D. T. 1976 (QPR) 5
Clough, B. H. 1960 (Middlesbrough) 2
Clough, N. H. 1989 (Nottingham F) 14
Coates, R. 1970 (Burnley, Tottenham H) 4
Cobbold, W. N. 1883 (Cambridge University, Old Carthusians) 9
Cock, J. G. 1920 (Huddersfield T, Chelsea) 2
Cockburn, H. 1947 (Manchester U) 13
Cohen, G. R. 1964 (Fulham) 37
Cole, A. 2001 (Arsenal, Chelsea) 64
Cole, A. A. 1995 (Manchester U) 15
Cole, J. J. 2001 (West Ham U, Chelsea) 50
Colclough, H. 1914 (C Palace) 1
Coleman, E. H. 1921 (Dulwich Hamlet) 1
Coleman, J. 1907 (Woolwich Arsenal) 1
Collymore, S. V. 1995 (Nottingham F, Aston Villa) 3
Common, A. 1904 (Sheffield U, Middlesbrough) 3
Compton, L. H. 1951 (Arsenal) 2
Conlin, J. 1906 (Bradford C) 1
Connelly, J. M. 1960 (Burnley, Manchester U) 20
Cook, T. E. R. 1925 (Brighton) 1
Cooper, C. T. 1995 (Nottingham F) 2

Cooper, N. C. 1893 (Cambridge University) 1
Cooper, T. 1928 (Derby Co) 15
Cooper, T. 1969 (Leeds U) 20
Coppell, S. J. 1978 (Manchester U) 42
Copping, W. 1933 (Leeds U, Arsenal, Leeds U) 20
Corbett, B. O. 1901 (Corinthians) 1
Corbett, R. 1903 (Old Malvernians) 1
Corbett, W. S. 1908 (Birmingham) 3
Corrigan, J. T. 1976 (Manchester C) 9
Cottee, A. R. 1987 (West Ham U, Everton) 7
Cotterill, G. H. 1891 (Cambridge University, Old Brightonians) 4
Cottle, J. R. 1909 (Bristol C) 1
Cowan, S. 1926 (Manchester C) 3
Cowans, G. S. 1983 (Aston Villa, Bari, Aston Villa) 10
Cowell, A. 1910 (Blackburn R) 1
Cox, J. 1901 (Liverpool) 3
Cox, J. D. 1892 (Derby Co) 1
Crabtree, J. W. 1894 (Burnley, Aston Villa) 14
Crawford, J. F. 1931 (Chelsea) 1
Crawford, R. 1962 (Ipswich T) 2
Crawshaw, T. H. 1895 (Sheffield W) 10
Crayston, W. J. 1936 (Arsenal) 8
Creek, F. N. S. 1923 (Corinthians) 1
Cresswell, W. 1921 (South Shields, Sunderland, Everton) 7
Crompton, R. 1902 (Blackburn R) 41
Crooks, S. D. 1930 (Derby Co) 26
Crouch, P. J. 2005 (Southampton, Liverpool) 28
Crowe, C. 1963 (Wolverhampton W) 1
Cuggy, F. 1913 (Sunderland) 2
Cullis, S. 1938 (Wolverhampton W) 12
Cunliffe, A. 1933 (Blackburn R) 2
Cunliffe, D. 1900 (Portsmouth) 1
Cunliffe, J. N. 1936 (Everton) 1
Cunningham, L. 1979 (WBA, Real Madrid) 6
Curle, K. 1992 (Manchester C) 3
Currey, E. S. 1890 (Oxford University) 2
Currie, A. W. 1972 (Sheffield U, Leeds U) 17
Cursham, A. W. 1876 (Notts Co) 6
Cursham, H. A. 1880 (Notts Co) 8

Daft, H. B. 1889 (Notts Co) 5
Daley, A. M. 1992 (Aston Villa) 7
Danks, T. 1885 (Nottingham F) 1
Davenport, P. 1985 (Nottingham F) 1
Davenport, J. K. 1885 (Bolton W) 2
Davis, G. 1904 (Derby Co) 2
Davis, H. 1903 (Sheffield W) 3
Davison, J. E. 1922 (Sheffield W) 1
Dawson, J. 1922 (Burnley) 2
Day, S. H. 1906 (Old Malvernians) 3
Dean, W. R. 1927 (Everton) 16
Deane, B. C. 1991 (Sheffield U) 3
Deeley, N. V. 1959 (Wolverhampton W) 2
Defoe, J. C. 2004 (Tottenham H, Portsmouth) 28
Devey, J. H. G. 1892 (Aston Villa) 2
Devonshire, A. 1980 (West Ham U) 8
Dewhurst, F. 1886 (Preston NE) 9
Dewhurst, G. P. 1895 (Liverpool Ramblers) 1
Dickinson, J. W. 1949 (Portsmouth) 48
Dimmock, J. H. 1921 (Tottenham H) 3
Ditchburn, E. G. 1949 (Tottenham H) 6
Dix, R. W. 1939 (Derby Co) 1
Dixon, J. A. 1885 (Notts Co) 1
Dixon, K. M. 1985 (Chelsea) 8
Dixon, L. M. 1990 (Arsenal) 22
Dobson, A. T. C. 1882 (Notts Co) 4
Dobson, C. F. 1886 (Notts Co) 1
Dobson, J. M. 1974 (Burnley, Everton) 5
Doggart, A. G. 1924 (Corinthians) 1
Dorigo, A. R. 1990 (Chelsea, Leeds U) 15
Dorrell, A. R. 1925 (Aston Villa) 4
Douglas, B. 1958 (Blackburn R) 36
Downing, S. 2005 (Middlesbrough) 18
Downs, R. W. 1921 (Everton) 1
Doyle, M. 1976 (Manchester C) 5
Drake, E. J. 1935 (Arsenal) 5
Dublin, D. 1998 (Coventry C, Aston Villa) 4
Ducat, A. 1910 (Woolwich Arsenal, Aston Villa) 6
Dunn, A. T. B. 1883 (Cambridge University, Old Etonians) 4
Dunn, D. J. I. 2003 (Blackburn R) 1
Duxbury, M. 1984 (Manchester U) 10
Dyer, K. C. 2000 (Newcastle U, West Ham U) 33

Earle, S. G. J. 1924 (Clapton, West Ham U) 2
Eastham, G. 1963 (Arsenal) 19
Eastham, G. R. 1935 (Bolton W) 1
Eckersley, W. 1950 (Blackburn R) 17
Edwards, D. 1955 (Manchester U) 18
Edwards, J. H. 1874 (Shropshire Wanderers) 1
Edwards, W. 1926 (Leeds U) 16
Ehiogu, U. 1996 (Aston Villa, Middlesbrough) 4
Ellerington, W. 1949 (Southampton) 2
Elliott, G. W. 1913 (Middlesbrough) 3
Elliott, W. H. 1952 (Burnley) 5
Evans, R. E. 1911 (Sheffield U) 4
Ewer, F. H. 1924 (Casuals) 2

Fairclough, P. 1878 (Old Foresters) 1
Fairhurst, D. 1934 (Newcastle U) 1
Fantham, J. 1962 (Sheffield W) 1
Fashanu, J. 1989 (Wimbledon) 2
Felton, W. 1925 (Sheffield W) 1
Fenton, M. 1938 (Middlesbrough) 1
Fenwick, T. W. 1984 (QPR, Tottenham H) 20
Ferdinand, L. 1993 (QPR, Newcastle U, Tottenham H) 17
Ferdinand, R. G. 1998 (West Ham U, Leeds U, Manchester U) 68
Field, E. 1876 (Clapham Rovers) 2
Finney, T. 1947 (Preston NE) 76
Fleming, H. J. 1909 (Swindon T) 11
Fletcher, A. 1889 (Wolverhampton W) 2
Flowers, R. 1955 (Wolverhampton W) 49
Flowers, T. D. 1993 (Southampton, Blackburn R) 11
Forman, Frank 1898 (Nottingham F 9
Forman, F. R. 1899 (Nottingham F) 3
Forrest, J. H. 1884 (Blackburn R) 11
Fort, J. 1921 (Millwall) 1
Foster, B. 2007 (Manchester U) 1
Foster, R. E. 1900 (Oxford University, Corinthians) 5
Foster, S. 1982 (Brighton & HA) 3
Foulke, W. J. 1897 (Sheffield U) 1
Foulkes, W. A. 1955 (Manchester U) 1
Fowler, R. B. 1996 (Liverpool, Leeds U) 26
Fox, F. S. 1925 (Millwall) 1
Francis, G. C. J. 1975 (QPR) 12
Francis, T. 1977 (Birmingham C, Nottingham F, Manchester C, Sampdoria) 52
Franklin, C. F. 1947 (Stoke C) 27
Freeman, B. C. 1909 (Everton, Burnley) 5
Froggatt, J. 1950 (Portsmouth) 13
Froggatt, R. 1953 (Sheffield W) 4
Fry, C. B. 1901 (Corinthians) 1
Furness, W. I. 1933 (Leeds U) 1

Galley, T. 1937 (Wolverhampton W) 2
Gardner, A. 2004 (Tottenham H) 1
Gardner, T. 1934 (Aston Villa) 2
Garfield, B. 1898 (WBA) 1
Garraty, W. 1903 (Aston Villa) 1
Garrett, T. 1952 (Blackpool) 3
Gascoigne, P. J. 1989 (Tottenham H, Lazio, Rangers, Middlesbrough) 57

Gates, E. 1981 (Ipswich T) 2
Gay, L. H. 1893 (Cambridge University, Old Brightonians) 3
Geary, F. 1890 (Everton) 2
Geaves, R. L. 1875 (Clapham Rovers) 1
Gee, C. W. 1932 (Everton) 3
Geldard, A. 1933 (Everton) 4
George, C. 1977 (Derby Co) 1
George, W. 1902 (Aston Villa) 3
Gerrard, S. G. 2000 (Liverpool) 67
Gibbins, W. V. T. 1924 (Clapton) 2
Gidman, J. 1977 (Aston Villa) 1
Gillard, I. T. 1975 (QPR) 3
Gilliat, W. E. 1893 (Old Carthusians) 1
Goddard, P. 1982 (West Ham U) 1
Goodall, F. R. 1926 (Huddersfield T) 25
Goodall, J. 1888 (Preston NE, Derby Co) 14
Goodhart, H. C. 1883 (Old Etonians) 3
Goodwyn, A. G. 1873 (Royal Engineers) 1
Goodyer, A. C. 1879 (Nottingham F) 1
Gosling, R. C. 1892 (Old Etonians) 5
Gosnell, A. A. 1906 (Newcastle U) 1
Gough, H. C. 1921 (Sheffield U) 1
Goulden, L. A. 1937 (West Ham U) 14
Graham, L. 1925 (Millwall) 2
Graham, T. 1931 (Nottingham F) 2
Grainger, C. 1956 (Sheffield U, Sunderland) 7
Gray, A. A. 1992 (C Palace) 1
Gray, M. 1999 (Sunderland) 3
Greaves, J. 1959 (Chelsea, Tottenham H) 57
Green, F. T. 1876 (Wanderers) 1
Green, G. H. 1925 (Sheffield U) 8
Green, R. P. 2005 (Norwich C) 1
Greenhalgh, E. H. 1872 (Notts Co) 2
Greenhoff, B. 1976 (Manchester U, Leeds U) 18
Greenwood, D. H. 1882 (Blackburn R) 2
Gregory, J. 1983 (QPR) 6
Grimsdell, A. 1920 (Tottenham H) 6
Grosvenor, A. T. 1934 (Birmingham) 3
Gunn, W. 1884 (Notts Co) 2
Guppy, S. 2000 (Leicester C) 1
Gurney, R. 1935 (Sunderland) 1

Hacking, J. 1929 (Oldham Ath) 3
Hadley, H. 1903 (WBA) 1
Hagan, J. 1949 (Sheffield U) 1
Haines, J. T. W. 1949 (WBA) 1
Hall, A. E. 1910 (Aston Villa) 1
Hall, G. W. 1934 (Tottenham H) 10
Hall, J. 1956 (Birmingham C) 17
Halse, H. J. 1909 (Manchester U) 1
Hammond, H. E. D. 1889 (Oxford University) 1
Hampson, J. 1931 (Blackpool) 3
Hampton, H. 1913 (Aston Villa) 4
Hancocks, J. 1949 (Wolverhampton W) 3
Hapgood, E. 1933 (Arsenal) 30
Hardinge, H. T. W. 1910 (Sheffield U) 1
Hardman, H. P. 1905 (Everton) 4
Hardwick, G. F. M. 1947 (Middlesbrough) 13
Hardy, H. 1925 (Stockport Co) 1
Hardy, S. 1907 (Liverpool, Aston Villa) 21
Harford, M. G. 1988 (Luton T) 2
Hargreaves, F. W. 1880 (Blackburn R) 3
Hargreaves, J. 1881 (Blackburn R) 2
Hargreaves, O. 2002 (Bayern Munich, Manchester U) 42
Harper, E. C. 1926 (Blackburn R) 1
Harris, G. 1966 (Burnley) 1
Harris, P. P. 1950 (Portsmouth) 2
Harris, S. S. 1904 (Cambridge University, Old Westminsters) 6
Harrison, A. H. 1893 (Old Westminsters) 2
Harrison, G. 1921 (Everton) 2
Harrow, J. H. 1923 (Chelsea) 2
Hart, C. 2008 (Manchester C) 1
Hart, E. 1929 (Leeds U) 8
Hartley, F. 1923 (Oxford C) 1
Harvey, A. 1881 (Wednesbury Strollers) 1
Harvey, J. C. 1971 (Everton) 1
Hassall, H. W. 1951 (Huddersfield T, Bolton W) 5
Hateley, M. 1984 (Portsmouth, AC Milan, Monaco, Rangers) 32
Hawkes, R. M. 1907 (Luton T) 5
Haworth, G. 1887 (Accrington) 5
Hawtrey, J. P. 1881 (Old Etonians) 2
Haygarth, E. B. 1875 (Swifts) 1
Haynes, J. N. 1955 (Fulham) 56
Healless, H. 1925 (Blackburn R) 2
Hector, K. J. 1974 (Derby Co) 2
Hedley, G. A. 1901 (Sheffield U) 1
Hegan, K. E. 1923 (Corinthians) 4
Hellawell, M. S. 1963 (Birmingham C) 2
Hendrie, L. A. 1999 (Aston Villa) 1
Henfrey, A. G. 1891 (Cambridge University, Corinthians) 5
Henry, R. P. 1963 (Tottenham H) 1
Heron, F. 1876 (Wanderers) 1
Heron, G. H. H. 1873 (Uxbridge, Wanderers) 5
Heskey, E. W. I. 1999 (Leicester C, Liverpool, Birmingham C, Wigan Ath) 45
Hibbert, W. 1910 (Bury) 1
Hibbs, H. E. 1930 (Birmingham) 25
Hill, F. 1963 (Bolton W) 2
Hill, G. A. 1976 (Manchester U) 6
Hill, J. H. 1925 (Burnley, Newcastle U) 11
Hill, R. 1983 (Luton T) 3
Hill, R. H. 1926 (Millwall) 1
Hillman, J. 1899 (Burnley) 1
Hills, A. F. 1879 (Old Harrovians) 1
Hilsdon, G. R. 1907 (Chelsea) 8
Hinchcliffe, A. G. 1997 (Everton, Sheffield W) 7
Hine, E. W. 1929 (Leicester C) 6
Hinton, A. T. 1963 (Wolverhampton W, Nottingham F) 3
Hirst, D. E. 1991 (Sheffield W) 3
Hitchens, G. A. 1961 (Aston Villa, Internazionale) 7
Hobbis, H. H. F. 1936 (Charlton Ath) 2
Hoddle, G. 1980 (Tottenham H, Monaco) 53
Hodge, S. B. 1986 (Aston Villa, Tottenham H, Nottingham F) 24
Hodgetts, D. 1888 (Aston Villa) 6
Hodgkinson, A. 1957 (Sheffield U) 5
Hodgson, G. 1931 (Liverpool) 3
Hodkinson, J. 1913 (Blackburn R) 3
Hogg, W. 1902 (Sunderland) 3
Holdcroft, G. H. 1937 (Preston NE) 2
Holden, A. D. 1959 (Bolton W) 5
Holden, G. H. 1881 (Wednesbury OA) 4
Holden-White, C. 1888 (Corinthians) 2
Holford, T. 1903 (Stoke) 1
Holley, G. H. 1909 (Sunderland) 10
Holliday, E. 1960 (Middlesbrough) 3
Hollins, J. W. 1967 (Chelsea) 1
Holmes, R. 1888 (Preston NE) 7
Holt, J. 1890 (Everton, Reading) 10
Hopkinson, E. 1958 (Bolton W) 14
Hossack, A. H. 1892 (Corinthians) 2
Houghton, W. E. 1931 (Aston Villa) 7
Houlker, A. E. 1902 (Blackburn R, Portsmouth, Southampton) 5
Howarth, R. H. 1887 (Preston NE, Everton) 5
Howe, D. 1958 (WBA) 23
Howe, J. R. 1948 (Derby Co) 3
Howell, L. S. 1873 (Wanderers) 1
Howell, R. 1895 (Sheffield U, Liverpool) 2
Howey, S. N. 1995 (Newcastle U) 4

Hudson, A. A. 1975 (Stoke C) 2
Hudson, J. 1883 (Sheffield) 1
Hudspeth, F. C. 1926 (Newcastle U) 1
Hufton, A. E. 1924 (West Ham U) 6
Hughes, E. W. 1970 (Liverpool, Wolverhampton W) 62
Hughes, L. 1950 (Liverpool) 3
Hulme, J. H. A. 1927 (Arsenal) 9
Humphreys, P. 1903 (Notts Co) 1
Hunt, G. S. 1933 (Tottenham H) 3
Hunt, Rev. K. R. G. 1911 (Leyton) 2
Hunt, R. 1962 (Liverpool) 34
Hunt, S. 1984 (WBA) 2
Hunter, J. 1878 (Sheffield Heeley) 7
Hunter, N. 1966 (Leeds U) 28
Hurst, G. C. 1966 (West Ham U) 49

Ince, P. E. C. 1993 (Manchester U, Internazionale, Liverpool, Middlesbrough) 53
Iremonger, J. 1901 (Nottingham F) 2

Jack, D. N. B. 1924 (Bolton W, Arsenal) 9
Jackson, E. 1891 (Oxford University) 1
Jagielka, P. N. 2008 (Everton) 1
James. D. B. 1997 (Liverpool, Aston Villa, West Ham U, Manchester C, Portsmouth) 39
Jarrett, B. G. 1876 (Cambridge University) 3
Jefferis, F. 1912 (Everton) 2
Jeffers, F. 2003 (Arsenal) 1
Jenas, J. A. 2003 (Newcastle U, Tottenham H) 18
Jezzard, B. A. G. 1954 (Fulham) 2
Johnson, A. 2005 (C Palace, Everton) 8
Johnson, D. E. 1975 (Ipswich T, Liverpool) 8
Johnson, E. 1880 (Saltley College, Stoke) 2
Johnson, G. M. C. 2004 (Chelsea, Portsmouth) 8
Johnson, J. A. 1937 (Stoke C) 5
Johnson, S. A. M. 2001 (Derby Co) 1
Johnson, T. C. F. 1926 (Manchester C, Everton) 5
Johnson, W. H. 1900 (Sheffield U) 6
Johnston, H. 1947 (Blackpool) 10
Jones, A. 1882 (Walsall Swifts, Great Lever) 3
Jones, H. 1923 (Nottingham F) 1
Jones, H. 1927 (Blackburn R) 6
Jones, M. D. 1965 (Sheffield U, Leeds U) 3
Jones, R. 1992 (Liverpool) 8
Jones, W. 1901 (Bristol C) 1
Jones, W. H. 1950 (Liverpool) 2
Joy, B. 1936 (Casuals) 1

Kail, E. I. L. 1929 (Dulwich Hamlet) 3
Kay, A. H. 1963 (Everton) 1
Kean, F. W. 1923 (Sheffield W, Bolton W) 9
Keegan, J. K. 1973 (Liverpool, SV Hamburg, Southampton) 63
Keen, E. R. L. 1933 (Derby Co) 4
Kelly, R. 1920 (Burnley, Sunderland, Huddersfield T) 14
Kennedy, A. 1984 (Liverpool) 2
Kennedy, R. 1976 (Liverpool) 17
Kenyon-Slaney, W. S. 1873 (Wanderers) 1
Keown, M. R. 1992 (Everton, Arsenal) 43
Kevan, D. T. 1957 (WBA) 14
Kidd, B. 1970 (Manchester U) 2
King, L. B. 2002 (Tottenham H) 19
King, R. S. 1882 (Oxford University) 1
Kingsford, R. K. 1874 (Wanderers) 1
Kingsley, M. 1901 (Newcastle U) 1
Kinsey, G. 1892 (Wolverhampton W, Derby Co) 4
Kirchen, A. J. 1937 (Arsenal) 3
Kirkland, C. E. 2007 (Liverpool) 1
Kirton, W. J. 1922 (Aston Villa) 1
Knight, A. E. 1920 (Portsmouth) 1
Knight, Z. 2005 (Fulham) 2
Knowles, C. 1968 (Tottenham H) 4
Konchesky, P. M. 2003 (Charlton Ath, West Ham U) 2

Labone, B. L. 1963 (Everton) 26
Lampard, F. J. 2000 (West Ham U, Chelsea) 61
Lampard, F. R. G. 1973 (West Ham U) 2
Langley, E. J. 1958 (Fulham) 3
Langton, R. 1947 (Blackburn R, Preston NE, Bolton W) 11
Latchford, R. D. 1978 (Everton) 12
Latheron, E. G. 1913 (Blackburn R) 2
Lawler, C. 1971 (Liverpool) 4
Lawton, T. 1939 (Everton, Chelsea, Notts Co) 23
Leach, T. 1931 (Sheffield W) 2
Leake, A. 1904 (Aston Villa) 5
Lee, E. A. 1904 (Southampton) 1
Lee, F. H. 1969 (Manchester C) 27
Lee, J. 1951 (Derby Co) 1
Lee, R. M. 1995 (Newcastle U) 21
Lee, S. 1983 (Liverpool) 14
Leighton, J. E. 1886 (Nottingham F) 1
Lennon, A. J. 2006 (Tottenham H) 9
Lescott, J. P. 2008 (Everton) 5
Le Saux, G. P. 1994 (Blackburn R, Chelsea) 36
Le Tissier, M. P. 1994 (Southampton) 8
Lilley, H. E. 1892 (Sheffield U) 1
Linacre, H. J. 1905 (Nottingham F) 2
Lindley, T. 1886 (Cambridge University, Nottingham F) 13
Lindsay, A. 1974 (Liverpool) 4
Lindsay, W. 1877 (Wanderers) 1
Lineker, G. 1984 (Leicester C, Everton, Barcelona, Tottenham H) 80
Lintott, E. H. 1908 (QPR, Bradford C) 7
Lipsham, H. B. 1902 (Sheffield U) 1
Little, B. 1975 (Aston Villa) 1
Lloyd, L. V. 1971 (Liverpool, Nottingham F) 4
Lockett, A. 1903 (Stoke) 1
Lodge, L. V. 1894 (Cambridge University, Corinthians) 5
Lofthouse, J. M. 1885 (Blackburn R, Accrington, Blackburn R) 7
Lofthouse, N. 1951 (Bolton W) 33
Longworth, E. 1920 (Liverpool) 5
Lowder, A. 1889 (Wolverhampton W) 1
Lowe, E. 1947 (Aston Villa) 3
Lucas, T. 1922 (Liverpool) 3
Luntley, E. 1880 (Nottingham F) 2
Lyttelton, Hon. A. 1877 (Cambridge University) 1
Lyttelton, Hon. E. 1878 (Cambridge University) 1

Mabbutt, G. 1983 (Tottenham H) 16
Macaulay, R. H. 1881 (Cambridge University) 1
McCall, J. 1913 (Preston NE) 5
McCann, G. P. 2001 (Sunderland) 1
McDermott, T. 1978 (Liverpool) 25
McDonald, C. A. 1958 (Burnley) 8
Macdonald, M. 1972 (Newcastle U) 14
McFarland, R. L. 1971 (Derby Co) 28
McGarry, W. H. 1954 (Huddersfield T) 4
McGuinness, W. 1959 (Manchester U) 2
McInroy, A. 1927 (Sunderland) 1
McMahon, S. 1988 (Liverpool) 17
McManaman, S. 1995 (Liverpool, Real Madrid) 37
McNab, R. 1969 (Arsenal) 4
McNeal, R. 1914 (WBA) 2
McNeil, M. 1961 (Middlesbrough) 9
Macrae, S. 1883 (Notts Co) 5
Maddison, F. B. 1872 (Oxford University) 1
Madeley, P. E. 1971 (Leeds U) 24
Magee, T. P. 1923 (WBA) 5
Makepeace, H. 1906 (Everton) 4
Male, C. G. 1935 (Arsenal) 19
Mannion, W. J. 1947 (Middlesbrough) 26
Mariner, P. 1977 (Ipswich T, Arsenal) 35
Marsden, J. T. 1891 (Darwen) 1

Marsden, W. 1930 (Sheffield W) 3
Marsh, R. W. 1972 (QPR, Manchester C) 9
Marshall, T. 1880 (Darwen) 2
Martin, A. 1981 (West Ham U) 17
Martin, H. 1914 (Sunderland) 1
Martyn, A. N. 1992 (C Palace, Leeds U) 23
Marwood, B. 1989 (Arsenal) 1
Maskrey, H. M. 1908 (Derby Co) 1
Mason, C. 1887 (Wolverhampton W) 3
Matthews, R. D. 1956 (Coventry C) 5
Matthews, S. 1935 (Stoke C, Blackpool) 54
Matthews, V. 1928 (Sheffield U) 2
Maynard, W. J. 1872 (1st Surrey Rifles) 2
Meadows, J. 1955 (Manchester C) 1
Medley, L. D. 1951 (Tottenham H) 6
Meehan, T. 1924 (Chelsea) 1
Melia, J. 1963 (Liverpool) 2
Mercer, D. W. 1923 (Sheffield U) 2
Mercer, J. 1939 (Everton) 5
Merrick, G. H. 1952 (Birmingham C) 23
Merson, P. C. 1992 (Arsenal, Middlesbrough, Aston Villa) 21
Metcalfe, V. 1951 (Huddersfield T) 2
Mew, J. W. 1921 (Manchester U) 1
Middleditch, B. 1897 (Corinthians) 1
Milburn, J. E. T. 1949 (Newcastle U) 13
Miller, B. G. 1961 (Burnley) 1
Miller, H. S. 1923 (Charlton Ath) 1
Mills, D. J. 2001 (Leeds U) 19
Mills, G. R. 1938 (Chelsea) 3
Mills, M. D. 1973 (Ipswich T) 42
Milne, G. 1963 (Liverpool) 14
Milton, C. A. 1952 (Arsenal) 1
Milward, A. 1891 (Everton) 4
Mitchell, C. 1880 (Upton Park) 5
Mitchell, J. F. 1925 (Manchester C) 1
Moffat, H. 1913 (Oldham Ath) 1
Molyneux, G. 1902 (Southampton) 4
Moon, W. R. 1888 (Old Westminsters) 7
Moore, H. T. 1883 (Notts Co) 2
Moore, J. 1923 (Derby Co) 1
Moore, R. F. 1962 (West Ham U) 108
Moore, W. G. B. 1923 (West Ham U) 1
Mordue, J. 1912 (Sunderland) 2
Morice, C. J. 1872 (Barnes) 1
Morley, A. 1982 (Aston Villa) 6
Morley, H. 1910 (Notts Co) 1
Morren, T. 1898 (Sheffield U) 1
Morris, F. 1920 (WBA) 2
Morris, J. 1949 (Derby Co) 3
Morris, W. W. 1939 (Wolverhampton W) 3
Morse, H. 1879 (Notts Co) 1
Mort, T. 1924 (Aston Villa) 3
Morten, A. 1873 (C Palace) 1
Mortensen, S. H. 1947 (Blackpool) 25
Morton, J. R. 1938 (West Ham U) 1
Mosforth, W. 1877 (Sheffield W, Sheffield Albion, Sheffield W) 9
Moss, F. 1922 (Aston Villa) 5
Moss, F. 1934 (Arsenal) 4
Mosscrop, E. 1914 (Burnley) 2
Mozley, B. 1950 (Derby Co) 3
Mullen, J. 1947 (Wolverhampton W) 12
Mullery, A. P. 1965 (Tottenham H) 35
Murphy, D. B. 2002 (Liverpool) 9

Neal, P. G. 1976 (Liverpool) 50
Needham, E. 1894 (Sheffield U) 16
Neville, G. A. 1995 (Manchester U) 85
Neville, P. J. 1996 (Manchester U, Everton) 59
Newton, K. R. 1966 (Blackburn R, Everton) 27
Nicholls, J. 1954 (WBA) 2
Nicholson, W. E. 1951 (Tottenham H) 1
Nish, D. J. 1973 (Derby Co) 5
Norman, M. 1962 (Tottenham H) 23
Nugent, D. J. 2007 (Preston NE) 1
Nuttall, H. 1928 (Bolton W) 3

Oakley, W. J. 1895 (Oxford University, Corinthians) 16
O'Dowd, J. P. 1932 (Chelsea) 3
O'Grady, M. 1963 (Huddersfield T, Leeds U) 2
Ogilvie, R. A. M. M. 1874 (Clapham R) 1
Oliver, L. F. 1929 (Fulham) 1
Olney, B. A. 1928 (Aston Villa) 2
Osborne, F. R. 1923 (Fulham, Tottenham H) 4
Osborne, R. 1928 (Leicester C) 1
Osgood, P. L. 1970 (Chelsea) 4
Osman, R. 1980 (Ipswich T) 11
Ottaway, C. J. 1872 (Oxford University) 2
Owen, J. R. B. 1874 (Sheffield) 1
Owen, M. J. 1998 (Liverpool, Real Madrid, Newcastle U) 89
Owen, S. W. 1954 (Luton T) 3

Page, L. A. 1927 (Burnley) 7
Paine, T. L. 1963 (Southampton) 19
Pallister, G. A. 1988 (Middlesbrough, Manchester U) 22
Palmer, C. L. 1992 (Sheffield W) 18
Pantling, H. H. 1924 (Sheffield U) 1
Paravicini, P. J. de 1883 (Cambridge University) 3
Parker, P. A. 1989 (QPR, Manchester U) 19
Parker, S. M. 2004 (Charlton Ath, Chelsea, Newcastle U) 3
Parker, T. R. 1925 (Southampton) 1
Parkes, P. B. 1974 (QPR) 1
Parkinson, J. 1910 (Liverpool) 2
Parlour, R. 1999 (Arsenal) 10
Parr, P. C. 1882 (Oxford University) 1
Parry, E. H. 1879 (Old Carthusians) 3
Parry, R. A. 1960 (Bolton W) 2
Patchitt, B. C. A. 1923 (Corinthians) 2
Pawson, F. W. 1883 (Cambridge University, Swifts) 2
Payne, J. 1937 (Luton T) 1
Peacock, A. 1962 (Middlesbrough, Leeds U) 6
Peacock, J. 1929 (Middlesbrough) 3
Pearce, S. 1987 (Nottingham F, West Ham U) 78
Pearson, H. F. 1932 (WBA) 1
Pearson, J. H. 1892 (Crewe Alex) 1
Pearson, J. S. 1976 (Manchester U) 15
Pearson, S. C. 1948 (Manchester U) 8
Pease, W. H. 1927 (Middlesbrough) 1
Pegg, D. 1957 (Manchester U) 1
Pejic, M. 1974 (Stoke C) 4
Pelly, F. R. 1893 (Old Foresters) 3
Pennington, J. 1907 (WBA) 25
Pentland, F. B. 1909 (Middlesbrough) 5
Perry, C. 1890 (WBA) 3
Perry, T. 1898 (WBA) 1
Perry, W. 1956 (Blackpool) 3
Perryman, S. 1982 (Tottenham H) 1
Peters, M. 1966 (West Ham U, Tottenham H) 67
Phelan, M. C. 1990 (Manchester U) 1
Phillips, K. 1999 (Sunderland) 8
Phillips, L. H. 1952 (Portsmouth) 3
Pickering, F. 1964 (Everton) 3
Pickering, J. 1933 (Sheffield U) 1
Pickering, N. 1983 (Sunderland) 1
Pike, T. M. 1886 (Cambridge University) 1
Pilkington, B. 1955 (Burnley) 1
Plant, J. 1900 (Bury) 1
Platt, D. 1990 (Aston Villa, Bari, Juventus, Sampdoria, Arsenal) 62
Plum, S. L. 1923 (Charlton Ath) 1
Pointer, R. 1962 (Burnley) 3
Porteous, T. S. 1891 (Sunderland) 1
Powell, C. G. 2001 (Charlton Ath) 5

Priest, A. E. 1900 (Sheffield U) 1
Prinsep, J. F. M. 1879 (Clapham Rovers) 1
Puddefoot, S. C. 1926 (Blackburn R) 2
Pye, J. 1950 (Wolverhampton W) 1
Pym, R. H. 1925 (Bolton W) 3

Quantrill, A. 1920 (Derby Co) 4
Quixall, A. 1954 (Sheffield W) 5

Radford, J. 1969 (Arsenal) 2
Raikes, G. B. 1895 (Oxford University) 4
Ramsey, A. E. 1949 (Southampton, Tottenham H) 32
Rawlings, A. 1921 (Preston NE) 1
Rawlings, W. E. 1922 (Southampton) 2
Rawlinson, J. F. P. 1882 (Cambridge University) 1
Rawson, H. E. 1875 (Royal Engineers) 1
Rawson, W. S. 1875 (Oxford University) 2
Read, A. 1921 (Tufnell Park) 1
Reader, J. 1894 (WBA) 1
Reaney, P. 1969 (Leeds U) 3
Redknapp, J. F. 1996 (Liverpool) 17
Reeves, K. P. 1980 (Norwich C, Manchester C) 2
Regis, C. 1982 (WBA, Coventry C) 5
Reid, P. 1985 (Everton) 13
Revie, D. G. 1955 (Manchester C) 6
Reynolds, J. 1892 (WBA, Aston Villa) 8
Richards, C. H. 1898 (Nottingham F) 1
Richards, G. H. 1909 (Derby Co) 1
Richards, J. P. 1973 (Wolverhampton W) 1
Richards, M. 2007 (Manchester C) 11
Richardson, J. R. 1933 (Newcastle U) 2
Richardson, K. 1994 (Aston Villa) 1
Richardson, K. E. 2005 (Manchester U) 8
Richardson, W. G. 1935 (WBA) 1
Rickaby, S. 1954 (WBA) 1
Ricketts, M. B. 2002 (Bolton W) 1
Rigby, A. 1927 (Blackburn R) 5
Rimmer, E. J. 1930 (Sheffield W) 4
Rimmer, J. J. 1976 (Arsenal) 1
Ripley, S. E. 1994 (Blackburn R) 2
Rix, G. 1981 (Arsenal) 17
Robb, G. 1954 (Tottenham H) 1
Roberts, C. 1905 (Manchester U) 3
Roberts, F. 1925 (Manchester C) 4
Roberts, G. 1983 (Tottenham H) 6
Roberts, H. 1931 (Arsenal) 1
Roberts, H. 1931 (Millwall) 1
Roberts, R. 1887 (WBA) 3
Roberts, W. T. 1924 (Preston NE) 2
Robinson, J. 1937 (Sheffield W) 4
Robinson, J. W. 1897 (Derby Co, New Brighton Tower, Southampton) 11
Robinson, P. W. 2003 (Leeds U, Tottenham H) 41
Robson, B. 1980 (WBA, Manchester U) 90
Robson, R. 1958 (WBA) 20
Rocastle, D. 1989 (Arsenal) 14
Rooney, W. 2003 (Everton, Manchester U) 43
Rose, W. C. 1884 (Swifts, Preston NE, Wolverhampton W) 5
Rostron, T. 1881 (Darwen) 2
Rowe, A. 1934 (Tottenham H) 1
Rowley, J. F. 1949 (Manchester U) 6
Rowley, W. 1889 (Stoke) 2
Royle, J. 1971 (Everton, Manchester C) 6
Ruddlesdin, H. 1904 (Sheffield W) 3
Ruddock, N. 1995 (Liverpool) 1
Ruffell, J. W. 1926 (West Ham U) 6
Russell, B. B. 1883 (Royal Engineers) 1
Rutherford, J. 1904 (Newcastle U) 11

Sadler, D. 1968 (Manchester U) 4
Sagar, C. 1900 (Bury) 2
Sagar, E. 1936 (Everton) 4
Salako, J. A. 1991 (C Palace) 5
Sandford, E. A. 1933 (WBA) 1
Sandilands, R. R. 1892 (Old Westminsters) 5
Sands, J. 1880 (Nottingham F) 1
Sansom, K. G. 1979 (C Palace, Arsenal) 86
Saunders, F. E. 1888 (Swifts) 1
Savage, A. H. 1876 (C Palace) 1
Sayer, J. 1887 (Stoke) 1
Scales, J. R. 1995 (Liverpool) 3
Scattergood, E. 1913 (Derby Co) 1
Schofield, J. 1892 (Stoke) 3
Scholes, P. 1997 (Manchester U) 66
Scott, L. 1947 (Arsenal) 17
Scott, W. R. 1937 (Brentford) 1
Seaman, D. A. 1989 (QPR, Arsenal) 75
Seddon, J. 1923 (Bolton W) 6
Seed, J. M. 1921 (Tottenham H) 5
Settle, J. 1899 (Bury, Everton) 6
Sewell, J. 1952 (Sheffield W) 6
Sewell, W. R. 1924 (Blackburn R) 1
Shackleton, L. F. 1949 (Sunderland) 5
Sharp, J. 1903 (Everton) 2
Sharpe, L. S. 1991 (Manchester U) 8
Shaw, G. E. 1932 (WBA) 1
Shaw, G. L. 1959 (Sheffield U) 5
Shea, D. 1914 (Blackburn R) 2
Shearer, A. 1992 (Southampton, Blackburn R, Newcastle U) 63
Shellito, K. J. 1963 (Chelsea) 1
Shelton A. 1889 (Notts Co) 6
Shelton, C. 1888 (Notts Rangers) 1
Shepherd, A. 1906 (Bolton W, Newcastle U) 2
Sheringham, E. P. 1993 (Tottenham H, Manchester U, Tottenham H) 51
Sherwood, T. A. 1999 (Tottenham H) 3
Shilton, P. L. 1971 (Leicester C, Stoke C, Nottingham F, Southampton, Derby Co) 125
Shimwell, E. 1949 (Blackpool) 1
Shorey, N. 2007 (Reading) 2
Shutt, G. 1886 (Stoke) 1
Silcock, J. 1921 (Manchester U) 3
Sillett, R. P. 1955 (Chelsea) 3
Simms, E. 1922 (Luton T) 1
Simpson, J. 1911 (Blackburn R) 8
Sinclair, T. 2002 (West Ham U, Manchester C) 12
Sinton, A. 1992 (QPR, Sheffield W) 12
Slater, W. J. 1955 (Wolverhampton W) 12
Smalley, T. 1937 (Wolverhampton W) 1
Smart, T. 1921 (Aston Villa) 5
Smith, A. 1891 (Nottingham F) 3
Smith, A. 2001 (Leeds U, Manchester U, Newcastle U) 19
Smith, A. K. 1872 (Oxford University) 1
Smith, A. M. 1989 (Arsenal) 13
Smith, B. 1921 (Tottenham H) 2
Smith, C. E. 1876 (C Palace) 1
Smith, G. O. 1893 (Oxford University, Old Carthusians, Corinthians) 20
Smith, H. 1905 (Reading) 4
Smith, J. 1920 (WBA) 2
Smith, Joe 1913 (Bolton W) 5
Smith, J. C. R. 1939 (Millwall) 2
Smith, J. W. 1932 (Portsmouth) 3
Smith, Leslie 1939 (Brentford) 1
Smith, Lionel 1951 (Arsenal) 6
Smith, R. A. 1961 (Tottenham H) 15
Smith, S. 1895 (Aston Villa) 1
Smith, S. C. 1936 (Leicester C) 1
Smith, T. 1960 (Birmingham C) 2
Smith, T. 1971 (Liverpool) 1
Smith, W. H. 1922 (Huddersfield T) 3
Sorby, T. H. 1879 (Thursday Wanderers, Sheffield) 1
Southgate, G. 1996 (Aston Villa, Middlesbrough) 57

Southworth, J. 1889 (Blackburn R) 3
Sparks, F. J. 1879 (Herts Rangers, Clapham Rovers) 3
Spence, J. W. 1926 (Manchester U) 2
Spence, R. 1936 (Chelsea) 2
Spencer, C. W. 1924 (Newcastle U) 2
Spencer, H. 1897 (Aston Villa) 6
Spiksley, F. 1893 (Sheffield W) 7
Spilsbury, B. W. 1885 (Cambridge University) 3
Spink, N. 1983 (Aston Villa) 1
Spouncer, W. A. 1900 (Nottingham F) 1
Springett, R. D. G. 1960 (Sheffield W) 33
Sproston, B. 1937 (Leeds U, Tottenham H, Manchester C) 11
Squire, R. T. 1886 (Cambridge University) 3
Stanbrough, M. H. 1895 (Old Carthusians) 1
Staniforth, R. 1954 (Huddersfield T) 8
Starling, R. W. 1933 (Sheffield W, Aston Villa) 2
Statham, D. J. 1983 (WBA) 3
Steele, F. C. 1937 (Stoke C) 6
Stein, B. 1984 (Luton T) 1
Stephenson, C. 1924 (Huddersfield T) 1
Stephenson, G. T. 1928 (Derby Co, Sheffield W) 3
Stephenson, J. E. 1938 (Leeds U) 2
Stepney, A. C. 1968 (Manchester U) 1
Sterland, M. 1989 (Sheffield W) 1
Steven, T. M. 1985 (Everton, Rangers, Marseille) 36
Stevens, G. A. 1985 (Tottenham H) 7
Stevens, M. G. 1985 (Everton, Rangers) 46
Stewart, J. 1907 (Sheffield W, Newcastle U) 3
Stewart, P. A. 1992 (Tottenham H) 3
Stiles, N. P. 1965 (Manchester U) 28
Stoker, J. 1933 (Birmingham) 3
Stone, S. B. 1996 (Nottingham F) 9
Storer, H. 1924 (Derby Co) 2
Storey, P. E. 1971 (Arsenal) 19
Storey-Moore, I. 1970 (Nottingham F) 1
Strange, A. H. 1930 (Sheffield W) 20
Stratford, A. H. 1874 (Wanderers) 1
Streten, B. 1950 (Luton T) 1
Sturgess, A. 1911 (Sheffield U) 2
Summerbee, M. G. 1968 (Manchester C) 8
Sunderland, A. 1980 (Arsenal) 1
Sutcliffe, J. W. 1893 (Bolton W, Millwall) 5
Sutton, C. R. 1998 (Blackburn R) 1
Swan, P. 1960 (Sheffield W) 19
Swepstone, H. A. 1880 (Pilgrims) 6
Swift, F. V. 1947 (Manchester C) 19

Tait, G. 1881 (Birmingham Excelsior) 1
Talbot, B. 1977 (Ipswich T, Arsenal) 6
Tambling, R. V. 1963 (Chelsea) 3
Tate, J. T. 1931 (Aston Villa) 3
Taylor, E. 1954 (Blackpool) 1
Taylor, E. H. 1923 (Huddersfield T) 8
Taylor, J. G. 1951 (Fulham) 2
Taylor, P. H. 1948 (Liverpool) 3
Taylor, P. J. 1976 (C Palace) 4
Taylor, T. 1953 (Manchester U) 19
Temple, D. W. 1965 (Everton) 1
Terry, J. G. 2003 (Chelsea) 44
Thickett, H. 1899 (Sheffield U) 2
Thomas, D. 1975 (QPR) 8
Thomas, D. 1983 (Coventry C) 2
Thomas, G. R. 1991 (C Palace) 9
Thomas, M. L. 1989 (Arsenal) 2
Thompson, A. 2004 (Celtic) 1
Thompson, P. 1964 (Liverpool) 16
Thompson, P. B. 1976 (Liverpool) 42
Thompson T. 1952 (Aston Villa, Preston NE) 2
Thomson, R. A. 1964 (Wolverhampton W) 8
Thornewell, G. 1923 (Derby Co) 4
Thornley, I. 1907 (Manchester C) 1
Tilson, S. F. 1934 (Manchester C) 4
Titmuss, F. 1922 (Southampton) 2
Todd, C. 1972 (Derby Co) 27
Toone, G. 1892 (Notts Co) 2
Topham, A. G. 1894 (Casuals) 1
Topham, R. 1893 (Wolverhampton W, Casuals) 2
Towers, M. A. 1976 (Sunderland) 3
Townley, W. J. 1889 (Blackburn R) 2
Townrow, J. E. 1925 (Clapton Orient) 2
Tremelling, D. R. 1928 (Birmingham) 1
Tresadern, J. 1923 (West Ham U) 2
Tueart, D. 1975 (Manchester C) 6
Tunstall, F. E. 1923 (Sheffield U) 7
Turnbull, R. J. 1920 (Bradford) 1
Turner, A. 1900 (Southampton) 2
Turner, H. 1931 (Huddersfield T) 2
Turner, J. A. 1893 (Bolton W, Stoke, Derby Co) 3
Tweedy, G. J. 1937 (Grimsby T) 1

Ufton, D. G. 1954 (Charlton Ath) 1
Underwood, A. 1891 (Stoke C) 2
Unsworth, D. G. 1995 (Everton) 1
Upson, M. J. 2003 (Birmingham C, West Ham U) 8
Urwin, T. 1923 (Middlesbrough, Newcastle U) 4
Utley, G. 1913 (Barnsley) 1

Vassell, D. 2002 (Aston Villa) 22
Vaughton, O. H. 1882 (Aston Villa) 5
Veitch, C. C. M. 1906 (Newcastle U) 6
Veitch, J. G. 1894 (Old Westminsters) 1
Venables, T. F. 1965 (Chelsea) 2
Venison, B. 1995 (Newcastle U) 2
Vidal, R. W. S. 1873 (Oxford University) 1
Viljoen, C. 1975 (Ipswich T) 2
Viollet, D. S. 1960 (Manchester U) 2
Von Donop 1873 (Royal Engineers) 2

Wace, H. 1878 (Wanderers) 3
Waddle, C. R. 1985 (Newcastle U, Tottenham H, Marseille) 62
Wadsworth, S. J. 1922 (Huddersfield T) 9
Wainscoat, W. R. 1929 (Leeds U) 1
Waiters, A. K. 1964 (Blackpool) 5
Walcott, T. J. 2006 (Arsenal) 2
Walden, F. I. 1914 (Tottenham H) 2
Walker, D. S. 1989 (Nottingham F, Sampdoria, Sheffield W) 59
Walker, I. M. 1996 (Tottenham H, Leicester C) 4
Walker, W. H. 1921 (Aston Villa) 18
Wall, G. 1907 (Manchester U) 7
Wallace, C. W. 1913 (Aston Villa) 3
Wallace, D. L. 1986 (Southampton) 1
Walsh, P. A. 1983 (Luton T) 5
Walters, A. M. 1885 (Cambridge University, Old Carthusians) 9
Walters, K. M. 1991 (Rangers) 1
Walters, P. M. 1885 (Oxford University, Old Carthusians) 13
Walton, N. 1890 (Blackburn R) 1
Ward, J. T. 1885 (Blackburn Olympic) 1
Ward, P. 1980 (Brighton & HA) 1
Ward, T. V. 1948 (Derby Co) 2
Waring, T. 1931 (Aston Villa) 5
Warner, C. 1878 (Upton Park) 1
Warnock, S. 2008 (Blackburn R) 1
Warren, B. 1906 (Derby Co, Chelsea) 22
Waterfield, G. S. 1927 (Burnley) 1
Watson, D. 1984 (Norwich C, Everton) 12
Watson, D. V. 1974 (Sunderland, Manchester C, Werder Bremen, Southampton, Stoke C) 65
Watson, V. M. 1923 (West Ham U) 5
Watson, W. 1913 (Burnley) 3
Watson, W. 1950 (Sunderland) 4
Weaver, S. 1932 (Newcastle U) 3

Webb, G. W. 1911 (West Ham U) 2
Webb, N. J. 1988 (Nottingham F, Manchester U) 26
Webster, M. 1930 (Middlesbrough) 3
Wedlock, W. J. 1907 (Bristol C) 26
Weir, D. 1889 (Bolton W) 2
Welch, R. de C. 1872 (Wanderers, Harrow Chequers) 2
Weller, K. 1974 (Leicester C) 4
Welsh, D. 1938 (Charlton Ath) 3
West, G. 1969 (Everton) 3
Westwood, R. W. 1935 (Bolton W) 6
Whateley, O. 1883 (Aston Villa) 2
Wheeler, J. E. 1955 (Bolton W) 1
Wheldon, G. F. 1897 (Aston Villa) 4
White, D. 1993 (Manchester C) 1
White, T. A. 1933 (Everton) 1
Whitehead, J. 1893 (Accrington, Blackburn R) 2
Whitfeld, H. 1879 (Old Etonians) 1
Whitham, M. 1892 (Sheffield U) 1
Whitworth, S. 1975 (Leicester C) 7
Whymark, T. J. 1978 (Ipswich T) 1
Widdowson, S. W. 1880 (Nottingham F) 1
Wignall, F. 1965 (Nottingham F) 2
Wilcox, J. M. 1996 (Blackburn R, Leeds U) 3
Wilkes, A. 1901 (Aston Villa) 5
Wilkins, R. C. 1976 (Chelsea, Manchester U, AC Milan) 84
Wilkinson, B. 1904 (Sheffield U) 1
Wilkinson, L. R. 1891 (Oxford University) 1
Williams, B. F. 1949 (Wolverhampton W) 24
Williams, O. 1923 (Clapton Orient) 2
Williams, S. 1983 (Southampton) 6
Williams, W. 1897 (WBA) 6
Williamson, E. C. 1923 (Arsenal) 2
Williamson, R. G. 1905 (Middlesbrough) 7
Willingham, C. K. 1937 (Huddersfield T) 12
Willis, A. 1952 (Tottenham H) 1
Wilshaw, D. J. 1954 (Wolverhampton W) 12
Wilson, C. P. 1884 (Hendon) 2
Wilson, C. W. 1879 (Oxford University) 2
Wilson, G. 1921 (Sheffield W) 12
Wilson, G. P. 1900 (Corinthians) 2
Wilson, R. 1960 (Huddersfield T, Everton) 63
Wilson, T. 1928 (Huddersfield T) 1
Winckworth, W. N. 1892 (Old Westminsters) 2
Windridge, J. E. 1908 (Chelsea) 8
Wingfield-Stratford, C. V. 1877 (Royal Engineers) 1
Winterburn, N. 1990 (Arsenal) 2
Wise, D. F. 1991 (Chelsea) 21
Withe, P. 1981 (Aston Villa) 11
Wollaston, C. H. R. 1874 (Wanderers) 4
Wolstenholme, S. 1904 (Everton, Blackburn R) 3
Wood, H. 1890 (Wolverhampton W) 3
Wood, R. E. 1955 (Manchester U) 3
Woodcock, A. S. 1978 (Nottingham F, Cologne, Arsenal) 42
Woodgate, J. S. 1999 (Leeds U, Newcastle U, Real Madrid, Tottenham H) 7
Woodger, G. 1911 (Oldham Ath) 1
Woodhall, G. 1888 (WBA) 2
Woodley, V. R. 1937 (Chelsea) 19
Woods, C. C. E. 1985 (Norwich C, Rangers, Sheffield W) 43
Woodward, V. J. 1903 (Tottenham H, Chelsea) 23
Woosnam, M. 1922 (Manchester C) 1
Worrall, F. 1935 (Portsmouth) 2
Worthington, F. S. 1974 (Leicester C) 8
Wreford-Brown, C. 1889 (Oxford University, Old Carthusians) 4
Wright, E. G. D. 1906 (Cambridge University) 1
Wright, I. E. 1991 (C Palace, Arsenal, West Ham U) 33
Wright, J. D. 1939 (Newcastle U) 1
Wright, M. 1984 (Southampton, Derby Co, Liverpool) 45
Wright, R. I. 2000 (Ipswich T, Arsenal) 2
Wright, T. J. 1968 (Everton) 11
Wright, W. A. 1947 (Wolverhampton W) 105
Wright-Phillips, S. C. 2005 (Manchester C, Chelsea) 19
Wylie, J. G. 1878 (Wanderers) 1

Yates, J. 1889 (Burnley) 1
York, R. E. 1922 (Aston Villa) 2
Young, A. 1933 (Huddersfield T) 9
Young, A. S. 2008 (Aston Villa) 3
Young, G. M. 1965 (Sheffield W) 1
Young, L. P. 2005 (Charlton Ath) 7

NORTHERN IRELAND

Addis, D. J. 1922 (Cliftonville) 1
Aherne, T. 1947 (Belfast Celtic, Luton T) 4
Alexander, T. E. 1895 (Cliftonville) 1
Allan, C. 1936 (Cliftonville) 1
Allen, J. 1887 (Limavady) 1
Anderson, J. 1925 (Distillery) 1
Anderson, T. 1973 (Manchester U, Swindon T, Peterborough U) 22
Anderson, W. 1898 (Linfield, Cliftonville) 4
Andrews, W. 1908 (Glentoran, Grimsby T) 3
Armstrong, G. J. 1977 (Tottenham H, Watford, Real Mallorca, WBA, Chesterfield) 63

Baird, C. P. 2003 (Southampton, Fulham) 32
Baird, G. 1896 (Distillery) 3
Baird, H. C. 1939 (Huddersfield T) 1
Balfe, J. 1909 (Shelbourne) 2
Bambrick, J. 1929 (Linfield, Chelsea) 11
Banks, S. J. 1937 (Cliftonville) 1
Barr, H. H. 1962 (Linfield, Coventry C) 3
Barron, J. H. 1894 (Cliftonville) 7
Barry, J. 1888 (Cliftonville) 3
Barry, J. 1900 (Bohemians) 1
Baxter, R. A. 1887 (Distillery) 1
Baxter, S. N. 1887 (Cliftonville) 1
Bennett, L. V. 1889 (Dublin University) 1
Best, G. 1964 (Manchester U, Fulham) 37
Bingham, W. L. 1951 (Sunderland, Luton T, Everton, Port Vale) 56
Black, K. T. 1988 (Luton T, Nottingham F) 30
Black, T. 1901 (Glentoran) 1
Blair, H. 1928 (Portadown, Swansea T) 4
Blair, J. 1907 (Cliftonville) 5
Blair, R. V. 1975 (Oldham Ath) 5
Blanchflower, J. 1954 (Manchester U) 12
Blanchflower, R. D. 1950 (Barnsley, Aston Villa, Tottenham H) 56
Blayney, A. 2006 (Doncaster R) 1
Bookman, L. J. O. 1914 (Bradford C, Luton T) 4
Bothwell, A. W. 1926 (Ards) 5
Bowler, G. C. 1950 (Hull C) 3
Boyle, P. 1901 (Sheffield U) 5
Braithwaite, R. M. 1962 (Linfield, Middlesbrough) 10
Breen, T. 1935 (Belfast Celtic, Manchester U) 9
Brennan, B. 1912 (Bohemians) 1
Brennan, R. A. 1949 (Luton T, Birmingham C, Fulham) 5
Briggs, W. R. 1962 (Manchester U, Swansea T) 2
Brisby, D. 1891 (Distillery) 1
Brolly, T. H. 1937 (Millwall) 4
Brookes, E. A. 1920 (Shelbourne) 1
Brotherston, N. 1980 (Blackburn R) 27
Brown, J. 1921 (Glenavon, Tranmere R) 3
Brown, J. 1935 (Wolverhampton W, Coventry C, Birmingham C) 10

Brown, N. M. 1887 (Limavady) 1
Brown, W. G. 1926 (Glenavon) 1
Browne, F. 1887 (Cliftonville) 5
Browne, R. J. 1936 (Leeds U) 6
Bruce, A. 1925 (Belfast Celtic) 1
Bruce, W. 1961 (Glentoran) 2
Brunt, C. 2005 (Sheffield W, WBA) 17
Buckle, H. R. 1903 (Cliftonville, Sunderland, Bristol R) 3
Buckle, J. 1882 (Cliftonville) 1
Burnett, J. 1894 (Distillery, Glentoran) 5
Burnison, J. 1901 (Distillery) 2
Burnison, S. 1908 (Distillery, Bradford, Distillery) 8
Burns, J. 1923 (Glenavon) 1
Burns, W. 1925 (Glentoran) 1
Butler, M. P. 1939 (Blackpool) 1

Campbell, A. C. 1963 (Crusaders) 2
Campbell, D. A. 1986 (Nottingham F, Charlton Ath) 10
Campbell, James 1897 (Cliftonville) 14
Campbell, John 1896 (Cliftonville) 1
Campbell, J. P. 1951 (Fulham) 2
Campbell, R. M. 1982 (Bradford C) 2
Campbell, W. G. 1968 (Dundee) 6
Capaldi, A. C. 2004 (Plymouth Arg, Cardiff C) 22
Carey, J. J. 1947 (Manchester U) 7
Carroll, E. 1925 (Glenavon) 1
Carroll, R. E. 1997 (Wigan Ath, Manchester U, West Ham U) 19
Casey, T. 1955 (Newcastle U, Portsmouth) 12
Caskey, W. 1979 (Derby Co, Tulsa R) 8
Cassidy, T. 1971 (Newcastle U, Burnley) 24
Caughey, M. 1986 (Linfield) 2
Chambers, R. J. 1921 (Distillery, Bury, Nottingham F) 12
Chatton, H. A. 1925 (Partick Th) 3
Christian, J. 1889 (Linfield) 1
Clarke, C. J. 1986 (Bournemouth, Southampton, QPR, Portsmouth) 38
Clarke, R. 1901 (Belfast Celtic) 2
Cleary, J. 1982 (Glentoran) 5
Clements, D. 1965 (Coventry C, Sheffield W, Everton, New York Cosmos) 48
Clingan, S. G. 2006 (Nottingham F) 15
Clugston, J. 1888 (Cliftonville) 14
Clyde, M. G. 2005 (Wolverhampton W) 3
Cochrane, D. 1939 (Leeds U) 12
Cochrane, G. 1903 (Cliftonville) 1
Cochrane, G. T. 1976 (Coleraine, Burnley, Middlesbrough, Gillingham) 26
Cochrane, M. 1898 (Distillery, Leicester Fosse) 8
Collins, F. 1922 (Celtic) 1
Collins, R. 1922 (Cliftonville) 1
Condy, J. 1882 (Distillery) 3
Connell, T. E. 1978 (Coleraine) 1
Connor, J. 1901 (Glentoran, Belfast Celtic) 13
Connor, M. J. 1903 (Brentford, Fulham) 3
Cook, W. 1933 (Celtic, Everton) 15
Cooke, S. 1889 (Belfast YMCA, Cliftonville) 3
Coote, A. 1999 (Norwich C) 6
Coulter, J. 1934 (Belfast Celtic, Everton, Grimsby T, Chelmsford C) 11
Cowan, J. 1970 (Newcastle U) 1
Cowan, T. S. 1925 (Queen's Island) 1
Coyle, F. 1956 (Coleraine, Nottingham F) 4
Coyle, L. 1989 (Derry C) 1
Coyle, R. I. 1973 (Sheffield W) 5
Craig, A. B. 1908 (Rangers, Morton) 9
Craig, D. J. 1967 (Newcastle U) 25
Craigan, S. J. 2003 (Partick Th, Motherwell) 35
Crawford, A. 1889 (Distillery, Cliftonville) 7
Croft, T. 1922 (Queen's Island) 3
Crone, R. 1889 (Distillery) 4
Crone, W. 1882 (Distillery) 12
Crooks, W. J. 1922 (Manchester U) 1
Crossan, E. 1950 (Blackburn R) 3
Crossan, J. A. 1960 (Sparta-Rotterdam, Sunderland, Manchester C, Middlesbrough) 24
Crothers, C. 1907 (Distillery) 1
Cumming, L. 1929 (Huddersfield T, Oldham Ath) 3
Cunningham, W. 1892 (Ulster) 4
Cunningham, W. E. 1951 (St Mirren, Leicester C, Dunfermline Ath) 30
Curran, S. 1926 (Belfast Celtic) 4
Curran, J. J. 1922 (Glenavon, Pontypridd, Glenavon) 5
Cush, W. W. 1951 (Glenavon, Leeds U, Portadown) 26

Dalrymple, J. 1922 (Distillery) 1
Dalton, W. 1888 (YMCA, Linfield) 11
D'Arcy, S. D. 1952 (Chelsea, Brentford) 5
Darling, J. 1897 (Linfield) 22
Davey, H. H. 1926 (Reading, Portsmouth) 5
Davis, S. 2005 (Aston Villa, Fulham) 28
Davis, T. L. 1937 (Oldham Ath) 1
Davison, A. J. 1996 (Bolton W, Bradford C, Grimsby T) 3
Davison, J. R. 1882 (Cliftonville) 8
Dennison, R. 1988 (Wolverhampton W) 18
Devine, A. O. 1886 (Limavady) 4
Devine, J. 1990 (Glentoran) 1
Dickson, D. 1970 (Coleraine) 4
Dickson, T. A. 1957 (Linfield) 1
Dickson, W. 1951 (Chelsea, Arsenal) 12
Diffin, W. J. 1931 (Belfast Celtic) 1
Dill, A. H. 1882 (Knock, Down Ath, Cliftonville) 9
Doherty, I. 1901 (Belfast Celtic) 1
Doherty, J. 1928 (Portadown) 1
Doherty, J. 1933 (Cliftonville) 2
Doherty, L. 1985 (Linfield) 2
Doherty, M. 1938 (Derry C) 1
Doherty, P. D. 1935 (Blackpool, Manchester C, Derby Co, Huddersfield T, Doncaster R) 16
Doherty, T. E. 2003 (Bristol C) 9
Donaghey, B. 1903 (Belfast Celtic) 1
Donaghy, M. M. 1980 (Luton T, Manchester U, Chelsea) 91
Donnelly, L. 1913 (Distillery) 1
Doran, J. F. 1921 (Brighton) 3
Dougan, A. D. 1958 (Portsmouth, Blackburn R, Aston Villa, Leicester C, Wolverhampton W) 43
Douglas, J. P. 1947 (Belfast Celtic) 1
Dowd, H. O. 1974 (Glenavon, Sheffield W) 3
Dowie, I. 1990 (Luton T, West Ham U, Southampton, C Palace, West Ham U, QPR) 59
Duff, M. J. 2002 (Cheltenham T, Burnley) 20
Duggan, H. A. 1930 (Leeds U) 8
Dunlop, G. 1985 (Linfield) 4
Dunne, J. 1928 (Sheffield U) 7

Eames, W. L. E. 1885 (Dublin U) 3
Eglington, T. J. 1947 (Everton) 6
Elder, A. R. 1960 (Burnley, Stoke C) 40
Elleman, A. R. 1889 (Cliftonville) 2
Elliott, S. 2001 (Motherwell, Hull C) 39
Elwood, J. H. 1929 (Bradford) 2
Emerson, W. 1920 (Glentoran, Burnley) 11
English, S. 1933 (Rangers) 2
Enright, J. 1912 (Leeds C) 1
Evans, J. G. 2007 (Manchester U) 10

Falloon, E. 1931 (Aberdeen) 2
Farquharson, T. G. 1923 (Cardiff C) 7
Farrell, P. 1901 (Distillery) 2
Farrell, P. 1938 (Hibernian) 1
Farrell, P. D. 1947 (Everton) 7
Feeney, J. M. 1947 (Linfield, Swansea T) 2

Feeney, W. 1976 (Glentoran) 1
Feeney, W. J. 2002 (Bournemouth, Luton T, Cardiff C) 24
Ferguson, G. 1999 (Linfield) 5
Ferguson, W. 1966 (Linfield) 2
Ferris, J. 1920 (Belfast Celtic, Chelsea, Belfast Celtic) 6
Ferris, R. O. 1950 (Birmingham C) 3
Fettis, A. W. 1992 (Hull C, Nottingham F, Blackburn R) 25
Finney, T. 1975 (Sunderland, Cambridge U) 14
Fitzpatrick, J. C. 1896 (Bohemians) 2
Flack, H. 1929 (Burnley) 1
Fleming, J. G. 1987 (Nottingham F, Manchester C, Barnsley) 31
Forbes, G. 1888 (Limavady, Distillery) 3
Forde, J. T. 1959 (Ards) 4
Foreman, T. A. 1899 (Cliftonville) 1
Forsythe, J. 1888 (YMCA) 2
Fox, W. T. 1887 (Ulster) 2
Frame, T. 1925 (Linfield) 1
Fulton, R. P. 1928 (Larne, Belfast Celtic) 21

Gaffikin, G. 1890 (Linfield Ath) 15
Galbraith, W. 1890 (Distillery) 1
Gallagher, P. 1920 (Celtic, Falkirk) 11
Gallogly, C. 1951 (Huddersfield T) 2
Gara, A. 1902 (Preston NE) 3
Gardiner, A. 1930 (Cliftonville) 5
Garrett, J. 1925 (Distillery) 1
Gaston, R. 1969 (Oxford U) 1
Gaukrodger, G. 1895 (Linfield) 1
Gault, M. 2008 (Linfield) 1
Gaussen, A. D. 1884 (Moyola Park, Magherafelt) 6
Geary, J. 1931 (Glentoran) 2
Gibb, J. T. 1884 (Wellington Park, Cliftonville) 10
Gibb, T. J. 1936 (Cliftonville) 1
Gibson W. K. 1894 (Cliftonville) 14
Gillespie, K. R. 1995 (Manchester U, Newcastle U, Blackburn R, Leicester C, Sheffield U) 81
Gillespie, S. 1886 (Hertford) 6
Gillespie, W. 1889 (West Down) 1
Gillespie, W. 1913 (Sheffield U) 25
Goodall, A. L. 1899 (Derby Co, Glossop) 10
Goodbody, M. F. 1889 (Dublin University) 2
Gordon, H. 1895 (Linfield) 3
Gordon R. W. 1891 (Linfield) 7
Gordon, T. 1894 (Linfield) 2
Gorman, W. C. 1947 (Brentford) 4
Gough, J. 1925 (Queen's Island) 1
Gowdy, J. 1920 (Glentoran, Queen's Island, Falkirk) 6
Gowdy, W. A. 1932 (Hull C, Sheffield W, Linfield, Hibernian) 6
Graham, W. G. L. 1951 (Doncaster R) 14
Gray, P. 1993 (Luton T, Sunderland, Nancy, Luton T, Burnley, Oxford U) 26
Greer, W. 1909 (QPR) 3
Gregg, H. 1954 (Doncaster R, Manchester U) 25
Griffin, D. J. 1996 (St Johnstone, Dundee U, Stockport Co) 29

Hall, G. 1897 (Distillery) 1
Halligan, W. 1911 (Derby Co, Wolverhampton W) 2
Hamill, M. 1912 (Manchester U, Belfast Celtic, Manchester C) 7
Hamill, R. 1999 (Glentoran) 1
Hamilton, B. 1969 (Linfield, Ipswich T, Everton, Millwall, Swindon T) 50
Hamilton, G. 2003 (Portadown) 5
Hamilton, J. 1882 (Knock) 2
Hamilton, R. 1928 (Rangers) 5
Hamilton, W. D. 1885 (Dublin Association) 1
Hamilton, W. J. 1885 (Dublin Association) 1
Hamilton, W. J. 1908 (Distillery) 1
Hamilton, W. R. 1978 (QPR, Burnley, Oxford U) 41
Hampton, H. 1911 (Bradford C) 9
Hanna, J. 1912 (Nottingham F) 2
Hanna, J. D. 1899 (Royal Artillery, Portsmouth) 1
Hannon, D. J. 1908 (Bohemians) 6
Harkin, J. T. 1968 (Southport, Shrewsbury T) 5
Harland, A. I. 1922 (Linfield) 2
Harris, J. 1921 (Cliftonville, Glenavon) 2
Harris, V. 1906 (Shelbourne, Everton) 20
Harvey, M. 1961 (Sunderland) 34
Hastings, J. 1882 (Knock, Ulster) 7
Hatton, S. 1963 (Linfield) 2
Hayes, W. E. 1938 (Huddersfield T) 4
Healy, D. J. 2000 (Manchester U, Preston NE, Leeds U, Fulham) 64
Healy, P. J. 1982 (Coleraine, Glentoran) 4
Hegan, D. 1970 (WBA, Wolverhampton W) 7
Henderson, J. 1885 (Ulster) 3
Hewison, G. 1885 (Moyola Park) 2
Hill, C. F. 1990 (Sheffield U, Leicester C, Trelleborg, Northampton T) 27
Hill, M. J. 1959 (Norwich C, Everton) 7
Hinton, E. 1947 (Fulham, Millwall) 7
Holmes, S. P. 2002 (Wrexham) 1
Hopkins, J. 1926 (Brighton) 1
Horlock, K. 1995 (Swindon T, Manchester C) 32
Houston, J. 1912 (Linfield, Everton) 6
Houston, W. 1933 (Linfield) 1
Houston, W. J. 1885 (Moyola Park) 2
Hughes, A. W. 1998 (Newcastle U, Aston Villa, Fulham) 59
Hughes, J. 2006 (Lincoln C) 2
Hughes, M.A. 2006 (Oldham Ath) 2
Hughes, M. E. 1992 (Manchester C, Strasbourg, West Ham U, Wimbledon, C Palace) 71
Hughes, P. A. 1987 (Bury) 3
Hughes, W. 1951 (Bolton W) 1
Humphries, W. M. 1962 (Ards, Coventry C, Swansea T) 14
Hunter, A. 1905 (Distillery, Belfast Celtic) 8
Hunter, A. 1970 (Blackburn R, Ipswich T) 53
Hunter, B. V. 1995 (Wrexham, Reading) 15
Hunter, R. J. 1884 (Cliftonville) 3
Hunter, V. 1962 (Coleraine) 2

Ingham, M. G. 2005 (Sunderland, Wrexham) 3
Irvine, R. J. 1962 (Linfield, Stoke C) 8
Irvine, R. W. 1922 (Everton, Portsmouth, Connah's Quay, Derry C) 15
Irvine, W. J. 1963 (Burnley, Preston NE, Brighton & HA) 23
Irving, S. J. 1923 (Dundee, Cardiff C, Chelsea) 18

Jackson, T. A. 1969 (Everton, Nottingham F, Manchester U) 35
Jamison, J. 1976 (Glentoran) 1
Jenkins, I. 1997 (Chester C, Dundee U) 6
Jennings, P. A. 1964 (Watford, Tottenham H, Arsenal, Tottenham H) 119
Johnson, D. M. 1999 (Blackburn R, Birmingham C) 48
Johnston, H. 1927 (Portadown) 1
Johnston, R. S. 1882 (Distillery) 5
Johnston, R. S. 1905 (Distillery) 1
Johnston, S. 1890 (Linfield) 4
Johnston, W. 1885 (Oldpark) 2
Johnston, W. C. 1962 (Glenavon, Oldham Ath) 2
Jones, J. 1930 (Linfield, Hibernian, Glenavon) 23
Jones, J. 1956 (Glenavon) 3
Jones, S. 1934 (Distillery, Blackpool) 2
Jones, S. G. 2003 (Crewe Alex, Burnley) 29
Jordan, T. 1895 (Linfield) 2

Kavanagh, P. J. 1930 (Celtic) 1

Keane, T. R. 1949 (Swansea T) 1
Kearns, A. 1900 (Distillery) 6
Kee, P. V. 1990 (Oxford U, Ards) 9
Keith, R. M. 1958 (Newcastle U) 23
Kelly, H. R. 1950 (Fulham, Southampton) 4
Kelly, J. 1896 (Glentoran) 1
Kelly, J. 1932 (Derry C) 11
Kelly, P. J. 1921 (Manchester C) 1
Kelly, P. M. 1950 (Barnsley) 1
Kennedy, A. L. 1923 (Arsenal) 2
Kennedy, P. H. 1999 (Watford, Wigan Ath) 20
Kernaghan, N. 1936 (Belfast Celtic) 3
Kirk, A. R. 2000 (Hearts, Boston U, Northampton T) 8
Kirkwood, H. 1904 (Cliftonville) 1
Kirwan, J. 1900 (Tottenham H, Chelsea, Clyde) 17

Lacey, W. 1909 (Everton, Liverpool, New Brighton) 23
Lafferty, K. 2006 (Burnley) 16
Lawther, R. 1888 (Glentoran) 2
Lawther, W. I. 1960 (Sunderland, Blackburn R) 4
Leatham, J. 1939 (Belfast Celtic) 1
Ledwidge, J. J. 1906 (Shelbourne) 2
Lemon, J. 1886 (Glentoran, Belfast YMCA) 3
Lennon, N. F. 1994 (Crewe Alex, Leicester C, Celtic) 40
Leslie, W. 1887 (YMCA) 1
Lewis, J. 1899 (Glentoran, Distillery) 4
Lockhart, H. 1884 (Rossall School) 1
Lockhart, N. H. 1947 (Linfield, Coventry C, Aston Villa) 8
Lomas, S. M. 1994 (Manchester C, West Ham U) 45
Loyal, J. 1891 (Clarence) 1
Lutton, R. J. 1970 (Wolverhampton W, West Ham U) 6
Lynas, R. 1925 (Cliftonville) 1
Lyner, D. R. 1920 (Glentoran, Manchester U, Kilmarnock) 6
Lytle, J. 1898 (Glentoran) 1

McAdams, W. J. 1954 (Manchester C, Bolton W, Leeds U) 15
McAlery, J. M. 1882 (Cliftonville) 2
McAlinden, J. 1938 (Belfast Celtic, Portsmouth, Southend U) 4
McAllen, J. 1898 (Linfield) 9
McAlpine, S. 1901 (Cliftonville) 1
McArthur, A. 1886 (Distillery) 1
McAuley, G. 2005 (Lincoln C, Leicester C) 10
McAuley, J. L. 1911 (Huddersfield T) 6
McAuley, P. 1900 (Belfast Celtic) 1
McBride, S. D. 1991 (Glenavon) 4
McCabe, J. J. 1949 (Leeds U) 6
McCabe, W. 1891 (Ulster) 1
McCambridge, J. 1930 (Ballymena, Cardiff C) 4
McCandless, J. 1912 (Bradford) 5
McCandless, W. 1920 (Linfield, Rangers) 9
McCann, G. S. 2002 (West Ham U, Cheltenham T, Barnsley, Scunthorpe U) 16
McCann, P. 1910 (Belfast Celtic, Glentoran) 7
McCarthy, J. D. 1996 (Port Vale, Birmingham C) 18
McCartney, A. 1903 (Ulster, Linfield, Everton, Belfast Celtic, Glentoran) 15
McCartney, G. 2002 (Sunderland) 25
McCashin, J. W. 1896 (Cliftonville) 5
McCavana, W. T. 1955 (Coleraine) 3
McCaw, J. H. 1927 (Linfield) 6
McClatchey, J. 1886 (Distillery) 3
McClatchey, T. 1895 (Distillery) 1
McCleary, J. W. 1955 (Cliftonville) 1
McCleery, W. 1922 (Cliftonville, Linfield) 10
McClelland, J. 1980 (Mansfield T, Rangers, Watford, Leeds U) 53
McClelland, J. T. 1961 (Arsenal, Fulham) 6
McCluggage, A. 1922 (Cliftonville, Bradford, Burnley) 13

McClure, G. 1907 (Cliftonville, Distillery) 4
McConnell, E. 1904 (Cliftonville, Glentoran, Sunderland, Sheffield W) 12
McConnell, P. 1928 (Doncaster R, Southport) 2
McConnell, W. G. 1912 (Bohemians) 6
McConnell, W. H. 1925 (Reading) 8
McCourt, F. J. 1952 (Manchester C) 6
McCourt, P. J. 2002 (Rochdale) 1
McCoy, R. K. 1987 (Coleraine) 1
McCoy, S. 1896 (Distillery) 1
McCracken, E. 1928 (Barking) 1
McCracken, R. 1921 (C Palace) 4
McCracken, R. 1922 (Linfield) 1
McCracken, W. R. 1902 (Distillery, Newcastle U, Hull C) 16
McCreery, D. 1976 (Manchester U, QPR, Tulsa R, Newcastle U, Hearts) 67
McCrory, S. 1958 (Southend U) 1
McCullough, K. 1935 (Belfast Celtic, Manchester C) 5
McCullough, W. J. 1961 (Arsenal, Millwall) 10
McCurdy, C. 1980 (Linfield) 1
McDonald, A. 1986 (QPR) 52
McDonald, R. 1930 (Rangers) 2
McDonnell, J. 1911 (Bohemians) 4
McElhinney, G. M. A. 1984 (Bolton W) 6
McEvilly, L. R. 2002 (Rochdale) 1
McFaul, W. S. 1967 (Linfield, Newcastle U) 6
McGarry, J. K. 1951 (Cliftonville) 3
McGaughey, M. 1985 (Linfield) 1
McGibbon, P. C. G. 1995 (Manchester U, Wigan Ath) 7
McGrath, R. C. 1974 (Tottenham H, Manchester U) 21
McGregor, S. 1921 (Glentoran) 1
McGrillen, J. 1924 (Clyde, Belfast Celtic) 2
McGuire, E. 1907 (Distillery) 1
McGuire, J. 1928 (Linfield) 1
McIlroy, H. 1906 (Cliftonville) 1
McIlroy, J. 1952 (Burnley, Stoke C) 55
McIlroy, S. B. 1972 (Manchester U, Stoke C, Manchester C) 88
McIlvenny, P. 1924 (Distillery) 1
McIlvenny, R. 1890 (Distillery, Ulster) 2
McKeag, W. 1968 (Glentoran) 2
McKeague, T. 1925 (Glentoran) 1
McKee, F. W. 1906 (Cliftonville, Belfast Celtic) 5
McKelvey, H. 1901 (Glentoran) 2
McKenna, J. 1950 (Huddersfield T) 7
McKenzie, H. 1922 (Distillery) 2
McKenzie, R. 1967 (Airdrieonians) 1
McKeown, N. 1892 (Linfield) 7
McKie, H. 1895 (Cliftonville) 3
Mackie, J. A. 1923 (Arsenal, Portsmouth) 3
McKinney, D. 1921 (Hull C, Bradford C) 2
McKinney, V. J. 1966 (Falkirk) 1
McKnight, A. D. 1988 (Celtic, West Ham U) 10
McKnight, J. 1912 (Preston NE, Glentoran) 2
McLaughlin, J. C. 1962 (Shrewsbury T, Swansea T) 12
McLean, B. S. 2006 (Rangers) 1
McLean, T. 1885 (Limavady) 1
McMahon, G. J. 1995 (Tottenham H, Stoke C) 17
McMahon, J. 1934 (Bohemians) 1
McMaster, G. 1897 (Glentoran) 3
McMichael, A. 1950 (Newcastle U) 40
McMillan, G. 1903 (Distillery) 2
McMillan, S. T. 1963 (Manchester U) 2
McMillen, W. S. 1934 (Manchester U, Chesterfield) 7
McMordie, A. S. 1969 (Middlesbrough) 21
McMorran, E. J. 1947 (Belfast Celtic, Barnsley, Doncaster R) 15
McMullan, D. 1926 (Liverpool) 3
McNally, B. A. 1986 (Shrewsbury T) 5
McNinch, J. 1931 (Ballymena) 3
McParland, P. J. 1954 (Aston Villa, Wolverhampton W) 34

McShane, J. 1899 (Cliftonville) 4
McVeigh, P. M. 1999 (Tottenham H, Norwich C) 20
McVicker, J. 1888 (Linfield, Glentoran) 2
McWha, W. B. R. 1882 (Knock, Cliftonville) 7
Madden, O. 1938 (Norwich C) 1
Magee, G. 1885 (Wellington Park) 3
Magill, E. J. 1962 (Arsenal, Brighton & HA) 26
Magilton, J. 1991 (Oxford U, Southampton, Sheffield W, Ipswich T) 52
Maginnis, H. 1900 (Linfield) 8
Mahood, J. 1926 (Belfast Celtic, Ballymena) 9
Mannus, A. 2004 (Linfield) 1
Manderson, R. 1920 (Rangers) 5
Mansfield, J. 1901 (Dublin Freebooters) 1
Martin, C. 1882 (Cliftonville) 3
Martin, C. 1925 (Bo'ness) 1
Martin, C. J. 1947 (Glentoran, Leeds U, Aston Villa) 6
Martin, D. K. 1934 (Belfast Celtic, Wolverhampton W, Nottingham F) 10
Mathieson, A. 1921 (Luton T) 2
Maxwell, J. 1902 (Linfield, Glentoran, Belfast Celtic) 7
Meek, H. L. 1925 (Glentoran) 1
Mehaffy, J. A. C. 1922 (Queen's Island) 1
Meldon, P. A. 1899 (Dublin Freebooters) 2
Mercer, H. V. A. 1908 (Linfield) 1
Mercer, J. T. 1898 (Distillery, Linfield, Distillery, Derby Co) 12
Millar, W. 1932 (Barrow) 2
Miller, J. 1929 (Middlesbrough) 3
Milligan, D. 1939 (Chesterfield) 1
Milne, R. G. 1894 (Linfield) 28
Mitchell, E. J. 1933 (Cliftonville, Glentoran) 2
Mitchell, W. 1932 (Distillery, Chelsea) 15
Molyneux, T. B. 1883 (Ligoniel, Cliftonville) 11
Montgomery, F. J. 1955 (Coleraine) 1
Moore, C. 1949 (Glentoran) 1
Moore, P. 1933 (Aberdeen) 1
Moore, R. 1891 (Linfield Ath) 3
Moore, R. L. 1887 (Ulster) 2
Moore, W. 1923 (Falkirk) 1
Moorhead, F. W. 1885 (Dublin University) 1
Moorhead, G. 1923 (Linfield) 4
Moran, J. 1912 (Leeds C) 1
Moreland, V. 1979 (Derby Co) 6
Morgan, G. F. 1922 (Linfield, Nottingham F) 8
Morgan, S. 1972 (Port Vale, Aston Villa, Brighton & HA, Sparta Rotterdam) 18
Morrison, R. 1891 (Linfield Ath) 2
Morrison, T. 1895 (Glentoran, Burnley) 7
Morrogh, D. 1896 (Bohemians) 1
Morrow, S. J. 1990 (Arsenal, QPR) 39
Morrow, W. J. 1883 (Moyola Park) 3
Muir, R. 1885 (Oldpark) 2
Mulholland, T.S. 1906 (Belfast Celtic) 2
Mullan, G. 1983 (Glentoran) 4
Mulligan, J. 1921 (Manchester C) 1
Mulryne, P. P. 1997 (Manchester U, Norwich C, Cardiff C) 27
Murdock, C. J. 2000 (Preston NE, Hibernian, Crewe Alex, Rotherham U) 34
Murphy, J. 1910 (Bradford C) 3
Murphy, N. 1905 (QPR) 3
Murray, J. M. 1910 (Motherwell, Sheffield W) 3

Napier, R. J. 1966 (Bolton W) 1
Neill, W. J. T. 1961 (Arsenal, Hull C) 59
Nelis, P. 1923 (Nottingham F) 1
Nelson, S. 1970 (Arsenal, Brighton & HA) 51
Nicholl, C. J. 1975 (Aston Villa, Southampton, Grimsby T) 51
Nicholl, H. 1902 (Belfast Celtic) 3
Nicholl, J. M. 1976 (Manchester U, Toronto B, Sunderland, Toronto B, Rangers, Toronto B, WBA) 73
Nicholson, J. J. 1961 (Manchester U, Huddersfield T) 41
Nixon, R. 1914 (Linfield) 1
Nolan, I. R. 1997 (Sheffield W, Bradford C, Wigan Ath) 18
Nolan-Whelan, J. V. 1901 (Dublin Freebooters) 5

O'Boyle, G. 1994 (Dunfermline Ath, St Johnstone) 13
O'Brien, M. T. 1921 (QPR, Leicester C, Hull C, Derby Co) 10
O'Connell, P. 1912 (Sheffield W, Hull C) 5
O'Connor, M. J. 2008 (Crewe Alex) 1
O'Doherty, A. 1970 (Coleraine) 2
O'Driscoll, J. F. 1949 (Swansea T) 3
O'Hagan, C. 1905 (Tottenham H, Aberdeen) 11
O'Hagan, W. 1920 (St Mirren) 2
O'Hehir, J. C. 1910 (Bohemians) 1
O'Kane, W. J. 1970 (Nottingham F) 20
O'Mahoney, M. T. 1939 (Bristol R) 1
O'Neill, C. 1989 (Motherwell) 3
O'Neill, J. 1962 (Sunderland) 1
O'Neill, J. P. 1980 (Leicester C) 39
O'Neill, M. A. M. 1988 (Newcastle U, Dundee U, Hibernian, Coventry C) 31
O'Neill, M. H. M. 1972 (Distillery, Nottingham F, Norwich C, Manchester C, Norwich C, Notts Co) 64
O'Reilly, H. 1901 (Dublin Freebooters) 3

Parke, J. 1964 (Linfield, Hibernian, Sunderland) 14
Paterson, M. A. 2008 (Scunthorpe U) 2
Patterson, D. J. 1994 (C Palace, Luton T, Dundee U) 17
Peacock, R. 1952 (Celtic, Coleraine) 31
Peden, J. 1887 (Linfield, Distillery) 24
Penney, S. 1985 (Brighton & HA) 17
Percy, J. C. 1889 (Belfast YMCA) 1
Platt, J. A. 1976 (Middlesbrough, Ballymena U, Coleraine) 23
Pollock, W. 1928 (Belfast Celtic) 1
Ponsonby, J. 1895 (Distillery) 9
Potts, R. M. C. 1883 (Cliftonville) 2
Priestley, T. J. M. 1933 (Coleraine, Chelsea) 2
Pyper, Jas. 1897 (Cliftonville) 7
Pyper, John 1897 (Cliftonville) 9
Pyper, M. 1932 (Linfield) 1

Quinn, J. M. 1985 (Blackburn R, Swindon T, Leicester C, Bradford C, West Ham U, Bournemouth, Reading) 46
Quinn, S. J. 1996 (Blackpool, WBA, Willem II, Sheffield W, Peterborough U, Northampton T) 50

Rafferty, P. 1980 (Linfield) 1
Ramsey, P. C. 1984 (Leicester C) 14
Rankine, J. 1883 (Alexander) 2
Rattray, D. 1882 (Avoniel) 3
Rea, R. 1901 (Glentoran) 1
Redmond, R. 1884 (Cliftonville) 1
Reid, G. H. 1923 (Cardiff C) 1
Reid, J. 1883 (Ulster) 6
Reid, S. E. 1934 (Derby Co) 3
Reid, W. 1931 (Hearts) 1
Reilly, M. M. 1900 (Portsmouth) 2
Renneville, W. T. J. 1910 (Leyton, Aston Villa) 4
Reynolds, J. 1890 (Distillery, Ulster) 5
Reynolds, R. 1905 (Bohemians) 1
Rice, P. J. 1969 (Arsenal) 49
Roberts, F. C. 1931 (Glentoran) 1
Robinson, P. 1920 (Distillery, Blackburn R) 2
Robinson, S. 1997 (Bournemouth, Luton T) 7
Rogan, A. 1988 (Celtic, Sunderland, Millwall) 18
Rollo, D. 1912 (Linfield, Blackburn R) 16

Roper, E. O. 1886 (Dublin University) 1
Rosbotham, A. 1887 (Cliftonville) 7
Ross, W. E. 1969 (Newcastle U) 1
Rowland, K. 1994 (West Ham U, QPR) 19
Rowley, R. W. M. 1929 (Southampton, Tottenham H) 6
Rushe, F. 1925 (Distillery) 1
Russell, A. 1947 (Linfield) 1
Russell, S. R. 1930 (Bradford C, Derry C) 3
Ryan, R. A. 1950 (WBA) 1

Sanchez, L. P. 1987 (Wimbledon) 3
Scott, E. 1920 (Liverpool, Belfast Celtic) 31
Scott, J. 1958 (Grimsby) 2
Scott, J. E. 1901 (Cliftonville) 1
Scott, L. J. 1895 (Dublin University) 2
Scott, P. W. 1975 (Everton, York C, Aldershot) 10
Scott, T. 1894 (Cliftonville) 13
Scott, W. 1903 (Linfield, Everton, Leeds C) 25
Scraggs, M. J. 1921 (Glentoran) 2
Seymour, H. C. 1914 (Bohemians) 1
Seymour, J. 1907 (Cliftonville) 2
Shanks, T. 1903 (Woolwich Arsenal, Brentford) 3
Sharkey, P. G. 1976 (Ipswich T) 1
Sheehan, Dr G. 1899 (Bohemians) 3
Sheridan, J. 1903 (Everton, Stoke C) 6
Sherrard, J. 1885 (Limavady) 3
Sherrard, W. C. 1895 (Cliftonville) 3
Sherry, J. J. 1906 (Bohemians) 2
Shields, R. J. 1957 (Southampton) 1
Shiels, D. 2006 (Hibernian) 4
Silo, M. 1888 (Belfast YMCA) 1
Simpson, W. J. 1951 (Rangers) 12
Sinclair, J. 1882 (Knock) 2
Slemin, J. C. 1909 (Bohemians) 1
Sloan, A. S. 1925 (London Caledonians) 1
Sloan, D. 1969 (Oxford U) 2
Sloan, H. A. de B. 1903 (Bohemians) 8
Sloan, J. W. 1947 (Arsenal) 1
Sloan, T. 1926 (Cardiff C, Linfield) 11
Sloan, T. 1979 (Manchester U) 3
Small, J. M. 1887 (Clarence, Cliftonville) 4
Smith, A. W. 2003 (Glentoran, Preston NE) 18
Smith, E. E. 1921 (Cardiff C) 4
Smith, J. E. 1901 (Distillery) 2
Smyth, R. H. 1886 (Dublin University) 1
Smyth, S. 1948 (Wolverhampton W, Stoke C) 9
Smyth, W. 1949 (Distillery) 4
Snape, A. 1920 (Airdrieonians) 1
Sonner, D. J. 1998 (Ipswich T, Sheffield W, Birmingham C, Nottingham F, Peterborough U) 13
Spence, D. W. 1975 (Bury, Blackpool, Southend U) 29
Spencer, S. 1890 (Distillery) 6
Spiller, E. A. 1883 (Cliftonville) 5
Sproule, I. 2006 (Hibernian, Bristol C) 11
Stanfield, O. M. 1887 (Distillery) 30
Steele, A. 1926 (Charlton Ath, Fulham) 4
Stevenson, A. E. 1934 (Rangers, Everton) 17
Stewart, A. 1967 (Glentoran, Derby Co) 7
Stewart, D. C. 1978 (Hull C) 1
Stewart, I. 1982 (QPR, Newcastle U) 31
Stewart, R. K. 1890 (St Columb's Court, Cliftonville) 11
Stewart, T. C. 1961 (Linfield) 1
Swan, S. 1899 (Linfield) 1

Taggart, G. P. 1990 (Barnsley, Bolton W, Leicester C) 51
Taggart, J. 1899 (Walsall) 1
Taylor, M. S. 1999 (Fulham, Birmingham C) 68
Thompson, F. W. 1910 (Cliftonville, Linfield, Bradford C, Clyde) 12
Thompson, J. 1897 (Distillery) 1
Thompson, P. 2006 (Linfield) 5
Thompson, R. 1928 (Queen's Island) 1
Thompson, W. 1889 (Belfast Ath) 1
Thunder, P. J. 1911 (Bohemians) 1
Todd, S. J. 1966 (Burnley, Sheffield W) 11
Toner, C. 2003 (Leyton Orient) 2
Toner, J. 1922 (Arsenal, St Johnstone) 8
Torrans, R. 1893 (Linfield) 1
Torrans, S. 1889 (Linfield) 26
Trainor, D. 1967 (Crusaders) 1
Tully, C. P. 1949 (Celtic) 10
Turner, A. 1896 (Cliftonville) 1
Turner, E. 1896 (Cliftonville) 1
Turner, W. 1886 (Cliftonville) 3
Twomey, J. F. 1938 (Leeds U) 2

Uprichard, W. N. M. C. 1952 (Swindon T, Portsmouth) 18

Vernon, J. 1947 (Belfast Celtic, WBA) 17

Waddell, T. M. R. 1906 (Cliftonville) 1
Walker, J. 1955 (Doncaster R) 1
Walker, T. 1911 (Bury) 1
Walsh, D. J. 1947 (WBA) 9
Walsh, W. 1948 (Manchester C) 5
Waring, J. 1899 (Cliftonville) 1
Warren, P. 1913 (Shelbourne) 2
Watson, J. 1883 (Ulster) 9
Watson, P. 1971 (Distillery) 1
Watson, T. 1926 (Cardiff C) 1
Wattie, J. 1899 (Distillery) 1
Webb, C. G. 1909 (Brighton & HA) 3
Webb, S. M. 2006 (Ross Co) 4
Weir, E. 1939 (Clyde) 1
Welsh, E. 1966 (Carlisle U) 4
Whiteside, N. 1982 (Manchester U, Everton) 38
Whiteside, T. 1891 (Distillery) 1
Whitfield, E. R. 1886 (Dublin University) 1
Whitley, Jeff 1997 (Manchester C, Sunderland, Cardiff C) 20
Whitley, Jim 1998 (Manchester C) 3
Williams, J. R. 1886 (Ulster) 2
Williams, M. S. 1999 (Chesterfield, Watford, Wimbledon, Stoke C, Wimbledon, Milton Keynes D) 36
Williams, P. A. 1991 (WBA) 1
Williamson, J. 1890 (Cliftonville) 3
Willighan, T. 1933 (Burnley) 2
Willis, G. 1906 (Linfield) 4
Wilson, D. J. 1987 (Brighton & HA, Luton T, Sheffield W) 24
Wilson, H. 1925 (Linfield) 2
Wilson, K. J. 1987 (Ipswich T, Chelsea, Notts Co, Walsall) 42
Wilson, M. 1884 (Distillery) 3
Wilson, R. 1888 (Cliftonville) 1
Wilson, S. J. 1962 (Glenavon, Falkirk, Dundee) 12
Wilton, J. M. 1888 (St Columb's Court, Cliftonville, St Columb's Court) 7
Wood, T. J. 1996 (Walsall) 1
Worthington, N. 1984 (Sheffield W, Leeds U, Stoke C) 66
Wright, J. 1906 (Cliftonville) 6
Wright, T. J. 1989 (Newcastle U, Nottingham F, Manchester C) 31

Young, S. 1907 (Linfield, Airdrieonians, Linfield) 9

SCOTLAND

Player	Caps
Adam, C. G. 2007 (Rangers)	2
Adams, J. 1889 (Hearts)	3
Agnew, W. B. 1907 (Kilmarnock)	3
Aird, J. 1954 (Burnley)	4
Aitken, A. 1901 (Newcastle U, Middlesbrough, Leicester Fosse)	14
Aitken, G. G. 1949 (East Fife, Sunderland)	8
Aitken, R. 1886 (Dumbarton)	2
Aitken, R. 1980 (Celtic, Newcastle U, St Mirren)	57
Aitkenhead, W. A. C. 1912 (Blackburn R)	1
Albiston, A. 1982 (Manchester U)	14
Alexander, D. 1894 (East Stirlingshire)	2
Alexander, G. 2002 (Preston NE, Burnley)	33
Alexander, N. 2006 (Cardiff C)	3
Allan, D. S. 1885 (Queen's Park)	3
Allan, G. 1897 (Liverpool)	1
Allan, H. 1902 (Hearts)	1
Allan, J. 1887 (Queen's Park)	2
Allan, T. 1974 (Dundee)	2
Ancell, R. F. D. 1937 (Newcastle U)	2
Anderson, A. 1933 (Hearts)	23
Anderson, F. 1874 (Clydesdale)	1
Anderson, G. 1901 (Kilmarnock)	1
Anderson, H. A. 1914 (Raith R)	1
Anderson, J. 1954 (Leicester C)	1
Anderson, K. 1896 (Queen's Park)	3
Anderson, R. 2003 (Aberdeen, Sunderland)	11
Anderson, W. 1882 (Queen's Park)	6
Andrews, P. 1875 (Eastern)	1
Archibald, A. 1921 (Rangers)	8
Archibald, S. 1980 (Aberdeen, Tottenham H, Barcelona)	27
Armstrong, M. W. 1936 (Aberdeen)	3
Arnott, W. 1883 (Queen's Park)	14
Auld, J. R. 1887 (Third Lanark)	3
Auld, R. 1959 (Celtic)	3
Baird, A. 1892 (Queen's Park)	2
Baird, D. 1890 (Hearts)	3
Baird, H. 1956 (Airdrieonians)	1
Baird, J. C. 1876 (Vale of Leven)	3
Baird, S. 1957 (Rangers)	7
Baird, W. U. 1897 (St Bernard)	1
Bannon, E. J. 1980 (Dundee U)	11
Barbour, A. 1885 (Renton)	1
Barker, J. B. 1893 (Rangers)	2
Barrett, F. 1894 (Dundee)	2
Battles, B. 1901 (Celtic)	3
Battles, B. jun. 1931 (Hearts)	1
Bauld, W. 1950 (Hearts)	3
Baxter, J. C. 1961 (Rangers, Sunderland)	34
Baxter, R. D. 1939 (Middlesbrough)	3
Beattie, A. 1937 (Preston NE)	7
Beattie, C. 2006 (Celtic, WBA)	7
Beattie, R. 1939 (Preston NE)	1
Begbie, I. 1890 (Hearts)	4
Bell, A. 1912 (Manchester U)	1
Bell, J. 1890 (Dumbarton, Everton, Celtic)	10
Bell, M. 1901 (Hearts)	1
Bell, W. J. 1966 (Leeds U)	2
Bennett, A. 1904 (Celtic, Rangers)	11
Bennie, R. 1925 (Airdrieonians)	3
Bernard, P. R. J. 1995 (Oldham Ath)	2
Berra, C. 2008 (Hearts)	1
Berry, D. 1894 (Queen's Park)	3
Berry, W. H. 1888 (Queen's Park)	4
Bett, J. 1982 (Rangers, Lokeren, Aberdeen)	25
Beveridge, W. W. 1879 (Glasgow University)	3
Black, A. 1938 (Hearts)	3
Black, D. 1889 (Hurlford)	1
Black, E. 1988 (Metz)	2
Black, I. H. 1948 (Southampton)	1

Player	Caps
Blackburn, J. E. 1873 (Royal Engineers)	1
Blacklaw, A. S. 1963 (Burnley)	3
Blackley, J. 1974 (Hibernian)	7
Blair, D. 1929 (Clyde, Aston Villa)	8
Blair, J. 1920 (Sheffield W, Cardiff C)	8
Blair, J. 1934 (Motherwell)	1
Blair, J. A. 1947 (Blackpool)	1
Blair, W. 1896 (Third Lanark)	1
Blessington, J. 1894 (Celtic)	4
Blyth, J. A. 1978 (Coventry C)	2
Bone, J. 1972 (Norwich C)	2
Booth, S. 1993 (Aberdeen, Borussia Dortmund, Twente)	21
Bowie, J. 1920 (Rangers)	2
Bowie, W. 1891 (Linthouse)	1
Bowman, D. 1992 (Dundee U)	6
Bowman, G. A. 1892 (Montrose)	1
Boyd, J. M. 1934 (Newcastle U)	1
Boyd, K. 2006 (Rangers)	14
Boyd, R. 1889 (Mossend Swifts)	2
Boyd, T. 1991 (Motherwell, Chelsea, Celtic)	72
Boyd, W. G. 1931 (Clyde)	2
Bradshaw, T. 1928 (Bury)	1
Brand, R. 1961 (Rangers)	8
Brandon, T. 1896 (Blackburn R)	1
Brazil, A. 1980 (Ipswich T, Tottenham H)	13
Breckenridge, T. 1888 (Hearts)	1
Bremner, D. 1976 (Hibernian)	1
Bremner, W. J. 1965 (Leeds U)	54
Brennan, F. 1947 (Newcastle U)	7
Breslin, B. 1897 (Hibernian)	1
Brewster, G. 1921 (Everton)	1
Brogan, J. 1971 (Celtic)	4
Brown, A. 1890 (St Mirren)	2
Brown, A. 1904 (Middlesbrough)	1
Brown, A. D. 1950 (East Fife, Blackpool)	14
Brown, G. C. P. 1931 (Rangers)	19
Brown, H. 1947 (Partick Th)	3
Brown, J. B. 1939 (Clyde)	1
Brown, J. G. 1975 (Sheffield U)	1
Brown, R. 1884 (Dumbarton)	2
Brown, R. 1890 (Cambuslang)	1
Brown, R. 1947 (Rangers)	3
Brown, R. jun. 1885 (Dumbarton)	1
Brown, S. 2006 (Hibernian, Celtic)	9
Brown, W. D. F. 1958 (Dundee, Tottenham H)	28
Browning, J. 1914 (Celtic)	1
Brownlie, J. 1909 (Third Lanark)	16
Brownlie, J. 1971 (Hibernian)	7
Bruce, D. 1890 (Vale of Leven)	1
Bruce, R. F. 1934 (Middlesbrough)	1
Buchan, M. M. 1972 (Aberdeen, Manchester U)	34
Buchanan, J. 1889 (Cambuslang)	1
Buchanan, J. 1929 (Rangers)	2
Buchanan, P. S. 1938 (Chelsea)	1
Buchanan, R. 1891 (Abercorn)	1
Buckley, P. 1954 (Aberdeen)	3
Buick, A. 1902 (Hearts)	2
Burchill, M. J. 2000 (Celtic)	6
Burke, C. 2006 (Rangers)	2
Burley, C. W. 1995 (Chelsea, Celtic, Derby Co)	46
Burley, G. E. 1979 (Ipswich T)	11
Burns, F. 1970 (Manchester U)	1
Burns, K. 1974 (Birmingham C, Nottingham F)	20
Burns, T. 1981 (Celtic)	8
Busby, M. W. 1934 (Manchester C)	1
Cairns, T. 1920 (Rangers)	8
Calderhead, D. 1889 (Q of S Wanderers)	1
Calderwood, C. 1995 (Tottenham H)	36
Calderwood, R. 1885 (Cartvale)	3
Caldow, E. 1957 (Rangers)	40

Caldwell, G. 2002 (Newcastle U, Hibernian, Celtic) 27
Caldwell, S. 2001 (Newcastle U, Sunderland) 9
Callaghan, P. 1900 (Hibernian) 1
Callaghan, W. 1970 (Dunfermline Ath) 2
Cameron, C. 1999 (Hearts, Wolverhampton W) 28
Cameron, J. 1886 (Rangers) 1
Cameron, J. 1896 (Queen's Park) 1
Cameron, J. 1904 (St Mirren, Chelsea) 2
Campbell, C. 1874 (Queen's Park) 13
Campbell, H. 1889 (Renton) 1
Campbell, Jas 1913 (Sheffield W) 1
Campbell, J. 1880 (South Western) 1
Campbell, J. 1891 (Kilmarnock) 2
Campbell, John 1893 (Celtic) 12
Campbell, John 1899 (Rangers) 4
Campbell, K. 1920 (Liverpool, Partick Th) 8
Campbell, P. 1878 (Rangers) 2
Campbell, P. 1898 (Morton) 1
Campbell, R. 1947 (Falkirk, Chelsea) 5
Campbell, W. 1947 (Morton) 5
Canero, P. 2004 (Leicester C) 1
Carabine, J. 1938 (Third Lanark) 3
Carr, W. M. 1970 (Coventry C) 6
Cassidy, J. 1921 (Celtic) 4
Chalmers, S. 1965 (Celtic) 5
Chalmers, W. 1885 (Rangers) 1
Chalmers, W. S. 1929 (Queen's Park) 1
Chambers, T. 1894 (Hearts) 1
Chaplin, G. D. 1908 (Dundee) 1
Cheyne, A. G. 1929 (Aberdeen) 5
Christie, A. J. 1898 (Queen's Park) 3
Christie, R. M. 1884 (Queen's Park) 1
Clark, J. 1966 (Celtic) 4
Clark, R. B. 1968 (Aberdeen) 17
Clarke, S. 1988 (Chelsea) 6
Clarkson, D. 2008 (Motherwell) 1
Cleland, J. 1891 (Royal Albert) 1
Clements, R. 1891 (Leith Ath) 1
Clunas, W. L. 1924 (Sunderland) 2
Collier, W. 1922 (Raith R) 1
Collins, J. 1988 (Hibernian, Celtic, Monaco, Everton) 58
Collins, R. Y. 1951 (Celtic, Everton, Leeds U) 31
Collins, T. 1909 (Hearts) 1
Colman, D. 1911 (Aberdeen) 4
Colquhoun, E. P. 1972 (Sheffield U) 9
Colquhoun, J. 1988 (Hearts) 2
Combe, J. R. 1948 (Hibernian) 3
Conn, A. 1956 (Hearts) 1
Conn, A. 1975 (Tottenham H) 2
Connachan, E. D. 1962 (Dunfermline Ath) 2
Connelly, G. 1974 (Celtic) 2
Connolly, J. 1973 (Everton) 1
Connor, J. 1886 (Airdrieonians) 1
Connor, J. 1930 (Sunderland) 4
Connor, R. 1986 (Dundee, Aberdeen) 4
Cook, W. L. 1934 (Bolton W) 3
Cooke, C. 1966 (Dundee, Chelsea) 16
Cooper, D. 1980 (Rangers, Motherwell) 22
Cormack, P. B. 1966 (Hibernian, Nottingham F) 9
Cowan, J. 1896 (Aston Villa) 3
Cowan, J. 1948 (Morton) 25
Cowan, W, D. 1924 (Newcastle U) 1
Cowie, D. 1953 (Dundee) 20
Cox, C. J. 1948 (Hearts) 1
Cox, S. 1949 (Rangers) 24
Craig, A. 1929 (Motherwell) 3
Craig, J. 1977 (Celtic) 1
Craig, J. P. 1968 (Celtic) 1
Craig, T. 1927 (Rangers) 8
Craig, T. B. 1976 (Newcastle U) 1
Crainey, S. D. 2002 (Celtic, Southampton) 6
Crapnell, J. 1929 (Airdrieonians) 9
Crawford, D. 1894 (St Mirren, Rangers) 3
Crawford, J. 1932 (Queen's Park) 5
Crawford, S. 1995 (Raith R, Dunfermline Ath, Plymouth Arg) 25
Crerand, P. T. 1961 (Celtic, Manchester U) 16
Cringan, W. 1920 (Celtic) 5
Crosbie, J. A. 1920 (Ayr U, Birmingham) 2
Croal, J. A. 1913 (Falkirk) 3
Cropley, A. J. 1972 (Hibernian) 2
Cross, J. H. 1903 (Third Lanark) 1
Cruickshank, J. 1964 (Hearts) 6
Crum, J. 1936 (Celtic) 2
Cullen, M. J. 1956 (Luton T) 1
Cumming, D. S. 1938 (Middlesbrough) 1
Cumming, J. 1955 (Hearts) 9
Cummings, G. 1935 (Partick Th, Aston Villa) 9
Cummings, W. 2002 (Chelsea) 1
Cunningham, A. N. 1920 (Rangers) 12
Cunningham, W. C. 1954 (Preston NE) 8
Curran, H. P. 1970 (Wolverhampton W) 5

Dailly, C. 1997 (Derby Co, Blackburn R, West Ham U, Rangers) 67
Dalglish, K. 1972 (Celtic, Liverpool) 102
Davidson, C. I. 1999 (Blackburn R, Leicester C) 17
Davidson, D. 1878 (Queen's Park) 5
Davidson, J. A. 1954 (Partick Th) 8
Davidson, S. 1921 (Middlesbrough) 1
Dawson, A. 1980 (Rangers) 5
Dawson, J. 1935 (Rangers) 14
Deans, J. 1975 (Celtic) 2
Delaney, J. 1936 (Celtic, Manchester U) 13
Devine, A. 1910 (Falkirk) 1
Devlin, P. J. 2003 (Birmingham C) 10
Dewar, G. 1888 (Dumbarton) 2
Dewar, N. 1932 (Third Lanark) 3
Dick, J. 1959 (West Ham U) 1
Dickie, M. 1897 (Rangers) 3
Dickov, P. 2001 (Manchester C, Leicester C, Blackburn R) 10
Dickson, W. 1888 (Dundee Strathmore) 1
Dickson, W. 1970 (Kilmarnock) 5
Divers, J. 1895 (Celtic) 1
Divers, J. 1939 (Celtic) 1
Dobie, R. S. 2002 (WBA) 6
Docherty, T. H. 1952 (Preston NE, Arsenal) 25
Dodds, D. 1984 (Dundee U) 2
Dodds, J. 1914 (Celtic) 3
Dodds, W. 1997 (Aberdeen, Dundee U, Rangers) 26
Doig, J. E. 1887 (Arbroath, Sunderland) 5
Donachie, W. 1972 (Manchester C) 35
Donaldson, A. 1914 (Bolton W) 6
Donnachie, J. 1913 (Oldham Ath) 3
Donnelly, S. 1997 (Celtic) 10
Dougal, J. 1939 (Preston NE) 1
Dougall, C. 1947 (Birmingham C) 1
Dougan, R. 1950 (Hearts) 1
Douglas, A. 1911 (Chelsea) 1
Douglas, J. 1880 (Renfrew) 1
Douglas, R. 2002 (Celtic, Leicester C) 19
Dowds, P. 1892 (Celtic) 1
Downie, R. 1892 (Third Lanark) 1
Doyle, D. 1892 (Celtic) 8
Doyle, J. 1976 (Ayr U) 1
Drummond, J. 1892 (Falkirk, Rangers) 14
Dunbar, M. 1886 (Cartvale) 1
Duncan, A. 1975 (Hibernian) 6
Duncan, D. 1933 (Derby Co) 14
Duncan, D. M. 1948 (East Fife) 3
Duncan, J. 1878 (Alexandra Ath) 2
Duncan, J. 1926 (Leicester C) 1
Duncanson, J. 1947 (Rangers) 1
Dunlop, J. 1890 (St Mirren) 1
Dunlop, W. 1906 (Liverpool) 1

Dunn, J. 1925 (Hibernian, Everton) 6
Durie, G. S. 1988 (Chelsea, Tottenham H, Rangers) 43
Durrant, I. 1988 (Rangers, Kilmarnock) 20
Dykes, J. 1938 (Hearts) 2

Easson, J. F. 1931 (Portsmouth) 3
Elliott, M. S. 1998 (Leicester C) 18
Ellis, J. 1892 (Mossend Swifts) 1
Evans, A. 1982 (Aston Villa) 4
Evans, R. 1949 (Celtic, Chelsea) 48
Ewart, J. 1921 (Bradford C) 1
Ewing, T. 1958 (Partick Th) 2

Farm, G. N. 1953 (Blackpool) 10
Ferguson, B. 1999 (Rangers, Blackburn R, Rangers) 43
Ferguson, D. 1988 (Rangers) 2
Ferguson, D. 1992 (Dundee U, Everton) 7
Ferguson, I. 1989 (Rangers) 9
Ferguson, J. 1874 (Vale of Leven) 6
Ferguson, R. 1966 (Kilmarnock) 7
Fernie, W. 1954 (Celtic) 12
Findlay, R. 1898 (Kilmarnock) 1
Fitchie, T. T. 1905 (Woolwich Arsenal, Queen's Park) 4
Flavell, R. 1947 (Airdrieonians) 2
Fleck, R. 1990 (Norwich C) 4
Fleming, C. 1954 (East Fife) 1
Fleming, J. W. 1929 (Rangers) 3
Fleming, R. 1886 (Morton) 1
Fletcher, D. B. 2004 (Manchester U) 35
Fletcher, S. 2008 (Hibernian) 1
Forbes, A. R. 1947 (Sheffield U, Arsenal) 14
Forbes, J. 1884 (Vale of Leven) 5
Ford, D. 1974 (Hearts) 3
Forrest, J. 1966 (Rangers, Aberdeen) 5
Forrest, J. 1958 (Motherwell) 1
Forsyth, A. 1972 (Partick Th, Manchester U) 10
Forsyth, C. 1964 (Kilmarnock) 4
Forsyth, T. 1971 (Motherwell, Rangers) 22
Foyers, R. 1893 (St Bernards) 2
Fraser, D. M. 1968 (WBA) 2
Fraser, J. 1891 (Moffat) 1
Fraser, M. J. E. 1880 (Queen's Park) 5
Fraser, J. 1907 (Dundee) 1
Fraser, W. 1955 (Sunderland) 2
Freedman, D. A. 2002 (C Palace) 2
Fulton, W. 1884 (Abercorn) 1
Fyfe, J. H. 1895 (Third Lanark) 1

Gabriel, J. 1961 (Everton) 2
Gallacher, H. K. 1924 (Airdrieonians, Newcastle U, Chelsea, Derby Co) 20
Gallacher, K. W. 1988 (Dundee U, Coventry C, Blackburn R, Newcastle U) 53
Gallacher, P. 1935 (Sunderland) 1
Gallacher, P. 2002 (Dundee U) 8
Gallagher, P. 2004 (Blackburn R) 1
Galloway, M. 1992 (Celtic) 1
Galt, J. H. 1908 (Rangers) 2
Gardiner, I. 1958 (Motherwell) 1
Gardner, D. R. 1897 (Third Lanark) 1
Gardner, R. 1872 (Queen's Park, Clydesdale) 5
Gemmell, T. 1955 (St Mirren) 2
Gemmell, T. 1966 (Celtic) 18
Gemmill, A. 1971 (Derby Co, Nottingham F, Birmingham C) 43
Gemmill, S. 1995 (Nottingham F, Everton) 26
Gibb, W. 1873 (Clydesdale) 1
Gibson, D. W. 1963 (Leicester C) 7
Gibson, J. D. 1926 (Partick Th, Aston Villa) 8
Gibson, N. 1895 (Rangers, Partick Th) 14
Gilchrist, J. E. 1922 (Celtic) 1
Gilhooley, M. 1922 (Hull C) 1
Gillespie, G. 1880 (Rangers, Queen's Park) 7
Gillespie, G. T. 1988 (Liverpool) 13
Gillespie, Jas 1898 (Third Lanark) 1
Gillespie, John 1896 (Queen's Park) 1
Gillespie, R. 1927 (Queen's Park) 4
Gillick, T. 1937 (Everton) 5
Gilmour, J. 1931 (Dundee) 1
Gilzean, A. J. 1964 (Dundee, Tottenham H) 22
Glass, S. 1999 (Newcastle U) 1
Glavin, R. 1977 (Celtic) 1
Glen, A. 1956 (Aberdeen) 2
Glen, R. 1895 (Renton, Hibernian) 3
Goram, A. L. 1986 (Oldham Ath, Hibernian, Rangers) 43
Gordon, C. S. 2004 (Hearts, Sunderland) 31
Gordon, J. E. 1912 (Rangers) 10
Gossland, J. 1884 (Rangers) 1
Goudle, J. 1884 (Abercorn) 1
Gough, C. R. 1983 (Dundee U, Tottenham H, Rangers) 61
Gould, J. 2000 (Celtic) 2
Gourlay, J. 1886 (Cambuslang) 2
Govan, J. 1948 (Hibernian) 6
Gow, D. R. 1888 (Rangers) 1
Gow, J. J. 1885 (Queen's Park) 1
Gow, J. R. 1888 (Rangers) 1
Graham, A. 1978 (Leeds U) 11
Graham, G. 1972 (Arsenal, Manchester U) 12
Graham, J. 1884 (Annbank) 1
Graham, J. A. 1921 (Arsenal) 1
Grant, J. 1959 (Hibernian) 2
Grant, P. 1989 (Celtic) 2
Gray, A. 1903 (Hibernian) 1
Gray, A. D. 2003 (Bradford C) 2
Gray, A. M. 1976 (Aston Villa, Wolverhampton W, Everton) 20
Gray, D. 1929 (Rangers) 10
Gray, E. 1969 (Leeds U) 12
Gray, F. T. 1976 (Leeds U, Nottingham F, Leeds U) 32
Gray, W. 1886 (Pollokshields Ath) 1
Green, A. 1971 (Blackpool, Newcastle U) 6
Greig, J. 1964 (Rangers) 44
Groves, W. 1888 (Hibernian, Celtic) 3
Gulliland, W. 1891 (Queen's Park) 4
Gunn, B. 1990 (Norwich C) 6

Haddock, H. 1955 (Clyde) 6
Haddow, D. 1894 (Rangers) 1
Haffey, F. 1960 (Celtic) 2
Hamilton, A. 1885 (Queen's Park) 4
Hamilton, A. W. 1962 (Dundee) 24
Hamilton, G. 1906 (Port Glasgow Ath) 1
Hamilton, G. 1947 (Aberdeen) 5
Hamilton, J. 1892 (Queen's Park) 3
Hamilton, J. 1924 (St Mirren) 1
Hamilton, R. C. 1899 (Rangers, Dundee) 11
Hamilton, T. 1891 (Hurlford) 1
Hamilton, T. 1932 (Rangers) 1
Hamilton, W. M. 1965 (Hibernian) 1
Hammell, S. 2005 (Motherwell) 1
Hannah, A. B. 1888 (Renton) 1
Hannah, J. 1889 (Third Lanark) 1
Hansen, A. D. 1979 (Liverpool) 26
Hansen, J. 1972 (Partick Th) 2
Harkness, J. D. 1927 (Queen's Park, Hearts) 12
Harper, J. M. 1973 (Aberdeen, Hibernian, Aberdeen) 4
Harper, W. 1923 (Hibernian, Arsenal) 11
Harris, J. 1921 (Partick Th) 2
Harris, N. 1924 (Newcastle U) 1
Harrower, W. 1882 (Queen's Park) 3
Hartford, R. A. 1972 (WBA, Manchester C, Everton, Manchester C) 50
Hartley, P. J. 2005 (Hearts, Celtic) 19
Harvey, D. 1973 (Leeds U) 16

Hastings, A. C. 1936 (Sunderland) 2
Haughney, M. 1954 (Celtic) 1
Hay, D. 1970 (Celtic) 27
Hay, J. 1905 (Celtic, Newcastle U) 11
Hegarty, P. 1979 (Dundee U) 8
Heggie, C. 1886 (Rangers) 1
Henderson, G. H. 1904 (Rangers) 1
Henderson, J. G. 1953 (Portsmouth, Arsenal) 7
Henderson, W. 1963 (Rangers) 29
Hendry, E. C. J. 1993 (Blackburn R, Rangers, Coventry C, Bolton W) 51
Hepburn, J. 1891 (Alloa Ath) 1
Hepburn, R. 1932 (Ayr U) 1
Herd, A. C. 1935 (Hearts) 1
Herd, D. G. 1959 (Arsenal) 5
Herd, G. 1958 (Clyde) 5
Herriot, J. 1969 (Birmingham C) 8
Hewie, J. D. 1956 (Charlton Ath) 19
Higgins, A. 1885 (Kilmarnock) 1
Higgins, A. 1910 (Newcastle U) 4
Highet, T. C. 1875 (Queen's Park) 4
Hill, D. 1881 (Rangers) 3
Hill, D. A. 1906 (Third Lanark) 1
Hill, F. R. 1930 (Aberdeen) 3
Hill, J. 1891 (Hearts) 2
Hogg, G. 1896 (Hearts) 2
Hogg, J. 1922 (Ayr U) 1
Hogg, R. M. 1937 (Celtic) 1
Holm, A. H. 1882 (Queen's Park) 3
Holt, D. D. 1963 (Hearts) 5
Holt, G. J. 2001 (Kilmarnock, Norwich C) 10
Holton, J. A. 1973 (Manchester U) 15
Hope, R. 1968 (WBA) 2
Hopkin, D. 1997 (C Palace, Leeds U) 7
Houliston, W. 1949 (Queen of the South) 3
Houston, S. M. 1976 (Manchester U) 1
Howden, W. 1905 (Partick Th) 1
Howe, R. 1929 (Hamilton A) 2
Howie, H. 1949 (Hibernian) 1
Howie, J. 1905 (Newcastle U) 3
Howieson, J. 1927 (St Mirren) 1
Hughes, J. 1965 (Celtic) 8
Hughes, R. D. 2004 (Portsmouth) 5
Hughes, W. 1975 (Sunderland) 1
Humphries, W. 1952 (Motherwell) 1
Hunter, A. 1972 (Kilmarnock, Celtic) 4
Hunter, J. 1909 (Dundee) 1
Hunter, J. 1874 (Third Lanark, Eastern, Third Lanark) 4
Hunter, W. 1960 (Motherwell) 3
Hunter, R. 1890 (St Mirren) 1
Husband, J. 1947 (Partick Th) 1
Hutchison, D. 1999 (Everton, Sunderland, West Ham U) 26
Hutchison, T. 1974 (Coventry C) 17
Hutton, A. 2007 (Rangers, Tottenham H) 7
Hutton, J. 1887 (St Bernards) 1
Hutton, J. 1923 (Aberdeen, Blackburn R) 10
Hyslop, T. 1896 (Stoke, Rangers) 2

Imlach, J. J. S. 1958 (Nottingham F) 4
Imrie, W. N. 1929 (St Johnstone) 2
Inglis, J. 1883 (Rangers) 2
Inglis, J. 1884 (Kilmarnock Ath) 1
Irons, J. H. 1900 (Queen's Park) 1
Irvine, B. 1991 (Aberdeen) 9

Jackson, A. 1886 (Cambuslang) 2
Jackson, A. 1925 (Aberdeen, Huddersfield T) 17
Jackson, C. 1975 (Rangers) 8
Jackson, D. 1995 (Hibernian, Celtic) 28
Jackson, J. 1931 (Partick Th, Chelsea) 8
Jackson, T. A. 1904 (St Mirren) 6
James, A. W. 1926 (Preston NE, Arsenal) 8
Jardine, A. 1971 (Rangers) 38
Jarvie, A. 1971 (Airdrieonians) 3
Jenkinson, T. 1887 (Hearts) 1
Jess, E. 1993 (Aberdeen, Coventry C, Aberdeen) 18
Johnston, A. 1999 (Sunderland, Rangers, Middlesbrough) 18
Johnston, L. H. 1948 (Clyde) 2
Johnston, M. 1984 (Watford, Celtic, Nantes, Rangers) 38
Johnston, R. 1938 (Sunderland) 1
Johnston, W. 1966 (Rangers, WBA) 22
Johnstone, D. 1973 (Rangers) 14
Johnstone, J. 1888 (Abercorn) 1
Johnstone, J. 1965 (Celtic) 23
Johnstone, Jas 1894 (Kilmarnock) 1
Johnstone, J. A. 1930 (Hearts) 3
Johnstone, R. 1951 (Hibernian, Manchester C) 17
Johnstone, W. 1887 (Third Lanark) 3
Jordan, J. 1973 (Leeds U, Manchester U, AC Milan) 52

Kay, J. L. 1880 (Queen's Park) 6
Keillor, A. 1891 (Montrose, Dundee) 6
Keir, L. 1885 (Dumbarton) 5
Kelly, H. T. 1952 (Blackpool) 1
Kelly, J. 1888 (Renton, Celtic) 8
Kelly, J. C. 1949 (Barnsley) 2
Kelso, R. 1885 (Renton, Dundee) 7
Kelso, T. 1914 (Dundee) 1
Kennaway, J. 1934 (Celtic) 1
Kennedy, A. 1875 (Eastern, Third Lanark) 6
Kennedy, J. 1897 (Hibernian) 1
Kennedy, J. 1964 (Celtic) 6
Kennedy, J. 2004 (Celtic) 1
Kennedy, S. 1905 (Partick Th) 1
Kennedy, S. 1975 (Rangers) 5
Kennedy, S. 1978 (Aberdeen) 8
Ker, G. 1880 (Queen's Park) 5
Ker, W. 1872 (Queen's Park) 2
Kerr, A. 1955 (Partick Th) 2
Kerr, B. 2003 (Newcastle U) 3
Kerr, P. 1924 (Hibernian) 1
Key, G. 1902 (Hearts) 1
Key, W. 1907 (Queen's Park) 1
King, A. 1896 (Hearts, Celtic) 6
King, J. 1933 (Hamilton A) 2
King, W. S. 1929 (Queen's Park) 1
Kinloch, J. D. 1922 (Partick Th) 1
Kinnaird, A. F. 1873 (Wanderers) 1
Kinnear, D. 1938 (Rangers) 1
Kyle, K. 2002 (Sunderland) 9

Lambert, P. 1995 (Motherwell, Borussia Dortmund, Celtic) 40
Lambie, J. A. 1886 (Queen's Park) 3
Lambie, W. A. 1892 (Queen's Park) 9
Lamont, W. 1885 (Pilgrims) 1
Lang, A. 1880 (Dumbarton) 1
Lang, J. J. 1876 (Clydesdale, Third Lanark) 2
Latta, A. 1888 (Dumbarton) 2
Law, D. 1959 (Huddersfield T, Manchester C, Torino, Manchester U, Manchester C) 55
Law, G. 1910 (Rangers) 3
Law, T. 1928 (Chelsea) 2
Lawrence, J. 1911 (Newcastle U) 1
Lawrence, T. 1963 (Liverpool) 3
Lawson, D. 1923 (St Mirren) 1
Leckie, R. 1872 (Queen's Park) 1
Leggat, G. 1956 (Aberdeen, Fulham) 18
Leighton, J. 1983 (Aberdeen, Manchester U, Hibernian, Aberdeen) 91
Lennie, W. 1908 (Aberdeen) 2
Lennox, R. 1967 (Celtic) 10
Leslie, L. G. 1961 (Airdrieonians) 5
Levein, C. 1990 (Hearts) 16

Liddell, W. 1947 (Liverpool) 28
Liddle, D. 1931 (East Fife) 3
Lindsay, D. 1903 (St Mirren) 1
Lindsay, J. 1880 (Dumbarton) 8
Lindsay, J. 1888 (Renton) 3
Linwood, A. B. 1950 (Clyde) 1
Little, R. J. 1953 (Rangers) 1
Livingstone, G. T. 1906 (Manchester C, Rangers) 2
Lochhead, A. 1889 (Third Lanark) 1
Logan, J. 1891 (Ayr) 1
Logan, T. 1913 (Falkirk) 1
Logie, J. T. 1953 (Arsenal) 1
Loney, W. 1910 (Celtic) 2
Long, H. 1947 (Clyde) 1
Longair, W. 1894 (Dundee) 1
Lorimer, P. 1970 (Leeds U) 21
Love, A. 1931 (Aberdeen) 3
Low, A. 1934 (Falkirk) 1
Low, J. 1891 (Cambuslang) 1
Low, T. P. 1897 (Rangers) 1
Low, W. L. 1911 (Newcastle U) 5
Lowe, J. 1887 (St Bernards) 1
Lundie, J. 1886 (Hibernian) 1
Lyall, J. 1905 (Sheffield W) 1

McAdam, J. 1880 (Third Lanark) 1
McAllister, B. 1997 (Wimbledon) 3
McAllister, G. 1990 (Leicester C, Leeds U, Coventry C) 57
McAllister, J. R. 2004 (Livingston) 1
Macari, L. 1972 (Celtic, Manchester U) 24
McArthur, D. 1895 (Celtic) 3
McAtee, A. 1913 (Celtic) 1
McAulay, J. 1884 (Arthurlie) 1
McAulay, J. D. 1882 (Dumbarton) 9
McAulay, R. 1932 (Rangers) 2
Macauley, A. R. 1947 (Brentford, Arsenal) 7
McAvennie, F. 1986 (West Ham U, Celtic) 5
McBain, E. 1894 (St Mirren) 1
McBain, N. 1922 (Manchester U, Everton) 3
McBride, J. 1967 (Celtic) 2
McBride, P. 1904 (Preston NE) 6
McCall, A. 1888 (Renton) 1
McCall, A. S. M. 1990 (Everton, Rangers) 40
McCall, J. 1886 (Renton) 5
McCalliog, J. 1967 (Sheffield W, Wolverhampton W) 5
McCallum, N. 1888 (Renton) 1
McCann, N. 1999 (Hearts, Rangers, Southampton) 26
McCann, R. J. 1959 (Motherwell) 5
McCartney, W. 1902 (Hibernian) 1
McClair, B. 1987 (Celtic, Manchester U) 30
McClory, A. 1927 (Motherwell) 3
McCloy, P. 1924 (Ayr U) 2
McCloy, P. 1973 (Rangers) 4
McCoist, A. 1986 (Rangers, Kilmarnock) 61
McColl, I. M. 1950 (Rangers) 14
McColl, R. S. 1896 (Queen's Park, Newcastle U, Queen's Park) 13
McColl, W. 1895 (Renton) 1
McCombie, A. 1903 (Sunderland, Newcastle U) 4
McCorkindale, J. 1891 (Partick Th) 1
McCormack, R. 2008 (Motherwell) 1
McCormick, R. 1886 (Abercorn) 1
McCrae, D. 1929 (St Mirren) 2
McCreadie, A. 1893 (Rangers) 2
McCreadie, E. G. 1965 (Chelsea) 23
McCulloch, D. 1935 (Hearts, Brentford, Derby Co) 7
McCulloch, L. 2005 (Wigan Ath, Rangers) 15
MacDonald, A. 1976 (Rangers) 1
McDonald, J. 1886 (Edinburgh University) 1
McDonald, J. 1956 (Sunderland) 2
MacDougall, E. J. 1975 (Norwich C) 7
McDougall, J. 1877 (Vale of Leven) 5
McDougall, J. 1926 (Airdrieonians) 1
McDougall, J. 1931 (Liverpool) 2
McEveley, J. 2008 (Derby Co) 3
McFadden, J. 2002 (Motherwell, Everton) 37
McFadyen, W. 1934 (Motherwell) 2
Macfarlane, A. 1904 (Dundee) 5
Macfarlane, W. 1947 (Hearts) 1
McFarlane, R. 1896 (Greenock Morton) 1
McGarr, E. 1970 (Aberdeen) 2
McGarvey, F. P. 1979 (Liverpool, Celtic) 7
McGeoch, A. 1876 (Dumbreck) 4
McGhee, J. 1886 (Hibernian) 1
McGhee, M. 1983 (Aberdeen) 4
McGinlay, J. 1994 (Bolton W) 13
McGonagle, W. 1933 (Celtic) 6
McGrain, D. 1973 (Celtic) 62
McGregor, A. 2007 (Rangers) 1
McGregor, J. C. 1877 (Vale of Leven) 4
McGrory, J. 1928 (Celtic) 7
McGrory, J. E. 1965 (Kilmarnock) 3
McGuire, W. 1881 (Beith) 2
McGurk, F. 1934 (Birmingham) 1
McHardy, H. 1885 (Rangers) 1
McInally, A. 1989 (Aston Villa, Bayern Munich) 8
McInally, J. 1987 (Dundee U) 10
McInally, T. B. 1926 (Celtic) 2
McInnes, D. 2003 (WBA) 2
McInnes, T. 1889 (Cowlairs) 1
McIntosh, W. 1905 (Third Lanark) 1
McIntyre, A. 1878 (Vale of Leven) 2
McIntyre, H. 1880 (Rangers) 1
McIntyre, J. 1884 (Rangers) 1
MacKay, D. 1959 (Celtic) 14
Mackay, D. C. 1957 (Hearts, Tottenham H) 22
Mackay, G. 1988 (Hearts) 4
Mackay, M. 2004 (Norwich C) 5
McKay, J. 1924 (Blackburn R) 1
McKay, R. 1928 (Newcastle U) 1
McKean, R. 1976 (Rangers) 1
McKenzie, D. 1938 (Brentford) 1
Mackenzie, J. A. 1954 (Partick Th) 9
McKeown, M. 1889 (Celtic) 2
McKie, J. 1898 (East Stirling) 1
McKillop, T. R. 1938 (Rangers) 1
McKimmie, S. 1989 (Aberdeen) 40
McKinlay, D. 1922 (Liverpool) 2
McKinlay, T. 1996 (Celtic) 22
McKinlay, W. 1994 (Dundee U, Blackburn R) 29
McKinnon, A. 1874 (Queen's Park) 1
McKinnon, R. 1966 (Rangers) 28
McKinnon, R. 1994 (Motherwell) 3
MacKinnon, W. 1883 (Dumbarton) 4
MacKinnon, W. W. 1872 (Queen's Park) 9
McLaren, A. 1929 (St Johnstone) 5
McLaren, A. 1947 (Preston NE) 4
McLaren, A. 1992 (Hearts, Rangers) 24
McLaren, A. 2001 (Kilmarnock) 1
McLaren, J. 1888 (Hibernian, Celtic) 3
McLean, A. 1926 (Celtic) 4
McLean, D. 1896 (St Bernards) 2
McLean, D. 1912 (Sheffield W) 1
McLean, G. 1968 (Dundee) 1
McLean, T. 1969 (Kilmarnock) 6
McLeish, A. 1980 (Aberdeen) 77
McLeod, D. 1905 (Celtic) 4
McLeod, J. 1888 (Dumbarton) 5
MacLeod, J. M. 1961 (Hibernian) 4
MacLeod, M. 1985 (Celtic, Borussia Dortmund, Hibernian) 20
McLeod, W. 1886 (Cowlairs) 1
McLintock, A. 1875 (Vale of Leven) 3
McLintock, F. 1963 (Leicester C, Arsenal) 9
McLuckie, J. S. 1934 (Manchester C) 1

McMahon, A. 1892 (Celtic) 6
McManus, S. 2007 (Celtic) 13
McMenemy, J. 1905 (Celtic) 12
McMenemy, J. 1934 (Motherwell) 1
McMillan, I. L. 1952 (Airdrieonians, Rangers) 6
McMillan, J. 1897 (St Bernards) 1
McMillan, T. 1887 (Dumbarton) 1
McMullan, J. 1920 (Partick Th, Manchester C) 16
McNab, A. 1921 (Morton) 2
McNab, A. 1937 (Sunderland, WBA) 2
McNab, C. D. 1931 (Dundee) 6
McNab, J. S. 1923 (Liverpool) 1
McNair, A. 1906 (Celtic) 15
McNamara, J. 1997 (Celtic, Wolverhampton W) 33
McNamee, D. 2004 (Livingston) 4
McNaught, W. 1951 (Raith R) 5
McNaughton, K. 2002 (Aberdeen, Cardiff C) 4
McNeill, W. 1961 (Celtic) 29
McNiel, H. 1874 (Queen's Park) 10
McNiel, M. 1876 (Rangers) 2
McPhail, J. 1950 (Celtic) 5
McPhail, R. 1927 (Airdrieonians, Rangers) 17
McPherson, D. 1892 (Kilmarnock) 1
McPherson, D. 1989 (Hearts, Rangers) 27
McPherson, J. 1875 (Clydesdale) 1
McPherson, J. 1879 (Vale of Leven) 8
McPherson, J. 1888 (Kilmarnock, Cowlairs, Rangers) 9
McPherson, J. 1891 (Hearts) 1
McPherson, R. 1882 (Arthurlie) 1
McQueen, G. 1974 (Leeds U, Manchester U) 30
McQueen, M. 1890 (Leith Ath) 2
McRorie, D. M. 1931 (Morton) 1
McSpadyen, A. 1939 (Partick Th) 2
McStay, P. 1984 (Celtic) 76
McStay, W. 1921 (Celtic) 13
McSwegan, G. 2000 (Hearts) 2
McTavish, J. 1910 (Falkirk) 1
McWattie, G. C. 1901 (Queen's Park) 2
McWilliam, P. 1905 (Newcastle U) 8
Madden, J. 1893 (Celtic) 2
Main, F. R. 1938 (Rangers) 1
Main, J. 1909 (Hibernian) 1
Maley, W. 1893 (Celtic) 2
Maloney, S. R. 2006 (Celtic, Aston Villa) 11
Malpas, M. 1984 (Dundee U) 55
Marshall, D. J. 2005 (Celtic) 2
Marshall, G. 1992 (Celtic) 1
Marshall, H. 1899 (Celtic) 2
Marshall, J. 1885 (Third Lanark) 4
Marshall, J. 1921 (Middlesbrough, Llanelly) 7
Marshall, J. 1932 (Rangers) 3
Marshall, R. W. 1892 (Rangers) 2
Martin, B. 1995 (Motherwell) 2
Martin, F. 1954 (Aberdeen) 6
Martin, N. 1965 (Hibernian, Sunderland) 3
Martis, J. 1961 (Motherwell) 1
Mason, J. 1949 (Third Lanark) 7
Massie, A. 1932 (Hearts, Aston Villa) 18
Masson, D. S. 1976 (QPR, Derby Co) 17
Mathers, D. 1954 (Partick Th) 1
Matteo, D. 2001 (Leeds U) 6
Maxwell, W. S. 1898 (Stoke C) 1
May, J. 1906 (Rangers) 5
Meechan, P. 1896 (Celtic) 1
Meiklejohn, D. D. 1922 (Rangers) 15
Menzies, A. 1906 (Hearts) 1
Mercer, R. 1912 (Hearts) 2
Middleton, R. 1930 (Cowdenbeath) 1
Millar, J. 1897 (Rangers) 3
Millar, J. 1963 (Rangers) 2
Miller, A. 1939 (Hearts) 1
Miller, C. 2001 (Dundee U) 1
Miller, J. 1931 (St Mirren) 5
Miller, K. 2001 (Rangers, Wolverhampton W, Celtic, Derby Co) 37
Miller, L. 2006 (Dundee U) 1
Miller, P. 1882 (Dumbarton) 3
Miller, T. 1920 (Liverpool, Manchester U) 3
Miller, W. 1876 (Third Lanark) 1
Miller, W. 1947 (Celtic) 6
Miller, W. 1975 (Aberdeen) 65
Mills, W. 1936 (Aberdeen) 3
Milne, J. V. 1938 (Middlesbrough) 2
Mitchell, D. 1890 (Rangers) 5
Mitchell, J. 1908 (Kilmarnock) 3
Mitchell, R. C. 1951 (Newcastle U) 2
Mochan, N. 1954 (Celtic) 3
Moir, W. 1950 (Bolton W) 1
Moncur, R. 1968 (Newcastle U) 16
Morgan, H. 1898 (St Mirren, Liverpool) 2
Morgan, W. 1968 (Burnley, Manchester U) 21
Morris, D. 1923 (Raith R) 6
Morris, H. 1950 (East Fife) 1
Morrison, J. C. 2008 (WBA) 1
Morrison, T. 1927 (St Mirren) 1
Morton, A. L. 1920 (Queen's Park, Rangers) 31
Morton, H. A. 1929 (Kilmarnock) 2
Mudie, J. K. 1957 (Blackpool) 17
Muir, W. 1907 (Dundee) 1
Muirhead, T. A. 1922 (Rangers) 8
Mulhall, G. 1960 (Aberdeen, Sunderland) 3
Munro, A. D. 1937 (Hearts, Blackpool) 3
Munro, F. M. 1971 (Wolverhampton W) 9
Munro, I. 1979 (St Mirren) 7
Munro, N. 1888 (Abercorn) 2
Murdoch, J. 1931 (Motherwell) 1
Murdoch, R. 1966 (Celtic) 12
Murphy, F. 1938 (Celtic) 1
Murray, I. 2003 (Hibernian, Rangers) 6
Murray, J. 1895 (Renton) 1
Murray, J. 1958 (Hearts) 5
Murray, J. W. 1890 (Vale of Leven) 1
Murray, P. 1896 (Hibernian) 2
Murray, S. 1972 (Aberdeen) 1
Murty, G. S. 2004 (Reading) 4
Mutch, G. 1938 (Preston NE) 1

Naismith, S. J. 2007 (Kilmarnock, Rangers) 2
Napier, C. E. 1932 (Celtic, Derby Co) 5
Narey, D. 1977 (Dundee U) 35
Naysmith, G. A. 2000 (Hearts, Everton, Sheffield U) 40
Neil, R. G. 1896 (Hibernian, Rangers) 2
Neill, R. W. 1876 (Queen's Park) 5
Neilson, R. 2007 (Hearts) 1
Nellies, P. 1913 (Hearts) 2
Nelson, J. 1925 (Cardiff C) 4
Nevin, P. K. F. 1986 (Chelsea, Everton, Tranmere R) 28
Niblo, T. D. 1904 (Aston Villa) 1
Nibloe, J. 1929 (Kilmarnock) 11
Nicholas, C. 1983 (Celtic, Arsenal, Aberdeen) 20
Nicholson, B. 2001 (Dunfermline Ath) 3
Nicol, S. 1985 (Liverpool) 27
Nisbet, J. 1929 (Ayr U) 3
Niven, J. B. 1885 (Moffat) 1

O'Connor, G. 2002 (Hibernian, Lokomotiv Moscow, Birmingham C) 15
O'Donnell, F. 1937 (Preston NE, Blackpool) 6
O'Donnell, P. 1994 (Motherwell) 1
Ogilvie, D. H. 1934 (Motherwell) 1
O'Hare, J. 1970 (Derby Co) 13
O'Neil, B. 1996 (Celtic, Wolfsburg, Derby Co, Preston NE) 7
O'Neil, J. 2001 (Hibernian) 1
Ormond, W. E. 1954 (Hibernian) 6
O'Rourke, F. 1907 (Airdrieonians) 1

Orr, J. 1892 (Kilmarnock) 1
Orr, R. 1902 (Newcastle U) 2
Orr, T. 1952 (Morton) 2
Orr, W. 1900 (Celtic) 3
Orrock, R. 1913 (Falkirk) 1
Oswald, J. 1889 (Third Lanark, St Bernards, Rangers) 3

Parker, A. H. 1955 (Falkirk, Everton) 15
Parlane, D. 1973 (Rangers) 12
Parlane, R. 1878 (Vale of Leven) 3
Paterson, G. D. 1939 (Celtic) 1
Paterson, J. 1920 (Leicester C) 1
Paterson, J. 1931 (Cowdenbeath) 3
Paton, A. 1952 (Motherwell) 2
Paton, D. 1896 (St Bernards) 1
Paton, M. 1883 (Dumbarton) 5
Paton, R. 1879 (Vale of Leven) 2
Patrick, J. 1897 (St Mirren) 2
Paul, H. McD. 1909 (Queen's Park) 3
Paul, W. 1888 (Partick Th) 3
Paul, W. 1891 (Dykebar) 1
Pearson, S. P. 2004 (Motherwell, Celtic, Derby Co) 10
Pearson, T. 1947 (Newcastle U) 2
Penman, A. 1966 (Dundee) 1
Pettigrew, W. 1976 (Motherwell) 5
Phillips, J. 1877 (Queen's Park) 3
Plenderleith, J. B. 1961 (Manchester C) 1
Porteous, W. 1903 (Hearts) 1
Pressley, S. J. 2000 (Hearts) 32
Pringle, C. 1921 (St Mirren) 1
Provan, D. 1964 (Rangers) 5
Provan, D. 1980 (Celtic) 10
Pursell, P. 1914 (Queen's Park) 1

Quashie, N. F. 2004 (Portsmouth, Southampton, WBA) 14
Quinn, J. 1905 (Celtic) 11
Quinn, P. 1961 (Motherwell) 4

Rae, G. 2001 (Dundee, Rangers, Cardiff C) 13
Rae, J. 1889 (Third Lanark) 2
Raeside, J. S. 1906 (Third Lanark) 1
Raisbeck, A. G. 1900 (Liverpool) 8
Rankin, G. 1890 (Vale of Leven) 2
Rankin, R. 1929 (St Mirren) 3
Redpath, W. 1949 (Motherwell) 9
Reid, J. G. 1914 (Airdrieonians) 3
Reid, R. 1938 (Brentford) 2
Reid, W. 1911 (Rangers) 9
Reilly, L. 1949 (Hibernian) 38
Rennie, H. G. 1900 (Hearts, Hibernian) 13
Renny-Tailyour, H. W. 1873 (Royal Engineers) 1
Rhind, A. 1872 (Queen's Park) 1
Richmond, A. 1906 (Queen's Park) 1
Richmond, J. T. 1877 (Clydesdale, Queen's Park) 3
Ring, T. 1953 (Clyde) 12
Rioch, B. D. 1975 (Derby Co, Everton, Derby Co) 24
Riordan, D. G. 2006 (Hibernian) 1
Ritchie, A. 1891 (East Stirlingshire) 1
Ritchie, H. 1923 (Hibernian) 2
Ritchie, J. 1897 (Queen's Park) 1
Ritchie, P. S. 1999 (Hearts, Bolton W, Walsall) 7
Ritchie, W. 1962 (Rangers) 1
Robb, D. T. 1971 (Aberdeen) 5
Robb, W. 1926 (Rangers, Hibernian) 2
Robertson, A. 1955 (Clyde) 5
Robertson, D. 1992 (Rangers) 3
Robertson, G. 1910 (Motherwell, Sheffield W) 4
Robertson, G. 1938 (Kilmarnock) 1
Robertson, H. 1962 (Dundee) 1
Robertson, J. 1931 (Dundee) 2
Robertson, J. 1991 (Hearts) 16
Robertson, J. N. 1978 (Nottingham F, Derby Co) 28
Robertson, J. G. 1965 (Tottenham H) 1
Robertson, J. T. 1898 (Everton, Southampton, Rangers) 16
Robertson, P. 1903 (Dundee) 1
Robertson, T. 1889 (Queen's Park) 4
Robertson, T. 1898 (Hearts) 1
Robertson, W. 1887 (Dumbarton) 2
Robinson, R. 1974 (Dundee) 4
Robson, B. 2008 (Dundee U) 2
Ross, M. 2002 (Rangers) 13
Rough, A. 1976 (Partick Th, Hibernian) 53
Rougvie, D. 1984 (Aberdeen) 1
Rowan, A. 1880 (Caledonian, Queen's Park) 2
Russell, D. 1895 (Hearts, Celtic) 6
Russell, J. 1890 (Cambuslang) 1
Russell, W. F. 1924 (Airdrieonians) 2
Rutherford, E. 1948 (Rangers) 1

St John, I. 1959 (Motherwell, Liverpool) 21
Sawers, W. 1895 (Dundee) 1
Scarff, P. 1931 (Celtic) 1
Schaedler, E. 1974 (Hibernian) 1
Scott, A. S. 1957 (Rangers, Everton) 16
Scott, J. 1966 (Hibernian) 1
Scott, J. 1971 (Dundee) 2
Scott, M. 1898 (Airdrieonians) 1
Scott, R. 1894 (Airdrieonians) 1
Scoular, J. 1951 (Portsmouth) 9
Sellar, W. 1885 (Battlefield, Queen's Park) 9
Semple, W. 1886 (Cambuslang) 1
Severin, S. D. 2002 (Hearts, Aberdeen) 15
Shankly, W. 1938 (Preston NE) 5
Sharp, G. M. 1985 (Everton) 12
Sharp, J. 1904 (Dundee, Woolwich Arsenal, Fulham) 5
Shaw, D. 1947 (Hibernian) 8
Shaw, F. W. 1884 (Pollokshields Ath) 2
Shaw, J. 1947 (Rangers) 4
Shearer, D. 1994 (Aberdeen) 7
Shearer, R. 1961 (Rangers) 4
Sillars, D. C. 1891 (Queen's Park) 5
Simpson, J. 1895 (Third Lanark) 3
Simpson, J. 1935 (Rangers) 14
Simpson, N. 1983 (Aberdeen) 5
Simpson, R. C. 1967 (Celtic) 5
Sinclair, G. L. 1910 (Hearts) 3
Sinclair, J. W. E. 1966 (Leicester C) 1
Skene, L. H. 1904 (Queen's Park) 1
Sloan, T. 1904 (Third Lanark) 1
Smellie, R. 1887 (Queen's Park) 6
Smith, A. 1898 (Rangers) 20
Smith, D. 1966 (Aberdeen, Rangers) 2
Smith, G. 1947 (Hibernian) 18
Smith, H. G. 1988 (Hearts) 3
Smith, J. 1924 (Ayr U) 1
Smith, J. 1935 (Rangers) 2
Smith, J. 1968 (Aberdeen, Newcastle U) 4
Smith, J. 2003 (Celtic) 2
Smith, J. E. 1959 (Celtic) 2
Smith, Jas 1872 (Queen's Park) 1
Smith, John 1877 (Mauchline, Edinburgh University, Queen's Park) 10
Smith, N. 1897 (Rangers) 12
Smith, R. 1872 (Queen's Park) 2
Smith, T. M. 1934 (Kilmarnock, Preston NE) 2
Somers, P. 1905 (Celtic) 4
Somers, W. S. 1879 (Third Lanark, Queen's Park) 3
Somerville, G. 1886 (Queen's Park) 1
Souness, G. J. 1975 (Middlesbrough, Liverpool, Sampdoria) 54
Speedie, D. R. 1985 (Chelsea, Coventry C) 10
Speedie, F. 1903 (Rangers) 3
Speirs, J. H. 1908 (Rangers) 1
Spencer, J. 1995 (Chelsea, QPR) 14

Stanton, P. 1966 (Hibernian)	16
Stark, J. 1909 (Rangers)	2
Steel, W. 1947 (Morton, Derby Co, Dundee)	30
Steele, D. M. 1923 (Huddersfield)	3
Stein, C. 1969 (Rangers, Coventry C)	21
Stephen, J. F. 1947 (Bradford)	2
Stevenson, G. 1928 (Motherwell)	12
Stewart, A. 1888 (Queen's Park)	2
Stewart, A. 1894 (Third Lanark)	1
Stewart, D. 1888 (Dumbarton)	1
Stewart, D. 1893 (Queen's Park)	3
Stewart, D. S. 1978 (Leeds U)	1
Stewart, G. 1906 (Hibernian, Manchester C)	4
Stewart, J. 1977 (Kilmarnock, Middlesbrough)	2
Stewart, M. J. 2002 (Manchester U)	3
Stewart, R. 1981 (West Ham U)	10
Stewart, W. G. 1898 (Queen's Park)	2
Stockdale, R. K. 2002 (Middlesbrough)	5
Storrier, D. 1899 (Celtic)	3
Strachan, G. D. 1980 (Aberdeen, Manchester U, Leeds U)	50
Sturrock, P. 1981 (Dundee U)	20
Sullivan, N. 1997 (Wimbledon, Tottenham H)	28
Summers, W. 1926 (St Mirren)	1
Symon, J. S. 1939 (Rangers)	1
Tait, T. S. 1911 (Sunderland)	1
Taylor, J. 1872 (Queen's Park)	6
Taylor, J. D. 1892 (Dumbarton, St Mirren)	4
Taylor, W. 1892 (Hearts)	1
Teale, G. 2006 (Wigan Ath, Derby Co)	11
Telfer, P. N. 2000 (Coventry C)	1
Telfer, W. 1933 (Motherwell)	2
Telfer, W. D. 1954 (St Mirren)	1
Templeton, R. 1902 (Aston Villa, Newcastle U, Woolwich Arsenal, Kilmarnock)	11
Thompson, S. 2002 (Dundee U, Rangers)	16
Thomson, A. 1886 (Arthurlie)	1
Thomson, A. 1889 (Third Lanark)	1
Thomson, A. 1909 (Airdrieonians)	1
Thomson, A. 1926 (Celtic)	3
Thomson, C. 1904 (Hearts, Sunderland)	21
Thomson, C. 1937 (Sunderland)	1
Thomson, D. 1920 (Dundee)	1
Thomson, J. 1930 (Celtic)	4
Thomson, J. J. 1872 (Queen's Park)	3
Thomson, J. R. 1933 (Everton)	1
Thomson, R. 1932 (Celtic)	1
Thomson, R. W. 1927 (Falkirk)	1
Thomson, S. 1884 (Rangers)	2
Thomson, W. 1892 (Dumbarton)	4
Thomson, W. 1896 (Dundee)	1
Thomson, W. 1980 (St Mirren)	7
Thornton, W. 1947 (Rangers)	7
Toner, W. 1959 (Kilmarnock)	2
Townsley, T. 1926 (Falkirk)	1
Troup, A. 1920 (Dundee, Everton)	5
Turnbull, E. 1948 (Hibernian)	8
Turner, T. 1884 (Arthurlie)	1
Turner, W. 1885 (Pollokshields Ath)	2
Ure, J. F. 1962 (Dundee, Arsenal)	11
Urquhart, D. 1934 (Hibernian)	1
Vallance, T. 1877 (Rangers)	7
Venters, A. 1934 (Cowdenbeath, Rangers)	3
Waddell, T. S. 1891 (Queen's Park)	6
Waddell, W. 1947 (Rangers)	17

Wales, H. M. 1933 (Motherwell)	1
Walker, A. 1988 (Celtic)	3
Walker, F. 1922 (Third Lanark)	1
Walker, G. 1930 (St Mirren)	4
Walker, J. 1895 (Hearts, Rangers)	5
Walker, J. 1911 (Swindon T)	9
Walker, J. N. 1993 (Hearts, Partick Th)	2
Walker, R. 1900 (Hearts)	29
Walker, T. 1935 (Hearts)	20
Walker, W. 1909 (Clyde)	2
Wallace, I. A. 1978 (Coventry C)	3
Wallace, W. S. B. 1965 (Hearts, Celtic)	7
Wardhaugh, J. 1955 (Hearts)	2
Wark, J. 1979 (Ipswich T, Liverpool)	29
Watson, A. 1881 (Queen's Park)	3
Watson, J. 1903 (Sunderland, Middlesbrough)	6
Watson, J. 1948 (Motherwell, Huddersfield T)	2
Watson, J. A. K. 1878 (Rangers)	1
Watson, P. R. 1934 (Blackpool)	1
Watson, R. 1971 (Motherwell)	1
Watson, W. 1898 (Falkirk)	1
Watt, F. 1889 (Kilbirnie)	4
Watt, W. W. 1887 (Queen's Park)	1
Waugh, W. 1938 (Hearts)	1
Webster, A. 2003 (Hearts)	22
Weir, A. 1959 (Motherwell)	6
Weir, D. G. 1997 (Hearts, Everton, Rangers)	61
Weir, J. 1887 (Third Lanark)	1
Weir, J. B. 1872 (Queen's Park)	4
Weir, P. 1980 (St Mirren, Aberdeen)	6
White, John 1922 (Albion R, Hearts)	2
White, J. A. 1959 (Falkirk, Tottenham H)	22
White, W. 1907 (Bolton W)	2
Whitelaw, A. 1887 (Vale of Leven)	2
Whyte, D. 1988 (Celtic, Middlesbrough, Aberdeen)	12
Wilkie, L. 2002 (Dundee)	11
Williams, G. 2002 (Nottingham F)	5
Wilson, A. 1907 (Sheffield W)	6
Wilson, A. 1954 (Portsmouth)	1
Wilson, A. N. 1920 (Dunfermline, Middlesbrough)	12
Wilson, D. 1900 (Queen's Park)	1
Wilson, D. 1913 (Oldham Ath)	1
Wilson, D. 1961 (Rangers)	22
Wilson, G. W. 1904 (Hearts, Everton, Newcastle U)	6
Wilson, Hugh 1890 (Newmilns, Sunderland, Third Lanark)	4
Wilson, I. A. 1987 (Leicester C, Everton)	5
Wilson, J. 1888 (Vale of Leven)	4
Wilson, P. 1926 (Celtic)	4
Wilson, P. 1975 (Celtic)	1
Wilson, R. P. 1972 (Arsenal)	2
Winters, R. 1999 (Aberdeen)	1
Wiseman, W. 1927 (Queen's Park)	2
Wood, G. 1979 (Everton, Arsenal)	4
Woodburn, W. A. 1947 (Rangers)	24
Wotherspoon, D. N. 1872 (Queen's Park)	2
Wright, K. 1992 (Hibernian)	1
Wright, S. 1993 (Aberdeen)	2
Wright, T. 1953 (Sunderland)	3
Wylie, T. G. 1890 (Rangers)	1
Yeats, R. 1965 (Liverpool)	2
Yorston, B. C. 1931 (Aberdeen)	1
Yorston, H. 1955 (Aberdeen)	1
Young, A. 1905 (Everton)	2
Young, A. 1960 (Hearts, Everton)	8
Young, G. L. 1947 (Rangers)	53
Young, J. 1906 (Celtic)	1
Younger, T. 1955 (Hibernian, Liverpool)	24

WALES

Adams, H. 1882 (Berwyn R, Druids) 4
Aizlewood, M. 1986 (Charlton Ath, Leeds U, Bradford C, Bristol C, Cardiff C) 39
Allchurch, I. J. 1951 (Swansea T, Newcastle U, Cardiff C, Swansea T) 68
Allchurch, L. 1955 (Swansea T, Sheffield U) 11
Allen, B. W. 1951 (Coventry C) 2
Allen, M. 1986 (Watford, Norwich C, Millwall, Newcastle U) 14
Arridge, S. 1892 (Bootle, Everton, New Brighton Tower) 8
Astley, D. J. 1931 (Charlton Ath, Aston Villa, Derby Co, Blackpool) 13
Atherton, R. W. 1899 (Hibernian, Middlesbrough) 9

Bailiff, W. E. 1913 (Llanelly) 4
Baker, C. W. 1958 (Cardiff C) 7
Baker, W. G. 1948 (Cardiff C) 1
Bale, G. 2006 (Southampton, Tottenham H) 11
Bamford, T. 1931 (Wrexham) 5
Barnard, D. S. 1998 (Barnsley, Grimsby T) 22
Barnes, W. 1948 (Arsenal) 22
Bartley, T. 1898 (Glossop NE) 1
Bastock, A. M. 1892 (Shrewsbury T) 1
Beadles, G. H. 1925 (Cardiff C) 2
Bell, W. S. 1881 (Shrewsbury Engineers, Crewe Alex) 5
Bellamy, C. D. 1998 (Norwich C, Coventry C, Newcastle U, Blackburn R, Liverpool, West Ham U) 51
Bennion, S. R. 1926 (Manchester U) 10
Berry, G. F. 1979 (Wolverhampton W, Stoke C) 5
Blackmore, C. G. 1985 (Manchester U, Middlesbrough) 39
Blake, N. A. 1994 (Sheffield U, Bolton W, Blackburn R, Wolverhampton W) 29
Blew, H. 1899 (Wrexham) 22
Boden, T. 1880 (Wrexham) 1
Bodin, P. J. 1990 (Swindon T, C Palace, Swindon T) 23
Boulter, L. M. 1939 (Brentford) 1
Bowdler, H. E. 1893 (Shrewsbury T) 1
Bowdler, J. C. H. 1890 (Shrewsbury T, Wolverhampton W, Shrewsbury T) 4
Bowen, D. L. 1955 (Arsenal) 19
Bowen, E. 1880 (Druids) 2
Bowen, J. P. 1994 (Swansea C, Birmingham C) 2
Bowen, M. R. 1986 (Tottenham H, Norwich C, West Ham U) 41
Bowsher, S. J. 1929 (Burnley) 1
Boyle, T. 1981 (C Palace) 2
Britten, T. J. 1878 (Parkgrove, Presteigne) 2
Brookes, S. J. 1900 (Llandudno) 2
Brown, A. I. 1926 (Aberdare Ath) 1
Brown, J. R. 2006 (Gillingham, Blackburn R) 2
Browning, M. T. 1996 (Bristol R, Huddersfield T) 5
Bryan, T. 1886 (Oswestry) 2
Buckland, T. 1899 (Bangor) 1
Burgess, W. A. R. 1947 (Tottenham H) 32
Burke, T. 1883 (Wrexham, Newton Heath) 8
Burnett, T. B. 1877 (Ruabon) 1
Burton, A. D. 1963 (Norwich C, Newcastle U) 9
Butler, J. 1893 (Chirk) 3
Butler, W. T. 1900 (Druids) 2

Cartwright, L. 1974 (Coventry C, Wrexham) 7
Carty, T. See McCarthy (Wrexham).
Challen, J. B. 1887 (Corinthians, Wellingborough GS) 4
Chapman, T. 1894 (Newtown, Manchester C, Grimsby T) 7
Charles, J. M. 1981 (Swansea C, QPR, Oxford U) 19
Charles, M. 1955 (Swansea T, Arsenal, Cardiff C) 31
Charles, W. J. 1950 (Leeds U, Juventus, Leeds U, Cardiff C) 38
Clarke, R. J. 1949 (Manchester C) 22
Coleman, C. 1992 (C Palace, Blackburn R, Fulham) 32
Collier, D. J. 1921 (Grimsby T) 1
Collins, D. L. 2005 (Sunderland) 7
Collins, J. M. 2004 (Cardiff C, West Ham U) 24
Collins, W. S. 1931 (Llanelly) 1
Collison, J. D. 2008 (West Ham U) 2
Conde, C. 1884 (Chirk) 3
Cook, F. C. 1925 (Newport Co, Portsmouth) 8
Cornforth, J. M. 1995 (Swansea C) 2
Cotterill, D. R. G. B. 2006 (Bristol C, Wigan Ath) 11
Coyne, D. 1996 (Tranmere R, Grimsby T, Leicester C, Burnley, Tranmere R) 16
Crofts, A. L. 2006 (Gillingham) 12
Crompton, W. 1931 (Wrexham) 3
Cross, E. A. 1876 (Wrexham) 2
Crosse, K. 1879 (Druids) 3
Crossley, M. G. 1997 (Nottingham F, Middlesbrough, Fulham) 8
Crowe, V. H. 1959 (Aston Villa) 16
Cumner, R. H. 1939 (Arsenal) 3
Curtis, A. T. 1976 (Swansea C, Leeds U, Swansea C, Southampton, Cardiff C) 35
Curtis, E. R. 1928 (Cardiff C, Birmingham) 3

Daniel, R. W. 1951 (Arsenal, Sunderland) 21
Darvell, S. 1897 (Oxford University) 2
Davies, A. 1876 (Wrexham) 2
Davies, A. 1904 (Druids, Middlesbrough) 2
Davies, A. 1983 (Manchester U, Newcastle U, Swansea C, Bradford C) 13
Davies, A. O. 1885 (Barmouth, Swifts, Wrexham, Crewe Alex) 9
Davies, A. R. 2006 (Yeovil T) 1
Davies, A. T. 1891 (Shrewsbury T) 1
Davies, C. 1972 (Charlton Ath) 1
Davies, C. M. 2006 (Oxford U, Verona, Oldham Ath) 5
Davies, D. 1904 (Bolton W) 3
Davies, D. C. 1899 (Brecon, Hereford) 2
Davies, D. W. 1912 (Treharris, Oldham Ath) 2
Davies, E. Lloyd 1904 (Stoke, Northampton T) 16
Davies, E. R. 1953 (Newcastle U) 6
Davies, G. 1980 (Fulham, Manchester C) 16
Davies, Rev. H. 1928 (Wrexham) 1
Davies, Idwal 1923 (Liverpool Marine) 1
Davies, J. E. 1885 (Oswestry) 1
Davies, Jas 1878 (Wrexham) 1
Davies, John 1879 (Wrexham) 1
Davies, Jos 1888 (Newton Heath, Wolverhampton W) 7
Davies, Jos 1889 (Everton, Chirk, Ardwick, Sheffield U, Manchester C, Millwall, Reading) 11
Davies, J. P. 1883 (Druids) 2
Davies, Ll. 1907 (Wrexham, Everton, Wrexham) 13
Davies, L. S. 1922 (Cardiff C) 23
Davies, O. 1890 (Wrexham) 1
Davies, R. 1883 (Wrexham) 3
Davies, R. 1885 (Druids) 1
Davies, R. O. 1892 (Wrexham) 2
Davies, R. T. 1964 (Norwich C, Southampton, Portsmouth) 29
Davies, R. W. 1964 (Bolton W, Newcastle U, Manchester C, Manchester U, Blackpool) 34
Davies, S. 2001 (Tottenham H, Everton, Fulham) 50
Davies, S. I. 1996 (Manchester U) 1
Davies, Stanley 1920 (Preston NE, Everton, WBA, Rotherham U) 18
Davies, T. 1886 (Oswestry) 1
Davies, T. 1903 (Druids) 4
Davies, W. 1884 (Wrexham) 1
Davies, W. 1924 (Swansea T, Cardiff C, Notts Co) 17
Davies, William 1903 (Wrexham, Blackburn R) 11
Davies, W. C. 1908 (C Palace, WBA, C Palace) 4
Davies, W. D. 1975 (Everton, Wrexham, Swansea C) 52

Davies, W. H. 1876 (Oswestry) 4
Davis, G. 1978 (Wrexham) 3
Davis, W. O. 1913 (Millwall Ath) 5
Day, A. 1934 (Tottenham H) 1
Deacy, N. 1977 (PSV Eindhoven, Beringen) 12
Dearson, D. J. 1939 (Birmingham) 3
Delaney, M. A. 2000 (Aston Villa) 36
Derrett, S. C. 1969 (Cardiff C) 4
Dewey, F. T. 1931 (Cardiff Corinthians) 2
Dibble, A. 1986 (Luton T, Manchester C) 3
Doughty, J. 1886 (Druids, Newton Heath) 8
Doughty, R. 1888 (Newton Heath) 2
Duffy, R. M. 2006 (Portsmouth) 13
Durban, A. 1966 (Derby Co) 27
Dwyer, P. J. 1978 (Cardiff C) 10

Eardley, N, 2008 (Oldham Ath) 7
Earnshaw, R. 2002 (Cardiff C, WBA, Norwich C, Derby Co) 38
Easter, J. M. 2007 (Wycombe W, Plymouth Arg) 7
Eastwood, F. 2008 (Wolverhampton W) 9
Edwards, C. 1878 (Wrexham) 1
Edwards, C. N. H. 1996 (Swansea C) 1
Edwards, D. 2008 (Wolverhampton W) 5
Edwards, G. 1947 (Birmingham C, Cardiff C) 12
Edwards, H. 1878 (Wrexham Civil Service, Wrexham) 8
Edwards, J. H. 1876 (Wanderers) 1
Edwards, J. H. 1895 (Oswestry) 3
Edwards, J. H. 1898 (Aberystwyth) 1
Edwards, L. T. 1957 (Charlton Ath) 2
Edwards, R. I. 1978 (Chester, Wrexham) 4
Edwards, R. O. 2003 (Aston Villa, Wolverhampton W) 15
Edwards, R. W. 1998 (Bristol C) 4
Edwards, T. 1932 (Linfield) 1
Egan, W. 1892 (Chirk) 1
Ellis, B. 1932 (Motherwell) 6
Ellis, E. 1931 (Nunhead, Oswestry) 3
Emanuel, W. J. 1973 (Bristol C) 2
England, H. M. 1962 (Blackburn R, Tottenham H) 44
Evans, B. C. 1972 (Swansea C, Hereford U) 7
Evans, C. M. 2008 (Manchester C) 2
Evans, D. G. 1926 (Reading, Huddersfield T) 4
Evans, H. P. 1922 (Cardiff C) 6
Evans, I. 1976 (C Palace) 13
Evans, J. 1893 (Oswestry) 3
Evans, J. 1912 (Cardiff C) 8
Evans, J. H. 1922 (Southend U) 4
Evans, Len 1927 (Aberdare Ath, Cardiff C, Birmingham) 4
Evans, M. 1884 (Oswestry) 1
Evans, P. S. 2002 (Brentford, Bradford C) 2
Evans, R. 1902 (Clapton) 1
Evans, R. E. 1906 (Wrexham, Aston Villa, Sheffield U) 10
Evans, R. O. 1902 (Wrexham, Blackburn R, Coventry C) 10
Evans, R. S. 1964 (Swansea T) 1
Evans, S. J. 2007 (Wrexham) 6
Evans, T. J. 1927 (Clapton Orient, Newcastle U) 4
Evans, W. 1933 (Tottenham H) 6
Evans, W. A. W. 1876 (Oxford University) 2
Evans, W. G. 1890 (Bootle, Aston Villa) 3
Evelyn, E. C. 1887 (Crusaders) 1
Eyton-Jones, J. A. 1883 (Wrexham) 4

Farmer, G. 1885 (Oswestry) 2
Felgate, D. 1984 (Lincoln C) 1
Finnigan, R. J. 1930 (Wrexham) 1
Fletcher, C. N. 2004 (Bournemouth, West Ham U, C Palace) 29
Flynn, B. 1975 (Burnley, Leeds U, Burnley) 66
Ford, T. 1947 (Swansea T, Aston Villa, Sunderland, Cardiff C) 38
Foulkes, H. E. 1932 (WBA) 1
Foulkes, W. I. 1952 (Newcastle U) 11
Foulkes, W. T. 1884 (Oswestry) 2
Fowler, J. 1925 (Swansea T) 6
Freestone, R. 2000 (Swansea C) 1

Gabbidon, D. L. 2002 (Cardiff C, West Ham U) 40
Garner, G. 2006 (Leyton Orient) 1
Garner, J. 1896 (Aberystwyth) 1
Giggs, R. J. 1992 (Manchester U) 64
Giles, D. C. 1980 (Swansea C, C Palace) 12
Gillam, S. G. 1889 (Wrexham, Shrewsbury, Clapton) 5
Glascodine, G. 1879 (Wrexham) 1
Glover, E. M. 1932 (Grimsby T) 7
Godding, G. 1923 (Wrexham) 2
Godfrey, B. C. 1964 (Preston NE) 3
Goodwin, U. 1881 (Ruthin) 1
Goss, J. 1991 (Norwich C) 9
Gough, R. T. 1883 (Oswestry White Star) 1
Gray, A. 1924 (Oldham Ath, Manchester C, Manchester Central, Tranmere R, Chester) 24
Green, A. W. 1901 (Aston Villa, Notts Co, Nottingham F) 8
Green, C. R. 1965 (Birmingham C) 15
Green, G. H. 1938 (Charlton Ath) 4
Green, R. M. 1998 (Wolverhampton W) 2
Grey, Dr W. 1876 (Druids) 2
Griffiths, A. T. 1971 (Wrexham) 17
Griffiths, F. J. 1900 (Blackpool) 2
Griffiths, G. 1887 (Chirk) 1
Griffiths, J. H. 1953 (Swansea T) 1
Griffiths, L. 1902 (Wrexham) 1
Griffiths, M. W. 1947 (Leicester C) 11
Griffiths, P. 1884 (Chirk) 6
Griffiths, P. H. 1932 (Everton) 1
Griffiths, T. P. 1927 (Everton, Bolton W, Middlesbrough, Aston Villa) 21
Gunter, C. 2007 (Cardiff C, Tottenham H) 6

Hall, G. D. 1988 (Chelsea) 9
Hallam, J. 1889 (Oswestry) 1
Hanford, H. 1934 (Swansea T, Sheffield W) 7
Harrington, A. C. 1956 (Cardiff C) 11
Harris, C. S. 1976 (Leeds U) 24
Harris, W. C. 1954 (Middlesbrough) 6
Harrison, W. C. 1899 (Wrexham) 5
Hartson, J. 1995 (Arsenal, West Ham U, Wimbledon, Coventry C, Celtic) 51
Haworth, S. O. 1997 (Cardiff C, Coventry C) 5
Hayes, A. 1890 (Wrexham) 2
Hennessey, W. R. 2007 (Wolverhampton W) 10
Hennessey, W. T. 1962 (Birmingham C, Nottingham F, Derby Co) 39
Hersee, A. M. 1886 (Bangor) 2
Hersee, R. 1886 (Llandudno) 1
Hewitt, R. 1958 (Cardiff C) 5
Hewitt, T. J. 1911 (Wrexham, Chelsea, South Liverpool) 8
Heywood, D. 1879 (Druids) 1
Hibbott, H. 1880 (Newtown Excelsior, Newtown) 3
Higham, G. G. 1878 (Oswestry) 2
Hill, M. R. 1972 (Ipswich T) 2
Hockey, T. 1972 (Sheffield U, Norwich C, Aston Villa) 9
Hoddinott, T. F. 1921 (Watford) 2
Hodges, G. 1984 (Wimbledon, Newcastle U, Watford, Sheffield U) 18
Hodgkinson, A. V. 1908 (Southampton) 1
Holden, A. 1984 (Chester C) 1
Hole, B. G. 1963 (Cardiff C, Blackburn R, Aston Villa, Swansea C) 30
Hole, W. J. 1921 (Swansea T) 9

Hollins, D. M. 1962 (Newcastle U) 11
Hopkins, I. J. 1935 (Brentford) 12
Hopkins, J. 1983 (Fulham, C Palace) 16
Hopkins, M. 1956 (Tottenham H) 34
Horne, B. 1988 (Portsmouth, Southampton, Everton, Birmingham C) 59
Howell, E. G. 1888 (Builth) 3
Howells, R. G. 1954 (Cardiff C) 2
Hugh, A. R. 1930 (Newport Co) 1
Hughes, A. 1894 (Rhos) 2
Hughes, A. 1907 (Chirk) 1
Hughes, C. M. 1992 (Luton T, Wimbledon) 8
Hughes, E. 1899 (Everton, Tottenham H) 14
Hughes, E. 1906 (Wrexham, Nottingham F, Wrexham, Manchester C) 16
Hughes, F. W. 1882 (Northwich Victoria) 6
Hughes, I. 1951 (Luton T) 4
Hughes, J. 1877 (Cambridge University, Aberystwyth) 2
Hughes, J. 1905 (Liverpool) 3
Hughes, J. I. 1935 (Blackburn R) 1
Hughes, L. M. 1984 (Manchester U, Barcelona, Manchester U, Chelsea, Southampton) 72
Hughes, P. W. 1887 (Bangor) 3
Hughes, W. 1891 (Bootle) 3
Hughes, W. A. 1949 (Blackburn R) 5
Hughes, W. M. 1938 (Birmingham) 10
Humphreys, J. V. 1947 (Everton) 1
Humphreys, R. 1888 (Druids) 1
Hunter, A. H. 1887 (FA of Wales Secretary) 1

Jackett, K. 1983 (Watford) 31
Jackson, W. 1899 (St Helens Rec) 1
James, E. 1893 (Chirk) 8
James, E. G. 1966 (Blackpool) 9
James, L. 1972 (Burnley, Derby Co, QPR, Burnley, Swansea C, Sunderland) 54
James, R. M. 1979 (Swansea C, Stoke C, QPR, Leicester C, Swansea C) 47
James, W. 1931 (West Ham U) 2
Jarrett, R. H. 1889 (Ruthin) 2
Jarvis, A. L. 1967 (Hull C) 3
Jenkins, E. 1925 (Lovell's Ath) 1
Jenkins, J. 1924 (Brighton & HA) 8
Jenkins, R. W. 1902 (Rhyl) 1
Jenkins, S. R. 1996 (Swansea C, Huddersfield T) 16
Jenkyns, C. A. L. 1892 (Small Heath, Woolwich Arsenal, Newton Heath, Walsall) 8
Jennings, W. 1914 (Bolton W) 11
John, R. F. 1923 (Arsenal) 15
John, W. R. 1931 (Walsall, Stoke C, Preston NE, Sheffield U, Swansea T) 14
Johnson, A. J. 1999 (Nottingham F, WBA) 15
Johnson, M. G. 1964 (Swansea T) 1
Jones, A. 1987 (Port Vale, Charlton Ath) 6
Jones, A. F. 1877 (Oxford University) 1
Jones, A. T. 1905 (Nottingham F, Notts Co) 2
Jones, Bryn 1935 (Wolverhampton W, Arsenal) 17
Jones, B. S. 1963 (Swansea T, Plymouth Arg, Cardiff C) 15
Jones, Charlie 1926 (Nottingham F, Arsenal) 8
Jones, Cliff 1954 (Swansea T, Tottenham H, Fulham) 59
Jones, C. W. 1935 (Birmingham) 2
Jones, D. 1888 (Chirk, Bolton W, Manchester C) 14
Jones, D. E. 1976 (Norwich C) 8
Jones, D. O. 1934 (Leicester C) 7
Jones, Evan 1910 (Chelsea, Oldham Ath, Bolton W) 7
Jones, F. R. 1885 (Bangor) 3
Jones, F. W. 1893 (Small Heath) 1
Jones, G. P. 1907 (Wrexham) 2
Jones, H. 1902 (Aberaman) 1
Jones, Humphrey 1885 (Bangor, Queen's Park, East Stirlingshire, Queen's Park) 14
Jones, Ivor 1920 (Swansea T, WBA) 10
Jones, Jeffrey 1908 (Llandrindod Wells) 3
Jones, J. 1876 (Druids) 1
Jones, J. 1883 (Berwyn Rangers) 3
Jones, J. 1925 (Wrexham) 1
Jones, J. L. 1895 (Sheffield U, Tottenham H) 21
Jones, J. Love 1906 (Stoke, Middlesbrough) 2
Jones, J. O. 1901 (Bangor) 2
Jones, J. P. 1976 (Liverpool, Wrexham, Chelsea, Huddersfield T) 72
Jones, J. T. 1912 (Stoke, C Palace) 15
Jones, K. 1950 (Aston Villa) 1
Jones, Leslie J. 1933 (Cardiff C, Coventry C, Arsenal) 11
Jones, M. A. 2007 (Wrexham) 2
Jones, M. G. 2000 (Leeds U, Leicester C) 13
Jones, P. L. 1997 (Liverpool, Tranmere R) 2
Jones, P. S. 1997 (Stockport Co, Southampton, Wolverhampton W, QPR) 50
Jones, P. W. 1971 (Bristol R) 1
Jones, R. 1887 (Bangor, Crewe Alex) 3
Jones, R. 1898 (Leicester Fosse) 1
Jones, R. 1899 (Druids) 1
Jones, R. 1900 (Bangor) 2
Jones, R. 1906 (Millwall) 2
Jones, R. A. 1884 (Druids) 4
Jones, R. A. 1994 (Sheffield W) 1
Jones, R. S. 1894 (Everton) 1
Jones, S. 1887 (Wrexham, Chester) 2
Jones, S. 1893 (Wrexham, Burton Swifts, Druids) 6
Jones, T. 1926 (Manchester U) 4
Jones, T. D. 1908 (Aberdare) 1
Jones, T. G. 1938 (Everton) 17
Jones, T. J. 1932 (Sheffield W) 2
Jones, V. P. 1995 (Wimbledon) 9
Jones, W. E. A. 1947 (Swansea T, Tottenham H) 4
Jones, W. J. 1901 (Aberdare, West Ham U) 4
Jones, W. Lot 1905 (Manchester C, Southend U) 20
Jones, W. P. 1889 (Druids, Wynnstay) 4
Jones, W. R. 1897 (Aberystwyth) 1

Keenor, F. C. 1920 (Cardiff C, Crewe Alex) 32
Kelly, F. C. 1899 (Wrexham, Druids) 3
Kelsey, A. J. 1954 (Arsenal) 41
Kenrick, S. L. 1876 (Druids, Oswestry, Shropshire Wanderers) 5
Ketley, C. F. 1882 (Druids) 1
King, J. 1955 (Swansea T) 1
Kinsey, N. 1951 (Norwich C, Birmingham C) 7
Knill, A. R. 1989 (Swansea C) 1
Koumas, J. 2001 (Tranmere R, WBA, Wigan Ath) 29
Krzywicki, R. L. 1970 (WBA, Huddersfield T) 8

Lambert, R. 1947 (Liverpool) 5
Latham, G. 1905 (Liverpool, Southport Central, Cardiff C) 10
Law, B. J. 1990 (QPR) 1
Lawrence, E. 1930 (Clapton Orient, Notts Co) 2
Lawrence, S. 1932 (Swansea T) 8
Lea, A. 1889 (Wrexham) 4
Lea, C. 1965 (Ipswich T) 2
Leary, P. 1889 (Bangor) 1
Ledley, J. C. 2006 (Cardiff C) 22
Leek, K. 1961 (Leicester C, Newcastle U, Birmingham C, Northampton T) 13
Legg, A. 1996 (Birmingham C, Cardiff C) 6
Lever, A. R. 1953 (Leicester C) 1
Lewis, B. 1891 (Chester, Wrexham, Middlesbrough, Wrexham) 10
Lewis, D. 1927 (Arsenal) 3
Lewis, D. 1983 (Swansea C) 1
Lewis, D. J. 1933 (Swansea T) 2
Lewis, D. M. 1890 (Bangor) 2
Lewis, J. 1906 (Bristol R) 1
Lewis, J. 1926 (Cardiff C) 1

Lewis, T. 1881 (Wrexham) 2
Lewis, W. 1885 (Bangor, Crewe Alex, Chester, Manchester C, Chester) 27
Lewis, W. L. 1927 (Swansea T, Huddersfield T) 6
Llewellyn, C. M. 1998 (Norwich C, Wrexham) 6
Lloyd, B. W. 1976 (Wrexham) 3
Lloyd, J. W. 1879 (Wrexham, Newtown) 2
Lloyd, R. A. 1891 (Ruthin) 2
Lockley, A. 1898 (Chirk) 1
Lovell, S. 1982 (C Palace, Millwall) 6
Lowndes, S. R. 1983 (Newport Co, Millwall, Barnsley) 10
Lowrie, G. 1948 (Coventry C, Newcastle U) 4
Lucas, P. M. 1962 (Leyton Orient) 4
Lucas, W. H. 1949 (Swansea T) 7
Lumberg, A. 1929 (Wrexham, Wolverhampton W) 4

McCarthy, T. P. 1889 (Wrexham) 1
McMillan, R. 1881 (Shrewsbury Engineers) 2
Maguire, G. T. 1990 (Portsmouth) 7
Mahoney, J. F. 1968 (Stoke C, Middlesbrough, Swansea C) 51
Mardon, P. J. 1996 (WBA) 1
Margetson, M. W. 2004 (Cardiff C) 1
Marriott, A. 1996 (Wrexham) 5
Martin, T. J. 1930 (Newport Co) 1
Marustik, C. 1982 (Swansea C) 6
Mates, J. 1891 (Chirk) 3
Matthews, R. W. 1921 (Liverpool, Bristol C, Bradford) 3
Matthews, W. 1905 (Chester) 2
Matthias, J. S. 1896 (Brymbo, Shrewsbury T, Wolverhampton W) 5
Matthias, T. J. 1914 (Wrexham) 12
Mays, A. W. 1929 (Wrexham) 1
Medwin, T. C. 1953 (Swansea T, Tottenham H) 30
Melville, A. K. 1990 (Swansea C, Oxford U, Sunderland, Fulham, West Ham U) 65
Meredith, S. 1900 (Chirk, Stoke, Leyton) 8
Meredith, W. H. 1895 (Manchester C, Manchester U) 48
Mielczarek, R. 1971 (Rotherham U) 1
Millership, H. 1920 (Rotherham Co) 6
Millington, A. H. 1963 (WBA, C Palace, Peterborough U, Swansea C) 21
Mills, T. J. 1934 (Clapton Orient, Leicester C) 4
Mills-Roberts, R. H. 1885 (St Thomas' Hospital, Preston NE, Llanberis) 8
Moore, G. 1960 (Cardiff C, Chelsea, Manchester U, Northampton T, Charlton Ath) 21
Morgan, C. 2007 (Milton Keynes D, Peterborough U) 8
Morgan, J. R. 1877 (Cambridge University, Derby School Staff) 10
Morgan, J. T. 1905 (Wrexham) 1
Morgan-Owen, H. 1902 (Oxford University, Corinthians) 4
Morgan-Owen, M. M. 1897 (Oxford University, Corinthians) 13
Morley, E. J. 1925 (Swansea T, Clapton Orient) 4
Morris, A. G. 1896 (Aberystwyth, Swindon T, Nottingham F) 21
Morris, C. 1900 (Chirk, Derby Co, Huddersfield T) 27
Morris, E. 1893 (Chirk) 3
Morris, H. 1894 (Sheffield U, Manchester C, Grimsby T) 3
Morris, J. 1887 (Oswestry) 1
Morris, J. 1898 (Chirk) 1
Morris, R. 1900 (Chirk, Shrewsbury T) 6
Morris, R. 1902 (Newtown, Druids, Liverpool, Leeds C, Grimsby T, Plymouth Arg) 11
Morris, S. 1937 (Birmingham) 5
Morris, W. 1947 (Burnley) 5
Moulsdale, J. R. B. 1925 (Corinthians) 1
Murphy, J. P. 1933 (WBA) 15
Myhill, G. O. 2008 (Hull C) 1

Nardiello, D. 1978 (Coventry C) 2
Nardiello, D. A. 2007 (Barnsley, QPR) 3
Neal, J. E. 1931 (Colwyn Bay) 2
Neilson, A. B. 1992 (Newcastle U, Southampton) 5
Newnes, J. 1926 (Nelson) 1
Newton, L. F. 1912 (Cardiff Corinthians) 1
Nicholas, D. S. 1923 (Stoke, Swansea T) 3
Nicholas, P. 1979 (C Palace, Arsenal, C Palace, Luton T, Aberdeen, Chelsea, Watford) 73
Nicholls, J. 1924 (Newport Co, Cardiff C) 4
Niedzwiecki, E. A. 1985 (Chelsea) 2
Nock, W. 1897 (Newtown) 1
Nogan, L. M. 1992 (Watford, Reading) 2
Norman, A. J. 1986 (Hull C) 5
Nurse, M. T. G. 1960 (Swansea T, Middlesbrough) 12
Nyatanga, L. J. 2006 (Derby Co) 21

O'Callaghan, E. 1929 (Tottenham H) 11
Oliver, A. 1905 (Bangor, Blackburn R) 2
Oster, J. M. 1998 (Everton, Sunderland) 13
O'Sullivan, P. A. 1973 (Brighton & HA) 3
Owen, D. 1879 (Oswestry) 1
Owen, E. 1884 (Ruthin Grammar School) 3
Owen, G. 1888 (Chirk, Newton Heath, Chirk) 4
Owen, J. 1892 (Newton Heath) 1
Owen, T. 1879 (Oswestry) 1
Owen, Trevor 1899 (Crewe Alex) 2
Owen, W. 1884 (Chirk) 16
Owen, W. P. 1880 (Ruthin) 12
Owens, J. 1902 (Wrexham) 1

Page, M. E. 1971 (Birmingham C) 28
Page, R. J. 1997 (Watford, Sheffield U, Cardiff C, Coventry C) 41
Palmer, D. 1957 (Swansea T) 3
Parris, J. E. 1932 (Bradford) 1
Parry, B. J. 1951 (Swansea T) 1
Parry, C. 1891 (Everton, Newtown) 13
Parry, E. 1922 (Liverpool) 5
Parry, M. 1901 (Liverpool) 16
Parry, P. I. 2004 (Cardiff C) 11
Parry, T. D. 1900 (Oswestry) 7
Parry, W. 1895 (Newtown) 1
Partridge, D. W. 2005 (Motherwell, Bristol C) 7
Pascoe, C. 1984 (Swansea C, Sunderland) 10
Paul, R. 1949 (Swansea T, Manchester C) 33
Peake, E. 1908 (Aberystwyth, Liverpool) 11
Peers, E. J. 1914 (Wolverhampton W, Port Vale) 12
Pembridge, M. A. 1992 (Luton T, Derby Co, Sheffield W, Benfica, Everton, Fulham) 54
Perry, E. 1938 (Doncaster R) 3
Perry, J. 1994 (Cardiff C) 1
Phennah, E. 1878 (Civil Service) 1
Phillips, C. 1931 (Wolverhampton W, Aston Villa) 13
Phillips, D. 1984 (Plymouth Arg, Manchester C, Coventry C, Norwich C, Nottingham F) 62
Phillips, L. 1971 (Cardiff C, Aston Villa, Swansea C, Charlton Ath) 58
Phillips, T. J. S. 1973 (Chelsea) 4
Phoenix, H. 1882 (Wrexham) 1
Pipe, D. R. 2003 (Coventry C) 1
Poland, G. 1939 (Wrexham) 2
Pontin, K. 1980 (Cardiff C) 2
Powell, A. 1947 (Leeds U, Everton, Birmingham C) 8
Powell, D. 1968 (Wrexham, Sheffield U) 11
Powell, I. V. 1947 (QPR, Aston Villa) 8
Powell, J. 1878 (Druids, Bolton W, Newton Heath) 15
Powell, Seth 1885 (Oswestry, WBA) 7
Price, H. 1907 (Aston Villa, Burton U, Wrexham) 5
Price, J. 1877 (Wrexham) 12
Price, L. P. 2006 (Ipswich T, Derby Co) 6
Price, P. 1980 (Luton T, Tottenham H) 25
Pring, K. D. 1966 (Rotherham U) 3

Pritchard, H. K. 1985 (Bristol C) 1
Pryce-Jones, A. W. 1895 (Newtown) 1
Pryce-Jones, W. E. 1887 (Cambridge University) 5
Pugh, A. 1889 (Rhostyllen) 1
Pugh, D. H. 1896 (Wrexham, Lincoln C) 7
Pugsley, J. 1930 (Charlton Ath) 1
Pullen, W. J. 1926 (Plymouth Arg) 1

Rankmore, F. E. J. 1966 (Peterborough U) 1
Ratcliffe, K. 1981 (Everton, Cardiff C) 59
Rea, J. C. 1894 (Aberystwyth) 9
Ready, K. 1997 (QPR) 5
Reece, G. I. 1966 (Sheffield U, Cardiff C) 29
Reed, W. G. 1955 (Ipswich T) 2
Rees, A. 1984 (Birmingham C) 1
Rees, J. M. 1992 (Luton T) 1
Rees, R. R. 1965 (Coventry C, WBA, Nottingham F) 39
Rees, W. 1949 (Cardiff C, Tottenham H) 4
Richards, A. 1932 (Barnsley) 1
Richards, D. 1931 (Wolverhampton W, Brentford, Birmingham) 21
Richards, G. 1899 (Druids, Oswestry, Shrewsbury T) 6
Richards, R. W. 1920 (Wolverhampton W, West Ham U, Mold) 9
Richards, S. V. 1947 (Cardiff C) 1
Richards, W. E. 1933 (Fulham) 1
Ricketts, S. 2005 (Swansea C, Hull C) 28
Roach, J. 1885 (Oswestry) 1
Robbins, W. W. 1931 (Cardiff C, WBA) 11
Roberts, A. M. 1993 (QPR) 2
Roberts, D. F. 1973 (Oxford U, Hull C) 17
Roberts, G. W. 2000 (Tranmere R) 9
Roberts, I. W. 1990 (Watford, Huddersfield T, Leicester C, Norwich C) 15
Roberts, Jas 1913 (Wrexham) 2
Roberts, J. 1879 (Corwen, Berwyn R) 7
Roberts, J. 1881 (Ruthin) 2
Roberts, J. 1906 (Bradford C) 2
Roberts, J. G. 1971 (Arsenal, Birmingham C) 22
Roberts, J. H. 1949 (Bolton W) 1
Roberts, N. W. 2000 (Wrexham, Wigan Ath) 4
Roberts, P. S. 1974 (Portsmouth) 4
Roberts, R. 1884 (Druids, Bolton W, Preston NE) 9
Roberts, R. 1886 (Wrexham) 3
Roberts, R. 1891 (Rhos, Crewe Alex) 2
Roberts, R. L. 1890 (Chester) 1
Roberts, S. W. 2005 (Wrexham) 1
Roberts, W. 1879 (Llangollen, Berwyn R) 6
Roberts, W. 1883 (Rhyl) 1
Roberts, W. 1886 (Wrexham) 4
Roberts, W. H. 1882 (Ruthin, Rhyl) 6
Robinson, C. P. 2000 (Wolverhampton W, Portsmouth, Sunderland, Norwich C, Toronto Lynx) 46
Robinson, J. R. C. 1996 (Charlton Ath) 30
Rodrigues, P. J. 1965 (Cardiff C, Leicester C, Sheffield W) 40
Rogers, J. P. 1896 (Wrexham) 3
Rogers, W. 1931 (Wrexham) 2
Roose, L. R. 1900 (Aberystwyth, London Welsh, Stoke, Everton, Stoke, Sunderland) 24
Rouse, R. V. 1959 (C Palace) 1
Rowlands, A. C. 1914 (Tranmere R) 1
Rowley, T. 1959 (Tranmere R) 1
Rush, I. 1980 (Liverpool, Juventus, Liverpool) 73
Russell, M. R. 1912 (Merthyr T, Plymouth Arg) 23

Sabine, H. W. 1887 (Oswestry) 1
Saunders, D. 1986 (Brighton & HA, Oxford U, Derby Co, Liverpool, Aston Villa, Galatasaray, Nottingham F, Sheffield U, Benfica, Bradford C) 75
Savage, R. W. 1996 (Crewe Alex, Leicester C, Birmingham C) 39
Savin, G. 1878 (Oswestry) 1
Sayer, P. A. 1977 (Cardiff C) 7
Scrine, F. H. 1950 (Swansea T) 2
Sear, C. R. 1963 (Manchester C) 1
Shaw, E. G. 1882 (Oswestry) 3
Sherwood, A. T. 1947 (Cardiff C, Newport Co) 41
Shone, W. W. 1879 (Oswestry) 1
Shortt, W. W. 1947 (Plymouth Arg) 12
Showers, D. 1975 (Cardiff C) 2
Sidlow, C. 1947 (Liverpool) 7
Sisson, H. 1885 (Wrexham Olympic) 3
Slatter, N. 1983 (Bristol R, Oxford U) 22
Smallman, D. P. 1974 (Wrexham, Everton) 7
Southall, N. 1982 (Everton) 92
Speed, G. A. 1990 (Leeds U, Everton, Newcastle U, Bolton W) 85
Sprake, G. 1964 (Leeds U, Birmingham C) 37
Stansfield, F. 1949 (Cardiff C) 1
Stevenson, B. 1978 (Leeds U, Birmingham C) 15
Stevenson, N. 1982 (Swansea C) 4
Stitfall, R. F. 1953 (Cardiff C) 2
Sullivan, D. 1953 (Cardiff C) 17
Symons, C. J. 1992 (Portsmouth, Manchester C, Fulham, C Palace) 37

Tapscott, D. R. 1954 (Arsenal, Cardiff C) 14
Taylor, G. K. 1996 (C Palace, Sheffield U, Burnley, Nottingham F) 15
Taylor, J. 1898 (Wrexham) 1
Taylor, O. D. S. 1893 (Newtown) 4
Thatcher, B. D. 2004 (Leicester C, Manchester C) 7
Thomas, C. 1899 (Druids) 2
Thomas, D. A. 1957 (Swansea T) 2
Thomas, D. S. 1948 (Fulham) 4
Thomas, E. 1925 (Cardiff Corinthians) 1
Thomas, G. 1885 (Wrexham) 2
Thomas, H. 1927 (Manchester U) 1
Thomas, Martin R. 1987 (Newcastle U) 1
Thomas, Mickey 1977 (Wrexham, Manchester U, Everton, Brighton & HA, Stoke C, Chelsea, WBA) 51
Thomas, R. J. 1967 (Swindon T, Derby Co, Cardiff C) 50
Thomas, T. 1898 (Bangor) 2
Thomas, W. R. 1931 (Newport Co) 2
Thomson, D. 1876 (Druids) 1
Thomson, G. F. 1876 (Druids) 2
Toshack, J. B. 1969 (Cardiff C, Liverpool, Swansea C) 40
Townsend, W. 1887 (Newtown) 2
Trainer, H. 1895 (Wrexham) 3
Trainer, J. 1887 (Bolton W, Preston NE) 20
Trollope, P. J. 1997 (Derby Co, Fulham, Coventry C, Northampton T) 9
Tudur-Jones, O. 2008 (Swansea C) 2
Turner, H. G. 1937 (Charlton Ath) 8
Turner, J. 1892 (Wrexham) 1
Turner, R. E. 1891 (Wrexham) 2
Turner, W. H. 1887 (Wrexham) 5

Van Den Hauwe, P. W. R. 1985 (Everton) 13
Vaughan, D. O. 2003 (Crewe Alex, Real Sociedad) 13
Vaughan, Jas 1893 (Druids) 4
Vaughan, John 1879 (Oswestry, Druids, Bolton W) 11
Vaughan, J. O. 1885 (Rhyl) 4
Vaughan, N. 1983 (Newport Co, Cardiff C) 10
Vaughan, T. 1885 (Rhyl) 1
Vearncombe, G. 1958 (Cardiff C) 2
Vernon, T. R. 1957 (Blackburn R, Everton, Stoke C) 32
Villars, A. K. 1974 (Cardiff C) 3
Vizard, E. T. 1911 (Bolton W) 22
Vokes, S. M. 2008 (Bournemouth) 2

Walley, J. T. 1971 (Watford) 1
Walsh, I. P. 1980 (C Palace, Swansea C) 18
Ward, D. 1959 (Bristol R, Cardiff C) 2

Ward, D. 2000 (Notts Co, Nottingham F) 5
Warner, J. 1937 (Swansea T, Manchester U) 2
Warren, F. W. 1929 (Cardiff C, Middlesbrough, Hearts) 6
Watkins, A. E. 1898 (Leicester Fosse, Aston Villa, Millwall) 5
Watkins, W. M. 1902 (Stoke, Aston Villa, Sunderland, Stoke) 10
Webster, C. 1957 (Manchester U) 4
Weston, R. D. 2000 (Arsenal, Cardiff C) 7
Whatley, W. J. 1939 (Tottenham H) 2
White, P. F. 1896 (London Welsh) 1
Wilcock, A. R. 1890 (Oswestry) 1
Wilding, J. 1885 (Wrexham Olympians, Bootle, Wrexham) 9
Williams, A. 1994 (Reading, Wolverhampton W, Reading) 13
Williams, A. E. 2008 (Stockport Co) 3
Williams, A. L. 1931 (Wrexham) 1
Williams, A. P. 1998 (Southampton) 2
Williams, B. 1930 (Bristol C) 1
Williams, B. D. 1928 (Swansea T, Everton) 10
Williams, D. G. 1988 (Derby Co, Ipswich T) 13
Williams, D. M. 1986 (Norwich C) 5
Williams, D. R. 1921 (Merthyr T, Sheffield W, Manchester U) 8
Williams, E. 1893 (Crewe Alex) 2
Williams, E. 1901 (Druids) 5
Williams, G. 1893 (Chirk) 6
Williams, G. E. 1960 (WBA) 26
Williams, G. G. 1961 (Swansea T) 5
Williams, G. J. 2006 (West Ham U, Ipswich T) 2
Williams, G. J. J. 1951 (Cardiff C) 1
Williams, G. O. 1907 (Wrexham) 1
Williams, H. J. 1965 (Swansea T) 3
Williams, H. T. 1949 (Newport Co, Leeds U) 4
Williams, J. H. 1884 (Oswestry) 1
Williams, J. J. 1939 (Wrexham) 1
Williams, J. T. 1925 (Middlesbrough) 1
Williams, J. W. 1912 (C Palace) 2
Williams, R. 1935 (Newcastle U) 2
Williams, R. P. 1886 (Caernarvon) 1
Williams, S. G. 1954 (WBA, Southampton) 43
Williams, W. 1876 (Druids, Oswestry, Druids) 11
Williams, W. 1925 (Northampton T) 1
Witcomb, D. F. 1947 (WBA, Sheffield W) 3
Woosnam, A. P. 1959 (Leyton Orient, West Ham U, Aston Villa) 17
Woosnam, G. 1879 (Newtown Excelsior) 1
Worthington, T. 1894 (Newtown) 1
Wynn, G. A. 1909 (Wrexham, Manchester C) 11
Wynn, W. 1903 (Chirk) 1

Yorath, T. C. 1970 (Leeds U, Coventry C, Tottenham H, Vancouver W) 59
Young, E. 1990 (Wimbledon, C Palace, Wolverhampton W) 21

REPUBLIC OF IRELAND

Aherne, T. 1946 (Belfast Celtic, Luton T) 16
Aldridge, J. W. 1986 (Oxford U, Liverpool, Real Sociedad, Tranmere R) 69
Ambrose, P. 1955 (Shamrock R) 5
Anderson, J. 1980 (Preston NE, Newcastle U) 16
Andrews, P. 1936 (Bohemians) 1
Arrigan, T. 1938 (Waterford) 1

Babb, P. A. 1994 (Coventry C, Liverpool, Sunderland) 35
Bailham, E. 1964 (Shamrock R) 1
Barber, E. 1966 (Shelbourne, Birmingham C) 2
Barrett, G. 2003 (Arsenal, Coventry C) 6
Barry, P. 1928 (Fordsons) 2
Beglin, J. 1984 (Liverpool) 15
Bennett, A. J. 2007 (Reading) 2
Bermingham, J. 1929 (Bohemians) 1
Bermingham, P. 1935 (St James' Gate) 1
Bonner, P. 1981 (Celtic) 80
Braddish, S. 1978 (Dundalk) 2
Bradshaw, P. 1939 (St James' Gate) 5
Brady, F. 1926 (Fordsons) 2
Brady, T. R. 1964 (QPR) 6
Brady, W. L. 1975 (Arsenal, Juventus, Sampdoria, Internazionale, Ascoli, West Ham U) 72
Branagan, K. G. 1997 (Bolton W) 1
Breen, G. 1996 (Birmingham C, Coventry C, West Ham U, Sunderland) 63
Breen, T. 1937 (Manchester U, Shamrock R) 5
Brennan, F. 1965 (Drumcondra) 1
Brennan, S. A. 1965 (Manchester U, Waterford) 19
Brown, J. 1937 (Coventry C) 2
Browne, W. 1964 (Bohemians) 3
Bruce, A. 2007 (Ipswich T) 1
Buckley, L. 1984 (Shamrock R, Waregem) 2
Burke, F. 1952 (Cork Ath) 1
Burke, J. 1929 (Shamrock R) 1
Burke, J. 1934 (Cork) 1
Butler, P. J. 2000 (Sunderland) 1
Butler, T. 2003 (Sunderland) 2
Byrne, A. B. 1970 (Southampton) 14
Byrne, D. 1929 (Shelbourne, Shamrock R, Coleraine) 3
Byrne, J. 1928 (Bray Unknowns) 1
Byrne, J. 1985 (QPR, Le Havre, Brighton & HA, Sunderland, Millwall) 23
Byrne, J. 2004 (Shelbourne) 2
Byrne, P. 1931 (Dolphin, Shelbourne, Drumcondra) 3
Byrne, P. 1984 (Shamrock R) 8
Byrne, S. 1931 (Bohemians) 1

Campbell, A. 1985 (Santander) 3
Campbell, N. 1971 (St Patrick's Ath, Fortuna Cologne) 11
Cannon, H. 1926 (Bohemians) 2
Cantwell, N. 1954 (West Ham U, Manchester U) 36
Carey, B. P. 1992 (Manchester U, Leicester C) 3
Carey, J. J. 1938 (Manchester U) 29
Carolan, J. 1960 (Manchester U) 2
Carr, S. 1999 (Tottenham H, Newcastle U) 44
Carroll, B. 1949 (Shelbourne) 2
Carroll, T. R. 1968 (Ipswich T, Birmingham C) 17
Carsley, L. K. 1998 (Derby Co, Blackburn R, Coventry C, Everton) 39
Cascarino, A. G. 1986 (Gillingham, Millwall, Aston Villa, Celtic, Chelsea, Marseille, Nancy) 88
Chandler, J. 1980 (Leeds U) 2
Chatton, H. A. 1931 (Shelbourne, Dumbarton, Cork) 3
Clarke, C. R. 2004 (Stoke C) 2
Clarke, J. 1978 (Drogheda U) 1
Clarke, K. 1948 (Drumcondra) 2
Clarke, M. 1950 (Shamrock R) 1
Clinton, T. J. 1951 (Everton) 3
Coad, P. 1947 (Shamrock R) 11
Coffey, T. 1950 (Drumcondra) 1
Colfer, M. D. 1950 (Shelbourne) 2
Colgan, N. 2002 (Hibernian, Barnsley) 9
Collins, F. 1927 (Jacobs) 1
Conmy, O. M. 1965 (Peterborough U) 5
Connolly, D. J. 1996 (Watford, Feyenoord, Wolverhampton W, Excelsior, Feyenoord, Wimbledon, West Ham U, Wigan Ath) 41
Connolly, H. 1937 (Cork) 1
Connolly, J. 1926 (Fordsons) 1
Conroy, G. A. 1970 (Stoke C) 27

Conway, J. P. 1967 (Fulham, Manchester C) 20
Corr, P. J. 1949 (Everton) 4
Courtney, E. 1946 (Cork U) 1
Coyle, O. C. 1994 (Bolton W) 1
Coyne, T. 1992 (Celtic, Tranmere R, Motherwell) 22
Crowe, G. 2003 (Bohemians) 2
Cummins, G. P. 1954 (Luton T) 19
Cuneen, T. 1951 (Limerick) 1
Cunningham, K. 1996 (Wimbledon, Birmingham C) 72
Curtis, D. P. 1957 (Shelbourne, Bristol C, Ipswich T, Exeter C) 17
Cusack, S. 1953 (Limerick) 1

Daish, L. S. 1992 (Cambridge U, Coventry C) 5
Daly, G. A. 1973 (Manchester U, Derby Co, Coventry C, Birmingham C, Shrewsbury T) 48
Daly, J. 1932 (Shamrock R) 2
Daly, M. 1978 (Wolverhampton W) 2
Daly, P. 1950 (Shamrock R) 1
Davis, T. L. 1937 (Oldham Ath, Tranmere R) 4
Deacy, E. 1982 (Aston Villa) 4
Delaney, D. F. 2008 (QPR) 2
Delap, R. J. 1998 (Derby Co, Southampton) 11
De Mange, K. J. P. P. 1987 (Liverpool, Hull C) 2
Dempsey, J. T. 1967 (Fulham, Chelsea) 19
Dennehy, J. 1972 (Cork Hibernians, Nottingham F, Walsall) 11
Desmond, P. 1950 (Middlesbrough) 4
Devine, J. 1980 (Arsenal, Norwich C) 13
Doherty, G. M. T. 2000 (Luton T, Tottenham H, Norwich C) 34
Donnelly, J. 1935 (Dundalk) 10
Donnelly, T. 1938 (Drumcondra, Shamrock R) 2
Donovan, D. C. 1955 (Everton) 5
Donovan, T. 1980 (Aston Villa) 2
Douglas, J. 2004 (Blackburn R, Leeds U) 8
Dowdall, C. 1928 (Fordsons, Barnsley, Cork) 3
Doyle, C. 1959 (Shelbourne) 1
Doyle, Colin 2007 (Birmingham C) 1
Doyle, D. 1926 (Shamrock R) 1
Doyle, K. E. 2006 (Reading) 18
Doyle, L. 1932 (Dolphin) 1
Doyle, M. P. 2004 (Coventry C) 1
Duff, D. A. 1998 (Blackburn R, Chelsea, Newcastle U) 68
Duffy, B. 1950 (Shamrock R) 1
Duggan, H. A. 1927 (Leeds U, Newport Co) 5
Dunne, A. P. 1962 (Manchester U, Bolton W) 33
Dunne, J. 1930 (Sheffield U, Arsenal, Southampton, Shamrock R) 15
Dunne, J. C. 1971 (Fulham) 1
Dunne, L. 1935 (Manchester C) 2
Dunne, P. A. J. 1965 (Manchester U) 5
Dunne, R. P. 2000 (Everton, Manchester C) 42
Dunne, S. 1953 (Luton T) 15
Dunne, T. 1956 (St Patrick's Ath) 3
Dunning, P. 1971 (Shelbourne) 2
Dunphy, E. M. 1966 (York C, Millwall) 23
Dwyer, N. M. 1960 (West Ham U, Swansea T) 14

Eccles, P. 1986 (Shamrock R) 1
Egan, R. 1929 (Dundalk) 1
Eglington, T. J. 1946 (Shamrock R, Everton) 24
Elliott, S. W. 2005 (Sunderland) 9
Ellis, P. 1935 (Bohemians) 7
Evans, M. J. 1998 (Southampton) 1

Fagan, E. 1973 (Shamrock R) 1
Fagan, F. 1955 (Manchester C, Derby Co) 8
Fagan, J. 1926 (Shamrock R) 1
Fairclough, M. 1982 (Dundalk) 2
Fallon, S. 1951 (Celtic) 8
Fallon, W. J. 1935 (Notts Co, Sheffield W) 9
Farquharson, T. G. 1929 (Cardiff C) 4
Farrell, P. 1937 (Hibernian) 2
Farrell, P. D. 1946 (Shamrock R, Everton) 28
Farrelly, G. 1996 (Aston Villa, Everton, Bolton W) 6
Feenan, J. J. 1937 (Sunderland) 2
Finnan, S. 2000 (Fulham, Liverpool) 50
Finucane, A. 1967 (Limerick) 11
Fitzgerald, F. J. 1955 (Waterford) 2
Fitzgerald, P. J. 1961 (Leeds U, Chester) 5
Fitzpatrick, K. 1970 (Limerick) 1
Fitzsimons, A. G. 1950 (Middlesbrough, Lincoln C) 26
Fleming, C. 1996 (Middlesbrough) 10
Flood, J. J. 1926 (Shamrock R) 5
Fogarty, A. 1960 (Sunderland, Hartlepools U) 11
Foley, D. J. 2000 (Watford) 6
Foley, J. 1934 (Cork, Celtic) 7
Foley, M. 1926 (Shelbourne) 1
Foley, T. C. 1964 (Northampton T) 9
Foy, T. 1938 (Shamrock R) 2
Fullam, J. 1961 (Preston NE, Shamrock R) 11
Fullam, R. 1926 (Shamrock R) 2

Gallagher, C. 1967 (Celtic) 2
Gallagher, M. 1954 (Hibernian) 1
Gallagher, P. 1932 (Falkirk) 1
Galvin, A. 1983 (Tottenham H, Sheffield W, Swindon T) 29
Gamble, J. 2007 (Cork C) 2
Gannon, E. 1949 (Notts Co, Sheffield W, Shelbourne) 14
Gannon, M. 1972 (Shelbourne) 1
Gaskins, P. 1934 (Shamrock R, St James' Gate) 7
Gavin, J. T. 1950 (Norwich C, Tottenham H, Norwich C) 7
Geoghegan, M. 1937 (St James' Gate) 2
Gibbons, A. 1952 (St Patrick's Ath) 4
Gibson, D. T. D. 2008 (Manchester U) 2
Gilbert, R. 1966 (Shamrock R) 1
Giles, C. 1951 (Doncaster R) 1
Giles, M. J. 1960 (Manchester U, Leeds U, WBA, Shamrock R) 59
Given, S. J. J. 1996 (Blackburn R, Newcastle U) 86
Givens, D. J. 1969 (Manchester U, Luton T, QPR, Birmingham C, Neuchatel X) 56
Gleeson, S. M. 2007 (Wolverhampton W) 2
Glen, W. 1927 (Shamrock R) 8
Glynn, D. 1952 (Drumcondra) 2
Godwin, T. F. 1949 (Shamrock R, Leicester C, Bournemouth & BA) 13
Golding, J. 1928 (Shamrock R) 2
Goodman, J. 1997 (Wimbledon) 4
Goodwin, J. 2003 (Stockport Co) 1
Gorman, W. C. 1936 (Bury, Brentford) 13
Grace, J. 1926 (Drumcondra) 1
Grealish, A. 1976 (Orient, Luton T, Brighton & HA, WBA) 45
Gregg, E. 1978 (Bohemians) 8
Griffith, R. 1935 (Walsall) 1
Grimes, A. A. 1978 (Manchester U, Coventry C, Luton T) 18

Hale, A. 1962 (Aston Villa, Doncaster R, Waterford) 14
Hamilton, T. 1959 (Shamrock R) 2
Hand, E. K. 1969 (Portsmouth) 20
Harrington, W. 1936 (Cork) 5
Harte, I. P. 1996 (Leeds U, Levante) 64
Hartnett, J. B. 1949 (Middlesbrough) 2
Haverty, J. 1956 (Arsenal, Blackburn R, Millwall, Celtic, Bristol R, Shelbourne) 32
Hayes, A. W. P. 1979 (Southampton) 1
Hayes, W. E. 1947 (Huddersfield T) 2
Hayes, W. J. 1949 (Limerick) 1
Healey, R. 1977 (Cardiff C) 2
Healy, C. 2002 (Celtic, Sunderland) 13

Heighway, S. D. 1971 (Liverpool, Minnesota Kicks) 34
Henderson, B. 1948 (Drumcondra) 2
Henderson, W. C. P. 2006 (Brighton & HA, Preston NE) 6
Hennessy, J. 1965 (Shelbourne, St Patrick's Ath) 5
Herrick, J. 1972 (Cork Hibernians, Shamrock R) 3
Higgins, J. 1951 (Birmingham C) 1
Holland, M. R. 2000 (Ipswich T, Charlton Ath) 49
Holmes, J. 1971 (Coventry C, Tottenham H, Vancouver W) 30
Hoolahan, W. 2008 (Blackpool) 1
Horlacher, A. F. 1930 (Bohemians) 7
Houghton, R. J. 1986 (Oxford U, Liverpool, Aston Villa, C Palace, Reading) 73
Howlett, G. 1984 (Brighton & HA) 1
Hoy, M. 1938 (Dundalk) 6
Hughton, C. 1980 (Tottenham H, West Ham U) 53
Hunt, S. P. 2007 (Reading) 11
Hurley, C. J. 1957 (Millwall, Sunderland, Bolton W) 40
Hutchinson, F. 1935 (Drumcondra) 2

Ireland S .J. 2006 (Manchester C) 6
Irwin, D. J. 1991 (Manchester U) 56

Jordan, D. 1937 (Wolverhampton W) 2
Jordan, W. 1934 (Bohemians) 2

Kavanagh, G. A. 1998 (Stoke C, Cardiff C, Wigan Ath) 16
Kavanagh, P. J. 1931 (Celtic) 2
Keane, R. D. 1998 (Wolverhampton W, Coventry C, Internazionale, Leeds U, Tottenham H) 81
Keane, R. M. 1991 (Nottingham F, Manchester U) 67
Keane, T. R. 1949 (Swansea T) 4
Kearin, M. 1972 (Shamrock R) 1
Kearns, F. T. 1954 (West Ham U) 1
Kearns, M. 1971 (Oxford U, Walsall, Wolverhampton W) 18
Kelly, A. T. 1993 (Sheffield U, Blackburn R) 34
Kelly, D. T. 1988 (Walsall, West Ham U, Leicester C, Newcastle U, Wolverhampton W, Sunderland, Tranmere R) 26
Kelly, G. 1994 (Leeds U) 52
Kelly, J. 1932 (Derry C) 4
Kelly, J. A. 1957 (Drumcondra, Preston NE) 47
Kelly, J. P. V. 1961 (Wolverhampton W) 5
Kelly, M. J. 1988 (Portsmouth) 4
Kelly, N. 1954 (Nottingham F) 1
Kelly, S. M. 2006 (Tottenham H, Birmingham C) 11
Kendrick, J. 1927 (Everton, Dolphin) 4
Kenna, J. J. 1995 (Blackburn R) 27
Kennedy, M. F. 1986 (Portsmouth) 2
Kennedy, M. J. 1996 (Liverpool, Wimbledon, Manchester C, Wolverhampton W) 34
Kennedy, W. 1932 (St James' Gate) 3
Kenny, P. 2004 (Sheffield U) 7
Keogh, A. D. 2007 (Wolverhampton W) 7
Keogh, J. 1966 (Shamrock R) 1
Keogh, S. 1959 (Shamrock R) 1
Kernaghan, A. N. 1993 (Middlesbrough, Manchester C) 22
Kiely, D. L. 2000 (Charlton Ath, WBA) 10
Kiernan, F. W. 1951 (Shamrock R, Southampton) 5
Kilbane, K. D. 1998 (WBA, Sunderland, Everton, Wigan Ath) 87
Kinnear, J. P. 1967 (Tottenham H, Brighton & HA) 26
Kinsella, J. 1928 (Shelbourne) 1
Kinsella, M. A. 1998 (Charlton Ath, Aston Villa, WBA) 48
Kinsella, O. 1932 (Shamrock R) 2
Kirkland, A. 1927 (Shamrock R) 1

Lacey, W. 1927 (Shelbourne) 3
Langan, D. 1978 (Derby Co, Birmingham C, Oxford U) 26
Lapira, J. 2007 (Notre Dame) 1
Lawler, J. F. 1953 (Fulham) 8
Lawlor, J. C. 1949 (Drumcondra, Doncaster R) 3
Lawlor, M. 1971 (Shamrock R) 5
Lawrenson, M. 1977 (Preston NE, Brighton & HA, Liverpool) 39
Lee, A. D. 2003 (Rotherham U, Cardiff C, Ipswich T) 10
Leech, M. 1969 (Shamrock R) 8
Lennon, C. 1935 (St James' Gate) 3
Lennox, G. 1931 (Dolphin) 2
Long, S. P. 2007 (Reading) 8
Lowry, D. 1962 (St Patrick's Ath) 1
Lunn, R. 1939 (Dundalk) 2
Lynch, J. 1934 (Cork Bohemians) 1

McAlinden, J. 1946 (Portsmouth) 2
McAteer, J. W. 1994 (Bolton W, Liverpool, Blackburn R, Sunderland) 52
McCann, J. 1957 (Shamrock R) 1
McCarthy, J. 1926 (Bohemians) 3
McCarthy, M. 1932 (Shamrock R) 1
McCarthy, M. 1984 (Manchester C, Celtic, Lyon, Millwall) 57
McConville, T. 1972 (Dundalk, Waterford) 6
McDonagh, Jacko 1984 (Shamrock R) 3
McDonagh, J. 1981 (Everton, Bolton W, Notts Co, Wichita Wings) 25
McEvoy, M. A. 1961 (Blackburn R) 17
McGeady, A. 2004 (Celtic) 18
McGee, P. 1978 (QPR, Preston NE) 15
McGoldrick, E. J. 1992 (C Palace, Arsenal) 15
McGowan, D. 1949 (West Ham U) 3
McGowan, J. 1947 (Cork U) 1
McGrath, M. 1958 (Blackburn R, Bradford PA) 22
McGrath, P. 1985 (Manchester U, Aston Villa, Derby Co) 83
McGuire, W. 1936 (Bohemians) 1
Macken, A. 1977 (Derby Co) 1
Macken J. P. 2005 (Manchester C) 1
McKenzie, G. 1938 (Southend U) 9
Mackey, G. 1957 (Shamrock R) 3
McLoughlin, A. F. 1990 (Swindon T, Southampton, Portsmouth) 42
McLoughlin, F. 1930 (Fordsons, Cork) 2
McMillan, W. 1946 (Belfast Celtic) 2
McNally, J. B. 1959 (Luton T) 3
McPhail, S. 2000 (Leeds U) 10
McShane, P. D. 2007 (WBA, Sunderland) 11
Madden, O. 1936 (Cork) 1
Maguire, J. 1929 (Shamrock R) 1
Mahon, A. J. 2000 (Tranmere R) 2
Malone, G. 1949 (Shelbourne) 1
Mancini, T. J. 1974 (QPR, Arsenal) 5
Martin, C. 1927 (Bo'ness) 1
Martin, C. J. 1946 (Glentoran, Leeds U, Aston Villa) 30
Martin, M. P. 1972 (Bohemians, Manchester U, WBA, Newcastle U) 52
Maybury, A. 1998 (Leeds U, Hearts, Leicester C) 10
Meagan, M. K. 1961 (Everton, Huddersfield T, Drogheda) 17
Meehan, P. 1934 (Drumcondra) 1
Miller, L. W. P. 2004 (Celtic, Manchester U, Sunderland) 18
Milligan, M. J. 1992 (Oldham Ath) 1
Monahan, P. 1935 (Sligo R) 2
Mooney, J. 1965 (Shamrock R) 2
Moore, A. 1996 (Middlesbrough) 8
Moore, P. 1931 (Shamrock R, Aberdeen, Shamrock R) 9
Moran, K. 1980 (Manchester U, Sporting Gijon, Blackburn R) 71
Moroney, T. 1948 (West Ham U, Evergreen U) 12

Morris, C. B. 1988 (Celtic, Middlesbrough) 35
Morrison, C. H. 2002 (C Palace, Birmingham C, C Palace) 36
Moulson, C. 1936 (Lincoln C, Notts Co) 5
Moulson, G. B. 1948 (Lincoln C) 3
Muckian, C. 1978 (Drogheda U) 1
Muldoon, T. 1927 (Aston Villa) 1
Mulligan, P. M. 1969 (Shamrock R, Chelsea, C Palace, WBA, Shamrock R) 50
Munroe, L. 1954 (Shamrock R) 1
Murphy, A. 1956 (Clyde) 1
Murphy, B. 1986 (Bohemians) 1
Murphy, D. 2007 (Sunderland) 8
Murphy, J. 1980 (C Palace) 3
Murphy, J. 2004 (WBA) 1
Murphy, P. M. 2007 (Carlisle U) 1
Murray, T. 1950 (Dundalk) 1

Newman, W. 1969 (Shelbourne) 1
Nolan, R. 1957 (Shamrock R) 10

O'Brien, A. 2007 (Newcastle U) 5
O'Brien, A. J. 2001 (Newcastle U, Portsmouth) 26
O'Brien, F. 1980 (Philadelphia F) 3
O'Brien J. M. 2006 (Bolton W) 3
O'Brien, L. 1986 (Shamrock R, Manchester U, Newcastle U, Tranmere R) 16
O'Brien, M. T. 1927 (Derby Co, Walsall, Norwich C, Watford) 4
O'Brien, R. 1976 (Notts Co) 5
O'Byrne, L. B. 1949 (Shamrock R) 1
O'Callaghan, B. R. 1979 (Stoke C) 6
O'Callaghan, K. 1981 (Ipswich T, Portsmouth) 21
O'Cearuill, J. 2007 (Arsenal) 2
O'Connell, A. 1967 (Dundalk, Bohemians) 2
O'Connor, T. 1950 (Shamrock R) 4
O'Connor, T. 1968 (Fulham, Dundalk, Bohemians) 7
O'Driscoll, J. F. 1949 (Swansea T) 3
O'Driscoll, S. 1982 (Fulham) 3
O'Farrell, F. 1952 (West Ham U, Preston NE) 9
O'Flanagan, K. P. 1938 (Bohemians, Arsenal) 10
O'Flanagan, M. 1947 (Bohemians) 1
O'Halloran, S. E. 2007 (Aston Villa) 2
O'Hanlon, K. G. 1988 (Rotherham U) 1
O'Kane, P. 1935 (Bohemians) 3
O'Keefe, E. 1981 (Everton, Port Vale) 5
O'Keefe, T. 1934 (Cork, Waterford) 3
O'Leary, D. 1977 (Arsenal) 68
O'Leary, P. 1980 (Shamrock R) 7
O'Mahoney, M. T. 1938 (Bristol R) 6
O'Neill, F. S. 1962 (Shamrock R) 20
O'Neill, J. 1952 (Everton) 17
O'Neill, J. 1961 (Preston NE) 1
O'Neill, K. P. 1996 (Norwich C, Middlesbrough) 13
O'Neill, W. 1936 (Dundalk) 11
O'Regan, K. 1984 (Brighton & HA) 4
O'Reilly, J. 1932 (Brideville, Aberdeen, Brideville, St James' Gate) 20
O'Reilly, J. 1946 (Cork U) 2
O'Shea, J. F. 2002 (Manchester U) 45

Peyton, G. 1977 (Fulham, Bournemouth, Everton) 33
Peyton, N. 1957 (Shamrock R, Leeds U) 6
Phelan, T. 1992 (Wimbledon, Manchester C, Chelsea, Everton, Fulham) 42
Potter, D. M. 2007 (Wolverhampton W) 5

Quinn, A. 2003 (Sheffield W, Sheffield U) 8
Quinn, B. S. 2000 (Coventry C) 4
Quinn, N. J. 1986 (Arsenal, Manchester C, Sunderland) 91

Reid, A. M. 2004 (Nottingham F, Tottenham H, Charlton Ath, Sunderland) 27
Reid, C. 1931 (Brideville) 1
Reid, S. J. 2002 (Millwall, Blackburn R) 20
Richardson, D. J. 1972 (Shamrock R, Gillingham) 3
Rigby, A. 1935 (St James' Gate) 3
Ringstead, A. 1951 (Sheffield U) 20
Robinson, J. 1928 (Bohemians, Dolphin) 2
Robinson, M. 1981 (Brighton & HA, Liverpool, QPR) 24
Roche, P. J. 1972 (Shelbourne, Manchester U) 8
Rogers, E. 1968 (Blackburn R, Charlton Ath) 19
Rowlands, M. C. 2004 (QPR) 3
Ryan, G. 1978 (Derby Co, Brighton & HA) 18
Ryan, R. A. 1950 (WBA, Derby Co) 16

Sadlier, R. T. 2002 (Millwall) 1
Savage, D. P. T. 1996 (Millwall) 5
Saward, P. 1954 (Millwall, Aston Villa, Huddersfield T) 18
Scannell, T. 1954 (Southend U) 1
Scully, P. J. 1989 (Arsenal) 1
Sheedy, K. 1984 (Everton, Newcastle U) 46
Sheridan, J. J. 1988 (Leeds U, Sheffield W) 34
Slaven, B. 1990 (Middlesbrough) 7
Sloan, J. W. 1946 (Arsenal) 2
Smyth, M. 1969 (Shamrock R) 1
Squires, J. 1934 (Shelbourne) 1
Stapleton, F. 1977 (Arsenal, Manchester U, Ajax, Le Havre, Blackburn R) 71
Staunton, S. 1989 (Liverpool, Aston Villa, Liverpool, Aston Villa) 102
Stevenson, A. E. 1932 (Dolphin, Everton) 7
Stokes, A. 2007 (Sunderland) 3
Strahan, F. 1964 (Shelbourne) 5
Sullivan, J. 1928 (Fordsons) 1
Swan, M. M. G. 1960 (Drumcondra) 1
Synnott, N. 1978 (Shamrock R) 3

Taylor, T. 1959 (Waterford) 1
Thomas, P. 1974 (Waterford) 2
Thompson, J. 2004 (Nottingham F) 1
Townsend, A. D. 1989 (Norwich C, Chelsea, Aston Villa, Middlesbrough) 70
Traynor, T. J. 1954 (Southampton) 8
Treacy, R. C. P. 1966 (WBA, Charlton Ath, Swindon T, Preston NE, WBA, Shamrock R) 42
Tuohy, L. 1956 (Shamrock R, Newcastle U, Shamrock R) 8
Turner, C. J. 1936 (Southend U, West Ham U) 10
Turner, P. 1963 (Celtic) 2

Vernon, J. 1946 (Belfast Celtic) 2

Waddock, G. 1980 (QPR, Millwall) 21
Walsh, D. J. 1946 (Linfield, WBA, Aston Villa) 20
Walsh, J. 1982 (Limerick) 1
Walsh, M. 1976 (Blackpool, Everton, QPR, Porto) 21
Walsh, M. 1982 (Everton) 4
Walsh, W. 1947 (Manchester C) 9
Waters, J. 1977 (Grimsby T) 2
Watters, F. 1926 (Shelbourne) 1
Weir, E. 1939 (Clyde) 3
Whelan, G. D. 2008 (Stoke C) 2
Whelan, R. 1964 (St Patrick's Ath) 2
Whelan, R. 1981 (Liverpool, Southend U) 53
Whelan, W. 1956 (Manchester U) 4
White, J. J. 1928 (Bohemians) 1
Whittaker, R. 1959 (Chelsea) 1
Williams, J. 1938 (Shamrock R) 1

BRITISH AND IRISH INTERNATIONAL GOALSCORERS SINCE 1872

Where two players with the same surname and initials have appeared for the same country, and one or both have scored, they have been distinguished by reference to the club which appears *first* against their name in the international appearances section.

ENGLAND

Player	Goals
A'Court, A.	1
Adams, T. A.	5
Adcock, H.	1
Alcock, C. W.	1
Allen, A.	3
Allen, R.	2
Amos, A.	1
Anderson, V.	2
Anderton, D. R.	7
Astall, G.	1
Athersmith, W. C.	3
Atyeo, P. J. W.	5
Bache, J. W.	4
Bailey, N. C.	2
Baily, E. F.	5
Baker, J. H.	3
Ball, A. J.	8
Bambridge, A. L.	1
Bambridge, E. C.	11
Barclay, R.	2
Barmby, N. J.	4
Barnes, J.	11
Barnes, P. S.	4
Barry, G.	1
Barton, J.	1
Bassett, W. I.	8
Bastin, C. S.	12
Beardsley, P. A.	9
Beasley, A.	1
Beattie, T. K.	1
Beckham, D. R. J.	17
Becton, F.	2
Bedford, H.	1
Bell, C.	9
Bentley, R. T. F.	9
Bishop, S. M.	1
Blackburn, F.	1
Blissett, L.	3
Bloomer, S.	28
Bond, R.	2
Bonsor, A. G.	1
Bowden, E. R.	1
Bowers, J. W.	2
Bowles, S.	1
Bradford, G. R. W.	1
Bradford, J.	7
Bradley, W.	2
Bradshaw, F.	3
Brann, G.	1
Bridge, W. M.	1
Bridges, B. J.	1
Bridgett, A.	3
Brindle, T.	1
Britton, C. S.	1
Broadbent, P. F.	2
Broadis, I. A.	8
Brodie, J. B.	1
Bromley-Davenport, W.	2
Brook, E. F.	10
Brooking, T. D.	5
Brooks, J.	2
Broome, F. H.	3
Brown, A.	4
Brown, A. S.	1
Brown, G.	5
Brown, J.	3
Brown, W.	1
Buchan, C. M.	4
Bull, S. G.	4
Bullock, N.	2
Burgess, H.	4
Butcher, T.	3
Byrne, J. J.	8
Campbell, S. J.	1
Camsell, G. H.	18
Carter, H. S.	7
Carter, J. H.	4
Chadwick, E.	3
Chamberlain, M.	1
Chambers, H.	5
Channon, M. R.	21
Charlton, J.	6
Charlton, R.	49
Chenery, C. J.	1
Chivers, M.	13
Clarke, A. J.	10
Cobbold, W. N.	6
Cock, J. G.	2
Cole, A.	1
Cole, J. J.	7
Common, A.	2
Connelly, J. M.	7
Coppell, S. J.	7
Cotterill, G. H.	2
Cowans, G.	2
Crawford, R.	1
Crawshaw, T. H.	1
Crayston, W. J.	1
Creek, F. N. S.	1
Crooks, S. D.	7
Crouch, P. J.	14
Currey, E. S.	2
Currie, A. W.	3
Cursham, A. W.	2
Cursham, H. A.	5
Daft, H. B.	3
Davenport, J. K.	2
Davis, G.	1
Davis, H.	1
Day, S. H.	2
Dean, W. R.	18
Defoe, J. C.	5
Devey, J. H. G.	1
Dewhurst, F.	11
Dix, W. R.	1
Dixon, K. M.	4
Dixon, L. M.	1
Dorrell, A. R.	1
Douglas, B.	11
Drake, E. J.	6
Ducat, A.	1
Dunn, A. T. B.	2
Eastham, G.	2
Edwards, D.	5
Ehiogu, U.	1
Elliott, W. H.	3
Evans, R. E.	1
Ferdinand, L.	5
Ferdinand, R. G.	2
Finney, T.	30
Fleming, H. J.	9
Flowers, R.	10
Forman, Frank	1
Forman, Fred	3
Foster, R. E.	3
Fowler, R. B.	7
Francis, G. C. J.	3
Francis, T.	12
Freeman, B. C.	3
Froggatt, J.	2
Froggatt, R.	2
Galley, T.	1
Gascoigne, P. J.	10
Geary, F.	3
Gerrard, S. G.	13
Gibbins, W. V. T.	3
Gilliatt, W. E.	3
Goddard, P.	1
Goodall, J.	12
Goodyer, A. C.	1
Gosling, R. C.	2
Goulden, L. A.	4
Grainger, C.	3
Greaves, J.	44
Grovesnor, A. T.	2
Gunn, W.	1
Haines, J. T. W.	2
Hall, G. W.	9
Halse, H. J.	2
Hampson, J.	5
Hampton, H.	2
Hancocks, J.	2
Hardman, H. P.	1
Harris, S. S.	2
Hassall, H. W.	4
Hateley, M.	9
Haynes, J. N.	18
Hegan, K. E.	4
Henfrey, A. G.	2
Heskey, E. W.	5
Hilsdon, G. R.	14
Hine, E. W.	4
Hinton, A. T.	1
Hirst, D. E.	1
Hitchens, G. A.	5
Hobbis, H. H. F.	1
Hoddle, G.	8
Hodgetts, D.	1
Hodgson, G.	1
Holley, G. H.	8
Houghton, W. E.	5
Howell, R.	1
Hughes, E. W.	1
Hulme, J. H. A.	4
Hunt, G. S.	1
Hunt, R.	18
Hunter, N.	2
Hurst, G. C.	24
Ince, P. E. C.	2
Jack, D. N. B.	3
Jeffers, F.	1
Jenas, J. A.	1
Johnson, D. E.	6
Johnson, E.	2
Johnson, J. A.	2
Johnson, T. C. F.	5
Johnson, W. H.	1
Kail, E. I. L.	2
Kay, A. H.	1
Keegan, J. K.	21
Kelly, R.	8
Kennedy, R.	3
Kenyon-Slaney, W. S.	2
Keown, M. R.	2
Kevan, D. T.	8
Kidd, B.	1
King, L. B.	1
Kingsford, R. K.	1
Kirchen, A. J.	2
Kirton, W. J.	1
Lampard, F. J.	14
Langton, R.	1
Latchford, R. D.	5
Latheron, E. G.	1
Lawler, C.	1
Lawton, T.	22
Lee, F.	10
Lee, J.	1
Lee, R. M.	2
Lee, S.	2
Le Saux, G. P.	1
Lindley, T.	14
Lineker, G.	48
Lofthouse, J. M.	3
Lofthouse, N.	30
Hon. A. Lyttelton	1
Mabbutt, G.	1
Macdonald, M.	6
Mannion, W. J.	11
Mariner, P.	13
Marsh, R. W.	1
Matthews, S.	11
Matthews, V.	1
McCall, J.	1
McDermott, T.	3
McManaman, S.	3
Medley, L. D.	1
Melia, J.	1
Mercer, D. W.	1
Merson, P. C.	3
Milburn, J. E. T.	10
Miller, H. S.	1
Mills, G. R.	3
Milward, A.	3
Mitchell, C.	5
Moore, J.	1
Moore, R. F.	2
Moore, W. G. B.	2
Morren, T.	1
Morris, F.	1
Morris, J.	3
Mortensen, S. H.	23
Morton, J. R.	1
Mosforth, W.	3
Mullen, J.	6
Mullery, A. P.	1
Murphy, D. B	1
Neal, P. G.	5
Needham, E.	3
Nicholls, J.	1
Nicholson, W. E.	1
Nugent, D. J.	1
O'Grady, M.	3
Osborne, F. R.	3
Owen, M. J.	40
Own goals	28
Page, L. A.	1
Paine, T. L.	7

Palmer, C. L. 1
Parry, E. H. 1
Parry, R. A. 1
Pawson, F. W. 1
Payne, J. 2
Peacock, A. 3
Pearce, S. 5
Pearson, J. S. 5
Pearson, S. C. 5
Perry, W. 2
Peters, M. 20
Pickering, F. 5
Platt, D. 27
Pointer, R. 2

Quantrill, A. 1

Ramsay, A. E. 3
Revie, D. G. 4
Redknapp, J. F. 1
Reynolds, J. 3
Richards, M. 1
Richardson, K. E. 2
Richardson, J. R. 2
Rigby, A. 3
Rimmer, E. J. 2
Roberts, F. 2
Roberts, H. 1
Roberts, W. T. 2
Robinson, J. 3
Robson, B. 26
Robson, R. 4
Rooney, W. 14
Rowley, J. F. 6
Royle, J. 2
Rutherford, J. 3

Sagar, C. 1
Sandilands, R. R. 3
Sansom, K. 1
Schofield, J. 1
Scholes, P. 14
Seed, J. M. 1
Settle, J. 6
Sewell, J. 3
Shackleton, L. F. 1
Sharp, J. 1
Shearer, A. 30
Shelton, A. 1
Shepherd, A. 2
Sheringham, E. P. 11
Simpson, J. 1
Smith, A. 1
Smith, A. M. 2
Smith, G. O. 11
Smith, Joe 1
Smith, J. R. 2
Smith, J. W. 4
Smith, R. 13
Smith, S. 1
Sorby, T. H. 1
Southgate, G. 2
Southworth, J. 3
Sparks, F. J. 3
Spence, J. W. 1
Spiksley, F. 5
Spilsbury, B. W. 5
Steele, F. C. 8
Stephenson, G. T. 2
Steven, T. M. 4
Stewart, J. 2
Stiles, N. P. 1
Storer, H. 1
Stone, S. B. 2
Summerbee, M. G. 1

Tambling, R. V. 1
Taylor, P. J. 2
Taylor, T. 16
Terry, J. G. 4
Thompson, P. B. 1
Thornewell, G. 1
Tilson, S. F. 6
Townley, W. J. 2
Tueart, D. 2

Vassell, D. 6
Vaughton, O. H. 6
Veitch, J. G. 3
Viollet, D. S. 1

Waddle, C. R. 6
Walker, W. H. 9
Wall, G. 2
Wallace, D. 1
Walsh, P. 1
Waring, T. 4
Warren, B. 2
Watson, D. V. 4
Watson, V. M. 4
Webb, G. W. 1
Webb, N. 4
Wedlock, W. J. 2
Weller, K. 1
Welsh, D. 1
Whateley, O. 2
Wheldon, G. F. 6
Whitfield, H. 1
Wignall, F. 2
Wilkes, A. 1
Wilkins, R. G. 3
Willingham, C. K. 1
Wilshaw, D. J. 10
Wilson, G. P. 1
Winckworth, W. N. 1
Windridge, J. E. 7
Wise, D. F. 1
Withe, P. 1
Wollaston, C. H. R. 1
Wood, H. 1
Woodcock, T. 16
Woodhall, G. 1
Woodward, V. J. 29
Worrall, F. 2
Worthington, F. S. 2
Wright, I. E. 9
Wright, M. 1
Wright, W. A. 3
Wright-Phillips, S. C. 4
Wylie, J. G. 1

Yates, J. 3

NORTHERN IRELAND

Anderson, T. 4
Armstrong, G. 12

Bambrick, J. 12
Barr, H. H. 1
Barron, H. 3
Best, G. 9
Bingham, W. L. 10
Black, K. 1
Blanchflower, D. 2
Blanchflower, J. 1
Brennan, B. 1
Brennan, R. A. 1
Brotherston, N. 3
Brown, J. 1
Browne, F. 2

Campbell, J. 1
Campbell, W. G. 1
Casey, T. 2
Caskey, W. 1
Cassidy, T. 1
Chambers, J. 3
Clarke, C. J. 13
Clements, D. 2
Cochrane, T. 1
Condy, J. 1
Connor, M. J. 1
Coulter, J. 1
Croft, T. 1
Crone, W. 1
Crossan, E. 1
Crossan, J. A. 10
Curran, S. 2
Cush, W. W. 5

Dalton, W. 4
D'Arcy, S. D. 1
Darling, J. 1
Davey, H. H. 1
Davis, S. 1
Davis, T. L. 1
Dill, A. H. 1
Doherty, L. 1
Doherty, P. D. 3
Dougan, A. D. 8
Dowie, I. 12
Dunne, J. 4

Elder, A. R. 1
Elliott, S. 4
Emerson, W. 1
English, S. 1

Feeney, W. 1
Feeney, W. J. 3
Ferguson, W. 1
Ferris, J. 1
Ferris, R. O. 1
Finney, T. 2

Gaffkin, J. 4
Gara, A. 3
Gaukrodger, G. 1
Gibb, J. T. 2
Gibb, T. J. 1
Gibson, W. 1
Gillespie, K. R. 2
Gillespie, W. 13
Goodall, A. L. 2
Griffin, D. J. 1
Gray, P. 6

Halligan, W. 1
Hamill, M. 1
Hamilton, B. 4
Hamilton, W. R. 5
Hannon, D. J. 1
Harkin, J. T. 2
Harvey, M. 3
Healy, D. J. 34
Hill, C. F. 1
Hughes, M. E. 5
Humphries, W. 1
Hunter, A. (*Distillery*) 1
Hunter, A. (*Blackburn R*) 1
Hunter, B. V. 1

Irvine, R. W. 3
Irvine, W. J. 8

Johnston, H. 2
Johnston, S. 2
Johnston, W. C. 1
Jones, S. 1
Jones, S. (*Crewe Alex*) 1
Jones, J. 1

Kelly, J. 4
Kernaghan, N. 2
Kirwan, J. 2

Lacey, W. 3
Lafferty, K. 5
Lemon, J. 2
Lennon, N. F. 2
Lockhart, N. 3
Lomas, S. M. 3

Magilton, J. 5
Mahood, J. 2
Martin, D. K. 3
Maxwell, J. 2
McAdams, W. J. 7
McAllen, J. 1
Mcauley, J. L. 1
McCann, G. S. 1
McCartney, G. 1
McCandless, J. 2
McCandless, W. 1
McCaw, J. H. 1
McClelland, J. 1
McCluggage, A. 2
McCracken, W. 1
McCrory, S. 1
McCurdy, C. 1
McDonald, A. 3
McGarry, J. K. 1
McGrath, R. C. 4
McIlroy, J. 10
McIlroy, S. B. 5
McKenzie, H 1
McKnight, J. 2
McLaughlin, J. C. 6
McMahon, G. J. 2
McMordie, A. S. 3
McMorran, E. J. 4
McParland, P. J. 10
McWha, W. B. R. 1
Meldon, P. A 1
Mercer, J. T. 1
Millar, W. 1
Milligan, D. 1
Milne, R. G. 2
Molyneux, T. B. 1
Moreland, V. 1
Morgan, S. 3
Morrow, S. J. 1
Morrow, W. J. 1
Mulryne, P. P. 3
Murdock, C. J. 1
Murphy, N. 1

Neill, W. J. T. 2
Nelson, S. 1
Nicholl, C. J. 3
Nicholl, J. M. 1
Nicholson, J. J. 6

O'Boyle, G. 1
O'Hagan, C. 2
O'Kane, W. J. 1
O'Neill, J. 2
O'Neill, M. A. 4
O'Neill, M. H. 8
Own goals 7

Patterson, D. J. 1
Peacock, R. 2
Peden, J. 7
Penney, S. 2
Pyper, James 2
Pyper, John 1

Quinn, J. M. 12
Quinn, S. J. 4

Reynolds, J. 1
Rowland, K. 1
Rowley, R. W. M. 2
Rushe, F. 1

Sheridan, J. 2
Sherrard, J. 1
Sherrard, W. C. 2
Simpson, W. J. 5
Sloan, H. A. de B. 4
Smyth, S. 5
Spence, D. W. 3
Sproule, I. 1
Stanfield, O. M. 11
Stevenson, A. E. 5
Stewart, I. 2

Taggart, G. P. 7
Thompson, F. W. 2
Torrans, S. 1
Tully, C. P. 3
Turner, A. 1

Walker, J.	1
Walsh, D. J.	5
Welsh, E.	1
Whiteside, N.	9
Whiteside, T.	1
Whitley, Jeff	2
Williams, J. R.	1
Williams, M. S.	1
Williamson, J.	1
Wilson, D. J.	1
Wilson, K. J.	6
Wilson, S. J.	7
Wilton, J. M.	2
Young, S.	1

N.B. In 1914 Young goal should be credited to Gillespie W v Wales

SCOTLAND

Aitken, R. (*Celtic*)	1
Aitken, R. (*Dumbarton*)	1
Aitkenhead, W. A. C.	2
Alexander, D.	1
Allan, D. S.	4
Allan, J.	2
Anderson, F.	1
Anderson, W.	4
Andrews, P.	1
Archibald, A.	1
Archibald, S.	4
Baird, D.	2
Baird, J. C.	2
Baird, S.	2
Bannon, E.	1
Barbour, A.	1
Barker, J. B.	4
Battles, B. Jr	1
Bauld, W.	2
Baxter, J. C.	3
Beattie, C.	1
Bell, J.	5
Bennett, A.	2
Berry, D.	1
Bett, J.	1
Beveridge, W. W.	1
Black, A.	3
Black, D.	1
Bone, J.	1
Booth, S.	6
Boyd, K	7
Boyd, R.	2
Boyd, T.	1
Boyd, W. G.	1
Brackenridge, T.	1
Brand, R.	8
Brazil, A.	1
Bremner, W. J.	3
Brown, A. D.	6
Buchanan, P. S.	1
Buchanan, R.	1
Buckley, P.	1
Buick, A.	2
Burke, C.	2
Burley, C. W.	3
Burns, K.	1
Cairns, T.	1
Caldwell, G.	2
Calderwood, C.	1
Calderwood, R.	2
Caldow, E.	4
Cameron, C.	2
Campbell, C.	1
Campbell, John (*Celtic*)	5
Campbell, John (*Rangers*)	4
Campbell, J. (*South Western*)	1
Campbell, P.	2
Campbell, R.	1
Cassidy, J.	1
Chalmers, S.	3
Chambers, T.	1
Cheyne, A. G.	4
Christie, A. J.	1
Clarkson, D.	1
Clunas, W. L.	1
Collins, J.	12
Collins, R. Y.	10
Combe, J. R.	1
Conn, A.	1
Cooper, D.	6
Craig, J.	1
Craig, T.	1
Crawford, S.	4
Cunningham, A. N.	5
Curran, H. P.	1
Dailly, C.	6
Dalglish, K.	30
Davidson, D.	1
Davidson, J. A.	1
Delaney, J.	3
Devine, A.	1
Dewar, G.	1
Dewar, N.	4
Dickov, P.	1
Dickson, W.	4
Divers, J.	1
Dobie, R. S.	1
Docherty, T. H.	1
Dodds, D.	1
Dodds, W.	7
Donaldson, A.	1
Donnachie, J.	1
Dougall, J.	1
Drummond, J.	2
Dunbar, M.	1
Duncan, D.	7
Duncan, D. M.	1
Duncan, J.	1
Dunn, J.	2
Durie, G. S.	7
Easson, J. F.	1
Elliott, M. S.	1
Ellis, J.	1
Ferguson, B.	3
Ferguson, J.	6
Fernie, W.	1
Fitchie, T. T.	1
Flavell, R.	2
Fleming, C.	2
Fleming, J. W.	3
Fletcher, D.	4
Fraser, M. J. E.	3
Freedman, D. A.	1
Gallacher, H. K.	23
Gallacher, K. W.	9
Gallacher, P.	1
Galt, J. H.	1
Gemmell, T. (*St Mirren*)	1
Gemmell, T. (*Celtic*)	1
Gemmill, A.	8
Gemmill, S.	1
Gibb, W.	1
Gibson, D. W.	3
Gibson, J. D.	1
Gibson, N.	1
Gillespie, Jas.	3
Gillick, T.	3
Gilzean, A. J.	12
Gossland, J.	2
Goudie, J.	1
Gough, C. R.	6
Gourlay, J.	1
Graham, A.	2
Graham, G.	3
Gray, A.	7
Gray, E.	3
Gray, F.	1
Greig, J.	3
Groves, W.	4
Hamilton, G.	4
Hamilton, J. (*Queen's Park*)	3
Hamilton, R. C.	15
Harper, J. M.	2
Hartley, P. J.	1
Harrower, W.	5
Hartford, R. A.	4
Heggie, C. W	4
Henderson, J. G.	1
Henderson, W.	5
Hendry, E. C. J.	3
Herd, D. G.	3
Herd, G.	1
Hewie, J. D.	2
Higgins, A. (*Newcastle U*)	1
Higgins, A. (*Kilmarnock*)	4
Highet, T. C.	1
Holt, G.J.	1
Holton, J. A.	2
Hopkin, D.	2
Houliston, W.	2
Howie, H.	1
Howie, J.	2
Hughes, J.	1
Hunter, W.	1
Hutchison, D.	6
Hutchison, T.	1
Hutton, J.	1
Hyslop, T.	1
Imrie, W. N.	1
Jackson, A.	8
Jackson, C.	1
Jackson, D.	4
James, A. W.	4
Jardine, A.	1
Jenkinson, T.	1
Jess, E.	2
Johnston, A.	2
Johnston, L. H.	1
Johnston, M.	14
Johnstone, D.	2
Johnstone, J.	4
Johnstone, Jas.	1
Johnstone, R.	10
Johnstone, W.	1
Jordan, J.	11
Kay, J. L.	5
Keillor, A.	3
Kelly, J.	1
Kelso, R.	1
Ker, G.	10
King, A.	1
King, J.	1
Kinnear, D.	1
Kyle, K.	1
Lambert, P.	1
Lambie, J.	1
Lambie, W. A.	5
Lang, J. J.	2
Latta, A.	2
Law, D.	30
Leggat, G.	8
Lennie, W.	1
Lennox, R.	3
Liddell, W.	6
Lindsay, J.	6
Linwood, A. B.	1
Logan, J.	1
Lorimer, P.	4
Love, A.	1
Low, J. (*Cambuslang*)	1
Lowe, J. (*St Bernards*)	1
Macari, L.	5
MacDougall, E. J.	3
MacFarlane, A.	1
MacLeod, M.	1
Mackay, D. C.	4
Mackay, G.	1
MacKenzie, J. A.	1
MacKinnon, W. W.	5
Madden, J.	5
Maloney, S.	1
Marshall, H.	1
Marshall, J.	1
Mason, J.	4
Massie, A.	1
Masson, D. S.	5
McAdam, J.	1
McAllister, G.	5
McAulay, J. D.	1
McAvennie, F.	1
McCall, J.	1
McCall, S. M.	1
McCalliog, J.	1
McCallum, N.	1
McCann, N.	3
McClair, B. J.	2
McCoist, A.	19
McColl, R. S.	13
McCulloch, D.	3
McCulloch, L.	1
McDougall, J.	4
McFadden, J.	13
McFadyen, W.	2
McGhee, M.	2
McGinlay, J.	4
McGregor, J.	1
McGrory, J.	6
McGuire, W.	1
McInally, A.	3
McInnes, T.	2
McKie, J.	2
McKimmie, S.	1
McKinlay, W.	4
McKinnon, A.	1
McKinnon, R.	1
McLaren, A.	4
McLaren, J.	1
McLean, A.	1
McLean, T.	1
McLintock, F.	1
McMahon, A.	6
McManus, S.	1
McMenemy, J.	5
McMillan, I. L.	2
McNeill, W.	3
McNiel, H.	5
McPhail, J.	3
McPhail, R.	7
McPherson, J.	5
McPherson, J. (*Vale of Leven*)	1
McPherson, R.	1
McQueen, G.	5
McStay, P.	9
McSwegan, G.	1
Meiklejohn, D. D.	3
Millar, J.	2
Miller, K.	11
Miller, T.	2
Miller, W.	1
Mitchell, R. C.	1
Morgan, W.	1
Morris, D.	1
Morris, H.	3
Morton, A. L.	5
Mudie, J. K.	9
Mulhall, G.	1
Munro, A. D.	1
Munro, N.	2
Murdoch, R.	5
Murphy, F.	1
Murray, J.	1
Napier, C. E.	3
Narey, D.	1
Naysmith, G. A.	1
Neil, R. G.	2

Nevin, P. K. F. 5
Nicholas, C. 5
Nisbet, J. 2

O'Connor, G. 4
O'Donnell, F. 2
O'Hare, J. 5
Ormond, W. E. 2
O'Rourke, F. 1
Orr, R. 1
Orr, T. 1
Oswald, J. 1
Own goals 16

Parlane, D. 1
Paul, H. McD. 2
Paul, W. 5
Pettigrew, W. 2
Provan, D. 1

Quashie, N. F. 1
Quinn, J. 7
Quinn, P. 1

Rankin, G. 2
Rankin, R. 2
Reid, W. 4
Reilly, L. 22
Renny-Tailyour, H. W. 1
Richmond, J. T. 1
Ring, T. 2
Rioch, B. D. 6
Ritchie, J. 1
Ritchie, P. S. 1
Robertson, A. 2
Robertson, J. 3
Robertson, J. N. 8
Robertson, J. T. 2
Robertson, T. 1
Robertson, W. 1
Russell, D. 1

Scott, A. S. 5
Sellar, W. 4
Sharp, G. 1
Shaw, F. W. 1
Shearer, D. 2
Simpson, J. 1
Smith, A. 5
Smith, G. 4
Smith, J. 1
Smith, John 13
Somerville, G. 1
Souness, G. J. 4
Speedie, F. 2
St John, I. 9
Steel, W. 12
Stein, C. 10
Stevenson, G. 4
Stewart, A. 1
Stewart, R. 1
Stewart, W. E. 1
Strachan, G. 5
Sturrock, P. 3

Taylor, J. D. 1
Templeton, R. 1
Thompson, S. 3
Thomson, A. 1
Thomson, C. 4
Thomson, R. 1
Thomson, W. 1
Thornton, W. 1

Waddell, T. S. 1
Waddell, W. 6
Walker, J. 2
Walker, R. 7
Walker, T. 9
Wallace, I. A. 1
Wark, J. 7
Watson, J. A. K. 1
Watt, F. 2
Watt, W. W. 1
Webster, A. 1
Weir, A. 1
Weir, D. 1
Weir, J. B. 2
White, J. A. 3
Wilkie, L. 1
Wilson, A. 2
Wilson, A. N. 13
Wilson, D. (*Queen's Park*) 2
Wilson, D. (*Rangers*) 9
Wilson, H. 1
Wylie, T. G. 1

Young, A. 5

WALES
Allchurch, I. J. 23
Allen, M. 3
Astley, D. J. 12
Atherton, R. W. 2

Bale, G. 2
Bamford, T. 1
Barnes, W. 1
Bellamy, C. D. 15
Blackmore, C. G. 1
Blake, N. A. 4
Bodin, P. J. 3
Boulter, L. M. 1
Bowdler, J. C. H. 3
Bowen, D. L. 1
Bowen, M. 3
Boyle, T. 1
Bryan, T. 1
Burgess, W. A. R. 1
Burke, T. 1
Butler, W. T. 1

Chapman, T. 2
Charles, J. 1
Charles, M. 6
Charles, W. J. 15
Clarke, R. J. 5
Coleman, C. 4
Collier, D. J. 1
Collins, J. 1
Crosse, K. 1
Cumner, R. H. 1
Curtis, A. 6
Curtis, E. R. 3

Davies, D. W. 1
Davies, E. Lloyd 1
Davies, G. 2
Davies, L. S. 6
Davies, R. T. 9
Davies, R. W. 6
Davies, Simon 6
Davies, Stanley 5
Davies, W. 6
Davies, W. H. 1
Davies, William 5
Davis, W. O. 1
Deacy, N. 4
Doughty, J. 6
Doughty, R. 2
Durban, A. 2
Dwyer, P. 2

Earnshaw, R. 13
Eastwood, F. 4
Edwards, G. 2
Edwards, R. I. 4
England, H. M. 4
Evans, C. 1
Evans, I. 1
Evans, J. 1
Evans, R. E. 2
Evans, W. 1
Eyton-Jones, J. A. 1

Fletcher, C. 1
Flynn, B. 7
Ford, T. 23
Foulkes, W. I. 1
Fowler, J. 3

Giles, D. 2
Giggs, R. J. 12
Glover, E. M. 7
Godfrey, B. C. 2
Green, A. W. 3
Griffiths, A. T. 6
Griffiths, M. W. 2
Griffiths, T. P. 3

Harris, C. S. 1
Hartson, J. 14
Hersee, R. 1
Hewitt, R. 1
Hockey, T. 1
Hodges, G. 2
Hole, W. J. 1
Hopkins, I. J. 2
Horne, B. 2
Howell, E. G. 3
Hughes, L. M. 16

James, E. 2
James, L. 10
James, R. 7
Jarrett, R. H. 3
Jenkyns, C. A. 1
Jones, A. 1
Jones, Bryn 6
Jones, B. S. 2
Jones, Cliff 16
Jones, C. W. 1
Jones, D. E. 1
Jones, Evan 1
Jones, H. 1
Jones, I. 1
Jones, J. L. 1
Jones, J. O. 1
Jones, J. P. 1
Jones, Leslie J. 1
Jones, R. A. 2
Jones, W. L. 6

Keenor, F. C. 2
Koumas, J. 9
Krzywicki, R. L. 1

Ledley, J. 1
Leek, K. 5
Lewis, B. 4
Lewis, D. M. 2
Lewis, W. 8
Lewis, W. L. 3
Llewelyn, C. M 1
Lovell, S. 1
Lowrie, G. 2

Mahoney, J. F. 1
Mays, A. W. 1
Medwin, T. C. 6
Melville, A. K 3
Meredith, W. H. 11
Mills, T. J. 1
Moore, G. 1
Morgan, J. R. 2
Morgan-Owen, H. 1
Morgan-Owen, M. M. 2
Morris, A. G. 9
Morris, H. 2
Morris, R. 1
Morris, S. 2

Nicholas, P. 2

O'Callaghan, E. 3
O'Sullivan, P. A. 1
Owen, G. 2
Owen, W. 4
Owen, W. P. 6
Own goals 14

Palmer, D. 3
Parry, P. I. 1
Parry, T. D. 3
Paul, R. 1
Peake, E. 1
Pembridge, M. 6
Perry, E. 1
Phillips, C. 5
Phillips, D. 2
Powell, A. 1
Powell, D. 1
Price, J. 4
Price, P. 1
Pryce-Jones, W. E. 3
Pugh, D. H. 2

Reece, G. I. 2
Rees, R. R. 3
Richards, R. W. 1
Roach, J. 2
Robbins, W. W. 4
Roberts, J. (*Corwen*) 1
Roberts, Jas. 1
Roberts, P. S. 1
Roberts, R. (*Druids*) 1
Roberts, W. (*Llangollen*) 2
Roberts, W. (*Wrexham*) 1
Roberts, W. H. 1
Robinson, C. P. 1
Robinson, J. R. C. 3
Rush, I. 28
Russell, M. R. 1

Sabine, H. W. 1
Saunders, D. 22
Savage, R. W. 2
Shaw, E. G. 2
Sisson, H. 4
Slatter, N. 2
Smallman, D. P. 1
Speed, G. A. 7
Symons, C. J. 2

Tapscott, D. R. 4
Taylor, G. K. 1
Thomas, M. 4
Thomas, T. 1
Toshack, J. B. 12
Trainer, H. 2

Vaughan, John 2
Vernon, T. R. 8
Vizard, E. T. 1

Walsh, I. 7
Warren, F. W. 3
Watkins, W. M. 4
Wilding, J. 4
Williams, A. 1
Williams, D. R. 2
Williams, G. E. 1
Williams, G. G. 1
Williams, W. 1
Woosnam, A. P. 3
Wynn, G. A. 1

Yorath, T. C. 2
Young, E. 1

REPUBLIC OF IRELAND
Aldridge, J. 19
Ambrose, P. 1
Anderson, J. 1

Barrett, G. 2
Bermingham, P. 1
Bradshaw, P. 4

Player	Goals
Brady, L.	9
Breen, G.	7
Brown, J.	1
Byrne, D.	1
Byrne, J.	4
Cantwell, J.	14
Carey, J.	3
Carroll, T.	1
Cascarino, A.	19
Coad, P.	3
Connolly, D. J.	9
Conroy, T.	2
Conway, J.	3
Coyne, T.	6
Cummins, G.	5
Curtis, D.	8
Daly, G.	13
Davis, T.	4
Dempsey, J.	1
Dennehy, M.	2
Doherty, G. M. T.	4
Donnelly, J.	4
Donnelly, T.	1
Doyle, K. E.	5
Duff, D. A.	7
Duffy, B.	1
Duggan, H.	1
Dunne, J.	13
Dunne, L.	1
Dunne, R. P.	5
Eglington, T.	2
Elliott, S. W.	1
Ellis, P.	1
Fagan, F.	5
Fallon, S.	2
Fallon, W.	2
Farrell, P.	3
Finnan, S.	2
Fitzgerald, P.	2
Fitzgerald, J.	1
Fitzsimons, A.	7
Flood, J. J.	4
Fogarty, A.	3
Foley, D.	2
Fullam, J.	1
Fullam, R.	1
Galvin, A.	1
Gavin, J.	2
Geoghegan, M.	2
Giles, J.	5
Givens, D.	19
Glynn, D.	1
Grealish, T.	8
Grimes, A. A.	1
Hale, A.	2
Hand, E.	2
Harte, I. P.	11
Haverty, J.	3
Healy, C.	1
Holland, M. R.	5
Holmes, J.	1
Horlacher, A.	2
Houghton, R.	6
Hughton, C.	1
Hurley, C.	2
Ireland, S. J.	4
Irwin, D.	4
Jordan, D.	1
Kavanagh, G. A.	1
Keane, R. D.	33
Keane, R. M.	9
Kelly, D.	9
Kelly, G.	2
Kelly, J.	2
Kennedy, M.	4
Keogh, A.	1
Kernaghan, A. N.	1
Kilbane, K. D.	7
Kinsella, M. A.	3
Lacey, W.	1
Lawrenson, M.	5
Leech, M.	2
Long, S. P.	3
McAteer, J. W.	3
McCann, J.	1
McCarthy, M.	2
McEvoy, A.	6
McGee, P.	4
McGrath, P.	8
McLoughlin, A. F.	2
McPhail, S. J. P.	1
Mancini, T.	1
Martin, C.	6
Martin, M.	4
Miller, L. W. P.	1
Mooney, J.	1
Moore, P.	7
Moran, K.	6
Morrison, C. H.	9
Moroney, T.	1
Mulligan, P.	1
O'Brien, A. J.	1
O'Callaghan, K.	1
O'Connor, T.	2
O'Farrell, F.	2
O'Flanagan, K.	3
O'Keefe, E.	1
O'Leary, D. A.	1
O'Neill, F.	1
O'Neill, K. P.	4
O'Reilly, J. (*Brideville*)	2
O'Reilly, J. (*Cork*)	1
O'Shea, J. F.	1
Own goals	10
Quinn, N.	21
Reid, A. M.	4
Reid, S. J.	2
Ringstead, A.	7
Robinson, M.	4
Rogers, E.	5
Ryan, G.	1
Ryan, R.	3
Sheedy, K.	9
Sheridan, J.	5
Slaven, B.	1
Sloan, J.	1
Squires, J.	1
Stapleton, F.	20
Staunton, S.	7
Strahan, J.	1
Sullivan, J.	1
Townsend, A. D.	7
Treacy, R.	5
Touhy, L.	4
Waddock, G.	3
Walsh, D.	5
Walsh, M.	3
Waters, J.	1
White, J. J.	2
Whelan, R.	3

David Healy of Northern Ireland (left) in action against Bulgaria in a friendly international at Windsor Park in February. Healy's total of 13 goals in the Euro 2008 qualifying campaign broke the record of 12 previously held by Croatia's Davor Šuker. (Action Images/Lee Mills)

SOUTH AMERICA

COPA SUDAMERICANA 2007

FIRST PHASE
Byes to second phase:
Boca Juniors, River Plate, America, Guadalajara, Pachuca (Holders), DC United..

SECTION 1 (ARGENTINA)
Arsenal 1, San Lorenzo 1
Lanus 2, Estudiantes 0
San Lorenzo 0, Arsenal 3
Estudiantes 2, Lanus 1

SECTION 2 (BRAZIL)
Fiqueirense 2, Sao Paulo 2
Goias 2, Cruzeiro 0
At Paranaense 2, Vasco da Gama 4
Botafogo 3, Corinthians 1
Sao Paulo 1, Fiqueirense 1
Cruzeiro 1, Goias 0
Vasco da Gama 2, At Paranaense 0
Corinthians 1, Botafogo 2

SECTION 3 (CHILE, BOLIVIA)
FIRST STAGE
Audax Italiano 2, Jorge Wilstermann 0
Real Potosi 1, Colo Colo 1
Jorge Wilstermann 1, Audax Italiano 1
Colo Colo 3, Real Potosi 1

SECOND STAGE
Colo Colo 0, Audax Italiano 0
Audax Italiano 1, Colo Colo 1

SECTION 4 (ECUADOR, VENEZUELA)
FIRST STAGE
Olmedo 1, Zamora 0
Carabobo 0, El Nacional 1
Zamora 1, Olmedo 2
El Nacional 4, Carabobo 0

SECOND STAGE
El Nacional 2, Olmedo 0
Olmedo 0, El Nacional 1

SECTION 5 (COLOMBIA, PERU)
FIRST STAGE
Milionarios 0, Coronel Bolognesi 1
Universitario 0, At Nacional 1
Coronel Bolognesi 0, Milionarios 1
Milionarios won 5-4 on penalties.
At Nacional 1, Universitario 0

SECOND STAGE
At Nacional 2, Milionarios 3
Milionarios 0, At Nacional 0

SECTION 6 (URUGUAY, PARAGUAY)
FIRST STAGE
Defensor 2, Libertad 1
Libertad 2, Defensor 2
Tacuary 1, Danubio 1
Libertad 2, Defensor 2
Danubio 1, Tacuary 1
Tacuary won 4-1 on penalties.

SECOND STAGE
Tacuary 1, Defensor 1
Defensor 3, Tacuary 0

SECOND PHASE
Lanus 2, Vasco da Gama 0
Boca Juniors 2, Sao Paulo 1
Goias 2, Arsenal 3
Botafogo 1, River Plate 0
Defensor 3, El Nacional 0
Pachuca 1, America 4
Milionarios 1, Colo Colo 1
DC United 2, Guadalajara 1
Vasco da Gama 3, Lanus 0
Sao Paulo 1, Boca Juniors 0
Arsenal 1, Goias 1
River Plate 4, Botafogo 2
El Nacional 2, Defensor 0
America 0, Pachuca 2
Colo Colo 1, Milionarios 1
Milionarios won 7-6 on penalties.
Guadalajara 1, DC United 0

QUARTER-FINALS
America 2, Vasco da Gama 0
Sao Paulo 0, Milionarios 1
Arsenal 0, Guadalajara 0
Defensor 2, River Plate 2
Vasco da Gama 1, America 0
Milionarios 2, Sao Paulo 0
Guadalajara 1, Arsenal 3
River Plate 0, Defensor 0

SEMI-FINALS FIRST LEG
Milionarios 2, America 3
River Plate 0, Arsenal 0

SEMI-FINALS SECOND LEG
America 2, Milionarios 0
Arsenal 0, River Plate 0
Arsenal won 4-2 on penalties.

FINAL
America 2, Arsenal 3
Arsenal 1, America 2
Arsenal won on away goals.

COPA LIBERTADORES 2008

PRELIMINARY ROUND FIRST LEG
Arsenal 2, Mineros 0
Cruzeiro 3, Cerro Porteno 1
Atlas 2, La Paz 0
Olmedo 1, Lanus 0
Cienciano 1, Wanderers 0
Boyaca Chico 4, Audax Italiano 3

PRELIMINARY ROUND SECOND LEG
Mineros 2, Arsenal 1
Cerro Porteno 2, Cruzeiro 3
(Abandoned 65 minutes; crowd trouble, result stood.)
La Paz 1, Atlas 2
Lanus 3, Olmedo 0
Wanderers 0, Cienciano 0
Audax Italiano 1, Boyaca Chico 0

Group 1	*P*	*W*	*D*	*L*	*F*	*A*	*Pts*
Cruzeiro	6	3	2	1	11	7	11
San Lorenzo	6	3	1	2	8	7	10
Caracas	6	2	1	3	6	11	7
Real Potosi	6	2	0	4	11	11	6

Group 2	*P*	*W*	*D*	*L*	*F*	*A*	*Pts*
Estudiantes	6	3	2	1	9	5	11
Lanus	6	2	4	0	9	6	10
Dep Cuenca	6	1	3	2	2	5	6
Danubio	6	1	1	4	5	9	4

Group 3	*P*	*W*	*D*	*L*	*F*	*A*	*Pts*
Atlas	6	3	2	1	11	6	11
Boca Juniors	6	3	1	2	12	9	10
Colo Colo	6	3	1	2	11	9	10
UA Maracaibo	6	0	2	4	3	13	2

Group 4	*P*	*W*	*D*	*L*	*F*	*A*	*Pts*
Flamengo	6	4	1	1	9	4	13
Nacional	6	4	0	2	9	5	12
Cienciano	6	2	1	3	5	9	7
Coronel Bolognesi	6	0	2	4	0	5	2

Group 5	*P*	*W*	*D*	*L*	*F*	*A*	*Pts*
River Plate	6	4	0	2	14	8	12
America	6	3	0	3	10	10	9
Univ Catolica	6	3	0	3	6	6	9
Univ San Martin	6	2	0	4	4	10	6

Group 6	*P*	*W*	*D*	*L*	*F*	*A*	*Pts*
Cucuta	6	3	2	1	7	4	11
Santos	6	3	1	2	13	6	10
Guadalajara	6	3	0	3	8	5	9
San Jose	6	1	1	4	4	17	4

Group 7	*P*	*W*	*D*	*L*	*F*	*A*	*Pts*
Sao Paulo	6	3	2	1	6	4	11
At Nacional	6	2	2	2	8	5	8
Sp Luqueno	6	2	1	3	8	10	7
Audax Italiano	6	2	1	3	6	9	7

Group 8	*P*	*W*	*D*	*L*	*F*	*A*	*Pts*
Fluminense	6	4	1	1	11	3	13
LDU Quito	6	3	1	2	10	5	10
Arsenal	6	3	0	3	6	14	9
Libertad	6	1	0	5	5	10	3

SECOND ROUND FIRST LEG
Lanus 0, Atlas 1
LDU Quito 2, Estudiantes 0
At Nacional 1, Fluminense 2
Boca Juniors 2, Cruzeiro 1
America (Mex) 2, Flamengo 4
Nacional 0, Sao Paulo 0
San Lorenzo 2, River Plate 1
Santos 2, Cucuta 0

SECOND ROUND SECOND LEG
Atlas 2, Lanus 2
Estudiantes 2, LDU Quito 1
Fluminense 1, At Nacional 0
Cruzeiro 1, Boca Juniors 2
Flamengo 0, America (Mex) 3
Sao Paulo 2, Nacional 0

QUARTER-FINALS FIRST LEG
Sao Paulo 1, Fluminense 0
Boca Juniors 2, Atlas 2
America (Mex) 2, Santos 0
San Lorenzo 1, LDU Quito 1

QUARTER-FINALS SECOND LEG
Fluminense 3, Sao Paulo 1
Atlas 0, Boca Juniors 3
Santos 1, America (Mex) 0
LDU Quito 1, San Lorenzo 1
(LDU Quito won 5-3 on penalties.)

SEMI-FINALS FIRST LEG
America (Mex) 1, LDU Quito 1
Boca Juniors 2, Fluminense 2

SEMI-FINALS SECOND LEG
LDU Quito 0, America (Mex) 0
Fluminense 3, Boca Juniors 1

FINAL FIRST LEG
LDU Quito 4, Fluminense 2

FINAL SECOND LEG
Fluminense 3, LDU Quito 1
(LDU Quito won 3-1 on penalties.)

LEADING GOALSCORERS

Salvador Cabanas (America)	8
Marcelo Moreno (Cruzeiro)	8

ASIA

EAST ASIAN CHAMPIONSHIP

FINAL TABLE	P	W	D	L	F	A	Pts
South Korea	3	1	2	0	5	4	5
Japan	3	1	2	0	3	2	5
China	3	1	0	2	5	5	3
North Korea	3	0	2	1	3	5	2

SOUTH ASIAN CHAMPIONSHIP

FINAL
India 0, Maldives 1

ASIAN CUP

FINAL
Iraq 1, Saudi Arabia 0

ASIAN CHAMPIONS CUP

FINAL
Urawa 2, Sepahan 0
Sepahan 1, Urawa 1

AFRICAN NATIONS CUP 2008

FINAL TOURNAMENT IN GHANA

Group A	P	W	D	L	F	A	Pts
Ghana	3	3	0	0	5	1	9
Guinea	3	1	1	1	5	5	4
Morocco	3	1	0	2	7	6	3
Namibia	3	0	1	2	2	7	1
Group B	P	W	D	L	F	A	Pts
Ivory Coast	3	3	0	0	8	1	9
Nigeria	3	1	1	1	2	1	4
Mali	3	1	1	1	1	3	4
Benin	3	0	0	3	1	7	0
Group C	P	W	D	L	F	A	Pts
Egypt	3	2	1	0	8	3	7
Cameroon	3	2	0	1	10	5	6
Zambia	3	1	1	1	5	6	4
Sudan	3	0	0	3	0	9	0
Group D	P	W	D	L	F	A	Pts
Tunisia	3	1	2	0	5	3	5
Angola	3	1	2	0	4	2	5
Senegal	3	0	2	1	4	6	2
South Africa	3	0	2	1	3	5	2

QUARTER-FINALS
Ghana 2, Nigeria 1
Ivory Coast 5, Guinea 0
Egypt 2, Angola 1
Tunisia 2, Cameroon 3

SEMI-FINALS
Ghana 0, Cameroon 1
Ivory Coast 1, Egypt 4

MATCH FOR THIRD PLACE
Ghana 4, Ivory Coast 2

FINAL
Egypt 1, Cameroon 0

NORTH AMERICA

MAJOR LEAGUE SOCCER 2007

EASTERN CONFERENCE	P	W	D	L	F	A	Pts
DC United	30	16	7	7	56	34	55
New England Rev	30	14	8	8	51	43	50
New York Red Bulls	30	12	7	11	47	45	43
Kansas City Wizards	30	11	7	12	45	45	40
Chicago Fire	30	10	10	10	31	36	40
Columbus Crew	30	9	10	11	39	44	37
Toronto	30	6	7	17	25	49	25

WESTERN CONFERENCE	P	W	D	L	F	A	Pts
Chivas USA	30	15	8	7	46	28	53
Houston Dynamo	30	15	7	8	43	23	52
FC Dallas	30	13	5	12	37	44	44
Colorado Rapids	30	9	8	13	29	34	35
Los Angeles Galaxy	30	9	7	14	38	48	34
Real Salt Lake	30	6	9	15	31	45	27

SEMI-FINALS EASTERN CONFERENCE
Chicago Fire 1, DC United 0
New York Red Bulls 0, New England Rev 0
DC United 2, Chicago Fire 2
New England Rev 1, New York Red Bulls 0

SEMI-FINALS WESTERN CONFERENCE
FC Dallas 1, Houston Dynamo 0
Kansas City Wizards 1, Chivas USA 0
Houston Dynamo 4, FC Dallas 1
Chivas USA 0, Kansas City Wizards 0

EASTERN CONFERENCE FINAL
New England Rev 1, Chicago Fire 0

WESTERN CONFERENCE FINAL
Houston Dynamo 2, Kansas City Wizards 0

MLS CUP 2007
New England Rev 1, Houston Dynamo 2

UEFA UNDER-21 CHAMPIONSHIP 2007–09

QUALIFYING ROUND

GROUP 1
Italy 4, Albania 0
Greece 4, Azerbaijan 1
Croatia 2, Faeroes 0
Croatia 3, Greece 2
Albania 1, Faeroes 0
Azerbaijan 0, Greece 2
Italy 2, Faeroes 1
Albania 1, Croatia 0
Albania 0, Italy 1
Croatia 3, Azerbaijan 2
Faeroes 0, Greece 2
Italy 2, Croatia 0
Faeroes 1, Azerbaijan 0
Greece 2, Italy 2
Azerbaijan 1, Albania 1
Faeroes 1, Croatia 2
Italy 5, Azerbaijan 0
Faeroes 0, Albania 5
Greece 3, Croatia 4
Azerbaijan 0, Croatia 1
Faeroes 0, Italy 1
Greece 2, Albania 1
Azerbaijan 0, Italy 2

GROUP 2
Armenia 1, Liechtenstein 0
Ukraine 1, Turkey 2
Ukraine 4, Armenia 0
Armenia 1, Czech Republic 1
Liechtenstein 2, Turkey 3
Czech Republic 8, Liechtenstein 0
Armenia 0, Ukraine 2
Liechtenstein 0, Czech Republic 4
Turkey 2, Ukraine 0
Liechtenstein 1, Armenia 4
Turkey 3, Liechtenstein 0

GROUP 3
Bulgaria 1, Montenegro 2
Republic of Ireland 0, Portugal 2
Montenegro 0, England 3
Bulgaria 0, England 2
Portugal 4, Montenegro 0
Bulgaria 1, Portugal 0
England 1, Montenegro 0
Montenegro 1, Portugal 2
Republic of Ireland 0, England 3
Montenegro 1, Republic of Ireland 0
England 2, Bulgaria 0
Republic of Ireland 1, Bulgaria 0
England 3, Republic of Ireland 0
Republic of Ireland 1, Montenegro 1
Portugal 2, Bulgaria 0

GROUP 4
Georgia 0, Spain 1
Kazakhstan 0, Russia 3
Poland 3, Georgia 1
Georgia 2, Kazakhstan 1
Russia 1, Poland 0
Poland 1, Kazakhstan 0
Spain 4, Georgia 0
Russia 4, Kazakhstan 0
Poland 0, Spain 2
Kazakhstan 4, Georgia 1
Poland 0, Russia 1
Spain 3, Poland 0
Georgia 2, Russia 0
Spain 5, Kazakhstan 0

GROUP 5
Estonia 0, Norway 1
Macedonia 0, Holland 1
Norway 0, Holland 1
Switzerland 1, Macedonia 1
Macedonia 1, Estonia 0
Norway 2, Switzerland 1
Macedonia 1, Norway 1
Estonia 0, Switzerland 4
Holland 1, Macedonia 0
Switzerland 5, Estonia 0
Norway 2, Estonia 0
Macedonia 2, Switzerland 1
Holland 3, Estonia 0
Holland 0, Switzerland 1

GROUP 6
Slovenia 2, Lithuania 1
Denmark 0, Finland 1
Denmark 4, Lithuania 0
Finland 3, Scotland 2
Lithuania 0, Slovenia 0
Scotland 0, Denmark 0
Scotland 3, Lithuania 0
Finland 1, Slovenia 0
Slovenia 1, Denmark 3
Lithuania 0, Finland 1
Lithuania 0, Denmark 3
Slovenia 0, Scotland 4
Denmark 1, Slovenia 0
Finland 2, Lithuania 1
Scotland 2, Finland 1

GROUP 7
Iceland 0, Cyprus 1
Slovakia 2, Iceland 2
Belgium 0, Austria 1
Slovakia 1, Austria 1
Iceland 0, Belgium 0
Austria 2, Cyprus 1
Belgium 4, Slovakia 2
Iceland 1, Austria 1
Slovakia 4, Cyprus 1
Cyprus 1, Slovakia 2
Austria 3, Belgium 2
Cyprus 1, Austria 2
Belgium 1, Iceland 2
Cyprus 2, Iceland 0
Cyprus 0, Belgium 2
Austria 1, Slovakia 0

GROUP 8
Serbia 1, Latvia 1
Belarus 1, Hungary 0
Hungary 1, Latvia 0
San Marino 0, Belarus 3
Belarus 2, Latvia 1
San Marino 1, Hungary 6
Serbia 3, Belarus 1
Latvia 2, San Marino 0
Hungary 2, Serbia 1
Serbia 3, San Marino 0
Hungary 0, Belarus 1
Belarus 6, San Marino 0
Latvia 1, Hungary 0
Belarus 1, Serbia 1
San Marino 0, Serbia 5

GROUP 9
Moldova 0, Northern Ireland 1
Israel 3, Luxembourg 0
Northern Ireland 0, Germany 3
Moldova 1, Israel 0
Luxembourg 1, Northern Ireland 2
Israel 2, Germany 2
Luxembourg 0, Moldova 2
Germany 3, Moldova 0
Northern Ireland 1, Israel 3
Northern Ireland 5, Luxembourg 0
Northern Ireland 3, Moldova 0
Israel 2, Northern Ireland 1
Germany 6, Luxembourg 0
Israel 1, Moldova 0

GROUP 10
France 1, Romania 1
Malta 0, Romania 1
France 1, Wales 0
Bosnia 4, Malta 0
Romania 3, Bosnia 0
Malta 0, France 2
France 4, Bosnia 0
Romania 0, France 0
Wales 3, Malta 1
Romania 4, Malta 0
Wales 4, Bosnia 0
Malta 2, Bosnia 1
Wales 4, France 2
Malta 0, Wales 4
Bosnia 1, Wales 2

Competition still being played.

UEFA UNDER-17 CHAMPIONSHIP 2008

(Finals in Turkey)

GROUP A
Scotland 0, Serbia 2
Turkey 3, Holland 0
Turkey 1, Scotland 0
Holland 1, Serbia 0
Serbia 0, Turkey 0
Holland 2, Scotland 0

GROUP B
France 2, Republic of Ireland 1
Spain 2, Switzerland 0
Republic of Ireland 0, Switzerland 1
France 3, Spain 3
Switzerland 0, France 2
Republic of Ireland 1, Spain 3

SEMI-FINALS
Spain 2, Holland 1
Turkey 1, France 1
(France won 4-3 on penalties).

FINAL
France 0, Spain 4

FIFA UNDER-17 WORLD CUP 2007

(Finals in South Korea)

GROUP A

	P	W	D	L	F	A	Pts
Peru	3	2	1	0	2	0	7
Costa Rica	3	1	1	1	3	2	4
South Korea	3	1	0	2	2	4	3
Togo	3	0	2	1	2	3	2

GROUP B

	P	W	D	L	F	A	Pts
England	3	2	1	0	8	2	7
Brazil	3	2	0	1	14	3	6
North Korea	3	1	1	1	3	7	4
New Zealand	3	0	0	3	0	13	0

GROUP C

	P	W	D	L	F	A	Pts
Spain	3	2	1	0	7	4	7
Argentina	3	1	2	0	5	2	5
Syria	3	1	1	1	3	2	4
Honduras	3	0	0	3	3	10	0

GROUP D

	P	W	D	L	F	A	Pts
Nigeria	3	3	0	0	9	2	9
France	3	1	1	1	4	4	4
Japan	3	1	0	2	4	6	3
Haiti	3	0	1	2	3	8	1

GROUP E

	P	W	D	L	F	A	Pts
Tunisia	3	3	0	0	8	3	9
USA	3	1	0	2	6	7	3
Tajikistan	3	1	0	2	4	5	3
Belgium	3	1	0	2	3	6	3

GROUP F

	P	W	D	L	F	A	Pts
Germany	3	2	1	0	11	5	7
Ghana	3	2	0	1	8	5	6
Colombia	3	1	1	1	9	5	4
Trinidad & Tobago	3	0	0	3	1	14	0

FIRST ROUND

Tunisia 1, France 3
Spain 3, North Korea 0
Ghana 1, Brazil 0
Peru 1, Tajikistan 1
Peru won 5-4 on penalties.
Argentina 2, Costa Rica 0
Nigeria 2, Colombia 1
England 3, Syria 1
Germany 2, USA 1

QUARTER-FINALS

France 1, Spain 1
Spain won 5-4 on penalties.
Ghana 2, Peru 0
Argentina 0, Nigeria 2
England 1, Germany 4

SEMI-FINALS

Spain 2, Ghana 1
Nigeria 3, Germany 1

MATCH FOR THIRD PLACE

Ghana 1, Germany 2

FINAL

Spain 0, Nigeria 0
Nigeria won 3-0 on penalties.

FIFA UNDER-20 WORLD CUP 2007

(Finals in Canada)

GROUP A

	P	W	D	L	F	A	Pts
Chile	3	2	1	0	6	0	7
Austria	3	1	2	0	2	1	5
Congo	3	1	1	1	3	4	4
Canada	3	0	0	3	0	6	0

GROUP B

	P	W	D	L	F	A	Pts
Spain	3	2	1	0	8	5	7
Zambia	3	1	1	1	4	3	4
Uruguay	3	1	1	1	3	4	4
Jordan	3	0	1	2	3	6	1

GROUP C

	P	W	D	L	F	A	Pts
Mexico	3	3	0	0	7	2	9
Gambia	3	2	0	1	3	4	6
Portugal	3	1	0	2	4	4	3
New Zealand	3	0	0	3	1	5	0

GROUP D

	P	W	D	L	F	A	Pts
USA	3	2	1	0	9	3	7
Poland	3	1	1	1	3	7	4
Brazil	3	1	0	2	4	5	3
South Korea	3	0	2	1	4	5	2

GROUP E

	P	W	D	L	F	A	Pts
Argentina	3	2	1	0	7	0	7
Czech Republic	3	1	2	0	4	3	5
North Korea	3	0	2	1	2	3	2
Panama	3	0	1	2	1	8	1

GROUP F

	P	W	D	L	F	A	Pts
Japan	3	2	1	0	4	1	7
Nigeria	3	2	1	0	3	0	7
Costa Rica	3	1	0	2	2	3	3
Scotland	3	0	0	3	2	7	0

FIRST ROUND

Austria 2, Gambia 1
USA 2, Uruguay 1
Spain 4, Brazil 2
Japan 2, Czech Republic 2
Czech Republic won 4-3 on penalties.
Chile 1, Portugal 0
Zambia 1, Nigeria 2
Argentina 3, Poland 1
Mexico 3, Congo 0

QUARTER-FINALS

Austria 2, USA 1
Spain 1, Czech Republic 1
Czech Republic won 4-3 on penalties.
Chile 4, Nigeria 0
Argentina 1, Mexico 0

SEMI-FINALS

Austria 0, Czech Republic 2
Chile 0, Argentina 3

MATCH FOR THIRD PLACE

Austria 0, Chile 1

FINAL

Czech Republic 1, Argentina 2

ENGLAND UNDER-21 RESULTS 1976–2008

EC UEFA Competition for Under-21 Teams

Year	Date		Venue		
			v ALBANIA	Eng	Alb
EC1989	Mar	7	Shkroda	2	1
EC1989	April	25	Ipswich	2	0
EC2001	Mar	27	Tirana	1	0
EC2001	Sept	4	Middlesbrough	5	0
			v ANGOLA	Eng	Ang
1995	June	10	Toulon	1	0
1996	May	28	Toulon	0	2
			v ARGENTINA	Eng	Arg
1998	May	18	Toulon	0	2
2000	Feb	22	Fulham	1	0
			v AUSTRIA	Eng	Aus
1994	Oct	11	Kapfenberg	3	1
1995	Nov	14	Middlesbrough	2	1
EC2004	Sept	3	Krems	2	0
EC2005	Oct	7	Leeds	1	2
			v AZERBAIJAN	Eng	Az
EC2004	Oct	12	Baku	0	0
EC2005	Mar	29	Middlesbrough	2	0
			v BELGIUM	Eng	Bel
1994	June	5	Marseille	2	1
1996	May	24	Toulon	1	0
			v BRAZIL	Eng	B
1993	June	11	Toulon	0	0
1995	June	6	Toulon	0	2
1996	June	1	Toulon	1	2
			v BULGARIA	Eng	Bul
EC1979	June	5	Pernik	3	1
EC1979	Nov	20	Leicester	5	0
1989	June	5	Toulon	2	3
EC1998	Oct	9	West Ham	1	0
EC1999	June	8	Vratsa	1	0
EC2007	Sept	11	Sofia	2	0
EC2007	Nov	16	Milton Keynes	2	0
			v CROATIA	Eng	Cro
1996	Apr	23	Sunderland	0	1
2003	Aug	19	West Ham	0	3
			v CZECHOSLOVAKIA	Eng	Cz
1990	May	28	Toulon	2	1
1992	May	26	Toulon	1	2
1993	June	9	Toulon	1	1
			v CZECH REPUBLIC	Eng	CzR
1998	Nov	17	Ipswich	0	1
EC2007	June	11	Arnhem	0	0
			v DENMARK	Eng	Den
EC1978	Sept	19	Hvidovre	2	1
EC1979	Sept	11	Watford	1	0
EC1982	Sept	21	Hvidovre	4	1
EC1983	Sept	20	Norwich	4	1
EC1986	Mar	12	Copenhagen	1	0
EC1986	Mar	26	Manchester	1	1
1988	Sept	13	Watford	0	0
1994	Mar	8	Brentford	1	0
1999	Oct	8	Bradford	4	1
2005	Aug	16	Herning	1	0
			v EAST GERMANY	Eng	EG
EC1980	April	16	Sheffield	1	2
EC1980	April	23	Jena	0	1
			v FINLAND	Eng	Fin
EC1977	May	26	Helsinki	1	0
EC1977	Oct	12	Hull	8	1
EC1984	Oct	16	Southampton	2	0
EC1985	May	21	Mikkeli	1	3
				Eng	Fin
EC2000	Oct	10	Valkeakoski	2	2
EC2001	Mar	23	Barnsley	4	0
			v FRANCE	Eng	Fra
EC1984	Feb	28	Sheffield	6	1
EC1984	Mar	28	Rouen	1	0
1987	June	11	Toulon	0	2
EC1988	April	13	Besancon	2	4
EC1988	April	27	Highbury	2	2
1988	June	12	Toulon	2	4
1990	May	23	Toulon	7	3
1991	June	3	Toulon	1	0
1992	May	28	Toulon	0	0
1993	June	15	Toulon	1	0
1994	May	31	Aubagne	0	3
1995	June	10	Toulon	0	2
1998	May	14	Toulon	1	1
1999	Feb	9	Derby	2	1
EC2005	Nov	11	Tottenham	1	1
EC2005	Nov	15	Nancy	1	2
			v GEORGIA	Eng	Geo
EC1996	Nov	8	Batumi	1	0
EC1997	April	29	Charlton	0	0
2000	Aug	31	Middlesbrough	6	1
			v GERMANY	Eng	Ger
1991	Sept	10	Scunthorpe	2	1
EC2000	Oct	6	Derby	1	1
EC2001	Aug	31	Frieburg	2	1
2005	Mar	25	Hull	2	2
2005	Sept	6	Mainz	1	1
EC2006	Oct	6	Coventry	1	0
EC2006	Oct	10	Leverkusen	2	0
			v GREECE	Eng	Gre
EC1982	Nov	16	Piraeus	0	1
EC1983	Mar	29	Portsmouth	2	1
1989	Feb	7	Patras	0	1
EC1997	Nov	13	Heraklion	0	2
EC1997	Dec	17	Norwich	4	2
EC2001	June	5	Athens	1	3
EC2001	Oct	5	Ewood Park	2	1
			v HOLLAND	Eng	H
EC1993	April	27	Portsmouth	3	0
EC1993	Oct	12	Utrecht	1	1
2001	Aug	14	Reading	4	0
EC2001	Nov	9	Utrecht	2	2
EC2001	Nov	13	Derby	1	0
2004	Feb	17	Hull	3	2
2005	Feb	8	Derby	1	2
2006	Nov	14	Alkmaar	1	0
EC2007	June	20	Heerenveen	1	1
			v HUNGARY	Eng	Hun
EC1981	June	5	Keszthely	2	1
EC1981	Nov	17	Nottingham	2	0
EC1983	April	26	Newcastle	1	0
EC1983	Oct	11	Nyiregyhaza	2	0
1990	Sept	11	Southampton	3	1
1992	May	12	Budapest	2	2
1999	April	27	Budapest	2	2
			v REPUBLIC OF IRELAND	Eng	RoI
1981	Feb	25	Liverpool	1	0
1985	Mar	25	Portsmouth	3	2
1989	June	9	Toulon	0	0
EC1990	Nov	13	Cork	3	0
EC1991	Mar	26	Brentford	3	0
1994	Nov	15	Newcastle	1	0
1995	Mar	27	Dublin	2	0

				Eng	RoI
EC2007	Oct	16	Cork	3	0
EC2008	Feb	5	Southampton	3	0

			v ITALY	Eng	Italy
EC1978	Mar	8	Manchester	2	1
EC1978	April	5	Rome	0	0
EC1984	April	18	Manchester	3	1
EC1984	May	2	Florence	0	1
EC1986	April	9	Pisa	0	2
EC1986	April	23	Swindon	1	1
EC1997	Feb	12	Bristol	1	0
EC1997	Oct	10	Rieti	1	0
EC2000	May	27	Bratislava	0	2
2000	Nov	14	Monza*	0	0
2002	Mar	26	Valley Parade	1	1
EC2002	May	20	Basle	1	2
2003	Feb	11	Pisa	0	1
2007	Mar	24	Wembley	3	3
EC2007	June	14	Arnhem	2	2

**Abandoned 11 mins; fog.*

			v ISRAEL	Eng	Isr
1985	Feb	27	Tel Aviv	2	1

			v LATVIA	Eng	Lat
1995	April	25	Riga	1	0
1995	June	7	Burnley	4	0

			v LUXEMBOURG	Eng	Lux
EC1998	Oct	13	Greven Macher	5	0
EC1999	Sept	3	Reading	5	0

			v MACEDONIA	Eng	M
EC2002	Oct	15	Reading	3	1
EC2003	Sept	5	Skopje	1	1

			v MALAYSIA	Eng	Mal
1995	June	8	Toulon	2	0

			v MEXICO	Eng	Mex
1988	June	5	Toulon	2	1
1991	May	29	Toulon	6	0
1992	May	25	Toulon	1	1
2001	May	24	Leicester	3	0

			v MOLDOVA	Eng	Mol
EC1996	Aug	31	Chisinau	2	0
EC1997	Sept	9	Wycombe	1	0
EC2006	Aug	15	Ipswich	2	2

			v MONTENEGRO	Eng	M
EC2007	Sept	7	Podgorica	3	0
EC2007	Oct	12	Leicester	1	0

			v MOROCCO	Eng	Mor
1987	June	7	Toulon	2	0
1988	June	9	Toulon	1	0

			v NORWAY	Eng	Nor
EC1977	June	1	Bergen	2	1
EC1977	Sept	6	Brighton	6	0
1980	Sept	9	Southampton	3	0
1981	Sept	8	Drammen	0	0
EC1992	Oct	13	Peterborough	0	2
EC1993	June	1	Stavanger	1	1
1995	Oct	10	Stavanger	2	2
2006	Feb	28	Reading	3	1

			v POLAND	Eng	Pol
EC1982	Mar	17	Warsaw	2	1
EC1982	April	7	West Ham	2	2
EC1989	June	2	Plymouth	2	1
EC1989	Oct	10	Jastrzebie	3	1
EC1990	Oct	16	Tottenham	0	1
EC1991	Nov	12	Pila	1	2
EC1993	May	28	Zdroj	4	1
EC1993	Sept	7	Millwall	1	2
EC1996	Oct	8	Wolverhampton	0	0

				Eng	Pol
EC1997	May	30	Katowice	1	1
EC1999	Mar	26	Southampton	5	0
EC1999	Sept	7	Plock	1	3
EC2004	Sept	7	Rybnik	3	1
EC2005	Oct	11	Hillsborough	4	1
2008	Mar	25	Wolverhampton	0	0

			v PORTUGAL	Eng	Por
1987	June	13	Toulon	0	0
1990	May	21	Toulon	0	1
1993	June	7	Toulon	2	0
1994	June	7	Toulon	2	0
EC1994	Sept	6	Leicester	0	0
1995	Sept	2	Lisbon	0	2
1996	May	30	Toulon	1	3
2000	Apr	16	Stoke	0	1
EC2002	May	22	Zurich	1	3
EC2003	Mar	28	Rio Major	2	4
EC2003	Sept	9	Everton	1	2
EC2008	Nov	20	Agueda	1	1

			v ROMANIA	Eng	Rom
EC1980	Oct	14	Ploesti	0	4
EC1981	April	28	Swindon	3	0
EC1985	April	30	Brasov	0	0
EC1985	Sept	10	Ipswich	3	0
2007	Aug	21	Bristol	1	1

			v RUSSIA	Eng	Rus
1994	May	30	Bandol	2	0

			v SAN MARINO	Eng	SM
EC1993	Feb	16	Luton	6	0
EC1993	Nov	17	San Marino	4	0

			v SENEGAL	Eng	Sen
1989	June	7	Toulon	6	1
1991	May	27	Toulon	2	1

			v SERBIA	Eng	Ser
EC2007	June	17	Nijmegen	2	0

			v SERBIA-MONTENEGRO	Eng	S-M
2003	June	2	Hull	3	2

			v SCOTLAND	Eng	Sco
1977	April	27	Sheffield	1	0
EC1980	Feb	12	Coventry	2	1
EC1980	Mar	4	Aberdeen	0	0
EC1982	April	19	Glasgow	1	0
EC1982	April	28	Manchester	1	1

				Eng	Sco
EC1988	Feb	16	Aberdeen	1	0
EC1988	Mar	22	Nottingham	1	0
1993	June	13	Toulon	1	0

			v SLOVAKIA	Eng	Slo
EC2002	June	1	Bratislava	0	2
EC2002	Oct	11	Trnava	4	0
EC2003	June	10	Sunderland	2	0
2007	June	5	Norwich	5	0

			v SLOVENIA	Eng	Slo
2000	Feb	12	Nova Gorica	1	0

			v SOUTH AFRICA	Eng	SA
1998	May	16	Toulon	3	1

			v SPAIN	Eng	Spa
EC1984	May	17	Seville	1	0
EC1984	May	24	Sheffield	2	0
1987	Feb	18	Burgos	2	1
1992	Sept	8	Burgos	1	0
2001	Feb	27	Birmingham	0	4
2004	Nov	16	Alcala	0	1
2007	Feb	6	Derby	2	2

			v SWEDEN	Eng	Swe
1979	June	9	Vasteras	2	1
1986	Sept	9	Ostersund	1	1
				Eng	Swe
EC1988	Oct	18	Coventry	1	1
EC1989	Sept	5	Uppsala	0	1
EC1998	Sept	4	Sundvall	2	0
EC1999	June	4	Huddersfield	3	0
2004	Mar	30	Kristiansund	2	2
			v SWITZERLAND	Eng	Swit
EC1980	Nov	18	Ipswich	5	0
EC1981	May	31	Neuenburg	0	0
1988	May	28	Lausanne	1	1
1996	April	1	Swindon	0	0
1998	Mar	24	Brugglifeld	0	2
EC2002	May	17	Zurich	2	1
EC2006	Sept	6	Lucerne	3	2
			v TURKEY	Eng	Tur
EC1984	Nov	13	Bursa	0	0
EC1985	Oct	15	Bristol	3	0
EC1987	April	28	Izmir	0	0
EC1987	Oct	13	Sheffield	1	1
EC1991	April	30	Izmir	2	2
1991	Oct	15	Reading	2	0
EC1992	Nov	17	Orient	0	1
EC1993	Mar	30	Izmir	0	0
EC2000	May	29	Bratislava	6	0
EC2003	April	1	Newcastle	1	1
EC2003	Oct	10	Istanbul	0	1

			v UKRAINE	Eng	Uk
2004	Aug	17	Middlesbrough	3	1
			v USA	Eng	USA
1989	June	11	Toulon	0	2
1994	June	2	Toulon	3	0
			v USSR	Eng	USSR
1987	June	9	Toulon	0	0
1988	June	7	Toulon	1	0
1990	May	25	Toulon	2	1
1991	May	31	Toulon	2	1
			v WALES	Eng	Wales
1976	Dec	15	Wolverhampton	0	0
1979	Feb	6	Swansea	1	0
1990	Dec	5	Tranmere	0	0
EC2004	Oct	8	Blackburn	2	0
EC2005	Sept	2	Wrexham	4	0
2008	May	5	Wrexham	2	0
			v WEST GERMANY	Eng	WG
EC1982	Sept	21	Sheffield	3	1
EC1982	Oct	12	Bremen	2	3
1987	Sept	8	Ludenscheid	0	2
			v YUGOSLAVIA	Eng	Yugo
EC1978	April	19	Novi Sad	1	2
EC1978	May	2	Manchester	1	1
EC1986	Nov	11	Peterborough	1	1
EC1987	Nov	10	Zemun	5	1
EC2000	Mar	29	Barcelona	3	0
2002	Sept	6	Bolton	1	1

ENGLAND C 2007–2008

15 November 2007 *(in Helsinki)*

Finland 0

England C 2 *(Morrison 34, Tubbs 58)*

England: Cronin; Brayford, Brownhill, Chalmers, Henry, Morrison, Penn, Lewes, Constable, Tubbs (Harrad), Okay (Gleeson).

21 February 2008 *(at Exeter)*

England 2 *(Cole 39, Morrison 51)*

Wales 1 *(Lawless 49)* 2443

England: Cronin; Brayford, Brownhill, Harding, Henry, Morrison, Penn (Gleeson 81), Chalmers, Harrad (Holmes 87), Cole (Goulding 74), Moxey.
Wales: Morris; Critchell, Gross (Davies 79), Lawless, Parslow, Surman (Rewbury 72), Byrne (Edwards 70), Fowler, Bond, Fleetwood, Jones (Stephens 87).

FOUR NATIONS TOURNAMENT

20 May 2008 *(in Colwyn Bay)*

England 1 *(Cole 35)*

Gibraltar 0

England: Bartlett; McPhee, Brayford, Morrison, Nicholson, Harding, Chalmers (Martin 72), Penn (Gleeson 68), Burgess, Cole (Harrad 80), Morrison (Shaw 75).

22 May 2008 *(in Colwyn Bay)*

England 1 *(Morison 75)*

Scotland 0

England: Tynan; Brayford, Morrison, Hatswell, Nicholson, McPhee, Martin, Gleeson (Cole 70), Moxey (Burgess 46), Harrad, Shaw (Morrison 70).

24 May 2008 *(in Rhyl)*

England 3 *(Burgess 27 (pen), Morrison 34, Harrad 65)*

Wales 0 659

England: Bartlett; Brayford, Nicholson, Harding, Hatswell, Morrison (McPhee 72), Penn, Cole (Harrad 61), Martin (Chalmers 20), Burgess, Morison (Shaw 67).

	P	*W*	*D*	*L*	*F*	*A*	*Pts*
England	3	3	0	0	5	0	9
Wales	3	1	1	1	7	6	4
Scotland	3	1	1	1	5	4	4
Gibraltar	3	0	0	3	4	11	0

FRIENDLIES

31 May 2008 *(at St George's)*

Grenada 1 *(Langaigne 30)*

England 1 *(Morison 77)* 2700

England: Tynan; Brayford, Morrison, Hatswell, Nicholson, Burgess, Gleeson (Penn 67), Chalmers, Woolford (Harrad 67), Morrison (Shaw 82), Cole.

2 June 2008 *(at Bridgetown)*

Barbados 0

England 2 *(Shaw 16, Penn 75)* 3100

England: Bartlett; Brayford, Morrison, Smith (Hatswell 85), Nicholson, Burgess, Penn, Chalmers (Gleeson 75), Cole (Woolford 67), Shaw (Morrison 77), Harrad.

BRITISH AND IRISH UNDER-21 TEAMS 2007–08

■ *Denotes player sent off.*

ENGLAND

Bristol City, 21 August 2007, 18,640

England (1) 1 *(Derbyshire 8)*

Romania (1) 1 *(Hart 25 (og)) Scutaru*■

England: Hart (Alnwick 46); Gardner (Mancienne 46), Onuoha, Wheater, Cranie, Kightly (Johnson A 46), Johnson M (Huddlestone 65), Noble (Muamba 65), Walcott, Derbyshire (Milner 78), Agbonlahor (Moore 78).

Podgorica, 7 September 2007

Montenegro (0) 0

England (2) 3 *(Onuoha 6, Agbonlahor 10, Surman 90)*

England: Hart; Cranie, Taylor A, Noble, Taylor S, Onuoha, Milner, Gardner (Surman 80), Derbyshire (Blackstock 90), Agbonlahor, Walcott (Muamba 63).

Sofia, 11 September 2007, 1000

Bulgaria (0) 0

England (2) 2 *(Huddlestone 25, Noble 32)*

England: Hart; Cranie, Taylor A, Noble, Taylor S, Onuoha, Milner, Huddlestone, Derbyshire (Moore 81), Agbonlahor (Kightly 70), Walcott (Muamba 55).

Leicester, 12 October 2007, 20,022

England (1) 1 *(Derbyshire 20)*

Montenegro (0) 0

England: Hart; Cranie, Taylor A, Surman (Muamba 30), Taylor S, Onuoha, Milner, Huddlestone, Derbyshire (Jerome 79), Agbonlahor (Kightly 83), Walcott.

Cork, 16 October 2007

Republic of Ireland (0) 0

England (3) 3 *(Noble 10, 17, Milner 26)*

Republic of Ireland: Randolph; Nolan, O'Halloran, Keogh R, O'Dea, Garvan, O'Brien J, Quinn S, Rooney (Powell 66), Stokes, Clarke (Gleeson 88).
England: Hart; Cranie, Taylor A, Noble, Taylor S, Onuoha (Wheater 77), Milner, Huddlestone, Derbyshire (Moore 66), Agbonlahor (Johnson A 75), Walcott.

Milton Keynes, 16 November 2007, 20,222

England (1) 2 *(Agbonlahor 40, Milner 81 (pen))*

Bulgaria (0) 0

England: Hart; Gardner, Mattock, Cattermole, Taylor S, Wheater, Milner, Huddlestone (Johnson A 85), Derbyshire (Muamba 46), Abgonlahor (Leadbitter 79), Walcott.

Agueda, 20 November 2007, 5468

Portugal (1) 1 *(Vieirinha 3 (pen))*

England (0) 1 *(Johnson A 49)*

England: Hart; Gardner, Mattock, Cattermole, Taylor S (Mancienne 46), Wheater, Milner, Huddlestone, Johnson A, Muamba, Walcott.

Southampton, 5 February 2008, 31,473

England (0) 3 *(O'Halloran 59 (og), Milner 68, Walcott 78)*

Republic of Ireland (0) 0

England: Hart; Gardner, Mattock, Noble (Surman 86), Taylor S, Wheater, Milner, Huddlestone (Jerome 79), Lennon, Muamba, Walcott (Johnson A 86).
Republic of Ireland: Randolph; Nolan, O'Halloran, O'Cearuill, O'Dea, Quinn S (Morris 83), Garvan, O'Toole, Keogh A, Stokes (O'Brien J 87), Clarke (Rooney 65).

Wolverhampton, 25 March 2008, 28,178

England (0) 0

Poland (0) 0

England: Hart (Heaton 46); Mancienne, Fox, Surman (Mattock 88), Onuoha, Shawcross (Dann 65), Gardner (Leadbitter 46), O'Hara, Jerome (Campbell 65), Moore (Derbyshire 65), Johnson A.

SCOTLAND

Falkirk, 21 August 2007, 1685

Scotland (1) 1 *(Naismith 4)*

Czech Republic (0) 0

Scotland: MacDonald; Cuthbert, Dixon (Scobbie 82), Hamill (Quinn 57), O'Leary, Reynolds, McCormack, Mulgrew (McDonald K 66), Fletcher (McAllister 66), Stevenson (Fitzpatrick 57), Naismith (Campbell 72).

Vaasa, 8 September 2007

Finland (1) 3 *(Sadik, Petrescu 48, Jalisto 89)*

Scotland (1) 2 *(Fletcher 45, Mulgrew 80)*

Scotland: MacDonald; Kenneth, Wallace, Reynolds, Cuthbert, Stevenson, McCormack (Scobbie 86), Hamill (Fitzpatrick 65), Fletcher, Mulgrew■, Naismith.

Dunfermline, 12 September 2007, 1041

Scotland (0) 0

Denmark (0) 0

Scotland: MacDonald; Kenneth, Wallace, Reynolds, Cuthbert, Stevenson (Fitzpatrick 69), McCormack (Campbell 81), Hamill, Fletcher, Robertson (Quinn 57), Naismith.

Easter Road, 11 October 2007

Scotland (2) 3 *(McCormack 44, Mulgrew 45, Fletcher 59)*

Lithuania (0) 0

Scotland: MacDonald; Kenneth, Considine, Reynolds, Cuthbert (McCann 86), Hamill, McCormack, McDonald, Fletcher (Campbell 83), Mulgrew (Stevenson 68), Naismith.

16 October 2007, 4500

Holland (1) 4 *(Bruins 14, 72, Bakkal 77, George 88)*

Scotland (0) 0

Scotland: Smith (McLean 46); McCann, Considine (Dixon 54), Reynolds, Kenneth, Hamill (McDonald 78), Campbell, Quinn (Arfield 78), Elliot (Cuthbert 57), Mulgrew (Stevenson 68), Naismith (Cameron 54).

Nova Gorica, 17 November 2007

Slovenia (0) 0

Scotland (1) 4 *(Hamill 33, McCormack 51, Naismith 57 (pen), Fletcher 62)*

Scotland: MacDonald; McCann, Wallace, Hamill (Cameron 50), Kenneth, Reynolds, McCormack, Arfield, Fletcher, Mulgrew (Stevenson 81), Naismith (Quinn 76).

Abrantes, 5 February 2008

Portugal (1) 2 *(Saleiro 33, Pele 67)*

Scotland (0) 1 *(Quinn 82)*

Scotland: MacDonald; Wallace, Hamill, Cuthbert, Scobbie, Elliot, Naismith, Caddis, Dorrans (Conroy 83), Quinn, Stevenson.

Cartaxo, 6 February 2008

Ukraine (1) 2 *(Stepanenko 42, L'opa 51)*

Scotland (0) 2 *(Arfield 65, Conroy 71)*

Scotland: Smith; McCann, Cuthbert, O'Leary, Mulgrew, Arfield, Cameron, McArthur, Snodgrass (Conroy 66), Campbell, Lennon (Elliot 85).

Aberdeen, 26 March 2008, 4700

Scotland (1) 2 *(Naismith 29, McDonald 83)*

Finland (1) 1 *(Hamalainen 40)*

Scotland: MacDonald; Cuthbert, Wallace, Hamill, Kenneth, Reynolds, McCormack, McDonald, Campbell (Dorrans 56), Arfield (Mulgrew 71), Naismith.

Kilmarnock, 20 May 2008, 3036

Scotland (0) 1 *(Cuthbert 70)*

Norway (1) 4 *(Skjelbred 27, Mathisen 55, Elyounossi 74, Kleiven 90)*

Scotland: McLean (Fleming 46); Mitchell, Cuthbert, Pearce (McAllister 86), Wallace, Dorrans (Lennon 62), Arfield, Hamill (McCormack 76), Mulgrew, Elliot, Conroy (Snodgrass 58).

WALES

Helstad, 21 August 2007, 1717

Sweden (3) 3 *(Toivonen 11 (pen), 31 (pen), 44)*

Wales (2) 4 *(Cotterill 27, Edwards 45, Vokes 58, Allen 61)*

Wales: Williams O (Taylor R 46); Blake, Jacobson, Collins M (Ramsey 46), Williams R (Taylor N 57), Mike Williams, Allen (Warlow 83), Edwards, Evans C (Church 76), Cotterill, MacDonald.

France, 7 September 2007, 2000

France (0) 1 *(Erdley 50 (og))*

Wales (0) 0

Wales: Williams O; Erdley, Jacobson, Ramsey (James 81), Gunter, Mike Williams, Allen (Vokes 67), Edwards, Evans C, Cotterill, MacDonald (Taylor N 67).

Wrexham, 17 October 2007, 1112

Wales (2) 3 *(Mike Williams 16, Church 41, Vokes 72)*

Malta (0) 1 *(Zammit 79)*

Wales: Williams O; Gunter, Jacobson (Taylor N 75), Williams D, Ramsey, Mike Williams, Allen, Bradley (MacDonald 68), Church, Vokes, Cotterill.

Wrexham, 17 November 2007, 759

Wales (1) 4 *(MacDonald 29, Vokes 54, Evans C 72, Collison 86)*

Bosnia (0) 0

Wales: Williams O; Blake, Jacobson, Ramsey (Bradley 65), Mike Williams, Rhys Williams (Ribeiro 38), Allen (Adams 82), Vokes, Evans C, MacDonald, Collison.

Cardiff, 20 November 2007, 564

Wales (1) 4 *(Evans C 44, 79 (pen), 90 (pen))*

France (0) 2 *(Gourcuff 72 (pen), Payet 76)*

Wales: Williams O; Blake, Jacobson, Ramsey (Bradley 58), Mike Williams, Allen, Vokes (Church 70), Evans C, MacDonald, Ribeiro, Collison.

Paola, 5 February 2008

Malta (0) 0

Wales (0) 4 *(Evans C 62, 90 (pen), Church 80, Williams R 88)*

Wales: Williams O; Blake, Jacobson, Collison, Williams R, Mike Williams, Allen (King 84), Ramsey (Brown 57), Vokes (Church 70), Evans C, MacDonald.

Sarajevo, 26 March 2008, 1030

Bosnia (0) 1 *(Dialiba 58)*

Wales (0) 2 *(Church 86, Evans 88)*

Wales: Williams O; Jacobson, Collison, Gunter, Williams R, Allen (Brown 55), Ramsey (Bradley 72), Vokes (Church 72), Evans C, MacDonald, Mike Williams.

Wrexham, 15 May 2008, 6831

Wales (0) 0

England (2) 2 *(Huddlestone 19 (pen), Walcott 25)*

Wales: Hennessey; Eardley (Ribeiro 62), Jacobson, Collison, Gunter, Nyatanga, Cotterill (Adams 77), Edwards D, Vokes (Church 63), Evans C (Davies C 77), MacDonald.

England: Hart (Lewis 46); Cranie, Taylor A (O'Hara 57), Cattermole, Mancienne, Wheater (Dann 46), Walcott, Huddlestone, Agbonlahor (Blackstock 57), Leadbitter (Muamba 73), Johnson A (Shawcross 86).

NORTHERN IRELAND

Ballymena, 21 August 2007

Northern Ireland (0) 2 *(McKenna 79, Taylor 84)*

Finland (1) 1 *(Puustinen 18)*

Northern Ireland: Tuffey; Callaghan, Taylor, McArdle, Casement, Garrett, Mulgrew (Hazley), McKenna, Stewart (McAllister), Fordyce (Waterworth), Buchanan (Carvill).

Lurgan, 7 September 2007

Northern Ireland (0) 0

Germany (0) 3 *(Ebert 78, Ozil 89, Hennings 90)*

Northern Ireland: Tuffey; Buchanan (McCaffrey 85), Callaghan, Casement, Fordyce, Garrett, McArdle, Stewart (Waterworth 89), Taylor, Turner (Carvill 80), McKenna.

Beggen, 12 September 2007

Luxembourg (1) 1 *(Sagramola 9)*

Northern Ireland (0) 2 *(Fordyce 63, Waterworth 74)*

Northern Ireland: Tuffey; Callaghan, Taylor, McArdle, Casement, Garrett, Turner (Mulgrew), McKenna, Stewart (Waterworth), Fordyce, Buchanan (Carvill).

Lurgan, 17 October 2007

Northern Ireland (0) 1 *(Turner 57)*

Israel (1) 3 *(Bozaglo 1, Shechter 51, Azriel 81)*

Northern Ireland: Tuffey; Kane, Taylor, McArdle, Casement, Chapman (Mulgrew 55), Turner, Fordyce, Stewart (Waterworth 55), Carvill, Buchanan (McAllister 77).

Lurgan, 16 November 2007

Northern Ireland (4) 5 *(Buchanan 2, Waterworth 5, O'Connor 8, Ward 27, Turner 56)*

Luxembourg (0) 0

Northern Ireland: Tuffey (Carson 46); Kane, Callaghan, McArdle, Cathcart, Garrett (Howland 46), Turner, O'Connor, Waterworth, Ward (Carvill 71), Buchanan.

Lurgan, 20 November 2007

Northern Ireland (3) 3 *(O'Connor 3, Ward 10, Buchanan 11)*

Moldova (0) 0

Northern Ireland: Tuffey; Kane, Callaghan, McArdle, Cathcart, Garrett, Turner, O'Connor (Stewart 70), Waterworth, Ward (Fordyce 60), Buchanan.

Tel Aviv, 6 February 2008

Israel (0) 2 *(Sahar 65, Srur 87)*

Northern Ireland (0) 1 *(Stewart 82)*

Northern Ireland: Tuffey; Buchanan, Callaghan (Carvill 89), Garrett (Fordyce 78), McArdle, Stewart, Turner (Mulgrew 82), O'Connor, Kane, Ward, Cathcart.

Ballymena, 26 March 2008

Northern Ireland (0) 1 *(Stewart 65)*

Romania (2) 3 *(Deac 32, Keseru 45, 70)*

Northern Ireland: Carson (Tuffey 46); Kane, McCaffrey, Casement, McArdle (Callaghan 46), Garrett, Turner (McVey 79), Howland (Buchanan 46), Waterworth (Fordyce 62), Carvill (Stewart 62), Meenan (Mulgrew 60).

REPUBLIC OF IRELAND

Furth, 21 August 2007, 5000

Germany (1) 2 *(Hennings 17, Beck 85)*

Republic of Ireland (1) 2 *(Gleeson 38, 66)*

Republic of Ireland: Randolph; Kane (Nolan 46), O'Halloran, Keogh R, O'Dea, Cregg (McFaul 70), Gleeson, Quinn S (Collins M 46), Rooney, O'Brien J (Kelly 75), Clarke (Powell 70).

Dublin, 7 September 2007, 2759

Republic of Ireland (0) 0

Portugal (1) 2 *(Paulo Machado 4, Veloso 54)*

Republic of Ireland: Randolph; Nolan, Keogh R, O'Dea, O'Halloran, Gleeson (Collins M 68), Cregg (Garvan 46), Quinn S, O'Brien J, Rooney (Sammon 74), Clarke.

Uppsala, 12 October 2007

Sweden (0) 2 *(Oremo 55, Wernbloom 86)*

Republic of Ireland (1) 3 *(Quinn S 20, Sheehan 62, Downes 71)*

Republic of Ireland: Randolph (Henderson 46); Nolan (Coleman 58), Spillane, O'Dea, O'Halloran, Cregg, Garvan (Power 46), Quinn S (Sheehan 46), O'Brien J (Judge 68), Downes, Stokes.

Podgorica, 16 November 2007

Montenegro (1) 1 *(Vujovic 4)*

Republic of Ireland (0) 0

Republic of Ireland: Quigley; Nolan, Powell, O'Cearuill, Keogh R, O'Toole (Downes 69), Gleeson, Quinn S, Rooney, O'Brien J (Sammon 88), Treacy.

Athlone, 20 November 2007, 1251

Republic of Ireland (0) 1 *(O'Toole 90)*

Bulgaria (0) 0

Republic of Ireland: Quigley; Nolan, Powell, O'Cearuill, O'Dea, Gleeson, Sheehan, Quinn S (O'Toole 83), O'Brien J (Downes 88), Rooney (Sammon 73), Stokes.

Galway, 25 March 2008

Republic of Ireland (0) 1 *(Keogh 73)*

Montenegro (0) 1 *(Bojovic 68)*

Republic of Ireland: Supple; Nolan, O'Cearuill, O'Dea, Powell, Gibson, O'Toole (Best 60), Stokes, Clarke (Scannell 46), Quinn S, Keogh A.

REPUBLIC OF IRELAND UNDER-23 INTERNATIONALS

Dublin, 13 November 2007

Republic of Ireland (2) 2 *(Peers 26, Brennan 33)*

Slovakia (0) 0

Republic of Ireland: Murphy; O'Brien G, Powell, Kenna, Peers, Keegan, Kelly (Kavanagh 86), Rice (O'Donnell 71), Behan (Rowe 65), Mooney (Sammon 76), Brennan.

Lurgan, 13 May 2008

Northern Ireland (0) 0

Republic of Ireland (0) 1 *(Price 90)*

Northern Ireland: Nelson; Holland, McClean, Mulgrew, Watson, Lindsay, Ward S, Clarke, Thompson, Stewart (McAllister 73), Scullion (Garrett 57).
Republic of Ireland: Murphy (Shamrock R); O'Brien, Guthrie, Kenna (Murphy (Cork City) 78), Powell, Kelly (Behan 46), Keegan, Rice, Brennan, Quigley (Rowe 65), Mooney.

INTERNATIONAL TROPHY CHALLENGE

Belgium, 11 Dec 2007

Belgium (0) 2 *(Hubert 56, Lutun 85)*

Northern Ireland (0) 1 *(Thompson 46)*

Northern Ireland: Nelson; Holland, Lindsay, Watson, Ogilby, Mulgrew (Scullion 67), Ward S, Clarke, Waterworth (Stewart 67), Thompson, McGinn.

INTERCONTINENTAL CUP

Malaysia, 15 May 2008

Malaysia (0) 1 *(Sale 90)*

Republic of Ireland (2) 3 *(Collins 2, Ward)*

Republic of Ireland: Redmond; Nolan, Dennehy (Ryan 73), Spillane, Lowry, Elebert (Maher 69), Collins, Berrett, Treacy (Judge 84), Clarke, Ward.

Malaysia, 17 May 2008

Nigeria (2) 3 *(Jerimiah 12, Okorowanta 28, Moses 54)*

Republic of Ireland (0) 1 *(Clarke 90)*

Republic of Ireland: Skinner; Madden, Dennehy, Lowry, Elebert, Ryan, Maher (Collins 58), Salmon (Treacy 85), Moore (Ward 72), Judge, Clarke.

Malaysia, 19 May 2008

Iraq (0) 0

Republic of Ireland (0) 0

Republic of Ireland: Redmond; Nolan, Dennehy, Elebert, Lowry, Ryan, Berrett (Judge 67), Collins, Treacy, Clarke, Ward.

SEMI-FINAL

Malaysia, 23 May 2008

Australia (2) 3 *(Simon 7, 17, 75)*

Republic of Ireland (0) 1 *(Judge 84)*

Republic of Ireland: Redmond; Madden, Elebert, Lowry, Spillane, Ryan (Maher 84), Collins (Salmon 23), Treacy, Judge, Clarke, Ward (Moore 25).

BRITISH UNDER-21 APPEARANCES 1976–2008

ENGLAND

Player	Apps
Ablett, G. 1988 (Liverpool)	1
Adams, N. 1987 (Everton)	1
Adams, T. A. 1985 (Arsenal)	5
Agbonlahor, G. 2007 (Aston Villa)	10
Allen, B. 1992 (QPR)	8
Allen, C. 1980 (QPR, C Palace)	3
Allen, C. A. 1995 (Oxford U)	2
Allen, M. 1987 (QPR)	2
Allen, P. 1985 (West Ham U, Tottenham H)	3
Allen, R. W. 1998 (Tottenham H)	3
Alnwick, B. R. 2008 (Tottenham H)	1
Ambrose, D. P. F. 2003 (Ipswich T, Newcastle U, Charlton Ath)	10
Ameobi, F. 2001 (Newcastle U)	19
Anderson, V. A. 1978 (Nottingham F)	1
Anderton, D. R. 1993 (Tottenham H)	12
Andrews, I. 1987 (Leicester C)	1
Ardley, N. C. 1993 (Wimbledon)	10
Ashcroft, L. 1992 (Preston NE)	1
Ashton, D. 2004 (Crewe Alex, Norwich C)	9
Atherton, P. 1992 (Coventry C)	1
Atkinson, B. 1991 (Sunderland)	6
Awford, A. T. 1993 (Portsmouth)	9
Bailey, G. R. 1979 (Manchester U)	14
Baines, L. J. 2005 (Wigan Ath)	16
Baker, G. E. 1981 (Southampton)	2
Ball, M. J. 1999 (Everton)	7
Barker, S. 1985 (Blackburn R)	4
Barmby, N. J. 1994 (Tottenham H, Everton)	4
Bannister, G. 1982 (Sheffield W)	1
Barnes, J. 1983 (Watford)	2
Barnes, P. S. 1977 (Manchester C)	9
Barrett, E. D. 1990 (Oldham Ath)	4
Barry, G. 1999 (Aston Villa)	27
Barton, J. 2004 (Manchester C)	2
Bart-Williams, C. G. 1993 (Sheffield W)	16
Batty, D. 1988 (Leeds U)	7
Bazeley, D. S. 1992 (Watford)	1
Beagrie, P. 1988 (Sheffield U)	2
Beardsmore, R. 1989 (Manchester U)	5
Beattie, J. S. 1999 (Southampton)	5
Beckham, D. R. J. 1995 (Manchester U)	9
Bent, D. A. 2003 (Ipswich T, Charlton Ath)	14
Bent, M. N. 1998 (C Palace)	2
Bentley, D. M. 2004 (Arsenal, Blackburn R)	8
Beeston, C 1988 (Stoke C)	1
Benjamin, T. J. 2001 (Leicester C)	1
Bertschin, K. E. 1977 (Birmingham C)	3
Birtles, G. 1980 (Nottingham F)	2
Blackstock, D. A. 2008 (QPR)	2
Blackwell, D. R. 1991 (Wimbledon)	6
Blake, M. A. 1990 (Aston Villa)	8
Blissett, L. L. 1979 (Watford)	4
Booth, A. D. 1995 (Huddersfield T)	3
Bothroyd, J. 2001 (Coventry C)	1
Bowyer, L. D. 1996 (Charlton Ath, Leeds U)	13
Bracewell, P. 1983 (Stoke C)	13
Bradbury, L. M. 1997 (Portsmouth, Manchester C)	3
Bramble, T. M. 2001 (Ipswich T, Newcastle U)	10
Branch, P. M. 1997 (Everton)	1
Bradshaw, P. W. 1977 (Wolverhampton W)	4
Breacker, T. 1986 (Luton T)	2
Brennan, M. 1987 (Ipswich T)	5
Bridge, W. M. 1999 (Southampton)	8
Bridges, M. 1997 (Sunderland, Leeds U)	3
Brightwell, I. 1989 (Manchester C)	4
Briscoe, L. S. 1996 (Sheffield W)	5
Brock, K. 1984 (Oxford U)	4
Broomes, M. C. 1997 (Blackburn R)	2
Brown, M. R. 1996 (Manchester C)	4
Brown, W. M. 1999 (Manchester U)	8
Bull, S. G. 1989 (Wolverhampton W)	5
Bullock, M. J. 1998 (Barnsley)	1
Burrows, D. 1989 (WBA, Liverpool)	7
Butcher, T. I. 1979 (Ipswich T)	7
Butt, N. 1995 (Manchester U)	7
Butters, G. 1989 (Tottenham H)	3
Butterworth, I. 1985 (Coventry C, Nottingham F)	8
Bywater, S. 2001 (West Ham U)	6
Cadamarteri, D. L. 1999 (Everton)	3
Caesar, G. 1987 (Arsenal)	3
Cahill, G. J. 2007 (Aston Villa)	3
Callaghan, N. 1983 (Watford)	9
Camp, L. M. J. 2005 (Derby Co)	5
Campbell, A. P. 2000 (Middlesbrough)	4
Campbell, F. L. 2008 (Manchester U)	1
Campbell, K. J. 1991 (Arsenal)	4
Campbell, S. 1994 (Tottenham)	11
Carbon, M. P. 1996 (Derby Co)	4
Carr, C. 1985 (Fulham)	1
Carr, F. 1987 (Nottingham F)	9
Carragher, J. L. 1997 (Liverpool)	27
Carlisle, C. J. 2001 (QPR)	3
Carrick, M. 2001 (West Ham U)	14
Carson, S. P. 2004 (Leeds U, Liverpool)	29
Casper, C. M. 1995 (Manchester U)	1
Caton, T. 1982 (Manchester C)	14
Cattermole, L. B. 2008 (Middlesbrough)	3
Chadwick, L. H. 2000 (Manchester U)	13
Challis, T. M. 1996 (QPR)	2
Chamberlain, M. 1983 (Stoke C)	4
Chaplow, R. D. 2004 (Burnley)	1
Chapman, L. 1981 (Stoke C)	1
Charles, G. A. 1991 (Nottingham F)	4
Chettle, S. 1988 (Nottingham F)	12
Chopra, R, M. 2004 (Newcastle U)	1
Clark, L. R. 1992 (Newcastle U)	11
Clarke, P. M. 2003 (Everton)	8
Christie, M. N. 2001 (Derby Co)	11
Clegg, M. J. 1998 (Manchester U)	2
Clemence, S. N. 1999 (Tottenham H)	1
Clough, N. H. 1986 (Nottingham F)	15
Cole, A. 2001 (Arsenal)	4
Cole, A. A. 1992 (Arsenal, Bristol C, Newcastle U)	8
Cole, C. 2003 (Chelsea)	19
Cole, J. J. 2000 (West Ham U)	8
Coney, D. 1985 (Fulham)	4
Connor, T. 1987 (Brighton & HA)	1
Cooke, R. 1986 (Tottenham H)	1
Cooke, T. J. 1996 (Manchester U)	4
Cooper, C. T. 1988 (Middlesbrough)	8
Corrigan, J. T. 1978 (Manchester C)	3
Cort, C. E. R. 1999 (Wimbledon)	12
Cottee, A. R. 1985 (West Ham U)	8
Couzens, A. J. 1995 (Leeds U)	3
Cowans, G. S. 1979 (Aston Villa)	5
Cox, N. J. 1993 (Aston Villa)	6
Cranie, M. J. 2008 (Portsmouth)	6
Cranson, I. 1985 (Ipswich T)	5
Cresswell, R. P. W. 1999 (York C, Sheffield W)	4
Croft, G. 1995 (Grimsby T)	4
Crooks, G. 1980 (Stoke C)	4
Crossley, M. G. 1990 (Nottingham F)	3
Crouch, P. J. 2002 (Portsmouth, Aston Villa)	5
Cundy, J. V. 1991 (Chelsea)	3
Cunningham, L. 1977 (WBA)	6
Curbishley, L. C. 1981 (Birmingham C)	1
Curtis, J. C. K. 1998 (Manchester U)	16
Daniel, P. W. 1977 (Hull C)	7
Dann, S. 2008 (Coventry C)	2
Davenport, C. R. P. 2005 (Tottenham H)	8
Davies, A. J. 2004 (Middlesbrough)	1
Davies, C. E. 2006 (WBA)	3
Davies, K. C. 1998 (Southampton, Blackburn R, Southampton)	3
Davis, K. G. 1995 (Luton T)	3
Davis, P. 1982 (Arsenal)	11
Davis, S. 2001 (Fulham)	11
Dawson, M. R. 2003 (Nottingham F, Tottenham H)	13
Day, C. N. 1996 (Tottenham H, C Palace)	6
D'Avray, M. 1984 (Ipswich T)	2

Deehan, J. M. 1977 (Aston Villa) 7
Defoe, J. C. 2001 (West Ham U) 23
Dennis, M. E. 1980 (Birmingham C) 3
Derbyshire, M. A. 2007 (Blackburn R) 11
Dichio, D. S. E. 1996 (QPR) 1
Dickens, A. 1985 (West Ham U) 1
Dicks, J. 1988 (West Ham U) 4
Digby, F. 1987 (Swindon T) 5
Dillon, K. P. 1981 (Birmingham C) 1
Dixon, K. M. 1985 (Chelsea) 1
Dobson, A. 1989 (Coventry C) 4
Dodd, J. R. 1991 (Southampton) 8
Donowa, L. 1985 (Norwich C) 3
Dorigo, A. R. 1987 (Aston Villa) 11
Downing, S. 2004 (Middlesbrough) 8
Dozzell, J. 1987 (Ipswich T) 9
Draper, M. A. 1991 (Notts Co) 3
Duberry, M. W. 1997 (Chelsea) 5
Dunn, D. J. I. 1999 (Blackburn R) 20
Duxbury, M. 1981 (Manchester U) 7
Dyer, B. A. 1994 (C Palace) 10
Dyer, K. C. 1998 (Ipswich T, Newcastle U) 11
Dyson, P. I. 1981 (Coventry C) 4

Eadie, D. M. 1994 (Norwich C) 7
Ebbrell, J. 1989 (Everton) 14
Edghill, R. A. 1994 (Manchester C) 3
Ehiogu, U. 1992 (Aston Villa) 15
Elliott, P. 1985 (Luton T) 3
Elliott, R. J. 1996 (Newcastle U) 2
Elliott, S. W. 1998 (Derby Co) 3
Etherington, N, 2002 (Tottenham H) 3
Euell, J. J. 1998 (Wimbledon) 6
Evans, R. 2003 (Chelsea) 2

Fairclough, C. 1985 (Nottingham F, Tottenham H) 7
Fairclough, D. 1977 (Liverpool) 1
Fashanu, J. 1980 (Norwich C, Nottingham F) 11
Fear, P. 1994 (Wimbledon) 3
Fenton, G. A. 1995 (Aston Villa) 1
Fenwick, T. W. 1981 (C Palace, QPR) 11
Ferdinand, A. J. 2005 (West Ham U) 17
Ferdinand, R. G. 1997 (West Ham U) 5
Fereday, W. 1985 (QPR) 5
Flitcroft, G. W. 1993 (Manchester C) 10
Flowers, T. D. 1987 (Southampton) 3
Ford, M. 1996 (Leeds U) 2
Forster, N. M. 1995 (Brentford) 4
Forsyth, M. 1988 (Derby Co) 1
Foster, S. 1980 (Brighton & HA) 1
Fowler, R. B. 1994 (Liverpool) 8
Fox, D. J. 2008 (Coventry C) 1
Froggatt, S. J. 1993 (Aston Villa) 2
Futcher, P. 1977 (Luton T, Manchester C) 11

Gabbiadini, M. 1989 (Sunderland) 2
Gale, A. 1982 (Fulham) 1
Gallen, K. A. 1995 (QPR) 4
Gardner, A. 2002 (Tottenham H) 1
Gardner, C. 2008 (Aston Villa) 6
Gascoigne, P. J. 1987 (Newcastle U) 13
Gayle, H. 1984 (Birmingham C) 3
Gernon, T. 1983 (Ipswich T) 1
Gerrard, P. W. 1993 (Oldham Ath) 18
Gerrard, S. G. 2000 (Liverpool) 4
Gibbs, N. 1987 (Watford) 5
Gibson, C. 1982 (Aston Villa) 1
Gilbert, W. A. 1979 (C Palace) 11
Goddard, P. 1981 (West Ham U) 8
Gordon, D. 1987 (Norwich C) 4
Gordon, D. D. 1994 (C Palace) 13
Grant, A. J. 1996 (Everton) 1
Grant, L. A. 2003 (Derby Co) 4
Granville, D. P. 1997 (Chelsea) 3
Gray, A. 1988 (Aston Villa) 2
Greening, J. 1999 (Manchester U, Middlesbrough) 18
Griffin, A. 1999 (Newcastle U) 3
Guppy, S. A. 1998 (Leicester C) 1

Haigh, P. 1977 (Hull C) 1
Hall, M. T. J. 1997 (Coventry C) 8
Hall, R. A. 1992 (Southampton) 11
Hamilton, D. V. 1997 (Newcastle U) 1
Harding, D. A. 2005 (Brighton & HA) 4
Hardyman, P. 1985 (Portsmouth) 2
Hargreaves, O. 2001 (Bayern Munich) 3
Harley, J. 2000 (Chelsea) 3
Hart, C. 2007 (Manchester C) 12
Hateley, M. 1982 (Coventry C, Portsmouth) 10
Hayes, M. 1987 (Arsenal) 3
Hazell, R. J. 1979 (Wolverhampton W) 1
Heaney, N. A. 1992 (Arsenal) 6
Heath, A. 1981 (Stoke C, Everton) 8
Heaton, T. D. 2008 (Manchester U) 1
Hendon, I. M. 1992 (Tottenham H) 7
Hendrie, L. A. 1996 (Aston Villa) 13
Hesford, I. 1981 (Blackpool) 7
Heskey, E. W. I. 1997 (Leicester C, Liverpool) 16
Hilaire, V. 1980 (C Palace) 9
Hill, D. R. L. 1995 (Tottenham H) 4
Hillier, D. 1991 (Arsenal) 1
Hinchcliffe, A. 1989 (Manchester C) 1
Hinshelwood, P. A. 1978 (C Palace) 2
Hirst, D. E. 1988 (Sheffield W) 7
Hislop, N. S. 1998 (Newcastle U) 1
Hoddle, G. 1977 (Tottenham H) 12
Hodge, S. B. 1983 (Nottingham F, Aston Villa) 8
Hodgson, D. J. 1981 (Middlesbrough) 6
Holdsworth, D. 1989 (Watford) 1
Holland, C. J. 1995 (Newcastle U) 10
Holland, P. 1995 (Mansfield T) 4
Holloway, D. 1998 (Sunderland) 1
Horne, B. 1989 (Millwall) 5
Howe, E. J. F. 1998 (Bournemouth) 2
Hoyte, J. R. 2004 (Arsenal) 18
Hucker, P. 1984 (QPR) 2
Huckerby, D. 1997 (Coventry C) 4
Huddlestone, T. A. 2005 (Derby Co, Tottenham H) 26
Hughes, S. J. 1997 (Arsenal) 8
Humphreys, R. J. 1997 (Sheffield W) 3
Hunt, N. B. 2004 (Bolton W) 10

Impey, A. R. 1993 (QPR) 1
Ince, P. E. C. 1989 (West Ham U) 2

Jackson, M. A. 1992 (Everton) 10
Jagielka, P. N. 2003 (Sheffield U) 6
James, D. B. 1991 (Watford) 10
James, J. C. 1990 (Luton T) 2
Jansen, M. B. 1999 (C Palace, Blackburn R) 6
Jeffers, F. 2000 (Everton, Arsenal) 16
Jemson, N. B. 1991 (Nottingham F) 1
Jenas, J. A. 2002 (Newcastle U) 9
Jerome, C. 2006 (Cardiff C, Birmingham C) 10
Joachim, J. K. 1994 (Leicester C) 9
Johnson, A. 2008 (Middlesbrough) 7
Johnson, G. M. C. 2003 (West Ham U, Chelsea) 14
Johnson, M. 2008 (Manchester C) 1
Johnson, S. A. M. 1999 (Crewe Alex, Derby Co, Leeds U) 15
Johnson, T. 1991 (Notts Co, Derby Co) 7
Johnston, C. P. 1981 (Middlesbrough) 2
Jones, D. R. 1977 (Everton) 1
Jones, C. H. 1978 (Tottenham H) 1
Jones, D. F. L. 2004 (Manchester U) 1
Jones, R. 1993 (Liverpool) 2

Keegan, G. A. 1977 (Manchester C) 1
Kenny, W. 1993 (Everton) 1
Keown, M. R. 1987 (Aston Villa) 8
Kerslake, D. 1986 (QPR) 1
Kightly, M. J. 2008 (Wolverhampton W) 3
Kilcline, B. 1983 (Notts C) 2
Kilgallon, M. 2004 (Leeds U) 5
King, A. E. 1977 (Everton) 2
King, L. B. 2000 (Tottenham H) 12
Kirkland, C. E. 2001 (Coventry C, Liverpool) 8
Kitson, P. 1991 (Leicester C, Derby Co) 7
Knight, A. 1983 (Portsmouth) 2
Knight, I. 1987 (Sheffield W) 2
Knight, Z. 2002 (Fulham) 4
Konchesky, P. M. 2002 (Charlton Ath) 15
Kozluk, R. 1998 (Derby Co) 2

Lake, P. 1989 (Manchester C) 5
Lampard, F. J. 1998 (West Ham U) 19

Langley, T. W. 1978 (Chelsea) 1
Leadbitter, G. 2008 (Sunderland) 3
Lee, D. J. 1990 (Chelsea) 10
Lee, R. M. 1986 (Charlton Ath) 2
Lee, S. 1981 (Liverpool) 6
Lennon, A. J. 2006 (Tottenham H) 3
Le Saux, G. P. 1990 (Chelsea) 4
Lescott, J. P. 2003 (Wolverhampton W) 2
Lewis, J. P. 2008 (Peterborough U) 1
Lita, L. H. 2005 (Bristol C, Reading) 9
Lowe, D. 1988 (Ipswich T) 2
Lukic, J. 1981 (Leeds U) 7
Lund, G. 1985 (Grimsby T) 3

McCall, S. H. 1981 (Ipswich T) 6
McDonald, N. 1987 (Newcastle U) 5
McEveley, J. 2003 (Blackburn R) 1
McGrath, L. 1986 (Coventry C) 1
MacKenzie, S. 1982 (WBA) 3
McLeary, A. 1988 (Millwall) 1
McLeod, I. M. 2006 (Milton Keynes D) 1
McMahon, S. 1981 (Everton, Aston Villa) 6
McManaman, S. 1991 (Liverpool) 7
Mabbutt, G. 1982 (Bristol R, Tottenham H) 7
Makin, C. 1994 (Oldham Ath) 5
Mancienne, M. I. 2008 (Chelsea) 4
Marney, D. E. 2005 (Tottenham H) 1
Marriott, A. 1992 (Nottingham F) 1
Marsh, S. T. 1998 (Oxford U) 1
Marshall, A. J. 1995 (Norwich C) 4
Marshall, L. K. 1999 (Norwich C) 1
Martin, L. 1989 (Manchester U) 2
Martyn, A. N. 1988 (Bristol R) 11
Matteo, D. 1994 (Liverpool) 4
Mattock, J. W. 2008 (Leicester C) 4
Matthew, D. 1990 (Chelsea) 9
May, A. 1986 (Manchester C) 1
Merson, P. C. 1989 (Arsenal) 4
Middleton, J. 1977 (Nottingham F, Derby Co) 3
Miller, A. 1988 (Arsenal) 4
Mills, D. J. 1999 (Charlton Ath, Leeds U) 14
Mills, G. R. 1981 (Nottingham F) 2
Milner, J. P. 2004 (Leeds U, Newcastle U) 36
Mimms, R. 1985 (Rotherham U, Everton) 3
Minto, S. C. 1991 (Charlton Ath) 6
Moore, I. 1996 (Tranmere R, Nottingham F) 7
Moore, L. I. 2006 (Aston Villa) 5
Moran, S. 1982 (Southampton) 2
Morgan, S. 1987 (Leicester C) 2
Morris, J. 1997 (Chelsea) 7
Mortimer, P. 1989 (Charlton Ath) 2
Moses, A. P. 1997 (Barnsley) 2
Moses, R. M. 1981 (WBA, Manchester U) 8
Mountfield, D. 1984 (Everton) 1
Muamba, F. N. 2008 (Birmingham C) 8
Muggleton, C. D. 1990 (Leicester C) 1
Mullins, H. I. 1999 (C Palace) 3
Murphy, D. B. 1998 (Liverpool) 4
Murray, P. 1997 (QPR) 4
Murray, M. W. 2003 (Wolverhampton W) 5
Mutch, A. 1989 (Wolverhampton W) 1
Myers. A. 1995 (Chelsea) 4

Naylor, L. M. 2000 (Wolverhampton W) 3
Nethercott, S. H. 1994 (Tottenham H) 8
Neville, P. J. 1995 (Manchester U) 7
Newell, M. 1986 (Luton T) 4
Newton, A. L. 2001 (West Ham U) 1
Newton, E. J. I. 1993 (Chelsea) 2
Newton, S. O. 1997 (Charlton Ath) 3
Nicholls, A. 1994 (Plymouth Arg) 1
Noble, M. J. 2007 (West Ham U) 10
Nolan, K. A. J. 2003 (Bolton W) 1
Nugent, D. J. 2006 (Preston NE) 14

Oakes, M. C. 1994 (Aston Villa) 6
Oakes, S. J. 1993 (Luton T) 1
Oakley, M. 1997 (Southampton) 4
O'Brien, A. J. 1999 (Bradford C) 1
O'Connor, J. 1996 (Everton) 3
O'Hara, J. D. 2008 (Tottenham H) 2
Oldfield, D. 1989 (Luton T) 1
Olney, I. A. 1990 (Aston Villa) 10
O'Neil, G. P. 2005 (Portsmouth) 9
Onuoha, C. 2006 (Manchester C) 14
Ord, R. J. 1991 (Sunderland) 3
Osman, R. C. 1979 (Ipswich T) 7
Owen, G. A. 1977 (Manchester C, WBA) 22
Owen, M. J. 1998 (Liverpool) 1

Painter, I. 1986 (Stoke C) 1
Palmer, C. L. 1989 (Sheffield W) 4
Parker, G. 1986 (Hull C, Nottingham F) 6
Parker, P. A. 1985 (Fulham) 8
Parker, S. M. 2001 (Charlton Ath) 12
Parkes, P. B. F. 1979 (QPR) 1
Parkin, S. 1987 (Stoke C) 5
Parlour, R. 1992 (Arsenal) 12
Parnaby, S. 2003 (Middlesbrough) 4
Peach, D. S. 1977 (Southampton) 6
Peake, A. 1982 (Leicester C) 1
Pearce, I. A. 1995 (Blackburn R) 3
Pearce, S. 1987 (Nottingham F) 1
Pennant, J. 2001 (Arsenal) 24
Pickering N. 1983 (Sunderland, Coventry C) 15
Platt, D. 1988 (Aston Villa) 3
Plummer, C. S. 1996 (QPR) 5
Pollock, J. 1995 (Middlesbrough) 3
Porter, G. 1987 (Watford) 12
Potter, G. S. 1997 (Southampton) 1
Pressman, K. 1989 (Sheffield W) 1
Proctor, M. 1981 (Middlesbrough, Nottingham F) 4
Prutton, D. T. 2001 (Nottingham F, Southampton) 25
Purse, D. J. 1998 (Birmingham C) 2

Quashie, N. F. 1997 (QPR) 4
Quinn, W. R. 1998 (Sheffield U) 2

Ramage, C. D. 1991 (Derby Co) 3
Ranson, R. 1980 (Manchester C) 10
Redknapp, J. F. 1993 (Liverpool) 19
Redmond, S. 1988 (Manchester C) 14
Reeves, K. P. 1978 (Norwich C, Manchester C) 10
Regis, C. 1979 (WBA) 6
Reid, N. S. 1981 (Manchester C) 6
Reid, P. 1977 (Bolton W) 6
Reo-Coker, N. S. A. 2004 (Wimbledon, West Ham U) 23
Richards, D. I. 1995 (Wolverhampton W) 4
Richards, J. P. 1977 (Wolverhampton W) 2
Richards, M. 2007 (Manchester C) 3
Richards, M. L. 2005 (Ipswich T) 1
Richardson, K. E. 2005 (Manchester U)
Rideout, P. 1985 (Aston Villa, Bari) 5
Ridgewell, L. M. 2004 (Aston Villa) 8
Riggott, C. M. 2001 (Derby Co) 8
Ripley, S. E. 1988 (Middlesbrough) 8
Ritchie, A. 1982 (Brighton & HA) 1
Rix, G. 1978 (Arsenal) 7
Roberts, A. J. 1995 (Millwall, C Palace) 5
Roberts, B. J. 1997 (Middlesbrough) 1
Robins, M. G. 1990 (Manchester U) 6
Robinson, P. P. 1999 (Watford) 3
Robinson, P. W. 2000 (Leeds U) 11
Robson, B. 1979 (WBA) 7
Robson, S. 1984 (Arsenal, West Ham U) 8
Rocastle, D. 1987 (Arsenal) 14
Roche, L. P. 2001 (Manchester U) 1
Rodger, G. 1987 (Coventry C) 4
Rogers, A. 1998 (Nottingham F) 3
Rosario, R. 1987 (Norwich C) 4
Rose, M. 1997 (Arsenal) 2
Rosenior, L. J. 2005 (Fulham) 7
Routledge, W. 2005 (C Palace, Tottenham H) 12
Rowell, G. 1977 (Sunderland) 1
Ruddock, N. 1989 (Southampton) 4
Rufus, R. R. 1996 (Charlton Ath) 6
Ryan, J. 1983 (Oldham Ath) 1
Ryder, S. H. 1995 (Walsall) 3

Samuel, J. 2002 (Aston Villa) 7
Samways, V. 1988 (Tottenham H) 5
Sansom, K. G. 1979 (C Palace) 8
Scimeca, R. 1996 (Aston Villa) 9
Scowcroft, J. B. 1997 (Ipswich T) 5
Seaman, D. A. 1985 (Birmingham C) 10
Sedgley, S. 1987 (Coventry C, Tottenham H) 11

Sellars, S. 1988 (Blackburn R) 3
Selley, I. 1994 (Arsenal) 3
Serrant, C. 1998 (Oldham Ath) 2
Sharpe, L. S. 1989 (Manchester U) 8
Shaw, G. R. 1981 (Aston Villa) 7
Shawcross, R. J. 2008 (Stoke C) 2
Shearer, A. 1991 (Southampton) 11
Shelton, G. 1985 (Sheffield W) 1
Sheringham, E. P. 1988 (Millwall) 1
Sheron, M. N. 1992 (Manchester C) 16
Sherwood, T. A. 1990 (Norwich C) 4
Shipperley, N. J. 1994 (Chelsea, Southampton) 7
Sidwell, S. J. 2003 (Reading) 5
Simonsen, S. P. A. 1998 (Tranmere R, Everton) 4
Simpson, P. 1986 (Manchester C) 5
Sims, S. 1977 (Leicester C) 10
Sinclair, T. 1994 (QPR, West Ham U) 5
Sinnott, L. 1985 (Watford) 1
Slade, S. A. 1996 (Tottenham H) 4
Slater, S. I. 1990 (West Ham U) 3
Small, B. 1993 (Aston Villa) 12
Smith, A. 2000 (Leeds U) 10
Smith, D. 1988 (Coventry C) 10
Smith, M. 1981 (Sheffield W) 5
Smith, M. 1995 (Sunderland) 1
Smith, T. W. 2001 (Watford) 1
Snodin, I. 1985 (Doncaster R) 4
Soares, T. J. 2006 (C Palace) 4
Statham, B. 1988 (Tottenham H) 3
Statham, D. J. 1978 (WBA) 6
Stead, J. G. 2004 (Blackburn R, Sunderland) 11
Stein, B. 1984 (Luton T) 3
Sterland, M. 1984 (Sheffield W) 7
Steven, T. M. 1985 (Everton) 2
Stevens, G. A. 1983 (Brighton & HA, Tottenham H) 8
Stewart, J. 2003 (Leicester C) 1
Stewart, P. 1988 (Manchester C) 1
Stockdale, R. K. 2001 (Middlesbrough) 1
Stuart, G. C. 1990 (Chelsea) 5
Stuart, J. C. 1996 (Charlton Ath) 4
Suckling, P. 1986 (Coventry C, Manchester C, C Palace) 10
Summerbee, N. J. 1993 (Swindon T) 3
Sunderland, A. 1977 (Wolverhampton W) 1
Surman, A. R. E. 2008 (Southampton) 4
Sutch, D. 1992 (Norwich C) 4
Sutton, C. R. 1993 (Norwich C) 13
Swindlehurst, D. 1977 (C Palace) 1

Talbot, B. 1977 (Ipswich T) 1
Taylor, A. D. 2007 (Middlesbrough) 7
Taylor, M. 2001 (Blackburn R) 1
Taylor, M. S. 2003 (Portsmouth) 3
Taylor, R. A. 2006 (Wigan Ath) 4
Taylor, S. J. 2002 (Arsenal) 3
Taylor, S. V. 2004 (Newcastle U) 25
Terry, J. G. 2001 (Chelsea) 9
Thatcher, B. D. 1996 (Millwall, Wimbledon) 4
Thelwell, A. A. 2001 (Tottenham H) 1
Thirlwell, P. 2001 (Sunderland) 1
Thomas, D. 1981 (Coventry C, Tottenham H) 7
Thomas, J. W. 2006 (Charlton Ath) 2
Thomas, M. 1986 (Luton T) 3
Thomas, M. L. 1988 (Arsenal) 12
Thomas, R. E. 1990 (Watford) 1
Thompson, A. 1995 (Bolton W) 2
Thompson, D. A. 1997 (Liverpool) 7
Thompson, G. L. 1981 (Coventry C) 6

Thorn, A. 1988 (Wimbledon) 5
Thornley, B. L. 1996 (Manchester U) 3
Tiler, C. 1990 (Barnsley, Nottingham F) 13
Tonge, M. W. E. 2004 (Sheffield U) 2

Unsworth, D. G. 1995 (Everton) 6
Upson, M. J. 1999 (Arsenal) 11

Vassell, D. 1999 (Aston Villa) 11
Vaughan, J. O. 2007 (Everton) 1
Venison, B. 1983 (Sunderland) 10
Vernazza, P. A. P. 2001 (Arsenal, Watford) 2
Vinnicombe, C. 1991 (Rangers) 12

Waddle, C. R. 1985 (Newcastle U) 1
Walcott, T. J. 2007 (Arsenal) 15
Wallace, D. L. 1983 (Southampton) 14
Wallace, Ray 1989 (Southampton) 4
Wallace, Rod 1989 (Southampton) 11
Walker, D. 1985 (Nottingham F) 7
Walker, I. M. 1991 (Tottenham H) 9
Walsh, G. 1988 (Manchester U) 2
Walsh, P. A. 1983 (Luton T) 4
Walters, K. 1984 (Aston Villa) 9
Ward, P. 1978 (Brighton & HA) 2
Warhurst, P. 1991 (Oldham Ath, Sheffield W) 8
Watson, B. 2007 (C Palace) 1
Watson, D. 1984 (Norwich C) 7
Watson, D. N. 1994 (Barnsley) 5
Watson, G. 1991 (Sheffield W) 2
Watson, S. C. 1993 (Newcastle U) 12
Weaver, N. J. 2000 (Manchester C) 10
Webb, N. J. 1985 (Portsmouth, Nottingham F) 3
Welsh, J. J. 2004 (Liverpool, Hull C) 8
Wheater, D. J. 2008 (Middlesbrough) 6
Whelan, P. J. 1993 (Ipswich T) 3
Whelan, N. 1995 (Leeds U) 2
Whittingham, P. 2004 (Aston Villa, Cardiff C) 17
White, D. 1988 (Manchester C) 6
Whyte, C. 1982 (Arsenal) 4
Wicks, S. 1982 (QPR) 1
Wilkins, R. C. 1977 (Chelsea) 1
Wilkinson, P. 1985 (Grimsby T, Everton) 4
Williams, D. 1998 (Sunderland) 2
Williams, P. 1989 (Charlton Ath) 4
Williams, P. D. 1991 (Derby Co) 6
Williams, S. C. 1977 (Southampton) 14
Wilson, M. A. 2001 (Manchester U, Middlesbrough) 6
Winterburn, N. 1986 (Wimbledon) 1
Wise, D. F. 1988 (Wimbledon) 1
Woodcook, A. S. 1978 (Nottingham F) 2
Woodgate, J. S. 2000 (Leeds U) 1
Woodhouse, C. 1999 (Sheffield U) 4
Woods, C. C. E. 1979 (Nottingham F, QPR, Norwich C) 6
Wright, A. G. 1993 (Blackburn R) 2
Wright, M. 1983 (Southampton) 4
Wright, R. I. 1997 (Ipswich T) 15
Wright, S. J. 2001 (Liverpool) 10
Wright, W. 1979 (Everton) 6
Wright-Phillips, S. C. 2002 (Manchester C) 6

Yates, D. 1989 (Notts Co) 5
Young, A. S. 2007 (Watford, Aston Villa) 10
Young, L. P. 1999 (Tottenham H, Charlton Ath) 12

Zamora, R. L. 2002 (Brighton & HA) 6

NORTHERN IRELAND

Armstrong, D. T. 2007 (Hearts) 1

Bailie, N. 1990 (Linfield) 2
Baird, C. P. 2002 (Southampton) 6
Beatty, S. 1990 (Chelsea, Linfield) 2
Black, J. 2003 (Tottenham H) 1
Black, K. T. 1990 (Luton T) 1
Black, R. Z. 2002 (Morecambe) 1
Blackledge, G. 1978 (Portadown) 1
Blayney, A. 2003 (Southampton) 4
Boyle, W. S. 1998 (Leeds U) 7
Braniff, K. R. 2002 (Millwall) 11
Brotherston, N. 1978 (Blackburn R) 1
Browne, G. 2003 (Manchester C) 5
Brunt, C. 2005 (Sheffield W) 2
Buchanan, D. T. H. 2006 (Bury) 15
Buchanan, W. B. 2002 (Bolton W, Lisburn Distillery) 5
Burns, L. 1998 (Port Vale) 13

Callaghan, A. 2006 (Limavady U, Ballymena U, Derry C) 15
Campbell, S. 2003 (Ballymena U) 1
Capaldi, A. C. 2002 (Birmingham C, Plymouth Arg) 14
Carlisle, W. T. 2000 (C Palace) 9
Carroll, R. E. 1998 (Wigan Ath) 11
Carson, S. 2000 (Rangers, Dundee U) 2

Carson, T. 2007 (Sunderland) 6
Carvill, M. D. 2008 (Wrexham) 7
Casement, C. 2007 (Ipswich T) 9
Cathcart, C. 2007 (Manchester U) 6
Catney, R. 2007 (Lisburn Distillery) 1
Chapman, A. 2008 (Sheffield U) 1
Clarke, L. 2003 (Peterborough U) 4
Clarke, R. 2006 (Newry C) 7
Clarke, R. D. J. 1999 (Portadown) 5
Clingan, S. G. 2003 (Wolverhampton W, Nottingham F) 11
Close, B. 2002 (Middlesbrough) 10
Clyde, M. G. 2002 (Wolverhampton W) 5
Connell, T. E. 1978 (Coleraine) 1
Coote, A. 1998 (Norwich C) 12
Convery, J. 2000 (Celtic) 4

Davey, H. 2004 (UCD) 3
Davis, S. 2004 (Aston Villa) 3
Devine, D. 1994 (Omagh T) 1
Devine, J. 1990 (Glentoran) 1
Dickson, H. 2002 (Wigan Ath) 1
Doherty, M. 2007 (Hearts) 2
Dolan, J. 2000 (Millwall) 6
Donaghy, M. M. 1978 (Larne) 1
Donnelly, M. 2007 (Sheffield U) 1
Dowie, I. 1990 (Luton T) 1
Duff, S. 2003 (Cheltenham T) 1

Elliott, S. 1999 (Glentoran) 3
Ervin, J. 2005 (Linfield) 2
Evans, J. G. 2006 (Manchester U) 3

Feeney, L. 1998 (Linfield, Rangers) 8
Feeney, W. 2002 (Bournemouth) 8
Ferguson, M. 2000 (Glentoran) 2
Fitzgerald, D. 1998 (Rangers) 4
Fordyce, D. T. 2007 (Portsmouth, Glentoran) 12
Friars, E. C. 2005 (Notts Co) 7
Friars, S. M. 1998 (Liverpool, Ipswich T) 21

Garrett, R. 2007 (Stoke C) 10
Gault, M. 2005 (Linfield) 2
Gilfillan, B. J. 2005 (Gretna, Peterhead) 9
Gillespie, K. R. 1994 (Manchester U) 1
Glendinning, M. 1994 (Bangor) 1
Graham, G. L. 1999 (C Palace) 5
Graham, R. S. 1999 (QPR) 15
Gray, P. 1990 (Luton T) 1
Griffin, D. J. 1998 (St Johnstone) 10

Hamilton, G. 2000 (Blackburn R, Portadown) 12
Hamilton, W. R. 1978 (Linfield) 1
Harkin, M. P. 2000 (Wycombe W) 9
Harvey, J. 1978 (Arsenal) 1
Hawe, S. 2001 (Blackburn R) 2
Hayes, T. 1978 (Luton T) 1
Hazley, M. 2007 (Stoke C) 3
Healy, D. J. 1999 (Manchester U) 8
Herron, C. J. 2003 (QPR) 2
Higgins, R. 2006 (Derry C) 1
Holmes, S. 2000 (Manchester C, Wrexham) 13
Howland, D. 2007 (Birmingham C) 4
Hughes, J. 2006 (Lincoln C) 7
Hughes, M. A. 2003 (Tottenham H, Oldham Ath) 12
Hughes, M. E. 1990 (Manchester C) 1
Hunter, M. 2002 (Glentoran) 1

Ingham, M. G. 2001 (Sunderland) 4

Johnson, D. M. 1998 (Blackburn R) 11
Johnston, B. 1978 (Cliftonville) 1
Julian, A. A. 2005 (Brentford) 1

Kane, A. M. 2008 (Blackburn R) 5
Kee, P. V. 1990 (Oxford U) 1
Kelly, D. 2000 (Derry C) 11
Kelly, N. 1990 (Oldham Ath) 1
Kirk, A. R. 1999 (Hearts) 9

Lafferty, K. 2006 (Burnley) 2
Lennon, N. F. 1990 (Manchester C, Crewe Alex) 2
Lindsay, K. 2006 (Larne) 1
Lyttle, G. 1998 (Celtic, Peterborough U) 8

Magee, J. 1994 (Bangor) 1
Magilton, J. 1990 (Liverpool) 1
Matthews, N. P. 1990 (Blackpool) 1
McAllister, M. 2007 (Dungannon Swifts) 3
McArdle, R. A. 2006 (Sheffield W, Rochdale) 19
McAreavey, P. 2000 (Swindon T) 7
McBride, J. 1994 (Glentoran) 1
McCaffrey, D. 2006 (Hibernian) 8
McCallion, E. 1998 (Coleraine) 1
McCann, G. S. 2000 (West Ham U) 11
McCann, P. 2003 (Portadown) 1
McCann, R. 2002 (Rangers, Linfield) 2
McCartney, G. 2001 (Sunderland) 5
McChrystal, M. 2005 (Derry C) 9
McCourt, P. J. 2002 (Rochdale, Derry C) 8
McCoy, R. K. 1990 (Coleraine) 1
McCreery, D. 1978 (Manchester U) 1
McEvilly, L. R. 2003 (Rochdale) 9
McFlynn, T. M. 2000 (QPR, Woking, Margate) 19
McGibbon, P. C. G. 1994 (Manchester U) 1
McGlinchey, B. 1998 (Manchester C, Port Vale, Gillingham) 14
McGovern, M. 2005 (Celtic) 10
McGowan, M. V. 2006 (Clyde) 2
McIlroy, T. 1994 (Linfield) 1
McKenna, K. 2007 (Tottenham H) 6
McKnight, P. 1998 (Rangers) 3
McLean, B. S. 2006 (Rangers) 1
McMahon, G. J. 2002 (Tottenham H) 1
McVeigh, A. 2002 (Ayr U) 1
McVeigh, P. M. 1998 (Tottenham H) 11
McVey, K. 2006 (Coleraine) 8
Meenan, D. 2007 (Finn Harps, Monaghan U) 3
Melaugh, G. M. 2002 (Aston Villa, Glentoran) 11
Millar, W. P. 1990 (Port Vale) 1
Miskelly, D. T. 2000 (Oldham Ath) 10
Moreland, V. 1978 (Glentoran) 1
Morgan, M. P. T. 1999 (Preston NE) 1
Morris, E. J. 2002 (WBA, Glentoran) 8
Morrison, O. 2001 (Sheffield W, Sheffield U) 7
Morrow, A. 2001 (Northampton T) 1
Morrow, S. 2005 (Hibernian) 4
Mulgrew, J. 2007 (Linfield) 10
Mulryne, P. P. 1999 (Manchester U, Norwich C) 5
Murray, W. 1978 (Linfield) 1
Murtagh, C. 2005 (Hearts) 1

Nicholl, J. M. 1978 (Manchester U) 1
Nixon, C. 2000 (Glentoran) 1

O'Connor, M. J. 2008 (Crewe Alex) 3
O'Hara, G. 1994 (Leeds U) 1
O'Neill, J. P. 1978 (Leicester C) 1
O'Neill, M. A. M. 1994 (Hibernian) 1

Paterson, M. A. 2007 (Stoke C) 2
Patterson, D. J. 1994 (C Palace) 1

Quinn, S. J. 1994 (Blackpool) 1

Ramsey, K. 2006 (Institute) 1
Robinson, S. 1994 (Tottenham H) 1

Scullion, D. 2006 (Dungannon Swifts) 8
Shiels, D. 2005 (Hibernian) 6
Simms, G. 2001 (Hartlepool U) 14
Skates, G. 2000 (Blackburn R) 4
Sloan, T. 1978 (Ballymena U) 1
Smylie, D. 2006 (Newcastle U, Livingston) 6
Stewart, T. 2006 (Wolverhampton W, Linfield) 19

Taylor, J. 2007 (Hearts) 8
Taylor, M. S. 1998 (Fulham) 1
Teggart, N. 2005 (Sunderland) 2
Thompson, P. 2006 (Linfield) 4
Toner, C. 2000 (Tottenham H, Leyton Orient) 17
Tuffey, J. 2007 (Partick T) 13
Turner, C. 2007 (Sligo R, Bohemians) 12

Ward, J. J. 2006 (Aston Villa, Chesterfield) 6
Ward, M. 2006 (Dungannon Swifts) 1
Ward, S. 2005 (Glentoran) 10
Waterman, D. G. 1998 (Portsmouth) 14

Waterworth, A. 2008 (Lisburn Distillery, Hamilton A) 7
Webb, S. M. 2004 (Ross Co, St Johnstone, Ross Co) 6
Wells, D. P. 1999 (Barry T) 1
Whitley, J. 1998 (Manchester C) 17
Willis, P. 2006 (Liverpool) 1

SCOTLAND

Adam, C. G. 2006 (Rangers) 5
Adams, J. 2007 (Kilmarnock) 1
Aitken, R. 1977 (Celtic) 16
Albiston, A. 1977 (Manchester U) 5
Alexander, N. 1997 (Stenhousemuir, Livingston) 10
Anderson, I. 1997 (Dundee, Toulouse) 15
Anderson, R. 1997 (Aberdeen) 15
Anthony, M. 1997 (Celtic) 3
Archdeacon, O. 1987 (Celtic) 1
Archibald, A. 1998 (Partick Th) 5
Archibald, S. 1980 (Aberdeen, Tottenham H) 5
Arfield, S. 2008 (Falkirk) 5

Bagen, D. 1997 (Kilmarnock) 4
Bain, K. 1993 (Dundee) 4
Baker, M. 1993 (St Mirren) 10
Baltacha, S. S. 2000 (St Mirren) 3
Bannon, E. J. 1979 (Hearts, Chelsea, Dundee U) 7
Beattie, C. 2004 (Celtic) 7
Beattie, J. 1992 (St Mirren) 4
Beaumont, D. 1985 (Dundee U) 1
Bell, D. 1981 (Aberdeen) 2
Bernard, P. R. J. 1992 (Oldham Ath) 15
Berra, C. 2005 (Hearts) 6
Bett, J. 1981 (Rangers) 7
Black, E. 1983 (Aberdeen) 8
Blair, A. 1980 (Coventry C, Aston Villa) 5
Bollan, G. 1992 (Dundee U, Rangers) 17
Bonar, P. 1997 (Raith R) 4
Booth, S. 1991 (Aberdeen) 14
Bowes, M. J. 1992 (Dunfermline Ath) 1
Bowman, D. 1985 (Hearts) 1
Boyack, S. 1997 (Rangers) 1
Boyd, K. 2003 (Kilmarnock) 8
Boyd, T. 1987 (Motherwell) 5
Brazil, A. 1978 (Hibernian) 1
Brazil, A. 1979 (Ipswich T) 8
Brebner, G. I. 1997 (Manchester U, Reading, Hibernian) 18
Brighton, T. 2005 (Rangers, Clyde) 7
Broadfoot, K. 2005 (St Mirren) 5
Brough, J. 1981 (Hearts) 1
Brown, A. H. 2004 (Hibernian) 1
Brown, S. 2005 (Hibernian) 10
Browne, P. 1997 (Raith R) 1
Bryson, C. 2006 (Clyde) 1
Buchan, J. 1997 (Aberdeen) 13
Burchill, M. J. 1998 (Celtic) 15
Burke, A. 1997 (Kilmarnock) 4
Burke, C. 2004 (Rangers) 3
Burley, C. W. 1992 (Chelsea) 7
Burley, G. E. 1977 (Ipswich T) 5
Burns, H. 1985 (Rangers) 2
Burns, T. 1977 (Celtic) 5

Caddis, P. 2008 (Celtic) 1
Caldwell, G. 2000 (Newcastle U) 19
Caldwell, S. 2001 (Newcastle U) 4
Cameron, G. 2008 (Dundee U) 3
Campbell, R. 2008 (Hibernian) 6
Campbell, S. 1989 (Dundee) 3
Campbell, S. P. 1998 (Leicester C) 15
Canero, P. 2000 (Kilmarnock) 17
Carey, L. A. 1998 (Bristol C) 1
Casey, J. 1978 (Celtic) 1
Christie, M. 1992 (Dundee) 3
Clark, R. B. 1977 (Aberdeen) 3
Clarke, S. 1984 (St Mirren) 8
Clarkson, D. 2004 (Motherwell) 13
Cleland, A. 1990 (Dundee U) 11
Collins, J. 1988 (Hibernian) 8
Collins, N. 2005 (Sunderland) 7
Connolly, P. 1991 (Dundee U) 3
Connor, R. 1981 (Ayr U) 2
Conroy, R. 2007 (Celtic) 4
Considine, A. 2007 (Aberdeen) 3
Cooper, D. 1977 (Clydebank, Rangers) 6
Cooper, N. 1982 (Aberdeen) 13
Crabbe, S. 1990 (Hearts) 2
Craig, M. 1998 (Aberdeen) 2
Craig, T. 1977 (Newcastle U) 1
Crainey, S. D. 2000 (Celtic) 7
Crainie, D. 1983 (Celtic) 1
Crawford, S. 1994 (Raith R) 19
Creaney, G. 1991 (Celtic) 11
Cummings, W. 2000 (Chelsea) 8
Cuthbert, S. 2007 (Celtic) 10

Dailly, C. 1991 (Dundee U) 34
Dalglish, P. 1999 (Newcastle U, Norwich C) 6
Dargo, C. 1998 (Raith R) 10
Davidson, C. I. 1997 (St Johnstone) 2
Davidson, H. N. 2000 (Dundee U) 3
Dawson, A. 1979 (Rangers) 8
Deas, P. A. 1992 (St Johnstone) 2
Dempster, J. 2004 (Rushden & D) 1
Dennis, S. 1992 (Raith R) 1
Diamond, A. 2004 (Aberdeen) 12
Dickov, P. 1992 (Arsenal) 4
Dixon, P. 2008 (Dundee) 2
Dodds, D. 1978 (Dundee U) 1
Dods, D. 1997 (Hibernian) 5
Doig, C. R. 2000 (Nottingham F) 13
Donald, G. S. 1992 (Hibernian) 3
Donnelly, S. 1994 (Celtic) 11
Dorrans, G. 2007 (Livingston) 4
Dow, A. 1993 (Dundee, Chelsea) 3
Dowie, A. J. 2003 (Rangers, Partick Th) 14
Duff, S. 2003 (Dundee U) 9
Duffy, D. A. 2005 (Falkirk, Hull C) 8
Duffy, J. 1987 (Dundee) 1
Durie, G. S. 1987 (Chelsea) 4
Durrant, I. 1987 (Rangers) 4
Doyle, J. 1981 (Partick Th) 2

Easton, C. 1997 (Dundee U) 21
Elliot, B. 1998 (Celtic) 2
Elliot, C. 2006 (Hearts) 6
Esson, R. 2000 (Aberdeen) 7

Fagan, S. M. 2005 (Motherwell) 1
Ferguson, B. 1997 (Rangers) 12
Ferguson, D. 1987 (Rangers) 5
Ferguson, D. 1992 (Dundee U) 7
Ferguson, D. 1992 (Manchester U) 5
Ferguson, I. 1983 (Dundee) 4
Ferguson, I. 1987 (Clyde, St Mirren, Rangers) 6
Ferguson, R. 1977 (Hamilton A) 1
Findlay, W. 1991 (Hibernian) 5
Fitzpatrick, A. 1977 (St Mirren) 5
Fitzpatrick, M. 2007 (Motherwell) 4
Flannigan, C. 1993 (Clydebank) 1
Fleck, R. 1987 (Rangers, Norwich C) 6
Fleming, G. 2008 (Gretna) 1
Fletcher, D. B. 2003 (Manchester U) 2
Fletcher, S. 2007 (Hibernian) 6
Foster, R. M. 2005 (Aberdeen) 5
Fotheringham, M. M. 2004 (Dundee) 3
Fowler, J. 2002 (Kilmarnock) 3
Foy, R. A. 2004 (Liverpool) 5
Fraser, S. T. 2000 (Luton T) 4
Freedman, D. A. 1995 (Barnet, C Palace) 8
Fridge, L. 1989 (St Mirren) 2
Fullarton, J. 1993 (St Mirren) 17
Fulton, M. 1980 (St Mirren) 5
Fulton, S. 1991 (Celtic) 7

Gallacher, K. W. 1987 (Dundee U) 7
Gallacher, P. 1999 (Dundee U) 7
Gallagher, P. 2003 (Blackburn R) 11
Galloway, M. 1989 (Hearts, Celtic) 2
Gardiner, J. 1993 (Hibernian) 1
Geddes, R. 1982 (Dundee) 5
Gemmill, S. 1992 (Nottingham F) 4
Germaine, G. 1997 (WBA) 1

Gilles, R. 1997 (St Mirren) 7
Gillespie, G. T. 1979 (Coventry C) 8
Glass, S. 1995 (Aberdeen) 11
Glover, L. 1988 (Nottingham F) 3
Goram, A. L. 1987 (Oldham Ath) 1
Gordon, C. S. 2003 (Hearts) 5
Gough, C. R. 1983 (Dundee U) 5
Graham, D. 1998 (Rangers) 8
Grant, P. 1985 (Celtic) 10
Gray, S. 1987 (Aberdeen) 1
Gray S. 1995 (Celtic) 7
Gunn, B. 1984 (Aberdeen) 9

Hagen, D. 1992 (Rangers) 8
Hamill, J. 2008 (Kilmarnock) 9
Hamilton, B. 1989 (St Mirren) 4
Hamilton, J. 1995 (Dundee, Hearts) 14
Hammell, S. 2001 (Motherwell) 11
Handyside, P. 1993 (Grimsby T) 7
Hannah, D. 1993 (Dundee U) 16
Harper, K. 1995 (Hibernian) 7
Hartford, R. A. 1977 (Manchester C) 1
Hartley, P. J. 1997 (Millwall) 1
Hegarty, P. 1987 (Dundee U) 6
Hendry, J. 1992 (Tottenham H) 1
Hetherston, B. 1997 (St Mirren) 1
Hewitt, J. 1982 (Aberdeen) 6
Hogg, G. 1984 (Manchester U) 4
Hood, G. 1993 (Ayr U) 3
Horn, R. 1997 (Hearts) 6
Howie, S. 1993 (Cowdenbeath) 5
Hughes, R. D. 1999 (Bournemouth) 9
Hughes, S. 2002 (Rangers) 12
Hunter, G. 1987 (Hibernian) 3
Hunter, P. 1989 (East Fife) 3
Hutton, A. 2004 (Rangers) 7

Irvine, G. 2006 (Celtic) 2

James, K. F. 1997 (Falkirk) 1
Jardine, I. 1979 (Kilmarnock) 1
Jess, E. 1990 (Aberdeen) 14
Johnson, G. I. 1992 (Dundee U) 6
Johnston, A. 1994 (Hearts) 3
Johnston, F. 1993 (Falkirk) 1
Johnston, M. 1984 (Partick Th, Watford) 3
Jordan, A. J. 2000 (Bristol C) 3
Jupp, D. A. 1995 (Fulham) 9

Kennedy, J. 2003 (Celtic) 15
Kenneth, G. 2008 (Dundee U) 6
Kerr, B. 2003 (Newcastle U) 14
Kerr, M. 2001 (Kilmarnock) 1
Kerr, S. 1993 (Celtic) 10
Kinniburgh, W. D. 2004 (Motherwell) 3
Kirkwood, D. 1990 (Hearts) 1
Kyle, K. 2001 (Sunderland) 12

Lambert, P. 1991 (St Mirren) 11
Langfield, J. 2000 (Dundee) 2
Lappin, S. 2004 (St Mirren) 10
Lauchlan, J. 1998 (Kilmarnock) 11
Lavety, B. 1993 (St Mirren) 9
Lavin, G. 1993 (Watford) 7
Lawson, P. 2004 (Celtic) 10
Leighton, J. 1982 (Aberdeen) 1
Lennon, S. 2008 (Rangers) 2
Levein, C. 1985 (Hearts) 2
Leven, P. 2005 (Kilmarnock) 2
Liddell, A. M. 1994 (Barnsley) 12
Lindsey, J. 1979 (Motherwell) 1
Locke, G. 1994 (Hearts) 10
Love, G. 1995 (Hibernian) 1
Lynch, S. 2003 (Celtic, Preston NE) 13

McAllister, G. 1990 (Leicester C) 1
McAllister, R. 2008 (Inverness CT) 2
McAlpine, H. 1983 (Dundee U) 5
McAnespie, K. 1998 (St Johnstone) 4
McArthur, J. 2008 (Hamilton A) 1
McAuley, S. 1993 (St Johnstone) 1
McAvennie, F. 1982 (St Mirren) 5
McBride, J. 1981 (Everton) 1
McBride, J. P. 1998 (Celtic) 2
McCall, A. S. M. 1988 (Bradford C, Everton) 2
McCann, K. 2008 (Hibernian) 4
McCann, N. 1994 (Dundee) 9
McClair, B. 1984 (Celtic) 8
McCluskey, G. 1979 (Celtic) 6
McCluskey, S. 1997 (St Johnstone) 14
McCoist, A. 1984 (Rangers) 1
McConnell, I. 1997 (Clyde) 1
McCormack, D. 2008 (Hibernian) 1
McCormack, R. 2006 (Rangers, Motherwell) 9
McCracken, D. 2002 (Dundee U) 5
McCulloch, A. 1981 (Kilmarnock) 1
McCulloch, I. 1982 (Notts Co) 2
McCulloch, L. 1997 (Motherwell) 14
McCunnie, J. 2001 (Dundee U, Ross Co, Dunfermline Ath) 20
MacDonald, J. 1980 (Rangers) 8
MacDonald, J. 2007 (Hearts) 8
McDonald, C. 1995 (Falkirk) 5
McDonald, K. 2008 (Dundee) 4
McEwan, C. 1997 (Clyde, Raith R) 17
McEwan, D. 2003 (Livingston) 2
McFadden, J. 2003 (Motherwell) 7
McFarlane, D. 1997 (Hamilton A) 3
McGarry, S. 1997 (St Mirren) 3
McGarvey, F. P. 1977 (St Mirren, Celtic) 3
McGarvey, S. 1982 (Manchester U) 4
McGhee, M. 1981 (Aberdeen) 1
McGinnis, G. 1985 (Dundee U) 1
McGlinchey, M. R. 2007 (Celtic) 1
McGregor, A. 2003 (Rangers) 6
McGrillen, P. 1994 (Motherwell) 2
McGuire, D. 2002 (Aberdeen) 2
McInally, J. 1989 (Dundee U) 1
McKenzie, R. 1997 (Hearts) 2
McKimmie, S. 1985 (Aberdeen) 3
McKinlay, T. 1984 (Dundee) 6
McKinlay, W. 1989 (Dundee U) 6
McKinnon, R. 1991 (Dundee U) 6
McLaren, A, 1989 (Hearts) 11
McLaren, A. 1993 (Dundee U) 4
McLaughlin, B. 1995 (Celtic) 8
McLaughlin, J. 1981 (Morton) 10
McLean, E. 2008 (Dundee U, St Johnstone) 2
McLean, S. 2003 (Rangers) 4
McLeish, A. 1978 (Aberdeen) 6
MacLeod, A. 1979 (Hibernian) 3
McLeod, J. 1989 (Dundee U) 2
MacLeod, M. 1979 (Dumbarton, Celtic) 5
McManus, T. 2001 (Hibernian) 14
McMillan, S. 1997 (Motherwell) 4
McNab, N. 1978 (Tottenham H) 1
McNally, M. 1991 (Celtic) 2
McNamara, J. 1994 (Dunfermline Ath, Celtic) 12
McNaughton, K. 2002 (Aberdeen) 1
McNeil, A. 2007 (Hibernian) 1
McNichol, J. 1979 (Brentford) 7
McNiven, D. 1977 (Leeds U) 3
McNiven, S. A. 1996 (Oldham Ath) 1
McParland, A. 2003 (Celtic) 1
McPhee, S. 2002 (Port Vale) 1
McPherson, D. 1984 (Rangers, Hearts) 4
McQuilken, J. 1993 (Celtic) 2
McStay, P. 1983 (Celtic) 5
McWhirter, N. 1991 (St Mirren) 1
Main, A. 1988 (Dundee U) 3
Malcolm, R. 2001 (Rangers) 1
Maloney, S. 2002 (Celtic) 21
Malpas, M. 1983 (Dundee U) 8
Marshall, D. J. 2004 (Celtic) 10
Marshall, S. R. 1995 (Arsenal) 5
Mason, G. R. 1999 (Manchester C, Dunfermline Ath) 2
Mathieson, D. 1997 (Queen of the South) 3
May, E. 1989 (Hibernian) 2
Meldrum, C. 1996 (Kilmarnock) 6
Melrose, J. 1977 (Partick Th) 8
Miller, C. 1995 (Rangers) 8
Miller, J. 1987 (Aberdeen, Celtic) 7
Miller, K. 2000 (Hibernian, Rangers) 7
Miller, W. 1978 (Aberdeen) 2
Miller, W. 1991 (Hibernian) 7
Milne, K. 2000 (Hearts) 1

Milne, R. 1982 (Dundee U) 3
Mitchell, C. 2008 (Falkirk) 1
Money, I. C. 1987 (St Mirren) 3
Montgomery, N. A. 2003 (Sheffield U) 2
Morrison, S. A. 2004 (Aberdeen, Dunfermline Ath) 12
Muir, L. 1977 (Hibernian) 1
Mulgrew, C. P. 2006 (Celtic, Wolverhampton W) 11
Murray, H. 2000 (St Mirren) 3
Murray, I. 2001 (Hibernian) 15
Murray, N. 1993 (Rangers) 16
Murray, R. 1993 (Bournemouth) 1
Murray, S. 2004 (Kilmarnock) 2

Narey, D. 1977 (Dundee U) 4
Naismith, S. J. 2006 (Kilmarnock, Rangers) 15
Naysmith, G. A. 1997 (Hearts) 22
Neilson, R. 2000 (Hearts) 1
Nevin, P. 1985 (Chelsea) 5
Nicholas, C. 1981 (Celtic, Arsenal) 6
Nicholson, B. 1999 (Rangers) 7
Nicol, S. 1981 (Ayr U, Liverpool) 14
Nisbet, S. 1989 (Rangers) 5
Noble, D. J. 2003 (West Ham U) 2
Notman, A. M. 1999 (Manchester U) 10

O'Brien, B. 1999 (Blackburn R, Livingston) 6
O'Connor, G. 2003 (Hibernian) 8
O'Donnell, P. 1992 (Motherwell) 8
O'Leary, R. 2008 (Kilmarnock) 2
O'Neil, B. 1992 (Celtic) 7
O'Neil, J. 1991 (Dundee U) 1
O'Neill, M. 1995 (Clyde) 6
Orr, N. 1978 (Morton) 7

Parker, K. 2001 (St Johnstone) 1
Parlane, D. 1977 (Rangers) 1
Paterson, C. 1981 (Hibernian) 2
Paterson, J. 1997 (Dundee U) 9
Payne, G. 1978 (Dundee U) 3
Peacock, L. A. 1997 (Carlisle U) 1
Pearce, A. J. 2008 (Reading) 1
Pearson, S. P. 2003 (Motherwell) 8
Pressley, S. J. 1993 (Rangers, Coventry C, Dundee U) 26
Provan, D. 1977 (Kilmarnock) 1
Prunty, B. 2004 (Aberdeen) 6

Quinn, P. C. 2004 (Motherwell) 3
Quinn, R. 2006 (Celtic) 9

Rae, A. 1991 (Millwall) 8
Rae, G. 1999 (Dundee) 6
Redford, I. 1981 (Rangers) 6
Reid, B. 1991 (Rangers) 4
Reid, C. 1993 (Hibernian) 3
Reid, M. 1982 (Celtic) 2
Reid, R. 1977 (St Mirren) 3
Reilly, A. 2004 (Wycombe W) 1
Renicks, S. 1997 (Hamilton A) 1
Reynolds, M. 2007 (Motherwell) 8
Rice, B. 1985 (Hibernian) 1
Richardson, L. 1980 (St Mirren) 2
Riordan, D. G. 2004 (Hibernian) 5
Ritchie, A. 1980 (Morton) 1
Ritchie, P. S. 1996 (Hearts) 7
Robertson, A. 1991 (Rangers) 1
Robertson, C. 1977 (Rangers) 1
Robertson, D. 1987 (Aberdeen) 7
Robertson, D. 2007 (Dundee U) 2
Robertson, G. A. 2004 (Nottingham F, Rotherham U) 15
Robertson, H. 1994 (Aberdeen) 2
Robertson, J. 1985 (Hearts) 2
Robertson, L. 1993 (Rangers) 3
Robertson, S. 1998 (St Johnstone) 2
Roddie, A. 1992 (Aberdeen) 5
Ross, G. 2007 (Dunfermline Ath) 1
Ross, T. W. 1977 (Arsenal) 1
Rowson, D. 1997 (Aberdeen) 5
Russell, R. 1978 (Rangers) 3

Salton, D. B. 1992 (Luton T) 6
Samson, C. I. 2004 (Kilmarnock) 6
Scobbie, T. 2008 (Falkirk) 3
Scott, M. 2006 (Livingston) 1
Scott, P. 1994 (St Johnstone) 4
Scrimgour, D. 1997 (St Mirren) 3
Seaton, A. 1998 (Falkirk) 1
Severin, S. D. 2000 (Hearts) 10
Shannon, R. 1987 (Dundee) 7
Sharp, G. M. 1982 (Everton) 1
Sharp, R. 1990 (Dunfermline Ath) 4
Sheerin, P. 1996 (Southampton) 1
Shields, G. 1997 (Rangers) 2
Simmons, S. 2003 (Hearts) 1
Simpson, N. 1982 (Aberdeen) 11
Sinclair, G. 1977 (Dumbarton) 1
Skilling, M. 1993 (Kilmarnock) 2
Smith, B. M. 1992 (Celtic) 5
Smith, C. 2008 (St Mirren) 2
Smith, D. L. 2006 (Motherwell) 2
Smith, G. 1978 (Rangers) 1
Smith, G. 2004 (Rangers) 8
Smith, H. G. 1987 (Hearts) 2
Smith, S. 2007 (Rangers) 1
Sneddon, A. 1979 (Celtic) 1
Snodgrass, R. 2008 (Livingston) 2
Soutar, D. 2003 (Dundee) 11
Speedie, D. R. 1985 (Chelsea) 1
Spencer, J. 1991 (Rangers) 3
Stanton, P. 1977 (Hibernian) 1
Stark, W. 1985 (Aberdeen) 1
Stephen, R. 1983 (Dundee) 1
Stevens, G. 1977 (Motherwell) 1
Stevenson, L. 2008 (Hibernian) 7
Stewart, C. 2002 (Kilmarnock) 1
Stewart, J. 1978 (Kilmarnock, Middlesbrough) 3
Stewart, M. J. 2000 (Manchester U) 17
Stewart, R. 1979 (Dundee U, West Ham U) 12
Stillie, D. 1995 (Aberdeen) 14
Strachan, G. D. 1980 (Aberdeen) 1
Strachan, G. D. 1998 (Coventry C) 7
Sturrock, P. 1977 (Dundee U) 9
Sweeney, P. H. 2004 (Millwall) 8
Sweeney, S. 1991 (Clydebank) 7

Tarrant, N. K. 1999 (Aston Villa) 5
Teale, G. 1997 (Clydebank, Ayr U) 6
Telfer, P. N. 1993 (Luton T) 3
Thomas, K. 1993 (Hearts) 8
Thompson, S. 1997 (Dundee U) 12
Thomson, K. 2005 (Hibernian) 6
Thomson, W. 1977 (Partick Th, St Mirren) 10
Tolmie, J. 1980 (Morton) 1
Tortolano, J. 1987 (Hibernian) 2
Turner, I. 2005 (Everton) 6
Tweed, S. 1993 (Hibernian) 3

Wales, G. 2000 (Hearts) 1
Walker, A. 1988 (Celtic) 1
Wallace, I. A. 1978 (Coventry C) 1
Wallace, L. 2007 (Hearts) 7
Wallace, R. 2004 (Celtic, Sunderland) 4
Walsh, C. 1984 (Nottingham F) 5
Wark, J. 1977 (Ipswich T) 8
Watson, A. 1981 (Aberdeen) 4
Watson, K. 1977 (Rangers) 2
Watt, M. 1991 (Aberdeen) 12
Watt. S. M. 2005 (Chelsea) 5
Webster, A. 2003 (Hearts) 2
Whiteford, A. 1997 (St Johnstone) 1
Whittaker, S. G. 2005 (Hibernian) 18
Whyte, D. 1987 (Celtic) 9
Wilkie, L. 2000 (Dundee) 6
Will, J. A. 1992 (Arsenal) 3
Williams, G. 2002 (Nottingham F) 9
Wilson, M. 2004 (Dundee U, Celtic) 19
Wilson, S. 1999 (Rangers) 7
Wilson, T. 1983 (St Mirren) 1
Wilson, T. 1988 (Nottingham F) 4
Winnie, D. 1988 (St Mirren) 1
Woods, M. 2006 (Sunderland) 2
Wright, P. 1989 (Aberdeen, QPR) 3
Wright, S. 1991 (Aberdeen) 14
Wright, T. 1987 (Oldham Ath) 1

Young, Darren 1997 (Aberdeen) 8
Young, Derek 2000 (Aberdeen) 5

WALES

Adams, N. W. 2008 (Bury) 2
Aizlewood, M. 1979 (Luton T) 2
Allen, J. M. 2008 (Swansea C) 7
Anthony, B. 2005 (Cardiff C) 8

Baddeley, L. M. 1996 (Cardiff C) 2
Balcombe, S. 1982 (Leeds U) 1
Bale, G. 2006 (Southampton) 3
Barnhouse, D. J. 1995 (Swansea C) 3
Bater, P. T. 1977 (Bristol R) 2
Beevers, L. J. 2005 (Boston U, Lincoln C) 7
Bellamy, C. D. 1996 (Norwich C) 8
Birchall, A. S. 2003 (Arsenal, Mansfield T) 12
Bird, A. 1993 (Cardiff C) 6
Blackmore, C. 1984 (Manchester U) 3
Blake, D. J. 2007 (Cardiff C) 6
Blake, N. A. 1991 (Cardiff C) 5
Blaney, S. D. 1997 (West Ham U) 3
Bodin, P. J. 1983 (Cardiff C) 1
Bowen, J. P. 1993 (Swansea C) 5
Bowen, M. R. 1983 (Tottenham H) 3
Boyle, T. 1982 (C Palace) 1
Brace, D. P. 1995 (Wrexham) 6
Bradley, M. S. 2007 (Walsall) 5
Brough, M. 2003 (Notts Co) 3
Brown, J. D. 2008 (Cardiff C) 2
Brown, J. R. 2003 (Gillingham) 7
Byrne, M. T. 2003 (Bolton W) 1

Calliste, R. T. 2005 (Manchester U, Liverpool) 15
Carpenter, R. E. 2005 (Burnley) 1
Cegielski, W. 1977 (Wrexham) 2
Chapple, S. R. 1992 (Swansea C) 8
Charles, J. M. 1979 (Swansea C) 2
Church, S. R. 2008 (Reading) 6
Clark, J. 1978 (Manchester U, Derby Co) 2
Coates, J. S. 1996 (Swansea C) 5
Coleman, C. 1990 (Swansea C) 3
Collins, J. M. 2003 (Cardiff C) 7
Collins, M. J. 2007 (Fulham, Swansea C) 2
Collison, J. D. 2008 (West Ham U) 5
Cotterill, D. R. G. B. 2005 (Bristol C, Wigan Ath) 11
Coyne, D. 1992 (Tranmere R) 7
Critchell, K. A. R. 2005 (Southampton) 3
Crofts, A. L. 2005 (Gillingham) 10
Crowell, M. T. 2004 (Wrexham) 7
Curtis, A. T. 1977 (Swansea C) 1

Davies, A. 1982 (Manchester U) 6
Davies, A. G. 2006 (Cambridge U) 6
Davies, A. R. 2005 (Southampton, Yeovil T) 14
Davies, C. M. 2005 (Oxford U, Verona, Oldham Ath) 9
Davies, D. 1999 (Barry T) 1
Davies, G. M. 1993 (Hereford U, C Palace) 7
Davies, I. C. 1978 (Norwich C) 1
Davies, L. 2005 (Bangor C) 1
Davies, R. J. 2006 (WBA) 4
Davies, S. 1999 (Peterborough U, Tottenham H) 10
Day, R. 2000 (Manchester C, Mansfield T) 11
Deacy, N. 1977 (PSV Eindhoven) 1
De-Vulgt, L. S. 2002 (Swansea C) 2
Dibble, A. 1983 (Cardiff C) 3
Doyle, S. C. 1979 (Preston NE, Huddersfield T) 2
Duffy, R. M. 2005 (Portsmouth) 7
Dwyer, P. J. 1979 (Cardiff C) 1

Eardley, N. 2007 (Oldham Ath) 4
Earnshaw, R. 1999 (Cardiff C) 10
Easter, D. J. 2006 (Cardiff C) 1
Ebdon, M. 1990 (Everton) 2
Edwards, C. N. H. 1996 (Swansea C) 7
Edwards, D. A. 2006 (Shrewsbury T, Luton T, Wolverhampton W) 8
Edwards, R. I. 1977 (Chester) 2
Edwards, R. W. 1991 (Bristol C) 13
Evans, A. 1977 (Bristol R) 1
Evans, C. 2007 (Manchester C) 8
Evans, K. 1999 (Leeds U, Cardiff C) 4
Evans, P. S. 1996 (Shrewsbury T) 1
Evans, S. J. 2001 (C Palace) 2
Evans, T. 1995 (Cardiff C) 3

Fish, N. 2005 (Cardiff C) 2
Fleetwood, S. 2005 (Cardiff C) 5
Flynn, C. P. 2007 (Crewe Alex) 1
Folland, R. W. 2000 (Oxford U) 1
Foster, M. G. 1993 (Tranmere R) 1
Fowler, L. A. 2003 (Coventry C, Huddersfield T) 9
Freestone, R. 1990 (Chelsea) 1

Gabbidon, D. L. 1999 (WBA, Cardiff C) 17
Gale, D. 1983 (Swansea C) 2
Gall, K. A. 2002 (Bristol R, Yeovil T) 8
Gibson, N. D. 1999 (Tranmere R, Sheffield W) 11
Giggs, R. J. 1991 (Manchester U) 1
Gilbert, P. 2005 (Plymouth Arg) 12
Giles, D. C. 1977 (Cardiff C, Swansea C, C Palace) 4
Giles, P. 1982 (Cardiff C) 3
Graham, D. 1991 (Manchester U) 1
Green, R. M. 1998 (Wolverhampton W) 16
Griffith, C. 1990 (Cardiff C) 1
Griffiths, C. 1991 (Shrewsbury T) 1
Grubb, D. 2007 (Bristol C) 1
Gunter, C. 2006 (Cardiff C, Tottenham H) 7

Haldane, L. O. 2007 (Bristol R) 1
Hall, G. D. 1990 (Chelsea) 1
Hartson, J. 1994 (Luton T, Arsenal) 9
Haworth, S. O. 1997 (Cardiff C, Coventry C, Wigan Ath) 12
Hennessey, W. R. 2006 (Wolverhampton W) 5
Hillier, I. M. 2001 (Tottenham H, Luton T) 5
Hodges, G. 1983 (Wimbledon) 5
Holden, A. 1984 (Chester C) 1
Holloway, C. D. 1999 (Exeter C) 2
Hopkins, J. 1982 (Fulham) 5
Hopkins, S. A. 1999 (Wrexham) 1
Huggins, D. S. 1996 (Bristol C) 1
Hughes, D. 2005 (Kaiserslautern, Regensburg) 2
Hughes, D. R. 1994 (Southampton) 1
Hughes, I. 1992 (Bury) 11
Hughes, L. M. 1983 (Manchester U) 5
Hughes, R. D. 1996 (Aston Villa, Shrewsbury T) 13
Hughes, W. 1977 (WBA) 3

Jackett, K. 1981 (Watford) 2
Jacobson, J. M. 2006 (Cardiff C, Bristol R) 14
James, L. R. S. 2006 (Southampton) 8
James, R. M. 1977 (Swansea C) 3
Jarman, L. 1996 (Cardiff C) 10
Jeanne, L. C. 1999 (QPR) 8
Jelleyman, G. A. 1999 (Peterborough U) 1
Jenkins, L. D. 1998 (Swansea C) 9
Jenkins, S. R. 1993 (Swansea C) 2
Jones, C. T. 2007 (Swansea C) 1
Jones, E. P. 2000 (Blackpool) 1
Jones, F. 1981 (Wrexham) 1
Jones, J. A. 2001 (Swansea C) 3
Jones, L. 1982 (Cardiff C) 3
Jones, M. A. 2004 (Wrexham) 4
Jones, M. G. 1998 (Leeds U) 7
Jones, P. L. 1992 (Liverpool) 12
Jones, R. A. 1994 (Sheffield W) 3
Jones, S. J. 2005 (Swansea C) 1
Jones, V. 1979 (Bristol R) 2

Kendall, L. M. 2001 (C Palace) 2
Kendall, M. 1978 (Tottenham H) 1
Kenworthy, J. R. 1994 (Tranmere R) 3
King, A. 2008 (Leicester C) 1
Knott, G. R. 1996 (Tottenham H) 1

Law, B. J. 1990 (QPR) 2
Lawless, A. 2006 (Torquay U) 1
Ledley, J. C. 2005 (Cardiff C) 5
Letheran, G. 1977 (Leeds U) 2
Letheran, K. C. 2006 (Swansea C) 1
Lewis, D. 1982 (Swansea C) 9
Lewis, J. 1983 (Cardiff C) 1
Llewellyn, C. M. 1998 (Norwich C) 14
Loveridge, J. 1982 (Swansea C) 3
Low, J. D. 1999 (Bristol R, Cardiff C) 1
Lowndes, S. R. 1979 (Newport Co, Millwall) 4

MacDonald, S. B. 2006 (Swansea C)	12
McCarthy, A. J. 1994 (QPR)	3
McDonald, C. 2006 (Cardiff C)	3
Mackin, L. 2006 (Wrexham)	1
Maddy, P. 1982 (Cardiff C)	2
Margetson, M. W. 1992 (Manchester C)	7
Martin, A. P. 1999 (C Palace)	1
Martin, D. A. 2006 (Notts Co)	1
Marustik, C. 1982 (Swansea C)	7
Maxwell, L. J. 1999 (Liverpool, Cardiff C)	14
Meaker, M. J. 1994 (QPR)	2
Melville, A. K. 1990 (Swansea C, Oxford U)	2
Micallef, C. 1982 (Cardiff C)	3
Morgan, A. M. 1995 (Tranmere R)	4
Morgan, C. 2004 (Wrexham, Milton Keynes D)	12
Moss, D. M. 2003 (Shrewsbury T)	6
Mountain, P. D. 1997 (Cardiff C)	2
Mumford, A. O. 2003 (Swansea C)	4
Nardiello, D. 1978 (Coventry C)	1
Neilson, A. B. 1993 (Newcastle U)	7
Nicholas, P. 1978 (C Palace, Arsenal)	3
Nogan, K. 1990 (Luton T)	2
Nogan, L. M. 1991 (Oxford U)	1
Nyatanga, L. J. 2005 (Derby Co)	9
Oster, J. M. 1997 (Grimsby T, Everton)	9
Owen, G. 1991 (Wrexham)	8
Page, R. J. 1995 (Watford)	4
Parslow, D. 2005 (Cardiff C)	4
Partridge, D. W. 1997 (West Ham U)	1
Pascoe, C. 1983 (Swansea C)	4
Pearce, S. 2006 (Bristol C)	3
Pejic, S. M. 2003 (Wrexham)	6
Pembridge, M. A. 1991 (Luton T)	1
Perry, J. 1990 (Cardiff C)	3
Peters, M. 1992 (Manchester C, Norwich C)	3
Phillips, D. 1984 (Plymouth Arg)	3
Phillips, G. R. 2001 (Swansea C)	3
Phillips, L. 1979 (Swansea C, Charlton Ath)	2
Pipe, D. R. 2003 (Coventry C, Notts Co)	12
Pontin, K. 1978 (Cardiff C)	1
Powell, L. 1991 (Southampton)	4
Powell, L. 2004 (Leicester C)	3
Powell, R. 2006 (Bolton W)	1
Price, J. J. 1998 (Swansea C)	7
Price, L. P. 2005 (Ipswich T)	10
Price, M. D. 2001 (Everton, Hull C, Scarborough)	13
Price, P. 1981 (Luton T)	1
Pritchard, M. O. 2006 (Swansea C)	4
Pugh, D. 1982 (Doncaster R)	2
Pugh, S. 1993 (Wrexham)	2
Pulis, A. J. 2006 (Stoke C)	5
Ramasut, M. W. T. 1997 (Bristol R)	4
Ramsey, A. J. 2008, (Cardiff C)	7
Ratcliffe, K. 1981 (Everton)	2
Ready, K. 1992 (QPR)	5
Rees, A. 1984 (Birmingham C)	1
Rees, J. M. 1990 (Luton T)	3
Rees, M. R. 2003 (Millwall)	4
Ribeiro, C. M. 2008 (Bristol C)	3
Roberts, A. M. 1991 (QPR)	2
Roberts, C. J. 1999 (Cardiff C)	1
Roberts, G. 1983 (Hull C)	1
Roberts, G. W. 1997 (Liverpool, Panionios, Tranmere R)	11
Roberts, J. G. 1977 (Wrexham)	1
Roberts, N. W. 1999 (Wrexham)	3
Roberts, P. 1997 (Porthmadog)	1
Roberts, S. I. 1999 (Swansea C)	13
Roberts, S. W. 2000 (Wrexham)	3
Robinson, C. P. 1996 (Wolverhampton W)	6
Robinson, J. R. C. 1992 (Brighton & HA, Charlton Ath)	5
Rowlands, A. J. R. 1996 (Manchester C)	5
Rush, I. 1981 (Liverpool)	2
Savage, R. W. 1995 (Crewe Alex)	3
Sayer, P. A. 1977 (Cardiff C)	2
Searle, D. 1991 (Cardiff C)	6
Slatter, D. 2000 (Chelsea)	6
Slatter, N. 1983 (Bristol R)	6
Somner, M. J. 2004 (Brentford)	2
Speed, G. A. 1990 (Leeds U)	3
Spender, S. 2005 (Wrexham)	6
Stevenson, N. 1982 (Swansea C)	2
Stevenson, W. B. 1977 (Leeds U)	3
Stock, B. B. 2003 (Bournemouth)	4
Symons, C. J. 1991 (Portsmouth)	2
Taylor, G. K. 1995 (Bristol R)	4
Taylor, N. J. 2008 (Wrexham)	3
Taylor, R. F. 2008 (Chelsea)	1
Thomas, D. G. 1977 (Leeds U)	3
Thomas, D. J. 1998 (Watford)	2
Thomas, J. A. 1996 (Blackburn R)	21
Thomas, Martin R. 1979 (Bristol R)	2
Thomas, Mickey R. 1977 (Wrexham)	2
Thomas, S. 2001 (Wrexham)	5
Tibbott, L. 1977 (Ipswich T)	2
Tipton, M. J. 1998 (Oldham Ath)	6
Tolley, J. C. 2001 (Shrewsbury T)	12
Tudur-Jones, O. 2006 (Swansea C)	3
Twiddy, C. 1995 (Plymouth Arg)	3
Valentine, R. D. 2001 (Everton, Darlington)	8
Vaughan, D. O. 2003 (Crewe Alex)	8
Vaughan, N. 1982 (Newport Co)	2
Vokes, S. M. 2007 (Bournemouth)	9
Walsh, D. 2000 (Wrexham)	8
Walsh, I. P. 1979 (C Palace, Swansea C)	2
Walton, M. 1991 (Norwich C.)	1
Ward, D. 1996 (Notts Co)	2
Warlow, O. J. 2007 (Lincoln C)	2
Weston, R. D. 2001 (Arsenal, Cardiff C)	4
Whitfield, P. M. 2003 (Wrexham)	1
Wiggins, R. 2006 (C Palace)	5
Williams, A. P. 1998 (Southampton)	9
Williams, A. S. 1996 (Blackburn R)	16
Williams, D. 1983 (Bristol R)	1
Williams, D. I. L. 1998 (Liverpool, Wrexham)	9
Williams, D. T. 2006 (Yeovil T)	1
Williams, E. 1997 (Caernarfon T)	2
Williams, G. 1983 (Bristol R)	2
Williams, G. A. 2003 (C Palace)	5
Williams, M. 2001 (Manchester U)	10
Williams, M. P. 2006 (Wrexham)	13
Williams, M. R. 2006 (Wrexham)	2
Williams, O. Fon 2007 (Crewe Alex)	8
Williams, R. 2007 (Middlesbrough)	6
Williams, S. J. 1995 (Wrexham)	4
Wilmot, R. 1982 (Arsenal)	6
Worgan, L. J. 2005 (Milton Keynes D, Rushden & D)	5
Wright, A. A. 1998 (Oxford U)	3
Young, S. 1996 (Cardiff C)	5

FA SCHOOLS & YOUTH GAMES 2007–08

■ *Denotes player sent off.*

ENGLAND UNDER-19

Gibbs, Lansbury (Arsenal); Clark (Aston Villa); Aluko, Pearce (Birmingham C); Obadeyi (Bolton W); Wright (Charlton Ath); Bertrand, Cork, Hutchinson, Sawyer, Sinclair (Chelsea); Moses (Crystal Palace); Atkins (Derby Co); Eastwood (Huddersfield T); Upson (Ipswich T); Delph (Leeds U); Mattock (Leicester C); Obeng (Manchester C); Brandy, Welbeck (Manchester U); Steele, Walker (Middlesbrough); Carroll (Newcastle U); Henry (Reading); Beevers (Sheffield W); Robson-Kanu (Southend U); Chandler (Sunderland); Button (Tottenham H); Sears, Spence, Stanislaus, Tomkins (West Ham U).

11 September 2007 *(at Notts Co)*

England 4 *(Brandy 5, Carroll 15, Sawyer 19, Obadeyi 60)*

Belarus 0 4266

England: Eastwood; Cork, Bertrand, Sawyer■, Hutchinson, Clark, Henry, Chandler, Carroll (Sears 63), Brandy (Obadeyi 46), Aluko (Upson 85).

12 October 2007 *(at Doncaster)*

England 5 *(Brandy 46, Carroll 60, Henry 69, Pearce 73, Sinclair 78)*

Iceland 1 *(Gunnarsson 53)* 5752

England: Steele; Hutchinson, Bertrand, Cork, Pearce, Clark, Henry, Chandler (Wright 80), Carroll (Obadeyi 68), Brandy (Gibbs 82), Sinclair.

14 October 2007 *(at Scunthorpe)*

England 6 *(Clark 2, Obadeyi 30, 70, 86, Chandler 29, Brandy 49)*

Romania 0 3370

England: Steele; Hutchinson, Cork, Pearce, Clark, Henry (Spence 87), Chandler (Wright 55), Brandy (Upson 62), Obadeyi, Mattock, Gibbs.

17 October 2007 *(at Barnsley)*

England 3 *(Obadeyi 30, Henry 69, Pearce 76)*

Belgium 1 *(Odjidja-Ofoe 73)* 5993

England: Atkins; Hutchinson, Cork, Clark, Henry, Brandy, Obadeyi, Wright (Chandler 57), Upson (Gibbs 78), Mattock (Pearce 46), Spence.

14 November 2007 *(in Elversberg)*

Germany 1 *(Nsereko 34)*

England 0

England: Button; Gibbs, Cork, Clark, Tomkins, Aluko, Chandler, Sawyer, Robson-Kanu, Lansbury, Obadeyi.

5 February 2008 *(at Swindon)*

England 2 *(Sinclair 22 (pen), Clark 74)*

Croatia 0 11,303

England: Steele (Button 46); Obeng, Bertrand, Cork, Tomkins, Clark, Henry (Upson 79), Gibbs, Robson-Kanu (Carroll 46), Brandy (Sears 74), Sinclair.

25 March 2008 *(at Milton Keynes)*

England 3 *(Tomkins 19, 59, Carroll 64)*

Russia 1 *(Pesegov 61)* 8814

England: Button (Steele 46); Obeng, Cork, Tomkins (Beevers 66), Clark, Sinclair (Delph 78), Walker, Carroll (Obadeyi 75), Upson (Stanislas 66), Aluko, Henry.

26 May 2008 *(in Minsk)*

England 2 *(Sears 29, 85 (pen))*

Poland 0

England: Button; Obeng, Clark, Tomkins, Mattock, Sinclair, Cork, Gibbs, Moses (Bertrand), Sears, Carroll.

28 May 2008 *(in Minsk)*

England 1 *(Henry 56)*

Serbia 0

England: Button; Obeng (Walker), Tomkins, Pearce, Mattock, Sinclair (Welbeck), Gibbs, Cork, Henry, Sears (Bertrand), Carroll.

31 May 2008 *(in Minsk)*

Belarus 0

England 0

England: Steele; Cork, Tomkins, Clark, Sinclair, Gibbs (Walker 46), Carroll (Sears 72), Moses, Bertrand, Welbeck (Pearce 90), Chandler.

ENGLAND UNDER-18

Hoyte, Thomas (Arsenal); Clancy (Aston Villa); Plummer (Bristol C); Ofori-Twumasi (Chelsea); Elito (Colchester U); Hills (Crystal Palace); Bennett R (Grimsby T); Smithies (Huddersfield T); Elliott (Leeds U); Chambers A (Leicester C); Tripper (Manchester C); Amos, Drinkwater, Welbeck, Woods (Manchester U); Franks, Porritt, Smallwood (Middlesbrough); Reid (Nottingham F); Gosling (Plymouth Arg, Everton); Oxley (Rotherham U); Rose (Tottenham H); Spence (West Ham U); Bennett K (Wolverhampton W).

20 November 2007 *(at Gillingham)*

England 2 *(Welbeck 38, Drinkwater 82)*

Ghana 0 5297

England: Smithies (Woods 46); Ofori-Twumasi (Tripper 83), Reid, Gosling, Spence, Hoyte, Franks (Plummer 46), Rose (Clancy 80), Welbeck (Chambers 72), Thomas (Drinkwater 67), Porritt (Elito 46).

16 April 2008 *(at Hartlepool)*

England 2 *(Welbeck 10, Drinkwater 90)*

Austria 0 2306

England: Amos (Oxley 46); Hoyte, Hills (Reid 71), Gosling (Smallwood 46), Bennett R, Spence, Franks (Bennett K 46), Drinkwater, Welbeck, Rose (Chambers 71), Elito (Elliott 79).

ENGLAND UNDER-17

Bartley, Cruise, Henderson, Watt, Wilshere (Arsenal); Delfounesco, Forrester (Aston Villa); Lyness, McPike, Sammons, Sheldon (Birmingham C); Eckersley, Stokes (Bolton W); Solly (Charlton Ath); Gordon, Mellis, Nouble, Phillip, Philliskirk (Chelsea); Bostock (Crystal Palace); Mutch, Severn (Derby Co); Rodwell (Everton); Briggs, Foderingham (Fulham); John, O'Neill (Leicester C); Highdale, Wootton (Liverpool); Ajose, James, Norwood, Stewart (Manchester U); Walker (Millwall); Donaldson (Newcastle U); Rudd (Norwich C); Noble (Sunderland); Parrett, Smith, Townsend (Tottenham H); Hemmings (Wolverhampton W).

30 July 2007 *(in Fredericia)*

England 2 *(Donaldson 60, 67)*

Iceland 0

England: Lyness; Solly, Rodwell, Stokes, Briggs, Highdale, Bostock (Mutch 73), Hemmings (Sammons 63), Henderson, Donaldson (John 80), Philliskirk (Sheldon 80).

31 July 2007 *(at Kolding)*

England 2 *(Donaldson 15, Sheldon 41)*

Finland 1

England: Walker; Briggs (Solly), Rodwell, Wootton, Donaldson (Philliskirk 64), Henderson (Highdale 53), Sammons, O'Neill, Mutch (Stokes 70), John, Sheldon (Hemmings 77).

2 August 2007 *(in Ikast)*

England 0

Sweden 2 *(Soder 18, 67)*

England: Lyness; O'Neill, Stokes, Wootton, Solly, Highdale, Bostock, Hemmings (Sammons 69), Philliskirk (Donaldson 46) (Rodwell 80), John (Briggs 59), Sheldon (Henderson 74).

4 August 2007 *(in Fredericia)*

England 4 *(Philliskirk 17, Donaldson 33, Sheldon 43, Briggs 73)*

Norway 1 *(Hedenstad 53 (pen))*

England: Walker; Solly, Stokes, Wootton, Briggs, Highdale, Mutch (Sheldon) (John), Sammons, Henderson, Donaldson (Hemmings), Philliskirk.

THE ALGARVE TOURNAMENT

2 February 2008 *(in the Algarve)*

Denmark 0

England 3 *(Donaldson 27, Briggs 48, Parrett 70)*

England: Severn; Smith, Briggs (Rodwell 48), James (Parrett 55), Bartley, Watt (Townsend 48), Mutch, Donaldson (Bostock 55), Eckersley, Noble, Nouble.

3 February 2008 *(in Portimao)*

France 0

England 2 *(Mellis 15, Donaldson 34 (pen))*

England: Rudd; Briggs (Smith 70), Rodwell, Bartley (Eckersley 40), O'Neill, Parrett, Bostock (Mutch 65), Mellis (James 44), Watt (Nouble 40), Donaldson, Townsend (Noble 70).

5 February 2008 *(in Silves)*

Portugal 0

England 0

England: Severn; Smith, Rodwell (Parrett 40), Briggs, O'Neill, Bostock (Watt 40), James, Mellis (Donaldson 68), Mutch, Townsend, Noble (Nouble 40).

EUROPEAN CHAMPIONSHIP

QUALIFIERS

21 October 2007 *(in Estonia)*

England 6 *(Donaldson 18, 68, Delfounesco 22, 24, 56, James 80)*

Malta 0

England: Foderingham; Solly, Cruise, Rodwell, Gordon, Wilshere, James, Bostock, Forrester (Norwood 61), Delfounesco (Parrett 55), Donaldson (Townsend 70).

23 October 2007 *(in Estonia)*

England 6 *(James 10, Delfounesco 33, Briggs 38, Parrett 55, Wilshere 72, Rodwell 80)*

Estonia 0

England: Lyness; Briggs, Cruise, Rodwell, O'Neill, Townsend, Parrett, Norwood (Wilshere 68), Stewart, James (Bostock 41), Delfounesco (Donaldson 51).

26 October 2007 *(in Estonia)*

England 0

Portugal 0

England: Foderingham; Gordon, James, Briggs, Solly, Norwood, Parrett, Wilshere (Bostock), Townsend (Delfounesco), Forrester (Rodwell), Donaldson.

ELITE QUALIFYING ROUND

25 March 2008 *(in Rishon)*

France 1 *(Mezui 78)*

England 1 *(Rodwell 58)*

England: Foderingham; Solly, O'Neill, Rodwell, Briggs, Parrett, James, Mutch, Forrester (Mellis 75), Donaldson (Delfounesco 79), Wilshere.

27 March 2008 *(in Rishon)*

Russia 3 *(Kolkorin 35, Stolyarenko 39, Pugachev 66)*

England 2 *(James 45, Delfounesco 72)*

England: Foderingham; Gordon, Briggs, Rodwell, Solly, Mellis (Forrester 72), James, Wilshere, Bostock (Parrett 41), Stewart (Donaldson 41), Delfounesco.

30 March 2008 *(in Tel Aviv)*

Israel 2 *(Gadir 38, Hakim 62)*

England 2 *(Mellis 11, Delfounesco 80)*

England: Rudd; O'Neill, Briggs (Gordon 60), Bartley, Rodwell, Bostock, Mutch, Mellis (James 29), Forrester (Stewart 77), Donaldson, Delfounesco.

UNDER-17 INTERNATIONAL TOURNAMENT

29 August 2007 *(at Brentford)*

England 6 *(Townsend 30, 33, O'Neil 34, Stewart 64, Parrett 68, Mellis 80)*

Northern Ireland 1 *(Stokes 78 (og))*

England: Rudd; O'Neil, James, Stokes, Briggs, Stewart, Norwood, McPike (Mellis 70), Bostock (Parrett 61), Phillip, Townsend (Ajose 62).

31 August 2007 *(at Wycombe)*

England 1 *(Phillip)*

Turkey 1 *(Soner)*

England: Lyness; Solly, Gordon, Stokes, O'Neill, James, Parrett, Bostock, Mellis (Phillip 53), Donaldson, Ajose (Townsend 73).

2 September 2007 *(at Luton)*

England 3 *(Townsend 20, Donaldson 30, Stewart 50)*

Italy 0 3272

England: Rudd; Gordon, Solly, James, Briggs, Mellis, Norwood (O'Neill 68), McPike, Stewart (Ajose 51), Townsend, Donaldson (Phillip 59).

ENGLAND UNDER-16

Aneke, Banton, Byles, Freeman, Frimpong, Nicholas (Arsenal); Bowen (Blackburn R); McGeechan (Bolton W); Shelvey (Charlton Ath); Knott, McEachran (Chelsea); Grandison (Coventry C); Sekajja (Crystal Palace); Baxter, Davies (Everton); Marsh-Brown (Fulham); Garbutt (Leeds U); Benali (Manchester C); Fryers, Lampkin, Tunnicliffe (Manchester U); Pilatos (Middlesbrough); Steer (Norwich C); Head (Plymouth Arg); Baggie, Browne, Macdonald, Mills, Walcott (Reading); Oshodi (Watford); Elford-Alliyu, Hurst (WBA); Mendez-Laing, Reckord (Wolverhampton W).

SKY SPORTS VICTORY SHIELD

11 October 2007 *(at Blackpool)*

England 2 *(Shelvey 62, Banton 79)*

Northern Ireland 2 *(Duffy 73 (pen), Burke 80)* 3114

England: Steer; Byles (Oshodi 58), Browne (Marsh-Brown 46), Frimpong (Pilatos 76), Macdonald, Fryers, Lampkin (Banton 62), Tunnicliffe, Baxter, Shelvey, McEachran (Walcott 46).

2 November 2007 *(at Telford)*

England 2 *(Shelvey 33, Baxter 38)*

Wales 0 3610

England: Davies; Marsh-Brown (Garbutt 46), Hurst, Shelvey, Nicholas, Oshodi, Baggie (Bowen 57), Tunnicliffe (Frimpong 66), Baxter, Head (Aneke 66), Knott (Alliyu 25).

29 November 2007 *(at Falkirk)*

Scotland 1 *(Naismith 69 (pen))*

England 2 *(Shelvey 40, Baxter 68 (pen))* 2005

England: Steer; Byles (Marsh-Brown 46), Hurst, Frimpong, MacDonald (Garbutt 30), Oshodi, Shelvey (McEachran 70), Tunnicliffe, Baxter, Head (Alliyu 67), Baggie (Sekajja 52).

Wales 1, Scotland 0
Northern Ireland 1, Scotland 3
Wales 0, Northern Ireland 1

	P	*W*	*D*	*L*	*F*	*A*	*Pts*
England	3	2	1	0	6	3	7
Northern Ireland	3	1	1	1	4	5	4
Scotland	3	1	0	2	4	4	3
Wales	3	1	0	2	1	4	3

FRIENDLY

21 February 2008 *(in Katwijk)*

Holland 2

England 1 *(Fryers)*

England: Steer (Davies 46); Marsh-Brown, Reckord (Mills 62), Frimpong (Benali 63), Oshodi (Fryers 5), Nicholas, Grandison (McEachran 46), Tunnicliffe, Baxter, Walcott (Knott 73), Mendez-Laing (McGeechan 73).

MONTAIGU TOURNAMENT

19 March 2008 *(in Le Poire Sur Vie)*

England 3 *(Baxter 41 (pen), Fryers 48, Freeman 63)*

Japan 1

England: Davies; Fryers, Frimpong, Nicholas, Macdonald, Shelvey (Walcott 80), Tunnicliffe, Freeman (Mendez-Laing 69), Baxter (Head 72), McEachran, Byles (Marsh-Brown 72).

20 March 2008 *(in Le Poire Sur Vie)*

England 1 *(Frimpong 71)*

Germany 0

England: Steer; Marsh-Brown (Mendez-Laing 70), Fryers, Frimpong, Macdonald, Shelvey (Reckord 80), Tunnicliffe, Baxter, Head (Byles 60), Garbutt, Walcott (Freeman 55).

22 March 2008 *(in Les Brouzils)*

England 0

USA 1

England: Davies; Marsh-Brown, Fryers, Macdonald, Tunnicliffe, Mendez-Laing (Byles 68), McEachran, Reckord, Walcott (Shelvey 73), Head (Freeman 65), Garbutt.

24 March 2008 *(in Montaigu)*

France 0

England 0

(England won 5-4 on penalties).
England: Steer; Fryers, Frimpong, Macdonald, Shelvey, Tunnicliffe, Freeman (Reckord 78), Baxter, Byles, Head (Mendez-Laing 40), Garbutt.

WOMEN'S FOOTBALL 2007–08

The most important event in the women's football calendar for 2007–08 was undoubtedly the Women's World Cup held in China in September 2007. England's head coach Hope Powell led a strong contingent with the desire to at least qualify from their difficult group. They were very successful drawing 2-2 with Japan; 0-0 with the strongest team in the competition Germany and finally destroying Argentina 6-1. Unfortunately they were drawn in the quarter-finals with another very strong team losing 0-3 to the USA and thus went out of the competition. Ms Powell indicated that although she was disappointed at exiting the World Cup at that stage she was nonetheless proud at what had been achieved and the style in which the team had played. Germany went on to lift the trophy beating Brazil in the final by 2-0 their scorers being Birgit Prinz and Simone Laudehr. Third place went to the USA with Norway fourth. Both the Adidas Golden Boot and Golden Shoe were won by Marta of Brazil and the Fair Play Award went to Norway. Germany made history by becoming the first country to successfully defend their title having won in the USA in 2003. They are now provisionally set to host the next World Cup in 2011. Currently the ever improving England women are on course to qualify for the European Championships in 2009 whilst their younger counterparts the Under 19's have already got to the Championship Finals in France where they will play in the group stages, Germany, Sweden and Scotland.

So far as the domestic scene is concerned it is arguably wearisome to once more start with and be yet again praising the Arsenal Ladies for another brilliant season, but such is their domination of the women's game that this seems inevitable. They completed a Premier League and Women's FA Cup double for the second year in succession and remained undefeated in the League again for two seasons in a row. However they could not avoid two defeats, one being in the Premier League Cup at the feet of Everton and the other was in the Women's Uefa Cup and being holders they were disappointingly eliminated from that competition. As indicated the Premier League Cup went to Everton by a 1-0 victory over the Gunners at Leyton Orient's ground on the evening of the 28th February 2008. The match was decided by a goal from Amy Kane after only 7 minutes and the most improving women's team held on despite great pressure to gain what their manager Mo Marley described as a fantastic victory. Arsenal of course bounced back to win the Women's FA Cup defeating Leeds United by 4-1 on the City Ground Nottingham on the 5th May 2008. No early goals in this final with Kelly Smith giving Arsenal the lead in the 53rd minute which was followed 6 minutes later by the Gunners doubling their tally through Jane Ludlow. The game was put beyond United when just a minute after their second goal, Lianne Sanderson netted to give Arsenal an unassailable lead. Although Jess Clarke pulled one back for Leeds on 69 minutes, Kelly Smith scored her second and Arsenal's fourth in the 83rd minute to give the Gunners yet another triumph. Their manager Vic Akers had more cause for celebration when his team also annexed the Premier League Reserve Section Cup defeating Chelsea 1-0 after extra time on Bishop Stortford's ground.

In the FA Women's Premier League it was Arsenal again, this time they achieved their fifth League title in a row when they beat Chelsea 4-1 in April '08. They had to settle for two draws this campaign in another unbeaten run which at one time saw a winning streak of 51 matches. Their total of points was 62 and their goal difference 70; but it is clear to see why Everton are undoubtedly on their heels because the Merseysiders finished second with 57 points, a goal difference of 55 and were only defeated once. Cardiff with 12 points and Charlton Athletic with just 4 were relegated.

In the Northern Division the winners Nottingham Forest secured promotion with 59 points comfortably ahead of Lincoln City who notched 55; Stockport County and Crewe Alexandra were the relegated clubs. The Southern Division was won by WFC Fulham who also gained promotion, with a tally of 50 points from Millwall Lionesses who achieved 44 points. The number of clubs now participating in women's football grows apace which has created a very vibrant Reserve League Section. In the Southern Division One, the winners were Chelsea with 40 points, four more than runners-up Arsenal. In Division Two, WFC Fulham came top with 43 points, the same number as Barnet who were second on goal difference. The Midlands/North Division One, saw Leeds out in front with 54 points and Everton second on 39; whilst the Division Two Champions were Blackburn Rovers with 39 points with Newcastle United 3 points behind.

A number of players and officials were honoured at the annual FA Awards in London in May '08, Sir Trevor Brooking being one of those who took part in the presentation ceremonies. The full list of awards is as follows:

Umbro Top Goal Scorer – National Division	Lianne Sanderson (Arsenal).
Umbro Top Goal Scorer – Southern Division	Ann-Marie Heatherson (Fulham).
Umbro Top Goal Scorer – Northern Division	Melanie Raey (Newcastle U).
The FA Young Player of the Year	Fern Whelan.
The FA Club Media Award	Birmingham City LFC.
The FA Club Marketing Award	Leeds United LFC.
Tesco Manager of the Year	Mark Saunderson (Fulham).
Tesco Club of the Year	Nottingham Forest LFC.
Best Programme Award	Barnet LFC.
The FA Fair Play Award	Crewe Alexandra LFC.
The FA National Media Award	Fairgame.
The FA Regional Media Award	Lincolnshire Echo.
Nationwide International Player of the Year	Casey Stoney.
Tesco Players' Player of the Year	Jill Scott.

Special Award for contribution to Women's Football
Presented by Faye White, England Captain, to Lance Hardy of BBC Sport.

The FA Special Achievement Award
Presented by Ray Kiddell of The FA Women's Committee to Sheila Edmunds.

KEN GOLDMAN

FA WOMEN'S PREMIER LEAGUE 2007–08

NATIONAL DIVISION

	P	W	D	L	F	A	GD	Pts
Arsenal	22	20	2	0	85	15	70	62
Everton	22	18	3	1	69	14	55	57
Leeds U	22	12	4	6	45	33	12	40
Bristol Academy	22	10	4	8	45	35	10	34
Chelsea	22	9	5	8	40	35	5	32
Doncaster R Belles	22	8	5	9	44	42	2	29
Watford	22	9	2	11	53	52	1	29
Blackburn R	22	8	4	10	50	45	5	28
Birmingham C	22	7	4	11	34	39	–5	25
Liverpool	22	6	4	12	31	51	–20	22
Cardiff C	22	3	3	16	19	69	–50	12
Charlton Ath	22	0	4	18	6	91	–85	4

SOUTHERN DIVISION

	P	W	D	L	F	A	GD	Pts
WFC Fulham	22	15	5	2	70	19	51	50
Millwall Lionesses	22	13	5	4	50	21	29	44
Barnet	22	13	4	5	61	21	40	43
Portsmouth	22	13	3	6	63	26	37	42
West Ham U	22	12	0	10	63	46	17	36
Crystal Palace	22	10	4	8	45	30	15	34
Colchester U	22	10	1	11	51	54	–3	31
Keynsham T	22	8	6	8	51	31	20	30
Newquay	22	9	2	11	50	45	5	29
Brighton & HA	22	6	2	14	35	57	–22	20
AFC Team Bath	22	5	4	13	39	53	–14	19
Reading Royals	22	0	0	22	8	183	–175	0

NORTHERN DIVISION

	P	W	D	L	F	A	GD	Pts
Nottingham F	22	18	4	0	80	26	54	58
Lincoln C	22	18	1	3	66	16	50	55
Sunderland	22	16	2	4	52	30	22	50
Newcastle U	22	10	3	9	58	46	12	33
Preston NE	22	10	1	11	39	39	0	31
Sheffield W	22	8	2	12	38	48	–10	26
Manchester C	22	7	4	11	29	41	–12	25
Tranmere R	22	7	3	12	36	57	–21	24
Rotherham U	22	7	1	14	41	62	–21	22
Aston Villa	22	6	3	13	49	59	–10	21
Stockport Co	22	6	1	15	21	54	–33	19
Crewe Alex	22	5	4	14	30	61	–31	18

NATIONAL DIVISION RESULTS 2007–08

	Arsenal	Birmingham C	Blackburn R	Bristol Academy	Cardiff C	Charlton Ath	Chelsea	Doncaster R Belles	Everton	Leeds U	Liverpool	Watford
Arsenal	—	3–0	5–1	2–0	9–0	5–0	4–1	4–3	0–0	1–1	5–2	4–1
Birmingham C	0–3	—	1–0	1–1	2–1	6–1	1–3	3–3	1–1	2–3	1–2	2–3
Blackburn R	1–3	4–1	—	1–3	6–0	6–0	1–2	3–2	0–2	2–1	2–3	4–2
Bristol Academy	0–1	2–1	2–2	—	4–1	7–0	2–2	0–1	1–3	0–0	4–3	2–0
Cardiff C	0–6	2–3	1–3	1–3	—	2–1	0–1	0–1	0–4	0–4	1–1	1–2
Charlton Ath	0–7	0–4	0–5	0–3	0–4	—	0–0	1–1	0–6	0–5	1–1	0–6
Chelsea	0–3	0–1	1–1	3–4	5–0	4–0	—	3–4	1–2	1–2	4–1	4–3
Doncaster R Belles	2–4	2–0	3–0	0–3	1–1	4–0	1–1	—	1–2	2–3	3–2	2–2
Everton	0–2	2–2	5–1	3–0	6–0	7–0	3–0	3–1	—	4–0	2–1	3–0
Leeds U	0–4	2–1	4–4	1–0	2–3	2–2	0–1	3–1	1–2	—	2–0	2–1
Liverpool	1–4	1–0	1–1	3–2	4–0	2–0	0–0	0–3	1–5	0–3	—	1–4
Watford	2–6	0–1	3–2	6–2	1–1	4–0	2–3	4–3	1–4	2–4	4–1	—

NATIONAL DIVISION LEAGUE – PREVIOUS WINNERS

1992–93 Arsenal
1993–94 Doncaster Belles
1994–95 Arsenal
1995–96 Croydon
1996–97 Arsenal
1997–98 Everton
1998–99 Croydon
1999–00 Croydon
2000–01 Arsenal
2001–02 Arsenal
2002–03 Fulham
2003–04 Arsenal
2004–05 Arsenal
2005–06 Arsenal
2006–07 Arsenal
2007–08 Arsenal

THE FA WOMEN'S CUP 2007–08

SPONSORED BY E.ON

PRELIMINARY ROUND

Durham City v Team Northumbria 0-1
Bolton Ambassadors v Penrith United 1-5
Bury Girls & Ladies v Windscale 3-1
Nottingham United v Heather St Johns 1-0
Worcester City v Bourne United 0-1
Copsewood (Coventry) v Tamworth FC Lionesses 15-0
Kingsthorpe Ladies & Girls v Bedford Ladies 0-9
Rayleigh Raiders v Brentwood Town 1-7
Saffron Walden Town v Garston 3-2
Crowborough Athletic v Haywards Heath Town 1-4
Bexhill United v Canterbury City 0-4
Eastbourne Town v Rottingdean Village 0-6
Tooting & Mitcham United v Havant & Waterlooville 0-4
Chichester City United withdrew v Abbey Rangers w.o.
Carterton v Aylesbury United 5-0
Banbury United v Brize Norton 0-2
Penzance v Launceston 7-1

FIRST QUALIFYING ROUND

Team Northumbria v Gateshead Cleveland Hall 4-0
Killingworth YPC v Blyth Spartans 1-4
Spennymoor Town v Lumley Ladies 3-0
York City v Norton & Stockton Ancients 6-1
Whitley Bay v Pelton Newfield 4-1
Darlington RA v Glendale 11-2
Bolton Wanderers v Liverpool Feds 2-4
Bury Girls & Ladies v Wirral 4-1
Blackpool Wren Rovers v Denton Town 4-0
Penrith United v Wigan 3-5
Kirklees w.o. v Pudsey Juniors withdrew.
Huddersfield Town v Sheffield 2-1
Keighley v Morley Spurs 3-5
Barnsley v Ossett Albion 3-1
Linby CW v West Bridgford 1-2
Rise Park v Sandiacre Town 5-1
Huncote Sports & Social v Buxton 3-3
Buxton won 4-3 on penalties.
Nottingham United v Mansfield Town 6-5
Winterton Rangers v Radcliffe Olympic 3-4
Chesterfield withdrew v Friar Lane & Epworth w.o.
Rolls Royce Leisure v Loughborough Foxes 4-2
Oadby Town Women v Loughborough Dynamo 2-0
Bourne United v Birmingham Athletic 0-1
Lichfield Diamonds w.o. v AFC Telford United Ladies withdrew.
Solihull v Dudley United 4-1
Stratford Town v Leamington Lions 3-1
Farefield Villa v Rugby Town 4-1
Copsewood (Coventry) v Allscott 6-0
Norwich City v Woodbridge Town 3-1
Cambridge United v March Town United 11-0
Peterborough v West Lynn 4-3
Cambridge University v Haverhill Rovers 4-0
Corby S&L v Thorplands United 12-0
Arlesey Town v Kings Sports Luton 2-0
Leighton Linslade v Daventry Town 1-4
Bedford Ladies v Kettering Town 3-2
Barking v Tring Athletic 2-0
Braintree Town v Harlow Athletic 6-0
Billericay v Chelmsford City 2-0
Runwell Hospital v Hoddesdon Owls 1-3
Brentwood Town v Saffron Walden Town 5-1
Basildon United v C&K Basildon 4-2
London Colney v Stevenage Borough 5-0
Thurrock & Tilbury v Harpenden Colts 2-2
Harpenden Colts won 5-3 on penalties.
Hemel Hempstead Town v Dagenham & Redbridge 0-1
Royston Town v Hannakins 2-3
Acton Sports Club v Corinthian Casuals 3-1
Hendon v Haringey Borough 3-3
Hendon won 4-3 on penalties.
Petts Wood v Dynamo North London 3-1
Battersea v Brentford 2-0
Tower Hamlets v Denham United 1-3
Staines Town v Tottenham Hotspur 3-4
London Women v The Comets 3-2
Dover Athletic v Eastbourne Borough 1-3
Canterbury City v Rottingdean Village 4-1
Ashford Girls v Ebbsfleet United 2-6
Haywards Heath Town w.o. v Sheerness East failed to fulfil fixture.
Woking v Salisbury City 2-2
Salisbury City won 5-2 on penalties.
Abbey Rangers v Aldershot Town 0-6
Horley Town v Littlehampton Town 3-3
Horley Town won 3-1 on penalties.
Havant & Waterlooville v Upper Beeding 8-0
Gloucester City v Oxford City 0-2
Chinnor v Burnham 1-2
Newbury Ladies & Girls v Brize Norton 11-1
Carterton v Stoke Lane Athletic 2-1
Wycombe Wanderers v Tetbury Town 8-0
Bracknell Town v MK Wanderers 3-1
Henley Town v Woodley Saints 3-0
Marlow Girls & Ladies v Slough 2-6
Penzance v Saltash United 8-1
Taunton Town v Weymouth 6-1
Cullompton Rangers v St Blazey 8-0
Poole Town v Alphington 5-2
Larkhall Athletic v Barnstaple Town 8-0
Keynsham Town Development v Ilminster Town 1-3
Hampstead v Long Lane 1-3

SECOND QUALIFYING ROUND

Team Northumbria v Whitley Bay 0-2
Spennymoor Town v Blyth Spartans 2-3
Darlington RA v York City 3-1
Bury Girls & Ladies v Blackpool Wren Rovers 1-6
Liverpool Feds v Wigan 3-2
Huddersfield Town v Morley Spurs 2-7
Kirklees v Barnsley 1-5
Radcliffe Olympic v Oadby Town Women 7-1
Rise Park v Buxton 2-0
Nottingham United v Friar Lane & Epworth 1-6
West Bridgford v Rolls Royce Leisure 0-8
Birmingham Athletic v Farefield Villa 2-2
Birmingham Athletic won 5-4 on penalties.
Solihull v Lichfield Diamonds 3-3
Solihull won 7-6 on penalties.
Copsewood (Coventry) v Straford Town 3-1
Cambridge United v Peterborough 0-5
Norwich City v Cambridge University 4-2
Arlesey Town v Daventry Town 4-0
Corby S&L v Bedford Ladies 3-3
Corby S&L won 4-2 on penalties.
Barking v Hannakins 7-2
Dagenham & Redbridge v Basildon United 11-0
London Colney v Hoddesdon Owls 8-3
Billericay v Brentwood Town 0-1
Harpenden Colts v Braintree Town 0-3
Denham United v London Women 7-0
Hendon v Petts Wood 1-4
Battersea v Long Lane 0-2
Acton Sports Club v Tottenham Hotspur 3-1
Canterbury City v Ebbsfleet United 0-1
Eastbourne Borough v Haywards Heath Town 3-1
Aldershot Town v Horley Town 1-6
Salisbury City v Havant & Waterlooville 3-1
Wycombe Wanderers withdrew v Slough w.o.
Burnham v Newbury Ladies & Girls 1-6
Carterton v Bracknell Town 0-6
Oxford City v Henley Town 4-0
Penzance v Larkhall Athletic 6-0
Cullompton Rangers v Taunton Town 6-0
Ilminster Town v Poole Town 0-3

THIRD QUALIFYING ROUND

Barnsley v Radcliffe Olympic 0-1
Blackpool Wren Rovers v Blyth Spartans 3-0
Morley Spurs v Liverpool Feds 1-0
Darlington RA v Whitley Bay 3-3
Whitley Bay won 7-6 on penalties.
Peterborough v Norwich City 1-3
Birmingham Athletic v Friar Lane & Epworth 0-2
Copsewood (Coventry) v Solihull 6-1
Rolls Royce Leisure v Rise Park 1-4
Braintree Town v Denham United 1-4
Dagenham & Redbridge v Corby S&L 2-1
Brentwood Town v London Colney 2-4
Barking v Arlesey Town 1-1
Barking won 2-0 on penalties.
Newbury Ladies & Girls v Long Lane 2-4
Petts Wood v Horley Town 2-1
Salisbury City v Eastbourne Borough 6-1
Ebbsfleet United v Slough 2-0
Bracknell Town v Acton Sports Club 3-4
Poole Town v Oxford City 0-6
Cullompton Rangers v Penzance 3-3
Penzance won 4-2 on penalties.

FIRST ROUND

Curzon Ashton v Hull City 9-3
Salford SV v Middlesbrough 0-1
West Auckland Town v Chester City 2-1
Leeds City Vixens v Rochdale 1-2
Morley Spurs v Scunthorpe United 1-5
Blackpool Wren Rovers v Whitley Bay 2-0
Bradford City v Peterlee Town 1-2
Leafield Athletic Triplex v Leicester City 0-7
Norwich City v West Bromwich Albion 0-4
Loughborough Students v Rushden & Diamonds 2-0
Coventry City v Leicester City 2-1
Wolverhampton Wanderers v Radcliffe Olympic 1-3
Hereford Pegasus v TNS Ladies 0-4
Friar Lane & Epworth v Derby County 1-6
Copsewood (Coventry) v Alfreton Town 4-0
Northampton Town v Rise Park 4-0
Whitehawk v Bedford Town Bells 1-0
London Colney v Lewes 1-9
Chesham United v Petts Wood 7-1
Long Lane v Luton Town 1-5
Welwyn Garden City v Dagenham & Redbridge 2-0
Queens Park Rangers v Reading Women 3-1
Denham United v Acton Sports Club 2-2
Acton Sports Club won 4-2 on penalties.

AFC Wimbledon v Barking	5-4
Gillingham v Ipswich Town	1-0
Enfield Town v Ebbsfleet United	3-0
AFC Bournemouth v Plymouth Argyle	1-2
Frome Town v Penzance	2-0
Oxford City v Salisbury City	8-1
Yeovil Town v Team Western	3-1
Forest Green Rovers v Southampton Saints	1-0

SECOND ROUND

Scunthorpe United v Curzon Ashton	0-4
Middlesbrough v Radcliffe Olympic	5-0
Peterlee Town v Rochdale	3-4
Blackpool Wren Rovers v West Auckland Town	2-2
West Auckland Town won 4-3 on penalties.	
Northampton Town v Leicester City	0-4
Coventry City v Derby County	2-1
West Bromwich Albion v Loughborough Students	2-1
TNS Ladies v Copsewood (Coventry)	2-3
Whitehawk v AFC Wimbledon	3-0
Luton Town v Enfield Town	2-2
Luton Town won 3-2 on penalties.	
Lewes v Welwyn Garden City	1-5
Queens Park Rangers v Acton Sports Club	3-0
Chesham United v Gillingham	3-3
Chesham United won 6-5 on penalties.	
Frome Town v Forest Green Rovers	0-1
Yeovil Town v Swindon Town	4-4
Swindon Town won 4-3 on penalties.	
Plymouth Argyle v Oxford City	3-1

THIRD ROUND

Newcastle United v Stockport County	1-0
West Auckland Town v Manchester City	1-4
Sheffield Wednesday v Middlesbrough	0-2
Rotherham United v Rochdale	6-3
Preston North End v Curzon Ashton	5-1
Sunderland v Tranmere Rovers	5-1
Aston Villa v West Bromwich Albion	2-1
Copsewood (Coventry) v Crewe Alexandra	0-1
Leicester City v Nottingham Forest	1-0
Coventry City v Lincoln City	0-1
West Ham United v Queens Park Rangers	5-0
Barnet v Reading Royals	10-2
Brighton & Hove Albion v Welwyn Garden City	2-1
Whitehawk v Fulham	1-5
Colchester United v Luton Town	3-1
Millwall Lionesses v Crystal Palace	2-1
Chesham United v Portsmouth	0-5
AFC Team Bath v Newquay	1-2
Forest Green Rovers v Keynsham Town	3-3
Forest Green Rovers won 3-2 on penalties.	
Swindon Town v Plymouth Argyle	1-1
Swindon Town won 7-6 on penalties.	

FOURTH ROUND

Millwall Lionesses v Leicester City	0-1
Preston North End v Newcastle United	1-3
Sunderland v Birmingham City	1-4
Liverpool v Forest Green Rovers	6-0
Barnet v Everton	0-9
West Ham United v Colchester United	7-0
Arsenal v Newquay	11-1
Bristol Academy v Leeds United	1-1
Leeds United won 4-3 on penalties.	
Swindon Town v Doncaster Rovers Belles	0-5
Crewe Alexandra v Cardiff City	0-4
Rotherham United v Portsmouth	3-4
Chelsea v Middlesbrough	5-2
Manchester City v Watford	1-4
Charlton Athletic v Fulham	0-3
Blackburn Rovers v Brighton & Hove Albion	4-1
Aston Villa v Lincoln City	0-6

FIFTH ROUND

Chelsea v Leeds United	1-1
Leeds United won 6-5 on penalties.	
Cardiff City v Doncaster Rovers Belles	3-2
Watford v Newcastle United	3-3
Newcastle United won 2-1 on penalties.	
Lincoln City v Portsmouth	5-1
Leicester City v Everton	0-3
Blackburn Rovers v Liverpool	4-1
Fulham v Birmingham City	0-2
Arsenal v West Ham United	8-1

SIXTH ROUND

Arsenal v Birmingham City	5-1
Newcastle United v Everton	1-3
Cardiff City v Leeds United	1-5
Lincoln City v Blackburn Rovers	3-2

SEMI-FINALS

Lincoln City v Arsenal	1-5
Everton v Leeds United	0-0
Leeds United won 5-4 on penalties.	

FINAL (at Nottingham Forest)

Monday 5 May, 2008

Arsenal 4 *(Smith K 53, 83, Ludlow 59, Sanderson 60)*

Leeds U 1 *(Clarke 69)* 24,582

Arsenal: Byrne; Scott, Ludlow, White, Grant (Tracy 74), Smith K, Sanderson (Fleeting 74), Yankey (Davison 74), Carney, Asante, Phillip.
Leeds U: Telford; Bradley, Wright (Bonner 86), Holtham, Smith S, Houghton, Clarke, Moore (Sutcliffe 60), Barr, Culvin (Thackray 86), Walton.

THE FA WOMEN'S PREMIER LEAGUE CUP 2007–08

PRELIMINARY ROUND

Lincoln City v Millwall Lionesses	3-1
Fulham v Team Bath	6-1
Newcastle United v Sheffield Wednesday	6-3
Nottingham Forest v Sunderland	0-1

FIRST ROUND

Watford v Manchester City	4-0
Colchester United v Tranmere Rovers	4-2
Stockport County v Lincoln City	1-2
Blackburn Rovers v Brighton & Hove Albion	8-0
Everton v Barnet	6-0
Preston North End v Fulham	2-1
Reading Royals v West Ham United	0-9
Sunderland w.o. v Charlton Athletic w.d.	
Doncaster Rovers Belles v Crystal Palace	2-0
Newquay v Keynsham Town	4-3
Newcastle United v Bristol Academy	0-3
Rotherham United v Portsmouth	3-6
Liverpool v Leeds United	2-0
Crewe Alexandra v Chelsea	1-9
Cardiff City v Arsenal	0-4
Aston Villa v Birmingham City	1-4

SECOND ROUND

Watford v Doncaster Rovers Belles	3-2
Blackburn Rovers v Bristol Academy	2-1
Preston North End v Sunderland	3-4
Colchester United v Liverpool	2-3
Birmingham City v Portsmouth	3-0
Chelsea v Lincoln City	5-1
West Ham United v Everton	1-4
Newquay v Arsenal	1-11

THIRD ROUND

Blackburn Rovers v Liverpool	2-3
Watford v Birmingham City	3-2
Arsenal v Chelsea	3-1
Everton v Sunderland	3-0

SEMI-FINALS

Arsenal v Liverpool	4-0
Watford v Everton	1-2

FINAL (at Leyton Orient)

Everton (1) *(Kane 7)*

Arsenal (0) 5008

Everton: Hill; Easton (Hinnigan 88), Unitt, Williams, Westwood, Johnson, Handley, Scott, Dowie (Duggan 77), Kane, Evans.
Arsenal: Byrne; Scott, Ludlow, White (Davison 86), Smith, Sanderson (Grant 64), Fleeting, Yankey, Carney, Asante, Phillip.
Referee: M. McLaughlin.

UEFA WOMEN'S CHAMPIONSHIP 2006–08

PRELIMINARY ROUND

GROUP A1
Northern Ireland 5, Croatia 1
Turkey 9, Georgia 0
Croatia 2, Turkey 1
Georgia 0, Northern Ireland 4
Croatia 6, Georgia 0
Northern Ireland 0, Turkey 1

GROUP A2
Bosnia 2, Israel 5
Armenia 1, Latvia 0
Israel 1, Armenia 0
Latvia 1, Bosnia 4
Israel 3, Latvia 0
Bosnia 1, Armenia 1

GROUP A3
Malta 0, Slovakia 8
Lithuania 1, Luxembourg 1
Slovakia 3, Lithuania 0
Luxembourg 4, Malta 2
Slovakia 4, Luxembourg 0
Malta 0, Lithuania 0

GROUP A4
Estonia 0, Romania 5
Bulgaria 3, Azerbaijan 0
Azerbaijan 3, Estonia 2
Romania 1, Bulgaria 0
Romania 4, Azerbaijan 1
Estonia 0, Bulgaria 5

GROUP A5
Kazakhstan 1, Wales 2
Macedonia 0, Faeroes 7
Wales 6, Macedonia 0
Faeroes 0, Kazakhstan 1
Wales 2, Faeroes 1
Kazakhstan 1, Macedonia 0

QUALIFYING ROUND

GROUP 1
England 4, Northern Ireland 0
Northern Ireland 1, Czech Republic 3
Belarus 0, Spain 3
Belarus 5, Northern Ireland 0
Belarus 1, Czech Republic 4
Czech Republic 2, Spain 2
England 4, Belarus 0
England 1, Spain 0
Spain 4, Northern Ireland 0
Northern Ireland 0, England 2
England 0, Czech Republic 0
Czech Republic 4, Northern Ireland 0
Spain 6, Belarus 1
Spain 4, Czech Republic 1
Belarus 1, England 6
Northern Ireland 0, Spain 3

GROUP 2
Republic of Ireland 2, Hungary 1
Hungary 3, Romania 3
Italy 0, Sweden 2
Republic of Ireland 1, Italy 2
Romania 0, Sweden 7
Sweden 7, Hungary 0
Romania 0, Republic of Ireland 2
Hungary 1, Italy 3
Italy 5, Romania 0
Republic of Ireland 2, Romania 1
Italy 4, Republic of Ireland 1
Hungary 0, Republic of Ireland 2
Hungary 0, Sweden 6
Sweden 1, Italy 0
Romania 1, Italy 6
Romania 3, Hungary 1

GROUP 3
France 6, Greece 0
Slovenia 0, Serbia 5
France 6, Slovenia 0
Greece 0, Iceland 3
Iceland 1, France 0
Iceland 5, Serbia 0
Slovenia 2, Iceland 1
Serbia 0, France 8
Slovenia 0, France 2
Serbia 1, Greece 2
Greece 0, France 5
Serbia 0, Slovenia 3
France 2, Serbia 0
Slovenia 3, Greece 1
Serbia 0, Iceland 4

GROUP 4
Germany 5, Holland 1
Switzerland 1, Belgium 0
Switzerland 2, Holland 2
Wales 0, Germany 6
Germany 7, Switzerland 0
Holland 2, Wales 1
Wales 0, Switzerland 2
Germany 3, Belgium 0
Belgium 1, Wales 0
Holland 0, Germany 1
Wales 0, Belgium 1
Wales 0, Holland 1
Belgium 2, Holland 2
Belgium 3, Switzerland 1
Belgium 0, Germany 5
Switzerland 2, Wales 0
Germany 4, Wales 0

GROUP 5
Slovakia 2, Portugal 1
Scotland 0, Portugal 0
Slovakia 0, Ukraine 4
Ukraine 2, Scotland 1
Ukraine 5, Slovakia 0
Denmark 5, Portugal 1
Slovakia 0, Scotland 3
Portugal 0, Slovakia 1
Portugal 0, Ukraine 1
Scotland 0, Denmark 1
Slovakia 1, Denmark 4
Denmark 2, Scotland 1
Portugal 1, Scotland 4
Portugal 0, Denmark 4
Scotland 0, Ukraine 1
Denmark 6, Slovakia 1

GROUP 6
Austria 0, Poland 1
Israel 2, Poland 2
Israel 0, Russia 6
Israel 0, Norway 3
Poland 4, Israel 1
Austria 1, Russia 5
Austria 5, Israel 0
Norway 3, Russia 0
Russia 3, Poland 1
Norway 3, Austria 0
Norway 7, Israel 0
Norway 3, Poland 0
Poland 2, Austria 4
Russia 4, Israel 0
Competition still being played.

ENGLAND WOMEN'S INTERNATIONAL MATCHES 2007–08

WORLD CUP

11 September 2007 *(in Shanghai)* 27.146

Japan 2 *(Miyama 55, 90)*

England 2 *(Smith K 81, 83)*

England: Brown; Scott A (Johnson 89), Stoney, Chapman, White, Phillip, Carney, Williams, Aluko (Scott J 74), Smith K, Yankey.

14 September 2007 *(in Shanghai)* 27,730

England 0 Germany 0

England: Brown; Scott A, Stoney, Chapman, White, Phillip, Carney (Yankey 56), Williams, Smith K, Asante, Scott J.

17 September 2007 *(in Chengdu)* 30,730

England 6 *(Gonzalez 9 (og), Scott J 10, Williams 51 (pen), Smith K 64, 77, Exley 90 (pen))*

Argentina 1 *(Gonzalez 60)*

England: Brown; Scott A (Smith S 68), Stoney, White, Phillip, Williams, Aluko (Handley 79), Smith K (Exley 79), Yankey, Asante, Scott J.

22 September 2007 *(in Tianjin)* 29,586

England 0

USA 3 *(Wambach 48, Boxx 57, Lilly 60)*

England: Brown; Scott A, Stoney, Chapman, White, Phillip (Sanderson 81), Carney, Aluko (Yankey 46), Smith K, Asante, Scott J.

27 October 2007 *(at Walsall)* 8632

England 4 *(Scott A 11, 64, Smith K 33, Aluko 49)*

Belarus 0

England: Brown; Scott A, Stoney, Chapman (Scott J), Phillip, Asante, Carney (Smith S 46), Williams, Aluko, Smith K (Sanderson 55), Yankey.

25 November 2007 *(at Shrewsbury)* 8753

England 1 *(Carney 65)* **Spain 0**

England: Brown; Scott A, Stoney, Scott J, White, Asante, Carney, Williams, Aluko (Sanderson 55), Smith K, Yankey.

12 February 2008 *(in Larnaca)*

England 0

Sweden 2 *(Schelin 44, 81)*

England: Chamberlain; Scott A (Handley 80), White (Bassett 80), Phillip, Stoney (Unitt 62), Asante, Scott J (Aluko 40), Williams, Carney (Smith S 40) (Johnson 69), Smith K (Westwood 62), Yankey.

14 February 2008 *(in Larnaca)*

Norway 1 *(Stensland 53)*

England 2 *(Williams 47, Smith K 64 (pen)*

England: Chamberlain (Hawke 73); Scott A, White, Phillip, Stoney, Asante, Williams, Smith K, Carney, Sanderson (Aluko 73), Yankey.

6 March 2008 *(in Lurgan)*

Northern Ireland 0

England 2 *(Williams 18, White 84)*

England: Chamberlain; Scott A (Johnson 71), Stoney, Asante, White, Phillip, Carney, Scott J, Smith K, Williams, Yankey.

20 March 2008 *(at Doncaster)* 5975

England 0

Czech Republic 0

England: Chamberlain; Scott A, Stoney, Asante, White, Phillip (Johnson 46), Carney, Williams, Sanderson (Aluko 46), Westwood, Yankey.

8 May 2008 *(in Minsk)*

Belarus 1 *(Ryzhevich 30)*

England 6 *(Scott J 1, Williams 6, 25, 86, Sanderson 43, White 90).*

England: Chamberlain; Scott A (Johnson 46), Stoney, Scott J, White, Asante, Carney (Handley 46), Williams, Sanderson, Smith K (Bassett 59), Yankey.

Arsenal's Kelly Smith (8) and Leeds United's Jade Moore do battle during the FA Women's FA Cup Final at the City Ground, Nottingham. (Empics Sport/PA Photos/Mike Egerton)

UNIBOND LEAGUE 2007–08

UNIBOND PREMIER DIVISION 2007–08

			Home					Away					Total						
		P	*W*	*D*	*L*	*F*	*A*	*W*	*D*	*L*	*F*	*A*	*W*	*D*	*L*	*F*	*A*	*GD*	*Pts*
1	Fleetwood Town	40	14	4	2	43	23	14	3	3	38	16	28	7	5	81	39	42	91
2	Witton Albion	40	17	1	2	54	15	10	7	3	30	13	27	8	5	84	28	56	89
3	Gateshead	40	14	2	4	43	16	12	5	3	50	26	26	7	7	93	42	51	85
4	Eastwood Town	40	13	4	3	40	24	7	5	8	21	21	20	9	11	61	45	16	69
5	Buxton	40	10	3	7	36	27	10	5	5	24	23	20	8	12	60	50	10	68
6	Guiseley	40	9	6	5	29	21	10	4	6	36	22	19	10	11	65	43	22	67
7	Marine	40	11	0	9	37	30	8	4	8	33	35	19	4	17	70	65	5	61
8	Hednesford Town	40	9	4	7	36	32	6	4	10	26	33	15	8	17	62	65	–3	53
9	Worksop Town	40	6	8	6	31	32	7	4	9	28	30	13	12	15	59	62	–3	51
10	Ashton United	40	6	8	6	31	31	5	7	8	32	42	11	15	14	63	73	–10	48
11	Kendal Town	40	7	8	5	36	27	5	3	12	25	43	12	11	17	61	70	–9	47
12	Whitby Town	40	9	2	9	41	37	4	5	11	27	38	13	7	20	68	75	–7	46
13	Prescott Cables	40	8	4	8	21	24	5	4	11	27	38	13	8	19	48	62	–14	46
14	Frickley Athletic	40	8	6	6	29	22	3	7	10	21	46	11	13	16	50	68	–18	46
15	North Ferriby United	40	7	3	10	26	40	6	4	10	27	36	13	7	20	53	76	–23	46
16	Matlock Town	40	9	6	5	34	24	3	3	14	21	44	12	9	19	55	68	–13	45
17	Ilkeston Town	40	6	6	8	40	39	4	8	8	24	33	10	14	16	64	72	–8	44
18	Ossett Town	40	6	4	10	21	28	6	4	10	27	32	12	8	20	48	60	–12	44
19	Leek Town	40	5	8	7	27	30	6	3	11	27	38	11	11	18	54	68	–14	44
20	Stamford	40	6	6	8	30	38	5	4	11	29	48	11	10	19	59	86	–27	43
21	Lincoln United	40	2	4	14	18	39	5	4	11	26	46	7	8	25	44	85	–41	29

Gateshead promoted via play-offs; Prescot Cables deducted 1 point for playing ineligible player.

UNIBOND FIRST DIVISION NORTH 2007–08

	P	*W*	*D*	*L*	*F*	*A*	*GD*	*Pts*
Bradford Park Avenue	42	25	7	10	91	43	48	82
FC United of Manchester	42	24	9	9	91	49	42	81
Skelmersdale United	42	23	9	10	94	46	48	78
Curzon Ashton	42	23	9	10	78	48	30	78
Bamber Bridge	42	22	8	12	70	54	16	74
Ossett Albion	42	20	10	12	77	65	12	70
Wakefield	42	19	7	16	58	49	9	64
Newcastle Blue Star	42	17	12	13	71	58	13	63
Rossendale United	42	16	11	15	66	74	–8	59
Garforth Town	42	16	8	18	60	63	–3	56
Lancaster City	42	15	9	18	54	70	–16	54
Harrogate Railway Ath	42	13	12	17	51	58	–7	51
Clitheroe	42	13	11	18	63	77	–14	50
Chorley	42	10	12	20	56	80	–24	42
Mossley	42	12	6	24	60	100	–40	42
Radcliffe Borough	42	9	11	22	53	75	–22	38
Woodley Sports –1	42	7	13	22	38	65	–27	33
Bridlington Town	42	8	8	26	42	99	–57	32

FC United of Manchester promoted via play-offs. Woodley Sports 1 pt deducted for playing an ineligible player.

UNIBOND FIRST DIVISION SOUTH 2007–08

	P	*W*	*D*	*L*	*F*	*A*	*GD*	*Pts*
Retford United	42	31	6	5	93	35	58	99
Cammell Laird	42	27	5	10	82	54	28	86
Nantwich Town	42	25	4	13	90	45	45	79
Sheffield FC	42	22	10	10	82	53	29	76
Stocksbridge Park Steels	42	21	9	12	72	61	11	72
Grantham Town	42	22	4	16	74	58	16	70
Colwyn Bay	42	19	8	15	86	65	21	65
Belper Town	42	17	13	12	73	64	9	64
Goole	42	18	10	14	77	69	8	64
Carlton Town	42	16	11	15	86	82	4	59
Gresley Rovers	42	18	5	19	53	69	–16	59
Quorn	42	15	8	19	69	76	–7	53
Warrington Town	42	13	8	21	51	78	–27	47
Alsager Town	42	12	7	23	58	88	–30	43
Shepshed Dynamo	42	10	8	24	44	75	–31	38
Brigg Town	42	8	12	22	56	86	–30	36
Kidsgrove Athletic	42	7	10	25	61	90	–29	31
Spalding United	42	3	10	29	46	105	–59	19

Cammell Laird take the automatic promotion due to Retford United not satisfying ground grading conditions. League position 6 qualifies for a play off place. Nantwich town promoted via play-offs.

LEADING GOALSCORERS (in order of league goals)

Premier Division	*Lge*	*Cup*	*Total*
Warlow (Witton Albion)	25	5	30
Sanasay (Worksop Town/ Bradford Park Avenue)	21	2	23
Brunskill (Whitby Town)	20	8	28
Hanson (Guiseley)	20	5	25
Armstrong (Gateshead)	17	3	20
Briscoe (Leek Town)	17	2	19
Dyer (Hednesford Town)	17	1	18
Cumiskey (Marine)	16	8	24
Milligan (Fleetwood Town)	16	5	21
Ross (Buxton/Ilkeston Town)	16	4	20
Barraclough (Matlock Town)	16	3	19
Towler (Frickley Ath/ BridlingtonTown)	16	3	19
Bradley (Buxton)	16	0	16

First Division North	*Lge*	*Cup*	*Total*
Patterson (FC United of Manchester)	33	8	41
Norton (Curzon Ashton)	32	7	39
Eastwood (Rossendale United)	23	2	25
Howson (Radcliffe Borough)	22	14	36
Novak (Newcastle Blue Star)	20	2	22
Salmon (Bamber Bridge)	19	9	28
Kelsey (Ossett Albion)	19	5	24
Donnelly (Skelmersdale United)	18	9	27
Moseley (Bradford Park Avenue)	17	3	20
Howarth (Wakefield)	16	2	18
Murt (Skelmersdale United/ Colwyn Bay)	16	2	18
Kelly (Garforth Town)	16	0	16

First Division South	*Lge*	*Cup*	*Total*
Harvey (Retford United)	29	6	35
Black (Colwyn Bay)	25	5	30
Hay (Cammell Laird)	22	2	24
Thomas (Carlton Town)	21	5	26
Hannah (Belper Town)	19	7	26
Carter (Nantwich Town)	19	6	25
Kinsey (Nantwich Town)	19	6	25
Bray (Goole)	19	3	22
Blenkinsopp (Gresley Rovers)	18	6	24
Bignall (Carlton Town)	17	5	22
Godber (Retford United)	16	5	21
Whittaker (Alsager Town)	16	4	20
Riley (Stocksbridge Park Steels)	16	2	18

All play-off goals included under Cup.

ATTENDANCES

Premier Division – Highest Attendances
2666 Fleetwood Town v Frickley Athletic
1074 Fleetwood Town v Buxton
1014 Witton Albion v Fleetwood Town

First Division North – Highest Attendances
3348 FC United of Manchester v Bamber Bridge
2704 FC United of Manchester v Lancaster City

First Division South – Highest Attendances
927 Nantwich Town v Goole
664 Nantwich Town v Alsager Town

UNIBOND LEAGUE CHALLENGE CUP 2007–08

FIRST ROUND
Bamber Bridge 2, Chorley 1
Cammell Laird 3, Rossendale United 4
Clitheroe 4, Colwyn Bay 4
Colwyn Bay won 4-2 on penalties.
FC United of Manchester 0, Alsager Town 1
Goole 2, Wakefield 0
Nantwich Town 1, Radcliffe Borough 1
Nantwich Town won 7-6 on penalties.
Ossett Albion 4, Harrogate Railway Ath 2
Quorn 2, Belper Town 1
Sheffield 6, Gresley Rovers 5
Shepshed Dynamo 3, Grantham Town 3
Grantham Town won 5-4 on penalties.
Skelmersdale United 5, Lancaster City 0
Spalding United 2, Carlton Town 1
Stocksbridge Park Steels 2, Mossley 1
Woodley Sports 1, Curzon Ashton 2

SECOND ROUND
Alsager Town 1, Curzon Ashton 4
Newcastle Blue Star 2, Bradford Park Avenue 1
Bridlington Town 4, Brigg Town 2
Garforth Town 2, Ossett Albion 1
Goole 1, Sheffield 1
Sheffield won 5-3 on penalties.
Nantwich Town 5, Stocksbridge Park Steels 1
Retford United 1, Quorn 2
Spalding United 3, Grantham Town 6
Warrington Town 2, Rossendale United 0
Colwyn Bay 2, Bamber Bridge 1
Kidsgrove Athletic 0, Skelmersdale United 3

THIRD ROUND
Colwyn Bay 2, Witton Albion 2
Witton Albion won 4-2 on penalties.
Fleetwood Town 7, Warrington Town 3
Kendal Town 3, Skelmersdale United 5
Bridlington Town 1, Guiseley 4
Eastwood Town 4, Matlock Town 3
Garforth Town 0, Whitby Town 6
Gateshead 2, Newcastle Blue Star 0
Hednesford Town 3, Ashton United 1
Ilkeston Town 2, Grantham Town 1
Leek Town 2, Buxton 1
Marine 3, Prescot Cables 1
North Ferriby United 2, Stamford 1
Ossett Town 0, Frickley Athletic 2
Sheffield 4, Lincoln United 2
Worksop Town 3, Quorn 0
Curzon Ashton 1, Nantwich Town 1
Curzon Ashton won 5-4 on penalties.

FOURTH ROUND
Fleetwood Town 2, Marine 3
Gateshead 3, Sheffield 2
Guiseley 3, Eastwood Town 4
Ilkeston Town 1, Hednesford Town 0
North Ferriby United 2, Worksop Town 2
Worksop Town won 5-4 on penalties.
Skelmersdale United 3, Leek Town 1
Whitby Town 0, Frickley Athletic 1
Witton Albion 2, Curzon Ashton 1

QUARTER-FINALS
Ilkeston Town 1, Eastwood Town 1
Eastwood Town won 4-3 on penalties.
Skelmersdale United 2, Marine 0
Witton Albion 0, Gateshead 1
Worksop Town 0, Frickley Athletic 1

SEMI-FINALS
Eastwood Town 3, Frickley Athletic 1
Skelmersdale United 2, Gateshead 2
Skelmersdale United won 4-2 on penalties.

FINAL
Eastwood Town 3, Skelmersdale United 0

PRESIDENT'S CUP 2007–08

FIRST ROUND
Garforth Town 3, Wakefield 3
Wakefield won 3-2 on penalties.
Lancaster City 0, Chorley 2
Quorn 1, Carlton Town 4
Kidsgrove Athletic 1, Radcliffe Borough 3

SECOND ROUND
Brigg Town 1, Carlton Town 1
Brigg Town won 4-2 on penalties.
Cammell Laird 3, Alsager Town 2
Belper Town 2, Gresley Rovers 1
Bridlington Town 2, Ossett Albion 3
Chorley 1, Nantwich Town 2
Colwyn Bay 2, Woodley Sports 2
Colwyn Bay won 4-3 on penalties.
Curzon Ashton 1, Stocksbridge Park Steels 4
FC United of Manchester 5, Bamber Bridge 0
Goole 3, Spalding United 1
Harrogate Railway 0, Bradford Park Avenue 1
Mossley 0, Skelmersdale United 0
Skelmersdale United won 6-5 on penalties.
Newcastle Blue Star 1, Wakefield 2
Radcliffe Borough 4, Warrington Town 1
Rossendale United 3, Clitheroe 2
Sheffield 1, Grantham Town 0
Shepshed Dynamo 0, Retford United 2

THIRD ROUND
Brigg Town 3, Bradford Park Avenue 2
FC United of Manchester 2, Rossendale United 1
Goole 2, Stocksbridge Park Steels 1
Nantwich Town 5, Cammell Laird 1
Ossett Albion 1, Colwyn Bay 0
Retford United 5, Sheffield 0
Skelmersdale United 1, Radcliffe Borough 2
Wakefield 2, Belper Town 1

QUARTER-FINALS
Goole 2, Wakefield 1
Nantwich Town 5, FC United of Manchester 1
Nantwich Town disqualified for fielding an ineligible player.
Radcliffe Borough 5, Brigg Town 1
Retford United 4, Ossett Albion 4
Ossett Albion won 6-5 on penalties.

SEMI-FINALS
Goole 1, FC United of Manchester 3
Ossett Albion 0, Radcliffe Borough 1

FINAL
FC United of Manchester 2, Radcliffe Borough 0

UNIBOND LEAGUE PROMOTION PLAY-OFFS 2007–08

PREMIER DIVISION

SEMI-FINALS
Gateshead 4, Eastwood Town 0
Witton Albion 1, Buxton 1
Buxton won 6-5 on penalties.

FINAL
Gateshead 2, Buxton 0

FIRST DIVISION NORTH

SEMI-FINALS
Skelmersdale United 3, Curzon Ashton 0
FC United of Manchester 3, Bamber Bridge 2

FINAL
FC United of Manchester 4, Skelmersdale United 1

FIRST DIVISION SOUTH

SEMI-FINALS
Nantwich Town 2, Grantham Town 1
Sheffield 4, Stocksbridge Park Steels 1

FINAL
Nantwich Town 2, Sheffield 2
Nantwich Town won 4-1 on penalties.

SOUTHERN LEAGUE 2007–08

BRITISH GAS BUSINESS LEAGUE PREMIER DIVISION 2007–08

			Home			*Away*			*Total*						
		P	*W*	*D*	*L*	*W*	*D*	*L*	*W*	*D*	*L*	*F*	*A*	*GD*	*Pts*
1	King's Lynn	42	14	6	1	10	7	4	24	13	5	91	36	55	85
2	Team Bath	42	12	4	5	13	4	4	25	8	9	71	41	30	83
3	Halesowen Town	42	13	4	4	9	9	3	22	13	7	80	46	34	79
4	Chippenham Town	42	11	8	2	9	5	7	20	13	9	73	44	29	73
5	Bashley	42	12	7	2	7	5	9	19	12	11	60	46	14	69
6	Gloucester City	42	10	5	6	9	6	6	19	11	12	81	50	31	68
7	Hemel Hempstead Town	42	8	6	7	11	5	5	19	11	12	67	50	17	68
8	Brackley Town	42	9	5	7	7	7	7	16	12	14	57	53	4	60
9	Banbury United	42	7	8	6	7	8	6	14	16	12	55	57	–2	58
10	Yate Town	42	9	3	9	7	7	7	16	10	16	71	76	–5	58
11	Clevedon Town	42	7	9	5	6	9	6	13	18	11	49	46	3	57
12	Swindon Supermarine	42	7	8	6	7	4	10	14	12	16	51	67	–16	54
13	Merthyr Tydfil	42	10	5	6	3	9	9	13	14	15	65	70	–5	53
14	Mangotsfield United	42	8	9	4	4	7	10	12	16	14	38	42	–4	52
15	Rugby Town	42	7	5	9	6	7	8	13	12	17	55	66	–11	51
16	Corby Town	42	8	3	10	6	5	10	14	8	20	60	67	–7	50
17	Tiverton Town	42	10	6	5	3	5	13	13	11	18	45	60	–15	50
18	Hitchin Town	42	8	5	8	4	6	11	12	11	19	46	61	–15	47
19	Bedford Town	42	7	6	8	5	3	13	12	9	21	54	73	–19	45
20	Bromsgrove Rovers	42	5	9	7	5	3	13	10	12	20	46	67	–21	42
21	Cirencester Town	42	6	3	12	2	5	14	8	8	26	44	80	–36	32
22	Cheshunt	42	3	5	13	2	3	16	5	8	29	42	103	–61	23

BRITISH GAS BUSINESS LEAGUE ONE MIDLANDS DIVISION 2007–08

			Home			*Away*			*Total*						
		P	*W*	*D*	*L*	*W*	*D*	*L*	*W*	*D*	*L*	*F*	*A*	*GD*	*Pts*
1	Evesham United	40	15	2	3	13	5	2	28	7	5	68	24	44	91
2	Leamington	40	14	4	2	13	4	3	27	8	5	74	27	47	89
3	Stourbridge	40	14	1	5	11	2	7	25	3	12	97	48	49	78
4	Sutton Coldfield Town	40	14	4	2	9	4	7	23	8	9	93	52	41	77
5	Rushall Olympic	40	12	4	4	11	3	6	23	7	10	68	23	45	76
6	Chesham United	40	9	4	7	14	3	3	23	7	10	78	40	38	76
7	Chasetown	40	11	4	5	12	2	6	23	6	11	71	38	33	75
8	Aylesbury United	40	12	3	5	7	6	7	19	9	12	64	49	15	66
9	Leighton Town	40	8	7	5	9	5	6	17	12	11	59	42	17	63
10	Romulus	40	11	4	5	7	4	9	18	8	14	60	53	7	62
11	Barton Rovers	40	9	5	6	5	11	4	14	16	10	54	45	9	58
12	Bishops Cleeve	40	9	5	6	8	2	10	17	7	16	63	61	2	58
13	Dunstable Town	40	7	1	12	7	4	9	14	5	21	63	65	–2	47
14	Willenhall Town*	40	8	5	7	4	8	8	12	13	15	53	58	–5	46
15	Bedworth United	40	9	6	5	3	4	13	12	10	18	40	51	–11	46
16	Cinderford Town	40	6	5	9	6	1	13	12	6	22	47	82	–35	42
17	Stourport Swifts	40	5	4	11	5	4	11	10	8	22	40	81	–41	38
18	Rothwell Town	40	3	4	13	6	1	13	9	5	26	34	69	–35	32
19	Woodford United	40	3	3	14	4	3	13	7	6	27	30	88	–58	27
20	Malvern Town	40	1	6	13	2	3	15	3	9	28	34	95	–61	18
21	Berkhamsted Town	40	2	1	17	0	3	17	2	4	34	27	126	–99	10

Willenhall Town deducted 3 points.

BRITISH GAS BUSINESS LEAGUE ONE SOUTH & WEST DIVISION 2007–08

			Home			*Away*			*Total*						
		P	*W*	*D*	*L*	*W*	*D*	*L*	*W*	*D*	*L*	*F*	*A*	*GD*	*Pts*
1	Farnborough	42	14	5	2	13	3	5	27	8	7	120	48	72	89
2	Fleet Town	42	14	3	4	12	4	5	26	7	9	78	48	30	85
3	Didcot Town	42	9	9	3	15	2	4	24	11	7	99	42	57	83
4	Oxford City	42	13	3	5	11	6	4	24	9	9	82	41	41	81
5	Uxbridge	42	13	4	4	9	5	7	22	9	11	72	50	22	75
6	Bridgwater Town	42	12	5	4	7	8	6	19	13	10	74	45	29	70
7	Paulton Rovers	42	12	4	5	8	6	7	20	10	12	77	57	20	70
8	Windsor & Eton	42	11	3	7	9	6	6	20	9	13	75	66	9	69
9	Marlow	42	12	4	5	8	2	11	20	6	16	74	54	20	66
10	Burnham	42	8	5	8	10	4	7	18	9	15	67	55	12	63
11	Gosport Borough	42	11	4	6	7	4	10	18	8	16	69	67	2	62
12	Godalming Town	42	13	1	7	4	8	9	17	9	16	70	70	0	60
13	Hillingdon Borough	42	12	2	7	4	6	11	16	8	18	68	70	–2	56
14	AFC Hayes	42	8	2	11	9	2	10	17	4	21	75	99	–24	55
15	Thatcham Town	42	8	7	6	5	3	13	13	10	19	59	62	–3	49
16	Abingdon United	42	8	7	6	5	2	14	13	9	20	64	75	–11	48
17	Winchester City	42	9	4	8	4	5	12	13	9	20	58	71	–13	48
18	Taunton Town	42	7	7	7	5	4	12	12	11	19	66	79	–13	47
19	Andover	42	7	5	9	4	2	15	11	7	24	62	101	–39	40
20	Bracknell Town	42	5	5	11	3	5	13	8	10	24	45	93	–48	34
21	Slough Town	42	6	2	13	3	3	15	9	5	28	44	87	–43	32
22	Newport IOW	42	1	2	18	1	3	17	2	5	35	25	143	–118	11

SOUTHERN LEAGUE PLAY-OFFS 2007–08

PREMIER DIVISION PLAY-OFF FINAL

Saturday 3 May 2008
Team Bath 2 *(Cooper 50, Canham S 89)* 838
Halesowen Town 1 *(Brennan 59 pen)*

DIVISION ONE MIDLANDS PLAY–OFF FINAL

Saturday 3 May 2008
Leamington 1 *(Mackey 17)*
Stourbridge 2 *(Bennett 20, Broadhurst L 117)* 1634
aet.

DIVISION ONE SOUTH & WEST PLAY-OFF FINAL

Saturday 3 May 2008
Oxford City 1 *(Bell 34)*
Uxbridge 0 646

SOUTHERN LEAGUE LEADING GOALSCORERS 2007–08

(Includes League and League Cup goals only)

PREMIER DIVISION

Sean Canham (Team Bath)	36
Dean Brennan (Halesowen Town)	29
Stephen Diggin (Corby Town)	25
Jospeh Francis (King's Lynn)	22
Nicholas Gordon (Banbury United)	21
Aaron Blakemore (Yate Town)	19

DIVISION ONE MIDLANDS

Daniel Burnell (Chesham United)	27
Dean Perrow (Chasetown)	27
Ben Mackey (Leamington)	24
Mark Owen (Evesham United)	23
Tyrone Barnett (Willenhall Town)	22
Mark Bellingham (Stourbridge)	22
Leon Broadhurst (Stourbridge)	21

DIVISION ONE SOUTH & WEST

Justin Bennett (Gosport Borough)	30
Danny Jordan (AFC Hayes)	25
Michael Bartley (Farnborough)	22
Robert Claridge (Paulton Rovers)	22
Jack King (Didcot Town)	22

SOUTHERN LEAGUE ATTENDANCES 2007–08

PREMIER	**Highest Average**	1148	King's Lynn
	Division Highest	2336	King's Lynn 0 Team Bath 0 (5 April 2008)
DIVISION ONE MIDLANDS	**Highest Average**	576	Leamington
	Division Highest	860	Leamington 2 Chasetown 4 (8 March 2008)
DIVISION ONE SOUTH & WEST	**Highest Average**	595	Farnborough
	Division Highest	951	Farnborough 5 Fleet Town 1 (26 December 2007)

ERREA SOUTHERN LEAGUE CUP 2007–08

FIRST ROUND

Willenhall Town v Sutton Coldfield Town	0-3
Bishop's Cleeve v Cinderford Town	1-2
Rothwell Town v Leamington	1-3
Taunton Town v Newport (IOW)	2-1
AFC Hayes v Slough Town	6-1
Barton Rovers v Uxbridge	0-1
Berkhamsted Town v Woodford United	4-2
Chasetown v Bedworth United	1-2
Didcot Town v Andover	4-2
Dunstable Town v Leighton Town	1-0
Farnborough v Abingdon United	2-2
Farnborough won 3-2 on penalties.	
Godalming Town v Thatcham Town	3-2
Hillingdon Borough v Bracknell Town	3-0
Marlow v Burnham	4-3
Oxford City v Fleet Town	4-2
Romulus v Rushall Olympic	2-1
Stourbridge v Malvern Town	0-1
Stourport Swifts v Evesham United	1-2
Windsor & Eton v Winchester City	1-0
Aylesbury United v Chesham United	2-1
Paulton Rovers v Gosport Borough	2-2
Gosport Borough won 7-6 on penalties.	

SECOND ROUND

Berkhamsted Town v Aylesbury United	1-1
Berkhamsted Town won 5-4 on penalties.	
Bridgwater Town v Chippenham Town	2-3
Cinderford Town v Malvern Town	2-0
Evesham United v Gloucester City	2-4
Hillingdon Borough v Windsor & Eton	2-0
Leamington v Bedworth United	1-0
Marlow v AFC Hayes	3-2
Oxford City v Didcot Town	3-4
Romulus v Sutton Coldfield Town	0-2
Taunton Town v Gosport Borough	0-2
Uxbridge v Dunstable Town	1-0
Godalming Town v Farnborough	1-1
Godalming Town won 3-1 on penalties.	

THIRD ROUND

Banbury United v Brackley Town	2-0
Bedford Town v Corby Town	3-1
Cirencester Town v Cinderford Town	2-1
Clevedon Town v Tiverton Town	2-1
Gosport Borough v Didcot Town	0-2
Hillingdon Borough v Berkhamsted Town	3-0
King's Lynn v Hitchin Town	3-1
Mangotsfield United v Yate Town	4-1
Marlow v Cheshunt	1-3
Rugby Town v Halesowen Town	2-0
Swindon Supermarine v Merthyr Tydfil	5-1
Team Bath v Chippenham Town	2-1
Uxbridge v Hemel Hempstead Town	2-2
Hemel Hempstead Town won 4-3 on penalties.	
Sutton Coldfield Town v Gloucester City	3-1
Bashley v Godalming Town	1-0
Bromsgrove Rovers v Leamington	2-2
Bromsgrove Rovers won 4-2 on penalties.	

FOURTH ROUND

Bashley v Hillingdon Borough	3-3
Hillingdon Borough won 4-3 on penalties.	
Bromsgrove Rovers v Banbury United	2-4
Cirencester Town v Sutton Coldfield Town	3-2
Didcot Town v Cheshunt	4-0
Mangotsfield United v Swindon Supermarine	0-2
Rugby Town v Bedford Town	1-0
Team Bath v Clevedon Town	0-1
King's Lynn v Hemel Hempstead Town	1-1
King's Lynn won 5-3 on penalties.	

QUARTER-FINALS

Banbury United v Hillingdon Borough	0-1
Didcot Town v Cirencester Town	2-2
Didcot Town won 4-3 on penalties.	
King's Lynn v Rugby Town	4-1
Swindon Supermarine v Clevedon Town	0-6

SEMI-FINALS

Didcot Town v Clevedon Town	1-2
King's Lynn v Hillingdon Borough	0-1

FINAL FIRST LEG

Hillingdon Borough v Clevedon Town (att 115)	1-1

FINAL SECOND LEG

Clevedon Town v Hillingdon Borough (att 233)	0-3

RYMAN LEAGUE 2007–08

RYMAN LEAGUE PREMIER DIVISION 2007–08

			Home					Away					Total						
		P	W	D	L	F	A	W	D	L	F	A	W	D	L	F	A	GD	Pts
1	Chelmsford City	42	15	5	1	53	16	11	4	6	31	23	26	9	7	84	39	45	87
2	Staines Town	42	12	6	3	50	23	10	6	5	35	31	22	12	8	85	54	31	78
3	AFC Wimbledon	42	12	3	6	40	21	10	6	5	41	26	22	9	11	81	47	34	75
4	AFC Hornchurch	42	13	2	6	38	20	7	8	6	30	24	20	10	12	68	44	24	70
5	Ramsgate	42	13	5	3	43	21	6	6	9	24	32	19	11	12	67	53	14	68
6	Ashford Town (Middx)	42	14	3	4	51	29	6	3	12	28	36	20	6	16	79	65	14	66
7	Hendon	42	9	8	4	32	28	9	3	9	47	39	18	11	13	79	67	12	65
8	Tonbridge Angels	42	11	6	4	40	24	6	6	9	37	33	17	12	13	77	57	20	63
9	Margate	42	11	5	5	46	35	6	6	9	25	33	17	11	14	71	68	3	62
10	Billericay Town	42	10	6	5	40	26	6	6	9	26	31	16	12	14	66	57	9	60
11	Horsham	42	12	1	8	37	26	6	4	11	26	37	18	5	19	63	63	0	59
12	Heybridge Swifts	42	10	6	5	38	27	4	7	10	26	37	14	13	15	64	64	0	55
13	Wealdstone	42	8	5	8	37	37	7	4	10	31	38	15	9	18	68	75	–7	54
14	Hastings United	42	11	2	8	35	26	4	6	11	23	41	15	8	19	58	67	–9	53
15	Harlow Town	42	6	8	7	31	28	7	5	9	25	24	13	13	16	56	52	4	52
16	Harrow Borough	42	11	0	10	38	37	4	7	10	23	37	15	7	20	61	74	–13	52
17	Maidstone United	42	7	4	10	30	33	9	0	12	26	46	16	4	22	56	79	–23	52
18	Carshalton Athletic	42	7	7	7	21	21	7	1	13	31	44	14	8	20	52	65	–13	50
19	Boreham Wood	42	9	4	8	30	27	6	1	14	26	46	15	5	22	56	73	–17	50
20	East Thurrock United (–1)	42	9	3	9	24	29	5	6	10	24	38	14	9	19	48	67	–19	50
21	Folkestone Invicta	42	7	7	7	24	31	6	3	12	25	39	13	10	19	49	70	–21	49
22	Leyton	42	2	3	16	20	60	2	1	18	15	63	4	4	34	35	123	–88	16

East Thurrock United deducted 1 point.

RYMAN LEAGUE DIVISION ONE NORTH 2007–08

		P	W	D	L	F	A	W	D	L	F	A	W	D	L	F	A	GD	Pts
1	Dartford	42	16	2	3	61	17	11	6	4	46	25	27	8	7	107	42	65	89
2	AFC Sudbury	42	13	4	4	55	17	11	4	6	31	23	24	8	10	86	40	46	80
3	Redbridge (–1)	42	13	5	3	35	14	11	4	6	35	29	24	9	9	70	43	27	80
4	Ware	42	15	2	4	65	27	8	8	5	45	31	23	10	9	110	58	52	79
5	Canvey Island	42	10	6	5	37	18	13	4	4	45	21	23	10	9	82	39	43	79
6	Brentwood Town	42	11	6	4	38	22	11	5	5	32	27	22	11	9	70	49	21	77
7	Bury Town	42	14	4	3	43	17	8	5	8	33	36	22	9	11	76	53	23	75
8	Edgware Town	42	14	6	1	35	12	6	8	7	18	27	20	14	8	53	39	14	74
9	Maldon Town	42	12	5	4	45	29	7	5	9	33	34	19	10	13	78	63	15	67
10	Northwood	42	12	5	4	41	25	6	7	8	30	36	18	12	12	71	61	10	66
11	Aveley	42	11	6	4	33	25	7	6	8	35	40	18	12	12	68	65	3	66
12	Enfield Town	42	6	6	9	20	27	12	3	6	40	36	18	9	15	60	63	–3	63
13	Great Wakering Rovers	42	5	5	11	38	35	8	4	9	26	31	13	9	20	64	66	–2	48
14	Waltham Abbey	42	6	6	9	18	36	6	4	11	24	42	12	10	20	42	78	–36	46
15	Arlesey Town	42	9	2	10	40	42	3	7	11	24	42	12	9	21	64	84	–20	45
16	Witham Town	42	8	2	11	45	51	4	3	14	30	58	12	5	25	75	109	–34	41
17	Potters Bar Town	42	4	5	12	29	40	6	4	11	16	37	10	9	23	45	77	–32	39
18	Wingate & Finchley	42	5	6	10	27	35	3	5	13	18	37	8	11	23	45	72	–27	35
19	Waltham Forest	42	3	7	11	23	35	4	5	12	21	39	7	12	23	44	74	–30	33
20	Tilbury (–1)	42	4	9	8	29	36	3	3	15	20	60	7	12	23	49	96	–47	32
21	Ilford	42	6	3	12	28	36	2	5	14	19	59	8	8	26	47	95	–48	32
22	Wivenhoe Town	42	5	5	11	28	43	3	2	16	18	43	8	7	27	46	86	–40	31

Redbridge deducted 1 point. Tilbury deducted 1 point.

RYMAN LEAGUE DIVISION ONE SOUTH 2007–08

		P	W	D	L	F	A	W	D	L	F	A	W	D	L	F	A	GD	Pts
1	Dover Athletic	42	15	4	2	41	13	15	4	2	43	16	30	8	4	84	29	55	98
2	Tooting & Mitcham United	42	13	4	4	41	14	13	4	4	47	27	26	8	8	88	41	47	86
3	Cray Wanderers	42	14	5	2	47	21	11	6	4	40	21	25	11	6	87	42	45	86
4	Metropolitan Police	42	15	1	5	36	20	9	2	10	33	27	24	3	15	69	47	22	75
5	Worthing	42	12	1	8	43	24	10	6	5	34	25	22	7	13	77	49	28	73
6	Dulwich Hamlet	42	9	7	5	36	25	11	3	7	32	22	20	10	12	68	47	21	70
7	Kingstonian	42	13	3	5	39	21	7	7	7	27	31	20	10	12	66	52	14	70
8	Ashford Town	42	9	4	8	30	24	10	6	5	34	27	19	10	13	64	51	13	67
9	Sittingbourne	42	10	5	6	30	27	10	2	9	26	31	20	7	15	56	58	–2	67
10	Walton & Hersham	42	10	6	5	39	30	5	6	10	26	32	15	12	15	65	62	3	57
11	Whyteleafe	42	9	4	8	33	27	8	1	12	24	35	17	5	20	57	62	–5	56
12	Burgess Hill Town (–8)	42	11	2	8	35	27	7	6	8	26	30	18	8	16	61	57	4	54
13	Croydon Athletic	42	9	4	8	35	28	5	5	11	30	48	14	9	19	65	76	–11	51
14	Whitstable Town	42	7	6	8	36	38	7	2	12	33	46	14	8	20	69	84	–15	50
15	Chipstead	42	7	3	11	36	39	8	2	11	22	37	15	5	22	58	76	–18	50
16	Walton Casuals	42	6	10	5	31	30	5	5	11	24	38	11	15	16	55	68	–13	48
17	Leatherhead	42	8	2	11	24	26	5	5	11	28	37	13	7	22	52	63	–11	46
18	Chatham Town	42	7	4	10	26	30	5	6	10	32	40	12	10	20	58	70	–12	46
19	Eastbourne Town	42	5	7	9	33	42	6	4	11	25	42	11	11	20	58	84	–26	44
20	Corinthian Casuals	42	6	5	10	27	38	5	6	10	24	39	11	11	20	51	77	–26	44
21	Horsham YMCA	42	3	2	16	18	47	4	4	13	18	38	7	6	29	36	85	–49	27
22	Molesey	42	0	6	15	19	54	3	3	15	17	46	3	9	30	36	100	–64	18

Burgess Hill Town deducted 8 points.

RYMAN LEAGUE PLAY-OFFS 2007–08

PREMIER DIVISION PLAY-OFF FINAL
Staines Town 1, AFC Wimbledon 2

DIVISION ONE NORTH PLAY-OFF FINAL
Redbridge 1, Canvey Island 1
Canvey Island won 5-4 on penalties.

DIVISION ONE SOUTH PLAY-OFF FINAL
Tooting & Mitcham United 1, Cray Wanderers 0

RYMAN LEAGUE ATTENDANCES 2007–08

Premier Division Highest Average	2597	AFC Wimbledon
Ryman Division One North Highest Average	1135	Dartford
Ryman Division One South Highest Average	943	Dover Athletic

RYMAN LEAGUE LEADING GOALSCORERS 2007–08

PREMIER LEAGUE		*Games played*	*Goals scored*
Nwokeji M	Staines Town	34	25
Pinnock J	Margate	41	24
Woods-Garness B	Billericay Town	39	19
Main J	AFC Wimbledon	26	18
Parker S	AFC Hornchurch	33	18
Haule B	Hendon	37	17
Bricknell B	Billericay Town	39	16
Browne S	Heybridge Swifts	34	16
Holmes R	Chelmsford City	38	16
Brayley A	Chelmsford City	41	15
Lee K	AFC Hornchurch	30	15
Thomas S	Boreham Wood	42	15
Olorunda A	Hastings United	38	14
DIVISION ONE NORTH			
Frendo J	Ware	40	32
Cass B	Dartford	42	31
Rowe J	AFC Sudbury	35	26
Reed S	Bury Town	36	22
McDonald C	Witham Town	31	20
Wareham S	Maldon Town	32	20
Smith K	Tilbury	34	19
Tuohy M	Great Wakering Rovers	33	19
Ricks J	Maldon Town	38	18
DIVISION ONE SOUTH			
Baitup L	Eastbourne Town	40	23
Carley C	Metropolitan Police	38	23
Harper S	Burgess Hill Town	33	21
Henry-Hayden J	Tooting & Mitcham U	40	21
Traynor B	Kingstonian	37	21
Dryden J	Dover Athletic	41	19
Vines P	Tooting & Mitcham U	32	19
Collin F	Dover Athletic	40	18
Ademola M	Croydon Athletic	36	17
Stevens D	Leatherhead	34	17

ISTHMIAN LEAGUE CUP 2007–08

FIRST ROUND
Redbridge 2, Brentwood Town 0
Waltham Forest 2, Arlesey Town 3

SECOND ROUND
Dover Athletic 2, Eastbourne Town 3
Kingstonian 3, Cray Wanderers 1
AFC Wimbledon 0, Whyteleafe 2
Ashford Town (Middlesex) 2, Walton & Hersham 1
Ashford Town 1, Burgess Hill Town 3
Billericay Town 0, AFC Sudbury 3
Bury Town 2, Chelmsford City 3
Carshalton Athletic 4, Corinthian Casuals 0
Dulwich Hamlet 0, Tooting & Mitcham United 0
Tooting & Mitcham United won 5-3 on penalties.
Edgware Town 3, Staines Town 1
Great Wakering Rovers 4, Ilford 1
Harlow Town 1, Ware 3
Harrow Borough 0, Metropolitan Police 5
Horsham 4, Hastings United 0
Leatherhead 3, Croydon Athletic 2
Margate 2, East Thurrock United 3
Molesey 2, Wealdstone 3
Potters Bar Town 3, Leyton 1
Ramsgate 4, Chatham Town 2
Redbridge 2, Sittingbourne 1
Waltham Abbey 3, Wingate & Finchley 1
Walton Casuals 1, Northwood 0
Whitstable Town 4, Worthing 3
Maidstone United 5, Canvey Island 2
Arlesey Town 4, Enfield Town 0
Hendon 2, Boreham Wood 3
Tonbridge Angels 4, Chipstead 1
Witham Town 1, Maldon Town 0
Wivenhoe Town 0, Heybridge Swifts 2
Horsham YMCA 4, Folkestone Invicta 3
Dartford 3, Aveley 0
AFC Hornchurch 3, Tilbury 0

THIRD ROUND
Ashford Town (Middlesex) 2, Metropolitan Police 0
Potters Bar Town 1, Edgware Town 4
Walton Casuals 2, Ware 1
Kingstonian 1, Tooting & Mitcham United 2
AFC Sudbury 2, Chelmsford City 1
Arlesey Town 4, Witham Town 2
Burgess Hill Town 1, Whyteleafe 3
Carshalton Athletic 1, Leatherhead 0
East Thurrock United 0, Ramsgate 1
Redbridge 2, Great Wakering Rovers 1
Waltham Abbey 0, Heybridge Swifts 4
Eastbourne Town 1, Horsham 5
Dartford 3, Whitstable Town 0
AFC Hornchurch 3, Maidstone United 0
Boreham Wood 2, Wealdstone 3
Tonbridge Angels 4, Horsham YMCA 2

FOURTH ROUND
Arlesey Town 1, Edgware Town 4
Tooting & Mitcham United 1, Whyteleafe 0
Redbridge 0, AFC Sudbury 1
Horsham 1, Walton Casuals 2
AFC Hornchurch 1, Ramsgate 2
Heybridge Swifts 3, Dartford 0
Wealdstone 1, Ashford Town (Middlesex) 0
Tonbridge Angels 1, Carshalton Athletic 3

QUARTER-FINALS
AFC Sudbury 1, Edgware Town 0
Ramsgate 1, Tooting & Mitcham United 1
Ramsgate won 4-3 on penalties.
Wealdstone 0, Heybridge Swifts 1
Carshalton Athletic 1, Walton Casuals 1
Walton Casuals won 5-4 on penalties.

SEMI-FINALS
Heybridge Swifts 0, AFC Sudbury 6
Walton Casuals 0, Ramsgate 1

FINAL
AFC Sudbury 0, Ramsgate 0 568
aet; Ramsgate won 5-4 on penalties.

THE FA TROPHY 2007–08

IN PARTNERSHIP WITH CARLSBERG

FIRST QUALIFYING ROUND

Prescot Cables v Frickley Athletic 2-3
Buxton v Leek Town 2-1
Romulus v Warrington Town 0-1
Stocksbridge Park Steels v Skelmersdale United 3-1
Stamford v Matlock Town 2-2, 0-1
Harrogate Railway v Radcliffe Borough 2-4
Gateshead v Shepshed Dynamo 2-1
Mossley v Rushall Olympic 0-1
Colwyn Bay v Newcastle Blue Star 2-1
Gresley Rovers v Guiseley 0-1
Witton Albion v Ashton United 6-1
North Ferriby United v Ilkeston Town 1-1, 1-4
Grantham Town v Kendal Town 1-3
Clitheroe v Lancaster City 0-0, 2-1
Fleetwood Town v Worksop Town 1-0
Chasetown w.o. v Scarborough removed.
Willenhall Town v Hednesford Town 1-3
Eastwood Town v Bamber Bridge 0-1
Chorley v Curzon Ashton 1-2
Bradford (Park Avenue) v Sheffield 0-2
Bridlington Town v Retford United 0-2
Wakefield v Nantwich Town 1-1, 3-2
Ossett Town v Whitby Town 3-2
Marine v Lincoln United 5-0
Billericay Town v Ilford 2-1
Tonbridge Angels v Harrow Borough 3-2
Brentwood Town v Harlow Town 1-1, 1-0
Ashford Town v Leyton 1-4
Chatham Town v Witham Town 0-3
Walton & Hersham v Folkestone Invicta 2-1
Chesham United v Bedford Town 2-1
Bury Town v Maidstone United 1-1, 1-3
Metropolitan Police v Great Wakering Rovers 3-0
Leighton Town v Wealdstone 0-0, 1-2
Ware v Ashford Town (Middlesex) 4-1
Sittingbourne v Northwood 0-2
Cheshunt v Heybridge Swifts 1-2
Boreham Wood v Chelmsford City 1-2
Chipstead v Worthing 1-3
Dunstable Town v Hemel Hempstead Town 1-1, 1-2
Ramsgate v Horsham 2-3
East Thurrock United v Cray Wanderers 3-3, 3-2
Horsham YMCA v Canvey Island 1-3
AFC Hornchurch v Dartford 0-0, 3-0
Edgware Town v Hastings United 1-2
Carshalton Athletic v Corinthian Casuals 2-1
AFC Wimbledon v Hendon 2-1
Maldon Town v Dover Athletic 1-2
Hitchin Town v Eastbourne Town 3-0
AFC Sudbury v King's Lynn 0-0, 1-2
Corby Town v Barton Rovers 4-1
Leatherhead v Arlesey Town 3-0
Halesowen Town v Brackley Town 0-2
Cinderford Town v Cirencester Town 2-1
Mangotsfield United v Fleet Town 0-0, 2-0
Chippenham Town v Merthyr Tydfil 3-0
Slimbridge withdrew v Bashley w.o.
Swindon Supermarine v Farnborough 1-1, 0-1
Tiverton Town v Burnham 0-1
Oxford City v Windsor & Eton 0-1
Winchester City v Gosport Borough 2-2, 1-2
Stourbridge v Gloucester City 1-1, 0-2
Leamington v Banbury United 2-0
Hillingdon Borough v Bedworth United 1-1, 2-1
Yate Town v Didcot Town 2-1
Woodford United v Bracknell Town 2-0
Rugby Town v Clevedon Town 1-3
Uxbridge v Andover 4-1
Staines Town v Abingdon United 0-0, 2-5
Aylesbury United v Margate 0-0, 1-3
Evesham United v Bromsgrove Rovers 1-0
Team Bath v Taunton Town 1-0

SECOND QUALIFYING ROUND

Stocksbridge Park Steels v Witton Albion 2-5
Curzon Ashton v Ilkeston Town 1-3
Warrington Town v Ossett Town 0-3
Bamber Bridge v Marine 1-1, 3-2
Hednesford Town v Guiseley 1-2
Fleetwood Town v Retford United 1-1, 1-5
Frickley Athletic v Colwyn Bay 1-2
Chasetown v Radcliffe Borough 0-0, 1-2
Wakefield v Buxton 0-2
Matlock Town v Gateshead 1-2
Rushall Olympic v Clitheroe 1-1
Tie awarded to Rushall Olympic, Clitheroe removed.
Sheffield v Kendal Town 3-2
Hitchin Town v Cinderford Town 2-1
Chippenham Town v Heybridge Swifts 3-2
Leatherhead v Mangotsfield United 1-1, 1-1
Leatherhead won 3-1 on penalties.
AFC Wimbledon v Chelmsford City 4-0
Abingdon United v Maidstone United 2-2, 3-5
Woodford United v Wealdstone 1-4
Bashley v Leyton 3-1
Tonbridge Angels v East Thurrock United 2-0
Brentwood Town v Canvey Island 0-2
Yate Town v Carshalton Athletic 0-3
Farnborough v Windsor & Eton 1-3
Burnham v Ware 2-1
AFC Hornchurch v Northwood 2-2, 1-2
Gloucester City v Hillingdon Borough 3-3, 1-0
Worthing v Walton & Hersham 0-0, 3-1
Corby Town v Evesham United 2-2, 2-4
Gosport Borough v Metropolitan Police 3-2
Witham Town v Horsham 3-2
King's Lynn v Billericay Town 2-2, 3-1
Uxbridge v Hastings United 1-0
Hemel Hempstead Town v Clevedon Town 2-1
Leamington v Margate 1-1, 1-0
Dover Athletic v Brackley Town 2-1
Chesham United v Team Bath 3-5

THIRD QUALIFYING ROUND

Gateshead v Boston United 2-1
Solihull Moors v Cambridge City 1-4
Retford United v Radcliffe Borough 3-1
Guiseley v Worcester City 1-0
Evesham United v Redditch United 1-1, 0-1
Rushall Olympic v Ossett Town 0-0, 2-3
Bamber Bridge v Ilkeston Town 2-1
Hinckley United v Alfreton Town 1-3
Colwyn Bay v Sheffield 1-1, 2-2
Colwyn Bay won 5-4 on penalties.
Vauxhall Motors v Hyde United 1-0
Blyth Spartans v Gainsborough Trinity 2-2, 1-1
Blyth Spartans won 3-1 on penalties.
Barrow v Southport 2-3
Burscough v Leigh RMI 2-3
Hucknall Town v Witton Albion 1-1, 2-1
Nuneaton Borough v Workington 0-0, 1-2
Buxton v AFC Telford United 0-1
Stalybridge Celtic v Tamworth 0-2
Harrogate Town v Kettering Town 0-2
Bromley v Chippenham Town 2-1
Bishop's Stortford v Hampton & Richmond Borough 2-1
Hemel Hempstead Town v Team Bath 3-0
AFC Wimbledon v Northwood 2-1
Maidstone United v Canvey Island 0-1
Basingstoke Town v Lewes 1-4
Gosport Borough v Braintree Town 1-4
Dorchester Town v Worthing 1-1, 2-1
Fisher Athletic v Leamington 1-2
Bognor Regis Town v Havant & Waterlooville 2-1
Bashley v Leatherhead 4-0
Gloucester City v Uxbridge 1-0
Hayes & Yeading United v Witham Town 4-2
Carshalton Athletic v Hitchin Town 1-1, 2-1
Eastleigh v Weston-Super-Mare 4-2
Windsor & Eton v Newport County 1-2
Bath City v Thurrock 2-0
Tonbridge Angels v Burnham 1-0
Wealdstone v Welling United 1-0
King's Lynn v Eastbourne Borough 3-1
Maidenhead United v St Albans City 2-0
Dover Athletic v Sutton United 1-1, 0-1

FIRST ROUND

AFC Telford United v Blyth Spartans	1-2
Vauxhall Motors v Northwich Victoria	2-1
Alfreton Town v Southport	1-0
Halifax Town v Leamington	2-1
Stafford Rangers v Ossett Town	3-1
Colwyn Bay v Burton Albion	1-2
Bamber Bridge v Rushden & Diamonds	2-3
Droylsden v Redditch United	2-1
Histon v Retford United	5-2
Gateshead v Farsley Celtic	1-1, 1-4
Cambridge United v King's Lynn	5-0
Hucknall Town v Tamworth	0-1
Leigh RMI v Workington	1-3
Guiseley v Kidderminster Harriers	1-2
Cambridge City v Kettering Town	3-2
Altrincham v York City	1-3
Gloucester City v Braintree Town	0-2
Hemel Hempstead Town v Woking	0-1
Grays Athletic v Lewes	3-0
Maidenhead United v AFC Wimbledon	0-2
Dorchester Town v Stevenage Borough	2-1
Bishop's Stortford v Canvey Island	8-0
Torquay United v Bashley	1-0
Crawley Town v Bromley	1-0
Newport County v Bath City	3-0
Ebbsfleet United v Carshalton Athletic	4-1
Oxford United v Tonbridge Angels	0-0, 0-1
Wealdstone v Weymouth	0-1
Sutton United v Forest Green Rovers	1-4
Hayes & Yeading United v Aldershot Town	0-5
Exeter City v Salisbury City	3-0
Eastleigh v Bognor Regis Town	1-0

SECOND ROUND

Vauxhall Motors v Burton Albion	1-4
Woking v Aldershot Town	2-4
Tonbridge Angels v AFC Wimbledon	0-4
Droylsden v Cambridge City	1-0
Weymouth v Kidderminster Harriers	0-0, 2-2
Weymouth won 3-0 on penalties.	
Farsley Celtic v Alfreton Town	1-1, 2-0
Rushden & Diamonds v Exeter City	3-0
Dorchester Town v Ebbsfleet United	0-2
Histon v Cambridge United	2-0
Braintree Town v Workington	1-1, 2-1
Bishop's Stortford v Halifax Town	2-2, 1-4
Newport County v Torquay United	1-2
Stafford Rangers v Forest Green Rovers	2-1
Crawley Town v Eastleigh	2-1
York City v Grays Athletic	1-1, 4-1
Blyth Spartans v Tamworth	0-1

THIRD ROUND

Ebbsfleet United v Weymouth	1-0
Burton Albion v Histon	1-1, 1-0
Aldershot Town v Braintree Town	3-0
Farsley Celtic v York City	0-2
Stafford Rangers v Tamworth	2-2, 1-2
Crawley Town v Droylsden	8-0
AFC Wimbledon v Torquay United	0-2
Halifax Town v Rushden & Diamonds	0-2

FOURTH ROUND

Tamworth v Aldershot Town	1-2
Rushden & Diamonds v York City	0-1
Torquay United v Crawley Town	4-1
Burton Albion v Ebbsfleet United	0-0, 0-1

SEMI-FINALS (two legs)

Torquay United v York City	2-0, 0-1
Ebbsfleet United v Aldershot Town	3-1, 1-1

FINAL (at Wembley)

Saturday 10 May 2008

Ebbsfleet United (1) 1 *(McPhee 45)*

Torquay United (0) 0 40,186

Ebbsfleet United: Cronin; Hawkins, Opinel, Bostwick, Smith, McCarthy, McPhee, Barrett, Moore, Akinde, Long (MacDonald).

Torquay United: Rice; Adams, Nicholson, Mansell, Woods, Todd, Phillips (Stevens), Hargreaves, D'Sane (Benyon), Sills (Hill), Zebroski.

Referee: M. Atkinson (West Riding).

THE FA COUNTY YOUTH CUP 2007–08

FIRST ROUND

Isle of Man v Lancashire	2-1
Birmingham v Staffordshire	1-0
Shropshire v East Riding	1-3
Manchester v North Riding	1-2
Cheshire v Northumberland	4-3
Derbyshire v Nottinghamshire	0-3
Oxfordshire v London	1-3
Jersey v Cornwall	3-2
Cambridgeshire v Dorset	6-0
Herefordshire v Huntingdonshire	2-4
Hertfordshire v Worcestershire	3-1
Middlesex v Guernsey	2-1
Hampshire v Norfolk	4-2
Devon v Kent	1-4
Somerset v Essex	0-3

SECOND ROUND

East Riding v Birmingham	0-3
Lincolnshire v Nottinghamshire	3-0
Isle of Man v Westmorland	1-2
Cheshire v West Riding	1-2
Leicestershire & Rutland v Sheffield & Hallamshire	3-3
Sheffield & Hallamshire won 4-3 on penalties.	
North Riding v Durham	1-2
Cumberland v Liverpool	1-2
Wiltshire v Hampshire	2-2
Wiltshire won 5-3 on penalties.	
Surrey v Gloucestershire	2-1
Huntingdonshire v Essex	4-0
Northamptonshire v London	3-2
Middlesex v Berks & Bucks	5-0
Cambridgeshire v Kent	4-0
Hertfordshire v Suffolk	0-1
Sussex w.o. v Army withdrew	
Jersey v Bedfordshire	1-2

THIRD ROUND

Cambridgeshire v Sheffield & Hallamshire	6-2
Westmorland v Sussex	0-1
Lincolnshire v Liverpool	0-1
Durham v Suffolk	1-2
West Riding v Surrey	2-0
Birmingham v Middlesex	0-5
Wiltshire v Huntingdonshire	5-3
Bedfordshire v Northamptonshire	2-1

FOURTH ROUND

Bedfordshire v Cambridgeshire	0-3
Sussex v Suffolk	1-2
West Riding v Wiltshire	2-0
Liverpool v Middlesex	0-3

SEMI-FINALS

Suffolk v West Riding	2-0
Middlesex v Cambridgeshire	1-4

FINAL (at Ipswich Town FC)

Suffolk (2) 2 *(Read 4, Garnham 16)*

Cambridgeshire (1) 1 *(Marriott 18)* 948

THE FA VASE 2007–08

IN PARTNERSHIP WITH CARLSBERG

FIRST QUALIFYING ROUND

Bishop Auckland v Esh Winning 1-0
Thackley v South Shields 1-1, 2-1
Hall Road Rangers v Yorkshire Amateur 2-0
Crook Town v Ashington 2-1
Silsden v Leeds Met Carnegie 4-2
Morpeth Town v North Shields 5-0
Ryton v Winterton Rangers 0-3
Kirkham & Wesham v Worsborough Bridge Athletic 3-1
Ashton Athletic v Rossington Main 6-0
Nostell MW v Abbey Hey 2-0
Holker Old Boys v Chadderton 1-5
Cheadle Town v St Helens Town 1-0
Oadby Town v Blackwell MW 4-3
Hinckley Downes v Gornal Athletic 2-0
South Normanton Athletic v Newark Town 1-0
Radford v Staveley MW 1-3
Highgate United v Shirebrook Town 2-1
Barrow Town v Holwell Sports 2-1
Heanor Town v Kimberley Town 2-0
Borrowash Victoria v Tividale 3-1
Arnold Town v Westfields 1-3
Bromyard Town v Walsall Wood 2-4
Rothley Imperial v Goodrich 1-5
Brockton v Clipstone Welfare 4-1
Lye Town v Southam United 3-3, 0-3
Cradley Town v Meir KA 4-3
Ellistown v Gedling MW 1-2
Biddulph Victoria v Studley 0-3
Stapenhill v New Mills 0-2
Oldbury United v Ibstock United 3-0
Pershore Town v Glossop North End 1-3
Coventry Copsewood v Radcliffe Olympic 0-3
Shifnal Town v Anstey Nomads 4-3
Friar Lane & Epworth v Dudley Sports 3-2
Pelsall Villa v Blaby & Whetstone Athletic 4-2
Norwich United v Huntingdon Town 6-0
Stowmarket Town v Dereham Town 0-1
Hadleigh United v Godmanchester Rovers 0-1
Tiptree United removed v Sileby Rangers w.o.
Basildon United v Raunds Town 0-1
North Greenford United v Wootton Blue Cross 3-2
Biggleswade United v Rothwell Corinthians 3-1
Royston Town v FC Clacton 2-1
Cockfosters v Southend Manor 3-2
Langford v Stewarts & Lloyds 2-3
Arlesey Athletic v Stanway Rovers 1-8
Hullbridge Sports v AFC Kempston Rovers 3-1
Haringey Borough v Harwich & Parkeston 1-3
St Margaretsbury v Northampton Spencer 3-2
Concord Rangers v London Colney 5-1
Hythe Town v Slade Green 3-0
Horley Town v Selsey 2-1
Ringmer v Lingfield 4-2
Three Bridges v Saltdean United 1-0
East Preston v Eastbourne United 1-4
Cobham v Newhaven 6-0
Peacehaven & Telscombe v Pagham 2-3
Rye United v Frimley Green 3-2
Fareham Town v Lymington Town 1-2
Andover New Street v Clanfield 85 3-1
Cove v Christchurch 3-3, 3-4
Reading Town v Henley Town 1-5
Westbury United v Malmsbury Victoria 3-1
Farnborough North End v Chalfont St Peter 1-3
Wantage Town v Hamble ASSC 2-2, 0-1
Bournemouth v Abingdon Town 2-0
Ringwood Town v Calne Town 1-2
United Services Portsmouth v Milton United 2-2, 1-2
Melksham Town v Alton Town 2-0
AFC Wallingford v Devizes Town 1-2
Highworth Town v Aylesbury Vale 3-1
Buckingham Town v Blackfield & Langley 0-2
Shepton Mallet v Barnstaple Town 3-1
Shaftesbury v Bodmin Town 2-3
Larkhall Athletic v Liskeard Athletic 0-1
Torrington removed v Dawlish Town w.o.
Hallen v Bristol Manor Farm 5-2
Penryn Athletic v Falmouth Town 0-2
Keynsham Town v Newton Abbot 0-1
Penzance v Bishop Sutton 1-0
Radstock Town v Welton Rovers 0-3

SECOND QUALIFYING ROUND

Washington v Barton Town Old Boys 3-0
Morpeth Town v Bedlington Terriers 1-2
Pontefract Colleries v Tadcaster Albion 3-2
Silsden v Dunston Federation 1-3
Guisborough Town v Hebburn Town 0-1
Norton & Stockton Ancients v Thornaby 0-4
West Allotment Celtic v Shildon 2-5
Seaham Red Star v Sunderland RCA 7-0
Bishop Auckland v Winterton Rangers 2-4
Willington v Selby Town 0-4
Marske United v Hall Road Rangers 4-2
Team Northumbria v Stokesley SC 2-4
Northallerton Town v Darlington Railway Athletic 4-0
Eccleshill United v Horden CW 3-1
Armthorpe Welfare v Chester-le-Street Town 5-5, 2-1
Easington Colliery v Thackley 1-4
Whickham v Jarrow Roofing Boldon CA 1-3
Crook Town v Durham City 3-6
Spennymoor Town v Liversedge 5-1
Bottesford Town v Tow Law Town 1-2
Brandon United v Pickering Town 0-5
Runcorn Linnets v Daisy Hill 3-0
Parkgate v Atherton Colleries 2-1
Maltby Main v Maine Road 2-1
Blackpool Mechanics v Paulton Victoria 1-0
Chadderton v Atherton LR 1-3
Bootle v Padiham 3-0
Oldham Town v Ashville 5-4
Formby v Dinnington Town 2-1
Colne v Bacup Borough 1-0
Cheadle Town v Ashton Town 2-3
Darwen v Penrith Town 2-1
Winsford United v Hallam 0-1
Trafford v Nostell MW 2-1
Squires Gate v Nelson 4-2
Kirkham & Wesham v Brodsworth MW 4-3
AFC Emley v Ramsbottom United 4-3
Congleton Town v Ashton Athletic 1-1, 2-3
Bewdley Town v Pelsall Villa 7-0
Leek CSOB v Greenwood Meadows 3-0
Heath Hayes v Loughborough Dynamo 1-0
Rocester v Tipton Town 2-3
Goodrich v Pilkington XXX 2-7
Glapwell v Boldmere St Michaels 2-0
Oadby Town v Hinckley Downes 1-2
Coleshill Town v Bolehall Swifts 2-2, 1-0
Sporting Khalsa v Barnt Green Spartak 1-2
Cadbury Athletic v AFC Wulfrunians 2-1
Kirby Muxloe v St Andrews 3-1
Ludlow Town v Mickleover Sports 1-2
Pegasus Juniors v Graham St Prims 3-1
Brierley Hill & Withymoor v Heanor Town 0-1
Newcastle Town v Wolverhampton Casuals 2-1
Calverton MW v Teversal 1-0
Barrow Town v Market Drayton Town 2-3
Radcliffe Olympic v Rainworth MW 0-2
Gedling Town v Castle Vale 4-3
Shifnal Town v Birstall United 3-1
Heather St John v Coventry Sphinx 0-3
Norton United v Eccleshall 1-0
Cradley Town v Elsmere Rangers 1-0
Westfields v Shawbury United 2-3
Holbrook MW v Walsall Wood 1-0
Friar Lane & Epworth v Dudley Town 1-0
South Normanton Athletic v Dunkirk 2-2, 0-3
Coalville Town v Oldbury United 1-2
Staveley MW v Studley 0-1
Borrowash Victoria v Highgate United 3-2
Glossop North End v Racing Club Warwick 2-0
Sutton Town v Highfield Rangers 3-2
Alvechurch v Brockton 4-3
Gedling MW v Atherstone Town 3-2
Wellington v Ledbury Town 4-1
Southam United v Stone Dominoes 2-4
Nuneaton Griff v Long Eaton United 3-3, 0-1

Bridgnorth Town v New Mills 3-2
Dereham Town v Great Yarmouth Town 6-0
Eynesbury Rovers v Whitton United 1-4
Kirklee & Pakefield v St Ives Town 0-1
Bourne Town v Yaxley 2-6
Diss Town v Fakenham Town 6-0
March Town United v Woodbridge Town 1-2
Thetford Town v Newmarket Town 2-5
Ely City v Lincoln Moorlands Railway 3-3, 4-1
Holbeach United v Godmanchester Rovers 2-0
Felixstowe & Walton United v Sleaford Town 3-4
Norwich United v Blackstones 0-0, 0-3
Debenham LC v Long Melford 2-1
Gorleston v Cornard United 3-0
Walsham Le Willows v Wisbech Town 5-0
St Neots Town v Soham Town Rangers 1-3
Haverhill Rovers v Leiston 2-4
Ampthill Town v Beaumont Athletic 6-1
Desborough Town v Hoddesdon Town 4-3
Tring Athletic v Bedford 3-0
Barking v Sileby Rangers 4-0
St Margaretsbury v Harwich & Parkeston 1-1, 2-2
St Margaretsbury won 4-3 on penalties.
London APSA v Bedfont Green 0-3
Stanway Rovers v Hullbridge Sports 4-2
Long Buckby v Broxbourne Borough V&E 2-0
Sawbridgeworth Town v Sun Postal 2-1
Sawbridgeworth Town removed for fielding ineligible players.
Cockfosters v Sporting Bengal United 3-2
Biggleswade United v Clapton 2-1
Ruislip Manor v Colney Heath 2-3
Leverstock Green v Halstead Town 3-0
Raunds Town v Stotfold 0-5
Stansted v Daventry United 1-2
Stewarts & Lloyds v Brimsdown Rovers 0-2
Royston Town v Bedfont 3-2
Thrapston Town v Harpenden Town 1-3
Eton Manor v Saffron Walden Town 3-0
Biggleswade Town v Bugbrooke St Michaels 3-4
Hatfield Town v Kingsbury London Tigers 2-3
Kingsbury London Tigers removed for fielding an ineligible player.
North Greenford United v Cranfield United 6-0
Concord Rangers v Oxhey Jets 3-0
Ringmer v Sidlesham 5-2
Broadbridge Heath v Three Bridges 1-2
Bookham v Dorking 0-1
Lancing v Raynes Park Vale 2-3
Epsom & Ewell v Tunbridge Wells 2-2, 0-3
Worthing United v Banstead Athletic 4-2
Farnham Town v Littlehampton Town 1-0
Guildford City v Pagham 2-1
Herne Bay v Colliers Wood United 1-4
Chichester City United v Westfield 2-0
Eastbourne United v Hassocks 2-4
Faversham Town v Hailsham Town 2-3
Cobham v Lordswood 3-1
Sevenoaks Town v Egham Town 3-1
Chertsey Town v Erith Town 3-0
Wealden v Erith & Belvedere 1-1, 0-1
Southwick v Camberley Town 0-4
Mile Oak v Crawley Down 2-2, 1-3
Deal Town v Redhill 4-1
Haywards Heath Town v Chessington & Hook United1-4
Wick v East Grinstead Town 3-1
Hythe Town v Shoreham 2-0
Rye United v Sidley United 2-1
Horley Town v Greenwich Borough 1-2
Lymington Town v Blackfield & Langley 2-1
Amesbury Town v Christchurch 0-5
Devizes Town v Brockenhurst 0-1
Melksham Town v Thame United 2-1
Marlow United v Buckingham Athletic 4-0
Witney United v Calne Town 2-1
Brading Town v Highworth Town 2-2, 1-2
Downton v Moneyfields 0-1
Hamble ASSC v Kidlington 2-2,4-1
Holmer Green v Andover New Street 4-1
Milton United v Henley Town 0-2
Westbury United v Chalfont St Peter 3-4
Bicester Town v Shrewton United 2-1
Carterton v Shrivenham 1-1, 1-3
Arlesford Town v Cowes Sports 1-2
Bournemouth v Wootton Bassett Town 12-0
Hartley Wintney v Newport Pagnell Town 0-2
Sandhurst Town v Pewsey Vale 2-1
Shepton Mallet v St Blazey 5-3
Chard Town v Liskeard Athletic 1-2
Porthleven v Bridport 3-1
Newquay v Shortwood United 2-3
Collompton Rangers v Wadebridge Town 2-4
Brislington v Welton Rovers 1-1, 2-2
Brislington won 4-3 on penalties.
Willand Rovers v Saltash United 4-1
Clevedon United v Almondsbury Town 0-4
Newton Abbot v Harrow Hill 1-0
Budleigh Salterton v Bodmin Town 4-1
Launceston v Dawlish Town 1-6
Hallen v Falmouth Town 3-0
Bitton v Odd Down 2-1
Fairford Town v Plymouth Parkway 1-3
Tavistock v Gillingham Town 0-4
Penzance v Wellington Town 1-4
Hamworthy United v Elmore 4-0
Ilfracombe Town v Minehead 3-1

FIRST ROUND

Seaham Red Star v Selby Town 2-1
Durham City v Sunderland Nissan 5-0
Billingham Town v Hebburn Town 0-1
Northallerton Town v Pontefract Colleries 3-1
Tow Law Town v Pickering Town 2-3
Armthorpe Welfare v Jarrow Roofing Boldon CA 0-1
Eccleshill United v Thackley 2-1
Bedlington Terriers v Consett 1-7
Washington v Shildon 0-3
Dunston Federation v Stokesley SC 4-2
Winterton Rangers v Thornaby 1-0
Spennymoor Town v Marske United 3-1
Squires Gate v Maltby Main 3-1
Darwen v Atherton LR 2-3
Trafford v Oldham Town 2-0
Runcorn Linnets v Salford City 1-2
Ashton Town v Hallam 1-3
Blackpool Mechanics v Formby 0-2
Ashton Athletic v Colne 2-1
Kirkham & Wesham v Parkgate 5-0
Bootle v AFC Emley 2-0
Hinckley Downes v Long Eaton United 2-3
Friar Lane & Epworth v Kirby Muxloe 3-2
Leek CSOB v Coleshill Town 0-2
Holbrook MW v Heath Hayes 0-1
Gedling Town v Pegasus Juniors 4-0
Wellington v Calverton MW 4-0
Shifnal Town v Borrowash Victoria 2-4
Newcastle Town v Alvechurch 1-2
Pilkington XXX v Bewdley Town 0-3
Coventry Sphinx v Glossop North End 4-3
Glapwell v Oldbury United 1-3
Sutton Town v Tipton Town 1-6
Stone Dominoes v Rainworth MW 0-2
Barnt Green Spartak v Market Drayton Town 2-3
Shawbury United v Bridgnorth Town 2-1
Cadbury Athletic v Norton United 1-3
Studley v Heanor Town 1-0
Dunkirk v Gedling MW 2-1
Cradley Town v Mickleover Sports 1-0
Deeping Rangers v Woodbridge Town 1-2
Gorleston v St Ives Town 0-3
Boston Town v Holbeach United 3-2
Dereham Town v Soham Town Rangers 1-2
Leiston v Debenham LC 3-0
Newmarket Town v Yaxley 3-2
Wroxham v Whitton United 2-1
Sleaford Town v Walsham Le Willows 5-1
Ely City v Needham Market 1-4
Blackstones v Diss Town 3-1
Desborough Town v Bugbrooke St Michaels 9-0
Long Buckby v Welwyn Garden City 3-2
Hanwell Town v Sun Postal 7-1
Leverstock Green v Biggleswade United 0-1
Royston Town v Harpenden Town 2-1
St Margaretsbury v Wembley 0-1
Hatfield Town v Romford
after FA investigation. *0-3*
Barking v Daventry United 4-2
Stotfold v Tring Athletic 0-1
Barkingside v Brimsdown Rovers 0-2
Ampthill Town v Colney Heath 4-1
Concord Rangers v Hertford Town 2-0

Eton Manor v North Greenford United 4-2
Wellingborough Town v Stanway Rovers 1-1, 0-1
Cockfosters v Bedfont Green 2-1
Bowers & Pitsea v Harefield United 1-3
Worthing United v Chessington & Hook United 2-3
Three Bridges v Sevenoaks Town 4-3
Greenwich Borough v Chichester City United 7-0
Merstham v Dorking 2-0
Rye United v Farnham Town 2-1
Tunbridge Wells v Thamesmead Town 2-2, 0-1
Hassocks v Ash United 2-0
Crawley Down v Croydon 3-2
Camberley Town v Colliers Wood United 2-1
Raynes Park Vale v Cobham 0-3
Deal Town v Chertsey Town 5-1
Erith & Belvedere v Guildford City 4-5
Wick v Ringmer 0-2
Arundel v Hythe Town 5-0
Hailsham Town v Crowborough Athletic 3-4
Witney United v Ardley United 1-5
VT v North Leigh 2-1
Bournemouth v Melksham Town 1-2
Highworth Town v Beaconsfield SYCOB 3-2
Henley Town v Shrivenham 2-3
Christchurch v Sandhurst Town 4-1
Chalfont St Peter v Bicester Town 3-2
New Milton Town v Hungerford Town 0-2
Hamble ASSC v Flackwell Heath 2-3
Holmer Green v Brockenhurst 0-4
Cowes Sports v Corsham Town 3-2
Marlow United v Lymington Town 1-1, 1-5
Moneyfields v Newport Pagnell Town 3-2
Ilfracombe Town v Brislington 4-0
Bitton v Porthleven 3-0
Hamworthy United v Newton Abbot 8-1
Shepton Mallet v Gillingham Town 1-5
Wellington Town v Hallen 0-2
Willand Rovers v Shortwood United 2-1
Poole Town v Liskeard Athletic 5-1
Budleigh Salterton v Plymouth Parkway 2-2, 0-2
Almondsbury Town v Frome Town 1-0
Dawlish Town v Wadebridge Town 2-1

SECOND ROUND
Squires Gate v Northallerton Town 2-2, 3-4
Salford City v Shildon 5-1
Billingham Synthonia v Ashton Athletic 2-1
Eccleshill United v Pickering Town 1-1, 2-3
Atherton LR v Newcastle Benfield 0-0, 2-3
Flixton v Rainworth MW 1-0
Formby v Jarrow Roofing Boldon CA 4-1
Durham City v Consett 0-4
Kirkham & Wesham v West Auckland Town 3-0
Bootle v Winterton Rangers 3-4
Spennymoor Town v Dunston Federation 0-0, 1-3
Seaham Red Star v Trafford 2-3
Hebburn Town v Whitley Bay 1-4
Hallam v Glasshoughton Welfare 1-0
Alvechurch v Causeway United 1-1, 0-1
Shawbury United v Stratford Town 1-0
Bewdley Town v Coventry Sphinx 1-2
Wellington v Friar Lane & Epworth 2-3
Studley v Sleaford Town 4-1
Heath Hayes v Borrowash Victoria 3-0
Boston Town v Long Eaton United 2-0
Barwell v Coleshill Town 1-3
Gedling Town v Cradley Town 2-1
Tipton Town v Market Drayton Town 2-0
Oldbury United v Dunkirk 0-0, 2-1
Norton United v Blackstones 0-2
Leiston v St Ives Town 2-3
Concord Rangers v Potton United 5-0
Lowestoft Town v Desborough Town 1-0
Stanway Rovers v Barking 6-1
Soham Town Rangers v Long Buckby 0-1
Hanwell Town v Cogenhoe United 0-1
Newmarket Town v Biggleswade United 1-0
Needham Market v Eton Manor 4-1
Ampthill Town v Burnham Ramblers 3-0
Mildenhall Town v Wroxham 2-1
Wembley v Woodbridge Town 2-2, 2-0
Brimsdown Rovers v Tring Athletic 3-1
Romford v Cockfosters 3-0
Royston Town v Ipswich Wanderers 0-2
VT v Guildford City 4-2
Lymington Town v Hassocks 1-0
Brockenhurst v Crawley Down 4-1
Thamesmead Town v Greenwich Borough 0-2
AFC Totton v VCD Athletic 0-1
Chessington & Hook United v Crowborough Athletic 2-2, 3-4
Three Bridges v Camberley Town 0-1
Deal Town v Moneyfields 3-4
Whitehawk v Flackwell Heath 2-3
Christchurch v Merstham 1-7
Cowes Sports v Arundel 4-2
Chalfont St Peter v Harefield United 1-5
Ringmer v Ardley United 4-1
Rye United v Cobham 2-2, 3-2
Bemerton Heath Harlequins v Bideford 2-3
Hamworthy United v Poole Town 1-2
Willand Rovers v Sherborne Town 0-3
Hungerford Town v Gillingham Town 5-0
Melksham Town v Street 4-1
Shrivenham v Dawlish Town 3-2
Wimborne Town v Hallen 3-2
Bitton v Highworth Town 3-2
Almondsbury Town v Truro City 2-4
Plymouth Parkway v Ilfracombe Town 2-0

THIRD ROUND
Winterton Rangers v Pickering Town 2-1
Winterton Rangers removed for fielding an ineligible player.
Billingham Synthonia v Dunston Federation 1-3
Consett v Trafford 2-1
Salford City v Hallam 3-0
Newcastle Benfield v Kirkham & Wesham 2-5
Whitley Bay v Flixton 6-0
Northallerton Town v Formby 0-6
Tipton Town v Friar Lane & Epworth 3-1
Coventry Sphinx v Oldbury United 4-0
Coleshill Town v Blackstones 1-2
Shawbury United v Cogenhoe United 2-1
Studley v Gedling Town 4-3
Long Buckby v Heath Hayes 3-2
Causeway United v Boston Town 0-1
Merstham v VT 2-2, 1-1
Merstham won 4-3 on penalties.
St Ives Town v Romford 1-1, 4-2
Lowestoft Town v Rye United 4-2
Concord Rangers v Newmarket Town 7-1
Greenwich Borough v Wembley 2-1
Crowborough Athletic v Brimsdown Rovers 2-1
Ampthill Town v VCD Athletic 1-3
Ringmer v Needham Market 1-3
Mildenhall Town v Stanway Rovers 0-5
Camberley Town v Flackwell Heath 2-1
Ipswich Wanderers v Harefield United 0-3
Plymouth Parkway v Hungerford Town 0-1
Sherborne Town v Lymington Town 1-3
Bitton v Brockenhurst 3-1
Poole Town v Cowes Sports 1-0
Melksham Town v Truro City 0-3
Moneyfields v Shrivenham 1-2
Bideford v Wimborne Town 1-0

FOURTH ROUND
Whitley Bay v Long Buckby 1-0
Truro City v Bideford 3-2
Hungerford Town v Boston Town 1-0
Concord Rangers v Shawbury United 4-1
Kirkham & Wesham v Studley 3-0
St Ives Town v Bitton 3-2
VCD Athletic v Needham Market 0-2
Merstham v Pickering Town 4-2
Camberley Town v Tipton Town 3-1
Coventry Sphinx v Salford City 3-1
Dunston Federation v Shrivenham 8-0
Stanway Rovers v Formby 4-2
Greenwich Borough v Harefield United 2-1
Poole Town v Consett 1-1, 1-4
Lymington Town v Crowborough Athletic 1-4
Lowestoft Town v Blackstones 3-2

FIFTH ROUND
Hungerford Town v Greenwich Borough 2-2, 2-1
Concord Rangers v Camberley Town 2-0
St Ives Town v Needham Market 2-2, 0-4
Merstham v Consett 5-4

Lowestoft Town v Dunston Federation 2-1
Truro City v Whitley Bay 0-3
Crowborough Athletic v Kirkham & Wesham 0-2
Stanway Rovers v Coventry Sphinx 1-3

SIXTH ROUND
Concord Rangers v Lowestoft Town 0-1
Kirkham & Wesham v Coventry Sphinx 2-2, 1-0
Hungerford Town v Whitley Bay 0-1
Merstham v Needham Market 2-3

SEMI-FINALS (two legs)
Lowestoft Town v Whitley Bay 4-0, 0-3
Kirkham & Wesham v Needham Market 3-2, 1-0

FINAL (at Wembley)

Sunday 11 May 2008

Kirkham & Wesham (0) 2 *(Walwyn 84, 90)*
Lowestoft Town (1) 1 *(Thompson 10)* 19,537

Kirkham & Wesham: Summerfield; Jackson (Walwyn 80), Keefe (Allen 54), Thompson, Shaw, Eastwood, Clark, Blackwell, Wane, Paterson (Sheppard 90), Smith.
Lowestoft Town: Reynolds; Poppy, Potter, Woodrow, Saunders, Plaskett (McGee 79), Godbould, Darren Cockrill (Dale Cockrill 46), Stock, King (Hunn 54).
Referee: A. D'Urso (Essex).

THE FA YOUTH CUP 2007–08

SPONSORED BY E.ON

PRELIMINARY ROUND
Moneyfields v Weymouth 3-0
Horley Town v Margate 1-0
Chester-le-Street Town v Wallsend BC 1-2
Eccleshill United v Harrogate Railway 1-2
Gornal Athletic v Sutton Coldfield Town 0-4
Stratford Town v Stafford Rangers 1-4
Soham Town Rangers v Stowmarket Town 5-4
Walsham Le Willows v Bury Town 0-2
Thrapston Town v Wellingborough Town 0-1
AFC Hornchurch v Romford 0-2
Saltdean United v Camberley Town 0-2
Westbury United v Wootton Bassett Town 1-3
Tiverton Town v Bristol Manor Farm 7-1
West Allotment Celtic v Sunderland RCA 3-3
Sunderland RCA won 4-3 on penalties.
AFC Kempston Rovers v Stotfold 0-2
Beaconsfield SYCOB v Marlow 0-2
Yorkshire Amateur v Armthorpe Welfare 2-1
Rossington Main v North Ferriby United 1-2
Stone Dominoes v Coventry Sphinx 7-2
Cradley Town v Newcastle Town 3-0
Eccleshall v Bromyard Town 4-0
Nuneaton Borough v Burton Albion 2-0
Nuneaton Griff v Wellington 0-2
Redditch United v Highgate United 1-0
Wroxham v Newmarket Town 3-2
Arlesey Town v Cranfield United 2-5
Stevenage Borough v Berkhamsted Town 4-0
Sun Postal v Colney Heath 0-1
St Margaretsbury v Tring Athletic 3-0
FC Clacton v Witham Town 1-2
Chelmsford City v Hoddesdon Town 1-0
Brentwood Town v Canvey Island 2-1
Royston Town v Boreham Wood 0-7
Haringey Borough v Leyton 1-4
Hastings United v Dover Athletic 4-2
Sutton United v Arundel 2-1
Bashley v Bournemouth 1-2
Bedworth United v Alvechurch 2-3
VT v Winchester City 3-1
Farsley Celtic v Stocksbridge Park Steels 2-1
Liversedge v Sheffield 2-5
Bowers & Pitsea v Clapton 5-1
Faversham Town v Maidstone United 0-6
VCD Athletic v Tunbridge Wells 3-1
Eastbourne Borough v Erith & Belvedere 2-0
Ramsgate v Rye United 5-2
Poole Town v Dorchester Town 1-1
Poole Town won 3-2 on penalties.
Gillingham Town v Hamworthy United 1-1
Gillingham Town won 11-10 on penalties.
Bridgwater Town v Bath City 2-6
Seaham Red Star v Gateshead 5-2
Cambridge United v Witton United 11-1
St Albans City v Sawbridgeworth Town 8-0
AFC Totton v Eastleigh 1-2
Exeter City v Gloucester City 0-3
Ringmer v Haywards Heath Town 1-7
Ossett Albion v Worksop Town 1-0
Selby Town v Hall Road Rangers 0-3
Eastwood Town v Hinckley United 6-3
Corby Town v Cogenhoe United 2-0
Horsham v Godalming Town 2-1
Salisbury City v Shaftesbury 11-0
York City v Dunston Federation 4-0
Pickering Town v Whitley Bay 0-5
Solihull Moors v Boldmere St Michaels 0-2
Stourbridge v Tipton Town 4-0
Rothwell Corinthians v Bedford 4-4
Bedford won 5-3 on penalties.
Bishop's Stortford v Leverstock Green 2-5
Worthing v Leatherhead 2-3
Colliers Wood United v Carshalton Athletic 1-7
Burgess Hill Town v Epsom & Ewell 6-1
Weston-Super-Mare v Bishop's Cleeve 2-1
Guisborough Town w.o. v Scarborough removed.
Hampton & Richmond Borough w.o. v Kingsbury London Tigers withdrew.
Peacehaven & Telscombe withdrew v South Park w.o.
Tooting & Mitcham United w.o. v Farnham Town withdrew.

FIRST QUALIFYING ROUND
Bowers & Pitsea v Chelmsford City 1-3
Moneyfields v Gillingham Town 5-1
St Albans City v Leverstock Green 0-4
Silsden AFC v Guiseley AFC 3-0
Salisbury City v Eastleigh 1-1
Eastleigh won 5-3 on penalties.
Vauxhall Motors v Nantwich Town 3-3
Vauxhall Motors won 4-3 on penalties.
Ashton Town AFC v Trafford 4-3
Calne v Prescot Cables 1-2
Hall Road Rangers v Bradford Park Avenue 1-0
Loughborough Dynamo v Stamford 2-3
Long Eaton United v Deeping Rangers 1-1
Long Eaton United won 4-2 on penalties.
Stafford Rangers v Stone Dominoes 0-1
Leiston v Diss Town 3-4
Woodbridge Town v Long Melford 4-0
Debenham LC v Fakenham Town 3-0
Cambridge United v Wroxham 8-3
Raunds Town v Northampton Spencer 2-1
Cranfield United v Wellingborough Town 1-2
Bedford v Corby Town 0-3
Romford v Ilford 1-0
Brentwood Town v Heybridge Swifts 5-2
Dulwich Hamlet v AFC Wimbledon 1-2
Lordswood v Whyteleafe 1-4
Ebbsfleet United v Croydon 5-0
Sittingbourne v Chatham Town 0-2
South Park v Hastings United 0-7
Tooting & Mitcham United v Horsham 7-0
Milton United v Witney United 6-0
Aylesbury United v Chalfont St Peter 5-1
Didcot Town v Marlow 2-1
Christchurch v VT 1-0
Tiverton Town v Wootton Bassett Town 5-0
Woodley Sports v Altrincham 1-1
Woodley Sports won 3-2 on penalties.
Ashville v Marine 1-2
Alvechurch v AFC Telford United 4-3
Kettering Town v Daventry United 21-0
Leatherhead v Sutton United 3-2

Carterton v Oxford United 0-5
Gloucester City v Forest Green Rovers 3-0
Bootle v Workington 3-0
Northwich Victoria v Warrington Town 0-1
Stalybridge Celtic v Burscough 0-6
Garforth Town v Thackley 1-7
Sheffield v Halifax Town 6-2
Stapenhill v Eastwood Town 2-1
Boston United v Teversal 3-0
Blackstones v Carlton Town 1-0
Shirebrook Town v Retford United 0-1
Matlock Town v Glossop North End 2-1
Bourne Town v Barrow Town 2-3
Gresley Rovers v Mickleover Sports 0-2
Blaby & Whetstone Athletic v Arnold Town 2-0
Racing Club Warwick v Worcester City 1-4
Coleshill Town v Bromsgrove Rovers 1-3
Redditch United v Hednesford Town 2-1
Rugby Town v Stourbridge 0-1
Atherstone Town v Malvern Town 0-3
Cradley Town v Chasetown 2-4
Great Yarmouth Town v Histon 2-1
Stotfold v Leighton Town 1-0
Biggleswade United v Dunstable Town 0-5
Southend Manor v Burnham Ramblers 1-2
Thurrock v Stevenage Borough 1-6
Hitchin Town v Buntingford Town 1-4
Witham Town v Hullbridge Sports 0-4
Cheshunt v Ware 3-4
Redbridge v Leyton 2-3
Hanwell Town v Staines Town 1-3
Wingate & Finchley v Enfield Town 1-2
Corinthian Casuals v Erith Town 2-2
Erith Town won 4-1 on penalties.
Ashford Town (Middx) v Northwood 3-2
Hampton & Richmond Borough v Hillingdon Borough 1-0
Croydon Athletic v Hayes & Yeading United 4-2
Ramsgate v East Grinstead Town 0-0
East Grinstead Town won 3-1 on penalties.
Dartford v Folkestone Invicta 0-1
Deal Town v Lingfield 1-0
Horley Town v Tonbridge Angels 0-3
Three Bridges v Westfield 1-0
Chertsey Town v Cobham 4-2
Binfield v Andover 4-2
North Leigh v Henley Town 5-4
Sandhurst Town v Basingstoke Town 1-5
Cove v Reading Town 1-5
Banbury United v Buckingham Town 0-1
Farnborough v Abingdon United 0-3
Newport Pagnell Town v Bracknell Town 2-2
Bracknell Town won 4-1 on penalties.
Fleet Town v Oxford City 3-5
Thatcham Town v Maidenhead United 0-5
Witton Albion v Salford City 0-4
Barwell v Oadby Town 0-2
Grays Athletic v Maldon Town 3-2
Braintree Town v Colney Heath 2-4
Harefield United v Wealdstone 2-6
Edgware Town v North Greenford United 4-1
Harrow Borough v Thamesmead Town 3-5
Yate Town v Mangotsfield United 1-3
West Allotment Celtic v Ryton 3-1
Dinnington Town v Hallam 3-0
Carshalton Athletic v Horsham YMCA 4-1
Burnham v Alton Town 3-1
Farsley Celtic v Ossett Albion 5-3
Yorkshire Amateur v Harrogate Railway 1-1
Yorkshire Amateur won 3-0 on penalties.
Bugbrooke St Michaels v Huntingdon Town 0-3
Billericay Town v Welwyn Garden City 0-2
Fisher Athletic v Uxbridge 7-4
Eastbourne Borough v Haywards Heath Town 6-1
VCD Athletic v Chipsted 0-2
Chesham United v Aldershot Town 0-3
Bournemouth v Poole Town 2-4
Chard Town v Brislington 4-3
Newcastle Benfield v Wallsend BC 1-2
Seaham Red Star v Guisborough Town 2-0
Sevenoakes Town v Lewes 0-8
Newport County v Merthyr Tydfil 1-2
Radstock Town v Paulton Rovers 1-4
Southport v Curzon Ashton 0-1
Ashton Athletic v Lancaster City 7-2
North Ferriby United v Ossett Town 1-4
Alfreton Town v Lincoln United 4-2
Lye Town v Pershore Town 1-3
Wellington v Stourport Swifts 3-2
Sutton Coldfield Town v Nuneaton Borough 1-3
Bury Town v Soham Town Rangers 5-0
March Town United v Kirkley & Pakefield 2-1
King's Lynn v Lowestoft Town 3-3
Lowestoft Town won 3-0 on penalties.
Wivenhoe Town v St Margaretsbury 2-0
Bromley v Maidstone United 1-3
Camberley Town v Molesey 4-0
Kidlington v Biscester Town 4-1
York City v Whitley Bay 4-0
Boldmere St Michaels v Eccleshall 0-1
Bitton AFC v Cirencester Town 3-2
Weston-Super-Mare v Bath City 1-1
Bath City won 6-5 on penalties.
Burgess Hill Town v Woking 4-5
Rushden & Diamonds v Rothwell Town 3-0
Atherton LR w.o. v Chadderton withdrew.
London Colney withdrew v Hemel Hempstead Town w.o.
Waltham Abbey w.o. v Potters Bar Town withdrew.
Harlow Town withdrew v Boreham Wood w.o.
Walton & Hersham w.o. v Wick withdrew.

SECOND QUALIFYING ROUND

Buckingham Town v Oxford City 1-2
Bracknell Town v Aylesbury United 1-0
Barrow Town v Boston United 1-7
Debenham LC v Great Yarmouth Town 2-1
Christchurch v Moneyfields 2-1
Boreham Wood v Buntingford Town 4-1
Mickleover Sports v Blackstones 3-0
Hall Road Rangers v Silsden 0-3
Long Eaton United v Retford United 2-2
Retford United won 4-3 on penalties.
Bury Town v Lowestoft Town 3-2
Cambridge United v Diss Town 11-0
Stotfold v Huntingdon Town 6-0
Burnham Ramblers v Hemel Hempstead Town 0-2
Wivenhoe Town v Waltham Abbey 1-2
Hullbridge Sports v Ware 4-2
Maidstone United v Eastbourne Borough 3-1
Chatham Town v Lewes 0-5
Milton United v Didcot Town 4-3
Tiverton Town v Bitton 5-2
Woodley Sports v Vauxhall Motors 3-1
Alvechurch v Wellington 6-0
Colney Heath v Chelmsford City 2-2
Colney Heath won 5-3 on penalties.
Croydon Athletic v Fisher Athletic 2-1
Chipstead v Deal Town 1-2
Leatherhead v Walton & Hersham 1-0
Burnham v Oxford United 0-3
Wallsend BC v West Allotment Celtic 1-2
Warrington Town v Curzon Ashton 0-3
Burscough v Salford City 3-4
Bootle v Ashton Town 4-5
Prescot Cables v Ashton Athletic 0-1
Yorkshire Amateur v Thackley 4-1
Alfreton Town v Blaby & Whetstone Athletic 3-1
Stapenhill v Matlock Town 4-0
Stamford v Oadby Town 2-2
Stamford won 3-1 on penalties.
Chasetown v Malvern Town 2-1
Nuneaton Borough v Pershore Town 2-0
Stone Dominoes v Eccleshall 2-1
Wellingborough Town v Dunstable Town 1-2
Stevenage Borough v Brentwood Town 4-1
Hampton & Richmond Borough v Ashford Town (Middx) 0-2
Leyton v AFC Wimbledon 1-0
Thamesmead Town v Wealdstone 0-1
Edgware Town v Enfield Town 0-3
Hastings United v Whyteleafe 0-1
Ebbsfleet United v Folkestone Invicta 4-1
Tooting & Mitcham United v Chertsey Town 8-2
Maidenhead United v Kidlington 3-0
Binfield v Basingstoke Town 0-4
Marine v Atherton LR 2-0
Carshalton Athletic v Woking 2-1
Farsley Celtic v Dinnington Town 1-4
Reading Town v North Leigh 2-0
Abingdon United v Aldershot Town 1-2
Poole Town v Eastleigh 2-1
Chard Town v Merthyr Tydfil 1-3
Seaham Red Star v York City 2-5

Ossett Town v Sheffield	0-0
Sheffield won 5-4 on penalties.	
Kettering Town v Rushden & Diamonds	2-2
Rushden & Diamonds won 5-3 on penalties.	
Bath City v Paulton Rovers	3-2
Woodbridge Town v March Town United	5-0
Bromsgrove Rovers v Redditch United	3-2
Corby Town v Raunds Town	2-2
Corby Town won 4-1 on penalties.	
Tonbridge Angels v East Grinstead Town	1-0
Camberley Town v Three Bridges	4-0
Stourbridge v Worcester City	2-1
Welwyn Garden City v Leverstock Green	2-4
Erith Town v Staines Town	0-3
Gloucester City v Mangotsfield United	3-2
Romford v Grays Athletic	0-3

THIRD QUALIFYING ROUND

Mickleover Sports v Retford United	3-3
Retford United won 5-4 on penalties.	
Stapenhill v Boston United	0-3
Debenham LC v Woodbridge Town	2-9
Grays Athletic v Leverstock Green	2-1
Waltham Abbey v Stevenage Borough	1-2
Colney Heath v Boreham Wood	0-2
Enfield Town v Ashford Town (Middx)	2-0
Camberley Town v Carshalton Athletic	3-0
Oxford City v Aldershot Town	0-4
Bracknell Town v Maidenhead United	2-1
Merthyr Tydfil v Gloucester City	0-1
Rushden & Diamonds v Stotfold	4-1
Corby Town v Dunstable Town	5-1
Ashton Athletic v Marine	1-2
Bath City v Tiverton Town	0-3
York City w.o. v West Allotment Celtic removed.	
Staines Town v Croydon Athletic	1-2
Curzon Ashton v Salford City	4-0
Yorkshire Amateur v Dinnington Town	1-2
Stamford v Alfreton Town	0-2
Nuneaton Borough v Alvechurch	4-0
Bromsgrove Rovers v Chasetown	4-1
Leyton v Wealdstone	5-0
Whyteleafe v Tonbridge Angels	1-0
Basingstoke Town v Milton United	1-0
Poole Town v Christchurch	1-2
Woodley Sports v Ashton Town	1-4
Cambridge United v Bury Town	11-1
Leatherhead v Tooting & Mitcham United	2-0
Stone Dominoes v Stourbridge	2-2
Stourbridge won 6-5 on penalties.	
Hemel Hempstead Town v Hullbridge Sports	3-1
Maidstone United v Lewes	0-1
Reading Town v Oxford United	1-3
Silsden v Sheffield	3-1
Ebbsfleet United v Deal Town	3-1

FIRST ROUND

Marine v Chester City	0-4
Grimsby Town v Tranmere Rovers	0-1
Bury v Silsden	3-0
Huddersfield Town v Hartlepool United	4-3
York City v Dinnington Town	5-1
Darlington v Leeds United	0-1
Doncaster Rovers v Rochdale	3-1
Bradford City v Macclesfield Town	1-2
Oldham Athletic v Wrexham	1-1
Oldham Athletic won 3-2 on penalties.	
Carlisle United v Stockport County	2-0
Morecambe v Rotherham United	2-3
Curzon Ashton v Chesterfield	1-1
Curzon Ashton won 7-6 on penalties.	
Ashton Town v Crewe Alexandra	1-6
Mansfield Town v Alfreton Town	5-0
Lincoln City v Boston United	2-2
Lincoln City won 5-4 on penalties.	
Nuneaton Borough v Port Vale	1-3
Retford United v Stourbridge	6-0
Nottingham Forest v Walsall	1-2
Shrewsbury Town v Bromsgrove Rovers	1-1
Shrewsbury Town won 5-4 on penalties.	
Luton Town v Leyton Orient	2-1
Dagenham & Redbridge v Gillingham	2-1
Stevenage Borough v Enfield Town	5-1
Camberley Town v Millwall	0-5
Rushden & Diamonds v Grays Athletic	6-1
Cambridge United v Hemel Hempstead Town	5-1
Leatherhead v Wycombe Wanderers	0-3
Corby Town v Leyton	2-0
Whyteleafe v Barnet	0-0
Barnet won 5-4 on penalties.	
Southend United v Croydon Athletic	3-1
Brentford v Lewes	3-1
Ebbsfleet United v Northampton Town	0-3
Boreham Wood v Woodbridge Town	3-2
Brighton & Hove Albion v Milton Keynes Dons	4-3
Swansea City v Gloucester City	5-0
Yeovil Town v Tiverton Town	0-0
Tiverton Town won 3-2 on penalties.	
Basingstoke Town v Hereford United	4-6
Bracknell Town v Aldershot Town	1-2
Christchurch v Bristol Rovers	1-3
Oxford United v AFC Bournemouth	2-1
Cheltenham Town v Swindon Town	0-1

SECOND ROUND

Mansfield Town v Carlisle United	1-4
Macclesfield Town v Rotherham United	3-0
Tranmere Rovers v Huddersfield Town	1-2
Oldham Athletic v Lincoln City	4-1
Curzon Ashton v Chester City	1-1
Chester City won 6-5 on penalties.	
Retford United v Shrewsbury Town	0-2
Cambridge United v Crewe Alexandra	1-2
Bury v York City	0-2
Port Vale v Doncaster Rovers	2-1
Walsall v Leeds United	1-2
Boreham Wood v Swansea City	1-5
Wycombe Wanderers v Dagenham & Redbridge	5-0
Luton Town v Corby Town	4-1
Stevenage Borough v Oxford United	2-1
Southend United v Barnet	7-3
Brentford v Swindon Town	1-2
Northampton Town v Tiverton Town	6-2
Bristol Rovers v Brighton & Hove Albion	0-3
Hereford United v Millwall	3-5
Aldershot Town v Rushden & Diamonds	0-3

THIRD ROUND

Port Vale v Swansea City	4-0
Luton Town v Leeds United	0-3
Stoke City v Wigan Athletic	1-1
Stoke City won 4-3 on penalties.	
Everton v Bristol City	0-2
Blackpool v Macclesfield Town	2-3
Oldham Athletic v Sheffield United	0-1
Manchester City v Millwall	5-1
Huddersfield Town v Birmingham City	1-2
Wolverhampton Wanderers v Charlton Athletic	2-3
Chester City v York City	3-0
Portsmouth v Fulham	1-0
Swindon Town v Barnsley	2-1
Queens Park Rangers v Ipswich Town	3-5
Burnley v Arsenal	1-5
Stevenage Borough v Chelsea	0-1
Newcastle United v Shrewsbury Town	0-1
Carlisle United v Sheffield Wednesday	1-1
Carlisle United won 4-2 on penalties.	
Leicester City v Blackburn Rovers	1-0
Wycombe Wanderers v Liverpool	0-5
Plymouth Argyle v Coventry City	3-0
Sunderland v Norwich City	6-1
Northampton Town v Reading	0-1
West Ham United v Bolton Wanderers	0-2
Manchester United v Brighton & Hove Albion	2-1
Crystal Palace v Hull City	1-0
Scunthorpe United v Watford	1-2
Preston North End v West Bromwich Albion	3-1
Southend United v Derby County	4-1
Southampton v Tottenham Hotspur	0-1
Rushden & Diamonds v Colchester United	1-3
Aston Villa v Crewe Alexandra	3-1
Middlesbrough v Cardiff City	1-0

FOURTH ROUND

Portsmouth v Plymouth Argyle	1-2
Bristol City v Leeds United	2-1
Manchester United v Carlisle United	1-2
Swindon Town v Middlesbrough	2-0
Southend United v Stoke City	3-1
Sunderland v Macclesfield Town	2-1
Bolton Wanderers v Port Vale	2-3
Colchester United v Aston Villa	0-1

Ipswich Town v Watford 3-1
Charlton Athletic v Sheffield United 6-0
Leicester City v Crystal Palace 3-2
Birmingham City v Preston North End 3-1
Tottenham Hotspur v Chester City 2-1
Liverpool v Arsenal 1-0
Reading v Manchester City 1-3
Chelsea v Shrewsbury Town 4-0

FIFTH ROUND
Plymouth Argyle v Birmingham City 3-2
Sunderland v Liverpool 5-3
Aston Villa v Ipswich Town 5-0
Chelsea v Leicester City 3-1
Charlton Athletic v Swindon Town 5-1
Carlisle United v Southend United 2-0
Port Vale v Tottenham Hotspur 1-0
Bristol City v Manchester City 2-4

SIXTH ROUND
Port Vale v Chelsea 2-5
Plymouth Argyle v Manchester City 1-4
Charlton Athletic v Sunderland 1-2
Carlisle United v Aston Villa 0-2

SEMI-FINALS (two legs)
Chelsea v Aston Villa 1-1, 3-2
Sunderland v Manchester City 0-2, 1-0

FINAL (first leg)

Thursday 3 April 2008

Chelsea (0) 1 *(Kakuta 66)*

Manchester City (0) 1 *(Sturridge 49)* 11,890

Chelsea: Taylor; Ofori-Twumasi, Gordon, Woods, Bruma, Van Aanholt, Stoch, Mellis, Nielsen (Phillip 62), Kakuta, Tejera Rodriguez.
Manchester City: Hartley; Trippier, McGivern, Tutte, Boyata, Mee, Weiss, Kay, Ball (Ibrahim 86), Sturridge, McDermott (Tsiaklis 71).
Referee: P. Walton (Northamptonshire).

FINAL (second leg)

Wednesday 16 April 2008

Manchester City (2) 3 *(Mee 24, Weiss 35, Ball 87 (pen))*

Chelsea (1) 1 *(McGivern 6 (og))* 19,780

Manchester City: Hartley; Trippier (Ibrahim 90), Boyata (Tsiaklis 82), Kay, Mee, McGivern, Tutte, Weiss, Mak, Ball, McDermott.
Chelsea: Taylor; Ofori-Twumasi, Gordon (Nouble 73), Woods, Bruma, Van Aanholt, Stoch, Mellis, Tejera, Kakuta, Nielsen (Phillip 54).
Referee: P. Walton (Northamptonshire).

THE FA SUNDAY CUP 2007–08

IN PARTNERSHIP WITH CARLSBERG

PRELIMINARY ROUND
AFC Pudsey withdrew v Penny Lane w.o.
Irlam MS v Britannia 0-2
Dawdon CW v Jolly Miller 3-0
Swanfield v Hartlepool Rovers Quoit 2-1
Queensbury v Home & Bargain 4-4
Queensbury won 3-2 on penalties.
Oak Tree Jacks v Obiter Fabs 4 1-4
Halton Moor v Seymour KFCA 1-2
Heyford United v Barcabullona 2-1
Travellers v Sporting Dynamo 4-3
Oadby United v Loft Style Sinners 0-3
Moggerhanger Sunday v Belstone 1-6
London Maccabi Lions v AC Sportsmen 1-3
Club Lewsey v Pardon Royals 2-0
Loughton Nu Bar v Postels 2000 (Kents) 4-4
Loughton Nu Bar won on penalties.
Greenbridge MOT Centre v Ashton 1-1
Greenbridge MOT Centre won on penalties.
CB Hounslow United v St Josephs (Luton) 1-3
Richfield Rovers v FC Houghton Centre 3-1
Scafftech UK Bristol v Woolston T&L 1-0
Reading Irish withdrew v GL Sports w.o.
Broadfields United v Sutton Athletic 2-3
Lashings v Millburn 2-3
Rettendon FC withdrew v Wainscott Arrows w.o.
Lakeside Athletic v The Black Dog FC (Weymouth) 1-0

FIRST ROUND
Portland (Carlisle) v Brow 3-2
Stanley Royal v Shankhouse United 4-0
Dock v BRNESC 4-2
Portland (Workington) v Barry's 2-3
Penny Lane v Britannia 2-1
Royal Clayton v Canada 0-6
Hartlepool Lion Hillcarter v Queens Park 0-1
Dengo United v Drum 5-4
Seaburn v Hartlepool Athletic Rugby 2-1
Hetton Lyons Cricket Club v Hessle Rangers 12-0
Ford Motors v Elland AFC 6-5
Dawdon CW v Swanfield 3-2
West Lee v Murton Victoria 2-4
Hartlepool Supporters Athletic v Lobster 0-4
Oyster Martyrs v Ring o'Bells (Shipley) 7-0
Rawdon v Sunderland RCA Wavendon 3-3
Rawdon won 3-0 on penalties.
Allerton v Queensbury 0-3
Paddock v Albion Sports 3-1
Shipley Town withdrew v JOB w.o.
Sandon Dock v Nicosia 1-6
Silsden (Sunday) v Fforde Green 2-0
Heywood Irish Centre v Sandstone 3-1
Norcoast Farmers v Bolton Woods 2-5
Seymour KFCA v Obiter Fabs 4 3-5
Buttershaw Whitestar v Copplehouse 1-2
Abandoned 51 minutes due to player and spectator misconduct; both clubs removed from competition.
Western Approaches v Crossflatts 4-2
Magnet Tavern v Advance Couriers 4-1
Scots Grey v Springfield Lions 13-0
Marden v Beaufort 3-0
Bartley Green Social v Bartley Green Sunday 1-2
Pertemps v Heyford United 2-2
Pertemps won on penalties.
Grosvenor Park v Belt Road 3-1
Mackadown Lane S&S v Leicester Polska 1-2
Birstall Stamford v Diffusion 3-0
Loft Style Sinners v Travellers 7-2
Punch Bowl v Ounsdale Albion 1-1
Punch Bowl won on penalties.
Hawkins Sports w.o. v Wernley & Smethwick Town removed.
Gossoms End v St Margarets 0-3
Bedford FC Sunday v 61 FC (Sunday) 2-4
AC Sportsmen v Belstone 1-2
Partizan v Nirankari Sports Sabha 1-2
St Andrews (Sunday) v Brache Green Man 3-0
Enfield Rangers v Cube 4-0
Hammer v Bury Park SC 1-5
Liscombe Park Pipers v Aris 4-3
Celtic SC (Luton) v QOB 2-1
Loughton Nu Bar v Club Lewsey 1-2
Crawley Green (Sunday) v Greengate 2-3
Skew Bridge v Moat 3-4
Albion Manor v Luton Old Boys (Sunday) 6-0
Brantham Athletic v Risden Wood 6-2
Coopers Kensington v Greenbridge MOT Centre 8-0
St Josephs (Luton) v Richfield Rovers 3-1
Bedes Lea 97 v Bournemouth Electric 2-4
Corsham Centre v Bloomfield Sports 5-0
Scafftech UK Bristol v GL Sports 4-0
Golden Lion v Livingstone Rara 3-4
Bedfont Sunday v Sutton Athletic 0-3
Quested v Millburn 3-2
Nicholas Wybacks v Wainscott Arrows 3-1
Hamworthy United (Sunday) v Lakeside Athletic 4-3

SECOND ROUND

Penny Lane v Stanley Royal 1-0
Portland (Carlisle) v Barry's 0-2
Seaburn v Queens Park 2-2
Seaburn won 7-6 on penalties.
Canada v Dengo United 2-1
Coundon Conservative v Ford Motors 3-0
Dawdon CW v Bolton Woods 6-3
Obiter Fabs 4 v Dock 0-6
Rawdon v Lobster 1-2
Murton Victoria v Oyster Martyrs 0-0
Oyster Martyrs won 5-3 on penalties.
Heywood Irish Centre v Paddock 1-6
Queensbury v JOB 4-1
Hetton Lyons Cricket Club v Buttershaw White Star or Copplehouse
Tie awarded to Hetton Lyons Cricket Club; opponents removed.
Nicosia v Western Approaches 4-3
Bartley Green Sunday v Magnet Tavern 0-2
Silsden (Sunday) v Scots Grey 3-2
Birstall Stamford v Grosvenor Park 5-3
Pertemps v Leicester Polska 4-1
St Margarets v Punch Bowl 4-1
Loft Style Sinners v Hawkins Sports 5-0
Liscombe Park Pipers v Enfield Rangers 3-2
61 FC (Sunday) v Bury Park SC 1-3
Sutton Athletic v Nirankari Sports Sabha 2-3
St Andrews (Sunday) v Moat 4-2
Celtic SC (Luton) v Belstone 1-3
Brantham Athletic v Greengate 4-2
Club Lewsey v Albion Manor 5-3
Scafftech UK Bristol v Marden 2-1
Corsham Centre v Lebeq Tavern Courage 1-2
Mayfair United v Nicholas Wybacks 3-1
Quested v St Josephs (Luton) 1-5
Hamworthy United (Sunday) v Livingstone Rara 4-2
Coopers Kensington v Bournemouth Electric 3-1

THIRD ROUND

Canada v Lobster 1-0
Seaburn v Penny Lane 1-1
Seaburn won 5-4 on penalties.
Coundon Conservative v Queensbury 2-1
Silsden (Sunday) v Dawdon CW 2-0
Nicosia v Dock 4-3
Hetton Lyons Cricket Club v Oyster Martyrs 3-1
Paddock v Barry's 4-1
Pertemps v Magnet Tavern 0-4
Bury Park SC v Club Lewsey 1-2
St Margarets v Birstall Stamford 1-4
Brantham Athletic v Loft Style Sinners 6-3
St Andrews (Sunday) v Nirankari Sports Sabha 4-3
St Josephs (Luton) v Liscombe Park Pipers 2-1
Coopers Kensington v Scafftech UK Bristol 0-2
Hamworthy United (Sunday) v Mayfair United 1-2
Belstone v Lebeq Tavern Courage 1-2

FOURTH ROUND

Canada v Coundon Conservative 0-2
Nicosia v Magnet Tavern 1-2
Silsden (Sunday) v Paddock 1-2
Hetton Lyons Cricket Club v Seaburn 1-1
Hetton Lyons Cricket Club won 5-3 on penalties.
Birstall Stamford v St Andrews (Sunday) 1-2
Scafftech UK Bristol v Brantham Athletic 0-4
St Josephs (Luton) v Lebeq Tavern Courage 6-0
Mayfair United v Club Lewsey 0-2

FIFTH ROUND

St Andrews (Sunday) v Hetton Lyons Cricket Club 0-4
Coundon Conservative v St Josephs (Luton) 2-1
Paddock v Club Lewsey 4-0
Magnet Tavern v Brantham Athletic 1-2

SEMI-FINALS

Paddock v Hetton Lyons Cricket Club 0-2
Brantham Athletic v Coundon Conservative 1-2

FINAL

Coundon Conservative 2 *(Thompson 2, Houlahan 24)*
Hetton Lyons Cricket Club 3 *(Clarke 12, Irvine 55, Pearson 84 (pen))*
(at Liverpool FC) 1052

NATIONAL LEAGUE SYSTEMS CUP 2007–08

PRELMINARY ROUND

Liverpool County Premier League v Teesside League 2-0
Cheshire Association League v West Cheshire League 2-1
Northern Football Alliance v Lancashire Amateur League 3-2
Brighton Hove & District League v Sussex County League Div 3 1-4
Southern Amateur Football League v Kent County League 6-3
Essex & Suffolk Border League v Middlesex County League 0-2
Mid Sussex League v Spartan South Midlands League Div 2 3-1

FIRST ROUND

Northern Football Alliance v Wearside League 0-2
Manchester Football League v Cumberland County League 0-0
Cumberland County League won 4-2 on penalties.
Cheshire Association League v Liverpool County Premier League 1-2
Hertfordshire Senior County League v Peterborough & District League 4-2
Cambridgeshire County League v Northamptonshire Combination 2-3
Central Midlands League v Midland Football Combination Div 1 1-1
Midland Football Combination Div 1 won 5-3 on penalties.
Northampton Town League v Anglian Combination 1-3
Essex Olympian League v Mid Sussex League 4-0
Tie awarded to Mid Sussex League; Essex Olympian League fielded ineligible player.
Southern Amateur Football League v Middlesex County League 3-1
Amateur Football Combination v Bedfordshire Football League 4-0
North Berks League v Sussex County League Div 3 0-6
Wiltshire Football League v Reading Football League 2-3
Somerset County League v Gloucestershire County League 2-2
Gloucestershire County League won 4-3 on penalties.
Jersey Football Combination v Guernsey Priaulx League 1-3
Dorset Premier League v Hampshire League 2004 1-2
Tie awarded to Dorset Premier League, Hampshire League 2004 withdrew.

SECOND ROUND

Wearside League v The Isle of Man League 1-2
Cumberland County League v Liverpool County Premier League 0-2
Anglian Combination v Northamptonshire Combination 3-2
Midland Football Combination Div 1 v Hertfordshire Senior County League 3-1
Mid Sussex League v Southern Amateur Football League 0-3
Sussex County League Div 3 v Amateur Football Combination 1-2
Guernsey Priaulx League v Gloucestershire County League 2-0
Dorset Premier League v Reading Football League 3-2

THIRD ROUND

Liverpool County Premier League v The Isle of Man League 0-1
Anglian Combination v Midland Football Combination Div 1 0-4
Southern Amateur Football League v Dorset Premier League 3-1
Guernsey Priaulx League v Amateur Football Combination 2-2
Amateur Football Combination won 10-9 on penalties.

SEMI-FINALS

Isle of Man League v Midland Football Combination (Div 1) 1-1
Midland Football Combination (Div 1) won 4-1 on penalties.
Southern Amateur Football League v Amateur Football Combination 2-0

FINAL

Midland Football Combination v Southern Amateur Football League 1-1
Southern Amateur Football League won 4-2 on penalties.

FA PREMIER RESERVE LEAGUES 2007–08

FA PREMIER RESERVE LEAGUE – NORTH SECTION

	P	W	D	L	F	A	GD	Pts
Liverpool	18	13	4	1	31	8	23	43
Manchester C	18	8	6	4	34	29	5	30
Manchester U	18	8	5	5	25	19	6	29
Sunderland	18	9	2	7	28	24	4	29
Blackburn R	18	8	4	6	32	25	7	28
Newcastle U	18	5	7	6	31	27	4	22
Middlesbrough	18	5	7	6	23	26	–3	22
Everton	18	4	4	10	21	31	–10	16
Wigan Ath	18	4	3	11	19	36	–17	15
Bolton W	18	3	4	11	13	32	–19	13

Leading Goalscorers *(includes Play-off final)*

Nemeth K	Liverpool	9
Brouwer J	Liverpool	8
Judge A	Blackburn R	7
Grimes A	Manchester C	7
Carroll A	Newcastle U	7
Clarke A	Blackburn R	6
Craddock T	Middlesbrough	6
Hutchinson B	Middlesbrough	6
Godsmark J	Newcastle U	6
Stokes A	Sunderland	6

RESULTS 2007–08	BR	BW	E	L	MC	MU	M	NU	S	WA
Blackburn R	—	1-2	3-0	0-1	1-1	1-0	4-1	1-3	5-0	0-0
Bolton W	0-1	—	0-1	0-3	1-1	0-2	1-3	2-2	1-0	0-4
Everton	3-2	2-3	—	0-1	2-0	2-2	0-0	1-1	1-2	1-2
Liverpool	0-0	1-0	3-0	—	2-1	2-0	4-0	2-1	0-1	3-1
Manchester C	3-2	2-1	4-2	2-3	—	3-1	1-1	2-2	1-0	3-2
Manchester U	1-2	1-1	1-0	1-1	4-1	—	2-1	3-1	2-0	1-1
Middlesbrough	1-1	0-0	3-1	1-1	1-1	1-2	—	0-5	4-1	0-0
Newcastle U	2-4	3-0	3-0	0-0	1-1	1-1	0-2	—	1-3	3-1
Sunderland	7-2	3-0	0-0	0-1	1-3	1-0	2-0	2-2	—	1-0
Wigan Ath	0-2	2-1	1-5	0-3	2-4	0-1	0-4	2-0	1-4	—

FA PREMIER RESERVE LEAGUE – SOUTH SECTION

	P	W	D	L	F	A	GD	Pts
Aston Villa	18	10	5	3	38	17	21	35
West Ham U	18	9	4	5	32	21	11	31
Reading	18	8	7	3	32	16	16	31
Arsenal	18	8	6	4	26	17	9	30
Fulham	18	8	4	6	27	25	2	28
Chelsea	18	5	7	6	23	21	2	22
Birmingham C	18	6	4	8	25	33	–8	22
Tottenham H	18	5	6	7	22	24	–2	21
Portsmouth	18	5	4	9	12	25	–13	19
Derby Co	18	1	3	14	13	51	–38	6

Leading Goalscorers

Mikaelsson T	Aston Villa	8
Lita L	Reading	8
Di Santo F	Chelsea	7
Barazite N	Arsenal	6
Danns N	Birmingham C	6
Forssell M	Birmingham C	5
Brown W	Fulham	5
Henry J	Reading	5
Pekhart T	Tottenham H	5

RESULTS 2007–08	A	AV	BC	C	DC	F	P	R	TH	WH
Arsenal	—	1-0	2-3	1-1	5-1	0-2	2-0	0-1	1-1	2-0
Aston Villa	1-1	—	1-0	6-0	4-1	4-1	2-0	1-1	3-1	2-1
Birmingham C	2-1	0-2	—	0-0	3-2	5-1	0-0	0-6	3-3	3-1
Chelsea	0-1	1-1	0-2	—	3-1	2-2	0-0	1-2	1-1	3-0
Derby Co	1-2	0-6	1-0	0-2	—	1-1	0-2	1-1	2-2	0-8
Fulham	1-2	2-0	2-2	3-2	2-0	—	3-0	2-0	1-0	1-1
Portsmouth	0-2	2-2	1-0	0-4	2-1	1-0	—	1-1	1-0	0-1
Reading	1-1	1-1	5-1	1-0	5-0	0-2	2-0	—	2-2	1-1
Tottenham H	0-0	3-0	1-0	0-3	1-0	3-1	3-1	0-1	—	1-3
West Ham U	2-2	1-2	4-1	0-0	2-1	2-0	2-1	2-1	1-0	—

PREMIER RESERVE LEAGUE PLAY-OFF

Liverpool 3 *(Nemeth, Brouwer, Leiva)*
Aston Villa 0 7,580

at Anfield, Liverpool.

Liverpool: Gulacsi; Darby, Insua, San Jose, Huth, Plessis, El Zhar (Simon), Pezzini, Brouwer (Pacheco), Nemeth (Lindfield), Flynn.
Aston Villa: Taylor; Lund (Bannan), Baker (Delfouneso), Osbourne, Clark, Lowry, Salifou, Routledge, Harewood, Herd, Maloney (Albrighton).

Referee: Mark Clattenburg (Tyne & Wear)

PONTIN'S RESERVE LEAGUES 2007–08

PONTIN'S HOLIDAYS LEAGUE

DIV. ONE CENTRAL	P	W	D	L	F	A	GD	Pts
Nottingham F	22	19	2	1	67	21	46	59
Port Vale	22	11	4	7	38	30	8	37
Coventry C	22	10	6	6	42	27	15	36
Leicester C	22	10	4	8	49	39	10	34
WBA	22	9	6	7	51	45	6	33
Wolverhampton W	22	9	5	8	41	34	7	32
Walsall	22	10	2	10	35	36	–1	32
Shrewsbury T	22	9	4	9	35	39	–4	31
Stoke C	22	9	3	10	25	36	–11	30
Bradford C	22	7	2	13	30	43	–13	23
Huddersfield T	22	5	5	12	21	34	–13	20
Oldham Ath	22	1	3	18	20	70	–50	6

DIV. ONE WEST	P	W	D	L	F	A	GD	Pts
Morecambe	22	14	4	4	43	31	12	46
Manchester C	22	13	3	6	61	35	26	42
Carlisle U	22	11	5	6	43	30	13	38
Preston NE	22	11	2	9	41	39	2	35
Wrexham	22	11	2	9	46	45	1	35
Burnley	22	10	4	8	37	33	4	34
Blackpool	22	9	4	9	43	33	10	31
Tranmere R	22	9	2	11	23	31	–8	29
Bury	22	6	6	10	30	40	–10	24
Chester C	22	6	5	11	23	44	–21	23
Rochdale	22	6	3	13	41	46	–5	21
Accrington S	22	5	2	15	29	53	–24	17

DIV. ONE EAST	P	W	D	L	F	A	GD	Pts
Hartlepool U	22	13	3	6	53	31	22	42
Sheffield U	22	11	5	6	35	28	7	38
Sheffield W	22	11	4	7	37	23	14	37
Hull C	22	11	4	7	30	26	4	37
Rotherham U	22	10	2	10	33	39	–6	32
Leeds U	22	8	6	8	33	29	4	30
Scunthorpe U	22	7	8	7	35	40	–5	39
Grimsby T	22	8	3	11	34	43	–9	27
Darlington	22	8	3	11	21	31	–10	27
York C	22	8	2	12	30	31	–1	26
Barnsley	22	7	5	10	29	44	–15	26
Lincoln C	22	7	1	14	37	42	–5	22

PONTIN'S HOLIDAYS LEAGUE CUP

GROUP ONE	P	W	D	L	F	A	GD	Pts
Morecambe	3	1	2	0	7	5	2	5
Huddersfield T	3	1	2	0	5	4	1	5
Tranmere R	3	1	1	1	3	3	0	4
Chester C	3	0	1	2	3	6	–3	1

GROUP TWO*	P	W	D	L	F	A	GD	Pts
WBA	3	3	0	0	13	2	11	9
Leicester C	4	3	0	1	6	8	–2	9
Rotherham U	3	0	2	1	4	5	–1	2
Lincoln C	3	0	1	2	3	7	–4	1
Sheffield U	3	0	1	2	2	6	–4	1

**Remaining group matches – Rotherham U v WBA, Sheffield U v Lincoln C were not played and declared void.*

GROUP THREE	P	W	D	L	F	A	GD	Pts
Barnsley	3	2	1	0	15	5	10	7
Bradford C	3	2	0	1	8	7	1	6
Hartlepool U	3	0	2	1	7	8	–1	2
Grimsby T	3	0	1	2	3	13	–10	1

SEMI-FINALS

Morecambe 1, Leicester C 0
WBA 6, Barnsley 1

FINAL

Morecambe 1, WBA 1
Morecambe won 4-2 on penalties.

PONTIN'S HOLIDAY COMBINATION

CENTRAL DIVISION	P	W	D	L	GD	Pts
Southampton	18	12	3	3	20	39
Charlton Ath	18	11	4	3	22	37
Watford	18	9	4	5	5	31
Crystal Palace	18	5	8	5	–2	23
Leyton Orient	18	7	2	9	–5	23
Wycombe W	18	7	2	9	–5	23
Brighton & HA	18	6	3	9	3	21
Millwall	18	5	5	8	–14	20
Aldershot T	18	5	4	9	–12	19
QPR	18	3	5	10	–12	14

EAST DIVISION	P	W	D	L	GD	Pts
Ipswich T	18	16	1	1	49	49
Norwich C	18	9	5	4	19	32
Southend U	18	9	3	6	12	30
Colchester U	18	5	10	3	3	25
Peterborough U	18	6	5	7	–4	23
Luton T	18	6	3	9	–11	21
Milton Keynes D	18	6	2	10	–13	20
Northampton T	18	5	4	9	–13	19
Stevenage B	18	3	6	9	–20	15
Grays Ath	18	3	5	10	–22	14

WALES AND WEST DIVISION	P	W	D	L	GD	Pts
Bristol C	18	14	1	3	33	43
Yeovil T	18	11	4	3	20	37
Plymouth Arg	18	10	3	5	16	33
Swindon T	18	8	6	4	6	30
Exeter C	18	6	5	7	–7	23
Swansea C	18	6	2	10	–13	20
Bournemouth	18	6	2	10	–14	20
Bristol R	18	5	4	9	–9	19
Forest Green R	18	4	2	12	–8	14
Cheltenham T	18	3	5	10	–24	14

FA ACADEMY UNDER 18 LEAGUE 2007–08

GROUP A	P	W	D	L	F	A	GD	Pts
Arsenal	28	17	5	6	74	31	43	56
West Ham U	28	16	3	9	63	38	25	51
Fulham	28	14	7	7	39	28	11	49
Portsmouth	28	15	4	9	44	44	0	49
Crystal Palace	28	14	5	9	59	41	18	47
Southampton	28	13	4	11	43	52	–9	43
Chelsea	28	11	6	11	58	52	6	39
Charlton Ath	28	9	8	11	47	51	–4	35
Ipswich T	28	9	5	14	39	53	–14	32
Norwich C	28	6	9	13	45	56	–11	27
Millwall	28	4	6	18	30	64	–34	18

GROUP B	P	W	D	L	F	A	GD	Pts
Aston Villa	28	22	2	4	84	33	51	68
Tottenham H	28	18	5	5	69	35	34	59
Leicester City	28	18	4	6	70	41	29	58
Reading	28	13	5	10	40	42	–2	44
Bristol C	28	11	5	12	50	51	–1	38
Milton Keynes D	28	9	2	17	33	54	–21	29
Watford	28	7	6	15	30	54	–24	27
Birmingham C	28	5	8	14	31	54	–23	23
Coventry C	28	4	6	18	31	58	–27	18
Cardiff C	28	3	7	18	30	68	–38	16

GROUP C	P	W	D	L	F	A	GD	Pts
Manchester C	28	21	4	3	75	22	53	67
Everton	28	17	7	4	56	24	32	58
Manchester U	28	14	6	8	47	44	3	48
Crewe Alex	28	14	6	8	50	51	–1	48
Liverpool	28	11	10	7	49	34	15	43
Blackburn R	28	10	5	13	36	38	–2	35
WBA	28	8	7	13	44	66	–22	31
Wolverhampton W	28	7	8	13	29	37	–8	29
Bolton W	28	6	9	13	42	47	–5	27
Stoke C	28	6	7	15	28	42	–14	25

GROUP D	P	W	D	L	F	A	GD	Pts
Sunderland	28	20	3	5	68	31	37	63
Nottingham F	28	16	5	7	58	42	16	53
Leeds U	28	13	6	9	53	38	15	45
Middlesbrough	28	11	9	8	39	37	2	42
Sheffield U	28	10	6	12	33	34	–1	36
Huddersfield T	28	9	7	12	30	42	–12	34
Derby Co	28	10	2	16	26	53	–27	32
Newcastle U	28	7	6	15	41	49	–8	27
Sheffield W	28	5	7	16	24	53	–29	22
Barnsley	28	3	4	21	20	73	–53	13

PUMA YOUTH ALLIANCE 2007–08

NORTH WEST CONFERENCE

	P	W	D	L	F	A	GD	Pts
Walsall	27	18	5	4	61	34	27	59
Wigan Ath	27	17	5	5	65	25	40	56
Carlisle U	27	16	4	7	61	37	24	52
Macclesfield T	27	15	5	7	61	32	29	50
Blackpool	27	15	4	8	62	52	10	49
Burnley	27	14	3	10	63	46	17	45
Chester C	27	12	5	10	36	33	3	41
Preston NE	27	12	3	12	51	50	1	39
Tranmere R	27	10	8	9	42	38	4	38
Wrexham	27	10	7	10	40	35	5	37
Oldham Ath	27	11	4	12	60	63	–3	37
Port Vale	27	10	7	10	41	46	–5	37
Bury	27	11	4	12	47	54	–7	37
Stockport Co	27	11	3	13	50	55	–5	36
Morecambe	27	5	5	17	42	64	–22	20
Accrington S	27	5	4	18	32	83	–51	19
Rochdale	27	4	6	17	49	76	–27	18
Shrewsbury T	27	4	4	19	27	67	–40	16

NORTH EAST CONFERENCE

	P	W	D	L	F	A	GD	Pts
Hull C	24	16	3	5	62	28	34	51
Doncaster R	24	15	3	6	49	27	22	48
Hartlepool U	24	13	4	7	49	38	11	43
Lincoln C	24	12	5	7	42	35	7	41
York C	24	12	2	10	36	25	11	38
Grimsby T	24	10	4	10	34	47	–13	34
Mansfield T	24	9	5	10	44	49	–5	32
Bradford C	24	9	4	11	32	37	–5	31
Rotherham U	24	7	9	8	36	32	4	30
Darlington	24	6	5	13	19	36	–17	23
Chesterfield	24	4	10	10	31	42	–11	22
Scunthorpe U	24	6	4	14	28	49	–21	22
Boston U	24	4	8	12	29	46	–17	20

SOUTH WEST CONFERENCE

	P	W	D	L	F	A	GD	Pts
Plymouth Arg	18	14	3	1	59	17	42	45
Swansea C	18	10	4	4	30	18	12	34
Swindon T	18	9	4	5	34	17	17	31
Cheltenham T	18	9	3	6	33	30	3	30
Bournemouth	18	8	5	5	34	25	9	29
Bristol R	18	8	3	7	29	27	2	27
Oxford U	18	6	2	10	27	26	1	20
Yeovil T	18	4	3	11	15	37	–22	15
Hereford U	18	4	3	11	14	45	–31	15
Exeter C	18	1	4	13	7	40	–33	7

SOUTH EAST CONFERENCE

	P	W	D	L	F	A	GD	Pts
QPR	19	13	3	3	45	18	27	42
Gillingham	18	11	2	5	32	23	9	35
Leyton Orient	18	10	3	5	32	26	6	33
Luton T	19	9	4	6	31	27	4	31
Northampton T	19	8	3	8	29	29	0	27
Rushden & D	18	7	4	7	22	19	3	25
Wycombe W	18	6	6	6	33	26	7	24
Southend U	19	6	5	8	30	39	–9	23
Brighton & HA	18	6	4	8	31	23	8	22
Peterborough U	18	6	4	8	21	22	–1	22
Colchester U	19	6	3	10	20	34	–14	21
Barnet	19	6	2	11	20	42	–22	20
Brentford	18	2	5	11	18	36	–18	11

THE PUMA YOUTH ALLIANCE CUP 2007–08

SOUTHERN SECTION

GROUP 1	P	W	D	L	F	A	GD	Pts
Wycombe W	6	4	2	0	21	7	14	14
Hereford U	6	3	0	3	10	16	–6	9
Cheltenham T	6	2	2	2	10	8	2	8
Peterborough U	6	1	4	1	7	8	–1	7
Rushden & D	6	2	1	3	12	14	–2	7
Northampton T	6	2	1	3	7	9	–2	7
Exeter C	6	1	2	3	5	10	–5	5

GROUP 2	P	W	D	L	F	A	GD	Pts
Gillingham	7	6	1	0	18	6	12	19
Swindon T	7	5	0	2	16	13	3	15
Colchester U	7	3	2	2	11	8	3	11
Southend U	7	3	2	2	11	9	2	11
Bristol R	7	3	0	4	14	15	–1	9
Oxford U	7	2	1	4	9	12	–3	7
Leyton Orient	7	2	1	4	11	15	–4	7
Yeovil T	7	0	1	6	6	18	–12	1

GROUP 3	P	W	D	L	F	A	GD	Pts
Plymouth Arg	7	7	0	0	26	7	19	21
Luton T	7	5	1	1	13	10	3	16
QPR	7	5	0	2	16	5	11	15
Brighton & HA	7	3	0	4	8	8	0	9
Brentford	7	1	3	3	7	14	–7	6
Bournemouth	7	1	2	4	4	9	–5	5
Swansea C	7	0	3	4	9	17	–8	3
Barnet	7	0	3	4	7	20	–13	3

SECOND ROUND
Bristol R 0, Colchester U 5
Cheltenham T 3, Oxford U 3
Gillingham 0, Brentford 1
Peterborough U 2, Southend U 1
Plymouth Arg 0, Brighton & HA 5
QPR 2, Luton T 0
Swindon T 1, Rushden & D 2
Wycombe W 8, Hereford U 0

QUARTER-FINALS
Peterborough U 1, QPR 5
Brighton & HA 3, Wycombe W 1
Oxford U 0, Colchester U 1
Rushden & D 0, Brentford 0
(Brentford won 4–1 on penalties.)

SEMI-FINALS
Colchester U 3, QPR 0
Brighton & HA 2, Brentford 0

SOUTHERN FINAL
Colchester U 3, Brighton & HA 0

NORTHERN SECTION

FIRST ROUND
Blackpool 2, Boston U 0
Hartlepool U 2, Scunthorpe U 0

SECOND ROUND
Blackpool 0, Preston NE 2
Burnley 5, Shrewsbury T 1
Bury 2, Hartlepool U 4
Carlisle U 5, Chesterfield 2
Lincoln C 0, Mansfield T 1
Rotherham U 1, Rochdale 3
Stockport Co 1, Hull C 2
Wigan Ath 3, Morecambe1

QUARTER-FINALS
Burnley 3, Rochdale 1
Carlisle U 0, Wigan Ath 3
Hull C 2, Preston NE 0
Mansfield T 0, Hartlepool U 2

SEMI-FINALS
Burnley 2, Hartlepool U 2
(Hartlepool U win 5-4 on penalties.)
Hull C 4, Wigan Ath 0

NORTHERN FINAL
Hartlepool U 2, Hull C 3

PUMA YOUTH ALLIANCE CUP FINAL

Colchester U 0 Hull C 3

NON-LEAGUE TABLES 2007–08

NATIONAL LEAGUE SYSTEM – STEP 5

ARNGROVE NORTHERN LEAGUE DIVISION ONE

	P	W	D	L	F	A	GD	Pts
Durham City	42	32	6	4	106	42	64	102
Consett	42	26	8	8	105	43	62	86
Whitley Bay	42	26	7	9	99	55	44	85
Newcastle Benfield	42	22	7	13	67	51	16	73
Shildon	42	22	6	14	80	53	27	72
Dunston Federation	42	19	11	12	67	59	8	68
Tow Law Town	42	21	5	16	70	63	7	68
Morpeth Town	42	18	10	14	78	64	14	64
Billingham Synthonia	42	19	7	16	63	63	0	64
Billingham Town	42	19	6	17	80	73	7	63
Sunderland Nissan	42	17	12	13	70	64	6	63
Spennymoor Town	42	14	14	14	68	52	16	56
West Allotment Celtic	42	16	8	18	75	80	–5	56
Seaham Red Star	42	14	10	18	78	83	–5	52
Bedlington Terriers	42	12	10	20	60	80	–20	46
West Auckland Town	42	12	9	21	65	81	–16	45
Ashington	42	12	9	21	50	77	–27	45
Chester-Le-Street Town	42	12	9	21	51	86	–35	45
Northallerton Town	42	13	4	25	53	85	–32	43
Bishop Auckland	42	12	6	24	55	82	–27	42
Washington	42	12	5	25	53	97	–44	41
Jarrow Roofing Boldon CA	42	4	7	31	36	96	–60	19

SUSSEX COUNTY LEAGUE DIVISION ONE

	P	W	D	L	F	A	GD	Pts
Crowborough Athletic	38	30	5	3	99	33	66	95
Whitehawk	38	21	12	5	61	34	27	75
Arundel	38	20	10	8	90	49	41	70
East Preston	38	19	10	9	48	40	8	67
Wick	38	19	7	12	77	55	22	64
Three Bridges	38	17	9	12	74	60	14	60
Hassocks	38	15	13	10	57	46	11	58
Redhill	38	16	8	14	59	56	3	56
Pagham	38	15	8	15	60	55	5	53
Ringmer	38	14	9	15	81	73	8	51
Eastbourne United Ass	38	14	8	16	67	62	5	50
Shoreham	38	12	14	12	54	50	4	50
Hailsham Town	38	13	11	14	54	58	–4	50
St Francis Rangers	38	13	6	19	56	62	–6	45
Selsey	38	10	12	16	67	72	–5	42
Chichester City United	38	12	3	23	66	100	–34	39
Worthing United	38	9	8	21	53	84	–31	35
Oakwood	38	7	12	19	52	85	–33	33
Rye United	38	8	6	24	46	86	–40	30
Sidley United	38	8	5	25	39	100	–61	29

CHERRY RED COMBINED COUNTIES PREMIER DIVISION

	P	W	D	L	F	A	GD	Pts
Merstham	41	35	5	1	114	21	93	110
Guildford City	42	25	7	10	88	45	43	82
Camberley Town	42	24	7	11	83	54	29	79
Cove	42	22	6	14	75	58	17	72
Horley Town	42	20	9	13	66	59	7	69
North Greenford United	42	20	8	14	75	58	17	68
Colliers Wood United	42	18	10	14	86	75	11	64
Chertsey Town	42	19	5	18	81	85	–4	62
Bedfont Green	42	17	10	15	82	67	15	61
Epsom & Ewell	42	16	13	13	66	58	8	61
Chessington & Hook	42	17	9	16	76	68	8	60
Egham Town	42	15	13	14	80	75	5	58
Reading Town	41	16	7	18	67	62	5	55
Wembley	42	14	10	18	49	55	–6	52
Ash United	42	15	6	21	78	87	–9	51
Sandhurst Town	42	14	9	19	63	89	–26	51
Banstead Athletic	42	14	8	20	79	99	–20	50
Bookham	42	12	8	22	64	94	–30	44
Raynes Park Vale	42	9	14	19	56	85	–29	41
Bedfont	42	11	8	23	55	101	–46	41
Cobham	42	10	7	25	60	93	–33	37
Dorking	42	6	5	31	45	100	–55	23

Reading Town v Merstham match not played.

EAGLE BITTER UNITED COUNTIES LEAGUE PREMIER DIVISION

	P	W	D	L	F	A	GD	Pts
Stotfold	40	28	7	5	117	45	72	91
Long Buckby	40	23	12	5	99	49	50	81
Desborough Town	40	23	12	5	78	44	34	81
Blackstones	40	24	7	9	90	50	40	79
St Ives Town	40	22	8	10	78	59	19	74
Boston Town	40	21	9	10	73	53	20	72
Deeping Rangers (–3)	40	20	12	8	80	39	41	69
St Neots Town	40	16	12	12	67	48	19	60
Cogenhoe United	40	15	12	13	61	52	9	57
Wellingborough Town	40	16	8	16	56	52	4	56
Holbeach United	40	16	7	17	72	73	–1	55
Stewarts & Lloyds Corby	40	15	8	17	65	64	1	53
Northampton Spencer	40	13	12	15	60	51	9	51
Sleaford Town	40	15	6	19	73	76	–3	51
Newport Pagnell Town	40	15	6	19	60	73	–13	51
Yaxley	40	11	8	21	51	78	–27	41
Raunds Town	40	9	10	21	58	75	–17	37
Bourne Town	40	9	7	24	49	85	–36	34
Potton United	40	9	5	26	45	90	–45	32
Wootton Blue Cross	40	7	9	24	56	109	–53	30
AFC Kempston Rovers (–1)	40	3	3	34	26	149	–123	11

SPORT ITALIA HELLENIC LEAGUE PREMIER DIVISION

	P	W	D	L	F	A	GD	Pts
North Leigh	42	29	9	4	123	53	70	96
Almondsbury Town	42	29	9	4	98	30	68	96
Hungerford Town	42	28	8	6	118	47	71	92
Witney United	42	25	10	7	97	51	46	85
Shortwood United	42	23	8	11	93	50	43	77
Highworth Town	42	22	8	12	75	52	23	74
Milton United	42	19	10	13	75	67	8	67
Shrivenham	42	19	7	16	72	72	0	64
Flackwell Heath	42	19	6	17	95	86	9	63
Lydney Town	42	19	6	17	71	71	0	63
Badshot Lea	42	17	9	16	92	91	1	60
Wantage Town	42	17	7	18	80	78	2	58
Ardley United	42	15	9	18	90	76	14	54
Hook Norton	42	14	12	16	55	74	–19	54
Kidlington	42	14	11	17	86	73	13	53
Bicester Town	42	13	12	17	57	70	–13	51
Pegasus Juniors (–3)	42	12	12	18	61	78	–17	45
Carterton	42	11	9	22	59	93	–34	42
Abingdon Town	42	11	8	23	65	87	–22	41
Fairford Town	42	8	8	26	52	100	–48	32
Harrow Hill	42	2	8	32	36	117	–81	14
AFC Wallingford (–1)	42	2	2	38	30	164	–134	7

POLYMAC SERVICES MIDLAND FOOTBALL ALLIANCE

	P	W	D	L	F	A	GD	Pts
Atherstone Town	42	25	11	6	94	36	58	86
Loughborough Dynamo	42	25	10	7	90	47	43	85
Market Drayton Town	42	25	7	10	96	54	42	82
Boldmere St Michaels	42	20	11	11	75	49	26	71
Rocester	42	18	13	11	77	72	5	67
Causeway United	42	18	12	12	59	42	17	66
Stratford Town	42	17	12	13	88	63	25	63
Coalville Town	42	18	7	17	64	56	8	61
Tipton Town	42	19	4	19	58	63	–5	61
Barwell	42	16	12	14	61	60	1	60
Westfields	42	17	8	17	66	56	10	59
Biddulph Victoria	42	17	8	17	65	65	0	59
Studley	42	17	8	17	58	73	–15	59
Alvechurch	42	17	7	18	68	68	0	58
Shifnal Town	42	15	11	16	64	64	0	56
Friar Lane & Epworth	42	15	11	16	72	77	–5	56
Oadby Town	42	14	9	19	71	68	3	51
Racing Club Warwick	42	14	8	20	65	82	–17	50
Coventry Sphinx	42	14	3	25	62	97	–35	45
Stapenhill	42	8	11	23	53	97	–44	35
Oldbury United (–1)	42	7	12	23	48	71	–23	32
Cradley Town	42	6	5	31	31	125	–94	23

VODKAT NORTH WEST COUNTIES LEAGUE DIVISION ONE

	P	W	D	L	F	A	GD	Pts
Trafford	38	30	5	3	102	35	67	95
Salford City	38	26	6	6	75	35	40	84
Newcastle Town	38	24	7	7	95	45	50	79
Maine Road	38	20	8	10	75	45	30	68
Colne	38	19	11	8	69	45	24	68
Squires Gate	38	19	9	10	52	43	9	66
Glossop North End	38	20	5	13	72	46	26	65
Flixton	38	17	7	14	65	65	0	58
Congleton Town	38	17	6	15	73	60	13	57
Winsford United	38	16	8	14	60	47	13	56

	P	W	D	L	F	A	GD	Pts
Silsden	38	15	10	13	65	57	8	55
Runcorn Linnets	38	14	6	18	53	64	−11	48
Formby (−3)	38	14	3	21	52	60	−8	42
St Helens Town	38	11	8	19	64	93	−29	41
Atherton Collieries	38	10	10	18	44	67	−23	40
Ramsbottom United	38	9	10	19	41	59	−18	37
Abbey Hey	38	6	9	23	45	106	−61	27
Bacup Borough	38	5	11	22	35	69	−34	26
Atherton LR	38	5	9	24	38	86	−48	24
Nelson	38	5	8	25	42	90	−48	23

NORTHERN COUNTIES EAST PREMIER LEAGUE

	P	W	D	L	F	A	GD	Pts
Winterton Rangers	38	29	4	5	116	37	79	91
Glapwell	38	23	9	6	86	38	48	78
Pickering Town	38	22	7	9	68	42	26	73
Liversedge	38	20	8	10	73	41	32	68
Nostell Miners Welfare	38	19	7	12	81	64	17	64
Hallam	38	19	5	14	82	69	13	62
Selby Town	38	16	12	10	76	52	24	60
Parkgate	38	18	4	16	80	54	26	58
Armthorpe Welfare	38	17	7	14	73	69	4	58
Arnold Town	38	16	9	13	54	48	6	57
Eccleshill United	38	15	5	18	57	74	−17	50
Long Eaton United	38	14	7	17	48	63	−15	49
Brodsworth Welfare (−2)	38	14	5	19	61	91	−30	45
Mickleover Sports	38	11	10	17	58	78	−20	43
Shirebrook Town	38	11	9	18	38	63	−25	42
Thackley	38	11	7	20	54	75	−21	40
South Normanton Ath (−3)	38	10	10	18	42	64	−22	37
Maltby Main	38	9	9	20	52	72	−20	36
Lincoln Moorlands Railway	38	9	6	23	53	83	−30	33
Glasshoughton Welfare	38	4	6	28	26	101	−75	18

RIDGEONS EASTERN COUNTIES LEAGUE PREMIER DIVISION

	P	W	D	L	F	A	GD	Pts
Soham Town Rangers	42	31	6	5	108	34	74	99
Needham Market	42	29	7	6	114	56	58	94
Wroxham	42	27	6	9	103	44	59	87
Dereham Town	42	23	7	12	92	59	33	76
Mildenhall Town	42	22	10	10	75	47	28	76
Kirkley & Pakefield	42	21	10	11	82	54	28	73
Stanway Rovers	42	20	10	12	82	62	20	70
Felixstowe & Walton	42	20	7	15	82	74	8	67
Leiston	42	17	11	14	65	57	8	62
Haverhill Rovers	42	19	5	18	72	66	6	62
Lowestoft Town	42	18	4	20	88	91	−3	58
Wisbech Town	42	18	4	20	60	83	−23	58
CRC	42	16	9	17	77	63	14	57
King's Lynn Reserves	42	15	9	18	66	64	2	54
Norwich United	42	13	8	21	49	75	−26	47
Walsham le Willows	42	14	5	23	54	98	−44	47
Woodbridge Town	42	13	7	22	67	96	−29	46
Harwich & Parkeston	42	13	4	25	62	98	−36	43
Histon Reserves	42	12	4	26	67	84	−17	40
Swaffham Town (−1)	42	10	9	23	59	99	−40	38
Newmarket Town	42	8	6	28	62	107	−45	30
Ipswich Wanderers	42	7	4	31	44	119	−75	25

MOLTEN SPARTAN SOUTH MIDLANDS LEAGUE PREMIER DIVISION

	P	W	D	L	F	A	GD	Pts
Beaconsfield SYCOB	42	31	5	6	102	36	66	98
Chalfont St Peter	42	26	11	5	104	45	59	89
Biggleswade Town	42	28	5	9	93	51	42	89
Hertford Town	42	25	6	11	95	45	50	81
Harefield United	42	25	5	12	86	52	34	80
Langford	42	23	4	15	97	67	30	73
Leverstock Green	42	21	10	11	86	57	29	73
Brimsdown Rovers	42	21	7	14	85	51	34	70
Hanwell Town	42	21	7	14	79	65	14	70
Tring Athletic	42	19	6	17	77	76	1	63
St Margaretsbury	42	18	8	16	66	52	14	62
Broxbourne Borough V&E (−10)	42	20	9	13	81	73	8	59
Aylesbury Vale	42	16	8	18	64	73	−9	56
Kingsbury London Tigers	42	15	8	19	57	73	−16	53
Colney Heath	42	14	6	22	47	82	−35	48
Welwyn Garden City	42	14	3	25	64	95	−31	45
Cockfosters	42	11	9	22	61	92	−31	42
Biggleswade United	42	11	8	23	60	97	−37	41
Oxhey Jets	42	9	10	23	64	87	−23	37
Holmer Green	42	8	9	25	49	99	−50	33
Ruislip Manor	42	6	6	30	43	105	−62	24
London Colney	42	3	4	35	27	114	−87	13

SYDENHAMS WESSEX LEAGUE PREMIER DIVISION

	P	W	D	L	F	A	GD	Pts
AFC Totton	44	33	7	4	120	39	81	106
VT FC	44	32	6	6	106	35	71	102
Wimborne Town	44	30	6	8	125	33	92	96
Poole Town	44	29	9	6	120	35	85	96
Bournemouth	44	27	12	5	92	40	52	93
Brockenhurst	44	23	11	10	87	55	32	80
Moneyfields	44	24	7	13	82	45	37	79
Fareham Town	44	22	9	13	87	65	22	75
Cowes Sports	44	20	13	11	91	59	32	73
Hamworthy United	44	19	8	17	55	54	1	65
Horndean	44	15	13	16	76	73	3	58
Hayling United	44	15	9	20	66	101	−35	54
Bemerton Heath H	44	15	8	21	74	101	−27	53
Alton Town	44	15	7	22	66	89	−23	52
Brading Town	44	13	12	19	67	85	−18	51
Christchurch	44	15	5	24	67	80	−13	50
Hamble ASSC	44	11	14	19	47	72	−25	47
Romsey Town	44	12	7	25	68	98	−30	43
New Milton Town	44	11	8	25	58	88	−30	41
Lymington Town (−1)	44	11	7	26	63	103	−40	39
Alresford Town	44	9	8	27	48	88	−40	35
Ringwood Town	44	5	9	30	45	124	−79	24
Downton	44	1	3	40	29	177	−148	6

TOOLSTATION WESTERN LEAGUE PREMIER DIVISION

	P	W	D	L	F	A	GD	Pts
Truro City	40	33	4	3	132	39	93	103
Dawlish Town	40	25	11	4	103	45	58	86
Willand Rovers	40	22	10	8	78	48	30	76
Frome Town	40	21	11	8	86	41	45	74
Corsham Town	40	20	11	9	71	63	8	71
Bideford	40	17	17	6	85	46	39	68
Bitton	40	19	7	14	71	46	25	64
Ilfracombe Town	40	19	7	14	76	69	7	64
Welton Rovers	40	17	10	13	44	35	9	61
Devizes Town	40	16	12	12	68	70	−2	60
Melksham Town	40	13	12	15	51	57	−6	51
Barnstaple Town	40	14	8	18	71	67	4	50
Brislington	40	12	13	15	55	61	−6	49
Calne Town	40	15	4	21	57	70	−13	49
Hallen	40	13	10	17	64	81	−17	49
Bristol Manor Farm	40	10	9	21	64	84	−20	39
Radstock Town	40	10	8	22	60	83	−23	38
Street	40	8	9	23	36	80	−44	33
Bishop Sutton	40	7	8	25	41	99	−58	29
Chard Town	40	8	4	28	53	104	−51	28
Odd Down	40	5	7	28	30	108	−78	22

ESSEX SENIOR LEAGUE

	P	W	D	L	F	A	GD	Pts
Concord Rangers	32	25	2	5	94	26	68	77
Enfield	32	24	5	3	88	29	59	77
Barkingside	32	24	2	6	79	25	54	74
Eton Manor	32	20	5	7	81	44	37	65
Romford	32	19	7	6	75	41	34	64
Southend Manor	32	18	4	10	50	31	19	58
Bowers & Pitsea	32	17	5	10	57	41	16	56
Burnham Ramblers	32	15	7	10	69	45	24	52
Barking	32	14	6	12	54	43	11	48
Stansted	32	10	8	14	50	50	0	38
Clapton	32	8	9	15	38	57	−19	33
Sawbridgeworth Town	32	8	4	20	34	69	−35	28
Mauritius Sports & Pennant	32	7	5	20	41	70	−29	26
Hullbridge Sports	32	4	12	16	35	66	−31	24
Beaumont Athletic	32	6	3	23	36	113	−77	21
Basildon United	32	3	8	21	26	82	−56	17
London APSA	32	2	4	26	24	99	−75	10

KENT LEAGUE PREMIER DIVISION

	P	W	D	L	F	A	GD	Pts
Thamesmead Town	32	24	6	2	87	36	51	78
VCD Athletic	32	22	5	5	73	33	40	71
Beckenham Town	32	21	7	4	80	41	39	70
Hythe Town	32	20	5	7	85	35	50	65
Erith Town	32	13	12	7	61	35	26	51
Herne Bay	32	14	8	10	60	46	14	50
Erith & Belvedere	32	13	10	9	68	49	19	49
Greenwich Borough	32	12	10	10	44	36	8	46
Deal Town	32	12	5	15	62	66	−4	41
Tunbridge Wells	32	12	5	15	53	60	−7	41
Sevenoaks Town	32	9	6	17	57	64	−7	33
Croydon	32	9	5	18	38	61	−23	32
Faversham Town	32	9	4	19	43	79	−36	31
Slade Green	32	8	6	18	38	75	−37	30
Holmesdale	32	6	10	16	40	59	−19	28
Lordswood	32	7	6	19	39	69	−30	27
Sporting Bengal United	32	4	4	24	31	115	−84	16

NATIONAL LEAGUE SYSTEM – STEP 6

ARNGROVE NORTHERN LEAGUE DIVISION TWO

	P	W	D	L	F	A	GD	Pts
Penrith Town	38	24	7	7	78	40	38	79
South Shields	38	24	5	9	98	52	46	77
Ryton	38	24	3	11	83	41	42	75
Sunderland Ryhope CA	38	22	4	12	83	54	29	70
Horden CW	38	21	5	12	71	57	14	68
Whickham	38	20	6	12	87	73	14	66
Thornaby	38	18	7	13	78	64	14	61
Marske United	38	17	8	13	69	43	26	59
Stokesley SC	38	17	5	16	68	71	–3	56
Norton & Stockton Ancients	38	17	3	18	66	46	20	54
Birtley Town	38	16	6	16	57	66	–9	54
Guisborough Town	38	16	5	17	73	64	9	53
Esh Winning	38	15	7	16	73	58	15	52
Crook Town	38	14	9	15	60	74	–14	51
Hebburn Town	38	14	7	17	55	72	–17	49
Prudhoe Town	38	13	9	16	61	68	–7	48
North Shields	38	11	4	23	50	87	–37	37
Darlington RA	38	10	6	22	51	78	–27	36
Team Northumbria (–3)	38	6	8	24	43	90	–47	23
Brandon United	38	2	4	32	26	132	–106	10

SUSSEX COUNTY LEAGUE DIVISION TWO

	P	W	D	L	F	A	GD	Pts
East Grinstead Town	34	26	6	2	89	41	48	84
Lingfield	34	20	6	8	73	40	33	66
Rustington	34	19	8	7	70	29	41	65
Peacehaven & Telscombe	34	20	5	9	93	59	34	65
Mile Oak	34	17	8	9	79	56	23	59
Crawley Down	34	19	1	14	59	60	–1	58
Westfield	34	18	3	13	71	64	7	57
Littlehampton Town	34	16	5	13	66	54	12	53
Wealden	34	14	7	13	69	56	13	49
Midhurst & Easebourne	34	15	4	15	52	67	–15	49
Steyning Town	34	12	6	16	51	53	–2	42
Lancing	34	10	8	16	64	61	3	38
Sidlesham	34	11	5	18	61	65	–4	38
Southwick	34	11	5	18	44	62	–18	38
Seaford Town	34	12	1	21	61	79	–18	37
Storrington	34	9	7	18	48	67	–19	34
Broadbridge Heath	34	8	5	21	45	75	–30	29
Pease Pottage Village	34	3	2	29	39	146	–107	11

CHERRY RED COMBINED COUNTIES LEAGUE DIVISION ONE

	P	W	D	L	F	A	GD	Pts
Staines Lammas	37	28	3	6	111	28	83	87
Hanworth Villa	38	25	9	4	124	38	86	84
Hartley Wintney	38	24	8	6	87	38	49	80
Westfield	38	24	6	8	86	40	46	78
Farnham Town	38	19	10	9	88	57	31	67
Frimley Green	38	19	6	13	71	53	18	63
Knaphill	37	18	7	12	77	72	5	61
Worcester Park	37	17	5	15	70	57	13	56
CB Hounslow United	37	17	5	15	76	65	11	56
Warlingham	35	14	10	11	80	64	16	52
Chobham	36	15	5	16	70	76	–6	50
South Park	37	12	9	16	79	75	4	45
Feltham	38	12	7	19	57	77	–20	43
Neasden Foundation	26	14	0	12	49	45	4	42
Crescent Rovers	37	12	4	21	50	84	–34	40
Sheerwater	37	10	6	21	63	113	–50	36
Tongham	37	9	5	23	58	93	–35	32
Farleigh Rovers	37	8	7	22	38	74	–36	31
Coulsdon United	37	8	4	25	51	99	–48	28
Merrow	35	1	2	32	24	161	–137	5

Neasden Foundation were expelled from the League. (None of their remaining fixtures were played.)

EAGLE BITTER UNITED COUNTIES LEAGUE DIVISION ONE

	P	W	D	L	F	A	GD	Pts
Daventry Town	30	26	3	1	106	26	80	81
Peterborough Northern Star	30	18	7	5	68	26	42	61
Rothwell Corinthians	30	15	7	8	60	42	18	52
Huntingdon Town	30	16	4	10	51	40	11	52
Daventry United	30	16	4	10	67	59	8	52
Northampton ON Cheneks	30	15	3	12	56	56	0	48
Bugbrooke St Michaels	30	13	4	13	54	47	7	43
Buckingham Town	30	11	9	10	60	60	0	42
Whitworths	30	11	8	11	63	60	3	41
Olney Town	30	11	7	12	44	48	–4	40
Thrapston Town	30	11	3	16	52	59	–7	36
Northampton Sileby Rangers	30	9	6	15	47	64	–17	33
Eynesbury Rovers	30	8	8	14	46	67	–21	32
Rushden & Higham U	30	7	6	17	32	51	–19	27
Burton Park Wanderers	30	5	4	21	29	76	–47	19
Irchester United	30	3	7	20	37	91	–54	16

SPORT ITALIA HELLENIC LEAGUE DIVISION ONE EAST

	P	W	D	L	F	A	GD	Pts
Chalfont Wasps	32	24	5	3	102	30	72	77
Marlow United	32	21	7	4	65	29	36	70
Englefield Green Rovers	32	19	4	9	61	39	22	61
Ascot United	32	18	4	10	73	46	27	58
Kintbury Rangers	32	18	3	11	71	48	23	57
Henley Town	32	17	6	9	57	39	18	57
Holyport	32	17	4	11	80	59	21	55
Bisley	32	17	4	11	75	55	20	55
Binfield (–1)	32	13	10	9	60	37	23	48
Thame United	32	14	5	13	57	41	16	47
Penn & Tylers Green	32	12	7	13	40	40	0	43
Wokingham & Emmbrook	32	12	4	16	43	58	–15	40
Rayners Lane	32	9	8	15	45	69	–24	35
Finchampstead	32	6	7	19	36	67	–31	25
Chinnor	32	6	4	22	29	69	–40	22
Prestwood	32	3	7	22	33	99	–66	16
Eton Wick	32	0	3	29	22	124	–102	3

SPORT ITALIA HELLENIC LEAGUE DIVISION ONE WEST

	P	W	D	L	F	A	GD	Pts
Winterbourne United	34	22	5	7	90	36	54	71
Old Woodstock Town	34	21	4	9	77	36	41	67
Letcombe	34	20	5	9	83	41	42	65
Trowbridge Town	34	20	5	9	76	46	30	65
Cheltenham Saracens	34	18	9	7	89	33	56	63
Easington Sports	34	17	7	10	74	40	34	58
Pewsey Vale	34	17	7	10	51	36	15	58
Tytherington Rocks	34	15	11	8	70	38	32	56
Oxford City Nomads	34	16	6	12	66	49	17	54
Cricklade Town	34	16	6	12	63	56	7	54
Purton	34	14	2	18	55	78	–23	44
Clanfield	34	12	5	17	66	79	–13	41
Launton Sports	34	12	4	18	49	79	–30	40
Headington Amateurs	34	10	8	16	50	63	–13	38
Wootton Bassett Town	34	11	3	20	43	66	–23	36
Malmesbury Victoria	34	9	9	16	35	62	–27	36
Banbury United Reserves	34	4	3	27	32	119	–87	15
Cirencester United	34	2	1	31	16	128	–112	7

MIDLAND COMBINATION PREMIER DIVISION

	P	W	D	L	F	A	GD	Pts
Coleshill Town	42	30	5	7	124	47	77	95
Highgate United	42	29	8	5	95	49	46	95
Southam United	42	22	9	11	83	63	20	75
Loughborough University	42	21	10	11	78	55	23	73
Castle Vale (–1)	42	20	11	11	85	62	23	70
Pilkington XXX	42	19	11	12	83	75	8	68
Heather St John	42	19	10	13	80	64	16	67
Pershore Town (–3)	42	21	7	14	77	61	16	67
Brocton	42	18	12	12	77	65	12	66
Heath Hayes	42	18	10	14	99	80	19	64
Walsall Wood	42	17	11	14	62	53	9	62
Cadbury Athletic	42	16	11	15	80	72	8	59
Nuneaton Griff	42	16	11	15	69	66	3	59
Bartley Green	42	14	6	22	70	83	–13	48
Massey Ferguson	42	14	6	22	65	94	–29	48
Barnt Green Spartak	42	13	7	22	67	75	–8	46
Bolehall Swifts	42	11	11	20	57	77	–20	44
Continental Star	42	11	9	22	79	99	–20	42
Feckenham	42	11	9	22	52	96	–44	42
Meir KA (–3)	42	11	9	22	51	73	–22	39
Coventry Copsewood	42	9	11	22	57	84	–27	38
Brereton Social	42	2	6	34	25	122	–97	12

VODKAT NORTH WEST COUNTIES LEAGUE DIVISION TWO

	P	W	D	L	F	A	GD	Pts
New Mills	34	28	3	3	107	23	84	87
Kirkham & Wesham	34	24	5	5	88	31	57	77
Ashton Athletic	34	20	7	7	68	35	33	67
Oldham Town	34	19	7	8	79	44	35	64
Chadderton	34	19	4	11	55	52	3	61
Bootle	34	18	6	10	86	53	33	60
Leek CSOB	34	16	7	11	57	51	6	55
Norton United	34	13	11	10	47	52	–5	50
Blackpool Mechanics	34	11	12	11	47	45	2	45
Stone Dominoes	34	12	8	14	60	59	1	44
Darwen	34	13	5	16	55	65	–10	44
Padiham	34	11	8	15	50	48	2	41
Ashton Town	34	12	4	18	53	80	–27	40
Cheadle Town (–3)	34	10	6	18	44	80	–36	33
Eccleshall	34	8	6	20	41	69	–28	30
Holker Old Boys	34	8	2	24	41	82	–41	26
Castleton Gabriels	34	6	6	22	46	97	–51	24
Daisy Hill	34	2	5	27	28	86	–58	11

NORTHERN COUNTIES EAST LEAGUE DIVISION ONE

	P	W	D	L	F	A	GD	Pts
Dinnington Town	32	24	6	2	88	40	48	78
Hall Road Rangers	32	22	1	9	65	42	23	67
Bottesford Town	32	19	5	8	62	40	22	62
Rainworth Miners Welfare	32	16	9	7	60	38	22	57
Scarborough Athletic (–6)	32	18	7	7	80	45	35	55
Gedling Town	32	16	7	9	70	45	25	55
Leeds Met Carnegie	32	17	4	11	67	45	22	55
Staveley Miners Welfare	32	14	4	14	49	53	–4	46
Barton Town Old Boys (–3)	32	13	9	10	82	62	20	45
Teversal	32	10	12	10	58	66	–8	42
AFC Emley	32	10	8	14	59	66	–7	38
Tadcaster Albion	32	9	7	16	48	66	–18	34
Borrowash Victoria	32	8	6	18	49	76	–27	30
Yorkshire Amateur	32	7	8	17	37	67	–30	29
Worsbrough Bridge Ath	32	7	6	19	40	67	–27	27
Rossington Main	32	7	3	22	47	87	–40	24
Pontefract Collieries	32	1	6	25	29	85	–56	9

RIDGEONS EASTERN COUNTIES LEAGUE DIVISION ONE

	P	W	D	L	F	A	GD	Pts
Tiptree United	36	28	2	6	88	39	49	86
Ely City	36	22	8	6	81	42	39	74
Whitton United	36	18	10	8	94	42	52	64
Diss Town	36	19	6	11	86	47	39	63
Hadleigh United	36	18	9	9	71	42	29	63
Halstead Town (–1)	36	18	10	8	72	45	27	63
Saffron Walden Town	36	17	10	9	49	36	13	61
Gorleston	36	17	9	10	87	62	25	60
Debenham LC (–3)	36	17	10	9	66	38	28	58
FC Clacton	36	16	10	10	73	59	14	58
Great Yarmouth Town	36	12	8	16	58	71	–13	44
Downham Town	36	11	10	15	42	67	–25	43
Thetford Town	36	9	12	15	59	71	–12	39
Stowmarket Town	36	10	9	17	61	76	–15	39
March Town United	36	6	14	16	54	82	–28	32
Godmanchester Rovers	36	8	6	22	36	76	–40	30
Fakenham Town	36	6	6	24	40	112	–72	24
Cornard United	36	4	9	23	36	94	–58	21
Long Melford	36	5	4	27	35	87	–52	19

MOLTEN SPARTAN SOUTH MIDLANDS LEAGUE DIVISION ONE

	P	W	D	L	F	A	GD	Pts
Kentish Town	36	23	6	7	92	52	40	75
Haringey Borough	36	22	7	7	87	55	32	73
Hoddesdon Town	36	20	9	7	77	49	28	69
Stony Stratford Town	36	20	7	9	89	58	31	67
Royston Town	36	19	8	9	92	44	48	65
New Bradwell St Peter	36	17	11	8	63	43	20	62
Ampthill Town	36	18	6	12	90	64	26	60
Sport London E Benfica	36	16	8	12	67	50	17	56
Bedford	36	16	2	18	69	82	–13	50
Cheshunt Reserves	36	13	10	13	59	55	4	49
Amersham Town	36	14	5	17	66	72	–6	47
Brache Sparta	36	12	6	18	55	81	–26	42
Buckingham Athletic	36	10	11	15	45	56	–11	41
Bedford Town Reserves	36	10	8	18	49	74	–25	38
Arlesey Athletic	36	10	7	19	52	79	–27	37
Harpenden Town	36	8	10	18	44	66	–22	34
Sun Postal Sports	36	9	7	20	49	81	–32	34
Winslow United	36	8	7	21	64	107	–43	31
Cranfield United	36	8	3	25	58	99	–41	27

SYDENHAMS WESSEX LEAGUE DIVISION ONE

	P	W	D	L	F	A	GD	Pts
Tadley Calleva	40	33	3	4	134	45	89	102
Laverstock & Ford	40	29	3	8	124	59	65	90
Farnborough North End	40	26	9	5	101	30	71	87
Verwood Town	40	23	6	11	94	63	31	75
Totton & Eling	40	22	8	10	80	50	30	74
Fawley	40	22	5	13	94	44	50	71
Warminster Town	40	20	11	9	89	48	41	71
Petersfield Town	40	21	7	12	90	53	37	70
United Services Portsmouth	40	21	6	13	98	65	33	69
Blackfield & Langley	40	18	10	12	70	57	13	64
Amesbury Town	40	16	5	19	100	86	14	53
Shaftesbury	40	14	9	17	73	63	10	51
Stockbridge	40	11	12	17	47	61	–14	45
AFC Portchester	40	11	9	20	59	86	–27	42
Fleet Spurs	40	12	6	22	64	95	–31	42
Liss Athletic	40	8	10	22	58	95	–37	34
Whitchurch United	40	8	10	22	51	97	–46	34
East Cowes Vics	40	8	10	22	50	103	–53	34
Andover New Street	40	9	5	26	54	117	–63	32
Hythe & Dibden	40	6	9	25	42	125	–83	27
AFC Aldermaston	40	4	3	33	31	161	–130	15

TOOLSTATION WESTERN LEAGUE DIVISION ONE

	P	W	D	L	F	A	GD	Pts
Wellington	40	27	8	5	124	45	79	89
Sherborne Town	40	26	7	7	111	41	70	85
Larkhall Athletic	40	26	7	7	87	43	44	85
Shrewton United	40	23	5	12	82	71	11	74
Cadbury Heath	40	22	7	11	82	59	23	73
Hengrove Athletic	40	20	9	11	83	61	22	69
Westbury United	40	20	8	12	92	62	30	68
Longwell Green Sports	40	19	11	10	71	47	24	68
Portishead	40	17	12	11	81	59	22	63
Roman Glass St George	40	15	10	15	70	55	15	55
Shepton Mallet	40	16	5	19	71	79	–8	53
Oldland Abbotonians	40	13	11	16	80	77	3	50
Bradford Town	40	14	8	18	62	84	–22	50
Keynsham Town	40	14	7	19	51	67	–16	49
Clevedon United	40	12	8	20	50	75	–25	44
Elmore	40	11	7	22	73	106	–33	40
Minehead	40	10	10	20	55	96	–41	40
Bridport	40	10	6	24	64	77	–13	36
Backwell United	40	7	10	23	48	101	–53	31
Almondsbury	40	6	12	22	44	82	–38	30
Weston St Johns	40	5	6	29	54	148	–94	21

SPORT ITALIA WEST MIDLANDS LEAGUE PREMIER DIVISION

	P	W	D	L	F	A	GD	Pts
Bridgnorth Town	40	31	4	5	97	33	64	97
Bewdley Town	40	23	6	11	83	57	26	75
Shawbury United	40	21	9	10	86	59	27	72
Wednesfield	40	20	9	11	68	51	17	69
Dudley Town	40	20	9	11	56	48	8	69
AFC Wulfrunians	40	19	10	11	83	43	40	67
Ellesmere Rangers	40	20	7	13	71	52	19	67
Dudley Sports (–3)	40	19	12	9	64	46	18	66
Darlaston Town	40	17	12	11	71	57	14	63
Lye Town	40	18	8	14	80	58	22	62
Tividale	40	13	12	15	72	65	7	51
Pelsall Villa	40	14	9	17	67	71	–4	51
Wellington	40	13	11	16	63	79	–16	50
Ludlow Town	40	13	11	16	50	73	–23	50
Goodrich	40	13	6	21	72	83	–11	45
Gornal Athletic	40	10	12	18	46	63	–17	42
Brierley Hill & Withymoor	40	12	5	23	62	89	–27	41
Wolverhampton Casuals (–1)	40	8	15	17	58	80	–22	38
Ledbury Town	40	10	3	27	56	100	–44	33
Bromyard Town	40	8	7	25	46	87	–41	31
Bustleholme	40	7	5	28	55	112	–57	26

SCOTTISH

SCOT-ADS HIGHLAND FOOTBALL LEAGUE

	P	W	D	L	F	A	GD	Pts
Cove Rangers	28	19	7	2	85	33	52	64
Keith	28	18	7	3	80	27	53	61
Deveronvale	28	17	7	4	85	33	52	58
Buckie Thistle	28	17	6	5	54	24	30	57
Fraserburgh	28	16	3	9	65	43	22	51
Inverurie Loco Works	28	15	4	9	67	39	28	49
Huntly	28	13	6	9	60	44	16	45
Forres Mechanics	28	13	5	10	67	46	21	44
Nairn County	28	12	4	12	44	49	–5	40
Clachnacuddin	28	10	7	11	49	50	–1	37
Wick Academy	28	9	5	14	49	60	–11	32
Rothes	28	5	4	19	49	75	–26	19
Lossiemouth	28	4	5	19	22	66	–44	17
Brora Rangers	28	4	4	20	29	74	–45	16
Fort William	28	1	0	27	16	158	–142	3

TYREMAN EAST OF SCOTLAND LEAGUE PREMIER DIVISION

	P	W	D	L	F	A	GD	Pts
Whitehill Welfare	22	16	2	4	56	21	35	50
Edinburgh University	22	15	4	3	41	14	27	49
Spartans	22	14	5	3	57	23	34	47
Edinburgh City	22	12	4	6	50	34	16	40
Preston Athletic	22	11	7	4	41	28	13	40
Dalbeattie Star	22	11	2	9	45	37	8	35
Annan Athletic	22	7	7	8	40	33	7	28
Lothian Thistle	22	7	5	10	30	44	–14	26
Easthouses Lily	22	6	2	14	31	50	–19	20
Coldstream	22	5	4	13	26	62	–36	19
Selkirk	22	3	3	16	22	44	–22	12
Craigroyston	22	2	1	19	21	70	–49	7

AMATEUR FOOTBALL ALLIANCE 2007–08

AFA SENIOR CUP

**aet*
†won after extra time and penalties

ROUND ONE
Bank of England 1, Hale End Athletic 2
Old Belgravians 1, Alexandra Park† 1
Old Chigwellians 0, Old Aloysians 3
Old Challoners FC 9, Wandsworth Borough 1
Broomfield 5, Southgate County 2
Old Finchleians 3, Old Manorians 0
Old Buckwellians 0, Old Westminster Citizens 5
South Bank Cuaco 3, HSBC 6
†Old Cholmeleians 3, Mill Hill County Old Boys 3
Albanian 4, William Fitt 3
Latymer Old Boys w.d. Parkfield w.o.
†Economicals 3, Old Brentwoods 3
Old Latymerians 7, Old Malvernian 0
Old Parmiterians 2, Old Ignatians 3
Old Salvatorians 1, Old Actonians Association* 2
Old Guildfordians 0, Old Tiffinians 4
Old Stationers 0, Alleyn Old Boys 11
†Leyton County Old Boys 3, Weirside Rangers 3
Old Esthameians 3, Old Foresters 0

ROUND TWO
Alleyn Old Boys 2, Old Ignatians 0
Albanian 2, Hale End Athletic 4
Leyton County Old Boys 3, Old Isleworthians 1
Broomfield 3, Bromleians Sports 0
Sinjuns Grammarians 1, Parkfield 0
Alexandra Park 4, Wood Green Old Boys 3
Old Latymerians 0, Winchmore Hill 2
Old Bradfieldians 1, Wake Green Amateur 2
Polytechnic 4, Old Finchleians 0
Merton 0, Old Wilsonians 1
Old Owens 6, Old Lyonian 1
Old Hamptonians 2, Southgate Olympic 0
Economicals 5, Old Edmontonians 2
Bealonians 6, Old Westminster Citizens 1
Old Actonians Association 1, Nottsborough 2
Norsemen 3, HSBC 0
Kew Association w.o. Old Cholmeleians w.d.
Ibis 2, Enfield Old Grammarians 1
Honourable Artillery Company 2, Fulham Compton Old Boys 0
East Barnet Old Grammarians 4, Old Challoners FC 3
Old Esthameians 4, Crouch End Vampires 1
Carshalton 0, UCL Academicals 3
BB Eagles 6, Lancing Old Boys 3
*Old Meadonians 2, Civil Service 1
Lloyds TSB Bank 2, Old Tiffinians 4
†Old Parkonians 2, Old Danes 2
Mill Hill Village 2, Glyn Old Boys 3
Old Salesians 0, Old Aloysians 3
West Wickham 4, Old Salopians 0
Old Carthusian 4, Old Wokingians 3
Old Vaughanians 0, Old Suttonians 5
Brent 0, Old Minchendenians 1

ROUND THREE
Old Suttonians 4, Glyn Old Boys 1
Alexandra Park 4, Kew Association 2
UCL Academicals 2, Polytechnic 0
Old Owens 3, Bealonians 1
Old Hamptonians 2, Old Parkonians 3
Alleyn Old Boys 5, Ibis 0
Old Meadonians 3, Hale End Athletic 0
Economicals 2, Broomfield 3
Old Minchendenians 4, Sinjuns Grammarians 0
Old Esthameians 2, Honourable Artillery Company 0
Winchmore Hill 1, Old Carthusian 2
Old Wilsonians 3, East Barnet Old Grammarians 1
BB Eagles 3, Wake Green Amateur 5
Old Aloysians 3, Old Tiffinians 0
West Wickham 3, Leyton County Old Boys 0
Nottsborough 2, Norsemen 0

ROUND FOUR
Old Parkonians 1, UCL Academicals 3
Old Meadonians 2, Old Suttonians 1
Old Wilsonians 1, Alexandra Park 2
†Old Carthusian 2, Wake Green Amateur 2
Old Esthameians 1, Old Aloysians 3
West Wickham 2, Nottsborough 3
Alleyn Old Boys 1, Old Owens 0
Old Minchendenians 5, Broomfield 2

QUARTER-FINALS
Nottsborough 5, Alexandra Park 0
Old Aloysians 2, Old Minchendenians 0
Old Meadonians 3, UCL Academicals 2
Alleyn Old Boys 4, Old Carthusian 1

SEMI-FINALS
Old Aloysians 1, Nottsborough 3
Alleyn Old Boys 1, Old Meadonians 2

FINAL
†Old Meadonians 2, Nottsborough 2

SOUTHERN AMATEUR LEAGUE

SENIOR SECTION

DIVISION 1	P	W	D	L	F	A	Pts
West Wickham	20	13	6	1	33	16	45
Nottsborough	20	9	6	5	41	33	33
Old Owens*	20	9	5	6	36	27	29
Old Salesians	20	7	8	5	33	27	29
Winchmore Hill	20	6	8	6	24	19	26
Polytechnic	20	7	4	9	35	41	25
Alleyn Old Boys	20	5	8	7	31	31	23
Old Wilsonians	20	6	5	9	33	38	23
Old Actonians Association	20	5	8	7	27	32	23
Broomfield	20	6	5	9	38	51	23
Civil Service	20	3	5	12	20	36	14

**Penalty points deducted*

DIVISION 2	P	W	D	L	F	A	Pts
Old Esthameians	20	14	3	3	50	20	45
Weirside Rangers	20	13	1	6	47	22	40
Merton	20	11	3	6	49	28	36
Norsemen	20	11	3	6	43	23	36
Carshalton	20	10	3	7	41	36	33
East Barnet Old Gramm.	20	9	2	9	43	36	29
HSBC	20	7	5	8	33	37	26
Kew Association	20	6	5	9	34	42	23
BB Eagles	20	7	2	11	28	46	23
Old Lyonians	20	4	4	12	27	58	16
South Bank Cuaco*	20	1	3	16	17	64	1

**Penalty points deducted*

DIVISION 3	P	W	D	L	F	A	Pts
Old Parkonians	20	15	4	1	78	28	49
Crouch End Vampires	20	12	5	3	48	22	41
Bank of England	20	11	4	5	36	26	37
Old Finchleians*	20	11	4	5	60	29	36
Lloyds TSB Bank	20	11	1	8	37	41	34
Ibis	20	8	6	6	46	37	30
Old Latymerians*	20	7	4	9	35	31	24
Old Westminster Citizens	20	7	3	10	35	43	24
Alexandra Park	20	5	2	13	40	54	17
Old Stationers	20	3	2	15	21	72	11
Southgate Olympic	20	2	1	17	15	68	7

**Penalty points deducted*

INTERMEDIATE SECTION
Div 1 – 11 teams – Won by Carshalton Res
Div 2 – 11 teams – Won by Old Salesians Res
Div 3 – 11 teams – Won by Old Parkonians Res

JUNIOR SECTION
Div 1 – 11 teams – Won by Alleyn Old Boys 3rd
Div 2 – 11 teams – Won by Carshalton 3rd
Div 1 – 11 teams – Won by Old Wilsonians 3rd

MINOR SECTION
Div 1 – 11 teams – Won by Winchmore Hill 4th
Div 2 North – 12 teams – Won by Norsemen 4th
Div 2 South – 10 teams – Won by Carshalton 4th
Div 3 North – 11 teams – Won by Norsemen 6th
Div 3 South – 10 teams – Won by Polytechnic 5th
Div 4 North – 11 teams – Won by Winchmore Hill 8th
Div 4 South – 10 teams – Won by Alleyn Old Boys 4th

Div 5 North – 11 teams – Won by Old Esthameians 5th
Div 5 South – 10 teams – Won by Kew Association 6th
Div 6 South – 10 teams – Won by Kew Association 7th
Div 7 South – 9 teams – Won by Polytechnic 9th
Div 8 South – 9 teams – Won by Kew Association 9th

AMATEUR FOOTBALL COMBINATION

PREMIER DIVISION	*P*	*W*	*D*	*L*	*F*	*A*	*Pts*
Old Aloysians	18	12	4	2	50	20	40
Albanian	18	11	5	2	41	22	38
Old Parmiterians	18	10	3	5	33	27	33
Bealonians	18	7	5	6	31	26	26
Old Meadonians	18	7	4	7	41	35	25
UCL Academicals	18	6	5	7	31	39	23
Honorable Artillery Co.	18	4	8	6	34	35	20
Old Hamptonians	18	4	6	8	29	37	18
Hale End Athletic	18	4	4	10	22	44	16
Enfield Old Grammarians	18	2	2	14	18	45	8

SENIOR DIVISION 1	*P*	*W*	*D*	*L*	*F*	*A*	*Pts*
Parkfield	20	12	5	3	56	31	41
Old Meadonians Res	20	13	2	5	56	36	41
Old Salvatorians	20	9	5	6	37	26	32
Old Challoners	20	9	4	7	41	36	31
Old Suttonians	20	9	3	8	37	33	30
Old Ignatians	20	8	4	8	38	38	28
Glyn Old Boys	20	8	4	8	36	39	28
Clapham Old Xaverians	20	7	4	9	38	48	25
Sinjuns Grammarians	20	7	3	10	38	56	24
Southgate County	20	5	3	12	40	49	18
Old Tiffinians	20	3	3	14	27	52	12

SENIOR DIVISION 2	*P*	*W*	*D*	*L*	*F*	*A*	*Pts*
Old Minchendenians	20	17	3	0	84	24	54
Old Belgravians	20	14	3	3	70	27	45
Hon Artillery Co Res	20	13	0	7	62	35	39
Old Danes	20	12	1	7	67	45	37
Wood Green Old Boys	20	10	4	6	65	51	34
Shene Old Grammarians	20	7	3	10	50	56	24
Old Dorkinians	20	7	2	11	45	43	23
Old Vaughanians	20	6	2	12	43	72	20
Old Pauline	20	4	7	9	47	52	19
Kings Old Boys	20	5	2	13	32	68	17
Mill Hill Village	20	1	1	18	11	103	4

SENIOR DIVISION 3 NORTH

	P	*W*	*D*	*L*	*F*	*A*	*Pts*
UCL Academicals Res	20	11	5	4	49	23	38
Old Edmontonians	20	10	7	3	46	28	37
Old Kolsassians	20	10	5	5	55	36	35
Old Aloysians Res	20	10	3	7	50	45	33
Old Salvatorians Res	20	10	2	8	50	36	32
Enfield Old Grammarians Res	20	9	5	6	42	41	32
Latymer Old Boys	20	7	4	9	44	57	25
Old Manorians	20	6	6	8	36	34	24
Albanian Res	20	6	5	9	32	45	23
Old Isleworthians	20	4	6	10	38	58	18
Brent	20	2	2	16	26	65	8

SENIOR DIVISION 3 SOUTH

	P	*W*	*D*	*L*	*F*	*A*	*Pts*
Centymca	20	16	2	2	90	30	50
Old Hamptonians Res	20	14	2	4	54	26	44
Economicals	20	11	5	4	49	29	38
Fulham Compton Old Boys	20	9	4	7	40	34	31
Hampstead Heathens	20	7	6	7	31	38	27
Old Guildfordians	20	7	6	7	33	41	27
Fitzwilliam Old Boys	20	7	6	7	28	40	27
Old Meadonians 3rd	20	7	2	11	38	48	23
John Fisher Old Boys	20	5	1	14	30	65	16
Wandsworth Borough	20	4	2	14	32	59	14
Kings Old Boys Res	20	2	6	12	30	45	12

INTERMEDIATE DIVISION NORTH

	P	*W*	*D*	*L*	*F*	*A*	*Pts*
Egbertian	20	18	0	2	75	18	54
Parkfield Res	20	17	2	1	81	24	53
William Fitt	20	14	2	4	70	30	44
Leyton County Old Boys	20	11	0	9	56	27	33
Bealonians Res	20	10	3	7	53	39	33
Old Aloysians 3rd	20	7	5	8	47	42	26
Hale End Athletic Res	20	5	5	10	24	39	20
Old Buckwellians	20	5	2	13	45	59	17
Old Woodhouseians	20	4	4	12	34	67	16
Southgate County Res	20	4	4	12	25	63	16
Old Parmiterians Res*	20	1	1	18	19	121	1

**Points deducted – breach of rules.*

INTERMEDIATE DIVISION SOUTH

	P	*W*	*D*	*L*	*F*	*A*	*Pts*
Old Thorntonians	22	14	5	3	65	33	47
Old Bromleians	22	15	2	5	71	40	47
Credit Suisse	22	14	3	5	79	43	45
National Westminster Bank	22	14	3	5	56	45	
Royal Bank of Scotland	22	12	2	8	52	53	38
Old Tenisonians	22	7	9	6	64	42	30
Chislehurst Sports	22	6	7	9	50	69	25
Mickleham Old Boxhillians	22	7	3	12	40	57	24
Old Josephians	22	6	3	13	65	71	21
Pegasus	22	5	6	11	41	63	21
Old Sedcopians	22	5	1	16	43	76	16
Witan	22	3	4	15	41	71	13

INTERMEDIATE DIVISION WEST

	P	*W*	*D*	*L*	*F*	*A*	*Pts*
Old Hamptonians III	18	14	1	3	58	29	43
Old Uffingtonians	18	10	3	5	71	47	33
Old Magdalenians	18	8	4	6	48	37	28
London Welsh	18	9	1	8	53	47	28
Old Kingsburians	18	9	1	8	45	45	28
Chertsey Old Salesians	18	6	4	8	49	45	22
Old Manorians II	18	5	5	8	38	47	20
Parkfield III	18	5	4	9	29	47	19
Old Vaughanians II	18	5	4	9	21	58	19
Old Challoners II	18	4	3	11	37	47	15

NORTHERN REGIONAL

Division 1 – 9 teams – Won by Enfield Old Grammarians 3rd
Division 2 – 11 teams – Won by Old Aloysians 4th
Division 3 – 11 teams – Won by Mill Hill County Old Boys Res
Division 4 – 10 teams – Won by Mill Hill Village Res
Division 5 – 10 teams – Won by Mill Hill County Old Boys 3rd
Division 6 – 11 teams – Won by Mayfield Athletic Res
Division 7 – 9 teams – Won by Mill Hill County Old Boys 5th
Division 8 – 9 teams – Won by Old Minchendenians 4th
Division 9 – 11 teams – Won by Old Ignatians 5th

SOUTHERN REGIONAL

Division 1 – 10 teams – Won by Old Wokingians
Division 2 – 9 teams – Won by Old Josephians Res
Division 3 – 10 teams – Won by Marsh
Division 4 – 10 teams – Won by Old Tenisonians 3rd
Division 5 (SW) – 11 teams – Old Dorkinians 3rd
Division 5 (SE) – 9 teams – Won by Royal Sun Alliance
Division 6 (SW) – 10 teams – Won by Economicals 3rd
Division 6 (SE) – 9 teams – Won by City of London Res
Division 7 (SW) – 10 teams – Won by Teddington
Division 7 (SE) – 9 teams – Won by Old Bromleians 3rd
Division 8 (SW) – 9 teams – Won by Old Suttonians 8th

WESTERN REGIONAL

Division 1 – 10 teams – Won by Old Meadonians 4th
Division 2 – 9 teams – Won by Old Manorians 3rd
Division 3 – 9 teams – Won by Old Kingsburians 3rd
Division 4 – 8 teams – Won by Old Meadonians 6th
Division 5 – 8 teams – Won by Ealing Association Res

WESTERN SPRING CUP

Cardinal Manning Res 5 Old Manorians 5th 4

ARTHURIAN LEAGUE

PREMIER DIVISION	*P*	*W*	*D*	*L*	*F*	*A*	*Pts*
Old Carthusians	18	16	1	1	61	11	49
Old Brentwoods	18	14	2	2	54	20	44
Old Westminsters*	18	10	2	6	41	33	29
Lancing Old Boys	18	7	5	6	35	26	26
Old Etonians	18	7	1	10	34	30	22
Old Foresters	18	6	4	8	35	45	22
Old Harrovians	18	5	5	8	38	41	20
Old Cholmeleians	18	5	5	8	20	35	20
Old Bradfieldians	18	3	2	13	20	71	11
Old Tonbridgians	18	2	3	13	22	48	9

DIVISION 1	*P*	*W*	*D*	*L*	*F*	*A*	*Pts*
Old Malvernians	16	12	0	4	44	29	36
King's Wimbledon Old Boys	16	8	4	4	39	24	28
Old Aldenhamians	16	8	3	5	40	33	27
Old Haileyburians	16	5	7	4	28	30	22
Old Reptonians	16	6	2	8	45	42	20
Old Radleians	16	6	2	8	29	34	20
Old Wykehamists	16	5	3	8	26	37	18
Old Salopians	16	5	2	9	39	38	17
Old Chigwellians	16	5	1	10	21	44	16

DIVISION 2	P	W	D	L	F	A	Pts
Old Carthusians II	16	11	2	3	43	18	35
Old King's Scholars	16	10	2	4	33	14	32
Old Haberdashers	16	7	2	7	41	32	23
Old Etonians II	16	7	2	7	37	36	23
Old Aldenhamians II	16	7	2	7	35	35	23
Old Brentwoods II*	16	7	1	8	36	31	19
Old Chigwellians II	16	5	4	7	19	29	19
Old Foresters II	16	6	1	9	30	46	19
Old Westminsters II*	16	3	2	11	19	52	8

DIVISION 3	P	W	D	L	F	A	Pts
Old Harrovians II	14	8	3	3	43	28	27
Old Bradfieldians II	14	8	1	5	34	28	25
Old Foresters III	14	7	3	4	38	30	24
Old Oundelians	14	7	2	5	34	29	23
Old Wellingtonians	14	5	4	5	37	31	19
Old Etonians III	14	5	2	7	41	39	17
Old Salopians II	14	3	4	7	27	41	13
Old Chigwellians III	14	3	1	10	17	45	10

DIVISION 4	P	W	D	L	F	A	Pts
Old Carthusians III	12	8	2	2	37	13	26
Lancing Old Boys II	12	6	4	2	26	16	22
Old Cholmeleians II	12	5	1	6	23	29	16
Old Westminsters III	12	3	5	4	31	35	14
Old Foresters IV*	12	5	2	5	28	33	14
Old Malvernians II	12	4	1	7	27	44	13
Old Brentwoods III	12	2	3	7	32	34	9

DIVISION 5	P	W	D	L	F	A	Pts
Old Harrovians III	12	10	0	2	36	12	30
Old Eastbournians	12	10	0	2	37	16	30
Old Amplefordians	12	5	2	5	28	23	17
Old Wykehamists II*	12	5	4	3	22	16	16
Old Cholmeleians III	12	3	1	8	18	19	10
Old Brentwoods IV	12	2	2	8	15	33	8
Old Cholmeleians IV*	12	2	1	9	7	44	4

**Points deducted – breach of rules.*

JUNIOR LEAGUE CUP
Old Oundelians 3 Old Etonians Res 2

DERRICK MOORE VETERANS CUP
Old Carthusians 2 Lancing Old Boys 1

UNIVERSITY OF LONDON MEN'S INTER-COLLEGIATE LEAGUE

WEEKEND ONE DIVISION	P	W	D	L	F	A	Pts
Royal Holloway College	11	9	1	1	29	5	28
Royal Holloway	12	10	2	0	37	6	32
University College	12	8	2	2	28	10	26
Imperial College	12	7	2	3	23	11	23
School of Oriental & African Studies	12	6	4	2	31	14	22
London School of Economics	12	5	2	5	17	25	17
Royal Holloway Res	12	5	1	6	22	26	16
St Bart's & Royal London	12	4	1	7	16	18	13
London School of Economics 3rd	12	4	1	7	10	23	13
Royal Free & University College Medical School	12	4	0	8	20	22	12
University College Res	12	3	3	6	18	21	12
London School of Economics Res	12	4	0	8	13	28	12
Imperial College Res	12	3	2	7	15	28	11
King's College *	12	4	2	6	11	29	11

**Points deducted/awarded.*

WEEKEND TWO DIVISION	P	W	D	L	F	A	Pts
Queen Mary	12	11	0	1	42	10	33
Imperial Medicals	12	9	2	1	47	10	29
King's College Medical Schools	11	7	3	1	46	12	24
University College 4th	12	6	2	4	40	26	20
Queen Mary Res	11	6	1	4	25	18	19
University College 3rd	12	5	2	5	19	27	17
King's College Res	12	4	4	4	31	22	16
Goldsmiths	12	5	1	6	30	36	16
Royal Holloway 3rd	12	4	2	6	13	21	14
King's College Medical Schools Res	11	3	1	7	19	32	10
Imperial College 3rd	12	3	1	8	15	40	10
St George's Hospital Medical School	12	3	0	9	13	49	9
Imperial Medicals Res	11	0	1	10	9	46	1

**Points deducted/awarded.*

DIVISION ONE	P	W	D	L	F	A	Pts
University College 6th	20	12	3	5	63	28	39
University College 5th	20	10	3	7	54	45	33
Royal Veterinary College	20	9	6	5	39	32	33
Queen Mary 3rd	20	10	1	9	55	54	31
Royal Holloway 4th	19	9	4	6	32	31	31
Imperial College 5th	20	9	1	10	35	40	28
Royal Free & University College Medical School Res	20	7	4	9	46	47	25
King's College Medical Schools 3rd	20	7	4	9	39	50	25
Imperial College 4th	20	6	5	9	62	61	23
St Bart's & Royal London Res	20	7	2	11	45	47	23
King's College 3rd*	19	3	7	9	25	60	13

**Points deducted/awarded.*

DIVISION TWO	P	W	D	L	F	A	Pts
London School of Economics 4th	20	14	5	1	63	21	47
London School of Economics 5th	20	15	2	3	53	17	47
University College 7th	20	11	4	5	47	46	37
University of the Arts	17	10	4	3	59	24	34
Royal Holloway 5th	19	8	5	6	49	35	29
St George's Hospital Medical School Res	20	5	6	9	28	41	21
King's College 4th	20	5	6	9	28	35	21
King's College5th	20	6	2	12	41	47	20
Royal Free & University College Medical School 3rd	19	5	2	12	26	70	17
School of Pharmacy*	18	5	1	12	24	40	13
Imperial Medicals 3rd	19	2	3	14	20	62	9

**Points deducted/awarded.*

DIVISION THREE

	P	*W*	*D*	*L*	*F*	*A*	*Pts*
Imperial College at Wye	19	16	3	0	63	19	51
London School of Economics 6th	20	15	0	5	66	26	45
Queen Mary 4th	20	13	3	4	63	26	42
School of Oriental & African Studies Res	20	11	4	5	56	41	37
Imperial College 6th	20	9	1	10	44	47	28
King's College Medical Schools 4th	20	7	2	11	48	59	23
Royal Holloway 6th	19	7	1	11	34	55	22
King's College Medical Schools 5th	19	5	3	11	37	50	18
Royal Free & University College Medical School 4th	20	4	6	10	21	34	18
Imperial College 7th	19	4	5	10	35	53	17
Royal School of Mines	20	1	4	15	26	83	7

***Points deducted/awarded.*

DIVISION FOUR

	P	*W*	*D*	*L*	*F*	*A*	*Pts*
School of Slavonic & East European Studies	20	16	3	1	82	21	51
London School of Economics 7th	20	16	2	2	76	16	50
Queen Mary 5th	20	15	1	4	63	25	46
Goldsmiths Res	20	14	3	3	92	28	45
King's College 6th*	20	8	2	10	42	60	23
Royal Veterinary College Res	20	7	1	12	41	65	22
Goldsmiths 3rd	20	5	4	11	40	72	19
St Bart's & Royal London 3rd	20	6	1	13	33	65	19
Imperial Medicals 4th	20	5	3	12	30	47	18
St Bart's & Royal London 4th	19	3	4	12	22	57	13
St George's Hospital Medical School 3rd	19	2	0	17	23	88	6

***Points deducted/awarded.*

CHALLENGE CUP
Imperial College 1 Royal Holloway 2

RESERVES CHALLENGE CUP
King's College Medical School Res 1 King's College Res 2

PLATE CUP
King's College 4th 2 London School of Economics 5th 1

UNIVERSITY OF LONDON WOMEN'S INTER-COLLEGIATE LEAGUE

PREMIER DIVISION	*P*	*W*	*D*	*L*	*F*	*A*	*Pts*
Royal Holloway	10	9	1	0	33	4	28
King's College Medical Schools	8	6	1	1	38	9	19
University College	10	4	1	5	27	22	13
Queen Mary	10	2	2	6	21	43	8
Goldsmiths	10	2	1	7	10	37	7
Imperial College	8	2	0	6	12	26	6

***Points deducted/awarded.*

DIVISION ONE	*P*	*W*	*D*	*L*	*F*	*A*	*Pts*
Royal Veterinary College	9	7	0	2	42	12	21
Royal Free & University College Medical School	9	6	2	1	41	8	20
London School of Economics	9	6	1	2	44	7	19
King's College	8	5	1	2	30	8	16
School of Oriental & African Studies	9	4	3	2	22	7	15
St George's Hospital Medical School	9	4	2	3	21	26	14
City University	9	4	1	4	26	32	13
University College Res	9	2	0	7	10	35	6
King's College Medical Schools Res	9	1	0	8	11	53	3
Royal Free & University College Medical School Res*	8	0	0	8	1	60	–3

***Points deducted/awarded.*

WOMEN'S CHALLENGE CUP
University College 1 King's College Medical School 7

124th UNIVERSITY MATCH

(at Craven Cottage, 29 March 2008)

Cambridge 5 Oxford 3

Cambridge: *J Dean; *A Murphy, N Pantelides, A Hakimi, *C Turnbull, *D Mills, *A Coleman (Capt.), L Pendlebury, M Stock, *M Johnson, *J Rutt.

Substitutes: J Chavkin, S Ferguson (GK), M Baxter, M Amos, W Lalande.

Scorers: Stock (4), Amos.

Oxford: D Robinson; *M Rigby, *P Rainford (Capt.), T Hodgson, *T Wherry, *H Sullivan, L Farr, *C Knight, *J Kelly, *A Toogood, N de Walden.

Substitutes: S. Hall, T Howell, K Desai.

Scorers: Sullivan, Toogood, Kelly.

**denotes Old Blue*
Cambridge have won 49 games, Oxford 47 and 28 have been drawn.

IMPORTANT ADDRESSES

The Football Association: The Secretary, 25 Soho Square, London W1D 4FA. *020 7745 4545*

Scotland: David Taylor, Hampden Park, Glasgow G42 9AY. *0141 616 6000*

Northern Ireland (Irish FA): Chief Executive: Howard J. C. Wells, 20 Windsor Avenue, Belfast BT9 6EG. *028 9066 9458*

Wales: D. Collins, 3 Westgate Street, Cardiff, South Glamorgan CF10 1DP. *029 2037 2325*

Republic of Ireland B. Menton (FA of Ireland): 80 Merrion Square South, Dublin 2. *00353 16766864*

International Federation (FIFA): P. O. Box 85 8030 Zurich, Switzerland. *00 411 384 9595. Fax: 00 411 384 9696*

Union of European Football Associations: Secretary, Route de Geneve 46, Case Postale CH-1260 Nyon, Switzerland. *0041 22 994 44 44. Fax: 0041 22 994 44 88*

THE LEAGUES

The Premier League: M. Foster, 11 Connaught Place, London W2 2ET. *020 7298 1600*

The Football League: Secretary, The Football League, Unit 5, Edward VII Quay, Navigation Way, Preston, Lancashire PR2 2YF. *0870 442 0 1888. Fax 0870 442 0 1188*

Scottish Premier League: R. Mitchell, Hampden Park, Somerville Drive, Glasgow G42 9BA. *0141 646 6962*

The Scottish League: P. Donald, Hampden Park, Glasgow G42 9AY. *0141 616 6000*

The Irish League: Secretary, 96 University Street, Belfast BT7 1HE. *028 9024 2888*

Football League of Ireland: D. Crowther, 80 Merrion Square, Dublin 2. *00353 16765120*

Blue Square UK: PO Box 37354, London N1 2WT. Alan Alger. *E-mail:* alan.alger@bluesquare.com

Eastern Counties League: B. A. Badcock, 18 Calford Drive, Hanchett Drive, Haverhill, Suffolk CB9 7WQ. *01440 708064*

Hellenic League: B. King, 83 Queens Road, Carterton, Oxon OX18 3YF. *01993 212738*

Kent League: R. Vinter, Bakery House, The Street, Chilham, Canterbury, Kent CT4 8BX. *01227 730457*

Leicestershire Senior League: R. J. Holmes, 9 Copse Close, Hugglescote, Coalville, Leicestershire LE67 2GL. *01530 831818*

Midland Combination: N. Harvey, 115 Millfield Road, Handsworth Wood, Birmingham B20 1ED. *0121 357 4172*

Northern Premier: R. D. Bayley, 22 Woburn Drive, Hale, Altrincham, Cheshire WA15 8LZ. *0161 980 7007*

Northern League: T. Golightly, 85 Park Road North, Chester-le-Street, Co Durham DH3 3SA. *0191 3882056*

Isthmian League: N. Robinson, Triumph House, Station Approach, Sanderstead Road, South Croydon, Surrey CR2 0PL. *020 8409 1978*

Southern League: D. J. Strudwick, 8 College Yard, Worcester WR1 2LA. *01905 330444.*
J. Mills. *E-mail:* secretary@southern-football-league.co.uk

Spartan South Midlands League: M. Mitchell, 26 Leighton Court, Dunstable, Beds LU6 1EW. *01582 667291*

United Counties League: R. Gamble, 8 Bostock Avenue, Northampton NN1 4LW. *01604 637766*

Western League: K. A. Clarke, 32 Westmead Lane, Chippenham, Wilts SN15 3HZ. *01249 464467*

West Midlands League: N. R. Juggins, 14 Badger Way, Blackwell, Bromsgrove, Worcs B60 1EX. *0121 445 2953*

Northern Counties (East): B. Wood, 6 Restmore Avenue, Guiseley, Leeds LS20 9DG. *01943 874558*

Central Midlands Football League: J. Worrall, 36 Spilsby Close, Cantley, Doncaster DN4 6TJ. *01302 370188*

Combined Counties League: L. Pharo, 17 Nigel Fisher Way, Chessington, Surrey KT9 2SN. *020 8391 0297*

Essex Senior League: D. Walls, 2 Hillsfield Cottage, Layer, Breton, Essex CO2 0PS. *01206 330146*

Midland Football Alliance: P. Dagger, 11 The Oval, Bicton, Nr Shrewsbury, Shropshire SY3 8ER. *01742 850859*

North West Counties Football League: G. J. Wilkinson, 46 Oaklands Drive, Penwortham, Preston, Lancs PR1 0XY. *01772 746312*

Wessex League: I. Craig, 7 Old River, Denmead, Hampshire PO7 6UX. *02392 230973*

South Western League: P. Lowe, 14 Anderton Court, Whitchurch, Tavistock, Devon PL19 9EX. *01822 613715*

Devon League: P. Hiscox, 19 Ivy Close, Wonford, Exeter, Devon EX2 5LX. *01392 493995*

Northern Alliance: J. McLackland, 92 Appletree Gardens, Walkerville, Newcastle-upon-Tyne NE6 4SX. *0191 262 6665*

Sussex County League: P. Beard, 2 Van Gogh Place, Bersted, Bognor Regis, West Sussex PO22 9BG. *01243 822063.*

Wearside League: T. Clark, 55 Vicarage Close, Silksworth, Sunderland, Tyne & Wear SR3 1UF. *0191 521 1242*

West Cheshire League: A. Green, 46 Bertram Drive, Meols, Wirral, Cheshire CH47 0LH. *0151 632 4946*

OTHER USEFUL ADDRESSES

Amateur Football Alliance: M. L. Brown, 55 Islington Park Street, London N1 1QB. *020 7359 3493*

English Schools FA: Mike Spinks, 1/2 Eastgate Street, Stafford ST16 2NQ. *01785 251142*

British Universities Sports Association: G. Gregory-Jones, Chief Executive: BUSA, 20-24 King's Bench Street, London SE1 0QX. *0207 633 5050*

The Football Supporters Federation: Chairman: Malcolm Clarke, 20 Woodlands Road, Sale, Cheshire M33 2DW. *0161 962 7337 . Mobile: 07939 594730.* National Secretary: Mike Williamson, 2 Repton Avenue, Torrishome, Morecambe, Lancs LA4 6RZ. *01524 425242, 07729 906329 (mobile).* National Administrator: Mark Agate, 'The Stadium', 14 Coombe Close, Lordswood, Chatham, Kent ME5 8NU. *01634 319461 (and fax) 07931 635637 (mobile)*

National Playing Fields Association: Col. R. Satterthwaite, O.B.E., 578b Catherine Place, London, SW1

Professional Footballers' Association: G. Taylor, 2 Oxford Court, Bishopsgate, Off Lower Mosley Street, Manchester M2 3WQ. *0161 236 0575*

Referees' Association: A. Smith, 1 Westhill Road, Coundon, Coventry CV6 2AD. *024 7660 1701*

Women's Football Alliance: Miss K. Doyle, The Football Association, 25 Soho Square, London W1D 4FA. *020 7745 4545*

League Managers Association: The Camkin Suite, 1 Pegasus House, Pegasus Court, Tachbrook Park, Warwick CV34 6LW. *01926 831 556. Fax: 01926 429 781*

Institute of Football Management and Administration; Commercial and Marketing Managers Association; Technical and Development Staffs Association; LMA Web Limited: as above

The Football Programme Directory: David Stacey, 'The Beeches', 66 Southend Road, Wickford, Essex SS11 8EN. *01268 732041 (and fax)*

England Football Supporters Association: Publicity Officer, David Stacey, 'The Beeches', 66 Southend Road, Wickford, Essex SS11 8EN. *01268 732041 (and fax)*

World Cup (1966) Association: Hon. Secretary, David Duncan, 96 Glenlea Road, Eltham, London SE9 1DZ

The Ninety-Two Club: 104 Gilda Crescent, Whitchurch, Bristol BS14 9LD

The Football Trust: Second Floor, Walkden House, 10 Melton Street, London NW1 2EJ. *020 7388 4504*

Association of Provincial Football Supporters Clubs in London: Stephen Moon, 32 Westminster Gardens, Barking, Essex IG11 0BJ. *020 8594 2367*

World Association of Friends of English Football: Carlisle Hill, Gluck, Habichthof 2, D24939 Flensburg, Germany. *0049 461 4700222*

Football Postcard Collectors Club: PRO: Bryan Horsnell, 275 Overdown Road, Tilehurst, Reading RG31 6NX. *0118 942 4448 (and fax)*

UK Programme Collectors Club: Secretary, John Litster, 46 Milton Road, Kirkcaldy, Fife KY1 1TL. *01592 268718. Fax: 01592 595069*

Programme Monthly & Football Collectable Magazine: P.O. Box 3236 Norwich NR7 7BE

Scottish Football Historians Association: 43 Lady Nairn Avenue, Kirkcaldy KY1 2AW

Phil Gould (Licensed Football Agent), c/o Whoppit Management Ltd, P. O. Box 27204, London N11 2WS. *07071 732 468. Fax: 07070 732 469*

The Scandinavian Union of Supporters of British Football: Postboks, 15 Stovner, N-0913 Oslo, Norway

Football Writers' Association: Executive Secretary, Ken Montgomery, 6 Chase Lane, Barkingside, Essex IG6 1BH. *0208 554 2455 (and fax)*

Programme Promotions: 47 The Beeches, Lampton Road, Hounslow, Middlesex TW3 4DF.
Web: www.footballprogrammes.com

FOOTBALL CLUB CHAPLAINCY

"You'll be missed dreadfully." It was the Chairman's first utterance since his friend the chaplain had told him, a full couple of minutes earlier, of his intention to retire from his honorary position at the club at the end of the season.

"By some, perhaps so," smiled the chaplain, "but I've found you a top-class replacement who can take over in the summer and being much younger than me, he'll soon become a great asset to the club I feel sure."

"We will trust your judgement on that," said the Chairman, "but bring him along to meet me sometime. It will surely help him to know that he has my backing here."

"Of course," returned the chaplain, "and he'll certainly appreciate that. But he is a local clergyman and has followed the club as a fan for many years, so he's not without knowledge of our situation."

"Don't let us lose contact with you though, will you?" insisted the Chairman. "You know you'll always be welcome here – for a match or if you find yourself in the area."

"You've always been most supportive towards me," said the chaplain, "and thank you for the kind offer. I won't forget it. And it does seem to be the case that the arrival of a new chaplain usually revitalises the role when his predecessor has been around for a long time."

The Chairman kept his thoughts to himself on that matter, but he was confident that he and his family would make sure that they maintained the friendship that had grown up between them and the man sitting before him.

THE REV

OFFICIAL CHAPLAINS TO FA PREMIERSHIP AND FOOTBALL LEAGUE CLUBS

Rev Ken Baker – Aston Villa; Rev Ken Howles – Blackburn R; Rev Philip Mason – Bolton W; Rev Matt Baker – Charlton Ath; Rev Henry Corbett – Everton; Rev Gary Piper – Fulham; Rev Bill Bygroves – Liverpool; Rev Chris Howitz – Manchester C; Rev John Boyers – Manchester U; Rev David Tully – Newcastle U; Rev Jonathan Jeffrey and Mr Mick Mellows (Co-Chaplains) – Portsmouth; Rev Elwin Cockett – West Ham United; Rev Peter Amos – Barnsley; Rev Michael Ward – Blackpool; Rev John Moore – Boston U; Rev Andy Rimmer – Bournemouth; Rev Andy Bowerman – Bradford C; Rev Lewis Allen – Brentford; Rev Derek Cleave – Bristol C; Rev Dave Jeal – Bristol R; Rev Mark Hirst – Burnley; Rev John O'Dowd – Bury; Rev Alun Jones – Carlisle U; Mr Paul Bennett and Rev John O'Dwyer (Co-Chaplains) – Cheltenham T; Rev Jim McGlade – Chesterfield; Rev Simon Lawton – Crewe Alexandra; Rev Chris Roe – Crystal Palace; Pastor Jon Burns – Darlington; Rev Tony Luke – Derby Co; Rev Brian Quar – Doncaster R; Rev Richard Hayton – Gillingham; Rev Allen Bagshawe – Hull C; Rev Kevan McCormack – Ipswich T; Rev Paul C. Welch and Fr Steven Billington (Co-Chaplains) – Leeds U; Rev Bruce Nadin – Leicester C; Rev Alan Comfort – Leyton Orient; Rev Andrew Vaughan – Lincoln C; Rev Jeremy Tear – Macclesfield T; Rev Timothy Mitchell – Mansfield T; Fr Owen Beament – Millwall; Rev Ron Smith – Milton Keynes D; Rev Ken Baker – Northampton T; Revs Bert Cadmore and Arthur W. Bowles (Co-Chaplains) – Norwich C; Rev Simon Cansdale – Nottingham F; Rev Mark Tanner – Notts Co; Rev Richard Longfoot – Peterborough U; Rev Jeff Howden – Plymouth Arg; Rev John M Hibberts – Port Vale; Rev Chris Nelson – Preston NE; Rev Bob Mayo and Rev Cameron Collington (Co-Chaplains) – Queens Park Rangers; Steve Prince – Reading; Rev Alan Wright – Scunthorpe U; Rev Peter Allen – Sheffield W; Rev Ian Johnson – Southampton; Rev Billy Montgomery – Stockport Co; Rev Kevin Johns – Swansea C; Rev Simon Stevenette – Swindon T; Fr Gerald Courell – Tranmere R; Rev Martin Butt – Walsall; Rev Clive Ross – Watford; Rev John Hall-Matthews and Rev Steve Davies (Co-Chaplains) – Wolverhampton W; Rev Jim Pearce – Yeovil T; Rev Peter Wyatt – Dagenham & Redbridge; Rev Stephen Clark – Doncaster Rovers; Rev Chris Sims – Shrewsbury Town; Rev Stephen Taylor – Sunderland; Rev Ken Hipkiss – West Bromwich Albion; Rev John Roberts and Rev Tim O'Brien (Co-Chaplains) – Wycombe Wanderers; Rev Mike Pusey – Aldershot Town.

The chaplains hope that those who read this page will see the value and benefit of chaplaincy work in football and will take appropriate steps to spread the word where this is possible. They would also like to thank the editors of the Football Yearbook *for their continued support for this specialist and growing area of work.*

For further information, please contact: SCORE (Sports Chaplaincy Offering Resources and Encouragement), PO Box 123, Sale, Cheshire M33 4ZA). Telephone 0161-969-1762 or email JKBSCOREUK@aol.com.

Obituary

The Rev Canon John Hester chaplain at Brighton & Hove Albion FC 1975–97 died 10 February 2008 aged 80.

OBITUARIES

Paul Aimson (Born Prestbury, Macclesfield, Cheshire, 3 August 1943. Died Christchurch, Dorset, 9 January 2008.) Paul Aimson was a much-travelled centre forward, who began his career with Manchester City in the early 1960s. He was best known for his performances in two spells for York City, for whom he scored 113 goals in 248 appearances. He also played for Bury, Bradford City, Huddersfield, Bournemouth and Colchester.

Charlie Aitken (Born Gorebridge, Midlothian, 19 July 1932. Died Dalkeith, Midlothian, 12 January 2008.) Charlie Aitken was one of the all-time greats in the history of Motherwell FC. He joined the club as a 17-year-old and remained a stalwart figure at Fir Park for almost two decades. A key figure at right half in the side during the late 1950s and early '60s, he made over 400 first-team appearances and was the club's Player of the Year in 1957 and 1958. Charlie was capped once by Scotland B and represented the Scottish League XI on two occasions.

Jack Ansell (Born Newport Pagnell, Beds., 4 August 1921. Died 12 April 2008.) Jack Ansell was a goalkeeper who made 142 appearances for Northampton Town between 1948 and 1952. He later played for Headington United (now Oxford United) helping them win the Southern League title in 1952–53.

Mick Atkin (Born Scunthorpe, 14 February 1948. Died Grimsby, 15 January 2008.) Mick Atkin was a central defender who made over 100 first-team appearances for Scunthorpe United, helping them win promotion from the Fourth Division in 1971–72. For most of his career he was a part-time professional, combining football with a job as a PE teacher.

Giuseppe Baldo (Born Piombino Dese, nr. Padua, Italy, 27 July 1914.Died Montecatini Terme, nr. Pistoia, Italy, 31 July 2007.) Giuseppe Baldo represented Italy at the 1936 Olympic Games tournament, earning a gold medal after his team defeated Austria in the final. A half back, he featured for Padova and Lazio at club level.

Bobby Bark (Born Stranraer, 27 January 1926. Died Barrow in Furness, 1 July 2007.) Bobby Bark joined Barrow as an inside forward towards the end of the 1947–48 campaign, but his senior action was limited to just a single appearance against Oldham in September 1948.

Keith Barker (Born Stoke-on-Trent, 22 February 1949. Died 1 January 2008.) Goalkeeper Keith Barker joined Cambridge United, then members of the Southern League, during the 1967–68 season and featured regularly prior to the club's election to the Football League in 1970. However, he failed to break into the line-up during the 1970–71 campaign, and later joined Barnsley, where he made nine first-team appearances before losing his place in the side.

Jack Barnes (Born Atherstone, Warwickshire, 28 April 1908. Died Coleshill, Warwickshire, 1 April 2008.) Jack Barnes joined Coventry City early in 1928, making his Football League debut against Crystal Palace in February of that year. A speedy left winger he went on to play for Walsall, Watford, Exeter and York, making over 200 senior appearances. One of the highlights of his career was playing in the Exeter team that lifted the Division Three South Cup in the 1933–34 season. At the time of his death, just weeks short of his 100th birthday, Jack was believed to be the oldest surviving former Football League professional.

Jan Bekker (Born Cardiff, 24 December 1951. Died Bridgend, 26 December 2007.) Jan Bekker was a forward who spent 18 months on the books of Swansea City in the mid-1970s, scoring 5 goals in 25 senior appearances. A Wales Amateur international, he later played for Southern League club Bridgend Town.

Danny Bergara (Born Rocha, Uruguay, 24 July 1942. Died Sheffield, 25 July 2007.) Danny Bergara played as a youngster with Racing Club of Montevideo before moving to Spain's Real Mallorca in 1962. A useful striker, he also turned out for Sevilla and Tenerife before retiring in the early 1970s. He subsequently came to England and after coaching with Luton Town and Sheffield United he had spells as manager of Rochdale (1988–89), Stockport (1989–1995) and Rotherham (1996–1997). His main successes came at Edgeley Park, where he led Stockport to promotion from the Fourth Division in 1990–91 and successive Autoglass Trophy finals at Wembley in 1992 and 1993. Danny also coached England U18s and U20s in the early 1980s.

Eric Binns (Born Halifax, 13 August 1924. Died September 2007.) Defender Eric Binns joined Halifax Town shortly before the end of the 1945–46 season, but was never able to establish himself in the line-up at The Shay. After a spell in non-League football with Goole Town, he spent six years with Burnley, but here too he was mostly a reserve, before concluding his senior career with two seasons at Blackburn, where he made 23 appearances.

Barney Bircham (Born Philadelphia, Co. Durham, 31 August 1924. Died 11 October 2007.) Barney Bircham featured regularly in goal for Sunderland during the wartime emergency competitions, making 63 first-team appearances, but he failed to make the first team during a spell at Chesterfield and although he was later on the books of Grimsby and Colchester United, he was mainly a reserve for both clubs.

Jeroen Boere (Born Arnhem, Netherlands, 18 November 1967. Died Marbella, Spain, 16 August 2007.) Jeroen made his name playing in the Netherlands with a string of clubs including De Graafschap, VVV Venlo and Go Ahead Eagles before being sold to West Ham in September 1993. A tall and effective striker, he was hampered by injuries during his time at Upton Park. After spells with Crystal Palace and Southend Jeroen moved to Japan where he played for the Omiya Ardija club. In May 1999 he was attacked outside a Tokyo bar and lost an eye, which brought his playing career to an end. His death came in tragic circumstances after he had moved to Spain where he worked in real estate.

Jimmy Bonthrone (Born Kinglassie, Fife, 1929. Died Kirkcaldy, Fife, 7 June 2008.) Jimmy Bonthrone was a forward who joined East Fife in the summer of 1947 and went on to become one of the stars of their successful team in the 1950s, helping the Fifers win the Scottish League Cup in October 1953. Capped by Scotland at B international level, he went on to play for Dundee, Stirling Albion and Queen of the South, scoring a career total of 153 goals in 373 senior appearances. He later managed East Fife (1963 to 1969) and Aberdeen (1971 to 1975) before returning to East Fife as commercial manager for 14 years up until his retirement in 1994.

Len Boyd (Born Plaistow, London, 11 November 1923. Died Melton Mowbray, 14 February 2008.) Len Boyd signed for Plymouth as an inside forward at the end of the war, but it was only when he dropped back to wing half that his career progressed. In 1949 he was sold to Birmingham City for what was a record fee for Argyle and he went on to play in more than 250 senior games for the Blues. He led the club to promotion back to the top flight in 1954–55 and the following season helped them achieve their best-ever performances: sixth place in Division One and runners-up to Manchester City in the FA Cup. Len was capped by England against Netherlands at B international level in March 1952.

Gordon Bradley (Born Easington, Co. Durham, 23 November 1933. Died Manassas, Virginia, USA, 29 April 2008.) Gordon Bradley had been on Sunderland's books as a youngster, but after suffering a serious injury he left the club. However, he later developed as a right half with Bradford Park Avenue and Carlisle, before moving to Canada where he played in the Eastern Canada Professional League. Gordon subsequently settled in the USA, playing in the NASL for New York Generals, Baltimore Bays and New York Cosmos, for whom he was player-coach from 1971 until 1977. During his time with the Cosmos he signed a number of star players including Pelé and Franz Beckenbauer.

Des Broomfield (Born Hove, Sussex, 6 October 1921. Died June 2007.) Wing half Des Broomfield featured in a handful of wartime games for Brighton, and remained with the club in the early post-war years, adding a further 20 Football League appearances.

Tom Burlison (Born Edmondsley, Co. Durham, 23 May 1936. Died 20 May 2008.) Tom Burlison made almost 200 senior appearances as a wing half or outside left for Hartlepools United and Darlington between 1957 and 1965. He subsequently developed a successful career as a trade union official with the General & Municipal Workers Union, rising to become Deputy General Secretary. He was also active in the Labour Party, serving on the NEC and as national treasurer, and in 1997 was made a Life Peer, taking on the title of Baron Burlison of Rowlands Gill. He is the only former professional footballer to sit in the House of Lords.

Tommy Burns (Born Glasgow, 16 December 1956. Died Glasgow, 15 May 2008.) A product of Celtic's youth policy, Tommy Burns joined the professional ranks at Parkhead in August 1973 and went on to become one of the club's most influential players over the next 15 years. A thoughtful left-footed midfielder with fine vision and an inch-perfect pass, he made a total of 510 competitive appearances for the Bhoys, assisting the club to six Scottish League titles, two Scottish Cup wins and a Scottish League Cup trophy. Tommy also won representative honours for Scotland with 8 full caps, 5 at U21 level and a single appearance for the Scottish League XI. In 1989 he moved on to Kilmarnock, where he eventually became player-manager, leading the club to promotion to the Premier Division in 1992–93. Later he managed Celtic (1994 to 1997) and Reading (1998 to 1999) before returning to Parkhead where he had most recently been first-team coach. His death followed a lengthy battle against skin cancer.

Wattie Carlyle (Born Grangemouth, Stirlingshire, 23 May 1938. Died 31 December 2007.) Winger Wattie Carlyle was on Rangers' books as a youngster, but he failed to break into the first team at Ibrox. However, he went on to make over 150 senior appearances for Dundee United, Motherwell, St Johnstone, Queen of the South, East Stirlingshire and Alloa during the 1960s.

Tim Carter (Born Bristol, 5 October 1967. Died Manchester, 19 June 2008.) Tim Carter was a strong and fearless goalkeeper who made almost 250 senior appearances in a career that spanned the period 1985 to 1999. After starting out as an apprentice with Bristol Rovers, he spent five years on the books of Sunderland before going on to play for Hartlepool, Millwall (two spells), Blackpool, Oxford and Halifax. Tim later worked as a goalkeeping coach most recently with the Academy players at Sunderland, as well as assisting the Estonia national team on a part-time basis. His death occurred in tragic circumstances, shortly after he had been reported missing by his family.

Nigel Cassidy (Born Sudbury, Suffolk, 7 December 1945. Died 19 May 2008.) Nigel Cassidy was a popular centre forward who began his career with Norwich City, moving on to Scunthorpe in December 1968. He scored the goal that knocked Sheffield Wednesday out of the FA Cup in a giant-killing act in January 1970 and later that year he was sold to Oxford United. Nigel also played for Cambridge United, achieving a career tally of 81 Football League goals from 261 appearances.

George Christie (Born circa 1920. Died Aberdeen, 22 January 2008.) George Christie was a talented winger who spent seven seasons as a regular for Dundee during the 1950s, assisting the club to two Scottish League Cup victories (1951–52, 1952–53) and also gaining a Scottish Cup runners-up medal in 1952. He later had a brief spell with Third Lanark.

Derek Clark (Born Newcastle upon Tyne, 10 August 1931. Died 9 June 2008.) Derek Clark was an inside forward who spent four years on the books of Lincoln City in the early 1950s. He scored within two minutes of his Football League debut against Tranmere in February 1953, but received only three more first-team outings for the Imps. He was the uncle of England cricketer Paul Collingwood.

Len Comley (Born Swansea, 25 January 1922. Died Mumbles, Swansea, 5 August 2007.) Len Comley was a versatile forward who played in over 100 wartime games for Swansea, and remained with the club for the first three seasons of peacetime football, during which time he added a further 28 Football League appearances.

Ernie Coombs (Born Writhington, Somerset, 21 December 1912. Died Taunton, Somerset, 1 April 2008.) Ernie Coombs was a forward who received a solitary outing for Bristol Rovers in the 1931–32 season. He later had a season on the books of Bristol City, without making a first-team appearance, and also turned out for Bath before returning to senior football with Blackburn in November 1933. However, he featured in just a handful of games for Rovers before returning to the Southern League with Bath once more.

Ken Cousins (Born Bristol, 6 August 1922. Died 11 October 2007.) Goalkeeper Ken Cousins made 12 appearances for Bristol City during the 1945–46 season, but once peacetime football resumed he was mostly confined to the reserves, save for a brief run in the line-up during January 1947.

David Crawford (Born circa 1942. Died August 2007.) David Crawford was a key figure for Linfield FC, acting as a committee member for more than 40 years and treasurer for over 20 years. He was club chairman from 2003 until the time of his death.

Ian Crawford (Born Edinburgh, 14 July 1934. Died Peterborough, 30 November 2007.) After spending the early years of his career with Hibernian and Hamilton Academical, winger Ian Crawford signed for Hearts in August 1954. He did well at Tynecastle, gaining a Scottish Cup winners medal in 1956 and assisting the team to the League Championship in 1957–58 and two League Cup triumphs. He later played for West Ham and Scunthorpe, before spending five years as a regular with Peterborough United, by which time he had converted to full back. He was capped once by Scotland at U23 level. Ian later enjoyed a successful career in coaching working in many parts of the world.

Dermot Cross (Born Dublin, Ireland, 30 January 1931. Died Dublin, Ireland, 13 December 2007.) Dermot Cross was an inside forward who played for a string of League of Ireland clubs in the 1950s and early 1960s. He won League titles with Drumcondra (1957–58) and Dundalk (1962–63) and made three appearances for the League of Ireland representative side.

Willie Cunningham (Born Mallusk, Co. Antrim, 20 February 1930. Died Dunfermline, 31 August 2007.) Willie Cunningham was a dependable and versatile defender who developed with St Mirren before being sold to Leicester City towards the end of 1954. He helped the Foxes win the Second Division title in 1956–57 before returning north to end his career at Dunfermline. Willie remained with the Pars after retiring as a player, eventually succeeding Jock Stein as manager, and he also managed Falkirk and St Mirren. He was a regular with Northern Ireland in the 1950s, gaining 30 caps and contributing to their success in the 1958 World Cup when they reached the quarter-final stage.

William Curzon (Born Sunderland, 1921. Died 2007.) William Curzon signed amateur forms for Sunderland in May 1939 and went on to make two first-team appearances for the club during the war.

John Cushley (Born Hamilton, Lanarkshire, 21 January 1943. Died Bothwell, Lanarkshire, 24 March 2008.) John Cushley spent seven years on the books of Celtic in the 1960s, where he was a stand-in centre half for Billy McNeill. He subsequently played alongside the likes of Bobby Moore and Martin Peters at West Ham, before moving back to Scotland for successful spells with Dunfermline and Dumbarton. More recently he had returned to Celtic as the club's education and welfare officer.

Ron Davies (Born Merthyr Tydfil, 21 September 1932. Died Mountain Hare, Merthyr Tydfil, 8 December 2007.) Ron Davies was mostly a second choice at right back during six seasons at Cardiff in the 1950s, but when he dropped down a division to sign for Southampton in 1958 he gained regular first-team football. An ever-present in Saints' Third Division championship-winning side of 1959–60, he initially adjusted well to Second Division football, but eventually lost out to Stuart Williams. Ron concluded his career with a spell at Aldershot.

Eric Davis (Born Stonehouse, Devon, 26 February 1932. Died Plymouth, 21 July 2007.) Eric Davis was a big powerful centre forward who spent eight years as a professional for Plymouth Argyle, Scunthorpe, Chester and Oldham. His goals helped the Iron clinch the Division Three North title in 1957–58, when he found the net in each of the final six games of the campaign.

Bobby Davison (Born Kimblesworth, Co. Durham, circa 1923. Died July 2007.) Bobby Davison was one of the stars of amateur football in the 1950s. A big, powerful centre half he played for Bishop Auckland in both the 1950 and 1951 FA Amateur Cup finals, ending on the losing side on each occasion, before gaining a winners' medal when Crook won the trophy in 1954. Bobby gained a single cap for England Amateurs during a spell with Shildon.

Norman Deeley (Born Wednesbury, Staffs, 30 November 1933. Died Wednesbury, West Midlands, 7 September 2007.) Norman Deeley had represented England at Schoolboy international level before joining the groundstaff at Molineux. He eventually broke into the Wolves line-up after several years on the fringes of the squad, gaining Football League Championship medals in 1957–58 and 1958–59. He also scored twice in the 1960 FA Cup final when Blackburn Rovers were defeated 3–0. Capped twice by England during the 1959 tour of South America, he later played for Leyton Orient and Worcester City.

John Dewsbury (Born Port Tennant, Swansea, 16 February 1932. Died Swansea, 6 October 2007.) John Dewsbury signed for Swansea Town as an 18-year old, but in five years on the books at the Vetch Field, he enjoyed only a brief run in the first team. He subsequently followed manager Billy Lucas to Newport County, but here too he was mostly a reserve before moving into non-League football.

Tommy Dickson (Born Belfast, 16 July 1929. Died Belfast, 31 December 2007.) Tommy Dickson was one of the great stars of the Linfield team in the post-war period, scoring 451 goals in 650 appearances for the Windsor Park club. Predominantly an inside left, he won eight Irish League titles and five Irish Cup winners' medals, while he also gained a solitary cap for Northern Ireland against Scotland in November 1956.

Ray Dixon (Born Denaby, Yorkshire, 31 December 1930. Died Mexborough, Yorkshire, 10 April 2008.) Although a regular scorer at reserve-team level for Rotherham, Ray Dixon was never more than a second choice at centre forward for the first team, making just 14 appearances in two seasons at Millmoor. He subsequently joined Southern League club King's Lynn for whom he proved to be a prolific scorer and helped the club reach the third round of the FA Cup in 1961–62.

George Dobson (Born Chiswick, Middlesex, 24 August 1949. Died 10 September 2007.) George Dobson graduated from apprentice to full-time professional at Brentford in the summer of 1967. A useful winger, he spent some three years on the club's books, featuring in 92 first-team games, before injury brought on a premature retirement. Later George returned to Griffin Park to work in the Centre of Excellence.

Peter Dobson (Born Frimley, Surrey, 13 June 1925. Died 5 February 2008.) Peter Dobson was a forward who joined Ipswich Town shortly after the start of the 1949–50 season. However, despite spending five years on the books at Portman Road, he failed to make the breakthrough to regular first-team football and in the summer of 1954 he moved on to join Cambridge United, then members of the Eastern Counties League.

John Doherty (Born Barton in Irwell, Manchester, 12 March 1935. Died Heald Green, Cheshire, 13 November 2007.) John Doherty signed amateur forms for Manchester United at the age of 15 and graduated to the professional ranks two years later. A highly promising young inside forward possessing tremendous skill, his career was affected by a string of injuries although he managed 16 first-team appearances for United when they won the Football League title in the 1955–56 season. Soon afterwards he moved on to Leicester but then succumbed to a combination of illness and injury and left the full-time game when just 23 years of age. In recent years John held the post of chairman of the Manchester United Former Players' Association, helping to raise over half a million pounds for charitable causes.

Derek Dooley, MBE (Born Pitsmoor, Sheffield, 13 December 1929. Died Norton, Sheffield, 5 March 2008.) Derek Dooley began his senior career as an amateur on the books of Lincoln City, but it was only after he turned professional with Sheffield Wednesday that he showed his full potential. He burst on the first-team scene at Hillsborough with some sensational goalscoring feats in the 1951–52 season when he scored 46 Football League goals, a club record for a single season and one that has yet to be broken. His career ended in tragedy in February

Derek Dooley

1953 when a broken leg became infected with gangrene and the limb was amputated to save his life. Derek subsequently worked in football administration, running the Development Fund at Hillsborough for several years and serving Wednesday briefly as manager, before changing his allegiance to Sheffield United where he was commercial manager, managing director and finally chairman.

Ray Drinkwater (Born Jarrow, 18 May 1931. Died Guildford, Surrey, 25 March 2008.) Ray Drinkwater joined Portsmouth from Guildford City in November 1955, but was generally a back-up goalkeeper at Fratton Park. He moved on to Queens Park Rangers in 1958 as a replacement for Peter Springett, and went on to become the club's regular 'keeper over the next five years, making more than 200 first-team appearances.

Jimmy Dugdale (Born Liverpool, 15 January 1932. Died 25 February 2008.) A calm and efficient defender, Jimmy Dugdale was one of the finest uncapped centre halves of his generation. He was in exceptional form during the 1953–54 season, winning representative honours for England B and the Football League and assisting Albion to victory over Preston in the FA Cup final. Early in 1956 Jimmy opted for a move to local rivals Aston Villa, where he went on to gain a second Cup winners' medal, featuring in the 1957 final when Manchester United were defeated. He also helped Villa to victory in the first-ever Football League Cup final against Rotherham in 1961, before winding down his career with a season at Queens Park Rangers.

John Dumsday (Born Pontypridd, 1921. Died Southborne, Bournemouth, 2007.) John Dumsday signed amateur forms for Queens Park Rangers in April 1940 and went on to make a single wartime appearance in the away game at Aldershot on 10 May 1941 before enlisting with the RAF.

Billy Elliott

Shaun Dunlop (Born Ballymoney, Co. Antrim, 6 October 1945. Died 27 December 2007.) Shaun Dunlop was an apprentice on Arsenal's books in the early 1960s without making the grade, but in a decade with Coleraine he made over 400 first-team appearances, gaining an Irish Cup winners' medal in 1965. An inside forward or winger, he was capped for Northern Ireland at Youth and U23 levels, and also won representative honours for the Irish League.

Frank Eccleshare, OBE (Born 1912. Died Lincoln, 23 January 2008.) Frank Eccleshare was a local builder who was chairman of Lincoln City from 1963 until 1967. He took over at a time when the Imps were close to collapse and transformed the club finances, paving the way for a revival of the team's performances at the end of the 1960s.

Billy Elliott (Born Bradford, 20 March 1925. Died Sunderland, 21 January 2008.) Billy Elliott began his career as a wing half and featured regularly for Bradford Park Avenue during the wartime emergency competitions. He shone when transformed into an outside left, netting the goal to knock Arsenal out of the FA Cup at Highbury in January 1948. In September 1951 he was sold to Burnley, where he gained five full caps for England, and he then enjoyed a successful spell at Sunderland, earning a reputation as one of the most effective wingers of his era. After retiring as a player Billy went into coaching and worked throughout the world, including spells in charge of the Libya national team, Daring (Brussels) and Brann Bergen. He was also manager of Darlington between 1979 and 1983.

John Eves (Born Sunderland, 28 February 1922. Died 2007.) A member of the Sunderland Boys team that reached the semi-final of the ESFA Trophy in 1935–36, full back John Eves went on to sign for his hometown club and made 123 wartime appearances. In September 1946 he joined Darlington where he was a regular in the line-up in the early post-war seasons.

Cyril Fairclough (Born Radcliffe, Manchester, 21 April 1923. Died 20 February 2008.) Cyril Fairclough was a full back who spent 13 years on the books of Bury, making in excess of 200 first-team appearances during his stay at Gigg Lane. He later had a successful spell as coach of Lancashire Combination outfit Chorley.

Wally Fielding (Born Edmonton, Middlesex, 26 November 1919. Died Cornwall, 18 January 2008.) Wally Fielding signed for Everton in September 1945 and went on to establish himself as a key figure in the club's line-up over the next 14 years, making over 400 appearances. An intelligent inside forward, he was a member of the side that won promotion from the Second Division in 1953–54 and he came close to international honours, appearing for England against Scotland in an unofficial fixture in aid of the victims of the Burnden Park disaster. Wally was player-manager of Southport for almost 18 months, then after a spell out of the game worked for Luton and Watford on the backroom staff.

Roy Finch (Born Barry Island, Glamorgan, 7 April 1922. Died Lincoln, 14 August 2007.) Roy Finch signed for West Bromwich Albion during the war, but it was only when he moved on to join Lincoln City in February 1949 that he experienced regular first-team football. He became a key figure on the left wing for the Imps in the 1950s, assisting the club to the Division Three North title in 1951–52, and making almost 300 appearances before retiring in 1959.

Jim Finney (Born 17 August 1924. Died Hereford, 1 April 2008.) Jim Finney was one of the top English referees of the 1960s and took charge of the 1962 FA Cup final and the 1971 Football League Cup final. He also refereed in the 1966 World Cup finals. Jim was later assistant secretary of Hereford United and then secretary of Cardiff City.

John Fleming (Born Kilrenny, Fife, circa 1923. Died Edinburgh, 9 September 2007.) John Fleming was a Fife businessman who was appointed as chairman of East Fife in 1961, helping to rescue the club at a time of severe financial problems. He stayed in post for a number of years, serving on the committee of the Scottish FA.

Reg Flewin (Born Portsmouth, 28 November 1920. Died Shanklin, Isle of Wight, 24 May 2008.) Reg Flewin made his debut for Portsmouth in the final home game of the 1938–39 season, but then war intervened. He featured regularly for

Pompey during the hostilities, making almost 200 appearances in the emergency competitions and being capped by England in the unofficial international against Wales in September 1944. Reg went on to captain Portsmouth to the Football League title in 1948–49 and 1949–50, eventually retiring to become assistant manager in 1953. He later became manager of Stockport County (1960–1963) and Bournemouth (1963–1965).

Reg Flewin

Johnny Gavin (Born Limerick, Ireland, 20 April 1928. Died September 2007.) Johnny Gavin was a prolific outside right, best known for his two spells at Norwich in the 1950s. His tally of 122 Football League goals from 312 appearances remains a club record for the Canaries. In between he had a season at Tottenham and he later played for Watford and Crystal Palace before leaving the game in the summer of 1961. Johnny also won seven caps for the Republic of Ireland.

Eric Gemmell (Born Prestwich, Manchester, 7 April 1921. Died February 2008.) Eric Gemmell was a centre forward who made a couple of appearances for Manchester City during the war before moving on to Oldham in 1947. Over the next seven seasons he netted 109 Football League goals for the Latics (a club record at the time) including 7 in an 11–2 victory over Chester in January 1952. Eric helped the club win the Division Three North title in 1952–53 and concluded his career with spells at Crewe and Rochdale.

Ray Goddard (Born Fulham, London, 13 February 1949. Died Spain, 11 December 2007.) Goalkeeper Ray Goddard began his senior career with Fulham, but failed to break into the first team at Craven Cottage. He fared better in a seven-year spell at Orient, accumulating more than 300 appearances and being a near ever-present in the side that won the Third Division title in 1969–70. Ray later played for Millwall and Wimbledon, featuring in promotion campaigns for both clubs.

Len Graham (Born Belfast, 17 October 1925. Died Blackpool, 30 September 2007.) Len Graham joined Doncaster shortly after the start of the 1949–50 season and went on to establish himself as the club's regular left back for the next eight years, making more than 300 Football League appearances. He was a regular for Northern Ireland during this period, winning 14 caps, thus making him the club's most capped player. He later had a brief spell at Torquay, managed Ards and then acted as trainer for Port Vale and Blackpool.

David Grant (Born Edinburgh, 31 July 1943. Died Edinburgh, 30 April 2008.) David Grant was a versatile forward who was mostly on the periphery of first-team action in the early years of his career with Third Lanark and Reading. However, he was a regular performer for almost a decade for Stirling Albion and East Stirling, taking his tally of senior appearances beyond the 250-mark in the process.

Willie Grant (Born Alloa, 27 January 1936. Died Garmouth, Moray, 26 July 2007.) Willie Grant made his senior debut for Hearts in April 1955, but that proved to be his only appearance for the Tynecastle club and in subsequent spells at Alloa and Stirling Albion he never really established himself as a regular. However, when switching to Highland League football he proved a revelation, becoming one of the most prolific centre forwards in the history of the competition. He scored some 348 goals in 255 appearances for Elgin City between 1961 and 1967, before finishing his career with a spell as player-coach of Inverness Thistle.

Davie Gray (Born Coupar Angus, 8 February 1922. Died Dundee, 17 May 2008.) Davie Gray was a right back who joined Rangers in January 1945 and played in the famous fixture against the touring Moscow Dynamo team in November 1945. However, he struggled to establish himself in a competitive environment at Ibrox and moved south to join Preston. A lengthy spell at Blackburn followed before he returned to Scotland to play for Dundee and Dundee United. Davie later had a spell as manager of Forfar Athletic.

Jack Gregory (Born Southampton, 25 January 1925. Died Southampton, 17 March 2008.) Although Jack Gregory spent 11 seasons on the books of Southampton, he was mostly a reserve. A full back who could play on either flank, he moved on to Leyton Orient in the summer of 1955, enjoying three seasons of regular first-team football before winding down his career with a 12-month spell at Bournemouth.

Phil Gunter (Born Portsmouth, 6 January 1932. Died Australia, 10 July 2007.) Phil Gunter was one of the stars of the Portsmouth team of the 1950s. A talented defender, he made 359 first-team appearances for Pompey between 1951 and 1964, gaining a Third Division championship medal in 1961–62. He also won representative honours for England B and England U23. Phil concluded his career with two seasons at Aldershot before joining Southern League outfit Guildford City.

Jack Haigh (Born Rotherham, 10 September 1928. Died Balby, Doncaster, 17 September 2007.) Jack Haigh briefly played for Gainsborough Trinity before joining Liverpool shortly after the start of the 1949–50 season. However, it was at Scunthorpe that he made his name, making over 350 first-team appearances and helping the Iron win the Division Three North title in 1957–58. Two seasons at Doncaster followed, before he concluded his career at Buxton.

Wilf Hall (Born St Helens, Lancs., 14 October 1934. Died 6 August 2007.) Wilf Hall was a goalkeeper who spent seven years on the books of Stoke City without ever really established himself as a regular in the first team. He subsequently had a spell with Ipswich Town where he was mostly employed as a back-up to Roy Bailey. On leaving Portman Road Wilf signed for Macclesfield Town, then members of the Cheshire League, where he spent more than 30 years, serving as player, coach, trainer, director and, most recently, as match-day commissionaire.

David Halford (Born Crossley Green, Herts., 19 October 1915. Died Tadcaster, Yorks, July 2007.) David Halford won two caps for England Schools in 1930 and later joined Derby County, but received few senior opportunities at the

Baseball Ground and it was only after he dropped into Division Three North with Oldham that he experienced regular first-team football. An outside left, he also appeared as a guest for Queens Park Rangers and Watford during the war.

Dave Hancock (Born Exeter, 24 July 1938. Died South Africa, July 2007.) Dave Hancock was a versatile wing half who began his career with Plymouth Argyle. However, he managed only a couple of appearances for the Pilgrims before moving on to Torquay where he was a first-team regular for five seasons, helping the club win promotion from Division Four in 1959–60. Dave subsequently joined Exeter in time to help the Grecians gain promotion from the Fourth Division in 1963–64, before emigrating to South Africa, where he played for a string of clubs including Durban United, Corinthians and Southern Suburbs.

Jack Hannaway (Born Bootle, 22 October 1927. Died 2007.) Jack Hannaway became Manchester City's regular left back in the 1951–52 season, but thereafter he was in and out the side. After seven years at Maine Road he moved on to join Gillingham, where he made over 100 appearances, then returned to the North West for a season as captain of Southport.

Tommy Harmer (Born Hackney, London, 2 February 1928. Died Edmonton, London, 25 December 2007.) Tommy Harmer was a talented inside forward and although possessing a frail physique he had great technical ability. A tremendous dribbler of the ball he made over 200 first-team appearances for Tottenham in the 1950s, probably his greatest game in the club colours coming on the day Bill Nicholson was appointed manager in 1958. Everton were defeated 10–4 with Tommy scoring one goal and having a hand in most of the others. He concluded his playing career with spells at Watford and Chelsea (where he was also youth-team coach). Tommy was capped for England B against Netherlands B in March 1952.

Brian Harris (Born Bebington, Cheshire, 16 May 1935. Died Chepstow, 17 February 2007.) Brian Harris was a wing half who spent over a decade at Everton, making more than 350 first-team appearances. He contributed to the Football League title campaign in 1962–63 and gained an FA Cup winners' medal following the Toffees' dramatic victory over Sheffield Wednesday in the 1966 final. Soon afterwards he moved on to Cardiff City, where he was a member of the team that reached the semi-finals of the European Cup Winners' Cup in 1967–68. Brian finished his career at Newport County, later managing the club from January 1974 to March 1975.

Bobby Harrop (Born Manchester, 25 August 1936. Died Margate, Kent, 8 November 2007.) Bobby Harrop was a member of the Manchester United team that won the FA Youth Cup in 1953–54 and also gained representative honours for England Youths. One of several youngsters thrust into first-team action for United in the wake of the Munich Air Disaster, he made 11 first-team appearances at Old Trafford before moving on for a spell with Tranmere Rovers. Bobby subsequently joined Margate and went on to make over 500 first-team appearances for the Kent club.

Albert Henderson (Born Aberdeen. Died Arbroath, 30 April 2008.) Albert Henderson was an inside forward or wing half who made almost 300 appearances for Dundee during the 1950s, helping the team to victory over Kilmarnock in the 1952–53 Scottish League Cup final. He went on to play briefly for St Mirren before a knee injury brought his playing career to a close. Albert subsequently served Arbroath as manager from September 1962 until January 1980.

Gordon Henry (Born Troon, Ayrshire, 9 October 1930. Died December 2007.) Gordon Henry spent the early years of his career with St Mirren, but it was only when he moved south and signed for Aldershot that he played first-team football on a regular basis. A versatile player who could turn out at centre forward, centre half or full back, he made exactly 200 senior appearances for the Shots.

John Hepple (Born Middlesbrough, 12 March 1970. Died South Bank, Middlesbrough, 10 March 2008.) John Hepple spent two seasons as a professional with Sunderland in the late 1980s. Principally a striker with the club's reserve and youth teams, his only experience of senior football came during a spell on loan with Hartlepool at the end of the 1988–89 campaign.

Cecil Heydon (Born Birkenhead, 24 May 1919. Died Brent, London, August 2007.) Cecil Heydon was a wing half who spent most of his career as a reserve. He managed just a handful of appearances despite playing for four different clubs: New Brighton, Derby, Doncaster and Rochdale. Like many of his generation, his best years were lost to the war, although in 1945–46 he enjoyed 24 outings for Doncaster Rovers in that season's emergency competitions.

Carl Hoddle (Born Harlow, Essex, 8 March 1967. Died Sawbridgeworth, Herts., 2 March 2008.) Carl Hoddle began his career as an apprentice with Tottenham Hotspur, but failed to make the grade at White Hart Lane. He later played in Malaysia and for a number of English non-League clubs, before returning to senior football with Leyton Orient in the summer of 1989. Over the next six seasons the tall midfield player went on to make over 100 Football League appearances with the O's and then Barnet before leaving the full-time game. Carl was the younger brother of former Tottenham star Glenn Hoddle.

John Hollowbread (Born Enfield, Middlesex, 2 January 1934. Died Torrevieja, Alicante, Spain, 7 December 2007.) John Hollowbread signed amateur forms for Tottenham in June 1950, and turned professional two years later, but it was not until 1958 that he made his bow in senior football. A solid goalkeeper, he made over 70 first-team appearances for Spurs and then spent two seasons with Southampton before a knee injury effectively ended his career.

Frankie Howard (Born Acton, Middlesex, 30 January 1931. Died 11 October 2007.) Outside left Frankie Howard made over 200 appearances for Brighton during the 1950s before injury brought his playing career to a close. Soon afterwards he was appointed as groundsman at the Goldstone Ground, and, with the exception of a short break, he remained in post for the next 41 years before being made redundant in 2007.

John Hulme (Born Mobberley, Cheshire, 6 February 1945. Died 26 May 2008.) John Hulme was a committed and dependable centre half who made his senior debut for Bolton Wanderers against Nottingham Forest in October 1962 and went on to make some 200 appearances during a decade on the books at Burnden Park. He later served Reading as club captain before winding down his career with spells at Bury and Swiss club La Chaux de Fonds, where he was player-coach.

Forbes Johnston (Born Aberdeen, 3 August 1971. Died Murray Bridge, Adelaide, Australia, 12 July 2007.) Forbes Johnston was a resolute defender who made over 150 senior appearances for Falkirk and Airdrieonians between 1990 and 2000. He subsequently emigrated to Australia to focus on his career in accountancy. Forbes won representative honours for Scotland at Youth and U21 levels and also represented Great Britain in the World Student Games.

Jimmy Johnston (Born Aberdeen, 12 April 1923. Died North Berwick, 16 September 2007.) A tough tackling left half, Jimmy Johnston was a member of the successful Peterhead team of 1946–47, before moving south to sign for Leicester City. He never really established himself at Filbert Street but later went on to make over 200 Division Three South appearances for Reading and Swindon.

Keith Jones (Born Nantyglo, Monmouthshire, 23 October 1928. Died Redditch, August 2007.) Keith Jones joined Aston Villa from Kidderminster Harriers in the summer of 1946, but it was not until the mid-1950s that he became a regular in the line-up. He went on to make 199 appearances for Villa and subsequently featured regularly for both Port Vale and Crewe. He was capped for Wales against Scotland in November 1949.

Ray Jones (Born East Ham, London, 28 August 1988. Died London, 25 August 2007.) Ray Jones joined Queens Park Rangers' Centre of Excellence at the age of 15, progressing to become a trainee on leaving school, and stepping up to the professional ranks in January 2007. A tall, skilful front man who used the ball intelligently, he scored six goals from a total of 35 appearances during the 2006–07 season. He also won representative honours for England U19s, featuring against the Netherlands in September 2006. Ray was tragically killed in a car accident when on the threshold of his career.

Ray Jones (Born Chester, 4 June 1944. Died 16 July 2007.) Ray Jones was a right back who made his debut for Chester in December 1962. He went on to make over 150 first-team appearances for the club over the next seven years before switching to the non-League game.

Ron Jukes (Born Walsall, 1928. Died Walsall, 13 January 2008.) Ron Jukes was a well-known scout in the West Midlands for over 40 years. A local schoolteacher, he is credited with discovering many players who went on to enjoy successful careers including Colin Taylor, Allan Clarke and Steve Bull.

Terry Kelly (Born Luton, 16 January 1932. Died Luton, 2 August 2007.) Terry Kelly was a centre half who was on Luton Town's books between 1950 and 1963. Although he spent much of his time as a back up to Syd Owen, he accumulated over 100 senior appearances for the Hatters and was a member of the team that won the Southern Professional Floodlit Cup in 1956–57.

Steve Kemp (Born Shrewsbury, 2 May 1955. Died January 2008.) Steve Kemp stepped up to the professional ranks with Shrewsbury Town in the summer of 1973 after completing an apprenticeship at Gay Meadow. A defender, he went on to make eight senior appearances for the club before moving to play in Australia.

Mark Kendall (Born Tredegar, Monmouthshire, 20 September 1958. Died Blackwood, Monmouthshire, 1 May 2008.) Mark Kendall was a goalkeeper who made 36 first-team appearances during a four-year spell with Tottenham. He went on to play in over 300 games for Newport County, leaving for Wolves shortly before the club lost their Football League status. At Molineux he was an ever-present as Wolves won the Fourth Division title in 1987–88, also featuring in their Sherpa Van Trophy winning side against Burnley at Wembley and gaining a Third Division Championship medal the following year. He also played briefly for Swansea, gaining a Welsh Cup winners' medal in 1991. Mark was capped by Wales at Youth and U21 levels.

Davie Kinnear (Born 22 February 1917. Died Newton Mearns, East Renfrewshire, 3 February 2008.) Davie Kinnear shone as a 16-year-old outside left with Raith Rovers in the 1933–34 season and was soon on his way to Rangers. At Ibrox he was a near ever-present in the side that won the Scottish League title in 1936–37 and also won a champions' medal in 1938–39 before war intervened. Davie had spells with Third Lanark, Dunfermline and Stirling after the war. Later he returned to Ibrox and he went on to serve the club as trainer and physio from 1956 until 1970. He made one appearance for Scotland, against Czechoslovakia in December 1937.

Harry Kirtley (Born Washington, Co. Durham, 23 May 1930. Died December 2007.) Harry Kirtley was an inside forward who made over 100 appearances for Sunderland between 1948 and 1955. He later played for both Cardiff City and Gateshead, featuring for the latter club in their final season of League football.

Brian Lambert (Born Sutton-in-Ashfield, Notts, 10 July 1936. Died Kirkby-in-Ashfield, Notts, 27 December 2007.) Brian Lambert spent six years as a professional with Mansfield Town in the 1950s. Principally a full back, he made 30 first-team appearances for the Stags.

Eric Lancelotte (Born Jhansi, India, 26 February 1917. Died Canterbury, 1 September 2007.) Born in India, where his father was stationed in the Royal Artillery, Eric Lancelotte joined the groundstaff at Charlton Athletic in 1933. After four years at The Valley he eventually made his first-team debut, but soon afterwards war intervened to put his career on hold. An effective forward, he later spent two seasons as a regular with Brighton in the old Division Three South before switching to non-League football.

Jim Langley (Born Kilburn, London, 7 February 1929. Died Yiewsley, Hillingdon, London, 9 December 2007.) Although originally an outside left when he joined Leeds United in 1952, Jim Langley quickly converted to left back with great success. He went on to make more than 600 senior appearances for Brighton, Fulham and Queens Park Rangers up until his retirement in 1967. Jim won representative honours for the Football League against the Irish League in October 1956 and later won three full England caps during his stay at Fulham. In the twilight of his career he helped QPR sensationally defeat West Brom to win the Football League Cup in 1967.

Ken Leek (Born Ynysybwl, Glamorgan, 26 July 1935. Died Daventry, Northamptonshire, 19 November 2007.) Ken Leek was a hard running, robust centre forward who developed with Northampton Town before he was sold to Leicester in the summer of 1958. A brief spell at Newcastle followed before he signed for Birmingham, for whom he enjoyed the distinction of scoring two goals in the first leg of the Football League Cup final in 1962–63 as the Blues won their only senior trophy to date. He later returned to Northampton to assist the club's promotion to the top flight in 1964–65 and then wound down his career with a couple of seasons at Bradford City. Ken also won 13 caps for Wales between 1960 and 1965.

Bobby Leishman (Born Edinburgh. Died Edinburgh, 31 March 2008.) Bobby Leishman was an inside left who made 110 first-team appearances for East Fife between 1954 and 1959. He subsequently had the briefest of spells with Falkirk and Raith before switching to East of Scotland League side Ferranti Thistle.

Dai Lewis (Born Cardigan, 12 February 1936. Died Swansea, 30 October 2007.) A winger or inside forward, Dai Lewis played for Swansea Town and Torquay United during the period 1957 to 1961, making a total of 37 senior appearances.

Tom Liddell (Born Edinburgh, 15 January 1931. Died Edinburgh, 1 June 2008.) Tom Liddell was a wing half who joined East Fife from Musselburgh Athletic in December 1952 and went on to make 12 Scottish League appearances before retiring due to injuries in the summer of 1956.

Nils Liedholm (Born: Valdemarsvik, Sweden, 18 October 1922. Died: Cuccaro Monferrato, Italy, 5 November 2007.) Nils Liedholm was one of the all-time greats of Swedish football. At club level he starred as an inside forward with IFK Norrköping before moving to Italy where he spent 12 years as a professional with AC Milan, making over 350 appearances and helping them win the Serie A title on four occasions. Although his international career was limited by Sweden's reluctance to play professional players, he won 23 full caps, gaining an Olympic Gold medal in 1948 and a World Cup runners-up medal in 1958. Nils remained in Italy when his playing days were over and coached a number of clubs including Fiorentina, Roma and AC Milan.

Jackie Little (Born Gateshead, 17 May 1912. Died Ipswich, 15 October 2007.) Jackie Little joined Ipswich Town in their non-League days, playing in the Eastern Counties and Southern Leagues before their elevation to senior status. A left-sided forward, he featured in the club's first-ever Football League fixture against Southend United in August 1938 and went on to play in over 150 senior games during his stay at Portman Road, scoring 24 goals.

Bert Lister (Born Manchester, 4 October 1939. Died Manchester, 16 July 2007.) Bert Lister is best known for his exploits with Oldham Athletic in the early 1960s, scoring almost a century of goals for the Latics including six in an 11–0 victory over Southport on Boxing Day 1962. A talented forward, he had begun his career at Manchester City, and later turned out for Rochdale and Stockport before leaving the full-time game in 1967.

Norrie McArthur (Born St Andrews, Fife, 6 September 1947. Died Cellardyke, Fife, 15 April 2008.) Norrie McArthur was an inside forward who played for several Highland League clubs including Elgin and Clachnacuddin before spending part of the 1973–74 season with Berwick Rangers. He later played at Junior level in Scotland for many years.

Dougie McBain (Born Blantyre, 22 September 1924. Died 1 February 2008.) Dougie McBain featured at right half for Queen's Park in the 1947–48 season, also earning selection for the Great Britain squad for the 1948 Olympic Games tournament. Shortly afterwards he signed for Queen of the South, for whom he went on to make just short of 200 first-team appearances before retiring from the game at the end of the 1954–55 season.

Jack McDonald (Born Maltby, Yorkshire, 27 August 1921. Died 28 June 2007.) Jack McDonald made his name as a goal-scoring left winger in wartime, when he guested for a string of clubs and assisted Chelsea in their defeat of Millwall in the Football League War Cup South final at Wembley in April 1945. Later he helped Fulham win the Second Division title in 1948–49. Jack had begun his career with spells at Wolves and Bournemouth before the war, and later turned out for both Southampton and Southend before retiring at the end of the 1954–55 campaign.

Derek McKay (Born Banff, 13 December 1949. Died Pattaya, Thailand, 19 April 2008.) Derek McKay was playing Highland League football with Deveronvale at the age of 15, later spending time on the books of Dundee without achieving a great deal of success. He shone during a couple of seasons at Aberdeen, scoring the winner in the Scottish Cup semi-final against Kilmarnock in 1970, and then netting two in the final when the Dons defeated Celtic 3–1 to take the trophy. He subsequently had a spell with Barrow before eventually emigrating to live in Australia.

George McKay (Born Dundee, circa 1921. Died Dundee. 14 October 2007.) George 'Piper' McKay signed for Dundee United during the war, later playing for Dundee, East Fife and Morton. An outside left, he subsequently had a spell in Canada where he played for Montreal Vickers of the Eastern Division of the National Soccer League.

Jimmy McKnight (Died May 2008.) Jimmy McKnight spent four seasons on the books of Queen of the South and a further two with Ayr United, although he only managed a handful of outings for both clubs. However, he experienced regular first-team football after joining Stranraer in the summer of 1955, making over 150 appearances before leaving the club at the end of the 1959–60 campaign.

Jimmy McStay (Born Newry, 4 August 1922. Died January 2007.) Jimmy McStay featured for a number of Irish clubs including Newry Town, Limerick, Ballymena and Dundalk before signing for Grimsby Town in August 1948. A talented outside right, he made 65 first-team appearances for the Mariners. Earlier in his career he had been capped for the League of Ireland representative side.

Michael Maidens (Born Middlesbrough, 7 May 1987. Died Redcar, Cleveland, 19 October 2007.) Michael Maidens joined Hartlepool United as a trainee on leaving school and went on to make his first-team debut at the age of 17. A winger who was effective on either flank, Michael featured regularly in the first-team squad during the 2005–06 season, and later spent time on loan with York City and Blyth Spartans. At the time of his death he was a member of Hartlepool's reserve team. Michael was tragically killed when the car in which he was a passenger was involved in a collision on Teesside.

Keith Matthews (Born Wrexham, 7 March 1934. Died January 2008.) Keith Matthews was a winger who joined Wrexham from Llay United in December 1952, but although he spent three seasons with the Racecourse club he made just nine first-team appearances.

Harry May (Born Glasgow, 15 October 1928. Died July 2007.) Harry May made his debut for Cardiff at centre forward, but most of his subsequent career was spent at left back. After two seasons with Swindon he joined Barnsley, where he was an ever-present in the team that won the Division Three North title in 1954–55. Harry later played for Southend and Gloucester City.

Ron Mitchell (Born Dundee, 22 June 1921. Died Dundee, 22 November 2007.) Ron Mitchell made his debut for St Johnstone in 1946, but spent most of his career in Scotland's C Division, making over 200 appearances for Brechin City and Berwick Rangers. Initially an inside left, he later dropped back to left half. Away from football he enjoyed a successful academic career and for many years he was a Professor of Mathematics at Dundee University.

Alan Moore (Born Hebburn, 7 March 1927. Died 7 April 2008.) Alan Moore was a tricky winger who amassed over 275 senior appearances in a career that saw him play for Chesterfield, Hull, Nottingham Forest, Coventry, Swindon and Rochdale during the 1950s. He was later player-manager of Cambridge United, then members of the Southern League, from December 1959 through to 1963.

Bill Morgan (Born Rotherham, 26 September 1926. Died Halifax, 12 July 2007.) Left half Bill Morgan played reserve-team football for Wolverhampton Wanderers and Sheffield United, before joining Halifax Town in the summer of 1948. Bill went over to make over a century of appearances for the Shaymen before injuries took their toll. He ended his career with a couple of seasons at Rochdale.

Malcolm Musgrove (Born Lynemouth, Northumberland, 8 July 1933. Died 14 September 2007.) Malcolm Musgrove was a pacy, direct left winger who made over 300 appearances for West Ham between 1953 and 1962. A near ever-present in 1957–58 campaign, when the Second Division title was won, he was also Hammer of the Year in 1959–60. Malcolm subsequently spent three seasons at Leyton Orient before moving into coaching with Charlton and Aston Villa, then linking up with his former West Ham colleague Frank O'Farrell at Leicester. He followed O'Farrell to Manchester United as coach and then managed Torquay (1973 to 1976), later coaching a number of clubs. He also served as Chairman of the PFA from 1963 until 1966.

Wilf Nash (Born circa 1913. Died 11 March 2008.) Wilf Nash was a winger who made two appearances for Coventry City in the wartime emergency competitions during the 1943–44 season.

Ken Nethercott (Born Bristol, 22 July 1925. Died Norwich, 14 December 2007.) Ken Nethercott signed for Norwich City in April 1947 after being demobilised from military service and went on to become one of the greatest goalkeepers in the club's history. Over the next 12 years he made over 400 first-team appearances before his career was effectively ended after he suffered a shoulder injury in the FA Cup sixth round tie against Sheffield United in February 1959. Ken was capped for England B against Scotland B in March 1953.

Phil O'Donnell (Born Bellshill, Lanarkshire, 25 March 1972. Died Wishaw, Lanarkshire, 29 December 2007.) Phil O'Donnell was a talented left-sided midfield player who progressed through the youth scheme with Motherwell to sign professional forms at the age of 18. Soon afterwards he made his first-team debut and at the end of his first season he gained a Scottish Cup winners' medal, scoring one of the goals as 'Well defeated Dundee United 4–3. Thereafter he was a regular in the line-up, attracting wider attention with representative honours for the national team and twice winning the Scottish PFA Young Player of the Year title (1992 and 1994). Early in the 1994–95 season he was sold to Celtic for a fee of £1.75 million, but although he gained another Scottish Cup winners' medal in 1995, he was hampered by a string of injuries. A move to Sheffield Wednesday in the summer of 1999 did not see Phil return to full fitness, and he spent much of his time at Hillsborough in the treatment room due to knee injuries. After leaving Wednesday he eventually linked up with Motherwell once more and in the summer of he was appointed player-coach. Phil tragically collapsed and died whilst playing for Motherwell against Dundee United on 29 December 2007.

Phil O'Donnell

Fred Ogden (Born Oldham, 13 April 1925. Died February 2008.) Fred Ogden spent three seasons as Oldham Athletic's regular goalkeeper, but then fractured a collarbone in September 1951. He remained at Boundary Park until the summer of 1955, then had a season with Chesterfield, where he was limited to reserve-team football, before returning to Oldham briefly once more. Later, Fred joined the backroom staff at Boundary Park, taking charge of the junior players and also serving as trainer to the A and reserve teams for several years.

Jimmy O'Neill (Born Dublin, Ireland, 13 October 1931. Died Southport, 15 December 2007.) Jimmy O'Neill made over 200 first-team appearances for Everton between 1949 and 1960, featuring in the side that won promotion from the Second Division in 1953–54. He added a further century of appearances for Stoke and also played for Darlington and Port Vale before retiring in 1967. Jimmy was also a regular for the Republic of Ireland international team, winning 17 caps between 1952 and 1959.

Roy Onslow (Born Swindon, 12 September 1928. Died 31 July 2007.) Roy Onslow was an inside forward who made almost 150 senior appearances for Swindon Town in two spells during the 1950s separated by a season in the Southern League with Kidderminster. He later played for a number of non-League clubs including Chippenham Town, Bath and Salisbury.

Cyril Ordish (Born Basford, Notts., 23 May 1915. Died Bakewell, Derbyshire, August 2007.) Full back Cyril Ordish had spells as a professional with both Chesterfield and Wolverhampton Wanderers, but it was only when he signed for Reading in February 1938 that he experienced regular first-team football. He went on to appear 23 times for the Royals before the war intervened to effectively end his career.

Graham Paddon (Born Manchester, 24 August 1950. Died Norfolk, 19 November 2007.) Graham Paddon began his senior career with Coventry City, but he struggled to break into a strong squad at Highfield Road and in October 1969 he joined Norwich City. Here he developed into a hard-running midfield player with a tremendous left-foot shot, helping City win the Second Division title in 1971–72 before being sold to West Ham. The three years Graham spent with the Hammers were probably the best of his career, and in May 1975 he was a member of the team that defeated Fulham to win the FA Cup final. The following season he won a runners-up medal in the European Cup Winners' Cup as the Hammers lost out to Anderlecht in the final. Graham eventually returned to Norwich, but suffered a broken leg just weeks after re-signing for the club. Thereafter he played briefly in Hong Kong before leaving football for a while, only to return to the game as a coach with Portsmouth and Stoke City. Earlier in his career he had earned a single cap for England at U23 level.

Harold Peace (Born Darlaston, Staffs., 1923. Died 29 December 2007.) Harold Peace was a centre forward who made 23 wartime appearances for Walsall, scoring four goals. Short and with plenty of pace, he went on to play for Darlaston and Hednesford Town.

Eric Perkins (Born West Bromwich, 19 August 1934. Died Walsall, 30 January 2008.) Eric Perkins was a full back who made a couple of senior appearances for West Bromwich Albion before moving on to Walsall in the summer of 1956. He enjoyed greater success with the Saddlers, receiving over 70 first-team outings in three seasons at the club.

Bill Perry (Born Johannesburg, South Africa, 10 September 1930. Died Blackpool, 27 September 2007.) Bill Perry was playing in South Africa for Johannesburg Rangers when he was spotted by Blackpool and signed up shortly after the start of the 1949–50 campaign. He quickly became the club's regular outside left, retaining his position for some eight seasons and making over 400 first-team appearances. A short stocky man blessed with tremendous pace, he had appeared for Blackpool in the 1951 FA Cup final when they were defeated by Newcastle United. Two years later came his finest hour in football, when he netted the winning goal as the Seasiders defeated Bolton 4–3 to win the trophy in a game that is always referred to as 'The Matthews Final'. Bill won three caps for England and also played for the Football League representative side. He concluded his career with a season at Southport.

Billy Pointon (Born Hanley, Staffs., 25 November 1920. Died Portsmouth, 6 January 2008.) Billy Pointon was a centre forward who joined Port Vale in 1940 and went on to make over 100 appearances, including wartime games, before being sold to Queens Park Rangers for what was then a record fee for Vale. He also had a spell with Brentford before switching to the non-League game.

Bill Perry

Ian Porterfield (Born Dunfermline, 11 February 1946. Died Surrey, 11 September 2007.) Ian Porterfield made his bow in senior football as a teenaged triallist with Cowdenbeath. However, he signed for Raith Rovers soon afterwards, moving on to Sunderland in January 1968. He developed into an intelligent forward at Roker Park, making over 250 first-team appearances. His finest moment in football came when he scored the decisive goal in the 1973 FA Cup final, providing one of the greatest shocks of all time as Sunderland, then members of the Second Division, defeated odds-on favourites Leeds United to take the trophy. The following year Ian was badly injured in a car accident, but fought his way back to fitness with great determination and subsequently enjoyed three successful seasons with Sheffield Wednesday. He later turned to management with Rotherham, Sheffield United, Aberdeen, Reading and Chelsea before coaching at international level in a number of countries including Zambia, Saudi Arabia, Trinidad & Tobago and, most recently, Armenia.

David Preece (Born Bridgnorth, Shropshire, 28 May 1963. Died 20 July 2007.) David Preece made his name as an all-action midfield player with Walsall, where he was a member of the side that reached the semi-final of the Football League Cup in 1983–84. The following December he was sold to Luton and went on to become a mainstay of the Hatters' side for ten years, making a total of almost 400 senior appearances during his stay at Kenilworth Road. He won a League Cup winners' medal in 1987–88, and a runners-up medal in the same competition the following season. After a brief spell at Derby he spent five seasons at Cambridge, where he was also involved in a coaching role and he later had a spell as assistant manager of Torquay United. David also won three caps for England B in the summer of 1989.

Antonio Puerta (Born 26 November 1984. Died 28 August 2007.) Antonio Puerta was a left-sided midfield player who developed through the Sevilla youth policy. A member of the team that won back-to-back UEFA Cup finals in 2006 and 2007, he had made his full international debut for Spain against Sweden in October 2006. His death came in tragic circumstances: he collapsed during the Liga fixture with Getafe after suffering a heart attack and although rushed to hospital he died shortly afterwards.

Freddie Pye (Born Stockport, 11 March 1928. Died 31 March 2008.) Freddie Pye spent a season-and-a-half on the books of Accrington Stanley in the late 1940s, making a handful of Football League appearances. He subsequently turned out for a string of non-League clubs in the North West. Away from football he developed a successful scrap metal business, enabling him to become chairman of Stockport County (late 1970s), chairman of Wigan Athletic (early 1980s) and vice-chairman of Manchester City (1988–1993).

Eddie Quinlan (Born Clapton, London, 15 August 1931. Died Reading, 10 March 2008.) Outside left Eddie Quinlan joined Tottenham from Great Yarmouth Town in March 1952, but never made it past the reserve team at White Hart Lane. However, he fared better at Reading, for whom he made 53 appearances between 1953 and 1956.

John Reames (Born Lincoln, 19 February 1942. Died 6 May 2008.) John Reames was appointed chairman of Lincoln City in March 1985 and remained in post until November 2000, becoming the club's longest serving chairman. For the period November 1998 until the summer of 2000 he was also the team manager, enjoying a degree of success when he won the Division Three Manager of the Month award for October 1999. John also had a spell on the Football League Management Committee during the 1990s.

Anton Reid (Born 20 September 1990. Died 20 August 2007.) A promising young left back or central defender, Anton Reid joined Walsall's Centre of Excellence as a 13-year-old. He tragically collapsed and died during a training session shortly after stepping up to become a trainee with the club.

David Reid (Born 1938. Died Tasmania, Australia, December 2007.) David Reid was a centre forward who was capped by Scotland Juniors against Ireland in 1959 before Dunfermline stepped in to sign him from Luncarty Juniors. However, he made just two appearances for the Pars and another two for Dundee United before leaving the senior game. He later emigrated to Australia.

Jack Rennie (Died Melrose, 4 December 2007.) Jack Rennie had a trial with Dundee during 1933–34 and later spent three seasons on the books of Hibernian without making the first team. He went on to sign for Leyton Orient, where he made six appearances at full back in the 1938–39 season.

Graham Reynolds (Born Newport, 23 January 1937. Died Cardiff, 27 February 2008.) Graham Reynolds was a versatile forward who made a handful of appearances as a young amateur for Newport County, becoming the club's youngest-ever League player at the time, before moving away to study. He returned to Somerton Park in 1963, making a further 43 appearances for the club and eventually switching to professional status. Graham was also a talented cricketer, making two First Class and 11 Sunday League appearances for Glamorgan. At the time of his death he was President of the Gwent Football Association.

Tony Richardson (Born Cleethorpes, Lincs., 5 November 1943. Died Spain, 29 August 2007.) Tony Richardson had a spell on the books of Nottingham Forest without making the first team, and then drifted off to sign for Cheltenham Town before returning to the senior ranks with Bradford City, where he made two first-team appearances during the 1962–63 season. He later served Grimsby Town as commercial manager for 15 years until his retirement in May 2006.

John Riley (Born Glasgow, 20 July 1920. Died November 2007.) Winger John Riley made 22 wartime appearances for Celtic between 1941 and 1943, then had a spell in Junior football before returning to the seniors with Clyde in 1945. He made 19 Scottish League appearances during his stay at Shawfield and later had a brief association with Arbroath before leaving the game.

Eddie Rutherford (Born Glasgow, 8 February 1921. Died 29 June 2007.) Eddie Rutherford guested for Lincoln City and Bradford City during the war, then returned to Rangers where he was a member of the first team to complete a domestic treble of League, Cup and League Cup in 1948–49. A talented winger, he also helped the Ibrox club to a League and Cup double in 1949–50 and the following September won representative honours for the Scottish League against the Irish League. He subsequently had spells with Hearts, Raith Rovers and Hamilton. Eddie won a single cap for Scotland, lining up against France in May 1948.

Óscar Sánchez (Born Cochabamba, Bolivia, 16 July 1971. Died Bolivia, 23 November 2007.) Óscar Sánchez was a central defender who won 78 caps for Bolivia, appearing in the side that lost out to Brazil in the 1997 Copa America final. He had originally been selected to play for his country in the 2007 Copa America tournament but withdrew and died within a matter of months from cancer of the kidney. At club level he played for The Strongest and Bolívar in Bolivia, and Gimnasia Jujuy and Independiente de Avellaneda in Argentina.

Donald Saunders (Born 23 May 1922. Died 29 April 2008.) Donald Saunders was a journalist who worked on a number of regional newspapers including the *Western Mail*, *Derby Evening Telegraph* and Brighton's *Evening Argus* before joining the sports desk of the *Daily Telegraph* in 1955. He covered football and boxing for the *Telegraph* for some 30 years, and also reported on seven Olympic Games.

Ian Porterfield

Les Shannon (Born Liverpool, 12 March 1926. Died Dunstable, 2 December 2007.) Les Shannon enjoyed a brief run in the Liverpool line-up at the start of the 1948–49 campaign but otherwise made little impact during his time at Anfield. After moving to Burnley in November 1949 he converted to wing half and went on to make over 250 appearances for the Clarets. He also won three England B caps during his time at Turf Moor. On retiring as a player Les coached Everton and Arsenal, then served as manager of Bury (1966–69) and Blackpool (1969–70). Following this he enjoyed a spell in Greece coaching PAOK, Iraklis, Olympiakos Piraeus and OFI Crete, then in Norway with Brann Bergen before returning to England and a post with Luton Town,

Joe Shaw (Born Murton, Co. Durham, 23 June 1928. Died Sheffield, 18 November 2007.) Joe Shaw signed for Sheffield United in July 1945, but he had to wait three years for his senior debut. After converting from wing half to centre half during the 1954–55 season he developed as an excellent, skilful defender and came close to international honours, being capped for the Football League against both the Scottish League and the Irish League in 1958. Joe spent 20 years on the club's books and his total of 629 Football League appearances still stands as a record for the Blades. After retiring as a player he had spells as manager of York City (1967–68) and Chesterfield (1973–76).

Paddy Shortt (Born circa 1949. Died Cork, Ireland, 5 September 2007.) Paddy Shortt was an orthodox right winger who enjoyed a successful career in the League of Ireland, gaining successive championships with Waterford (1972–73) and Cork City (1973–74) as well as winning the FAI Cup with Limerick in 1971. He also represented the Republic of Ireland at Amateur and U23 levels.

Dave Simmons (Born Ryde, Isle of Wight, 24 October 1948. Died Cambridgeshire, 3 July 2007.) Dave Simmons was a big, powerful centre forward whose career only really got going when he signed for Colchester United midway through the 1970–71 season. Within a matter of months he had helped create history when he scored the third and final goal as the U's defeated Leeds United to create one of the greatest-ever FA Cup shocks. His career had begun with spells at Arsenal and Aston Villa, and after leaving Layer Road in 1973 he turned out for Cambridge United and Brentford.

Gordon Skeech (Born Warrington, 15 May 1924. Died Newton-le-Willows, Merseyside, 13 May 2008.) Gordon Skeech joined Shrewsbury Town from Runcorn in November 1954. He made his debut at the end of the 1954–55 season, but it was another three years before he won a regular place in the line-up at left back. Gordon went on to make 223 Football League appearances for the Shrews before returning to Runcorn in the summer of 1963.

Les Smith (Born Halesowen, 24 December 1927. Died Stourbridge, 8 March 2008.) Les Smith was a talented winger who spent a decade on the books of Wolves for whom he was generally used as back-up for Jimmy Mullen and Johnny Hancocks. On moving to neighbours Aston Villa in February 1956 he gained a greater level of first-team exposure, featuring in the side that defeated Manchester United to win the FA Cup in 1957.

Ellis Stafford (Born Sheffield, 17 August 1929. Died 31 October 2007.) Ellis Stafford made almost 200 appearances for Peterborough United in their Midland League days, converting from centre forward to the right-back position soon after his arrival. He went on to appear in the club's first-ever Football League fixture against Wrexham in August 1960 but soon lost his place in the side through injury. He later returned to London Road to serve Posh for another 20 years in the capacity of pools and commercial manager.

Johnny Steele (Born Glasgow, 24 November 1916. Died 14 January 2008.) Johnny Steele developed as an inside left with East Fife and Ayr United in the 1930s, also enjoying a loan spell with Raith Rovers. In the summer of 1938 he moved south to sign for Barnsley, where he proved to be a great success, scoring 17 goals as the club romped away with the Division Three North title in his first season. After retiring as a player he joined the coaching staff at Oakwell in 1951 and went on to manage the club from 1960 to 1971 and again in 1972–73. He also held the posts of general manager and secretary from 1970 until 1982, and for a while was a director of the club.

Byron Stevenson (Born Llanelli, 7 September 1956. Died 6 September 2007.) Byron Stevenson was a versatile defender or midfield player who made over 150 senior appearances for Leeds United and Birmingham City in a decade from 1975. He later wound down his career with a season at Bristol Rovers. Byron was capped 15 times by Wales and also won international honours at U23 level.

Ken Sykes (Born Darlington, 29 January 1926. Died 2008.) Ken Sykes was a big centre forward who played six times for Darlington in the 1946–47 season. He later had spells with Middlesbrough (0 appearances) and Hartlepools United (1 outing) before leaving the full time game in 1950.

Derek Tapscott (Born Barry, 30 June 1932. Died 12 June 2008.) Derek Tapscott joined Arsenal from Barry Town in 1953 and went on to score 62 goals from 119 Football League appearances for the Gunners. A pacy, direct centre forward, he later had a successful spell with Cardiff City, helping them win promotion to the old First Division in 1959–60 before concluding his career with a season at Newport County. Derek also won 14 caps for Wales between 1954 and 1959.

Ken Teasdale (Born circa 1922. Died 21 February 2008.) Ken Teasdale was a goalkeeper who made 71 appearances for Bradford City in the emergency competitions during World War Two. He later spent the 1947–48 season on the books of Accrington Stanley without making a first-team appearance. After retiring as a player he turned to refereeing and remained active in local football in the Bradford area until reaching the age of 75.

Garry Telfer (Born 19 January 1965. Died Dumfries, 17 July 2007.) Garry Telfer was a striker who had two spells with Queen of the South, featuring in over 50 first-team games. He also played for Annan Athletic and Dalbeattie Star. Away from football Garry worked as a fire fighter and he died suddenly after being taken ill while attending a fire in the Dumfries area.

Matt Thomson, MBE (Born circa 1938. Died 15 April 2008.) Matt Thomson was a committed defender who joined Motherwell from Ardeer Thistle in 1960 and went on to make over 200 first-team appearances during a nine-year spell at Fir Park. He later set up his own business, Thomson Litho, which became Scotland's largest independent printing firm and his personal wealth put him in the top 100 of the Rich List for Scotland. Matt also served Motherwell as a director for several years.

Jimmy Todd (Born Belfast, 19 March 1921. Died Stoke-on-Trent, 19 December 2007.) Jimmy Todd was a wing half who featured in wartime for Blackpool before moving on to Port Vale in October 1946. He spent seven seasons with the Potteries club, making over 150 League and Cup appearances.

Ken Tucker (Born Poplar, London, 2 October 1925. Died Southend, May 2008.) Outside left Ken Tucker joined West Ham from Finchley in August 1946, and went on to score a hat-trick on his debut for the Hammers against Chesterfield some 12 months later. Although often a reserve at Upton Park, he scored 31 goals from 83 games during his stay and later played for Notts County and Margate before leaving football.

Alan Tyrer (Born Liverpool, 8 December 1942. Died Middlesbrough, January 2008.) Alan Tyrer featured briefly for Everton as a 17-year old, but it was not until he moved on to Mansfield Town that he experienced regular first-team football. A small, slightly built forward, he helped the Stags win promotion in 1964–65, and then played for Arsenal and Bury, failing to establish himself at either club. Alan later became one of the key players for Workington in the 1970s, making over 250 first-team appearances.

Lawrence Wallace (Born Sandown, Isle of Wight, 1917. Died Eastleigh, Hants., 13 September 2007.) Lawrence Wallace was an amateur forward who played in a solitary first-team game for Southampton against Manchester City at Maine Road in March 1939. He was also a capable sprinter, representing England at the 1938 Empire Games when he was a member of the team that won a silver medal in the 4 x 110 yards relay contest.

Peter Walsh (Born Dublin, Ireland, 18 October 1922. Died Ballybough, Dublin, Ireland, 23 October 2007.) A bustling centre forward, Peter Walsh enjoyed a successful spell with Dundalk in the late 1940s, gaining an FAI Cup winners' medal in 1949 when Shelbourne were defeated in the final. In August 1949 he signed for Luton Town, but although he scored in his first two appearances for the Hatters he was unable to establish himself in the line-up and after a season at Kenilworth Road he moved on to join Brighton, where he failed to make the first team.

Cyril Watkin (Born Stoke-on-Trent, 21 July 1926. Died Stoke-on-Trent, 3 July 2007.) Cyril Watkin was an outside left who joined Stoke City during the war and went on to make 86 first-team appearances for the club. He later had a spell with Bristol City before leaving full-time football and returning to live in the Potteries.

Pat Watters (Born circa 1939. Died April 2008.) Pat Watters was a versatile forward who spent the early 1960s as a fringe player with Stirling Albion, Stranraer and Forfar. He went on to experience regular first-team football during spells with Stenhousemuir (1963–65) and East Stirling (1965–67) taking his tally of senior appearances close to the 150-mark.

Frank Wayman (Born Bishop Auckland, Co. Durham, 30 December 1931. Died Ferryhill, Co. Durham, 7 February 2008.) Frank Wayman was a skilful outside right who joined Preston North End from West Auckland in the summer of 1953, but failed to make a senior appearance during his stay at Deepdale. He later featured regularly during a season with Chester and also spent time on the books of Darlington. His death came in tragic circumstances after he received serious head injuries when he was struck by a motor cycle whilst out walking his dog.

John Wilkinson (Born Worksop, 1 April 1949. Died 22 September 2007.) John Wilkinson made nine appearances for Grimsby Town in the mid-1960s, mostly when deputising for the club's regular left back, Graham Taylor. He later played for Nantwich Town before moving to live in the Mansfield area where he worked in the licensed trade.

George Wright (Born Plymouth, 10 October 1919. Died Tarleton, Lancashire, 23 April 2008.) Goalkeeper George Wright made 12 Football League appearances for Plymouth Argyle either side of the Second World War before moving on to Colchester United, then a Southern League club. He remained at Layer Road after the club was elected to the League in 1950 and went on to add a further 151 appearances for the U's before retiring at the end of the 1954–55 campaign.

Reg Wyatt (Born Plymouth, 18 September 1932. Died Plymouth, 16 November 2007.) Reg Wyatt played as an inside forward at the beginning of his career, but went on to make his name in the professional game as a defender for Plymouth Argyle. A member of the team that won the Third Division title in 1958–59, he made 217 senior appearances for Argyle before finishing his career with a spell at Torquay.

Ian Nannestad
Soccer History Magazine

THE FOOTBALL RECORDS

BRITISH FOOTBALL RECORDS

ALL-TIME PREMIER LEAGUE CHAMPIONSHIP SEASONS ON POINTS AVERAGE

	Team	*Season*	*P*	*W*	*D*	*L*	*F*	*A*	*Pts*	*Pts Av*
1	Chelsea	2004–05	38	29	8	1	72	15	95	2.50
2	Manchester U	1999–2000	38	28	7	3	97	45	91	2.39
3	Chelsea	2005–06	38	29	4	5	72	22	91	2.39
4	Arsenal	2003–04	38	26	12	0	73	26	90	2.36
5	Manchester U	2006–07	38	28	5	5	83	27	89	2.34
6	Arsenal	2001–02	38	26	9	3	79	36	87	2.28
	Manchester U	2007–08	38	27	6	5	80	22	87	2.28
8	Manchester U	2002–03	38	25	8	5	74	34	83	2.18
9	Manchester U	1995–96	38	25	7	6	73	35	82	2.15
10	Blackburn R	1994–95	42	27	8	7	80	39	89	2.11
11	Manchester U	2000–01	38	24	8	6	79	31	80	2.10
12	Manchester U	1998–99	38	22	13	3	80	37	79	2.07
13	Arsenal	1997–98	38	23	9	6	68	33	78	2.05
14	Manchester U	1992–93	42	24	12	6	67	31	84	2.00
15	Manchester U	1996–97	38	21	12	5	76	44	75	1.97

PREMIER LEAGUE EVER-PRESENT CLUBS

	P	*W*	*D*	*L*	*F*	*A*	*Pts*
Manchester U	620	394	137	89	1220	539	1319
Arsenal	620	332	168	120	1048	548	1164
Chelsea	620	310	168	142	977	606	1098
Liverpool	620	306	157	157	992	607	1075
Aston Villa	620	230	187	203	782	724	877
Tottenham H	620	223	165	232	839	847	834
Everton	620	211	167	242	758	808	800

TOP TEN PREMIERSHIP APPEARANCES

1	Gary Speed	535	**6**	Gareth Southgate	426
2	David James	511	**7**	Teddy Sheringham	418
3	Ryan Giggs	495	**8**	Andy Cole	414
4	Sol Campbell	453	**9**	Emile Heskey	404
5	Alan Shearer	441	**10**	Paul Scholes and Frank Lampard	395

TOP TEN PREMIERSHIP GOALSCORERS

1	Alan Shearer	260	**6**	Teddy Sheringham	146
2	Andy Cole	187	**7**	Michael Owen	136
3	Thierry Henry	174	**8**	Jimmy Floyd Hasselbaink	127
4	Robbie Fowler	163	**9**	Dwight Yorke	123
5	Les Ferdinand	149	**10**	Ian Wright	113

PREMIERSHIP GOAL MILESTONES

Goal	**Date**	**Scorer**	**Match**
1	15.8.92	Brian Deane	Sheffield U v Manchester U
100	25.8.92	Mark Walters	Liverpool v Ipswich T
1000	7.4.93	Mike Newell	Blackburn R v Nottingham F
5000	7.12.96	Andy Townsend	Aston Villa v Southampton
10,000	15.12.01	Les Ferdinand	Tottenham H v Fulham
11,000	7.12.02	Jay-Jay Okocha	Bolton W v Blackburn R
12,000	13.12.03	Alan Shearer	Newcastle U v Tottenham H
13,000	28.11.04	Frederic Kanoute	Tottenham H v Middlesbrough
14,000	26.12.05	Jermain Defoe	Tottenham H v Birmingham C
15,000	30.12.06	Moritz Volz	Fulham v Chelsea

EUROPEAN CUP AND CHAMPIONS LEAGUE RECORDS

CHAMPIONS LEAGUE ATTENDANCES AND GOALS FROM GROUP STAGES ONWARDS

Season	*Attendances*	*Average*	*Goals*	*Games*
1992–93	873,251	34,930	56	25
1993–94	1,202,289	44,529	71	27
1994–95	2,328,515	38,172	140	61
1995–96	1,874,316	30,726	159	61
1996–97	2,093,228	34,315	161	61
1997–98	2,868,271	33,744	239	85
1998–99	3,608,331	42,451	238	85
1999–2000	5,490,709	34,973	442	157
2000–01	5,773,486	36,774	449	157
2001–02	5,417,716	34,508	393	157
2002–03	6,461,112	41,154	431	157
2003–04	4,611,214	36,890	309	125
2004–05	4,946,820	39,575	331	125
2005–06	5,291,187	42,330	285	125
2006–07	5,591,463	44,732	309	125
2007–08	5,454,718	43,638	330	125

HIGHEST AVERAGE ATTENDANCE IN ONE EUROPEAN CUP SEASON
1959–60 50,545 from a total attendance of 2,780,000.

HIGHEST SCORE IN A EUROPEAN CUP MATCH
Feyenoord (Holland)12, KR Reykjavik (Iceland) 0
(First Round First Leg 1969–70)

HIGHEST AGGREGATE
Benfica (Portugal) 18, Dudelange (Luxembourg) 0
(Preliminary Round 1965–66)

MOST GOALS OVERALL
61 Raul (Real Madrid) 1995–2008.
59 Ruud Van Nistelrooy (PSV Eindhoven, Manchester United and Real Madrid) 1998–2008.
56 Andriy Shevchenko (Dynamo Kiev, AC Milan and Chelsea) 1994–2008.

CHAMPIONS LEAGUE BIGGEST WINS
Liverpool 8 Besiktas 0 6.11.07
Juventus 7, Olympiakos 0 10.12.2003
Marseille 6, CKSA Moscow 0 17.3.93

FIRST TEAM TO SCORE SEVEN GOALS
Paris St Germain 7, Rosenborg 2 24.10.2000

HIGHEST AGGREGATE OF GOALS
Monaco 8, La Coruna 3 05.11.2003

HIGHEST SCORING DRAW
Hamburg 4, Juventus 4 13.9.2000

GREATEST COMEBACKS
Werder Bremen beat Anderlecht 5-3 after being three goals down in 33 minutes on 8.12.1993. They scored five goals in 23 second-half minutes.
La Coruna beat Paris St Germain 4-3 after being three goals down in 55 minutes on 7.3.2001. They scored four goals in 27 second-half minutes.
Liverpool after being three goals down in the first half on 25.5.2005 in the Champions League Final. They scored three goals in five second-half minutes and won the penalty shoot-out after extra time 3-2.
Liverpool 3 goals down to Basle in 29 minutes on 12.11.2002. They scored three second half goals in 24 minutes to draw 3-3.

MOST GOALS IN CHAMPIONS LEAGUE MATCH
4, Marco Van Basten AC Milan v IFK Gothenburg (33, 53 (pen), 61, 62 mins) 4-0 25.11.1992.
4, Simone Inzaghi Lazio v Marseille (17, 37, 38, 71 mins) 5-1 14.3.2000.
4, Ruud Van Nistelrooy Manchester U v Sparta Prague (14, 25 (pen), 60, 90 mins) 4-1 3.11.2004.
4, Dado Prso, Monaco v La Coruna (26, 30, 45, 49, 23 mins) 8-3 5.11.2003.
4, Andriy Shevchenko, AC Milan at Fenerbahce (16, 52, 70, 76,60 mins) 4-0 23.11.2005.

WINS WITH TWO DIFFERENT CLUBS
Miodrag Belodedici (Steaua) 1986; (Red Star Belgrade) 1991.
Ronald Koeman (PSV Eindhoven) 1988; (Barcelona) 1992.
Dejan Savicevic (Red Star Belgrade) 1991; (AC Milan) 1994.
Marcel Desailly (Marseille) 1993; (AC Milan) 1994.
Frank Rijkaard (AC Milan) 1989, 1990; (Ajax) 1995.
Vladimir Jugovic (Red Star Belgrade) 1991; (Juventus) 1996.
Didier Deschamps (Marseille) 1993; (Juventus) 1996.
Paulo Sousa (Juventus) 1996; (Borussia Dortmund) 1997.
Christian Panucci (AC Milan) 1994; (Real Madrid) 1998.
Jimmy Rimmer (Mancheser U) 1968, (Aston Villa) 1982 but as a non-playing substitute.

MOST WINS WITH DIFFERENT CLUBS
Clarence Seedorf (Ajax) 1995; (Real Madrid) 1998; (AC Milan) 2003, 2007.

MOST WINNERS MEDALS
6 Francisco Gento (Real Madrid) 1956, 1957, 1958, 1959, 1960, 1966.
5 Alfredo Di Stefano (Real Madrid) 1956, 1957, 1958, 1959, 1960.
5 Jose Maria Zarraga (Real Madrid) 1956, 1957, 1958, 1959, 1960.
4 Jose-Hector Rial (Real Madrid) 1956, 1957, 1958, 1959.
4 Marquitos (Real Madrid) 1956, 1957, 1959, 1960.
4 Phil Neal (Liverpool) 1977, 1978, 1981, 1984.

MOST GOALS SCORED IN FINALS
7 Alfredo Di Stefano (Real Madrid), 1956 (1), 1957 (1 pen), 1958 (1), 1959 (1), 1960 (3).
7 Ferenc Puskas (Real Madrid), 1960 (4), 1962 (3).

MOST FINAL APPEARANCES PER COUNTRY
Italy 25 (11 wins, 14 defeats).
Spain 20 (11 wins, 9 defeats).
England 16 (11 wins, 5 defeats).
Germany 13 (6 wins, 7 defeats).

MOST CLUB FINAL WINNERS
Real Madrid (Spain)	9	1956, 1957, 1958, 1959, 1960, 1966, 1998, 2000, 2002.
AC Milan (Italy)	7	1963, 1969, 1989, 1990, 1994, 2003, 2007.

MOST APPEARANCES IN FINAL
Real Madrid 12; AC Milan 11.

MOST EUROPEAN CUP APPEARANCES
Paolo Maldini (AC Milan)

Season	*European Cup*	*UEFA Cup*	*Super Cup*	*WCC*
1985–86	0	6	0	0
1987–88	0	2	0	0
1988–89	7	0	0	0
1989–90	8	0	2	1
1990–91	4	0	1	1
1992–93	10	0	0	0
1993–94	10	0	2	1
1994–95	11	0	1	1
1995–96	0	8	0	0
1996–97	6	0	0	0
1999–2000	6	0	0	0
2000–01	14	0	0	0
2001–02	0	4	0	0
2002–03	19	0	0	0
2003–04	9	0	1	1
2004–05	13	0	0	0
2005–06	9	0	0	0
2006–07	9	0	0	0
2007–08	4	0	0	0
Total	139	20	7	5

MOST SUCCESSFUL MANAGER
Bob Paisley (Liverpool) 1977, 1978, 1981.

FASTEST GOALS SCORED IN CHAMPIONS LEAGUE
10.2 sec	Roy Makaay for Bayern Munich v Real Madrid 7 March 2007.
20.07 sec	Gilberto Silva for Arsenal at PSV Eindhoven 25 September 2002.
20.12 sec	Alessandro Del Piero for Juventus at Manchester United 1 October 1997.

YOUNGEST CHAMPIONS LEAGUE GOALSCORER
Peter Ofori-Quaye for Olympiakos v Rosenborg at 17 years 195 days in 1997-98.

FASTEST HAT-TRICK SCORED IN CHAMPIONS LEAGUE
Mike Newell, 9 mins for Blackburn R v Rosenborg (4-1) 6.12.95.

MOST SUCCESSIVE CHAMPIONS LEAGUE APPEARANCES
Rosenborg (Norway) 11 1995–96 – 2005–06.

MOST SUCCESSIVE WINS IN THE CHAMPIONS LEAGUE
Barcelona (Spain) 11 2002–03.

TOP TEN PREMIER LEAGUE AVERAGE ATTENDANCES 2007–08

1	Manchester U	75,691
2	Arsenal	60,070
3	Newcastle U	51,321
4	Liverpool	43,532
5	Sunderland	43,344
6	Manchester C	42,126
7	Chelsea	41,397
8	Aston Villa	40,029
9	Everton	36,955
10	Tottenham H	35,967

TOP TEN FOOTBALL LEAGUE AVERAGE ATTENDANCES 2007–08

1	Leeds U	26,543
2	Sheffield U	25,631
3	Norwich C	24,527
4	Leicester C	23,509
5	Wolverhampton W	23,499
6	Charlton Ath	23,191
7	WBA	22,311
8	Ipswich T	21,935
9	Sheffield W	21,418
10	Southampton	21,254

TOP TEN AVERAGE ATTENDANCES

1	Manchester United	2006–07	75,826
2	Manchester United	2007–08	75,691
3	Manchester United	2005–06	68,765
4	Manchester United	2004–05	67,871
5	Manchester United	2003–04	67,641
6	Manchester United	2002–03	67,630
7	Manchester United	2001–02	67,586
8	Manchester United	2000–01	67,544
9	Manchester United	1999–2000	58,017
10	Manchester United	1967–68	57,552

TOP TEN AVERAGE WORLD CUP FINAL CROWDS

1	In USA	1994	68,604
2	In Brazil	1950	60,772
3	In Germany	2006	52,416
4	In Mexico	1970	52,311
5	In England	1966	50,458
6	In Italy	1990	48,368
7	In Mexico	1986	46,956
8	In West Germany	1974	46,684
9	In France	1998	43,366
10	In Argentina	1978	42,374

TOP TEN ALL-TIME ENGLAND CAPS

1	Peter Shilton	125
2	Bobby Moore	108
3	Bobby Charlton	106
4	Billy Wright	105
5	David Beckham	102
6	Bryan Robson	90
7	Michael Owen	89
8	Kenny Sansom	86
9	Gary Neville	85
10	Ray Wilkins	84

TOP TEN ALL-TIME ENGLAND GOALSCORERS

1	Bobby Charlton	49
2	Gary Lineker	48
3	Jimmy Greaves	44
4	Michael Owen	40
5	Tom Finney	30
6	Nat Lofthouse	30
7	Alan Shearer	30
8	Vivian Woodward	29
9	Steve Bloomer	28
10	David Platt	27

GOALKEEPING RECORDS

(without conceding a goal)

BRITISH RECORD (all competitive games)
Chris Woods, Rangers, in 1196 minutes from 26 November 1986 to 31 January 1987.

FA PREMIER LEAGUE
Peter Cech (Chelsea) in 1025 minutes from 12 December 2004 to 5 March 2005.

FOOTBALL LEAGUE
Steve Death, Reading, 1103 minutes from 24 March to 18 August 1979.

MOST CLEAN SHEETS IN A SEASON

Peter Cech (Chelsea) 24 2004–05

MOST CLEAN SHEETS OVERALL IN PREMIER LEAGUE

David James (Liverpool, Aston Villa, West Ham U, Manchester C and Portsmouth) 160 games.

MOST GOALS FOR IN A SEASON

FA PREMIER LEAGUE		*Goals*	*Games*
1999–2000	Manchester U	97	38
FOOTBALL LEAGUE			
Division 4			
1960–61	Peterborough U	134	46
SCOTTISH PREMIER LEAGUE			
2003–04	Celtic	105	38
SCOTTISH LEAGUE			
Division 2			
1937–38	Raith R	142	34

MOST GOALS AGAINST IN A SEASON

FA PREMIER LEAGUE		*Goals*	*Games*
1993–94	Swindon T	100	42
FOOTBALL LEAGUE			
Division 2			
1898–99	Darwen	141	34
SCOTTISH PREMIER LEAGUE			
1999–2000	Aberdeen	83	36
SCOTTISH LEAGUE			
Division 2			
1931–32	Edinburgh C	146	38

MOST LEAGUE GOALS IN A SEASON

FA PREMIER LEAGUE		*Goals*	*Games*
1993–94	Andy Cole (Newcastle U)	34	40
1994–95	Alan Shearer (Blackburn R)	34	42
FOOTBALL LEAGUE			
Division 1			
1927–28	Dixie Dean (Everton)	60	39
Division 2			
1926–27	George Camsell (Middlesbrough)	59	37
Division 3(S)			
1936–37	Joe Payne (Luton T)	55	39
Division 3(N)			
1936–37	Ted Harston (Mansfield T)	55	41
Division 3			
1959–60	Derek Reeves (Southampton)	39	46
Division 4			
1960–61	Terry Bly (Peterborough U)	52	46
FA CUP			
1887–88	Jimmy Ross (Preston NE)	20	8
LEAGUE CUP			
1986–87	Clive Allen (Tottenham H)	12	9
SCOTTISH PREMIER LEAGUE			
2000–01	Henrik Larsson (Celtic)	35	37
SCOTTISH LEAGUE			
Division 1			
1931–32	William McFadyen (Motherwell)	52	34
Division 2			
1927–28	Jim Smith (Ayr U)	66	38

MOST FA CUP FINAL GOALS

Ian Rush (Liverpool) 5: 1986(2), 1989(2), 1992(1)

SCORED IN EVERY PREMIERSHIP GAME

Arsenal 2001–02 38 matches

FEWEST GOALS FOR IN A SEASON

FA PREMIER LEAGUE		*Goals*	*Games*
2007–08	Derby Co	20	38
FOOTBALL LEAGUE			
Division 2			
1899–1900	Loughborough T	18	34
SCOTTISH PREMIER LEAGUE			
2001–02	St Johnstone	24	38
SCOTTISH LEAGUE			
New Division 1			
1980–81	Stirling Alb	18	39

FEWEST GOALS AGAINST IN A SEASON

FA PREMIER LEAGUE		*Goals*	*Games*
2004–05	Chelsea	15	38
FOOTBALL LEAGUE			
Division 1			
1978–79	Liverpool	16	42
SCOTTISH PREMIER LEAGUE			
2001–02	Celtic	18	38
SCOTTISH LEAGUE			
Division 1			
1913–14	Celtic	14	38

MOST LEAGUE GOALS IN A CAREER

FOOTBALL LEAGUE			
Arthur Rowley	*Goals*	*Games*	*Season*
WBA	4	24	1946–48
Fulham	27	56	1948–50
Leicester C	251	303	1950–58
Shrewsbury T	152	236	1958–65
	434	619	
SCOTTISH LEAGUE			
Jimmy McGrory			
Celtic	1	3	1922–23
Clydebank	13	30	1923–24
Celtic	396	375	1924–38
	410	408	

MOST HAT-TRICKS

Career
34 Dixie Dean (Tranmere R, Everton, Notts Co, England)

Division 1 (one season post-war)
6 Jimmy Greaves (Chelsea), 1960–61

Three for one team one match
West, Spouncer, Hooper, Nottingham F v Leicester Fosse, Division 1, 21 April 1909
Barnes, Ambler, Davies, Wrexham v Hartlepools U, Division 4, 3 March 1962
Adcock, Stewart, White, Manchester C v Huddersfield T, Division 2, 7 Nov 1987
Loasby, Smith, Wells, Northampton T v Walsall, Division 3S, 5 Nov 1927
Bowater, Hoyland, Readman, Mansfield T v Rotherham U, Division 3N, 27 Dec 1932

MOST CUP GOALS IN A CAREER

FA CUP (Pre-Second World war)
Henry Cursham 48 (Notts Co)

FA CUP (post-war)
Ian Rush 43 (Chester, Liverpool)

LEAGUE CUP
Geoff Hurst 49 (West Ham U, Stoke C)
Ian Rush 49 (Chester, Liverpool, Newcastle U)

GOALS PER GAME (Football League to 1991–92)

Goals per game	Division 1		Division 2		Division 3		Division 4		Division 3(S)		Division 3(N)	
	Games	Goals	Games	Goals	Games	Goals	Games	Goals	Games	Goals	Games	Goals
0	2465	0	2665	0	1446	0	1438	0	997	0	803	0
1	5606	5606	5836	5836	3225	3225	3106	3106	2073	2073	1914	1914
2	8275	16550	8609	17218	4569	9138	4441	8882	3314	6628	2939	5878
3	7731	23193	7842	23526	3784	11352	4041	12123	2996	8988	2922	8766
4	6229	24920	5897	23588	2837	11348	2784	11136	2445	9780	2410	9640
5	3752	18755	3634	18170	1566	7830	1506	7530	1554	7770	1599	7995
6	2137	12822	2007	12042	769	4614	786	4716	870	5220	930	5580
7	1092	7644	1001	7007	357	2499	336	2352	451	3157	461	3227
8	542	4336	376	3008	135	1080	143	1144	209	1672	221	1768
9	197	1773	164	1476	64	576	35	315	76	684	102	918
10	83	830	68	680	13	130	8	80	33	330	45	450
11	37	407	19	209	2	22	7	77	15	165	15	165
12	12	144	17	204	1	12	0	0	7	84	8	96
13	4	52	4	52	0	0	0	0	2	26	4	52
14	2	28	1	14	0	0	0	0	0	0	0	0
17	0	0	0	0	0	0	0	0	0	0	1	17
	38164	**117061**	**38140**	**113030**	**18768**	**51826**	**18631**	**51461**	**15042**	**46577**	**14374**	**46466**

New Overall Totals (since 1992)		Totals (up to1991–92)		Complete Overall Totals (since 1888–89)	
Games	32552	Games	143119	Games	175671
Goals	83720	Goals	426421	Goals	510141

Extensive research by statisticians has unearthed seven results from early years of the Football League which differ from the original scores. These are 26 January 1889 Wolverhampton W 5 Everton 0 (not 4-0), 16 March 1889 Notts Co 3 Derby Co 5 (not 2-5), 4 January 1896 Arsenal 5 Loughborough 0 (not 6-0), 28 November 1896 Leicester Fosse 4 Walsall 2 (not 4-1), 21 April 1900 Burslem Port Vale v Lincoln City 2-1 (not 2-0), 25 December 1902 Glossop NE 3 Stockport Co 0 (not 3-1), 26 April 1913 Hull C 2 Leicester C 0 (not 2-1).

GOALS PER GAME (from 1992–93)

Goals per game	Premier		Championship/Div 1		League One/Div 2		League Two/Div 3	
	Games	Goals	Games	Goals	Games	Goals	Games	Goals
0	550	0	743	0	714	0	703	0
1	1202	1202	1659	1659	1659	1659	1675	1675
2	1580	3160	2239	4478	2274	4548	2187	4374
3	1282	3846	1878	5634	1927	5781	1869	5607
4	894	3576	1206	4824	1218	4872	1123	4492
5	443	2215	671	3355	634	3170	587	2935
6	227	1362	301	1806	250	1500	266	1596
7	94	658	95	665	112	784	102	714
8	43	344	30	240	28	224	36	288
9	9	81	5	45	13	117	10	90
10	1	10	3	30	3	30	3	30
11	1	11	2	22	0	0	1	11
	6326	**16465**	**8832**	**22758**	**8832**	**22685**	**8562**	**21812**

A CENTURY OF LEAGUE AND CUP GOALS IN CONSECUTIVE SEASONS

George Camsell	*League*	*Cup*	*Season*
Middlesbrough	59	5	1926–27
(101 goals)	33	4	1927–28

(*Camsell's cup goals were all scored in the FA Cup.*)

Steve Bull			
Wolverhampton W	34	18	1987–88
(102 goals)	37	13	1988–89

(*Bull had 12 in the Sherpa Van Trophy, 3 Littlewoods Cup, 3 FA Cup in 1987–88; 11 Sherpa Van Trophy, 2 Littlewoods Cup in 1988–89.*)

PENALTIES

Most in a Season (individual)

Division 1	*Goals*	*Season*
Francis Lee (Manchester C)	13	1971–72

Most awarded in one game

Five Crystal Palace (4 – 1 scored, 3 missed) v Brighton & HA (1 scored), Div 2 1988–89

Most saved in a Season

Division 1		
Paul Cooper (Ipswich T)	8 (of 10)	1979–80

MOST GOALS IN A GAME

FA PREMIER LEAGUE
19 Sept 1999 Alan Shearer (Newcastle U) 5 goals v Sheffield W
4 Mar 1995 Andy Cole (Manchester U) 5 goals v Ipswich T

FOOTBALL LEAGUE
Division 1
14 Dec 1935 Ted Drake (Arsenal) 7 goals v Aston V
Division 2
5 Feb 1955 Tommy Briggs (Blackburn R) 7 goals v Bristol R
23 Feb 1957 Neville Coleman (Stoke C) 7 goals v Lincoln C
Division 3(S)
13 April 1936 Joe Payne (Luton T) 10 goals v Bristol R
Division 3(N)
26 Dec 1935 Bunny Bell (Tranmere R) 9 goals v Oldham Ath
Division 3
16 Sept 1969 Steve Earle (Fulham) 5 goals v Halifax T
24 April 1965 Barrie Thomas (Scunthorpe U) 5 goals v Luton T
20 Nov 1965 Keith East (Swindon T) 5 goals v Mansfield T
2 Oct 1971 Alf Wood (Shrewsbury T) 5 goals v Blackburn R
10 Sept 1983 Tony Caldwell (Bolton W) 5 goals v Walsall
4 May 1987 Andy Jones (Port Vale) 5 goals v Newport Co
3 April 1990 Steve Wilkinson (Mansfield T) 5 goals v Birmingham C
5 Sept 1998 Giuliano Grazioli (Peterborough U) 5 goals v Barnet
6 April 2002 Lee Jones (Wrexham) 5 goals v Cambridge U
Division 4
26 Dec 1962 Bert Lister (Oldham Ath) 6 goals v Southport

FA CUP
20 Nov 1971 Ted MacDougall (Bournemouth) 9 goals v Margate (*1st Round*)

LEAGUE CUP
25 Oct 1989 Frankie Bunn (Oldham Ath) 6 goals v Scarborough

SCOTTISH LEAGUE
Premier Division
17 Nov 1984 Paul Sturrock (Dundee U) 5 goals v Morton
Premier League
23 Aug 1996 Marco Negri (Rangers) 5 goals v Dundee U
Division 1
14 Sept 1928 Jimmy McGrory (Celtic) 8 goals v Dunfermline Ath
Division 2
1 Oct 1927 Owen McNally (Arthurlie) 8 goals v Armadale
2 Jan 1930 Jim Dyet (King's Park) 8 goals v Forfar Ath
18 April 1936 John Calder (Morton) 8 goals v Raith R
20 Aug 1937 Norman Hayward (Raith R) 8 goals v Brechin C

SCOTTISH CUP
12 Sept 1885 John Petrie (Arbroath) 13 goals v Bon Accord (*1st Round*)

LONGEST SEQUENCE OF CONSECUTIVE SCORING (Individual)

FA PREMIER LEAGUE
Ruud Van Nistelroy (Manchester U) 15 in 10 games 2003–04

FOOTBALL LEAGUE RECORD
Tom Phillipson (Wolverhampton W) 23 in 13 games 1926–27

LONGEST UNBEATEN SEQUENCE

FA PREMIER LEAGUE	*Team*	*Games*
May 2003–October 2004	Arsenal	49
FOOTBALL LEAGUE		
Division 1		
Nov 1977–Dec 1978	Nottingham F	42

LONGEST UNBEATEN CUP SEQUENCE

Liverpool 25 rounds League/Milk Cup 1980–84

LONGEST UNBEATEN SEQUENCE IN A SEASON

FA PREMIER LEAGUE	*Team*	*Games*
2003–04	Arsenal	38
FOOTBALL LEAGUE		
Division 1		
1920–21	Burnley	30

LONGEST UNBEATEN START TO A SEASON

FA PREMIER LEAGUE	*Team*	*Games*
2003–04	Arsenal	38
FOOTBALL LEAGUE		
Division 1		
1973–74	Leeds U	29
1987–88	Liverpool	29

LONGEST SEQUENCE WITHOUT A WIN IN A SEASON

FOOTBALL LEAGUE	*Team*	*Games*
Division 2		
1983–84	Cambridge U	31

LONGEST SEQUENCE WITHOUT A WIN FROM SEASON'S START

FOOTBALL LEAGUE	*Team*	*Games*
Division 4		
1970–71	Newport Co	25

LONGEST SEQUENCE OF CONSECUTIVE DEFEATS

FOOTBALL LEAGUE	*Team*	*Games*
Division 2		
1898–99	Darwen	18

East Stiling 24 in 2003–04.

LONGEST WINNING SEQUENCE

FA PREMIER LEAGUE	*Team*	*Games*
2001–02 and 2002–03	Arsenal	14
FOOTBALL LEAGUE		
Division 2		
1904–05	Manchester U	14
1905–06	Bristol C	14
1950–51	Preston NE	14
FROM SEASON'S START		
Division 3		
1985–86	Reading	13
SCOTTISH PREMIER LEAGUE		
2003–04	Celtic	25

HIGHEST WINS

Highest win in a First-Class Match
(*Scottish Cup 1st Round*)

Arbroath	36	Bon Accord	0	12 Sept 1885

Highest win in an International Match

England	13	Ireland	0	18 Feb 1882

Highest win in a FA Cup Match

Preston NE (*1st Round*)	26	Hyde U	0	15 Oct 1887

Highest win in a League Cup Match

West Ham U (*2nd Round, 2nd Leg*)	10	Bury	0	25 Oct 1983
Liverpool (*2nd Round, 1st Leg*)	10	Fulham	0	23 Sept 1986

Highest win in an FA Premier League Match

Manchester U	9	Ipswich T	0	4 Mar 1995
Nottingham F	1	Manchester U	8	6 Feb 1999

Highest win in a Football League Match

Division 2 – highest home win				
Newcastle U	13	Newport Co	0	5 Oct 1946
Division 3(N) – highest home win				
Stockport Co	13	Halifax T	0	6 Jan 1934
Division 2 – highest away win				
Burslem Port Vale	0	Sheffield U	10	10 Dec 1892

Highest wins in a Scottish League Match

Scottish Premier League – highest home win				
Rangers	7	St Johnstone	0	8 Nov 1998
Celtic	7	Aberdeen	0	16 Oct 1999
Celtic	7	Aberdeen	0	2 Nov 2002
Hibernian	7	Livingston	0	8 Feb 2006
Scottish Division 2 – highest home win				
Airdrieonians	15	Dundee Wanderers	1	1 Dec 1894
Scottish Premier League – away home win				
Hamilton A	0	Celtic	8	5 Nov 1988

MOST HOME WINS IN A SEASON

Brentford won all 21 games in Division 3(S), 1929–30

RECORD AWAY WINS IN A SEASON

Doncaster R won 18 of 21 games in Division 3(N), 1946–47

CONSECUTIVE AWAY WINS

FA PREMIER LEAGUE
Chelsea 9 games 2004–05

MOST WINS IN A SEASON

		Wins	*Games*
FA PREMIER LEAGUE			
2004–05	Chelsea	29	38
2005–06	Chelsea	29	38
FOOTBALL LEAGUE Division 3(N)			
1946–47	Doncaster R	33	42
SCOTTISH PREMIER LEAGUE			
2001–02	Celtic	33	38
SCOTTISH LEAGUE Division 1			
1920–21	Rangers	35	42

MOST POINTS IN A SEASON
(under old system of two points for a win)

		Points	*Games*
FOOTBALL LEAGUE Division 4			
1975–76	Lincoln C	74	46
SCOTTISH LEAGUE Division 1			
1920–21	Rangers	76	42

FEWEST WINS IN A SEASON

		Wins	*Games*
FA PREMIER LEAGUE			
2007–08	Derby Co	1	38
FOOTBALL LEAGUE Division 2			
1899–1900	Loughborough T	1	34
SCOTTISH PREMIER LEAGUE			
1998–99	Dunfermline Ath	4	36
SCOTTISH LEAGUE Division 1			
1891–92	Vale of Leven	0	22

UNDEFEATED AT HOME OVERALL

Liverpool 85 games (63 League, 9 League Cup, 7 European, 6 FA Cup), Jan 1978–Jan 1981

UNDEFEATED AT HOME LEAGUE

Chelsea 82 games, March 2004–May 2008 continuing

UNDEFEATED IN A SEASON

FA PREMIER LEAGUE		
2003–04	Arsenal	38 games
FOOTBALL LEAGUE		
1889–90	Preston NE	22 games
Division 2		
1893–94	Liverpool	22 games

UNDEFEATED AWAY

Arsenal 19 games FA Premier League 2001–02 and 2003–04 (only Preston NE with 11 in 1888–89 had previously remained unbeaten away) in the top flight

HIGHEST AGGREGATE SCORES

FA PREMIER LEAGUE

Portsmouth	7	Reading	4	29 Sept 2007

Highest Aggregate Score England
Division 3(N)

Tranmere R	13	Oldham Ath	4	26 Dec 1935

Highest Aggregate Score Scotland
Division 2

Airdrieonians	15	Dundee Wanderers	1	1 Dec 1894

MOST POINTS IN A SEASON
(three points for a win)

		Points	*Games*
FA PREMIER LEAGUE			
2004–05	Chelsea	95	38
FOOTBALL LEAGUE Championship			
2005–06	Reading	106	46
SCOTTISH PREMIER LEAGUE			
2001–02	Celtic	103	38
SCOTTISH LEAGUE New Division 3			
2004–05	Gretna	98	36

FEWEST POINTS IN A SEASON

		Points	*Games*
FA PREMIER LEAGUE			
2007–08	Derby Co	11	38
FOOTBALL LEAGUE Division 2			
1904–05	Doncaster R	8	34
1899–1900	Loughborough T	8	34
SCOTTISH PREMIER LEAGUE			
2005–06	Livingston	18	38
SCOTTISH LEAGUE Division 1			
1954–55	Stirling Alb	6	30

ONE DEFEAT IN A SEASON

FA PREMIER LEAGUE		Defeats	Games
2004–05	Chelsea	1	38
FOOTBALL LEAGUE			
Division 1			
1990–91	Arsenal	1	38
SCOTTISH PREMIER LEAGUE			
2001–02	Celtic	1	38
SCOTTISH LEAGUE			
Premier Division			
Division 1			
1920–21	Rangers	1	42
Division 2			
1956–57	Clyde	1	36
1962–63	Morton	1	36
1967–68	St Mirren	1	36
New Division 2			
1975–76	Raith R	1	26

MOST DRAWN GAMES IN A SEASON

FA PREMIER LEAGUE		Draws	Games
1993–94	Manchester C	18	42
1993–94	Sheffield U	18	42
1994–95	Southampton	18	42
FOOTBALL LEAGUE			
Division 1			
1978–79	Norwich C	23	42
Division 3			
1997–98	Cardiff C	23	46
1997–98	Hartlepool U	23	46
Division 4			
1986–87	Exeter C	23	46
SCOTTISH PREMIER LEAGUE			
1998–99	Dunfermline Ath	16	38
SCOTTISH LEAGUE			
Premier Division			
1993–94	Aberdeen	21	44
New Division 1			
1986–87	East Fife	21	44

MOST DEFEATS IN A SEASON

FA PREMIER LEAGUE		Defeats	Games
1994–95	Ipswich T	29	42
2005–06	Sunderland	29	38
2007–08	Derby Co	29	38
FOOTBALL LEAGUE			
Division 3			
1997–98	Doncaster R	34	46
SCOTTISH PREMIER LEAGUE			
2005–06	Livingston	28	38
SCOTTISH LEAGUE			
New Division 1			
1992–93	Cowdenbeath	34	44

NEW WEMBLEY RECORDS

ENGLAND UNDER-21 INTERNATIONALS
24.3.07 England Under-21 v Italy Under-21 55,700

TROPHY FINAL
12.5.07 Stevenage B v Kidderminster H 53,262

VASE FINAL
13.5.07 Truro C v AFC Totton 27,754

FA CUP FINAL
19.5.07 Chelsea v Manchester U 89,826

CONFERENCE PLAY-OFF
20.5.07 Morecambe v Exeter C 40,043

LEAGUE 2 PLAY-OFF
26.5.07 Bristol R v Shrewsbury T 61,589

LEAGUE 1 PLAY-OFF
27.5.07 Blackpool v Yeovil T 59,313

CHAMPIONSHIP PLAY-OFF
28.5.07 Derby Co v WBA 74,993

ENGLAND INTERNATIONALS
1.6.07 England v Brazil 88,745

NO DEFEATS IN A SEASON

FA PREMIER LEAGUE		
2003–04	Arsenal	won 26, drew 12
FOOTBALL LEAGUE		
Division 1		
1888–89	Preston NE	won 18, drew 4
Division 2		
1893–94	Liverpool	won 22, drew 6
SCOTTISH LEAGUE DIVISION 1		
1898–99	Rangers	won 18

MOST SUCCESSFUL MANAGERS

Sir Alex Ferguson CBE
Manchester U
20 major trophies in 17 seasons:
10 Premier League, 5 FA Cup, 2 League Cup, 2 European Cup, 1 Cup-Winners' Cup.

Aberdeen
1976–86 – 9 trophies:
3 League, 4 Scottish Cup, 1 League Cup, 1 Cup-Winners' Cup.

Bob Paisley
Liverpool
1974–83 – 13 trophies:
6 League, 3 European Cup, 3 League Cup, 1 UEFA Cup.

SENDINGS-OFF

SEASON
451 (League alone) 2003–04
(Before rescinded cards taken into account)

DAY
19 (League) 13 Dec 2003

FA CUP FINAL
Kevin Moran, Manchester U v Everton 1985
Jose Antonio Reyes, Arsenal v Manchester U 2005

QUICKEST
FA Premier League
Andreas Johansson Wigan Ath v Arsenal 7 May 2006 and Keith Gillespie Sheffield U v Reading 20 January 2007 both in 10 seconds
Football League
Walter Boyd, Swansea C v Darlington Div 3 as substitute in zero seconds 23 Nov 1999

MOST IN ONE GAME
Five: Chesterfield (2) v Plymouth Arg (3) 22 Feb 1997
Five: Wigan Ath (1) v Bristol R (4) 2 Dec 1997
Five: Exeter C (3) v Cambridge U (2) 23 Nov 2002

MOST IN ONE TEAM
Wigan Ath (1) v Bristol R (4) 2 Dec 1997
Hereford U (4) v Northampton T (0) 6 Sept 1992

LEAGUE CHAMPIONSHIP HAT-TRICKS

Huddersfield T	1923–24 to 1925–26
Arsenal	1932–33 to 1934–35
Liverpool	1981–82 to 1983–84
Manchester U	1998–99 to 2000–01

MOST LEAGUE MEDALS

Ryan Giggs (Manchester U) 10: 1993, 1994, 1996, 1997, 1999, 2000, 2001, 2003, 2007 and 2008

MOST LEAGUE APPEARANCES (750+ matches)

1005 Peter Shilton (286 Leicester City, 110 Stoke City, 202 Nottingham Forest, 188 Southampton, 175 Derby County, 34 Plymouth Argyle, 1 Bolton Wanderers, 9 Leyton Orient) 1966–97

931 Tony Ford (355 Grimsby T, 9 Sunderland (loan), 112 Stoke C, 114 WBA, 68 Grimsby T, 5 Bradford C (loan), 76 Scunthorpe U, 103 Mansfield T, 89 Rochdale) 1975–2002

909 Graeme Armstrong (204 Stirling A, 83 Berwick R, 353 Meadowbank T, 268 Stenhousemuir, 1 Alloa) 1975–2001

863 Tommy Hutchison (165 Blackpool, 314 Coventry City, 46 Manchester City, 92 Burnley, 178 Swansea City, 68 Alloa) 1965–91

824 Terry Paine (713 Southampton, 111 Hereford United) 1957–77

790 Neil Redfearn (35 Bolton W, 10 Lincoln C (loan), 90 Lincoln C, 46 Doncaster R, 57 Crystal Palace, 24 Watford, 62 Oldham Ath, 292 Barnsley, 30 Charlton Ath, 17 Bradford C, 22 Wigan Ath, 42 Halifax T, 54 Boston U, 9 Rochdale) 1982–2004

782 Robbie James (484 Swansea C, 48 Stoke C, 87 QPR, 23 Leicester C, 89 Bradford C, 51 Cardiff C) 1973–94

777 Alan Oakes (565 Manchester C, 211 Chester C, 1 Port Vale) 1959–84

774 Dave Beasant (340 Wimbledon, 20 Newcastle U, 133 Chelsea, 6 Grimsby T (loan), 4 Wolverhampton W (loan), 88 Southampton, 139 Nottingham F, 27 Portsmouth, 1 Tottenham H (loan), 16 Brighton & HA) 1979–2003

771 John Burridge (27 Workington, 134 Blackpool, 65 Aston Villa, 6 Southend U (loan), 88 Crystal Palace, 39 QPR, 74 Wolverhampton W, 6 Derby Co (loan), 109 Sheffield U, 62 Southampton, 67 Newcastle U, 65 Hibernian, 3 Scarborough, 4 Lincoln C, 3 Aberdeen, 3 Dumbarton, 3 Falkirk, 4 Manchester C, 3 Darlington, 6 Queen of the South) 1968–96

770 John Trollope (all for Swindon Town) 1960–80†

764 Jimmy Dickinson (all for Portsmouth) 1946–65

763 Stuart McCall (395 Bradford C, 103 Everton, 194 Rangers, 71 Sheffield U) 1982–2004

761 Roy Sproson (all for Port Vale) 1950–72

760 Mick Tait (64 Oxford U, 106 Carlisle U, 33 Hull C, 240 Portsmouth, 99 Reading, 79 Darlington, 139 Hartlepool U) 1975–97

758 Ray Clemence (48 Scunthorpe United, 470 Liverpool, 240 Tottenham Hotspur) 1966–87

758 Billy Bonds (95 Charlton Ath, 663 West Ham U) 1964–88

757 Pat Jennings (48 Watford, 472 Tottenham Hotspur, 237 Arsenal) 1963–86

757 Frank Worthington (171 Huddersfield T, 210 Leicester C, 84 Bolton W, 75 Birmingham C, 32 Leeds U, 19 Sunderland, 34 Southampton, 31 Brighton & HA, 59 Tranmere R, 23 Preston NE, 19 Stockport Co) 1966–88

† record for one club

CONSECUTIVE

401 Harold Bell (401 Tranmere R; 459 in all games) 1946–55

MOST SENIOR MATCHES

1390 Peter Shilton (1005 League, 86 FA Cup, 102 League Cup, 125 Internationals, 13 Under-23, 4 Football League XI, 20 European Cup, 7 Texaco Cup, 5 Simod Cup, 4 European Super Cup, 4 UEFA Cup, 3 Screen Sport Super Cup, 3 Zenith Data Systems Cup, 2 Autoglass Trophy, 2 Charity Shield, 2 Full Members Cup, 1 Anglo-Italian Cup, 1 Football League play-offs, 1 World Club Championship)

MOST FA CUP APPEARANCES

88 Ian Callaghan (79 Liverpool, 7 Swansea C, 2 Crewe Alex)

YOUNGEST PLAYERS

FA Premier League appearance
Matthew Briggs, 16 years 65 days, Fulham v Middlesbrough, 13.5.2007.

FA Premier League scorer
James Vaughan, 16 years 271 days, Everton v Crystal Palace 10.4.2005

Football League appearance
Albert Geldard, 15 years 158 days, Bradford Park Avenue v Millwall, Division 2, 16.9.29; and
Ken Roberts, 15 years 158 days, Wrexham v Bradford Park Avenue, Division 3N, 1.9.51
If leap years are included, Ken Roberts was 157 days

Football League scorer
Ronnie Dix, 15 years 180 days, Bristol Rovers v Norwich City, Division 3S, 3.3.28.

Division 1 appearance
Derek Forster, 15 years 185 days, Sunderland v Leicester City, 22.8.64.

Division 1 scorer
Jason Dozzell, 16 years 57 days as substitute Ipswich Town v Coventry City, 4.2.84

Division 1 hat-tricks
Alan Shearer, 17 years 240 days, Southampton v Arsenal, 9.4.88
Jimmy Greaves, 17 years 10 months, Chelsea v Portsmouth, 25.12.57

FA Cup appearance (any round)
Andy Awford, 15 years 88 days as substitute Worcester City v Boreham Wood, 3rd Qual. rd, 10.10.87

FA Cup proper appearance
Luke Freeman, 15 years 273 days, Gillingham v Barnet 10.11.2007

FA Cup Final appearance
Curtis Weston, 17 years 119 days, Millwall v Manchester U, 2004

FA Cup Final scorer
Norman Whiteside, 18 years 18 days, Manchester United v Brighton & Hove Albion, 1983

FA Cup Final captain
David Nish, 21 years 212 days, Leicester City v Manchester City, 1969

League Cup appearance
Chris Coward, 16 years 30 days, Stockport Co v Sheffield W, 2005

League Cup Final scorer
Norman Whiteside, 17 years 324 days, Manchester United v Liverpool, 1983

League Cup Final captain
Barry Venison, 20 years 7 months 8 days, Sunderland v Norwich City, 1985

OLDEST PLAYERS

FA Premier League appearance
John Burridge 43 years 5 months, Manchester C v QPR 14.5.1995

Football League appearance
Neil McBain, 52 years 4 months, New Brighton v Hartlepools United, Div 3N, 15.3.47 (McBain was New Brighton's manager and had to play in an emergency)

Division 1 appearance
Stanley Matthews, 50 years 5 days, Stoke City v Fulham, 6.2.65

INTERNATIONAL RECORDS

MOST GOALS IN AN INTERNATIONAL

Record/World Cup	Archie Thompson (Australia) 13 goals v American Samoa	11.4.2001
England	Malcolm Macdonald (Newcastle U) 5 goals v Cyprus, at Wembley	16.4.1975
	Willie Hall (Tottenham H) 5 goals v Ireland, at Old Trafford	16.11.1938
	Steve Bloomer (Derby Co) 5 goals v Wales, at Cardiff	16.3.1896
	Howard Vaughton (Aston Villa) 5 goals v Ireland, at Belfast	18.2.1882
Northern Ireland	Joe Bambrick (Linfield) 6 goals v Wales, at Belfast	1.2.1930
Wales	John Price (Wrexham) 4 goals v Ireland, at Wrexham	25.2.1882
	Mel Charles (Cardiff C) 4 goals v Ireland, at Cardiff	11.4.1962
	Ian Edwards (Chester) 4 goals v Malta, at Wrexham	25.10.1978

MOST GOALS IN AN INTERNATIONAL CAREER

		Goals	*Games*
England	Bobby Charlton (Manchester U)	49	106
Scotland	Denis Law (Huddersfield T, Manchester C, Torino, Manchester U)	30	55
	Kenny Dalglish (Celtic, Liverpool)	30	102
Northern Ireland	David Healy (Manchester U, Preston NE, Leeds U, Fulham)	34	64
Wales	Ian Rush (Liverpool, Juventus)	28	73
Republic of Ireland	Robbie Keane (Wolverhampton W, Coventry C, Internazionale, Leeds U, Tottenham H)	33	81

HIGHEST SCORES

Record/World Cup Match	Australia	31	American Samoa	0	2001
European Championship	San Marino	0	Germany	13	2006
Olympic Games	Denmark	17	France	1	1908
	Germany	16	USSR	0	1912
Other International Match	Libya	21	Oman	0	1966
European Cup	Feyenoord	12	K R Reykjavik	2	1969
European Cup-Winners' Cup	Sporting Lisbon	16	Apoel Nicosia	1	1963
Fairs & UEFA Cups	Ajax	14	Red Boys	0	1984

GOALSCORING RECORDS

World Cup Final	Geoff Hurst (England) 3 goals v West Germany	1966
World Cup Final tournament	Just Fontaine (France) 13 goals	1958
Career	Artur Friedenreich (Brazil) 1329 goals	1910–30
	Pele (Brazil) 1281 goals	*1956–78
	Franz 'Bimbo' Binder (Austria, Germany) 1006 goals	1930–50
World Cup Finals fastest	Hakan Sukur (Turkey) 10.8 secs v South Korea	2002

**Pele subsequently scored two goals in Testimonial matches making his total 1283.*

MOST CAPPED INTERNATIONALS IN THE BRITISH ISLES

England	Peter Shilton	125 appearances	1970–90
Northern Ireland	Pat Jennings	119 appearances	1964–86
Scotland	Kenny Dalglish	102 appearances	1971–86
Wales	Neville Southall	92 appearances	1982–97
Republic of Ireland	Steve Staunton	102 appearances	1988–2002

LONDON INTERNATIONAL VENUES

Eleven different venues in the London area have staged full England international games: Kennington Oval, Richmond Athletic Ground, Queen's Club, Crystal Palace, Craven Cottage, The Den, Stamford Bridge, Highbury, Wembley, Selhurst Park, White Hart Lane and Upton Park.

FOOTBALL TITLES FOR YOUR REFERENCE LIBRARY

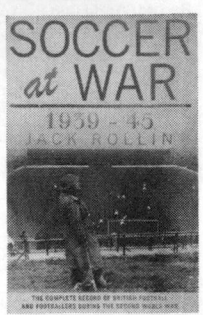

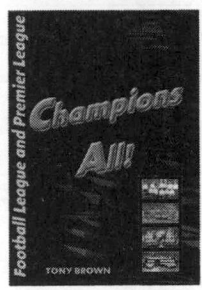

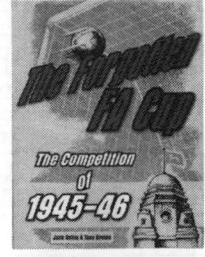

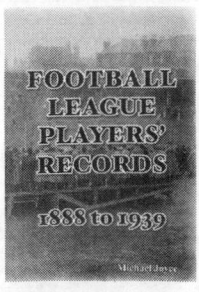

THE FA BARCLAYS PREMIERSHIP AND COCA-COLA FOOTBALL LEAGUE FIXTURES 2008–09

**Sky Sports*

Saturday, 9 August 2008
Coca-Cola Football League Championship
Birmingham C v Sheffield U* (12.45)
Blackpool v Bristol C
Cardiff C v Southampton
Charlton Ath v Swansea C
Coventry C v Norwich C
Crystal Palace v Watford
Derby Co v Doncaster R
Ipswich T v Preston NE
Plymouth Arg v Wolverhampton W
QPR v Barnsley
Sheffield W v Burnley

Coca-Cola Football League One
Bristol R v Carlisle U
Crewe Alex v Brighton & HA
Hartlepool U v Colchester U
Huddersfield T v Stockport Co
Leicester C v Milton Keynes D
Leyton Orient v Hereford U
Northampton T v Cheltenham T
Oldham Ath v Millwall
Scunthorpe U v Leeds U
Southend U v Peterborough U
Swindon T v Tranmere R
Yeovil T v Walsall

Coca-Cola Football League Two
Accrington S v Aldershot T
Barnet v Chesterfield
Bournemouth v Gillingham
Bradford C v Notts Co
Bury v Brentford
Dagenham & R v Chester C
Darlington v Exeter C
Grimsby T v Rochdale
Luton T v Port Vale
Rotherham U v Lincoln C
Shrewsbury T v Macclesfield T
Wycombe W v Morecambe

Sunday, 10 August 2008
Coca-Cola Football League Championship
Nottingham F v Reading* (1.15)

Saturday, 16 August 2008
Barclays Premier League
Arsenal v WBA* (12.45)
Aston Villa v Manchester C
Bolton W v Stoke C
Everton v Blackburn R
Hull C v Fulham
Middlesbrough v Tottenham H
Sunderland v Liverpool
West Ham U v Wigan Ath

Coca-Cola Football League Championship
Barnsley v Coventry C
Bristol C v Derby Co* (5.20)
Burnley v Ipswich T
Doncaster R v Cardiff C
Norwich C v Blackpool
Preston NE v Crystal Palace
Reading v Plymouth Arg
Sheffield U v QPR
Southampton v Birmingham C
Swansea C v Nottingham F
Watford v Charlton Ath
Wolverhampton W v Sheffield W

Coca-Cola Football League One
Brighton & HA v Bristol R
Carlisle U v Crewe Alex
Cheltenham T v Swindon T
Colchester U v Huddersfield T
Hereford U v Yeovil T
Leeds U v Oldham Ath
Millwall v Southend U
Milton Keynes D v Northampton T
Peterborough U v Leyton Orient
Stockport Co v Leicester C
Tranmere R v Hartlepool U
Walsall v Scunthorpe U

Coca-Cola Football League Two
Aldershot T v Bournemouth
Brentford v Grimsby T
Chester C v Wycombe W
Chesterfield v Bury
Exeter C v Shrewsbury T
Gillingham v Luton T
Lincoln C v Dagenham & R
Macclesfield T v Bradford C
Morecambe v Rotherham U
Notts Co v Darlington
Port Vale v Accrington S
Rochdale v Barnet

Sunday, 17 August 2008
Barclays Premier League
Chelsea v Portsmouth* (1.30)
Manchester U v Newcastle U* (4.00)

Saturday, 23 August 2008
Barclays Premier League
Blackburn R v Hull C
Fulham v Arsenal
Liverpool v Middlesbrough
Newcastle U v Bolton W
Stoke C v Aston Villa
Tottenham H v Sunderland
WBA v Everton
Wigan Ath v Chelsea

Coca-Cola Football League Championship
Birmingham C v Barnsley
Blackpool v Sheffield U
Cardiff C v Norwich C
Charlton Ath v Reading
Coventry C v Bristol C
Crystal Palace v Burnley
Derby Co v Southampton
Ipswich T v Wolverhampton W
Nottingham F v Watford
Plymouth Arg v Swansea C
QPR v Doncaster R
Sheffield W v Preston NE

Coca-Cola Football League One
Bristol R v Hereford U
Crewe Alex v Walsall
Hartlepool U v Stockport Co
Huddersfield T v Milton Keynes D
Leicester C v Tranmere R
Leyton Orient v Carlisle U
Northampton T v Millwall
Oldham Ath v Cheltenham T
Scunthorpe U v Peterborough U
Southend U v Brighton & HA
Swindon T v Colchester U
Yeovil T v Leeds U

Coca-Cola Football League Two
Accrington S v Macclesfield T
Barnet v Brentford
Bournemouth v Exeter C
Bradford C v Rochdale
Bury v Morecambe
Dagenham & R v Port Vale
Darlington v Gillingham
Grimsby T v Chesterfield
Luton T v Notts Co
Rotherham U v Chester C
Shrewsbury T v Aldershot T
Wycombe W v Lincoln C

Sunday, 24 August 2008
Barclays Premier League
Manchester C v West Ham U* (4.00)

Monday, 25 August 2008
Barclays Premier League
Portsmouth v Manchester U* (8.00)

Saturday, 30 August 2008
Barclays Premier League
Arsenal v Newcastle U
Bolton W v WBA
Everton v Portsmouth
Hull C v Wigan Ath
Manchester U v Fulham
Middlesbrough v Stoke C
Sunderland v Manchester C
West Ham U v Blackburn R

Coca-Cola Football League Championship
Barnsley v Derby Co
Bristol C v QPR
Burnley v Plymouth Arg
Doncaster R v Coventry C
Norwich C v Birmingham C
Preston NE v Charlton Ath

Reading v Crystal Palace
Sheffield U v Cardiff C
Southampton v Blackpool
Swansea C v Sheffield W
Watford v Ipswich T* (5.20)
Wolverhampton W v Nottingham F

Coca-Cola Football League One
Brighton & HA v Leyton Orient
Carlisle U v Yeovil T
Cheltenham T v Leicester C
Colchester U v Oldham Ath
Hereford U v Crewe Alex
Leeds U v Bristol R
Millwall v Huddersfield T
Milton Keynes D v Swindon T
Peterborough U v Hartlepool U
Stockport Co v Scunthorpe U
Tranmere R v Northampton T
Walsall v Southend U

Coca-Cola Football League Two
Aldershot T v Bradford C
Brentford v Rotherham U
Chester C v Barnet
Chesterfield v Wycombe W
Exeter C v Luton T
Gillingham v Accrington S
Lincoln C v Grimsby T
Macclesfield T v Darlington
Morecambe v Dagenham & R
Notts Co v Shrewsbury T
Port Vale v Bournemouth
Rochdale v Bury

Sunday, 31 August 2008
Barclays Premier League
Aston Villa v Liverpool* (4.00)
Chelsea v Tottenham H* (1.30)

Saturday, 6 September 2008
Coca-Cola Football League One
Brighton & HA v Scunthorpe U
Carlisle U v Southend U
Cheltenham T v Huddersfield T
Colchester U v Leicester C
Hereford U v Swindon T
Leeds U v Crewe Alex
Millwall v Hartlepool U
Milton Keynes D v Yeovil T
Peterborough U v Bristol R
Stockport Co v Northampton T
Tranmere R v Oldham Ath
Walsall v Leyton Orient

Coca-Cola Football League Two
Aldershot T v Darlington
Brentford v Dagenham & R
Chester C v Bury
Chesterfield v Rotherham U
Exeter C v Accrington S
Gillingham v Grimsby T
Lincoln C v Barnet
Macclesfield T v Luton T
Morecambe v Shrewsbury T
Notts Co v Bournemouth
Port Vale v Bradford C
Rochdale v Wycombe W

Saturday, 13 September 2008
Barclays Premier League
Blackburn R v Arsenal
Fulham v Bolton W
Liverpool v Manchester U* (12.45)
Manchester C v Chelsea
Newcastle U v Hull C
Portsmouth v Middlesbrough
Tottenham H v Aston Villa
WBA v West Ham U
Wigan Ath v Sunderland

Coca-Cola Football League Championship
Birmingham C v Doncaster R
Blackpool v Barnsley
Cardiff C v Bristol C
Charlton Ath v Wolverhampton W
Coventry C v Preston NE
Crystal Palace v Swansea C
Derby Co v Sheffield U
Ipswich T v Reading
Nottingham F v Burnley
Plymouth Arg v Norwich C
QPR v Southampton
Sheffield W v Watford

Coca-Cola Football League One
Bristol R v Walsall
Crewe Alex v Colchester U
Hartlepool U v Cheltenham T
Huddersfield T v Tranmere R
Leicester C v Millwall
Leyton Orient v Stockport Co
Northampton T v Peterborough U
Oldham Ath v Milton Keynes D
Scunthorpe U v Carlisle U
Southend U v Hereford U
Swindon T v Leeds U
Yeovil T v Brighton & HA

Coca-Cola Football League Two
Accrington S v Notts Co
Barnet v Morecambe
Bournemouth v Macclesfield T
Bradford C v Exeter C
Bury v Lincoln C
Dagenham & R v Chesterfield
Darlington v Port Vale
Grimsby T v Chester C
Luton T v Aldershot T
Rotherham U v Rochdale
Shrewsbury T v Gillingham
Wycombe W v Brentford

Sunday, 14 September 2008
Barclays Premier League
Stoke C v Everton* (1.30)

Tuesday, 16 September 2008
Coca-Cola Football League Championship
Barnsley v Cardiff C
Bristol C v Birmingham C
Burnley v Blackpool
Doncaster R v Charlton Ath
Norwich C v QPR
Preston NE v Nottingham F
Reading v Sheffield W
Sheffield U v Coventry C
Southampton v Ipswich T
Swansea C v Derby Co
Watford v Plymouth Arg
Wolverhampton W v Crystal Palace

Saturday, 20 September 2008
Barclays Premier League
Blackburn R v Fulham
Bolton W v Arsenal
Hull C v Everton
Liverpool v Stoke C
Manchester C v Portsmouth
Sunderland v Middlesbrough
Tottenham H v Wigan Ath
West Ham U v Newcastle U

Coca-Cola Football League Championship
Birmingham C v Blackpool
Bristol C v Doncaster R
Coventry C v QPR
Crystal Palace v Plymouth Arg
Derby Co v Cardiff C
Norwich C v Sheffield U
Nottingham F v Charlton Ath
Preston NE v Wolverhampton W
Sheffield W v Ipswich T
Southampton v Barnsley
Swansea C v Burnley
Watford v Reading

Coca-Cola Football League One
Brighton & HA v Walsall
Carlisle U v Leeds U
Colchester U v Milton Keynes D
Crewe Alex v Southend U
Hartlepool U v Oldham Ath
Hereford U v Scunthorpe U
Huddersfield T v Northampton T
Leyton Orient v Leicester C
Millwall v Cheltenham T
Peterborough U v Tranmere R
Stockport Co v Swindon T
Yeovil T v Bristol R

Coca-Cola Football League Two
Aldershot T v Gillingham
Barnet v Bury
Bradford C v Bournemouth
Brentford v Lincoln C
Chester C v Shrewsbury T
Darlington v Accrington S
Exeter C v Notts Co
Morecambe v Grimsby T
Port Vale v Macclesfield T
Rochdale v Chesterfield
Rotherham U v Luton T
Wycombe W v Dagenham & R

Sunday, 21 September 2008
Barclays Premier League
Chelsea v Manchester U* (2.00)
WBA v Aston Villa* (12.00)

Saturday, 27 September 2008
Barclays Premier League
Arsenal v Hull C
Aston Villa v Sunderland
Everton v Liverpool* (12.45)
Fulham v West Ham U
Manchester U v Bolton W
Middlesbrough v WBA
Newcastle U v Blackburn R
Stoke C v Chelsea

Coca-Cola Football League Championship
Barnsley v Norwich C
Blackpool v Coventry C
Burnley v Preston NE
Cardiff C v Birmingham C
Charlton Ath v Sheffield W
Doncaster R v Southampton
Ipswich T v Crystal Palace
Plymouth Arg v Nottingham F
QPR v Derby Co
Reading v Swansea C
Sheffield U v Watford
Wolverhampton W v Bristol C

Coca-Cola Football League One
Bristol R v Crewe Alex
Cheltenham T v Stockport Co
Leeds U v Hereford U
Leicester C v Hartlepool U

Milton Keynes D v Peterborough U
Northampton T v Brighton & HA
Oldham Ath v Huddersfield T
Scunthorpe U v Yeovil T
Southend U v Leyton Orient
Swindon T v Millwall
Tranmere R v Colchester U
Walsall v Carlisle U

Coca-Cola Football League Two
Accrington S v Rochdale
Bournemouth v Darlington
Bury v Wycombe W
Chesterfield v Brentford
Dagenham & R v Rotherham U
Gillingham v Port Vale
Grimsby T v Barnet
Lincoln C v Morecambe
Luton T v Chester C
Macclesfield T v Exeter C
Notts Co v Aldershot T
Shrewsbury T v Bradford C

Sunday, 28 September 2008
Barclays Premier League
Portsmouth v Tottenham H* (1.30)
Wigan Ath v Manchester C* (4.00)

Tuesday, 30 September 2008
Coca-Cola Football League Championship
Bristol C v Plymouth Arg
Burnley v Watford
Cardiff C v Coventry C
Crystal Palace v Charlton Ath
Derby Co v Birmingham C
Doncaster R v Sheffield U
Ipswich T v Barnsley
Preston NE v Swansea C
QPR v Blackpool
Sheffield W v Nottingham F
Southampton v Norwich C
Wolverhampton W v Reading

Saturday, 4 October 2008
Barclays Premier League
Blackburn R v Manchester U
Chelsea v Aston Villa
Manchester C v Liverpool
Portsmouth v Stoke C
Sunderland v Arsenal
Tottenham H v Hull C
WBA v Fulham
Wigan Ath v Middlesbrough

Coca-Cola Football League Championship
Barnsley v Doncaster R
Birmingham C v QPR
Blackpool v Cardiff C
Charlton Ath v Ipswich T
Coventry C v Southampton* (5.20)
Norwich C v Derby Co
Nottingham F v Crystal Palace
Plymouth Arg v Sheffield W
Reading v Burnley
Sheffield U v Bristol C
Swansea C v Wolverhampton W
Watford v Preston NE

Coca-Cola Football League One
Brighton & HA v Cheltenham T
Carlisle U v Tranmere R
Colchester U v Bristol R
Crewe Alex v Northampton T
Hartlepool U v Swindon T
Hereford U v Walsall
Huddersfield T v Leicester C
Leyton Orient v Scunthorpe U
Millwall v Milton Keynes D
Peterborough U v Leeds U
Stockport Co v Oldham Ath
Yeovil T v Southend U

Coca-Cola Football League Two
Aldershot T v Bury
Barnet v Accrington S
Bradford C v Luton T
Brentford v Macclesfield T
Chester C v Lincoln C
Darlington v Shrewsbury T
Exeter C v Gillingham
Morecambe v Chesterfield
Port Vale v Notts Co
Rochdale v Dagenham & R
Rotherham U v Grimsby T
Wycombe W v Bournemouth

Sunday, 5 October 2008
Barclays Premier League
Everton v Newcastle U* (4.00)
West Ham U v Bolton W* (1.30)

Saturday, 11 October 2008
Coca-Cola Football League One
Bristol R v Leyton Orient
Cheltenham T v Colchester U
Leeds U v Brighton & HA
Leicester C v Yeovil T
Milton Keynes D v Carlisle U
Northampton T v Hartlepool U
Oldham Ath v Hereford U
Scunthorpe U v Crewe Alex
Southend U v Stockport Co
Swindon T v Huddersfield T
Tranmere R v Millwall
Walsall v Peterborough U

Coca-Cola Football League Two
Accrington S v Bradford C
Bournemouth v Rotherham U
Bury v Exeter C
Chesterfield v Chester C
Dagenham & R v Barnet
Gillingham v Morecambe
Grimsby T v Wycombe W
Lincoln C v Rochdale
Luton T v Darlington
Macclesfield T v Aldershot T
Notts Co v Brentford
Shrewsbury T v Port Vale

Saturday, 18 October 2008
Barclays Premier League
Arsenal v Everton
Aston Villa v Portsmouth
Bolton W v Blackburn R
Fulham v Sunderland
Hull C v West Ham U
Liverpool v Wigan Ath
Manchester U v WBA
Middlesbrough v Chelsea* (12.45)
Newcastle U v Manchester C

Coca-Cola Football League Championship
Bristol C v Norwich C
Burnley v Birmingham C
Cardiff C v Charlton Ath
Crystal Palace v Barnsley
Derby Co v Plymouth Arg
Doncaster R v Blackpool
Ipswich T v Swansea C
Preston NE v Reading
QPR v Nottingham F
Sheffield W v Sheffield U
Southampton v Watford
Wolverhampton W v Coventry C

Coca-Cola Football League One
Brighton & HA v Hereford U
Carlisle U v Peterborough U
Cheltenham T v Scunthorpe U
Crewe Alex v Milton Keynes D
Huddersfield T v Bristol R
Leyton Orient v Tranmere R
Millwall v Leeds U
Northampton T v Yeovil T
Oldham Ath v Leicester C
Southend U v Swindon T
Stockport Co v Colchester U
Walsall v Hartlepool U

Coca-Cola Football League Two
Aldershot T v Brentford
Bradford C v Gillingham
Chester C v Port Vale
Dagenham & R v Bury
Exeter C v Grimsby T
Lincoln C v Chesterfield
Luton T v Accrington S
Morecambe v Rochdale
Notts Co v Macclesfield T
Rotherham U v Barnet
Shrewsbury T v Bournemouth
Wycombe W v Darlington

Sunday, 19 October 2008
Barclays Premier League
Stoke C v Tottenham H* (4.00)

Tuesday, 21 October 2008
Coca-Cola Football League Championship
Barnsley v Sheffield W
Birmingham C v Crystal Palace
Blackpool v Derby Co
Charlton Ath v Bristol C
Coventry C v Burnley
Norwich C v Wolverhampton W
Nottingham F v Ipswich T
Plymouth Arg v Preston NE
Reading v Doncaster R
Sheffield U v Southampton
Swansea C v QPR
Watford v Cardiff C

Coca-Cola Football League One
Bristol R v Oldham Ath
Colchester U v Millwall
Hartlepool U v Huddersfield T
Hereford U v Carlisle U
Leeds U v Leyton Orient
Leicester C v Walsall
Milton Keynes D v Stockport Co
Peterborough U v Brighton & HA
Scunthorpe U v Southend U
Swindon T v Northampton T
Tranmere R v Cheltenham T
Yeovil T v Crewe Alex

Coca-Cola Football League Two
Accrington S v Shrewsbury T
Barnet v Wycombe W
Bournemouth v Dagenham & R
Brentford v Morecambe
Bury v Rotherham U
Darlington v Bradford C
Gillingham v Notts Co
Grimsby T v Luton T
Macclesfield T v Lincoln C
Port Vale v Exeter C
Rochdale v Chester C

Wednesday, 22 October 2008
Coca-Cola Football League Two
Chesterfield v Aldershot T

Saturday, 25 October 2008

Barclays Premier League
Blackburn R v Middlesbrough
Everton v Manchester U
Manchester C v Stoke C
Portsmouth v Fulham
Sunderland v Newcastle U* (12.45)
Tottenham H v Bolton W
WBA v Hull C
Wigan Ath v Aston Villa

Coca-Cola Football League Championship
Barnsley v Bristol C
Birmingham C v Sheffield W
Blackpool v Crystal Palace
Charlton Ath v Burnley
Coventry C v Derby Co
Norwich C v Doncaster R
Nottingham F v Cardiff C
Plymouth Arg v Ipswich T
Reading v QPR* (5.20)
Sheffield U v Preston NE
Swansea C v Southampton
Watford v Wolverhampton W

Coca-Cola Football League One
Bristol R v Southend U
Colchester U v Carlisle U
Hartlepool U v Brighton & HA
Hereford U v Stockport Co
Leeds U v Walsall
Leicester C v Northampton T
Milton Keynes D v Cheltenham T
Peterborough U v Huddersfield T
Scunthorpe U v Millwall
Swindon T v Oldham Ath
Tranmere R v Crewe Alex
Yeovil T v Leyton Orient

Coca-Cola Football League Two
Accrington S v Wycombe W
Barnet v Exeter C
Bournemouth v Lincoln C
Brentford v Shrewsbury T
Bury v Luton T
Chesterfield v Notts Co
Darlington v Dagenham & R
Gillingham v Chester C
Grimsby T v Bradford C
Macclesfield T v Rotherham U
Port Vale v Morecambe
Rochdale v Aldershot T

Sunday, 26 October 2008

Barclays Premier League
Chelsea v Liverpool* (1.30)
West Ham U v Arsenal* (4.00)

Tuesday, 28 October 2008

Barclays Premier League
Bolton W v Everton
Hull C v Chelsea
Manchester U v West Ham U
Middlesbrough v Manchester C
Stoke C v Sunderland* (8.00)

Coca-Cola Football League Championship
Bristol C v Sheffield U
Burnley v Reading
Cardiff C v Blackpool
Crystal Palace v Nottingham F
Derby Co v Norwich C
Doncaster R v Barnsley
Ipswich T v Charlton Ath
Preston NE v Watford
QPR v Birmingham C
Sheffield W v Plymouth Arg
Southampton v Coventry C
Wolverhampton W v Swansea C

Coca-Cola Football League One
Brighton & HA v Leicester C
Carlisle U v Hartlepool U
Cheltenham T v Bristol R
Crewe Alex v Peterborough U
Huddersfield T v Yeovil T
Leyton Orient v Milton Keynes D
Millwall v Hereford U
Northampton T v Colchester U
Oldham Ath v Scunthorpe U
Southend U v Leeds U
Stockport Co v Tranmere R
Walsall v Swindon T

Coca-Cola Football League Two
Aldershot T v Port Vale
Bradford C v Bury
Chester C v Brentford
Dagenham & R v Grimsby T
Exeter C v Chesterfield
Lincoln C v Gillingham
Luton T v Bournemouth
Morecambe v Accrington S
Notts Co v Rochdale
Rotherham U v Darlington
Shrewsbury T v Barnet
Wycombe W v Macclesfield T

Wednesday, 29 October 2008

Barclays Premier League
Arsenal v Tottenham H* (8.00)
Aston Villa v Blackburn R
Fulham v Wigan Ath
Liverpool v Portsmouth
Newcastle U v WBA

Saturday, 1 November 2008

Barclays Premier League
Chelsea v Sunderland
Everton v Fulham* (12.45)
Manchester U v Hull C
Middlesbrough v West Ham U
Newcastle U v Aston Villa
Portsmouth v Wigan Ath
Stoke C v Arsenal
Tottenham H v Liverpool
WBA v Blackburn R

Coca-Cola Football League Championship
Birmingham C v Coventry C
Bristol C v Reading
Burnley v Norwich C
Cardiff C v Wolverhampton W
Charlton Ath v Barnsley
Crystal Palace v Sheffield W
Derby Co v Nottingham F
Doncaster R v Swansea C
Ipswich T v QPR
Preston NE v Southampton
Sheffield U v Plymouth Arg
Watford v Blackpool

Coca-Cola Football League One
Brighton & HA v Millwall
Cheltenham T v Leeds U
Huddersfield T v Crewe Alex
Leicester C v Bristol R
Leyton Orient v Hartlepool U
Milton Keynes D v Tranmere R
Oldham Ath v Yeovil T
Peterborough U v Hereford U
Scunthorpe U v Swindon T
Southend U v Colchester U
Stockport Co v Carlisle U
Walsall v Northampton T

Coca-Cola Football League Two
Bournemouth v Chesterfield
Bradford C v Barnet
Brentford v Rochdale
Dagenham & R v Accrington S
Exeter C v Chester C
Grimsby T v Darlington
Lincoln C v Port Vale
Macclesfield T v Gillingham
Morecambe v Aldershot T
Notts Co v Bury
Rotherham U v Wycombe W
Shrewsbury T v Luton T

Sunday, 2 November 2008

Barclays Premier League
Bolton W v Manchester C* (4.00)

Saturday, 8 November 2008

Barclays Premier League
Arsenal v Manchester U* (12.45)
Aston Villa v Middlesbrough
Hull C v Bolton W
Liverpool v WBA
Manchester C v Tottenham H
Sunderland v Portsmouth
West Ham U v Everton
Wigan Ath v Stoke C

Coca-Cola Football League Championship
Barnsley v Sheffield U
Blackpool v Ipswich T
Coventry C v Crystal Palace
Norwich C v Preston NE
Nottingham F v Birmingham C
Plymouth Arg v Charlton Ath
QPR v Cardiff C
Reading v Derby Co
Sheffield W v Doncaster R
Southampton v Bristol C* (5.20)
Swansea C v Watford
Wolverhampton W v Burnley

Sunday, 9 November 2008

Barclays Premier League
Blackburn R v Chelsea* (1.30)
Fulham v Newcastle U* (4.00)

Saturday, 15 November 2008

Barclays Premier League
Arsenal v Aston Villa
Blackburn R v Sunderland
Bolton W v Liverpool* (12.45)
Fulham v Tottenham H
Manchester U v Stoke C
Newcastle U v Wigan Ath
WBA v Chelsea
West Ham U v Portsmouth

Coca-Cola Football League Championship
Barnsley v Watford
Birmingham C v Charlton Ath
Blackpool v Preston NE
Bristol C v Nottingham F
Cardiff C v Crystal Palace
Coventry C v Plymouth Arg
Derby Co v Sheffield W
Doncaster R v Ipswich T
Norwich C v Swansea C
QPR v Burnley
Sheffield U v Reading
Southampton v Wolverhampton W

Coca-Cola Football League One
Bristol R v Scunthorpe U
Carlisle U v Brighton & HA
Colchester U v Walsall

Crewe Alex v Leyton Orient
Hartlepool U v Milton Keynes D
Hereford U v Cheltenham T
Leeds U v Huddersfield T
Millwall v Stockport Co
Northampton T v Oldham Ath
Swindon T v Leicester C
Tranmere R v Southend U
Yeovil T v Peterborough U

Coca-Cola Football League Two
Accrington S v Bournemouth
Aldershot T v Exeter C
Barnet v Notts Co
Bury v Grimsby T
Chester C v Morecambe
Chesterfield v Shrewsbury T
Darlington v Lincoln C
Gillingham v Rotherham U
Luton T v Dagenham & R
Port Vale v Brentford
Rochdale v Macclesfield T
Wycombe W v Bradford C

Sunday, 16 November 2008
Barclays Premier League
Everton v Middlesbrough* (1.30)
Hull C v Manchester C* (4.00)

Saturday, 22 November 2008
Barclays Premier League
Aston Villa v Manchester U
Chelsea v Newcastle U
Liverpool v Fulham
Manchester C v Arsenal
Middlesbrough v Bolton W
Portsmouth v Hull C
Stoke C v WBA
Wigan Ath v Everton

Coca-Cola Football League Championship
Burnley v Doncaster R
Charlton Ath v Sheffield U
Crystal Palace v Bristol C
Ipswich T v Derby Co
Nottingham F v Norwich C* (5.20)
Plymouth Arg v Cardiff C
Preston NE v Barnsley
Reading v Southampton
Sheffield W v Coventry C
Swansea C v Birmingham C
Watford v QPR
Wolverhampton W v Blackpool

Coca-Cola Football League One
Brighton & HA v Huddersfield T
Bristol R v Swindon T
Carlisle U v Cheltenham T
Crewe Alex v Stockport Co
Hereford U v Northampton T
Leeds U v Hartlepool U
Leyton Orient v Millwall
Peterborough U v Colchester U
Scunthorpe U v Leicester C
Southend U v Oldham Ath
Walsall v Milton Keynes D
Yeovil T v Tranmere R

Coca-Cola Football League Two
Barnet v Macclesfield T
Brentford v Darlington
Bury v Gillingham
Chester C v Aldershot T
Chesterfield v Accrington S
Dagenham & R v Notts Co
Grimsby T v Bournemouth
Lincoln C v Shrewsbury T
Morecambe v Exeter C
Rochdale v Luton T
Rotherham U v Bradford C
Wycombe W v Port Vale

Sunday, 23 November 2008
Barclays Premier League
Sunderland v West Ham U* (4.00)
Tottenham H v Blackburn R* (1.30)

Tuesday, 25 November 2008
Coca-Cola Football League Championship
Barnsley v Burnley
Birmingham C v Ipswich T
Blackpool v Sheffield W
Bristol C v Watford
Cardiff C v Reading
Coventry C v Swansea C
Derby Co v Preston NE
Doncaster R v Nottingham F
Norwich C v Crystal Palace
QPR v Charlton Ath
Sheffield U v Wolverhampton W
Southampton v Plymouth Arg

Coca-Cola Football League One
Cheltenham T v Southend U
Colchester U v Yeovil T
Hartlepool U v Bristol R
Huddersfield T v Leyton Orient
Leicester C v Crewe Alex
Millwall v Carlisle U
Milton Keynes D v Hereford U
Northampton T v Leeds U
Oldham Ath v Walsall
Stockport Co v Brighton & HA
Swindon T v Peterborough U
Tranmere R v Scunthorpe U

Coca-Cola Football League Two
Accrington S v Bury
Aldershot T v Lincoln C
Bournemouth v Morecambe
Bradford C v Chesterfield
Darlington v Chester C
Exeter C v Rotherham U
Gillingham v Rochdale
Luton T v Brentford
Macclesfield T v Grimsby T
Notts Co v Wycombe W
Port Vale v Barnet
Shrewsbury T v Dagenham & R

Saturday, 29 November 2008
Barclays Premier League
Aston Villa v Fulham
Liverpool v West Ham U
Middlesbrough v Newcastle U
Portsmouth v Blackburn R
Stoke C v Hull C
Sunderland v Bolton W
Tottenham H v Everton
Wigan Ath v WBA

Coca-Cola Football League Championship
Burnley v Derby Co
Charlton Ath v Southampton
Crystal Palace v QPR
Ipswich T v Sheffield U
Nottingham F v Barnsley
Plymouth Arg v Blackpool
Preston NE v Bristol C
Reading v Coventry C
Sheffield W v Norwich C
Watford v Doncaster R
Wolverhampton W v Birmingham C

Sunday, 30 November 2008
Barclays Premier League
Chelsea v Arsenal* (4.00)
Manchester C v Manchester U* (1.30)

Coca-Cola Football League Championship
Swansea C v Cardiff C* (11.30)

Saturday, 6 December 2008
Barclays Premier League
Arsenal v Wigan Ath
Blackburn R v Liverpool
Bolton W v Chelsea
Everton v Aston Villa
Fulham v Manchester C
Hull C v Middlesbrough
Manchester U v Sunderland
Newcastle U v Stoke C
WBA v Portsmouth
West Ham U v Tottenham H

Coca-Cola Football League Championship
Barnsley v Reading
Birmingham C v Watford
Blackpool v Charlton Ath
Bristol C v Swansea C
Cardiff C v Preston NE
Coventry C v Nottingham F
Derby Co v Crystal Palace
Doncaster R v Plymouth Arg
Norwich C v Ipswich T
QPR v Wolverhampton W
Sheffield U v Burnley
Southampton v Sheffield W

Coca-Cola Football League One
Cheltenham T v Crewe Alex
Colchester U v Hereford U
Hartlepool U v Yeovil T
Huddersfield T v Walsall
Leicester C v Southend U
Millwall v Bristol R
Milton Keynes D v Scunthorpe U
Northampton T v Leyton Orient
Oldham Ath v Brighton & HA
Stockport Co v Peterborough U
Swindon T v Carlisle U
Tranmere R v Leeds U

Coca-Cola Football League Two
Accrington S v Brentford
Aldershot T v Wycombe W
Bournemouth v Chester C
Bradford C v Dagenham & R
Darlington v Rochdale
Exeter C v Lincoln C
Gillingham v Chesterfield
Luton T v Barnet
Macclesfield T v Bury
Notts Co v Morecambe
Port Vale v Grimsby T
Shrewsbury T v Rotherham U

Tuesday, 9 December 2008
Coca-Cola Football League Championship
Burnley v Cardiff C
Charlton Ath v Coventry C
Crystal Palace v Southampton
Ipswich T v Bristol C
Nottingham F v Sheffield U
Plymouth Arg v Birmingham C
Preston NE v Doncaster R
Reading v Blackpool
Sheffield W v QPR
Swansea C v Barnsley
Watford v Norwich C
Wolverhampton W v Derby Co

Saturday, 13 December 2008

Barclays Premier League
Aston Villa v Bolton W
Chelsea v West Ham U
Liverpool v Hull C
Manchester C v Everton
Middlesbrough v Arsenal
Portsmouth v Newcastle U
Stoke C v Fulham
Sunderland v WBA
Tottenham H v Manchester U
Wigan Ath v Blackburn R

Coca-Cola Football League Championship
Burnley v Southampton
Charlton Ath v Derby Co
Crystal Palace v Doncaster R
Ipswich T v Cardiff C
Nottingham F v Blackpool
Plymouth Arg v QPR
Preston NE v Birmingham C
Reading v Norwich C
Sheffield W v Bristol C
Swansea C v Sheffield U
Watford v Coventry C
Wolverhampton W v Barnsley

Coca-Cola Football League One
Brighton & HA v Milton Keynes D
Bristol R v Tranmere R
Carlisle U v Leicester C
Crewe Alex v Swindon T
Hereford U v Hartlepool U
Leeds U v Colchester U
Leyton Orient v Cheltenham T
Peterborough U v Oldham Ath
Scunthorpe U v Northampton T
Southend U v Huddersfield T
Walsall v Millwall
Yeovil T v Stockport Co

Coca-Cola Football League Two
Barnet v Gillingham
Brentford v Bradford C
Bury v Port Vale
Chester C v Notts Co
Chesterfield v Macclesfield T
Dagenham & R v Exeter C
Grimsby T v Shrewsbury T
Lincoln C v Accrington S
Morecambe v Darlington
Rochdale v Bournemouth
Rotherham U v Aldershot T
Wycombe W v Luton T

Saturday, 20 December 2008

Barclays Premier League
Arsenal v Liverpool
Blackburn R v Stoke C
Bolton W v Portsmouth
Everton v Chelsea
Fulham v Middlesbrough
Hull C v Sunderland
Manchester U v Wigan Ath
Newcastle U v Tottenham H
WBA v Manchester C
West Ham U v Aston Villa

Coca-Cola Football League Championship
Barnsley v Plymouth Arg
Birmingham C v Reading
Blackpool v Swansea C
Bristol C v Burnley
Cardiff C v Sheffield W
Coventry C v Ipswich T
Derby Co v Watford
Doncaster R v Wolverhampton W
Norwich C v Charlton Ath
QPR v Preston NE
Sheffield U v Crystal Palace
Southampton v Nottingham F

Coca-Cola Football League One
Cheltenham T v Walsall
Colchester U v Scunthorpe U
Hartlepool U v Southend U
Huddersfield T v Hereford U
Leicester C v Peterborough U
Millwall v Crewe Alex
Milton Keynes D v Leeds U
Northampton T v Carlisle U
Oldham Ath v Leyton Orient
Stockport Co v Bristol R
Swindon T v Yeovil T
Tranmere R v Brighton & HA

Coca-Cola Football League Two
Accrington S v Rotherham U
Aldershot T v Grimsby T
Bournemouth v Bury
Bradford C v Chester C
Darlington v Barnet
Exeter C v Rochdale
Gillingham v Brentford
Luton T v Morecambe
Macclesfield T v Dagenham & R
Notts Co v Lincoln C
Port Vale v Chesterfield
Shrewsbury T v Wycombe W

Friday, 26 December 2008

Barclays Premier League
Aston Villa v Arsenal
Chelsea v WBA
Liverpool v Bolton W
Manchester C v Hull C
Middlesbrough v Everton
Portsmouth v West Ham U
Stoke C v Manchester U
Sunderland v Blackburn R
Tottenham H v Fulham
Wigan Ath v Newcastle U

Coca-Cola Football League Championship
Burnley v Barnsley
Charlton Ath v QPR
Crystal Palace v Norwich C
Ipswich T v Birmingham C
Nottingham F v Doncaster R
Plymouth Arg v Southampton
Preston NE v Derby Co
Reading v Cardiff C
Sheffield W v Blackpool
Swansea C v Coventry C
Watford v Bristol C
Wolverhampton W v Sheffield U

Coca-Cola Football League One
Brighton & HA v Colchester U
Bristol R v Milton Keynes D
Carlisle U v Huddersfield T
Crewe Alex v Oldham Ath
Hereford U v Tranmere R
Leeds U v Leicester C
Leyton Orient v Swindon T
Peterborough U v Millwall
Scunthorpe U v Hartlepool U
Southend U v Northampton T
Walsall v Stockport Co
Yeovil T v Cheltenham T

Coca-Cola Football League Two
Barnet v Aldershot T
Brentford v Bournemouth
Bury v Darlington
Chester C v Accrington S
Chesterfield v Luton T
Dagenham & R v Gillingham
Grimsby T v Notts Co
Lincoln C v Bradford C
Morecambe v Macclesfield T
Rochdale v Shrewsbury T
Rotherham U v Port Vale
Wycombe W v Exeter C

Sunday, 28 December 2008

Barclays Premier League
Arsenal v Portsmouth
Blackburn R v Manchester C
Bolton W v Wigan Ath
Everton v Sunderland
Fulham v Chelsea
Hull C v Aston Villa
Manchester U v Middlesbrough
Newcastle U v Liverpool
WBA v Tottenham H
West Ham U v Stoke C

Coca-Cola Football League Championship
Barnsley v Preston NE
Birmingham C v Swansea C
Blackpool v Wolverhampton W
Bristol C v Crystal Palace
Cardiff C v Plymouth Arg
Coventry C v Sheffield W
Derby Co v Ipswich T
Doncaster R v Burnley
Norwich C v Nottingham F
QPR v Watford
Sheffield U v Charlton Ath
Southampton v Reading

Coca-Cola Football League One
Cheltenham T v Peterborough U
Colchester U v Leyton Orient
Hartlepool U v Crewe Alex
Huddersfield T v Scunthorpe U
Leicester C v Hereford U
Millwall v Yeovil T
Milton Keynes D v Southend U
Northampton T v Bristol R
Oldham Ath v Carlisle U
Stockport Co v Leeds U
Swindon T v Brighton & HA
Tranmere R v Walsall

Coca-Cola Football League Two
Accrington S v Grimsby T
Aldershot T v Dagenham & R
Bournemouth v Barnet
Bradford C v Morecambe
Darlington v Chesterfield
Exeter C v Brentford
Gillingham v Wycombe W
Luton T v Lincoln C
Macclesfield T v Chester C
Notts Co v Rotherham U
Port Vale v Rochdale
Shrewsbury T v Bury

Saturday, 3 January 2009

Coca-Cola Football League One
Brighton & HA v Northampton T
Carlisle U v Walsall
Colchester U v Tranmere R
Crewe Alex v Bristol R
Hartlepool U v Leicester C
Hereford U v Leeds U
Huddersfield T v Oldham Ath
Leyton Orient v Southend U
Millwall v Swindon T
Peterborough U v Milton Keynes D
Stockport Co v Cheltenham T
Yeovil T v Scunthorpe U

Coca-Cola Football League Two
Aldershot T v Notts Co
Barnet v Grimsby T
Bradford C v Shrewsbury T
Brentford v Chesterfield
Chester C v Luton T
Darlington v Bournemouth
Exeter C v Macclesfield T
Morecambe v Lincoln C
Port Vale v Gillingham
Rochdale v Accrington S
Rotherham U v Dagenham & R
Wycombe W v Bury

Saturday, 10 January 2009
Barclays Premier League
Arsenal v Bolton W
Aston Villa v WBA
Everton v Hull C
Fulham v Blackburn R
Manchester U v Chelsea
Middlesbrough v Sunderland
Newcastle U v West Ham U
Portsmouth v Manchester C
Stoke C v Liverpool
Wigan Ath v Tottenham H

Coca-Cola Football League Championship
Barnsley v Southampton
Blackpool v Birmingham C
Burnley v Swansea C
Cardiff C v Derby Co
Charlton Ath v Nottingham F
Doncaster R v Bristol C
Ipswich T v Sheffield W
Plymouth Arg v Crystal Palace
QPR v Coventry C
Reading v Watford
Sheffield U v Norwich C
Wolverhampton W v Preston NE

Coca-Cola Football League One
Bristol R v Yeovil T
Cheltenham T v Millwall
Leeds U v Carlisle U
Leicester C v Leyton Orient
Milton Keynes D v Colchester U
Northampton T v Huddersfield T
Oldham Ath v Hartlepool U
Scunthorpe U v Hereford U
Southend U v Crewe Alex
Swindon T v Stockport Co
Tranmere R v Peterborough U
Walsall v Brighton & HA

Coca-Cola Football League Two
Accrington S v Darlington
Bournemouth v Bradford C
Bury v Barnet
Chesterfield v Rochdale
Dagenham & R v Wycombe W
Gillingham v Aldershot T
Grimsby T v Morecambe
Lincoln C v Brentford
Luton T v Rotherham U
Macclesfield T v Port Vale
Notts Co v Exeter C
Shrewsbury T v Chester C

Saturday, 17 January 2009
Barclays Premier League
Blackburn R v Newcastle U
Bolton W v Manchester U
Chelsea v Stoke C
Hull C v Arsenal
Liverpool v Everton
Manchester C v Wigan Ath
Sunderland v Aston Villa
Tottenham H v Portsmouth
WBA v Middlesbrough
West Ham U v Fulham

Coca-Cola Football League Championship
Birmingham C v Cardiff C
Bristol C v Wolverhampton W
Coventry C v Blackpool
Crystal Palace v Ipswich T
Derby Co v QPR
Norwich C v Barnsley
Nottingham F v Plymouth Arg
Preston NE v Burnley
Sheffield W v Charlton Ath
Southampton v Doncaster R
Swansea C v Reading
Watford v Sheffield U

Coca-Cola Football League One
Brighton & HA v Leeds U
Carlisle U v Milton Keynes D
Colchester U v Cheltenham T
Crewe Alex v Scunthorpe U
Hartlepool U v Northampton T
Hereford U v Oldham Ath
Huddersfield T v Swindon T
Leyton Orient v Bristol R
Millwall v Tranmere R
Peterborough U v Walsall
Stockport Co v Southend U
Yeovil T v Leicester C

Coca-Cola Football League Two
Aldershot T v Macclesfield T
Barnet v Dagenham & R
Bradford C v Accrington S
Brentford v Notts Co
Chester C v Chesterfield
Darlington v Luton T
Exeter C v Bury
Morecambe v Gillingham
Port Vale v Shrewsbury T
Rochdale v Lincoln C
Rotherham U v Bournemouth
Wycombe W v Grimsby T

Saturday, 24 January 2009
Coca-Cola Football League One
Bristol R v Colchester U
Cheltenham T v Brighton & HA
Leeds U v Peterborough U
Leicester C v Huddersfield T
Milton Keynes D v Millwall
Northampton T v Crewe Alex
Oldham Ath v Stockport Co
Scunthorpe U v Leyton Orient
Southend U v Yeovil T
Swindon T v Hartlepool U
Tranmere R v Carlisle U
Walsall v Hereford U

Coca-Cola Football League Two
Accrington S v Barnet
Bournemouth v Wycombe W
Bury v Aldershot T
Chesterfield v Morecambe
Dagenham & R v Rochdale
Gillingham v Exeter C
Grimsby T v Rotherham U
Lincoln C v Chester C
Luton T v Bradford C
Macclesfield T v Brentford
Notts Co v Port Vale
Shrewsbury T v Darlington

Tuesday, 27 January 2009
Barclays Premier League
Portsmouth v Aston Villa
Sunderland v Fulham
Tottenham H v Stoke C
WBA v Manchester U
West Ham U v Hull C
Wigan Ath v Liverpool

Coca-Cola Football League Championship
Barnsley v Ipswich T
Birmingham C v Derby Co
Blackpool v QPR
Charlton Ath v Crystal Palace
Coventry C v Cardiff C
Norwich C v Southampton
Nottingham F v Sheffield W
Plymouth Arg v Bristol C
Reading v Wolverhampton W
Sheffield U v Doncaster R
Swansea C v Preston NE
Watford v Burnley

Coca-Cola Football League One
Bristol R v Cheltenham T
Colchester U v Northampton T
Hartlepool U v Carlisle U
Hereford U v Millwall
Leeds U v Southend U
Leicester C v Brighton & HA
Milton Keynes D v Leyton Orient
Peterborough U v Crewe Alex
Scunthorpe U v Oldham Ath
Swindon T v Walsall
Tranmere R v Stockport Co
Yeovil T v Huddersfield T

Coca-Cola Football League Two
Accrington S v Morecambe
Barnet v Shrewsbury T
Bournemouth v Luton T
Brentford v Aldershot T
Bury v Bradford C
Darlington v Rotherham U
Gillingham v Lincoln C
Grimsby T v Dagenham & R
Macclesfield T v Wycombe W
Port Vale v Chester C
Rochdale v Notts Co

Wednesday, 28 January 2009
Barclays Premier League
Blackburn R v Bolton W
Chelsea v Middlesbrough
Everton v Arsenal
Manchester C v Newcastle U

Coca-Cola Football League Two
Chesterfield v Exeter C

Saturday, 31 January 2009
Barclays Premier League
Arsenal v West Ham U
Aston Villa v Wigan Ath
Bolton W v Tottenham H
Fulham v Portsmouth
Hull C v WBA
Liverpool v Chelsea
Manchester U v Everton
Middlesbrough v Blackburn R
Newcastle U v Sunderland
Stoke C v Manchester C

Coca-Cola Football League Championship
Bristol C v Barnsley
Burnley v Charlton Ath
Cardiff C v Nottingham F
Crystal Palace v Blackpool
Derby Co v Coventry C
Doncaster R v Norwich C

Ipswich T v Plymouth Arg
Preston NE v Sheffield U
QPR v Reading
Sheffield W v Birmingham C
Southampton v Swansea C
Wolverhampton W v Watford

Coca-Cola Football League One
Brighton & HA v Hartlepool U
Carlisle U v Colchester U
Cheltenham T v Milton Keynes D
Crewe Alex v Tranmere R
Huddersfield T v Peterborough U
Leyton Orient v Yeovil T
Millwall v Scunthorpe U
Northampton T v Leicester C
Oldham Ath v Swindon T
Southend U v Bristol R
Stockport Co v Hereford U
Walsall v Leeds U

Coca-Cola Football League Two
Aldershot T v Rochdale
Bradford C v Grimsby T
Chester C v Gillingham
Dagenham & R v Darlington
Exeter C v Barnet
Lincoln C v Bournemouth
Luton T v Bury
Morecambe v Port Vale
Notts Co v Chesterfield
Rotherham U v Macclesfield T
Shrewsbury T v Brentford
Wycombe W v Accrington S

Tuesday, 3 February 2009
Coca-Cola Football League Championship
Bristol C v Charlton Ath
Burnley v Coventry C
Cardiff C v Watford
Crystal Palace v Birmingham C
Derby Co v Blackpool
Doncaster R v Reading
Ipswich T v Nottingham F
Preston NE v Plymouth Arg
QPR v Swansea C
Sheffield W v Barnsley
Southampton v Sheffield U
Wolverhampton W v Norwich C

Coca-Cola Football League One
Brighton & HA v Peterborough U
Carlisle U v Hereford U
Cheltenham T v Tranmere R
Crewe Alex v Yeovil T
Huddersfield T v Hartlepool U
Leyton Orient v Leeds U
Millwall v Colchester U
Northampton T v Swindon T
Oldham Ath v Bristol R
Southend U v Scunthorpe U
Stockport Co v Milton Keynes D
Walsall v Leicester C

Coca-Cola Football League Two
Aldershot T v Chesterfield
Bradford C v Darlington
Chester C v Rochdale
Dagenham & R v Bournemouth
Exeter C v Port Vale
Lincoln C v Macclesfield T
Luton T v Grimsby T
Morecambe v Brentford
Notts Co v Gillingham
Rotherham U v Bury
Shrewsbury T v Accrington S
Wycombe W v Barnet

Saturday, 7 February 2009
Barclays Premier League
Blackburn R v Aston Villa
Chelsea v Hull C
Everton v Bolton W
Manchester C v Middlesbrough
Portsmouth v Liverpool
Sunderland v Stoke C
Tottenham H v Arsenal
WBA v Newcastle U
West Ham U v Manchester U
Wigan Ath v Fulham

Coca-Cola Football League Championship
Barnsley v Crystal Palace
Birmingham C v Burnley
Blackpool v Doncaster R
Charlton Ath v Cardiff C
Coventry C v Wolverhampton W
Norwich C v Bristol C
Nottingham F v QPR
Plymouth Arg v Derby Co
Reading v Preston NE
Sheffield U v Sheffield W
Swansea C v Ipswich T
Watford v Southampton

Coca-Cola Football League One
Bristol R v Huddersfield T
Colchester U v Stockport Co
Hartlepool U v Walsall
Hereford U v Brighton & HA
Leeds U v Millwall
Leicester C v Oldham Ath
Milton Keynes D v Crewe Alex
Peterborough U v Carlisle U
Scunthorpe U v Cheltenham T
Swindon T v Southend U
Tranmere R v Leyton Orient
Yeovil T v Northampton T

Coca-Cola Football League Two
Accrington S v Luton T
Barnet v Rotherham U
Bournemouth v Shrewsbury T
Brentford v Chester C
Bury v Dagenham & R
Chesterfield v Lincoln C
Darlington v Wycombe W
Gillingham v Bradford C
Grimsby T v Exeter C
Macclesfield T v Notts Co
Port Vale v Aldershot T
Rochdale v Morecambe

Saturday, 14 February 2009
Coca-Cola Football League Championship
Birmingham C v Nottingham F
Bristol C v Southampton
Burnley v Wolverhampton W
Cardiff C v QPR
Charlton Ath v Plymouth Arg
Crystal Palace v Coventry C
Derby Co v Reading
Doncaster R v Sheffield W
Ipswich T v Blackpool
Preston NE v Norwich C
Sheffield U v Barnsley
Watford v Swansea C

Coca-Cola Football League One
Brighton & HA v Carlisle U
Cheltenham T v Hereford U
Huddersfield T v Leeds U
Leicester C v Swindon T
Leyton Orient v Crewe Alex
Milton Keynes D v Hartlepool U
Oldham Ath v Northampton T
Peterborough U v Yeovil T
Scunthorpe U v Bristol R
Southend U v Tranmere R
Stockport Co v Millwall
Walsall v Colchester U

Coca-Cola Football League Two
Bournemouth v Accrington S
Bradford C v Wycombe W
Brentford v Port Vale
Dagenham & R v Luton T
Exeter C v Aldershot T
Grimsby T v Bury
Lincoln C v Darlington
Macclesfield T v Rochdale
Morecambe v Chester C
Notts Co v Barnet
Rotherham U v Gillingham
Shrewsbury T v Chesterfield

Saturday, 21 February 2009
Barclays Premier League
Arsenal v Sunderland
Aston Villa v Chelsea
Bolton W v West Ham U
Fulham v WBA
Hull C v Tottenham H
Liverpool v Manchester C
Manchester U v Blackburn R
Middlesbrough v Wigan Ath
Newcastle U v Everton
Stoke C v Portsmouth

Coca-Cola Football League Championship
Barnsley v Charlton Ath
Blackpool v Watford
Coventry C v Birmingham C
Norwich C v Burnley
Nottingham F v Derby Co
Plymouth Arg v Sheffield U
QPR v Ipswich T
Reading v Bristol C
Sheffield W v Crystal Palace
Southampton v Preston NE
Swansea C v Doncaster R
Wolverhampton W v Cardiff C

Coca-Cola Football League One
Bristol R v Leicester C
Carlisle U v Stockport Co
Colchester U v Southend U
Crewe Alex v Huddersfield T
Hartlepool U v Leyton Orient
Hereford U v Peterborough U
Leeds U v Cheltenham T
Millwall v Brighton & HA
Northampton T v Walsall
Swindon T v Scunthorpe U
Tranmere R v Milton Keynes D
Yeovil T v Oldham Ath

Coca-Cola Football League Two
Accrington S v Dagenham & R
Aldershot T v Morecambe
Barnet v Bradford C
Bury v Notts Co
Chester C v Exeter C
Chesterfield v Bournemouth
Darlington v Grimsby T
Gillingham v Macclesfield T
Luton T v Shrewsbury T
Port Vale v Lincoln C
Rochdale v Brentford
Wycombe W v Rotherham U

Saturday, 28 February 2009
Barclays Premier League
Arsenal v Fulham
Aston Villa v Stoke C
Bolton W v Newcastle U
Chelsea v Wigan Ath
Everton v WBA
Hull C v Blackburn R
Manchester U v Portsmouth
Middlesbrough v Liverpool
Sunderland v Tottenham H
West Ham U v Manchester C

Coca-Cola Football League Championship
Barnsley v QPR
Bristol C v Blackpool
Burnley v Sheffield W
Doncaster R v Derby Co
Norwich C v Coventry C
Preston NE v Ipswich T
Reading v Nottingham F
Sheffield U v Birmingham C
Southampton v Cardiff C
Swansea C v Charlton Ath
Watford v Crystal Palace
Wolverhampton W v Plymouth Arg

Coca-Cola Football League One
Brighton & HA v Crewe Alex
Carlisle U v Bristol R
Cheltenham T v Northampton T
Colchester U v Hartlepool U
Hereford U v Leyton Orient
Leeds U v Scunthorpe U
Millwall v Oldham Ath
Milton Keynes D v Leicester C
Peterborough U v Southend U
Stockport Co v Huddersfield T
Tranmere R v Swindon T
Walsall v Yeovil T

Coca-Cola Football League Two
Aldershot T v Accrington S
Brentford v Bury
Chester C v Dagenham & R
Chesterfield v Barnet
Exeter C v Darlington
Gillingham v Bournemouth
Lincoln C v Rotherham U
Macclesfield T v Shrewsbury T
Morecambe v Wycombe W
Notts Co v Bradford C
Port Vale v Luton T
Rochdale v Grimsby T

Tuesday, 3 March 2009
Barclays Premier League
Portsmouth v Chelsea
Stoke C v Bolton W
Tottenham H v Middlesbrough
WBA v Arsenal
Wigan Ath v West Ham U

Coca-Cola Football League Championship
Birmingham C v Bristol C
Blackpool v Burnley
Cardiff C v Barnsley
Charlton Ath v Doncaster R
Coventry C v Sheffield U
Crystal Palace v Wolverhampton W
Derby Co v Swansea C
Ipswich T v Southampton
Nottingham F v Preston NE
Plymouth Arg v Watford
QPR v Norwich C
Sheffield W v Reading

Coca-Cola Football League One
Bristol R v Brighton & HA
Crewe Alex v Carlisle U
Hartlepool U v Tranmere R
Huddersfield T v Colchester U
Leicester C v Stockport Co
Leyton Orient v Peterborough U
Northampton T v Milton Keynes D
Oldham Ath v Leeds U
Scunthorpe U v Walsall
Southend U v Millwall
Swindon T v Cheltenham T
Yeovil T v Hereford U

Coca-Cola Football League Two
Accrington S v Port Vale
Barnet v Rochdale
Bournemouth v Aldershot T
Bradford C v Macclesfield T
Bury v Chesterfield
Dagenham & R v Lincoln C
Darlington v Notts Co
Grimsby T v Brentford
Luton T v Gillingham
Rotherham U v Morecambe
Shrewsbury T v Exeter C
Wycombe W v Chester C

Wednesday, 4 March 2009
Barclays Premier League
Blackburn R v Everton
Fulham v Hull C
Liverpool v Sunderland
Manchester C v Aston Villa
Newcastle U v Manchester U

Saturday, 7 March 2009
Coca-Cola Football League Championship
Birmingham C v Southampton
Blackpool v Norwich C
Cardiff C v Doncaster R
Charlton Ath v Watford
Coventry C v Barnsley
Crystal Palace v Preston NE
Derby Co v Bristol C
Ipswich T v Burnley
Nottingham F v Swansea C
Plymouth Arg v Reading
QPR v Sheffield U
Sheffield W v Wolverhampton W

Coca-Cola Football League One
Bristol R v Leeds U
Crewe Alex v Hereford U
Hartlepool U v Peterborough U
Huddersfield T v Millwall
Leicester C v Cheltenham T
Leyton Orient v Brighton & HA
Northampton T v Tranmere R
Oldham Ath v Colchester U
Scunthorpe U v Stockport Co
Southend U v Walsall
Swindon T v Milton Keynes D
Yeovil T v Carlisle U

Coca-Cola Football League Two
Accrington S v Gillingham
Barnet v Chester C
Bournemouth v Port Vale
Bradford C v Aldershot T
Bury v Rochdale
Dagenham & R v Morecambe
Darlington v Macclesfield T
Grimsby T v Lincoln C
Luton T v Exeter C
Rotherham U v Brentford
Shrewsbury T v Notts Co
Wycombe W v Chesterfield

Tuesday, 10 March 2009
Coca-Cola Football League Championship
Barnsley v Birmingham C
Bristol C v Coventry C
Burnley v Crystal Palace
Doncaster R v QPR
Norwich C v Cardiff C
Preston NE v Sheffield W
Reading v Charlton Ath
Sheffield U v Blackpool
Southampton v Derby Co
Swansea C v Plymouth Arg
Watford v Nottingham F
Wolverhampton W v Ipswich T

Coca-Cola Football League One
Brighton & HA v Southend U
Carlisle U v Leyton Orient
Cheltenham T v Oldham Ath
Colchester U v Swindon T
Hereford U v Bristol R
Leeds U v Yeovil T
Millwall v Northampton T
Milton Keynes D v Huddersfield T
Peterborough U v Scunthorpe U
Stockport Co v Hartlepool U
Tranmere R v Leicester C
Walsall v Crewe Alex

Coca-Cola Football League Two
Aldershot T v Shrewsbury T
Brentford v Barnet
Chester C v Rotherham U
Exeter C v Bournemouth
Gillingham v Darlington
Lincoln C v Wycombe W
Macclesfield T v Accrington S
Morecambe v Bury
Notts Co v Luton T
Port Vale v Dagenham & R
Rochdale v Bradford C

Wednesday, 11 March 2009
Coca-Cola Football League Two
Chesterfield v Grimsby T

Saturday, 14 March 2009
Barclays Premier League
Arsenal v Blackburn R
Aston Villa v Tottenham H
Bolton W v Fulham
Chelsea v Manchester C
Everton v Stoke C
Hull C v Newcastle U
Manchester U v Liverpool
Middlesbrough v Portsmouth
Sunderland v Wigan Ath
West Ham U v WBA

Coca-Cola Football League Championship
Barnsley v Blackpool
Bristol C v Cardiff C
Burnley v Nottingham F
Doncaster R v Birmingham C
Norwich C v Plymouth Arg
Preston NE v Coventry C
Reading v Ipswich T
Sheffield U v Derby Co
Southampton v QPR
Swansea C v Crystal Palace
Watford v Sheffield W
Wolverhampton W v Charlton Ath

Coca-Cola Football League One
Brighton & HA v Yeovil T
Carlisle U v Scunthorpe U
Cheltenham T v Hartlepool U

Colchester U v Crewe Alex
Hereford U v Southend U
Leeds U v Swindon T
Millwall v Leicester C
Milton Keynes D v Oldham Ath
Peterborough U v Northampton T
Stockport Co v Leyton Orient
Tranmere R v Huddersfield T
Walsall v Bristol R

Coca-Cola Football League Two
Aldershot T v Luton T
Brentford v Wycombe W
Chester C v Grimsby T
Chesterfield v Dagenham & R
Exeter C v Bradford C
Gillingham v Shrewsbury T
Lincoln C v Bury
Macclesfield T v Bournemouth
Morecambe v Barnet
Notts Co v Accrington S
Port Vale v Darlington
Rochdale v Rotherham U

Saturday, 21 March 2009
Barclays Premier League
Blackburn R v West Ham U
Fulham v Manchester U
Liverpool v Aston Villa
Manchester C v Sunderland
Newcastle U v Arsenal
Portsmouth v Everton
Stoke C v Middlesbrough
Tottenham H v Chelsea
WBA v Bolton W
Wigan Ath v Hull C

Coca-Cola Football League Championship
Birmingham C v Norwich C
Blackpool v Southampton
Cardiff C v Sheffield U
Charlton Ath v Preston NE
Coventry C v Doncaster R
Crystal Palace v Reading
Derby Co v Barnsley
Ipswich T v Watford
Nottingham F v Wolverhampton W
Plymouth Arg v Burnley
QPR v Bristol C
Sheffield W v Swansea C

Coca-Cola Football League One
Bristol R v Peterborough U
Crewe Alex v Leeds U
Hartlepool U v Millwall
Huddersfield T v Cheltenham T
Leicester C v Colchester U
Leyton Orient v Walsall
Northampton T v Stockport Co
Oldham Ath v Tranmere R
Scunthorpe U v Brighton & HA
Southend U v Carlisle U
Swindon T v Hereford U
Yeovil T v Milton Keynes D

Coca-Cola Football League Two
Accrington S v Exeter C
Barnet v Lincoln C
Bournemouth v Notts Co
Bradford C v Port Vale
Bury v Chester C
Dagenham & R v Brentford
Darlington v Aldershot T
Grimsby T v Gillingham
Luton T v Macclesfield T
Rotherham U v Chesterfield
Shrewsbury T v Morecambe
Wycombe W v Rochdale

Saturday, 28 March 2009
Coca-Cola Football League One
Brighton & HA v Tranmere R
Bristol R v Stockport Co
Carlisle U v Northampton T
Crewe Alex v Millwall
Hereford U v Huddersfield T
Leeds U v Milton Keynes D
Leyton Orient v Oldham Ath
Peterborough U v Leicester C
Scunthorpe U v Colchester U
Southend U v Hartlepool U
Walsall v Cheltenham T
Yeovil T v Swindon T

Coca-Cola Football League Two
Barnet v Darlington
Brentford v Gillingham
Bury v Bournemouth
Chester C v Bradford C
Chesterfield v Port Vale
Dagenham & R v Macclesfield T
Grimsby T v Aldershot T
Lincoln C v Notts Co
Morecambe v Luton T
Rochdale v Exeter C
Rotherham U v Accrington S
Wycombe W v Shrewsbury T

Saturday, 4 April 2009
Barclays Premier League
Arsenal v Manchester C
Blackburn R v Tottenham H
Bolton W v Middlesbrough
Everton v Wigan Ath
Fulham v Liverpool
Hull C v Portsmouth
Manchester U v Aston Villa
Newcastle U v Chelsea
WBA v Stoke C
West Ham U v Sunderland

Coca-Cola Football League Championship
Barnsley v Nottingham F
Birmingham C v Wolverhampton W
Blackpool v Plymouth Arg
Bristol C v Preston NE
Cardiff C v Swansea C
Coventry C v Reading
Derby Co v Burnley
Doncaster R v Watford
Norwich C v Sheffield W
QPR v Crystal Palace
Sheffield U v Ipswich T
Southampton v Charlton Ath

Coca-Cola Football League One
Cheltenham T v Leyton Orient
Colchester U v Leeds U
Hartlepool U v Hereford U
Huddersfield T v Southend U
Leicester C v Carlisle U
Millwall v Walsall
Milton Keynes D v Brighton & HA
Northampton T v Scunthorpe U
Oldham Ath v Peterborough U
Stockport Co v Yeovil T
Swindon T v Crewe Alex
Tranmere R v Bristol R

Coca-Cola Football League Two
Accrington S v Lincoln C
Aldershot T v Rotherham U
Bournemouth v Rochdale
Bradford C v Brentford
Darlington v Morecambe
Exeter C v Dagenham & R
Gillingham v Barnet
Luton T v Wycombe W
Macclesfield T v Chesterfield
Notts Co v Chester C
Port Vale v Bury
Shrewsbury T v Grimsby T

Saturday, 11 April 2009
Barclays Premier League
Aston Villa v Everton
Chelsea v Bolton W
Liverpool v Blackburn R
Manchester C v Fulham
Middlesbrough v Hull C
Portsmouth v WBA
Stoke C v Newcastle U
Sunderland v Manchester U
Tottenham H v West Ham U
Wigan Ath v Arsenal

Coca-Cola Football League Championship
Burnley v QPR
Charlton Ath v Birmingham C
Crystal Palace v Cardiff C
Ipswich T v Doncaster R
Nottingham F v Bristol C
Plymouth Arg v Coventry C
Preston NE v Blackpool
Reading v Sheffield U
Sheffield W v Derby Co
Swansea C v Norwich C
Watford v Barnsley
Wolverhampton W v Southampton

Coca-Cola Football League One
Brighton & HA v Swindon T
Bristol R v Northampton T
Carlisle U v Oldham Ath
Crewe Alex v Hartlepool U
Hereford U v Leicester C
Leeds U v Stockport Co
Leyton Orient v Colchester U
Peterborough U v Cheltenham T
Scunthorpe U v Huddersfield T
Southend U v Milton Keynes D
Walsall v Tranmere R
Yeovil T v Millwall

Coca-Cola Football League Two
Barnet v Bournemouth
Brentford v Exeter C
Bury v Shrewsbury T
Chester C v Macclesfield T
Chesterfield v Darlington
Dagenham & R v Aldershot T
Grimsby T v Accrington S
Lincoln C v Luton T
Morecambe v Bradford C
Rochdale v Port Vale
Rotherham U v Notts Co
Wycombe W v Gillingham

Monday, 13 April 2009
Coca-Cola Football League Championship
Barnsley v Swansea C
Birmingham C v Plymouth Arg
Blackpool v Reading
Bristol C v Ipswich T
Cardiff C v Burnley
Coventry C v Charlton Ath
Derby Co v Wolverhampton W
Doncaster R v Preston NE
Norwich C v Watford
QPR v Sheffield W
Sheffield U v Nottingham F
Southampton v Crystal Palace

Coca-Cola Football League One
Cheltenham T v Yeovil T
Colchester U v Brighton & HA
Hartlepool U v Scunthorpe U
Huddersfield T v Carlisle U
Leicester C v Leeds U
Millwall v Peterborough U
Milton Keynes D v Bristol R
Northampton T v Southend U
Oldham Ath v Crewe Alex
Stockport Co v Walsall
Swindon T v Leyton Orient
Tranmere R v Hereford U

Coca-Cola Football League Two
Accrington S v Chester C
Aldershot T v Barnet
Bournemouth v Brentford
Bradford C v Lincoln C
Darlington v Bury
Exeter C v Wycombe W
Gillingham v Dagenham & R
Luton T v Chesterfield
Macclesfield T v Morecambe
Notts Co v Grimsby T
Port Vale v Rotherham U
Shrewsbury T v Rochdale

Saturday, 18 April 2009
Barclays Premier League
Aston Villa v West Ham U
Chelsea v Everton
Liverpool v Arsenal
Manchester C v WBA
Middlesbrough v Fulham
Portsmouth v Bolton W
Stoke C v Blackburn R
Sunderland v Hull C
Tottenham H v Newcastle U
Wigan Ath v Manchester U

Coca-Cola Football League Championship
Burnley v Sheffield U
Charlton Ath v Blackpool
Crystal Palace v Derby Co
Ipswich T v Norwich C
Nottingham F v Coventry C
Plymouth Arg v Doncaster R
Preston NE v Cardiff C
Reading v Barnsley
Sheffield W v Southampton
Swansea C v Bristol C
Watford v Birmingham C
Wolverhampton W v QPR

Coca-Cola Football League One
Brighton & HA v Oldham Ath
Bristol R v Millwall
Carlisle U v Swindon T
Crewe Alex v Cheltenham T
Hereford U v Colchester U
Leeds U v Tranmere R
Leyton Orient v Northampton T
Peterborough U v Stockport Co
Scunthorpe U v Milton Keynes D
Southend U v Leicester C
Walsall v Huddersfield T
Yeovil T v Hartlepool U

Coca-Cola Football League Two
Barnet v Luton T
Brentford v Accrington S
Bury v Macclesfield T
Chester C v Bournemouth
Chesterfield v Gillingham
Dagenham & R v Bradford C
Grimsby T v Port Vale
Lincoln C v Exeter C
Morecambe v Notts Co
Rochdale v Darlington
Rotherham U v Shrewsbury T
Wycombe W v Aldershot T

Saturday, 25 April 2009
Barclays Premier League
Arsenal v Middlesbrough
Blackburn R v Wigan Ath
Bolton W v Aston Villa
Everton v Manchester C
Fulham v Stoke C
Hull C v Liverpool
Manchester U v Tottenham H
Newcastle U v Portsmouth
WBA v Sunderland
West Ham U v Chelsea

Coca-Cola Football League Championship
Barnsley v Wolverhampton W
Birmingham C v Preston NE
Blackpool v Nottingham F
Bristol C v Sheffield W
Cardiff C v Ipswich T
Coventry C v Watford
Derby Co v Charlton Ath
Doncaster R v Crystal Palace
Norwich C v Reading
QPR v Plymouth Arg
Sheffield U v Swansea C
Southampton v Burnley

Coca-Cola Football League One
Cheltenham T v Carlisle U
Colchester U v Peterborough U
Hartlepool U v Leeds U
Huddersfield T v Brighton & HA
Leicester C v Scunthorpe U
Millwall v Leyton Orient
Milton Keynes D v Walsall
Northampton T v Hereford U
Oldham Ath v Southend U
Stockport Co v Crewe Alex
Swindon T v Bristol R
Tranmere R v Yeovil T

Coca-Cola Football League Two
Accrington S v Chesterfield
Aldershot T v Chester C
Bournemouth v Grimsby T
Bradford C v Rotherham U
Darlington v Brentford
Exeter C v Morecambe
Gillingham v Bury
Luton T v Rochdale
Macclesfield T v Barnet
Notts Co v Dagenham & R
Port Vale v Wycombe W
Shrewsbury T v Lincoln C

Saturday, 2 May 2009
Barclays Premier League
Aston Villa v Hull C
Chelsea v Fulham
Liverpool v Newcastle U
Manchester C v Blackburn R
Middlesbrough v Manchester U
Portsmouth v Arsenal
Stoke C v West Ham U
Sunderland v Everton
Tottenham H v WBA
Wigan Ath v Bolton W

Coca-Cola Football League One
Brighton & HA v Stockport Co
Bristol R v Hartlepool U
Carlisle U v Millwall
Crewe Alex v Leicester C
Hereford U v Milton Keynes D
Leeds U v Northampton T
Leyton Orient v Huddersfield T
Peterborough U v Swindon T
Scunthorpe U v Tranmere R
Southend U v Cheltenham T
Walsall v Oldham Ath
Yeovil T v Colchester U

Coca-Cola Football League Two
Barnet v Port Vale
Brentford v Luton T
Bury v Accrington S
Chester C v Darlington
Chesterfield v Bradford C
Dagenham & R v Shrewsbury T
Grimsby T v Macclesfield T
Lincoln C v Aldershot T
Morecambe v Bournemouth
Rochdale v Gillingham
Rotherham U v Exeter C
Wycombe W v Notts Co

Sunday, 3 May 2009
Coca-Cola Football League Championship
Burnley v Bristol C
Charlton Ath v Norwich C
Crystal Palace v Sheffield U
Ipswich T v Coventry C
Nottingham F v Southampton
Plymouth Arg v Barnsley
Preston NE v QPR
Reading v Birmingham C
Sheffield W v Cardiff C
Swansea C v Blackpool
Watford v Derby Co
Wolverhampton W v Doncaster R

Saturday, 9 May 2009
Barclays Premier League
Arsenal v Chelsea
Blackburn R v Portsmouth
Bolton W v Sunderland
Everton v Tottenham H
Fulham v Aston Villa
Hull C v Stoke C
Manchester U v Manchester C
Newcastle U v Middlesbrough
WBA v Wigan Ath
West Ham U v Liverpool

Saturday, 16 May 2009
Barclays Premier League
Bolton W v Hull C
Chelsea v Blackburn R
Everton v West Ham U
Manchester U v Arsenal
Middlesbrough v Aston Villa
Newcastle U v Fulham
Portsmouth v Sunderland
Stoke C v Wigan Ath
Tottenham H v Manchester C
WBA v Liverpool

Sunday, 24 May 2009
Barclays Premier League
Arsenal v Stoke C
Aston Villa v Newcastle U
Blackburn R v WBA
Fulham v Everton
Hull C v Manchester U
Liverpool v Tottenham H
Manchester C v Bolton W
Sunderland v Chelsea
West Ham U v Middlesbrough
Wigan Ath v Portsmouth

BLUE SQUARE PREMIER FIXTURES 2008–09

Friday, 8 August 2008
Barrow v Oxford U

Saturday, 9 August 2008
Crawley T v York C
Eastbourne B v Rushden & D'monds
Ebbsfleet U v Mansfield T
Histon v Torquay U
Kettering T v Forest Green R
Kidderminster H v Lewes
Northwich Vic v Cambridge U
Salisbury C v Burton Alb
Weymouth v Grays Ath
Woking v Altrincham T
Wrexham v Stevenage B

Tuesday, 12 August 2008
Altrincham T v Barrow
Burton Alb v Northwich Vic
Cambridge U v Kidderminster H
Forest Green R v Salisbury C
Grays Ath v Kettering T
Lewes v Crawley T
Mansfield T v Histon
Oxford U v Weymouth
Rushden & D'monds v Ebbsfleet U
Stevenage B v Eastbourne B
Torquay U v Woking

Thursday, 14 August 2008
York C v Wrexham

Saturday, 16 August 2008
Altrincham T v Kettering T
Burton Alb v Woking
Cambridge U v Barrow
Forest Green R v Crawley T
Grays Ath v Northwich Vic
Lewes v Salisbury C
Mansfield T v Kidderminster H
Oxford U v Eastbourne B
Rushden & D'monds v Wrexham
Stevenage B v Weymouth
York C v Histon

Monday, 18 August 2008
Torquay U v Ebbsfleet U

Thursday, 21 August 2008
Wrexham v Oxford U

Saturday, 23 August 2008
Barrow v Mansfield T
Crawley T v Torquay U
Eastbourne B v Cambridge U
Ebbsfleet U v Stevenage B
Histon v Burton Alb
Kettering T v Rushden & D'monds
Kidderminster H v Altrincham T
Northwich Vic v York C
Salisbury C v Grays Ath
Weymouth v Lewes
Woking v Forest Green R

Monday, 25 August 2008
Altrincham T v Wrexham
Burton Alb v Kidderminster H
Cambridge U v Kettering T
Forest Green R v Weymouth
Grays Ath v Eastbourne B
Lewes v Ebbsfleet U
Mansfield T v Northwich Vic
Oxford U v Woking
Rushden & D'monds v Histon
Stevenage B v Crawley T
Torquay U v Salisbury C
York C v Barrow

Thursday, 28 August 2008
Torquay U v York C

Saturday, 30 August 2008
Barrow v Stevenage B
Burton Alb v Lewes
Crawley T v Northwich Vic
Eastbourne B v Altrincham T
Ebbsfleet U v Oxford U
Histon v Forest Green R
Kettering T v Woking
Kidderminster H v Rushden & D'monds
Mansfield T v Grays Ath
Salisbury C v Wrexham
Weymouth v Cambridge U

Tuesday, 2 September 2008
Barrow v Rushden & D'monds
Crawley T v Grays Ath
Eastbourne B v Forest Green R
Ebbsfleet U v Cambridge U
Histon v Altrincham T
Kettering T v Stevenage B
Kidderminster H v Torquay U
Northwich Vic v Oxford U
Salisbury C v Weymouth
Woking v Lewes
Wrexham v Burton Alb
York C v Mansfield T

Saturday, 6 September 2008
Altrincham T v Salisbury C
Cambridge U v Wrexham
Forest Green R v Ebbsfleet U
Grays Ath v Kidderminster H
Lewes v Barrow
Mansfield T v Eastbourne B
Oxford U v Kettering T
Rushden & D'monds v Crawley T
Stevenage B v Burton Alb
Torquay U v Northwich Vic
Weymouth v Histon
York C v Woking

Saturday, 13 September 2008
Burton Alb v Weymouth
Cambridge U v Torquay U
Crawley T v Mansfield T
Eastbourne B v Histon
Kettering T v York C
Kidderminster H v Oxford U
Lewes v Rushden & D'monds
Northwich Vic v Forest Green R
Salisbury C v Barrow
Stevenage B v Altrincham T
Woking v Grays Ath
Wrexham v Ebbsfleet U

Saturday, 20 September 2008
Altrincham T v Lewes
Barrow v Kettering T
Ebbsfleet U v Woking
Forest Green R v Stevenage B
Grays Ath v Wrexham
Histon v Northwich Vic
Mansfield T v Cambridge U
Oxford U v Crawley T
Rushden & D'monds v Burton Alb
Torquay U v Eastbourne B
Weymouth v Kidderminster H
York C v Salisbury C

Tuesday, 23 September 2008
Altrincham T v Mansfield T
Ebbsfleet U v Eastbourne B
Forest Green R v Torquay U
Grays Ath v Stevenage B
Histon v Lewes
Kettering T v Burton Alb
Kidderminster H v York C
Northwich Vic v Barrow
Oxford U v Cambridge U
Weymouth v Crawley T
Woking v Salisbury C
Wrexham v Rushden & D'monds

Saturday, 27 September 2008
Barrow v Ebbsfleet U
Burton Alb v Forest Green R
Cambridge U v Grays Ath
Crawley T v Kettering T
Eastbourne B v Kidderminster H
Lewes v Oxford U
Northwich Vic v Weymouth
Rushden & D'monds v Altrincham T
Salisbury C v Mansfield T
Stevenage B v York C
Woking v Histon
Wrexham v Torquay U

Saturday, 4 October 2008
Altrincham T v Ebbsfleet U
Burton Alb v Crawley T
Forest Green R v Wrexham
Grays Ath v Lewes
Histon v Salisbury C
Kettering T v Northwich Vic
Kidderminster H v Barrow
Mansfield T v Woking
Oxford U v Rushden & D'monds
Torquay U v Stevenage B
Weymouth v Eastbourne B
York C v Cambridge U

Tuesday, 7 October 2008
Barrow v Burton Alb
Cambridge U v Lewes
Crawley T v Forest Green R
Eastbourne B v Kettering T
Ebbsfleet U v Histon
Northwich Vic v Kidderminster H
Rushden & D'monds v Grays Ath
Salisbury C v Altrincham T
Stevenage B v Mansfield T
Torquay U v Oxford U
Woking v Weymouth
Wrexham v York C

Saturday, 11 October 2008
Altrincham T v Oxford U
Burton Alb v Mansfield T
Cambridge U v Weymouth
Crawley T v Barrow
Eastbourne B v Stevenage B
Kidderminster H v Ebbsfleet U
Lewes v Forest Green R
Northwich Vic v Grays Ath

Rushden & D'monds v Torquay U
Salisbury C v Kettering T
Woking v York C
Wrexham v Histon

Saturday, 18 October 2008
Barrow v Eastbourne B
Ebbsfleet U v Torquay U
Forest Green R v Cambridge U
Grays Ath v Woking
Histon v Crawley T
Kettering T v Kidderminster H
Lewes v Northwich Vic
Mansfield T v Wrexham
Oxford U v Burton Alb
Stevenage B v Salisbury C
Weymouth v Altrincham T
York C v Rushden & D'monds

Saturday, 1 November 2008
Altrincham T v Histon
Barrow v Forest Green R
Burton Alb v Ebbsfleet U
Cambridge U v Rushden & D'monds
Kettering T v Weymouth
Kidderminster H v Grays Ath
Northwich Vic v Eastbourne B
Oxford U v York C
Salisbury C v Crawley T
Torquay U v Mansfield T
Woking v Stevenage B
Wrexham v Lewes

Saturday, 15 November 2008
Crawley T v Cambridge U
Eastbourne B v Woking
Ebbsfleet U v Barrow
Forest Green R v Altrincham T
Grays Ath v Oxford U
Histon v Kettering T
Lewes v Burton Alb
Mansfield T v Salisbury C
Rushden & D'monds v Kidderminster H
Stevenage B v Northwich Vic
Weymouth v Wrexham
York C v Torquay U

Tuesday, 18 November 2008
Cambridge U v York C
Crawley T v Ebbsfleet U
Eastbourne B v Salisbury C
Grays Ath v Rushden & D'monds
Kettering T v Barrow
Mansfield T v Altrincham T
Northwich Vic v Burton Alb
Oxford U v Kidderminster H
Stevenage B v Histon
Torquay U v Lewes
Weymouth v Woking
Wrexham v Forest Green R

Saturday, 22 November 2008
Altrincham T v Cambridge U
Barrow v Weymouth
Burton Alb v Stevenage B
Ebbsfleet U v Kettering T
Forest Green R v Mansfield T
Histon v Oxford U
Kidderminster H v Wrexham
Lewes v Grays Ath
Rushden & D'monds v Eastbourne B
Salisbury C v Northwich Vic
Woking v Torquay U
York C v Crawley T

Saturday, 29 November 2008
Altrincham T v Rushden & D'monds
Barrow v Histon
Burton Alb v Eastbourne B
Cambridge U v Ebbsfleet U
Grays Ath v Torquay U
Kettering T v Lewes
Northwich Vic v Crawley T
Oxford U v Forest Green R
Salisbury C v York C
Stevenage B v Wrexham
Weymouth v Mansfield T
Woking v Kidderminster H

Saturday, 6 December 2008
Crawley T v Altrincham T
Eastbourne B v Northwich Vic
Ebbsfleet U v Weymouth
Forest Green R v Burton Alb
Histon v Woking
Kidderminster H v Salisbury C
Lewes v Stevenage B
Mansfield T v Oxford U
Rushden & D'monds v Barrow
Torquay U v Cambridge U
Wrexham v Kettering T
York C v Grays Ath

Tuesday, 9 December 2008
Barrow v Altrincham T
Burton Alb v Cambridge U
Eastbourne B v Torquay U
Ebbsfleet U v Forest Green R
Histon v York C
Kettering T v Crawley T
Kidderminster H v Mansfield T
Northwich Vic v Wrexham
Salisbury C v Lewes
Stevenage B v Grays Ath
Weymouth v Oxford U
Woking v Rushden & D'monds

Saturday, 20 December 2008
Altrincham T v Burton Alb
Cambridge U v Salisbury C
Crawley T v Kidderminster H
Forest Green R v Kettering T
Grays Ath v Barrow
Lewes v Woking
Mansfield T v Weymouth
Oxford U v Stevenage B
Rushden & D'monds v Northwich Vic
Torquay U v Histon
Wrexham v Eastbourne B
York C v Ebbsfleet U

Friday, 26 December 2008
Barrow v Wrexham
Burton Alb v York C
Eastbourne B v Lewes
Ebbsfleet U v Grays Ath
Histon v Cambridge U
Kettering T v Mansfield T
Kidderminster H v Forest Green R
Northwich Vic v Altrincham T
Salisbury C v Oxford U
Stevenage B v Rushden & D'monds
Weymouth v Torquay U
Woking v Crawley T

Sunday, 28 December 2008
Cambridge U v Stevenage B
Crawley T v Eastbourne B
Forest Green R v Barrow
Grays Ath v Histon
Lewes v Kettering T
Mansfield T v Burton Alb
Northwich Vic v Salisbury C
Oxford U v Ebbsfleet U
Rushden & D'monds v Weymouth
Torquay U v Kidderminster H
Wrexham v Woking
York C v Altrincham T

Thursday, 1 January 2009
Altrincham T v Northwich Vic
Cambridge U v Histon
Crawley T v Woking
Forest Green R v Kidderminster H
Grays Ath v Ebbsfleet U
Lewes v Eastbourne B
Mansfield T v Kettering T
Oxford U v Salisbury C
Rushden & D'monds v Stevenage B
Torquay U v Weymouth
Wrexham v Barrow
York C v Burton Alb

Saturday, 3 January 2009
Altrincham T v Forest Green R
Barrow v Cambridge U
Burton Alb v Torquay U
Eastbourne B v Oxford U
Ebbsfleet U v Wrexham
Histon v Mansfield T
Kettering T v Grays Ath
Kidderminster H v Crawley T
Salisbury C v Rushden & D'monds
Stevenage B v Lewes
Weymouth v York C
Woking v Northwich Vic

Saturday, 17 January 2009
Cambridge U v Woking
Ebbsfleet U v Rushden & D'monds
Forest Green R v Eastbourne B
Grays Ath v Burton Alb
Kettering T v Salisbury C
Kidderminster H v Weymouth
Mansfield T v Crawley T
Northwich Vic v Histon
Oxford U v Altrincham T
Stevenage B v Barrow
Torquay U v Wrexham
York C v Lewes

Saturday, 24 January 2009
Altrincham T v Torquay U
Barrow v Kidderminster H
Burton Alb v Kettering T
Crawley T v Oxford U
Eastbourne B v York C
Histon v Grays Ath
Lewes v Mansfield T
Rushden & D'monds v Forest Green R
Salisbury C v Stevenage B
Weymouth v Northwich Vic
Woking v Ebbsfleet U
Wrexham v Cambridge U

Tuesday, 27 January 2009
Altrincham T v York C
Burton Alb v Barrow
Cambridge U v Oxford U
Ebbsfleet U v Crawley T
Grays Ath v Weymouth
Kidderminster H v Histon
Lewes v Torquay U
Mansfield T v Rushden & D'monds

Salisbury C v Forest Green R
Stevenage B v Kettering T
Woking v Eastbourne B
Wrexham v Northwich Vic

Saturday, 31 January 2009
Barrow v Salisbury C
Crawley T v Wrexham
Eastbourne B v Mansfield T
Ebbsfleet U v Kidderminster H
Forest Green R v Histon
Kettering T v Altrincham T
Northwich Vic v Woking
Oxford U v Lewes
Rushden & D'monds v Cambridge U
Torquay U v Grays Ath
Weymouth v Burton Alb
York C v Stevenage B

Saturday, 7 February 2009
Altrincham T v Eastbourne B
Barrow v Torquay U
Burton Alb v Rushden & D'monds
Grays Ath v Crawley T
Histon v Weymouth
Kettering T v Oxford U
Kidderminster H v Cambridge U
Lewes v Wrexham
Mansfield T v York C
Northwich Vic v Ebbsfleet U
Salisbury C v Woking
Stevenage B v Forest Green R

Saturday, 14 February 2009
Cambridge U v Mansfield T
Eastbourne B v Crawley T
Ebbsfleet U v Burton Alb
Kidderminster H v Northwich Vic
Oxford U v Barrow
Rushden & D'monds v Lewes
Salisbury C v Histon
Torquay U v Altrincham T
Weymouth v Stevenage B
Woking v Kettering T
Wrexham v Grays Ath
York C v Forest Green R

Saturday, 21 February 2009
Altrincham T v Woking
Barrow v Grays Ath
Burton Alb v Wrexham
Crawley T v Salisbury C
Forest Green R v Northwich Vic
Histon v Eastbourne B
Kettering T v Torquay U
Lewes v Cambridge U
Mansfield T v Ebbsfleet U
Stevenage B v Kidderminster H
Weymouth v Rushden & D'monds
York C v Oxford U

Tuesday, 24 February 2009
Burton Alb v Altrincham T
Crawley T v Lewes
Eastbourne B v Ebbsfleet U
Grays Ath v Cambridge U
Histon v Barrow
Northwich Vic v Kettering T
Oxford U v Mansfield T
Rushden & D'monds v York C
Stevenage B v Woking
Torquay U v Forest Green R
Wrexham v Kidderminster H

Saturday, 28 February 2009
Altrincham T v Stevenage B
Barrow v Northwich Vic
Cambridge U v Crawley T
Forest Green R v Grays Ath
Kidderminster H v Eastbourne B
Lewes v Histon
Oxford U v Torquay U
Rushden & D'monds v Mansfield T
Woking v Burton Alb
Wrexham v Salisbury C
York C v Weymouth

Saturday, 7 March 2009
Cambridge U v Burton Alb
Crawley T v Weymouth
Eastbourne B v Wrexham
Ebbsfleet U v York C
Forest Green R v Oxford U
Grays Ath v Altrincham T
Kettering T v Histon
Mansfield T v Lewes
Northwich Vic v Stevenage B
Salisbury C v Kidderminster H
Torquay U v Rushden & D'monds
Woking v Barrow

Tuesday, 10 March 2009
Weymouth v Salisbury C

Saturday, 14 March 2009
Altrincham T v Weymouth
Burton Alb v Salisbury C
Crawley T v Rushden & D'monds
Histon v Ebbsfleet U
Lewes v Kidderminster H
Mansfield T v Forest Green R
Oxford U v Grays Ath
Stevenage B v Cambridge U
Torquay U v Barrow
Woking v Wrexham
York C v Kettering T

Saturday, 21 March 2009
Barrow v Lewes
Eastbourne B v Burton Alb
Ebbsfleet U v Altrincham T
Forest Green R v York C
Grays Ath v Mansfield T
Histon v Stevenage B
Kidderminster H v Woking
Northwich Vic v Torquay U
Rushden & D'monds v Oxford U
Weymouth v Kettering T
Wrexham v Crawley T

Tuesday, 24 March 2009
Cambridge U v Northwich Vic
Kettering T v Eastbourne B
Salisbury C v Ebbsfleet U

Saturday, 28 March 2009
Altrincham T v Crawley T
Burton Alb v Grays Ath
Forest Green R v Lewes
Histon v Wrexham
Kettering T v Ebbsfleet U
Mansfield T v Torquay U
Northwich Vic v Rushden & D'monds
Salisbury C v Eastbourne B
Stevenage B v Oxford U
Weymouth v Barrow
Woking v Cambridge U
York C v Kidderminster H

Saturday, 4 April 2009
Barrow v Woking
Cambridge U v Forest Green R
Crawley T v Burton Alb
Eastbourne B v Weymouth
Ebbsfleet U v Northwich Vic
Grays Ath v York C
Kidderminster H v Stevenage B
Lewes v Altrincham T
Oxford U v Histon
Rushden & D'monds v Salisbury C
Torquay U v Kettering T
Wrexham v Mansfield T

Saturday, 11 April 2009
Altrincham T v Kidderminster H
Burton Alb v Histon
Cambridge U v Eastbourne B
Forest Green R v Woking
Grays Ath v Salisbury C
Lewes v Weymouth
Mansfield T v Barrow
Oxford U v Wrexham
Rushden & D'monds v Kettering T
Stevenage B v Ebbsfleet U
Torquay U v Crawley T
York C v Northwich Vic

Monday, 13 April 2009
Barrow v York C
Crawley T v Stevenage B
Eastbourne B v Grays Ath
Ebbsfleet U v Lewes
Histon v Rushden & D'monds
Kettering T v Cambridge U
Kidderminster H v Burton Alb
Northwich Vic v Mansfield T
Salisbury C v Torquay U
Weymouth v Forest Green R
Woking v Oxford U
Wrexham v Altrincham T

Saturday, 18 April 2009
Altrincham T v Grays Ath
Barrow v Crawley T
Burton Alb v Oxford U
Forest Green R v Rushden & D'monds
Histon v Kidderminster H
Kettering T v Wrexham
Northwich Vic v Lewes
Salisbury C v Cambridge U
Stevenage B v Torquay U
Weymouth v Ebbsfleet U
Woking v Mansfield T
York C v Eastbourne B

Saturday, 25 April 2009
Cambridge U v Altrincham T
Crawley T v Histon
Eastbourne B v Barrow
Ebbsfleet U v Salisbury C
Grays Ath v Forest Green R
Kidderminster H v Kettering T
Lewes v York C
Mansfield T v Stevenage B
Oxford U v Northwich Vic
Rushden & D'monds v Woking
Torquay U v Burton Alb
Wrexham v Weymouth

THE SCOTTISH PREMIER LEAGUE AND FOOTBALL LEAGUE FIXTURES 2008–09

Saturday, 2 August 2008

Irn-Bru First Division
Clyde v Morton
Partick Th v Dunfermline Ath
Queen of the S v Airdrie U
Ross Co v Dundee
St Johnstone v Livingston

Irn-Bru Second Division
Arbroath v Alloa Ath
Ayr U v Raith R
Brechin C v Stirling Alb
East Fife v Peterhead
Queen's Park v Stranraer

Irn-Bru Third Division
Albion R v Forfar Ath
Berwick R v East Stirlingshire
Cowdenbeath v Annan Ath
Dumbarton v Montrose
Stenhousemuir v Elgin C

Saturday, 9 August 2008

Clydesdale Bank Premier League
Aberdeen v Inverness CT
Falkirk v Rangers
Hearts v Motherwell
Kilmarnock v Hibernian

Irn-Bru First Division
Airdrie U v Partick Th
Dundee v Clyde
Dunfermline Ath v Queen of the S
Livingston v Ross Co
Morton v St Johnstone

Irn-Bru Second Division
Alloa Ath v Ayr U
Peterhead v Arbroath
Raith R v Queen's Park
Stirling Alb v East Fife
Stranraer v Brechin C

Irn-Bru Third Division
Annan Ath v Stenhousemuir
East Stirlingshire v Albion R
Elgin C v Dumbarton
Forfar Ath v Cowdenbeath
Montrose v Berwick R

Sunday, 10 August 2008

Clydesdale Bank Premier League
Celtic v St Mirren

Monday, 11 August 2008

Clydesdale Bank Premier League
Hamilton A v Dundee U

Saturday, 16 August 2008

Clydesdale Bank Premier League
Dundee U v Celtic
Hibernian v Falkirk
Inverness CT v Hamilton A
Motherwell v Aberdeen
Rangers v Hearts
St Mirren v Kilmarnock

Irn-Bru First Division
Airdrie U v Dundee
Clyde v Ross Co
Morton v Livingston
St Johnstone v Dunfermline Ath

Irn-Bru Second Division
Alloa Ath v Raith R
Ayr U v Arbroath
Brechin C v Peterhead
East Fife v Queen's Park
Stranraer v Stirling Alb

Irn-Bru Third Division
Berwick R v Dumbarton
Annan Ath v East Stirlingshire
Cowdenbeath v Albion R
Forfar Ath v Elgin C
Stenhousemuir v Montrose

Sunday, 17 August 2008

Irn-Bru First Division
Queen of the S v Partick Th

Saturday, 23 August 2008

Clydesdale Bank Premier League
Aberdeen v Rangers
Celtic v Falkirk
Hearts v St Mirren
Inverness CT v Hibernian
Kilmarnock v Hamilton A
Motherwell v Dundee U

Irn-Bru First Division
Dundee v Morton
Dunfermline Ath v Airdrie U
Livingston v Clyde
Partick Th v St Johnstone
Ross Co v Queen of the S

Irn-Bru Second Division
Arbroath v East Fife
Peterhead v Alloa Ath
Queen's Park v Brechin C
Raith R v Stranraer
Stirling Alb v Ayr U

Irn-Bru Third Division
Albion R v Berwick R
Dumbarton v Stenhousemuir
East Stirlingshire v Forfar Ath
Elgin C v Cowdenbeath
Montrose v Annan Ath

Saturday, 30 August 2008

Clydesdale Bank Premier League
Celtic v Rangers
Dundee U v Kilmarnock
Falkirk v Inverness CT
Hamilton A v Hearts
Hibernian v Motherwell
St Mirren v Aberdeen

Irn-Bru First Division
Airdrie U v Morton
Dunfermline Ath v Livingston
Partick Th v Ross Co
St Johnstone v Clyde

Irn-Bru Second Division
Alloa Ath v Stranraer
Arbroath v Stirling Alb
Ayr U v Queen's Park
East Fife v Brechin C
Peterhead v Raith R

Irn-Bru Third Division
Berwick R v Forfar Ath
Annan Ath v Albion R
Dumbarton v East Stirlingshire
Montrose v Elgin C
Stenhousemuir v Cowdenbeath

Sunday, 31 August 2008

Irn-Bru First Division
Queen of the S v Dundee

Saturday, 13 September 2008

Clydesdale Bank Premier League
Aberdeen v Hamilton A
Falkirk v Hearts
Hibernian v Dundee U
Inverness CT v St Mirren
Motherwell v Celtic
Rangers v Kilmarnock

Irn-Bru First Division
Clyde v Partick Th
Dundee v Dunfermline Ath
Livingston v Airdrie U
Morton v Queen of the S
Ross Co v St Johnstone

Irn-Bru Second Division
Brechin C v Arbroath
Queen's Park v Peterhead
Raith R v East Fife
Stirling Alb v Alloa Ath
Stranraer v Ayr U

Irn-Bru Third Division
Albion R v Dumbarton
Cowdenbeath v Berwick R
East Stirlingshire v Stenhousemuir
Elgin C v Annan Ath
Forfar Ath v Montrose

Saturday, 20 September 2008

Clydesdale Bank Premier League
Aberdeen v Dundee U
Hamilton A v Hibernian
Hearts v Inverness CT
Kilmarnock v Celtic
St Mirren v Falkirk

Irn-Bru First Division
Airdrie U v Clyde
Dundee v Livingston
Dunfermline Ath v Ross Co
Partick Th v Morton
Queen of the S v St Johnstone

Irn-Bru Second Division
Alloa Ath v East Fife
Arbroath v Queen's Park
Peterhead v Stranraer
Raith R v Stirling Alb

Irn-Bru Third Division
Annan Ath v Forfar Ath
Dumbarton v Cowdenbeath
Elgin C v Albion R
Montrose v East Stirlingshire
Stenhousemuir v Berwick R

Sunday, 21 September 2008
Clydesdale Bank Premier League
Rangers v Motherwell

Irn-Bru Second Division
Ayr U v Brechin C

Saturday, 27 September 2008
Clydesdale Bank Premier League
Celtic v Aberdeen
Dundee U v Hearts
Falkirk v Hamilton A
Hibernian v Rangers
Inverness CT v Kilmarnock
Motherwell v St Mirren

Irn-Bru First Division
Clyde v Queen of the S
Livingston v Partick Th
Morton v Dunfermline Ath
Ross Co v Airdrie U
St Johnstone v Dundee

Irn-Bru Second Division
Brechin C v Raith R
East Fife v Ayr U
Queen's Park v Alloa Ath
Stirling Alb v Peterhead
Stranraer v Arbroath

Irn-Bru Third Division
Albion R v Stenhousemuir
Berwick R v Annan Ath
Cowdenbeath v Montrose
East Stirlingshire v Elgin C
Forfar Ath v Dumbarton

Saturday, 4 October 2008
Clydesdale Bank Premier League
Aberdeen v Hibernian
Celtic v Hamilton A
Dundee U v Inverness CT
Hearts v Kilmarnock
St Mirren v Rangers

Irn-Bru First Division
Clyde v Dunfermline Ath
Partick Th v Dundee
Queen of the S v Livingston
Ross Co v Morton
St Johnstone v Airdrie U

Irn-Bru Second Division
Arbroath v Raith R
Ayr U v Peterhead
Brechin C v Alloa Ath
East Fife v Stranraer
Queen's Park v Stirling Alb

Irn-Bru Third Division
Albion R v Montrose
Berwick R v Elgin C
Cowdenbeath v East Stirlingshire
Dumbarton v Annan Ath
Stenhousemuir v Forfar Ath

Sunday, 5 October 2008
Clydesdale Bank Premier League
Motherwell v Falkirk

Saturday, 18 October 2008
Clydesdale Bank Premier League
Falkirk v Aberdeen
Hamilton A v St Mirren
Hibernian v Hearts
Inverness CT v Celtic
Kilmarnock v Motherwell
Rangers v Dundee U

Irn-Bru First Division
Airdrie U v Queen of the S
Dundee v Ross Co
Dunfermline Ath v Partick Th
Livingston v St Johnstone
Morton v Clyde

Irn-Bru Second Division
Alloa Ath v Arbroath
Peterhead v East Fife
Raith R v Ayr U
Stirling Alb v Brechin C
Stranraer v Queen's Park

Irn-Bru Third Division
Annan Ath v Cowdenbeath
East Stirlingshire v Berwick R
Elgin C v Stenhousemuir
Forfar Ath v Albion R
Montrose v Dumbarton

Saturday, 25 October 2008
Clydesdale Bank Premier League
Celtic v Hibernian
Dundee U v St Mirren
Hamilton A v Rangers
Hearts v Aberdeen
Inverness CT v Motherwell
Kilmarnock v Falkirk

Irn-Bru First Division
Airdrie U v Dunfermline Ath
Clyde v Livingston
Morton v Dundee
Queen of the S v Ross Co
St Johnstone v Partick Th

Irn-Bru Second Division
Alloa Ath v Peterhead
Ayr U v Stirling Alb
Brechin C v Queen's Park
East Fife v Arbroath
Stranraer v Raith R

Saturday, 1 November 2008
Clydesdale Bank Premier League
Aberdeen v Kilmarnock
Falkirk v Dundee U
Hearts v Celtic
Motherwell v Hamilton A
Rangers v Inverness CT
St Mirren v Hibernian

Irn-Bru First Division
Dundee v Airdrie U
Dunfermline Ath v St Johnstone
Livingston v Morton
Partick Th v Queen of the S
Ross Co v Clyde

Irn-Bru Second Division
Arbroath v Ayr U
Peterhead v Brechin C
Queen's Park v East Fife
Raith R v Alloa Ath
Stirling Alb v Stranraer

Irn-Bru Third Division
Albion R v Cowdenbeath
Dumbarton v Berwick R
East Stirlingshire v Annan Ath
Elgin C v Forfar Ath
Montrose v Stenhousemuir

Saturday, 8 November 2008
Clydesdale Bank Premier League
Celtic v Motherwell
Dundee U v Aberdeen
Hamilton A v Falkirk
Hibernian v Inverness CT
Kilmarnock v Rangers
St Mirren v Hearts

Irn-Bru First Division
Airdrie U v Livingston
Dunfermline Ath v Dundee
Partick Th v Clyde
Queen of the S v Morton
St Johnstone v Ross Co

Irn-Bru Second Division
Alloa Ath v Stirling Alb
Arbroath v Brechin C
Ayr U v Stranraer
East Fife v Raith R
Peterhead v Queen's Park

Irn-Bru Third Division
Berwick R v Albion R
Annan Ath v Montrose
Cowdenbeath v Elgin C
Forfar Ath v East Stirlingshire
Stenhousemuir v Dumbarton

Wednesday, 12 November 2008
Clydesdale Bank Premier League
Aberdeen v St Mirren
Celtic v Kilmarnock
Dundee U v Hibernian
Hearts v Hamilton A
Inverness CT v Falkirk
Motherwell v Rangers

Saturday, 15 November 2008
Clydesdale Bank Premier League
Falkirk v Motherwell
Hamilton A v Celtic
Hibernian v Aberdeen
Inverness CT v Hearts
Kilmarnock v Dundee U
Rangers v St Mirren

Irn-Bru First Division
Clyde v St Johnstone
Dundee v Queen of the S

Livingston v Dunfermline Ath
Morton v Airdrie U
Ross Co v Partick Th

Irn-Bru Second Division
Brechin C v East Fife
Queen's Park v Ayr U
Raith R v Peterhead
Stirling Alb v Arbroath
Stranraer v Alloa Ath

Irn-Bru Third Division
Albion R v Annan Ath
Cowdenbeath v Stenhousemuir
East Stirlingshire v Dumbarton
Elgin C v Montrose
Forfar Ath v Berwick R

Saturday, 22 November 2008
Clydesdale Bank Premier League
Dundee U v Hamilton A
Hearts v Falkirk
Kilmarnock v Inverness CT
Motherwell v Hibernian
Rangers v Aberdeen
St Mirren v Celtic

Irn-Bru First Division
Airdrie U v Ross Co
Dunfermline Ath v Morton
Partick Th v Livingston
Queen of the S v Clyde

Irn-Bru Second Division
Alloa Ath v Queen's Park
Arbroath v Stranraer
Ayr U v East Fife
Peterhead v Stirling Alb
Raith R v Brechin C

Irn-Bru Third Division
Berwick R v Cowdenbeath
Annan Ath v Elgin C
Dumbarton v Albion R
Montrose v Forfar Ath
Stenhousemuir v East Stirlingshire

Saturday, 29 November 2008
Clydesdale Bank Premier League
Aberdeen v Motherwell
Celtic v Inverness CT
Falkirk v Hibernian
Hamilton A v Kilmarnock
Hearts v Rangers
St Mirren v Dundee U

Irn-Bru First Division
Dundee v St Johnstone

Saturday, 6 December 2008
Clydesdale Bank Premier League
Falkirk v St Mirren
Hibernian v Celtic
Inverness CT v Dundee U
Kilmarnock v Aberdeen
Motherwell v Hearts
Rangers v Hamilton A

Irn-Bru First Division
Clyde v Airdrie U
Livingston v Dundee
Morton v Partick Th
Ross Co v Dunfermline Ath
St Johnstone v Queen of the S

Irn-Bru Second Division
Brechin C v Ayr U
East Fife v Alloa Ath
Queen's Park v Arbroath
Stirling Alb v Raith R
Stranraer v Peterhead

Irn-Bru Third Division
Albion R v Elgin C
Berwick R v Stenhousemuir
Cowdenbeath v Dumbarton
East Stirlingshire v Montrose
Forfar Ath v Annan Ath

Saturday, 13 December 2008
Clydesdale Bank Premier League
Aberdeen v Falkirk
Celtic v Hearts
Dundee U v Rangers
Hibernian v Hamilton A
Motherwell v Kilmarnock
St Mirren v Inverness CT

Irn-Bru First Division
Clyde v Dundee
Partick Th v Airdrie U
Queen of the S v Dunfermline Ath
Ross Co v Livingston
St Johnstone v Morton

Irn-Bru Second Division
Arbroath v Peterhead
Ayr U v Alloa Ath
Brechin C v Stranraer
East Fife v Stirling Alb
Queen's Park v Raith R

Irn-Bru Third Division
Annan Ath v Berwick R
Dumbarton v Forfar Ath
Elgin C v East Stirlingshire
Montrose v Cowdenbeath
Stenhousemuir v Albion R

Saturday, 20 December 2008
Clydesdale Bank Premier League
Falkirk v Celtic
Hamilton A v Motherwell
Hearts v Dundee U
Inverness CT v Aberdeen
Kilmarnock v St Mirren
Rangers v Hibernian

Irn-Bru First Division
Airdrie U v St Johnstone
Dundee v Partick Th
Dunfermline Ath v Clyde
Livingston v Queen of the S
Morton v Ross Co

Irn-Bru Second Division
Alloa Ath v Brechin C
Peterhead v Ayr U
Raith R v Arbroath
Stirling Alb v Queen's Park
Stranraer v East Fife

Irn-Bru Third Division
Annan Ath v Dumbarton
East Stirlingshire v Cowdenbeath
Elgin C v Berwick R
Forfar Ath v Stenhousemuir
Montrose v Albion R

Saturday, 27 December 2008
Clydesdale Bank Premier League
Aberdeen v Hearts
Dundee U v Falkirk
Hibernian v Kilmarnock
Motherwell v Inverness CT
Rangers v Celtic
St Mirren v Hamilton A

Irn-Bru First Division
Airdrie U v Morton
Dunfermline Ath v Livingston
Partick Th v Ross Co
Queen of the S v Dundee
St Johnstone v Clyde

Irn-Bru Second Division
Alloa Ath v Stranraer
Arbroath v Stirling Alb
Ayr U v Queen's Park
East Fife v Brechin C
Peterhead v Raith R

Irn-Bru Third Division
Albion R v East Stirlingshire
Berwick R v Montrose
Cowdenbeath v Forfar Ath
Dumbarton v Elgin C
Stenhousemuir v Annan Ath

Saturday, 3 January 2009
Clydesdale Bank Premier League
Celtic v Dundee U
Falkirk v Kilmarnock
Hamilton A v Aberdeen
Hearts v Hibernian
Inverness CT v Rangers
St Mirren v Motherwell

Irn-Bru First Division
Clyde v Partick Th
Dundee v Dunfermline Ath
Livingston v Airdrie U
Morton v Queen of the S
Ross Co v St Johnstone

Irn-Bru Second Division
Brechin C v Arbroath
Queen's Park v Peterhead
Raith R v East Fife
Stirling Alb v Alloa Ath
Stranraer v Ayr U

Irn-Bru Third Division
Albion R v Dumbarton
Cowdenbeath v Berwick R
East Stirlingshire v Stenhousemuir
Elgin C v Annan Ath
Forfar Ath v Montrose

Saturday, 10 January 2009
Irn-Bru Third Division
Berwick R v Forfar Ath
Annan Ath v Albion R
Dumbarton v East Stirlingshire
Montrose v Elgin C
Stenhousemuir v Cowdenbeath

Saturday, 17 January 2009
Clydesdale Bank Premier League
Aberdeen v Celtic
Dundee U v Motherwell
Hamilton A v Inverness CT
Hibernian v St Mirren

Kilmarnock v Hearts
Rangers v Falkirk

Irn-Bru First Division
Dundee v Morton
Dunfermline Ath v Airdrie U
Livingston v Clyde
Partick Th v St Johnstone
Ross Co v Queen of the S

Irn-Bru Second Division
Arbroath v East Fife
Peterhead v Alloa Ath
Queen's Park v Brechin C
Raith R v Stranraer
Stirling Alb v Ayr U

Irn-Bru Third Division
Albion R v Berwick R
Dumbarton v Stenhousemuir
East Stirlingshire v Forfar Ath
Elgin C v Cowdenbeath
Montrose v Annan Ath

Saturday, 24 January 2009
Clydesdale Bank Premier League
Aberdeen v Rangers
Celtic v Hibernian
Dundee U v St Mirren
Hearts v Inverness CT
Kilmarnock v Hamilton A
Motherwell v Falkirk

Irn-Bru First Division
Airdrie U v Dundee
Clyde v Ross Co
Morton v Livingston
Queen of the S v Partick Th
St Johnstone v Dunfermline Ath

Irn-Bru Second Division
Alloa Ath v Raith R
Ayr U v Arbroath
Brechin C v Peterhead
East Fife v Queen's Park
Stranraer v Stirling Alb

Irn-Bru Third Division
Berwick R v Dumbarton
Annan Ath v East Stirlingshire
Cowdenbeath v Albion R
Forfar Ath v Elgin C
Stenhousemuir v Montrose

Saturday, 31 January 2009
Clydesdale Bank Premier League
Falkirk v Aberdeen
Hamilton A v Hearts
Hibernian v Motherwell
Inverness CT v Celtic
Rangers v Dundee U
St Mirren v Kilmarnock

Irn-Bru First Division
Airdrie U v Partick Th
Dundee v Clyde
Dunfermline Ath v Queen of the S
Livingston v Ross Co
Morton v St Johnstone

Irn-Bru Second Division
Arbroath v Alloa Ath
Ayr U v Raith R
Brechin C v Stirling Alb
East Fife v Peterhead
Queen's Park v Stranraer

Irn-Bru Third Division
Albion R v Forfar Ath
Berwick R v East Stirlingshire
Cowdenbeath v Annan Ath
Dumbarton v Montrose
Stenhousemuir v Elgin C

Saturday, 7 February 2009
Irn-Bru Second Division
Alloa Ath v Ayr U
Peterhead v Arbroath
Raith R v Queen's Park
Stirling Alb v East Fife
Stranraer v Brechin C

Irn-Bru Third Division
Annan Ath v Stenhousemuir
East Stirlingshire v Albion R
Elgin C v Dumbarton
Forfar Ath v Cowdenbeath
Montrose v Berwick R

Saturday, 14 February 2009
Clydesdale Bank Premier League
Celtic v Rangers
Dundee U v Inverness CT
Hearts v Aberdeen
Kilmarnock v Hibernian
Motherwell v Hamilton A
St Mirren v Falkirk

Irn-Bru First Division
Clyde v Morton
Partick Th v Dunfermline Ath
Queen of the S v Airdrie U
Ross Co v Dundee
St Johnstone v Livingston

Irn-Bru Second Division
Brechin C v Raith R
East Fife v Ayr U
Queen's Park v Alloa Ath
Stirling Alb v Peterhead
Stranraer v Arbroath

Irn-Bru Third Division
Albion R v Stenhousemuir
Berwick R v Annan Ath
Cowdenbeath v Montrose
East Stirlingshire v Elgin C
Forfar Ath v Dumbarton

Saturday, 21 February 2009
Clydesdale Bank Premier League
Aberdeen v Dundee U
Falkirk v Hamilton A
Hearts v St Mirren
Inverness CT v Hibernian
Motherwell v Celtic
Rangers v Kilmarnock

Irn-Bru First Division
Airdrie U v Clyde
Dundee v Livingston
Dunfermline Ath v Ross Co
Partick Th v Morton
Queen of the S v St Johnstone

Irn-Bru Second Division
Alloa Ath v East Fife
Arbroath v Queen's Park
Ayr U v Brechin C
Peterhead v Stranraer
Raith R v Stirling Alb

Irn-Bru Third Division
Annan Ath v Forfar Ath
Dumbarton v Cowdenbeath
Elgin C v Albion R
Montrose v East Stirlingshire
Stenhousemuir v Berwick R

Saturday, 28 February 2009
Clydesdale Bank Premier League
Aberdeen v Kilmarnock
Celtic v St Mirren
Dundee U v Hearts
Hamilton A v Rangers
Hibernian v Falkirk
Inverness CT v Motherwell

Irn-Bru First Division
Clyde v Queen of the S
Livingston v Partick Th
Morton v Dunfermline Ath
Ross Co v Airdrie U
St Johnstone v Dundee

Irn-Bru Second Division
Brechin C v East Fife
Queen's Park v Ayr U
Raith R v Peterhead
Stirling Alb v Arbroath
Stranraer v Alloa Ath

Irn-Bru Third Division
Albion R v Annan Ath
Cowdenbeath v Stenhousemuir
East Stirlingshire v Dumbarton
Elgin C v Montrose
Forfar Ath v Berwick R

Wednesday, 4 March 2009
Clydesdale Bank Premier League
Falkirk v Dundee U
Hamilton A v Hibernian
Hearts v Motherwell
Kilmarnock v Celtic
Rangers v Inverness CT
St Mirren v Aberdeen

Saturday, 7 March 2009
Irn-Bru First Division
Airdrie U v Livingston
Dunfermline Ath v Dundee
Partick Th v Clyde
Queen of the S v Morton
St Johnstone v Ross Co

Irn-Bru Second Division
Alloa Ath v Stirling Alb
Arbroath v Brechin C
Ayr U v Stranraer
East Fife v Raith R
Peterhead v Queen's Park

Irn-Bru Third Division
Berwick R v Cowdenbeath
Annan Ath v Elgin C
Dumbarton v Albion R
Montrose v Forfar Ath
Stenhousemuir v East Stirlingshire

Tuesday, 10 March 2009
Irn-Bru First Division
Clyde v St Johnstone
Dundee v Queen of the S

Livingston v Dunfermline Ath
Morton v Airdrie U
Ross Co v Partick Th

Saturday, 14 March 2009

Clydesdale Bank Premier League
Aberdeen v Hamilton A
Celtic v Falkirk
Hibernian v Hearts
Inverness CT v Kilmarnock
Motherwell v Dundee U
St Mirren v Rangers

Irn-Bru First Division
Airdrie U v Queen of the S
Dundee v Ross Co
Dunfermline Ath v Partick Th
Livingston v St Johnstone
Morton v Clyde

Irn-Bru Second Division
Alloa Ath v Arbroath
Peterhead v East Fife
Raith R v Ayr U
Stirling Alb v Brechin C
Stranraer v Queen's Park

Irn-Bru Third Division
Annan Ath v Cowdenbeath
East Stirlingshire v Berwick R
Elgin C v Stenhousemuir
Forfar Ath v Albion R
Montrose v Dumbarton

Saturday, 21 March 2009

Clydesdale Bank Premier League
Dundee U v Celtic
Falkirk v Inverness CT
Hamilton A v St Mirren
Hibernian v Aberdeen
Kilmarnock v Motherwell
Rangers v Hearts

Irn-Bru First Division
Clyde v Dunfermline Ath
Partick Th v Dundee
Queen of the S v Livingston
Ross Co v Morton
St Johnstone v Airdrie U

Irn-Bru Second Division
Arbroath v Raith R
Ayr U v Peterhead
Brechin C v Alloa Ath
East Fife v Stranraer
Queen's Park v Stirling Alb

Irn-Bru Third Division
Albion R v Montrose
Berwick R v Elgin C
Cowdenbeath v East Stirlingshire
Dumbarton v Annan Ath
Stenhousemuir v Forfar Ath

Saturday, 4 April 2009

Clydesdale Bank Premier League
Celtic v Hamilton A
Dundee U v Hibernian
Falkirk v Rangers
Hearts v Kilmarnock
Inverness CT v St Mirren
Motherwell v Aberdeen

Irn-Bru First Division
Airdrie U v Dunfermline Ath
Clyde v Livingston
Morton v Dundee
Queen of the S v Ross Co
St Johnstone v Partick Th

Irn-Bru Second Division
Alloa Ath v Peterhead
Ayr U v Stirling Alb
Brechin C v Queen's Park
East Fife v Arbroath
Stranraer v Raith R

Irn-Bru Third Division
Berwick R v Albion R
Annan Ath v Montrose
Cowdenbeath v Elgin C
Forfar Ath v East Stirlingshire
Stenhousemuir v Dumbarton

Saturday, 11 April 2009

Clydesdale Bank Premier League
Aberdeen v Inverness CT
Hamilton A v Dundee U
Hearts v Celtic
Kilmarnock v Falkirk
Rangers v Motherwell
St Mirren v Hibernian

Irn-Bru First Division
Dundee v Airdrie U
Dunfermline Ath v St Johnstone
Livingston v Morton
Partick Th v Queen of the S
Ross Co v Clyde

Irn-Bru Second Division
Arbroath v Ayr U
Peterhead v Brechin C
Queen's Park v East Fife
Raith R v Alloa Ath
Stirling Alb v Stranraer

Irn-Bru Third Division
Albion R v Cowdenbeath
Dumbarton v Berwick R
East Stirlingshire v Annan Ath
Elgin C v Forfar Ath
Montrose v Stenhousemuir

Saturday, 18 April 2009

Clydesdale Bank Premier League
Celtic v Aberdeen
Dundee U v Kilmarnock
Falkirk v Hearts
Hibernian v Rangers
Inverness CT v Hamilton A
Motherwell v St Mirren

Irn-Bru First Division
Clyde v Airdrie U
Livingston v Dundee
Morton v Partick Th
Ross Co v Dunfermline Ath
St Johnstone v Queen of the S

Irn-Bru Second Division
Brechin C v Ayr U
East Fife v Alloa Ath
Queen's Park v Arbroath
Stirling Alb v Raith R
Stranraer v Peterhead

Irn-Bru Third Division
Albion R v Elgin C
Berwick R v Stenhousemuir
Cowdenbeath v Dumbarton
East Stirlingshire v Montrose
Forfar Ath v Annan Ath

Saturday, 25 April 2009

Irn-Bru First Division
Airdrie U v Ross Co
Dundee v St Johnstone
Dunfermline Ath v Morton
Partick Th v Livingston
Queen of the S v Clyde

Irn-Bru Second Division
Alloa Ath v Queen's Park
Arbroath v Stranraer
Ayr U v East Fife
Peterhead v Stirling Alb
Raith R v Brechin C

Irn-Bru Third Division
Annan Ath v Berwick R
Dumbarton v Forfar Ath
Elgin C v East Stirlingshire
Montrose v Cowdenbeath
Stenhousemuir v Albion R

Saturday, 2 May 2009

Irn-Bru First Division
Clyde v Dundee
Partick Th v Airdrie U
Queen of the S v Dunfermline Ath
Ross Co v Livingston
St Johnstone v Morton

Irn-Bru Second Division
Arbroath v Peterhead
Ayr U v Alloa Ath
Brechin C v Stranraer
East Fife v Stirling Alb
Queen's Park v Raith R

Irn-Bru Third Division
Albion R v East Stirlingshire
Berwick R v Montrose
Cowdenbeath v Forfar Ath
Dumbarton v Elgin C
Stenhousemuir v Annan Ath

Saturday, 9 May 2009

Irn-Bru First Division
Airdrie U v St Johnstone
Dundee v Partick Th
Dunfermline Ath v Clyde
Livingston v Queen of the S
Morton v Ross Co

Irn-Bru Second Division
Alloa Ath v Brechin C
Peterhead v Ayr U
Raith R v Arbroath
Stirling Alb v Queen's Park
Stranraer v East Fife

Irn-Bru Third Division
Annan Ath v Dumbarton
East Stirlingshire v Cowdenbeath
Elgin C v Berwick R
Forfar Ath v Stenhousemuir
Montrose v Albion R

OTHER FIXTURES 2008–09

AUGUST 2008

Tue 5 UEFA Champions League 2Q (2)
Wed 6 UEFA Champions League 2Q (2)
Sat 9 FL Season starts
Sun 10 FA Community Shield
Tue 12 UEFA Champions League 3Q (1)
Wed 13 UEFA Champions League 3Q (1)
Thu 14 UEFA Cup 2Q (1)
Sat 16 FA Cup EP
PL Season starts
Wed 20 England v Czech Republic (F)
Mon 25 Bank Holiday
Tue 26 UEFA Champions League 3Q (2)
Wed 27 UEFA Champions League 3Q (2)
Thu 28 UEFA Cup 2Q (2)
Fri 29 UEFA Super Cup Final
Sat 30 FA Cup P

SEPTEMBER 2008

Sat 6 Andorra v England (WCQ)
FA Vase 1Q
Sun 7 FA Women's Cup P
Mon 8 FA Youth Cup P**
Wed 10 Croatia v England (WCQ)
Sat 13 FA Cup 1Q
Tue 16 UEFA Champions League MD 1
Wed 17 UEFA Champions League MD 1
Thu 18 UEFA Cup 1 (1)
Sat 20 FA Vase 2Q
Sun 21 FA Sunday Cup P
Mon 22 FA Youth Cup 1Q**
Sat 27 FA Cup 2Q
Sun 28 Czech Republic v England (Women's ECQ)
FA Women's Cup 1Q
Tue 30 UEFA Champions League MD 2

OCTOBER 2008

Wed 1 UEFA Champions League MD 2
Thu 2 UEFA Cup 1 (2)
Spain v England (Women's ECQ)
Sat 4 FA Trophy P
FA Vase 1P
Mon 6 FA Youth Cup 2Q**
Sat 11 England v Kazakhstan (WCQ)
FA Cup 3Q
Sun 12 FA Women's Cup 2Q
Wed 15 Belarus v England (WCQ)
Sat 18 FA Trophy 1Q
Sun 19 FA Sunday Cup 1
FA County Youth Cup 1*
Mon 20 FA Youth Cup 3Q**
Tue 21 UEFA Champions League MD 3
Wed 22 UEFA Champions League MD 3
Thu 23 UEFA Cup MD 1
Sat 25 FA Cup 4Q
Sun 26 FA Women's Cup 3Q

NOVEMBER 2008

Sat 1 FA Trophy 2Q
Tue 4 UEFA Champions League MD 4
Wed 5 UEFA Champions League MD 4
Thu 6 UEFA Cup MD 2
Sat 8 FA Cup 1P
FA Youth Cup 1P*
Sun 9 FA Women's Cup 1P
Sat 15 FA Vase 2P
Sun 16 FA Sunday Cup 2
FA County Youth Cup 2*
Wed 19 Germany v England (F)
Sat 22 FA Trophy 3Q
FA Youth Cup 2P*
Sun 23 FA Women's Cup 2P
Tue 25 UEFA Champions League MD 5
Wed 26 UEFA Champions League MD 5
Thu 27 UEFA Cup MD 3
Sat 29 FA Cup 2P

DECEMBER 2008

Wed 3 UEFA Cup MD 4
Thu 4 UEFA Cup MD 4
Sat 6 FA Vase 3P
Sun 7 FA Sunday Cup 3
Tue 9 UEFA Champions League MD 6
Wed 10 UEFA Champions League MD 6
Sat 13 FA Trophy 1P
FA Youth Cup 3P*
Sun 14 FA Women's Cup 3P
Wed 17 UEFA Cup MD 5
Thu 18 UEFA Cup MD 5
Sun 21 FA County Youth Cup 3*

JANUARY 2009

Sat 3 FA Cup 3P
Sun 4 FA Women's Cup 4P
Sat 10 FA Trophy 2P
Sun 11 FA Sunday Cup 4
Sat 17 FA Vase 4P
FA Youth Cup 4P*
Sat 24 FA Cup 4P
Sun 25 FA County Youth Cup 4*
FA Women's Cup 5P
Sat 31 FA Trophy 3P
FA Youth Cup 5P*

FEBRUARY 2009

Sat 7 FA Vase 5P
Wed 11 International Friendly
Sat 14 FA Cup 5P
FA Youth Cup 6P*
Wed 18 UEFA Cup 32 (1)

Thu 19 UEFA Cup 32 (1)
Sat 21 FA Trophy 4P
Sun 22 FA Sunday Cup 5
FA Women's Cup 6P
Tue 24 UEFA Champions League 16 (1)
Wed 25 UEFA Champions League 16 (1)
Thu 26 UEFA Cup 32 (2)
Sat 28 FA Vase 6P

MARCH 2009
Sun 1 FA County Youth Cup SF*
Sat 7 FA Cup 6P
FA Youth Cup SF1*
Tue 10 UEFA Champions League 16 (2)
Wed 11 UEFA Champions League 16 (2)
Thu 12 UEFA Cup 16 (1)
Sat 14 FA Trophy SF1
Wed 18 UEFA Cup 16 (2)
Thu 19 UEFA Cup 16 (2)
Sat 21 FA Trophy SF2
FA Youth Cup SF2*
Sun 22 FA Sunday Cup SF
FA Women's Cup SF
Sat 28 FA Vase SF1

APRIL 2009
Wed 1 England v Ukraine (WCQ)
Sat 4 FA Vase SF2
Tue 7 UEFA Champions League QF (1)
Wed 8 UEFA Champions League QF (1)
Thu 9 UEFA Cup QF (1)
Fri 10 Good Friday
Mon 13 Easter Monday
Tue 14 UEFA Champions League QF (2)
Wed 15 UEFA Champions League QF (2)
Thu 16 UEFA Cup QF (2)
Sat 18 FA Cup SF
Sun 19 FA Cup SF
Sat 25 FA County Youth Cup Final (prov)
Sun 26 FA Sunday Cup Final (prov)
Tue 28 UEFA Champions League SF (1)
Wed 29 UEFA Champions League SF (1)
Thu 30 UEFA Cup SF (1)

MAY 2009
Sat 2 FL Season ends
FA County Youth Cup Final (prov)
Sun 3 FA Sunday Cup Final (prov)
Mon 4 Bank Holiday
FA Women's Cup Final
Tue 5 UEFA Champions League SF (2)
Wed 6 UEFA Champions League SF (2)
Thu 7 UEFA Cup SF (2)
Sat 9 FA Trophy Final
Sun 10 FA Vase Final
Wed 20 UEFA Cup Final
Sat 23 PL Season ends
FL Play-Off Final League 2
Sun 24 FL Play-Off Final League 1
Mon 25 Bank Holiday
FL Play-Off Final Championship
Wed 27 UEFA Champions League Final
Sat 30 FA Cup Final

JUNE 2009
Sat 6 Kazakhstan v England (WCQ)
Wed 10 England v Andorra (WCQ)

* *closing date of round*
** *ties to be played in the week commencing*
FA Youth Cup Final 1st & 2nd Legs – dates to be confirmed

STOP PRESS

Ronaldo "slave" – Blatter ... Luton to start 30 pts deducted! ... Barry and Villa at loggerheads ... Pompey's little England ... Palace fury over "baby-snatching" ... Spurs unhappy over alleged "tapping" ... England U-19s fail to reach knock-out stage ... Germans might be Euro sub for Ukraine ...

Summer transfers completed and pending:
Premier League: Arsenal: Aaron Ramsey (Cardiff C) undisclosed; Samir Nasri (Marseille). **Aston Villa:** Steve Sidwell (Chelsea) undisclosed; Curtis Davies (WBA) undisclosed. **Blackburn R:** Robbie Fowler (Cardiff C) undisclosed. **Bolton W:** Johan Elmander (Toulouse) undisclosed; Fabrice Muamba (Birmingham C) undisclosed. **Chelsea:** Jose Bosingwa (Porto) £16.2m; Deco (Barcelona) £7.9m. **Fulham:** Andranik Teimourian (Bolton W) Free; Zoltan Gera (WBA) Free; David Stockdale (Darlington) undisclosed; Mark Schwarzer (Middlesbrough) Free; Toni Kallio (Young Boys) undisclosed; Bobby Zamora and John Pantsil (West Ham U) joint fee £6.3m. **Hull C:** Craig Fagan (Derby Co) £750,000; Bernard Mendy (Paris St Germain); Geovanni (Manchester C) Free; Peter Halmosi (Plymouth Arg) undisclosed; Tony Warner (Fulham) Free; George Boateng (Middlesbrough) £1m. **Liverpool:** Philip Degen (Borussia Dortmund) Free; Diego Cavalieri (Palmeiras) undisclosed; Andrea Dossena (Udinese) undisclosed. **Manchester C:** Jo (CSKA Moscow) £19m. **Middlesbrough:** Didier Digard (Paris St Germain) £4m; Marvin Emnes (Sparta Rotterdam) £3.2m. **Newcastle U:** Jonas Gutierrez (Mallorca) undisclosed; Danny Guthrie (Liverpool) undisclosed. **Portsmouth:** Ben Sahar (Chelsea) Loan; Glen Little (Reading) undisclosed; Peter Crouch (Liverpool) £11m. **Stoke C:** Dave Kitson (Reading) £5.5m. **Tottenham H:** Heurelho Gomes (PSV Eindhoven) undisclosed; Giovanni (Barcelona) undisclosed; Luka Modric (Dinamo Zagreb) £16.5m; John Bostock (Crystal Palace) £700,000. **WBA:** Gianni Zuiverloon (Heerenveen) undisclosed; Luke Moore (Aston Villa) £3m; Marek Cech (Porto) £1.4m; Scott Carson (Liverpool) £3.25m. **West Ham U:** Balint Bajner (Liberty Arad) undisclosed. **Wigan Ath:** Daniel De Ridder (Birmingham C) Free; Olivier Kapo (Birmingham C) £3.5m.

Football League Championship: Barnsley: Darren Moore (Derby Co) Free; Iain Hume (Leicester C) £1.2m; Hugo Colace (Newell's Old Boys); Mounir El Haimour (Neuchatel Xamax). **Birmingham C:** Lee Carsley (Everton) Free; Kevin Phillips (WBA) Free; Marcus Bent (Charlton Ath). **Blackpool:** Alex John-Baptiste (Mansfield T); Matthew Gilks (Norwich C); Marlon Broomes (Stoke C) Free; Joe Martin (Tottenham H); Steven Kabba (Watford) Loan; Jermaine Wright (Southampton) Free; Adam Hammill (Liverpool) Loan. **Bristol C:** Gavin Williams (Ipswich T); Emad Meteb (Al Ahly) £1.5m. **Burnley:** Kevin McDonald (Dundee) £500,000; Martin Paterson (Scunthorpe U) £1m; Remco Van der Schaaf (Vitesse) Free; Christian Kalvenes (Dundee U). **Cardiff C:** Tom Heaton (Manchester U) Loan; Miquel Comminges (Swindon T); Mark Kennedy (Crystal Palace) Free. **Charlton Ath:** Mark Hudson (Crystal Palace) Free; Stuart Fleetwood (Forest Green R). **Coventry C:** Guillaume Beuzelin (Hibernian) Free; Kieren Westwood (Carlisle U); Freddy Eastwood (Wolverhampton W); Aron Gunnarsson (AZ). **Crystal Palace:** Johannes Ertl (FK Austria); Nick Carle (Bristol C); Patrick McCarthy (Charlton Ath); Calvin Andrew (Luton T). **Derby Co:** Martin Albrechtsen (WBA) Free; Kris Commons (Nottingham F) Free; Paul Green (Doncaster R) Free; Nathan Ellington (Watford) Loan; Jordan Stewart (Watford) Free; Liam Dickinson (Stockport Co) £750,000; Paul Connolly (Plymouth Arg) Free; Steve Davies (Tranmere R); Przemyslaw Kazmierczak (Porto) Loan; Rob Hulse (Sheffield U) £1.75m. **Doncaster R:** John Spicer (Burnley) Free. **Ipswich T:** Kevin Lisbie (Colchester U). **Norwich C:** Wes Hoolahan (Blackpool); Ryan Bertrand (Chelsea) Loan; Dejan Stefanovic (Fulham); Elliot Omozusi (Fulham) Loan. **Nottingham F:** Paul Anderson (Swansea C) Loan; Guy Moussi (Angers); Robert Earnshaw (Derby Co) £2.65m; Andy Cole (Sunderland) Free. **Plymouth Arg:** Karl Duguid (Colchester U); Jason Puncheon (Barnet) Free. **Preston NE:** Barry Nicholson (Aberdeen) Free. **QPR:** Radek Cerny (Slavia Prague) Free; Peter Ramage (Newcastle U) Free. **Sheffield U:** Greg Halford (Sunderland) Loan; Sun Jihai (Manchester C) Free. **Sheffield W:** James O'Connor (Burnley) Free. **Southampton:** Lee Holmes (Derby Co) Free; Tommy Forecast (Tottenham H); Paul Wotton (Plymouth Arg) Free. **Swansea C:** Mark Gower (Southend U) Free; Albert Serran (Espanyol). **Wolverhampton W:** David Jones (Derby Co); Sam Vokes (Bournemouth); Chris Iwelumo (Charlton Ath).

Football League 1: Brighton & HA: Adam Virgo (Celtic) Free; Colin Hawkins (Chesterfield) Free; Kevin McLeod (Colchester U) Free; Matthew Richards (Ipswich T) Loan. **Bristol R:** Jeff Hughes (Crystal Palace); Darryl Duffy (Swansea C) £100,000. **Carlisle U:** Ben Williams (Crewe Alex) Free; Josh Gowling (Bournemouth) Free. **Cheltenham T:** Alex Russell (Bristol C) Free. **Colchester U:** Paul Reid (Barnsley) Free; Matt Lockwood (Nottingham F); David Perkins (Rochdale); Steven Gillespie (Cheltenham T) £400,000. **Crewe Alex:** Steve Collis (Southend U) Free; Joel Grant (Aldershot T) £130,000; Jake Livermore (MK Dons) Loan; Calvin Zola (Tranmere R) £400,000. **Hartlepool U:** Ritchie Jones (Yeovil T) Free; Alan Power (Nottingham F) Free. **Hereford U:** Matt Done (Wrexham); Darren Randolph (Charlton Ath) Loan; Toumani Diagouraga (Watford); Robbie Threlfall (Liverpool) Loan. **Huddersfield T:** Jim Goodwin

(Scunthorpe U) Free; Chris Lucketti (Southampton) Free. **Leeds U:** Enoch Showunmi (Bristol C) Free; Alan Sheehan (Leicester C) Free; Andy Robinson (Swansea C) Free. **Leicester C:** Michael Morrison (Cambridge U); Lloyd Dyer (MK Dons) Free; Kelvin Etuhu (Manchester C) Loan; Kerrea Gilbert (Arsenal) Loan. **Leyton Orient:** Simon Dawkins (Tottenham H) Loan; Danny Granville (Colchester U) Free. **Millwall:** Nadjim Abdou (Plymouth Arg) Free; David Forde (Luton T) Free. **Northampton T:** Leon Constantine (Leeds U) Free; Liam Davis (Coventry C); Mark Haines (Grays Ath) Free. **Oldham Ath:** Danny Whitaker (Port Vale) Free; Greg Fleming (Gretna) Free. **Peterborough U:** Russell Martin (Wycombe W). **Scunthorpe U:** Kenny Milne (Falkirk) Free; Garry Thompson (Morecambe) Free. **Southend U:** Paul Furlong (Luton T) Free; Osei Sankofa (Charlton Ath) Free; Steve Mildenhall (Yeovil T) Free; Ian Joyce (Watford) Free. **Stockport Co:** Johnny Mullins (Mansfield T); Owain fon Williams (Crewe Alex) Free; Peter Thompson (Linfield). **Swindon T:** Kevin Amankwaah (Swansea C). **Tranmere R:** George O'Callaghan (Cork C); Bas Savage (Millwall) Free; Edrissa Sonko (Walsall) Free; Gareth Edds (Milton Keynes D) Free; Luke Waterfall (Barnsley) Free. **Walsall:** Dwayne Mattis (Barnsley) Free; Stephen Roberts (Doncaster R) Free; Jabo Ibehre (Leyton Orient) Free. **Yeovil T:** Kieran Murtagh (Fisher Ath); Danny Schofield (Huddersfield T) Free; Darren Way (Swansea C) £50,000.

Football League 2: Aldershot T: Dean Howell (Rushden & D) Free; Chris Blackburn (Swindon T); Marvin Morgan (Woking). **Barnet:** Luke Medley (Bradford C) Free. **Bradford C:** Paul McLaren (Tranmere R) Free; Graeme Lee (Shrewsbury T); Chris Brandon (Huddersfield T) Free. **Brentford:** Marvin Williams (Yeovil T); Marcus Bean (Blackpool) Free; Charlie MacDonald (Southend U). **Bury:** Efetobor Sodje (Bury) Free; Wayne Brown (Hereford U) Free; Ryan Cresswell (Sheffield U) Free. **Chester C:** Ryan Lowe (Crewe Alex) Free; David Mannix (Accrington S) Free; James Harris (Accrington S) Free; Anthony Barry (Yeovil T) Free. **Chesterfield:** Zavon Hines (West Ham U) Loan; Paul Harsley (Port Vale) Free; Robert Page (Huddersfield T) Free; Darren Currie (Luton T) Free. **Dagenham & R:** Mark Nwokeii (Staines T) Free. **Darlington:** David Poole (Stockport Co) Free; Adam Griffin (Stockport Co) Free; Adam Proudlock (Stockport Co) Free. **Exeter C:** Marcus Stewart (Yeovil T) Free; Ryan Harley (Weston-Super-Mare) Free. **Gillingham:** Mark McCammon (Doncaster R) Free. **Grimsby T:** Robbie Stockdale (Tranmere R); Matthew Heywood (Brentford); Richard Hope (Wrexham) Free; Chris Llewellyn (Wrexham) Free. **Lincoln C:** Robert Burch (Sheffield W) Free; Aaron Brown (Gillingham) Free; Janos Kovacs (Chesterfield) Free; Stefan Oakes (Wycombe W) Free. **Macclesfield T:** Paul Morgan (Bury) Loan. **Morecambe:** Michael Carr (Northwich Vic) Free. **Notts Co:** Matt Hamshaw (Mansfield T) Free; Michael Johnson (Derby Co) Free; Jason Beardsley (Derby Co) Loan. **Port Vale:** John McCombe (Hereford U) Free; David Howland (Birmingham C) Free; Steve Thompson (Middlesbrough); Louis Dodds (Leicester C). **Rochdale:** Scott Wiseman (Darlington) Free; Clark Keltie (Darlington) Free; Ciaran Toner (Grimsby T) Free; Jon Shaw (Halifax T). **Rotherham U:** Alex Rhodes (Bradford C). **Shrewsbury T:** Shane Cansdell-Sherriff (Tranmere R) Free; Grant Holt (Nottingham F) £170,000; Stephen Hindmarch (Carlisle U); Paul Murray (Gretna) Free. **Wycombe W:** Lewis Spence (Crystal Palace) Free; John Mousinho (Brentford) Free.

Scottish Premier League: Aberdeen: Bertrand Bossu (Walsall) Free; Stuart Duff (Dundee U) Free. **Celtic:** Georgios Samaras (Manchester C) undisclosed. **Dundee U:** Warren Feeney (Cardiff C) Loan; Paul Dixon (Dundee) Nominal; Michael McGovern (Celtic) Free. **Falkirk:** Neil McCann (Hearts) Free. **Hibernian:** David van Zanten (St Mirren) Free. **Kilmarnock:** Allan Russell (Airdrie U) Free. **Rangers:** Kyle Lafferty (Burnley) £3m; Kenny Miller (Derby Co) £2m; Andrius Velicka (Viking) £1m. **St Mirren:** Tom Brighton (Millwall) Free.

Leaving the country: Mathieu Flamini Arsenal to AC Milan; Jens Lehmann Arsenal to Stuttgart; Alexander Hleb Arsenal to Barcelona; Gilberto Silva Arsenal to Panathinaikos; Patrik Berger Aston Villa to Sparta Prague; Daniel Braaten Bolton W to Toulouse; Slobodan Rajkovic Chelsea to Twente; Khalid Boulahrouz Chelsea to Stuttgart; Claude Makelele Chelsea to Paris St Germain; Brian McBride Fulham to Toronto; Ricardo Batista Fulham to Sporting Lisbon; Harry Kewell Liverpool to Galatasaray; Anthony Le Tallec Liverpool to Le Mans; John Arne Riise Liverpool to Roma £3.96m; Andreas Isaksson Manchester City to PSV Eindhoven; Gerrard Pique Manchester U to Barcelona; Fabio Rochemback Middlesbrough to Sporting Lisbon; Emre Newcastle U to Fenerbahce £2m; David Rozehnal Newcastle to Lazio; Andreas Granqvist Wigan Ath to Groningen £600,000; Julius Aghahowa Wigan Ath to Kayseri; Mikael Forssell Birmingham C to Hannover 96; Rafael Schmitz Birmingham C to Valenciennes; Ellery Cairo Coventry C to NAC Breda; Junior Agogo Nottingham F to Zanzibar £565,000; Emerse Fae Reading to Nice Loan; Dominik Werling Barnsley to Erzgebirge; Rohan Ricketts Barnsley to Toronto; Kim Christensen Barnsley to Midtyjlland.

Colin Kazim-Richards was transferred to Fenerbahce in June 2007, but still appears on Sheffield United's retain list.

Daily Round-Up clarification: items featured on May 4 and May 21 concerning Fernando Torres and Ryan Giggs were as reported at the time. In both instances, the club pages for Liverpool and Manchester United reflected a more accurate interpretation.